P9-CQO-171

HARRAP'S
New Standard
FRENCH AND ENGLISH DICTIONARY

VOLUME THREE

ENGLISH—FRENCH

A—K

SUB-EDITORS

Hazel Curties, B.A. (née Catterall)
Flora Elphick, B.A.
H. R. Elphick
Muriel Holland Smith
Elizabeth A. H. Strick, M.A.
Helen Zarb, B.A.

PRINCIPAL COLLABORATORS AND TECHNICAL ADVISERS

Jean Bétesta, *Chevalier de la Légion d'Honneur*
Reginald Bowen, B.A., *Docteur de l'Université de Strasbourg*
Commander Ian Forbes, DSC, RN
F. G. S. Parker, M.A.

HARRAP'S New Standard

FRENCH AND ENGLISH DICTIONARY

by

J. E. MANSION, M.A.

Revised and Edited by

R. P. L. LEDÉSERT, *Licencié-ès-Lettres*, *Licencié en Droit*,

and

MARGARET LEDÉSERT, M.A.

VOLUME THREE

ENGLISH—FRENCH

A—K

HARRAP

LONDON AND PARIS

Published in Great Britain
by HARRAP LIMITED
19–23 Ludgate Hill, London EC4M 7PD
Fourth impression: 1983

ISBN 0 245-51859-2

Text set in 8/7½ pt Photon Times, printed and bound in Great Britain at The Pitman Press, Bath

Preface

"Forty Years On"

The late J. E. Mansion, author of *Harrap's Standard French English Dictionary*, began work on his project in the years immediately preceding World War I, and Part I (French–English) was published in 1934. Part II (English–French) appeared in February 1939 and, precisely forty years on, in February 1979, we completed the manuscript of the revised edition of it. Research work on the revision of the dictionary as a whole was begun in 1945, when a card index was compiled by the wearisome task of cutting up copies of the original edition. In a very short space of time thousands of new cards had been added, representing words not appearing in the original dictionary and new acceptations of existing words. The mass of new material increased with even greater rapidity once the compilation of the manuscript of the first part was begun, as in a very large percentage of cases an addition to it meant a new card for the second part. The new material has been derived from a number of sources: the examination of the most modern unilingual dictionaries; the reading of periodicals and recently published books; the study of advertisements and public notices; suggestions sent in by users of the dictionary; and words or expressions gleaned quite fortuitously in the course of conversation. We should like in this context to express our gratitude to our friends living in and around Holyport, where we have our permanent home, and Les Pilles, the village in southern France where we have a house that was the scene of much of our labours, for the help they so frequently gave us, often unconsciously, in finding the word we were looking for.

When the French–English part of the *Harrap's New Standard French and English Dictionary* was published in the autumn of 1972 we had already begun work on the compilation of the second part. Our preliminary studies and consultations had already confirmed our fears that we were undertaking a task even more formidable than the revision of the first part, so that it was hardly encouraging when some of our friends (not lexicographers) said to us, "Well, now that you've done the French–English the English–French shouldn't take all that much time!". If one is compiling a bilingual technical dictionary it is true to say that the second part is to a considerable extent, though by no means completely, the mirror image of the first. When one is tackling the second part of a large *general* bilingual dictionary, there are additional complications; the straight translations of scientific words or the names of concrete objects will have in the main been solved in the compilation of the first part; but a very important element in a general dictionary is the translation of idiomatic phrases, only some of which can be rendered by an equally idiomatic phrase in the second language. For this English–French part we have therefore devoted a considerable amount of time to studying idioms from the standpoint of English usage, particularly in view of the large number of expressions which have been introduced into the language since 1939, and of the fact that many phrases which were Americanisms then are standard English in Britain today.

A further complication of the English language is that it is the mother tongue not only of most of the British Isles, but also of Australia and New Zealand, almost the entire North American continent and much of South Africa. This naturally implies regional differences of vocabulary and usage, and we have endeavoured to increase considerably our selection of words used in these countries, going beyond the widely known American **elevator** (lift), **automobile** (car), **gasoline** (petrol), the South African **outspan** or the Australian slang **to waltz Matilda** made popular in Britain by the song *Waltzing Matilda*. American vocabulary presents further difficulties as there are words which are used throughout the North American continent, while others are current only in the United States or in Canada; we have distinguished them as far as possible by the symbols *NAm:*, *U.S:*, and *Can:* respectively. Moreover, the English spoken in different parts of the globe differs at times not only in the vocabulary but in structure. It is easy to record that the Americans have two past participles for the verb **to get, got** and **gotten**; or that they **fill out a form** while the British **fill in a form**. But what cannot adequately be recorded in a bilingual dictionary is the somewhat greater formality of American written English. Take, for example, the frequent use of the subjunctive where British usage favours a modal auxiliary. In an American detective novel, written largely in conversation style, we found, "It was important to him that his son follow him (in the business)". In Britain one would say, "It was important to him that his son should succeed (or follow) him (in the business)".

No dictionary can contain a complete word list, and selection must always be to a certain extent a matter of personal choice. What we have aimed at is to produce a work of manageable dimensions and of wide scope. The material added includes words and expressions introduced into the language since 1939, with particular attention to modern technical, scientific and industrial development. Modern colloquial and idiomatic expressions have been introduced, and some of the original examples which seem stilted or oldfashioned deleted. This must not be taken to mean that all words or expressions which are not in current use have been removed; this dictionary is intended not only for users who require an extensive vocabulary of modern English, but also for those reading literary, scientific or technical works published in the past. Three category indications are used for such words or expressions: *Lit:* denotes words occurring only in literary works or formal style; *A:* is used for obsolete or archaic words and expressions, and *O:* for obsolescent ones, now used frequently only by the older generations.

We have included a wide range of colloquialisms (marked *F:*) and a large number of widely used slang words and expressions (marked *P:*), together with a few vulgar words (marked *V:*) which, though not in use in polite conversation, are widely encountered. We should like to point out that *P:* is also used for expressions which betray uneducated speech, and that *P:Pej:* indicates words used derogatively, usually with a deliberate intention to hurt or insult, for example **nigger, wog,** or **Yid**. We have also introduced the abbreviation *Fig:* where words are not used in their literal sense, to distinguish them from colloquialisms.

It is perhaps important to indicate where economies in the word list have been introduced, either by deletion from the original dictionary or by deliberate omission. It would clearly be impossible to list all the compound words and combined forms deriving from prefixes such as **auto-, anti-, psycho-, sub-,** etc., so a broad representative selection has been made of the most widely used and those which present difficulties in translation which the user might not be able to solve by reference to comprehensive or specialized unilingual dictionaries. Proper names (personal, geographical, or historical) have often been omitted where they have exactly the same form in both languages, unless they are used attributively or occur in some idiomatic phrase or traditional saying. Some of the less well known proper names appearing in the original dictionary have been deleted, as have some of the more obscure classical allusions, the study of the classics being less widespread than it was forty years ago. Lengthy explanations in the original dictionary of the origins of words or phrases have been severely pruned or cut out altogether, on the principle that a bilingual dictionary is not an encyclopaedia.

Orthography

Orthography also presented its problems. It would obviously increase the length of the dictionary beyond reasonable limits were we to give all possible alternatives, so the spelling given in our headwords is that which appears to be the most current in the British Isles, though we have listed what seem to be the most widely used variants, and have naturally recorded American spellings which show considerable differences with British usage, e.g. **plow** (plough), **maneuver** (manoeuvre), **catalog** (catalogue). We would, moreover, use such spellings in an example with an American background or illustrating an American construction. For words with the alternative suffixes **-ise** or **-ize** and **-isation** or **-ization** the forms **-ize** and **-ization** have been adopted throughout, as, though English usage is about equally divided between the two, American practice favours **-ize** and **-ization**. To save space, however, we have listed only the British spelling for words for which the American variants fall within the scope of clearly defined rules, and draw the attention of the American user or the French user more conversant with the American form of spelling to the following salient differences:

(*a*) the British use of the final **-our** where the American usage is **-or** (e.g. *U.K:* behavi**our,** col**our,** fav**our;** *U.S:* behavi**or,** col**or,** fav**or**);

(*b*) the British use of the final **-re** where American usage is **-er** (e.g. *U.K:* theat**re,** kilomet**re,** cent**re;** *U.S:* theat**er,** kilomet**er,** cent**er**); in this context it should be noted that British English distinguishes between **metre,** a measure of length (or a term of prosody), and **meter,** a machine (as in **gas meter, speedometer,** etc.);

(*c*) the doubling of the final **l** in British usage before a vowel in derivative adjectives or participles, irrespective of accentuation (e.g. *U.K:* woo**ll**en, trave**ll**ing; *U.S:* woo**l**en, trave**l**ing);

(*d*) the single **l** in British usage in derivatives before a final syllable beginning with a consonant, where American usage is **ll** (*e.g. U.K:* ski**l**ful, enro**l**ment; *U.S:* ski**ll**ful, enro**ll**ment);

(*e*) the British use of a final **-ce** in certain words for which the American usage is **-se** (*e.g. U.K:* defen**ce,** preten**ce;** *U.S:* defen**se,** preten**se**);

(*f*) the greater, though not exclusive, use in scientific words of **ae** where American usage prefers **e** (*e.g. U.K:* an**ae**mia; *U.S:* an**e**mia);

(*g*) the British preference for **ph** in scientific words such as sul**ph**ur, sul**ph**uric, in contrast with the American use of **f** (sul**f**ur, sul**f**uric); in recent years there have been some indications that Britain might be about to follow the American lead, but the **ph** spelling still appears to be usual one.

In the examples quoted above we have described the American spellings as *U.S:* rather than *NAm:* as Canadian usage seems still to be divided between the two possible spellings.

Layout

Users familiar with the layout conceived by Mr Mansion in the original edition of *Harrap's Standard French and English Dictionary* will notice a certain number of changes. We have maintained the minor differences introduced into the French–English part of abandoning the use of capital letters in the text except where they are essential and, in order to save space, representing headwords which appear in examples in exactly the same form by their initial letter only. But the radical change has been the presentation of the headwords in strictly alphabetical order. In the original dictionary adverbs ending in **-ly** came at the end of the adjectives from which they were formed, verbs were followed by their compound verbs and participial adjectives or nouns, and nouns and adjectives were followed by hyphenated derivative nouns or adjectives, irrespective of alphabetical order. Adverbs ending in **-ly**, participial adjectives and nouns are now to be found in their correct alphabetical position, but the compound verbs still follow the main verb, constituting the one real exception to strict alphabetical order. This decision was taken because the user will obviously wish at times, in order to find an adequate translation of a phrase, to consult concurrently both the simple verb and the compound, and alphabetical order would often place them very far apart; if the user has any doubts about this statement, he has only to consult the text to see the number of intervening articles between the verb **go** and the alphabetical place of **go up**—though we admit that this is an extreme example.

The problem of the hyphenated nouns and adjectives is far more complex. It is true that the hyphen is used much less today than it was forty years ago, and many of these formerly hyphenated words are now written in a single word, so that they naturally transfer to their alphabetical position. The same applies to certain adjectives which retain the traditional hyphen, *e.g.* **blue-eyed, white-haired,** and nouns or adjectives for which most people (at least in Britain) continue to prefer the hyphen because of the juxtaposition of two vowels or two consonants, *e.g.* **co-operative, co-ownership, de-icer, ferro-alloy, book-keeping, wash-house,** etc. But the real problem is the fact that there are no strict rules for the use of the hyphen in English. As far as compound adjectives are concerned, the use or omission of the hyphen appears to vary according to the preference of the writer, although the scales are tipped in favour of the hyphen; here it is perhaps pertinent to remark that in the case of a compound adjective consisting of **well** plus a participle, the use of the hyphen is incorrect (though not infrequently seen) if the adjective follows the verb, and optional if it precedes the noun, *e.g.* **the phrase was well chosen; a well chosen** (or **well-chosen**) **phrase**. There are, moreover, cases where a hyphen is absolutely essential to make the meaning clear; for example, **a little used car** is a small vehicle which has seen service on the roads, while **a little-used car** is a vehicle of any size, even a Rolls, which spends most of its life in the garage.

Hyphenated nouns are fairly rare in modern English; when they occur the users of the dictionary will find them in their proper alphabetical place, as they will those formerly hyphenated and now written in one word. Where the usage is not yet established, and this is often the case with recently coined compound nouns, we have occasionally bracketed a hyphen (*e.g.* **spin(-)off**). There remains the not inconsiderable number of formerly hyphenated words now written as two separate words. To what extent can they be considered as nouns in their own right and listed as headwords? In spite of the practice in several dictionaries, including *Webster's Third New International*, we consider that in many cases the "word" involved consists of one noun prefaced by another used attributively, and such "words" are listed with the attributive uses of the first noun. The user, however, should note that certain "two-word words" have been placed under the second element, where they appear to be classified more appropriately. A long list of examples would be unlikely to prove helpful, but the problems involved can be explained by examining **back-door,** *s*., a form which would not be used in modern English. There are four possibilities:

(*a*) **backdoor,** *s*. Though this is a logical development we have rarely seen it used except adjectivally.
(*b*) **back door,** *s*. But why should **back door** qualify as a noun any more than **oak door** or **green door?**
(*c*) Place it under **back,** adjective, with **back room,** etc.
(*d*) Place it under **door,** in juxtaposition to **front door.**

Either (*c*) or (*d*) is acceptable, and in this particular case it might have been preferable that the example should appear under both **back** and **door;** the reason why it is only under **door** is that with the example of the figurative use the entry is too long to appear in both places.

As far as the arrangement of the material under each headword is concerned, we have continued Mr. Mansion's plan of using the subdivisions **1., 2., 3.,** etc. to denote important differences in the meaning or use of a word, and (*a*), (*b*), (*c*), etc. to show differences of lesser importance. In general the divisions (i), (ii), (iii), etc. are used to show different meanings of the same phrase (*e.g.* **vital statistics,** (i) statistiques démographiques; (ii) *F:* mensurations (d'une femme)), though in longer articles and in the case of the compound verbs they may occur as subdivisions of (*a*), (*b*), etc.; any further subdivisions needed are then marked (*α*), (*β*), (*γ*), etc. In addition the divisions **I, II, III,** etc. are also used when the headword in question has several different grammatical functions such as adjective, adverb and/or noun, and in long articles to separate the transitive and intransitive verbs or the simple and compound verbs.

We have virtually dispensed with cross references; they can be very exasperating to the user, and their inclusion could not but delay the publication of a large dictionary, as it would be impossible to check them all with any degree of accuracy until the whole of the manuscript was completed. As far as the reference to irregular plurals and parts of irregular verbs are concerned, we consider that the users of *Harrap's New Standard French and English Dictionary* are sufficiently familiar with the English language not to need them. The longer idiomatic phrases are listed under the headword which to us appears to be the key word of the phrase, though shorter examples often appear under each of the main headwords concerned. There are, however, some cross references for variants in spelling of a headword when the article is of considerable length.

Editorial Methods

For the compilation of the manuscript of the dictionary we had a team of six sub-editors working with us, the maximum which appeared practical if a reasonable uniformity in layout and style were to be achieved. We were particularly fortunate in having as members of our team H. R. ("John") Elphick and his wife Flora, both of whom worked with Mr Mansion on the compilation of the original dictionary. Their personal experience of the principles underlying the conception of the original work has been of the utmost value.

The orchestration of the physical production of the work was not without its problems. As substantial sections of the manuscript were completed, they were sent to two readers, Dr Reginald Bowen and Mr F. G. S. Parker, to check for inconsistencies, errors and omissions. The manuscript was then sent letter by letter to the printers, who duly supplied us with galley proofs. The galley proofs were then read, the corrections collated, and the work set up in page proof letter by letter. From the time that each letter was in page, only minor amendments could be made, and additions were possible only if some existing item of lesser importance were deleted.

Acknowledgements

Though the compilation of the manuscript has been the work of ourselves and our six sub-editors, the task would have been impossible without the assistance of the large army of helpers working in the Harrap offices and in all parts of the globe who have over the years assisted us in our research work. Some of them have worked with us for a relatively short time, others for a considerable number of years, and we would like to express our sincere thanks to them. We cannot name them all, but among those who were members of the office research team we wish to mention particularly Mr P. H. Collin, Mrs Françoise Collin, Mrs E. A. H. Strick, Mrs Valerie Deane, Mlle Christine Fontan and Miss Vivien Flynn. Outside contributors to whom we owe special thanks include MM. Jean Bétesta, Michel Ginguay and Roland Ginguay for their valuable assistance in the military and technical fields; Commander Ian Forbes for his help with naval and nautical terms; Mr H. T. Porter and M. F. Bourlière for a valuable contribution on the names of birds; Mrs Patricia Forbes for additions to the vocabulary of natural history and the petroleum industry; M. D. Fortin (Canada) for his contribution to agricultural terms; M. J. Augier for his technical advice; Dr I. Feldblum who supplied us with medical terms; and to our late advisers M. Marcel Ferlin and Professor Lewis Harmer, whose contributions ranged over a wide field.

We also thank Mr C. B. Johnson, Mrs Aileen Kent and Mr Olaf Anderson, former Chairman of George G. Harrap & Co., for their help in reading the proofs; and, last but by no means least, The Pitman Press for setting the dictionary.

September, 1979

RENÉ LEDÉSERT
MARGARET LEDÉSERT

Préface

Quarante ans plus tard

J. E. Mansion (1870–1942), auteur du *Harrap's Standard French and English Dictionary*, a entrepris son travail dans les années qui ont immédiatement précédé la guerre de 1914–1918. La première partie (français-anglais) a été publiée en 1934. La deuxième partie (anglais-français) a paru en février 1939 et, exactement quarante ans plus tard, en février 1979, nous avons complété le manuscrit de l'édition révisée de cette deuxième partie. C'est en 1945 que nous avons commencé la révision du dictionnaire Mansion, par la constitution d'un fichier de base: travail fastidieux qui a consisté à découper mot par mot l'édition originale pour établir une fiche par mot-clef. Ce fichier était déjà fort important, mais nos recherches l'ont rapidement augmenté de milliers de fiches nouvelles représentant soit des mots introduits dans la langue depuis 1939, soit les sens nouveaux de certains mots qui figuraient déjà dans l'édition originale. Pour la partie anglais-français, les mots ou exemples à ajouter ont augmenté plus rapidement encore lorsque la partie français-anglais a été commencée, une addition à la première partie entraînant très souvent la constitution d'une fiche nouvelle pour la seconde partie. Ces additions proviennent de sources variées: l'étude des dictionnaires anglais-anglais les plus récents; la lecture de revues et de livres récemment publiés; l'examen des prospectus publicitaires et des avis au public; des suggestions envoyées par les usagers du dictionnaire; et des mots et des expressions recueillis par hasard au cours de la conversation. Nous voudrions ici exprimer notre reconnaissance aux amis qui nous ont souvent aidés, parfois inconsciemment, dans nos recherches pour trouver le mot juste, ceux qui vivent à Holyport où se trouve notre demeure permanente, ou ceux des Pilles, village du midi de la France où notre maison a vu se dérouler beaucoup de nos travaux.

Quand la première partie (français-anglais) du *Harrap's New Standard French and English Dictionary* a été publiée à l'automne 1972, nous avions déjà commencé le travail de compilation de la deuxième partie. Nos recherches avaient confirmé nos craintes, car nous étions déjà conscients du fait que la révision de la deuxième partie représentait une tâche infiniment plus vaste que la révision de la première partie. Il était alors plutôt décourageant d'entendre nos amis nous dire: "Maintenant que vous avez terminé la partie français–anglais, la partie anglais–français devrait être rapidement terminée". Quand on fait un dictionnaire bilingue technique il est exact de dire que la seconde partie est jusqu'à un certain point le miroir de la première. Mais, quand on entreprend la seconde partie d'un gros dictionnaire bilingue général, il y a des complications supplémentaires. La traduction d'un nom scientifique ou d'un objet (comme une table) a été généralement résolue lors de la compilation de la première partie, mais un élément très important d'un dictionnaire général est la traduction d'idiotismes, dont quelques-uns seulement se traduisent par un idiotisme analogue dans la deuxième langue. Un grand nombre de nouvelles expressions se sont introduites dans la langue anglaise depuis 1939, et beaucoup d'idiotismes qui étaient alors des américanismes sont maintenant d'usage courant en Grande-Bretagne. C'est pourquoi, dans cette seconde partie anglais–français, nous avons consacré beaucoup de temps à l'étude de l'évolution de ces idiotismes dans l'anglais britannique actuel.

L'anglais est la langue maternelle, outre la plupart des habitants des Îles Britanniques, des Australiens, des Néo-Zélandais, des habitants de la plus grande partie de l'Amérique du Nord et d'une grande partie de l'Afrique du Sud, ce qui complique singulièrement la tâche du lexicographe. Ceci implique des différences régionales de vocabulaire et nous avons donc essayé d'augmenter considérablement le nombre des mots utilisés dans ces divers pays. Le vocabulaire américain présente des difficultés supplémentaires, car certains mots sont utilisés dans l'ensemble du continent nord-américain, tandis que d'autres sont courants seulement aux États-Unis ou bien au Canada; nous les avons distingués autant que possible par les symboles *NAm:, U.S:* ou *Can:* selon le cas. De plus, l'anglais parlé dans les différentes parties du globe est différent non seulement par le vocabulaire mais parfois par la syntaxe. Il est facile de mentionner que les Américans ont deux formes du participe passé pour le verbe **to get, got** et **gotten,** qu'en Amérique on dit **fill out a form,** tandis que les Britanniques disent **fill in a form.** Néanmoins il est impossible d'indiquer dans un dictionnaire bilingue certaines nuances, par exemple le style plus formel que l'on trouve parfois dans l'américain écrit, comme l'usage plus répandu du subjonctif dans des phrases où l'anglais britannique emploie de préférence un verbe auxiliaire à valeur modale. Citons par exemple une phrase prise dans un roman policier américain: "it was important to him that his son follow him (in the business)" (il tenait beaucoup à ce que son fils prenne sa suite (dans l'affaire)); en Grande-Bretagne on dirait plutôt: "it was important to him that his son should succeed (or follow) him (in the business)".

Nul dictionnaire ne peut contenir tout le vocabulaire d'une langue; et les mots qui y figurent représentent jusqu'à un certain point le choix personnel de l'auteur. Nous avons essayé de faire un ouvrage de dimensions acceptables dont le vocabulaire soit aussi étendu que possible. Nos additions comprennent des mots et des expressions qui sont introduits dans la langue depuis 1939 surtout en ce que concerne les progrès scientifiques et techniques. Nous avons ajouté des idiotismes et des expressions familières modernes et nous avons supprimé certains des exemples originaux que semblaient désuets ou forcés. Cela ne signifie pas, cependant, que tous les mots ou expressions qui ne sont plus d'usage courant ont disparu. Ce dictionnaire s'adresse non seulement aux usagers qui désirent un vocabulaire étendu de l'anglais moderne, mais aussi à ceux qui lisent des ouvrages littéraires, scientifiques ou techniques publiés dans le passé. Il y a trois symboles utilisés pour avertir l'usager: *Lit:* indique des mots employés essentiellement dans des ouvrages littéraires; *A:* les mots ou expressions archaïques; *O:* ceux qui ont vieilli et qui sont utilisés seulement par les générations plus âgées.

Le dictionnaire contient un nombre considérable d'expressions familières (*F:*) et populaires (*P:*), ainsi que quelques expressions de style trivial (*V:*) qui se rencontrent assez souvent. Il faut ajouter que le symbole *P:* s'emploie également pour des expressions qui trahissent un manque d'instruction et que *P:Pej:* indique des mots utilisés dans un sens péjoratif, généralement avec l'intention de blesser ou d'insulter, par exemple **nigger, wog, yid.** Nous avons ajouté le symbole *Fig:* pour indiquer un sens figuré d'un mot.

Il est peut-être de quelque importance d'indiquer où nous avons limité le nombre des mots-clefs, soit en supprimant certains mots qui figuraient dans le dictionnaire original, soit en limitant le nombre d'additions. Il serait certainement impossible de faire la liste de tous les mots composés qui dérivent de préfixes, *p.ex.*, **auto-, anti-, psycho-, sub-,** etc.; par conséquent nous avons fait un choix de ceux qui sont les plus usités, ou de ceux qui présentent des difficultés de traduction. Des noms propres (de personnes, géographiques, historiques) ne figurent souvent pas quand ils ont exactement la même forme dans les deux langues, à moins qu'ils ne soient employés comme attributs ou qu'ils ne se rencontrent dans des idiotismes (*p.ex.*, **to meet one's Waterloo**). Nous avons supprimé aussi un certain nombre de noms propres peu usités, ainsi que des allusions classiques peu connues, puisque l'étude des classiques est maintenant moins répandue qu'il y a quarante ans. Certaines longues explications du dictionnaire original concernant l'origine des mots ou des idiotismes ont été élaguées ou supprimées, car nous avons adopté le principe qu'un dictionnaire bilingue n'est pas une encyclopédie.

Orthographe

L'orthographe nous a conduit à différents problèmes. Si nous avions mis toutes les variantes possibles pour chaque mot le dictionnaire aurait atteint des proportions démesurées; par conséquent l'orthographe donnée pour les mots-clefs suit l'usage britannique, y compris les variantes les plus usitées. Nous avons naturellement noté l'orthographe américaine qui diffère considérablement de l'usage britannique, par exemple **plow** (plough), **maneuver** (manoeuvre), **catalog** (catalogue), etc.; et nous nous servons de l'orthographe américaine dans les exemples dont le contexte est américain. Dans le cas des suffixes **-ise** ou **ize** et **isation** ou **-ization** nous avons retenu les formes **ize** et **ization,** car l'usage anglais hésite entre les deux orthographes, alors que l'usage américain préfère **ize** et **ization.**

L'usager trouvera seulement l'orthographe britannique des mots pour lesquels l'usage américain suit des règles déterminées et nous attirons l'attention des Français plus habitués à l'orthographe américaine sur les différences suivantes:

(*a*) l'usage britannique de la terminaison -**our** alors que l'américain se sert de -**or** (*U.K:* behavi**our,** col**our,** fav**our;** *U.S:* behavi**or,** col**or,** fav**or**);

(*b*) la terminaison britannique **-re** est remplacée par **-er** an américain (*U.K:* theat**re,** kilomet**re,** cent**re;** *U.S:* theat**er,** kilomet**er,** cent**er**); dans ce contexte il faut noter que l'anglais britannique distingue entre **metre** pour signifier une mesure de longueur ou un terme de prosodie et **meter** pour un appareil (**gas meter, speedometer,** etc.);

(*c*) dans l'usage britannique la lettre **l** est redoublée quand la dernière syllabe commence par une voyelle, quelle que soit l'accentuation, alors que l'usage américain met un seul **l** (*U.K:* woo**ll**en, trave**ll**ing; *U.S:* woo**l**en, trave**l**ing);

(*d*) l'usage britannique met un seul **l** devant une syllabe terminale commençant par une consonne, alors que l'usage américain demande **ll** (*U.K:* skilful, enrolment; *U.S:* ski**ll**ful, enro**ll**ment);

(*e*) pour certains mots qui en anglais britannique ont la terminaison -**ce** l'américain écrit -**se** (*U.S:* defen**ce,** preten**ce;** *U.S:* defen**se,** preten**se**);

(*f*) l'usage plus généralisé dans le vocabulaire scientifique de **ae** en anglais britannique alors qu'en Amérique on préfère **e** (*U.K:* an**ae**mia; *U.S:* an**e**mia);

(*g*) dans le vocabulaire scientifique l'usage britannique est de mettre **ph** dans, par exemple, **sulphur, sulphuric,** alors que l'orthographe américaine est **sulfur, sulfuric.**

Dans les exemples ci-dessus nous avons mis *U.S:* et non pas *NAm:* parce que l'usage canadien semble suivre soit l'orthographe américaine soit l'orthographe britannique.

Disposition typographique

L'usager qui connaît la disposition typographique de l'édition originale du *Harrap's Standard French and English Dictionary* remarquera un certain nombre de changements. Nous avons conservé les petites modifications faites dans la première partie (français–anglais) en supprimant les majuscules dans le texte sauf dans les cas où elles sont essentielles et en représentant les mots-clefs dans les articles seulement par leur lettre initiale lorsque leur orthographe ne comporte pas de variante. Le changement radical est la présentation des mots clefs dans un ordre strictement alphabétique, exception faite pour les verbes à postposition (**come down, go away, take up,** etc.). Dans l'édition originale les adverbes se terminant en -**ly** suivaient les adjectifs dont ils dérivaient, les verbes étaient suivis par les verbes à postposition et les participes pris substantivement ou adjectivement, les substantifs ou adjectifs par des noms ou des adjectifs écrits avec un trait d'union, système qui pouvait déconcerter l'usager qui les cherchait dans l'ordre alphabétique.

L'usage du trait d'union a présenté de nombreuses difficultés, car il n'existe pas de règle absolue en anglais à cet égard. Le trait d'union s'emploie beaucoup moins qu'il y a quarante ans et beaucoup de mots à trait d'union sont maintenant écrits en un seul mot, de sorte qu'ils se trouvent transférés automatiquement à leur place alphabétique. C'est également le cas de certains adjectifs toujours écrits avec un trait d'union, par exemple **blue-eyed, white-haired** et des substantifs ou adjectifs que la plupart des gens, au moins en Grande-Bretagne, écrivent avec un trait d'union à cause de la juxtaposition de deux voyelles ou de deux consonnes, par exemple

co-operative, co-ownership, de-icer, ferro-alloy, book-keeping, wash-house, etc. En ce qui concerne les adjectifs composés, l'emploi du trait d'union varie selon l'auteur, quoique, d'une manière générale, on semble préférer mettre un trait d'union. Il est peut-être à propos de dire que dans le cas d'un adjectif composé comprenant **well** plus un participe, l'usage du trait d'union est incorrect si l'adjectif suit le verbe, mais permis, sans être obligatoire, s'il le précède (*p.ex.*, **the phrase was well chosen, a well chosen** (ou **well-chosen**) **phrase**). Il y a en outre des cas où le trait d'union est absolument essentiel pour différencier deux sens; par exemple, **a little used car** est une petite voiture qui a beaucoup roulé tandis que **a little-used car** est une voiture de n'importe quelle taille, même une Rolls, qui passe la plupart de son temps au garage.

Les substantifs à trait d'union sont plutôt rares dans l'anglais moderne; l'usager les trouvera à leur place alphabétique. Là où l'usage n'est pas encore établi, ce qui est souvent le cas pour les noms composés de formation récente, nous avons parfois mis un trait d'union entre parenthèses (*p.ex.* **spin(-)off**). Il reste toujours un nombre considérable de mots écrits avec un trait d'union autrefois et maintenant en deux mots séparés. Doit-on les traiter comme de vrais substantifs et en faire des mots-clefs? En dépit de ce que l'on trouve dans certains dictionnaires, y compris *Webster's Third New International*, nous considérons que souvent le "mot" en question comprend deux substantifs dont l'un s'emploie attributivement; dans ces cas le "mot" figure sous le mot-clef qui forme son premier élément ou, si plus approprié, le deuxième. On peut éclaircir tant soit peu ce problème en examinant le mot **back-door,** qu'aujourd'hui on n'écrit plus avec un trait d'union. Quatre solutions se présentent:

(*a*) l'écrire en un seul mot: **backdoor.** Ceci semble logique, mais cette forme ne se rencontre que rarement et seulement dans un sens attributif;

(*b*) mettre (en deux mots) un mot-clef **back door;** mais ces deux mots ne constituent pas un vrai substantif, pas plus que **green door** ou **oak door;**

(*c*) le mettre sous **back,** adjectif, comme on l'a fait pour **back room,** etc.;

(*d*) le mettre sous **door,** en juxtaposition avec **front door.** La meilleure solution aurait peut-être été de le mettre sous **back** et également sous **door.** La raison pour laquelle nous avons opté pour **door** seulement est que le sens figuré de l'expression y est l'objet d'un long exemple.

Nous n'avons pas changé la classification établie par J. E. Mansion pour la présentation du texte: les différences importantes du sens ou de l'usage d'un mot sont indiquées par les numéros **1., 2., 3.,** etc., tandis que (*a*), (*b*), (*c*), etc. montrent des différences moindres. D'une manière générale (i), (ii), (iii), etc. marquent seulement les différents sens d'une locution (*p.ex.* **vital statistics,** (i) statistiques démographiques; (ii) *F:* mensurations (d'une femme)), mais dans de longs articles nous nous en sommes servis parfois comme subdivisions de (*a*), (*b*), etc.; dans ces cas nous avons utilisé (*α*), (*β*), (*γ*), etc. pour indiquer les différents sens des locutions. Pour les très longs articles nous avons conservé les sub-divisions **I, II, III,** etc. quand le mot en question a plusieurs fonctions grammaticales: verbe transitif et intransitif et verbes à postposition, ou adjectif, adverbe et substantif.

Exception faite d'un certain nombre de variantes orthographiques, nous avons éliminé les renvois, qui peuvent être exaspérants pour l'usager; d'autre part, en eussions-nous mis, la publication du dictionnaire en eût été retardée, la vérification de tous avant la terminaison du manuscrit étant presque impossible. Nous avons supprimé également tout renvoi aux pluriels irréguliers et aux formes de la conjugaison des verbes, car nous estimons que l'usager du *Harrap's New Standard French and English Dictionary* connaît assez bien la langue anglaise pour ne pas en avoir besoin. Les idiotismes paraissent en général sous un seul mot-clef, celui qui nous semble le plus significatif de l'expression en question.

Méthodes de travail

Une équipe de six rédacteurs travaillaient avec nous à la compilation du manuscrit, ce qui était, à notre avis, le nombre maximum assurant le plus d'uniformité possible. Nous avons été particulièrement heureux d'avoir comme membres de notre équipe M. et Mme H. R. Elphick, qui l'un et l'autre ont travaillé avec M. Mansion à la compilation du dictionaire original. Leur connaissance personnelle des méthodes utilisées dans cet ouvrage a été un apport précieux.

Afin de pouvoir publier ce nouveau dictionnaire dans un délai raisonnable, nous avons dû travailler lettre par lettre. Au fur et à mesure que nous avions rédigé le manuscrit d'une lettre, nous l'avons envoyé à deux collaborateurs, MM.Reginald Bowen et F. G. S. Parker, qui ont vérifié le texte. Le manuscrit a alors été envoyé lettre par lettre à l'imprimeur qui nous a expédié les épreuves en placard. Celles-ci ont été corrigées alors par plusieurs lecteurs, et quand leurs corrections ont été collationnées, l'ouvrage a été mis en page. Dès qu'une lettre était en page, seuls des changements d'importance typographique minime ont pu être effectués et des additions n'ont été possibles que quand nous avons pu les mettre à la place d'articles moins importants.

Remerciements

Quoique la compilation du manuscrit ait été notre travail et celui de nos six rédacteurs, notre tâche aurait été impossible sans l'aide, au cours des années, de tous les collaborateurs qui ont fait un gros travail de recherche et nous tenons à les en remercier. Parmi ceux qui ont travaillé dans les bureaux de la maison Harrap, nous voudrions mentionner particulièrement M. P. H. Collin, Mme Françoise Collin, Mme E. A. H. Strick, Mme Valerie Deane, Mlle Christine Fontan et Mlle Vivien Flynn. Parmi nos collaborateurs extérieurs, qui ont été très nombreux, nous remercions tout particulièrement MM. Jean Bétesta, Michel Ginguay et Roland Ginguay pour leur aide surtout dans des domaines militaires et techniques; Commander Ian Forbes pour sa contribution aux expressions maritimes; MM. H. T. Porter et F. Bourlière qui nous ont apporté une contribution importante pour les noms des oiseaux; Mme Patricia Forbes qui nous a fourni un vocabulaire étendu dans le domaine de l'histoire naturelle et de l'industrie du pétrole; M. D. Fortin (Canada) qui nous a fourni des termes agricoles; M. J. Augier, pour des termes techniques; le Dr I. Feldblum qui nous a aidés pour le vocabulaire médical; et nos anciens collaborateurs, maintenant décédés, M. Marcel Ferlin et le Professeur Lewis Harmer.

Nous remercions également M. C. B. Johnson, Mme Aileen Kent et M. Olaf Anderson, ancien directeur général de la maison Harrap, de nous avoir aidés à la lecture des épreuves; et The Pitman Press qui a imprimé l'ouvrage.

Septembre, 1979

RENÉ LEDÉSERT
MARGARET LEDÉSERT

Principal Works Consulted—Principaux Ouvrages Consultés

Webster's Third New International Dictionary
Webster's New Collegiate Dictionary (1974)
Supplement to the Oxford English Dictionary
The Concise Oxford Dictionary of Current English (1976)
Oxford Advanced Learner's Dictionary of Current English (1976)
Chambers Twentieth Century Dictionary (1972)
Chambers Dictionary of Science and Technology (1971)
The Penguin English Dictionary
The Penguin Dictionaries of Biology, Building, Civil Engineering, Computers, Electronics, Geology, Geography, Psychology and Science
The Senior Dictionary of Canadian English (Gage, Toronto, 1973)
H. W. Fowler: A Dictionary of Modern English Usage (Gower's revised edition 1965) (O.U.P.)
Daniel Jones: Everyman's English Pronouncing Dictionary (revised by A. C. Gimson) (Dent)

P. Robert: Dictionnaire alphabétique et analogique de la langue française (with supplement) (Société du nouveau Littré)
Le Petit Robert
Grand Larousse Encyclopédique (and supplement)
Grand Larousse de la langue française
Petit Larousse
Dictionnaire Encyclopédique (Quillet)

Stedman's Medical Dictionary (E. & S. Livingstone Ltd)
Butterworth's Medical Dictionary
Monkhouse: A Dictionary of Geography (Edward Arnold)
L. Dudley Stamp: A glossary of Geographical Terms (Longman)
P. George: Dictionnaire de la Géographie (Presses Universitaires de France)
H. Baulig: Vocabulaire franco-anglo-allemand de Géomorphologie (Soc. d'édition: les Belles Lettres)
J. Noorduijn en Zoon & N. Gorinchen: Geological Nomenclature (Ed. A. A. G. Schieferdecker)
Camille & Dehaine: Dictionary of Data Processing (Harrap)
M. Ginguay: Dictionnaire d'Informatique (Masson, Paris)
G. A. Marks & C. B. Johnson: Harrap's English–French Dictionary of Slang & Colloquialisms
E. Partridge: A Dictionary of Historical Slang (Penguin)

Pronunciation

WHILE we wish to emphasize from the outset that this is not a phonetic dictionary, we have maintained the principle adopted by Mr Mansion in the original edition of giving the pronunciation of each headword, *tant bien que mal*, by means of phonetic symbols. From the point of view of the user whose mother tongue is not English, some guidance is obviously desirable for a language in which the words **bough**, **cough**, **dough**, **rough**, **through** and **thorough** are pronounced respectively [bau], [kɔf], [dou], [rʌf], [θru:] and ['θʌrə], and in which the word spelt **bow** can be [bau] or [bou] according to the meaning. Another difficulty is the change of stress according to the part of speech; for example, **permit** is pronounced ['pə:mit] when a noun and [pə'mit] when a verb. Native English speakers, too, have their difficulties, especially for the less well known scientific words; here, we may add, there is often no real solution; for example, the pronunciation by a group of students of a recently invented scientific word may very well depend on the pronunciation used by their professor. This difficulty can also occur in highly literary language; a graduate in English may easily hesitate over the pronunciation of the word **soughing**, in a phrase like **the wind soughing through the branches**.

A further difficulty about the pronunciation of words in isolation in English is sentence stress. In rapid speech the virtual disappearance of certain vowels, consonants or even syllables is not necessarily an indication of uneducated or even slovenly speech; ['hi:wəzəkən'tempri (*not* kən'tempərəri) əv'main] (**he was a contemporary of mine**) is unlikely to shock even the purist; and while many novelists write **'im** for **him** to indicate uneducated speech, we wonder how many people when speaking rapidly would pronounce the **h** in **don't tell him** [dount'telim], as opposed to **tell him, but not her** [tel'himbətnɔt'hə:]. As in general the phonetics given are intended primarily for the user whose mother tongue is not English, we have given mainly the more careful pronunciation of the word in question, as the use of this cannot constitute a real fault.

The phonetic symbols used are those of the International Phonetic Association as given in the Daniel Jones *English Pronouncing Dictionary* and as revised by Professor Gimson, *using a broad transcription*. In a few cases we have deliberately deviated from changes introduced by Professor Gimson:

(*a*) for the symbol [ou] (as in **go**) he substituted [əu]; the phonetics of this dictionary are designed primarily for French-speaking users, and we consider that [əu] would suggest to them the rather "cramped" vowel sound characteristic of the semi-educated speech of some parts of South-Eastern England; we have therefore maintained [ou];

(*b*) the symbol [*o*] has not been used; we have opted for either [ə] as in **November** [nə'vembə*r*] or [ou] as in **photo-** ['foutou] or **coherent** [kou'hiərənt];

(*c*) in the Gimson revision the symbol [*] has been used at the end of words terminating in **-r** to indicate that the **r** is pronounced only when the following word begins with a vowel; we consider that the italic [-*r*] (e.g. **ever** ['evə*r*]) is a symbol which the user will find easier to remember, and we have therefore maintained it.

Word stress is indicated by a stress mark preceding the stressed syllable, e.g. **abbot** ['æbət]; **address** [ə'dres]. It should however be noted that in American English there is a tendency to stress some two-syllable words on the first syllable instead of on the second as in British English, e.g. **address** ['ædres], **research** ['ri:sə:tʃ] (not [ri'sə:tʃ]); what the future pronunciation will be is open to doubt; ['ri:sə:tʃ], though not approved by purists (or by ourselves) is nevertheless now often heard in England.

In general, we have not indicated secondary stress on a word; in our opinion the careful pronunciation of the vowel in a syllable with secondary stress is enough to guarantee correct pronunciation.

Having used the term "correct pronunciation", we now find ourselves faced with a problem: what is really the correct pronunciation of English? It is impossible within the scope of this dictionary to give a range of variants, so we have confined ourselves largely to the "received pronunciation" (R.P.) of the educated Englishman who speaks in a way which reveals little or no regional background. While we do not in any way suggest that we are in the same class as G. B. Shaw's Professor Higgins, we have enough experience to agree with him that such people are few. Slight variations in vowel sounds suggest different backgrounds or ancestry, and the user of this dictionary must therefore assume that certain symbols represent a fairly wide range of pronunciation. For example, the symbol [æ] represents the **a** as in **hat** or in **add**, the symbol [ɑ:] the **a** as in **baa, father**, etc.; but [æ] and [ɑ:] vary somewhat in length according to the speaker and in some words, moreover, there is a sound which is intermediate between [æ] and [ɑ:], *e.g.* the **a** in **castle**, **glass**, etc.; in Southern England the pronunciation is usually [ɑ:], in Northern England, Scotland and North America it is usually nearer [æ]; for this dictionary we have chosen the pronunciation [ɑ:] (**castle** ['kɑ:sl]). In connection with this same vowel sound, we wish to draw particular attention to words with the prefix **trans-** and those containing the element **graph**; as these are both large groups of words we decided that we could not give alternative pronunciations, so we have opted throughout for the sound [æ]. Before coming to any decision we listened to many speakers and made some recordings on tape; we reached the conclusion that for **trans-** the approximation [trænz, træns] is the more usual, though for most words [trɑ:nz, trɑ:ns] is acceptable. The simple noun **graph** is more often [græf]; for **graphic** we have heard only ['græfik]; the real difficulty is **-graph** as a final syllable, as in **telegraph**, **photograph**; in such words the **a** is not usually as broad as [ɑ:], nor as "clipped" a sound as the [æ] of **hat**; we have adopted the solution of using [græf] throughout, but are fully aware of the imperfections of such a convention.

The following points should also be noted:

(*a*) words such as **art**, **bark**, **perfect**, **learn**, **girl**, **curl**, etc. have been transcribed as [ɑ:t], [bɑ:k], ['pə:fikt], [lə:n], [gə:l], [kə:l], etc.; the **r** is not normally pronounced at all by English speakers, though it can be heard in varying degrees, especially in speakers from Scotland or North America;

(*b*) words such as **which**, **why**, **what** have been shown with the [h] symbol in parentheses, *i.e.* [(h)witʃ], [(h)wai], [(h)wɔt]; most English (as opposed to Scottish or American) speakers drop the [h] when speaking rapidly, though they frequently pronounce it in careful speech or when emphasizing the word;

(*c*) words such as **picture**, **departure** are, as in Mr Mansion's original edition, transcribed as ['piktjər], [di'pɑ:tjər], not ['piktʃər], [di'pɑ:tʃər], as the more cultivated pronunciation [jə] appears preferable to us;

(*d*) the vowel combination [ju(:)] calls for some explanations:

(i) in words such as **durable**, where the [ju:] sound is followed by an [r], we have opted for ['dju:rəbl] rather than ['dju:ərəbl]; while we agree with the phoneticians who maintain that there is a slight component or "glide" preceding the [r], the addition of the [ə] would suggest an additional syllable to users whose mother tongue is not English;

(ii) some difficulties occurred about the transcription of the syllables **su** and **lu**; in many cases the usual pronunciation is indubitably [su:] and [lu:], in others [sju:] and [lju:]; nevertheless there are words for which our tape recordings revealed a diversity of practice which is in no way regional, so for these we have used [s(j)u:] and [l(j)u:], *e.g.* **suit** [s(j)u:t], **suicide** ['s(j)u:isaid]; **lurid** ['l(j)u:rid];

(*e*) parentheses around [t] before a final [ʃ] also indicate that this sound is dropped by some speakers; but [(ə)] means that the vowel is elided in rapid speech and [(:)] that the previous vowel is not always, or only slightly, lengthened;

(*f*) we have given American variants of pronunciation only for words for which there is a marked difference, *e.g.* **tomato** [*Eng:* tə'mɑ:tou, *NAm:* tə'meitou], **clerk** [*Eng:* klɑ:k, *NAm:* klə:k].

The appended table gives a list of the phonetic symbols used, with examples of words in which they appear, to illustrate the spelling variants which occur.

Prononciation

Quoique cet ouvrage ne soit pas un dictionnaire de phonétique nous avons suivi l'exemple de M. Mansion en donnant la notation phonétique de chaque mot-clef. La prononciation de l'anglais est compliquée et l'étranger n'est pas seul à hésiter sur la prononciation d'un mot qu'il ne connaît pas. Pensons à **bough** [bau], **cough** [kɔf], **dough** [dou], **rough** [rʌf], **through** [θru:] et **thorough** ['θʌrə]; à **bow**, qui se prononce [bau] ou [bou] selon le sens du mot; ou **permit** (comme substantif ['pə:mit] et comme verbe [pə'mit]).

Comme la notation phonétique est destinée principalement à l'usager dont la langue maternelle n'est pas l'anglais, nous avons donné la prononciation soignée du mot en question, car son usage ne peut jamais constituer une faute véritable. Mais un mot prononcé séparément ne peut pas tenir compte de l'accent oratoire, qui est très important en anglais. Quand on parle rapidement, l'élision de certaines voyelles, consonnes ou même de syllabes ne doit pas nécessairement être interprétée comme un manque d'instruction. Prenons la phrase **he was a contemporary of mine**; en conversation tout le monde dirait ['hi:wəzəkən'tempriəv'main], et ne se servirait pas de la prononciation soignée [kən'tempərəri]. Beaucoup de romanciers écrivent **'im** au lieu de **him** pour indiquer le manque d'instruction de la personne qui parle, mais peu de gens prononceraient l'**h** de **don't tell him** [dount'telim], ce qui serait incorrect dans **tell him but not her** [tel'himbətnɔt'hə:].

Nous avons donné la notation phonétique selon les principes de l'Association phonétique internationale en suivant l'*English Pronouncing Dictionary* de Daniel Jones, révisé par le Professeur Gimson. Mais dans certains cas nous avons préféré ne pas nous servir des changements de M. Gimson:

(*a*) il a remplacé le symbole [ou] par [əu] (**go** [gəu]); nous avons conservé [ou], parce qu'il nous semble que [əu] inciterait l'usager francophone à prononcer la voyelle "pointue" caractéristique de la mauvaise prononciation dans certaines parties du sud-est de l'Angleterre;

(*b*) nous avons décidé de ne pas employer le symbole [*o*] et de choisir entre [ə] (**November** [nə'vembər]) et [ou] (**photo** ['foutou], **coherent** [kou'hiərənt]) selon l'accentuation;

(*c*) à cause de l'appel visuel, nous préférons le symbole [*r*] à [*] pour indiquer que, quand un mot se termine en **r**, l'**r** se prononce seulement quand le mot suivant commence par une voyelle.

La syllabe accentuée est précédée par l'indication ['] (*p.ex.* **abbot** ['æbət], **address** [ə'dres]). Il faut cependant noter qu'en anglais américain l'accent tonique des mots à deux syllabes tombe sur la première plutôt que sur la deuxième (*p.ex.* **address**, *U.K:* [ə'dres], *NAm:* ['ædres]; **research** *U.K:* [ri'sə:tʃ], *NAm:* ['ri:sə:tʃ]); mais peut-on savoir ce qui se dira à l'avenir, car dès maintenant on entend parfois ['ri:sə:tʃ] en Grande-Bretagne, sans toutefois que les puristes l'acceptent. Quoique certains mots puissent avoir un accent tonique secondaire, nous ne l'avons pas indiqué, en estimant que la prononciation soignée de la voyelle est suffisante pour assurer une prononciation correcte.

Nous avons employé le terme "prononciation correcte"—mais que signifie-t-il? Il est impossible dans ce dictionnaire de mettre toutes les nuances possibles et nous avons donc choisi ce que les Anglais appellent "received pronunciation", l'anglais de l'homme cultivé qui ne trahit pas (ou guère) ses origines régionales. Mais il y a néanmoins, surtout en ce qui concerne les voyelles, des prononciations différentes qui indiquent des différences de milieu ou de région et l'usager de ce dictionnaire doit donc comprendre que certains symboles ont des variantes de prononciation. Par exemple, [æ] représente l'**a** de **hat** ou d'**add**, [ɑ:] celui de **baa** ou de **father**. Mais [æ] et [ɑ:] varient souvent selon celui qui parle; dans des mots tels que **castle**, **glass**, etc. la voyelle est prononcée généralement [ɑ:] dans le sud de l'Angleterre, mais au nord, en Écosse et en Amérique du Nord elle approche de [æ]; pour ce dictionnaire nous avons choisi [ɑ:] (**castle** ['kɑ:sl]). Nous attirons également l'attention de l'usager sur le préfixe **trans-** et sur les mots qui contiennent l'élément **graph**. Comme ce sont de grands groupes de mots il n'était pas possible de donner des variantes et nous avons choisi [æ]. En écoutant des enregistrements sur bandes magnétiques nous avons constaté que la prononciation [træns, trænz] est plus répandue, quoique, dans la plupart des cas, [trɑ:ns, trɑ:nz] est également acceptable. Le substantif **graph** se prononce généralement [græf], **graphic** toujours ['græfik]; mais quand **-graph** constitue la syllabe finale d'un mot (**telegraph**, **photograph**) la prononciation de la voyelle est généralement intermédiaire entre [æ] et [ɑ:]; nous avons choisi [æ], tout en nous rendant compte que c'est une imperfection.

Nous attirons, d'autre part, l'attention de l'usager sur les détails suivants:

(*a*) nous avons donné aux mots tels que **art**, **bark**, **perfect**, **learn**, **girl**, **curl**, etc. la notation [ɑ:t], [bɑ:k], ['pə:fikt], [lə:n], [gə:l], [kə:l], etc.; en Angleterre on ne prononce généralement pas l'**r**, que l'on peut cependant remarquer surtout chez des Écossais ou des Américains;

(*b*) des mots tels que **which**, **why**, **what** sont représentés avec l'**h** entre parenthèses, [(h)witʃ], [(h)wai], [(h)wɔt]; la plupart des Écossais et des Américains le prononcent toujours mais les Anglais l'escamotent quand ils parlent rapidement;

(*c*) pour des mots tels que **picture** ou **departure** nous avons conservé la notation de M. Mansion ['piktjə*r*], [di'pɑ:tjə*r*], qui nous semble indiquer une prononciation plus cultivée que ['piktʃə*r*] ou [di'pɑ:tʃə*r*];

(*d*) l'usage du symbole [ju:] mérite des explications:
(i) dans un mot comme **durable**, où le son [ju:] est suivi par un **r**, nous avons choisi ['dju:rəbl] plutôt que ['dju:ərəbl]; quoique nous soyons d'accord avec les phonéticiens qu'il y a un léger son de transition avant l'**r**, l'addition d'un [ə] serait susceptible de suggérer une syllabe supplémentaire;
(ii) en ce qui concerne les syllabes **su** et **lu**, nous avons constaté que très souvent la prononciation courante est [su:] et [lu:]; il y a cependant des cas où, sans avoir aucun accent régional, certaines personnes disent [su:] et [lu:] et d'autres [sju:] et [lju:]; pour ces mots nous utilisons les symboles [s(j)u:] et [l(j)u:] (**suit** [s(j)u:t]; **suicide** ['s(j)u:isaid]; **lurid** ['l(j)u:rid]);

(*e*) un [t] entre parenthèses avant un [ʃ] final indique que cette consonne n'est pas toujours prononcée; mais [(ə)] signifie que la voyelle est élidée quand on parle rapidement et [(:)] que la voyelle précédente n'est pas toujours allongée;

(*f*) nous avons donné les variantes américaines de prononciation seulement pour les mots pour lesquels il y a une différence marquée, par exemple, **tomato** [*U.K:* tə'mɑ:tou, *NAm:* tə'meitou], **clerk** [*U.K:* klɑ:k, *NAm:* klə:k].

Le tableau qui suit donne une liste des symboles phonétiques utilisés avec des mots pour illustrer des variantes orthographiques de chaque son.

Table of Phonetic Symbols—Tableau des Symboles Phonétiques

CONSONANTS AND SEMICONSONANTS

[p] pat [pæt]; top [tɔp]; pepper ['pepər]
[b] but [bʌt]; tab [tæb]; robber ['rɔbər]
[m] mat [mæt]; ram [ræm]; hammer ['hæmər]; prism ['priz(ə)m]; bomb [bɔm]; calm [kɑ:m]
[f] fat [fæt]; laugh [lɑ:f]; ruff, rough [rʌf]; physics ['fiziks]; elephant ['elifənt]
[v] vat [væt]; avail [ə'veil]; rave [reiv]
[t] tap [tæp]; pat [pæt]; patter ['pætər]; trap [træp]; tight [tait]; time, thyme [taim]; act [ækt]; pest [pest]; debt [det]
[d] dab [dæb]; mad [mæd]; madder ['mædər]; build [bild]
[n] no, know [nou]; ban [bæn]; banner ['bænər]; pancake ['pænkeik]; nab [næb]; gnat [næt]; pneumonia [nju:'mouniə]
[s] sat [sæt]; scene [si:n]; sent, scent [sent]; science ['saiəns]; socks [sɔks]; mouse [maus]; toss [tɔs]; kudos ['kju:dɔs]; ceiling ['si:liŋ]; coincide [kouin'said]; ice [ais]; psychology [sai'kɔlədʒi]
[θ] thatch [θætʃ]; ether ['i:θər]; faith [feiθ]; breath [breθ]
[z] zinc [ziŋk]; zone [zoun]; buzz [bʌz]; houses ['hauziz]; business ['biznis]; adze [ædz]; odds [ɔdz]
[ð] that [ðæt]; there [ðɛər]; mother ['mʌðər]; breathe [bri:ð]
[l] lad [læd], all [ɔ:l]; faithful ['feiθful]; table ['teibl]; chisel ['tʃizl]
[ʃ] sham [ʃæm]; dish [diʃ]; sugar ['ʃugər]; chef [ʃef]; ocean ['ouʃ(ə)n]; nation ['neiʃ(ə)n]; machine [mə'ʃi:n]; action ['ækʃ(ə)n]; conviction [kən'vikʃ(ə)n]; lunch [lʌnʃ]
[tʃ] chat [tʃæt]; search [sə:tʃ]; chisel ['tʃizl]; thatch [θætʃ]; rich [ritʃ]
[ʒ] pleasure ['pleʒər]; vision ['viʒ(ə)n]; beige [beiʒ]
[dʒ] jam [dʒæm]; jail, gaol [dʒeil]; gem [dʒem]; gin [dʒin]; rage [reidʒ]; edge [edʒ]; badger ['bædʒər]
[k] cup [kʌp]; cat [kæt]; kitten ['kitn]; clap [klæp]; crack [kræk]; choir, quire ['kwaiər]; queen [kwi:n]; kick [kik]; key, quay [ki:]; khaki ['kɑ:ki]; cue, queue [kju:]; antic ['æntik]; arctic ['ɑ:ktik]; pique [pi:k]; accept [ək'sept]; exercise ['eksəsaiz]; expect [iks'pekt]; cox [kɔks]
[g] get [get]; give [giv]; go [gou]; ghost [goust]; grain [grein]; guard [gɑ:d]; guess [ges]; guilt, gilt [gilt]; again [ə'gen]; egg [eg]; exist [eg'zist]; exact [eg'zækt]; hungry ['hʌŋgri]
[h] hat [hæt]; cohere [kou'hiər]
[χ] loch [lɔχ]; pibroch ['pi:brɔχ]
[ŋ] bang [bæŋ]; sing [siŋ]; singer ['siŋər]; anchor ['æŋkər]; anger ['æŋgər]; link [liŋk]
[r] rat [ræt]; arise [ə'raiz]; barring ['bɑ:riŋ]
[*r*] (*sounded only when a final* **r** *is carried on to the next word*) far [fɑ:*r*]; sailor ['seilə*r*]; finger ['fiŋgə*r*]
[j] yam [jæm]; yet [jet]; youth [ju:θ]; picture ['piktjər]
[w] wall [wɔ:l]; await [ə'weit]; choir, quire ['kwaiər]; quite [kwait]
[(h)w] what [(h)wɔt]; why [(h)wai]

VOWELS and VOWEL COMBINATIONS

[i:] bee [bi:]; fever ['fi:vər]; see, sea [si:]; ceiling ['si:liŋ]; ski [ski:]; release [ri'li:s]; chlorine ['klɔ:ri:n]
[iə] beer, bier [biər]; appear [ə'piər]; really ['riəli]
[i] bit [bit]; added ['ædid]; drastic ['dræstik]; sieve [siv]; helplessness ['helplisnis]; begin [bi'gin]; elect [i'lekt]; manage ['mænidʒ]
[e] bet [bet]; meant [ment]; deaf [def]; leopard ['lepəd]; menace ['menəs]; said [sed]; coalesce [kouə'les]; manageress [mænidʒə'res]
[ei] date [deit]; day [dei]; railing ['reiliŋ]; feign [fein]; rain, rein, reign [rein];
[ɛə] bear, bare [bɛər], there, their [ðɛər]; airy ['ɛəri]
[æ] bat [bæt]; add [æd]; graph [græf]; transact [træn'zækt]
[ai] aisle, isle [ail]; height [hait]; life [laif]; fly [flai]; beside [bi'said]; aniline ['ænilain]; guide [gaid]; guy [gai]
[ɑ:] art [ɑ:t]; ask [ɑ:sk]; car [kɑ:*r*]; father ['fɑ:ðər]; glass [glɑ:s]; castle ['kɑ:sl]; palm [pɑ:m]
[au] fowl, foul [faul]; house [haus]; cow [kau]; renounce [ri'nauns]
[ɔ] wad [wɔd]; wash [wɔʃ]; lot [lɔt]; what [(h)wɔt]
[ɔ:] all [ɔ:l]; haul [hɔ:l]; saw [sɔ:]; caught, court [kɔ:t]; coarse, course [kɔ:s]; short [ʃɔ:t]; wart [wɔ:t]; thought [θɔ:t]; thwart [θwɔ:t]
[ɔi] boil [bɔil]; toy [tɔi]; oyster ['ɔistər]; loyal ['lɔiəl]
[ou] low [lou]; soap [soup]; rope [roup]; road, rode, rowed [roud]; sew, so, sow (*verb*) [sou]; though [ðou]; cohere [kou'hiər]; coalesce [kouə'les]
[u:] shoe [ʃu:]; clue [klu:]; prove [pru:v]; room [ru:m]; to, two [tu:]; threw, through [θru:]; true [tru:]; frugal ['fru:g(ə)l]; coupon ['ku:pɔn]; wounded ['wu:ndid]; (*slightly shorter*) Rumania [ru(:)'meiniə]
[ju:] few [fju:]; hew, hue [hju:]; huge [hju:dʒ]; humour ['hju:mər]; nuisance ['nju:s(ə)ns]
[(j)u:] suit [s(j)u:t]; suicide ['s(j)u:isaid]
[(j)uə] lurid ['l(j)uərid]; lure [l(j)uər]
[u] put [put]; wool [wul]; wood, would [wud]; full [ful]
[ju] incubate ['inkjubeit]; regulate ['regjuleit]; duplicity [dju'plisiti]
[uə] poor [puər]; sure [ʃuər]
[ʌ] cut [kʌt]; sun, son [sʌn]; cover ['kʌvər]; rough [rʌf]
[ə:] curl [kə:l]; pearl, purl [pə:l]; herb [hə:b]; terse [tə:s]; girl [gə:l]; learn [lə:n]; turgid ['tə:dʒid]; purr [pə:*r*]; myrrh [mə:*r*]; interment [in'tə:mənt]
[ə] decency ['di:sənsi]; obey [ə'bei]; Atlantic [ət'læntik]; ferment (*verb*) [fə'ment]; amend [ə'mend]; upon [ə'pɔn]; delicate ['delikət]

Abbreviations Used in the Dictionary

Abréviations Utilisées dans le Dictionnaire

A:	archaism; ancient; in former use	désuet
a., adj.	adjective	adjectif
abbr.	abbreviation	abréviation
abs.	absolutely; absolute use	emploi absolu
Ac:	acoustics	acoustique
acc.	accusative	accusatif
Adm:	administration; civil service	administration
adv.	adverb	adverbe
adv.phr.	adverbial phrase	locution adverbiale
Aedcs:	aerodynamics	aérodynamique
Aer:	aeronautics	aéronautique
Agr:	agriculture	agriculture
A. Hist:	ancient history	histoire ancienne
Alch:	alchemy	alchimie
Algae:	algae	algues
Amph:	Amphibia	amphibiens
Anat:	anatomy	anatomie
Ann:	Annelida, worms	annelés
Ant:	antiquity, antiquities	antiquité
Anthr:	anthropology	anthropologie
Ap:	apiculture	apiculture
approx.	approximately	sens approché
Arach:	Arachnida	arachnides
Arb:	arboriculture	arboriculture; sylviculture
Arch:	architecture	architecture
Archeol:	archaeology	archéologie
Arm:	armour	armure
Arms:	arms; armaments	armes; armements
art.	article	article
Art:	art	beaux-arts
Artil:	artillery	artillerie
Astr:	astronomy	astronomie
Astrol:	astrology	astrologie
Astro-Ph:	astrophysics	astrophysique
Atom. Ph:	atomic, nuclear, physics	sciences atomiques
attrib.	attributive	attributif
Austr:	Australia; Australian(ism)	Australie; australien; expression australienne
Aut:	motoring; automobile industry	automobilisme; industrie automobile
aux.	auxiliary	auxiliaire
Av:	aviation; aircraft	aviation; avions
B:	Bible; biblical	Bible; biblique
Bac:	bacteriology	bactériologie
Bak:	baking	boulangerie
Ball:	ballistics	ballistique
Bank:	banking	opérations de banque
Belg:	Belgium; Belgian	Belgique; belge
B. Hist:	Bible history	histoire sainte
Bib:	bibliography	bibliographie
Bill:	billiards	jeu de billard
Bio-Ch:	biochemistry	biochimie
Biol:	biology	biologie
Bookb:	bookbinding	reliure
Book-k:	book-keeping	comptabilité
Bootm:	boot and shoe industry	cordonnerie; industrie de la chaussure
Bot:	botany	botanique
Box:	boxing	boxe
Breed:	breeding	élevage
Brew:	brewing	brasserie
Brickm:	brickmaking	briqueterie
Can:	Canada, Canadian(ism)	Canada; canadien; expression canadienne
card.a.	cardinal adjective	adjectif cardinal
Cards:	card games	jeux de cartes
Carp:	carpentry	charpenterie; menuiserie du bâtiment
Cer:	ceramics	céramique
cf.	refer to	conferatur
Ch:	chemistry	chimie
Chess:	chess	jeu d'échecs
Ch. of Eng:	Church of England	Église anglicane
Chr:	chronology	chronologie
Cin:	cinema	cinéma
Civ:	civilization	civilisation
Civ. E:	civil engineering	génie civil
Cl:	classical; Greek or Roman antiquity	classique, antiquité grecque ou romaine
Clockm:	clock and watch making	horlogerie
Cmptr:	computers; data processing	ordinateurs; informatique
Coel:	Coelenterata	cœlentérés
cogn.acc.	cognate accusative	accusatif de l'objet interne
Cokem:	cokemaking	industrie du coke
coll.	collective	collectif
Com:	commerce; business term	(terme du) commerce
comb.fm.	combining form	forme de combinaison
Comest:	comestibles, food	comestibles
comp.	comparative	comparatif
Conch:	conchology	conchyliologie
condit.	conditional	conditionnel
conj.	conjunction	conjonction
Const:	construction, building industry	industrie du bâtiment
Coop:	cooperage	tonnellerie
Corr:	correspondence, letters	correspondance, lettres
Cost:	costume; clothing	costume; habillement
cp.	compare	comparer
Cr:	cricket	cricket
Crust:	Crustacea	crustacés
Cryst:	crystallography	cristallographie
Cu:	culinary; cooking	culinaire; cuisine
Cust:	customs	douane
Cy:	bicycles; cycling	bicyclettes; cyclisme
Danc:	dancing	danse
dat.	dative	datif
def.	(i) definite; (ii) defective (verb)	(i) défini; (ii) (verbe) défectif
dem.	demonstrative	démonstratif
Dent:	dentistry	art dentaire
Dial:	dialectal	dialectal
dim.	diminutive	diminutif
Dipl:	diplomacy; diplomatic	diplomatie; diplomatique
Dist:	distilling	distillation
Dom. Ec:	domestic economy; household equipment	économie domestique; ménage

Abbreviations Used in the Dictionary

Draw:	*drawing*	dessin
Dressm:	*dressmaking*	couture (mode)
Dy:	*dyeing*	teinture
Dyn:	*dynamics*	dynamique
E.	*east*	est
E:	*engineering*	industries mécaniques
Ecc:	*ecclesiastical*	église et clergé
Echin:	*Echinodermata*	échinodermes
e.g.	*for example*	par exemple
El:	*electricity; electrical engineering*	électricité; électrique; électrotechnique
Elcs:	*electronics*	électronique
Eng.	*England; English*	Angleterre; anglais, britannique
Engr:	*engraving*	gravure
Ent:	*entomology*	entomologie
Equit:	*equitation*	équitation
esp.	*especially*	surtout
etc.	*et cetera*	et cætera
Eth:	*ethics*	morale
Ethn:	*ethnology*	ethnologie
Exp:	*explosives*	explosifs
f.	*feminine*	féminin
F:	*colloquial(ism)*	familier; style de la conversation
Farr:	*farriery*	maréchalerie
Fb:	*(Association) football*	football
Fenc:	*fencing*	escrime
Fig:	*figurative*	sens figuré
Fin:	*finance*	finances
Fish:	*fishing*	pêche
For:	*forestry*	forêts
Fort:	*fortification*	fortification
Fr.	*France; French*	France; français
Fr.C:	*French Canadian*	canadien français
Fung:	*fungi*	champignons
Furn:	*furniture*	mobilier
Games:	*games*	jeux
Gaming:	*gaming; gambling*	le jeu; jeux d'argent
Gasm:	*gasmaking*	industrie du gaz
Geog:	*geography*	géographie
Geol:	*geology*	géologie
ger.	*gerund*	gérondif
Glassm:	*glassmaking*	verrerie
Golf:	*golf*	golf
Gr.	*Greek*	grec
Gr.Alph:	*Greek alphabet*	alphabet grec
Gr.Ant:	*Greek antiquity*	antiquité grecque
Gr.Civ:	*Greek civilization*	civilisation grecque
Gr.Hist:	*Greek history*	histoire grecque
Gram:	*grammar*	grammaire
Gym:	*gymnastics*	gymnastique
Hairdr:	*hairdressing*	coiffure
Harn:	*harness; saddlery*	sellerie; harnais
Hatm:	*hatmaking*	chapellerie
Her:	*heraldry*	blason
Hist:	*history; historical*	histoire; historique
Hor:	*horology*	horométrie
Hort:	*horticulture*	horticulture
Hum:	*humorous*	humoristique
Husb:	*animal husbandry*	élevage
Hyd.E:	*hydraulic engineering*	hydromécanique
Hyg:	*hygiene; sanitation*	hygiène; installations sanitaires
i.	*intransitive*	intransitif
I.C.E:	*internal combustion engines*	moteurs à combustion interne
Ich:	*ichthyology; fish*	ichtyologie; poissons
Ill:	*illuminants; lighting*	illuminants; éclairage
imp.	*imperative*	impératif
impers.	*impersonal*	impersonnel
ind.	*indicative*	indicatif
Ind:	*industry; industrial*	industrie; industriel
indef.	*indefinite*	indéfini
ind.tr.	*indirectly transitive*	transitif avec régime indirect
inf.	*infinitive*	infinitif
Ins:	*insurance*	assurance
int.	*interjection*	interjection
Internat:	*international*	international
interr.	*interrogative*	interrogatif
inv.	*invariable*	invariable

Iron:	*ironic(ally)*	ironique(ment)
Jap:	*Japanese*	japonais
Jew:	*Jewish*	juif, juive
Jewel:	*jewellery*	bijouterie
Join:	*joinery*	menuiserie
Journ:	*journalism; journalistic*	journalisme; style journalistique
Jur:	*jurisprudence; legal term*	droit; terme de palais
Knit:	*knitting*	tricot
Lacem:	*lacemaking*	dentellerie
Lap:	*lapidary arts*	arts lapidaires; taillerie
Laund:	*laundering*	blanchissage
Leath:	*leatherwork*	travail du cuir
Ling:	*linguistics; language*	linguistique; langue
Lit:	*literary use; literature; literary*	forme littéraire; littérature; littéraire
Lith:	*lithography*	lithographie
Locksm:	*locksmithery*	serrurerie
Log:	*logic*	logique
Lt.	*Latin*	latin
m.	*masculine*	masculin
Magn:	*magnetism*	magnétisme
Mapm:	*mapmaking*	cartographie
Mch:	*machines; machinery*	machines; machines à vapeur
Mch.Tls:	*machine tools*	machines-outils
Meas:	*weights and measures*	poids et mesures
Mec:	*mechanics*	mécanique
Mec.E:	*mechanical engineering*	industries mécaniques
Med:	*medicine; illnesses; medical*	médecine; maladies; médical
Metall:	*metallurgy*	métallurgie
Metalw:	*metalworking*	travail des métaux
Metaph:	*metaphysics*	métaphysique
Meteor:	*meteorology*	météorologie
Mil:	*military; army*	militaire; armée de terre
Mill:	*milling*	meunerie
Min:	*mining and quarrying*	exploitation des mines et carrières
Miner:	*mineralogy*	minéralogie
M.Ins:	*marine insurance*	assurance maritime
Moll:	*molluscs*	mollusques
Moss:	*mosses and lichens*	muscinées
Mount:	*mountaineering*	alpinisme
Mth:	*mathematics*	mathématiques
Mus:	*music*	musique
Myr:	*Myriapoda*	myriapodes
Myth:	*mythology*	mythologie
N.	*north*	nord
NAm:	*North American*	de l'Amérique du Nord
N.Arch:	*naval architecture*	architecture navale
Nat.Hist:	*natural history*	histoire naturelle
Nau:	*nautical*	terme de marine
Nav:	*navigation*	navigation
Navy:	*Navy*	marine militaire
Needlew:	*needlework*	couture (travaux d'aiguille)
neg.	*negative*	négatif
nom.	*nominative*	nominatif
Num:	*numismatics*	numismatique
num.a.	*numeral adjective*	adjectif numéral
N.Z:	*New Zealand*	(de la) Nouvelle-Zélande
O:	*obsolescent*	vieilli
Obst:	*obstetrics*	obstétrique
Oc:	*oceanography*	océanographie
occ.	*occasionally*	parfois
onomat.	*onomatopoeia*	onomatopée
Opt:	*optics*	optique
Orn:	*ornithology; birds*	ornithologie; oiseaux
Ost:	*ostreiculture; oysters*	ostréiculture; huîtres
p.	(i) *past;* (ii) *participle*	(i) passé; (ii) participe
P:	*uneducated speech; slang*	expression populaire; argot
Paint:	*painting trade*	peinture en bâtiment
Pal:	*paleography*	paléographie
Paleont:	*paleontology*	paléontologie
Paperm:	*papermaking*	fabrication du papier
Parl:	*parliament*	parlement
Pej:	*pejorative*	péjoratif
pers.	*person(s); personal*	personne(s); personnel
Petr:	*petroleum industry*	industrie pétrolière
Ph:	*physics*	physique

Pharm:	*pharmacy*	pharmacie
Phil:	*philosophy*	philosophie
Phot:	*photography*	photographie
Phot. Engr:	*photo-engraving; process work*	procédés photomécaniques; photogravure
phr.	*phrase*	locution
Physiol:	*physiology*	physiologie
Pisc:	*pisciculture*	pisciculture
pl.	*plural*	pluriel
Plumb:	*plumbing*	plomberie
P.N:	*public notice*	affichage; avis au public
Poet:	*poetical*	poétique
Pol:	*politics; political*	politique
Pol. Ec:	*political economy, economics*	économie politique
poss.	*possessive*	possessif
Post:	*postal services*	postes et télécommunications
p.p.	*past participle*	participe passé
pr.	*present (tense)*	présent (de l'indicatif)
pref.	*prefix*	préfixe
Prehist:	*prehistory*	préhistoire
prep.	*preposition*	préposition
prep.phr.	*prepositional phrase*	locution prépositive
Pr.n.	*proper name*	nom propre
pron.	*pronoun*	pronom
Pros:	*prosody*	prosodie; métrique
Prot:	*Protozoa*	protozoaires
Prov:	*proverb*	proverbe
pr.p.	*present participle*	participe présent
Psy:	*psychology*	psychologie
Psychics:	*psychics*	métapsychisme
p.t.	*past tense*	passé défini
Publ:	*publishing*	édition
Pyr:	*pyrotechnics*	pyrotechnie
qch.	(*something*)	quelque chose
qn	(*someone*)	quelqu'un
q.v.	*which see*	se reporter à ce mot
Rac:	*racing*	courses
Rad:	*radar*	radar
Rad.-A:	*radioactivity*	radioactivité
Rail:	*railways, railroads*	chemins de fer
R.C.Ch:	*Roman Catholic Church*	Église catholique
Rec:	*tape recorders; record players*	magnétophones; tourne-disques
rel.	*relative*	relatif
Rel:	*religion(s)*	religion(s)
Rel. H:	*religious history*	histoire des religions
Rept:	*reptiles*	reptiles
Rh:	*rhetoric*	rhétorique
Rom:	*Roman*	romain
Ropem:	*ropemaking*	corderie
Row:	*rowing*	aviron
R.t.m:	*registered trademark*	marque déposée
Rubberm:	*rubber manufacture*	industrie du caoutchouc
Rugby Fb:	*Rugby (football)*	rugby
Russ:	*Russian*	russe
S.	*south*	sud
s., sb.	*substantive, noun*	substantif, nom
s.a.	*see also*	voir
Sch:	*schools and universities; students (slang, etc.)*	écoles; universités; (argot, etc.) scolaire
Scot:	*Scotland; Scottish*	Écosse; écossais
Scout:	*Scout and Guide Movements*	scoutisme
Sculp:	*sculpture*	sculpture
Ser:	*sericulture*	sériciculture
sg., sing.	*singular*	singulier
Ski:	*skiing*	ski
Sm.a:	*small arms*	armes portatives
s.o.	*someone*	(quelqu'un)
Soapm:	*soapmaking*	savonnerie
Sp:	*sport*	sport
Space:	*astronautics; space travel*	astronautique; voyages interplanétaires
Spong:	*sponges*	spongiaires
Stat:	*statistics*	statistique
St.Exch:	*Stock Exchange*	terme de Bourse
sth.	*something*	(quelque chose)
Stonew:	*stoneworking*	taille de la pierre
sub.	*subjunctive*	subjonctif
suff.	*suffix*	suffixe
Sug.-R:	*sugar refining*	raffinerie du sucre
sup.	*superlative*	superlatif
Surg:	*surgery*	chirurgie
Surv:	*surveying*	géodésie et levé de plans
Swim:	*swimming*	natation
Sw.Fr:	*Swiss French*	mot utilisé en Suisse
Switz:	*Switzerland*	Suisse
Tail:	*tailoring*	mode masculine
Tan:	*tanning*	tannage des cuirs
Tchn:	*technical*	terme technique, terme de métier
Telecom:	*telecommunications*	télécommunications
Ten:	*tennis*	tennis
Ter:	*teratology*	tératologie
Tex:	*textiles; textile industry*	industries textiles
Tg:	*telegraphy*	télégraphie
Th:	*theatre; theatrical*	théâtre
Theol:	*theology*	théologie
thg.	*thing(s)*	(chose(s))
Tls:	*tools*	outils
Toil:	*toilet; makeup*	toilette; maquillage
Town P:	*town planning*	urbanisme
Toys:	*toys*	jouets
Tp:	*telephony*	téléphonie
tr.	*transitive*	transitif
Trans:	*transport*	transports
Turf:	*turf, horse racing*	turf
T.V:	*television*	télévision
Typ:	*typography*	typographie
Typew(r):	*typing; typewriters*	dactylographie; machines à écrire
U.S:	*United States; American*	États-Unis; américain
usu.	*usually*	d'ordinaire
usu. with sg. const.	*usually with singular construction*	verbe généralement au singulier
v.	*verb*	verbe
V:	*vulgar; not in polite use*	trivial
Veh:	*vehicles*	véhicules
Ven:	*venery; hunting*	chasse
Vet:	*veterinary science*	art vétérinaire
v.i.	*intransitive verb*	verbe intransitif
v.ind.tr.	*indirectly transitive verb*	verbe transitif indirect
Vit:	*viticulture*	viticulture
v.pr.	*pronominal verb*	verbe pronominal
v.tr.	*transitive verb*	verbe transitif
W.	*west*	ouest
Wine-m:	*wine making*	industrie du vin
with sg. or pl. const.	*with singular or plural construction*	verbe au singulier ou au pluriel
Woodw:	*woodworking*	menuiserie
Wr:	*wrestling*	lutte
W.Tel:	*wireless telegraphy and telephony; radio*	téléphonie et télégraphie sans fil; radio
W.Tg:	*wireless telegraphy*	télégraphie sans fil
W.Tp:	*wireless telephony*	téléphonie sans fil
X-Rays:	*X Rays*	Rayons X
Y:	*yachting*	yachting
Z:	*zoology; mammals*	zoologie; mammifères
—	*nearest equivalent* (*of an institution, an office, etc., when systems vary in the different countries*)	équivalent le plus proche (d'un terme désignant une institution, une charge, etc., dans les cas où les systèmes varient dans les différents pays)

A, a[1] [ei]. **1.** (*a*) (la lettre) A, a *m*; **it's spelt with two a's,** cela s'écrit avec deux a; *Tp:* **A for Andrew,** A comme Anatole; *Geol:* **A horizon,** horizon A; *F:* **he doesn't know A from B,** il est absolument nul; **he knows the case from A to Z,** il connaît l'affaire à fond, d'un bout à l'autre; **A 1** ['ei'wʌn], (i) *Nau:* **A 1 (at Lloyd's),** de première cote (au Lloyd); (ii) *F:* (*NAm: also* **A number 1**) de première classe, catégorie, qualité; de premier rang, de premier ordre; *F:O:* **he's A 1,** il se porte à merveille; **A 1!** excellent! parfait! à la bonne heure! *Nau:* **A.B.** ['ei'bi:], (i) matelot *m* de deuxième classe; (ii) bon matelot; (*b*) (*in house numbering*) **51 A,** 51 bis; (*c*) *Sch:* **A stream** = classe *f* de type 1; **to pass, get, one's A levels** = être reçu au baccalauréat, *F:* au bac; (*d*) **A road** = route nationale. **2.** *Mus:* la *m*; **in A flat,** en la bémol; **to give the tuning A to the orchestra,** donner le la, le ton, à l'orchestre. **3.** *Cin:* (*adult*) **A film,** film interdit aux moins de seize ans.

a[2], **an** [ə, ən], *indef. art.* NOTE: (i) **a** *is used before words with an initial consonant* (*including* [j] *and* [w]), *and* **an** *before a vowel sound;* **an** *is occ. used before* **hotel, historic(al),** *and* **historian** (*but never before* **history**), *though generally only by older people or as a conscious literary device*; (ii) *the stressed pronunciation* [ei, æn], *is rare, and occurs only in sentences such as* **this word should be written with an a** [ən'ei] **not an an** [ən'æn], ce mot s'écrit avec *a,* pas avec *an.* **1.** un, une; (*a*) **a man,** un homme; **an old man,** un vieillard; **a history,** une histoire; **a historian** [əhis'tɔ:riən], **an historian** [ənis'tɔ:riən], un historien; **a hotel** [əhou'tel], **an hotel** [ənou'tel], un hôtel; **an heiress** [ən'ɛəres], une héritière; **an hour** [ən'auər], une heure; **a unit** [ə'ju:nit], une unité; **an M.P.** [ən'em'pi:], un député; **the months with an r in them** [ən'ɑ:rinðəm], les mois en R; **a man and (a) woman,** un homme et une femme; **a wife and mother,** une épouse et mère; **come and see me, but not on a Monday,** venez me voir, mais pas un lundi; (*b*) (*following* **such, too, so,** *etc.*) **such a stupid man,** un homme si stupide; **such a difficult job,** une tâche si difficile; **too long a book,** un livre trop long; **too high a price,** un prix trop élevé; **so resolute a tone,** un ton si résolu; **how unlikely a story!** quelle histoire invraisemblable! **many an artist,** bien des artistes; *Lit:* **many a time and oft,** maintes et maintes fois; **half a pound,** une demi-livre. **2.** (*usu. def. art. in Fr.*) (*a*) **to have an aquiline nose,** avoir le nez aquilin; **to have a good ear,** avoir l'oreille juste; **I have a sore throat,** j'ai mal à la gorge; (*b*) **to have a taste for sth.,** avoir le goût de qch.; **to have a flair for sth.,** avoir du flair pour qch.; **he has a contempt for fools,** il a du dédain pour les imbéciles; **the town has lost a quarter, a third, of its inhabitants,** la ville a perdu le quart, le tiers, de ses habitants; **he had a leg amputated,** il a été amputé de la jambe; **he hasn't a penny,** il n'a pas le sou; **I have a right to live,** j'ai le droit de vivre; *Iron:* **a fine excuse!** la belle excuse! (*c*) (*generalizing use*) **a woman takes life too seriously,** les femmes prennent la vie trop au sérieux; **a dead calm often precedes great storms,** le calme plat précède souvent les grandes tempêtes. **3.** (*distributive use*) (*a*) **apples at fifteen pence a pound,** pommes à quinze pence la livre; **five francs a head,** cinq francs par tête; **ten a side,** dix de chaque côté; (*b*) (*time*) **three times a week, a month, a year,** trois fois par semaine, par mois, par an; **fifty kilometres an hour,** cinquante kilomètres à l'heure. **4.** (*partitive in Fr.*) **I haven't a book,** je n'ai pas de livre (*but* **I haven't a single book,** je n'ai pas un seul livre); **the walk has given me an appetite,** la promenade m'a donné de l'appétit. **5.** (*a*) (= **a certain, a particular**) **I know a doctor who . . .,** je connais un certain médecin qui . . .; **it was a Mr Martin who told me,** c'était un certain M. Martin qui me l'a dit; **in a sense, in a way,** dans un certain sens; d'un certain point de vue; (*b*) (*with* **at, of** = **the same**) **to come in two at a time,** entrer deux par deux; **they're all of an age,** ils sont tous du même âge; **all of a size,** tous de la même grandeur, de la même taille; *Lit:* **we are (all) of a mind,** nous sommes tous du même avis; (*c*) (= **a single**) **they were killed to a man,** ils furent tués jusqu'au dernier; **he emptied the glass at a draught,** il a vidé le verre d'un seul coup; **I haven't understood a word,** je n'ai pas compris un seul mot. **6.** (*omitted in Fr.*) (*a*) **he is an Englishman, a father,** il est anglais, père; **he was a barrister,** il était avocat; (*but* **it was a barrister who . . .,** c'était un avocat qui . . .); **an Englishman who was staying there,** un Anglais de passage; (*b*) (*before nouns in apposition*) **Caen, a large town in Normandy,** Caen, ville importante de Normandie; **Mr Thomas, a very good dentist,** M. Thomas, dentiste réputé; **he was made a colonel, a well merited honour,** il fut nommé colonel, honneur qu'il méritait bien; (*c*) (*in titles*) **A New English Dictionary,** Nouveau Dictionnaire anglais; (*d*) **to put an end to sth.,** mettre fin à qch.; **to have a right to sth.,** avoir droit à qch.; **to make a fortune,** faire fortune; (*e*) **what a man!** quel homme! **what a pity!** quel dommage! (*f*) **as a rule,** en règle générale; **to live like a prince,** vivre en prince; **to sell sth. at a loss,** vendre qch. à perte; **within a short time,** à bref délai; **three and a half,** trois et demi.

a-[1] [ə], *pref.* (*a*) *A: & Lit:* (*with gerund*) **to set the bells a-ringing,** mettre les cloches en branle; **a-dancing round the maypole,** qui dansent autour de l'arbre de mai; (*b*) (i) *forming adjs.* **asleep,** endormi; (ii) *forming advs.* **aloud,** à haute voix; tout haut; **ashore,** à terre; *Dial:* **a-purpose,** exprès, à dessein.

a-[2] [ei; æ], *pref.* (= **not**) **amoral** [ei-], amoral; **asymmetry** [æ-], asymétrie *f.*

aa ['ɑ:ɑ:], *s. Geol:* aa *m.*

Aachen ['ɑ:χən, 'ɑ:kən], *Pr.n. Geog:* Aix-la-Chapelle.

aandblom ['ɑ:ndblɔm], *s. Bot:* hesperantha *m.*

aardvark ['ɑ:dvɑ:k], *s. Z:* oryctérope *m* (du Cap).

aardwolf, *pl.* **-wolves** ['ɑ:dwulf, -wulvz], *s. Z:* protèle *m.*

Aargau ['ɑ:gau], *Pr.n. Geog:* l'Argovie *f.*

Aaron ['ɛərən], *Pr.n.m. B.Hist:* Aaron, Aharon; **Aaron's rod,** (i) *B:* la verge d'Aaron; (ii) *Bot:* molène commune, bouillon-blanc *m, pl.* bouillons-blancs, cierge maudit; (iii) *Bot:* verge d'or; *Bot:* **Aaron's beard,** (i) mille-pertuis *m inv* velu; (ii) cymbalaire *f.*

Aaronic [ɛə'rɔnik], *a. B:* d'Aaron.

aasvoel ['ɑ:sfoul], **aasvogel** ['ɑ:sfougəl], *s. Orn:* (*S. Africa*) vautour *m.*

abac ['æbæk], *s. Mth:* abaque *m.*

abaca ['æbəkə], *s. Bot:* abaca *m,* bananier *m* textile, des Philippines.

aback [ə'bæk], *adv.* (*a*) *Nau:* (*of sail*) masqué, coiffé; sur le mât; (*of ship*) **to be a.,** avoir le vent dessus; **to be caught a., taken a.,** être pris devant, vent dessus; être masqué; **all a.,** masqué partout; **to brace a.,** brasser à culer; (*b*) *Fig:* **to be taken a.,** être, rester, déconcerté, interdit, interloqué; se déconcerter; **he seemed somewhat taken a.,** il avait l'air tant soit peu déconcerté; **you seem taken a. by it,** cela a l'air de vous surprendre, dé vous déconcerter; **very much taken a.,** complètement déconcerté; ahuri.

abaculus, *pl.* **-li** [ə'bækjuləs, -li:], *s.* abacule *m.*

abacus, *pl.* **-ci, -cuses** ['æbəkəs, -sai, -si:; -kəsiz], *s.* **1.** *Mth:* abaque *m,* boulier *m* compteur. **2.** *Arch:* abaque, tailloir *m* (de chapiteau). **3.** *Min: etc:* **a. major,** augette *f,* sébile *f.*

Abaddon [ə'bædn], *Pr.n. B:* (*a*) Abaddon *m,* l'Ange *m* de l'abîme; (*b*) abaddon, l'abîme *m,* l'enfer *m.*

abaft [ə'bɑ:ft], *Nau:* **1.** *adv.* sur l'arrière; vers l'arrière; **right a.,** droit arrière; (*of wind*) **to draw, veer, a.,** adonner. **2.** *prep.* **a. the mast,** sur l'arrière du mât; en arrière du mât; **a. the beam,** sur l'arrière du travers.

abaissé [ə'beisei], *a. Her:* abaissé.

abalienate [æb'eiljəneit], *v.tr. Jur:* aliéner (un bien).

abalienation [æb'eiljəneiʃ(ə)n], *s. Jur:* aliénation *f* (d'un bien).

abalone [æbə'louni], *s. Moll:* ormeau *m.*

abampere [æbæm'pɛər], *s. El.Meas:* unité *f* électromagnétique C.G.S. d'intensité.

abandon[1] [ə'bændən, *O: occ.* abɑ̃dɔ̃], *s.* (*a*) abandon *m,* laisser-aller *m,* expansion *f;* (*b*) désinvolture *f,* entrain *m.*

abandon[2] [ə'bænd(ə)n], *v.tr.* abandonner; délaisser (sa famille, etc.); renoncer à (un projet); *Nau:* **to a. ship,** abandonner, évacuer, le bâtiment; **to a. a new-born child,** exposer un nouveau-né; **to a. all hope of success,** abandonner tout espoir de réussite; **to a. the attempt,** y renoncer; **to a. oneself to despair,** s'abandonner, se livrer, se laisser aller, au désespoir; *Jur:* **to a. a prosecution, a mortgaged estate,** renoncer à des poursuites; délaisser un bien hypothéqué; *Ins:* **to a. property covered by a policy,** faire délaissement aux assureurs des biens, de la cargaison, du navire sinistré, etc.

abandoned [ə'bændənd], *a.* **1.** abandonné; délaissé; *Adm:* **a. road,** route désaffectée. **2.** *O:* dévergondé; dépravé; (femme) perdue (d'honneur).

abandonee [əbændə'ni:], *s. Jur: Ins:* abandonnataire *mf.*

abandoning [ə'bænd(ə)niŋ], *s.,* **abandonment** [ə'bændənmənt], *s.* **1.** abandon(nement) *m* (de qn, de qch.); cession *f* (de biens); délaissement *m* (de sa famille, *Jur:* de terre hypothéquée, *Nau: etc:* d'objets ou de navire assurés); **a. of a claim, of a request,** retrait *m* d'une réclamation, d'une demande; *Mil:* **a. of post in face of the enemy,** abandon de poste en présence de l'ennemi. **2.** *A:* **abandonment,** abandon *m,* laisser-aller *m.*

abarthrosis [æbɑ:'θrousis], *s. Anat:* diarthrose *f.*

abase [ə'beis], *v.tr. Lit:* abaisser, ravaler (qn); humilier, rabattre (qn); **to a. oneself,** s'abaisser, s'humilier, se dégrader; **to a. oneself so far as to . . .,** s'abaisser jusqu'à. . . .

abased [ə'beist], *a. Her:* abaissé.

abasement [ə'beismənt], *s. Lit:* **1.** abaissement *m*, ravalement *m*; humiliation *f*, abjection *f*. **2.** abaissement, humilité *f*.

abash [ə'bæʃ], *v.tr.* (*usu. passive*) confondre, interloquer, décontenancer, interdire, démonter (qn); **to be abashed,** perdre contenance; **to be abashed at sth.,** être confus, interloqué, tout interdit, de qch.; **it made me feel terribly abashed,** j'en étais tout confus; je ne savais pas où me mettre.

abashment [ə'bæʃmənt], *s. O:* confusion *f*, décontenancement *m*, embarras *m*.

abasia [ə'beiziə], *s. Med:* abasie *f*.

abatable [ə'beitəbl], *a.* qui peut être diminué, annulé, etc.

abate[1] [ə'beit]. **1.** *v.tr.* (*a*) *A:* diminuer (l'orgueil, le zèle, etc.); affaiblir (le courage); relâcher, ralentir (son activité); diminuer, faire cesser (la douleur, le bruit, etc.); **to a. one's pretensions,** réduire ses prétentions; (*b*) *A:* **to a. sth. of the price,** rabattre qch. sur le prix; (*c*) *Jur:* (i) abolir, faire cesser, mettre fin à (un abus, etc.); arrêter (une action); (ii) (faire) annuler, rendre nul et non avenu (un ordre judiciaire). **2.** *v.i.* (*a*) (*of storm, etc.*) diminuer, faiblir, s'affaiblir; (*of storm, fear, pain*) se calmer, s'apaiser; se modérer; (*of epidemic*) s'enrayer; (*of flood*) baisser, diminuer; **the wind abated,** le vent mollit, tomba; (*b*) *Jur:* (*of writ, appeal*) s'annuler; s'éteindre; (*of claim*) devenir caduc; (*c*) *O:* (*of wages, rent, etc.*) baisser, diminuer de valeur.

abate[2], *v.tr. & i. Jur:* prendre possession (d'un immeuble) (appartenant à un héritier).

abatement[1] [ə'beitmənt], *s.* **1.** (*a*) (*also* **abating** [ə'beitiŋ]) diminution *f*, affaiblissement *m*; apaisement *m* (d'une tempête); relâchement *m* (du temps); abaissement *m*, rabais *m* (des eaux); *Med:* (i) décours *m*, rémission *f*, (ii) diminution *f* (d'une fièvre); (*b*) abolition *f* (d'un abus); **noise a. campaign,** campagne *f* contre le bruit; (*c*) *Her:* brisure (déshonorante). **2.** (*a*) *Adm:* abattement *m* (sur le chiffre des revenus); défalcation *f* (sur l'impôt sur le revenu); dégrèvement *m*; (*b*) *Com:* rabais, réduction *f*, déduction *f*, remise *f* (sur le prix); **without a.,** sans déduction, sans remise. **3.** *Jur:* réduction; annulation *f* (d'un ordre judiciaire); **plea in a.,** demande *f* en nullité; **action in a. (by heirs),** action *f* en réduction.

abatement[1] [ə'beitmənt], *s.* **1.** (*a*) (*also* **abating** partenant à un héritier).

abatis [æbæ'ti:], *s. Mil:* abat(t)is *m*; **portable a.,** abatis rapporté; **live a.,** abatis sur place.

abatised [æbæ'ti:zd], *a. Mil:* à abat(t)is.

abat-jour [æbæ'ʒu:ər], *s.* abat-jour *m inv.*

abator[1] [ə'beitər], *s.* abolisseur *m*; personne *f* qui abolit (un abus).

abator[2], *s. Jur:* personne *f* qui prend possession (d'un immeuble) (appartenant à un héritier).

abattis [æbæ'ti:] *s. Mil:* = ABATIS.

abattoir ['æbətwɑ:r], *s.* abattoir *m*.

abature ['æbətju:r], *s. Ven:* abattures *fpl.*

abaxial [æb'æksiəl], *a. Bot:* désaxé.

abb [æb], *s. Tex:* **1.** fil *m* de trame. **2.** déchets *mpl* de toison.

abba ['æbə], *s. B:Ecc:* abba *m*.

abbacy ['æbəsi], *s.* **1.** dignité abbatiale, dignité d'abbé, d'abbesse. **2.** (*term of office*) abbatiat *m*. **3.** droits, privilèges, abbatiaux; juridiction abbatiale. **4.** abbaye *f*, bénéfice *m*.

Abbas(s)id(e) [æ'bæsid, 'æbəsid], *a. & s. Hist:* Abbas(s)ide (*m*).

abbatial [æb'eiʃl], *a.* abbatial, -aux.

Abbe ['æbei], *Pr.n. Ch:* **A. refractometer,** réfractomètre *m* d'Abbe.

abbé ['æbei], *s. Ecc:* abbé *m*.

abess ['æbes, -is], *s.* **1.** abbesse *f*; supérieure *f* (de couvent); mère abbesse. **2.** *A:* maquerelle *f*.

Abbevillian [æb'viliən], *a. Prehist:* abbevillien.

abbey ['æbi], *s.* (*a*) abbaye *f*; *attrib.* **a. lands,** terres abbatiales; *Hist:* **a. counter, a. piece,** pièce donnée à qn qui a fait un pèlerinage à une abbaye; *Hist: Pej:* **a. lubber,** moine paresseux; (*b*) **a. (church),** (église) abbatiale (*f*).

abbot ['æbət], *s.* abbé *m* (d'un couvent, d'un monastère); (père) supérieur *m*; **mitred a.,** abbé mitré; *Hist:* (*in mediaeval revels*) **a. of unreason, of misrule,** évêque *m* de la déraison, pape *m* des fous.

abbotship ['æbətʃip], *s.* = ABBACY.

abbreviate[1] [ə'bri:viət], *a. Nat.Hist:* de peu d'extension; court.

abbreviate[2] [ə'bri:vieit], *v.tr.* abréger (un mot, etc.); **metre is abbreviated to m.,** l'abréviation de mètre est m.; **abbreviated edition,** édition abrégée, tronquée; *Mth: A:* **abbreviated multiplication, division,** multiplication, division, abrégée.

abbreviation [əbri:vi'eiʃ(ə)n], *s.* abréviation *f*.

abbreviator [ə'bri:vieitər], *s. Ecc:* abréviateur *m* (des lettres apostoliques).

abbreviatory [ə'bri:viətri], *a.* abréviatif.

ABC, abc ['eibi:'si:], *s.* (*a*) ABC, abc *m*; **he doesn't know his ABC,** il ne sait pas son alphabet; **as easy, simple, as ABC,** simple comme bonjour; (*b*) *Sch:* abécédaire *m*; (*c*) *Geol:* **ABC soil,** sol où les horizons A, B, C sont bien marqués.

abcoulomb [æb'ku:lɔmb], *s. El.Meas:* unité *f* électromagnétique C.G.S. (u.é.m. C.G.S.) de quantité.

Abdera [æbdiərə], *Pr.n. A.Geog:* Abdère *f*.

Abderhalden [æbdə'hɔ:ld(ə)n, æpdə:'hæld(ə)n], *Pr.n. Ch:* **A. reaction,** réaction *f* d'Abderhalden.

Abderian [æb'diəriən], *a.* d'Abdère.

Abderite ['æbdərait], *s.* **1.** Abdéritain, -aine. **2.** *A:* homme à esprit obtus; innocent *m*.

abdicable ['æbdikəbl], *a.* qui peut être abdiqué, renoncé.

abdicant ['æbdikənt], *a. & s.* abdicataire (*mf*).

abdicate ['æbdikeit], *v.tr.* (*a*) abdiquer (un trône); se démettre de, renoncer à (une charge); renoncer à (un droit); **abdicating, abdicated, king,** roi abdicataire; (*b*) *abs.* abdiquer; résigner le pouvoir.

abdication [æbdi'keiʃ(ə)n], *s.* abdication *f* (d'un trône); renonciation *f* (à un droit); démission *f* (d'une charge).

abdicator ['æbdikeitər], *s.* abdicataire *mf* (d'un trône); renonciateur, -trice (à un droit).

abdomen ['æbdəmən, *occ.* æb'doumən], *s.* abdomen *m*; *Med:* **acute a.,** ventre aigu chirurgical.

abdominal [əb'dɔminl], *a.* abdominal, -aux; *Anat:* **a. wall,** paroi abdominale; **a. regions,** régions de l'abdomen; *s. Med:* **an a.,** une opération abdominale; *Med:* **a. belt,** ceinture abdominale, hypogastrique; *Ich:* **a. fins,** nageoires abdominales, ventrales.

abdominally [əb'dɔminəli], *adv.* à, dans, l'abdomen.

abdomino- [əb'dɔminou], *pref.* abdomino-.

abdominogenital [əb'dɔminou'dʒenitl], *a. Anat:* abdomino-génital, -aux.

abdominothoracic [əb'dɔminouθɔr'æsik], *a. Anat:* abdominothoracique.

abdominous [əb'dɔminəs], *a. A:* ventru, à gros ventre; pansu; corpulent.

abducens, *pl.,* **-centes** [əb'dju:sens, -'senti:z], *a. & s. Anat:* **a. (nerve),** (nerf) abducteur *m* (de l'œil).

abducent [əb'dju:sənt], *a. & s. Anat:* abducteur (*m*); **a. nerve,** nerf abducteur de l'œil.

abduct [əb'dʌkt], *v.tr.* **1.** *Jur:* (*a*) enlever (qn); (*b*) détourner (une mineure). **2.** *Surg: etc:* opérer l'abduction (d'un organe, etc.); dévier (un organe).

abduction [əb'dʌkʃ(ə)n], *s.* **1.** *Jur:* (*a*) enlèvement *m* (de qn); (*b*) détournement *m* (de mineure); **a. by force, menace, fraud,** rapt *m:* **a. by consent,** rapt par séduction. **2.** *Physiol:* abduction *f*, déplacement *m*. **3.** *Surg:* séparation *f*, solution *f* de continuité (des parties contiguës après fracture transversale); écartement *m* (des lèvres d'une plaie). **4.** *Log:* abduction.

abductor [əb'dʌktər]. **1.** *s. Jur:* (*a*) ravisseur *m*; auteur *m* d'un enlèvement; (*b*) détourneur, -euse (de mineure). **2.** *a. & s. Anat:* **a. (muscle),** (muscle) abducteur (*m*); **a. pollicis,** abducteur du pouce.

abeam [ə'bi:m], *adv. Nau: Av:* par le travers; en belle; **with the wind a.,** sur la perpendiculaire du vent; **right a.,** droit par le travers; **we are a. of the lighthouse,** nous sommes par le travers du phare; **the lighthouse was a. of us,** le phare était par notre travers.

abecedarian ['eibi:si:'dɛəriən]. **1.** *a.* (*a*) (ordre) alphabétique, abécédaire; (*b*) ignorant; (*c*) (connaissance) rudimentaire. **2.** *s.* commençant, -ante.

abed [ə'bed], *adv. A:* (*a*) au lit, couché; **to lie late a.,** faire la grasse matinée; (*b*) alité (par une maladie); **to be brought a. of a child,** accoucher d'un enfant.

abele [ə'bi:l, 'eibl], *s. Bot:* peuplier blanc; ypréau *m*.

Abelian [ə'bi:liən], *a. Mth:* **A. function, A. group, A. question,** fonction abélienne, groupe abélien, équation abélienne; **A. integrals,** intégrales abéliennes.

abelmosk ['eiblmɔsk], **abelmusk** ['eiblmʌsk], *s. Bot:* ambrette *f*, abelmosch *m*.

abeltree ['eibltri:], *s.* = ABELE.

aberdevine [æbədə'vain], *s. Orn:* tarin *m*.

Aberdonian [æbə'douniən], *a. & s.* (originaire, habitant, -ante) d'Aberdeen.

Abernethy [æbə'neθi], *Pr.n. Comest:* **A. biscuit,** (sorte de) biscuit digestif.

aberrance [æb'erəns], *s.* aberrance *f*.

aberrancy [æb'erənsi], *s.* déviation *f*.

aberrant [æb'erənt]. **1.** *a.* (*a*) égaré (du droit chemin); dévoyé; (*b*) *Biol:* aberrant; anormal, -aux. **2.** *s.* (*a*) dévoyé, -ée; (*b*) *Biol:* individu aberrant.

aberrate ['æbəreit], *v.i.* dévier; s'égarer (du droit chemin).

aberration [æbər'eiʃ(ə)n], *s.* **1.** (*a*) aberration *f*, déviation *f* (de qn, d'un navire); (*b*) **phenomena that appeared to be aberrations from nature,** phénomènes qui semblaient s'écarter de la nature. **2.** (*a*) égarement *m* (des passions, etc.); **mental a.,** égarement d'esprit; aberration; confusion mentale; *Jur:* démence *f*; **in a moment of mental a.,** dans un moment d'absence; (*b*) écart *m* (de conduite). **3.** *Astr: Mth: Opt: etc:* aberration; *Opt:* **chromatic a.,** aberration chromatique; **spherical a.,** aberration sphérique, de sphéricité. **4.** *Biol:* aberration (autosomique, sexuelle); structure aberrante, anormale; développement aberrant, anormal; anomalie *f*; sport *m*.

aberrational [æbər'eiʃənl], *a.* excentrique.

abet [ə'bet], *v.tr.* (**abetted**). **1. to a. s.o. in a crime,** encourager qn à un crime; *Jur:* **to aid and a. s.o.,** être le complice premier de qn; **aided and abetted by . . .,** avec la complicité de. . . . **2.** encourager (un vice, le crime); s'associer à (un crime), se faire, se rendre, complice (d'un crime); prêter assistance à (un trafic).

abetment [ə'betmənt], *s.* **a. in crime,** encouragement *m* au crime; **a. of a crime,** complicité *f* dans un crime.

abetter [ə'betər], *s.* = ABETTOR.

abetting[1] [ə'betiŋ], *a.* complice, fauteur, -trice.

abetting[2], *s.* (**aiding and**) **a.,** complicité *f* (dans un crime).

abettor [ə'betər], *s.* **a. of a crime,** complice *mf* d'un crime; **a. of disturbances,** fauteur, -trice, de désordres; **his abettors in crime,** les complices de ses crimes.

abeyance [ə'beiəns], *s.* (*a*) suspension *f* (d'une loi); vacation *f* (de droits); vacance *f* (d'un poste); **work in a.,** travail en souffrance; **to leave a decree in a.,** suspendre un décret; **the matter is still in a.,** la question est toujours pendante, en suspens; **law in a.,** loi inappliquée; **to fall into a.,** tomber en désuétude; (*b*) *Jur:* **land in a.,** biens jacents, vacants; **estate in a.,** succession vacante; **to call (a title) out of a.,** relever (un titre).

abeyant [ə'beiənt], *a.* en suspens, en désuétude.

abfarad [æb'færæd], *s. El.Meas:* unité *f* électromagnétique C.G.S (u.é.m. C.G.S) de capacité.

abhenry [æb'henri], *s. El.Meas:* unité *f* électromagnétique C.G.S. (u.é.m. C.G.S.) d'inductance.

abhor [əb'hɔ:r], *v.tr.* (**abhorred**) abhorrer; détester; avoir horreur de (qn, qch.); avoir (qn, qch.) en horreur.

abhorrence [əb'hɔrəns], *s.* **1.** horreur *f* (**of,** de); extrême aversion *f* (**of,** pour, de); **to hold sth. in a.,** avoir qch. en horreur; **to be held in a. by s.o.,** être en horreur, en abomination, à qn. **2.** aversion, bête noire.

abhorrent [əb'hɔrənt], *a.* **1.** (*of pers., thg*) **to be a. to s.o.,** être répugnant, en horreur, à qn; répugner à qn; **there is nothing about him that I find either a. or attractive,** il n'y a rien en lui qui me repousse ou qui m'attire. **2.** *A:* (*of thg*) **to be a. to, from, sth.,** être contraire, opposé, à qch.; être incompatible avec qch.; **theory a. to reason,** théorie opposée à la raison, qui répugne à la raison. **3.** *A:* (*of pers.*) **to be a. of, from, sth.,** avoir horreur de qch.; être opposé à qch.; être ennemi de qch.

abhorrently [əb'hɔrəntli], *adv.* détestablement; exécrablement; d'une façon répugnante.

abhorrer [əb'hɔ:rər], *s.* **1.** personne *f* qui tient qn, qch., en horreur; **a. of lies,** haïsseur, -euse, de mensonges. **2.** *Eng.Hist:* **the Abhorrers,** les signataires d'une protestation au roi en 1679.

abidance [ə'baid(ə)ns], *s.* **1.** *A:* séjour *m* (**in,** dans). **2. a. by the truth, by the law,** respect *m* de la vérité; soumission *f* à la loi.

abide [ə'baid]. **1.** *v.i.* (*a*) *A: & Lit:* (*p.t. & p.p. usu.* **abode** [ə'boud]) rester, demeurer (**with s.o.,** avec qn); **to a. at, in, a place,** demeurer, séjourner, dans un lieu; habiter un lieu; (*b*) **to a. by a promise,** rester fidèle à, tenir, une promesse; **to a. by a rule, a decision, a law,** se conformer à, s'incliner devant, se soumettre à, respecter, une règle, une décision, une loi; **to a. by one's agreement,** tenir parole; **I shall a. by your decision,** je me soumets à votre décision; je m'en rapporte à vous; **to a. by one's own decision,** s'en tenir à, maintenir, sa décision; **we a. by the treaty,** nous nous en tenons à l'exécution du traité; **he will a. by his opinion,** il ne démordra pas de son opinion; **I a. by what I said,** je maintiens mon dire; (*c*) (*of thg*) durer, subsister, demeurer. **2.** *v.tr.* (*a*) **to a. the test,** subir l'épreuve; (*b*) *A: & Lit:* attendre; **I will a. the coming of my lord,** j'attendrai la venue de mon seigneur; **I a. my time,** j'attends l'occasion; je me réserve; **to a. the event,** attendre l'issue; (*c*) *A: & Lit:* soutenir; *B:* **who may a. the day of his coming?** qui soutiendra le jour de son arrivée? (*d*) *F:* (*neg. & interr.*) **I can't a. him,** je ne peux pas le sentir, le souffrir, le supporter; *A:* **he couldn't a. to look at it,** il ne pouvait pas en supporter la vue.

abider [ə'baidər], *s. A:* **a. in a place,** habitant, -ante, d'un lieu.

abiding[1] [ə'baidiŋ], *a.* permanent, durable, constant, immuable.

abiding[2], *s. A: & Lit:* **a. place,** lieu *m* de séjour; domicile *m.*

abietate [ei'baiəteit], *s. Ch:* abiétate *m.*

abietic [eibai'etik], *a. Ch:* abiétique.

Abietineae [æbie'tinii:], *s. pl. Bot:* abiétinées *f.*

Abigail ['æbigeil]. **1.** *Pr.n.f.* Abigaïl. **2.** *s. A:* femme *f* de chambre; *Th:* suivante *f*, soubrette *f.*

ability [ə'biliti], *s.* **1.** (*a*) capacité *f*, pouvoir *m* (**to do sth.,** de faire qch.); (*b*) *Jur:* habilité *f* (à succéder, à tester, etc.); capacité légale (pour tester, etc.); (*c*) *Scot: A:* puissance *f* physique; force *f.* **2.** habilité, capacité, compétence *f*, intelligence *f*, talent *m*, aptitude *f*; **man of a.,** homme capable; **man of great a.,** homme très doué; homme d'une grande capacité; **to do sth. to the best of one's a.,** faire qch. dans la mesure de ses moyens, de ses forces; faire qch. de son mieux; **salary commensurate with one's abilities,** appointements proportionnels à ses compétences.

abiogenesis [eibaiou'dʒenisis], *s.* abigénèse *f.*

abiosis [eibai'ousis], *s. Biol:* abiose *f.*

abiotic [eibai'ɔtik], *a.* abiotique.

abiotropic [eibaio'trɔfik], *a. Biol: Med:* abiotropique.

abiotrophy [eibaiou'trɔfi], *s. Biol: Med:* abiotrophie *f.*

abirritant [æb'iritənt], **abirritative** [æb'iriteitiv], *a. Med:* calmant.

abject ['æbdʒekt], *a.* **1.** abject, déchu, misérable; pitoyable; **to live in a. poverty,** ramper dans la misère. **2.** (*a*) bas, vil; (*b*) servile (**to,** envers).

abjection [æb'dʒekʃ(ə)n], *s.* **1.** abjection *f*, misère *f*, abaissement *m.* **2.** *Bot:* projection *f* (des spores d'un sporophore).

abjectly ['æbdʒektli], *adv.* **1.** abjectement, misérablement. **2.** bassement, avec servilité.

abjectness ['æbdʒektnis], *s.* abjection *f*; misère *f.*

abjuration [æbdʒu'reiʃ(ə)n], *s.* abjuration *f* (**of,** de); reniement *m* (de sa foi); renonciation *f* (sous serment); rétraction solennelle.

abjure [əb'dʒuər], *v.tr.* abjurer (sa foi, ses erreurs); faire abjuration de (sa foi, etc.); renier (sa religion); renoncer (sous serment à (ses droits); **to a. lying,** renoncer au mensonge; *Hist:* **to a. the realm,** s'engager sous serment à s'exiler (après avoir commis un crime).

abjurer [əb'dʒurər], *s.* renieur *m* (**of,** de).

ablactation [æblæk'teiʃ(ə)n], *s.* ablactation *f.*

ablate [æb'leit]. **1.** *v.tr. Surg:* pratiquer l'ablation (d'une tumeur, etc.). **2.** *v.i. Geol:* subir l'ablation.

ablation [æb'leiʃ(ə)n], *s. Geol: Surg:* ablation *f* (d'un glacier, d'une tumeur); *attrib. Geol:* **a. moraine,** moraine d'ablation.

ablatival [æblə'taivl], *a. Gram:* ablatif.

ablative[1] ['æblətiv], *a. & s. Gram:* **a. (case),** (cas) ablatif (*m*); **in the a.,** à l'ablatif; **a. absolute,** ablatif absolu.

ablative[2] [ə'bleitiv], *a.* qui subit l'ablation.

ablaut ['æblaut], *s. Ling:* ablaut *m*, apophonie *f*, alternance *f* (de la voyelle radicale du verbe).

ablaze [ə'bleiz], *adv.* & *a.* en feu, en flammes; enflammé, embrasé; **to be a.,** flamber; **a. with light, with colour,** resplendissant de lumière, de couleur; **a. with anger,** enflammé de colère; **the house was a.,** la maison flambait; le feu avait pris à la maison; **the house was a. with light,** la maison étincelait de lumière; **to set Europe a.,** mettre l'Europe en feu, en flammes; incendier, embraser, l'Europe.

able ['eibl], *a.* **1.** (*a*) capable, compétent; expert, habile; **a. worker,** bon travailleur; compétent; **he's the most a., the ablest, man I know,** c'est l'homme le plus capable que je connaisse; **a very a. man,** un homme de haute capacité; **he's not very a.,** il est peu capable; il n'est pas très fort; *Jur:* **a. in body and mind,** sain de corps et d'esprit; *Nau:* **a. seaman,** matelot de deuxième classe; (*b*) **to be a. to do sth.,** (i) savoir, être capable de, faire qch.; (ii) (*as infin. of the verb* **can**) pouvoir, être en mesure de, être à même de, être en état de, faire qch.; **I shan't be a. to come today,** je ne pourrai pas venir aujourd'hui; **better a. to do sth.,** plus capable, mieux à même, de faire qch.; **I was a. to master my anger,** j'ai su maîtriser ma colère; **I'll do it if I'm a.,** je le ferai si possible; **I'll go when I'm a.,** j'irai quand je pourrai; **I go to see her when I'm a.,** je vais la voir selon mes possibilités, quand j'ai le temps; **a. to pay,** en mesure de payer; (*c*) *Jur:* **a. to devise property, to inherit,** apte, habile, à léguer, à succéder. **2. a. piece of work,** travail compétent; travail bien fait, **your a. assistance,** votre aide efficace.

able-bodied ['eibl'bɔdid], *a.* fort, robuste, vigoureux; *Mil:* (i) valide; (ii) bon pour le service; *Nau:* **a.-b. seaman,** matelot *m* de deuxième classe.

ablegate ['æbligeit], *s. R.C.Ch:* ablégat *m.*

able-minded ['eibl'maindid], *a.* intelligent; de haute capacité intellectuelle.

ablepharia [æbli'fɛəriə], *s.* abléphario *f.*

ablepsia [æb'lepsiə], *s. Med:* ablepsie *f.*

ablet ['æblit], *s. Ich:* ablette *f.*

abloom [ə'blu:m], *adv. & a. A: & Lit:* en fleur(s); **all nature is a. once more,** toute la nature est refleurie.

abluent ['æbluənt], *s.* détergent *m.*

ablush [ə'blʌʃ], *adv. & a. A: & Lit:* (en) rougissant.

ablution [ə'blu:ʃ(ə)n], *s.* ablution *f*; *Ecc:* **to perform the a. of the chalice,** ablutionner le calice; *Adm: etc:* **a. facilities,** *Mil: F:* **the ablutions,** lavabos *mpl*; *F:* **to perform one's ablutions,** faire ses ablutions, se laver.

ably ['eibli], *adv.* habilement; expertement; avec talent; avec maîtrise; **he a. supported our efforts,** il nous a prêté une aide efficace, une aide considérable; son aide nous a rendu grand service.

abnegate ['æbnigeit], *v.tr.* renoncer à (une croyance, un privilège); faire abnégation de (sa volonté, ses droits, etc.); **to a. one's faith,** renoncer (à) sa foi.

abnegation [æbni'geiʃ(ə)n], *s.* **1.** abnégation *f* (de soi, de ses intérêts); renoncement *m*, renonciation *f.* **2.** désaveu *m*, reniement *m* (d'une doctrine, etc.).

abnegator ['æbnigeitər], *s.* renonciateur, -trice (**of,** de).

abnormal [æb'nɔ:ml]. **1.** *a.* (*a*) anormal, -aux; qui échappe à la norme; (*b*) *Cmptr:* **a. exit,** sortie anormale; **a. condition,** anomalie *f.* **2.** (*a*) *a. Pej:* perverti; (*b*) *s.* anormal, -ale; perverti, -ie.

abnormalcy [æb'nɔ:məlsi], **abnormalism** [æb'nɔ:məlizm], *s.* = ABNORMALITY.

abnormality [æbnɔ:'mæliti], *s.* **1.** caractère anormal (de qch.); anomalie *f.* **2.** (*a*) difformité *f*; (*b*) bizarrerie *f*; aberration *f.*

abnormalize [æb'nɔ:məlaiz], *v.tr.* rendre anormal.

abnormally [æb'nɔ:məli], *adv.* anormalement.

abnormity [æb'nɔ:miti], *s.* **1.** *A:* = ABNORMALITY. **2.** (*a*) monstruosité *f*; (*b*) monstre *m.*

abo ['æbou], *s. Austr: F:* aborigène *m* (d'Australie).

aboard [ə'bɔ:d]. **1.** *adv.* à bord; **to go a.,** aller, monter, à bord; s'embarquer; **to have s.o. a.,** avoir qn à son bord; **life a.,** la vie à bord; **to take goods a.,** embarquer des marchandises; **to haul the tacks a.,** amurer; mettre les amures à bloc; **all a.!** (i) *Nau:* embarquez! (ii) *Rail: esp. U.S:* en voiture! **2.** *adv.* (*a*) **to fall a. (of) a ship, to run a. a ship,** aborder un navire (par le travers); se heurter contre un navire; entrer en collision avec un navire; (*b*) *A:* **to lay the enemy a.,** aborder l'ennemi; (*c*) **to keep the land a.,** ranger la terre. **3.** *prep.* **a. ship,** à bord (d'un navire); **a. a train, a bus, an aircraft,** dans un train, un autobus, un avion.

abode [ə'boud], *s.* **1.** *Lit:* demeure *f*, habitation *f*, résidence *f.* **2.** *Lit:* (lieu *m* de) séjour *m*; **to take up one's a. in the country,** s'installer à la campagne; *Jur:* **place of a.,** domicile *m*; **to make one's a. at . . .,** élire domicile à . . .; fixer sa résidence à . . .; **of, with, no fixed a.,** sans domicile fixe. **3.** *A:* séjour (dans un endroit).

abohm [æb'oum], *s. El.Meas:* unité *f* électromagnétique C.G.S. (u.é.m. C.G.S.) de résistance.

aboideau [æ'bwædou], **aboiteau** [æ'bwætou], *s. Hyd.E: Can:* aboiteau *m* (*Fr.C.*).

aboil [ə'bɔil], *a. & adv. A: & Lit:* **1.** bouillant; en ébullition. **2.** (*of pers.*) furieux; en ébullition.

abolish [ə'bɔliʃ], *v.tr.* abolir, supprimer (un usage, un abus); abolir, éteindre (des droits); abroger (une loi).

abolishable [ə'bɔliʃəbl], *a.* abolissable.

abolisher [ə'bɔliʃər], *s.* abolisseur *m.*

abolishing [ə'bɔliʃiŋ], **abolishment** [ə'bɔliʃmənt], *s.* abolition *f.*

abolition [æbə'liʃ(ə)n], *s.* abolition *f*; suppression *f* (d'un abus); abrogation *f* (d'une loi).

abolitionism [æbə'liʃənizm], *s. Hist:* abolitionnisme *m.*

abolitionist [æbə'liʃənist], *s. & a.* abolitionniste (*mf*); antiesclavagiste (*mf*).

aboma [ə'boumə], *s. Rept:* aboma *m.*

abomasitis [ə'boumə'saitis], *s. Vet:* abomasite *f.*

abomasum [æbou'meisəm], *s. Z:* caillette *f*, abomasum *m* (d'un ruminant).

A-bomb[1] ['eibɔm], *s.* bombe *f* atomique, bombe A.

A-bomb[2], *v.tr.* détruire (qch.) à la bombe atomique; atomiser (qch.).

abominable [ə'bɔminəbl], *a.* (*a*) abominable; odieux; haïssable; (*b*) *F:* exécrable, au-dessous de tout; **his writing's a.,** son écriture est terrible, il écrit comme un chat; (*c*) **the a. snowman,** l'abominable homme des neiges.

abominably [ə'bɔminəbli], *adv.* (*a*) abominablement; odieusement; (*b*) *F:* très mal; **he plays a.,** il joue abominablement, comme un pied.

abominate[1] [ə'bɔminət], *a. A: & Lit:* (*a*) exécrable; (*b*) exécré.

abominate[2] [ə'bɔmineit], *v.tr.* abominer, abhorrer, exécrer, haïr, détester; avoir (qch.) en abomination, en horreur.

abomination [əbɔmin'eiʃ(ə)n], *s.* **1.** (*a*) abomination *f* (**of,** de); **to be held in a. by s.o., to be an a. to s.o.,** être en abomination, en horreur, à qn; (*b*) *B:* **the a. of desolation,** l'abomination de la désolation; **for all that do such things are an a. unto the Lord,** car quiconque fait ces choses-là est en abomination à l'Éternel; **it is an a. before the Lord to . . .,** c'est un sacrilège de. . . . **2.** *F:* **this coffee's an a.,** ce café est une abomination, est abominable, est au-dessous de tout.

abominator [ə'bɔmineitər], *s.* haïsseur *m* (de qch.); personne qui déteste, qui exècre (qch.); **to be an a. of meanness,** détester, haïr, l'avarice; avoir l'avarice en abomination.

aboriginal [æbə'ridʒinl]. **1.** *a.* (*a*) primitif; (*b*) indigène, autochtone, aborigène. **2.** *s.* aborigène *m*, indigène *mf.*

aborigine [æbə'ridʒini:], *s.* (*a*) aborigène *m* d'Australie; (*b*) *pl.* aborigènes, indigènes *mpl.*

abort[1] [ə'bɔ:t], *s.* (*a*) *Mil.Av:* mission non accomplie; (*of rocket, spacecraft*) **launch a.,** termination prématurée d'un lancement; (*b*) *Cmptr:* arrêt *m*, suspension *f*, d'exécution (d'un programme).

abort[2], *v.* **1.** *v.i.* (*a*) *Biol:* avorter; (*b*) (*of project*) avorter. **2.** *v.tr.* (*a*) pratiquer un avortement sur (une femme); faire avorter (une femme); (*b*) *Biol:* faire avorter (des fruits, etc.); (*c*) faire avorter (un projet); (*d*) *Cmptr:* abandonner (un programme), suspendre l'exécution d'(un programme).

aborted [ə'bɔ:tid], *a.* **1.** avorté. **2.** imparfait, rudimentaire.

aborticide [ə'bɔ:tisaid], *s.* fœticide *m.*

abortifacient [əbɔ:ti'feiʃənt], *a. & s. Obst:* abortif (*m*).

aborting [ə'bɔ:tiŋ], *s.* avortement *m.*

abortion [ə'bɔ:ʃ(ə)n], *s.* **1.** (*a*) *Obst:* avortement *m*, *esp.* avortement provoqué; **to procure an a.,** faire avorter (qn); **procuring of a.,** manœuvres abortives; *Med:Vet:* **infectious, contagious, a.,** brucellose *f*; avortement épizootique; *Vet:* **vibrionic a.,** vibriose *f*; *Obst:* **missed a.,** rétention *f* intra-utérine de l'œuf mort; (*b*) *Bot:* contabescence *f* (du pollen); rachitis *m*, rachitisme *m* (de la graine); (*c*) avortement (d'un projet). **2.** *F:* (*a*) (*dwarfed creature*) avorton *m*, monstre *m*, *P:* fausse couche; (*b*) œuvre mal venue, manquée; **what an a.!** quelle horreur!

abortionist [ə'bɔ:ʃənist], *s.* médecin avorteur; avorteuse *f*; *F:* **back-street a.,** faiseuse *f* d'anges.

abortive [ə'bɔ:tiv], *a.* **1.** (*a*) *Biol: A:* abortif; (*b*) *Bot:* abortif, rudimentaire; (*c*) *Obst:* **a. treatment,** traitement abortif. **2.** (*of plan, etc.*) avorté, mort-né, manqué; **to prove a.,** ne pas aboutir; n'aboutir à rien; échouer, avorter; **a. attempt, effort,** essai, effort, qui échoue, qui n'aboutit à rien; coup manqué; *Mil: etc:* **a. attack,** attaque avortée; **a. mission,** mission non accomplie.

abortively [ə'bɔ:tivili], *adv.* **1.** *A:* (naître) avant terme, prématurément. **2.** sans succès; sans aboutir à rien; **after trying a. to help them,** après avoir essayé sans (aucun) succès de les aider.

abortiveness [ə'bɔ:tivnis], *s.* insuccès *m*, non-réussite *f* (d'un projet).

abortogenic [ə'bɔ:tou'dʒenik], *a. Obst:* abortif.

aboulia [ə'bu:liə], *s. Med:* aboulie *f.*

aboulic [ə'bu:lik], *a.* aboulique.

abound [ə'baund], *v.i.* abonder, affluer; être en abondance; foisonner; **river abounding in fish,** rivière qui abonde en poissons; **country abounding in wheat,** pays abondant, riche, en blé.

abounding [ə'baundiŋ], *a. Lit:* abondant, illimité, infini; **a. energy,** énergie infinie; **a. generosity,** générosité illimitée.

about [ə'baut], *adv. & prep.* **1.** (*a*) autour (de); *O:* **to gather a. the fire,** s'assembler autour du feu; **he looked a. him,** il regarda autour de lui; **the hills (round) a. the town,** les collines autour de la ville, à l'entour de la ville; **the people a. us,** les gens auprès de nous, qui nous entourent; *U.S:* **the lake is a mile a.,** le lac a un mille de circonférence; **he went a long way a.,** il fit un long détour; (*b*) de côté et d'autre; **to stroll a.,** se promener de ci, de là; se promener de côté et d'autre; **there was nobody a.,** il n'y avait personne dans le voisinage; il n'y avait personne (de visible); **to follow s.o. a.,** suivre qn partout; **don't leave those papers lying a.,** ne laissez pas traîner ces papiers; **a. here,** par ici, dans ces parages; **to walk a. the streets,** marcher par les rues; **there's a great deal of influenza a. at present,** il y a beaucoup de grippe actuellement; **there's plenty of money a.,** il y a beaucoup d'argent en circulation; **he's a. again,** il est de nouveau sur pied; **to be a. early,** être matinal; **to have one's eyes a. one,** avoir l'œil ouvert; (*c*) **there is no vanity a. him,** la vanité n'est pas son fait; **there is something unusual a. him,** il y a dans sa personne quelque chose de pas ordinaire; **there's something a. a horse that . . .,** il y a chez le cheval un je ne sais quoi qui . . .; *O:* **I have no money a. me,** je n'ai pas d'argent sur moi; (*d*) **to do sth. turn and turn a.,** faire qch. à tour de rôle, tour à tour; **day and day a.,**

tous les deux jours; **we take duty week and week a.,** nous prenons la semaine à tour de rôle. **2. the other way a.,** en sens inverse; **to turn a., face a.,** faire demi-tour; faire volte-face; se retourner; *Mil:* **a. turn!** *U.S:* **a. face!** demi-tour! *Nau:* **ready a.!** pare à virer! paré à virer! **a. ship!** envoyez! *O:* **to turn sth. a.,** retourner qch.; tourner qch. de l'autre côté. **3.** environ, presque; **there are a. thirty,** il y en a environ trente; il y en a une trentaine; **she is a. sixty,** elle a environ soixante ans; elle a dans les soixante ans; **he's a. my age,** il a à peu près mon âge; **it will cost you (somewhere) a. a hundred francs,** ça vous coûtera dans les cent francs; **to have a. a hundred pounds,** avoir une centaine de livres; **a. as big,** à peu près, presque, aussi grand; **that's a. right,** c'est à peu près cela; **the work's a. done,** le travail est à peu près achevé; **he's much a. the same,** il va à peu près de même; **it's a. time,** (i) il est presque temps, il commence à être temps; (ii) *Iron:* il est grand temps, vous y avez mis du temps; **haven't we had a. enough of this?** ça va durer longtemps (cette plaisanterie)? *F:* **I'm just a. fed up!** j'en ai complètement marre! **he came a. three o'clock,** il est venu vers trois heures, sur les trois heures; **a. midday, a. one o'clock,** vers midi, vers, *F:* sur, une heure; **it's a. three months since we had any news,** ça va faire dans les trois mois qu'on est sans nouvelles. **4.** au sujet de; **to make inquiries a. sth.,** se renseigner sur, au sujet de, qch.; **to quarrel a. nothing,** se quereller à propos de rien; *Lit:* **much ado a. nothing,** beaucoup de bruit pour rien; **there was a fight a. who should remain,** on se battit pour décider qui devait rester; **a. that,** là-dessus, à ce sujet, à cet égard; **a. what? what a.?** à quel sujet? à quel propos? **what's it all a.?** de quoi s'agit-il? **I know what it's all a.,** je sais de quoi il retourne; **I have come a. that,** je viens pour cela, à ce propos; **he has come a. the rent,** (i) il vient pour le loyer, pour toucher son terme; (ii) il vient à propos du loyer, du terme; **to speak a. sth.,** parler de qch.; **there is a great deal a. love in his essays,** il est fort question d'amour dans ses essais; **it was a. her that the quarrel arose,** c'est elle qui fut l'occasion de la dispute; **to be uneasy a. s.o.,** être inquiet à l'égard de qn, sur le compte de qn; **what I admire a. that man, a. him, a. that book, is . . .,** ce que j'admire chez cet homme, en lui, dans ce livre, c'est . . .; **he told me all a. it,** il m'a mis au courant; **the doubts I had a. his intelligence,** les doutes que j'ai éprouvés quant à son intelligence; **I told him what I thought a. him,** je lui ai dit son fait, ses quatre vérités; **how a. a game of bridge?** si on faisait un bridge? **what a. my bath?** et mon bain? **well, what a. it?** eh bien, et puis après? (*news vendor's cry*) **read all a. it!** lisez tous les détails! **5.** (*a*) **to be a. to do sth.,** être sur le point de, près de, faire qch.; **what were you a. to say?** qu'est-ce que vous alliez dire? **when he was a. to die,** quand il fut sur le point de mourir; **he is a. to start,** il est sur son départ; **just as he was a. to leave,** quand il fut pour partir; (*b*) **to go a. one's work,** faire sa besogne; **this is how I go a. it,** voici comment je m'y prends; **to know what one is a.,** savoir, connaître, son affaire; **I know what I'm a.,** je sais ce que je fais; **what are you a.?** (i) que faites-vous? (ii) à quoi songez-vous? qu'est-ce que vous faites là? **mind what you're a.!** faites attention! **you haven't been long a. it,** il ne vous a pas fallu longtemps (pour le faire); **while you are a. it,** pendant que vous y êtes; **there are no two ways a. it,** de deux choses l'une; **be quick a. it!** dépêchez-vous! **to go a. one's business,** vaquer à ses affaires; *F:* **to send s.o. a. his business,** envoyer promener qn. **6.** *for the use of* **about** *in the formation of compound verbs, e.g.* **come about, get about, go about, stand about,** *etc., see these verbs.*

about-face[1] [ə'baut'feis], *s.* revirement *m* (d'opinion).

about-face[2], *v.i.* **1.** faire demi-tour. **2.** changer d'opinion.

about-ship [ə'baut'ʃip], *v.i. Nau:* virer (de bord).

aboutsledge [ə'bautsledʒ], *s. Metalw:* marteau *m* à (frapper) devant; marteau à deux mains.

about-turn[1] [ə'baut'tə:n], *s.* **to do an a.-t.,** faire demi-tour.

about-turn[2], *v.i.* faire demi-tour.

above [əb'ʌv], *adv., prep., a. & s.*

I. *adv. & prep.* **1.** au dessus (de); (*a*) **the water reached a. their knees,** l'eau leur montait jusqu'au-dessus des genoux; *Book-k:* **a. the line,** au-dessus de la ligne; (*b*) **to hover a. the town,** planer au-dessus de la ville; **we live one a. the other,** nous demeurons l'un au-dessus de l'autre; **the tenants of the flat a.,** les locataires du dessus; **underground passages arranged one a. the other,** souterrains disposés en saut de mouton; **to watch the clouds a.,** regarder les nuages au-dessus de soi, au ciel; **in the heavens a.,** là-haut, aux cieux; **heavens a.!** juste ciel! **the powers a.,** les puissances célestes; **a voice from a.,** une voix d'en haut; **view from a.,** vue plongeante; **policy imposed on me from a.,** politique que mes supérieurs m'imposent, qui me vient d'en haut; (*c*) **a mountain rises a. the lake,** une montagne s'élève au-dessus du lac, domine le lac; **his voice was heard a. the din,** on entendait sa voix par-dessus le tumulte; sa voix dominait le fracas; **to fish a. the bridge,** pêcher en amont, au-dessus, du pont; **the Seine valley a. Paris,** la vallée de la Seine à l'amont de Paris; **a. lock,** en amont de l'écluse; **a. ground,** sur terre; sorti, sortant, de la terre; *Min:* au jour, à la surface; *F:* **he's still a. ground,** il est toujours en vie, il reste encore sur terre; (*d*) **he is a. me in rank,** il est mon supérieur hiérarchique, il est d'un rang supérieur au mien; **a. par,** au-dessus du pair; **a. one's station,** au-dessus de sa condition; **he thinks himself a. business,** il se croit trop grand seigneur pour s'occuper de ses affaires; **to show oneself a. prejudice,** se montrer supérieur aux préjugés; **to live a. one's means,** vivre au-dessus de ses moyens; avoir un train de vie qui dépasse ses moyens; **temperature a. normal,** température supérieure à la normale; **a. criticism,** hors de l'atteinte de la critique; **a. my understanding,** au-dessus, au delà, de ma portée; **that is a. my comprehension, that's a. me,** cela dépasse mon entendement; cela me dépasse; **a. all. . .,** surtout . . ., sur toutes choses . . ., (surtout et) avant tout . . ., par-dessus tout . . ., au-dessus de toutes choses . . .; (*e*) *F:* **to be a bit a. oneself,** être un peu monté, déborder, *F:* être gonflé à bloc; **to get a. oneself,** s'en faire accroire; être très satisfait de sa petite personne; *Turf:* **horse that is a. itself,** cheval trop ardent. **2.** (*in book, document*) ci-dessus; **see the paragraph a.,** voir le paragraphe ci-dessus; **as a.,** comme ci-dessus; **the article referred to a.,** l'article susvisé; **the articles referred to a.,** les articles précédemment énumérés. **3.** (*of pers.*) **to be a. suspicion, meanness,** être au-dessus de tout soupçon, incapable de bassesse; **I am a. doing that,** je suis trop fier pour faire cela; je me respecte trop pour faire cela; je dédaigne de faire cela; **he is a. deception, a. telling a lie,** il ne saurait s'abaisser jusqu'à vous tromper, jusqu'à mentir. **4.** (*a*) **a. twenty,** plus de vingt; **she must be a. forty,** elle doit avoir passé la quarantaine; **over and a. that,** en plus de cela; (*b*) **I can't go a. B flat,** je ne monte pas plus haut que le si bémol; (*c*) **tickets numbered 200 and a.,** billets qui portent le numéro 200 et au-delà.

II. *a.* (*in book, etc.*) **the a. decree,** le décret précité; **the a. circumstances,** les circonstances sus-énoncées; **the a. quotation,** la citation ci-dessus.

III. *s.* **the a. is a quotation from** *Hamlet,* le passage ci-dessus est une citation de *Hamlet;* **the a. was the driver of the vehicle,** le susdit était le conducteur du véhicule.

aboveboard [ə'bʌvbɔ:d]. **1.** *adv.* **to play fair and a.,** jouer cartes sur table, montrer son jeu; agir ouvertement, franchement, loyalement, sans rien cacher. **2.** *a.* loyal; franc, franche; **everything is a.,** tout est franc et loyal; **everything is open and a. in this transaction,** il n'y a rien de caché, de louche, dans cette affaire; **his conduct was completely a.,** il a agi en tout bien (et) tout honneur.

above-line [ə'bʌv'lain], *a. Book-k:* (*of surplus, etc.*) au-dessus de la ligne.

above-mentioned [ə'bʌv'menʃənd], **above-named** [ə'bʌv'neimd], *a.* susmentionné, sus-dénommé, susnommé, susdit; mentionné, cité, énoncé, ci-dessus; indiqué plus haut; précité.

aboveproof [ə'bʌvpru:f], *a. Dist: NAm:* au-dessus de preuve.

abovestairs [ə'bʌvstɛəz]. *NAm:* **1.** *a.* (*of room*) d'en haut, du haut, (situé) à l'étage supérieur. **2.** *adv.* en haut; aux étages supérieurs.

above-water [ə'bʌv'wɔ:tər], *a.* (*a*) *Nau:* **a.-w. repairs,** réparations dans les œuvres mortes; (*b*) à la surface; à flot; surnageant.

abracadabra [æbrəkə'dæbrə], *s.* (*a*) (*magic formula*) abracadabra *m;* (*b*) jargon *m.*

abradant [ə'breid(ə)nt], *a. & s.* abrasif (*m*); (poudre *f*) à égriser, à roder.

abrade [ə'breid]. **1.** *v.tr.* (*a*) user (qch.) par le frottement, par abrasion; abraser; écorcher (la peau, etc.); scarifier; éroder (un rocher, etc.); arracher (des particules); **abrading wheel,** meule *f* à user, à roder; (*b*) *Fig: A:* irriter, épuiser (qn). **2.** *v.i.* s'user par le frottement; s'éroder; (*of bearings*) gripper.

abrader [ə'breidər], *s.* machine *f* à roder.

Abraham ['eibrəhæm, 'eibrəm], *Pr.n.m.* Abraham; *A:* **to sham A.,** faire le malade, l'épileptique; *Bot:* **A.'s balm,** agnus-castus *m.*

abranchial [ei'bræŋkiəl], **abranchian** [ei'bræŋkiən], **abranchiate** [ei'bræŋkieit], **abranchious** [ei'bræŋkiəs], *a. Z:* abranche, dépourvu de branchies.

abrase [ə'breiz], *v.tr.* abraser, user par le frottement, par abrasion.

abrasijet [ə'breizidʒet], *s. Min:* abrasijet *m.*

abrasin [ə'breizin], *s.* **a. oil,** huile *f* d'abrasin.

abrasion [ə'breiʒ(ə)n], *s.* **1.** (usure *f* par le) frottement *m;* attrition *f;* abrasion *f;* usure; frai *m* (des monnaies); *Mec.E:* grippure *f* (d'un palier); *Cin:* (*on film*) **abrasions,** éraflures *f; Phot:* **a. marks,** marques d'abrasion; *Geol:* **a. platform,** plate-forme *f* d'abrasion. **2.** *Med:* écorchure *f,* éraflure, excoriation *f* (de la peau); abrasion (d'une muqueuse); *Dent:* abrasion.

abrasive [ə'breisiv], *a. & s.* abrasif (*m*).

abraxas [ə'bræksəs], *s.* **1.** *Archeol: Lap:* abraxas *m.* **2.** *Ent:* abraxas.

abreact [æbri'ækt], *v.tr. & i. Psy:* abréagir, manifester une abréaction.

abreaction [æbri'ækʃ(ə)n], *s. Psy:* abréaction *f.*

abreast [ə'brest], *adv.* **1.** (*a*) (*of horses, etc.*) de front; sur la même ligne; *Navy:* **line a.,** en ligne de front; *Mil:* **units disposed a.,** unités accolées; **to come a. of a car,** arriver à la hauteur d'une voiture; (*b*) (*of people*) **to walk a.,** marcher côte à côte; **to march two a.,** marcher par deux; **four a.,** par rangs de quatre; *Aut:* **to overtake three a.,** doubler en troisième position; **to keep a. of a science,** suivre les progrès d'une science; **to keep wages a. of the cost of living,** maintenir les salaires au niveau du coût de la vie; **to keep a. of the times,** marcher de pair avec son époque; se maintenir à la page; suivre son temps; vivre avec son temps, avec son époque; **to be a. of the times,** être de son temps; être dans le mouvement, dans le train; être à la hauteur des idées actuelles; être à la page. **2.** *Nau:* **to be a. of a ship, of a landmark,** être par le travers, à la hauteur, d'un navire, d'un amer. **3.** *a. El:* **a. connection,** couplage *m* en parallèle; accouplement *m* en quantité.

abreuvoir [æbrə:v'wa:r], *s. Const:* abreuvoir *m.*

abridge [ə'bridʒ], *v.tr.* **1.** abréger (un ouvrage, etc.); raccourcir (un livre, un chapitre); **this history course is abridged from his work in six volumes,** ce cours d'histoire est extrait de, est un abrégé de, son ouvrage en six volumes. **2.** *A:* diminuer, restreindre, retrancher (l'autorité, les droits, de qn). **3.** *A:* **to a. s.o. of a right, of a power,** priver qn (partiellement ou complètement) d'un droit, d'un pouvoir.

abridged [ə'bridʒd], *a.* **a. edition,** édition réduite; **a. version (of a narrative, etc.),** abrégé *m,* résumé *m* (d'un récit, etc.); **to give an a. account of sth.,** raconter qch. en raccourci.

abridg(e)ment [ə'bridʒmənt], *s.* **1.** (*a*) (*also* **abridging** [ə'bridʒiŋ]), raccourcissement *m* (d'un ouvrage, etc.); (*b*) *A:* diminution *f* (d'autorité); restriction *f* (d'un droit). **2.** abrégé *m,* précis *m,* résumé *m.*

abridger [ə'bridʒər], *s.* abréviateur, -trice (d'un ouvrage).

abroach [ə'broutʃ], *adv.* (*a*) (*of cask*) en perce; (*b*) *A:* (*of ideas, etc.*) en circulation.

abroad [ə'brɔ:d], *adv.* **1.** (*a*) à l'étranger; en voyage; **to live a.,** vivre à l'étranger; **he is just back from a.,** il revient de l'étranger; **our colleagues from a.,** nos collègues étrangers; nos collègues d'outremer; **capital invested a.,** capitaux placés dehors; **customers who have come from a.,** clients venus du dehors, des pays étrangers; (*b*) *A:* (*of pers.*) sorti, (au) dehors; **he ventured a. only once a day,** il ne sortait qu'une fois par jour; **a lion at home, a mouse a.,** rogue chez lui, timide dans le monde. **2.** au loin, de tous côtés; **scattered a.,** éparpillé de tous côtés; **the news spread a.,** la nouvelle se répandit; **there is a rumour a. that. . .,** le bruit court que. . .; *O:* **there are evil reports a. about him,** de mauvais bruits courent sur son compte. **3.** (*a*) *A:* **he is, his mind is, all a.,** il est tout désorienté; *A: & NAm:* **I'm all a.,** je n'y suis pas, j'y perds mon latin; **you're all a.,** vous n'y êtes pas du tout; vous divaguez, *F:* tu dérailles; (*b*) *Row:* **the crew was all a.,** l'équipe avait perdu son ensemble, *F:* l'équipe cafouillait.

abrocome ['æbrəkoum], *s. Z:* abrocome *m.*

Abrocomidae [æbrə'kɔmidi:], *s.pl. Z:* abrocomidés *m.*

abrogate ['æbrəgeit], *v.tr.* (*a*) abroger (une loi); (*b*) *Lit:* **I cannot a. my principles,** je ne saurais renoncer à mes principes.

abrogation [æbrə'geiʃ(ə)n], *s.* abrogation *f.*

abrogative ['æbrəgeitiv], *a. Jur:* abrogatif; abrogatoire.

abrogator ['æbrəgeitər], *s.* signataire *mf* d'une abrogation.

abroma [ə'broumə], *s. Bot:* abrome *m;* (*genus*) abroma *m.*

abrotanum [ə'brɔtənəm], *s. Bot:* abrotone *f,* auron(n)e *f.*

abrupt [ə'brʌpt], *a.* **1.** abrupt; (départ, personne) brusque; (départ) brusqué, précipité; (attaque) brusquée; (ton) cassant; (style) heurté, décousu, saccadé; **the evening came to an a. end,** la soirée s'acheva brusquement. **2. a. slope,** pente abrupte, raide, rude; **a. headland,** cap escarpé, à pic; **a. ascent,** montée ardue, raide.

abruption [ə'brʌpʃ(ə)n], *s.* brusque rupture *f.*

abruptly [ə'brʌptli], *adv.* **1.** (*a*) brusquement, tout à coup, sans transition; (*b*) (parler) abruptement, avec brusquerie. **2. path that climbs a.,** sentier qui monte abruptement, à pic, en pente raide. **3.** *Bot:* **a. pinnate,** abruptipenné.

abruptness [ə'brʌptnis], *s.* **1.** (*a*) brusquerie *f*, rudesse *f*; (*b*) précipitation *f* (d'un départ); (*c*) décousu *m* (du style). **2.** raideur *f* (d'un sentier, etc.).

abrus ['æbrəs], *s. Bot:* abre *m*; (*genus*) abrus *m*.

Abruzzi (the) [ðiə'brutsi:], *Pr.n.pl. Geog:* les Abruzzes *f*; **the people of the A.,** les Abruzzains, Abruzzais.

Absalom ['æbsələm], *Pr.n.m. B:* Absalon.

abscess ['æbses], *s.* abcès *m*; dépôt *m* (dans le poumon); foyer purulent; **fixation a.,** abcès de fixation; **to form an a.,** abcéder; **formation of an a.,** abcédation *f*; **to lance, drain, an a.,** ouvrir, percer, vider, un abcès.

abscessed ['æbsest], *a.* qui est le siège d'un abcès.

abscessroot ['æbsesru:t], *s. Bot: U.S:* (espèce de) polémonie *f*.

abscind [æb'sind], *v.tr.* exciser.

abscise [æb'saiz], *v.tr. & i. Bot:* (se) séparer par abscission.

absciss[1] ['æbsis], *a. Bot:* **a. layer,** assise génératrice.

absciss[2], *v.tr. & i. Bot:* (se) séparer par abscission.

abscissa, *pl.* **-ae, -as** [æb'sisə, -i:, -əz], *s. Mth:* abscisse *f*; **to plot the a. of a point,** porter un point en abscisse.

abscission [æb'siʃ(ə)n], *s.* **1.** *Surg:* abscission *f*, excision *f*. **2.** *Bot:* **a. layer,** assise génératrice.

abscond [æb'skɔnd], *v.i.* se soustraire à la justice; s'enfuir, s'évader (**from,** de); *F:* décamper, déguerpir, filer; disparaître; prendre la clef des champs, lever le pied, mettre la clef sous le paillasson, faire un trou à la lune, s'éclipser.

absconder [æb'skɔndər], *s.* **1.** fugitif, -ive; évadé, -ée. **2.** *Jur:* contumace *m*, défaillant *m*.

absconding[1] [æb'skɔndiŋ], *a.* en fuite.

absconding[2], *s.* fuite *f*, évasion *f*, *F:* décampement *m*.

abseil [æb'zail], *v.i. Mount:* descendre en rappel.

abseiling [æb'zailiŋ], *s. Mount:* rappel *m*.

absence ['æbs(ə)ns], *s.* **1.** absence *f*, éloignement *m* (**from,** de); **a. makes the heart grow fonder,** l'éloignement renforce l'affection; **to be conspicuous by one's a.,** briller par son absence; *Jur:* **sentenced in his, her, a.,** condamné(e) par contumace; **leave of a.,** congé *m*; *Mil: etc:* **a. with, without, leave,** absence régulière, illégale. **2. a. of taste, of frankness,** manque *m* de goût, de franchise; **in the a. of definite information,** faute de, à défaut de, renseignements précis. **3. a. of mind,** distraction *f*, préoccupation *f*. **4.** *Med:* (*in epilepsy*) absence. **5.** *Sch:* (*esp. at Eton*) appel *m* des élèves.

absent[1] ['æbs(ə)nt], *a.* **1.** (*a*) absent (**from,** de); *Mil: etc:* **a. with leave,** en (position d') absence régulière, en permission; **a. without leave,** en (position d') absence illégale, porté manquant; (*toast*) **(to our) a. friends!** à nos amis absents! **why were you a. from school?** pourquoi n'étiez-vous pas en classe? *s.* **the a. are always (in the) wrong,** les absents ont toujours tort; (*b*) manquant; **in this animal the teeth are a.,** chez cet animal les dents sont absentes, manquent. **2.** *occ.* distrait.

absent[2] [æb'sent], *v.pr.* **to a. oneself,** s'absenter (**from,** de).

absentee [æbsən'ti:], *s.* **1.** (*a*) absent, -ente; (*b*) manquant, -ante (à l'appel); *Mil:* insoumis *m*; *Navy: etc:* absent (illégalement); (*c*) *Ind: etc:* absentéiste *mf*. **2.** *Hist:* **a. landlord** (propriétaire foncier) absentéiste.

absenteeism [æbsən'ti:izm], *s.* **1.** *Ind: etc:* absentéisme *m*. **2.** *Hist:* absentéisme (d'un propriétaire).

absently ['æbsəntli], *adv.* distraitement, d'un air distrait.

absentminded ['æbsənt'maindid], *a.* distrait, préoccupé; **to be a.,** avoir, être sujet à, des absences (d'esprit).

absentmindedly ['æbsənt'maindidli], *adv.* distraitement; d'un air distrait; d'un ton préoccupé.

absentmindedness ['æbsəntmaindidnis], *s.* distraction *f*, préoccupation *f*.

absidiole [æb'sidiɔl], *s. Arch:* absidiole *f*.

absinthe ['æbsinθ, absɛ̃:t], *s.* absinthe *f*.

absinthin, absinthiin ['æbsinθin, æb'sinθi:in], *s. Ch:* absinthine *f*.

absinthism ['æbsinθizm], *s.* absinthisme *m*.

absinthol [æbsin'θɔl], *s. Ch:* thuyone *f*.

absit omen ['æbsit'oumen], *Lt. phr.* **1.** *A:* (*said to s.o. who sneezes*) (que) Dieu vous bénisse! **2.** Dieu nous en préserve!

absolute ['æbsəlu:t]. **1.** *a.* (*a*) absolu; **a. ignorance,** ignorance absolue; **case of a. necessity,** cas de nécessité absolue, de force majeure; **a. power,** pouvoir absolu, illimité; **a. monarchy,** monarchie absolue; *Pol:* **a. majority,** majorité absolue; **a. veto,** veto formel; **a. alcohol,** alcool absolu, anhydre; *Rail:* **a. block (system),** bloc absolu; *Jur:* **decree a.,** décret irrévocable; **a. liability,** obligation inconditionnelle; **a. owner,** propriétaire incommutable; *Gram:* **a. construction,** construction absolue; **ablative a.,** ablatif absolu; **a. superlative,** superlatif absolu; *Mus:* **to have a. pitch,** avoir l'oreille absolue; *Ph:* **a. error,** erreur absolue; **a. humidity,** humidité absolue; **a. temperature,** température absolue; **a. scale (of temperature),** échelle absolue, échelle K(elvin); **a. zero,** zéro absolu; **system of a. units, a. system,** système d'unités absolu; *Av:* **a. ceiling,** plafond absolu; **a. altimeter,** altimètre indicateur d'altitude absolue; *Mth:* **a. value,** valeur absolue; **a. value computer,** calculateur à valeurs réelles; *Cmptr:* **a. address,** adresse absolue, réelle; **a. code,** code réel, langage *m* machine; **a. coding,** codage absolu, programmation *f* en langage machine; **a. instruction,** instruction absolue, réelle; (*b*) autoritaire; **don't be so a.,** ne soyez pas si autoritaire, si outrecuidant; (*c*) **they are in a. distress,** ils sont dans une véritable misère, une misère complète; **it's an a. scandal,** c'est un véritable scandale; c'est ni plus ni moins qu'un scandale; *F:* **he's an a. fool,** c'est un parfait imbécile; **he's the a. end, limit,** c'est le dernier des derniers. **2.** *s. Phil:* **the a.,** l'absolu *m*.

absolutely [æbsə'lu:tli], *adv.* absolument; en valeur absolue; **to reign a.,** régner absolument; **a. correct, true,** rigoureusement exact, on ne peut plus vrai; **you're a. right,** vous avez entièrement, complètement, tout à fait, raison; **it is a. forbidden to . . .,** il est formellement interdit de . . .; **we a. must do it,** de toute force il nous faut le faire, il nous faut absolument le faire; *Jur:* **a. void,** radicalement nul; *Gram:* **verb used a.,** verbe employé absolument, dans un sens absolu; *Mth:* **a. convergent,** absolument convergent.

absoluteness ['æbsəlu:tnis], *s.* **1.** pouvoir absolu. **2.** caractère absolu (de qch.); réalité *f*. **3.** *Phil:* absoluité *f*.

absolution [æbsə'lu:ʃ(ə)n], *s.* **1.** *Ecc:* (*a*) absolution *f*; **the power of a.,** le pouvoir de délier; (*b*) **a. (of the dead),** absoute *f*. **2.** *A: & Lit:* acquittement *m*; pardon *m*.

absolutism ['æbsəlu:tizm], *s.* **1.** *Pol:* absolutisme *m*. **2.** *Phil:* absoluité *f*.

absolutist ['æbsəlu:tist], *a. & s.* absolutiste (*mf*).

absolutory [æb'sɔlut(ə)ri], *a.* absolutoire.

absolve [əb'zɔlv, -'sɔlv], *v.tr.* **1.** (*a*) absoudre (**s.o. of a sin,** qn d'un péché); **he was absolved from all blame for . . .,** il fut reconnu qu'il n'était aucunement responsable de . . ., (*b*) remettre (un péché). **2. to a. s.o. from an obligation, from a vow, etc.,** affranchir, dégager, délier, relever, dispenser, qn d'une obligation, d'un vœu, etc.

absolving[1] [əb'zɔlviŋ, -sɔl-], *a.* absolutoire.

absolving[2], *s.* dispensation *f* (**from,** de).

absolvitor [əb'sɔlvitər], *s. Scot: Jur:* acquittement *m*.

absonant ['æbsənənt], *a.* (*a*) dissonant; en désaccord (**from, to,** avec); (*b*) contraire (à la raison).

absorb [əb'sɔ:b, -'zɔ:b], *v.tr.* **1.** (*a*) absorber (un liquide, la chaleur, etc.); **measures taken to a. the surplus wheat,** mesures prises pour résorber les excédents de blé; (*b*) **to a. a shock, a sound,** amortir un choc, un son; (*c*) incorporer, absorber, intégrer, assimiler (des immigrants, etc.); **the business has been absorbed by a competitor,** l'entreprise a été absorbée par un concurrent. **2.** (*a*) **his business absorbs him,** ses affaires l'absorbent; (*b*) **to become absorbed in sth.,** s'absorber dans qch.; **he is entirely absorbed in his business,** il est complètement absorbé dans ses affaires; il est (tout) entier à son commerce; **to listen with absorbed interest,** écouter avec un intérêt profond.

absorbable [əb'sɔ:bəbl, -'zɔ:b], *a. Ch: etc:* absorbable.

absorbedly [əb'sɔ:bidli, -'zɔ:b-], *adv.* d'un air absorbé; **to gaze at sth. a.,** s'absorber, être absorbé, dans la contemplation de qch.

absorbedness [əb'sɔ:bidnis, -zɔ:b], *s.* absorbement *m* (d'esprit).

absorbefacient [əbsɔ:bi'feiʃjənt, -zɔ:b-], *a. & s. Med:* résorbant (*m*).

absorbency [əb'sɔ:bənsi, -zɔ:b-], *s.* capacité *f* d'absorption.

absorbent [əb'sɔ:bənt, -zɔ:b-], *a. & s.* absorbant (*m*); **a. of water,** avide d'eau; *s:* **a. cotton,** coton *m* hydrophile, ouate *m*.

absorber [əb'sɔ:bər, -zɔ:b-], *s.* **1.** *Ch: Ph: etc:* absorbeur *m*. **2.** amortisseur *m* (de son, d'oscillations, etc.); **shock a.,** *Aut: etc:* amortisseur; *Artil:* amortisseur de chute; (*on gun carriage*) amortisseur de crosse.

absorbing [əb'sɔ:biŋ, -zɔ:b-], *a.* (*a*) absorbant; *Bot:* **a. trichome, a. hair,** poil absorbant; *Hyd.E:* **a. well,** puits perdu, absorbant; (*b*) absorbant, intéressant, passionnant.

absorptiometer [əbsɔ:pʃi'ɔmitər, -zɔ:b-], *s.* absorptiomètre *m*.

absorption [əb'sɔ:pʃ(ə)n, -zɔ:b-], *s.* **1.** absorption *f*; *Ph:* **a. spectrum,** spectre *m* d'absorption; **a. lines,** raies *f* d'absorption; **a. coefficient,** coefficient *m* d'absorption; **a. factor,** absorptivité *f*; **a. of radiation,** absorption des radiations; *Elcs:* **a. range,** intervalle *m* d'absorption; **a. wavemeter,** ondemètre *m* d'absorption; *Mth:* **law of a.,** loi *f* d'absorption; *Miner:* **a. figures,** houppes *f*. **2.** absorbement *m* (de l'esprit). **3.** (*a*) amortissement *m* (de sons, d'un coup, etc.); (*b*) absorption, assimilation *f*, intégration *f* (des immigrants, etc.); absorption (d'une entreprise par une autre).

absorptive [əb'sɔ:ptiv, -zɔ:b-], *a.* absorptif; absorbant; **a. power,** force *f* d'absorption, absorptivité *f*.

absorptiveness [əb'sɔ:ptivnis, -zɔ:b-], **absorptivity** [əbsɔ:p'tiviti, -zɔ:b-], *s.* absorptivité *f*.

absquatulate [əb'skwɔtjuleit], *v.i. Hum: A:* ficher le camp.

absquatulation [əbskwɔtju'leiʃ(ə)n], *s. Hum: A:* décampement *m*.

abstain [əb'stein], *v.i.* **1.** s'abstenir (**from (doing) sth.,** de (faire) qch.); **to a. from meat,** faire maigre. **2.** *abs.* (*a*) s'abstenir de boissons alcooliques, ne boire que de l'eau; (*b*) **to a. (from voting),** s'abstenir, ne pas voter.

abstainer [əb'steinər], *s.* (*a*) celui, celle, qui s'abstient (de qch.); *Pol:* celui, celle, qui ne vote pas; (*b*) abstème *mf*; buveur, -euse, d'eau; **to be a total a.,** ne boire que de l'eau.

abstaining [əb'steiniŋ], *s.* abstinence *f* (**from,** de).

abstatampere ['æbstæt'æmpɛər], *s. El.Meas:* unité *f* électrostatique C.G.S (u.é.s. C.G.S.) d'intensité.

abstatfarad ['æbstætfæræd], *s.* unité *f* électrostatique C.G.S. (u.é.s. C.G.S.) de capacité.

abstemious [əb'sti:miəs], *a.* (*a*) sobre, tempérant, abstinent; (*b*) **an a. meal,** un repas frugal.

abstemiously [əb'sti:miəsli], *adv.* sobrement; frugalement.

abstemiousness [əb'sti:miəsnis], *s.* sobriété *f*, tempérance *f*; abstinence *f*.

abstention [əb'stenʃ(ə)n], *s.* **1.** abstention *f*; abstinence *f* (**from,** de). **2.** *Pol:* abstention (en matière électorale); abstentionnisme *m*.

abstentionist [əb'stenʃənist], *s. Pol:* abstentionniste *mf*.

absterge [æb'stə:dʒ], *v.tr. Med: A:* absterger.

abstergent [æb'stə:ʒənt], *a. & s.* abstergent (*m*); détersif (*m*).

abstersion [æb'stə:ʃ(ə)n], *s.* abstersion *f*; détersion *f*.

abstersive [æb'stə:siv], *a. & s.* abstersif (*m*); détersif (*m*).

abstinence ['æbstinəns], *s.* (*a*) abstinence *f* (**from,** de); *Ecc:* **day of a.,** jour *m* d'abstinence; (*b*) **(total) a.,** abstinence (complète) de boissons alcooliques.

abstinency ['æbstinənsi], *s.* habitudes *fpl* de tempérance, de frugalité.

abstinent ['æbstinənt], *a.* abstinent, tempérant, sobre; frugal.

abstinently ['æbstinəntli], *adv.* d'une manière abstinente; sobrement; modérément; frugalement.

abstract[1] ['æbstrækt]. **1.** *a.* (*a*) abstrait; **a. number,** nombre abstrait, nombrant; **a. mechanics,** mécanique rationnelle; *Cmptr:* **a. symbol,** symbole abstrait; *Gram:* **a. noun,** nom abstrait; **a. art,** art abstrait; **a. artist,** abstrait *m*; (*b*) abstrait, abstrus; **lost in a. speculations,** perdu dans des spéculations abstruses. **2.** *s.* (*a*) **the a.,** l'abstrait *m*; **to consider sth. in the a.,** considérer qch. dans l'abstrait, du point de vue abstrait; **to know sth. in the a.,** avoir une connaissance théorique, abstraite, de qch.; **justice in the a. is nothing,** la justice en soi n'est rien; (*b*) **an a.,** une peinture, une sculpture, abstraite.

abstract[2] ['æbstrækt], *s.* résumé *m*, abrégé *m*, sommaire *m*, précis *m*, extrait *m*, analyse *f*; **a. of statistics,** précis de statistiques; **to make an a. of an account,** faire le relevé d'un compte; analyser un compte; **to make an a. of a document,** faire le dépouillement d'un document; résumer un document; *Jur:* **a. of title,** intitulé *m* (d'un acte, etc.).

abstract[3] [æb'strækt], *v.tr.* **1.** (*a*) soustraire, dérober, voler (**sth. from s.o.** qch. à qn); détourner (de l'argent); distraire, soustraire (des documents); **the letter had been abstracted from the bag,** la lettre avait été volée dans la sacoche; (*b*) détourner (l'attention de qn); **to a. one's mind from sth.,** détacher son esprit de qch. **2.** (*a*) **to a. a quality, a conception,** abstraire une qualité, une conception, faire abstraction d'une qualité, d'une conception; (*b*) *Ch: Ind:* extraire (par distillation). **3.** résumer, abréger, dépouiller (un livre); relever (un compte).

abstracted [æb'stræktid], *a.* distriat, rêveur, -euse; (regard) concentré, perdu dans le vague; (air) pensif.

abstractedly [æb'stræktidli], *adv.* **1.** *Lit:* (*b*) **to consider an occurrence a. from the issue,** considérer un événement abstraction faite, en faisant abstraction, du résultat; (*b*) **to consider a problem a.,** considérer un problème par abstraction, abstraitement, dans l'abstrait. **2.** distraitement, d'un air distrait; d'un ton préoccupé.

abstractedness [æb'stræktidnis], *s.* absence *f* (d'esprit); préoccupation *f.*

abstracter [æb'stræktər], *s.* **1.** abstracteur *m*; détourneur, -euse (de documents, etc.). **2.** (*a*) abréviateur, -trice (d'un ouvrage); (*b*) *Adm: approx.* = rédacteur, -trice (dans un ministère).

abstraction [æb'strækʃ(ə)n], *s.* **1.** (*a*) soustraction *f* d'argent, de papiers, etc.); distraction *f*, détournement *m*, vol *m*; *Jur:* **a. of documents,** soustraction frauduleuse; (*b*) **a. of heat from a body,** perte *f* de chaleur d'un corps; (*c*) *Ch: Ind:* extraction *f* (par distillation). **2.** (*a*) *Phil:* abstraction *f*; (*b*) idée abstraite; **to lose oneself in abstractions,** se perdre dans les abstractions. **3. a. (of mind),** distraction, préoccupation *f* (d'esprit); **in a moment of a.,** dans un moment d'abstraction, d'inattention; **with an air of a.,** d'un air distrait; avec un regard vague. **4.** *Art:* dessin abstrait, non figuratif; abstraction.

abstractionism [æb'strækʃənizm], *s.* **1.** *Phil: etc:* abstractionnisme *m.* **2.** l'art abstrait.

abstractionist [æ'strækʃənist], *a. & s.* **1.** *Phil: etc:* abstractionniste (*mf*); abstracteur *m.* **2.** *Art:* abstrait (*m*); **a. painting,** peinture abstraite.

abstractive [æb'stræktiv], *a.* abstractif.

abstractively [æb'stræktivli], *adv.* abstractivement.

abstractiveness [æb'stræktivnis], *s.* abstractivité *f.*

abstractly ['æbstræktli], *adv.* abstraitement, d'une manière abstraite; **considered a.,** considéré dans l'abstrait, abstraitement.

abstractor [æb'stræktər], *s.* = ABSTRACTER.

abstruse [æb'stru:s], *a.* abstrus; abscons; obscur.

abstrusely [æb'stru:sli], *adv.* d'une manière abstruse, compliquée.

abstruseness [æb'stru:snis], *s.* caractère abstrus (de qch.); complexité *f.*

abstrusity [æb'stru:siti], *s.* complexité *f.*

absurd [əb'sə:d]. **1.** *a.* absurde; **it is a. to suspect him,** il est absurde de le soupçonner; **you're (being) a.!** vous êtes ridicule, absurde, fou! vous déraisonnez! **what an a. question!** quelle question ridicule, saugrenue! **it's a.!** c'est ridicule, absurde! **the a. part of the matter is that . . .,** l'absurde *m* de l'affaire c'est que . . .. **2.** *s.* **the a.,** l'absurde.

absurdity [əb'sə:diti], *s.* absurdité *f*; **speech full of absurdities,** discours plein d'absurdités, de propos ridicules; **the a. of such a situation,** l'absurde *m*, l'absurdité, d'une pareille situation; ce qu'une pareille situation offre d'absurde; **to carry sth. to the point of a.,** pousser qch. jusqu'à l'absurdité; **it's the height of a.,** c'est le comble de l'absurdité; *Cmptr:* **a. check,** contrôle *m* de vraisemblance.

absurdly [əb'sə:dli], *adv.* (*a*) absurdement; (*b*) *F:* **she's a. rich,** elle est ridiculement riche.

absurdness [əb'sə:dnis], *s.* absurdité *f.*

Abt rack ['æbtræk], *s. Rail:* crémaillère *f* (de l'ingénieur suisse Roman Abt).

abuilding [ə'bildiŋ], *a. & adv. A: & U.S:* (*of house*) en construction; **there's discontent a.,** le mécontentement des esprits s'accroît.

abulia [ə'bu:liə], *s. Med:* aboulie *f.*

abulic [ə'bu:lik], *a. Med:* aboulique.

abundance [ə'bʌndəns], *s.* **1.** (*a*) abondance *f*; grande quantité; **he has an a. of friends,** il a des amis en abondance; **there is an a. of people who . . .,** il y a quantité de gens, une multitude de gens, qui . . .; **in a.,** en abondance, à profusion; (*b*) *Lit:* épanchement *m*; *B:* **out of the a. of the heart the mouth speaketh,** c'est de la plénitude, de l'abondance, du cœur que la bouche parle; (*c*) **to live in a.,** vivre dans l'abondance. **2.** *Biol: etc:* abondance (d'une espèce, etc.). **3.** *Cards:* (*solo whist*) abondance; **a. déclarée, declared, royal a.,** chelem *m*, abondance déclarée.

abundant [ə'bʌndənt], *a.* abondant **(in,** en); fertile (en blé, etc.); **when money is a.,** lorsque la monnaie est abondante; **there is a. evidence that . . .,** les preuves abondent que . . .; il a été amplement démontré que . . .; *Mth:* **a. number,** nombre abondant; *Chr:* **a. year,** année abondante.

abundantly [ə'bʌndəntli], *adv.* abondamment; en abondance; copieusement; **garden in which everything yields a.,** jardin où tout donne à foison.

aburton [ə'bə:t(ə)n], *adv. Nau:* **stowed a.,** arrimé en breton, à travers.

abusable [ə'bju:zəbl], *a.* (autorité, etc.) dont on peut abuser.

abusage [ə'bju:zidʒ], *s.* emploi abusif (d'un mot).

abuse[1] [ə'bju:s], *s.* **1.** (*a*) abus *m* **(of,** de); *Jur:* **a. of administrative authority,** abus d'autorité, de pouvoir; **a. of discretion,** abus de pouvoir; **a. of process,** abus de procédure; **a. of trust,** prévarication *f*; (*b*) **to remedy an a.,** redresser un abus; (*c*) emploi abusif (d'un terme, etc.); (*d*) dommage (infligé); **a. of the highway,** dommage, dégradations *fpl*, à la route; (*e*) *Jur:* viol *m.* **2.** (*a*) insultes *fpl*, injures *fpl*; **term of a.,** injure; **to shower a. on s.o.,** accabler qn d'injures; (*b*) dénigrement *m*, médisance *f.*

abuse[2] [ə'bju:z], *v.tr.* **1.** abuser de (son autorité, la confiance de qn, etc.); mésuser de (son pouvoir); faire abus de (qch.); **a much abused word,** mot employé abusivement; mot trop, mal, employé; **this permission was abused,** il a été fait abus de cette permission. **2.** (*a*) maltraiter, houspiller (qn); (*b*) *Jur:* violer (une femme). **3.** (*a*) médire, dire du mal, de (qn); déblatérer contre (qn); dénigrer (qn); **I was the most abused man in the country,** j'ai été plus que tout autre poursuivi par la vindicte publique; (*b*) injurier, dire des injures à (qn); **to a. s.o. left and right,** injurier qn tant et plus; agonir qn d'injures. **4.** *A:* abuser, tromper, duper; (*still so used occ. in passive*) **you have been abused,** on vous a trompé; **I am not to be abused by empty promises,** je ne me laisserai pas abuser par de vaines promesses.

abuser [ə'bju:zər], *s.* **1.** séducteur *m* (de jeunes filles). **2.** détracteur, -trice. **3.** *A:* trompeur, -euse. **4.** personne *f* qui emploie (un mot, etc.) abusivement.

abusing [ə'bju:ziŋ], *s.* abus *m* **(of,** de).

abusive [ə'bju:siv], *a.* **1.** (emploi) abusif (d'un mot). **2.** (propos) injurieux, offensant; (homme) grossier, mal embouché; **to use a. language to s.o.,** injurier, invectiver, qn. **3.** *A:* trompeur, -euse. **4.** (traitement, etc.) brutal.

abusively [ə'bju:sivli], *adv.* **1. to use a word a.,** employer un mot abusivement. **2.** (parler) injurieusement, grossièrement. **3.** (traiter qn, qch.) brutalement.

abusiveness [ə'bju:sivnis], *s.* grossièreté *f* (de langage).

abut [ə'bʌt], *v.i. & tr.* **(abutted, abutting). 1. to a. (sth.), to a. on, against (sth.),** aboutir à, confiner à (un endroit); donner sur (la rivière, etc.); **our fields a.,** nos champs sont limitrophes, se touchent, sont attenants. **2.** *Const:* **to a. on, against (a wall, etc.),** s'appuyer, buter, contre (une paroi); s'arc-bouter contre (un mur, etc.). **3.** *Carp:* (*a*) *v.i.* (s')abouter; (*b*) *v.tr.* abouter (deux pièces).

abutilon [ə'bju:tilən], *s. Bot: Hort:* abutilon *m.*

abutment [ə'bʌtmənt], *s.* **1.** *Carp:* aboutement *m*; *NAm:* **a. piece,** seuil *m*; semelle *f.* **2.** *Arch: Civ.E:* (*a*) arc-boutant *m*, *pl.* arcs-boutants (d'une muraille); contrefort *m*; (*b*) butée *f*, culée *f* (d'un pont); piédroit *m*; pied-droit *m*, *pl.* pieds-droits (d'une voûte, d'une arcade); *attrib.* **a. wall (of a bridge),** mur *m* de culée; **a. pier,** arc-boutant, pied-droit, pile culée; (*c*) point *m* de poussée (d'une voûte, etc.). **3.** *Dent:* pilier *m.*

abuttals [ə'bʌtlz], *s.pl. Jur:* (tenants et) aboutissants *mpl.*

abutter [ə'bʌtər], *s. Jur:* propriétaire *m* limitrophe; (propriétaire) riverain (*m*).

abutting [ə'bʌtiŋ], *a.* **1.** aboutissant, attenant **(on,** à); **gardens a. on the river,** jardins aboutissants à la rivière; **lands a. on an estate,** aboutissants *mpl*; **a. owner,** riverain *m.* **2. a. joint,** assemblage *m* en about; **a. surface,** surface *f* de contact.

abuzz [ə'bʌz]. *a. & adv.* en commotion; **Paris is a. over the case,** le procès a un grand retentissement à Paris.

abvolt ['æbvoult], *s. El.Meas:* unité *f* électromagnétique C.G.S. (u.é.m. C.G.S.) de force.

abysm [ə'bizm], *s. A: & Lit:* abîme *m.*

abysmal [ə'bizml], *a.* **1.** (*a*) sans fond; insondable; **a. ignorance, ignorance profonde;** (*b*) *F:* atroce; **to live in a. conditions,** vivre dans une misère insondable. **2.** *Oc:* abyssal.

abysmally [ə'bizməli]. *adv.* **a. ignorant,** d'une ignorance profonde; **she plays the part a.,** elle interprète le rôle d'une façon atroce; **in a. bad taste,** d'un goût exécrable.

abyss [ə'bis], *s.* **1.** abîme *m*, gouffre *m.* **2.** *Oc:* abysse *m*, zone abyssale. **3.** *Her:* abîme.

abyssal [ə'bisl], *a.* **1.** (*a*) *Oc:* abyssal, abyssique; **a. fauna,** faune abyssale; **a. zone,** zone abyssale; (*b*) *Geol:* **a. rocks,** roches abyssales. **2.** *A:* sans fond, insondable.

abyssalbenthic [əbisəl'benθik], *a.* = ABYSSOBENTHIC.

abyssalpelagic [əbisəlpe'lædʒik], *a.* = ABYSSOPELAGIC.

Abyssinia [æbi'siniə], *Pr.n. Geog:* Abyssinie *f*, Éthiopie *f.*

Abyssinian [æbi'siniən]. **1.** *a. Geog:* abyssinien, abyssin, éthiopien; **the A. Empire,** l'empire *m* d'Éthiopie; *Z:* **A. cat,** chat abyssin. **2.** *s.* Abyssinien, -ienne; Éthiopien, -ienne. **3.** *s. Ling:* l'abyssinien *m.* **4.** *a.* **A. well,** abyssinienne *f.*

abyssobenthic [əbisou'benθik], *a.* abyssobenthique; **a. fauna,** faune benthique profonde.

abyssopelagic [əbisoupe'lædʒik], *a.* abyssopélagique; **a. fauna,** faune pélagique profonde.

acacia [ə'keiʃə], *s.* **1.** *Bot:* acacia *m*; **false a., a. robinia,** faux acacia; robinier *m.* **2.** (*timber*) caroube *m*, carouge *m.* **3. a. (gum),** gomme *f* arabique; (suc *m* d') acacia.

academe [ækə'di:m], *s. esp. U.S:* (*a*) ambiance *f*, milieu *m*, universitaire; (*b*) *Pej:* pédant, -ante.

academia [ækə'di:miə], *s. esp. U.S:* ambiance *f*, milieu *m*, universitaire.

academic [ækə'demik]. **1.** *a.* (*a*) *Phil:* académique, platonicien; (*b*) **a. discussion,** débat *m* académique; discussion abstraite, sans portée pratique; **a. principles,** principes *m* d'école; **it is of a. interest only,** cela n'a aucun intérêt pratique; **of purely a. interest,** qui n'est intéressant qu'au point de vue (i) académique, intellectuel, (ii) historique; **out of purely a. interest,** par simple curiosité; (*c*) *Pej:* **a. style,** style compassé, guindé; (*d*) (carrière, etc.) universitaire; (vie) d'érudit; **a. costume,** costume *m* académique; (*e*) *Art:* (peinture, etc.) académique. **2.** *s.* universitaire *mf*; érudit, -ite. **3.** (*a*) *s.* **taste for the a.,** goût *m* pour l'académique; (*b*) *s.pl.* arguments *m* stériles; arguties *f.*

academical [ækə'demikl]. **1.** *a.* universitaire; **he had received an a. education,** il avait fait des études universitaires; **a. books,** livres *m* classiques. **2.** *s.pl.* **(full) academicals,** toge *f*, épitoge *f* et bonnet *m* universitaires.

academically [ækə'demik(ə)li], *adv.* académiquement.

academician [əkædə'miʃ(ə)n], *s.* académicien *m*; *esp.* **Royal A.,** membre de la *Royal Academy* (des Beaux-Arts).

academicism [ækə'demisizm], **academism** [ə'kædəmizm], *s.* académisme *m.*

academize [ə'kædəmaiz], *v.tr. Art:* académiser (une pose, etc.).

academy [ə'kædəmi], *s.* **1.** (*a*) *Gr.Phil:* l'Académie *f* (de Platon); (*b*) *U.S: Pej:* **the new wave has rapidly become an a.,** la nouvelle vague est devenue rapidement un classicisme étroit, un académisme. **2.** (*a*) académie; **the Royal A. (of Arts),** (i) l'Académie royale des Beaux-Arts; (ii) le Salon (de Londres); **a. of music,** conservatoire *m*; **fencing a.,** salle *f* d'escrime; (*b*) **military a.,** école *f* militaire. **3.** (*a*) *A:* (*high-sounding title of private school*) école (privée); pension *f*, pensionnat *m*; (*b*) *Scot:* = lycée *m*; *U.S:* collège (privé). **4.** *Art:* **a. (figure),** académie (d'après le modèle nu); **a. board,** carton encollé (pour peinture à l'huile).

Acadia [ə'keidiə], *Pr.n. Hist: Geog:* Acadie *f*, Nouvelle-Écosse *f.*

Acadian [ə'keidiən]. **1.** *Geog:* (*a*) *a.* acadien; (*b*) *s.* Acadien, -ienne. **2.** *Geol:* acadien *m.*

acaena [ə'si:nə], *s. Bot:* acène *f*, acæna *f.*

acajou ['ækəʒu:], *s. Bot:* acajou *m.*

acaleph(e) ['ækəlef], *s. Coel:* acalèphe *m.*

Acalephae [ækə'li:fi:], *s.pl. Coel:* acalèphes *m.*

acalycine [ə'kælisain], *a. Bot:* sans calice.

acanaceous [ækə'neiʃəs], *a. Bot:* épineux.

Acanthaceae [ækæn'θeisi:i:], *s. pl. Bot:* acanthacées *f.*

acanthaceous [ækæn'θeiʃəs], *a. Bot:* (*a*) épineux; (*b*) des acanthacées.

acanthine [ə'kænθain], *a.* (*a*) *Bot:* de l'acanthe; (*b*) orné de feuilles d'acanthe.

acanthite ['ækənθait], *s. Miner:* acanthite *f.*

acanthocarpous [əkænθou'ka:pəs], *a. Bot:* acanthocarpe.

Acanthocephala [əkænθou'sefələ], **Acanthocephali** [əkænθou'sefəlai], *s.pl. Ann:* acanthocéphales *m.*

acanthocephalan [ə'kænθou'sefələn], **acanthocephalid** [əkænθou'sefəlid], *a. & s. Ann:* acanthocéphale (*m*).

acanthocladous [ə'kænθou'kleidəs], *a. Bot:* à branches épineuses.

Acanthodii [ækæn'θoudiai], *s.pl. Paleont:* acanthodes *m.*

acanthoid [ə'kænθɔid], *a. Bot:* acanthoïde.

acanthopanax [æ,kæθou'pænæks], *s. Bot:* acanthopanax *m.*

acanthophis [ækæn'θoufis], *s. Rept:* acanthophis *m.*

acanthopt ['ækənθɔpt], **acanthopteran** [ækæn'θɔptərən], **acanthopterygian** [ækænθɔptə'ridʒiən], *s. Ich:* acanthoptère *m*; acanthoptérygien *m.*

Acanthopteri [ækæn'θɔptərai], **Acanthopterygii** [ækænθɔptə'ridʒiai], *s.pl. Ich:* acanthoptères *m*; acanthoptérygiens *m.*

acanthosis [ækæn'θousis], *s. Med:* **a. nigricans,** acanthosis *f* (nigricans).

acanthosoma, *pl.* **-ata** [ə'kænθou'soumə, -a:tə], *s. Ent:* acanthosome *m.*

acanthous [əˈkænθəs], *a. Nat.Hist:* épineux.

Acanthuridæ [ækænˈθjuridiː], *s.pl. Ich:* acanthuridés *m.*

acanthurus [əˈkænθərəs], *s. Ich:* acanthure *m,* poisson chirurgien.

acanthus [əˈkænθəs], *s.* **1.** *Bot:* acanthe *f.* **2.** *Arch:* (feuille *f* d')acanthe.

acapnia [æˈkæpniə], *s. Med:* acapnie *f,* hypocapnie *f.*

acardiac [eiˈkaːdiæk], *a. Ter:* acardiaque.

acarian [əˈkɛəriən]. **1.** *s. Arach:* acaride *m,* acarien *m.* **2.** *a.* dû aux acarides.

acariasis [ækəˈraiəsis], *s. Med:* acariasis *f,* acariose *f.*

acarid [ˈækərid], **acaridan** [əˈkærid(ə)n], **acaridian** [ækəˈridiən], *s.* acaride *m.*

Acarida [æˈkæridə], **Acarina** [ækəˈrainə], *s.pl. Arach:* acarides *m,* acariens *m.*

acarinosis [ækærinˈousis], **acariosis** [ækæriˈousis], *s. Med:* acariose *f,* acariasis *f.*

Acarnania [ækaːˈneiniə], *Pr.n. Geog:* Acarnanie *f.*

Acarnanian [ækaːˈneiniən], *Geog:* **1.** *a.* acarnanien. **2.** *s.* Acarnanien, -ienne.

acaroid [ˈækərɔid], *a.* **1.** *Bot:* **a. resin, a. gum,** acroïde *f,* accroïde *f,* acchroïde *f.* **2.** qui ressemble à un acaride.

acarpous [eiˈkaːpəs], *a. Bot:* acarpe.

acarus, *pl.* **-ri** [ˈækərəs, -rai], *s. Arach:* acare *m.*

acatalectic [eikætəˈlektik], *Pros:* **1.** *a.* acatalectique. **2.** *s.* acatalecte *m.*

acatalepsy [eiˈkætəlepsi], *s. Phil:* acatalepsie *f.*

acataleptic [eikætəˈleptik], *a.* acataleptique.

acaudate [eiˈkɔːdeit], *a. Anat: Z:* acaudé.

acaulescent [eikɔːlˈesənt], **acauline** [eiˈkɔːlain], **acaulous** [eiˈkɔːləs], *a. Bot:* acaule.

Accadian [æˈkeidiən], *A.Hist:* **1.** *a.* akkadien. **2.** *s.* Akkadien, -ienne. **3.** *s. Ling:* l'akkadien *m.*

accede [ækˈsiːd], *v.i.* **1. to a. to an office,** entrer en possession d'une charge; **to a. to the throne,** monter sur le trône. **2.** (*a*) **to a. to a treaty,** donner son adhésion à un traité; **to a. to s.o.'s wishes,** donner suite, accéder, aux désirs de qn; **to a. to a request,** accueillir, faire droit à, une demande; (*b*) **to a. to a party,** adhérer, se joindre, à un parti. **3.** *Jur:* **property which accedes,** propriété qui s'acquiert par accession.

accelerant [əkˈselərənt]. **1.** *a.* accélérateur, -trice. **2.** *s.* accélérateur *m.*

accelerate [əkˈseləreit]. **1.** *v.tr.* (*a*) accélérer (la marche, le pouls, un travail); presser (un mouvement, un travail); précipiter (les événements); activer (un travail); *abs. Aut:* accélérer; (*b*) hâter, précipiter (le départ, la mort, de qn); **to a. proceedings,** hâter une procédure. **2.** *v.i.* (*of motion, etc.*) s'accélérer.

accelerated [əkˈseləreitid], *a.* (mouvement, etc.) accéléré.

accelerating[1] [əkˈseləreitiŋ], *a.* accélérateur, -trice; *Elcs:* **a. anode,** anode accélératrice.

accelerating[2], *s.* accélération *f.*

acceleration [əkseləˈreiʃ(ə)n], *s.* (*a*) accélération *f*; **negative a.,** accélération retardatrice, négative; retardation *f*; **constant a.,** accélération uniforme; **uniform a.,** vitesse uniformément accélérée; **a. time,** temps d'accélération, de montée en vitesse; **lighting a.,** accélération foudroyante; *Aut:* reprise foudroyante; *Elcs:* **post-deflexion a.,** post(-)accélération *f*; (*b*) *Cin:* accéléré *m.*

accelerative [əkˈselərətiv], *a.* accélérateur, -trice.

accelerator [əkˈseləreitər]. **1.** *a. & s.* accélérateur, -trice; *Physiol:* **a. nerves,** nerfs accélérateurs. **2.** *s. Aut: Atom.Ph: Clockm: Phot: etc:* accélérateur *m*; (*electric pump for heating system*) accélérateur, circulateur *m*; *El:* anode accélératrice (d'un tube oscillographique); *Tchn:* (**vulcanization**) **a.,** vulcanite *f,* accélérateur (de vulcanisation); *Aut:* **a. pedal,** pédale *f* d'accélération; **to depress the a.,** donner un coup d'accélérateur; **to release the a.,** lâcher l'accélérateur.

accelerograph [əkˈselərougræf], *s.* accélérographe *m.*

accelerometer [əkseləˈrɔmitər], *s. Mec:* accéléromètre *m*; **statistical a.,** accéléro-compteur *m, pl.* accéléro-compteurs.

accent[1] [ˈæks(ə)nt], *s.* **1.** (*a*) accent *m*; **to have a German a.,** avoir l'accent allemand; **to speak with an a.,** parler avec un accent; (*b*) **with an a. of anger,** d'un ton irrité, fâché; **he related, in broken accents, that. . .,** il raconta, d'une voix brisée, entrecoupée, que. . . . **2.** (*a*) *Pros:* accent, temps marqué; *Ling:* **a. shift,** déplacement *m* de l'accent d'intensité; (*b*) *Mus:* (i) temps fort; (ii) accent (mélodique); **a. mark,** accent (de mode d'exécution); (*c*) **with the a. on . . .,** en mettant l'accent sur . . .; **fashion with the a. on youth,** mode qui met l'accent sur la jeunesse. **3.** (*a*) **sentence a.,** accent oratoire; (*b*) **grammatical accents,** accents grammaticaux; **acute, grave a.,** accent aigu, accent grave. **4.** *Art:* accent (de lumière, etc.).

accent[2] [ækˈsent], *v.tr.* **1.** accentuer (une syllabe, une voyelle, etc.); appuyer sur (une syllabe, etc.). **2.** = ACCENTUATE.

accented [ækˈsentid], *a.* accentué; *Ling:* accentuel.

accentor [ækˈsentər], *s. Orn:* accenteur *m*; **hedge a.,** accenteur mouchet; **alpine a.,** accenteur alpin, *F:* pégot *m*; **mountain a.,** accenteur montanelle.

accentuable [ækˈsentjuəbl], *a. Ling:* accentuable.

accentual [ækˈsentjuəl], *a. Ling:* accentuel.

accentuate [ækˈsentjueit], *v.tr.* accentuer, souligner, appuyer sur, faire ressortir, rehausser, mettre en relief (un détail, etc.); accuser (un contraste); attirer l'attention sur (qch.).

accentuated [ækˈsentjueitid], *a.* fortement marqué; accentué.

accentuation [æksentjuˈeiʃ(ə)n], *s.* accentuation *f* (d'une voyelle, d'un détail, etc.).

accept [əkˈsept], *v.tr. & ind.tr.* **1.** (*a*) accepter (un cadeau, une offre); agréer (les salutations, les prières, de qn); admettre (les raisons, les excuses, de qn); agréer (un prétendant); donner son adhésion à (un traité); **to a. battle,** accepter la bataille; **to a. an invitation,** accepter une invitation; **to a. an invitation to dinner,** accepter à dîner; **to a. s.o. as a companion,** accepter qn pour, comme, compagnon; **to be accepted,** être accepté; passer; **she is accepted everywhere,** tout le monde l'accepte; **contrary to accepted opinion,** à l'encontre des idées reçues; contrairement à l'opinion courante; **the accepted custom,** l'usage admis; **doctrine which has become universally accepted,** doctrine devenue classique; *Com:* **to a. a bill,** accepter un effet; **to a. (delivery of) goods,** prendre des marchandises en recette; *NAm:* **surface that does not a. ink,** surface qui ne prend pas l'encre; (*b*) **to a. the inevitable,** se soumettre au destin; **it's not pleasant, but we shall have to a. it,** ce n'est pas agréable, mais il nous faut nous y résigner; (*c*) *A: & Lit:* **to a. persons,** montrer de la partialité pour qn; (*d*) (*of female animal*) **to a. the male, to a. coitus,** accepter l'approche du mâle. **2.** *A:* **to a. of a gift,** daigner accepter un cadeau.

acceptability [əkseptəˈbiliti], *s.* acceptabilité *f.*

acceptable [əkˈseptəbl], *a.* (*a*) acceptable, agréable; bienvenu; **sacrifice a. to God,** sacrifice *m* agréable à Dieu; **your letters are always most a.,** vos lettres sont toujours les bienvenues; **your cheque was most a.,** votre chèque est arrivé fort à propos; **his speech was more a. than those that came before,** son discours était mieux venu que les précédents; (*b*) admissible, acceptable; possible; **she considered him as an a. husband,** elle le considérait comme un mari possible; *F:* **just about a.,** tolérable, supportable; (boisson) potable.

acceptableness [əkˈseptəblnis], *s.* acceptabilité *f.*

acceptably [əkˈseptəbli], *adv.* acceptablement; d'une manière acceptable; *O:* **she plays very a.,** elle joue (i) assez bien, (ii) très agréablement.

acceptance [əkˈseptəns], *s.* **1.** (*a*) acceptation *f*; consentement *m* à recevoir (qch.); accueil *m* favorable (de qch.); **a. of a proposal,** agrément donné à une proposition; **to beg s.o.'s a. of sth.,** prier qn d'accepter qch.; **to secure a. of sth.,** faire accepter qch.; (*of story, etc.*) **to find a.,** trouver créance; **that is unworthy of your a.,** cela ne mérite pas que vous l'acceptiez; cela ne mérite pas, n'est pas digne, de vous être offert; **this proposal met with general a.,** cette proposition a rallié tous les suffrages; **to gain a. for one's opinion,** faire prévaloir son opinion; *Com:* **to present a bill for a.,** présenter une traite à l'acceptation; **a. bank, house,** banque *f* d'escompte d'effets étrangers; *Jur:* **a. of a judgment,** acquiescement *m* à un jugement; (*b*) *Th:* réception *f* (d'une pièce par le comité de lecture); (*c*) *Com: Ind:* réception (d'un article commandé); **qualified a.,** acceptation sous réserve; **unconditional a.,** acceptation sans réserve; **partial a.,** acceptation restreinte; **a. test, trial,** essai *m* de réception, de recette, d'homologation; **a. firing test,** tir *m* de recette (d'un canon); *Mil: Adm:* **formal a.,** réception définitive; (*d*) *A: & Lit:* **a. of persons,** partialité *f*; **without a. of persons,** sans faire acception de personne; (*e*) *Turf:* engagement *m*; **a. fee,** droit *m* d'entrée; (*f*) (*of female animal*) accouplement *m.* **2.** *A: Journ:* **he spoke with a.,** son discours fut bien accueilli; **she played a gavotte with great a.,** elle a joué une gavotte fort agréablement.

acceptant [əkˈseptənt], *a. & s.* acceptant, -ante.

acceptation [æksepˈteiʃ(ə)n], *s.* (*a*) acception *f,* signification *f* (d'un mot); **in the full a. of the word,** dans toute l'acception du mot; (*b*) *B: & Lit:* acceptation *f.*

accepter [əkˈseptər], *s.* acceptant, -ante.

accepting [əkˈseptiŋ], *s.* acceptation *f*; *attrib.* **a. house,** banque *f* d'escompte d'effets étrangers.

acceptive [əkˈseptiv], *a.* prêt à accepter (une idée, etc.).

acceptor [əkˈseptər], *s.* **1.** (*a*) *Com:* tiré *m*; accepteur *m* (d'une lettre de change); **a. for honour, a. supra protest,** intervenant *m*; avaliste *mf*; donneur *m* d'aval; (*b*) *Ch:* accepteur; *Elcs:* **a. (impurity),** accepteur, impureté acceptrice; *El:* **a. (circuit),** circuit *m* résonance-série; *Tex:* **to be a dye a.,** prendre la teinture. **2.** *Turf:* coureur *m.*

access[1] [ˈækses], *s.* **1.** (*a*) accès *m,* abord *m*; **means of a.,** moyens *m* d'accès; **difficult of a.,** d'un accès difficile, d'une approche difficile; difficile à approcher; **easy of a.,** abordable, accostable, facilement accessible; **door that gives a. to a room,** porte qui donne accès à, qui commande, une pièce; **a. to the door is by a flight of steps,** on accède à la porte par un escalier; *P.N: Aut:* **a. only,** sauf riverains et livreurs; **manholes that give easy a. to the mains,** trous *m* d'homme qui facilitent la visite des canalisations; *Const:* **a. eye, maintenance a.,** trou d'accès; trou d'inspection; **a. road,** route *f* d'accès; *Cmptr:* **a. time,** temps *m* d'accès, de prise; **parallel, simultaneous, a.,** accès parallèle, simultané; **a. arm,** bras *m* d'accès, bras de lecture/écriture; **a. mode,** mode *m* d'accès; **random a. storage,** mémoire *m* à accès sélectif; **to obtain, gain, a. to s.o.,** trouver accès auprès de qn; accéder à qn; **to have a. to s.o.,** avoir accès chez, auprès de, qn; avoir son entrée, ses entrées, chez, auprès de, qn; *Com:* **to have a. to the books of a company,** prendre communication des livres d'une société; (*b*) **the a. and recess of the sea,** le flux et le reflux de la mer. **2. a. of fever, of rage,** accès de fièvre, de rage; **a. of joy,** saisissement *m* de joie.

access[2], *v.tr. Cmptr:* accéder à.

accessary [ækˈsesəri], *a. & s.* = ACCESSORY.

accessibility [æksesiˈbiliti], *s.* accessibilité *f*; commodité *f,* facilité *f,* d'accès (**of,** de).

accessible [ækˈsesəbl], *a.* **1.** (*a*) (endroit, personne, etc.) accessible, abordable, approchable; **knowledge a. to everyone,** connaissances *fpl* à la portée de tout le monde, accessibles à tous; **this collection is not a. to the public,** cette collection n'est pas ouverte au public, n'est pas visible; (*b*) *Cmptr:* accessible, adressable. **2.** (*of pers.*) (*a*) accueillant; (*b*) **a. to pity,** accessible à la pitié; **he was a. to bribery,** il n'était pas incorruptible.

accessibleness [ækˈsesəblnis], *s.* = ACCESSIBILITY.

accession [ækˈseʃ(ə)n], *s.* **1. a. of light, of air,** admission *f* de lumière, d'air. *Fin:* **a. of funds from abroad,** arrivage *m* de fonds de l'étranger. **2.** (*a*) accroissement *m* (par addition); **a. to one's income,** augmentation *f,* accroissement *m,* de revenus; addition *f* à ses revenus; **accession(s) book,** registre *m* des additions (à une bibliothèque); **a. number,** numéro *m* matricule; (*b*) adhésion *f* (à un parti); **there have been many accessions to our party,** notre parti s'est augmenté de nombreuses recrues, de nombreux adhérents; (*c*) **a. to a treaty,** accession *f,* assentiment *m,* adhésion, à un traité. **3.** (*a*) **a. to manhood,** arrivée *f* à l'âge d'homme; (*b*) **a. to power,** accession au pouvoir; **a. to office,** entrée *f* en fonctions; **a. to the throne,** avènement *m* au trône; **a. to an estate,** entrée en possession, en jouissance, d'un patrimoine. **4.** *Cmptr:* consultation *f*; **a. rate,** vitesse *f* de consultation; **a. number,** numéro de référence (de document). **5.** *NAm:* **a. of feeling,** accès *m* d'émotion.

accession[2], *v.tr.* inscrire (un livre) au registre des additions (à une bibliothèque).

accessional [ækˈseʃənl], *a.* additionnel.

accessioning [ækˈseʃəniŋ], *s.* inscription *f* (d'un livre) au registre des additions (à une bibliothèque).

accessorial [æksesˈɔːriəl], *a.* (*a*) auxiliaire, supplémentaire, subsidiaire; *Cmptr:* **a. equipment,** matériel *m* annexe; (*b*) **a. guilt,** culpabilité *f* comme complice.

accessorily [ækˈsesərili], *adv.* accessoirement, subsidiairement.

accessorize [ækˈsesəraiz], *v.tr.* munir d'accessoires.

accessory [ækˈsesəri]. **1.** *a.* accessoire, subsidiaire (**to,** à); **a. minerals,** minéraux accessoires; **a. equipment,** matériel annexe; *Anat:* **a. nerve,** nerf *m* accessoire; *Bot:* **a. bud, shoot,** prompt-bourgeon *m, pl.* prompts-bourgeons; *Jur:* **a. clause,** clause *f* accessoire. **2.** *s.* (*a*) accessoire *m*; organe *m* accessoire, auxiliaire; **car accessories,** accessoires d'automobile, automobiles; **toilet accessories,** accessoires de toilette; *Cost:* **accessories,** accessoires; (*b*) *pl.* appareillage *m* (d'une usine, etc.); *Th:* accessoires *mpl* (d'une pièce. **3.** *s. & a.*; **a. to a crime,** complice *m,* d'un crime; *Jur:* **a. before the fact,** complice par instigation; **a. after the fact,** complice par assistance, complice après coup.

acciaccatura [æˈtʃækəˈtuərə], *s. Mus:* acciaccatura *f.*

accidence [ˈæksid(ə)ns], *s.* (*a*) *Gram:* morphologie *f,* lexicologie *f*; (*b*) rudiments *mpl,* éléments *mpl* (d'une science, etc.).

accident [ˈæksid(ə)nt], *s.* **1.** (*a*) accident *m*; *Jur:* cas fortuit; **by a.**, accidentellement; **by a mere a.**, par pur hasard; **nothing was left to a.**, rien n'était laissé au hasard; on avait paré à toute éventualité; **by a fortunate a.**, par un heureux accident; (*b*) **serious a.**, accident grave; **fatal a.**, accident mortel; fatalité *f*; *Jur:* **a. to third parties**, accident causé aux tiers; **to meet with, to have, an a.**, être, se trouver, victime d'un accident; **car a.**, accident d'automobile; **road a.**, accident de la route, de la circulation; **industrial a.**, accident du travail; **the victims of the a. were taken to hospital**, on a transporté les victimes de l'accident, les accidentés, à l'hôpital; **a. insurance**, assurance *f* contre les accidents; **a. policy**, police *f* d'assurance accidents; *Jur:* **accidents at sea**, fortunes *fpl* de mer; **accidents will happen**, tout le monde est faillible; on ne peut pas parer à tout; on ne saurait tout prévoir; **chapter of accidents**, suite *f*, succession *f*, de mésaventures, de malheurs; *F:* **the child has had an a.**, l'enfant a fait pipi dans sa culotte; (*c*) *Med:* **cerebral a.**, congestion cérébrale. **2.** accident, inégalité *f*, irrégularité *f* (du terrain). **3.** (*a*) *Phil:* accident; (*b*) **accidents of presentation**, présentation *f* linguistique et typographique (d'un livre).

accidental [æksi'dentl]. **1.** *a.* (*a*) accidentel, fortuit; **a. meeting**, rencontre *f* de hasard; *Surv: etc:* **a. errors**, erreurs accidentelles, erreurs fortuites; (*b*) accessoire, subsidiaire; non-essentiel; *Art:* **a. light**, *s.* **accidental**, contre-jour *m*; reflet *m*; *Mus:* **a. sharp, flat**, dièse, bémol, accidentel. **2.** *s. Mus:* accident *m*; signe accidentel.

accidentality [æksiden'tæliti], *s.* nature fortuite (d'un événement, etc.).

accidentally [æksi'dentəli], *adv.* (*a*) accidentellement, par hasard, fortuitement; (*b*) accidentellement, par mégarde; *F:Hum:* **a. on purpose** (exprès, mais) comme s'il s'agissait d'un accident; comme par hasard.

accident-prone ['æksid(ə)ntproun], *a.* prédisposé aux accidents.

accident-proneness ['æksid(ə)nt'prounnis], *s.* prédisposition *f* aux accidents.

accipiter [æk'sipitər], *s. Orn:* accipiter *m*.

accipitral [æk'sipitrəl], *a.* **1.** d'une rapacité d'épervier; (oiseau) rapace. **2.** aux yeux d'aigle.

Accipitres [æk'sipitri:z], *s.pl. Orn:* accipitres *mpl*.

Accipitridae [æksipi'tri:di:], *s.pl. Orn:* accipitridés *m*.

accipitrine [æk'sipitrin, -ain]. *Orn:* **1.** *a.* accipitrin. **2.** *s.* accipiter *m*.

acclaim[1] [ə'kleim], *v.tr.* (*a*) acclamer; accueillir (qn) par des acclamations; applaudir (qn); (*b*) **Charlemagne was acclaimed emperor**, Charlemagne fut acclamé, proclamé, salué, empereur.

acclaim[2], *s. Lit:* acclamation *f*, acclamations.

acclaimer [ə'kleimər], *s.* acclamateur *m*.

acclamation [æklə'meiʃ(ə)n], *s.* acclamation *f*; **carried by a., with a.**, adopté par acclamation.

acclamatory [ə'klæmət(ə)ri], *a.* acclamatif.

acclimatation [əklaimə'teiʃ(ə)n]. **1.** *s.* acclimatement *m* (**to**, à). **2.** acclimatation *f*.

acclimate [ə'klaimət, 'æklimeit], *v.tr. esp. U.S:* = ACCLIMATIZE.

acclimated [ə'klaimətid, 'æklimeitid], *a.* acclimaté; **a. tropical plants**, plantes tropicales acclimatées.

acclimation [ækli'meiʃ(ə)n], *s.* **1.** acclimatement *m*. **2.** acclimatation *f*.

acclimatizable [ə'klaimətaizəbl], *a.* acclimatable.

acclimatization [əklaimətai'zeiʃ(ə)n], *s.* **1.** acclimatement *m* (**to**, à). **2.** acclimatation *f*.

acclimatize [ə'klaimətaiz], *v.tr.* acclimater; naturaliser (une plante, etc.); **to become acclimatized**, *v.i.* **to a.**, s'acclimater.

acclimatizer [ə'klaimətaizər], *s.* acclimateur *m*.

acclivitous [ə'klivitəs], *a.* escarpé; en pente.

acclivity [ə'kliviti], *s.* montée *f*, côte *f*; rampe *f*; escarpement *m*.

acclivous [ə'klaivəs[, *a.* escarpé; en pente.

accolade ['ækəleid], *s.* **1.** accolade *f*; (i) coup du plat de l'épée; (ii) embrassade cérémoniale. **2.** *Arch:* (arc *m* en) accolade. **3.** *Mus:* accolade.

accollated ['ækəleitid], *a. Her: Num:* accolé.

accollé(e) [æ'kolei], *a. Her:* accolé.

accolled [æ'kəld], *a. Num: Her:* accolé.

accommodate [ə'kəmədeit], *v.tr.* **1.** (*a*) accommoder, approprier, conformer (ses goûts à ceux d'un autre); **to a. oneself to circumstances**, s'accommoder, s'adapter, aux circonstances; (*b*) ajuster, adapter (qch. à qch.); *Mec.E:* **to a. the difference in assembly**, rattraper les différences de montage; (*c*) arranger (une querelle); concilier (des opinions, des personnes). **2.** (*a*) **to a. s.o.**, accommoder, servir, obliger, qn; **to a. a client**, rendre service à, obliger, un client; **to do sth. to a. s.o.**, faire qch. pour arranger qn; (*b*) **to a. s.o. with sth.**, donner, fournir, qch. à qn; fournir qn de qch; **to a s.o. with a loan**, faire un prêt à qn; prêter une somme à qn. **3.** loger, recevoir (tant de personnes); **his car can a. six**, on tient à six dans sa voiture, il y a de la place pour six (personnes) dans sa voiture; **how am I to a. my guests?** comment vais-je loger mes invités? **restaurant that can a. 50 people**, restaurant en mesure de servir 50 personnes, où il y a de la place pour 50 personnes. **4.** *v.i.* (*a*) *esp. U.S:* s'accommoder (aux circonstances, etc.); (*b*) (*of the eye*) accommoder.

accommodating[1] [ə'kəmədeitiŋ], *a.* (*a*) complaisant, obligeant, serviable, accommodant; peu difficile (**about**, sur); **a. man (in business)**, homme coulant en affaires; (*b*) *Pej:* (*of morals, religion, etc.*); accommodant, commode, arrangeant; **a. morals**, morale *f* facile; **a. husband**, mari complaisant.

accommodating[2], *s.* ajustement *m*, adaptation *f* (**to**, à).

accommodatingly [əkəmə'deitiŋli], *adv.* complaisamment.

accommodation [əkəmə'deiʃ(ə)n], *s.* **1.** (*a*) ajustement *m*, adaptation *f* (**to**, à); *Bot: Z:* accommodation *f*; *Physiol:* accommodation (de l'œil); (*b*) accommodement *m*, arrangement *m*, ajustement (d'une dispute); **to come to an a.**, arriver à un compromis; s'arranger (à l'amiable). **2.** (*of pers*) complaisance *f*, accommodement; *A:* **through the friendly a. of Messrs X**, grâce à l'amabilité de MM. X. **3.** (*a*) commodité *f*, facilités *fpl*; **for your a.**, pour votre commodité; *Com:* **a. bill**, billet *m* de complaisance; *Nau:* **a. ladder**, échelle *f* de commandement, de coupée; *Rail: U.S:* **a. (train)**, (train *m*) omnibus (*m*); *NAm:* **a. ramp**, rampe *f* d'accès; **a. road**, chemin *m* de terre, de moisson, d'exploitation, de desserte; **a. address**, adress *f* de convention; (*b*) logement *m*, installation matérielle; chambre *f* d'hôtel; *Nau:* emménagements *mpl*; aménagements *mpl*; **furnished a.**, chambres garnies; *Pej:* **a. house**, hôtel; garni; *Adm:* **a. unit**, logement (pour une famille); appartement *m*; **a. of a railway carriage**, contenance *f* d'un wagon; *A:* **a. for man and beast** (ici) on loge à pied et à cheval; *Austr: N.Z:* **a. paddock**, pré *m* à l'usage des transhumants, etc.; **we have found a.**, nous avons trouvé à nous loger; *NAm:* **we had very good accommodations in Italy**, nous avons trouvé de très bons hôtels, de très bons logements, en Italie; **we haven't a. for so many people**, nous ne pouvons pas loger tant de gens; **ample a. for visitors**, de nombreuses facilités de logement pour les voyageurs; **we have no sleeping a.**, nous n'avons pas de chambres; **there is a. in this restaurant for 50 people**, il y a des places pour, on peut servir, 50 personnes dans ce restaurant; *Adm: A:* **assistance and a.**, secours *m* et refuge *m*; (*c*) avance *f*, prêt *m* (d'argent).

accommodative [ə'kəmədeitiv], *a.* = ACCOMMODATING[1].

accommodativeness [ə'kəmədeitivnis], *s.* facilité *f*, complaisance *f* (en affaires, etc.).

accommodator [ə'kəmədeitər], *s.* (*a*) remplacant, -ante; (*b*) *NAm:* domestique *mf* qui travaille (i) à mi-temps, (ii) par occasion; **a. who goes anywhere to cook and serve dinners**, cuisinier, -ière, qui va chez divers clients pour préparer et servir le dîner; traiteur *m*.

accompaniment [ə'kʌmp(ə)nimənt], *s.* (*a*) accompagnement *m*; accessoires *mpl*; (*b*) *Her:* accompagnement (de l'écu); (*c*) *Mus:* accompagnement (**on the piano**, au piano); **a. figure**, contre-chant *m*.

accompanist [ə'kʌmp(ə)nist], *s. Mus:* accompagnateur, -trice.

accompany [ə'kʌmp(ə)ni], *v.tr.* **1.** accompagner (qn); **to be accompanied by s.o.**, être accompagné de (*occ.* par) qn; **the president was accompanied by his secretary, by a general**, le président était accompagné de son secrétaire, par un général; **accompanied by numerous servants**, suivi, escorté, de nombreux domestiques. **2.** (*a*) **he accompanied these words with a smile**, il accompagna ces mots d'un sourire; (*b*) **fever accompanied by, with, delirium**, fièvre accompagnée de délire. **3.** *Mus:* (*a*) **to a. s.o. on the piano**, accompagner qn au piano; **accompanied by Miss X**, accompagné par Mlle X; (*b*) *abs.* accompagner.

accompanying[1], [ə'kʌmp(ə)niiŋ], *a.* (symptôme, etc.) concomitant.

accompanying[2], *s. Mus:* **to be good at a.**, être bon accompagnateur, bonne accompagnatrice.

accompanyist [ə'kʌmp(ə)niist], *s. Mus:* accompagnateur, -trice.

accomplice [ə'kəmplis, -'kʌm-], *s.* complice *mf*, coauteur *m*, compère *m* (d'un escamoteur, etc.); **his accomplices in crime**, les complices de ses crimes.

accomplish [ə'kəmpliʃ, -'kʌm-], *v.tr.* **1.** accomplir, exécuter, achever, effectuer; venir à bout de (qch.); mener à bonne fin (une tâche); consommer (une œuvre, un crime); effectuer (un voyage, une traversée); réaliser (une prédiction); **to a. one's object**, atteindre son but; **he will never a. anything**, il ne fera jamais rien qui vaille; **we know what Mr X has accomplished**, on sait le bel effort réalisé par M. X.; **mission accomplished**, mission accomplie. **2.** *A:* parachever, parfaire (son éducation, etc.).

accomplishable [ə'kəmpliʃəbl, -'kʌm-], *a.* exécutable; (projet) réalisable.

accomplished [ə'kəmpliʃt, -'kʌm-] *a.* **1.** accompli, achevé; **a. fact**, fait accompli. **2. she is an a. dancer**, c'est une danseuse accomplie; elle danse à (la) perfection; **he is very a.**, il possède de nombreux talents; il est très accompli, très cultivé.

accomplishing [ə'kəmpliʃiŋ, -'kʌm], *s.* accomplissement *m*, réalisation *f*.

accomplishment [ə'kəmpliʃmənt, -'kʌm-], *s.* **1.** (*a*) accomplissement *m*, achèvement *m*, exécution *f*, consommation *f* (d'une tâche, d'un devoir); réalisation *f* (d'un projet); **difficult of a.**, d'un accomplissement difficile; difficile à réaliser; (*b*) chose accomplie, réalisée; **when we realize the greatness of his a.**, quand on se rend compte de l'effort qu'il a réalisé. **2.** *usu.pl.* art(s) *m* d'agrément, talent(s) *m* (d'agrément); **she has many accomplishments**, elle est très accomplie; elle possède de nombreux talents; **his only a. was playing the flute**, il jouait de la flûte; c'était son seul talent.

accord[1] [ə'kɔ:d], *s.* **1.** (*a*) accord *m*, consentement *m*; **with one a.**, d'un commun accord; **to be in a., out of a., with sth.**, être d'accord, en désaccord, avec qch.; *NAm:* **in a. with modern techniques**, en conformité avec la technique moderne; (*b*) *Lit: & NAm:* pacte *m*; entente *f*; (*c*) *Com:* **a. and satisfaction**, libération *f* (d'une obligation) à titre onéreux. **2. to do sth. of one's own a.**, faire qch. de son plein gré, de son propre gré, de sa propre volonté, de son propre mouvement; faire qch. d'office, de soi-même, spontanément; **I came of my own a.**, je suis venu de moi-même. **3.** *Mus: Art: Poet:* harmonie *f*, accord accord (de sons, de couleurs).

accord[2]. **1.** *v.i.* s'accorder, être d'accord, concorder (**with**, avec); *Lit:* **his conduct and his principles do not a. well together**, sa conduite et ses principes ne s'accordent pas, ne vont pas bien ensemble; **the result did not a. with our calculations**, le résultat a trompé nos calculs. **2.** *v.tr.* (*a*) accorder, concéder, octroyer (**to**, **a**); (*b*) *Lit:* accorder, mettre d'accord (des personnes, des faits).

accordance [ə'kɔd(ə)ns], *s.* **1.** accord *m*, rapport *m*, conformité; **in a. with your instructions**, en conformité avec, en conformité de, conformément à, vos ordres; nous conformant à vos ordres; d'après vos ordres; suivant vos ordres; **in a. with the decision**, aux termes de la décision; **statement in a. with the facts**, affirmation *f* conforme à la vérité, d'accord avec la vérité, en harmonie avec la vérité. **2.** octroi *m*, concession *f* (d'un privilège, etc.).

accordant [ə'kɔ:d(ə)nt], *a.* **1.** concordant; d'accord. **2.** d'accord (**to, with**, avec); conforme (**to, with**, à); en harmonie (avec). **3.** *Geog:* concordant; **a. junction (of rivers)**, concordance *f* des confluents.

according [ə'kɔ:diŋ], *adv. used only in:* **1.** *conj. phrs.* (*a*) *O:* **a. as**, selon que, suivant que, comme, + *ind.*; **we see things differently a. as we are rich or poor**, on voit les choses différemment selon qu'on est riche ou pauvre; (*b*) **a. to how, the way in which, it is done**, suivant la façon dont on le fait; **a. to whether it rains or is fine**, selon qu'il pleut ou qu'il fait beau; **a. to whether one is rich or poor**, selon qu'on est riche ou pauvre; **a. to why he came**, selon la raison pour laquelle il est venu; **a. to what you decide**, comme vous déciderez, selon votre décision. **2.** *prep. phr.* (*a*) **a. to instructions**, selon, suivant, d'après, les ordres; conformément aux ordres; **a. to age, height**, par rang d'âge, de taille; **a. to plan**, conformément au plan; (*b*) **a. to him**, d'après lui; à l'entendre; à l'en croire; à ce qu'il dit; **a. to that**, d'après cela; à ce compte-là; **a. to what everyone says, a. to all accounts**, au dire de tout le monde; **the Gospel a. to St Luke**, l'Évangile selon saint Luc; **a. to this author . . .**, d'après, au rapport de, cet auteur . . .; **we give each a. to our means**, nous donnons chacun selon nos moyens.

accordingly [ə'kɔ:diŋli], *adv.* **1.** (*a*) **to act a.**, agir en conséquence; **they soon saw what had happened and acted a.**, ils se rendirent vite compte de ce qui était arrivé et ils se conduisirent à l'avenant; **he began to understand and his face changed a.**, il commençait à comprendre, et son expression changeait à mesure; (*b*) *A:* **a. as** = **according as. 2.** donc; **a. I wrote to him**, je lui ai donc écrit; aussi lui ai-je écrit; en conséquence je lui ai écrit.

accordion [ə'kɔ:diən], *s.* accordéon *m*; **piano a.**, accordéon à touches; **a. player**, accordéoniste *mf*, joueur, -euse, d'accordéon; *Dressm: etc:* **a. pleats**, plis *m* en accordéon; **a.-pleated**, (plié) en accordéon; en plis d'accordéon; **a. door, partition,** porte *f,* cloison *m,* repliable; cloison extensible; *F:* porte accordéon.

accordionist [ə'kɔ:diənist], *s.* accordéoniste *mf.*

accost[1] [ə'kɔst], *v.tr.* **1.** (*a*) accoster, aborder (qn, un navire); **to be accosted by a stranger,** être abordé par un inconnu; (*b*) (*of prostitute*) racoler, raccrocher (qn). **2.** *A:* être contigu à (qch.).

accost[2], *s. A:* abord *m,* abordée *f.*

accostable [ə'kɔstəbl], *a.* abordable; (personne) à l'abord facile.

accosted [ə'kɔstid], *a. Her:* (*a*) (*of animals, etc.*) accosté; (*b*) (*of shields*) accolé.

accosting [ə'kɔstiŋ], *s. Jur:* racolage *m,* raccrochage *m.*

accouchement [ə'ku:ʃmɑ̃], *s. Obst:* accouchement *m.*

account[1] [ə'kaunt], *s.* **1. to be quick at accounts,** être un calculateur rapide; *A:* **to cast an a.,** faire un calcul; **money of a.,** monnaie *f* de compte. **2.** (*a*) *Com:* compte *m,* note *f*; **let me have your a.,** envoyez-moi votre note, votre compte; **detailed, itemized, a.,** compte spécifié, détaillé; **accounts payable,** dettes passives; **accounts receivable,** dettes actives; **to have an a.,** *U.S:* **a charge a., with s.o.,** avoir un compte chez qn; **put it on, down to, charge it to, my a.,** inscrivez-le, mettez-le, à mon compte; **cash or a.?** avez-vous un compte chez nous? **in a. with s.o.,** en compte avec qn; **to pay a sum on a.,** payer une somme en acompte, à compte, à valoir; payer un acompte, un à valoir; **to pay ten pounds on a.,** donner un acompte de dix livres; **on, for, a. of s.o.,** pour le compte de qn, à valoir sur qn; **to buy sth. on one's own a.,** acheter qch. pour son (propre) compte; **to a. rendered, as per a. rendered,** suivant compte remis; suivant relevé remis; **to settle an a.,** régler une note, un compte; (*b*) **the accounts (of a firm, etc.),** la comptabilité (d'une entreprise, etc.); **accounts department,** (service *m* de) la comptabilité; **profit and loss a.,** compte des profits et pertes; **income and expenditure a.,** compte des dépenses et recettes; **capital a.,** compte capital; **sales a.,** compte des ventes; **advertising a.,** budget *m* de publicité; **contra a.,** compte d'autre part; **a. book,** livre *m* de comptes; registre *m* de la comptabilité; **to keep the accounts,** tenir les livres, les écritures, les comptes, la comptabilité; **to keep separate accounts,** faire bourse à part; **to keep strict a. of expenses,** tenir un compte rigoureux des dépenses; (*c*) *Bank:* **bank a.,** compte en banque; **name of an a.,** intitulé *m* d'un compte, **current a.,** compte courant; **deposit a.,** compte de dépôt; **joint a.,** compte joint; **loan a.,** compte de prêt; crédit *m*; compte d'avances; **credit a.,** compte créditeur; **debit a.,** compte débiteur; **to open an a.,** ouvrir un compte; **to overdraw an a.,** mettre un compte à découvert; **statement of a.,** relevé *m* de compte; (*d*) *St.Exch:* **the A.,** la liquidation (mensuelle); **current a.,** liquidation courante; **next a.,** liquidation prochaine; **a. day,** (jour *m* de) liquidation; (jour de) règlement *m*; **dealings for the a.,** négociations *f* à terme; **securities dealt in for the a.,** valeurs *f* à terme; **bull a.,** position *f* acheteur; position à la hausse; **bear a.,** position vendeur; position à la baisse; (*e*) exposé *m,* état *m,* mémoire *m,* note *f*; **a. of expenses,** état, note, de dépenses; **a. of one's transactions,** état, exposé, de ses opérations; *Jur:* **a. of liabilities and assets,** état des dettes actives et passives; (*f*) **to turn sth. to a.,** tirer parti, avantage, de qch.; faire valoir qch.; mettre qch. à profit, profiter de qch.; utiliser qch.; **I turned it to a.,** j'y ai trouvé mon compte; **to turn sth. to good a.,** tirer un bon parti de qch.; **to turn sth. to the best a.,** tirer tout le profit, tout le parti possible, de qch.; **he turns everything to good a.,** il fait profit de tout; il fait flèche de tout bois; (*g*) **to call s.o. to a. (for (doing) sth.),** demander une explication de qn; demander compte à qn (de qch.); prendre qn à partie (d'avoir fait qch.); **to bring s.o. to a.,** faire payer ses méfaits à qn; *A:* & *Lit:* **he has gone to his a.,** il est mort; il a payé sa dette à la nature; **to give a. of sth.,** rendre raison, compte, de qch.; **to give a good a. of oneself,** (i) justifier de sa bonne conduite; (ii) s'acquitter bien; **he gave quite a good a. of himself,** il s'est acquitté assez bien; il s'en est bien tiré. **3.** (*a*) **(person, thing) of some a., of no (great) a.,** (personne *f,* chose *f*) qui compte, qui ne compte guère; **he is of very little a.,** il a peu d'influence; **competitors of no great a.,** des concurrents peu dangereux, peu sérieux; **man of no a.,** homme insignifiant, de peu d'importance, qui ne compte pas; **to be of some a.,** être tenu en estime; **to hold one's life of little a.,** faire bon marché de sa vie; ne pas marchander sa vie; compter sa vie pour rien; **to take sth. into a., to take a. of sth.,** tenir compte de qch.; avoir égard à qch.; faire état de qch.; faire entrer qch. en ligne de compte; **taking everything into a.,** tout calcul fait, tout bien calculé; **to take the circumstances into a.,** faire la part des circonstances; **to leave (sth.) out of a., to take no a. of** (sth.), ne pas tenir compte de (qch.); ne pas compter (qch.); ne faire aucun cas de (qch.); faire abstraction de (qch.); négliger (une circonstance); **in this budget moneys owing to us are not taken into a.,** dans ce budget nos créances n'entrent pas en ligne de compte; (*b*) **on a. of s.o.,** à cause de qn; **I was nervous on his a.,** j'avais peur pour lui; **I did it on your account,** c'est pour vous que je l'ai fait; **I did it on a. of you,** je l'ai fait à cause de vous; **on a. of sth.,** à cause de, pour cause de, en raison de, par suite de, en considération de, qch.; **absent on a. of ill health,** absent pour raison de santé; **persecuted on a. of . . .,** poursuivi sous le chef de . . .; **on every a.,** sous tous les rapports; **on many accounts,** sous divers titres; **on what a.?** à propos de quoi? à quel propos? **on no a., not on any a.,** dans aucun cas, sous aucun prétexte, en aucune manière, pour rien au monde; **I won't have it on any a.,** je m'y oppose absolument, formellement; je le défends absolument; (*c*) **to act on one's own a.,** agir de sa propre initiative, de soi-même; **I did it entirely on my own a.,** je l'ai fait de mon propre chef; **she writes a great deal on her own a.,** elle écrit beaucoup de son côté; **if he is to succeed in his examination he must read a great deal on his own a.,** s'il veut être reçu à son examen il lui faut faire beaucoup de lectures personnelles; **although employed by a firm, he is allowed to work in his spare time on his own a.,** quoique employé par une entreprise, on lui permet de travailler à son propre compte pendant ses heures libres; **to set up in business on one's own a.,** s'établir à son compte; *Iron:* **please don't bother on my a.,** je vous en prie je ne compte pas. **4.** récit *m,* relation *f,* narration *f* (d'un fait); description *f* (d'une personne); **to give an a. of sth.,** faire le récit, la relation, de qch.; **to give an a. of the situation,** faire un exposé de la situation; **to give an a. of oneself,** (i) rendre compte de ses faits et gestes; (ii) *A:* décliner ses titres et qualités; **to give the reader an a. of . . .,** renseigner le lecteur sur . . .; **to receive an a. of sth.,** recevoir un rapport sur qch.; **according to his a.,** (i) d'après lui, d'après ses dires, selon lui, à ce qu'il dit; (ii) à l'en croire; **according to his a. of it, the disaster is serious,** d'après le récit qu'il en fait, c'est un désastre; **by all accounts,** au dire de tout le monde; **that's quite a different a.,** voilà une toute autre histoire, un tout autre son de cloche.

account[2], *v.tr. & ind.tr.* **1.** (*a*) **to a. s.o. (to be) wise, guilty,** tenir qn pour sage, coupable, regarder, considérer, qn comme sage, coupable; **to be accounted rich,** être regardé comme riche; passer pour riche; **to a. oneself lucky,** s'estimer heureux; **I a. it a piece of good fortune that . . .,** je considère que nous pouvons nous estimer heureux que . . .; (*b*) *Lit:* **to be much, little, accounted of,** être beaucoup, peu, estimé. **2.** (*a*) **to a. for (sth.),** rendre compte de, rendre raison de, justifier (de) (sa conduite); expliquer (une circonstance); **he has been called upon to a. for his conduct,** on lui a demandé raison de sa conduite; **to a. for a sum of money, for an expenditure,** rendre compte d'une somme; justifier une dépense; **there is still much to be accounted for,** il reste encore beaucoup de faits qui demandent une explication; **he has a great deal to a. for,** il a beaucoup de choses à justifier; (*b*) **I can't a. for it,** je n'y comprends rien, je ne me l'explique pas; **there is no accounting for it,** c'est inexplicable; **there is no accounting for tastes,** des goûts et des couleurs, on ne discute pas; les goûts diffèrent tellement; chacun son goût; (*c*) *F:* **to a. for (= kill) s.o.,** faire son affaire à qn; **to have accounted for five brace of partridge,** avoir cinq couples de perdrix à son actif, au tableau; (*d*) *Turf: etc:* **Gladiator should a. for Monarch,** Gladiator devrait remporter la victoire sur Monarch; (*e*) *Book-k:* comptabiliser (une dépense, etc.).

accountability [əkauntə'biliti], *s.* responsabilité *f.*

accountable [ə'kauntəbl], *a.* **1. to be a. to s.o. for sth.,** être responsable de qch. envers qn; être comptable à qn de qch.; **to be a. for a sum of money,** être redevable d'une somme d'argent; avoir à rendre compte d'une somme d'argent; **he is not a. for his actions,** il est irresponsable; **I am not (to be held) a. for my brother's actions,** je ne suis pas responsable des actions de mon frère; **I am a. to no man,** je ne dois rendre compte à personne. **2.** (*a*) **event that is a. (for),** événement qui est explicable; (*b*) *Adm: Jur:* **a. receipt,** reçu certifié; pièce *f* comptable.

accountableness [ə'kauntəblnis], *s.* responsabilité *f.*

accountably [ə'kauntəbli], *adv.* d'une manière explicable.

accountancy [ə'kauntənsi], *s.* **1.** comptabilité *f*; expertise *f* comptable. **2.** tenue *f* des livres.

accountant [ə'kauntənt], *s.* **1.** *Jur:* défendeur *m* (dans une action en reddition de comptes). **2.** (*a*) agent *m* comptable; comptable *m*; teneur *m* de livres; **chief a.,** chef *m* de (la) comptabilité; chef comptable; (*b*) **chartered a.,** *U.S:* **certified public a.,** = (i) expert *m* comptable; (ii) conseiller fiscal; (*c*) *Adm:* **the A. General** (*pl.* **Accountants General**), le Chef de la comptabilité.

accountantship [ə'kauntəntʃip], *s.* situation *f* de (i) comptable, (ii) chef de la comptabilité.

accounting [ə'kauntiŋ], *s.* comptabilité *f*; expertise *f* comptable; **cost a.,** comptabilité de prix de revient; **the a. department,** (le service de) la comptabilité, les services comptables; **a. machine,** machine *f* comptable; tabulatrice *f*; **automatic a.,** mécanographie *f*; **automatic a. machine, equipment,** machine, matériel *m,* mécanographique; **a. machine operator,** mécanographe *mf.*

accouplement [ə'kʌpəlm(ə)nt], *s. Carp: Const:* tirant *m* de charpente en bois.

accoutre [ə'ku:tər], *v.tr.* (*used chiefly in p.p.*) (*a*) *Hist:* accoutrer (un chevalier, etc.); caparaçonner (un destrier); (*b*) **accoutred with pistols,** armé de pistolets; (*c*) *Pej:* accoutrer, affubler **(with,** de).

accoutrement(s) [ə'ku:trəmənt(s)], *s.* (*pl.*); (*a*) *Hist:* harnachement *m*; caparaçon *m* (d'un destrier); (*b*) équipement *m,* fourniment *m* (du soldat); **a. maker,** fabricant *m* d'équipements militaires; (*c*) *Pej:* affublements *mpl,* oripeaux *mpl.*

accredit [ə'kredit], *v.tr.* **1.** accréditer (qn, qch.); mettre (qn, qch.) en crédit, en réputation. **2. to a. an ambassador to a government,** accréditer un ambassadeur auprès d'un gouvernement. **3.** *A:* **to a. sth. to s.o., to a. s.o. with sth.,** mettre qch. sur le compte de qn; **he was accredited with having said . . .,** il était censé avoir dit . . ..

accreditation [əkredi'teiʃ(ə)n], *s.* accréditation *f* (d'un ambassadeur).

accredited [ə'kreditid], *a.* **1.** (*of pers.*) accrédité, autorisé. **2.** *A:* **a. opinions, beliefs,** opinions, croyances, reçues, orthodoxes, admises; **a. rumour,** bruit accrédité, auquel l'on attache croyance. **3.** *Adm:* *A:* **a. milk** = lait *m* provenant des troupeaux tuberculinés.

accrediting[1] [ə'kreditiŋ], *s.* accréditation *f*; accréditement *m.*

accrediting[2], *a.* accréditif.

accrementition [ækrimen'tiʃ(ə)n], *s. Biol:* accrémentition *f.*

accrescence [ə'kres(ə)ns], *s.* **1.** *Bot:* accroissement *m.* **2.** accrétion *f.*

accrescent [ə'kres(ə)nt], *a. Bot:* accrescent.

accrete [ə'kri:t]. **1.** *v.i.* (*a*) s'accroître par (i) addition, (ii) concrétion; (*b*) s'ajouter **(to,** à); **the lands that accreted to the Crown,** les terres dont s'enrichit la Couronne; *Geol: Jur:* **accreted land,** accrue *f.* **2.** *v.tr. Lit:* **to a. followers to one's party,** s'attirer des partisans; enrôler des partisans.

accretion [ə'kri:ʃ(ə)n], *s.* **1.** (*a*) accroissement *m* organique; (*b*) accrétion *f*; accroissement par alluvion, par addition; addition *f* **(to,** à); **beach a.,** crue *f,* engraissement *m,* de plage; (*c*) *Jur:* accroissement, majoration *f* (d'héritage). **2.** (*a*) *Physiol:* apposition *f*; *Bot:* accrétion; (*b*) *Med:* soudure *f* (des doigts, des orteils).

accretionary [ə'kri:ʃ(ə)nəri], **accretive** [ə'kri:tiv], *a.* qui s'accroît (i) organiquement, (ii) par addition; **a. process,** procédé *m* d'addition.

accroides [æ'krɔidi:z], *s.* **a. (resin), a. (gum),** acroïde *f,* accroïde *f,* acchroïde *f.*

accrual [ə'kru:əl], *s.* accumulation *f*; **on an a. basis,** d'après la méthode de comptabilité patrimoniale.

accrue [ə'kru:]. **1.** *v.i.* (*a*) provenir, dériver **(from,** de); (*b*) (*of moneys, land, etc.*); **to a. to s.o.,** revenir à qn; **the advantages that a. to society from the liberty of the press,** les avantages que la société retire de la liberté de la presse. **2.** *v.i.* (*of interest*) courir, s'accumuler; **interest accrues from . . .,** les intérêts courent à partir de. . . . **3.** *v.tr.* **to a. leave,** accumuler son congé.

accrued [ə'kru:d], *a. Fin:* (intérêt) couru; (intérêts) (ac)cumulés.

accruing [ə'kru:iŋ], *a, Fin:* (*a*) **portion a. to each heir,** portion afférente à chaque héritier; (*b*) (intérêts) à échoir, venant à échéance.

acculturate [ə'kʌltjureit], *v.tr.* acculturer.

acculturation [əkʌltjur'eiʃ(ə)n], *s. Pol.Ec: esp. U.S:* acculturation *f.*

acculturize [ə'kʌltjuraiz], *v.tr.* acculturer.

accumbent [ə'kʌmb(ə)nt], *a.* (*a*) à demi couché, étendu; (*b*) *Bot:* accombant, appliqué.

accumulate [ə'kju:mjuleit]. **1.** *v.tr.* (*a*) accumuler, amasser (une fortune, etc.); amonceler, entasser; **to a. electricity,** emmagasiner, accumuler, de l'électricité; (*b*) *Cmptr:* accumuler, totaliser, cumuler (dans un registre, etc.). **2.** *v.i.* s'accumuler, s'amonceler, s'entasser, s'amasser; to **allow one's dividends to a.,** laisser accumuler ses dividendes.

accumulated [ə'kju:mjuleitid], *a.* accumulé; **a. dividends,** dividendes accumulés; *Cmptr:* **a. error,** erreur cumulée; **a. register,** registre *m* de cumul.

accumulating [ə'kju:mjuleitiŋ], *s.* accumulation *f*; *Cmptr:* cumul *m.*

accumulation [əˌkju:mju'leiʃ(ə)n], *s.* **1.** (*a*) accumulation *f*, amoncellement , entassement *m*; **a. of heat, of electricity,** accumulation, emmagasinage *m*, de la chaleur, de l'électricité; **a. of money,** thésaurisation *f*; **a. of capital, capital a.,** accumulation du capital; **rate of capital a.,** taux *m* d'accumulation, de formation, du capital; (*b*) *Jur:* cumul *m*; (*c*) *Cmptr:* accumulation, cumul. **2.** (*a*) amas *m*, monceau *m*, tas *m*, accumulation; **an untidy a. of books,** un tas de livres en désordre; (*b*) *Med:* dépôt *m* (de pus, etc.).

accumulative [ə'kju:mjulətiv], *a.* **1.** qui s'accumule; *Cmptr:* **a. card,** carte *f* cumul; **a. error,** erreur cumulée. **2.** (*of pers.*) qui aime à accumuler, à thésauriser; thésauriseur.

accumulator [ə'kju:mjuleitər], *s.* **1.** (*pers.*) accumulateur, -trice (de richesses, etc.). **2.** (*a*) *Mec.E: Civ.E:* accumulateur *m* (d'énergie); **steam a.,** accumulateur de vapeur; accumulateur thermique; **hydraulic a.,** accumulateur hydraulique; (*b*) *El:* accumulateur, *F:* accu *m*; **pasted-plate a.,** accu(mulateur) à oxydes rapportés; **ferro-nickel a.,** accu(mulateur) au fer-nickel; **alkaline a.,** accu(mulateur) alcalin; **lead (-acid)a.,** accu(mulateur) au plomb; **fluid a.,** accu(mulateur) à électrolyte liquide; **pressure a.,** accu(mulateur) de pression; **grid-type a.,** accu(mulateur) à grillage; **a. box,** bac *m*, cuve *f* d'accu(mulateur); **a. capacity indicator,** accumètre *m*; (*c*) *Cmptr:* accumulateur; **a. register,** registre *m* accumulateur; registre de cumul. **3.** *Turf:* **a. (bet),** pari *m* avec report.

accuracy ['ækjurəsi], *s.* (*a*) exactitude *f*; degré *m* de justesse; justesse *f*, précision *f*; **a. of 0·5 per cent.,** précision de 0,5 pour cent; **a. of a prediction,** justesse d'une prédiction; **mathematical a.,** exactitude mathématique; *Artil:* **a. of fire,** justesse, précision, du tir; *Mus:* **a. of intonation,** justesse de la voix; (*b*) fidélité *f* (de mémoire, d'une traduction); exactitude (d'une citation); correction *f*, fidélité (d'un dessin); (*c*) *Cmptr:* **a. control character,** caractère *m* de contrôle de précision; **a. control system,** système *m* de contrôle de précision.

accurate ['ækjurət], *a.* (*a*) exact, juste, précis; **a. scales,** balance *f* juste; **he is quick and a. at figures,** il calcule vite et correctement; **to be (strictly) a . . .,** à proprement parler . . ., pour être tout à fait exact. . . . **to take a. aim,** viser juste; **to have an a. eye,** avoir le coup d'œil sûr; *F:* avoir le compas dans l'œil; (*b*) (mémoire, traduction) fidèle; (citation) exacte; (dessin) correct, fidèle.

accurately ['ækjurətli], *adv.* (*a*) exactement, avec justesse, avec précision; **to define a. the meaning of sth.,** préciser le sens, la portée, de qch.; **to answer a.,** (i) répondre avec précision; (ii) donner une réponse correcte; (*b*) **to translate a.,** traduire fidèlement; **to draw sth. a.,** dessiner qch. correctement.

accurateness ['ækjurətnis], *s.* exactitude *f*; précision *f*.

accursed [ə'kə:sid], *a. Lit:* maudit, exécrable, détestable.

accurst [ə'kə:st], *a. Poet:* maudit.

accusable [ə'kju:zəbl], *a.* accusable (of, de).

accusal [ə'kju:zl], *s.* accusation *f*.

accusant [ə'kju:z(ə)nt], *s.* accusateur, -trice.

accusation [ækju'zeiʃ(ə)n], *s.* **1.** accusation *f*; *Jur:* incrimination *f*; **to bring an a. against s.o.,** porter, proférer, une accusation contre qn. **2.** *Jur:* (*indictment*) acte *m* d'accusation.

accusative [ə'kju:zətiv], *a. & s. Gram:* **a. (case),** (cas) accusatif *m*; régime direct; **word in the a.,** mot à l'accusatif; **cognate a.,** accusatif de qualification, de l'objet interne.

accusatorial [əkju:zə'tɔ:riəl], *a. Jur:* accusatoire.

accusatory [ə'kju:zət(ə)ri], *a.* (langage, etc.) accusateur, -trice.

accuse [ə'kju:z], *v.tr.* accuser (**s.o. of sth., of doing sth.,** qn de qch., de faire qch.); *Jur:* incriminer (qn); **to a. s.o. of cowardice,** taxer qn de lâcheté.

accused [ə'kju:zd], *s. Jur:* **the a.,** l'inculpé(e) (*in all cases*); le, la, prévenu(e) (d'un délit); l'accusé(e) (d'un crime); l'incriminé(e).

accuser [ə'kju:zər], *s.* accusateur, -trice.

accusing[1] [ə'kju:ziŋ], *a.* accusateur, -trice.

accusing[2], *s.* accusation *f* (de qn).

accusingly [ə'kju:ziŋli], *adv.* d'une manière accusatrice; **he pointed a. at me,** il me désigna d'un doigt accusateur.

accusive [ə'kju:siv], *a. U.S:* = ACCUSATORY.

accustom [ə'kʌstəm], *v.tr.* accoutumer, habituer (**s.o. to sth., to do sth.,** qn à qch., à faire qch.); aguerrir (qn à, contre, la fatigue, etc.); **to a. oneself to sth.,** s'accoutumer, s'habituer, se faire, s'aguerrir, à qch.; **to a. oneself to discipline,** se faire à la discipline.

accustomed [ə'kʌstəmd], *a.* **1.** accoutumé, habitué (**to,** à); **to be a. to . . .,** (i) avoir coutume de . . ., (ii) être accoutumé à. . . . **I am a. to getting up early,** j'ai coutume, j'ai l'habitude, de me lever de bonne heure; **to get a. to sth.,** s'accoutumer à qch.; se faire à qch.; **to get a. to doing sth.,** s'accoutumer à faire qch.; prendre l'habitude de faire qch.; **the cat soon got a. to us,** le chat ne fut pas long à s'apprivoiser; **you get a. to anything,** on se fait à tout; **a. to fatigue,** aguerri à la fatigue; **that is not what I am a. to,** (i) ce n'est pas dans mes habitudes, (ii) ce n'est pas à quoi je suis accoutumé. **2.** *O:* habituel, coutumier, ordinaire; d'usage.

ace[1] [eis], *s.* **1.** (*a*) (*at dice, dominoes, cards*) as *m*; **a. point,** première flèche (du jeu de jacquet); *F:* **to have an a. up one's sleeve,** avoir un as dans sa manche, avoir plus d'un tour dans son sac; **to hold all the aces,** avoir tous les atouts en main; (*b*) *Ten:* **(service) a.,** ace *m*. **2.** (pers.) (*a*) as; **flying a.,** as de l'aviation; *attrib;* **a. reporter,** journaliste d'élite; **a. players,** joueurs de premier ordre; (*b*) *F:* personne généreuse, *F:* épée *f*; bon type. **3. within an a. of sth.,** à deux doigts de qch.; **to be within an a. of death, of being killed,** toucher la mort du doigt. **4.** *F:* **on one's a.,** tout seul. **5.** *U.S: P:* billet *m* d'un dollar. **6.** *P:* cigarette *f* de marijuana, reefer *m*, stick *m*.

ace[2]. *P:* **1.** *v.tr.* **a. it!** ça suffit! **2.** *v.i.* **to a. in,** jouer des coudes; **to a. in on s.o.'s conversation,** piger la conversation de qn.

Aceldama [ə'keldəmə, -'sel-]. **1.** *Pr.n. B:* Le Champ du sang; Haceldama *m*. **2.** *s. Lit:* Champ de carnage.

acellular [ei'seljulər], *a. Biol:* sans formation cellulaire.

acenaphthene [æsinæf'θi:n], *s. Ch:* acénaphtène *m.*

acenaphthylene [æsi'næfθili:n], *s. Ch:* acénaphtylène *m.*

acentric [ei'sentrik], *a.* (*a*) *Mth:* sans centre; (*b*) *Biol:* acentrique.

Acephala [æ'sefələ], *s.pl. Moll:* acéphales *m.*

acephalan [æ'sefələn], *s. Moll:* acéphale *m.*

acephalia [æse'feiliə], **acephalism** [æ'sefəlizm], *s. Ter:* acéphalie *f*.

acephalic [æse'fælik], *a. Moll:* acéphale.

acephalous [æ'sefələs], *a.* **1.** (*a*) *Moll:* acéphale; (*b*) *Pros:* (vers) acéphale, auquel manque la première syllabe. **2.** (État, assemblée) sans chef; *Ecc:* acéphale.

acephalus [æ'sefələs], *s. Ter:* acéphale *m*, acéphalien, -ienne.

acephaly [æ'sefali], *s.* acéphalie *f*.

acer ['eisər], *s. Bot:* acer *m.*

Aceraceae [eisə'reisi:i:], *s.pl. Bot:* acéracées *fpl.*, acérinées *fpl.*

acerb [ə'sə:b], *a.* (*a*) (*of fruit, etc.*) aigre, sur: (*b*) (*of pers. etc.*) acerbe, aigre, mordant.

acerbate[1] [ə'sə:bət], *a.* acerbe, exacerbé, aigri.

acerbate[2] ['æsəbeit], *v.tr.* irriter, exaspérer.

acerbic [ə'sə:bik], *a.* = ACERB.

acerbity [ə'sə:biti], *s.* acerbité *f*; aigreur *f* (de ton).

aceric [æ'serik], *a. Ch:* (acide) acérique.

acerose ['æsərous], *a.* (*a*) *Bot:* acéré; (feuille de pin) en forme d'aiguille; (*b*) acéreux.

acerous[1] ['æsərəs], *a.* acéreux.

acerous[2] [ei'si:rəs], *a. Ent:* acère.

acervate ['æsəveit], *a. Bot:* qui croît en grappes.

acervulus [æ'sə:vjuləs], *s.* **1.** *Fung:* acervule *m*, acervulus *m*. **2.** *Anat:* **a. (cerebri),** acervule, acervulus.

acescence [ə'ses(ə)ns], **acescency** [ə'ses(ə)nsi], *s.* acescence *f*.

acescent [ə'ses(ə)nt], *a.* acescent.

Acestes [ə'sesti:z], *Pr.n.m. Lt.Lit:* Aceste.

acetabular [æse'tæbjulər], *a. Anat:* acétabulaire.

acetabulum [æse'tæbjuləm], *s.* **1.** *Anat: Z:* acétabule *f*, acetabulum *m*; cavité *f* cotyloïde (de l'os iliaque); cotyle *f*; ventouse postérieure (de la sangsue). **2.** *Rom.Ant:* acétabule, acetabulum.

acetal ['æsitl], *s. Ch:* acétal *m.*

acetaldehyde [æsi'tældihaid], *s. Ch:* acétaldéhyde *f*.

acetalization [æsi:təlai'zeiʃ(ə)n], *s. Ch:* acétalisation *f*.

acetamide [æ'setəmaid, -mid], *s. Ch:* acétamide *m.*

acetanilide [æset'ænilaid, -id], *s. Ch:* acétanilide *m.*

acetarsol [æ'setəsɔl], *s. Pharm:* acétarsol *m.*

acetate ['æsiteit], *s.* (*a*) *Ch:* acétate *m*; **amyl, copper, ethyl, lead, a.,** acétate d'amyle, de cuivre, d'éthyle, de plomb; *Phot:* **a. toning bath,** bain *m* de virage à l'acétate de sodium; *Tex:* **cellulose a.,** acétate de cellulose; acétocellulose *f*, acétycellulose *f*; (*b*) *Rec: F:* disque *m* souple.

acetazolamide [æsetæ'zoulæmaid], *s. Med:* acétazolamide *m.*

acetic [æ'si:tik, -'set-], *a. Ch:* acétique; **a. acid,** acide *m* acétique, éthanoïque *m*; **glacial a. acid,** acide acétique concentré, cristallisable, glacial; **a. anhydride,** anhydride *m* acétique; **a. ester,** ester *m* acétique; **a.. fermentation,** fermentation *f* acétique.

acetification [æsi:tifi'keiʃ(ə)n, -set-], *s.* acétification *f*.

acetify [æ'si:tifai, -set-]. **1.** *v.tr.* acétifier. **2.** *v.i.* s'acétifier; tourner au vinaigre.

acetimeter [æsetimitər], *s. Ind:* acétimètre *m*; burette *f* acétimétrique.

acetin [æ'si:tin], *s. Ch:* acétine *f*.

acetoin ['æsitɔin], *s. Ch:* acétoïne *f*.

acetol ['æsitɔl], *s. Ch:* acétol *m*, propanolone *m*, acétylcarbinol *m*.

acetolysis [æsi'tɔlisis], *s. Ch:* acétolyse *f*.

acetometer [æsi'tɔmitr], *s.* acétomètre *m.*

aceton(a)emia [æsitou'ni:miə], *s. Med:* acétonémie *f*; *Vet:* acétose *f*, toxémie *f* de gestation (de la brebis).

aceton (a)emic [æsitou'ni:mik], *a. Med:* acétonémique.

acetonaphthone [æsi:tou'næfθoun], *s. Ch:* acétonaphtone *f*, acétylnaphtalène *m*, méthylnaphtylcétone *f*.

acetone ['æsitoun], *s. Ch:* acétone *f*; éther *m* pyroacétique; propanone *m*, diméthylcétone *f*; **a. chloroform,** acétone-chloroforme *m*.

acetonitrile [ˌæsitou'naitril], *s. Ch:* acétonitrile *m.*

acetonuria [ˌæsitou'njuriə], *s. Med:* acétonurie *f*.

acetonylacetone [ˌæsitounil'æsitoun], *s. Ch:* acétonylacétone *f*.

acetophenone [ˌæsitoufe'noun], *s. Ch:* acétophénone *f*, acétylbenzène *m*.

acetose ['æsitous], **acetous** ['æsitəs], *a.* acéteux.

acetosity [æsi'tɔsiti], *s.* acétosité *f*.

acetyl ['æsitil], *s. Ch:* acétyle *m*; **a. chloride, bromide,** chlorure *m*, bromure *m*, d'acétyle; *Tex:* **a. cellulose,** acétylcellulose *f*, acétocellulose *f*.

acetylacetone ['æsitil'æsitoun], *s. Ch:* acétylacétone *f*.

acetylate [æ'setileit], *v.tr. Ch:* acétyler.

acetylation [æsiti'leiʃ(ə)n], *s. Ch: Tex:* acétylation *f*.

acetylcholine [ˌæsitil'kouli:n, -lin], *s. Ch: Biol:* acétylcholine *f*.

acetylcyanide [ˌæsitil'saiənaid], *s. Ch:* cyanure *m* d'acétyle.

acetylene [æ'setili:n], *s. Ch:* acétylène *m*; **a. lamp,** lanterne *f* à acétylène; **a. blowpipe,** chalumeau *m* à acétylène; **a. welding,** soudure *f* autogène.

acetylenic [æseti'lenik], *a. Ch:* acétylénique.

acetylide [æ'setilaid], *s. Ch:* acétylure *m*; **cuprous a.,** acétylure cuivreux.

acetyliodide [ˌæsetil'aioudaid], *s. Ch:* iodure *m* d'acétyle.

acetylsalicylic [ˌæsetilsæli'silik], *a. Ch:* acétylsalicylique; **a. acid,** acide *m* acétylsalicylique; aspirine *f*.

acetyltannic [æsetil'tænik], *a. Pharm:* **a. acid,** acétyltanin *m*.

acetylurea [æsetilju'riə], *s. Ch:* acétylurée *f*, acétyluréide *m*.

Achae [æ'ki:ə], **Achaia** [æ'kaiə], *Pr.n. A.Geog:* Achaïe *f*.

Achaean [æ'ki:ən], **Achaian** [æ'kaiən], *A.Hist:* **1.** *a.* achaïen, achéen, achaïque; **the A. League,** la Ligue achéenne. **2.** *s.* Achaïen, -enne; Achéen, -éenne.

Achaemenid [æ'keminid]. *A.Hist:* **1.** *a.* achéménide. **2.** *s.* Achéménide *mf*.

achaenocarp [æ'ki:noukɑ:p], *s. Bot:* akène *m.*

Achates [æ'keiti:z], *Pr.n.m. Lt.Lit:* Achate; *Lit:* **the fidus A. of s.o.,** le fidèle Achate de qn.

Achatinidae [ækæ'ti:nidi:], *s.pl. Moll:* achatinidés *m.*

ache[1] [eik], *s.* mal *m*, douleur *f*; *F:* **I'm all aches and pains,** je suis tout courbaturé, tout moulu; j'ai mal partout.

ache[2], *v.i.* **my head aches,** la tête me fait mal; j'ai mal à la tête; **it makes my head a.,** cela me donne le, un, mal de tête; cela me donne mal à la tête; **I'm aching all over, in every limb,** je me sens des douleurs par tout le corps; je me sens moulu; je suis tout brisé; tous les membres me font mal; **which tooth aches?** quelle est la dent qui vous fait mal? **the exercise has made my legs a.,** l'exercice m'a fatigué, courbaturé, les jambes; **it made my arms a.,** j'en avais les bras endoloris; **it makes my heart a.,** cela me fait mal au cœur; cela me serre le cœur; cela me fend le cœur; **I laughed until my sides ached,** j'ai ri à m'en rendre malade; *F:* **he was aching to join in the fight,** il brûlait de prendre part au combat.

Achelous [æke'louəs], *Pr.n. Geog: Myth:* Achéloüs *m*, Achéloos *m*.

achene [ə'ki:n], **achenium** [ə'ki:niəm], *s. Bot:* akène *m*, achaine *m*, achène *m*.

Acheron ['ækərɔn], *Pr.n.* (*a*) *Myth:* l'Achéron *m*; (*b*)

Lit: les Enfers *m.*

Acheulean [ə'ʃu:liən], *a. & s. Paleont:* acheuléen (*m*).

à-cheval [aʃə'val], *a. Mil:* **to take up an à-c. position on a river, a railway,** achevaler un fleuve, une ligne de chemin de fer.

achievable [ə'tʃi:vəbl], *a.* faisable, exécutable.

achieve [ə'tʃi:v], *v.tr.* **1.** (*a*) accomplir (un exploit); exécuter, réaliser (une entreprise); (*b*) *A:* achever, consommer (un ouvrage, un voyage, etc.). **2.** acquérir (de l'honneur); parvenir (aux honneurs); se faire (une réputation). **3.** atteindre (à), arriver à (un but); **to a. a result,** obtenir un résultat; **to a. one's purpose, one's ends,** parvenir, en venir, à ses fins; **he has achieved the impossible,** il a fait l'impossible; **he will never a. anything,** il n'arrivera jamais à rien; **with courage one can a. anything,** avec du courage on arrive à tout.

achievement [ə'tʃi:vmənt], *s.* **1.** accomplissement *m,* réalisation *f,* exécution *f* (d'un projet, etc.). **2.** (*a*) exploit *m,* (haut) fait; (*b*) **when we consider his a.,** lorsque nous considérons (i) son œuvre, (ii) l'effort qu'il a accompli. **3.** *Her:* armoiries *fpl.*

achieving [ə'tʃi:viŋ], *s.* **1.** accomplissement *m,* exécution *f.* **2.** obtention *f* (d'un résultat).

achillea [æki'li:ə], *s. Bot:* achillée *f.*

Achilles [ə'kili:z], *Pr.n.m.* Achille; **Achilles' tendon, tendon of A.,** tendon *m* d'Achille; corde *f* d'Hippocrate; **gambling is his Achilles' heel,** le jeu c'est là son faible, c'est son talon d'Achille.

aching[1] ['eikiŋ], *a.* douloureux, endolori; **an a. tooth,** une dent malade. *Lit:* **a. heart,** cœur endolori, dolent; **to do sth. with an a. heart,** faire qch. avec un arrachement de cœur; *F:* **to have an a. void,** avoir l'estomac dans les talons.

aching[2], mal *m,* douleur *f.*

achlamydeous [æklæ'midiəs], *a. Bot:* achlamydé.

acholia [æ'kouliə], *s. Med:* acholie *f.*

acholuric [ækə'ljuːrik], *a. Med:* **a. jaundice,** ictère *m* acholurique.

achondroplasia [ækɔndrou'pleisiə], *s. Med:* achondroplasie *f.*

achondroplastic [ækɔndrou'plæstik], *a. Med: Vet:* achondroplasique.

achorion [æ'kouriən], *s. Fung:* achorion *m.*

achroite ['ækrɔit], *s. Miner:* achroïte *f.*

achromasia [ækrou'meiziə], *s. Med:* achromasie *f.*

achromatic [ækrou'mætik], *a.* **1.** *Opt:* achromatique. **2.** **a. vision,** achromatopsie *f.* **3.** *Biol:* **a. spindle,** fuseau *m* achromatique.

achromatin [æ'kroumətin], *s. Biol:* achromatine *f.*

achromatism [æ'kroumətizm], *s.* **1.** *Opt:* achromatisme *m.* **2.** *Med:* achromatopsie *f*; daltonisme *m.*

achromatization [ækroumətai'zeiʃ(ə)n], *s.* achromatisation *f.*

achromatize [æ'kroumətaiz], *v.tr.* achromatiser (un objectif, etc.).

achromatopsia [ækroumə'tɔpsiə], **achromatopsy** [ækroumə'tɔpsi], *s. Med:* achromatopsie *f*; daltonisme *m.*

achromatous [æ'kroumətəs], **achromous** [æ'krouməs], *a.* achrome.

achromia [ei'kroumiə], *s. Med:* achromie *f.*

achy ['eiki], *a. F:* **I feel rather a.,** je me sens des douleurs par tout le corps; j'ai mal un peu partout; **my throat's rather a.,** j'ai un peu mal à la gorge.

achylia [ei'kiliə], *s. Med:* achylie *f.*

acicula, *pl.* **-ae** [æ'sikjulə, -i:], *s. Nat.Hist:* acicule *m.*

acicular [æ'sikjulər], *a. Nat.Hist:* aciculaire, aiguillé.

aciculate [æ'sikjulət], **aciculated** [æ'sikjuleitid], *a.* aciculé.

aciculiforme [æsi'kju:lifɔ:m], *a.* aciculiforme, aiguillé.

acid ['æsid], **1.** *a.* acide; **slightly a. wine,** vin verdelet; *Comest:* **a. drop,** bonbon acidulé, anglais; **a. solution,** solution *f* acide; **a. soil,** sol acide; **a. rock,** roche acide; *Metall:* **a. process,** procédé *m* acide; (*b*) revêche, rechigné; **his expression was as a. as ever,** son visage était aussi revêche que jamais; il avait un air renfrogné comme toujours; **a. answer,** réponse acide, aigre-douce; verte réponse; **to give an a. flavour to one's praise,** vinaigrer sa louange; *s. P:* **to come the a.,** parler d'un ton acide, caustique. **2.** *s.* (*a*) acide *m*; **amino a.,** aminoacide *m,* acide aminé; **fatty a.,** acide gras; **green acids,** acides verts; **dead a.,** acide mort; *attrib.* **a. determination,** dosage *m* de l'acidité; **a. value, number,** indice *m* d'acide; **a. vat,** cuve *f* à acide; **a. test,** (i) épreuve à la pierre de touche; (ii) épreuve décisive, concluante; **a. tester,** acidimètre *m,* acidomètre *m*; **a. heat test,** essai *m* d'échauffement sulfurique; **a. bath,** bain *m* acide; *Phot:* **a. fixer,** fixateur *m* acide; (*b*) *P:* (= L.S.D.) sucre *m*; **a. funk,** trouille acidulée.

acid(a)emia [æsi'di:miə], *s. Med:* acidose *f.*

acid-fast ['æsidfɑ:st], *a. Biol:* (bacille) acido-résistant; *pl.* acido-résistants.

acid-fastness ['æsidfɑ:stnis], *s. Biol:* acido-résistance *f.*

acid-forming ['æsidfɔ:miŋ], *a.* acidogène.

acid-head ['æsidhed], *s. P:* acidulé, -ée.

acidic [æ'sidik], *a.* acide; **a. rocks,** roches acides.

acidiferous [æsi'difərəs], *a.* acidifère.

acidifiable [æsidi'faiəbl], *a.* acidifiable.

acidification [æ'sidifi'keiʃ(ə)n], *s.* (*a*) acidification *f*; (*b*) *Tex:* acidage *m.*

acidifier [æ'sidifaiər], *s.* acidifiant *m.*

acidify [æ'sidifai]. **1.** *v.tr.* acidifier; *Pharm:* aiguiser (un médicament). **2.** *v.i.* s'acidifier.

acidifying [æ'sidifaiiŋ], *a.* acidifiant.

acidimeter [æsi'dimitər], *s.* acidimètre *m,* acidomètre *m*; pèse-acide *m, pl.* pèse-acides.

acidimetric [æsidi'metrik], *a.* acidimétrique.

acidimetry [æsi'dimitri], *s.* acidimétrie *f.*

acidity [æ'siditi], *s.* **1.** (*a*) acidité *f*; verdeur *f* (des fruits, du vin); (*b*) *Med:* aigreurs *fpl.* **2.** aigreur, verdeur (d'une réponse).

acidize ['æsidaiz], *v.tr.* **1.** acidifier. **2.** traiter à l'acide; *Min:* acidifier (un puits).

acidizing ['æsidaiziŋ], *s. Min:* acidification *f.*

acidly ['æsidli], *adv.* aigrement, avec aigreur, avec acerbité.

acidness ['æsidnis], *s.* aigreur *f,* verdeur *f* (d'une réponse).

acidoid ['æsidɔid], *a. Ch:* acidoïde.

acidolysis [æsi'dɔlisis], *s. Ch:* acidolyse *f.*

acidometer [æsi'dɔmitər], *s.* acidomètre *m,* acidimètre *m,* pèse-acide *m, pl.* pèse-acides.

acidophil(e) [æ'sidoufi:l, -fail], *a. Bot:* **a. leucocytes,** leucocytes *m* acidophiles.

acidosis [æsi'dousis], *s. Med:* acidose *f.*

acid-proof ['æsidpru:f], **acid-resisting** ['æsidri'zistiŋ], *a.* acido-résistant; qui résiste aux acides; résistant à l'acide; réfractaire aux acides, inattaquable, par les acides; (vernis) antiacide, inattaquable par les acides.

acidulate [æ'sidjuleit], *v.tr.* aciduler.

acidulated [æ'sidjuleitid], *a.* acidulé; *Com:* **a. drops,** bonbons acidulés, anglais.

acidulent[1] [æ'sidjulənt], **acidulous** [æ'sidjuləs], *a.* acidulé.

acidulent[2], *s.* acidulent *m.*

acierage ['æsiəridʒ], **acieration** [æsiə'reiʃ(ə)n], *s. El: Metall:* aciérage *m,* aciération *f.*

acierate ['æsiəreit], *v.tr. Metall:* aciérer (par cémentation).

aciform ['æsifɔ:m], *a. Nat.Hist:* aciculiforme; aciforme.

acinaciform [,æsi'næsifɔ:m], *a. Bot:* acinaciforme.

acineta [æsi'ni:tə], *s.* **1.** *Bot:* acineta *m.* **2.** *Z:* acinète *m.*

Acinetae [æsi'ni:ti:], *s.pl. Z:* acinétides *m.*

aciniform [æ'sinifɔ:m], *a.* aciniforme; acineux.

acinose ['æsinouz], **acinous** ['æsinəs], *a. Anat: Bot:* acineux; *Anat:* **a. glands,** glandes acineuses, conglomérées, en grappes.

acinus ['æsinəs], *s. Anat: Bot:* acine *m,* acinus *m.*

Acipenseridae [æsipen'seridi:], *s.pl. Ich:* acipensérides *m.*

ack-ack ['æk'æk]. *Mil:* (*a*) *s.* (i) Forces terrestres anti-aériennes (F.T.A.); (ii) artillerie anti-aérienne; (iii) Défense contre avions (D.C.A.); (*b*) *attrib.* **a.-a. fire,** tir anti-aérien.

ack emma ['æk 'emə], *adv. A:* **1.** *Mil: Tp: & P:* (= A.M.) du matin. **2.** *P:* (= *air mechanic*) mécanicien *m* d'avion.

acknowledge [ək'nɔlidʒ], *v.tr.* **1.** (*a*) reconnaître, avouer (qch.); reconnaître (qn); **he acknowledges his debt, his mistake,** il reconnaît sa dette; il reconnaît, avoue, confesse, convient de, son erreur; **he acknowledged having organized the plot,** il reconnut avoir organisé le complot; **he refused to a. his son,** il refusa de reconnaître son fils; **to a. s.o. as one's chief, to be one's chief,** reconnaître qn pour chef; **he was acknowledged as king,** il fut reconnu pour roi; **to a. s.o. as one's brother,** avouer qn pour frère; **to a. sth. as a fact,** faire la constatation de qch.; **to a. oneself beaten, to a. defeat,** s'avouer, se reconnaître, vaincu; rendre les armes; **his genius is acknowledged,** on lui reconnaît du génie; *Fenc:* **to a. a hit,** accuser un coup; annoncer à haute voix un coup reçu; (*b*) reconnaître, récompenser (un service); (*c*) se montrer reconnaissant, exprimer sa reconnaissance (d'un service). **2.** répondre à (une courtoisie, un salut, etc.); **to a. (receipt of) a letter,** accuser réception d'une lettre; **I a. receipt of your letter,** je vous accuse réception de votre lettre; *Nau:* **to a. a signal,** faire l'aperçu. **3.** *attrib. Cmptr:* **a. character,** caractère *m* d'accusé de réception affirmatif.

acknowledged [ək'nɔlidʒd], *a.* **1.** (*a*) (fait) reconnu, avéré, notoire; (*b*) **an a. thief,** un voleur reconnu. **2.** qui fait autorité.

acknowledg(e)ment [ək'nɔlidʒm(ə)nt], *s.* **1.** (*a*) constatation *f*; reconnaissance *f* (d'un bienfait); *Com:* reçu *m,* quittance *f* (d'un payement); **a. (of receipt),** accusé *m* de réception (d'une lettre, d'un colis); **formal a.,** simple accusé de réception; **we have had no a. of our invitation,** on ne nous a pas même accusé réception de notre invitation; *Adm:* **a. of a complaint,** récépissé *m* d'une réclamation; *Jur:* **a. of debt, of indebtedness,** reconnaissance de dette; *Cmptr:* **a. signal,** signal *m* d'accusé de réception; **to make an a. of sth.,** reconnaître qch.; **in a. of this service,** pour témoigner ma, sa, reconnaissance de ce service; pour récompenser ce service; (*b*) aveu *m* (d'une faute); *Jur:* **a. by record,** aveu. **2.** **acknowledgements,** remerciements *mpl*; *O:* **to bow one's acknowledgements to s.o.,** remercier qn d'une inclinaison de tête; **to lift one's hat in a. to s.o.,** remercier qn d'un salut, d'un coup de chapeau.

acknowledging [æk'nɔlidʒiŋ], *s.* constatation *f*; reconnaissance *f* (d'une dette, etc.); accusé *m* de réception (d'une lettre).

aclinic [ə'klinik], *a.* (ligne *f*) aclinique.

acme ['ækmi], *s.* (*a*) *Lit:* acmé *m,* plus haut point; comble *m,* summum *m* (de la perfection, du bonheur); sommet *m,* faîte *m* (de la gloire, des honneurs); apogée *m* (de la puissance); plus haut période (de la gloire, de l'éloquence); **to reach the a. of one's desires,** parvenir au comble de ses désirs; **to attain the a. of perfection,** arriver à la perfection même; **to be at the a. of one's glory,** être à l'apogée de la gloire; (*b*) *Med:* acmé (d'une maladie).

acmite ['ækmait], *s. Miner:* acmite *f.*

acne ['ækni], *s. Med:* acné *f*; **a. rosacea,** couperose *f,* rosacée *f.*

acnode ['æknoud], *s. Mth:* point acnodal, point conjugué.

acock [ə'kɔk], *adv. O:* **with hat (set) a.,** le chapeau (rejeté) en arrière (d'un air de défi); le chapeau sur l'oreille.

a-cock-bill [ə'kɔkbil], *adv. Nau: A:* **yards a-c.-b.,** vergues *f* en pantenne; **anchor a-c.-b.,** ancre *f* en veille, en péneau.

Acoela [æ'si:lə], *s.pl. Ann:* acœles *m.*

Acoelomata [æsilou'mɑ:tə], *s.pl. Nat.Hist:* acœlomates *m.*

acoelomate [æ'si:loumeit], **acoelomatous** [æsi:lou'meitəs], *a. Ann:* dépourvu de cœlome.

acoelous [æ'si:ləs], *a. Nat.Hist:* dépourvu de tube digestif.

acolyte ['ækəlait], *s.* **1.** *Ecc: & F:* acolyte *m.* **2.** *Ecc:* répondant *m* (à la messe).

acolythate [æ'kɔliθeit], *s. R.C.Ch:* acolytat *m.*

acone ['eikoun], *a. Ent:* acône.

aconitase [æ'kɔniteiz], *s. Ch:* aconitase *f.*

aconitate [æ'kɔniteit], *s. Ch:* aconitate *m.*

aconite ['ækənait], *s. Bot: Pharm:* aconit *m.*

aconitic [ækə'nitik], *a. Ch:* aconitique.

aconitin(e) [ə'kɔniti(:)n, -tain], *s. Ch:* aconitine *f.*

acontium, *pl.* **-ia** [æ'kɔntiəm, -iə], *s. Coel:* acontie *f.*

acorn ['eikɔ:n], *s.* **1.** (*a*) *Bot:* gland *m* (du chêne); **a. cup,** cupule *f*; **the a. crop, the a. harvest,** la glandée; **to gather, get in, the acorns,** faire la glandée; (*b*) *El:* **a. tube,** tube *m,* valve *f,* à vide gland. **2.** *Nau:* pomme *f* (de girouette).

acorn barnacle ['eikɔ:n'bɑ:nəkl], *s. Crust:* balane *m,* gland *m* de mer, turban *m* rouge.

acorn-bearing ['eikɔ:n'bɛəriŋ], *a.* balanophore, glandifère.

acorn-eating ['eikɔ:n'i:tiŋ], *a.* balanophage.

acorned ['eikɔ:nd], *a. Her:* englanté.

acorn-shaped ['eikɔ:n'ʃeipt], *a.* glandiforme.

acorn shell ['eikɔ:nʃel], *s. Crust:* = ACORN BARNACLE.

acorus ['ækərəs], *s. Bot:* acore *m,* acorus *m,* galanga *m,* *F:* poivre *m* des abcilles.

acosmism [ei'kɔsmizm], *s. Phil:* acosmisme *m.*

acotyledon [eikɔti'li:d(ə)n], *s. Bot:* acotylédone *f,* acotylédonée *f.*

acotyledonous [eikɔti'li:dənəs], *a. Bot:* acotylédone, acotylédoné.

acoumeter [ə'ku:mitər], **acousimeter** [æku:'simitər], *s. Med: etc:* acoumètre *m.*

acoumetry [ə'ku:mitri], *s. Med:* acoumétrie *f.*

acousma [ə'ku:zmə], *s. Med:* acousmie *f.*

acoustic(al) [ə'ku:stik(l)], *a.* acoustique; sonore; phonique; **a. construction,** échométrie *f*; **a. tile,** carreau *m,* panneau *m,* insonorisant; **a. treatment,** insonorisation *f*; *Anat:* **a. nerve,** nerf acoustique, auditif; *El: Elcs:* **a. velocity,** vitesse *f* des ondes sonores; *Cmptr:* **a. delay line,** ligne *f* à retard acoustique; **a. memory, store, storage,** mémoire *f* acoustique.

acoustically [ə'ku:stik(ə)li], *adv.* acoustiquement; *Elcs:* **a. coupled,** à couplage acoustique.

acoustician [æku:s'tiʃ(ə)n], *s.* acousticien, -ienne.
acousticolateral [æku:stikou'lætərəl], *a. Ich: Ann:* **a. system,** ligne latérale.
acoustics [ə'ku:stiks], *s.pl.* (*with sg. or pl. const.*) acoustique *f*; **a. is the science of sound,** l'acoustique est la science des sons; **the a. of this hall are excellent,** cette salle a une bonne acoustique.
acquaint [ə'kweint], *v.tr.* **1. to a. s.o. with sth., a fact,** informer, avertir, qn de qch.; faire savoir qch. à qn; faire part à qn de qch.; apprendre un fait à qn; **to a. s.o. with the facts (of the case),** mettre qn au courant (des faits); instruire qn des faits; mettre qn au fait (de la situation); **to a. s.o. with his duties,** mettre qn au courant de ses fonctions; **to a. oneself with the circumstances,** prendre connaissance des faits; se mettre au courant des faits; se mettre au fait des circonstances; se renseigner sur les faits. **2. to be acquainted with s.o., sth.,** connaître qn; connaître, savoir, qch.; **to become, make oneself, aquainted with s.o.,** faire, lier, connaissance avec qn; **they became acquainted in 1972,** ils se sont connus en 1972; **to become better acquainted with s.o.,** faire plus ample connaissance avec qn; **to make two persons acquainted,** faire faire connaissance à deux personnes; mettre deux personnes en relation; **to be intimately acquainted with s.o.,** être très lié avec qn; **to become, make oneself, acquainted with sth.,** prendre connaissance (des faits); apprendre, s'initier à, étudier (une langue, une science); **to be acquainted with the facts of the case,** être au fait, au courant, de la question; avoir connaissance des faits en cause.
acquaintance [ə'kweintəns], *s.* **1.** connaissance *f* (**with,** de); (*a*) **his a. with the classical languages,** sa connaissance des langues classiques; (*b*) **long a. with s.o.,** relations *f* de longue date avec qn; **to make s.o.'s a.,** faire la connaissance de qn; **to make a.,** faire connaissance; **to make a. with s.o.,** faire connaissance avec qn; **to claim a. with s.o.,** (i) se vanter de connaître qn; (ii) rappeler à qn que l'on se connaît, que l'on s'est déjà vu; **to drop a. with s.o.,** cesser de voir qn; **I have not the honour of his a.,** je n'ai pas l'honneur de le connaître; **he improves upon a.,** il gagne à être connu; **upon further a., I got to like him,** lorsque je l'ai connu davantage, il m'est devenu sympathique. **2.** (*pers.*) personne *f* de connaissance; connaissance; **he is an a., nothing more,** c'est une connaissance, rien de plus; **the face of an old a.,** une figure de connaissance; **to have a wide circle of acquaintances,** avoir des relations très étendues; **to enlarge one's circle of acquaintances,** étendre le cercle de ses relations.
acquaintanceship [ə'kweintənsʃip], *s.* **1.** relations *fpl,* rapports *mpl.* **2.** *coll.* cercle *m* de connaissances, relations; **wide a.,** relations étendues.
acquest [æ'kwest], *s. Jur:* acquêt *m.*
acquiesce [ækwi'es], *v.i.* acquiescer (**in a request,** à une demande); donner son assentiment (**in,** à); **to a. in a doctrine, in an arrangement,** accepter, se ranger à, une doctrine; accepter un arrangement; **the nation acquiesced more and more to the papal claims,** la nation se pliait de plus en plus aux exigences de la papauté.
acquiescence [ækwi'esns], *s.* **1.** acquiescement *m* (**in,** à); assentiment *m,* consentement *m*; **he signified his a. by a nod,** il inclina la tête en signe d'assentiment; **he smiled a.,** il eut un sourire d'approbation. **2.** soumission *f* (**in,** à).
acquiescent [ækwi'esnt], *a.* disposé à acquiescer; consentant.
acquiescing [ækwi'esiŋ], *s.* = ACQUIESCENCE.
acquirable [ə'kwaiərəbl], *a.* qui peut s'acquérir, s'obtenir.
acquire [ə'kwaiər], *v.tr.* (*a*) acquérir (qch.); se rendre propriétaire de (qch.); **he acquired a handsome fortune,** il acquit une belle fortune; **to a. a habit,** prendre, contracter, une habitude; **to a. a taste for sth.,** prendre goût à qch.; **to a. knowledge,** apprendre; élargir ses connaissances; **he has acquired a certain knowledge of the language,** il possède une certaine connaissance de la langue; (*b*) *Cmptr:* saisir (des données).
acquired [ə'kwaiərd], *a.* acquis; **a. taste,** goût acquis; **whisky is an a. taste,** le goût du whisky ne s'acquiert qu' avec l'habitude; *Biol:* **a. characteristics,** caractères acquis.
acquirement [ə'kwaiəmənt], *s.* **1.** acquisition *f* (**of,** de). **2.** (*a*) talent (acquis); **knowledge of a foreign language is no mean a.,** la connaissance d'une langue étrangère n'est pas peu de chose; (*b*) *pl.* connaissances *fpl,* acquis *m*; **his acquirements were considerable,** il avait beaucoup d'acquis.
acquirer [ə'kwaiərər], *s.* (*a*) acquéreur *m*; (*b*) **he was always a great a. of knowledge,** il a toujours aimé à s'instruire.
acquiring [ə'kwaiəriŋ], *s.* acquisition *f.*
acquisition [ækwi'ziʃ(ə)n], *s.* acquisition *f* ((i) action d'acquérir, (ii) chose acquise); **devoted to the a. of wealth,** âpre à s'enrichir; ne songeant qu'à s'enrichir; **come and see my new acquisitions,** venez voir mes nouvelles acquisitions; **in less than a year Napoleon lost all his acquisitions,** en moins d'un an Napoléon perdit toutes ses conquêtes; **he is a great a. to our party,** c'est une recrue précieuse pour notre parti; *Cmptr:* **data a.,** saisie *f,* collecte *f,* rassemblement *m,* de données; *Adm:* **compulsory a. of property,** expropriation *f.*
acquisitive [ə'kwizitiv], *a.* **1.** thésauris(at)eur, -euse. **2.** âpre au gain.
acquisitively [ə'kwizitivli], *adv.* avidement, avec rapacité.
acquisitiveness [ə'kwizitivnis], *s.* (*a*) acquisivité *f*; (*b*) avidité *f,* âpreté *f* au gain, rapacité *f.*
acquit [ə'kwit], *v.tr.* (**acquitting, acquitted**). **1. to a. a debt,** s'acquitter d'une dette, acquitter une dette; régler une dette. **2.** acquitter (un accusé); **to a. s.o. of sth.,** absoudre qn de qch.; **to a. s.o. of a debt,** acquitter qn d'une dette; **to a. s.o. of a charge,** décharger qn d'une accusation; **he was acquitted on two of the charges,** il fut acquitté sur deux des chefs. **3.** (*a*) **to a. oneself of a duty, of a task,** s'acquitter d'un devoir, d'une tâche; (*b*) **to a. oneself well,** se bien comporter; se bien acquitter; **he acquitted himself like a man,** il y a mis du sien.
acquittal [ə'kwitl], *s.* **1.** *Jur:* acquittement *m* (d'un accusé, d'un débiteur); décision *f* absolutoire; décharge *f* (d'un accusé); absolution *f* (d'un coupable); **for the a. of my conscience,** pour décharger ma conscience; par acquit de conscience. **2.** (*a*) exécution *f,* accomplissement *m* (d'un devoir); (*b*) *Jur:* acquittement (d'une dette).
acquittance [ə'kwit(ə)ns], *s.* **1.** (*a*) *Com: Jur:* acquit *m,* acquittement *m* (d'une dette); (*b*) *A. Jur:* quittance *f*; décharge *f.* **2.** *A:* = ACQUITTAL I.
acquitting [ə'kwitiŋ], *s.* = ACQUITTAL.
Acraeidae [æ'kreiidi:], *s.pl. Ent:* acraeides *m.*
Acrania [ei'kreiniə], *s.pl. Ich:* acraniens *m.*
Acrasiales [æ'kreizi'a:liz], *s. pl. Fung:* acrasiés *m.*
acraspedote [æ'kræspidouti], *a. Coel:* acraspède, acraspédote.
acrawl [ə'krɔ:l], *adv. & a. A:* **1.** rampant; en rampant. **2.** grouillant (**with,** de).
acre[1] ['eikər], *s.* **1.** (*a*) *A:* champ *m,* pré *m;* **God's a.,** le champ de repos, le cimetière; (*b*) *pl.* **proud of his broad acres,** fier de ses terres, de ses arpents. **2.** *Meas:* acre *f* (0·4 hectare); (*approx.* =) arpent *m,* demi-hectare *m;* **he owns acres of land,** il a des terres étendues; il a du bien au soleil.
Acre[2], *Pr.n. Geog:* Saint-Jean-d'Acre *m.*
acreage ['eikəridʒ], *s.* superficie *f* (en mesures agraires).
acrid ['ækrid], *a.* **1.** (goût *m,* fumée *f*) âcre. **2.** (style) mordant; (critique *f*) acerbe; (humeur *f*) âcre.
acridian [æ'kridiən], *a. Ent:* acridien.
Acrididae [æ'kridid:], **Acridiidae** [æ'kridiidi:], *s.pl. Ent:* acridiens *m.*
acridine ['ækridi:n], *s. Ch:* acridine *f*; **a. dye,** colorant *m* acridinique.
acridity [æ'kriditi], **acridness** ['ækridnis], *s.* âcreté *f*; acerbité *f.*
acridly ['ækridli], *adv.* avec âcreté; avec acerbité.
acriflavine [ækri'fleivi:n], *s. Ch:* acriflavine *f.*
acrimonious [ækri'mouniəs], *a.* acrimonieux, atrabilaire; (*of woman*) acariâtre; **the discussion became a.,** la discussion s'envenimait.
acrimoniously [ækri'mouniəsli], *adv.* acrimonieusement, avec acrimonie.
acrimony ['ækriməni], **acrimoniousness** [ækri'mouniəsnis], *s.* acrimonie *f*; amertume *f* (de caractère); aigreur *f* (de ton, de caractère).
acro- ['ækrou], *pref.* acro-.
acrobat ['ækrəbæt], *s.* acrobate *mf.*
acrobatic [ækrə'bætik]. **1.** *a.* acrobatique; **a. feat,** acrobatie *f,* tour *m* d'acrobate, d'acrobatie. **2.** *s.pl.* **acrobatics,** acrobatie *f.*
acrobatism ['ækrəbætizm], *s.* acrobatisme *m,* acrobatie *f.*
acrocarpous [ækrou'ka:pəs], *a. Bot:* acrocarpe.
acrocephalia [ækrouse'feiliə], *s.* acrocéphalie *f.*
acrocephalic [ækrouse'fælik], **acrocephalous** [ækrou'sefələs], *a.* acrocéphale.
acrocephaly [ækrou'sefəli], *s.* acrocéphalie *f.*
acrocyanosis [ækrousaiə'nousis], *s. Med:* acrocyanose *f.*
acrodont ['ækroudɔnt], *s. Rept:* acrodonte *m.*
acrodynia [ækrou'diniə], *s. Med:* acrodynie *f.*
acrolein [æ'krouliin, 'ækrəlin], *s. Ch:* acroléine *f,* accroi *f,* aldéhyde *m* acrylique, propénal *m.*
acromegalic [ækroume'gælik], *a. Med:* acromégalique.
acromegaly [ækrou'megəli], *s. Med:* acromégalie *f*; mégalacrie *f.*
acromial [æ'kroumiəl], *a. Anat:* acromial.
acromion [æ'kroumiən], *s. Anat:* **the a. (process),** l'acromion *m.*
acron ['ækrɔn], *s. Ent:* acron *m.*
acronychal [æ'krɔnikl], *a. Astr:* acronyque.
acronym ['ækrənim], *s.* sigle *m* (qui peut être prononcé comme un mot).
acropar(a)esthesia [ækroupæ:res'θi:siə], *s. Med:* acroparesthésia *f.*
acropetal [ækrou'petl], *a. Bot:* acropète.
acrophobia [ækrou'foubiə], *s.* acrophobie *f.*
acrophonic [ækrou'fɔnik], *a. Ling:* acrophonique.
acrophony [ə'krɔfəni], *s. Ling:* acrophonie *f.*
acropodium [ækrou'poudiəm], *s. Sculp:* acropodium *m.*
acropolis [ə'krɔpəlis], *s.* acropole *f.*
acrose ['ækrous], *s. Ch:* acrose *m.*
acrosome ['ækrousoum], *s. Biol:* acrosome *m*; bouton *m,* coiffe *f,* céphalique.
acrospore ['ækrouspɔər], *s. Fung:* acrospore *f.*
across [ə'krɔs], *adv. & prep.* **1.** en travers (de); en croix; *Nau:* **with yards a.,** les vergues en croix; **with his arms folded a. his chest,** les bras croisés sur la poitrine. **2.** (*a*) **to walk a. (a street),** traverser (une rue); **to run a. the street,** traverser la rue en courant; **to run a. the fields,** courir à travers (les) champs; **pursuit a. country,** poursuite à travers champs; **to swim a. a river,** traverser, passer, franchir, une rivière à la nage; **to go a. a bridge,** passer (sur) un pont; franchir un pont; **how, when, did you come a.?** comment, quand, avez-vous fait la traversée? **we shall soon be a.,** (i) nous serons bientôt de l'autre côté; (ii) la traversée sera bientôt faite; **an idea came a. my mind that . . .,** l'idée m'a traversé l'esprit, m'a passé par l'esprit, que . . .; *Th:* **to get a. the footlights,** passer la rampe; (*of play*) **to get, come, a.,** plaire à l'assistance; être bien reçu du public; **he managed to get, put, it a.,** il a réussi (i) à se faire comprendre, (ii) à faire adopter sa proposition, (iii) à convaincre les autres, ses adversaires; **to get sth. a. to s.o.,** faire comprendre qch. à qn; (*b*) **to lay sth. a. (sth.),** mettre qch. en travers (de qch.); **to throw a bridge a. a river,** jeter un pont sur une rivière; **line drawn a. the page,** ligne tirée en travers de la page; **the road lies a. the plain,** la route traverse la plaine; *F:* **I'll put you a. my knee!** je vais te donner une fessée; **the wind blew a. me,** j'avais le vent de côté; (*of clouds*) **to blow a. the wind,** chasser à contre; *F:* **to get a. s.o.,** irriter, exaspérer, qn; *Ten:* **ball played a. the court,** balle croisée; (*c*) **to come a. a person, a passage in a book,** rencontrer (par hasard) une personne, un passage dans un livre; **we ran a. each other,** nous nous sommes rencontrés; nous nous sommes trouvés nez à nez; (*d*) *F:* **to come a. with the money,** payer; *F:* **the police finally persuaded him to come a.,** finalement la police l'a persuadé de parler; *P:* **you'd better come a.!** il faut vider ton sac! (*e*) *F:* **to put sth. a. on s.o.,** faire croire, faire avaler, qch. à qn; **to put it a. s.o.,** (i) régler son compte à qn; (ii) faire une rosserie à qn; (iii) tromper, balancer, qn. **3.** (*a*) **the distance a.,** (i) la distance en largeur; (ii) la longueur de la traversée; **the river is more than a mile a.,** le fleuve a plus d'un mille de large; **tree that is two metres a.,** arbre qui a deux mètres de coupe; **beam 50 centimetres a.,** poutre de 50 centimètres d'épaisseur; **he is wide a. the shoulders,** il est large d'épaules; (*b*) **he lives a. the street,** il habite de l'autre côté de la rue; **countries a. the seas,** les pays de l'autre côté de la mer; les pays d'outremer; **they talked to each other a. the table,** ils se parlaient d'un côté de la table à l'autre; (*c*) (*in crosswords*) horizontalement.
across-the-board [ə'krɔsðə'bɔ:d], *a.* général; qui s'applique à tout le monde; **an a.-t.-b. wage increase,** une augmentation générale des salaires; **a.-t.-b. cuts,** réduction linéaire générale (des droits de douane).
acrostic [ə'krɔstik], *a. & s.* acrostiche (*m*).
acrostolion [ækrɔ'stouliən], **acrostolium** [ækrɔ'stouliəm], *s. N.Arch:* acrostole *m.*
acroter [æ'kroutər], **acroterion** [ækrou'teriən], **acroterium,** *pl.* **-ia** [ækrou'teriəm, -iə], *s. Arch:* acrotère *m.*
Acrothoracica [ækrouθɔ'ræsikə], *s.pl. Crust:* acrothoraciques *m.*
acrylaldehyde ['ækril'ældihaid], *s. Ch:* aldéhyde *m* acrylique, acroléine *f,* propénal *m.*
acrylate ['ækrileit], *a. & s.* **a. (resin),** résine *f* acrylique.
acrylic [ə'krilik], *a. Ch:* acrylique; **a. acid,** acide *m* acrylique, propénoïque *m*; **a. resin, plastic,** résine *f* acrylique.
acrylonitrile [ˌækrilou'naitr(a)il], *s. Ch:* acrylonitrile *m,*

-nitrile *m* acrylique.

act[1] [ækt], *s.* **1.** (*a*) acte *m*; **a. of justice, of kindness,** acte de justice, de bonté; **a. of grace, of indemnity,** mesure *f* de grâce, d'amnistie; **a. of war,** acte de guerre; (*b*) *Theol:* **a. of faith, of contrition,** acte de foi, de contrition; (*c*) **A. of Parliament,** loi *f*, décret *m*; **Companies A.,** loi sur les sociétés; **factory a.,** législation industrielle; loi sur les accidents du travail; **finance a.,** loi de finances; **land a.,** loi agraire; **provisions of an a.,** provisions *f* d'une loi; (*d*) **the Acts of the Apostles,** les Actes des Apôtres; *Jur:* **a. of substitution,** acte subrogatoire; **I deliver this (as) my a. and deed,** signé de ma main; fait de ma main; **to take a. of a confession,** prendre acte d'un aveu. **2.** action *f*; **the a. of walking,** l'action de marcher; **my first a. was to open the window,** la première chose que j'ai faite a été d'ouvrir la fenêtre; **an a. of folly,** une folie; **a stupid a.,** une action stupide, *F:* une bêtise; **as an a. of courtesy,** par politesse; **it is the a. of an ill-bred person,** c'est le fait d'un homme mal élevé; **to catch s.o. in the (very) a.,** prendre qn sur le fait, en flagrant délit, *F:* la main dans le sac; **he was in the a. of picking it up when he fell,** en se baissant pour le ramasser il est tombé; *Jur: Ins:* **a. of God,** (i) (cas *m* de) force majeure; (ii) cas fortuit; cause naturelle. **3.** *Th: etc:* (*a*) acte (d'une pièce); **in the second a.,** au second acte; (*b*) numéro *m* (d'un artiste); **circus a.,** numéro de cirque; *F:* **it's a real circus a.,** il y a de quoi vous faire rigoler; **to put on an a.,** jouer la comédie, poser, frimer; **he likes to do his little a.,** il aime à faire son petit numéro; **it's all an a.,** c'est du cinéma; **to get in on the a.,** se mettre dans le mouvement; **to be in on the a.,** être dans le coup; **to let s.o. in on the a.,** mettre qn dans le coup. **4.** *Sch: A:* **to keep the a.,** soutenir sa thèse; **keeping of the acts,** soutenance *f* de thèses.

act[2]. **1.** *v.tr. A:* (*a*) accomplir (un acte); **to a. enormities,** commettre des énormités; (*b*) (*with passive force*) **at the very moment when this piece of perfidy was acting,** au moment même où s'accomplissait cette perfidie. **2.** *v.tr.* (*a*) **to a. a play, a character,** jouer, représenter, une pièce, un personnage; **to a. a part,** remplir un rôle; **to a. Hamlet,** jouer, faire, Hamlet; **to a. the hero,** jouer, faire, le héros; jouer les héros; **to a. the fool, the goat, the idiot,** faire l'imbécile, *F:* le zigoto; *Pej:* **to a. the part,** se carrer (dans un rôle); (*b*) **to a. a part,** feindre; faire, jouer, la comédie; **to a. fear,** feindre, simuler, la crainte; **he was only acting,** il ne faisait que feindre; il faisait semblant; (*c*) **to a. the part of an honest man,** se conduire, agir, en honnête homme; **to a. the part of a judge,** remplir, exercer, les fonctions de juge. **3.** *v.i.* (*a*) agir, prendre des mesures; **it is time to a.,** il est temps d'agir; **he is slow to a.,** il est lent à agir; **he did not know how to a.,** (i) il ne savait quoi faire, comment se conduire; (ii) il ne savait quel parti prendre; **to a. prudently,** agir prudemment; **diplomats a. with extreme punctiliousness towards one another,** les diplomates en usent entre eux avec une extrême délicatesse; **to a. like, as, a friend,** agir, se conduire, en ami; se comporter comme un ami; **I acted for the best,** j'ai fait pour le mieux; **to a. for s.o.,** agir au nom de qn; représenter qn; **to a. as (secretary, etc.),** exercer les fonctions de (secrétaire, etc.); **his daughter acts as his secretary,** sa fille lui sert de secrétaire; **to a. from a sense of duty,** agir par devoir; **to a. on advice,** agir d'après un conseil; suivre un conseil; **to a. on an order,** exécuter un ordre; **to a. on a letter,** donner suite à une lettre; **to a. on one's principles, according to one's principles,** agir conformément à ses principes; mettre ses principes en pratique; *Cmptr:* **to a. (up)on data,** effectuer un traitement (sur les données); (*b*) **the police refused to a.,** la police refusa d'intervenir; **the pump is not acting properly,** la pompe ne fonctionne, ne marche, pas bien; **the brake refuses to a.,** le frein ne fonctionne pas; **fuse that acts as a switch,** fusible qui fait l'office de commutateur; **the engine acts as a brake,** le moteur fait fonction de frein; (*c*) **to a. on the brain, the bowels,** agir, exercer une action, sur le cerveau, sur l'intestin; **acted upon by gravity,** sollicité par la pesanteur; **acid that acts on metals,** acide qui mord sur les métaux, qui entame les métaux; (*d*) *Th: Cin:* jouer; **he doesn't a. well,** il ne joue pas bien; ce n'est pas un bon acteur; **to a. for the films,** faire du cinéma; **to a. in a film,** tourner dans un film; **this play will not a.,** cette pièce est impossible à jouer, ne passera pas la rampe; (*of play*) **will it a.?** est-ce que c'est jouable?

actable ['æktəbl], *a. Th: etc:* jouable.

Actaeon [æk'ti:ən]. **1.** *Pr.n.m. Myth:* Actéon. **2.** *s. Moll:* actéon *m*.

actinal ['æktinl], *a. Z:* actinal, -aux.

acting[1] ['æktiŋ], *a.* **1.** remplissant les fonctions de . . .; suppléant; intérimaire; **a. manager,** (i) directeur gérant; (ii) directeur intérimaire; gérant *m* provisoire; **lieutenant a. captain,** lieutenant faisant fonction de capitaine; **the a. president of the council,** le président du conseil en exercise, en fonctions. **2.** *Th:* **a. company,** troupe *f* de comédiens.

acting[2], *s.* **1.** action *f*. **2.** (*a*) *Th:* jeu *m* (d'un acteur); exécution *f*, production *f* (d'une pièce de théâtre); **a. play,** pièce destinée à la scène; pièce jouable; **a. copy, version (of a play),** exemplaire *m* (d'une pièce) à l'usage des acteurs; (*b*) fait *m* de faire du théâtre, de jouer la comédie; **to go in for a.,** faire du théâtre; **at school we did a lot of a.,** au collège nous avons monté pas mal de pièces, nous avons souvent joué des comédies; (*c*) **it's just a.,** c'est de la comédie; il fait semblant; c'est une comédie qu'il nous joue.

actinia, *pl.* **-ias, -iae** [æk'tiniə, -iəz, -ii:], *s. Coel:* actinie *f*.

actinian [æk'tiniən], *s. Coel:* actinie *f*, anémone *f* de mer.

Actin(i)aria [æktin(i)'εəriə], *s.pl.* actin(i)aires *m*.

actinic [æk'tinik], *a. Ph:* actinique; **a. spectrum,** spectre *m* chimique; **a. rays,** rayons *m* actiniques, chimiques; **a. balance,** bolomètre *m*.

actinide ['æktinaid], *s. Ch:* actinide *m*; **the a. series,** les actinides.

actiniferous [ækti'nifərəs], *a. Ph:* actinifère.

actinism ['æktiniźm], *s. Ph:* actinisme *m*.

actinium [æk'tiniəm], *s. Ch:* actinium *m*; **the a. series,** la série de l'actinium, les actinides *m*; **a. emanation,** actinon *m*.

actinobacillosis [,æktinoubæsi'lousis], *s. Vet:* actinobacillose *f*.

actinograph [æk'tinougræf], *s. Ph:* actinographe *m*.

actinoid ['æktinɔid], *s. Ch:* actinide *m*.

actinolite [æk'tinoulait], *s. Miner:* actinolite *f*, actinote *f*.

actinology [ækti'nɔlədʒi], *s.* **1.** *Z:* actinologie *f*. **2.** *Ph:* étude *f* de l'action chimique de la lumière.

actinometer [ækti'nɔmitər], *s. Ph: etc:* actinomètre *m*; photomètre *m* de tirage, de pose; **recording a.,** actinographe *m*.

actinometric(al) [,æktinou'metrik(l)], *a.* actinométrique.

actinometry [ækti'nɔmitri], *s.* actinométrie *f*.

actinomorphic [,æktinou'mɔ:fik], *a. Bot:* actinomorphe.

actinomyces [,æktinou'maisi:z], *s. Bac:* actinomycès *m*.

Actinomycetales [,æktinoumaisə'teili:z], *s.pl. Bac:* actinomycétales *f*.

actinomycete [,æktinou'maisi:t], *s. Bac:* actinomycète *f*.

actinomycin [,æktinou'maisin], *s. Med:* actinomycine *f*.

actinomycosis [,æktinoumai'kousis], *s. Vet: Med:* actinomycose *f*.

actinon ['æktinɔn], *s. Ch:* actinon *m*.

Actinophrys [ækti'nɔfris], *s. Prot:* actinophrys *f*.

Actinopoda [æktinou'poudə], *s.pl. Prot:* actinopodes *m*.

Actinopterygii [æktinɔpte'ridʒii:], *s.pl. Ich:* actinoptérygiens *m*.

actinotherapy [æktinou'θerəpi], *s.* actinothérapie *f*.

actino-uranium [æk,tinouju'reiniəm], *s. Ch:* actino-uranium *m*.

Actinozoa [æktinou'zouə], *s.pl. Coel:* anthozoaires *m*.

action ['ækʃ(ə)n], *s.* **1.** action *f* (d'une personne, d'un remède, etc.); **the a. of water (on the banks of a stream, etc.),** le travail des eaux, l'action de l'eau (sur la berge d'une rivière, etc.); **to take a.,** agir; intervenir; prendre des mesures; **to take a. about, on, sth.,** prendre une initiative au sujet de qch.; **industrial a.,** (i) grève *f*; (ii) action revendicative; **line of a.,** ligne *f* de conduite; **man of a.,** homme d'action; **to make s.o. take a.,** forcer qn à agir; *Com: etc:* **(passed to you) for a.,** pour suite à donner; **sphere of a.,** sphère *f* d'activité; **to suit the a. to the word,** joindre le geste à la parole; joindre l'exemple au précepte; **to put, set, sth. in action, to bring, call, sth. into a.,** mettre qch. en action, en œuvre, en jeu, en mouvement; faire agir, faire marcher, faire jouer, faire fonctionner, qch.; actionner (une machine); **to put a plan into a.,** mettre un projet à exécution, à l'effet; **to come into a.,** entrer en action, en jeu; (*of machine*) **in a.,** en marche; en état de service; **machines in full a.,** machines tournant à plein; **to bring the law into a.,** faire intervenir la loi; **through the a. of this law,** par le jeu de cette loi; **out of a.,** hors de service; en panne; **to put a machine out of a.,** détraquer une machine; *Mec:* **principle of least a.,** principe de moindre action; *Ch:* **law of mass a.,** loi d'action de masse; **to have an a. on sth.,** avoir, exercer, une action sur qch.; agir sur qch.; *Cmptr:* **a. code,** code *m* d'intervention; **a. switch,** touche *f*, bouton *m*, de service; *Art:* **a. painting,** peinture gestuelle. **2.** (*deed*) action, acte *m*, fait *m*; **splendid a.,** action d'éclat; *Lit:* haut fait; **impulsive a.,** action irréfléchie; coup *m* de tête. **3.** *Th:* action (d'une pièce); **unity of a.,** unité *f* d'action; **time of a.,** durée *f* de l'action; **the scene of the a. is . . .,** la scène se passe à. . . . **4.** (*a*) action, gestes *mpl* (d'un joueur); train *m*, allure *f*, action (d'un cheval); *Equit:* **high a.,** allure relevée; *Ten: etc:* **to perfect one's a.,** perfectionner son jeu; (*b*) mécanisme *m* (d'une montre, etc.); jeu *m* (d'une pompe, d'une serrure); mécanique *f* (d'un piano, d'un orgue). **5.** *Jur:* **a. at law,** action en justice; procès *m* (civil ou criminel); **legal a.,** action juridique; procès; **right of a.,** droit *m* d'ester en jugement; **direct a.,** action directe; **indirect a.,** action indirecte, oblique; **a. for libel,** procès, plainte *f*, en diffamation; **a. for damages,** action en dommages et intérêts; **a. for payment,** action en paiement; **a. for an account,** action en reddition de compte; **a. in expropriation of real property,** poursuite *f* en expropriation d'immeubles; **the subject of the a.,** l'objet en litige; **to institute an a.,** introduire une instance (en justice); **to bring an a. against s.o.,** intenter une action, un procès, à, contre, qn; exercer des poursuites contre qn; porter, déposer, une plainte contre qn; (faire) appeler qn en justice; **to bring an a. against s.o. for infringement of patent,** assigner qn en contrefaçon; **the a. is pending,** l'action est en cours; **to take a. against s.o.,** (i) poursuivre, citer, attaquer, qn en justice; engager, entamer, initier, commencer, des poursuites (judiciaires) contre qn; agir contre qn; (ii) prendre des mesures contre qn. **6.** (*a*) *Mil: etc:* **a. operation,** combat *m*, engagement *m*; **combined a.,** action combinée, combat de toutes armes; **concerted a.,** action d'ensemble; **containment a., delaying a.,** action retardatrice; **joint a.,** action interarmes, action combinée; **naval a.,** engagement naval, opération navale; **surprise a.,** action de surprise; **action!** en batterie! **a. front, rear, right, left!** en batterie face en avant, face en arrière, face à droite, face à gauche! **to come into a.,** entrer en action, engager le combat; **to break off the a.,** rompre le combat, décrocher; **ready for a.,** prêt(s) à combattre, à intervenir; **to send troops into a.,** faire intervenir des troupes; jeter des troupes dans la bataille; **out of a.,** (i) hors de combat; (ii) hors de service, *F:* de cause; **killed in a.,** tué à l'ennemi, mort au champ d'honneur; **the artillery was in a.,** on tirait au canon; **battery in a.,** batterie en action; (*b*) activité *f*; **let's have a bit of a.!** un peu d'activité! *F:* grouillez-vous!

actionable ['ækʃənəbl], *a. Jur:* (mot, action) qui expose à des poursuites; actionnable; sujet(te) à procès, à une action judiciaire.

actionless ['ækʃənlis], *a. Ch: etc:* inerte.

activable ['æktivəbl], *a. Atom.Ph: etc:* activable.

activate ['æktiveit], *v.tr.* **1.** (*a*) *Ch: Biol: etc:* activer; (*b*) accélérer, presser; (*c*) *Cmptr:* rendre actif, déclencher (les marteaux d'impression); lancer (un programme); actionner (un bouton). **2.** *Ph:* rendre (un corps) radio(-) actif.

activated ['æktiveitid], *a. Ch:* activé; **a. alumina,** alumine activée; **a. carbon,** charbon actif, activé; **a. (sewage) sludge,** boues activées.

activation [ækti'veiʃ(ə)n], *s.* (*a*) activation *f*; (*b*) *Cmptr:* déclenchement *m*; commande *f*.

activator ['æktiveitər], *s. Ch: etc:* activeur *m*; activateur *m*; accélérateur *m*.

active ['æktiv], *a.* **1.** (*a*) actif; alerte; agile; **a. man,** homme actif, allant, remuant; **he is always a.,** il est toujours en train de se démener; **to be still a.,** être encore alerte, allant, actif, ingambe; **a. life,** vie active; **a. in the defence of his friends,** actif à défendre ses amis; **a. collaboration,** collaboration agissante, active; **a. volcano,** volcan actif; (*of volcano*) **to become a.,** entrer en activité; *Jur: Adm: etc:* **a. consideration (of a document, etc.),** examen approfondi (d'un document, etc.); *Med:* **a. immunity,** immunité *f* par (les) anticorps; **a. poison,** poison *f* rapide; *Fin:* **a. balance,** balance *f* excédentaire; **a. money,** monnaie circulante; monnaie active; *St.Exch:* **these shares are very a.,** ces valeurs sont très allantes; **there is an a. demand for wool,** les laines sont très recherchées; *Pol.Ec:* **a. population,** population active; **a. tonnage,** tonnage actif, en service; **a. brain,** cerveau éveillé; **a. imagination,** imagination vive; (*b*) *Cmptr:* (compte, fichier) mouvementé, ayant fait l'objet d'un mouvement; (programme) en cours d'exécution; **a. store,** mémoire active; **a. transducer,** transducteur actif; (*c*) *Ph:* radio(-)actif; (*d*) **a. charcoal,** charbon actif, activé; **a. sewage sludge,** boues activées. **2.** *Gram:* **verb in the a. (voice),** verbe *m* à l'actif, à la voix active. **3.** (*a*) *Mec:* **a. pressure,** pression effective; *El:* **a. cell,** élément (d'accu) chargé; **cell**

no longer a., élément déchargé, à plat; (*b*) **to be an a. party to sth., to take an a. part in sth.,** prendre une part active, effective, à qch.; **these laws are a. in every realm of nature,** ces lois s'exercent dans tous les domaines de la nature. **4.** (*a*) *Mil: etc:* **a. duty,** service actif, activité *f* de service; **a. list,** (i) annuaire *m* de l'armée active; (ii) personnel *m* de l'armée active; **to be on the a. list,** (i) être sur l'annuaire de l'armée active; (ii) être en service actif, en activité de service; **a. service,** (i) service aux armées, service sur un théâtre d'opérations, service en campagne; (ii) service actif; **to see a. service for the first time,** (i) faire sa première campagne; (ii) recevoir le baptême du feu; **to be called up for a. service,** être appelé sous les drapeaux; (*b*) (*of official*) **to be in a. employment,** être en activité (de service), être en pied.

actively ['æktivli], *adv.* activement.

activism ['æktivizm], *s. Pol:* activisme *m.*

activist ['æktivist], *s. Pol:* activiste *mf.*

activistic [ækti'vistik], *a. Pol:* activiste.

activity [æk'tiviti], *s.* **1.** activité *f*; **man of a.,** homme actif; **the a. of a large town,** le mouvement d'une grande ville; **in full a.,** en pleine activité; **economic a.,** activité économique. **2.** activité, action *f,* branche *f* d'activité; **that does not come within the sphere of my activities,** cela ne rentre pas dans mes fonctions; c'est en dehors de ma sphère d'action; **his numerous activities leave him little leisure,** ses nombreuses occupations lui laissent peu de loisirs; **anti-national activities,** menées antinationales. **3.** *Ph:* (*a*) radio(-)activité *f*; (*b*) (*of a source*) activité. **4.** *Cmptr:* mouvement *m* (portant sur un fichier); mouvementation *f* (d'un fichier); **a. factor, a. ratio,** taux *m* d'activité, de mouvement (d'un fichier).

acton ['æktən], *s. A.Arm:* hoqueton *m.*

actor ['æktər], *s.* **1.** (*a*) acteur *m*; artiste *m* (dramatique); comédien *m*; **tragic a.,** tragédien *m*; **actors in a farce,** joueurs *m* d'une farce; **film a.,** acteur de cinéma; **to be an a., a film a.,** faire du théâtre, du cinéma; **a.-producer,** acteur et metteur *m* en scène; (*b*) *U.S: F:* **bad a.,** mauvais type. **2.** *Ch:* réactif *m* (à action rapide).

actress ['æktris], *s.* actrice *f*; artiste *f* (dramatique); comédienne *f*; **tragic a.,** tragédienne *f*; **film a.,** actrice de cinéma; **she is a film a.,** elle fait du cinéma.

actressy ['æktrisi], *a. F: Pej:* théâtral; **her voice was a.,** elle parlait (toujours) d'un ton théâtral.

actual ['æktjuəl], *a.* **1.** réel, véritable; **it's an a. fact,** c'est un fait positif; **to take an a. case,** pour prendre un cas concret; **a. size,** grandeur réelle, vraie grandeur; **to give the a. figures,** donner les chiffres mêmes; **a. numbers of an army,** effectif réel d'une armée; **a. possession,** possession *f* de fait; **the a. provisions of an act,** les dispositions expresses d'une loi; **in a. fact . . .,** pratiquement . . ., effectivement . . ., en fait . . .; **there is no a. recruiting of labour,** il n'y a pas, à proprement parler, de recrutement de main-d'œuvre; **a. employment,** emploi effectif; **on the basis of the a. value,** sur la base de la valeur réelle; *Com:* **a. cost,** prix *m* (i) d'achat, (ii) de revient; *Pol.Ec:* **a. and theoretical distributions,** distributions *f* empiriques et théoriques; *Cmptr:* **a. address,** adresse absolue, réelle; **a. key,** indicatif *m* interne; adresse réelle (en COBOL); **a. coding,** codage absolu; **a. instruction,** instruction réelle, effective; **a. stock,** stock réel, les existants; *Med:* **a. cautery,** cautère actuel; *Theol:* **a. sin,** péché actuel; **a. grace,** grâce actuelle. **2.** (*present*) actuel, présent; **the a. position of affairs,** l'état de choses actuel.

actuality [æktju'æliti], *s.* **1.** (*a*) réalité *f*; (*b*) actualité *f,* le temps présent; **play that lacks a.,** pièce qui n'a aucun rapport avec la vie d'aujourd'hui; (*c*) *W.Tel: T.V:* programme *m* documentaire. **2.** *pl.* **actualities,** (i) conditions réelles; (ii) conditions actuelles.

actualization [æktjuəlai'zeiʃ(ə)n], *s.* **1.** actualisation *f*. **2.** réalisation *f* (d'une idée, d'un projet, etc.). **3.** *Psy:* actuation *f.*

actualize ['æktjuəlaiz], *v.tr.* **1.** réaliser (une conception). **2.** faire revivre (une scène). **3.** actualiser, rendre actuel.

actually ['æktjuəli], *adv.* **1.** (*a*) réellement, véritablement, effectivement; à vrai dire; de fait; en fait, en réalité; **profits a. realized,** bénéfice effectivement réalisé; **do you a. mean it?** êtes-vous réellement sérieux? **I do not a. love her,** je ne ressens pas d'amour pour elle, à proprement parler; **I was invited to dinner at eight, but the dinner didn't a. begin until nine,** on m'a invité à dîner à huit heures, mais le repas proprement dit n'a commencé qu'à neuf heures; (*b*) **I a. found the door open,** à mon grand étonnement j'ai trouvé la porte ouverte; **he a. swore,** il alla (même) jusqu'à lâcher un juron; **he's a. getting married again!** voilà qu'il se remarie! (*redundant*) **a., I rather like it,** à vrai dire, ça me plaît (plutôt); **are you living in London?—I am, a.,** est-ce que vous habitez à Londres?—mais oui! **2.** *occ.* actuellement, à présent.

actuarial [ˌæktju'ɛəriəl], *a.* actuariel; **modern a. science,** la science actuarielle moderne.

actuarially [æktju'ɛəriəli], *adv.* au, du, point de vue actuariel.

actuary ['æktjuəri], *s.* **1.** *Ins:* actuaire *m*; **actuaries' tables,** tables *f* de mortalité. **2.** = chef-comptable *m, pl.* chefs-comptables, d'une caisse d'épargne.

actuate ['æktjueit] *v.tr.* **1.** mettre en action, mettre en mouvement, mener, commander, faire marcher (une machine); **the force that actuates the machine, the bullet,** la force qui anime la machine, la balle. **2.** animer, pousser, faire agir (qn); **actuated by jealousy,** poussé, inspiré, par la jalousie.

actuating ['æktjueitiŋ], *a.* **1.** (mécanisme) de commande, de manœuvre. **2.** (motif) qui fait agir (qn).

actuation [æktju'eiʃ(ə)n], *s.* mise *f* en action (d'une machine, etc.); commande *f,* manœuvre *f* (d'une machine).

actuator ['æktjueitər], *s. Mec: etc:* actionneur *m*; vérin *m*; *Cmptr:* (i) dispositif *m,* mécanisme *m,* de commande; (ii) bras *m* (de lecture/écriture); *Mec.E:* **(electrical) a.,** moteur *m* (électrique) d'asservissement; *Av:* **trim a.,** actionneur de trim.

acuity [ə'kju(:)iti], *s.* acuité *f* (d'une pointe, de l'esprit, de la douleur, etc.); **visual a.,** acuité visuelle.

Aculeata [əkjuli'eitə], *s.pl. Ent:* aculéates *m,* aculés *m.*

aculeate [æ'kju:liət], **aculeated** [əkjuli'eitid], *a.* **1.** *Bot: Ent:* aculé; porte-aiguillon *inv. Bot:* épineux. **2.** *Lit:* (mot) piquant.

aculeiform [æ'kju:liifɔ:m], *a.* aculéiforme.

aculeus [æ'kju:liəs], *s. Ent: Bot:* aiguillon *m* (d'une abeille, d'un rosier, etc.).

acumen [ə'kju:men], *s.* **1.** pénétration *f,* finesse *f* (d'esprit), clairvoyance *f,* perspicacité *f.* **2.** *Bot:* pointe *f.*

acuminate[1] [æ'kju:minət], **acuminated** [æ'kju:mineitid], *a. Nat.Hist:* acuminé, acumineux; pointu, alêné.

acuminate[2] [æ'kju:mineit]. **1.** *v.i.* être acuminé, pointu. **2.** *v.tr.* rendre pointu.

acumination [ækjumi'neiʃ(ə)n], *s.* terminaison *f* en pointe.

acuminous [æ'kju:minəs], *a.* **1.** *Lit:* perspicace, doué de finesse. **2.** *Nat.Hist:* acuminé.

acupunctor [ækju'pʌŋktər], *s. Med:* acupuncteur *m,* acuponcteur *m.*

acupuncture [ækju'pʌŋktjər], *s. Med:* acupuncture *f,* acuponcture *f.*

acushla [ə'ku:ʃlə], *s. Dial:* (*Irish*) mon chéri, ma chérie; ma mignonne.

acustico-lateralis [ə'kustikoulætə'reilis], *a. Ich:* acousticolatéral, -aux.

acutangular [ə'kju:t'æŋgjulər], *a.* (*a*) *Mth:* acutangulaire; (*b*) *Bot:* acutangulé.

acute [ə'kju:t], *a.* **1.** (*a*) (angle) aigu; (pointe) aiguë; *Bot:* (*of leaf*) terminé en pointe aiguë; (*b*) *Gram:* **a. accent,** accent aigu. **2.** (*a*) (son) aigu; (douleur) aiguë, intense; vive (douleur); **a. remorse,** remords cruels, poignants; (*of anxiety, etc.*) **to become more a.,** s'aviver; (*b*) **a. stage of a disease,** période aiguë d'une maladie; **he was operated on for a. appendicitis,** on l'a opéré à chaud pour l'appendicite; **the present a. crisis,** la crise qui sévit actuellement. **3.** (*a*) **a. ear,** oreille fine, ouïe fine; **a. sight,** vue perçante; (*b*) (esprit) fin, pénétrant, perspicace, vif, subtil, délié, aiguisé; **an a. observer,** un observateur pénétrant; **an a. businessman,** un homme d'affaires avisé, perspicace.

acute-angled [ə'kju:tæŋgld], *a.* acutangulé; à angle(s) aigu(s); (triangle) acutangle.

acutely [ə'kju:tli], *adv.* **1.** vivement; intensément. **2.** avec une intelligence aiguisée; avec finesse; finement; avec perspicacité.

acuteness [ə'kju:tnis], *s.* **1.** aiguïté *f* (d'un angle). **2.** (*a*) acuité *f* (d'une douleur, d'un son); intensité *f* (d'une douleur, d'un remords); (*b*) caractère aigu (d'une maladie, d'un accès). **3.** (*a*) finesse *f* (d'ouïe); acuité (de la vision); vivacité *f* (d'un sentiment); (*b*) pénétration *f,* perspicacité *f* (de l'esprit).

acutifoliate [əkjuti'foulieit], *a. Bot:* acutifolié.

acutilobate [əkjuti'loubeit], *a. Bot:* acutilobé.

acuyari palm [æ'kwɑ:ri'pɑ:m], *s. Bot:* acrocomia *m.*

acyanopsia [eisaiə'nopsiə], *s. Med:* acyanopsie *f.*

acyclic [ei'saiklik, -'sik-], *a.* acyclique.

acyl ['eisi:l], *s. Ch:* acyle *m.*

acylate [ˌæsileit], *v.tr. Ch:* acyler.

acylation [æsi'leiʃ(ə)n], *s. Ch:* acylation *f.*

acyloin ['æsiloin], *s. Ch:* acyloïne *f.*

ad [æd], *s. F:* annonce *f*; **to put an ad in the papers,** insérer une annonce dans les journaux; **small ads,** petites annonces.

adactylous [eidæk'tiləs], *a.* adactyle.

adage ['ædidʒ], *s.* adage *m*; maxime *f.*

adagio [ə'dɑ:(d)ʒiou], *adv. & s.* adagio (*m*).

Adam[1] ['ædəm], *Pr.n.m.* Adam; **Adam's apple,** pomme *f* d'Adam; *F:* **Adam's ale,** château *m* la Pompe; vin *m* de grenouilles, sirop *m* de grenouille; **dressed like A. and Eve,** dans le costume du père Adam; **not to know s.o. from A.,** ne connaître qn ni d'Ève ni d'Adam; **the old A.,** le vieil Adam; le vieil homme; **to cast off the old A.,** dépouiller le vieil homme; quitter sa peau; **it's as old as A., it's been there since A. was a boy,** cela remonte au déluge; **the new A.,** le Christ; *Geog:* **Adam's Peak,** pic *m* d'Adam; *Bot: F:* **Adam's fig,** (i) banane *f* des Antilles; (ii) bananier *m* du Paradis, figuier *m* d'Adam; **Adam's flannel,** bouillon-blanc *m*; **Adam's needle,** yucca *m*; *Cu: F:* **A. and Eve on a raft,** deux œufs servis sur un toast.

Adam[2], *Pr.n: Hist. of Arch:* **the A. brothers,** les frères Adam; **A. style,** style *m* des frères Adam (en bâtiment et en meubles); **A. house,** maison construite par les frères Adam.

adamant ['ædəmənt]. **1.** *s. A:* (*a*) diamant *m*; **heart of a.,** cœur *m* de bronze, de pierre; **frame of a.,** corps *m* d'acier; (*b*) aimant *m.* **2.** *a.* dur; inflexible, intransigeant; **he is a. on this point,** sur ce point il est intransigeant, il ne transige pas.

adamantine [ædə'mæntain], *a.* adamantin; **a. spar,** diamant *m* spathique, corindon *m,* spath adamantin; *Dent:* **a. substance,** substance adamantine; *A: & Lit:* **a. chains,** d'infrangibles chaînes; **a. ties,** liens indissolubles; **a. fortitude,** courage indomptable; **a. state.** État invincible.

adamantly ['ædəməntli], *adv.* inflexiblement; avec tenacité; d'une manière intransigeante.

adamantoblast [ædə'mæntoublɑ:st], *s. Anat:* adamantoblaste *m.*

Adamic [æ'dæmik], *a.* adamique.

adamine ['ædəmain], *s. Miner:* adamine *f.*

adamite[1] ['ædəmait], *s. Miner:* adamine *f.*

Adamite[2], *s. Rel.H:* Adamien *m,* Adamite *m.*

Adamitic [ædə'mitik], *a. Rel.H:* adamien.

Adamitism ['ædəmitizm], *s. Rel.H:* adamisme *m.*

Adams-Stokes ['ædəmz'stouks], *Pr.n: Med:* **A.-S. syndrome,** syndrome *m* d'Adams-Stokes, pouls lent permanent.

adansonia [ædən'souniə], *s. Bot:* adansonia *m.*

Adapis ['ædəpis], *s. Paleont:* adapis *m.*

adapt [ə'dæpt]. **1.** *v.tr.* adapter, ajuster, approprier, accommoder (**sth. to sth.,** qch. à qch.); remanier (une œuvre); **to a. (two things) to each other,** coadapter (deux choses); **to a. a novel for the stage,** adapter un roman à la scène; **text adapted from Cicero,** texte d'après Cicéron; **to a. a shed to make a garage,** adapter, reconstruire, un hangar pour en faire un garage; **to a. oneself to circumstances,** s'adapter, s'ajuster, s'accommoder, se conformer, se faire, aux circonstances; **to a. one's language to the circumstances,** approprier son langage aux circonstances; **we must a. ourselves to circumstances,** selon le vent la voile; **to a. oneself to one's company,** s'adapter à, se mettre au diapason de, la compagnie; **he can't a. himself to his audience,** il ne sait pas se mettre à la portée de son auditoire; **the beech adapts itself to any soil,** le hêtre s'accommode de n'importe quel sol. **2.** *v.i.* **you will need time to a. to your new environment,** il vous faudra un certain temps pour vous adapter à votre nouveau milieu; **in adapting to new techniques,** en s'adaptant à de nouvelles techniques; **failure to a.,** refus *m* de s'adapter; **birds a. to urban life,** les oiseaux s'adaptent à la vie des villes.

adaptability [ədæptə'biliti], *s.* faculté *f* d'adaptation; souplesse *f*; **to show great a.,** s'arranger de tout, s'accommoder à toutes les circonstances; *Bot: etc:* **a. to environment,** adaptabilité *f* au milieu.

adaptable [ə'dæptəbl], *a.* **1.** (*a*) adaptable, ajustable, qui peut s'adapter, être adapté (to, à); (*b*) susceptible d'être utilisé (**for,** pour; **to an end,** dans un but). **2. a. person,** personne qui s'arrange de tout, qui s'accommode à toutes les circonstances; **he is very a.,** il sait s'adapter aux circonstances; il s'accommode partout, à toutes les circonstances; il s'arrange de tout; **a. disposition,** tempérament *m* commode; **a. mind,** esprit *m* souple.

adaptation [ædæp'teiʃ(ə)n], *s.* (*a*) adaptation *f,* appropriation *f* (**of sth. to sth.,** de qch. à qch.); **a. of a room to office use,** transformation *f* d'une pièce en bureau; **a. for the stage,** adaptation à la scène; **rate of a.,** vitesse d'adaptation; (*b*) *Biol:* adaptation, finalité *f*; (*c*) *Opt:* **dark a.,** adaptation à l'obscurité.

adaptative [ædæp'teitiv], *a.* qui s'adapte; *Nat.Hist:* adaptatif.

adapted [ə'dæptid], *a.* **a. to sth.,** approprié à, fait pour, qch.; **a. for doing sth.,** propre à faire qch.; **well a. for a**

purpose, bien adapté à un but; qui se prête à un but; **a. to the needs of . . .,** correspondant aux besoins de . . .

adapter, adaptor [ə'dæptər], *s.* **1.** adaptateur *m*, auteur *m* d'une adaptation; remanieur *m*. **2.** intermédiaire *m* de raccord; (*a*) *Ch:* allonge *f* (d'alambic); *El:* adapteur *m*, adaptateur, raccord *m* (de lampe); **hose a.,** raccord de tuyau flexible; *I.C.E:* **sparking-plug a.,** culot *m* pour bougie; **(syringe) a.,** embout *m* (d'une seringue); (*b*) *Phot:* parquet *m* d'adaptation (de l'appareil); **plate a.,** (i) cadre *m* intermédiaire; (ii) châssis-adaptateur *m, pl.* châssis-adaptateurs, de, à, plaques; **lens a.,** bague *f* porte-objectif; (*c*) *Aut:* **bumper a.,** montage *m* pour pare-choc; (*d*) *Cmptr:* **communication a.,** adapteur de communication; **data a. unit,** unité *f* de contrôle et d'adaptation; (*e*) *Rec:* centreur *m*.

adapting[1] [ə'dæptiŋ], *a. Cmptr:* auto-adapteur, -trice.

adapting[2], *s.* adaptation *f*.

adaptive [ə'dæptiv], *a.* adaptif; souple; *Biol:* **a. mechanism,** mécanisme adaptif.

adaptiveness [ə'dæptivnis], *s.* adaptation *f*; **economic a.,** souplesse *f* économique.

adaxial [æd'aksiəl], *a. Bot:* ventral.

add[1] [æd], *v.tr.* **1.** (*a*) ajouter, joindre (**to,** à); **to a. s.o. to a committee,** adjoindre qn à un comité; **if we a. his evidence to that of the others . . .,** si nous joignons son témoignage à celui des autres . . .; **to a. the interest to the capital,** ajouter l'intérêt au capital; **to a. to a building,** faire une addition à un bâtiment; **to a. a piece to one's garden,** agrandir son jardin; **an old house, added to from time to time,** une vieille maison, agrandie à des époques successives; **to a. to s.o.'s difficulties,** ajouter aux embarras de qn; **this measure added to the unemployment,** cette mesure accentua le chômage; **this news adds to our joy,** cette nouvelle augmente, accroît, notre joie, ajoute à notre joie, redouble notre joie; **to a. to s.o.'s beauty,** rehausser la beauté de qn; **added to which,** en outre de quoi; ajoutez que; **(in order) to give an added effect to the scene,** pour rehausser l'effet de la scène; pour corser la scène; **to a. to my work,** par surcroît de besogne; **to a. to my distress . . .,** pour mettre le comble à mon malheur, à mon chagrin . . .; **to a. sth. in,** ajouter, inclure, qch.; faire entrer qch. en ligne de compte; *Mth:* **to a. a nought,** apposer un zéro; *Mus:* **added lines,** lignes *f* supplémentaires; **as an added inducement,** en surcroît, en surplus; (*b*) (*say besides*) ajouter; **he added that . . .,** il ajouta que. . . . **2.** *Mth:* (*a*) **to a. (up, together) ten numbers,** additionner dix nombres, faire la somme, l'addition, de dix nombres; **to a. six to eight,** additionner six avec huit, ajouter six à huit; **if we a. these figures and the others together . . .,** si nous additionnons ces chiffres avec les autres . . .; **to a. up a column of figures,** totaliser une colonne de chiffres; *abs.* **to a. correctly,** additionner correctement; faire des additions justes; calculer juste; (*b*) *v.i.* **the assets a. up to two millions,** l'actif se totalise par deux millions; **the figures don't a. up,** les chiffres sont faux; **the accounts won't a. up,** je n'arrive pas à faire accorder les comptes; *Cmptr:* **to a. short, to a. over,** additionner un chiffre trop faible, trop élevé; *Fig:* **what does it all a. up to?** qu'est-ce que cela signifie? **it just doesn't a. up,** cela n'a ni queue ni tête, ni sens ni raison; **his story just doesn't a. up,** ce qu'il dit ne tient pas debout; **I've tried to make it mean something else but it doesn't a. up any other way,** j'ai essayé d'en trouver une autre interprétation, mais en vain; **the evidence doesn't a. up to much,** l'évidence est peu convaincante, ne vaut pas grand-chose. **3.** *Carp: Needlew: etc:* rapporter (une pièce à une autre).

add[2], *s. Cmptr:* addition *f*; **Boolean a., logical a.,** réunion *f* logique, mélangeur *m*; **false a.,** addition sans report(s); **a. instruction,** instruction *f* d'addition; **a. time,** durée *f* d'addition, temps *m* d'addition; **a. subtract time,** durée d'addition/soustraction.

adda ['ædə], *s. Rept:* scinque officinal, scinque des boutiques.

addax ['ædæks], *s. Z:* addax *m*.

addend ['ædend], *s. Mth:* second nombre (d'une addition); *Cmptr:* cumulateur *m*, second terme (d'une somme); deuxième opérande *f* (d'une addition); nombre à ajouter.

addendum, *pl.* **-a** [æ'dendəm, -ə], *s.* **1.** (*a*) addenda *m*; (*b*) addition *f* (à un livre, etc.); supplément *m*. **2.** *Mec.E:* saillie *f* au delà de la ligne d'engrènement (d'une roue dentée); **a. line, circle,** ligne *f* de couronne, cercle *m* de tête de dent.

adder[1] ['ædər], *s.* **1.** (*pers.*) additionneur, -euse. **2.** (*a*) machine *f* à additionner; additionneuse *f*; (*b*) *Cmptr:* addeur *m*, additionneur; **one-digit a., half a.,** demi-additionneur *m*; **binary half a.,** demi-additionneur binaire; **serial full a.,** additionneur série.

adder[2], *s.* **1.** vipère *f*; **European common a.,** vipère péliade; **horned a.,** vipère cornue, céraste *m*; **deaf a.,** orvet *m*, serpent *m* de verre; **death a.,** acanthophis *m*; **puff a.,** vipère clotho; **banded a.,** bongare bleu; *U.S:* **puffing a., flatheaded a.,** hétérodon *m*; **young a.,** vipereau *m*. **2.** *Ent: F:* **flying a.,** a. **fly,** libellule *f*, demoiselle *f*.

adder-spit ['ædəspit], *s. Bot:* fougère commune, arborescente; fougère à l'aigle.

adder's tongue ['ædəːztʌŋ], *s. Bot:* (*a*) ophioglosse *m* vulgaire, langue *f* de serpent, herbe *f* sans couture; (*b*) érythrone *m*, dent-de-chien *f, pl.* dents-de-chien.

adder-subtractor ['ædəsəb'træktər], *s.* additionneur-soustracteur *m, pl.* additionneurs-soustracteurs.

adderwort ['ædəwəːt], *s. Bot:* bistorte *f*.

addible ['ædibl], *a.* (somme, etc.) additionnable (**to,** à).

addict [1] ['ædikt], *s.* (*a*) personne adonnée à (l'opium, etc.); *Med:* intoxiqué, -ée; **a drug a.,** un(e) toxicomane; **morphia a.,** morphinomane; **cocaine a.,** cocaïnomane; **he is a drug a.,** il s'adonne aux stupéfiants; *F:* il se pique; (*b*) *F:* fanatique *m* (du football, de la danse, etc.).

addict[2] [ə'dikt], *v.tr.* (*used in passive*) **to be addicted to drink, etc.,** s'adonner, se livrer, être adonné, être livré, à la boisson, etc.; **to become addicted to vice,** s'abandonner au vice; *Lit:* **addicted to the Muses,** adonné aux Muses.

addiction [ə'dikʃ(ə)n], *s.* (*a*) inclination *f* (**for,** à), penchant *m* (**for,** pour); *Med:* manie *f* pathologique, intoxication *f*; assuétude *f*; **a. to morphia,** morphinomanie *f*; (*b*) dépendance *f* (morphique, barbiturique, cannabique, etc.).

addictive [ə'diktiv], *a. Med:* (drogue) susceptible de provoquer le phénomène de dépendance.

adding ['ædiŋ], *s.* addition *f*; **a. machine,** additionneuse *f*; machine *f* à calculer, à additionner; calculateur *m* mécanique; *Cmptr:* **a. circuit,** circuit additionneur, d'addition; **a. counter,** compteur additif; **a. lister,** additionneuse imprimante.

Addis-Ababa ['ædis'æbəbə], *Pr.n. Geog:* Addis-Abéba.

Addisonism ['ædisənizm], *s. Med:* addisonisme *m*.

Addison's disease ['ædis(ə)nzdi,ziːz], *s. Med:* maladie *f* d'Addison; maladie bronzée.

additament [æd'itəmənt], *s.* addition *f*.

addition [ə'diʃ(ə)n], *s.* **1.** (*a*) addition *f*; ajout *m*; **a. to a law,** addition à une loi; **he has just had an a. to his family,** sa famille vient d'augmenter; **a welcome a. to my salary,** un heureux surcroît d'appointements; un heureux complément de mes appointements; **additions to the staff,** adjonction *f* de personnel; **in a.,** en outre, en sus, de plus, par surcroît, **in a. to sth.,** en plus, en sus, de qch; **in a. to this question,** en dehors de cette question; **in a. to that sum he still owes me . . .,** outre cette somme il me redoit . . .; **in a. to these misfortunes,** pour surcroît de malheur; pour comble de malheur; **to pay sth. in a.,** payer un supplément; (*b*) *Const:* **a. to a building,** rajout *m*, extension *f*, à un bâtiment; (*c*) *Fin:* **a. to the stock,** augmentation *f* de capital (par incorporation de réserves); (*d*) *Cmptr:* **destructive, non-destructive, a.,** addition avec, sans, effacement; **a. circuit,** circuit *m* d'addition; **a. record,** article *m* supplémentaire; adjonction *f*, nouvel article (dans un fichier). **2.** *Mth:* addition; **simple a.,** addition de nombres de même espèce; **compound a.,** addition de nombres complexes; **a. of probabilities,** addition des probabilités. **3.** *attrib. Ch:* **a. compound, product,** composé, produit, additif; **a. agent,** matière *f* d'apport.

additional [ə'diʃənl], *a.* additionnel, supplémentaire; **a. postage,** surtaxe *f*; *Post:* **for each a. 50 gr.,** au-dessus, par 50 gr.; (*taxis, etc.*) **a. charges,** suppléments; *Adm:* **a. tax,** impôt additionnel; supplément d'imposition; *Mch:* **a. port,** lumière *f* auxiliaire; **a. reason,** nouvelle raison, raison de plus; **to put a. work on s.o.,** imposer à qn un surcroît de besogne; **without a. remarks,** sans faire d'autre observation; **to take a. care,** prendre encore plus de soin; *Fin: Com: etc:* **a. investment,** investissement *m* supplémentaire; **a. payment,** supplément; **a. clause,** avenant *m*; *Ins:* **a. security,** nantissement *m*; sûreté *f*; contre-caution *f*; **call for a. cover,** appel *m* de marge; *Cmptr:* **a. character,** caractère spécial.

additionally [ə'diʃənəli], *adv.* en outre (**to,** de); en sus; par addition; en supplément (**to,** de).

additive ['æditiv]. **1.** *a.* additif; **a. agent,** matière *f* d'apport; *Med:* **a. effect,** effet *m* synergique. **2.** *s.* additif *m*, produit *m* d'addition; *Petr:* adjuvant *m*, dope *m*; *I.C.E:* **anti-carbon a.,** additif anti-calamine, anticalaminant *m*; *Rubber Ind:* **vulcanized oil a.,** factice *m*.

additively ['æditivli], *adv.* additivement.

additivity [ædi'tiviti], *s.* additivité *f*.

addle[1] ['ædl], *a. A:* = ADDLED.

addle[2]. **1.** *v.tr.* (*a*) pourrir, gâter, rendre couvi (un œuf); (*b*) *F:* troubler, brouiller (le cerveau, la tête); gâter (une affaire). **2.** *v.i.* (*of egg*) se pourrir, se gâter.

addlebrained ['ædlbreind], *a. F:* écervelé; qui a le cerveau vide, trouble; (esprit) brouillon.

addled ['ædld], *a.* **1.** (œuf) pourri, gâté, couvi. **2.** *F:* (cerveau) trouble, brouillé.

addlehead ['ædlhed], *s. F:* écervelé, -ée; quelqu'un qui a le cerveau vide, trouble; esprit *m* brouillon.

addleheaded [ædl'hedid], *a.* = ADDLEBRAINED.

add-lister ['ædlistər], *s. Com:* caisse enregistreuse (avec colonne de référence).

addorsed [ə'dɔːst], *a. Her:* adossé.

address[1] [ə'dres], *s.* **1.** adresse *f*, habileté *f*, dextérité *f*, savoir-faire *m*. **2.** (*a*) adresse (d'une personne, d'une lettre); *Jur:* **a. for service,** domicile élu; **what is your a.?** où habitez-vous? **of no (known) a.,** sans domicile connu; **business a.,** adresse du siège commercial; **home, private, a.,** adresse privée, personnelle; **to have a good a.,** habiter un quartier chic; **a. plate,** plaque-adresse *f*, *pl.* plaques-adresse; **a. book,** carnet *m* d'adresses; (*b*) *Cmptr:* **base a.,** adresse de base, adresse origine; **absolute a.,** adresse absolue, réelle; **arithmetic a.,** adresse arithmétique; **seek a.,** adresse de recherche; **zero a. instruction format,** format *m* d'instruction sans adresse. **3.** *A: & Lit:* (*a*) abord *m*; **to be of pleasing a.,** avoir l'abord aimable, agréable; **a man of good a.,** un homme à l'abord distingué, qui se présente bien; (*b*) **to pay one's addresses to a lady,** faire la cour à une femme; rechercher une femme en mariage; **to reject s.o.'s addresses,** repousser les avances de qn. **4.** (*a*) adresse (de félicitations, de sympathie); requête *f*, supplique *f* (au roi); (*b*) discours *m*, allocution *f*, conférence *f*, causerie *f*; **to deliver a short a.,** faire, prononcer, une courte allocution. **5. form of a.,** titre *m* (à donner en s'adressant à qn); **forms of a.,** titres de politesse.

address[2], *v.tr.* **1.** (*a*) **to a. a letter to s.o.,** adresser une lettre à qn.; **to a. a ship to s.o.,** consigner un navire à qn.; (*b*) **to a. a letter,** mettre, écrire, l'adresse sur une lettre. **2.** (*a*) **to a. one's prayers to God,** adresser ses prières à Dieu; **to a. reproaches, criticisms, to s.o.,** adresser des reproches, des critiques, à qn; (*b*) **to a. s.o.,** (i) aborder, accoster, qn; (ii) adresser la parole à qn; **he addressed me as 'Colonel,'** il m'a appelé "Colonel;" **I am too young to be addressed as 'Mademoiselle,'** je suis trop jeune pour qu'on m'appelle "mademoiselle;" **to a. oneself to s.o.,** (i) s'adresser à qn; (ii) apostropher qn; (*c*) **to a. a crowd,** haranguer une foule; **he is to a. the meeting,** il doit prendre la parole à la réunion; **when he addresses the House,** quand il parle à la Chambre; **please a. your remarks to the chair** = veuillez vous adresser au président; **to a. s.o. at length,** tenir un long discours à qn; (*d*) *Cmptr:* adresser, accéder à, désigner. **3.** *Golf:* viser (la balle). **4.** *O:* **to a. oneself to a task,** se mettre en devoir d'accomplir une tâche; se mettre à une tâche; entreprendre une tâche; **let us now a. ourselves to the business in hand,** venons-en maintenant à l'affaire qui nous occupe; *A: F:* **he addressed himself to the pie,** il attaqua le pâté.

addressable [ə'dresəbl], *a. Cmptr:* **a. store,** mémoire *f* adressable.

addressed [ə'drest], *a.* (enveloppe) qui porte l'adresse (du destinataire); **please send a stamped a. envelope,** envoyez, s'il vous plaît, une enveloppe timbrée avec votre adresse; *Cmptr:* **a. system,** système adressé.

addressee [ædre'siː], *s.* destinataire *mf*; receveur *m* (d'un télégramme, etc.).

addresser [ə'dresər], *s.* **1.** (*a*) pétitionnaire *m*; (*b*) *O:* **my a.,** la personne qui me parle, qui me parlait. **2.** expéditeur, -trice (d'une lettre, etc.).

addressing [ə'dresiŋ], *s.* (*a*) mise *f* de l'adresse (sur une enveloppe); **a. machine,** machine *f* à adresser; (*b*) *Cmptr:* adressage *m*; **absolute a.,** adressage absolu, réel; **one-ahead, stepped, a.,** adressage à progression automatique avancée; **symbolic a.,** adressage symbolique.

addressless [ə'dreslis], *a.* sans adresse; *Cmptr:* **a. instruction format,** format *m* d'instruction sans adresse.

Addressograph [ə'dresougræf], *s.* (*R.t.m. of machines manufactured by Addressograph Multigraph Corporation*) Adressographe *m*; machine *f* à imprimer les adresses.

adduce [ə'djuːs], *v.tr.* alléguer, apporter (des raisons, des preuves, etc.); produire (un témoin); invoquer, citer (une autorité); **to a. proof,** fournir la preuve; alléguer, apporter, une preuve.

adducer [ə'djuːsər], *s.* celui, celle, qui allègue (des raisons), qui cite (une autorité).

adducible [ə'djuːsibl], *a.* (exemple, etc.) qui peut être allégué, apporté.

adduct[1] [æ'dʌkt], *v.tr. Physiol:* déterminer l'adduction (d'un muscle, etc.).

adduct[2] [ˈædʌkt], *s. Ch:* additif *m.*

adducting [æˈdʌktiŋ], *a. Anat:* (muscle) adducteur.

adduction [æˈdʌkʃ(ə)n], *s.* **1.** allégation *f* (d'une raison); citation *f,* invocation *f* (d'une autorité). **2.** *Physiol:* adduction *f.*

adductive [æˈdʌktiv], *a. Anat:* (muscle) adducteur.

adductor [æˈdʌktər], *s. Anat:* adducteur *m.*

ade [eid], *s. U.S:* boisson fruitée.

Adela [ˈædilə]. **1.** *Pr.n.f.* Adèle. **2.** *s. Ent:* adèle *f.*

Adelaide [ˈædəleid]. **1.** *Pr.n.f.* Adélaïde. **2.** *Pr.n. Geog:* Adélaïde.

Adelidae [æˈdelidiː], *s.pl. Ent:* adélides *m.*

Adelie [ˈædili], *Pr.n. Geog:* **A. Land,** terre *f* Adélie; *Orn:* **A. penguin,** manchot *m* Adélie.

adelite [ˈædilait], *s. Miner:* adélite *f.*

adelomorphic [ædelouˈmɔːfik], **adelomorphous** [ædelouˈmɔːfəs], *a.* adélomorphe.

Adelphi [æˈdelfi], *Pr.n.pl. Lt.Lit:* **the A.,** les Adelphes *m* (de Térence).

Adelphian [æˈdelfiən]. *Rel.H:* **1.** *a.* messalien. **2.** *s.* Messalien, -ienne.

adelphophagy [ædelfouˈfɑːdʒi], *s. Nat.Hist:* adel-phophagie *f.*

adelphous [æˈdelfəs], *a. Bot:* adelphe.

ademption [æˈdemʃ(ə)n], *s. Jur:* ademption *f* (d'un legs) (le légateur ayant déjà fait au bénéficiaire une donation pour les mêmes raisons).

adenalgia [ædiˈnældʒiə], *s. Med:* adénalgie *f.*

adenase [ˈædineiz], *s. Bio.-Ch:* adénase f.

adenectomy [ædiˈnektəmi], *s. Surg:* adénectomie *f.*

Adeni [ˈeidini], *a. & s. Geog:* (natif, -ive, habitant, -ante) d'Aden.

adenia [æˈdiːniə], *s. Med:* adénie *f.*

adenine [ˈædinain], *s. Bio.-Ch:* adénine *f.*

adenitis [ædiˈnaitis], *s. Med:* adénite *f.*

adenocarcinoma [ˈædinoukɑːsiˈnoumə], *s. Med:* adénocarcinome *m,* adéno-cancer *m,* épithélioma *m* adénoïde.

adenofibroma [ˈædinoufaiˈbroumə], *s. Med:* adéno-fibrome *m.*

adenoid [ˈædinɔid], *a. Anat:* adénoïde; *Med:* **a. growths,** *s. F:* **adenoids,** adénomes *m* naso-pharyngiens, végétations *f* adénoïdes.

adenoidal [ædiˈnɔidl], *a.* adénoïdien.

adenoidectomy [ædinɔidˈektəmi], *s. Surg:* adénoïdectomie *f,* adénectomie *f.*

adenolymphocele [ˈædinouˈlimfousiːl], *s. Med:* adénolymphocèle *m.*

adenoma [ædiˈnoumə], *s. Med:* adénome *m.*

adenomyoma [ˈædinoumaiˈoumə], *s. Med:* adénomyome *m,* endométriose *f.*

adenopathy [ædinouˈpæθi], *s. Med:* adénopathie *f.*

adenopharyngitis [ˈædinoufærinˈdʒaitis], *s. Med:* adénopharyngite *f.*

adenophlegmon [ˈædinouˈflegmən], *s. Med:* adénophlegmon *m.*

adenosarcoma [ˈædinousɑːˈkoumə], *s. Med:* adénosarcome *m.*

adenose [ˈædinous], **adenous** [ˈædinəs], *a. Anat:* glandulaire.

Adephaga [ædiˈfeigə], *s.pl. Ent:* adéphages *m.*

adept [ˈædept]. **1.** *a.* **to be a. in sth., at doing sth.,** être expert, habile, à qch., à faire qch.; être versé dans (une science); connaître qch. à fond. **2.** *s.* adepte *mf*; initié, -ée; expert *m* **(in,** en).

adequacy [ˈædikwəsi], *s.* adéquation *f*; suffisance *f* (d'une récompense, etc.); justesse *f* (d'une expression); congruité *f* (d'une théorie); **to question the a. of . . .,** mettre en doute le bien-fondé de . . .

adequate [ˈædikwət], *a.* **1.** *(a)* adéquat, suffisant (to, à); **a. supply of meat,** quantité suffisante de viande; **production a. to the demand,** production adéquate à la demande; **a. reward,** récompense adéquate, suffisante; **a. help,** aide *f* efficace; **room of a. size,** pièce *f* d'une grandeur raisonnable; **a. idea of . . .,** idée juste, exacte, de . . .; idée adéquate de . . .; *(b)* proportionné (to, à); **a. remuneration for the work carried out,** rémunération proportionnée, correspondant, au travail accompli; *(c)* **my pen is not a. to describe the scene,** ma plume est impuissante à décrire la scène; **I can find nobody a. to the task,** je ne trouve personne (qui soit) à la hauteur de la tâche; *(d)* **this material is scarcely a. for a winter suit,** ce tissu n'est guère approprié à un costume d'hiver; *(e) Pej:* adéquat, acceptable; médiocre; **it can hardly be called a.,** ce n'est guère acceptable; **the play was what the critics call a., meaning inadequate,** les critiques ont décrit la pièce comme acceptable, ce qui veut dire inacceptable. **2.** *Jur:* **a. judge,** juge compétent.

adequately [ˈædikwətli], *adv.* suffisamment, convenablement; en juste proportion; **to reward s.o. a.,** récompenser qn dignement; donner à qn une récompense suffisante; **a. expressible in words,** adéquatement exprimable par des mots; qu'on peut décrire en mots d'une manière raisonnable; *Pej:* **he can hardly be said to do it a.,** on ne peut guère dire qu'il le fait d'une manière acceptable, d'une manière compétente.

adequateness [ˈædikwətnis], *s.* suffisance *f*; justesse *f* (d'une expression, etc.).

adequation [ædiˈkweiʃ(ə)n], *s.* adéquation *f*; équivalence (parfaite).

adermin(e) [ˈædəmin, -main], *s. Bio.-Ch:* adermine *f.*

adfected [ædˈfektid], *a. Mth:* **a. equation,** équation affectée.

adhere [ədˈhiər], *v.i.* **1.** *(of thg)* adhérer, se coller (to, à); **to a. to the tongue, to the lips,** happer à la langue, aux lèvres; **the scab adheres to the wound,** la croûte tient à la plaie. **2.** *(of pers.) (a)* **to a. to a proposal, to a party,** adhérer, donner son adhésion, à une proposition, à un parti; s'attacher à un parti; *(b)* **to a. to one's decision,** persister dans sa décision; s'en tenir à, maintenir, sa décision; **I a. to my statement,** je maintiens mon dire; **to a. to a promise,** observer une promesse; **to a. strictly to a clause,** se montrer irréducible sur un article.

adherence [ədˈhiərəns], *s.* **1.** *(of thg)* adhérence *f* (to, à); happement *m* (à la langue). **2.** *(of pers.) (a)* attachement *m,* fidélité *f* (à un parti); *(b)* accession *f,* adhésion (à un parti).

adherend [ədˈhiərənd], *s.* surface *f* d'adhérence.

adherent [ədˈhiərənt]. **1.** *a. (a)* adhérent (to, à); collé, attaché (to, à); *(b) Nat.Hist:* connexe (to, avec); adhérent; *Bot:* **a. ovary,** ovaire adhérent. **2.** *s.* adhérent *m*; partisan *m*; **to win adherents,** faire secte; **idea that is gaining adherents,** idée *f* qui fait école.

adhering[1] [ədˈhiəriŋ], *a.* = ADHERENT I.

adhering[2], *s.* adhérence *f,* attachement *m.*

adhesion [ədˈhiːʒ(ə)n], *s.* **1.** adhésion *f* (to, à); accession *f* (à un parti); approbation *f* (d'un projet); *Lit:* **to give, signify, one's a. to a plan,** donner son adhésion à un projet. **2.** *Mec: Med: Surg: Bot:* adhérence *f*; **ground a., road a.,** adhérence au sol (des roues, etc.); *Rail:* **a. (weight),** poids adhérent.

adhesive [ədˈhiːsiv]. **1.** adhésif, collant; agglutinant, agglutinateur, -trice; tenace; **a. stamp,** timbre adhésif, mobile; **a. envelope,** enveloppe gommée; **a. tape,** ruban adhésif. **2.** *a.* adhérent; *Mec:* **a. capacity,** pouvoir adhérent; *Ph:* **a. attraction,** attraction *f* moléculaire. **3.** *s.* colle *f,* produit adhérent, adhésif *m.*

adhesiveness [ədˈhiːsivnis], *s.* **1.** adhérence *f,* adhésion *f*; force *f* d'adhésion; tendance *f* à se coller, à s'attacher. **2.** *Psy:* adhésivité.

ad hoc [ˈædˈhɔk], *Lt. adv. & adj. phr.* ad hoc; **ad h. committee,** comité spécial, ad hoc.

ad hominem [ˈædˈhɔminem], *Lt. adj.phr.* **ad h. argument,** argument *m* ad hominem.

adiabat [ˈædiəbæt], *s. Ph: Meteor:* (courbe) adiabatique *f*; **condensation a.,** adiabatique humide; **dry a.,** adiabatique sèche; **pseudo a.,** pseudo-adiabatique *f,* adiabatique saturée; **wet a.,** adiabatique humide.

adiabatic [ædiəˈbætik]. **1.** *a. Ph: Meteor:* adiabatique; **a. curve, line,** courbe *f,* ligne *f,* adiabatique; **a. chart,** diagramme *m* adiabatique; **a. coefficient,** rapport *m* des chaleurs spécifiques; **a. lapse rate,** vitesse *f* (i) de refroidissement adiabatique, (ii) d'échauffement adiabatique; **a. process,** transformation *f* adiabatique; **a. expansion,** détente *f* adiabatique. **2.** *s.* (courbe) adiabatique *f.*

adiabatically [ædiəˈbætik(ə)li], *adv.* adiabatiquement.

adiantum [ædiˈæntəm], *s. Bot:* adiante *m,* capillaire *m* de Montpellier.

adiaphoresis [ædiəfɔˈriːsis], *s. Med:* adiaphorèse *f,* adiapneustie *f.*

adieu [əˈdjuː]. **1.** *int.* adieu! **2.** *s.* **to bid s.o. a.,** dire adieu *m,* faire ses adieux, à qn; **to make, take, one's adieu(s),** faire ses adieux.

ad infinitum [ˈædinfiˈnaitəm], *Lt.adv.phr.* à l'infini; *F:* **he went on talking ad i.,** il parlait à n'en plus finir.

ad interim [ædˈintərim], *Lt.adv. & adj.phr. Jur:* par intérim; **judgment ad i.,** sentence *f* provisoire; **ad i. copyright,** protection *f* intérimaire d'un ouvrage; **duties ad i.,** intérimat *m.*

adipic [əˈdipik], *a. Ch:* (acide) adipique.

adipocere [ædipouˈsiər], *s. Ch:* adipocire *f.*

adipocerite [ædiˈpɔsərait], *s. Geol:* adipocérite *f.*

adipolysis [ædiˈpɔlisis], *s. Physiol:* adipolyse *f.*

adipopexia [ædipouˈpeksiə], *s. Med:* adipopexie *f.*

adipose [ˈædipous]. **1.** *a.* adipeux; **a. tissue,** tissu adipeux. **2.** *s.* graisse animale.

adiposis [ædiˈpousis], *s. Med:* adipose *f*; adiposité *f*; **a. dolorosa,** adipose douloureuse, maladie *f* de Dercum.

adiposity [ædiˈpɔsiti], *s.* adiposité *f.*

adiposogenital [ædipɔsouˈdʒenitl], *a. Med:* adiposo-génital, -aux.

adit [ˈædit], *s.* **1.** *Min: (a)* galerie *f* (d'accès) à flanc de coteau; *(b)* galerie d'écoulement. **2.** *A: & Lit:* accès *m* d'un lieu; **to have free a.,** avoir libre accès.

aditus [ˈæditəs], *s. Anat:* **a. ad antrum,** aditus *m* ad antrum (de l'oreille).

adjacency [əˈdʒeis(ə)nsi], *s.* **1.** contiguïté *f* **(to a place,** à un lieu); confinité *f* (de deux pays). **2.** *(a)* **a. of a place,** proximité *f,* voisinage immédiat, d'un lieu; *(b)* **a. of two angles,** adjacence *f* de deux angles; *(c) Cmptr:* proximité; **a. matrix,** matrice *f* d'incidence.

adjacent [əˈdʒeis(ə)nt], *a.* (angle, terrain) adjacent; contigu, -uë, attenant (to, à); avoisinant; (pays) limitrophe (to, de); **a. rooms,** chambres contiguës; **a. parts of an estate,** tenants *m* et aboutissants *m*; **to be a. to sth.,** être contigu à qch.; avoisiner qch.; *Jur:* **a. owner,** riverain *m*; *Cmptr:* **a. channel,** voie adjacente; **a. channel interference,** interférence adjacente; **a. vertex,** sommet adjacent; *Sp: F:* **that's very a.,** nous l'avons, vous l'avez, manqué de près.

adjacently [əˈdʒeis(ə)ntli], *adv.* en contiguïté.

adjectival [ædʒikˈtaivl], *a. (a) Gram:* adjectif, adjectival; **a. clause,** proposition adjective; **a. use (of participle, etc.),** emploi adjectif (d'un participe, etc.); *(b) P:O:* **what an a. nerve!** quel sacré culot!

adjectivally [ædʒikˈtaivəli], *adv. Gram:* adjectivement; **present participle used a.,** participe présent adjectivé.

adjective [ˈædʒiktiv]. **1.** *a. (a) (of clause, etc.)* adjectif; *(b) Dy:* (couleur) adjective; *(c) Jur:* **law a.,** procédure *f*; code *m* de procédure. **2.** *s. Gram:* adjectif *m.*

adjectively [ˈædʒiktivli], *adv. Gram:* adjectivement.

adjectivize [æˈdʒektivaiz], *v.tr.* adjectiver; **adjectivized noun,** nom adjectivé.

adjoin [əˈdʒɔin]. **1.** *v.tr. (a) A:* adjoindre **(s.o. to s.o., sth. to sth.,** qn à qn, qch. à qch.); *(b)* avoisiner (un lieu); être contigu à (qch.); toucher, attenir à (qch.); **his house adjoins mine,** sa maison est tout contre la mienne. **2.** *v.i.* **the two houses a.,** les deux maisons sont contiguës, se touchent.

adjoining [əˈdʒɔiniŋ], *a. (a)* contigu, -uë; avoisinant; **house with a. garden,** maison *f* avec jardin y attenant; **garden a. mine,** jardin attenant au mien; **house a. ours,** maison contiguë à la nôtre, qui touche à la nôtre; **meadow a. the river,** prairie attenante (à) la rivière; *(b)* **the a. room,** la pièce voisine.

adjoint [ˈædʒɔint], *a. Mth:* adjoint; **a. matrix,** matrice adjointe; **determinant a.,** déterminant adjoint.

adjourn [əˈdʒəːn]. **1.** *v.tr.* **to a. sth. to, until, the next day, for a week, for a fortnight,** ajourner, différer, remettre, renvoyer, qch. au lendemain, à huitaine, à quinzaine; *Jur:* **to a. the case to the following Monday,** renvoyer la cause au lundi suivant. **2.** *v.i. (a) (of meeting, etc.)* (i) s'ajourner **(until,** à); (ii) lever la séance; clore les débats; **to a. over the holidays,** suspendre les séances jusqu'à la fin des vacances; **the meeting adjourned at 3 o'clock,** la séance a été levée à 3 heures; *(b)* (of group of persons); **to a. to the drawing room,** passer au salon.

adjourning [əˈdʒəːniŋ], **adjournment** [əˈdʒəːnmənt], *s. (a)* ajournement *m,* suspension *f* (d'une séance, etc.); *(b)* renvoi *m,* remise *f* (d'une affaire, etc.); **a. for a week,** remise à huitaine.

adjudge [əˈdʒʌdʒ], *v.tr.* **1.** prononcer sur, juger, décider judiciairement (une querelle, une question de droit, etc.). **2. to a. s.o. (to be) guilty,** déclarer qn coupable. **3.** *A:* **to a. s.o. to a penalty, to suffer a penalty,** condamner qn à une peine, à souffrir une peine. **4.** *(a)* **to a. a prize to s.o.,** adjuger, décerner, une récompense à qn; *(b) (of arbitrator)* accorder (une réduction, etc.); **to a. damages,** adjuger, accorder, des dommages-intérêts.

adjudg(e)ment [əˈdʒʌdʒmənt], *s.* jugement *m,* décision *f.*

adjudicate [əˈdʒuːdikeit], *v.tr. & i.* juger, décider (une affaire); prononcer sur (une affaire); rendre un arrêt; rendre une sentence arbitrale; adjuger, décerner (un prix); **to a. a claim,** juger une réclamation; **magistrates entitled to a.,** magistrats compétents; **to a. s.o. (to be) bankrupt,** déclarer, mettre, qn en faillite; **to a. on a question,** prononcer sur une question.

adjudication [ədʒuːdiˈkeiʃ(ə)n], *s.* jugement *m,* décision *f,* arrêt *m*; **a. of bankruptcy,** jugement déclaratif de faillite; **a. of a bankrupt's debts,** répartition *f* des dettes d'un failli.

adjudicative [əˈdʒuːdikətiv], *a. Jur:* (acte, etc.) déclaratif, déclaratoire.

adjudicator [əˈdʒuːdikeitər], *s. (a)* arbitre *m*; juge *m*; *(b) (in musical competitions, etc.)* membre *m* du jury.

adjunct [ˈædʒʌŋkt], *s.* **1.** *(a) (pers.)* adjoint, -ointe, (to, de); auxiliaire *mf*; *(b) (thg)* accessoire *m* (of, de). **2.** *Gram:* complément *m* (du verbe, etc.). **3.** *a.* auxiliaire; *U.S:* **a. professor,** professeur adjoint.

adjunction [əˈdʒʌŋkʃ(ə)n], *s.* adjonction *f* **(of,** de; **to,** à);

Mth: **field obtained by a.,** corps obtenu par adjonction.

adjunctive [ə'dʒʌŋktiv], *a.* accessoire (*to*, à).

adjunctively [ə'dʒʌŋktivli], *adv.* par addition.

adjuration [,ædʒuə'reiʃ(ə)n], *s.* **1.** adjuration *f.* **2.** *Jur:* engagement *m* sous serment.

adjure [ə'dʒuər], *v.tr. Lit:* **to a. s.o. to do sth.,** adjurer, conjurer, supplier, qn de faire qch.

adjust [ə'dʒʌst], *v.tr.* **1.** arranger (une affaire, une querelle); concilier, régler (un différend); vider (une querelle); arrêter, redresser (un compte); *M.Ins:* **to a. an average,** répartir une avarie. **2.** (*a*) ajuster (qch. à qch.); **to a. oneself to new conditions,** s'adapter aux conditions nouvelles; *Mec.E: etc:* **the valve adjusts itself to the ports,** le tiroir épouse la surface; (*b*) régler, ajuster (une balance, les freins, une montre, un compas, etc.); caler (les balais d'une dynamo); monter (un appareil); agencer (les parties d'une machine); étalonner (un instrument); rectifier, centrer (un outil); tarer (une soupape); mettre (un microscope, un moteur) au point; égaliser (la pression, etc.); *Fin:* **to a. prices,** ajuster les prix; **income adjusted for inflation,** revenu réel compte tenu de l'inflation; *Nau:* **to a. the compasses,** compenser, corriger, les compas; (*c*) ajuster, arranger (son chapeau, ses vêtements, etc.); **to a. oneself,** s'ajuster; *esp.* se reboutonner; *Chess:* **to a. a piece,** adouber une pièce. **3.** *v.i.* **to a. (to new conditions, etc.),** s'adapter (aux nouvelles conditions, etc.).

adjustable [ə'dʒʌstəbl], *a.* (*a*) (différend) susceptible d'accommodement; (*b*) *Mec.E: Cmptr: etc:* ajustable, réglable; *Aut:* **a. front seats,** sièges *m* avant réglables; **a. brake cable,** câble *m* de frein de longueur réglable; **a. spanner,** clef anglaise, clef à molette; *Cmptr:* **a. point,** virgule *f* réglable.

adjusted [ə'dʒʌstid], *a. Psy:* **(well) a.,** bien équilibré.

adjuster [ə'dʒʌstər], *s.* **1.** (*pers.*) ajusteur *m*; régleur *m*; metteur *m* au point; *M.Ins:* **average a.,** répartiteur *m* d'avaries; dispacheur *m.* **2.** appareil *m*, organe *m*, de réglage.

adjusting [ə'dʒʌstiŋ], *s.* (*a*) mise *f* au point; réglage *m*, tarage *m*; centrage *m*; **a. screw,** vis *f* de réglage, de rappel, de serrage, de butée; **a. nut,** écrou tendeur, de serrage; *Ind:* **a. shop,** atelier *m* de mise au point; (*b*) *Fin:* **a. of prices,** ajustement *m* des prix.

adjustment [ə'dʒʌstmənt], *s.* **1.** (*a*) ajustement *m* (d'un différend, etc.); arrangement *m* (d'une affaire); règlement *m* (d'un compte, etc.); **to bring about an a.,** amener un accommodement, une entente; *M.Ins:* **average a.,** répartition *f* d'avaries; dispache *f*; (*b*) adaptation *f*; **period of a.,** période *f* d'adaptation; **time a.,** ajustement chronologique; **trend a.,** ajustement au trend; **a. for stock valuation,** ajustement pour plus-value des stocks. **2.** ajustement (d'une balance); rectification *f* (d'un outil, d'un instrument); réglage *m* (d'un mécanisme); tarage *m* (d'une soupape); mise *f* au point (d'un microscope, etc.); *Nau:* compensation *f*, correction *f* (des compas); *El.E:* calage *m* (des balais); **rough a., coarse a.,** réglage approximatif; **final a.,** mise au point; **fine a.,** réglage de précision; *Mec.E: etc:* **out of a.,** déréglé, décalé.

adjustor [ə'dʒʌstər], *s.* = ADJUSTER.

adjutage ['ædʒutidʒ], *s. Hyd.E:* ajutage *m.*

adjutancy ['ædʒətənsi], *s. Mil:* fonctions *fpl* de capitaine adjudant major, de capitaine adjoint.

adjutant ['ædʒətənt], *s.* **1.** *Mil:* (i) capitaine *m* adjudant major, *F:* le major; (ii) officier adjoint; *Artil:* **a. officer,** lieutenant adjoint; **garrison a.,** adjudant *m* de garnison; **a. general,** adjudant général. **2.** *Orn:* **a. (stork),** marabout *m* des Indes, *F:* adjudant *m.*

adjuvancy ['ædʒuvənsi], *s. Lit:* aide *f*, secours *m.*

adjuvant ['ædʒuvənt]. **1.** *A:* (*of pers.*) (*a*) *a.* auxiliaire; (*b*) *s.* auxiliaire *m*, adjuteur *m*, aide *m.* **2.** *a.* & *s. Med: Ch: etc.* adjuvant (*m*).

Adlerian [æd'leəriən], *a. Psy:* **A. psychologists,** psychologues adlériens.

ad lib ['æd'lib], *adv.phr. F:* à volonté; (*of food, drink*) à discrétion.

ad-lib[1] ['æd'lib], *v.i.* & *tr.* **(ad-libbed, ad-libbing)**; *F:* improviser.

ad lib[2], *a. F:* improvisé.

ad-libber ['æd'libər], *s. F:* improvisateur, -trice.

ad-libbing ['æd'libiŋ], *s. F:* improvisation *f.*

ad libitum ['æd'libitəm], *Lt. adv.phr.* à volonté; à discrétion.

adman, *pl.* **-men** ['ædmæn, -men], *s. F:* publicitaire *m.*

admass ['ædmæs], *s. F:* le grand public.

admeasure [æd'meʒər], *v.tr. Jur:* effectuer un partage; partager (un legs, une propriété, parmi les héritiers).

admeasurement [æd'meʒəm(ə)nt], *s. Jur:* **1.** partage *m* (de terrains communs, etc.). **2.** mesurage *m*, action *f* de mesurer (un terrain, etc.).

Admetus [æd'mi:təs], *Pr.n.m. Gr.Lit:* Admète.

admin [əd'min], *s. F:* administration *f.*

adminicle [æd'minikl], *s. Jur:* adminicule *m.*

administer [əd'ministər], *v.tr.* (*a*) administrer, régir (un pays); administrer, gérer (des affaires, des biens); appliquer (les lois); **to a. justice,** dispenser, rendre, la justice; **judges a. the laws,** les juges sont les organes de la loi; (*b*) **to a. the last sacraments, a remedy, to s.o.,** administrer les derniers sacrements, un médicament, à qn; **to a. an oath, the oath, to s.o.,** faire prêter serment à qn; assermenter qn; **to a. a rebuke to s.o.,** faire, adresser, une réprimande à qn; (*c*) **administered price,** prix administré, imposé.

administrable [əd'ministrəbl], *a.* qui peut être administré.

administrant [əd'ministrənt], *s.* administrateur, -trice.

administrate [əd'ministreit], *v.tr.* = ADMINISTER.

administration [ədmini'streiʃ(ə)n], *s.* **1.** (*a*) administration *f*, gestion *f* (des affaires, d'une fortune, etc.); régie *f* (d'une succession, etc.); (*b*) *Jur:* curatelle *f* (des biens d'un mineur); (*c*) *Jur:* **letters of a.,** lettres *f* d'administration (désignant un administrateur à la succession d'un défunt intestat); **to take out letters of a.,** se faire nommer administrateur de la succession; (*d*) administration (de la justice, des sacrements, d'un remède); **after the a. of the oath,** après que (le témoin, etc.) eut prêté serment; après la prestation de serment; (*e*) *Mil:* **a. officer,** officier *m* d'administration. **2.** *coll.* **the A.,** l'administration, le gouvernement, le ministère.

administrative [əd'ministrətiv], *a.* administratif; **a. unit,** circonscription administrative; **a. details,** détails *m* d'ordre administratif; *Ind:* **a. expenses,** dépenses *f* de direction; frais *m* d'administration; (*in civil service*) **the a. grade,** les fonctionnaires supérieurs; *Cmptr:* **a. data processing,** informatique *f* de gestion, traitement *m* de l'information en gestion; **a. information,** information *f* de gestion.

administratively [əd'ministrətivli], *adv.* administrativement.

administrator [əd'ministreitər], *s.* **1.** administrateur *m*; gérant *m* (d'une entreprise); gestionnaire *m.* **2.** *Jur:* curateur *m* (des biens d'un mineur, etc.); conseil *m* judiciaire (d'un prodigue); **a. to child unborn,** curateur au ventre; **a. of an estate,** administrateur d'une succession.

administratorship [əd'ministreitəʃip], *s.* gestion *f*, gérance *f*, administration *f*; *Jur:* curatelle *f* (des biens d'un mineur); **during his a.,** pendant, sous, son administration.

administratrix, -trices [əd'ministreitriks, -trisi:z], *s.f.* **1.** administratrice; gestionnaire. **2.** *Jur:* curatrice (des biens d'un mineur, etc.).

admirable ['ædmərəbl], *a.* admirable, excellent, parfait; **a. in quality,** admirable par la qualité.

admirably ['ædmərəbli], *adv.* admirablement; **he succeeded a.,** il a réussi à merveille; **a. suited to sth.,** éminemment propre à qch.

admiral ['ædmərəl], *s.* **1.** (*a*) (i) amiral *m*; (ii) vice-amiral *m* d'escadre; **A. Nelson,** l'amiral Nelson; **Lord High A.,** (ancien titre du) chef suprême de la Marine (aujourd'hui tenu par le souverain britannique); **admiral's bridge,** pont *m* de majorité, de l'amiral; **A. Superintendant (of dockyard),** major-général *m*, commandant *m* (d'arsenal); *Nau: F:* **to broach, tap, the a.,** faire un piquage de fût; (*b*) commandant en chef (d'une flotte marchande). **2.** *Ent:* **red a.,** vulcain *m*; **white a.,** petit sylvain.

admiral shell ['ædmərəlʃel], *s. Conch:* amiral *m*, amadis *m.*

admiralty ['ædm(ə)rəlti], *s.* **1.** (*a*) *Hist:* **the A.** = le Ministère de la Marine; **First Lord of the A.** = Ministre *m* de la Marine; (*b*) **A. Board** = division navale du ministère de la Défense; **court of A.,** tribunal *m* maritime. **2.** *Poet:* maîtrise *f* des mers. **3.** *Geog:* **The A. Islands,** les îles de l'Amirauté; **A. Island** (*British Columbia*), île de l'Amirauté.

admiration [ædmə'reiʃ(ə)n], *s.* (*a*) admiration *f* (**of, for,** pour); **to fill s.o. with a.,** remplir qn d'admiration, émerveiller qn; **to stand in a. before s.o., to be lost in a. of s.o.,** être en admiration devant qn; **to be struck with a.,** être saisi d'admiration; tomber en admiration; **to cry out in a.,** crier merveille; **to look at s.o. with a.,** regarder qn avec admiration; **note of a.,** point admiratif; (*b*) **to be the a. of everyone,** être, faire, l'admiration de tous.

admirative ['ædmərətiv], *a.* admiratif.

admire [əd'maiər], *v.tr.* **1.** admirer; **to a. a woman,** admirer une femme; **to a. oneself in a glass,** se mirer dans une glace. **2.** exprimer son admiration de (qch.); **don't forget to a. the baby,** n'oubliez pas de vous extasier devant le bébé; *Iron: F:* **I a. your cheek!** vous avez du toupet! **3.** *U.S: Dial:* désirer (faire qch.); **I'd a. to see . . .,** je voudrais bien voir. . . .

admirer [əd'maiərər], *s.* (*a*) admirateur, -trice; (*b*) *O:* adorateur *m* soupirant *m* (d'une femme); **faithful a.,** chevalier servant.

admiring [əd'maiəriŋ] (regard, ton, etc.) admiratif.

admiringly [əd'maiəriŋli], *adv.* avec admiration, admirativement.

admissibility [ədmisi'biliti], *s.* admissibilité *f* (d'une preuve, etc.); *Jur:* recevabilité *f* (d'un pourvoi, d'un témoignage).

admissible [əd'misibl], *a.* (*a*) (idée, projet) admissible; *Jur:* (pourvoi) recevable; **a. hypothesis,** hypothèse *f* admissible; (*b*) *Mec.E: etc:* **a. play,** jeu permis, admis.

admission [əd'miʃ(ə)n], *s.* **1.** (*a*) admission *f*, accès *m* (à une école, à un emploi, etc.); **to gain a. to a society,** se faire recevoir dans une société; obtenir l'entrée d'une société; **to gain a. to s.o., to a place,** trouver accès auprès de qn; se faire admettre dans un endroit; **to have free a. to a theatre,** avoir son entrée libre à un théâtre; **a. free,** entrée libre; accès gratuit; **a. to the stalls is 50 fr.,** le prix des fauteuils est de 50 fr.; (*b*) *Cust:* **free a.,** admission en franchise; **temporary a.,** admission temporaire. **2.** (*a*) admission, acceptation *f* (d'un argument, d'une preuve); (*b*) *Jur:* reconnaissance *f* (d'un fait allégué); confession *f* (d'un crime, etc.); aveu *m*; **to make full admissions (of guilt),** faire des aveux complets; avouer tout; **to make admissions,** faire des aveux; admettre certains faits; **by, on, his own a.,** de son propre aveu. **3.** *Mch: I.C.E:* admission, adduction *f*, introduction *f*, entrée *f*, arrivée *f*, aspiration *f* (de la vapeur, des gaz, etc.); injection *f* (de l'eau); **retarded, late, a.,** retard *m* à l'admission; **a. pipe,** tuyau *m*, conduite *f*, d'amenée; **a. valve,** soupape *f* d'admission; *I.C.E:* **a. stroke,** course aspirante; **a. port,** lumière *f* d'admission.

admit [əd'mit], *v.* **(admitted; admitting) 1.** *v.tr.* (*a*) admettre (qn à qch., dans un endroit); laisser entrer (qn); livrer passage à (qn); **I gave orders that he was not to be admitted,** je lui ai consigné ma porte; **children, dogs, not admitted,** les enfants ne sont pas admis; il est défendu d'entrer avec des chiens; **a. bearer,** laissez passer le porteur de la présente; laissez passer; **the key admits one to the garden,** la clé donne entrée au jardin; **he was admitted to hospital,** il a été admis à l'hôpital; **to a. s.o. to one's friendship,** admettre qn dans son intimité; **to be admitted to the Academy,** entrer à l'Académie; (*b*) **the windows do not a. enough air,** les fenêtres ne laissent pas entrer assez d'air; (*c*) **harbour that admits large ships,** port qui reçoit de grands bâtiments; (*d*) admettre (une vérité, des excuses); consentir (un fait); reconnaître (un principe, sa faute); convenir de (ses torts); concéder (qu'on a tort); **I a. receipt of your letter, I a. receiving your letter,** je reconnais avoir reçu votre lettre; **it must be admitted that . . .,** il faut reconnaître que + *ind*; **it is generally admitted that . . .,** on admet, on reconnaît, généralement que . . .; on s'accorde à reconnaître que . . .; **everyone admits that . . .,** il est certain, de l'aveu de tout le monde, que . . .; **I a. that you are right,** j'admets, je conviens, que vous avez raison; **no one would a. having done it,** personne ne reconnaissait, n'avouait, l'avoir fait; **to a. one's guilt,** se reconnaître, s'avouer, coupable; faire des aveux; avouer; **I was wrong, I a.,** j'ai eu tort, j'en conviens, je n'en disconviens pas, je l'avoue; **I do not a. that it is so,** je me refuse à admettre cela; **I had to a. to myself that . . .,** j'ai dû m'avouer à moi-même que . . .; (*e*) **to a. a claim,** faire droit à, accueillir, une réclamation. **2.** *v.ind.tr.* **his conduct admits of no excuse, of no explanation,** sa conduite est sans excuse, est inexplicable; **it admits of no doubt,** cela ne souffre aucun doute; **the passage admits of several interpretations,** le passage admet, est susceptible de, plusieurs interprétations; **a jet aircraft does not a. of careless handling,** un avion à réaction ne peut pas être manœuvré à la légère.

admittable [əd'mitəbl], *a.* admissible (dans un endroit).

admittance [əd'mit(ə)ns], *s.* **1.** permission *f* d'entrer; entrée *f* (**to,** dans); accès *m* (à un endroit, auprès de qn); **to give s.o. a.,** laisser entrer qn; admettre qn; **to gain, get, a. to a place,** parvenir à entrer dans un lieu; **to refuse s.o. a.,** refuser de laisser entrer qn; **he was denied, refused, a.,** on ne voulut pas le laisser entrer; **no a. (except on business),** entrée interdite, défense *f* d'entrer dans les chantiers, *Nau:* défense de monter à bord (sauf pour affaires). **2.** *El:* admittance *f*; *Cmptr:* **transfer a.,** admittance de transfert.

admitted [əd'mitid], *a.* **1.** admis; **a. custom,** usage admis. **2. a. truth,** vérité reconnue, avouée; **an a. thief,** un voleur reconnu pour tel; un voleur avéré.

admittedly [əd'mitidli], *adv.* **a. incorrect,** reconnu (pour, comme) incorrect; **the country is a. badly governed,** le pays de l'aveu général est mal gouverné; **he is a. a socialist,** (i) il est socialiste et il ne s'en cache pas; (ii) il est exact que c'est un socialiste; **he's a bad lot, a., but how charming!** c'est un mauvais garçon, il est vrai, mais si charmant!

admix [əd'miks]. 1. *v.tr.* **to a. sth. with sth.,** mélanger qch. avec qch. 2. *v.i.* (*of substances*) se mélanger.

admixture [əd'mikstjər], *s.* 1. mélange *m*; dosage *m*. 2. *Pharm:* (ad)mixtion *f*; **water with an a. of alcohol,** eau additionnée d'alcool. 3. *Const:* (*in concrete, plaster*) additif *m*.

admonish [əd'mɔniʃ], *v.tr.* 1. (*a*) admonester, reprendre (qn); faire une remontrance, des remontrances, à (qn); (*b*) *A:* **to a. s.o. to do sth.,** exhorter qn à faire qch. 2. *A:* (*a*) **to a. s.o. of a danger,** avertir, prévenir, qn d'un danger; (*b*) **to a. s.o. of an obligation, of an occurrence,** rappeler à qn une obligation, instruire qn d'un événement.

admonisher [əd'mɔniʃər], *s.* admoniteur, -trice.

admonishing [əd'mɔniʃiŋ], **admonishment** [əd'mɔniʃmənt], **admonition** [ædmə'niʃ(ə)n], *s.* 1. remontrance *f*, admonestation *f*, réprimande *f*, blâme *m*; *Ecc:* admonition *f*, exhortation *f*. 2. *Adm:* avertissement *m*.

admonitive [əd'mɔnitiv], *a.* = ADMONITORY.

admonitor [əd'mɔnitər], *s.* = ADMONISHER.

admonitory [əd'mɔnit(ə)ri], *a.* (lettre, etc.) (i) de remontrances, (ii) *A:* d'avertissement.

adnate ['ædneit], *a. Nat.Hist:* adné, adhérent, coadné.

ad nauseam [æd'nɔːsiæm], *Lt.adv.phr.* à satiété; jusqu'à la nausée.

adnexa [æd'neksə], *s.pl. Biol:* annexes *f, esp.* annexes embryonnaires; **a. oculi,** glandes lacrymales; **a. uteri,** oviductes *mpl* et ovaires *mpl*.

adnexectomy, [ædneks'ektəmi], *s. Surg:* salpingo-ovariectomie *f*.

adnexitis [ædneks'aitis], *s. Med:* annexite *f*.

adnexopexy [ædneksou'peksi], *s. Surg:* salpingo-ovariopexie *f*.

adnominal [æd'nɔminl], *a. Ling:* adnominal.

ado [ə'duː], *s.* 1. agitation *f*, activité *f*, bruit *m*, embarras *m*, affairement *m*; **without (any) more a., without further a.,** sans plus de façons, de cérémonie, d'embarras; sans autre forme de procès; **she signed the contract without further a.,** elle signa le contrat sans plus (faire) de difficulté; **he made no more a., but . . .,** il n'hésita plus, mais . . .; **to make much a. about nothing,** (i) faire beaucoup de bruit pour rien; faire bien du tapage pour peu de chose; (ii) faire un crime à qn d'une bagatelle. 2. *O:* difficulté *f*, peine *f*; **he had much a. to get through the work,** il eut du mal, de la peine, à venir à bout du travail.

adobe [ə'doub(i)], *s. Const:* adobe *m* (brique ou maison).

adolesce [ædə'les], *v.i. F: esp. U.S:* être adolescent.

adolescence [ædə'les(ə)ns], *s.* adolescence *f*; *Geog:* jeunesse *f* (d'un cycle d'érosion).

adolescent [ædə'les(ə)nt], *a. & s.* adolescent, -ente.

adolescently [ædə'lesəntli], *adv.* comme un adolescent, une adolescente.

Adolphus [ə'dɔlfəs], *Pr.n.m.* Adolphe.

Adonia [ə'douniə], *s. Gr.Civ:* Adonies *fpl*.

Adonian [ə'douniən], **Adonic** [ə'dɔnik], *a.* adonien, adonique; *Pros:* **A. verse,** *s.* **Adonic,** adonien *m*, adonique *m*.

adonidin [ə'dɔnidin], *s. Pharm:* adonidine *f*.

Adonis [ə'dounis]. 1. (*a*) *Pr.n.m. Myth:* Adonis; (*b*) *s.m.* Adonis; *O:* **he's a regular A.,** c'est un véritable Adonis. 2. *s. Ent:* adonis *m. Bot:* adonis *f*.

adonite ['ædənait], **adonitol** [ə'dɔnitɔl], *s. Ch:* adonite *f*, adonitol *m*.

adonize ['ædənaiz], *v.i. A: & Lit:* faire l'Adonis.

adopt [ə'dɔpt], *v.tr.* 1. adopter (un enfant); **to a. s.o. as one's son,** adopter qn pour fils. 2. (*a*) adopter (une ligne de conduite); choisir, embrasser (une carrière); **the course to a.,** la marche à suivre; **to a. measures, a method,** instaurer des mesures, une méthode; **to a. a view, advice,** se rallier à une opinion; suivre un conseil; **the Council is sure to a. this proposal,** il n'est pas douteux que le Conseil adopte, fera sienne, cette proposition; **to a. a patronizing tone,** prendre un ton protecteur; (*b*) approuver (les minutes d'un conseil d'administration); (*c*) **this road should have been adopted,** cette rue aurait dû être prise en charge par la municipalité.

adoptability [ə'dɔptəbiliti], *s.* aptitude *f* pour être adopté.

adoptable [ə'dɔptəbl], *a.* adoptable.

adopted [ə'dɔptid], *a.* (*a*) (enfant, mot) adopté; **a. son,** fils adoptif; **my a. country,** mon pays d'adoption; (*b*) **a. road,** rue prise en charge par la municipalité.

adoptee [ədɔp'tiː], *s. Jur:* adopté, -ée.

adopter [ə'dɔptər], *s.* 1. *Jur:* adoptant, -ante (d'un enfant, etc.). 2. **of an opinion,** personne *f* qui se range à une opinion.

adoptianism, adoptionism [ə'dɔpʃənizm], *s. Rel.H:* adoptianisme *m*.

adoption [ə'dɔpʃ(ə)n], *s.* 1. adoption *f* (d'un enfant, d'une coutume, d'un pays); **I am an American by a.,** je suis américain d'adoption. 2. (*a*) adoption (d'une loi); choix *m* (d'une carrière); **the a. of this opinion, of this theory, would involve . . .,** pour qui se rallierait à cette opinion, à cette théorie, cela entraînerait . . .; (*b*) adoption (des minutes à un conseil d'administration, etc.); (*c*) **a. of a street (by the council),** prise *f* en charge d'une rue (par la municipalité).

adoptionist [ə'dɔpʃənist], *a. & s. Rel.H:* adoptien, -ienne.

adoptive [ə'dɔptiv], *a.* 1. (enfant, père) adoptif. 2. (langue) qui adopte facilement des termes étrangers.

adoptively [ə'dɔptivli], *adv.* par adoption.

adorable [ə'dɔːrəbl], *a.* adorable.

adorableness [ə'dɔːrəblnis], *s.* nature *f*, caractère *m*, adorable (de qn, de qch.).

adorably [ə'dɔːrəbli], *adv.* adorablement; à ravir.

adoral [æ'dɔːrəl], *a. Z:* adoral, -aux.

adoration [ædə'reiʃ(ə)n], *s.* adoration *f*; **the a. of the Cross,** l'adoration de la Croix; **Act of A.,** acte d'adoration; **his a. for my cousin,** l'amour, le culte, qu'il portait à ma cousine.

adore [ə'dɔːr], *v.tr.* adorer (qn, qch.); aimer (qn) à l'adoration; **the adorer and the adored,** l'adorateur, -trice, et l'adoré(e); **I a. riding,** j'adore monter a cheval.

adorer [ə'dɔːrər], *s.* adorateur, -trice; **her adorers,** ses adorateurs; ses soupirants; *Lit:* **he has long been her a.,** voilà longtemps qu'il l'adore, qu'il est à ses genoux.

adoretus [ædə'riːtəs], *s. Ent:* adorète *m*.

adoring [ə'dɔːriŋ], *a.* (*a*) adorant; **a. eyes,** yeux adorants; (*b*) (*of pers.*) adorateur, -trice.

adoringly [ə'dɔːriŋli], *adv.* avec adoration.

adorn [ə'dɔːn], *v.tr.* orner, parer, embellir (**with,** de); **the walls were adorned with . . .,** les murs s'agrémentaient de . . ., s'enjolivaient de . . . *O:* **to a. oneself,** se parer (**with,** de); se faire beau, se faire belle; *Hum:* **face adorned with a red nose,** visage (ad)orné d'un nez rouge.

adorning[1] [ə'dɔːniŋ], *a.* embellissant, enjolivant.

adorning[2], *s.* = ADORNMENT I.

adornment [ə'dɔːnmənt], *s.* 1. ornementation *f*. 2. ornement *m*, parure *f*. *O:* **in all her adornments,** dans tous ses atours.

adpressed [æd'prest], *a. Bot:* apprimé.

Adrastus [ə'dræstəs], *Pr.n.m.* Adraste.

adrenal [æ'driːnl]. 1. *a.* surrénal, -aux. 2. *s.* (glande *f*, capsule *f*) surrénale (*f*).

adrenalectomy [ædriːnə'lektəmi], *s. Surg:* surrénalectomie *f*.

adrenalin(e) [ə'drenəlin, -ain], *s.* adrénaline *f*; **a. secretion,** sécrétion *f* adrénalique.

adrenalitis [ædrenə'laitis], *s. Med:* surrénalite *f*.

adrenergic [ædren'əːdʒik], *a. Anat:* adrénergique.

adrenin [ə'drenin], *s. Physiol:* adrénaline *f*.

adreno- [æd'riːnou], *pref.* adréno-.

adrenocortical [ædriːnou'kɔːtikl], *a.* corticosurrénal, -aux.

adrenocorticotrophic [ædriːnoukɔːtikou'trɔfik], *a.* **a. hormone,** hormone adrénocorticotrophique, A.C.T.H.

adrenocorticotrophin [ædriːnoukɔːtikou'trɔfin], *s.* adrénocorticotrophine *f*, hormone *f* adrénocorticotrophique.

adrenolytic [ædriːnou'litik], *a. Med:* adrénolytique.

adret ['ædret], *s. Geog:* adret *m*.

Adrian ['eidriən], *Pr.n.m.* Adrien.

Adrianople [eidriə'noupl], *Pr.n. Geog: A:* Andrinople (*now*) Edirne; **A. red,** rouge *m* d'Andrinople.

Adriatic [eidri'ætik], *a. Geog:* **the A. Sea,** *s.* **the Adriatic,** la mer Adriatique, l'Adriatique *f*; **the A. coast,** le littoral de l'Adriatique.

adrift [ə'drift], *adv. Nau:* à la dérive; (*of ship*) **to run, go, a.,** aller à la dérive; dériver; **to break a.,** rompre ses amarres; partir en dérive; **to be a.,** être en dérive, à l'abandon; *F: O:* **you are all a.,** vous êtes loin du compte; vous divaguez! **I am all a.,** je ne m'y reconnais plus; **to turn a vessel a.,** abandonner, laisser aller, un navire à la dérive; *F:* **to turn s.o. a.,** abandonner qn; renvoyer qn; mettre qn sur le pavé; **he was turned a. in the world,** il fut abandonné à ses propres ressources; il fut lâché dans le monde; **to cut a boat a.,** couper l'amarre; laisser aller un bateau à la dérive; **to cut oneself a. from s.o.,** rompre avec qn; se séparer de qn.

adroit [ə'drɔit], *a.* (discours) adroit; (politique, personne) adroite, habile.

adroitly [ə'drɔitli], *adv.* adroitement, habilement.

adroitness [ə'drɔitnis], *s.* adresse *f*, dextérité *f*; **his a. in getting out of a difficulty,** son adresse à se tirer d'une difficulté.

adscititious [ˌædsi'tiʃəs], *a. Lit:* adventice; surajouté.

adscript ['ædskript], *a. Ling:* **iota a.,** iota adscrit.

adsorb [æd'sɔːb], *v.tr. Ph:* adsorber.

adsorbable [æd'sɔːbəbl], *a. Ch: Ph:* qui peut être adsorbé.

adsorbate [æd'sɔːbeit], *s. Ch: Ph:* adsorbat *m*.

adsorbent [æd'sɔːb(ə)nt], *a. & s. Ch: Ph:* adsorbant (*m*).

adsorption [æd'sɔːpʃ(ə)n], *s. Ch: Ph:* adsorption *f*.

adularia [ædju'lɛəriə], *s. Miner:* adulaire *f*.

adulate ['ædjuleit], *v.tr. Lit:* aduler, flatter, flagorner.

adulation [ædju'leiʃ(ə)n], *s. Lit:* adulation *f*, flatterie *f*, flagornerie *f*.

adulator ['ædjuleitər], *s. Lit:* adulateur, -trice; louangeur, -euse.

adulatory ['ædjuleitəri], *a. Lit:* adulateur, -trice; adulatif; louangeur, -euse.

Adullam [ə'dʌləm], *Pr.n. B:* Hadullam; **the cave of A.,** (i) la caverne d'Hadullam, (ii) *Pol: Hist: F:* = **the Adullamites.**

Adullamite [ə'dʌləmait], *s.* 1. *B.Lit:* Hadullamite *mf*. 2. *pl. Pol.Hist: F:* **the Adullamites,** les dissidents *m* du parti libéral (1866).

adult ['ædʌlt, ə'dʌlt]. 1. *s.* adulte *mf*. 2. *a.* adulte; **a. baptism,** baptême *m* des adultes; **a. education,** enseignement *m* des adultes; **a. behaviour,** comportement *m* adulte; adultisme *m*; **a serious a. love affair,** un amour sérieux et adulte.

adulterant [ə'dʌltərənt], *a. & s.* adultérant (*m*).

adulterate[1] [ə'dʌltərət], *a. Lit:* 1. (*of substance*) adultéré, falsifié, frelaté, sophistiqué. 2. = ADULTEROUS.

adulterate[2] [ə'dʌltəreit], *v.tr.* adultérer (une substance); altérer, falsifier (les monnaies); frelater, sophistiquer, frauder (du vin, du lait); altérer (de la nourriture); corrompre (une langue); **adulterated milk,** lait additionné d'eau.

adulterating [ə'dʌltəreitiŋ], *a.* adultérant, altératif.

adulteration [ədʌltə'reiʃ(ə)n], *s.* adultération *f* (des médicaments); altération *f*, falsification *f* (des monnaies); frelatage *m* (des boissons); sophistication *f*, altération *f* (des aliments).

adulterator [ə'dʌltəreitər], *s.* falsificateur, -trice; sophistiqueur *m*, adultérateur *m*, frelateur *m* (d'aliments, etc.).

adulterer [ə'dʌltərər], *s.* adultère *m*.

adulteress [ə'dʌltəris], *s.* (*pers.*) adultère *f*.

adulterine [ə'dʌltərain], *a.* 1. (enfant) adultérin. 2. faux, frelaté; contrefait. 3. *Eng.Hist:* (*of castle, guild*) illicite.

adulterous [ə'dʌlt(ə)rəs], *a.* adultère.

adulterously [ə'dʌlt(ə)rəsli], adv. 1. par adultère. 2. (vivre) en état d'adultère.

adultery [ə'dʌltəri], *s.* adultère *m* (violation *f* de la foi conjugale); **single a., double a.,** adultère simple, double.

adulthood [ə'dʌlthud], *s.* âge *m* adulte.

adulticide [ə'dʌltisaid], *s.* pesticide *m* (qui détruit les insectes adultes).

adultness [ə'dʌltnis], *s.* (*a*) caractère *m* adulte; (*b*) adultisme *m*.

adumbrate ['ædʌmbreit], *v.tr. Lit:* 1. ébaucher, esquisser (un plan, un système). 2. faire pressentir, laisser pressentir, laisser entrevoir (de nouvelles démarches). 3. jeter son ombre sur (qch.); voiler, obscurcir.

adumbration [ædʌm'breiʃ(ə)n], *s. Lit:* 1. ébauche *f*, esquisse *f* (d'un plan, etc.). 2. (*a*) signes précurseurs (d'un événement); (*b*) pressentiment *m*. 3. obscurcissement *m*.

adurol ['ædjurɔl], *s. Ch: Phot:* adurol *m*.

adust [ə'dʌst], *a. A:* 1. brûlé par le soleil; desséché, aduste. 2. (*a*) *Med:* aduste; (*b*) *Lit:* atrabilaire, maussade.

ad valorem ['ædvæ'lɔːrem], *Lt.phr. Com: Ind:* **ad. v. duty,** droit *m* sur la valeur; droit ad valorem, droit proportionnel; **to pay a duty ad v.,** payer un droit sur, d'après, la valeur des marchandises.

advance[1] [əd'vaːns], *s.* 1. (*a*) marche *f* en avant, mouvement *m* en avant, approche *f*; **to check the a. of the locusts,** arrêter la marche des sauterelles; **to make an a.,** avancer; **a. towards sth.,** acheminement *m* à, vers, qch.; *Adm:* **a. in seniority,** majoration *f* d'ancienneté; **to slow down the enemy a.,** ralentir l'avance ennemie; *Mil:* **a. party,** (i) détachement *m* d'avant-garde; (ii) détachement précurseur; **a. guard,** avant-garde *f*; **leading element of the a. guard,** pointe *f* de l'avant-garde; **the a. guard of the drama,** les auteurs dramatiques d'avant-garde; **a. guard Americans think that . . .,** les Américains d'avant-garde pensent que . . .; **a. technology industry,** industrie *f* de pointe; (*b*) *adv.phr.* **in a.,** (i) en avant; (ii) en avance; (iii) d'avance, à l'avance, par avance; (iv) avant la lettre; **distributed in a. of the conference,** distribué avant le congrès; **we must look in a.,** il faut regarder en avant; **to arrive in a.,** arriver en avance; **to arrive in a. of the others,** arriver avant les autres, en avant des autres; **to go off in a. of the party,** partir en avance, en éclaireurs; **to be in a. of one's time,** être en avance sur son temps; devancer son époque; **to pay in a.,** payer d'avance; **to pay a sum in a.,** verser une provision, des provisions; avancer un paiement; **duty payable in a.,** droit exigible d'avance; **fixed in a.,** fixé à l'avance; (prix, etc.) forfaitaire; **to spend one's income in a.,** anticiper sur ses revenus; *Corr:* **thanking you in a.,** en vous remerciant d'avance; avec mes remerciements anticipés; *Th: etc:* **to book in a.,** louer à l'avance; **to book a seat a week in a.,** retenir une place huit jours à l'avance; (*c*) **a. notice,** préavis *m*; **a. payment,** paiement par anticipation; *Publ:* **a. copy,** exemplaire *m* précédant la mise en vente; exemplaire de lancement; **a. proofs, sheets,** bonnes feuilles (de publicité); *For:* **a. cutting,** coupe *f* préparatoire; (*d*) *I.C.E:* **a. of the ignition, of the spark,** avance *f* à l'allumage; **automatic a.,** dispositif *m* automatique d'avance; **to cut down the a.,** réduire l'avance; **a. diagram,** graphique *m* d'avance. **2.** (*a*) avancement *m*, progrès *m*, développement *m* (des sciences, etc.); **there have been great advances in gas turbines,** on a fait des progrès décisifs, de grands pas en avant, dans le domaine des turbines à gaz; *Lit:* **the a. of thought,** le cheminement, le progrès, de la pensée; (*b*) *Cmptr:* = ADVANCEMENT. **3. to make an a., advances, the first advances, to s.o.,** faire une avance, des avances, les premières avances, à, auprès de, qn; faire les premières démarches de politesse ou de réconciliation; **to respond to s.o.'s advances,** répondre aux invites de qn; (*of man*) **to make advances (to a woman),** faire des avances (à une femme); (*of woman*) **to make advances to a man,** provoquer, *F:* aguicher, un homme; faire des coquetteries, des avances, à un homme. **4.** *Com: Fin:* (*a*) avance (de fonds); à-bon-compte *m inv*; à-valoir *m inv*; **to make an a. of a hundred pounds to s.o.,** faire à qn une avance de cent livres; avancer cent livres à qn; **a. account,** compte *m* d'avances; **a. on a contract,** acompte *m* sur contrat; **a. against security,** avance contre garantie; **advances on securities,** prêts *m* sur titres; **standing a.,** avance permanente; **secured advances,** avances contre garanties; **unsecured advances,** avances à découvert, avances sur notoriété; (*b*) augmentation *f* (de prix), renchérissement *m*; hausse *f*; **the general a. in prices,** la hausse, l'augmentation, générale des prix; **there is an a. on wheat,** il y a hausse sur les blés; **to be on the a.,** être en hausse, (*at an auction sale*) **any a.?** qui dit mieux?

advance², *v.tr. & i.*

I. *v.tr.* **1.** (*a*) avancer (le pied, *Chess:* un pion, etc.); (*b*) avancer (l'heure d'un paiement, etc.); *I.C.E:* **to a. the ignition,** mettre de l'avance à l'allumage; **to a. the ignition fully,** mettre toute l'avance; (*c*) avancer (une idée, une opinion); présenter, mettre en avant (une opinion, une observation); risquer (une observation, une objection); alléguer (un prétexte). **2.** (*a*) faire progresser, faire avancer (les sciences, etc.); faire avancer (des troupes jusqu'à la nouvelle ligne); reculer (une frontière); (*b*) *Cmptr:* faire progresser (le compteur); faire défiler (la bande magnétique); faire avancer (le papier sur l'imprimante, la carte dans la piste); (*c*) élever, porter, faire avancer (qn à un grade supérieur); **incident likely to a. his interests,** incident *m* favorable à ses intérêts; (*d*) accélérer (la croissance, le développement, etc.). **3.** augmenter, hausser (le prix de qch.). **4. to a. s.o. money,** avancer de l'argent à qn; **I will a. him £100 on your note of hand,** je lui avancerai cent livres sur un billet de vous, si vous me signez un billet; **the farmers were advanced money for the purchase of cattle,** on avança de l'argent aux éleveurs, on fit aux éleveurs une avance d'argent, pour leur permettre d'acheter du bétail; **sums advanced,** avances *f*; mises *f* hors.

II. *v.i.* **1.** s'avancer (**towards,** vers); (*of troops*) se porter en avant; **to a. on a military objective,** avancer sur un objectif militaire; **he advanced on me (threateningly),** il vint sur moi; **the season is advancing,** la saison s'avance; **to a. to victory,** marcher à la victoire; **to a. two steps, two paces,** faire deux pas en avant; *Mil:* **a. and be recognized!** avance au ralliement! **2.** (*a*) avancer (en âge, dans ses études); *Biol: etc:* évoluer; **the work is advancing,** l'ouvrage avance, fait des progrès; **the flood is advancing,** l'inondation fait des progrès; (*b*) (*of officers, etc.*) recevoir de l'avancement; monter (en grade). **3.** *Fin:* (*of shares, etc.*) augmenter de prix, hausser, monter; **prices are advancing,** les prix sont à la hausse, augmentent.

advanced [əd'vɑːnst], *a.* **1.** (*a*) (poste) avancé; (études, opinions) avancées; **an a. liberal,** un libéral avancé, un ultra-libéral; **an a. book,** un livre d'avant-garde; **a more a. civilization,** une civilisation plus évoluée; **a. economy,** économie développée; **a. country,** pays développé, industrialisé; *Mil:* **a. guard,** avant-garde *f*; **a. party,** (i) détachement *m* d'avant-garde; (ii) détachement précurseur; *Fort:* **a. work,** ouvrage avancé; **to be very a., to hold very a. ideas,** avoir des idées très avancées; (*b*) **a. course,** cours supérieur; cours de perfectionnement; **a. mathematics,** mathématiques supérieures; **the sections in small type are for a. students,** les sections en petits caractères s'adressent aux étudiants déjà avancés; (*c*) *Tchn:* perfectionné; d'avant-garde; **a. technology,** technologie de pointe; *Av.* **a. fanjet,** réacteur *m* à double flux perfectionné. **2.** (*a*) **the night is far a.,** il est tard dans la nuit; **the season is a.,** c'est la fin de saison; (*b*) **he died at an a. age,** il est mort très vieux.

advancement [əd'vɑːnsmənt], *s.* **1.** (*a*) avancement *m* (d'une personne, des sciences); progrès *m* (des sciences); **to work for the a. of backward races,** travailler au progrès des races arriérées; **economic a.,** essor *m* économique; (*b*) *Cmptr:* progression *f* (du compteur); avancement, défilement *m* (du papier, de la bande). **2.** *Jur:* avance *f* d'hoirie (à un enfant).

advancer [əd'vɑːnsər], *s.* **1. a. of funds,** avanceur *m* de fonds. **2.** *El:* **phase a.,** avanceur de phase.

advancing [əd'vɑːnsiŋ], *a.* qui s'avance; **a. storm,** orage qui s'avance; **a. economy,** économie progressive.

advantage¹ [əd'vɑːntidʒ], *s.* **1.** avantage *m*; **absolute a.,** avantage absolu; **dubious a.,** avantage contestable; **law of comparative a.,** loi *f* des avantages comparés, comparatifs; **to have the a., of, over, s.o., to gain the a. over s.o.,** avoir, remporter, l'avantage sur qn; l'emporter sur qn; avoir le dessus; *A:* **to take s.o. at a.,** prendre qn au dépourvu; *O:* **you have the a. of me, sir,** à qui ai-je l'honneur de parler, monsieur? **to have the a. of, in, numbers,** avoir l'avantage du nombre; **this article offers the a. of cheapness,** cet article se recommande par son bon marché; **to enjoy many advantages over others,** être fort avantagé par rapport aux autres; **to retain the a.,** garder l'avantage; **I gained little a. from it,** j'en ai eu, j'en ai remporté, peu de profit; **he knows where his a. lies,** il sait où se trouve son intérêt; **to see the a. of a compromise,** reconnaître l'intérêt d'un compromis; **to find it an a. to have done sth.,** se trouver bien d'avoir fait qch.; **this would tend to their a.,** cela leur serait avantageux; ce serait à leur avantage; **you will find it an a. to act as they do,** vous aurez avantage à faire comme eux; **you might with a. apply to . . .,** vous pourriez utilement vous adresser à . . .; **to take a. of sth.,** profiter, abuser, de qch.; tirer avantage, profit, de qch.; **to take a. of s.o.,** abuser de la crédulité, de la bonne volonté, de la naïserie, de qn; exploiter qn; **to take a. of a mistake,** prendre avantage de la faute d'un adversaire; **to take the fullest a. of a success,** exploiter un succès; **he took a. of the fact that everyone was asleep to slip away,** il profita de ce que tout le monde dormait encore pour s'esquiver; **to turn sth. to a.,** tirer parti de qch.; mettre qch. à profit; faire tourner qch. à son avantage; **to make a mistake to one's own a.,** se tromper à son profit; (*of event*) **to turn out to s.o.'s a.,** tourner à l'avantage de qn; profiter à qn; **to show off sth. to a.,** faire valoir qch.; **to show sth. to its best a.,** donner toute sa valeur à qch.; **to show to (great) a.,** faire (très) bonne figure; faire bien; **to lay out one's money to a.,** faire fructifier son argent; **to sell sth. to (good) a.,** vendre qch. à son avantage, avantageusement; **to sell sth. to the best a.,** vendre qch. le plus avantageusement possible; **to dress to the best a.,** s'habiller à son avantage; *Ten:* **a. server,** avantage dedans, au servant; **a. striker,** avantage dehors, au relanceur. **2.** *Mec:* multiplication *f* (d'un levier); **mechanical a.,** bras *m* de levier, effet *m* mécanique.

advantage², *v.tr.* avantager, favoriser (qn, qch.); procurer des avantages à (qn); *A: & Lit:* **what shall it a. you to . . .?** quel profit trouverez-vous à. . . .?

advantageous [ædvən'teidʒəs], *a.* avantageux (to, pour); profitable, utile (to, à).

advantageously [ædvən'teidʒəsli], *adv.* avantageusement; utilement.

advantageousness [ædvən'teidʒəsnis], *s.* avantage *m*, utilité *f*.

advection [æd'vekʃən], *s. Meteor:* advection *f*; **a. fog,** brouillard *m* d'advection.

advective [æd'vektiv], *a. Meteor:* d'advection.

advehent [æd'viːh(ə)nt], *a. Anat:* afférent.

advent ['ædvənt], *s.* **1.** *Ecc:* (*a*) **Advent,** l'Avent *m*; **A. Sunday,** le premier dimanche de l'Avent; **during A.,** pendant l'Avent; (*b*) **the second A.,** le second Avènement. **2.** arrivée *f* (d'une chose importante); venue *f*, apparition *f*, avènement *m* (d'un personnage); **the a. of a new art,** l'avènement d'un art nouveau; **since the a. of the motor car,** depuis l'avènement de l'automobile.

Adventist ['ædvəntist], *s. Rel.H:* Adventiste *mf*; **Seventh-day A.,** adventiste du septième jour.

adventitious [ædven'tiʃəs], *a.* **1.** adventice; (*a*) (fait *m*) accessoire; (*b*) accidentel, fortuit; **a. find,** trouvaille accidentelle, découverte fortuite; *Jur:* **a. property,** biens adventifs. **2.** *Bot:* (*a*) (plante) adventice; (*b*) **a. organ,** organe adventif; **a. roots are produced by layering,** on obtient des racines adventives par marcottage.

adventitiously [ædven'tiʃəsli], *adv.* d'une manière adventice; (*a*) accessoirement; (*b*) accidentellement; fortuitement.

adventive [æd'ventiv]. **1.** *a. & s. Nat.Hist:* (*a*) **a. (plant),** (plante) adventice (*f*); (*b*) **a. (root),** (racine) adventive (*f*). **2.** *a. Geol:* **a. cone,** cône adventif.

adventure¹ [əd'ventjər], *s.* **1.** aventure *f*; (*a*) entreprise hasardeuse; **life of a.,** vie *f* d'aventure, vie aventureuse; **a. story,** roman d'aventure(s); (*b*) événement *m* (qui arrive à qn); **after many adventures,** après bien des péripéties; **he told us about his adventures,** il nous a raconté ses aventures. **2.** (*a*) spéculation hasardée; (*b*) *Com: A:* pacotille *f* (embarquée par un marin ou un passager).

adventure². **1.** *v.tr.* aventurer, hasarder, risquer (sa fortune, sa vie, etc.); **to a. an opinion,** risquer, avancer, une opinion. **2.** *v.i.* (*a*) **to a. in(to) a place, (up)on an undertaking,** s'aventurer, se hasarder, dans un endroit, dans une entreprise; (*b*) *A:* **to a. to do sth.,** se hasarder à faire qch.

adventurer [əd'ventjərər], *s.* (*in all senses*) aventurier *m*; homme *m* d'aventures; *Pej:* chevalier *m* d'industrie; intrigant *m*; rastaquouère *m*, aigrefin *m*.

adventuresome [əd'ventjəsəm], *a.* aventureux; téméraire.

adventuresomeness [əd'ventjəsəmnis], *s.* témérité *f*; goût *m* des aventures; esprit *m* d'aventure.

adventuress [əd'ventjəris], *s.f. Pej:* aventurière; intrigante.

adventurism [əd'ventjərizm], *s. Pol: etc:* aventurisme *m*.

adventuristic [ədventjə'ristik], *a. Pol:* aventuriste.

adventurous [əd'ventjərəs], *a.* aventureux; audacieux; **a. man,** homme *m* d'aventures; homme entreprenant.

adventurously [əd'ventjərəsli], *adv.* aventureusement.

adventurousness [əd'ventjərəsnis], *s.* hardiesse *f*, audace *f*; esprit *m* d'aventures.

adverb ['ædvəːb], *s. Gram:* adverbe *m*.

adverbial [əd'vəːbiəl], *a. Gram:* adverbial; **a. phrase,** locution adverbiale.

adverbialize [əd'vəːbiəlaiz], *v.tr.* adverbialiser.

adverbially [əd'vəːbiəli], *adv.* adverbialement; **adjective used a.,** adjectif adverbialisé.

adversary ['ædvəs(ə)ri], *s.* adversaire *mf*; **the A.,** Satan *m*.

adversative [əd'vəːsətiv], *a. Gram:* adversatif.

adverse ['ædvəːs], *a.* **1.** adverse; (*a*) contraire, opposé (to, à); **a. wind,** vent *m* contraire; **to be a. to a policy,** être opposé à une politique; *Jur:* **the a. party,** la partie adverse; (*b*) ennemi (to, de); hostile (to, à, envers); **a. fortune,** fortune *f* adverse; (*c*) défavorable; **a. days,** jours *m* d'adversité; **a. to health,** contraire à la santé; **a. budget,** budget *m* déficitaire; **a. balance,** balance déficitaire; **a. report,** rapport *m* défavorable. **2. the a. slope,** la pente opposée; **the a. page,** la page ci-contre.

adversely ['ædvəːsli, əd'vəːsli], *adv.* (*a*) **to act a. to s.o.,** agir (tout) au contraire de qn; prendre le contre-pied de ce que fait qn; (*b*) **to influence s.o. a.,** exercer une influence défavorable sur qn; **to act a. to s.o.'s interests,** agir contre les intérêts de qn; **to report a. (on s.o., sth.),** faire un rapport défavorable (sur qn, qch.).

adversity [əd'vəːsiti], *s.* adversité *f*; **companions in a.,** compagnons *m* d'infortune; **after many adversities,** après bien des adversités, bien des traverses.

advert¹ [əd'vəːt], *v.i. A: & Lit:* **to a. to sth.,** faire allusion à qch.; parler de qch.; citer qch.; **I shall now a. to another matter,** je vais maintenant vous entretenir d'autre chose.

advert² ['ædvəːt], *s. F:* réclame *f*; annonce *f*.

advertence [əd'vəːt(ə)ns], *s. A: & Lit:* **1.** attention *f* (to, à); **it is right that a. should be had to this fact,** il est bon de tenir compte de ce fait, de prendre garde à ce fait. **2.** = ADVERTENCY.

advertency [əd'vəːt(ə)nsi], *s. A: & Lit:* attention (habituelle); **lack of a.,** inadvertence *f*.

advertent [əd'vəːt(ə)nt], *a. A: & Lit:* attentif, vigilant.

advertently [əd'vəːtəntli], *adv. A: & Lit:* attentivement, avec attention, avec vigilance.

advertise ['ædvətaiz], *v.tr. & i.* **1.** *A:* avertir, informer (s.o. of sth., qn de qch.). **2.** (*a*) (i) (faire) annoncer, faire savoir, faire connaître (un événement dans les journaux); (ii) afficher (une vente, etc.); **to a. in a paper,** (faire) insérer une annonce dans un journal; **to a. for sth.,** chercher qch. par la voie des annonces, par voie d'annonce; demander qch. dans les journaux; **it pays to a.,** la publicité fait gagner de l'argent; **house advertised for sale,** maison *f* dont la mise en vente est (i) annoncée, (ii) affichée; (*b*) faire de la réclame, de la publicité, de la propagande (pour un produit); **to a. widely to launch sth. on the market,** faire appel à la grande publicité pour lancer un article; **(goods) as advertised (on television)** (marchandises *f*) conformes à la spécification publicitaire (télévisée); **to a. oneself or one's work,** se faire valoir; *F:* **you needn't a. the fact,** vous n'avez pas besoin de le crier sur les toits, d'annoncer ça à coups de grosse caisse; (*c*) **the advertised time of departure,** l'heure prévue pour le départ; l'heure du départ indiquée sur l'horaire.

advertisement [əd'vəːtismənt], *s.* **1.** publicité *f,* réclame *f;* **demonstration with a view to a.,** manifestation entreprise dans un but publicitaire; **bad a.,** contre-publicité *f;* **this has perhaps not been a very good a. for such a project,** la publicité d'un tel projet aurait pu être mieux faite; **it's no a. for him,** cela ne lui fait pas de réclame. **2.** (*a*) (*in newspaper*) annonce *f;* **front-page a.,** annonce en première page; **classified advertisements,** petites annonces; **a. manager,** annoncier *m;* **I put an a. in the paper,** j'ai fait passer une annonce dans le journal; (*b*) (*on wall, etc.*) affiche *f.* **3.** *A:* **a. to the reader,** avis *m,* avertissement *m,* au lecteur; préface *f.*

advertiser ['ædvətaizər], *s.* **1.** (*a*) annonceur *m;* (*b*) faiseur *m* de réclame. **2.** *A:* journal *m* d'annonces; feuille *f* d'annonces.

advertising ['ædvətaiziŋ], publicité *f,* réclame *f;* annonces *fpl; attrib.* **a. medium,** organe *m* de publicité; **a. agency,** bureau *m,* agence *f,* de publicité; **a. agent,** agent *m* de publicité; annoncier *m;* **a. manager,** chef *m* de la publicité; **a. sheet,** feuille *f* d'annonces; **a. space,** emplacement réservé à la publicité; **a. account,** budget *m* de publicité; **a. media,** supports *m* publicitaires; **a. schedule,** programme *m* des annonces; **cheapness can be a bad a. point,** le bon marché peut être une contre-publicité.

advice [əd'vais], *s.* (*the pl is rare, except in 3*). **1.** conseil(s) *m* (*pl*), avis *m;* **piece of a.,** conseil; **to give s.o. a sound piece of a.,** donner un bon conseil, un bon avis, *F:* un bon tuyau, à qn; **to ask for a.,** demander des conseils; **to take a. from s.o.; to ask, seek, s.o.'s a.,** prendre conseil de qn; prendre l'avis de qn; demander conseil à qn; **to take s.o.'s a.,** suivre le conseil de qn; se conformer à l'avis de qn; écouter les avis de qn; en croire qn; **to act on s.o.'s a.,** agir selon, sur, le conseil de qn; **to take medical, legal, a.,** consulter un médecin, un homme de loi; **doctor, barrister, who gives a.,** médecin, avocat, qui consulte; **you ought to take a.,** vous devriez consulter; **he will take nobody's a.,** il n'en fait qu'à sa tête; **at, by, on, under, s.o.'s a.,** sur l'avis, le conseil, de qn; suivant les conseils de qn. **2.** avis; *Com:* **a. note, letter of a.,** lettre *f,* note *f,* d'avis; **as per a.,** suivant avis; **payable without preliminary a.,** payable sans préavis, sans avis préalable; **until further a.,** jusqu'à nouvel avis. **3.** *pl.* nouvelles *f,* avis; **we have advices from abroad,** nous avons reçu des informations, des avis, de l'étranger.

advice-boat [əd'vaisbout], *s. Navy: A:* aviso *m,* mouche *f* (d'escadre).

advisability [ədvaizə'biliti], *s.* opportunité *f,* convenance *f;* **a. of doing sth.,** utilité *f* qu'il y aurait à faire qch.

advisable [əd'vaizəbl], *s.* **1.** (démarche) recommandable, conseillable, à conseiller, judicieuse; **it would be a. to lock up these papers,** il serait prudent de mettre ces papiers sous clef; **it would be more a. to see him again,** il serait préférable de le revoir. **2.** opportun, à propos; convenable (for, pour); **it might be a. to . . .,** peut-être conviendrait-il de . . .; peut-être serait-il opportun de . . .; il y aurait peut-être lieu de . . .; **as shall be deemed a.,** ainsi qu'on le jugera utile, ainsi qu'il appartiendra; **he thought it a. to retire,** il crut devoir se retirer; il crut, il jugea, à propos de se retirer; **if you consider it a.,** si bon vous semble; **if you think it a. to wait,** si vous jugez bon d'attendre.

advisableness [əd'vaizəblnis], *s.* = ADVISABILITY.

advise [əd'vaiz], *v.tr. & i.*

I. *v.tr.* **1.** (*a*) **to a. s.o.,** conseiller qn; **to a. s.o. to do sth.,** conseiller à qn de faire qch.; engager qn à faire qch.; **I am advised to wait,** on me conseille d'attendre; **I strongly a. you to . . .,** je vous recommande (instamment) de. . . . **what do you a. me to do?** que me conseillez-vous? **be advised by me,** suivez mes conseils; croyez-m'en; (*b*) **to a. sth.,** recommander qch. (à qn); conseiller une ligne de conduite (à qn); (*c*) **to a. s.o. against sth., against doing sth.,** déconseiller qch. à qn; déconseiller à qn de faire qch.; mettre qn en garde contre qch. **2. to a. s.o. on a question,** renseigner qn sur une question; **to a. on a question,** servir de conseil pour une question. **3.** (*a*) **to a. s.o. of sth.,** avertir, prévenir, instruire, qn de qch., faire part à qn de qch.; mettre qn au courant de qch.; porter qch. à la connaissance de qn; **to a. s.o. that . . .,** avertir, prévenir, qn que. . . . **to keep s.o. advised of sth.,** tenir qn au courant de qch.; (*b*) *Com:* **to a. a draft,** aviser d'une traite, donner avis d'une traite.

II. *v.i. A:* **1. to a. with s.o.,** (i) consulter qn; demander conseil à qn; (ii) se consulter avec qn. **2. the King will a.,** le roi avisera.

advised [əd'vaizd], *a.* **1.** (acte) réfléchi, délibéré. **2.** judicieux; *esp.* **well-, ill-a. action,** action judicieuse, peu judicieuse.

advisedly [əd'vaizidli], *adv.* **1.** de propos délibéré; à dessein. **2.** en connaissance de cause, après mûre considération.

advisedness [əd'vaizidnis], *s.* **1.** caractère judicieux (d'une action). **2.** opportunité *f* (d'une action).

adviser, advisor [əd'vaizər], *s.* conseiller, -ère; **legal a.,** conseiller juridique; avocat *m* conseil; **spiritual a.,** directeur *m* de conscience; **he is literary a. to a firm of publishers,** il est conseiller littéraire d'une maison d'édition.

advisory [əd'vaizəri]. **1.** *a.* (conseil) consultatif; (voix) consultative; **in an a. capacity,** à titre consultatif; **a. services,** services *m* de documentation. **2.** *s. U.S:* bulletin *m* de renseignements, *esp.* bulletin météorologique.

advocacy ['ædvəkəsi], *s.* **1.** profession *f,* fonction *f,* d'avocat. **2. a. of a cause,** plaidoyer *m* en faveur d'une cause; appui donné à une cause; **to speak in a. of sth., of s.o.,** prononcer un plaidoyer en faveur de qch., de qn; appuyer (une cause); se faire l'avocat d'une cause.

advocate[1] ['ædvəkət, -eit], *s.* **1.** *Jur:* (*in Scot.*) avocat *m;* **the Faculty of Advocates,** le Barreau écossais; **the Advocates' Library,** la Bibliothèque du barreau et Bibliothèque nationale d'Écosse (à Édimbourg); **the Lord A.** = le Procureur général (en Écosse). **2.** avocat; défenseur *m* (d'une cause, d'une doctrine, etc.); **the advocates of free trade,** ceux qui préconisent le libre-échange; les partisans du libre-échange; **to become the a. of a cause,** se faire l'apôtre d'une cause; **he is a good a.,** il plaide bien; *Ecc. & F:* **Devil's a.,** avocat du diable. **3.** *Mil:* **Judge a. (before a court-martial),** rapporteur *m* (d'un conseil de guerre); **Judge a. general,** président *m* (du conseil de guerre).

advocate[2] ['ædvəkeit], *v.tr.* (*a*) plaider en faveur de (qch.); soutenir, appuyer (une cause); (*b*) préconiser (l'emploi de qch.); **I wouldn't a. a divorce,** je ne vous conseille pas, je déconseille, le divorce.

advocator ['ædvəkeitər], *s.* conseiller, -ère (d'une ligne de conduite, etc.).

advowee [ædvau'iː], *s. Ecc:* collateur *m* (d'un bénéfice).

advowson [əd'vauz(ə)n], *s. Ecc:* droit *m* de présentation (à un bénéfice ecclésiastique); collation *f* (d'un bénéfice); patronage *m.*

adynamia [eidai'neimiə], *s. Med:* adynamie *f.*

adynamic [eidai'næmik], *a. Med: Ph:* adynamique.

adytum, *pl.* **-a** ['æditəm, -ə], *s.* (*a*) *Gr.Ant:* adytum *m;* (*b*) *A:* sanctuaire *m,* sanctum sanctorum *m.*

adze[1] [ædz], *s.* (*U.S: also* **adz**); *Tls:* (*a*) (H)erminette *f;* **Cooper's a.,** cochoir *m,* doloire *f,* aisceau *m,* aissette *f,* hachotte *f,* tille *f;* **rounding a.,** herminette à gouge; (*b*) **a. of an ice axe,** sape *f* d'un piolet.

adze[2], *v.tr.* (*U.S: also* **adz**); entailler (le bois) à l'herminette; doler; aplanir (une poutre, etc.).

Aeacus ['iːəkəs], *Pr.n.m. Gr.Myth:* Éaque.

aecidial [i'sidiəl], *U.S:* **aecial** ['iːʃiəl], *a. Fung:* de l'écidie.

aecidiospore [i'sidiouspɔər], *U.S:* **aeciospore** ['isiouspɔər], *s. Fung:* écidiospore *f.*

aecidium, *pl.* **-ia** [i'sidiəm, -iə], *U.S:* **aecium,** *pl.* **-ia,** ['iːsiəm, -iə], *s. Fung:* écidie *f,* æcidie *f.*

aëdes ['eiidiːz], *s. Ent:* æde *m,* aède *m.*

aedicule ['iːdikjul], *s.* édicule *m.*

aedile ['iːdail, -dil], *s. Rom.Ant:* édile *m.*

aedileship ['iːdailʃip, -dil-], *s. Rom.Ant:* édilité *f.*

aedilitian [iːdə'liʃ(ə)n], *a. Rom.Ant:* édilitaire.

aegagrus [iː'gægrəs], *s. Z:* ægagre *f.*

aegagropila [iːgægrou'pailə], **aegagropile** [iːgægrou'pail], *s. Vet:* ægagropile *m,* égagropile *m.*

Aegean [i'dʒiːən], *a.* **1.** *Geog:* **the A. sea,** *s.* **the Aegean,** la mer Égée. **2.** *A.Hist:* égéen, -enne.

Aegeria [i'dʒiəriə], *Pr.n.f. Rom.Myth:* Égérie.

Aegeriidae [iːdʒə'riidiː], *s.pl. Ent:* ægériidés *m,* sésiidés *m.*

Aegeus ['iːdʒiəs], *Pr.n.m. Gr.Mth:* Égée.

aegilops ['iːdʒilɔps], *s. Bot:* ægilops *m.*

Aegina [i'dʒainə], *Pr.n. Geog:* Égine *f.*

Aeginetan [iːdʒi'niːt(ə)n]. *Geog:* **1.** *a.* éginète; *Art:* **the A. Marbles,** les marbres *m* d'Égine. **2.** *s.* Éginète *mf.*

Aeginetic [iːdʒi'netik], *a.* éginétique.

aegirine ['iːdʒirain], **aegirite** ['iːdʒirait], *s. Miner:* ægirine *f,* ægyrine *f.*

aegis ['iːdʒis], *s.* (*a*) *Gr.Myth:* égide *f;* (*b*) égide; protection *f;* **under the a. of . . .,** sous l'égide de . . .; sous les auspices de. . . .

Aegisthus [i'dʒisθəs], *Pr.n.m. Gr.Lit:* Égisthe.

aegithalos [iːdʒi'θeiləs], *s. Orn:* ægithale *m;* mésange *f* à longue queue.

aegle ['iːgli, 'egli], *s. Bot:* ægle *m.*

aegolius [i'gouliəs], *s. Orn:* ægolie *f,* chouette pattue.

aegophony [i'gɔfəni], *s. Med:* égophonie *f.*

aegopodium [iːgou'poudiəm], *s. Bot:* ægopodium *m.*

Aegos-potami [i'gɔs'pɔtəmai], *Pr.n. A.Hist:* Ægos-Potamos.

aegre ['iːgər], *s. Oc:* mascaret *m.*

aegrotat [i(ː)'groutæt], *s. Sch:* certificat *m* d'indisposition (délivré par le médecin); **he got an a.** = il était malade lors de l'examen, mais l'université lui a quand même accordé son diplôme.

aegyrite ['iːdʒərait], *s. Miner:* ægirine *f,* ægyrine *f.*

Aelian ['iːliən], *Pr.n.m. Gr.Lit:* Élien.

Aeneas [i'niːəs], *Pr.n.m. Lt.Lit:* Énée.

Aeneid (the) [ðiː'iːniid], *s. Lt.Lit:* l'Énéide *f.*

Aeneolithic [iːniou'liθik], *a. Prehist:* énéolithique.

aenigmatite [iː'nigmətait], *s. Miner:* ænigmatite *f,* cossyrite *f.*

Aeolia [iː'ouliə], *Pr.n. A.Geog:* Éolie *f.*

Aeolian[1] [iː'ouliən]. **1.** *a.* (*a*) *A.Geog:* éolien; (*b*) *Mus:* **A. mode,** mode éolien. **2.** *s. A.Geog:* Éolien, -ienne.

aeolian[2], *a.* éolien; *Mus:* **a. harp,** *also* **A. harp,** harpe éolienne; *Geog:* **a. drift,** dérive éolienne; **a. erosion,** érosion éolienne.

Aeolic [iː'oulik], *Ling:* **1.** *a.* éolien, éolique. **2.** *s.* éolien *m.*

aeoliopile, aeolipyle [iː'oulipail], *s. Ph:* éolipyle *m.*

Aeolis[1] ['iːoulis], *Pr.n. A.Geog:* Éolie *f.*

aeolis[2], *s. Moll:* éolide *f;* (*genus*) éolis *f;* **plumed a.,** éolis mauve, nudibranche *m* mauve.

aeolotropic [iːolou'trɔpik], *a. Ph:* anisotropique, anisotrope.

aeolotrophy [iːɔ'lɔtrəpi], *s. Ph:* anisotropie *f.*

Aeolus ['iːouləs], *Pr.n.m. Gr.Myth:* Éole.

aeon ['iːən], *s.* **1.** *Phil:* éon *m.* **2.** période *f* de temps sans mesure; éternité *f;* **for aeons upon aeons,** pendant des siècles, des éternités.

aepyceros [iː'pisərəs], *s. Z:* æpycéros *m;* impala *m.*

aepyornis, *pl.* **-es** [iːpi'ɔːnis, -iz], *s. Paleont:* æpyornis *m.*

aeraemia [iː'riːmiə], *s. Med:* aérémie *f.*

aerate ['ɛəreit], *v.tr.* **1.** (*a*) aérer, ventiler; (*b*) *Physiol:* artérialiser (le sang). **2.** gazéifier (de l'eau, une eau minérale).

aerated [ɛə'reitid], *a.* (*a*) aéré; (*b*) (*of water*) gazeux; (*c*) *Const:* **a. concrete,** béton *m* cellulaire, béton au gaz, béton mousse.

aerating[1] [ɛə'reitiŋ], *a.* aérateur, -trice; qui aère; *Bot:* **a. tissue,** aérenchyme *m.*

aerating[2], **aeration** [ɛə'reiʃ(ə)n], *s.* (*a*) aération *f;* (*b*) *Physiol:* artérialisation *f* (du sang).

aerator [ɛə'reitər], *s.* aérateur *m;* gazéificateur *m* (d'eau, etc.).

aeremia [iː'riːmiə], *s. Med:* aérémie *f.*

aerenchyma [ɛə'reŋkimə], *s. Bot:* aérenchyme *m.*

aerial ['ɛəriəl]. **1.** *a.* aérien; *Bot:* **a. root,** racine aérienne; **a. (orchid, etc.),** (orchidée, etc.) aéricole; **a. railway,** voie ferrée aérienne; **a. cable,** câble aérien; **a. perspective,** perspective aérienne. **2.** *s. W.Tel: T.V: etc:* antenne *f;* **sending a., transmitting a.,** antenne d'émission; **receiving a.,** antenne réceptrice; **twin (wire) a.,** antenne à deux fils, bifilaire; **frame a., loop a.,** (i) (antenne en) cadre (*m*); (ii) antenne fermée; **cage a.,** antenne en cage; **trailing a.,** antenne pendante; *T.V:* **H aerial,** antenne (de télévision) en forme de H; **a. base,** support *m* d'antenne; **a. tap,** prise *f* d'antenne; **a. wire,** fil *m* d'antenne.

aerialist ['ɛəriəlist], *s.* acrobate (aérien).

aerially ['ɛəriəli], *adv.* d'une manière aérienne.

Aerian ['ɛəriən], *s. Rel.H:* Aérien *m.*

aeride [ɛərid], *s. Bot:* aéride *f.*

aerie, aery ['ɛəri, 'iəri], *s.* aire *f* (d'un aigle).

aeriferous [ɛə'rifərəs], *a.* aérifère.

aerification [ɛərifi'keiʃ(ə)n], *s.* aération *f.*

aeriform ['ɛərifɔːm], *a.* aériforme; gazeux.

aero- ['ɛərou], *comb.fm.* aéro-.

aerobatics [ɛərou'bætiks], *s.pl. Av:* acrobaties (aériennes), voltige *f.*

aerobe ['ɛəroub]. *Biol:* **1.** *a.* aérobie. **2.** *s.* aérobie *m;*

facultative a., aérobie facultatif; **obligate a.**, aérobie strict.

aerobian [ɛə'roubiən], *a. & s. Biol:* aérobie (*m*).

aerobic [ɛə'roubik], *a.* **1.** *Biol:* aérobie. **2.** *Mec.E:* **a. engine**, moteur *m*, réacteur *m*, aérobie.

aerobiologic(al) [ɛəroubaiə'lɔdʒik(l)], *a.* aérobiologique.

aerobiology [ɛəroubai'ɔlədʒi], *s.* aérobiologie *f.*

aerobiont [ɛə'roubaiɔnt], *s. Biol:* aérobie *m.*

aerobiosis [ɛə'roubaiousis], *s.* aérobiose *f.*

aerobiotic [ɛəroubai'ɔtik], *a. Biol:* aérobie.

aerobium, *pl.* **-ia** [ɛər'oubiəm, -iə], *s. Biol:* aérobie *m.*

aerocamera [ɛərou'kæm(ə)rə], *s.* appareil *m* de photographie aérienne.

aerocartograph [ɛərou'ka:təgræf], *s.* aérocartographe *m.*

aerocartography [ɛərouka:'tɔgrəfi], *s.* aérocartographie *f.*

aerochemical [ɛərou'kemikl], *a.* aérochimique; **a. warfare**, guerre *f* aérochimique; **a. attack**, attaque aérochimique.

aero club ['ɛərouklʌb], *s.* aéro-club *m*, *pl.* aéro-clubs.

aerocolia [ɛərou'kouliə], **aerocoly** [ɛərou'kouli], *s. Med:* aérocolie *f.*

aerocondenser, [ɛəroukən'densər], *s. Mec:* aérocondenseur *m.*

aerocyst ['ɛərousist], *s. Algae:* aérocyste *f.*

aerodontalgia [ɛəroudɔn'tældʒiə], *s.* aérodontalgie *f.*

aerodontia [ɛərou'dɔntiə], **aerodontics** [ɛərou'dɔntiks], *s. Dent:* aérodontie *f.*

aerodrome ['ɛəroudroum], *s.* aérodrome *m.*

aerodynamic [ɛəroudai'næmik]. **1.** *a.* aérodynamique; *Ph:* **a. axis**, axe *m* de poussée; **a. centre**, centre *m* aérodynamique, de poussée; **a. damping**, résistance *f* à l'avancement, aux forces aérodynamiques; **a. efficiency**, finesse *f* (rapport de la portance à la traînée); **a. heating**, échauffement *m* cinétique; **a. missile**, engin doté de surfaces aérodynamiques; **a. surfaces**, voilure *f*, volets *mpl* aérodynamiques; **a. trajectory**, trajectoire *f* balistique; **a. volume**, volume total d'un aérostat; *Ph: Mec:* **a. centre**, centre *m* aérodynamique; *Av.* **a. centre (of wing section)**, foyer *m* (de profil d'aile). **2.** *s.pl.* (*usu. with sing. const.*) **aerodynamics**, aérodynamique *f.*

aerodynamicist [ɛəroudai'næmisist], *s.* aérodynamicien, -ienne; aérodynamiste *mf.*

aerodyne ['ɛəroudain], *s. Aer:* aérodyne *m.*

aeroelastic [ɛəroui'læstik], *a.* aéroélastique.

aeroelasticity [ɛərouilæs'tisiti], *s.* aéroélasticité *f.*

aeroembolism [ɛərou'embəlizm], *s. Med:* aéroembolisme *m.*

aero(-)engine ['ɛərouendʒin], *s.* moteur *m* d'avion.

aerofoil ['ɛəroufɔil], *s. Av:* plan *m* à profil d'aile; voilure *f*; surface portante, sustentrice.

aerogenic [ɛərou'dʒenik], **aerogenous** [ɛər'ɔdʒinəs], *a. Med:* aérogène.

aerogeography [ɛəroudʒi:'ɔgrəfi], *s.* aérogéographie *f.*

aerogeology [ɛəroudʒi:'ɔlədʒi], *s.* aérogéologie *f.*

aerogram(me) ['ɛərougræm], *s.* aérogramme *m.*

aerograph ['ɛərougræf], *s.* **1.** *Meteor: U.S:* météorographe *m.* **2.** aérographe *m*, pinceau vaporisateur (de peinture, etc.), pistolet *m.*

aerographer [ɛə'rɔgrəfər], *s.* (*pers.*) **1.** *Meteor: U.S:* aérographe *m.* **2.** peintre *m* (qui utilise un aérographe).

aerography [ɛə'rɔgrəfi], *s.* aérographie *f.*

aerolite ['ɛəroulait], **aerolith** ['ɛərouliθ], *s.* (*a*) aérolithe *m*, aérolite *m*; (*b*) asidère *m.*

aerolithic [ɛərou'liθik], **aerolitic** [ɛərou'litik], *a.* aérolithique.

aerologic(al) [ɛərou'lɔdʒik(l)], *a.* aérologique.

aerologist [ɛə'rɔlədʒist], *s.* aérologue *mf*, aérologiste *mf.*

aerology [ɛə'rɔlədʒi], *s.* aérologie *f.*

aeromagnetic [ɛəroumæg'netik], *a.* aéromagnétique.

aeromancy [ɛərou'mænsi], *s.* aéromancie *f.*

aeromarine [ɛəroumə'ri:n], *a.* aéro(-)maritime, *pl.* aéro(-)maritimes.

aeromechanic [ɛəroumi'kænik], *s.* mécanicien *m* d'aviation, d'avion.

aeromechanics [ɛəroumi'kæniks], *s.* mécanique *f* des gaz, des fluides.

aerometal [ɛərou'metl], *s.* laiton *m* d'aluminium.

aerometer [ɛə'rɔmitər], *s.* aéromètre *m.*

aerometric [ɛərou'metrik], *a.* aérométrique.

aerometry [ɛə'rɔmitri], *s.* aérométrie *f.*

aeronaut ['ɛərounɔ:t], *s.* aéronaute *mf.*

aeronautic(al) [ɛərou'nɔ:tik(l)], *a.* aéronautique; **a. chart, map**, carte *f* aéronautique; **a. equipment**, équipement *m*, matériel *m*, aéronautique; **a. engineer**, ingénieur *m* de l'aéronautique; **a. light**, feu *m* aéronautique; **a. station**, station *f* radio-aéronautique.

aeronautics [ɛərou'nɔ:tiks], *s.pl.* (*usu. with sg. const.*) (*a*) aéronautique *f*; (*b*) navigation aérienne.

aeronaval ['ɛərou'neivl], *a.* aéronaval, -als; **a. base**, base aéronavale; **a. war**, guerre aéronavale.

aeroneurosis [ɛərounju'rousis], *s. Med:* aéronévrose *f*, névrose *f* des aviateurs.

aeronomy [ɛə'rɔnəmi], *s.* aéronomie *f.*

aero-otitis [ɛərouou'taitis], *s. Med:* aéro-otite *f.*

aerophagia [ɛərou'feidʒiə], *s. Med:* aérophagie *f.*

aerophagist [ɛə'rɔfədʒist], *s. Med:* aérophage *mf.*

aerophilately [ɛəroufi'lætəli], *s.* aérophilatélie *f.*

aerophobia [ɛərou'foubiə], *s.* aérophobie *f.*

aerophone ['ɛəroufoun], *s. Tp:* aérophone *m.*

aerophore ['ɛəroufɔər], *s.* aérophore *m.*

aerophotograph [ɛərou'foutəgræf], *s.* photographie aérienne.

aerophotography [ɛəroufə'tɔgrəfi], *s.* aérophotographie *f.*

aerophyte ['ɛəroufait], *s. Bot:* aérophyte *f*; plante *f* aéricole, épiphyte.

aeroplane ['ɛərəplein], *s.* avion *m.*

aeroplankton [ɛərou'plæŋktən], *s. Nat.Hist:* aéroplancton *m.*

aeropulse ['ɛəroupʌls], *s. Av:* pulsoréacteur *m.*

aeroresonator ['ɛərou'rezəneitər], *s. Av:* pulsoréacteur *m.*

aeroscope ['ɛərouskoup], *s. Bac: Meteor:* aéroscope *m.*

aeroscopy [ɛə'rɔskəpi], *s.* aéroscopie *f.*

aerosiderite [ɛərou'sidərait], *s.* sidérolit(h)e *f.*

aerosite ['ɛərousait], *s. Miner:* argyrythrose *f*, pyrargyrite *f*, argent rouge antimonial.

aerosol ['ɛərousɔl], *s.* aérosol *m*; *Com:* bombe *f*; *Med:* **a. therapy**, aérosolthérapie *f.*

aerospace ['ɛərouspeis]. **1.** *a.* aérospatial, -aux; **a. industries**, industries aérospatiales. **2.** *s.* (*a*) l'espace aérien et interplanétaire; (*b*) les activités aérospatiales, l'aérospatiale *f*; **Minister for A.**, Ministre *m* de l'Aérospatiale; **the world of a.**, le monde aérospatial.

aerosphere ['ɛərousfi:ər], *s.* aérosphère *f.*

aerostat ['ɛəroustæt], *s. Av:* aérostat *m.*

aerostatic [ɛərou'stætik]. **1.** *a.* aérostatique. **2.** *s.pl.* (*usu. with sg. const.*) **aerostatics**, aérostatique *f.*

aerostation ['ɛərousteiʃ(ə)n], *s.* aérostation *f.*

aerotechnical ['ɛərou'teknikl], *a.* aérotechnique.

aerotechnics ['ɛərou'tekniks], *s.* (*usu. with sg. const.*) aérotechnique *f.*

aerotherapeutics ['ɛərouθerə'pju:tiks], *s.pl.* (*usu. with sg. const.*), **aerotherapy** [ɛərou'θerəpi], *s.* aérothérapie *f.*

aerothermic ['ɛərou'θə:mik], *a.* aérothermique.

aerothermodynamics [ɛərouθə:moudai'næmiks], *s.pl.* (*usu. with sg. const.*) aérothermodynamique *f.*

aerotitis [ɛərou'taitis], *s. Med:* aéro-otite *f.*

aerotonometer [ɛəroutə'nɔmitər], *s. Med:* aérotonomètre *m.*

aerotonometry [ɛəroutə'nɔmitri], *s. Med:* aérotonométrie *f.*

aerotrain ['ɛəroutrein], *s.* aérotrain *m.*

aerotropism [ɛə'rɔtrəpizm], *s. Biol:* aérotropisme *m.*

aeruginous [ɛə'ru:dʒinəs], *a.* érugineux.

Aeschines ['i:skini:z], *Pr.n.m.* Eschine.

Aeschylus ['i:skiləs], *Pr.n.m.* Eschyle.

Aesculapian [i:skju'leipiən], *a.* l'Esculape; médicinal, -aux; *Rept:* **A. snake**, couleuvre *f* d'Esculape.

Aesculapius [i:skju'leipiəs]. **1.** *Pr.n.m. Myth:* Esculape; **Aesculapius's staff**, caducée *m.* **2.** *s. Rept:* esculape *m.*

aesculin ['i:skjulin], *s. Bio-Ch:* æsculine *f* esculine *f.*

Aesop ['i:sɔp], *Pr.n.m. Gr.Lit:* Ésope; *Crust:* **A. prawn**, hippolyte *m.*

Aesopian [i:'soupiən], **Aesopic** [i:'sɔpik], *a.* (apologue, etc.) ésopique.

aesthesia [i:s'θi:ziə], *s.* esthésie *f.*

aesthesiogenic [i:sθi:ziou'dʒenik], *a.* esthésiogène.

aesthesiology [i:sθi:zi'ɔlədʒi], *s.* esthésiologie *f.*

aesthesiometer [i:sθi:zi'ɔmitər], *s.* esthésiomètre *m.*

aesthesis [i:s'θi:sis], *s.* esthésie *f.*

aesthete ['i:sθi:t], *s.* esthète *mf.*

aesthetic(al) [i:s'θetik(l)], *a.* **1.** esthétique. **2.** (*a*) de bon goût; (*b*) *Pej:* prétentieux; qui affiche des prétentions artistiques.

aesthetically [i:s'θetikəli], *adv.* esthétiquement.

aesthetician [i:sθe'tiʃ(ə)n], *s.* esthéticien, -ienne.

aestheticism [i:s'θetisizm], *s.* (*a*) esthétisme *m*; (*b*) esthéticisme *m.*

aesthetics [i:s'θetiks], *s.pl.* (*usu. with sg.const.*) esthétique *f.*

aestival [is'ti:vl, es-], *a. Bot: etc:* estival, -aux.

aestivate ['i:stiveit, 'es-], *v.i. & tr.* estiver.

aestivation [i:sti'veiʃ(ə)n, es-], *s.* **1.** *Bot:* estivation *f*, préfloraison *f.* **2.** *Z:* estivation.

aethogen ['i:θoudʒen], *s. Ch:* éthogène *m.*

aethrioscope ['i:θriouskoup], *s. Meteor:* éthrioscope *m.*

aethusa [i:'θjuzə], *s. Bot:* æthuse *f.*

aetiological [i:tiou'lɔdʒikl], *a.* étiologique.

aetiology [i:ti'ɔlədʒi], *s.* étiologie *f.*

Aetius ['i:tiəs], *Pr.n.m. Hist:* Aétius.

Aetolia [i:'touliə], *Pr.n. Geog:* Étolie *f.*

Aetolian [i:'touliən]. **1.** *a. Geog:* étolien. **2.** *s. Geog:* Étolien, -ienne. **3.** *s. A.Ling:* étolien *m.*

afar [ə'fa:r], *adv. chiefly Lit:* **from a.**, de loin; **a. off**, au loin; éloigné.

affability [æfə'biliti], *s.* affabilité *f* (**towards**, envers, avec); aménité *f*, courtoisie *f*, gracieuseté *f.*

affable ['æfəbl], *a.* affable, courtois, gracieux (**to, with**, envers, avec).

affableness ['æfəblnis], *s.* = AFFABILITY.

affably ['æfəbli], *adv.* avec courtoisie, avec affabilité, gracieusement.

affair [ə'fɛər], *s.* (*a*) affaire *f*; **that's my a.**, ça, c'est mon affaire; **a difficult a. to handle**, un problème délicat, une affaire délicate; **to put one's affairs in order**, mettre de l'ordre dans ses affaires; **his affairs are in a muddle**, ses affaires sont en désordre; **he's very young to be at the head of affairs**, il est bien jeune pour être à la tête de l'entreprise, de l'affaire; **to talk about one's own affairs**, raconter ses affaires; **in the present state of affairs**, du train où vont les choses; *F:* **what a ghastly a.! that's a nice, fine, state of affairs!** en voilà du propre! (*b*) **affairs of state**, les affaires de l'État; **foreign affairs**, les affaires étrangères; *Can:* **External Affairs**, les Affaires Extérieures (*Fr.C*); (*c*) (love) **a.**, affaire (de cœur); intrigue *f*; aventure *f*; **unhappy love a.**, déception sentimentale; *A:* **a. of honour**, affaire d'honneur, duel *m.*

affaire [æ'fɛər], *s.* affaire *f* (de cœur); intrigue *f.*

affect[1] [ə'fekt], *v.tr.* **1.** (*a*) *A:* affecter (une forme); **these plants a. strange shapes**, ces plantes affectent des formes étranges; (*b*) *A:* affecter (une manière, une vertu, etc.); **to a. to do sth., to be sth.**, affecter de faire qch., d'être qch.; **he affects liberality**, il fait parade de générosité; (*c*) **to a. indifference, grief**, simuler l'indifférence, la douleur. **2.** *A:* (*of plants, animals*) fréquenter (une région).

affect[2], *v.tr.* **1.** (*a*) atteindre, attaquer, toucher (qn); affecter (un organe, etc.); influer sur (qch.); **these restrictions a. woollens particularly**, ces restrictions atteignent particulièrement les lainages; **to be affected by a fall in prices**, être atteint par une baisse de prix; **articles of food are not affected by this order**, les denrées alimentaires ne sont pas visées par ce décret; **the price of glue affects the cost of binding**, le prix de la colle intervient, entre, dans le coût de la reliure; **the economic crisis which is affecting the country at present**, la crise économique qui frappe le pays en ce moment; **the climate has affected his health**, le climat a altéré sa santé; **it affects me personally**, cela me touche, m'intéresse, personnellement; **to a. s.o.'s interests**, porter atteinte aux intérêts de qn; **it closely affects my interests**, cela touche de très près mes intérêts; **I fail to see how this affects you**, je ne vois pas en quoi cela vous intéresse; **those most directly affected**, les premiers intéressés; **this gas affects the lungs**, ce gaz affecte, atteint, les poumons; **the epidemic did not a. the troops**, l'épidémie n'a pas gagné les troupes; **this will a. business**, cela influera sur les affaires; (*b*) *Med:* intéresser; **bowel complaint that also affects the liver**, maladie intestinale qui intéresse le foie; (*c*) **he affected indifference**, il affectait, simulait, l'indifférence. **2.** affecter, affliger, toucher (qn); **to be much affected by sth.**, être très affecté, affligé, de qch.; **to be affected at the sight of sth.**, se laisser attendrir au spectacle de qch.; **he is easily affected**, il s'affecte aisément; **nothing affects him**, rien ne le touche; il ne s'émeut de rien. **3.** (*a*) toucher, concerner (qn, qch.); **his failure does not a. our firm**, sa faillite ne touche pas notre maison; **that does not a. the matter**, cela ne fait rien à l'affaire; **to a. the result**, influer sur le résultat; (*b*) **to a. events**, influer sur les événements; *Jur:* **fact that affected the findings**, fait qui a exercé une influence sur les conclusions. **4.** *A:* **to be affected to a service**, être affecté à un service. **5.** *Jur:* affecter (une terre, etc.).

affect[3], *s. Psy:* phénomène affectif; affect *m.*

affectation [æfek'teiʃ(ə)n], *s.* **1. a. of interest, of indifference, etc.**, affectation *f*, simulation *f*, d'intérêt, d'indifférence, etc. **2.** affectation; manque *m* de naturel; afféterie *f*, apprêt *m* (de langage); **to avoid a.**, éviter le recherché. **3.** *Mil: A:* **a. to a service**, affectation à un service.

affected[1] [ə'fektid], *a.* (*of pers., manners*) (*a*) affecté, maniéré, affété; **a. style**, style maniéré, (re)cherché, apprêté, style qui sent l'étude; **a. courtesies**, simagrées de politesse; (*b*) **a. indifference, a. interest**, indifférence simulée, intérêt simulé; **a. cheerfulness**, gaieté *f* d'emprunt.

affected[2], *a.* **1.** (*a*) *A:* **to be well, ill, a. towards s.o.**, être bien, mal, disposé pour qn; (*b*) **to be a. with a disease,** être atteint d'une maladie; **the lung is a.,** le poumon est atteint, attaqué, touché; **the lungs are becoming a.,** les poumons commencent à se prendre; **a. part (of the body),** partie atteinte, intéressée, souffrante; (*c*) ému, touché; **to be much a. by sth.,** ressentir vivement qch.; **too much a. to answer,** trop ému pour répondre. 2. *Jur:* **a. estate,** domaine affecté (d'hypothèques).

affectedly [ə'fektidli], *adv.* avec affectation.

affectedness [ə'fektidnis], *s.* affectation *f*; manque *m* de naturel; apprêt *m* (de langage, etc.); afféterie *f.*

affecting [ə'fektiŋ], *a.* (spectacle, etc.) touchant, attendrissant.

affection [ə'fekʃ(ə)n], *s.* 1. affection *f*, tendresse *f*; amitié *f*, attachement *m*; **to have an a. for s.o., to feel a. towards s.o.,** avoir, ressentir, de l'affection pour qn; **he is held in great a.,** on l'aime beaucoup; il est très aimé; **to gain, win, s.o.'s a.,** se faire aimer de qn; gagner l'affection, le cœur, de qn; **to set one's affections on s.o.,** placer son affection sur qn; **to trifle with s.o.'s affections,** badiner avec l'amour de qn. 2. *Med:* affection (de poitrine, de la peau, etc.); **nervous a.,** affection nerveuse. 3. *pl. Phil:* attributs *m*, qualités *f* (des corps).

affectional [ə'fekʃənəl], *a. A:* 1. capable d'affection. 2. = AFFECTIVE.

affectionate [ə'fekʃənət], *a.* affectueux; **she nursed him with a. care,** elle l'a soigné tendrement, avec affection; *Corr:* **your a. daughter,** votre fille affectueuse.

affectionately [ə'fekʃənətli], *adv.* affectueusement; **she greeted him a.,** elle l'a salué d'un ton affectueux; *Corr:* **yours a.,** bien affectueusement.

affectionateness [ə'fekʃənətnis], *s.* affectuosité *f.*

affective [ə'fektiv], *a. Psy:* affectif.

affectivity [æfek'tiviti], *s. Psy:* affectivité *f.*

afferent ['æfərənt], *a. Physiol:* (vaisseau) afférent.

affiance[1] [ə'faiəns], *s. A. & Lit:* 1. foi *f*, confiance *f* (**in,** en). 2. fiançailles *fpl.*

affiance[2], *v.tr. A: & Lit:* fiancer (**s.o. to s.o.,** qn avec qn).

affianced [ə'faiənst], *a. A: & Lit:* **to be a. to s.o.,** être fiancé(e) à qn; **the a. couple,** les deux fiancés; **a. bride,** fiancée *f.*

affidavit [ˌæfi'deivit], *s. Jur:* déclaration *f* par écrit et sous serment, enregistrée sur acte timbré; attestation *f* par écrit; déposition *f* (de témoin) sous serment; affirmation *f*; **a. made by process server,** constat *m* d'huissier; (*of deponent*) **to swear an a.,** certifier sous serment une déclaration (écrite); **to take an a.,** (i) (*of judge*) obtenir une déclaration (écrite) sous serment, (ii) faire une déclaration sous serment; **evidence taken on a.,** dépositions recueillies sous serment; dépositions rigoureuses en témoignage.

affiliate [ə'filieit], *v.tr.* 1. (*of a society*) **to a. members,** s'affilier des membres. 2. (*a*) **to a. a member to, with, a society,** affilier un membre à une société; **to a. (oneself) to, with, a society,** s'affilier à une société; **affiliated company,** filiale *f*; (*b*) *v.i. U.S:* entrer en relations, fraterniser (**with,** avec). 3. *Jur:* **to a. a child (up)on, to, a putative father,** assigner un enfant à un père putatif.

affiliation [əfili'eiʃ(ə)n], *s.* 1. (*a*) affiliation *f* (à une société) (*b*) **political affiliations,** attaches *f* politiques. 2. *Jur:* (*a*) *A:* légitimation *f*, reconnaissance *f* (d'un enfant); (*b*) *A:* adoption *f* (d'un enfant); (*c*) procédure *f* en recherche de paternité; recherche *f* de la paternité; **action (by bastard) for a.,** recherche de paternité; **a. order,** assignation *f* d'enfant à un père putatif.

affine[1] ['æfain], *a. Mth:* affine; **a. geometry,** géométrie *f* affine.

affine[2] [æ'fain], *v.tr.* 1. *Lit: Metall: etc: A:* affiner. 2. *Sug.R:* affiner.

affinity [ə'finiti], *s.* (*a*) affinité *f* (**with, to,** avec; **between,** entre); **spiritual a.,** affinité spirituelle; (*b*) conformité *f* de caractère; (*c*) *Mth: Biol:* affinité; *Ch:* **a. for a body,** affinité pour un corps; (*d*) parenté *f* par alliance.

affirm [ə'fə:m], *v.tr.* 1. affirmer, soutenir (**that,** que); **to a. sth. to s.o.,** affirmer qch. à qn; assurer qch. à qn; assurer qn de qch. 2. *Jur:* confirmer, homologuer (un jugement).

affirmable [ə'fə:məbl], *s.* qui peut s'affirmer; (conclusion) valide.

affirmant [ə'fə:mənt]. 1. *a.* affirmatif. 2. *s. Jur:* personne *f* qui fait une déclaration solennelle (tenant lieu de serment).

affirmation [æfə'meiʃ(ə)n], *s.* 1. (*a*) affirmation *f*, assertion *f*; (*b*) *Jur:* déclaration solennelle (tenant lieu de serment). 2. *Jur:* confirmation *f*, homologation *f* (d'un jugement).

affirmative [ə'fə:mətiv]. 1. *a.* affirmatif; **to make an a. sign,** faire un signe affirmatif; faire signe que oui; *Nau:* **a. signal,** triangle *m* oui. 2. *s.* **if he replies in the a.,** s'il répond affirmativement; s'il répond par, dans, l'affirmative; si sa réponse est affirmative; s'il dit oui; **the answer is in the a.,** la réponse est oui.

affirmatively [ə'fə:mətivli], *adv.* affirmativement; *Log:* assertivement.

affirmatory [ə'fə:mət(ə)ri], *a.* affirmatif.

affix[1] ['æfiks], *s.* 1. addition *f* (à un mémoire). 2. *Ling:* affixe *m.*

affix[2] [ə'fiks], *v.tr.* attacher (**sth. to sth.,** qch. à qch.); **to a. a seal, a stamp, to a document,** apposer un sceau, un timbre, à, sur, un document.

affixal [ə'fiksl], *a. Ling:* affixal, -aux.

afflation [ə'fleiʃ(ə)n], *s.* 1. inspiration *f* d'air. 2. inspiration (de génie).

afflatus [ə'fleitəs], *s.* souffle (divin, du génie).

afflict [ə'flikt], *v.tr.* affliger, tourmenter, désoler; **to be afflicted with rheumatism,** être affligé de rhumatismes; **to be afflicted at, by, a piece of news,** être affligé, s'affliger, d'une nouvelle.

afflicted [ə'fliktid], (*a*) *a.* affligé; (*b*) *s.pl.* **the a.,** les affligés.

afflicting [ə'fliktiŋ], *a.* affligeant.

affliction [ə'flikʃ(ə)n], *s.* 1. affliction *f*; malheur *m*; **deafness is a great a.,** la surdité est une grande affliction; *Lit:* **to eat the bread of a.,** manger le pain d'affliction; **these forms to be filled in are a real a.,** ces formules à remplir font mon désespoir. 2. calamité *f*, revers *m*; **we survived all these afflictions,** nous avons survécu à tous ces revers de fortune. 3. **the afflictions of old age,** les infirmités *f* de la vieillesse.

afflictive [ə'fliktiv], *a. A:* pénible; **to be a. to s.o.,** affliger, peiner, qn.

affluence ['æfluəns], *s.* 1. affluence *f*; grand concours (de gens, etc.). 2. abondance *f*, richesse *f*; **to live in a.,** vivre dans l'opulence *f*; **to rise to a.,** arriver à la fortune.

affluent[1] ['æfluənt], *a.* 1. abondant, riche (**in,** en). 2. opulent, riche; **in a. circumstances,** très à l'aise; **to be in a. circumstances,** jouir d'une large aisance; **a. society,** société *f* d'abondance.

affluent[2]. 1. *a. Physiol:* **a. blood,** sang affluent. 2. *s. Geog: A:* affluent *m* (d'une rivière).

affluently ['æfluəntli], *adv.* avec opulence; (vivre) dans l'aisance.

afflux ['æflʌks], *s.* 1. afflux *m*, affluence *f* (du sang, etc.). 2. concours *m* (de gens); **a sudden a. of strangers,** une affluence inopinée d'étrangers.

afford [ə'fɔ:d], *v.tr.* 1. (*usu. with* **can**) (*a*) avoir les moyens (pécuniaires) (de faire qch.); être en mesure (de faire qch.); **a piece of extravagance I could ill a.,** une extravagance qui n'était guère dans mes moyens; **I can, cannot, a. to be generous,** mes moyens me permettent, ne me permettent pas, d'être généreux; *Fig:* **you can a. to be generous,** vous pouvez vous permettre d'être généreux; **I cannot a. to be idle,** je ne suis pas à même de ne rien faire; **he can(not) a. wine,** ses moyens (ne) lui permettent (pas) de boire du vin; il ne peut pas se payer le luxe de boire du vin; **I can't a. it,** mes moyens ne le permettent pas; c'est trop cher pour moi; **I can't a. so much, as much as that,** je ne peux pas y mettre tant que ça, donner tant d'argent que cela; **he can easily a. to build a house,** il a largement les moyens de faire construire une maison; (*b*) **I can a. to wait,** je peux attendre; **we can't a. to lose a minute,** il n'y a pas une minute à perdre; **can you a. the time?** disposez-vous du temps (nécessaire)? **I cannot a. to create a bad impression,** cela me nuirait de faire une mauvaise impression; **I cannot a. to die yet,** je ne suis pas encore prêt à mourir. 2. (*give, provide*) (*a*) *Lit:* (*of pers.*) donner, accorder (qch. à qn); **kind heaven a. him everlasting rest,** que Dieu dans sa miséricorde lui donne le repos éternel; (*b*) (*of thg*) fournir, offrir; **these trees afforded us very little shelter,** ces arbres ne nous fournissaient qu'un piètre abri; *Lit:* **this will a. me an opportunity to . . .,** cela me fournira l'occasion de . . .; **history affords several examples of it,** l'histoire en offre plusieurs exemples; **this affords me great pleasure,** cela me procure un grand plaisir, me fait grand plaisir.

afforest [æ'fɔrist, ə-], *v.tr.* 1. *A:* convertir (une région) en grande chasse gardée. 2. boiser (une terre, une région); soumettre (une région) au régime forestier.

afforestation [æfɔris'teiʃ(ə)n, ə-], *s.* 1. *A:* conversion *f* (d'une région) en chasse gardée. 2. boisement *m*, afforestation *f*; plantation *f* en bois; soumission *f* (d'une région) au régime forestier.

affranchise [ə'fræn(t)ʃaiz], *v.tr.* 1. affranchir (un serf, un esclave). 2. *Lit:* **to a. s.o. from an oath,** dégager, délier, qn d'un serment.

affranchisement [ə'fræn(t)ʃizmənt], *s.* affranchissement *m* (d'un serf, d'un esclave).

affray [ə'frei], *s. O: & Jur:* 1. bagarre *f*, échauffourée *f*. 2. (*between two men*) rixe *f.*

affreightment [ə'freitmənt], *s. Com:* affrètement *m.*

affricate ['æfrikət], **affricative** [ə'frikətiv], *s. Ling:* affriquée *f.*

affront[1] [ə'frʌnt], *s.* affront *m*, offense *f.*

affront[2], *v.tr.* 1. (*a*) insulter, offenser; faire (un) affront à (qn); (*b*) *O:* faire rougir (qn); faire honte à (qn). 2. *A. & Lit:* affronter, braver (un danger, la mort).

affronté(e) [æ'frʌnteil], **affrontee** [æ'frʌnti:], *a. Her: Num:* affronté.

affronter [ə'frʌntər], *s. A:* insulteur *m*, offenseur *m.*

affronting [ə'frʌntiŋ], *a.* insultant, offensant.

affusion [ə'fju:ʒ(ə)n], *s.* 1. *Med: etc:* affusion *f*, aspersion *f*. 2. *Ecc:* (*form of baptism*) infusion *f.*

Afghan ['æfgæn]. 1. *a. Geog:* afghan; *Z:* **A. Hound,** lévrier afghan. 2. *s. Geog:* Afghan, -ane. 3. *s. Ling:* afghan *m*. 4. *s.* (*no cap.*) *A: & NAm:* (i) couverture *f*, (ii) châle *m*, en tricot.

Afghanistan [æf'gænista:n], *s. Pr.n. Geog:* Afghanistan *m.*

afield [ə'fi:ld], *adv.* (*a*) *A:* **to be a.,** (*of labourer*) être aux champs; (*of warrior*) être en campagne; **to go, walk, a.,** aller, se promener, dans les champs; (*b*) **to go far a., farther a.,** aller très loin, plus loin.

afire [ə'faiər], *adv. & a. A. & Lit:* en feu; **the chimney is a.,** le feu est à la cheminée; **to be (all) a. with the desire to . . .,** brûler du désir de. . . . **to set sth. a.,** mettre le feu à qch.

aflame [ə'fleim], *adv. & a. Lit:* en flammes, embrasé, **to be a. with colour,** briller de vives couleurs; rutiler; **to be a. with curiosity,** brûler de curiosité; **to set sth. a.,** mettre qch. en feu, en combustion; embraser, enflammer (les cœurs, le pays); mettre le feu à qch; **this rumour had set Vendée a.,** cette rumeur avait mis le feu à la Vendée.

afloat [ə'flout], *adv. & a.* 1. (*a*) à flot, sur l'eau; à la mer; (*of ship, F: of pers.*) **to be a.,** être à flot; **to set a ship a.,** lancer, mettre à la mer, mettre à l'eau, un navire; *F:* **to set a newspaper, etc., a.,** lancer un journal, etc.; **to get, set, a ship, F: s.o., a. again,** renflouer un navire; remettre un navire, qn, à flot; (*of ship*) **to get a. (after running aground),** se déséchouer; détoucher; **to keep a ship a.,** maintenir un navire à flot; **what had remained a. from the wreck,** ce qui avait surnagé au naufrage; *F:* (*of pers.*) **to keep a.,** se maintenir à flot; surnager; *Com:* **to keep bills a.,** faire circuler des effets; **to keep s.o. a. (financially),** *F:* renflouer qn; (*b*) **service a.,** service *m* à bord; **to serve a.,** servir sur mer; *Navy:* **officer serving a.,** officier embarqué; (*c*) **to be a. in space, in the atmosphere,** planer dans l'espace, dans l'atmosphère. 2. (*of rumour, etc.*) **to be a.,** courir, circuler; **to set rumours a. (about s.o.),** mettre des bruits en circulation, faire courir des histoires, donner cours à un bruit, semer des bruits (sur le compte de qn); **this idea is a. again,** cette idée revient sur l'eau.

afoot [ə'fut], *adv.* 1. **to be, to go, to come, a.,** aller, venir, à pied. 2. **to be afoot:** (*a*) être sur pied, en mouvement; (*b*) *A:* **he was a. in a moment,** (i) il se releva, (ii) il mit pied à terre, sur-le-champ. 3. **a plan is a. to . . .,** on envisage, on a formé, un projet pour . . .; on a formé le projet de . . .; **there's something a.,** il se prépare quelque chose; il se trame quelque chose; *F:* il se tripote quelque chose (en train); **there's mischief a.,** il se prépare un mauvais coup; **I wish I knew what was a.,** je voudrais bien savoir ce qui se prépare; **go and see what's a.,** allez voir ce qui se passe; **to set a rumour a.,** mettre un bruit en circulation.

afore [ə'fɔ:r], *adv. & prep.* 1. *Nau:* **a. (the mast),** sur l'avant (du mât); **look out a. there!** veillez devant! 2. *A. & Dial:* avant.

aforementioned [ə'fɔ:menʃənd], *a. Jur:* susmentionné, susnommé, susdit, mentionné ci-dessus.

aforesaid [ə'fɔ:sed], *a. & adv. Jur:* susmentionné, susdit, précité, mentionné ci-dessus; **as a.,** ainsi qu'il a été spécifié plus haut.

aforethought [ə'fɔ:θɔ:t], *a. Jur:* **with, of, malice a.,** avec préméditation, avec intention criminelle.

afraid [ə'freid], *a.* pris de peur; **to be a. of (s.o., sth.),** avoir peur de (qn, qch.), craindre (qn, qch.); **don't be a.,** n'ayez pas peur; ne craignez rien; **to make s.o. a.,** faire peur à qn; effrayer qn; **to be a. of the dark,** craindre l'obscurité, **to be a. to do, of doing, sth.,** ne pas oser faire, qch.; avoir peur, craindre, de faire qch.; **I should be a. to ask him for help,** je n'oserais pas lui demander du secours; **I was a. of offending him,** j'avais peur, je craignais, de l'offenser; **I am afraid he will die,** je crains qu'il ne meure; **I am not a. of his dying,** je ne crains pas qu'il meure; **I'm a. he won't come,** j'ai peur qu'il ne vienne pas; **I'm a. we shall be very late,** j'ai bien peur que nous allions arriver très en retard; **it's too late, I'm a.,** c'est trop tard, j'en ai peur; **I'm a. so,** j'ai bien peur que oui; **I'm a. it *is* so!** j'en ai (bien) peur; **I'm a. I can't**

tell you, je le regrette, mais je ne saurais guère vous le dire; **I'm a. he's out,** (i) je crois bien qu'il est sorti; (ii) je regrette, mais il est sorti; **I'm a. that it's only too true,** je crains bien que ce ne soit que trop vrai; **to be a. of (hard) work,** bouder à la besogne; **he's not a. of work,** il ne renâcle pas devant la besogne.

Aframerican ['æfrə'merik(ə)n], *s. U.S:* = AFRO-AMERICAN.

Afrasian [əf'reiʒ(ə)n, -ʃ(ə)n], *a. & s. U.S:* = AFRO-ASIAN.

afreet ['æfri:t], *s. Arab Myth:* afrite *m.*

afresh [ə'freʃ], *adv.* de nouveau, à nouveau; **her tears had started a.,** ses larmes coulaient de nouveau, de plus belle; **to start sth. a.,** recommencer qch.

Africa ['æfrikə], *Pr.n. Geog:* Afrique *f.*

African ['æfrik(ə)n], *a. Geog:* africain; *Bot:* **A. violet,** saintpaulia *m.* 2. *s. Geog:* Africain, -aine.

Africanist ['æfrikənist], *s.* africaniste *mf.*

Africanization [æfrikənai'zeiʃ(ə)n], *s.* africanisation *f.*

Africanize ['æfrikənaiz], *v.tr.* africaniser.

Afrikaans [æfri'kɑ:ns], *s. Ling:* afrika(a)ns *m.*

Afrikander [æfri'kændər], *s. A:* = AFRIKANER.

Afrikaner [æfrikɑ:nər]. 1. *a.* afrikaner. 2. *s.* Afrikaner *mf.*

afrit(e) ['æfri:t], *s. Arab Myth:* afrite *m.*

Afro-American ['æfrouə'merik(ə)n]. 1. *a.* afro-américain. 2. *s.* Afro-américain, -aine.

Afro-Asian ['æfrou'eiʃ(ə)n, -'eiʒ(ə)n]. 1. *a.* afro-asiatique, *pl.* afro-asiatiques. 2. *s.* Afro-asiatique *mf.*

afrormosia [æfrɔ:'mouziə], *s. Bot:* afrormosia *m.*

aft [ɑ:ft]. 1. *adv. Nau: Av:* sur, à, vers, l'arrière; **to berth a.,** coucher à l'arrière; **to go a.,** aller à l'arrière; **a. of the mast, of the funnel,** sur l'arrière du mât, de la cheminée; (*of wind*) **to draw a.,** adonner; **to have the wind dead a.,** avoir le vent en poupe, entre deux écoutes. 2. *a.* **a. end,** extrémité *f* arrière; *Av:* **a. fan,** soufflante *f* arrière; *Hyd.E:* **a. bay,** bief *m* d'aval, de fuite (d'une écluse); **a. gate,** porte *f* aval (d'une écluse).

after ['ɑ:ftər], *adv., prep., conj. & a.*

I. *adv.* après. 1. (*place, order*) **to come a.,** venir après, venir à la suite; **and Jill came tumbling a.,** et Jill dégringola après lui, derrière lui; **you speak first and I shall speak a.,** parlez d'abord et (moi) je parlerai ensuite. 2. (*time*) **I never spoke to him a.,** je ne lui ai jamais parlé ensuite, depuis; **I heard of it a.,** je l'ai appris plus tard; **he was ill for months a.,** il en est resté malade pendant des mois; **I was never treated like that before or a.,** je n'ai jamais été traité de cette façon ni avant ni depuis; **soon a.,** bientôt après; **long a.,** longtemps après; **the night, the week, a.,** la nuit, la semaine, d'après; **a year a.,** un an après, plus tard; **the day a.,** le lendemain; **the morning a.,** (i) le lendemain matin; (ii) *F:* la gueule de bois.

II. *prep.* après. 1. (*place*) **to walk a. s.o.,** marcher après qn; **he closed the door a. me,** il referma la porte sur moi; **close the door a. you,** fermez la porte après vous; **the chemist's is just a. the church,** la pharmacie est tout de suite après l'église; *F:* **to be a. s.o., sth.,** être après qn, qch.; être en quête de qn, de qch.; **she's a. a husband,** elle fait la chasse au mari; **the hounds were a. the fox,** les chiens étaient à la poursuite du renard; **the police are a. you,** la police est à vos trousses; **to be a. a job,** chercher un emploi; être à la recherche d'un emploi; **we're both a. the same thing,** nous courons le même lièvre; **nobody comes a. her,** elle n'est recherchée, courtisée, de personne; **what's he a.?** (i) qu'est-ce qu'il a en tête? (ii) qu'est-ce qu'il cherche? **I see what you're a.,** je vois où vous voulez en venir; *F:* je te vois venir; **money's what he's a.,** c'est l'argent qu'il lui faut, qu'il cherche. 2. (*time*) (*a*) **to reign a. s.o.,** régner après qn; **a. dinner,** après dîner; **I shall be free a. three o'clock,** je serai libre à partir de trois heures; **a. this date,** passé cette date; **on and a. the 15th.,** à partir du 15; **a. hours,** après le travail; après les heures du service; après l'heure de fermeture; **a. all, a. all's said and done,** au bout du compte, à la fin (des fins), somme toute, tout compte fait, au demeurant; enfin; **a. all, what does it matter?** après tout, qu'est-ce que ça fait? **the day a. the battle,** le lendemain de la bataille; **the day a. tomorrow,** après-demain; **it is a. five (o'clock),** il est cinq heures passées; il est passé cinq heures; *U.S:* **twenty a. four,** quatre heures vingt; **they came in one a. the other,** ils sont entrés à la file, les uns après les autres; **he read page a. page,** il lut page sur page; **to commit blunder a. blunder,** faire sottise sur sottise; **charge a. charge,** des assauts répétés; **I've told you that time a. time,** je vous ai dit cela maintes (et maintes) fois; **day a. day,** jour après jour; **year a. year,** une année après l'autre, tous les ans, chaque année; **he spent his holidays there year a. year,** il y passait ses vacances tous les ans, chaque année; (*b*) (*in compounds forming adjs.*) **a.-dinner speech,** discours *m* d'après dîner; **a.-school activities,** activités *f* extra-scolaires; **the a.-war years,** les années *f* qui suivaient la guerre, les années d'après-guerre. 3. (*order*) (*a*) **the first a. the king,** le premier après le roi; **a. you, sir,** après vous, monsieur; *F:* **a. you with the butter,** après vous le beurre; (*b*) **I put Milton a. Dante,** je mets Milton au-dessous de Dante. 4. (*manner*) **he's a man a. my own heart,** c'est un homme qui a les mêmes idées que moi, qui m'est sympathique; **landscape a. Turner,** paysage d'après Turner, à la (manière de) Turner; *F:* **a. a fashion,** tant bien que mal; *O:* **a. the old style, a. the Russian fashion,** à la vieille mode, à la russe; **a. a pattern,** d'après, suivant, selon, un modèle. 5. *Dial:* (*Irish*) **to be a. doing sth.,** (i) être en train de faire qch.; (ii) être disposé à faire qch.; **you won't be a. doing that,** vous n'allez quand même pas le faire.

III. *conj.* (*a*) après que + *ind.*; **I come a. he has gone,** je viens après qu'il est parti; **I shall come a. he goes, a. he has gone,** je viendrai après qu'il sera parti; **I came a. he went, a. he had gone,** je suis venu après qu'il fut parti; (*b*) après + *infin.*; **a. I had seen him I went out,** après l'avoir vu, je suis sorti; **a. dining, a. he had had his dinner, he went out,** après avoir dîné il est sorti; **a. (he had been) drinking he was bad tempered,** il était méchant après boire, quand il buvait il devenait méchant; il avait le vin mauvais; **a. the peace had been made,** (après) la paix faite.

IV. *a.* (*a*) à venir; **in a. days,** (i) dans les jours à venir; (ii) dans la suite; plus tard dans la vie; **the a. years,** le temps à venir; **in the a. years,** plus tard (dans la vie); (*b*) *Nau: Veh:* arrière; **a. cabin,** cabine *f* sur l'arrière; **a. hold,** cale *f* arrière; **a. body,** arrière *m,* arrière-train *m.*

after-ages ['ɑ:ftəreidʒiz], *s.pl. A:* 1. les siècles futurs; la postérité. 2. les époques postérieures.

after-beat ['ɑ:ftəbi:t], *a. Mus:* **a.-b. accompaniment,** accompagnement *m* à contretemps.

afterbirth ['ɑ:ftəbə:θ], *s.* 1. *Obst:* arrière-faix *m,* délivre *m,* secondines *fpl.* 2. *Jur:* naissance (i) posthume, (ii) postérieure au testament.

afterblow ['ɑ:ftəblou], *s. Tchn:* sursoufflage *m.*

afterbrain ['ɑ:ftəbrein], *s. Anat:* moelle allongée.

afterburner ['ɑ:ftəbə:nər], *s.* (appareil *m,* dispositif *m,* de) postcombustion (*f*).

afterburning ['ɑftəbə:niŋ], *s.* (*of rockets, turbojets*) postcombustion *f.*

after-care, aftercare ['ɑ:ftəkɛər], *s.* soins post-natals, post-opératoires, etc.; soins ultérieurs (donnés à un convalescent); surveillance *f* (de convalescents, de jeunes criminels, etc.).

afterclap ['ɑ:ftəklæp], *s.* contrecoup *m* (d'un événement, etc.).

aftercooler ['ɑ:ftəku:lər], *s.* refroidisseur *m* complémentaire.

aftercrop ['ɑ:ftəkrɔp], *s.* regain *m* (de foin); seconde récolte.

after-culture ['ɑ:ftəkʌltjər], *s. For: etc:* regarnissage *m*; restauration *f* des vides.

afterdamp ['ɑ:ftədæmp], *s. Min:* gaz *m* délétères (provenant d'une explosion de grisou); mofette *f.*

after effect(s) ['ɑftərifekt(s)], *s.* suites *fpl,* contrecoup *m,* répercussion *f* (d'un événement); *Med:* séquelles *fpl,* reliquat *m* (d'une maladie); résultat *m* secondaire (d'un traitement).

after-fame ['ɑ:ftəfeim], *s. Lit:* renommée *f* posthume; gloire *f* posthume.

after-felling ['ɑ:ftəfeliŋ], *s. For:* coupe *f* secondaire.

aftergas ['ɑ:ftəgæs], *s. Min:* gaz *m* délétères (provenant d'une explosion).

afterglow ['ɑ:ftəglou], *s.* 1. dernières lueurs, derniers reflets (du soleil couchant). 2. incandescence résiduelle; **radarscope a.,** rémanence *f* de l'écran radar. 3. réaction *f* (après un bain froid, etc.).

aftergrass ['ɑ:ftəgrɑ:s], *s. Agr:* regain *m* (d'herbe).

aftergrowth ['ɑ:ftəgrouθ], *s.* 1. regain *m* (de foin); seconde récolte. 2. *Fig:* développement *m.*

afterlife ['ɑ:ftəlaif], *s.* 1. la vie après la mort. 2. suite *f* de la vie; **in a.,** plus tard dans la vie.

afterlight ['ɑ:ftəlait], *s.* 1. derniers reflets (de lumière). 2. sagesse tardive, d'après coup.

aftermath ['ɑ:ftəmæθ, mɑ:θ], *s.* 1. *Agr:* regain *m* (de foin); arrière-foin *m.* 2. suites *fpl* (d'un événement); **the a. of war,** (i) les répercussions *f* de la guerre; (ii) l'après-guerre *m.*

after-mentioned ['ɑ:ftə'menʃ(ə)nd], *a.* mentionné ci-après.

aftermost ['ɑ:ftəmoust], *a. Nau:* **the a. part,** la partie la plus en arrière, la plus à l'arrière.

afternoon ['ɑ:ftə'nu:n]. 1. *s.* après-midi *m or f inv.*; *A: & Dial:* après-dîner *m*; **I shall see him this a.,** je le verrai cet(te) après-midi; **in the a.,** (pendant) l'après-midi; **at half-past two in the a.,** à deux heures et demie de l'après-midi; *Jur: etc:* à deux heures et demie du soir, de relevée; **every a.,** tous les après-midi; **I saw him (on) Tuesday a.,** je l'ai vu mardi après-midi; **come and have tea with us this a.,** venez prendre le thé tantôt, cet après-midi. 2. *attrib.* **a. tea,** thé *m,* goûter *m.* 3. *adv. esp. U.S:* **afternoons,** (pendant) l'après-midi.

afterpains ['ɑ:ftəpeinz], *s.pl. Obst:* tranchées utérines.

afterpiece ['ɑ:ftəpi:s], *s.* 1. *Th:* divertissement *m* (de fin de représentation). 2. *N.Arch:* safran *m* (du gouvernail).

after-ripening ['ɑ:ftəraipniŋ], *s. Bot:* maturation *f* (des graines, des fruits) après la récolte.

afters ['ɑ:ftəz], *s.pl. F:* dessert *m.*

after-sales, aftersales ['ɑ:ftəseilz], *a. Com:* **a.-s. service,** service *m* après-vente.

after(-)sensation ['ɑ:ftəsen'seiʃən], *s.* image consécutive.

aftershaft ['ɑ:ftəʃɑ:ft], *s. Orn:* plume *f* secondaire; formation *f* secondaire à la base du rachis principal.

aftershave ['ɑ:ftəʃeiv], *a.* **a. lotion,** lotion *f* après-rasage.

aftershock ['ɑ:ftəʃɔk], *s. Geol:* réplique *f* (d'un séisme).

after-supper ['ɑ:ftə'sʌpər], *s. A:* (*a*) dessert *m*; (*b*) souper tardif; second souper.

afterswarm ['ɑ:ftəswɔ:m], *s. Ap:* jet *m,* rejet *m* (d'abeilles).

after-tack ['ɑ:ftətæk], *s. Paint:* surface collante (qui reparaît sur une couche de peinture sèche).

aftertaste ['ɑ:ftəteist], *s.* arrière-goût *m*; (of wine) déboire *m.*

afterthought ['ɑ:ftəθɔ:t], *s.* (*a*) réflexion *f* après coup; **to add a condition as an a.,** ajouter une condition après coup; (*b*) *F:* (*of child*) enfant *m* sur le tard, *P:* revenez-y *m.*

after-treatment ['ɑ:ftətri:tmənt], *s.* soins ultérieurs (à donner à un convalescent); traitement ultérieur (d'un produit).

afterwards ['ɑ:ftəwədz], *adv.* (*U.S: occ.* **afterward**) après, plus tard, ensuite, dans la suite, par la suite; **I only heard of it a.,** je ne l'ai su qu'après coup; **a long time a.,** longtemps après; **they lived happily ever a.,** depuis lors ils vécurent toujours heureux.

after-wit ['ɑ:ftəwit], *s. A:* sagesse *f* après coup, esprit *m* de l'escalier.

afterword ['ɑftəwə:d], *s.* postface *f,* épilogue *m.*

afterworld ['ɑftəwə:ld], *s.* l'au-delà *m,* la vie après la mort.

aga ['ɑ:gə, ə'gɑ:], *s.* (*Turkish title*) aga *m,* agha *m.*

again [ə'gen, *occ.* ə'gein], *adv.* 1. (*a*) de nouveau, encore; **once a.,** encore une fois, une fois de plus; **here we are a.!** nous revoilà! nous voilà de nouveau; *F:* **not you a.!** (c'est) toi encore! **don't do it a.!** ne recommencez pas, plus! **they're at it a.!** les voilà qui recommencent! **there's the dog howling a.,** voilà encore, revoilà, le chien qui hurle; **never a.,** (ne . . .) jamais plus; plus jamais (. . . ne); **such a thing will never happen a.,** pareille chose ne se reproduira plus; **a. and a., time and (time) a.,** maintes et maintes fois; à plusieurs reprises; **I have told you so a. and a.,** je vous l'ai dit vingt fois, cent fois; **now and a.,** *Lit:* **ever and a.,** de temps en temps; de temps à autre; **as much a.,** deux fois autant; **half as much a.,** de moitié plus; **half as long a.,** de moitié plus long; **he is as old a. as Mary (is),** il a deux fois l'âge de Marie; (*b*) (*with vb.*) re-; **to begin a.,** recommencer; **to come a.,** revenir; **I've seen him a.,** je l'ai revu; **I hope I shall find it a.,** j'espère bien le retrouver; (*c*) **what was your name a.?** rappelez-moi votre nom; **what's his name a.?** comment s'appelle-t-il déjà? encore? (*d*) *A: & Lit:* (*intensive*) **the blow made his ears ring a.,** ce fut un coup à lui faire tinter les oreilles; **the loaded table groaned a.,** la table chargée gémissait sous le poids. 2. (*a*) de plus, d'ailleurs, en outre; **a. I am not sure that . . .,** d'ailleurs je ne suis pas sûr que . . .; (*b*) **(then) a., (and) a.,** d'autre part; d'un autre côté.

against [ə'genst, *occ.* ə'geinst], *prep.* contre. 1. (*a*) **to fight a. s.o.,** se battre contre qn; **to march a. the enemy,** marcher à l'ennemi; **I have nothing to say a. it,** je n'ai rien à dire là-contre; **to argue a. sth.,** plaider à contre-pied de qch.; **I'm a. having him here,** je ne veux pas qu'il vienne; **it was done a. my will,** cela s'est fait contre mon gré; **I did it a. my will,** je l'ai fait malgré moi, à contre-cœur; **to act a. the law,** agir contrairement à la loi; **action that is a. the rules,** action contraire aux règlements; **he is dead a. persecution,** il est l'ennemi irréductible des persécutions; **fate is a. him,** le destin lui est contraire; **conditions are a. us,** les conditions nous sont défavorables; *Book-k:* **to make an entry a. s.o.,** débiter qn; **to maintain an opinion a. the whole world,** soutenir une opinion envers et contre tous; **his manner is a. him,** sa façon de se comporter lui est préjudiciable; **her age is a. her,** on peut lui objecter son âge; **his appearance is, goes, a. him,** il ne paie pas de mine;

there is no law a. it, il n'y a pas de loi qui s'y oppose; **a. the nap, a. the hair,** à contre-poil, à rebours, à rebrousse-poil; **a. the grain,** contre le fil, à contre-fil, à rebours; *Fig:* à contre-cœur; **a. the light,** à contre-jour; **a. the tide,** à contre-marée; **to go a. the tide,** prendre le contre-sens de la marée; **it was a race a. time,** on n'avait guère le temps de le faire; *Mec:* **to act a. a force,** contrarier une force; (*b*) **to warn s.o. a. s.o., sth.,** mettre qn en garde contre qn, qch.; (*c*) **to run up a. a wall,** courir, aller, donner, contre un mur; *Aut: F:* aller s'emboutir contre un mur; **to come up a. sth.,** se heurter contre qch.; *F:* **to run, come, up a. s.o.,** rencontrer qn par hasard; (*d*) **leaning a. the wall,** appuyé contre le mur; **to place sth. a. a wall,** adosser qch. à un mur; (*e*) à l'encontre de; **never go a. nature,** il ne faut jamais aller à l'encontre de la nature; (*f*) **(a standard weight) a. which all weights can be checked,** (un poids étalon) d'après lequel, sur lequel, on peut vérifier les poids; (*g*) **the symbol N is placed against each new rule,** le symbole N est placé en regard de chaque nouvelle règle; *Ph:* **graph of viscosity a. temperature,** courbe *f* de la viscosité en fonction de la température. **2.** (*a*) **my rights (as) a. the government,** mes droits vis-à-vis du gouvernement; (*b*) *A:* **over a. the school,** en face de l'école, vis-à-vis de l'école. **3. to show up a. a background,** se détacher sur un fond. **4.** *Lit:* **to make preparations a. his return,** faire des préparatifs pour son retour; **to buy preserves a. the winter,** acheter des conserves en prévision de l'hiver. **5. three deaths this year as a. thirty in 1970,** trois morts cette année contre trente, comparées à trente, en 1970.

agalacia [ægə'leisiə], **agalactia** [ægə'læktiə], **agalaxy** ['ægəlæksi], *s. Vet: Med:* agalactie *f*, agalaxie *f*.

agalite ['ægəlait], *s. Miner:* agalite *f*.

agalloch [ə'gælək], **agalwood** ['ægəlwud], *s. Bot:* calambac *m*, calambour *m*, calambouc *m*.

agalmatolite [ægəl'mætoulait], *s. Geol:* agalmatolit(h)e *f*.

agama ['ægəmə], *s. Rept:* agame *m*; **Caucasian a.,** agame du Caucase; **sand a.,** agame à tête de crapaud (asiatique); **common (African) a.,** agame(-)colon *m*.

agami [ə'gɑːmi], *s. Orn:* agami *m*, *F:* oiseau-trompette *m*, *pl.* oiseaux-trompettes.

agamic [ə'gæmik], **agamous** ['ægəməs], *a. Biol:* agame.

agamid ['ægəmid], *s. Rept:* agamidé *m*.

Agamidae [æ'gæmidiː], *s.pl. Rept:* agamidés *m*.

agamogenesis [ægəmou'dʒenisis], *s. Biol:* agamie *f*.

agamogony [ægə'mɔgəni], *s. Biol:* schizogonie *f*.

agamoid ['ægəmɔid], *s. Rept:* agamidé *m*.

agamont ['ægəmɔnt], *s. Prot:* agamonte *m*, schizonte *m*.

agapanthus [ægə'pænθəs], *s. Bot:* agapanthe *f*.

agape[1] [ə'geip], *adv. & a.* bouche bée; **to stand a.,** rester bouche bée; **mouth a. with astonishment,** bouche arrondie par l'étonnement.

agape[2], *pl.* **-ae** ['ægəpiː], *s. Rel.H:* agape *f*.

agapetae [ægə'piːtiː], *s.f.pl.* **agapeti** [ægə'piːtai], *s.m.pl. Rel.H:* agapètes *mf*.

agapornis [ægə'pɔːnis], *s. Orn:* agapornis *m*.

agar-agar ['ɑːgər'ɑːgər, 'eigər'eigər], *s.* agar-agar *m*, gélose *f*.

agaric ['ægərik], *s.* **1.** *Fung:* agaric *m*; **royal a.,** oronge *f*; **fly a.,** (amanite *f*) tue-mouches *m*, fausse oronge; **St George's a.,** mousseron *m*, tricholome *m* de la Saint-Georges; **fairy-ring a.,** faux mousseron. **2.** *Miner:* **a. mineral,** agaric minéral, agaric fossile, agarice *f*.

Agaricaceae [ægəri'keisiiː], *s.pl. Fung:* agaricacées *f*.

Agaricales [ægəri'keiliːz], *s.pl. Fung:* agaricales *f*.

Agaristidae [ægə'ristidiː], *s.pl. Ent:* agaristides *m*.

agate ['ægət], *s.* **1.** (*a*) *Miner:* agate *f*; **eye a.,** agate œillée; onyx œillé; **tree a., dendritic a.,** agate arborisée; (*b*) *Moll:* **a. snail,** achatine *f*. **2.** *Tls:* agate à brunir. **3.** *Typ: U.S:* corps *m* 5½.

Agatha ['ægəθə], *Pr.n.f.* Agathe.

Agathocles [ə'gæθəkliːz], *Pr.n.m. Gr.Hist:* Agathocle.

agatiferous [ægə'tifərəs], *a.* agatifère.

agatine ['ægətin, -tain], *a.* agatin.

agatise ['ægətaiz], *v.tr.* agatiser, agatifier.

agatoid ['ægətɔid], *a.* agatoïde.

agave ['ægeiv, ə'geivi], *s. Bot:* agave *m*.

agaze [ə'geiz], *a. A: & U.S:* en contemplation.

agba ['ægbə], *s. Bot:* agba *m*; **a. (wood),** tola *m*.

age[1] [eidʒ], *s.* **1.** âge *m*; (*a*) **(of) middle a.,** (d')âge mûr; entre deux âges; **to be past middle a.,** être sur le retour, sur le déclin de la vie; **of uncertain a.,** entre deux âges; **twenty years of a.,** âgé de vingt ans; **what a. is he?** quel âge a-t-il? **when I was your a.,** quand j'avais votre âge; **when I was a little girl your a.,** quand j'étais une petite fille de ton âge; **he has a daughter your a.,** il a une fille de votre âge; **at his a. he ought to be able to earn his own living,** à son âge il devrait être capable de gagner sa vie; *F:* **be your a.!** voyons, tu n'es plus un enfant! **to be under a.,** être mineur; **to be under a. to hold a driving licence,** être trop jeune pour passer son permis de conduire; **full a.,** âge légal; (état *m* de) majorité *f*; **to be of a.,** être majeur; **to come of a.,** atteindre sa majorité; **coming of a.,** entrée *f* en majorité; **at his, her, coming of a.,** à sa majorité; **to be over a. to do sth.,** être trop âgé pour faire qch.; **they are of an a.,** ils sont à peu près du même âge; **to be of an a. to marry,** être en âge de se marier; **a. of discretion,** âge de raison, de discrétion; **mental a.,** âge mental; **he doesn't look his a.,** il ne porte pas son âge; **she might be any a.,** elle n'a pas d'âge; elle est sans âge; **he might be any a. between 40 and 60,** il pouvait, peut, avoir entre 40 and 60 ans; *Adm: Mil:* **a. group,** classe *f*; **he comes into the 15 to 20 a. group,** il fait partie du groupe, de la classe, des 15 à 20 ans; **to be promoted in order of a.,** avancer à l'ancienneté; **pensionable a., retirement a.,** âge de (la mise à) la retraite; **retirement on account of a.,** retraite *f* par limite d'âge; **waiving of a. limit,** dispense *f* d'âge; **school-leaving a.,** âge de fin de scolarité; *Pol.Ec:* **a. distribution, structure (of the population),** répartition *f*, structure *f*, par âge (de la population); **a. pyramid,** pyramide *m* des âges; *Ind: etc:* **a.-life method of depreciation,** méthode *f* d'amortissement par tranches annuelles égales; *Bot:* **a. ring,** cerne *m* (d'un arbre); (*b*) **(old) a.,** vieillesse *f*; **the house is falling to pieces with a.,** la maison tombe de vieillesse, de vétusté. **2.** (*a*) âge, époque *f*, siècle *m*; **from a. to a.,** d'âge en âge; *Lit:* **to all ages,** à tout jamais; *Lit:* **throughout all ages,** dans tous les temps; **the a. we live in,** notre siècle, le siècle où nous vivons; **in our a.,** à notre époque; **the present a.,** l'époque actuelle; la génération actuelle; *Hist: Prehist:* **the stone a.,** l'âge de pierre; **the neolithic a.,** le néolithique, l'âge de la pierre polie; **the bronze a.,** l'âge du bronze; **the dark ages,** les premiers siècles du moyen âge; le premier moyen âge; le haut moyen âge; *Lit: etc:* **the Augustan A.,** (i) le siècle d'Auguste; (ii) le siècle de Louis XIV; (iii) (*in Eng.*) l'époque de la reine Anne; *Myth:* **the golden a.,** l'âge d'or; **the brazen a.,** l'âge d'airain; **the iron a.,** l'âge de fer; (*b*) *F:* **it's ages, an a., since I saw him, I haven't seen him for ages,** il y a un siècle, une éternité, des éternités, que je ne l'ai vu. **3.** *Cards:* (*at poker*) joueur *m* à gauche, qui parle le dernier.

age[2], *v.* **(aged** [eidʒd], **ageing** ['eidʒiŋ]). **1.** *v.i.* vieillir, prendre de l'âge; **he had aged beyond his years,** il avait vieilli et paraissait plus que son âge; **he had aged beyond belief,** il avait vieilli d'une façon inconcevable; **he had aged beyond recognition,** il avait vieilli à ne plus le reconnaître. **2.** *v.tr.* vieillir; rendre (qn) vieux; **that hat ages you,** ce chapeau vous vieillit. **3.** *v.tr. Ind: etc:* mûrir (un produit; vieillir (un métal).

aged, *a.* **1.** ['eidʒid] (*a*) âgé; vieux, vieil, vieille; **an a. man,** un vieillard; *s.* **the a.,** les vieillards, les vieux; (*b*) (*of horse*) hors d'âge. **2.** [eidʒd] (*a*) **a. twenty,** âgé de vingt ans; (*b*) **I found him greatly a.,** je l'ai trouvé bien vieilli.

ageing[1] ['eidʒiŋ], *a.* (*a*) vieillissant; **a. population,** population viellissante; (*b*) **her hat is very a.,** son chapeau la vieillit.

ageing[2], *s.* **1.** vieillissement *m* (d'une personne, de la population). **2.** vieillissement (d'un métal, d'un vin, etc.).

ageless ['eidʒlis], *a.* **1.** toujours jeune. **2.** éternel.

agelong ['eidʒlɔŋ], *a.* (coutume, etc.) séculaire.

agency ['eidʒənsi], *s.* **1.** (*a*) action *f*, opération *f*; **through the a. of water,** par l'action de l'eau; (*b*) agent *m*; **natural agencies,** agents naturels; (*c*) entremise *f*; **through s.o.'s a.,** par l'entremise, par l'intermédiaire *m*, de qn; (*d*) *O:* **man has free a.,** l'homme peut agir selon son libre arbitre. **2.** (*a*) *Com:* agence *f*, bureau *m*; **sole a. for a firm,** représentation exclusive d'une maison; **advertising a.,** agence de publicité; **news, press, a.,** agence de presse; **employment a.,** agence de placement; **estate a.,** agence immobilière; **land a.,** agence foncière; **customs a.,** agence en douane; **shipping a.,** agence maritime; **travel a.,** agence de tourisme; **literary a.,** agence littéraire; *Adm:* **government a.,** service gouvernemental; **public a.,** agence gouvernementale; (*b*) *Bank:* (i) succursale *f*, agence (de banque); (ii) direction *f* d'une succursale de banque; (*c*) *Com:* comptoir *m* (à l'étranger).

agenda [ə'dʒendə], *s.* (*formerly pl., now considered as sg.*) (*a*) ordre *m* du jour, programme *m* (d'une réunion); **to draw up an a.,** dresser l'ordre du jour; **to place a question on the a.,** inscrire une question à l'ordre du jour; (*b*) *Ecc:* agende *f*, rituel *m*.

agenesia [ædʒə'niːziə], *s. Med:* agénésie *f*.

agenesic [ædʒə'niːzik], *a. Med:* agénésique.

agenesis [ædʒə'niːsis], *s. Med:* agénésie *f*.

agent ['eidʒənt], *s.* **1.** (*a*) agent, -ente; **to be a free a.,** avoir (le droit d'agir selon) son libre arbitre; (*in telepathy*) **a. and percipient,** agent et patient; (*b*) homme *m* d'affaires; régisseur *m* (d'une propriété); *Com: etc:* agent, représentant *m*; **a. for the firm of . . .,** représentant de la maison . . .; **a. on the spot,** agent à demeure; **we are agents for Messrs X & Co.,** nous représentons la maison X et Cie.; **sole a.,** agent exclusif; **to be sole a. for . . .,** avoir la représentation exclusive de . . .; **sole a. for a brand,** seul dépositaire, concessionnaire, d'une marque; **appointed a.,** agent titré; **commission a.,** commissionnaire *m* en marchandises; **forwarding a., transit a.,** transitaire *m*; **advertising a.,** agent de publicité; **insurance a.,** agent d'assurances; **(real-)estate a.,** agent immobilier; **landlord's a.,** gérant, -ante, d'immeubles; **bank a.,** directeur *m* d'une succursale de banque; *U.S:* **station a.,** chef *m* de gare; *U.S: F:* **road a.,** voleur *m* de grand chemin; (*c*) **secret a.,** agent secret; **double a.,** agent double; (*d*) *Jur:* mandataire *mf*, commis *m*; fondé(e) de pouvoir. **2. chemical a.,** agent chimique; **therapeutical a.,** agent thérapeutique.

agent-general ['eidʒənt'dʒen(ə)rl], *s.* (*pl.* **agents-general**) *Dipl:* représentant fondé de pouvoirs.

age-old ['eidʒould], *a.* séculaire; qui n'a pas de date.

ageratum [æ'dʒerətəm, ædʒə'reitəm], *s. Bot:* agérate *mf*, ageratum *m*.

agglomerate[1] [ə'glɔmərət]. **1.** *a.* aggloméré. **2.** *s. Geol:* agglomérat *m*.

agglomerate[2] [ə'glɔməreit]. **1.** *v.tr.* agglomérer. **2.** *v.i.* s'agglomérer.

agglomeration [əglɔmə'reiʃ(ə)n], *s.* **1.** agglomération *f*, agrégation *f*. **2.** (*built-up area*) agglomération.

agglomerative [ə'glɔmərətiv], *a.* agglomératif.

agglutinant [ə'gluːtinənt], *a. & s.* agglutinant (*m*).

agglutinate[1] [ə'gluːtinət], *a.* agglutiné.

agglutinate[2] [ə'gluːtineit]. **1.** *v.tr.* agglutiner. **2.** *v.i.* s'agglutiner.

agglutinating [ə'gluːtineitiŋ], *a. Ling:* agglutinant.

agglutination [əgluːti'neiʃ(ə)n], *s.* agglutination *f*.

agglutinative [ə'gluːtinətiv], *a.* (*a*) agglutinatif, agglutinant; (*b*) *Ling:* agglutinant.

agglutinin [æ'gluːtinin], *s. Physiol:* agglutinine *f*.

agglutinogen [æglu:'tiːnədʒen], *s. Physiol:* agglutinogène *m*.

aggradation [ægrə'deiʃ(ə)n], *s. Geol:* alluvionnement *m*.

aggrade [æ'greid], *v.tr. Geol:* élever le niveau du (lit d'une rivière, etc.) par alluvionnement.

aggrandize [ə'grændaiz], *v.tr.* agrandir (un État, l'importance de qn); rendre (qn) plus puissant; exagérer (un incident).

aggrandizement [ə'grændizmənt], *s.* agrandissement *m* (d'un État, etc.); **he does it for his own a.,** il le fait pour se mettre en avant, pour se pousser dans le monde.

aggravate ['ægrəveit], *v.tr.* **1.** (*a*) aggraver (une faute, une difficulté); empirer (un mal); envenimer (une plaie, une querelle); **burglary aggravated by murder,** cambriolage aggravé de meurtre; *Jur:* **aggravated larceny,** vol qualifié; (*b*) augmenter (l'indignation, la douleur); (*c*) *A:* exagérer (un danger). **2.** *F:* agacer, exaspérer (qn); **to a. s.o. beyond the limits of endurance,** pousser qn à bout.

aggravating ['ægrəveitiŋ], *a.* **1. a. circumstance,** circonstance aggravante. **2.** *F:* exaspérant, assommant; **a. child,** enfant insupportable, désespérant, exaspérant.

aggravatingly ['ægrəveitiŋli], *adv. F:* d'une manière exaspérante; **he's a. smug,** il est d'une suffisance insupportable.

aggravation [ægrə'veiʃ(ə)n], *s.* **1.** (*a*) aggravation *f* (d'un crime, d'une maladie); envenimement *m* (d'une plaie, d'une querelle); (*b*) *F:* exaspération *f*, agacement *m*. **2.** circonstance aggravante.

aggregate[1] ['ægrigət]. **1.** *a.* (*a*) collectif; *Pol.Ec:* global, -aux; **for an a. period of three years,** pendant trois ans en tout; **a. economic activity,** ensemble *m* des activités économiques; **a. output,** production globale; **a. demand function,** fonction *f* de la demande globale; **a. employment,** emploi global; **a. market supply,** offre agrégative, globale, du marché; **a. market demand,** demande agrégative, globale, du marché; **a. net increment,** accroissement global net; **a. supply function,** fonction de l'offre globale; **a. variables,** variables globales; (*b*) *Bot: Geol: Z:* agrégé; **a. animals,** agrégés *mpl*; *Bot:* **a. species,** espèce agrégée. **2.** *s.* (*a*) ensemble *m*, total *m*; **world aggregates,** totaux mondiaux; **value aggregates,** agrégats *m* de valeurs; **in the a.,** en somme, dans l'ensemble; à tout prendre, somme toute; **reckoned in the a.,** calculé globalement; **man in the a.,** l'humanité prise dans sa totalité; l'homme moyen; (*b*) masse *f*, assemblage *m*, agrégation *f*; *Ch: Miner:* agrégat; **a rock is an a. of mineral particles,** les roches sont des agrégats composés de minéraux; (*c*) *Civ.E:* granulat *m*.

aggregate[2] ['ægrigeit]. **1.** *v.tr.* (*a*) *Ph:* agréger; (*b*) **to a.**

s.o. to an association, agréger qn à une association; (*c*) s'élever à (un nombre); monter à (un total). **2.** *v.i. Ph:* s'agréger.

aggregately ['ægrigətli], *adv.* collectivement; en masse; globalement.

aggregation [ægri'geiʃ(ə)n], *s.* **1.** (*a*) *Ph:* agrégation *f*, agglomération *f*; (*b*) *Pol.Ec:* **a. of production functions,** agrégation de fonctions de production; (*c*) agrégation (de qn à une société); (*d*) *Lit:* assemblage *m* (de personnes). **2.** agrégat *m*.

aggregative ['ægrigətiv], *a. Ph:* agrégatif.

aggress [ə'gres], *v.i. & tr.* attaquer, agresser; **the aggressed party,** la victime de l'agression.

aggression [ə'greʃ(ə)n], *s.* agression *f*; **war of a.,** guerre *f* d'agression; **victim of an a.,** victime *f* d'une agression; *Psy:* **(innate tendency to) a.,** l'instinct *m* d'agression.

aggressive [ə'gresiv], *a.* agressif; (regard, air) cassant; **a. speech,** discours agressif; **a. policy,** politique militante; *Psy:* **a. impulse,** impulsion agressive.

aggressively [ə'gresivli], *adv.* d'une manière agressive; d'un ton agressif; **a. virtuous man,** homme d'une vertu agressive, farouche.

aggressiveness [ə'gresivnis], *s.* caractère agressif; agressivité *f*.

aggressor [ə'gresər], *s.* agresseur *m*; *attrib.* **a. nation,** pays *m* agresseur.

aggrieve [ə'gri:v], *v.tr.* (*usu. passive*) chagriner, blesser; **to be aggrieved, feel aggrieved, at, by, sth.,** être chagriné, blessé, de qch.; se sentir sous le coup d'une injustice; se sentir lésé; **I feel aggrieved when I see such things,** cela me chagrine de voir de telles choses; *Jur:* **the aggrieved party,** la partie lésée.

agha ['ɑ:gə, ə'gɑ:], *s.* (*Turkish title*) aga *m*, agha *m*.

aghast [ə'gɑ:st], *a.* consterné; sidéré; stupéfait; ahuri; pantois; **to stand a.,** en être tout pantois.

agile ['ædʒail], *a.* agile; leste.

agilely ['ædʒailli], *adv.* agilement.

agility [ə'dʒiliti], *s.* agilité *f*.

agin [ə'gin], *prep. Dial: F: & Hum:* contre.

Agincourt ['ædʒinkɔ:t], *Pr.n. Geog: Hist:* Azincourt *m*.

aging ['eidʒiŋ], *a. & s. esp. U.S:* = AGEING.

agio ['ædʒiou], *s. Fin:* **1.** agio *m*; prix *m* du change; **a. account,** compte *m* d'agio. **2.** commerce *m* du change.

agiotage ['ædʒioutidʒ], *s. Fin:* agiotage *m*.

agitate ['ædʒiteit], *v.tr.* **1.** agiter, remuer (qch.); tourmenter (la surface de l'eau). **2.** agiter, troubler (qn, l'esprit de qn). **3.** (*a*) **to a. a question,** agiter une question; (*b*) *v.i.* **to a. for, against, sth.,** faire de l'agitation, mener une campagne, en faveur de, contre, qch.; **he's always agitating,** il sème toujours la discorde; c'est un contestataire.

agitated ['ædʒiteitid], *a.* agité; ému; troublé; *Med:* **a. melancholia,** mélancolie anxieuse.

agitating ['ædʒiteitiŋ], *a.* **1.** agitateur, -trice; émotionnant; troublant. **2.** *Civ.E:* **a. truck, lorry,** camion *m* bétonnière.

agitation [ædʒi'teiʃ(ə)n], *s.* **1.** agitation *f* (de l'air, de la mer); mouvement *m*. **2.** (*a*) agitation, émotion *f*, trouble *m*; **in a state of a.,** agité; (*b*) agitation (ouvrière, etc.); troubles. **3.** *A:* discussion *f* (d'une question).

agitato [ædʒi'tɑ:tou], *a. & adv. Mus:* agitato.

agitator ['ædʒiteitər], *s.* **1.** (*pers.*) agitateur, -trice; contestataire *m*. **2.** *Ind:* (appareil) brasseur *m*; agitateur *m*.

Aglaia [ə'glaiə], *Pr.n.f. Gr.Myth:* Aglaé.

agleam [ə'gli:m], *a. Lit:* luisant; **eyes a. with . . .,** yeux brillants de. . . .

aglet ['æglit], *s. A:* **1.** ferret *m* (de lacet). **2.** *Cost:* aiguillette *f*. **3.** chaton *m* (de noisetier, de bouleau).

agley [ə'glei], *adv. Dial: Scot:* de travers.

aglobulia [eiglɔ'bju:liə], **aglobulism** [ei'glɔbjulizm], *s. Med:* aglobulie *f*.

Aglossa [ei'glɔsə], *s.pl. Amph:* aglosses *m*.

aglossal [ei'glɔsl], **aglossate** [ei'glɔseit], *a. Nat.Hist:* aglosse.

aglossia [ei'glɔsiə], *s.* aglossie *f*.

aglow [ə'glou], *a.* **1.** (*of thg*) enflammé, embrasé; **to be a. with colour,** briller de vives couleurs; **the sun sets the peaks a.,** le soleil embrase les pics; **sky a. with the sunset,** ciel qu'embrase le soleil couchant. **2.** (*of pers.*) **I was all a. with the exercise,** l'exercise m'avait fouetté le sang; **face a. with delight,** visage rayonnant de joie, tout épanoui; **a. with health,** resplendissant de santé.

Aglypha ['æglifə], *s.pl. Rept:* aglyphes *m*.

aglyphous ['æglifəs], *a. Rept:* aglyphe.

agnail ['ægneil], *s.* envie *f* (filet de peau qui s'est détaché de l'ongle).

agnate ['ægneit], *a. & s. Jur:* agnat (*m*).

Agnatha ['ægnəθə], *s.pl. Z:* agnathes *m*.

agnathia [æg'neiθiə], *s. Med:* agnathie *f*.

agnatic [æg'nætik], *a.* agnatique.

agnation [æg'neiʃ(ə)n], *s. Jur:* agnation *f*.

Agnes ['ægnis], *Pr.n.f.* Agnès.

agnomen [æg'noumen], *s. Rom.Ant:* agnomen *m*, surnom *m*.

agnosia [æg'nousiə], *s. Med:* agnosie *f*; **auditory, gustatory, olfactory, optic, tactile, a.,** agnosie auditive, gustative, olfactive, visuelle, tactile.

agnostic [æg'nɔstik], *a. & s.* agnosticiste (*mf*); agnostique (*mf*).

agnosticism [æg'nɔstisizm], *s.* agnosticisme *m*.

agnus castus ['ægnəs'kæstəs], *s. Bot:* agnus-castus *m*; gattilier *m* d'Europe; petit-poivre *m*; poivre *m* sauvage.

agnus dei ['æɲus'deii, 'ægnus-], *s. Ecc:* agnus-Dei *m inv*.

ago [ə'gou]. **1.** *a.* (*always follows the noun*) **ten years a.,** il y a dix ans; **that was thirty years a.,** il y a de cela trente ans; cela date de trente ans; **he arrived an hour a.,** il est arrivé il y a une heure; il est là depuis une heure; **weeks a.,** il y a des semaines; **that was a good while a.,** il y a de cela pas mal de temps; il y a longtemps de tout cela; tout cela date de loin; **a little while a.,** tout à l'heure; tantôt, il y a peu de temps; **a few minutes a.,** il y a quelques minutes; tout à l'heure; il y a un instant. **2.** *adv.* **long a.,** il y a longtemps; **not long a.,** il n'y a pas longtemps; **not so long ago there was a monastery here,** il n'y a pas si longtemps, il y avait ici un couvent; **how long a. is it since . . .?** combien de temps y a-t-il que . . .? depuis combien de temps . . .? **as long a. as 1840,** déjà en 1840; dès 1840; **I knew him long a.,** je l'ai connu dans le temps; **I saw him no longer a. than last week,** je l'ai vu pas plus tard que la semaine dernière.

agog [ə'gɔg], *adv. & a.* **to be (all) a. for sth.,** attendre qch. avec impatience; **to be all a. (with excitement),** être en l'air, en émoi (à cause de qch.); **to be all a. to do sth.,** être impatient, griller d'envie, de faire qch.; **the whole town was a.,** toute la ville était en émoi.

agogic [ə'gɔdʒik], *a. Mus:* agogique.

agoing [ə'gouiŋ], *adv. A:* **to set sth., s.o., a.,** mettre qch., qn, en marche, en train, en branle; faire aller qch.; amorcer qch.

agonic [ə'gɔnik], *a. Magn:* agone, agonique; **a. lines,** agones *f*, agoniques *f*.

agonist ['ægənist], *s.* **1.** *Gr.Ant:* athlète *m*. **2.** *Lit:* protagoniste *mf*.

agonistic [ægə'nistik], *a.* **1.** *Gr.Ant:* agonistique, athlétique. **2.** *A. & Lit:* combatif.

agonistics [ægə'nistiks], *s.pl.* (*with sg. const.*) agonistique *f*.

agonize ['ægənaiz]. **1.** *v.tr.* (*a*) torturer; mettre (qn) au supplice, au martyre, à la torture; (*b*) (*passive use*) **I was agonized by the idea that . . .,** j'étais au supplice, angoissé, à l'idée que. . . . **2.** *v.i. Lit:* être au supplice, au martyre.

agonized ['ægənaizd], *a.* (cri) d'angoisse; **with an a. expression (on her face),** d'un regard plein d'angoisse.

agonizing ['ægənaiziŋ], *a.* (*of pain*) atroce; (*of spectacle*) navrant, poignant, angoissant; **a. cry,** cri déchirant; **a. fear of . . .,** peur *f* atroce de . . .; *F:* **it was simply a.,** c'était à vous rendre fou; c'était atroce.

agonizingly ['ægənaiziŋli], *adv.* avec angoisse.

agony ['ægəni], *s.* **1.** angoisse *f*; **to look on in a.,** regarder avec angoisse; **to be in an a. of pain,** être en proie à des douleurs atroces; **to suffer agonies, to be in agonies,** être au supplice, au martyre; *Journ:* **a. column,** annonces personnelles, particulières, petite correspondance; *F:* **it was a.!** j'en ai bavé; *F:* **to pile on the a.,** forcer la dose. **2. (death) a.,** agonie *f*; **he entered into his last a.,** il entra en agonie. **3. in an a. of fear,** saisi d'une peur atroce, en proie à une peur atroce; *O:* **a. of joy,** paroxysme *m* de joie; **in an a. of joy,** pris d'une joie délirante; **to be in an a. of anticipation,** se mourir d'impatience.

agora ['ægərə], *s.* (*pl.* **agorae** [-ri:], *or* **agoras**) *Gr.Ant:* agora *m*.

agoraphobia [ægərə'foubiə], *s. Psy:* agoraphobie *f*.

agoraphobic [ægərə'foubik], *a. & s. Psy:* agoraphobe (*mf*).

agouti [ə'gu:ti], *s. Z:* agouti *m*.

agraf(f)e [ə'græf], *s.* agrafe *f*.

agrammatism [æ'græmətizm], *s. Psy:* agrammatisme *m*.

agranulocytosis [eigrænjulousai'tousis], *s. Med:* agranulocytose *f*.

agraphia [ə'græfiə], *s. Med:* agraphie *f*.

agrarian [ə'greəriən]. **1.** *a.* (loi, mesure) agraire. **2.** *a. & s. Pol:* agrarien (*m*).

agrarianism [ə'greəriənizm], *s.* agrarianisme *m*.

agravic [ei'grævik], *a. Ph:* à gravité nulle.

agree [ə'gri:]. **1.** *v.i. & tr.* consentir, donner son adhésion (**to a proposal,** à une proposition); faire droit (à une requête); **to a. formally to sth.,** approuver qch. officiellement; **to a. to do sth.,** accepter, convenir, de faire qch.; consentir à faire qch.; **if France agrees to abandon her rights . . .,** si la France consent à abandonner ses droits. . . . **I a. that he was mistaken,** je vous accorde, j'admets, qu'il s'est trompé; **to a. to certain conditions,** convenir de, accepter, tomber d'accord sur, certaines conditions; **this was agreed,** il en fut convenu ainsi; *Jur:* **conditions agreed upon,** conditions acceptées d'un commun accord; *Jur:* **it is this day mutually agreed that . . .,** il a été ce jour mutuellement convenu que. . . . **they have, are, agreed about the prices,** ils sont convenus des prix; **let's a. to differ,** différons à l'amiable; **to a. to sth. being done,** accepter que qch. se fasse; **unless otherwise agreed,** sauf arrangement contraire; **we agreed that I should write to him,** il a été convenu que je lui écrirais; **agreed!** convenu! entendu! soit! d'accord! **2.** *v.i.* (*of pers.*) (*a*) s'accorder; être d'accord, être bien ensemble; tomber d'accord; **to make two people a.,** mettre deux personnes d'accord; **they cannot a.,** ils ne s'accordent pas ensemble; ils ne s'entendent pas (bien) ensemble; **we shall never a.,** jamais nous ne nous mettrons d'accord; (*b*) **to a. with s.o.,** entrer dans les idées de qn; donner raison à qn; penser comme qn; **to a. with s.o. about sth.,** être du même avis que qn sur une question; s'accorder, être d'accord, avec qn sur une question; **I do not a. with you in thinking her right to refuse,** je ne suis pas d'accord avec vous qu'elle ait raison de refuser; to **a. with s.o.'s opinion,** partager, se ranger à, l'opinion de qn; **I quite a. with you on that point,** je suis tout à fait de votre avis là-dessus; **I quite a.,** bon, d'accord! **I quite a., and if . . .,** bon, entendu, et si . . .; **he entirely agrees with you,** il est entièrement de votre avis; *F:* **I couldn't a. (with you) more!** tu l'as bien dit! **I don't a. with this theory,** je n'accepte pas cette théorie; **everyone agrees that . . ., it is generally agreed that . . .,** tout le monde accepte que . . .; au dire de tout le monde . . .; (*c*) **'you're right!' he agreed,** 'vous avez raison', acquiesça-t-il. **3.** *v.i.* (*of thgs*) (*a*) s'accorder, être d'accord, concorder (ensemble); (*of ideas, opinions*) se rencontrer; **that does not a. with what he said,** cela ne s'accorde pas, n'est pas d'accord, ne concorde pas, ne se concilie pas, avec ce qu'il a dit; (*b*) *Gram:* s'accorder; **the verb agrees with the subject in number,** le verbe s'accorde en nombre avec le sujet; (*c*) convenir (**with,** à); réussir; **his work, the climate, doesn't a. with him,** son emploi, le climat, ne lui convient pas, ne lui va pas; **hot weather doesn't a. with me,** la chaleur m'incommode; **lobster doesn't a. with me,** le homard ne me réussit pas; je ne digère pas le homard; **the treatment didn't a. with me,** le traitement ne m'a pas réussi. **4.** *v.tr. Book-k:* **to a. the accounts, the books,** faire accorder les livres; **to a. an account,** faire cadrer un compte; **the figures were agreed between the accountants,** les chiffres ont été acceptés (d'un commun accord) par les experts comptables.

agreeable [ə'griəbl], *a.* **1.** agréable (**to,** à); (*of pers.*) aimable (**to,** envers); **if that is a. to you,** si cela vous convient. **2.** (*a*) (*of pers.*) consentant; **to be a. to sth., to do sth.,** consentir à qch.; à faire qch.; accepter qch., accepter de faire qch.; **I am (quite) a.,** je veux bien; je ne demande pas mieux; (*b*) *A:* (*of thg*) conforme (**to,** à).

agreeableness [ə'griəblnis], *s.* (*a*) (*of pers.*) amabilité *f*; (*b*) (*of place, etc.*) agrément *m*, charme *m*.

agreeably [ə'griəbli], *adv.* agréablement.

agreed [ə'gri:d], *a.* convenu; forfaitaire; **a. price,** prix convenu; **contract at an a. price,** contrat *m* à forfait; **a. consideration,** (i) prix convenu; (ii) contrepartie convenue.

agreement [ə'gri:mənt], *s.* **1.** *Com: Jur: etc:* convention *f*, acte *m*, contrat *m*, traité *m*, arrangement *m*; *Jur:* **real a.,** bail *m*, (à long terme); **written a.,** convention par écrit; **a. for sale,** contrat, convention, acte, de vente; **collective a.,** contrat collectif; **collective wage a.,** convention collective des salaires; **to work by a.,** entreprendre un travail à prix convenu, à forfait; **to enter into, conclude, an a. with s.o.,** passer un traité, un contrat, avec qn; **an a. has been concluded between the two parties,** une convention est intervenue entre les deux parties; **to sign a legal a.,** s'engager par devant notaire (**to do sth.,** à faire qch.); **to abide by the a.,** s'en tenir aux conventions, à ce qui a été convenu. **2.** (*a*) accord *m* (**on, about,** sur); **to be in a. with s.o.,** être d'accord avec qn; **to be in a. with a decision,** se rallier à, approuver, une décision; **to come to an a.,** tomber d'accord; **to come to, arrive at, an a. with s.o.,** se mettre d'accord avec qn; s'accommoder, s'arranger, avec qn; **an a. was soon reached,** on arriva bientôt à une entente, à un modus vivendi; **an a. has been reached, by which . . .,** un accord est intervenu, d'après lequel . . .; *Com:* **as per a.,** comme (il a été) convenu; **by mutual a.,** de gré à gré; à l'amiable; d'un commun accord; *Jur:* **to bring about an a.,** obtenir une conciliation; (*b*) *Com: Ind:* **a. between producers, etc.,** entente *f* entre producteurs, etc.; **marketing a.,** accord de commercialisation; **General A. on Tariffs and Trade (G.A.T.T.),** Accord général sur les tarifs douaniers et le commerce; (*c*) (= **collusion**) **to have an a. with s.o.,** avoir une entente, un arrangement, avec qn. 3. (*a*) conformité *f,* concordance *f* (de différentes choses, entre qch. et qch.); (*b*) *Gram:* accord **(with,** avec); **a. of adjectives,** concordance des adjectifs.

agressin [ə'gresin], *s. Biol:* agressine *f.*

agrestal [ə'grestl], *a.* (*of plant*) agreste.

agrestic [ə'grestik], *a. Lit:* agreste, rustique; rural, -aux.

agricultural [ægri'kʌltʃər(ə)l, -'kʌltjə-], *a.* (produit, etc.) agricole; (peuple) agriculteur; **a. economics,** économie *f* agricole, agraire; **a. engineer,** ingénieur *m* agronome; **a. labourer, worker,** ouvrier *m* agricole; **a. college,** école *f* d'agriculture; **a. show,** comice *m* agricole; **a. implement,** instrument *m* aratoire; **a. machinery,** machines *fpl* agricoles; **a. holding,** exploitation *f* agricole.

agricultur(al)ist [ægri'kʌltʃər(əl)ist, -tjə-], *s.* agriculteur *m.*

agriculture ['ægrikʌltʃər, -tjər], *s.* agriculture *f*; **extensive, intensive, a.,** agriculture extensive, intensive; **Food and A. Organization (F.A.O.),** Organisation *f* pour l'alimentation et l'agriculture.

Agrigenti [ægri'dʒenti], *s.pl. A.Geog:* Agrigentins *m.*

Agrigento [ægri'dʒentou], *s. Pr.n. Geog:* Agrigente *f.*

Agrigentum [ægri'dʒentəm], *Pr.n. A.Geog:* Agrigente *f.*

agrilus ['ægriləs], *s. Ent:* agrile *m*; agrilus *m.*

agrimony ['ægriməni], *s. Bot:* 1. **(common) a.,** aigremoine *f* (d'Europe). 2. **hemp a.,** eupatoire *f* à feuilles de chanvre; **water a.,** chanvre *m* d'eau.

agrion ['ægriən], *s. Ent:* agrion *m.*

Agrionidae [ægri'ɔnidiː], *s.pl. Ent:* agrionides *m,* agrionidés *m.*

agriotes [ægri'outiːz], *s. Ent:* agriot(t)e *m.*

Agrippina [ægri'painə], *Pr.n.f. Hist:* Agrippine.

agro- ['ægrou], *pref.* agro-.

agrobiology [ægroubai'ɔlədʒi], *s.* agrobiologie *f.*

agro-city ['ægrou'siti], **agrogorod,** *pl.* **-goroda** ['ægrou'gɔrɔd, -gɔrɔ'daː], *s.* (*in U.S.S.R.*) agroville *f.*

agrology [ə'grɔlədʒi], *s.* agrologie *f.*

agronome ['ægrənoum], *s.* agronome *m.*

agronomic [ægrə'nɔmik], *a.* agronomique.

agronomist [ə'grɔnəmist], *s.* agronome *m.*

agronomy [ə'grɔnəmi], *s.* agronomie *f.*

agrostemma [ægrou'stemə], *s. Bot:* agrostemme *f*; agrostemma *f.*

agrostis [ə'grɔstis], *s. Bot:* agrostis *m,* agrostide *f.*

agrostology [ægrɔs'tɔlədʒi], *s. Bot:* agrostologie *f.*

agrostologist [ægrɔs'tɔlədʒist], *s.* agrostologue *m.*

agrotis [ə'groutis], *s. Ent:* agrotide *f.*

agrotown ['ægroutaun], *s.* (*in U.S.S.R.*) agroville *f.*

aground [ə'graund], *adv. Nau:* échoué; au sec, amorti; **to run a ship a.,** (faire) échouer un navire; mettre un navire à la côte; (*of ship*) **to run a.,** échouer (à la côte), faire côte, s'échouer; toucher au banc; **running a.,** échouage *m*; **to be (fast) a.,** être échoué, à la côte, à la terre, au sec; **we are a.,** le navire touche (le fond).

ague ['eigjuː], *s. Med: A:* fièvre (paludéenne) intermittente; **fit of a.,** accès *m* de fièvre; tremblement *m* de fièvre; **to shake with a.,** trembler la fièvre; **a.(-)cake,** rate hypertrophiée.

aguish ['eigjuiʃ], *a. A:* 1. (*of condition*) fiévreux, fébrile. 2. (*of climate*) paludéen. 3. (*of pers.*) sujet à des accès de fièvre paludéenne; impaludé.

aguti [ə'guːti], *s. Z:* agouti *m.*

agynous [ei'dʒainəs], *a. Bot:* agynique.

ah [ɑː], *int.* ah! ha! heu!

aha [ə'haː], *int.* haha!

Ahab ['eihæb], *Pr.n.m. B.Hist:* Achab.

Ahaggar [ə'hægər], *Pr.n. Geog:* Hoggar *m.*

Ahasuerus [əhæzju'iərəs], *Pr.n.m.* 1. *B.Hist:* Assuérus. 2. Ahasvérus (le Juif errant).

Ahaz ['eihæz], *Pr.n.m. B.Hist:* Achaz.

Ahaziah [eiə'zaiə], *Pr.n.m. B.Hist:* Ochosias, Achazia.

ahead [ə'hed], *adv.* 1. *Nau:* (*a*) **to be a.,** être sur l'avant, en avant (du navire); **the ship was a. of us,** le navire était devant nous; **the ship was right a.,** le navire était droit devant; **to draw a. of s.o., a ship,** dépasser qn, un navire; gagner l'avant d'un navire; **to keep a. of a ship,** se tenir sur l'avant d'un navire; **to go a.,** aller de l'avant; avancer; faire route; **full speed a.!** en avant toute! **half speed, slow speed, a.!** en avant à demi-vitesse, doucement! **next a.,** matelot *m* d'avant; **a ship breakers, (right) a.!** un navire, des brisants, (droit) devant! *Navy:* **firing a.,** tir *m* en pointe; feu *m* de chasse; (*b*) **wind a.,** vent debout; (*c*) *Navy:* **line a.,** en ligne de file, en colonne; **to form single line a.,** prendre la ligne de file. 2. (*of pers., car, etc.*) (*a*) **to get a.,** prendre de l'avance; (*of runner, cyclist, etc.*) **to draw a.,** se décoller; **to be a. of the bunch,** mener le peloton; **to go on a.,** prendre les devants; **go on a.!** filez devant! **you go on a., I'll follow,** continuez, je vous suis; **a. of s.o.,** en avant de qn; **to go on a. of s.o.,** devancer qn; **to get a. of s.o.,** dépasser qn; **to be two hours a. of s.o.,** avoir deux heures d'avance sur qn; **he is a. of his form,** il est en avance sur sa classe; **he is going a.,** il fait des progrès, il va de l'avant; **to be a. of one's time,** être en avance sur son temps, son époque; **to be a. of time,** (i) être, arriver, avoir fini, avant l'heure; (ii) (*of clock*) avancer sur l'heure; **to be a. of schedule,** être en avance sur les prévisions; **I'm well a. with my work,** je suis très en avance dans mon travail; **you've got your best years a. of you,** vous avez vos meilleures années devant vous; **to look a.,** penser à l'avenir; **we must look a.,** il faut voir venir les choses; **mind that looks, sees, far a.,** esprit prévoyant; **to see things a long time, way, a.,** prévoir les choses de loin; **how far a. should one book?** combien de temps faut-il retenir d'avance? (*b*) **they went straight a.,** ils allaient (tout) droit devant eux; **go a.!** (i) allez! marchez! continuez (tout droit)! (ii) vas-y! allez-y! *F:* **to give s.o. the go a.,** donner le feu vert à qn.

ahem [(h)m'mm], *int.* hum!

ahimsa [ə'himsə], *s. Hindu Phil:* ahimsa *f.*

ahoy [ə'hɔi], *int. Nau:* **boat, ship, a.!** oh(é) du canot! du navire!

ahull [ə'hʌl], *adv. Nau: A:* **to lie a.,** être à la cape sèche; **to run a.,** filer à sec (de toile).

ai ['ɑːi], *s. Z:* aï *m,* paresseux *m.*

aiblins ['eiblinz], *adv. Dial: Scot:* peut-être.

aid[1] [eid], *s.* 1. aide *f,* assistance *f,* secours *m,* appui *m*; **with, by, the a. of s.o., sth.,** avec l'aide de qn; à l'aide de qch.; **to call in s.o.'s a.,** avoir recours à qn, à l'aide de qn; **to go to s.o.'s a.,** aller, se porter, au secours de qn; **collection in a. of . . .,** quête *f* au profit de . . .; *F:* **what's (all) this in a. of?** c'est en l'honneur de quoi? à quoi ça rime? *Pol.Ec:* **a. to the developing countries,** aide aux pays en voie de développement; **mutual a.,** entraide *f*; **mutual-a. society,** société *f* de secours mutuels, d'assistance mutuelle; **legal a.,** assistance judiciaire; **medical a.,** soins médicaux; **first a.,** premiers secours (aux blessés); soins d'urgence. 2. (*a*) **aids to health,** conseils *m* pour se bien porter; **aids and appliances,** moyens *m* de secours; **hearing a., deaf a.,** aide-ouïe *m inv,* appareil *m* de correction auditive, prothèse auditive; *Sch:* **visual aids,** pièces *f* de démonstration avec éléments graphiques, visuels; (*b*) *pl. Hist:* aides, subsides *m*; **the Court of Aids,** la cour des aides; (*c*) *pl. Equit:* aides. 3. (*pers.*) aide *mf.*

aid[2], *v.tr.* 1. aider, assister, secourir (qn); donner aide à (qn); venir en aide à (qn); venir à l'aide de (qn); prêter son concours, son appui, à (qn); **to a. one another,** s'aider les uns les autres, s'entraider; *Lit:* **Heaven aiding . . .,** Dieu aidant . . .; *Jur:* **to a. and abet s.o.,** être le complice de qn. 2. soutenir, venir en aide à (une entreprise); **their contribution greatly aided the progress of the undertaking,** leur contribution a aidé considérablement aux progrès de l'entreprise; **the treatment did little to a. his recovery,** le traitement n'a guère contribué à sa guérison.

aide [eid], **aide-de-camp** ['eid(d)əkɑ̃], *s.* (*pl.* **aides-de-camp** ['eid(d)əkɑ̃]), *Mil:* aide *m* de camp; officier *m* d'ordonnance.

aide-mémoire ['eidmemwɑːr], *s. Dipl:* aide-mémoire *m inv.*

aiding ['eidiŋ], *s.* aide *f*; **a. and abetting,** complicité *f.*

aiglet ['eiglit], *s.* = AGLET.

aigrette ['eigret], *s.* aigrette *f.*

aiguille [ei'gwiːl], *s.* 1. *Geog:* aiguille *f* (d'une montagne). 2. *Tchn:* aiguille (de marteau piqueur, etc.).

aiguillette [eigwi'let], *s.* 1. *Cost:* aiguillette *f.* 2. *Cu:* aiguillette (de canard, etc.).

aikenite ['eikənait], *s. Miner:* aikenite *f.*

ail [eil]. 1. *v.tr. A:* (*with indef. subject, esp. in interr.*) faire souffrir (qn); **what ails you?** (i) de quoi souffrez-vous? qu'est-ce que vous avez? (ii) à qui en avez-vous? à qui en voulez-vous? qu'avez-vous? **he doesn't know what ails him,** il ne sait pas ce qu'il a, de quoi il souffre. 2. *v.i.* être souffrant.

ailantho [ei'lænθou], **ailanthus** [ei'lænθəs], **ailantus** [ei'læntəs], *s.* (*a*) *Bot:* ailant(h)e *m*; vernis *m* du Japon; (*b*) *Ent:* **Chinese a. moth,** attacus chinois de l'ailant(h)e.

aileron ['eilərɔn], *s. Av:* aileron *m*; **balanced a.,** aileron compensé; **built-in, pander type, a.,** aileron encastré; **skew a.,** aileron en biais; **a. chord,** profondeur *f* d'aileron; **a. lever,** guignol *m* d'aileron; **a. turn,** tonneau *m* en descendant.

ailing ['eiliŋ], *a.* souffrant, malade, indisposé, mal portant; **she has been a. for a long time,** elle souffre depuis longtemps; **he's always a.,** il a une petite santé.

ailment ['eilmənt], *s.* mal *m*; maladie (légère); **childish ailments,** maladies d'enfants; **ailments due to teething,** troubles *m* de dentition.

ailurophobia [eiljurou'foubiə], *s. Med:* ailourophobie *f.*

aim[1] [eim], *s.* 1. (*a*) action *f* de viser; **to miss one's a.,** (i) (*with firearm*) manquer le but, manquer son coup; (ii) frapper à faux; **to take a. at s.o.,** viser qn; coucher, mettre, qn en joue; **to take a.,** mettre en joue; prendre sa visée; **to take a true a., to take accurate a.,** viser juste, exactement; bien viser; **if I had a better a.,** si je pouvais mieux viser, ajuster; (*b*) but *m*; **missiles that fall short of their a.,** projectiles *m* qui n'atteignent pas le but. 2. but, objet *m,* dessein *m*; visées *fpl*; **ambitious aims,** visées ambitieuses, projets ambitieux; **his a. was to . . .,** il avait pour but de . . .; il visait à. . . . **he has one a. and object in life,** sa vie n'a qu'un (seul) but; **what is the a. of these questions?** où tendent ces questions? **with the a. of doing sth.,** dans le dessein de faire qch.

aim[2]. 1. *v.tr.* (*a*) **to a. a stone, a blow, at s.o.,** lancer une pierre à qn; porter, allonger, un coup à qn; (*b*) ajuster (un fusil, etc.); *Mil:* pointer; **to a. a gun, a pistol, at s.o.,** coucher qn en joue avec un fusil, un pistolet; **the bullet was aimed at you,** la balle vous était destinée; **well-aimed fire,** feu bien ajusté; *Artil:* **the target to a. at,** le but à battre; (*c*) **to a. one's remarks at s.o.,** parler à l'adresse de qn; **remark aimed at s.o.,** remarque adressée à qn; **to a. a criticism at s.o.,** porter une critique sur qn; **measures aimed against our trade,** mesures dirigées contre notre commerce; **that was aimed at you!** à vous la balle! c'était une pierre dans votre jardin. 2. *v.ind.tr.* (*a*) **to a. at s.o. (with a gun),** ajuster, viser, qn; mettre, coucher, qn en joue; (*b*) **to a. at becoming sth.,** *NAm:* **to a. to become sth.,** aspirer, viser, à devenir qch; **the kind of novel which people a. at writing now,** le genre de roman qu'on s'efforce d'écrire aujourd'hui; **to a. at absolute power,** viser au pouvoir absolu; **what are you aiming at?** quel but poursuivez-vous? où voulez-vous en venir? **the thing to be aimed at is . . .,** le but à atteindre, qu'il faut viser, c'est. . . . **decree that aims at altering . . .,** arrêt *m* qui vise à changer . . .; *NAm: F:* **I a. to go,** j'ai l'intention d'y aller; **he aims to be helpful,** il croit rendre service; (*c*) **to a. for a place,** diriger ses pas vers un endroit; **I'm aiming for Paris,** Paris est mon but.

aimer ['eimər], *s.* 1. (*pers.*) viseur, -euse. 2. *Av:* **bomb a.,** viseur *m* de bombardement.

aiming ['eimiŋ], *s.* visée *f*; *Mil:* pointage *m*; **a. post,** jalon *m*; **a. rest,** chevalet *m* de pointage.

aimless ['eimlis], *a.* sans but, sans objet; **an a. sort of life,** une vie désœuvrée, qui ne mène à rien; **an a. way of doing sth.,** une façon confuse de faire qch.

aimlessly ['eimlisli], *adv.* sans but, sans objet, sans dessein; **to wander about a.,** aller, errer, à l'aventure.

aimlessness ['eimlisnis], *s.* manque *m* de but à atteindre; manque d'ambition; **the a. of his remarks,** le manque de portée, l'inanité *f,* de ses observations.

ain't [eint] *A. & P:* = **am not, is not, are not.**

Ainu ['einuː]. 1. *a. Ethn:* aïnou. 2. *s. Ethn:* Aïnou, -oue. 3. *s. Ling:* aïnou *m.*

air[1] [ɛər], *s.* 1. air *m*; (*a*) **ambient a.,** air ambiant; **atmospheric a.,** air atmosphérique; **calm a.,** air calme; **moving a.,** air agité; **breath of a.,** souffle *m* d'air; **bad a., foul a., stale a.,** air vicié; **pure a.,** air pur; **fresh a.,** air frais; **this room needs some fresh a.,** il faut aérer, ventiler, cette pièce; cette pièce manque d'air; **to take the a., go out for a breath of (fresh) a.,** sortir prendre l'air, le frais; **fresh-a. fiend,** pleinairiste *mf*; **in the open a.,** en plein air, au grand air, à ciel ouvert; **to expose water to the a.,** aérer l'eau; *attrib.* **a. density,** masse *f* spécifique de l'air; **a. draught,** courant *m* d'air; **a. friction,** frottement *m* de l'air; **a. pressure,** (i) pression *f* d'air; (ii) pression atmosphérique; **a. resistance,** résistance *f* de l'air; **a. temperature,** température ambiante; *Med:* **a. cure,** cure *f* d'air; *F:* **I can't live on a.,** je ne vis pas de l'air du temps; **to walk on a.,** être aux anges; ne pas se sentir de joie; **he's walking on a.!** il ne touche pas à la terre; **since she heard the news she's been walking, treading, on a.,** depuis qu'elle a appris la nouvelle, elle est aux anges, elle ne se connaît plus; **there's something in the a.,** il y a quelque chose dans l'air; il se prépare quelque chose; il se trame quelque chose; **there are rumours in the a.,** il y a des bruits qui circulent; **the idea was in the a.,** l'idée était dans l'air; **it's all in the a. as yet,** ce ne sont encore que de vagues projets; il n'y a rien de décidé pour le moment; *Mil:* **their left flank was entirely in the a.,** le flanc gauche était entièrement exposé, découvert; *F:* **to beat the a.,** (i) donner des coups d'épée dans l'eau; taper dans le vide; (ii) disserter dans le vide; *F:* **it's all**

hot a., ce sont des discours en l'air; **castles in the a.,** châteaux *m* en Espagne; **to melt, vanish, into thin a.,** s'anéantir, s'évanouir, disparaître (aux yeux de qn); **all that money has vanished into thin a.,** tout cet argent a complètement disparu, a passé au bleu; **it seemed as though everybody had vanished into thin a.,** on aurait dit que tout le monde s'était évaporé; (*b*) *Poet: Nau:* brise *f*, vent *m*; **still a.,** vent nul; (*c*) *Tchn:* **auxiliary a., extra a.,** air additionnel; **compressed a.,** air comprimé; *Med:* **compressed-a. disease,** mal *m* des caissons; *Mec:* **ram a.,** air de pression aérodynamique, air de surpuissance; *Ch: Ind:* **liquid a.,** air liquide; (*d*) *attrib. Mec.E:* **a. cleaner, a. filter, a. screen, a. strainer,** filtre *m* à air, épurateur *m* d'air; **a. cock,** robinet *m* d'air; **a. compressor,** compresseur *m* d'air; **a. channel, a. flue,** conduit *m* d'air, conduit à vent; *Min:* buse *f* d'aérange; **a. duct,** conduite *f* d'air, amenée *f* d'air, manche *f* à air; **a. heater,** (i) réchauffeur *m* d'air; (ii) calorifère *m* à air chaud; **a. inlet, a. intake,** admission *f* d'air, entrée *f* d'air; *Mch:* reniflard *m*; **a. outlet,** sortie *f* d'air; **a. vane, a. wing,** moulinet *m* (régulateur); **a. jacket,** chemise *f*, enveloppe *f*, à circulation d'air; **a. manifold,** collecteur *m* d'air; *Aut:* **a. surface,** surface *f* de léchage (d'un radiateur); *Metall:* **a. bubble,** bulle *f* d'air, soufflure *f*; **a. gate,** (i) *Metall:* porte *f* d'aérage; (*in mould*) évent *m*; (ii) *Min:* porte d'aérage; *El:* **a. gap,** entrefer *m*; *Elcs:* **a. buffer,** tampon *m* atmosphérique, à air; **a. break,** isolement *m* par air; (*e*) *attrib.* (= *compressed air*) à air comprimé, pneumatique; **a. conveyor,** convoyeur *m*, transporteur *m*, pneumatique; **a. gun,** fusil *m*, carabine *f*, à air comprimé; **a. engine,** (i) moteur *m* à air comprimé; (ii) moteur à air chaud; **a. hammer,** marteau *m* pneumatique; **a. hoist, a. winch,** treuil *m* à air comprimé; *Av: Nau:* **a. raft,** radeau *m* pneumatique; *Min:* **a. drive,** puisage *m* à air comprimé; **a. gauge,** micromètre *m* pneumatique; **a. starter,** démarreur *m* pneumatique. **2.** (*a*) **high up in the a.,** très haut audessus de nous, très haut dans le ciel; **in the a.,** en l'air, dans les airs; **to throw sth. (up) in the a.,** jeter qch. en l'air; *F:* **he went up in the a. when I mentioned it,** quand je lui en ai parlé, il a sauté en l'air, il a explosé; *Lit:* **the fowl(s) of the a.,** les habitants *m* de l'air, la gent ailée; (*b*) *Meteor:* **upper a.,** haute atmosphère, couches *pl.* supérieures de l'atmosphère; **upper-a. station,** station *f* d'observation en altitude; **upper-a. equipment,** matériel *m* d'observation en altitude; **upper-a. soundings,** sondages *m* atmosphériques en altitude; **upper-a. data,** observations *f* en altitude; **upper-a. report,** (bulletin *m* d') observation en altitude; (*c*) *Av:* **freedom of the a.,** liberté *f* de l'espace aérien; **by a.,** par avion, par air, par voie aérienne; *attrib.* **a. traffic,** circulation aérienne, trafic aérien; **a. traffic control,** contrôle *m* de la circulation aérienne; **a. traffic controller, officer,** contrôleur *m* de la circulation aérienne, *F:* aiguilleur *m* du ciel; **a. traffic control station,** station *f*, centre *m*, de contrôle de la circulation aérienne; **a. traffic clearance,** autorisation *f* de circuler (dans l'espace aérien); **a. traffic rules,** règlements *m* de circulation aérienne; **a. cargo, a. freight,** frêt aérien; **a. transport,** transports aériens, par avion; **a. carrier,** (i) transporteur aérien; (ii) compagnie aérienne; **a. travel,** voyages *mpl* par avion; **a. trip,** voyage par avion; **a. hostess,** hôtesse *f* de l'air; **a. route,** route, ligne, aérienne; itinéraire aérien; **a. terminal,** aérogare *f*; **a. display, a. show,** exposition aérienne, salon *m* de l'aéronautique, de l'aviation; **a. pageant,** manifestation, fête, aérienne; (*d*) *Adm:* **the Air Division (of the Ministry of Defence),** *Hist:* (*or for countries other than U.K.*) **the Air Ministry** = le Ministère de l'Air; *Mil.Av:* **the Royal Air Force, the U.S. Air Force,** l'Aviation *f*, l'Aéronautique *f* (militaire); **the Army Air Force,** l'Aviation Légère de l'Armée de Terre (ALAT); **the Fleet Air Arm, the Naval Air Force,** l'Aéronavale *f*; **the a. forces supported the ground troops,** les forces aériennes ont soutenu les effectifs terrestres; **a. personnel, a. staff,** personnel *m* de l'aviation, de l'aéronautique; **a. cadet,** élève *m* officier d'aviation, de l'aéronautique; **a. officer,** officier *m* d'aviation, de l'aéronautique; **a. alert,** alerte aérienne; **a. attack,** attaque aérienne; **a. reconnaissance,** reconnaissance aérienne; **a. cover,** couverture aérienne, (force de) protection aérienne; **(tactical) a. support,** soutien aérien (tactique); **control of the a.,** contrôle *m* de l'espace aérien, maîtrise *f* de l'air; **a. control,** contrôle (tactique) aérien; **a. control centre,** centre *m* de contrôle tactique air; *Navy: U.S:* **a. controlman** (*pl.* **-men**), officier marinier contrôleur du trafic (aérien); **a. superiority, a. supremacy,** supériorité aérienne, maitrise de l'air; **the a. and sea supremacy of the Allies,** la maîtrise aéronavale des Alliés; *Mil:* **a. concealment,** dissimulation *f* aux vues de l'aviation ennemie, à l'observation aérienne. **3.** *W.Tel: F:* les ondes *fpl*; **to be on the a.,** parler à la radio; **his speech will be on the a. on Thursday,** son discours sera radiodiffusé jeudi; **to put a play on the a.,** mettre une pièce en ondes; *attrib.* **a. time,** temps *m* d'antenne; durée *f* de l'émission, des émissions. **4.** *Mus:* air. **5.** (= *appearance*) air, mine *f*, apparence *f*; **there is an a. of comfort everywhere,** il y a partout une apparence, un air, de confort; **this has the a. of being . . .,** cela a l'air d'être . . .; **he has an a. about him,** il a beaucoup de cachet, il s'impose; **there is an evil a. about him,** il a mauvais air, mauvaise mine; **to carry sth. off with an a.,** faire qch. avec assurance, avec aplomb; **to give oneself airs, to put on airs,** se donner des airs; faire le suffisant, la suffisante; **to put on airs with s.o.,** traiter qn de haut; **don't put on airs!** ne prenez pas cet air supérieur, suffisant! ne faites pas le grand seigneur, la grande dame!

air[2], *v.tr.* **1.** (*a*) **to a. a room,** aérer une pièce; renouveler l'air d'une pièce; **to hang clothes out to a.,** éventer des vêtements; mettre des vêtements à l'air, au vent, à l'évent; **to a. linen,** aérer du linge; **to a. a bed,** bassiner un lit; (*b*) **the question needs to be aired,** la question demande à être discutée ouvertement; **to a. one's grievances,** exposer des griefs (personnels); conter ses doléances; (*c*) *A:* **to a. oneself,** prendre de l'air (au jardin, etc.). **2. to a. one's opinions, one's knowledge,** faire parade de, faire étalage de, afficher, ses opinions, son savoir; **to a. one's feelings,** donner libre cours à ses sentiments.

air ambulance ['ɛər'æmbjul(ə)ns], *s.* avion *m* sanitaire.

air base ['ɛəbeis], *s.* base aérienne.

air blast ['ɛəblɑːst], *s.* (*a*) *Meteor:* bourrasque *f*, vent violent; (*b*) *Mec.E:* jet *m* d'air; pression *f* d'air; soufflage *m*, souffle *m*, soufflerie *f*; *Metall:* vent; *Min:* chasse *f* d'air; (*c*) *attrib.* (i) à air comprimé; (ii) à refroidissement par air; *El:* **a.-b. transformer,** transformateur *m* à refroidissement par air.

air bleed ['ɛəbliːd], *s. Mec.E:* **1.** (*a*) prise *f* d'air; (*b*) chasse *f*, évacuation *f*, d'air; purge *f* (d'air); *attrib.* **a.-b. valve,** soupape *f*, clapet *m*, de prélèvement d'air. **2.** orifice *m* de ventilation.

airborne ['ɛəbɔːn], *a.* **1.** en suspension dans l'air; **a. dust,** poussière(s) *f*(*pl*) en suspension dans l'air; **a. radioactivity,** radioactivité *f* des matières en suspension dans l'air. **2.** *Aedcs:* (*a*) (*of aircraft*) en vol, sustenté; (*of captive balloon*) en l'air; (*of free balloon, of dirigible*) vogant, évoluant, dans les airs; (*of aircraft*) **to become a.,** décoller, commencer à voler; (*b*) *Mil:* (i) aéroporté; (ii) exécuté par des troupes aéroportées; **a. troops, a. units,** troupes, unités, aéroportées; **a. infantry,** infanterie *f* de l'air; **a. assault, a. attack,** attaque exécutée par des troupes aéroportées, assaut vertical; (*c*) *Av:* de bord, d'avion; **a. equipment,** équipement(s) *m*(*pl*), matériel *m*, de bord; **a. direction-finder,** radiogoniomètre *m* de bord; **a. radar,** radar *m* de bord, d'avion.

air brake ['ɛəbreik], *s.* (*a*) *Veh:* frein *m* pneumatique, à air comprimé; (*b*) *Av:* frein aérodynamique, aérofrein *m*.

air-breathing ['ɛəbriːðiŋ], *a. I.C.E:* **a.-b. engine,** moteur réacteur aérobie; moteur réacteur utilisant l'air ambiant.

air bridge ['ɛəbridʒ], *s. Av:* pont aérien.

airbrush ['ɛəbrʌʃ], *s. Paint:* aérographe *m*; pinceau *m* à air; pistolet vaporisateur.

airbus ['ɛəbʌs], *s.* aérobus *m*.

air cell ['ɛəsel], *s.* **1.** *Anat:* alvéole *f* pulmonaire. **2.** chambre *f* à air (d'un œuf).

air chamber ['ɛə'tʃeimbər], *s.* **1.** *Tchn:* chambre *f* à air, réservoir *m* d'air; (*of torpedo*) réservoir d'air comprimé; *Hyd.E:* cloche *f* d'air (d'une pompe); réservoir d'air (d'un bélier hydraulique); chambre de détente; (*in water conduit*) ventouse *f*; *Metall:* boîte *f* à vent (du cubilot). **2.** *Conch:* loge *f* (de nautile, etc.).

air coach ['ɛəkoutʃ], *s. U.S:* avion *m* à classe unique.

air-commodore ['ɛəkɔmədɔər], *s. Mil.Av:* = général *m* de brigade (aérienne).

air-condition ['ɛəkən'diʃ(ə)n], *v.tr.* climatiser, conditionner.

air-conditioned ['ɛəkən'diʃ(ə)nd], *a.* climatisé, à air conditionné.

air-conditioner ['ɛəkən'diʃ(ə)nər], *s.* conditionneur *m* d'air, climatiseur *m*.

air-conditioning ['ɛəkən'diʃ(ə)niŋ], *s.* climatisation *f*, conditionnement *m* (de l'air); **a.-c. equipment,** matériel *m* de climatisation; **a.-c. system,** (i) système *m* de climatisation; (ii) circuit *m* d'air conditionné.

air-cool ['ɛə'kuːl], *v.tr.* refroidir par l'air.

air-cooled ['ɛəkuːld], *a.* refroidi par l'air; *I.C.E:* **a.-c. engine,** moteur *m* à refroidissement par air.

air-cooler ['ɛəkuːlər], *s.* refroidisseur *m* à air.

air-cooling ['ɛəkuːliŋ], *s.* refroidissement *m* par l'air.

air-core ['ɛəkɔːər], *a. El:* **a.-c. coil,** bobine *f* à air, sans noyau; **a.-c. inductance,** self-inductance *f* sans fer; *W.Tel:* **a.-c. transformer,** transformateur *m* à air.

air corridor ['ɛə'kɔridɔər], *s. Av:* couloir aérien, couloir de franchissement.

aircraft ['ɛəkrɑːft], *s.* **1.** *A:* navigation aérienne (en tant que science). **2.** (*pl.* **aircraft**) avion *m*, appareil *m* (d'aviation), aéronef *m*; (*a*) **heavier-than-air a.,** aéronef plus lourd que l'air, aérodyne *m*; **lighter-than-air a.,** aéronef plus léger que l'air, aérostat *m*; (*b*) **all-wing a.,** aile volante; **fixed-wing a.,** appareil à voilure fixe; **rotary-wing, rotating-wing, rotor, a.,** appareil à voilure tournante; **high-wing a.,** avion à voilure haute, à ailes surélevées; **semi-high-wing a.,** avion à voilure mi-haute, à ailes mi-surélevées; **low-wing a.,** avion à voilure basse, à ailes surbaissées; **semi-low-wing a.,** avion à voilure mi-basse, à ailes mi-surbaissées; **swing-wing a.,** avion à voilure variable, à ailes variables; **variable-geometry a.,** avion à géométrie, à flèche, variable; **STOL (short-take-off-and-landing) a.,** avion à décollage et à atterrissage court; **VTOL (vertical-take-off-and-landing) a.,** avion à décollage et à atterrissage vertical; **lifting-body a.,** avion à fuselage porteur; (*c*) **single-seat(er) a.,** avion à une place, (avion) monoplace *m*; **two-seat(er) a.,** avion à deux places, (avion) biplace *m*; **three-seat a.,** avion à trois places, (avion) triplace *m*; **four-seat a.,** avion à quatre places, (avion) quadriplace *m*; (*d*) **jet(-propelled) a.,** avion à réaction; **twin-jet, three-jet, four-jet, a.,** (avion) biréacteur *m*, triréacteur *m*, quadriréacteur *m*; **piston-engine(d) a.,** avion à moteur à piston; **twin-engine a.,** (avion) bimoteur *m*; **nuclear-powered a.,** avion (à propulsion) atomique, à propulsion nucléaire; (*e*) **civil a.,** avion civil; **private a.,** avion de tourisme; **business a.,** avion d'affaires; **charter a.,** (i) avion affrété au voyage; *F:* avion charter; (ii) avion-taxi *m*, *pl.* avions-taxis; **commercial a.,** avion commercial; **transport a.,** avion de transport; **light-transport, medium-transport, a.,** avion petit, moyen, porteur; **heavy-transport, heavy-lift, large-capacity, a.,** avion gros porteur; **passenger a.,** avion (de transport) de passagers; **long-haul, medium-haul, short-haul, a.,** avion long, moyen, court, courrier; **short-haul transport a.,** avion de transport à courte distance; **tanker a.,** avion-citerne *m*, *pl.* avions-citernes; **utility a.,** avion utilitaire, avion de travail; (*f*) **military a.,** avion, appareil, militaire; **combat a.,** avion de combat; **artillery co-operation a.,** avion de réglage de tir; **artillery reconnaissance a.,** avion (de repérage) d'artillerie; **ground-attack a.,** avion d'attaque au sol; **(ground) strike a.,** avion d'assaut; **interceptor a.,** avion d'interception, intercepteur *m*; **reconnaissance a.,** avion de reconnaissance; **multi mission a.,** avion plyvalent; **long-range, medium-range, short-range, a.,** (i) avion à grand, à moyen, à petit, rayon d'action; (ii) avion long, moyen, court, courrier; **ambulance a.,** avion sanitaire; **general-purpose a., utility a.,** avion (à) toutes fins; **liaison a.,** avion de liaison; **messenger a.,** avion estafette; **target-practice a.,** avion-cible *m*, *pl.* avions-cibles; **training a., trainer a.,** avion-école *m*, *pl.* avions-écoles; avion d'entraînement; **troop-carrier a.,** avion de transport de troupe; **manned a.,** avion piloté; **unmanned, pilotless, a.,** avion sans pilote; avion-robot *m*, *pl.* avions-robot; **radio-controlled a.,** avion télécommandé; (*g*) **naval a., fleet a.,** appareil de l'aéronavale; **carrier-based a.,** avion embarqué; **land-based a.,** avion basé à terre; **anti-submarine (attack) a.,** avion de lutte anti-sous-marine; **maritime-reconnaissance a.,** avion de reconnaissance maritime; **torpedo a.,** avion torpilleur; (*h*) **a. factory,** usine d'aviation; **a. manufacturer, a. constructor,** constructeur *m* d'avions, avionneur *m*; **a. engineer,** ingénieur *m* de l'aéronautique; **a. engineering,** ingénierie *f* aéronautique, génie *m* aéronautique; **a. operator,** exploitant *m* de matériel d'aviation; **pre-production a.,** avion de présérie; **production a.,** avion de série; **a. prototype,** (appareil) prototype *m*.

aircraft carrier ['ɛəkrɑːft'kæriər], *s.* porte-avions *m inv.*

aircraftman, *pl.* **-men** ['ɛəkrɑːftmən], *s. Mil.Av:* (soldat *m* de) deuxième classe *m*; **leading a., senior a.,** (soldat de) première classe *m*.

aircraftwoman, *pl.* **-women** ['ɛəkrɑːftwumən, -wimen], *s.* femme soldat de la W.R.A.F.; **leading a.,** femme caporal de la W.R.A.F.

aircrew ['ɛəkruː], *s. Av:* équipage *m*.

air cushion ['ɛəkuʃ(ə)n], *s.* **1.** coussin *m* à air; coussin élastique, pneumatique. **2.** *Mec.E: etc:* matelas *m* d'air, tampon *m* d'air (d'un mouton à vapeur, etc.). **3.** *attrib.* **a.-c. craft, vehicle,** appareil *m*, véhicule *m*, à coussin d'air.

air defence ['ɛədi'fens], *s. Mil:* défense aérienne; **active**

a.d., défense aérienne active; **passive a.d.,** défense aérienne passive, protection aérienne; **mobile, static, a.d.,** défense aérienne mobile, statique; *attrib.* **a.d. command,** commandement *m* de défense aérienne; **a.d. controller,** contrôleur *m* de défense aérienne, contrôleur "AIR"; **a.d. operation centre,** centre *m* d'opération de la défense aérienne; *Navy:* **a.d. ship,** bâtiment directeur de défense aérienne.

air-dried ['ɛədraid], *a.* séché à l'air.

airdrome ['ɛədroum], *s. NAm:* aérodrome *m.*

airdrop ['ɛədrɔp], *s. Av:* largage *m* (de charges).

air-drop ['ɛədrɔp], *v.tr. Av:* larguer (des charges).

air-dry ['ɛədrai], *a.* séché à l'air.

air-drying ['ɛədraiiŋ], *a.* siccatif à l'air.

Airedale ['ɛədeil], *s.* chien *m* airedale; airedale (-terrier) *m.*

airer ['ɛərər], *s.* chevalet *m* (pour linge); séchoir *m* (de cuisine); chauffe-linge *m inv.*

air-exhauster ['ɛərig'zɔ:stər], *s.* aspirateur *m*; ventilateur aspirant.

airfield ['ɛəfi:ld], *s.* champ *m* d'aviation, terrain *m* d'aviation, aérodrome *m*; **alternate a.,** aérodrome auxiliaire, de remplacement; **alternative a.,** aérodrome de diversion; **dispersal a.,** aérodrome de dispersion; **emergency a.,** aérodrome de secours; **underground a.,** aérodrome souterrain.

airflow ['ɛəflou], *s.* (*a*) écoulement *m* d'air; **smooth a.,** écoulement régulier; **turbulent a.,** écoulement turbulent; *attrib.* **a. speed,** vitesse *f* de l'écoulement de l'air; (*b*) *attrib. U.S: Aut:* **a. body,** carrosserie *f* aérodynamique.

airfoam ['ɛəfoum], *s.* mousse *f* de latex.

airfoil ['ɛəfɔil], *s. NAm:* = AEROFOIL.

air force *see* AIR[1] 2(*d*).

airframe ['ɛəfreim], *s.* cellule *f* d'avion, fuselage *m*; **a. designer,** avionneur *m.*

air freight [ɛə'freit], *s.* transport *m* par air; **sent by a. f.,** envoyé par avion, par air.

airfreight ['ɛəfreit], *v.tr. esp. NAm:* acheminer, transporter, par avion, par air.

airgraph ['ɛəgræf], *s.* lettre *f* microphotographique.

air hole ['ɛəhoul], *s.* **1.** (*ventilator*) aspirail *m*, soupirail *m*; trou *m* d'évent; évent *m*; prise *f* d'air; venteau *m* (d'un soufflet). **2.** (*in metal*) soufflure *f*; bulle *f* d'air, globule *m.*

airily ['ɛərili], *adv.* légèrement; d'un ton dégagé, cavalier; avec désinvolture.

airiness ['ɛərinis], *s.* **1.** (*a*) situation aérée (d'un bâtiment); (*b*) bonne ventilation (d'une pièce). **2.** légèreté *f* (d'esprit); insouciance *f*; désinvolture *f.*

airing ['ɛəriŋ], *s.* **1.** (*a*) ventilation *f*, renouvellement *m* de l'air (d'une salle, etc.); aérage *m*, aération *f*; (*b*) éventage *m* (de vêtements); exposition *f* à l'air; **a. cupboard,** armoire chauffante. **2.** (*a*) (petite) promenade; **to take an a.,** prendre l'air; se promener (à l'air); faire un petit tour; **to take horses for an a.,** promener des chevaux; **a. yard,** promenoir *m*, préau *m* (de prison); (*b*) **to give a project an a.,** lancer un ballon d'essai.

air letter ['ɛə:letər], *s.* aérogramme *m.*

airless ['ɛəlis], *a.* **1.** privé d'air, renfermé. **2.** sans air. **3.** (temps, soirée) sans vent, lourd(e).

airlessness ['ɛəlisnis], *s.* manque *m* d'air (d'une pièce); lourdeur *f* (du temps, etc.).

airlift[1] ['ɛəlift], *s.* **1.** *Av:* pont aérien; transport aérien; emport (aérien). **2.** *Min:* air-lift *m*, extraction *f* pneumatique, à air comprimé.

airlift[2], *v.tr.* transporter par avion.

airline ['ɛəlain], *s.* ligne aérienne; compagnie aérienne; service *m* de transports aériens, de transport par avion.

air line ['ɛəlain], *s. esp. NAm:* ligne directe; trajet *m* à vol d'oiseau.

airliner ['ɛəlainər], *s.* avion *m* de ligne.

airlock ['ɛəlɔk], *s.* **1.** (*a*) *Civ.E:* écluse *f*, sas *m* pneumatique, à air, clapet *m* à air (d'un caisson); (*b*) *Nau:* sas (de la chaufferie); (*c*) *Space:* sas (d'entrée, de sortie). **2.** *Mch: etc:* (*in pipe*) bouchon *m* d'air; cantonnement *m* d'air; poche *f* d'air, retenue *f* d'air.

airmail[1] ['ɛəmeil], *s.* (*a*) poste aérienne; service postal aérien; **by a.,** par avion; (*b*) courrier *m* par avion; **a. letter,** lettre (envoyée) par avion.

airmail[2], *v.tr.* envoyer (une lettre, etc.) par avion.

airman, *pl.* **-men** ['ɛəmən], *s.m.* (*a*) aviateur; (*b*) *Mil.Av:* **a. (basic),** soldat (de l'armée de l'air).

airmanship ['ɛəmənʃip], *s.* qualités requises de l'aviateur; habileté *f* (d'un aviateur).

air-minded ['ɛəmaindid], *a.* (*a*) qui s'intéresse à l'aviation; (*b*) qui aime les voyages par avion.

airmobile ['ɛəmɔbi:l], *a. Mil.Av:* (division *f*, unité *f*) aéromobile.

air photogrammetry ['ɛəfoutou'græmitri], *s. Mapm:* aérophotogrammétrie *f.*

airplane ['ɛəplein], *s. NAm:* avion *m.*

air pocket ['ɛəpɔkit], *s.* **1.** *Av:* trou *m* d'air. **2.** (*a*) *Hyd.E: etc:* cantonnement *m* d'air, poche *f* d'air (dans une canalisation); (*b*) collecteur *m* à air; poche à air.

air poise ['ɛəpɔiz], *s. Ph:* aéromètre *m.*

airport ['ɛəpɔ:t], *s. Av:* aéroport *m.*

air port ['ɛəpɔ:t], *s. Nau:* sabord *m* d'aérage; hublot *m.*

airproof ['ɛəpru:f], *a.* étanche (à l'air).

air raid ['ɛəreid], *s.* raid aérien; attaque, incursion, aérienne; **a.r. precautions,** défense passive; **a.r. precaution service,** service de défense passive, la Défense Passive; **a.r. warden,** agent *m*, volontaire *m*, de la défense passive; chef *m* d'abri, d'îlot; **a.r. warning district,** secteur de défense passive; **a.r. warning system,** dispositif *m* d'alerte aérienne.

air rifle ['ɛə'raifl], *s.* fusil *m* à air comprimé.

air scoop ['ɛəsku:p], *s. Av: Nau:* prise *f* d'air, manche *f* à air; bossette *f* d'entrée d'air.

airscrew ['ɛəskru:], *s. Av: O:* hélice *f.*

air-sea ['ɛə'si], *a.* aéro-maritime, *pl.* aéro-maritimes; **a.-s. rescue,** sauvetage *m* aéro-maritime, sauvetage aérien en mer.

airship ['ɛəʃip], *s.* (ballon) dirigeable *m*, aéronef *m*; **non-rigid a.,** dirigeable, aéronef, à enveloppe souple; **rigid, semi-rigid, a.,** dirigeable, aéronef, à enveloppe rigide, semi-rigide.

airsick ['ɛəsik], *a.* **to be a.,** avoir le mal de l'air.

airsickness ['ɛəsiknis], *s.* mal *m* de l'air.

airspace ['ɛərspeis], *s. Av: etc:* espace aérien.

air space ['ɛərspeis], *s.* **1.** cubage *m* (d'une pièce, etc.). **2.** *Elcs:* isolement *m* par air.

airspeed ['ɛərspi:d], *s. Av:* vitesse *f* (d'un avion); **true a.,** vitesse propre; **indicated a.,** vitesse indiquée; **a. indicator,** (anémomètre) badin *m*; **a. recorder,** enregistreur *m* de vitesse.

air spray ['ɛəsprei], *s.* = AIRBRUSH.

airstop ['ɛəstɔp], *s. Av:* héliport *m.*

airstream ['ɛəstri:m], *s.* écoulement *m* d'air.

airstrip ['ɛəstrip], *s. Av:* bande *f* d'envol, piste *f* de fortune.

airtight ['ɛərtait], *a.* (clôture) hermétique; (récipient, etc.) à clôture hermétique; étanche (à l'air).

airtightness ['ɛətaitnis], *s.* herméticité *f*; étanchéité *f* (à l'air).

air-to-air ['ɛətu'ɛər], *a. Mil:* (engin *m*) air-air *inv*; *Av:* **a.-to-a. homing,** autoguidage *m* entre avions.

air-to-ground ['ɛətə'graund], *a. Mil:* (projectile *f*) avion-à-terre *inv.*

air-to-surface ['ɛətə'sɔ:fəs], *a.* (engin *m*) *Mil:* air-sol *inv*, *Navy:* air-surface *inv.*

air-transported ['ɛətræns'pɔ:tid], *a.* aérotransporté.

air tunnel ['ɛətʌnl], *s.* tunnel *m* aérodynamique (d'une soufflerie).

airway ['ɛəwei], *s.* **1.** *Min:* voie *f* d'air, d'aérage; galerie *f* d'aérage; airage *m*, maillage *m*, troussage *m*; carnet *m* (d'aérage). **2.** *Av:* (*a*) route, ligne, voie, aérienne; **a. marker,** balise *f* d'entrée de piste; (*b*) radio-alignement *m*; **to fly airways,** radiobaliser, voler par radio-alignement; **flying airways,** radio-balisage *m.* **3.** *W.Tel: T.V: U.S:* chaîne *f.*

airwoman, *pl.* **-women** ['ɛəwumən, -wimin], *s.f.* aviatrice.

airworthiness ['ɛəwə:ðinis], *s. Av.* tenue *f* en l'air, navigabilité *f*; **a. certificate,** certificat *m* de navigabilité.

airworthy ['ɛəwə:ði], *a. Av:* (i) en état de prendre l'air, en bon état de vol, de navigabilité; (ii) muni d'un certificat de navigabilité; **to be a.,** tenir l'air.

airy ['ɛəri], *a.* **1.** bien aéré, ouvert à l'air; **a. room,** pièce bien aérée. **2.** *Lit:* (*a*) élevé, aérien; (*b*) élancé. **3.** léger, éthéré, impalpable; **a. phantoms,** fantômes immatériels, impalpables. **4.** *Lit:* (pas, etc.) léger; *Hum:* **his a. tread,** son pas éléphantin. **5.** (*a*) (*of conduct, etc.*) léger, insouciant, désinvolte, dégagé, cavalier; (*b*) **a. promises,** promesses vaines, illusoires; promesses en l'air.

airy-fairy ['ɛəri'fɛəri], *a. F:* (*a*) (*of girl, movement*) gracieux et léger; (*b*) (*of ideas, etc.*) impraticable, irréalisable.

aisle [ail], *s.* **1.** *Ecc.Arch:* bas-côté *m*, *pl.* bas-côtés; nef latérale, collatérale; collatéral *m*, *pl.* -aux. **2.** (*a*) **the bride was walking up the a. on her father's arm,** la mariée remontait l'allée centrale (de l'église) au bras de son père; (*b*) passage *m* (entre bancs); couloir central (d'un autobus, etc.); allée (de cinéma, etc.); *NAm:* couloir étroit; *Th: F:* **to have them (rolling) in the aisles,** avoir un succès fou.

aisled [aild], *a.* (église) à bas-côtés.

ait [eit], *s.* îlot *m* (dans une rivière).

aitch [eitʃ], *s.* (*a*) (la lettre) h *m*; **to drop one's aitches,** ne pas aspirer les h; (*b*) *Cu:* **a. bone,** culotte *f* (de bœuf).

Aizoaceae [eizou'eisii:], *s.pl. Bot:* mésembryanthémées *f*, aizoacées *f.*

aizoon [ei'zu:n], *s. Bot:* aizoon *m.*

ajar [ə'dʒɑ:r], *adv. & a.* (*of door, window*) entrouvert, entrebâillé, entre-clos; **to leave the door a.,** entrebâiller la porte; **the door was, stood, a.,** la porte était entrouverte, entrebâillée.

Ajax ['eidʒæks]. **1.** *Pr.n.m. Gr.Lit:* (*a*) Ajax, fils de Télamon; (*b*) **A. the Less,** Ajax, fils d'Oïlée. **2.** *s. P: A:* **the a.,** les lieux *m* d'aisance, les cabinets *m.*

ajowan [ə'dʒauən], **ajwan** ['ædʒwən], *s. Bot:* ajowan *m*; *Ch:* **a. oil,** essence *f* d'ajowan.

ajutage ['ædʒutidʒ], *s.* ajutage *m* (d'une fontaine, etc.).

Akan ['ɑ:kɑwqn], *s. Ling:* akan *m.*

akathisia [ækə'θi:ziə], *s. Psy:* akatathisie *f.*

akee [ə'ki:], *s. Bot:* akee *f.*

akene [ə'ki:n], *s. Bot:* akène *m*, achène *m*, achaine *m.*

akimbo [ə'kimbou], *adv.* **with arms a.,** les (deux) poings sur les hanches; **to stand with arms a.,** faire le pot à deux anses.

akin [ə'kin], *adv. & a.* **1. a. to s.o.,** parent de qn; apparenté à, avec, qn; **the two words are a.,** ces deux mots sont apparentés. **2. to be a. to sth.,** ressembler à qch.; rejoindre qch.; avoir des rapports avec qch.; **feeling a. to fear,** sentiment voisin, approchant, qui approche, de l'effroi, ressemblant à l'effroi; **passion a. to love,** passion *f* qui tient de, qui rejoint, qui touche à, qui frise, l'amour.

akinesia [æki'ni:siə], **akinesis** [æki'ni:sis], *s. Med:* acinèse *f.*

Akkadian [æ'keidiən]. **1.** *A.Hist:* (*a*) *a.* akkadien; (*b*) *s.* Akkadien, -ienne. **2.** *s. Ling:* akkadien *m.*

Akromyodi [ækroumai'oudai], *s.pl. Orn:* akromyodés *m.*

ala, *pl.* **-ae** ['eilə, -i:], *s. Anat: Nat.Hist:* aile *f*; **the alae of the nose,** les ailes du nez.

alabandine [ælə'bændin, -ain], *s. Lap: A:* almandine *f*, almandin *m*, alamandin *m.*

alabandite [ælə'bændait], *s. Miner:* alabandite *f*, alabandine *f.*

alabaster ['æləbæstər, -bɑ:-], *s.* **1.** albâtre *m*; **gypseous, modern, a.,** alabastrite *f*; **as white as a.,** d'une blancheur d'albâtre; **a. vase,** vase *m* d'albâtre. **2.** *Archeol:* alabastron *m*, alabastre *m.*

alabastrine [ælə'bæstrain], *a. Lit:* **1.** d'albâtre. **2.** d'une blancheur d'albâtre.

alabastron [ælə'bæstrən], *s. Archeol:* alabastron *m*, alabastre *m.*

alack [ə'læk], *int. A. & Poet:* hélas! **a. the day! a.-a-day!** ô jour malheureux!

alacritous [ə'lækritəs], *a. Lit:* prompt, empressé.

alacrity [ə'lækriti], *s.* empressement *m*, promptitude *f*; **he accepted with a.,** il a accepté avec enthousiasme.

Aladdin [ə'lædin], *Pr.n.m. Myth:* Aladin; **Aladdin's lamp,** la lampe d'Aladin.

alalia [ə'leiliə], *s. Med:* aphasie *f*, aphémie *f.*

alamandine [ælə'mændin, -ain], *s. Miner:* alamandin *m*, almandine *f.*

Alamannia [ælə'mæniə], *Pr.n.* = ALEMANNIA.

à la mode [ælæ'mɔd], *a.phr. Cu:* **beef à la m.,** bœuf *m* à la mode.

Alan ['æl(ə)n], *Pr.n.m.* Alain.

alanine ['ælənin], *s. Ch:* alanine *f.*

alapeen ['æləpi:n], *s. Tex: A:* alépine *f.*

alar ['eilər], *a.* **1.** *Anat: etc:* alaire. **2.** *Bot:* **A:** axillaire.

alarm[1] [ə'lɑ:m], *s.* **1.** alarme *f*, alerte *f*; **to raise the a.,** donner l'éveil; **to give the a. to s.o.,** donner l'alarme, l'alerte, à qn, alerter qn; **to spread (the) a.,** répandre l'alarme; **to spread a. and despondency,** répandre des bruits alarmistes; **to sound the a.,** sonner l'alarme, le tocsin, l'appel aux armes; **alarms and excursions,** (i) *Th: etc:* alertes et échauffourées *fpl*; (ii) alertes, incursions *fpl*, agitation *f*, remue-ménage *m*; **to take a.,** prendre l'alarme; s'alarmer; **general a. was felt when he failed to reappear,** on s'alarmait de ce qu'il ne reparaissait pas; **to put the camp into a state of a.,** jeter l'alarme dans le camp; **false a.,** fausse alerte; **he ran and hid in a.,** effrayé, il a couru se cacher; *attrib.* **a. call, a. note (of bird),** cri *m* d'alarme. **2.** *Fenc:* appel *m* du pied. **3.** (*a*) avertisseur *m*, signal *m*, sonnette *f* d'alarme; **burglar a.,** signalisateur *m* anti-vol; **fire a.,** avertisseur d'incendie; *Mch:* **low-water a.,** sifflet-avertisseur *m*, *pl.* sifflets-avertisseurs, de bas niveau; (*b*) sonnerie *f* (du réveil); **a. (clock),** réveille-matin *m inv*, réveil *m*; **to wind up the a.,** remonter la sonnerie; **to set the a. for six (o'clock),** mettre le réveil à six heures; **I slept right through the a.,** je n'ai pas entendu sonner le réveil. **4.** *attrib.* **a. bell,** (i) tocsin *m*, cloche *f* d'alarme; (ii) timbre avertisseur, sonnerie d'alarme; **a. signal,** signal *m* d'alarme; **a. whistle,** sifflet *m* d'alarme; **a. gun,** canon *m* d'alarme; *Rail:* **a. contact,** crocodile *m*; *Mch:* **a. gauge,** avertisseur (i) de bas niveau, (ii) de pression exagérée;

Mil: **a. post,** quartier *m* d'assemblée; point *m* de ralliement; *El:* **a. relay,** relais *m* de contrôle.
alarm[2], *v.tr.* **1.** *(a)* alarmer, donner l'alarme à (qn); *(b)* alerter (des troupes). **2.** alarmer, effrayer; **nobody was alarmed by it,** personne ne s'en est ému; **to be alarmed at sth.,** s'alarmer, s'effrayer, s'émouvoir, de qch.; être alarmé de qch.; **don't be alarmed,** ne craignez rien; soyez sans crainte; ne vous effrayez pas.
alarming [ə'lɑːmiŋ], *a.* alarmant; angoissant; effrayant.
alarmingly [ə'lɑːmiŋli], *adv.* d'une manière alarmante, effrayante; **a. stupid,** d'une stupidité effarante.
alarmism [ə'lɑːmizm], *s.* esprit *m* alarmiste, tendances *fpl* alarmistes.
alarmist [ə'lɑːmist], *a. & s.* alarmiste *(mf).*
alarum [ə'lærəm], *s.* **1.** *A:* = ALARM[1] **1. 2.** *(a)* réveille-matin *m inv,* réveil *m*; *(b)* timbre *m,* sonnerie *f* (du réveil).
alary ['eiləri], *a.* alaire.
alas [ə'læs], *int.* hélas! **a. for his hopes!** quelle déception pour lui!
Alaska [ə'læskə], *Pr.n. Geog:* Alaska *m*; **the A. Highway,** la route de l'Alaska.
alastrim [æ'læstrim], *s. Med:* alastrim *m.*
alate(d) ['eileit(id)], *a. Nat.Hist:* ailé.
alatern(us) ['ælətəːn(əs)], *s. Bot:* alaterne *m.*
Alaudidae [æ'laudidiː], *s.pl. Orn:* alaudidés *m,* les alouettes *f.*
alb [ælb], *s. Ecc.Cost:* aube *f.*
Alba ['ælbə], *Pr.n.* **1.** *Geog:* Alba. **2.** *A.Geog:* **A. Longa,** Albe la Longue.
albacore ['ælbəkɔːr], *s. Ich:* germon *m,* thon blanc.
Albania [æl'beiniə], *Pr.n. Geog:* Albanie *f.*
Albanian [æl'beiniən]. *Geog:* **1.** *a.* albanais. **2.** *s.* Albanais, -aise. **3.** *s. Ling:* albanais *m.*
Albany ['ɔːlbəni], *Pr.n. Lit: A:* Écosse *f.*
albarello [ælbə'relou], *s. Cer:* albarelle *f.*
albata [æl'beitə], *s. Metall:* maillechort *m.*
albatross ['ælbətrɔs], *s. Orn:* albatros *m*; **black-browed a.,** albatros à sourcils noirs; **black-footed a.,** albatros à pattes noires; **grey headed a.,** albatros à tête grise; **wandering a.,** albatros hurleur; **short-tailed a.,** albatros de Chine, *Fr.C:* albatros à queue courte; **yellow-nosed a.,** albatros à bec jaune, *Fr.C:* albatros à nez jaune; **light-mantled sooty a.,** albatros fuligineux.
albedo [æl'biːdou], *s. Ph: Astr:* albédo *m* (d'une planète, de la neige, etc.).
albedometer [ælbi'dɔmitər], *s.* albédomètre *m.*
albeit [ɔːl'biːit], *conj. Lit:* quoique, bien que, + *sub.*; **a. he failed,** quoiqu'il ait échoué; **a brilliant, a. slipshod, writer,** écrivain brillant, bien que négligeant; **she had become a woman, a. a very young woman,** elle était devenue femme, encore que très jeune femme.
Albert ['ælbəːt]. **1.** *Pr.n.m.* Albert. **2.** *s. Cost: A:* chaîne (de montre) **giletière.**
Albertan [æl'bəːtən], *a. & s. Geog:* (habitant, -ante, natif, -ive) de l'Alberta; albertain, -aine.
albertite ['ælbətait], *s. Miner:* albertite *f.*
albescent [æl'bes(ə)nt], *a. Lit:* qui tend vers le blanc; pâlissant.
Albian ['ælbiən], *a. & s. Geol:* albien *(m).*
Albigenses [ælbi'dʒensiːz], *s.pl. Rel.H:* Albigeois *m.*
Albigensian [ælbi'dʒensiən], *Rel.H:* **1.** *a.* albigeois; **the A. Crusade,** la croisade des Albigeois. **2.** *s.* Albigeois, -oise.
Albigensianism [ælbi'dʒensiənizm], *s. Rel.H:* albigéisme *m.*
albinic ['ælbinik], *a.* albinos *inv.*; atteint d'albinisme.
albinism ['ælbinizm], *s.* albinisme *m.*
albinistic [ælbi'nistik], *a.* albinos *inv.*
albino, *pl.* **-os** [æl'biːnou, -ouz], *a. & s.* albinos *(mf)*; *a.* dépigmenté; **a. negro,** nègre blanc; **a. rabbit,** lapin *m* russe.
Albion ['ælbiən], *Pr.n. A. Geog: Lit:* Albion *f*; **perfidious A.,** la perfide Albion.
albite ['ælbait], *s. Miner:* albite *f.*
albitization [ælbitai'zeiʃ(ə)n], *s. Miner:* albitisation *f.*
Albuginaceae [ælbjudʒi'neisiiː], *s.pl. Fung:* albuginacées *f.*
albuginea [ælbju'dʒiniə], *s. Anat:* membrane albuginée; tunique albuginée (de l'œil); albuginée *f* (du testicule).
albuginean [ælbju'dʒiniən], **albugineous** [æl'bjuːdʒiniəs], *a.* albugineux; *(of tissue, etc.)* albuginé.
albuginitis [ælbjudʒi'naitis], *s. Med:* albuginite *f.*
albugo [æl'bjuːgou], *s.* **1.** *Med:* leucome *m*; albugo *m,* albuginé *f, F:* taie *f,* maille *f* (de l'œil). **2.** *Fung:* albugo.
albula [æl'bjuːlə], *s. Ich:* albula *m, F:* banane *f* de mer.
album ['ælbəm], *s.* **1.** album *m*; **loose-leaf a.,** album à feuilles mobiles. **2.** *Rec:* album; 33 tours *m.*
albumen ['ælbjumin, æl'bjuːmin], *s.* **1.** albumen *m,* blanc *m* d'œuf. **2.** albumine *f* (du sérum du sang). **3.** *Bot:* albumen (de l'embryon).
albumenize [æl'bjuːminaiz], *v.tr. esp.Phot:* enduire (qch.) d'albumen.
albumin ['ælbjumin, æl'bjuːmin], *s. Biol: Ch:* albumine *f.*
albuminate [æl'bjuːmineit], *s. Ch:* albuminate *m.*
albuminimeter [ælbjumi'nimitər], *s. Med:* albuminimètre *m.*
albuminoid [æl'bjuːminɔid], *a. & s.* albuminoïde *(m).*
albuminometer [ælbjumi'nɔmitər], *s.* albuminimètre *m.*
albuminose [æl'bjuːminous], **albuminous** [æl'bjuːminəs], *a.* albumineux.
albuminuria [ælbjumi'njuːriə], *s. Med:* albuminurie *f.*
albuminuric [ælbjumi'njuːrik], *a. Med:* albuminurique.
albumose ['ælbjumous], *s. Ch: Physiol:* albumose *f.*
albumosuria [ælbjumou'sjuːriə], *s. Med:* albumosurie *f.*
alburn[1] ['ælbəːn], **alburnum** [æl'bəːnəm], *s. Bot: Ind:* aubier *m*; faux bois.
alburn[2], *s. Ich:* ablette *f.*
Alcaeus [æl'siːəs], *Pr.n.m. Gr.Lit:* Alcée.
Alcaic [æl'keiik]. **1.** *a. Pros:* alcaïque. **2.** *s.pl.* **Alcaics,** (vers *m*) alcaïques *(m).*
alcaligenes [ælkə'lidʒiniːz], *s.pl. Bac:* alcaligènes *m.*
alcalizing ['ælkəlaiziŋ], *a.* alcalifiant.
alcalosis [ælkə'lousis], *s. Med:* alcalose *f.*
alcapton [æl'kæptɔn], *s. Ch:* alcaptone *f.*
alcaptonuria [ælkæptɔ'njuːriə], *s. Med:* alcaptonurie *f.*
Alcedinidae [ælsi'dinidiː], *s.pl. Orn:* alcédinidés *m,* les martins-pêcheurs *m.*
Alcelaphinae [ælsi'læfiniː], *s.pl. Z:* alcélaphinés *m.*
Alcestis [æl'sestis], *Pr.n.f. Gr.Lit:* Alceste.
alchemic(al) [æl'kemik(l)], *a.* alchimique.
alchemilla [ælkə'milə], *s. Bot:* alchemille *f,* alchimille *f, F:* manteau *m* de Notre-Dame.
alchemist ['ælkəmist], *s.* alchimiste *m.*
alchemistic [ælkə'mistik], *a.* alchimique.
alchemize ['ælkəmaiz], *v.tr.* transmuer.
alchemy ['ælkəmi], *s.* alchimie *f.*
Alcibiades [ælsi'baiədiːz], *Pr.n.m. Gr.Hist:* Alcibiade.
Alcidae ['ælsidiː], *s.pl. Orn:* alcidés *m,* les pingouins *m.*
alcohol ['ælkəhɔl], *s.* alcool *m*; **pure a.,** alcool absolu; **denatured a.,** alcool dénaturé; **ethyl, ordinary, a.,** alcool éthylique, ordinaire; **wood a.,** méthanol *m*; **industrial a.,** alcool industriel; **a. content,** teneur *m* en alcool, pourcentage *m* d'alcool; *Med: U.S:* **rubbing a.** = alcool à 90°; *U.S:* **a. lamp,** lampe *f* à alcool.
alcohol(a)emia [ælkəhɔ'liːmiə], *s. Med:* alcoolémie *f.*
alcoholate ['ælkəhɔleit], *s.* alcoolat *m.*
alcoholature [ælkə'hɔlətjər], *s. Pharm:* alcoolature *f.*
alcoholic [ælkə'hɔlik]. **1.** *a.* alcoolique; **a. drink,** boisson alcoolisée; *Pharm:* **a. tincture,** alcoolé *m.* **2.** *s. (pers.)* alcoolique *mf.*
alcoholism ['ælkəhɔlizm], *s.* alcoolisme *m.*
alcoholizable [ælkəhɔ'laizəbl], *a.* alcoolisable.
alcoholization [ælkəhɔlai'zeiʃ(ə)n], *s.* alcoolisation *f.*
alcoholize ['ælkəhɔlaiz], *v.tr.* alcooliser.
alcoholomania [ælkəhɔlou'meiniə], *s. Med:* alcoolomanie *f.*
alcohol(o)meter ['ælkəhɔl'mitər, ælkəhɔ'lɔmitər], *s.* alcoomètre *m,* alcoolomètre *m*; pèse-alcool *m, pl.* pèse-alcools; pèse-liqueur *m, pl.* pèse-liqueurs.
alcoholometry [ælkəhɔ'lɔmitri], *s.* alcoométrie *f,* alcoolométrie *f.*
Alcoran (the) [ðiːælkɔ'rɑːn], *s.* le Coran, le Koran, l'Alcoran *m.*
alcove ['ælkouv], *s.* **1.** alcôve *f*; niche *f,* enfoncement *m* (dans un mur); **dining a.,** coin *m* des repas, coin salle à manger. **2.** *A:* berceau *m,* tonnelle *f* (de jardin).
alcoved ['ælkouvd], *a.* en alcôve.
alcyon[1] ['ælsiən], *s. Orn:* halcyon *m,* martin-chasseur *m, pl.* martins-chasseurs.
alcyon[2], *s. Coel:* alcyonaire *m.*
Alcyonacea [ælsiə'neisiə], *s.pl. Coel:* alcyonidés *m.*
Alcyonaria [ælsiə'nɛəriə], *s.pl. Coel:* alcyonaires *m.*
alcyonarian [ælsiə'nɛəriən], *a. & s. Coel:* alcyonaire *(m).*
aldehyde ['ældihaid], *s. Ch:* aldéhyde *f.*
aldehydic [ældi'haidik], *a. Ch:* aldéhydique.
alder ['ɔːldər], *s. Bot:* **1.** aune *m,* aulne *m*; **common a., silver-leaved a.,** aune grisâtre; **black a.,** verne *m,* vergne *m.* **2. a. blackthorn, black a.,** bourdaine *f,* frangule *f.* **3.** *NAm:* **white a.,** clèthre *m* à feuilles d'aune.
alderman, *pl.* **-men** ['ɔːldəmən], *s.m. Adm:* (i) = conseiller municipal; (ii) = conseiller général; **she has been made an a.** = elle a été nommée (i) au conseil municipal, (ii) au conseil départemental.
aldermanship ['ɔːldəmənʃip], *s.* = fonctions *fpl,* dignité *f* (i) de conseiller municipal, (ii) de conseiller général.
Alderney ['ɔːldəni], *Pr.n. Geog:* Aurigny *m*; *Husb:* **A. cow,** vache *f* d'Aurigny.
Aldine ['ɔːldain], *a. Typ.Hist:* aldin; **A. edition,** édition aldine, Alde *m.*
aldohexose [ældou'heksous], *s. Ch:* aldohexose *m.*
aldol ['ældɔl, -doul], *s. Ch:* aldol *m.*
aldolization [ældɔlai'zeiʃ(ə)n], *s. Ch:* aldolisation *f.*
aldopentose [ældou'pen'tous], *s. Ch:* aldopentose *m.*
aldose ['ældous], *s. Ch:* aldose *m.*
aldosterone [ældou'stiːroun], *s. Physiol:* aldostérone *f,* électrocortine *f.*
aldoxim(e) [æl'dɔksim], *s. Ch:* aldoxime *f.*
Aldus ['ɔːldəs], *Pr.n. & s. Typ:* Alde *m.*
ale [eil], *s.* **1.** bière anglaise (légère); ale *f*; **pale a.,** bière blonde; pale-ale *m*; **brown ale,** bière brune; *F:* **Adam's a.,** = château *m* la pompe. **2. ginger a.,** boisson gazeuse au gingembre.
aleatory ['eiliət(ə)ri], *a.* (contrat, etc.) aléatoire.
Alec(k) ['ælik], *Pr.n.m. (dim. of* **Alexander)** Alexandre; *F:* **a smart A.,** (i) un finaud; un combinard; (ii) un je-sais-tout.
alecithal [ei'lesiθəl], *a. Biol:* alécithe.
alecost ['eilkɔst], *s. Bot:* balsamite *f*; baume *m* des jardins; herbe *f* au coq; menthe-coq *f.*
alee [ə'liː], *adv. Nau:* sous le vent; **to put the helm a.,** mettre la barre dessous, au vent; **hard a.!** la barre dessous toute! loffez rondement!
alegar ['æligər, 'eiligər], *s.* vinaigre *m* de bière.
alehouse ['eilhaus], *s. A:* cabaret *m*; *Prov:* **everyone has a penny to spend at a new a.,** tout nouveau tout beau.
Alemanni [ælə'mænai], *s.pl. Hist:* Alemans *m,* Alamans *m.*
Alemannia [ælə'mæniə], *Pr.n. A.Geog:* Aléman(n)ie *f.*
Alemannian [ælə'mæniən], **Alemannic** [ælə'mænik], *a. Hist:* Aléman(n)ique.
alembic [ə'lembik], *s.* alambic *m.*
alembicated [ə'lembikeitid], *a.* alambiqué.
alepine ['ælipiːn], *s. Tex: A:* alépine *f.*
Aleppo [ə'lepou], *Pr.n. Geog:* Alep *m*; *Med: A:* **A. ulcer, boil, gall,** bouton *m* d'Alep, ulcère *m* d'Orient; *Bot:* **A. pine,** pin *m* d'Alep, de Jérusalem; *Bot: (on oak)* **A. gall,** noix *f* de galle.
alerion [ə'liəriən], *s. Her:* alérion *m.*
alert[1] [ə'ləːt]. **1.** *a.* *(a)* alerte, vigilant, éveillé; *(b)* actif, vif, preste, ingambe; **a. mind,** esprit présent, vif, éveillé. **2.** *s.* alerte *f*; **to be on the a.,** être sur le qui-vive, être en état d'alerte; **to be on the a. against an attack,** veiller en prévision d'une attaque; **to keep s.o. on the a.,** tenir qn en haleine, en éveil, toujours éveillé; **that put me on the a.,** cela me fit ouvrir l'œil; *F:* cela m'a mis la puce à l'oreille; *Mil:* **simple a.,** alerte simple; **general a.,** alerte générale; **reinforced a.,** alerte renforcée; *Cmptr:* **read a.,** incident *m* de lecture.
alert[2], *v.tr.* alerter; **troops have been alerted,** les troupes sont en état d'alerte.
alertly [ə'ləːtli], *adv.* d'une manière alerte; prestement.
alertness [ə'ləːtnis], *s.* **1.** *(a)* vigilance *f*; *(b)* promptitude *f* **(in doing sth.,** à faire qch.). **2.** vivacité *f.*
alette [ə'let], *s. Arch:* membrette *f* (d'une arche, etc.).
aleukaemic [eilju'kiːmik], *a. Med:* aleucémique; **a. leukaemia,** leucémie *f* aleucémique.
aleuri(o)spore [ə'ljuːri(ou)spɔər], *s. Fung:* aleuriospore *f,* aleurie *f.*
Aleurites [ælju'raitiːz], *s. Bot:* aleurite *m.*
aleurone [ə'ljuːroun], *s. Bot: Ch:* aleurone *f,* céréaline *f*; *Bot:* **a. layer,** assise *f* protéique; **a. grains,** grains *m* d'aleurone.
Aleut [æli'uːt], *s.* **1.** *Geog:* Aléoute *mf.* **2.** *Ling:* aléoute *m,* aleut *m.*
Aleutian [ə'ljuːʃ(ə)n]. *Geog:* **1.** *a.* Aléoute; aléoutien; **the A. Islands,** les (îles) Aléoutiennes. **2.** *s.* Aléoute *mf.*
alevin ['ælvin], *s. Ich:* alevin *m.*
alewife ['eilwaif], *s.* **1.** *Ich:* *(pl.* **alewife** *or* **alewives** [-waivz]) (variété *f* d')alose *f.* **2.** *A:* *(pl.* **-wives)** cabaretière *f.*
Alexander [ælig'zɑːndər], *Pr.n.m.* Alexandre.
Alexandra [ælig'zɑːndrə], *Pr.n.f.* Alexandra; *Geog:* **A. Land,** Terre Alexandra.
Alexandretta [æligzɑːn'dretə], *Pr.n. Geog:* Alexandrette *f.*
Alexandria [ælig'zɑːndriə], *Pr.n. Geog:* Alexandrie *f.*
Alexandrian [ælig'zɑːndriən]. *A.Hist: Geog:* **1.** *a.* alexandrin; *A.Hist:* **the A. Library,** la bibliothèque d'Alexandrie; *Phil:* **the A. School,** l'école *f* d'Alexandrie. **2.** *s.* Alexandrin, -ine.
Alexandrine [ælig'zɑːndrain], *a. & s. Pros:* alexandrin *(m).*
Alexandrinism [ælig'zɑːndrinizm], *s. Phil: Lit:* alexandrinisme *m.*
alexandrite [ælig'zɑːndrait], *s. Miner:* alexandrite *f.*
alexia [ə'leksiə], *s. Med:* alexie *f.*
alexin(e) [ə'leksin, -ɑin], *s. Bio-Ch:* alexine *f.*
alexipharmic [əleksi'fɑːmik], *a. & s. A:* antivénéneux,

alexipharmaque (*m*).

Alexius [ə'leksiəs], *Pr.n.m.* Alexis.

alfa ['ælfə], *s. Bot:* **a. (grass),** alfa *m.*

alfalfa [æl'fælfə], *s. Bot:* luzerne *f.*

alfilaria [ælfilə'riə], *s. Bot:* érodium *m.*

Alfol ['ælfɔl], *s. Const. R.t.m:* alfol *m.*

Alfonso [æl'fɔnsou], *Pr.n.m.* Alphonse.

alfresco [æl'freskou], *a. & adv.* **1.** en plein air; **a. lunch,** déjeuner *m.* **2. a. painting,** peinture *f* à fresque.

alga, *pl.* **-ae** ['ælgə, 'ældʒi:], *s. Bot:* algue *f*; **green algae,** spyrogyres *m*; **brown algae,** goémon *m* jaune.

algaecide ['ældʒisaid] *s.* = ALGICIDE.

algal ['ælgl], *a.* **1.** des algues. **2.** *Fung:* (*of cells in lichen*) gonidial, -aux; gonimique.

Algaroth ['ælgərɔθ], *Pr.n. A.Pharm:* **powder of A.,** algaroth *m.*

algarroba [ælgə'roubə], *s. Bot:* **1.** caroubier *m.* **2.** algarobie *f* (de l'Amérique du Sud).

algazel [ælgə'zel], *s. Z:* algazelle *f.*

algebra ['ældʒibrə], *s.* algèbre *f*; **modern a.,** algèbre moderne; **elementary a.,** rudiments *mpl* d'algèbre; **Boolean a.,** algèbre booléenne, de Boole; **logical a.,** algèbre logique; **matrix a.,** algèbre matricielle; **a. of subsets,** clan *m*; **central simple a.,** algèbre simple centrale.

algebraic(al) [ældʒi'breiik(l)], *a.* algébrique; **algebraical expression,** expression *f,* formule *f,* algébrique; **algebraic(al) sign, symbol,** signe *m,* symbole *m,* algébrique; **algebraic sum,** somme *f* algébrique; **algebraic identities,** identités *f* algébriques; **algebraic function, theory,** fonction *f,* théorie *f,* algébrique; **algebraic singularity (of analytic function),** point *m* critique, point de branchement.

algebraically [ældʒi'breiik(ə)li], *adv.* algébriquement; en valeur algébrique.

algebr(a)ist ['ældʒibr(ei)ist], *s.* algébriste *mf.*

Algeciras [ældʒi'siərəs], *Pr.n. Geog:* Algésiras *m.*

algedonic [ældʒi'dɔnik], *a. Psy:* alghédonique.

Algeria [æl'dʒiəriə], *Pr.n. Geog:* l'Algérie *f.*

Algerian [æl'dʒiəriən]. **1.** (*of Algeria*) (*a*) *a.* algérien; (*b*) *s.* Algérien, -ienne. **2.** (*of Algiers*) (*a*) *a.* algérois; (*b*) *s.* Algérois, -oise. **3. A. onyx,** marbre *m* onyx.

Algerine ['ældʒirain], *s. A:* **1.** *Geog:* Algérois, -oise. **2.** *Hist:* pirate *m* de la côte d'Alger; pirate barbaresque.

algesia [æl'dʒi:ziə, -siə], *s. Med:* algésie *f.*

algesimeter [ældʒi'zimitər], *s.* algésimètre *m.*

algesis [æl'dʒi:sis], *s. Med:* douleur *f.*

algic ['ældʒik], *a. Ch:* (acide) algénique.

algicide ['ældʒisaid], *s.* algicide *m.*

algid ['ældʒid], *a. Med:* algide; **a. cholera,** choléra *m* algide.

algidity [æl'dʒiditi], *s. Med:* algidité *f.*

Algiers [æl'dʒiəz], *Pr.n. Geog:* Alger *m.*

algin(e) ['ældʒin, -ain], *s. Ch:* algine *f.*

alginate ['ældʒineit], *s. Ch:* alginate *m.*

alginic [æl'dʒinik], *a. Ch:* (acide) alginique.

algodonite [æl'gɔdənait], *s. Miner:* algodonite *f.*

algoid ['ælgɔid], *a.* algoïde.

Algol[1] ['ælgɔl], *Pr.n. Astr:* Algol *m.*

algol[2], *s. Cmptr:* algol *m.*

algolagnia [ælgə'lægniə], *s. Med:* algolagnie *f.*

algological [ælgou'lɔdʒikl], *a.* algologique.

algologist [æl'gɔlədʒist], *s.* algologue *mf.*

algology [æl'gɔlədʒi], *s.* algologie *f.*

Algonkian [æl'gɔŋkiən], **Algonquian** [æl'gɔŋkwiən]. **1.** *a. & s. Geol:* algonkien (*m*), algonquien (*m*). **2.** *s. Ethn:* Algonquien, -ienne; Algonkien, -ienne. **3.** *a. & s. Ling:* algonkien, algonquien.

Algonkin [æl'gɔŋkin], **Algonquin** [æl'gɔŋkwin], *s.* **1.** *Ethn:* Algonquien, -ienne; Algonkien, -ienne; **the Algonkins, Algonquins,** les Algonquins *m,* Algonkins *m.* **2.** *Ling:* algonquien *m,* algonkien *m.*

algophilia [ælgou'filiə], *s. Med:* algophilie *f.*

algophobia [ælgou'foubiə], *s. Med:* algophobie *f.*

algorithm ['ælgəriðm], *s. Mth:* algorithme *m*; **Euclidean a.,** algorithme d'Euclide; *Cmptr:* **a. translation,** traduction *f* algorithmique.

algorithmic [ælgə'riðmik], *a. Mth:* algorithmique; *Cmptr:* **a. language,** langage *m* algorithmique.

algorithmically [ælgə'riðmikəli], *adv. Cmptr:* de façon algorithmique.

algous ['ælgəs], *a.* (*a*) rempli d'algues; (*b*) qui ressemble, semblable, aux algues.

alias ['eiliəs]. **1.** *adv.* alias, autrement dit, autrement nommé; **the woman X, a. Y,** la femme X, dite Y, connue sous le nom de Y. **2.** *s.* (*pl.* **aliases** ['eiliəsiz]) (*a*) nom emprunté, nom d'emprunt, faux nom; **his a. was . . .,** il était connu sous le nom de . . .; **he has several aliases,** il a plusieurs noms de rechange; **to travel under an a.,** voyager sous un faux nom; (*b*) *Cmptr:* pseudonyme *m,* étiquette équivalente.

aliasing ['eiliəsiŋ], *s. Cmptr:* **a. error,** erreur *f* d'échantillonnage.

alibi[1] ['ælibai], *s.* (*a*) *Jur:* alibi *m;* **to plead, fall back on, set up, an a.,** plaider l'alibi; invoquer un alibi; **to produce an a.,** produire, fournir, un alibi; **to establish an a.,** prouver, établir, son alibi; (*b*) *F:* prétexte *m,* excuse *f*; **he's always looking for an a.,** il est toujours prêt à s'excuser.

alibi[2], *v.tr. & i.* (**alibied, alibiing**) *F:* (*a*) **X is alibied by Y,** c'est Y qui prouve, établit, l'alibi d'X; (*b*) s'excuser (à cause de qch.).

alicant(e) ['ælikænt], *s.* vin *m* d'Alicante; alicante *m.*

Alice ['ælis], *Pr.n.f.* Alice.

Alick ['ælik], *Pr.n.m.* = ALEC(K).

alicyclic [æli'saiklik], *a. Ch:* alicyclique.

alidad(e) ['ælidæd, -deid], *s. Surv: etc:* alidade *f*; graphomètre *m;* **open-sight a.,** alidade à pinnules; **telescopic a.,** alidade à lunette; **clinometer a.,** alidade à éclimètre; **triangular a.,** alidade de triangulation.

alien[1] ['eiliən]. **1.** *a. & s. Jur:* étranger, -ère (non naturalisé(e)); **resident, non-resident, a.,** étranger résident, non résident; **enemy a.,** sujet, sujette, d'un pays ennemi; **Enemy A. Property Act,** loi *f* sur les biens ennemis; **undesirable a.,** étranger indésirable. **2.** *a.* étranger (à qch.), éloigné (de qch.); contraire, opposé (à qch.); qui répugne (à qch.); **such an action would be entirely a. to her nature,** une telle action serait entièrement contraire à sa nature. **3.** *s.* (*a*) *Bot:* plante introduite (dans une région), qui n'est pas indigène (à la région); (*b*) *Ling:* mot étranger (qui n'a pas entièrement droit de cité dans une langue); **it is sheer a. hunting to try to find a pure English equivalent for** ***tête-à-tête,*** il faut être chauvin au plus haut degré pour essayer de trouver un mot d'origine anglaise pour remplacer *tête-à-tête.*

alien[2], *v.tr.* **1.** *A: & Lit:* = ALIENATE 2. **2.** *Jur:* = ALIENATE 1.

alienability [eiliənə'biliti], *s. Jur:* aliénabilité *f,* mutabilité *f* (d'une terre, etc.).

alienable ['eiliənəbl], *a. Jur:* (bien) aliénable, mutable.

alienage ['eiliənidʒ], *s.* qualité *f* d'étranger, d'étrangère.

alienate ['eiliəneit], *v.tr.* **1.** *Jur:* aliéner (des biens, etc.). **2.** détacher, éloigner, désaffectionner, (s')aliéner (qn, les esprits); **to a. s.o. from his friends,** détacher qn de ses amis. **3. to a. a sum from its proper destination,** détourner une somme de sa destination propre.

alienation [eiliə'neiʃ(ə)n], *s.* **1.** *Jur:* aliénation *f* (de biens). **2.** aliénation (de cœurs); désaffection *f.* **3. mental a.,** aliénation (mentale); égarement *m* d'esprit. **4.** *Th:* **a. effect,** distanciation *f.*

alienator ['eiliəneitər], *s. Jur:* aliénateur, -trice.

alienee [eiliə'ni:], *s. Jur:* aliénataire *mf.*

alienism ['eiliənizm], *s.* **1.** qualité *f* d'étranger. **2.** *Med:* aliénisme *m.*

alienist ['eiliənist], *s. Med:* (médecin) *m* aliéniste (*mf*).

alienor ['eiliənər], *s. Jur:* aliénateur, -trice.

aliferous [æ'lifərəs], *a. Ent:* alifère.

aliform ['eilifɔ:m], *a. Nat.Hist: etc:* aliforme.

aligerous [æ'lidʒərəs], *a. Ent:* alifère.

alight[1] [ə'lait], *v.i.* (**alighted,** *occ. Lit:* **alit**) **1.** descendre (de cheval, *Lit:* de voiture). **2.** (*a*) (*of bird*) s'abattre, se poser; *Ven:* se remiser; (*b*) *Av: A:* atterrir.

alight[2], *a.* allumé, en feu; **to catch a.,** s'allumer; prendre feu; **to set sth. a.,** mettre le feu à qch.; mettre qch. en feu; **all a. with the morning sun,** tout embrasé par le soleil du matin.

alighting [ə'laitiŋ], *s. Av: A:* atterrissage *m*; amérissage *m,* amerrissage *m.*

align [ə'lain]. **1.** *v.tr.* (*a*) aligner (des soldats, etc.); mettre (des objets) en ligne; *Cmptr:* aligner, cadrer (des cartes); (*b*) *Mec.E:* dresser (des arbres, etc.); faire coïncider les axes; (*c*) dégauchir, redresser (des organes faussés ou gauchis); *Elcs:* aligner, redresser, régler; *Aut:* régler le parallélisme (des roues); (*d*) *Fin:* aligner; **Belgium aligns her currency on France,** la Belgique aligne sa monnaie sur la France. **2.** *v.i.* (*a*) s'aligner, se mettre en ligne; prendre position; (*b*) (*of shafts, etc.*) coïncider.

aligner [ə'lainər], *s.* mécanisme *m,* dispositif *m,* d'alignement; *Cmptr:* dispositif de cadrage (des cartes).

aligning [ə'lainiŋ], *s.* alignement *m*; *Elcs:* **a. indicator,** indicateur *m* d'alignement; *Aut:* **wheel a.,** réglage *m* du parallélisme des roues.

alignment [ə'lainm(ə)nt], *s.* (*a*) alignement *m*; tracé *m* (d'une voie ferrée, etc.); *Cmptr:* alignement, cadrage *m*; (*of optical instrument*) **zero a.,** ligne *f* de foi; **out of a.,** (i) désaligné; (ii) *Const:* hors d'œuvre; (iii) *Typ:* (ligne) sortante; **irregular a.,** désalignement *m*; *Mth: etc:* **a. chart,** nomogramme *m*; *Fin:* **a. of currencies,** alignement des monnaies; **the sharp a. of political parties,** la démarcation nette des partis politiques; (*b*) redressage *m,* dégauchissement *m* (d'organes faussés, etc.); (*c*) centrage *m,* équerrage *m*; (*d*) *Elcs:* alignement, redressage, réglage *m*; **a. input,** accord *m* d'antenne; **antenna a.,** réglage du circuit d'antenne; **a. fixture,** dispositif *m* de vérification d'alignement; (*e*) *Aut:* parallélisme *m* (des roues); **front wheel a.,** parallélisme des roues avant.

alike [ə'laik]. **1.** *a.* semblable, pareil, ressemblant; **they are very much a.,** ils sont très ressemblants; ils se ressemblent beaucoup; **they're as a. as two peas,** ils se ressemblent comme deux gouttes d'eau; **no two are a.,** il n'y en a pas deux de pareils, pas deux qui se ressemblent; **you are all a.!** vous vous ressemblez tous! vous êtes tous les mêmes! vous êtes tous pareils! *F:* vous êtes tous du même tonneau; **all things are a. to him,** tout lui est égal, indifférent; *Nau:* **two boats a.,** deux canots bâtards. **2.** *adv.* pareillement; de même; de la même manière; également; **to treat everybody a.,** traiter tout le monde de la même manière, de la même façon; traiter tout le monde également; **in everything they think a.,** ils sont toujours du même avis; **dressed a.,** habillés de même; vêtus uniformément; **to go out every day, summer and winter a.,** sortir tous les jours, été comme hiver.

aliment[1] ['ælimənt], *s.* **1.** aliment *m.* **2.** *Scot: Jur:* = ALIMONY.

aliment[2] ['æliment], *v.tr.* **1.** alimenter. **2.** *Scot: Jur:* faire une pension alimentaire à (qn).

alimental [æli'mentl], *a.* **1.** nourrissant, nutritif; *Med:* alimenteux. **2.** *Jur:* alimentaire.

alimentary [æli'mentəri], *a.* **1.** *Anat:* **a. canal,** tube *m,* conduit *m,* canal *m,* alimentaire; tube digestif. **2. a. substances,** substances *f* alimentaires. **3.** (= ALIMENTAL) *Jur:* **a. endowment,** pension *f* alimentaire.

alimentation [ælimen'teiʃ(ə)n], *s.* alimentation *f.*

alimony ['æliməni], *s. Jur:* pension *f* alimentaire (faite à l'épouse après séparation de corps); **obligation to pay a.,** obligation *f* alimentaire; **claim of a.,** demande *f* d'aliments; **to provide one's wife with a.,** fournir des aliments à son épouse.

aline [ə'lain], *v.,* **alinement** [ə'lainm(ə)nt], *s.esp. U.S:* = ALIGN, ALIGNMENT.

aliped ['æliped]. **1.** *a.* (*a*) *Z:* aux ailes membraneuses; (*b*) *Lit:* (*of Mercury, etc.*) aux pieds ailés. **2.** *s. Z:* ch(é)iroptère *m.*

aliphatic [æli'fætik], *a. Ch:* aliphatique, acyclique.

aliquot ['ælikwɔt], *a. & s. Mth:* **a. (part),** (partie *f*) aliquote (*f*).

alisma [ə'lizmə], *s. Bot:* wiesnérie *f,* alisme *m,* alisma *m*; *F:* plantain *m* d'eau.

Alismaceae [æliz'meisii:], *s.pl. Bot:* alismacées *f.*

alison ['ælisn], *s. Bot: F:* **sweet a.,** alysson *m,* alysse *m.*

alite ['eilait], *s. Const:* alite *f.*

aliturgic(al) [eili'tə:dʒik(l)], *a. Ecc:* aliturgique.

alive [ə'laiv], *a.* (*never used unqualified before a noun*) **1.** (*a*) (*of pers.*) **to be (still) a.,** être (encore) vivant, en vie; vivre (encore); **if he is still a.,** s'il est encore de ce monde; **to keep s.o. a.,** maintenir qn en vie; **to come a.,** (i) naître à la vie; (ii) s'animer; **to come a. again,** revenir à la vie; ressusciter; **to be burnt, buried, a.,** être brûlé, enterré, vif; **we found them a.,** nous les avons trouvés vivants; *F:* **to be a. and kicking,** être plein de vie; être gai et dispos; être en pleine forme; **he was a. and kicking when I saw him last week,** il était en (très) bonne forme quand je l'ai vu la semaine dernière; **it's good to be a.!** il fait bon vivre! **dead or a.,** mort ou vif; **more dead than a.,** plus mort que vif; **that's not going to happen while I'm a.,** cela ne se fera pas de mon vivant; **when your father was a.,** du vivant de votre père; **the best man a.,** le meilleur homme du monde; **no man a.,** personne, aucun homme, au monde; **he will do it better than any man a.,** il le fera mieux que personne, que qui que ce soit; *F: O:* **man a.!** par exemple! **man a.! where have you come from?** c'est vous, grand Dieu! et d'où venez-vous? **man a.!** *U.S:* **sakes a.! is it you?** c'est vous? pas possible! (*b*) (*of thg*) **to keep a memory a.,** garder, entretenir, un souvenir; **to keep the conversation a.,** entretenir la conversation; ne pas laisser languir la conversation. **2. to be fully a. to the danger,** avoir pleinement conscience du danger; **to be a. to one's own interests,** veiller à ses intérêts, être soucieux de ses (propres) intérêts; **to be a. to the importance of . . .,** se rendre compte de, comprendre (bien), en sentir, l'importance de . . .; **I am a. to the fact that . . .,** je n'ignore pas que. . . . **3. he is very much a.,** (i) il est très remuant; (ii) il a l'esprit très éveillé; **look a.!** remuez-vous (donc)! faites vite! dépêchez-vous! *P:* grouille-toi! **4. the cheese was a. with maggots,** le fromage grouillait de vers; **the heath is a. with game,** la lande foisonne de gibier; **the street was a. with people,**

la rue fourmillait de monde; **town a. with soldiers,** ville grouillante de soldats. 5. *El: esp. U.S:* **the wire was a.,** le fil était sous tension.

alizarin(e) [ə'lizərin, -ain], *s. Ch:* alizarine *f.*

alkalescence [ælkə'lesns], *s. Ch:* alcalescence *f.*

alkalescent [ælkə'lesnt], *a. Ch:* alcalescent.

alkali ['ælkəlai], *s. Ch:* alcali *m;* **a. strength,** force *f* d'alcalinité (d'une solution, etc.); **a.-resisting,** inattaquable par les alcalis, **a. metal,** métal alcalin.

alkali-cellulose ['ælkəlai'seljulouz], *s.* alcalicellulose *f.*

alkalify ['ælkəlifai]. *Ch:* **1.** *v.tr.* alcal(in)iser; **alkalifying principle,** principe alcalifiant. **2.** *v.i.* devenir alcalin; s'alcaliser.

alkalimeter [ælkə'limitər], *s. Ch:* alcalimètre *m.*

alkalimetric [ælkəli'metrik], *a. Ch:* alcalimétrique.

alkalimetry [ælkə'limitri], *s. Ch:* alcalimétrie *f.*

alkaline ['ælkəlain], *a. Ch:* alcalin; **to make a solution a.,** alcaliser une solution; **a. metals, earths,** métaux alcalins, terres alcalines; **a. earth metals,** métaux alcalino-terreux.

alkalinity [ælkə'liniti], *s. Ch:* alcalinité *f.*

alkalization [ælkəlai'zeiʃ(ə)n], *s. Ch:* alcal(in)isation *f.*

alkalize ['ælkəlaiz], *v.tr. Ch:* alcal(in)iser.

alkaloid ['ælkəlɔid], *a. & s. Ch:* alcaloïde (*m*).

alkalosis [ælkə'lousis], *s. Med:* alcalose *f.*

alkane ['ælkein], *s. Ch:* alcane *m.*

alkanet ['ælkənet], *s. Bot:* buglosse *f.* **field a.,** lycopside *f* des champs; **dyer's a.,** buglosse des teinturiers; orcanète *f.*

alkannin [æl'kænin], *s. Ch:* alcannine *f,* alkannine *f.*

alkapton [æl'kæptɔn], *s. Ch:* alcaptone *f.*

alkaptonuria [ælkæptə'nju:riə], *s. Med:* alcaptonurie *f.*

alkekengi [ælki'kendʒi], *s. Bot:* alkékenge *f.*

alkene [ælki:n], *s. Ch:* alcène *m.*

alkyd ['ælkid], *s. Ch:* alkyd *m.*

alkyl ['ælkil], *s. Ch:* alcoyle *m,* alkyle *m.*

alkylate[1] ['ælkileit], *s. Ch:* alcoylat *m,* alkylat *m.*

alkylate[2], *v.tr. Ch:* alcoyler, alkyler.

alkylated ['ælkileitid], *a. Ch:* alkylé, alcoylé.

alkylating ['ælkileitiŋ], *a. Med:* **a. agent,** alkylant *m.*

alkylation [ælki'leiʃ(ə)n], *s. Ch:* alcoylation *f,* alkylation *f.*

alkylene ['ælkili:n], *s. Ch:* alcoylène *m.*

alkylhalide [ælkil'hælaid], *s. Ch:* alcoylhalogène *m,* halogénure *m* d'alkyle, d'alcoyle.

alkylic [æl'kilik], *a. Ch:* alkylique.

alkylidene [æl'kilidi:n], *s. Ch:* alcoylidène *m.*

alkylogen [æl'kiloudgen], *s. Ch:* = AKYLHALIDE.

alkyne ['ælkain], *s. Ch:* alcyne *f.*

all [ɔ:l]. **1.** *a. & pron.* tout, tous; (*a*) *a.* **a. France,** toute la France; **a. day,** (pendant) toute la journée; **a. men,** tous les hommes; **that you, of a. men, should do such a thing!** vous êtes la dernière personne dont on attendrait une pareille action! **a. the others,** tous les autres; **to be a. things to a. men,** être tout à tous; **a. his life,** toute sa vie; **a. the way,** tout le long du chemin; **to go a. the way,** aller tout le long du chemin, jusqu'au bout; **it isn't roses a. the way,** la vie n'est pas tout roses; **is that a. the luggage you're taking?** c'est tout ce que vous emportez de bagages? **for a. his wealth,** en dépit de, malgré, sa fortune; **with a. his faults I'm fond of him,** en dépit de, malgré, tous ses défauts je l'aime bien; **with a. speed,** au plus vite, à toute vitesse; **at a. hours,** à toute heure; *F:* **he comes home at a. hours,** il rentre à des heures indues; **they used to play bridge until a. hours of the night,** ils jouaient au bridge jusqu'à pas d'heures; **in a. sorts of ways,** de toutes les façons; **a. that's nonsense,** tout ça, c'est des bêtises; **you're not as ill as a. that,** vous n'êtes pas malade à ce point-là; vous n'êtes pas (aus) si malade que ça; **1066 and a. that,** 1066 et le reste, et la suite; (*b*) *a. & pron.* **almost a.,** presque tous; **a. are agreed that . . .,** tous, toutes, sont d'accord, chacun est d'accord, que . . .; **not a. are agreed,** tous ne sont pas d'accord; **a. of us,** nous tous; tous tant que nous sommes; **you must a. of you work hard,** vous devez tous travailler dur; **a. this is beside the point,** tout ceci est en dehors de la question; *F:* **it cost him a. of 1,000 dollars,** cela lui a coûté au moins 1,000 dollars; *F:* **he must be a. of sixty,** il doit avoir au moins soixante ans; **a. together,** tous, toutes, à la fois, ensemble; **a. but he, him,** tous sauf, excepté, lui; **a. and sundry,** tous sans exception; **a. whom I saw,** tous ceux, toutes celles, que j'ai vu(e)s; (*c*) *pron.* **we a. love him,** nous l'aimons tous; **she wanted to open them a.,** elle voulait tous les ouvrir, les ouvrir tous; **I know it a.,** (i) je sais tout cela; (ii) (*of poem, etc.*) je le sais en entier; **I gave you it a.,** je vous ai tout donné; **take it a.,** prenez le tout; **in the middle of it a.,** au milieu de tout cela; (*d*) *adv. Games:* **five a.,** cinq à cinq; *Ten:* **four a.,** quatre jeux partout; **five a.,** à deux de jeu; **fifteen a.,** quinze à, quinze A; **set a.,** set *m* partout; **they are set a.,** ils sont à égalité de sets; (*at dominoes*) **three a., five a.,** trois partout, cinq partout; (*e*) *pron.* **almost a.,** presque tout; **a. that glitters is not gold,** tout ce qui brille n'est pas or; **a. that happens,** tout ce qui arrive; **a. (that) I say,** tout ce que je dis; **for a. he may say,** en dépit de ce qu'il dit; quoi qu'il en dise; **that's a.,** c'est tout; voilà tout; **is that a.?** (i) est-ce tout? (ii) *Iron:* n'est-ce que cela? ce n'est que ça? la belle affaire! **if that's a.,** si ce n'est que cela; s'il ne tient qu'à cela; **if that's a. there is new,** s'il n'y a que cela de nouveau; **all's well,** tout va bien; **I think that's about a.,** je crois que c'est tout; **it was a. I could do not to laugh,** je me tenais à quatre pour ne pas rire; **when all's said and done, a. said and done,** somme toute, au bout du compte, en fin de compte, quand tout est dit; tout compte fait, en dernière analyse; **after a.,** au bout du compte, tout compte fait. **2.** (*a*) *pron.* **once and for a.,** une fois pour toutes; **for a. I know,** autant que je sache; **for a. I care,** pour (tout) ce que cela me fait; **thirty men in a.,** trente hommes en tout; **I spent a hundred francs in a.,** j'ai dépensé cent francs en tout; **above a.,** surtout; **most of a.,** surtout, le plus; **the best of a. would be to . . .,** le mieux serait de . . .; **when I was busiest of a.,** au moment où j'étais le plus occupé; (*b*) *adv.phr.* **at all: did you speak at a.?** avez-vous dit quoi que ce soit? **do you know him at a.?** le connaissez-vous aucunement? **I didn't speak at a.,** je n'ai pas parlé du tout; je n'ai rien dit; **I'm not at a. astonished,** je n'en suis aucunement étonné; **not at a.,** (i) pas du tout, *F:* du tout; (ii) (*when thanked*) je vous en prie; **nothing at a.,** rien du tout; **I don't know at a.,** je n'en sais rien (du tout); **without at a. wishing to criticize you,** sans aucunement vouloir vous faire des critiques, sans aucune prétention de critique; **if he comes at a.,** si tant est qu'il vienne; s'il lui arrive de venir; si par hasard il vient; **he will write to you tomorrow, if at a.,** il vous écrira demain, si tant est qu'il vous écrive; s'il vous écrit (du tout), ce sera demain; **if you go there at a.,** si vous faites tant que d'y aller; **if you hesitate at a.,** pour peu que vous hésitiez; **if he coughs at a. she runs upstairs,** pour si peu qu'il tousse elle monte en courant; **if you are at a. anxious,** si vous êtes tant soit peu inquiet; **if it is at a. cold,** pour peu qu'il fasse froid; s'il fait le moindre froid; **if there is any wind at a.,** s'il y a le moindre vent; **if you have any intelligence at a. you can see that . . .,** pour peu qu'on ait d'intelligence on s'aperçoit que . . .; **why do it at a.?** pourquoi se donner la peine de le faire? (*c*) *adv.phr.* **all but: a. but impossible,** presque impossible; **I a. but fell,** j'ai failli tomber; **he a. but embraced her,** c'est tout juste s'il ne l'a pas embrassée; peu s'en fallut qu'il ne l'embrassât; il était sur le point de l'embrasser; **I'm a. but certain of it,** j'en ai la quasi-certitude; **it was a. but certain that . . .,** il était à peu près certain que . . .; **it's a. but done,** c'est pour ainsi dire fini, fait; c'est comme fait; **the play was a. but ended,** la pièce touchait à sa fin; (*d*) *adv. or adj.phr.* **all in all: taking it a. in a.,** à tout prendre; **they were a. in a. to each other,** ils ne vivaient que l'un pour l'autre; ils étaient dévoués l'un à l'autre; **she was a. in a. to him,** elle était ce qu'il avait de plus cher au monde; (*e*) *pron.* **and a.,** et (tout) le reste; **and down will come cradle and baby and a.,** berceau, bébé, tout fera patatras; **I'll sell you the house, the furniture, the carpets, the television and a.,** je vous vends la maison, y compris les meubles, les tapis, la télévision et tout le bataclan; (*f*) *pron. P:* **damn a.,** rien du tout, rien de rien; **how much did you understand?- damn a.!** qu'est-ce que tu y as compris?- rien de rien, deux fois rien; **what do they pay you?-damn a.!** qu'est-ce qu'ils vous payent?-des clopinettes; **I've done damn a. today,** je n'ai rien fichu aujourd'hui. **3.** *adv.* tout; **he, she, is a. alone,** il est tout seul, elle est toute seule; **to be (dressed) a. in black,** être habillé(e) tout en noir, tout de noir; *Lit:* être tout de noir vêtu; **his hands were a. tar,** ses mains étaient couvertes de goudron, il avait les mains couvertes de goudron; **he was a. blood and sweat,** il était couvert de sang et de sueur; **she is a. ears, a. impatience,** elle est tout oreilles, tout impatience; **a. in one piece,** tout d'une pièce; **I'm a. for staying here,** je ne demande qu'à rester ici; **to be a. for a course of action,** être tout entier pour une ligne de conduite; **I'm a. for liberty,** je tiens à, j'en suis pour, la liberté; **she's a. for making money,** elle ne songe qu'à gagner de l'argent; **she is a. for accepting this offer,** elle est tout en faveur d'accepter cette offre; **my wife was a. for calling in a doctor,** ma femme voulait à toute force, à tout prix, appeler un médecin; **he's not a. bad,** il n'est pas entièrement mauvais; **the old grudges are not a. gone,** les anciennes rancunes ne sont pas entièrement dissipées; **a. the better, a. the worse (for me),** tant mieux, tant pis (pour moi); **you will be a. the better for it,** vous vous en trouverez (d'autant) mieux; **I love him a. the better for his faults,** ses défauts me le rendent d'autant plus cher; **I think a. the less of him for it,** je l'en estime d'autant moins; **the army was giving way a. along the line,** l'armée cédait sur toute la ligne; **the hour came a. too soon,** l'heure n'arriva que trop tôt; **a. at once,** (i) (*suddenly*) tout à coup, subitement; (ii) (*at one time*) tout d'un coup, tous à la fois; **that's a. nonsense,** tout cela est absurde; **that's a. very well, but . . .,** tout cela est bel et bien mais . . .; *F:* **he's a. there,** il a les yeux en face des trous; **he's not a. there,** il est un peu simple d'esprit; **is he a. there?** est-ce qu'il a perdu la tête? est-ce qu'il sait ce qu'il fait? est-ce qu'il est fou? NOTE: *For numerous other expressions with* **all,** *e.g.* **all clear, all fours, all over, all round, all up,** *see the second word.* **4.** *s.* tout *m,* totalité *f;* **to stake one's a.,** jouer son va-tout; **we must stake our a.,** il faut risquer le tout pour le tout; **I have given you my a.,** tout ce que j'avais à donner, tu l'as eu; **music is my life, my a.,** la musique est ma vie, mon seul amour; **to lose one's a.,** perdre son pécule.

all-absorbing [ɔ:ləb'sɔ:biŋ], *a.* absorbant, du plus haut intérêt, passionnant.

allactite ['ælɔktait], *s. Miner:* allactite *f.*

Allah ['ælə], *Pr.n.m.* Allah.

Allan ['ælən], *Pr.n.m.* Alain.

allantoic [ælæn'tɔik], *a. Anat:* allantoïdien; allantoïque.

Allantoidea [æləntɔ'i:diə], *s.pl. Z:* allantoïdiens *m.*

allantoin [ə'læntɔin], *s. Ch:* allantoïne *f.*

allantois [ə'læntɔis], *s. Anat:* membrane *f* allantoïde; allantoïde *f.*

all-around ['ɔ:lə'raund], *a. NAm:* (athlète) complet; (homme) universel.

allative ['ælətiv], *a. Ling:* allatif.

allay [ə'lei], *v.tr.* (*a*) apaiser, calmer (une tempête, une colère); tempérer, modérer (l'ardeur du soleil); (*b*) apaiser (une querelle); calmer (la frayeur); endormir, dissiper (les soupçons); (*c*) alléger, adoucir, calmer, soulager, amortir, assoupir (la douleur); apaiser (la soif, la faim); couper, apaiser (la fièvre).

allaying [ə'leiiŋ], apaisement *m,* adoucissement *m,* soulagement *m,* assoupissement *m,* amortissement *m.*

all-bountiful ['ɔ:l'bauntifl], *a. Lit:* infiniment bon.

all(-)clear ['ɔ:l'kliər], *s.* (signal *m* de) fin *f* d'alerte.

all-conquering ['ɔ:l'kɔnk(ə)riŋ], *a.* (amour, etc.) qui triomphe de tout; toujours victorieux.

all-devouring ['ɔ:ldi'vau(ə)riŋ], *a.* (temps) qui consume tout; (*of passion*) dévorant.

allegation [æli'geiʃ(ə)n], *s.* allégation *f;* **to make an a.,** alléguer qch.

allege [ə'ledʒ], *v.tr.* **1.** alléguer, prétendre (**that,** que + *ind.*); **to a. ill health as a reason,** alléguer la mauvaise santé comme motif; donner comme raison sa mauvaise santé; **to a. an urgent appointment,** prétexter un rendez-vous urgent; **the words alleged to have been spoken by . . .,** les propos qui auraient été tenus par . . .; **he was alleged to be dead,** on le prétendait mort, on le disait mort. **2.** *A:* plaider, citer (un exemple); *Jur:* **to a. one's good faith,** exciper de sa bonne foi.

alleged [ə'ledʒd], *a.* **a. reason,** raison alléguée; **a. information,** prétendu renseignement; **the a. thief,** le voleur présumé.

allegedly [ə'ledʒidli], *adv.* prétendument; présumément.

Allegheny [æli'geini], *Pr.n. Geog:* **the A. Mountains, the Alleghenies,** les Monts Alléghani.

allegiance [ə'li:dʒ(ə)ns], *s.* **1.** fidélité *f,* obéissance *f* (**to,** à); **profession of a.,** soumission *f;* **to owe a. to the sovereign,** devoir fidélité et obéissance au souverain; **to own a. to a party,** être inféodé à un parti; **to renounce one's a. to a party,** se détacher d'un parti. **2. to take the oath of a.,** prêter serment *m* d'allégeance.

allegoric(al) [æli'gɔrik(l)], *a.* allégorique.

allegorically [æli'gɔrikəli], *adv.* allégoriquement, par allégorie, sous forme d'allégorie.

allegorist ['æligərist], *s.* allégoriste *m.*

allegorize ['æligəraiz], *v.tr. & i.* allégoriser.

allegory ['æligəri], *s.* **1.** allégorie *f.* **2.** *A:* emblème *m,* symbole *m.*

allegro [ə'legrou, -'lei-], *adv. & s.* allégro (*m*).

allegretto [æli'gretou], *adv. & s.* allégretto (*m*).

allel(e) [æ'li:l], **allelomorph** [æ'li:loumɔrf], *s. Biol:* allèle *m.*

allelic [æ'li:lik], **allelomorphic** [əli:lou'mɔ:fik], *a. Biol:* allélomorphe.

allelomorphism [æli:lou'mɔ:fizm], *s. Biol:* allélomorphisme *m.*

allelotropic [æli:lou'trɔpik], *a. Ch:* allélotrope.

allelotropism [æli:lou'troupizm], **allelotropy** [æli'loutrəpi], *s. Ch:* allélotropie *f.*

alleluia, -luja [æli'lu:jə], *int. & s.* alléluia (*m*).

all-embracing ['ɔ:lim'breisiŋ], *a.* qui embrasse tout; **a.-e. knowledge,** vaste érudition.

allene ['æli:n], *s. Ch:* allène *m.*

allergen ['ælədʒen], *s. Med:* allergène *m.*

allergenic [ælə'dʒenik], *a. Med:* allergénique.
allergic [ə'lə:dʒik], *a. Med:* allergique; *F:* **I'm a. to fish,** je suis allergique au poisson, le poisson ne me convient pas, ne me réussit pas; *Med:* **a. infection,** allergide *f*; *F:* **I'm a. to him,** il me répugne.
allergist ['ælədʒist], *s. Med:* allergologiste *mf.*
allergy ['ælədʒi], *s. Med:* (*a*) allergie *f*; (*b*) *F:* **he has an a. for work,** il déteste travailler; **I have a positive a. for him,** il me répugne.
allerion [æ'leriən], *s. Her:* alérion *m.*
alleviate [ə'li:vieit], *v.tr.* alléger, soulager (la douleur); adoucir (le chagrin); apaiser (la soif); **pain-alleviating medicine,** potion *f* anodine.
alleviation [əli:vi'eiʃ(ə)n], *s.* allègement *m* (de la douleur); soulagement *m,* adoucissement *m*; **a. factor,** facteur *m* d'atténuation.
alleviative [ə'li:viətiv], *a. & s.* adoucissant (*m*), calmant (*m*); *Med:* anodin (*m*), lénitif (*m*).
alleviator [ə'li:vieitər], *s.* (*a*) personne *f* (ou chose *f*) qui apporte un soulagement (of, à); (*b*) *Med:* **pain a.,** anodin *m.*
alley[1] ['æli], *s.* (*a*) (*in park, etc.*) allée *f*; (*b*) ruelle *f*; **blind a.,** impasse *m*; **that's only a blind a. job,** c'est une situation sans avenir; *F:* **a. cat,** chat *m* de gouttière; **thieves' a.,** coupe-gorge *m inv*; (*c*) **bowling a.,** boulodrome *m, F:* bowling *m.*
alley[2], *s.* = ALLY[3].
Alleynian [ə'leiniən], *s.* **old A.,** ancien élève de Dulwich College (fondé par Edward Alleyn).
alleyway ['æliwei], *s.* **1.** ruelle *f*; passage étroit. **2.** *N.Arch:* coursive *f.*
alliaceous [æli'eiʃəs], *a. Bot: Ch:* alliacé.
alliance [ə'laiəns], *s.* **1.** alliance *f. Hist:* **the Triple A.,** la Triple Alliance; la Triplice; **to enter into an a.,** s'allier (with, avec); **to fight in a. with s.o.,** combattre avec qn pour allié; **to re-enter into an a. with a country,** renouer alliance avec un pays; **political a.,** apparentement *m*; **to make a political a. with a party,** s'apparenter avec un parti. **2. a. by marriage,** alliance; apparentage *m.*
alliaria [æli'ɛəriə], *s. Bot:* alliaire *f.*
allice shad ['ælisʃæd], *s. Ich:* grande alose, alose commune.
allied ['ælaid], *a.* **1.** allié (to, with, à, avec); **the a. Powers,** les Puissances alliées; **the a. nations,** les nations coalisées; **closely a. industries,** industries connexes. **2.** *Biol: Med: etc:* de la même famille, du même ordre, de la même nature; *Nat.Hist:* **a. species,** espèces voisines.
alligator ['æligeitər], *s.* **1.** (*a*) *Rept:* alligator *m*; (*b*) *Leath:* crocodile *m.* **2.** *Can:* (*a*) bateau utilisé pour le transport du bois (sur une rivière); (*b*) *Mil:* véhicule *m* amphibie. **3.** (*a*) *Min:* crocodile; **a. grab,** foène *f,* gueule *f* de crocodile; (*b*) *Tls:* **a. wrench,** pince universelle crocodile; **a. clip,** pince crocodile. **4.** *Bot: esp. N.Am:* **a. pear,** (poire *f* d')avocat *m.* **5.** *P:* enragé, -ée, du swing.
alligatoring [æli'geit(ə)riŋ], *s. Const:* crocodilage *m,* formation *f* de frisures, fendillement *m* (du vernis, de la peinture).
all-important ['ɔ:lim'pɔ:t(ə)nt], *a.* de la plus haute importance, de toute importance.
all-in ['ɔ:lin], *a.* **1.** *Com:* **a.-in price,** prix *m* tout compris; prix forfaitaire; *El:* **a.-in agreement,** police *f* mixte (force et lumière); *Ins:* **a.-in policy,** police *f* tous risques. **2.** *Sp:* **a.-in wrestling,** catch *m.*
all-inclusive ['ɔ:lin'klu:siv], *a.* vaste, compréhensif; qui embrasse tout.
alliterate [ə'litəreit], *v.i.* allitérer.
alliteration [əlitə'reiʃ(ə)n], *s.* allitération *f.*
alliterative [ə'litərətiv, -reit-], *a.* allitératif.
all-merciful ['ɔ:l'mə:siful], *a.* infiniment miséricordieux.
all-metal ['ɔ:l'metl], *a.* entièrement métallique.
all-night ['ɔ:lnait], *a.* (veillée, etc.) de la nuit entière; *Adm: etc.* **a.-n. service,** permanence *f* de nuit; *Mil: etc:* **a.-n. pass,** permission *f* de la nuit.
allocate ['æləkeit], *v.tr.* **1.** (*a*) allouer, assigner (qch. à qn, à qch.); **to a. a sum to sth.,** affecter, assigner, une somme à qch.; (*b*) **to a. a sum amongst several people,** répartir une somme entre plusieurs personnes; **to a. duties,** attribuer, distribuer, des fonctions (to, à). **2.** *Ph: etc:* déterminer la position de (qch.).
allocating ['æləkeitiŋ], *s.* = ALLOCATION I.
allocation [ælə'keiʃ(ə)n], *s.* **1.** (*a*) allocation *f,* affectation *f* (d'une somme); **a. of capital,** affectation des investissements; **a. to reserve funds,** affectation aux fonds de réserve; (*b*) répartition *f* (de dépenses, etc.); attribution *f* (de fonctions); **a. of labour,** répartition de la main-d'œuvre; **a. of resources,** répartition des moyens; (*c*) **a. of contract,** adjudication *f*; **a. to lowest tender,** adjudication au mieux-disant; **a. to the highest bidder,** adjudication à la surenchère. **2.** part assignée; somme assignée.
allocatur [ælou'keitər], *s. Jur:* état certifié des frais.
allocentric [ælou'sentrik], *a. Psy:* allocentriste.
alloch(e)iria [ælou'ki:riə], *s. Med:* allochirie *f.*
allochtone ['æləktən, -toun], *s. Geol:* allochtone *m.*
allocht(h)onous [æ'lɔktənəs, -θənəs], *a. Geol:* allochtone.
allocinnamic [ælousi'næmik], *a. Ch:* (acide *m*) allocinnamique.
allocution [ælou'kjuʃ(ə)n], *s.* allocution *f.*
al(l)odial [ə'loudiəl]. *Hist:* **1.** *a.* allodial, -aux; (bien) tenu en franc-alleu. **2.** *s.* bien allodial.
al(l)odiality [əloudi'æliti], *s. Hist:* allodialité *f.*
al(l)odium [ə'loudiəm], *s. Hist:* (franc-)alleu *m, pl.* (francs-)alleux.
allogamy [ə'lɔgəmi], *s. Bot:* allogamie *f,* fécondation croisée.
allogeneous [ælou'dʒiniəs], *a.* allogène.
allogenic [ælou'dʒi:nik], *a. Geol: etc:* allogène, allothigène.
allometric [ælou'metrik], *a. Biol:* allométrique.
allometry [æ'lɔmitri], *s. Biol:* allométrie *f.*
allomorph ['æloumɔ:f], *s.* **1.** *Ch: Cryst:* allomorphe *m,* forme *f* allotropique. **2.** *Ling:* allomorphe.
allomorphic [ælou'mɔ:fik], *a.* **1.** *Ch: Cryst:* allomorphe. **2.** *Ling:* allomorphe.
allomorphism [ælou'mɔ:fizm], *s. Ch: Cryst:* allomorphie *f.*
allomorphite [ælou'mɔ:fait], *s. Miner:* allomorphite *f.*
allomucic [ælou'mju:sik], *a. Ch:* (acide *m*) allomucique.
allonge [ə'lɔn(d)ʒ], *s. Com: Fin:* allonge *f* (d'une lettre de change, etc.).
allonym ['ælounim], *s.* **1.** (*pers.*) allonyme *mf.* **2.** allonyme *m,* livre *m* allonyme.
allonymous [æ'lɔniməs], *a.* allonyme.
allopathic [ælou'pæθik], *a. Med:* allopathique.
allopathically [ælou'pæθikəli], *adv.* allopathiquement.
allopathist [æ'lɔpəθist], *s. Med:* allopathe *m.*
allopathy [ə'lɔpəθi], *s. Med:* allopathie *f.*
allopatric [ælou'pætrik], *a. Biol:* allopatrique.
allophane ['æloufein], *s. Miner:* allophane *f.*
allophone ['æloufoun], *s.m. Ling:* allophone *m.*
allopolyploid [ælou'pɔliplɔid], *a. & s. Biol:* allopolyploïde (*m*).
allopolyploidy [æloupɔli'plɔidi], *s. Biol:* allopolyploïdie *f.*
allot [ə'lɔt], *v.tr.* (**allotted**) **1. a. sth. to s.o.,** attribuer, assigner, qch. à qn; lotir qn de qch.; **to a. sth. to, for, an object,** affecter, destiner, qch. à un but; **Lombardy was alloted to him,** la Lombardie lui échut en partage; *Mil: Navy:* **to a. a portion of pay to a relative, etc.,** déléguer une portion de solde à un parent, etc. **2.** répartir, distribuer (des fonctions, des sièges, *Fin:* des actions).
allotetraploid [ælou'tetrəplɔid], *a. Biol:* amphidiploïde.
allothigenic [ælouθi'dʒenik], **allothigenous** [ælou'θidʒinəs], **allothogenous** [ælou'θɔdʒinəs], *a. Geol:* allothigène, allogène.
allotment [ə'lɔtm(ə)nt], *s.* **1.** (*a*) attribution *f* (de qch. à qn); affectation *f* (d'une somme à un but); *Mil: Navy:* **a. of pay (to wife, etc.),** délégation *f* de solde (à une épouse, etc.); (*b*) partage *m,* répartition *f*; distribution *f* (des cabines, de fonctions, etc.); lotissement *m* (de parts, d'une propriété); **a. of time,** emploi *m* du temps; *For:* **a. of areas,** assiette *f* des coupes; aménagement *m* des coupes; *Fin:* **a. of shares,** attribution d'actions; **letter of a.,** (lettre *f* d')avis (*m*) de répartition; lettre d'allocation; bulletin *m* de souscription; **to pay so much on a.,** payer tant lors de la répartition. **2.** (*a*) portion *f,* part *f,* lot *m*; (*b*) lopin *m* de terre; **allotments,** jardins ouvriers.
allotriomorphic [æˌlɔtriou'mɔ:fik], *a. Miner:* allotriomorphe.
allotropic(al) [ælou'trɔpik(l)], *a. Ch:* allotropique.
allotrope ['æloutroup], *s. Ch:* variété *f,* forme *f* allotropique.
allotropism [æ'lɔtrəpizm], *s. Ch:* allotropisme *m.*
allotropy [æ'lɔtrəpi], *s. Ch:* allotropie *f.*
allottable [ə'lɔtəbl], *a.* **1.** assignable. **2.** répartissable.
allottee [ælɔ'ti:], *s.* **1.** *Fin:* attributaire *mf.* **2.** *Mil: Navy:* parent(e) à qui un combattant a délégué sa solde; bénéficiaire *mf* d'une délégation de solde.
all-out ['ɔ:l'aut], *F:* **1.** *a.* **a.-o. effort,** effort *m* suprême, maximum; **a.-o. attack,** attaque *f* à fond, avec tous ses moyens. **2.** *adv.* (*usu. without hyphen*) complètement, entièrement; **to go a.o.,** ne pas s'épargner; **he's going a.o. to succeed,** il se démène pour réussir.
all-over ['ɔ:l'ouvər], *a.* **with an a.-o. pattern,** dont le dessin couvre toute la surface.
all-overish ['ɔ:l'ouvəriʃ], *a. F: A:* **to feel a.-o.,** se sentir vaguement indisposé, se sentir tout chose.
allow [ə'lau], *v.tr.* **1.** (*a*) *A: & Lit:* admettre; **to a. sth. to be true,** admettre, reconnaître, qch. pour vrai; **he allows it to be true,** il admet, il convient, que c'est vrai; **he is allowed to have genius,** on lui reconnaît du génie; **he allowed that she was well bred,** il m'accorda qu'elle était bien élevée; **I a. that you are right,** j'admets que vous avez raison; **I was wrong, I a.,** j'ai eu tort, j'en conviens, je l'avoue; (*b*) **to a. a request, a claim,** faire droit à une demande, à une réclamation; admettre une requête; (*c*) *N.Am: F:* juger, opiner, affirmer (**that,** que). **2.** (*a*) (*permit*) permettre, souffrir, tolérer, admettre (qch.); **to a. no discussion on sth.,** ne pas admettre, ne pas souffrir, de discussion sur qch.; **to a. s.o. sth.,** permettre qch. à qn; **a. me to . . .,** permettez-moi de . . .; **I am allowed wine,** le vin m'est permis; **passengers are not allowed on the bridge,** la passerelle est interdite aux voyageurs; **shooting is not allowed here,** ici la chasse n'est pas permise; **no dogs allowed,** il est défendu d'introduire des chiens; **he is not allowed any whim,** on ne lui souffre, passe, aucune fantaisie; **to a. s.o. to do sth.,** permettre à qn de, autoriser qn à, faire qch; **a. me to tell you the truth,** souffrez que je vous dise la vérité; **as soon as circumstances a. . . .,** dès que les circonstances le permettront; **circumstances will not a. it,** les circonstances s'opposent; **to be allowed to compete,** être admis à concourir; **I am allowed to do it,** il m'est permis, on me permet, de le faire; **a. me!** permettez (-moi)! **perhaps I may be allowed to speak now,** à moi de parler, à moi la parole, maintenant, s'il vous plaît; **to a. oneself to do sth.,** se permettre de faire qch.; **the law allows you twenty days grace,** la loi vous impartit, vous accorde, un délai de vingt jours; **at the end of the six months allowed,** à l'expiration du délai de six mois; **to a. an item of expenditure,** allouer une dépense; (*b*) **to a. sth. to be lost,** laisser perdre qch.; **to a. oneself to be led, to be deceived,** se laisser mener, se laisser tromper; **I will not a. you to be ill-treated,** je ne vous laisserai pas maltraiter; (*c*) *ind.tr. O:* (*of thg*) **tone which allowed of no reply,** ton qui n'admettait pas de réplique; **the matter allows of no delay,** l'affaire ne souffre pas de retard; **comedy allows of a certain familiarity,** la comédie autorise une certaine familiarité; **his condition would not a. of his going out,** son état ne lui permettait pas de sortir. **3.** (*a*) **to a. s.o. £100 a year,** faire, accorder, allouer, à qn une rente de £100; **he allows his sister £500 a year,** il fait à sa sœur une pension de £500; **to a. a debtor time to pay,** accorder un délai à un débiteur; **we must a. one hour for dressing,** il faut compter une heure pour nous habiller; (*b*) *Com: Fin:* **to a. s.o. a discount,** consentir, accorder, faire, un escompte, une remise, à qn; faire bénéficier, bonifier, qn d'une remise; **to a. 5%,** déduire 5%; **to a. 5% interest on deposits,** allouer 5% d'intèret aux dépôts; (*c*) *ind.tr.* **to a. for sth.,** tenir compte de qch.; faire la part de qch.; avoir égard à qch.; **to a. for sums paid in advance,** faire déduction des sommes payées d'avance; **packing is not allowed for,** l'emballage ne peut être déduit; **after allowing for . . .,** déduction faite de . . .; **to a. for the wind, for shrinkage,** tenir compte du vent, du rétrécissement; **to a. for heat expansion,** ménager du jeu pour la dilatation; **to a. space for an accumulator,** ménager de la place pour un accumulateur; **to a. for accidents,** faire la part des accidents; **to a. for readjustments,** prévoir des rectifications; **delays are allowed for,** les retards sont prévus; **to a. for the tare,** défalquer la tare; **to a. so much for carriage,** (i) ajouter, (ii) déduire, tant pour le port; **allowing for the circumstances,** eu égard aux circonstances; **you must a. for his being ill,** il faut tenir compte de ce qu'il est malade.
allowable [ə'lauəbl], *a.* admissible, admis, permis, légitime; *Jur:* (legs *m,* etc.) autorisable; (réclamation *f*) recevable; *Com: etc:* **a. expense,** dépense *f* déductible; dépense remboursable.
allowably [ə'lauəbli], *adv.* d'une manière admissible; légitimement.
allowance[1] [ə'lauəns], *s.* **1.** (*a*) tolérance *f* (d'un abus, etc.); (*b*) *Jur:* **a. of items in an account,** allocation *f* des articles dans un compte. **2.** (*a*) pension *f* alimentaire (donnée volontairement); rente *f*; **to make one's mother, one's daughter, an a. of £1000 a year,** faire à sa mère, à sa fille, une rente de £1000 par an; **to give one's daughter an a. of £10 a month,** donner à sa fille £10 par mois (en argent de poche); **to stop, cut off, s.o.'s a.,** couper les vivres à qn; *Jur:* **allowance for necessaries,** pension alimentaire; (*b*) *Adm: etc:* allocation; dégrèvement *m* (pour charges de famille, etc.); **cost-of-living a.,** indemnité *f* de vie chère, de cherté de vie; **family allowances,** allocations familiales; **supplementary allowances,** majorations *fpl* de pension; *Fin:* **personal a.,** abattement personnel (sur l'impôt); **earned income a.,** déduction *f* au titre de revenus salariaux ou professionnels; *Mil: etc:* **field a.,** indemnité de campagne; **mess a.,** indemnité, traitement

m, de table; **daily(subsistence) a.**, indemnité journalière; **acting a.**, indemnité de fonctions; **married a.**, indemnité de chef de famille, d'homme marié; **allowances in kind, in money**, prestations *f* en nature, en deniers; *Adm: Com:* **office, entertainment, a.**, frais *mpl* de bureau, de représentation; **travel, travelling, a.**, allocation de voyage; indemnité de déplacement; **foreign currency a.**, allocation en devises; (*c*) *A:* ration *f*; **to put s.o. on (short) a.**, mettre qn à la ration; rationner qn; mesurer la nourriture à qn; (*d*) *Trans:* **(free) luggage a.**, bagages *mpl* en franchise; (*e*) *Rac:* **time a.**, rendement *m* de temps; *Turf:* (*of horse, jockey*) **to have an a. of five pounds (weight)**, avoir droit à une décharge de cinq livres. **3.** *Com: Fin:* remise *f*, rabais *m*, déduction *f*, concession *f*; **to make an a. on an article**, faire, accorder, un rabais sur un article; **a. for loss**, réfaction *f*; *Com:* **a. to cashier for errors**, tare *f* de caisse; passe *f* de caisse; **a. for exchange fluctuations**, prévisions *fpl* pour fluctuations du change; **depreciation a., wear-and-tear a.**, prévision pour amortissement. **4.** (*a*) *Mec.E: etc:* tolérance; (*in minting coins*) faiblage *m*; *Mec.E:* **a. in width**, gras *m* sur la largeur; **a. for machining**, surépaisseur *f* pour usinage; **a. for heat expansion**, jeu *m* à ménager pour la dilatation; **to make a generous a. for waste**, laisser une bonne marge pour les déchets; **to make a. for the tare**, défalquer la tare; *Artil: etc:* **a. for lateral deviation, for deflection**, dérive *f*; (*b*) **to make allowance(s) for sth.**, tenir compte de, faire la part de, avoir égard à, qch.; **to make allowances for s.o.**, avoir de l'indulgence pour qn; se montrer indulgent, être d'une grande indulgence, envers qn; **we must make allowances for youth**, il faut faire la part de la jeunesse; **after making all allowances, every a.**, tout bien considéré; **due a. being made**, toute proportion gardée.

allowance[2], *v.tr. A:* **1.** (*a*) faire une rente, une pension, à (qn); (*b*) rationner (qn). **2.** rationner (le pain, etc.).

allowedly [ə'lauidli], *adv.* de l'aveu de tous; de l'aveu général.

alloy[1] ['ælɔi], *s.* alliage *m*; (*of gold*) carature *f*; (*with low percentage of gold*) billon *m*; *attrib.* **a. steel**, acier allié, acier spécial, acier compound; *Lit:* **happiness without a.** [ə'lɔi], bonheur *m* sans mélange.

alloy[2]. **1.** *v.tr.* allier (l'or avec l'argent, etc.); *Lit:* **nothing happened to a.** [ə'lɔi] **our happiness**, rien ne vint altérer, diminuer, notre bonheur, porter atteinte à notre bonheur. **2.** *v.i.* (*of metals*) s'allier (l'un avec l'autre).

alloyage [ə'lɔiidʒ], *s.* alliage *m*.

alloyed ['ælɔid], *a.* (*of metal, joy, etc.*) allié (**with**, à, avec).

alloying [ə'lɔiiŋ], *s.* alliage *m*; carature *f* (de l'or).

all-powerful ['ɔːl'pauəful], *a.* tout-puissant, toute-puissante, *pl.* tout-puissants, toutes-puissantes.

all-purpose ['ɔːl'pəːpəs], *a.* répondant à tous les besoins; universel; à tout faire; **a.-p. computer**, calculateur universel.

all-round ['ɔːl'raund], *a.* (*a*) (athlète, etc.) complet; **an a.-r. man**, un homme universel; **a.-r. improvement**, amélioration générale, sur toute la ligne; (*b*) *Mil:* **a.-r. defence**, défense *f* en point d'appui fermé; défense circulaire; *Artil:* **a.-r. traverse**, (affût *m*, canon *m*) tous azimuts; **a.-r. fire**, tir *m* tous azimuts.

all-rounder ['ɔːl'raundər], *s.* homme universel; athlète complet.

allspice ['ɔːlspais], *s. Bot:* piment *m*, poivron *m*; poivre *m* de la Jamaïque; toute-épice *f*.

all-star ['ɔːl'stɑːr], *a. Th: etc:* **a.-s. performance**, spectacle joué exclusivement par des vedettes.

all-time ['ɔːltaim], *a. F:* (record) sans précédent, inouï, jamais atteint auparavant; **a.-t. high**, record le plus élevé; **a.-t. low**, record de médiocrité, le plus bas.

allude [ə'l(j)uːd], *v.ind.tr.* **to a. to sth., to s.o.**, (*of pers.*) faire allusion à qch., à qn; (*of phrase*) avoir trait à, se rapporter à, qch., qn; **I a. to my parents**, je veux parler de, je veux dire, mes parents; **I am not alluding to anybody in particular**, je ne vise personne.

all-up ['ɔːlʌp], *a. Av:* **a.-up weight**, poids global en vol.

allure[1] [ə'l(j)u(ə)r], *s. A: & Lit:* attrait *m*, attirance *f*, charme *m*.

allure[2], *v.tr.* **1.** *A:* **to a. s.o. to(wards) oneself, (in)to a party, (in)to a place**, attirer qn à, vers, soi; attirer qn à, dans, un parti, un endroit; **to a. a fish**, amorcer un poisson; **to a. customers**, amadouer, amorcer, les clients; **to a. s.o. from his duty**, débaucher qn; détourner qn de son devoir. **2.** (*fascinate*) attirer, séduire (qn, les yeux, etc.); **to a. s.o. with promises**, attirer, allécher, séduire, entraîner, qn par des promesses.

allurement [ə'l(j)u(ə)mənt], *s.* attrait *m*; appât *m*, amorce *f*; allèchement *m*, séduction *f*, entraînement *m*.

alluring [ə'l(j)u(ə)riŋ], *a.* attrayant, attirant, tentant, alléchant, séduisant, entraînant.

alluringly [ə'l(j)u(ə)riŋli], *adv.* d'une manière attrayante, attirante, séduisante.

allusion [ə'l(j)uːʒ(ə)n], *s.* allusion *f*; **to make an a., some a., to sth.**, faire allusion à qch.; **in a. to sth.**, par allusion à qch.; *F:* **who are you making allusions to, about?** c'est moi que tu vises?

allusive [ə'l(j)uːsiv], *a.* (style, etc.) allusif, plein d'allusions; *Her:* **a. arms**, armes parlantes.

allusively [ə'l(j)uːsivli], *adv.* allusivement; par allusion(s).

allusiveness [ə'l(j)uːsivnis], *s.* **a. of style**, style plein d'allusions.

alluvial [ə'luːviəl]. **1.** *a. Geol:* alluvial, -aux, d'alluvion; alluvien; **a. plain**, plaine alluviale, d'alluvions; **a. cone, fan**, cône *m* d'accumulation, de déjection; **a. deposits**, alluvions *fpl*; **a. diamonds**, diamants alluviens. **2.** *s. Austr:* alluvions aurifères.

alluviate [ə'luːvieit], *v.tr. & i.* alluvionner; couvrir d'alluvions.

alluviation [əluːvi'eiʃ(ə)n], *s.* alluvionnement *m*.

alluvion [ə'luːviən], *s.* **1.** *Jur:* alluvion *f*. **2.** *occ. Geol:* alluvions.

alluvium [ə'luːviəm], *s.* (*the pl.* **alluvia** *is rare*) *Geol:* (*a*) alluvions *fpl*; (*b*) (*in restricted sense*) limon *m*.

all-weather ['ɔːlweðər], *a.* tous temps; *Av:* **a.-w. aircraft, fighter**, avion *m*, chasseur *m*, tous temps; **a.-w. landing**, atterrissage *m* tout temps.

ally[1] ['ælai], *s.* (*a*) allié, -ée; coallié, -ée; *Hist:* (*World War I, II*) **the Allies**, les Alliés; **to become allies**, s'allier (ensemble); se coaliser; (*b*) partisan, -ane; **he found plenty of allies in his campaign against . . .**, il a trouvé beaucoup de partisans, d'adhérents, pour sa campagne contre . . .. **2.** *Nat.Hist: NAm:* espèce voisine.

ally[2] [ə'lai]. **1.** *v.tr.* (*a*) allier (qn, qch.) (**to, with**, à, avec); (*b*) **this newspaper is allied with three others**, ce journal est associé avec trois autres. **2.** *v.i.* (*a*) s'allier (**to**, à; **with**, avec); (*b*) **dogs are allied** ['ælaid] **to wolves**, les chiens sont de la même famille que les loups.

ally[3] ['æli], *s. Games:* **(a. taw)** (grosse) bille (en marbre, en albâtre); cal(l)ot *m*; pouce *m*.

allyl ['ælil], *s. Ch:* allyle *m*; **a. alcohol**, alcool *m* allylique.

allylen ['ælailin], *s. Ch:* allylène *m*.

allylic [æ'lilik], *a.* allylique.

allylthiourea [ælailθiouju'riə], *s. Ch:* allylthiourée *f*.

almagest ['ælmədʒest], *s. A.Astr:* almageste *m*.

alma(h) ['ælmə], *s.* almée *f*.

Alma Mater, alma mater ['ælmə'meitər, -'mɑːtər], *s.* l'université *f*, l'école *f*, où l'on a fait ses études; alma mater *f*.

almanac ['ɔlːmənæk, 'æl-], *s.* almanach *m*.

almandine ['ælməndiːn, -dain], **almandite** ['ælmən dait], *s. Miner:* almandine *f*, almandite *f*.

almeh ['ælmei], *s.* almée *f*.

almightiness [ɔːl'maitinis], *s.* toute-puissance *f*, omnipotence *f*.

almighty [ɔːl'maiti]. **1.** (*a*) *a. & s.* tout-puissant, toute-puissante, *pl.* tout-puissants, toutes-puissantes; **the A.**, le Tout-Puissant, le Très-Haut; (*b*) *a.* **the a. dollar**, le dollar tout-puissant. **2.** *F:* (*a*) *a. esp. NAm:* (*intensive*) **to be in an a. fix**, être dans le pétrin; **an a. row**, un fracas de tous les diables; (*b*) *adv. F: NAm:* très; **he's a. stubborn**, il est têtu comme une mule.

almond ['ɑːmənd], *s.* **1.** (*a*) amande *f*; **sweet a.**, amande douce; **bitter a.**, amande amère; **burnt almonds**, amandes grillées; pralines *f*; **shelled almonds**, amandes décortiquées; **ground almonds**, amandes pilées; **a. oil**, huile *f* d'amande; **sweet a. oil**, huile d'amandes douces; **oil of bitter almonds**, essence *f* d'amandes amères; **a. paste, a. icing**, pâte *f* d'amandes; **a. cake**, (i) *Cu:* gâteau *m* d'amandes, aux amandes; (ii) *Husb:* tourteau *m* d'amandes, **a.(-shaped) eyes**, yeux *m* en amande; (*b*) **a. (tree)**, amandier *m*; **a. grove**, amandaie *f*; (*c*) **a. willow**, osier brun; osier-amandier *m*, *pl.* osiers-amandiers. **2.** *Orn:* **a. tumbler**, pigeon *m* tumbler. **3.** *Anat: A:* amygdale *f*.

almond-eyed ['ɑːmənd'aid], *a.* aux yeux en amande.

almoner ['ɑːmənər, 'æl-], *s.* **1.** aumônier *m*, distributeur *m* d'aumônes; *Hist:* **Lord High A.**, Grand Aumônier (du Roi). **2.** *O:* **(hospital) a.**, assistant(e) social(e) (d'un hôpital).

almonry ['ɑːmənri, 'æl-], *s.* aumônerie *f*.

almost ['ɔːlmoust], *adv.* presque; à peu près, quasi; **a. blind**, quasi aveugle; **a. always**, presque toujours; **a. nothing**, presque rien; **it's a. six (o'clock)**, il est presque, à peu près, six heures; **it's a. lunch time**, il est presque l'heure du déjeuner; **he a. fell**, il a failli tomber.

alms [ɑːmz], *s.sg or pl.* aumône *f*; **to give a. to s.o.**, donner, faire, l'aumône à qn; faire la charité à qn; **to ask an a. of s.o.**, demander l'aumône, la charité, à qn; **a. box**, tronc *m* pour les pauvres.

almsgiver ['ɑːmzgivər], *s.* distributeur, -trice, d'aumônes.

almsgiving ['ɑːmzgiviŋ], *s.* l'aumône *f*.

almshouse ['ɑːmzhaus], *s.* (*a*) fondation *f*, maison *f* de retraite, pour vieillards; (*b*) *U.S: A:* hospice *m*.

almsman, *pl.* **-men** ['ɑːmzmən], *s.m.* vieillard (qui habite dans une fondation, une maison de retraite).

almswoman, *pl.* **-women** ['ɑːmzˌwumən, -ˌwimin], *s.f.* vieille femme (qui habite dans une fondation, une maison de retraite).

almucantar [ælmju'kæntər], *s. Astr:* almicantarat *m*.

alocasia [ælou'keisiə], *s. Bot:* alocasia *m*.

aloe ['ælou], *s.* **1.** *Bot:* (*a*) aloès *m*; **tongue-shaped a.**, bec-de-cane *m*; **aloes wood**, bois *m* d'aloès, bois d'aigle; (*b*) **American a.**, agave *m* d'Amérique; pite *f*. **2.** *pl.* (*usu. with sg. constr.*) *Pharm:* **aloes**, aloès; **bitter aloes**, amer *m* d'aloès.

aloetic [ˌælou'etik], *a. & s. Pharm:* aloétique (*m*).

aloft [ə'lɔft], *adv.* (*a*) *Nau:* en haut (dans la mâture); dans la mâture; **a. there!** oh(é) de la hune! **away a.!** en haut les gabiers! (*b*) en l'air; (*c*) *A:* **to go a.**, aller au paradis.

alogical [ei'lɔdʒikl], *a.* alogique.

aloin ['æləin], *s. Ch:* aloïne *f*.

alone [ə'loun], *a.* (*not used before noun*) **1.** seul; **he lives (all) a.**, il demeure (tout) seul; **I like being a.**, j'aime la solitude; **he stands a. in his opinion**, il est seul de son opinion; **we are not a. in thinking that . . .**, nous ne sommes pas seuls à trouver que . . .; **he a. saw it**, lui seul l'a vu; il n'y a que lui qui l'ait vu; **an expert a. could advise us**, seul un expert pourrait nous conseiller; **you a. can help me**, vous êtes le seul qui puissiez m'aider; **I did it a.**, je l'ai fait tout seul, à moi seul; **London a. has a population equal to . . .**, Londres à lui seul a une population égale à . . .; **I have a hiding place that I a. know**, j'ai une cachette que moi seul connais, connue de moi seul; *B:* **man does not live by bread a.**, l'homme ne vit pas que de pain; **to believe s.o. on his word a.**, croire qn sur (sa) simple parole; **a. at last!** enfin seul(s)! **they sometimes spoke of it when a. together**, ils en parlaient parfois seul à seul; **I want to speak to you a.**, je voudrais vous parler seul à seul; **he was a. with his own thoughts**, il était seul à seul avec lui-même; **for the month of June a. sixty deaths have been reported**, dans le seul mois de juin, rien qu'au cours du mois de juin, on a signalé soixante cas de mort; **his silence a. is sufficient proof against him**, rien que son silence le condamne; **with that charm which is his a.**, avec ce charme qui lui est propre, qui n'appartient qu'à lui; **work, incident, that stands a.**, ouvrage *m*, incident *m*, unique (en son genre); *F:* **to go it a.**, y aller d'autorité; faire cavalier seul; **if nobody will help me I'll go it a.**, si personne ne m'aide je le ferai tout seul. **2.** (*a*) **to let, leave, s.o., sth., a.**, (i) laisser qn tranquille, en paix; (ii) laisser (qn) faire; (iii) ne pas se mêler de qch.; **leave these things a.**, ne touchez pas à tout ça; **leave me a.!** laissez-moi donc! *F:* fichez-moi la paix! **let it a.**, n'y touchez pas; ne vous en mêlez pas; laissez cela; **it is a subject better left a.**, c'est un sujet qu'il ne faut toucher que du bout du doigt; **leave him a. to finish his work**, laissez-le finir son travail; **your work is all right, leave it a.**, votre travail est bien, n'y retouchez pas; *Prov:* **let well a., leave well a.**, le mieux est (souvent) l'ennemi du bien; ne touchez pas à ce qui est bien; ne réveillez pas le chat qui dort; (*b*) **let a. . . .**, sans parler de . . ., sans compter . . .; **they were six in the car, let a. the dogs**, ils étaient six dans l'auto, sans compter les chiens, sans parler des chiens. **3.** *adv.* seulement.

along [ə'lɔŋ]. **1.** *prep.* le long de; (*a*) **to walk a. the shore**, longer la plage, se promener (tout) le long de la plage; **to go a. a street**, suivre une rue; passer par une rue; **to sail a. the land, the coast**, serrer la terre; naviguer près de terre; longer, suivre, la côte; côtoyer le rivage; **to creep a. the wall**, se faufiler le long du mur; **to crawl a. the ground**, ramper à la surface du sol; **victorious all a. the line**, victorieux sur toute la ligne; **section a. the line MN**, coupe *f* suivant la ligne MN; (*b*) **trees a. the river**, arbres *m* qui bordent la rivière, sur le bord de la rivière; *F:* **you'll find it a. by the church**, vous le trouverez près de l'église, du côté de l'église. **2.** *adv.* (*often expletive, with a general implication of progress*) (*a*) **to move a.**, avancer; **to walk, stride, a.**, avancer à grandes enjambées; **fetch it a.!** apportez-le! **come a. with me**, venez-vous-en avec moi; **come a.!** arrivez donc! venez donc! *F:* **come a. now!** sois, soyez, raisonnable! **he'll be a. in ten minutes**, il va s'amener dans dix minutes; (*redundant*) **bring a tent a. with you**, apportez une tente; **he took his dog a.**, il y a amené son chien; (*b*) *NAm:* **a. about four o'clock**, vers quatre heures; **the afternoon was well a.**, l'après-midi tirait à sa fin; **were you a.!** est-ce que vous étiez là? **he was a. toward fifty**, il allait sur les cinquante ans, il approchait la cinquantaine; (*c*) **I knew that all a.**, je le savais dès, depuis, le commencement, depuis longtemps; **I said so all a.,** c'est ce que j'ai toujours dit; (*d*) *F:* **to get a.,** (i) **he manages to get a.,** il s'en tire tant bien que mal; (ii) **I can't get a. with him,** il ne m'est pas sympathique; on ne s'accorde pas ensemble; (iii) **get a. (with you)!** (*a*) allez, filez! allez, ouste! (*b*) *Iron:* allons donc! ça c'est un peu fort!

alongshore [ə'lɔŋ'ʃɔːr], *adv.* le long de la côte; **to sail a.,** longer la terre.

alongside [ə'lɔŋ'said], *adv. & prep. Nau:* accosté (le long de . . .); **to make a boat fast (close) a. a ship,** amarrer un canot le long du bord, à toucher le bord; **to come a. (a ship), a. of a ship,** accoster, aborder (un navire); **come a.!** accostez! **a. the quay,** le long du quai, bord à quai; **to come a. (the quay),** aborder à quai; **it is difficult to get a.,** l'accostage *m* est difficile; **to be a.,** être accosté; **to tow a ship a.,** remorquer un navire à couple; **the ships lay a. of each other,** les navires étaient bord à bord, contre à contre; **to moor a. (of) a ship,** s'amarrer à couple d'un navire; **to moor, lay, berth, a boat a. (the quay, etc.),** accoster un bateau le long du quai; **to pass a. (of a ship),** élonger un navire; *Com:* **delivery a. ship,** livraison *f* sous palan; **free a. ship,** franco sous palan; **to walk a. s.o.,** marcher côte à côte avec qn; **he stood a. of me,** il se tenait à mon côté, à côté de moi; **the car stopped a. the kerb,** l'auto s'arrêta au bord du trottoir, le long du trottoir.

aloof [ə'luːf], *adv. & a.* **1.** *Nau:* au large et au vent; **keep a.!** passez au large! **2.** (*a*) **to keep, hold, a. (from sth.),** se tenir (visiblement) à l'écart, à distance, éloigné (de qch.); s'abstraire (de qch.); se tenir sur la réserve; **he stands a. from the crowd,** il se tient à l'écart de la foule; **to keep a. from politics,** ne pas se mêler de politique, se désintéresser de la politique; ne pas faire de politique; **to stand a. from a cause,** se tenir en dehors d'une cause; **to hold, stand, a.,** s'abstenir (lorsqu'il s'agit de faire qch.); **he kept very much a.,** il s'est montré très distant; **to live a. from the world,** vivre dans l'éloignement du monde; (*b*) (*of pers.*) **she was reserved and a.,** elle était réservée et distante.

aloofly [ə'luːfli], *adv.* d'une manière réservée, distante.

aloofness [ə'luːfnis], *s.* attitude distante; réserve *f* **(from,** à l'égard de).

alopecia [ælou'piːʃə], *s. Med:* alopécie *f.*

alose [ə'lous], *s. Ich:* alose *f.*

Alouattae [ælə'wæti], *s.pl. Z:* alouatinés *m.*

aloud [ə'laud], *adv.* à haute voix; (tout) haut; **to read a.,** lire à haute voix; *Lit:* **to cry a. for vengeance,** crier vengeance; **half a.,** entre haut et bas.

alp [ælp], *s. Geog:* (*a*) alpe *f*; pâturage *m* de montagne; *Dial:* alp *m;* (*b*) **the Alps,** les Alpes; **the Swiss, French, Austrian, Alps,** les Alpes suisses, françaises, autrichiennes; **the Australian Alps,** les Alpes australiennes; **the Southern Alps,** les Alpes néo-zélandaises, méridionales.

alpaca [æl'pækə], *s.* **1.** *Z:* alpaca *m,* alpaga *m.* **2.** *Tex:* alpaga *m*; **a. wool,** laine *f* d'alpaga.

alpax ['ælpæks], *s. Metall:* alpax *m.*

alpenglow ['ælpənglou], *s.* alpenglühen *m.*

alpenhorn ['ælpənhɔːn], *s.* cor *m* des Alpes.

alpenstock ['ælpənstɔk], *s.* alpenstock *m*; bâton ferré.

alpestrine [æl'pestrin], *a.* (plante) alpestre.

alpha ['ælfə], *s.* (*a*) *Gr.Alph:* alpha *m*; *Fig:* **a. and omega,** l'alpha et l'oméga, le commencement et la fin; (*b*) *Ph:* **a. rays,** rayons *mpl,* rayonnement *m,* alpha; **a. particle,** particule *f* alpha; **a. radiator, emitter,** émetteur *m* alpha; **a. (radio)activity,** radioactivité *f* alpha; (*c*) *Cmptr:* **a. type-in,** message *m* alphabétique d'entrée.

alphabet ['ælfəbet], *s.* alphabet *m*; **a. soup,** (i) potage *m* aux pâtes alphabet; (ii) *F:* abus *m* des sigles.

alphabetic(al) [ælfə'betik(l)], *a.* alphabétique; *Cmptr;* **a. code, coding,** code *m* alphabétique; **a. item,** donnée *f* alphabétique.

alphabetically [ælfə'betik(ə)li], *adv.* alphabétiquement; par ordre alphabétique.

alphabetism ['ælfəbetizm], *s.* alphabétisme *m.*

alphabetization [ælfəbetai'zeiʃ(ə)n], *s.* classement *m* par ordre alphabétique.

alphabetize ['ælfəbetaiz], *v.tr.* classer par ordre alphabétique.

alphameric(al) [ælfə'merik(l)], *a.* alphanumérique.

alphamethylnaphthalene ['ælfəmeθil'næfθəliːn], *s. Ch:* alphaméthylnaphtalène *m.*

alphanumeric(al) [ælfənju'merik(l)], *a.* alphanumérique; **a. code,** code *m* alphanumérique.

alphanumerics [ælfənju'meriks], *s.pl.* (*usu. with sg. const.*) caractères *m* alphanumériques.

Alpheus [æl'fi(ː)əs]. **1.** *Pr.n.m. Gr.Myth:* Alphée. **2.** *s. Crust:* alphée *m.*

Alphonso [æl'fɔnsou, -zou], *Pr.n.m.* Alphonse.

alpia ['ælpiə], *s. Bot:* alpiste *m.*

alpine ['ælpain], *a.* (club, chasseur) alpin; (site, paysage, climat) alpestre; **a. range,** chaîne *f* de montagnes alpique; **a. horn,** cor *m* des Alpes; **the A. foreland,** les Préalpes *fpl*; **a. climbing,** alpinisme *m*; *Bot:* **a. plant,** *s.* **alpine,** plante alpine, alpicole; **a. poppy,** pavot *m* des Alpes; *Ethn:* **A. race,** race alpine.

alpinism ['ælpinizm], *s.* alpinisme *m.*

alpinist ['ælpinist], *s.* alpiniste *mf.*

alpist ['ælpist], *s. Bot:* alpiste *m.*

alquifou [ˌælki'fuː], *s. Cer:* alquifoux *m.*

already [ɔːl'redi], *adv.* déjà; dès à présent: **ten o'clock a.!** déjà dix heures!

alright [ɔːl'rait], *adv. F:* (*incorrect spelling*) = **all right** (*see* RIGHT[1]).

Alsace ['ælzæs, -sæs], *Pr.n. Geog:* Alsace *f.*

Alsatia [æl'seiʃiə], *Pr.n.* **1.** *Geog: A:* l'Alsace *f.* **2.** (*a*) *A:* quartier *m* de Londres (avec droit d'asile) qui servait de refuge aux voleurs, aux gueux; cour *f* des miracles; (*b*) *Lit:* refuge *m.*

Alsatian [æl'seiʃ(ə)n]. **1.** *a.* alsacien; (vin) d'Alsace; (littérature) alsatique. **2.** *s.* (*a*) Alsacien, -ienne; (*b*) (*dog*) (*formerly* **Alsatian wolf-hound, wolf-dog**) berger *m* d'Alsace, alsacien, allemand.

alsine ['ælsain], *s. Bot:* alsine *f.*

also ['ɔːlsou], *adv.* aussi; **I a. discovered that . . .,** (i) moi aussi j'ai trouvé que . . ., (ii) j'ai encore trouvé que . . .; **it should a. be stated that . . .,** il faut ajouter que . . .; **he saw it a.,** il l'a vu également; lui aussi l'a vu; *Turf:* **a. ran,** non classés, ont couru aussi; *F:* **an a. ran,** (i) concurrent qui n'a pas été classé; (ii) une non-valeur; **not only . . . but a. . . .,** non seulement . . . mais encore . . ., mais aussi. . . .

alstonite ['ælstənait], *s. Miner:* alstonite *f.*

alstrœmeria [ælstrə'meəriə], *s. Bot:* alstrœmère *f.*

alt [ælt], *s.* **1.** *Mus:* **(notes) in a.,** (notes) au-dessus de la portée. **2.** *F: A:* **in a.,** exalté.

Altaic [æl'teiik], *a. Ethn: Ling:* altaïque.

altaite [æl'teiait], *s. Miner:* altaïte *f,* élasmose *f.*

altar ['ɔːltər], *s.* **1.** (*a*) autel *m*; **high a.,** maître-autel *m, pl.* maîtres-autels; **side a.,** autel latéral; **table a.,** autel improvisé; **a. curtain,** custode *f* d'autel; **a. cloth,** nappe *f* d'autel; **a. stone,** pierre *f* d'autel; **a. rail,** balustrade *f,* grille *f,* (du sanctuaire) de l'autel; (*of communicant*) **to kneel at the a. rail,** s'approcher de la sainte table; **a. screen,** retable *m*; **a. bread,** pain *m* d'autel; pain à chanter; **a. boy,** enfant *m* de chœur; **to set up an a.,** dresser un autel; **to lead s.o. to the a.,** conduire qn à l'autel; *Fig:* **to lay one's ambitions on the a.,** sacrifier, faire le sacrifice de, ses ambitions; (*b*) *Nau:* gradin *m* (d'une cale de radoub). **2.** *Astr:* **the A.,** l'Autel.

altarpiece ['ɔːltəpiːs], *s.* tableau *m* d'autel; retable *m.*

altazimuth [ælt'æziməθ], *s.* altazimut *m*; **a. theodolite,** théodolite altazimutal.

alter ['ɔːltər]. **1.** *v.tr.* (*a*) changer; modifier; remanier; retoucher (un vêtement, etc.); (*b*) **to a. the place of sth.,** changer qch. de place; **your translation would be better if you altered the word order,** votre traduction serait meilleure si vous changiez l'ordre des mots; **I cannot a. my plans for you,** je ne peux pas changer, modifier, mes projets à cause de vous; **they had to a. the plans of the house to comply with official regulations,** ils ont dû faire des modifications aux plans de la maison en raison des règlements; **they altered the kitchen to include a dining alcove,** ils ont transformé la cuisine pour y aménager un coin-repas; **the play was altered to make it suitable for the young actors,** on a remanié la pièce pour l'adapter aux possibilités des jeunes acteurs; **that alters the case, the situation,** voilà qui change les choses, la situation; **a man cannot a. his nature,** on ne peut pas se refaire; **the time of the train has been altered,** on a changé l'heure du train; **what date do we a. the clocks?** à quelle date est-ce qu'on change l'heure? **to a. sth. for the better,** améliorer qch.; **to a. sth. for the worse,** changer qch. pour le pire; **she altered her hairstyle,** elle a changé de coiffure; **I shall have to a. this dress before I can wear it,** il me faudra faire des retouches à cette robe avant de la porter; **by expressing it that way you a. the facts,** en l'exprimant de cette façon vous faussez les faits; **to a. one's course,** changer de route; *Nau:* **to a. course,** changer la route, modifier la route; **the river has altered its course,** la rivière a changé de cours; (*b*) *NAm: Austr:* châtrer. **2.** *v.i.* **he has greatly altered,** il a bien changé; **he has altered for the better,** il a changé en mieux; **he will never a.,** il ne changera jamais; il mourra dans sa peau; **her whole outlook has altered,** elle a complètement changé d'horizon; **the weather has altered for the better, for the worse,** le temps s'est amélioré, s'est détérioré; *B:* **the law of the Medes and Persians which altereth not,** la loi des Mèdes et des Perses qui demeure immuable.

alterability [ɔːltərə'biliti], *s.* variabilité *f.*

alterable ['ɔːlt(ə)rəbl], *a.* (*a*) sujet à changer; variable; (*b*) modifiable.

alteration ['ɔːltə'reiʃ(ə)n], *s.* (*a*) remaniement *m* (de qch.); retouche *f* (à qch.); modification (apportée à qch.); changement *m*; **slight a.,** petite modification; **he made frequent alterations to his novels,** il remaniait sans cesse ses romans; *Sch:* **the frequent alterations in the syllabus,** le remaniement incessant des programmes; les modifications continuelles faites aux programmes; *Typ:* **alterations in the layout of a page,** remaniement de la disposition typographique d'une page; **a. in a plan,** changement apporté à un projet; **a. in articles of association,** modification aux statuts (d'une société, etc.); *Com: etc:* **a. in a clause,** changement à une clause; **timetable subject to a.,** (i) horaire *m* susceptible de révisions; (ii) programme *m* sauf modifications; **we have made a lot of alterations in the house,** nous avons fait beaucoup de transformations chez nous; *Tail: Dressm:* **alterations in three days,** retouches (aux vêtements) dans un délai de trois jours; **to make an a. to a dress,** faire une modification, une retouche, à une robe; **a. hand,** pompier, -ière; *Th: etc:* **to accept a play subject to a.,** recevoir une pièce à correction; *Nau:* **a. of course,** (i) dérangement *m* de route; abattée *f*; (ii) changement de route; (*b*) *Cmptr:* modification; **a. switch,** inverseur *m*; (*c*) **marginal alterations,** corrections *f* en marge.

alterative ['ɔːltəreitiv], *a. & s. Med:* altératif (*m*), altérant (*m*).

altercate ['ɔːltəkeit], *v.i.* se quereller **(with,** avec); **to a. about sth.,** disputer de, sur, qch.

altercation [ɔːltə'keiʃ(ə)n], *s.* altercation *f,* dispute *f,* querelle *f*; *Jur:* contestation *f*; plaidoirie *f* contradictoire; **to have an a.,** se disputer.

altered ['ɔːltəːd], *a.* **he is greatly a.,** il est bien changé; **a. appearance,** changement *m* de visage, d'aspect.

alter ego ['æltər'egou], *Lt.phr. used as s.* alter ego *m;* **he is my a.e.,** c'est mon alter ego; c'est un autre moi-même.

altering[1] ['ɔːlt(ə)riŋ], *a.* **1.** changeant, variable. **2.** en train de changer.

altering[2], *s.* = ALTERATION.

alterity [ɔːl'teriti], *s. Phil:* altérité *f.*

alternance [ɔːl'təːnəns], *s. Ling:* alternance *f.*

alternant [ɔːl'təːnənt], *a.* alternant; *Geol:* **a. layers,** dépôts alternants, couches alternantes.

Alternaria [ɔːltə'nɛəriə], *s. Fung:* alternaria *m.*

alternariose [ɔːltə'nɛəriouz], *s. Fung:* alternariose *f.*

alternate[1] [ɔː'təːnət]. **1.** *a.* (*a*) alternatif, alterné, alternant; **the a. action of sun and rain,** l'action alternative, alternée, du soleil et de la pluie; **to come on a. days,** venir tous les deux jours; **a. laughter and tears,** rires et pleurs successifs, alternés; **a. layers of stone and timber,** couches alternantes, alternées, de pierre et de bois; **professors lecturing on a. days,** professeurs alternants; *Biol:* **a. generation,** alternance *f* des générations; (*b*) *Mil: etc:* **a. position,** position *f* de rechange, de remplacement; *Av: etc:* **a. routing,** déviation *f*; **a. route,** parcours *m* de rechange; **a. airfield,** aérodrome *m* de déroutement, de dégagement; **a. gross weight,** poids maximum autorisé en surcharge occasionnelle; (*c*) *Cmptr:* **a. action switch,** bouton *m* à double effet; **a. area,** deuxième zone, zone utilisée en bascule; **a. operation,** travail *m* en bascule; **a. routing,** voie *f* de déroutement; **a. track** piste *f* de remplacement, de réserve. **2.** *a. Mth: Bot:* (angles, feuilles) alternes; **exterior, interior, a. angles,** angles *m* alternes externes, internes. **3.** *a. Pros:* (rimes) croisées. **4.** *s. esp. NAm:* (*a*) remplaçant, -ante; (*b*) **Gatwick is an a. to London Airport,** Gatwick sert d'aérodrome de dégagement pour l'aéroport de Londres.

alternate[2] ['ɔːltəneit]. **1.** *v.tr.* (*a*) faire alterner (deux choses); employer (deux choses) tour à tour, alternativement; (*b*) *Agr:* **to a. crops,** alterner des récoltes; (*c*) *Cmptr:* utiliser en bascule. **2.** *v.i.* (*a*) alterner **(with,** avec); se succéder (tour à tour); **to a. between laughter and tears,** passer du rire aux larmes; **to a. between wealth and poverty,** basculer de la richesse à la pauvreté; (*b*) *El:* (*of current*) varier selon une sinusoïde, changer périodiquement de sens.

alternate-leaved [ɔːl'təːnətliːvd], *a. Bot:* alternifolié.

alternately [ɔː'təːnətli], *adv.* **1.** alternativement, tour à tour; en alternance. **2.** *Bot:* **leaves placed a.,** feuilles alternes.

alternating ['ɔːltəneitiŋ], *a.* **1.** alternant, alterné; *Mth:* **a. series,** série alternée. **2.** (*a*) *El.E:* (courant) alternatif; **a.-current dynamo, generator,** alternateur *m*; machine alternative; **a.-current motor,** alternomoteur *m;* (*b*) *Mec.E:* (mouvement) alternatif, de va-et-vient; **a. saw,** scie alternative; (*c*) *Cmptr:* **a. operation,** travail *m* en bascule.

alternation [ɔːltə'neiʃ(ə)n], *s.* **1.** alternation *f* (d'un mouvement). **2.** (*a*) alternance *f* (du jour et de la nuit, *Biol:* de générations, *Geol:* des couches); (*b*) **alternations of rain and sun, of optimism and despair,** alternatives *f* de pluie et de soleil, d'optimisme et de désespoir; (*c*) roulement *m,* alternance (de personnes qui se remplacent). **3.** (*a*) *El:* alternance; (*b*) *Cmptr:* alternance; bascule *f* de tampons.

alternative [ɔː'təːnətiv]. **1.** *a.* (*a*) alternatif; **an a. proposal,** une contre-proposition; (*b*) **a. road,** route *f* d'emprunt; **I'll give you an a. route,** je vais vous indiquer un second, un autre, itinéraire; **a. airfield,** aérodrome *m* de dégagement; *Mil: etc:* **a. position,** position *f* secondaire, auxiliaire. **2.** *s.* (*a*) alternative *f*; **the a. of a fine or a month's imprisonment,** l'alternative d'une amende ou d'un mois de prison; (*b*) **the a. would be to . . .,** l'alternative, une autre solution, serait de . . .; **to have no a.,** ne pas avoir le choix; **this leaves us no a.,** cela nous ôte toute alternative; **he had no a. but to obey,** il n'a pu faire autrement que d'obéir; **there is no a.,** il n'y a pas d'alternative. NOTE: *Correctly used,* **alternative** *implies a choice between two things only.*

alternatively [ɔː'təːnətivli], *adv.* avec l'alternative de . . .; **fine of £20, or a. one month's imprisonment,** amende *f* de vingt livres, avec l'alternative d'un mois de prison; **a., you could agree to this solution,** ou bien vous pourriez accepter cette solution.

alternator ['ɔːltəneitər], *s. El:* alternateur *m;* **single-phase a.,** alternateur monophasé; **three-phase a.,** alternateur triphasé.

alternifoliate [ɔːltəːni'foulieit], *a. Bot:* alternifolié.

alternipinnate [ɔːltəːni'pineit], *a. Bot:* alternipenné.

alternisepalous [ɔːltəːni'sepələs], *a. Bot:* alternisépale.

Althea [æl'θiːə]. **1.** *Pr.n.f.* Althée. **2.** *s. Bot:* althée *m,* althæa *m.*

althorn ['ælthɔːn], *s. Mus:* (saxhorn) alto *m.*

although [ɔːl'ðou], *conj.* (*a*) quoique, bien que, encore que, + *sub;* **a. I have never seen him I often write to him,** quoique je ne l'aie jamais vu je lui écris souvent; (*b*) **a. I am a father,** tout père que je suis; **a. (I am) unmarried I am happy,** je suis contente, quoique célibataire; **a. not beautiful, she was attractive,** sans être belle elle plaisait.

altigraph ['æltigræf], *s. Av:* barographe enregistreur, baromètre enregistreur.

altimeter ['æltimiːtər], *s. Av:* altimètre *m;* **absolute a.,** indicateur *m* d'altitude absolue; **pressure a.,** altimètre barométrique; **electrical-capacity a.,** altimètre électrostatique; **radio a.,** radiosonde *f;* **a. setting,** réglage *m* altimétrique.

altimetric [ælti'metrik], *a.* altimétrique.

altimetry [æl'timitri], *s.* altimétrie *f.*

altiplanation [æltiplæ'neiʃ(ə)n], *s. Geol:* altiplanation *f.*

altitude ['æltitjuːd], *s.* (*a*) altitude *f,* élévation *f* (au-dessus du niveau de la mer); **at these altitudes the snow never melts,** à cette altitude la neige ne fond jamais; **at an a. of 500 metres,** à une altitude de 500 mètres; **at a high a.,** en altitude; **absolute a.,** altitude absolue; **relative a.,** altitude relative; **actual, true, a.,** altitude vraie; *Med:* **high-a. treatment,** cure *f* d'altitude; *Av:* **a. flight,** vol à haute altitude; **pull-up, critical a.,** altitude de rétablissement; **cruising a.,** altitude de croisière; **a. recorder,** enregistreur *m* d'altitude; **a. control, controller,** commande *f* altimétrique, contrôleur *m* d'altitude; **a. compensator,** correcteur *m* d'altitude; **a. chamber,** caisson *m* d'altitude; **a. engine,** moteur suralimenté; **a. sickness, a. anoxia,** mal *m* d'altitude; mal des aviateurs; **a. narcosis,** ivresse *f* d'altitude; (*b*) hauteur *f* (d'un astre, d'un triangle).

altitudinal [ælti'tjuːdinl], *a.* altitudinaire.

alto ['æltou], *s. Mus:* **1.** alto *m;* **a. clef,** clef *f* d'ut troisième ligne. **2.** (*a*) (*male voice*) haute-contre *f, pl.* hautes-contre; (*b*) (*female voice*) contralto *m,* contralte *m;* (*in choral singing*) **to sing a.,** chanter la partie d'alto. **3.** (*a*) alto (à cordes); quinte *f;* (*b*) *attrib.* **a. trombone, saxophone,** trombone *m,* saxophone *m,* alto.

altocumulus [æltou'kjuːmjuləs], *s. Meteor:* altocumulus *m.*

altogether [ɔːltə'geðər]. **1.** *adv.* (*a*) (*wholly*) entièrement, tout à fait, complètement; **you are a. right,** vous avez entièrement, grandement, raison; **to change sth. a.,** changer qch. de fond en comble, radicalement; **it's a. out of the question,** c'est absolument impossible; **I don't a. agree,** je ne suis pas entièrement de votre avis; (*b*) (*on the whole*) somme toute . . .; **taking things a.,** à tout prendre; **a., I'm sorry about it,** à tout prendre, somme toute, je le regrette; (*c*) **how much a.?** combien en tout? combien tout compris? **a. we did not spend £5,** nous n'avons pas dépensé cinq livres en tout; **a. there were a thousand books,** il y avait mille livres, un millier de livres, en tout. **2.** *s. F:* **in the a.,** complètement nu, dans le costume d'Adam.

alto-relievo ['æltouri'liːvou], *s.* haut-relief *m, pl.* hauts-reliefs; **in a.-r.,** en haut-relief.

altostratus [æltou'strɑːtəs, -'strei-], *s. Meteor:* altostratus *m.*

altricial [æl'triʃ(ə)l], *a. Orn:* nidicole.

altrose ['æltrouz], *s. Ch:* altrose *m.*

altruism ['æltruizm], *s.* altruisme *m.*

altruist ['æltruist], *s.* altruiste *mf.*

altruistic [æltru'istik], *a.* altruiste.

alucita [ə'ljuːsitə], *s. Ent:* alucite *f.*

aludel ['æljud(ə)l], *s. Tchn:* aludel *m.*

alula ['æljulə], *s.* **1.** *Orn:* alule *f;* aile bâtarde. **2.** *Ent:* (*also* **alulet** ['æljulit]) cuilleron *m* (de diptère).

alum[1] ['æləm], *s.* alun *m;* **chrome a.,** alun de chrome; **potash a.,** alun ordinaire; **ammonia a.,** sulfate *m* double d'aluminium et d'ammonium; alun ammoniacal; **iron a., a. feather, feather a.,** alun de fer, alun de plume; halotrichite *f;* **a. mine,** carrière *f* d'alun; **a. shales,** schistes *m* alunifères; **a. stone,** alunite *f;* *Phot:* **a. bath,** bain aluné.

alum[2], *v.tr.* aluminer, aluner; *Phot:* **alumed fixing bath,** bain de fixage aluné.

Alumel ['æljumel], *s. Metall: R.t.m:* Alumel *m.*

alumina [ə'l(j)uːminə], *s. Miner:* alumine *f.*

aluminate[1] [ə'l(j)uːminət], *s.* aluminate *m.*

aluminate[2] [ə'l(j)uːmineit], *v.tr.* **1.** (*to mix with alum*) aluminer. **2.** *Dy: etc:* (*to steep in alum*) aluner.

alumination [əl(j)uːmi'neiʃ(ə)n], *s.Ch:Dy:* aluminage *m.*

aluming ['æləmiŋ], *s.* alunation *f,* alunage *m.*

aluminiferous [əl(j)uːmi'nifərəs], *a.* aluminifère.

aluminite [ə'l(j)uːminait], *s. Miner:* aluminite *f,* aluminaire *f.*

aluminium [ælju'miniəm], *s.* aluminium *m;* **a. oxide,** alumine *f;* **a. sheet,** tôle *f* d'aluminium; **a. powder,** aluminium en poudre; **a. paint,** peinture *f* à l'aluminium; **a. works,** aluminerie *f;* **a. bronze,** cupro-aluminium *m.*

aluminize [ə'l(j)uːminaiz], *v.tr.* **1.** *Metall:* combiner avec de l'aluminium; **aluminized steel,** acier *m* à l'aluminium. **2.** *Tchn:* recouvrir d'une couche d'aluminium; métalliser avec de l'aluminium; aluminiser; *Opt:* aluminer (un miroir); *Elcs:* **aluminized screen (of cathode ray tube),** écran aluminisé (d'un tube cathodique). **3.** (*a*) *Ch:* aluminer; (*b*) *Dy:* aluner.

aluminizing [ə'l(j)uːminaiziŋ], *s.* **1.** *Metall:* combinaison *f,* alliage *m* (d'un métal) avec de l'aluminium. **2.** *Tchn:* métallisation *f* à l'aluminium; aluminisation *f;* *Opt:* aluminiage *m,* aluminure *f* (d'un miroir). **3.** *Ch: Dy:* aluminage *m,* alunage *m* (d'un tissu).

aluminosilicate [ə'l(j)uːminou'silikeit], *s. Ch:* aluminosilicate *m.*

aluminothermy [ə'l(j)uːminou'θəːmi], *s. Metall: Ind:* aluminothermie *f.*

aluminous [ə'l(j)uːminəs], *a.* alumineux; **a. cement,** ciment alumineux.

aluminum [ə'luːminəm], *s. NAm:* = ALUMINIUM.

alumna, *pl.* **-ae** [ə'lʌmnə, -iː], *s.f. NAm:* ancienne élève (d'un collège); ancienne étudiante, diplômée, (=) licenciée (d'une université).

alumniate [ə'lʌmnieit], *s. Sch: NAm:* alumnat *m.*

alumniferous [æləm'nifərəs], *a.* alunifère.

alumnus, *pl.* **-i** [ə'lʌmnəs, -ai], *s.m. NAm:* ancien élève (d'un collège); ancien étudiant, diplômé, (=) licencié (d'une université).

Alundum [ə'lʌndəm], *s. Ind: R.t.m:* Alundum *m.*

alunite ['æljunait], *s. Miner:* alunite *f.*

alunogen [ə'luːnoudʒen], *s. Miner:* alunogène *m.*

alurgite ['ælədʒait], *s. Miner:* alurgite *f.*

alutaceous [ælju'teiʃəs], *a.* alutacé.

Alva ['ælvə], *Pr.n. Hist:* **the Duke of A.,** le duc d'Albe.

alveolar [ælvi'oulər], *a.* alvéolaire; *Anat:* **a. point,** point *m* alvéolaire (du maxillaire supérieur); **a. process, ridge,** bord *m* alvéolaire (du maxillaire supérieur ou inférieur); *Ling:* **a. consonant, s. alveolar,** (consonne *f*) alvéolaire *f.*

alveolate ['ælviələt], *a. Biol:* alvéolé, alvéolaire.

alveolation [ælviou'leiʃ(ə)n], *s. Geol:* alvéolisation *f.*

alveole ['ælvioul], *s.* alvéole *m* or *f;* favéole *f.*

alveolectomy [ælviou'lektəmi], *s. Dent:* alvéolectomie *f.*

alveolite ['ælvioulait], *s. Paleont:* alvéolite *m.*

alveolitis [ælviou'laitis], *s. Med:* alvéolite *f.*

alveolodental ['ælviəlou'dentl], *a. Anat:* alvéolodentaire.

alveolus, *pl.* **-i** ['ælviələs, -ai], *s.* alvéole *m* or *f.*

alvine ['ælvain], *a.* alvin; du bas-ventre.

alvite ['ælvait], *s. Miner:* alvite *f.*

always ['ɔːlwəz, -wiz, *stressed* 'ɔːlweiz], *adv.* (*a*) toujours; **water a. has some air in it,** l'eau contient toujours de l'air; **he's nearly a. here,** il est presque toujours ici; **he's a. out,** il est toujours sorti; **he a. comes on Thursdays,** il vient toujours le jeudi; **a. smiling,** toujours riant; **the office is a. open,** le bureau est ouvert en permanence; **I wish you weren't a. bringing up your age,** si seulement vous ne mettiez pas tout le temps votre âge en avant; **he's a. spying,** il est toujours à vous épier; (*b*) **I can a. try,** je puis toujours, quand même, essayer; **there's a. a first time,** on peut toujours s'y mettre; il ne faut jamais dire 'jamais'; *P:* **'let sleeping dogs lie', I a. say,** 'il ne faut pas réveiller le chien qui dort', voilà ce que je dis; **if he gives you £5, it's a. something,** s'il vous donne cinq livres, c'est toujours ça; **there's a. the old age pension,** en tout cas on aura la retraite de vieillesse; **if you can't have the** *Standard Dictionary* **there's a.** the *Shorter,* si l'on ne peut pas avoir le *Standard Dictionary* il y a toujours le *Shorter.*

alyssum ['ælis(ə)m], *s. Bot:* alysson *m,* alysse *m;* **rock a.,** corbeille *f* d'or, thlaspi *m* jaune; **sweet a.,** corbeille d'argent.

alytes ['æletiːz], *s. Amph:* alyte *m,* alytes *m.*

amadavat [æmədə'væt], *s. Orn:* bengali *m* rouge, bengali de l'Inde.

Amadeus [æmə'diːəs], *Pr.n.m.* Amédée.

Amadis ['æmədis], *Pr.n.m. Lit:* **A. of Gaul,** Amadis de Gaule.

amadou ['æmədu:], *s.* amadou *m.*

amah ['ɑːmə], *s.f.* (*in India, etc.*) (*a*) nourrice; (*b*) bonne d'enfants; (*c*) bonne (indigène).

amain [ə'mein], *adv. A: & Poet:* **to smite sth. a.,** frapper qch. avec violence, de toutes ses forces; **to ride a.,** aller à toute bride; **to flee a.,** fuir précipitamment, à toutes jambes; *Nau:* **lower a.!** amenez en grand!

Amalek ['æməlek], *Pr.n.m. B.Hist:* Amalech.

Amalekite [ə'mæləkait], *s. B.Hist:* Amalécite *mf.*

Amalfitan [ə'mælfit(ə)n], *a. & s. Geog:* **1.** *a.* amalfitain. **2.** *s.* Amalfitain, -aine.

amalgam [ə'mælgəm], *s.* amalgame *m;* *Ind:* **a. solution,** bain *m* d'amalgamation.

amalgamate[1] [ə'mælgəmət, -eit], *a.* (métal, langage) amalgamé.

amalgamate[2] [ə'mælgəmeit]. **1.** *v.tr.* (*a*) amalgamer (l'or, l'étain); (*b*) amalgamer (des idées); fusionner (des sociétés, etc.); unifier (les industries); *Fin:* **to a. shares,** fusionner des actions. **2.** *v.i.* (*a*) (*of metals*) s'amalgamer; (*b*) (*of ideas*) s'amalgamer; (*of companies*) fusionner; opérer une fusion; (*of races*) se mélanger, fusionner.

amalgamating [ə'mælgəmeitiŋ], *s.* **1.** amalgamation *f* (des métaux); *attrib.* **a. mill,** moulin *m* à, pour, amalgamer. **2.** fusion *f,* fusionnement *m;* mélange *m.*

amalgamation [əmælgə'meiʃ(ə)n], *s.* **1.** amalgamation *f* (des métaux), (*of gold, silver*) **a. process,** procédé *m* par amalgamation. **2.** fusion *f,* fusionnement *m* (de deux sociétés, *Fin:* d'actions); mélange *m* (de races, etc.); **a. of industries,** unification industrielle.

amalgamator [ə'mælgəmeitər], *s. Tchn:* (*for gold and silver*) amalgamateur *m;* **pan a.,** amalgamateur à cuve.

Amalthaea [æmæl'θiːə], *Pr.n.f. Myth:* Amalthée.

amanita [æmə'naitə], *s. Fung:* amanite *f;* **a. phalloides** [fæ'lɔidiːz], **deadly a.,** amanite phalloïde, oronge-ciguë verte.

amanuensis, *pl.* **-es** [əmænju'ensis, -iːz], *s. Lit:* secrétaire *m* (à la main); **I act as a.,** c'est moi qui tiens la plume.

amarant(h) ['æmərænt, -ænθ], *s. Bot:* amarante *f;* **a.(-coloured) ribbons,** des rubans amarante.

Amarant(h)aceae [æmərən'teisiː, -'θeisiː], *s.pl. Bot:* amarantacées *f.*

amarant(h)ine [æmə'ræntain, -θain], *a.* **1.** (d')amarante. **2.** *Lit: A:* impérissable, immortel.

amarantite [æmə'ræntait], *s. Miner:* amarantite *f.*

amaril ['æməril], *a. Med:* amaril.

amarine ['æmərin, -ain], *s. Ch:* amarine *f.*

Amaryllidaceae [æmərili'deisiː], *s.pl. Bot:* amaryllidacées *f,* amaryllidées *f.*

Amaryllis [æmə'rilis]. **1.** *Pr.n.f.* Amaryllis. **2.** *s. Bot:* amaryllis *f* (belle-dame); lis *m* de Saint-Jacques.

amass [ə'mæs], *v.tr.* amasser; **to a. a fortune,** amasser une fortune; accumuler une fortune.

amateur ['æmətəːr, æmə'təːr, 'æmətjuər], *s.* (*a*) amateur *m;* **he is an a. of painting,** c'est un amateur de belles peintures; il s'intéresse à la peinture; (*b*) amateur, dilettante *m;* **he paints as an a.,** il peint en amateur, la peinture est son violon d'Ingres; *Pej:* **he's an a. at painting,** il peint en amateur, *F:* il barbouille, c'est un barbouilleur; **she plays well for an a.,** elle joue bien pour un amateur; (*c*) *Sp:* amateur; (*d*) *attrib.* **a. painter,** peintre *m* amateur; **a. work,** travail *m* d'amateur, de dilettante; **a. championship,** championnat *m* d'amateur; *Turf:* **a. rider,** gentleman rider *m.*

amateurish [æmə'tə:riʃ], *a. Pej:* (travail, etc.) d'amateur, maladroit; **a. painting,** barbouillage *m*; **a. playing of the piano,** pianotage *m*.

amateurishly [æmə'tə:riʃli], *adv.* en amateur, maladroitement.

amateurishness [æmə'tə:riʃnis], *s.* manque *m* de maîtrise, maladresse *f*.

amateurism ['æmətərizm], *s.* **1.** dilettantisme *m*. **2.** *Sp:* amateurisme *m*.

amative ['æmətiv], *a. Lit:* (*of pers.*) porté à aimer, à l'amour; passionné.

amativeness ['æmətivnis], *s. Phren:* amativité *f*.

amatol ['æmətɔl], *s. Exp:* amatol *m*.

amatory ['æmət(ə)ri], *a.* (sentiment) amoureux; (lettre) d'amour; (poète, poème) érotique, anacréontique.

amaurosis [æmɔ:'rousis], *s. Med:* amaurose *f*.

amaurotic [æmɔ:'rɔtik], *a. Med:* amaurotique.

amaze[1] [ə'meiz], *v.tr.* confondre, stupéfier, étonner, ébahir, *F:* renverser; **his courage amazed me,** j'ai été stupéfait de son courage; **her stupidity amazes me,** sa stupidité me renverse; **it amazes me that he could have done such a thing,** il m'étonne qu'il ait pu faire une telle chose; *Iron:* **you a. me!** voilà qui m'étonne! vraiment?

amaze[2], *s. A: & Poet:* étonnement *m*.

amazed [ə'meizd], *a.* confondu, stupéfait, ébahi, *F:* renversé; **to be a.,** rester stupéfait, ébahi; tomber des nues; **I was a. at his courage,** j'ai été stupéfait, stupéfié, de son courage; **I am a. at it,** j'en reste confondu; **I am a. at you,** vous m'étonnez; **I am a. to find that. . .,** je suis stupéfait de découvrir que . . .; **I was a.!** j'étais complètement renversé!

amazedly [ə'meizidli], *adv.* avec stupéfaction; d'un air stupéfait.

amazement [ə'meizm(ə)nt], *s.* stupéfaction *f*; stupeur *f*; (grand) étonnement; ébahissement *m*; **to recover from one's a.,** revenir de son étonnement; **to listen in a.,** écouter avec stupeur; **I heard with a. that. . .,** j'ai été stupéfait d'apprendre que . . .; à mon grand étonnement j'ai appris que. . . .

amazing [ə'meiziŋ], *a.* stupéfiant, étonnant, *F:* renversant; **a. dexterity,** dextérité prestigieuse; **it's a.!** je n'en reviens pas! *Com:* **a. offer!** offre exceptionnelle!

amazingly [ə'meiziŋli], *adv.* étonnamment; **he's doing a. well,** il réussit à merveille; il fait des affaires merveilleuses; **a. generous,** d'une générosité exceptionnelle; **a. stupid,** d'une stupidité incroyable.

Amazon ['æməz(ə)n]. **1.** *s.f.* (*a*) *Myth:* Amazone, (femme) guerrière; (*b*) femme forte et athlétique. **2.** *Pr.n. Geog:* **the (river) A.,** l'Amazone *f*; *attrib.* **the A. basin,** le bassin amazonien. **3.** *s. Ent:* **a. (ant),** (fourmi *f*) amazone *f*. **4.** *s. Orn:* **blue-faced a.,** amazone *m* à queue rouge; **blue-fronted a.,** amazone à front bleu; **Cuban a.,** amazone à tête blanche; **Levaillant's a.,** amazone de Levaillant.

Amazonia [ˌæmə'zouniə], *Pr.n. Geog:* Amazonie *f*.

Amazonian [æmə'zouniən], *a.* **1.** (*a*) d'Amazone; (*b*) (*of woman*) forte et athlétique. **2.** *Geog:* de l'Amazone, amazonien.

amazonite ['æməzənait], **amazonstone** ['æməzən'stoun], *s. Miner:* amazonite *f*.

ambages [æm'beidʒi:z], *s.pl. Lit:* ambages *m*, équivoques *f*; détours *m*.

ambary ['æmbəri], *s. Bot:* ketmie *f* à chanvre; *Tex:* chanvre *m* de Gombo.

ambassador [æm'bæsədər], *s.* (*a*) ambassadeur *m*, (*woman*) ambassadrice *f*; **the ambassador's wife,** l'ambassadrice; **a. extraordinary, a. at large,** ambassadeur extraordinaire; **the British A. in Paris,** l'ambassadeur d'Angleterre à Paris; **the French A. to Japan,** l'ambassadeur de France auprès du Japon; **A. to the Court of St. James's,** ambassadeur auprès de la reine (du roi) d'Angleterre; (*b*) ambassadeur, -drice (de l'art, du goût, de la mode, etc.).

ambassadorial [æmbæsə'dɔ:riəl], *a.* ambassadorial, -aux; d'ambassadeur.

ambassadorship [æm'bæsədəʃip], *s.* ambassade *f*, charge *f* d'ambassadeur.

ambassadress [æm'bæsdris], *s.f.* (= *ambassador's wife, incorrectly used for woman ambassador*) ambassadrice.

amber[1] ['æmbər], *s.* **1.** (*a*) ambre *m*; **yellow a.,** ambre jaune; succin *m*; (*b*) *Ich:* **a. fish,** sériole *f* (de Duméril); (*c*) *Moll:* **a. snail,** succinée *f*, ambrette *f*; (*d*) *Miner:* **a. potch,** (variété jaune d') opale *f* de feu. **2.** *a.* (*a*) d'ambre, en ambre; **a. varnish,** vernis *m* au succin; (*b*) **a. (-coloured),** ambré; *Adm:* **a. light,** feu *m* orange; *F:* **to shoot the a.,** passer à, brûler, l'orange.

amber[2], *v.tr.* ambrer; parfumer d'ambre.

ambergris ['æmbəgri:s], *s.* ambre gris.

amberjack ['æmbədʒæk], *s. Ich:* **1.** séricole *f* (de Duméril). **2.** cavaille *f*.

amberoid ['æmbərɔid], *s. Ind:* ambroïne *f*.

amber-tipped ['æmbə'tipt], *a.* **1.** (porte-cigarette) à bout d'ambre. **2.** *O:* (cigarette) à bout ambré.

ambetti [æm'beti], *s. Glassm:* verre ambité.

ambiance ['æmbiəns], *s.* = AMBIENCE.

ambidexter ['æmbi'dekstər], *a. & s.* **1.** ambidextre (*mf*). **2.** *A:* homme *m* de mauvaise foi; fourbe *m*.

ambidext(e)rous ['æmbi'dekstrəs], *a.* ambidextre.

ambidextrousness ['æmbi'dekstrəsnis], **ambidexterity** ['æmbidek'steriti], *s.* ambidextérité *f*.

ambience ['æmbiəns], *s.* ambiance *f*.

ambient ['æmbiənt], *a.* (air) ambiant; (température) ambiante; *Tchn:* **a. thermoresistor,** sonde *f* thermométrique d'ambience.

ambiguity [æmbi'gju:iti], *s.* **1.** ambiguïté *f*. **2.** équivoque *f*.

ambiguous [æm'bigjuəs], *a.* **1.** ambigu, -uë, équivoque. **2.** incertain; **an a. conflict,** un conflit d'issue douteuse. **3.** obscur; difficile à comprendre; **a. style,** style confus.

ambiguously [æm'bigjuəsli], *adv.* avec ambiguïté, d'une manière ambiguë, équivoque.

ambiguousness [æm'bigjuəsnis], *s.* ambiguïté *f*.

ambiparous [æm'bipərəs], *a. Bot:* ambipare.

ambit ['æmbit], *s. Lit:* **1.** circuit *m*, tour *m* (d'une ville, etc.). **2.** bornes *fpl*, limites *fpl* (d'un terrain, etc.). **3.** étendue *f*, portée *f* (d'une action, d'un pouvoir, etc.).

ambition [æm'biʃ(ə)n], *s.* ambition *f*; **the a. to shine, to succeed,** l'ambition de briller, de réussir; **eaten up with a.,** dévoré d'ambition; **to have great ambitions,** avoir de hautes visées; **to make it one's a. to do sth.,** mettre son ambition à faire qch; **the summit of my a. is. . .,** ma plus haute ambition c'est . . .; **to be a lawyer's clerk was not the height of my a.,** être clerc de notaire, ce n'était pas mon rêve; **unscrupulous a.,** arrivisme *m*.

ambitious [æm'biʃəs], *a.* ambitieux. **1. to be a. of power,** ambitionner le pouvoir; **to be a. to do sth.,** ambitionner de faire qch. **2. a. plans,** projets ambitieux.

ambitiously [æm'biʃəsli], *adv.* ambitieusement.

ambitiousness [æmbiʃəsnis], *s.* caractère ambitieux.

ambitti, ambitty ['æmbiti], *a. Glassm:* ambité.

ambivalence [æm'bivələns], *s.* ambivalence *f*.

ambivalent [æm'bivələnt], *a.* ambivalent.

ambivert ['æmbivə:t], *s. Psy:* ambiéqual *m*, -aux.

ambiverted [æmbi'və:tid], *a. Psy:* ambiéqual, -aux.

amble[1] ['æmbl], *s.* **1.** *Equit:* amble *m*, entre-pas *m*; **I saw him coming along at an a.,** je le vis qui arrivait à l'amble. **2.** (*of pers.*) pas *m* tranquille; allure *f* tranquille.

amble[2], *v.i.* **1.** *Equit:* (*a*) aller (à) l'amble; **to a. along,** chevaucher à l'amble; (*b*) (*of horse*) **to make a horse a.,** mettre un cheval à l'amble. **2.** *F:* (*of pers.*) **to a. along,** aller, marcher, d'un pas tranquille; flâner.

ambler ['æmblər], *s.* **1.** cheval ambleur. **2.** promeneur, -euse sans but; flâneur, -euse.

ambling[1] ['æmbliŋ], *a.* (cheval) ambleur, qui va (à) l'amble; **a. mare,** haquenée *f*; **with an a. gait,** (i) à l'amble; (ii) *F:* au petit trot.

ambling[2], *s.* = AMBLE[1]

Amblycephalidae [æmblisi'fælidi:], *s.pl. Rept:* amblycéphalidés *m*.

amblygonite [æm'bligənait], *s. Miner:* amblygonite *f*.

amblyope ['æmblioup], *a. & s. Med:* amblyope (*mf*).

amblyopia [æmbli'oupiə], *s. Med:* amblyopie *f*.

amblyopic [æmbli'oupik], *a. Med:* amblyope.

Amblyopsidae [æmbli'ɔpsidi:], *s.pl. Ich:* amblyopsidés *m*, amblyopsides *m*.

amblyopsis [æmbli'ɔpsis], *s. Ich:* amblyopsis *m*.

amblypod ['æmblipɔd], *s. Paleont:* amblypode *m*.

Amblypoda [æm'blipɔdə], *s.pl. Paleont:* amblypodes *m*.

amblyrhynchus [æmbli'riŋkəs], *s. Z:* amblyrhynque *m*.

Amblystoma [æm'blistoumə], *s. Amph:* amblystome *m*.

Amblystomidae [æmblis'tɔmidi:], *s.pl. Amph:* amblystomidés *m*.

ambo ['æmbou], *s. Ecc. Arch:* ambon *m*.

amboceptor [æmbou'septər], *s. Bio-Ch:* ambocepteur *m*.

ambon ['æmbən], *s.* **1.** *Anat:* ambon *m*. **2.** *Ecc. Arch:* ambon.

Amboyna [æm'bɔinə], *Pr.n. Geog:* Amboine *f*; *Com:* **A. wood,** bois *m* d'Amboine; amboine *m*.

ambrain ['æmbrein], *s. Ch:* ambréine *f*.

ambrette [æm'bret], *s.* **1.** *Bot: etc:* ambrette *f*. **2.** *Hort:* poire *f* d'ambrette.

ambrite ['æmbrait], *s. Miner:* ambrite *f*.

ambroid ['æmbrɔid], *s. Ind:* ambroïne *f*.

Ambrose ['æmbrouz], *Pr.n.m.* Ambroise.

ambrosia [æm'brouziə], *s.* (*a*) *Myth:* ambroisie *f*; (*b*) *Bot:* ambroisie, ambrosia *f*; (*c*) *Fung:* ambrosia *m*.

ambrosial [æm'brouziəl], *a.* ambrosiaque; au parfum d'ambroisie.

Ambrosian [æm'brouziən], *a.* Ambrosien; de saint Ambroise; *esp. Ecc: Mus:* **A. rite, chant,** rite, chant, ambrosien.

ambry ['æmbri], *s. A:* armoire *f*, placard *m*.

ambsace ['eimzeis], *s. Games:* (*dicing: etc:*) besas *m*, ambesas *m*, beset *m*.

ambulacral [æmbju'leikrl], *a. Echin:* ambulacraire, ambulacral, -aux.

ambulacralia [æmbjulə'kreiliə], *s.pl. Echin:* trous *m* ambulacraires.

ambulacrum, *pl.* **-a** [æmbju'leikrəm, -ə], *s. Echin:* ambulacre *m*.

ambulance ['æmbjuləns], *s.* ambulance *f*; **a. train,** train *m* sanitaire; **a. ship,** navire *m* hôpital; **flying a., a. plane,** avion *m* sanitaire; **a. post,** poste *m* d'ambulance; **a. man,** ambulancier(-brancardier) *m*; infirmier *m*; *Mil:* **a. company,** compagnie *f* sanitaire; **field a.,** ambulance divisionnaire; *U.S: F:* **a. chaser,** homme de loi (peu digne) qui arrive à la scène d'un accident pour chercher la clientèle.

ambulant ['æmbjulənt], *a. Med:* ambulatoire; **a. typhoid,** fièvre *f* typhoïde ambulatoire; *a. & s.* **a. (patient),** malade ambulant.

ambulate ['æmbjuleit], *v.i.* déambuler; aller et venir; se promener.

ambulation [æmbju'leiʃ(ə)n], *s.* déambulation *f*.

ambulatory[1] ['æmbjulət(ə)ri, -leit-], *a.* **1.** ambulant, mobile; *Jur:* (tribunal) ambulatoire. **2.** *Med:* (*a*) ambulatoire; **a. typhoid,** fièvre *f* typhoïde ambulatoire; (*b*) (malade) ambulant, sur pied. **3.** *s. Z:* patte *f*, etc., ambulatoire.

ambulatory[2], *s.* promenoir *m*, préau *m*; *Ecc. Arch:* déambulatoire *m*.

ambuscade[1] [æmbəs'keid], *s.* = AMBUSH[1].

ambuscade[2], *v.tr. & i.* = AMBUSH[2].

ambush[1] ['æmbuʃ], *s.* embuscade *f*; guet-apens *m*, *pl.* guets-apens; traquenard *m*; **to be, lie, in a.,** être, se tenir, en embuscade; être à l'affût; **to be attacked from a.,** être victime d'un guet-apens; **troops in a.,** troupes embusquées; **to drive troops out of a.,** débusquer des troupes.

ambush[2]. **1.** *v.tr.* (*a*) **to a. the enemy,** attirer l'ennemi dans un piège, dans un traquenard; **to be ambushed,** tomber dans une embuscade; (*b*) *A:* embusquer (des troupes); *now used only in p.p.* **ambushed troops,** troupes embusquées. **2.** *v.i.* s'embusquer; se tenir en embuscade.

ambusher ['æmbuʃər], *s.* personne *f* qui dresse un guet-apens, un traquenard.

Ambystomatidae [æmbistou'mætidi:], *s.pl. Amph:* ambystomatidés *m*.

ameba, amebic, *etc. NAm:* = AMOEBA, AMOEBIC, etc.

ameer [ə'miər], *s.m. A:* émir.

amelanchier [æmə'læŋkiər], *s. Bot:* amélanchier *m*.

Amelia[1] [ə'mi:liə], *Pr.n.f.* Amélie.

amelia[2], *s. Med:* amélie *f*.

ameliorant [ə'mi:liərənt], *s. Agr:* engrais *m*, amendement *m*.

ameliorate [ə'mi:liəreit]. **1.** *v.tr.* améliorer. **2.** *v.i.* s'améliorer, s'amender.

ameliorating [ə'mi:liəreitiŋ], *a.* améliorant.

amelioration [əmi:liə'reiʃ(ə)n], *s.* amélioration *f*.

ameliorative [ə'mi:liərətiv], *a.* amélioratif; améliorateur, -trice.

ameliorator [ə'mi:liəreitər], *s. Agr:* engrais *m*, amendement *m*.

amen ['ɑ:men, 'ei'men], *int.* amen; ainsi soit-il; *O:* **and we all say a. to that,** c'est ce que nous souhaitons tous; c'est aussi notre avis.

amenability [əmi:nə'biliti], *s.* **1.** *Jur:* justiciabilité *f* (**to,** de), responsabilité *f* (**to,** envers). **2.** soumission *f*, docilité *f*.

amenable [ə'mi:nəbl], *a.* **1.** (*a*) *Jur:* justiciable, ressortissant, relevant (**to a court,** d'un tribunal); responsable (**to s.o.,** envers qn); sujet (**to,** à); **a. to a fine,** passible d'une amende; **the case is not a. to ordinary rules,** ce cas n'est pas justiciable des règles ordinaires, n'est pas sujet aux règles ordinaires; (*b*) **ore a. to profitable treatment,** minerai susceptible d'être traité à profit. **2.** (*a*) **a. to the law, to discipline,** soumis à la loi, à la discipline; **a. to advice,** docile aux conseils; **a. to kindness,** sensible à la bonté; **a. to reason,** raisonnable; disposé à entendre raison; (*b*) **a. child,** enfant soumis, docile.

amenableness [ə'mi:nəbəlnis], *s.* = AMENABILITY.

amenably [ə'mi:nəbli], *adv.* **1.** d'une façon soumise, docile. **2.** *A:* **a. to your instructions,** conformément à vos ordres.

amend [ə'mend]. **1.** *v.tr.* (*a*) amender, modifier (un projet de loi); apporter, faire, une modification à (un projet); rectifier (un compte); corriger (un texte); (*b*) réformer (sa vie); **to a. one's ways,** s'amender. **2.** *v.i.* s'amender, se corriger.

amendable [ə'mendəbl], *a.* amendable, capable d'amendement; **a. error,** erreur *f* réparable.

amending [ə'mendiŋ], *a.* correctif; *A:* **the a. hand,** la plume du censeur.

amendment [ə'mendmənt], *s.* **1.** (*a*) modification *f* (d'un projet de loi); rectification *f* (d'un compte); correction *f* (d'un texte); redressement *m* (d'une erreur); (*b*) *Pol: etc:* amendement *m*; **a. to an a.**, sous-amendement *m*, *pl.* sous-amendements; **to move an a.**, proposer un amendement (**to a bill,** à un projet de loi). **2.** *A:* amélioration *f* (de la santé, etc.).

amends [ə'mendz], *s.pl.* réparation *f*, dédommagement *m*, compensation *f*; **to make a.**, faire amende honorable; **to make a. for an injury,** réparer un tort; **to make a. to s.o. for sth.,** dédommager qn de qch.; faire réparation à qn de qch.; **I shall make a.,** je réparerai; **to make a. for this wrong,** en réparation de ce tort; **to make a. for your disappointment,** pour vous consoler de votre déception; **his good qualities make a. for his shortcomings,** ses bonnes qualités compensent ses défauts; **by way of making a. for sth.,** en dédommagement de qch.; **to make a. for one's rudeness,** réparer son incivilité; **that will make some a.,** ce sera en quelque sorte une compensation, un dédommagement.

amenity [ə'mi:niti], *s.* **1.** aménité *f*, agrément *m*, charme *m* (d'un lieu). **2.** aménité, amabilité *f*, affabilité *f*. **3.** *pl.* **amenities:** (*a*) aménités *fpl*, civilités *fpl*; **exchange of amenities,** échange *m* de courtoisies, de civilités; (*b*) **the amenities of home life,** le charme, les douceurs, de la vie intime; **the amenities of life,** les agréments de l'existence; **amenities of a place,** agréments d'un lieu; **to interfere with the amenities of a town,** nuire au charme, aux agréments, aux attraits, d'une ville; **amenities of an hotel,** aménagements *m* d'un hôtel; **a new district requires amenities such as schools, public houses and a cinema,** un nouveau quartier demande des ressources telles que des écoles, des cafés et un cinéma; *Jur:* **compensation for loss of amenities,** dommages-intérêts *mpl* pour atteinte portée à l'agrément (d'une propriété); (*c*) *attrib.* **a. centre,** centre *m* de récréations (y compris un terrain de jeux); **houses of a. value,** maisons bien situées; (*in hospital*) **a. bed** = chambre privée (payante).

amenorrhoea [əmenə'riə], *s. Med:* aménorrhée *f*.

ament[1] ['æmənt, 'eimənt], **amentum** [ə'mentəm], *s. Bot:* chaton *m*; iule *m*.

ament[2] ['eimənt], *s.* idiot *m* de naissance.

amentaceous [æmen'teiʃəs], *a. Bot:* (*a*) amentifère; (*b*) amental, -aux.

amental [æ'mentl], *a. Bot:* amental, -aux.

Amentales [æmen'teili:z], *s.pl. Bot:* amentales *f*.

amentia [ə'menʃiə], *s.* idiotie congénitale.

Amentiferae [æmen'tifəri:], *s.pl. Bot:* amentifères *m*.

amentiferous [æmen'tifərəs], *a. Bot:* amentifère.

amentiform [æ'mentifɔ:m], *a. Bot:* amentiforme.

amerce [ə'mə:s], *v.tr. A:* **1. to a. an estate to the Crown,** confisquer une terre au profit de la Couronne. **2.** mettre (qn) à l'amende; infliger une amende à qn; exiger une amende de qn; **to a. s.o. in a week's labour,** infliger huit jours de corvée à qn (en guise de réparation).

amercement [ə'mə:smənt], *s. A:* **1.** mise *f* à l'amende. **2.** amende *f*.

America [ə'merikə], *Pr.n. Geog:* Amérique *f*; **North A.,** Amérique du Nord; **South A.,** Amérique du Sud; **Latin A.,** Amérique latine.

American [ə'merik(ə)n]. **1.** *a.* (*a*) *Geog:* (i) américain; (ii) américain, des États-Unis; **North A.,** nord-américain, de l'Amérique du Nord; **South A.,** sud-américain, de l'Amérique du Sud; **A. Indian,** Amérindien, -ienne; (*b*) *Ling:* **A. English,** américain *m*; (*c*) **A. blight,** puceron *m* lanigère; **A. leopard,** jaguar *m*; **A. cloth,** toile cirée; **A. organ,** harmonium *m*. **2.** *s.* Américain, -aine; **North A.,** Nord-Américain, -aine; **South A.,** Sud-Américain, -aine; (*b*) *Ling:* américain *m*.

Americana [əmeri'kɑ:nə], *s.pl.* collection *f* de livres, documents, etc. au sujet de l'histoire et de la civilisation américaines.

Americanism [ə'merikənizm], *s. Ling: etc:* américanisme *m*.

Americanist [ə'merikənist], *s.* américaniste *mf*.

Americanization [əmerikənai'zeiʃ(ə)n], *s.* américanisation *f*.

Americanize [ə'merikənaiz]. **1.** *v.tr.* américaniser. **2.** *v.i.* s'américaniser.

americium [æmer'iʃiəm], *s. Ch:* américium *m*.

Amerigo Vespucci [æmə'ri:gouves'pu:tʃi], *Pr.n.m.* Améric Vespuce.

Amerind ['æmərind], *a. & s.*, **Amerindian** [æmər'indiən], *a. & s.*, **Amerindic** [æmər'indik], *a.* **1.** *a.* amérindien. **2.** *s.* Amérindien, -ienne.

amesace ['eimzeis], *s.* = AMBSACE.

Ametabola [æmi'tæbələ], *s.pl. Ent:* amétaboles *m*.

ametabolic [æmetə'bɔlik], **ametabolous** [eimi'tæbələs], *a. Ent:* amétabole.

amethyst ['æmiθist], *s.* améthyste *f*; **oriental a.,** saphir violet; **a. ring,** bague *f* d'améthyste; **the a. ring (of a bishop),** l'anneau d'améthyste.

amethystine [æmi'θistain], *a.* d'améthyste.

ametropia [æme'troupiə], *s. Med:* amétropie *f*.

Amharic [æm'hɑ:rik], *a. & s. Ling:* amharique (*m*).

amiability [eimiə'biliti], *s.* **1.** amabilité *f* (to, envers). **2.** **after a few amiabilities,** après quelques paroles aimables; après quelques amabilités.

amiable ['eimiəbl], *a.* aimable (to, envers); **to be most a.,** être d'une grande amabilité; **to make oneself a. to s.o.,** faire l'aimable auprès de qn.

aimiably ['eimiəbli], *adv.* aimablement; avec amabilité.

amiableness ['eimiəblnis], *s.* amabilité *f*.

amiantosis [æmiæn'tousis], *s. Med:* amiantose *f*, asbestose *f*.

amiant(h)us [æmi'æntəs, -θəs], *s. Miner:* amiante *m*.

amicability [æmikə'biliti], *s.* **1.** nature, disposition, amicale. **2.** concorde *f*; **a. being now restored,** la concorde étant dès lors rétablie.

amicable ['æmikəbl], *a.* **1.** (*of manner, etc.*) amical; (*of pers.*) bien disposé; **a. designs,** desseins *m* pacifiques; **a. relations,** relations amicales. **2.** amiable; (*a*) *Jur:* **a. settlement,** arrangement *m* à l'amiable; (*b*) *Mth:* (nombres) amiables.

amicably ['æmikəbli], *adv.* (i) amicalement; (ii) à l'amiable; **to live a. together,** vivre en harmonie; **to settle a matter a.,** s'arranger à l'amiable.

amicableness ['æmikəbəlnis], *s.* = AMICABILITY.

amice[1] ['æmis], *s. Ecc:* amict *m* (de prêtre).

amice[2], *s. Ecc:* aumusse *f*, aumuce *f* (de chanoine).

amicron [æ'maikrɔn], *s. Ph:* ultramicron *m*.

amid [ə'mid], *prep. Lit:* au milieu de; parmi; entre; **unseen a. the throng,** inaperçu au milieu de la foule.

amide ['æmaid], *s. Ch:* amide *f*.

amidic [ə'midik], *a. Ch:* amidique.

amidin(e) ['æmidin, -dain], *s. Ch:* amidine *f*.

amidogen [æ'midoudʒen], *s. Ch:* amidogène *m*.

amidol ['æmidɔl], *s. Phot:* amidol *m*.

amidopyrin [æmidou'pairin], *s. Pharm:* amidopyrine *f*.

amidoxime [æmi'dɔksim], *s. Ch:* amidoxime *f*.

amidships [ə'midʃips], *adv. Nau:* **1.** au milieu du navire; **cabin a.,** cabine *f* par le travers; **the boat parted a.,** le navire s'ouvrit par le milieu; *Aer:* **diameter a.,** diamètre *m* au maître-couple (d'un dirigeable). **2. to put the helm a.,** mettre la barre droite; **helm a.!** barre à zéro! zéro (la barre)!

amidst [ə'midst], *prep.* = AMID.

amimia [ə'mi:miə], *s. Med:* amimie *f*.

amination [æmi'neiʃ(ə)n], *s. Ch:* amination *f*.

amine ['æmin, ə'mi:n], *s. Ch:* amine *f*.

aminic [æ'minik], *a. Ch:* aminé.

amino- [ə'minou, ə'mi:nou], *pref. Ch:* amino-.

amino acid [æ'mi:nou'æsid, ə'mi:nou], *s. Ch:* aminoacide *m*, acide aminé.

aminoazo ['æminou'eizou, ə'mi:nou-], *a. Ch:* azoamidé, azoaminé.

aminobenzoic ['æminoubenzoik, ə'mi:nou-], *a. Ch:* aminobenzoïque.

aminophenol ['æminoufenɔl, ə'mi:nou-], *s. Ch:* aminophénol *m*.

aminoplast(ic) ['æminouplæst(ik), ə'minou-], *s. Ch:* aminoplaste *m*.

amir [ə'miər], *s.m.* émir.

Amish ['æmiʃ], *s. Rel:* Amish *m*.

amiss [ə'mis], *adv. & a.* **1.** (*wrongly*) mal, de travers; **to take sth. a.,** prendre qch. de travers, en mal, en mauvaise part; **he never takes anything a.,** il prend tout du bon côté; il ne se froisse jamais; **do not take these remarks a.,** il ne faut pas mal interpréter ces observations; **he took it very much a.,** il a très mal pris la chose. **2.** (*out of order*) mal à propos; **it would not be a. for you to . . .,** vous ne feriez pas mal de . . .; **that would not come a.,** cela n'arriverait pas mal (à propos); **nothing comes a. to him,** il s'arrange de tout; il fait feu de tout bois; *O:* **what's a. with you?** qu'avez-vous? qu'est-ce qui ne va pas? quelle mouche vous pique? **something is a.,** il y a quelque chose qui cloche; **nothing is a. (with the machine),** il n'y a rien de détraqué, rien qui cloche.

amissibility [əmisi'biliti], *s. Jur:* amissibilité *f*.

amissible [ə'misibl], *a. Jur:* amissible.

amitosis [æmi'tousis], *s. Biol:* amitose *f*.

amitotic [æmi'tɔtik], *a. Biol:* amitotique.

amity ['æmiti], *s.* amitié *f*, concorde *f*, bonne intelligence; **a. between two countries,** bons rapports, bonnes relations, entre deux pays; **to live in a. with s.o.,** vivre en amitié, en bonne intelligence, en paix, sur un pied d'amitié, avec qn; **treaty of a.,** traité *m* d'amitié; *A:* **our ancient amities,** nos relations amicales, qui datent de si loin; notre vieille amitié.

amixia [ei'miksiə], *s. Biol:* amixie *f*.

amman ['æmən], *s.* amman *m*.

ammeter ['æmitər], *s.* ampèremètre *m*; **dead-beat a.,** ampèremètre apériodique; **hot-wire a.,** ampèremètre thermique; **charging a.,** ampèremètre de courant de charge; **load a.,** ampèremètre de courant débité; **ironclad a.,** ampèremètre blindé; **moving-iron a.,** ampèremètre à fer mobile; **moving-coil a.,** ampèremètre à bobine mobile; **recording a.,** ampèremètre enregistreur.

ammiolite ['æmioulait], *s. Miner:* ammiolit(h)e *f*.

ammo ['æmou], *s. F:* = AMMUNITION.

ammobium [æ'moubiəm], *s. Bot:* ammobium *m*.

ammocoete ['æmousi:t], *s. Ich:* ammocète *m*.

ammodyte ['æmoudait], *s. Rept:* ammodyte *m*; *Ich:* ammodyte, lançon *m*.

ammonal ['æmənl], *s. Exp:* ammonal *m*.

Ammonea [æ'mouniə], *s.pl. Paleont:* ammonées *m*.

ammonia [ə'mouniə], *s. Ch:* ammoniaque *f*, gaz ammoniac; **a. alum,** alun ammoniacal; **a. hydrate, a. solution,** *F:* **ammonia,** (solution aqueuse d') ammoniaque; *F:* alcali volatil; **a. liquor, a. water,** eau ammoniacale.

ammoniac [ə'mouniæk]. **1.** *a.* ammoniac, -aque; **sal a.,** sel ammoniac. **2.** *s.* **(gum) a.,** gomme ammoniaque.

ammoniacal [æmou'naiəkl], *a.* ammoniacal, -aux.

ammoniate [ə'mounieit], *s.* **rough ammoniates,** ammoniacates bruts, déchets organo-azotés industriels, déchets (organiques) amminés.

ammoniated [ə'mounieitid], *a. Pharm: etc:* ammoniacé, ammoniaqué; **a. (tincture of) quinine,** (teinture de) quinine ammoniaquée.

ammonification [əmounifi'keiʃ(ə)n], *s.* ammonisation *f*.

ammonite ['æmənait], *s. Paleont:* ammonite *f*.

Ammonite[2], *s. A.Geog:* Ammonite *mf*.

Ammonitoidea [æməni'tɔidiə], *s.pl. Paleont:* ammonitidés *m*.

ammonium [ə'mouniəm], *s. Ch:* ammonium *m*; **a. hydrate,** (solution aqueuse d')ammoniaque *f*; **a. carbonate,** carbonate *m* d'ammoniaque; **a. chloride,** chlorure *m* d'ammonium; chlorhydrate *m* d'ammoniaque; **a. sulphate,** sulfate *m* d'ammoniaque; **a. hydroxide,** hydroxide *m* d'ammonium.

ammoniuria [əmouni'ju:riə], *s. Med:* ammoniurie *f*.

ammonization [əmouni'zeiʃ(ə)n], *s.* ammonisation *f*.

ammonoid ['æmənɔid], *s. Paleont:* ammonoïde *m*.

Ammonoidea ['æmənɔidiə], *s.pl. Paleont:* ammonoïdes *m*.

ammonolysis, *pl.* **-es** [æmə'nɔlisis, -i:z], *s. Ch:* ammoniolyse *f*.

ammophila [æ'mɔfilə], *s.* **1.** *Bot:* ammophile *f*. **2.** *Ent:* (guêpe *f*) ammophile *m*.

ammophilous [æ'mɔfiləs], *a. Nat.Hist:* ammophile.

ammunition [æmju'niʃ(ə)n], *s. Mil:* **1.** (*a*) munitions *fpl*; **service a.,** munitions de guerre; **emergency a.,** munitions de réserve; **training a.,** munitions d'instruction; **target-practice a.,** munitions d'exercice; **live a.,** munitions réelles, pour tir réel; **blank a.,** munitions à blanc; **dummy a.,** fausses munitions; **consumption, expenditure, of a.,** consommation *f* de munitions; **replenishment of a.,** recomplètement *m* en munitions; *Fig:* **to provide one's enemies with a.,** s'offrir en proie à l'opposition; (*b*) projectile *m*, cartouche *f*; **chambered a., fixed a.,** projectile complet, serti; **semi-fixed a.,** projectile en pièces séparées; **blank a.,** cartouche, obus *m*, à blanc; **dummy a.,** fausse cartouche, faux obus; **live a.,** cartouche réelle, obus réel. **2.** *attrib:* (*a*) à, de, munitions; **a. box,** coffre *m* à munitions; **a. chest, a. container,** caisse *f* à munitions; *Av:* **a. container,** conteneur *m* à munitions (pour parachutage); **a. carrier,** chenillette *f*, véhicule *m*, porte-munitions; **a. trailer,** remorque *f* porte-munitions; **a. waggon,** caisson *m* à munitions; **a. train,** (i) *Artil: etc:* train *m* de combat; (ii) *Rail:* train de munitions; **a. depot, a. dump,** dépôt *m* de munitions; **a. park,** parc *m* à munitions; **a. supply,** ravitaillement *m* en munitions; **a. supply column,** colonne *f* de ravitaillement en munitions; **a. supply point,** centre avancé de ravitaillement en munitions, point *m* de distribution des munitions; *Ind:* **a. factory,** usine *f* à munitions; (*b*) *Artil: etc:* (*in gun detachment*) **a. number,** pourvoyeur *m*; (*c*) *Navy:* **a. lighter,** bugalet *m*; (*d*) réglementaire; de l'intendance; *O:* de munition, d'ordonnance; **a. boots,** chaussures *f*, brodequins *m*, réglementaires, de l'intendance; **a. bread,** pain de l'intendance, de munition.

amnesia [æm'ni:ziə], *s. Med:* amnésie *f*.

amnesiac [æm'ni:ziæk], *s. Med:* amnésique *mf*.

amnesic [æm'ni:zik], *a.* amnésique.

amnesty[1] ['æmnisti], *s.* amnistie *f*; pardon collectif; **a. ordinance,** décret *m*, ordonnance *f*, d'amnistie; **to return to one's country under an a.,** rentrer dans sa patrie en vertu d'une amnistie.

amnesty[2], *v.tr.* amnistier.
amniography [æmni'ɔgrəfi], *s. Obst:* amniographie *f.*
amnion, *pl.* -ia ['æmniən, -iə], *s. Physiol:* amnios *m.*
amniorrh(o)ea [æmniɔ'riə], *s. Obst:* amniorrhée *f.*
amnios ['æmniɔs], *s.* 1. *Physiol: A:* = AMNION. 2. *Bot:* amnios *m.*
Amniota [æmni'outə], *s.pl. Z:* amniotes *m.*
amniote ['æmniout], *s. Z:* amniote *m.*
amniotic [æmni'ɔtik], *a. Anat:* amniotique; **a. fluid,** liquide *m* amniotique.
amoeba, *pl.* -as, -ae [ə'mi:bə, -əz, -i:], *s. Prot:* (*a*) amibe *f*; (*b*) *pl.* **Amoebae,** amibiens *mpl.*
amoebaean [æ'mi:biən], *a. Gr.Lit:* **a. verse,** vers *mpl* stichomythiques.
amoebiasis [əmi:bi'eisis], *s. Med:* amibiase *f.*
amoebic [ə'mi:bik], *a. Med:* amibien; **a. dysentery,** dysenterie amibienne.
amoebiform [ə'mi:bifɔ:m], *a.* amibiforme.
amoeboid [ə'mi:bɔid], *a.* amiboïde.
amok [ə'mʌk]. 1. *a.* amok. 2. *adv.* **to run a.,** (i) tomber dans une folie furieuse; (ii) *F:* devenir fou furieux; (iii) *F:* perdre son sang-froid; voir rouge. 3. *s.* amok *m.*
amomum [ə'moumǝm], *s. Bot:* amome *m.*
among [ə'mʌŋ], **amongst** [ə'mʌŋst], *prep.* NOTE: *though there is no clear distinction in meaning or use between the two words,* **among** *is the more normal, but* **amongst** *is used frequently before a vowel;* parmi, entre; (*a*) **house standing a. trees,** maison située au milieu des arbres, environnée d'arbres; **sitting a. her children,** assise au milieu de ses enfants; **to play a. the bushes,** jouer parmi les buissons; **to wander a. the ruins,** errer dans les ruines; **I caught sight of him a. the crowd,** je l'aperçus au milieu de la foule, parmi la foule; **someone sprang up from a. the crowd,** quelqu'un surgit de la foule; (*b*) **we are not a. savages,** nous ne sommes pas chez des sauvages; **to live a. savages,** vivre au milieu des sauvages; **we are a. friends,** nous sommes entre amis, en pays de connaissance; **this expression is current a. young people,** cette expression est courante chez les jeunes; *Lit:* **he fell a. thieves,** il tomba entre les mains des voleurs; (*c*) **to count s.o. a. one's friends,** mettre, compter, qn au nombre de ses amis; **numbered a. the dead,** compté parmi les morts, au nombre des morts; *Ecc:* **blessed art thou amongst women,** vous êtes bénie entre toutes les femmes; **several a. the audience heard it,** plusieurs d'entre les assistants l'ont entendu; **a. the guests were . . .,** au nombre des invités se trouvaient . . .; **a. them are several . . .,** parmi eux il y en a plusieurs . . .; *Sch:* **these papers are fair, but there are some good ones a. them,** ces compositions sont passables, mais il y en a de bonnes parmi elles, dans le nombre; **not one a. them,** pas un d'entre eux, parmi eux; **he is one a. many,** (i) il n'est pas le seul; (ii) il n'a pas son pareil; **he is one a. a thousand,** il est un entre mille; **a. other things he said that . . .,** il a dit entre autres que . . .; **a. his works will be found . . .,** parmi ses œuvres on trouvera . . .; (*d*) **nations divided a. themselves,** nations divisées entre elles; **£1000 to be divided a. them,** £1000 à partager entre eux; **they haven't ten pounds a. them,** à eux tous ils n'ont pas (même) une dizaine de livres; **they quarrel a. themselves,** ils se disputent entre eux; **you must agree a. yourselves,** il faut vous entendre entre vous; **do it a. you,** faites-le entre vous; **you have made a nice mess of it a. you,** à vous tous vous avez fait un beau gâchis.
amoral [ei'mɔrəl], *a.* amoral, -aux.
amoralism [ei'mɔrəlizm], *s.* amoralisme *m.*
amoralist [ei'mɔrəlist], *s.* amoraliste *mf.*
amorality [eimɔ'ræliti], *s.* amoralité *f.*
Amorites ['æmǝraits], *s.pl. B.Hist:* Amorrhéens *m.*
amorous ['æmərəs], *a.* 1. amoureux (**of s.o.,** de qn); porté vers l'amour; **an a. youth,** un jeune amoureux; **a. verse,** poésie *f* érotique. 2. **to be of an a. disposition,** être d'un tempérament amoureux; avoir un tempérament amoureux.
amorously ['æmərəsli], *adv.* amoureusement; avec amour.
amorousness ['æmərəsnis], *s.* tempérament amoureux.
amorphism [ə'mɔ:fizm], *s.* amorphie *f.*
amorphous [ə'mɔ:fəs], *a.* 1. *Biol: Ch: Geol: Miner:* amorphe. 2. (esprit) mal organisé; (opinions) sans forme; (projet) vague, amorphe.
amorphousness [ə'mɔ:fəsnis], *s.* état *m* amorphe; *Biol:* amorphie *f.*
amortizable [ə'mɔrtizəbl], *a.* amortissable.
amortization [əmɔ:ti'zeiʃ(ə)n], *s.* 1. *Com: Fin:* amortissement *m* (d'une dette, etc.); *Ind:* **a. quota,** cote *f,* taux *m,* d'amortissement. 2. *Jur:* aliénation *f* en mainmorte.
amortize [ə'mɔ:taiz], *v.tr.* 1. *Com: Fin:* amortir (une dette). 2. *Jur:* aliéner (une terre) en mainmorte.
amortizement [ə'mɔ:tizmənt]. 1. = AMORTIZATION. 2. *Arch:* amortissement *m.*
amount[1] [ə'maunt], *s.* 1. *Com:* somme *f,* montant *m,* total *m* (d'une facture, etc.); **have you the right a.?** avez-vous votre compte? **I haven't the exact a.,** je n'ai pas la monnaie; (*on bus, etc.*) **please tender the exact a.,** on est prié de faire l'appoint; donnez la monnaie juste, s'il vous plaît; **a. of expenses,** chiffre *m* de la dépense; **what is the a. of their turnover?** quel est leur chiffre d'affaires? **a. invested (in a company),** mise *f* de fonds; **amounts of stock negotiable,** quotités *fpl* de titres négociables; **(up) to the a. of. . .,** jusqu'à concurrence de . . .; *Book-k:* **a. brought in,** report *m* des exercices antérieurs; **a. carried forward,** report à nouveau. 2. (*a*) quantité *f*; **a. of work that an engine will do,** somme de travail que peut rendre, fournir, une machine; **in small amounts,** par petites quantités; **he drank a great a. of beer,** il buvait beaucoup de bière; **a greater a. of. . .,** une plus grande quantité de . . .; (*b*) *F:* **to spend any a. of money,** dépenser énormément d'argent; dépenser de l'argent à profusion; **he has any a. of money,** il a de l'argent tant et plus; **to make any a. of money,** ramasser de l'argent à la pelle; **we have any a. of books,** nous avons des livres en masse; (*c*) (*percentage*) teneur *f*; **a. of grease in a leather,** teneur en graisse d'un cuir. 3. *A:* valeur *f,* importance *f* (d'une affirmation, etc.); **these facts are of little a.,** ces faits ne signifient pas grand'chose.
amount[2], *v.i.* 1. (*of money, etc.*) s'élever, (se) monter (to, à); *Com:* **the stocks a. to so much,** les stocks s'élèvent à tant, atteignent tant; **transactions amounting to several million pounds,** opérations qui se chiffrent par plusieurs millions de livres; **his fortune did not a. to ten thousand pounds,** sa fortune n'allait pas à dix mille livres; **I don't know what my debts a. to,** j'ignore le montant de mes dettes. 2. (*be equivalent*) équivaloir, se réduire, revenir, se résumer, se borner, se ramener (to, à); **these conditions a. to a refusal,** ces conditions équivalent à un refus; **this is what his argument amounts to,**voici à quoi se réduit son raisonnement; **it amounts to the same thing,** cela revient au même, *F:* c'est tout comme; **it amounts to this, that . . .,** cela revient à dire que . . .; **this doesn't a. to saying that . . .,** cela ne va pas à dire que . . .; **all that amounts to very little, to nothing,** tout cela a peu d'importance, ne signifie pas grand'chose, se réduit à rien; *F:* **he'll never a. to much,** il ne sera, ne fera, jamais grand-chose; il ne fera jamais parler de lui.
amour [ə'muər], *s. usu. Pej:* intrigue galante.
amour propre ['æmuə'prɔpr], *s.* amour-propre *m.*
amp [æmp], *s. El.Meas: F:* ampère *m.*
Ampelidaceae [æmpeli'deisii:], *s.pl. Bot:* ampélidacées *f.*
Ampelidae [æm'pelidi:], *s.pl. Orn:* ampélidés *m.*
ampelite ['æmpilait], *s. Miner:* ampélite *m.*
ampelography [æmpi'lɔgrəfi], *s. Vit:* ampélographie *f.*
ampelopsis [æmpi'lɔpsis], *s. Bot:* ampélopsis *m.*
amperage ['æmpəridʒ], *s. El:* ampérage *m.*
ampere ['æmpεər], *s. El.Meas:* ampère *m.*
ampere-hour ['æmpεər'auər], *s.* (*pl.* **ampere-hours**) ampère(-)heure *m, pl.* ampères-heures, ampèreheures.
ampere meter ['æmpεəmi:tər], *s. A:* = AMMETER.
ampere turn ['æmpεə'tə:n], *s.* ampère(-)tour *m, pl.* ampère(-)tours.
ampersand ['æmpəsænd], *s. Typ:* et *m* commercial.
amphetamine [æm'fetəmin, -main]. *Pharm:* (*a*) *s.* amphétamine *f*; (*b*) *attrib.* amphétaminique.
amphi- ['æmfi], *pref.* amphi-.
amphiarthrosis [æmfiɑ:θrousis], *s. Anat:* amphiarthrose *f.*
amphiaster ['æmfiæstər], *s. Biol:* amphiaster *m.*
Amphibia [æm'fibiə], *s.pl. Z:* amphibiens *m*; **tailed A.,** urodèles *m*; **tailless A.,** anoures *m.*
amphibian [æm'fibiən], *a. & s.* 1. *Z:* amphibie (*m*). 2. *Trans:* (voiture *f,* etc.) amphibie (*m*).
amphibiotic [æmfibai'ɔtik], *a. Ent:* amphibiotique.
Amphibiotica [æmfibai'ɔtikə], *s.pl. Ent:* amphibiotiques *m.*
amphibious [æm'fibiəs], *a.* amphibie.
amphibiousness [æm'fibiəsnis], *s.* nature *f* amphibie.
amphiblastula [æmfi'blæstjulə], *s. Biol:* amphiblastula *f.*
amphibola [æm'fibələ], *s. Moll:* amphibola *f.*
amphibole ['æmfiboul], *s. Miner:* amphibole *f.*
amphibolic[1] [æmfi'bɔlik], *a. Geol:* amphibolique.
amphibolic[2], *a. Med: etc:* amphibole.
amphibolite [æm'fibəlait], *s. Miner:* amphibolite *f.*
amphibological [æmfibə'lɔdʒikl], *a.* amphibologique.
amphibologically [æmfibə'lɔdʒikəli], *adv.* amphibologiquement.
amphibology [æmfi'bɔlədʒi], *s.* amphibologie *f.*
amphibrach ['æmfibræk], *a. & s. Pros:* amphibraque (*m*).
amphicarpic [æmfi'kɑ:pik], *a. Bot:* amphicarpe.
amphicoelous [æmfi'si:ləs], *a. Z: Anat:* amphicœle, amphcœlien, amphicœlique.
Amphictyon [æm'fiktiən], *s. Gr.Hist:* amphictyon *m.*
amphictyonic [æmfikti'ɔnik], *a. Gr.Hist:* (conseil *m*) amphictyonique.
amphictyony [æm'fiktiəni], *s.* amphictyonie *f.*
amphidiploid [æmfi'diplɔid], *a. Biol:* amphidiploïde.
amphidisc ['æmfidisk], *s. Spong:* amphidisque *m.*
amphidromic [æmfi'droumik], *a. Oc:* amphidrome.
amphigam ['æmfigæm], *s. Bot:* amphigame *m.*
amphigamous [æm'figəməs], *a. Bot:* amphigame.
amphigastrium, *pl.* -ia [æmfi'gæstriəm, -iə], *s. Bot:* amphigastre *m.*
amphigenous [æm'fidʒənəs], *a. Bot: etc:* amphigène.
amphigoric [æmfi'gɔrik], *a.* amphigourique.
amphigory ['æmfigəri], **amphigouri** [æmfi'guəri], *s.* amphigouri *m.*
amphimacer [æm'fiməsər], *s. Pros:* amphimacre *m,* crétique *m.*
amphimixis [æmfi'miksis], *s. Biol:* amphimixie *f.*
Amphineura [æmfi'nju:rə], *s.pl. Moll:* amphineures *m.*
amphioxus [æmfi'ɔksəs], *s. Z:* amphioxus *m.*
amphipneustic [æmfi'(p)nju:stik], *a. Amph:* amphipneuste.
amphipod ['æmfipɔd], *s. Crust:* amphipode *m.*
Amphipoda [æm'fipədə], *s.pl. Crust:* amphipodes *m.*
amphipodan [æm'fipədən], *a. & s.* amphipode.
amphipodous [æm'fipədəs], *a.* amphipode.
amphiprostyle [æmfi'proustail], *a. & s. Arch:* amphiprostyle (*m*).
amphisarca [æmfi'sɑ:kə], *s. Bot:* amphisarque *m.*
amphisbaena [æmfiz'bi:nə], *s. Myth: Rept: Her:* amphisbène *m.*
Amphisbaenidae [æmfis'bi:nidi:], *s.pl. Rept:* amphisbaenidés *m,* amphisbénidés *m.*
amphiscian [æm'fiʃ(ə)n], *s. Geog:* amphiscien *m.*
amphistome ['æmfistoum], *s. Ann:* amphistome *m.*
amphitheatre ['æmfiθiətər], *s. Arch: Th: etc:* amphithéâtre *m*; **the mountains formed an a.,** les montagnes s'élevaient en amphithéâtre.
amphitheatrical [æmfiθi'ætrikl], *a.* (combat, spectacle) d'amphithéâtre; amphithéâtral, -aux.
Amphitryon [æm'fitriən]. 1. *Pr.n.m. Myth:* Amphitryon. 2. *s.m. A:* (*from Molière's play,* Amphitryon) Amphitryon, hôte.
amphiuma [æmfi'ju:mə], *s. Amph:* amphiume *m,* amphiuma *m.*
Amphiumidae [æmfi'ju:midi:], *s.pl. Amph:* amphiumidés *m.*
ampholyte ['æmfəlait], *s. Ch:* ampholyte *m.*
amphora, *pl.* -ae ['æmfərə, -i:], *s.* amphore *f.*
amphoric [æm'fɔrik], *a. Med:* (respiration, toux) amphorique.
amphoteric [æmfə'terik], *a. Ch:* amphotère.
ample ['æmpl], *a.* (*a*) (*large, roomy*) **an a. garment,** un ample, large, vêtement; **man of a. proportions,** homme corpulent; (*b*) (*abundant, more than enough*) **a. resources,** d'abondantes ressources; **to have a. means,** avoir de la fortune; **he has a. means for building,** il a largement les moyens de bâtir, de construire; **they have had a. opportunities for doing it,** ils ont eu de nombreuses occasions de le faire; **an a. supply of coal, a. coal, for the winter,** largement assez de charbon pour l'hiver; **she has a. material to make a dress,** elle a largement assez, bien assez, de tissu pour faire une robe; **a. proof,** preuve évidente; **I have a. reason to think that . . .,** j'ai de fortes raisons de penser que . . .; (*c*) (*enough*) **to have a. time (to do sth.),** avoir amplement, grandement, largement, le temps (de faire qch.); **fifty pence should be a. pocket money for a boy of his age,** cinquante pence d'argent de poche devrait suffire à un garçon de son âge.
ampleness ['æmpəlnis], *s.* ampleur *f,* abondance *f* (de ressources).
amplexicaudate [æmpleksi'kɔ:deit], *a. Z:* amplexicaude.
amplexicaul [æm'pleksikɔ:l], *a. Bot:* amplexicaule, embrassant.
amplexifoliate [æmpleksi'foulieit], *a. Bot:* amplexifolié.
amplexus [æm'pleksəs], *s. Amph:* amplexus *m.*
ampliation [æmpli'eiʃ(ə)n], *s.* 1. ampliation *f.* 2. *Jur:* (*a*) remise *f,* ajournement *m* (d'un procès criminel); (*b*) prorogation *f* de délai.
ampliative ['æmplieitiv], *a. Log:* ampliatif; **a. inference,** induction amplifiante.
amplidyne ['æmplidain], *s. El:* amplidyne *m.*
amplification [æmplifi'keiʃ(ə)n], *s.* 1. augmentation *f,* extension *f*; **he added some details in a. of his report,** il

aujouta des détails supplémentaires à son compte rendu; *Gram:* **a. of the predicate,** extension de l'attribut. **2.** *Opt:* grossissement *m* (d'une lentille, etc.). **3.** amplification *f*; *Elcs:* **energy, power, a.,** amplification de puissance; **linear a.,** amplification linéaire; *W.Tel:* **low-frequency, audio-frequency, a.,** amplification à basse fréquence; **high-frequency, radio-frequency, a.,** amplification à haute fréquence; *El:* **voltage a.,** amplification de tension; *attrib:* **a. constant,** constante *f* d'amplification; **a. factor,** coefficient *m* d'amplification.

amplifier ['æmplifaiər], *s.* **1.** (*a*) *Phot:* (lentille) amplificatrice *f*; (*b*) *Artil:* **torque a.,** amplificateur de couple; (*c*) *Med:* **ear a.,** amplificateur contre la surdité. **2.** *El: Elcs: W.Tel:* (*a*) **balanced a.,** amplificateur compensé; **feed-back a.,** amplificateur à réaction; **negative feed-back a.,** amplificateur à contre-réaction; **high-frequency, radio-frequency, a.,** amplificateur haute fréquence; **low-frequency, audio-frequency, a.,** amplificateur basse fréquence; **high-gain a.,** amplificateur à gain élevé; **linear a.,** amplificateur linéaire; **multi-channel, multi-way, a.,** amplificateur à plusieurs voies; **multi-range a.,** amplificateur à plusieurs sensibilités; **multi-stage, cascade, a.,** amplificateur à plusieurs étages, en cascade; **one-stage a.,** amplificateur à un étage; **two-stage, three-stage, etc., a.,** amplificateur à deux, trois, etc., étages; **push-pull a.,** amplificateur push-pull, à montage symétrique; **resonance, tuned, a.,** amplificateur à résonance; **transistor a.,** amplificateur à transistors; **direct-coupled a.,** amplificateur à liaison directe; (*b*) **booster, power, a.,** amplificateur de puissance; **chopper a.,** (amplificateur) hacheur *m*; **input a.,** amplificateur d'entrée; pré-amplificateur *m*; **pulse a.,** amplificateur d'impulsions; **relay a.,** amplificateur relais; **shut-down a.,** amplificateur de sécurité; **voltage a.,** amplificateur de tension; **wash-out a.,** amplificateur d'effacement; *T.V:* **stabilising a.,** amplificateur de stabilisation, stabilisateur *m*; **video a.,** ampli(ficateur) vidéo; (*c*) *attrib.* **a. chain,** chaîne *f* d'amplificateurs; **a. circuit,** circuit *m* d'amplification; **a. noise,** bruit *m,* souffle *m,* d'amplification; **a. output,** puissance *f* de sortie d'un amplificateur; **a. tube,** lampe amplificatrice.

amplify ['æmplifai]. **1.** *v.tr.* (*a*) amplifier (un exposé, etc.); ajouter des détails à (un rapport, etc.); **to a. knowledge,** étendre, développer, ses connaissances; (*b*) *El:* amplifier (le courant). **2.** *v.i. O:* discourir.

amplifying ['æmplifaiiŋ], amplificateur, -trice; amplificatif; *W.Tel:* **a. stage,** étage amplificateur; *Log:* **a. proposition,** proposition ampliative.

amplitude ['æmplitju:d], *s.* **1.** (*a*) amplitude *f*; étendue *f* (de l'espace); ampleur *f* (des dimensions, des ressources, etc.); *Pol.Ec:* **a. ratio of seasonal variations,** rapport *m* d'amplitude des mouvements saisonniers; (*b*) *Astr:* **western, occiduous, a. of a star,** amplitude occase d'un astre; **ortive a.,** amplitude ortive; (*c*) *Ph:* **a. of oscillations, of vibrations,** amplitude des oscillations, des vibrations; **peak-to-peak a.,** amplitude de crête à crête (d'un mouvement ondulatoire); *Atom.Ph:* **scattering a.,** amplitude de diffusion; **a. analyser,** analyseur *m* d'amplitude; **magnetic a.,** déclinaison *f* magnétique; amplitude; *Elcs: etc:* **a. characteristic,** courbe *f* de réponse; **a. distortion,** distortion *f* harmonique, d'amplitude; **a. limiter,** écrêteur *m* (d'onde); **a. modulation,** modulation *f* d'amplitude; **a. modulated,** modulé en amplitude; (*d*) **tidal a.,** amplitude de marée; *Nau:* **a. of pitch, of roll,** amplitude du tangage, du roulis; (*e*) **a. of accommodation,** amplitude d'accommodation (de l'œil). **2.** *Lit:* abondance *f*, ampleur (de style, etc.).

amply ['æmpli], *adv.* amplement, grandement; largement (récompensé).

ampoule ['æmpu:l], *s. Med:* ampoule *f.*

ampulla, *pl.* **-ae** [æm'pulə, -i:], *s.* **1.** (*flask*) ampoule *f.* **2.** *Anat:* ampoule (d'un canal).

ampullaceal [æmpu'leisiəl], *a. Bot:* ampullacé.

ampullaceous [æmpu'leiʃəs], *a.* (*a*) en forme d'ampoule; *esp.* (*b*) *Bot:* ampullacé.

ampullar ['æmpulər], **ampullary** [æm'puləri], *a.* ampullaire.

Ampullariidae [æmpuləri'i:di:], *s.pl. Moll:* ampullariidés *m.*

amputate ['æmpjuteit], *v.tr.* amputer, faire l'amputation de (la jambe, etc.); **his right leg was amputated,** il a été amputé, il a subi l'amputation, de la jambe droite.

amputation [æmpju'teiʃ(ə)n], *s. Surg:* amputation *f*; **flap a.,** amputation à lambeaux; **a. through a bone,** amputation dans la continuité; **a. through a joint,** amputation dans la contiguïté, dans l'article; désarticulation *f.*

amputator ['æmpjuteitər], *s.* opérateur, -trice (d'une amputation).

amputee [æmpju'ti:], *s.* amputé, -ée.

amtrack ['æmtræk], *s. Veh: Mil:* véhicule chenillé amphibie; amtrack *m.*

amuck [ə'mʌk], *a. & adv.* = AMOK.

amulet ['æmjulet], *s.* amulette *f.*

amusable [ə'mju:zəbl], *a.* amusable.

amuse [ə'mju:z], *v.tr.* (*a*) amuser, divertir, égayer, faire rire (qn); **he must be amused,** il faut le distraire; **hard to a.,** difficilement amusable; **to a. oneself,** s'amuser, se divertir; **to a. oneself by, with, doing sth.,** s'amuser, se récréer, à faire qch., en faisant qch.; **to a. oneself with sth.,** s'amuser avec qch.; **to keep the company amused (before main event),** amuser le tapis; **try to keep the audience amused for another ten minutes,** tâchez d'amuser le public encore dix minutes; (*b*) *A:* **to a. the enemy,** amuser l'ennemi; tromper la vigilance de l'ennemi.

amused [ə'mju:zd], *a.* amusé; diverti; **to be a. at, by, sth.,** être amusé de qch.; s'amuser de qch.; **I was a. at him,** il m'a fait rire; **we were greatly a. by it,** nous en avons beaucoup ri.

amusedly [ə'mju:zidli], *adv.* avec amusement; en riant.

amusement [ə'mju:zmənt], *s.* **1.** amusement *m*; (*a*) divertissement *m*; **place of a.,** lieu *m* de divertissement; **this gave me a great deal of a.,** cela m'a beaucoup amusé; cela m'a fort diverti; **smile of a.,** sourire amusé; **to the great a. of the company,** au grand amusement de la compagnie; (*b*) distraction *f*; **we have few amusements here,** nous avons ici peu de distractions; **to do sth. for a.,** faire qch. par jeu, par amusement, pour son amusement, pour se distraire; **a. park,** parc *m* d'attractions. **2. money for one's amusements,** argent pour ses menus plaisirs.

amuser [ə'mju:zər], *s.* amuseur, -euse.

amusia [æ'mju:ziə], *s. Med:* amusie *f*; **sensory a.,** tonaphasie *f.*

amusing [ə'mju:ziŋ], *a.* amusant, divertissant; **highly a.,** désopilant; **the a. part of the business, the a. thing about it, is that . . .,** le plus beau, le plaisant, de l'affaire c'est que . . .; *Iron:* **how a.!** comme c'est amusant!

amusingly [ə'mju:ziŋli], *adv.* d'une manière amusante, divertissante.

Amy ['eimi], *Pr.n.f.* Aimée.

Amygdalaceae [æmigdə'leisii:], *s.pl. Bot:* amygdalées *f.*

amygdale ['æmigdæl], *s. Geol:* amygdale *f.*

amygdalectomy [æmigdə'lektəmi], *s. Surg:* amygdalectomie *f.*

amygdalic [æmig'dælik], *a.* **1.** = AMYGDALINE. **2.** *Ch:* amygdalique.

amygdalin [æ'migdəlin], *s. Ch:* amygdaline *f.*

amygdaline [ə'migdəlain], *a.* amygdalin; qui a rapport aux amygdales.

amygdaloid [æ'migdəlɔid], *a. & s. Geol:* amygdaloïde (*f*).

amygdule [æ'migdju:l], *s. Geol:* amygdale *f.*

amyl ['æmil], *s. Ch:* amyle *m*; **a. acetate,** acétate *m* d'amyle; **a. alcohol,** alcool *m* amylique.

amylaceous [æmi'leiʃəs], *a.* amylacé.

amylase ['æmileiz], *s. Ch:* amylase *f.*

amylene ['æmili:n], *s. Ch:* amylène *m.*

amylic [ə'milik], *a. Ch:* amylique.

amylin(e) ['æmilin, -lain], *s.* amyline *f.*

amylobacter [æmilou'bæktər], *s. Bac:* amylobacter *m.*

amyloid ['æmilɔid], *a. & s. Bio-Ch:* amyloïde (*f*); *Med:* **a. degeneration,** maladie *f* amyloïde; dégénérescence *f* amyloïde; dégénérescence cireuse, lardacée; amylose *f.*

amyloidosis [æmilɔi'dousis], *s. Med:* amylose *f.*

amylolysis [æmi'lɔlisis], *s. Bio-Ch:* amylolyse *f.*

amylolytic [æmilou'litik], *a. Bio-Ch:* amylolytique.

amylopectin [æmilou'pektin], *s. Bio-Ch:* amylopectine *f.*

amyloplast ['æmilouplɑ:st], *s. Bot:* amyloplaste *m,* amyloleucite *m,* leucoplaste *m.*

amylose ['æmilous], *s. Ch:* amylose *m.*

amyotrophia [æmiou'troufiə], **amyotrophy** [æmiou'troufi], *s. Med:* amyotrophie *f.*

an [æn], *conj.A:* (*a*) et; (*b*) si; **an it please your Majesty,** s'il plaît à votre Majesté.

an- [æn], *pref.* an-.

ana ['ɑ:nə], *s. Lit.Hist:* ana *m*; **to collect anas,** recueillir des ana.

ana- ['ænə], *pref.* ana-.

anabaena [ænə'bi:nə], *s. Bot:* sphérozyge *m.*

anabantid [ænə'bæntid], *a. & s. Ich:* anabante (*m*).

anabaptism [ænə'bæptizm], *s. Rel.H:* anabaptisme *m.*

anabaptist [ænə'bæptist], *a. & s. Rel.H:* anabaptiste (*mf*).

anabaptistical [ænəbæp'tistikl], *a.* anabaptiste.

anabas ['ænəbæs], *s. Ich:* anabas *m.*

anabasis, *pl.* **-es** [ə'næbəsis, -i:z], *s.* **1.** *Mil.Hist:* anabase *f,* avance *f*; *Gr.Lit:* **the A. (of Xenophon),** l'Anabase (de Xénophon). **2.** *Med:* anabase. **3.** *Bot:* anabase.

anabatic [ænə'bætik], *a. Meteor:* (vent) anabatique.

anabiosis [ænəbai'ousis], *s. Biol:* anabiose *f.*

anableps ['ænəbleps], *s. Ich:* anableps *m.*

anabolic [ænə'bɔlik], *a. Biol:* anabolique.

anabolism [ə'næbəlizm], *s. Biol;* anabolisme *m.*

anabranch ['ænəbrɑ:ntʃ], *s. Geog: esp. Austr:* bras anastomosé (d'une rivière).

anacamptic [ænə'kæmptik], *a.* anacamptique.

anacard ['ænəkɑ:d], *s. Bot:* anacarde *m.*

Anacardiaceae [ænəkɑ:di'eisii:], *s.pl. Bot:* térébinthacées *f.*

anacardium [ænə'kɑ:diəm], *s. Bot:* anacardier *m.*

anacathartic [ænəkæ'θɑ:tik], *a. Med:* anacathartique.

anachromatic [ænəkrou'mætik], *a. Opt: Phot:* (objectif) anachromatique.

anachronism [ə'nækrənizm], *s.* anachronisme *m.*

anachronistic [ənækrə'nistik], *a.* anachronique; **a. errors,** fautes *f* d'anachronisme.

anachronistically [ənækrə'nistik(ə)li], *adv.* anachroniquement.

anaclastic [ænə'klæstik], *a. Opt:* (courbe) anaclastique.

anaclitic [ænə'klitik], *a. Psy:* anaclitique.

anacoluthon, *pl.* **-a** [ænəkou'lju:θɔn, -ə], *s. Gram:* anacoluthe *f.*

anaconda [ænə'kɔndə], *s. Rept:* anaconda *m,* eunecte *m.*

Anacreon [ə'nækriən], *Pr.n.m.* Anacréon.

Anacreontic [ənækri'ɔntik], *a.* anacréontique.

anacrusis, *pl.* **-es** [ænə'kru'sis, -i:z], *s. Pros: Mus:* anacrouse *f,* anacruse *f.*

anacyclus [ænəsaikləs], *s. Bot:* anacycle *m.*

anadiplosis [ænədi'plousis], *s. Rh:* anadiplose *f.*

anadromous [ə'nædrəməs], *a.* (poisson) anadrome.

Anadyomene [ænədai'ɔmini], *a. Myth:* (Vénus) Anadyomène *f.*

anaemia [ə'ni:miə], *s.* anémie *f*; **pernicious a.,** anémie pernicieuse progressive; **hypoferric, iron-deficiency, a.,** anémie ferriprive; **cerebral a.,** anémie cérébrale; **miner's a.,** anémie des mineurs, ankylostomiase *f.*

anaemic [ə'ni:mik], *a.* (*a*) *Med:* anémique; **to become a.,** s'anémier; (*b*) faible, sans énergie; **a. literature,** littérature *f* exsangue.

anaerobe, *pl.* **-ia** [æ'nεəroub, -iə], *s. Bac:* anaérobie *f.*

anaerobic [ænεə'roubik], *a.* anaérobie; *Mec.E:* **a. engine,** (i) moteur *m,* réacteur *m,* anaérobie; (ii) moteur à réaction pure, réacteur pur.

anaerobiont [æ'nεəroubaiɔnt], *s. Bac:* anaérobie *f.*

anaerobiosis, *pl.* **-es** [ænεəroubai'ousis, -i:z], *s.* anaérobiose *f.*

anaerobiotic [ænεəroubai'ɔtik], *a.* anaérobie.

anaesthesia [ænəs'θi:ziə], *s.* anesthésie *f*; **general, local, a.,** anesthésie générale, locale; **spinal a.,** anesthésie rachidienne

anaesthesiologist [ænəsθi:zi'ɔlədʒist], *s.* anesthésiologiste *mf.*

anaesthesiology [ænəsθi:zi'ɔlədʒi], *s.* anesthésiologie *f.*

anaesthesis [ænəs'θi:sis], *s.* anasthécinésie *f.*

anaesthetic [ænis'θetik], *a. & s.* anesthésique (*m*); anesthésiant *m*; **under the a.,** sous l'effet *m* de l'anesthésique.

anaesthetist [ə'ni:sθətist], *s.* anesthésiste *mf.*

anaesthetization [əni:sθətai'zeiʃ(ə)n], *s. Med:* administration *f* d'un anesthésique; insensibilisation *f.*

anaesthetize [ə'ni:sθətaiz], *v.tr. Med:* anesthésier; insensibiliser.

anagallis [ænə'gælis], *s. Bot:* anagallide *f,* anagallis *f.*

anagenesis [ænə'dʒenisis], *s.* anagénèse *f.*

anaglyph ['ænəglif], *s.* anaglyphe *m.*

anaglyphic [ænə'glifik], **anaglyptique** [ænə'gliptik], *a.* anaglyphique, anaglyptique.

anagoge ['ænəgɔdʒi], *s. Theol:* anagogie *f.*

anagogic(al) [ænə'gɔdʒik(l)], *a. Theol:* anagogique.

anagogy ['ænəgɔdʒi], *s. Theol:* anagogie *f.*

anagram ['ænəgræm], *s.* anagramme *f.*

anagrammatic(al) [ænəgrə'mætik(l)], *a.* anagrammatique.

anagrammatically [ænəgrə'mætik(ə)li], *adv.* anagrammatiquement; par l'entremise d'une anagramme.

anagrammatist [ænə'græmətist], *s.* anagrammatiste *mf*; faiseur, -euse, d'anagrammes.

anagrammatize [ænə'græmətaiz], *v.tr.* anagrammatiser.

anagyris [ænə'dʒairis], *s. Bot:* anagyre *m.*

Anak ['einæk], *Pr.n.m. B.Lit:* Hanak; *Lit:* **a son of A.,** un géant.

anal ['einl], *a. Anat:* anal, -aux; *Z:* **a. glands,** glandes anales; *Ich:* **a. fin,** nageoire anale; *Ent:* **a. appendages,** cerques *m.*

analcime ['ænælsaim], **analcite** ['ænælsait], *s. Miner:*

analcime *f*, analcite *f*.

analecta [ænə'lektə], **analects** ['ænəlekts], *s.pl. Lit:* analectes *m*.

analemma [ænə'lemə], *s. Mth: Astr:* analemme *m*; planisphère *m*.

analeptic [ænə'leptik], *a. & s. Med:* analeptique (*m*).

analgesia [ænæl'dʒi:ziə], *s. Med:* analgésie *f*, analgie *f*.

analgesic [ænæl'dʒi:sik, -zik], **analgetic** [ænæl'dʒetik], *a. & s. Med:* analgésique (*m*); anodin (*m*).

anallagmatic [ænælæg'mætik], *a. Mth:* anallagmatique; **a. curve,** anallagmatique *f*.

Anallantoidea [ænælæn'tɔidiə], *s.pl. Ich: Amph:* anallantoïdiens *m*.

anallatic [ænə'lætik], *a. Surv:* (lunette *f*) anallatique.

anallatism [æ'nælətizm], *s.* anallatisme *m*.

analog ['ænəlɔg], *a. & s. esp. NAm:* = ANALOGUE.

analogical [ænə'lɔdʒikl], *a.* analogique.

analogically [ænə'lɔdʒik(ə)li], *adv.* analogiquement; par analogie.

analogism [ə'nælədʒizm], *s.* analogisme *m*.

analogist [ə'nælədʒist], *s.* analogiste *mf*.

analogize [ə'nælədʒaiz]. **1.** *v.tr* (*a*) représenter, expliquer, (qch.) par analogie; (*b*) **to a. sth. with sth.,** établir, trouver, découvrir, une analogie entre qch. et qch. **2.** *v.i.* (*a*) (*of pers.*) raisonner par analogie; (*b*) (*of thg*) **to a. with sth.,** avoir, offrir, présenter, de l'analogie avec qch.

analogous [ə'næləgəs], *a.* analogue (to, with, à).

analogously [ə'næləgəsli], *adv.* d'une manière analogue (**to, with,** à).

analogue ['ænəlɔg], *s.* analogue *m*; *Cmptr:* **a. computer,** calculateur *m*, calculatrice *f*, analogique; **a./digital, a.-to-digital converter,** convertisseur *m* analogique-numérique (*pl.* analogiques-numériques); codeur *m* analogique-digital (*pl.* analogiques-digitaux); **a. adder,** additionneur *m* analogique; **a. network, channel,** réseau *m*, voie *f*, analogique; **a. representation,** représentation *f* analogique.

analogy [ə'nælədʒi], *s.* analogie *f* (**to, with,** avec; **between,** entre); **to argue from a.,** raisonner par analogie; **argument by, from, a.,** analogisme *m*; **on the a. of . . . by a. with . . .,** par analogie avec. . . .

analphabet [ænælfəbet], *a. & s.* analphabète (*mf*).

analphabetic [ænælfə'betik], *a.* analphabète.

analysable ['ænəlaizəbl], *a.* analysable.

analyse ['ænəlaiz], *v.tr.* **1.** *esp. Ch: Mth: etc:* analyser; faire l'analyse de (qch.); *Com:* **to a. an account,** dépouiller, décomposer, un compte; *Gram:* **to a. a sentence,** analyser une phrase, faire l'analyse logique d'une phrase. **2.** *Psy:* psychanalyser.

analyser ['ænəlaizər], *s.* **1.** (*pers.*) celui, celle, qui analyse (une idée, une émotion, etc.); *Pej:* analyseur *m*. **2.** (*apparatus*) (*a*) *Ph:* **high-sensitive a.,** analyseur à sensibilité élevée; **mass, speed, a.,** analyseur de masse, de vitesse; *Ac:* **harmonic a.,** analyseur harmonique, d'harmoniques; **sound a.,** analyseur de son; **vibration a.,** analyseur de vibration; *Ph: Elcs:* **frequency a.,** analyseur de fréquence; **wave a.,** analyseur d'onde; *Atom.Ph:* **multi-channel a.,** analyseur à plusieurs canaux; **60-channel a.,** analyseur à 60 canaux; **pulse-amplitude a.,** analyseur d'amplitude (d'impulsions); **time a.,** analyseur de temps, de minutage (d'impulsions); (*b*) *Opt:* analyseur (de polariscope, etc.); **spectrum a.,** appareil *m* pour analyse spectrale, analyseur de spectre; (*c*) *Av:* **flight a.,** analyseur de vol; (*d*) *Ind:* **exhaust-gas, flue-gas, a.,** analyseur de gaz d'échappement, de gaz de combustion; *Petr:* **viscosity a.,** analyseur de viscosité; *Hyd.E: Mec.E:* **delivery-rate, flow, a.,** analyseur de débit; (*e*) *Cmptr:* (i) analyseur; (ii) programme *m* d'analyse; **network a.,** analyseur de réseau, simulateur *m* (d'étude) de réseaux; **digital, electronic, differential a.,** analyseur différentiel numérique, électronique.

analysis, *pl.* **-es** [ə'næləsis, -i:z], *s.* analyse *f*; (*a*) *Ch:* **qualitative a.,** analyse qualitative; **quantitative a.,** analyse quantitative; dosage *m*; **volumetric a.,** analyse volumétrique; **proximate, ultimate, a.,** analyse immédiate, élémentaire; **wet, dry, a.,** analyse par voie humide, sèche; **check a.,** analyse contradictoire; (*b*) *Ph:* **physical a.,** analyse physique; **dimensional a.,** analyse dimensionnelle; **harmonic a.,** analyse harmonique (d'une forme d'onde); **spectral a., spectrum a.,** analyse spectrale; **spectrographic, spectroscopic, a.,** analyse spectrographique, spectroscopique; (*c*) *Meteor:* **master a.,** analyse maîtresse; **advisory a.,** analyse auxiliaire, bulletin *m* analytique d'orientation; **surface a.,** analyse en surface; **upper air a.,** analyse en altitude; **main a. centre,** centre *m* d'analyse principal; **subsidiary a. centre,** centre d'analyse secondaire, sous-centre *m*, *pl.* sous-centres, d'analyse; (*d*) **mathematical a.,** analyse mathématique; **numerical a.,** analyse numérique, calcul *m* numérique; **differential a.,** analyse différentielle; **parametric a.,** analyse paramétrique; **transcendental a.,** analyse transcendante; *Mec:* **stress a.,** calcul de résistance, analyse des efforts supportés (par une pièce mécanique, etc.); *Cmptr: etc:* **systems a.,** analyse fonctionnelle; **critical path a.,** analyse de chemin critique; **operations a.,** recherche opérationnelle; **sequential a.,** analyse séquentielle; (*e*) *Com: Pol.Ec:* **a. of an account,** dépouillement *m*, décomposition *f*, d'un compte; **economic a.,** analyse économique; **statistical a.,** analyse statistique; **cost-benefit a.,** analyse des coûts et rendements; **cost-effectiveness a.,** étude *f* de coût et d'efficacité; **operating costs a.,** comptabilité *f* analytique d'exploitation; **supply and demand a.,** analyse de l'offre et de la demande; (*f*) *Gram: etc:* **a. of a sentence,** analyse logique d'une phrase; **in the last a.,** en dernière analyse.

analyst ['ænəlist], *s.* **1.** *Ch: Mth: etc:* analyste *mf*; *Pol.Ec:* économiste-statisticien *m*, *pl.* économistes-statisticiens; *Cmptr:* **systems a.,** analyste de systèmes, analyste fonctionnel(le). **2.** *Psy:* (psych)analyste *mf*.

analytic(al) [ænə'litik(l)], *a.* analytique; **analytical mind,** esprit *m* d'analyse; **analytic language,** langue analytique; *Phil:* **analytic judgement,** jugement *m* analytique; **analytic psychology,** psychologie introspective; **analytical chemistry,** chimie *f* analytique; **analytical chemist,** chimiste *m* analyste, expert; *Mth:* **analytic(al) geometry,** géométrie *f* analytique; **analytic function,** fonction *f* analytique, holomorphe; *Cmptr:* **analytical function generator,** générateur *m* de fonctions analytiques; **analytical table,** (i) table *f* analytique (des matières); (ii) tableau *m* analytique (de l'histoire, etc.).

analytics [ænə'litiks], *s.pl.* (*usu. with sg. const.*) **1.** l'analytique *f*. **2. Aristotle's A.,** les Analytiques d'Aristote.

anamesite [ænə'mi:zait], *s. Miner:* anamésite *f*.

anamirta [ænə'mɑ:tə], *s. Bot:* anamirte *m*.

anamnesis [ænæm'ni:sis], *s.* **1.** *Med:* anamnésie *f*; retour *m* de mémoire. **2.** (*a*) *Med:* anamnèse *f*; souvenirs *mpl* du malade; (*b*) *Ecc:* (*prayer*) anamnèse.

anamnestic [ænæm'nestik], *a. Med:* anamnestique.

Anamniota [ænæmni'outə], *s.pl. Ich: Amph:* anamniés *m*, anamniotes *m*, anamniens *m*.

anamniote [æ'næmniɔt], **anamniotic** [ænæmni'ɔtik], *a. & s. Ich: Amph:* anamniote (*m*), anamnien (*m*), anamnié (*m*).

Anamorpha [ænə'mɔ:fə], *s.pl. Myr:* anamorphes *m*.

anamorphosis [ænə'mɔ:fəsis], *s.* **1.** *Opt:* anamorphose *f*. **2.** *Bot:* dégénérescence *f* morbide.

anamorph(ot)ic [ænə'mɔ:fik, ænəmɔ:'fɔtik], *a. Opt:* anamorphoseur, anamorphotique; *Cin: T.V:* **a. lens,** objectif *m* anamorphoseur.

ananas [ə'neinəs, ə'nɑ:nəs], *s. Bot:* ananas *m*.

anandrous [ə'nændrəs], *a. Bot:* anandre, anandraire, anandrique.

Ananias [ænə'naiəs]. **1.** *Pr.n.m.B.Hist:* Ananias. **2.** *s. Lit:* menteur.

anapaest ['ænəpi:st], *s. Pros:* anapeste *m*.

anapaestic [ænə'pi:stik], *a. Pros:* anapestique, anapeste.

anaphase ['ænəfeiz], *s. Biol:* anaphase *f*.

anaphora [ə'næfərə], *s. Rh: Ecc:* anaphore *f*.

anaphoresis [ænəfə'ri:sis], *s. Ch:* anaphorèse *f*.

anaphoric [ænə'fɔrik], *a. Gram:* (pronom) anaphorique.

anaphrodisia [ænæfrə'di:ziə], *s. Med:* anaphrodisie *f*.

anaphrodisiac [ænæfrə'di:ziæk], *a. & s. Pharm:* anaphrodisiaque (*m*).

anaphylactia [ænəfi'læktiə], *s. Med:* anaphylactique *m*; état *m* anaphylactique.

anaphylactic [ænəfi'læktik], *a. Med:* anaphylactique; **a. shock,** choc *m* anaphylactique.

anaphylactogen [ænəfi'læktədʒən], *s. Med:* anaphylactogène *m*.

anaphylactoid [ænəfi'læktɔid], *a. Med:* anaphylactoïde.

anaphylaxis [ænəfi'læksis], **anaphylaxy** [ænəfi'læksi], *s. Med:* anaphylaxie *f*.

anaplasia [ænə'pleiziə], *s. Biol:* anaplasie *f*.

anaplasmosis [ænəplæz'mousis], *s. Vet:* anaplasmose *f*.

anaplastic [ænə'plæstik], *a.* (chirurgie) anaplastique.

anaplasty [ænə'plæsti], **anaplastics** [ænə'plæstiks], *s. Surg:* autoplastie *f*.

anaptyctic [ænæp'tiktik], *a. Ling:* anaptyctique.

anaptyxis [ænæp'tiksis], *s. Ling:* anaptyxe *f*.

anarchic(al) [æ'nɑ:kik(l)], *a.* anarchique.

anarchically [æ'nɑ:kik(ə)li], *adv.* anarchiquement.

anarchism ['ænəkizm], *s.* anarchisme *m*.

anarchist ['ænəkist], *a. & s.* anarchiste (*mf*).

anarchize ['ænɑ:kaiz], *v.tr.* anarchiser.

anarcho-syndicalism [æ'nɑ:kou'sindikəlizm], *s. Pol:* anarcho-syndicalisme *m*.

anarcho-syndicalist [æn'ɑ:kou'sindikəlist], *a. & s. Pol:* anarcho-syndicaliste (*mf*), *pl.* anarcho-syndicalistes.

anarchy ['ænəki], *s.* anarchie *f*.

anarthria [æ'nɑ:θriə], *s. Med:* anarthrie *f*.

anasarca [ænə'sɑ:kə], *s.* **1.** *Med:* anasarque *f*; leucophlegmasie *f*; œdème généralisé. **2.** *Med: Vet:* anasarque; purpura *m* hémorragique; fièvre pétéchiale.

anasarcous [ænə'sɑ:kəs], *a.* hydropique.

Anaspidacea [ænæspi'deisiə], *s.pl. Crust:* anaspidacés *m*.

Anastasia [ænə'steiziə], *Pr.n.f.* Anastasie.

Anastasius [ænə'steiʃəs], *Pr.n.m.* Anastase.

anastatic [ænə'stætik], *a. Engr:* (gravure) anastatique, en relief.

anastatica [ænæs'tætikə], *s. Bot:* anastatica *f*, anastatique *f*, rose *f* de Jéricho.

anastigmat [æ'næstigmæt], *a. & s. Opt: Phot:* **a. (lens),** objectif *m* anastigmat, anastigmatique; anastigmat *m*; **convertible a.,** anastigmat dédoublable.

anastigmatic [ænæstig'mætik], *a. Opt:* anastigmat, anastigmatique.

anastigmatism [ænæs'tigmətizm], *s.* anastigmatisme *m*.

anastomic [ænæs'toumik], *a.* **a. ulcer,** ulcère *m* peptique.

anastomose [æ'næstəmouz]. **1.** *v.tr. & i. Anat: etc:* (s')anastomoser. **2.** *Geog: v.i.* (*of river*) s'anastomoser.

anastomosed [æ'næstəmouzd], *a. Geog:* anastomosé.

anastomosing [æ'næstəmouziŋ], *a. Geog:* anastomosé, qui s'anastomose.

anastomosis [ænæstə'mousis], *s.* **1.** *Anat: Nat.Hist:* anastomose *f*. **2.** *Geog:* (*a*) anastomose; (*b*) lit (d'une rivière) anastomosé.

anastomotic [ænæstə'mɔtik], *a. Anat: Nat.Hist:* anastomotique.

anastrophe [æ'næstrəfi], *s. Rh:* anastrophe *f*.

anastylosis [ænæsti'lousis], *s. Arch:* anastylose *f*.

anatase ['ænəteiz], *s. Miner:* anatase *f*.

anatexis [ænə'teksis], *s. Geol:* anatexie *f*.

anathema [ə'næθəmə], *s.* anathème *m* ((i) malédiction; (ii) personne frappée de malédiction); **here his name is a.,** ici son nom est maudit; **it's, he's a. to me,** c'est ma bête noire.

anathematization [ənæθəmətai'zeiʃ(ə)n], *s.* anathématisation *f*.

anathematize [ə'næθəmətaiz], *v.tr.* (*a*) anathématiser (qn); frapper (qn) d'anathème; (*b*) maudire (qn).

anatidae [ə'nætidi:], *s.pl. Orn:* anatidés *m*.

anatocism [ə'nætəsizm], *s. Fin: A:* anatocisme *m*; intérêts composés.

Anatolia [ænə'touliə], *Pr.n. Geog:* Anatolie *f*.

Anatolian [ænə'touliən]. *Geog:* **1.** *a.* anatolien. **2.** *s.* Anatolien, -ienne.

Anatolius [ænə'touliəs], *Pr.n.m.* Anatole.

anatomical [ænə'tɔmikl], *a.* anatomique; **a. specimen,** pièce *f* d'anatomie; préparation *f* anatomique; **a. theatre,** amphithéâtre *m* d'anatomie.

anatomically [ænə'tɔmik(ə)li], *adv.* anatomiquement; **a. speaking,** en termes d'anatomie.

anatomist [ə'nætəmist], *s.* anatomiste *mf*.

anatomize [ə'nætəmaiz], *v.tr.* anatomiser; faire l'anatomie de (qch.); disséquer.

anatomy [ə'nætəmi], *s.* **1.** structure *f* anatomique; **the a. of an earthworm is much simpler than that of a man,** la structure anatomique du ver de terre est beaucoup plus simple que celle de l'homme. **2.** (*a*) (*the science*) l'anatomie *f*; **comparative a.,** anatomie comparée; **human a.,** anatomie humaine; (*b*) (*textbook*) cours *m* d'anatomie. **3.** anatomie, dissection *f*. **4.** (*a*) pièce *f* d'anatomie; (*b*) *A:* (i) squelette *m*, momie *f*; (ii) personnage *m* squelettique.

anatoxin [ænə'tɔksin], *s. Bio-Ch:* anatoxine *f*.

anatropous [æn'ætrəpəs], *a. Bot:* (ovule *m*) anatrope.

anatta [ə'nætə], **anatto** [ə'nætou], *s.* **1.** *Dy:* rocou *m*. **2. a. (tree),** rocouyer *m*.

anauxite ['ænɔ:ksait], *s. Miner:* anauxite *f*.

Anaxagoras [ænæk'sægəræs], *Pr.n.m. Gr.Phil:* Anaxagore.

Anaximander [ænæksi'mændər], *Pr.n.m. Gr.Phil:* Anaximandre.

Anaximenes [ænæk'simini:z], *Pr.n.m. Gr.Hist:* Anaximène.

anbury ['ænbri], *s.* **1.** *Hort:* hernie *f*. **2.** *Vet:* papillome *m* (rempli de sang).

ancestor ['ænsestər], *s.* ancêtre *m*; aïeul *m*, *pl.* aïeux; **an a. of mine,** un de mes ancêtres; **our ancestors,** nos ancêtres, nos aïeux; nos pères; **Saint Louis, the common a. of the Bourbons,** saint Louis, tige *f* de la branche des Bourbons; **a. worship,** culte *m* des ancêtres; nécrolâtrie *f*.

ancestral [æn'sestrl], *a.* (*a*) héréditaire, de famille; **his a. home,** la demeure de ses ancêtres; *NAm:* **black hair is an a. trait in that family,** les cheveux noirs sont héréditaires dans cette famille; (*b*) *Biol:* ancestral, -aux.

ancestrally [æn'sestrəli], *adv.* héréditairement.

ancestress ['ænsestris], *s.f.* ancêtre, aïeule.

ancestry ['ænsestri], *s.* **1.** race *f*; lignée *f*, lignage *m*; longue suite d'ancêtres; ascendance *f*; **both families were of French a.,** l'une et l'autre famille avait une ascendance française. **2.** *Coll:* ancêtres *mpl*; ascendants *mpl*; aïeux *mpl*.

Anchises [æŋ'kaisi:z], *Pr.n.m. Lt.Lit:* Anchise.

anchor[1] ['æŋkər], *s.* **1.** (*a*) *Nau: etc:* ancre *f*; **bower a.,** ancre de bossoir; **sea a.,** ancre flottante; ancre de cape, du large; **kedge a.,** ancre d'embossage, ancre de touée; **sheet a.,** ancre de veille; *Fig:* ancre, planche *f*, de salut; **stockless a.,** ancre brevetée, ancre sans jas; **stream a.,** ancre de détroit; **mooring a.,** ancre de corps-mort; **a. buoy,** bouée *f* de mouillage, d'ancre; bouée de corps-mort; plateau *m* d'ancre; **a. light,** feu *m* de mouillage; **a. ring,** organeau *m*, cigale *f*; **a. stock,** jas *m*; **a. watch,** garde *f* de l'ancre; quart *m* de rade; **stand by to a.!** pare à mouiller! **to let go, drop, the a.,** jeter, mouiller, l'ancre; **let go the a.!** mouillez! **to weigh a.,** lever l'ancre; appareiller; **to come to a., to cast a.,** s'ancrer, mouiller; (*of pers.*) s'ancrer (quelque part); se fixer; **to lie, ride, at a.,** être à l'ancre; mouiller; **at a.,** au mouillage; **the a. comes home,** l'ancre chasse; **to slip the a.,** filer (sa chaîne) par le bout; **foul a.,** ancre surjalée, engagée; (*of ship*) **to drag her a.,** chasser sur son ancre, sur ses ancres; *Geog:* **a. ice,** glaces *fpl* de fond; *Aer:* **balloon a.,** ancre de ballon; ancre-chaîne *f*, *pl.* ancres-chaînes; herse *f*; (*b*) *Const:* **a. block, a. wall,** ancrage *m*; point m d'attache (d'un tirant); **a. iron, tie,** grappin *m*; **a. plate,** plaque *f* d'ancrage; contre-plaque *f*, *pl.* contre-plaques; **a. stake,** pieu *m*, piquet *m*, de retenue; **a. stay,** câble *m* d'ancrage; **a. nut,** écrou *m* à river, écrou à patte; (*c*) **a. man,** (i) *Sp:* dernier coureur, joueur (d'une équipe); (ii) *W.Tel: T.V:* pilote *m* d'émission.

anchor[2], *v.* **1.** *v.tr.* (*a*) *Nau:* ancrer, mouiller (un navire), mettre (un navire) à l'ancre, au mouillage; (*b*) *Nau: etc:* hauban(n)er (un mât, etc.); *Const:* affermir (qch.) par des ancres; *Mil:* abattre (une pièce). **2.** *v.i.* (*a*) jeter l'ancre; mouiller, prendre son mouillage; **to a. by the stern,** mouiller par l'arrière; **to a. in the open sea,** mouiller au large; **to a. off Deal,** mouiller au large de Deal; (*b*) *F:* s'ancrer (dans un lieu).

anchorage[1] ['æŋkəridʒ], *s.* **1.** *Nau:* (*a*) ancrage *m*, mouillage *m*; **there is a safe a. at . . .,** il y a un bon mouillage à . . .; **to leave the a.,** dérader; (*b*) droits *mpl* d'ancrage, de stationnement. **2.** *Surg:* fixation *f* (d'un viscère déplacé, etc.). **3.** *Civ.E: Const:* ancrage; point *m* d'attache (d'un tirant, etc.). **4.** *Cmptr:* accrochage *m*; adhérence *f*.

anchorage[2], *s.* retraite *f* d'anachorète.

anchored ['æŋkə:d], *a.* **1.** (*a*) *Nau:* ancré, mouillé; à l'ancre; *Fish:* **a. net,** rets sédentaire; (*b*) **firmly a. faith,** foi solidement ancrée. **2.** en forme d'ancre; *Her:* ancré.

anchoress ['æŋkəres], *s. Ecc:* recluse *f*.

anchoret ['æŋkəret], **anchorite** ['æŋkərait], *s.* anachorète *m*; **he isn't exactly an anchorite,** ce n'est pas un saint Antoine.

anchoretic [æŋkə'retik], *a.* anachorétique; d'anachorète(s).

anchoring ['æŋk(ə)riŋ], *s.* ancrage *m*, mouillage *m*; **a. gear,** apparaux *mpl* de mouillage; **a. ground, place, berth,** ancrage, mouillage.

anchorless ['æŋkəlis], *a.* (*a*) *Nau:* sans ancre; (*b*) (*of pers.*) désemparé; qui se laisse aller; qui n'a pas de racines.

anchovy ['æntʃəvi, æn'tʃouvi], *s.* **1.** *Ich: Cu:* anchois *m*; **a. butter, paste,** beurre *m*, pâte *f*, d'anchois; **a. sauce,** sauce *f* aux anchois; **a. toast,** toast *m* aux anchois, au beurre d'anchois. **2.** *Bot:* **a. pear,** poire *f* d'anchois; (*tree*) grias *m*.

anchylose ['æŋkilouz]. **1.** *v.tr.* ankyloser. **2.** *v.i.* s'ankyloser.

anchylosed ['æŋkilouzd], *a.* ankylosé; *F:* (*of pers.*) perclus; (*of bones*) **to become a.,** s'ankyloser, se souder.

anchylosis [æŋki'lousis], *s. Med:* ankylose *f*.

ancient[1] ['einʃ(ə)nt], *a.* (*a*) ancien; âgé; de vieille date; **it reminds one of a. times,** cela vous rappelle le bon vieux temps; **family of a. descent,** famille ancienne, de longue lignée; **a. monument,** monument *m* historique; **a. oak,** chêne *m* centenaire; *Geol:* **a. rocks,** roches primitives; *Jur:* **a. lights,** servitude *f* de vue; *B:* **the A. of Days,** l'Ancien des jours, l'Éternel *m*; (*b*) **A. Rome,** la Rome antique; **the a. world,** le monde antique; *s.* **the Ancients,** les anciens; **a. history,** l'histoire ancienne; *F:* **that's a. history,** ça, c'est vieux, c'est une vieille histoire.

ancient[2], *s. A:* **1.** (*standard*) enseigne *f*. **2.** (*standard-bearer*) enseigne *m*.

anciently ['einʃəntli], *adv.* anciennement; au temps des anciens; **China, a. called Cathay,** la Chine, appelée autrefois le Cathay.

ancientry ['einʃ(ə)ntri], *s. A: & Lit:* **1.** ancienneté *f* (de race, de famille). **2. tales of a.,** contes *mpl* de l'ancien temps.

ancillary [æn'siləri], *a.* (*a*) subordonné, ancillaire, accessoire, (to, à); **an a. undertaking,** une entreprise auxiliaire; une filiale; (*b*) auxiliaire; **a. equipment,** matériel *m* annexe, d'appoint; accessoires *mpl*.

ancipital [æn'sipitl], **ancipitous** [æn'sipitəs], *a. Bot:* ancipité.

ancon, *pl.* **-es** ['æŋkən, -i:z], *s. Anat: Arch:* ancon *m*; *Husb: A:* **a. sheep,** la race ancon.

Ancona[1] [æŋ'kounə], *Pr.n. Geog:* Ancône *f*.

ancona[2], *s. Ecc.Arch:* tableau *m* d'autel en panneaux séparés.

anconeus [æŋ'kouniəs], *s. Anat:* anconé *m*.

ancred ['æŋkə:d], *a. Her:* ancré.

Ancyloceras [ænsi'lɔsərəs], *s. Paleont:* ancylocère *m*, ancyloceras *m*.

ancylostomiasis [ænsilɔstoumai'æsis], *s. Med:* ankylostomiase *f*, uncinariose *f*.

Ancyra [æn'sairə], *Pr.n. A.Geog:* ancyre *f*.

and[1] [*stressed,* ænd, *unstressed* ənd, ən, n], *conj.* et. **1.** (*a*) (*connecting words*) **a knife a. fork,** un couteau et une fourchette; **father a. mother are out,** mon père et ma mère sont sortis; **father, mother a. the maid are all out,** mon père, ma mère et la bonne sont tous sortis; **the president a./or the secretary,** le président ou le secrétaire ou tous les deux; **four a. five make(s) nine,** quatre plus cinq font neuf; (*b*) (*with numerals*) (i) *A: & Lit:* **five a. twenty** (= twenty-five), vingt-cinq; **four a. twenty blackbirds baked in a pie,** vingt-quatre merles cuits dans un pâté; (ii) **two hundred a. two,** deux cent deux; **four and a half,** quatre et demi; **four a. three quarters,** quatre trois quarts; **an hour and twenty minutes,** une heure vingt minutes; *A:* **three (shillings) a. six(pence),** trois shillings six pence; (*c*) **ham a. eggs,** des œufs au jambon; **carriage a. pair,** voiture *f* à deux chevaux; **now a. then,** de temps en temps; **he goes for a walk summer a. winter alike,** hiver comme été il fait une promenade; (*d*) (*after* **without**) ni; **he came without pencils a. paper,** il est venu sans crayons ni papier; (*e*) **he speaks English, a. very well too,** il parle anglais et même très bien; **it is a mere farce, a. a poor one,** c'est une simple farce, et qui est médiocre; **he is a capable leader, a. a man of energy,** c'est un chef capable, et qui a de l'énergie; **a. what about the invalids?** et les malades? (*f*) (*intensive repetition*) **for miles a. miles,** pendant des milles et des milles; **better a. better,** de mieux en mieux; **worse a. worse,** de pis en pis, de pire en pire; **smaller a. smaller,** de plus en plus petit; **her cheeks burned redder a. redder,** elle rougissait de plus en plus; **I knocked a. knocked, but . . .,** je frappai tant et plus, mais . . .; **over a. over again,** maintes et maintes fois; **through a. through,** de bout en bout; de part en part; (*g*) **there are books a. books, dogs a. dogs,** il y a livres et livres, chiens et chiens; il y a fagots et fagots. **2.** (*connecting clauses*) (*a*) **he sang a. danced,** il chantait et dansait; **he could read a. write,** il savait lire et écrire; (*b*) **move (an inch) a. you're a dead man,** un pas et vous êtes mort; (*c*) **go a. look for it,** allez le chercher; **come a. see me,** venez me voir; **wait a. see,** attendez voir; **try a. help me,** tâchez de m'aider; **divide a. rule,** diviser pour régner; (*d*) **a. not,** sans (que); **to look for sth. a. not see it,** chercher qch. sans le voir; **he could go through an earthquake a. show no emotion,** il passerait par un tremblement de terre sans montrer d'émotion; **can a man disappear like that, a. no questions be asked?** un homme peut-il disparaître de la sorte sans qu'on s'en inquiète? **he could stuff his pockets a. no one notice,** il avait le truc pour bourrer ses poches sans que personne y prît garde. **3.** *A:* (*conditional*) **but a. thou wilt enter into life,** mais si tu veux entrer dans la vie; **let her change her place a. need be,** qu'elle change de place s'il est besoin. **4.** *s.* (*a*) **without ifs a. ands,** sans si ni mais; (*b*) *Cmptr:* (*often written* AND) **a. circuit, element, gate,** circuit *m* ET, élément *m* ET.

and[2], *v.i. Cmptr:* faire une intersection logique; **to a. into,** introduire par intersection logique.

Andalusia [ændə'lu:siə, -ziə], *Pr.n. Geog:* Andalousie *f*.

Andalusian [ændə'lu:siən, -ziən]. **1.** *Geog:* (*a*) *a.* andalou; (*b*) *s.* Andalou, -ouse. **2.** *s. Ling:* andalou *m*. **3.** *s.* (cheval) andalou *m*.

andalusite [ændə'lu:sait], *s. Miner:* andalousite *f*.

Andaman ['ændəmən]. **1.** *Pr.n. Geog:* **the A. Islands,** les îles Andaman. **2.** (*also* **Andamanese** [ændəmæ'ni:z]) (*a*) *a.* andaman; **Andaman Islander,** Andaman, -ane; (*b*) *s.* Andaman, -ane; (*c*) *s. Ling:* andaman *m*.

andante [æn'dænti], *adv. & s. Mus:* andante (*m*), andanté (*m*).

andantino [ændæn'ti:nou], *adv. & s. Mus:* andantino (*m*).

Andean ['ændiən], *a. Geog:* andin; des Andes; **the A. Cordillera,** la Cordillère des Andes.

Andes ['ændi:z], *Pr.n. Geog:* **the A.,** les Andes *f*, la Cordillère des Andes.

andesine ['ændisain], *s. Miner:* andésine *f*.

andesite ['ændisait], *s. Miner:* andésite *f*.

andesitic [ændi'sitik], *a. Geol:* andésitique.

Andine ['ændain], *a. Geog:* andin.

andiron ['ændaiən], *s.* (*a*) landier *m*; (*b*) chenet *m*; chevrette *f*; marmouset *m*.

andorite ['ædərait], *s. Miner:* andorite *f*.

Andorra [æn'dɔrə], *Pr.n. Geog:* (La république d')Andorre *f*; **A. (City),** Andorre la Vieille.

Andorran [æn'dɔrən]. *Geog:* **1.** *a.* andorran. **2.** *s.* Andorran, -ane.

andradite ['ændrədait], *s. Miner:* andradite *f*.

andrena [æn'dri:nə], *s. Ent:* andrène *m*.

Andrew ['ændru:], *Pr.n.m.* **1.** André. **2.** *Nau: P: A:* la Marine britannique.

androcephalous [ændrou'sefələs], *a.* androcéphale.

Androcles ['ændrəkli:z], *Pr.n.m. Rom.Hist:* Androclès.

androconium, *pl.* **-ia** [ændrou'kouniəm, -iə], *s. Ent:* androconie *f*.

androecium [æn'dri:siəm], *s. Bot:* androcée *m*, andrœcie *f*.

androgen ['ændroudʒin], *s.m. Biol:* androgène.

androgenesis [ændrou'dʒenəsis], *s. Biol:* androgénèse *f*.

androgenic [ændrou'dʒenik], *a.* androgène.

androgynary [æn'drɔdʒinəri], *a. Bot:* androgynaire.

androgyne ['ændroudʒin, -dʒain], *s. Bot: Z:* androgyne *m*.

androgynia [ændrou'dʒini'], *s.* androgynie *f*.

androgynous [æn'drɔdʒinəs], *a.* **1.** *Bot:* androgyne. **2.** *Z:* hermaphrodite, androgyne.

androgyny [æn'drɔdʒini], *s.* androgynie *f*.

android ['ændrɔid], *s.* androïde *m*.

Andromache [æn'drɔməkil], *Pr.n.f.* Andromaque.

Andromeda [æn'drɔmidə]. **1.** *Pr.n.f. Myth: Astr:* Andromède; *Astr:* **A. nebula,** Grande Nébuleuse d'Andromède. **2.** *s. Bot:* andromeda *m*, andromède *f*.

Andromedes [æn'drɔmidi:z], **Andromedids** [æn'drɔmədidz], *Pr.n. pl. Astr:* Biélides *f*, Andromédides *f*.

andromonoecious [ændroumə'niʃəs], *a. Bot:* andromonoïque.

Andronicus [ændrə'naikəs], *Pr.n.m.* (*a*) *Lt.Lit:* (Livius) Andronicus; (*b*) *Hist:* **A. Comnenus,** Andronic Comnène.

andropetalar [ændrou'petələr], **andropetalous** [ændrou'petələs], *a. Bot:* andropétalaire.

androphore ['ændroufɔ:r], *s. Bot:* androphore *m*.

andropogon [ændrou'pougən], *s. Bot:* andropogon *m*, *F:* barbon *m*.

androsace [æn'drouseis], *s. Bot:* androsace *m*.

androsphinx ['ændrousfinks], *s. Myth:* androsphinx *m*.

androspore ['ændrouspɔ:r], *s. Bot:* androspore *f*.

androsterone [ændrou'steroun], *s. Physiol:* androstérone *f*.

Andy ['ændi], *Pr.n.m. F:* (*dim. of* **Andrew**) Dédé.

anecdotage ['ænikdoutidʒ], *s.* **1.** recueil *m* d'anecdotes. **2.** *F:* radotage *m*; **in his a.,** dans sa vieillesse conteuse.

anecdotal [ænik'doutl], *a.* anecdotique.

anecdotalist [ænik'doutəlist], *s.* anecdotier *m*.

anecdote ['ænikdout], *s.* anecdote *f*.

anecdotic(al) [ænik'dɔtik(l)], *a.* anecdotique.

anecdotist ['ænikdoutist], *s.* anecdotier *m*.

anechoic [æni'kouik], *a. Ac:* anéchoïque, anéchoïde; **a. chamber, a. wall,** chambre *f*, cloison *f*, anéchoïque.

anele [ə'ni:l], *v.tr. A:* oindre; *esp. Ecc:* administrer l'extrême onction à (qn).

anelectrotonus [ænilek'trɔtənəs], *s. Med:* anélectrotonus *m*.

anemia [ə'ni:miə], *s.*, etc. = ANAEMIA, etc.

anemochorous [əni:mou'kɔ:rəs], *a. Bot:* anémochore.

anemogram [ə'nemougræm], *s. Meteor:* anémogramme *m*.

anemograph [ə'nemougræf], *s. Meteor:* anémographe *m*.

anemographic [ənemou'græfik], *a.* anémographique.

anemometer [æne'mɔmitər], *s. Meteor:* anémomètre *m*; **speed and direction a.,** girouette-anémomètre *f*, *pl.*

girouettes-anémomètres.
anemometric [ænemou'metrik], *a.* anémométrique.
anemometry [æne'mɔmitri], *s. Meteor:* anémométrie *f.*
anemone [ə'nemәni], *s.* 1. *Bot:* anémone *f*; **white a.,** albanaise *f*; **star a.,** anémone des jardins; **blue mountain a.,** anémone des Apennins; **poppy a.,** anémone couronnée; **wood a.,** anémone des bois, sylvie *f.* 2. *Coel:* **sea a.,** anémone de mer; **opelet a.,** anémone de mer (toujours ouverte); **beadlet a.,** petite actinie; **dahlia a.,** grande actinie; **jewel a.,** (petite) anémone des grottes; **plumose a.,** anémone plumeuse.
anemophilous [æne'mɔfiləs], *a. Bot:* anémophile, anémogame.
anemophily [æne'mɔfili], *s. Bot:* anémophilie *f,* anémogamie *f.*
anemoscope [ə'neməskoup], *s. Meteor:* anémoscope *m.*
anemotropism [ænemou'troupizm], *s. Biol:* anémotropisme *m.*
anencephalous [ænen'sefələs], *a. Ter:* anencéphale, anencéphalique.
anencephalus [ænen'sefələs], *s. Ter:* anencéphale *m,* anencéphalien *m.*
anencephaly [ænen'sefəli], *s. Ter:* anencéphalie *f.*
anent [ə'nent], *prep. A: & Scot:* touchant, concernant, sur, au sujet de, à propos de.
aner ['ænər], *s. Ent:* fourmi *f* mâle.
anergia [æ'nə:dʒiə], **anergy** ['ænədʒi], *s. Med:* anergie *f.*
aneroid ['ænərɔid], *a. Ph:* anéroïde; **a. barometer,** baromètre *m* anéroïde.
aneroidograph [ænə'rɔidougræf], *s. Meteor:* barographe *m.*
anesthesia [ænes'θi:ziə], *s.* = ANAESTHESIA.
anethum [ə'ni:θəm], *s. Bot:* anet(h) *m.*
aneuploid [æ'nju:plɔid], *a. Biol:* aneuploïde.
aneuploidy [ænju'plɔidi], *s. Biol:* aneuploïdie *f.*
aneurin [æ'nju:rin], *s. Bio-Ch:* aneurine *f.*
aneurism, aneurysm ['ænjurizm], *s. Med:* anévrisme *m,* anévrysme *m.*
aneurismal, aneurysmal [ænju'rizml], *a. Med:* anévrismal, anévrysmal, -aux.
anew [ə'nju:, *NAm: also* ə'nu:], *adv. O: & NAm:* 1. (*once more*) de nouveau; **to begin a.,** commencer de nouveau, recommencer; **to take up a task a.,** reprendre une tâche; **to build a wall a.,** refaire un mur à neuf. 2. (*in a new way*) à nouveau; **to create sth. a.,** créer qch. à nouveau, sous une forme nouvelle; recréer qch.
anfractuosity [ænfræktju'ɔsiti], *s. (a) Lit:* anfractuosité *f*; *(b) pl.* sinuosités *f*; détours *m*; *Anat:* **anfractuosities of the brain,** anfractuosités cérébrales.
angary ['æŋgəri], *s. Jur:* angarie *f.*
angel[1] ['eindʒl], *s.* 1. *(a)* ange *m*; **little a.,** angelet *m*; **the a. of darkness,** l'ange des ténèbres; **the a. of death,** l'ange de la mort; **guardian a.,** ange gardien; **a. worship,** angélolâtrie *f*; *F:* **he's on the side of the angels,** (i) il a une attitude traditionnelle, il est conservateur; (ii) il est des nôtres; **fallen a.,** (i) ange déchu; (ii) *F: A:* femme déchue; *F:* **an a. passes,** un ange passe; *F:* **you a.! you're an a.!** tu es un amour! *F:* **be an a. and do up my dress,** sois gentil et agrafe-moi ma robe; *Prov:* **talk of angels and you will hear the flutter of their wings,** quand on parle du loup on en voit la queue; *(b) Th: etc: F:* bailleur *m* de fonds; commanditaire *m*; *(c) Av: F:* altitude *f* de mille pieds; *(d) F:* écho radar non identifié. 2. *attrib.* *(a)* **a. face,** (i) visage *m* d'ange, visage angélique; (ii) *F:* un, une, Marie-Louise; *A.Furn:* **a. bed,** lit *m* d'ange (sans colonnes); *A.Cost:* **a. sleeves,** manches *f* d'ange; *Tex:* **a. skin,** peau *f* d'ange; *Arch:* **a. beam,** blochet décoré d'un ange sculpté; *(b) Cu:* **a. cake, a. food (cake),** (variété de) gâteau *m* de Savoie; *(c) Toil: A:* **a. water,** (eau *f* de) Portugal *m*; *(d) Ich:* **a. ray, a. shark,** ange de mer, angelot *m.* 3. *Num: A:* angelot *m.* 4. *Fish:* cuiller *f* (à ailes); hélice *f* (pour la pêche du brochet, de la truite). 5. *Cu:* **angels on horseback,** friture *f* d'huîtres bardées de tranches de lard. 6. *Fung: F:* **destroying a.,** amanite printanière.
angel[2], *F:* 1. *v.tr. Th: etc:* commanditer, financer (une pièce, etc.). 2. *v.i. Av:* prendre de l'altitude.
Angela ['ændʒələ], *Pr.n.f.* Angèle.
angelfish ['eindʒəlfiʃ], *s. Ich:* (i) ange *m* de mer, angelot *m*; (ii) échippe *m*; (iii) spatule *f*; (iv) scalaire *m*; **(black) a.,** ange (noir, de mer); **Brazilian a.,** ange noir du Brésil; scalaire.
angelic [æn'dʒelik], *a.* angélique; **an a. smile,** un sourire d'ange; *Ecc:* **the A. Salutation,** la Salutation angélique.
Angelica [æn'dʒelikə]. 1. *Pr.n.f.* Angélique. 2. *s. Bot: Cu: etc:* angélique *f*; *Bot:* **wild a.,** angélique sauvage; *Ch:* **a. oil,** essence *f* d'angélique.
angelical [æn'dʒelikl], *s.* angélique.
angelically [æn'dʒelik(ə)li], *adv.* angéliquement.
Angelina [ændʒə'li:nə], *Pr.n.f.* Angéline.
angelize ['eindʒəlaiz], *v.tr.* angéliser.
angelolatry [eindʒəl'ɔlətri], *s.* angélolâtrie *f.*
angelus ['ændʒələs], *s. Ecc:* angélus *m.*
anger[1] ['æŋgər], *s.* colère *f*; emportement *m*; **fit of a.,** accès *m* de colère; **terrible fits of a.,** des colètres terribles; **in a fit, a moment, of a.,** dans un accès de colère; dans un moment d'emportement; transporté de colère; **in a state of blind a.,** dans une colère folle, aveugle; **to provoke s.o. to a.,** exciter la colère de qn; **to act in a.,** agir sous le coup de la colère; **to speak in a.,** parler sous le coup de la colère.
anger[2], *v.tr.* irriter (qn); mettre (qn) en colère; **he is easily angered,** il se met facilement en colère; il est irascible.
angered ['æŋgə:d], *a.* irrité, furieux.
Angevin ['ændʒəvin], *a. Geog: Hist:* Angevin; d'Anjou.
angina [æn'dʒainə], *s. Med: (a)* angine *f*; **Vincent's a.,** angine de Vincent; *(b)* **a. pectoris** ['pektəris] angine de poitrine, angor *m* pectoris.
anginal ['ændʒinl], **anginose** ['ændʒinous], **anginous** ['ændʒinəs], *a.* angineux.
angio- ['ændʒiou], *pref.* angio-.
angiocardiogram ['ændʒiou'kɑ:diougræm], *s. Med:* angiocardiographie *f.*
angiocarditis ['ændʒioukɑ:'daitis], *s. Med:* angiocardite *f.*
angiocarp ['ændʒioukɑ:p], *s. Fung:* angiocarpe *m.*
angiocarpic [ændʒiou'kɑ:pik], **angiocarpous** [ændʒiou'kɑ:pəs], *a. Fung:* angiocarpe.
angiocholitis [ændʒioukə'laitis], *s. Med:* angiocholite *f.*
angiogram ['ændʒiougræm], *s. Med:* angiographie *f.*
angiographic [ændʒiou'græfik], *a. Med:* ang(é)iographique.
angiography [ændʒi'ɔgrəfi], *s. Med:* ang(é)iographie *f.*
angiology [ændʒi'ɔlədʒi], *s. Med:* angiologie *f.*
angioma, *pl.* **-mata** [ændʒi'oumə, -mɑ:tə], *s. Med:* angiome *m,* angiose *f*; nævus *m* vasculaire.
angioneurosis [ændʒiounju'rousis], *s. Med:* angioneurose *f.*
angioneurotic [ændʒiounju'rɔtik], *a. Med:* angioneurotique; **a. œdema,** œdème *m* angioneurotique.
angioscope ['ændʒiouskoup], *s. Med:* angioscope *m.*
angiosperm ['ændʒiouspə:m], *s. Bot:* angiosperme *f.*
Angiospermae [ændʒiou'spə:mi:], *s.pl. Bot:* angiospermes *f.*
angiospermal [ændʒiou'spə:ml], **angiospermous** [ændʒiou'spə:məs], *a. Bot:* angiosperme.
angiotomy [ændʒi'ɔtəmi], *s.* angiotomie *f.*
angiotonin [ændʒiou'tounin], *s. Physiol:* angiotensine *f.*
angle[1] ['æŋgl], *s.* 1. *(a) Mth:* angle *m*; **acute a.,** angle aigu; **obtuse a.,** angle obtus; **reflex a.,** angle plein; **right a.,** angle droit, angle de 90°; **at right angles to . . .,** à angle droit avec . . ., perpendiculaire à . . .; **straight a.,** angle plat, angle de 180°; **steady a.,** angle constant; **adjacent, contiguous, angles,** angles adjacents; **exterior, external, a.,** angle externe; **interior, internal, a.,** angle interne; **opposite, vertical, angles,** angles opposés par le sommet; **curvilinear a.,** angle curviligne; **dihedral, trihedral, a.,** angle dièdre, trièdre; **solid a.,** angle polyèdre; **spheric a.,** angle sphérique; (*in spherical coordinates*) **a. of elevation,** latitude *f*; (*of ellipse*) **excentric a.,** anomalie *f* excentrique; (*in polar coordinates*) **polar a.,** angle polaire, anomalie; (*in logarithmic calculus*) **related a., reference a.,** angle auxiliaire; **at an a. of . . .,** sous un angle de . . .; **curves that meet at an a.,** courbes *f* qui se coupent à un angle; **at an a.,** de biais; **the house stands at an a. to the street,** la maison fait angle sur la rue; **to wear one's hat at an a.,** porter son chapeau de travers, de guingois; **to take an a.,** relever un angle; **to plot an a.,** reporter un angle; *(b) Astr:* **hour a.,** angle horaire; **local, sideral, hour a.,** angle horaire local, sidéral; **meridian a.,** angle méridien; **parallactic a.,** angle parallactique; **zenith(al) a.,** angle zénithal; *(c) Opt:* **a. of incidence,** angle d'incidence; **a. of polarization, polarizing a.,** angle de polarisation; **a. of reflection, specular a.,** angle de réflexion; **a. of refraction, refracting a.,** angle de réfraction; angle réfringent (d'un prisme); **a. of vision, visual a., viewing a.,** angle de vision, angle visuel; *Ph:* **beam a., wave a.,** angle de radiation; **radiation a.,** angle de rayonnement; *Phot:* **a. of view,** angle de champ; **wide a.,** grand angle; **wide-a. lens,** objectif grand angulaire; *Cin:* **a. shot,** prise *f* de vue oblique; *(d)* angle, point *m* de vue; **to study a problem from every a., from all angles,** étudier un problème sur toutes ses faces, sous tous les angles; **to consider a problem from the economic a.,** considérer un problème du point de vue économique; **to give a tendentious a. to a report,** orienter un compte-rendu d'une façon tendancieuse; *F:* **we shall need a special selling a. to market these goods,** une publicité spéciale sera nécessaire pour vendre ces marchandises; *F:* **what's your a. on this?** qu'est-ce que vous pensez de cela? comment vois-tu la chose? *F:* **to know all the angles,** connaître la musique; la connaître dans les coins; *(e) F:* **his a. was selling off photographs to magazines,** son métier était de vendre des photos aux revues. 2. *Mil: (a) Artil: Ball:* **apex a., displacement a.,** parallaxe *f* de but, de repère; **a. of convergence, of divergence,** angle de convergence, de divergence; **a. of deflection,** angle de dérive; **a. of departure, of projection,** angle de départ, de projection; **a. of depression,** angle de dépression, de tir négatif; **a. of elevation, of altitude,** angle de hausse, de tir positif; **a. of fall, of impact,** angle de chute, d'arrivée (d'un projectile); **a. of fire, firing a., a. of quadrant elevation, quadrant a.,** angle de tir, angle au niveau; **a. of shift,** (angle de) transport *m*; **a. of sight,** angle de mire, de visée; **a. of site,** angle de site; **a. of traverse,** angle de fauchage; **clearance a.,** angle de dégagement; *Artil:* **(target) aspect a.,** angle de présentation (de la cible); **a. of lead,** angle de visée en avant (de la cible); *Ball:* (*of gun barrel*) **a. of jump,** angle de relèvement; **a. of negative jump,** angle d'abaissement; *(b) Mil.Av:* **dropping a.,** angle de visée (de bombardement); *(c) Navy:* (*of torpedo*) **a. of entry,** incidence *f* d'entrée (d'une torpille). 3. *Av: (a) Aerdcs:* **a. of attack, of incidence,** (i) *Av: etc:* angle d'attaque, d'incidence (d'un plan dans l'atmosphère); (ii) *Nau:* (angle d') incidence du vent sur une voile; **critical a. (of attack), stalling a., burble a.,** angle (d'attaque ou d'incidence) critique; **a. of crab, drift a.,** angle de dérive; **a. of sideslip,** angle de dérapage; **a. of pitch,** angle de tangage; **a. of roll,** angle de roulis; **a. of yaw,** angle de lacet; **lift a.,** angle de portance; **zero lift a.,** angle de portance nulle; *(b) Av: Ball:* **a. of ascent, of climb,** angle de montée (d'un avion, d'un projectile); **a. of descent,** angle de descente; **a. of flight path,** angle d'inclinaison de la trajectoire de vol (d'un avion), de la trajectoire (d'un projectile); *(c)* (*flight*) **a. of heading,** angle de cap; **flying a.,** angle de vol; **a. of glide, gliding a.,** angle de plané, de pente; **a. of bank,** angle d'inclinaison; **a. of dive, dive a.,** angle de piqué; **zero dive a.,** angle de piqué nul; **landing a.,** angle d'atterrissage; *(d)* (*control and lifting surfaces*) **a. of stabilizer setting,** angle d'attache, de calage, du plan fixe horizontal; **a. of wing setting,** angle d'attache, de calage, de l'aile; **aileron a.,** angle de braquage d'aileron; **helm, steering, a.,** angle de braquage; **rudder, elevator, a.,** angle de braquage de gouverne de direction, de gouverne de profondeur; **sweepback a.,** angle de flèche, flèche *f* (de l'aile); **trim a.,** angle d'assiette, de réponse; *(e)* **(propeller, rotor) blade a.,** angle (de calage) de pale; (*of helicopter*) **flapping a.,** angle de levée de pale (de rotor); **lag a.,** angle de décalage de pale (de rotor). 4. *Nau:* **a. of heel, of list; listing a.,** angle de gîte; **upsetting a.,** angle de chavirement; **course a.,** angle de route; **drift a.,** angle de dérive. 5. *Ski:* **stemming a.,** angle de freinage. 6. *(a) Civ.E:* **a. of gradient, of slope,** angle de déclivité; **a. of repose, of rest,** angle naturel de repos, angle de talus; *Fort:* **dead a.,** angle mort; **re-entrant a.,** angle rentrant; **salient a.,** angle saillant; *(b) Const:* coin *m,* encoignure *f,* angle (d'une pièce); *(c) Mec.E:* **a. of torque,** angle de torsion; **camber a.,** angle de carrossage (d'auto, d'avion, etc.); **contact a. (of belt),** angle d'enroulement (d'une courroie); **fleet a.,** angle d'attaque (d'un câble); *(d) Mch.Tls:* **a. of clearance, relief a.,** angle d'incidence, de dépouille; **a. of dip,** angle d'inclinaison (de l'outil); **(back) rake a.,** angle d'attaque (de l'outil); **cutting a.,** angle de coupe; **dig-in a.,** angle de coupe antérieur; **drag a.,** angle de coupe postérieur; **lip a., tool a.,** angle de taillant, du tranchant; *(e) attrib. Const:* **a. bar, a. iron, a. piece, a. plate,** cornière *f,* équerre *f*; **a. bracket,** équerre; *Mec.E: etc:* **a. block,** coin, taquet *m*; **a. brace,** (i) *Tls:* foret *m* à angle; (ii) *Const:* aisselier *m,* contrefiche *f* (de ferme de toit); **a. flange,** bride *f* angulaire; **a. lever,** levier coudé, brisé; **a. pipe,** tuyau cintré; *Surv:* **a. gauge,** goniomètre *m.* 7. *El: Elcs:* **a. of loss, loss a.,** angle de pertes; **phase a.,** angle de phase; **a. of lag,** angle de décalage des phases, angle de retard; **a. of brush lag,** angle de décalage des balais (d'une dynamo). 8. *Anat:* **cranial base a.,** angle de la base du crâne; **facial a.,** angle facial; **goniac a.,** angle goniaque; **incisal a.,** angle incisif (d'une dent); **labial a., a. of the mouth,** commissure *f* des lèvres.
angle[2]. 1. *v.i. (a)* obliquer; faire des angles; *(b) Ten:* jouer la diagonale. 2. *v.tr. (a) Tchn:* angler (une moulure, etc.); *(b)* orienter (un compte-rendu); présenter (des faits) d'une façon tendancieuse, d'un point de vue préjugé.
angle[3], *v.i. (a)* pêcher à la ligne; **to a. for trout,** pêcher la truite; *(b) F:* **to a. for compliments, for an invitation,** quêter des compliments, une invitation; **to a. for a hus-**

band, faire la chasse au mari.

Angle[4], *s. Hist:* Angle *mf*; **the Angles and Saxons settled in England,** les Angles et les Saxons s'établirent en Angleterre.

angled ['æŋgld], *a.* (*a*) à angle, aux angles; **acute-a.,** acutangle, aux angles aigus; (*b*) *Her:* anglé; (*c*) *Sp:* **a. shot,** coup *m* en diagonale; (*d*) (*of report, etc.*) partial, -aux; tendancieux.

Angledozer ['æŋgldouzər], *s. Civ.E: R.t.m.* Angledozer *m.*

angler ['æŋglər], *s.* **1.** pêcheur *m* à la ligne. **2.** *Ich:* **a. (fish),** poisson-grenouille *m, pl.* poissons-grenouilles; baudroie *f*; lophie pêcheuse; crapaud *m* de mer, crapaud pêcheur.

anglesite ['æŋglsait], *s. Miner:* anglésite *f.*

anglewise ['æŋglwaiz], *adv.* obliquement, diagonalement, en travers.

Anglian ['æŋgliən]. **1.** *a.* anglien; des Angles. **2.** *s. Ling:* anglien *m.*

Anglican ['æŋglikən]. *Ecc:* **1.** *a.* anglican; **the A. Church,** l'Église anglicane. **2.** *s.* Anglican, -ane.

Anglicanism ['æŋglikənizm], *s.* **1.** *Ecc:* anglicanisme *m.* **2.** *U.S:* anglomanie *f.*

anglice ['æŋglisi(:)], *Lt.adv.* en anglais.

Anglicism ['æŋglisizm], *s.* anglicisme *m.*

Anglicist ['æŋglisist], *s.* angliciste *mf,* anglicisant, -ante.

Anglicize ['æŋglisaiz], *v.tr.* Angliciser.

Anglo- ['æŋglou], *comb.fm.* Anglo-.

Anglo-American ['æŋglouə'merikən]. **1.** *a.* anglo-américain. **2.** *s.* Anglo-Américain, -aine, *pl.* Anglo-Américains, -aines.

Anglo-Arab ['æŋglou'ærəb], *a. & s.* (cheval) anglo-arabe *m, pl.* anglo-arabes.

Anglo-Canadian ['æŋgloukə'neidiən], *s.* Canadien, -ienne, anglophone.

Anglo-Catholic ['æŋglou'kæθ(ə)lik], *a. & s. Ecc:* anglo-catholique (*mf*).

Anglo-Catholicism ['æŋgloukə'θɔlisizm], *s. Ecc:* anglo-catholicisme *m.*

Anglo-French ['æŋglou'frenʃ]. **1.** *a.* franco-britannique, *pl.* franco-britanniques; *Hist:* **the A.-F. wars,** les guerres avec la France; les guerres de France. **2.** *s. Ling:* anglo-normand *m.*

Anglo-Indian ['æŋglou'indjən]. **1.** *a.* anglo-indien, *pl.* anglo-indiens. **2.** *s.* (*a*) *Adm:* Eurasien, -ienne (qui a du sang indien); (*b*) Anglo-Indien, -ienne (Anglais, aise (i) né(e) dans l'Inde, aux Indes; (ii) qui habite, travaille, dans l'Inde).

Anglo-Irish ['æŋglou'airiʃ]. **1.** *a.* anglo-irlandais. **2.** *s.pl.* **the A.-I.,** les Anglo-Irlandais *m.*

Anglo-Irishman, -woman, *pl.* **-men, -women** ['æŋglou'airiʃmən, -wumən, -mən, -wimin], *s.* Anglo-Irlandais, -aise, *pl.* Anglo-Irlandais, -aises.

Anglomania ['æŋglou'meiniə], *s.* anglomanie *f.*

Anglomaniac ['æŋglou'meiniæk], *s.* anglomane *mf.*

Anglo-Norman ['æŋglou'nɔ:mən]. **1.** *a.* anglo-normand. **2.** *s.* Anglo-Normand, -ande, *pl.* Anglo-Normand(e)s. **3.** *s. Ling:* anglo-normand *m.*

Anglophile ['æŋgloufail], *s.* **1.** anglophile *mf.* **2.** *Can:* Canadien, -ienne, francophone qui apprécie la civilisation du Canada anglophone.

Anglophilia ['æŋglou'filiə], *s.* **1.** anglophilie *f.* **2.** *Can:* (*of French Canadians*) appréciation *f* de la civilisation du Canada anglophone.

Anglophobe ['æŋgloufoub], *a. & s.* anglophobe (*mf*).

Anglophobia ['æŋglou'foubiə], *s.* anglophobie *f.*

Anglo-Roman ['æŋglou'roumən], *a. Ecc:* anglo-catholique.

Anglo-Saxon ['æŋglou'sæks(ə)n]. **1.** *a.* anglo-saxon. **2.** *s.* Anglo-Saxon, -onne, *pl.* Anglo-Saxon(ne)s. **3.** *s. Ling:* anglo-saxon *m.*

Angola [æŋ'goulə]. **1.** *Pr.n. Geog:* Angola *m.* **2.** *Tex: A:* angora *m.*

angolar [æŋgou'la:r], *s. Num:* angolar *m.*

angon ['æŋgɔn], *s. Prehist:* angon *m.*

angor ['æŋgɔ:r], *s. Med:* angor *m.*

Angora [æŋ'gɔ:rə]. **1.** *Pr.n. Geog: A:* Angora (*now* Ankara). **2.** *a. & s.* **A. (goat),** chèvre *f* angora (*usu. inv*); **A. (cat),** chat, chatte, angora; **A. (rabbit),** lapin *m* Angora. **3.** *s. Tex:* angora.

angostura [æŋgɔs'tjuərə], *s. Pharm: etc:* angosture *f,* angusture *f.*

angrily ['æŋgrili], *adv.* en colère; avec colère; avec emportement.

angry ['æŋgri], *a.* (*a*) fâché, irrité courroucé, *F:* furieux (**with s.o.,** *NAm:* **at s.o., about sth.,** contre qn de qch.); **he is very a.,** il est fort en colère, très fâché; **to be a. about sth.,** être fâché de qch.; **he was a. at being kept waiting,** il était irrité qu'on le fît attendre, de ce qu'on le faisait attendre; **to be a. with oneself,** être mécontent de soi; s'en vouloir; **I am a. with myself for forgetting you,** je m'en veux de vous avoir oublié; **who are you a. with?** après qui en avez-vous? **inclined to be a.,** coléreux, colérique; porté à la colère; **to get a.,** se mettre en colère; se fâcher, s'irriter; *F:* prendre la mouche; **to get a. with s.o.,** se fâcher contre qn; **to get thoroughly a.,** se fâcher tout rouge; **to feel a.,** ressentir de la colère; **to make s.o. a.,** fâcher, exaspérer, qn; mettre qn en colère; (*b*) **a. voices,** voix irritées, colères; **to come to a. words,** en venir à des paroles violentes; *Lit:* **the a. sea,** la mer courroucée, en courroux; **a. sky,** ciel *m* sombre; ciel à l'orage; **he sent me an a. letter,** il m'a envoyé une lettre courroucée, *F:* furieuse; **an a. young man,** un contestataire; (*c*) *Med:* **a. sore,** plaie irritée, enflammée.

angstrom, Angström ['æŋstrəm], *s. Ph.Meas:* angström *m.*

Anguidae ['æŋgwidi:], *s.pl. Rept:* anguidés *m, F:* les orvets *m.*

anguiform ['æŋgwifɔ:m], *a.* anguiforme.

Anguillidae [æŋ'gwilidi:], *s.pl. Ich:* anguillidés *m.*

anguilliform [æŋ'gwilifɔ:m], *a.* anguilliforme.

anguillula [æŋgwi'lju:lə], *s. Ann:* anguillule *f.*

anguine ['æŋgwin], *a.* (*a*) anguiforme; (*b*) sinueux.

anguish[1] ['æŋgwiʃ], *s.* **1.** angoisse *f*; douleur *f*; déchirement *m* de cœur; **to be in a.,** être dans l'angoisse; être à la torture, au supplice; **to cause s.o. a.,** angoisser qn. **2.** *Med:* angoisse.

anguish[2]. *esp. NAm:* **1.** *v.tr.* angoisser; accabler (qn) de douleur. **2.** *v.i.* éprouver de l'angoisse.

anguished ['æŋgwiʃt], *a.* angoissé, tourmenté, accablé (de douleur).

angular ['æŋgjulər], *a.* **1.** (vitesse, etc.) angulaire; **a. distance between two points,** distance angulaire de deux points. **2.** (*a*) (rocher, visage) anguleux; (corps) décharné, osseux; (*b*) (mouvement) saccadé.

angularity [æŋgju'læriti], *s.* angularité *f.*

angularly ['æŋgjuləli], *adv.* **1.** angulairement, en forme d'angle. **2.** diagonalement, obliquement, en travers.

angulate ['æŋgjuleit], *a.* angulé.

angulation [æŋgju'leiʃ(ə)n], *s.* forme *f* angulaire.

anguloa [æŋgju'louə], *s. Bot:* anguloa *f.*

angustifoliate [æŋgʌsti'foulieit], *a. Bot:* angustifolié.

angustirostrate [æŋgʌsti'rɔstreit], *a. Orn:* angustirostre.

angustiseptal [æŋgʌsti'septl], **angustiseptate** [æŋgʌsti'septeit], *a. Bot:* angustiseptė.

angustura [æŋgʌs'tjuərə], *s.* angusture *f,* angosture *f.*

angwantibo [æŋ'gwæntibou], *s. Z:* angwantibo *m,* potto *m.*

anharmonic [ænha:'mɔnik], *a. Mth:* **a. ratio,** rapport *m* anharmonique, birapport *m*

anhelation [ænhi'leiʃ(ə)n], *s. Med:* anhélation *f*; respiration anhélante, anhéleuse.

anhelous [æn'hi:ləs], *a.* anhéleux.

anhidrosis [ænhi'drousis], *s. Med:* anhidrose *f,* anidrose *f.*

Anhimidae [æn'himidi:], *s.pl. Orn:* anhimidés *m.*

anhinga [æn'hiŋgə], *s. Orn:* anhinga *m, F:* oiseau-serpent, *pl.* oiseaux-serpents.

anhistous [æn'histəs], *a. Biol:* anhiste.

anhydraemia [ænhai'dri:miə], *s. Med:* anhydrémie *f.*

anhydration [ænhai'dreiʃ(ə)n], *s. Ch:* anhydrisation f.

anhydride [æn'haidraid], *s. Ch:* anhydride *m.*

anhydrite [æn'haidrait], *s. Miner:* anhydrite *f.*

anhydromyelia [ænhaidroumai'i:liə], *s. Med:* anhydromyélie *f.*

anhydrous [æn'haidrəs], *a. Ch:* anhydre.

ani ['æni], *s. Orn:* ani *m, F:* merle-corbeau *m, pl.* merles-corbeaux; **white a.,** guira *m.*

anicut ['ænikʌt], *s.* (*in India*) barrage *m* de prise, de dérivation.

anil ['ænil], *s.* **1.** (*a*) *Bot:* anil *m,* indigotier *m*; (*b*) *Dy:* indigo *m.* **2.** *Ch:* anil.

anile ['einail], *a. Lit:* **1.** de vieille femme. **2.** imbécile.

anilide ['ænilaid], *s. Ch:* anilide *f.*

Aniliidae [æni'li:di:], *s.pl. Rept:* aniliidés *m.*

aniline ['ænilain], *s. Ch:* aniline *f,* phénilamine *f. attrib.* **a. dyes,** colorants *m* azoïques; **a. purple,** aniléine *f.*

anilism ['ænilizm], *s. Med:* anilisme *m.*

anility [æ'niliti], *s. Lit:* radotage *m*; faiblesse *f* d'esprit sénile (chez une vieille femme).

animadversion [ænimæd'və:ʃ(ə)n], *s. Lit:* animadversion *f,* censure *f,* blâme *m*; **general a.,** improbation générale; **to make animadversions on sth.,** critiquer qch.; se répandre en critiques sur qch.

animadvert [ænimæd'və:t], *v.i. Lit:* **to a. on s.o.'s action,** critiquer, blâmer, censurer, l'action de qn; **his conduct has been generally animadverted (up)on,** sa conduite a encouru l'animadversion générale, l'improbation générale.

animal ['æniml]. **1.** *s.* animal *m, pl.* aux; **a. house,** animalerie *f*; *Husb:* **live animals, animals on the hoof,** animaux sur pied; **animals slaughtered,** animaux abattus; **draught a.,** bête *f* de trait; **a. feeding stuffs,** aliments *mpl* pour bétail; *Art:* **a. painter,** animalier *m.* **2.** *a.* **the a. kingdom,** le règne animal; **a. life,** vie animale; **a. nature,** animalité *f*; **a. husbandry,** élevage *m*; **food of a. origin,** aliments d'origine animale; **a. manure,** engrais animal; **a. pole,** pôle animal (d'un œuf); **a. starch,** glycogène *f*; **a. black,** noir animal; **a. glue,** colle animale; **a. spirits,** exubérance *f.*

animalcular [æni'mælkjulər], *a.* animalculaire.

animalcule, *pl;* **-cula, -cules** [æni'mælkju:l, -kjulə, -kju:lz], *s.* animalcule *m*; *Prot:* **bell a.,** vorticelle *f*; **globe a.,** volvox globuleux.

animalism ['æniməlizm], *s.* **1.** *Biol:* animalisme *m.* **2.** activité animale. **3.** animalité *f,* sensualité *f.*

animalist ['ænimə1ist], *s.* **1.** animaliste *m.* **2.** *Art:* animalier *m.*

animality [æni'mæliti], *s.* **1.** animalité *f.* **2.** *coll.* les animaux *m.*

animalization [ænimәlai'zeiʃ(ə)n], *s. Physiol:* animalisation *f* (des aliments végétaux).

animalize ['æniməlaiz], *v.tr.* **1.** *Physiol:* animaliser (les aliments). **2.** (*a*) sensualiser (une passion, etc.); (*b*) **to become animalized,** s'animaliser.

animate[1] ['ænimət], *a.* animé; doué de vie; *s.* **the live and the a.,** le vivant et l'animé; **to become a.,** s'animer.

animate[2] ['ænimeit], *v.tr.* animer; encourager, stimuler (qn); mouvementer (la conversation).

animated ['ænimeitid], *a.* animé; **a. discussion,** discussion animée; **to become a.,** s'animer; **the discussion was getting a.,** la discussion s'échauffait; *Cin:* **a. cartoons,** dessins animés.

animatedly ['ænimeitidli], *adv.* d'un ton animé; d'un regard animé; vivement; avec vivacité; avec entrain.

animating ['ænimeitiŋ], *a.* qui anime, qui a de l'entrain; vif.

animation [æni'meiʃ(ə)n], *s.* **1.** animation *f*; vivacité *f*; chaleur *f* (du style); feu *m,* entrain *m,* verve *f* (d'un orateur); **play that lacks a.,** pièce *f* qui manque de vie, d'entrain. **2.** stimulation *f,* encouragement *m.* **3.** *Cin:* animation.

animator ['ænimeitər], *s.* animateur, -trice.

anime, animé ['ænimei], *s. Bot:* animé *f.*

animism ['ænimizm], *s.* **1.** *Phil:* animisme *m*; attribution d'une âme aux objets inanimés. **2.** *Phil: Theol:* spiritualisme *m.*

animist ['ænimist], *a. & s. Phil:* animiste *mf.*

animistic [æni'mistik], *a. Phil:* animiste.

animosity [æni'mɔsiti], *s.* animosité *f*; **to feel a. against s.o.,** avoir, ressentir, de l'animosité contre qn.

animus ['æniməs], *s.* **1.** stimulation *f.* **2.** animosité *f,* hostilité *f.*

anion ['ænaiən], *s. Ph: El:* anion *m.*

anionic [ænai'ɔnik], *a. Ph: El:* anionique.

anionotropy [ænaiɔnou'troupi], *s. Ch:* anionotropie *f.*

aniridia [æni'ridiə], *s. Med:* aniridie *f.*

anisaldehyde [ænis'ældihaid], *s. Ch:* aldéhyde *m* anisique.

anisated ['æniseitid], *a.* anisé.

anise ['ænis], *s. Bot:* anis *m*; **star a., Chinese a., a. tree,** badiane *f*; anis étoilé, anis de la Chine; **to flavour sth. with a.,** aniser qch.

aniseed ['ænisi:d], *s.* (graine *f* d')anis *m*; *Cu:* **a. cake,** gâteau *m* à l'anis.

aniseikonia [ænisei'kouniə], *s. Med:* aniséiconie *f.*

anisette [æni'zet], *s.* anisette *f* (liqueur).

anisic [ə'nisik], *a. Ch:* (acide, série) anisique.

anisidine [ə'nisidain], *s. Ch:* anisidine *f.*

anisochromia [ænisou'kroumiə], *s. Med:* anisochromie *f.*

anisocoria [ænieou'kɔ:riə], *s. Med:* anisocorie *f.*

anisocytosis [ænisousi'tousis], *s. Med:* anisocytose *f.*

anisodactyl(ous) [ænisou'dæktil(əs)], *a. Nat.Hist:* anisodactyle.

anisogamy [æni'sɔgəmi], *s. Biol:* anisogamie *f.*

anisol(e) ['ænisɔl], *s. Ch:* anisol(e) *m.*

anisomeric [ænisou'merik], *a. Ch:* anisomère.

anisomerous [æni'sɔmərəs], *a. Bot:* anisomère.

anisometropia [ænisoume'troupiə], *s. Opt: Med:* anisométropie *f.*

anisomyarian [ænisoumai'εəriən], *s. Moll:* anisomyaire *m.*

anisopetalous [ænisou'petələs], *a. Bot:* anisopétale.

anisophyllous [ænisou'filəs], *a. Bot:* anisophylle.

Anisoptera [æni'sɔptərə], *s.pl. Ent:* anisoptères *m.*

anisostemonous [ænisou'stemənəs], *a. Bot:* anisostémone.

anisosthenia [ænisou'sθi:niə], *s. Med:* anisosthénie *f.*

anisosthenic [ænisou'sθi:nik], *a. Med:* anisosthène.

anisotropic [ænisou'trɔpik], *a. Biol: Ph:* anisotropique; anisotrope.

anisotropism [ænisou'trɔpizm], **anisotropy** [æni'sɔtrəpi], *s. Biol: Ph:* anisotropie *f.*
anker ['æŋkər], *s. A.Meas: (about 38 litres)* anker *m.*
ankerite ['æŋkərait], *s. Miner:* ankérite *m*; spath brunissant.
ankh [æŋk], *s. Archeol:* croix ansée (d'Égypte), (croix) ankh (*m*).
ankle ['æŋkl], *s.* cheville *f* (du pied); **a. bone,** astragale *m*; **a. joint,** cheville *f*, attache *f* du pied; **a. boots,** bottillons *m*; **a. socks,** socquettes *f*; **a. strap,** barrette *f* (de chaussure); **a. support,** chevillière *f*; **a. ring,** anneau *m* de cheville; **a.-length dress,** robe *f* qui descend jusqu'à la cheville.
anklet ['æŋklət], *s.* **1.** anneau *m* attaché autour de la cheville; (*a*) manille *f* (de forçat); (*b*) *Toil:* bracelet *m* de jambe, de cheville. **2.** (*a*) guêtron *m* (de chasseur); (*b*) molletière *f* cycliste. **3.** *NAm:* socquette *f.*
ankyloblepharon [æŋkilou'blefərən], *s. Med:* ankyloblépharon *m.*
ankyloglossia [æŋkylou'glɔsiə], *s. Med:* ankyloglossie *f.*
ankylorrhinia [æŋkilou'rainiə], *s. Med:* ankylorrhinie *f.*
ankylose ['æŋkilouz]. *Med:* **1.** *v.tr.* ankyloser. **2.** *v.i.* s'ankyloser.
ankylosis [æŋki'lousis], *s. Med:* ankylose *f.*
ankylostoma [æŋki'lɔstoumə], *s. Ann:* ankylostome *m.*
ankylostomiasis ['æŋkiloustou'maiəsis], *s. Med:* ankylostomiase *f*, ankylostomose *f*, anémie *f* des mineurs.
ankyroid ['æŋkirɔid], *a. Anat:* ankyroïde.
Anna[1] ['ænə], *Pr.n.f.* Anna, Anne; *Hist:* **A. Comnena,** Anne Comnène.
anna[2], *s. Num:* ($\frac{1}{16}$ *rupee*) Anna *m.*
annabergite [ænə'bɔ:dʒait], *s. Miner:* annabergite *f.*
annalist ['ænəlist], *s.* annaliste *m.*
annals ['æn(ə)lz], *s.pl.* **1.** annales *f.* **2.** *Ecc:* messes dites pendant la durée d'une année.
Annam [æ'næm], *Pr.n. Geog:* Annam *m.*
Annamese [ænə'mi:z], **Annamite** ['ænəmait], *s. Geog:* Annamite *mf.*
Annas ['ænəs], *Pr.n.m. B.Hist:* Anne, Ananos.
annate ['æneit, 'ænət], *s. Ecc.Hist:* annate *f.*
Ann(e) [æn], *Pr.n.f.* (*a*) Anne; *Hist:* **Anne of Austria,** Anne d'Autriche; **Anne of Cleves,** Anne de Clèves; (*b*) *F:* **Queen Anne's dead,** (i) c'est de l'histoire ancienne; (ii) ta combinaison passe, tu cherches une belle-mère.
anneal [ə'ni:l], *v.tr. Metall:* recuire, adoucir (un métal, le verre); détremper (un métal).
annealing [ə'ni:liŋ], *s.* recuit *m*, recuite *f* (d'un métal, du verre); *Metall:* adoucissement *m*; **black a.,** recuit noir; **blue a.,** recuit bleu; **box a.,** recuit en vase clos; **bright a.,** recuit blanc; **close a.,** recuit en vase clos; **differential a.,** recuit différentiel; **flame a.,** adoucissement à la flamme; **full a.,** recuit complet; **normalizing a.,** normalisation *f*; **process a.,** revenu *m*; **skin a.,** recuit de surface; **soft a.,** recuit adoucissant; **stress-release a.,** recuit de libération des tensions; **a. furnace,** (i) four *m* à recuire; (ii) four à cloche.
annectent [ə'nektənt], *a. Biol:* connectif.
annelid ['ænəlid], *s. Nat.Hist:* annélide *f.*
Annelida [ə'nelidə], *s.pl. Nat.Hist:* annélides *f.*
annex[1] [ə'neks], *v.tr.* **1.** annexer (**sth. to sth.,** qch. à qch.); ajouter, joindre (une pièce à un mémoire). **2. to a. a province,** annexer une province.
annex[2], *s.* = ANNEXE.
annexation [æneks'eiʃ(ə)n], *s.* annexion *f* (**of,** de), mainmise *f* (**of,** sur).
annexationism [æneks'eiʃənizm], *s. Pol:* annexionnisme *m.*
annexationist [æneks'eiʃənist], *a. & s.* annexionniste (*mf*).
annexe ['æneks], *s.* annexe *f*; **a. to a hotel,** dépendance *f*, annexe, d'un hôtel.
annexed ['ænekst], *a.* annexé; *Com:* **the a. memorandum,** le mémoire ci-joint, ci-contre.
annexitis [æneks'aitis], *s. Med:* annexite *f.*
annexive [ə'neksiv], *s. Gram:* conjonctif.
Annie ['æni], *Pr.n.f. (dim. of Ann)* Annette, Annie.
Anniellidae [æni'elidi:], *s.pl. Amph:* anniellidés *m.*
annihilable [ə'naiələbl], *a.* annihilable.
annihilate [ə'naiəleit], *v.tr.* anéantir, réduire à néant (une flotte, une armée); annihiler, supprimer (le temps, l'espace).
annihilating [ə'naiəleitiŋ], *a.* annihilant; annihilateur, -trice.
annihilation [ənaiə'leiʃ(ə)n], *s.* (*a*) anéantissement *m* (d'une flotte, d'un peuple, d'une ville); annihilation *f*; (*b*) *Atom.Ph:* annihilation; dématérialisation *f.*
annihilationism [ənaiə'leiʃənizm], *s. Theol:* annihilationnisme *m.*
annihilationist [ənaiə'leiʃənist], *a. & s. Theol:* annihilationniste *m.*
annihilator [ə'naiəleitər], *s.* **1.** (*pers.*) annihilateur, -trice; destructeur *m.* **2.** *Mth:* annulateur *m*; **a. in the dual space of a given subspace,** orthogonal *m* d'un sous-espace vectoriel dans le dual.
anniversary [æni'və:s(ə)ri], *s.* anniversaire *m*; **it's our wedding a.,** c'est l'anniversaire de notre mariage; **it happened on the a. of . . .,** c'est arrivé le jour (de l')anniversaire de . . ..
Anno Domini ['ænou'dɔminai, -ni:]. **1.** *Lt.phr.* (*abbr.* **A.D.** ['ei'di:]) en l'an du Seigneur, de grâce; **in 1066 A.D.,** en 1066 apr. J.-C. (après Jésus-Christ). **2.** *s. F:* les ans *m*; la vieillesse qui vient; **I'm not ill, it's just a.d.,** je ne suis pas souffrant, c'est la vieillesse.
annona [æ'nounə], *s.* **1.** *Bot:* an(n)one *f.* **2.** *Rom.Civ:* annone.
Annonaceae [ænou'neisii:], *s.pl. Bot:* annonacées *f.*
annotate ['ænəteit], *v.tr.* annoter (un livre, etc.); accompagner (un texte) de remarques; commenter (un texte); **annotated text,** texte avec commentaire.
annotating ['ænəteitiŋ], **annotation** [ænə'teiʃ(ə)n], *s.* (*a*) annotation *f*; (*b*) *Cmptr:* **annotation,** annotation.
annotator ['ænəteitər], *s.* annotateur, -trice; commentateur, -trice.
announce [ə'nauns], *v.tr.* annoncer (qn, qch.); **to a. the guests,** annoncer les invités; **to a. a marriage,** annoncer un mariage; faire l'annonce d'un mariage; **he announced himself as sent by . . .,** il annonça qu'il était envoyé par . . .; **the Prime Minister has announced his cabinet,** le premier ministre a fait connaître la composition de son ministère.
announcement [ə'naunsmənt], *s.* **1.** annonce *f*, avis *m*; (*of birth, marriage, etc.*) faire-part *m inv*; **a. of death,** avis mortuaire (passé dans les journaux). **2.** *Jur:* affiche *f* judiciaire.
announcer [ə'naunsər], *s.* **1.** annonceur *m.* **2.** *W.Tel: T.V:* annonceur; speaker *m*, speakerine *f.*
annoy [ə'nɔi], *v.tr.* (*a*) contrarier, chagriner (qn); (*b*) gêner, irriter, fâcher, *F:* embêter (qn); **he annoys me,** il me fâche, il m'exaspère; **flies a. horses,** les mouches gênent les chevaux; **stop annoying your little sister,** cesse de taquiner ta petite sœur; **it annoys me to have to work on Sundays,** cela me fâche, me rend furieux, d'être obligé de travailler le dimanche; (*c*) harceler (l'ennemi).
annoyance [ə'nɔiəns], *s.* **1.** contrariété *f*, chagrin *m*; **look of a.,** air contrarié, fâché. **2.** désagrément *m*, ennui *m*, *F:* embêtement *m*; **source of a.,** désagrément, cause *f* d'ennuis; **petty annoyances,** petits ennuis.
annoyed [ə'nɔid], *a.* contrarié, ennuyé; fâché; **to be very much a. (at, about, sth.),** être très contrarié (de qch.); en être furieux; **to get a. at sth.,** se vexer, se fâcher, de qch.; **to be a. with s.o. about sth., for doing sth.,** se fâcher contre qn au sujet de qch., d'avoir fait qch.
annoying [ə'nɔiiŋ], *a.* contrariant, fâcheux, ennuyeux, *F:* embêtant; **the a. thing about it is that . . .,** le fâcheux de l'affaire c'est que . . .; **how a.!** que c'est fâcheux, *F:* embêtant!
annoyingly [ə'nɔiiŋli], *adv.* d'une manière fâcheuse, *F:* embêtante.
annual ['ænjuəl]. **1.** *a.* annuel; **a. leave,** congé annuel; **a. instalment,** annuité *f*; **debt repayable by a. instalments,** dette annuitaire; **a. abstract of statistics,** annuaire *m* de statistiques; **a. report (of a company),** rapport *m* de gestion (d'une compagnie); **he has an a. salary of £5000,** il gagne £5000 par an; **the club's a. dinner will be held on March 15,** le dîner annuel du club aura lieu le 15 mars; *Bot:* (*of tree*) **a. ring, a. zone,** couche annuelle. **2.** *s.* (*a*) *Bot:* plante annuelle; (*b*) *Publ:* annuaire; publication annuelle; (*c*) *Ecc:* (i) (*mass said daily for a year*) annuel *m*; (ii) messe *f* de bout de l'an.
annually ['ænjuəli], *adv.* annuellement; tous les ans.
annuitant [ə'nju:it(ə)nt], *s.* **1.** pensionnaire *mf* (de l'État, etc.). **2.** rentier, -ière (en viager); **life a.,** rentier viager, rentière viagère.
annuity [ə'nju:iti], *s.* **1. a. in redemption of debt,** annuité *f.* **2.** rente (annuelle); **government a.,** rente sur l'État; **perpetual a.,** rente perpétuelle; rente en perpétuel; **terminable a.,** rente à terme; annuité résiliable; **life a.,** rente viagère, pension viagère; **a. in reversion, reversionary a.,** rente réversible; **survivorship a.,** rente viagère avec réversion; **deferred a.,** annuité différée; **contingent a.,** annuité contingente; **to invest, sink, money in an a., to buy an a.,** placer son argent en viager, à fonds perdu; **to pay s.o. an a.,** servir, faire, une rente à qn.
annul [ə'nʌl], *v.tr.* (**annulled**) annuler, résilier (un acte); résoudre (un contrat); annihiler (un testament); dénoncer (un traité); dissoudre (un mariage); abroger (une loi); casser, infirmer (une décision); **his marriage was annulled,** son mariage a été déclaré nul.
annular ['ænjulər], *a.* (éclipse, doigt, espace) annulaire; *Cmptr:* **a. magnet,** aimant *m* torique.
annularia [ænju'lɛəriə], *s. Bot: Paleont:* annularia *f.*
annulary ['ænjuləri], *a. & s.* (doigt) annulaire *m.*
annulate ['ænjulət], **annulated** ['ænjuleitid], *a.* **1.** *Bot: Z:* annelé. **2.** *Arch:* armillé.
annulation [ænju'leiʃ(ə)n], *s.* **1.** formation *f* d'anneaux. **2.** anneau *m.*
annulet ['ænjulit], *s.* (*a*) *Arch:* annelet *m*, filet *m*, armille *f*; (*b*) *Her:* annelet; (*c*) *Ent:* (papillon *m* hétérocère) grophos *m.*
annullable [ə'nʌləbl], *a.* annulable, annihilable; (contrat *m*) résoluble.
annulling[1] [ə'nʌliŋ], *a.* qui annule; annulatif; **a. clause,** clause *f* abrogatoire; *Nau:* **a. signal,** signal *m* d'annulement.
annulling[2], **annulment** [ə'nʌlmənt], *s.* annulation *f*, résiliation *f*, résiliement *m*, résolution *f* (d'un contrat, etc.); annihilation *f*, cassation *f* (d'un testament); dissolution *f* (d'un mariage); abrogation *f* (d'une loi); abolition *f* (d'un décret); **decree of a.,** décret abolitif.
annulose ['ænjulous], *a.* annelé.
annulus ['ænjuləs], *s.* **1.** *Bot:* anneau *m* (de capsule de fougère, etc.); bague *f* (d'un champignon); collerette *f* (de chapeau de champignon). **2.** *Mth:* (*a*) anneau (sphérique), couronne *f*; (*b*) espace *f* annulaire. **3.** *Min:* **a. pressure,** pression *f* annulaire.
annunciate [ə'nʌnsieit, -ʃieit], *v.tr.* annoncer, proclamer (une nouvelle, la venue du Messie, etc.).
annunciation [ənʌnsi'eiʃ(ə)n], *s.* **1.** *Ecc:* **the A.,** l'Annonciation *f.* **2.** proclamation *f*, annonce *f* (d'un fait).
annunciator [ə'nʌnsieitər, -ʃi-], *s.* **1.** annonciateur, -trice (du Messie, etc.). **2.** (*a*) *Tp:* avertisseur *m*, annonciateur; **a. board,** tableau indicateur; (*b*) *Rail:* **electrical a.** (*used in signalling*), correspondance *f*; (*c*) *Nau:* transmetteur *m* d'ordres; (*d*) *Cmptr:* annonciateur *m.*
anoa [ə'nouə], *s. Z:* anoa *m*, buffle-pygmée *m*, *pl.* buffles-pygmées, des Célèbes.
Anobiidae [ænou'bi:idi:], *s.pl. Ent:* anobiidés *m.*
anobium [ə'noubiəm], *s. Ent:* anobie *m*, anobion *m*, anobium *m.*
anoci-association [ə'nousiəsousi'eiʃ(ə)n], *s. Med:* anoci(e)-association *f.*
anodal [ə'noudl], **anodic** [ə'noudik], *a. El:* anodique; **anodic oxidation,** oxydation *f* anodique.
anode ['ænoud], *s. El:* anode *f*; électrode positive; plaque *f*; **discharge at a.,** décharge *f* de l'anode; **a. voltage,** tension *f* de plaque; **a. current,** courant *m* anodique; *W.Tel:* **a. screen,** écran *m* de plaque.
anodization [ænoudai'zeiʃ(ə)n], *s. Metall:* anodisation *f.*
anodize ['ænoudaiz], *v.tr. Metall:* anodiser.
anodizing ['ænoudaiziŋ], *s. Metall:* anodisation *f.*
anodonta [ænou'dɔntə], *s. Moll:* anodonte *m.*
anodontia [ænou'dɔntiə], *s.* anodontie *f.*
anodyne ['ænoudain], *a. & s.* (*a*) *Med: etc:* anodin (*m*); calmant (*m*); antalgique (*m*); (*b*) **a. remark,** remarque *f* qui ne peut blesser personne.
anoint [ə'nɔint], *v.tr.* **1.** oindre; **to a. s.o. with oil,** oindre qn d'huile; **to a. s.o. king, bishop,** sacrer qn roi, évêque; **the Lord's Anointed,** l'Oint *m* du Seigneur. **2.** mettre un onguent, une pommade, sur (une plaie).
anointing [ə'nɔintiŋ], *s.* **1.** onction *f.* **2.** sacre *m* (d'un roi, d'un évêque).
anole [ə'noul], **anoli(s)** [ə'nouli(s)], **anolian** [ə'nouliən], *s. Rept:* anolis *m*; **giant anole of Haiti,** anolis géant d'Haïti; **common green anole,** anolis à gorge rouge.
anolyte ['ænoulait], *s. El:* anolyte *m.*
anomalistic [ənɔmə'listik], *a.* **1.** = ANOMALOUS. **2.** *Astr:* (année, mois) anomalistique.
anomalous [ə'nɔmələs], *a.* **1.** *Bot: Med: etc:* anomal, -aux; *Opt:* **a dispersion,** dispersion anomale; *Gram:* **a. verb,** verbe anomal. **2.** exceptionnel, irrégulier; anormal, -aux.
anomalously [ə'nɔmələsli], *adv.* irrégulièrement.
anomalousness [ə'nɔmələsnis], *s.* caractère anormal, exceptionnel (de qch.).
anomalure [ənɔmə'lju:ər], *s. Z:* anomalure *m*, écureuil volant.
Anomaluridae [ənɔmə'lju:ridi:], *s.pl. Z:* Anomaluridés *m.*
anomaly [ə'nɔməli], *s.* (*a*) *Ph: etc:* anomalie *f*; **Bouguer a.,** anomalie de Bouguer; **a. of temperature, temperature a.,** anomalie thermique; *Astr:* **truce a., mean a., eccentric a.,** anomalie vraie, moyenne, excentrique; (*b*) *Biol: etc:* anomalie, irrégularité *f*, aberration *f.*
anomia [ə'noumiə], *s. Moll:* anomie *f*, anomia *f.*
anomic ['ænəmik], *a.* anomique; **a. suicide,** suicide *m* anomique.

anomie ['ænəmi], *s. Phil:* anomie *f.*

anomocarpous [ənɔmou'kɑ:pəs], *a. Bot:* anomocarpe.

anomodont [ə'nɔmoudɔnt], *s. Rept:* anomodonte *m.*

Anomodontia [ənɔmou'dɔntiə], *s.pl. Rept:* anomodontes *m.*

anomophyllous [ənɔmou'filəs], *a. Bot:* anomophylle.

Anomura [ænɔ'mju:rə], *s.pl. Crust:* anomures *m.*

anomuran [ænɔ'mju:rən], **anomurous** [ænɔ'mju:rəs], *a. Crust:* anomure.

anomy ['ænəmi], *s. Phil:* anomie *f.*

anon[1] [ə'nɔn], *adv. A: & Hum:* **1.** tout à l'heure, bientôt; à l'instant. **2.** plus tard; **but more of this a.,** je reviendrai sur cela.

anon[2], *a.* anonyme.

anona [æ'nounə], *s. Bot:* anone *f.*

Anonaceae [ænou'neisii:], *s.pl. Bot:* anonacées *f.*

anonaceous [ænou'neiʃəs], *a. Bot:* anonacé.

anonychia [ænou'nikiə], *s. Med:* anonychie *f.*

anonym ['ænənim], *s.* **1.** (*pers.*) anonyme *m.* **2.** faux nom; pseudonyme *m.*

anonymity [ænə'nimiti], *s.* anonyme *m,* anonymat *m.*

anonymous [ə'nɔniməs], *a.* anonyme; **a. writer,** anonyme *m;* **to remain a.,** garder l'anonyme, l'anonymat.

anonymously [ə'nɔniməsli], *adv.* anonymement; **to write a.,** écrire sous (le couvert de) l'anonymat, en gardant l'anonyme.

anonymousness [ə'nɔniməsnis], *s.* = ANONYMITY.

anoöpsia [ænou'ɔpsiə], *s. Med:* anopsie *f.*

anopheles [ə'nɔfili:z], *s. Ent:* anophèle *m.*

anophthalmia [ænɔf'θælmiə], *s. Ter:* anophthalmie *f.*

anophthalmus [ænɔf'θælməs], *s. Ent:* anophthalme *m.*

anopisthographic [ænɔpisθou'græfik], *a.* anopisthographique; **a. book,** anopisthographe *m.*

Anopleura [ænou'plju:rə], *s.pl. Ent:* anoploures *m.*

Anoplotheridae [ænouplɔ'θeridi:], *s.pl. Paleont:* anoplothéridés *m.*

anoplotherium [ænouplɔ'θeriəm], *s. Paleont:* anoplothérium *m.*

Anoplura [ænou'pl(j)u:rə], *s.pl. Ent:* anoploures *m.*

anopsia [æ'nɔpsiə], *s. Med:* anopsie *f.*

anorak ['ænəræk], *s. Cost:* anorak *m.*

anorchia [æ'nɔ:kiə], **anorchism** ['ænɔ:kiʒm], *s. Med:* anorchidie *f.*

anorchous [æ'nɔ:kəs], *a. Med:* anorchide.

anorchus [æ'nɔ:kəs], *s. Med:* anorchide *m.*

anorexia [ænə'reksiə], *s. Med:* anorexie *f.*

anorthite ['ænəθait], *s. Miner:* anorthite *f.*

anorthose ['ænəθouz], *s. Miner:* anorthose *f.*

anosmatic [ænɔz'mætik], *a. Z:* anosmatique.

anosmia [æ'nɔsmiə], *s. Med:* anosmie *f.*

Anostraca [ænɔs'treikə], *s.pl. Crust:* anostracés *m.*

another [ə'nʌðər], *a. & pron.* **1.** (*an additional*) encore (un); **a. cup of tea,** encore une tasse de thé; **a. fifty years,** encore cinquante ans; **in a. ten years,** dans dix ans d'ici; **a. two minutes and I should have missed the boat,** deux minutes plus tard, deux minutes de plus, et je manquais le bateau; **I have received a. three hundred francs,** j'ai reçu trois cents autres francs; *Rail:* **to put on a. coach,** rajouter une voiture; **without a. word,** sans plus; sans un mot de plus. **2.** (*a similar*) (*a*) un(e) autre, un(e) second(e); *F:* **have a. (drink)!** encore un(e)? **such a.,** un autre du même genre, du même modèle; **there is not a. such man,** il n'a pas son pareil; **he will be a. Picasso,** ce sera un second Picasso; (*b*) **you're a liar! and you're a.!** menteur! toi aussi! **3.** (*a*) (*a different*) un(e) autre; **a. person was there before me,** un autre m'avait devancé; **take this cup away and bring me a. (one),** enlevez cette tasse et apportez-m'en une autre; **that's (quite) a. matter,** c'est tout autre chose; *F:* c'est une autre paire de manches, voilà bien une autre chanson; **I feel a. man,** je me sens tout autre, tout rajeuni; **a. time,** une autre fois; **couldn't we do that a. time?** est-ce que cela ne peut pas se remettre à plus tard? **we shall reserve that for a. occasion,** ce sera pour une autre fois; *Parl: F:* **a. place,** l'autre Chambre *f;* **he sat in the Commons before he went to a. place,** il siégea à la Chambre des Communes avant de passer aux Lords; **let's do it a. way,** faisons autrement; *F:* **tell me a.!** ce n'est pas vrai! quelle histoire! (*b*) **she now has a. husband,** elle a maintenant un nouveau mari. **4. one . . . a.:** (*a*) **science is one thing, art is a.,** la science est une chose, l'art en est une autre; **one would blame him, a. would excuse him,** tel l'en blâmait, tel autre l'en excusait; **I have heard it from one source and a. during the week,** j'en ai entendu parler de part et d'autre au courant de la semaine; (*b*) **one way or a.,** d'une façon ou d'une autre; **(taking) one year with a.,** bon an mal an; **taking one thing with a., we just manage,** l'un dans l'autre, on arrive à joindre les deux bouts; (*c*) (*reciprocal pron.*) **one a.,** l'un l'autre, les uns les autres; **love one a.,** aimez-vous les uns les autres; **he and his wife adore one a.,** lui et sa femme s'adorent (l'un l'autre); **they give one a. presents,** ils se donnent des cadeaux (l'un à l'autre); **near one a.,** l'un près de l'autre; près l'un de l'autre; **to kiss one a.,** s'embrasser; **to help one a.,** s'entraider.

anoura [ə'nuərə, ə'nuərə], **anourous** [ə'nuərəs, ə'nauərəs], = ANURA, ANUROUS.

anox(a)emia [ænɔk'si:miə], *s. Med:* anoxémie *f,* anoxhémie *f.*

anoxia [æ'nɔksiə], *s. Med:* anoxie *f;* **altitude a.,** mal *m* des aviateurs.

Ansaphone ['ɑ:nsəfoun], *s. R.t.m: Tp:* répondeur *m* téléphonique, enregistreur.

ansate(d) ['ænseit(id)], *a. Her: etc:* muni d'une anse; ansé; **ansate cross,** croix ansée.

Anseridae [æn'seridi:], *s.pl. Orn:* ansérides *m,* anatidés *m,* les oies *f.*

Anseriformes [ˌænseri'fɔ:mi:z], *s.pl. Orn:* ansériformes *m.*

Anserinae [æn'serini:], *s.pl. Orn:* ansérinés *m.*

anserine ['ænsərain], *a.* **1.** ansérin, qui a rapport aux oies; **a. skin,** peau ansérine, *F:* chair *f* de poule. **2.** *F: A:* stupide; bête (comme une oie).

answer[1] ['ɑ:nsər], *s.* **1.** (*a*) réponse *f* (à une question, à une lettre); réplique *f* (à une observation, à une critique); **back a.,** réplique impertinente; **his a. was that he knew nothing about it,** il a répondu qu'il n'en savait rien; **she made no a.,** elle n'a pas répondu; **he's always got an a.,** il a la réplique vive, facile; **he has an a. to everything,** il a réponse à tout; *F:* **to know all the answers,** (i) être au courant de tout; être à la page; (ii) se vanter de son savoir; (iii) savoir se tirer d'affaire; connaître les trucs; être combinard; **her only a. was to burst into tears,** pour toute réponse elle a fondu en larmes; **the a. to magnetic mines was found within a few weeks,** la parade aux mines magnétiques a été trouvée en quelques semaines; **his a. to the insult was a blow,** il a répondu à l'insulte par un coup de poing; *F:* **it's the a. to a maiden's prayer,** c'est exactement ce qu'il nous fallait, ce qu'il nous faut; c'est ce que nous cherchions, attendions, voulions; *F:* **he's hardly the a. to a maiden's prayer,** il n'est guère celui dont rêvent les jeunes filles; *Corr:* **in a. to your letter,** en réponse à votre lettre; **will you please let me have an a. before the end of the week,** je vous prie de me donner une réponse, de me répondre, avant la fin de la semaine; (*b*) *Jur: etc:* **a. to a charge,** réfutation *f* à une accusation; **I have a complete a. to the charge,** je suis prêt à réfuter entièrement cette accusation; (*c*) *Cmptr:* **a. mode,** mode *f* réponse; **a.-back drum,** tambour *m* réponse; (*d*) *Mus:* (*In counterpoint*) réplique; **real a. (of a fugue),** réponse; (*e*) *Fenc:* riposte *f.* **2.** *Mth:* solution *f* (d'un problème); **what is the correct a. to the problem?** quelle est la solution correcte du problème? **arithmetic with answers,** manuel *m* d'arithmétique avec solutions; **a. book,** livre *m* du maître.

answer[2], *v.tr. & i.* **1.** répondre; (*a*) **to a. s.o.,** répondre, faire réponse, à qn; **to a. back,** répliquer; répondre; **don't a. back!** pas de réplique! (*of dog*) **answers to the name of Rover,** répond au nom de Rover; *F:* (*of pers.*) **to a. to the name of Martin,** s'appeler Martin; (*b*) **to a. a question, a letter,** répondre à une question, à une lettre; **letters to be answered,** lettres à répondre; **letters answered,** lettres répondues; **the question was not answered,** la question est restée sans réponse; **the question is not easy to a.,** c'est une question à laquelle il n'est pas facile de répondre, qui ne comporte pas une solution facile; *Sch:* **few of the candidates answered the question well,** très peu des candidats ont bien traité la question; **I can't a. for him,** (i) je ne peux pas répondre pour lui, de sa part; (ii) je ne peux pas garantir ce qu'il va faire, qu'il le fera; *Turf:* (*of horse*) **to a. the question,** se montrer à la hauteur de l'effort à fournir; (*c*) **to a. the roll, to a. (to) one's name,** répondre à l'appel; **to a. the bell,** répondre à un coup de sonnette; **to a. the door,** aller ouvrir; venir ouvir; (*d*) (*of ship*) **to a. the helm,** obéir à la barre; sentir la barre; **ship that answers the helm,** navire obéissant; **ship that no longer answers the helm,** navire qui ne gouverne plus; **horse that answers the spur,** cheval qui répond, qui obéit, à l'éperon; (*e*) **to a. a charge,** répondre à, réfuter, une accusation; (*f*) **to a. a description,** répondre à un signalement; (*g*) **to a. a prayer,** exaucer une prière. **2. to a. the requirements of . . .,** répondre aux besoins de . . .; **to a. the purpose,** remplir le but; **that will a. my purpose,** cela fera mon affaire; **to a. several purposes,** servir à plusieurs usages; **a saucepan will a. the purpose just as well as a kettle,** une casserole convient, fera l'affaire, aussi bien qu'une bouilloire; **that won't a.,** cela ne fera pas l'affaire; cela n'est guère une bonne solution. **3. to a.** (= *vouch*) **for s.o., for s.o.'s honesty,** répondre de qn; se porter, se rendre, garant de qn, de l'intégrité de qn; (*s. a.* 1(*b*)) **to a. for the truth of sth.,** garantir l'exactitude de qch.; **to a. for one's actions,** prendre la responsabilité de ses propres actes; **he has a lot to a. for,** il est responsable de bien des choses; *F:* **you'll a. for that!** vous me payerez ça! **I can't a. for your getting it this week,** je ne garantis pas que vous l'aurez cette semaine.

answerable ['ɑ:nsərəbl], *a.* **1.** (*a*) garant, responsable, comptable (**to s.o. for sth.,** envers qn de qch.); **the Company is not a. for . . .,** la Compagnie ne répond pas de . . .; (*b*) **to be a. to an authority,** relever d'une autorité; **he is a. to nobody,** il ne doit de comptes à personne; il n'est solidaire de personne; **I am a. only to my husband,** je ne relève que de mon mari. **2.** (*a*) **the question is not a.,** c'est une question (i) à laquelle on ne peut pas répondre, (ii) que l'on ne peut pas résoudre; (*b*) **a. charge,** accusation *f* réfutable.

answerer ['ɑ:nsərər], *s.* **1.** (*pers.*) répondant, -ante. **2.** (*instrument*) **telephone a.,** répondeur *m* téléphonique.

answering ['ɑ:nsəriŋ], *a.* **1. an a. cry,** un cri jeté en réponse. **2.** (*equivalent*) qui répond, correspond, est équivalent (**to,** à); **I saw someone a. to your description,** j'ai vu quelqu'un qui répondait à votre description. **3.** *Tp:* **a. jack,** jack *m* de réponse; **a. service,** répondeur *m* téléphonique.

ant[1] [ænt], *s.* (*a*) fourmi *f;* **wood a., red a.,** fourmi rouge, fauve; **winged a., a. fly,** fourmi ailée; **amazon a., warrior a.,** fourmi amazone; **slave a.,** fourmi esclavagiste; **honey a.,** fourmi à miel; **mason a.,** fourmi maçonne; **market-gardening a.,** fourmi champignonniste; **harvesting a.,** fourmi moissonneuse; **visiting a.,** fourmi de visite; **spider a., velvet a.,** mutille *f;* **soldier a.,** soldat *m* des bois; **white a.,** fourmi blanche; termite *m;* **ant('s) eggs,** œufs *m* de fourmi; *F:* **to have ants in one's pants,** avoir la bougeote; (*b*) *F:* **a. cow,** puceron *m.*

ant[2], *v.i. Orn: F:* (*of bird*) prendre un bain de fourmis; se frictionner à l'aide de fourmis.

ant- [ænt], *pref.* = ANTI-, ANTE-, *before a vowel.*

anta, *pl.* **-ae** ['æntə, -i:], *s. Arch:* ante *f;* **a. cap,** chapiteau *m* d'ante.

antacid [ænt'æsid]. **1.** *a. & s. Med:* antiacide (*m*); alcalin (*m*). **2.** *a.* résistant aux acides.

Antaeus [æn'ti(:)əs], *Pr.n.m. Myth:* Antée.

antagonism [æn'tægənizm], *s.* (*a*) antagonisme *m,* opposition *f;* **a. between two people,** antagonisme, rivalité *f,* de, entre, deux personnes; (*b*) *Bio-Ch:* **bacterial a.,** antagonisme microbien.

antagonist [æn'tægənist], *s.* **1.** antagoniste *mf,* adversaire *m.* **2.** *Physiol:* (muscle) antagoniste *m.* **3.** *Bio-Ch:* antagoniste *m.*

antagonistic [æntægə'nistik], *a.* (*a*) opposé, contraire (**to,** à); **a. environment,** milieu *m* antagonique; *Biol:* **a. symbiosis,** symbiose *f* dysharmonique; antibiose *f;* parasitisme *m; Physiol:* **a. muscles,** muscles *m* antagonistes; (*b*) hostile (**to,** à); **cats and dogs are a.,** le chat et le chien sont des adversaires traditionnels; les chats détestent les chiens.

antagonize [æn'tægənaiz], *v.tr.* **1.** (*a*) (*of a force*) s'opposer à (une autre force); contrarier (une force); (*b*) *Physiol:* (*of muscle*) neutraliser l'effort (d'un autre muscle). **2.** éveiller l'antagonisme, l'hostilité, de (qn), éloigner (qn); **to a. the public,** ranger l'opinion contre soi; **cats a. dogs,** les chats éveillent l'hostilité des chiens.

antalgic [ænt'ældʒik], *a. & s. Med:* antalgique (*m*); anodin (*m*).

antalkali [ænt'ælkəlai], *s. Med:* médicament *m* qui corrige l'alcalinité.

antalkaline [ænt'ælkəlain], *a. & s.* antialcalin (*m*).

antanaclasis [æntænə'kleisis], *s. Rh:* antanaclase *f.*

Antananarivo ['æntænænə'ri:vou], *Pr.n. Geog:* Tananarive.

antaphrodisiac ['æntæfrou'diziæk], *a. & s. Pharm:* antiaphrodisiaque (*m*).

antapoplectic ['æntæpə'plektik], *a. & s. Med:* antiapoplectique (*m*).

antarctic [æn'tɑ:ktik]. **1.** *a.* (pôle, faune, etc.) antarctique. **2.** *s.* **the A.,** l'Antarctique *m.*

Antarctica [æn'tɑ:ktikə], *Pr.n. Geog:* Antarctique *m,* Antarctide *f.*

Antares [æn'tɛəri:z], *Pr.n. Astr:* Antarès *m;* le Cœur du Scorpion.

antarthritic ['æntɑ:'θritik], *a. & s. Med:* antiarthritique (*m*).

antasthmatic ['æntæsθ'mætik], *a. & s. Med:* antiasthmatique (*m*).

ant bear ['æntbɛər], *s. Z:* **1.** tamanoir *m.* **2.** oryctérope *m* (du Cap).

antbird ['æntbə:d], **antcatcher** ['æntkætʃər], *s. Orn:*

fourmilier *m.*

ante[1] ['ænti], *s. Cards: (at poker)* **1.** première mise. **2.** ouvreur (primitif).

ante[2], *v.tr. & i.* **to a. (up) 1.** *Cards: (at poker)* ouvrir le jeu; déposer la première mise. **2.** *P: (a)* payer, s'exécuter; *(b)* **to a. up money on . . .,** ponter sur . . ..

ante- ['ænti], *pref.* anté-; pré-; *occ.* anti-.

anteater ['ænti:tər], *s. Z:* fourmilier *m*; **great a.,** tamanoir *m*; myrmécophage *m*; **scaly a.,** pangolin *m*; **spiny a., porcupine a.,** échidné *m*; **marsupial a., banded a.,** myrmécobie *m*; fourmilier-marsupial *m, pl.* fourmiliers-marsupiaux; *F:* fourmilier à poche; **two-toed a.,** cyclope *m*, petit fourmilier arboricole; **tamandua a.,** tamandua *m.*

anteating ['ænti:tiŋ], *a. Z:* myrmécophage.

ante bellum ['ænti'beləm], *Lt.adj.phr. (a)* d'avant-guerre; *(b) U.S:* d'avant la guerre civile.

antébrachial [ænti'breikiəl], *a. Z: Anat:* antébrachial, -aux.

antecedence [ænti'si:d(ə)ns], *s.* **1.** *(a)* antériorité *f*; *(b)* priorité *f.* **2.** *Astr:* antécédence *f.*

antecedent [ænti'si:d(ə)nt]. **1.** *a.* antécédent (to, à); **a. signs of a disease,** symptômes précurseurs d'une maladie; *Geog:* **a. river, stream,** antécédent *m.* **2.** *s. (a) Gram: Log: Mth:* antécédent *m*; *(b) Mus:* thème *m* (d'une fugue); *(c) pl.* **his antecedents,** ses antécédents; son passé; ses ancêtres; **to be proud of one's antecedents,** être fier de ses ancêtres.

antechamber ['æntitʃeimbər], *s.* **1.** antichambre *f.* **2.** *I.C.E:* préchambre *f*; **Diesel engine with a.,** moteur *m* Diesel à chambre de précombustion, à préchambre.

antechapel ['æntitʃæpl], *s. Ecc.Arch:* avant-corps *m* d'une chapelle, d'une église.

antecolic ['æntikɔlik], *a. Med:* précolique.

anteconsonantal ['ænti'kɔnsənæntl], *a. Ling:* anteconsonantique.

antedate[1] ['æntideit], *s.* antidate *f.*

antedate[2] ['ænti'deit], *v.tr.* **1.** *(a)* antidater (une nomination, un document); *(b)* faire remonter (un événement) trop loin dans le passé. **2.** *(a)* précéder; venir avant (un événement); *(b)* hâter, avancer (un événement); provoquer (un accouchement) avant terme.

antediluvian [æntidi'lu:viən], *a.* antédiluvien.

antedon ['æntidɔn], *s. Echin:* antedon *m.*

ante fix, *pl.* **-fixes, -fixa** ['æntifiks, -fiksiz, -fiksə], *s. Arch:* antéfixe *f.*

anteflexion [ænti'flekʃ(ə)n], *s.* antéflexion *f* (de l'utérus).

antehypophysis, *pl.* **-physes** [æntihai'pɔfisis, -fisi:z], *s. Anat:* antéhypophyse *f.*

antelope ['æntiloup], *s. (pl.* **antelopes,** *occ.* **antelope)** *Z:* antilope *f*; **Indian a.,** cervicapre *m*; **Barbary a.,** gazelle *f*; **royal a.,** néotrague *m*, antilope royale, pygmée; **roan a.,** antilope rouane; **sable a.,** antilope noire géante; **(Indian) four-horned a.,** antilope tétracère; **saiga a.,** saïga *m*; **harnessed a.,** guib (harnaché); **antelope are very attractive creatures,** les antilopes sont de fort jolies bêtes; *U.S:* **the A. State,** le Nébraska.

antemeridian ['æntimə'ridiən], *a.* de la matinée.

ante meridiem ['æntimə'ridiem], *Lt.phr. (abbr.* **a.m.** ['ei'em]) avant midi; **five a.m.,** cinq heures du matin.

antemundane [ænti'mʌndein], *a.* préexistant au monde.

antenatal [ænti'neitl], *a.* prénatal, -als.

antenna [æn'tenə], *s.* **1.** *(pl.* **-ae** [-i:]) *Ent: Crust:* antenne *f*; *Moll:* tentacule *m*; corne *f* (de limaçon). **2.** *(pl. usu.* **-as** [-əz]) *W.Tel: T.V:* antenne; **beam a., directional a.,** antenne dirigée; **fishbone a.,** antenne directionnelle en arête de poisson; **balancing a.,** antenne de compensation; **radar a., horn a.,** antenne (de) radar; **built-in, suppressed a.,** antenne noyée; **flush a.,** antenne encastrée; **a. coil,** bobine *f*, bobinage *m*, d'antenne; **a. alignment,** réglage *m* de circuit d'antenne.

antennal [æn'ten(ə)l], *a.* d'antenne.

Antennaria [ænte'nɛəriə], *s.pl. Bot:* antennaria *f.*

Antennariidae [æntenɛəri'idi:], *s.pl. Ich:* antennariidés *m.*

antennarius [ænte'nɛəriəs], *s. Ich:* antennaire *m.*

antennary [æn'tenəri], *a.* antennaire.

Antennata [ænte'neitə], *s.pl. Z:* antennates *m.*

antennate [æn'teneit], *a.* antenné, pourvu d'antennes.

antenniferous [ænte'nifərəs], *a.* antennifère.

antenniform [ænteni'fɔ:m], *a.* antenniforme.

antennularia [æntenju'lɛəriə], *s. Coel:* antennulaire *f.*

antennule [æn'tenju:l], *s. Crust:* antennule *f.*

antenuptial [ænti'nʌpʃ(ə)l], *a.* anténuptial, -aux; prénuptial, -aux; **a. settlement, a. contract,** contrat *m* de mariage.

antepalatal [ænti'pælətl], *a. Ling:* prépalatal, -aux.

antependium [ænti'pendiəm], *s. Ecc:* devant *m* d'autel.

antepenult [æntipe'nʌlt], **antipenultimate** [æntipe'nʌltimət], *a. & s.* antépénultième *f.*

antepodal [ænti'poudl], *a. Bot:* **a. cells,** antipodes *m.*

anteposition [æntipə'ziʃ(ə)n], *s. Gram:* antéposition *f*, inversion *f.*

anterior [æn'tiəriər], *a. (a)* antérieur, -eure (to, à); *Gram:* **past a.,** passé antérieur; *(b) Anat:* (muscle, etc.) antérieur.

anteriority [æntiəri'ɔriti], *s.* antériorité *f.*

anterograde ['æntərougreid], *a. Med:* antérograde.

anteroinferior ['æntərouin'fiəriər], *a. Anat:* antéroinférieur.

anterointernal ['æntərouin'tə:n(ə)l], *a. Anat:* antérointerne.

anteroom ['æntiru(:)m], *s.* antichambre *f*, vestibule *m.*

anteroposterior ['æntəroupɔs'tiəriər], *a. Anat:* antéropostérieur.

anterosuperior ['æntərousu'piəriər], *a. Anat:* antérosupérieur.

anteversion [ænti'və:ʃ(ə)n], *s. Med:* antéversion *f* (de l'utérus).

anthela ['ænθilə], *s. Bot:* anthèle *f.*

anthelion, *pl.* **-ia** [æn'θi:liən, -iə], *s. Meteor:* anthélie *f.*

anthelix [æn'θi:liks], *s. Anat:* anthélix *m.*

anthelmintic, anthelminthic [ænθel'mintik, -θik], *a. & s. Med:* anthelmint(h)ique *(m)*, vermifuge *(m).*

anthem ['ænθəm], *s.* **1.** *Ecc.Mus: (a) A: (antiphon)* antienne *f*; *(b)* motet *m.* **2.** *(a)* **national a.,** hymne national; *(b) A. & Lit:* chant *m* d'allégresse.

anthemis ['ænθimis], *s.* **1.** *Bot:* anthémis *m.* **2.** *Pharm:* fleurs *fpl* de camomille.

anther ['ænθər], *s. Bot:* anthère *f.*

anthericum [æn'θerik(ə)m], *s. Bot:* anthericum *m.*

antheridiophore [ænθə'ridioufɔ:r], *s. Bot:* anthéridiophore *m.*

antheridium, *pl.* **-ia** [ænθə'ridiəm, -iə], *s. Bot:* anthéridie *f.*

antheriferous [ænθə'rifərəs], *a. Bot:* anthérifère.

antherozoid [ænθərou'zɔid], *s. Bot:* anthérozoïde *m.*

anthesis, *pl.* **-es** [æn'θi:sis, -i:z], *s. Bot:* anthèse *f*, floraison *f.*

anthidium [æn'θidiəm], *s. Ent:* anthidie *f.*

anthill ['ænthil], *s.* fourmilière *f.*

anthoceros [æn'θɔsərəs], *s. Bot:* anthocéros *m.*

Anthocerotales [ænθousərə'teili:z], *s.pl. Bot:* anthocérotales *f.*

Anthocoridae [ænθou'kɔridi:], *s.pl. Ent:* anthocorides *m.*

anthocyan [ænθou'saiən], **anthocyanin** [ænθou'saiənin], *s. Bio-Ch:* anthocyane *f*, anthocyanine *f.*

anthocyanidin [ænθousai'ænedin], *s. Bio-Ch:* anthocyanidine *f.*

anthodium, *pl.* **-ia** [æn'θoudiəm, -iə], *s. Bot:* anthode *m*; capitule *m.*

anthogenesis [ænθou'dʒenisis], *s.* anthogénèse *f.*

anthological [ænθə'lɔdʒikl], *a.* anthologique.

anthologist [æn'θɔlədʒist], *s.* anthologue *m.*

anthologize [æn'θɔlədʒaiz]. *(a) v.tr.* mettre (un poème, etc.) dans une anthologie; **a much anthologized poem,** poème qu'on trouve dans toutes les anthologies; *(b) v.i.* faire une anthologie.

anthology [æn'θɔlədʒi], *s.* anthologie *f.*

Anthomedusae [ænθoumi'dju:zi:], *s.pl. Coel:* tubularidés *m.*

anthonomus [ænθou'nouməs], *s. Ent:* anthonome *m.*

Anthony ['æntəni], *Pr.n.m.* Antoine; *A:* **(St) Anthony's fire,** érysipèle *m*; *A:* feu *m* Saint-Antoine; feu céleste; *F: O:* **an A. Eden,** un chapeau de feutre noir.

anthophagous [æn'θɔfəgəs], *a.* anthophage.

anthophilian [ænθə'filiən], **anthophilous** [æn'θɔfiləs], *a. Ent:* anthophile.

Anthophora [æn'θɔfərə], *s.pl. Ent:* anthophores *m.*

anthophore ['ænθəfɔ:r], *s. Ent:* anthophore *m.*

anthophyllite [ænθou'filait], *s. Miner:* anthophyllite *f.*

Anthophyta [ænθou'faitə], *s.pl. Bot:* anthophytes *f.*

anthoxanthin [ænθɔks'ænθin], *s. Bot:* anthoxanthine *f.*

Anthozoa [ænθou'zouə], *s.pl. Coel:* anthozoaires *m.*

anthozoan, anthozoon [ænθou'zouən], *s. Coel:* anthozoaire *m.*

anthracene ['ænθrəsi:n], *s. Ch:* anthracène *m*, anthracine *f*; *attrib.* **a. dyes,** colorants *m* anthracéniques; **a. oil,** huile *f* anthracénique.

anthracic [æn'θræsik], *a. Med:* charbonneux.

anthraciferous [ænθrə'sifərəs], *a. Geol:* anthracifère.

anthracite ['ænθrəsait], *s. Min:* anthracite *m.*

anthracitic [ænθrə'sitik], **anthracitous** ['ænθrəsaitəs], *a. Geol:* anthraciteux, anthracifère.

anthracnose [æn'θræknous], **anthracnosis** [ænθræk'nousis], *s. Bot:* anthracnose *f.*

anthracoid ['ænθrəkɔid], *a. Med:* charbonneux, anthracoïde.

anthracolithic [ænθrəkɔ'liθik], *a. Geol:* anthracifère.

anthraconite [æn'θrækənait], *s. Miner:* anthraconite *f or m.*

anthracosis [ænθrə'kousis], *s. Med:* anthracose *f*, anthracosis *f.*

anthracotherium [ænθrəkou'θeriəm], *s. Paleont:* anthracotherium *m.*

anthracotic [ænθrə'kɔtik], *a. Med:* anthracosique.

anthranilate [ænθrə'naileit], *s. Ch:* anthranilate *m.*

anthranilic [ænθrə'nailik], *a. Ch:* anthranilique.

anthranol ['ænθrənɔl], *s. Ch:* anthranol *m.*

anthraquinone [ænθrə'kwinoun], *s. Ch:* anthraquinone *f.*

anthrax ['ænθræks], *s.* **1.** *Vet: Med: (a)* anthrax *m*; furoncle malin; pustule, tumeur, charbonneuse; *(b)* charbon *m*; fièvre charbonneuse; **a. bacillus,** bactéridie charbonneuse, de charbon; **a.-carrying flies,** mouches charbonneuses. **2.** *Ent:* anthrax.

anthrenus [æn'θri:nəs], *s. Ent:* anthrène *m.*

Anthribidae [æn'θribidi:], *s.pl. Ent:* anthribidés *m.*

anthriscus [æn'θriskəs], *s. Bot:* anthrisque *f*, persil *m* sauvage.

anthrone ['ænθroun], *s. Ch:* anthrone *f.*

anthropo- ['ænθrəpou, -pə, ænθrə'pɔ], *pref.* anthropo-.

anthropobiology ['ænθrə:poubai'ɔlədʒi], *s.* anthropobiologie *f.*

anthropocentric ['ænθrəpou'sentrik], *a. Phil:* anthropocentrique; **a. outlook,** anthropocentrisme *m.*

anthropocentrism ['ænθrəpou'sentrizm], *s. Phil:* anthropocentrisme *m.*

anthropoclimatology ['ænθrəpouklaimə'tɔlədʒi], *s.* anthropoclimatologie *f.*

anthropogenesis ['ænθrəpou'dʒenisis], *s.* anthropogénèse *f*, anthropogénésie *f*, anthropogénie *f.*

anthropogeography ['ænθrəpoudʒi'ɔgrəfi], *s.* anthropogéographie *f.*

anthropography [ænθrə'pɔgrəfi], *s.* anthropographie *f.*

anthropoid ['ænθrəpɔid], *a. & s. (a)* anthropoïde *(m)*; *(b) Z:* (singe *m*) anthropomorphe; anthropoïde *(m).*

Anthropoidea [ænθrə'pɔidiə], *s.pl. Z:* anthropoïdes *m.*

anthropolite [æn'θrɔpəlait], **anthropolith** [æn'θrɔpəliθ], *s.* anthropolithe *m.*

anthropological ['ænθrəpə'lɔdʒikl], *a.* anthropologique.

anthropologist [ænθrə'pɔlədʒist], *s.* anthropologiste *mf*, anthropologue *mf.*

anthropology [ænθrə'pɔlədʒi], *s.* anthropologie *f.*

anthropometer [ænθrə'pɔmitər], *s.* anthropomètre *m.*

anthropometric(al) [ænθrəpə'metrik(l)], *a.* anthropométrique.

anthropometry [ænθrə'pɔmitri], *s.* anthropométrie *f*; **criminal a. department,** service *m* anthropométrique.

anthropomorphic [ænθrəpou'mɔ:fik], *a.* anthropomorphe.

anthropomorphism [ænθrəpou'mɔ:fizm], *s. Phil:* anthropomorphisme *m.*

anthropomorphist [ænθrəpou'mɔ:fist], **anthropomorphite** [ænθrəpou'mɔ:fait], *s. Phil:* anthropomorphiste *mf*, anthropomorphite *mf.*

anthropomorphize [ænθrəpou'mɔ:faiz], *v.tr.* anthropomorphiser.

anthropomorphous [ænθrəpou'mɔ:fəs], *a.* anthropomorphe.

anthroponymy [ænθrə'pɔnimi], *s. Ling:* anthroponymie *f.*

Anthropophagi [ænθrə'pɔfədʒai], *s.pl.* anthropophages *m.*

anthropophagous [ænθrə'pɔfəgəs], *a.* anthropophage.

anthropophagy [ænθrə'pɔfədʒi], *s.* anthropophagie *f.*

anthropophilism [ænθrə'pɔfilizm], *s. Biol:* anthropophilie *f.*

anthropophobia [ænθrəpou'foubiə], *s.* anthropophobie *f.*

anthropopithecus ['ænθrəpoupi'θi:kəs], *s. Paleont:* anthropopithèque *m.*

anthroposomatology ['ænθrəpousomə'tɔlədʒi], *s.* anthroposomatologie *f.*

anthropotomy [ænθrə'pɔtəmi], *s.* anthropotomie *f.*

anthropozoic ['ænθrəpou'zouik], *a. Geol:* anthropozoïque.

anthurium [æn'θjuəriəm], *s. Bot:* anthure *m*, anthurium *m.*

anthyllis [æn'θilis], *s. Bot:* anthyllide *f*, anthyllis *f.*

anti ['ænti], *a. F:* **he's just a.,** c'est un contestataire.

anti- ['ænti], *pref.* anti-; anté-; contre.

antiacid [ænti'æsid], *s.* antiacide *m.*

anti-aircraft ['ænti'ɛəkrɑ:ft], *a.* antiaérien, contre avions; **a.-a. gun, etc.,** canon, etc., antiaérien; **a.-a. artillery,** artillerie antiaérienne; **a.-a. defence,** (i) défence antiaérienne, contre avions; (ii) les Forces Terrestres Antiaériennes; **A.-A. Operations Centre,** Centre de

Renseignements et de Direction de Tir.
antialcohol(ic) ['æntiælkə'hɔl(ik)], *a.* antialcoolique.
antialcoholist ['æntiælkə'hɔlist], *s.* antialcoolique *mf.*
antiar ['æntiɑ:r], *s. Bot: Pharm:* antiar *m.*
antiarthritic ['æntiɑ:'θritik], *a.* antiarthritique.
antiasthmatic ['æntiæs(θ)'mætik], *a.* antiasthmatique.
antiatomic ['æntiə'tɔmik], *a.* antiatomique.
anti-attrition ['æntiə'triʃ(ə)n], *a. & s. Mec.E:* antifriction (*m*).
antiauxin [ænti'ɔ:ksin], *s. Bio-Ch:* antiauxine *f.*
antibacterial ['æntibæk'tiəriəl], *a. Med:* antibactérien.
antiballistic ['æntibə'listik], *a.* antiballistique, antimissile; **a. missile,** engin *m* antimissile, fusée *f* antimissile.
antibilious ['ænti'biliəs], *a. Med:* (remède) antibilieux.
antibiosis ['æntibai'ousis], *s.* antibiose *f.*
antibiotic ['æntibai'ɔtik], *a. & s.* antibiotique (*m*).
anti-blistering ['ænti'blistəriŋ], *a. Med:* antivésicant.
antibody ['æntibɔdi], *s. Physiol:* anticorps *m.*
antibrachial ['ænti'breikiəl], *a. Anat:* antibrachial, -aux.
antic ['æntik]. **1.** *s.* (*usu.pl.*) (*a*) bouffonnerie *f*, singerie *f*; **he's up to his antics again,** le voilà de nouveau qui fait le bouffon, qui fait des farces; (*b*) *pl.* gambades *f*, cabrioles *f*. **2.** *a. A:* (*a*) grotesque; (*b*) gai, folichon. **3.** *s.m. A:* bouffon, farceur.
anti-carbon ['ænti'kɑ:bən], *a. Ch: I.C.E:* (additif) anticalaminant.
anticatarrhal ['æntikə'tɑ:r(ə)l], *a. & s. Med:* anticatarrhal, -aux (*m*).
anticathode ['ænti'kæθoud], *s. El:* anticathode *f.*
anticatholic ['ænti'kæθ(ə)lik], *a. & s.* anticatholique (*mf*).
antichlor ['æntiklɔ:r], *s. Tex: etc:* antichlore *m.*
anticholeraic ['æntikɔlə'reiik], *a. & s. Pharm:* anticholérique (*m*).
antichresis [ænti'kri:sis], *s. Jur:* antichrèse *f.*
antichrist ['æntikraist], *s.* antéchrist *m.*
antichristian ['ænti'kristjən], *a.* antichrétien.
antichristianism ['ænti'kristjənizm], *s.* antichristianisme *m.*
anticipate [æn'tisipeit], *v.tr.* **1.** (*a*) **to a. events, one's income, etc.,** anticiper sur les événements, sur son revenu, etc.; **to a. a pleasure,** se réjouir d'avance d'un bonheur; savourer un plaisir d'avance; (*b*) escompter (un résultat, un vote, etc.). **2. to a. s.o.,** prévenir, devancer, qn; **to a. s.o.'s wishes, s.o.'s thought, an objection,** aller au-devant des désirs de qn, de la pensée de qn, d'une objection; **to a. s.o.'s orders, s.o.'s desires,** prévenir les ordres de qn, devancer les désirs de qn; aller au-devant des désirs de qn. **3.** anticiper, avancer (un paiement, l'heure de son arrivée). **4.** prévoir, envisager, s'attendre à (une difficulté, un plaisir, etc.); se promettre (un plaisir); **this event was not anticipated,** on n'avait pas prévu, envisagé, cet événement; **I did not a. that he would come,** je ne m'attendais pas à ce qu'il vînt, à sa venue; **I anticipated as much,** je m'y attendais; **to a. the worst,** s'attendre au pire; pronostiquer au plus grave.
anticipation [æntisi'peiʃ(ə)n], *s.* **1.** (*a*) anticipation *f*; **we bought some coal in a. of a strike,** nous avons acheté du charbon en pensant à la possibilité d'une grève; **to enjoy sth. by a.,** jouir de qch. par anticipation; goûter (un plaisir) d'avance; *Corr:* **thanking you in a.,** avec mes remerciements anticipés; en vous remerciant d'avance; (*b*) *Mus:* anticipation (d'un accord). **2.** prévision *f*; **the general a. was that . . .,** on prévoyait que + *ind.*; on s'attendait à ce que + *sub.*; **to save in a. of the future,** économiser en prévision de l'avenir. **3.** attente *f*, expectation *f*, expectative *f.*
anticipative [æn'tisipeitiv], *a.* **1.** anticipé. **2.** *Lit:* **to be a. of sth.,** s'attendre à qch.; être dans l'expectative de qch.
anticipator [æn'tisipeitər], *s.* personne *f* qui anticipe (**of,** sur).
anticipatory [æntisi'peitəri], *a.* anticipé, anticipatif; par anticipation.
anticivic ['ænti'sivik], *a.* anticivique.
Anticlea [ænti'kli:ə], *Pr.n.f. Gr.Lit:* Anticlée.
anticlerical ['ænti'klerikl], *a. & s.* anticlérical, -ale, -aux.
anticlericalism ['ænti'klerikəlizm], *s.* anticléricalisme *m.*
anticlimactic ['æntiklai'mæktik], *a.* (dénouement, etc.) où l'action retombe dans l'ordinaire.
anticlimax ['ænti'klaimæks], *s.* **1.** *Rh:* anticlimax *m*; gradation inverse, descendante. **2. the fifth act forms an a.,** avec le cinquième acte nous retombons dans l'ordinaire, nous retombons sur terre, on passe du sublime au terre à terre; **the arrival of the mayor was an a.,** l'arrivée du maire nous a fait revenir au terre à terre.
anticlinal ['ænti'klainl], *a. Geol:* anticlinal, -aux; **a. fold,** pli anticlinal.
anticline ['æntiklain], *s. Geol:* anticlinal, -aux *m.*
anticlinorium ['æntiklai'nɔ:riəm], *s. Geol:* anticlinorium *m.*
anticlockwise ['ænti'klɔkwaiz], *adv. & a.* en sens inverse des aiguilles d'une montre.
anticoagulant ['æntikou'ægjulənt], *a. & s. Med:* anticoagulant (*m*).
anticoincidence ['æntikou'insid(ə)ns], *s. Atom.Ph:* **a.-c. unit,** montage *m* à anticoïncidence.
anticolonialism ['æntikə'louniəlizm], *s.* anticolonialisme *m.*
anticolonialist ['æntikə'louniəlist], *s.* anticolonialiste *mf.*
anticonformism ['æntikən'fɔ:mizm], *s.* anticonformisme *m.*
anticonformist ['æntikən'fɔ:mist], *s.* anticonformiste *mf.*
anticonstitutional ['æntikɔnsti'tju:ʃn(ə)l], *a.* anticonstitutionnel.
anticonstitutionally ['æntikɔnsti'tju:ʃn(ə)li], *adv.* anticonstitutionnellement.
anticonvulsant ['æntikən'vʌls(ə)nt], *a. & s. Med:* anticonvulsant (*m*).
anticorrosive ['æntikə'rousiv, -ziv], *a. & s.* anticorrosif (*m*).
Anticosti [ænti'kɔsti], *Pr.n. Geog:* Anticosti *m*; l'île *f* de l'Assomption.
anticyclic [ænti'saiklik], *a.* anticyclique.
anticyclone [ænti'saikloun], *s. Meteor:* anticyclone *m.*
anticyclonic [æntisai'klɔnik], *a. Meteor:* anticyclonique; anticyclonal, -aux.
anti-dazzle ['ænti'dæzl], **anti-dazzling** ['ænti'dæzliŋ], *a.* anti-aveuglant, *pl.* anti-aveuglants; anti-éblouissant, *pl.* anti-éblouissants.
antidemocratic ['æntidemə'krætik], *a.* antidémocratique.
antidiuretic ['æntidaiju'retik], *a. Med:* antidiurétique.
antidotal [ænti'doutl], *a.* qui peut servir d'antidote; antivénéneux.
antidote ['æntidout], *s.* antidote *m*, contrepoison *m.*
anti-dramatic ['æntidrə'mætik], *a.* antidramatique.
antidromous [æn'tidrəməs], *a. Bot:* antidrome.
antiemetic ['æntii'metik], *a.* antiémétique.
anti-enzyme ['ænti'enzaim], *s. Bio-Ch:* antienzyme *m.*
antifading ['ænti'feidiŋ], *a. W.Tel: etc:* antifading *inv.*
antifascism ['ænti'fæʃizm], *s. Pol:* antifascisme *m.*
antifascist ['ænti'fæʃist], *a. & s. Pol:* antifasciste (*mf*).
antifebrile ['ænti'febril], *a. & s. Med:* antifébrile (*m*); fébrifuge (*m*)
antifebrin [ænti'fi:brin], *s. Pharm:* antifébrine *f.*
antifeminism ['ænti'feminizm], *s.* antiféminisme *m.*
antifeminist ['ænti'feminist], *s.* antiféministe *mf.*
antiferment ['ænti'fə:mənt], *s. Ch:* antiferment *m.*
antiferromagnetic ['ænti'feroumæg'netik], *a. Ph:* antiferromagnétique.
antiferromagnetism ['ænti'ferou'mægnitizm], *s. Ph:* antiferromagnétisme *m.*
anti-flu ['ænti'flu:], *a.* antigrippal, -aux.
anti-fouling ['ænti'fauliŋ], *a.* préservatif; (peinture *f*) anti-fouling; *Nau:* **a.-f. composition,** enduit préservatif; corroi *m.*
antifreeze ['ænti'fri:z], *a. & s. Aut:* antigel (*m*).
anti-French ['ænti'fren(t)ʃ], *a.* (démonstration *f*, etc.) francophobe, gallophobe.
anti-Freudism ['ænti'frɔidizm], *s. Psy:* anti-freudisme *m.*
antifriction ['ænti'frikʃ(ə)n], *a. Mec.E:* (garniture, etc.) antifriction; **a. grease,** savon *m* métallique; **a. metal,** métal *m* antifriction.
anti-G ['ænti'dʒi:], *a. Av:* **a.-G suit,** vêtement *m*, combinaison *f*, anti-g.
antigen ['æntidʒen], *s. Med:* antigène *m.*
antigenic [ænti'dʒenik], *a.* antigènique.
anti-glare ['ænti'gleər], *a.* = ANTI-DAZZLE.
Antigone [æn'tigəni], *Pr.n.f.* Antigone.
antigorite [æn'tigərait], *s. Miner:* antigorite *f.*
anti government(al) ['ænti'gʌvə:nmənt, -gʌvə:n'mentl], *a.* antigouvernemental, -aux.
Antigua [æn'tigə], *Pr.n. Geog:* Antigua *m*, Antigoa *m.*
anti-hail ['ænti'heil], *a. Agr: etc:* paragrêle; **a.-h. rocket,** fusée *f* paragrêle.
antihalation ['æntihə'leiʃ(ə)n], **antihalo** ['ænti'heilo], *a. & s. Phot:* antihalo (*m inv.*).
antihelix ['ænti'hi:liks], *s.* = ANTHELIX.
anti-hero, anti-heroine [ænti'hiərou, -'herouin], *s. Lit:* anti-héros *m, pl.* anti-héros, anti-héroïne *f, pl.* anti-héroïnes.
antihistamine ['ænti'histəmin], **antihistaminic** ['æntihistə'minik], *a. & s. Med:* antihistaminique (*m*).
antihormone ['ænti'hɔ:moun], *s. Med:* antihormone *f.*
anti-icer ['ænti'aisər], *s.* antigivreur *m.*
anti-icing ['ænti'aisiŋ]. **1.** *s.* antigivrage *m.* **2.** *a.* antigivre *inv.*
anti-incrustator ['ænti'inkrʌsteitər], *s. Mec.E:* anti-incrustant *m, pl.* anti-incrustants.
anti-jam(ming) ['ænti'dʒæm(iŋ)], *s. W.Tel: etc:* antibrouillage *m.*
anti-jammer ['ænti'dʒæmər], *s. W.Tel: etc:* antibrouilleur *m.*
anti-Jewish ['ænti'dʒu:iʃ], *a.* antijuif, -ive; antisémitique.
anti-kink ['ænti'kiŋk], *a.* antivrilleur, -euse.
anti-knock ['ænti'nɔk], *a. & s. I.C.E:* antidétonnant (*m*).
anti-liberal ['ænti'libərəl], *a. Pol:* antilibéral, -aux.
Antilles (the) [ði:æn'tili:z], *Pr.n.pl. Geog:* les Antilles *f*; **the Greater, Lesser, A.,** les Grandes, Petites, Antilles.
antilocapra [æntilou'kæprə], *s. Z:* antilocapre *f*, antilocapra *f.*
Antilocapridae [æntilou'kæpridi:], *s.pl. Z:* antilocapridés *m.*
Antilochus [æn'tiləkəs], *Pr.n.m. Gr.Lit:* Antiloque.
antilog ['æntilɔg], *s. Mth: F:* antilog *m.*
antilogarithm ['ænti'lɔgəriθm], *s. Mth:* antilogarithme *m.*
antilogical ['ænti'lɔdʒikl], *a.* antilogique.
antilogous [æn'tiləgəs], *a.* antilogue.
antilogy [æn'tilədʒi], *s.* antilogie *f.*
Antilopinae [ænti'lɔpini:], *s.pl. Z:* antilopinés *m.*
antimacassar [æntimə'kæsər], *s.* têtière *f* (de fauteuil, de canapé).
Antimachus [æn'timəkəs], *Pr.n.m.* Antimaque.
antimagnetic ['æntimæg'netik], *a.* antimagnétique.
antimalarial ['æntimə'lɛəriəl], *a. Med:* antimalarique.
antimasonic ['æntimə'sɔnik], *a.* antimaçonnique.
antimatter ['æntimætər], *s.* antimatière *f.*
antimephitic ['æntime'fitik], *a. & s. Med:* antiméphitique (*m*).
antimetabolite ['æntime'tæbəlait], *s. Med:* antimétabolite *m.*
antimetathesis ['æntime'tæθəsis], *s.* antimétathèse *f.*
antimicrobial ['æntimai'kroubiəl], **antimicrobic** ['æntimai'kroubik], *a.* antimicrobien.
antimilitarism ['ænti'militərizm], *s.* antimilitarisme *m.*
antimilitarist ['ænti'militərist], *s.* antimilitariste *mf.*
antiministerial ['æntiminis'tiəriəl], *a.* antiministériel.
anti-missile ['ænti'misail], *a.* antimissile; **a.-m. missile,** missile *m* antimissile.
antimonarchical ['æntimə'nɑ:kikl], *a.* antimonarchique.
antimonarchism ['ænti'mɔnəkizm], *s.* antimonarchisme *m.*
antimonarchist ['ænti'mɔnəkist], *a. & s.* antimonarchiste (*mf*).
antimonial [ænti'mouniəl], *a. Med: Pharm:* antimonial, -aux; stibial, -aux; antimonié; stibié; *A:* **a. wine,** vin *m* émétique.
antimoniate [ænti'mounieit], *s. Ch:* antimoniate *m.*
antimonic [ænti'mɔnik], *a.* antimonique, stibique.
antimonide ['æntimənaid], *s. Ch:* antimoniure *m.*
antimonious [ænti'mouniəs], *a. Ch:* antimonieux, stibieux.
antimonite ['æntimənait], *s. Ch:* antimonite *m.*
antimoniuretted [ænti'mɔnjuəretid], *a. Ch:* **a. hydrogen,** hydrogène antimonié.
antimony ['æntiməni], *s.* antimoine *m*; **a. sulfide, black a.,** antimoine cru, sulfuré; sulfure noir d'antimoine; **grey a.,** stibine *f*, stibnite *f*; **red a.,** kermès minéral; kermésite *f*; *Pharm:* **tartarated a.,** tartre stibié.
antimonyl [æn'timonil], *s. Ch:* antimonyle *m.*
antimoral ['ænti'mɔr(ə)l], *a.* antimoral, -aux.
antinational ['ænti'næʃən(ə)l], *a.* antinational, -aux.
anti-natural ['ænti'nætjər(ə)l], *a.* contre nature.
antinazi ['ænti'nɑ:tsi], *a. & s. Pol:* antinazi, -ie.
antinephritic ['æntine'fritik], *a. Pharm:* antinéphrétique.
antineuralgic ['æntinju'rældʒik], *a. & s. Pharm:* antinévralgique (*m*).
antineutron ['ænti'nju:trɔn], *s. Atom.Ph:* antineutron *m.*
anting ['æntiŋ], *s. Orn:* formicage *m.*
antinode ['æntinoud], *s. Ph:* antinœud *m*, ventre *m* (d'onde); (*in circuit or aerial*) **a. of potential,** antinœud, ventre, de potentiel, de tension.
antinomian ['ænti'noumiən], *a. & s. Phil:* antinomien, -ienne.
antinomic ['ænti'nɔmik], *a. Phil:* antinomique.
antinomy [æn'tinəmi], *s. Phil:* antinomie *f.*
Antinous [æn'tinouəs], *Pr.n. Rom.Ant:* Antinoüs *m.*
anti-novel ['æntinɔvl], *s. Lit:* antiroman *m*, nouveau roman.
antinuclear ['ænti'nju:kliər], *a.* antiatomique.

Antioch ['æntiɔk], *Pr.n. A.Geog:* Antioche *f.*
Antiochus [æn'taiəkəs], *Pr.n.m. A.Hist:* Antiochus.
Antiope [æn'taiəpi], *Pr.n.f. Myth:* Antiope.
antioxidant ['ænti'ɔksidənt], *a. & s.* antioxydant (*m*).
antioxygen ['ænti'ɔksidʒən], *s. Ch:* antioxygène *m.*
antipapal ['ænti'peip(ə)l], *a.* antipapiste.
antipapist ['ænti'peipist], *s.* antipapiste *m.*
antiparallel ['ænti'pærəlel], *a. Myth:* antiparallèle.
antiparalytic ['æntipærə'litik], *a. Med:* antiparalytique.
antiparliamentary ['æntipɑ:lə'ment(ə)ri], *a.* antiparlementaire.
antiparticle ['ænti'pɑ:tikl], *s. Atom.Ph:* antiparticule *f.*
antipatharians [æntipæ'θɛəriənz], *s.pl. Coel:* antipathaires *m.*
antipathetic(al) ['æntipə'θetik(l)], *a.* antipathique (to, à).
antipathetic(al)ly ['æntipə'θetik(ə)li], *adv.* par antipathie.
antipathid [ænti'pæθid], *s. Coel:* antipathe *m,* corail noir.
antipathy [æn'tipəθi], *s.* antipathie *f*; **to feel a. for s.o.,** avoir de l'antipathie pour, contre, qn; avoir de l'aversion pour qn.
antipatriot ['ænti'peitriət, -'pæt-], *s.* antipatriote *mf.*
antipatriotic ['æntipætri'ɔtik], *a.* antipatriotique.
antipatriotism ['ænti'pætriətizm], *s.* antipatriotisme *m.*
antiperistalsis ['æntiperi'stælsis], *s. Physiol:* mouvement *m* antipéristaltique.
antiperistaltic ['æntiperi'stæltik], *a. Physiol:* (mouvement *m*) antipéristaltique.
antipersonnel ['æntipə:sə'nel], *a.* **a. bombs,** bombes *f* antipersonnel.
antiphilosophical ['æntifilə'sɔfikl], *a.* antiphilosophique.
antiphlogistic ['æntiflə'dʒistik], *a.* antiphlogistique.
antiphon ['æntifən], *s. Ecc.Mus:* antienne *f.*
antiphonal [æn'tifənl], *Ecc.Mus:* **1.** *a.* (*a*) (en forme) d'antienne; (*b*) en contre-chant. **2.** *s.* = ANTIPHONARY.
antiphonally [æn'tifənəli], *adv. Ecc.Mus:* en contrechant.
antiphonary [æn'tifənəri], *s. Ecc.Mus:* antiphonaire *m,* antiphonal *m.*
antiphony [æn'tifəni], *s.* = ANTIPHON.
antiphrasis [æn'tifrəsis], *s. Rh:* antiphrase *f.*
antiplague ['ænti'pleig], *a.* antipestilentiel; **a. serum,** sérum antipesteux.
antipodal [æn'tipədl]. **1.** *a. Geog:* antipodal, -aux. **2.** *a. & s. Bot:* **a. (cell),** antipode *f.*
antipodean [æntipə'di(:)ən], *a.* **1.** *Geog:* antipode; antipodal, -aux. **2.** diamétralement opposé (to, à).
antipodes [æn'tipədi:z], *s.pl. Geog:* **the a.,** les antipodes *m*; **at the a.,** aux antipodes.
antipoetic ['æntipou'etik], *a.* antipoétique.
antipoints ['æntipɔints], *s.pl. Mth:* antipoints *m.*
antipoison ['ænti'pɔizn], *s.* antivénéneux *m*; contrepoison *m, pl.* contre-poisons.
antipole ['æntipoul], *s. Mth:* antipôle *m.*
antipope ['æntipoup], *s. Ecc.Hist:* antipape *m.*
antipopery ['ænti'poupəri], *s.* antipapisme *m.*
antipopular ['ænti'pɔpjulər], *a.* antipopulaire.
antiprogressive ['æntiprə'gresiv], *a.* antiprogressif.
antiprohibitionism ['æntiprouhi'biʃənizm], *s.* antiprohibitionnisme *m.*
antiprohibitionist ['æntiprouhi'biʃənist], *s.* antiprohibitionniste *mf.*
antiprotectionist ['æntiprə'tekʃənist], *s. Pol:* antiprotectionniste *mf.*
antiproton [ænti'proutən], *s. Ph:* antiproton *m.*
antiputrefactive ['æntipju:tri'fæktiv], *a.* antiputride.
antipyretic ['æntipai'retik], *a. & s. Med:* antipyrétique (*m*); fébrifuge (*m*).
antipyrin(e) ['ænti'pairi(:)n], *s. Pharm:* antipyrine *f,* analgésine *f.*
antiquarian [ænti'kwɛəriən]. **1.** *a.* ancien; **a. taste,** goût *m* de l'antique; **a. collection,** collection *f* d'antiquités; **a. bookseller,** libraire *mf* qui vend des vieilles éditions; **a. bookshop,** librairie spécialisée dans les vieilles éditions. **2.** *s.* (*a*) antiquaire *mf*; (*b*) *Paperm:* format *m* de papier à dessin (134 × 79 cm.).
antiquarianism [ænti'kwɛəriənizm], *s.* **1.** métier *m* d'antiquaire. **2.** goût *m* des antiquités.
antiquary ['æntikwəri], *s.* amateur *m* d'antiquités; antiquaire *m.*
antiquated ['æntikweitid], *a.* vieilli; désuet; suranné; vieillot, -otte; **a little old woman in a. clothes,** une petite vieille habillée à l'ancienne mode; **an a. kitchen range,** une cuisinière (à charbon) d'autrefois; **he has such a. ideas,** il est tellement vieux jeu.
antique[1] [æn'ti:k]. **1.** *a.* (*a*) *A:* antique, des anciens; (*b*) antique, ancien; vénérable; **a. statue,** statue ancienne; **(genuine) a. furniture,** meubles *mpl* d'époque; *F:* **he was carrying an a. umbrella,** il avait un parapluie de très ancien modèle. **2.** *s.* (*a*) *Art:* **the a.,** l'antique *m*; (*b*) **antiques,** antiquités *f*; **a. shop,** magasin *m* d'antiquités; **a. dealer,** antiquaire *mf*; **their house is furnished entirely with antiques,** dans leur maison il n'y a que des meubles d'époque; (*of piece of furniture*) **it isn't a genuine a.,** ce n'est pas d'époque; *F:* **this stove's a real a.!** cette cuisinière remonte au déluge! **3.** *s. Typ:* antique *f.*
antique[2], *v.tr. Bookb:* relier (un livre) à l'antique; antiquer (la reliure).
antiquely [æn'ti:kli], *adv.* antiquement.
antiqueness [æn'ti:knis], *s.* ancienneté *f.*
antiquity [æn'tikwiti], *s.* (*a*) ancienneté *f* (d'un usage, etc.); (*b*) l'antiquité (grecque, romaine); **the works of art of classical a.,** les antiquités; **the status of women in a.,** la condition de la femme dans l'antiquité, dans le monde ancien; (*c*) **Roman antiquities in Provence,** les antiquités romaines, les monuments romains, en Provence; **the Egyptian antiquities in the British Museum,** les antiquités égyptiennes du British Museum.
anti-rabic ['ænti'ræbik], *a. Med:* antirabique.
antirachitic ['æntiræ'kitik], *a. Med:* (vitamine *f,* etc.) antirachitique.
antiracialism ['ænti'reiʃəlizm], **antiracism** ['ænti'reisizm], *s.* antiracisme *m.*
anti-radar ['ænti'reidɑ:r], *a. & s.* antiradar (*m inv*).
antiradiation ['æntireidi'eiʃ(ə)n], *a.* **a. suit,** vêtement *m* antiradiations.
antirational ['ænti'ræʃən(ə)l], *a.* antirationnel.
antirationalism ['ænti'ræʃənəlizm], *s.* antirationalisme *m.*
antireflecting ['æntiri'flektiŋ], *a. Opt:* antireflet *inv.*
anti-religious ['æntiri'lidʒəs], *a.* antireligieux.
anti-republican ['æntiri'pʌblikən], *a. & s.* antirépublicain, -aine.
antirevolutionary ['æntirevə'lu:ʃən(ə)ri], *a. & s.* antirévolutionnaire (*mf*).
antirrhinum [ænti'rainəm], *s. Bot:* antirrhinum *m,* muflier *m*; *F:* gueule-de-lion *f, pl.* gueules-de-lion; gueule-de-loup *f, pl.* gueules-de-loup; mufle *m* de veau, de bœuf.
anti-rust ['ænti'rʌst], *a. & s.* **a.-r. (composition),** (enduit *m*) antirouille (*m inv*).
anti-scale ['ænti'skeil], *a.* **a.-s. (boiler) composition,** désincrustant *m.*
antiscians [æn'tiʃənz], *s.pl. Geog:* antisciens *m.*
antiscorbutic ['æntiskɔ:'bju:tik], *a. & s. Pharm:* antiscorbutique (*m*).
antiscriptural ['ænti'skriptjər(ə)l], *a.* antibiblique, antiscripturaire.
antisegregationist ['æntisegri'geiʃənist], *s.* antiségrégationniste *mf.*
anti-Semite ['ænti'si:mait], *s.* antisémite *mf.*
anti-Semitic ['æntisi'mitik], *a.* antisémitique.
anti-Semitism ['ænti'semitizm], *s.* antisémitisme *m.*
antisepsis [ænti'sepsis], *s. Med:* antisepsie *f.*
antiseptic [ænti'septik], *a. & s. Med:* antiseptique (*m*).
antiseptically [ænti'septik(ə)li], *adv.* d'une façon antiseptique; en se servant des antiseptiques; à l'aide de procédés antiseptiques.
antisepticism [ænti'septisizm], *s.* traitement chirurgical antiseptique.
antisepticize [ænti'septisaiz], *v.tr.* antiseptiser.
antiserum ['ænti'siərəm], *s. Med:* antisérum *m.*
anti-shock ['ænti'ʃɔk], *a.* antichoc *inv*; *Med:* **a.-s. treatment,** traitement *m* antichoc.
antiskating ['ænti'skeitiŋ], *a. Rec:* **a. device,** antiskating *m.*
anti-skid ['ænti'skid], *a. Aut: etc:* antidérapant.
antislavery ['ænti'sleivəri], *s.* antiesclavagisme *m*; *attrib.* **a. campaign,** campagne *f* antiesclavagiste.
antisocial ['ænti'souʃl], *a.* antisocial, -aux.
antisocialist ['ænti'souʃəlist], *a. & s.* antisocialiste.
anti-Soviet ['ænti'souviət], *a.* antisoviétique.
antispasmodic ['æntispæz'mɔdik], *a. & s.* antispasmodique (*m*).
antispark ['ænti'spɑ:k], *a.* anti-étincelles *inv.*
anti-spin ['ænti'spin], *a. Av:* antivrille, antivrilleur.
anti-splash ['ænti'splæʃ], *a.* **a.-s. (tap-)nozzle,** (ajutage *m*) brise-jet *m inv.*
anti-Stalinist ['ænti'stɑ:linist], *a. & s.* anti-Stalinien, -enne.
Antisthenes [æn'tisθini:z], *Pr.n.m. Gr.Phil:* Antisthène.
anti-strike ['ænti'straik], *a.* antigréviste.
antistrophe [æn'tistrəfi], *s. A.Th: Rh:* antistrophe *f.*
anti-submarine ['ænti'sʌbməri:n], *a.* anti-sous-marin; **a.-s. warfare,** guerre anti-sous-marine.
antisyphilitic ['æntisifi'litik], *a. & s. Med:* antisyphilitique (*m*).
anti-tank ['ænti'tæŋk], *a. Mil:* antiblindé, antichar(s), anti-tank; **a.-t. defence,** défense *f* antichars; **a.-t. weapon, rocket, etc.,** engin *m,* fusée *f,* etc., antichars.
antitetanic ['æntite'tænik], *a. & s. Med:* antitétanique (*m*).
anti-theatre ['æntiθi:ətər], *s. Lit:* anti-théâtre *m, pl.* antithéâtres.
anti-theft ['ænti'θeft], *a.* (serrure *f,* etc.) antivol *inv*; **a.-t. device,** antivol *m inv.*
antithermic ['ænti'θə:mik], *a. Med:* antithermique.
antithesis, *pl.* **-es** [æn'tiθisis, -i:z], *s.* **1.** antithèse *f* **(between,** entre; **to, of,** de). **2.** opposé *m,* contraire *m* (de); **he is the a. of a radical,** il est tout l'opposé d'un radical.
antithetic(al) [ænti'θetik(l)], *a.* antithétique.
antithetically [ænti'θetik(ə)li], *adv.* par antithèse.
antithrombin ['ænti'θrɔmbin], *s. Med:* antithrombine *f.*
anti-torpedo ['æntitɔ:'pi:dou], *a. & s. Navy:* antitorpilleur (*m*).
antitoxic ['ænti'tɔksik], *a. Med:* antitoxique; antivénéneux.
antitoxin ['ænti'tɔksin], *s. Med:* antitoxine *f.*
anti-trade ['ænti'treid], *a. & s. Meteor:* (vent) contre-alizé (*m*).
antitragal [æn'titrəg(ə)l], **antitragic** [ænti'trædʒik], *a. Anat:* antitragien.
antitragus [æn'titrəgəs, ænti'treigəs], *s. Anat:* antitragus *m.*
antitropic [ænti'trɔpik], *a. Nat.Hist:* antitrope.
antitrust ['ænti'trʌst], *a.* anti-trust *inv.*
antitubercular ['æntitju'bə:kjulər], *a. Med:* antituberculeux.
antitussive ['ænti'tʌsiv], *a. Med:* anti-toux *inv.,* béchique.
antitype ['æntitaip], *s.* antitype *m*; contrepartie *f.*
antivaccinationist ['æntivæksi'neiʃənist], *s.* antivaccinateur, -trice.
antivariolar ['æntiværi'oulər], *a. Med:* antivariolique.
antivenin [ænti'venin], *s. Med:* **a. treatment,** traitement antivénéneux, antivenin.
antivenomous ['ænti'venəməs], *a.* antivenimeux.
antivermicular ['æntivə'mikjulər], *a. Physiol:* (mouvement *m*) antipéristaltique.
antivirus ['ænti'vaiərəs], *s.* antivirus *m.*
antivitamin ['ænti'vitəmin], *s.* antivitamine *m.*
antivivisection ['æntivivi'sekʃ(ə)n], *s.* antivivisection(n)isme *m.*
antivivisectionist ['æntivivi'sekʃənist], *s.* antivivisection(n)iste *mf.*
anti-waste ['ænti'weist], *a.* **1.** *Physiol:* (*of food, etc.*) antidéperditeur, -trice. **2.** **a.-w. campaign,** campagne *f* contre le gaspillage.
antizymic ['ænti'zaimik], *a. Biol:* antizymique.
antler ['æntlər], *s.* **1.** andouiller *m* (d'un cerf, etc.); **the antlers,** le bois, les bois; **first a.,** dague *f.* **2.** *Ent:* **a. moth,** charæas *f.*
antlered ['æntləd], *a.* (cerf) portant son bois.
antlerite ['æntlərait], *s. Miner:* antlérite *f.*
ant lion ['æntlaiən], *s. Ent:* fourmi-lion *m, pl.* fourmis-lions.
Antonia [æn'tounjə], *Pr.n.f.* Antoinette.
Antonines ['æntənainz], *Pr.n.m.pl. A.Hist:* les Antonins.
Antoninus [æntə'nainəs], *Pr.n.m.* Antonin; *A.Hist:* **A. Pius,** Antonin le Pieux.
Antonius [æn'touniəs], **Antony** ['æntəni], *Pr.n.m.* Antoine; **Marcus A., Mark Antony,** Marc Antoine.
antonomasia [æntənə'meiziə], *s. Rh:* antonomase *f.*
antonym ['æntənim], *s.* antonyme *m.*
antonymous [æn'tɔniməs], *a.* antonyme.
antonymy [æn'tɔnimi], *s.* antonymie *f.*
ant-pitta ['æntpitə], *s. Orn:* grallaire *f.*
antrectomy [æn'trektəmi], **antroduodenectomy** ['æntroudjuoudə'nektəmi], *s. Surg:* antrectomie *f.*
antritis [æn'traitis], *s. Med:* antrite *f.*
antrotomy [æn'trɔtəmi], *s. Surg:* antrotomie *f.*
antrum ['æntrəm], *s. Anat:* antre *m,* sinus *m*; **a. of Highmore,** sinus maxillaire; antre d'Highmore.
ant-shrike ['æntʃraik], *s. Orn:* **1.** batara *m,* thamnophile *m.* **2.** grallaire *f.*
ant-thrush ['ænt'θrʌʃ], *s. Orn:* **1.** fourmilier *m*; **Boddaert's a.-t.,** fourmilier tétéma. **2.** brève *f,* grive *f* superbe.
Antwerp ['æntwə:p], *Pr.n. Geog:* Anvers *m*; *Orn:* **A. pigeon,** anversois *m.*
anuclear [ei'nju:kliər], *a. Atom.Ph:* anucléaire.
anucleate [æ'nju:kliət], *a. Biol:* anucléé.
Anura [æ'nju:rə], *s.pl. Amph:* Anoures *m.*
anuran [æ'nju:rən]. *Amph:* **1.** *a.* anoure, sans queue. **2.** *s.* anoure *m.*
anuresis [ænju'ri:sis], **anuria** [ə'nju:riə], *s. Med:*

anurèse *f*, anurie *f*.

anurous [ə'nju:rəs], *a. Amph:* anoure; sans queue.

anus ['einəs], *s. Anat:* anus *m*.

anvil ['ænvil], *s.* 1. (*a*) *Metalw:* enclume *f*; **two-horned a., two-beaked a.,** bigorne *f*; **small a., hand a.,** tasseau *m*, bigorneau *m*, enclumette *f*, tas *m*; **a. beak,** bec *m* d'enclume; **a. bed, block,** (i) billot *m* d'enclume; semelle *f*, souche *f*, d'enclume; (ii) chabotte *f* (de marteau-pilon); javotte *f*; (*b*) *Lit:* (*of project, etc.*) **on the a.,** à l'étude, en préparation. 2. *Anat:* enclume (de l'oreille).

anxiety [æŋ'zaiəti], *s.* 1. (*a*) inquiétude *f*; **deep a.,** anxiété *f*, angoisse *f*; **to cause s.o. great a.,** donner de grandes inquiétudes, bien des soucis, à qn; **to be in a state of mortal a.,** être dans des transes mortelles; **to relieve s.o.'s a.,** tirer qn d'inquiétude; **to remove all anxieties,** rassurer toutes les inquiétudes; *Pol:* donner tous apaisements voulus; **to be full of a.,** être anxieux; (*b*) **a. for s.o.'s safety,** sollicitude *f* pour la sûreté de qn; (*c*) désir *m*; **a. to please s.o.,** désir de plaire à qn. 2. *Med:* anxiété.

anxious ['æŋkʃəs], *a.* 1. (*a*) (*of pers.*) inquiet, -ète, soucieux, ennuyé, (**about,** sur, de; au sujet de); **very a., extremely a.,** tourmenté, angoissé; **don't be a. about . . .,** ne vous inquiétez pas de . . .; **to be over-a.,** être porté à se tourmenter; être de tempérament inquiet; **to be a. for s.o., for s.o.'s safety,** (i) être plein de sollicitude pour qn, pour la sûreté de qn; (ii) craindre pour qn; **I am a. about his health,** sa santé me préoccupe; (*b*) (*of thg*) inquiétant; **an a. business,** une affaire qui nous cause bien des préoccupations, bien du souci; **we had an a. time of it,** cela nous a causé bien des inquiétudes; **an a. moment,** un moment d'anxiété; **one of the most a. moments of his life,** un des moments les plus angoissants de sa vie; *Ecc: U.S:* **the a. seat,** le banc des pénitents; *U.S:* **to be on the a. seat,** (i) être inquiet; (ii) être au supplice (pour savoir . . .). 2. désireux; **to be a. for sth.,** désirer vivement qch.; **to be a. to do sth.,** tenir à faire qch.; être désireux, soucieux, avide, impatient, de faire qch.; **a. to start,** pressé de partir; **a. to make his way,** impatient de percer; **I can't say that I'm a. to see him,** je ne peux pas dire que je brûle d'envie de le voir; **I'm not very a. to see him,** je n'ai pas particulièrement envie de le voir; **why are you so a. to go?** (i) pourquoi êtes-vous si impatient de partir? (ii) pourquoi tenez-vous tant à y aller? **he is a. for her to return,** il attend son retour avec impatience, il lui tarde qu'elle revienne; **I am very a. for him to come,** je tiens beaucoup à ce qu'il vienne. 3. *Med:* anxieux

anxiously ['æŋ(k)ʃəsli], *adv.* 1. (*a*) avec inquiétude; (*b*) anxieusement, avec anxiété. 2. avec sollicitude. 3. avec impatience; **to await news a.,** attendre avec impatience des nouvelles.

any ['eni], *a. pron. & adv.* I *a. qualifying phrs.* (*such as* **a. more, a. of the, . . .**) 1. (*some; one out of many*) (*a*) **have you a. milk, a. books?** avez-vous du lait, des livres? **have you a. more milk?** avez-vous encore du lait? **have you a. more books?** avez-vous d'autres livres? **is there a. hope?** y a-t-il de l'espoir, quelque espoir? (*with implied negation*) y a-t-il aucun espoir? **in a. village of a. importance,** dans tout village tant soit peu considérable; **if it's in a. way inconvenient,** pour peu que cela vous dérange; **if there is still a. idea that . . .,** s'il subsiste aucune idée que . . .; (*b*) **is there a. Englishman who . . .?** y a-t-il un Anglais qui . . .? **can a. man think that?** y a-t-il un (seul) homme qui pense cela? **he knows French if a. man does,** il sait le français comme pas un. 2. (*a*) **not a.,** ne . . . aucun, nul; **he hasn't a. reason to complain,** il n'a aucune raison de se plaindre; **I owe nothing to a. man,** je ne dois rien à qui que ce soit; **he hasn't a. money,** il n'a pas d'argent; **he hasn't a. more money (left),** il n'a plus d'argent; **she looked at the windows but didn't go into a. shop, a. of the shops,** elle a regardé toutes les devantures, mais elle n'est entrée dans aucun magasin; **I don't think a. guests, a. of the guests have arrived yet,** je ne pense pas qu'aucun des invités soit encore arrivé; (*b*) (*with implied negation*) **he is forbidden to do a. work,** tout travail lui est interdit; **it is difficult to find a. explanation for it,** il est difficile d'en trouver aucune explication; **he will be very reluctant to give up a. of his duties,** c'est à contre-cœur qu'il renoncera à quelque partie que ce soit de ses fonctions. 3. (*a*) (*no matter which*) n'importe (le)quel; **come a. day (you like),** venez n'importe quel jour; **a. of these books,** n'importe lequel de ces livres; **come at a. time you like,** venez à n'importe quelle heure, n'importe quand, quand bon vous semblera; **a. man, woman, or child,** qui que ce soit, homme, femme, ou enfant; **under a. pretext,** sous n'importe quel prétexte; **not under a. pretext,** sous aucun prétexte; **if for a. reason (whatever) . . .,** si pour n'importe quelle raison . . .; **bring a. friend you like,** amenez n'importe qui de vos amis; **a. doctor will tell you that,** n'importe quel médecin vous le dira; **a. man will tell you that,** n'importe qui, le premier venu, vous le dira; **a. serious-minded person will tell you that . . .,** n'importe qui de sérieux vous dira que . . .; **that may happen a. day, at a. time,** cela peut arriver d'un jour à l'autre, n'importe quand, à n'importe quel moment; **I expect him a. minute, a. moment now,** je l'attends d'un instant à l'autre; **take a. two cards,** prenez deux cartes quelconques; **the ingredients may be in absolutely a. proportions,** les proportions sont absolument quelconques, sont au choix; *Mth:* **take a. three points,** prenez trois points quelconques; *F:* **a. old thing,** n'importe quoi; **a. old book,** un livre quelconque; (*b*) (*any and every*) **a. pupil who forgets his books will be punished,** tout élève qui oubliera ses livres sera puni; **at a. hour of the day,** à toute heure de la journée; **he took a holiday on a. (and every) occasion,** à toute occasion, à n'importe quelle occasion, il s'octroyait un congé.
II. *pron.* (*a*) **take the whole cake, I don't want a.,** prenez le gâteau entier, je n'en ai pas envie; **he has no money and no prospect of a.,** il est sans argent et sans l'espoir d'en avoir; **I'll lend you these books but please don't lose a.,** je vais vous prêter ces livres mais je vous prie de ne pas en perdre; (*b*) **I need some ink; have you a.?** il me faut de l'encre; en avez-vous? **is there a. more?** y en a-t-il encore? **I needn't say a. more,** pas besoin d'en dire davantage; **there is little, there are few, if a.,** il y en a peu, si tant est qu'il y en ait du tout; *F:* **he wasn't having a.,** il n'a pas marché; *F:* **I'm not putting up with a. of that!** ça, je ne peux pas le souffrir, l'avaler! *P:* **a. more for a. more?** qui veut du rabiot? (*c*) *pl. O:* (*now usu.* **anybody, anyone**) **will a. forget who have known these happy times?** de ceux qui ont connu ces temps heureux, y en a-t-il qui les oublieront?
III. *adv.* (*a*) **I'm not a. better,** je ne vais pas mieux; **I can't speak a. more plainly,** je ne peux pas parler plus clairement; **I can't go a. further,** je ne puis pas aller plus loin; **they did not behave a. too well,** leur conduite a laissé à désirer; **are you a. the better for it?** vous en portez-vous mieux? **I don't see him a. longer, a. more,** je ne le vois plus; *F:* **a. old how,** n'importe comment; (*b*) *NAm: F:* **that didn't help us a.,** cela ne nous a été d'aucun secours; (*of sick person*) **has he improved a.?** est-ce qu'il y a aucune amélioration? est-ce qu'il commence à aller mieux? **I'm not worrying a.!** si tu crois que je me donne des soucis! (*c*) *conj.phr.* **I didn't do it a. more than you did,** je ne l'ai pas fait plus que vous; **they haven't found the thief a. more than the jewels,** ils n'ont pas trouvé le voleur, ni les bijoux (non plus).

anybody ['enibɔdi], *pron & s.*, **anyone** ['eniwʌn], *pron.* (*no pl.*) NOTE: **anybody** *and* **anyone** *are not always interchangeable; in examples where one of the forms is either essential or preferred, the word has been printed in full*) 1. (*indeterminate*) quelqu'un; (*with implied negation*) personne; **can you see a. over there?** voyez-vous quelqu'un là-bas? **if only I knew a. to talk to,** si seulement je connaissais quelqu'un à qui parler; **does a. dare to say so?** y a-t-il personne qui ose le dire? **he is a scholar if anyone is,** c'est un savant s'il en fut jamais. 2. (*in neg. sentences*) **not a.,** ne . . . personne; **you needn't disturb a.,** il est inutile que vous dérangiez personne; **there was hardly a.,** il n'y avait presque personne; **I'm not doing a. any harm,** je ne fais de mal à personne; **I won't speak to a.,** je ne parlerai (pas) à qui que ce soit; **he doesn't care for a. or anything,** il se moque du tiers comme du quart. 3. (*no matter who*) n'importe qui; tout le monde; **a. will tell you so,** le premier venu vous le dira; **a. can afford that luxury,** tout le monde peut se permettre ce luxe-là; **anyone would think him mad, a. would think he was mad,** on le croirait fou; **a. but me,** tout autre que moi; **bring along a. you like,** amenez qui vous voudrez; **he knows London better than a.,** il connaît Londres mieux que pas un; **he speaks better than a.,** il parle mieux que quiconque; **it would be rash on anyone's part,** ce serait téméraire de la part de quiconque; **he is more to be pitied than a.,** il est plus à plaindre qu'aucun autre; **I challenge a. to . . .,** je défie qui que ce soit de . . .; **I haven't met a. else,** je n'ai rencontré personne d'autre; *Sp:* **it's anybody's match, game, race, etc.,** n'importe qui, n'importe quelle équipe, peut gagner, peut remporter la victoire; **it's anybody's, anyone's guess!** qui sait? 4. *F:* **is he anybody?** est-il quelqu'un? **he isn't just anybody,** ce n'est pas n'importe qui; **he never will be anybody,** il ne sera jamais rien; ce sera toujours une nullité; **everybody who was anybody was invited,** on avait invité toutes les personnalités marquantes. 5. *s. Pej: F: A:* (*pl.* **anybodies**) **just as anybody,** un homme quelconque, un rien du tout; **two or three anybodies,** deux ou trois hommes quelconques.

anyhow ['enihau]. 1. *adv. F:* **to do sth. (all) a.,** (i) faire qch. d'une manière quelconque, *F:* à la six-quatre-deux; (ii) faire qch. n'importe comment, tant bien que mal; **the room looks all a.,** la pièce est en désordre, en pagaille; **you look all a.,** vous paraissez tout chose; **it doesn't pay to do one's work a.,** vous ne gagnez rien à travailler n'importe comment, au petit bonheur. 2. *conj.* en tout cas, de toute façon; toujours est-il que . . .; **a. it's too late now,** en tout cas il est trop tard maintenant; **a. I must leave tomorrow,** de toute façon il me faut partir demain; **a. you can try,** vous pouvez toujours essayer; **a. tell us what you know,** dites toujours ce que vous savez; **a. it must be realised that there is no simple solution,** toujours est-il évident qu'il n'y a pas de solution facile.

anyone, *pron. See* ANYBODY.

anyplace ['enipleis], *adv. NAm: F:* n'importe où; (*in neg. sentences*) nulle part; **I can't find it a.,** je ne peux le trouver nulle part; **I would have looked for it a. else,** je l'aurais cherché n'importe où ailleurs.

anything ['eniθiŋ], *pron.* 1. (*something*) quelque chose; (*with implied negation*) rien; **can I do a. for you?** puis-je vous être utile à quelque chose? est-ce que je puis vous aider? **I'm going to the post; is there a. I can do for you?** je vais à la poste; vous n'avez besoin de rien? est-ce que vous avez besoin de quelque chose? **have you a. to write with?** avez-vous de quoi écrire? **is there a. more pleasant than . . .?** est-il rien de plus agréable que . . . ? **did you say a.?** avez-vous dit quoi que ce soit? (*in shop*) **a. else, madam?** et avec cela, madame? **he must be earning a. from £10000 to £15000 a year,** il doit gagner au moins dans les 10000 à 15000 livres par an; **if a. should happen to him,** (i) s'il lui arrivait quelque malheur; (ii) s'il mourait; **has he seen a. of life?** est-ce qu'il connaît rien à la vie? **do you see a. of your friend?** voyez-vous quelquefois votre ami? **is he a. of a critic?** est-ce qu'il vaut quoi que ce soit en tant que critique? **if he is a. of a gentleman he will apologize,** s'il est tant soit peu bien élevé il fera des excuses; **is (there) a. the matter?** y a-t-il quelque chose qui ne marche pas? 2. (*in neg. sentences*) **not a.,** ne . . . rien; **he doesn't do a.,** il ne fait rien; **without doing a. (whatever),** sans rien faire (du tout); sans faire quoi que ce soit; **I shan't give you a. at all,** je ne vous donnerai rien du tout; **hardly a.,** presque rien; **not that he knows a. about it,** non qu'il y connaisse rien; **it doesn't mean a.,** cela ne veut rien dire; **he isn't a. of a poet,** comme poète il est nul. 3. (*no matter what*) n'importe quoi; tout; **he eats a.,** il mange de tout; **a. you like,** tout ce que vous voudrez; **a. will do,** n'importe quoi fera l'affaire; **she looks good in a.,** un rien l'habille; **I love a. French,** j'aime tout ce qui est français; **he would do a. for me,** il ferait tout pour moi; il se mettrait en quatre pour me servir; **I would have given a. not to go,** j'aurais tout donné pour ne pas y aller; **I would give a. to know . . .,** je donnerais gros pour savoir . . .; **the two girls were a. but ordinary,** les deux jeunes filles n'étaient nullement quelconques; **he's a. but mad,** il n'est rien moins que fou; **he's not mad; a. but,** il n'est pas fou; loin de là; **I can't think of a. else,** je ne puis penser à rien d'autre; *U.S: F:* **he didn't do a. else,** voilà précisément ce qu'il a fait; *F:* **she's too silly for a.,** elle est bête comme ses pieds. 4. *adv.phr.* (*intensive*) *F:* **like a.: to work like a.,** travailler comme un fou; **to laugh like a.,** rire à se tordre, à pleins poumons; **it's raining like a.,** il pleut à torrents; **as easy as a.,** facile comme tout, simple comme bonjour.

anyway ['eniwei], *conj.* = ANYHOW 2.

anywhen ['enihwen], *adv. U.S: F:* n'importe quand.

anywhere ['eni(h)weər], *adv.* 1. n'importe où; dans quelque endroit que ce soit; **put it a.,** mettez-le n'importe où; **can you see it a.?** pouvez-vous le voir quelque part? **I'd know him a.,** je le reconnaîtrais entre mille; **it's miles from a.,** c'est au bout du monde, en plein bled; **a. else,** partout ailleurs; **here if a.,** dans ce lieu entre tous; **has he a. near finished?** est-il près d'avoir fini? **are you going a. this evening?** est-ce que vous sortez ce soir? est-ce que vous faites quelque chose ce soir? *U.S:* **he earns a. from 300 to 400 dollars a week,** il gagne dans les 300 à 400 dollars par semaine. 2. **not a.,** nulle part; en aucun endroit, en aucun lieu; **I can't find it a.,** je ne le trouve nulle part.

anywise ['eniwaiz], *adv. A: & Lit:* (*also* **in anywise**) 1. d'une manière quelconque. 2. en aucune façon; d'aucune façon; **the only thing a. important,** la seule chose d'aucune importance; **if he has in a. offended you,** s'il vous a offensé en aucune façon. 3. (*in neg. sentences*) **not a. essential,** pas du tout essentiel, aucunement essentiel.

Anzac ['ænzæk], *s.m. Mil:* Anzac.

Anzus ['ænzəs], *s. Pol.* Anzus *m*.

aorist ['ɛərist], *a. & s. Gram:* aoriste (*m*).

aorta [ei'ɔ:tə], *s. Anat:* aorte *f*; **bulb of the a.,** bulbe *m* aortique.

aortal [ei'ɔ:tl], *a. Anat:* aortique.

aortectomy [eiɔ:'tektəmi], *s. Surg:* aortectomie *f*.

aortic [ei'ɔ:tik], *a. Anat:* aortique; *Med:* **a. insufficiency, a. incompetence,** insuffisance *f* aortique; **a. arches,** arcs *m* aortiques.

aortitis [eiɔ:'taitis], *s. Med:* aortite *f*.

aortography [eiɔ:'tɔgrəfi], *s. Med:* aortographie *f*.

aortostenosis [ei'ɔ:touste'nousis], *s. Med:* aortosténose *f*.

Aosta [ɑ:'ɔstə], *Pr.n. Geog:* Aoste *f*.

aoudad ['ɑ:udæd], *s. Z:* arui *m*.

apace [ə'peis], *adv. A. & Lit:* à grands pas; vite, rapidement; **winter is coming on a.,** voici déjà l'hiver.

Apache[1] [ə'pætʃi], *s. Ethn:* Apache *mf*.

apache[2] [ə'pæʃ], *s.* (*gangster*) apache *m*.

apagoge [æpə'goudʒi], *s. Log:* apagogie *f*; réduction *f* à l'absurde.

Apalachee [æpə'lætʃi], *s.* **1.** *Ethn:* Apalache *mf*. **2.** *Geog:* **A. Bay,** la baie d'Apalachie.

apanage[1] ['æpənidʒ, 'æpænɑ:ʒ], *s. Hist:* apanage *m*; **to endow a prince with an a.,** apanager un prince; *Lit:* **reason is the a. of man,** la raison est l'apanage de l'homme.

apanage[2], *v.tr. Hist:* apanager (un prince, etc.).

apanaged ['æpənidʒd], *a. Hist:* apanagé.

apanagist [ə'pænədʒist], *s. Hist:* apanagiste *mf*.

apar ['æpɑ:r], **apara** ['æpərə], *s. Z:* apar *m*, tolypeute *m*.

apart [ə'pɑ:t], *adv.* **1.** (*a*) *A:* (*aside*) **to take s.o. a.,** prendre qn à part; **to set sth. a. for s.o.,** mettre qch. de côté pour qn; réserver qch. à qn; (*b*) **the garage stands a. from the house,** le garage est (i) séparé de la maison, (ii) à quelque distance de la maison; **he stood a. from the others,** il se tenait à l'écart des autres; *Lit:* **to live a. from the world,** vivre écarté du monde; (*c*) **a class a.,** un genre à part; **they consider themselves in a class a.,** ils se considèrent au-dessus des autres; **a place set a. for worship,** un endroit destiné au culte. **2.** (*a*) (*separated by distance*) **they are a mile a.,** ils sont à un mille l'un de l'autre; une distance d'un mille les sépare; **lines 10 centimetres a.,** lignes espacées de 10 centimètres; **the stakes should be placed 50 centimetres a.,** l'écartement des pieux devrait être de 50 centimètres; **the trees are not planted far enough a.,** les arbres sont plantés trop près; **to stand with one's feet wide a.,** se tenir les jambes (franchement) écartées; **towns as far a. as New York and Tokyo,** des villes aussi éloignées que New York et Tokyo; (*b*) (*separated in time*) **children born two years a.,** des enfants nés à un intervalle de deux ans; (*c*) **the boys and girls were kept a.,** on tenait séparés les garçons et les filles; **if you don't keep the dogs a. they'll fight,** si vous ne séparez pas les chiens ils vont se battre; **it is difficult to tell them a.,** il est difficile de les distinguer l'un de l'autre; **our ideas are not very far a.,** à quelque chose près nous avons le même point de vue; **this problem cannot be treated a.,** c'est un problème qu'on ne peut pas considérer séparément; **viewed a. his opinions appeared unsound,** vues indépendamment ses opinions paraissaient mal fondées. **3.** (*in pieces*) (*a*) **to take a machine a.,** démonter, désassembler, une machine; **I can't get it a.,** je n'arrive pas à le défaire, à le démonter; **my dress is coming a. at the seams,** ma robe commence à se découdre; (*b*) *F:* **to take s.o. a.,** rosser qn d'importance; **to take a room a.,** fouiller une pièce à fond. **4.** (*leaving out of consideration*) (*a*) **style a. the book has merit,** à part le style le livre a du mérite; **joking a.,** plaisanterie à part; sans blague; **these considerations a., I agree,** à part ces considérations je suis d'accord; (*b*) **a. from,** à part; sauf; **a. from these difficulties,** ces difficultés mises à part; **a. from the fact that . . .,** indépendamment du fait que . . .; outre que . . .; **a. from a few mistakes,** à part, sauf, quelques erreurs; **he has no interests a. from his profession,** à part sa profession il ne s'intéresse à rien; **his only interest a. from his office work was music,** en dehors de son bureau il ne s'intéressait qu'à la musique; **a. from him there is nobody who can do it,** à part lui personne ne peut le faire; il n'y a personne sauf lui qui puisse le faire.

apartheid [ə'pɑ:tait, -eit], *s.* (*in S. Africa*) apartheid *m*, ségrégation *f*.

apartment [ə'pɑ:tmənt], *s.* **1.** (*a*) salle *f*; chambre *f*; pièce *f*; **state apartments,** grands appartements; salons *m* d'apparat; (*b*) (*usu. pl.*) logement *m*; appartement *m*; **to take apartments,** retenir, prendre, un appartement, un logement; **to let furnished apartments,** louer en meublé, *Pej:* en garni; (**furnished**) **apartments to let,** chambres (meublées) à louer; *P: A:* **to have apartments to let,** être faible d'esprit; avoir le cerveau creux. **2.** *NAm:* (*flat*) appartement; **a. block, building, house,** immeuble *m* d'habitation, immeuble divisé en appartements; maison *f* de rapport.

apatelite [ə'pætəlait], *s. Miner:* apatélite *f*.

apathetic [æpə'θetik], *a.* apathique, indifférent.

apathetically [æpə'θetikli], *adv.* apathiquement; avec indifférence.

apathy ['æpəθi], *s.* apathie *f*; indifférence *f*.

apatite ['æpətait], *s. Miner:* apatite *f*.

apatosaurus [æpæto'sɔ:rəs], *s. Paleont:* apatosaure *m*.

ape[1] [eip], *s.* **1.** (*a*) *Z:* (grand) singe (sans queue); **barbary a.,** magot *m*; **the higher apes,** les primates *m*, les simiidés *m*; (*b*) *F:* singe; **to play the a.,** faire le singe; faire l'imbécile; *A:* **she will lead apes in hell,** elle mourra vieille fille. **2.** *Ich:* **sea a.,** renard marin.

ape[2], *v.tr.* singer; imiter; mimer; contrefaire; se calquer sur (qn).

apeak [ə'pi:k], *adv. & a. Nau:* **1.** (ancre) à pic. **2. yard arms a.,** vergues *f* en pantenne, apiquées; **to set the yards a.,** apiquer les vergues; **oars a.,** avirons mâtés.

apelike ['eiplaik], *a.* comme un singe; (visage *m*) simiesque.

Apelles [ə'peli:z], *Pr.n.m. Gr.Ant:* Apelle.

Apennines (the) [ði'æpinainz], *Pr.n.pl. Geog:* les Apennins *m*.

apepsia [ə'pepsiə], **apepsy** [ə'pepsi], *s. Med:* apepsie *f*.

aperient [ə'piəriənt], *a. & s. Med:* laxatif (*m*); relâchant(*m*).

aperiodic [eipiəri'ɔdik], *a. Mec: El: etc.* (galvanomètre, etc.) apériodique; *W.Tel:* **a. circuit,** circuit *m* apériodique.

aperispermic [əperi'spə:mik], *a. Bot:* apérispermé.

aperistalsis [eiperi'stælsis], *s. Med:* manque *m* de péristaltisme.

aperitif [ə'peritif], *s.* apéritif *m*.

aperitive [ə'peritiv]. **1.** *a. Med:* laxatif. **2.** *a. & s.* (vin, etc.) apéritif (*m*).

aperture ['æpətjuər], *s.* (*a*) ouverture *f*, fente *f*, orifice *f*; lumière *f* (d'une pinnule, etc.); regard *m*, fenêtrelle (de fourneau, etc.); **apertures of a building,** jours *m* d'un bâtiment; *Sm.a:* **aiming a.,** échancrure *f*, œilleton *m*, de visée; **a. sight,** hausse *f* à œilleton; *Cmptr:* **a. plate,** plaque *f* à trous; **a. card,** carte *f* à fenêtre, à microfilm; (*b*) *Phot:* ouverture (d'un objectif, du diaphragme); **full a.,** grande, pleine, ouverture; **working a., effective a.,** ouverture utile; **a. ratio, relative a.,** ouverture relative; *Cin:* **a. vignette,** cache *m*.

apery ['eipəri], *s.* singerie *f*.

apetalous [ei'petələs], *a. Bot:* apétale.

apex, *pl.* **apexes, apices** ['eipeks, -iz, 'eipisi:z], *s.* **1.** (*a*) sommet *m* (d'un triangle, d'un édifice, d'une montagne); *Arch:* **a. stone,** clausoir *m*; **a. of a career,** point culminant d'une carrière; apogée *m* d'une carrière; (*b*) *Nat.Hist:* pointe *f*, extrémité *f*; sommet (d'un organe, etc.); *esp. Fung:* apex *m*. **2.** *Astr:* **a. of the sun's motion,** apex de la sphère céleste; *Anat:* **a. of the heart,** apex du cœur; **a. of the lung,** sommet du poumon.

aph(a)eresis [æ'fiərisis], *s. Ling: Surg:* aphérèse *f*.

aphakia [æ'feikiə], *s. Med:* aphakie *f*.

aphakic [æ'feikik], *a. Med:* aphake.

Aphaniptera [æfæ'niptərə], *s.pl. Ent:* siphonaptères *m*, aphaniptères *m*.

aphanite ['æfənait], *s. Miner:* aphanite *f*.

aphanomyces [æfænou'maisi:z], *s. Fung:* aphanomyces *m*.

aphasia [ə'feiziə], *s. Med:* aphasie *f*; **auditory a., sensory a.,** surdité verbale, aphasie sensorielle; **motor a.,** aphasie motrice; aphémie *f*.

aphasiac [ə'feiziæk], **aphasic** [ə'feizik], *a. & s.* aphasique (*mf*).

aphelion [æ'fi:liən], *s. Astr:* aphélie *f*; apside supérieure (de l'orbite).

apheliotropic [ə'fi:lioutrɔpik], *a. Bot:* (feuille, etc.) à héliotropisme négatif.

aphemia [æ'fi:miə], *s. Med:* aphémie *f*.

aphesis ['æfisis], *s. Ling:* aphérèse *f* (d'une voyelle atone); déglutination *f*.

aphetic [ə'fetik], *a. Ling:* déglutiné.

Aphetohyoidea [æfi:touhai'ɔidiə], *s.pl. Paleont:* placodermes *m*.

aphid ['eifid, 'æfid], *s. Ent:* aphis *m*, puceron *m*.

Aphididae [ei'fididi:, ə'fid-], *s.pl. Ent:* aphididés *m*.

aphidian [ei'fidiən, ə'fid-], *a. & s. Ent:* aphidien (*m*).

aphidophagous [eifi'dɔfəgəs, æfid-], *a. Z:* aphidiphage.

aphis, *pl.* **-ides** ['eifis, 'æfis; -idi:z], *s. Ent:* aphis *m*; puceron *m*; **woolly a.,** puceron lanigère.

aphlebia [ei'fli:biə], *s. Bot: Paleont:* aphlébie *f*.

aphonia [æ'founiə, ei'foun-], *s. Med:* aphonie *f*; extinction *f* de voix.

aphonic [æ'fɔnik, ei-], **aphonous** ['æfənəs], *a.* **1.** *Med: etc:* aphone. **2.** *Ling:* (phonème) sourd.

aphony ['æfəni], *s.* aphonie *f*.

aphorism ['æfərizm], *s.* aphorisme *m*.

aphoristic [æfə'ristik], *a.* aphoristique.

aphoristically [æfə'ristik(ə)li], *adv.* par aphorisme.

aphotic [ei'foutik], *a. Oc:* aphotique; **a. region,** région aphotique.

aphrodisia [æfrou'di:ziə], *s. Med:* aphrodisie *f*.

aphrodisiac [æfrou'diziæk], *a. & s.* aphrodisiaque (*m*).

aphrodisiacal [æfroudizi'ækl], *a.* aphrodisiaque.

Aphrodite [æfrou'daiti]. **1.** *Pr.n.f. Gr.Myth:* Aphrodite. **2.** *s. Ent:* **A. (butterfly),** argynne *m*, nacré *m*. **3.** *Ann:* aphrodite *f*, *F:* souris *f*, taupe *f*, de mer.

Aphroditidae [æfrou'daitidi:], *s.pl. Ann:* aphroditiens *m*, aphroditidés *m*.

aphrosiderite [æfrou'sidərait], *s. Miner:* aphrosidérite *f*.

aphtha, *pl.* **-ae** ['æfθə, -i:], *s. Med: Vet:* (*a*) pustule aphteuse; (*b*) *pl.* aphte *m*.

aphthoid ['æfθɔid], *a. Med:* aphtoïde.

aphthongia [æf'θɔngiə], *s. Med:* apht(h)ongie *f*.

aphthous ['æfθəs], *a. Med: Vet:* aphteux; *Med:* **a. stomatitis,** stomatite aphteuse; *Vet:* **a. fever,** fièvre aphteuse.

aphyllous [ə'filəs], *a. Bot:* aphylle.

apiarian [eipi'ɛəriən], *a.* apicole; d'apiculture.

apiarist ['eipiərist], *s.* apiculteur *m*.

apiary ['eipiəri], *s.* rucher *m*.

apical ['æpik(ə)l, 'ei-], *a. Mth: Bot: etc:* apical, -aux.

apicifixed ['æpəsifikst], *a. Nat.Hist:* apicifixe.

apicodental [æpikou'dentl], *a. Ling:* apicodental, -aux.

apicopalatal [æpikou'pælətl], *a. Ling:* apicopalatal, -aux.

apiculate [ə'pikjulət], *a.* (*a*) *Bot:* apiculé; (*b*) *Cryst: etc:* apiciforme.

apicultural [eipi'kʌltjər(ə)l], *a.* apicole.

apiculture ['eipikʌltjər], *s.* apiculture *f*.

apiculturist [eipi'kʌltʃərist], *s.* apiculteur *m*.

apiculus [ə'pikjuləs], *s. Nat.Hist:* apicule *m*.

Apidae ['æpidi:], *s.pl. Ent:* apides *f*, apidés *m*.

apiece [ə'pi:s], *adv.* chacun; (*of thg*) **to cost ten pence a.,** coûter dix pence (la) pièce; (*of pers.*) **he gave them five francs a.,** il leur donna cinq francs chacun, cinq francs par personne, *F:* cinq francs chaque; **to be given, get, two apples a.,** recevoir chacun deux pommes.

apigenin [æ'pidʒənin], *s. Ch:* apigénine *f*.

apiin ['eipiən, 'æp-], *s. Ch:* apiine *f*.

apiol(e) ['æpiɔl], *s. Ch: Pharm:* apiol *m*.

apionol ['æpiənɔl], *s. Ch:* apionol *m*.

apios ['eipiəs], *s. Bot:* apios *m*.

apish ['eipiʃ], *a.* **1.** simiesque; **a. trick,** tour *m* de singe, singerie *f*. **2.** (*a*) imitateur, -trice; (*b*) *A:* affecté, poseur, -euse.

apishness ['eipiʃnis], *s.* singeries *fpl*; sotte imitation.

apivorous [ei'pivərəs], *a.* apivore.

Aplacentalia [eipleisen'teiliə], **Aplacentaria** [eipleisen'tɛəriə], *s.pl. Z:* aplacentaires *m*.

Aplacophora [æplə'kɔfərə], *s.pl. Moll:* aplacophores *m*.

aplanat ['æplənæt], *s. Phot:* (objectif) aplanat (*m*).

aplanatic [æplə'nætik], *a. Phot:* (objectif) aplanétique.

aplanatism [ə'plænətizm], *s. Opt:* aplanétisme *m*.

aplanospore [ə'plænəspɔər], *s. Bot:* aplanospore *f*.

aplasia [ei'pleiziə], *s. Med:* aplasie *f*.

aplastic [ei'plæstik], *a. Med:* (anémie *f*) aplastique.

aplenty [ə'plenti], *adv. NAm: F:* en abondance.

aplite ['æplait], *s. Miner:* aplite *f*.

aplodontia [æplou'dɔnʃiə], *s. Z:* aplodontie *f*, *F:* castor *m* de montagne.

Aplodontiidae [æploudɔn'ti:idi], *s.pl. Z:* aplodontidés *m*.

aplomb [ə'plɔm], *s.* aplomb *m*; sang-froid *m*; confiance *f* en soi.

aplome [æ'ploum], *s. Miner:* aplome *m*.

aplustre [æ'plustri], *s. Rom.Ant:* aplustre *m* (de la poupe d'un vaisseau).

aplysia [ə'pli:ziə], *s. Moll:* aplysie *f*, téthys *f*, *F:* lièvre marin.

apneic, apnoeic [æp'ni:ik], *a. Ent: Med:* apnéique.

apnoea [æp'ni:ə], *s. Med:* apnée *f*, apneustie *f*.

apocalypse [ə'pɔkəlips], *s.* apocalypse *f*; **the A. (of St John),** les Révélations *f* de saint Jean, l'Apocalypse; **the four horsemen of the A.,** les quatre cavaliers de l'Apocalypse.

apocalyptic [əpɔkə'liptik], *a.* apocalyptique.

apocalyptically [əpɔkə'liptik(ə)li], *adv.* d'une manière apocalyptique.

apocarpous [æpou'kɑ:pəs], *a. Bot:* apocarpé, apocarpe, dialycarpellé.

apocarpy [æpou'kɑ:pi], *s. Bot:* apocarpie *f*.

apochromat ['æpoukroumæt], *s. Phot:* objectif *m* apochromatique.

apochromatic [æpəkrou'mætik], *a. Opt:*

apochromatique.
apocopated [ə'pɔkəpeitid], *a. Ling:* apocopé.
apocope [ə'pɔkəpi], *s. Ling:* apocope *f.*
Apocrita [ə'pɔkritə], *s.pl. Ent:* apocrites *m.*
Apocrypha (the) [ðiə'pɔkrifə], *s.pl. B.Lit:* **1.** les livres *m* deutérocanoniques. **2.** les apocryphes *m.*
apocryphal [ə'pɔkrifl], *a.* apocryphe.
Apocynaceae [æpɔsi'neisii:], *s.pl. Bot:* apocynées *f*, apocynacées *f.*
apocynum [æpə'sainəm], *s. Bot:* apocyn *m*, apocynum *m.*
apod ['æpɔd], **apode** ['æpoud], *a. & s. Nat.Hist:* apode (*m*).
Apoda ['æpədə], *s.pl. Nat.Hist:* apodes *m.*
apodal ['æpədl], *a. Nat.Hist:* apode.
apodan ['æpədən], *s. Ich:* apode *m.*
apodeictic [æpou'daiktik], *a. Log: Phil:* apodictique.
apodeme ['æpədi:m], *s. Ent: Crust:* apodème *m.*
Apodes ['æpədi:z], *s.pl. Ich:* apodes *m.*
apodia [æ'poudiə], *s. Ter:* apodie *f.*
apodictic(al) [æpou'diktik(l)], *a. Log: Phil:* apodictique.
Apodidae [æ'pɔdidi:], *s.pl. Orn:* apodidés *m.*
Apodiformes [æpɔdi'fɔ:mi:z], *s.pl. Orn:* apodiformes *m.*
apodosis, *pl.* **-es** [ə'pɔdəsis, -i:z], *s. Gram: Rh:* apodose *f.*
apodous ['æpədəs], *a. Nat.Hist:* apode.
apoenzyme [æpou'enzaim], *s. Bio-Ch:* apoenzyme *f*, apodiastase *f.*
apogamous [ə'pɔgəməs], *a. Bot:* apogamique.
apogamy [ə'pɔgəmi], *s. Bot:* apogamie *f.*
apogean [æpou'dʒi:ən], *a. Astr:* (position *f*) à l'apogée.
apogee ['æpədʒi:], *s.* apogée *m*; **the moon is in a.,** la lune est à son apogée; *Space:* **a. motor,** moteur *m* d'apogée; *Lit:* **his fame had reached its a.,** son renom était à son apogée.
apogon ['æpəgən], *s. Ich:* apogon *m.*
apograph ['æpəgræf], *s.* apographe *m.*
apojove ['æpoudʒouv], *s. Astr:* apojove *m.*
apolar [ei'poulər], *a. Biol: Anat:* (cellule *f*) apolaire.
apolitical [eipə'litikl], *a.* apolitique.
Apollinian [æpə'liniən], *a. Phil: etc:* apollinien.
Apollo [ə'pɔlou]. **1.** *Pr.n.m. Myth:* Apollon; **A. Clarius,** le dieu de Claros; *Art:* **the A. (of the) Belvedere** [belvi'diːər], l'Apollon du Belvédère. **2.** *s. Ent:* **A. (butterfly),** (papillon *m*) apollon *m.*
Apollyon [ə'pɔliən], *Pr.n.m.* l'Ange *m* de l'abîme; Satan (dans le *Pilgrim's Progress* de Bunyan).
apologetic(al) [əpɔlə'dʒetik(l)], *a.* **1.** (ton, etc.) d'excuse; **to be very apologetic for coming so late,** se confondre en excuses d'arriver si tard; **he was quite a. about it,** il s'en est excusé vivement. **2.** (livre, etc.) apologétique.
apologetically [əpɔlə'dʒetik(ə)li], *adv.* **1.** en manière d'excuse; pour s'excuser; en s'excusant. **2.** sous forme d'apologie, de justification.
apologetics [əpɔlə'dʒetiks], *s.pl.* (*usu. with sg. construction*) *Theol:* apologétique *f.*
apologia [æpə'loudʒiə], *s. Lit:* apologie *f* (for, de); justification *f* (de sa vie, etc.).
apologist [ə'pɔlədʒist], *s.* apologiste *m*, défenseur *m.*
apologize [ə'pɔlədʒaiz], *v.i.* **to a. to s.o. for sth.,** s'excuser de qch. auprès de qn; faire, présenter, des excuses, ses excuses, à qn pour qch.; **to a. for doing sth.,** s'excuser de faire qch.; **to a. for one's attire,** s'excuser sur sa tenue; **I a. for having kept you waiting,** excusez-moi de vous avoir fait attendre.
apologue ['æpəlɔg], *s.* apologue *m.*
apology [ə'pɔlədʒi], *s.* **1.** (*a*) excuses *fpl*; **letter of a.,** lettre *f* d'excuses; lettre pour s'excuser; **to make, offer, an a.,** faire, présenter, des excuses; **to make a full a. to s.o.,** faire une réparation d'honneur à qn; faire amende honorable; **to demand an a.,** exiger des excuses; **to be profuse in one's apologies,** se répandre, se confondre, en excuses; **with apologies for troubling you,** avec toutes mes excuses pour la peine que je vous donne; (*b*) *F:* **an a. for a dinner,** un semblant de dîner; **an a. for a man,** (i) un petit bout d'homme; (ii) un piètre personnage. **2.** *Lit:* (*vindication*) apologie *f*, justification *f* (de sa vie).
apolysis [ə'pɔlisis], *s. Ecc:* (*Orthodox Church*) apolyse *f.*
apomict ['æpoumikt], *a. & s. Biol:* (espèce *f*) apomictique.
apomictic [æpou'miktik], *a. Biol:* apomictique.
apomixis [æpou'miksis], *s. Biol:* apomixie *f.*
apomorphia [æpou'mɔrfiə], **apomorphine** [æpou'mɔrfin, -fain], *s. Pharm:* apomorphine *f.*
aponeurosis, *pl.* **-es** [æpounju'rousis, -i:z], *s. Anat:* aponévrose *f*, fascia *m.*
aponeurositis [æpounjurou'saitis], *s. Med:* aponévrosite *f.*
aponeurotic [æpounju'rɔtik], *a. Anat:* aponévrotique; fascial, -aux.
aponeurotomy [æpounju'rɔtəmi], *s. Surg:* aponévrotomie *f.*
aponogeton [æpɔnou'dʒetən], *s. Bot:* aponogéton *m.*
Aponogetonaceae [æpɔnoudʒətə'neisii:], *s.pl. Bot:* aponogétonacées *f.*
apophony [ə'pɔfəni], *s. Ling:* alternance *f* (de voyelles); ablaut *m*; apophonie *f.*
apophthegm ['æpə(f)θem], *s.* apophtegme *m.*
apophyge [ə'pɔfidʒi], *s. Arch:* apophyge *f*, escape *f* (d'une colonne).
apophyllite [æpə'filait], *s. Miner:* apophyllite *f.*
apophysary [ə'pɔfisəri], *a. Anat:* apophysaire.
apophysate [ə'pɔfizeit], *a. Bot:* muni d'une apophyse.
apophysis [ə'pɔfisis], *s. Bot: Anat: etc:* apophyse *f*; **a. of the femur,** tête *f* du fémur.
apophysitis [æpɔfi'zaitis], *s. Med:* apophysite *f.*
apoplectic [æpə'plektik], *a.* (personne) apoplectique; (attaque) d'apoplexie; **he had an a. fit, an a. stroke,** il eut une attaque d'apoplexie; il fut frappé d'apoplexie; il tomba en apoplexie; il a eu un coup de sang, une congestion cérébrale, *F:* une attaque.
apoplectiform [æpə'plektifɔrm], *a. Med:* apoplectiforme.
apoplectoid [æpə'plektɔid], *a. Med:* apoplectoïde.
apoplexy ['æpəpleksi], *s.* (*a*) *Med:* apoplexie *f*; congestion (cérébrale); **heat a.,** coup *m* de chaleur; coup de soleil; (*b*) (*of vine*) esca *f.*
aporia [æ'pɔ:riə], *s. Phil: Rh:* aporie *f.*
aposaturn [æpou'sætə:n], *s. Astr:* aposaturne *m.*
aposematic [æpousə'mætik], *a. Nat.Hist:* (*of colour, etc.*) aposématique, avertissant, prémonitoire.
aposiopesis [æpəsaiou'pi:sis], *s. Rh:* apisiopèse *f.*
apospory [ə'pɔspəri], *s. Bot:* aposporie *f.*
apostasy [ə'pɔstəsi], *s.* apostasie *f.*
apostate [ə'pɔstət], *a. & s.* apostat, -ate; relaps, -se; **to become an a.,** apostasier.
apostatic [æpɔs'tætik], *a.* apostat.
apostatize [ə'pɔstətaiz], *v.i.* apostasier; **to a. from one's faith,** apostasier sa foi.
a posteriori [ɑ:pɔsteri'ɔri], *Lt. a. & adv.phr.* a posteriori.
apostil [ə'pɔstil], *s. A:* apostille *f*; annotation marginale.
apostle [ə'pɔsl], *s.* apôtre *m*; **the Apostles' Creed,** le Symbole des Apôtres; *attrib.* **a. spoon,** cuiller *f*, cuillère *f*, avec figurine d'apôtre; *Orn: Austr:* **a. bird,** struthidea *m*, oiseau-apôtre *m*, *pl.* oiseaux apôtres.
apostleship [ə'pɔslʃip], **apostolate** [ə'pɔstələt], *s.* apostolat *m.*
apostolic(al) [æpɔs'tɔlik(l)], *a. Ecc:* apostolique; **apostolic benediction,** bénédiction *f* apostolique; **the Apostolic Fathers,** les Pères apostoliques; **the Apostolic See,** le siège apostolique, le Saint-Siège; **the holy, catholic and apostolic church,** l'église sainte, catholique et apostolique; **apostolic(al) succession,** succession *f* apostolique.
apostolically [æpɔs'tɔlik(ə)li], *adv.* apostoliquement.
apostolicity [æpɔstə'lisiti], *s.* apostolicité *f.*
apostolize [æ'pɔstəlaiz], *v.tr.* apostoliser.
apostrophe [ə'pɔstrəfi], *s.* **1.** *Rh:* apostrophe *f.* **2.** *Gram:* apostrophe.
apostrophize [ə'pɔstrəfaiz], *v.tr.* **1.** *Lit:* apostropher (qn). **2.** mettre une apostrophe à (un mot).
apothecary [ə'pɔθik(ə)ri], *s. A:* apothicaire *m*, pharmacien *m*; **apothecaries' weight,** poids et mesures employés en pharmacie; **apothecary's shop,** apothicairerie *f*, pharmacie *f.*
apothecium [æpou'θi:siəm], *s. Fung:* apothécie *f.*
apothem ['æpouθem], *s. Mth:* apothème *m.*
apotheosis, *pl.* **-oses** [əpɔθi'ousis, -'ousi:z], *s.* apothéose *f.*
apotheosize [ə'pɔθiousaiz], *v.tr.* apothéoser.
apotropaic [æpɔtrou'peiik], *a. Lit:* apotropaïque.
apozymase [æpə'zaimeiz], *s. Bio.-Ch:* apozymase *f.*
appal [ə'pɔ:l] (*NAm: also* **appall**), *v.tr.* (**appalling; appalled**) consterner; épouvanter; plonger (le public, etc.) dans la consternation; **we were appalled at the thought of another war,** la pensée d'une autre guerre nous horrifiait, nous mettait au désespoir.
Appalachian [æpə'lætʃən, -'leitʃ-], *a.* **1.** *Geog:* **the A. Mountains,** *s.* **the Appalachians,** les (monts *m*) Appalaches (*m*); **A. relief, topography,** relief appalachien. **2.** *Bot:* **A. tea,** apalachine *f*, thé *m* des Apalaches.
appalling [ə'pɔ:liŋ], *a.* épouvantable, effroyable; **there has been an a. drop in the takings,** la recette a baissé dans des proportions impressionnantes, effrayantes; *F:* **to make an a. row,** faire un bruit de tous les diables.
appallingly [ə'pɔ:liŋli], *adv.* épouvantablement, effroyablement; **he's a. stupid,** il est d'une stupidité extraordinaire.
appanage[1] ['æpənidʒ], *s. Hist:* apanage *m.*
appanage[2], *v.tr. Hist:* apanager (un prince).
appanaged ['æpənidʒd], *a. Hist:* apanagé.
apparatus, *pl.* **-us, -uses** [æpə'reitəs, -əsiz], *s.* (*the pl. is rare, though the sg. is often used in coll. sense*) **1.** (*a*) appareil *m*, dispositif *m*, mécanisme *m*; **laboratory a.,** appareils de laboratoire; **I haven't the right a. to do it,** je n'ai pas l'équipement *m* nécessaire pour le faire; **surgical a.,** appareil(s) de chirurgie; *Cmptr:* **duplex a.,** appareil duplex; **start-stop a.,** appareil arythmique; *Gym:* **a. work,** gymnastique *f* aux agrès; *Physiol:* **the digestive a.,** l'appareil digestif; (*b*) **fishing a.,** attirail *m* de pêche; *Lit:* **the a. of war,** l'attirail de la guerre. **2.** *Lit:* **critical a., a. criticus** ['kritikəs], appareil, apparat *m*, critique (d'un texte).
apparel[1] [ə'pær(ə)l], *s.* **1.** *A: & Lit:* (*a*) vêtement(s) *m*, habillement *m*, habits *mpl*; **he is simple in his a.,** il est simple dans sa mise; *F:* **in the simplest a.,** nu(e) comme un ver; (*b*) ornement(s) *m*, parure *f*, accoutrement *m*, apparcil *m*; (*c*) *Nau:* équipement. **2.** *Ecc:* parements *mpl* (de chasuble, etc.).
apparel[2], *v.tr. A. & Lit:* (*p.p. & p.t.* **apparelled**) (*a*) (vêtir, revêtir (qn); (*b*) parer (qn); (*c*) *Nau:* équiper (un navire).
apparent [ə'pær(ə)nt, ə'pɛər(ə)nt], *a.* (*a*) (qui est, qui semble être) apparent, manifeste, évident; **the truth became a. to him,** la vérité lui apparut; **from what I have said it is a. that . . .,** de ce que j'ai dit il ressort que . . .; **as will soon become a.,** comme on le verra bientôt; **when he has studied the facts it becomes a. that . . .,** quand on a étudié les faits il est évident que . . .; **without its being a.,** sans qu'il y paraisse; **the difference, distinction, is a. rather than real,** la différence, la distinction, est apparente plutôt que réelle; **his jealousy was a. in his speech,** sa jalousie perçait son discours; **in spite of his a. indifference,** malgré son air d'indifférence; **it is quite a. that he will never be able to do it,** il est bien évident, bien clair, qu'il ne pourra jamais le faire; (*b*) *Pol.Ec:* **a. consumption,** consommation apparente; **a. available supplies,** disponibilités apparentes; *Cmptr: etc:* **a. power,** puissance apparente; *Astr:* **a. diameter,** diamètre apparent; **a. horizon,** horizon apparent; **a. time,** heure apparente, temps apparent; **local a. noon,** midi apparent local; *Jur:* **heir a.,** héritier présomptif; **a. easement,** servitude apparente; **in face of a. danger,** (i) face à un danger apparent, possible; (ii) *Jur:* en état de légitime défense.
apparently [ə'pærəntli, -'pɛər-], *adv.* (*a*) évidemment, manifestement; **this is a. the best solution,** ceci est clairement la meilleure solution; **a. I shall have to do it,** je serai évidemment obligé de le faire; (*b*) apparemment, en apparence, à ce qu'il semble; **this is a. true,** il paraît que c'est vrai; **he is a. going to Venice,** il semble qu'il va aller à Venise; **an a. difficult problem,** un problème qui paraît difficile.
apparentness [ə'pær(ə)ntnis, -'pɛər-], *s.* évidence *f.*
apparition [æpə'riʃ(ə)n], *s.* **1.** apparition *f.* **2.** fantôme *m*, revenant *m*, apparition.
apparitor [ə'pæritər], *s.m.* appariteur.
appaumé(e) [æ'poumei], *a. Her:* appaumée.
appeal[1] [ə'pi:l], *s.* **1.** appel *m*, recours *m*; **a. to arms,** recours aux armes; *Jur:* **a. at law,** appel; **a. from a sentence,** appel d'une condamnation; **Court of A.,** cour *f* d'appel; **Supreme Court of A.,** cour de cassation; **Final Court of A.,** cour souveraine; **to hear an a. from a decision,** juger en appel d'une décision; **without a.,** sans appel; en dernier ressort; **to judge without a.,** juger souverainement; **with possible a.,** en premier ressort; **notice of a.,** intimation *f* (d'appel); **to give notice of a. to s.o.,** faire intimer un appel à qn; **to lodge an a.,** interjeter appel, se pourvoir en appel; **to lodge an a. with the Supreme Court,** se pourvoir en cassation; **the condemned men have been informed of the rejection of their a.,** les condamnés ont été informés du rejet de leur recours en grâce; **acquitted on a.,** acquitté en seconde instance; **to quash a sentence on a.,** casser un jugement en appel; **a. to arbitration,** recours à l'arbitrage; **there is no a. from this court,** la décision de cette cour est sans appel; **military a. court.,** conseil de révision. **2.** (*a*) appel (en faveur d'une cause, etc.); **to make an a. to s.o.'s generosity,** faire appel à la générosité de qn; **to broadcast an a. to the public,** radiodiffuser un appel à la générosité du public; **I can only make a. to your reason,** je ne puis que faire appel à votre raison, à votre bon sens; (*b*) **the a. of the sea,** l'attrait de la mer; **this painting has great a.,** cette peinture est très attrayante; **she has great a.,** elle a beaucoup de charme; **sex a.,** charme sensuel, *F:* sex-appeal *m*; **emotional a.,** attrait sentimental; *Com:* **sales a.,** attraction commerciale. **3.** prière *f*, supplication *f*; **with a look of a.,** d'un air suppliant.
appeal[2], *v.i.* **1.** *Jur: etc:* (*a*) **to a. to the law,** invoquer l'aide de la justice, de la loi; **to a. from a judgment,**

appeler d'un jugement; **to a. to another court,** en appeler à un autre tribunal; introduire un recours devant un autre tribunal; **to a. to the Supreme Court,** se pourvoir en cassation; **to a. against a decision,** réclamer contre une décision; *Jur:* faire opposition à une décision; faire appel (à un tribunal) d'une décision; **I a. to your honour,** j'en appelle à votre honneur; **to a. to the country,** en appeler au pays; **to a. to arms,** recourir aux armes; **to a. to s.o.'s generosity,** faire appel à la générosité de qn; (*b*) interjeter appel; (*c*) *v.tr. NAm:* **to a. a case,** interjeter appel; en appeler d'une décision. **2. to a. to s.o. for help,** demander des secours à qn; avoir recours à qn; faire appel à qn; **to a. for a cause,** adresser, lancer, un appel en faveur d'une cause; **I a. to you to abandon this plan,** je vous supplie d'abandonner ce projet. **3. to a. to s.o., to s.o.'s imagination,** s'adresser à qn, à l'imagination de qn; (*of thg*) attirer, séduire, charmer, l'imagination; **the plan appeals to me,** le projet me sourit; **if it appeals to you,** si le cœur vous en dit; **subject that appeals to me,** sujet *m* qui m'intéresse, auquel je m'intéresse; **it doesn't a. to me,** cela ne me dit rien; **the idea did not a. to him,** l'idée ne l'enchantait guère; **this idea should a. to the practical mind,** cette idée devrait attirer les esprits positifs; **to a. to the emotions,** faire appel aux sentiments; **he appeals to me,** je le trouve sympathique, il m'est sympathique; **this offer should a. to him,** cette offre devrait lui plaire; *Com:* **styles that a. to the young,** modes *f* qui s'adressent aux jeunes; **play that appeals to the gallery,** pièce goûtée par la galerie.

appealable [ə'piːləbl], *a.* **1.** *Jur:* (*of action*) appelable; dont on peut appeler. **2.** (*of pers.*) **a. to,** sensible à un appel.

appealing [ə'piːliŋ], *a.* **1.** (regard, etc.) suppliant. **2.** (ton) émouvant. **3.** (personnalité) sympathique.

appealingly [ə'piːliŋli], *adv.* **1.** d'un ton, d'un regard, suppliant; **when she looks at me so a. I can refuse her nothing,** quand elle me regarde de ce petit air suppliant je ne puis rien lui refuser. **2. she smiles so a.,** elle a le sourire si sympathique, si attrayant.

appear [ə'piər], *v.i.* **1.** (*become visible*) paraître, apparaître; devenir visible; se montrer; **when Christ shall a.,** quand le Christ se montrera; **the stars are beginning to a.,** les étoiles commencent à se montrer; **the sun appeared from behind a cloud,** le soleil est sorti de derrière un nuage; **a head appeared at the window,** un visage s'est montré à la fenêtre; **a huge lorry suddenly appeared out of the fog,** un gros camion a surgi tout à coup dans le brouillard; **a ghost appeared to him,** un spectre lui apparut. **2.** (*present oneself publicly*) (*a*) se présenter; *Jur:* comparaître, paraître; **to a. before a court,** comparaître devant un tribunal; **to fail to a.,** faire défaut; **failure to a.,** défaut *m* de comparution; **to a. for s.o.,** répondre pour qn; représenter qn; (*of counsel*) plaider pour qn; **to a. against s.o.,** se présenter contre qn; se porter partie contre qn; **Mr X appeared to defend,** Me X défendait; **I don't want to a. in the business,** je ne veux pas paraître dans l'affaire; (*b*) (*of actor*) **to a. on the stage,** entrer en scène; paraître sur la scène; **she is to a. in** *Macbeth,* elle va jouer dans *Macbeth*; **that was when I appeared on the scene,** c'est à ce moment que je suis arrivé, que j'ai fait mon apparition; (*c*) (*of book*) paraître; **a new daily will a. in March,** un nouveau quotidien paraîtra, sortira, au mois de mars. **3.** (*a*) (*seem*) **to a. sad,** paraître, sembler, avoir l'air, triste; **he appears to be forty,** il paraît, semble, avoir quarante ans; **he appeared to hesitate,** il paraissait hésiter, il avait l'air d'hésiter; **he appears to have a lot of friends,** on lui voit beaucoup d'amis; **it appears to me that you are wrong,** il me paraît que vous avez tort; **there appears to be a mistake,** il semble(rait) qu'il y ait erreur; **so it appears, so it would a.,** il paraît que oui; **it appears not,** il paraît que non; **though the apple appeared sound it contained maggots,** tout en paraissant saine, la pomme contenait des vers; **he does not a. ever to have visited London,** il ne paraît pas qu'il ait jamais visité Londres; **it appears that the ship did not call at Naples,** le navire, à ce qu'il paraît, n'a pas fait escale à Naples; (*b*) (*be clear, evident*) **it appeared later that . . .,** on a vu par la suite, plus tard, que . . .; **if you are jealous, don't let it a.,** si vous êtes jaloux ne le faites pas voir; **as appears from these records,** comme il ressort de ces pièces; **as it appears from a judgment of the court,** comme il appert par jugement du tribunal; **to make it a. that . . .,** (i) faire voir que . . .; montrer, prouver, que . . .; rendre manifeste que . . .; (ii) prétendre que . . .; **the press made it a. that it was a national disaster,** selon la presse c'était un désastre national.

appearance [ə'piərəns], *s.* **1.** (*a*) apparition *f*; entrée *f*; **to make an a., one's a.,** paraître, faire son apparition, se montrer, se présenter, arriver; **to put in an a.,** (i) paraître (chez qn); (ii) faire acte de présence; **he failed to put in an a.,** il ne s'est pas montré (à la cérémonie); *Th:* **first a. of Miss X,** début *m* de Mlle X; **to make one's first a.,** débuter; faire ses débuts; **to make one's last a.,** paraître pour la dernière fois; (*b*) *Jur:* comparution *f* (devant un tribunal); (*c*) *Jur:* acte formel par lequel le défenseur signifie son intention de s'opposer à la demande; (*d*) *Publ:* parution *f* (d'un livre). **2.** (*a*) (*look, aspect*) apparence *f*, aspect *m*, air *m*, figure *f*, mine *f*, dehors *m*; **he has a pleasing a.,** il a un extérieur aimable, un air sympathique; **a young man of good a.,** un jeune homme qui se présente bien; **from his a. one would say . . .,** à son air, à son extérieur, on dirait . . .; **he congratulated her on her a.,** il l'a félicitée sur sa toilette; **one should not judge by appearances,** il ne faut pas juger selon les apparences; **judging by its a. the house was empty,** vue de l'extérieur la maison semblait vide; **the a. of the streets,** l'aspect des rues; **an a. of gaiety,** un air de gaieté; **at first a.,** à première vue; au premier coup d'œil; au premier abord; (*b*) (*semblance*) apparence; **appearances are against him,** les apparences sont contre lui; **to, by, all appearance(s),** selon toute apparence; apparemment; **to keep up appearances,** sauver, garder, les apparences; **for the sake of appearances,** pour sauver les apparences; pour la forme; **to keep up an a. on small means,** faire figure avec peu de fortune; (*c*) **there was not the slightest a. of one,** il n'y en avait pas un(e) de visible, *F:* pas la queue d'un(e). **3.** *A:* fantôme *m*; vision *f*.

appearer [ə'piərər], *s. Jur:* comparant, -ante.

appeasable [ə'piːzəbl], *a.* que l'on peut apaiser.

appease [ə'piːz], *v.tr.* (*a*) apaiser, calmer, tranquilliser (qn); (*b*) apaiser, satisfaire, assouvir (la faim, une passion).

appeasement [ə'piːzmənt], *s.* (*a*) apaisement *m*, adoucissement *m*; (*b*) assouvissement *m*; (*c*) **policy of a.,** politique *f* d'apaisement, de conciliation.

appeaser [ə'piːzər], *s.* conciliateur, -trice.

appeasing [ə'piːziŋ], *s.* = APPEASEMENT.

appellant [ə'pelənt]. **1.** *a. & s. Jur:* appelant, -ante. **2.** *a. Rel.H:* **A. Jansenists,** appelants *m*.

appellate [ə'pelət], *a. Jur:* **a. jurisdiction,** juridiction *f* d'appel.

appellation [æpe'leiʃ(ə)n], *s.* appellation *f*, nom *m*, titre *m*, désignation *f*; **Robert II hardly deserved his a. of the Pious,** Robert II ne mérita guère son surnom de Pieux.

appellative [ə'pelətiv]. **1.** *Gram:* (*a*) *a.* appellatif; (nom) commun; (*b*) *s.* nom commun; nom générique. **2.** *s.* appellation *f*.

append [ə'pend], *v.tr.* **1.** *Lit:* appendre, suspendre (des étendards à une voûte, etc.). **2.** (*a*) attacher, joindre (qch. à qch.); (*b*) **to a. one's signature to a document,** apposer sa signature sur un document; **to a. a seal to an act,** apposer, attacher, un sceau à, sur, un acte; **to a. a document to a dossier,** annexer un document à un dossier; **to a. marginal notes,** ajouter des notes marginales.

appendage [ə'pendidʒ], *s.* **1.** accessoire *m*, apanage *m* (to, de); **the house and its appendages,** la maison et ses dépendances *f*, et ses annexes *f*. **2.** *Anat: Nat.Hist:* appendice *m*; annexe *f* (d'un organe); **caudal a.,** appendice caudal; **paired appendages,** paire *f* d'appendices.

appendant [ə'pendənt]. **1.** *a.* (*a*) *Lit:* accessoire (**to, on,** à); (*b*) attaché (**to, on,** à); **seal a. by a silk cord,** sceau attaché par un cordon de soie. **2.** *s.* (*a*) accessoire *m*; (*b*) (*of country, etc.*) dépendance *f*; (*c*) *Anat:* **appendants of an organ,** annexes *f* d'un organe.

appendectomy [æpen'dektəmi], **appendicectomy** [əpendi'sektəmi], *s. Surg:* appendicectomie *f*.

appendicitis [əpendi'saitis], *s. Med:* appendicite *f*; **a. case, patient suffering from a.,** appendicitaire *mf*, appendiciteux, -euse.

appendicle [ə'pendikl], *s.* appendicule *m*.

appendicocele [æ'pendikousiːl], *s. Med:* appendicocèle *f*.

appendicostomy [əpendi'kɔstəmi], *s. Surg:* appendicostomie *f*.

appendicular [æpen'dikjulər], *a.* appendiculaire ((i) *Nat.Hist:* qui se rapporte aux organes latéraux; (ii) *Med:* qui se rapporte à l'appendice iléo-cæcal).

Appendicularia [æpendikju'lɛəriə], *s.pl. Z:* appendiculaires *m*.

appendiculate [æpen'dikjulət, -leit], *a. Bot: etc:* appendiculé.

appending[1] [ə'pendiŋ], *a.* = APPENDANT I.

appending[2], *s.* **1.** *Lit:* suspension *f* (des étendards à une voûte, etc.). **2.** apposition *f* (d'un sceau, etc.).

appendix[1], *pl.* **-ixes, -ices** [ə'pendiks, -iksiz, -isiːz], *s.* **1.** *Anat:* appendice *m*; **vermiform a.,** appendice vermiculaire, vermiforme, iléo-cæcal, *pl.* iléo-cæcaux; *Med:* **grumbling a.,** appendicite *f* chronique. **2.** annexe *f* (d'un rapport, etc.); appendice (d'un livre).

appendix[2], *v.tr. esp. U.S:* annexer, ajouter en appendice.

apperception [æpə(ː)'sepʃ(ə)n], *s. Psy:* aperception *f*, perception *f*.

apperceptive [æpə(ː)'septiv], **appercipient** [æpə(ː)'sipiənt], *a. Psy:* aperceptif.

appertain [æpə'tein], *v.i. Adm: & Lit:* **1.** appartenir (to, à); **lands appertaining to the Crown,** terres relevant de la Couronne, dépendantes de la Couronne. **2. duties appertaining to my office,** devoirs *m* qui incombent à mes fonctions; devoirs qui m'incombent en tant que magistrat, maire, etc.

appetence ['æpit(ə)ns], **appetency** ['æpit(ə)nsi], *s. A: & Lit:* (*a*) appétence *f*; (*b*) appétit *m*, désir *m* (**of, for, after,** de), convoitise *f* (pour); **he had an appetency for power,** il était travaillé par l'ambition du pouvoir.

appetent ['æpit(ə)nt], *a. A: & Lit:* avide, brûlant de convoitise.

appetite ['æpitait], *s.* (*a*) appétit *m*; **to have a good a.,** avoir bon appétit; **to have a small, poor a.,** avoir peu d'appétit, avoir un appétit d'oiseau; **to spoil, take away, s.o.'s a.,** couper l'appétit, la faim, à qn; **to give s.o. an a., to whet s.o.'s a.,** mettre qn en appétit; **the sea air gives me an a.,** l'air de la mer me donne de l'appétit; **to recover one's a.,** retrouver son appétit; **it's made me lose my a.,** j'en ai perdu le boire et le manger; **loss of a.,** manque *m* d'appétit, *Med:* inappétence *f*, anorexie *f*; *Lit:* **the a. grows with what it feeds on,** l'appétit vient en mangeant; (*b*) **a. for revenge,** soif *f* de vengeance.

appetition [æpi'tiʃ(ə)n], *s. Phil: etc:* appétition *f*.

appetitive [ə'petitiv], *a.* appétitif.

appetizer ['æpitaizər], *s.* **1.** (*a*) *O:* apéritif *m*; (*b*) *Comest:* (i) amuse-gueule *m*, *pl.* amuse-gueule(s); (ii) *O:* hors-d'œuvre *m inv.* **2. to take a walk as an a.,** faire une promenade pour se donner de l'appétit, se mettre en appétit.

appetizing ['æpitaiziŋ], *a.* appétissant, alléchant, affriandant.

appetizingly ['æpitaiziŋli], *adv.* d'une façon appétissante.

Appian[1] ['æpiən], *Pr.n.m. Rom.Hist:* Appien.

Appian[2], *a. Rom.Ant:* **the A. Way,** la Voie appienne.

applaud [ə'plɔːd], *v.tr. & i.* **1.** applaudir (qn); battre, claquer, des mains; **to a. to the echo,** applaudir à tout rompre; **to be applauded,** être applaudi; soulever les applaudissements. **2. to a. s.o.'s efforts,** applaudir aux efforts de qn.

applauder [ə'plɔːdər], *s.* **1.** applaudisseur *m*. **2.** approbateur, -trice (d'une politique, etc.).

applause [ə'plɔːz], *s.* **1.** applaudissements *mpl*; **to meet, be greeted, with a.,** être applaudi; soulever les applaudissements; **to win a.,** se faire applaudir (**from,** par, de); **to win the a. of the audience,** se faire applaudir du public; **great a.,** vifs applaudissements; applaudissements prolongés. **2.** approbation *f*.

apple ['æpl], *s.* **1.** (*a*) pomme *f*; **eating a., dessert a.,** pomme au couteau, pomme de dessert; **cooking a.,** pomme à cuire; *Lit:* **a. of discord,** pomme de discorde; **an a. a day keeps the doctor away** = chaque jour une pomme conserve son homme; **a. core,** trognon *m* de pomme; **a. corer,** vide-pomme *m*, *pl.* vide-pommes; *O:* **a. woman,** marchande *f* de pommes; *Cu:* **baked a.,** pomme cuite (au four); **stewed apples,** compote *f* de pommes; pommes en compote; **a. sauce,** (i) compote de pommes; (ii) *NAm: F:* absurdité *f*, bêtise *f*; **a. turnover,** chausson *m* aux pommes; **a. tart,** tarte *f* aux pommes; **a. pie** = tarte, tourte *f*, aux pommes; **in a.-pie order,** admirablement rangé, en ordre parfait; *F:* **a.-pie bed,** lit *m* en portefeuille; **a. brandy,** eau-de-vie *f* de cidre; = calvados *m*; (*b*) **a. (tree),** (i) pommier *m*; (ii) (*for graft stock*) doucin *m*; **a. orchard,** pommeraie *f*; (*c*) **crab a.,** pomme sauvage; **crab a. (tree),** pommier sauvage; (*d*) *Bot:* **bitter a.,** coloquinte *f*; **a. of Cain,** arbousier *m*, arbre *m* à fraises; **a. of Sodom, Dead Sea a.,** pomme de Sodome; **a. of Peru,** datura *m*, stramoine *f*; *Austr:* **a. tree,** (espèce d')eucalyptus *m*; **a. box,** eucalyptus bicolor, eucalyptus baueriana; **a. gum,** eucalyptus stuartiana; **emu a.,** owenia *m*. **2.** *Ent:* **a. blight, woolly a. aphid,** puceron *m* lanigère; **a. weevil,** anthonome *m*; **red-humped a. worm,** écureuil *m*; **a. tree borer,** saperde *f*. **3. a. of the eye,** prunelle *f* de l'œil; **he's, she's, it's, the a. of his eye,** c'est, il en prend soin comme de la prunelle de ses yeux.

appleberry ['æplberi], *s. Bot:* billardiera *f*.

applecart ['æplkɑːt], *s.* voiture *f* à bras (de marchand des quatre saisons); *F:* **to upset the a.,** tout bouleverser, déranger, chambarder; brouiller les cartes.

apple-cheeked ['æpltʃiːkt], *a.* aux joues pleines et

vermeilles; **little a.-c. old woman,** petite vieille aux pommettes rouges, à figure de pomme d'api.

apple-green ['æpl'gri:n], *a. & s.* vert pomme (*m*) *inv.*

applejack ['æpldʒæk], *s.* eau-de-vie *f* de cidre; = calvados *m.*

applenut ['æplnʌt], *s. Bot:* fruit *m* de l'arbre à ivoire.

apple-polish ['æplpɔliʃ], *v.i. & tr. NAm: F:* lécher les bottes (à qn).

apple-polisher ['æplpɔliʃər], *s. NAm: F:* lécheur, -euse, de bottes.

apple shell ['æplʃel], *s.* (*a*) *Moll:* ampullaire *f*, pila *f*; (*b*) *Conch:* cordon bleu.

apple snail ['æplsneil], *s. Moll:* ampullaire *f*, pila *f.*

appliance [ə'plaiəns], *s.* **1.** *A:* = APPLICATION I. **2.** (*a*) appareil *m*, instrument *m*, dispositif *m*, agencement *m*; **safety a.,** dispositif de sûreté; **rescue a.,** engin *m* de sauvetage; *A:* **appliances of war,** engins de guerre; **mechanical a.,** engin mécanique; **lifting appliances,** engins de levage; **orthopaedic appliances,** appareils orthopédiques; **household appliances,** appareils ménagers; **electric household appliances,** appareils électroménagers; (*b*) *pl.* accessoires *m* (d'une machine, etc.); attirail *m.*

applicability [æplikə'biliti], *s.* applicabilité *f.*

applicable [ə'plikəbl, 'æplikəbl], *a.* applicable, approprié (to, à).

applicant ['æplikənt], *s.* **1. a. for a job,** candidat *m* à un emploi; **a. for a patent,** demandeur *m* d'un brevet; *Fin:* **a. for shares,** souscripteur *m* à des actions; souscripteur d'actions. **2.** *Jur:* demandeur, -deresse; requérant, -ante; partie requérante.

application [æpli'keiʃ(ə)n], *s.* **1.** (*a*) application *f*, applicage *m* (*of sth. to sth.*, de qch. à, sur, qch.); **a. of a theory,** application d'une théorie; **a. of a coat of varnish,** apposition *f* d'une couche de vernis; **a. of a poultice,** application d'un cataplasme; *Pharm:* **for external a.,** pour l'usage externe; *Mec.E:* **gradual a. of power,** entraînement progressif; **a. of the brake,** freinage *m*; serrage *m* du frein; *Jur:* **a. of payments,** imputation *f* de paiements; **a debtor may specify a. of his payments,** un débiteur peut déterminer l'imputation de ses paiements; (*b*) (*thing applied*) application; enduit *m;* (*c*) **industrial applications of a discovery,** applications industrielles d'une découverte; **practical applications of a process,** réalisations *f* d'un procédé; (*d*) *Cmptr:* application; **standby a.,** exploitation *f* à plusieurs calculateurs; **a. audit,** guide *m* d'analyse (pour l'étude d'une application); **a. engineer,** ingénieur techno-commercial; **a. of power,** mise *f* sous tension; **a. program(me),** programme *m* d'applications; **a. programmer,** programmeur, -euse, d'applications; **a. software,** software *m* d'application. **2.** assiduité *f*, application (à l'étude, etc.); contention *f* d'esprit; **the close a. required for . . .,** la tension d'esprit requise pour . . .; **to lack a.,** manquer d'application, d'esprit de suite; **chess demands close a.,** les échecs demandent beaucoup d'application. **3.** (*a*) demande *f*, sollicitation *f*, requête *f*; **a. for a job, for help, for a patent,** demande d'emploi, de secours, de brevet; **to make an a. for sth.,** formuler une demande pour obtenir qch.; **to make a. to s.o. for sth.,** s'adresser à qn pour avoir qch.; **a. has been made to the court for an inquiry into the debtor's assets,** le tribunal est saisi d'une demande de discussion; **samples are sent on a.,** on envoie des échantillons sur demande; **a. form,** bulletin *m* de demande; (*b*) *Fin:* **a. for shares,** souscription *f* d'actions; demande de titres en souscription; **to make a. for shares,** souscrire (à) des actions; **payable on a.,** payable en souscrivant, à la souscription; **a. form,** bulletin *m* de souscription; **a. money,** versement *m* de souscription; **a. is covered,** la souscription est couverte.

applicational [æpli'keiʃənl], *a. Cmptr:* **a. software,** software *m* d'application.

applicator ['æplikeitər], *s. Pharm: etc:* applicateur *m*; dispositif *m* pour l'application (de médicaments, etc.).

applied [ə'plaid], *a.* **a. ornament,** applique *f*; **a. sciences,** sciences expérimentales, appliquées; **a. mathematics,** mathématiques appliquées; **a. psychology,** psychotechnique *f*; **a. art,** arts industriels, décoratifs.

appliqué [æ'pli:kei], *s. Needlew:* **1.** broderie *f* d'application *f*; **a. lace,** dentelle *f* princesse; **a. lacemaker,** striqueuse *f.* **2.** applique *f*, aplat *m.*

appliquéd [æ'pli:keid], *a.* appliqué; **a. ornament,** applique *f.*

apply [ə'plai], *v.tr. & i.* **1.** (*a*) appliquer (**sth. to sth.**, qch. sur qch.); faire l'application de (qch. à qch.); coller (qch. sur qch.); **to a. a poultice,** appliquer un cataplasme; **to a. a light to sth.,** mettre le feu à qch.; **to a. the brake,** freiner; serrer le frein; (*b*) **to a. a system,** appliquer un système, mettre un système en pratique; **this rule applies to all cases,** cette règle est applicable à tous les cas; **this applies to my case,** ceci s'applique à mon propre cas; **this law applies only to the future,** cette loi ne dispose que pour l'avenir; *Com: Fin:* **to a. a payment to a particular debt,** imputer, affecter, un paiement à une dette spécifiée; (*c*) **to a. one's mind to sth.,** appliquer son esprit à qch.; s'appliquer à qch.; **to a. oneself to one's work,** travailler avec application; s'attacher à son travail. **2.** (*a*) **to a. to s.o. for sth.,** s'adresser, recourir, avoir recours, à qn pour obtenir qch.; **I am applying to you,** j'ai recours à vous; je recours à vous; **to a. for help,** demander des secours; **to a. for a job,** poser sa candidature à un emploi; solliciter, postuler, un emploi; **a. within,** s'adresser ici; (*b*) *Fin:* **to a. for shares,** souscrire (à) des actions.

applying [ə'plaiiŋ], *s.* application *f*, applicage *m* (de qch. à, sur, qch.).

appoggiatura [əpɔdʒiə'tuərə], *s. Mus:* appog(g)iature *f.*

appoint [ə'pɔint], *v.tr.* **1.** nommer; (*a*) **to a. s.o. (to be) mayor,** nommer qn maire; **he was appointed headmaster of Eton (College),** il fut nommé directeur du collège d'Eton; **to a. s.o. (as) one's heir,** nommer, instituer, qn son héritier; (*b*) **to a. s.o. to sth., to do sth.,** nommer qn à qch.; désigner qn pour faire qch.; *Adm:* **to a. s.o. to an office,** préposer qn à une fonction; **to a. s.o. to a post,** désigner qn pour, à, un poste; **to a. a committee,** nommer, constituer, un comité; **to a. an expert,** désigner un expert; **to a. an heir,** instituer un héritier; **newly appointed officials,** fonctionnaires entrants, nouvellement nommés. **2.** (*a*) fixer, désigner, assigner (l'heure, l'endroit); arrêter (un jour); **to a. a day to meet again,** prendre jour pour se revoir; (*b*) *A:* **to a. that sth. shall be done,** décider que qch. se fera; prescrire que qch. se fasse. **3.** *Jur:* léguer, transmettre, (des biens) avec faculté de distribution.

appointé [ə'pɔintei], *a. Her:* appointé.

appointed [ə'pɔintid], *a.* **1.** désigné; (*a*) **at the a. time,** à l'heure dite, convenue, indiquée, fixée; au moment donné; **on the a. day,** au jour marqué; (*b*) **a. agent,** agent attitré. **2.** installé, équipé, monté; **well-a. house,** maison bien montée, bien agencée, bien installée.

appointee [æpɔin'ti:], *s.* délégué, -ée; nouveau, -elle, titulaire.

appointing [ə'pɔintiŋ], *s.* désignation *f*, nomination *f* (to, à).

appointive [ə'pɔintiv], *a. NAm:* **a. posts,** emplois obtenus par nomination.

appointment [ə'pɔintmənt], *s.* **1.** rendez-vous *m*; (*for business*) entrevue *f*; *Adm:* convocation *f*; **to make, fix, an a. with s.o.,** assigner, fixer, un rendez-vous, donner rendez-vous, à qn; prendre date, prendre jour, avec qn; **to make, accept, an a. with s.o. for three o'clock, for Monday,** prendre rendez-vous pour trois heures, pour lundi; **to break an a.,** manquer au rendez-vous; **to meet s.o. by a.,** se rencontrer avec qn sur rendez-vous; **have you an a.?** avez-vous un rendez-vous? *Adm:* êtes-vous convoqué? **2.** (*a*) *A:* **by the King's a.,** par ordre, par décret, du Roi; (*b*) *Jur:* **power of a.,** faculté *f* de distribution (de biens) (accordée à un légataire). **3.** (*a*) nomination *f* (de qn à un emploi); *Adm:* désignation *f* (de qn pour un emploi, un navire); *Mil: Navy:* affectation *f* (de qn à un navire, une unité); **a. of an official,** désignation, nomination, d'un fonctionnaire; (*of shop, etc.*) **by a. to His, Her, Majesty,** fournisseur breveté, attitré, de sa Majesté; *Navy:* **to receive one's a. (to a ship),** recevoir sa désignation; *Journ:* **appointments vacant,** offres *f* d'emploi; **appointments board,** (i) bureau *m* de placement; (ii) *Sch:* département *m* d'information et de prospective; (*b*) place *f*, charge *f*, emploi *m*; **to hold an a.,** être préposé à un emploi. **4.** (*a*) *A:* équipement *m* (de troupes); armement *m*, habillage *m* (d'un vaisseau); (*b*) *pl.* aménagement *m*, agencements *mpl*, installation *f* (d'une maison); (*c*) *pl.* *A:* **appointments of an office,** émoluments *m*, appointements *m*, attachés à une charge.

apport ['æpɔ:t], *s. Psychics:* apport *m.*

apportion [ə'pɔ:ʃ(ə)n], *v.tr. Fin:* répartir, ventiler (les frais); lotir (une propriété); **to a. sth. to s.o.,** assigner qch. à qn; **to a. (out) a sum among several people,** répartir, partager, distribuer, une somme entre plusieurs personnes.

apportionment [ə'pɔ:ʃ(ə)nmənt], *s.* partage *m*, répartition *f* (d'impôts, de dépenses, etc.); allocation *f* (des vivres, etc.); lotissement *m*, distribution *f* (de parts, d'une propriété); ventilation (de frais, etc.).

apposable [æ'pouzəbl], *a.* (*of the thumb*) apposable (aux autres doigts).

appose [æ'pouz], *v.tr. Jur: etc:* **to a. one's signature to a document,** apposer sa signature, à, sur un document; revêtir un document de sa signature.

apposite ['æpəzit], *a.* juste; approprié (**to,** à); (fait) à propos; **a. remark,** remarque bien amenée, faite à propos; observation *f* juste; **to be a. to a case,** s'appliquer, convenir, à un cas.

appositely ['æpəzitli], *adv.* à propos; convenablement.

appositeness ['æpəzitnis], *s.* justesse *f* (d'une observation); à-propos *m*, opportunité *f* (d'une action).

apposition [æpə'ziʃ(ə)n], *s.* **1.** *Gram: etc:* apposition *f*; **words in a.,** mots appositifs, en apposition. **2. to bring the ends of a broken bone into a.,** affronter les extrémités d'un os fracturé. **3.** *Bot: etc:* apposition.

appositional [æpə'ziʃənl], **appositive** [æ'pɔzitiv], *a.* appositif; en apposition.

appraisable [ə'preizəbl], *a.* évaluable.

appraisal [ə'preizl], **appraisement** [ə'preizmənt], *s.* évaluation *f*, estimation *f*, appréciation *f*; (*before auction*) prisée *f*; **official a.,** expertise *f*; **investment a.,** appréciation des investissements; **market a.,** évaluation du marché; **a. method of depreciation,** méthode *f* d'amortissement fondée sur la valeur du moment; **self a.,** autocritique *f.*

appraise [ə'preiz], *v.tr.* priser, estimer, évaluer (qch.) (**at so much,** à tant); faire l'appréciation de (qch.); apprécier la valeur de (qch.); faire l'expertise (des dégâts).

appraiser [ə'preizər], *s.* estimateur *m*, priseur *m*, évaluateur, -trice; appréciateur *m*; **official a.** (**of property, etc.**), commissaire-priseur *m*, *pl.* commissaires-priseurs; expert *m.*

appreciable [ə'pri:ʃiəbl], *a.* appréciable; sensible; **without a. change,** sans variation notable; **there is an a. difference between the two prices,** il y a une différence appréciable entre les deux prix.

appreciably [ə'pri:ʃiəbli], *adv.* à un degré appréciable; sensiblement.

appreciate [ə'pri:ʃieit, -sieit]. **1.** *v.tr.* (*a*) évaluer (des marchandises); estimer la valeur de (qch.); **he, it, was never appreciated at his, its, true value, worth,** il n'a jamais été apprécié à sa juste valeur; (*b*) apprécier; faire cas de (qch.); **he doesn't greatly a. your attentions,** il ne fait pas grand cas de vos attentions; **I deeply a. this honour,** je suis profondément sensible à cet honneur; **songs greatly appreciated,** chansons très goûtées; **I fully a. (the fact) that . . .,** je me rends clairement compte, je ne me dissimule pas, que . . .; **I fully a. all you have done,** je ne méconnais pas vos services; **I greatly a. your kindness,** je suis très sensible à votre gentillesse, à votre amabilité; **I a. your having done this,** je vous suis reconnaissant d'avoir fait cela; **I hope they'll a. having an expert's views,** j'espère qu'ils seront satisfaits d'avoir l'avis d'un expert; **the blind a. sound, but not colour,** les aveugles se rendent compte des sons mais non des couleurs, sont sensibles aux sons mais non aux couleurs. **2.** *Fin:* (*a*) *v.tr.* hausser la valeur de (qch.); **to a. the coinage,** rehausser les monnaies; (*b*) *v.i.* (*of goods, etc.*) augmenter de valeur; hausser de prix; monter; accuser une plus-value; **appreciated surplus,** plus-value, *pl.* plus-values; **the franc has appreciated in terms of other currencies,** le franc s'est apprécié par rapport aux autres monnaies. **3.** *v.i.* s'améliorer.

appreciation [əpri:ʃi'eiʃ(ə)n, -siei∫(ə)n], *s.* **1.** (*a*) appréciation *f* ((i) du prix, de la valeur, de qch., (ii) d'un service, de la situation, etc.); estimation *f* (de la valeur de qch.); évaluation *f*; (*b*) **to give, write, an a. of a new play, of a novel,** faire la critique d'une nouvelle pièce, d'un roman; **to have no a. of music,** être fermé à la musique; ne pas être connaisseur en musique; *Sch:* **literary a.,** explication *f* de texte, explication littéraire; **musical a.,** appréciation musicale; **I should like to express my a. of your kindness,** j'aimerais bien vous dire combien je suis sensible à, reconnaissant de, votre gentillesse; (*c*) *Cmptr:* **a. course,** cours *m* d'initiation. **2.** accroissement *m*, hausse *f* de valeur; amélioration *f*, valorisation *f*, plus value *f*, *pl.* plus-values; **these shares show an a.,** ces actions ont enregistré une plus-value; **a. of assets,** plus-value d'actif; **a. of the exchange,** plus-value du change; **a. in prices,** amélioration des cours, des prix.

appreciative [ə'pri:ʃiətiv, -siətiv], **appreciatory** [ə'pri:ʃiət(ə)ri, -siət(ə)ri], *a.* **1.** (jugement, etc.) élogieux; **after a few a. words,** après quelques paroles élogieuses. **2.** appréciateur, -trice; **to be appreciative of music,** être sensible à la musique; apprécier la musique; **don't think I'm not appreciative,** ne croyez pas que je n'en suis pas reconnaissant.

appreciatively [ə'pri:ʃiətivli], *adv.* (*a*) favorablement; (*b*) avec satisfaction; **the audience listened a.,** les assistants ont écouté avec appréciation.

appreciator [ə'pri:ʃieitər, -sieitər], *s.* appréciateur, -trice.

apprehend [æpri'hend], *v.tr.* **1.** *Jur:* arrêter (qn); appréhender (qn) (au corps); saisir (qn) au corps. **2.** *A: & Lit:* (*a*) percevoir (un son, etc.); (*b*) comprendre, saisir (le sens d'une phrase, etc.); **you are, I apprehend,**

related to . . ., vous êtes, si je ne me trompe, parent de . . .; **I had not apprehended that. . .**, je ne m'étais pas rendu compte que . . .. 3. *A: & Lit:* appréhender, redouter, craindre (un danger, etc.).

apprehensible [æpri'hensibl], *a.* appréhensible (**to the senses, by the senses,** par les sens); perceptible; saisissable.

apprehension [æpri'henʃ(ə)n], *s.* **1.** *Jur:* arrestation *f*; prise *f* de corps; **a. of a deserter,** arrestation *f* d'un déserteur. **2.** (*a*) perception *f* (d'un son, etc.); compréhension *f* (des faits); (*b*) *Psy:* entendement *m*, appréhension *f*; **to be slow of a.,** avoir l'intelligence, la conception, lente; avoir l'esprit, l'entendement, lent. **3.** appréhension, crainte *f*; **to give cause for a.,** motiver des craintes; **I am under no apprehensions about . . .,** je n'ai aucune crainte au sujet de . . ..

apprehensive [æpri'hensiv], *a.* **1. the a. faculty,** la faculté de comprendre, de percevoir; la faculté de compréhension; **the a. faculties,** les facultés perceptives. **2.** (*of pers.*) intelligent, fin; à l'esprit ouvert. **3.** timide, craintif; **to be a. of danger,** redouter, appréhender, le danger; **to be a. of failure,** craindre d'échouer; **to be a. for s.o., for s.o.'s safety,** craindre pour qn, pour la sûreté de qn.

apprehensively [æpri'hensivli], *adv.* avec appréhension, avec crainte; craintivement.

apprehensiveness [æpri'hensivnis], *s.* **1.** faculté *f* de comprendre, de percevoir. **2.** appréhension *f*; timidité *f*.

apprentice[1] [ə'prentis], *s.* (*a*) apprenti, -ie; (*b*) commençant, -ante; débutant, -ante.

apprentice[2], *v.tr.* **to a. s.o. to s.o.,** placer, mettre, qn en apprentissage chez qn.

apprenticed [ə'prentist], *a.* en apprentissage (**to,** chez).

apprenticeship [ə'prenti(s)ʃip], *s.* apprentissage *m*; **to serve one's a. with s.o.,** faire son apprentissage chez qn.

appressed [æ'prest], *a. Bot:* appressé, apprimé.

apprise [ə'praiz], *v.tr. Lit:* **to a. s.o. of sth.,** apprendre qch. à qn; prévenir, informer, qn de qch.; porter qch. à la connaissance de qn; donner connaissance de qch. à qn.

appro ['æprou], *s. Com: F:* **on a.,** à l'essai, à condition.

approach[1] [ə'proutʃ], *s.* approche *f.* **1.** (*a*) **the a. of the invaders,** l'approche des envahisseurs; *Aut: Jur:* **to give audible warning of a.,** annoncer son approche; **the a. of spring,** la venue du printemps; **the a. of death,** l'approche, les approches, de la mort; (*b*) abord *m*; *Lit:* **man easy of a.,** homme qui est d'un abord facile; homme abordable, affable; (*c*) **his a. to the problem,** sa méthode d'attaque du problème, la façon dont il aborde le problème; **I don't like his a.,** je n'aime pas sa façon de s'y prendre; **freshness of a.,** fraîcheur *f* d'imagination; **this book is an excellent a. to nuclear physics,** ce livre est une excellente initiation à la physique nucléaire; *Pol.Ec:* **systems a.,** approche par la théorie des systèmes; **top management a.,** optique *f* de la direction générale; (*d*) **to make approaches to s.o.,** faire des avances à qn. **2.** voie *f* d'accès; **the a. to a town,** les abords, les approches, les accès *m*, d'une ville; **a. to a harbour,** atterrage *m*, accès, d'un port; **a. to a house,** avenue *f*, chemin *m*, conduisant à une maison; **the a. to the station is up a slope,** on arrive, on accède, à la gare par une rampe. **3.** (*a*) rapprochement *m*; **it is the nearest a. to perfection,** cela approche le plus près de la perfection; **there was no a. to a riot,** il n'y a pas eu le moindre semblant d'émeute; **an a. to accuracy is not enough,** une approximation de l'exactitude ne suffit pas; (*b*) *Mth:* **method of continual approaches,** méthode *f* des approximations successives. **4.** *Arb:* **a. graft, grafting,** greffe *f* par approche. **5.** *Golf:* **a. shot,** coup *m* d'approche; **short a.,** approche piquée; **long a., running-up a.,** approche allongée. **6.** *Mil:* (*a*) **a. march,** marche *f* d'approche; **covered a.,** (marche d')approche couverte; **a. under cover,** (i) cheminement *m* à couvert; (ii) approche défilée aux vues adverses; (*b*) **approaches, a. works,** travaux *mpl* d'approche; **covered approaches,** abords couverts; **open approaches,** abords découverts; **to block the approaches,** bloquer les abords; **to deny the enemy the Baltic approaches,** interdire à l'ennemi les abords de la Baltique. **7.** *Av:* **a. aids,** moyens *m* d'approche; **overhead a.,** approche en spirale à 360°; **ground control a.,** atterrissage *m* par contrôle au sol; **a. end of runway,** entrée *f* de piste, seuil *m* de la piste.

approach[2]. **1.** *v.i.* approcher, s'approcher; *Golf:* jouer le coup d'approche; *Nau:* **to a. on opposite courses,** s'approcher à contre-bord; **this approaches perfection,** cela approche de la perfection, n'est pas loin de (toucher à) la perfection; **Christmas is approaching,** Noël est proche; Noël approche. **2.** *v.tr.* (*a*) approcher; **we are approaching London,** nous approchons de Londres; **he was approaching forty,** il approchait de la quarantaine; il allait sur la quarantaine; *Nau:* **to be approached by a ship,** être rejoint par un navire; **to a. (land),** atterrir; **the wind was approaching gale force,** le vent soufflait presque en tempête; **it was with something approaching a feeling of relief that . . .,** ce fut avec un sentiment presque de soulagement que . . .; **I've never seen anything approaching it,** je n'ai jamais rien vu d'approchant; *Mth:* **to a. a limit,** tendre vers une limite; (*b*) s'approcher de (qn); aborder, approcher (qn); entrer en communication avec qn; **to a. s.o. on the subject of . . .,** approcher qn, entrer en pourparlers avec qn, faire une démarche auprès de qn, au sujet de . . .; **they approached the general to arrange an armistice,** ils sont entrés en pourparlers avec le général au sujet d'un armistice; **to a. s.o. in a friendly spirit,** approcher qn avec des intentions de paix; **to be easy, difficult, to a.,** avoir l'abord facile, difficile; **when he is working it is impossible to a. him,** quand il est en train de travailler il est impossible de l'aborder; (*c*) tâter, pressentir (qn); (*d*) **to a. a question,** aborder, s'attaquer à, une question; (*e*) *A:* **to a. a chair to the fire,** approcher une chaise du feu.

approachability [əproutʃə'biliti], *s.* accessibilité *f*.

approachable [ə'proutʃəbl], *a.* (personne, endroit) accessible, approchable; (personne, côte) abordable.

approaching [ə'proutʃiŋ], *a.* approchant; **his a. death,** sa mort prochaine; **the a. spring,** le printemps tout proche; **the a. car,** la voiture qui vient, venait, en sens inverse; **an a. storm,** une tempête qui arrive.

approbate ['æproubeit], *v.tr. U.S:* approuver.

approbation [æprə'beiʃ(ə)n], *s.* **1.** approbation *f*, agrément *m*, consentement *m*; assentiment *m*; **nod of a.,** signe de tête approbatif. **2.** approbation, jugement *m* favorable; **to show one's a.,** manifester son approbation; **to earn the a. of the public,** mériter les suffrages *m* du public; **smile of a.,** sourire approbateur. **3.** *Com: A:* **goods on a.,** marchandises *f* à condition, à l'essai.

approbative [æ'prɔbətiv], **approbatory** [æprə'beitəri], *a.* **1.** consentant, approbatif. **2.** favorable; approbateur, -trice.

appropriable [ə'proupriəbl], *a.* appropriable.

appropriate[1] [ə'proupriət], *a.* **1.** (*a*) approprié; **style a. to the subject,** style qui convient au sujet; style approprié au sujet; **salary a. to an office,** traitement *m* applicable à une fonction, que comporte une fonction; **words a. to express our ideas,** mots propres à exprimer notre pensée; (*b*) *Ecc:* **a. benefice,** bénéfice approprié. **2.** propre, convenable, (**to, for,** à); **a. name,** nom bien choisi; **a. word,** mot *m* de situation; **the remark is a.,** l'observation est juste, à propos; **to take a. action,** agir comme il convient; prendre les mesures indiquées; **to make a. allowance(s),** faire les ajustements *m* nécessaires; **a. music, speech,** musique *f*, discours *m*, de circonstance.

appropriate[2] [ə'prouprieit], *v.tr.* **1.** (*a*) s'approprier (qch.); s'emparer de (qch.); prendre possession de (qch.); usurper (qch.); s'adjuger (qch.); **to a. the funds,** s'approprier, détourner, les fonds; **to a. s.o.'s ideas,** prendre, dérober, ses idées à qn; (*b*) s'attribuer, se destiner, se réserver (qch.). **2.** approprier, appliquer, affecter, consacrer (**sth. to, for, a purpose,** qch. à une destination); *Ecc:* **appropriated benefice,** bénéfice approprié.

appropriately [ə'proupriətli], *adv.* convenablement, proprement; à juste titre; à propos; comme il convient; congrûment; **she was not a. dressed for a wedding,** elle n'était pas en tenue convenable pour assister à un mariage.

appropriateness [ə'proupriətnis], *s.* convenance *f*, justesse *f*, à-propos *m*, applicabilité *f*.

appropriation [əproupri'eiʃ(ə)n], *s.* **1.** appropriation *f*, prise *f* de possession (of, de). **2.** (*a*) appropriation, application *f*, affectation *f*, (de qch. à un usage); (*b*) affectation de fonds; *Fin:* attribution *f*, distraction *f* (d'une somme); **to make an a. for a special purpose,** faire une distraction à des fins spéciales; **a. account,** compte *m* d'affectation; **a. to a debt,** imputation *f* sur une dette; **a. to the reserve,** dotation *f*, affectation, à la réserve; **prior a.,** prélèvement *m* prioritaire; *Ecc:* **a. of the tithes,** appropriation de la dîme. **3.** *Pol:* crédit *m* (budgétaire); budget *m*; **allotment of appropriations,** répartition *f* de budgets; **a. bill,** (projet *m* de) loi *f* de finances.

appropriator [ə'prouprieitər], *s.* usurpateur, -trice (of, de); **to be an a. of sth.,** s'approprier qch.

approvable [ə'pru:vəbl], *a.* digne d'approbation, qui mérite l'approbation.

approval [ə'pru:vl], *s.* **1.** approbation *f*, agrément *m*; **for a.,** pour approbation; **to meet with s.o.'s a., to receive a.,** recevoir, obtenir, l'approbation de qn; être approuvé; **I hope it will meet with your a.,** j'espère que vous en serez satisfait; **does my action meet with your a.?** approuvez-vous mon action? **gesture, sign, of a.,** geste, signe, approbatif; **to nod a.,** approuver de la tête; faire un signe de tête approbateur. **2.** *Adm:* ratification *f*, homologation *f*; **to stamp one's a. upon a document,** ratifier, homologuer, un document. **3.** *Com:* (*a*) **on a.,** à condition, à l'essai; **to buy sth. on a.,** acheter qch. à l'épreuve, à condition; **watch sent on a.,** montre envoyée à titre d'essai; **book sent on a.,** livre envoyé à l'examen, en communication; (*b*) *NAm:* **approvals,** marchandises envoyées à titre d'essai.

approve [ə'pru:v]. **1.** *v.tr.* (*a*) *A:* **to a. one's valour,** prouver son courage, faire preuve de courage; **to a. oneself a man of the world,** se montrer homme du monde; (*b*) approuver, sanctionner (une action); ratifier, homologuer (une décision); agréer (un contrat); **conduct approved by . . .,** conduite qui a obtenu l'approbation de . . .; **to be approved by all sensible people,** recueillir l'approbation de tous les gens raisonnables; **read and approved,** lu et approuvé; **type (of engine, etc.) approved by the government,** type agréé par l'État. **2.** *v.ind.tr.* **to a. of sth.,** approuver qch.; **he did not a. of our playing football on Sundays,** il n'approuvait pas que nous jouions au football le dimanche; **do you a. of his going away?** trouvez-vous bon qu'il parte? approuvez-vous son départ? **to a. of a method,** être partisan d'une méthode; **I don't a. of your friends,** vos amis ne me plaisent pas; **to a. of s.o.'s choice,** applaudir au choix de qn; féliciter qn de son choix; **the proposal was approved of,** la proposition a été approuvée, agréée; **I don't a. of the plan,** je ne suis pas d'accord avec ce projet.

approved [ə'pru:vd], *a.* (*a*) *A:* **an a. thief,** un voleur connu comme tel; un voleur notoire; (*b*) approuvé, agréé; réglementaire; **the old a. methods,** les méthodes classiques; *Adm:* **(officially) a.,** homologué; **a. stamp,** cachet *m* d'authentification; **a. type certificate,** certificat *m* d'homologation; *Av:* **a. maximum rate of descent,** vitesse de descente maximum autorisée; *Ins:* **a. society,** compagnie d'assurances agréée par l'État; *Breed:* **a. stallion,** étalon autorisé; *Sch: A:* **a. school,** école *f* pour les délinquants juvéniles.

approver [ə'pru:vər], *s.* **1.** approbateur, -trice. **2.** *Jur:* (*King's evidence*) complice *m* dénonciateur de ses camarades.

approving [ə'pru:viŋ], *a.* approbateur, -trice.

approvingly [ə'pru:viŋli], *adv.* avec approbation; d'un air, d'un ton, approbateur; **she smiled a.,** elle a eu un sourire approbateur.

approximate[1] [ə'prɔks(i)mət], *a.* **1.** *Biol: Ph:* rapproché, proche, voisin. **2.** (calcul, etc.) approximatif, approché; **a. calculation,** approximation *f*; **a. value,** valeur approximative; **a. estimate,** (i) appréciation, évaluation, approximative; (ii) devis approximatif; **the a. distance between A and B is 10 kilometres,** A est à à peu près 10 kilomètres de B.

approximate[2] [ə'prɔksimeit]. **1.** *v.tr.* rapprocher (deux cas, etc.); *Mth:* **uniformly approximated,** approché(s) uniformément; **to a. a decimal,** forcer une décimale; **to a. a case to another,** rapprocher un cas d'un autre; **conditions during the experiment approximated actual conditions as much as possible,** au cours de l'expérience on a établi des conditions aussi rapprochées que possible des conditions normales. **2.** *v.i.* **to a. to the truth,** approcher de la vérité; se rapprocher de la vérité; **to a. to a lie,** friser le mensonge.

approximately [ə'prɔksimətli], *adv.* approximativement, sensiblement; à peu près; en gros; **his account of what happened was a. correct,** sa version de ce qui s'était passé était à peu près correcte; **it's finished, or a.,** c'est terminé, ou presque; **five miles are a. eight kilometres,** cinq milles valent à peu près huit kilomètres; **his income is a. £5000,** son revenu est d'environ cinq mille livres.

approximation [əprɔksi'meiʃ(ə)n]. **1.** rapprochement *m* (d'opinions, etc.). **2.** approximation *f*; **a. to reality,** approximation de la réalité; **a. to a meaning,** approchant *m* d'un sens; **to be satisfied with an a.,** se contenter d'un résultat approximatif, d'un à-peu-près; **this figure is only an a.,** ceci n'est qu'un chiffre approximatif; *Mth:* **a. method,** méthode *f* par approximation; **to solve an equation by a.,** résoudre une équation par approximations successives, par approches successives.

approximative [ə'prɔksimətiv], *a.* approximatif.

appui [æ'pwi:], *s. Equit: Mil:* appui *m*; *Mil:* **point of a.,** point *m* d'appui.

appulse [ə'pʌls], *s.* choc *m*, rencontre *f*; *Astr:* appulse *f*; approche *f* (de deux planètes, etc.).

appurtenance [ə'pə:tinəns], *s.* **1.** *Jur:* (*a*) appartenance *f*; (*b*) droit *m* accessoire, servitude *f* (d'un immeuble); **house with all its appurtenances,** (i) immeuble avec ses appartenances et dépendances, ses circonstances et dépendances; (ii) immeuble avec ses servitudes. **2.** (*a*) *Tchn:* installation *f* subsidiaire; (*b*) *pl.* accessoires *m*, appareil *m*, attirail *m*, équipage *m*, équipement *m*.

appurtenant [ə'pə:tinənt], *a. Jur:* (*a*) **a. to sth.,** appartenant à qch.; dépendant de qch.; (*b*) propre, particulier (**to,** à); **the treaty and the a. ratifications,** le traité et les ratifications qui s'y rapportent.

apraxia [ei'præksiə], *s. Med:* apraxie *f*; **sensory a., agnostic a.,** apraxie psycho-sensorielle; **motor a.,** apraxie (idéo-)motrice.

apraxic [ei'præksik], *a. Med:* apraxique.

après-ski ['æprei'ski], *a.* **a.-s. outfit,** tenue *f* d'après-ski.

aprick [ə'prik], *adv. & a.* (*a*) *A: & Lit:* prêt à piquer; (*b*) (*of dog*) **with ears a.,** les oreilles dressées.

apricot ['eiprikɔt], *s.* (*a*) *Hort:* abricot *m*; **a. tree,** abricotier *m*; **a. plum,** abricotine *f*, prune abricotée, prune abricot; **a. peach,** pêche abricotée, pêche abricot; (*b*) (*colour*) abricot *m inv*.

April ['eipril], *s.* avril *m*; **in A.,** en avril, au mois d'avril; (**on**) **the first, the seventh, of A.,** le premier, le sept, avril; **A. showers** = giboulées *f* de mars; **A. Fool's Day,** le premier avril; **to make an A. fool of s.o.,** donner, faire, un poisson d'avril à qn; faire gober à qn un poisson d'avril; **A. fool!** poisson d'avril! **to be made an A fool (of),** recevoir un poisson d'avril.

a priori ['eiprai'ɔ:rai, æpri'ɔ:ri], *adv. & a.* a priori; **a p. reasoning,** raisonnement *m* a priori.

apriorism ['eiprai'ɔrizm, æp-], *s.* apriorisme *m*.

apriorist [eiprai'ɔ:rist, æp-], *s.* aprioriste *mf*.

aprioristic ['eipraiɔ'ristik, æp-], *a.* aprioristique.

apriority ['eiprai'ɔriti], *s.* apriorisme *m*.

aproctia [ei'prɔktiə], *s. Ter:* aproctie *f*, aproctose *f*.

apron ['eiprən], *s.* **1.** *Cost:* tablier *m*; *F:* **to be tied to one's mother's a. strings,** être pendu(e) aux jupes, aux jupons, de sa mère; **his mother keeps him tied to her a. strings,** sa mère le tient en laisse, le garde dans ses jupes. **2.** *Tchn:* (*a*) *Artil:* couvre-lumière *m*, *pl.* couvre-lumières (d'un canon); (*b*) *Hyd.E:* radier *m* (d'un bassin); **downstream a.,** arrière-radier *m*, *pl.* arrière-radiers; (*c*) *N.Arch:* contre-étrave *f*, *pl.* contre-étraves (d'un navire), (*d*) *A.Veh: A.Aut:* tablier; **side a.,** bavolet *m*; (*e*) *Av:* aire *f* de manœuvre, de stationnement; piste *f* (devant les hangars); tablier, aire en dur (pour révision et réparation des avions); **a. services,** services *m* en piste; (*f*) *Const:* **a. piece,** échiffre *m*; *U.S:* **a. wall,** écoinçon *m*; (*g*) *Tls:* **a. lathe,** tour *m* à tablier; *Ind.* **a. feed,** tablier sans fin; (*h*) *Th:* **a. (stage),** avant-scène *f*, *pl.* avant-scènes. **3.** (*a*) *Anat:* **(Hottentot) a.,** tablier; (*b*) peau *f* du cou (d'une oie, d'un bélier).

aproned ['eiprənd], *a.* qui porte un tablier.

apronful ['eiprənful], *s.* plein tablier; **with an a. of flowers,** des fleurs plein le tablier.

apropos ['æprə'pou]. **1.** *s.* à-propos *m*; opportunité *f* (d'une action, d'une observation). **2.** *a.* **a very a. remark,** une observation très à propos, très opportune. **3.** *prep.phr.* **it was mentioned a. of the holidays,** il en a été parlé à propos des vacances.

aprosexia [eiprou'seksiə], *s. Med:* aprosexie *f*.

apse [æps], *s.* **1.** *Ecc.Arch:* abside *f*, apside *f*. **2.** *Astr:* apside; **a. line,** ligne *f* des apsides.

apsidal ['æpsidl], *a.* **1.** *Ecc.Arch:* absidal, -aux. **2.** *Astr:* des apsides; apsidal.

apsidiole [æp'sidioul], *s. Ecc.Arch:* absidiole *f*; chapelle absidale.

apsis, *pl.* **apsides** ['æpsis, 'æpsidi:z, æp'saidi:z], *s.* **1.** *Astr:* apside *f*; **line of apsides,** ligne *f* d'apsides. **2.** *occ.* (*a*) *Ecc.Arch:* absidiole *f*; (*b*) *Ecc:* reliquaire *m*, absidiole.

apt [æpt], *a.* **1.** (mot) juste, fin; (expression) heureuse, qui convient. **2. a. to do sth:** (*a*) (*of pers.*) enclin, porté, sujet, à faire qch.; **he is a. to forget,** il lui arrive fréquemment d'oublier; il a une tendance à oublier; il oublie facilement; **we are a. to believe that . . .,** on croit volontiers que . . .; **I am a. to think that . . .,** j'incline à croire que . . .; **a careless person is a. to make mistakes,** quelqu'un de peu soigneux fait facilement des erreurs; (*b*) (*of thg*) sujet à, susceptible de, faire qch.; **toys a. to go wrong,** jouets sujets à se détraquer; **buttons a. to come off,** boutons qui ont une tendance à se détacher; **iron is a. to rust,** le fer se rouille facilement; (*c*) *U.S:* **he is a. to lose his job,** il va probablement perdre son emploi. **3.** apte, propre (**for,** à); **horse a. for reproduction,** cheval propre à la reproduction. **4.** (élève, etc.) intelligent, habile; **one of my aptest pupils,** un de mes meilleurs élèves; un de mes élèves les mieux doués.

aptenodytes [æptenou'daiti:z], *s. Orn:* aptenodytes *m*.

Aptera ['æptərə], *s.pl. Ent:* aptères *m*.

apteral ['æptərəl], *a.* **1.** *Ent: Orn: etc:* aptère, sans ailes. **2.** *Gk.Arch:* aptère.

apteran ['æptərən], *a. & s. Ent:* aptère (*m*).

apterous ['æptərəs], *a.* **1.** *Ent: Orn: etc:* aptère, sans ailes. **2.** *Bot:* aptère.

aptery ['æptəri], *s. Nat.Hist:* aptérisme *m*.

Apterygidae [æptə'ridʒidi:], *s.pl. Orn:* aptérygidés *m*.

Apterygiformes [æptəridʒi'fɔ:mi:z], *s.pl. Orn:* aptérygiformes *m*.

Apterygota [æpteri'goutə], *s.pl. Orn:* aptérygotes *m*.

apteryx ['æptəriks], *s. Orn:* aptéryx *m*, kiwi *m*.

Aptian ['æptiən, 'æpʃən], *a. & s. Geol:* aptien (*m*).

aptitude ['æptitju:d], *s.* **a. for sth.,** aptitude *f* à, pour, qch.; disposition(s) *f* pour qch.; **to have an a. for learning,** être apte à apprendre; avoir des dispositions pour l'étude; **he had a singular a. for dealing with difficulties,** il avait un talent particulier pour aviser aux difficultés; **to show great a.,** montrer de grandes dispositions; **a. test,** test *m* d'aptitude, d'intelligence pratique.

aptly ['æptli], *adv.* avec justesse; à propos, avec à-propos; **a.-timed remark,** remarque faite bien à propos; **he is a. called Fatty,** il mérite bien son surnom de Lardon.

aptness ['æptnis], *s.* **1.** justesse *f*, à-propos *m* (d'une expression, d'une citation, etc.). **2.** (*a*) (*of pers.*) penchant *m*, tendance *f* (**to do sth.,** à faire qch.); (*b*) (*of thg*) **the a. of iron to rust,** la tendance du fer à se rouiller. **3.** *occ.* = APTITUDE.

aptyalia [æptai'eiliə], **aptyalism** [æp'taiəlizm], *s. Med:* aptyalisme *m*, asialie *f*, xérostomie *f*.

aptychus, *-pl.* **-i** ['æptikəs, -ai], *s. Paleont:* aptychus *m*.

Apuleius [æpju'li:əs], *Pr.n.m. Lt.Lit:* Apulée.

Apulia [ə'pju:liə], *Pr.n. Geog:* la Pouille; *A.Geog:* l'Apulie *f*.

Apulian [ə'pju:liən]. *Geog:* (*a*) *a.* apulien; (*b*) *s.* Apulien, -ienne.

apus ['æpəs], *s. Crust:* apus *m*.

apyre(c)tic [eipai're(k)tik, æp-], *a. Med:* apyrétique.

apyrene [eipai'ri:n], *a. Nat.Hist:* apyrène.

apyrexia [eipai'reksiə, æp-], *s.* apyrexie *f*.

apyrous [ei'paiərəs], *a.* apyre.

aqua ['ækwə], *s.* (*used to form compounds in*) *Ch: Pharm:* **a. fortis,** eau-forte *f*; **a. regia** ['ri:dʒiə], eau régale; **a. vitae** ['vaiti:], eau-de-vie *f*; *F:* **a. pura** ['pju:rə], eau *f*.

aquabatics [ækwə'bætiks], *s.pl.* acrobatie *f* aquatique.

aquacade ['ækwəkeid], *s. NAm:* fête *f* aquatique.

aquadrome ['ækwədroum], *s.* centre *m* de ski nautique.

aquafer ['ækwəfεər], *s. Geol:* couche *f* aquifère.

aquafortist ['ækwə'fɔ:tist], *s. Engr:* aquafortiste *mf*.

aqualung ['ækwəlʌŋ], *s.* scaphandre *m* autonome.

aquamarine [ækwəmə'ri:n], *s. Miner:* aigue-marine *f*, *pl.* aigues-marines.

aquanaut ['ækwənɔ:t], *s.* aquanaute *mf*.

aquaplane[1] ['ækwəplein], *s.* aquaplane *m*.

aquaplane[2], *v.i.* faire de l'aquaplane.

aquaplaner ['ækwəpleinər], *s.* aquaplaniste *mf*.

aquaplaning [ækwə'pleiniŋ], *s.* **1.** *Sp:* l'aquaplane *m*. **2.** *Aut:* aquaplaning *m*, effet *m* d'hydroglisseur.

aquapuncture [ækwə'pʌŋktjər], *s.* aquapuncture *f*.

aquarelle [ækwə'rel], *s. Art:* **1.** aquarelle *f*. **2.** dessin (i) au trait aquarellé, (ii) colorié au pochoir; **to finish a drawing in a.,** (i) aquareller un dessin; (ii) colorier un dessin au pochoir.

aquarellist [ækwə'relist], *s.* **1.** aquarelliste *mf*. **2.** (*a*) colorieur *m*; (*b*) peintre au pochoir.

aquarist [ə'kwεərist], *s.* aquariophile *mf*.

aquarium, *pl.* **-iums, -ia** [ə'kwεəriəm, -iəmz, -iə], *s.* aquarium *m*.

Aquarius [ə'kwεəriəs], *Pr.n. Astr:* le Verseau.

Aquastat ['ækwəstæt], *s. Tchn: R.t.m:* aquastat *m*.

aquatic [ə'kwætik], *a.* **1.** (plante, etc.) aquatique. **2. a. sports,** *s.pl.* **aquatics,** sports *m* nautiques; sports pratiqués sur l'eau (polo, natation, canotage, joutes).

aquatile ['ækwətail], *a.* aquatile.

aquatint ['ækwətint], *s. Engr:* aquatinte *f*.

aquatinter ['ækwətintər], *s.* aquatintiste *mf*.

aqueduct ['ækwidʌkt], *s.* (*a*) *Civ.E:* aqueduc *m*; **a. bridge,** pont-aqueduc, *pl.* ponts-aqueducs; (*b*) *Anat:* aqueduc.

aqueous ['eikwiəs], *a.* **1.** aqueux; **a. humour,** humeur aqueuse (de l'œil); *Pharm:* **a. solution,** soluté *m*. **2.** *Geol:* (roche *f*) sédimentaire.

aquicultural [ækwi'kʌltjərl], *a.* aquicole.

aquiculture ['ækwikʌltjər], *s.* aquiculture *f*.

aquiculturist [ækwi'kʌltjərist], *s.* aquiculteur *m*.

aquifer ['ækwifεər], *s. Geol:* couche *f* aquifère.

aquiferous [æ'kwifərəs], *a. Geol:* aquifère.

Aquifoliaceae [ækwifouli'eisii:], *s.pl. Bot:* aquifoliacées *f*.

Aquila ['ækwilə], *Pr.n. Astr:* l'Aigle *m*.

aquilaria [ækwi'lεəriə], *s. Bot:* aquilaria *m*.

aquilegia [ækwi'li:dʒiə], *s. Bot:* aquilégie *f*, ancolie *f*; (*genus*) aquilegia *f*.

Aquileia [ækwi'li:ə], *Pr.n. Geog:* Aquilée *f*.

aquiline ['ækwilain], *a.* aquilin, d'aigle; **a. nose,** nez aquilin, busqué, en bec d'aigle.

Aquinas [ə'kwainæs], *a.* **Saint Thomas A.,** saint Thomas d'Aquin.

Aquitaine [ækwi'tein], *Pr.n. Geog: Hist:* Aquitaine *f*; **the basin of A.,** le bassin d'Aquitaine.

Aquitanian [ækwi'teiniən]. **1.** *Hist:* (*a*) *a.* aquitanique, aquitain; **the A. nobility,** la noblesse aquitaine; (*b*) *s.* Aquitain, -aine. **2.** *a. & s. Geol:* aquitanien (*m*).

aquiver [ə'kwivər], *a. NAm: & Lit:* tremblant, frémissant, palpitant (de joie, etc.).

aquosity [ə'kwɔsiti], *s.* aquosité *f*.

ara[1] ['ɑ:rə, 'εərə], *s. Orn:* ara *m*.

Ara[2] ['ɑ:rə], *Pr.n. Astr:* l'Autel *m*.

Arab ['ærəb]. **1.** *Ethn:* (*a*) *a.* arabe; **the A. world,** le monde arabe; *Pol:* **the A. League,** la Ligue arabe; (*b*) *s.* Arabe *mf*. **2.** *a. & s.* (cheval *m*) arabe (*m*). **3.** *s. F: O:* **street a.,** gamin *m* des rues.

araba[1] ['ærəbə], *s. Veh:* araba *f*.

araba[2], *s. Z:* alouat(t)e *m*, singe hurleur.

araban ['ærəbæn], *s. Ch:* arabanne *m*.

Arabella [ærə'belə], *Pr.n.f.* Arabelle.

arabesque [ærə'besk]. **1.** *a.* (*a*) *A:* = ARABIAN; (*b*) *Arch:* (décoration) arabesque, dans le style arabe. **2.** *s.* (*a*) *usu. pl. Arch:* arabesque(s) *f*; (*b*) *Danc:* arabesque.

Arabia [ə'reibiə], *Pr.n. Geog:* Arabie *f*; **Saudi A.,** Arabie Séoudite; *Hist:* **A. Felix** ['fi:liks], Arabie Heureuse; **A. Petraea** [pe'tri:ə], Arabie Pétrée.

Arabian [ə'reibiən]. **1.** *a.* (*a*) arabique, arabe de l'Arabie; **the A. Gulf,** le Golfe Arabique; **the A. peninsula,** la péninsule d'Arabie; **A. camel,** dromadaire *m*; (*b*) *Lit:* **The A. Nights,** les Mille et une Nuits. **2.** *s.* Arabe *mf* (d'Arabie).

Arabic ['ærəbik]. **1.** *a.* (*a*) (langue, littérature) arabe; **A. scholar,** arabisant *m*; **A. numerals,** chiffres *m* arabes; (*b*) **gum a.,** gomme *f* arabique. **2.** *s. Ling:* arabe *m*; **A.-speaking,** arabophone.

Arabicism [ə'ræbisizm], *s. Ling:* arabisme *m*.

Arabicize [ə'ræbisaiz], *v.tr.* arabiser.

Arabidopsis [æræbi'dɔpsis], *s. Bot:* arabidopsis *f*.

arabin ['ærəbin], *s. Phot:* **a. process,** procédé à la gomme bichromatée.

arabinose [ə'ræbinous], *s. Ch:* arabinose *f*.

arabis [rærəbis], *s. Bot:* arabette *f*, arabis *f*.

Arabist ['ærəbist], *s.* arabisant *m*.

arabitol [ə'ræbitɔl], *s. Ch:* arabite *f*, arabitol *m*.

Arabization [ærəbai'zeiʃ(ə)n], *s.* arabisation *f*.

Arabize ['ærəbaiz], *v.tr.* arabiser.

arable ['ærəbl], *a.* (terre, sol) arable; **a. farming,** culture *f* des terres).

Araby ['ærəbi], *Pr.n. Geog: A: & Poet:* Arabie *f*.

aracanga [ærə'kæŋgə], *s. Orn:* araracanga *m*.

aracari, araçari [ærə'sɑ:ri], *s. Orn:* aracari *m*.

Araceae [ə'reisii:], *s.pl. Bot:* aracées *f*.

arachic [æ'rætʃik], **arachidic** [æræ'kidik], *a. Ch:* (acide *m*) arachique, arachidique.

arachin ['ærəkin], *s. Bio-Ch:* arachine *m* or *f*.

arachis ['ærəkis], *s. Bot:* arachide *f*; *esp. U.S:* **a. oil,** huile *f* d'arachide.

arachnean [æræk'niən], *a. Lit:* (tissu, etc.) arachnéen.

arachnid [ə'ræknid], *s. Z:* arachnide *m*.

Arachnida [ə'ræknidə], *s.pl. Z:* arachnides *m*.

arachnidan [ə'ræknid(ə)n], *s. Z:* arachnide *m*.

arachnidism [ə'ræknidizm], *s. Med:* arachnidisme *m*.

arachnism [ə'ræknizm], *s. Med:* aranéisme *m*, arachnidisme *m*.

arachnites [æræk'naiti:z], *s. Bot:* **a. apifera** [æ'pifərə], ophrys *f* abeille.

arachnitis [æræk'naitis], *s. Med:* arachnitis *f*, arachnoïdite *f*.

arachnodactylia [æræknoudæk'tiliə], **arachnodactyly** [æræknou'dæktili], *s. Med:* arachnodactylie *f*.

arachnoid [æ'ræknɔid]. **1.** *Anat:* (*a*) *a.* arachnoïdien, arachnoïde; (*b*) *s.* arachnoïde *f* (du cerveau). **2.** *a. Bot:* arachnoïde. **3.** *s. Z:* arachnoïde *m*.

arachnoidal [æræk'nɔidl], **arachnoidean** [æræk'nɔidiən], *a. Anat:* arachnoïdien.

arachnoidism [æ'ræknɔidizm], *s. Med:* arachnidisme *m*.

arachnoiditis [æræknɔi'daitis], *s. Med:* arachnoïdite *f* arachnitis *f*.

arachnologist [æræk'nɔ:lədʒist], *s.* arachnologue *mf*.

arachnology [æræk'nɔ:lədʒi], *s.* arachnologie *f*.

araco-, *see* AREO-.

araeostyle [ə'ri:oustail], *s. Arch:* aréostyle *m*.

araeosystyle [ə'ri:ousistail], *s. Arch:* aréosystyle *m*.

Aragon ['ærəgən], *Pr.n. Geog:* Aragon *m.*
Aragonese [ærəgə'ni:z]. *Geog:* (*a*) *a.* aragonais; (*b*) *s.* Aragonais, -aise; (*c*) *s. Ling:* aragonais *m.*
aragonite [ə'rægənait], *s. Miner:* aragonite *f*; **twin a.,** aragonite confluente.
aralia [ə'reiliə], *s. Bot:* aralia *m.*
Araliaceae [əreili'eisii:], *s.pl. Bot:* araliacées *f.*
Aramaean [ærə'mi(:)ən]. **1.** *B.Hist:* (*a*) *a.* araméen; (*b*) *s.* Araméen, -enne. **2.** *s. Ling:* araméen *m.*
Aramaic [ærə'meiik], *a. & s. Ling:* aramaïque (*m*), araméen (*m*); syro-chaldaïque (*m*).
Araneida [ærə:'ni:idə], *s.pl. Arach:* aranéides *m.*
araneiform [ærə'ni:ifɔ:m], *a.* aranéiforme.
araneologist [æreini'ɔlədʒist], *s.* aranéologue *mf.*
araneology [æreini'ɔlədʒi], *s.* aranéologie *f.*
arapaima [ærə'paimə], *s. Ich:* arapaïma *m.*
araponga [ærə'pɔŋgə], *s. Orn:* araponga *m,* oiseau-cloche *m, pl.* oiseaux-cloches, sonneur *m.*
araracanga [ærærə'kæŋgə], *s. Orn:* araracanga *m.*
araroba [ærə'oubə], *s. Bio-Ch:* araroba *f.*
Araucania [ærɔ:'keiniə], *Pr.n. Geog:* Araucanie *f.*
Araucanian [ærɔ:'keiniən]. *Geog:* (*a*) *a.* araucan, araucanien; (*b*) *s.* Araucan, -ane; Araucanien, -ienne.
araucaria [ærɔ:'kɛəriə], *s. Bot:* araucaria *m,* araucarie *f.*
Araucariaceae [ærɔkɛəri'eisii:], *s.pl. Bot:* auraucariées *f.*
arbalest ['ɑ:bəlest], *s. A:* arbalète *f.*
arbalester ['ɑ:bəlestər], **arbalestrier** [ɑ:bə'lestriər], **arbalister** ['ɑ:bəlistər], *s. A.Mil:* arbalétrier *m.*
arbiter ['ɑ:bitər], *s.* (*in non-technical senses*) arbitre *m*; **a. of taste,** arbitre des élégances; *Lit:* **he was the a. of the lives of his subjects,** il jugeait souverainement de la vie et de la mort de ses sujets.
arbitrage ['ɑ:bitridʒ], *s. Fin: St.Exch:* arbitrage *m*; **a. syndicate,** syndicat *m* arbitragiste.
arbitragist ['ɑ:bitrədʒist], *s. Fin:* arbitragiste *m.*
arbitral ['ɑ:bitr(ə)l], *a.* arbitral, -aux.
arbitrament [ɑ:'bitrəmənt], *s. A: & Lit:* arbitrage *m,* jugement arbitral, décision arbitrale; **to resort to the a. of war,** s'en remettre au sort des armes; **to trust to the a. of time,** s'en remettre à l'avenir.
arbitrarily ['ɑ:bitrərəli], *adv.* arbitrairement.
arbitrariness ['ɑ:bitrərinis], *s.* arbitraire *m* (d'une décision, etc.).
arbitrary ['ɑ:bitrəri], *a.* arbitraire; **a. decision,** décision *f* arbitraire; **a. classification,** classification arbitraire, artificielle; *Mth:* **a. constants,** *s.pl.* **arbitraries,** quantités *f* arbitraires (d'une équation); **a. element,** élément *m* arbitraire, générique; **a. solution,** solution indéterminée (d'un système d'équations).
arbitrate ['ɑ:bitreit]. **1.** *v.tr.* arbitrer, juger, trancher (un différend). **2.** *v.i.* décider en qualité d'arbitre; arbitrer.
arbitration [ɑ:bi'treiʃ(ə)n], *s.* **1.** arbitrage *m*; **procedure by a.,** procédure arbitrale; **settlement by a.,** règlement *m* par arbitrage; solution arbitrale; **to refer a question to a.,** soumettre une question à un arbitrage; **to submit an affair for a.,** mettre une affaire en compromis; **difference submissible to a.,** litige *m* arbitrable; **a. treaty,** traité *m* d'arbitrage; **a. court, court of a.,** tribunal arbitral; **a. board,** conseil arbitral; **a. clause,** clause *f* d'arbitrage; clause compromissoire; **a. analysis,** analyse arbitrale. **2.** *Fin:* **a. of exchange,** arbitrage du change.
arbitrationist [ɑ:bi'treiʃənist], *s.* partisan *m* de l'arbitrage.
arbitrator ['ɑ:bitreitər], *s. Jur:* arbitre *m*; arbitre-juge *m, pl.* arbitres-juges; amiable compositeur *m*; compromissaire *m.*
arbitress ['ɑ:bitris], *s.f. Lit:* arbitre *m or f*; **she was the absolute a. of fashion,** elle était l'arbitre absolu de la mode.
arbor[1] ['ɑ:bər], *s. Mec.E:* (*a*) arbre *m* (de roue); arbre, axe *m* (de meule); **a. shaft,** joint *m* de cardan; (*b*) mandrin *m* (de tour); **cutter a., milling a.,** mandrin de fraisage; mandrin, arbre, porte-fraises; **a. press,** presse *f* à mandriner; (*c*) *Hor:* **barrel a.,** arbre de barillet.
arbor[2], *s.* **1.** (*forming compounds in botany, chemistry, etc.*) arbre *m, Bot:* **a. Judae** ['dʒu:di:], arbre de **Judée; a. vitae** ['vaiti:], arbre de vie; thuia, thuya *m*; *A.Ch:* **a. Dianae** [dai'eini:], arbre de Diane; **a. Saturni,** arbre de Saturne. **2.** *NAm:* **A. Day,** jour (désigné par l'Administration) où chacun est tenu de planter un arbre.
arbor[3], *s. U.S:* = ARBOUR.
arboreal [ɑ:'bɔ:riəl], *a.* **1.** d'arbre(s). **2.** (animal) arboricole; (existence) sur les arbres.
arboreous [ɑ:'bɔ:riəs], *a.* **1.** (terrain, etc.) arbreux, boisé. **2.** = ARBOREAL. **3.** = ARBORESCENT.
arborescence [ɑ:bə'res(ə)ns], *s.* arborescence *f.*
arborescent [ɑ:bə'res(ə)nt], *a.* **1.** arborescent; **a. shrub,** arbuste *m*; *A.Ch:* **a. silver,** arbre *m* de Diane; **a. lead,** arbre de Saturne. **2.** *Miner:* (*of agate, etc.*) herborisé, arborisé; **a. growth,** arborisation *f.*
arboretum [ɑ:bə'ri:təm], *s.* arborétum *m*; collection *f* d'arbres et arbustes.
arboricole [ɑ:'bɔrikɔl], **arboricolous** [ɑ:bə'rikələs], *a.* arboricole.
arboriculture ['ɑ:bərikʌltjər], *s.* arboriculture *f.*
arboriculturist [ɑ:bəri'kʌltjərist], *s.* arboriculteur *m,* arboriste *m*; pépiniériste *m.*
arborist ['ɑ:bərist], *s.* arboriculteur *m,* arboriste *m.*
arborization [ɑ:bərai'zeiʃ(ə)n], *s.* arborisation *f.*
arborized ['ɑ:bəraizd], *a. Miner:* arborisé, herborisé.
arbour ['ɑ:bər], *s. Hort:* berceau *m* de verdure; salle *f* de verdure; tonnelle *f,* charmille *f,* gloriette *f*; **vine a.,** treille *f.*
arboured ['ɑ:bəd], *a.* couvert d'un berceau; sous un berceau; ombreux.
arbuscle ['ɑ:bʌsl], **arbuscula** [ɑ:'bʌskjulə], *s. Bot:* arbuscule *f.*
arbuscule ['ɑ:bʌskjul], *s. Nat.Hist:* arbuscule *f.*
arbutin ['ɑ:bjutin], *s. Bio-Ch:* arbutine *f.*
arbutus [ɑ:'bju:təs], *s. Bot:* **1. a. (unedo),** arbousier *m*; **a. berry,** arbouse *f.* **2.** *NAm:* **(trailing) a.,** épigée rampante.
arc[1] [ɑ:k], *s.* **1.** (*a*) *Mth: etc:* arc *m*; **a. of a circle,** arc de cercle; **a. length,** longueur *f* d'arc; *Geog: Nau:* **great circle a.,** arc de grand cercle; **to describe an a.,** décrire un arc; *Pol.Ec:* **a. elasticity of demand,** élasticité *f* d'arc de la demande; *Artil:* **a. of fire, of training,** champ *m* de tir (d'un canon, etc.); **dead a.,** angle mort, arc privé de feu; (*b*) *Mec:* secteur *m*; **toothed a.,** secteur denté, secteur à crémaillère; *Artil:* **elevating a.,** secteur (denté) de hausse, de pointage en hauteur; **traversing a.,** secteur (denté) de pointage en direction; **graduated a.,** limbe *m.* **2.** *El:* **electric a., voltaic a.,** arc électrique, voltaïque; **break a.,** arc de rupture; **a. converter,** arc oscillant; **a. back,** allumage *m,* arc en retour; **a. suppression coil,** bobine *f* d'équilibrage; **a. lamp,** lampe *f* à arc; **a. cutting,** coupage *m* à l'arc; **a. welding,** soudure *f* à l'arc; **a. brazing,** soudo-brasage *m* à l'arc.
arc[2], *v.i.* **(arked, arced** [ɑ:kt]) *El:* faire jaillir un arc, amorcer l'arc; (*of dynamo, commutator*) **to a. (over),** cracher; projeter des étincelles.
arca, *pl.* **-ae** ['ɑ:kə, -i:], *s. Moll:* arche *f.*
arcade [ɑ:'keid], *s.* **1.** (*a*) arcade(s) *f* (en bord de rue); (*b*) galerie *f* (marchande); passage (couvert). **2.** *Arch:* **(blind) a.,** arcature *f.* **3.** *Anat:* arcade *f.*
arcaded [ɑ:'keidid], *a.* couvert, bordé, d'arcades.
Arcadia [ɑ:'keidiə], *Pr.n. A.Geog: & Lit:* Arcadie *f.*
Arcadian [ɑ:'keidiən], *a. Lit:* arcadien; d'une simplicité pastorale; **a. days,** jours *m* d'innocence et de bonheur.
arcading [ɑ:'keidiŋ], *s. coll.* arcades *fpl.*
arcana [ɑ:'keinə], *s.pl. Lit:* arcanes *m.*
arcane [ɑ:'kein], *a. Lit:* mystérieux.
arcanite ['ɑ:kənait], *s. Miner:* arcanite *m.*
arcature ['ɑ:kətjər], *s. Arch:* arcature *f.*
arcella [ɑ:'selə], *s. Prot:* arcelle *f.*
Arcesilaus [ɑ:kesi'leiəs], *Pr.n.m. Gr.Phil:* Arcésilas.
arch[1] [ɑ:tʃ], *s.* **1.** *Arch: Const:* voûte *f*; arc *m*; cintre *m*; **a. of a vault,** arceau *m*; **semicircular a.,** arc en plein cintre; **pointed, gothic, a.,** arc brisé; **flat a.,** voûte plate; arc déprimé; **rampant a.,** arc rampant; **lancet a.,** arc lancéolé; **triangular a.,** arc angulaire; **horseshoe, Moorish, a.,** arc en fer à cheval, arc outrepassé; **raised a.,** arc surhaussé; **obtuse, depressed, a., drop a.,** arc surbaissé; **splayed a.,** arc ébrasé; **Tudor a.,** arc en carène; **inflected, inverted, a.,** arc renversé; **basket-handled a.,** voûte en anse de panier; **a. band,** nervure *f*; **a. stone,** voussoir *m*; **a. brace,** arc-boutant *m, pl.* arcs-boutants; **window a., door a.,** remenée *f*; **small a.,** voûtin *m*; *Lit:* **the a. of the heavens,** la voûte du ciel, des cieux; *Ecc:* **the Court of Arches,** la Cour d'appel ecclésiastique de la Province de Cantorbéry; la Cour archiépiscopale. **2.** (*a*) *Civ.E:* arche *f* (d'un pont, d'un viaduc); **trussed a.,** arc en treillis; **a. girder,** ferme *f* en arc; **navigation a.,** arche marinière; *Hyd.E:* **a. dam,** barrage *m* voûte; **a. gravity dam,** barrage voûte-poids; **to sleep under the arches,** dormir sur les quais; (*b*) *Min:* estau *m*; (*c*) **a. of a furnace,** voûte d'un fourneau; **fire a.,** four *m* à fritte. **2.** (*a*) **a. of a saddle,** arcade *f* d'une selle; (*b*) *Anat:* **a. of the eyebrows,** arc des sourcils; **the orbital arches,** les arcades orbitaires; **dental a.,** arc, arcade, dentaire; **a. of the aorta,** crosse *f,* arc, de l'aorte; **a. (of the instep),** cambrure *f* (du pied); **a. support,** cambrure *f* (pour chaussures); **to suffer from fallen arches,** avoir le pied plat.
arch[2]. **1.** *v.tr.* (*a*) voûter (une porte, un passage); (*b*) arquer, cintrer; cambrer; **the cat is arching its back,** le chat bombe, arque, le dos, fait le dos rond, fait le gros dos. **2.** *v.i.* se voûter, former voûte, bomber.
arch[3], *a. O:* (*usu. attrib., and only of women and children*) espiègle; malin, -igne; malicieux; **she threw me an a. glance,** elle me lança un coup d'œil espiègle et moqueur.
arch(-), *a. & pref.* archi-; grand; insigne; **a. enemy,** grand adversaire; **a. traitor,** traître *m* insigne; architraître; **a. villain,** scélérat achevé.
Archaen [ɑ:'ki:ən], *a. & s. Geol:* archéen (*m*).
Archæoceti ['ɑ:kiou'seti], *s.pl. Paleont:* archéocètes *m.*
Archæocyathidae ['ɑ:kiousi'æθidi:], *s.pl. Paleont:* archæocyathidés *m.*
archaeocyte ['ɑ:kiousait], *s. Biol:* archéocyte *m.*
archaeological [ɑ:kiə'lɔdʒikl], *a.* archéologique.
archaeologically [ɑ:kiə'lɔdʒik(ə)li], *adv.* archéologiquement.
archaeologist [ɑ:ki'ɔlədʒist], *s.* archéologue *mf.*
archaeology [ɑ:ki'ɔlədʒi], *a.* archéologie *f*; **underwater a.,** archéologie sous-marine; **post-mediaeval a.,** *U.S:* **historical a.,** archéologie des temps modernes.
archaeopteryx [ɑ:ki'ɔptəriks], *s. Paleont:* archéoptéryx *m,* archéoptérix *m.*
Archaeornithes [ɑ:kiɔ:'naiθi:z], *s.pl. Paleont:* archéornithes *m.*
archaic [ɑ:'keiik], *a.* archaïque.
archaism ['ɑ:keiizm], *s.* archaïsme *m.*
archaist ['ɑ:keiist], *s.* archaïste *mf*; archaïsant, -ante.
archaistic [ɑ:kei'istik], *a.* qui affecte l'archaïsme.
archaize ['ɑ:keiaiz]. **1.** *v.i. Lit:* se servir d'archaïsmes; affecter l'archaïsme; archaïser. **2.** *v.tr.* donner à (qch.) une tournure, une allure, archaïque.
archangel[1] ['ɑ:keindʒl], *s.* **1.** archange *m.* **2.** (*a*) *Bot:* lamier *m*; **yellow a.,** ortie *f* jaune; **red a.,** lamier pourpre; (*b*) *Orn:* pigeon bouvreuil *m.*
Archangel[2], *Pr.n. Geog:* Arkhangel(sk) *m*; *Com: A:* **A. mats,** paillassons *m* en écorce de tilleul.
archangelic [ɑ:kæn'dʒelik], *a.* archangélique.
archbishop ['ɑ:tʃ'biʃəp], *s.m.* archevêque; métropolitain; **archbishop's palace,** palais *m* archiépiscopal.
archbishopric [ɑ:tʃ'biʃəprik], *s.* **1.** archevêché *m,* archidiocèse *m*; circonscription archiépiscopale. **2.** archiépiscopat *m* (dignité ou durée des fonctions).
archconfraternity ['ɑ:tʃkɔnfrə'tə:niti], *s. Ecc:* archiconfrérie *f.*
archdeacon ['ɑ:tʃ'di:k(ə)n], *s.m.* archidiacre.
archdeaconate [ɑ:tʃ'di:k(ə)nət], *s.* archidiaconat *m.*
archdeaconry [ɑ:tʃ'di:k(ə)nri], *s.* **1.** (*jurisdiction of archdeacon*) archidiaconé *m.* **2.** archidiaconat *m* (dignité ou durée des fonctions). **3.** résidence archidiaconale.
archdeaconship [ɑ:tʃ'di:k(ə)nʃip], *s.* archidiaconat *m.*
archdiocesan ['ɑ:tʃdai'ɔsiz(ə)n], *a. Ecc:* archidiocésain.
archdiocese ['ɑ:tʃ'daiəsi:z, -sis], *s. Ecc:* archidiocèse *m,* archevêché *m.*
archducal [ɑ:tʃ'dju:kl], *a.* archiducal, -aux.
archduchess ['ɑ:tʃ'dʌtʃis], *s.f.* archiduchesse.
archduchy ['ɑ:tʃ'dʌtʃi], *s.* archiduché *m.*
archduke ['ɑ:tʃ'dju:k], *s.m.* archiduc.
arched ['ɑ:tʃt], *a.* (*a*) à arc, en voûte; voûté; voussé; surélevé; **a. window,** fenêtre (i) cintrée; (ii) en arc brisé; **a. girder,** poutre *f,* ferme *f,* en arc; (*b*) arqué, cintré; busqué, cambré; **a. nose,** nez busqué; **a. eyebrows,** sourcils arqués; **a. foot, instep,** pied, cou de pied, cambré; (*of horse*) **a. neck,** encolure rouée; (*c*) *Her:* (*of fess*) voûté, courbé; (*of arm, leg*) courbé.
archegonial [ɑ:ki'gouniəl], *a. Bot:* archégoniate.
Archegoniata(e) [ɑ:kigouni'eitə, -ti:], *s.pl. Bot:* archégoniates *f.*
archegoniate [ɑ:ki'gounieit], *a. & s. Bot:* archégoniate (*f*).
archegoniophore [ɑ:ki'gounioufɔ:r], *s. Bot:* archégoniophore *m.*
archegonium [ɑ:ki'gouniəm], *s. Bot:* archégone *m.*
Archegosaurus [ɑ:kigou'sɔ:rəs], *s. Paleont:* archégosaure *m.*
archencephalic [ɑ:kensə'fælik], *a.* archencéphale.
archencephalon [ɑ:ken'sefələn], *s. Biol:* archencéphale *m.*
archenteric [ɑ:ken'terik], *a.* archentérique.
archenteron, *pl.* **-a** [ɑ:k'entərən, -ə], *s. Biol:* archentéron *m.*
archer ['ɑ:tʃər], *s.* **1.** archer *m.* **2.** *Ich:* archer, toxote *m,* poisson cracheur. **3.** *Astr:* **the a.,** le Sagittaire.
archery ['ɑ:tʃəri], *s.* tir *m* à l'arc.
archetypal [ɑ:ki'taipl], **architypical** [ɑ:ki'tipikl], *a.* archétypal, -aux.
archetype ['ɑ:kitaip], *s.* archétype *m.*
archfiend ['ɑ:tʃ'fi:nd], *s.* (*a*) archidémon *m*; (*b*) Satan *m.*
archiater [ɑ:kieitər], *s. Gr. & Rom.Ant:* archiâtre *m.*
Archibald ['ɑ:tʃibɔ:ld]. **1.** *Pr.n.* Archambaud. **2.** *s.* (*also* **Archie**) *Mil.Hist: P:* canon anti-aérien; canon contre-avions.
archicarp ['ɑ:kikɑ:p], *s. Fung:* archicarpe *f.*

archidiaconal [ɑ:kidai'ækənl], *a.* d'archidiacre.

archiepiscopacy [ɑ:kii'piskəpəsi], *s.* archiépiscopat *m.*

archiepiscopal [ɑ:kii'piskəpl], *a.* archiépiscopal, -aux; métropolitain.

archiepiscopate [ɑ:kii'piskəpeit], *s.* archiépiscopat *m.*

archil ['ɑ:kil, 'ɑ:tʃil], *s. Bot: Dy:* orseille *f.*

Archilochus [ɑ:'kiləkəs], *Pr.n.m. Gr.Lit:* Archiloque.

archimandrite [ɑ:ki'mændrait], *s. Ecc:* archimandrite *m.*

Archimedean [ɑ:ki'mi:diən, -mi'di:ən], *a.* archimédien, d'Archimède; *Mec:* **A. screw,** vis *f* d'Archimède, vis sans fin, hélice *f,* limace *f,* escargot *m;* **A. drill,** foret *m* à vis d'Archimède.

Archimedes [ɑ:ki'mi:di:z], *Pr.n.m. Gr.Hist:* Archimède; *Ph:* **Archimedes' principle,** le principe d'Archimède; **Archimedes' screw,** vis d'Archimède, vis sans fin, hélice *f,* limace *f,* escargot *m.*

Archimycetes [ɑ:kimai'si:ti:z], *s.pl. Fung:* archimycètes *m.*

arching ['ɑ:tʃiŋ]. **1.** voussure *f* (d'une voûte). **2.** arcades *fpl* (d'un édifice); série *f* d'arcades.

archipallium [ɑ:ki'pæliəm], *s. Anat:* archipallium *m.*

archipelago, *pl.* **-o(e)s** [ɑ:ki'peləgou, -ouz], *s. Geog:* archipel *m.*

archipterygium [ɑ:kip'teridʒiəm], *s. Ich:* archiptérygie *f.*

architect ['ɑ:kitekt], *s.* architecte *m;* **naval a.,** ingénieur *m* des constructions navales, du génie maritime; **a.-designed house,** maison *f* construite selon les plans d'un architecte; *Lit:* **to be the a. of one's fortunes,** être l'artisan de sa fortune, le fils de ses œuvres.

architectonic [ɑ:kitek'tɔnik], *a.* architectonique.

architectonics [ɑ:kitek'tɔniks], *s.pl.* (*usu. with sg. const.*) architectonique *f.*

architectural [ɑ:ki'tektʃərəl], *a.* architectural, -aux.

architecturally [ɑ:ki'tektʃərəli], *adv.* au point de vue architecture; **a. the house leaves much to be desired,** au point de vue architecture la maison laisse beaucoup à désirer.

architecture ['ɑ:kitektʃər], *s.* architecture *f;* **naval a.,** architecture navale.

architeuthis [ɑ:ki'tju:θis], *s. Moll:* archit(h)eut(h)is *m,* poulpe géant.

architrave ['ɑ:kitreiv], *s.* **1.** *Arch:* architrave *f,* épistyle *m.* **2.** *Const.* encadrement *m* (d'une porte, d'une fenêtre).

architraved ['ɑ:kitreivd], *a. Arch:* architravé.

architype ['ɑ:kitaip], *s. Biol:* archétype *m.*

archival ['ɑ:kivl, ɑ:'kaivl], *a. Cmptr:* **a. file,** fichier d'archives; **a. records,** archives *f;* **a. storage,** archivage *m.*

archive ['ɑ:kaiv], *v.tr.* archiver.

archives ['ɑ:kaivz], *s.pl.* archives *f* ((i) le local, (ii) les documents).

archiving ['ɑ:kaiviŋ], *s.* archivage *m.*

archivist ['ɑ:kivist], *s.* archiviste *mf.*

archivistic [ɑ:ki'vistik], *a.* archivistique.

archivolt ['ɑ:kivoult], *s. Arch:* archivolte *f.*

archlute ['ɑ:tʃ'lju:t], *s. Mus:* archiluth *m.*

archly ['ɑ:tʃli], *adv. O:* d'un air espiègle, malin; malicieusement; **she smiled a.,** elle fit un sourire malicieux.

archness ['ɑ:tʃnis], *s. O:* (*of women and children*) malice *f,* espièglerie *f* (du regard, du sourire).

archon ['ɑ:kən], *s.m. Gr.Hist:* archonte.

archpriest ['ɑ:tʃ'pri:st], *s.m. Ecc:* archiprêtre; *Gr.Ch:* archipope.

archsee ['ɑ:tʃ'si:], *s.* archevêché *m.*

archway ['ɑ:tʃwei], *s.* passage voûté; porte cintrée, voûte *f* d'entrée; arcade *f;* **you go in under, through, an a.,** on entre, passe, sous une voûte, sous un portail.

Arcidae ['ɑ:sidi:], *s.pl. Moll:* arcidés *m.*

Arcifera [ɑ:'sifərə], *s.pl. Amph:* arcifères *m.*

arciferous [ɑ:'sifərəs], *s. Amph:* arcifère.

arciform ['ɑ:sifɔ:m], *a.* arciforme.

arcing ['ɑ:kiŋ], *s. El:* amorçage *m* (d'arc); crachement *m;* jaillissement *m* d'étincelles; projection *f* d'étincelles; **a. time,** durée *f* de l'arc; **a. test,** essai *m* de claquage; **a. back,** allumage *m,* arc *m,* en retour; **a. contacts,** pare-étincelles *mpl;* **a. horn,** cornet *m* de soufflage d'étincelles.

arcosolium, *pl.* **-ia** [ɑ:kou'souliəm, -iə], *s. Archeol:* arcosolium *m.*

arctation [ɑ:k'teiʃ(ə)n], *s. Med:* arctation *f.*

arctic ['ɑ:ktik]. **1.** *a.* arctique; **a. circle,** cercle *m* arctique; *s.* **the A.,** l'Arctique *m,* **a. temperature,** température arctique, glaciale. **2.** *s. U.S:* couvre-chaussure *m, pl.* couvre-chaussures; caoutchouc *m.*

Arctiidae [ɑ:k'tiidi:], *s.pl. Ent:* arctiidés *m.*

arctostaphylos [ɑ:ktou'stæfiləs], *s. Bot:* arctostaphylos *m,* raisin *m* d'ours.

arcuate ['ɑ:kjuət], **arcuated** ['ɑ:kjueitid], *a.* arqué; courbé en arc; en forme d'arc.

arcuation [ɑ:kju'eiʃ(ə)n], *s.* **1.** incurvation *f.* **2.** *Arch:* système *m,* ensemble *m,* d'arcs, d'arcades.

arc-weld [ɑ:k'weld], *v.tr. Tchn:* souder à l'arc (électrique).

arc welding ['ɑ:k'weldiŋ], *s. Metalw:* soudure *f* à l'arc (électrique), en arc.

Ardeidae [ɑ:'deiidi:], *s.pl. Orn:* ardéidés *m,* les hérons *m.*

ardency ['ɑ:dənsi], *s. Lit:* ardeur *f.*

ardent ['ɑ:d(ə)nt], *a.* **1.** ardent; **a. heat,** chaleur ardente; *A:* **a. spirits,** liqueurs fortes; alcool *m,* spiritueux *mpl.* **2.** ardent, passionné; *Lit:* **a. in pursuit of the enemy,** ardent à poursuivre l'ennemi.

ardently ['ɑ:dəntli], *adv.* ardemment, avec ardeur; de toute son âme.

ardisia [ɑ:'di:siə], *s. Bot:* ardisia *f.*

ardour ['ɑ:dər], *s.* ardeur *f.*

arduous ['ɑ:djuəs], *a.* (sentier, travail) ardu, pénible, malaisé; (chemin) escarpé; (calcul) laborieux; (travail) rude, pénible; (travail) acharné.

arduously ['ɑ:djuəsli], *adv.* péniblement, difficilement.

arduousness ['ɑ:djuəsnis], *s.* arduité *f,* difficulté *f.*

area ['ɛəriə], *s.* **1.** (*a*) aire *f,* superficie *f* (d'un cercle, d'un champ, etc.); **the floor a. of the room is 20 square metres,** la superficie de la pièce est de 20 mètres carrés; **country larger in a. than France,** pays dont la superficie est plus grande que celle de la France; (*b*) surface *f; Const:* **dining a.,** coin *m* des repas, coin salle à manger; **wall a.,** surface de paroi; **this house has a large kitchen a.,** cette maison a une grande cuisine; *Mec.E: etc:* **bearing a.,** surface de contact; **carrying a.,** surface portante; **grate a.,** surface de grille; **slewing a.,** champ *m* de rotation (d'une grue); **a. served by a crane,** champ de travail d'une grue; *Av:* **wing a.,** surface d'ailes, des plans de sustentation; **design wing a.,** surface alaire; *Nau:* **blade a.,** surface des ailes (de l'hélice); **sail a.,** surface de voilure; *Typ:* **type a.,** justification *f;* **if this product should come in contact with the skin, wash the affected a. immediately,** si ce produit vient en contact avec la peau, lavez la partie atteinte immédiatement; (*c*) *Civ.E: etc:* **hard surfaced a.,** aire en dur; *Av:* **landing a.,** aire d'atterrissage; **servicing a.,** aire d'entretien; *Aut:* (**free**) **parking a.,** parking (gratuit); (*on motorway*) **service a.,** aire de service principale, aire de ravitaillement; **picnic a.,** aire (de stationnement, de pique-nique); (*in park*) **play a.,** aire de jeu; (*d*) plage *f; Opt:* **light a.,** plage lumineuse; **dark a.,** plage sombre, plage d'ombre; *Metalw:* **areas showing roughness,** plages présentant des aspérités. **2.** étendue *f* (de pays), territoire *m,* région *f;* zone *f;* périmètre *m* (d'influence, etc.); (*a*) **densely populated a.,** région à population dense; **mining a.,** région minière; **cotton (growing) a.,** région du coton; *Geog:* **drainage, catchment, a.,** aire de drainage; (*in a town*) **residential a.,** quartier résidentiel; **shopping a.,** quartier commerçant; **industrial, factory, a.,** zone industrielle; **sales a.,** territoire de vente; **free trade a.,** zone de libre-échange; **customs a.,** territoire douanier; **currency a.,** zone monétaire; **sterling, dollar, franc, a.,** zone sterling, dollar, franc; **postal a.,** zone postale; **surburban a.,** zone suburbaine; **the Greater London a.,** l'agglomération londonienne; le grand Londres; *Tp:* **the London a.,** le réseau de Londres; (*b*) *Pol.Ec: etc:* **economic a.,** secteur *m* économique; **growth a.,** secteur de croissance; **problem a.,** domaine *m* problématique; zone critique; (*c*) *Mil: etc:* **forward a.,** zone de l'avant, zone avancée; **forward maintenance a.,** zone logistique avancée; **rear (maintenance) a.,** zone (logistique) arrière; **concentration a.,** zone de concentration; **lying up a., assembly a.,** zone de stationnement; **fighting, combat, battle, a.,** zone d'engagement, de combat, de bataille; **prohibited, restricted, a.,** zone prohibée; **regulated stay a.,** zone à séjour réglementé; **a. bombing,** bombardement *m* sur zone; (*d*) *Cmptr:* **storage a.,** zone de mémoire; **alternate a.,** deuxième zone, zone utilisée en bascule; **input a.,** zone d'entrée, zone d'introduction; **output a.,** zone de sortie; **work, working, a.,** zone de manœuvre (en mémoire); (*e*) *Rad:* **interference a., mush a.,** zone de brouillage; (*f*) *Anat:* **areas of the brain,** territoires cérébraux; *Biol:* **germinal a.,** aire germinative, embryonnaire. **3.** *Const:* (*also NAm:* **areaway** ['ɛəriəwei]) (*a*) cour *f* d'entrée en sous-sol (sur la rue); **a. steps,** escalier *m* de service (du sous-sol); (*b*) *NAm:* passage *m* (entre des immeubles).

areca ['ærikə], *s. Bot:* **a. (nut),** (noix *f* d')arec *m;* **a. palm (tree),** aréquier *m;* **a. catechu,** arec cachou.

arecaine ['ærikain], *s. Ch:* arécaïne *f.*

arecoline [æ'ri:kouli:n, -lain], *s. Ch:* arécoline *f.*

arena, *pl.* **-as** [ə'ri:nə, -əz], *s.* **1.** (*a*) arène *f;* (*b*) champ *m* (d'une activité, etc.); **the a. of the war,** le théâtre de la guerre. **2.** *Med: A:* sable *m,* gravelle *f.*

arenaceous [æri'neiʃəs], *a.* (*a*) *Geol:* arénacé, arénifère; (*b*) *Bot: Z:* arénicole, arénaire.

arenaria [æri'nɛəriə], *s. Bot:* arénaire *f.*

arenicola [æri'nikələ], *s. Ann:* arénicole *f.*

arenicolous [æri'nikələs], *a. Bot: Z:* arénaire, arénicole.

arenite ['ærinait], *s. Geol:* arénite *f,* arényte *f.*

areography [æri'ɔgrəfi], *s.* aréographie *f.*

areola, *pl.* **-ae** [æ'ri:ələ, -i:], *s.* (*a*) *Anat: Biol: etc:* aréole *f; Med:* zone *f* rouge (de vaccination); (*b*) *Anat:* halo *m,* aréole (du mamelon).

areolar [æ'ri:ələr], *a. Anat:* aréolaire; cellulaire; **a. tissue,** tissu connectif; *esp.* tissu cellulaire sous-cutané; tissu lamineux.

areolate [æ'ri:ələt, -leit], **areolated** [æ'ri:əleitid], *a. Biol:* aréolé.

areolation [æriə'leiʃ(ə)n], *s.* aréolation *f.*

areometer [æri'ɔmitər], *s. Ph: etc:* aréomètre *m.*

areometric(al) [æriə'metrik(l)], *a. Ph:* aréométrique.

areometry [æri'ɔmitri], *s. Ph:* aréométrie *f.*

Areopagite [æri'ɔpəgait], *s.m. Gr.Hist:* aréopagite.

Areopagus [æri'ɔpəgəs]. **1.** *Pr.n. A.Geog:* Aréopage *m.* **2.** *s. Gr.Ant: etc:* aréopage.

areostyle ['ærioustail], *s. Arch:* aréostyle *m.*

Ares ['ɛəri:z], *Pr.n.m. Gr.Myth:* Arès.

arête [æ'ret], *s. Geog:* arête *f.*

Arethusa [æri'θju:zə]. **1.** *Pr.n.f. Gr.Myth: etc:* Aréthuse. **2.** *s. Bot:* aréthuse *f.*

Aretino [æri'ti:nou], *Pr.n.m. Italian Lit:* l'Arétin.

arfvedsonite ['ɑ:vədsənait], *s. Miner:* arfvedsonite *f.*

argala ['ɑ:gələ], *s. Orn:* marabout *m* des Indes, *F:* adjudant *m.*

argali ['ɑ:gəli, -lai], *s. Z:* argali *m.*

argan ['ɑ:gæn], *s. Bot:* argan *m;* **a. tree,** arganier *m;* **a. oil,** huile *f* d'argan.

Argand ['ɑ:gænd], *s.* **A. lamp,** lampe *f* d'Argand; quinquet *m.*

argas ['ɑ:gəs], *s. Arach:* argas *m.*

argent ['ɑ:dʒ(ə)nt]. *Her: & Poet:* **1.** *s.* argent *m.* **2.** *a.* argenté; *Her:* d'argent, argent *inv;* **a. a lion gules,** d'argent à un lion de gueules.

argental [ɑ:'dʒentl], *a.* **a. mercury,** mercure argental.

Argentan[1] ['ɑ:dʒ(ə)ntæn], *Pr.n. Geog:* Argentan; **A. lace,** point *m* d'Argentan.

argentan[2], *s. Metall:* argentan *m,* argenton *m,* maillechor(t) *m.*

argentic [ɑ:'dʒentik], *a. Ch:* argentique.

argentiferous [ɑ:dʒən'tifərəs], *a.* argentifère.

Argentina[1] [ɑ:dʒ(ə)n'ti:nə], *Pr.n. Geog:* Argentine *f;* la République Argentine.

argentina[2], *s. Ich:* argentine *f.*

argentine[1] ['ɑ:dʒ(ə)ntain]. **1.** *a.* argentin. **2.** *s.* (*a*) *Ich:* argentine *f;* (*b*) *Miner:* spath schisteux; feldspath nacré; argentine *f.*

Argentine[2], *a. Geog:* **the A. Republic,** *s.* **the A.,** la République Argentine, l'Argentine *f.*

Argentinean, Argentinian [ɑ:dʒən'tiniən]. *Geog:* (*a*) *a.* argentin; (*b*) *s.* Argentin, -ine.

argentite ['ɑ:dʒ(ə)ntait], *s. Miner:* argentite *f,* argyrose *f,* argyrite *f.*

argentometry [ɑ:dʒən'tɔmitri], *s. Ch:* argentométrie *f.*

argenton ['ɑ:dʒəntɔn], *s.* = ARGENTAN[2].

argie-bargie ['ɑ:dʒi'bɑ:dʒi], *s. & v.i. F:* = ARGY-BARGY.

argil ['ɑ:dʒil], *s. Cer:* argile *f* (de potier).

argillaceous [ɑ:dʒi'leiʃəs], *a.* argileux, argillacé.

argilliferous [ɑ:dʒi'lifərəs], *a.* argilifère.

arginin(e) ['ɑ:dʒinin, -ain], *s. Bio-Ch:* arginine *f.*

argiope [ɑ:'dʒaiəpi], *s. Arach:* argiope *m,* argyope *m.*

Argiopidae [ɑ:dʒi'ɔpidi:], *s.pl. Arach:* argiopidés *m.*

argle-bargle ['ɑ:gl'bɑ:gl], *s. & v.i. F:* = ARGY-BARGY.

argol[1] ['ɑ:gɔl], *s.* tartre brut.

argol[2], *s.* argol *m* (excréments desséchés des yaks employés comme combustible).

Argolis ['ɑ:gəlis], *Pr.n. Geog:* Argolide *f.*

argon ['ɑ:gɔn], *s. Ch:* argon *m;* **a. arc welding,** soudage *m* à l'argon.

Argonaut ['ɑ:gənɔ:t], *s.* **1.** *Gr.Myth:* Argonaute *m.* **2.** *Moll:* voilier *m,* argonaute.

Argos ['ɑ:gɔs], *Pr.n. Geog:* Argos *f.*

argosy ['ɑ:gəsi], *s. A: & Poet:* **1.** caraque *f.* **2.** flotte *f.*

Argovian [ɑ:'gouviən], *a. & s. Geog:* argovien (*m*).

arguable ['ɑ:gjuəbl], *a.* (opinion) discutable, soutenable, défendable.

argue ['ɑ:gu(:)]. **1.** *v.tr.* (*a*) (*indicate*) *O: & Lit:* prouver, indiquer, démontrer; **his actions a. him to be a coward,** ses actions prouvent, accusent, décèlent, sa lâcheté; (*b*) discuter, débattre, raisonner sur (une question, etc.); **to a. that sth. is impossible,** soutenir, prétendre, maintenir, que qch. est impossible; **to a. s.o. into, out of, doing sth.,** persuader à qn, dissuader qn, de faire qch. (à force d'arguments); **I argued him into coming,**

je l'ai finalement convaincu qu'il lui fallait venir; *F:* **to a. the toss,** disputailler. **2.** *v.i.* (*a*) argumenter (**against s.o.,** contre qn); *Phil:* **to a. from the effect to the cause,** arguer, argumenter, de l'effet à la cause; **to a. about everything,** arguer sur tout; **he's always arguing,** c'est un argumentateur; (*b*) discuter, (se) disputer, raisonner (**with s.o. about sth.,** avec qn sur qch.); plaider (**for, against sth.,** pour, contre, qch.); **to a. as to whether . . .,** disputer de savoir si . . .: **to obey without arguing (the point),** obéir sans discussion; **to go on arguing,** faire des raisonnements à perte de vue; **all this argues in his favour,** tout ceci témoigne en sa faveur; **this argues for a Greek origin of the word,** ceci nous mène à croire que le mot est d'origine grecque; **don't a.!** pas de raisonnements! *F:* tais-toi!

arguer ['ɑːgjuər], *s.* argumentateur, -trice; argueur *m*; disputeur, -euse; *Pej:* raisonneur, -euse; ergoteur, -euse.

Arguesian [ɑː'gweisiən], *a. Mth:* **A. transformation,** transformation arguésienne inverse, conjugé isogonal.

argufier ['ɑːgjufaiər], *s. Pej:* (*a*) raisonneur, -euse; ergoteur, -euse; (*b*) disputailleur, -euse.

argufy ['ɑːgjufai], *v.i. F: Pej:* (*a*) argumenter, raisonner; faire le raisonneur; ergoter; (*b*) disputailler.

arguing ['ɑːgjuiŋ], *s.* argumentation *f*; **and there's no a. about it!** il n'y a pas à discuter!

argulus, *pl.* **-li** ['ɑːgjuləs, -lai], *s. Crust:* argule *m*, argulus *m*.

argument ['ɑːgjum(ə)nt], *s.* **1.** argument *m* (**for, against,** en faveur de, contre); **to follow s.o.'s (line of) a.,** suivre le raisonnement de qn; **his a. is that gold should be done away with,** sa thèse est qu'il faudrait abolir l'or; **that is another a. for dismissing him,** c'est une raison de plus pour le congédier; **to put forward an opinion for argument's sake,** avancer une opinion pour le plaisir de discuter; **let us suppose for argument's sake that . . .,** supposons à titre d'exemple que . . .; **it is beyond a. that . . .,** il est indiscutable que . . .. **2.** discussion *f*, dispute *f*, débat *m*; **to get the best of an a.,** l'emporter dans une discussion; **to obey without a.,** obéir sans argument; **youth will brook no a.,** la jeunesse est tranchante. **3.** (*a*) *A:* argument *m*, thèse *f* (d'un discours, d'une pièce de théâtre); *Jur:* **my a. shows that . . .,** mon plaidoyer démontre que . . .; (*b*) *Lit:* (*synopsis, outline, summary*) argument (d'un ouvrage); sommaire *m*. **4.** *Astr: Myth:* argument (d'une quantité imaginaire, etc.).

argumentation [ɑːgjumen'teiʃ(ə)n], *s.* argumentation *f*.

argumentative [ɑːgju'mentətiv], *a.* **1.** (ouvrage) raisonné, critique; (faculté) d'argumentation. **2.** (*of pers.*) raisonneur; disposé à argumenter, à disputailler; **don't be so a.,** ne raisonnez pas tant.

argumentatively [ɑːgju'mentətivli], *adv.* d'un esprit raisonneur; en se disputant.

argumentativeness [ɑːgju'mentətivnis], *s.* disposition *f* à argumenter; esprit raisonneur.

Argus ['ɑːgəs]. **1.** *Pr.n.m. Gr.Myth:* Argus. **2.** *s. Lit:* Argus *m*; gardien *m* à l'œil vigilant; **A. -eyed,** aux yeux d'Argus; vigilant. **3.** *s.* (*a*) *Ent:* (papillon *m*) argus; (*b*) *Orn:* (faisan *m*) argus.

argy-bargy[1] ['ɑːdʒi'bɑːdʒi], *s. F:* chamaillerie *f*.

argy-bargy[2], *v.i. F:* argumenter, raisonner; disputailler, discutailler.

argynnis [ɑː'ginis], *s. Ent:* argynne *m*.

argyranthous [ɑːdʒi'rænθəs], *a. Bot:* argyranthème.

argyria [ɑː'dʒiriə], *s. Med:* argyrisme *m*, argyrose *f*.

argyric [ɑː'dʒirik], *a. Ch:* argyrique.

argyrite ['ɑːdʒirait], *s.* (*a*) *Miner:* argyrite *f*; (*b*) *Med:* argyrite, argyrose *f*.

argyrodite [ɑː'dʒiroudait], *s. Miner:* argyrodite *f*.

argyrol [ɑː'dʒairɔl], *s. Pharm:* argyrol *m*.

argyroneta [ɑːdʒi'rɔnitə], *s. Arach:* argyronète *f*.

argyrophyllous [ɑːdʒirou'filəs], *a. Bot:* argyrophylle.

argyrose ['ɑːdʒirouz], *s. Miner: Med:* argyrose *f*, argyrite *f*.

argyrythrose [ɑː'dʒiriθrouz], *s. Miner:* argyrythrose *f*, pyrargyrite *f*.

aria ['ɑːriə], *s. Mus:* aria *f*.

Ariadne [æri'ædni], *Pr.n.f. Gr.Myth:* Ariane.

Arian ['ɛəriən], *Rel.H:* (*a*) *a.* arien; (*b*) *s.* Arien,-ienne.

Arianism ['ɛəriənizm], *s. Rel.H:* arianisme *m*.

arid ['ærid], *a.* (terre, sujet) aride.

aridity [æ'riditi], **aridness** ['æridnis], *s.* aridité *f*.

aridly ['æridli], *adv.* aridement.

Aries ['ɛər(i)iːz, 'æreiːs], *Pr.n. Astr:* le Bélier; **first point of A.,** point *m* gamma, point vernal.

arietta [æri'etə], *s. Mus:* ariette *f*.

aright [ə'rait], *adv. A: & Lit:* bien, juste, correctement; **to judge a.,** bien juger; **to think a.,** penser juste; **if I heard a.,** si j'ai bien entendu.

aril ['æril], **arillus** [æ'riləs], *s. Bot:* arille *m* (d'une graine).

arillate ['ærilət, -eit], *a. Bot:* (graine) arillée.

arillode ['æriloud], *s. Bot:* arillode *m*.

Arimathaea [ærimə'θiə], *Pr.n. A.Geog:* Arimathie *f*.

arion ['ɛəriən], *s. Moll:* arion *m*.

arioso [ɑːri'ousou], *a., adv. & s. Mus:* arioso (*m*).

Ariosto [æri'ɔstou], *Pr.n.m. Lit.Hist:* l'Arioste.

Ariovistus [æriou'vistəs], *Pr.n.m. Hist:* Arioviste.

arise [ə'raiz], *v.i.* (**arose** [ə'rouz], **arisen** [ə'riz(ə)n]). **1.** *Lit:* s'élever; (*a*) (*of pers.*) **a prophet, a poet, arose,** un prophète, un poète, surgit, se révéla; (*b*) *O:* (*of thg*) **along the road buildings soon arose,** le long de la route s'élevèrent bientôt des bâtiments; (*c*) *B: Ecc:* **to a. from the dead,** ressusciter (des morts); **the prophet bade him a.,** le prophète lui dit: "levez-vous." **2.** (*of thg*) (*a*) s'élever, surgir, survenir, s'offrir, se présenter, se produire; **a murmur, a quarrel, arose,** un murmure, une querelle, s'éleva; **a storm arose,** il survint une tempête; **incidents might a.,** il pourrait naître, se produire, des incidents; **there arose a great cry,** de grands cris se firent entendre; **another difficulty then arose,** alors survint, surgit, se présenta, une nouvelle difficulté; il se produisit alors une nouvelle difficulté; **if complications a . . .,** s'il survient des complications . . .; **when the case arises,** quand le cas adviendra, se produira; **the question has not arisen,** la question ne s'est pas encore posée; le cas ne s'est pas encore présenté; **should the occasion a. . . .,** le cas échéant . . .; (*b*) émaner, provenir, résulter (**from,** de); **obligations that a. from a clause,** obligations qui émanent d'une clause; **diseases that a. from the unhealthiness of a country,** maladies qui proviennent, qui procèdent, de l'insalubrité d'un pays, qui sont dues à l'insalubrité d'un pays; **thence it arises that . . .,** de là vient que . . ., de là il résulte que . . .; **conditions arising out of the war,** conditions nées de la guerre; **arising from (this proposal, etc.),** comme suite à (cette proposition, etc.).

arista, *pl.* **-ae** [ə'ristə, -iː], *s. Bot:* arête *f*.

Aristaeus [æris'tiːəs], *Pr.n.m. Gr.Myth:* Aristée.

Aristarchus [æris'tɑːkəs], *Pr.n.m. Gr.Ant:* Aristarque.

aristate ['æristeit, -ət], *a. Bot:* aristé, barbu.

aristida [æ'ristidə], *s. Bot:* aristide *f*.

Aristides [æ'ristidiːz, æris'taidiːz], *Pr.n.m. Gr.Hist:* Aristide.

Aristippus [æris'tipəs], *Pr.n.m. Gr.Ant:* Aristippe.

aristocracy [æris'tɔkrəsi], *s.* **1.** aristocratie *f*. **2.** (*a*) gouvernement *m* par une aristocratie; (*b*) état gouverné par une aristocratie.

aristocrat ['æristəkræt, ə'ris-], *s.* aristocrate *mf*.

aristocratic [æristə'krætik], *a.* aristocratique; distingué.

aristocratically [æristə'krætik(ə)li], *adv.* aristocratiquement.

aristogenesis [æristou'dʒenisis], *s. Biol:* aristogénèse *f*.

aristol ['æristɔl], *s. Pharm:* aristol *m*.

aristolochia [æristou'loukiə], *s. Bot:* aristoloche *f*.

Aristolochiaceae [æristoulouki'eisiiː], *s.pl. Bot:* aristolochi(ac)ées *f*.

Aristophanes [æris'tɔfəniːz], *Pr.n.m. Gr.Lit:* Aristophane.

Aristotelian [æristɔ'tiːliən], *a.* aristotélicien, -ienne; (doctrine) aristotélique; **an A. philosopher,** un philosophe de l'école d'Aristote; **A. logic,** la logique d'Aristote.

Aristotelianism [æristɔ'tiːliənizm], *s.* aristotélisme *m*.

Aristotle ['æristɔtl], *Pr.n.m.* **1.** *Gr.Phil:* Aristote. **2.** *Echin:* **A.'s lantern,** lanterne *f* d'Aristote.

arite ['ɛərait], *s. Miner:* arite *f*.

arithmetic [ə'riθmətik], *s.* arithmétique *f*; calcul *m*; **mental a.,** calcul mental, calcul de tête; **to buy an a. (book),** acheter une arithmétique.

arithmetic(al) [æriθ'metik(l)], *a.* (NOTE: *the two forms are largely interchangeable, though in computer language* **arithmetic** *is usual*) arithmétique; (*a*) **a. mean,** moyenne *f* arithmétique; **a. proportion,** proportion *f* arithmétique; **a. ratio,** raison *f*, proportion, arithmétique; **a. progression,** progression *f* arithmétique; *Pol.Ec:* **a. discount,** (i) escompte en dedans; (ii) escompte rationnel; (*b*) *Cmptr:* **a. check,** contrôle *m* arithmétique; **a. computer,** calculateur *m* arithmétique; **a. operator,** opérateur *m* arithmétique; **a. shift,** décalage *m* arithmétique; **a. statement,** instruction *f* de calcul.

arithmetically [æriθ'metik(ə)li], *adv.* arithmétiquement.

arithmetician [æriθmə'tiʃ(ə)n], *s.* arithméticien, -ienne; calculateur, -trice.

arithmography [æriθ'mɔgrəfi], *s.* arithmographie *f*.

arithmology [æriθ'mɔlədʒi], *s.* arithmologie *f*.

arithmometer [æriθ'mɔmitər], *s. A:* arithmomètre *m*; machine *f* à calculer.

Arizona [æri'zounə], *Pr.n. Geog:* Arizona *m*.

arizonite [æri'zounait], *s. Miner:* arizonite *f*.

arjun ['ɑːdʒ(ə)n], *s. Bot:* badamier *m*.

ark [ɑːk], *s.* **1.** arche *f*; **Noah's a.,** l'arche de Noé; *F:* **it looks as if it has come out of the a.,** ça a l'air de remonter au déluge. **2. the A. of the Covenant,** l'Arche d'alliance, l'Arche sainte. **3.** *NAm: F:* péniche *f*; bateau peu manœuvrable. **4.** *Moll:* **a. shell,** arche de Noé.

Arkansas ['ɑːkənsɔː], *Pr.n. Geog:* Arkansas.

Arkansan [ɑː'kænz(ə)n], *U.S: F:* **Arkansawyer** ['ɑːk(ə)nsɔːjər], *s. Geog:* habitant, -ante, de l'Arkansas.

arkansite ['ɑːkənsait], *s. Miner:* arkansite *f*.

arkose ['ɑːkouz], *s. Miner:* arkose *f*.

arles [ɑːlz], *s.pl. Scot: Dial:* arrhes *fpl*.

arm[1] [ɑːm], *s.* **1.** (*a*) bras *m* (de personne, de vertébré, de brachiopode); **upper a.,** haut *m* du bras, arrière-bras *m inv*; **to carry a child in one's arms,** porter un enfant au bras, dans ses bras; **infant in arms,** bébé, enfant, porté au bras; **to carry sth. under one's a.,** porter qch. sous le bras, sous l'aisselle; **to carry a basket over one's a.,** porter un panier au bras; **to walk a. in a.,** marcher en se donnant le bras; marcher bras dessus bras dessous; **she took my a.,** elle m'a pris le bras; elle a passé la main à mon bras; **she flung her arms round me,** elle m'a entouré de ses bras; elle s'est jetée à mon cou; **to put one's a. round s.o.,** prendre qn par la taille; **sitting with her arms on the table,** assise le coude sur la table, accoudée à la table; **to greet, receive, s.o. with open arms,** recevoir qn à bras ouverts; ouvrir, tendre, les bras à qn; faire à qn un accueil cordial; faire fête à qn; **to carry sth. at arm's length,** porter qch. à bras tendu; **to keep s.o. at arm's length,** tenir qn à distance; **he has a long a.,** il a le bras long; *F:* **make a long a. and reach me down that book,** étends le bras et descends-moi ce bouquin; (*as traffic signal*) **to put out one's a.,** étendre, sortir, le bras; *attrib:* **a. band,** brassard *m* (de deuil); (*in archery, etc.*) **a. guard,** brassard; *Veh:* **a. loop, sling, strap,** appuie-bras *m inv*, embrasse *f*, brassière *f*, porte-bras *m inv*; *Aut: etc:* **a. rest,** accoudoir *m*, appuie-bras; **concealable a. rest,** accoudoir escamotable; (*b*) **the secular a.,** le bras séculier; (*c*) *F:* **a. of the law,** représentant *m* de la loi. **2.** bras (de mer, d'un fleuve, de fauteuil, de levier, de manivelle); fléau *m* (de balance); rayon *m* (de roue); bras, patte *f* (d'ancre); branche *f* (d'arbre, de tenailles, d'un fer à cheval); tige *f* (de défourneuse); accoudoir *m* (de fauteuil); potence *f* (d'enseigne de boutique, etc.); **long a.,** (i) croc *m* de boucherie; (ii) échenilloir-élagueur *m* (à long manche); **sail a.,** (i) châssis *m* de l'aile (d'un moulin à vent); (ii) *Moll:* tentacule *m* (du nautile); *Nau:* **the chain is round the arms,** l'ancre est surpattée; **yard a.,** fusée *f*, bout *m*, de vergue; *Mec.E:* **linked a.,** billette articulée; *Civ.E:* (*of bascule bridge*) **front a. lever,** avant-bras *m inv*; **back a.,** arrière-bras *m inv*; *Rec:* **pick-up a.,** bras de lecture.

arm[2], *s.* **1.** (*weapon*) *usu. pl.* arme *f*; (*a*) **side arms,** armes blanches; **small arms,** armes portatives; *Mil:* **a. of close combat,** arme de combat rapproché; *attrib.* **arms control,** contrôle *m* des armements; **arms race,** course *f* aux armements; **arms factory,** armurerie *f*, fabrique *f* d'armes, usine *f* d'armements; **arms manufacturer,** armurier *m*, fabricant *m* d'armes; **arms trade,** commerce *m* des armes, d'armes; **to provide (s.o., sth.) with arms,** armer (qn, qch.); **to quell a rising by force of arms,** réprimer une insurrection, un soulèvement, par les armes; **a. in hand,** à main armée; **bearing of arms,** port *m* d'armes; **right to keep and bear arms,** autorisation *f* de port d'armes; **call to arms,** appel *m* aux armes; **to arms!** aux armes! **nation in arms,** nation *f* en armes; **to bear, carry, arms,** porter les armes; **(to be) under arms,** (être) sous les armes; **parade under arms,** prise *f* d'armes; **to parade under arms,** défiler avec armes; *O:* prendre les armes; **to take up arms,** prendre les armes, s'armer (**against,** contre); **to take up arms again,** reprendre les armes; **to rise up in arms (against s.o., sth.),** se dresser en armes (contre, qn, qch.); **to lay down one's arms,** déposer, mettre bas, les armes; *Fig:* désarmer, rendre les armes; *Fig:* **to be up in arms against s.o.,** être insurgé, en révolte, en rébellion ouverte, contre qn; *F:* se gendarmer contre qn; **everyone is up in arms about it,** tout le monde proteste, est indigné; c'est une levée de boucliers générale; **unions up in arms against employers,** les syndicats dressés contre le patronat; (*b*) *Mil:* **the profession of arms,** le métier, la carrière, des armes; le métier militaire; (*c*) *Mil:* (*branch of service*) arme; **the Air A.,** l'arme aérienne, l'aviation *f*; **the Fleet Air Arm,** l'aéronavale *f*; **the fourth a.,** la quatrième arme (les troupes aéroportées, aéromobiles); **combatant a.,** arme combattante; **associated arms,** armes participant à une même opération, armes adaptées; **twelve thousand men of all arms,** douze mille hommes de toutes armes.

2. *pl. Her:* armoiries *f*, armes; **undifferenced arms,** armes pleines; **arms of alliance,** armoiries d'alliance; **arms of community,** armoiries de communauté, de corporation; **arms of dominion,** armoiries de domaine, de souveraineté; **arms of pretension,** armoiries de prétention; **arms of succession,** armoiries de succession; **painted, emblazoned, with the arms of the town,** peint aux armes de la ville.

arm[3]. **1.** *v.tr.* (*a*) (*to provide with weapons*) armer (qn, un régiment, une place forte, etc.); **to a. oneself with an umbrella,** s'armer, se nantir, d'un parapluie; **he was armed with every conceivable tool,** il était pourvu de tous les outils imaginables; *Lit:* **to a. oneself with patience,** s'armer de patience; (*b*) (*to make ready for detonation*) **to a. a bomb, a fuse, a torpedo, a mine,** armer une bombe, une fusée, une torpille, une mine; (*c*) *Tchn:* armer (un aimant, une poutre, etc.); renforcer (une poutre, etc.). **2.** *v.i.* s'armer (**against s.o.,** contre qn); prendre les armes.

armada [ɑ:'mɑ:də], *s.* (*a*) *Hist:* armada *f*; **the Invincible A.,** l'Invincible Armada; (*b*) grande flotte de guerre; (*c*) **air a.,** flotte aérienne.

armadillo [ɑ:mə'dilou], *s.* **1.** *Z:* tatou *m*; cochon cuirassé; **mataco a.,** tolypeute *m*; **hairy a.,** tatou velu, peludo *m*; **giant a.,** tatou géant; **nine-banded a.,** tatou à neuf bandes. **2.** *Crust:* (*woodlouse*) armadille *m or f*.

Armageddon [ɑ:mə'ged(ə)n], *s.* (*a*) *B.Lit:* Armageddon *m*; (*b*) *Lit:* la lutte suprême; la grande mêlée des peuples.

armament ['ɑ:məmənt], *s.* **1.** (*equipping*) armement *m* (d'une troupe, etc.). **2.** (*equipment*) armement; (*of ship*) artillerie *f*, munitions *fpl* de guerre; **naval armaments,** armements navals; **the armaments race,** la course aux armements; **a. maker,** fabricant *m* de matériel de guerre; *Navy:* **heavy a.,** artillerie de gros calibre; **light a.,** artillerie légère; **main a.,** artillerie principale; grosse artillerie; **secondary a.,** artillerie moyenne. **3.** (*force equipped*) forces *fpl*; armée *f*, flotte navale.

armangite ['ɑ:məŋgait], *s. Miner:* armangite *f*.

armature ['ɑ:mətjər], *s.* **1.** *Biol: etc:* armure *f*. **2.** *El:* induit *m* (d'un condensateur, d'une dynamo); armature *f* (d'une magnéto, d'une petite dynamo); **a. winding,** enroulement *m*, bobinage *m*, de l'induit; **bar-wound a.,** induit à barres; **ring a.,** induit en anneau, anneau *m* de gramme; **drum(-wound) a.,** induit en tambour, en cylindre; **disc a.,** induit en disques, en anneau plat; **girder a.,** induit Siemens; **shuttle type a.,** induit en double T, en navette; **a. structure,** corps *m* de l'induit. **3.** *Const:* armature (d'un édifice en ciment, etc.).

armchair ['ɑ:m'tʃɛər], *s.* fauteuil *m*; **a. strategist, tactician, politician,** stratégiste *m*, tacticien *m*, politicien *m*, en chambre, du café du commerce.

armed ['ɑ:md], *a.* **1.** (*furnished with weapons*) armé (**with,** de); **a. with a gun, with teeth, etc.,** armé d'un fusil, de dents, etc.; **a. to the teeth,** armé jusqu'aux dents; **fully a.,** *A:* **a. at all points,** armé de toutes pièces, de pied en cap; **a. man,** homme armé; **a. party,** groupe *m* d'hommes armés, bande armée; *Mil:* détachement *m* en armes; *Mil:* **a. forces,** forces armées; *Nau:* **a. merchant cruiser, a merchantman,** croiseur *m* auxiliaire, navire de commerce armé en guerre; **a. ship,** (i) *Nau:* navire armé en guerre; (ii) *Navy:* bâtiment cuirassé; **a. trawler,** chalutier armé (en guerre); **a. with full powers,** armé de pleins pouvoirs. **2.** (*a*) (*with the use of weapons or armed forces*) **a. conflict,** conflit armé; **a. warfare,** guerre *f* par les armes; **to offer a. resistance,** résister par les armes, se défendre les armes à la main; *Mil:* **a. demonstration,** démonstration *f* (de forces armées, de forces navales); *Mil.Av:* **a. reconnaissance,** reconnaissance armée, offensive; (*b*) (*with armed forces in readiness*) **a. neutrality,** neutralité armée; **a. peace,** paix armée; **a. truce,** suspension *f* d'armes. **3.** (*ready for detonation*) (*of bomb, fuse, torpedo, mine, etc.*) armé. **4.** *Tchn:* (*of beam, magnet, etc.*) armé. **5.** *Ann:* **a. tapeworm,** ténia armé.

armeline ['ɑ:məli:n], *s.* armeline *f*.

Armenia [ɑ:'mi:niə], *Pr.n. Geog:* Arménie *f*.

armenian [ɑ:'mi:niən]. **1.** *a.* (*a*) arménien; **A. stone,** lapis-lazuli *m inv*; *A.Pharm:* **A. bole,** bol *m* d'Arménie; (*b*) *s.* Arménien, -ienne. **2.** *s. Ling:* arménien *m*.

armet ['ɑ:met], *s. A.Arms:* armet *m*.

armful ['ɑ:mful], *s.* brassée *f*; **to bring flowers in armfuls, by the a.,** apporter des fleurs à bras pleins, à pleins bras, plein les bras; *F:* (*of girl*) **that's a nice a!** elle est bien carrossée!

armhole ['ɑ:mhoul], *s.* emmanchure *f*, entournure *f*.

armiger ['ɑ:midʒər], *s.m. Hist:* écuyer, gentilhomme (portant écu de chevalier).

armigerous [ɑ:'midʒərəs], *a.* portant écu de chevalier.

armilla [ɑ:'milə], *s.* armille *f*.

Armillaria [ɑ:mi'lɛəriə], *s. Fung:* armillaire *f*.

armillary ['ɑ:miləri, ɑ:'miləri], *a.* armillaire; *Astr:* **a. sphere,** sphère *f* armillaire.

armillate ['ɑ:milət, -leit], *a. Bot:* armillaire.

arming ['ɑ:miŋ], *s.* **1.** (*a*) armement *m*; (*b*) **a. of a bomb, of a fuse, of a torpedo, of a mine,** armement *m* d'une bombe, d'une fusée, d'une torpille, d'une mine; *attrib.* **a. device, system,** dispositif *m*, système *m*, d'armement. **2.** *Nau:* suif *m* (de la grande sonde). **3.** *Bookb:* **a. press,** presse *f* à estamper.

Arminian [ɑ:'miniən]. *Rel.H:* (*a*) *a.* arminien; (*b*) *s.* Arminien, -ienne.

Arminianism [ɑ:'miniənizm], *s. Rel.H:* arminianisme *m*.

armistice ['ɑ:mistis], *s.* armistice *m*; **A. day,** l'anniversaire *m* de l'Armistice (de 1918).

armless ['ɑ:mlis], *a.* sans bras.

armlet ['ɑ:mlit], *s.* **1.** bracelet (porté au-dessus du coude). **2.** brassard *m*. **3.** petit bras de mer.

armoire [ɑ:m'wɑ:r], *s. Furn:* armoire *f*.

armoracia [ɑ:mə'reisiə], *s. Bot:* armoracia *f*.

armorial [ɑ:'mɔ:riəl]. **1.** *a.* armorial, -aux; héraldique; **a. bearings,** armoiries *fpl*. **2.** *s.* armorial *m*.

Armorica [ɑ:'mɔrikə], *Pr.n. Geog:* Armorique *f*.

Armorican [ɑ:'mɔrikən], *a. Geog:* armoricain; **A. peninsula,** péninsule armoricaine; **A. massif,** massif armoricain.

armoried ['ɑ:mərid], *a. Her:* armorié.

armorist ['ɑ:mərist], *s.* armoriste *m*, héraldiste *m*.

armory[1] ['ɑ:məri], *s.* (science *f* du) blason *m*; l'art *m* héraldique.

armory[2], *s.* = ARMOURY.

armour[1] ['ɑ:mər], *s.* **1.** *Hist:* armure *f* (de chevalier, etc.); **mail a.,** cotte annelée, de mailles; **suit of a.,** armure complète; **knights in a.,** chevaliers revêtus de leur armure; **in full a.,** armé de pied en cap; **a. bearer,** écuyer *m*. **2.** (*a*) *N.Arch:* cuirasse *f*, cuirassement *m*, blindage *m* (d'un bâtiment); **side a.,** cuirasse verticale, cuirasse des flancs, blindage de flanc; (*b*) blindage (d'un véhicule, d'un train blindé, d'un char de combat, etc.); *Mil:* (*of tank*) **front, rear, side a.,** blindage avant, arrière, latéral; (*c*) *Mil: coll.* **armour,** l'arme blindée, les blindés *m*. **3.** *Tp:* armure *f*, armature *f* (de câble); *El:* blindage (d'un transformateur, etc.). **4.** scaphandre *m*.

armour[2], *v.tr.* cuirasser (un navire); blinder (un train, etc.); *El:* armer (un câble).

armour-clad ['ɑ:məklæd], *a.* blindé, cuirassé.

armoured ['ɑ:məd], *a.* **1.** (*a*) *Navy:* cuirassé; **a. cruiser, deck,** croiseur, pont, cuirassé; (*b*) *Mil:* blindé, cuirassé; **a. infantry, cavalry,** infanterie, cavalerie, blindée, **a. units,** unités blindées, cuirassées; **a. battalion, regiment,** bataillon *m*, régiment *m*, de chars; **a. brigade,** brigade blindée; **a. brigade group,** groupement blindé; **a. division,** division blindée; **a. troops,** troupes blindées, les blindés *m*; *U.S:* **a. corps,** l'arme blindée, les blindés; **a. vehicle,** véhicule blindé; **a. combat vehicle,** engin blindé; **a. car,** (i) engin blindé de reconnaissance; (ii) voiture blindée (de police, etc.); (iii) fourgon *m* bancaire; **light a. car,** automitrailleuse *f*, engin léger de reconnaissance; **a. personnel carrier,** véhicule blindé de transport de troupe; **a. train,** train blindé; (*c*) *Ich:* **a. catfish,** poisson chat cuirassé. **2.** (*a*) *Tchn:* **a. hose,** tuyau (souple) armé; *El: Tp:* **a. cable,** câble armé, revêtu d'une armure, d'une armature; *El:* **a. transformer,** transformateur blindé; *Tp:* **a. cord,** cordon armé, revêtu d'une spirale protectrice; (*b*) *Const:* **a. concrete,** béton armé.

armourer ['ɑ:mərər], *s. Ind: Mil: Navy:* armurier *m*.

armouring ['ɑ:məriŋ], *s.* **1.** cuirassement *m*, blindage *m* (d'un navire, etc.). **2.** armature *f*, armure *f* (d'un câble électrique); *El:* blindage *m* (d'un transformateur, etc.); **iron a.,** armature en feuillard.

armour-piercing ['ɑ:mə'piəsiŋ], *a.* (obus) perforant, de rupture.

armour plate ['ɑ:mə'pleit], *s. N.Arch: etc:* plaque *f* d'acier, de blindage; tôle *f* de blindage.

armour-plated ['ɑ:mə'pleitid], *a.* **1.** *N.Arch: etc:* cuirassé; blindé. **2.** *F:* (*of pers.*) blindé; pachydermique; insensible aux injures.

armour plating ['ɑ:mə'pleitiŋ], *s. N.Arch: etc:* **1.** blindage *m*, cuirassement *m*. **2.** cuirasse *f*.

armoury ['ɑ:məri], *s.* **1.** (*a*) magasin *m* d'armes; (*b*) *U.S:* fabrique *f* d'armes. **2.** (*in barracks*) armurerie *f*. **3.** (*armourer's craft*) armurerie. **4.** (*in museum, etc.*) salle *f* d'armes. **5.** *Mil: NAm:* salle *f* d'exercice.

armozeen [ɑ:mou'zi:n], *s. Tex: A:* armoisin *m*.

armpit ['ɑ:mpit], *s.* aisselle *f*.

army ['ɑ:mi], *s.* **1.** (*a*) armée *f* (de terre); *Iron:* **a toy a.,** une petite armée pour rire; **to be in the a.,** être dans l'armée, au service, au régiment; être soldat, militaire; **to go into, join, the a.,** (i) s'engager, s'enrôler, se faire soldat; (ii) (*conscription*) partir au régiment, entrer au service; **that wasn't the way in the a.,** ça ne se faisait pas comme ça, ce n'était pas comme ça, au régiment; **standing a., regular a.,** armée permanente, active; **professional a.,** armée de métier; *Jur:* **the A. Act,** (i) le code (de justice) militaire; (ii) la loi organique de l'armée; *attrib.* **a. corps,** corps *m* d'armée; **A. list,** Annuaire *m* militaire; Cadres *m* de l'armée; **a. contractor,** fournisseur *m* de l'armée; **a. lorry, truck,** camion *m* militaire; (*b*) **a. group,** groupe *m* d'armées; **the eighth a.,** la huitième armée; **relieving a.,** armée de secours; **an a. twenty thousand strong,** une armée de vingt mille hommes; **a. of occupation,** armée d'occupation; (*c*) **the Salvation A.,** l'Armée du Salut. **2.** foule *f*, multitude *f* (d'hommes, etc.); **a whole a. of officials,** toute une armée de fonctionnaires. **3.** *Ent: NAm:* **a. worm,** chenille *f* de la leucanie, *F:* ver *m* militaire.

arna ['ɑ:nə], *s. Z:* arni *m*.

arnebia [ɑ:'ni:biə], *s. Bot:* arnebia *f*.

arnee ['ɑ:ni], *s. Z:* arni *m*.

arnica ['ɑ:nikə], *s.* **1.** *Bot:* arnica *f*, arnique *f*; bétoine *f* des montagnes, des Vosges. **2.** *Pharm:* (teinture *f* d')arnica.

Arnold ['ɑ:nəld], *Pr.n.m.* Arnaud, Arnoul.

arnotto [ɑ:'nɔtou], *s.* = ANATTO.

arolla [ə'rɔlə], *s. Bot:* arolle *f*; pin *m* cembro.

aroma [ə'roumə], *s.* arôme *m*; bouquet *m* (d'un vin, d'un cigare); **to give sth. an a.,** aromatiser qch.

aromatic [ærou'mætik]. **1.** *a.* (*a*) aromatique; (parfum) balsamique; (*b*) *Ch:* **a. series,** série *f* aromatique; **a. compounds,** composés *m* aromatiques; **a. ring,** noyau *m* aromatique, benzénique. **2.** *s.* (*a*) aromate *m*; (*b*) *pl. Ch:* **aromatics,** carbures *m* aromatiques, à noyau.

aromatization [æroumətai'zeiʃ(ə)n], *s.f. Ch:* aromatisation *f*.

aromatize [ə'roumətaiz], *v.tr. Ch:* aromatiser.

aronia [ə'rouniə], *s. Bot:* aronia *f*.

around [ə'raund]. **1.** *adv.* (*a*) autour, à l'entour; **all a.,** tout autour, de tous côtés, de toutes parts; **for ten miles a.,** à dix milles à l'entour, à la ronde; **the woods (all) a.,** les bois d'alentour; (*b*) **to wander a.,** rôder; *P:* **to sleep a.,** coucher (avec n'importe qui); couchailler; (*c*) *F:* sur pied, debout, levé; **he's now able to get a. again,** il est de nouveau sur pied; (*d*) (*of thg*) **this product has been a. for a long time,** ce produit est en circulation depuis longtemps; *F:* **she's been a.,** elle est avertie; **where have you been?—a.!** où est-ce que tu t'es traîné?—par ci, par là! **2.** *prep.* (*a*) autour de; **his arms were a. her neck,** il avait les bras autour de son cou; **the people a. him,** son entourage, les gens qui l'entourent; **a. London,** à la périphérie de Londres; (*b*) **to travel a. the country,** parcourir le pays; **a. the world in 80 days,** le tour du monde en 80 jours; (*c*) **the meeting adjourned at a. four o'clock,** on a levé la séance sur les quatre heures; *NAm:* **it cost a. five dollars,** cela a coûté environ cinq dollars.

arouse [ə'rauz], *v.tr.* **1.** (*a*) réveiller, éveiller (qn); **to a. s.o. from his sleep,** tirer qn de son sommeil; (*b*) secouer (qn) (de sa paresse, de sa torpeur); stimuler (qn). **2.** exciter, éveiller, susciter (un sentiment); soulever (des passions); piquer, éveiller, provoquer (la jalousie); chatouiller (la curiosité); appeler (le mépris); éveiller (des soupçons); **he could a. all that was worst in a man,** il savait éveiller les pires instincts de l'homme; **his jealousy was aroused,** sa jalousie fut mise en éveil; **the incident aroused his suspicions,** l'incident a éveillé ses soupçons.

arpeggiated [ɑ:'pedʒieitid], *a. Mus:* (accord) arpégé.

arpeggio[1] [ɑ:'pedʒiou], *s. Mus:* arpège *m*; **to play arpeggios,** (i) faire des arpèges, arpéger (sur le piano); (ii) exécuter un passage en arpèges.

arpeggio[2], *v. Mus:* **1.** *v.i.* arpéger. **2.** *v.tr.* arpéger (un accompagnement); exécuter (un passage) en arpèges.

arquebus ['ɑ:kwibəs], *s.* arquebuse *f*.

arquebusier [ɑ:kwibə'siər], *s. A.Mil:* arquebusier *m*.

arquerite ['ɑ:kwərait], *s. Miner:* arquérite *f*.

arracacha [ærə'kætʃə], **arracacia** [ærə'keiʃə], *s. Bot:* arracacha *m*, arracacia *m*.

arrack ['ærək], *s. Dist:* arack *m*.

arraign [ə'rein], *v.tr. Jur: & Lit:* (*a*) mettre (qn) en accusation; accuser, inculper (qn) (**for,** de); traduire (qn) devant un tribunal; traduire (qn) en justice; (*b*) attaquer (qn, une opinion); s'en prendre à (qn); blâmer ouvertement.

arraigner [ə'reinər], *s. Jur:* accusateur, -trice.

arraignment [ə'reinmənt], *s.* **1.** *Jur:* (*a*) mise *f* en accusation; mise en jugement; (*b*) acte *m* d'accusation; (*c*) interpellation *f* de l'accusé (qui doit répondre "coupable" ou "non coupable"). **2.** *Lit:* censure *f*, critique *f* hostile (d'un livre, d'une action).

arrange [ə'rein(d)ʒ], *v.tr.* arranger, aménager. **1.** (*a*) (*set in order*) disposer, mettre en ordre, ranger, arranger (les meubles, etc.); ordonner (un cortège, etc.); **to a. books on a shelf,** ranger des livres sur un rayon; **to a. them in alphabetical order,** les ranger par ordre alphabétique; **to a. one's affairs,** régler ses affaires; **artist who is good at arranging the subjects of his picture,** peintre *m* qui sait camper ses personnages; **the stage effects are arranged with skill,** les effets de scène sont ménagés avec habileté; **she spent the morning arranging the flowers,** elle a passé la matinée à fleurir la maison; *Mth:* **to a. terms** (*in ascending or descending order*), ordonner les termes (d'un polynôme); **to a. in (a) sequence,** ordonner, classer; *Mil:* **to a. troops in extended order, in fan order,** disposer les troupes en ordre dilué, en éventail; *Chess:* **arranging!** j'adoube! (*b*) (*adapt*) **piece arranged for the piano,** morceau adapté, arrangé, pour piano; **to a. a score for the piano,** réduire une partition (pour piano). **2.** (*plan beforehand*) **to a. the drawing room for the party,** préparer, arranger, aménager, le salon pour la soirée; **to a. a marriage,** arranger un mariage; **a marriage has been arranged between . . . and . . .,** on annonce les fiançailles de Mlle. . . avec M. . . .; **to a. a treaty,** (i) préparer, (ii) conclure, un traité; **to a. to do sth.,** (i) s'arranger, prendre ses dispositions, pour faire qch.; faire en sorte de faire qch.; (ii) s'arranger avec qn pour faire qch.; convenir de faire qch.; **to a. a time for sth.,** fixer une heure pour qch.; **to a. a concert,** organiser un concert; **I shall a. it,** j'y pourvoirai; je prendrai les dispositions nécessaires; *F:* je vais arranger ça; **to a. for sth. to be done,** prendre des dispositions, des mesures, pour que qch. se fasse; **I have arranged for somebody to escort her,** j'ai pris des dispositions pour qu'on l'accompagne; **to a. with s.o. about sth.,** s'accorder, tomber d'accord, avec qn au sujet de qch.; **everything is arranged,** tout est en ordre; **we arranged to meet at ten,** nous avons convenu de nous retrouver à dix heures; **it was arranged that . . .,** il fut convenu que . . .; **try to a. it,** tâchez d'arranger la chose; **a. it among yourselves,** arrangez cela entre vous; entendez-vous là-dessus; **I arranged it so that nobody heard of his departure,** je m'arrangeai, j'arrangeai les choses, de façon que personne n'apprît son départ; **they arranged a scheme by which . . .,** ils concertèrent un projet par lequel . . .; **one cannot a. for everything,** on ne peut pas tout prévoir; **the meeting arranged for tomorrow,** la réunion prévue pour demain. **3.** (*settle*) accommoder, ajuster, arranger (un différend).

arrangeable [ə'rein(d)ʒəbl], *a.* arrangeable.

arrangement [ə'rein(d)ʒmənt], *s.* **1.** (*a*) arrangement *m*, disposition *f*, aménagement *m*, mise *f* en ordre (**of,** de); **to make arrangements for sth., to make arrangements to do sth., to make arrangements for sth. to be done,** prendre des dispositions, des mesures, faire des préparatifs, pour qch., pour faire qch., pour que qch. se fasse; **to make all necessary arrangements,** prendre toutes les dispositions utiles, nécessaires; **to make arrangements for a journey,** faire ses préparatifs pour un voyage; (*b*) **flower, floral, arrangements,** l'art *m* de disposer les fleurs; **the flower arrangements were exceptionally beautiful,** les fleurs étaient disposées avec un goût exquis; (*c*) *Mus:* **a. for piano,** arrangement, adaptation *f*, réduction *f*, pour piano. **2.** accommodement *m* (d'un différend); accord *m*, entente *f*; *Jur:* transaction *f*; *Com: etc:* **to make an a., to come to an a., with s.o.,** entrer en arrangement, faire un arrangement, prendre un arrangement, passer un compromis, avec qn; **price by a.,** prix à débattre; **to come to an a. with one's creditors,** parvenir à un accord avec ses créanciers; **private a.,** accord à l'amiable. **3.** *F:* chose *f*, affaire *f*; **what's that a.?** qu'est-ce que c'est que cette machine-là? que ce machin-là? que ce truc-là?

arranger [ə'rein(d)ʒər], *s. esp. Mus:* arrangeur, -euse.

arranging [ə'rein(d)ʒiŋ], *s.* arrangement *m*, aménagement *m*, ajustement *m*, règlement *m*.

arrant ['ær(ə)nt], *a.* insigne, achevé; franc, *f.* franche; **a. liar,** menteur achevé.

arras ['ærəs], *s. A:* tenture(s) *f*; tapisserie(s) *f*.

array[1] [ə'rei], *s.* **1.** (*a*) rangs *mpl;* **in close a.,** en rangs serrés; **in battle a.,** en ordre de bataille; (*b*) étalage *m*; **an imposing a. of tools,** un imposant déploiement d'outils; **a great a. of people,** bon nombre de gens; une foule considérable; (*c*) *Mth:* rangée *f*, tableau *m* (de chiffres); *Cmptr:* **core a.,** matrice *f* de tores; **disc a.,** pile *f* de disques; **type a.,** jeu *m* de caractères; **a. pitch,** pas *m* longitudinal; (*d*) *W.Tel: T.V:* **antenna a.,** (i) système *m* d'antennes; (ii) dispositif *m* d'antenne. **2.** *Hist:* mobilisation des milices, etc. **3.** *Jur:* (*a*) appel nominal (des jurés); (*b*) tableau *m* (des jurés). **4.** *Lit:* parure *f*, appareil *m*; **in rich a.,** parée de tous ses atours, de ses plus beaux atours.

array[2], *v.tr.* **1.** (*a*) ranger, mettre en ordre; disposer, déployer (des troupes, etc.) (en ordre de bataille); *A:* **they arrayed themselves against the King,** ils se rangèrent au parti hostile au roi; ils prirent les armes contre le roi; (*b*) *Mth: Elcs: etc:* aligner; **arrayed wires,** nappe *f* de câbles. **2.** *Jur:* **to a. a panel,** (i) dresser le tableau des jurés; (ii) faire l'appel nominal des jurés. **3.** *Lit:* revêtir, orner, parer (**s.o. in sth.,** qn de qch.).

arrayment [ə'reimənt], *s. A:* disposition *f* (des troupes en ordre de bataille, etc.).

arrearage [ə'riəridʒ], *s.* **1.** retard *m* (dans le travail, etc.). **2.** *pl. A: & NAm:* arriéré *m*, arrérages *mpl*; solde *m* de compte encore dû; reliquat *m* de compte.

arrear(s) [ə'riər, ə'riəz], *s.* **1.** arriéré *m*, arrérages *mpl*; **arrears of rent,** arriéré de loyer; **arrears of wages,** arrérages de salaires, rappel *m* de salaires; **rent in arrear(s),** loyer *m* en arrière, arriéré, en retard; **work in a.,** travail *m* en retard; **ratepayer in arrears,** contribuable en retard; **I am three months in arrears with the rent,** je suis en retard de trois mois pour mon terme; **to get, fall, into arrears,** (i) (*of pers.*) se mettre en retard, s'arriérer; (ii) (*of moneys*) arrérager; **to be in arrear(s) with one's correspondence,** avoir de l'arriéré, être en retard, en arrière, dans sa correspondance; **to make up arrears (of work),** se remettre au courant, à flot; **arrears of interest,** intérêts moratoires, de retard, arriérés, échus et non payés; arrérages; **salary with arrears as from 1st March,** traitement *m* avec rétroactivité au 1er mars, avec effet rétroactif à compter du 1er mars. **2.** *prep.phr. A:* **to walk in arrear of the procession,** marcher derrière le cortège.

arrector [ə'rektər], *s. Anat:* muscle arrecteur; **a. pili muscle,** muscle pilomoteur.

arrest[1] [ə'rest], *s.* **1.** (*a*) arrestation *f* (d'un malfaiteur); *Jur:* prise *f* de corps; **under a.,** en état d'arrestation; **to effect an a.,** opérer une arrestation; **wholesale arrests,** arrestations en masse; **warrant of a.,** mandat *m* d'arrêt; (*b*) *Mil: Navy:* arrêts *mpl*; **open a.,** arrêts simples; **close a.,** arrêts forcés, de rigueur; consigne *f* à la chambre; **house a.,** (i) *Mil: Navy:* arrêts à la chambre; (ii) *Pol: etc:* résidence surveillée; **under a.,** aux arrêts; **to be, remain, under a.,** garder les arrêts; **to put an officer under a.,** mettre un officier aux arrêts; consigner un officier; *Navy:* envoyer un officier à sa chambre. **2.** (*a*) arrêt *m*, suspension *f* (d'un mouvement, du progrès, etc.); **a. of the vital functions,** arrêt dans les fonctions vitales; (*b*) *Jur:* **a. of judgment,** sursis *m*, surséance *f*, à l'exécution d'un jugement; suspension de jugement.

arrest[2], *v.tr.* **1.** arrêter (le mouvement, le progrès, de qn, de qch.); **arrested growth, development (of s.o., of sth.),** arrêt *m* dans la croissance (de qn), dans le développement (de qch.). **2.** arrêter (un malfaiteur); mettre (qn) en état d'arrestation; appréhender (qn) au corps; s'assurer de la personne de (qn). **3.** arrêter, fixer, retenir (l'attention, les regards). **4.** *Jur:* **to a. judgment,** suspendre l'exécution d'un jugement; surseoir à un jugement. **5.** *Jur:* (*Scot: & Admiralty Law*) saisir (des biens mobiliers, un navire).

arrestation [æres'teiʃ(ə)n], *s.* **1.** (*a*) arrêt *m*; (*b*) *Jur:* saisie-arrêt *m*; opposition *f*. **2.** *U.S:* arrestation *f*; prise *f* de corps.

arrester [ə'restər], *s.* **1.** celui qui arrête (un malfaiteur). **2.** *Scot: Jur:* saisissant *m* (de biens mobiliers). **3.** *Tchn:* (*a*) intercepteur *m*, séparateur *m*; **fly ash a.,** séparateur d'escarbilles; **fire a., flame a.,** pare-flammes *m inv*; **lightning a.,** parafoudre *m*, paratonnerre *m*; **spark a.,** pare-étincelles *m inv*; (*b*) *attrib. Av:* **a. gear,** (i) (*on runway*) dispositif *m* d'arrêt; (ii) (*on carrier deck*) dispositif d'appontage; **a. hook,** crosse *f*, crochet *m*, d'arrêt, d'appontage; **a. net,** filet *m* d'arrêt, d'appontage; **a. wire,** brin *m* d'arrêt, d'appontage.

arresting[1] [ə'restiŋ], *a.* attachant, impressionnant, frappant; qui arrête l'attention; **a. picture,** tableau qui tire l'œil; **an a. sight,** un spectacle frappant; **she is not beautiful, but she has an a. smile,** sans être belle, elle a un sourire attrayant.

arresting[2], *s.* **1.** *Jur:* arrestation *f*; prise *f*, appréhension *f*, de corps. **2.** *Mec.E: etc:* arrêt *m*; **a. device,** dispositif *m* d'arrêt; *Av:* **a. gear,** dispositif *m* (i) d'arrêt, (ii) d'appontage.

arrestingly [ə'restiŋli], *adv.* **a. beautiful, ugly,** qui frappe par sa beauté, par sa laideur.

arrhenatherum [ærə'næθərəm], *s. Bot:* arrhenatherum *m*.

arrhenoblastoma [ærənou'blɑ:stoumə], *s. Med:* arrhénoblastome *m*.

arrhenotokous [ærə'nɔtəkəs], *a. Biol:* arrhénotoque.

arrhenotoky [ærə'nɔtəki], *s. Biol:* arrhénotoquie *f*.

arrhizal [ə'raizl], **arrhizous** [ə'raizəs], *a. Bot:* arrhize.

arrhythmia [ə'riθmiə], **arrhythmy** ['æriθmi], *s. Med:* arythmie *f* (du pouls, etc.).

arrhythmic [ə'riθmik], *a.* (pouls) arythmique.

Arrian ['æriən], *Pr.n.m. Gr.Lit:* Arrien.

arrière-ban ['æriɛəbæn], *s. Hist:* arrière-ban *m*, *pl.* arrière-bans.

arrière-fief ['æriɛəfi:f], *s. Hist:* arrière-fief *m*, *pl.* arrière-fiefs.

arrière-pensée ['æriɛəpɑ̃sei], *s.* arrière-pensée *f*, *pl.* arrière-pensées.

arrière-vassal, *pl.* **arrière-vassals** ['æriɛə'væsəl, -əlz], *s. Hist:* arrière-vassal, -ale, *pl.* arrière-vassaux, -ales.

arrière-voussure ['æriɛə'vu:sjuɛr], *s. Arch:* arrière-voussure *f*, *pl.* arrière-voussures.

arris ['æris], *s.* arête vive (d'un prisme, d'une cannelure); *Const:* **a. gutter,** gouttière *f* en V; **a. rafter,** arêtier *m*; **a. tile,** arêtière *f*, faîtière *f*.

arrisways, arriswise ['ærisweiz, -waiz], *adv.* angulairement; en pointe, en arête.

arrival [ə'raivl], *s.* **1.** (*a*) arrivée *f*; **on a.,** à l'arrivée (de qn, de qch.); *Post:* **to await a.,** ne pas faire suivre; *Nau:* **for a.,** à livrer à l'arrivée; (*b*) *Com:* arrivage *m* (de marchandises); **daily arrivals,** arrivages quotidiens; (*c*) *Nau:* entrée *f* (d'un navire); **port of a.,** port *m* d'arrivée; (*d*) *Trans:* débarquement *m* (de voyageurs); **on a.,** au débarquement; **arrivals and departures,** (i) mouvement *m* des trains, des avions, etc.; (ii) tableaux *m* d'affichage. **2.** (*pers.*) **a new a.,** (i) un nouveau venu, une nouvelle venue; (ii) *F:* un nouveau-né, une nouvelle-née; **late arrivals,** retardataires *m*.

arrive [ə'raiv], *v.i. O:* (*a*) arriver (**at, in,** à, dans); **we arrived at three o'clock,** nous sommes arrivés à trois heures; **he has just arrived,** il arrive à l'instant; il ne fait que d'arriver; **he is expected to a. next week,** on attend son arrivée pour la semaine prochaine; **as soon as he arrived in London,** dès son arrivée à Londres; **to a. just at the right moment, in the nick of time,** arriver juste à temps, au bon moment; *F:* arriver comme marée en carême; **the third to a. was Helen,** la troisième arrivante fut Hélène; **to a. on the scene,** to **a. unexpectedly,** survenir; **a client arrived and stopped me from going out,** l'arrivée d'un client m'a empêché de sortir; (*b*) **to a. at the age of sixty,** atteindre, parvenir à, arriver à, l'âge de soixante ans; **to a. at perfection,** atteindre, arriver à, la perfection; **to a. at a decision, a conclusion,** arriver, en venir, aboutir, à une décision, à une conclusion; **to a. at a price,** calculer, fixer, un prix; parvenir à un prix; convenir d'un prix.

arrogance ['ærəgəns], *s.* arrogance *f*; morgue *f*.

arrogant ['ærəg(ə)nt], *a.* arrogant; **a. tone of voice,** ton arrogant, rogue.

arrogantly ['ærəgəntli], *adv.* arrogamment; avec arrogance.

arrogate ['ærougeit], *v.tr. Lit: & Jur:* **1. to a. sth. to oneself,** s'arroger qch., usurper qch., s'attribuer qch. **2. to a. sth. to s.o.,** attribuer injustement, à tort, qch. à qn.

arrogation [ærou'geiʃ(ə)n], *s. Lit: & Jur:* prétention mal fondée; **a. of sth.,** usurpation *f* de qch.

arrow[1] ['ærou], *s.* **1.** (*a*) flèche *f*; **to shoot, let fly, an a.,** lancer, décocher, une flèche; **to fly straight as an a.,** voler droit comme une flèche; **as swift as an a.,** vif comme l'éclair; **the a. has hit the mark,** le trait est arrivé à son adresse; *Adm: A:* **broad a.** = marque *f* de l'État; *Arch:* **a. slit,** archère *f*, archière *f*; (*b*) flèche (indicatrice, de direction); (*c*) *Const:* **a. point bracing,** entretoisement *m* à triangles. **2.** (*a*) *Surv:* fiche *f* (d'arpenteur); zéro *m* (d'un vernier); **drop a.,** fiche plombée; (*b*) *Mth:* **vector a.,** flèche, segment orienté.

arrow[2], *v.tr.* indiquer au moyen d'une flèche; flécher (une route, une direction).

arrow grass ['ærougrɑ:s], *s. Bot:* (*a*) triglochin *m*, troscart *m*; **seaside a. g.,** triglochin maritime; (*b*) aristide *f*.

arrowhead ['ærouhed], *s.* **1.** tête *f*, fer *m*, pointe *f*, de flèche. **2.** flèche (indicatrice, de direction). **3.** *Bot:* fléchière *f*, sagittaire *f*, sagette *f*, flèche *f* d'eau, queue-d'aronde *f*, *pl.* queues-d'aronde. **4.** *Needlw:* abeille *f*.

arrowheaded ['ærouhedid], *a.* en forme de tête de flèche; cunéiforme.

arrowing ['ærouiŋ], *s.* fléchage *m*.

arrowroot ['ærouru:t], *s.* **1.** *Bot:* marante *f*. **2.** *Cu:* arrowroot *m*.

arrow-shaped ['ærouʃeipt], *a.* en forme de flèche; sagitté.

arrowstone ['æroustoun], *s. Paleont:* bélemnite.

arroyo [ə'rɔijou], *s.* arroyo *m*.

arse [ɑ:s], *s. P:* **1.** (*not in polite use*) cul *m*, derrière *m*; **a. over tip,** à la renverse; cul par-dessus tête; **a. up,** le cul en l'air. **2.** cul (d'une poulie).

arse about ['ɑ:se'bout], *v.i. P:* (*not in polite use*) **don't you go arsing about in there,** va pas faire le con là-dedans.

arse-crawler ['ɑːskrɔːlər], **arse-licker** ['ɑːslikər], *s. P:* (*not in polite use*) lèche-cul *m inv.*
arsehole ['ɑːshoul], *s. P:* (*not in polite use*) trou *m* de balle, du cul.
arsenal ['ɑːsənl], *s.* arsenal *m*, -aux.
arsenate ['ɑːsənət], *s. Ch:* arséniate *m*; **acid lead a.,** arséniate diplombique, arséniate acide de plomb; **basic lead a.,** arséniate triplombique, arséniate basique de plomb.
arsenated ['ɑːsəneitid], *a. Ch:* arsénié, arsénifère, arsénique.
arseniasis [ɑːsə'naiəsis], *s. Med:* arseniciase *f*, arsenicisme *m*.
arseniate [ɑː'senieit], *s. Ch:* arséniate *m*.
arsenic[1] ['ɑːs(ə)nik], *s.* arsenic *m*; **white a., flaky a., flowers of a.,** arsenic blanc, acide arsénieux; anhydride arsénieux; **red a., ruby a.,** arsenic sulfure rouge, rubis *m* d'arsenic réalgar *m*; **yellow a., sulphide of a.,** sulfure *m* jaune d'arsenic; orpiment *m*, orpin *m*; **a. eating,** arsénicophage; **a. eater,** arsénicophage *mf.*
arsenic [2] [ɑː'senik], *a. Ch:* (acide) arsénique.
arsenical [ɑː'senikl], *a.* arsenical; *Med:* **a. intoxication,** arséniciase *f*, arsénicisme *m*.
arsenide ['ɑːsənaid], *s. Ch:* arséniure *m*.
arseniferous [ɑːsə'nifərəs], *a.* arsénifère.
arsenious [ɑː'siːniəs], *a.* arsénieux; **a. oxide,** acide arsénieux.
arsenism ['ɑːsənizm], *s. Med:* arsénicisme *m*.
arsenite ['ɑːsənait], *s.* **1.** *Ch:* arsénite *m*. **2.** *Miner:* arsénite arsénolit(h)e *m*.
arseniuretted [ɑː'senjuəretid], *a. Ch:* (hydrogène, etc.) arsénié.
arsenobismite ['ɑːsənou'bizmait], *s. Miner:* arsenbismuth *m*.
arsenolite [ɑː'senoulait], *s. Miner:* arsénolit(h)e *m*, arsénite *m*.
arsenopyrite ['ɑːsənou'paiərait], *s. Miner:* arsénopyrite *f*; pyrite arsenicale; fer arsenical; mispickel *m*.
arsenotherapy ['ɑːsənou'θerəpi], *s.* arsénothérapie *f.*
arsine ['ɑːsiːn], *s. Ch:* arsine *f*, arsénamine *f.*
arsis, *pl.* **arses** ['ɑːsis, 'ɑːsiːz], *s. Mus: Pros:* arsis *f*; ictus *m*; *Mus:* temps fort; *Pros:* syllabe accentuée.
arson ['ɑːs(ə)n], *s.* incendie *m* volontaire, par malveillance; *Jur:* crime *m* d'incendie; **to commit a.,** provoquer (volontairement) un incendie.
arsonist ['ɑːsənist], *s.* incendiaire *mf.*
arsonvalization [ɑːs(ə)nvæli'zeiʃ(ə)n], *s. Med:* arsonvalisation *f*; diathermie *f.*
arsphenamine [ɑːs'fenəmiːn], *s. Med:* salvarsan *m*.
art [ɑːt], *s.* **1.** art *m*; (*a*) **the (fine) arts,** les beaux-arts *m*; **a. school,** école *f* des beaux arts; **a. student,** élève *mf*, étudiant, -ante, d'une école des beaux-arts; **a. critic,** critique *mf* d'art; **a. for art's sake,** l'art pour l'art; (*b*) *Sch:* **faculty of arts,** faculté des lettres; **arts student,** étudiant, -ante, en lettres; **bachelor of arts** = licencié, -ée, ès lettres; (*c*) **arts and crafts,** (i) artisanat *m* d'expression; (ii) *Sch:* travaux manuels; *attrib.* **a. pottery,** poterie *f* d'art; **a. needlework,** travail *m* (à l'aiguille) de fantaisie; (*d*) **the a. of war,** l'art militaire; l'art de la guerre; **the black a.,** la magie noire; **the noble a.,** le noble art, la boxe. **2.** (*a*) adresse *f*, habileté *f*, artifice *m*, art, **she has the a. of pleasing,** elle a l'art de plaire; **the whole a. of government lies in persuading other people,** le secret de gouverner se ramène à persuader les autres; **to use every a. in order to . . .,** user de tous les artifices, de tous les stratagèmes, pour . . .; (*b*) *Jur:* **to have a. and part in sth.,** être fauteur et complice de qch.
Artaxerxes [ɑːtæg'zɔːksiːz], *Pr.n.m. A.Hist:* Artaxerxès.
artefact ['ɑːtifækt], *s.* **1.** produit œuvré; *Archeol:* objet (caillou, etc.) façonné. **2.** *Biol:* artefact *m*.
Artemis ['ɑːtimis], *Pr.n.f. Gr.Myth:* Artémis.
Artemisia [ɑːti'miziə]. **1.** *Pr.n. Gr.Hist:* Artémise. **2.** *s. Bot:* armoise *f*; artemisia *f*.
arterial [ɑː'tiəriəl], *a.* **1.** *Anat: Med: etc:* artériel; **a. haemorrhage,** artériorragie *f*; **a. pressure,** pression artérielle. **2. a. road,** grande voie de communication; **a. system,** réseau artériel; **a. navigation,** navigation fluviale.
arterialization [ɑːtiəriəlai'zeiʃ(ə)n], *s.* artérialisation *f* (du sang veineux).
arterialize [ɑː'tiəriəlaiz], *v.tr.* **1.** artérialiser (le sang veineux); (*of blood*) **to become arterialized,** s'artérialiser. **2.** établir de grandes artères dans (un réseau de communications, de voies ferrées, etc.).
arteriectomy [ɑːtiəri'ektəmi], *s. Surg:* artériectomie *f.*
arteriograph [ɑː'tiəriougraːf], *s. Med:* artériographe *m*.
arteriography [ɑːtiəri'ɔgrəfi], *s. Med:* artériographie *f.*
arteriole [ɑː'tiərioul], *s. Anat:* artériole *f.*
arteriology [ɑːtiəri'ɔlədʒi], *s.* artériologie *f.*
arteriopathy [ɑːtiəri'ɔpəθi], *s.* artériopathie *f.*
arteriosclerosis [ɑː'tiəriousklə'rousis], *s.* artériosclérose *f*; sclérose *f* vasculaire; sclérose des artères.
arteriosclerotic [ɑː'tiəriousklə'rɔtik], *a.* artérioscléreux.
arteriotomy [ɑːtiəri'ɔtəmi], *s. Surg:* artériotome *m*.
arteritis [ɑːtə'raitis], *s. Med:* artérite *f.*
artery ['ɑːtəri], *s.* **1.** *Anat:* artère *f*; **small a.,** artériole *f.* **2. main arteries,** grandes voies de communication, grandes artères.
artesian [ɑː'tiːziən, -'tiːʒən], *a.* artésien; de l'Artois; *Hyd.E:* **a. well,** puits artésien; *Geol:* **a. layer,** nappe jaillissante.
artful ['ɑːtful], *a.* **1.** (*of pers.*) (*a*) *A:* adroit, habile, ingénieux; (*b*) rusé, artificieux, astucieux; malin, -igne; **a. as a monkey,** malin comme un singe. **2.** (*of thg*) (*a*) *A:* artificiel; (*b*) ingénieux, habile; **an a. dodge,** un truc ingénieux.
artfully ['ɑːtfuli], *adv.* astucieusement, avec artifice.
artfulness ['ɑːtfulnis], *s.* **1.** *A:* art *m*, adresse *f*, habileté *f*, ingéniosité *f.* **2.** astuce *f* (de qn, de langage).
arthralgia [ɑː'θrældʒiə], *s. Med:* arthralgie *f.*
arthralgic [ɑː'θrældʒik], *a. Med:* arthralgique.
arthrectomy [ɑː'θrektəmi], *s. Surg:* arthrectomie *f.*
arthritic [ɑː'θritik], *a. Med:* arthritique; **a. diathesis,** arthritisme *m*; **a. rheumatism,** rhumatisme noueux.
arthritis [ɑː'θraitis], *s. Med:* arthrite *f*; **rheumatoid a.,** rhumatisme articulaire, noueux, déformant; arthrite sèche, déformante; polyarthrite chronique évolutive.
arthritism ['ɑːθritizm], *s. Med:* arthritisme *m*.
arthro- ['ɑːθrou], *pref.* arthro-.
arthrobranch(ia) [ɑːθrou'bræŋk(iə)], *s. Crust:* arthrobranchie *f.*
arthrodesis [ɑːθrou'diːsis], *s. Surg:* arthrodèse *f.*
arthrodia [ɑː'θroudiə], *s. Anat:* arthrodie *f.*
arthrology [ɑː'θrɔlədʒi], *s. Anat:* arthrologie *f.*
arthroplasty [ɑːθrou'plæsti], *s. Surg:* arthroplastie *f.*
arthropod ['ɑːθroupɔd], *s. Z:* arthropode *m*.
Arthropoda [ɑː'θrɔpədə], *s.pl. Z:* arthropodes *m*.
arthropodal [ɑː'θrɔpədl], **arthropodous** [ɑː'θrɔpədəs], *a. Z:* propre aux arthropodes.
arthrosis [ɑː'θrousis], *s.* **1.** *Anat:* articulation *f.* **2.** *Med:* arthrose *f*; ostéo-arthropathie dystrophique, dégénérative, déformante.
arthrospore ['ɑːθrouspɔːr], *s. Bot:* arthrospore *f.*
arthrotomy [ɑː'θrɔtəmi], *s. Surg:* arthrotomie *f.*
Arthur ['ɑːθər], *Pr.n.m.* Arthur.
Arthurian [ɑː'θjuəriən], *a. Lit.Hist:* (cycle *m*, etc.) d'Arthur, du roi Arthur, (roman) arthurien.
artichoke ['ɑːtitʃouk], *s.* **1. globe a.,** artichaut *m*; **prickly a.,** chardonnette *f*; **a. bed,** artichautière *f*; *Cu:* **a. hearts, hearts of a.,** fonds *mpl*, cœurs *mpl*, d'artichaut. **2. Jerusalem a.,** topinambour *m*; **Chinese, Japanese, a.,** crosne *m* (du Japon).
article[1] ['ɑːtikl], *s.* **1.** (*a*) *Bot: Ent:* article *m*; point *m* d'articulation; (*b*) *A:* moment *m*, conjoncture *f*; **in the a. of death,** à l'article de la mort. **2.** (*a*) *Com: Jur:* article, clause *f* (d'une convention, d'un traité); **articles of apprenticeship, of a partnership,** contrat *m* d'apprentissage, de société; acte *m* de société, d'association; **articles of marriage,** conventions matrimoniales; contrat de mariage; **the articles of a contract,** les stipulations *f* d'un contrat; **articles of association,** statuts *m* (d'une société à responsabilité limitée); **appointed, provided, by the articles,** statutaire; **under the articles, in accordance with the articles,** statutairement; (*of sale, contract*) **articles and conditions,** cahier *m* des charges; **articles of war,** *Mil:* code *m* (de justice) militaire; *Navy:* code de justice maritime; *Nau:* **ship's articles,** (i) contrat *m* d'engagement, conditions *fpl* d'embarquement; (ii) rôle *m* de l'équipage, rôle d'équipage; (*b*) **a. of faith,** article de foi; *Theol:* **the Articles of Religion, the Thirty-nine Articles,** les Articles de religion (de l'Église anglicane); (*c*) *Jur:* (*count of indictment*) chef *m* d'accusation. **3.** *Journ: etc:* article (de journal, de revue, d'encyclopédie); papier *m*; **feature a.,** article d'intérêt général; **leading a.,** éditorial *m*, -aux. **4.** article, objet *m*; *P: O:* **the a.,** le vase de nuit; **a. of clothing,** vêtement *m*, article d'habillement; *Com:* **to put an a. on the market,** lancer un produit sur le marché; **returned a.,** rendu *m*, laissé *m* pour compte; *F: O:* **that's the very a.!** c'est exactement ce qu'il (me) faut! **5.** *A:* (*subject*) **I have no anxiety on that a.,** je n'ai aucune inquiétude sur ce point. **6.** *Gram:* **definite, indefinite, a.,** article défini, indéfini.
article[2], *v.tr.* **1.** *Jur:* (*a*) **to a. an offence against s.o.,** *v.i.* **to a. against s.o.,** dresser un acte d'accusation, formuler une accusation, contre qn; (*b*) **to a. s.o. for an offence,** accuser qn d'un crime. **2. to a. s.o. to an attorney, to an architect,** placer qn (comme élève) chez un avoué, chez un architecte; **articled clerk,** clerc *m* d'avoué, de *solicitor*, lié par un contrat d'apprentissage; **I was an articled clerk with Mr X,** j'ai fait mon apprentissage chez M. X, avoué.
articular [ɑː'tikjulər], *a. Nat.Hist: Anat:* articulaire; **a. disc,** ménisque *m* articulaire.
Articulata [ɑːtikju'leitə], *s.pl. Z:* articulés *m*.
articulate[1] [ɑː'tikjulət]. **1.** *a.* & *s. Z:* articulé (*m*). **2.** *a.* (*a*) **a. speech,** langage articulé; (*b*) (*of manner of speaking*) net, distinct; (*c*) **millions of people were becoming a.,** des millions de gens se faisaient désormais entendre (par suite d'émancipation politique).
articulate[2] [ɑː'tikjuleit], *v.tr.* & *i.* **1.** *Anat:* articuler (un squelette, etc.); (*in passive*) s'articuler; **bone that articulates, is articulated, with another,** os qui s'articule, est articulé, avec un autre. **2.** articuler, énoncer (un mot, etc.); **he doesn't a. his words,** son énonciation est mauvaise.
articulated [ɑː'tikjuleitid], *a. Nat.Hist: Ling: etc:* articulé; *Const:* **a. girder,** poutre articulée; *Veh:* **a. vehicle,** semi-remorque *f*, *pl.* semi-remorques.
articulately [ɑː'tikjulətli], *adv.* (parler) (i) d'une voix articulée; (ii) distinctement, clairement, nettement.
articulateness [ɑː'tikjulətnis], *s.* **1.** caractère articulé (d'un langage). **2.** articulation nette; netteté *f* d'énonciation.
articulation [ɑːtikju'leiʃ(ə)n], *s. Nat.Hist: Mec.E: Ling: etc:* articulation *f*; *Ling:* **faulty a.,** défaut *m* de prononciation; *Tp:* **band a.,** netteté *f* pour les bandes.
articulator [ɑː'tikjuleitər], *s. Dent:* articulateur *m*.
articulatory [ɑː'tikjulət(ə)ri], *a.* articulatoire.
artifact ['ɑːtifækt], *s.* **1.** produit ouvré; *Archeol:* objet (caillou, etc.) façonné. **2.** *Biol:* artefact *m*.
artifice ['ɑːtifis], *s.* **1.** artifice *m*, ruse *f*; combinaison *f*; **a. of war,** ruse de guerre, artifice de guerre; stratagème *m*. **2.** art *m*, habileté *f*, adresse *f.*
artificer [ɑː'tifisər], *s.* **1.** artisan *m*, ouvrier *m*; mécanicien *m*; *Mil:* artificier *m*; *Navy:* **engine-room a.,** mécanicien; **chief engine-room a.,** maître mécanicien. **2.** *A:* artisan (de sa fortune, du malheur d'autrui); auteur *m* (de sa propre ruine); architecte *m* (de l'univers).
artificial [ɑːti'fiʃ(ə)l], *a.* **1.** artificiel; **a. flowers,** fleurs artificielles; **a. wood,** similibois *m*; **a. stone,** similipierre *f*; **a. respiration,** respiration artificielle; **a. leg,** jambe artificielle; **a. limb,** prothèse *f* orthopédique; **a. hair,** cheveux *m* postiches; **a. teeth,** fausses dents, prothèse dentaire; **a. kidney,** rein artificiel; *Agr:* **a. meadow,** prairie artificielle; **a. manure,** engrais *mpl* chimiques; *Astr: etc:* **a. horizon,** horizon artificiel; *Cmptr:* **a. intelligence,** intelligence artificielle; **a. language,** langage artificiel. **2.** factice, simulé; **a. style,** style factice, recherché, qui sent l'étude; **a. manners,** manières affectées.
artificiality [ɑːtifiʃi'æliti], **artificialness** [ɑːti'fiʃ(ə)lnis], *s.* artificialité *f*; nature artificielle (d'un produit, etc.); caractère artificiel, manque *m* de naturel (d'un jardin, d'un décor).
artificially [ɑːti'fiʃəli], *adv.* artificiellement.
artillerist [ɑː'tilərist], *s. Mil:* artilleur *m*; expert *m* en balistique.
artillery [ɑː'tiləri], *s.* **1.** (*a*) artillerie *f*; **field a.,** (i) *Mil:* artillerie de campagne; (ii) *Navy:* artillerie de débarquement; **heavy a.,** artillerie lourde; **light a.,** artillerie légère; **medium a.,** artillerie de moyen calibre, artillerie moyenne; **superheavy a.,** artillerie à grande puissance; **coast a.,** artillerie de côte; **fortress a.,** artillerie de forteresse, de place; **marine a.,** artillerie de marine; **mountain a.,** artillerie de montagne; **naval a.,** artillerie navale; **railway a.,** artillerie sur voie ferrée; **pack a.,** artillerie sur bât; **self-propelled a.,** artillerie automotrice; **tractor-drawn a.,** artillerie tractée; **anti-aircraft a.,** artillerie anti-aérienne; **anti-tank a.,** artillerie anti-chars, *Belg:* anti-blindés; **corps a.,** artillerie de corps d'armée; **divisional a.,** artillerie divisionnaire; **accompanying a.,** artillerie d'accompagnement; **a. covering the infantry,** *U.S:* **direct support a.,** artillerie d'appui direct; **a. detailed for general work,** *U.S:* **general support a.,** artillerie d'action d'ensemble; **to serve in the a.,** servir dans l'artillerie; **the a. was in action,** on tirait au canon; (*b*) *attrib.* **a. fire,** tir *m* d'artillerie; **a. duel,** duel *m* d'artillerie; **a. park,** parc *m* d'artillerie; **a. train,** train *m* d'artillerie; *A:* **a. waggon,** caisson *m*; *A:* **a. company,** corps *m* d'artillerie; (*still so used in*) **the Honourable A. Company,** régiment territorial (infanterie et artillerie) recruté parmi les citoyens de Londres; *Aut: A:* **a. type wheel,** roue *f* type artillerie. **2.** *Bot:* **a. plant,** plante *f* au feu d'artifice.
artilleryman, *pl.* **-men** [ɑː'tilərimən], *s.m.* artilleur.
artiness ['ɑːtinis], *s. Pej:* recherche *f* de l'effet artistique.
artinite ['ɑːtinait], *s. Miner:* artinite *f.*

artiodactyl [ɑːtiou'dæktil], *a. & s. Z:* (ongulé) artiodactyle (*m*).

Artiodactyla [ɑːtiou'dæktilə], *s.pl.Z:* artiodactyles *m*.

artiodactylous [ɑːtiou'dæktiləs], *a. Z:* artiodactyle.

artisan [ɑːti'zæn], *s.* artisan *m*, ouvrier *m*; **the a. class,** l'artisanat *m*.

artist ['ɑːtist], *s.* (*a*) artiste *mf* (peintre); **he is an a.,** il est artiste, il est peintre; il fait de la peinture; **pavement a.,** barbouilleur, -euse, de trottoir; (*b*) **this dancer is really an a.,** ce danseur est un vrai artiste.

artiste [ɑː'tiːst], *s. Th:* artiste *mf*.

artistic [ɑː'tistik], *a.* (arrangement) artistique; (style, goût, tempérament) artiste; (toilette) de bon goût.

artistically [ɑː'tistik(ə)li], *adv.* (*a*) artistement, avec art, en artiste, artistiquement; (*b*) du point de vue artistique.

artistry ['ɑːtistri], *s.* art *m* (avec lequel qch. a été ordonné, truqué, etc.); *Lit:* **the a. of the Goncourt brothers,** l'écriture *f* artiste des Goncourt.

artless ['ɑːtlis], *a.* **1.** sans art, dénué d'art. **2.** naturel, simple; sans artifice. **3.** naïf, ingénu, candide, bon.

artlessly ['ɑːtlisli], *adv.* **1.** sans art. **2.** naturellement, simplement; sans artifice. **3.** naïvement, ingénument.

artlessness ['ɑːtlisnis], *s.* **1.** naturel *m*, simplicité *f*. **2.** naïveté *f*, ingénuité *f*, candeur *f*.

art nouveau ['ɑːnuːvou], *a. & s. Art:* modern style (*m*).

artocarpus [ɑːtou'kɑːpəs], *s. Bot:* artocarpe *m* ((i) arbre *m* à pain, (ii) jaquier *m*).

arty ['ɑːti], *a. Pej:* (mobilier, etc.) qui affiche des goûts artistiques; prétentieux.

arty-crafty ['ɑːti'krɑːfti], *a. F: Pej:* bohême, artiste (genre St Germain des Prés).

arui ['ærui], *s. Z:* arui *m*.

arum ['ɛərəm], *s. Bot:* arum *m*, *F:* gouet *m*, pied-de-veau, *m*, *pl.* pieds-de-veau; **a. lily,** arum; richardie *f*; **water a.,** calle *f*; **bog a.,** calle des marais.

arundo [ə'rʌndou], *s. Bot:* arundo *m*.

aruspex ['ærjuspeks], *s. Rom.Ant:* aruspice *m*.

Arval ['ɑːv(ə)l], *a. Rom.Ant:* **the A. Brethren,** les frères *m* Arvales.

Arvicolinae [ɑːvikə'liːniː], *s.pl. Z:* arvicolinés *m*.

arvicoline [ɑː'vikəlain], *a. Z:* arvicole.

Aryan ['ɛəriən]. *Ethn: Ling: etc:* (*a*) *a.* aryen; (*b*) *s.* Aryen, -enne.

aryl ['æril], *s. Ch:* aryle *f*.

arylamine [æ'riləmain], *s. Ch:* arylamine *f*.

arytenoid [æri'tiːnɔid], *a. & s. Anat:* aryténoïde (*m*).

arytenoiditis [æritinɔi'daitis], *s. Med:* aryténoïdite *f*.

as [əz, *stressed* æz], *adv., conj. & rel.pron.*

I. *adv.* **1.** (*in principal clause*) aussi, si; **I am as tall as you,** je suis aussi grand que vous; **I can do that (quite) as well as you,** je peux faire cela (tout) aussi bien que vous; **is it as high as that?** est-ce si haut que ça? **one is as bad as the other,** l'un vaut l'autre; (*intensive*) *F:* **he was as deaf as deaf,** il était sourd comme tout, sourd comme un pot; **she lay as still as still,** elle reposait dans une immobilité absolue. **2. I shall help you as far as I can,** je vous aiderai autant que je pourrai; **I worked as hard, as long, as I could,** j'ai travaillé tant que j'ai pu; **as much for your sake as for mine,** tant pour vous que pour moi; **as soon as possible,** aussitôt que possible. **3. as for that, as to that,** quant à cela, pour cela; **as far as you are concerned,** quant à (ce qui est de) vous; **to question s.o. as to his motives,** interroger qn sur ses motifs; **as for you . . .,** quant à vous . . .; pour ce qui est de vous . . ..

II. *conj. & adv.* (*in subordinate clause*) **1.** (*degree*) (*a*) que; **you are as tall as he is,** vous êtes aussi grand que lui; **I came down as fast as I could,** je suis descendu aussi vite que possible; **I shouted as loudly as I could,** j'ai crié de toutes mes forces; **you are not as, not so, tall as he is,** vous n'êtes pas si, aussi, grand que lui; **he is not so rich as you imagine,** il n'est pas si riche que vous vous l'imaginez; **he's not such a fool as he looks,** il n'est pas si bête qu'il en a l'air; **I want a house twice as large as this,** il me faut une maison deux fois plus grande que celle-ci; **Alaska is three times as big as France,** l'Alaska est grand comme trois fois la France; **she was as good as she was pretty,** elle était aussi sage que jolie; elle était sage autant que jolie; **she was now as fat as she had been thin,** autant elle avait été maigre, autant elle était maintenant obèse; **he is as generous as he is wealthy,** il est libéral autant que riche; **to be as good as one's word,** tenir ses promesses; **by day as well as by night,** le jour comme la nuit de jour comme de nuit; (*b*) (*in intensifying similes*) comme; **as pale as death,** pâle comme un mort; **quick as thought,** vite comme la pensée; **as white as a sheet,** blanc comme un linge; **it's as easy as anything,** c'est simple comme bonjour; c'est facile comme tout. **2.** (*a*) (*concessive*) **delightful as London is,** si agréable que soit Londres; **ignorant as he is,** tout ignorant qu'il est; **Londonder as I am, this is new to me,** tout Londonien que je suis, cela m'est nouveau; **much as I like him,** quelle que soit mon affection pour lui; **short as it is, the book is very interesting,** si court qu'il soit, tout court qu'il est, *Lit:* pour court qu'il soit, le livre est très intéressant; **be that as it may,** quoi qu'il en soit; **laugh as they would, he maintained that it was true,** ils avaient beau rire, il affirmait que c'était vrai; (*b*) **covered with dust as he was, he didn't want to come in,** couvert qu'il était de poussière, il ne voulait pas entrer. **3.** (*manner*) (*a*) comme; **do as you like,** faites comme vous voulez, comme vous voudrez; **pronounce the *a* as in father,** prononcez l'*a* comme dans *father;* **it happened as I told you,** cela s'est passé comme je vous l'ai dit, ainsi que je vous l'ai dit; **I remembered him as having served in the army,** je me souvenais de lui comme ayant servi dans l'armée; **as often happens,** comme il arrive souvent; ainsi qu'il arrive souvent; **as stated yesterday, the meeting will be held . . .,** comme il a été annoncé hier, comme nous l'annoncions hier, la réunion se tiendra . . .; **you don't hold your pen as I do,** vous ne tenez pas votre plume comme moi, de la même façon que moi; *Tchn:* **as cast,** brut de fonderie; **as drawn,** brut d'étirage; **as machined,** brut d'usinage; *Mth:* **A is to B as C is to D,** A est à B comme C est à D; **ten francs just as it stands,** dix francs tel quel; **leave it as it is,** laissez-le tel quel, tel qu'il est; **as it is, we must . . .,** les choses étant ainsi, comme il en est, en l'occurrence, il nous faut . . .; **you have too many friends as it is,** vous avez déjà trop d'amis; **as was also the case with me,** comme il en était, en fut, de moi; **yesterday as it were,** comme qui dirait hier; **as you were!** (i) *Mil: Gym:* revenez! au temps! *F:* remettez ça! (ii) *F:* pardon, ce n'est pas cela que je voulais dire! (*b*) **as . . ., so . . .: (just) as we must know how to command, so must we know how to obey,** de même qu'il faut savoir commander, (de même) il faut savoir obéir; **as a man lives, so he dies,** comme on a vécu, ainsi l'on meurt; **as it is with the parents, so it is with the children,** il en est des enfants comme des parents; (*c*) **they rose as one man,** ils se levèrent comme un seul homme; (*d*) **as I live, I saw him strike the blow!** aussi vrai que je suis en vie, je l'ai vu frapper le coup! **if I had been present, as I was not, I should have voted against him,** si j'avais été présent, ce qui n'est pas le cas, j'aurais voté contre lui; (*e*) (*introducing a predicate complement*) **to consider s.o. as a friend,** considérer qn comme un ami; **to describe s.o. as having exceptional talent,** décrire qn comme ayant un talent exceptionnel; **to treat s.o. as a stranger,** traiter qn en étranger; **to recognize s.o. as one's son,** reconnaître qn pour son fils; **I had him as a master,** je l'ai eu pour maître; **I suspect my nephew as the author of the mischief,** je soupçonne mon neveu d'être l'auteur du méfait; **he was often ill as a child,** enfant il fut souvent malade; il fut souvent malade dans son enfance; **to use sth. as a flag,** se servir de qch. comme drapeau, en guise de drapeau; **he was there as a relative,** il était là à titre de parent; *F:* **X is coming too.—What as?** X vient aussi—à quel titre? **to send sth. as a present,** envoyer qch. en, comme, cadeau; *Th:* **X as Hamlet,** X dans le rôle de Hamlet; **to act as interpreter,** servir d'interprète; **to act as secretary,** (i) servir de secrétaire; (ii) agir en qualité de secrétaire; **the letter I wrote as president,** la lettre que j'ai écrite en ma qualité de président; **I acted in my capacity as a magistrate,** j'ai agi en ma qualité de magistrat; **a study of Dumas as writer and as man,** une étude de Dumas en tant qu'écrivain et en tant qu'homme; **to act as a father,** agir en père; **to be dressed as a page,** être habillé en page; **what will you go to the fancy-dress ball as?—as a pierrot, as Henry VIII,** en quoi serez-vous au bal costumé?—en pierrot, en costume de Henri VIII; **as a nation, we do not care for books,** en tant que nation, dans l'ensemble de notre nation, nous n'estimons guère les livres; **as a very old friend of your father's,** en tant que vieil ami de votre père; **my rights as a father,** mes droits de père; **as one doctor to another,** soit dit entre médecins; **its value as literature,** sa valeur en tant qu'œuvre littéraire; **a patois, as distinct from a dialect,** un patois, en tant qu'il diffère d'un dialecte; **as a revenge for . . .,** pour se venger de . . .. **4.** (*time*) (*a*) **as I was opening the door,** comme j'ouvrais la porte; au moment où j'ouvrais la porte; **he went out (just) as I came in,** il est sorti comme, au moment (même) où, j'entrais; **one day as I was sitting . . .,** un jour que j'étais assis . . .; **they were murdered as they lay asleep,** ils furent assassinés pendant qu'ils dormaient, pendant leur sommeil; (*b*) **he grew more charitable as he grew older,** il devenait plus charitable à mesure qu'il vieillissait; **the child grows handsomer as she grows older,** l'enfant embellit en grandissant; **as he met her more often and knew her better, they became good friends,** à la rencontrer plus souvent et à la mieux connaître, ils devinrent bons amis; **he drew back as I advanced,** à mesure que j'avançais, il reculait; **I shall order the volumes as published,** je commanderai les volumes au fur et à mesure de leur publication; **as and when required,** à discrétion; **as and when I want,** à mon bon plaisir; **as and when they are needed,** au moment où on en a besoin. **5.** (*reason*) **as you are not ready, we cannot go,** comme vous n'êtes pas prêt, nous ne pouvons pas partir; **as I am going that way, I shall fetch them,** puisque j'y passe, je les rapporterai. **6.** (*result*) **he arranged matters so as to please everyone,** il arrangea les choses de manière, de façon, à contenter tout le monde; **be so good as to come,** soyez assez bon pour venir; veuillez (bien) avoir la bonté de venir; **he is not so foolish as to believe it,** il n'est pas assez stupide pour le croire; **put on your gloves so as to be ready,** mettez vos gants pour être prêt, de manière à être prêt. **7.** *O:* **mother is well, as are the children, as also the children,** maman va bien, de même que les enfants, et les enfants de même.

III. *rel.pron.* **I had the same trouble as you,** j'ai eu les mêmes difficultés que vous; **beasts of prey, (such) as the lion or tiger,** les bêtes fauves, telles que, comme, le lion ou le tigre; **I am old, as you can see,** je suis âgé, comme vous pouvez le voir; **he was a foreigner, as they noticed from his pronunciation,** il était étranger, ce qui se percevait à sa prononciation.

asafoetida [æsə'fetidə, -'fiː-], *s.* **1.** *Bot:* férule *f* persique. **2.** *Pharm: etc:* assa fœtida *f*.

asarabacca [æsərə'bækə], *s. Bot:* asaret *m* d'Europe; oreille *f* d'homme; oreillette *f*.

asarum ['æsərəm], *s. Bot:* asaret *m*.

asbestine [æz'bestin], *a.* **1.** *Miner:* asbestin, amiantin. **2.** semblable à l'amiante; incombustible.

asbestos [æz'bestəs], *s. Miner:* amiante *m*; **flaked a.,** amiante floconneux; *Ind:* **brass-reinforced a.,** amiante armé de laiton; **sprayed (limpet) a.,** amiante projeté; **woven a.,** amiante tissé; **a. cement,** Fibrociment *m* (*R.t.m.*), amiante-ciment *m*; **a. cord,** tresse *f* d'amiante (pour chaudières); **a. twine,** corde *f* d'amiante; **a. board, sheet,** carton *m* d'amiante; **a. joint,** joint *m* à l'amiante au carton d'amiante; **a.-faced,** à surface amiantée.

asbestosis [æzbes'tousis], *s. Med:* asbestose *f*.

asbolan ['æzboulæn], **asbolite** ['æzboulait], *s. Miner:* asbolane *f*, wad *m*.

Ascanius [æs'keiniəs], *Pr.n.m. Lt.Lit:* Ascagne.

Ascaphidae [æs'kæfidiː], *s.pl. Amph:* ascaphidés *m*.

ascariasis [æskə'raiəsis], **ascaridiasis** [æskəri'daiəsis], *s. Med:* ascaridiose *f*.

ascarid ['æskərid], *s. Ann: Med:* ascaride *m*, ascaris *m*, lombric (intestinal).

Ascaridae [æs'kæridiː], *s.pl. Ann: Med:* ascaridés *m*.

ascaris, *pl.* **ascarides** ['æskəris, æs'kæridiːz], *s.* = ASCARID.

ascend [ə'send]. **1.** *v.i.* (*a*) monter; **the balloon was ascending,** le ballon montait; *Ecc:* **He ascended into Heaven,** il monta aux Cieux; (*b*) *A:* (*of genealogical line*) remonter. **2.** *v.tr.* (*a*) **to a. the throne,** monter sur le trône; *Lit:* **to a. the pulpit,** monter en chaire; (*b*) *A:* **to a. a mountain, a hill,** faire l'ascension d'une montagne; gravir une colline; *A: & Lit:* **to a. a stair,** monter un escalier; **to a. a tree,** grimper, monter, à un arbre; (*c*) **to a. a river,** remonter un fleuve.

ascendancy, -ency [ə'sendənsi], *s. Lit:* **1.** ascendant *m*, pouvoir *m*, influence *f* (**over s.o.,** sur qn); **he had gained such an a. over them that . . .,** il avait pris sur eux un tel ascendant que . . .; **to exercise an a. over s.o.,** exercer une influence sur qn. **2.** (*of nation, etc.*) **to rise to a.,** arriver à la suprématie.

ascendant, -ent [ə'sendənt]. **1.** *a.* (*a*) *Astrol: Mth: etc:* ascendant; **a. star,** astre ascendant; (*b*) *Bot:* **a. stem,** tige montante. **2.** *s.* (*a*) *Astrol:* ascendant *m*; **to be in the a.,** (i) (*of point of the ecliptic*) être à l'ascendant; (ii) *Fig:* avoir le dessus, s'affirmer; prédominer, avoir une grande autorité; **his star is in the a.,** son étoile est à l'ascendant; son étoile grandit; (*b*) *Jur:* ascendant; **our ascendants and our descendants,** nos ascendants et nos descendants.

ascender [ə'sendər], *s. Typ:* tête *f* d'une lettre montante.

ascending [ə'sendiŋ], *a.* **1.** *Astr: Mth: etc:* ascendant; **a. series,** progression croissante; **in a. order,** en ordre croissant; *Mus:* **a. scale,** gamme ascendante, montante; *Anat:* **a. colon,** côlon ascendant. **2.** (*a*) *Meteor:* **a. current,** courant ascendant; *Av:* **a. power,** puissance *f* de montée, force ascensionnelle; (*b*) *Min:* **a. working,** battage remontant; (*c*) *Bot:* **a. stem,** tige montante. **3.** *Jur:* **a. line,** ascendance *f*; ligne ascendante (de parenté).

ascension [ə'senʃ(ə)n]. **1.** *s.* ascension *f*; *esp. Ecc:* **A. Day,** jour *m,* fête *f,* de l'Ascension; *Astr:* **right a.,** ascension droite (d'un astre); **oblique a.,** ascension oblique. **2.** *Pr.n. Geog:* **A. (Island),** (l'île *f* de l')Ascension.

ascensional [ə'senʃənl], *a.* (mouvement) ascensionnel.

ascensionist [ə'senʃ(ə)nist], *s. Aer:* ascension(n)iste *mf.*

Ascensiontide [ə'senʃəntaid], *s. Ecc:* l'Ascension *f.*

ascensive [ə'sensiv], *a.* (*a*) ascendant, montant; (*b*) *Gram:* emphatique.

ascent [ə'sent], *s.* **1.** (*a*) ascension *f* (d'une montagne); **first a.,** première *f*; **balloon a.,** ascension en ballon; **to make an a.,** faire une ascension; (*b*) ascension (d'un ballon); **the a. of Napoleon,** l'ascension, l'essor *m,* de Napoléon; (*c*) montée *f,* remontée *f* (d'un piston, etc.); (*d*) **a. of salmon (from sea to river),** remonte *f.* **2.** montée, pente *f,* rampe *f*; **there is a steep a. to the top,** il y a une forte montée jusqu'au sommet; la montée est très raide avant le sommet. **3.** *Jur:* **line of a.,** ascendance *f.*

ascertain [æsə'tein], *v.tr.* constater (un fait); s'assurer, s'informer, de (la vérité de qch.); se rendre compte de (sa position); **to a. sth. from s.o.,** s'informer de qch. auprès de qn; **to a. whether a piece of news is true,** vérifier une nouvelle; s'assurer si une nouvelle est vraie; **it is difficult to a. whether . . .,** il est difficile de savoir si . . .; **to a. that all danger is over,** s'assurer que tout danger est écarté, qu'il n'y a plus de danger; **when we had ascertained that there were no casualties . . .,** quand nous eûmes acquis la certitude qu'il n'y avait pas de blessés . . .

ascertainable [æsə'teinəbl], *a.* (fait) que l'on peut constater, dont on peut s'assurer, s'informer; (fait) vérifiable.

ascertained [æsə'teind], *a.* (fait) constaté, établi; **a. damages,** dégâts constatés.

ascertainment [æsə'teinmənt], *s.* **1.** constatation *f* (d'un fait). **2.** vérification *f.*

ascesis [ə'si:sis], *s. Phil:* ascèse *f.*

ascetic [ə'setik]. **1.** *a.* ascétique, **a. books,** *s.pl.* **ascetics,** ascétiques *m.* **2.** *s.* ascète *mf,* ascétique *mf.*

ascetical [ə'setik(ə)l], *a.* **1. a. theology,** l'ascétique *f.* **2.** ascétique.

ascetically [ə'setik(ə)li], *adv.* ascétiquement; (vivre) en ascète; **a. minded,** enclin à l'ascétisme.

asceticism [ə'setisizm], *s.* ascétisme *m*; ascétique *f.*

ascians ['æʃianz], *s.pl. Geog:* asciens *m.*

Ascidiacea [æsidi'eisiə], *s.pl. Coel:* ascidiacés *m.*

ascidian [ə'sidiən], *a.* & *s. Coel:* ascidien (*m*), tunicier (*m*); **colonial ascidians,** didemnidés *m.*

ascidiform [ə'sidifɔ:m], *a. Bot: etc:* ascidiforme.

ascidium, *pl.* **-a** [ə'sidiəm, -ə], *s.* **1.** *Bot:* ascidie *f.* **2.** *Coel:* ascidie, *F:* outre *f* de mer.

ascites [ə'saiti:z], *s. Med: Vet:* ascite *f*; hydropisie *f* ascite.

ascitic(al) [ə'saitik(l)], *a. Med: Vet:* ascite, ascitique.

asclepiad [æs'kli:piæd], *s.* **1.** *Pros:* asclépiade *m.* **2.** *Bot:* asclépiadée *f.*

Asclepiadaceae [æskli:piə'deisii:], *s.pl. Bot:* asclépiad(ac)ées *f.*

Asclepiades [æs'kli:piədi:z], *Pr.n.m. Gr.Ant:* Asclépiade.

asclepias [æs'kli:piəs], *s. Bot:* asclépiade *f.*

ascochyta [æs'kɔkitə], *s. Fung:* ascochyta *m.*

ascogenous [æs'kɔdʒənəs], *a. Fung:* ascogène.

ascogone ['æskɔgoun], **ascogonium,** *pl.* **-ia** [æskə'gouniəm, -iə], *s. Fung:* ascogone *m.*

ascolichen [æskou'laikən], *s.* ascolichen *m.*

ascoloy ['æskəlɔi], *s.* acier américain au chrome.

Ascomycetes [æskoumai'si:ti:z], *s.pl. Fung:* ascomycètes *m.*

ascophyllum [æskou'filəm], *s. Algae:* ascophylle *f.*

ascorbic [əs'kɔ:bik], *a.* ascorbique; **a. acid,** acide *m* ascorbique.

ascospore ['æskouspɔər], *s. Fung:* ascospore *f.*

Ascothoracica [æskouθɔ'reisikə], *s.pl. Crust:* ascothoraciques *m.*

ascribable [ə'skraibəbl], *a.* attribuable, imputable **(to,** à).

ascribe [ə'skraib], *v.tr.* **1.** attribuer, imputer **(to,** à); **to a. a disaster to s.o.'s carelessness,** attribuer, imputer, référer, un malheur à la négligence de qn; **he ascribes my election to his influence,** il attribue, rapporte, mon élection à son influence. **2. to a. a characteristic to s.o., a meaning to a word,** attribuer, prêter, un trait à qn, un sens à un mot.

ascription [ə'skripʃ(ə)n], *s.* attribution *f,* imputation *f* **(of sth. to sth.,** de qch. à qch.).

ascus ['æskəs], *s. Biol: Bot:* asque *m* or *f*; thèque *f.*

asdic ['æzdik], *s. Nav:* (*from anti-submarine detection investigation committee*) asdic *m.*

aseismic [ei'saizmik], *a. Geol:* aséismique.

aseismicity [eisaiz'misiti], *s. Geol:* aséismicité *f.*

aseitas [ei'si:itæs], **aseity** [ei'si:iti], *s. Theol:* aséité *f.*

asemia [ei'si:miə], *s. Med:* asémie *f.*

asepsis [ei'sepsis], *s. Med:* asepsie *f.*

aseptic [ei'septik], *a.* & *s. Med:* aseptique (*m*).

asepticism [ei'septisizm], *s. Med:* asepsie *f.*

asepticize [ei'septisaiz], *v.tr. Med:* aseptiser (une plaie, etc.).

asepticizing [ei'septisaiziŋ], *s. Med:* aseptisation *f.*

asexual [ei'seksjuəl], *a. Biol:* asexué, asexuel; *Bot:* **a. flower,** fleur *f* neutre.

asexuality ['eiseksju'æliti], *s.* caractère asexuel **(of,** de).

ash[1] [æʃ], *s.* **1.** *Bot:* (*a*) **a. (tree),** frêne *m*; **a. grove,** frênaie *f*; (*b*) **manna a., flowering a.,** frêne à fleurs; orne *m*; **bitter a.,** quassier *m* de (la) Jamaïque; **mountain a.,** sorbier commun, sauvage, des oiseaux, des oiseleurs. **2.** *O:* bâton *m* de route.

ash[2], *s.* **1.** (*a*) cendre(s) *f*(*pl*); **cigar a.,** cendre de cigare; **he dropped some (cigar) a. on his trousers,** il a laissé tomber de la cendre sur son pantalon; **to reduce, burn, sth. to ashes,** réduire qch. en cendres; **a. content of a fuel,** résidu *m* en cendres d'un combustible; **to rake out the ashes,** enlever les cendres; **a. constituents,** principes minéraux (d'une plante, etc.); **volcanic a.,** cendres volcaniques; **a. cloud,** nuée *f* de cendres (au-dessus d'un volcan); **incandescent a. cloud,** nuée ardente; *Lit:* **to rake over the ashes of the past,** tisonner les cendres du passé; *Ecc:* **A. Wednesday,** le mercredi des Cendres; (*b*) *Mch: etc:* **ashes,** escarbilles *f*; **a. ejector, hoist,** escarbilleur *m*; éjecteur *m* d'escarbilles; **a. hole, pit,** cendrier *m,* fosse *f* aux cendres, à escarbilles; *Metall:* **a. spot,** cendrure *f* (dans le fer, etc.); **a. heap,** crassier *m*; (*c*) *a.* & *s.* (*also* **ash grey**) cendré (*m*), gris cendré (*m*) *inv.* **2.** *pl.* (*a*) **(mortal remains)** cendres (des morts); dépouille mortelle; **peace to his ashes!** paix à ses cendres! (*b*) *Cr:* **the Ashes,** le trophée que les équipes anglaises et australiennes se disputent. **3.** *Ch: Ind:* **blue ashes, a. blue,** cendre bleue; **lead ash(es),** cendre de plomb; cendrée *f.*

ash[3], *v.tr.* **1.** couvrir (qch.) de cendres; *Metall:* **to a. a mould,** cendrer un moule à fonte. **2.** *Ch:* minéraliser.

ashamed [ə'ʃeimd], *a.* **1.** honteux, confus; **to be a. of s.o., of sth.,** avoir honte de qn, de qch.; **I am a. of you,** vous me faites honte; **to feel a.,** être couvert de confusion; **to be, feel, a. to do sth., of doing sth.,** avoir honte, être honteux, de faire qch.; éprouver de la honte à faire qch.; avoir honte à faire qch.; **I am a. to have to ask you this favour,** je suis confus d'avoir à vous demander cette faveur; **you make me feel a.,** (i) vous me rendez confus; (ii) vous me faites honte; **I am a. to say that . . .,** j'avoue à ma confusion que . . .; **I am a. that you were forgotten,** je suis confus qu'on vous ait oublié; **you ought to be a. of yourself,** vous devriez avoir honte, être honteux; **there is nothing to be a. of,** il n'y a pas de quoi avoir honte; **I told him he ought to be a. of his ingratitude,** je lui ai dit qu'il devrait avoir honte de son ingratitude. **2. unable to work and a. to beg,** incapable de travailler et trop fier pour mendier.

Ashanti [ə'ʃænti], *s.* **1.** *Ethn:* Achanti, -ie. **2.** *Ling:* achanti *m.*

ashbin ['æʃbin], *s. esp. NAm:* boîte *f* à ordures; poubelle *f.*

ash-blond ['æʃ'blɔnd], *a.* blond cendré *inv.*

ash boat ['æʃbout], *s. Nau:* allège *f,* bette *f,* chaland *m,* à escarbilles.

ashcake ['æʃkeik], *s. U.S:* gâteau (de maïs) cuit sous la cendre.

ashcan ['æʃkæn], *s. NAm:* = ASHBIN.

ashen[1] ['æʃn], *a.* de frêne, en frêne.

ashen[2], *a. Lit:* **1.** (pluie, etc.) de cendres. **2.** (*of colour*) cendré; couleur de cendres; (gris) pâle; (*of face*) pâle comme la mort; blanc comme un linge; **a. complexion,** visage terreux.

ash-grey ['æʃ'grei], *a.* gris cendré *inv*; cendré; cendreux, -euse.

ash grub ['æʃgrʌb], *s. Fish:* larve *f* du cynips des feuilles de chêne.

ash key ['æʃki:], *s. Bot:* samare *f* de frêne.

ashlar[1] ['æʃlər], *s. Const: Arch:* (*a*) pierre *f* de taille; moellon *m* d'appareil; **bastard a., rough a.,** moellonage *m,* libage *m*; **a. work,** appareil *m* en moellons; moellonage; (*b*) parements *mpl,* revêtement *m* (des murs d'un édifice).

ashlar[2], *v.tr.* donner à (un édifice) un parement en pierre de taille.

ashlaring ['æʃləriŋ], *s. Const:* **1.** parement *m* en pierre de taille. **2.** cloison verticale (d'une mansarde).

ashore [ə'ʃɔ:r], *adv. Nau:* **1.** à terre; **to be a.,** être à terre; **to go a.,** aller, descendre, à terre; débarquer; **to set, put, (passengers, etc.) a.,** débarquer (des passagers, etc.). **2.** échoué; **to be driven a.,** être jeté à la côte; (*of ship*) **to run a.,** s'échouer; faire côte; se jeter à la côte; **we're a.,** nous sommes à la côte.

ashpan ['æʃpæn], *s.* cendrier *m* (de poêle); garde-cendres *m inv.*

ashplant ['æʃplɑ:nt], *s.* bâton *m* de route.

ashtray ['æʃtrei], *s.* cendrier *m* (de fumeur).

ashy ['æʃi], *a.* **1.** cendreux, couvert de cendres. **2.** cendré, couleur de cendres; **his face went a. pale,** il devint blême, pâle comme la mort; son visage blêmit.

Asia ['eiʃə], *Pr.n. Geog:* Asie *f*; **A. Minor,** Asie Mineure.

asialia [æzi'eiliə], *s. Med:* asialie *f.*

Asian ['eiʃn, 'eiʒn]. **1.** *a.* asiatique, asiate; *Med:* **A. flu,** grippe *f* asiatique. **2.** *s.* Asiatique *mf.*

Asianic [eisi'ænik], *a. Ling:* asianique.

Asiarch ['eisiɑ:k], *s. Rom.Ant:* asiarque *m.*

Asiatic [eisi'ætik, eiʃi-]. **1.** *a.* asiatique; d'Asie; **A. cholera,** choléra *m* asiatique. **2.** *s.* Asiatique *mf.*

aside [ə'said]. **1.** *adv.* de côté; à l'écart; à part; **to pull (a curtain, etc.) a.,** écarter (un rideau, etc.); **to push sth. a.,** écarter qch. d'une poussée; **to lay, put, sth. a.,** mettre qch. de côté; **to stand a.,** (i) se tenir à l'écart, à part; (ii) se ranger; **to step a.,** s'écarter, se ranger; **to draw a. to let s.o. pass,** s'effacer pour laisser passer qn; **to slip a.,** se dérober **(from,** à); **to turn a.,** se détourner **(from,** de); **putting that a.,** à part cela; laissant cela de côté; **I took, drew, him a.,** je le pris à part, à l'écart, en particulier; **leaving patriotism a., I should not like to . . .,** patriotisme à part, je ne voudrais pas . . .; *Th:* **(words spoken) a.,** (paroles dites) en aparté. **2.** *prep.phr. NAm:* **aside from:** (*a*) à part; **a. from my own interest,** mon propre intérêt à part; (*b*) en plus de; **a. from being a plane stop it is a river port,** c'est un port fluvial aussi bien qu'une escale aérienne; (*c*) excepté, sauf; **a. from the fright I was unhurt,** j'en ai été quitte pour la peur. **3.** *s.* remarque faite à l'écart; à-côté *m, pl.* à-côtés; *Th:* aparté *m.*

asiderite [æ'sidərait], *s. Miner:* asidère *f,* asidérite *f.*

Asilidae [ə'sailidi:], *s.pl. Ent:* asilidés *m.*

asilus [ə'sailəs], *s. Ent:* asile *m.*

asimina [æ'siminə], *s. Bot:* asiminier *m.*

asinine ['æsinain], *a.* (*a*) (race) asine; (type) asinien; (*b*) *F:* stupide, sot; digne d'un âne; **that was an a. thing to do,** ça, c'était vraiment une bêtise.

asininity [æsi'niniti], *s. F:* stupidité *f,* bêtise *f.*

asiphonate [ei'saifəneit], *a.* & *s. Moll:* asiphoné (*m*).

asity ['æsiti], *s. Orn:* philépitte *f.*

ask [ɑ:sk], *v.tr.* & *i.* **(asked** [ɑ:skt]) demander. **1.** (*inquire*) **to a. s.o. sth.,** demander qch. à qn; **a. him his name,** demandez-lui son nom; **to a. the time,** demander l'heure; **to a. s.o. a question,** poser une question à qn; **a. any questions you like,** posez toutes les questions que vous voulez; *Turf:* (*of jockey*) **to a. the question,** pousser le cheval; **a. him how old he is,** demandez-lui son âge; **she asked him how he was,** elle lui a demandé des nouvelles de sa santé; **a. a policeman,** adressez-vous à un agent de police; **it may be asked whether . . .,** on peut se demander si . . .; **to a. s.o. the way,** demander son chemin à qn; *F:* **if you a. me,** à mon avis; *F:* (*intensive*) **he says he paid £500 for it; I a. you!** il dit qu'il l'a payé £500; je vous demande (un peu)! *F:* **a. me another!** je n'ai pas la moindre idée! **2.** (*a*) (*beg for, request to be given*) **to a. a favour of s.o., to a. s.o. a favour,** demander une faveur à qn; **if it isn't asking too much,** si ce n'est pas une trop grande faveur à vous demander; **it's asking too much of me, too much to a. of me,** c'est trop me demander; **he's always asking for sth.,** il est toujours à demander qch.; ce sont des quémanderies sans fin; **to a. s.o.'s permission to do sth.,** demander à qn la permission de faire qch.; (*b*) (*of price*) **how much are you asking for it?** combien en voulez-vous? **to ask 600 francs for sth.,** demander 600 francs pour qch., de qch.; **to ask too much for an article,** surfaire un article; **they are asking too much for this house,** ils demandent trop pour cette maison. **3.** (*request*) (*a*) **to a. to do sth.,** demander à faire qch.; demander la permission, l'autorisation, de faire qch.; **he asked to be admitted,** il demanda à être admis; **to a. to be excused,** (i) s'excuser de partir; (ii) *Sch:* demander la permission de sortir; (*b*) **to a. s.o. to do sth.,** demander à qn, prier qn, solliciter qn, de faire qch.; **to ask s.o. to attend,** requérir la présence de qn; convoquer qn; **I have been asked to show you these samples,** je suis chargé de vous soumettre ces échantillons; **I will now a. Mr Martin to address the meeting, move the resolution, etc.,** la parole est à M. Martin; **ask him to wait,** priez-le d'attendre; **ask him to come in,** priez-le d'entrer; faites-le entrer; **being asked to speak . . .,** étant prié de parler . . .; **a. her to sing,** demandez-lui de chanter. **4.** (*a*) **to a. about sth.,** se renseigner sur qch.; **to ask s.o. about sth.,** interroger qn sur qch.; se renseigner sur qch. auprès de qn; **he asked me all about my work,** il m'a demandé toutes sortes de renseignements, m'a interrogé longuement, sur mon travail; (*b*) **to a. after, about, s.o., about s.o.'s health,** demander des nouvelles de (la santé de) qn; **he asked me about him, her,** il m'a demandé de ses nouvelles. **5.** (*a*) **to a. for s.o.,** demander à voir qn; **I asked for the manager,** je demandai à parler au gérant; j'ai demandé le gérant; (*b*) **to a. for sth.,** demander qch.; faire la demande de qch.; solliciter qch.; **you'll get nothing without asking,** vous n'obtiendrez rien sans demander; **to a. s.o. for sth.,** demander qch. à qn; **we were asked for our passports,** on nous demanda nos passeports; **to a. for work,** demander du travail; **to a. for leave of absence,** demander un congé; **to a. for something to eat, to drink,** demander à manger, à boire; **to a. for something to read,** demander qch. à lire; **to a. for time,** demander un délai; **to a. for a rise,** demander une augmentation; **to a. for security,** demander une caution, une garantie; **to a. for more,** en redemander; **to a. for sth. back,** redemander (un objet prêté, etc.); **to be asking for trouble,** aller au-devant des ennuis; *F:* ne demander que plaies et bosses; *F:* **he's been asking for it!** il l'a bien cherché! il ne l'a pas volé! (*c*) (*of thg*) **it asks for attention, for care,** cela demande de l'attention, du soin. **6.** *Ecc:* (*a*) *A:* **to ask the banns,** publier les bans; (*b*) (*usu. passive*) **to a. s.o. in church,** publier les bans de qn; **she was asked in church yesterday,** ses bans ont été publiés hier; **this is the first time of asking,** c'est ici la première publication. **7.** inviter; **to a. s.o. to lunch,** inviter qn à déjeuner; **to a. s.o. back,** rendre une invitation, rendre la politesse; **it was you who asked him here,** c'est vous qui l'avez invité à venir ici; **I have written asking him to come,** je lui ai écrit de venir; **to a. s.o. in, out, up,** demander à qn, prier qn, d'entrer, de sortir, de monter; inviter qn à entrer, à sortir, à monter; **he was asked into the drawing room,** on le fit entrer au salon; **I am asked out for the evening,** je suis invité chez des amis, en ville, pour la soirée; **I have asked him** (i) **up,** (ii) **down, for the weekend,** je l'ai invité à passer le week-end (i) en ville, (ii) à la campagne; **as we hadn't been asked we have asked ourselves,** comme nous n'étions pas invités nous nous sommes invités nous-mêmes.

askance [ə'skæns, -ɑːns], *A:* **askant** [ə'skænt], *adv.* de côté, du coin de l'œil, obliquement; **to look a. at s.o., at sth.,** regarder qn, qch., de travers, avec méfiance, d'un œil malveillant.

askari ['æskəri], *s.m. Mil: etc:* (*in Africa*) askari, ascari.

askeletal [ei'skelətl], *a. Z:* sans squelette.

asker ['ɑːskər], *s.* **1.** interrogateur, -trice. **2.** quémandeur, -euse.

askew [ə'skjuː], *adv.* (*a*) de biais, de côté; **to put one's clothes on a.,** s'habiller de guingois; **his nose is a.,** il a le nez de travers; **to look a. at s.o.,** jeter à qn un regard de côté, un regard fuyant; (*b*) **to cut (a plank, etc.) a.,** couper (une planche, etc.) à fausse équerre.

asking ['ɑːskiŋ], *s.* **1.** *A:* **a. of the banns,** publication *f* des bans. **2. you may have it, it's yours for the a.,** il ne vous en coûtera que la peine de le demander; il n'y a qu'à (le) demander; **this privilege is to be had for the a.,** ce privilège s'obtient très facilement; **it can be had for the a.,** cela se donne. **3. a. price,** prix demandé.

aslant [ə'slɑːnt]. **1.** *adv.* obliquement, de travers, de biais; **the rain was falling a.,** la pluie tombait obliquement. **2.** *prep.* **the engine lay a. the track,** la locomotive était couchée en travers de la voie.

asleep [ə'sliːp], *adv.* & *a.* **1.** endormi; **to be a.,** dormir, sommeiller; **to be fast, sound, a.,** être profondément endormi, plongé dans le sommeil; dormir profondément, sur les deux oreilles; dormir d'un profond sommeil; **he lay a.,** il dormait; **to fall, drop a.,** s'endormir; **I was so tired that I was falling a. on my feet,** j'étais si fatigué que je dormais debout; **to fall a. again,** se rendormir; (*euphemism for* **die**) **to fall a.,** entrer dans le repos éternel. **2.** (*a*) **my foot is a.,** j'ai le pied engourdi, endormi; (*b*) *Games:* **top that is a.,** toupie qui dort.

asmanite ['æsmənait], *s. Miner:* asmanite *f.*

Asmodeus [æs'moudiəs, æsmou'diːəs], *Pr.n.m. B:* Asmodée.

asocial ['ei'souʃiəl, -'souʃəl], *a.* asocial, -aux.

asomatognosia [eisəmatəg'nouziə], *s. Med:* asomatognosie *f.*

asp [æsp], *s. Rept:* **1.** *Hist:* aspic *m* de Cléopâtre; serpent *m* à lunettes. **2.** (vipère *f*) aspic.

asparaginase [æspə'rædʒineiz], *s. Bio-Ch:* asparaginase *f.*

asparagine [æs'pærədʒiːn], *s. Bio-Ch:* asparagine *f.*

asparagus [əs'pærəgəs], *s. Bot:* (*genus*) asparagus *m*; *coll. Hort: Cu:* asperges *fpl*; **a stick of a.,** une asperge; **a.-bed,** plant *m* d'asperges; **a. tongs,** pince *f* à asperges; *Bot:* **a. fern,** asparagus, asperge plumeuse; *Ent:* **a. beetle,** criocère *m* de l'asperge; *Miner:* **a. stone,** asparagolite *f.*

aspartic [æs'pɑːtik], *a. Ch:* (acide *m*) aspartique.

aspect ['æspekt], *s.* **1.** exposition *f,* vue *f*; orientation *f*; **to have a northern a.,** être exposé au nord; avoir une exposition nord; faire face au nord; être orienté au nord; **flats with southern a.,** appartements *m* côté midi. **2.** aspect *m,* air *m*; (*a*) **to examine the different aspects of a subject,** examiner les différents aspects d'un sujet; **to see sth. in its true a.,** voir qch. sous son véritable point de vue, sous son vrai jour; **to wear quite another a.,** changer tout à fait de face; prendre un air tout autre; **to study every a. of a question,** étudier une question sous toutes ses faces; étudier le fort et le faible, le pour et le contre, d'une question; (*b*) *Astrol:* **a. of the planets,** aspect des planètes. **3.** *Ling: Gram:* aspect *m* (du verbe). **4.** *attrib.* (*a*) *Av:* **a. ratio,** allongement *m* (d'une aile); **wing with an a. ratio of 10·75,** voilure *f* d'allongement 10,75; (*b*) *Cmptr:* **a. card,** carte *f* de recherche.

aspectual [æs'pektjuəl], *a. Gram:* aspectuel.

aspen ['æspən]. **1.** *s. Bot:* (peuplier *m*) tremble *m.* **2.** a. **a. leaf,** feuille *f* de tremble; **a. grove,** tremblaie *f.*

asperge [æs'pəːdʒ], *v.tr.* asperger.

asperges [æs'pəːdʒiːz], *s. Ecc:* asperges *m.*

Aspergillales [æspərdʒi'leiliːz], *s.pl. Fung:* aspergillales *f.*

aspergilliform [æspə'dʒilifɔːm], *a. Bot:* aspergilliforme.

aspergillin [æspə'dʒilin], *s. Fung: Pharm:* aspergilline *f.*

aspergillosis [æspədʒi'lousis], *s. Med:* aspergillose *f.*

aspergillum [æspə'dʒiləm], *s.* **1.** *Ecc:* goupillon *m,* aspergès *m.* **2.** *Moll:* aspergillum *m,* bréchite *m.*

aspergillus [æspə'dʒiləs], *s. Fung:* aspergille *f*; aspergillus *m.*

asperifoliate [æspəri'foulieit], **asperifolious** [æspəri'fouliəs], *a. Bot:* aspérifolié.

asperity [æs'periti], *s.* **1.** (*a*) âpreté *f* (d'un reproche, de la voix); **to speak with a.,** parler d'une voix sèche, âpre; parler âprement; (*b*) rigueur *f,* sévérité *f* (du climat); (*c*) rudesse *f* (de caractère); aspérité *f* (de style). **2.** (*rough excrescence*) aspérité. **3.** *pl.* duretés *f,* rudesses; **having exchanged some asperities,** après avoir échangé des paroles dures.

aspermatism [ei'spəːmətizm], **aspermia** [ei'spəːmiə], *s. Bot: Med:* aspermie *f*; aspermatisme *m.*

aspermous [ei'spəːməs], *a. Bot:* asperme.

asperse [ə'spəːs], *v.tr.* **1.** *A:* **to a. s.o. with water,** (i) asperger qn d'eau; (ii) éclabousser qn. **2.** *Lit:* (*a*) calomnier, diffamer, vilipender (qn); (*b*) **the calumnies with which I have been aspersed,** les calomnies qu'on a répandues sur mon compte; (*c*) **to a. s.o.'s honour, s.o.'s good name,** porter atteinte à l'honneur, à la réputation, de qn; salir, éclabousser, la réputation de qn.

aspersed [ə'spəːst], *a. Her:* semé.

aspersion [əs'pəːʃ(ə)n], *s.* **1.** (*sprinkling*) aspersion *f.* **2.** calomnie *f*; **to cast aspersions on s.o.,** répandre des calomnies sur qn; dire des noirceurs de qn; **to cast aspersions on s.o.'s honour,** porter atteinte à l'honneur de qn.

aspersorium [æspə'sɔːriəm], *s. Ecc:* bénitier portatif.

asperula [æ'sperjulə], *s. Bot:* asperula *f.*

asphalt[1] ['æsfælt], *s. Miner: Civ.E:* asphalte *m*; (*often loosely*) bitume *m*; goudron minéral; poix *f* de Judée; **poured a.,** asphalte coulé; **compressed, rolled, a.,** asphalte comprimé, damé; **mastic a.,** mastic *m* d'asphalte; **a. covering,** revêtement *m* d'asphalte; revêtement bitumé, asphaltique; **a. distributor,** goudronneuse *f*; **a. roadway,** chaussée asphaltée.

asphalt[2], *v.tr. Civ.E:* asphalter, bitumer (une route, etc.).

asphaltene [æsfæl'tiːn], *s. Civ.E:* asphaltène *m.*

asphaltic [æs'fæltik], *a.* asphaltique; **a. (roofing) felt,** carton bitumé (pour toitures); **a. concrete,** béton *m* asphaltique.

asphalting ['æsfæltiŋ], *s.* asphaltage *m,* bitumage *m.*

asphaltite ['æsfæltait], *s. Miner:* asphaltite *m.*

aspheric(al) [ei'sferik(l)], *a.* asphérique.

asphodel ['æsfədel], *s. Bot:* asphodèle *m*; bâton royal; **yellow a.,** bâton de Jacob.

asphygmia [æs'figmiə], *s. Med:* asphygmie *f.*

asphyxia [æs'fiksiə], *s.* asphyxie *f.*

asphyxiant [æs'fiksiənt], *s.* agent asphyxiant.

asphyxiate [æs'fiksieit], *v.tr.* & *i.* (s')asphyxier.

asphyxiating [æs'fiksieitiŋ], *a.* asphyxiant.

asphyxiation [æsfiksi'eiʃ(ə)n], *s.* asphyxie *f.*

aspic[1] ['æspik], *s.* **1.** *A:* = ASP. **2.** *A.Artil:* aspic *m.*

aspic[2], *s. Cu:* aspic *m.*

aspic[3], *s. Bot:* aspic *m*; grande lavande.

aspidiotus [æspidi'outəs], *s. Ent:* aspidiote *m.*

aspidistra [æspi'distrə], *s. Bot:* aspidistra *m.*

aspidium [æs'pidiəm], *s. Bot:* aspidium *m.*

Aspidobranchia [æspidou'bræŋkiə], *s.pl. Moll:* aspidobranches *m.*

aspidosperma [æspidou'spəːmə], *s. Bot:* aspidosperma *m.*

aspirant ['æspir(ə)nt]. **1.** *s.* aspirant, -ante (**to, after,** *A:* **for,** à); candidat, -ate. **2.** *a. A:* & *Lit:* = ASPIRING[1].

aspirate[1] ['æspirət]. *Ling:* **1.** *a.* aspiré. **2.** *s.* (*a*) (lettre) aspirée *f*; (*b*) (la lettre) h; **look after your aspirates,** n'oubliez pas d'aspirer les h.

aspirate[2] ['æspireit], *v.tr.* **1.** aspirer (une voyelle, l'h). **2.** aspirer (un gaz, un liquide).

aspirating ['æspireitiŋ], *a.* aspirant; **a. filter,** filtre *m* à vide.

aspiration [æspi'reiʃ(ə)n], *s.* aspiration *f*; *Med:* **a. biopsy,** ponction-biopsie *f.*

aspirator ['æspireitər], *s.* **1.** *Ph: Med:* aspirateur *m.* **2.** *Agr:* tarare *m*; van *m* mécanique; cribleur *m.* **3.** (*filter-pump*) trompe *f.*

aspiratory [æspi'reit(ə)ri], *a.* aspirateur, -trice; aspiratoire.

aspire [ə'spaiər], *v.i.* **1.** (*a*) aspirer; **to a. to, after, sth.,** aspirer, prétendre, viser, à qch.; ambitionner qch.; soupirer après qch.; **to a. to do sth.,** aspirer à, ambitionner de, faire qch.; (*b*) avoir de l'ambition. **2.** *A:* & *Lit:* (*of smoke, thought, etc.*) monter; s'élever.

aspirin ['æsp(i)rin], *s. Pharm:* aspirine *f*; **take two aspirins,** prenez deux comprimés *m* d'aspirine.

aspiring[1] [ə'spaiəriŋ], *a.* **1.** ambitieux. **2.** *A:* & *Lit:* qui monte vers les nues.

aspiring[2], *s.* aspiration *f.*

Asplenium [æ'spliːniəm], *s. Bot:* asplenium *m,* asplénie *f.*

asporogenic [eeiiiispɔrou'dʒenik], **asporogenous** [eispɔ'rɔdʒənəs], *a. Bot:* asporogène.

asportation [æspɔː'teiʃ(ə)n], *s. Jur:* emport *m* (d'objets volés).

aspredo [æ'spriːdou], *s. Ich:* asprède *m.*

ass[1], *s.* **1.** [æs], âne *m*; **she a.,** ânesse *f*; **ass's foal, ass's colt,** ânon *m*; **ass's milk,** lait *m* d'ânesse; (*b*) **wild a.,** hémione *m*; onagre *m.* **2.** [æs, *occ.* ɑːs], âne; idiot, -ote; sot, sotte; **he's a perfect a.,** c'est un âne bâté; il est bête à manger du foin, bête comme ses pieds; **don't be a silly a.,** ne fais pas l'imbécile, l'idiot; **to make an a. of oneself,** (i) faire l'idiot, l'imbécile; (ii) se donner en spectacle; se faire moquer de soi.

ass[2] [æs, *occ.* ɑːs], *v.i. F:* **to a. about,** faire l'imbécile, l'idiot; faire des bêtises.

ass[3] [æs], *s. U.S: P:* (*not in polite use*) cul *m,* derrière *m*; **a. backwards,** sens dessus dessous.

assacu ['æsəkju], *s. Bot:* assacu *m.*

assafoetida [æsə'fetidə], *s.* = ASAFOETIDA.

assagai ['æsəgai], *s.* = ASSEGAI.

assail [ə'seil], *v.tr. A:* & *Lit:* **1.** (*a*) assaillir, attaquer (l'ennemi, une place forte, etc.); **they assailed us with a volley of stones,** ils nous assaillirent à coups de pierres; **when nations a. each other,** lorsque les nations s'entre-déchirent; **to a. s.o. with insult,** accabler, agonir, qn d'injures; **to a. s.o. with questions,** accabler qn de questions; **the evils that might a. us,** les maux qui pourraient nous atteindre; (*b*) (*of critics, etc.*) **to a. an author,** s'attaquer à un auteur. **2.** (*a*) (*of noise*) **to a. the ear,** frapper l'oreille, les oreilles; (*b*) **when fear assails us,** quand la crainte nous saisit, nous envahit.

assailable [ə'seiləbl], *a. Lit:* (position, doctrine) attaquable; (théorie) qui prête aux attaques, mal défendable.

assailant [ə'seilənt], **assailer** [ə'seilər], *s.* **1.** assaillant, -ante; agresseur *m.* **2.** *Lit:* **the assailants of this new doctrine,** ceux qui s'attaquent à cette nouvelle doctrine.

Assam [æ'sæm], *Pr.n. Geog:* Assam *m.*

Assamese [æsæ'miːz]. **1.** *Geog:* (*a*) *a.* assamais; (*b*) *s.* Assamais, -aise. **2.** *s. Ling:* assamais *m.*

assapan(ic) ['æsəpæn(ik)], *s. Z:* glaucomys *m.*

assart[1] [ə'sɑːt], *s. Agr:* **1.** essart *m.* **2.** essartage *m.*

assart[2], *v.tr. Agr:* essarter (le terrain).

assassin [ə'sæsin], *s.* **1.** assassin *m* (d'un homme d'État, etc.). **2.** *pl. Hist:* **Assassins,** assassins, Ismaïliens *m.* **3.** *attrib. Ent:* **a. bug,** triatome *m*; réduve *m*; **a. fly,** asile *m.*

assassinate [ə'sæsineit], *v.tr.* assassiner.

assassination [əsæsi'neiʃ(ə)n], *s.* assassinat *m.*

assassinator [ə'sæsineitər], *s.* assassin *m.*

assault [ə'sɔːlt], *s.* **1.** (*a*) assaut *m*; attaque (brusquée); **to make an a. on a position,** attaquer, assaillir, une position; **to take, carry, a town by a.,** prendre une ville d'assaut; **a. craft,** engin *m* d'assaut; **a. vehicle,** véhicule *m* de combat; **a. boat, ship,** embarcation *f,* bâtiment *m,* d'assaut; **a. bridge,** pont *m* d'assaut; **a. gun,** canon *m* d'assaut; **a. course,** (i) parcours *m* du combattant; (ii) piste *f* d'assaut; (*b*) *Fenc:* **a. of, at, arms,** assaut d'armes. **2.** (*a*) *Jur:* tentative *f* de voie de fait; **unprovoked a.,** agression *f*; **aggravated a.,** voies *fpl* de fait des plus graves; violence *f*; **a. and battery,** (menaces *fpl* et) voies de fait; coups *mpl* et blessures *fpl*; **to commit an a.,** se porter, se livrer, à des voies de fait (**on,** sur), à une tentative de voies de fait; **criminal a.,** (i) tentative de viol; (ii) viol *m*; **indecent a.,** attentat *m* à la pudeur; outrage *m* aux mœurs.

assault[2], *v.tr.* **1.** attaquer, assaillir (une position); donner l'assaut à (une ville, etc.). **2.** (i) attaquer (qn); (ii) violenter (une femme); **charged with assaulting s.o.,** accusé de s'être porté, livré, à des voies de fait sur qn; **to be assaulted,** être victime (i) d'une agression, (ii) d'un attentat à la pudeur.

assaultable [ə'sɔːltəbl], *a.* attaquable.

assaulter [ə'sɔːltər], *s.* assaillant *m*, agresseur *m*.

assay[1] [ə'sei], *s.* **1.** *Metall: etc:* essai *m* (d'un métal précieux, d'un minerai); *Ch:* dosage *m*; **cold a.,** essai à froid; **dry a.,** essai par voie sèche; **a. value,** teneur *f* (d'un minerai); **a. balance, a. scales,** balance *f* d'essai; trébuchet *m*; pesette *f*; **a. furnace,** fourneau *m* d'essai, four *m* d'essayeur, four à coupelle; **a. spoon,** éprouvette *f*; **to make an a. of. . .,** faire l'essai de. . .; *Adm:* **a. office,** bureau *m* d'essai, de garantie (des métaux précieux); bureau des garanties; **a. master,** essayeur. **2.** *A:* vérification *f* des poids et mesures.

assay[2], *v.tr.* **1.** (*a*) **to a. a precious metal, an ore,** essayer, titrer, analyser, un métal précieux, un minerai; faire l'essai d'un métal; mettre un métal à l'essai; passer un métal à la coupelle; coupeller un métal; (*b*) (*with passive force and adv. extension*) **ore that assays ten per cent of silver,** minerai qui titre dix pour cent d'argent. **2.** *A:* (*try, attempt*) essayer (**to do sth.,** de faire qch.).

assayable [ə'seiəbl], *a. Metall:* titrable.

assayer [ə'seiər], *s. Ch: etc:* essayeur *m*.

assaying [ə'seiiŋ], *s.* essai *m*, titrage *m*, analyse *f* (d'un minerai, etc.); coupellation *f* (de l'or, etc.).

assegai ['æsigai], *s.* zagaie *f*, sagaie *f*.

assemblage [ə'semblidʒ], *s.* **1.** assemblage *m* (de pièces de menuiserie, etc.). **2.** (*a*) assemblage, réunion *f*, concours *m* (de personnes); rassemblement *m*; (*b*) collection *f* (d'objets).

assemble[1] [ə'sembl], *s. Mil:* (signal *m* de) rassemblement *m*.

assemble[2]. **1.** *v.tr.* (*a*) assembler (des personnes); ameuter (des révoltés, etc.); convoquer (un parlement); *Mil:* rassembler (des troupes); (*b*) *Tchn:* assembler (des pièces de menuiserie, etc.); *Mec.E:* ajuster, assembler, monter, construire (une machine); habiller (une montre, etc.); **factory assembled,** monté en usine; (*in foundry*) **to a. the moulds,** mouler les creux. **2.** *v.i.* s'assembler; se rassembler; se réunir (dans un endroit); (*of insurgents, etc.*) s'ameuter.

assemblé [æ'sɑ̃blei], *s. Danc:* assemblé *m*.

assembler [ə'semblər], *s.* **1.** *Ind:* monteur, -euse; ajusteur, -euse; **major a.,** monteur de grosses pièces. **2.** *Cmptr:* assembleur *m*, programme *m* d'assemblage; **one-to-one a.,** traducteur *m* ligne à ligne.

assembling [ə'sembliŋ], *s.* **1.** assemblage *m*; rassemblement *m* (de personnes, de troupes); convocation *f* (d'un parlement); *Mil:* **a. point,** lieu *m* (i) de rassemblement, (ii) de déploiement. **2.** assemblage (d'un meuble, etc.); ajustage *m*, montage *m* (d'une machine); habillage *m* (d'une montre); *Mec.E:* **a. pressure,** pression *f* d'emmanchement.

assembly [ə'sembli], *s.* **1.** assemblement *m*; réunion *f*; (*a*) **place of a.,** lieu *m* de réunion; *Jur:* **unlawful a.,** attroupement *m*; **in open a.,** en séance publique; (*b*) *A:* soirée dansante (par souscription); **a. rooms,** salle *f* des fêtes, salle de danse; (*c*) *Sch: etc:* rassemblement *m*; *Mil:* **a. area,** zone *f* d'attente. **2.** *Pol: etc:* assemblée *f*; **the National A.,** l'Assemblée nationale; *Ecc:* **the General A.,** la réunion annuelle des représentants de l'Église d'Écosse. **3.** (*a*) *Ind: etc:* montage *m*; **a. shop, hall, room,** salle, atelier *m*, de montage; **a. line,** banc *m*, chaîne *f*, de montage; **a. bench,** banc de montage; **a. drawing,** plan *m* de montage; **continuous a.,** montage à la chaîne; **mass a.,** montage en série; **a. line trolley,** chariot *m* de chaîne; *Mil:* **a. area,** aire *f* de montage (des missiles); (*b*) *Cmptr:* **a. language,** langage *m* d'assemblage; **a. process,** assemblage *m*; **a. run,** phase *f* d'assemblage; **a. time,** moment *m* de l'assemblage; **a. programme, routine,** assembleur *m*, programme *m* d'assemblage.

assemblyman, *pl.* **-men** [ə'sembliman], *s. NAm:* membre *m* d'une assemblée (législative).

assent[1] [ə'sent], *s.* assentiment *m*, consentement *m*, acquiescement *m*; *Jur:* agrément *m*; **verbal a.,** consentement verbal; **the royal a.,** le consentement, la sanction, du souverain; la sanction royale; **by common a. he is . . .,** du consentement de tous, il est . . .; **with one a., he was chosen chief,** à l'unanimité il fut choisi pour chef.

assent[2], *v.i.* **1.** (*a*) accéder, acquiescer, donner son assentiment (**to,** à); (*b*) (*of sovereign, etc.*) sanctionner (une loi, etc.). **2.** *Lit:* **to a. to the truth of sth.,** reconnaître la vérité de qch.; reconnaître qch. pour vrai; **to a. to a theory,** admettre une théorie; approuver une théorie.

assentation [æsen'teiʃ(ə)n], *s. A: & Lit:* assentiment obséquieux.

assenter [ə'sentər], *s.* approbateur, -trice.

assentient [ə'senʃənt], *a. & s.* approbateur, -trice.

assenting[1] [ə'sentiŋ], *a.* consentant.

assenting[2], *s.* consentement *m*; approbation *f*.

assentor [ə'sentər], *s. Pol:* signataire *mf* à l'appui (de la mise en avant d'un candidat au Parlement).

assert [ə'səːt], *v.tr.* **1.** (*a*) revendiquer; **to a. one's rights,** revendiquer ses droits; **to a. one's claims to . . .,** faire valoir ses droits à . . .; (*b*) **to a. oneself,** s'imposer; s'affirmer; soutenir, faire respecter, ses droits; **you must a. your authority,** il vous faut imposer votre autorité. **2. to a. that. . .,** affirmer, prétendre, soutenir, que . . .; **to a. one's innocence, one's good faith,** protester de son innocence, de sa bonne foi.

assertion [ə'səːʃ(ə)n], *s.* **1. a. of one's rights,** revendication *f* de ses droits. **2.** assertion *f*, affirmation *f*; **to make an a.,** affirmer qch.; **that bears out my a.,** cela confirme mon dire. **3.** *Cmptr:* **a. box,** pavé *m* d'organigramme.

assertive [ə'səːtiv], *a.* **1.** (*a*) autoritaire; impérieux; dominateur, -trice; outrecuidant; (*b*) (ton, etc.) péremptoire, autoritaire, cassant. **2.** *Gram: Log:* assertif.

assertively [ə'səːtivli], *adv.* **1.** d'une façon autoritaire; péremptoirement; d'un ton cassant. **2.** *Gram: Log:* assertivement.

assertiveness [ə'səːtivnis], *s.* ton *m*, manière *f*, autoritaire.

assertorial [æsəː'tɔːriəl], **assertoric(al)** [æsəː'tɔrik(l)], *a. Phil:* assertoire, assertorique.

assertory [ə'səːtəri], *a.* assertif.

assess [ə'ses], *v.tr.* **1.** (*a*) répartir, établir (un impôt); **to a. the expenses to be paid by each of the members,** répartir les dépenses entre les membres; (*b*) estimer, inventorier; *Jur:* **to a. the damages,** fixer les dommages et intérêts; **to a. a fine,** fixer le montant d'une amende; **to a. the damage,** évaluer les dégâts; *Nau:* évaluer l'avarie; **compensation to be assessed,** compensation à déterminer; (*c*) **to a. the quality of a commodity,** juger de la qualité d'un produit. **2. to a. a loan upon s.o., upon a community,** imposer un prêt à qn, à une société. **3.** *Adm:* **to a. s.o. in, at, so much,** coter, imposer, taxer, qn à tant; fixer la cote de qn à tant; **persons assessed for surtax,** personnes assujetties à la surtaxe. **4.** (*a*) **to a. a property (for taxation),** évaluer une propriété; **to a. a building,** évaluer la valeur locative d'un immeuble; (*b*) **if we a. this speech at its true worth,** si nous estimons ce discours à sa juste valeur.

assessable [ə'sesəbl], *a.* **1.** (impôt) répartissable. **2.** (dommage) évaluable. **3.** (propriété) imposable.

assessed [ə'sest], *a.* **a. taxes,** impôts directs.

assessment [ə'sesmənt], *s.* **1.** (*a*) répartition *f*, assiette *f* (d'un impôt); (*b*) évaluation *f* (de dégâts, *Nau:* d'avarie, *Adm:* d'une propriété); *Jur:* **a. of damages,** fixation *f* de dommages et intérêts; **a. of the value of sth.,** estimation *f* de la valeur de qch.; *Pol.Ec:* **a. of market prospects,** évaluation des perspectives du marché; **demand a.,** évaluation de la demande; **risk a.,** appréciation *f* des risques; (*c*) imposition *f* (d'une commune, d'un immeuble); (*d*) cotisation *f* (du contribuable); **basis of a.,** assiette *f* des impôts; **notice of a.,** avertissement *m* des contributions; **year of a.,** année *f* d'imposition. **2.** (*amount*) cote *f*, taxe officielle; **a. on landed property,** cote foncière; **a. on income,** cote mobilière; impôt *m* sur le revenu; **to claim a reduction of a.,** demander une réduction d'impôts; faire une demande de dégrèvement; **to reduce the a. on a building,** dégrever un immeuble.

assessor [ə'sesər], *s.* **1.** *Jur:* assesseur (adjoint à un juge); juge assesseur. **2.** répartiteur *m* (d'un impôt, etc.); *Adm:* **a. of taxes,** inspecteur *m* des contributions (directes).

assessorial [æse'sɔːriəl], *a. Jur:* (fonctions, etc.) d'assesseur; assessor(i)al, -aux.

assessorship [ə'sesəʃip], *s.* **1.** *Jur:* assessor(i)at *m*. **2.** *Adm.* charge *f* de contrôleur.

asset ['æset], *s.* **1.** chose *f* dont on peut tirer avantage; possession *f*; avoir *m*; **his knowledge of French is a great a. to him,** sa connaissance du français lui est un avantage précieux; **he is a great a. to our party,** c'est un atout dans notre jeu; **he is one of our assets,** c'est une de nos valeurs. **2.** *Fin: etc:* (*a*) *pl.* **assets,** actif *m*, avoir(s) *m* (*pl*); *Jur:* masse *f* d'une succession, d'une société; masse active (d'une liquidation après faillite); **available assets,** actif disponible, liquide; **capital assets,** actif immobilisé; **circulating assets,** capitaux circulants; **frozen assets,** fonds bloqués, non liquides; **liquid assets,** actif liquide; **realizable assets,** actif réalisable; **personal assets,** biens *m* meubles; **real assets,** biens immobiliers; **excess of assets over liabilities,** excédent *m* de l'actif sur le passif; (*b*) *attrib.* **a. turnover,** rotation *f* des capitaux; **a. value,** valeurs *fpl* des actifs; **a. valuation reserve,** provision *f* pour évaluation d'actif.

asseverate [ə'sevəreit], *v.tr.* affirmer (solennellement) (**that,** que + *ind.*); **to a. one's innocence,** protester de son innocence.

asseveration [əsevə'reiʃ(ə)n], *s.* affirmation (solennelle); protestation *f* (d'innocence).

assibilate [ə'sibileit], *v.tr. Ling:* assibiler (un son).

assibilation [əsibi'leiʃ(ə)n], *s. Ling:* assibilation *f*.

assiduity [æsi'djuiti], *s.* **1.** assiduité *f*, diligence *f* (**in doing sth.,** à faire qch.). **2.** *pl. A:* petits soins (**to,** auprès de); prévenances *f* (envers qn); **the assiduities of courtiers,** les assiduités des courtisans.

assiduous [ə'sidjuəs], *a.* **1.** (*of pers.*) assidu; diligent. **2.** (*a*) **a. work,** travail assidu; (*b*) *A:* **a. complaints,** plaintes assidues; plaintes sans fin.

assiduously [ə'sidjuəsli], *adv.* assidûment.

assiduousness [ə'sidjuəsnis], *s.* assiduité *f*.

as(s)iento [æsi'entou], *s. Hist:* asiento *m*.

assign[1] [ə'sain], *s. Jur:* ayant cause *m*, ayant droit *m* (*pl.* ayants cause, ayants droit); délégué, -ée; mandataire *mf*, attributaire *mf*.

assign[2], *v.tr.* **1.** assigner (**to,** à); (*a*) donner (qch.) en partage (à qn); **Paris was assigned to Charibert, Orleans to Clodomir,** Paris fut donné en partage, fut attribué, à Caribert, Orléans à Clodomir; *Mil:* **to a. men to an arm,** verser des hommes dans une arme; (*b*) **to a. a reason for,** *occ.* **to, sth.,** donner la raison de qch.; **to a. a meaning to a word,** attribuer un sens à un mot; **to a. a salary to an office,** attribuer un traitement à un emploi; (*c*) **to a. an hour, a place,** fixer, assigner, une heure, un lieu; (*d*) **to a. a task, a duty, to s.o.,** assigner, attribuer, une tâche, une fonction, à qn; **the duty assigned to me,** la tâche qui m'incombe. **2.** *Jur:* **to a. a property to s.o.,** céder, transférer, une propriété à qn; **to a. a right to s.o.,** attribuer un droit à qn; faire cession d'un droit à qn; **to a. shares, a patent, to s.o.,** transmettre des actions, un brevet, à qn; céder des actions, un brevet, à qn.

assignable [ə'sainəbl], *a.* **1.** (*a*) assignable, attribuable (**to,** à); (*b*) **rates a. to an estate,** contributions afférentes à une terre; (*c*) (date, etc.) que l'on peut fixer, que l'on peut déterminer. **2.** *Jur:* (bien) cessible, transférable.

assignat [æsin'jɑː, 'æsignæt], *s. Fr.Hist:* assignat *m*.

assignation [æsig'neiʃ(ə)n], *s.* **1.** distribution *f*, répartition *f*, attribution *f* (de biens). **2.** *Jur:* cession *f*, transfert *m* (de biens, de dettes, etc.); **a. of those in action,** cession-transport *f*; **a. of shares, of patent,** transmission *f* d'actions, de brevet; **a. of a claim,** transport *m* d'une créance (*in bankruptcy*); **deed of a.,** acte *m* de transfert; acte attributif. **3.** (*a*) fixation *f* (d'une heure, d'un lieu de rendez-vous); (*b*) rendez-vous *m*; (*c*) rendez-vous galant.

assignee [æsai'niː], *s. Jur:* **1.** (*a*) = ASSIGN[1]; (*b*) (administrateur-)séquestre *m*; syndic *m*; **assignees in bankruptcy,** syndics de faillite. **2.** cessionnaire *mf* (d'une créance, etc.).

assigning [ə'sainiŋ], *s.* **1.** distribution *f*, répartition *f*, attribution *f* (de biens). **2.** fixation *f* (d'un rendez-vous, etc.).

assignment [ə'sainmənt], *s.* **1.** (*a*) distribution *f*, répartition *f*, attribution *f* (de biens); (*b*) affectation *f*, allocation *f*, attribution (de qch. à qn); **a. of s.o. to a post,** affectation de qn à, désignation *f* de qn pour, un poste; **job a.,** affectation des tâches; (*c*) *Jur: etc:* cession *f*, transfert *m* (de biens, de dettes, etc.); **a. of property to creditors,** cession de biens à des créanciers; **deed of a.,** acte attributif, acte de transfert; **a. of a patent,** (i) cession *f* d'un brevet; (ii) concession *f* de licence d'exploitation d'un brevet; (*d*) citation *f*, production *f* (de raisons); attribution *f* (de cause) (**to,** à). **2.** *Sch: etc:* tâche assignée; *Journ:* reportage assigné (à un tel); **to take on a dangerous a.,** accepter (i) une tâche dangereuse, un reportage dangereux, (ii) un poste dangereux.

assignor [ə'sainər], *s.* **1.** *Com: Jur:* cédant, -ante. **2.** *St.Exch:* **official a.,** liquidateur officiel.

assimilable [ə'similəbl], *a.* **1.** *Physiol:* (aliment) assimilable; **the stomach renders food a.,** l'estomac élabore les aliments. **2.** comparable, assimilable (**to,** à).

assimilate [ə'simileit]. **1.** *v.tr.* (*a*) (*make alike*) **to a. the laws of two countries,** assimiler les lois de deux pays; (*b*) (*compare*) *A:* assimiler, comparer (**to,** à); **these two cases cannot be assimilated,** on ne peut pas ranger ces deux cas dans la même catégorie; (*c*) *Physiol:* **to a. food,** assimiler des aliments; (*d*) **Canada has assimilated people from many countries,** le Canada a assimilé des gens de beaucoup de pays; **she reads too quickly to a. everything,** elle lit trop vite pour tout assimiler, tout retenir. **2.** *v.i.* (*a*) **to a. to, with, sth.,** s'assimiler à qch.; (*b*) *Ling:* (*of consonants*) s'assimiler; (*c*) **in this country foreigners find it difficult to a.,** dans ce pays les étrangers s'adaptent difficilement.

assimilation [əsimi'leiʃ(ə)n], *s.* **1.** (*a*) (*making or becoming alike*) assimilation *f* (**to, with,** à); *Ling:* assimilation (de consonnes); (*b*) (*comparison*) assimilation (**to,** à); comparaison *f* (**to,** avec). **2.** (*a*) *Physiol:* assimilation (des aliments); (*b*) *Bot:* assimilation chlorophyllienne, photosynthèse *f*.

assimilative [ə'simileitiv, -lətiv], *a.* **1.** assimilateur, -trice. **2.** *Physiol:* (aliment) assimilatif, qui s'assimile facilement.

assimilatory [əsimi'leit(ə)ri], *a.* = ASSIMILATIVE I.

Assimineidae [æsimini'idi:], *s.pl. Moll:* assiminéidés *m*.

Assisi [ə'si:zi, ə'si:si], *Pr.n.* (*a*) *Geog:* Assise *f*; (*b*) **St. Francis of A.,** Saint François d'Assise.

assist [ə'sist]. NOTE: *in current English the verb* **to assist** *has been largely superseded by* **to help. 1.** *v.tr.* aider (qn); prêter son concours, son assistance, à (qn); seconder (qn) (dans son travail); **to a. s.o. in (doing) sth.,** aider qn à faire qch.; **a glass of wine assists digestion,** un verre de vin aide (à) la digestion. **2.** *v.i.* prendre part (à une cérémonie, etc.).

assistance [ə'sistəns], *s.* aide *f*, secours *m*, assistance *f*; **technical a.,** assistance technique; *Adm: A:* **National A.** = aide sociale; **to give s.o. a.,** prêter aide, assistance, (son) concours, à qn; prêter main-forte (à la police, etc.); **to come to s.o.'s a.,** venir à l'aide de, en aide à, au secours de, qn; **with the a. of sth., of s.o.,** à l'aide de qch., avec l'aide de qn; **to be of a. to s.o.,** aider qn, être utile à qn.

assistant [ə'sistənt]. **1.** *a.* qui aide; auxiliaire; adjoint; sous-; **a. manager,** sous-directeur *m*, *pl.* sous-directeurs; sous-gérant *m*, *pl.* sous-gérants; **a. master, mistress,** professeur *m* (dans l'enseignement secondaire); **a. lecturer,** *esp. NAm:* **a. professor** = maître assistant (à une université); *Ecc:* **a. curate** = sous-vicaire *m*, *pl.* sous-vicaires; *Ind: etc:* **a. machine-operator,** aide-opérateur *m*, *pl.* aides-opérateurs. **2.** *s.* aide *mf*; adjoint, -ointe; auxiliaire *mf*; collaborateur, -trice; **(shop) a.,** vendeur, -euse; **laboratory a.,** assistant, -ante, de laboratoire; laborantin, -ine.

assistantship [ə'sistəntʃip], *s. Sch: esp. NAm:* assistanat *m*.

assize [ə'saiz], *s.* **1.** *Adm: A:* (*statutory price*) taxe *f*, tarif *m*, barème *m* (du blé, du pain, de la bière). **2.** (*a*) (*usu. in pl.*) *Jur:* **(court of) assizes, a. court,** (cour *f* d')assises *fpl*; **to be brought before the assizes,** être traduit en cour d'assises; *A:* **the great a., the last a.,** le jugement dernier; (*b*) *Scot: Jur:* (i) jugement *m* par jury; (ii) **the a.,** le jury. **3.** *Hist:* **the Assizes of Jerusalem,** les Assises de Jérusalem.

asslicker ['æslikər], *s. U.S: P:* (*not in polite use*) lèche-cul *m inv*.

associability [əsouʃə'biliti], *s.* associabilité *f* (**with,** à).

associable [ə'souʃəbl], *a.* associable (**with,** à).

associate[1] [ə'souʃiət]. **1.** *a.* associé; *Ind: etc:* **a. company,** société affiliée, apparentée; *Sch: esp. NAm:* **a. professor** = professeur *m* de faculté. **2.** *s.* (*a*) associé, -ée; adjoint, -ointe; **a. of an academy,** membre correspondant, associé(e), d'une académie; **associates in crime,** consorts *m*; (*b*) compagnon *m*, camarade *mf*; **I don't like his associates,** je n'aime pas ses fréquentations; (*c*) (*of thg*) accessoire *m* (de qch.).

associate[2] [ə'souʃieit]. **1.** *v.tr.* associer (**with,** avec qn, à qch.); **to be associated with s.o. in an undertaking,** s'associer avec qn pour une entreprise; **to be associated with a plot,** tremper dans un complot; *Phil:* **to a. ideas,** associer des idées. **2.** *v.i.* (*a*) **to a. with s.o. in sth., in doing sth.,** s'associer, s'unir, avec qn pour qch., pour faire qch.; (*b*) **to a. with s.o.,** fréquenter qn; **to a. with bad companions,** faire de mauvaises fréquentations; **he associated with a gang of robbers,** il s'est affilié à une bande de voleurs.

associated [ə'souʃieitid], *a.* associé; **a. sciences,** disciplines associées; *Adm:* **a. territories,** territoires associés; *Mil:* **a. unit,** unité adaptée; **a. headquarters,** état-major adapté.

association [əsousi'eiʃ(ə)n], *s.* **1.** (*a*) association *f*; **a. of ideas,** association d'idées; **land full of historic associations,** pays *m* fertile en souvenirs historiques; *Jur:* **deed of a.,** acte *m* d'association, acte de société; (*b*) fréquentation *f* (**with s.o.,** de qn); **to form associations,** se faire des relations; **through long a. with . . .,** à force de fréquenter . . .; (*c*) **a. football,** football *m* association. **2.** (*a*) association, société *f*; amicale *f* (de professeurs, etc.); **to form an a.,** constituer une société; **trade a.,** association professionnelle; **(restrictive) trade associations,** ententes industrielles; **producers' a.,** syndicat *m* de producteurs; **Young Men's, Young Women's, Christian A.,** Union chrétienne de jeunes gens, de jeunes femmes; Association des jeunes gens chrétiens, des jeunes femmes chrétiennes; *Sch:* **Parents' A.,** association de parents d'élèves; **to form an a.,** constituer une société; (*b*) *Bot:* association végétale.

associationism [əsousi'eiʃ(ə)nizm], *s.* **1.** *Phil:* association(n)isme *m*. **2.** *Pol.Ec:* fouriérisme *m*.

associationist [əsousi'eiʃ(ə)nist], *s.* **1.** *Phil:* association(n)iste *m*. **2.** *Pol.Ec:* fouriériste *m*.

associative [ə'sousiətiv], *a.* (principe, pouvoir) d'association; associatif; *Mth:* **a. law,** loi associative; *Cmptr:* **a. memory, storage, store,** mémoire associative.

associativity [əsousiə'tiviti], *s. Mth:* associativité *f*.

associator [ə'sousieitər], *s. A:* **1.** complice *mf*, affilié, -ée (**with,** de). **2.** adjoint, -e (**with,** de).

assonance ['æsənəns], *s. Ling:* assonance *f*.

assonant ['æsənənt], *a. Ling:* assonant.

assonate ['æsəneit], *v.i. Ling:* assoner.

assonia [ə'souniə], *s. Bot:* dombéya *m*.

assort [ə'sɔ:t], (*rarely used in modern spoken Eng.*) **1.** *v.tr.* (*a*) assortir (**with,** à); assortir, marier (des couleurs); (*b*) classer, ranger (**with,** parmi); (*c*) *A:* assortir (un magasin) (**with,** de). **2.** *v.i.* (*a*) (s')assortir (bien, mal, avec qch.); (*b*) *A:* **to a. with s.o.,** fréquenter qn.

assorted [ə'sɔ:tid], *a.* (*a*) assorti; **well a. couple,** époux assortis, ménage heureux; (*b*) **a. colours,** couleurs variées; **box of a. screws,** boîte *f* de vis assorties; **a. chocolates,** chocolats fourrés assortis.

assortment [ə'sɔ:tmənt], *s.* **1.** assortiment *m*, choix *m* (de marchandises, d'outils, etc.); jeu *m* (d'outils); *Typ:* **scale of a.,** police *f*. **2.** *A:* classement *m*, classification *f* (par sortes).

assuage [ə'sweidʒ], *v.tr. Lit:* apaiser, adoucir, calmer, soulager, assoupir (les souffrances de qn); apaiser, satisfaire (un appétit, un désir); (*of pain*) **to be assuaged,** se calmer.

assuagement [ə'sweidʒmənt], *s. Lit:* apaisement *m*, adoucissement *m*, soulagement *m*, assoupissement *m* (de la douleur).

assuaging [ə'sweidʒiŋ], *s. Lit:* **1.** = ASSUAGEMENT. **2.** satisfaction *f* (d'un appétit).

Assuan [æs'wæn], *Pr.n. Geog:* Assouan *m*.

assumable [ə'sju:məbl], *a.* **1.** (*a*) (titre, etc.) appropriable; (*b*) **a. responsibility,** responsabilité *f* dont on peut se charger. **2.** supposable, présumable; **it is a. that . . .,** il est à supposer, à présumer, que . . ..

assume [ə'sju:m], *v.tr.* **1.** (*a*) prendre, se donner (un air, une mine, un ton); affecter, revêtir (une forme, un caractère); **the judges a. their robes,** les juges revêtent leur toge; les juges se revêtent de leurs toges; **to a. a holiday appearance,** prendre un air de fête; **things are assuming a better complexion,** les choses prennent meilleure tournure; (*b*) **the casing assumes the shape of the engine,** le carter épouse la forme du moteur. **2.** (*a*) prendre sur soi, prendre à son compte, assumer (une charge, une responsabilité); se charger (d'un devoir); *Com:* **to a. all risks,** assumer tous les risques; (*b*) **to a. power, authority,** prendre le pouvoir, prendre possession du pouvoir; **to a. command,** prendre le commandement; *Lit:* **to a. the crown,** ceindre la couronne, le diadème; **to a. the direction of affairs,** prendre en main la conduite des affaires. **3.** s'attribuer, s'arroger, s'approprier (un droit, un titre, etc.); **to a. a name,** adopter, emprunter, un nom; *Jur:* **to a. ownership,** faire acte de propriétaire; (*of heir*) **to a. a succession,** s'immiscer dans une succession. **4.** simuler, affecter; **to a. a virtue,** se parer d'une vertu; affecter une vertu; prétendre à une vertu; feindre une vertu. **5.** présumer, supposer (qch.); tenir (qch.) comme établi; *Phil: Mth:* admettre (qch.) en postulat; **I a. that he will come,** je présume qu'il viendra; **the author assumes everything and proves nothing,** l'auteur suppose tout et ne prouve rien; **he was assumed to be rich,** on le supposait riche; il était censé être riche; **the man who is assumed to have stolen it,** l'homme que l'on présume l'avoir volé; **in the absence of proof he must be assumed to be innocent,** en l'absence de preuves, il doit être présumé innocent; **you have no right to a. this to be any concern of yours,** vous n'avez pas le droit de présumer que cela vous regarde; **to a. the existence of sth.,** présumer l'existence de qch.; **let us a. that . . .,** prenons, mettons, supposons, que . . .; **assuming that the story is true,** en supposant, en admettant, que l'histoire soit vraie; **assuming free competition,** en cas de libre concurrence; **to a. the worst,** mettre les choses au pis.

assumed [ə'sju:md], *a.* **1.** supposé, feint, faux; **with a. nonchalance,** avec une affectation d'indifférence; **a. piety,** fausse dévotion; **a. virtues,** vertus d'occasion, d'emprunt; **a. name,** pseudonyme *m*; nom supposé, nom d'emprunt, nom de guerre. **2. a. load (on a bridge, etc.),** surcharge *f* hypothétique; **a. rate of increase,** taux *m* d'accroissement présumé; *Cmptr:* **a. decimal point,** virgule décimale implicite; **a. option,** option implicite, systématique, par défaut.

assuming [ə'sju:miŋ], *a.* présomptueux, prétentieux, arrogant.

assumpsit [ə'sʌm(p)sit], *s. Jur: A:* **1.** contrat *m*. **2.** action *f* en exécution de contrat ou en dommage-intérêt pour rupture de contrat.

assumption [ə'sʌm(p)ʃ(ə)n], *s.* **1.** *Ecc:* assomption *f* (de la Vierge); **Feast of the A.,** fête *f* de l'Assomption. **2.** (*a*) action *f* de prendre (une forme, un caractère); *Jur:* **a. of a succession,** immixtion *f* dans une succession; **unauthorized a. of a right,** usurpation *f* d'un droit; *Her:* **arms of a.,** armes assomptives; (*b*) **a. of office,** entrée *f* en fonctions; **a. of holy orders,** susception *f* des ordres sacrés; entrée dans les ordres. **3.** (*a*) affectation *f* (de vertu); **he turned away with an a. of indifference,** il se détourna en feignant l'indifférence; (*b*) arrogance *f*, prétention(s) *f*, présomption *f*; **to make no a. of special knowledge,** n'afficher aucune prétention à des connaissances spéciales. **4.** (*a*) supposition *f*, hypothèse *f*; *Phil:* postulat *m*; **I am going on the a. that . . .,** je me fonde sur l'hypothèse que . . .; **basic a.,** hypothèse de base, hypothèse fondamentale; **groundless, gratuitous, a.,** supposition gratuite; (*b*) *Log:* mineure *f* (d'un syllogisme); assomption.

assumptive [ə'sʌm(p)tiv], *a.* **1.** *Her:* **a. arms,** armes assomptives. **2.** (*a*) (raisonnement) hypothétique; (*b*) (fait) que l'on peut admettre; (fait) admis. **3.** *A:* présomptueux, arrogant.

assurable [ə'ʃuərəbl], *a.* assurable.

assurance [ə'ʃuər(ə)ns], *s.* **1.** (*a*) (*certainty*) assurance *f*; **I have every a. that he will help us,** j'ai la ferme assurance qu'il nous aidera; **in full a. of his good faith,** en toute assurance de sa bonne foi; **to make a. double, doubly, sure,** pour plus de sûreté; pour surcroît de sûreté; par surcroît de précaution; (*b*) promesse (formelle); **I have his distinct a. that . . .,** j'ai sa promesse formelle que . . .; (*c*) affirmation *f*; **a. to the contrary,** affirmation contraire; **I have his a. to the contrary,** il m'a affirmé le contraire; **I can give you the a. that . . .,** je peux vous assurer, vous affirmer, que . . .. **2.** *Jur:* **a. (of property),** (i) constitution *f* de droits; (ii) transfert *m* de droits (à une propriété). **3.** (*a*) *Ins:* **life a.,** assurance sur la vie; assurance-vie, *pl.* assurances-vie; **a. company,** compagnie *f* d'assurances; (*b*) *Cmptr:* taux *m* de service; **quality a.,** contrôle *m* de qualité. **4.** (*a*) assurance, fermeté *f*, confiance *f*; aplomb *m*; (*b*) hardiesse *f*, présomption *f*; **to answer with a.,** répondre (i) d'un ton assuré, avec assurance; (ii) d'un ton hardi, hardiment; **he had the a. to tell me that . . .,** *F:* il a eu le toupet de me dire que . . ..

assure [ə'ʃuər], *v.tr.* **1.** (*a*) *Ins:* **to a. s.o.'s life,** assurer la vie de qn; **to a. one's life,** s'assurer (sur la vie); **to have one's life assured,** se faire assurer sur la vie; *v.i.* **to a. with a company,** s'assurer à une compagnie; (*b*) **(make certain) to a. the peace, the happiness, of s.o.,** assurer la paix, le bonheur, de qn; (*c*) (*affirm*) **to a. s.o. of the truth of sth., of one's devotion,** assurer qn de la vérité de qch., de son dévouement; **to a. s.o. of a fact,** assurer, affirmer, un fait à qn; **he assures me that it is true,** il me certifie que c'est vrai; **he assured me that he was willing to do it,** il m'assura qu'il voulait bien le faire; **she assures me that she has enough to live on,** elle m'assure avoir de quoi vivre; **he will do it, I can a. you!** il le fera, je vous en réponds! **2.** *A: & Lit:* rassurer, encourager (qn); donner du cœur à (qn).

assured [ə'ʃuə:d]. **1.** *a.* (succès, etc.) assuré. **2.** *s. Ins:* assuré, -ée.

assuredly [ə'ʃuəridli], *adv.* assurément, à coup sûr; sans contredit.

assurer [ə'ʃuərər], *s.* **1.** *A:* affirmateur, -trice (d'un fait). **2.** *Ins:* (*also* **assuror**) assureur *m*.

assurgent [ə'sə:dʒ(ə)nt], *a.* **1.** (*a*) *Lit:* ascendant; (*b*) *Bot:* assurgent. **2.** *A: & Lit:* agressif.

Assyria [ə'siriə], *Pr.n. A.Geog:* Assyrie *f*.

Assyrian [ə'siriən]. **1.** *A.Hist:* (*a*) *a.* assyrien; (*b*) *s.* Assyrien, -ienne. **2.** *Ling:* assyrien *m*.

Assyriologist [əsiri'ɔlədʒist], *s.* Assyriologue *m*.

Assyriology [əsiri'ɔlədʒi], *s.* Assyriologie *f.*

astable [ei'steibl], *a. Elcs:* astable, instable.

Astacidea [æstæ'sidiə], *s.pl. Crust:* astacidés *m.*

astacene ['æstəsi:n], **astacin** ['æstəsin], *s. Ch:* astacine *f.*

Astacura [æstæ'kju:rə], *s.pl. Crust:* astacoures *m.*

Astarte [æs'tɑ:ti]. **1.** *Pr.n.f. Myth:* Astarté. **2.** *s. Moll:* astarte *f*, astarté *f.*

Astartidae [æs'tɑ:tidi:], *s.pl. Moll:* astartidés *m.*

astasia [æs'teiziə], *s. Med:* astasie *f.*

astatic [ei'stætik], *a. El:* astatique; **a. needles,** aiguilles astatiques; **a. couple, a. system,** système *m* astatique; **a. galvanometer,** galvanomètre *m* astatique.

astatine ['æstəti:n], *s. Atom.Ph:* astatine *m.*

asteism ['æstiizm], *s.* astéisme *m.*

aster ['æstər], *s.* **1.** *Bot:* (*a*) aster *m*; **China a.,** aster de Chine; reine-marguerite *f*, *pl.* reines-marguerites; (*b*) *U.S:* marguerite *f* d'automne, aster œil-du-Christ, *pl.* œils-du-Christ. **2.** *Biol:* aster.

astereognosis [æstiəriɔg'nousis], *s. Med:* astéréognosie *f.*

asteria [æ'stiəriə], *s. Cryst:* astérie *f.*

asterias, *pl.* **-ae** [æ'stiəriəs, -i:], *s. Echin:* astérie *f*; *F:* étoile *f* de mer.

asteriated [æ'stiərieitid], *a. Miner:* (pierre) astérique; **a. opal,** astérie *f.*

Asteriidae [æstəri'idi:], *s.pl. Echin:* astéries *f*, astérides *f.*

Asterinidae [æstə'rinidi:], *s.pl. Echin:* astérinidés *m.*

asterion [æ'steriən], *s. Anat:* astérion *m.*

asterisk[1] ['æst(ə)risk], *s.* astérisque *m*; *Cmptr:* **a. protection,** protection *f* par astérisques.

asterisk[2], *v.tr.* astériser; mettre un astérisque à (un mot); marquer (un mot) d'un astérisque.

asterism ['æstərizm], *s.* **1.** *Astr:* astérisme *m.* **2.** *Cryst:* astérisme; astérie *f.* **3.** *Typ:* astérisques *mpl* en triangle.

astern [ə'stə:n]. *Nau: Av:* **1.** *adv.* (*a*) (*position on ship, etc.*) à l'arrière, sur l'arrière; **we had two guns a.,** nous avions deux canons à l'arrière, en poupe; (*b*) (*backwards*) **to go, come, a.,** culer; aller de l'arrière; faire machine, marche, arrière; mettre en arrière; marcher en arrière; **to drop a.,** culer; **motion a., a. motion,** marche *f* (en) arrière; mouvement *m* en arrière; **full speed a.!** en arrière à toute vitesse! en arrière toute! **to go full speed a.,** mettre route en arrière; **a. turbine,** turbine *f* de marche arrière; (*c*) (*behind*) **to make a boat fast a.,** amarrer un canot derrière; **to fall, drop, a.** (**of another ship**), rester en arrière; perdre; culer; **ship slightly a.,** navire *m* un peu à la traîne; **ship right a.,** navire droit derrière; *Navy:* **in close order a.,** beaupré sur poupe; **the ship next a.,** le matelot d'arrière; **to have the wind a.,** avoir le vent en arrière; **the wind is a.,** le vent empoupe le navire; *Navy:* **to fire a.,** tirer en retraite. **2.** *prep.phr.* **a. of a ship,** derrière un navire; sur l'arrière d'un navire; à la traîne; **to follow a. of a ship,** se trouver en poupe d'un navire; faire route dans les eaux d'un navire; **to pass a. of a ship,** passer sur l'arrière d'un navire.

asternal [ə'stə:nl], *a. Anat:* **a. ribs,** côtes asternales; fausses côtes.

asterococcus, *pl.* **-cocci** [æstərou'kɔkəs, -kɔk(s)i], *s. Bac:* asterococcus *m.*

asteroid ['æstərɔid]. **1.** *a.* en forme d'étoile. **2.** *s.* (*a*) *Astr:* astéroïde *m*; (*b*) *Echin:* astérie *f*, étoile *f* de mer.

asterolepis [æstə'rɔləpis], *s. Paleont:* asterolepis *m.*

Asterophyllites [æstəroufi'laiti:z], *s.pl. Paleont:* astérophyllitées *f.*

Asterozoa [æstərou'zouə], *s.pl. Echin:* astérozoaires *m.*

asthenia [æs'θi:niə], *s. Med:* asthénie *f.*

asthenic [æs'θenik], *a. Med:* asthénique.

asthenopia [æsθe'noupiə], *s. Med:* asthénopie *f.*

asthenospermia [æsθenou'spə:miə], *s. Med:* asthénospermie *f.*

asthenosphere ['æsθənousfiər], *s. Geol:* asthénosphère *f.*

asthma ['æs(θ)mə], *s.* asthme *m*; **to suffer from a.,** être asthmatique; souffrir de l'asthme.

asthmatic(al) [æs(θ)'mætik(l)]. **1.** *a.* asthmatique. **2.** *s.* **asthmatic,** asthmatique *mf.*

asthmogenic [æs(θ)mə'dʒenik], *a.* asthmogène.

Astian ['æstiən], *a.* & *s. Geol:* astien *m.*

astigmat [æ'stigmæt], *s. Opt:* astigmate *mf.*

astigmatic [æstig'mætik], *Opt:* **1.** *a.* astigmate, astigmatique. **2.** *s.* astigmate *mf.*

astigmatism [æ'stigmətizm], *s. Opt:* astigmatisme *m.*

astigmatizer [æ'stigmətaizər], *s.* astigmatiseur *m* (de télémètre).

astigmometer [æstig'mɔmitər], *s. Med:* astigmomètre *m.*

astir [ə'stə:r], *adv.* & *a.* **1.** (*in motion*) actif; en mouvement; animé; **to set sth. a.,** mettre qch. en mouvement, en branle; **it was he who set everything a.,** c'est lui qui a donné le branle. **2.** *O:* (*up and about*) debout, levé; **to be a. at six o'clock,** être debout à six heures; **I could hear no one a.,** je n'entendais bouger personne. **3.** (*in excitement*) en émoi, agité; **the whole town was a.,** toute la ville était en émoi.

astomatal [ei'stɔmətl], *a. Bot:* sans stomates.

astomatous [ei'stɔmətəs], *a. Prot:* astome.

astomia [ei'stoumiə], *s. Ter:* astomie *f.*

astomous [ei'stouməs], *a. Moss:* astome; *Bot:* sans stomates.

astonish [ə'stɔniʃ], *v.tr.* étonner, surprendre; jeter (qn) dans l'étonnement; **you a. me,** vous m'étonnez; **to be astonished at seeing sth.,** être étonné, s'étonner, de voir qch.; **I am astonished that. . .,** cela m'étonne que + *sub.*; **to look astonished,** avoir l'air étonné; ouvrir de grands yeux.

astonishing [ə'stɔniʃiŋ], *a.* étonnant, surprenant; **it is a. to me that. . .,** je m'étonne que . . .; **that is a., coming from him,** cela étonne de sa part.

astonishingly [ə'stɔniʃiŋli], *adv.* étonnamment; à mon, notre, grand étonnement, à ma grande surprise; **a. enough, he arrived,** chose étonnante, il y est arrivé.

astonishment [ə'stɔniʃmənt], *s.* étonnement *m*; (grande) surprise; **to my great a.,** à mon grand étonnement, à ma grande surprise; **look of a.,** air, regard, étonné; **I fell back in a.,** j'ai eu un sursaut d'étonnement, d'ébahissement; **I have heard to my a. that . . .,** j'ai appris, à mon grand étonnement, que . . .; **I can't get over my a.,** je n'en reviens pas.

astound [ə'staund], *v.tr.* confondre, abasourdir; frapper de stupeur; stupéfier; ébahir; **I was astounded by it,** j'en demeurai (i) stupéfait, (ii) atterré; **it astounds me! I'm astounded!** j'en reste abasourdi; cela me renverse; j'en suis renversé; je n'en reviens pas!

astounding [ə'staundiŋ], *a.* (*a*) abasourdissant, renversant; (*b*) (*calamitous*) (désastre) épouvantable; (nouvelle) atterrante.

Astraea [æ'stri(:)ə], *Pr.n.f. Myth:* Astrée.

Astraeidae [æ'striidi:], *s.pl. Z:* astræidés *m.*

astragal ['æstrəg(ə)l], *s. Arch: etc:* astragale *m* (d'une colonne, d'une pièce d'artillerie); chapelet *m* (d'une colonne).

astragalectomy [æstrəgæ'lektəmi], *s. Surg:* astragalectomie *f.*

astragalus, *pl.* **-i** [æ'strægələs, -ai], *s. Anat: Bot:* astragale *m.*

Astrak(h)an [æstrə'kæn]. **1.** *Pr.n. Geog:* astrak(h)an. **2.** *s.* (*fur*) astrakan *m.*

astral ['æstr(ə)l], *a.* astral, -aux; **a. lamp,** lampe astrale; *Psychics:* **a. body,** corps astral.

astrantia [æ'stræntiə, -tʃə], *s. Bot:* astrance *f*, astrantia *f.*

astra(po)phobia [æstrə(pɔ)'foubiə], *s. Med:* astraphobie *f.*

astray [ə'strei], *adv.* & *a.* (i) égaré; (ii) *Pej:* dévoyé; **to go a.,** (i) s'égarer, s'écarter de la route, faire fausse route; (ii) *Pej:* se dévoyer; se débaucher; **to lead s.o. a.,** (i) égarer qn; induire qn en erreur; (ii) débaucher, dévoyer, qn; détourner qn de la bonne voie; entraîner qn hors du droit chemin; **to keep s.o. from being led a.,** préserver qn de mauvais entraînements.

astrict [ə'strikt], *v.tr. A:* & *Lit:* astreindre (**to,** à).

astriction [ə'strikʃ(ə)n], *s. Med:* astriction *f.*

astrictive [ə'striktiv], *a.* & *s. Med:* astrictif, -ive; astringent (*m*).

astride [ə'straid], *adv., a.* & *prep.* **1.** à califourchon; jambe deçà jambe delà (sur qch.); **to ride a.,** monter à califourchon (sur un cheval, etc.); **to get a. a horse,** enfourcher un cheval; **to sit a. sth.,** être à cheval, chevaucher, être à califourchon, sur qch.; **the old bridge a. the river,** le vieux pont qui enjambe la rivière; **the enemy was a. our main line of supply,** l'ennemi était des deux côtés de notre axe de ravitaillement. **2. to stand a.,** se tenir (debout) les jambes écartées.

astrild ['æstrild], *s. Orn:* astrild *m*, *F:* queue-de-vinaigre *f*, *pl.* queues-de-vinaigre.

astringency [ə'strin(d)ʒ(ə)nsi], *s.* astringence *f.*

astringent [ə'strin(d)ʒ(ə)nt], *a.* & *s.* astringent (*m*); styptique (*m*).

astrionics [æstri'ɔniks], *s.* électronique appliquée à l'astronautique.

astro- ['æstrou], *pref.* astro-.

astrobiology ['æstroubai'ɔlədʒi], *s.* astrobiologie *f.*

astrocaryum ['æstrou'keəriəm], *s. Bot:* astrocarye *f*, astrocaryum *m.*

astro-compass ['æstrou'kʌmp'əs], *s.* compas *m* astronomique.

astrocyte ['æstrousait], *s. Biol:* astrocyte *f.*

astrodome ['æstroudoum], *s. Av:* astrodôme *m*; coupole vitrée avant.

astrodynamics ['æstroudai'næmiks], *s.* astrodynamique *f.*

astrogation [æstrou'geiʃ(ə)n], *s.* navigation *f* interplanétaire, astronautique *f.*

astrograph ['æstrougræf], *s.* astrographe *m.*

astroid ['æstrɔid], *a.* & *s.* astroïde (*f*).

astroite ['æstrɔit], *s. Miner:* astroïte *f.*

astrolabe ['æstrouleib, -læb], *s. Astr:* astrolabe *m.*

astrolater [ə'strɔlətər], *s.* astrolâtre *mf.*

astrolatry [ə'strɔlətri], *s.* astrolâtrie *f.*

astrologer [ə'strɔlədʒər], *s.* astrologue *m.*

astrologic(al) [æstrə'lɔdʒik(l)], *a.* astrologique.

astrologically [æstrə'lɔdʒik(ə)li], *adv.* astrologiquement.

astrology [ə'strɔlədʒi], *s.* astrologie *f*; **judicial a.,** astrologie judiciaire; **natural a.,** astrologie naturelle.

astromancy ['æstroumænsi], *s.* astromancie *f.*

astrometeorological ['æstroumi:tiərou'lɔdʒikl], astrométérologique.

astrometeorology ['æstroumi:tiə'rɔlədʒi], *s.* astrométéorologie *f.*

astrometer [æ'strɔmitər], *s.* astromètre *m.*

astrometrical [æstrou'metrikl], *a.* astrométrique.

astrometry [æ'strɔmitri], *s.* astrométrie *f.*

astronaut ['æstrənɔ:t], *s.* astronaute *m.*

astronautic [æstrə'nɔ:tik], *a.* astronautique.

astronautics [æstrə'nɔ:tiks], *s.* astronautique *f.*

astronavigation [æstrounævi'geiʃ(ə)n], *s.* astronavigation *f.*

astronomer [ə'strɔnəmər], *s.* astronome *m*; **the A. Royal,** (i) le Directeur de l'Observatoire de Greenwich; (ii) *Scot:* le Directeur de l'Observatoire d'Édimbourg.

astronomic(al) [æstrə'nɔmik(l)], *a.* astronomique; **a. time, year,** heure *f*, année *f*, astronomique; **a. numbers,** *s.pl.* **astronomicals,** fractions *f* astronomiques, sexagésimales; **a. unit,** unité *f* astronomique; *F:* **the sales reach astronomical figures,** la vente atteint des chiffres astronomiques.

astronomically [æstrə'nɔmik(ə)li], *adv.* astronomiquement.

astronomy [ə'strɔnəmi], *s.* astronomie *f.*

Astropectinidae ['æstroupek'tinidi:], *s.pl. Echin:* astropectinidés *m.*

astrophotograph ['æstrou'foutəgræf], *s.* astrophotographie *f.*

astrophotographic ['æstroufoutə'græfik], astrophotographique.

astrophotography ['æstroufə'tɔgrəfi], *s.* astrophotographie *f.*

astrophyllite ['æstrou'filait], *s. Miner:* astrophyllite *f.*

astrophysical ['æstrou'fizikl], *a.* astrophysique.

astrophysicist ['æstrou'fizisist], *s.* astrophysicien, -ienne.

astrophysics ['æstrou'fiziks], *s.pl.* (*usu. with sg.const.*) astrophysique *f.*

astroscope ['æstrəskoup], *s.* astroscope *m.*

Asturian [æs'tjuəriən], *a. Geog:* asturien, -ienne.

Asturias (the) [ði:æs'tjuəriæs], *Pr.n. Geog:* les Asturies *f.*

astute [əs'tju:t], *a.* **1.** fin, avisé, pénétrant. **2.** *Pej:* astucieux, matois, rusé.

astutely [əs'tju:tli], *adv.* **1.** avec finese; avec une grande pénétration. **2.** *Pej:* astucieusement; avec ruse.

astuteness [əs'tju:tnis], *s.* **1.** finesse *f*, sagacité *f*; pénétration *f.* **2.** *Pej:* astuce *f.*

Asuncion [əsunθi'oun, əsunsi'oun], *Pr.n. Geog:* Assomption *f* (capitale du Paraguay).

asunder [ə'sʌndər], *adv. A:* & *Lit:* **1.** (*apart*) éloignés, écartés (l'un de l'autre). **2.** (*in pieces*) **to tear sth. a.,** déchirer qch. en deux; **to break a.,** se casser en deux; (*of parts*) **to come, fall, a.,** se désunir, se disjoindre.

Aswan [æs'wæn], *Pr.n. Geog:* Assouan *m.*

aswirl [ə'swə:l], *adv.* & *a. Lit:* tourbillonnant.

asyllabia [eisi'leibiə], *s. Med:* asyllabie *f.*

asylum [ə'sailəm], *s.* **1.** (*a*) *Hist:* asile *m* (inviolable); (*b*) asile, (lieu *m* de) refuge *m*; **political, diplomatic, a.,** asile politique, diplomatique. **2.** *A:* (*a*) hospice *m*; (*b*) (**lunatic**) **a.,** maison *f*, hospice, asile, d'aliénés; *F:* maison de fous; (*c*) **orphan a.,** orphelinat *m.*

asymbolia [eisim'bouliə], *s. Med:* asymbolie *f.*

asymmetric(al) [eisi'metrik(l)], *a.* asymétrique; *Geol:* **a. fold,** pli déjeté; **a. valley,** vallée monoclinale; *Meteor:* **a. gusts,** rafales *f* dissymétriques; *Pol.Ec: etc:* **a. distribution,** distribution *f* dissymétrique; **a. income effect,** effet *m* de revenu asymétrique.

asymmetry [ei'simitri], *s.* asymétrie *f*, dissymétrie *f*; *Pol.Ec:* **a. between supply and demand,** asymétrie entre l'offre et la demande.

asymptomatic [eisimptə'mætik], *a. Med:* asymptomatique.

asymptote ['æsimptout], *s. Myth:* asymptote *f*; **lower, upper, a.,** asymptote inférieure, supérieure.

asymptotic(al) [æsimp'tɔtik(l)], *a. Myth:* asymptotique, asymptote; **a. line, curve,** ligne *f*, courbe *f*, asymptote; **a. direction,** direction *f* asymptotique.
asynapsis [ei'sinæpsis], *s.* asynapsis *f.*
asynchronism [ei'siŋkrənizm], *s. Mec:* asynchronisme *m.*
asynchronous [ei'siŋkrənəs], *a. Mec:* asynchrone; *El:* **a. motor,** moteur *m* asynchrone, d'induction; *Cmptr:* **a. computer, a. working,** calculateur *m*, fonctionnement *m*, asynchrone.
asynchronization [eisiŋkrənai'zeiʃ(ə)n], *s. Av:* **a. light,** voyant de désynchronisation.
asynclitism [ei'sinklitizm], *s. Med:* asynclitisme *m.*
asyndesis [ei'sindəsis], *s. Biol:* asyndèse *f.*
asyndeton [æ'sinditən], *s. Rh:* asyndète *m*, asyndéton *m.*
asynergia [eisi'nə:dʒiə], **asynergy** [ei'sinədʒi], *s. Med:* asynergie *f.*
asystole [ei'sistəli], **asystolia** [eisis'touliə], **asystolism** [ei'sistəlizm], *s. Med:* asystolie *f.*
at [æt, *unstressed* ət], *prep.* à. **1.** (*position*) (*a*) **at the centre, at the top,** au centre, au sommet; **at table, at church, at the concert, at school, at the station,** à table, à l'église, au concert, à l'école, à la gare; **the dog was at his heels,** le chien marchait sur ses talons; **at my side,** à mes côtés, à côté de moi; **at hand,** sous la main; **at Oxford, at le Havre,** à Oxford, au Havre; **at sea,** en mer; **after four days at sea,** après quatre jours de mer; **the Conference at Spa,** la Conférence de Spa; **ambassador at the court of James I,** ambassadeur *m* auprès de la cour de Jacques Ier; (*b*) **at home,** à la maison, chez soi; **at my uncle's, at the tailor's,** chez mon oncle, chez le tailleur; **we met at her father's,** nous nous sommes rencontrés chez son père; (*c*) **to sit at the window,** se tenir (au)près de la fenêtre; **he came in at the front door, at the window,** il entra par la grande porte, par la fenêtre; **to warm oneself at the fire,** se chauffer devant le feu; (*d*) *U.S: F:* **where are we at?** où en sommes-nous? **2.** (*time*) **at six o'clock,** à six heures; **at present,** à présent; **at that time,** à cette époque, en ce temps-là; **at a time when . . .,** dans un moment où . . .; **two at a time,** deux par deux, deux à la fois; **at the beginning of the year,** au commencement de l'année; **at the beginning,** dès le commencement; **at night,** la nuit, le soir; **at first,** d'abord; **at last,** enfin, à la fin; **at the latest,** au plus tard; **at three months after date,** à trois mois de date; **bill at three months,** papier *m* à trois mois d'echéance; **at once,** immédiatement. **3.** (*price*) **at two francs a pound,** à deux francs la livre; **apples are sold at tenpence a pound,** les pommes se vendent à dix pence la livre. **4. at my request,** sur ma demande; **boys at play,** élèves *m* en récréation; **at all events,** en tout cas. **5. quick at repartee,** prompt à la repartie; **to be good, bad, at mathematics;** être fort, faible, en mathématiques; **to be good at games,** être sportif. **6.** (*a*) **to look at sth.,** regarder qch.; **to be surprised at sth.,** être étonné de qch.; **to catch at sth.,** s'accrocher à qch.; **to aim at s.o.,** viser qn; **to play at cricket,** jouer au cricket; (*b*) **to laugh at s.o.,** se moquer de qn; **to talk at s.o.,** faire des allusions peu voilées à qn (qui se trouve présent); persifler qn (à son su ou à son insu); **to swear at s.o.,** jurer contre qn; **what are you driving at?** où voulez-vous en venir? (*c*) **to be at work,** être au travail; **to work hard at doing sth.,** travailler ferme à faire qch.; **to be at sth.,** être occupé à faire qch., s'occuper de qch.; *F:* **what are you at?** que faites-vous! **he is at it,** il y travaille; il est à la besogne; **he longs to be at it,** il lui tarde de s'y mettre; *F:* **to keep s.o. at it,** faire trimer qn; **I watched him at it,** je le regardais faire; **there were two of us at it,** (i) nous étions deux à la besogne; (ii) nous l'avons fait à deux; *F:* **let me see you at it again!** que je te voie encore faire cela! que je t'y reprenne! **she's at it again,** voilà qu'elle recommence! la voilà qui recommence! **while we are at it, why not . . .,** pendant que nous y sommes, pourquoi ne pas . . .; **he's a liar, and a poor one at that!** il est menteur et, qui plus est, un menteur médiocre; (*d*) **to be at s.o.,** être acharné contre qn, rudoyer, tancer, qn; **she is always at him,** (i) elle ne peut pas le laisser tranquille; (ii) elle le harcèle de querelles, elle est toujours après lui; *F:* **she's always on at me,** elle s'en prend toujours à moi; **they're at me again,** voilà encore qu'on s'en prend à moi; on m'attaque de nouveau; *Mil:* **at them!** chargez! en avant! tombez dessus! (*to dog*) **at him!** pille! pille!
atacamite [ə'tækəmait], *s. Miner:* atacamite *f.*
Atalanta [ætə'læntə], *Pr.n.f. Gr.Myth:* Atalante.
ataractic [ætə'ræktik], **ataraxic** [ætə'ræksik], *a. Med:* (tranquillisant) ataraxique.
ataraxia [ætə'ræksiə], **ataraxy** [ætə'ræksi], *s. Phil: Med:* ataraxie *f.*
atavism ['ætəvizm], *s.* atavisme *m.*
atavistic [ætə'vistik], *a.* atavique.
ataxia [ə'tæksiə], *s. Med:* = ATAXY.
ataxic [ə'tæksik], *a. & s. Med:* ataxique (*mf*).
ataxite [ə'tæksait], *s. Miner:* ataxite *f.*
ataxy [ə'tæksi], *s. Med:* ataxie *f*; incoordination *f*; **locomotor a.,** ataxie locomotrice progressive; tabes *m* dorsalis.
atelectasis [ætə'lektəsis], *s. Med:* atélectasie *f.*
ateles ['ætəli:z], *s. Z:* atèle *m*, singe *m* araignée.
atelia [ə'tiliə], *s. Biol:* atélie *f.*
atelic [ei'telik], *a. Biol:* atélique.
atelier [æ'teliei], *s.* atelier *m*, studio *m.*
atelomitic [eitelə'mitik], *a. Biol:* atélomitique.
Athalia [æ'θeiliə]. **1.** *Pr.n.f. B.Hist:* Athalie. **2.** *s. Ent:* athalia *f.*
Athanasian [æθə'neiʃ(ə)n], *a.* athanasien; **the A. Creed,** le Symbole de saint Athanase.
Athanasius [æθə'neiʃəs], *Pr.n.m. Rel.H:* Athanase.
athanor ['æθənɔər], *s. Alch:* athanor *m.*
Athecae [ə'θi:si:], *s.pl. Rept:* athèques *m.*
atheism ['eiθiizm], *s.* athéisme *m.*
atheist ['eiθiist], *s.* athée *mf.*
atheistic(al) [eiθi'istik(l)], *a.* **1.** (doctrine) athéistique. **2.** (personne) athée.
atheistically [eiθi'istik(ə)li], *adv.* en athée.
athelia [ei'θi:liə], *s. Med:* athélie *f.*
atheling ['æθiliŋ], *s. Hist:* prince, noble, anglo-saxon.
athematic [eiθi:'mætik], *a. Ling:* athématique.
Athena [ə'θi:nə], *Pr.n.f. Myth:* Athéné, Athéna.
athenaeum [æθi'ni(:)əm], *s.* **1.** *Gr.Ant:* l'Athénée *m.* **2.** athénée (cercle littéraire).
Athene [ə'θi:ni(:)], *Pr.n.f. Myth:* Athéné, Athéna.
Athenian [ə'θi:niən]. *Geog:* (*a*) *a.* athénien; d'Athènes; (*b*) *s.* Athénien, -ienne.
Athens ['æθənz], *Pr.n. Geog:* Athènes *f*; *Lit:* **the A. of the North,** l'Athènes du Nord (Édimbourg).
Athericera [æθə'ri:sərə], *s.pl. Ent:* athéricères *m.*
atherine ['æθərain], *s. Ich:* athérine *f*, faux éperlan.
athermal [ei'θə:m(ə)l], *a:* (*of mineral springs*) athermal, -aux.
athermancy [ei'θə:mənsi], *s. Ph:* athermanéité *f.*
athermanous [ei'θə:mənəs], *a. Ph:* athermane.
athermic [ei'θə:mik], *a. Ph:* athermique.
atheroma [æθə'roumə], *s. Med:* athérome artériel.
atheromatic ['æθərou'mætik], **atheromatose** [æθə'rɔmətəs], *a. Med:* athéromateux.
atheromatosis ['æθəroumæ'tousis], *s. Med:* athéromatose *f.*
atherosclerosis ['æθərousklə'rousis], *s. Med:* athérosclérose *f.*
atherosperma ['æθərou'spə:mə], *s. Bot:* athérosperme *m.*
atherurus [æθə'ruərəs], *s. Z:* athérure *m.*
athetesis [æθə'ti:sis], *s. Ling:* athétèse *f.*
athetosis [æθə'tousis], *s. Med:* athétose *f.*
athirst [ə'θə:st], *a. Lit:* altéré, assoiffé (**for,** de); **to be a. for blood,** avoir soif de sang; être altéré de sang; **a. for news, for wealth,** assoiffé de nouvelles, de richesses.
athlete ['æθli:t], *s.* athlète *mf*; *Med:* **athlete's foot,** pied *m* de l'athlète.
athletic [æθ'letik], *a.* (*a*) athlétique; **a. club,** société *f* d'athlétisme; *Med:* **a. type,** type athlétoïde; *F:* **a. heart,** cœur claqué; (*b*) **he's, she's, very a.,** c'est un sportif, une sportive.
athleticism [æθ'letisizm], *s.* athlétisme *m.*
athletics [æθ'letiks], *s.pl.* (*usu. with sg.const.*) **1.** *Gr.Civ: etc:* athlétique *f.* **2.** sports *m* athlétiques; athlétisme *m*; **I went in for athletics in my day,** je suis un vieux sportif.
at-home [ət'houm], *s. A:* réception *f*; (*in the evening*) soirée *f*; **Mrs X holds her at-homes on Tuesdays,** Madame X reçoit le mardi; **at.-h. day,** jour *m* de réception.
Athos ['æθɔs, 'eiθɔs], *Pr.n. Geog:* le mont Athos.
athrepsia [ei'θrepsiə], *s. Med:* athrépsie *f.*
athrombia [ei'θrɔmbiə], *s. Med:* athrombasie *f.*
athwart [ə'θwɔ:t]. **1.** *adv.* en travers; *Nau:* par le travers; *Nau:* **the current is a.,** le courant est en travers. **2.** *prep.* en travers de; *Nau:* **to run a. a ship's course,** croiser la route d'un navire; (*of ship*) **to lie a. hawse,** se trouver en travers sur l'avant d'un autre navire; *attrib. N.Arch:* **a. ribs,** membrures transversales; **the a. plane,** le plan transversal.
athwartship(s) [ə'θwɔ:tʃip(s)], *adv. Nau:* en travers du navire; par le travers (du navire); dans le sens latitudinal, transversal; transversalement; *N.Arch:* **the a. plane,** le plan transversal.
athyreosis [eiθairi'ousis], *s. Med:* athyroïdie *f.*
athyrium [ə'θiriəm], *s. Bot:* athyrium *m.*
atishoo [ə'tiʃu:], *int.* (*sneeze*) atchoum!
atlanta [æt'læntə], *s. Moll:* atlante *m*, atlanta *m.*
atlantal [æt'læntl], *a. Anat:* atloïdé, atloïdien.
atlantean [ætlæn'ti:ən], *a.* **1.** (force, etc.) digne d'un Atlas; (force) de géant. **2.** de l'Atlantide.
Atlantic [ət'læntik], *a. & s. Geog:* **the A. (Ocean),** l'(océan) Atlantique *m*; **the A. coastline,** le littoral atlantique; **an A. liner,** un transatlantique; *Hist:* **A. Charter,** Charte *f* atlantique.
Atlantides [ət'læntidi:z], *s.f.pl. Myth:* les Atlantides; les Pléiades.
Atlantis [ət'læntis], *Pr.n. Myth:* l'Atlantide *f.*
atlantosaurus [ətlæntou'sɔ:rəs], *s. Paleont:* atlantosaure *m.*
Atlas ['ætləs]. **1.** *Pr.n.m. Gr.Myth:* Atlas; **the daughters of A.,** les Atlantides *f.* **2.** *Pr.n. Geog:* **the A. Mountains,** l'Atlas *m.* **3.** *s.* (*a*) *Anat:* atlas; (*b*) *Paperm:* atlas; **an a. folio,** un in-folio format atlas, format atlantique; (*c*) *Geog: etc:* atlas; **historical a.,** atlas historique. **4.** *s. Arch:* (*pl.* **atlantes** [ət'lænti:z]) atlante *m*, télamon *m.* **5.** *attrib. Ent:* **a. beetle,** chalcosome *m*; **a. moth,** atlas.
atloid ['ætlɔid], **atloidean** [æt'lɔidiən], *a. Anat:* atloïdé, atloïdien.
atmidometer [ætmi'dɔmitər], *s. Ph:* atm(id)omètre *m*, évaporimètre *m.*
atmo ['ætmou], *s. Mec: Ph:* (*pressure of 760 mm of mercury*) atmosphère *f.*
atmolysis [æt'mɔlisis], *s. Ph:* atmolyse *f.*
atmometer [æt'mɔmitər], *s. Ph:* atm(id)omètre *m*, évaporimètre *m.*
atmosphere ['ætməsfiər], *s.* **1.** atmosphère *f* (terrestre, planétaire etc.); **sensible a.,** atmosphère permettant la sustentation aérodynamique. **2.** atmosphère, ambiance *f*; *F:* **there's plenty of a. here,** il y a de l'ambiance ici; **I don't like atmospheres,** je n'aime pas les milieux où l'on se dispute. **3.** *Mec: Ph:* (*pressure of 760 mm of mercury*) atmosphère.
atmospheric [ætməs'ferik]. **1.** *a.* atmosphérique; **a. pressure,** pression *f* atmosphérique; **a. conditions, disturbances,** conditions *f*, perturbations *f*, atmosphériques; **a. absorption,** absorption *f* atmosphérique; **a. electricity,** électricité *f* atmosphérique; *Mch:* **a. line,** ligne *f* atmosphérique (du diagramme); *Ph:* **a. lines,** raies *f* telluriques. **2.** *s.pl. W.Tel: etc:* **atmospherics,** (parasites *m*) atmosphériques *f.*
atoll ['ætɔl], *s. Geog:* atoll *m.*
atom ['ætəm], *s.* (*a*) *Ph:* atome *m*; (*b*) **not an a. of common sense,** pas l'ombre, pas un grain, de bon sens; **smashed to atoms,** réduit en miettes, en poudre, en poussière.
atom bomb ['ætəm'bɔm], *s.* bombe *f* atomique.
atom-bomb ['ætəm'bɔm], *v.tr.* lancer une bombe atomique sur (une ville, etc.); détruire (une ville) à la bombe atomique.
atom-free ['ætəmfri:], *a.* dénucléarisé.
atomic [ə'tɔmik], *a.* atomique; **a. energy,** énergie *f* atomique; **a. reactor,** pile *f* atomique; **a. warfare,** guerre *f* atomique; **a. number,** numéro *m*, nombre *m*, atomique; **a. physicist, scientist,** atomiste *m*; **the a. age,** l'ère *f*, l'âge *m*, atomique; **the a. theory,** (i) *Phil:* atomisme *m*; (ii) *Atom.Ph:* atomistique *f*, théorie *f* atomique.
atomically [ə'tɔmik(ə)li], *adv.* atomiquement.
atomicity [ætə'misiti], *s. Ch:* **1.** atomicité *f.* **2.** valence *f.*
atomic-powered [ə'tɔmik'pauə:d], *a.* à propulsion atomique.
atomics [ə'tɔmiks], *s.pl.* (*usu. with sg. const.*) sciences *f* atomiques.
atomism ['ætəmizm], *s.* **1.** *A.Phil:* atomisme *m*, atomistique *f.* **2.** *Atom.Ph:* atomisme.
atomist ['ætəmist], *s. A.Phil:* atomiste *m.*
atomistic [ætə'mistik], *a.* atomistique.
atomistics [ætə'mistiks], *s.pl.* (*usu. with sg. const.*) atomistique *f.*
atomization [ætəmai'zeiʃ(ə)n], *s.* atomisation *f*; pulvérisation *f*; vaporisation *f.*
atomize ['ætəmaiz], *v.tr.* atomiser; pulvériser; vaporiser.
atomizer ['ætəmaizər], *s.* atomiseur *m*; pulvérisateur *m*; vaporisateur *m*; *I.C.E:* gicleur *m.*
atomizing ['ætəmaiziŋ], *s.* = ATOMIZATION.
atonable [ə'tounəbl], *a.* expiable; (faute *f*) réparable, rachetable.
atonal [ei'toun(ə)l], *a. Mus:* atonal, -aux.
atonality [eitou'næliti], *s. Mus:* atonalité *f.*
atone [ə'toun]. **1.** *v.tr. or ind.tr.* **to a. (for) a fault by sth., by doing sth.,** expier, racheter, réparer, une faute par qch., en faisant qch.; *Theol:* **atoning act,** acte *m* satisfactoire. **2.** *A:* (*a*) *v.tr.* **to a. two persons,** accorder, réconcilier, deux personnes; (*b*) *v.i.* **to a. with s.o.,** se remettre d'accord, se réconcilier, avec qn.
atonement [ə'tounmənt], *s.* expiation *f*, réparation *f* (**for,** de); *Theol:* rachat *m*; **to make a. for a fault,** réparer une faute; **in a. for a wrong,** en réparation d'un tort; *Theol:* **to make a.,** satisfaire; **a. money,** offrande *f* expiatoire;

Jew.Rel: **Day of A.,** Fête *f* du Grand Pardon.
atonic [æ'tɔnik]. **1.** *a. Med:* (*of muscle, etc.*) atonique. **2.** *a. & s. Ling:* (syllabe) atone (*f*).
atony ['ætəni], *s. Med:* atonie *f*; aveulissement *m.*
atopite ['ætəpait], *s. Miner:* atopite *f.*
atopognosis [ætoupɔg'nousis], *s. Med:* atopognosie *f.*
atrabilious [ætrə'biliəs], *a.* atrabilaire, atrabilieux.
atrabiliousness [ætrə'biliəsnis], *s.* humeur noire.
atractaspis [ætræk'tæspis], *s. Rept:* atractaspis *m.*
Atremata [ætri'meitə], *s.pl. Z:* atremata *m.*
atresia [ə'tri:ziə], *s. Med:* (*a*) atrésie *f*; (*b*) occlusion *f.*
atresic [ə'tri:zik], **atretic** [ə'tri:tik], *a. Med:* atrésique, atrésié, atrétique.
Atreus ['ætriəs], *Pr.n.m. Gr.Lit:* Atrée.
atrichia [ei'trikiə], **atrichosis** [eitri'kousis], *s. Med:* atrichie *f*, atrichiasis *f.*
Atridae (the) [ðiə'traidi:], *Pr.n.mpl. Gr.Lit:* les Atrides.
atrip [ə'trip], *adv. Nau:* **with anchor a.,** l'ancre dérapée; **sails a.,** voiles prêtes à déferler; **yards a.,** vergues prêtes à border.
atriplex ['ætripleks], *s. Bot:* atriplex *m*, arroche *f.*
atrium, *pl.* **-a, -ums** ['ætriəm, -ə, -əmz; 'ei-], *s.* **1.** *Rom.Ant:* atrium *m.* **2.** *Anat:* (orifice *m* de l')oreillette *f* (du cœur).
atrocious [ə'trouʃəs], *a.* **1.** (crime *m*) atroce; **a. act,** atrocité *f.* **2.** *F:* (jeu *m* de mots, etc.) exécrable; (chapeau) affreux.
atrociously [ə'trouʃəsli], *adv.* **1.** atrocement. **2.** *F:* exécrablement; **a. bad,** exécrable.
atrociousness [ə'trouʃəsnis], *s.* atrocité *f.*
atrocity [ə'trɔsiti], *s.* **1.** atrocité *f* (d'un crime, d'un calembour). **2. to witness atrocities,** assister à des atrocités.
atropa ['ætrəpə], *s. Bot:* atrope *f.*
atrophic [æ'trɔfik], **atrophous** ['ætrəfəs], *a.* atrophique.
atrophied ['ætrəfid], atrophié.
atrophy[1] ['ætrəfi], *s.* atrophie *f*; contabescence *f*; **a. of the mind,** étiolement *m* de l'esprit.
atrophy[2] ['ætrəfi, -fai]. **1.** *v.tr.* atrophier. **2.** *v.i.* s'atrophier.
atrophying ['ætrəfiiŋ], atrophiant.
atropic [ei'trɔpik], *a. Ch:* atropique.
atropine ['ætrəpi(:)n], *s. Ch: Pharm:* atropine *f.*
atrop(in)ism ['ætrəp(in)izm], *s. Med:* atropisme *m.*
atropinization [ætrɔpinai'zeiʃ(ə)n], *s. Med:* atropinisation *f.*
Atropos ['ætrəpɔs], *Pr.n.f. Gr.Myth:* Atropos.
atrypa ['ætripə], *s. Paleont:* atrypa *m.*
atta ['ætə], *s. Ent:* atte *f*, fourmi *f* à parasol.
attaboy ['ætəbɔi], *int.esp. U.S:* bravo! à la bonne heure!
attach [ə'tætʃ]. **1.** *v.tr.* (*a*) attacher, lier, nouer, fixer, accrocher, connecter (**sth. to sth.,** qch. à qch.); interconnecter (deux choses); annexer (un document); **to a. oneself to s.o., to a party,** s'attacher à qn, à un parti; **the sample attached to your letter,** l'échantillon joint à votre lettre; (*b*) *Jur:* arrêter (qn); contraindre (qn) par corps; saisir (des biens mobiliers); mettre une saisie-arrêt, faire arrêt, sur (des biens mobiliers); mettre opposition sur (un traitement); (*c*) **I a. no importance to it,** je n'y prête, attache, aucune importance; **one cannot a. any blame to him (for the accident),** on ne peut lui imputer aucune responsabilité (de l'accident). **2.** *v.i.* s'attacher; **there is no suspicion attaching to him,** il n'est aucunement suspect.
attachable [ə'tætʃəbl], *a.* **1.** qui peut être attaché (**to,** à); facile à attacher, à fixer; **quickly a. part,** pièce *f* à montage rapide. **2.** *Jur:* (*a*) (*of property*) saisissable; **not a.,** insaisissable; (*b*) (*of persons*) contraignable par corps.
attaché [ə'tæʃei], *s.* **1.** *Dipl:* attaché *m*; **military a. to . . .,** attaché militaire auprès de . . . . **2. a. case,** porte-documents *m inv*; attaché-case *m.*
attached [ə'tætʃt], *a. & p.p.* **1.** (*a*) attaché (**to,** à); adjoint (à un personnel); sous les ordres (de qn); **official temporarily a. to another department,** fonctionnaire détaché à un autre service; **officer a. to the Staff as interpreter,** officier détaché auprès de l'état-major en qualité d'interprète; **advocate a. to the tribunal,** avocat *m* auprès du tribunal; **he is a. to the embassy,** il fait partie de l'ambassade; *Mil:* **a. unit,** unité rattachée; (*of ship*) **to be a. to a squadron,** faire partie d'une escadre; **salary attached to a post,** traitement afférent à un emploi; **house with garage a.,** maison *f* avec garage attenant; (*b*) **to be deeply a. to s.o.,** être fortement attaché à qn; avoir beaucoup d'attachement pour qn; **to become a. to s.o.,** s'attacher à qn; se prendre d'affection pour qn; **to be foolishly a. to the past,** avoir la superstition du passé; (*c*) *Cost:* **shirt with collar a.,** chemise col tenant. **2.** *Jur:* **debtor a.,** débiteur saisi(-arrêté).
attachment [ə'tætʃmənt], *s.* **1.** (*a*) action *f* d'attacher (qch. à qch.); attachement *m*; *Civ.E: etc:* attelage *m*, fixation *f*; *attrib. Tchn:* **a. fitting,** attache *f*; ferrure *f* d'attache, de fixation, de jonction; **a. point,** point *m* d'attache; **a. flange,** collerette *f* de fixation; **a. clamp,** collier *m* de fixation; **a. plate,** plaque *f* support; (*b*) attache *f*, lien *m*; **attachments of a muscle,** attaches d'un muscle; *Rail:* **tongue a. (of points),** patte *f* d'attache. **2.** accessoire *m* (d'un tour, d'une machine à coudre, etc.); **lathe with drilling a.,** tour avec accessoire pour foret. **3.** *Mil:* rattachement *m*, stage *m*; **to serve an a. with the French army,** faire un stage dans l'armée française. **4.** (*affection*) attachement *m* (**of s.o. for s.o., to sth.,** de qn pour qn, à qch.); affection *f* (**for,** pour); *O:* **to have another a.,** aimer ailleurs. **5.** *Jur:* (*a*) arrêt *m*, saisie *f*, saisie-arrêt *f*, opposition *f*; **a. of real property,** saisie immobilière; **foreign a.,** saisie foraine; **a. against securities,** opposition sur titre; **to issue an a. against s.o.'s person and goods,** faire arrêt, mettre arrêt, sur la personne et les biens de qn; (*b*) contrainte *f* par corps (pour offense à la Cour); (*c*) mandat *m* d'amener.
attack[1] [ə'tæk], *s.* **1.** attaque *f*, assaut *m*; (*a*) **to make an a. on s.o., sth.,** attaquer qn, qch.; *Jur:* **a. on honour,** atteinte *f* à l'honneur; **a. on the rights of property,** mesure *f* attentatoire à la propriété; (*b*) *Mil:* **deliberate a.,** attaque mûrement préparée, montée en détail; **encounter a.,** attaque de rencontre; **combined a.,** attaque combinée; **concerted a.,** attaque concertée; **disconnected a.,** attaque décousue, non coordonnée; **enveloping a.,** attaque enveloppante, d'enveloppement; **hit and run a.,** coup *m* de main de va-et-vient; **holding a.,** attaque de fixation, d'arrêt; **large scale a.,** attaque de grande envergure, de grand style; **night a.,** attaque de nuit; **piecemeal a.,** attaque par petits paquets, attaque fragmentaire; **renewed a.,** reprise *f* d'attaque, retour offensif; **rush a.,** attaque brusquée, inopinée; **a. formation,** formation *f*, dispositif *m*, d'attaque, de combat; **a. in the open,** attaque à découvert; **a. centring on Verdun,** attaque concentrée sur Verdun, ayant Verdun pour objectif principal; **to launch an a.,** lancer une attaque; **to push forward to the a.,** prendre l'offensive; **to rush to the a.,** se précipiter à l'assaut; **to push the a. home,** pousser l'attaque à fond; **to return to the a.,** revenir à la charge; **to break up, disrupt, an a.,** briser, dissocier, une attaque. **2.** (*a*) attaque, crise *f* (de goutte, etc.); **liver a.,** crise de foie, crise hépatique; **he has had another a. of gout,** la goutte l'a repris; **a. of nerves,** crise nerveuse, crise de nerfs; **to have an a. (of nerves),** piquer une crise (de nerfs); (*b*) attentat *m* (sur la vie, la personne, de qn). **3.** *Mus:* attaque (d'une note); **he has a fine a. (on the violin),** il attaque bien la corde.
attack[2], *v.tr.* **1.** (*a*) *Mil:* attaquer, assaillir (l'ennemi); **to be attacked,** subir une attaque; être attaqué; **the nations that attacked France,** les nations *f* agresseurs de la France; (*b*) **to a. s.o., s.o.'s rights,** attaquer qn, les droits de qn; s'en prendre à qn; s'attaquer à qn; **to a. s.o. violently,** diriger de violentes attaques contre qn; **to a. abuses, prejudices,** s'attaquer aux abus, aux préjugés; (*c*) **to a. a job,** s'attaquer à un travail; se mettre à un travail; aborder un travail; *F:* **to a. the dinner,** s'attaquer au diner. **2.** (*a*) **disease that attacks children,** maladie qui s'attaque aux enfants; (*b*) **rust attacks iron,** la rouille attaque le fer.
attackable [ə'tækəbl], *a.* attaquable.
attacker [ə'tækər], *s.* attaquant, -ante, agresseur *m*, assaillant, -ante.
attacking [ə'tækiŋ], *a.* attaquant, assaillant; **the a. forces,** les troupes engagées dans l'attaque; **a. party,** corps *m* d'attaque.
attacolite [æ'tækoulait], *s. Miner:* attacolite *f.*
attacus ['ætəkəs], *s. Ent:* attacus *m.*
attain [ə'tein]. **1.** *v.tr.* atteindre, arriver à (un endroit); s'élever jusqu'à (un haut rang); atteindre, parvenir à, arriver à (un grand âge); atteindre (à), arriver à, parvenir à (ses fins); **to a. one's majority,** arriver à, atteindre, sa majorité; **to a. the end (which we have) in view,** pour aboutir, arriver, aux fins que nous poursuivons; **to a. happiness,** atteindre au bonheur; **to a. the Crown,** s'élever, parvenir, jusqu'à la couronne; **to a. knowledge,** acquérir des connaissances. **2.** *v.ind.tr.* **to a. to perfection, power, honours,** atteindre à la perfection, arriver au pouvoir, parvenir aux honneurs.
attainability [əteinə'biliti], *s.* accessibilité *f* (d'un but, etc.).
attainable [ə'teinəbl], *a.* accessible; réalisable; que l'on peut atteindre; à la portée (**by,** de); *Pol.Ec:* **a. rate of growth,** taux *m* de croissance réalisable.
attainder [ə'teindər], *s. Jur: A:* (condamnation *f* à mort ou mise *f* hors la loi entraînant la) confiscation des biens (pour crime d'État, de haute trahison); mise *f* hors la loi; mort civile; **Act, Bill, of A.,** décret *m* de confiscation de biens et de mort civile.
attainment [ə'teinmənt], *s.* **1.** (*no pl.*) arrivée *f* (à ses fins); obtention *f*, réalisation *f*; **for the a. of his purpose,** pour atteindre, arriver, à ses fins; **I derived as much pleasure from the effort as from the a.,** j'ai trouvé autant de plaisir à fournir l'effort qu'à le voir aboutir; **end easy, difficult, of a.,** but facile, difficile, à atteindre. **2.** (*often in pl.*) acquisition(s) *f* de l'esprit; connaissance(s); savoir *m*; **man of considerable, of small, attainments,** homme qui a beaucoup d'instruction, de talent, d'acquis; homme peu instruit; **his legal, linguistic, attainments,** sa connaissance du droit, des langues; **low standard of a.,** niveau de connaissances, d'études, peu élevé.
attaint[1] [ə'teint], *a. A:* prévenu, accusé (**of,** de).
attaint[2], *v.tr. A:* **1.** *Jur:* frapper (qn) de mort civile. **2.** (*of disease*) atteindre, frapper, attaquer (qn). **3.** souiller, flétrir (qn, la gloire de qn). **4.** accuser (**of,** de).
attalea [ə'teiliə], *s. Bot:* attalea *f.*
Attalus ['ætələs], *Pr.n.m. A.Hist:* Attale.
attapulgite [ætæ'puldʒait], *s. Miner:* attapulgite *f.*
attar ['ætər], *s.* **a. of roses,** essence *f* de roses.
attempt[1] [ə'tempt], *s.* **1.** tentative *f*, essai *m*, effort *m*; **a. at theft,** tentative de vol; **an a. at a smile,** l'ébauche *f* d'un sourire; **without (making) any a. at concealment,** sans chercher à se cacher; **a. to escape,** tentative d'évasion; **to make an a. at sth., at doing sth., to do sth.,** essayer, tâcher, de faire qch.; s'essayer à faire qch.; **you made a very good a. at it,** (i) vous vous en êtes très bien acquitté; (ii) vous êtes arrivé fort près du but; **a. to commit a crime,** tentative de crime; **attempts to do sth.,** tentatives, efforts, pour faire qch.; **no a. will be made to . . .,** on n'essaiera pas de . . .; **to make useless attempts to do sth.,** tenter d'inutiles efforts pour faire qch.; **a lock that baffled all attempts by burglars,** une serrure qui a déjoué toutes les tentatives des cambrioleurs; **he made a. after a. to save him,** il s'est multiplié en tentatives pour le sauver; **to encourage s.o.'s attempts,** encourager les essais, les efforts, de qn; **first a.,** coup *m* d'essai; première tentative; **at the first a.,** du premier coup; **my first a. at a French essay,** mon premier essai de dissertation française; **to make one's first a.,** faire son coup d'essai; **he was making his first a. at swimming, to swim,** il s'essayait à, essayait de, nager pour la première fois; **to be successful at the first a.,** réussir du premier coup; emporter une affaire d'emblée; **this is not his first a.,** il n'en est pas à son coup d'essai; **I will make an a.,** je tâcherai de le faire; **to make another a.,** renouveler ses tentatives; revenir à la charge; **to make several attempts before succeeding,** s'y reprendre à plusieurs fois avant de réussir; **to fail in all one's attempts,** échouer dans toutes ses entreprises, dans tous ses efforts; **I'll do it or perish in the a.,** je le ferai ou j'y perdrai la vie; je vais le tenter dussé-je y perdre la vie; **to give up the a.,** y renoncer; se rebuter. **2.** attentat *m*; **a. on s.o.'s life,** attentat contre la vie de qn; **to make an a. on s.o.'s life,** attenter à la vie de qn; attenter sur qn; **to make an a. on the state,** attenter contre l'État; **a. on, against, liberty,** entreprise *f* contre la liberté; atteinte *f* à la liberté; **measure that constitutes an a. on liberty,** mesure *f* attentatoire à la liberté.
attempt[2], *v.tr.* **1.** (*a*) **to a. to do sth.,** essayer, tenter, tâcher, de faire qch.; chercher à faire qch.; s'efforcer de faire qch.; **he attempted to get up,** il essaya de se lever; il voulut se lever; (*b*) **to a. resistance,** essayer de résister; **he attempted a smile,** il essaya un sourire, il s'efforça de sourire; il ébaucha, esquissa, un sourire; **to a. a piece of work,** entreprendre un travail; s'attaquer à un travail; **to a. the impossible, to a. impossibilities,** tenter l'impossible; **attempted murder, theft,** tentative *f* d'assassinat, de vol. **2.** *A:* **to a. s.o.'s life,** attenter à la vie de qn; **to a. a fortress,** tenter l'assaut d'une forteresse. **3.** *A:* s'attaquer à la vertu de (qn); tenter de séduire (qn).
attemptable [ə'temptəbl], *a.* qui peut être essayé, tenté; (tâche) abordable, entreprenable.
attend [ə'tend]. **1.** *v.ind.tr.* (*give one's attention*) (*a*) **to a. to sth.,** faire, prêter, attention à qch.; **I was not attending to the conversation,** je n'étais pas à la conversation; (*b*) **to a. to s.o.,** écouter qn; **I shall a. to you in a minute,** je serai à vous dans une minute; **a. to what I say,** soyez attentif à mes paroles; *v.i.* **please a.!** veuillez me prêter (votre) attention! veuillez bien m'écouter! faites attention! (*c*) **to a. to sth.,** s'occuper, se charger, se préoccuper, de qch.; **to a. to one's duties, to the household duties,** vaquer à ses occupations, aux soins du ménage; **to a. to one's business,** s'occuper de ses affaires; **to a. to one's studies,** s'appliquer à ses études; **to a. to one's interests,** veiller, vaquer, à ses intérêts; **to a. to one's health,** veiller à, soigner, sa santé; **to a. to one's style,** soigner son style; **to a. to s.o.'s wants,** pour-

voir, subvenir, aux besoins de qn; **I shall a. to it,** je m'en occuperai; j'aurai soin que cela se fasse; *Com:* **to a. to an order,** exécuter une commande; **to a. to the correspondence,** faire la correspondance; s'occuper du courrier; (*d*) **to a. to s.o.,** s'occuper de qn; veiller sur qn; **to a. to a customer,** servir un client; **are you being attended to?** est-ce qu'on vous sert? est-ce qu'on s'occupe de vous? **2.** *v.tr.* (*of doctor*) soigner, donner des soins à (un malade); **to a. the injured,** s'empresser auprès des blessés; donner des soins aux blessés; **I was called to a. a child,** je fus appelé auprès d'un enfant. **3.** *v.tr. & ind.tr.* (*a*) **to a. s.o.,** (i) servir qn, être au service de qn, être de service auprès de qn; (ii) se rendre auprès de qn, se rendre aux ordres de qn; **we were attended by three waiters,** nous étions servis par trois garçons; **to a. (on) a prince,** suivre, accompagner, un prince; (*b*) *Lit:* **measure attended by unexpected consequences,** mesure suivie, accompagnée, de conséquences inattendues, qui a entraîné des conséquences inattendues, qui a eu des suites inattendues; **method attended by great difficulties,** méthode *f* qui comporte de grandes difficultés; **success attended my efforts,** mes efforts furent couronnés de succès; **our best wishes a. you,** nos meilleurs vœux vous accompagnent. **4.** *v.tr.* (*a*) **to a. church, school,** aller à l'église, à l'école; **I attended a small day school,** je fréquentais un petit externat; j'ai fait mes études à un petit externat; **to a. a lecture, a meeting,** assister à une conférence, à une réunion; **to a. (a course of) lectures,** suivre un cours; **the lectures are well attended,** les cours sont très suivis; **he never fails to a. a first performance,** il ne manque jamais une première; (*b*) *Ind:* **attended operation,** fonctionnement *m* sous surveillance (d'une machine).

attendance [ə'tendəns], *s.* **1.** (*a*) (*in boarding house, etc.*) service *m*; (*b*) (*of doctor*) **a. on s.o.,** soins *mpl* pour qn; visites *fpl* à qn; (*c*) *A:* **to be in a. (up)on a king, etc.,** être de service auprès d'un roi, etc. **2. a. (at a meeting, etc.),** présence *f*, assistance *f* (à une réunion, etc.); **school a.,** scolarisation *f*; fréquentation *f* scolaire; **regular a.,** assiduité *f*, régularité *f*, de présence; **a. prize,** prix *m* d'assiduité; **a. register,** registre *m* de présence; **non a.,** absence *f*; **his record of a. at the board meetings is bad,** il ne figure presque jamais au registre de présence du conseil d'administration; *Ind:* **a. bonus,** prime *f* d'assiduité; **a. card,** carte *f* de présence, de pointage; **a. (time) recorder,** pendule *f* de pointage; enregistreur *m* de (temps de) présence. **3.** assistance *f*; **there was a good a. at the meeting,** il y avait une assistance nombreuse à la réunion. **4.** *Ind:* conduite *f*, surveillance *f* (d'une machine).

attendant [ə'tendənt]. **1.** *a.* (*a*) *A:* **a. on s.o.,** qui escorte, qui suit, qui accompagne, qui sert, qn; *Jur:* **a. circumstances (of a crime, etc.),** circonstances *f* qui ont accompagné (un crime, etc.), circonstances concomitantes (d'un crime, etc.); *Lit:* **old age and its a. ills,** la vieillesse et les maux qui l'accompagnent; la vieillesse et son cortège d'infirmités; (*b*) *Mus:* **a. keys,** tons relatifs. **2.** *s.* (*a*) serviteur *m*, domestique *mf*; surveillant, -ante; *Adm:* préposé, -ée; (*in museum, etc.*) gardien *m*, gardienne *f*; (*in theatre*) ouvreuse *f*; (*in laboratory*) préparateur, -trice; (*b*) (*usu.pl.*) suivants *m*, gens *m*, satellites *m* (d'un roi, etc.); personnel *m* (d'un magasin, etc.); personnel de service; **the prince and his attendants,** le prince et sa suite, et son cortège; (*c*) **my medical a.,** mon médecin; (*d*) **to be a regular a. at school, at church,** être assidu à l'école, aller régulièrement à l'église.

attender [ə'tendər], *s. Ecc:* **(regular) a.,** pratiquant, -ante.

attending [ə'tendiŋ], *a.* **a. physician,** médecin traitant; *U.S:* (*in hospital*) **large a. staff,** important personnel médical.

attention [ə'tenʃ(ə)n], *s.* **1.** (*a*) attention *f* (**to,** à); **a. to truth, to detail,** préoccupation *f* de la vérité, des détails; **to give one's a. to sth.,** se préoccuper de qch; **to give one's whole a. to . . .,** se donner entièrement à . . .; *Com:* **your orders shall have our best a.,** vos ordres seront exécutés avec le plus grand soin; *Adm: Com:* **for the a. of Mr X,** à l'attention de M. X; **to turn one's a. to sth.,** diriger son attention vers qch.; porter son attention sur qch.; **we will now turn our a. to . . .,** nous allons maintenant nous occuper de . . .; **to pay a. to sth.,** faire attention à qch.; s'arrêter à, sur, qch.; avoir égard à qch.; tenir compte de qch.; **to pay particular a. to sth.,** s'attacher (surtout) à qch., à faire qch.; **nobody paid any a. to what I said,** on n'accorda aucune attention à mes paroles; **he pays no a. to style,** il n'attache aucune importance au style; **you are not paying a. to what I say,** vous n'êtes pas à ce que je dis; **to pay a. to s.o., to give one's a. to s.o.,** prêter (son) attention à qn; **pay a.!** faites attention! **he knew how to keep the a. of his pupils,** il savait se faire écouter de ses élèves; **to call, attract, draw, (s.o.'s) a. to sth.,** appeler, attirer, l'attention (de qn) sur qch.; signaler, recommander, qch. à l'attention de (qn); désigner qch. à l'attention de (qn); faire observer qch. à (qn); faire remarquer qch. (à qn); **to call a. to a fault,** relever une erreur; **a. must be drawn to the fact that . . .,** nous ferons remarquer que . . .; **to catch s.o.'s a.,** attirer, fixer, l'attention de qn; **to attract everybody's a.,** fixer tous les regards; **poster that attracts a.,** affiche *f* qui attire les regards, qui tire l'œil; **to attract a. by sth.,** se faire remarquer par qch.; **to attract a. by one's oddities,** se singulariser par ses bizarreries; **to hold, engage, s.o.'s a.,** retenir l'attention de qn; **book that holds the a.,** livre attachant; **to draw away s.o.'s a.,** détourner l'attention de qn; **to be all a.,** être (tout yeux et) tout oreilles; (*b*) soins *mpl*, entretien *m*; **the batteries require daily a., monthly a.,** les accus exigent un entretien journalier, des soins mensuels; **the instruments should have occasional a.,** les instruments doivent de temps en temps être soumis à une vérification, doivent être vérifiés de temps en temps. **2.** (*often in pl.*) attention(s), soins *mpl*, prévenance(s) *f*; **to be full of attentions for s.o.,** être attentionné, plein d'attentions, plein d'égards, avoir de la prévenance, pour qn; être aux petits soins pour qn; se dépenser en soins pour qn; **to show s.o. a.,** s'occuper de qn; **to require a great deal of a.,** demander beaucoup de soins; *F: O:* **to pay one's attentions to a lady,** faire la cour à une dame; être attentif auprès d'une dame; **to press one's attentions on s.o.,** poursuivre qn de ses assiduités *f*. **3.** *Mil:* **a.!** garde-à-vous! **to come to a.,** se mettre au garde-à-vous; **to spring to a.,** se mettre vivement au garde-à-vous; **to stand at a.,** être, se tenir au garde-à-vous.

attentive [ə'tentiv], *a.* **1.** attentif (**to,** à); soigneux (**to,** de); **a. to one's own interests,** soucieux de ses intérêts. **2. a. to s.o.,** assidu, empressé, auprès de qn; prévenant pour qn; plein d'égards, d'attentions, pour qn; **to be very a. to s.o.,** être aux petits soins pour qn; être très attentionné pour qn; se montrer galant (auprès d'une femme).

attentively [ə'tentivli], *adv.* attentivement; **to listen a.,** écouter avec attention.

attentiveness [ə'tentivnis], *s.* **1.** attention *f*. **2.** prévenances *fpl*, soins *mpl* (**to, for, s.o.,** pour qn).

attenuate[1] [ə'tenjueit]. **1.** *v.tr.* atténuer; (*a*) amincir; (*b*) raréfier (un gaz, etc.); *A.Med:* **to a. the humours,** atténuer les humeurs; (*c*) *Med:* atténuer (un virus); (*d*) **to a. a statement,** atténuer une affirmation. **2.** *v.i.* s'atténuer; (*of gas, etc.*) se raréfier; **his attenuated body,** son corps amaigri.

attenuate[2] [ə'tenjuət], *a.* atténué; aminci, amaigri; ténu; *Bot:* **a. leaf,** feuille atténuée.

attenuation [ətenju'eiʃ(ə)n], *s.* **1.** atténuation *f* (d'un virus, d'une affirmation, etc.). **2.** *A:* **a. of body,** exténuation *f* du corps; amaigrissement *m*. **3.** *El:* affaiblissement *m*; **a. constant,** constante *f* d'affaiblissement; **a. distortion,** distorsion *f* non uniforme; distorsion amplitude-fréquence.

attenuator [ə'tenjueitər], *s. El: Ac:* atténuateur *m*; amortisseur *m*; **acoustical a.,** panneau *m* acoustique, insonore.

attermine [ə'tə:min], *v.i. Jur: A:* octroyer des termes et délais.

attest [ə'test]. **1.** *v.tr.* (*a*) attester, certifier (un fait); **facts that a. his competence,** faits *m* qui témoignent de sa compétence; **to a. that . . .,** attester, certifier, que + *ind.*; **the document attests the fact that . . .,** le document fait foi que . . .; *Husb:* **attested herds,** troupeaux tuberculinés; (*b*) affirmer sous serment; **I relate nothing that I am not prepared to a.,** je ne raconte rien que je ne sois prêt à affirmer sous serment; **attesting notary,** notaire instrumentaire; notaire certificateur; **attested copy,** copie certifiée; **to a. a signature,** légaliser une signature; **duly attested declaration,** déclaration légalisée; (*c*) *v.ind.tr.* **to a. to sth.;** (i) témoigner de qch.; (ii) attester qch., se porter garant, témoin, de qch. **2.** (*a*) *Jur:* assermenter (qn); (*b*) *Mil:* faire prêter serment à (des volontaires); (*c*) *v.i. Mil:* prêter serment, s'inscrire (comme volontaire). **3.** *A:* **to a. the gods,** prendre les dieux à témoin (**that,** que + *ind.*); attester les dieux.

attestant [ə'testənt], *a. & s. Jur:* déposant, -ante, témoin *m*.

attestation [ætes'teiʃ(ə)n], *s.* **1.** *Jur:* (*a*) déposition *f* (d'un témoin); témoignage *m*; (*b*) attestation *f*; légalisation *f* (d'une signature); **a. clause,** clause *f* d'attestation (de l'authenticité d'une signature). **2.** *Jur:* intervention *f* (d'un témoin dans un acte). **3.** (*a*) assermentation *f* (d'une recrue, etc.); *Mil:* **a. paper,** formule *f*, feuille *f*, d'engagement; (*b*) prestation *f* de serment.

attestor [ə'testər], *s. Jur:* certificateur *m*; témoin *m* instrumentaire.

Attic[1] ['ætik], *a.* attique; **A. salt, wit,** sel *m* attique; *Arch:* **A. order,** ordre *m* attique.

attic[2], *s.* **1.** *Arch: Const:* (*a*) attique *m*; (*b*) mansarde *f*, chambre mansardée; grenier *m*; **a. storey,** étage mansardé; **he has an a. bedroom,** il couche dans une mansarde; **a. window,** (i) fenêtre *f* en mansarde; (ii) lucarne *f*; **to live in the attics,** loger sous les combles, sous les toits. **2.** *Anat:* attique.

Attica ['ætikə], *Pr.n. Geog: Hist:* Attique *f*.

atticism ['ætisizm], *s.* **1.** *Ling: Lit:* atticisme *m*. **2.** *Gr.Hist:* adhésion *f* au parti athénien.

atticist ['ætisist], *s.* atticiste *m*.

atticize ['ætisaiz]. *Gr.Hist:* **1.** *v.i.* se mettre du parti athénien. **2.** (*a*) *v.i.* affecter l'atticisme; (*b*) *v.tr.* **atticized cult,** culte modifié par les Athéniens.

Attidae ['ætidi:], *s.pl. Arach:* attides *f*.

Attila ['ætilə], *Pr.n.m. Hist:* Atilla.

attire[1] [ə'taiər], *s.* **1.** (*a*) vêtements *mpl;* costume *m*; **night a.,** vêtements de nuit; (*b*) *A: & Lit:* parure *f*, atours *mpl* (d'une femme). **2.** (*a*) *Ven:* ramure *f* (d'un cerf); (*b*) *Her:* **attires,** ramure.

attire[2], *v.tr. A: & Lit:* (*usu. passive or reflexive*) vêtir; parer; **to a. oneself in sth.,** (i) se parer de qch.; (ii) *Pej:* s'attifer, s'affubler, de qch.; **neatly attired,** vêtu, mis, avec soin.

attired [ə'taiə:d], *a. Her: Ven:* **stag a.,** cerf ramé.

attitude ['ætitju:d], *s.* **1.** (*a*) attitude *f*, pose *f*; port *m* (de la tête); **indecent a.,** posture peu convenable; **to strike an a.,** prendre une attitude dramatique; poser; (*b*) **a. of mind,** manière *f* de penser, de voir; disposition *f* d'esprit; état *m* d'esprit; comportement *m*; **a. of hostility,** attitude hostile; **a. of authority,** air *m* d'autorité; **to maintain a firm a.,** (i) rester ferme; (ii) garder bonne contenance; *F:* **if that's your a. there's nothing more to be said,** si tu penses comme ça il n'y a plus rien à dire; (*c*) *Pol.Ec:* **a. survey,** enquête *f* d'opinion; **user a.,** attitude des utilisateurs; *Psy:* **family a. test,** test *m* des attitudes familiales. **2.** (*of horse*) station *f*. **3.** *Av: etc:* attitude (d'un avion, d'un missile, etc. sur sa trajectoire); tenue *f*, comportement (d'un appareil); **a. control,** contrôle *m* d'attitude; **a. control system,** dispositif *m* de contrôle d'attitude; **a. indicator,** indicateur *m*, contrôleur *m*, d'attitude; **landing a.,** position *f* d'atterrissage; **a. of flight,** tenue en vol; **steep a.,** vol cabré; **a. relative to wind,** tenue par rapport au vent.

attitudinal [æti'tju:dinl], *a.* relatif au comportement; **a. research,** recherche *f* sur les comportements.

attitudinarian [ætitju:di'nɛəriən], *s.* poseur, -euse.

attitudinize [æti'tju:dinaiz], *v.i.* poser; faire des grâces; *F:* la faire à la pose; **without attitudinizing,** sans pose; sans affectation.

attitudinizer [æti'tju:dinaizər], *s.* poseur, -euse.

attle ['ætl], *s. Min: Miner:* gangue *f*.

atto- ['ætou], *pref.* atto- (10^{-18}e partie d'une unité).

attorney [ə'tə:ni], *s. Jur:* (*a*) *A: & NAm:* **a. (at law)** = avoué *m*; *U.S:* **District A.** = procureur *m* de la République; (*b*) **A. General** = (i) *Eng:* Procureur général; (ii) Procureur général d'un État; (iii) *Can:* Ministre *m* de la Justice; (*c*) *Com:* agréé, -éée (au tribunal de commerce); (*d*) procureur *m*, fondé *m* de pouvoir(s); **a. in fact,** mandataire *m*; **power of a.,** procuration *f*, mandat *m*, pouvoirs *mpl*; **to confer powers of a. on s.o.,** donner (la) procuration à qn; **full power of a.,** procuration générale; **to exercise power of a.,** exercer un pouvoir; **to execute a power of a.,** signer une procuration.

attorneyship [ə'tə:niʃip], *s. Jur:* **1.** procuration *f*, mandat *m*. **2.** (*a*) charge *f* de procureur; (*b*) *A: & NAm:* charge d'avoué.

attornment [ə'tə:nmənt], *s. Jur:* reconnaissance *f* des droits du nouveau propriétaire (par un locataire, etc.).

attract [ə'trækt], *v.tr.* **1.** (*a*) attirer (**to,** à, vers); **a magnet attracts iron,** l'aimant attire le fer; **the heavenly bodies a. one another,** les corps célestes s'attirent les uns les autres; **body attracted by a force,** corps sollicité, appelé, par une force; **to a. s.o.'s attention,** attirer l'attention de qn; (*b*) *Jur:* (*of crime, etc.*) **to a. a penalty,** entraîner une peine. **2.** séduire, attirer; exercer une attraction sur (qn); allécher (qn); avoir de l'attrait pour (qn); **the plan does not a. him,** ce projet ne lui sourit pas; **to feel attracted to s.o.,** ressentir un mouvement sympathique pour qn; **he is not attracted to her,** elle ne lui plaît pas; il ne ressent rien pour elle; *F:* elle ne lui dit rien.

attractable [ə'træktəbl], *a.* attirable.

attraction [ə'trækʃ(ə)n], *s.* **1.** attraction *f*, *Lit:* attirance *f* (**to,** vers); *Ph:* **a. of a magnet,** attraction, sollicitation *f* d'un aimant; **molecular a.,** attraction moléculaire; **the a. of gravity,** l'attraction; *Biol:* **a. sphere,** sphère attractive. **2.** (*usu. in pl.*) séduction *f*; attractions *fpl*, charme *m*, attraits *mpl*, appas *mpl*; **the a. of a good dish,** l'allèchement *m* d'un bon plat; **physical attractions,** séductions physiques. **3. the chief a. (at a party, a show, etc.),** le clou (de la fête, du spectacle, etc.); **the great a. of the day,** la grande attraction du jour.

attractive [ə'træktiv], *a.* **1.** (*of magnet, etc.*) attractif, attirant; *Ph:* **a. effect,** phénomène *m* d'attraction. **2.** (*of pers., offer, manner*) attrayant, attirant, séduisant; alléchant; **she is a.,** elle est séduisante; **the offer is a.,** la proposition est alléchante, a des attraits; **this prospect was a.,** cette perspective me souriait, m'attirait, me semblait intéressante; **to make an a. dish,** préparer un plat appétisant; **a. flat,** appartement coquet; *Com:* **a. prices,** prix intéressants.

attractively [ə'træktivli], *adv.* d'une manière attrayante, séduisante.

attractiveness [ə'træktivnis], *s.* attrait *m*, charme *m*, agrément *m*, attraction *f*.

attractivity [ətræk'tiviti], *s. Ph:* attractivité *f*.

attributable [ə'tribjutəbl], *a.* attribuable, imputable, dû (**to,** à).

attribute[1] ['ætribju:t], *s.* **1.** attribut *m*, qualité *f*; apanage *m*; **speech is an a. of man,** la parole est un attribut de l'homme. **2.** symbole *m*, attribut; *Lit:* **the sword, as an a. of justice,** le glaive, en tant qu'attribut de la justice. **3.** *Gram:* épithète *f*.

attribute[2] [ə'tribju(:)t], *v.tr.* attribuer, imputer, référer (**to,** à); **comedy attributed to Shakespeare,** comédie attribuée à Shakespeare; **you a. to him qualities that he does not possess,** vous lui prêtez des qualités qu'il n'a pas; **to a. a crime to s.o.,** mettre un crime sur le compte de qn; **to a. a disaster to s.o.'s carelessness,** attribuer, imputer, référer, un malheur à la négligence de qn.

attribution [ætri'bju:ʃ(ə)n], *s.* **1.** attribution *f*, imputation *f* (**to,** à); **a. of sth. to a purpose,** affectation *f* de qch. à un but. **2. that lies within, outside of, my attributions,** cela rentre dans, sort de, mes attributions, mes fonctions.

attributive [ə'tribjutiv]. *Gram:* **1.** *a.* **a. adjective,** épithète *f*; adjectif qualificatif. **2.** *s.* épithète.

attributively [ə'tribjutivli], *adv. Gram:* (employé) avec force qualificative; (employé) comme épithète.

attrition [ə'triʃ(ə)n], *s.* **1.** attrition *f*; usure *f* par le frottement; **war of a.,** guerre *f* d'usure; **a. rate,** (i) *Mil: etc:* taux *m* d'usure (du matériel, des effectifs); (ii) *Pol.Ec:* taux de perte de la clientèle; *Artil:* **a. fire,** tir *m* d'usure. **2.** *Theol:* attrition.

attune [ə'tju:n], *v.tr.* **1.** *Mus: A:* accorder (des instruments). **2.** *Lit:* accorder, harmoniser (**to,** avec); **ear attuned to every sound,** oreille exercée à saisir tous les sons; **tastes attuned to mine,** goûts *m* à l'unisson des miens; **the manner is perfectly attuned to the matter,** la forme est en parfaite harmonie avec le fond.

attunement [ə'tju:nmənt], *s.* harmonisation *f* (**to,** à, avec); mise *f* au diapason.

Aturian [ə'tju:riən], *a. & s. Geol:* aturien *m*.

atypic(al) [ei'tipik(l)], *a. Med: etc:* atypique.

aubade [ou'bɑ:d], *s. Mus:* aubade *f*.

aubaine [ou'bein], *s. A.Jur:* (**droit d'**) **a.,** (droit d') aubaine *f*.

aubergine ['oubə(d)ʒi:n], *s. Bot: Cu:* aubergine *f*.

aubr(i)etia [ɔ:'bri:ʃiə], *s. Bot:* aubriétie *f*, aubrietia *f*.

auburn ['ɔ:bən], *a.* auburn *inv*; **a. hair,** cheveux *mpl* châtain roux, aux reflets cuivrés.

au courant [ou'kuərɑ̃], *adv.* au courant (**of, with,** de).

auction[1] ['ɔ:kʃ(ə)n], *s.* (*a*) (**sale by**) **a., a. sale,** vente *f* à l'enchère, aux enchères; vente à l'encan; (vente à la) criée *f*; adjudication publique, aux enchères, vente publique; **Dutch a.,** vente à la baisse; enchère *f* au rabais; **by a.,** par voie d'adjudication; **to sell goods by a.,** *U.S:* **at a.,** vendre des marchandises aux enchères; (*of fish, etc.*) vendre à la criée; **to put sth. up to, for, a.,** mettre qch. aux enchères; **a. room,** salle *f* des ventes; (*for the sale of fish, vegetables, etc.*) chambre *f* des criées; (*b*) *Cards:* **a.** (**bridge**), bridge *m* aux enchères.

auction[2], *v.tr.* vendre (qch.) aux enchères, à l'encan; mettre (qch.) aux enchères; vendre (des denrées, un immeuble par autorité de justice) à la criée.

auctioneer [ɔ:kʃə'niər], *s.* **1.** (*auctioneer and valuer*) commissaire priseur *m*, *pl.* commissaires-priseurs. **2.** (*at a sale*) directeur *m* de la vente; (*at fish, vegetable, market etc.*) crieur *m*.

aucuba ['ɔ:kjubə], *s. Bot:* aucuba *m*.

audacious [ɔ:'deiʃəs], *a.* **1.** audacieux, hardi, intrépide. **2.** *Pej:* effronté, hardi, cynique.

audaciously [ɔ:'deiʃəsli], *adv.* **1.** audacieusement; avec audace; hardiment. **2.** *Pej:* effrontément; avec cynisme.

audaciousness [ɔ:'deiʃəsnis], **audacity** [ɔ:'dæsiti], *s.* audace *f*. **1.** intrépidité *f*, hardiesse *f*; **audacities of style,** audaces, hardiesses, de style. **2.** *Pej:* effronterie *f*, hardiesse *f*, cynisme *m*; **the lies which he had the a. to spread,** les mensonges qu'il a osé répandre.

audad ['audɑd], *s. Z:* arui *m*.

audibility [ɔ:di'biliti], **audibleness** ['ɔ:diblnis], *s.* perceptibilité *f*, audibilité *f* (d'un son).

audible ['ɔ:dibl], *a.* (*of sound*) perceptible (à l'oreille); (*of speech, voice*) audible; distinct, intelligible; qu'on peut entendre; **he was scarcely a.,** on l'entendait à peine; **there was a. laughter,** des rires se firent entendre; *Tp:* **a. call,** appel phonique; *Ph:* **radiations above the a. range,** rayonnement *m* ultra-sonore; **a. frequency,** fréquence *f* audible; **a. machmeter,** avertisseur *m* de mach; machmètre *m* audible.

audibly ['ɔ:dibli], *adv.* distinctement; intelligiblement; **to speak a.,** parler de façon à être entendu.

audience ['ɔ:djəns], *s.* **1.** audience *f*; **to give a. to s.o.,** (i) accorder une audience à qn; (ii) *Lit:* écouter, entendre, qn; *Lit:* **to have (an) a. of s.o.,** avoir une audience, une entrevue, avec qn; **to grant s.o. an a.,** accorder audience à qn; **to hold an a.,** tenir une audience; **it happened in open a.,** cela s'est passé en audience publique; **a. chamber,** salle *f* d'audience. **2.** (*at meeting, etc.*) assistance *f*, assistants *mpl*; (*at theatre*) spectateurs *mpl*, auditoire *m*, public *m*; (*at concert*) auditeurs *mpl*; **the whole a. applauded,** toute la salle applaudit; **to perform before a large a.,** jouer, chanter, etc., devant un nombreux public.

audile ['ɔ:dail], *a. & s.* auditif, -ive.

audio ['ɔ:diou], *a.* sonore; **a. tape,** bande *f* magnétique pour enregistrement sonore; **a. response unit,** unité *f* de réponse vocale; **a. range,** gamme *f* des fréquences audibles; *W.Tel: etc:* **a. switch,** clef *f* d'écoute.

audiofrequency ['ɔ:diou'fri:kwənsi], *s. W.Tel: etc:* audiofréquence *f*; basse fréquence, fréquence audible; acoustique musicale; **a. stage,** étage *m* basse fréquence; **a. wave,** onde *f* audiofréquence.

audiogram ['ɔ:diougræm], *s.* audiogramme *m*.

audio-lingual ['ɔ:diou'liŋgwəl], *a.* audio-vocal, -aux, audio-oral, -aux.

audiology [ɔ:di'ɔlədʒi], *s.* audiologie *f*.

audiometer [ɔ:di'ɔmitər], *s.* audiomètre *m*.

audiometry [ɔ:di'ɔmitri], *s.* audiométrie *f*.

Audion ['ɔ:diən], *s. R.t.m: W.Tel:* Audion *m*, tube *m* à vide.

audio-visual ['ɔ:diou'vizjuəl], *a.* audiovisuel.

audiphone ['ɔ:difoun], *s.* audi(o)phone *m*.

audit[1] ['ɔ:dit], *s.* (*a*) vérification *f*, apurement *m*, censure *f* (de comptes); vérification(s) comptable(s); *Adm:* **A. Office** = la Cour des comptes; **Commissioner of A.** = auditeur *m* à la Cour des comptes, *A.* **a. (ale),** bière *f* de qualité supérieure (offerte par certains collèges universitaires au règlement des fermages); *Ecc: A:* **a. house,** maison *f* du chapitre (d'une cathédrale); (*b*) *Pol.Ec:* **internal a.,** contrôle *m* interne; **management a.,** contrôle de gestion; **manpower a.,** inventaire *m* des effectifs; (*c*) *Space:* **a. list,** liste *f* de contrôle; **a. trail,** vérification à rebours; **a. roll,** bande *f* de contrôle.

audit[2], *v.tr.* vérifier, apurer, examiner (des comptes); **to a. the accounts of a company,** vérifier et certifier la comptabilité d'une société.

auditability [ɔ:ditə'biliti], *s.* contrôlabilité *f*.

auditing ['ɔ:ditiŋ], *s.* (*a*) vérification *f* et certification *f* des écritures; apurement *m*; (*b*) *Space:* **a. trail,** vérification à rebours.

audition[1] [ɔ:'diʃ(ə)n], *s.* **1.** ouïe *f*; faculté *f* d'entendre; **beyond the limit of a.,** au-delà des limites de l'ouïe. **2.** séance *f* d'essai (d'un chanteur, etc.); audition *f*.

audition[2], *v.tr. & i.* auditionner.

auditive ['ɔ:ditiv], *a.* auditif.

auditor ['ɔ:ditər], *s.* **1.** auditeur *m* (d'une conférence, etc.). **2.** (*a*) *Adm:* commissaire *m* aux comptes; vérificateur *m* des comptes; **A.-General,** Vérificateur général des Comptes (du Royaume-Uni); (*b*) *Com: Fin:* expert *m* comptable; vérificateur *m* comptable; réviseur *m*; commissaire aux comptes (d'une société); censeur *m* (d'une compagnie d'assurances); **auditor's final discharge,** quitus *m*.

auditorial [ɔ:di'tɔ:riəl], *a.* qui se rapporte à un Commissaire aux comptes, à une vérification de comptes.

auditorium [ɔ:di'tɔ:riəm], *s.* **1.** salle *f* (de théâtre, de concerts, de conférences, etc.); *NAm:* vaisseau *m* (d'une église). **2.** *Ecc:* parloir *m* (d'un couvent).

auditorship ['ɔ:ditəʃip], *s.* charge *f* de Commissaire aux comptes; commissariat *m*.

auditory ['ɔ:dit(ə)ri]. **1.** *a.* auditif; **the a. organ,** l'organe *m* de l'ouïe; *Anat:* **the external, internal, a. meatus,** le conduit auditif externe, interne. **2.** *s. NAm:* = AUDITORIUM 1.

Augean [ɔ:'dʒi(:)ən], *a. Lit:* (*a*) **the A. stables,** les écuries *f* d'Augias; (*b*) d'une saleté infecte.

Augeas [ɔ:'dʒi:æs], *Pr.n.m. Gr.Myth:* Augias.

augelite ['ɔ:dʒəlait], *s. Miner:* augélite *f*.

augend ['ɔ:dʒend], *s. Mth:* premier nombre, premier opérande (d'une addition).

auger[1] ['ɔ:gər], *s.* **1.** *Tls:* perçoir *m*, foret *m*; (*carpenter's also*) rouanne *f*; **small a.,** laceret *m*; **Smith's a.,** tarière *f*; **a.-bit,** mèche torse, hélicoïdale; mèche pour bois; mèche de tarière; queue-de-cochon *f*, *pl.* queues-de-cochon; **shell a., spoon a.,** tarière à bout rond; tarière à cuiller; **a. smith,** vrillier *m*; **a. smithery,** vrillerie *f*. **2.** *Min: Civ.E:* sonde (anglaise); tarière (de sondage); **earth-boring a.,** sonde trépan. **3.** *attrib. Moll: Conch:* **a. shell,** terebra *m*, turitelle *f*, vis *f*; **a. worm,** chenille *f* du gâte-bois.

auger[2], *v.i. U.S: Av: F:* (*a*) descendre en vrille; (*b*) s'écraser après une descente en vrille.

Auger[3] ['ouʒei], *Pr.n. Atom.Ph:* **A. effect,** effet *m* Auger.

aught [ɔ:t], *s. A: & Lit:* quelque chose *m*, quoi que ce soit; **for a. I care,** pour ce qui m'importe; (*still occ. used in*) **for a. I know,** (pour) autant que je sache; à ce que je sache.

augite ['ɔ:dʒait], *s. Miner:* augite *f*.

augment[1] ['ɔ:gmənt], *s. Gram:* augment *m*; **syllabic, temporal, a.,** augment syllabique, temporel.

augment[2] [ɔ:g'ment]. **1.** *v.tr.* (*a*) augmenter, accroître (qch.) (**with, by,** de); ajouter à (qch.); augmenter (une pénalité); **he augmented his income by working on Sundays,** il augmentait son revenu en travaillant le dimanche; (*b*) *Cmptr:* compléter; faire progresser; (*c*) *Mus:* **augmented interval,** intervalle augmenté. **2.** *v.i.* augmenter, s'accroître.

augmentable [ɔ:g'mentəbl], *a.* augmentable.

augmentation [ɔ:gmen'teiʃ(ə)n], *s.* **1.** augmentation *f*, accroissement *m* (de fortune, etc.); aggravation *f* (des impôts); **a. in the revenue,** augmentation des revenus. **2.** *Her:* augmentation.

augmentative [ɔ:g'mentətiv], *a.* (suffixe, etc.) augmentatif.

augmenter [ɔ:g'mentər], *s.* **1.** augmentateur, -trice (d'un livre, etc.). **2.** *Cmptr:* (*a*) incrément *m*; (*b*) décrément *m*.

Augsburg ['augzbə:g], *Pr.n. Geog:* Augsbourg *m*; *Rel.H:* **Confession of A., A. Confession,** Confession *f* d'Augsbourg; *Hist:* **League of A.,** Ligue *f* d'Augsbourg.

augur[1] ['ɔ:gər], *s. Rom. Ant:* augure *m*; **the College of Augurs,** le Collège des augures.

augur[2], *v.tr. & i. Lit:* (*a*) augurer, présager, prédire; **from all that I a. no good,** de tout cela je ne présage, je n'augure, rien de bon; (*b*) (*of thg*) **it augurs no good,** cela ne présage, n'annonce, rien de bon; **the matter augurs well for us,** l'affaire s'annonce bien pour nous; **it augurs well, ill,** cela est de bon, de mauvais, augure.

augural ['ɔ:gjurəl], *a.* augural, -aux; **a. staff,** bâton augural; **a. science,** science augurale.

augury ['ɔ:gjuri], *s.* **1.** augure *m*; présage *m*; **the priests took the auguries,** les prêtres prirent les augures; **to draw auguries from . . .,** tirer des augures de . . .. **2.** science *f* des augures; science augurale.

august[1] [ɔ:'gʌst], *a.* (assemblée) auguste; (maintien) imposant, majestueux.

August[2] ['ɔ:gəst], *s.* août *m*; **in A.,** au mois d'août, en août; (**on**) **the first, the seventh, of A.,** le premier, le sept, août.

Augusta [ɔ:'gʌstə], *Pr.n.f.* Augusta; Augustine.

Augustan [ɔ:'gʌstən], *a.* **1.** (*a*) *Rom.Hist:* augustal, -aux; (*b*) **the A. age,** (i) *Lt.Lit:* le siècle d'Auguste; (ii) *Eng.Lit:* l'époque de la reine Anne. **2.** *Rel.H:* **the A. Confession,** la Confession d'Augsbourg.

auguste [au'gust], *s.* auguste *m* (dans un cirque).

Augustin [ɔ:'gʌstin], *a. Rel.H:* **A. Friars,** Augustins *m*.

Augustine [ɔ:'gʌstin]. **1.** *Pr.n.m.* Augustin. **2.** *a. & s.* = AUGUSTINIAN.

Augustinian [ɔ:gəs'tiniən]. *Rel.H:* **1.** *a.* (*a*) augustin; de l'ordre de Saint-Augustin; **the A. Canons,** les chanoines réguliers de Saint-Augustin; **A. hermit,** petit-père *m*, *pl.* petits-pères; (*b*) (*of doctrine*) augustinien. **2.** *s.* Augustin, -ine.

Augustinianism [ɔ:gəs'tiniənizm], *s. Ecc:* augustinisme *m*.

augustly [ɔ:'gʌstli], *adv.* majestueusement, augustement; d'un air auguste.

augustness [ɔ:'gʌstnis], *s.* majesté *f* (de maintien, etc.); caractère *m* auguste (d'une cérémonie, etc.).

Augustus [ɔ:'gʌstəs], *Pr.n.m.* Auguste.

auk [ɔ:k], *s. Orn:* alque *f*; **great a.,** grand pingouin; **razor-billed a.,** petit pingouin, pingouin torda, *Fr.C:* gode *m*; **little a.,** mergule nain.

auklet ['ɔ:klit], *s. Orn:* **Cassin's a.,** *Fr.C:* alque *f* de Cassin; **parakeet a.,** macareux *m* starik, *Fr.C:* alque perroquet; **rhinoceros a.,** *Fr.C:* alque à bec cornu; **crested a.,** macareux huppé.

aulacomnium [ɔːlə'kɔmniəm], *s. Moss:* aulacomnium *m.*
auld [ɔːld], *a. Scot:* vieux, vieil, vieille; **a. lang syne,** le temps jadis; le bon vieux temps; **A. Reekie,** la vieille Enfumée, (Édimbourg).
aulic ['ɔːlik], *a.* aulique; *Hist:* **the A. Council,** le Conseil aulique.
Aulularia (the) [ðiɔːluː'lɛəriə], *Pr.n. Lt.Lit:* l'Aululaire *f* (de Plaute).
Aulus Gellius ['ɔːləs'dʒeliəs], *Pr.n.m. Lt.Lit:* Aulu-Gelle.
aumbry ['ɔːmbri], *s.* = AMBRY.
aunt [ɑːnt], *s.f.* **1.** (*a*) tante; **a. by marriage,** tante par alliance; (*b*) (*of person other than true aunt*) (i) tante (à la mode de Bretagne); (ii) *A:* marraine de guerre; *F: O:* **my sainted a.!** mon Dieu! **2.** *F:* (*a*) **A. Sally,** (i) = jeu *m* de massacre, passe-boules *m inv;* (ii) objet *m* de dérision; *O:* **to go to the a.,** aller aux cabinets, au petit coin.
auntie, aunty ['ɑːnti], *s.f. F:* tantine.
au pair ['ou'pɛər]. **1.** *a.* **au p. student,** *F:* **au p. girl,** étudiante au pair. **2.** *adv.* **she's staying with them au p.,** elle est chez eux au pair.
aura ['ɔːrə], *s.* **1.** *A:* exhalaison *f;* effluve *m.* **2.** *Med: etc:* aura *f;* **epileptic a.,** aura épileptique.
aural[1] ['ɔːrəl], *a. Med:* de l'aura.
aural[2], *a.* de l'oreille; auditif, sonore; **a. memory,** mémoire auditive; **a. surgeon, specialist,** auriste *m; W.Tel: T.V: etc:* **a. reception,** réception *f* du son; **a. signal,** signal *m* son; **a. transmitter,** appareil transmetteur de la partie sonore; **a. channel,** voie *f* écoute; **a. null,** accord silencieux; **a. nulling,** extinction auditive.
auramin ['ɔːrəmin], **auramine** ['ɔːrəmain], *s. Ch:* auramine *f.*
aurantia [ɔː'rænʃiə], *s. Ch: Phot:* aurantia *f.*
aurate ['ɔːreit], *s. Ch:* aurate *m.*
aureate ['ɔːriət], *a. Lit:* d'or, doré.
Aurelia [ɔː'riːljə]. **1.** *Pr.n.f.* Aurélie. **2.** *s.* (*a*) *Coel:* aurélie *f,* aurelia *f;* (*b*) *Ent:* chrysalide *f.*
Aurelius [ɔː'riːljəs], *Pr.n.m.* Aurèle; *Hist:* **Marcus A.,** Marc-Aurèle.
aureola [ɔː'riələ], **aureole**[1] ['ɔːrioul], *s.* **1.** *Art:* auréole *f,* gloire *f* (d'un saint). **2. aureole,** auréole (du soleil).
aureole[2], *v.tr.* auréoler.
aureoled ['ɔːriould], *a.* auréolé.
aureomycin ['ɔːriou'maisin], *s. Pharm:* auréomycine *f.*
auric ['ɔːrik], *a. Ch:* (sel *m,* etc.) aurique.
aurichalcite [ɔːri'kælsait], *s. Miner:* aurichalcite *f,* auricalcite *f.*
auricle ['ɔːrikl], *s.* **1.** *Anat:* (*a*) auricule *f,* pavillon *m* (de l'oreille); (*b*) oreillette *f* (du cœur). **2.** (*a*) *Bot: Conch:* auricule (d'un pétale, d'un coquillage).
auricled ['ɔːrikld], *a.* = AURICULATE.
auricula, *pl.* **-ae, -as** [ɔː'rikjulə, -iː, -əz], *s.* **1.** *Anat:* = AURICLE I. **2.** *Bot:* auricule *f,* oreille *f* d'ours. **3.** (*a*) *Moll:* auricule, oreille de Midas; (*b*) *Echin:* auricule.
auricular [ɔː'rikjulər]. **1.** *a.* auriculaire; (*a*) de l'oreille; des oreillettes du cœur; **a. duct,** conduit *m* auriculaire; **a. appendix,** appendice *m* auriculaire (du cœur); (*b*) perceptible par l'oreille; *Ecc:* **a. confession,** confession *f* auriculaire; *Jur:* **a. witness,** témoin *m* auriculaire. **2.** *s.* (*a*) (*little finger*) (doigt) auriculaire *m;* (*b*) *pl. Orn:* (*tuft of feathers*) auricules *f.*
auricularia[1] [ɔːrikju'lɛəriə], *s. Echin:* auricularia *f.*
auricularia[2], *s. Fung:* auricularia *m.*
Auriculariales [ɔːrikjulɛəri'eiliːz], *s.pl. Fung:* auriculariales *f.*
auriculate [ɔː'rikjulət], *a. Bot: Conch:* auriculé.
Auriculidae [ɔːri'kjuːlidiː], *s.pl. Moll:* auriculidés *m.*
auriculo- [ɔː'rikjulou], *pref. Anat:* auriculo-.
auriculotemporal [ɔː'rikjulou'tempərəl], *a. Anat:* auriculo-temporal, -aux.
auriculoventricular [ɔː'rikjulouven'trikjulər], *a. Anat:* (orifice) auriculo-ventriculaire.
auride ['ɔːraid], *s. Miner:* auride *m.*
auriferous [ɔː'rifərəs], *a.* aurifère.
aurific [ɔː'rifik], *a.* aurifique.
aurification [ɔːrifi'keiʃ(ə)n], *s. Dent:* aurification *f* (d'une dent).
auriform ['ɔːrifɔːm], *a.* auriforme.
Auriga [ɔː'raigə], *Pr.n.m. Astr:* Auriga, Aurige, le Cocher.
Aurignacian [ɔːrig'neiʃ(ə)n], *a.* & *s. Prehist:* aurignacien (*m*).
aurin ['ɔːrin], *s. Ch:* aurine *f.*
auriscope ['ɔːriskoup], *s. Med:* otoscope *m.*
aurist ['ɔːrist], *s. Med:* (*ear specialist*) auriste *m,* auriculiste *m;* otologiste *m.*
aurochs ['ɔːrɔks], *s.* aurochs *m;* bœuf *m* urus.
aurocyanide ['ɔːrou'saiənaid], *s. Ch:* aurocyanure *m.*
Aurora [ɔː'rɔːrə]. **1.** *Pr.n.f. Myth:* Aurore. **2.** *s.* aurore *f;* **a. borealis,** aurore boréale; **a. australis,** aurore australe; *Ecc:* **mass for the a.,** messe aurorale.
auroral [ɔː'rɔːr(ə)l], *a. Lit:* auroral, -aux; de l'aurore.
aurous ['ɔːrəs], *a. Ch:* aureux.
auscult [ɔː'skʌlt], **auscultate** ['ɔːsk(ə)lteit], *v.tr. Med:* ausculter.
auscultation [ɔːsk(ə)l'teiʃ(ə)n], *s. Med:* auscultation *f;* **immediate a.,** auscultation immédiate; **mediate a.,** auscultation médiate; **to examine a patient by a.,** ausculter un malade.
auscultator ['ɔːsk(ə)lteitər], *s. Med:* auscultateur *m.*
Ausonius [ɔː'souniəs], *Pr.n.m. Lt.Lit:* Ausone.
auspicate ['ɔːspikeit], *v.tr.* **1.** *A:* présager, prédire. **2.** *U.S:* inaugurer; initier.
auspices ['ɔːspisiz], *s.pl.* auspices *m;* (*a*) *Rom.Ant:* **to take the a.,** prendre les auspices; **favourable a.,** d'heureux auspices; (*b*) **under the a. of the United Nations,** sous les auspices, des Nations Unies.
auspicious [ɔːs'piʃəs], *a.* **1.** (*a*) (vent *m,* etc.) propice, favorable; **the a. hour,** l'heure *f* propice; (*for lovers*) l'heure du berger; (*b*) (signe *m*) de bon augure. **2.** (âge) heureux, prospère; **for five a. years,** pendant cinq années de prospérité; **on this a. occasion,** en ce jour mémorable.
auspiciously [ɔːs'piʃəsli], *adv.* (*a*) sous d'heureux auspices; (*b*) favorablement; (*c*) **to begin a.,** commencer heureusement.
auspiciousness [ɔːs'piʃəsnis], *s.* heureux auspices; aspect *m* favorable, propice (d'une entreprise, etc.).
Aussie ['ɔzi]. *F:* (*a*) *a.* australien; (*b*) *s.* Australien, -ienne; **the Aussies,** les Australiens; (*c*) l'Australie *f;* (*d*) *Ling:* l'anglais australien.
austempering [ɔs'temp(ə)riŋ], *s. Metall:* trempe *f* bainitique (conjuguée).
austenite ['ɔstənait], *s. Metall:* austénite *f.*
austenitic [ɔstə'nitik], *a. Metall:* austénitique.
austenitizing ['ɔstəni'taiziŋ], **austenizing** ['ɔstənaiziŋ], *s. Metall:* austéni(ti)sation *f.*
Auster ['ɔːstər], *Pr.n. Myth: Poet:* Auster *m;* le vent du midi.
austere [ɔːs'tiər], *a.* **1.** austère; (repas) frugal, -aux; (appartement *m*) sans luxe, d'un goût sévère; (vie *f*) cénobitique; **to lead an a. life,** vivre en ascète. **2.** *A:* âpre (au goût).
austerely [ɔːs'tiəli], *adv.* austèrement; avec austérité; frugalement; sévèrement.
austereness [ɔːs'tiənis], *s.* austérité *f.*
austerity [ɔːs'teriti], *s.* austérité *f;* absence *f* de luxe; sévérité *f* de goût; **a. measures, policy,** mesures *f,* politique *f,* d'austérité; **the days of a.,** la période d'austérité, le temps des restrictions.
Austin ['ɔːstin], *a.* (= **Augustin**) *Ecc: A:* **A. Friars,** Augustins *m.*
austral ['ɔːstrəl], *a.* **1.** austral; *Astr:* **the a. signs,** les constellations australes; les signes australs, austraux. **2.** de l'Australie; **A. English,** l'anglais *m* de l'Australie (et de la Nouvelle-Zélande).
Australasia [ɔstrə'leiʒə, -'leiʃə], *Pr.n. Geog:* Australasie *f.*
Australasian [ɔstrə'leiʒ(ə)n, -'leiʃ(ə)n], (*a*) *a.* australasien; (*b*) *s.* Australasien, -ienne.
Australia [ɔs'treiliə], *Pr.n. Geog:* Australie *f;* **South A.,** Australie méridionale; **Western A., Australie occidentale.**
Australian [ɔs'treilien], (*a*) *a.* australien; (*b*) *s.* Australien, -ienne.
Australianism [ɔs'treiliənizm], *s.* australianisme *m,* tournure *f* de phrase australienne, mot australien.
australite ['ɔstrəlait], *s. Miner:* tectite *f.*
Australoid ['ɔstrəlɔid], *a. Ethn:* australoïde.
australopithecus ['ɔːstrəlou'piθəkəs], *s. Paleont:* australopithèque *m.*
Austrasia [ɔs'treiʃə], *Pr.n. Hist:* Austrasie *f.*
Austrasian [ɔs'treiʃ(ə)n]. *Hist:* (*a*) *a.* austrasien; (*b*) *s.* Austrasien, -ienne.
Austria ['ɔstriə], *Pr.n. Geog:* Autriche *f.*
Austria-Hungary ['ɔstriə'hʌŋg(ə)ri], *Pr.n. Hist:* Autriche-Hongrie *f.*
Austrian ['ɔstriən]. (*a*) *a.* autrichien; *Pol.Ec:* **A. economists, economists of the A. school,** économistes *m* de l'école autrichienne; (*b*) *s.* Autrichien, -ienne.
austringer ['ɔːstrindʒər], *s. A:* autoursier *m.*
Austro-Hungarian ['ɔstrouhʌŋ'gɛəriən]. *Hist:* (*a*) *a.* austro-hongrois; **the A.-H. Empire,** l'empire d'Autriche-Hongrie; (*b*) *s.* Austro-Hongrois, -oise.
Austronesian [ɔːstrou'niːziən], *a.* de l'Austronésie; malayo-polynésien, *pl.* malayo-polynésiens.
autacoid ['ɔːtəkɔid], *s. Physiol:* autacoïde *m.*
autacoidal [ɔːtə'kɔidl], *a. Physiol:* autacoïde.
autarchy ['ɔːtɑːki], *s.* autarchie *f.*
autarkic(al) [ɔː'tɑːkik(l)], *a.* autarcique.
autarky ['ɔːtɑːki], *s.* autarcie *f.*
autecology [ɔːti'kɔlədʒi], *s. Biol:* autécologie *f.*
authentic [ɔː'θentik], *a.* (*a*) authentique; digne de foi; *Jur:* **a. act,** acte *m* authentique; **a. text,** texte *m* qui fait foi; (*b*) *Ecc.Mus:* **a. mode,** mode *m* authentique; **a. cadence,** cadence *f* authentique.
authentically [ɔː'θentik(ə)li], *adv.* authentiquement.
authenticate [ɔː'θentikeit], *v.tr.* **1.** certifier, homologuer, légaliser, valider, viser (un acte, etc.). **2.** (*a*) établir l'authenticité de (qch.); vérifier; (*b*) *Mil:* (*signals*) identifier (un correspondant).
authenticated [ɔː'θentikeitid], *a.* **1.** authentique. **2.** d'une authenticité établie; avéré.
authentication [ɔːθenti'keiʃ(ə)n], *s.* **1.** authentification *f;* certification *f* (d'une signature, etc.) homologation *f,* législation *f,* validation *f.* **2.** (*a*) découverte *f;* preuve *f* de l'authenticité (d'un document, etc.); (*b*) *Mil: W.Tel: etc:* identification *f* (d'un correspondant); **a. code,** code *m* d'identification; **a. signal,** signal *m* d'identification.
authenticator [ɔː'θentikeitər], *s. W.Tel: etc:* signal *m* d'identification.
authenticity [ɔːθen'tisiti], *s.* authenticité *f.*
authigenic [ɔːθi'dʒenik], **authigenous** [ɔː'θidʒənəs], *a. Geol:* authigène.
author ['ɔːθər], *s.* (*a*) auteur *m* (d'un livre); **she is the a. of several novels,** elle est l'auteur de plusieurs romans; elle a écrit plusieurs romans; **you must read this a.!** il vous faut absolument lire des livres de cet auteur! (*b*) auteur (d'une théorie, etc.); **to be the a. of one's own misfortunes,** être l'auteur de sa ruine; *Lit:* **the a. of his being,** l'auteur de ses jours.
authoress ['ɔːθəres], *s.f.* femme *f* auteur; femme écrivain.
authoritarian [ɔːθɔri'tɛəriən], *a.* & *s.* autoritaire (*m*); partisan *m* de l'autorité.
authoritarianism [ɔːθɔri'tɛəriənizm], *s.* autoritarisme *m.*
authoritative [ɔː'θɔritətiv], *a.* **1.** (caractère *m*) autoritaire; (ton *m*) d'autorité; (ton) péremptoire. **2.** revêtu d'autorité; (*a*) **a. document,** document *m* qui fait foi, qui fait autorité; **body sufficiently a. to . . .,** corps doué de l'autorité suffisante pour . . .; (*b*) **a. information,** renseignement *m* de bonne source; **to have sth. from an a. source,** avoir qch. de source autorisée, de bonne source.
authoritatively [ɔː'θɔritətivli], *adv.* **1.** autoritairement; péremptoirement. **2.** avec autorité; **I can state it a.,** je puis l'affirmer de bonne source.
authoritativeness [ɔː'θɔritətivnis], *s.* **1.** air *m* d'autorité; ton *m* autoritaire, péremptoire. **2.** autorité *f* (d'un document, etc.).
authority [ɔː'θɔriti], *s.* autorité *f.* **1. to have, exercise, a. over s.o.,** (i) avoir, exercer, une autorité sur qn; (ii) avoir de l'ascendant sur qn; **who is in a. here?** qui est-ce qui commande ici? **to make one's a. felt,** faire sentir sa main; **to be under s.o.'s a.,** être sous les ordres, sous la domination, de qn; **to be under paternal a.,** être sous l'obéissance paternelle, sous la puissance paternelle. **2.** autorisation *f,* mandat *m;* **to have a. to act,** avoir qualité *f* pour agir; **to give s.o. a. to do sth.,** autoriser qn à faire qch., donner autorisation à qn de faire qch.; **to act on s.o.'s a.,** agir sur l'autorité de qn; **to do sth. on one's own a.,** faire qch. de sa propre autorité; **to do sth. without a.,** faire qch. sans autorisation, sans mandat. **3.** (*a*) **to be an a. on sth.,** faire autorité, être autorisé à parler, en matière de qch.; être expert dans la matière; (*b*) **to advance a statement on the a. of s.o.,** attester l'autorité de qn en faveur d'une affirmation; **to have sth. on good a.,** tenir, savoir, qch. de bonne part, de bonne source, de source autorisée; **to quote s.o. as one's a. (for a statement),** se réclamer de qn; **to quote one's authorities,** citer ses sources, ses auteurs. **4.** *Adm:* **public a., administrative a.,** corps constitué; service administratif; **the authorities,** l'administration *f;* les autorités; **the health authorities,** les services d'hygiène; **the military authorities,** les autorités militaires.
authorization [ɔːθ(ə)rai'zeiʃ(ə)n], *s.* autorisation *f* (**to do sth.,** de faire qch.); pouvoir *m;* mandat *m;* **a. in writing, written a.,** autorisation écrite.
authorize ['ɔːθəraiz], *v.tr.* (*a*) autoriser (qch.); **to a. s.o. to do sth.,** autoriser qn à faire qch.; donner pouvoir, donner mandat, à qn de faire qch.; **to be authorized to act,** avoir qualité pour agir; **authorized by custom,** sanctionné par l'usage; *Jur:* **to a. the sale of effects,** consentir la vente des effets; (*b*) *Med:* homologuer (des drogues, etc.).
authorized ['ɔːθəraizd], *a.* (*a*) autorisé; **to apply to an a. person,** s'adresser à qui de droit; *Ecc:* **the a. version** (of

the Bible), la traduction anglaise de la Bible de 1611; *Adm:* **a. charges,** prix homologués; (*b*) *Mil: etc:* réglementaire; organique; théorique; **a. strength,** effectifs *m* théoriques; **a. equipment,** matériel *m* organique.

authorship [ˈɔːθəʃip], *s.* **1.** profession *f*, qualité *f*, d'auteur. **2. to establish the a. of a book,** identifier l'auteur d'un livre; **to confess to the a. of a poem,** s'avouer l'auteur d'un poème; **to claim, repudiate, the a. of a book, of an invention,** revendiquer, désavouer, la paternité d'un livre, d'une invention.

autism [ˈɔːtizm], *s. Med:* autisme *m.*

autist [ˈɔːtist], *a. Med:* autiste.

autistic [ɔːˈtistik], *a. Med:* autistique.

auto [ˈɔːtou], *s. NAm: F:* automobile *f*, voiture *f.*

auto- [ˈɔːtou], *pref.* auto-.

auto-abstract [ˈɔːtouˈæbstrækt], *s. Cmptr:* analyse *f* automatique (de documents).

autoanalysis [ˈɔːtouəˈnæləsis], *s. Psy:* autoanalyse *f.*

auto-answering [ˈɔːtouˈɑːnsəriŋ], *s. Cmptr:* réponse *f* automatique.

autoantibody [ˈɔːtouˈæntibɔdi], *s. Med:* auto-anticorps *m.*

autobiographer [ˈɔːtoubaiˈɔgrəfər], *s.* autobiographe *mf.*

autobiographic(al) [ˈɔːtoubaiəˈgræfik(l)], *a.* autobiographique.

autobiography [ˈɔːtoubaiˈɔgrəfi], *s.* autobiographie *f.*

autocade [ˈɔːtoukeid], *s. U.S:* cortège *m* de voitures.

autocatalysis [ˈɔːtoukəˈtælisis], *s. Ch:* autocatalyse *f.*

autocephalous [ɔːtouˈsefələs], *a. Ecc:* (évêque *m*, église *f*) autocéphale.

autocephaly [ɔːtouˈsefəli], *s. Ecc:* autocéphalie *f.*

autochrome [ˈɔːtoukroum], *a. & s. A.Phot:* (plaque *f*) autochrome (*f*).

autochthon, *pl.* **-s, -es** [ɔːˈtɔkθən, -z, iːz], *s.* autochtone *m.*

autochthonal [ɔːˈtɔkθən(ə)l], **autochthonous** [ɔːˈtɔkθənəs], *a.* autochtone.

autocht(h)onism [ɔːˈtɔkθənizm], *s.* autochtonisme *m.*

autocht(h)ony [ɔːˈtɔkθəni], *s. Geol:* autochtonie *f.*

autoclave[1] [ˈɔːtoukluːv, -kleiv], *s. Ch: Ind:* (marmite *f*) autoclave (*m*).

autoclave[2], *v.tr.* stériliser à l'autoclave.

autocode [ˈɔːtoukoud], *s. Cmptr:* autocode *m.*

autocoder [ˈɔːtoukoudər], *s. Cmptr:* autocodeur *m.*

autocorrection [ˈɔːtoukɔˈrekʃ(ɔ)n], *s. Cmptr:* autocorrection *f*, correction *f* automatique.

autocorrelation [ˈɔːtoukəriˈleiʃ(ə)n], *s.* autocorrélation *f.*

autocracy [ɔːˈtɔkrəsi], *s.* autocratie *f.*

autocrat [ˈɔːtəkræt], *s.* autocrate *m*; *Hist:* **a. of all the Russias,** autocrate de toutes les Russies.

autocratic(al) [ɔːtəˈkrætik(l)], *a.* autocratique; (*of pers.*) autocrate; (caractère) absolu; **don't be so a.,** ne faites pas l'absolu.

autocratically [ɔːtəˈkrætik(ə)li], *adv.* autocratiquement.

auto-cycle [ˈɔːtousaikl], *s.* cyclomoteur *m*; **a.-c. rider,** cyclomotoriste *mf.*

auto-da-fé, *pl.* **autos-da-fé** [ˈɔːtoudɑːˈfei, ˈɔːtouz-], *s.* autodafé *m.*

autodidact [ˈɔːtouˈdaidækt], *s.* autodidacte *mf.*

autodigestion [ˈɔːtoudaiˈdʒestʃ(ə)n], *s. Med:* autodigestion *f.*

autodyne [ˈɔːtoudain], *a. & s. W.Tel:* autodyne (*m*).

autoerotic [ˈɔːtouiˈrɔtik], *a. Psy:* auto-érotique, *pl.* auto-érotiques.

autoeroticism [ˈɔːtouiˈrɔtisizm], **autoerotism** [ˈɔːtouˈerɔtizm], *s. Psy:* auto-érotisme *m.*

autofrettage [ɔːtouˈfretidʒ], *s. Mec.E:* autofrettage *m.*

autogamy [ɔːˈtɔgəmi], *s. Bot:* autogamie *f*, autofécondation *f.*

autogenesis [ˈɔːtouˈdʒenisis], *s. Biol:* autogénèse *f.*

autogenous [ɔːˈtɔdʒinəs], *a.* autogène; **a. welding,** soudure *f* autogène.

autogeny [ɔːˈtɔdʒini], *s. Biol:* autogénie *f.*

autogiro [ˈɔːtouˈdʒairou], *s. Av:* autogyre *m.*

autognosis [ˈɔːtouˈgnousis], *s.* autognose *f*, autognosie *f.*

autograft [ˈɔːtougrɑːft], *s. Surg:* autogreffe *f.*

autograph[1] [ˈɔːtəgrɑːf, -græf]. **1.** *s.* (*a*) autographe *m*; **a. album,** album *m* de signatures, *F:* keepsake *m*; *Com:* **a. book,** livre *m* de signatures; (*b*) reproduction autographiée. **2.** *a.* **a. letter of Byron,** lettre *f* autographe de Byron.

autograph[2], *v.tr.* **1.** écrire (une lettre, etc.) de sa propre main. **2.** écrire son autographe dans (un livre); signer, dédicacer (un exemplaire); mettre son autographe, apposer sa signature, à (un document). **3.** *Lith:* autographier (un manuscrit, etc.); le reproduire par procédé autographique.

autographic(al) [ɔːtəˈgræfik(l)], *a.* **1.** (lettre *f*) autographe. **2.** *Lith:* (encre *f*, papier *m*) autographique.

autographism [ɔːˈtɔgrəfizm], *s. Med:* autographisme *m.*

autography [ɔːˈtɔgrəfi], *s.* **1.** (*a*) action *f* de signer de sa propre main; (*b*) *coll.* autographe *m*; collection *f* d'autographes. **2.** *Lith:* autographie *f.*

autogyro [ˈɔːtouˈdʒairou], *s. Av:* autogyre *m.*

autoh(a)emorrhage [ˈɔːtouˈhemɔridʒ], *s. Ent:* saignée *f* réflexe.

autoh(a)emotherapy [ˈɔːtouhiːmouˈθerəpi], *s. Med:* auto(-)hémothérapie *f.*

autoignition [ˈɔːtouigˈniʃ(ə)n], *s. I.C.E:* auto-allumage *m.*

autoimmunisation [ˈɔːtouimjunaiˈzeiʃ(ə)n], *s. Med:* auto-immunisation *f.*

autoimmunity [ˈɔːtouiˈmjuːniti], *s. Med:* auto-immunité *f.*

autoinfection [ˈɔːtouinˈfekʃ(ə)n], *s. Med:* auto-infection *f.*

autointoxication [ˈɔːtouintɔksiˈkeiʃ(ə)n], *s. Med:* auto-intoxication *f*; (*of food, etc.*) **to cause a.,** intoxiquer.

autokinesis [ˈɔːtoukaiˈniːsis], *s.* autocinésie *f.*

autokinetic [ˈɔːtoukaiˈnetik], *a.* automobile.

autolithography [ˈɔːtouliˈθɔgrəfi], *s.* autographie *f.*

autolysis [ɔːˈtɔlisis], *s. Physiol:* autolyse *f.*

autolytic [ɔːtɔˈlitik], *a. Physiol:* autolytique.

automat [ˈɔːtəmæt], *s.* **1.** *U.S:* restaurant *m* à distributeurs automatiques. **2.** *Phot:* obturateur toujours armé.

automate [ˈɔːtəmeit], *v.tr.* automatiser, rendre automatique.

automated [ˈɔːtəmeitid], *a.* automatisé; **semi-a.,** semi-automatisé; **a. management,** gestion automatisée; **a. production management,** organisation automatisée de la production.

automatic [ɔːtəˈmætik], *a.* (*a*) automatique; **a. vending machine,** distributeur *m* automatique; *Sm.a:* **a. pistol,** *s.* **automatic,** automatique *m*; **a. working,** automaticité *f* (d'un mécanisme); *Typewr:* **a. carriage,** mécanisme automatique d'entraînement du papier; *Cmptr:* **a. coding,** codage *m* automatique; **a. feed punch,** perforateur *m* à alimentation automatique; *Tp:* **a. (telephone),** (téléphone *m*) automatique *m*; *F:* **are you on the a.?** est-ce que vous avez l'automatique? *Av:* **a. pilot,** pilote *m* automatique; *I.C.E:* **a. transmission,** transmission *f* automatique; **I've just bought a Renault a.,** je viens d'acheter une Renault (avec boîte de vitesse) automatique; *s.* **be careful, it's an a.!** attention! c'est une automatique! (*b*) (mouvement) automatique, inconscient, machinal, -aux.

automatically [ɔːtəˈmætikli], *adv.* **1.** automatiquement; **this will be done a.,** cela se fera automatiquement, d'office. **2.** automatiquement, machinalement, d'un mouvement inconscient.

automatics [ɔːtəˈmætiks], *s.pl.* (*usu. with sg. const.*) l'automatique *f.*

automation [ɔːtəˈmeiʃ(ə)n], *s.* **1.** automatisation *f.* **2.** l'automatique *f.*

automatism [ɔːˈtɔmətizm], *s.* automatisme *m.*

automatist [ɔːˈtɔmətist], *s.* automatiste *mf.*

automatization [ɔːtɔmətaiˈzeiʃ(ə)n], *s.* automatisation *f.*

automatize [ɔːˈtɔmətaiz], *v.tr.* automatiser; **highly automatized,** à automatisme poussé.

automaton, *pl.* **-ons, -a** [ɔːˈtɔmətən, -ənz, -ə], *s.* automate *m.*

automatous [ɔːˈtɔmətəs], *a.* automatique.

automobile[1] [ˈɔːtəmoubiːl], *s.* (*a*) *NAm:* automobile *f*, voiture *f*; **a. traffic,** circulation *f* automobile; (*b*) **a. club,** club *m* automobile.

automobile[2], *v.i. U.S: F:* se promener en voiture.

automobilism [ɔːtəˈmoubilizm], *s.* automobilisme *m.*

automobilist [ˈɔːtəməˈbiːlist], *s.* automobiliste *mf.*

automolite [ɔːˈtɔməlait], *s. Miner:* automolite *f.*

automonitor[1] [ˈɔːtouˈmɔnitər], *s. Cmptr:* programme *m* d'enregistrement des opérations.

automonitor[2], *v.tr.* enregistrer (le déroulement des opérations).

automorphism [ˈɔːtouˈmɔːfizm], *s.* automorphisme *m.*

automotive [ˈɔːtouˈmoutiv], *a.* **1.** automoteur, -trice. **2.** *esp. NAm:* automobile; **a. engineering,** technique *f* automobile.

autonomic [ɔːtəˈnɔmik], **autonomous** [ɔːˈtɔnəməs], *a.* autonome.

autonomism [ɔːˈtɔnəmizm], *s.* autonomisme *m.*

autonomist [ɔːˈtɔnəmist], *s.* autonomiste *m.*

autonomy [ɔːˈtɔnəmi], *s.* autonomie *f.*

autonym [ˈɔːtənim], *s.* ouvrage *m* autonyme.

autonymous [ɔːˈtɔniməs], *a.* autonyme.

autopepsia [ɔːtouˈpepsiə], *s. Med:* autodigestion *f.*

autophagous [ɔːˈtɔfəgəs], *a.* autophagique.

autophagy [ɔːˈtɔfədʒi], *s.* autophagie *f.*

autopiesis [ˈɔːtoupaiəsis], *s. Med:* autopiésis *f.*

autopilot [ˈɔːtoupailət], *s. Av:* pilote *m* automatique.

autoplastic [ɔːtouˈplæstik], *a.* (chirurgie *f*) autoplastique.

autoplasty [ˈɔːtouplæsti], *s. Surg:* autoplastie *f.*

autopsy[1] [ˈɔːtɔpsi, ɔːˈtɔpsi], *s.* autopsie *f.*

autopsy[2], *v.tr. U.S:* autopsier.

autoptic(al) [ɔːˈtɔptik(l)], *a.* autoptique.

autoradiogram [ˈɔːtouˈreidiougræm], **autoradiograph** [ˈɔːtouˈreidiougræf], *s.* autoradiogramme *m*, autoradiographie *f.*

autoradiography [ˈɔːtoureidiˈɔgrəfi], *s.* autoradiographie *f.*

autorotation [ˈɔːtourouˈteiʃ(ə)n], *s. Aer:* autorotation *f.*

autoscopy [ɔːˈtɔskəpi], *s. Psy:* autoscopie *f.*

autoserotherapy [ˈɔːtouˈsiərouˈθerəpi], *s. Med:* autosérothérapie *f.*

autosomal [ɔːtouˈsoum(ə)l], *a. Med:* autosomique.

autosome [ˈɔːtousoum], *s. Biol:* autosome *m.*

autostacker [ˈɔːtoustækər], *s.* garage *m* automatique.

autosuggestion [ˈɔːtousəˈdʒestʃ(ə)n], *s.* autosuggestion *f.*

autotomize [ɔːˈtɔtəmaiz], *v.tr. Nat.Hist:* (*of lizard, etc.*) s'autotomiser de (sa queue, etc.).

autotomy [ɔːˈtɔtəmi], *s. Nat.Hist:* autotomie *f*, auto amputation *f* (des lézards, crabes, etc.); **caudal a.,** autotomie caudale.

autotoxin [ˈɔːtouˈtɔksin], *s. Med:* autotoxine *f.*

autotransformer [ˈɔːtoutrænsˈfɔːmər], *s. El:* auto(-)transformateur *m.*

autotroph [ˈɔːtoutrɔf], *s. Bot:* autotrophe *m.*

autotrophic [ˈɔːtouˈtrɔfik], *a. Bot:* autotrophe.

autotype[1] [ˈɔːtoutaip], *s.* **1.** (le) vrai type, (le) type même. **2.** *Typ:* phototypographie *f* (procédé ou image); *Phot:* **a. tissue,** papier *m* au charbon. **3.** reproduction *f*, copie *f* (de tableau, sculpture, etc.).

autotype[2], *v.tr. Typ:* reproduire (une image, etc.) par procédé phototypographique.

autovaccination [ˈɔːtouvæksiˈneiʃ(ə)n], *s. Med:* autovaccination *f.*

autovaccine [ˈɔːtouˈvæksiːn], *s. Med:* autovaccin *m.*

autoverify [ɔːtouˈverifai], *v.tr. Cmptr:* vérifier (la perforation des cartes).

autoxidizable [ɔːtɔksiˈdaizəbl], *a. Ch:* autoxydable.

autumn [ˈɔːtəm], *s.* **1.** automne *m*; **in a.,** en automne; à l'automne; **late a.,** l'arrière-automne *m*; **an a. evening,** une soirée d'automne; *Lit:* **the a. of life,** l'automne de la vie. **2.** *attrib. Bot:* **a. crocus,** colchique *m* d'automne; **a. bells,** gentiane *f* des marais; **a. adonis,** goutte de sang *f*, *pl.* gouttes-de-sang; **a. plants,** plantes automnales; *Arb:* **a. wood,** bois *m* d'automne.

autumnal [ɔːˈtʌmn(ə)l], *a.* automnal; d'automne; d'arrière saison; **a. equinox,** équinoxe *m* d'automne.

Autunian [ouˈt(j)uːniən], *a. & s. Geol:* autunien (*m*).

autunite [ˈoutənait], *s. Miner:* autunite *f.*

auxanometer [ɔːksəˈnɔmitər], *s. Bot:* auxanomètre *m.*

auxesis [ɔːkˈsiːsis], *s. Biol:* auxèse *f*, auxesis *f.*

auxiliary [ɔːgˈziliəri], *a. & s.* auxiliaire (*mf*); subsidiaire (**to,** à); supplémentaire; (machine, etc.) de secours; **a. heating, lighting,** chauffage *m*, éclairage *m*, d'appoint; *Gram:* **a. verb,** verbe *m* auxiliaire; *Mth:* **a. variable,** *s.* **auxiliary,** variable *f* auxiliaire; *Tchn:* **a. equipment,** équipement *m* auxiliaire; matériel *m* annexe; **a. tank,** réservoir *m* supplémentaire, nourrice *f*; **a. generation system,** génération *f* de servitude; **a. engine,** machine *f* auxiliaire; *Cmptr:* **a. memory, storage, store,** mémoire *f* auxiliaire; **a. operation,** opération *f* auxiliaire, de servitude; **a. routine,** sous-programme *m* de servitude, de service; **a. hopper,** rampe *f* de chargement; **a. stacker,** case *f* de réception auxiliaire; *Mil:* **a. troops,** *s.pl.* **auxiliaries,** (troupes *f*) auxiliaires (*m*); *Nau:* **a. cruiser,** auxiliaire *m.*

auximone [ˈɔːksimoun], *s. Bot:* auximone *f.*

auxin [ˈɔːksin], *s. Bot:* auxine *f.*

auxochrome [ˈɔːksoukroum], *s. Ch:* auxochrome *m.*

auxocyte [ˈɔːksousait], *s. Biol:* auxocyte *m.*

auxospore [ˈɔːksouspɔər], *s. Algae:* auxospore *f.*

auxotroph [ˈɔːksoutrɔf], *s. Biol:* souche *f* auxotrophe.

ava [ˈɑːvə], *s. Bot:* ava *m*, awa *m.*

avadavat [ˈævədəvæt], *s. Orn:* bengali *m* rouge, bengali de l'Inde; **green a.,** bengali vert.

avahi [əˈvɑː(h)i], *s. Z:* avahi (laineux).

avail[1] [əˈveil], *s.* **1.** *Lit:* avantage *m*, utilité *f*; **of no a.,** sans effet; **to be of little a. to s.o.,** être peu utile, peu avantageux, à qn; **that will be of little a.,** cela ne servira pas à grand-chose; **to work to little a.,** travailler sans grand résultat, sans grand profit; **to work to no a.,** travailler sans résultat; **my advice was of no a.,** mes conseils n'eurent aucun effet; **it is of no a.,** cela ne sert à rien; *adj. & adv.phr.* **without a.,** sans effet; inutile(ment); ineffectif, -ivement. 2. *pl. U.S: A:* **avails,** produit *m* (d'une terre, d'une vente); revenus *mpl.*

avail[2], *v.tr. & i.* 1. *Lit:* profiter, servir, être utile, à (qn); **what avails his youth?** à quoi sert, à quoi bon, sa jeunesse? que lui vaut sa jeunesse? **nothing availed against the storm,** contre la tempête nous ne pouvions rien, nos efforts restaient impuissants. 2. **to a. oneself of sth.,** se servir, s'aider, de qch.; user de qch.; profiter de qch.; **to a. oneself of a right,** user d'un droit; faire usage d'un droit; se prévaloir d'un droit; **to a. oneself of the opportunity to do sth.,** saisir l'occasion de faire qch.

availability [əveilə'biliti], *s.* 1. disponibilité *f* (de matériaux, d'hommes, etc.); *Cmptr:* **a. ratio,** taux *m* de disponibilité. 2. *Rail: etc:* (durée *f* et rayon *m* de) validité *f* (d'un billet).

available [ə'veiləbl], *a.* 1. (*a*) disponible; (*of pers.*) libre; *Bank:* réalisable; **have you a man a.?** avez-vous un homme de libre? *U.S:* **X said that he would not be a. at the elections,** X a déclaré qu'il ne se présenterait pas comme candidat aux élections; **to try every a. means,** essayer de tous les moyens dont on dispose, tous les moyens possibles; **a. time,** temps *m* disponible; *Ind: etc:* **a. power,** (i) puissance *f*, (ii) énergie *f*, disponible, utilisable; *Hyd.E:* **a. head (of water),** chute *f* disponible; *Pol.Ec: etc:* **apparent a. supplies,** disponibilités apparentes; **items a. in stock,** disponibilités du stock; **a. assets,** actif *m* disponible, liquide; **a. funds,** fonds *m* liquides, disponibles; disponibilités *f*; **capital that can be made a.,** capitaux *m* mobilisables; *Fin:* **sum a. for dividend,** affectation *f* aux actions; (*b*) accessible; **court a. at all times,** tribunal *m* accessible en tout temps; cour *f* siégeant en permanence; **a. for passengers covering a distance of. . .,** accessible aux voyageurs effectuant un parcours de . . .; (*c*) *U.S:* (*of MS, etc.*) utilisable. 2. (*of rail ticket, etc.*) valable, bon, valide (pour deux mois, etc.); utilisable (par tous les trains); **period for which a ticket is a.,** durée *f* de validité d'un billet; **ticket no longer a.,** billet périmé; **season tickets are not a. tonight,** les abonnements sont suspendus ce soir.

availableness [ə'veiləblnis], *s.* = AVAILABILITY.

avalanche[1] ['ævəlɑːnʃ], *s.* (*a*) avalanche *f* (de neige; *F:* de félicitations, de demandes d'emploi, etc.); **a. gallery,** galerie *f* de défense contre les avalanches; **mud a.,** coulée *f* de boue, avalanche boueuse; **a. of electrons, ions,** avalanche électrique, ionique; (*b*) *Bot:* **a. lily,** erythrone *m.*

avalanche[2], *v.i.* tomber en avalanche.

avalent [ei'veilənt], *a. Ch:* avalent.

avant-corps ['ævɑ̃'kɔːr], *s. Arch:* avant-corps *m inv.*

avant-garde ['ævɑ̃'gɑːd]. *Lit: etc:* 1. *s.* l'avant-garde *f.* 2. *a.* d'avant-garde, avant-gardiste; **an a.-g. film,** un film d'avant-garde.

avant-gardism ['ævɑ̃'gɑːdizm], *s. Lit: etc:* avant-gardisme *m.*

avant-gardist(e) ['ævɑ̃'gɑːdist], *s. Lit: etc:* avant-gardiste *mf, pl.* avant-gardistes.

avarice ['ævəris], *s.* avarice *f.*

avaricious [ævə'riʃəs], *a.* avare, avaricieux.

avariciously [ævə'riʃəsli], *adv.* avaricieusement.

avariciousness [ævə'riʃəsnis], *s.* avarice *f.*

avascular [ei'væskjulər], *a. Med:* avasculaire.

avast [ə'vɑːst], *int. Nau:* tiens bon! tenez bon! baste! **a. heaving!** tiens bon virer! tenez bon virer!

avatar [ærvə'tɑːr], *s.* 1. *Hindu Rel:* avatar *m.* 2. manifestation *f*, phase *f* (de l'esprit international, etc.).

avaunt [ə'vɔːnt], *int. A:* arrière! retire-toi! loin de moi! va-t'en!

ave ['ɑːvi, 'eivi]. 1. *Lt.int. Ecc. & Lit:* (*a*) salut! (*b*) adieu! 2. *s.* avé (Maria) *m.*

aven ['æven], *s. Geog:* aven *m.*

avena [ə'viːnə], *s. Bot:* avena *f.*

avenaceous [ævi'neiʃəs], *a. Bot:* avénacé.

avenage ['ævinidʒ], *s. A. Jur:* avenage *m.*

avenge [ə'ven(d)ʒ], *v.tr.* venger (qn, une injure); prendre la vengeance de (qn); *B:* **a. me of mine adversary,** venge-moi de mon adversaire; **to a. oneself, be avenged, on one's enemies,** se venger de, sur, ses ennemis; prendre, tirer, vengeance de ses ennemis; exercer sa vengeance sur ses ennemis; **I will a. myself,** je me ferai justice moi-même; **to a. an insult on s.o.,** venger une injure sur qn; **to a. s.o. for an insult,** venger qn d'une injure; **his death will be avenged,** sa mort trouvera des vengeurs.

avenger [ə'ven(d)ʒər], *s.* vengeur *m*, vengeresse *f.*

avenging[1] [ə'ven(d)ʒiŋ], *a.* vengeur, -eresse; **an a. God,** un Dieu qui punit les méchants.

avenging[2], *s.* vengeance *f.*

avenin(e) ['ævənin, -nain], *s. Ch:* avénine *f*, avénéine *f.*

avens ['ævənz], *s. Bot:* 1. **wood a.,** benoîte *f*; **water a.,** benoîte des ruisseaux, *F:* herbe *f* à la tache. 2. **mountain a.,** chêneau *m*, chênette *f*, dryade *f.*

aventail(e) ['ævənteil], *s. A.Arm:* ventail *m* (de casque).

Aventine (the) [ði'ævəntain], *Pr.n. Geog:* le mont Aventin.

aventurin(e) [ə'ventjurin], *s.* 1. *Glassm:* **artificial a., a. glass,** aventurine *f.* 2. *Miner:* aventurine.

avenue ['ævinjuː], *s.* (*a*) avenue *f*; (*b*) *esp. U.S:* (belle) rue; boulevard *m*; (*in New York*) rue orientée du nord au sud; (*c*) chemin *m* d'accès; *Mil:* **a. of approach,** voie *f* d'accès; approches *fpl*; **to prepare an a. of escape,** se ménager une issue, une voie de retraite, une porte de sortie; **to provide new avenues for industry,** assurer de nouveaux débouchés à l'industrie; **to explore every a., that might lead to an agreement,** explorer toutes les voies pouvant amener à un accord; (*d*) promenade plantée d'arbres.

aver [ə'vəːr], *v.tr.* (**averring, averred**) 1. *Lit:* avérer, déclarer, affirmer (que); **everyone avers that he was present,** au dire de chacun il était présent; **this is averred to be true,** on affirme que c'est vrai. 2. *Jur:* prouver (son dire).

average[1] ['ævəridʒ], *s.* 1. (*a*) moyenne *f*; **arithmetic, geometric, harmonic, a.,** moyenne arithmétique, géométrique, harmonique; **weighted a.,** moyenne pondérée; **rough a.,** moyenne approximative; **on an a.,** en moyenne; **above the a.,** au-dessus de la moyenne; **taking as basis the a. figures for the last five years,** en adoptant comme base la moyenne des cinq dernières années; (*b*) *Fb: etc:* **goal a.,** goal-average *m*, avérage *m.* 2. *M.Ins:* avarie(s) *f*; **particular a.,** avarie particulière; **general a.,** avaries communes; **free from a.,** franc d'avaries; **a. adjustment, a. statement,** dispache *f*; **a. bond,** compromis *m* d'avarie.

average[2], *a.* moyen; **the a. Englishman, Frenchman,** l'Anglais, le Français, moyen; **man of a. ability,** homme *m* ordinaire; **of a. height,** de taille moyenne; **a. capacity,** capacité moyenne; **a. speed,** vitesse moyenne; **the a. reader,** le lecteur moyen; *Pol.Ec: Com:* **a. cost per unit,** coût unitaire moyen; **of good a. quality,** de bonne qualité moyenne; **a. price,** prix moyen; **a. specimen,** échantillon normal; **a. sales,** moyenne *f* des ventes; **a. durability of capital equipment,** longévité moyenne de l'équipement; **a. tare,** tare commune; *Av:* **a. duration of flight,** temps moyen par vol; **a. flight stage,** moyenne d'étape.

average[3], *v.tr. & i.* 1. prendre, établir, faire, la moyenne (des résultats, des ventes, etc.); *St.Exch: etc:* **to a. (up),** (se) faire une moyenne; établir une moyenne. 2. (*a*) **to a. so much, to a. up to so much,** donner, atteindre, rendre, une moyenne de tant; **the sales a. a thousand copies a year,** la vente moyenne, la moyenne des ventes, est de mille exemplaires par an; il se vend en moyenne mille exemplaires par an; (*b*) **he averages eight hours' work a day,** il travaille en moyenne huit heures par jour.

averager ['ævəridʒər], *s.* 1. *St.Exch:* faiseur *m* de moyenne. 2. *M.Ins:* répartiteur *m* d'avaries.

averment [ə'vəːmənt], *s.* 1. *Lit:* affirmation *f*; *Jur:* allégation *f.* 2. *Jur:* preuve *f* (d'une allégation).

Avernus [ə'vəːnəs], *Pr.n. Geog: Myth:* l'Averne *m.*

averrhoa [ævə'rouə, ə'vɛərəwə], *s. Bot:* averrhoa *m.*

Averr(h)oes [æ'vɛərouiːz], *Pr.n.m. Hist:* Averr(h)oès.

averr(h)oism [æ'vɛərouizm], *s. Phil:* averroïsme *m.*

averse [ə'vəːs], *a.* opposé; **to be a. to, from, sth.,** répugner à qch.; être opposé à qch.; être ennemi de qch.; **I should not be a. to marrying him,** il ne me répugnerait pas de l'épouser; **he is not a. to a glass of beer,** un verre de bière ne lui répugne pas; il prend volontiers un verre de bière; **I am not a. to making a sacrifice,** je ne suis pas à un sacrifice près.

aversely [ə'vəːsli], *adv.* avec aversion; à contrecœur.

averseness [ə'vəːsnis], *s.* aversion *f* (**to, from,** pour); répugnance *f* (**to, from,** à).

aversion [ə'vəːʃ(ə)n], *s.* 1. (*a*) aversion *f*, répugnance *f*; **to feel an a. to, for, s.o.,** se sentir de l'aversion pour, envers, de l'antipathie pour, contre, qn; **to feel a. to doing sth.,** répugner à faire qch.; **to feel a great a. to sth., to doing sth.,** se sentir une grande répugnance pour qch., à faire qch.; **to have an a. to s.o.,** avoir qn en aversion; **he has a great a. for her,** elle lui est très antipathique; (*b*) *Bot:* antagonisme microbien. 2. objet *m* d'aversion; **my pet a.,** ma bête noire.

avert [ə'vəːt], *v.tr.* 1. détourner (les yeux, son regard, ses pensées) (**from,** de). 2. écarter, éloigner, prévenir (des soupçons, un danger, un malheur); conjurer (une catastrophe); détourner (un coup); parer à (un accident).

avertable, avertible [ə'vəːtəbl], *a.* que l'on peut détourner, écarter; (danger *m*) conjurable.

avertin [ə'vəːtin], *s. Pharm:* avertine *f.*

avgas ['ævgæs], *s. Av: NAm: F:* essence *f* (pour) avion.

avian ['eiviən], *a. Orn:* avien.

aviary ['eiviəri], *s.* volière *f.*

aviate ['eivieit], *v.i. Av: O:* voler; monter en avion; faire de l'aviation.

aviation [eivi'eiʃ(ə)n], *s.* aviation *f*; **civil, military, a.,** aviation civile, militaire; **naval a.,** aéronavale *f*; aviation aéronautique, navale; **land-based a.,** aviation terrestre; **strategic a., tactical a.,** aviation stratégique, tactique; **reconnaissance a.,** aviation de reconnaissance; **a. spirit,** *NAm:* **a. gasoline,** essence *f* (pour) avion, d'aviation; **a. kerosene,** kérosène *m* aviation.

aviator ['eivieitər], *s.* aviateur, -trice; *Med:* **aviator's ear,** aéro-otite *f.*

Avicenna [ævi'senə], *Pr.n.m. Hist:* Avicenne.

avicennia [ævi'seniə], *s. Bot:* avicennia *m.*

avicolous [ei'vikələs], *a.* avicole, aviculaire.

avicula [ə'vikjulə], *s. Moll:* avicule *f.*

Avicularia [əvikju'lɛəriə], *s. Arach:* aviculaire *m.*

avicularium, *pl.* **-ia** [əvikju'lɛəriəm, -iə], *s. Moll:* aviculaire *m.*

Aviculidae [ævi'kjuːlidiː], *s.pl. Moll:* aviculidés *m.*

aviculture ['eivikʌltjər], *s.* aviculture *f.*

avid ['ævid], *a.* avide (**of, for,** de).

avidly ['ævidli], *adv.* avidement; avec avidité.

avidity [ə'viditi], *s.* avidité *f* (**for,** de, pour); **he read with a.,** il lisait avidement, avec avidité.

avifauna ['eivifɔːnə], *s.* avifaune *f*, faune avienne.

avionics [eivi'ɔniks], *s.* (*usu. with sg. const.*) avionique *f*, aéro-électronique *f.*

aviso, *pl.* **-os** [ə'vaizou, -ouz], *s. Navy:* aviso *m.*

avitaminosis [eivitæmi'nousis], *s. Med:* avitaminose *f.*

avizandum [ævi'zændəm], *s. Scot: Jur:* **to make a., to take a case in(to) a.,** différer le jugement jusqu'à plus ample délibéré.

avocado [ævə'kɑːdou], *s. Bot:* 1. avocatier *m.* 2. **avocado (pear),** (poire *f* d') avocat *m.*

avocation [ævou'keiʃ(ə)n], *s.* 1. *A:* distraction *f* (**from,** de). 2. *esp. NAm:* (*a*) occupation *f*; (*b*) vocation *f*, métier *m*, état *m*, profession *f.*

avocatory [ə'vɔkət(ə)ri], *a. Dipl:* **letters a.,** lettres *f* avocatoires; lettre de rappel.

avocet ['ævouset], *s. Orn:* avocette *f* (à manteau noir); **American a.,** *Fr.C:* avocette américaine.

Avogadro [ævou'gædrou], *Pr.n. Ph:* **Avogadro's law, hypothesis,** hypothèse *f* d'Avogadro-Ampère; **Avogadro's number, constant,** nombre *m* d'Avogadro.

avoid [ə'vɔid], *v.tr.* 1. éviter (qn, qch.); **to a. doing sth.,** éviter de faire qch.; **I could not a. speaking to him,** je ne pus faire autrement que de lui parler; **to a. s.o.,** se cacher à qn; **a. being seen,** évitez qu'on ne vous voie; **I couldn't a. his hearing it,** je n'ai pas pu éviter qu'il l'entendît. 2. (*evade*) se soustraire (au châtiment, etc.); esquiver (les attentions de qn, un coup, une difficulté); *Mil: etc:* **to a. action,** éviter le combat; s'esquiver; **to a. a collision,** parer à, éviter, un abordage; **to a. notice,** se dérober aux regards; **to a. s.o.'s eye,** fuir le regard de qn; **to a. the issue,** contourner les difficultés. 3. *Jur:* résoudre, rescinder, résilier, annuler (un contrat, etc.); annuler (une sentence).

avoidable [ə'vɔidəbl], *a.* 1. évitable. 2. *Jur:* résoluble; annulable.

avoidance [ə'vɔidəns], *s.* 1. action *f* d'éviter. 2. *Jur:* **a. of an agreement (owing to breach, etc.),** résolution *f*, annulation *f*, résiliation *f*, résiliement *m*, d'un contrat; (*in a contract*) **condition of a.,** condition *f* résolutoire; **action for a. of contract,** action *f* en nullité; **a. of contract owing to mistake or misrepresentation,** rescision *f.* 3. *esp.Ecc:* vacance *f* (d'un bénéfice, d'une charge ecclésiastique).

avoirdupois [ævədə'pɔiz, ævwɑːdju'pwɑː], *s.* poids *m* du commerce; **ounce a.,** once *f* avoirdupois; once du commerce.

avouch [ə'vautʃ], *v.tr. Lit:* 1. affirmer, déclarer. 2. *v.tr. & i.* (*a*) **to a. (for) sth.,** garantir qch.; se porter garant de qch.; (*b*) *A:* **to a. s.o.'s action,** avouer, reconnaître, l'action de qn.

avouchment [ə'vautʃmənt], *s. Lit:* 1. affirmation *f*, déclaration *f.* 2. (*a*) garantie *f*; (*b*) aveu *m* (de l'action de qn).

avow [ə'vau], *v.tr.* 1. (*a*) *A:* reconnaître; **his father avowed him for his son,** son père le reconnut pour fils; (*b*) **to a. oneself a free trader,** se déclarer, s'avérer, partisan du libre-échange. 2. *A: & Lit:* déclarer, affirmer (que). 3. avouer, admettre (une faute); **to a. oneself in the wrong,** avouer son tort.

avowable [ə'vauəbl], *a.* avouable.

avowal [ə'vauəl], *s. Lit:* aveu *m*; **to make an a.,** faire un aveu.

avowant [ə'vauənt], *s. Jur:* déclarant *m.*

avowed [ə'vaud], *a.* (ennemi, etc.) avéré, notoire; **he is an a. atheist,** c'est un athée avoué; **her a. lover,** son amoureux déclaré.

avowedly [ə'vauidli], *adv.* ouvertement, franchement; **to be a. a socialist,** s'avouer franchement socialiste.

avowry [ə'vauri], *s. Jur:* déclaration *f* (en justification d'une saisie).

avtur ['ævtəːr], *s. Av: F:* kérosène *m*, kérosine *f*, aviation.

avulsion [ə'vʌlʃ(ə)n], *s.* (*a*) *A:* arrachement *m* **(from,** de); (*b*) *Jur:* avulsion *f*; **land removed through a.,** terrain arraché par avulsion; (*c*) *Surg:* avulsion.

avuncular [ə'vʌŋkjulər], *a.* avunculaire.

avunculate [ə'vʌŋkjuleit], *s. Anthr:* avunculat *m*.

await [ə'weit], *v.tr.* **1.** (*a*) *Lit:* (*of pers.*) attendre (qch., *occ.* qn); **to be awaiting sth.,** être dans l'attente de qch.; **let us a. events,** attendons les événements; *Com:* **awaiting your orders,** dans l'attente de vos ordres; (*b*) **soldiers awaiting discharge,** soldats *m* en instance de réforme; *Com:* **parcels awaiting delivery,** colis *m* en souffrance. **2.** (*of thg*) **the fate that awaits him,** le sort qui l'attend, qui lui est réservé.

awake[1] [ə'weik], *v.* (*p.t.* **awoke** [ə'wouk]; *p.p.* **awaked** [ə'weikt]) **1.** *v.i.* (*a*) s'éveiller, se réveiller; *B:* **and Jacob awaked out of his sleep, and he said . . .,** et quand Jacob fut réveillé de son sommeil, il dit . . .; **he awoke to find himself famous,** du jour au lendemain il devint célèbre; (*b*) **to a. to the danger,** se rendre compte du danger; prendre conscience du danger; **to a. from an illusion,** revenir d'une illusion; avoir les yeux dessillés; **suddenly I awoke to my surroundings,** brusquement je repris conscience de mon entourage, je compris, je me rappelai, où j'étais. **2.** *v.tr.* (*a*) éveiller, réveiller (qn, les remords de qn); éveiller (la curiosité, les soupçons); faire naitre (un espoir, une passion); **to a. a child's intelligence,** éveiller l'intelligence d'un enfant; (*b*) **to a. s.o. to a sense of sth.,** ouvrir les yeux à qn sur qch.

awake[2], *a.* **1.** éveillé; **to lie a., to keep a.,** rester éveillé; **I was a.,** je ne dormais pas; **I was still a.,** je ne m'étais pas encore endormi; **to keep s.o. a.,** tenir qn éveillé; **the noise keeps him a.,** le bruit l'empêche de dormir, le tient éveillé; **wide a.,** (i) bien éveillé, tout éveillé; (ii) *F:* averti; malin, -igne; avisé; **he's wide a.!** il a l'œil ouvert! **2.** attentif; **to be a. to a danger,** avoir conscience d'un danger, se rendre compte d'un danger; **to be a. to one's own interest,** (i) veiller à, sur, ses intérêts; avoir l'œil à ses intérêts; (ii) se rendre compte de ses intérêts; comprendre son intérêt.

awaken [ə'weik(ə)n], *v.tr. & i.* — AWAKE[1].

awakening [ə'weik(ə)niŋ], *s.* (*a*) réveil *m*; (*b*) **a rude a.,** une amère désillusion; un âcheux réveil; **what an a.!** quel réveil!

award[1] [ə'wɔːd], *s.* **1.** *Jur:* arbitrage *m*; sentence arbitrale; décision (arbitrale), adjudication *f*; **to make an a.,** rendre un jugement (arbitral), prononcer, rendre, un arrêt; **to set aside, enforce, an a.,** annuler, rendre obligatoire, une sentence. **2.** (*a*) *Jur:* dommages-intérêts *mpl*; (*b*) *Mil: etc:* distinction *f* honorifique; *Sch: etc:* récompense *f*; **to make an a.,** (i) décerner un prix, une récompense; (ii) juger un candidat (à un examen); **university a.,** bourse *f* universitaire.

award[2], *v.tr.* adjuger, décerner **(sth. to s.o.,** qch. à qn), adjuger (un marché); conférer (un bénéfice, une dignité); **to a. s.o. a sum as damages,** allouer, accorder, attribuer, à qn une somme à titre de dommages-intérêts; **to a. a wage increase,** accorder une augmentation de salaires; *Mil:* **to a. a punishment to s.o.,** donner une punition à qn.

awarder [ə'wɔːdər], *s.* (*a*) adjudicateur *m* (d'un contrat, etc.); (*b*) *Sch:* membre *m* du jury (d'un examen).

awarding[1] [ə'wɔːdiŋ], *a.* adjudicatif.

awarding[2], *s.* décernement *m* (d'une récompense); attribution *f* (de bourses, etc.); adjudication *f* (d'un marché).

aware [ə'wɛər], *a.* **1.** *A:* sur ses gardes; averti; l'œil ouvert. **2.** avisé, informé, instruit **(of sth.,** de qch.); **to be a. of sth.,** avoir connaissance, avoir conscience, être au courant, de qch.; être instruit de qch.; savoir, ne pas ignorer, qch.; **to be a. of sth. a long way off,** sentir qch. de loin; **I wasn't a. of him,** je ne savais pas qu'il était là; je ne m'étais pas aperçu qu'il était là, je ne m'étais pas aperçu de sa présence; **I am a. of all the circumstances,** je connais tous les détails; **I am quite a., well a., of what I am doing,** je sais, je comprends, parfaitement ce que je fais; je me rends bien compte de ce que je fais; **I am well, fully, a. that . . .,** je n'ignore pas que . . .; **fully a. of the gravity of . . .,** conscient de la gravité de . . .; **not that I am a. of,** pas que je sache; **without being a. of it, I had . . .,** sans m'en apercevoir, j'avais . . .; **to become a. of sth.,** apprendre qch.; prendre connaissance (d'un fait); **I became a. of a smell of burning,** j'ai perçu une odeur de brûlé; **to make s.o. a. of sth.,** faire savoir qch. à qn; instruire, informer, prévenir, qn de qch.; **to make s.o. a. that . . .,** faire savoir à qn que . . . .

awareness [ə'wɛənis], *s.* **1.** *A:* vigilance *f*, promptitude *f* (d'esprit). **2.** conscience *f* (de qch.); **a sudden a.,** une prise de conscience.

awash [ə'wɔʃ], *adv.* **1.** *Nau:* (*of submarine, etc.*) à fleur d'eau; **reef a.,** écueil ras; ras *m*; **rocks a. at low tide,** roches *f* qui découvrent à marée basse. **2.** flottant sur l'eau; surnageant; **the rising flood water set all the furniture a.,** l'eau montant, tout le mobilier se mit à flotter. **3.** inondé; **the street was a.,** la rue était inondée.

away [ə'wei], *adv.* loin; au loin. **1.** (*forming part of a compound verb as in* **go away, put away,** *etc.; the sense of* **away** *is either contained in the French verb itself, or shown by the prefix* **en-** *or* **em-;** *the verbs themselves should be consulted for translations and idiomatic phrases*) **to go a.,** partir, s'en aller; **to walk, drive, a.,** partir à pied, en voiture; **to roll a.,** rouler plus loin; **to run, fly, a.,** s'enfuir, s'envoler; **to take sth. a.,** emporter qch. **2.** (*elliptical uses*) (*a*) **a. with you!** allez-vous-en! filez! **a. with it, with them!** emportez-le(s)! **a. with him!** emmenez-le! **one, two, three and a.!** un, deux, trois, partez! *A: & Lit:* **we must a.,** il nous faut partir; *F:* **well a.,** (i) bien en train; (ii) ivre, éméché; **I introduced David to Louise, and they were soon well a.,** j'ai présenté David à Louise et ils s'entendirent tout de suite; *Nau:* **a. port!** avant bâbord! **a. aloft!** en haut les gabiers! (*b*) *A: & Lit:* **I cannot a. with him,** je ne peux pas le supporter, le sentir. **3.** (*continuousness*) (*a*) **to work a.,** travailler toujours; continuer à travailler; **to work a. for two days,** travailler deux jours d'arrache-pied; **to fire a. at the enemy,** maintenir un feu nourri contre l'ennemi; **to fritter one's time a.,** perdre son temps (à ne rien faire); (*b*) **to do sth. right a.,** faire qch. tout de suite, sur-le-champ; *Rail: etc:* **right a.!** en route! **4.** (*distant*) loin; (*a*) **far a.,** dans le lointain, au loin; **a. in the distance,** tout au loin; **a. inland,** bien loin à l'intérieur des terres; **we are five miles a. from the station,** nous sommes à huit kilomètres de la gare; **the town is five miles a.,** la ville est à (une distance de) cinq milles; **five paces a. stood . . .,** à cinq pas de là se tenait . . .; **it is ten minutes' walk a.,** c'est à dix minutes d'ici, de là; il y a dix minutes à pied; **please stand a little farther a.,** voudriez-vous vous éloigner un peu; **this is far and a. the best,** c'est de beaucoup, sans comparaison, sans contredit, le meilleur; **that is far and a. better,** cela vaut infiniment mieux; (*b*) **to hold sth. a. from sth.,** tenir qch. éloigné, loin, de qch.; **to turn (one's face) a. from sth.,** détourner la tête de qch.; **the axis is inclined a. from the sun,** l'inclinaison *f* de l'axe s'éloigne du soleil; **the signpost pointed a. from the village,** le bras du poteau indiquait une direction opposée à celle du village; (*c*) **a. from home,** absent (de chez soi); **he is a.,** (i) il est absent; (ii) *P: O:* il est en prison, à l'ombre; **when he is a.,** quand il est absent; pendant son absence; **to stay a.,** rester absent; ne pas venir; **to keep a.,** se tenir à l'écart; éviter (un endroit, etc.); (*d*) *a. Sp:* **a. ground,** terrain *m* adverse; **a. match,** match *m* à l'extérieur, sur terrain adverse, chez les adversaires; *adv.* **to play a.,** jouer à l'extérieur. **5.** (*time*) **a. back,** dès; **I knew him a. back in 1930,** je l'ai connu dès 1930.

awe[1] [ɔː], *s. Hyd:* aube *f* (d'une roue hydraulique).

awe[2], *s.* crainte *f*; respect *m*; révérence *f*; **to strike s.o. with a.,** (i) (*of pers.*) imposer à qn un respect mêlé de crainte; (ii) (*of object, phenomenon*) frapper qn d'une terreur mystérieuse; **to hold, keep, s.o. in a.,** (en) imposer à qn; tenir qn en respect; être redouté de qn; **to stand in a. of s.o.,** (i) craindre, redouter, avoir une grande peur de, qn; (ii) avoir une crainte respectueuse de qn; **we stood in a. of him,** il nous intimidait.

awe[3], *v.tr.* remplir de crainte; intimider (qn); **they were awed into silence,** intimidés, ils se turent; **we were awed by the majestic beauty of the mountains,** la beauté majestueuse des montagnes nous remplissait d'une crainte émerveillée.

aweather [ə'weðər], *adv. Nau:* au vent; du côté du vent; **to be a. of one's moorings,** être au vent de sa bouée.

aweigh [ə'wei], *adv. Nau:* **with anchor a.,** l'ancre dérapée, guindée.

awe-inspiring ['ɔːinspaiəriŋ], **awesome** ['ɔːsəm], *a.* terrifiant, d'une majesté émotionnante; imposant, impressionnant; **awe-inspiring sight,** spectacle *m* grandiose; **an awesome silence,** un silence qui inspire un effroi religieux.

awe-stricken ['ɔːstrikn], **awe-struck** ['ɔːstrʌk], *a.* **1.** frappé d'une terreur profonde, mystérieuse, religieuse, etc. **2.** intimidé.

awful ['ɔːful], *a.* **1.** terrible, redoutable, effroyable; **to die an a. death,** mourir d'une mort terrible; **that's the a. part of it,** c'est cela le terrible. **2.** (*a*) terrifiant; (*b*) imposant, solennel. **3.** (*intensive*) *F:* terrible, affreux, abominable; **it's simply a.,** c'est affreux, inimaginable, inouï, fantastique; **what an a. liar!** ce qu'il est menteur! **I had an a. fright,** j'ai eu une belle peur; **he's an a. fool,** il est bien bête, bête comme ses pieds; **what an a. bore!** (i) (*of pers.*) qu'il est assommant, rasoir! (ii) (*of thg*) quelle corvée; **what a. weather!** quel temps de chien! quel temps abominable! **an a. cold,** un rhume pharamineux, un rhume de tous les diables; *P:* **you** *are* **a.!** t'es impossible! *P:* **she carried on something a.,** elle a fait une scène terrible. **4.** *adv. P:* (*intensive*) terriblement; **I'm a. glad to see you,** je suis rudement content de vous voir.

awfully ['ɔːf(ə)li], *adv.* **1.** terriblement, effroyablement. **2.** solennellement. **3.** *F:* (*intensive*) **I'm a. sorry,** je regrette infiniment, énormément; **I'm a. glad,** je suis joliment content, rudement content; **a. funny,** amusant, drôle, comme tout; **a. ugly,** affreusement laid; terriblement laid; **she's a. nice,** elle est gentille comme tout; **thanks a.!** merci mille fois!

awfulness ['ɔːfulnis], *s.* caractère imposant, solennité *f* (d'un lieu); caractère terrible (d'une situation).

awhile [ə'(h)wail], *adv. Lit:* pendant quelque temps, pendant quelques instants; un moment, un peu; **wait a.,** attendez un peu; **she stood a. listening,** elle s'arrêta pendant un moment pour écouter; **not yet a.,** pas encore; pas de si tôt.

awkward ['ɔːkwəd], *a.* **1.** (*clumsy*) gauche, maladroit, disgracieux, balourd; **he's an a. boy,** c'est un jeune maladroit; **to be a. in company,** manquer de maintien; ne pas savoir se présenter; **the a. age,** l'âge ingrat; *Mil: F:* **the a. squad,** le peloton des arriérés; les bleus; **to be a. with one's hands,** avoir la main maladroite; **a. sentence,** phrase gauche, mal venue. **2.** (*ill at ease*) embarrassé, gêné; **at our first meeting I felt very a.,** à notre première rencontre je me suis senti très gêné, embarrassé. **3.** (*embarrassing*) fâcheux, malencontreux, embarrassant, gênant; **it would be a. if we met,** une rencontre serait embarrassante; **it would be a. for me to meet him,** cela me gênerait de le rencontrer; **an a. silence,** un silence gêné; **to arrive at an a. moment,** arriver mal à propos, dans un mauvais moment, dans un moment fâcheux; **to ask a. questions,** poser des questions embarrassantes; **an a. situation,** un mauvais pas. **4.** (*inconvenient*) incommode, peu commode; **a. tool,** outil *m* peu maniable; **small table a. for writing at,** petite table incommode pour écrire; **a. corner,** virage difficile, dangereux; *F:* **he's an a. customer,** c'est un homme difficile, qui ne plaisante pas; il n'est pas commode.

awkwardly ['ɔːkwədli], *adv.* **1.** (*a*) gauchement, maladroitement, disgracieusement; (*b*) **the word comes in very a.,** le mot est employé fort mal à propos. **2.** d'une manière embarrassée, d'un ton embarrassé, gêné. **3.** d'une façon gênante, embarrassante; **to be a. situated,** se trouver dans une situation embarrassante, une fausse position, un mauvais pas. **4. the control lever is a. placed,** le levier de commande est mal placé, dans un endroit peu commode.

awkwardness ['ɔːkwədnis], *s.* **1.** (*a*) gaucherie *f*; maladresse *f*; (*b*) manque *m* de grâce; balourdise *f*. **2.** embarras *m*, gêne *f*; **a moment of a., a momentary a.,** un moment de gêne; **her pleasant manner prevented any a.,** son amabilité a mis fin à tout sentiment de gêne; **the a. of having to put up with his attentions,** l'embarras où j'étais d'avoir à souffrir ses attentions. **3.** (*of situation*) inconvénient *m*, difficulté *f*, incommodité *f*; **to spare s.o. the a. of such a situation,** épargner à qn l'ennui d'une pareille situation.

awl [ɔːl], *s. Tls:* alêne *f*, poinçon *m*, perçoir *m*; **spile a.,** épitoir *m*; **tracing a.,** traceret *m*; **marking a.,** pointe *f* à tracer; **sailmaker's a.,** marprime *f*; **(saddler's) drawing a.,** passe-corde *m*, *pl.* passe-cordes; **scratch a.,** tire-ligne *m*, *pl.* tire-lignes; **stabbing a.,** tire-point *m*, *pl.* tire points; **sewing a.,** carrelet *m* (de cordonnier).

awl-shaped ['ɔːlʃeipt], *a. Nat.Hist:* alêné, subulé.

awn[1] [ɔːn], *s. Bot:* barbe *f*, barbelure *f* (d'avoine, etc.); arête *f*.

awn[2], *v.tr.* ébarber (l'orge, etc.).

awned [ɔːnd], *a.* **1.** ébarbé. **2.** *Bot:* à barbes; muni de barbes; barbu; aristé.

awning ['ɔːniŋ], *s.* (*a*) tente *f*, vélum *m*; banne *f* (de boutique, etc.); bâche *f* (de charrette); **a. (blind),** store *m* à l'italienne; (*b*) *Nau:* tente, tendelet *m*; cabane *f* (de canot); **rain a.,** taud *m*, taude *f* (de canot); **main a.,** grande-tente, *pl.* grandes-tentes, tente de pont; **bridge a.,** tente de passerelle; **a. deck,** pont-abri *m*, *pl.* ponts-abris; **a. stretcher,** arbalétrier *m*; **a. rope,** ralingue *f* (d'une tente); **to spread, stretch, the awnings,** faire les tentes; **to furl the awnings,** serrer les tentes; (*c*) marquise *f* (de théâtre, d'hôtel, etc.).

awnless ['ɔːnlis], *a. Bot:* sans barbes.

awry [ə'rai], *adv. & a. O:* de travers; de guingois; **his mouth is a.,** il a la bouche de travers; **to wear one's hat a.,** porter son chapeau de côté; **your hat is a.,** votre chapeau est (posé) de travers; **skirt a.,** jupe *f* de travers, de guingois; (*of plans, etc.*) **to go all a.,** aller tout de travers; avorter.

axe[1], *pl.* **axes** [æks, 'æksiz], *s.* (*NAm: also* **ax**) **1.** hache *f*; **woodman's a., felling a.,** hache d'abattage, cognée *f* de bûcheron, merlin *m*; **cleaving a.,** hache de fendage; **mortise a.,** piochon *m*; **broad a.,** doloire *m*; **chip a.,** épaule *f* de mouton; **cross a.,** hache à picot; **holing a.,** bisaiguë *f*, herminette *f*; *A. Arms:* **hand a.,** coup-de-poing *m, pl.* coups-de-poing; **(caulker's) hammer a.,** malebête *f*; **a. hammer,** marteau *m* de maçon têtu; **ice a.,** piolet *m*; **a. head,** fer *m* de hache; **to cleave sth. with an a.,** fendre qch. d'un coup de hache; **to set the a. to a tree,** mettre la cognée à l'arbre; *Lit:* **to put the a. in the helve,** résoudre la difficulté; *F:* **to have an a. to grind,** avoir un intérêt, des intérêts, personnel(s) à servir; agir dans un but intéressé. **2.** *Adm: F:* **the a.,** coupe *f* dans les prévisions budgétaires; réductions *fpl* sur les traitements; diminutions *fpl* de personnel; **to apply the a. to public expenditure,** porter la hache dans les dépenses publiques.

axe[2], *v.tr.* **1.** mettre la cognée à (un arbre); tailler, dresser, dégrossir (du bois). **2.** *Adm: F:* **to a. public expenditure,** porter la hache dans les dépenses publiques; **to a. officials, officers,** renvoyer des fonctionnaires, des officiers (pour des raisons d'économie).

axe-shaped ['æksʃeipt], *a.* sécuriforme; en forme de hache.

axial ['æksiəl], *a.* axial, -aux; *Mil: etc:* **a. route, a. road,** pénétrante *f*; *Tp: Tel:* **a. cable,** câble axial; **a. cone, a. sleeve,** manche *f* conique pour le câble axial.

Axifera [æk'sifərə], *s.pl. Coel:* axifères *m*.

axil ['æksil], *s. Bot:* aisselle *f* (d'une feuille).

axile ['æksail], *a. Bot:* axile.

axilla [æk'silə], *s.* **1.** *Orn:* axille *f*. **2.** *Bot:* aisselle *f* (d'une feuille).

axillary [æk'siləri], *a.* axillaire.

axinite ['æksinait], *s. Miner:* axinite *f*.

axiolite ['æksioulait], *s. Miner:* axiolite *m*.

axiological [æksiou'lɔdʒikl], *a. Phil:* axiologique.

axiology [æksi'ɔlədʒi], *s. Phil:* axiologie *f*.

axiom ['æksiəm], *s.* axiome *m*; **consistency of axioms,** cohérence *f* des axiomes; **a. set,** axiomatique *f*.

axiomatic(al) [æksiə'mætik(l)], *a.* (*a*) axiomatique; **a. proposition,** proposition *f*, thèse *f*, axiomatique; (*b*) évident.

axiomatics [æksiə'mætiks], *s.pl.* (*usu. with sg. const.*) axiomatique *f*.

axiomatization [æksiɔmətai'zeiʃ(ə)n], *s.* axiomatisation *f*.

axiomatize [æksi'ɔmətaiz], *v.tr.* axiomatiser.

axis[1], *pl.* **axes** ['æksis, 'æksi:z], *s.* **1.** (*a*) axe *m* (d'une sphère, d'une plante, d'un cristal, etc.); *Geol:* axe (d'un plissement); **anticlinal a.,** axe anticlinal; **a. of the equator,** axe équatorial de la terre; *Mec:* **principal axes of a body,** axes principaux d'un corps; *Mth:* **X a.,** axe des X, des abscisses; **Y a.,** axe des Y, des ordonnées; **a. of revolution,** axe de révolution; **a. of an ellipse,** axe d'une ellipse; **major, minor, a.,** grand, petit, axe; **symmetry a.,** axe de symétrie; *Opt:* **a. of vision,** axe visuel; **a. of a lens,** axe d'une lentille; (*b*) *Mil: etc:* **a. of advance,** axe de progression; **a. of march,** axe de marche; **a. of supply,** axe (principal) de ravitaillement; **a. of signal communication,** *U.S:* **main a. of communications,** axe (principal) des transmissions; *Av:* **lift a.,** axe de sustentation; (*c*) *Pol:* **the A. powers,** les Puissances de l'axe. **2.** *Anat:* axis *m*, seconde vertèbre du cou; **a. cylinder,** cylindraxe *m*.

axis[2], *s. Z:* **a. deer,** axis *m*, (cerf *m*) chital *m* (de l'Inde).

axle ['æksl], *s.* **1.** *Veh:* **a. (tree),** essieu *m*; **live a.,** essieu tournant; **dead a.,** essieu fixe; **bent a., cranked a.,** essieu coudé; **drop a.,** essieu surbaissé; **forked a.,** essieu chappé; **fixed a.,** essieu fixe, rigide; **loose a.,** essieu libre; *Rail:* **driving a.,** essieu moteur; (*of electric locomotive*) pont *m*; *Aut:* **front a.,** essieu avant; **rear a.,** pont arrière; **floating a.,** (i) essieu, (ii) pont arrière, flottant; *attrib.* **a. arm,** fusée *f* (d'essieu); **a. box,** boîte *f* de l'essieu; boîte à graisse; **a. cap,** chapeau *m*, capot *m*, de moyeu, d'essieu; **a. drop,** courbure *f* d'essieu; **a. flange,** flasque *m* d'essieu; **a. head,** portée *f* de calage de l'essieu; **a. housing,** carter *m* d'essieu; **a. journal,** fusée *f* d'essieu; **a. neck,** gorge *f*, fusée *f*, d'essieu; **a. shaft,** demi-essieu *m, pl.* demi-essieux (du pont arrière); demi-arbre *m, pl.* demi-arbres. **2.** tourillon *m*, arbre *m*, axe *m* (d'une roue, etc.); *Clockm:* barrette *f* (du barillet).

axoidian [æk'sɔidiən], *a. Anat:* axoïdien.

axolotl [æksə'lɔtl], *s. Amph:* axolotl *m*.

axon ['æksən], *s. Anat:* axone *m*.

axonometric ['æksənou'metrik], *a. Mch.Draw:* **a. projection,** perspective *f* axonométrique.

axonometry [æksə'nɔmitri], *s.* axonométrie *f*.

axoplasm ['æksouplæzm], *s.* axoplasma *m*.

axopod ['æksoupɔd], **axopodium,** *pl.* **-ia** [æksou'poudiəm, -iə], *s. Z:* axopode *m*.

axostyle ['æksoustail], *s. Prot:* axostyle *m*.

ay(e)[1] [ai]. **1.** *adv. & int.* (*a*) (*esp. in Scot.*) oui; mais oui; (*b*) *Nau:* **a., a., sir!** (i) oui, commandant! bien, capitaine! bien, monsieur! (ii) paré! (*c*) *A:* **a., but then . . .,** c'est vrai, vous avez raison, mais . . .. **2.** *s.* (*in voting*) **ayes and noes,** voix *f* pour et contre; **the ayes have it,** les voix pour l'emportent; le vote est pour; la majorité est favorable; **thirty ayes and twenty noes,** trente oui et vingt non; trente pour et vingt contre.

ay(e)[2] [ei], *adv. A: & Lit:* toujours; **for (ever and) a.,** pour toujours; à tout jamais.

ayah ['aiə], *s.f.* ayah; (*in Far East*) bonne d'enfant.

aye-aye ['aiai], *s. Z:* aye-aye *m, pl.* ayes-ayes; chéiromys *m*.

ayous [ei'ju:s], *s. Bot:* ayous *m*, tulipier *m* d'Afrique.

azalea [ə'zeiliə], *s. Bot:* azalée *f*.

azaline ['æzəlain], *s. Ch: Phot:* azaline *f*.

Azariah [æzə'raiə], *Pr.n.m. B:* Azarias.

azarole ['æzəroul], *s. Bot:* (*a*) azerolier *m*, néflier *m* de Naples; (*b*) (*fruit*) azerole *f*.

azedarach [ə'zedəræk], *s. Bot:* azédarac(h) *m*, *F:* arbre *m* à chapelets.

azelaic [æzə'leiik], *a. Ch:* azélaïque.

azeotropic [eiziou'trɔpik], *a. Ch:* (mélange) azéotrope.

azide ['æzaid], *s. Ch:* azide *m*, azoture *m*.

Azilian [ə'ziliən], *a. Prehist:* azilien, du Mas d'Azil.

azimuth ['æziməθ], *s. Astr: Surv: etc:* azimut *m*; **magnetic a.,** azimuth magnétique; **map a.,** azimut géographique; **grid a.,** azimut calculé sur le nord du quadrillage; **true a.,** azimut vrai; **back a.,** azimut, visée *f*, arrière; **reverse a.,** azimut, visée, inverse; *attrib.* **a. compass,** compas *m* de relèvement, compas azimutal; **a. circle,** cercle azimutal; **a. dial,** cadran azimutal.

azimuthal [æzi'mju:θl], *a.* azimutal, -aux; *Ph:* **a. quantum number,** nombre quantique azimutal; *Av:* **a. control,** commande *f* cyclique (d'un hélicoptère).

azine ['æzain], *s. Ch:* azine *f*.

azo ['æzou], *s. Ch:* **a. compounds,** composés *m* azoïques; **a. dyes,** colorants *m* azoïques.

azobenzene [æzou'benzi:n], *s. Ch:* azobenzène *m*.

azobenzoic [æzouben'zouik], *a.* azobenzoïque.

azoic [ə'zouik], *a. Geol: Ch:* azoïque.

azol(e) ['æzoul], *s. Ch:* azol(e) *m*.

azolla [ə'zɔlə], *s. Bot:* azolle *f*.

azonal [ei'zounl], **azonic** [ei'zounik], *a.* azonal, -aux.

azoospermia [æzɔou'spə:miə], **azoospermatism** [æzɔou'spə:mətizm], *s. Med: Physiol:* azoospermie *f*.

azorella [æzɔ'relə], *s. Bot:* azorelle *f*.

Azores (the) [ðiə'zɔ:z], *Pr.n.pl. Geog:* les Açores *f*.

azot(a)emia [æzɔ'ti:miə], *s. Med:* azotémie *f*.

azot(a)emic [æzɔ'ti:mik], *a. Med:* azotémique.

azote ['æzout], *s. Ch: A:* azote *m*.

azotic [æ'zɔtik], *a. Ch: A:* azotique.

azotobacter [ə'zoutoubæktər], *s. Bac:* azotobacter *m*.

azotometer [æzou'tɔmitər], *s. Ch:* azotimètre *m*.

azotorrhea [æzoutə'ri:ə], *s. Med:* azotorrhée *f*.

azoturia [æzou'tjuəriə], *s. Med:* azoturie *f*.

Azov ['æzɔv], *Pr.n. Geog:* **Sea of A.,** mer *f* d'Azov.

azoxy- [æ'zɔksi], *pref. Ch:* azoxy-; **a. compound,** azoxique *m*, azoxyque *m*.

azoxybenzene [æ'zɔksiben'zi:n], *s. Ch:* azoxybenzène *m*.

Aztec ['æztek]. **1.** *Ethn: Hist:* (*a*) *a.* aztèque; (*b*) *s.* Aztèque *mf*. **2.** *Ling:* aztèque *m*.

Aztecan ['æztekən], *a.* aztèque.

azulene ['æzjuli:n], *s. Ch:* azulène *m*.

azulin ['æzjulin], *s. Ch:* azuline *f*.

azulmin [æ'zʌlmin], *s. Ch:* azulmine *f*.

azure[1] ['æʒər, 'eiʒər]. **1.** *s. Lit:* azur *m*; *Her:* azur. **2.** *attrib. Lit:* d'azur, azuré, azural, -aux; **an a. sky,** un ciel d'azur; *Dy: Paint:* **a. blue,** azur; *Miner:* **a. spar, stone,** pierre *f* d'azur; lapis-lazuli *minv*; lazulite *f*.

azure[2], *v.tr. Lit:* azurer.

azurean [æzju'ri:ən], *a. Lit:* azural, -aux.

azurin(e) ['æʒurin, -ain]. **1.** *a. Lit:* azurin; bleu gris. **2.** *s.* (*a*) *Dy:* azurine *f*; (*b*) *Ich:* gardon bleu (du Lancashire).

azurite ['æʒurait], *s. Miner:* azurite *f*.

azygospore [ei'zigouspɔ:r], *s. Fung:* azygospore *f*.

azygo(u)s ['æzigəs], *a. Anat:* azygos *inv*; **a. vein,** azygos *f*.

azyme ['æzim, 'æzaim], *s.* pain *m* azyme; azymes *mpl*.

azymite ['æzimait], *s. Ecc:* azymite *m*.

azymous ['æziməs], *a.* azyme.

B

B, b [bi:], *s.* **1.** *(a)* (la lettre) B, b *m*; *Tp:* **B for Benjamin,** B comme Berthe; *(b) (in numbering)* **house number 51B,** maison *f* numéro 51 ter; *Mil:* **B company,** deuxième compagnie *f*; *Geol:* **B horizon,** horizon *m* B; *(c)* **grade B (oranges, etc.),** (oranges, etc.) de deuxième catégorie; **B road** = route *f* secondaire; *(d) Sch: (in marking exercises)* = assez bien. **2.** *Mus:* si *m*; **B flat,** si bémol.

baa[1] [bɑ:], *s.* bêlement *m*; **baa!** bê! *(child's language)* **baa-lamb,** petit agneau, agnelet *m*.

baa[2], *v.i.* **(baaed, baa'd** [bɑ:d]) bêler.

baaing[1] ['bɑ:iŋ], *a.* bêlant.

baaing[2], *s.* bêlement *m*.

Baal, *pl.* **Baalim** ['beiəl, bɑ:l, 'beiəlim, 'bɑ:lim], *s.* *(a) Rel.H:* Baal *m*; *(b)* faux dieu.

Baalism ['beiəlizm, 'bɑ:-], *s.* *(a) Rel.H:* adoration *f* de Baal; *(b)* idolâtrie *f*.

Baalist, Baalite ['beiəlist, 'beiəlait, 'bɑ:-], *s. Rel.H:* *(a)* adorateur, -trice, de Baal; *(b)* idolâtre *mf*.

baba ['bɑ:bə], *s. Cu:* baba *m*.

babacoote ['bæbəku:t], *s. Z:* indri(s) *m* babakoto; indri(s) sans queue.

babassu ['bɑ:bəsu:], *s. Bot:* attalée *f*.

babble ['bæbl], *s. Dial:* bébé *m*.

babbitt[1] ['bæbit], *s.* **babbitt, Babbitt('s) metal,** métal *m* antifriction; métal blanc (inventé par Babbitt); régule *m*.

babbitt[2], *v.tr. Mec.E:* garnir (un coussinet) de métal antifriction, de métal blanc; réguler (un coussinet).

Babbitt[3]. **1.** *Pr.n.* Babbitt (nom du héros d'un roman de Sinclair Lewis). **2.** *s.m. NAm: Pej:* homme d'affaires parvenu (et borné).

babbitting ['bæbitiŋ], *s.* garniture *f* de métal blanc.

babbit(t)ism ['bæbitizm], *s. NAm:* façon *f* de vivre d'un parvenu (d'après Babbitt).

babbitt-lined ['bæbit'laind], *a. Mec.E:* régulé.

babbit(t)ry ['bæbitri] = BABBIT(T)ISM.

babble[1] ['bæbl], *s.* **1.** babil *m*, babillage *m*, babillement *m*. **2.** jaserie *f*, bavardage *m*. **3.** murmure *m*, gazouillement *m* (d'un ruisseau). **4.** *Tp:* murmure confus. **5.** *Ven:* clabaudage *m* (d'un chien).

babble[2]. **1.** *v.i.* *(a)* babiller; *(b)* bavarder, jaser; **to b. on,** parler sans s'arrêter; *(c) (of stream)* murmurer, gazouiller, babiller; *(d) Ven: (of hound)* babiller, brailler, clabauder. **2.** *v.tr.* *(a)* raconter (qch.) en babiliant, **to b. (out) nonsense,** débiter des sottises; *(b)* **to b. (out) a secret, the truth,** laisser échapper un secret, la vérité.

babbler ['bæblər], *s.* **1.** babillard, -arde; bavard, -arde. **2.** jaseur, -euse (qui laisse échapper des secrets); bavard, -arde. **3.** *Orn:* timalie *f*, turdoïde *m*, cratérope *m*, grive bavarde, grive bruyante; **quaker b.,** alcippe *m*; **scimitar b.,** pomatorhin *m*; **wren b.,** turdinule *m*; **(Malayan) tit b.,** macronus *m*. **4.** *Ven:* chien bavard; babillard *m*, braillard *m*, clabaud *m*.

babbling[1] ['bæbliŋ], *a.* *(a)* babillard, bavard, jaseur; *(of stream)* murmurant, babillard, jaseur; *(b) Ven:* (chien) braillard, clabaud.

babbling[2], *s.* = BABBLE[1].

babbly ['bæbli], *a.* qui babille, jase, gazouille.

babby ['bæbi], *s. Dial:* bébé *m*.

Babcock ['bæbkɔk], *Pr.n. Agr:* **B. bottle, flask,** fiole *f* de Babcock.

babe [beib], *s.* **1.** *(a) Lit: etc:* enfant *m* (en bas âge), petit enfant, bambin *m*; **out of the mouth of babes and sucklings . . .,** la vérité sort de la bouche des enfants; *(b) F:* naïf, naïve; **what a b. she is!** ce qu'elle est ingénue! **babes in the wood,** de jeunes innocents; **story that is no food for babes,** histoire qui n'est pas pour les jeunes filles; *(c) F: (in the House of Commons)* **The B.,** le dernier élu, le plus récent, des membres de la Chambre. **2.** *NAm: F:* jolie fille; **hi, b.!** bonjour, ma jolie!

Babel ['beibl]. **1.** *Pr.n.* **the Tower of B.,** la Tour de Babel. **2.** *s.* *(a)* brouhaha *m*; **it was (an) absolute b.,** c'était un vacarme à ne pas s'entendre; c'était la tour de Babel; *(b)* gratte-ciel *m inv* (mal conçu); *(c)* projet *m* excessivement grandiose.

babesia [bə'bi:ziə], *s. Prot:* babésia *m*.

babesiasis, *pl.* **-es** [bæbi'zaiæsis, -i:z], **babesiosis,** *pl.* **-es** [bæbizai'ousis, -i:z], *s. Vet:* babésiose *f*.

babesiellosis, *pl.* **-es** [bæbizaiə'lousis, -i:z], *s. Vet:* babésiellose *f*.

Babiana [bæbi'ɑ:nə], *s. Bot:* babiane *f*.

babiche [bæ'bi:ʃ], *s. Can:* lanière *f*, fil *m*, courroie *f*, de cuir vert, de tendon, de boyau.

babies' breath ['beibiz'breθ], *s. Bot:* = BABY'S BREATH.

babingtonite ['bæbiŋtənait], *s. Miner:* babingtonite *f*.

Babinski [bə'binski], *Pr.n. Med:* **B.'s reflex, sign,** signe *m* de Babinski.

babir(o)ussa [bæbi'ru:sə], *s. Z:* babiroussa *m*.

bablah ['bæblɑ:], *s. Bot:* bablah *m*, bablad *m*.

baboen ['bɑ:bu:n], *s. Com:* **b. (wood),** virola *m*.

baboo ['bɑ:bu:], *s.* = BABU.

babool [bɑ:'bu:l], *s. Bot:* acacia *m* d'Arabie.

baboon [bə'bu:n], *s. Z:* babouin *m*; **dog-faced b.,** cynocéphale *m*; **Arabian b.,** hamadryas *m*, tartarini *m*; **West-African b.,** drill *m*; *F:* **he's a great b.,** c'est une espèce d'armoire à glace, c'est un vrai orang-outang.

baboonery [bə'bu:nəri], *s.* **1.** colonie *f* de babouins. **2.** *(a)* stupidité grossière; *(b)* humour *f* grotesque.

baboosh, babouche, babuche [bɑ:'bu:ʃ], *s.* babouche *f*.

babu ['bɑ:bu:], *s. (in India) (a) (form of address)* monsieur; *(b) O:* employé *m* de bureau (qui sait un peu d'anglais).

babul [bɑ:'bu:l], *s. Bot:* acacia *m* d'Arabie.

baby[1] ['beibi], *s.* **1.** *(a) (m, f or neut)* bébé *m*; poupon *m*; *(in long clothes)* poupelin *m*, poupard *m*; **she has a b. boy, a b. girl,** elle a un petit garçon, une petite fille; **I have known him from a b.,** je l'ai vu naître; **the b. of the family,** le benjamin, *F:* le culot; **to behave like a b.,** faire le bébé; *F:* **to leave s.o. holding, carrying, the b.,** laisser à qn l'affaire sur les bras; laisser payer les pots cassés à qn; *F:* **to throw out the b. with the bathwater,** se montrer plus zélé que prudent; faire mal plutôt que bien par excès de zèle; *U.S: F:* **to plead the b. act,** (i) plaider l'incapacité en tant que mineur; (ii) plaider son inexpérience; *(b) F:* **the dictionary is his b.,** le dictionnaire est (i) sa création, son enfant, (ii) sa marotte; (iii) sa responsabilité; **his new b.,** sa dernière invention, son dernier dada; **that's your b.,** (i) c'est votre affaire, tire-toi d'affaire tout seul; (ii) débrouille-toi avec les parents de la fille; *(c) U.S: F:* jeune fille *f*, nana *f*; *(as a form of address)* chéri(e); *(d) U.S: F:* (i) type *m*; **he's a tough b.,** c'est un dur (à cuire); (ii) machin *m*; **here's the b. I'm going to fly,** voici l'appareil que je vais piloter; **I've been driving this b. for a year,** je conduis cette voiture depuis un an; *(e) Bot:* **b. tears** [tiəz], **baby's tears,** helxine *f*. **2.** *attrib.* *(a)* d'enfant, de bébé; *F:* **b. face,** visage poupin, poupard; figure poupine, pouparde; *(b)* **b. calf,** petit veau; **b. lamb,** petit agneau, agnelet *m*; *(c)* petit, minuscule; **b. carrots,** de toutes petites carottes; *Mus:* **b. grand,** (piano *m*) quart *m* de queue; *Aut: O:* **b. car,** voiturette *f*, petite voiture; *Phot: O:* **b. camera,** appareil *m* de poche, minuscule.

baby[2], *v.tr.* **(babied)** *F:* traiter (qn) en bébé; dorloter (qn).

baby-blue-eyes ['beibi'blu:aiz], *s. Bot:* nemophila *m* insignis.

baby bonus ['beibibounəs], *s. Can: F:* allocations familiales.

baby carriage ['beibikæridʒ], *NAm: F:* **baby buggy** ['beibibʌgi], *s.* *(a)* voiture *f* d'enfant, landau *m*; *(b)* poussette *f*.

baby carrier ['beibikæriər], *s.* porte-bébé(s) *m*, moïse *m* de toile.

baby-faced ['beibifeist], *a.* à visage poupin, à figure poupine.

baby farm ['beibifɑ:m], *s. usu. Pej:* pouponnière *f*; garderie *f* d'enfants.

baby farmer ['beibifɑ:mər], *s. usu. Pej:* gardeuse *f* d'enfants.

baby farming ['beibifɑ:miŋ], *s. usu. Pej:* garde *f* d'enfants.

babyhood ['beibihud], *s.* première, petite, enfance; bas âge.

babyish ['beibiiʃ], *a.* de petit enfant; bébête; puéril.

babyishly ['beibiiʃli], *adv.* puérilement; comme un petit enfant.

babyishness ['beibiiʃnis], *s.* enfantillage *m*; puérilité *f*.

Babylon ['bæbilən], *Pr.n.* *(a)* Babylone *f*; *Pej: A:* **the Whore of B.,** la papauté; Rome; *(b)* **a modern B.,** une Babylone moderne.

Babylonia [bæbi'louniə], *Pr.n. A.Geog:* Babylonie *f*.

Babylonian [bæbi'louniən]. **1.** *a.* *(a) B.Hist:* babylonien; **the B. Captivity,** la Captivité de Babylone; *(b)* babylonien, immense; somptueux. **2.** *s.* Babylonien, -ienne.

baby-minder ['beibimaindər], *s.* = BABY-SITTER.

baby ribbon ['beibirib(ə)n], *s.* ruban *m* comète.

baby's breath ['beibiz'breθ], *s. Bot: F:* **1.** muscari *m* botryoïde, muscari raisin, jacinthe *f* botride. **2.** gypsophile *f*.

baby-sit ['beibisit], *v.i.* **(-sat, -sitting)** garder les bébés; *F:* faire du baby-sitting.

baby-sitter ['beibisitər], *s.* gardien, -ienne, d'enfants, garde-bébé *mf*, *pl* gardes-bébés.

baby-sitting ['beibisitiŋ], *s.* garde *f* des bébés; *F:* service *m* biberon.

baby-snatcher ['beibisnætʃər], *s.* *(a)* kidnappeur *m*; *(b)* (i) vieux barbeau; (ii) femme qui épouse un garçon beaucoup plus jeune qu'elle.

baby-snatching ['beibisnætʃiŋ], *s.* *(a)* enlèvement *m*, rapt *m*, d'enfant, kidnapping *m*; *(b) F:* **I don't go in for b.-s.,** moi, je ne les prends pas au berceau, au biberon.

baby talk ['beibitɔ:k], *s.* babil enfantin.

baby-walker ['beibiwɔ:kər], *s.* trotteuse *f*.

bacca, *pl.* **-ae** ['bækə, -i:], *s. Bot:* baie *f*.

baccalaureate [bækə'lɔːriət], *s. Sch: NAm:* = licence *f*.
baccara(t) ['bækərɑː], *s. Cards:* baccara *m*; **to have a game of b.,** faire une partie de baccara.
baccate ['bækeit], *a. Bot:* **1.** baccifère. **2.** bacciforme.
bacchanal ['bækən(ə)l]. **1.** *a.* bachique. **2.** *s.* (*a*) (i) prêtre, prêtresse, de Bacchus; (ii) *Fig:* noceur *m*, tapageur, -euse; (*b*) bacchanale *f*; danse *f*, chant, *m*, débauche *m*, bachique.
Bacchanalia [bækə'neiliə], *s.pl.* bacchanales *f*.
Bacchanalian [bækə'neiliən]. **1.** *a.* bachique. **2.** *s. F:* (*reveller*) tapageur, -euse; noceur *m*.
Bacchant ['bækənt]. **1.** *s.* (*a*) prêtre, prêtresse, de Bacchus; bacchante *f*; (*b*) adorateur *m* de Bacchus. **2.** *a.* bachique.
bacchante [bə'kænti], *s.f.* bacchante, ménade.
baccharis ['bækəris], *s. Bot:* baccharis *m*.
bacchiac [bə'kaiæk], *a. Gr.Pros:* bacchiaque.
Bacchian ['bækiən], **Bacchic** ['bækik], *a.* bachique.
bacchius [bə'kaiəs], *s. Gr.Pros:* bacchius *m*.
Bacchus ['bækəs], *Pr.n.m. Myth:* Bacchus; **son of B.,** adorateur *m*, enfant *m*, disciple *m*, de Bacchus; adorateur de la Dive Bouteille.
bacciferous [bæk'sifərəs], *a. Bot:* baccifère.
bacciform ['bæksifɔːm], *a.* bacciforme.
baccivorous [bæk'sivərəs], *a. Z:* baccivore.
baccy ['bæki], *s. F: O:* tabac *m*, *P:* perlot *m*.
bach[1] [bætʃ], *v.i. & tr. esp. NAm: N.Z: F:* **to b. (it),** vivre en célibataire.
bach[2], *s. N.Z:* cabane *f* (à la campagne ou dans le jardin).
bachelor ['bætʃələr], *s.m.* **1.** *Hist:* bachelier (aspirant à la chevalerie); **knight b.,** chevalier (n'appartenant à aucun ordre) (distinction honorifique dont l'usage s'est perpétué). **2.** célibataire, garçon; **to live as a b.,** *U.S: F:* **to keep bachelor's hall,** mener une vie de garçon; vivre en garçon; **b. flat,** appartement *m* pour célibataire; **bachelor's establishment,** garçonnière *f*; **old b.,** vieux garçon; *attrib.* **b. uncle,** oncle non marié; **b. girl,** jeune fille indépendante, qui vit en célibataire. **3.** *Sch:* = licencié, -ée; **B. of Arts, of Science,** *approx.* = licencié, -ée, ès lettres, ès sciences; **B. of laws** = licencié, -ée, en droit; **B. of Divinity** = licencié, -ée, en théologie. **4.** *Z:* jeune animal *m* mâle, *esp.* jeune phoque *m* mâle.
bachelordom ['bætʃələdəm], **bachelorhood** ['bætʃələhud], *s.* célibat *m*; vie *f*, état *m*, de garçon.
bachelorism ['bætʃələrizm], *s.* état de vieux garçon.
bachelor's breeches ['bætʃələz'britʃiz], *s. Bot:* adlumia *m*, adlumie *f*.
bachelor's button ['bætʃələz'bʌt(ə)n], *s.* **1.** bouton *m* mobile, bouton sans queue. **2.** *Bot:* renoncule *f* double; bouton d'or.
bacher ['bætʃər], *s. F: esp. Austr:* homme, femme, qui vit en célibataire.
bacillæmia [bæsi'liːmiə], *s. Med:* bacillémie *f*.
bacillar [bə'silər, 'bæsilər], *a. Biol:* bacillaire.
bacillaria [bæsi'lɛəriə], *s. Algae:* bacillaire *f*.
bacillary [bə'siləri], *a. Biol:* bacillaire.
bacilliform [bə'silifɔːm], *a.* bacilliforme.
bacilloscopy [bæsi'lɔskəpi], *s. Med:* bacilloscopie *f*.
bacillosis, *pl.* **-es** [bæsi'lousis, -iːz], *s. Med:* bacillose *f*.
bacilluria [bæsi'ljuːriə], *s. Med:* bacillurie *f*.
bacillus, *pl.* **-i** [bə'siləs, -əi], *s. Biol: Med:* bacille *m*; **comma b.,** bacille virgule; **b. botulinus,** bacille botulique; **gas b.,** vibrion *m* septique; **tubercle b.,** bacille de Koch; **Vincent's b.,** bacille de Vincent; **b. infection,** bacillisation *f*; bacillose *f*.
bacitracin [bæsi'treisin], *s. Med:* bacitracine *f*.
back[1] [bæk], *s. a. & adv.*
I. *s.* **1.** (*a*) dos *m* (de qn, d'un animal); **to fall on one's b.,** tomber à la renverse; *F:* **I haven't a rag to my b.,** je n'ai rien à me mettre sur le dos; **she wears her hair down her b.,** elle porte les cheveux sur le dos; **to carry, sling, sth. across one's b.,** porter, mettre, qch. en bandoulière; **mind your backs!** attention, s'il vous plaît! **to be at the b. of s.o., of sth.,** (i) être derrière qn, qch.; (ii) soutenir qn, qch.; **the government has a broad b.,** le gouvernement a bon dos; **to do sth. behind s.o.'s b.,** faire qch. deppière le dos de qn; à l'insu de qn; **he laughs at you behind your b.,** il se moque de vous quand vous avez le dos tourné; **to turn one's b. on s.o.,** (i) tourner le dos à qn; montrer le dos à qn; (ii) abandonner qn; **to turn one's b. on the world,** se détacher du monde; **to sit, stand, with one's b. to s.o.,** tourner le dos à qn; **sitting with one's b. to the light,** assis à contre-jour, le dos à la lumière; *Rail:* **to sit with one's b. to the engine,** faire face à l'arrière; voyager dans le sens contraire de la marche du train; **excuse my b.,** excusez-moi si je vous tourne le dos; **to be glad to see the b. of s.o.,** être content de voir partir qn, d'être débarrassé de qn; **I saw him only from the b.,** je ne l'ai vu que de dos; **to be on one's b.,** (i) être étendu sur le dos; (ii) (*to be ill*), être alité; *P:* **she earns her money on her b.,** elle fait l'horizontale; *F:* **he's always on my b.,** il est toujours sur mon dos; **get off my b.!** fiche-moi la paix! **the cat arches its b.,** le chat fait le gros dos, arque le dos; **to put, get, s.o.'s b. up,** mettre qn en colère; fâcher qn; faire rebiffer qn; **to get one's b. up,** se fâcher, se rebiffer, se hérisser; prendre la mouche; **when we mention it, it puts his b. up,** quand on lui en parle, il se hérisse; **to make a b. (at leapfrog),** faire le mouton; **to make a b. for s.o., to lend a b. to s.o.,** faire la courte échelle à qn; **b. to b.,** dos à dos; adossés; **b. to front,** sens devant derrière; **to put one's b. against a wall,** s'acculer, s'appuyer, à, contre, un mur; **with one's b. to the wall,** (i) adossé au mur, les épaules plaquées au mur; (ii) poussée au pied du mur; aux abois; **he is fighting with his b. to the wall,** il est acculé dans ses derniers retranchements; **to put one's b. into sth.,** se donner entièrement, s'appliquer, à qch.; **to put one's b. into it,** s'y mettre énergiquement; donner un coup de collier; tirer à plein collier; y aller de tout son cœur; **he's putting his b. into it,** il n'y va pas de main morte! (*b*) les reins *m*, *F:* l'échine *f*; **to straighten one's b.,** cambrer les reins; **to break one's b.,** se casser les reins; **to break a rabbit's b.,** échiner un lapin; **to break s.o.'s b.,** échiner qn; *F:* **he won't break his b. working,** il ne se casse pas, ne se foule pas, au travail; **to break the b. of the work,** faire le plus dur, le plus fort, le plus gros, du travail; **to break the b. of the work for s.o.,** mâcher, triturer, la besogne à qn; (*c*) (*of ship*) **to break her b.,** se briser en deux; se casser; (*d*) *Leath:* croupon *m*; (*e*) *Tex:* **b. wool,** laine *f* mère. **2.** (*a*) dos (d'un couteau, d'un outil, d'un livre); envers *m* (d'un tissu); verso *m* (d'une feuille de papier, verso *m* (d'une feuille) de papier, d'une page); dos, verso (d'un chèque); *Fin:* **bills as per b.,** effets *m* comme au verso; (*b*) dossier *m* (d'une chaise); **adjustable b.,** dossier inclinable; (*c*) revers *m* (d'une médaille); **the b. of the hand,** le revers, le dessus, de la main; **he knows London like the b. of his hand,** il connaît Londres comme (le fond de) sa poche; (*d*) derrière *m* (d'une maison); arrière *m* (d'une maison, d'une voiture); **the kitchen is at the b.,** *U.S:* **in b. (of the house),** la cuisine est à l'arrière (de la maison); **let's go round to the b.,** allons à l'arrière; **the third floor b.,** le troisième sur la cour, sur le derrière; **b. of the mouth,** arrière-bouche *f*, *pl.* arrière-bouches; **b. of the throat,** arrière-gorge *f*, *pl.* arrière-gorges; **b. of the tongue,** dos de la langue; **carriage at the b. of the train,** voiture *f* en queue de, du, train; **the vocabulary is at the b. of the book,** le vocabulaire est à la fin du livre; *Phot:* **b. of a camera,** corps *m* arrière, arrière-cadre *m*, *pl.* arrière-cadres; **reversing b.,** parquet *m* réversible, cadre arrière réversible; **hinged b.,** volet *m* à charnière; **the dress fastens at the b.,** *U.S:* **in b.,** la robe s'agrafe dans le dos; **hair cropped close at the b.,** cheveux coupés ras par derrière; **idea at the b. of one's mind,** idée *f* (de) derrière la tête; arrière-pensée *f*, *pl.* arrière-pensées; **there's something at the b. of it,** il y a quelque chose derrière cela, il se trame quelque chose en dessous; **to get to the b. of a policy,** pénétrer les raisons d'une ligne de conduite; voir le dessous des cartes; **we must see the b. of it,** il faut achever le travail; il faut en voir la fin; *F:* **to talk through the b. of one's neck,** dire des bêtises; (*e*) *esp.N.Eng: Scot:* **on the b. of (a misfortune),** en plus (d'un malheur); pour surcroît (de malheur); **on the b. of that her husband died,** pour comble de malheur elle perdit son mari. **3.** *Arch:* extrados *m* (d'une voûte); *Civ.E:* heurt *m* (d'un pont). **4.** (*a*) fond *m* (d'une armoire, d'une salle); *Th:* **the b. of the stage,** l'arrière-siène, le fond de la scène; **at the very b. of. . .,** au fin fond de. . .; **seated at the b. of the pit,** assis au dernier rang du parterre; **to live at the b. of beyond,** habiter un trou perdu; (*b*) table *f* du fond (d'un violon, etc.); (*c*) derrière *mpl* (de la ville); *Pr.n.* **the Backs,** les pelouses *f* de Cambridge derrière les collèges. **5.** *Fb:* arrière *m*; **the backs.** l'arrière-défense *f*.
II. *a.* (*a*) (place, etc.) arrière, de derrière; **b. room,** pièce *f*, chambre *f*, sur la cour, qui donne sur l'arrière; *F:* **b.-room boy,** expert *m* qui travaille (i) à l'arrière-plan, (ii) à des recherches secrètes; **b. premises,** arrière-corps *m* (d'un bâtiment); **the b. streets of a town,** les bas quartiers d'une ville; *Can:* **a farm on the b. concessions,** une ferme dans l'arrière-plays; *Mil:* **the b. area,** l'arrière *m*; *Dressm:* **b. seam,** couture *f* de derrière; *Veh:* **b. wheel,** roue *f* arrière; **b. axle,** essieu *m* arrière; *Aut:* pont *m* arrière; **b.-axle shaft,** arbre *m* arrière; **b. seat,** siège *m* arrière; **to take a b. seat,** (i) s'asseoir à l'arrière (d'une voiture); prendre une place au fond d'une salle; (ii) *F:* passer au second plan, s'effacer, prendre un rôle accessoire; se trouver relégué au deuxième rang, céder le pas aux autres; *Pej:* **b.-seat driver,** personne qui donne des conseils au conducteur (d'une voiture); **don't be such a b.-seat driver!** tais-toi, c'est moi qui conduis! (*b*) (*in opposite direction*) **b. action,** mouvement *m* inverse; **b.-and-forth motion,** mouvement de va-et-vient, d'avance et de recul; *El: etc:* **b. current,** courant *m* de retour; contre-courant *m*, *pl.* contre-courants; *Ling:* **b. formation,** dérivation régressive; *Ven:* **b. scent,** contre-pied *m*; (*c*) (*in time*) *Com:* **b. orders,** commandes *f* en retard; **b. interest,** arrérages *mpl*; **b. rent,** arriéré(s) *m*(*pl*) de loyer; *Adm:* **b. pay,** rappel *m* de traitement; *Journ:* **b. number,** ancien, vieux, numéro (d'un journal), numéro déjà paru; (**all**) **the b. numbers of** *Punch*, la collection du *Punch*; (*of pers.*) **to be a b. number,** être vieux jeu; **he's a b. number,** il n'est plus à la page, *F:* c'est un croulant.
III. *adv.* **1.** (*of place*) (*a*) en arrière; *Th:* derrière la scène; **stand b.!** rangez-vous! **to step b. a pace,** faire un pas en arrière; **far b.,** loin derrière (les autres, etc.); dans les derniers rangs; **would you please stand a little farther b.?** voudriez-vous vous éloigner un peu? **house standing b. from the road,** maison écartée du chemin; maison en retrait; *prep.phr. NAm:* **b. of sth.,** derrière qch.; **the houses b. of the harbour,** les maisons derrière le port, en arrière du port; *Can:* **Ontario is b. east,** Ontario se trouve à l'est (du pays); *U.S:* **b. home in the States,** chez nous aux États-Unis; (*b*) dans le sens contraire; **to hit, strike, b.,** rendre coup pour coup; **if anyone hits me, I hit b.,** si on me frappe, je rends la pareille; **he is the kind of man who will hit b.,** il est homme à se défendre; **it was a bit of his own b.,** c'était une revanche; *Ten:* **to drive a ball straight b.,** jouer le contre-pied; (*with a v. often rendered by the pref.* re-) **to call s.o. b.,** rappeler qn; *Tp:* **ring, call, me b. in an hour,** rappelez-moi dans une heure; **to come b.,** revenir; **to go, drive, ride, sail, walk, b.,** (i) retourner (to, à); (ii) rebrousser chemin; **I took the wrong road and had to go, come, turn, b.,** je me suis trompé de chemin, et j'ai dû revenir sur mes pas; **to drive, chase, s.o. b.,** faire rebrousser chemin à qn; **to make one's way b.,** s'en retourner; **ship chartered to Lisbon and b. to London,** navire affrété pour voyage à Lisbonne avec retour sur Londres; **I shall take a shorter way b.,** je reviendrai par un chemin plus court; je prendrai un raccourci pour revenir; **take the train out to Chesham and b. from Wendover,** pour l'aller descendre à Chesham; pour le retour prendre le train à Wendover; **to hurry b.,** retourner en toute hâte; **now it's b. to school,** maintenant c'est la rentrée (des classes); *F:* **b. to the grindstone!** maintenant au travail! (*c*) de retour; **to arrive, come, b.,** rentrer; **when will he be b.?** quand sera-t-il de retour? **I'll be b.,** (i) je vais rentrer; (ii) *F:* vous aurez de mes nouvelles; **I expect him b. tomorrow,** j'attends son retour pour demain, je pense qu'il sera de retour demain; **I shall see you as soon as I am b., as soon as I get b.,** je vous verrai dès mon retour; **if ever I am b. in Paris,** si un jour je me retrouve à Paris; **here is my husband, just b. from Paris,** voici mon mari, qui vient de rentrer de Paris; **he's just b. from a trip,** il arrive de voyage; (*d*) **a few pages b.,** quelques pages plus haut; **he left him three miles b.,** il l'a laissé à trois milles d'ici. **2.** (*of time*) **some few years b.,** il y a (déjà) quelques années; **far b. in the Middle Ages,** à une période reculée du moyen âge; **as far b. as 1914,** déjà en 1914, dès 1914; **to go further b.,** remonter plus haut (dans le temps); **it was (a)way b. in 1890,** cela remonte à 1890; **three centuries b.,** trois siècles auparavant.
back[2], *v.*
I. *v.tr. & i.* **1.** *v.tr.* (*a*) (i) renforcer (un mur, une carte, etc.); épauler (une route, un accotement); endosser (un livre); rentoiler (un tableau); maroufler (une toile); **to b. a wall with sheet iron,** endosser un mur en tôle; *Nau:* **to b. an anchor,** empenneler une ancre; (ii) **to b. s.o., sth. (up),** soutenir, appuyer, qn, qch., prêter son appui à qn, seconder qn, épauler qn, *F:* pistonner qn; **to be well backed,** *F:* avoir du piston; **to b. s.o. in an argument,** donner raison à qn; *Turf:* **to b. a horse,** parier pour, sur, miser sur, un cheval, jouer un cheval; **to b. a horse each way,** jouer un cheval gagnant et placé; **well-backed horse,** cheval très coté; **to b. Destrier for a place,** parier sur Destrier placé; *Turf: & F:* **to b. the wrong horse,** parier, miser, sur le mauvais cheval; *Com: etc:* **to b. s.o.,** financer, soutenir, qn; **to b. a bill,** avaliser, endosser, un effet, donner son aval à un effet; (*of magistrate*) **to b. a warrant,** contresigner un mandat (d'amener, de perquisition, etc.); (iii) *Phot:* revêtir (une plaque) d'antihalo; (iv) *U.S: Dial:* mettre l'adresse à (une lettre); (*b*) (i) reculer (une charrette); faire reculer (un cheval); *Mch:* mettre (une machine) en arrière, refouler (un train); **to b. one's car into a lane,** entrer à reculons, en marche arrière, dans un chemin; **to b. a lorry against a platform,** abut(t)er un camion à un quai; (ii) *Nau:* **to b. the oars, to b. water,** (*α*) ramer à rebours, déramer, nager à culer; (*β*) (*to stop way*) scier, dénager; **b. together!** sciez partout! **b. all!** dénage par-

tout! (iii) *Nau:* masquer, coiffer (une voile); **to b. and fill a sail,** coiffer et servir une voile; *NAm: F:* **to b. and fill,** hésiter, tergiverser; (*c*) **to b. a horse,** monter à cheval, enfourcher un cheval; (*d*) servir de fond à (qch.); **the hills that b. the town,** les collines qui s'élèvent derrière la ville. **2.** *v.i.* (*a*) (i) aller en arrière; marcher à reculons; (*of horse*) reculer; *Aut: etc:* mettre en (marche) arrière, faire marche arrière; reculer; **to b. into sth.,** reculer contre qch.; *Aut:* **to b. into the garage,** entrer dans le garage en marche arrière; (*of train*) **to b. into the station,** reculer dans la gare; (*of steamer*) **to b. astern,** faire machine arrière; (ii) *Nau:* (*of wind*) (re)descendre, ravaler; (*b*) **the house backs on the high road,** la maison donne par derrière sur le grand chemin; **the town backs on to the hills,** la ville est adossée aux collines.

II. (*compound verbs*) **1. back away,** *v.i.* reculer.

2. back down, *v.i.* (*a*) descendre (une échelle, etc.) à reculons; (*b*) **the engine is backing down,** la machine revient sur le train; (*c*) avouer qu'on est dans son tort; abandonner une réclamation, y renoncer; rabattre de ses prétentions; en rabattre; (*d*) reculer, *F:* caner, filer doux.

3. back off, *v.tr. Mec.E:* **to b.o. a tool,** dégager, dépouiller, détalonner, un outil.

4. back out, *v.i.* (*a*) (*of pers. etc.*) sortir à reculons; (*of car*) sortir en marche arrière; (*b*) *F:* retirer sa promesse, se dédire, se dérober; retirer son enjeu; **to b.o. of a bargain,** revenir sur sa parole; se dégager d'un marché; **to b.o. of an undertaking,** se retirer d'une entreprise; **he's trying to b.o. of it,** il voudrait se dédire; **to b.o. of an argument,** se soustraire d'une discussion; (*c*) *F:* se défiler; *P:* caler.

5. back up, *v.tr.* soutenir, appuyer (qn, qch.); prêter son appui à (qn); seconder (qn); épauler (qn); *Pej:* pistonner (qn); **to b. s.o. up in an argument,** donner raison à qn; **to be backed up by s.o.,** être secondé de, par, qn; **he has no one to b. him up,** il est sans soutien; **to quote facts in order to b. up one's assertion,** citer des faits pour appuyer son dire; *Typ:* **to b. up (a sheet),** mettre (une feuille) en retiration.

back[3], *s. Brew: Dy:* cuve *f.*

backache ['bækeik], *s.* (*a*) douleurs *fpl* de reins; maux *mpl* de reins; (*b*) courbature *f.*

back-balanced ['bæk'bælənst], *a. Mec.E:* en porte-à-faux.

backband ['bækbænd], *s. Harn:* **1.** dossière *f.* **2.** surdos *m.*

backbench ['bæk'ben(t)ʃ], *s. Pol: usu.pl.* banquette *f* des députés sans portefeuille.

back-bencher ['bæk'ben(t)ʃər], *s. Pol:* député *m* sans portefeuille (à la Chambre des Communes ou des Lords).

backbite ['bækbait], *v.tr.* médire de (qn); *P:* débiner (qn).

backbiter ['bækbaitər], *s.* médisant, -ante, mauvaise langue; calomniateur, -trice; détracteur, -trice; *P:* débineur, -euse.

backbiting[1] ['bækbaitiŋ], *s.* médisance *f*; *P:* débinage *m.*

backbiting[2], *a.* médisant.

backblocks (the) [ðə'bækblɔks], *s.pl. Can: N.Z: Austr:* les régions *f* de l'intérieur.

backboard ['bækbɔ:d], *s.* **1.** dossier *m* (de banc, de canot, etc.). **2.** *Med:* planche *f* (pour s'allonger dans la position droite). **3.** (*basketball*) panneau *m.*

backboiler ['bæk'bɔilər], *s.* chauffe-eau *minv* derrière un foyer domestique.

backbone ['bækboun], *s.* **1.** (i) épine dorsale, colonne vertébrale; échine *f*; (ii) grande arête (de poisson); **English to the b.,** anglais jusqu'à la moelle des os, jusqu'au bout des ongles; **he's got b.,** il a du caractère, *F:* du cran; **he's got no b.,** il n'a pas de moelle dans les os, il manque de fermeté, d'énergie, de caractère; *F:* c'est une chiffe; **if he had more b.,** s'il avait plus de force de caractère, plus d'énergie; **manufacturers are the b. of the country,** les fabricants sont la force, la clef de voûte, du pays, forment l'armature morale et sociale du pays; **he is the b. of the movement,** c'est lui qui mène le mouvement; **this is the very b. of the whole argument,** c'est là-dessus que pivote tout le raisonnement. **2.** filière *f* (de tente). **3.** *Bookb:* dos *m* (d'un livre).

backbreaker ['bækbreikər], *s.* **1.** *Agr: A:* premier valet; chef *m* d'équipe. **2.** *F:* travail éreintant. **3.** *Wr:* brise-reins *m inv.*

backbreaking ['bækbreikiŋ], *a.* (travail, etc.) éreintant.

backchat ['bæktʃæt], *s. F:* (*a*) impertinence *f*; **(I want) none of your b.!** ne répliquez pas! (*b*) reparties *fpl.*

backcloth ['bæ(k)klɔθ], *s. Th:* toile *f* de fond; arrière-scène *f, pl.* arrière-scènes.

back-comb[1] ['bæk'koum], *s. Toil:* peigne *m* à chignon, peigne (de) chignon.

back-comb[2], *v.tr. Hairdr:* crêper.

back coupling ['bæk'kʌpliŋ], *s. W.Tel:* rétroaction *f.*

backcross ['bæ(k)krɔs], *s. Biol:* rétrocroisement *m.*

backdate ['bæk'deit], *v.tr.* antidater; **increase backdated to July 1st,** augmentation avec effet rétroactif au ler juillet.

backdown ['bækdaun], *s. esp. U.S:* abandon *m* de ses prétentions; retraite *f*; défaite *f.*

backdrop ['bækdrɔp], *s.* (*a*) *Th:* toile *f* de fond; arrière-scène *f, pl.* arrière-scènes; (*b*) arrière-plan *m, pl.* arrière-plans.

backed [bækt], *a.* **1. b. on to sth.,** adossé à qch. **2.** (*a*) à dos, à dossier; **b. saw,** scie *f* à dosseret, à dossière; (*b*) (*in compounds*) **broad-b.,** à large dos, qui a le dos large; **high-b. chair,** chaise *f* à grand dossier. **3.** *Com:* **b. bills,** papier fait. **4.** *Phot:* **b. plate,** plaque *f* à enduit antihalo.

back-end ['bæk'end], *s. Dial:* automne *m*, arrière saison *f.*

backer ['bækər], *s.* **1.** *Sp: esp. Turf:* parieur, -euse. **2.** *Com:* (*a*) **b. of a bill,** donneur *m* d'aval; avaliste *m*; (*b*) commanditaire *m*; (*c*) **financial b.,** bailleur, -euse, de fonds. **3.** *Pol: etc:* partisan *m*; **bribed b.,** *F:* chéquard *m* (d'une entreprise). **4.** (*backing piece*) pièce d'appui.

backfall ['bækfɔ:l], *s.* **1.** *Wr:* chute *f* sur le dos. **2.** (*in organ*) balancier *m.* **3.** *Paperm:* saut *m* (de pile), montagne *f.*

backfield ['bækfi:ld], *s. Fb: NAm:* arrière-défense *f.*

backfill[1] ['bækfil], *v.tr. Civ.E: etc:* remblayer.

backfill[2], **backfilling** ['bæk'filiŋ], *s. Civ.E: etc:* remblai *m*, remblayage *m.*

backfiller ['bæk'filər], *s. Civ.E: etc:* **1.** (*pers.*) remblayeur *m.* **2.** (*machine*) remblayeuse *f.*

backfire[1] ['bæk'faiər], *s.* **1.** *I.C.E:* allumage prématuré, contre-feu *m, pl.* contre-feux; **b. kick,** retour *m* de manivelle. **2.** retour de flamme (au carburateur); pétarade *f.* **3.** *U.S:* contre-feu (d'incendie de forêt, etc.). **4.** *Fig:* **there was a strong b. of opinion,** il y a eu un soudain renversement d'opinion, un revirement d'opinion.

backfire[2], *v.i. I.C.E:* **1.** s'allumer prématurément; pétarder. **2.** donner des retours *m* de flamme; avoir des retours; pétarader. **3.** *Fig:* **the plan backfired,** le projet leur est retombé sur le dos.

backfiring ['bæk'faiəriŋ], *s.* retours *mpl* de flamme; pétarades *fpl.*

backflap ['bækflæp], *s. Bookb:* rabat *m* de la jaquette.

backfolding ['bæk'fouldiŋ], *s. Geol:* plissement *m* en retour.

backgammon ['bækgæmən], *s.* (jeu *m* de) trictrac *m*; (jeu de) jacquet *m*; **b. board,** trictrac, jacquet.

background ['bækgraund], *s.* **1.** fond *m*, arrière-plan *m, pl.* arrière-plans; arrière-corps *m inv* (d'un bas relief); **to serve as a b. to . . .,** servir de fond à . . .; **b. of mountains,** fond, *Th.* décor *m*, de montagnes, **in the b.,** dans le fond, à l'arrière-plan; dans le lointain; **against a dark b.,** sur (un) fond sombre; **to keep (oneself) in the b.,** s'effacer; se tenir dans l'ombre; **to keep s.o. in the b.,** tenir qn à l'écart; **to push s.o. into the b.,** (i) mettre, reléguer, qn au second plan; (ii) prendre le pas sur qn; **to be relegated to the b.,** se trouver relégué à l'arrière-plan; **this question has fallen into the b.,** cette question est tombée au second plan; **there's a b. of bitterness in his writing,** il y a un fond d'amertume dans ses écrits; **b. (music),** (i) *Th: Cin:* fond musical; (ii) musique *f* d'ambiance; musique de fond; **b. noise,** bruit *m* de fond; *Cin:* **b. projection,** projection *f* par transparence. **2.** (*a*) (*of pers.*) (i) origines *fpl*; **young man of good b.,** garçon *m* de bonne famille; **to be brought up in a middle-class b.,** être élevé dans un ambiance bourgeoise; (ii) **what's his b.?** quelle est sa formation? quel est son passé? qu'est-ce qu'il a fait jusqu'à présent? *Med:* **patient's b.,** antécédents *mpl* du malade; (iii) **(cultural, educational) b.,** fonds *m*, acquis *m*, de culture; culture générale; (*b*) contexte *m* historique (d'un événement); données *fpl* de base, éléments *mpl* (d'un problème); **to appreciate Athens one needs to know its historical b.,** pour apprécier Athènes il faut connaître son histoire. **3.** *Ph:* mouvement *m* propre.

backhand ['bækhænd], *s.* **1. b. blow,** coup *m* de revers; *Ten:* **b. (stroke),** (coup de) revers *m*; **to take the ball on the b.,** reprendre la balle en revers; **to be good on the b.,** être bon pour les revers; **to serve on to one's opponent's b.,** servir sur le revers adverse; **to run round one's b.,** prendre tout en coup droit. **2.** écriture renversée, penchée à gauche. **3. b. welding,** soudure *f* à droite (en arrière).

backhanded ['bæk'hændid], *a.* **1. b. blow,** coup inattendu, déloyal, coup fourré; **b. compliment,** compliment *m* à rebours; compliment équivoque; **in a b. way,** déloyalement. **2. b. answer** = BACKHANDER 2. **3. b. writing,** écriture renversée, penchée à gauche.

backhander [bæk'hændər], *s. F:* **1.** coup *m* de revers; coup du revers de la main. **2.** riposte inattendue; attaque indirecte, déloyale; **to give s.o. a b.,** (i) rembarrer qn; (ii) donner un coup déloyal à qn.

backing ['bækiŋ], *s.* **1.** (*a*) renforcement *m* (d'un mur, d'une carte, etc.); *Const: Civ.E:* remplage *m*; *Bookb:* endossage *m* (d'un livre); *Art: etc:* marouflage *m* (d'une toile); rentoilage *m* (d'un tableau); argenture *f* (d'un miroir); (*b*) *Nau:* **b. of an anchor,** empennelage *m* d'une ancre; (*c*) *Phot:* enduisage *m* (de la plaque); (*d*) *Sp:* **b. of a horse,** paris *mpl* pour un cheval; (*e*) *Fin:* **b. of the currency,** garantie *f* de la circulation; (*f*) *Mus:* accompagnement *m.* **2.** (*a*) renfort *m*, support *m*, soutien *m* (d'un mur); *N.Arch:* matelas *m*, matelassure *f*, contreforts *mpl* (de la cuirasse); *Furn:* dossier *m* (d'un tapis); **wooden b.,** parquet *m* (d'une toile, d'un miroir); *Art: etc:* **cloth b.,** marouflage; (*b*) *Phot:* **antihalation b.,** (enduit *m*, couche *f*) antihalo *m*; (*c*) *Tls:* dosseret *m*, dossière *f* (d'une scie); (*d*) support *m* de soudage. **3.** (*a*) recul *m*, reculement *m* (d'un cheval, d'une charrette); acculement *m* (d'un cheval); refoulement *m* (d'un train); mise *f* en arrière, marche *f* (en) arrière (d'une machine); *attrib.* **to have no b. room, no b. space,** manquer de reculée; (*b*) nage *f* à culer (d'un canot); (*c*) avalaison *f*, changement *m* (du vent d'amont); renversement *m* (du vent).

backing-off ['bækiŋ'ɔf], *s. Mec.E:* dégagement *m*, détalonnage *m*, dépouillement *m.*

backingpiece ['bækiŋpi:s], *s. Mec.E: etc:* pièce *f* d'appui.

backing up ['bækiŋ'ʌp], *s.* **1.** soutien *m*, appui *m* (d'un candidat, etc.). **2.** *Typ:* retiration *f.*

backland ['bæklænd], *s. Geog:* **1.** hinterland *m.* **2.** dépression latérale (humide).

backlash ['bæklæʃ], *s.* **1.** *Mec.E:* jeu *m* (nuisible); retour *m* (de dents, de la denture); secousse *f*, battement *m*, saccade *f*; *Aut: F:* coups *mpl* de raquette. **2.** contrecoup *m*, répercussion *f* (d'une explosion), effet *m* de boomerang *m*; **(political, etc.) b.,** contre-courant *m* (politique, etc.). **3.** *El:* effet unidirectionnel imparfait (dû aux ions résiduels); **b. current,** courant inverse (dû à la présence d'ions positifs); **b. potential,** tension résiduelle.

backless ['bæklis], *a.* (robe *f*, etc.) sans dos; (banc *m*, etc.) sans dossier.

backlighting ['bæk'laitiŋ], *s. Art: Phot:* (éclairage *m* à) contre-jour *m, pl.* contre-jours.

backline ['bæklain], *s. Ten: etc:* ligne *f* de fond; *Fb: etc:* **the b. defence,** l'arrière-défense *f.*

backlog ['bæklɔg], *s.* arriéré *m* (de travail); *Com:* **b. of orders,** commandes non exécutées.

back-mark ['bækmɑ:k], *v.tr. Sp: F:* **1.** priver (un coureur) de son handicap. **2.** donner des points à (ses concurrents).

back-marker ['bækmɑ:kər], *s. Sp: F:* scratch *m*; champion, -ionne; *Ten:* joueur, -euse, classé(é) à zéro (dans un tournoi).

backmost ['bækmoust], *a.* dernier; le plus éloigné, le plus reculé.

back-nut ['bæknʌt], *s.* contre-écrou *m, pl.* contre-écrous; écrou *m* de blocage, d'arrêt; écrou de sûreté; doubles écrous.

backpack[1] ['bækpæk], *s.* bal(l)uchon *m* (de touriste à pied, d'astronaute).

backpack[2], *v.tr. & i.* porter (ses effets, etc.) sur le dos.

back-patting ['bækpætiŋ], *s. F:* félicitations *fpl.*

back-pedal ['bæk'pedl], *v.i.* **(back-pedalled)** (*a*) rétropédaler; (*b*) y renoncer; en rabattre; faire marche arrière.

back-pedalling ['bæk'pedliŋ], *s.* rétropédalage *m*; **b.-p. brake,** frein *m* par rétropédalage, dans le moyeu.

back plate ['bækpleit], *s.* **1.** (*a*) *Const:* contrecœur *m*, contre-plaque *f, pl.* contre-plaques (de la cheminée, de l'âtre); (*b*) palastre *m* (de serrure). **2.** *Mch:* fond *m* arrière (de chaudière). **3.** *Metall:* haire *f* (de four d'affinage). **4.** *Mil:* couvre-culasse *m* (de mitrailleuse); plaque *f* arrière (d'arme automatique de petit calibre); *Artil:* plaque de fermeture arrière; plaque d'appui (de mortier).

back-porch ['bækpɔ:tʃ], *s. T.V:* palier *m* arrière, seuil *m* de dépassement.

back-pressure ['bækpreʃər], *s.* **1.** contre-pression *f*, *Mch:* contre-vapeur *f*; *Hyd.E: etc:* **b.-p. valve,** clapet *m* de retenue; soupape *f* de retenue. **2.** *El:* contre-tension *f.*

back-projection ['bækprə'dʒekʃ(ə)n], *s. Cin:* projection *f* par transparence.

backrest ['bækrest], *s.* **1.** *Tchn:* lunette *f* (de tour). **2.** *Furn:* dossier-lit *m, pl.* dossiers lits.

back-rope ['bækroup], *s.* **1.** *Harn:* = BACKBAND. **2.** *Nau:* moustache *f* (de martingale).

backscatter ['bækskætər], **backscattering** ['bækskæt(ə)riŋ], *s. Atom.Ph:* diffusion *f* rétrograde.

back-scratcher ['bækskrætʃər], *s.* **1.** gratte-dos *m inv*; *Ant:* strigile *m.* **2.** *P:* (*a*) flatteur, -euse; flagorneur, -euse; (*b*) personne qui prête à une autre une aide intéressée.

back-scratching ['bækskrætʃiŋ], *s. P:* **1.** flagornerie *f.* **2.** aide mutuellement avantageuse.

backset ['bækset], *s.* **1.** contre-courant *m, pl.* contre-courants. **2.** revers *m* (de fortune); échec *m.*

backsheesh, backshish [bæk'ʃi:ʃ], *s.* bakchich *m*; **to expect b. from s.o.,** attendre un pot-de-vin de qn.

backshore ['bæk'ʃɔ:r], *s. Geog:* arrière-plage *f, pl.* arrière-plages.

backside ['bæk'said], *s.* **1.** *F:* derrière *m,* postérieur *m, P:* cul *m.* **2.** *Rac:* ligne droite du côté opposé.

backsight ['bæksait], *s.* **1.** *Sm.a:* hausse *f*; **b. bed,** pied *m* de hausse; **b. leaf,** planche *f* de hausse; **b. slide,** curseur *m* de hausse; **b. slide catch,** poussoir *m* de curseur de hausse; **(sighting notch of) b.,** cran *m* de mire. **2.** *Surv:* coup *m* arrière.

back-slang ['bækslæŋ], *s.* argot *m* qui consiste à prononcer les mots à rebours: **tekram** = *market;* **nottub** = *button.*

back-slap ['bækslæp], *v.i. & tr.* faire preuve d'une cordialité exubérante (envers qn); faire des assauts d'amabilité (à qn).

back-slapper ['bækslæpər], *s.* homme *m* d'une cordialité exubérante.

back-slapping ['bækslæpiŋ], *s.* cordialité exubérante.

backslide ['bækslaid], *v.i.* (**backslid**) retomber dans l'erreur, dans le vice; rechuter; revenir à ses anciens errements.

backslider ['bækslaidər], *s.* relaps, *f* relapse.

backsliding ['bæk'slaidiŋ], *s.* rechute *f* dans le péché, dans le vice; récidive *f.*

backslope ['bæksloup], *s. Geog:* revers *m* (d'une cuesta).

backspace ['bækspeis], *v.i. Typew:* rappeler le chariot.

backspacer ['bæk'speisər], *s.* (*also* **backspace key**) *Typew:* rappel *m* de chariot; rappel arrière.

backspin ['bækspin], *s. Sp:* **to put b. on a ball,** couper une balle.

backstage ['bæk'steidʒ]. **1.** *adv.* (*a*) derrière la scène; dans les coulisses; (*b*) à l'arrière-plan. **2.** *attrib.* **b. life, film,** vie *f* des coulisses, film *m* de la vie des coulisses.

backstair(s) ['bæk'stɛər, -ɛəz], *s. & a.* (i) escalier *m* de service; (ii) escalier dérobé; **b. influence,** (i) protections *fpl* en haut lieu; *F:* pistonnage *m,* piston *m*; (ii) menées sourdes, secrètes; **to succeed through b. influence,** arriver à coups de piston; **b. gossip,** propos *mpl* d'antichambre.

backstay ['bækstei], *s.* **1.** *Nau:* galhauban *m*; **b. traveller,** gouvernail *m* de drisse. **2.** *Harn:* sous-barbe *f inv,* soubarbe *f* (de bride).

backstitch ['bækstitʃ], *s. Needlew:* point *m* arrière, arrière-point *m, pl.* arrière-points; point de piqûre.

backstop ['bækstɔp], *s. Sp:* (*in baseball*) attrapeur *m.*

back-strap ['bækstræp], *s. Harn:* dossière *f*; surdos *m.*

backstretch ['bækstretʃ], *s. Rac:* ligne droite du côté opposé.

backstroke ['bækstrouk], *s.* **1.** (*a*) coup *m* de revers; (*b*) contre-coup *m, pl.* contre-coups. **2.** course *f* arrière, course de retour (d'un piston, etc.). **3.** *Swim:* nage *f* sur le dos; **100 metres (ladies') b.,** 100 mètres dos (dames).

backswamp ['bækswɔmp], *s. Geog:* (*esp. of Mississippi*) marais *m* (derrière une levée).

back swimmer ['bækswimər], *s. Ent:* notonecte *f.*

backsword ['bæksɔ:d], *s.* **1.** sabre *m.* **2.** *Fenc:* (= SINGLESTICK) (*a*) canne *f*; (*b*) escrime *f* à la canne.

back-to-back ['bæktə'bæk], *a.* dos-à-dos.

back-to-the-lander ['bæktəðə'lændər], *s.* partisan *m* du retour à la terre, à l'agriculture.

backtrack ['bæktræk], *v.i. NAm:* revenir sur ses pas; **to b. home,** s'en retourner chez soi.

back trail ['bæk'treil], *v.tr. U.S:* remonter sur la piste (du gibier, de qn).

back wall ['bæk'wɔ:l], *s. Geol:* mur *m* de rimaye (d'un cirque).

backward ['bækwəd]. **1.** *a.* (*a*) **b. motion,** mouvement *m* rétrograde, en arrière; **b. glance,** regard *m* en arrière; **b. and forward motion,** mouvement de va-et-vient, d'avance et de recul; **b. slope,** rampe *f* en arrière, à rebours; **b. flow (of water, etc.),** contre-courant *m, pl.* contre-courants; remous *m*; refoulement *m*; *Geog:* **b. erosion,** érosion régressive; (*b*) **b. harvest,** moisson *f* en retard; **b. fruits,** fruits tardifs; **b. child,** enfant *m* (i) qui a peu grandi, (ii) attardé, arriéré; **b. pupils,** élèves *m* retardataires, en retard, peu avancés; **b. race,** race *f* retardataire, moins évoluée; **the b. state of the country,** le retard dont souffre le pays; (*c*) **to be b. in doing sth.,** être lent, peu empressé, peu disposé, à faire qch.; hésiter à faire qch.; se montrer timide à faire qch.; **don't be b.,** ne faites pas le modeste; (*d*) *O:* **I don't want to be b. in generosity,** je ne veux pas être en reste de générosité. **2.** *adv.* = BACKWARDS.

backwardation [bækwə'deiʃ(ə)n], *s. St.Exch:* déport *m.*

backwardness ['bækwədnis], *s.* **1.** retard *m* (d'un enfant, de la moisson); tardiveté *f* (des fruits); lenteur *f* d'intelligence, arriération mentale. **2. b. in doing sth.,** hésitation *f,* lenteur, timidité *f,* répugnance *f,* à faire qch.

backwards ['bækwədz], *adv.* en arrière; **to jump, lean, b.,** sauter, se pencher, en arrière; **to go, walk, b.,** aller, marcher, à reculons; *F:* marcher en écrevisse; **to be carried, swept, b.,** être refoulé en arrière; **to fall b.,** tomber à la renverse; **to look b.,** (i) jeter un coup d'œil en arrière; (ii) (*in time*) jeter un regard en arrière; remonter dans le passé; (*of water*) **to flow b.,** couler à contre-courant; refouler; **the gun rolled b.,** le canon revint en arrière; **to reckon b. to a date,** remonter jusqu'à une date; **to stroke the cat b.,** caresser le chat à contre-poil, à rebrousse-poil; **to say the alphabet b.,** réciter l'alphabet à rebours; **to know sth. b.,** connaître qch. parfaitement, comme le fond de sa poche; **b. and forwards,** d'avant en arrière et d'arrière en avant; **to walk b. and forwards,** aller et venir, se promener de long en large; faire les cent pas; **movement b. and forwards,** mouvement *m* de va-et-vient, d'avance et de recul; **to go b. and forwards between two places,** faire la navette entre deux endroits.

backwash ['bækwɔʃ], *s.* remous *m.*

backwater ['bækwɔ:tər], *s.* **1.** *Hyd.E:* eau arrêtée (par un bief, etc.). **2.** (i) bras *m* de décharge (d'une rivière); (ii) accul *m* (de la mer); **to live in a b.,** habiter un trou perdu; **cultural backwaters,** les mares stagnantes de la culture. **3.** remous *m* (d'une roue de moulin, etc.). **4.** ressac *m,* renvoi *m* (des vagues).

back wind ['bækwind], *s. Nau:* retour *m* de vent.

back-wind ['bæk'wind], *v.tr. & i. Nau:* masquer.

backwoods ['bækwudz], *s.pl.* (*a*) forêts *f* (de l'intérieur) (de l'Amérique du Nord); (*b*) *F:* **to live in the b.,** habiter un trou perdu, un bled; vivre dans la brousse.

backwoodsman, *pl.* **-men** [bæk'wudzmən], *s.m.* **1.** (*a*) colon des forêts (de l'Amérique du Nord); défricheur *m* de forêts; (*b*) *F:* rustre *m,* rustaud *m.* **2.** *Parl: F:* membre de la Chambre des Lords qui ne fait acte de présence que lorsqu'il s'intéresse à un vote.

backword [bæk'wɔ:d], *s.* (*a*) réplique *f*; (*b*) rétraction *f* (d'une promesse, d'une commande).

backyard ['bæk'jɑ:d], *s.* (*a*) arrière-cour *f, pl.* arrière-cours; *F:* **we went all the way to Italy to find an artist when we had one in our own b.,** nous avons été jusqu'en Italie pour chercher un artiste quand nous en avions un à notre porte; (*b*) *U.S:* jardin *m* de derrière.

bacon ['beik(ə)n], *s.* lard *m*; porc salé et fumé; bacon *m*; **streaky b.,** petit lard, lard maigre; **fat b.,** gros lard; lard gras; *F:* **to save one's b.,** sauver sa peau; se tirer d'affaire; échapper au désastre; *A:* **to pull b. at s.o.,** faire un pied de nez à qn; *F:* **to bring home the b.,** revenir victorieux, triomphant; décrocher la timbale.

Baconian [bei'kouniən], *a. & s. Phil: Lit.Hist:* baconiste (*mf*) (disciple de Lord Francis Bacon (1561–1626) ou partisan du BACONIANISM 2).

Baconianism [bei'kouniənizm], *s.* **1.** *Phil:* baconisme *m.* **2.** *Lit.Hist:* attribution *f* à Lord Bacon des œuvres de Shakespeare.

bacony ['beikəni], *a.* qui rappelle le lard; *Med:* **b. degeneration of the liver,** dégénérescence lardacée du foie.

bacter(a)emia [bæktə'ri:miə], **bacteri(a)emia** [bæktiəri'i:miə], *s. Med:* bactériémie *f.*

bacterial [bæk'tiəriəl], *a. Biol: Med:* bactérien; **b. contamination,** infection bactérienne.

bactericidal [bæktiəri'saidl], *a.* bactéricide.

bactericide [bæk'tiərisaid], *s.* bactéricide *m.*

bacterin ['bæktərin], *s. Med:* vaccin bactérien.

bacteriological [bæktiəriə'lɔdʒikl], *a.* bactériologique; **b. warfare,** guerre *f* bactériologique.

bacteriologist [bæktiəri'ɔlədʒist], *s.* bactériologiste *mf,* bactériologue *mf.*

bacteriology [bæktiəri'ɔlədʒi], *s.* bactériologie *f.*

bacteriolysin [bæktiəriou'laisin], *s. Med:* bactériolysine *f.*

bacteriolysis [bæktiəri'ɔlisis], *s. Med: etc:* bactériolyse *f.*

bacteriolytic [bæktiəriou'litik], *a.* bactériolytique.

bacteriophage [bæk'tiərioufeidʒ], *s.* bactériophage *m*; phage *m.*

bacteriophagic [bæktiəriou'feidʒik], **bacteriophagous** [bæktiəri'ɔfəgəs], *a.* bactériophagique.

bacteriophagy [bæktiəri'ɔfədʒi], *s.* bactériophagie *f.*

bacterioscopy [bæktiəri'ɔskəpi], *s. Med:* bactérioscopie *f.*

bacteriosis [bæktiəri'ousis], *s. Bot:* bactériose *f.*

bacteriostatic [bæktiəriou'stætik], *a.* bactériostatique.

bacteriotherapy [bæktiəriou'θerəpi], *s.* bactériothérapie *f.*

bacterium, *pl.* **-ia** [bæk'tiəriəm, -iə], *s.* bactérie *f.*

bacteriuria [bæktiəri'ju:riə], *s. Med:* bactériurie *f.*

bacteroid ['bæktərɔid], *a.* bactéroïde.

Bactria ['bæktriə], *Pr.n. A. Geog:* **1.** la Bactriane. **2.** (*town*) Bactres *f.*

Bactrian ['bæktriən]. **1.** *a. A.Geog:* bactrien; *Z:* **B. camel,** chameau *m* bactrien. **2.** *s.* Bactrien, -ienne.

baculiform [bə'kju:lifɔ:m], *a.* baculiforme, en forme de bâtonnet.

baculite ['bækjulait], *s. Paleont:* baculite *f.*

bad [bæd], *a. & s.*

I. *a.* (**worse** [wɔ:s], **worst** [wɔ:st]) mauvais. **1.** (*a*) (*inferior*) **b. food,** mauvaise nourriture; nourriture de mauvaise qualité; **b. air,** air vicié; **b. meat,** viande gâtée, avariée; **b. coin,** (i) pièce *f* de mauvais aloi; (ii) pièce fausse; *F:* **he's always turning up like a b. penny,** il revient à tout bout de champ; on ne voit que lui; **b. debt,** mauvaise créance; créance irrécouvrable, douteuse, véreuse; **very b. work,** travail *m* détestable; **it's not b., not so b.,** ce n'est pas mal du tout; c'est très passable, ce n'est pas si mal; *P:* **it isn't half b.,** (i) c'est pas mal du tout; (ii) c'est au-dessus de tout; *Nau:* **b. holding ground,** fond *m* sans tenue; (*of food, etc.*) **to go b.,** se gâter, s'avarier; (*b*) (*incorrect*) **b. translation,** mauvaise traduction, traduction incorrecte; **he speaks b. French,** il parle mal le français, son français est mauvais; *Nau:* **to be on a b. course,** faire mauvaise route; **b. shot,** (i) coup mal visé; coup qui manque, *F:* rate, le but; (ii) (*pers.*) mauvais tireur; **to be b. at (lying, etc.),** s'entendre mal à (mentir, etc.); **to get into b. habits, ways,** prendre de mauvaises habitudes; **to fall back into the old b. ways,** revenir à ses anciens errements; (*c*) (*unfortunate*) **it's a b. business!** *F:* **it's a b. job!** c'est une mauvaise affaire! c'est une triste affaire! **b. day (at races, etc.),** *F:* jour *m* de poisse; **to be in a b. way,** être en mauvais, piteux, état; être dans de beaux draps; (*health*) filer un mauvais coton; (*in business*) être en fâcheuse posture; être mal-en-point; ne voler, ne plus battre, que d'une aile; **he'll come to a b. end,** il finira mal; **he has a b. name,** il a une mauvaise réputation; **it wouldn't be a b. thing, a b. plan, to . . .,** on ne ferait pas mal de . . .; **this fire was not a b. thing,** cet incendie ne fut pas si néfaste; **things are going from b. to worse,** les choses vont de mal en pis; les affaires empirent de jour en jour; (*of business, etc.*) **to look b.,** *F:* sentir le brûlé; **that looks b.,** c'est (un) mauvais signe; (*d*) *Jur:* **b. claim,** réclamation mal fondée; **b. voting paper,** bulletin de vote nul; **this is b. law, b. history,** c'est fausser la loi, l'histoire; (*e*) **word taken, used, in a b. sense,** mot *m* avec un sens péjoratif; (*f*) **to feel b. (about sth.),** avoir du remords (au sujet de qch.); (*g*) **b. blood,** ressentiment *m,* rancune *f.* **2.** (*a*) (*wicked*) **b. man,** (i) méchant homme; (ii) *U.S:* bandit *m*; **b. book,** mauvais livre; **b. life,** mauvaise vie, vie déréglée; **don't call people b. names,** n'injuriez pas les gens; **to say everything that is b. about s.o.,** dire pis que pendre de qn; **b. language,** gros mots *mpl*; *F:* **he's a b. lot,** *O:* **a b. egg, a b. hat,** c'est un vilain personnage, un vilain oiseau, un vilain coco, un vaurien, une fripouille; **he isn't as b. as he looks,** il n'est pas si diable qu'il est noir; (*b*) (*unpleasant*) **b. news,** mauvaise nouvelle; **b. treatment,** mauvais traitement; **b. weather,** mauvais temps; *Nau:* gros temps; **b. smell,** mauvaise odeur; **b. temper,** mauvaise humeur; **to have a b. cold, a b. headache,** avoir un gros rhume, un violent mal de tête; **to be on b. terms with s.o.,** être mal avec qn, en mauvais termes avec qn; être en brouille avec qn; **they are on b. terms (with each other),** ils sont mal ensemble; **it is very b. of you to . . .,** c'est très mal à vous, de votre part, de . . .; **it's (really) too b.! that's too b.!** c'est (par) trop fort! par trop violent! ça c'est raide! **it's too b. of him!** ce n'est vraiment pas bien de sa part! **it's too b. your having to stay at home,** c'est dommage, c'est bien malheureux, que vous soyez obligé de rester à la maison; **(it's) too b.!** je te plains! *F:* **she was by no means b. to look at,** elle ne manquait pas de charme physique; elle avait de l'œil, du chien; (*c*) (*injurious*) **b. accident,** accident *m* grave; **b. mistake,** lourde méprise, faute *f* grave; **to be b. for s.o., for sth.,** ne rien valoir à qn, pour qch.; **it is b. for him to smoke,** ça ne lui vaut rien de fumer; **it is b. for the health,** cela ne vaut rien pour la santé; **food that is b. for dyspeptics,** aliment *m* néfaste aux dyspeptiques; (*d*) *F:* (*ill*) **she's very b. today,** elle est très mal aujourd'hui; **I feel b.,** je ne me sens pas bien; **he is b. with his rheumatism,** il est repris de ses rhumatismes; il a une crise de rhumatisme; **she has a b. finger,** elle a mal au doigt; **my b. leg,** ma jambe malade; **b. tooth,** dent cariée; **I'm not so b.,** je ne vais

pas trop mal; **and how's your grandfather?—not so b.,** et comment va le grand-père?—il se défend; **how's business?—not so b.,** comment vont les affaires?—pas si mal; *P:* **she took b., was taken b., in church,** elle a eu une indisposition, s'est sentie indisposée, a été prise d'un malaise, pendant l'office.
II. *s.* (*a*) **to take the b. with the good,** accepter la mauvaise fortune aussi bien que la bonne; prendre le bénéfice avec les charges; (*b*) (*of pers.*) **to go to the b.,** mal tourner; se galvauder; **his son went to the b.,** son fils a mal tourné; **his business is going to the b.,** ses affaires sont en mauvaise passe; (*c*) **I am 500 francs to the b.,** je suis en perte de 500 francs; (*d*) *NAm:* **to be in b. with s.o.,** être mal vu de qn.

baddeleyite ['bædliait], *s. Miner:* baddeleyite *f.*

badderlocks ['bædəlɔks], *s. Bot:* varech *m* alimentaire.

baddish ['bædiʃ], *a. F:* assez mauvais, plutôt mauvais, plutôt médiocre.

Baden ['bɑ:d(ə)n], *Pr.n. Geog:* Bade *m*; *Hist:* **the Grand Duchy of B.,** le Grand Duché de Bade.

badge [bædʒ], *s.* **1.** (*a*) insigne *m* (d'un membre d'une société); insigne de casquette; plaque *f* (de cocher); médaille *f* (de porteur, etc.); *Mil:* écusson *m* (d'un régiment, etc.); **sporting b.,** insigne sportif; *Adm:* **to issue a b. to s.o.,** délivrer une plaque, une médaille, à qn; médailler (un marchand des quatre saisons, etc.); (*b*) **arm b.,** brassard *m*; (*c*) (*of Scout*) brevet *m*; badge *m*; (*d*) **b. messenger** (*in the House of Commons*) = huissier *m.* **2.** symbole *m,* marque *f,* signe distinctif (de la liberté, etc.). **3.** *N.Arch:* fausse galerie.

badger[1] ['bædʒər], *s.* **1.** (*a*) *Z:* blaireau *m*; *F:* grisard; *Austr:* (i) wombat *m*; (ii) péramèle *m*; **American b.,** carcajou *m,* taxidé *m,* télédu *m*; **stinking b.,** télagon *m,* télédu *m*; **to draw the b.,** (i) faire débucher le blaireau, déterrer le blaireau; (ii) *F:* forcer ses adversaires à répondre; *P: A:* **to overdraw the b.,** dépasser son crédit en banque; (*b*) *U.S: F:* **badger,** habitant, -ante, du Wisconsin; **the B. State,** le Wisconsin. **2.** (*brush*) blaireau (pour la barbe); blaireau pied de biche (de doreur, etc.). **3.** *U.S: P:* **the b. game,** l'entôlage *m.*

badger[2], *v.tr.* harceler, tourmenter, tracasser, importuner, persécuter (qn); *F:* scier le dos à (qn); **to go and b. s.o.,** aller relancer qn; **to b. s.o. for sth.,** harceler qn pour obtenir qch.; **to b. s.o. into granting a favour, to b. a favour out of s.o.,** obtenir une faveur de qn à force d'importunités.

badger dog ['bædʒədɔg], *s.* basset *m.*

badgering[1] ['bædʒəriŋ], *a.* importun.

badgering[2], *s.* harcèlement *m.*

bad-hearted ['bæd'hɑ:tid], *a. F:* **he's not a b.-h. man,** ce n'est pas un mauvais homme.

badigeon [bə'didʒən], *s.* mastic *m* à reboucher; badigeon *m*; **to stop, plaster up, (defects) with b.,** badigeonner.

badinage ['bædinɑ:ʒ], *s.* badinage *m.*

badlands ['bædlændz], *s. Geog:* bad-lands *mpl.*

bad-looking ['bæd'lukiŋ], *a. F:* **he's not b.-l.,** il n'est pas mal (de sa personne); **she's not too b.-l.,** elle n'est pas trop mal tournée, *P:* trop mal fichue: elle est plutôt bien.

badly ['bædli], *adv.* (**worse** [wə:s], **worst** [wə:st]) **1.** mal; **b. dressed,** mal habillé; **you acted b.,** vous avez mal agi; **to do, come off, b.,** mal réussir; **I came off b. in that affair,** cette affaire a tourné à mon désavantage; **to be very b. off,** être dans la gêne, dans la misère; **to be doing b.,** faire de mauvaises affaires; **things are going, turning out, b.,** les choses vont mal, tournent mal; **he speaks English b.,** il parle mal l'anglais; **to behave b.,** se mal conduire, se conduire mal; **you have treated him b.,** vous avez des torts envers lui; **he took it very b.,** il a très mal pris la chose; (*of machine, etc.*) **to work b.,** mal fonctionner. **2. b. wounded,** gravement, grièvement, blessé; **the b. disabled,** les grands infirmes, les grands mutilés; **b. beaten,** battu à plate couture. **3. to want sth. b.,** avoir grand besoin, grande envie, de qch.; **I need it b.,** j'en ai diablement besoin, il me le faut absolument.

badminton ['bædmintən], *s.* **1.** *Games:* badminton *m*; volant *m* au filet. **2.** *A:* boisson sucrée au citron et au vin rouge.

badness ['bædnis], *s.* **1.** (*a*) mauvaise qualité; mauvais état (d'une route, etc.); (*b*) **the b. of the weather,** la saleté du temps; **the b. of the climate,** la sévérité du climat. **2.** (*of pers.*) méchanceté *f.*

bad-tempered ['bæd'tempəd], *a.* grincheux; acariâtre; au caractère mal fait; **to be b.-t.,** avoir le caractère mal fait; **he is a b.-t. man,** il a le caractère difficile, il a mauvais caractère; **how b.-t. she is today!** comme elle est de mauvaise humeur aujourd'hui!

Baetica ['bi:tikə], *Pr.n. A.Geog:* Bétique *f.*

Baffin ['bæfin], *Pr.n. Geog:* **B. Island,** la Terre de Baffin.

baffle[1] ['bæfl], *s.* **1.** chicane *f*; déflecteur *m*; réverbère *m,* masque *m* (en tôle); cloison *f*; **b. door,** contre-porte *f, pl.* contre-portes (d'un fourneau); **b. collar,** manchon *m* de cimentation; **b. plate,** plaque-chicane *f, pl.* plaques-chicanes; **b. plating,** cloisonnage *m*; **b. separation of water and steam,** séparation *f* de l'eau et de la vapeur par heurtement, par choc; **b. separator,** séparateur *m* à chicanes. **2.** *W.Tel:* **b. (board),** baffle *m,* écran *m* (de haut-parleur).

baffle[2], *v.tr.* **1.** (*a*) confondre, déconcerter, dérouter (qn); mettre (la police, etc.) en défaut; dépister (la police); dérouter (les soupçons); (*b*) confondre, déjouer, faire échouer (les projets de qn); frustrer, décevoir (les espoirs); tromper (les calculs); tromper, éluder (la vigilance); échapper à (la poursuite); **to b. all description,** défier toute description; **to b. the imagination,** confondre l'imagination; **to b. definition,** échapper à toute définition; **difficulties that b. the intelligence,** difficultés *f* qui déroutent l'esprit; **mystery that has baffled all investigators,** mystère *m* qui a déjoué toutes les recherches; **baffled in his hopes,** frustré, déçu, dans ses espérances. **2.** décaler (des ouvertures, etc.); établir des chicanes dans (un conduit, etc.).

baffled ['bæfld], *a.* en chicane; décalé.

baffler ['bæflər], *s.* = BAFFLE[1] I.

baffling ['bæfliŋ], *a.* (*a*) déconcertant; (*b*) *Nau:* **b. winds,** brises folles; brises qui ne font que sauter.

baffy ['bæfi], *s. Golf:* (variété de) crosse *f* en bois à face très inclinée.

bag[1] [bæg], *s.* **1.** sac *m*; (*for collections in church*) bourse *f*; **travel(ling) b.,** sac de voyage; **paper b.,** sac de, en, papier; *Com:* **tear string b.,** sac à fil, à bande d'ouverture; *Mil: A:* **to march out with b. and baggage,** sortir d'une ville avec armes et bagages (après capitulation); *F:* **to pack up b. and baggage,** plier bagage; emporter, prendre, ses cliques et ses claques; faire son baluchon; *NAm: F:* **to leave s.o. holding the b.,** laisser qn en plan; s'esquiver; *P:* **there are bags of it,** il y en a des tas; **there's bags of room,** la place ne manque pas; *U.S: F:* **to set one's b. for an office,** se mettre en avant pour un emploi. **2.** (*a*) *Nat.Hist:* sac, poche *f*; **tear** [tiər] **b.,** sac lacrymal; **poison bag,** glande *f,* vésicule *f,* à venin; *Geol:* **b.** (= *pocket*) **of ore,** sac de minerai; (*b*) *Husb:* pis *m,* mamelle *f* (de vache); **the four quarters of the b.,** les quatre quartiers de la mamelle; (*c*) *Obst:* **b. of waters,** poche des eaux; (*d*) *F:* **bags under the eyes,** poches sous les yeux, **bags at the knees,** poches aux genoux (d'un pantalon). **3.** *Ven:* **the b.,** le tableau; **what's the b.?** qu'y a-t-il au tableau? **to make, secure, a good b.,** faire un grand abattis de gibier; faire bonne chasse; (*of fighter pilot, etc.*) avoir un beau tableau de chasse; *F:* **in the b.,** dans le sac, dans la poche; *Av:* au tableau; **it's in the b.,** c'est couru d'avance, c'est du tout cuit. **4.** *pl. F:* (*trousers*) pantalon *m, P:* grimpant *m.* **5.** *P:* (*a*) **old b.,** vieille chipie; (*b*) prostituée *f, P:* pouffiasse *f.*

bag[2], *v.* (**bagged; bagging**) **1.** *v.tr.* (*a*) **to b. (up) sth.,** mettre qch. en sac; ensacher (du minerai, etc.); (*b*) *Ven:* abattre, tuer (du gibier); *Av: F:* abattre (des avions); (*c*) *F:* empocher; s'emparer de (qch.); mettre la main sur (qch.); **where did you b. that?** où as-tu cueilli ça? **to b. the best seats,** accaparer, mettre la main sur, les meilleures places; **bags I (that)!** à moi ça! (*d*) *F:* voler, chiper; **somebody's bagged my tobacco,** on m'a chauffé mon tabac. **2.** *v.i.* (*a*) (se) gonfler, s'enfler; (*of garment, etc.*) bouffer, avoir trop d'ampleur; *Nau:* (*of sail, etc.*) faire (le) sac; **trousers that b. at the knees,** pantalon bouffant aux genoux, qui fait des poches aux genoux, qui fait bosse aux genoux; (*b*) *Nau:* tomber sous le vent; se laisser sous-venter; naviguer en travers.

bagasse [bɔ'gæs], *s. Sug.-R:* bagasse *f.*

bagatelle [bægə'tel], *s.* **1.** (*a*) bagatelle *f*; (*b*) *Mus:* petite pièce; divertissement *m.* **2.** *Games:* billard anglais (se terminant en demi-cercle et avec neuf trous dans le tapis).

bag fox ['bægfɔks], *s. Ven:* renard apporté dans un sac (pour être chassé à courre).

bagful ['bægful], *s.* sac plein; plein sac; sachée *f*; (*of game*) plein carnier.

baggage ['bægidʒ], *s.* **1.** (*a*) *Mil:* bagage *m*; **b.-waggon,** fourgon *m* à bagages; *A:* **b. master,** vaguemestre *m*; (*b*) *F: A:* **a saucy b.,** une jeune, petite, effrontée; **she's a saucy b.,** c'est une délurée; **you little b.!** petite friponne! (*c*) *P: A:* prostituée *f.* **2.** *esp. NAm:* bagages; *Rail:* **b. car,** fourgon *m* à bagages; **b. room,** (i) *Nau:* soute *f* aux bagages; (ii) *Rail:* consigne *f*; *Rail: etc: F:* **b. smasher,** porteur *m.*

bagginess ['bæginis], *s.* ampleur *f* (de vêtements); **b. about the knees (of trousers),** poches *fpl* aux genoux.

bagging[1] ['bægiŋ], *a.* = BAGGY.

bagging[2], *s.* **1.** ensachement *m* (de minerai, etc.); mise *f* en sac. **2.** toile *f* à sac.

baggy ['bægi], *a.* (vêtement) trop ample, trop lâche, mal coupé; (pantalon) flottant, bouffant; **b. cheeks,** joues pendantes; bajoues *f*; **b. eyes,** yeux *m* avec des poches; **trousers b. at the knees,** pantalon qui fait des poches aux genoux, qui poche.

bagman, *pl.* **-men** ['bægmən], *s.m. F: A:* commis voyageur.

bagpipe(s)[1] ['bægpaip(s)], *s.* (*usu. in pl.*) cornemuse *f.*

bagpipe[2], *v.tr. & i. Nau:* (*a*) se mettre vent dessus; (*b*) mettre (les voiles d'artimon) vent dessus.

bagpiper ['bægpaipər], *s.* joueur, -euse, de cornemuse.

bag-shaped ['bægʃeipt], *a.* en forme de sac; *Nat.Hist:* sacciforme.

baguette [bæ'get], *s. Join:* baguette *f.*

baguio ['bægjou], *s. Meteor:* (*in Philippines*) baguio *m.*

bag-wig ['bægwig], *s. A:* perruque *f* à bourse.

bagworm ['bægwə:m], *s. Ent: F:* psyché *f.*

bah [bɑ:], *int.* bah!

bahada [bə'hɑ:də], *s. Geog:* bahada *f,* bajada *f.*

Bahadur [bə'hɑ:dər], *s.m.* (*in India*) Bahadur. **1.** homme important ou qui fait l'important. **2.** titre donné autrefois par les Indiens aux officiers européens.

Bahama [bə'hɑ:mə], *Pr.n. Geog:* **the B. Islands, the Bahamas,** les Lucayes *f,* les îles *f* Bahamas, l'archipel *m* des Bahamas.

Bahamian [bə'hɑ:miən], *a. & s.* (natif, habitant) des îles *f* Bahamas.

Bahrain, Bahrein [bɑ:'rein], *Pr.n. Geog:* Bahrain *m,* Bahreïn *m.*

bahut [bɑ:'ɥ], *s. Furn: Arch:* bahut *m.*

Baiae ['baii:], *Pr.n. A.Geog:* Baïes *f.*

baignoire [beiɲ'wɑ:r], *s. Th:* baignoire *f.*

baikalite ['baikəlait], *s. Miner:* baïkalite *f.*

baikerite ['baikərait], *s. Miner:* baïkérite *f.*

bail[1] [beil], *s. Jur:* (*a*) cautionnement *m*; (*b*) (*pers.*) caution *f,* garant *m,* répondant *m*; (*c*) somme fournie à titre de cautionnement; **to go, stand, b., for s.o.,** se porter, se rendre, garant de qn; fournir caution pour qn (pour sa libération provisoire); répondre de qn; cautionner qn; *F:* **I'll go b. for that!** je vous le garantis! je vous en réponds! **to grant b.,** admettre une caution; **to refuse b.,** rejeter la demande de mise en liberté provisoire; **to admit s.o. to b.,** *F:* **to let s.o. out on b.,** accorder la liberté provisoire à qn (sous caution, moyennant caution); **to find b.,** fournir caution; **to surrender to one's b.,** décharger ses cautions; comparaître en jugement; **to forfeit b.,** ne pas comparaître en jugement; *F:* **to jump one's b.,** se dérober à la justice (alors qu'on jouit de la liberté provisoire).

bail[2], *v.tr. Jur:* **1.** (*a*) accorder la liberté provisoire à (qn) sous caution; (*b*) **to b. s.o. (out),** se porter caution pour obtenir l'élargissement provisoire de qn; cautionner qn. **2. to b. goods to s.o.,** déposer des biens chez qn sous contrat.

bail[3], *s.* **1.** *A.Fort:* (*a*) *pl.* lices *f*; palissade *f* (d'un château fort); (*b*) mur *m* d'enceinte; (*c*) basse-cour *f, pl.* basses-cours (d'un château fort). **2. (swinging) b.,** (*in stable*) bat-flanc(s) *m.* **3.** *pl. Cr:* barrettes *f,* bâtonnets *m* (qui couronnent le guichet).

bail[4], *s.* **1.** cerceau *m,* arceau *m* (soutenant la bâche d'une charrette). **2.** anse *f,* poignée *f* (d'un baquet, d'une bouilloire, etc.). **3.** guide-papier *m inv* (d'une machine à écrire).

bail[5], *s. Nau:* écope *f.*

bail[6], **1.** *v.tr.* **to b. a boat (out), to b. (out) the water,** écoper, vider, agréner, un canot; vider, écoper, l'eau d'une embarcation. **2.** *v.i. Av:* **to b. out,** sauter (en parachute) d'un avion en perdition.

bailable ['beiləbl], *a. Jur:* qui a droit à la liberté provisoire (sous caution); **b. offence,** délit *m* comportant l'élargissement provisoire du délinquant moyennant cautionnement par un tiers; délit pour lequel la mise en liberté sous caution est possible.

bail bond ['beilbɔnd], *s. Jur:* engagement signé par la caution.

bailee [bei'li:], *s. Jur:* dépositaire *mf* (de biens sous contrat).

bailer[1] ['beilər], *s.* **1.** écope *f,* sasse *f* (d'un canot); épuisette *f.* **2.** *Civ.E:* tube *m* à sédiment, cuvette *f.*

bailer[2] = BAILOR.

bailey[1] [beili], *s.* **1.** = BAIL[3] 1. **2. the Old B.** (= *the Central Criminal Court*), le tribunal principal de Londres en matière criminelle (situé dans la rue ainsi nommée); la cour d'assises de Londres.

Bailey[2], *Pr.n.* **B. bridge,** pont *m* Bailey, pont de fortune.

bailie ['beili], *s. Scot:* conseiller municipal.

bailiery ['beiliəri], *s. Scot:* juridiction *f* d'un conseiller municipal.

bailieship ['beiliʃip], *s. Scot:* fonction *f* de conseiller municipal.

bailiff ['beilif], *s.* **1.** *Jur:* **sheriff's b.,** agent *m* de poursuites; huissier *m,* porteur *m* de contraintes; recors *m.*

2. (*a*) régisseur *m*, intendant *m* (d'un domaine); **farm b.,** régisseur; **water b.,** (i) (*of a river*) garde-pêche *m*, *pl.* gardes-pêche; (ii) *A:* (*of a port*) percepteur *m* des droits du port; (*b*) **the B. of Dover Castle,** le custode du château fort de Douvres. 3. (*a*) *Hist:* bailli *m*; (*b*) **the High B. of Westminster,** le premier magistrat de la Cité de Westminster (à Londres).

bailing out ['beiliŋ'aut], *s.* = BALING OUT.

bailiwick ['beiliwik], *s.* 1. *Hist:* bailliage *m.* 2. (*a*) *Lit:* juridiction *f*, domaine *m* (du clergé, etc.); (*b*) *U.S: F:* région *f* sous la domination d'un voleur armé ou d'un homme politique.

bailliage ['beiliedʒ], *s. Hist:* bailliage *m.*

baillоné ['beilənei], *a. Her:* baillonné.

baillonnella [beilə'nelə], *s. Bot:* baillonnella *m.*

bailment ['beilmənt], *s. Jur:* 1. (*a*) caution *f*, cautionnement *m*; (*b*) mise *f* en liberté (d'un prisonnier) sous caution. 2. (acte *m* de) dépôt *m*; contrat *m* de gage.

bailor ['beilər], *s. Jur:* 1. (*a*) déposant *m* (de biens sous contrat); (*b*) prêteur *m.* 2. (*pers.*) caution *f.*

bailsman, *pl.* **-men** ['beilzmən], *s.m. Jur:* **to act as b.,** servir de caution, de répondant.

Baily's beads ['beiliz'bi:dz], *s.pl. Astr:* grains *m* de Baily.

Bainbridge ['beinbridʒ], *Pr.n. Physiol:* **B. reflex,** réflexe *m* de Bainbridge.

bainite ['beinait], *s. Metall:* bainite *f.*

bainitic [bei'nitik], *a. Metall:* bainitique.

bain-marie ['bænmæ'ri:], *s.* bain-marie *m*, *pl.* bains-marie.

bairn [bɛə(r)n], *s. Dial: Scot:* enfant *mf.*

bait[1] [beit], *s.* 1. (*a*) *Fish:* amorce *f*, appât *m*, achée *f*, aiche *f*, boitte *f*, boëtte *f*; **live b.,** appât vivant; **ground b.,** amorce de fond; **ground-b. fishing,** pêche *f* au coup; **ledger b.,** appât de fond; **spinning b.,** cuiller *f*, hélice *f*; **spoon(-)b.,** cuiller *f*, cuillère *f*; **to remove the b. (from a line),** déboëtter; (*b*) *F:* appât, leurre *m*; **to take, nibble at, rise to, swallow, the b.,** mordre à l'hameçon, à l'appât; prendre l'hameçon; gober l'appât; *F:* gober le morceau; gober la mouche. 2. (*a*) *A:* arrêt *m* pour rafraîchissement et repos; (*b*) *Dial:* goûter *m*; morceau *m* sur le pouce.

bait[2]. 1. *v.tr.* (*a*) harceler (un animal); **to b. a bull with dogs,** lancer, faire combattre, des chiens contre un taureau; **to b. s.o.,** harceler, tourmenter, qn; (*b*) (*of dog*) se lancer sur (le taureau, etc.). 2. (*a*) *v.tr. A:* faire manger (un cheval pendant une halte); (*b*) *v.i. A:* s'arrêter pour se rafraîchir; se restaurer. 3. *v.tr.* amorcer, appâter, embecquer, garnir (un hameçon, etc.) **(with,** avec); *F:* boëtter; amorcer (un piège); **to b. the line,** mettre l'appât à la ligne; amorcer; **to b. a hook with worms,** aicher, escher, un hameçon; **to ground b.,** amorcer (un coup, etc.).

bait[3], *s. P:* **to be in an awful b.,** être fou, folle, de colère.

baiter ['beitər], *s. Fish:* amorceur, -euse.

baitfish ['beitfiʃ], *s. Fish:* 1. (poisson utilisé comme) appât *m.* 2. (poisson pêché à l')appât.

baiting ['beitiŋ], *s.* 1. harcèlement *m* (des animaux); **badger b.,** déterrage *m* du blaireau; chasse *f* au blaireau; **bull b.,** combat *m* de chiens contre un taureau. 2. amorçage *m* (d'un hameçon, d'un piège, etc.); *Fish:* **b. needle,** aiguille *f* à amorcer.

baize [beiz], *s.* (*a*) feutrine *f*; **green b.,** tapis vert; **b.-covered door, green b. door,** porte feutrée; (*b*) *A:* **oil b.,** toile cirée.

bajada [bə'hɑ:də], *s. Geog:* bajada *f*, bahada *f.*

bajan ['beidʒən], **bejant** ['bidʒənt], *s. Sch:* (*at St. Andrews, etc.*) bizut(h)(e).

Bajocian [bə'dʒousiən], *a. & s. Geol:* bajocien (*m*).

bake[1] [beik], *s.* 1. cuisson *f* (du pain, etc.). 2. (*batch*) fournée *f* (de pain). 3. *Scot:* espèce de biscuit.

bake[2]. 1. *v.tr.* (*a*) cuire, faire cuire (qch.) (au four); **to b. bread,** cuire, faire, le pain; (*in the army*) manutentionner le pain; (*b*) cuire (des briques); **earth baked by the sun,** sol durci, desséché, par le soleil; (*c*) *Metall:* étuver (un moule); (*d*) étuver, désinfecter (la correspondance d'un hôpital, etc.). 2. *v.i.* (*a*) (*of bread, etc.*) cuire (au four); *F:* **we're baking (in the heat),** nous brûlons par cette chaleur; **I'm baking, I'm baked,** je crève de chaleur; (*b*) **the earth was baking in the sun,** la terre se durcissait, se desséchait, au soleil. 3. *v.i.* (*of soil*) s'agglomérer; se mettre en mottes.

baked [beikt], *a.* (*a*) rôti; cuit au four; **baked meat,** viande(s) rôtie(s); **baked potatoes,** pommes *f* de terre (i) au four, (ii) en robe de chambre; (*b*) *Typ:* (*of type*) collé ensemble (et donc difficile à distribuer).

bakehouse ['beikhaus], *s.* fournil *m*, boulangerie *f*; *Mil: Nau:* manutention *f.*

Bakelite ['beikəlait], *s. R.t.m:* Bakélite *f*; **to coat with B.,** bakéliser; **B. insulation,** isolant bakélisé; **B. wood,** bois bakélisé.

bakelize ['beikəlaiz], *v.tr.* bakéliser.

baker ['beikər], *s.* (*a*) boulanger *m*; **the baker's wife,** la boulangère; **journeyman b.,** gindre *m*, geindre *m*; **baker's man, boy,** garçon boulanger, *F:* mitron *m*; **baker's trade,** la boulangerie; **baker's shop,** boulangerie *f*; **the baker's will be shut,** la boulangerie sera fermée; **baker's dozen,** treize douze, treize à la douzaine, une treizaine; *Med:* **baker's itch,** psoriasis *m*; (*b*) (fruit *m*, légume *m*, etc.) à cuire (au four); (*c*) *Brickm:* cuiseur *m*; (*d*) *Fish:* mouche artificielle pour la pêche au saumon.

bakery ['beikəri], *s.* (*a*) boulangerie *f*; (*b*) *Mil: etc:* manutention *f.*

bakestone ['beikstoun], *s. Cu: O:* plaque *f* de four.

baking ['beikiŋ], *s.* 1. (*a*) cuisson *f* (du pain, etc.); **b. apples, pears,** pommes *f*, poires *f*, à cuire (au four); **b. dish, pan,** plat *m*, à rôtir, plat allant au four; **b. sheet,** tôle *f* (à gâteaux), plaque *f*; **b. tin,** (i) plat à rôtir; (ii) moule *f* à gâteaux; **b. powder,** poudre *f* à lever, poudre levain, levure artificielle; **b. soda,** carbonate *m* de soude; *Mil:* **the b. section,** la boulangerie; *a. F:* **b. hot,** excessivement chaud; **b. hot day,** journée *f* torride; **we were b. hot,** on grillait; (*b*) cuisson, cuite *f* (des briques, de la porcelaine, etc.); (*c*) *Metall:* étuvage *m*, étuvement *m* (des moules). 2. (*batch*) (*a*) fournée *f* (de pain); (*b*) cuite (de briques, etc.).

baksheesh, bakshish ['bækʃi:ʃ], *s.* bakhchich *m*; **to expect b. from s.o.,** attendre un pot-de-vin de qn.

Baku [bæ'ku:], *Pr.n. Geog:* Bakou *m.*

Balaam ['beiləm], *Pr.n.m.* 1. Balaam. 2. *Journ: A:* paragraphes sans importance consacrés au remplissage d'un journal; **B. box, B. basket,** endroit *m* où l'on garde les paragraphes dits "Balaam".

Balaclava [bælə'klɑ:və], *Pr.n. Geog:* Balaklava; **B. cap, helmet,** *s.* **balaclava,** passe-montagne *m*, *pl.* passe-montagnes.

Balaenidae [bælei'nidi:], *s.pl. Z:* balénidés *m.*

balaenoptera [bælei'nɔptərə], *s. Z:* balénoptère *m.*

balafo ['bæləfou], *s. Mus:* balafo(n) *m.*

balalaika [bælə'laikə], *s. Mus:* balalaïka *f.*

balance[1] ['bæləns], *s.* 1. (*a*) balance *f*; **Roman b.,** balance romaine; **spring b.,** peson *m*; **analytical, chemical, precision, b.,** balance de précision; (*if small*) trébuchet *m*, balance-trébuchet *f*, *pl.* balances-trébuchets; **Roberval's b.,** balance de Roberval; **letter b.,** pèse-lettres *m inv*; **lever b.,** peson à contrepoids; **b. case,** lanterne *f*; **to turn the b.,** faire pencher la balance; **to be, hang, in the b.,** être, rester, en balance; **for a long time victory hung in the b.,** longtemps la victoire balança; *B:* **thou art weighed in the balances, and art found wanting,** tu as été pesé en la balance et tu as été trouvé léger; **he was weighed in the b. and found wanting,** il ne s'est pas montré à la hauteur (de l'épreuve); (*b*) *Clockm:* = BALANCE WHEEL 1; (*c*) *Mec.E: etc:* **b. (weight),** contrepoids *m*; masse *f* d'équilibrage. 2. équilibre *m*, aplomb *m*; stabilité *f*; pondération *f*; **to keep, lose, recover, one's b.,** se tenir en équilibre; perdre l'équilibre; retrouver, reprendre, son équilibre; **to throw s.o. off his b.,** (i) faire perdre l'équilibre à qn; (ii) *F:* interloquer qn; (*mind*) **off b.,** (esprit) désaxé, déséquilibré; **he's completely off b.,** il est complètement déséquilibré; **to throw an instrument out of b.,** déséquilibrer un instrument; **alcohol causes lack of b.,** l'alcool déséquilibre; **picture that lacks b.,** tableau *m* qui manque d'harmonie, de pondération; **he's gifted but he lacks b.,** il est doué mais il manque de pondération; *Phil: etc:* **the b. of nature,** l'équilibre de la nature; **the b. of power,** la balance des pouvoirs; *Hist:* la balance politique; **b. of parties,** balance politique; **the b. of good and evil,** la compensation du mal par le bien; *Mec.E:* **lack of b.,** balourd *m* (d'un volant, etc.); **b. pole,** brimbale *f*, bringuebale *f*; *W.Tel:* **noise b.,** équilibre antiparasite. 3. *Com: Fin:* (*a*) solde *m*, restant *m*, reste *m*, reliquat *m* (d'un compte); **credit b., b. in hand,** solde créditeur; boni *m*; **debit b.,** solde débiteur; **b. carried forward, b. to next account,** report *m* à nouveau, solde à nouveau; **b. due,** (i) solde débiteur; (ii) solde de compte; **the b. due from you,** le restant de votre dû; **unexpended b.,** reliquat sans emploi; **to pay the b. in instalments,** payer le reste par acomptes; **payment of b.,** paiement *m* pour solde; **b. book,** livre *m* d'inventaire; **trial b., rough b.,** balance *f* de vérification; **trial-b. book,** livre *m* de soldes; *U.S:* **he spent the b. of his life in travel,** il passa le reste de sa vie à voyager; (*b*) balance, bilan *m*; **to strike a b.,** (i) établir une balance; arrêter un compte; (ii) dresser, établir, le bilan; *Pol.Ec:* **b. of trade,** balance du commerce, balance commerciale; **b. of payments,** balance des paiements; **the b. of advantage lies with him,** à tout prendre, l'avantage est de son côté; **on b.,** à tout prendre, tout bien considéré; **to win a race with a nice b. in hand,** gagner une course sans avoir fait appel à tous ses moyens. 4. *Astr:* **the Balance,** la Balance. 5. *Cmptr:* balance, solde; **b. error,** erreur *f* d'équilibrage.

balance[2]. 1. *v.tr.* (*a*) balancer, peser (les conséquences de qch., etc.); (*b*) mettre, maintenir, (un objet) en équilibre; équilibrer (une embarcation); équilibrer, stabiliser, compenser (des forces, etc.); pondérer (des pouvoirs); faire contrepoids à (qch.); *Aut:* **to b. the steering gear,** stabiliser la direction; **to b. the wheels,** équilibrer les roues; **to b. oneself on one foot,** s'équilibrer, s'affermir, se caler, sur un seul pied; **to b. a cue on one's nose,** tenir, maintenir, une queue de billard en équilibre sur son nez; (*c*) **to b. a disadvantage by, with, an advantage,** compenser un désavantage par un avantage; **one thing balances another,** une chose balance, compense, l'autre; (*d*) *Com: Fin:* balancer, solder, aligner (un compte); compenser (une dette); *Book-k:* **to b. the books,** régler les livres; **to b. the budget,** parvenir à, rétablir, l'équilibre budgétaire; équilibrer le budget; **to b. an adverse budget,** rétablir un budget déficitaire. 2. *v.i.* (*a*) se faire contrepoids; (*of scales*) se faire équilibre; **do these scales b.?** cette balance est-elle juste? **the two things b.,** les deux choses se balancent, se font équilibre; (*b*) *Com: Fin:* (*of accounts*) se balancer, s'équilibrer, se solder; **account that balances,** compte en balance; **my accounts b.,** mes comptes sont d'accord; (*c*) osciller, balancer; (*of pers.*) hésiter; balancer (entre deux partis); (*d*) *Danc:* balancer.

balance bar ['bælənsbɑ:r], *s.* = BALANCE BEAM 1, 2.

balance beam ['bælənsbi:m], *s.* 1. fléau *m*, verge *f*, de balance. 2. *Hyd.E:* balancier *m*, flèche *f* (d'une porte d'écluse). 3. *El:* **b.-beam relay,** relais *m* balance.

balance bob ['bælənsbɔb], *s. Min:* contre-balancier *m* (d'une pompe), *pl.* contre-balanciers.

balanced ['bælənst], *a.* 1. équilibré; compensé; *Biol:* stabilisé; **b. valve,** soupape équilibrée; **b. slide valve,** tiroir compensé; **to have a well-, ill-b. mind,** avoir l'esprit bien, mal, équilibré; avoir l'esprit pondéré; **well-b. sentence,** phrase *f* qui a du nombre; **ill-b. sentences,** phrases mal agencées; **well-b. diet,** régime *m* synthétique; **to take a b. view of a question,** avoir des vues pondérées sur une question. 2. en nombre égal; de force ou de valeur égale; **the two parties are pretty well b.,** les deux partis sont à peu près en nombre égal.

balance gear ['bælənsgiər], *s. Turb:* compensateur différentiel.

balance lever ['bæləns'li:vər], *s.* 1. *Civ.E:* arrière-bras *m inv* (d'un pont à bascule). 2. = BALANCE BEAM 1.

balancelle [bælən'sel], *s. Nau:* balancelle *f.*

balancer ['bælənsər], *s.* 1. (*a*) balancier *m*; pendule *m* (d'une torpille); (*b*) *Aut: Mec.E:* **crankshaft b.,** balancier de vilebrequin; (*c*) *El:* dispositif *m* d'équilibrage, compensateur *m*, équilibreur *m.* 2. *Ent:* balancier, haltère *m*, aileron *m* (des diptères). 3. (*pers.*) acrobate *mf*, funambule *mf.*

balance sheet ['bæləns)ʃi:t], *s. Com:* bilan *m* (d'inventaire); exercice *m*; tableau *m* par doit et avoir.

balance spring ['bælənsspriŋ], *s. Clockm:* ressort *m.*

balance staff ['bælənsstɑ:f], *s. Clockm:* axe *m.*

balance wheel ['bæləns(h)wi:l], *s.* 1. *Clockm: etc:* balancier *m* (de montre); roue *f* de rencontre (d'une horloge); régulateur *m*; **compensation b. w.,** balancier compensateur. 2. *Mec.E:* volant régulateur.

balancing[1] ['bælənsiŋ], *a.* 1. (*a*) (mouvement *m*) basculaire, de bascule; (*b*) (caractère) hésitant. 2. (*a*) (pouvoir) pondérateur, (puissance) pondératrice; (*b*) *Tchn:* (*of spring, etc.*) compensateur, -trice; *W.Tel:* **b. aerial,** antenne *f* de compensation.

balancing[2], *s.* 1. *O:* balancement *m*, hésitation *f* (entre deux choses). 2. (*a*) mise *f* en équilibre; équilibrage *m*; stabilisation *f*; action régulatrice; *W.Tel:* neutralisation *f*; *Aut:* **wheel b.,** équilibrage des roues; **to perform b. tricks,** faire des équilibres; *Equit:* faire de la haute voltige; (*b*) pondération *f* (des pouvoirs); (*c*) **b. of accounts,** règlement *m*, solde *m*, alignement *m*, des comptes; (*d*) *Art:* balancement (des figures dans un tableau). 3. ajustement *m* (de deux choses); compensation *f* (de qch. par qch.); **the life of man is a perpetual b. of probabilities,** toute la vie humaine roule sur des probabilités.

balancing pole ['bælənsiŋ'poul], *s.* contrepoids *m* (de danseur de corde).

balaniferous [bælə'nifərəs], *a. Bot:* balanophore.

balaninus [bælə'nainəs], *s. Ent:* balanin *m.*

balanites [bælə'naiti:z], *s. Bot:* balanites *m.*

balanitis [bælə'naitis], *s. Med:* balanite *f.*

Balanoglossida ['bælənou'glɔsidə], *s. Z:* entéropneustes *mpl.*

Balanoglossus ['bælənou'glɔsəs], *s. Z:* balanoglosse *m*, balanoglossus *m.*

balanophora [bælə'nɔfərə], *s. Bot:* balanophore *f.*

Balanophoraceae [bælənɔfɔ'reisii:], *spl. Bot:* balanophoracées *f.*

balano-posthitis ['bælənoupɔs'θaitis], *s. Med:* balano-posthite *f.*

balanorrhagia ['bælənou'reidʒiə], *s. Med:* balanite *f* gonoccique avec forte émission de pus.

balantidium [bælən'tidiəm], *s. Prot:* balantidium *m.*

balanus ['bælənəs], *s. Crust:* balane *m.*

balaphon ['bæləfɔn], *s. Mus:* balafo(n).

balas ['bæləs], *s.* **b. (ruby),** rubis *m* balais.

balata ['bælətə], *s.* **1.** *Bot:* balata *f*; **b. tree,** balata *m.* **2.** *Mec.E:* **b. belt,** courroie *f* (en) balata.

balbuties [bæl'bju:ʃii:z], *s. Med:* **1.** balbutiement *m.* **2.** balbisme *m* (bégaiement idiopathique).

balconet [bælkɔ'net], *s. Arch:* balconnet *m.*

balconied ['bælkənid], *a.* (maison *f*) à balcon(s).

balcony ['bælkəni], *s.* **1.** balcon *m.* **2.** *Th:* fauteuils *mpl,* stalles *fpl,* de première ou deuxième galerie.

bald [bɔ:ld], *a.* **1.** (*a*) chauve, *F:* déplumé; **b. patch,** région *f* chauve; région dégarnie de cheveux, de poils, de plumes, d'herbes; (*on head*) petite tonsure, commencement *m* de tonsure; **to be b. at the temples,** avoir les tempes dégarnies; *F:* **b. as a coot,** *Austr:* **as a bandicoot,** chauve comme un œuf; (*b*) (sommet de montagne, etc.) dénudé, pelé; **b. barley,** orge *f* sans barbes; *Aut:* **b. tyre,** pneu *m* lisse. **2.** (*of style, etc.*) maigre, décharné; plat; sec, sèche; **to have a b. style,** écrire sèchement; **b. statement of the facts,** simple exposition *f* des faits; exposition des faits sans glose. **3.** (*marked with white*) **b. horse,** cheval *m* belle-face.

baldachin, baldaquin ['bældəkin], *s.* baldaquin *m*; *Ecc:* ciel *m* (d'autel, etc.); *Archeol:* ciborium *m* (de basilique).

bald coot ['bɔ:ld'ku:t], *s.* **1.** *Orn:* foulque noire. **2.** *F:* tête *f* chauve.

balderdash ['bɔ:ldədæʃ], *s.* bêtises *fpl,* balivernes *fpl,* fadaises *fpl*; **to write b.,** barbouiller du papier; tomber dans l'amphigourisme; **it's all b.,** cela n'a ni rime ni raison.

baldhead ['bɔ:ldhed], *s.* **1.** tête *f* chauve; *F:* caillou déplumé; genou *m, pl.* -oux; *F:* **an old b.,** un vieux pelé; un vieux déplumé. **2.** *Orn:* colombe *f* chauve.

bald-headed ['bɔ:ld'hedid], *a.* (à la tête) chauve; **b.-h. people,** gens *m* chauves; *F:* **to go at it b.-h.,** y aller tête baissée, de toutes ses forces, de toute son énergie; mettre tout en jeu.

balding ['bɔ:ldiŋ], *a. F:* devenant chauve; **he is a b. thirty,** c'est un homme d'une trentaine d'années un peu déplumé.

baldly ['bɔ:ldli], *adv.* platement, sèchement.

baldness ['bɔ:ldnis], *s.* **1.** (*a*) calvitie *f,* alopécie *f,* **incipient b.,** calvitie naissante; (*b*) nudité *f* (d'une montagne, etc.). **2.** platitude *f,* nudité, maigreur *f,* pauvreté *f,* sécheresse *f* (du style, etc.).

baldpate ['bɔ:ldpeit], *s.* **1.** tête *f* chauve; *F:* caillou déplumé; genou *m, pl.* -oux. **2.** *Orn: U.S:* canard siffleur d'Amérique.

baldric ['bɔ:ldrik], *s.* **1.** *A:* baudrier *m*; écharpe *f.* **2.** *F:* **the B.,** le Zodiaque.

baldricwise ['bɔ:ldrikwaiz], *adv. A:* en écharpe.

Baldwin ['bɔ:ldwin], *Pr.n.m.* Baudouin.

bale[1] [beil], *s. A. & Poet:* **1.** malheur *m*; **to bring tidings of b.,** apporter des nouvelles de malheur, de mort; **day of b. and bitterness,** journée *f* de malheur et d'amertume; **the Day of B.,** le jugement dernier. **2.** tourment *m*; **to pray for the souls in b.,** prier pour les âmes en peine. **3.** douleur *f,* tristesse *f.*

bale[2], *s. Com:* balle *f,* ballot *m* (de marchandises, etc.); **b. of cotton, of wool,** balle de coton, de laine, pesant de 160 à 500 livres; **b. of paper,** ballot de dix rames de papier; **b. goods,** marchandises *fpl* en balles.

bale[3], *v.tr.* emballotter, paqueter, empaqueter (des marchandises).

bale[4], *s.* = BAIL[5].

bale[5], **1.** *v.tr.* = BAIL[6]. **2.** *v.i. Av:* **to b. out,** sauter (en parachute) d'un avion en perdition.

Balearic [bæli'ærik], *a. Geog:* **the B. Islands,** les îles *f* Baléares.

balearica [bæli'ærikəl], *s. Orn:* baléarique *f.*

balection [bə'lekʃ(ə)n], *s. Join:* moulure *f* en relief (d'un panneau de porte).

baleen [bə'li:n], *s. Com:* fanon *m* de baleine; baleine *f* (de corset).

balefire ['beilfaiər], *s. A:* **1.** bûcher *m* (funéraire). **2.** *Scot:* feu *m* d'alarme. **3.** feu de joie.

baleful ['beilful], *a. Lit:* sinistre, maléfique, funeste; **b. influence,** influence pernicieuse, néfaste; **b. sight,** spectacle *m* lugubre.

balefully ['beilfuli], *adv.* fatalement, sinistrement; lugubrement.

balefulness ['beilfulnis], *s.* aspect *m,* caractère *m,* funèbre, maléfique.

baler[1] ['beilər], *s.* = BAILER[1].

baler[2], *s.* **1.** presse *f* à balles, à emballer; *Agr:* **pick-up b.,** ramasseuse-presse *f, pl.* ramasseuses-presses. **2.** *Com:* (*pers.*) emballeur, -euse.

Balinese [bæli'ni:z], *Geog:* **1.** *a.* balinais. **2.** *s.* Balinais, -aise. **3.** *Ling:* balinais *m.*

baling ['beiliŋ], *s.* mise *f* en balles; paquetage *m*; **b. press,** presse *f* à paqueter, à emballer; presse à balles; presse hydraulique; **b. pin,** drapière *f.*

baling out ['beiliŋ'aut], *s. Av:* saut *m* (en parachute) d'un avion en perdition.

balista [bə'listə], *s. Rom. Ant:* baliste *f.*

balistes [bə'listi:z], *Ich:* baliste *m.*

balk[1] [bɔ:k], *s.* **1.** *Agr:* (*a*) bande *f,* billon *m,* de délimitation entre deux champs; (*b*) billon. **2.** (*a*) (i) pierre *f* d'achoppement; obstacle *m*; contretemps *m*; (ii) déception *f*; (*b*) *Games:* (*croquet*) position *f* de départ; *Bill:* (i) ligne *f* de départ; quartier *m*; (ii) demi-cercle *m* de départ; **to make a b.,** ramener sa bille et la rouge derrière la ligne de départ (de façon à ne pas laisser de jeu à l'adversaire); **to give s.o. a miss in b.,** concéder un point plutôt que de se risquer. **3.** *Const:* (grosse) poutre, solive *f,* billon *m,* poutrelle *f,* madrier *m*; *Nau:* cabrion *m* (d'arrimage); **claw b.,** poutrelle à griffe; **jointed b.,** poutrelle articulée; **quarter-b.,** tronc scié en quatre (dans le sens de la longueur). **4.** *Fish:* ralingue supérieure, têtière *f* (de filet).

balk[2]. **1.** *v.tr.* contrarier; (*a*) **to b. s.o.'s plans,** déjouer, frustrer, contrarier, contrecarrer, les desseins de qn; **to b. s.o. of his prey,** frustrer qn de sa proie; (*b*) se mettre en travers de (qn qui va sauter, etc.); entraver (qn); (*c*) éviter (un sujet); se soustraire à (une obligation); laisser passer (une occasion). **2.** *v.i.* (*a*) (*of horse*) refuser; se dérober; **to b. at a difficulty, at an expense,** s'arrêter, reculer, hésiter, devant une difficulté, devant une dépense; regimber contre une dépense; **to b. at the work,** rechigner devant la besogne; (*b*) *U.S:* (*of engine, etc.*) défaillir; rester en panne.

Balkan ['bɔ:lkən], *a.* **1.** *Geog:* **the B. mountains,** *s.pl.* **the Balkans,** les (monts) Balkans *m*; **the B. States,** les États *m* balkaniques; **the B. Peninsula,** la péninsule des Balkans. **2.** *Med:* **B. frame,** appareil *m* pour extension continue des fractures du fémur.

balkanization [bɔ:lkənai'zeiʃ(ə)n], *s.* balkanisation *f.*

balkanize ['bɔ:lkənaiz], *v.tr.* balkaniser.

balking ['bɔ:lkiŋ], *s.* (*a*) refus *m* (de la part d'un cheval); hésitation *f*; (*b*) *U.S:* défaillance *f* (du moteur, etc.).

ball[1] [bɔ:l], *s.* **1.** (*a*) boule *f* (de croquet, de bilboquet, de neige); balle *f* (de cricket, de tennis, de hockey, etc.); ballon *m* (d'enfant, de football), bille *f* (de billard); balle (de fusil); boulet *m* (de canon); pelote *f,* peloton *m* (de laine, de ficelle); pompon *m* (d'une frange, etc.); *Aut: A:* boule, poignée *f* (du levier de vitesse); *U.S:* **b. (game),** baseball *m*; **to wind wool into a b.,** (em)peloter, pelotonner, de la laine; mettre (de la laine) en pelote; **the three (golden) balls,** *P:* **the three brass balls,** les trois boules (enseigne *f* du prêteur sur gages); **black b. (for voting),** boule noire; **(conjuror's) vanishing b.,** muscade *f*; *Meteor:* **b. of fire, b. lightning,** globe *m* de feu; éclair *m* en boule; *Nau:* **signal b.,** ballon, bombe *f,* de signaux; *Av:* **light b.,** bombe éclairante; *U.S:* **the b. and chain,** la peine du boulet; *P:* **my b. and chain,** la bourgeoise; *Sm.a:* **to load with b.,** charger à balle; **to knock the balls about,** *Ten: etc:* peloter; *Bill:* caramboler les billes; **knocking the balls about,** pelotage *m*; lancement *m* de la balle; *Fb:* **to kick the b. about,** s'amuser avec le ballon; *Cr:* **no b.,** balle nulle, pas bonne; **to play b.,** (i) jouer à la balle; (ii) *Fig:* coopérer, être en cheville (avec qn); jouer le jeu; *Games:* **boundary b.,** *U.S:* **catch b.,** balle au camp; **call b.,** balle nommée; *F:* **to be on the b.,** (i) avoir de la présence d'esprit; (ii) connaître son affaire; **to keep the b. rolling,** continuer, soutenir, la conversation; ne pas laisser languir la conversation, le jeu; **to start the b. rolling,** déclencher la conversation; mener le branle; mettre le bal en train; ouvrir le bal; **his article started the b. rolling,** son article donna le branle; **the b. is in your court,** c'est votre tour; c'est à vous; **to have the b. at one's feet,** avoir la balle belle, avoir la partie belle; n'avoir qu'à se baisser; n'avoir qu'à saisir l'occasion; *F:* **to catch the b. on the bound,** saisir la balle au bond; **darning b.,** œuf *m,* boule, à repriser, à passefiler; *U.S:* **sour b.,** bonbon acidulé; (*b*) *Mec.E:* bille (de roulement); *attrib.* **b. cage,** cage *f,* lanterne *f,* à billes; **b. race,** (i) chemin *m,* voie *f,* bague *f,* de roulement (pour billes); (ii) cage à billes; **b. check,** bille d'arrêt; **b. cup, b. socket,** cuvette *f,* cuvette-rotule *f, pl.* cuvettes rotules; rotule *f*; **b. head,** corps *m* de rotule; **b. lever,** levier *m* à rotule; **b. valve,** (i) soupape *f* à boulet; clapet *m* sphérique; bille clapet; (ii) robinet *m,* soupape, à flotteur; *Metall:* **b. test (for hardness),** essai *m* (de dureté) à la bille; **to put a steel bar through a b. test,** biller une barre d'acier; **b. testing,** billage *m*; (*c*) **b. (-and-socket) joint,** (i) *Anat:* emboîtement *m* réciproque; énarthrose *f*; (ii) *Mec.E:* joint *m* à rotule, à boulet, à genou; (joint à) calotte *f* sphérique; articulation *f* à genouillère; *Civ.E:* **b. mill,** moulin *m* à boulets; broyeur *m* à boules; (*d*) *V:* **a kick in the balls,** un coup de pied aux couilles; **balls!** les couilles! c'est de la couille! quelle connerie! quelle couillonnade! **to make a balls (up) of sth.,** foutre la merde dans qch. **2.** (*a*) lentille *f* (de pendule); (*b*) éminence métatarsienne (du pied); **to walk on the b. of the foot,** marcher sur la demi-pointe des pieds; (*c*) *A:* paume *f* (de la main); (*d*) globe *m* (de l'œil); (*e*) (*round roots of trees, etc.*) **b. of earth,** motte *f*; **b. planting,** plantation *f* en mottes; **b. of spent tan,** motte de tannée; (*f*) *Metall:* loupe *f* (de fer fondu); (*g*) *Glassm:* **b. of molten glass,** paraison *f.* **3.** (*a*) *Cu:* **(force)meat b.,** boulette *f*; (*b*) *Vet:* (*bolus*) boulette. **4.** *Phot:* **b. of pneumatic release,** poire *f.*

ball[2]. **1.** *v.tr.* (*a*) agglomérer; *Metall:* baller (le fer); (*b*) *Tex:* (em)peloter, pelotonner (la laine, etc.); mettre (la laine) en pelote; (*c*) **horse balled up.** cheval qui a de la neige bottée sous les sabots; *P:* **balled up,** embrouillé; **everything's balled up,** tout est mêli-mêlo; rien ne marche plus. **2.** *v.tr. Vet:* **to b. a horse,** administrer une boulette à un cheval. **3.** *v.i.* s'agglomérer; **the snow balled under my shoes,** mes souliers bottaient dans la neige.

ball[3], *s.* (*a*) *Danc:* bal *m, pl.* bals; **private b.,** bal privé; **evening-dress b.,** bal paré; **to open the b.,** (i) ouvrir le bal; mettre le bal en train; (ii) *F:* mettre les choses en branle; donner le branle; entamer la discussion; ouvrir le bal; **b. dress,** robe *f* de bal; (*b*) *P:* **to have a b.,** *U.S:* **to have (oneself) a b.,** se paillarder.

ballad ['bæləd], *s.* **1.** *Mus:* ballade *f,* romance *f.* **2.** *Lit:* récit en vers disposé par strophes régulières; légende mise en vers; ballade *f.*

ballade [bæ'lɑ:d], *s. Lit:* ballade *f* (en strophes suivies d'un envoi).

ballad-monger ['bæləd'mʌŋgər], *s.* (*a*) *A:* chansonnier *m*; (*b*) *F: Pej:* compositeur *m* de chansons (médiocres).

ballan-wrasse ['bælən'ræs], *s. Ich:* carpe *f* de mer.

ballast[1] ['bæləst], *s.* **1.** *Nau: Aer:* lest *m*; **ship in b.(-trim),** navire *m* sur lest; **to proceed to a port in b.,** se rendre sur lest à un port; **shifting b.,** lest volant; **sand b.,** lest en sable; **to take in b.,** faire son lest; **to discharge, throw out, b.,** se délester; jeter du lest; **cargo in b.,** cargaison *f* à fond de cale; *attrib.* **b. donkey,** pompe *f* des ballasts; **b. tank,** ballast *m* (de sous-marin); *F:* (*of pers.*) **to have b.,** avoir l'esprit rassis, de la jugeote, du plomb dans la cervelle; **to lack b.,** manquer de jugeot(t)e. **2.** (*a*) *Civ.E:* pierraille *f,* blocaille *f,* cailloutage *m*; (*b*) *Rail:* ballast, empierrement; (*c*) *attrib.* **b. bed,** (i) *Rail: etc:* coffre *m,* empierrement; (de la voie); (ii) encaissement *m* (d'une route); *Rail:* **b. truck, car, wagon,** wagon *m* de terrassement; *Min:* **b. pit,** ballastière *f.*

ballast[2], *v.tr.* **1.** *Nau: Aer:* lester. **2.** *Civ.E:* (*a*) empierrer, ensabler; caillouter; (*b*) *Rail:* ballaster.

ballasting ['bæləstiŋ], *s.* **1.** *Nau: Aer:* lestage *m.* **2.** *Civ.E:* (*a*) empierrement *m,* ensablement *m*; cailloutage *m*; (*b*) *Rail:* ballastage *m.*

ball bearing ['bɔ:l'beəriŋ], *s.* **1.** *Mec.E:* roulement *m* à billes; palier *m,* coussinets *mpl,* à billes; **b.-b. cup,** alvéole *m or f* d'une bille. **2.** *Civ.E:* appuis *m* sphériques (d'un pont d'acier, etc.).

ballboy ['bɔ:lbɔi], *s. m. Ten: etc:* ramasseur de balles.

ball-clay ['bɔ:lklei], *s. Cer:* argile figuline.

ball cock ['bɔ:lkɔk], *s.* robinet *m,* soupape *f,* à flotteur.

ballerina [bælə'ri:nə], *s.* **1.** *Danc:* ballerine *f.* **2.** *Bootm:* ballerine.

ballet ['bælei], *s.* ballet *m*; *attrib.* **b. dancer,** danseur, -euse, d'opéra, de ballet; *f.* ballerine; **b. girl,** danseuse de ballet; **b. master, mistress,** directeur, -trice, de ballet; **b. skirt,** tutu *m.*

balletomane ['bælitoumein], *s.* balletomane *mf.*

balletomania [bælitou'meiniə], *s.* balletomanie *f.*

ballflower ['bɔ:lflauər], *s. Arch:* petite rosette décorative (très employée au XIIIe siècle dans l'architecture gothique anglaise).

balling ['bɔ:liŋ], *s.* **1.** agglomération *f* (de la neige, de l'argile, sous les chaussures, etc.); *Metall:* **b. up,** ballage *m* (du fer). **2.** *Tex:* (em)pelotage *m* (de la laine); **b. machine,** peloteuse *f,* pelotonneuse *f.*

bal(l)ista [bə'listə], *s. Rom.Ant:* baliste *f.*

ballistic [bə'listik], *a.* balistique; **b. data,** renseignements *mpl,* données *fpl,* balistiques; **b. wave,** onde *f* balistique.

ballistics [bə'listiks], *s.pl.* (*usu. with sg. const.*) balistique *f*; **interior, exterior, b.,** balistique intérieure, extérieure.

ballistite ['bælistait], *s. Exp:* balistite *f.*
ballistocardiograph [bəlistou'kɑ:diougræf], *s. Med:* balistocardiographe *m.*
ballistocardiography [bəlistoukɑ:di'ɔgrəfi], *s. Med:* balistocardiographie *f.*
ballocks ['bɔləks], *s.pl. V:* testicules *f*, couilles *f*; **b.!** les couilles! c'est de la couille! quelle connerie! quelle couillonnade!
ballon ['bælɔ̃], *s. Geog:* (*in the Vosges*) ballon *m.*
ballon(n)et ['bælənet], *s. Aer:* ballonnet (compensateur).
balloon[1] [bə'lu:n], *s.* **1.** (*a*) *Aer:* ballon *m*; aérostat *m*; (*of globular type*) sphérique *m*; **small b.,** ballonnet *m*; **air b.,** ballon à air; aérostat; **captive b., kite b., observation b.,** *U.S:* **fixed b.,** ballon captif; captif *m*; ballon cerf-volant (*pl.* cerfs-volants); ballon observateur, d'observation; **dirigible b.,** (ballon) dirigeable *m*; **free b.,** ballon libre; **fire b., hot-air b.,** montgolfière *f*, ballon à air chaud; **pilot b.,** ballon d'essai; ballon pilote; **(meteorological) b.,** radiosonde *f*; **sounding b.,** ballon-sonde *m*, *pl.* ballons-sondes; **barrage b.,** ballon de protection; **b. barrage,** barrage *m* de ballons; *Hist:* **the B. Service,** l'Aérostation *f*; **b. park, b. section,** parc *m* aérostatique; **to go up in a b.,** monter en ballon; *F:* **when the b. goes up,** (i) quand les hostilités commencent; (ii) quand on en vient aux prises avec la situation; (*b*) (*toy*) ballon d'enfant. **2.** (*a*) *Ch:* **b. (flask),** ballon; **b. glass,** (verre *m*) ballon. **3.** *Arch:* pomme *f*, boule *f* (de pilier, etc.). **4.** (*in cartoons, comic strips*) banderole *f*. **5.** *Hort:* (arbre taillé en) ovoïde *m*. **6.** *Fb:* (*high kick*) chandelle *f*. **7.** *attrib. Aut: A:* **b. tyre,** pneu *m* ballon, pneu confort.
balloon[2]. **1.** *v.i.* (*a*) *Aer:* monter en ballon; faire une ascension en ballon; (*b*) (*swell out*) bouffer; se ballonner; (*c*) *St.Exch: U.S:* faire la hausse; faire bondir les prix. **2.** *v.tr.* (*a*) ballonner (l'abdomen, etc.); (*b*) *Fb:* **to b. the ball,** botter le ballon en chandelle.
balloonette [bælu:'net], *s.* = BALLON(N)ET.
ballooning [bə'lu:niŋ], *s.* **1.** aérostation *f*. **2.** ballonnement *m* (d'un vêtement, d'une voile, etc.).
balloonist [bə'lu:nist], *s.* aéronaute *m*, aérostier *m.*
ballot[1] ['bælət], *s.* **1. b. (ball),** boule *f* de scrutin. **2.** (*a*) tour *m* de scrutin; **to vote by b.,** voter au scrutin; **single b.,** élection *f* sans ballottage; **second b.,** ballottage *m*, deuxième tour de scrutin; **to subject candidates to a second b.,** ballotter les candidats; **the candidates were subjected to a second b.,** il y a eu ballottage; (*b*) scrutin *m*, vote *m*; **to take, hold, a b.,** procéder à un scrutin, à un vote; **b. paper,** bulletin *m* de vote; **b. box,** urne *f* de scrutin. **3.** (*in Parliament*) tirage *m* au sort (pour la priorité du droit de soumettre des résolutions, etc.); **to hold a b.,** procéder à un tirage au sort. **4. peace b.,** referendum *m* pour la paix.
ballot[2]. **1.** *v.i.* (*a*) voter au scrutin (secret); **to b. for s.o.,** voter pour qn; élire qn au scrutin; **to b. against s.o.,** voter contre qn; *F:* blackbouler qn; (*b*) tirer au sort; **to b. for a place, etc.,** tirer une place, etc., au sort; (*in House of Commons, etc.*) **to b. for precedence,** tirer au sort pour le droit de priorité. **2.** *v.tr.* **to b. workmen, etc., on a question,** appeler les ouvriers, etc., à voter sur une question.
ballot[3], *s. Com:* ballot *m* (de marchandises).
ballotade ['bælə'tɑ:d], *s. Equit:* ballotade *f.*
ballotage ['bælətidʒ], *s.* (*in Fr. Pol.*) ballottage *m.*
balloting ['bælətiŋ], *s.* **1.** élection *f* au scrutin. **2.** tirage *m* au sort.
ballottement [bə'lɔtmənt], *s. Med:* ballottement *m.*
ball point ['bɔ:l'pɔint], *s. Mec.E:* pointe *f* bille.
ballpoint ['bɔl:pɔint], *s.* **b. (pen),** stylo *m* (à) bille.
ballroom ['bɔ:lru:m], *s.* salle *f* de bal; salle de danse; *attrib.* **b. dancing,** danses *fpl* de bal, de salon.
ball-shaped ['bɔ:lʃeipt], *a.* sphérique.
ball-trap ['bɔ:ltræp], *s.* **1.** soupape *f* à boulet; clapet *m* sphérique; bille *f* clapet. **2.** projecteur *m* (pour le tir aux pigeons); **pistol b.-t.,** projecteur à main.
bally ['bæli], *a. F:* (*euphemism for* BLOODY) **it's a b. nuisance!** c'est un fichu embêtement! **b. idiot!** bougre d'idiot! **the whole b. lot,** tout le saint-frusquin, tout le bazar.
ballyhoo[1] [bæli'hu:], *s. P:* **1.** grosse réclame; battage *m.* **2.** barat(t)in *m.*
ballyhoo[2], *v.tr. P:* **1.** agir sur (qn). **2.** faire de la réclame en faveur de (qch.).
ballyrag ['bæliræg], *v.tr. F: A:* brimer (qn); chahuter (un professeur); se moquer de qn avec insolence.
ballyragging ['bæliræɡiŋ], *s. F: A:* brimades *fpl*, chahutage *m.*
balm [bɑ:m], *s.* **1.** *Pharm: etc:* baume *m*; **b. of Gilead,** baume de la Mecque; térébenthine *f* de Judée; *Lit:* **a kind word is a b. to a wounded soul,** une bonne parole est une baume pour une âme meurtrie; *Bot:* **(lemon) b.,** mélisse officinale; citronnelle *f*; **garden b.,** citragon *m*; **molucca b.,** moluque *f* odorante; **bastard b.,** herbe saine; **Abraham's b.,** petit poivre, poivre sauvage, agnus-castus *m.*
balm-cricket ['bɑ:mkrikit], *s. Ent:* cigale *f.*
Balmer ['bɑ:mər], *Pr.n. Ph:* **B. formula,** formule *f* de Balmer; **B. series,** série *f* de Balmer.
balmily ['bɑ:mili], *adv. Lit:* **the wind blows b.,** le vent est chargé de doux parfums.
balminess ['bɑ:minis], *s.* **1. the b. of the evening air,** l'air embaumé du soir. **2.** *F:* loufoquerie *f.*
Balmoral [bæl'mɔr(ə)l], *Pr.n. Geog:* Balmoral *m* (résidence royale en Écosse); *A: Cost:* **B. petticoat, boots, cap,** jupe *f*, brodequins *mpl*, béret *m*, Balmoral.
balmy ['bɑ:mi], *a.* **1.** balsamique. **2.** (*a*) (air, temps) embaumé, parfumé; d'une douceur délicieuse; *Lit:* **b. breeze,** zéphir *m*; (*b*) *Lit:* (*soothing*) doux, *f* douce; calmant, adoucissant; **b. sleep,** doux sommeil. **3.** *F:* toqué, timbré, maboul, loufoque, complètement marteau.
balneal ['bælniəl], *a.* balnéaire.
balneary ['bælniəri]. **1.** *a.* balnéaire. **2.** *s.* station *f* balnéaire.
balneation [bælni'eiʃ(ə)n], *s.* balnéation *f.*
balneology [bælni'ɔlədʒi], *s.* thermalisme *m.*
balneotherapy [bælniou'θerəpi], *s.* balnéothérapie *f*; emploi *m* des bains en thérapeutique; cure *f* de bains.
baloney [bə'louni], *s. F:* **it's all b.,** (i) c'est des histoires! c'est de la fantaisie; (ii) c'est du chiqué, du boniment, *P:* des conneries!
balsa ['bɔ(:)lsə], *s.* **1.** *Bot:* balsa *m.* **2.** radeau *m* (en balsa).
balsam ['bɔ:lsəm]. **1.** (*a*) baume *m*; *Pharm: etc:* **friar's b.,** baume de benjoin; **true b., b. of Mecca,** baume de la Mecque, térébenthine *f* de Judée; **Canada b.,** baume du Canada; **copaiba b.,** baume de Copahu; **b. of Peru,** baume de Pérou; **b. of Tolu,** baume de Tolu; **Calaba b.,** baume Marie, baume vert des Antilles; (*b*) *Ch: Ind:* oléorésine *f*. **2.** *Bot:* **garden, yellow, b.,** balsamine *f*; **b. apple,** momordique *f* balsamine, pomme *f* de merveille. **3.** *Arb:* **b. fir,** sapin baumier; **b. poplar,** peuplier baumier, peuplier de Giléad; **b. tree,** quina-quina *m*, quino-quino *m.*
balsamic [bɔ:l'sæmik], *a.* balsamique.
balsamiferous [bɔ:lsə'mifərəs], *a.* balsamifère.
Balsaminaceae [bɔlsæmi'neisii:], *s.pl. Bot:* balsaminacées *f.*
Balt [bɔ:lt], *s. Hist:* Balte *mf.*
Balthazar [bæl'θæzər]. **1.** *Pr.n.m. B:* Balthazar. **2.** *s.* (*wine bottle*) balthazar *m.*
Baltic ['bɔ:ltik]. **1.** *a. Geog:* balte, baltique; **the B. Sea,** *s.* **the Baltic,** la (mer) Baltique; **B. shield,** bouclier *m* scandinave; **B. trade,** commerce *m* de la Baltique; **B. port,** port *m* balte; *Com:* **B. timber,** bois *m* du nord; *Com:* **the B. Exchange,** bourse *f* du commerce étranger des houilles, des bois, des huiles, et des céréales (située à Londres). **2.** *s. Ling:* baltique *m.*
Baluchi [bə'lu:tʃi]. *Geog:* **1.** *a.* baloutchi; béloutche. **2.** *s.* Baloutchi, -ie; Béloutche *mf.*
Baluchistan [bə'lu:tʃistæn, -tɑ:n; -lu:ki'stɑ:n], *Pr.n. Geog:* Bélou(t)chistan *m*, Baloutchistan *m.*
baluchitherium [bəlu:tʃi'θi:riəm], *s. Z:* baluchithérium *m.*
balun ['bælən], *s. El:* transformateur *m* symétrique-dissymétrique.
baluster ['bæləstər], *s.* **1.** balustre *m*; **b. railing,** parapet *m* à balustres. **2.** *pl.* rampe *f* d'escalier.
balustered ['bæləstəd], *a.* à balustres.
balustrade [bæləs'treid], *s.* (*a*) balustrade *f*; (*b*) accoudoir *m*, allège *f*, appui *m* (de fenêtre, etc.); garde-corps *m inv.*
balustraded [bæləs'treidid], à balustrade.
bambino [bæm'bi:nou], *s.m. Art:* Enfant Jésus.
bamboo [bæm'bu:], *s.* bambou *m*; **b. cane,** bambou, bamboche *f*; *Cu:* **b. shoots,** pousses *fpl* de bambou; **b. salt, sugar of b.,** tabas(c)hir *m*; *Pol:* **b. curtain,** rideau *m* de bambou.
bamboozle [bæm'bu:zl], *v.tr. F:* mystifier, enjôler, embobeliner (qn); *P:* mettre (qn) dedans; **you've been bamboozled,** on vous a enfoncé, refait; **you can't b. me,** on ne me la fait pas; ça ne prend pas avec moi; on ne m'a pas comme ça; **to b. s.o. out of sth.,** (i) frauder qn de qch.; (ii) soutirer qch. à qn; **they bamboozled him into making a new will,** ils ont réussi à lui faire rédiger un nouveau testament.
bamboozlement [bæm'bu:zlmənt], *s. F:* enjôlement *m*, duperie *f*, tromperie *f.*
bamboozler [bæm'bu:zlər], *s. F:* mystificateur, -trice; farceur, -euse; enjôleur, -euse.
Bambuseae [bæm'bju:zi(:)i:], *s.pl. Bot:* bambusées *fpl.*
ban[1] [bæn], *s.* **1.** (*a*) (*sentence of banishment, of outlawry*) ban *m*, bannissement *m*, proscription *f*; (*b*) *Ecc:* interdit *m*; anathème *m*; **to place s.o. under the b. of the Empire, of public opinion,** mettre qn au ban de l'Empire, de l'opinion (publique); vouer qn à la malédiction publique; **customs that are under the b. of society,** mœurs bannies de la bonne société, proscrites par la bonne société; (*c*) **a year's driving b.,** suspension *f* pour un an du permis de conduire; **atomic test b.,** interdiction *f* des essais atomiques. **2.** *pl. A:* = BANNS.
ban[2], *v.tr.* (**banned**) interdire (qn, qch.); mettre (un livre) à l'index; **play banned by the censor,** pièce interdite par la censure; **to be banned by public opinion,** être au ban de l'opinion (publique); **he is banned by society,** la société lui a fermé ses portes; **to b. war,** mettre la guerre hors la loi; **b. the bomb!** plus de bombes atomiques! **to be banned from driving,** se voir retirer son permis de conduire.
ban[3], *s. Hist:* (*in Croatia*) ban *m.*
ban[4], *s. Num:* ban *m*, *pl.* bani.
banal [bæ'nɑ:l, bæ'næl, 'beinl, 'bænl], *a.* **1.** *A:* (four, moulin) banal, -aux. **2.** banal; ordinaire.
banality [bə'næliti], *s.* **1.** *A.Jur:* **right of b.,** droit *m* de banalité. **2.** banalité *f*; **he began his letter with a few banalities,** il a commencé sa lettre par quelques banalités.
banana [bə'nɑ:nə], *s.* **1.** banane *f*; (*as opposed to plantain*) figue *f* banane; **Canary b.,** banane des Canaries, de Chine; **b. boat,** bananier *m*; *F:* **b. republic,** petit pays qui dépend de capitaux étrangers. **2. b. (tree),** bananier; (*as opposed to plantain*) bananier des sages; **b. plantation,** bananeraie *f*. **3.** *El: Cmptr:* **b. plug,** fiche *f* banane; **b. jack,** jack *m* pour casque téléphonique. **4.** *Paint:* **b. oil,** acétate *m* d'amyle.
banana-producing [bə'nɑ:nəprə'dju:siŋ], *a.* (région, etc.) bananifère.
bananaquit [bə'nɑ:nəkwit], *s. Orn:* sucrier *m*; (*coereba flaveola*) sucrier flavéole, à ventre jaune.
Banbury ['bænbri], *Pr.n. Geog:* Banbury; *Cu:* **B. cake,** tartelette *f* aux raisins secs.
bancal ['bæŋkəl], *s. A.Mil:* bancal *m*, *pl.* -als.
banco ['bæŋkou], *s. Games:* banco *m*; **to go b.,** faire banco; **b.!** banco!
band[1] [bænd], *s.* **1.** (*a*) lien *m* (de fer); frette *f*; cercle *m* (d'un tonneau); bandage *m* (d'une roue); bride *f* (d'un ressort); bracelet *m* (d'un fourreau); **steel b.,** ruban *m* d'acier; **nave b.,** frette de moyeu; *Sm.a:* **upper b. (of rifle),** embouchoir *m* (à quillon); **lower b.,** grenadière *f*; *Artil:* **driving b.,** ceinture *f* d'obus, de forcement; (*b*) bande *f* (de papier, de toile); ruban (d'un chapeau); *Bookb:* nerf *m*, nervure *f*, accolure *f*; bague *f* (de cigare); **cigar with a gold b.,** cigare bagué d'or; **narrow b.,** bandelette *f*; **silk moire b.,** ruban de moire (pour montre); (*round arm*) **crêpe b.,** brassard *m* de crêpe, de deuil; *Mil:* **cap b.,** (i) bandeau *m* (de képi, de casquette d'uniforme); (ii) (*usu. white and worn by troops on one side in manoeuvres*) manchon *m*; *Nau:* (*in Merchant Service*) **bands,** galons *mpl*; **rubber, elastic, b.,** élastique *m*; *Nau:* **strain b.,** barate *f*; *Av:* **mooring b.,** sangle *f* d'ancrage; **suspension b.,** ralingue *f* de suspension; **trajectory b.,** ralingue; bande de renforcement; (*c*) bande, raie *f* (de couleur, etc.); *Opt:* **bands of the spectrum,** bandes du spectre; **absorption bands,** bandes d'absorption; (*d*) **the bands in onyx,** les zones *f* de l'onyx; (*e*) *Arch:* (i) bague (d'une colonne); (ii) cordon *m* (d'un mur); (*f*) *W.Tel: Elcs:* **frequency b.,** bande de fréquence; **side bands,** bandes latérales; **b. filter,** filtre *m* de bande; **b.-pass filter, b.-pass circuit,** filtre, circuit *m*, passe-bande; **amateur b.,** bande de fréquence réservée aux émissions d'amateurs; **in the 19 metre b.,** dans la bande des 19 mètres; **transmission b.,** bande passante; (*g*) *Cmptr:* piste *f*, bande de fréquence; **calling b.,** bande d'appel; **guard b.,** bande de garde; **pass b.,** bande passante; **voice frequency b.,** bande de fréquence vocale; (*h*) *Rec:* plage *f* (d'un disque). **2.** *Mec.E: etc:* bande, courroie *f* (de transmission); **b. wheel,** roue *f* de transmission; **canvas b. (of conveyor),** bâche *f*; *Ind:* **endless b. (in mass production), b. conveyor,** tapis roulant; transporteur *m* à toile sans fin; **moving-b. production,** travail *m* à la chaîne; **b. of a caterpillar tractor;** chenille *f* d'une autochenille. **3.** *pl. Ecc.Cost: etc:* **bands,** rabat *m.*
band[2], *v.tr.* **1.** bander (un ballot); fretter (un four, etc.); mettre (un journal, etc.) sous bande. **2.** rayer; zébrer de rayures. **3.** baguer (un pigeon).
band[3], *s.* **1.** (*a*) bande *f*, troupe *f*; **the black bands that ravaged the frontier,** les bandes noires qui ravageaient la frontière; **a little b. of fugitives,** une petite troupe de fugitifs; **a merry b. of revellers,** une bande de joyeux noceurs; (*b*) compagnie *f*; *Pej:* clique *f* (de personnes); **author dear to a growing b. of readers,** auteur cher à un nombre croissant de lecteurs; **B. of Hope,** société *f* de tempérance (pour la jeunesse). **2.** *Mus:* (*a*) (*orchestra*) orchestre *m*; (*b*) *Mil: etc:* musique *f*; **the regimental b.,**

la musique du régiment; **brass b.,** fanfare *f*; **jazz b.,** jazz-band *m*, *pl.* jazz-bands; *A:* **German b.,** troupe *f* de musiciens ambulants; *Mil:* **the drum and bugle b.,** la batterie; *F:* la clique; **the members of the b.,** les musiciens; *F:* **one-man b.,** homme-orchestre *m*, *pl.* hommes-orchestres; *F: O:* **when the b. begins to play,** quand les choses se corsent.

band⁴, *v.i. & pr.* **to b. (together),** (i) se liguer; se réunir en bande; (ii) s'ameuter.

bandage¹ ['bændidʒ], *s.* (*a*) *esp. Med:* bandage *m*, bande *f*, bandelette *f*; (*for blindfolding*) bandeau *m*; **triangular b.,** bandage en triangle; **crêpe b.,** bande Velpeau; *F:* velpeau *m*; **(surgical) b.,** bande de pansement; pansement *m*; (*for the jaw*) chevêtre *m*; **arm b.,** pansement brachial, -aux; **chin b.,** mentonnière *f*; **fenestrated b.,** bandage fenêtré; **figure-of-eight b.,** bandage en huit de chiffre; **suspensory b.,** suspensoir *m*; **head swathed in bandages,** tête enveloppée de linges; **to put a b. on s.o., sth.,** bander qn, qch.; mettre un pansement à qn; **to remove a b. from a wound,** débander une plaie; enlever l'appareil, le pansement; (*b*) *Vet:* **horse b.,** bande jambière.

bandage², *v.tr.* bander (un bras cassé, une plaie); poser un appareil, mettre un pansement, sur (une plaie).

bandaging ['bændidʒiŋ], *s.* bandage *m*; pose *f* de l'appareil; pansement *m*.

bandan(n)a [bæn'dænə], *s.* (i) foulard *m*, (ii) mouchoir *m* (à pois ou en couleurs).

bandar ['bʌndər], *s. Z:* bandar *m*; macaque *m* rhésus.

bandbox ['bændbɔks], *s.* carton *m* à chapeau(x); carton de modiste; *O:* **to look as if one had just stepped out of a b.,** être tiré à quatre épingles; avoir l'air de sortir d'une boîte.

bandeau, *pl.* **-eaux** ['bændou, -ouz], *s.* **1.** (*headband*) bandeau *m*; **she wears her hair in bandeaux,** elle porte les cheveux en bandeaux. **2.** *Cost:* barrette *f* d'entrée de tête (d'un chapeau).

banded ['bændid], *a.* (*a*) à bandes; rayé; *Nat.Hist:* fascié; (*b*) *Her:* **garb b. vert,** gerbe bandée de sinople; **orb b. or,** monde cintré d'or; **fish b. gules,** poisson sanglé de gueules; (*c*) *Geol:* rubané; zoné; **b. structure, b. texture,** structure, texture, rubanée; texture protogneissique; texture litée; *Miner:* **b. agate,** agate rubanée.

bandelet ['bændlet], *s. Arch:* bandelette *f*.

bandelier [bændə'liər], *s.* = BANDOLEER.

banderilla [bændə'riljə], *s.* (*bullfighting*) banderille *f*.

banderillero [bændəri'ljεərou], *s.* (*bull fighting*) banderillero *m*.

banderol(e) ['bændərol], *s.* (*a*) oriflamme *f*; *Art: Her: Arch:* banderole *f*; (*b*) *Surv:* banderole.

bandfish ['bændfiʃ], *s. Ich:* **red b.,** cépole *m*, ruban *m*.

bandicoot ['bændiku:t], *s. Z:* **1.** bandicoot *m*, péramèle *m* (de l'Australie); *pl.* **the Australian bandicoots,** péramélidés *mpl*; **rabbit b.,** macrotis *m*, lièvre *m* à bourse. **2.** rat géant (des Indes), (rat) perchal (*m*), nésocie *m*.

banding ['bændiŋ], *s.* **1.** ceinturage *m* (d'obus, etc.). **2.** *Geol:* zonation *f*; zonalité *f*; (*in glacier*) structure rubanée; bandure *f* lamellaire; **crustified, crustification, b.,** rubanement concrétionné; **zonary b.,** zonation, structure, zonée.

bandit ['bændit], *s.* bandit *m*; **a gang of bandits,** une troupe de bandits; **the Calabrian banditti** [bæn'diti], les brigands *m* de la Calabre; **one-armed b.,** (espèce de) machine *f* à sous; *F:* tire-pognon *m*, *pl.* tire-pognons.

banditism ['bænditizm], *s.* banditisme *m*, brigandage *m*.

banditry ['bænditri], *s.* brigandage *m*.

bandmaster ['bændma:stər], *s.* (*a*) *O:* chef *m* d'orchestre; (*b*) *Mil: etc:* chef de musique, de fanfare.

bandog ['bændɔg], *s. A:* gros chien de garde; mâtin *m*.

bandoleer, bandolier [bændə'liər], *s.* (*a*) bandoulière *f* à cartouches; (*b*) collier *m* à cartouches.

bandolero [bændə'lεərou], *s. Lit:* bandolier *m*, bandoulier *m*.

bandoline ['bændəli:n], *s. Toil: A:* bandoline *f*.

bandoneon, bandonion [bæn'douniən], *s. Mus:* bandonéon *m*.

bandook ['bændu:k], *s. Mil: P: A:* fusil *m*; *P:* flingot *m*.

bandura ['bændərə, bæn'dɔ:rə], **bandore** ['bændɔ:r, bæn'dɔ:r], *s. A.Mus:* bandoura *f*.

bandrol ['bændrəl], *s. Art: Her: Arch:* banderole *f*.

bandsaw ['bændsɔ:], *s. Carp:* scie *f* à ruban; scie sans fin; **b. pulley,** volant *m* porte lame.

bandsman, *pl.* **men** ['bændzmən], *s.m.* musicien (d'un orchestre, d'une harmonie); (*of brass band*) fanfariste.

band spread ['bændspred], *s. W.Tel:* étalement *m* de bande.

bandstand ['bændstænd], *s.* kiosque *m* à musique.

bandwag(g)on ['bændwæg(ə)n], *s.* (*a*) char *m* des musiciens (en tête de la cavalcade); (*b*) *F:* **to climb on, jump on, the b.,** se mettre dans le mouvement; se ranger du bon côté; prendre le train en marche.

bandwidth ['bændwidθ], *s. W.Tel: Cmptr:* largeur *f* de bande; **nominal b.,** largeur de bande nominale.

bandy¹ ['bændi], *s. Games:* **1.** *A:* (*a*) jeu *m* de crosse; (*b*) **b.(-ball),** hockey *m*. **2.** (*curved club*) crosse *f*.

bandy², *v.tr.* (se) renvoyer (des paroles); échanger (des plaisanteries, des coups); **these letters of complaint are bandied backwards and forwards,** on se renvoie ces lettres de plainte comme des volants; **to b. words,** faire assaut de paroles; se chamailler; **her name was being bandied about,** on faisait du bruit à son sujet.

bandy³, *a.* **1.** (*a*) **b. legs,** jambes arquées, bancales, en manches de veste; arqûre *f* (d'un cheval); (*b*) *Furn:* **b. leg,** pied-de-biche *m*, *pl.* pieds-de-biche. **2.** (*of pers.*) = BANDY-LEGGED.

bandy⁴, *s.* charrette *f*, boghei *m* (des Indes orientales).

bandy-bandy ['bændi'bændi], *s. Rept: Austr:* bandy-bandy *m*.

bandy chair ['bænditʃεər], *s.* **to carry s.o. in a b. c.,** **to give s.o. a b. c.,** porter qn en chaise, faire la chaise à qn.

bandy-legged ['bændi'legd, -'legid], *a.* (*of pers.*) bancal, aux jambes arquées; *F:* aux jambes en manches de veste; (*of horse*) brassicourt, arqué.

bane [bein], *s.* **1.** (*a*) *Lit:* fléau *m*, peste *f*; *F:* **he's the b. of my life,** il m'empoisonne l'existence; (*b*) *A:* assassin *m*; (*c*) *A:* poison *m* (*still so used in compounds, e.g.* DOG'S BANE). **2.** *Vet:* distomatose *f*.

baneberry ['beinbəri], *s. Bot:* herbe *f* de Saint-Christophe.

baneful ['beinful], *a. Lit:* funeste, fatal, -als, pernicieux, nuisible; **b. influence,** influence néfaste, pernicieuse.

banefully ['beinfuli], *adv. Lit:* pernicieusement, funestement, nuisiblement.

banefulness ['beinfulnis], *s. Lit:* nuisibilité *f*; effet désastreux.

bang¹ [bæŋ], *s.* **1.** coup (violent); détonation *f* (de fusil, etc.); fracas *m*; claquement *m* (de porte); *Av:* **double b.,** double bang *m*; (*of firework, etc.*) **to go off with a b.,** détoner; faire pétard; *F:* **to go (off, over) with a b.,** faire réussite. **2.** *F:* dynamisme *m*.

bang², *v.*

I. *v.i. & tr.* **1.** *v.i.* (*a*) **to b. at, on, the door,** frapper à la porte avec bruit; heurter à la porte; donner de grands coups dans la porte; **to b. on the table with one's fist,** frapper la table du poing; cogner du poing sur la table; **to b. up against s.o.,** se heurter à, contre, qn; (*b*) (*of door*) claquer, battre; **the door banged shut,** la porte s'est fermée avec fracas; (*c*) **the guns were banging (away),** les canons tonnaient (sans interruption); **to b. away at the enemy,** bombarder l'ennemi; tirer sans cesse sur l'ennemi. **2.** *v.tr.* (*a*) frapper (violemment); **to b. a mat against the wall,** battre un paillasson contre le mur; **he banged his head on a low beam,** il s'est cogné la tête sur une poutre basse; *v.ind.tr.* **to b. on the piano,** s'escrimer sur le piano; **to b. out an accompaniment,** faire ressortir bruyamment l'accompagnement; (*b*) **to b. the door,** (faire) claquer la porte; fermer la porte avec fracas; frapper les portes; (*c*) *St.Exch:* **to b. the market,** faire baisser les prix; écraser le marché; casser les cours.

II. (*compound verbs*) **1. bang about,** (*a*) *v.tr.* **to b. s.o. about,** houspiller qn; (*b*) *v.i.* faire du fracas, du tapage; tapager.

2. bang down, *v.tr.* **to b. d. the lid,** abattre violemment le couvercle; **he banged it down on the table,** il l'a posé avec violence sur la table.

bang³. **1.** *int.* pan! v'lan! boum! *F:* **b. went a fiver!** j'ai dépensé cinq livres d'un seul coup! **2.** (*a*) *adv.* **to go b.,** éclater; **I came b. up against a wall,** je me suis heurté le front contre un mur; **he crashed b. into the tree,** il est rentré pile dans l'arbre; **to fall b. in the middle,** tomber en plein milieu; *F:* **to do sth. b. off,** faire qch. sur-le-champ; **b. on time,** exactement à l'heure, à l'heure exacte; **it's b. on,** c'est au poil; (*b*) *F:* (*euphemism for* damned) **the whole b. lot,** (i) tout le bataclan; tout le bazar; (ii) (*of people*) toute la clique.

bang⁴, *s. esp. NAm:* cheveux coupés à la chien; coiffure *f* à la chien; **to wear a b.,** être coiffé à la chien.

bang⁵, *v.tr. esp. NAm:* **to b. one's hair,** (faire) couper ses cheveux à la chien; *O:* **to b. a horse's tail,** écourter (la queue d')un cheval.

Bang⁶, *Pr.n. Vet:* **Bang's disease,** brucellose *f*.

banger ['bæŋər], *s. F:* **1.** saucisse *f*. **2.** *Pyr:* pétard *m*. **3.** (vieux) tacot, (vieille) guimbarde.

banging¹ ['bæŋiŋ], *a.* **1.** (porte) qui claque. **2.** *P: A:* **b. lie,** mensonge *m* énorme.

banging², *s.* (*a*) coups violents; claquement *m*; (*b*) détonations *fpl*.

Bangladesh [bæŋglə'deʃ], *Pr.n. Geog:* Bangladesh *m*.

bangle ['bæŋgl], *s.* **1.** bracelet *m*; **slave b.,** bracelet esclave. **2.** anneau attaché autour de la cheville.

bang-tail ['bæŋteil], *s.* **1.** *O:* cheval *m* à la queue écourtée; cheval écourté. **2.** *U.S:* (*a*) cheval de course; (*b*) cheval sauvage.

bang-up ['bæŋʌp], *a. P: O:* **a b.-up dinner,** un dîner numéro un; un chic dîner; **a b.-up show,** quelque chose de très chic.

banish ['bæniʃ], *v.tr.* **1.** bannir, exiler (**s.o. from a place,** qn d'un lieu); proscrire (qn). **2. to b. fear, care, etc.,** bannir, chasser, la crainte, les soucis, etc.

banishment ['bæniʃmənt], *s.* bannissement *m*, proscription *f*, exil *m*; **to go into b.,** partir pour l'exil; *Jur:* **local b.,** interdiction *f* de séjour.

banister ['bænistər], *s.* (*usu. pl.*) **1.** balustres *m* (d'escalier). **2.** rampe *f* (d'escalier); appui *m* d'escalier; **to slide down the banisters,** glisser le long de la rampe.

banjo, *pl.* **-os, -oes** ['bændʒou, -ouz], *s.* **1.** *Mus:* banjo *m*. **2.** *Aut: etc:* banjo; **b. axle,** pont *m* banjo; *Av:* **b. oiler,** graisseur *m* centrifuge.

banjoist ['bændʒouist], *s.* joueur, -euse, de banjo.

bank¹ [bæŋk], *s.* **1.** (*a*) talus *m*; terrasse *f*; levée *f* de terre; (*in garden*) glacis *m*; *Civ.E:* banquette *f*, remblai *m*; *Rail:* rampe *f*; *Min:* (*coal face*) front *m* de taille; *Turf:* banquette (irlandaise); **b. of flowers,** tertre *m* de fleurs; **b. engine,** machine *f* de renfort (pour la montée des rampes); (*b*) (*in river, sea*) banc *m* (de sable, de coquillages, de roches); (*in river*) javeau *m*, allaise *f*; **ice b.,** banquise *f*; *Geog:* **the Banks of Newfoundland,** le Banc de Terre-Neuve; (*c*) digue *f*; (*d*) panne *f* (de nuages); **b. of fog,** banc de brouillard; (*e*) *Artil:* **gun b.,** épaulement *m* de pièce. **2.** (*a*) (*steep side*) berge *f* accotement *m*, banquette *f*, bas côté (d'une rivière, d'un canal, d'un chemin, d'un fossé); (*b*) (*side*) bord *m*, rive *f* (d'une rivière, d'un lac); **the banks,** le rivage; **the opposite b. of the canal,** la berge opposée du canal; *Mil:* (*in bridge building*) **near b.,** première rive; **further b.,** seconde rive; *Min:* **b. claim,** concession riveraine. **3.** *Min:* recette *f* du jour; **b. engine,** moteur *m* à la surface; moteur du jour. **4.** *Av:* inclinaison *f*; virage *m* sur l'aile, incliné; **angle of b.,** angle *m* d'inclinaison; **double b.,** virage double; **b. indicator,** indicateur *m* d'incidence; **turn and b. indicator,** indicateur *m* de virage et d'incidence.

bank². **1.** *v.tr.* (*a*) **to b. a river,** contenir une rivière par des berges, par une digue; endiguer une rivière; (*b*) **to b. up,** remblayer, terrasser, amonceler (de la terre, de la neige, etc.); **to b. up the foot of a tree,** rechausser un arbre; *Civ.E:* **to b. a road** (*at a corner*), surhausser, relever, un virage; **banked corner,** dévers *m*; virage relevé; relèvement *m* de virage; **banked edge (of road, etc.),** berge *f*; **banked-in road,** route encaissée; (*c*) **to b. up the fire,** recharger le feu; *Mch:* **to b. (up) fires,** couvrir, coucher, les feux; rester sur les feux; mettre les feux au fond; (*d*) *Min:* **to b. the cage,** atterrir la cage. **2.** *v.i.* (*of snow, clouds, mist, etc.*) s'entasser, s'accumuler, s'amonceler. **3.** *v.i. Av:* pencher l'avion; s'incliner sur l'aile; virer (sur l'aile); **to under-b.,** virer à plat; **to over-b.,** virer trop penché.

bank³, *s.* **1.** *Com: Fin:* (*a*) banque *f*; **land b.,** banque territoriale, banque hypothécaire; crédit foncier; **merchant b.,** banque d'affaires; *A:* **penny b.,** caisse *f* d'épargne qui accepte des versements d'un penny; **private b.,** banque privée; **savings b.,** caisse d'épargne; **the B. of England,** la Banque d'Angleterre; **the World B.,** la Banque Mondiale; **b. account,** compte *m* en banque; **b. annuities,** rente perpétuelle, fonds consolidés; **b. bill,** (i) effet (tiré par une banque sur une autre); (ii) *U.S:* billet *m* de banque; **b. book,** livret *m* de banque; carnet *m* de banque; **b. credit,** crédit *m* en banque, crédit bancaire; **b. clerk,** employé, -ée, de banque; **b. messenger,** garçon *m* de recettes; **b. holiday,** (jour *m* de) fête légale (où les banques n'ouvrent pas); **b. roll,** ressources *fpl* monétaires; (*b*) (bureau *m* de) banque; **branch b.,** succursale *f* (d'une banque). **2.** (*gaming*) banque (de celui qui tient le jeu); **to break the b.,** faire sauter la banque, débanquer le banquier; *U.S:* **b. night,** gala *m* cinématographique avec loterie. **3. b. (paper),** (i) billets de banque et papier *m* bancable; (ii) papier coquille; papier poste. **4.** (*a*) *Cmptr:* **data b.,** fichier central; (*b*) *Med:* **blood, eye, b.,** banque du sang, des yeux.

bank⁴, *v.tr. & i.* **1.** mettre, déposer, (de l'argent) en banque; déposer (qch.) dans une banque; **to b. with s.o.,** avoir qn pour banquier, avoir un compte de banque chez qn; **where do you b.?** qui est votre banquier? **2.** (*gaming*) tenir la banque. **3. to b. on sth.,** compter sur qch., caver, miser, sur (un événement); **to b. on a success,** escompter un succès; **to b. on human gullibility,** caver, miser, sur la bêtise humaine.

bank⁵, *s.* **1.** *A:* = BENCH¹, 1. **2.** *Nau: A:* (*a*) banc *m* (de rameurs); (*b*) rang *m* (de rames, d'avirons); (*c*) travée *f*;

three banks of three seats with two aisles, trois travées de trois sièges séparées par deux couloirs longitudinaux. **3.** (*a*) *Typewr:* rang *m*; **a three-b. machine,** une machine à trois rangs de touches; (*b*) *Cin:* **b. of projectors,** rampe *f* de projecteurs; (*c*) *Mus:* clavier *m* (d'un orgue); **organ with three banks,** orgue *m* à trois claviers. **4. optical b.,** banc d'optique. **5.** *Ind:* groupe *f*, batterie *f* (de chaudières, de cornues, de lampes électriques, de transformateurs, etc.); *I.C.E:* rangée *f*, assise *f* (de cylindres); *Tp:* groupe, bloc *m*, banc (de broches ou de contacts).

bankable ['bæŋkəbl], *a. Fin:* (effet *m*) bancable, négociable en banque.

banker[1] ['bæŋkər], *s.* **1.** *Fin:* banquier *m*; **banker's draft,** chèque *m* bancaire, de banque. **2.** (*gaming*) banquier, tailleur *m*.

banker[2], *s.* **1.** *Fish:* banquier *m*, banquais *m* (qui pêche la morue); morutier *m*; terreneuvien *m*. **2.** *Rail:* **b. (engine),** machine *f* de renfort, de refoulement (pour la montée des rampes). **3.** *Austr:* rivière pleine d'eau.

banket ['bæŋkit], *s. Min:* conglomérat *m* aurifère.

banking[1] ['bæŋkiŋ], *s.* **1.** (*a*) remblayage *m*; surhaussement *m*, relèvement *m* (d'un virage); (*b*) **b. up of a river,** haussement *m* du niveau d'une rivière; (*c*) *Min:* atterrissage *m* (de la cage). **2.** remblai *m*; **b. of a road at a bend,** dévers *m* d'un virage. **3.** *Av:* inclinaison *f*; virage *m* sur l'aile, incliné; dévers, relèvement de virage.

banking[2], *s.* **1.** (affaires *fpl*, opérations *fpl*, de) banque *f*; **b. house,** maison *f* de banque, banquière; établissement *m* bancaire; **big b. houses,** maisons de haute banque; **b. account,** compte *m* en banque; **to have a b. account with . . .,** avoir un compte de banque chez . . .; **b. hours,** heures *fpl* de la banque; **b. business,** trafic *m* bancaire. **2.** profession *f* de banquier; la banque.

Bankiva [bæŋ'kaivə], *Pr.n. Husb:* **B. jungle fowl,** race *f* de Bankiva.

banknote ['bæŋknout], *s.* **1.** billet *m* de banque. **2.** *Paperm:* **b. paper,** bank *f*.

bankrupt[1] ['bæŋkrʌpt], *a. & s.* **1.** (*a*) (commerçant) failli (*m*); **to go b.,** (i) faire faillite; (ii) (*of business*) *F:* sauter; (iii) (*fraudulently*) faire banqueroute; **to be b.,** être en faillite; **to adjudge, adjudicate, s.o. b.,** déclarer, mettre, qn en faillite; **bankrupt's certificate,** concordat *m*; *Jur:* **undischarged b.,** failli non réhabilité; (*b*) **fraudulent, negligent, b.,** banqueroutier *m*; (*c*) *O:* **to be b. in, of, intelligence,** être dépourvu d'intelligence; **a man b. of honour,** un homme perdu d'honneur. **2.** (homme) criblé de dettes, sans ressources.

bankrupt[2], *v.tr.* **1.** mettre (qn) en faillite. **2.** ruiner (qn).

bankruptcy ['bæŋkrəp(t)si], *s.* **1.** (*a*) faillite *f*; *Jur:* **act of b.,** acte *m* manifeste d'insolvabilité (entraînant la faillite); **the B. Act,** le code de procédure régissant les faillites; (*b*) **fraudulent b.,** banqueroute *f*. **2.** ruine *f*.

banksia ['bæŋksiə], *s. Bot:* banksie *f*.

banksman, *pl.* **-men** ['bæŋksmən], *s.m. Min:* receveur; porion *m* de surface.

bannal [bæ'næl], *a. A:* = BANAL 1.

banner ['bænər], *s.* **1.** (*a*) bannière *f*, étendard *m*; **to enlist under s.o.'s b.,** se ranger sous la bannière de qn; *U.S:* **the star-spangled b.,** la bannière étoilée; (*b*) *Ecc:* bannière. **2.** *Bot:* étendard, pavillon *m* (d'une papilionacée). **3.** *attrib. NAm:* excellent, exceptionnel; de première classe; *Com:* **we've had a b. year,** nous avons fait des affaires d'or cette année; *Journ:* **b. headlines,** des titres flamboyants.

bannered ['bænəd], *a.* garni de bannières.

banneret ['bænəret], *s. Hist:* banneret *m*.

bannerol ['bænərəl], *s. Art: Her: Arch:* banderole *f*.

bannister ['bænistər], *s.* = BANISTER.

bannock ['bænək], *s.* (*in Scot.*) pain plat et rond cuit sans levain.

banns [bænz], *s.pl.* bans *m* (de mariage); **to put up, publish, the b.,** (faire) publier les bans; **to forbid the b.,** faire, mettre, opposition à (la célébration d')un mariage.

banquet[1] ['bæŋkwit], *s.* banquet *m*; dîner *m* de gala, d'apparat; **wedding b.,** repas *m* de noces; *Ecc:* **the heavenly b.,** le banquet céleste.

banquet[2]. **1.** *v.tr.* offrir un banquet, un grand dîner, un dîner de gala, à (qn). **2.** *v.i.* banqueter; festiner, faire festin; festoyer.

banqueter ['bæŋkwitər], *s.* banqueteur *m*.

banqueting ['bæŋkwitiŋ], *attrib.* **b. hall,** salle *f* de banquet, la salle du banquet.

banquette [bæŋ'ket], *s.* **1.** (*a*) *Fort:* banquette *f* de tir; (*b*) *Veh: A:* banquette (d'une diligence); (*c*) *Furn:* banquette. **2.** *U.S:* (*a*) talus *m*; (*b*) trottoir *m*. **3.** *Const:* tablette *f* d'appui. **4.** *Civ.E:* banquette, berme *f*.

banshee [bæn'ʃi:], *s. Myth:* = dame blanche.

bant [bænt], *v.i. O:* suivre un régime amaigrissant.

bantam ['bæntəm], *s.* **1.** *Husb:* coq *m*, poule *f*, (de) bantam; coq nain. **2.** *Mil: F:* **bantams,** (bataillon composé d')hommes *m* au-dessous de la taille réglementaire. **3.** *Elcs:* **b. (tube),** tube *m* miniature. **4.** *a. Box:* **b. weight,** poids *m* coq, bantam *m*.

banteng ['bænteŋ], *s. Z:* banteng *m*.

banter[1] ['bæntər], *s.* (*a*) badinage *m*, badineries *fpl*; (*b*) ironie *f*, raillerie *f*, persiflage *m*.

banter[2]. **1.** *v.tr.* (*a*) taquiner; (*b*) gouailler, railler; (*ill-naturedly*) persifler. **2.** *v.i.* (*a*) taquiner; (*b*) gouailler, railler; faire de l'ironie.

banterer ['bæntərər], *s.* railleur, -euse, badin, -ine, gouailleur, -euse; (*ill-natured*) persifleur, -euse.

bantering ['bænt(ə)riŋ], *a.* railleur, -euse, goguenard; gouailleur, -euse.

banteringly ['bænt(ə)riŋli], *adv.* railleusement, d'un ton goguenard; d'un air, d'un ton, railleur.

ban-the-bomb ['bænðə'bɔm], *a.* **b.-t.-b. demonstration,** manifestation *f* antiatomique.

Banti ['bænti], *Pr.n. Med:* **Banti's disease,** maladie *f* de Banti.

banting ['bæntiŋ], *s. O:* (*also* **b. diet**) régime amaigrissant, antiobésique, obésifuge; cure *f* d'amaigrissement.

bantling ['bæntliŋ], *s. Lit:* (*a*) poupon *m*, bambin *m*, mioche *mf*; (*b*) *Pej:* marmot *m*.

Bantu ['bæn'tu:]. **1.** *a. Ethn:* bantou. **2.** *s. Ethn:* Bantou, -oue. **3.** *s. Ling:* bantou *m*.

banyan ['bæniən], *s. Bot:* **b. (tree),** arbre *m* des banians, figuier *m* des banians; banian *m*.

baobab ['beioubæb], *s. Bot:* baobab *m*.

bap [bæp], *s.* petit pain au lait (longtemps particulier à l'Écosse).

baphia ['bæfiə], *s. Bot:* baphier *m*.

baptism ['bæptizm], *s.* **1.** baptême *m*; **private, clinical, b.,** ondoiement *m*; **conditional b.,** baptême sous condition; **b. by desire,** baptême de désir; **b. for the dead,** baptême pour les morts; **the b. of blood, of fire,** le baptême du sang, du feu; **to receive b.,** recevoir le baptême; **register of baptisms,** registre *m* baptistaire; **certificate of b.,** extrait *m* de baptême, extrait baptistaire. **2.** baptême (d'une cloche, d'un navire).

baptismal [bæp'tizm(ə)l], *a.* (registre *m*) baptistaire; (nom *m*) de baptême; (fonts) baptismaux.

baptist ['bæptist], *s.* **1. (St.) John the Baptist,** saint Jean-Baptiste. **2.** *Ecc:* baptiste *mf*; **the B. doctrine,** baptisme *m*; **Seventh-day Baptists,** sabbataires *mpl*.

baptist(e)ry ['bæptistri], *s.* baptistère *m*.

baptize [bæp'taiz], *v.tr.* **1.** baptiser; administrer, conférer, le baptême à (qn); **to be baptized,** recevoir le baptême; **to be baptized by the name of John,** être baptisé du nom de Jean. **2.** baptiser, bénir (une cloche, un navire).

baptizer [bæp'taizər], *s.* baptiseur *m*.

bar[1] [bɑ:r], *s.* **1.** (*a*) barre *f* (de fer, de bois, de chocolat, etc.); tablette *f* (de chocolat); barre, brique *f* (de savon); lingot *m* (d'or); lame *f* (de commutateur, etc.); *Cmptr:* barre, barreau *m*; *Metalw:* bar(r)ette *f*, traverse *f* (d'un châssis de fonderie); *Ac:* microbar *m*; *Hist:* **b. (of city),** porte *f* (d'une ville); **b. of a chain link,** étai *m* d'une maille; *Needlew:* **b. of a buttonhole,** bride *f*; **b. of a medal,** barrette *f* d'une médaille; **with b.** = avec palme *f*; **b. of a door,** bâcle *f* d'une porte, barre de porte; **b. (of colour),** raie *f* (de couleur); *Gym:* **parallel bars,** barres parallèles; **horizontal b.,** barre fixe; **jumping b.,** barre de sautoir *m*; **to pull up to the b.,** faire une traction, des tractions; *Harn:* **lower b. of the bit,** entretoise *f* du mors; *Min:* **miner's b.,** barre de mine, fleuret *m*; **type b.,** (i) *Typew:* tige *f* à caractères; (ii) *Typ:* ligne-bloc *f*, *pl.* lignes-blocs (de Linotype); (iii) *Cmptr:* barre d'impression, barre porte-caractères; *Cmptr:* **print b.,** barre d'impression; **interchangeable type b.,** barre d'impression à caractères amovibles; *Mec.E:* **boring b.,** arbre *m*, tige, de foret, arbre d'alésage; *Mec.E: Metall:* **test b.,** barreau *m* d'essai; éprouvette *f*; (*b*) *pl.* barreaux *m* (d'une fenêtre, d'une grille, d'une cage, d'une chaise, d'une prison); **the bars of the grate,** la grille du foyer; **to be behind (prison) bars,** être derrière les barreaux, être sous les verrous; (*c*) barrette (de chaussure); (*d*) *pl.* barres (de la bouche d'un cheval); (*e*) (*in river, harbour*) barre (de sable), traverse *f*; **off-shore b.,** cordon littoral; **to cross the b.,** (i) passer, franchir, la barre; (ii) *Lit:* mourir; **sand b.,** (i) somme *f*, ensablement *m* (à l'embouchure d'un fleuve); (ii) lido *m*; (*f*) *A:* barrière *f*; **toll b.,** barrière (de péage); (*g*) *Her:* burelle *f*, burèle *f*; **b. sinister,** barre de bâtardise; (*h*) *Geog:* **rimstone b.,** barre de travertin. **2.** (*a*) empêchement *m*, obstacle *m*; **to fix, set, a b. against sth.,** mettre obstacle, mettre un empêchement, à qch.; **to be a b. to sth.,** être un empêchement, faire obstacle, à qch.; **the colour b.,** racisme *m*; ségrégation raciale; *Jur:* **b. to set-off,** obstacle à la compensation; (*b*) *Jur:* exception *f*; fin *f* de non-recevoir. **3.** *Jur:* (*a*) barre (des accusés); **the prisoner at the b.,** l'accusé; **to appear at the b.,** paraître à la barre; **the b. of conscience, of public opinion,** le tribunal de la conscience, de l'opinion publique; (*b*) barreau (des avocats); **to read for the b.,** faire son droit; **to be called, to come, go, to the b.,** être reçu, se faire inscrire, au barreau; être reçu avocat; **call to the b.,** inscription *f*, entrée *f*, au barreau; inscription au tableau; **before going to the b.,** avant d'être avocat; **to be called within the b.,** être nommé avocat de la Couronne; (*c*) *coll.* les avocats (constitués par une des parties d'un procès); (*d*) *coll.* l'Ordre *m* des avocats; **the B. Council,** le Conseil de l'Ordre des avocats. **4.** (*a*) bar *m*; café *m*; buvette *f*; (*in Ireland*) marchand *m* de boissons; **lounge b.,** bar salon; *F:* **b. lounger,** pilier *m* de café; (*b*) comptoir *m* (d'un café); **he's always propping up the b.,** c'est un vrai pilier de café, de bar. **5.** (*a*) barre, ligne *f*, trait *m*; (*b*) *Mus:* **b. (line),** barre; **double b.,** double barre; (*c*) *Mus:* mesure *f*. **6.** *Meteor: Meas:* bar *m*.

bar[2], *v.tr.* (**barred; barring**) **1.** barrer; bâcler (une porte, etc.); griller (une fenêtre); **to b. the door against s.o., to b. s.o. out,** barrer la porte à qn; **to b. oneself in,** assurer la porte; se barricader. **2.** (*a*) (*obstruct*) barrer (un chemin); **to b. s.o.'s way,** barrer la route à qn; couper (le) chemin à qn; **to b. the way to progress,** barrer la route au progrès; **to b. s.o. from doing sth.,** empêcher qn de faire qch.; (*b*) = DEBAR; (*c*) *Surg: Vet:* **to b. a vein,** barrer une veine. **3.** (*a*) (*prohibit*) défendre, prohiber, interdire (une action); exclure (un sujet de conversation); (*b*) *F:* (*dislike*) ne pas supporter, ne pas approuver (une personne, une habitude); **she barred smoking in the drawing room,** elle n'admettait pas qu'on fumât au salon; (*c*) *Jur:* opposer une fin de non-recevoir à (une action). **4.** (*stripe*) rayer (de lignes); barrer.

bar[3], *prep.* excepté, sauf, hors; à part; à l'exception de; **b. one,** sauf un, sauf une; **b. none,** sans exception; **excellent book b. one or two chapters,** livre excellent à part un ou deux chapitres.

bar[4], *s. Ich:* maigre *m*.

Barabbas [bə'ræbəs], *Pr.n.m. B.Hist:* Bar(r)abbas.

baracan ['bærəkæn], *s. Tex:* baracan *m*.

baralipton [bærə'liptɔn], *s. Log:* baralipton *m*.

Bárány [bə'rɑ:ni], *s. Med:* **Bárány's test,** épreuves *fpl* de Bárány.

barb[1] [bɑ:b], *s.* **1.** (*a*) barbillon *m*, dardillon *m* (d'un hameçon); barbelure *f* (d'une flèche); ardillon *m* (d'un crochet); *F:* **exposed to the barbs of the critic,** exposé aux traits acérés de la critique; (*b*) picot *m* (de fil de fer barbelé); (*c*) *Engr: Metalw:* barbe *f*, bavure *f* (de métal). **2.** *pl.* (*a*) *Ich: Vet:* barbillons; *Bot:* arêtes *f*; (*b*) barbes (d'une plume). **3.** *Cost:* barbette *f* (d'une religieuse).

barb[2], *v.tr.* garnir de barbelures, de barbillons; **to b. a hook,** relever le barbillon d'un hameçon.

barb[3], *s.* cheval *m* barbe; barbe *m*.

barbacou ['bɑ:bəku:], *s. Orn:* barbacou *m*.

Barbadian [bɑ:'beidiən], *a. & s.* (natif, habitant) de la Barbade.

Barbados [bɑ:'beidouz], *Pr.n. Geog:* Barbade *f*; **B. cherry,** cerise *f* des Antilles; **B. gooseberry,** groseillier *m* d'Amérique; **B. nut,** noix *f* des Barbades; pignon *m* d'Inde; *Med:* **B. leg,** éléphantiasis *f* des Arabes; *Dist:* **B. water,** eau *f* des Barbades; citronnelle *f*; *Bot:* **B. pride,** fleur *f* de paradis.

Barbara[1] ['bɑ:b(ə)rə], *Pr.n.f.* Barbe.

barbara[2], *s. Log:* barbara *m*.

Barbaresque [bɑ:bə'resk], *a. Ethn: Art:* barbaresque.

barbarian [bɑ:'bɛəriən], *a. & s.* barbare (*mf*).

barbaric [bɑ:'bærik], *a.* barbare; rude, primitif.

barbarism ['bɑ:bərizm], *s.* **1.** *Gram: Ling:* barbarisme *m*. **2.** barbarie *f*, grossièreté *f*, rudesse *f*.

barbarity [bɑ:'bæriti], *s.* **1.** barbarie *f*, cruauté *f*, inhumanité *f*. **2. barbarities associated with war,** cruautés qui accompagnent la guerre.

barbarize ['bɑ:bəraiz]. **1.** *v.tr.* barbariser (un peuple, une langue). **2.** *v.i.* (*a*) barbariser; commettre des barbarismes (de langue); (*b*) devenir barbare.

Barbarossa ['bɑ:bə'rɔsə], *Pr.n.m. Hist:* Barberousse.

barbarous ['bɑ:bərəs], *a.* **1.** barbare. **2.** cruel, barbare, inhumain.

barbarously ['bɑ:bərəsli], *adv.* cruellement.

barbarousness ['bɑ:bərəsnis], *s.* = BARBARITY I.

Barbary ['bɑ:bəri], *Pr.n. Geog:* **the B. States,** la Barbarie, les États *m* barbaresques; *Hist:* **the B. corsairs,** les corsaires *m* barbaresques; **B. duck,** canard *m* de Barbarie, canard turc; **B. horse,** cheval *m* barbe; **B. sheep,** mouton *m* de Barbarie, mouflon *m* à manchettes; **B. ape,** magot *m*.

barbastelle ['bɑːbəstel], *s. Z:* barbastelle *f.*

barbate ['bɑːbeit], *a.* **1.** *Bot:* barbé, aristé. **2.** *Z:* barbu.

barbecue ['bɑːbikjuː], *s.* **1.** *(a)* rôtissoire *f*; barbecue *f*; *(b)* bœuf, porc, rôti tout entier, à la broche. **2.** grande fête de plein air (où l'on rôtit des animaux tout entiers, de la viande à la broche).

barbecue², *v.tr.* rôtir à la broche.

barbed [bɑːbd], *a.* **1.** *Bot:* aristé; hameçonné. **2.** barbelé; **b. arrow,** flèche barbelée; **b. wire,** fil de fer barbelé; barbelé *m*; ronce artificielle; **b.-wire fence,** haie barbelée; haie de barbelé; *Mil:* **b.-wire entanglements, net,** réseau *m* de (fils de fer) barbelés; les barbelés *m.* **3.** *Fig:* barbelé; **b. words,** paroles *f* acerbes.

barbel ['bɑːb(ə)l], *s.* **1.** *Ich:* barbeau (commun) *m.* **2.** barbillon *m*, cirre *m*, palpe *f*, barbe *f* (d'un poisson).

bar bell ['bɑːbel], *s.* barre *f* à disques; *Gym:* barre à sphères, à boules.

barbel(l)ed ['bɑːb(ə)ld], *a.* (poisson *m*) à barbillons.

barber ['bɑːbər], *s.* barbier *m*, coiffeur *m*; **barber's pole,** enseigne *f* de barbier; *A:* **b.-surgeon,** chirurgien *m* barbier; **barber's rash, itch,** sycosis *m*; **barber's block,** tête *f* à perruque.

barberry ['bɑːb(ə)ri], *s. Bot:* épine-vinette *f*, *pl.* épine(s)-vinettes; vinette *f*; **(common) b.,** vinettier *m*; berbéris commun.

barbershop ['bɑːbəʃɔp], *s. NAm:* **1.** salon *m* de coiffure (pour hommes). **2.** *Mus:* **b. harmony** chants *mpl*; à quatre voix d'hommes.

barbet ['bɑːbit], *s.* **1.** *Orn:* *(a)* barbu *m*, capitonidé *m*, barbican *m*; **bearded b.,** barbican à poitrine rouge; *(b)* barbacou *m*, trappiste *m*, bucconidé *m.* **2.** *Z:* **b. (spaniel),** barbet *m*; **young b.,** barbichon *m.*

barbette [bɑː'bet], *s. Fort:* barbette *f*; **b. gun,** pièce *f* en barbette.

barbican¹ ['bɑːbikən], *s. Fort:* barbacane *f.*

barbican², *s. Orn:* barbican *m.*

barbicel ['bɑːbisel], *s. Z:* crochet *m.*

barbital ['bɑːbitl], *s. Ch:* barbital *m.*

barbitone ['bɑːbitoun], *s. Pharm:* véronal *m.*

barbiturate [bɑː'bitjuəreit], *s. Ch:* barbiturique *m*, barbiturate *m.*

barbituric [bɑːbi'tjuːrik], *a.* barbital, -aux; **b. acid,** acide *m* barbiturique, malonylurée *f.*

barbone [bɑː'bouni], *s.* *(a)* *Moss:* barbule *f*; *(b)* *Vet:* barbone *f.*

barbotine ['bɑːbətin], *s. Cer:* barbotine *f.*

barbula ['bɑːbjulə], *s. Moss:* barbule *f.*

barbule ['bɑːbjuːl], *s.* **1.** barbule *f* (d'une plume). **2.** = BARBEL 2.

barcarol(l)e ['bɑːkəroul], *s. Mus:* barcarolle *f.*

Barcelona [bɑːsi'lounə], *Pr.n. Geog:* Barcelone *f.*

barchan ['bɑːkən], *s. Geog:* barkhane *f.*

Barcoo rot ['bɑːkuːrɔt], *s. Med:* ulcère *m* du désert.

bard¹ [bɑːd], *s.* **1.** *(a)* *(Celtic, esp. of Wales)* barde *m*; *(b)* *(of ancient Greece)* aède *m.* **2.** poète *m*; *Lit:* **the B.,** Shakespeare.

bard², **barde** [bɑːd], *s.* **1.** *Arm:* barde *f* (de cheval d'armes). **2.** *Cu:* barde (de lard).

bard³, *v.tr.* **1.** *Arm:* barder (un chevalier, un cheval). **2.** *Cu:* barder (une volaille, etc.).

barded ['bɑːdid], *a.* **1.** *Arm:* bardé, cuirassé. **2.** *Cu:* bardé.

bardic ['bɑːdik], *a.* qui se rapporte (i) à la poésie celtique, (ii) aux concours de poésie du Pays de Galles.

bardolatry [bɑː'dɔlətri], *s. Lit:* culte *m* de Shakespeare.

bare¹ ['beər], *a.* **1.** nu; dénudé; **b. legs,** jambes nues; **b. as the back of my hand,** *F:* **as a baby's bottom,** nu comme la main, comme un ver; **to fight with b. hands,** se battre à mains nues; **b. countryside,** pays nu, dénudé, pelé; **the trees are already b.,** les arbres sont déjà dénudés, dépouillés; **b. cupboard, cupboard b. of food,** placard *m* vide; buffet dégarni; **room b. of furniture,** chambre vide ou à peine meublée; **to lie, sleep, on the b. ground, on the b. boards,** coucher sur la dure; **lying on the b. earth,** couché à même le sol; **the b. facts,** le fait brutal; *(of skin)* **to grow b.,** se peler; **to lay b.,** mettre à nu, exposer (une surface, des fautes, sa poitrine, son cœur); dévoiler (un secret, une fraude); déchausser (des roches, des fondations, des racines, etc.); **laying b.,** mise *f* à nu; déchaussement *m*; **b. chest,** poitrine découverte; *El:* **b. wire,** fil dénudé; **b. end (of a wire),** extrémité nue, mise à nu, déchaussée; *Nau:* **b. yard,** vergue sèche; **to run, scud, under b. poles,** filer, courir, fuir, à sec (de toiles), à mâts et à cordes; *Cards:* **ace b., king b.,** as sec, roi sec; *Jur:* **b. trustee,** fidéicommissaire *m* dont les pouvoirs sont arrivés à expiration; *Nau:* **b. boat charter,** affrètement *m* coque nue. **2.** *(scanty)* **to earn a b. living,** gagner tout juste, à peine, de quoi vivre; gagner sa vie et rien de plus; *Jur:* **(income providing a) b. living,** portion congrue; **the b. minimum,** le strict minimum; **the b. necessities (of life),** juste ce qu'il faut pour vivre; **b. majority,** faible majorité *f*; **b. measure,** mesure rase; **it is only b. justice to say that . . .,** la justice la plus élémentaire nous oblige à reconnaître que . . .; **to condemn s.o. on a b. suspicion,** condamner qn sur un simple soupçon; **the b. thought frightens me,** cette seule pensée m'effraie; **I shudder at the b. idea,** je frémis rien que d'y penser; **a b. thank you,** un merci tout sec; **they received me with b. politeness,** c'est tout juste s'ils ont été polis; **his success is a b. possibility,** son succès est tout juste possible, est possible, sans plus; *Sch:* **he got a b. pass,** il a été reçu sans mention.

bare², *v.tr.* mettre (qch.) à nu; découvrir (une plaie, etc.); se découvrir (la tête); dénuder, dépouiller (un arbre, etc.); déchausser (des racines, etc.); **to b. one's sword,** tirer son épée du fourreau; mettre l'épée à nu; dégainer; **to b. the end of a wire,** dénuder, dépouiller, l'extrémité d'un fil; mettre le bout d'un fil à nu; **columns bared of their capitals,** colonnes décoiffées de leurs chapiteaux; **to b. one's teeth,** montrer ses dents; *Dent:* **to b. a tooth,** déchausser une dent.

bare³, *s. Const:* pureau *m*, échantillon *m* (d'une tuile, d'une ardoise de toiture).

bareback ['beəbæk], *adv.* **to ride b.,** monter (un cheval) à nu, à cru, à poil.

bare-backed ['beəbækt]. **1.** *a.* à dos nu, le dos nu; **b.-b. horse,** cheval nu, à poil. **2.** *adv.* = BAREBACK.

bare-boned ['beə'bound], *a.* décharné, squelettique.

barebones ['beəbounz], *s. F: O:* personne maigre, décharnée; squelette ambulant.

barefaced ['beəfeist], *a.* **1.** à visage imberbe; glabre. **2.** *(a)* sans masque; *(b)* *F:* (mensonge, etc.) éhonté, effronté, cynique; **it's b. robbery,** ce n'est ni plus ni moins qu'un vol, que du vol.

barefacedly [beə'feisidli, 'feistli], *adv.* effrontément, avec effronterie; cyniquement.

barefacedness [beə'feisidnis, -'feistnis], *s.* effronterie *f*; cynisme *m.*

barefoot(ed) ['beəfut(id)]. **1.** *a.* aux pieds nus; les pieds nus; *Ecc:* **b. Carmelites,** carmes déchaussés. **2.** *adv.* nu-pieds; (à) pieds nus.

barege [bæ'reiʒ], *s. Tex:* barège *m.*

bare-headed ['beə'hedid], *a. & adv.* nu-tête, (la) tête nue; **they stood b.-h.,** ils se tenaient nu-tête, tête nue; **to stand b.-h. before s.o.,** rester découvert devant qn.

bare-legged ['beə'leg(i)d], *a. & adv.* nu-jambes, (les) jambes nues; aux jambes nues.

barely ['beəli], *adv.* **1. room b. furnished,** (i) pièce dont le mobilier se réduit à l'essentiel; (ii) pièce pauvrement meublée; **to state a fact b.,** donner un fait sans détails, sans broder. **2.** à peine, tout juste; **I b. know him,** je le connais à peine; c'est à peine si je le connais; **he can b. read and write,** c'est tout juste, tout au plus, s'il sait lire et écrire; **he b. escaped death,** il échappa tout juste à la mort; **he is b. thirty,** c'est tout juste s'il a trente ans; **to have b. time,** n'avoir que juste le temps.

bareness ['beənis], *s.* **1.** nudité *f*, dénuement *m* (d'une chambre, etc.). **2.** pauvreté *f*, sécheresse *f* (de style, etc.).

baresthesia [bæres'θiːziə], *s. Med:* baresthésie *f.*

barfly ['bɑːflai], *s. NAm: F:* pilier *m* de bar.

bargain ['bɑːgin], *s.* marché *m*, affaire *f*; **a good b.,** une bonne affaire, un bon marché, un marché avantageux; **a bad b.,** une mauvaise affaire; **to get the best of the b.,** avoir l'avantage (dans un marché); **to strike a b. with s.o.,** conclure, faire, un marché avec qn; **to drive a hard b.,** chercher à gagner le dernier centime; **to drive a hard b. with s.o.,** imposer, faire, à qn des conditions très dures; **into the b.,** par dessus le marché, en plus; **a bargain's a b.,** on ne revient pas sur un marché; marché conclu reste conclu; **Dutch, wet, b.,** marché conclu à la bouteille; **it's a b.!** c'est entendu! c'est convenu! c'est marché conclu! *St.Exch:* **bargains done,** cours faits; **time b.,** marché à terme, marché à livrer, vente *f* à livrer; *Jur:* **b. and sale,** contrat *m* de vente impliquant le transfert de la propriété à titre onéreux; *Com:* **b. sale,** solde *m*; **b. price(s),** prix *m* de solde, prix exceptionnels; **b. counter,** rayon *m* des soldes; **b. basement,** sous-sol *m* des bonnes affaires, des soldes; **b. hunter,** chercheur, -euse, d'occasions, acheteur, -euse, à la recherche de soldes; **b. hunting,** la recherche des occasions, des soldes; **to hunt for bargains, to be on the lookout for bargains,** être à la recherche des occasions; *(of article)* **to be a b.,** être (à un prix) intéressant; **a real b.,** une véritable occasion; **it's a great b.!** c'est une belle occasion! une occasion superbe!

bargain². **1.** *v.i.* *(a)* entrer en négociations, négocier **(with s.o.,** avec qn); **to b. with s.o. for sth.,** traiter, faire marché, de qch. avec qn; **I didn't b. for that,** ce n'était pas dans nos conventions; je ne m'attendais pas à cela; ça n'est pas de jeu; **I didn't b. for your bringing all your friends,** je ne m'attendais pas à ce que vous ameniez tous vos amis; **I didn't b. to do that,** je ne m'étais pas engagé à cela; cela n'est pas dans notre marché; **he got more than he bargained for,** il ne s'attendait pas à avoir affaire à si forte partie; il a eu du fil à retordre; *(b)* *(haggle)* **to b. with s.o.,** marchander qn; **to b. over an article,** marchander un article. **2.** *v.tr.* **to b. sth. away,** perdre qch. en marchandant.

bargainee [bɑːgi'niː], *s. Jur: Com:* acheteur *m*, preneur *m.*

bargainer ['bɑːginər], *s.* marchandeur, -euse.

bargaining ['bɑːginiŋ], *s.* marchandage *m*; **b. unit,** groupement négociateur; **collective b.** = convention collective.

bargainor ['bɑːginər], *s. Jur: Com:* vendeur *m*, bailleur *m.*

barge¹ [bɑːdʒ], *s.* *(a)* *(dumb barge)* chaland *m*, bateau plat; allège *f*, péniche *f*, toue *f*, accon *m*; **canal b.,** balandre *f*; **motor b.,** chaland à moteur; **mud b.,** marie-salope *f* (de drague), *pl.* maries-salopes; bateau vasier; *Mil:* **landing b.,** chaland d'accostage; **invasion b.,** péniche de débarquement; *(b)* *(with sails)* gabare *f*, barge *f*; *(c)* bateau-maison *m*, *pl.* bateaux-maisons (appartenant à un club de l'aviron); *(d)* *Navy:* deuxième canot *m* (d'un navire de guerre); **admiral's b.,** canot amiral; *(e)* **state b.,** barque *f* de cérémonie.

barge². **1.** *F:* *v.i.* **to b. into, against, s.o., sth.,** venir se heurter contre qn, qch.; bousculer qn; se cogner sur qn, contre qch.; donner contre qch.; *F:* rentrer dans qn; **to b. in,** intervenir mal à propos; **to b. into a room,** faire irruption dans une pièce; *v.tr.* **to b. one's way through the crowd,** bousculer la foule pour passer; foncer à travers la foule. **2.** *v.i.* *F:* **to b. about,** s'avancer avec maladresse, en bousculant. **3.** *v.tr.* *NAm:* transporter (qch.) en péniche.

bargeboard ['bɑːdʒbɔːd], *s. Arch: Const:* bordure *f* de pignon.

barge couple ['bɑːdʒkʌpl], *s. Const:* traverse *f.*

barge course ['bɑːdʒkɔːs], *s. Const:* cordon *m.*

bargee [bɑː'dʒiː], **bargeman**, *pl.* **-men** ['bɑːdʒmən], *s.* *(a)* chalandier *m*; *(b)* gabarier *m*; *(c)* *F:* batelier *m*, marinier *m.*

bargemaster ['bɑːdʒmɑːstər], *s.* patron *m* de chaland ou de gabare.

bargepole ['bɑːdʒpoul], *s.* gaffe *f*; *F:* **I wouldn't touch it with a b.,** je n'en veux à aucun prix; **I wouldn't touch him with a b.,** (i) il me dégoûte; il n'est pas à prendre avec des pincettes; (ii) je ne veux rien avoir à faire avec lui.

baric¹ ['beərik], *a. Ch:* barytique.

baric², *a. Ph: Meteor:* (pression *f*) barométrique.

barilla [bə'rilə], *s. Bot: Ind:* barille *f.*

baring [beəriŋ], *s.* mise *f* à nu; dépouillement *m* (d'un arbre, etc.); déchaussement *m* (d'une racine, etc.); dégainement *m* (d'une épée).

baritone ['bæritoun]. **1.** *Mus:* *(a)* *s.* *(pers.)* baryton *m*; **high b.,** baryton ténorisant; *(b)* *a.* **b. voice,** voix *f* de baryton; *(c)* *s.* *(saxhorn or saxophone)* baryton; *(stringed instrument)* baryton. **2.** *Gr.Gram:* *a. & s.* (mot) baryton *(m).*

barium ['beəriəm], *s. Ch:* baryum *m*; **b. hydrate,** baryte hydratée; **b. carbonate,** carbonate *m* de baryte; **b. oxide,** oxyde *m* de baryum; **b. sulphate,** sulfate *m* de baryte; *Med:* **b. meal,** bouillie barytée; *Const:* **b. plaster,** plâtre *m* au baryum.

bark¹ [bɑːk], *s.* **1.** *(a)* écorce *f* (d'arbre); **inner b.,** liber *m*; **to strip the b. off a tree,** écorcer un arbre; **Peruvian b.,** quinquina *m*; **red b.,** quinquina rouge; **ordeal b.,** écorce de mançône; **shell b.,** hickory *m*, noyer blanc; *For:* **b. coppice,** taillis *m* à écorce; *Ent:* **b. beetle,** bostryche *f*, scolyte *m*; *(b)* *(left on cut timber)* grume *f.* **2. (tanner's) b.,** tan *m*; **spent b.,** tannée *f*; *Hort:* **b. bed,** couche *f* de tannée; *Ind:* **b. mill,** moulin *m* à tan; **b. pit,** fosse *f* de tanneur, fosse à tan.

bark², *v.tr.* *(a)* écorcer, décortiquer (un arbre); dépouiller (un arbre) de son écorce; *(b)* **to b. one's shins,** se raboter, s'écorcher, s'érafler, les tibias.

bark³, *s.* **1.** *(a)* aboiement *m*, aboi *m*; **to give a b.,** pousser un aboiement; **his b. is worse than his bite,** il aboie plus qu'il ne mord; il fait plus de bruit que de mal; il n'est pas si méchant qu'il en a l'air; *(b)* glapissement *m* (du renard). **2.** *F:* toux sèche. **3.** détonation *f* (d'une arme à feu).

bark⁴, *v.i.* **1.** *(a)* aboyer **(at,** après, contre, à); **to b. at the moon,** aboyer à la lune; **to b. up the wrong tree,** suivre une fausse piste; accuser qn à tort; *(b)* *(of fox)* glapir. **2.** dire (qch.) d'un ton sec, cassant; **no, he barked out,** non, dit-il d'un ton sec; **to b. out an order,** donner un ordre d'un ton sec. **3.** *(of firearm)* détoner. **4.** *F:* tousser.

bark⁵, *s.* **1.** *Nau:* trois-mâts *m* barque; **four-mast b.,**

quatre-mâts barque; **jackass b.**, jackass *f*. **2.** *Poet:* barque *f*.
barkan ['bɑ:kən], *s. Geog:* barkhane *f*.
barkbound ['bɑ:kbaund], *a. Bot:* (*of tree*) serré dans son écorce.
barked [bɑ:kt], *s.* **1.** écorcé; *For:* **b. wood**, bois pelard. **2.** éraflé.
barkeep ['bɑ:ki:p], *s.m. U.S: F:* = BARKEEPER.
barkeeper ['bɑ:ki:pər], *s.m. NAm:* cafetier, tenancier d'un bar.
barkentine ['bɑ:kənti:n], *s. Nau:* barque *f* goélette; trois-mâts *m* goélette.
barker[1] ['bɑ:kər], *s.* **1.** aboyeur, -euse. **2.** *A: & NAm:* (*in front of booth*) aboyeur. **3.** *P:* pistolet *m*; revolver *m*; aboyeur.
barker[2], *s. For: Ind:* **1.** (*pers.*) écorceur *m*. **2.** (*machine*) écorceuse *f*.
barkery ['bɑ:kəri], *s. Leath:* magasin *m* d'écorces.
barkhan ['bɑ:kən], *s. Geog:* barkhane *f*.
Barkhausen ['bɑ:khauzn], *Pr.n. W.Tel:* **B. oscillator**, oscillateur *m* de Barkhausen; **B.-Kurz oscillations**, oscillations *f* de Barkhausen et Kurz; *Magn:* **B. effect**, effet *m* de Barkhausen.
barking[1] ['bɑ:kiŋ], *s.* écorçage *m*; décortication *f*; **b. iron**, (i) outil *m* à écorcer; (ii) *P: A:* (*par calembour sur* BARK[4]) pistolet *m*; revolver *m*.
barking[2], *a.* (*a*) (chien) aboyeur; *Prov:* **b. dogs seldom, never, bite**, chien *m* qui aboie ne mord pas; (*b*) (renard) glapissant; (*c*) **b. deer**, muntjac *m*, cerf aboyeur.
barking[3], *s.* **1.** (*a*) aboiement *m* (d'un chien, *F:* d'un critique); (*b*) glapissement *m* (d'un renard). **2.** toux sèche.
bark-rigged ['bɑ:k'rigd], *a. Nau:* gréé en trois-mâts barque.
bark tree ['bɑ:ktri:], *s. Bot:* cinchona *m*.
barley ['bɑ:li], *s.* (*a*) orge *f*, *but m. in:* **hulled b.**, orge mondé, *and* **pearl b.**, orge perlé; blé *m* d'Égypte, de mai; **bald b.**, orge *f* sans barbes; **two-rowed b.**, pamelle *f*, paumelle *f*; orge à deux rangs; **four-rowed b.**, orge à quatre rangs; **hooded b.**, orge trifurquée; **winter b.**, escourgeon *m*, orge de prime; **wall b.**, orge des rats, des murs; *Brew:* **bruised b.**, brai *m*; (*b*) *attrib.* **b. beer**, cervoise *f*; **b. gruel**, crème *f* d'orge; **b. meal**, farine *f* d'orge; **b. sugar**, sucre *m* d'orge; **b. water**, tisane *f* d'orge; **b. mow**, meule *f* d'orge.
barleycorn ['bɑ:likɔ:n], *s.* **1.** grain *m* d'orge; *F:* **John B.**, le whisky. **2.** *Carp:* grain-d'orge *m* (entre moulures).
Barlow ['bɑ:lou], *Pr.n.m.* **1.** *Med:* **Barlow's disease**, maladie *f* de Barlow; scorbut *m* infantile. **2.** *Ph:* **Barlow's wheel**, roue *f* de Barlow. **3.** *NAm:* **B. knife**, *F:* **barlow**, grand couteau de poche (à une ou à deux lames).
barm [bɑ:m], *s.* levure *f* (de bière); levain *m* de bière.
barmaid ['bɑ:meid], *s.f.* serveuse, verseuse, dans un bar, *F:* barmaid.
barman, -men ['bɑ:mən], *s.m.* garçon de comptoir (d'un débit de boisson); serveur du bar; barman.
Barmecide ['bɑ:misaid], *a. & s. Hist: Lit:* Barmécide; **B. feast**, festin *m* de Barmécide (où il n'y a que des plats vides).
barminess ['bɑ:minis], *s. F:* loufoquerie *f*.
barmy ['bɑ:mi], *a.* **1.** contenant de la levure; écumeux; en fermentation. **2.** *F:* toqué, timbré, maboul, loufoque.
barn [bɑ:n], *s.* **1.** (*a*) grange *f*; **b. floor**, aire *f* de grange; **b. door**, porte *f* de grange; **b.-door fowl**, volaille *f* de basse-cour; *F:* (*of a poor shot*) **he couldn't hit a b. door**, il raterait la cible à bout portant; il manquerait un éléphant dans un tunnel, une vache dans un couloir; (*b*) *NAm:* étable *f*; écurie *f*; (*c*) (*for tobacco*) **drying b.**, suerie *f*; (*d*) *NAm:* dépôt *m* de tramways. **2.** *Atom.Ph: Meas:* barn *m*.
Barnabas ['bɑ:nəbəs], **Barnaby** ['bɑ:nəbi], *Pr.n.m.* **1.** Barnabé; *A:* **Barnaby Day**, la Saint-Barnabé (11 juin). **2.** *Bot:* **Barnaby's thistle**, centaurée *f* du solstice.
Barnabite ['bɑ:nəbait], *s.m. Ecc:* Barnabite.
barnacle ['bɑ:nəkl], *s.* **1.** *Orn:* **b. (goose)**, bernacle *f*, bernache *f* (nonnette). **2.** (*a*) *Crust:* (i) **(stalked, ship, goose) b.**, anatif(e) *m*, *F:* bernache, bernacle, cravan(t) *m*; (ii) **(acorn) b.**, balane *m*, gland *m* de mer, turban *m* rouge; (*b*) *F:* (i) individu cramponnant; crampon *m*; (ii) fonctionnaire *m* qui se cramponne à son poste; (*c*) vieux matelot, *F:* vieux bourlingueur.
barnacled ['bɑ:nəkld], *a.* couvert d'anatifes.
barnacles ['bɑ:nəklz], *s.pl.* **1.** *Vet:* morailles *f*, mouchettes *f*. **2.** *F: A:* (*spectacles*) besicles *f*.
Barnett ['bɑ:nit], *Pr.n. El:* **B. effect**, aimantation *f* par rotation, effet *m* Barnett.
barney ['bɑ:ni], *s.* **1.** *P:* (*a*) tricherie *f*; fumisterie *f*; duperie *f*; (*b*) querelle *f*. **2.** *Min:* chariot *m*.
barnful ['bɑ:nful], *s.* grangée *f*.
barnstorm ['bɑ:nstɔ:m], *v.i. F:* (*a*) être comédien ambulant; (*b*) faire une tournée (théâtrale, électorale, etc.).
barnstormer ['bɑ:nstɔ:mər], *s.* **1.** *F:* (*a*) comédien ambulant; *A:* cabotin; (*b*) mauvais(e) comédien(ne); cabotin, -ine. **2.** orateur électoral.
barnstorming ['bɑ:nstɔ:miŋ], *s.* **1.** *F:* théâtre ambulant. **2.** tournée, campagne, électorale.
barnyard ['bɑ:njɑ:d], *s.* basse-cour *f*, *pl.* basses-cours; **b. fowl**, volaille *f* de basse-cour.
barocyclometer [bærousi'klɔmitər], *s. Meteor:* baromètre anticyclonal.
barogram ['bærougræm], *s.* barogramme *m*.
barograph ['bærougræf], *s.* barographe *m*; baromètre enregistreur; *Av:* altigraphe *m*.
barology [bæ'rɔlədʒi], *s.* barologie *f*.
barometer [bə'rɔmitər], *s.* baromètre *m*; **siphon b.**, baromètre à siphon; **wheel b.**, baromètre à cadran; **cup b.**, baromètre à cuvette; **self-registering b.**, baromètre enregistreur; **mountain b.**, oromètre *m*; **b. reading**, hauteur *f* barométrique; **the b. points to rain, to set fair**, le baromètre est à la pluie, au beau fixe; **b. of public opinion**, indication *f* des réactions du public.
barometric(al) [bærə'metrik(l)], *a.* barométrique; **b. gradient**, gradient *m* barométrique; **b. pressure**, pression *f* atmosphérique.
barometrically [bærə'metrikli], *adv.* barométriquement.
barometry [bə'rɔmitri], *s.* barométrie *f*.
barometz ['bærəmets], *s. Bot:* barometz *m*.
baron ['bærən], *s.* **1.** (*a*) baron *m*; (*b*) *A:* titre donné aux juges de la Cour de l'Échiquier; (*c*) *F:* grand manitou (industriel). **2.** **b. of beef**, double aloyau *m*; selle *f* de bœuf.
baronage ['bærənidʒ], *s.* **1.** baronnage *m*. **2.** liste *f* des barons; annuaire *m* de la noblesse.
baronarcosis [bærənɑ:'kousis], *s. Med:* baronarcose *f*.
baroness ['bærənes], *s.f.* baronne.
baronet ['bærənet], *s.m.* baronnet.
baronetage ['bærənitidʒ], *s.* **1.** les baronnets *m*. **2.** liste *f* des baronnets.
baronetcy ['bærənitsi], *s.* dignité *f* de baronnet; **to be given a b.**, être élevé au rang de baronnet; être créé baronnet.
baronial [bə'rouniəl], *a.* baronnial; **b. hall**, demeure seigneuriale.
barony ['bærəni], *s.* **1.** baronnie *f*. **2.** (*in Ireland*) subdivision *f* d'un comté. **3.** *Scot:* grande propriété terrienne.
baroque [bə'rɔk], *a. & s. Hist. of Art:* baroque (*m*).
baroscope ['bærəskoup], *s. Ph:* baroscope *m*.
Barosma [bæ'rɔzmə, -'rɔsmə], *s. Bot:* barosma *m*.
barostat ['bæroustæt], *s.* barostat *m*.
barotaxis [bærou'tæksis], *s.*, **barotaxy** [bærou'tæksi], *s. Biol:* barotaxie *f*.
barothermograph [bærou'θə:mougræf], *s.* barothermographe *m*.
barouche [bə'ru:ʃ], *s. A. Veh:* calèche *f*.
barque [bɑ:k], *s. Nau:* trois-mâts barque *m*.
barquentine ['bɑ:kənti:n], *s. Nau:* = BARKENTINE.
barrace ['bærəs], *s. A:* lice *f*; champ clos.
barrack(s)[1] ['bærək(s)], *s.* **1.** (*a*) *Mil:* (*usu. pl.*) caserne *f*; quartier *m*; (*of cavalry*) quartier; **detention b.**, locaux *mpl* disciplinaires; prison *f* militaire; **b. duties**, travaux *mpl* de service intérieur; **b. guard**, garde *m* de police, détachement *m* de garde (au quartier); **to live in barracks**, (i) (*of officers*) loger, vivre, à la caserne, au quartier; (ii) (*of the soldiers*) être casernés; **life in barracks**, la vie de caserne; **the squadron was on its way back to the barracks**, l'escadron rentrait au quartier; **casemated barrack**, casemate *f*, logement *m* caverne (d'un fort); **confinement to barracks**, consigne *f* au quartier; **to be confined to barracks**, être consigné; *attrib.* **barrack square**, cour *f* du quartier; **barrack master**, officier *m* de casernement; **barrack warden**, casernier *m*; (*b*) **naval barracks**, caserne maritime; dépôt *m* des équipages de la flotte; (*c*) *Can:* = gendarmerie *f*. **2.** *Pej:* (*a*) *F:* grand bâtiment qui ressemble à une caserne; *F:* caserne; (*b*) *A. & Dial:* baraque *f*, chaumière *f*, taudis *m*.
barrack[2], *v.tr. Mil:* caserner (des troupes).
barrack[3], (*a*) *v.tr.* conspuer, huer (une équipe de joueurs); (*b*) *v.i.* faire du chahut, chahuter.
barracking[1] ['bærəkiŋ], *s.* casernement *m* (des troupes).
barracking[2], *s. Sp: etc:* chahutage *m*.
barrackroom ['bærəkru:m], *s.* chambrée *f*; *attrib.* **b. joke**, plaisanterie *f* de corps-de-garde; **b. language, manners**, langage *m* de corps de garde, de caserne, comportement *m* de soudard, manières soldatesques.
barracoon [bærə'ku:n], *s. Hist:* (i) négrerie *f*, (ii) baraquements *mpl* de forçats (sur la côte d'Afrique).
barracouta [bærə'ku:tə], *s. Ich:* barracuda *m*.
barracuda [bærə'kju:də], *s. Ich:* barracuda *m*, bécune *f*.
barrage[1] ['bærɑ:ʒ, bæ'rɑ:ʒ], *s.* **1.** *Hyd.E:* barrage *m* (d'un fleuve). **2.** *Mil: Artil:* barrage; **b. fire**, tir *m* de barrage, d'arrêt; **standing, stationary, b.**, tir d'arrêt; barrage fixe; **moving b.**, barrage mobile; **creeping, rolling, b.**, barrage roulant; **balloon b.**, barrage de ballons; **b. balloon**, ballon *m* de barrage, de protection; **box b.**, tir d'encagement; **ladder b.**, tir échelonné; **to lay down a b.**, établir un barrage; **to lift the b.**, lever, reporter, le barrage. **3.** **a b. of questions, of insults**, un torrent de questions, d'injures.
barrage[2], *v.tr. & i. Mil:* établir un tir de barrage (sur une ligne).
barramunda [bærə'mʌndə], *s.*, **barramundi** [bærə'mʌndi], *s. Ich:* (*a*) ceratodus *m*; (*b*) latès *m*.
barranca [bæ'rænkə], **barranco** [bæ'rænkou], *s. Geog:* barranco *m*.
barras ['bærəs], *s.* **b. (resin)**, barras *m*.
barrater, barrator ['bærətər], *s. Jur: A:* **1.** chicaneur *m*, procédurier *m*; personne *f* qui excite aux procès. **2.** juge vénal.
barratrous ['bærətrəs], *a. Jur:* entaché de baraterie.
barratry ['bærətri], *s.* **1.** *Jur: A:* (*a*) esprit *m* de chicane; (*b*) vénalité *f* (d'un juge). **2.** *Nau:* baraterie *f*; acte de violence, de fraude (commis par le capitaine).
barré ['bærei], *s. Tex:* bayadère *f*.
barred [bɑ:d], *a.* **1.** (*a*) barré; muni d'une grille, de barreaux; **b. window**, fenêtre grillée; (*b*) *Mus:* **barred C**, C barré. **2.** (drap, etc.) rayé. **3.** (port) obstrué par une barre de sable. **4.** *Jur:* **b. by limitation**, (droit) périmé; **these debts are b. at the end of five years**, ces dettes se prescrivent par cinq ans; il y a prescription pour ces dettes au bout de cinq ans.
barrel[1] ['bær(ə)l], *s.* **1.** (*a*) tonneau *m*, barrique *f*, futaille *f*, fût *m* (de vin, etc.); caque *f*, baril *m* (de harengs, etc.); gonne *f* (de goudron); baril (de pétrole); **b. head**, fond *m* de tonneau, de fût, etc.; **b. bulk** = cinq pieds *m* cubes; **b. horse, stand**, porte-fût(s) *m inv*; *U.S: P:* **b. house**, café *m*, bar *m*, de bas étage; **goods in barrels**, marchandise *f* de tonnelage; *Nau:* **cargo in barrels**, barillage *m*; *U.S: P:* **to be over a b.**, être à la merci de qn; *F:* **we're scraping the bottom of the b.**, nous en sommes maintenant aux articles (candidats, etc.) de la pire qualité (ayant épuisé les meilleurs); (*b*) **biscuit b.**, *NAm:* **cracker b.**, (i) *A:* baril de biscuits; (ii) boîte *f* à biscuits (en forme de cylindre); seau *m* à biscuits; *U.S:* **cracker b. philosopher**, commentateur *m* un peu naïf mais plein d'un bon sens rustique; = philosophe en chambre, de Café du Commerce; *U.S: F:* **the pork b.**, postes *mpl*, subventions *fpl*, etc., à la nomination du gouvernement et consentis aux électeurs influents; (*c*) *NAm: F:* grande quantité (**of**, de). **2.** (*a*) cylindre *m*, partie *f* cylindrique; fût, caisse *f* (d'un tambour); canon *m* ((i) de fusil, (ii) de seringue; (iii) de poupée de tour, (iv) de serrure, de clef); faussure *f* (d'une cloche); corps *m*, barillet *m* (de pompe); cylindre, barillet (de serrure); fusée *f*, mèche *f*, tambour *m*, cloche *f* (de cabestan, de treuil); *Nau:* marbre *m* (de la roue du gouvernail); *Clockm:* barillet, boîte à ressort (de montre); *Mus:* cylindre noté (d'un orgue mécanique); *Artil:* tube *m* (de canon); **training b.**, tube d'exercice; *Sm.a:* **b. sleeve**, cheminée *f*; *Mec.E:* **b. type engine**, moteur *m* à barillet; *Phot:* **lens b.**, barillet; **to give a hare (etc.) both barrels**, faire feu des deux coups sur un lièvre (etc.); *attrib. Mus:* **b. organ**, (i) orgue mécanique; (ii) orgue de Barbarie; piano *m* mécanique (à cylindre); *El:* **b. plating**, revêtement *m* électrolytique à cuve rotative; électrodéposition *f* au tonneau; **b. winding**, enroulement *m* en manteau; *Av:* **b. roll**, tonneau *m*; *Arch:* **b. vault**, voûte *f* en berceau; **b. roof**, toit cintré; (*b*) *Anat:* **b. of the ear**, caisse du tympan; (*c*) *Cost:* (*button*) olive *f*. **3.** tronc *m* (d'un bœuf, d'un cheval, etc.). **4.** bombement *m* (d'une chaussée). **5.** *U.S: Pol:* fonds *mpl* (d'un parti).
barrel[2], *v.tr.* (**barrelled; barrelling**) **1.** mettre (qch.) en fût; entonner, enfutailler (du vin); (en)caquer, embariller, empiler, aliter (des harengs); caquer (de la poudre à canon). **2.** bomber (une route). **3.** *v.i. U.S:* rouler très vite.
barrelage ['bærəlidʒ], *s.* quantité (de bière, etc.) évaluée en fûts.
barrelful ['bær(ə)lful], *s.* (contenu *m* d'un) tonneau, fût.
barrelled ['bærəld], *a.* **1.** (vin *m*) en tonneau(x), en fût(s); (harengs *m*) en caque. **2.** en forme de tonneau; bombé.
barrelling ['bærəliŋ], *s.* embarillage *m*; entonnage *m*; encaquement *m*; caquage *m* (de la poudre à canon).
barrel-shaped ['bær(ə)lʃeipt], *a.* en forme de baril, de tonneau; **b.-s. distortion**, distorsion *f* en barillet.
Barremian [bæ'ri:miən], *a. & s. Geol:* barrémien (*m*); *occ.* irgonien (*m*).
barren ['bær(ə)n], *a.* (*a*) stérile, improductif, infertile; (terrain *m*) aride; **union b. of issue**, union *f* stérile; **b. mare**, jument *f* vide, bréhaigne; *Min:* **b. ground**, terrain *m* stérile; **b. measures**, morts-terrains *mpl*; **b. lands**, *s.*

NAm: **barrens,** terrains infertiles; lande(s) *f* (*pl*); **pine barrens,** landes à pins; *Geog:* **B. Grounds, Lands,** la toundra du Canada du Nord; (*b*) **to work on a b. subject,** travailler à un sujet maigre, ingrat, aride; **mind b. of ideas,** esprit dépourvu d'idées, peu fertile en idées; **the attempt was b. of results,** la tentative n'aboutit pas.

barrenly ['bærənli], *adv.* stérilement; sans résultat(s).

barrenness ['bærənnis], *s.* (*a*) stérilité *f*; (*b*) aridité *f* (d'une étude, etc.).

barrenwort ['bærənwəːt], *s. Bot:* épimède *f*; **Alpine b.,** épimède des Alpes; chapeau *m* d'évêque.

barret ['bærət], *s. Ecc.Cost:* barrette *f*.

barrette [bæ'ret], *s.* **1.** garde *f* (d'un fleuret, d'une épée). **2.** *Cost:* (*hair slide*) barrette *f*.

barretter [bə'retər], *s. El: W.Tel:* tube *m* régulateur ferhydrogène.

barricade[1] ['bærikeid, bæri'keid], *s.* barricade *f*; *Fort: NAm:* merlon *m*; **b. of piles,** estacade *f*.

barricade[2], *v.tr.* barricader.

barrico ['bærikou], *s.* barrique *f*.

barrier[1] ['bæriər], *s.* (*a*) barrière *f*; *Mil: etc:* barrage *m* (d'obstacles); *El:* arrêt *m*, barrage; *Min:* arrêt-barrage *m*, *pl.* arrêts-barrages; *Cin:* ligne *f* de séparation; *Mil:* **b. fort,** fort *m* d'arrêt; *Av:* **anti-blast b.,** barrière antisouffle; **sound, sonic, b.,** mur *m* du son; **the language b.,** le mur des langues; **b. to progress,** obstacle *m* au progrès; *Rail:* **ticket b.,** portillon *m* d'accès; **counterpoise b.,** tapecul *m*; *Geog:* **ice b.,** muraille *f*, falaise *f*, de glace; **b. ice,** banquise *f*; **the Great Ice B.,** la Banquise; **b. reef,** récif *m* en barrière; **the Great B. Reef,** la Grande Barrière; *Hist:* **the B. Treaties,** les Traités *m* de la Barrière (1709, 1713); (*b*) *A:* **barriers,** lice *f*, champ clos.

barrier[2], *v.tr.* fermer (un enclos) avec une barrière.

barring[1] ['bɑːriŋ], *s.* **1.** barrage *m* (d'une porte, etc.). **2.** interdiction *f* (d'une action). **3.** *Sch: A:* **b. out,** révolte *f* des élèves (qui barraient les portes pour interdire l'entrée aux professeurs). **4.** *Min:* **b. (down),** abattage *m* au moyen de pinces.

barring[2], *prep.* excepté, sauf, à part; **b. accidents,** sauf accident, sauf imprévu.

barring-engine ['bɑːriŋendʒin], *s. Mch: I.C.E:* moteur démarreur; vireur *m* (le démarrage s'accomplissait à l'origine au moyen d'une barre employée comme levier).

barrister ['bæristər], *s. Jur:* **b.-at-law,** avocat *m*; **consulting b.,** avocat consultant, avocat conseil; **revising b.,** contrôleur *m* des listes électorales; **to appear on the roll of barristers,** être inscrit au barreau.

bar room ['bɑːruːm], *s. NAm:* salon *m* du bar.

barrow[1] ['bærou], *s.* (*a*) brouette *f*; (*b*) baladeuse *f*, voiture *f* à bras; charrette *f* à bras; **b. boy,** marchand *m* des quatre saisons; (*c*) *Rail:* diable *m*; (*d*) *Min:* wagonnet *m*, her(s)che *f*; (*e*) *Artil:* **shell b.,** civière *f*, wagonnet, de chargement.

barrow[2], *v.tr.* **1.** brouetter. **2.** *Min:* her(s)cher.

barrow[3], *s.* (*a*) *Archeol:* tumulus *m*; tertre *m* (funéraire); tombeau *m*; (*in Brittany*) galgal *m*; **unchambered long b.,** tertre tumulaire allongé; (*b*) *Geog:* (*in place names*) colline *f*.

barrow[4], *s.* porc *m* châtré.

barrowful ['bærouful], *s.* brouettée *f*.

barrowload ['bærouloud], *s.* **1.** brouettée *f*. **2.** voiturée *f*.

barrowman, *pl.* **-men** ['bæroumæn, -men], *s.* **1.** marchand *m* des quatre saisons. **2.** *Min:* traîneur *m* de wagonnets; her(s)cheur *m*.

barrulet ['bærjulit], *s. Her:* burelle *f*, burèle *f*.

barruly ['bæruli], *a. Her:* burelé.

barry ['bɑːri], *a. Her:* barré, burelé; **b. of ten pieces,** burelé de dix pièces.

bartender ['bɑːtendər], *s.* (*a*) garçon *m* de comptoir; (*b*) tenancier *m* d'un bar.

barter[1] ['bɑːtər], *s.* échange *m*; troc *m*.

barter[2], (*a*) *v.tr.* **to b. sth. for sth.,** échanger, troquer, qch. contre qch.; donner qch. en troc pour qch.; *v.ind.tr.* **to b. away (one's rights, etc.),** vendre (ses droits, etc.); (*b*) *v.i.* faire le commerce d'échange; faire le troc.

barterer ['bɑːtərər], *s.* **1.** troqueur, -euse. **2.** *Pej:* trafiqueur *m*.

barthite ['bɑːθait], *s. Miner:* barthite *f*.

Bartholin ['bɑːtəlin], *Pr.n. Anat:* **Bartholin's glands,** glandes *fpl* de Bartholin.

bartholinitis ['bɑːtəli'naitis], *s. Med:* bartholinite *f*.

Bartholomew [bɑː'θɔləmjuː], *Pr.n.m.* Barthélemy; *Hist:* **the Massacre of St. B.,** le Massacre de la Saint-Barthélemy.

bartisan, bartizan [bɑːti'zæn], *s. Arch: Fort:* **1.** tourelle *f* en encorbellement; échauguette *f*. **2.** bretèche *f*.

barton ['bɑːt(ə)n], *s. A:* **1.** basse-cour *f*, *pl.* basses-cours. **2.** la ferme du château.

Bartonian [bɑː'tounion], *a. & s. Geol:* bartonien (*m*).

barwood ['bɑːwud], *s.* bois *m* de cam *m*.

barycentre ['bærisentə], *s. Ph:* barycentre *m*.

barycentric [bæri'sentrik], *a. Ph:* barycentrique.

barye ['bæri], *s. Ph.Meas:* barye *f*.

barylite ['bærilait], *s. Miner:* barilite *f*.

baryon ['bæriən], *s. Ph:* baryon *m*.

barysphere ['bærisfiər], *s. Geol:* barysphère *f*.

baryta [bə'raitə], *s. Ch:* baryte *f*; **b. water,** eau *f* de baryte; **b. paper,** papier baryté.

barytes [bə'raitiːz], **barytine** ['bæritin, -ain], *s. Miner:* barytine *f*.

barytic [bə'ritik], *a. Geol:* barytifère; *Miner:* barytique.

barytocalcite [bæ'raitou'kælsait], *s. Miner:* barytocalcite *f*.

barytone ['bæritoun], *a. & s. Mus:* = BARITONE 1.

basal ['beisl], *a.* basal, -aux; fondamental, -aux; qui appartient à la base; *Bot:* (style *m*) basilaire; *Cryst:* (clivage *m*) basique; *Biol:* **b. gemmation,** gemmation basale; *Geol:* **b. conglomerate,** conglomérat basal; *Med:* **b. metabolic rate,** taux métabolique basal; **b. metabolism,** métabolisme basal.

basalt ['bæsɔːlt], *s. Geol: Miner: Cer:* basalte *m*; **b. glass,** basalte vitreux.

basaltic [bə'sɔːltik], *a.* basaltique; **b. columns,** colonnes *f* de basalte; orgues *fpl*.

basaltiform [bə'sɔːltifɔːm], *a. Geol:* basaltiforme.

basan ['bæz(ə)n], *s. Leath:* basane *f*; peau *f* de mouton.

basanite ['bæsənait], *s. Miner:* basanite *f*.

bascule ['bæskjuːl], *s. Civ.E:* bascule *f*; *esp.* **b. bridge,** pont(-levis) *m* à bascule (*pl.* ponts-levis).

base[1] [beis], *s.* **1.** (*a*) base *f* (de triangle, etc.); **b. measurement,** mesure *f* d'une base; **b. terminal,** origine *f* d'une base; (*b*) *Mth:* base (logarithmique, d'un système de numération); *Cmptr:* (i) base; (ii) (= *radix*) base (de numération); **data b.,** fichier central; **floating point b.,** base (de numération) à virgule flottante; **Napierian b.,** base des logarithmes népériens; **time b.,** base de temps, rythme *m*; (*c*) *Ling:* base, racine *f*; (*d*) *Ch:* base (d'un sel); (*e*) *Ind:* base, fondant *m* (d'un émail); *Paint:* pigment *m*; (*f*) *Sp:* (*baseball*) base, piquet *m*; **b. hit,** coup *m* de base; **b. runner,** coureur *m* à la base; **b. running,** course *f* à la base; *Games:* **prisoner's b.,** (jeu *m* de) barres *fpl*. **2.** (*a*) partie inférieure; fondement *m*; base; *Geog:* **b. level (of erosion),** niveau *m* de base (d'érosion); *Arch: Const:* soubassement *m*; (*of apparatus*) socle *m*, pied *m*, embase *f*, assise *f*; **b. (plate),** sole *f*, embase, soubassement (de machine-outil, etc.); **b. of a crane,** socle d'une grue; *Sm.a:* **front sight b.,** embase de guidon; **back sight b.,** pied de hausse; *Const: Civ.E:* **b. (course),** couche *f* de base; *El:* **insulating b.,** socle isolant; *Phot: Cin:* **b. of the film,** support *m* du film, de l'émulsion; (*b*) *Her:* pied *m* (de l'écu); (*c*) *Toil:* **powder b.,** support de poudre; (*d*) *Fig:* (*fundamental principle, starting point*) base; **the b. of an argument, a proposition,** la base d'un raisonnement, d'une proposition; *NAm: F:* **to be off b.,** (i) se gourer; (ii) être cinglé, dérailler; *Ind: NAm:* **b. rate, b. pay,** salaire *m* de base. **3. (metal) b. (of electric lamp),** culot *m* (de lampe); *Artil: Sm.a:* culot (d'obus, de cartouche); **single contact b.,** culot à plot central; **double contact b.,** culot à deux plots; *Aedcs:* **b. pressure,** pression *f* de culot. **4.** *Rail:* patin *m* (de rail); **width of rail b.,** largeur *f* de patin; *Veh: Rail:* **wheel b.,** empattement *m*, distance *f* entre les essieux. **5.** *Mil: etc:* **b. of operations,** base d'opérations; **advanced b.,** base avancée; **b. area,** zone *f* de (la) base; *NAm:* **b. section,** district *m* de base; partie *f* arrière de la zone de communications; **repair b.,** base de réparations; **b. shop,** atelier *m* de base; **supply b.,** base de ravitaillement; **b. hospital,** hôpital *m* de l'intérieur; **naval b.,** port *m* de guerre, station navale; **air b.,** base aérienne, base d'aviation; *Space:* **rocket b.,** base de lancement (de fusées). **6.** cratère *m* (de bombe atomique); *Atom.Ph:* **b. surge,** onde *f* de raz de marée, onde de choc.

base[2], *v.tr.* **1.** baser, fonder (**on,** sur); **to b. oneself on sth.,** se baser sur qch.; **this novel is based on the events of 1939,** ce roman est basé, repose, sur les événements de 1939; **to b. one's opinion on the fact that . . .,** asseoir, fonder, appuyer, son opinion sur le fait que . . .; **to b. a decision on a fact,** motiver une décision sur un fait; **to b. taxation on income,** asseoir l'impôt sur le revenu. **2.** *Av:* **a British-based U.S. aircraft,** un avion américain basé en Grande-Bretagne; *Navy:* **land-, shore-based installation,** installation *f* terrestre.

base[3], *a.* (*a*) bas, vil; **b. motive,** motif bas, indigne; **b. mind,** âme basse; **b. action,** action *f* ignoble, indigne, lâche; (*b*) **b. metals,** métaux vils; (*c*) **b. coin(age),** (i) pièce *f*, monnaie *f*, de mauvais aloi; (ii) fausse monnaie.

baseball ['beisbɔːl], *s. Sp:* base-ball *m*; **b. player,** baseballeur *m*, joueur *m* de base-ball.

baseband ['beisbænd], *s. W.Tel: El: Cmptr:* bande *f* de base.

baseboard ['beisbɔːd], *s.* **1.** *Phot:* chariot *m* (de l'appareil). **2.** *Const: etc:* plinthe *f*; *NAm:* base *m*, socle *m*, de lambris.

baseborn ['beisbɔːn], *a. A:* **1.** de basse extraction, de basse naissance. **2.** bâtard.

base burner ['beis'bəːnər], *s. NAm:* poêle *m*, fourneau *m*, à feu continu.

Basedow ['bɑːzdou], *Pr.n. Med:* **Basedow's disease,** maladie *f* de Basedow.

Basel ['bɑːzl, bɑːl], *Pr.n. Geog:* Bâle *f*.

baseless ['beislis], *a.* sans base, sans fondement; (critique *f*) qui manque de fondement; (nouvelle *f*) de pure imagination; **b. suspicions,** soupçons *m* sans fondement, injustifiés; **b. charge,** accusation *f* sans fondement, non fondée.

baselessness ['beislisnis], *s.* manque *m* de fondement.

base line ['beislain], *s.* **1.** (*a*) *Surv:* base *f*; (*b*) *Mch:* ligne *f* zéro (du diagramme). **2.** (*a*) *Artil:* direction *f* de surveillance; (*anti-aircraft*) ligne de base; (*b*) *Ten:* ligne de fond; **b.l. play,** jeu *m* de fond. **3.** *Art:* ligne de fuite (de la perspective).

basella [bæ'zelə], *s. Bot:* baselle *f*.

basely ['beisli], *adv.* bassement, vilement, lâchement.

baseman, *pl.* **-men** ['beismən], *s.m. Sp:* (*baseball*) joueur à la base.

basement ['beismənt], *s.* **1.** (*a*) soubassement *m* (d'une construction); allège *f* (d'une fenêtre); (*b*) *Geol:* socle *m*; soubassement; **impervious b.,** soubassement imperméable; **b. complex,** soubassement de roches ignées (qui se trouve au-dessous des couches sédimentaires). **2.** sous-sol *m*; **b. house,** maison *f* avec cuisine et offices en sous-sol; **b. flat,** (appartement *m* de) sous-sol; **b. light,** verre *m* dalle.

baseness ['beisnis], *s.* bassesse *f*; *A:* **b. of birth,** (i) bassesse de naissance; (ii) illégitimité *f*.

bash[1] [bæʃ], *s. F:* (*a*) coup *m*, enfoncement *m*; **the teapot, your hat, has had a b.,** la théière est bosselée, cabossée, votre chapeau est cabossé; (*b*) coup (sur la figure); coup de poing violent; **to give s.o. a b. on the face,** coller son poing sur la figure de qn, à qn; **to have a b. at sth.,** s'attaquer à, s'essayer à, qch., *F:* tenter le coup; *P:* **on the b.,** en bringue, en nouba, en vadrouille.

bash[2], *v.tr. F:* **to b. one's head, etc.,** se cogner la tête, etc.; **to b. (in) a hat, etc.,** aplatir, cabosser, un chapeau, etc. (d'un coup de poing); **to b. in one's hat,** renfoncer son chapeau; **to b. in a box,** défoncer une boîte; **to b. s.o. about,** houspiller, maltraiter, qn; **he bashed him on the head,** il lui a flanqué un coup sur la tête; il l'assomma; **to b. s.o.'s brains out,** décerveler qn; **to b. s.o. on the jaw,** coller son poing sur la figure de qn, à qn.

Bashan ['beiʃæn], *Pr.n. B.* Basan *m*.

basher ['bæʃər], *s. F:* cogneur *m*, pugiliste *m*.

bashful ['bæʃf(u)l], *a.* (*a*) modeste, timide; **b. lover,** amoureux transi; (*b*) modeste, pudique.

bashfully ['bæʃfuli], *adv.* (*a*) modestement; timidement, avec timidité; (*b*) pudiquement; en rougissant; (*c*) d'un air honteux, embarrassé, penaud.

bashfulness ['bæʃf(u)lnis], *s.* modestie *f*; timidité *f*; fausse honte.

bashi-bazouk [bæʃibə'zuːk], *s. Hist:* bachi-bouzouk *m*.

bashing ['bæʃiŋ], *s. F.* volée *f* de coups, rossée *f*, *Mil. etc:* **to take, get, a b.,** prendre quelque chose; **the town took a, the, hell of a b.,** la ville a pris un sacré coup; **union b.,** mesures anti-syndicales réputées injustes par le parti travailliste.

Bashkir ['bæʃkiər], *s. Ethn:* Baskir *m*, Bachkir *m*.

basi- ['bæsi, 'beisi], *pref.* basi-.

basic ['beisik], *a.* **1.** (*a*) (principe, etc.) fondamental; **b. truth,** vérité première; *Ling:* **b. vocabulary,** vocabulaire *m* de base; **b. English,** l'anglais *m* de base; **you must learn some b. French before leaving,** il faut apprendre des éléments de français avant de partir; (*b*) *Adm:* **b. abatement,** abattement *m* (d'impôt) à la base; **b. pay,** salaire *m* de base; *Pol.Ec:* **b. commodity,** denrée *f* témoin; (*c*) *Mil: U.S:* simple (soldat); (soldat) de deuxième classe. **2.** *Ch: Geol:* basique; *Geol:* (*used loosely*) **b. rock,** roche ignée; **b. lava,** lave *f* basique; *Metall:* **b. lining,** garnissage *m* basique; **b. slag,** scorie *f* basique, scories de déphosphoration; (*b*) *Ch:* sous-; **b. salt,** sous-sel *m*; **b. nitrate,** sous-nitrate *m*. **3.** *s.pl.* **basics,** choses essentielles; éléments *mpl*.

basically ['beisikli], *adv.* fondamentalement; à la base; **b. she is good, she is b. good, but . . .,** au fond c'est une bonne fille, mais . . .

basicity [bei'sisiti], *s. Ch. Metall:* basicité *f*.

basicranial [bæsi'kreiniəl], *a. Anat:* à la base du crâne.

Basidiomycetes [bæ'sidioumai'siːtiːz], *s.pl. Fung:* basidiomycètes *m*.

basidiospore [bː'sidiouspɔːr], *s. Fung:* basidiospore *f*.

basidiosporous [bæsidiou'spɔːrəs], *a. Fung:*

basidiosporé.

basidium [bæ'sidiəm], *s. Fung:* baside *m.*

basification [beisifi'keiʃ(ə)n], *s. Ch:* basification *f.*

basifixed ['beisifikst], *a. Bot:* basifixe.

basifugal [bæsi'fju:gl], *a. Bot:* basifuge.

basify ['beisifai], *v.tr. Ch:* rendre basique.

basigamous [bei'sigəməs], *a. Bot:* basigame.

basihyal ['beisi'hai(ə)l], *a. Anat: etc:* basihyal.

basil[1] ['bæzl], *s. Bot:* basilic *m*; **common, sweet, b.,** basilic commun; **bush, lesser, b.,** basilic noir, à petites feuilles.

basil[2], *s. Leath:* basane *f.*

Basil[3], *Pr.n.m.* Basile; *Ecc.Hist:* **St. B. the Great,** saint Basile le Grand.

basil[4], *s.* = BEZEL.

basilar ['bæzilər], *a. Anat: Bot:* (artère *f*, etc.) basilaire; **b. membrane,** membrane *f* basilaire.

Basilian [bə'ziliən], *a. Ecc:* Basilien, -ienne ((i) de la règle de saint Basile; (ii) de l'ordre de Saint-Basile).

basilic [bə'zilik], *a. Anat:* (veine *f*) basilique.

basilica [bə'silikə, -'zi-], *s. Ecc.Arch:* basilique *f.*

basilical [bə'silikl, -'zi-], **basilican** [bə'silik(ə)n, -zi-], *a.* basilical, -aux.

basilicon [bə'zilikən], *s. A:* onguent souverain; basilicon *m,* basilicum *m.*

basilisk ['bæzilisk], *s. Myth: Rept:* basilic *m.*

basin ['beisn], *s.* **1.** (*a*) bassin *m*; (*for soup, etc.*) écuelle *f*, bol *m*; (*for milk*) jatte *f*; **sugar b.,** sucrier *m*; **b. of a pair of scales,** plateau *m* d'une balance; **barber's b.,** plat *m* à barbe; **b. of a fountain,** vasque *f*, coupe *f*, d'une fontaine; (*b*) (*for washing up, etc.*) bassine *f*; cuvette *f*; **(wash) b.,** lavabo *m*; (*c*) *Metall:* **pouring b.,** bassin de coulée. **2.** *Geol: Geog:* (*a*) bassin; cuvette; **b. of deposition,** bassin sédimentaire; **fault b.,** bassin de faille; **inland drainage b.,** bassin fermé; (*b*) **(river) b.,** bassin (hydrographique); **the Paris B.,** le Bassin parisien; **catchment b.,** bassin de réception, bassin versant; (*c*) **coal b.,** bassin houiller; **the Saar B.,** le bassin de la Sarre; **b.-and-range landscape,** série *f* de horsts séparés par des bassins de faille. **3.** (*a*) *Geog:* port naturel; rade fermée; (*b*) *Nau:* bassin; **outer b.,** avant-bassin *m,* avant-port *m*; **docking b.,** bassin de desserte; **careening b.,** bassin de carénage; **tidal b.,** bassin à flot, darse *f*; (*c*) (*in canal, river*) garage *m*; **dry b.,** garage à sec; **turning b.,** bassin d'évitage. **4.** *Bot:* **Venus's b.,** cardère *f* sauvage; chardon *m* à foulon; cabaret *m* des oiseaux; bain *m* de Vénus.

basinerved ['bæsi'nə:vd], *a. Bot:* basinerve.

bas(i)net ['bæs(i)net], *s. Arm:* bassinet *m*; heaume *m* en calotte.

basinful ['beis(ə)nful], *s.* **1.** plein bol, bolée *f*, écuellée *f* (de soupe, etc.); bolée *f* (de vin). **2.** pleine cuvette (d'eau). **3.** *P:* **to have had a b.,** en avoir marre; en avoir tout son saoul; en avoir ras le bol.

basining [beisəniŋ], *s. Geol:* affaissement *m* (en cuvette).

basioccipital ['bæsiɔk'sipitl], *s. Anat:* (os) *m* basioccipital, -aux.

basion ['bæsiən], *s. Anat:* basion *m.*

basipetal [bæ'sipetl], *a. Bot:* basipète.

basiphilic [bæ'sifilik], *a. Physiol:* basophile.

basiphilia [bæsi'filiə], *s. Med:* basophilie *f.*

basipodite [bæ'sipoudait], *s. Crust:* basipodite *m.*

basis, *pl.* **bases** ['beisis, -i:z], *s.* **1.** base *f* (de négociations, etc.); fondement *m* (d'une opinion, etc.); **to take a principle as a b.,** se baser, se fonder, sur un principe; **b. of a tax,** assiette *f* d'un impôt; **on the b. of . . .,** (en) prenant pour base . . .; sur la base, les bases, de . . .. **2. b. of support, of equilibrium,** base, trapèze *m,* polygone *m,* de sustentation. **3.** matrice *f* de base. **4.** piédestal *m.*

bask [bɑ:sk], *v.i.* (*a*) **to b. in the sun,** se chauffer (au soleil); prendre le soleil; *F:* faire le lézard, lézarder; **to b. in s.o.'s favour,** jouir de la faveur de qn; (*b*) **basking shark,** pèlerin *m.*

basket ['bɑ:skit], *s.* **1.** (*a*) (*without a handle*) corbeille *f*; (*with a handle*) panier *m*; (*carried in front*) éventaire *m*; (*carried on the back*) hotte *f*; (*for coal, etc.*) banne *f*, manne *f*; (*small*) banneau *m,* bannette *f*; (*plaited shopping basket*) cabas *m*; couffin *m*; *Sp:* (*basketball*) panier; **(vegetable) b.,** calais *m*; **oyster b.,** cloyère *f*; **b. of game,** bourriche *f* de gibier; **laundry b.,** corbeille à linge; **linen b.,** panier à linge; **sink b.,** passoire *f* de coin d'évier; **waste paper b.,** corbeille *f* à papier(s); **picnic b.,** (i) panier; (ii) mallette *f*, de pique-nique; *Rail:* **luncheon b.,** panier déjeuner; *F:* **bread b.,** estomac *m*; *Com:* **display b.,** maniveau *m* (pour fruits, etc.); *Typew:* **type b.,** corbeille à caractères; *Metall:* **ore b.,** conge *m*; *F: A:* **to be left in the b.,** rester au fond du panier; ne pas être choisi, invité; **b. handle,** anse *f* de panier; *Arch:* **b.-handle arch,** arc *m* en anse de panier; (*b*) *F:* (= BASTARD) **(you) silly b.!** espèce d'idiot! (*c*) *Bot:* **b. of gold,** corbeille d'argent. **2.** *attrib.* (*a*) **b. making,** vannerie *f*; **b. maker,** vannier *m*; *Needlew:* **b. stitch,** point *m* de vannerie; (*b*) *Furn: etc:* en rotin, en osier; (*c*) *Anat:* **b. cell,** cellule *f* en panier; (*d*) (*of sword*) **b. hilt,** (garde *f* en) coquille *f*. **3.** *Ent:* **pollen b. (of bee),** corbeille (d'abeille). **4.** *A:* siège extérieur (à l'arrière d'une diligence).

basketball ['bɑ:skitbɔ:l], *s. Games:* basket-ball *m, F:* basket *m*; **b. player,** basket(t)eur, -euse.

basketeer [bɑ:ski'tiər], *s. Sp:* basket(t)eur, -euse.

basket fern ['bɑ:skitfə:n], *s. Bot:* (*a*) dryopteris *m*; (*b*) nephrolepsis *m.*

basketful ['bɑ:skitful], *s.* plein panier; panerée *f.*

basketry ['bɑ:skitri], *s.* vannerie *f.*

basketwork ['bɑ:skitwə:k], *s.* **1.** vannerie *f.* **2.** *Const: etc:* clayonnage *m*; entrelacement *m.*

Basle [bɑ:l], *Pr.n. Geog:* Bâle *f.*

Basommatophora [bæsɔmæt'ə'fɔ:rə], *s.pl. Moll:* basommatophores *m.*

bason ['beisn], *v.tr. Tex:* bastir (du feutre).

basoning ['beisəniŋ], *s. Tex:* bastissage *m.*

basophile ['bæsoufil], *a.,* **basophilic** [bæ'sɔfilik], *a. Physiol:* basophile.

basophilia [bæsou'filiə], *s. Med:* basophilie *f.*

Basque [bæsk, bɑ:sk]. **1.** (*a*) *a. Ethn:* basque; (*b*) *s. Ethn:* Basque *mf*; (*c*) *s. Ling:* basque *m.* **2.** *s. Cost:* basque *f.*

bas-relief ['bæsrili:f, 'bɑ:rəli'ef], *s.* bas-relief *m, pl.* bas-reliefs.

bass[1] [bæs], *s. Ich:* **1.** (*a*) perche commune; (*b*) **green b.,** perche-truite *f, pl.* perches-truites; **sea b.,** serran *m.* **2.** bar *m*; **striped b.,** bar rayé.

bass[2] [bæs], *s.* **1.** (*a*) *Bot:* liber *m*; (*b*) tille *f*, filasse *f*; **African b.,** raphia *m.* **2.** (*a*) **b. (mat),** paillasson *m* en fibre, en tille, en écorce de tilleul, etc.; **b. rope,** bastin *m*; (*b*) (*basket*) **(workman's) b.,** cabas *m.* **3.** *Bot: Com:* tilleul *m* d'Amérique.

bass[3] [beis], *a. & s. Mus:* basse *f.* **1.** (*a*) **b. voice,** voix *f* de basse; **singing b.,** basse chantante, récitante; **deep b.,** basse profonde; basse-contre *f, pl.* basses-contre; (*b*) (*in brass bands*) **E-flat b., B-flat b.,** contrebasse *f* en mi bémol, en si bémol; (*of violin, etc.*) **b. bar,** barre *f* d'harmonie, ressort *m*; (*c*) **b. tones,** sons *m* graves; (*d*) *s.* **this singer is a b.,** ce chanteur est une basse. **2. figured b.,** basse chiffrée, figurée, continue.

bass-baritone ['beis'bæritoun], *s. Mus:* basse *f* chantante.

basset[1] ['bæsit], *s.* basset-hound *m.*

basset[2], *s. Geol:* affleurement *m* (d'un filon, d'une couche).

basset[3], *v.i. Geol:* affleurer.

basset[4], *s. Cards:* bassette *f.*

basset horn ['bæsithɔ:n], *s. Mus:* cor *m* de basset.

bassetite ['bæsitait], *s. Miner:* bassetite *f.*

bassinet(te) [bæsi'net], *s.* **1.** berceau *m*; bercelonnette *f*, moïse *m.* **2.** voiture *f* d'enfant.

bassist ['bæsist], *s. Mus:* bassiste *m.*

bassoon [bə'su:n], *s. Mus:* **1.** basson *m*; **double b.,** contrebasson *m.* **2.** (*organ stop*) jeu *m* de basson.

bassoonist [bə'su:nist], *s. Mus:* basson *m,* bassoniste *m.*

basso-profondo, -profundo ['bæsouprə'fʌndou], *s.* (voix *f* de) basse profonde.

basswood ['bæswud], *s. Bot: Com:* tilleul *m* (d'Amérique); bois blanc, bois de tilleul.

bast [bæst], *s.* = BASS[2] 1.

bastard ['bæstəd]. **1.** *a. & s.* bâtard, -arde; *Jur:* enfant naturel, -elle; *Her: F:* **b. bar,** barre *f* de bâtardise. **2.** *a.* faux, fausse; corrompu; bâtard; **b. sugar,** (sucre) bâtard *m*; **b. file,** lime bâtarde; (*of paper, book, etc.*) **b. size,** format bâtard; *Bookb:* **b. leather backing,** reliure *f* à dos brisé; *Typ:* **b. title,** faux titre; **b. hand,** (écriture) bâtarde; *Orn:* **b. wing,** alule *f*; **a b. dialect,** un dialecte corrompu. **3.** *s. P:* (*also* ['bɑ:stəd]) salaud, salope; **you b.!** espèce de salaud! **you silly b.!** espèce d'idiot! **that's a b.,** ça c'est drôlement con; **hello, you old b.!** bonjour, mon vieux!

bastard-cut ['bæstəd'kʌt], *a. Woodw: etc:* à taille bâtarde.

bastardism ['bæstədizm], *s.* bâtardise *f.*

bastardization [bæstədai'zeiʃ(ə)n], *s.* **1.** action *f* de déclarer bâtard. **2.** abâtardissement *m.*

bastardize ['bæstədaiz], *v.tr.* **1.** déclarer (un enfant) bâtard, illégitime. **2.** abâtardir.

bastardizing ['bæstədaiziŋ], *s. Jur:* **b. of issue,** désaveu *m* de paternité.

bastardy ['bæstədi], *s.* bâtardise *f*; *Jur:* **b. case,** action *f* en désaveu de paternité; **b. order,** ordre *m* au père putatif d'avoir à fournir aux besoins de l'enfant.

baste[1] [beist], *v.tr. Needlew:* bâtir, faufiler, baguer (un corsage, etc.); **to b. on a lining,** glacer une doublure.

baste[2], *v.tr.* **1.** *Cu:* arroser (de sa graisse, de son jus) (un rôti, une volaille). **2.** *F: O:* bâtonner (qn).

bastille ['bæs'ti:l], *s.* **1.** *Fort:* bastille *f.* **2.** *Hist:* **the Bastille,** la Bastille; **Bastille Day,** le quatorze juillet.

bastinado[1] [bæsti'nɑ:dou], *s.* bastonnade *f.*

bastinado[2], *v.tr.* donner la bastonnade à (qn).

basting[1] ['beistiŋ], *s. Needlew:* bâti *m,* faufilure *f*; glacis *m* (de doublure); **b. thread,** faufil *m,* bâti.

basting[2], *s.* **1.** arrosement *m,* arrosage *m* (d'un rôti); **b. ladle, spoon,** louche *f.* **2.** *F: O:* bastonnade *f*; rossée *f.*

bastion ['bæstiən], *s. Fort:* bastion *m*; **half-b., demi-b.,** demi-bastion *m, pl.* demi-bastions.

bastioned ['bæstiənd], *a.* bastionné, embastionné.

bastite ['bæstait], *s. Miner:* bastite *f.*

bastnasite ['bæstnəsait], *s. Miner:* bastnaésite *f.*

basto ['bæstou], *s. Cards:* baste *m* (as de trèfle au jeu de l'hombre, du quadrille).

Basuto [bə'su:tou], *s. Ethn:* Bassouto *mf,* Sotho *mf.*

Basutoland [bə'su:toulænd], *Pr.n. Hist:* Basutoland *m.*

bat[1] [bæt], *s.* (*a*) *Z:* chauve-souris *f, pl.* chauves-souris; **bulldog b., mastiff b.,** molosse *m*; **disc-wing(ed) b.,** thyroptère *m*; **Daubenton's b.,** vespertilion *m* de Daubenton; **horse-shoe b.,** rhinolophe *m*; **South American leaf-nosed b.,** rhinophylle *m*; **mouse-tailed b.,** rhinopome *m*; **the large fruit bats,** les mégachiroptères *mpl*; **the insectivorous bats,** les microchiroptères *mpl*; **the long-fingered bats,** les miniopteres *mpl*; **the bulldog, free-tailed, bats,** les molossidés *mpl*; **long-eared b.,** oreillard *m*; *F:* **he went down the road like a b. out of hell,** il a descendu la rue comme un bolide; **to have bats in the belfry,** avoir une araignée au plafond; être toqué; *F:* **he's bats,** il est cinglé; (*b*) *P: A:* prostituée *f*; (*c*) *P:* **old b.,** vieille bique.

bat[2], *s.* **1.** batte *f* (de cricket, de base-ball, etc.); *Cr:* **to carry one's b.,** rester au guichet jusqu'à la fin de la tournée; **he's a good b.,** il manie bien la batte; **to do sth. off one's own b.,** faire qch. de sa propre initiative, de son (propre) chef, par ses propres moyens; prendre sur soi de faire qch. **2.** raquette *f* (de ping-pong); **sponge b.,** raquette mousse; battoir (de blanchisseuse); tapette *f* (pour enfoncer les bouchons). **3. (Harlequin's) b.,** batte. **4.** = BRICKBAT. **5.** *Furn: etc:* ouate *f* en feuille.

bat[3], *v.i.* **(batted; batting)** manier la batte (au cricket, au base-ball); *Cr:* être au guichet.

bat[4], *s. F:* **1.** pas *m,* allure *f*; **he went off at a good b.,** il est parti à toute allure, en quatrième vitesse. **2.** fête *f*, noce *f*, bombe *f.*

bat[5], *v.* **1.** *v.tr.* **to b. the eyes,** battre des paupières; **he didn't b. an eyelid, an eyelash,** (i) il n'a pas sourcillé, tiqué; (ii) il n'a pas fermé l'œil de la nuit. **2.** *v.i. F:* **to b. along,** filer (à toute vitesse); **to b. round,** faire la bombe, la noce, d'un cabaret à l'autre.

bat[6], *s.* (*in India*) langage *m*; *A:* **to sling the b.,** parler la langue des indigènes.

batara [bə'tɑ:rə], *s. Orn:* batara *m.*

batardeau [bæ'tɑ:dou], *s. Fort: Const:* bâtardeau *m.*

batata [bə'tɑ:tə], *s. Hort:* patate *f.*

Batavi [bə'teivai], *s.pl. A.Hist:* les Bataves *m.*

batch[1] [bætʃ], *s.* **1.** fournée *f* (de pain); **b. of prisoners, of wounded,** fournée de prisonniers, arrivage *m* de blessés; **a whole b. of letters,** tout un tas, tout un paquet, de lettres. **2.** lot *m* (de marchandises, etc.); *Cmptr:* lot (de données). **3.** gâchée *f* (de ciment, de béton); mélange *m* (de matières premières pour la fabrication du verre).

batch[2], *v.tr.* **1.** *Ind: Tchn:* préparer un mélange (de matières premières) en vue d'une fabrication, d'une cuvée (de vin, de bière), d'une coulée (de béton, de verre), d'une gâchée (de mortier); (*b*) faire une cuvée (de vin, de bière), une coulée (de béton, de verre), une gâchée (de mortier). **2.** doser (un mélange, les matières premières); *Civ.E:* mesurer, doser (les agrégats du béton).

batch[3], *v.i. & tr. F:* **to b. (it),** vivre en célibataire.

batched [bætʃt], *a.* **b. consignment, dispatch,** envoi groupé.

batcher ['bætʃər], *s. F: esp. Austr:* homme, femme, qui vit en célibataire.

batching, *a.* **1. b. plant,** usine *f* de dosage des agrégats du béton (sur un chantier); **b. process,** pesage *m* automatique par charges dosées. **2.** *Cmptr:* (*a*) groupement *m*; (*b*) blocage *m.*

batchy ['bætʃi], *a. P: O:* toqué, cinglé.

bate[1] [beit], *v.tr.* (*a*) *A:* réduire, diminuer, retrancher; **he would not b. a shilling,** il n'en rabattrait pas d'un shilling; **he won't b. a jot of his claims,** il ne veut rien rabattre de ses prétentions; (*b*) **to speak with bated breath,** parler en baissant la voix, à voix basse, dans un souffle.

bate[2], *s. Leath:* confit *m.*

bate[3], *v.tr. Leath:* mettre en confit (les peaux).

bate[4], *s. P:* **to be in an awful b.,** être fou, folle, de colère.

batea [bə'teiə], *s. Min:* (*gold*) sébile *f*, auge *f.*

bateau ['bætou]. **1.** *s. NAm:* bateau *m* (à fond plat). **2.** *attrib. Dressm:* **b. décolletage, b. (neck)line,** décolleté *m* bateau.

batfowl ['bætfaul], *v.tr.* capturer les oiseaux la nuit.

batfowling ['bætfauliŋ], *s.* capture *f* nocturne des oiseaux.

bath[1], *pl.* **baths** [bɑ:θ, bɑ:ðz], *s.* **1.** (*a*) bain *m*; **cold b.,** bain froid; **to take, have, a b.,** prendre un bain, se baigner; **to give a child a b.,** baigner un enfant; **to give a patient a blanket b.,** laver un malade au lit; **b. heater,** chauffe-bain *m, pl.* chauffe-bains; **b. salts,** sels *m* de bain; **b. towel,** serviette *f* de bain; **b. wrap,** peignoir *m;* sortie *f,* de bain; **public baths,** (i) bains publics; établissement *m* de bains; (ii) (*swimming*) piscine *f*; **to go to the baths,** (i) aller à la piscine; (ii) aller aux bains; **Turkish b.,** bain turc, bain maure, bain de vapeur; **Turkish baths,** hammam *m,* bains turcs; **vapour b.,** (i) *Med:* bain de vapeur; (ii) étuve *f* humide (de hammam); *Min:* **pithead baths,** lavabo *m*; **the Order of the Bath,** l'Ordre *m* du Bain; **Knight Commander, Companion, of the Bath,** Chevalier Commandeur, Compagnon, de l'Ordre du Bain; (*b*) **he was in a b. of perspiration,** il était en sueur, baigné de sueur. **2.** (*a*) baignoire *f*; **hip-b., sitz b.,** bain de siège, demi-bain *m, pl.* demi-bains; (*b*) *Med:* **bed b.,** bassin *m* pour toilette féminine; (*c*) *Phot: etc:* cuvette *f.* **3.** (*liquid*) **acid, alkaline, b.,** bain acide, alcalin; *Ch:* **copper b.,** bain de cuivrage; *Metalw:* **hardening b.,** bain de trempe; **tempering b., reheating b.,** bain de revenu; *Phot:* **alum b., hardening b.,** bain aluné; bain d'alunage; *Dy:* **white b.,** bain d'huile; *Phot:* **fixing b.,** bain de fixage, fixateur *m*; **toning b.,** bain de virage, de chlorure; **toning and fixing b.,** (bain) viro-fixateur *m*; *Phot: etc:* **stop b.,** bain d'arrêt, bain acide pour arrêt (du développement); *Ch: Med:* **sand b.,** bain de sable; *Metalw:* (*for tinning iron*) **tin b.,** tain *m*; *Ch: Cu:* **water b.,** bain-marie *m, pl.* bains-marie.

bath[2], **1.** *v.tr.* baigner, donner un bain à (qn). **2.** *v.i.* prendre un bain.

Bath[3], *Pr.n. Geog:* Bath; **B. stone,** oolithe bathonienne; **B. chair,** voiture *f* de promenade, de malade; *Cu:* **B. chap,** béquet *m*; **B. Oliver,** biscuit digestif; *A:* **B. brick,** brique anglaise (à nettoyer); *F: A:* **go to B.!** va-t'en au diable! va te promener!

bath asparagus ['bɑ:θə'spærəgəs], *s. Bot: Cu:* aspergettes *fpl.*

bathe[1] [beið], *s.* bain *m* (de rivière, de mer); baignade *f*; **to go for a b.,** (aller) se baigner; *F:* faire trempette.

bathe[2], **1.** *v.tr.* (*a*) baigner; **to b. one's face,** se baigner la figure; **face bathed in tears,** visage arrosé, baigné, inondé, de larmes, de pleurs; **bathed in perspiration,** trempé de sueur, en nage; **town bathed in light,** ville inondée, baignée, de lumière; (*b*) *U.S:* baigner (un enfant); (*c*) laver, lotionner, bassiner (une plaie). **2.** *v.i.* (*a*) se baigner, prendre un bain (de mer, de rivière); (*b*) *U.S:* prendre un bain (dans la baignoire).

bather ['beiðər], *s.* baigneur, -euse.

bathers ['beiðəz], *s.pl. F: Austr:* maillot *m* de bain.

bathetic [bæ'θetik], *a. Lit:* qui offre un contraste ridicule avec la pensée qui précède.

bath-house ['bɑ:θhaus], *s.* (établissement *m* de) bains *mpl.*

bathing ['beiðiŋ], *s.* (*a*) bains *mpl* de mer, baignades *fpl*; **sea b.,** bains de mer; **the b. here is good,** on se baigne ici avec plaisir; **b. here is safe,** il n'y a pas de danger à se baigner ici; la plage est sûre; **b. fatalities,** baignades tragiques, mortelles; **b. establishment,** établissement *m* de bains; bains publics; **b. place,** baignade; **b. resort,** station *f* balnéaire, plage *f*; **b. season,** saison *f* des bains; **b. attendant,** maître-nageur *m, pl.* maîtres-nageurs; *A:* **b. attendant, b. man, woman,** baigneur, -euse; **b. hut, cabin,** cabine *f* de bains; *A:* **b. machine,** cabine (de bains) roulante; **b. costume, suit,** costume *m,* maillot *m,* de bain; **b. trunks,** *A:* **b. drawers,** caleçon *m* de bain; **b. cap,** bonnet *m* de bain; **b. shoes,** sandales *f* de bain, de plage; **b. wrap,** peignoir *m* de bain; (*b*) bassinage *m,* lotion *f* (d'une plaie, etc.); (*c*) baignage *m* (du chanvre, etc.).

bathmat ['bɑ:θmæt], *s.* descente *f,* tapis *m,* de bain.

bathmism ['bæθmizm], *s. Biol:* bathmisme *m.*

batho- ['bæθou], *pref.* batho-.

bathochrome ['bæθoukroum], *s. & a. Ph: Ch:* bathochrome (*m*).

batholith ['bæθəliθ], *s. Geol:* batholit(h)e *m.*

bathometer [bə'θɔmitər], *s. Oc:* bathomètre *m,* bathymètre *m.*

Bathonian [bɑ:'θounian], *s. & a. Geol:* bathonien (*m*).

bathophobia [bæθou'foubiə], *s. Psy:* acrophobie *f.*

bathorse ['bæthɔ:s], *s. Mil: A:* cheval *m* de bât (utilisé pour le transport des bagages d'un officier).

bathos ['beiθɔs], *s.* (*a*) descente *f* ridicule du sublime au terre à terre dans un style élevé; (*b*) sentimentalité excessive.

bathrobe ['bɑ:θroub], *s.* peignoir *m* de bain; sortie *f* de bain.

bathroom ['bɑ:θru:m], *s.* salle *f* de bain(s); **b. unit,** bloc-bain *m, pl.* blocs-bains.

Bathsheba ['bæθʃibə, bæθ'ʃi:bə], *Pr.n.f.* Bethsabée.

bathtub ['bɑ:θtʌb], *s.* baignoire *f*; tub *m.*

bathwater ['bɑ:θw:ɔtər], *s.* **to throw the baby out with the b.,** se montrer plus zélé que prudent; faire mal plutôt que bien par excès de zèle.

bathy- ['bæθi], *pref.* bathy-.

bathyal [bə'θiəl], *a. Oc:* bathyal.

bathybial [bə'θibiəl], **bathybic** [bə'θibik], *a.* bathydrique.

bathybius [bə'θibiəs], *s. Nat.Hist:* bathybius *m.*

Bathyergidae [bæθi:'jə:dʒidi:], *s.pl. Z:* bathyergidés *mpl.*

bathymeter ['bæθimi:tər], *s.* bathymètre *m.*

bathymetric(al) [bæθi'metrik(l)], *a. Oc:* bathymétrique.

bathymetry [bə'θimitri], *s. Oc:* bathymétrie *f.*

bathypelagic [bæθipe'lædʒik], *a. Oc:* bathypélagique.

bathyplankton [bæθi'plæŋktən], *s.* bathyplancton *m.*

bathyscaph(e) ['bæθiskæf], *s.* bathyscaphe *m.*

bathysmal [bæ'θizml], *a. Oc:* abyssal.

bathysphere ['bæθisfiər], *s.* bathysphère *f.*

bathythermograph [bæθi'θə:məgræf], *s. Oc:* bathythermographe *m.*

batik ['bætik], *s.* batik *m*; **to ornament with b.,** batiker.

bating ['beitiŋ], *s.* chipage *m* (des peaux).

batiste [bæ'ti:st], *s. Tex:* batiste *f.*

batman, *pl* **-men** ['bætmən], *s. Mil: O:* (soldat) ordonnance *m or f.*

Batoidei [bə'tɔidiai], *s.pl. Ich:* batoïdes *m.*

batology [bə'tɔlədʒi], *s. Bot:* l'étude *f* des ronces.

baton ['bætən], *s.* **1.** (*a*) bâton *m*; *Mus:* baguette *f* (de tambour); **conductor's b.,** baguette, bâton, de chef d'orchestre; **field-marshal's b.,** bâton de maréchal; (*b*) *Sp:* (*in relay race*) témoin *m.* **2.** bâton (d'agent de police); matraque *f*; casse-tête *m inv.* **3.** *Her:* bâton; **b. sinister,** bâton péri, en barre.

Batrachia [bə'treikiə], *s.pl. Z:* batraciens *m.*

batrachian [bə'treikiən], *a. & s. Z:* batracien (*m*).

batsman, *pl.* **-men** ['bætsmən], *s.m. Cr:* batteur.

battalion [bə'tæljən], *s.* (*a*) (*infantry, armour, engineers*); bataillon *m*; **independent, separate, b.,** bataillon format corps; **b. commander,** commandant *m* de bataillon; **training b.,** bataillon d'instruction; **tank b., armoured b.,** bataillon de chars; **reconnaissance b.,** bataillon de reconnaissance; **labour b.,** bataillon de travailleurs auxiliaires; **pioneer b.,** bataillon de pionniers; **pontoon b.,** bataillon de pontonniers, d'équipage de pont; **b. group,** sous-groupement *m,* groupement *m* tactique à l'échelon bataillon; (*b*) *Artil: U.S:* groupe *m* (d'artillerie); **there are three batteries in the 280 mm gun b.,** il y a trois batteries dans le groupe de 280; (*c*) **missile b.,** groupe d'engins.

battels ['bætlz], *s.pl.* (*Oxford University*) **1.** note *f* des dépenses de bouche. **2.** mémoire trimestriel de tous les frais universitaires.

batten[1] ['bætn], *s.* **1.** (*a*) *Carp: etc:* (i) (*bead or moulding*) couvre-joint *m, pl.* couvre-joints; baguette *f*; nervure *f*; listel *m*; (ii) latte *f,* liteau *m*; tasseau *m* (de tablette); **roof b.,** volige *f*; latte volige; **half-round b.,** baguette demi-ronde; (*b*) *Nau:* barre *f,* latte, tringle *f*; **b. door,** porte *f* à traverses; **cargo battens,** vaigrage *m* à claire-voie; **rigging b.,** allumette *f*; étrésillon *m*; (*c*) *Ropem:* **épée** *f*; (*d*) (*box making*) anglaise *f.* **2.** *Th:* **the battens,** les herses *f* (d'éclairage). **3.** *Carp: Const:* planche *f* (de parquet).

batten[2], *v.tr.* **1.** (*a*) *Carp:* latter, voliger; (*b*) *Nau:* **to b. down the hatches,** (i) mettre les panneaux en place; (ii) condamner les panneaux, les descentes; assujettir, coincer, les panneaux. **2.** *Const:* planchéier (un parquet).

batten[3], *s. Tex:* battant *m,* chasse *f* (d'un métier à soie); **spring b.,** battant à claquette.

batten[4], *v.i. Lit:* s'engraisser, se bourrer, se repaître (**on,** de), **to b. on s.o.,** mettre qn en coupe réglée; être comme une sangsue, comme une tique, après qn; **to b. on others,** s'enrichir aux dépens des autres; s'engraisser des misères d'autrui.

battening ['bæt(ə)niŋ], *s. Carp:* voligeage *m.*

batter[1] ['bætər], *s. Cr:* batteur *m.*

batter[2], *s.* **1.** *Cu:* pâte *f* lisse; pâte à frire. **2.** *Typ:* (*a*) écrasement *m* (des caractères); (*b*) caractère endommagé, écrasé; caractère défectif; tête *f* de clou.

batter[3], *v.*

I. *v.tr.* (*a*) battre; *Artil:* battre en brèche, canonner (une ville); (*b*) *Typ:* endommager (des caractères); (*c*) bossuer (une casserole, un chapeau, etc.).

II. (*compound verbs*)

1. batter about, *v.tr.* maltraiter (qn); rouer (qn) de coups; cogner sur (qn); endommager (qch.); mettre (qch.) en mauvais état.

2. batter down, *v.tr.* abattre, démolir (qch.); battre (un mur) en brèche.

3. batter in, *v.tr.* enfoncer (une porte, etc.); **the skull of the victim was battered in,** la victime a eu le crâne défoncé.

batter[4], *s. Civ.E:* (*a*) fruit *m,* recoupement *m,* reculement *m* (d'un mur, etc.); **inner b.,** contre-fruit *m, pl.* contre-fruits; (*b*) **b. of an embankment,** talus *m,* angle *m* de glissement, d'un remblai.

batter[5]. **1.** *v.tr. Civ.E:* donner du fruit à (une muraille); taluter (un remblai). **2.** *v.i.* (*a*) (*of wall*) avoir du fruit; (*b*) (*of revetment, etc.*) aller en talus.

batter[6], *s. P:* **to go on the b.,** tirer une bordée.

battered[1] ['bætəd], *a.* (*a*) délabré, bossué; **old b. hat,** vieux chapeau cabossé; **b. furniture,** mobilier délabré; **b. teapot,** théière toute bosselée; (*b*) **b. face,** visage meurtri; *Med:* **b. baby, infant,** enfant maltraité, meurtri.

battered[2], *a. Civ.E:* (mur, etc.) recoupé, qui a du fruit.

battering ['bæt(ə)riŋ], *s.* action *f* de battre en brèche, de démolir; *Artil:* **b. train,** équipage *m* de siège; **b. charge,** charge pleine; *A.Mil:* **b. ram,** bélier *m.*

battery ['bæt(ə)ri], *s.* **1.** *Jur:* (*a*) rixe *f*; (*b*) voie *f* de fait; **assault and b.,** (menaces *fpl* et) voies de fait; coups *mpl* et blessures *fpl.* **2.** (*a*) *Artil:* groupe *m* (d'artillerie); *NAm: A:* batterie *f*; *NAm:* **b. executive,** lieutenant *m* de tir; (*b*) *Artil:* **floating b.,** batterie flottante; **trench mortar b.,** batterie de (mortiers de) tranchée; **breaching b.,** batterie de brèche; **coast b.,** batterie de côte; **half-b.,** demi-batterie *f*; **field b.,** batterie de campagne; **masked b.,** batterie masquée; **b. fire,** tir *m* par salves; *Navy:* **the b. deck,** la batterie. **3.** (*a*) batterie (de fours à coke, de chaudières, de bouteilles de Leyde, etc.); (*b*) *Phot:* **b. of lenses,** trousse *f* d'objectifs; (*c*) *El:* pile *f,* batterie; **to set up a b.,** monter une pile; **dry b.,** (batterie de) piles sèches; *Tp:* **line b.,** pile de ligne; (*d*) *El:* **(storage) b.,** accumulateur *m, F:* accu *m*; pile secondaire; batterie d'accumulateurs, *F:* boîte *f* d'accus; **pasted-plate b.,** accu à oxydes rapportés; accu à pastilles; **floating b., balancing b.,** batterie-tampon *f, pl* batteries-tampons; **thermo-electric b.,** colonne *f* thermo-électrique; *W.Tel:* **grid b.,** pile de polarisation; **b. set,** poste fonctionnant sur accus, alimenté par batteries; **A b.,** batterie de chauffage; **anode b., B b.,** batterie de plaques, batterie anodique, pile anodique; **C b.,** batterie de grille; **central b.,** batterie centrale; **common b.,** batterie locale; **portable b.,** batterie portable, accumulateur léger; **stationary b.,** batterie fixe, batterie stationnaire; (*e*) *Husb:* éleveuse *f* (à poulets), batterie; **b. hen,** poulet *m* de batterie; (*f*) *Psy:* **b. of tests,** batterie de tests. **4.** *Sp:* (*baseball*) **the b.,** le lanceur et le receveur. **5.** *Civ.E:* exploseur *m.* **6.** (*set*) batterie (de cuisine, etc.).

batting ['bætiŋ], *s.* **1.** *Cr: etc:* maniement *m* de la batte. **2.** *Furn: etc:* ouate *f* en feuille.

battle[1] ['bætl], *s.* bataille *f,* combat *m*; **pitched b.,** bataille rangée; **army drawn up in b. array, in b. formation, in b. order,** armée rangée en bataille; **line of b.,** front *m* de bataille; **order of b.,** *Mil:* ordre de bataille; répartition générale des forces; *Navy:* ordre tactique; *Navy:* **b. fleet,** flotte *f* de ligne, de combat; corps *m* de bataille; **b. position,** position *f* de combat; **b. area,** zone *f* de bataille, d'engagement; **b. practice,** exercices *mpl* de combat; **b. group,** groupement *m* de combat; groupement tactique; **to fight a b.,** livrer une bataille, un combat; **to give, offer, b.,** donner, livrer, bataille; engager le combat; **to refuse b.,** refuser le combat; se dérober; **to win a b.,** gagner une bataille; remporter une victoire; **killed in b.,** tué à l'ennemi, dans la bataille; **b. scarred,** meurtri par la bataille; **b. cry,** cri *m* de guerre; **b. song,** chant *m* de guerre; **b. piece,** (i) *Art:* (tableau *m* de) bataille; (ii) *Lit:* description *f* de combat; *Hist:* **trial by b.,** combat judiciaire; *Lit:* **to do b. for, against, s.o.,** se battre pour, contre, qn; livrer bataille pour qn; livrer bataille à, contre, qn; **to join b. with s.o.,** entrer en lutte avec qn, livrer bataille à qn; **the b. is not to the strong,** la victoire n'est pas aux forts; **youth is half the b.,** il n'est rien de tel que d'être jeune; **that's half the b.,** c'est bataille à moitié gagnée; **the first blow is half the b.,** le premier coup en vaut deux; **to fight s.o.'s battles,** prendre le parti de qn; livrer bataille pour qn; **to fight one's battles over again,** revenir sur, revivre, ses anciens faits d'armes; **to start the b.,** *F.* ouvrir la danse, b. royal, (i) mêlée générale; bagarre *f,* échauffourée *f*; (ii) prise *f* de bec.

battle[2]. **1.** *v.i.* se battre, lutter, rivaliser (**with s.o. for sth.,** avec qn pour qch.); **to b. with, against, public opinion,** combattre l'opinion; se battre, batailler, lutter, contre l'opinion; **to b. with, against, a fire,** combattre un incendie; lutter contre un incendie; **to b. against the wind,** lutter contre le vent; **he was battling for breath,** il faisait effort pour respirer; *with cogn. acc.* **to b. one's way through difficulties, obstacles,** se frayer un chemin à travers les difficultés, les obstacles. **2.** *v.tr. U.S:* combattre (une doctrine, etc.).

battleaxe ['bætlæks], *s.* **1.** *Mil: A:* hache *f* d'armes. **2.** *F:* **what a b.!** quelle virago! quelle mégère!

battle cruiser ['bætlkru:zər], *s. Navy: Hist:* croiseur *m* de combat, de bataille.

battled ['bætld], *a. Her:* crénelé, bastillé.

battledore ['bætldɔ:r], *s.* **1.** *(a) Laund:* battoir *m*; *(b) Bak:* pelle *f* à enfourner. **2.** *Sp:* raquette *f* (de jeu de volant); **to play at b. and shuttlecock,** jouer au volant. **3.** *Nau:* paille *f* de bitte.

battledress ['bætldres], *s. Mil:* tenue *f* de campagne.

battlefield ['bætlfi:ld], *s.* champ *m* de bataille.

battle-horse ['bætlhɔ:s], *s. A:* cheval *m* de bataille.

battlemented ['bætlməntid], *a.* crénelé.

battlements ['bætlmənts], *s.pl. (a) Arch:* créneaux *m*; *(b)* parapet *m*, rempart *m*.

battleplane ['bætlplein], *s. Av: A:* avion *m* de combat, de guerre.

battler ['bætlər], *s. Box:* batailleur *m*, cogneur *m*.

battleship ['bætlʃip], *s. Navy: Hist:* bâtiment *m* de ligne; cuirassé *m*; **first-class b.,** cuirassé d'escadre; **pocket b.,** cuirassé de poche; *Games:* **battleships,** bataille navale; **built like a b.,** solidement construit; *F: (of person)* **she's built like a b.,** c'est une armoire à glace.

battle sight ['bætlsait], *s. Artil:* hausse *f* de combat.

battlewagon ['bætlwæg(ə)n], *s. Mil: etc: F:* char *m*, véhicule blindé.

battleworthiness ['bætl'wə:ðinis], *s.* état de préparation (militaire) en vue de la guerre (défensive ou offensive).

battleworthy ['bætlwə:ði], *a.* militairement fort.

battology [bæ'tɔlədʒi], *s.* battologie *f*.

battue [bæ'tu:], *s.* **1.** *Ven:* battue *f*. **2.** *Fig:* carnage *m*; massacre *m* en masse.

batty ['bæti], *a. F:* toqué, timbré, dingo *inv.*; cinglé.

batwing ['bætwiŋ], *a.* en forme d'aile de chauve-souris; **b. sleeves,** manches *f* kimono; **b. collar,** col cassé; **b. tie,** nœud *m* papillon.

batwoman, *pl.* **-women** ['bætwumən, -wimin], *s.f. Mil:* femme (civile ou militaire) employée comme ordonnance d'officier.

bauble ['bɔ:bl], *s.* **1.** *(trinket)* fanfreluche *f*. **2. jester's b.,** marotte *f*. **3.** *(worthless thing)* babiole *f*, brimborion *m*, bimbelot *m*, colifichet *m*.

baud [bɔ:d], *s. Tg:* baud *m*.

Baudot ['bɔ:dou], *Pr.n. Tg:* **B. code,** code *m* Baudot; **B. system,** système *m* Baudot.

bauera ['bauərə], *s. Bot:* bauère *f*.

bauhinia [bou'hiniə], *s. Bot:* bauhinia *f*.

baulk [bɔ:k], *s. & v.* = BALK.

Baumé ['boumei], *Pr.n. Meteor:* **B. scale,** échelle *f* de Baumé.

baumhauerite [baum'hauərait], *s. Miner:* baumhauérite *f*.

bauxite ['bɔ:ksait], *s. Miner:* bauxite *f*.

bauxitic [bɔ:k'sitik], *a. Geol:* bauxitique.

Bavaria [bə'vɛəriə], *Pr.n. Geog:* Bavière *f*.

Bavarian [bə'vɛəriən]. **1.** *a. Geog:* bavarois; *Bot:* **B. gentian,** gentiane *f* de Bavière; *Cu:* **B. cream,** bavaroise *f*. **2.** *s. Geog:* Bavarois, -oise.

bavin ['bævin], *s.* fagot *m*.

bawbee [bɔ:'bi:], *s.* **1.** *Scot: F:* = sou *m*; **he's careful of the bawbees,** il ménage son argent; il regarde à chaque sou. **2.** *U.S:* bagatelle *f*.

bawd [bɔ:d], *s.f. A: (a)* procureuse, entremetteuse, proxénète, pourvoyeuse; *(b)* propriétaire d'un lupanar; *(c)* prostituée.

bawdily ['bɔ:dili], *adv.* impudiquement; d'une manière obscène.

bawdiness ['bɔ:dinis], *s.* obscénité *f*.

bawdry ['bɔ:dri], *s. A:* **1.** propos orduriers. **2.** paillardise *f*; impudicité *f*.

bawdy ['bɔ:di], *a.* obscène, paillard, impudique; **b. talk,** *s.* **bawdy,** propos orduriers; **b. house,** maison *f* de prostitution.

bawl[1] [bɔ:l], *s.* braillement *m*, beuglement *m*; *P:* gueulement *m*.

bawl[2], *v.tr. & i. (a)* brailler; crier à tue-tête, *F:* beugler; *P:* gueuler **(at s.o.,** contre qn); **to b. out abuse,** brailler, hurler, des injures; **to b. out an order,** gueuler un ordre; *(b)* pleurer bruyamment, brailler; *(c) P:* **to b. s.o. out,** engueuler qn.

bawler ['bɔ:lər], *s.* braillard, -arde; brailleur, -euse; criard, -arde.

bawling[1] ['bɔ:liŋ], *a.* braillard, criard.

bawling[2], *s.* braillement *m*.

bay[1] [bei], *s. Bot: (a)* **sweet b., b. laurel,** laurier commun, laurier-sauce *m*, *pl.* lauriers-sauce, laurier d'Apollon, laurier des poètes; *Cu:* **b. leaf,** feuille *f* de laurier; **b. tree,** laurier *m*; **cherry b.,** laurier-cerise *m*, *pl.* lauriers-cerise(s); laurier amandier; **b. wreath, bays,** couronne *f* de laurier(s); **to carry off the bays,** remporter les lauriers, la couronne du vainqueur; *(b)* **sweet b. (of America), white b.,** arbre *m* de castor.

bay[2], *s. Geog:* **1.** baie *f*; *(if small)* anse *f*; **Hudson B.,** la Baie d'Hudson; **the B. of Biscay,** le golfe de Gascogne. **2.** échancrure *f* (parmi des montagnes). **3.** *U.S:* enclave *f* de prairie (dans les forêts).

bay[3], *s.* **1.** *(a) (of bridge, roof, etc.)* travée *f*; *(b) (of joists)* claire-voie *f*, *pl.* claires-voies. **2.** *(a)* enfoncement *m*; *(space for door, etc.)* baie *f*; *Mil: (in a trench)* niche *f*, évitement *m*; *Av: (in aircraft)* **bomb b.,** ouverture *f* du lance-bombes; *(b) Rail:* quai *m* subsidiaire; quai en cul-de-sac; *(c) Ind:* hall *m* (d'usine, etc.); *Nau: etc:* **sick b.,** infirmerie *f*; *(d)* **parking b.,** place *f* de stationnement (à un parcomètre); **loading b.,** quai *m* de chargement; *(e) attrib.* **b. window,** fenêtre *f* en baie, en saillie; baie; **b. stall,** banquette *f* (dans l'embrasure d'une fenêtre). **3.** *(a) W.Tel: (of registers, selectors, racks)* baie; *(b) Cmptr:* (i) bâti *m*; (ii) armoire *f*; (iii) section *f*.

bay[4], *s.* aboi *m*, aboiement *m* (d'un chien de chasse); **to bring a stag to b.,** mettre un cerf aux abois; forcer, acculer, un cerf; **bringing to b.,** acculement *m*; **to stand at b.,** s'acculer à, contre, qch., lutter en désespéré; *(of wild boar)* tenir le ferme; **to be at b.,** être aux abois, à l'acculer; **to keep, hold, the enemy at b.,** tenir l'ennemi en échec.

bay[5], *v.i. (a) (of hound)* aboyer; donner de la voix; *(b)* **to b. (at) the moon,** hurler, aboyer, à la lune; **to b. at s.o.,** aboyer après qn.

bay[6], *s. Hyd.E:* bief *m*; **head b.,** bief d'amont; **tail b.,** bief, biez *m*, d'aval, de fuite (d'une écluse).

bay[7], *v.tr. Hyd.E:* endiguer.

bay[8], *a. & s.* (cheval) bai *(m)*; **light b.,** bai châtain, bai clair; (cheval) isabelle *(m)*; **dark b.,** bai brun, bai foncé; **red b.,** roux alezan, alezan roux.

bay[9], *s. Ven:* **b. (antler),** sur-andouiller *m*.

bayadere [beiə'diər], *s.* **1.** *(dancing girl)* bayadère *f*. **2.** *Tex:* bayadère.

bayberry ['beibəri], *s. Bot:* **1.** baie *f* de laurier. **2.** piment *m* de la Jamaïque. **3.** *NAm:* cirier *m*; arbre *m* à cire.

Bayer ['baiər], *Pr.n. Metall:* **B. process,** procédé *m* Bayer.

baying ['beiiŋ], *a.* aboiement *m*, clabaudement *m*, clabaudage *m*.

bayonet[1] ['beiənit], *s. Mil:* baïonnette *f*; **to fix bayonets,** mettre (la) baïonnette au canon; **with fixed bayonets,** baïonnette au canon; **to unfix bayonets,** remettre la baïonnette; **b. charge,** charge *f* à la baïonnette; **to hurl back the enemy at the point of the b.,** culbuter l'ennemi à la baïonnette; **b. drill, exercise,** escrime *f* à la baïonnette; **b. assault course,** piste *f* d'assaut à la baïonnette; *Mec.E: etc:* **b. joint,** joint *m* en baïonnette; *El:* **b. holder, socket,** douille *f* à baïonnette (de lampe électrique); **b. cap, base,** culot *m* à baïonnette.

bayonet[2] **(bayoneted)** *(a) v.tr.* percer (qn) d'un coup de baïonnette; **all those who stood their ground were bayoneted,** tous ceux qui ont tenu pied ont été abattus à coups de baïonnette, ont été passés à la baïonnette; *(b) v.i.* manier une baïonnette.

bayou ['baiju:], *s. Geog:* bayou *m*.

bay rum ['bei'rʌm], *s. Toil:* tafia *m* de laurier.

bay salt ['bei'sɔ:lt], *s.* sel gris, sel marin, sel de mer; *Cu:* gros sel.

baza ['bɑ:zə], *s. Orn:* baza *m*, *F:* huppard *m*.

bazaar [bə'zɑ:r], *s.* **1.** *(a)* bazar *m* (oriental); **b. keeper,** mercanti *m*; *(b)* bazar; magasin *m* à bon marché; **cheap b. trade,** bimbeloterie *f*; *A:* **sixpenny b.,** magasin à prix fixe; *A:* boutique *f* à treize sous; *Fin: F:* **b. shares,** valeurs *f* de fantaisie. **2.** vente *f* de charité.

Bazin ['bæzɛ̃], *Pr.n. Med:* **Bazin's disease,** (i) psoriasis *m* interne de la joue; (ii) ulcère *m* scrofuleux de la jambe.

bazooka [bə'zu:kə], *s.* **1.** *Artil:* bazooka *m* lance-roquettes *m. inv.* **2.** *Mus:* bazooka.

bdellium ['deliəm], *s. Bot: etc:* bdellium *m*.

Bdelloidea [de'lɔidiə], *s.pl. Z:* bdelloïdes *mpl*.

Bdellostoma [de'lɔstəmə], *s. Ich:* bdellostome *m*.

be [*stressed* bi:, *unstressed* bi(:)], *v.i. (pr.ind.* **am, art, is,** *pl.* **are**; *past ind.* **was, wast, was,** *pl.* **were**; *pr.sub.* **be**; *past sub.* **were, wert, were**; *p.p.* **being,** *p.p.* **been**; *imp.* **be**; *I am, he is, she is, it is, we are, you are, they are, are frequently shortened into:* **I'm, he's, she's it's, we're, you're, they're**; *is not, are not, was not, were not, into:* **isn't, aren't, wasn't, weren't)** être. **1.** *(copulative) (a)* **Mary is pretty,** Marie est jolie; **the weather was fine,** le temps était beau; **they are short of money,** ils sont à court d'argent; **seeing is believing,** voir c'est croire; **time is money,** le temps, c'est de l'argent; **ten yards is a lot,** dix mètres c'est beaucoup; **yours, his, is a fine house,** c'est une belle maison que la vôtre, que la sienne; **he's a bit odd, is Bob,** c'est un drôle de garçon que Bob; **isn't he lucky?** il a vraiment beaucoup de chance! *P:* **you** *are* **a one!** tu es un drôle de numéro! *P:* **he's one of them,** c'est une tapette; il en est; *(b)* **his father is a doctor,** son père est médecin; **he will be a general some day,** il arrivera à être général; il finira par être général; **he is an Englishman,** il est anglais, c'est un Anglais; **are they English?—yes, they are,** sont-ils anglais?—oui, ils le sont; **not ready yet? it's time you were,** pas encore prêt? il serait temps de l'être, que vous le soyez; **if I were you,** à votre place; si j'étais (que de) vous; **as it is, we must. . .,** les choses étant ainsi, comme il en est, il nous faut . . .; *(c)* **what a practical joker you are!** quel farceur vous faites! **unity is strength,** l'union fait la force; **three and two are five,** trois et deux font cinq; **money isn't everything,** l'argent ne fait pas tout; **it would be as well to. . .,** vous feriez (aussi) bien de . . .; **she has been a mother to me,** elle m'a tenu lieu de mère; elle a été pour moi comme une mère; **"Pat," being the story of an Irish boy,** "Pat," ou l'Histoire d'un petit Irlandais. **2.** *(with adv. or adv.phr.) (a)* **the books are on the table,** les livres sont, se trouvent, sur la table; **she was in her best dress,** elle avait, portait, sa plus belle robe; **he was a long time reaching the shore,** il mit longtemps à gagner le rivage; **what a time you've been!** comme vous avez été longtemps! comme cela vous a pris longtemps! **don't be long,** ne tardez pas (à revenir); **to be in danger,** se trouver en danger; **be here at four o'clock,** soyez, trouvez-vous, ici à quatre heures; **I was at the meeting,** j'ai été, j'ai assisté, à la réunion; **to be on the committee,** être membre, faire partie, du comité; **where, at what page, are we?** où en sommes-nous? **I don't know where I am,** (i) je ne sais pas où je suis; (ii) je ne sais pas à quoi m'en tenir; je suis tout désorienté; je ne sais pas où j'en suis; **where was I?** où en étais-je? **you never know where you are with him,** avec lui on ne sait jamais à quoi s'en tenir, on ne sait jamais de quoi il retourne; **here I am,** me voici; **ah, there you are!** vous voilà donc! **so you are back again,** vous voilà donc de retour; **there are my shoes,** voilà mes souliers; *(b) (of health)* **how are you?** comment allez-vous? comment vous portez-vous? **I am (feeling) better,** je vais mieux, je me trouve mieux; je me sens mieux; *(c) (measure)* **how much is that?** combien cela coûte-t-il? combien cela fait-il? **how far is it to London?** combien y a-t-il d'ici à Londres? **it is a mile from here,** c'est à un mille (d'ici); *(d) (time)* **when is the concert?** quand le concert aura-t-il lieu? **the flower show was last week,** l'exposition horticole a eu lieu la semaine dernière; **Christmas is on a Sunday this year,** Noël tombe un dimanche cette année; **when is your birthday?** quel jour est votre anniversaire? **today is the tenth,** nous sommes (aujourd'hui) le dix (du mois); **tomorrow is Friday,** c'est demain vendredi. **3.** *(a)* **to be** *(=feel)* **cold, afraid, etc.,** avoir froid, peur, etc.; **don't be afraid,** n'ayez pas peur; **to be ashamed of s.o., of sth.,** avoir honte de qn, de qch.; **it is cold,** il fait froid; **to be hungry,** avoir faim, être affamé; **to be right,** avoir raison; **to be wrong,** avoir tort; se tromper; être dans l'erreur; **to be sleepy,** avoir envie de dormir; avoir sommeil; **to be thirsty,** avoir soif; **to be warm,** (i) *(of water, etc.)* être chaud; (ii) *(of pers.)* avoir chaud; **my hands are cold,** j'ai froid aux mains; **how cold your hands are!** comme vous avez les mains froides! *(b)* **to be twenty (years old),** avoir vingt ans, être âgé de vingt ans; **the wall is six foot high,** le mur a six pieds de haut, est haut de six pieds; *(c)* **he was so foolish as to. . .,** il a eu la sottise de . . .. **4.** *(exist, occur, remain) (a)* **to be or not to be,** être ou ne pas être; **God alone is,** Dieu seul est, existe; **the time of iron ships was not yet,** on n'en était pas encore au temps des navires d'acier; **business is not what it was,** les affaires ne sont plus ce qu'elles étaient autrefois; **the greatest genius that ever was,** le plus grand génie qui ait jamais existé, qui fût jamais; **that may be,** cela se peut; **so be it!** ainsi soit-il! **well, so be it!** eh bien, soit! **to see things as they are,** voir les choses comme elles sont; **everything must remain just as it is,** tout doit rester tel quel; **leave my things just as they are,** laissez mes affaires telles quelles; **however that may be,** quoi qu'il en soit; **how is it that. . .?** comment se fait-il que + *sub.*, d'où vient(-il) que . . .? **it is the same with all great authors,** il en est de même de tous les grands auteurs; **let me be!** laissez-moi tranquille! *(b) impers.* **there is, there are,** (i) il y a; **there is a man in the garden,** il y a un homme dans le jardin; **what is there to see?** qu'est-ce qu'il y a à voir? **for there to be life, there must be water,** pour qu'il y ait de la vie il faut qu'il y ait de l'eau; **there will be dancing,** on dansera; **there were a dozen of us,** nous étions une douzaine; **what can there be in this drawer?** qu'est-ce qu'il peut (bien) y avoir dans ce tiroir? **as there were no survivors, the cause of the accident will never be known,** comme il n'y a pas de survivants, on ne saura jamais la cause de l'accident; (ii) *Lit:* (*in a wide, permanent sense*) il est; **there are men on whom fortune always smiles,** il est des hommes à qui tout sourit; (iii) **there was once a princess,** il était une fois une princesse. **5.** (*go or come*) **are you for Bristol?** allez-vous à Bristol? **I have been to see David,** j'ai été voir David; **he had been to inspect the land,** il était allé inspecter le terrain; **I have been to the museum,** j'ai visité le musée; **I have never been to Venice,** je n'ai jamais été à Venise; **I have been into every room,** j'ai visité toutes les pièces; **he was into the room like a flash,** il est entré dans la pièce en coup de foudre; **where have you been?** d'où venez-vous? **where have you been all this time?** d'où sortez-vous? **has anyone been?** est-il venu quelqu'un? **has the post, the milkman, been?** est-ce que le facteur, le laitier, est passé? (*to child*) **have you been today?** es-tu allé aujourd'hui? as-tu fait tes besoins aujourd'hui? *F:* **I've been there!** ça me connaît! *P:* **I've been and dropped the cakes!** voilà-t-il pas que j'ai laissé tomber les gâteaux! **you've been and gone and done it!** vous en avez fait une belle! **he's been and gone and done it!** il a fait le coup! **to be off,** s'en aller, partir, *F:* décamper, filer; **I'm off to church, to London,** je pars à la messe, je pars pour Londres; **it's getting late, I'm off,** il se fait tard, je me sauve, je pars, je file. **6.** *impers,* (*a*) **it is six o'clock,** il est six heures; **it is late,** il est tard; **it is a fortnight since I saw him,** il y a quinze jours, voilà quinze jours, que je ne l'ai vu; (*b*) **it is fine, cold, etc.,** il fait beau (temps); il fait froid, etc.; (*c*) **it is easy to do it,** il est facile de le faire; **it is right that. . .,** il est juste que = *sub*; **it is said that . . .,** on dit que . . .; *A:* **be it known then to you that. . .,** sachez donc que. . .; **it is you I am speaking to,** c'est à vous que je parle; **it is for you to decide,** c'est à vous de décider; **what is it?** (i) que voulez-vous? (ii) de quoi s'agit il? qu'est ce qu'il y a? **as it were,** pour ainsi dire, en quelque sorte; **yesterday as it were,** comme qui dirait hier; **were it only to please me,** ne fût-ce que pour me plaire; **were it not for my rheumatism, I should go with you,** si ce n'était mon rhumatisme, je vous accompagnerais; **had it not been for the rain,** n'eût été la pluie; **had it not been for him,** sans lui, n'eût été lui; **I thought it might be Mary, and Mary it was,** je pensai que ce pouvait être Marie, et c'était elle en effet, et c'était bien elle; **well, well, if it isn't George!** Georges! en voilà une surprise! **will you have beer?—all right! beer it is!** voulez-vous de la bière?—va pour de la bière; *F:* **what's it to be?** (i) qu'est-ce que vous prenez? (ii) décidez donc! *F:* **what's yours?** qu'est-ce que vous prenez? **7.** (*auxiliary uses*) (*a*) (*forming continuous forms of verb tenses*) **I am, was, doing sth.,** je fais, je faisais, qch.; je suis, j'étais, en train de faire qch.; **they are always laughing,** ils sont toujours à rire; **the house is being built,** on est en train de bâtir la maison; **I have (just) been writing,** je viens d'écrire; **I have been reading all day,** je viens de passer ma journée à lire; **I have been waiting for a long time,** il y a longtemps que j'attends, j'attends depuis longtemps; **I would have given anything not to be going,** j'aurais tout donné pour ne pas avoir à y aller; (*emphatic*) **why aren't you working?—I *am* working!** pourquoi ne travaillez-vous pas?—mais si je travaille! mais je travaille, voyons! **well, you *are* going ahead!** eh bien, vous en faites, des progrès! (*b*) (*with a few intr. verbs as auxiliary of the perfect tenses*) **the sun is set,** le soleil est couché; **the guests were all gone,** les invités étaient tous partis; (*c*) (*forming passive voice*) (i) **he was killed,** il fut tué; **he is respected by all,** il est respecté de tous; **the loft was reached by means of a ladder,** on accédait au grenier au moyen d'une échelle; **the top was reached at ten o'clock,** nous sommes arrivés au sommet à dix heures; **the top was reached by ten o'clock,** à dix heures nous étions arrivés au sommet; **he is allowed to smoke,** on lui permet de fumer; **he was laughed at,** on s'est moqué de lui; *Lit:* **be it said without meaning to be rude,** soit dit sans offense; **I expected he would be hooted,** je m'attendais à le voir huer; **I would sacrifice everything rather than that you should be disgraced,** je sacrifierais tout plutôt que de vous voir déshonoré; (ii) **he is to be pitied,** il est à plaindre; **how is it to be done?** comment le faire? **what is to be done?** que faire? (*d*) (*denoting futurity*) **I am to see him tomorrow,** je dois le voir demain; **he was never to see them again,** il ne devait plus les revoir; **is the house going to be sold, let?** est-ce qu'on va vendre, louer, la maison? **I was to have come, but. . .,** je devais venir, mais . . .; **he is to be hanged,** il sera pendu; (*e*) (*necessity, duty*) **am I to do it or not?** faut-il que je le fasse ou non? **you are to be at school tomorrow,** il faut que vous soyez à l'école demain; **they are both to be congratulated,** il faut les féliciter tous les deux; des félicitations leur sont dues à tous les deux; **I came because you said I was to,** je suis venu parce que vous me l'avez dit; **smack his head—am I to really?** flanque-lui une taloche—faut-il vraiment? (*f*) (*possibility*) **the twins were to be distinguished by their voices,** on pouvait distinguer les jumeaux à leur voix. **8.** (*a*) **the bride to be,** la future; *s. A:* **the to-be,** l'avenir; *s.* **has-been,** *F:* (*a*) homme *m* vieux jeu; vieux ramolli; *Mil:* (vieux) ramollot, vieille culotte de peau; (*b*) homme dont la carrière est finie; homme fini; *s.* **might-have-been:** (i) **to talk of might-have-beens,** parler de tout ce qui aurait pu être, arriver; (ii) **he's a might-have-been,** il aurait pu être quelque chose; c'est un raté; (*b*) **to be at sth.,** être occupé à faire qch., s'occuper de qch.; **what are you at?** que faites-vous? **while we are at it, why not . . .?** pendant que nous y sommes, *F:* tant qu'à faire, pourquoi ne pas . . .? **she is always at him,** (i) elle ne peut pas le laisser tranquille; (ii) elle le harcèle de querelles, elle est toujours après lui; (*c*) **to be for s.o., sth.,** tenir pour qn, qch.; **I am all for reform,** je suis pour, je suis partisan de, la réforme; **I'm all for staying here,** je ne demande qu'à rester ici; (*d*) (*belong*) **the battle is to the strong,** la victoire est aux forts. **9.** (*elliptical*) **is your book published?-it is,** est-ce que votre livre est sorti?-oui; **are you happy?-I am,** êtes-vous heureux?-oui, je le suis; mais oui! **is Mr. X at home?-he is,** M. X y est-il?-oui, il y est; **isn't he running fast?-he is!** n'est-ce pas qu'il court vite?-pour sûr! **was he not listening?-he wasn't,** est-ce qu'il n'écoutait pas?–non; **you are angry-no, I'm not-oh, but you are!** vous voilà fâché-pas du tout-oh, mais si! **he's back-is he?** il est de retour-vraiment? **so you're back, are you?** alors vous voilà de retour?

beach[1] [biːtʃ], *s.* **1.** (*a*) plage *f*; grève *f*; rivage *m*; **shingly b., pebble b.,** plage de galets; **sandy b.,** plage de sable; *Nau:* plateau *m*; **graving b.,** (cale *f* d') échouage *m*; **you're not the only pebble on the b.,** vous n'êtes pas unique au monde; il n'y a pas que vous sur terre; *F:* **on the b.,** (i) en chômage; (ii) sans le sou; (*b*) *Geol:* **raised b.,** plage soulevée. **2.** *attrib.* (*a*) **b. hut,** cabine *f* (de bains, de plage); **b. guard,** brigade *f* de sauvetage (sur une plage); *Bot:* **b. grass,** gourbet *m*; roseau *m* des sables; (*b*) *Mil:* **b. landing,** débarquement *m* sur plage; **b. party,** détachement *m* de plage; **b. commander,** commandant *m* de plage; **b. master,** officier *m* régulateur de plage; **b. obstruction, obstacles,** obstacles *mpl* de plage.

beach[2]. **1.** *v.tr.* échouer, mettre à l'échouage (un navire). **2.** *v.tr.* tirer (une embarcation) à sec. **3.** *v.i. Mil:* débarquer sur plage; aborder la plage de débarquement.

beachcomber ['biːtʃkoumər], *s.* **1.** vague déferlante. **2.** *F:* (*of pers.*) (*a*) batteur *m* de grève; rôdeur *m* de grève; (*b*) propre *m* à rien.

beached [biːtʃt], *a.* échoué; à sec.

beachhead ['biːtʃhed], *s. Mil:* tête *f* de pont (de débarquement).

beaching ['biːtʃiŋ], *s.* **1.** échouage *m*; **b. strand,** échouage. **2.** *Mil:* débarquement *m* sur plage; abordage *m* de la plage de débarquement.

beach-la-mar ['biːtʃlə'mɑːr], *s.* **1.** *Echin:* trépang *m*; tripang *m*; bêche-de-mer *f, pl.* bêches-de-mer; biche-de-mer *f, pl.* biches-de-mer. **2.** *Ling:* (*a*) sabir polynésien; (*b*) (*l'anglais m*) bêche-de-mer (*m*).

beach wagon ['biːtʃwæg(ə)n], *s. Aut:* canadienne *f*; familiale *f.*

beachwear ['biːtʃwɛər], *s.* vêtements *mpl* de plage.

beachy ['biːtʃi], *a.* (*a*) couvert de galets, caillouteux; (*b*) *Geog:* **B. Head,** le cap Béveziers.

beacon[1] ['biːk(ə)n], *s.* **1.** (*a*) *A:* feu *m* d'alarme; (*b*) tour *f* du feu d'alarme; (*c*) colline *f* du feu d'alarme. **2.** feu de joie. **3.** (*a*) *Nau: Av:* phare *m*; balise *f*; feu; **landmark b.,** phare de repère; **flashing b.,** feu à éclats; **floating b.,** feu flottant, bouée lumineuse; **b. light,** feu de balisage; *Av:* **aerial b.,** aérophare *m*; **direction b.,** projecteur *m* de balisage; **boundary b.,** balise, feu, de délimitation de terrain; (*b*) *Nau: Av:* **radio b.,** radiophare *m*; **radio b. navigation, navigation by radio b.,** radiobalisage *m,* navigation *f* par radioguidage; **code b.,** balise à occultations codées; **radio-range b.,** radiophare directionnel, à alignement fixe; **marker b.,** radiobalise *f*; radiophare secondaire d'approche; **fan marker b.,** radiobalise en éventail; **rotating (radio) b.,** radiophare tournant; **voice rotating b.,** radiophare tournant à fréquence audible; **blind approach b. system,** radioguidage *m* d'aérodrome; **b. course,** droite *f* de balisage; **radar b.,** balise radar; radar *m* de radio-navigation; **responder b.,** balise répondeuse; **b. tracking,** poursuite *f* (radar) par signal réponse; (*c*) *Adm: Aut:* **Belisha b.,** sphère orange lumineuse (indiquant un passage clouté).

beacon[2]. **1.** *v.tr.* (*a*) *A:* échelonner des feux d'alarme sur (une région); (*b*) *Av: Nau:* baliser (une aéroroute, la piste d'un aéroport, un chenal). **2.** *v.tr. Lit:* éclairer (une région, une côte). **3.** *v.i.* briller comme un phare.

beaconage ['biːk(ə)nidʒ], *s.* **1.** balisage *m.* **2.** droits *mpl* de balisage.

beaconing ['biːkəniŋ], *s.* **1.** échelonnement *m* des phares d'aviation, des radiophares. **2.** balisage *m.*

bead[1] [biːd], *s.* **1.** (*for prayers*) grain *m*; **(string of) beads,** chapelet *m*; **to tell, count, one's beads,** égrener, dire, son chapelet; dire le rosaire; **the great b.,** le pater (du chapelet); *Arch:* **b. moulding,** patenôtre *f,* chapelet *m.* **2.** (*a*) (*for ornament*) perle *f* (de verroterie, d'émail, etc.); **(string of) beads,** collier *m*; **to thread beads,** enfiler des perles; (*b*) (*drop*) goutte *f,* perle; *Metall:* goutte (de matière en fusion); *Ch:* perle; **beads of dew,** perles de rosée; **there were beads of perspiration on his forehead,** la sueur perlait sur son front; il suait à grosses gouttes; (*c*) bulle *f* (sur le vin, l'eau-de-vie); **the beads,** le chapelet; **wine with a fine b.,** vin *m* qui donne un beau chapelet; (*d*) *Arch: Join:* perle, baguette *f,* congé *m*; arête *f* (de moulure); *Const:* (*of sheet lead*) **hlp b.,** arêtier *m*; *Tls:* **b. tool,** gouge *f*; **b. plane,** mouchette *f.* **3.** (*of tyre*) talon *m,* bourrelet *m*; accrochage *m*; **clincher b.,** talon à crochet. **4.** *Sm.a:* guidon *m,* mire *f* (de fusil); grain *m* d'orge; *F:* **to draw a b. on s.o.,** ajuster, viser, qn. **5.** *Metalw:* cordon *m* de soudure; **parallel beads,** soudure *f* en cordons parallèles déposés par passes longitudinales. **6.** *El:* perle. **7.** *Cmptr:* **ferrite b.,** tore *m* de ferrite.

bead[2]. **1.** *v.tr.* (*a*) couvrir, orner, (qch.) de perles; emperler (une robe, etc.); enfiler (des perles); (*b*) *Arch: Join:* appliquer une baguette sur (qch.); (*c*) dudgeonner (un tube). **2.** *v.i.* (*a*) **the sweat beaded on his forehead,** la sueur perlait sur son front; (*b*) (*of liquids*) perler, faire la perle, faire chapelet.

beaded ['biːdid], *a.* **1.** (*a*) *Tex:* (*of material*) perlé; (*b*) (éclair, etc.) en chapelet. **2. b. edge,** talon *m* (de pneu); **b. tyre,** pneu *m* à talons, à bourrelets; **b. rim,** jante *f* à rebord. **3.** *Arch: Join:* **b. strip,** chapelet *m.*

beader ['biːdər], *s. Tls:* **(tube) b.,** mandrin *m.*

beading ['biːdiŋ], *s.* **1.** garniture *f* de perles. **2.** (*a*) *Arch: Join:* baguette *f*; *Tls:* **b. plane,** mouchette *f*; (*b*) (*of tyre*) talon *m,* bourrelet *m*; (*c*) *Metalw:* soudure *f* en cordons parallèles déposés par passes longitudinales.

beadle ['biːdl], *s.m.* **1.** (*a*) *A:* fonctionnaire qui faisait la police de la paroisse; (*b*) (*in church*) bedeau. **2.** (*in university*) appariteur, massier.

beadleship ['biːdlʃip], *s.* charge *f* de bedeau, d'appariteur.

bead-roll ['biːd'roul], *s. A: & Lit:* **1.** liste *f,* catalogue *m.* **2.** lignage *m.* **3.** chapelet *m,* rosaire *m.*

beadsman, *pl.* **-men** ['biːdzmən], *s. A:* viellard *m* qui habite dans une fondation.

bead tree ['biːdtriː], *s. Bot:* **1.** azédarac(h) *m,* mélie *f,* faux sycomore, margousier *m,* arbre saint, arbre à chapelets. **2.** staphylier pinné, patenôtrier *m.*

beadwork ['biːdwəːk], *s.* travail *m* de perles.

beady ['biːdi], *a.* **1.** (yeux) percés en vrille; (yeux) en trou de vrille; (yeux) de lynx. **2.** (liquide) qui perle.

beady-eyed ['biːdi'aid], *a.* aux yeux en vrille.

beagle[1] ['biːgl], *s.* **1.** (*a*) *A:* (chien *m*) bigle (*m*); beagle *m*; briquet *m*; (*b*) *F:* espion *m* (de la police); mouchard *m.* **2.** *Ven:* meute *f,* équipage *m* (de chiens pour la chasse au lièvre). **3.** *El:* brouilleur *m* automatique.

beagle[2], *v.i.* chasser avec des briquets.

beagling ['biːgliŋ], *s.* chasse *f* au briquet.

beak[1] [biːk], *s.* **1.** bec *m* (d'oiseau, de tortue, d'enclume, de cruche, de vase etc.); *F:* nez crochu, *P:* pif *m* (d'une personne); **eagle's b.,** (i) bec d'aigle; (ii) (*of pers.*) nez aquilin. **2.** *N.Arch: A:* éperon *m.* **3. b. iron,** bec (d'enclume); bigorne *f.*

beak[2], *s.m. F:* (*a*) magistrat (du commissariat de police); = commissaire de police; **to be up before the b.,** paraître devant le tribunal; (*b*) agent *m* de police; (*c*) *Sch:* pion *m.*

beaked [biːkt], *a.* **1.** (animal *m*) à bec; *Bot:* rostré; *Her:* becqué; **b. anvil,** bigorne *f*; *Z:* **b. whale,** hyperoodon *m.* **2.** (nez) crochu.

beaker ['biːkər], *s.* **1.** (*a*) *Lit:* gobelet *m*; coupe *f*; (*b*) timbale *f.* **2.** *Ch:* vase *m* à filtration chaude; becher *m.* **3.** *Archeol:* **b. bell, b. pottery,** vases caliciformes, campaniformes.

beakful ['biːkful], *s.* becquée *f.*

beakhead ['biːkhed], *s.* **1.** *N.Arch:* coltis *m.* **2.** *Sculp:* tête plate.

be-all ['biːɔːl], *s.* **the be-all and (the) end-all,** le but suprême, la fin des fins.

beam[1] [bi:m], *s.* **1.** (*a*) *Const:* poutre *f* (en bois), solive *f*, madrier *m*; (*small*) poutrelle *f*; **b. and joists,** solivure *f*; **main b.,** maîtresse poutre; **longitudinal b.,** longeron *m*, longrine *f*; **auxiliary b.,** sous-longeron *m, pl.* sous-longerons; **ceiling b.,** doubleau *m*; **cross b.,** sommier *m*, traverse *f*; **straining b.,** entrait retroussé; poutre traversière (d'un comble, etc.); **tie b.,** moufle *f or m*; longrine, moise *f*; entrait *m*; blochet *m* (de toit); tirant *m* (de charpente de fer, etc.); **b. bearing,** lambourde *f*; (*b*) *Gym:* **cross b.,** portique *m*; (*c*) fléau *m*, verge *f*, joug *m*, traversant *m*, traversin *m* (d'une balance); **b. scales,** balance *f* à fléau; **b. compass,** compas *m* à trusquin, à verge (de dessinateur); (*d*) age *m*, timon *m*, flèche *f*, perche *f*, haie *f*, haye *f* (d'une charrue); (*e*) *Harn:* canon *m* (de mors); (*f*) *Mch:* **(walking) b.,** balancier *m* (d'une machine à vapeur); **pump b.,** balancier de pompe; **b. engine,** machine *f* à balancier; (*g*) *Nau:* verge (d'une ancre); **ice b.,** brise-glace(s) *m inv*; (*h*) *Tex:* rouleau *m*, ensouple *f* (d'un métier); **print(ing) b.,** colorieur *m*; **yarn b., warp b.,** ensouple dérouleuse; **fore b., cloth b.,** ensouple enrouleuse; **roller b.,** porte-cylindre *m inv*; **web b.,** ensouple enrouleuse (de métier à tisser); **b. warping,** ourdissage *m*; (*i*) *Leath:* chevalet *m* (de corroyeur); (*j*) *Ven:* merrain *m* (de bois de cerf). **2.** *Nau: N.Arch:* (*a*) bau *m, pl.* baux; **trussed b.,** bau composé; **deck b.,** barrot *m* du pont; **orlop b.,** bau du faux-pont; **half b.,** demi-bau *m, pl.* demi-baux; **midship b., main b.,** maître-bau *m, pl.* maîtres-baux; **breast b.,** fronteau *m*; **cross b.,** barrotin *m*; **hold b.,** barre sèche; **panting b.,** barrot de coqueron; **b. shelf,** bauquière *f*; **b. clamp,** serre-bauquière *m, pl.* serre-bauquières; (*b*) travers *m* (d'un navire); **on the port, starboard, b.,** par le travers bâbord, tribord; **on the weather b.,** par le travers au vent; **b. sea, wind,** mer *f*, vent *m*, de travers; (*c*) **(breadth of) b. (of a ship),** largeur *f* (d'un navire); **extreme b.,** largeur au fort; **broad in the b.,** (i) (navire) à larges baux; (ii) *F:* (personne *f*) aux larges hanches, large de bassin; **b. line,** livet *m* de pont. **3.** (*a*) rayon *m* (de lumière, de soleil); **stray b. of sunshine,** coulée *f* de soleil; **the sun darts its beams,** le soleil darde ses traits; **b. of satisfaction, of delight,** large sourire *m*, épanouissement *m*, de satisfaction, de joie; (*b*) **b. of rays,** faisceau lumineux; **b. of a lighthouse, of a headlight,** faisceau d'un phare; **to find oneself right in the b. of the searchlights,** se trouver en plein dans le faisceau des projecteurs; **parallel b.,** faisceau parallèle. **4.** *El:* faisceau *m*; **b. alignement,** alignement *m*; **b. angle,** angle *m* de radiation; **b. jitter,** vacillement *m*, balancement *m*, de faisceau; **b. rider,** engin guidé par un faisceau; **b. rider (guidance),** guidage *m* par faisceau; **b. switching,** commutation *f* de faisceau; **b. voltage,** tension *f* de faisceau; **b. width,** ouverture *f* de faisceau; **cathodic b.,** faisceau cathodique; **electronic b.,** faisceau électronique; **holding b.,** faisceau de régénération, d'accumulation; **radar b.,** faisceau radar; **radio b.,** faisceau hertzien; **sound b.,** faisceau sonore; **T.V. scanning (electronic) b.,** faisceau cathodique explorateur; *Av:* **radio landing b.,** axe balisé d'atterrissage; *F:* **off (the) b.,** écarté du droit chemin; **you are completely off b.,** tu dérailles.

beam[2], *v.tr.* **1.** *Leath:* chevaler (des cuirs). **2.** *Tex:* ourdir (la chaîne).

beam[3]. **1.** *v.tr.* (*a*) (*of the sun*) **to b. (forth) rays,** envoyer, lancer, darder, des rayons; (*b*) *W.Tg:* **to b. a message,** transmettre un message par ondes dirigées; *F:* **advertisement beamed at wives,** réclame adressée aux femmes, aux ménagères; (*c*) *Av:* (*of aircraft*) **to be beamed in on Orly,** être dirigé vers Orly. **2.** *v.i.* (*a*) (*of the sun*) rayonner; (*b*) (*of pers.*) **to b. (with satisfaction),** rayonner (de satisfaction); **she beamed at us, her face beamed,** (en nous voyant) son visage s'épanouit en un large sourire; **beaming with health,** resplendissant de santé.

beam ends ['bi:m'endz], *s.pl.* (*a*) *N.Arch:* (*of ship*) **to be on her b.e.,** être accoté sur le côté; être engagé; **to lie, to be laid, thrown, on her b.e.,** se coucher horizontalement; accoter; **to throw a ship on her b.e.,** coucher un navire; (*b*) *F:* **to be on one's b.e.,** être, se trouver, à bout de ressources; être à sec.

beaming[1] ['bi:miŋ], *s. Tex:* ourdissage *m*; **b. frame,** ourdissoir *m*.

beaming[2], *a.* rayonnant; (soleil, visage) radieux; resplendissant; **b. smile,** sourire radieux; large sourire.

beaming[3], *s.* rayonnement *m*.

beam tree ['bi:mtri:], *s.* **(white) b.t.,** alisier blanc; (alisier) allouchier (*m*).

beamy ['bi:mi], *a.* (*a*) massif; (*b*) (*of ship*) à larges baux.

bean[1] [bi:n], *s.* **1.** (*a*) *Hort: Cu:* **broad b.,** fève *f*; **French b.,** *NAm:* **string b.,** haricot vert, *Fr.C:* fève verte; **runner b.,** haricot d'Espagne; **wax b.,** haricot beurre; **Lima b., sugar b.,** haricot de Lima; **butter b.,** (i) haricot de Lima; (ii) haricot beurre; *U.S:* **bush b.,** haricot (blanc); **kidney b., haricot b.,** haricot, soissons *m*; **horse b., field b.,** féverole *f*, fève à cheval, gourgane *f*; **locust b.,** caroube *f*; **Mexican jumping b.,** haricot sauteur; **soya b.,** soya *m*, soja *m*, pois chinois; **asparagus b.,** dolic *m* asperge; **bog b.,** trèfle *m* d'eau; ményanthe *m*; *Cu:* **dried beans, haricot beans,** haricots secs; **baked beans,** haricots blancs (en conserve) à la sauce tomate; *Hort:* **b. stick,** rame *f* (pour haricots); (*b*) *F:* **to be full of beans,** être gaillard; être frais et dispos; se porter à merveille; être plein de verve, plein d'entrain, gonflé à bloc; **to give s.o. beans,** (i) attraper qn; donner un savon à qn; (ii) flanquer une râclée à qn; (iii) battre qn à plate couture; **to know how many beans make five,** savoir compter jusqu'à cinq; avoir le fil; **he knows how many beans make five,** c'est un malin; **it isn't worth a b.,** ça ne vaut pas un radis; *F:* **I don't care a b.,** je m'en moque, *F:* je m'en fiche; **he hasn't a b.,** il n'a pas le sou; *P:* il n'a pas un radis; *F:* **to spill the beans,** mettre les pieds dans le plat; gaffer; vendre la mèche; *F: O:* **hullo, old b.!** tiens c'est toi, mon vieux? c'est toi, ma vieille branche? **2.** grain *m* (de café); graine *f*, fève (de cacao). **3.** *P: U.S:* tête *f*, ciboulot *m*, boule *f*, caboche *f*. **4.** *Petr:* duse *f*.

bean[2], *v.tr. esp. U.S: F:* frapper (qn) sur la tête; donner une calotte à (qn); **b. him with a shoe!** flanque-lui un coup sur la tête avec une chaussure!

beanery ['bi:nəri], *s. U.S: P:* restaurant *m* de basse qualité; gargote *f*.

beanfeast ['bi:nfi:st], *s. F:* **1.** *A:* petite fête (annuelle) offerte aux ouvriers par le patron. **2.** régal *m*; bombe *f*.

bean goose ['bi:ngu:s], *s. Orn:* oie *f* des moissons.

beanie ['bi:ni], *s. NAm: Sch:* (petite) casquette (d'étudiant).

beano ['bi:nou], *s. F:* régal *m*; bombe *f*; **to have a good, rare, old b.,** s'offrir une vraie bombe.

beanpole ['bi:npoul], *s.* (*a*) rame *f* (pour haricots); (*b*) *F:* (*pers.*) manche *m* à balai, échalas *m*.

beanstalk ['bi:nstɔ:k], *s.* tige *f* de fève, de haricot.

bean tree ['bi:ntri:], *s. Bot:* **1.** catalpa *m*. **2.** caroubier *m*. **3.** érythrine *f* corail.

bean trefoil ['bi:n'tri:fɔil], *s. Bot:* anagyre *m*.

bear[1] ['bɛər], *s.* **1.** (*a*) ours *m*; **she b.,** ourse *f*; **young b., bear's cub,** ourson *m*; **brown b.,** ours brun; **polar b.,** ours blanc; **Malayan b., sun b.,** bruan *m*, ours malais, ours des cocotiers; **sloth b.,** prochile *m*; **grizzly b.,** ours gris d'Amérique; ours grizzlé; **honey b.,** kinkajou *m*; **American black b.,** baribal *m*; **Australian native b.,** koala *m*; *Paleont:* **cave b.,** ours des cavernes; **b. pit,** fosse *f* aux ours; **b. hug,** étreinte *f*; *A:* **bear's grease,** graisse d'ours (employée comme pommade); *F:* **to be like a b. with a sore head,** être d'une humeur massacrante, être d'une humeur de dogue, être maussade comme tout, ne pas décolérer; **he's like a b. with a sore head,** il n'est pas à prendre avec des pincettes; **what a b.!** quel maussade! quel ours! *U.S: F:* **I'm as hungry as a b.,** j'ai une faim de loup; *Geog:* **B. Island,** l'île *f* des Ours (au S.-E. du Spitzberg); **the Great B. Lake,** le grand lac de l'Ours; (*b*) *Astr:* **the Great, Little, B.,** la Grande, la Petite, Ourse; (*c*) *Bot:* **bear's bind,** liseron *m* des haies; **bear's breech,** branche-ursine *f, pl.* branches-ursines; branc-ursine *f, pl.* brancs-ursines; acanthe *f*; **bear's ear,** oreille *f* d'ours, auricule *f*; **bear's foot,** pied-de-griffon *m, pl.* pieds-de-griffon; ellébore *m* fétide. **2.** *St.Exch:* baissier *m*, joueur *m* à la baisse; **b. speculation,** spéculation *f* à la baisse; **to go a b.,** spéculer à la baisse; **b. rumours,** bruits alarmants; **to raid the bears,** pourchasser le découvert; **to sell a b.,** vendre à découvert; **to squeeze the bears,** étrangler les vendeurs à découvert. **3.** *Metall:* loup *m*.

bear[2], (*a*) *v.tr.* **(beared)** *St.Exch:* **to b. the market,** chercher à faire baisser les cours; (*b*) *v.i.* **to b.,** spéculer à la baisse; prendre position à la baisse.

bear[3], *v.*

I. *v.tr. & i.* (*p.t.* **bore** [bɔ:r], *A: & B:* **bare** ['bɛər]; *p.p.* **borne** [bɔ:n]) (*a*) (*carry*) porter (un fardeau, des armes, un nom, une date, etc.); **he came in bearing a large parcel,** il est arrivé avec un énorme paquet; **to b. the mark of blows,** porter les marques de coups; **the document bears your signature,** le document est revêtu de votre signature; *Her:* **to b. argent, a cross gules,** porter d'argent à la croix de gueules; *Mth:* **quantity bearing an index,** quantité affectée d'un exposant; **to b. a good character,** avoir une bonne réputation; jouir d'une bonne réputation; **to b. oneself well,** se bien comporter; **the love she bore him,** l'affection qu'elle lui portait; **to b. s.o. company,** tenir compagnie à qn; **to b. s.o. a grudge,** garder rancune à qn; en vouloir à qn; tenir rigueur à qn; avoir de la rancune contre qn; **to b. sth. in mind,** (i) se souvenir de qch.; songer à qch.; avoir soin de faire qch.; ne pas oublier qch.; (ii) tenir compte de qch.; **it bears no relation to . . .,** cela n'a aucun rapport avec . . .; **it bears no resemblance to . . .,** cela n'a aucune ressemblance avec . . .; **to b. witness to sth.,** rendre, porter, témoignage de qch.; témoigner de qch.; attester qch.; (*b*) (*sustain, endure*) supporter, soutenir (un poids); supporter, endurer (la souffrance); supporter (les frais, les conséquences); souffrir (la douleur, la fatigue, le froid, une perte); *v.i.* **I wonder whether the ice will b.,** je me demande si la glace porte; **to b. a loss,** supporter, endosser, une perte; **to b. the responsibility of sth.,** avoir la responsabilité de qch.; **to b. the penalty of one's misdeeds,** porter la peine de ses méfaits; **the cost of transport is borne by us,** les frais de transport sont à notre charge; *Lit:* **to b. a part in sth.,** jouer un rôle dans qch.; **to b. the test,** subir l'épreuve; **the charge will not b. examination,** cette accusation ne supporte pas l'examen; **all truths will not b. telling,** toutes les vérités ne sont pas bonnes à dire; **there are passages in the book that will b. skipping,** il y a dans ce livre des passages que l'on peut fort bien sauter; **his language will not b. repeating,** son langage n'est pas à répéter; **story that will b. repeating,** histoire *f* qui ne perdrait rien de son sel à être répétée; **he could b. it no longer,** il ne pouvait plus y tenir; **to grin and b. it,** (tâcher de) faire bonne contenance; faire bonne mine à mauvais jeu; garder le sourire; **I cannot b. him, b. the sight of him,** je ne peux pas le souffrir, le sentir; **I cannot b. that perfume,** j'exècre ce parfum; **I cannot b. to see it,** je ne peux pas en supporter la vue; **I can't b. the idea of it,** je ne peux pas en souffrir, en supporter, l'idée; l'idée m'en est trop pénible; **he can b. this secret no longer,** ce secret le suffoque; **I cannot b. to be disturbed,** je ne peux pas souffrir qu'on me dérange; **she could not b. him to laugh at her,** elle ne pouvait pas supporter qu'il se moquât d'elle; *v.ind.tr.* **to b. with s.o.,** être, se montrer, indulgent pour qn; **to b. with s.o.'s uncertain temper,** endurer, supporter, les inégalités d'humeur de qn; (*c*) (*press*) **we were borne backwards (by the crowd, etc.),** nous fûmes refoulés (par la foule, etc.); **it was gradually borne in upon him that . . .,** peu à peu il s'est laissé persuader que . . ., l'idée s'est implantée dans son esprit que . . .; **it has been borne in upon me more and more that . . .,** je suis de plus en plus convaincu que . . .; **to b. to the right,** prendre à droite; appuyer à droite; se rabattre sur la droite; **to b. on sth.,** buter, appuyer, sur qch.; **beam bearing upon two uprights,** poutre *f* qui s'appuie, qui porte, sur deux montants; **the whole building bears on these columns,** tout l'édifice porte sur ces colonnes; **roof that bears too heavily on the walls,** toiture *f* qui charge trop les murs; **to b. hard, heavily, on s.o.,** (i) (*of pers.*) être dur pour qn; (ii) (*of thg*) peser lourdement sur qn; **law that bears unjustly on s.o.,** loi *f* qui défavorise injustement qn; **resolution bearing on a matter,** résolution *f* portant sur une question; **question that bears on the welfare of the country,** question qui intéresse le bien-être du pays; **the question bears closely upon . . .,** la question a un rapport très étroit avec . . .; **that does not b. on the question,** cela n'a aucun rapport avec la question; (*of pers.*) **to b. on a lever,** peser sur un levier; (*d*) **bring to b.,** to **bring all one's strength to b. on a lever,** peser (de toutes ses forces) sur un levier; **to bring a crowbar to b. on a door,** exercer des pesées *f* sur une porte (avec une pince-monseigneur); **to bring all one's energies to b. on an object,** apporter, consacrer, toute son énergie à qch.; **to bring one's mind to b. on sth.,** porter son attention sur qch.; **to bring influence to b. on s.o.,** exercer une influence sur qn; influencer qn; agir sur qn; **to bring pressure to b. on s.o.,** exercer une pression sur qn; exercer, faire agir, son influence sur qn; agir sur, influencer, qn; **to bring a telescope to b. on sth.,** braquer, diriger, fixer, une lunette sur qch.; **to bring artillery fire to b. on enemy concentrations,** diriger, appliquer, le tir, les feux, de l'artillerie sur les concentrations ennemies; (*e*) *Nau:* **the cape bears north-north-west,** on relève le cap au nord-nord-ouest; **how does the land b.?** comment relève-t-on la terre? (*f*) (*of ship*) **to b. round,** arriver en grand; (*g*) (*produce*) **to b. a child,** donner naissance à un enfant, mettre au jour un enfant, avoir un enfant; **she has borne him three sons,** elle lui a donné trois fils; **animals that b. more than two young,** animaux *m* qui portent plus de deux petits; **capital that bears interest,** capital *m* qui porte intérêt; **to b. fruit,** (i) (*of tree*) fruiter; rapporter, donner des fruits; porter fruit; (ii) (*of work, etc.*) porter fruit, fructifier; **my enquiries bore fruit,** mes recherches ont été couronnées de succès.

II. (*compound verbs*) **1. bear away,** (*a*) *v.tr.* emporter, enlever (qch.); **to be borne away by a force,** être entraîné par une force; (*b*) *v.i. Nau:* **to b. a. (for a point),** laisser arriver, laisser porter (sur une pointe, sur un cap).

2. bear down, (*a*) *v.tr.* **to b. d. the enemy,** accabler, vaincre, l'ennemi; **borne down by misfortune,** accablé par le malheur; **to b. d. all resistance,** briser, vaincre, venir à bout de, toute résistance; **to b. d. all opposition,** passer outre à toute opposition; (*b*) *v.i. Nau:* **to b. d. (up)on sth.,** courir sur qch.; **to b. d. on the enemy,** foncer, laisser porter, fondre sur l'ennemi; *F:* **to b. d. on s.o.,** fondre sur qn.

3. bear off, (*a*) *v.tr.* = BEAR AWAY (*a*); (*b*) *v.i. Nau:* **to b. o. from the land,** s'éloigner, s'écarter, de la terre; se relever de la côte; courir au large; défier (de) la terre; alarguer; (*of jolly boat, etc.*) **to b. o. (from a vessel),** déborder (d'un vaisseau).

4. bear out, *v.tr.* (*a*) **to b. o. a body, etc.,** emporter un cadavre, etc.; (*b*) **to b. o. a statement,** confirmer, justifier, une assertion; **to b. s.o. o.,** corroborer le dire de qn; **you will b. me o. that . . .,** vous direz avec moi que . . . .

5. bear up, (*a*) *v.tr.* soutenir (qn, qch.); (*b*) *v.i.,* (i) **to b. up against pain,** résister à la douleur; **to b. u. against, under, misfortune,** faire face, tenir tête, au malheur; ne pas se laisser abattre par la mauvaise fortune; **b. up!** tenez bon! ne vous laissez pas abattre! du courage! *F:* **how are you?—(oh, I'm) bearing up,** comment ça va?—(eh bien), ça va; je me défends; (ii) *Nau:* = BEAR AWAY (*b*).

bearable ['bɛərəbl], *a.* supportable; **the situation is no longer b.,** la situation n'est plus tenable.

bearably ['bɛərəbli], *adv.* d'une façon, d'une manière, supportable.

bearbaiting ['bɛəbeitiŋ], *s.* combats *mpl* d'ours et de chiens.

bearberry ['bɛəb(ə)ri], *s. Bot:* busserole *f*; raisin *m* d'ours, cerise *f* d'ours; *Bot: Pharm:* uva-ursi *m*; **Alpine b.,** busserole des Alpes.

bearbind, -bine ['bɛəbaind, -bain], *s. Bot:* liseron *m* des haies; liset *m,* clochette *f.*

bearcat ['bɛəkæt], *s. Z:* binturong *m.*

beard[1] [biəd], *s.* (*a*) barbe *f*; **pointed b.,** barbe en pointe; **to have a b.,** avoir de la barbe; porter la barbe; **man with a b.,** homme barbu, portant barbe; **he had a week's b.,** il avait une barbe de huit jours; (*b*) *Nat.Hist:* barbe; (*c*) *Bot:* arête *f* (d'épi), (*d*) barbelure *f* (d'une flèche, d'un hameçon); (*e*) barbe (d'une pièce de fonte, etc.); (*f*) *Typ:* talus *m* (d'un caractère); (*g*) *Woodw:* arête; (*h*) *Ac: Mus:* oreille *f.*

beard[2], *v.tr.* **1.** braver, défier, narguer, qn; *F:* **to b. the lion in his den,** aller défier qn chez lui; affronter la colère de qn. **2.** *Carp:* **to b. a board,** abattre l'arête d'une planche. **3.** *Metalw:* **to b. off a casting,** ébarber, boësser, une pièce de fonte.

bearded ['biədid], *a.* **1.** (homme, blé, poisson) barbu; (blé) aristé; (*at fair*) **the b. woman,** la femme à barbe; **b. arrow,** flèche barbelée; *Astr:* **b. comet,** comète chevelue. **2.** (*with adj. prefixed, e.g.*) **black-b. man,** homme *m* à barbe noire; **full-b.,** portant toute sa barbe.

beardgrass ['biədgrɑ:s], *s. Bot:* polypogon *m.*

beardless ['biədlis], *a.* imberbe, sans barbe; **b. youth,** blanc-bec *m, pl.* blancs-becs.

beard tongue ['biədtʌŋ], *s. Bot:* pentstemon *m.*

beard wheat ['biəd(h)wi:t], *s. Bot:* blé barbu.

bearer ['bɛərər], *s.* **1.** (*pers.*) (*a*) porteur *m* (de nouvelles, *Mount: etc:* de bagages, etc.); **the b. of this letter is Mr . . .,** le porteur de cette lettre est M. . . .; cette lettre vous sera remise par M. . . .; *Mil:* **b. company,** compagnie *f* de brancardiers; (*b*) **b. of a cheque, of a passport,** porteur d'un chèque, titulaire *mf* d'un passeport; *Fin:* **b. bond, cheque,** titre *m,* chèque, au porteur; (*c*) (*at funeral*) **the bearers,** les porteurs, *F:* les croquemorts. **2.** (*of tree*) **to be a good b.,** être de bon rapport. **3.** *Const: Mec.E:* support *m*; **b. (bar),** sommier *m* (d'une grille de fourneau, etc.); *pl. N.Arch:* **bearers,** carlingage *m* (de la machine); **boiler bearers,** berceau *m* de chaudière; **bearers of a rolling mill,** colonnes *f* d'un laminoir; *Av:* **engine bearers,** carlingage, carlingue *f,* batimoteur *m*; *Const:* **b. joist,** lambourde *f* (de parquet); *Aut: Av:* **b. plates (of the engine),** berceau *m* (du moteur).

bearfight ['bɛəfait], *s. F:* scène *f* de désordre; tohu-bohu *m*; bousculade *f.*

beargarden ['bɛəgɑ:d(ə)n], *s.* **1.** fosse *f* aux ours. **2.** *F:* pétaudière *f*; **to turn the place into a b.,** mettre le désordre partout; **the place is a b.!** on ne s'entend pas ici!

bear grass ['bɛəgrɑ:s], *s.* yucca *m,* yucca filamenteux; aiguille *f* d'Adam.

bearing[1] ['bɛəriŋ], *a.* **1.** porteur, -euse; **b. axle,** essieu porteur; **b. bar (of furnace),** sommier *m* (d'un fourneau); **b. wall,** mur *m* d'appui; **b. surface,** surface *f* d'appui; tablette *f* (d'une solive); *Mec.E:* surface portante, de portage; *Min:* **b. set,** cadre porteur. **2.** (*in compounds*) (*a*) **fruit-b.,** fructifère, qui porte des fruits; (*b*) **interest-b. capital,** capital producteur d'intérêts, capital qui rapporte; (*c*) -fère; **lead-b.,** plombifère; **nickel-b.,** nickelifère; **silver-b.,** argentifère; **wool-b.,** lanifère.

bearing[2], *s.* **1.** (*a*) port *m* (d'armes, de nouvelles); *Ecc:* **the B. of the Cross,** le portement de croix; (*b*) (*of pers.*) port, maintien *m*; conduite *f*; **soldierly b.,** attitude *f,* allure *f,* militaire; (*c*) *Her:* pièce *f* (de l'écu); **(armorial) bearings,** armoiries *fpl,* blason *m.* **2.** (*a*) capacité *f* de supporter (des maux, des souffrances); **his conduct is past (all) b.,** sa conduite est insupportable; (*b*) *Civ.E: Const: etc:* (appareil *m* d')appui *m* (d'un pont métallique); surface *f* d'appui (d'une poutre); portée *f* (de poutres); chape *f* (d'une balance); *Arch:* dé *m*; *Harn:* grille *f* (de l'étrier); **surface b.,** appui simple; **b. plate,** plaque *f* d'appui; **end b. plate,** flasque *m* palier; (*of beam, etc.*) **to take its b. on sth.,** prendre appui sur qch.; **connecting rod taking its b. on a crank pin,** bielle articulée sur un maneton; (*c*) *Mec.E:* palier *m*; roulement *m*; coussinet *m*; **main b.,** palier principal; **half b.,** demi-coussinet *m, pl.* demi-coussinets; **plain, journal, b.,** palier lisse; **babbitted b., antifriction b., white-metal b.,** palier antifriction, palier anti-frottement, palier régulé; **gas b.,** palier fluide; **water b.,** palier glissant; **self-oiling b., self-lubricating b.,** palier graisseur; **ball b.,** roulement à billes; **roller b.,** coussinet, palier, roulement, à rouleaux; **needle b.,** roulement à aiguilles; **thrust b.,** (portée *f* de) palier de butée; **ball-thrust b.,** butée *f* à billes; crapaudine *f* à billes; roulement de butée; **outboard b.,** palier en porte-à-faux; **hanging b.,** chaise suspendue, chaise pendante; **pilot b.,** palier guide, roulement guide; **slide b.,** palier à glissement; **split b.,** palier en deux pièces; demi-coussinet; **taper b.,** palier, roulement, coussinet, conique, à rouleaux coniques; **pivoted-shoe b.,** palier à blochets articulés, palier Mitchell; **slipper b., tilting-pad b.,** palier à segments pivotants; **axle b.,** palier d'essieu; **spring b.,** palier d'arbre, palier support; **connecting rod b.,** palier de bielle; **big end b.,** coussinet de tête de bielle; **small end b.,** coussinet de pied de bielle; **hot b.,** coussinet échauffé; **burned b.,** coussinet grillé; **wiped b.,** emportement *m* d'antifriction; **b. brasses,** coussinet antifriction, **b. cap, b. keep,** chapeau *m,* couvercle *f,* de palier; **b. standard,** corps *m* de palier; **b. pedestal,** support *m,* chevalet *m,* de palier. **3.** (*a*) *Surv: etc:* gisement *m,* azimut *m*; orientation *f*; direction *f*; *esp. Nau: Av:* relèvement *m*; position *f*; **magnetic b.,** azimut, gisement, magnétique; **true b.,** azimut, gisement, géographique; relèvement vrai; **grid b.,** azimut, gisement, par rapport au (nord du) quadrillage; **back b.,** contre azimut; visée *f* arrière; **compass b.,** relèvement au compas; *Mil:* angle *m* de marche à la boussole; **to take a compass b.,** prendre un relèvement au compas; **to march on a compass b.,** marcher à la boussole; **to take a b.,** prendre un gisement, un azimut; effectuer un relèvement; calculer une position; **to take the ship's bearings,** faire le point; relever la position du navire; **bearings from the ship,** gisement (d'un amer, etc.); **to take the bearings of a coast,** relever une côte, faire un relèvement d'une côte; **to take one's bearings,** s'orienter; se repérer; amorcer (un sujet, une question); **to lose one's bearings,** perdre sa direction, sa route; se trouver désorienté, *F:* perdre le nord; **he made me lose my bearings,** il m'a désorienté, *F:* il m'a fait perdre le nord; **to find, get, one's bearings,** retrouver sa direction, sa route; s'y reconnaître, s'y retrouver; reprendre le vent; (*b*) portée (d'une question, d'un argument); rapport *m* (avec une question); **I had not understood the b. of the remark,** je n'avais pas saisi la portée de la remarque; **to consider a question in all its bearings,** examiner une question sous tous les rapports, sous tous les aspects. **4.** (*a*) (*of tree, etc.*) **to be in full b.,** être en plein rapport; **to be past b.,** ne plus porter; *Hort:* **alternate b.,** alternance *f*; (*b*) mise *f* au monde (d'un enfant); **to be past (child) b.,** ne plus être en âge d'avoir des enfants.

bearish ['bɛəriʃ], *a.* **1.** (*a*) (manières) d'ours; (*b*) (*of pers.*) bourru; **rather b.,** un peu ours; peu sociable. **2.** *St.Exch: F:* **b. tendency,** tendance *f* à la baisse.

bearishly ['bɛəriʃli], *adv.* d'une manière peu sociable.

bearishness ['bɛəriʃnis], *s.* caractère bourru.

bear leader ['bɛəli:dər], *s.* (*a*) montreur *m,* meneur *m,* d'ours; (*b*) *A: F:* précepteur *m* qui accompagne son élève en voyage.

bearskin ['bɛəskin], *s.* **1.** peau d'ours (garnie de son poil); oursin *m.* **2.** *Mil.Cost:* bonnet *m* à poil; bonnet d'oursin.

bearwarden ['bɛəwɔ:d(ə)n], *s. A:* gardeur *m* d'ours; *Astr:* **the B.,** le Bouvier; Boötès *m.*

beast [bi:st], *s.* **1.** (*a*) bête *f*; *esp.* quadrupède *m*; **wild b.,** (i) bête sauvage; (ii) bête féroce; **the brute beasts,** les brutes *f*; **the king of the beasts,** le roi des animaux; **a huge b. of a horse,** un grand diable de cheval; (*b*) *B:* **the B.,** l'Antéchrist *m*; la grande Bête de l'Apocalypse; *Lit:* **the mark of the B.,** le signe, l'empreinte *f,* de l'Antéchrist. **2.** (*a*) **b. (of burden),** bête de somme, de trait; bête à dos; **a good horseman looks after his b.,** un bon cavalier soigne sa monture, sa bête; (*b*) *pl. Husb:* bétail *m,* bestiaux *mpl*; cheptel *m*; **herd of forty beast(s),** troupeau *m* de quarante têtes de bétail; **heavy beasts,** gros bétail; **light beasts,** menu bétail. **3.** *F:* (*a*) **to make a b. of oneself,** s'abrutir; **to live like a b.,** vivre dans l'abrutissement; **to sink to the level of a b.,** s'avilir; **what a b.!** quel animal, quel abruti (que cet homme-là)! (*b*) **isn't he a b.!** quelle brute! quel goujat! **to behave like a b.,** se conduire en goujat; **he's a perfect b.!** c'est une rosse! **a perfect b. of a master,** un professeur rosse; **that b. of a foreman,** cette vache de contremaître; **that filthy old b. Marchal,** ce vieux sagouin, ce vieux cochon de père Marchal; **it was a perfect b. of a day,** il a fait un temps abominable, un chien de temps; **a b. of a job,** (i) un chien de métier; (ii) une besogne fâcheuse; (*c*) **poor, miserable, little b.,** pauvre petit diable.

beastie ['bi:sti], *s. Scot:* bestiole *f,* petite bête.

beastliness ['bi:stlinis]. **1.** bestialité *f,* brutalité *f.* **2.** *F:* saleté *f* (d'esprit); *P:* saloperie *f*; **the b. of the weather,** la saleté du temps.

beastly ['bi:stli]. **1.** *a.* (*a*) bestial, -iaux; brutal, -aux; (*b*) *F:* sale, dégoûtant, infect; **what b. weather!** quel sale temps! quel chien de temps! quel temps de chien! quel temps, crois-tu! **it's a b. hole of a place,** c'est un sale trou. **2.** *adv. F:* (*a*) *O:* **b. drunk,** soûl comme une bourrique; (*b*) (*intensive*) **it's b. cold,** il fait bigrement froid; *O:* **b. difficult,** terriblement difficile.

beat[1] [bi:t], *s.* **1.** (*a*) battement *m* (du cœur, etc., *Fenc:* d'épée); pulsation *f* (du cœur); batterie *f* (de tambour); son *m* (du tambour); *Hor:* battement (d'un mouvement); **the clock is off the b., out of b.,** la pendule n'est pas d'aplomb; (*b*) *Mus:* (i) mesure *f,* temps *m*; **strong b.,** temps fort; **weak b.,** temps secondaire; (ii) mouvement de la main en battant la mesure; (iii) be bop *m*; **big b.,** jazz *m* à rythme fort marqué. **2.** *Ph:* battement (d'ondes sonores, électriques, etc.); *W.Tel:* **b. between two impressed frequencies,** battement entre deux fréquences imprimées. **3.** *Cmptr:* battement. **4.** (*a*) ronde *f* (d'un agent de police); *Mil:* parcours imparti à une sentinelle; itinéraire *m* (d'une ronde); **policeman on the b.,** agent qui fait sa ronde; *F:* **it's off my b. altogether,** ce n'est pas de ma compétence, pas mon rayon; **prostitute on the b., walking her b.,** prostituée à la retape, faisant le trottoir; (*b*) *U.S:* circonscription électorale; (*c*) *For:* triage *m.* **5.** *Ven:* (terrain *m* de) battue *f.* **6.** *U.S: P:* (*a*) **did you ever hear the b. of that?** avez-vous jamais entendu plus fort que ça? (*b*) *Journ:* primeur *f* d'une grosse nouvelle. **7.** *U.S: P:* (*a*) vagabond *m,* chemineau *m*; (*b*) carotteur *m,* parasite *m*; (*c*) beatnik *m.*

beat[2], *v.tr. & i.* **(beat, beaten)**

I. *v.tr. & i.* battre (qn, qch.). **1.** (*a*) (*strike*) **to b. s.o. with a stick,** donner des coups de bâton à qn; *P:* astiquer qn; **to b. s.o. black and blue,** meurtrir, rouer, qn de coups; mettre qn en capilotade; **to b. s.o. to death,** assommer qn (à coups de trique, etc.); faire périr qn sous le bâton; **to b. sth. flat,** aplatir qch. à coups de marteau; **to b. one's breast,** se frapper la poitrine; **to b. a carpet,** battre un tapis; **to b. eggs,** battre des œufs; **to b. a post into the ground,** enfoncer un pieu dans la terre; **to b. a walnut tree,** gauler, chabler, un noyer; **to b. a path,** frayer un chemin; **to b. on the door,** frapper, cogner, à la porte; **to b. a drum,** battre du tambour; **to b. to arms,** battre la générale; **to b. the assembly,** battre le rappel; **to b. the retreat (on drum),** battre la retraite; **to b. a retreat,** (i) *Mil:* battre en retraite; (ii) *Fig:* se retirer, se dérober; se dédire; **to b. time (to music),** battre la mesure; *occ.* marquer le temps; **his heart is beating with joy,** son cœur bat de joie; **his heart was beating like mad,** son cœur battait à se rompre, battait à grands coups; **the rain was beating against the window panes,** la pluie battait contre les vitres; **the waves b. against the shore, against the rocks,** les vagues déferlent sur le rivage, contre les rochers; *Ven:* **to b. a wood (for game),** battre, traquer, un bois; *F:* **to b. about the bush,** tourner autour du pot; accumuler les mais, les si et les car; tergiverser; **not to b. about the bush,** (i) aller droit au but, droit au fait; ne pas y aller par quatre chemins, par trente-six chemins; (ii) répondre sans ambages, sans paraphrase, carrément; *Nau:* **to b. to windward, against the wind, off the wind,** louvoyer; tirer des bordées; remonter dans le vent; gagner au vent; s'élever (dans le vent); *U.S: F:* **to b. one's way to a place,** gagner un endroit; *F:* **to b. it,** tirer au large; se tirer, se barrer; **now then, b. it!** allons, file! décampe! fiche le camp! barre-toi! (*b*) (*of bird*) **to b. its wings,** battre des ailes. **2.** (*conquer, surpass*) (*a*) **to b. the enemy,** battre l'ennemi; **to b. s.o. at chess,** battre qn aux échecs; **to b. s.o. in chemistry,** dépasser, battre, qn en chimie; **they got beaten,** ils se firent battre; *F:* **to b. s.o. into fits,** battre qn à plate(s) couture(s); *P:* brosser (un concurrent); *F:* **that beats me!** cela me surpasse! ça me dépasse! **you can't b. the zoo,** il n'y a rien de tel que le jardin zoologique; **that beats everything! it beats the band!** (i) il n'y a rien au-dessus de cela! (ii) ça c'est fort! ça c'est pas banal! ça c'est le comble! c'est de plus en plus fort! c'est le bouquet! il ne manquait plus que ça! **can you b. it?** y a-t-il plus fort que ça? (*b*) (*arrive before, get ahead of*) devancer (qn); *F:* **he b. me to it,** il m'a fauché ma place; (*c*) **to b. the record,** battre le record; (*d*) *U.S: P:* rouler, refaire (qn); **to b. the customs,** frauder la douane.

II. (*compound verbs*) **1. beat about,** *v.i. Nau:* batailler.

2. beat back, *v.tr.* repousser, refouler (qn); **to b. back the enemy,** repousser l'ennemi; **to b. back the flames,** rabattre les flammes.

3. beat down, (*a*) *v.tr.* (i) **to b. sth. down,** (r)abattre qch.; **to b. down the soil,** damer la terre; **the rain has beaten down the corn,** la pluie a couché les blés; **to b. down the fire (on a moor),** battre le feu avec des branches, des battes, pour l'éteindre; (ii) **to b. down the price of sth.,** marchander sur le prix de qch.; **to b. s.o. down,** faire baisser le prix à qn; marchander (avec) qn; (*b*) *v.i.* **the sun is beating down on our heads,** le soleil donne (à plomb) sur nos têtes; le soleil nous tape sur la tête.

4. beat in, *v.tr.* enfoncer, défoncer (une porte, etc.).

5. beat off, *v.tr.* **to b. s.o. off,** repousser, chasser, qn; **to b. off an attack,** repousser un assaut.

6. beat out, *v.tr.* (*a*) **to b. out a path,** frayer un chemin; (*b*) **to b. out iron,** battre, aplatir, le fer; **to b. out gold,** étendre l'or sous le marteau; marteler, écolleter (l'or, etc.); (*c*) **to b. out a rhythm,** *F:* **to b. it out,** marquer un rythme; (*d*) **to b. s.o.'s brains out,** assommer qn, décerveler qn; (*e*) **to b. the dust out of sth.,** battre qch. pour en faire sortir la poussière.

7. beat up, (*a*) *v.tr.* **to b. up eggs,** battre, fouetter, les œufs; faire mousser les œufs; **to b. up cream,** battre, fouetter, étoffer, la crème; (*b*) *v.tr.* **to b. up game,** *F:* **customers,** rabattre, traquer, le gibier, des clients; **to b. up (for) supporters,** recruter, racoler, des partisans; (*c*) *v.tr.* **to b. up s.o.,** relancer qn; **to b. up s.o.'s quarters,** (aller) relancer qn chez lui; (*d*) *v.tr. F:* **to b. s.o. up,** assommer qn; tabasser qn; (*e*) *v.tr. F:* **to b. it up,** (i) faire la nouba, la fête, la bombe; (ii) (*habitually*) mener une vie de patachon; (*f*) *v.tr. Tex:* tasser (les fils de la trame); (*g*) *v.i. Nau:* **to b. up,** louvoyer vers la terre; s'élever au vent vers la terre; tirer des bordées; gagner vers la terre; **to b. up to windward,** remonter le vent.

beat[3], *a.* **1.** *F:* (= BEATEN) **you have me b.,** je ne suis pas de force, j'y renonce. **2. the b. generation,** la génération des beatniks. **3.** *Med: Min:* **b. hand, elbow, knee,** main enflée; coude, genou, enflé.

beaten [bi:tn], *a.* **1. the b. track,** le chemin battu; les vieux sentiers rebattus, *F:* le grand chemin des vaches; **house off the b. track,** maison écartée; **to follow the b. track,** suivre les sentiers battus; **that's off the b. track,** ça sort de l'ordinaire. **2.** (or, fer) battu, martelé; **cold b.,** écroui; **floor of b. earth,** sol *m* en terre battue. **3.** (ennemi) battu, vaincu.

beater ['bi:tər], *s.* **1.** (*pers.*) (*a*) batteur, -euse; **gold b.,** batteur d'or; (*b*) *Ven:* rabatteur *m,* traqueur *m.* **2.** (*a*) batte *f*; battoir *m* (de laveuse); fouloir *m* (de foulon); *Mus:* tringle *f* (de triangle); *For:* **fire b.,** batte à feu; *Husb:* **b.-drum,** batteur *m* (d'une batteuse); (*b*) *Paperm:* pilon *m*; (*c*) *Tex:* volant *m.*

beatific(al) [bi(:)ə'tifik(l)], *a.* (vision *f*, etc.) béatifique; **to wear a beatific smile,** (i) rire aux anges; (ii) sourire d'un air béat; avoir la figure épanouie.

beatifically [bi(:)ə'tifik(ə)li], *adv.* d'une façon, d'un air, béatifique.

beatification [bi(:)ætifi'keiʃ(ə)n], *s. Ecc:* béatification *f.*

beatify [bi(:)'ætifai], *v.tr. Ecc:* béatifier.

beating[1] ['bi:tiŋ], *a.* **1.** (cœur) palpitant. **2.** (pluie) battante.

beating[2], *s.* **1.** (*a*) battement *m* (d'ailes, du cœur, etc.); (*b*) *Tchn:* battage *m*; *Paperm:* **b. machine,** pilon *m*; (*c*) *Ven:* rabattage *m,* rabat *m* (du gibier); traque *f*; (*d*) *Nau:* louvoyage *m.* **2.** (*a*) coups *mpl*; raclée *f*, rossée *f*; **to give s.o. a b.,** donner des coups de bâton à qn, *F:* rosser qn; **to get a b.,** recevoir une raclée, une correction; (*b*) défaite *f*, *P:* pile *f* (dans un match, etc.); **to get a good b.,** être battu à plate(s) couture(s); *P:* se faire piler.

beating up ['bi:tiŋʌp], *s.* **1.** *F:* **to give s.o. a b. up,** assommer qn. **2.** *Tex:* tassement *m* (des fils de la trame).

beatitude [bi(:)'ætitju:d], *s.* béatitude *f.*

beatnik ['bi:tnik], *s.* beatnik *m.*

Beatrice, Beatrix ['biətris, 'biətriks], *Pr.n.f.* Béatrice, Béatrix.

beau, *pl.* **beaus, beaux** [bou, bouz], *s.* **1.** élégant *m,* dandy *m,* petit-maître *m, pl.* petits-maîtres; *Hist:* **B. Brummel,** Beau Brummel; **an old b.,** un vieux beau, un coquard. **2.** *A: & U.S:* prétendant *m* (d'une jeune fille); galant *m.*

Beaufort ['boufət], *Pr.n. Meteor:* **B. scale,** échelle *f* de Beaufort; **B. notation,** notation *f* de Beaufort.

beau-ideal [bouai'diəl], *s.* idéal *m*; **the b.-i. of a perfect knight,** le type achevé du chevalier.

Beaujolais ['bouʒəlei], *s. Wine-m:* beaujolais *m.*

beaumontage [bou'mɔntidʒ], *s. Woodw: etc:* mastic *m* à reboucher; badigeon *m.*

Beaune [boun], *s. Wine-m:* beaune *m.*

beaut [bju:t], *P:* **1.** *s.* (*of girl, car*) **isn't she a b.?** n'est-ce pas qu'elle est magnifique? **you're a b.!** tu es un drôle de type, toi! **a b. of a black eye,** un œil poché magnifique, formidable. **2.** *a. Austr:* magnifique, *P:* sensas(s).

beauteous ['bju:tiəs], *a. Poet:* (très) beau, (très) belle.

beauteously ['bju:tiəsli], *adv. Poet:* admirablement, sublimement.

beauteousness ['bju:tiəsnis], *s. Poet:* sublime beauté *f.*

beautician [bju(:)'tiʃ(ə)n], *s.* esthéticien, -ienne, cosmétologiste *mf.*

beautification [bju:tifi'keiʃ(ə)n], *s.* embellissement *m,* enjolivement *m.*

beautifier ['bju:tifaiər], *s.* **1.** (*pers.*) embellisseur, -euse. **2.** produit *m* de beauté.

beautiful ['bju:tif(u)l]. **1.** (très) beau, (très) belle; **a b. face,** un très beau visage; **at twenty she was b.,** à vingt ans c'était une beauté; **he has b. thoughts,** il a de belles pensées. **2. we had a b. dinner, a b. crossing,** nous avons eu un dîner magnifique; nous avons fait une traversée magnifique. **3.** *s.* **the b.,** le beau.

beautifully ['bju:tif(u)li], *adv.* admirablement; on ne peut mieux; **that will do b.,** cela fera l'affaire parfaitement, à merveille.

beautifulness ['bju:tifulnis], *s.* beauté *f.*

beautify ['bju:tifai]. **1.** *v.tr.* embellir, orner, enjoliver. **2.** *v.i.* (*of woman*) se faire belle; se bichonner.

beautifying[1] ['bju:tifaiiŋ], *a.* embellissant.

beautifying[2], *s.* embellissement *m,* enjolivement *m.*

beauty ['bju:ti], *s.* beauté *f.* **1.** (*a*) **to be in the flower of one's b.,** être dans toute sa beauté; **to keep one's b. in old age,** vieillir en beauté; **to find unsuspected beauties in a work,** trouver dans un ouvrage des beautés insoupçonnées; **the beauties of nature,** les beautés de la nature; *Prov:* **b. is in the eye of the beholder,** il n'y a point de laides amours; *P:* **I'm going to spoil his b. for him,** je vais lui abîmer le portrait; je vais l'amocher; **aids to b., b. preparations,** produits *mpl* de beauté; **b. treatment,** soins *mpl* de beauté; **b. specialist,** esthéticien, -ienne; **b. parlour, b. shop,** institut *m* de beauté; **b. competition,** concours *m* de beauté; **b. parade,** concours de beauté; (*of cars, etc.*) concours d'élégance; **b. queen,** reine *f* d'un concours de beauté; (*b*) **the b. of it is that . . .,** le beau côté, le joli, de l'affaire, c'est que . . .; **that's the b. of it,** (i) voilà ce qui en fait le charme; (ii) c'est là le plus beau de l'affaire; (iii) c'est là le plaisant de l'affaire. **2.** (*a*) **she was a b. in her day,** elle a été une beauté dans son temps; **she's no b. but you'll like her,** ce n'est pas une Vénus mais elle vous plaira; **B. and the Beast,** la Belle et la Bête; **the Sleeping B.,** la Belle au bois dormant; (*b*) *F:* **isn't it a b.?** (*of flower, etc.*) n'est-ce pas qu'elle est jolie? (*of car, etc.*) n'est-ce pas qu'elle est chic? **it's a b.,** c'est un rêve; *P:* **he fetched him a b. on the chin,** il lui a flanqué un coup magnifique, formidable, sensas(s), au menton; **a real b. of a black eye,** un œil poché magnifique, fantastique; **come on, my b.!** viens, ma jolie! *Iron:* **well, you're a b.!** eh bien, tu es encore un drôle de type, toi! **3.** *Bot:* (*a*) **meadow b.,** rhexia *f*; (*b*) **b. bush,** kolkwitzia *m* amabilis.

beauty spot ['bju:ti'spɔt], *s.* **1.** (*on skin*) (*a*) (*natural*) grain *m* de beauté; (*b*) (*artificial*) mouche *f.* **2.** site *m,* coin *m,* pittoresque.

beaver[1] ['bi:vər], *s.* **1.** *Z:* (*a*) castor *m*; **North American mountain b.,** castor de montagne nord-américain; *F:* **to work like a b.,** travailler comme quatre; *F:* **an eager b.,** un(e) zélé(e); (*b*) **b. rat,** rat musqué; ondatra *m.* **2.** (*fur*) castor; **b. lamb,** mouton doré; *A:* **b. (hat),** chapeau *m*; (en poil) de castor. **3.** *Tex:* castorine *f.* **4.** *F:* vieux barbu; *O:* **to play b.,** jouer à tennis barbe. **5.** *Bot:* **b. tree,** arbre *m* de castor.

beaver[2], *s. A.Arm:* visière *f* (de casque).

beaverboard ['bi:vəbɔ:d], *s. Const:* panneau *m* en fibre de bois feutre.

beaverette [bi:və'ret], *s. Com:* **1.** fourrure *f* imitation castor; fourrure façon castor. **2.** drap *m* castor.

beavery ['bi:vəri], *s.* (ferme *f* d')élevage *m* de castors.

bebeerine [bi'biri(:)n], *s. Pharm:* bébéerine *f.*

bebeeru [bə'bi:ru:], *s. Bot:* ébène vert (de la Guyane).

be-bop ['bi:bɔp], *s. Mus: Danc:* be-bop *m.*

becalm [bi'kɑ:m], *v.tr.* **1.** *Lit: A:* calmer, apaiser. **2.** *Nau:* abriter, déventer (un navire, un yacht).

becalmed [bi'kɑ:md], *a. Nau:* (*of ship*) **to be b.,** (i) être abrité, déventé; (ii) être accalminé, encalminé.

becard ['beikɑ:d], *s. Orn:* bécarde *f.*

because [bi'kɔ(:)z]. **1.** *conj.* (*a*) parce que; **I eat b. I'm hungry,** je mange parce que j'ai faim; (*b*) **if I said so it was b. it had to be said,** si je l'ai dit c'est qu'il fallait le dire; **I was the more astonished b. I had been told . . .,** j'en fus d'autant plus étonné qu'on m'avait assuré . . .; **life seemed more worth living b. she had had a glimpse of death,** la vie lui semblait d'autant meilleure qu'elle avait entrevu la mort; **b. he dashed off a sonnet he thinks himself a poet,** pour avoir bâclé un sonnet il se croit poète; **just b. I love my husband I do not necessarily hate my brothers,** pour aimer mon mari je ne hais pas mes frères; **just b. I say nothing it does not follow that I see nothing,** ce n'est pas parce que je ne dis rien que je ne vois rien. **2.** *prep.phr.* **b. of sth.,** à cause de qch.; **he has been retired b. of his infirmities,** on l'a mis à la retraite vu ses infirmités, en raison de ses infirmités; **I said nothing b. of the children being there,** je n'ai rien dit à cause de la présence des enfants.

beccafico [bekə'fi:kou], *s. Orn: Cu:* becfigue *m.*

béchamel ['beʃəmel], *s. Cu:* **b. sauce,** (sauce *f* (à la)) béchamel(le) *f.*

bêche-de-mer, *pl.* **bêches-de-mer** ['beʃdə'mɛər, 'beʃiz], *s.* **1.** *Echin:* trépang *m,* tripang *m,* bêche-de-mer *f, pl.* bêches-de-mer. **2.** *Ling:* **b.-de-m. (English),** (l'anglais *m*) bêche-de-mer *m.*

Bechuana [betʃu'ɑ:nə], *s. Ethn:* Betchuana *m.*

Bechuanaland [betʃu'ɑ:nəlænd], *Pr.n. Hist:* Betchuanaland *m.*

beck[1] [bek], *s.* (*in N. of Eng.*) ruisseau *m.*

beck[2], *s.* signe *m* (de tête, de la main); **to have s.o. at one's b. and call,** avoir qn à ses ordres, à sa disposition; **to be at s.o.'s b. and call,** obéir aux moindres volontés de qn; obéir à qn au doigt et à l'œil; être aux ordres de qn; subir la loi de qn; **to be at the b. and call of everyone,** être aux ordres de tout le monde.

becket ['bekit], *s. Nau:* garcette *f*, ganse *f*, patte *f*, ringot *m.*

beckon ['bek(ə)n], *v.tr. & i.* faire signe (**to s.o.,** à qn); appeler (qn) du doigt, de la main, d'un geste; faire approcher (qn); **to b. s.o. in,** faire signe à qn d'entrer; **he beckoned (to) me to approach,** il me fit signe d'approcher; **I beckoned him back, over,** je lui fis signe de revenir, de venir nous retrouver.

becloud [bi'klaud], *v.tr. Lit:* couvrir de nuages, ennuager; voiler, obscurcir.

become [bi'kʌm], *v.* (**became**) [bi'keim], **become**) **1.** *v.i.* devenir; se faire; (*a*) (i) **to b. great, king, s.o.'s enemy, etc.,** devenir grand, roi, l'ennemi de qn, etc.; **to b. old, thin,** vieillir, maigrir; **they have b. more amiable,** ils se sont faits plus aimables; **to b. suspicious of s.o.,** concevoir des soupçons contre qn; **by degrees he became more obedient,** il en arriva peu à peu à se montrer plus obéissant; **to b. a priest, a doctor,** devenir, se faire, prêtre, médecin; *Jur:* **to b. security for s.o.,** se porter caution pour qn; **the murmurs became louder,** les murmures se faisaient plus forts; **to b. bankrupt,** faire faillite; **to b. convalescent,** entrer en convalescence; **custom that has become law,** usage *m* qui a passé en loi; (ii) (*with p.p.*) **to b. accustomed, attached, interested, etc.,** s'accoutumer, s'attacher, s'intéresser, etc.; (*of pers.*) **to b. known,** commencer à être connu; se faire connaître; (*b*) **what has b. of X?** qu'est devenu X? qu'est-il advenu de X? **what will b. of him?** que va-t-il devenir? **I don't know what has b. of him,** je ne sais pas ce qu'il est devenu; **what has b. of my fountain pen?** qu'est-ce qu'on a fait de mon stylo? où (diable) est mon stylo? **2.** *v.tr.* convenir à, aller (bien) à, être propre à (qn, qch.); **hat that does not b. her,** chapeau *m* qui ne lui sied pas, qui ne lui va pas; **language that does not b. a man of his rank,** langage *m* indigne d'un homme de son rang; **he stood his ground, as became a gallant soldier,** il a tenu bon, en brave soldat qu'il est, qu'il était.

becoming [bi'kʌmiŋ], *a.* **1.** convenable, bienséant. **2.** (*of* *dress, etc.*) seyant (**to,** à); qui sied (à); qui va bien (à); **b. dress,** robe avantageuse; **it isn't very b.,** cela ne vous va pas très bien; **very b. style of hairdressing,** coiffure *f* du dernier chic.

becomingly [bi'kʌmiŋli], *adv.* convenablement; comme il convient; **she was most b. dressed,** elle était habillée à son avantage; sa robe lui allait admirablement; **b. furnished,** meublé avec goût.

becomingness [bi'kʌmiŋnis], *s.* **1.** convenance *f,* bienséance *f.* **2. the b. of her hat,** l'effet heureux, *F:* le chic, de son chapeau.

Becquerel ['bekər(ə)l], *Pr.n. Rad.-A:* **B. ray,** rayon *m* de Becquerel.

becquerelite ['bekərilait], *s. Miner:* becquerélite *f.*

becuna [be'kju:nə], *s. Ich:* bécune *f.*

bed[1] [bed], *s.* lit *m*; *Lit: Poet:* couche *f.* **1.** (*a*) **single b.,** lit pour une personne; **double b.,** lit à deux places, de, pour, deux personnes; grand lit; **twin beds,** lits jumeaux; **box b.,** lit clos; **camp b.,** lit de camp; **folding b.,** lit pl :, esamotable; **spare b.,** lit d'ami; *Lit:* **the narrow b.,** la tombe; **b. of state,** lit de parade; **their room was a three-b. attic,** leur chambre était une mansarde à trois lits; **b. chair,** chaise-lit *m, pl.* chaises-lits; fauteuil-lit *m, pl.* fauteuils-lits; **b. settee,** canapé-lit *m, pl.* canapés-lits; **to give s.o. b. and board,** donner à qn le logement et la nourriture, le vivre et le couvert; **the marriage b.,** le lit conjugal, matrimonial; **child of the second b.,** enfant *mf* du second lit; **the wedding b.,** le lit nuptial; *Lit:* **when she was called to share his b.,** lorsqu'elle fut appelée à partager sa couche; *Jur:* **separation from b. and board,** séparation *f* de corps (et de biens); **to sleep in separate beds,** faire lit à part; *A:* **to be brought to b. of a boy,** accoucher d'un petit garçon; **to be in b.,** (i) être couché; (ii) (*through illness*) être alité, être au lit; garder le lit; **to go to b.,** (i) se coucher; (ii) (*through illness*) s'aliter, prendre le lit; **to take to one's b.,** s'aliter, prendre le lit; **to take to one's b. again,** reprendre le lit; **to keep to one's b.,** garder le lit; **to keep s.o. in b.,** garder qn au lit; aliter qn; **b. of sickness,** lit de douleur; *Lit:* **to lie on a b. of sickness,** être alité, être cloué au lit, par la maladie; **three days in b.,** trois jours *m* d'alitement; **to get into b.,** se mettre au lit; **I'm going home to b.,** je rentre me coucher; **to get out of b.,** se lever; **to get out of b. again,** se relever (du lit); **to leap, jump, out of b.,** sauter à, en, bas du lit; **to put a child to b.,** coucher un enfant, mettre un enfant au lit; **to send,** *F:* **pack, the children off to b.,** envoyer coucher les enfants; **to make the beds,** faire les lits; **to make up a b. for s.o.,** préparer un lit pour qn; **b. feels very comfortable in the morning,** le matin on est joliment bien au lit; **I don't like staying in b.,** je n'aime pas rester au lit; je n'aime pas (à) faire la grasse matinée; **an hour's walk before b.,** une heure de promenade avant de se mettre au lit, se coucher; (*at hotel*) **b. and breakfast,** chambre *f* et petit déjeuner; *Prov:* **as you make your b. so you must lie on it,** comme on fait son lit on se couche; *F:* **he got out of b. the wrong side,** il s'est levé du pied gauche; **b.-jacket,** liseuse *f*; **b. linen,** (*on bed*) draps *mpl* de lit et taies *fpl* d'oreillers; (*in cupboard*) linge *m*; **b. rest,** dossier *m* de malade; **b. table,** table *f* de malade; **b. warmer,** chauffe-lit *m* (électrique, etc.), *pl.* chauffe-lit(s); *Med:* **b. wetter,** malade *mf,* enfant *mf,* sujet à l'incontinence, *F:* qui fait pipi au lit; **b. wetting,** incontinence *f* nocturne; *F:* pipi *m* au lit; (*b*) (*bedstead*) **b. boards,** fond *m* de lit; châlit *m*; **b. frame,** bois *m,* fer *m,* de lit; **b. key,** clef *f* (pour démonter un bois de lit, un lit de fer); **b. spring,** ressort *m* de lit; (*c*) **spring b.,** sommier *m* (à ressorts); **feather b.,** lit de plume; *Med:* **air b.,** matelas *m* pneumatique; **water b.,** matelas à eau; (*d*) *F:* **to go to b. with a woman,** coucher avec une femme; **all he thinks of is b.,** il ne pense qu'à faire l'amour. **2.** (*a*) lit (d'une rivière, de la mer); fond *m* (de billard, d'une voiture, etc.); *Geog:* **mean water b.,** lit mineur; **high water b.,** lit majeur; *Hyd.E:* **filter b.,** lit de filtrage; (*b*) *Hort:* (**rectangular**) **b.,** planche *f,* carré *m* (de fleurs, de légumes); (**flower**) **b.,** parterre *m*; plate-bande *f, pl.* plates-bandes; (*round*) corbeille *f*; *Ost:* **oyster b.,** huîtrière *f,* (i) banc *m* d'huîtres; (ii) parc *m* à huîtres; (*c*) *Geol:* assise *f,* couche, lit, banc; *Miner:* gisement *m*; **b. of rock,** assise rocheuse; **b.-vein,** filon-couche *m, pl.* filons-couches; (*d*) *Civ.E:* *Rail:* infrastructure *f,* encaissement *m,* assiette *f*; **b. of a road, road b.,** assiette d'une chaussée; *Rail:* terre-plein *m, pl.* terre-pleins; *Const:* **b. of mortar,** bain *m* de mortier; *Const:* *Civ.E:* *etc:* **b. of concrete,** assise, couchis *m,* lit, de béton; **b. of stones,** lit, assise, de pierres; *Mill:* **b. stone,** meule *f* de dessous; (meule) gisante; (*e*) *Mec.E:* banc (de tour); sommier *m* (d'une machine); table (de raboteuse); (**engine-**)**b.,** support *m,* bâti *m,* assise; *Av:* berceau *m* (de moteur), carlingue *f,* carlingage *m*; (*f*) *Typ:* marbre *m* (de la presse); *Journ:* **the paper has gone to b.,** le journal est tombé; (*g*) **b. of the ship's bottom** (**in the mud**), souille *f*; (*h*) *Cmptr:* **card b.,** chemin *m* de cartes.

bed[2], *v.* (**bedded**) **1.** *v.tr.* (*a*) **to b.** (**up, down**) **horses,** faire la litière aux chevaux; (*b*) *Hort:* **to b.** (**out**) **plants,** dépoter des plantes; **to b.** (**in**) **seedlings,** repiquer des plants; (*c*) parquer (des huîtres); (*d*) *Civ.E:* (i) enrocher (un bâtardeau); (ii) **macadam bedded on sand,** macadam *m* sur matelas *m* de sable; (*e*) *Const:* sceller (une poutre dans un mur, etc.); asseoir (une pierre, les fondations); **the bullet bedded itself in the wall,** la balle s'enfonça, se logea, dans le mur; *Mec.E:* **to b. the brasses,** assurer l'assise *f* des portées; *El.E:* **to b. the brushes,** roder les balais (d'une dynamo, etc.); **to b. the wires,** loger les fils; (*f*) *Metall:* **to b.** (**in**) **a mould,** enterrer un modèle (dans le sable); (*g*) *P:* **to b. a woman,** coucher avec une femme. **2.** *v.i.* (*a*) (*of animal*) se gîter; *F:* (*of pers.*) **to b. down,** se coucher; (*b*) (*of foundations, bridge, etc.*) **to b.** (**down**), prendre son assiette; se tasser, se caler (dans la terre, etc.); (*of ship*) **to b. in the sand,** s'engraver; **the boats were bedded in the mud,** les bateaux étaient enfoncés dans la vase.

bedabble [bi'dæbl], *v.tr.* éclabousser, souiller.

bedad [bi'dæd], *int.* (*Irish*) dame! ma foi!

bedaub [bi'dɔ:b], *v.tr.* barbouiller (de peinture); *F:* peinturer.

bedazzle [bi'dæzl], *v.tr.* éblouir; épater.

bedbug ['bedbʌg], *s.* punaise *f* des lits.

bedchamber ['bedtʃeimbər], *s. Lit:* chambre *f* à coucher; *A:* chambre; (*at court*) **Gentleman of the B.,** gentilhomme *m, pl.* gentilshommes, de la chambre; **Lady of the B.,** dame *f* du lit; **the privacies of the b.,** les secrets de l'alcôve.

bedclothes ['bedklouðz], *s.pl.* couvertures *f* et draps *m* de lit; couchage *m*; **to turn down the b.,** faire la couverture (de lit).

bedcover ['bedkʌvər], *s.* dessus *m* de lit.

-bedded ['bedid], *a.* (*with adj. prefixed, e.g.*) single-, double-b. room, chambre *f* à un lit, à deux lits.

bedder ['bedər], *s.* **1. early b.,** couche-tôt *m inv.,* **late b.,** couche-tard *m inv.* **2.** *Sch:* (*at Cambridge*) femme *f* de ménage. **3.** *Hort:* plant *m,* plante *f,* à repiquer.

bedding ['bediŋ], *s.* **1.** (*a*) parcage *m* (des huîtres); (*b*) *Civ.E:* enrochement *m* (d'un bâtardeau, etc.); *Nau:* engravement *m* (d'un navire); (*c*) *Const:* scellement *m* (d'une poutre dans un mur, etc.); assiette *f* (d'une pierre); (*d*) *El.E:* **b. of the brushes,** rodage *m* des balais (d'une dynamo, etc.); **b. of the wires,** logement *m* des fils; (*e*) *Metall:* enterrage *m* (d'un modèle); (*f*) *Husb:* préparation *f* de la litière; (*g*) *Hort:* **b. out,** dépotage *m,* dépotement *m* (de plantes); **b.** (**-out**) **plants,** plants *m* à repiquer; **b. roses,** roses *f* pour massifs, pour corbeilles; (*h*) *Metall:* (i) mise *f* en lit, étalement *m* (du minerai); **b. plant,** parc *m* d'homogénéisation. **2.** (*a*) literie *f,* fournitures *fpl* (d'un lit); (*b*) *Mil:* *Navy:* (matériel *m* de) couchage *m*; *U.S:* **b. roll** = BEDROLL. **3.** (*a*) *Husb:* litière *f*; (*b*) *Civ.E:* matériau *m* d'enrochement, d'assise. **4.** *Geol:* couche *f,* lit *m,* stratification *f*; **b. plane,** plan *m* de stratification. **5.** lit (d'une chaudière, etc.).

beddy-byes ['bedi'baiz], *s.* (*child's word*) **to go to b.-b.,** aller faire dodo.

Bede [bi:d], *Pr.n.m. Hist:* **the Venerable B.,** le Vénérable Bède.

bedeck [bi'dek], *v.tr. Lit:* parer, orner, chamarrer (**s.o. with sth.,** qn de qch.); **to b. oneself,** s'attifer.

bedeguar ['bedigɑ:r], *s. Hort:* bédégar *m*; éponge *f.*

bedesman, *pl.* **-men** ['bi:dzmən], *s.m. A:* vieillard qui habite dans une fondation, une maison de retraite.

bedevil [bi'devl], *v.tr.* **1.** ensorceler (qn). **2.** taquiner, tourmenter, lutiner (qn). **3.** gâcher (qch.); **industrial relations bedevilled by politics,** rapports entre patrons et ouvriers envenimés par la politique.

bedevilment [bi'devlmənt], *s.* **1.** ensorcellement *m.* **2.** taquinerie *f,* vexation *f.*

bedew [bi'dju:], *v.tr. Lit:* humecter de rosée; **cheeks bedewed with tears,** joues baignées de larmes; **pillow bedewed with tears,** oreiller arrosé, trempé, de pleurs, de larmes.

bedfast ['bedfɑ:st], *a. NAm:* cloué au lit.

bedfellow ['bedfelou], *s.* camarade *mf* de lit; associé(e), collègue *mf*; **he's an unpleasant b.,** il est mauvais coucheur; **they make strange bedfellows,** c'est une association inattendue; c'est un couple disparate.

Bedford ['bedfəd], *Pr.n. Geog:* Bedford; *Tex:* **B. cord,** bedford *m*; *Geol:* **B. limestone,** pierre *f* calcaire provenant de Bedford (Indiana).

bedgown ['bedgaun], *s. A:* **1.** chemise *f* de nuit (de femme). **2.** robe *f* de chambre d'hospitalisé.

bedhead ['bedhed], *s.* chevet *m*; tête *f* (du lit).

bedight [bi'dait], *a. Poet:* paré (**with,** de).

bedim [bi'dim], *v.tr.* (**bedimmed**) *Lit:* obscurcir (l'esprit, les yeux); **eyes bedimmed with tears,** yeux voilés de larmes.

bedizen [bi'daizn], *v.tr. O: Pej:* attifer, chamarrer (**with,** de).

Bedlam ['bedləm]. **1.** *Pr.n.* (*corrupt. of Bethlehem*) hôpital *m* (d'aliénés) de Ste-Marie-Bethléem; **you would think this was B.,** on se croirait dans une maison de fous; on se croirait à Charenton. **2.** *s. F:* (*a*) *A:* maison *f* de fous, d'aliénés; (*b*) charivari *m,* tohu-bohu *m,* tintamarre *m*; chahut *m* à tout casser.

bedlamite ['bedləmait], *s. F: A:* fou, *f* folle; échappé *m* de Charenton.

bedmaker ['bedmeikər], *s. Sch:* (*at Cambridge, etc.*) femme *f* de ménage.

bedmate ['bedmeit], *s.* camarade *mf* de lit.

Bedouin ['beduin], **1.** *a.* bédouin. **2.** *s.* (*pl.* **Bedouin(s)**) Bédouin, -ine.

bedpan ['bedpæn], *s. Hyg:* bassin *m* de lit; **slipper b.,** pantoufle *f.*

bed-plate ['bedpleit], *s. Mch:* bâti *m,* sole *f,* semelle *f,* embase *f,* socle *m*; (taque *f* d')assise (*f*); plaque *f* de fondation (d'une machine); écuelle *f* (de cabestan); *Metall:* sole *f* (du fourneau); *Rail:* plaque d'aiguille; *Artil:* **trunnion b.-p.,** sousbande *f.*

bedpost ['bedpoust], *s.* colonne *f* de lit; quenouille *f* (de lit à colonnes); *F:* **between you and me and the b.,** soit dit entre nous.

bedraggle [bi'drægl], *v.tr.* (*a*) crotter, tacher de boue; (*b*) tremper (d'eau).

bedraggled [bi'drægld], *a.* (*a*) crotté, taché de boue; (*b*) trempé (d'eau); (*c*) (vêtement) dépenaillé.

bedridden ['bedridn], *a.* cloué au lit.

bedrock ['bedrɔk], *s.* (*a*) *Geol:* roche *f* de fond; tuf *m*; soubassement *m*; (*b*) fondement *m* (de sa croyance, etc.); **to get down to b.,** descendre au fond des choses; **now let's get down to b.,** c'est assez tourner autour du pot; parlons peu mais parlons bien; **b. question,** question fondamentale; **b. price,** prix le plus bas.

bedroll ['bedroul], *s. U.S: Mil:* rouleau *m* de (matériel de) couchage.

bedroom ['bedru:m], *s.* chambre *f* à coucher; **spare b.,** chambre d'ami; **b. slippers,** pantoufles *f* en feutre; *Th:* **b. farce,** comédie *f* leste.

-bedroomed ['bedru:md], *a.* **three-b. house,** maison pourvue de trois chambres à coucher.

bedside ['bedsaid], *s.* chevet *m*; bord *m* du lit; **at s.o.'s b.,** au chevet de qn; **b. carpet, rug,** descente *f* de lit; **b. lamp,** lampe *f* de chevet; veilleuse *f*; **b. table,** table *f* de nuit, de chevet; **b. books, literature,** livres *m* de chevet; **the nurse never left his b.,** l'infirmière ne quittait pas son chevet; (*of doctor*) **to have a good b. manner,** avoir un comportement agréable au chevet du malade.

bed-sittingroom ['bedsitiŋru:m], *s., F:* **bed-sit(ter)** ['bed'sit(ər)], *s.* chambre meublée, garnie; garni *m*; studio *m.*

bedsock ['bedsɔk], *s.* chausson *m* de nuit.

bedsore ['bedsɔ:r], *s.* escarre (produite par le séjour au lit); eschare *f*; *Med:* décubitus *m.*

bedspread ['bedspred], *s.* courtepointe *f*; couverture *f* de parade; dessus *m* de lit.

bedstead ['bedsted], *s.* châlit *m,* bois *m* de lit; **iron, mahogany, b.,** lit *m* de fer, lit en acajou; **folding b.,** lit pliant; lit-cage *m, pl.* lits-cages; *Av:* *F:* *A:* **flying b.,** lit-cage volant; *Mil:* **b. trestle, b. foot,** pied *m* de châlit.

bedstraw ['bedstrɔ:], *s. Bot:* caille-lait *m inv,* gaillet *m*; **lady's b.,** gaillet, caille-lait, jaune.

bedtick[1] ['bedtik], *s. U.S:* punaise *f.*

bedtick[2], **bedticking** ['bedtikiŋ], *s.* toile *f* à matelas.

bedtime ['bedtaim], *s.* heure *f* du coucher; **it is b.,** il est l'heure de se coucher, d'aller se coucher; **what is your b.?** à quelle heure vous couchez-vous? **it's past your b.,** vous devriez être déjà couché; **b. stories,** histoires *f* pour l'heure du coucher, pour endormir.

bedward(s) ['bedwəd(z)], *adv. O:* **to go b.,** aller se coucher.

bedworthy ['bedwə:ði], *s. F:* (*of woman*) séduisante.

bee[1] [bi:], *s.* **1.** abeille *f*; **queen b.,** abeille mère, reine *f* des abeilles; **hive b.,** abeille domestique; **working b.,** abeille neutre; abeille ouvrière; cirière *f*; **honey b.,** abeille domestique; *F:* mouche *f* à miel; **the honey bees,** les mellifères *m*; **black b., German b.,** abeille âtre; **bumble b., humble b.,** bourdon *m*; **stone bumble b.,** bourdon des pierres; **carpenter b.,** abeille menuisière, rubicole; abeille perce-bois; xylocope *mf*; **giant b., rock b.,** abeille géante; **Indian b.,** abeille indienne; **leaf cutter b.,** (abeille) coupeuse (*f*) de feuilles; mégachile *f*; **little b.,** abeille naine; **mason b.,** abeille maçonne; **rufous b.,** abeille des sables; **wasp b.,** nomade *f*; **bees' nest,** nid *m* d'abeilles; **to keep bees,** élever des abeilles; *F:* **to be a busy b.,** faire la mouche du coche; **to have a b. in one's bonnet,** (i) être timbré; avoir un grain; avoir une araignée au plafond; avoir des lubies; *P:* travailler du chapeau; (ii) avoir une idée fixe. **2.** *attrib:* (*a*) **b. glue,** propolis *f, occ. m*; **b. lover,** apiphile *mf*; **b.-loving,** apiphile; **b. master,** apiculteur *m*; **b. skep,** ruche *f* en paille; (*b*) *Bot:* **b. balm,** monarde *f* d'Amérique; **b. orchis,** ophrys *f* abeille; **b. plant,** cléome épineuse, cléome rose; **b. tree,** tilleul *m* (d'Amérique); (*c*) *Ent:* **b. fly,** bombyle *m*; **b. moth,** pyrale *f*, gallérie *f*; (*d*) *Orn:* **b. eater,** guêpier *m* (d'Europe); **blue-cheeked b. eater,** guêpier de Perse; **b. kite,** bondrée *f* apivore. **3.** (*a*) réunion *f* (pour travaux en commun); (*b*) concours *m*; **spelling b.,** concours (oral) d'orthographe.

bee[2], *s. N.Arch:* violon *m* (du beaupré).

beebread [ˈbiːbred], *s. Ap:* pâtée de pollen et de miel (donnée au couvain).

beech [biːtʃ], *s.* hêtre *m*, fayard *m*, *F:* fouteau *m*; **copper b.,** hêtre rouge, pourpre; **evergreen b.,** nothofagus *m*; **weeping b.,** hêtre pleureur; **b. grove,** foutelaie *f*, hêtraie *f*; **b. mast,** faînes *fpl* (surtout comme nourriture de pourceaux); **b. nut,** faîne; **b. oil,** huile *f* de faîne. **2.** *Com:* **b. (wood),** bois *m* de hêtre; **b. furniture,** meubles *mpl* en hêtre; **evergreen b. (timber),** roble *m*, pellin *m*.

beechdrops [ˈbiːtʃdrɔps], *s. Bot:* orobanche *f* de Virginie.

beechen [ˈbiːtʃ(ə)n], *a. A. & Lit:* de hêtre.

beech fern [ˈbiːtʃfəːn], *s. Bot:* polypode *m* phégoptère.

beech marten [ˈbiːtʃmɑːtin], *s. Z:* fouine *f*.

beef[1] [biːf], *s.* **1.** (*no pl.*) (*a*) *Cu:* bœuf *m*; **chilled b.,** bœuf frigorifié; **roast b.,** rôti *m* de bœuf, rosbif *m*; **salt b.,** bœuf salé, mariné; **corned b.,** corned beef *m*, conserve *f* de bœuf, *F:* singe *m*; **stewed b.,** ragoût *m* de bœuf, bœuf (à la) mode; **tinned stewed b.,** endaubage *m*; **boiled b.,** bœuf mariné bouilli légèrement; **b. cattle, b. animals,** bœufs de boucherie; (*b*) *F:* **to have plenty of b.,** avoir du muscle; **he's got plenty of b.,** il est costaud; **to put some b. into the job,** y mettre de l'énergie, y aller de toutes ses forces. **2.** *U.S:* (*a*) **a b.,** un bœuf, une vache; (*b*) (*pl.* **beefs** [biːfs], **beaves** [biːvz]) bœuf(s), vache(s), à l'engrais. **3.** *P:* grief *m*, plainte *f*; **he enjoys a good b.,** il aime ronchonner, rouspéter.

beef[2], **1.** *v.i. P:* ronchonner, rouspéter; *P:* râler. **2.** *v.tr. NAm: P:* **to b. up a scheme,** gonfler l'importance d'un projet; **to b. up the army,** renforcer l'armée.

beef-brained [ˈbiːfbreind], *a. F:* bête, stupide.

beefburger [ˈbiːfbəːgər], *s.* boulette *f* de bœuf hâché (entre deux morceaux de pain); hamburger *m*.

beefcake [ˈbiːfkeik], *s. F:* poitrine (d'homme) nue, bombée; **magazine full of b.,** magazine plein de (photos de) caïds, de costauds.

beefeater [ˈbiːfiːtər], *s.* **1.** *A:* mangeur *m*, avaleur *m*, de bœuf; domestique nourri grassement. **2.** *F:* (= *yeoman of the guard*) hallebardier *m*, (i) de la garde du corps; (ii) de service à la Tour de Londres. **3.** *Orn:* pique-bœuf *m*, *pl.* pique-bœufs.

beefer [ˈbiːfər], *s. P:* ronchonneur *m*, rouspéteur *m*, *P:* râleur *m*.

beefiness [ˈbiːfinis], *s. F:* (abondance *f* de) muscle *m*.

beefing [ˈbiːfiŋ], *s. P:* ronchonnement *m*, rouspétance *f*.

beefsteak [ˈbiːfˈsteik], *s. Cu:* biftek *m*; *Fung:* **b. fungus,** langue-de-bœuf *f*, *pl.* langues-de-bœuf; foie-de-bœuf *m*, *pl.* foies-de-bœuf; fistuline *f*.

beeftea [ˈbiːfˈtiː], *s.* bouillon *m* de bœuf; thé *m* de viande.

beef-witted [ˈbiːfˈwitid], *a. F:* stupide, bête.

beefwood [ˈbiːfwud], *s.* (*a*) *Bot:* casuarine *f*, filao *m*; (*b*) (*timber*) filao.

beefy [ˈbiːfi], *a. F:* musculeux, musclé; bien en chair; solide; costaud.

beehive [ˈbiːhaiv], *s. Ap:* ruche *f*; *F:* **a (regular) b. of industry,** une ruche d'industrie; *Gr.Ant:* **b. tomb,** tombe *f* à coupole; *Ch:* **b. shelf,** têt *m* à gaz.

beekeeper [ˈbiːkiːpər], *s.* apiculteur *m*.

beekeeping [ˈbiːkiːpiŋ], *s.* apiculture *f*; l'exploitation *f* apicole; **b. industry,** industrie abeillère.

beeline [ˈbiːlain], *s.* ligne *f* à vol d'abeille, à vol d'oiseau; **in a b.,** à vol d'abeille, d'oiseau; *F:* **to make a b. for sth.,** aller droit, directement, vers qch.; s'avancer en droite ligne vers qch.; **he made a b. for the door,** il ne fit qu'un saut vers la porte.

Beelzebub [biˈelzibʌb], *Pr.n.m.* **1.** *B.Lit:* Belzébuth. **2.** le Diable.

beep[1] [biːp], *s.* bip-bip *m* (d'un satellite, etc.).

beep[2], *v.i.* (*of satellite, etc.*) faire bip-bip.

beer [biːər], *s.* bière *f*. **1.** (*a*) **bitter b.,** bière piquante, amère, fortement houblonnée; **draught b.,** bière au tonneau, à la pompe, détaillée du fût; **bottled b.,** bière en can(n)ette; **small b.,** petite bière; *F:* **to think no small b. of oneself,** ne pas se prendre pour de la petite bière; se croire sorti de la cuisse de Jupiter; le porter haut, *P:* se gober; **that's small b.,** c'est insignifiant; **to be in b.,** être ivre; **fortune made in b.,** fortune faite dans la brasserie; *F:* **life isn't all b. and skittles,** tout n'est pas rose(s) dans ce (bas) monde; *attrib.* **b. barrel,** tonneau *m* à bière; **b. bottle,** bouteille *f* à bière; **b. engine,** pompe *f* à bière (sous pression); **b. garden,** café *m* en plein air; guinguette *f*; **b. glass,** bock *m*, chope *f*; *A:* **b. house, b. shop,** cabaret *m*; brasserie *f*; café-brasserie *f*, *pl.* cafés-brasseries; taverne *f*; **b. mat,** sous-bock *m inv.*; **b. money,** supplément de gages (donné lorsque l'on ne fournit pas la bière aux domestiques); *Can:* **b. parlour,** bar *m*; **b. pull,** (levier *m* de la) pompe à bière; **b. pump,** pompe à bière; (*b*) **to order a b.,** demander une bière, un demi. **2. ginger b.,** boisson gazeuse au gingembre; **spruce b.,** bière de spruce; sapinette *f*.

beerily [ˈbiːrili], *adv.* d'une voix avinée, d'un air ahuri.

Beersheba [biəˈʃiːbə], *Pr.n.* (*a*) *B.Geog:* Bersabée *f*; (*b*) *Geog:* Birshéba *f*.

Beer stone [ˈbiəstoun], *s. Const:* pierre calcaire extraite à Beer Head.

beery [ˈbiəri], *a.* **1.** (atmosphère *f*) qui sent la bière; **b. face,** trogne *f* d'ivrogne. **2.** un peu gris; **b. voice** = voix avinée.

beestings [ˈbiːstiŋz], *s.* amouille *f*; colostrum *m* (de la vache).

beeswax[1] [ˈbiːzwæks], *s.* (*a*) cire *f* d'abeilles; (*b*) cire à parquet.

beeswax[2], *v.tr.* cirer, encaustiquer (le parquet); passer (le parquet) à la cire.

beeswaxing [ˈbiːzwæksiŋ], *s.* cirage *m*, encaustiquage *m*.

beeswing [ˈbiːzwiŋ], *s.* **1.** pellicules *fpl* (du vin de Porto). **2.** vieux porto.

beet [biːt], *s. Bot: etc:* betterave *f*; **tap-rooted b.,** betterave longue; **turnip-rooted b.,** betterave ronde; **fodder b.,** betterave fourragère; **white b.,** (i) (bette) poirée (*f*); carde poirée; (ii) betterave à sucre; **sea kale b.,** bette à carde (blanche); bette à côtes; **sugar b.,** betterave à sucre; **b. sugar,** sucre *m* de betterave; **b.-worker,** betteravier, -ière; **b. industry,** industrie betteravière; *Agr:* **b. puller, b. harvester,** arracheuse *f* de betteraves.

beetle[1] [ˈbiːtl], *s.* mailloche *f*, masse *f* (en bois); maillet *m*; (*for paving*) hie *f*, demoiselle *f*, dame *f*; (*for pile driving*) mouton *m*; *Cer:* batte *f*; *Laund:* battoir *m*; (*quarrying*) batterand *m*; *Civ.E: etc:* **b. head,** mouton (de sonnette).

beetle[2], *v.tr.* battre (qch.) à coups de mailloche, etc.

beetle[3], *s. Ent:* coléoptère *m*; hister *m*, escarbot *m*, scarabée *m*.

beetle[4], *v.i. F:* **to b. off, away,** décamper; s'en aller; **to b. off to America,** filer aux États-Unis; **b. off!** va-t-en! **to b. along,** se traîner; aller doucement; **to b. about, around,** flâner.

beetle[5], *a.* **b. brows,** (i) sourcils proéminents; (ii) sourcils touffus; (iii) front sourcilleux.

beetle[6], *v.i.* surplomber; **the rocks b. over the ravine,** les rochers *m* surplombent le ravin.

beetle-boat [ˈbiːtlbout], *s. Mil:* bateau *m* de débarquement à fond plat.

beetle-brain [ˈbiːtlbrein], *s. F:* cerveau épais.

beetle-browed [ˈbiːtlbraud], *a.* (i) aux sourcils proéminents; (ii) aux sourcils épais, touffus, broussailleux; (iii) sourcilleux.

beetle-crushers, -squashers [ˈbiːtlkrʌʃəz, -skwɔʃəz], *s.pl. P:* **1.** pieds *m*; *P:* arpions *m*, ripatons *m*. **2.** godillots *m*, bateaux *m*, croquenots *m*; *P:* écrase-merdes *m inv*.

beetlehead [ˈbiːtlhed], *s. F:* imbécile *mf*.

beetling[1] [ˈbiːtliŋ], *s.* battage *m* à coups de mailloche, masse, maillet, etc.; *Tex:* **b. machine,** moulin *m* à pilons.

beetling[2], *a.* **1.** (*of rock*) surplombant, menaçant; **the high b. cliffs,** les hautes falaises en surplomb; **b. height,** précipice *m*. **2.** = BEETLE[5].

beetroot [ˈbiːtruːt], *s.* betterave (potagère).

beeves [biːvz], *s.pl.* **1.** *Poet:* bétail *m*. **2.** *Husb:* bœufs *m*, vaches *f*, à l'engrais.

befall [biˈfɔːl], *v.tr. & i.* (*conj. like* FALL; *used only in 3rd pers.*) *Lit:* arriver, survenir (à qn); **a misfortune befell him,** un malheur lui survint; il lui arriva un malheur; **what has befallen him?** qu'est-il advenu de lui? **it so befell that . . .,** il arriva que . . .; **b. what may!** arrive, advienne, que pourra!

befit [biˈfit], *v.tr. esp. Lit:* (**befitted**) (*used only in 3rd pers.*) convenir, seoir à (qn, qch.); **it does not b. a knight to . . .,** ce n'est pas le fait d'un chevalier de . . ..

befitting [biˈfitiŋ], *a.* convenable, seyant (à qn, qch.).

befittingly [biˈfitiŋli], *adv.* convenablement; comme il convient.

befog [biˈfɔg], *v.tr.* (**befogged**) *Lit:* **1.** envelopper de brouillard. **2.** obscurcir (la pensée, etc.); **wine befogs the senses,** le vin offusque la raison.

befool [biˈfuːl], *v.tr. Lit:* mystifier, tromper, berner.

before [biˈfɔːr]. **1.** *adv.* (*a*) (*in space*) en avant, devant; **to go on b.,** marcher en avant, prendre les devants; (*take precedence*) passer le premier; **he has gone on b.,** il est parti en avant; **there were trees both b. and behind,** il y avait des arbres devant et derrière; **this page and the one b.,** cette page et la précédente, et celle d'avant, et celle qui précède; (*b*) (*in time*) auparavant, avant; **two days b.,** deux jours avant, deux jours auparavant; l'avant-veille *f*; **the day b.,** le jour d'avant, le jour précédent; la veille; **the evening b.,** la veille au soir; **the year b.,** l'année d'auparavant, d'avant; **she had come two years b.,** elle était venue il y avait deux ans; **a moment b.,** un moment auparavant, un moment d'auparavant; **I had seen him only a, the, minute b.,** je l'avais vu la minute d'avant; **I have seen him b.,** je l'ai déjà vu; **I have never seen him b.,** je le vois pour la première fois; je ne l'ai encore jamais vu; **he had never done it b.,** il ne l'avait jamais fait jusqu'alors; **he never did it b.,** il ne l'a jamais fait jusqu'ici; **to go on as b.,** faire comme par le passé; **you should have told me so b.,** vous auriez dû me le dire plus tôt. **2.** *prep.* (*a*) (*place*) devant; **to stand b. s.o., sth.,** se tenir devant qn, qch.; **I have the poem b. me,** j'ai le poème sous les yeux, devant moi; **to have sth. b. one's eyes,** avoir qch. sous les yeux; **b. my (very) eyes,** sous mes (propres) yeux; **he said so b. me,** il l'a dit en ma présence; **he fled b. us,** il fuyait à notre approche; **I have nothing but the old people's home b. me,** je n'ai d'autre perspective que l'hospice, la maison de retraite; **b. God and man,** devant Dieu et les hommes; **to appear b. the judge,** comparaître par-devant le juge; **to bring a question b. a court,** saisir un tribunal d'une question; **the question b. us,** la question qui nous occupe; **we have two questions b. us,** nous sommes saisis de deux questions; **that is the task b. us,** c'est là la tâche qui nous incombe; (*b*) (*time*) avant; **b. Christ, B.C.,** avant Jésus-Christ, av. J.-C.; **b. our era,** antérieurement à notre ère; **b. long,** avant longtemps, sous peu; **not b. Easter,** pas avant Pâques; **it ought to have been done b. now,** ce devrait être déjà fait; **b. (the battle of) Leipzig,** avant Leipzig (*cp.* devant Leipzig); **just b. the meeting,** (à) la veille de la réunion; **to arrive an hour b. time,** arriver (avec) une heure d'avance; **we are b. our time,** nous sommes en avance; *F:* **it's not b. time,** ce n'est pas trop tôt; **I got here b. you,** je vous ai devancé; **the generations which came b. us,** les générations qui nous ont devancés; **the day b. the battle,** la veille de la bataille; **two days b. Christmas,** l'avant-veille de Noël; **b. answering,** avant (que) de répondre; *Mil:* **evacuation of a region b. the date fixed,** évacuation anticipée; *Fin:* **redemption b. due date,** remboursement anticipé; *F:* **my b.-breakfast cigarette,** ma cigarette d'avant-déjeuner; (*c*) (*preference, order*) **b. everything (else) I must have . . .,** il me faut avant tout . . .; **death b. dishonour,** plutôt la mort que le déshonneur; **to put virtue b. wealth,** mettre la vertu avant les richesses; préférer la vertu aux richesses; **ladies b. gentlemen,** les dames avant les messieurs; **the welfare of the country comes b. everything,** le bien de la patrie prime tout. **3.** *conj.* avant que (ne) + *sub.* (*a*) **come and see me b. you leave,** venez me voir avant que vous (ne) partiez, avant de partir, avant votre départ; **don't come in b. I call you,** n'entrez pas avant que, sans que, je vous appelle; **it will be long b. we see him again,** on ne le reverra pas d'ici longtemps; **it was long b. he came,** il fut longtemps à venir; **I had not waited long b. he came,** il ne tarda pas à venir; **b. night comes I shall know . . .,** d'ici (que vienne) la nuit je saurai . . .; **you'll be ruined b. you know where you are,** vous allez vous ruiner en moins de rien; **I'll be with you b. you can say Jack Robinson,** je suis à vous en moins de rien; (*b*) **I will die b. I yield,** je préfère mourir plutôt que de céder; (*c*) **b. I forget, they expect you this evening,** j'oubliais de vous dire qu'on vous attend ce soir.

beforehand [biˈfɔːhænd], *adv.* préalablement, au préalable, à l'avance, par avance, d'avance, auparavant; **to come an hour b.,** venir une heure d'avance; **I must tell you b. that . . .,** il faut vous dire d'avance, au préalable, que . . .; **you ought to have told me b.,** vous auriez dû me prévenir; **if I come I shall let you know b.,** si je viens je vous préviendrai; to see **things a long time b.,** prévoir les choses de loin; **to pay b.,** payer d'avance, à l'avance; **to rejoice b.,** se réjouir par avance, à l'avance; **I knew it b.,** je le savais déjà; **to be b. with the rent,** payer son loyer avant le terme.

beforetime [biˈfɔːtaim], *adv. A: & Lit:* autrefois, jadis.

befoul [biˈfaul], *v.tr. A: & Lit:* souiller, salir, ((i) un endroit; (ii) le nom, l'honneur, de qn).

befriend [biˈfrend], *v.tr.* venir en aide à, à l'aide de (qn); donner aide à (qn); secourir (qn); se montrer l'ami de (qn); protéger (qn).

befuddle [bi'fʌdl], *v.tr.* (*a*) griser (qn); (*b*) brouiller les idées de (qn).

befuddlement [bi'fʌdlmənt], *s.* (*a*) ivresse *f*; (*b*) hébétement *m.*

beg [beg], *v.* (**begged**)
I. *v.tr. & i.* **1.** (*a*) mendier; tendre la main; tendre la sébile; **to b. (for) one's bread,** mendier son pain; **to live by begging,** vivre d'aumône; **to b. one's way to Paris,** aller, venir, à Paris en mendiant (le long du chemin); *F:* **if I can b., borrow or steal a car for the holidays,** si je peux acquérir une voiture pour les vacances, n'importe comment; (*with passive force*) **these jobs go begging,** ce sont des emplois qui trouvent peu d'amateurs; **these jobs don't go begging for long,** ce sont des situations qu'on s'arrache; (*b*) (*of dog*) **to sit up and b.,** faire le beau. **2. to b. a favour of s.o.,** solliciter une faveur de qn; demander une faveur à qn; **to b. (of) s.o. to do sth.,** prier, supplier, qn de faire qch.; **to b. s.o. to attend,** requérir la présence de qn; **he begs to be listened to,** il supplie qu'on veuille bien l'écouter; **I begged for Mary to stay on for a week,** j'ai supplié qu'on permît à Marie de rester encore huit jours; **I b. to inform you that . . .,** j'ai l'honneur de vous faire savoir que . . .; *Com: O:* **we b. to hand you a cheque for . . .,** nous avons l'avantage de vous remettre un chèque de . . .; **I b. to state, to observe, that . . .,** qu'il me soit permis de faire remarquer que . . .; **to b. for peace,** demander la paix; **I b. (of) you!** de grâce! je vous en prie! **be quiet, I b. you!** taisez-vous, je vous en supplie! **to b. the question,** faire une pétition de principe; supposer vrai ce qui est en question; prendre pour un axiome la question à prouver.
II. (*compound verb*) **beg off.** (*a*) *v.tr.* **to b. s.o. off,** demander grâce pour qn; (*b*) *v.i.* **to b. off for the afternoon,** demander la permission de s'absenter pour l'après midi; **he begged off on account of his wife's illness,** il s'est excusé à cause de la maladie de sa femme.

beg(a)- ['beg(ə)], *pref. El:* dix à la neuvième puissance.

begad [bi'gæd], *int. A:* (*softened form of* **by God**) **1.** ma foi! **2.** sacrebleu!

beget [bi'get], *v.tr.* (**begot**) [bi'gɔt], *B:* **begat** [bi'gæt]; **begotten** [bi'gɔtn]) **1.** engendrer, procréer; **Abraham begat Isaac,** Abraham engendra Isaac; **discord begets crime,** la discorde enfante le crime; *B:* **the only begotten Son of the Father,** le Fils unique du Père. **2.** causer, susciter; faire naître (des difficultés, etc.).

begetter [bi'getər], *s.* **1.** père *m,* auteur *m* (of, de). **2.** cause *f* (of, de).

begetting [bi'getiŋ], *s.* engendrement *m,* procréation *f.*

beggar[1] ['begər], *s.* **1. b.** (**-man, -woman**), mendiant, -e, gueux, -euse, pauvre, -esse; **b. girl,** jeune mendiante, petite mendiante; **sturdy b.,** truand *m*; *Prov:* **beggars can't be choosers,** ne choisit pas qui emprunte; faute de souliers on va nu pieds. **2.** *F:* individu *m,* **funny little b.,** drôle *m* de petit bonhomme; **poor b.!** pauvre diable! **he's a b. for work,** il n'a pas son pareil pour le travail; **lucky b.!** (i) chançard! veinard! (ii) il en a de la chance, cet animal-là! **you little b.!** petit coquin! petit espiègle! **3.** *Bot:* **beggar's lice,** caille-lait *m inv,* gaillet *m*; **beggar's ticks,** (i) aigremoine *f*; (ii) bidens *m,* bident *m*; **b. weed,** barbe-de-moine *f, pl.* barbes-de-moine; cheveux *mpl* du diable.

beggar[2], *v.tr.* (**beggared** ['begəd]) **1. to b. s.o.,** réduire qn à la mendicité; mettre qn sur la paille; **to leave s.o. beggared,** laisser qn sans le sou. **2. to b. description,** défier toute description, être indescriptible; **it beggars description,** cela ne peut pas se décrire.

beggardom ['begədəm], *s. O: coll.* les mendiants, les gueux; la mendicité.

beggarliness ['begəlinis], *s.* mesquinerie *f.*

beggarly ['begəli], chétif, minable, misérable, mesquin; **b. wage,** salaire *m* dérisoire; salaire de misère, de famine; **for a b. few thousand francs!** pour quelques malheureux mille francs!

beggar-my-neighbour ['begəmi'neibər], *s. Cards:* bataille *f.*

beggary ['begəri], *s.* mendicité *f,* misère *f*; **to be reduced to b.,** être réduit à la mendicité, à l'aumône; être dans la misère.

begging[1] ['begiŋ], *a.* (frère, ordre) mendiant; **b. letter,** lettre quémandant une contribution (à une œuvre de bienfaisance).

begging[2], *s.* **1.** mendicité *f*; **b. bowl,** sébile *f* de mendiant. **2. b. the question,** pétition *f* de principe; *F:* simplisme *m.*

begin [bi'gin], *v.tr. & i.* (**began** [bi'gæn], **begun** [bi'gʌn]) commencer (un discours, une tâche, etc.); entamer, amorcer (une conversation, la partie); attaquer (un repas, etc.); **to b. one's work,** commencer son travail; (*of official*) entrer en fonctions; (*of an assembly*) inaugurer ses travaux; **to b. at the beginning,** commencer par le commencement; **he began life as a ploughboy,** il débuta dans la vie comme valet de charrue; **just where the hair begins,** à la naissance des cheveux; **before winter begins,** avant le début de l'hiver; **the guns began,** les canons entrèrent en danse; **the day began well, badly,** la journée s'annonça bien, mal; **never since the world began,** jamais depuis le commencement du monde; *F:* jamais depuis que le monde est monde; **to b. a fresh chapter, another bottle,** entamer un nouveau chapitre; entamer, déboucher, une autre bouteille; **to b. to do sth., to b. doing sth.,** commencer à faire qch.; se mettre à faire qch.; **he began studying law, he began to study law,** il commença son droit; **to b. to laugh, to cry, to b. laughing, crying,** se mettre à rire, à pleurer; se prendre à pleurer; **to b. to sing,** se mettre à chanter; entonner une chanson; **to b. to boil, to melt,** entrer en ébullition, en fusion; **he soon began to complain,** il ne tarda pas à se plaindre; **we began to get hungry,** la faim nous gagnait; **this system of education was beginning to be criticized,** on commençait à attaquer ce système d'enseignement; *F:* **it doesn't b. to compare with . . .,** cela est loin d'être comparable à . . .; **to b. by doing sth.,** débuter, commencer, par faire qch.; **b. with me,** commencez par moi; **the play begins with a prologue,** la pièce débute par un prologue; **to b. with, I thought he was wrong,** pour commencer, au préalable, de premier abord, de prime abord, je pensais qu'il avait tort; **to b. with, he has got his facts wrong,** pour commencer, d'abord, tout d'abord, il se trompe sur les faits; **to b. again,** recommencer, reprendre; **let us b. again,** recommençons; *F:* remettons ça; **to b. to cry again,** se reprendre à pleurer; **there, it's beginning again!** voilà que ça reprend! voilà que ça recommence! *Prov:* **well begun is half done,** à moitié fait qui commence bien.

beginner [bi'ginər], *s.* **1.** premier *m* à agir; auteur *m,* cause *f* (d'une querelle, etc.); *Th:* **beginners please!** en scène pour le un! **2.** commençant, -ante; débutant, -ante; novice *mf*; **I'm only a b.,** je ne suis qu'un apprenti; **beginner's luck,** aux innocents les mains pleines.

beginning [bi'giniŋ], *s.* commencement *m*; début *m* (d'un discours, d'une carrière, etc.); origine *f,* naissance *f* (du monde, etc.); **in the b.,** au commencement, au début; **from the b.,** dès le commencement; dès le principe; **from b. to end,** depuis le commencement, le début, jusqu'à la fin; d'un bout à l'autre; de bout en bout; **at the b. of term,** à la rentrée des classes; **the first beginnings of civilization,** les rudiments *m* de la civilisation; **here Methodism had its beginnings,** ce fut ici le berceau du Méthodisme; **from modest beginnings he rose to be . . .,** parti de très bas, il en arriva à se trouver . . .; **since the b. of things,** depuis la naissance du monde; depuis que le monde est monde; **to make a b.,** commencer, débuter; **to start again from the very b.,** reprendre le travail à pied d'œuvre; *Mec.E: etc:* **b. of looseness, of play,** amorce *f* de desserrage, de jeu; *Aut:* **b. of a skid,** amorce de dérapage; *Civ.E:* **b. (of the cutting) of a road, of a tunnel,** amorce, amorçage *m,* d'une rue, d'un tunnel; **everything has a b.,** il y a un début à tout; **a good b. is half the battle,** à moitié fait qui commence bien; matines bien sonnées sont à moitié dites; **a bad b. makes a bad ending,** qui commence mal finit mal.

begird [bi'gə:d], *v.tr.* (*p.p.* **begirt** [bi'gə:t]) *Lit:* ceindre, entourer (**s.o. with sth.,** qn de qch.); **city begirt with ramparts,** ville ceinte de remparts.

begob [bi'gɔb], *int.* = BEGORRA.

begohm ['begoum], *s.* mille mégohms *m.*

begone [bi'gɔn], *p.p. A:* (*used as imp.*) va-t'en! allez-vous-en! partez! hors d'ici!

begonia [bi'gouniə], *s. Bot:* bégonia *m.*

Begoniaceae [bi'gounieisii:], *s.pl. Bot:* bégoniacées *f.*

begorra [bi'gɔrə], *int. Irish Dial:* (*by God*) **1.** sacrebleu! **2.** ma foi!

begrime [bi'graim], *v.tr. Lit:* noircir, salir, barbouiller; **begrimed with smoke, with soot,** noirci de fumée; barbouillé de suie.

begrudge [bi'grʌdʒ], *v.tr.* **1.** donner (qch.) à contrecœur; **to b. doing sth.,** faire qch. à contrecœur; *F:* rechigner à faire qch. **2. to b. s.o. sth.,** envier qch. à qn; **they b. him his food,** on lui mesure, on lui reproche, sa nourriture; **he had begrudged her nothing,** il ne lui avait rien refusé; **do you b. him this honour?** lui enviez-vous cet honneur?

begrudging [bi'grʌdʒiŋ], *a.* **1. b. acquiescence, smile,** assentiment, sourire, donné à contrecœur. **2. b. look,** regard envieux. **3. b. with one's compliments,** chiche, avare, de compliments.

begrudgingly [bi'grʌdʒiŋli], *adv.* **1.** à contrecœur; *F:* en rechignant. **2.** envieusement. **3.** chichement.

begti ['begti], *s. Ich:* latès *m.*

beguile [bi'gail], *v.tr. Lit:* **1.** enjôler, séduire, tromper (qn); *B:* **the serpent beguiled me,** le serpent m'a séduite; **to b. one's creditors,** amuser ses créanciers; **to b. s.o. with promises,** bercer qn de promesses; **to b. s.o. out of sth.,** soutirer qch. à qn; **to b. s.o. into doing sth.,** user de séduction pour faire faire qch. à qn; induire qn à faire qch. **2.** distraire, charmer, amuser; **to b. the time,** faire passer le temps; tromper son ennui; se désennuyer; **to b. the time doing sth.,** s'amuser à faire qch.; tromper son ennui en faisant qch.; **to b. the long night watches,** tromper les longues heures de veille; **to b. hunger** (*with tobacco, etc.*), tromper la faim; **to b. s.o.'s leisure,** charmer les loisirs de qn; **to b. one's sorrow,** se distraire de son chagrin.

beguilement [bi'gailmənt], *s. Lit:* enjôlement *m,* séduction *f.*

beguiler [bi'gailər], *s. Lit:* séducteur, -trice; trompeur, -euse.

beguiling [bi'gailiŋ], *a.* (sourire, etc.) enjôleur, séduisant.

beguilingly [bi'gailiŋli], *adv.* d'une manière séduisante, enjôleuse.

beguine[1] [bi'gi:n], *s.f. Rel:* béguine.

beguine[2], *s. Danc:* biguine *f.*

begum ['beigəm, *O:* 'bi:-], *s.f.* (*India & Pakistan*) bégum, reine, princesse.

behalf [bi'hɑ:f], *s.* **on b. of s.o.,** au nom de qn; *Com:* **payment on b. of s.o.,** versement *m* au compte, à l'acquit, de qn; **I come on b. of Mr. X,** je viens de la part de M. X; **he is acting on my b.,** il agit pour moi, pour mon compte; **on b. of my colleagues and myself,** en mon nom et au nom de mes collègues; **to do much on b. of the prisoners,** faire beaucoup pour les prisonniers; **don't be uneasy on my b.,** ne vous inquiétez pas à mon sujet.

behave [bi'heiv], *v.i.* **1.** (*usu. with adv.*) **to b. well, badly, wisely, like a man of honour,** se comporter, se conduire, bien, mal, prudemment, en homme d'honneur; **to b. well towards, to, s.o.,** bien agir envers qn, bien se comporter à l'égard de qn, envers qn, avec qn; bien se conduire à l'égard de, envers, qn; **what a way to b.!** quelle manière de se conduire! **the engine, the boat, behaves well, badly,** le moteur, le bateau, se comporte bien, mal; **ship that behaves well at sea,** navire qui tient bien la mer, qui navigue bien. **2.** (*also as v.pr.*) **to know how to b.,** savoir vivre; **we know how to b. in the presence of ladies,** on sait se tenir auprès des dames; **I'll teach him how to b.!** je lui apprendrai la politesse! (*to child, etc.*) **b. yourself!** de la tenue! tiens-toi (comme il faut)! sois sage! **3. how a salt behaves in the presence of water,** la manière dont un sel réagit à l'eau; **it is interesting to see how he behaves when faced with criticism,** il est intéressant d'observer la manière dont il réagit à la critique.

behaved [bi'heivd], *a.* (*with adv. prefixed, e.g.*) **well-b.,** sage; poli; qui se conduit bien; qui a de la conduite; qui a du maintien, de la tenue; **ill-b., badly b.,** qui se conduit mal; qui se tient mal; malhonnête; grossier; **the best-b. boy in the class,** l'élève le plus sage de la classe; **to become better b.,** s'assagir.

behaviour [bi'heivjər], *s.* **1.** façon *f* de se comporter, d'agir; comportement *m*; maintien *m*; conduite *f* (**to, towards, s.o.,** avec, envers, qn); procédé *m* (envers qn); **your b. is being watched,** on observe vos faits et gestes; **good b.,** bonne conduite; **to put s.o. on his best b.,** recommander à qn de se bien tenir, de se surveiller; **to be on one's best b.,** se surveiller; se conduire de son mieux; **be on your best b.!** tenez-vous! **sedate b.,** allure posée; *Mil:* **good b. certificate,** certificat *m* de bonne conduite; *Med:* **b. therapy,** traitement *m* de comportement. **2.** allure *f,* fonctionnement *m,* comportement (d'une machine); tenue *f* (d'une voiture); tenue en l'air (d'un avion). **3.** comportement (de particules atomiques, etc.).

behavioural [bi'heivjərəl], *a. Psy:* comportemental, -aux; **b. science,** science *f* de l'étude du comportement.

behaviourism [bi'heivjərizm], *s.* psychologie *f* du comportement; behavio(u)risme *m.*

behaviourist [bi'heivjərist], *a. & s. Psy:* behavio(u)riste.

behaviouristic [biheivjə'ristik], *a. Psy:* behavio(u)riste.

behaviouristics [biheivjə'ristiks], *s.* (*usu. with sg. const.*) science *f* du behavio(u)risme.

behead [bi'hed], *v.tr.* décapiter; faire tomber la tête de (qn); **he was beheaded,** on lui coupa la tête, le cou.

beheading [bi'hediŋ], *s.* décapitation *f*; *A:* décollation *f* (de saint Jean-Baptiste, etc.).

behemoth [bi'hi:məθ], *s. B: & Lit:* béhémoth *m*; monstre *m.*

behen ['bi:hen, -hən], *s. Bot:* **1.** béhen *m*; **white b.,** béhen blanc; silène enflé; **red b.,** béhen rouge; saladelle *f.* **2.**

ben *m*, béhen; *Pharm:* **oil of b.,** huile *f* de ben, de béhen; **b. nut,** noix *f* de ben.

behenic [bi'henik], *a. Ch:* (acide *m*) béhénique.

behenolic [bihe'noulik], *a. Ch:* (acide *m*) béhénolique.

behest [bi'hest], *s. Lit:* commandement *m*, ordre *m*; **to do sth. at s.o.'s b.,** faire qch. sur l'ordre de qn.

behind [bi'haind]. **1.** *adv.* derrière, par derrière; (*a*) **hair cropped close b.,** cheveux coupés ras par derrière; **to attack s.o. from b.,** attaquer qn par derrière; **to come b.,** venir derrière; suivre; **to fall, lag, b.,** s'attarder; traîner en arrière; se laisser distancer; ne pas pouvoir suivre; **to stay, remain, b.,** rester, demeurer, en arrière; **the servants had remained b.,** les domestiques n'étaient pas partis; *A:* **to get up b. (on a horse),** monter en croupe; monter par derrière; **to take s.o. up b. (on the crupper),** prendre qn en croupe; **the Alps and the plains b.,** les Alpes et les plaines au-delà; (*b*) **to be b. with one's studies, with one's work, with one's payments,** être en retard pour ses études, dans son travail, pour ses paiements; **we ate ravenously and were not b. with the drink,** nous mangeâmes comme quatre et bûmes d'autant; **we are b. in business this year,** nous ne ferons pas nos affaires cette année; **I don't want to be b.,** je ne veux pas être en retard; **special class for children who are b.,** classe spéciale pour les enfants qui sont en retard; *Sp:* **they are only three points b.,** ils ne sont qu'à trois points. **2.** *prep.* (*a*) derrière; **he hid b. it,** il se cacha derrière; **look b. you,** regardez derrière vous; retournez-vous; **garden b. the house,** jardin derrière la maison; **to walk, follow, close b. s.o.,** marcher sur les talons de qn; **to walk b. a guide,** suivre un guide; **their devotion carried them on b. him,** leur dévouement les entraîna sur ses pas; **he left an honoured name b. him,** il laissa (après lui) un nom honoré; **she will remain b. me,** elle demeurera après moi; **I can't understand their policy; there must be something b. (it),** je ne comprends rien à leur politique; il doit y avoir quelque chose (là-)dessous; **what's b. all this?** qu'y a-t-il derrière tout cela? *Th: etc:* **b. the scenes,** dans la coulisse; **to be b.** (= *to support*) **s.o.,** soutenir qn; **he has the minister b. him,** il a le ministre derrière, avec lui; il est épaulé, protégé, par le ministre; *F:* **he's right b. me,** (i) il me donne son appui; (ii) il est à mes trousses; (iii) *Iron:* il me suit de loin; **to put a thought b. one,** rejeter une pensée; **I put this offer b. me,** je ne voulus rien savoir de cette offre; **another day b. me!** encore une journée de faite! **it's all b. me now,** c'est passé pour moi; *B:* **get thee b. me, Satan!** retire-toi de moi, Satan! (*b*) en arrière de, en retard sur (qn, qch.); **country (far) b. its neighbours,** pays *m* (très) en arrière de ses voisins; **to be b. s.o. in knowledge,** le céder à qn en savoir; **here we are far b. Paris,** ici nous sommes très en retard sur Paris (en matière de modes, etc.). **3.** *s. F:* derrière *m*, *P:* cul *m*; *F:* **to kick s.o.'s b.,** botter le derrière de, à, qn, enlever le ballon à qn; **to fall on one's b.,** tomber sur le derrière.

behindhand [bi'haindhænd], *adv. & a.* (*a*) en arrière, en retard, attardé; **to be b. with the rent,** être en retard pour, avec, le loyer; **I am b. with my work,** mon travail est en retard; **to be b. in doing sth.,** apporter du retard à faire qch.; (*b*) arriéré, een retard (sur son siècle); (*c*) **he is not b. in generosity,** il n'est pas en reste de générosité; **so as not to be b. in politeness. . .,** pour ne pas être en reste de politesse . . ..

Behistan [behis'tɑ:n], **Behistun** [behis'tu:n], *Pr.n. Geog:* le Behistoun, le Bisoutoun; **the B. Inscription,** l'Inscription *f* de Behistoun.

behold [bi'hould], *v.tr.* (**beheld** [bi'held]; **beheld**) *Lit:* **1.** voir; apercevoir; **I beheld a strange sight,** je fus témoin d'un étrange spectacle. **2.** *imp.* **b.!** voyez! **b. he cometh!** voici qu'il vient! **b. I am with thee,** et voici, je suis avec toi; **b. thy servant,** voici ton serviteur; **and b. (how things turn out)!** et tenez!

beholden [bi'houldn], *a.* **to be b. to s.o.,** être redevable à qn (**for,** de); être obligé à, envers, qn; être reconnaissant à qn (**for,** de).

beholder [bi'houldər], *s.* spectateur, -trice; assistant, -ante; témoin *m*; **beauty is in the eye of the b.,** il n'y a point de laides amours.

behoof [bi'hu:f], *s. A:* **to, for, on, s.o.'s b.,** à l'avantage, au profit, de qn; **for one's own b.,** dans son propre intérêt, à l'intention.

behove [bi'houv], *NAm:* **behoove** [bi'hu:v], *v.tr. impers.* incomber à; **it behoves him to . . .,** il lui appartient de . . ..

beige [beiʒ], *a. & s.* **1.** *Tex:* (*material*) beige (*f*). **2.** (*colour*) beige (*m*); blond (*m*).

being[1] ['bi:iŋ], *a.* **for the time b.,** pour le moment, pour le quart d'heure, pour l'heure, actuellement, temporairement; **that's all we can do for the time b.,** c'est tout ce que nous pouvons faire pour le moment; **this is my home for the time b.,** voici où j'habite provisoirement; **the manager for the time b.,** le gérant actuel.

being[2], *s.* **1.** existence *f*, être *m*; (*a*) **those to whom you owe your b.,** ceux qui vous ont donné l'être, le jour; (*b*) **to come into b.,** prendre forme, prendre naissance, se produire, se développer, survenir; **the coming into b. of a new industry,** la naissance, l'éclosion *f*, d'une nouvelle industrie; **to bring, call, sth. into b.,** faire naître qch.; susciter qch.; **to bring a plan into b.,** réaliser un projet; **then in b.,** qui existait alors, alors existant; **the company is still in b.,** la société existe encore; **fleet in b.,** flotte vivante. **2.** être; (*a*) **all my b. revolts at the idea,** tout mon être se révolte à cette idée; (*b*) **a human b.,** un être humain; **human beings,** le genre humain, les humains *m*; **intelligent beings,** êtres intelligents; **the Supreme B.,** l'Être Suprême.

Beirut [bei'ru:t], *Pr.n. Geog:* Beyrouth *m*.

Beja ['beidʒə]. **1.** *Ethn:* (*a*) *s.inv.* Bedja, *pl.* Bedjas; (*b*) *a.* bedja. **2.** *Ling:* le bedja.

bejabbers [bi'dʒæbəz], **bejabers** [bi'dʒeibəz], *int. Irish:* sacrebleu!

bejewelled [bi'dʒu(:)əld], *a.* paré de bijoux; **she was heavily b.,** *F:* elle était parée comme une châsse.

bekra ['bekrə], *s. Z:* tétracère *m*.

bekti ['bekti], *s. Ich:* latès *m*.

bel [bel], *s. Ph.Meas:* bel *m*.

belabour [bi'leibər], *v.tr.* (*a*) battre (qn) à coups redoublés, rouer (qn) de coups; administrer une bonne rossée à (qn); rosser (qn) d'importance; *F:* flanquer une tannée à (qn); (*b*) accabler (qn) d'injures; assaillir (qn).

belah ['bi:lə], *s. Bot:* casuarina *m*.

belated [bi'leitid], *a.* **1.** (voyageur, etc.) attardé; surpris par la nuit. **2.** (repentir, renseignement, etc.) tardif; (invité, etc.) en retard; **b. measures,** mesures *f* en retard sur les événements.

belatedly [bi'leitidli], *adv.* un peu tard; tardivement, sur le tard, trop tard.

belatedness [bi'leitidnis], *s. A:* tardiveté *f*; **the b. of the hour,** l'heure tardive; **the b. of his repentance,** son repentir tardif.

belaud [bi'lɔ:d], *v.tr.* **1.** *Lit:* combler, couvrir, (qn) de louanges; porter (qn) aux nues; chanter les louanges de (qch.). **2.** *Pej: A:* louanger (qn).

belay[1] [bi'lei], *v.tr.* (*a*) *Nau:* tourner, amarrer, lacer (une manœuvre); **b.!** (i) amarrez! (ii) *A:* en voilà assez! (*b*) *Mount:* assurer (la corde).

belay[2], *s. Mount:* point *m* d'assurance.

belaying [bi'leiiŋ], *s.* (*a*) *Nau:* tournage *m*, amarrage *m*; **b. pin, cleat,** cabillot *m*, chevillot *m*, taquet *m*; poupée *f* d'amarrage; **range of b. pins,** râtelier *m* de cabillots; (*b*) *Mount:* assurance *f*.

bel canto ['bel'kæntou], *s. Mus:* bel canto *m*.

belch[1] [bel(t)ʃ], *s.* **1.** éructation *f*, renvoi *m*; *P:* rot *m*. **2.** vomissement *m* (de flammes, etc.).

belch[2]. **1.** *v.i.* avoir un renvoi; éructer; *P:* roter. **2.** *v.tr.* **to b. forth, b. out, blasphemies, flames, smoke,** vomir des blasphèmes, des flammes, de la fumée.

belcher ['beltʃər], *s. A:* foulard bleu à pois blancs (comme en porta le pugiliste Jim Belcher).

beldam(e) ['beldəm], *s.f. Lit:* vieille sorcière; mégère.

beleaguer [bi'li:gər], *v.tr.* assiéger, cerner, investir (une ville).

beleaguerer [bi'li:gərər], *s.* assiégeant *m*.

beleaguerment [bi'li:gəmənt], *s.* investissement *m* (d'une ville).

belemnite ['beləmnait], *s. Paleont:* bélemnite *f*.

Belemnitidae [belem'nitidi:], *s.pl. Paleont:* bélemnitidés *m*.

Belemnoidea [belem'nɔidiə], *s.pl. Paleont:* bélemnoïdes *m*.

belfried ['belfrid], *a.* (tour *f*) à beffroi.

belfry ['belfri], *s.* **1.** beffroi *m*, clocher *m*; *F:* **he's got bats in the b.,** il a une araignée au plafond; il est toqué. **2.** *Nau:* mouton *m*, potence *f* (de la cloche).

belga ['belgə], *s. Fin:* (*former Belgian unit of exchange*) belga *m*.

Belgian ['beldʒən]. **1.** *a.* (*a*) belge; de Belgique; (*b*) **B. hare,** léporide *m*; lapin-lièvre *m* (*pl.* lapins-lièvres) belge; **B. sheepdog,** berger *m* belge. **2.** *s.* Belge *mf*.

Belgic ['beldʒik], *a. Hist:* des Pays-Bas.

Belgium ['beldʒəm], *Pr.n. Geog:* Belgique *f*.

Belgo- ['belgou], *pref.* belgo-; **B.-Dutch,** belgo-hollandais.

Belial ['bi:liəl], *Pr.n.m.* Bélial; l'Esprit malin.

belie [bi'lai], *v.tr.* (*pr.p.* **belying** [bi'laiiŋ]) **1.** donner un démenti à (des paroles); démentir (une promesse, des espérances, des craintes); tromper (l'attente de qn); **his appearance belies him,** on le méjugerait sur sa mine; il ne paie pas de mine. **2.** *NAm:* démentir (qn); donner un démenti à (qn).

belief [bi'li:f], *s.* **1.** croyance *f*, conviction *f*; **b. in ghosts,** croyance aux revenants; **b. in God,** croyance en Dieu; **in his b. that he would get better . . .,** (étant) persuadé qu'il guérirait. . .; **to entertain the b. that. . .,** croire, être convaincu, que . . .; **it is past all b.,** c'est incroyable; c'est à n'y pas croire; **to the best of my b.,** à ce que je crois; autant que je sache; **it is my b. that. . .,** je suis convaincu que. . .; j'ai la conviction que. . .. **2. b. in s.o., in sth.,** foi *f*, confiance *f*, en qn, en qch.; **I have no b. in doctors,** je n'ai pas confiance dans les médecins, je fais peu de cas des médecins.

believable [bi'li:vəbl], *a.* croyable.

believableness [bi'li:vəblnis], *s.* crédibilité *f*.

believe [bi'li:v]. **1.** *v.tr.* (*a*) croire (une nouvelle, etc.); ajouter foi à (une rumeur); accorder créance à (une affirmation); **I b. that it is true,** je crois que c'est vrai; **I do not b. that it is true,** je ne crois pas que ce soit vrai; **I solemnly and sincerely b. that . . .,** en mon âme et conscience je suis convaincu que . . .; **I b. (that) I am right,** je crois avoir raison; **he believed he could succeed,** il pensait pouvoir réussir; **I b. him to be alive,** je le crois vivant; **he is believed to be in Paris,** on le croit à Paris; **these views we b. to be fair and true,** ces opinions, nous les tenons pour justes; **the house was believed to be haunted,** la maison passait pour être hantée; **he is believed to have a chance,** on lui croit des chances (de réussir); **he believes himself to have been unfairly treated,** il se croit (la) victime d'une injustice; **I b. not,** je crois que non; je ne le crois pas; **I b. so,** je crois que oui; je le crois; **I don't b. a word of it,** je n'en crois rien, pas un mot; **I don't know what to b.,** je ne sais que croire; je ne sais pas à quoi m'en tenir; **I could scarcely b. my eyes,** j'en croyais à peine mes yeux; *F:* j'ai cru avoir la berlue; **seeing is believing,** voir c'est croire; **one must not b. everything one hears,** il ne faut pas ajouter foi à tout ce que l'on entend; **to b. only what one sees,** ne s'en rapporter qu'au témoignage de ses yeux; **people ready to b. any rumour,** populace *f* crédule à tous les bruits; **to make s.o. b. sth.,** faire croire qch. à qn; **to make s.o. b. that. . .,** faire croire à qn que . . .; faire accroire à qn que . . .; **you would have us b. that all is lost,** à vous croire tout serait perdu; *F:* **don't you b. it!** n'en croyez rien! détrompez-vous! *F:* croyez ça et buvez de l'eau! **I can well b. it,** je suis prêt à le croire; **would you b. it, b. it or not, he fell for her!** il s'est épris d'elle, figure-toi! (*b*) **to b. s.o.,** croire qn, accorder créance au dire de qn; **to be believed,** trouver créance; **if he is to be believed . . .,** à l'en croire . . .; s'il faut l'en croire . . .; **he is not to be believed,** il n'est pas digne de foi; *F:* **he's a smart one, b. me** [bili:v'mi:]! *F:* **b. you me!** c'est un malin et pas d'erreur! **I have suffered much, b. me!** j'ai bien souffert, va! allez! **I b. you!** je vous crois! je (le) crois bien! **I b. so,** je crois que oui. **2.** *v.i.* (*a*) **to b. in (one) God,** croire en (un seul) Dieu; **to b. in ghosts,** croire aux revenants; (*b*) **to b. in s.o.'s word,** croire à la parole de qn; **I don't b. in his promises,** je me défie de ses promesses; **to b. in a method,** être partisan d'une méthode; **I don't b. in doctors,** je n'ai pas confiance dans les médecins; je fais peu de cas des médecins; **I don't b. in aspirin,** (i) je ne crois pas à l'efficacité de l'aspirine; (ii) je crois que l'emploi de l'aspirine est à éviter; **he believes in change,** il est pour le(s) changement(s). **3. to make b. to do sth.,** feindre, faire semblant, de faire qch.; **to make b. that . . .,** faire semblant que . . .; **let's make b. that we're Indians,** supposons que nous sommes, soyons, des Indiens.

believer [bi'li:vər], *s.* **1.** (*religious*) croyant, -ante. **2. to be a b. in sth.,** (i) croire à qch.; (ii) être partisan *m* de qch.; **to be a b. in ghosts,** croire aux revenants; **I am not a b. in patent medicines,** je fais peu de cas, je ne crois pas à l'efficacité, je ne suis pas partisan, des spécialités pharmaceutiques; **believers in the strong hand,** partisans de la main forte.

believing [bi'li:viŋ], *a.* croyant.

belike [bi'laik], *adv. A: & Lit:* probablement, peut-être, vraisemblablement; **b. he will consent,** il y a lieu de croire qu'il donnera son consentement.

Belisarius [beli'sɛəriəs], *Pr.n.m. Rom.Hist:* Bélisaire.

Belisha [bə'li:ʃə, bi'laiʃə], *Pr.n. Adm: Aut:* **B. beacon,** sphère orange lumineuse (indiquant un passage clouté).

belittle [bi'litl], *v.tr.* rabaisser, déprécier, amoindrir (le mérite de qn); rabaisser, amoindrir, déprécier, décrier (qn); méconnaître, décrier (un projet); **don't b. his advice,** ne faites pas fi de ses conseils; **to b. oneself,** (i) faire le modeste; se déprécier; (ii) se déconsidérer (aux yeux de qn, auprès de qn); **you must not b. yourself,** il ne faut pas vous amoindrir.

Belitzski [bi'litski], *Pr.n.m. Phot:* **Belitzski's reducer,**

affaiblisseur *m* de Belitzski.

bell[1] [bel], *s.* **1.** (*a*) **(clapper) b.,** (*in church, etc.*) cloche *f*; (*smaller*) clochette *f*; (*in house*) sonnette *f*; (*fixed*) timbre *m*; (*for cattle, etc.*) clochette, clarine *f*, sonnaille *f*; **sheep b.,** bélière *f*, clochette (de troupeaux); **globular b., sleigh b.,** grelot *m*; **electric b.,** sonnerie *f* (électrique); trembleuse *f*; *Tp:* timbre d'appel; **single-stroke b.** (*of front door, etc.*), sonnerie à un coup; timbre; **table b.,** timbre de table; **call b.,** (i) sonnerie, sonnette, d'appel; avertisseuse *f*; (ii) timbre de table; *Med: etc:* **night b.,** sonnette de nuit; **set of bells (of a church),** sonnerie (d'une église); **the heavy bells,** la grosse sonnerie; **great b.** (*of a church*), bourdon *m*; **chime of bells,** carillon *m*; **Bow bells,** les cloches de l'église de Saint Mary-le-Bow (Londres); **to be born within the sound of Bow bells,** naître dans la Cité de Londres; être un vrai *cockney;* **the telephone bell's ringing,** le téléphone sonne; on appelle au téléphone; **the b. rang for dinner,** la cloche donna le signal du dîner; **to pull the b.,** tirer la sonnette; donner un coup de sonnette; **there's a ring at the b., there's the b.,** on sonne; **to ring the b.,** (i) sonner; (ii) (*handbell*) agiter la sonnette; (iii) (*at a fair*) faire sonner le timbre de la tête de Turc; *F:* **to ring, bear away, carry off, the b.,** décrocher la timbale, remporter la palme, être le premier, être à la tête; l'emporter sur les autres; **that rings a b.,** cela me rappelle, dit, quelque chose; (*b*) **the dinner b.,** la cloche du dîner; **to ring the dinner b.,** sonner le dîner; **the dinner b. has gone,** on a sonné pour le dîner; **the first b. for vespers has gone, rung,** le premier coup des vêpres a sonné; **has the second b. rung?** a-t-on sonné le second coup? **no one answered the b.,** personne n'a répondu à mon coup de sonnette; **passing b.,** glas *m* (pour annoncer l'agonie de qn); (*c*) *Nau:* **to strike the bells,** piquer l'heure; **six bells,** six coups (de cloche); **to strike eight bells,** piquer midi. **2.** calice *m*, clochette (d'une fleur); pavillon *m* (d'une trompette, d'un haut-parleur, etc.); campane *f* (d'une colonne); vase *m* (de chapiteau); *Gasm:* cloche (de gazomètre); *Hort:* cloche; *Metall:* cône *m*, cloche (d'un haut fourneau); **diving b.,** cloche à, de, plongeurs. **3.** *attrib.* (*a*) **b. founder,** fondeur *m* de cloches; **b. foundry,** fonderie *f* de cloches; **b. crank, b.-crank lever,** levier coudé, à renvoi; renvoi *m*, bascule *f*, équerre *f*, de sonnette; articulation *f*; guignol *m* d'angle; **b.-crank linkage,** mécanisme *m* de renvoi; **b. handle,** (i) tirant *m* (de cloche, de sonnette); (ii) poignée *f* (de sonnette à main); **b. hanger,** poseur *m* de sonnettes; **b. hanging,** pose *f* de sonnettes; *Metall:* **b. metal,** métal *m*; bronze *m*, de cloches; **b.-metal ore,** stannite *f*; **b. ringer,** (i) sonneur *m*; (ii) carillonneur *m*; (iii) protagoniste *m* de l'art campanaire; **b. ringing,** (i) carillonnement *m*; (ii) art *m* campanaire; **b. tower,** clocher *m*, campanile *m*; **b. wire,** fil *m* à sonnerie; de sonnette; **b.-wire lever,** renvoi de sonnette; (*b*) (*bell-shaped*) **b.-bottomed trousers, b. bottoms,** pantalon *m* à pattes d'éléphant; *Hort: etc:* **b. glass,** cloche en verre; **to put a plant under a b. glass,** clocher une plante; mettre une plante sous cloche; *Aut:* **b. housing of the rear axle,** trompette *f* de pont arrière; *Ch:* **b. jar,** cloche; **b. mouth,** évasement *m*, égueulement *m*; **b. tent,** tente *f* conique; (*c*) (*with a bell*) **b. buoy,** bouée *f* à cloche; **b. punch,** poinçon *m* (de billet) à timbre sonore; (*d*) *Cmptr:* **b. character,** caractère *m* d'appel (d'attention); (*e*) *Ent:* **b. moth,** tordeuse *f*; (*f*) *Orn:* **b. magpie,** réveilleur *m*, strépère *m*; **b. miner,** manorine *f*. **4.** *Bot:* **bells of Ireland,** molucelle *f* lisse, mélisse *f* des Moluques.

bell[2]. **1.** *v.tr.* **to b. a cow,** attacher une clochette autour du cou d'une vache; *A: F:* **to b. the cat,** attacher le grelot. **2.** *v.i.* (*a*) (*of skirt, etc.*) faire cloche; ballonner; (*b*) (*of tube, etc.*) **to b. out,** s'évaser, renfler.

bell[3], *s.* bramement *m* (du cerf).

bell[4], *v.i.* (*of deer*) bramer; *A:* raire, réer.

bell[5], *s.* bulle *f*; *Paperm:* bulle, soufflure *f*, cloque *f*.

Bella ['belə], *Pr.n.f.* (*dim. of Arabella, Isabella*) Arabelle; Isabelle.

belladonna [belə'dɔnə], *s. Bot:* **1.** belladone *f*; *Pharm:* **b. liniment,** liniment *m* à la belladone. **2. b. lily,** amaryllis *f* belle-dame (*pl.* belles-dames); lis *m* de Saint-Jacques.

Bellatrix ['belətriks], *Pr.n. Astr:* Bellatrix.

bellbird ['belbə:d], *s. Orn:* oiseau-cloche *m*, *pl.* oiseaux-cloches; (i) (*S. America*) procnia *m*, araponga *m*; (ii) *N.Z:* anthornis *m*; *Austr:* **crested b.,** oréoïque *f*.

bellboy ['belbɔi], *s.m. NAm:* groom (d'hôtel); chasseur.

bell captain ['bel'kæptin], *s.m. NAm:* surveillant des grooms (à un hôtel).

belle [bel], *s.f.* (*pers.*) beauté; **the b. of the ball,** la reine, la beauté, du bal.

Bellerophon [bə'lerəf(ə)n]. **1.** *Pr.n.m.* Bellérophon. **2.** *s. Paleont:* **bellerophon,** bellérophon *m*.

belles-lettres ['bel'letr], *s.pl.* belles-lettres *f*.

bellet(t)rist ['bel'letrist], *s.* **1.** auteur *m* qui se spécialise dans les belles-lettres. **2.** amateur *m* de belles-lettres.

bellet(t)ristic(al) ['bel'letristik(l)], *a.* (journal, etc.) consacré aux belles-lettres; (discours) concernant les belles-lettres.

Belleville ['belvil], *s. Nau:* chaudière *f* Belleville (nom de l'inventeur).

bellflower ['belflauər], *s. Bot:* campanule *f*; **nettle-leaved b.,** campanule gantelée; gant *m* de bergère, de Notre-Dame; **giant b.,** campanule à grosses fleurs.

bellhop ['belhɔp], *s. NAm: F:* = BELLBOY.

bellicose ['belikous], *a.* belliqueux.

bellicosely ['belikousli], *adv.* agressivement.

bellicosity [beli'kɔsiti], *s.* humeur belliqueuse; caractère belliqueux; agressivité *f*.

-bellied ['belid], *a.* (*with adj. prefixed*) à ventre . . .; **big-b.,** à gros ventre; pansu, ventripotent.

belligerency [be'lidʒər(ə)nsi], *s.* belligérence *f*.

belligerent [be'lidʒər(ə)nt]. (*a*) *a.* & *s.* belligérant (*m*); (*b*) *a.* belliqueux, agressif, belligérant.

belling[1] ['beliŋ], *s.* bramement *m* (du cerf).

belling[2], *s. Paperm:* soufflure *f*, bulle *f*, cloque *f*.

Bellini [be'li:ni], *Pr.n. Anat:* **Bellini's ducts, tubes, tubules,** tubes *f* de Bellini.

Bellini-Tosi [be'li:ni'tosi], *Pr.n. W.Tel:* **B.-T. aerial, antenna,** antenne *f* Bellini-Tosi.

bellis ['belis], *s. Bot:* bellis *f*, pâquerette *f*.

bellite ['belait], *s. Exp:* bellite *f*.

bellman, *pl.* **-men** ['belmən], *s.m.* **1.** crieur public. **2.** *A:* veilleur de nuit.

bell-mouthed ['bel'mauðd], *a.* évasé; (entrée *f*) en entonnoir.

Bellona [be'lounə], *Pr.n.f. Myth:* Bellone.

bellow[1] ['belou], *s.* (*a*) beuglement *m*, mugissement *m*; (*b*) hurlement *m* (de douleur, etc.).

bellow[2]. **1.** *v.i.* (*of bull*) beugler, mugir; (*of pers., ocean*) mugir, hurler. **2.** *v.tr.* **to b. (out),** hurler (un ordre); *F:* beugler (une chanson).

bellower ['belouər], *s.* **1.** animal beuglant, mugissant. **2.** (*of pers.*) hurleur, -euse.

bellowing ['belouiŋ], *s.* **1.** beuglement *m*, mugissement *m* (d'un animal). **2.** hurlements *mpl* (d'une personne).

bellows ['belouz], *s.pl.* **1.** (*a*) soufflet *m* (pour le feu); **a pair of b.,** un soufflet; (*occ.sg.*) **a wheezy old b.,** un vieux soufflet poussif; *Hort:* **powder b.,** puceronnière *f*; (*b*) *F:* les poumons *m*; *O:* **it's b. to mend with me,** c'est ma poitrine qui n'est pas solide. **2.** soufflerie *f* (d'un orgue). **3.** *Phot:* soufflet (d'un appareil); **extension b.,** allonge *f*. **4.** *Ich:* **b. fish,** (i) centrisque *m*, *F:* bécasse *f* de mer; (ii) baudroie *f*, lotte *f* de mer; (iii) orbe épineux, diodon *m*.

bellpull ['belpul], *s.* **1.** cordon *m* de sonnette. **2.** poignée *f* de sonnette; pied-de-biche *m*, *pl.* pieds-de-biche.

bellpush ['belpuʃ], *s.* bouton *m* (de sonnerie électrique); bouton poussoir, bouton-pressoir *m*, *pl.* boutons-pressoirs; bouton d'appel.

bell-shaped ['belʃeipt], *a.* en forme de cloche.

bellwether ['belweðər], *s.m.* **1.** *Husb:* sonnailler; bélier meneur du troupeau. **2.** *O: Pej:* chef de bande; meneur.

bellwort ['belwə:t], *s. Bot:* campanule *f*.

belly[1] ['beli], *s.* **1.** (*a*) ventre *m* (de l'homme, d'un animal); *P:* panse *f*, bedaine *f*, bidon *m*; *Cu:* **b. of pork,** poitrine *f* de porc; *F:* **to make a god of one's b.,** être porté sur son ventre, sur sa bouche; se faire un dieu de son estomac; **to have an empty b.,** *F:* se brosser (le ventre); n'avoir rien dans le buffet, dans le fusil; **his eyes were bigger than his b.,** il a eu les yeux plus grands que le ventre; **to rob one's b. to cover one's back,** prendre sur sa nourriture pour couvrir ses frais de toilette; *A:* **clothe the back and starve the b.,** habit de velours, ventre de son; **an army fights on its b.,** pour être d'attaque, il faut que les troupes soient bien nourries; *Prov:* **the b. has no ears,** ventre affamé n'a point d'oreilles; *attrib. Med:* **b. belt,** ventrière *f*; *Anat: F:* **b. button,** nombril *m*; **b. dance,** danse *f* du ventre; **b. laugh,** rire rabelaisien, énorme; (*b*) *Leath:* flanc *m*. **2.** (*a*) ventre (d'une cruche, d'un avion, etc.); panse (d'une cruche); surface *f* convexe (d'une pierre, etc.); *Av:* **b. tank,** réservoir ventral; (*b*) *Mus:* table *f* d'harmonie (d'un violon, d'un piano). **3.** *Nau:* creux *m*, renflement *m*, dedans *m*, sein *m*, fond *m* (d'une voile).

belly[2]. **1.** *v.tr.* (*a*) (*of wind*) **to b. (out) the sails,** enfler, gonfler, les voiles; (*b*) *Mil:* **to b. a tank,** faire cabrer un char. **2.** *v.i. Nau:* (*of sail*) faire (le) sac; s'enfler, se gonfler; faire ventre.

bellyache[1] ['belieik], *s. F:* mal *m* de ventre; colique *f*; **to have the b.,** avoir mal au ventre; avoir la colique.

bellyache[2], *v.i. P:* ronchonner, rouspéter, bougonner, grogner; *P:* râler.

bellyacher ['belieikər], *s. P:* ronchonneur *m*, rouspéteur *m*; *P:* râleur *m*.

bellyband ['belibænd], *s.* **1.** *Harn:* sous-ventrière *m*, *pl.* sous-ventrières. **2.** *Med:* bandage *m* de corps.

bellyflop[1] ['beliflɔp], *s. Swim: F:* **to do a b.,** faire un plat.

bellyflop[2], *v.i. F:* **1.** *Swim:* faire un plat. **2.** *Can:* aller en traîneau à plat ventre.

bellyful ['beliful], *s.* plein ventre, *F:* ventrée *f*; *F:* **to have had a b. (of sth.),** (i) en avoir une gavée; en avoir marre; (ii) en avoir tout son soûl.

bellyland ['belilænd], *v.i. Av:* atterrir sur le ventre.

bellylanding ['belilændiŋ], *s. Av:* atterrissage *m* sur le ventre.

belone [bi'louni], *s. Ich:* belone *f*, orphie *f*.

belong [bi'lɔŋ], *v.i.* **1.** (*a*) appartenir, être (**to,** à); **that book belongs to me,** ce livre m'appartient, est à moi; **the future belongs to those who dare,** l'avenir appartient aux audacieux; *Jur:* **to b. to s.o. by right,** compéter à qn; (*b*) *impers. A:* **it belongs to me to decide,** il m'appartient de décider; (*c*) relever (de qn, qch.); **the governments to which we b.,** les gouvernements dont nous relevons; (*of land, etc.*) **to b. to the Crown,** dépendre de la Couronne. **2.** (*be appropriate*) être propre (à qch.); **such amusements do not b. to his age,** de tels amusements ne sont pas de son âge; **to what category do they b.?** à quelle catégorie appartiennent-ils? sous quelle catégorie faut-il les ranger? **things that b.,** choses *f* qui vont ensemble, qui font partie du même tout; **cheese belongs with salad,** le fromage va avec la salade. **3.** (*a*) **to b. to a society,** faire partie d'une société; **he belongs to the town council,** il est du conseil municipal; **do you b. to this club?** êtes vous membre de ce cercle? **to b. to a place,** (i) être (natif, originaire) d'un endroit; (ii) résider à un endroit; **I b. here,** je suis d'ici; je me sens chez moi ici; **to feel that one doesn't b.,** se sentir seul, isolé; **these amphibians b. to the arctic seas,** ces amphibies sont propres aux mers arctiques; *Jur:* **dossier to which a document belongs,** dossier auquel incombe une pièce; **these cases b. to a conciliation court,** ces affaires ressortissent de la justice de paix; (*b*) **this is where the spoons b.,** c'est ici qu'on range les cuillers; **to put sth. where it doesn't b.,** mal ranger, placer, qch.; **to put things back where they b.,** remettre les choses à leur place.

belongings [bi'lɔŋiŋz], *s.pl.* affaires *f*, effets *m* (appartenant à qn); **personal b.,** objets personnels; **I am moving with all my b.,** je m'en vais avec toutes mes affaires, *F:* avec armes et bagages; je déménage toutes mes affaires, tout ce qui m'appartient.

belonite ['belənait], *s. Miner:* bélonite *f*.

Belorussia [belou'rʌʃə], *Pr.n. Geog:* Biélorussie *f*, Russie Blanche.

Belorussian [belou'rʌʃən]. **1.** *Geog:* (*a*) *a.* biélorusse; (*b*) *s.* Biélorusse, Russe blanc, Blanc-russe, *pl.* Blancs-russes. **2.** *Ling:* *s.* biélorusse *m*.

belostoma [be'lɔstəmə], *s. Ent:* bélostome *m*.

Belostomatidae [beloustou'mætidi:], **Belostomidae** [belou'stoumidi:], *s.pl. Ent:* bélostomes *m*, bélostomatidés *m*.

beloved. 1. *p.p.* & *a.* [bi'lʌvd], aimé; **b. by all,** aimé de tous, par tout le monde; **b. of the gods,** aimé, chéri, des dieux; **to make oneself b. by all,** se faire aimer de tous. **2.** *a.* & *s.* [bi'lʌvid] bien-aimé(e), chéri(e); **the b. wife of . . .,** l'épouse bien-aimée de . . .; **my b.,** mon, ma, bien-aimé(e); *Ecc:* **dearly b. brethren,** mes bien chers frères.

below [bi'lou]. **1.** *adv.* (*a*) en bas, (au-)dessous; **remain b.,** restez en bas; **voices from b.,** des voix qui venaient d'en bas; **the tenants (of the flat) b.,** les locataires du dessous; **the road ran b.,** la route était située en contrebas; **here b. (on earth),** ici-bas; **down b.,** (i) en bas, en contre-bas; (ii) en enfer; *Nau:* **all hands b.!** tout le monde en bas! **b. there!** (i) gare dessous! attention en bas! (ii) *Nau:* la bordée sur le pont! (*b*) *Jur:* **the court b.,** le tribunal inférieur; (*c*) **the passage quoted b.,** le passage cité (i) ci-dessous; (ii) plus loin, ci-après; **signature affixed b.,** signature apposée ci-dessous; **please state b. . . .,** veuillez noter au bas . . .. **2.** *prep.* au-dessous de; (*a*) **b. the knee,** au-dessous du genou; **b. the snow-line,** au-dessous de la limite des neiges; **on the table and b. it,** sur la table et (au-)dessous; **struck b. the ribs,** frappé au défaut des côtes; **he never goes b. the surface,** il s'arrête à la surface des choses; (*b*) **b. (the) average,** au-dessous de la moyenne; **b. par,** au-dessous du pair; *F:* **I'm feeling a bit b. par,** je ne suis pas dans mon assiette; **temperature b. normal,** température inférieure à la normale; **ten degrees b. zero,** *F:* **ten degrees b.,** dix degrés au-dessous de zéro; moins dix; **b. sea level,** au-dessous du niveau de la mer; (*c*) **b. the surface,** sous la surface; *Th:* **b. stage,** les dessous *m*; (*d*) **b. the bridge,** en aval du pont; (*e*) **to be b. s.o. in rank,** occuper un rang inférieur à qn; **to set man b. dumb animals,** ravaler l'homme au-dessous des animaux; **it would be b. me to ask for that job,** je ne m'abaisserais pas jusqu'à demander cet emploi.

Belshazzar [bel'ʃæzər], *Pr.n.m.* Balthazar, Belshatsar; **Belshazzar's Feast,** le Festin de Balthazar.

belt[1] [belt], *s.* **1.** (*a*) (**waist-**)**b.,** ceinture *f*; *Mil:* ceinturon *m*; **to tighten one's b.,** (i) serrer sa ceinture, son ceinturon; (ii) *F:* se boucler la ceinture; se serrer le ventre; *P:* se la boucler; **to have too many whiskies under one's b.,** avoir bu trop de whisky; **to use the b. and braces approach (to a problem),** apporter toutes les précautions; *F:* se garder à carreau; **shoulder b.,** baudrier *m*, banderole *f*; (**flag-bearer's**) **colour-b.,** brayer *m*; (**ladies'**) **suspender b.,** porte-jarretelles *m inv*; *Tail:* **fixed b. at back,** martingale *f* au dos; *Aut: Av:* **seat b., safety b.,** ceinture de sécurité; (*judo*) **to have the brown b.,** être ceinture marron; *Box:* **to hold the b.,** être le champion; **blow below the b.,** coup bas; coup au-dessous de la ceinture; coup déloyal; *Fig:* **to hit s.o. below the b.,** donner à qn un coup en traître, un coup bas; frapper qn déloyalement; **that's hitting below the b.,** c'est de la déloyauté; c'est un sale coup; (*b*) *Cost:* (*foundation*) gaine *f*; (*c*) *N.Arch:* **armour b.,** ceinture cuirassée. **2.** (*a*) *Mec.E: etc:* courroie *f* (de transmission); corde plate; **V**(**-shaped**) **b.,** courroie en (forme de) coin, courroie trapézoïdale; **chain b.,** courroie articulée; **b.-driven,** mû, actionné, par une courroie; commandé par courroie; **b. fastener,** agrafe *f* de courroie, attache-courroie *m inv*; **b. guide, b. idler,** galet *m* de guidage de courroie, guide *m* de courroie, guide-courroie *m, pl.* guide-courroie(s); **b. punch,** perce-courroie(s) *m inv*; **b. shifter, b. slipper,** embrayeur *m*, monte-courroie *m inv*; fourchette *f* de courroie; **b. tension,** tension *f* de courroie; *Civ.E: etc:* **b. conveyor,** transporteur *m* à courroie, à ruban, à bande; **conveyor b.,** bande transporteuse, courroie de transport, ruban roulant; *Ind:* **endless b., continuous b., assembly b.,** courroie sans fin; chaîne de montage; tapis roulant; *Carp:* **b. saw,** scie *f* à ruban, sans fin; (*b*) *Mil:* **feed b., loading b.** (*of machine gun*), bande-chargeur *f* (souple), *pl.* bandes-chargeurs; **b.-loading, b.-filling, machine,** appareil *m* à approvisionner, garnir, les bandes-chargeurs. **3.** (*a*) **b. of hills,** ceinture de collines; **b. of land,** bande *f* de terre; *Town P:* **green b.,** ceinture, zone, verte, de verdure; **b. highway,** route de ceinture; ceinture périphérique; *NAm:* **b. line,** ligne *f* (de chemin de fer) de ceinture; **b. railway,** chemin *m* de fer de ceinture; **b. tram,** tramway *m* de ceinture; *Hort:* **b. of trees,** rideau protecteur; (*b*) *Arch: Astr:* bande; **the belts of Jupiter,** les zones, bandes, de Jupiter; (*c*) **the calm belts,** les zones des calmes; **trade-wind b.,** zone des (vents) alizés; **standard time b.,** fuseau *m* horaire; *U.S:* **corn b., cotton b.,** région *f* du maïs, du coton; **coal b.,** zone houillère; **the Black b.,** la zone des noirs, noire; **the mosquito b.,** la zone des moustiques. **4.** *Geog:* **the Great B., Little B.,** le Grand(-)Belt, Petit(-)Belt (de la Baltique).

belt[2], *v.*

I. *v.tr.* **1.** ceinturer, ceindre (qn, qch.); **to b. a knight,** ceindre l'épée à un chevalier. **2.** (*surround*) entourer (qch.) d'une ceinture; former une ceinture autour de (qch.). **3.** *Mec.E:* relier (deux machines, etc.) par une courroie. **4.** *F:* donner des coups de courroie à (qn); fustiger.

II. (*compound verbs*) **1. belt along,** *v.i. F:* courir, marcher, (*in car*) aller, conduire, à toute vitesse.

2. belt out, *v.tr.* vociférer, gueuler, (un ordre, une chanson).

3. belt up, *v.i. P:* se taire; **b. up!** ta gueule! boucle-la! la boucle!

belt[3], *s. P:* coup dur; *P:* gnon *m*; beigne *f*.

beltane ['beltein], *s. Scot:* le premier mai; **b. fire,** feu *m* de joie du premier mai.

belted ['beltid], *a.* ceinturé; **b. overcoat,** pardessus *m* avec ceinture; *F:* **b. earl,** seigneur haut et puissant.

belting ['beltiŋ], *s.* **1.** (*a*) ceinture(s) *f(pl)*, courroie(s) *f(pl)*; *Mec.E:* **round leather b.,** corde *f* en cuir; (*b*) matière *f* à courroies. **2.** *Mec.E:* transmission *f*. **3.** *F:* **to give a child a (good) b.,** administrer une correction à un enfant (avec une courroie); fustiger un enfant.

belt-shaped ['beltʃeipt], *a. Nat.Hist:* zoniforme.

beltway ['beltwei], *s. NAm:* ceinture *f* périphérique; route *f* de ceinture.

beluga [bi'lu:gə], *s.* **1.** *Ich:* bél(o)uga *m*, ichtyocolle *m*. **2.** *Z:* bél(o)uga.

belvedere ['belvidiər], *s.* **1.** *Arch:* belvédère *m*, mirador(e) *m*. **2.** *Bot:* belvédère; belle-à-voir *f, pl.* belles-à-voir; ansérine *f* à balais.

bembex ['bembeks], **bembix** ['bembiks], *s. Ent:* bembex *m*.

bementite ['bi:məntait], *s. Miner:* bémentite *f*.

bemired [bi'maiəd], *a. Lit:* crotté, embourbé.

bemoan [bi'moun], *v.tr.* pleurer, déplorer (qch.); gémir sur (qch.); **to b. the loss of sth.,** se lamenter de la perte de qch.; pleurer la perte de qch.

bemuse [bi'mju:z], *v.tr. Lit:* stupéfier; obnubiler, troubler les idées de (qn).

Ben[1] [ben], *Pr.n.m.* (*dim. of Benjamin*) **Big B.,** la grosse cloche des *Houses of Parliament* (à Londres).

ben[2], *Scot:* **1.** *adv.* à l'intérieur (de la maison); **come away b.,** (i) entrez; (ii) entrez dans la salle, dans la belle pièce; ne restez pas dans la salle commune, dans la cuisine; *s.* **a but and b.,** maison à deux pièces. **2.** *prep.* **b. the house,** (i) dans la maison; (ii) dans la salle de la maison.

ben[3], *s. Geog: Scot:* sommet *m*, pic *m*; **B. Nevis,** le mont Nevis.

ben[4], *s. Bot:* ben *m*, béhen *m*; **b. nut,** noix *f* de ben; *Pharm:* **oil of b.,** huile *f* de ben, de béhen.

Benares [bi'nɑ:riz], *Pr.n. Geog:* Bénarès.

bench[1] [ben(t)ʃ], *s.* **1.** (*a*) banc *m*, banquette *f*; gradin *m* (d'amphithéâtre); *Parl:* **the Treasury B., Front B.,** le banc ministériel; **the Front Benches,** les premières banquettes (occupées d'un côté par les ministres, de l'autre par les ex-ministres et membres "ministrables" de l'opposition); **Back Benches,** banquettes des membres n'ayant pas de portefeuille; **the episcopal b.,** le banc des évêques (à la Chambre des Lords); *Jur:* **the judge's b.,** le siège du juge; **the magistrates', witnesses', b.,** le banc des magistrats, des témoins; **The Court of King's B.,** *Fr.C:* la Cour du Banc du Roi; *Th: O:* **to play to empty benches,** jouer devant des banquettes vides, *F:* devant les banquettes; (*b*) *Jur:* **the B.,** la magistrature; le pouvoir judiciaire; **to be on the B.,** (i) être magistrat; (ii) siéger au tribunal; **to be raised to the b.,** être nommé, (i) juge; (ii) évêque; (*c*) (*the judges*) **the b.,** la Cour; **b. warrant,** mandat d'arrêt délivré par la Cour; (*d*) *Sp:* banc (pour les joueurs qui ne sont pas sur le terrain); **to be on the b.,** (i) attendre son tour; (ii) avoir été retiré du jeu, renvoyé du terrain. **2.** (*a*) établi *m* (de menuisier); banc, marbre *m* (d'ajusteur); selle *f* (de tonnelier); table *f* de travail (manuel); *Hort:* tablette *f* (de serre); **levelling b.,** marbre à tracer; *Mec.E:* **b. hand,** ajusteur *m* sur métaux, ajusteur mécanicien; **b. holdfast, b. hook,** valet *m* d'établi; **b. stop,** griffe *f* d'établi; (*b*) **optical b.,** banc optique; *Mec.E:* **testing b.,** banc d'essai, d'épreuve; **b. test,** essai *m* au banc; *Ch: etc:* **laboratory b.,** paillasse *f*; table de manipulation; (*c*) *Gasm:* **retort b.,** batterie *f* de cornues. **3.** banc; estrade *f* (sur laquelle on exhibe un chien, etc., à une exposition); **b. dog,** chien qui participe à une exposition canine; *U.S:* **b. show,** exposition canine. **4.** (*a*) banquette (de terre); *Const:* gradin; redan *m*; *Arch:* **b. table,** banc continu au socle; (*b*) *Civ.E:* accotement *m*, berme *f* (d'un chemin). **5.** *Geog:* (*also* **benchland**) terrasse *f* (au-dessus d'une vallée); plaine *f* de piémont; **wave-cut b.,** terrasse taillée par l'action des vagues.

bench[2]. **1.** *v.tr.* (*a*) fournir (une salle) de banquettes; (*b*) exhiber (un chien à une exposition); (*c*) *NAm:* renvoyer; retirer (un joueur) du jeu; (*d*) *Hort:* mettre (des plantes) sur la tablette. **2.** *v.i.* (*of sand, etc.*) former une banquette, un banc.

bencher ['ben(t)ʃər], *s. Jur:* avocat *m* appartenant au corps des doyens des *Inns of Court* (*q.v. under* INN); membre *m* du conseil d'une école de droit, du conseil d'une association légale.

benchman, *pl.* **-men** ['ben(t)ʃmən], *s.* (*a*) cordonnier *m*; (*b*) ajusteur mécanicien; ajusteur sur métaux; (*c*) *Bak:* pétrisseur *m*.

benchmark ['ben(t)ʃmɑ:k], *s.* **1.** *Surv:* repère *m* (de nivellement); cote *f* (de niveau); borne-repère *f, pl.* bornes-repères. **2.** *Cmptr:* point *m* de référence; **b. problem,** problème *m* de référence.

bend[1] [bend], *s.* nœud *m*; ajut *m*; **fisherman's b.,** nœud de grappin; **single, double, sheet b.,** nœud d'écoute simple, double; **carrick b.,** nœud de vache.

bend[2], *s.* **1.** *Her:* bande *f*; **b. sinister,** barre *f*; **party per b. sinister,** tranché, taillé. **2.** *Tan:* moitié *f* d'un croupon; demi-croupon, *pl.* demi-croupons; **b. leather,** cuir *m* à semelles.

bend[3], *s.* **1. forward, backward, b. of the body,** inclination *f* du corps en avant, en arrière. **2.** (*a*) courbure *f*; courbe *f*; (*of road, pipe*) coude *m*; (*of road*) tournant *m*, angle *m*, virage *m*, boucle *f*; (*of river*) méandre *m*, sinuosité *f*, boucle; *Arch:* voussure *f* (d'une voûte); **b. of the arm,** saignée *f* du bras; **b. of the back,** chute *f* des reins; *Farr;* **b. of the neck (of a horse),** pli *m* de l'encolure; *Cy:* **b. of the handlebar,** cintre *m* du guidon; *Mec.E:* **expansion b.,** arc compensateur; **return b., U b.,** (i) courbe de retour; (ii) tube *m* en U, coude en U; *P.N:* **bends for 3 miles,** virages sur 5 kilomètres; (*of road*) **to take, make, a b. to the right,** tourner, faire un tournant, vers la droite; *Aut:* **to take a sharp b.,** virer court; **to take a b. at speed,** prendre, effectuer, un virage à toute vitesse; (*b*) *P:* (i) **to get sth. on the b.,** obtenir qch. par des moyens détournés; (ii) **to go on the b.,** faire la noce, la bombe, la bringue; tirer une bordée; (iii) **to be round the b.,** être fou, *F:* marteau, cinglé. **3.** *Med: F:* **the bends,** le mal des caissons.

bend[4], *v.*

I. *v.tr. & i.* (**bent;** *p.p.* **bent,** *A:* **bended**) **1.** courber (un osier, le corps); plier (le coude, etc.); ployer, fléchir (le genou); baisser (la tête); arquer (le dos); cambrer, cintrer (un tuyau, un rail); cambrer, arquer (du bois, du fer); dévirer (du bois); *Ph:* réfracter (la lumière); infléchir (un rayon); **to b. a pipe (at a right angle),** couder un tuyau; **she was bending over the cradle,** elle était penchée sur le berceau; **to b. one's head over a book,** pencher la tête sur un livre; **to b. s.o. to one's will,** plier qn à sa volonté; **to b. s.o. to a strict discipline,** ployer qn à une discipline sévère; **to b. to s.o.'s will,** se plier à, fléchir devant, la volonté de qn; **better b. than break,** mieux vaut plier que rompre; **the road, river, bends to the right,** la route, la rivière, tourne, s'infléchit, fait un coude, un tournant, vers la droite; **to b. beneath a burden,** plier, fléchir, sous un fardeau; **old man bending under a heavy load,** vieillard courbé sous un pesant fardeau; **to b. low before s.o.,** se courber jusqu'à terre devant qn; *F:* **to catch s.o. bending,** surprendre qn en mauvaise posture; *P:* **to b. the elbow,** lever le coude (être adonné à la boisson). **2.** (*a*) *v.tr.* **to b. a rod, a key (out of shape),** forcer, fausser, une barre de fer, une clef; **chimney stack bent out of plumb,** cheminée dévoyée; (*b*) *v.i.* **to b. under a strain,** (*of wood, iron*) arquer; (*of steel plate, etc.*) s'envoiler; (*of rod, wheel*) (se) voiler; (*c*) *v.tr. P:* **to b. (the result of) a match,** arranger d'avance le résultat d'un match. **3.** *v.tr.* tendre, bander (un arc, un ressort). **4.** *v.tr.* (*a*) **to b. one's steps towards a place,** diriger, porter, ses pas vers un endroit; **to b. one's steps homewards,** se diriger vers sa demeure; regagner sa demeure; s'acheminer vers sa maison; **to b. one's mind to study,** s'appliquer, se plier, appliquer son esprit, à l'étude; **to b. one's efforts towards sth., towards doing sth.,** diriger tous ses efforts à qch., à faire qch.; (*b*) *Lit:* **to b. one's gaze on sth.,** fixer ses regards sur qch.; **all eyes were bent on her,** tous les yeux étaient fixés sur elle; **with his eyes bent on the ground,** les yeux attachés au sol. **5.** *v.tr. Nau:* (*a*) étalinguer (un câble); frapper (une manœuvre); enverguer (une voile); **to b. on a signal,** frapper un signal; (*b*) abouter (deux cordages).

II. (*compound verbs*) **1. bend back;** (*a*) *v.tr.* reployer en arrière; replier; recourber (une lame, etc.); réfléchir (la lumière); (*b*) *v.i.* (i) se recourber; se réfléchir; (*of fingernail, etc.*) se rebrousser; (ii) (*of pers.*) se pencher en arrière.

2. bend down; (*a*) *v.tr.* courber, ployer, affaisser (une branche); **the weight of the flowers bends down the stem,** le poids des fleurs fait ployer la tige; **the tree was bent down by the weight of the fruit,** l'arbre penchait sous le poids des fruits; (*b*) *v.i.* se courber, se baisser.

3. bend forward, *v.i.* se pencher en avant; pencher la tête en avant.

4. bend over; (*a*) *v.i.* (*of pers.*) se pencher; (*of rock, etc.*) surplomber; *F:* **he bent over backwards to help me,** il s'est mis en quatre pour m'aider; (*b*) *v.tr.* replier (une tôle, etc.).

5. bend round, *v.tr.* recourber.

Ben Day ['ben'dei], *Pr.n. Phot.Engr:* **B.D.** (*also* **benday**) **process,** procédé *m* benday.

bended ['bendid], *a. Lit:* **to receive sth. on b. knee,** recevoir qch. un genou à terre; *Fig:* **to beg for sth. on one's b. knees,** demander qch. à (deux) genoux.

bender ['bendər], *s.* **1.** (*pers.*) *Metalw: etc:* cintreur *m*. **2.** *Metalw: etc:* machine *f* à cintrer, plier, couder; cintreuse *f*. **3.** *P: O:* pièce *f* de sixpence (de l'ancienne monnaie). **4.** *P:* soûlerie *f*, ribote *f*, bordée *f*.

bending ['bendiŋ], *s.* **1.** (*a*) ployage *m*, cintrage *m*; **b. machine,** machine *f* à cintrer, plier, couder; cintreuse *f*; **b. press,** presse *f* à cintrer; (*b*) *Mec.E: etc:* arcure *f*, arqûre *f* (d'une partie métallique); envoilure *f* (de l'acier à la trempe, etc.); voilure *f* (d'une roue); flambage *m* (d'une colonne); (*c*) flexion *f*; *Mec:* **b. strength,** résistance *f* à la flexion; **b. test,** essai *m*, épreuve *f*, de ployage, de flexion; **b. stress under wind pressure,** effort *m* de flexion par le vent; **b. moment,** moment *m* de flexion; moment fléchissant; (*d*) *Geol:* plissement *m* (d'une couche); (*e*) bandage *m* (d'un arc). **2.** (*of pers.*) penchement *m*. **3.** *Nau:* aboutage *m* (de deux cordages). **4. bending back,** reploiement *m*, repliement *m*, recourbement *m*, rebroussement *m*.

Bendix ['bendiks], *Pr.n. Mec.E: Aut: etc:* **B. gear, B. drive,** pignon *m* Bendix, accouplement *m* Bendix; bendix *m*.

bendlet ['bendlit], *s. Her:* cotice *f*; **b. sinister,** traverse *f*.

bendways ['bendweiz], *a. Her:* en bande.

bendwise ['bendwaiz], *a. Her:* penché.

bendy[1] ['bendi], *a. Her:* bandé; **b. counterchanged per bend sinister,** bandé-contre-bandé; **b. sinister,** barré; **b. sinister per bend counter changed,** contre-barré.

bendy[2], *s. Bot:* okra *m.*

bendy tree ['benditri:], *s. Bot:* thespesia *m*; porcher *m.*

bene ['beni], *s. Bot:* = BENNE.

beneaped [bi'ni:pt], *a. Nau:* (navire) retenu par manque d'eau; échoué jusqu'aux vives eaux; amorti; au plein; **to get b.,** amortir.

beneath [bi'ni:θ]. **1.** *adv.* dessous, au-dessous; en bas; **from b.,** de dessous; *B:* **in the earth b.,** ici-bas sur la terre. **2.** *prep.* (*a*) (*lower than*) **to marry b. one,** se marier au-dessous de son rang; se mésallier; faire une mésalliance; **this is b. my notice,** cela est indigne de mon attention; **b. contempt,** souverainement méprisable, indigne d'attention; **he would consider it b. him to complain,** il dédaignerait de se plaindre; *Lit:* **the town lies b. the castle,** la ville est située au-dessous du château; (*b*) (*under*) **there is a Roman city b. the modern town,** il y a une ville romaine sous (les fondations de) la ville actuelle, moderne; **the plank gave way b. me,** la planche a cédé sous mon poids; *Lit:* **to bend b. a burden,** plier sous un fardeau; **to sink b. the waves,** disparaître, sombrer, sous les flots.

benedicite [beni'daisiti, -'di:tʃiti], *s.* (*a*) (*at meals*) bénédicité *m*; (*b*) *Ecc:* **the B.** (*omnia opera*), le Benedicite omnia *inv.*

benedick ['benidik], *s.m. Lit:* (*a*) vieux garçon nouveau marié (personnage de Shakespeare); (*b*) nouveau marié.

Benedict ['benidikt], *Pr.n.m.* Benoit, Benoist.

Benedictine [beni'diktin]. **1.** *Ecc:* (*a*) *a.* bénédictin; (*b*) *s.* Bénédictin, -ine. **2.** *s. R.t.m:* (*also* [-ti:n]) (*liqueur*) Bénédictine *f.*

benediction [beni'dikʃ(ə)n], *s.* **1.** bénédiction *f.* **2.** (*at meals*) bénédicité *m*; **to pronounce the b.,** dire le bénédicité. **3.** *R.C.Ch:* **B. of the Holy Sacrament,** salut *m.*

benedictional [beni'dikʃənəl], **benedictionary** [beni'dikʃənəri], *s. Ecc:* bénédictionnaire *m.*

benedictive [beni'diktiv], *a. Ling:* (*esp. in Sanskrit*) précatif.

benedictory [beni'diktəri], *a.* de bénédiction; **b. prayer,** bénédiction *f.*

benedictus [beni'diktəs], *s. Ecc:* benedictus *m.*

benefaction [beni'fakʃ(ə)n, 'beni-], *s.* **1.** *Lit:* bienfaisance *f.* **2.** (*a*) *Lit:* bienfait *m*; (*b*) œuvre *f* de bienfaisance, de charité; legs *m* charitable; donation *f.*

benefactor, -tress ['benifæktər, -tris], *s.* **1.** bienfaiteur, -trice. **2.** donateur, -trice.

benefic [bi'nefik], *a. Astrol:* (astre *m*) bénéfique.

benefice ['benifis], *s. Ecc: Hist:* bénéfice *m.*

beneficed ['benifist], *a. Ecc:* pourvu d'un bénéfice; **b. clergyman,** bénéficier *m.*

beneficence [bi'nefis(ə)ns], *s.* **1.** bienfaisance *f.* **2.** œuvre *f* de bienfaisance. **3.** *Astrol:* action *f* bénéfique.

beneficent [bi'nefis(ə)nt], *a.* **1.** bienfaisant. **2.** salutaire. **3.** *Astrol:* (astre *m*) bénéfique.

beneficently [bi'nefisəntli], *adv.* **1.** avec bienfaisance. **2.** salutairement.

beneficial [beni'fiʃ(ə)l], *a.* **1.** salutaire, profitable, utile, avantageux; **b. to the health,** salutaire pour la santé; **b. to business,** avantageux pour les affaires, aux affaires; **rain is b. to the soil,** la pluie fait du bien à la terre; la pluie est un bienfait pour la terre. **2.** *Jur:* **b. owner, b. occupant,** usufruitier, -ière.

beneficially [beni'fiʃəli], *adv.* avantageusement; salutairement; utilement.

beneficiary [beni'fiʃəri], *a.* & *s. Ecc: Jur:* bénéficier, -ière; bénéficiaire (*m*); ayant droit *m*, *pl.* ayants droit.

benefit[1] ['benifit], *s.* **1.** *A:* (*favour, blessing*) bienfait *m.* **2.** (*profit, advantage*) avantage *m*, profit *m*; **the public b.,** le bien public; **to derive b. from sth.,** profiter de qch.; se trouver bien de qch.; **one always feels the benefits of a good education,** on se sent toujours d'une bonne éducation; **take your coat off, otherwise you won't feel the b. of it when you go out (again),** enlevez votre pardessus, autrement vous aurez froid en sortant; **to share in the benefits of sth.,** recevoir sa part des avantages de qch. **I get, gain,** *Lit:* **reap, no b. from it,** il ne m'en revient aucun avantage; **fringe benefits,** avantages accessoires; (*for employees*) compléments *m* de salaire en nature; *Pej:* (*of official, etc.*) **to collect fringe benefits,** faire de la gratte; **performance for the b. of the blind,** représentation *f* au profit des aveugles; **I did it for your b.,** je l'ai fait pour votre bien; **don't do it just for my b.,** ne faites pas cela expressément pour moi; **she had put on her best clothes for his b.,** elle s'était endimanchée à son intention; **let me add for your b. that . . .,** j'ajouterai pour votre gouverne que . . .; **for the b. of one's health,** dans l'intérêt de sa santé; **to give s.o. the b. of one's advice,** aider qn de ses conseils; *Jur:* **b. of the doubt,** bénéfice *m* du doute; **to get the b. of the doubt,** bénéficier du doute; **to give s.o. the b. of the doubt,** faire bénéficier qn du doute; acquitter qn faute de preuves; *Hist:* **b. of clergy,** bénéfice de clergie; *F:* **to live with s.o. without b. of clergy,** se marier avec qn de la main gauche; *attrib.* **b. club, b. society,** société *f* de secours mutuels. **3.** *Th: Sp:* **b. (performance), b. (match),** représentation *f*, match *m*, au bénéfice de qn, à bénéfice; représentation extraordinaire. **4.** *Adm: Ins:* indemnité *f*, allocation *f*; **social security benefits,** prestations sociales; **unemployment b.,** indemnité de chômage; **industrial injuries b.,** indemnité pour accidents du travail; **sickness b., medical b.,** indemnité de maladie, secours médical; **maternity b.,** allocation de maternité; **to pay out benefits,** verser les prestations; *Ins:* **to be in, out of, b.,** être, ne pas, ne plus, être, en droit de revendiquer une allocation sur les fonds de sa société d'assurance sociale.

benefit[2]. **1.** *v.tr.* faire du bien, être avantageux, profiter, à (qn, qch.); **a steady exchange rate benefits trade,** un change stable est avantageux au commerce, favorise le commerce; **hoarders whose money benefits no one,** thésauriseurs *m* dont l'argent ne profite à personne. **2.** *v.i.* **to b. by sth.,** profiter de qch.; gagner à qch.; se trouver bien de qch., tirer avantage de qch.; **you will b. by a holiday,** un congé vous fera du bien; **what did he b. by your advice?** qu'a-t-il retiré de vos conseils? **to b. from a rise in prices,** profiter, tirer profit, d'une hausse de prix.

Benelux ['benilʌks], *s. Geog: Pol:* Benelux *m*; **B. problems,** problèmes beneluxiens.

Beneventum [beni'ventəm], *Pr.n. Geog:* Bénévent *m.*

benevolence [bi'nevələns], *s.* **1.** bienveillance *f*, bonté *f.* **2.** (*a*) **act of b.,** bienfait *m*; don *m* charitable; (*b*) *Hist:* don, prêt *m* (bénévole mais) obligatoire; emprunt forcé.

benevolent [bi'nevələnt], *a.* **1.** bienveillant (**to,** envers); **b. smile,** sourire plein de bonté. **2.** bienfaisant, charitable (**to,** envers); **b. society,** association *f* de bienfaisance; société *f* de secours mutuels.

benevolently [bi'nevələntli], *adv.* avec bienveillance.

Bengal [beŋ'gɔ:l, *occ.* 'beŋgɔ:l *when attrib.*], *Pr.n. Geog:* Bengale *m*; **B. light, B. fire,** feu *m* de Bengale; **B. isinglass,** agar agar *m*; *Bot:* **B. hemp,** chanvre *m* du Bengale, crotalaire *f.*

Bengali [beŋ'gɔ:li], **Bengalese** [beŋgə'li:z], *Geog:* **1.** *a.* bengali *inv*, bengalais. **2.** *s.* Bengali *mf inv*, Bengalais, -aise. **3.** *s. Ling:* le bengali, le bengalais. **4.** *s. Orn:* bengali *m*, moineau *m* du Japon.

bengaline ['beŋgəli:n], *s. Tex:* bengaline *f.*

Beni[1] ['beni], *a.* & *s.* = BENIN.

beni[2], *s. Bot:* = BENNE.

benighted [bi'naitid], *a.* **1.** (voyageur, etc.) anuité, surpris par la nuit. **2.** plongé dans (les ténèbres de) l'ignorance; *O:* **b. policy,** politique aveugle, faite d'incompétence; *F:* **b. idiot,** sacré imbécile.

benign [bi'nain], *a.* (*a*) bénin, *f*, bénigne; doux, *f*, douce; favorable; (*b*) *Med:* **b. fever,** fièvre bénigne; **b. tumour,** tumeur bénigne.

benignancy [bi'nignənsi], *s. Lit:* bienveillance *f*, bonté *f.*

benignant [bi'nignənt], *a.* bénin, *f* bénigne; bon, bienveillant; *Astrol:* **b. star,** astre propice, bénin; *Med:* **b. growth,** tumeur bénigne.

benignantly [bi'nignəntli], *adv. Lit:* avec bienveillance; bénignement.

benignity [bi'nigniti], *s.* **1.** *Lit:* bienveillance *f*, bonté *f.* **2.** bénignité *f* (du climat, d'une fièvre, d'un astre).

benignly [bi'nainli], *adv.* bénignement.

Benin, *pl.* **-ins, Beninese** ['benin, -inz, beni'ni:z], *a.* & *s. Ethn:* (indigène *mf*) du Bénin; *Art:* **B. bronze,** bronze *m* du Bénin.

benison ['benizn], *s. A:* bénédiction *f.*

Benjamin[1] ['ben(d)ʒ(ə)min], *Pr.n.m.* Benjamin; *Jew.Hist:* **the tribe of B.,** la tribu de Benjamin; les Benjam(in)ites; *F:* **the B. (of the family),** le Benjamin (de la famille); le tardillon; le favori, le gâté.

benjamin[2], *s. Tail: F: A:* pardessus collant.

benjamin[3], *s. Bot:* (i) benjoin *m*; (ii) trillium *m*; (iii) impatiente *f*, balsamine *f*; **b. tree,** (i) styrax *m* benjoin; (ii) lindère-benjoin *f*, *pl.* lindères-benjoins; laurier-benjoin *m*, *pl.* lauriers-benjoins.

Benjamite ['ben(d)ʒəmait], *s. Jew.Hist:* Benjam(in)ite *mf.*

benk [beŋk], *s. Coal Min:* taille *f.*

benne ['beni], *s. Bot:* sésame *m*; **b. oil,** huile *f* de sésame.

bennet ['benit], *s. Bot:* **herb b.,** benoite *f.*

Bennettitales [beneti'teili:z], *s.pl. Paleont:* bennettitales *f.*

benni, benny ['beni], *s. Bot:* = BENNE.

bent[1] [bent], *a.* **1.** (*a*) courbé, plié, arqué; (essieu, levier) coudé; **doubly b.,** bicoudé; **b. back,** dos voûté; **he went away with b. head,** il se retira le dos rond, tête basse; **b. ironwork,** serrurerie *f* d'art; (*b*) faussé, fléchi, gauchi; *Aut:* **b. chassis,** châssis tordu; **to become b.,** (i) s'arquer, se courber; (*with age*) se voûter, s'affaisser; (ii) (*of rod, spring*) fléchir, gauchir; (*c*) *Opt:* **b. ray,** rayon infléchi; (*d*) *P:* (i) malhonnête, déshonnête; **b. warder,** gardien de prison corrompu, vénal; (ii) **b. boxing match,** match de boxe truqué; (iii) **b. goods,** objets volés; (iv) (mécanisme) détraqué, dérangé; (v) homosexuel, inverti. **2.** (*determined*) déterminé, résolu, décidé (**on doing sth.,** à faire qch.); **he is b. on ruining you,** il est acharné à votre perte; **he is b. on seeing me,** il veut absolument me voir; il tient à me voir; **he is b. on learning French,** il veut absolument apprendre le français; **his mind is b. on perfecting the machine,** il est préoccupé de perfectionner la machine; **to be b. on mischief,** nourrir de mauvais desseins; **to be b. on gain,** être âpre au gain; **b. on self-destruction,** obstiné à se perdre. **3.** *Lit:* **to be homeward b.,** diriger ses pas, s'acheminer, vers la maison.

bent[2], *s.* penchant *m*, inclination *f*, disposition *f* (**for,** pour); **the general b. of his character,** la tendance générale de son caractère; **to follow one's b.,** suivre son penchant, son inclination; **to have a b. towards sth.,** avoir du goût pour qch., un penchant à qch.; **to have a natural b. for music,** avoir des dispositions naturelles pour la musique; *A:* **to enjoy oneself to the top of one's b.,** s'amuser tout son saoul, à souhait, tant qu'on peut.

bent[3], *s.* **1.** *Bot:* **b. (grass),** (i) jonc *m*; (ii) agrostide *f*; **sweet b.,** luzule *f* des champs; **way b.,** orge *f* des rats, des murs; **white b., wire b.,** nard *m* raide; **flying b.,** molinie *f.* **2.** lande *f*, prairie *f.*

benthal ['benθəl], **benthic** ['benθik], *Biol:* (faune *f*) benth(on)ique.

Benthamism ['benθəmizm], *s. Phil:* benthamisme *m.*

Benthamite ['benθəmait], *s.* adhérent, -ente, du benthamisme.

benthonic [ben'θɔnik], *a. Biol:* (faune *f*) benth(on)ique.

benthos ['benθɔs], *s. Oc: Biol:* benthos *m.*

benthoscope ['benθəskoup], *s. Oc:* bathysphère *f.*

bentonite ['bentənait], *s. Miner:* bentonite *f.*

bentwood ['bentwud], *a.* **b. chair,** chaise *f* en bois courbé.

benumb [bi'nʌm], *v.tr.* (*a*) engourdir, transir; **fingers benumbed with cold,** doigts engourdis par le froid; doigts gourds; **we were benumbed with cold,** nous étions transis de froid; (*b*) paralyser, engourdir (l'esprit, l'intelligence).

benz(o) ['benz(ou)], *pref. Ch:* benz(o)-.

benzal ['benz(ə)l], *s. Ch:* benzylidène *m.*

benzaldehyde [ben'zældihaid], *s.* benzaldéhyde *m.*

benzamide [ben'zæmaid], *s. Ch:* benzamide *m.*

benzanilide [ben'zænilaid], *s. Ch:* benzanilide *f.*

benzanthrone [benz'ænθroun], *s. Ch:* benzanthrone *f.*

benzazide [benz'æzaid], *s. Ch:* benzazide *f.*

benzazimide [benz'æzimaid], *s. Ch:* benzazimide *m.*

Benzedrine ['benzidri:n], *s. R.t.m:* Benzédrine *f.*

benzein ['benzeiin], *s. Ch:* benzéine *f.*

benzene ['benzi:n], *s. Ch:* benzène *m*; **b. ring, nucleus,** noyau *m* benzénique, hexagone *m* de Kekule; **b. hydrocarbons,** hydrocarbones *m* benzéniques; **methyl b.,** toluène *m.*

benzenoid ['benzənɔid], *a. Ch:* benzénoïde.

benzidine ['benzidi:n], *Ch:* **1.** *s.* benzidine *f.* **2.** *a.* (transformation *f*) benzidinique.

benzil ['benzil], *s. Ch:* benzile *m.*

benzine ['benzi:n, ben'zi:n], *s.* **1.** *Ch: A:* = BENZENE. **2.** *Ch: Ind:* benzine *f.*

benzoate ['benzoueit], *s. Ch:* benzoate *m*; **b. of soda,** benzoate de sodium.

benz(o)hydrol [benz(ou)'haidrɔl], *s. Ch:* benzhydrol *m.*

benzoic [ben'zouik], *a. Ch:* benzoïque.

benzoin ['benzouin], *s.* **1.** **(gum) b.,** benjoin *m.* **2.** *Ch:* benzoïne *f.*

benzol ['benzɔl], *s. Ch: Com:* benzol *m*; **b. scrubber,** épurateur *m* de benzol (à frôlement).

benzoleic [benzə'li:ik], *a. Ch:* benzoléique.

benzoline ['benzouli:n], *s.* benzoline *f.*

benzolism ['benzoulizm], *s. Med:* benzolisme *m*, benzénisme *m.*

benzonaphtol [benzou'næftɔl], *s. Ch:* benzonaphtol *m.*

benzonitrile [benzou'naitril], *s. Ch:* benzonitrile *m.*

benzophenone [benzou'fi:noun, -fi'noun], *s. Ch:* benzophénone *f.*

benzopyrene [benzou'pairi:n], *s. Ch:* benzopyrène *m.*

benzoquinone [benzou'kwinoun, -kwi'noun], *s. Ch:* benzoquinone *f.*

benzoyl ['benzɔil], *s. Ch:* benzoyle *m.*

benzyl ['benzil], *s. Ch:* benzyle *m*; **b. alcohol, b.**

cellulose, alcool *m*, cellulose *f*, benzylique.

benzylamine [ben'ziləmain], *s. Ch:* benzylamine *f*.

benzylic [ben'zilik], *a. Ch:* benzylique.

benzylidene [ben'zilidiːn], *s. Ch:* benzylidène *m*.

bequeath [bi'kwiːð], *v.tr.* léguer **(to,** à).

bequest [bi'kwest], *s.* legs *m*; **charitable b.,** legs de charité; (*in museum*) **picture purchased from the Chantry b.,** tableau acheté avec les fonds *m* de Sir Francis Chantry.

ber [bɛər], *s. Bot:* **b. (fruit),** jujube *m*; **b.(-fruit) tree,** jujubier *m*.

berate [bi'reit], *v.tr.* gronder, réprimander, morigéner (qn).

Berber ['bəːbər]. **1.** *Ethn:* (*a*) *a.* berbère; (*b*) *s.* Berbère *mf.* **2.** *s. Ling:* le berbère.

Berberidaceae [bəːbəri'ɔɪ'dɑːiː], *s.pl. Bot:* berbéridacées *f*.

berberin ['bəːbərin], **berberine** ['bəːbəriːn], *s. Ch: Physiol:* berbérine *f*.

berberis ['bəːbəris], **berberry** ['bəːbəri], *s. Bot:* épine-vinette *f, pl.* épines-vinettes; vinette *f*.

berceuse [bɛə'səːz], *s. Mus:* berceuse *f*.

bereave [bi'riːv], *v.tr.* (*p.t. & p.p.* **bereft** [bi'reft], **bereaved;** *usu.* **bereft** *in* 1 *and* **bereaved** *in* 2) priver, déposséder **(s.o. of sth.,** qn de qch.). **1. indignation had bereft him of speech,** l'indignation l'avait prive de la parole; **to be bereft of one's possessions,** se trouver dépossédé; être privé de ses biens; **bereft of all hope,** privé de tout espoir; ayant perdu tout espoir; **bereft of reason,** dénué, privé, de raison; **pedestal bereft of its statue,** piédestal veuf de sa statue. **2.** *Lit:* **an accident bereaved him of his father, of his parents,** un accident lui a ravi son père, l'a rendu orphelin.

bereaved [bi'riːvd], *a.* affligé (d'un deuil); *s.* **the b.,** l'affligé(e); les affligé(e)s; la famille du mort, de la morte.

bereavement [bi'riːvmənt], *s.* perte *f* (d'un parent); deuil *m*; **owing to a recent b.,** en raison d'un deuil récent.

Berengaria [beriŋ'gɛəriə], *Pr.n.f. Hist:* Bérengère.

Berengarius [beriŋ'gɛəriəs], *Pr.n.m. Hist:* Bérenger.

Berenice [beri'naisi(ː)], *Pr.n.f.* Bérénice; *Astr:* **Berenice's Hair,** la Chevelure de Bérénice.

beret ['berei, 'beri], *s. Cost:* béret *m*; *Mil:* **the red berets,** les bérets rouges, les parachutistes *m*; **the blue berets,** les bérets bleus, les troupes *f* de l'O.N.U.

berg [bəːg], *s.* **1.** iceberg *m*, montagne *f* de glace. **2.** (*in S. Africa*) montagne.

Bergamask ['bəːgəmæsk]. **1.** *Geog:* (*a*) *a.* bergamasque; (*b*) *s.* Bergamasque *mf.* **2.** *s. Danc:* bergamasque *f*.

Bergamo ['bəːgəmou], *Pr.n. Geog:* Bergame *f*.

bergamot[1] ['bəːgəmət], *s.* **1.** *Bot:* (*a*) (*orange*) bergamote *f*; **b. tree,** bergamotier *m*; (*b*) (i) menthe *f* aquatique; (ii) monarde *f.* **2.** (*perfume*) **(oil of) b.,** essence *f* de bergamote.

bergamot[2], *s.* (*pear*) bergamote *f*, crassane *f*.

Bergamot[3], *a.* **B. tapestry,** bergame *f*.

bergander [bəː'gændər], *s. Orn:* tadorne *m*.

berginization [bəːdʒinai'zeiʃ(ə)n], *s. Ind:* berginisation *f* (des hydrocarbures lourds).

Bergius ['bəːdʒiəs], *Pr.n. Ch:* **B. process,** procédé *m* Bergius.

bergschrund ['bɛəgʃrund], *s. Mount:* rimaye *f*.

Bergsonian [bəːg'souniən], *a. Phil:* bergsonien.

Bergsonism ['bəːgsənizm], *s. Phil:* bergsonisme *m*.

bergylt ['bəːgilt], *s. Ich:* sébaste *m*.

beribboned [bi'ribnd], *a.* enrubanné; **b. old soldier,** ancien militaire paré de ses rubans (de médaille).

beriberi ['beri'beri], *s. Med:* béribéri *m*.

Berkeleian [bɑː'kli(ː)ən]. **1.** *a.* (philosophie *f* idéaliste) de (l'evêque) Berkeley. **2.** *s.* adhérent, -ente, du berkeleyisme.

Berkeleianism [bɑː'kliənizm], *s. Phil:* berkeleyisme *m*.

berkelium [bəː'kiːliəm], *s. Ch:* berkélium *m*.

Berlin [bəː'lin]. **1.** *Pr.n. Geog:* Berlin; *A:* **B. wool,** laine *f* de Berlin, laine à tricoter, à tapisserie, à broder; **B. warehouse,** magasin *m* de laine à tricoter; **B. gloves,** gants *m* de laine de Berlin; *Metall:* **B. iron,** fonte *f* de Berlin; *Metalw:* **B. black,** vernis *m.* **2.** *s. Veh: A:* berline *f*.

berline [bə(ː)'liːn], *s. Veh: A:* berline *f*.

Berliner [bəː'linər], *s. Geog:* Berlinois, -oise.

berlinite ['bəːlinait], *s. Miner:* berlinite *f*.

berm [bəːm], *s.* **1.** *Fort:* berme *f* (d'un rempart); *Civ.E:* berme, banquette *f* (d'un canal); risberme *f* (d'un barrage). **2.** *Geol:* (*a*) replat *m* d'érosion, banquette d'érosion (*b*) (*Nile Valley*) plaine *f* d'inondation.

Bermuda [bəː'mjuːdə], *Pr.n. Geog:* **the B. Islands,** *s.* **the Bermudas,** les Bermudes *f*; *Bot:* **B. grass,** cynodon *m*; **B. lily,** bermudienne *f*; *Cost:* **B. shorts,** *s.* **bermudas,** bermuda *m*; *Y:* **B. rig,** gréement *m* Marconi.

Bermudian [bəː'mjuːdiən], *Geog:* **1.** *a.* bermudien; *Y:* **B. rig,** gréement *m* Marconi; **B. mainsail,** voile bermudienne. **2.** *s.* Bermudien, -ienne.

bernacle ['bəːnəkl], *s. Orn:* **b. (goose),** bernacle *f*, bernache *f*, oie marine, cane *f* à collier.

Bern(e) [bəːn], *Pr.n. Geog:* Berne *f*.

Bernardine ['bəːnədin], *Ecc:* **1.** *a.* bernardin. **2.** *s.* Bernardin, -ine.

Bernese [bəː'niːz, 'bəː-], *Geog:* **1.** *a.* bernois; **the B. Alps,** les Alpes bernoises. **2.** *s.* Bernois, -oise.

Bernice [bəː'naisi(ː), bəː'niːs], *Pr.n.f.* Bérénice.

bernicle ['bəːnikl], *s.* = BERNACLE.

Bernoulli [bəː'nuli], *Pr.n. Ch:* **Bernoulli's theorem,** theorème *m*, principe *m*, de Bernoulli.

Beroë ['berəwi]. **1.** *Pr.n. Myth:* Béroé *f.* **2.** *Coel:* béroé *m*.

Berriasian [beri'eisiən], *a. & s. Geol:* berriasien (*m*).

berried ['berid], *a.* **1.** *Bot:* à baies, couvert de baies. **2.** (crustacé) œuvé.

berry[1] ['beri], *s.* **1.** *Bot:* baie *f*; **coffee b.,** fruit *m* du caféier, cerise *f* de caféier; **holly b.,** cenelle *f.* **2.** *Com:* (*a*) **Avignon b., French b.,** grenette *f*; (*b*) **b. wax,** cire *f* de cirier. **3.** (*a*) frai *m* (de poisson); (*b*) œufs *mpl* (de crustacé); **lobster in b.,** homard œuvé. **4.** *Orn:* caroncule *f* (de cygne commun). **5.** *U.S: F:* (*a*) dollar *m*; (*b*) **he's the berries,** c'est un as, une perle.

berry[2], *v.i.* **1.** (*of shrub*) former des baies; se garnir de baies. **2. to go berrying,** aller à la cueillette des baies, des mûres, etc.

bersagliere, *pl* **-i** [bəːsɑːli'ɛəri(ː)], *s. Mil:* (*Italy*) bersaglier *m*.

berserk [bə(ː)'zəːk], *s.* berserk *m*; **to go b.,** devenir fou furieux.

berteroa [bəːtə'ouə], *s. Bot:* berteroa *m*.

berth[1] [bəːθ], *s.* **1.** *Nau:* (*a*) évitée *f*, évitage *m*; **we have a foul b.,** nous n'avons pas notre évitage; **to give a ship a wide b.,** éviter, parer, un navire; passer au large d'un navire; **to give a headland, etc., a wide b.,** prendre, donner, du tour; *F:* **to give s.o. a wide b.,** éviter qn; se garder d'approcher de qn; **give these people a wide b.,** défiez-vous de ces gens-là; (*b*) **(anchoring) b.,** poste *m* de mouillage, d'amarrage; **open b.,** mouillage forain; (*c*) poste *m* à quai; emplacement *m*; **loading b.,** emplacement de chargement. **2.** (*a*) *Nau: Rail:* couchette *f* (de passager, de voyageur); (*b*) *Nau:* cadre *m* (d'officier, d'homme d'équipage.). **3.** (*a*) emplacement (de qch.); (*b*) *F:* place *f*, position *f*, emploi *m*; **to find a b.,** arriver à se caser; trouver une situation **(with,** chez); **to find a soft b.,** trouver un emploi pépère; **to find a b. for s.o.,** caser qn. **4.** *Can: For:* peuplement *m*.

berth[2]. **1.** *v.tr.* (*a*) donner, assigner, un poste à (un navire); (*b*) accoster (un navire) le long du quai; amener, amarrer, (un navire) à quai; (*c*) donner une couchette à (qn). **2.** *v.i.* (*a*) (*of ship*) (i) mouiller; (ii) aborder à quai; se ranger à quai; (*b*) (*of passengers or crew*) **to b. forward, aft,** coucher à l'avant, à l'arrière; **I berthed forward,** j'avais une cabine à l'avant.

Bertha ['bəːθə]. **1.** *Pr.n.f.* Berthe; *Hist:* (1914–1918) (*gun bombarding Paris*). **Big B.,** la grosse Bertha. **2.** *A.Cost:* berthe *f* (de corsage décolleté).

berthage ['bəːθidʒ], *s. Nau:* **1.** (emplacement *m* de) mouillage *m.* **2.** droits *mpl* d'amarrage.

berthe [bɛəːt], *s. A.Cost:* berthe *f* (de corsage décolleté).

berthing ['bəːθiŋ], *s.* **1.** (*a*) mouillage *m*; (*b*) abordage *m* à quai. **2.** aménagements *mpl* (à bord); postes *mpl* de couchage.

bertholletia [bəːθə'liːʃə], *s. Bot:* berthollétie *f*.

Bert(ie) ['bəːt(i)], *Pr.n.m.* (*nom d'amitié pour* (i) **Bertrand, Bertram;** (ii) **Albert**) (i) Bertrand; (ii) Albert.

Bertillon [bəː'tijən], *Pr.n.* **B. system,** bertillonnage *m*.

bertillonnage [bəːtijə'nɑːʒ], *s.* bertillonnage *m*.

Bertram ['bəːtrəm], **Bertrand** ['bəːtrənd], *Pr.n.m.* Bertrand.

beryl ['beril], *s. Miner:* béryl *m*.

beryllia [be'riliə], *s. Ch:* glucine *f*.

berylline ['berilain, -liːn], *a.* qui ressemble au béryl; (couleur *f*) de béryl.

beryllium [be'riliəm], *s. Ch:* béryllium *m*, glucinium *m*; **b. oxide,** glucine *f*.

beryx ['beriks], *s. Ich:* béryx *m*.

berzelianite [bə(ː)'ziːliənait], *s. Miner:* berzélianite *f*.

berzelite ['bə(ː)zilait], *s. Miner:* berzélite *f*.

besant ['bez(ə)nt], *s.* = BEZANT.

beseech [bi'siːtʃ], *v.tr.* **(besought** [bi'sɔːt]; **besought)** *Lit:* **1.** supplier; adjurer, conjurer, implorer **(s.o. to do sth.,** qn de faire qch.); **I b. you for pardon,** je vous supplie de me pardonner. **2. to b. leave to do sth.,** implorer, solliciter, la permission de faire qch.; **to b. s.o.'s pardon,** implorer le pardon de qn.

beseeching[1] [bi'siːtʃiŋ], *s.* supplications *fpl*, instances *fpl*.

beseeching[2], *a.* (air, ton) suppliant.

beseechingly [bi'siːtʃiŋli], *adv.* d'un air, d'un ton, suppliant.

beseem [bi'siːm], *v.tr. A: Lit:* (*used only in 3rd pers.*) **to b. s.o. (well, ill),** convenir, seoir, (bien, mal) à qn; **it would ill b. me to . . .,** je serais mal venu à . . .; **it does not b. a knight to . . .,** il ne sied pas à un chevalier de . . .; ce n'est pas le fait d'un chevalier de . . ..

beseeming [bi'siːmiŋ], *a. A: Lit:* convenable, seyant; qui va bien à (qn).

beseemingly [bi'siːmiŋli], *adv. A: Lit:* convenablement; d'une façon appropriée; d'une manière qui sied (à qn).

beset [bi'set], *v.tr.* **(beset; beset; besetting)** *Lit:* **1.** cerner (des troupes); assaillir, obséder (qn); serrer (qn) de près; **we were close b.,** nous étions serrés de près; **b. with dangers, with difficulties,** environné, entouré, de dangers, de difficultés; **career b. with difficulties,** carrière hérissée de difficultés. **2.** assiéger (un endroit). **3.** (*of misfortunes, temptations, etc.*) assaillir (qn); **to be b. by doubts,** être assailli de doutes; **b. by hunger,** pressé par la faim. **4. crown b. with diamonds,** couronne ornée, incrustée, de diamants.

besetment [bi'setmənt], *s. A: & Lit:* **1.** (*a*) investissement *m* (d'une ville, etc.); (*b*) blocus *m.* **2.** faible *m*, côté *m* faible; défaut *m*.

besetting [bi'setiŋ], *a.* (*of idea, thought, etc.*) obsédant; **b. sin,** péché *m* d'habitude; **it's his b. sin,** c'est son grand défaut, son péché mignon.

beshrew [bi'ʃruː], *v.tr. A:* (*only as imprecation*) **b. the day!** maudit soit le jour! **b. me if . . .,** le diable m'emporte si . . ..

beside [bi'said], *prep.* **1.** (*a*) (*by the side of, close to*) à côté, auprès, de (qn, qch.); **close b. s.o., sth.,** tout auprès de qn, de qch.; **seated b. me,** assis à côté de moi, auprès de moi, à mes côtés; **a table with a chair b. it,** une table avec une chaise à côté; (*b*) (*compared with*) à côté de, auprès de (qn, qch.); **b. him everyone else appears slow,** à côté de lui tous les autres paraissent lents; (*c*) (*besides*) **I want nothing b. this,** je ne désire rien en dehors de cela; **other people b. ourselves have remarked on it,** d'autres personnes que nous en ont fait l'observation. **2.** (*a*) **b. the question, the point, the mark,** à côté de la question, étranger à la question, hors de propos, en dehors du sujet; **that is b. the point,** cela n'a rien à voir à l'affaire; **this criticism is b. the point,** cette critique porte à faux; (*b*) **to be b. oneself,** être hors de soi; **to be b. oneself with joy,** ne plus se sentir de joie; ne plus se posséder de joie; être fou, transporté, de joie; **b. himself with anger,** outré de colère; **he was b. himself with rage,** la colère l'emportait.

besides [bi'saidz]. **1.** *adv.* (*a*) en outre, en plus; **many more b.,** encore bien d'autres; **I have, b., two nephews,** j'ai, en outre, deux neveux; **nothing b.,** rien de plus; **he bought us a house and a drawing-room suite b.,** il nous a acheté une maison, et en plus de cela, un mobilier de salon; (*b*) **it is too late; b., I am tired,** il est trop tard; d'ailleurs, du reste, d'autre part, et en outre, je suis fatigué; **you must have patience; b., you are only twenty,** il faut patienter un peu; aussi bien n'avez-vous que vingt ans. **2.** *prep.* **there are others b. him,** il y en a d'autres que lui; **there are three others b. him,** il y en a trois en plus de lui; **we were four b. John,** nous étions quatre sans compter Jean; **I have another umbrella b. that one,** j'ai un autre parapluie que celui-là; **b. this gift he received others,** outre ce cadeau il en reçut d'autres; **b. which, he was unwell,** sans compter qu'il était indisposé; **no one b. you,** personne hormis, excepté, vous; **I want nothing b. this,** je ne désire rien en dehors de cela; **who b. him?** qui hormis lui, à part lui? qui si ce n'est lui? **b. the fact that . . .,** sans compter que . . ..

besiege [bi'siːdʒ], *v.tr.* assiéger; mettre le siège devant (une ville); faire le siège d(')une ville); **to b. s.o. with requests,** assiéger qn de demandes; **he was besieged after the meeting,** après la réunion il fut entouré, l'on se pressa autour de lui.

besieger [bi'siːdʒər], *s.* assiégeant *m*, assaillant *m*.

besieging [bi'siːdʒiŋ], *a.* assiégeant; **b. army,** armée *f* d'investissement, de siège.

beslaver [bi'slævər], *v.tr. A:* couvrir (qch.) de bave; baver sur (qch.).

beslobber [bi'slɔbər], *v.tr. A: F:* **1.** = BESLAVER. **2.** prodiguer des baisers (baveux) à (qn).

besmear [bi'smiər], *v.tr. Lit:* barbouiller, souiller **(with grease, etc.,** de graisse, etc.).

besmirch [bi'sməːtʃ], *v.tr. Lit:* salir, tacher, souiller (qch.); salir, ternir (la mémoire de qn, etc.); entacher, *F:* chiffonner (l'honneur de qn); **to b. one's name,** galvauder son nom; se galvauder; **to b. s.o.'s good name,** couvrir qn de boue.

besom ['biːzəm], *s.* **1.** balai *m* (de jonc, de bruyère); *F: O:* **to jump the b.,** remplir, jouer, un simulacre de mariage. **2.** (*also* ['bizəm]) *Dial: F:* (i) effrontée *f*; (ii) **an old b.,**

une vieille mégère.

besot [bi'sɔt], *v.tr.* (**besotted**) **1.** abrutir (**with,** de); **drink has besotted him,** l'ivrognerie l'a dégradé. **2.** affoler, envoûter.

besotted [bi'sɔtid], *a.* **1.** abruti (par l'opium, la boisson); **to become b.,** s'abrutir. **2.** affolé, entiché (de qn).

bespangle [bi'spæŋgl], *v.tr. Lit:* pailleter, parsemer (**with,** de).

bespangled [bi'spæŋgld], *a. Lit:* scintillant (**with,** de); **meadows b. with flowers,** prés parsemés, émaillés, de fleurs.

bespatter [bi'spætər], *v.tr.* éclabousser; **bespattered with mud,** tout couvert de boue; *F:* crotté jusqu'à l'échine, comme un barbet.

bespeak[1] [bi'spi:k], *v.tr. O:* (**bespoke; bespoken,** *A:* **bespoke**) **1.** *(a)* commander (des souliers, etc.); retenir, arrêter (une place, etc.); retenir (une chambre à l'hôtel); **to b. a book at the library,** s'inscrire pour un livre, retenir un livre, à la bibliothèque de prêt; *(b) Lit:* demander, solliciter (une faveur). **2.** accuser, annoncer; **the cut of his clothes bespeaks the provincial,** la coupe de ses vêtements accuse le provincial; **his conversation bespeaks intelligence,** sa conversation annonce de l'intelligence. **3.** *Lit:A:* **to b. s.o.,** parler, s'adresser, à qn.

bespeak[2], *s. Th: A:* **b. performance,** représentation *f* à bénéfice.

bespeckle [bi'spekl], *v.tr.* tacheter, moucheter.

bespectacled [bi'spektəkld], *a.* qui porte des lunettes; portant lunettes; à lunettes.

bespoke [bi'spouk], *a. (a)* **b. garment,** vêtement (fait) sur commande, sur mesure; *(b)* **b. tailor, shoemaker,** tailleur *m,* cordonnier *m,* qui travaille sur commande, sur mesure; tailleur, cordonnier, à façon.

besprinkle [bi'spriŋkl], *v.tr. Lit: (a)* arroser, asperger (**with,** de); *(b)* saupoudrer (**with,** de); *(c)* parsemer (**with,** de).

Bess [bes], *Pr.n.f. (dim. of Elizabeth)* Lisette, Babette; *F: A:* **brown B.,** fusil *m* à pierre; mousquet *m*; *Hist: F:* **Good Queen B.,** la bonne reine Élisabeth (1558–1603); **in the days of Good Queen B.,** du temps où Berthe filait.

Bessarabia [besə'reibiə], *Pr.n. Geog:* Bessarabie *f.*

Bessarabian [besə'reibiən], *a. & s. Geog:* (originaire, natif, -ive) de Bessarabie.

Bessemer ['besimər], *Pr.n. Metall:* **B. process,** procédé *m* Bessemer; **B. (converter),** convertisseur *m* Bessemer; **B. (steel),** acier *m* Bessemer.

bessemerize ['besiməraiz], *v.tr. Metall:* convertir (le minerai) par le procédé Bessemer.

bessemerizing ['besiməraiziŋ], *s. Metall:* bessemérisation *f.*

Bessie ['besi], *Pr.n.f.* = BESS.

best[1] [best]. **1.** *a. & s. (a)* (le) meilleur, (la) meilleure; *(neuter)* le mieux; **the b. man on earth,** le meilleur homme du monde; **he is the b. of men,** *F:* **one of the b.,** c'est la crème des hommes; **may the b. man win,** que le meilleur gagne; *(at a wedding)* **b. man,** garçon *m* d'honneur; *F:* **his b. girl,** sa bonne amie, la jeune fille de son choix; **my b. hat,** mon plus beau chapeau, *F:* mon chapeau numéro un; **the b. bedroom,** la meilleure chambre; **to manufacture under the b. conditions,** fabriquer au mieux; **acceptance test under the b. conditions,** essai de réception favorisé par des conditions optimales; **I am acting in your b. interests,** j'agis au mieux de vos intérêts; **the wine was of the b.,** le vin était des meilleurs; **we drank of the b., of his b.,** nous avons bu du meilleur, de son meilleur; **the b. is good enough for me,** croûte de pâté vaut bien pain; **(dressed) in one's b. (clothes),** endimanché; *(of woman)* dans ses plus beaux atours; *F:* sur son trente et un; **to put on one's b. clothes,** se mettre sur son trente et un; **I had dressed in my b.,** j'avais mis mes plus beaux habits, ma plus belle robe; **he can sing with the b.,** il chante comme pas un; **we are the b. of friends,** nous sommes les meilleurs amis du monde; **b. friend,** ami(e) intime, ami(e) de cœur; **our mothers were on b. friend terms,** nos mères étaient des amies intimes; **I am in the b. of health,** je me porte à merveille; je suis en excellente santé; **the b. of the matter, the b. of it, is that . . .,** le plus beau de l'affaire c'est que . . .; **the b. part of the way, of the year,** la plus grande partie du chemin, de l'année; **the b. part of his savings,** le plus clair de ses économies; **I waited for the b. part of an hour,** j'ai attendu une petite heure; **the b. part of £5,** cinq livres ou peu s'en faut; **this is the b. there is,** voici ce qu'il y a de meilleur, de mieux; *F:* **the b. of luck, all the b.!** bonne chance! meilleurs souhaits! *U.S:* **my brother sends his b.,** toutes sortes d'amitiés, bien des choses, de la part de mon frère; *F:* **the party was the b. ever,** la soirée était la meilleure qui fût jamais; **to know what is b. for s.o.,** savoir ce qui va, convient, le mieux à qn; **it is b. to . . .,** il y a avantage à . . ., le mieux c'est de . . .; **the b. thing you can do, the b. course to take, the b. way, is to . . .,** ce que vous avez de mieux à faire, ce qu'il y a de mieux à faire, c'est de . . .; **I asked him what was b. to be done,** je lui demandai ce qu'il y avait de mieux à faire; **it would be b., the b. plan would be, to . . .,** le mieux serait de . . .; **I thought it (would be) b. to stay,** j'ai pensé qu'il valait mieux rester; **the next b. thing would be to . . .,** à défaut de cela le mieux serait de . . .; **he's the next b.** = faute de X il y a Y; **he is b. at landscape painting,** ce qu'il réussit le mieux c'est le paysage; **to do one's b., the b. one can, the b. in one's power, to . . .,** faire ce qu'on peut, faire de son mieux, faire tout son possible, pour . . .; **I did my b. to comfort her,** je la consolai de mon mieux; **he did his b. to smile,** il s'efforça de sourire; **I am doing my (level) b., the b. I can, for you,** je fais tout ce que je peux pour vous; **they were doing their b. for the wounded,** ils s'empressaient autour des blessés; **do the b. you can,** (i) arrangez-vous; (ii) faites pour le mieux; **to look one's b.,** être, paraître, à son avantage; *(of woman)* être en beauté; **he looked his b. in uniform,** l'uniforme l'avantageait; **she looks her b. in the morning,** elle est à son avantage le matin; **to be at one's b.,** être en train, en forme; **when he is at his b. . . .,** quand il est bien en train; **she was at her b. at thirty,** c'est à trente ans qu'elle a été le plus belle; **that is Dickens at his b.,** voilà du meilleur Dickens; **to get the b. out of s.o.,** encourager qn à faire de son mieux; faire donner à qn tout ce qu'il peut; **to get the b. of s.o.,** remporter un avantage sur qn; *F:* enfoncer qn; **to get, have, the b. of it, of the bargain, to come off b.,** l'emporter, avoir l'avantage; avoir le dessus; remporter la victoire; tenir le bon bout; **you have the b. of it,** c'est vous le mieux partagé; **to have the b. of an argument,** l'emporter dans une discussion; *F:* **I give you b.,** je reconnais que vous êtes plus fort que moi; je vous donne gagné; **to have, get, the b. of the game,** dominer la partie; **to hope for the b.,** ne pas désespérer, avoir bon espoir; **to make the b. of sth.,** s'accommoder de qch.; **to make the b. of the matter, of it,** en prendre son parti; se tirer d'affaire le mieux possible, se faire une raison, se débrouiller; **to make the b. of a bad job, of a bad bargain,** faire bonne mine à mauvais jeu; faire contre mauvaise fortune bon cœur; **one must make the b. of things,** il faut se faire une raison; où la chèvre est attachée il faut qu'elle broute; **to make the b. of the circumstances,** s'adapter aux circonstances; **he made the b. of his way home,** il s'empressa, se hâta, de rentrer; il s'en retourna au plus vite, en toute hâte, sans perdre de temps; *Cards: etc:* **to play the b. of three games,** jouer en parties liées; jouer au meilleur de trois; *Sp: F:* **to beat one's previous b.,** battre son meilleur temps; *F:* **a new world's b.,** un nouveau record mondial; *F:* **six of the b.,** une fessée magistrale; *(b) adv.phr.* (i) **at (the) b.,** au mieux; *St.Exch:* **to sell at b.,** vendre au mieux; **at b. he will get 2000 votes,** (en mettant les choses) au mieux, il aura 2000 suffrages; **at (the) b. it is a poor piece of work,** pour dire le mieux, c'est un piètre travail; **at b. we cannot arrive before tomorrow,** c'est tout au plus si nous pourrons arriver demain; **at (the) b. it will bring you in . . .,** en mettant les choses au mieux cela vous rapportera . . .; **he was undemonstrative at the b. (of times),** même dans ses meilleurs moments il était peu démonstratif; (ii) **to act for the b.,** agir pour le mieux; **I did it for the b.,** j'ai fait pour le mieux; **it's all for the b.,** (α) tout est pour le mieux; (β) c'est dans la meilleure intention; (iii) **to do sth. to the b. of one's ability, abilities,** faire qch. de son mieux; agir dans la mesure de ses moyens; **to the b. of my belief, knowledge, recollection,** à ce que je crois, autant que je sache, (pour) autant que, d'autant que, je puis(se) m'en souvenir, autant qu'il m'en souvienne; **to the b. of my judgment,** à mon humble avis; autant que je peux en juger. **2.** *adv. (a)* **he does it (the) b.,** c'est lui qui le fait le mieux; **I comforted her as b. I could,** je la consolai de mon mieux; **I came, got, down as b. I could,** je suis descendu comme j'ai pu; **you know b.,** c'est vous (qui êtes) le mieux placé pour en juger; **do as you think b.,** faites comme bon vous semble(ra), ce que bon vous semble(ra); faites à votre idée, faites comme vous l'entendez; *(b)* **the b. dressed man,** l'homme le mieux habillé; **the b. known book,** le livre le mieux, le plus, connu; **the b. looking women,** les femmes les plus jolies; **she was the b. looking of the three sisters,** c'était la mieux des trois sœurs; **the b. tempered person,** la personne au meilleur caractère; le meilleur caractère; **b. selling novel,** roman *m* à succès, à fort tirage.

best[2], *v.tr. F:* l'emporter sur (qn); *F:* enfoncer, rouler (qn); circonvenir (qn); *P:* faire le poil à (qn); **he was hopelessly bested by . . .,** il a été roulé à plates coutures par . . ..

bestead[1] [bi'sted], *v.* (*p.t.* **besteaded;** *p.p.* **bestead, bested** [bi'sted]) *A: (a) v.tr.* aider, secourir (qn); *(b)* profiter, être avantageux (à qch., qn).

bestead[2], **bested** [bi'sted], *a. A: (a)* entouré (**by,** de); *(b)* **ill b.,** mal situé; en mauvaise posture.

bester ['bestər], *s. P: O:* dupeur, -euse.

bestial ['bestjəl], *a.* bestial, -aux; **to become b.,** se bestialiser.

bestialism ['bestiəlizm], *s.* déraison *f*; manque *m* de raison.

bestiality [besti'æliti], *s.* bestialité *f.*

bestialize ['bestjəlaiz], *v.tr.* bestialiser, abrutir.

bestially ['bestjəli], *adv.* bestialement.

bestiary ['bestiəri], *s. Lit.Hist:* bestiaire *m.*

bestir [bi'stə:r], *v.pr.* (**bestirred**) **to b. oneself,** se remuer, se démener, s'activer; *F:* se secouer, s'actionner; se grouiller.

bestow [bi'stou], *v.tr. Lit:* **1.** accorder, octroyer, donner, attribuer (**sth. upon s.o.,** qch. à qn); **to b. a favour on s.o.,** accorder une faveur à qn; **to b. a title on s.o.,** conférer un titre à qn; **to b. one's confidence on s.o.,** investir qn de sa confiance; placer sa confiance en qn; **to b. one's affection on s.o.,** placer son affection sur qn; **to b. one's hand on s.o.,** faire don de sa main à qn; **to b. the hand of one's daughter (in marriage) upon s.o.,** accorder à qn la main de sa fille; **to b. a title on oneself,** s'adjuger un titre. **2.** *A: (a)* **to b. sth. somewhere,** déposer qch. quelque part; **to b. one's money wisely,** placer sagement son argent; *(b)* **to b. s.o. somewhere,** loger qn quelque part.

bestowal [bi'stouəl], *s.* **1.** *Lit:* don *m,* octroi *m* (de qch.); *Theol:* **the b. of divine grace,** l'effusion *f* de la grâce divine. **2.** *A:* placement *m.*

bestower [bi'stouər], *s. Lit:* donateur, -trice.

bestowing [bi'stouiŋ], *s. Lit:* = BESTOWAL.

bestowment [bi'stoumənt], *s. Lit:* **1.** = BESTOWAL. **2.** don (octroyé).

bestrew [bi'stru:], *v.tr.* (*p.t.* **bestrewed;** *p.p.* **bestrewed** *or* **bestrewn** [bi'stru:n]) *Lit:* parsemer, joncher (**sth. with sth.,** qch. de qch.); **streets bestrewn with flowers,** rues jonchées de fleurs.

best seller ['best'selər], *s.* **1.** *(a)* livre *m* à succès, à fort tirage, à forte vente; best-seller *m, pl.* best-sellers; **it's a b. s.,** c'est un des grands succès de la librairie; **the b. s. of the season,** le gros succès, le grand tirage, de la saison; *(b)* auteur *m* d'un livre à succès. **2.** article *m* de grosse vente.

best-selling [best'seliŋ], *a.* à grand succès, de grosse vente.

bestudded [bi'stʌdid], *a. Lit:* **b. with flowers, stars,** (par)semé de fleurs, d'étoiles.

bet[1] [bet], *s.* pari *m,* gageure *f*; **even b.,** pari avec enjeu égal; **to make, lay, a b.,** parier, faire un pari; **to take (up) a b.,** tenir, accepter, un pari; **a good, safe, b.,** un coup sûr; **your best b. would be to . . .,** à votre place je . . ., ce que vous avez de mieux à faire c'est . . ..

bet[2], *v.tr. & i.* (*p.t.* **bet;** *p.p.* **bet,** *occ.* **betted**) *(a)* parier (une somme); **to b. on a horse,** miser sur, jouer, un cheval; **to b. ten to one that . . .,** parier à dix contre un que . . .; **to b. two to one,** parier le double contre le simple; **to b. on a certainty,** parier à coup sûr; *(b)* **to b. with s.o.,** parier avec qn; **to b. that one will do sth.,** parier de faire qch.; **I'll b. you that . . .,** je vous parierais que . . ., parions que . . .; **to b. against s.o., sth.,** parier contre qn, qch.; **to b. on sth.,** parier sur qch.; *F:* **you b.! you b. your boots!** pour sûr! je vous en réponds! *P:* tu parles! je te crois! un peu! **you b. we had a good time,** je vous promets qu'on s'est amusé; **I'll b. you anything (you like) (that . . .),** j'en donnerais ma tête à couper (que . . .); **taste this, I b. you'll like it,** goûtez ceci, vous m'en direz des nouvelles; **I b. you don't!** chiche (que tu ne le feras pas)! **b. you I will!** chiche (que je le fais); **I'll b. (you) it is!** gage que si!

beta[1] ['bi:tə], *s. Gr. Alph:* bêta *m*; *Atom.Ph:* **b. rays,** rayons *m* bêta; **b. particle,** particule *f* bêta; **b. radiator, emitter,** émetteur *m* bêta; **b. absorption gauge,** jauge *f* bêta; *Med:* **b. ray therapy,** bêtathérapie *f.*

beta[2], *s. Bot:* beta *f.*

betacism ['bi:təsizm], *s. Ling:* permutation *f* de b et v.

betafite ['bi:təfait], *s. Miner:* bétafite *f.*

betain(e) ['bi:tein], *s. Ch:* bétaïne *f.*

betake [bi'teik], *v.pr.* (*p.t.* **betook** [bi'tuk]; *p.p.* **betaken** [bi'teik(ə)n]) *Lit:* **to b. oneself to a place, to s.o.,** (s'en) aller, se transporter, se rendre, se retirer, dans, à, un endroit; aller chez qn, se rendre auprès de qn; **to b. oneself to flight,** prendre la fuite, se mettre en fuite.

betatron ['bi:tətrɔn], *s. Atom.Ph:* bêtatron *m.*

betel ['bi:t(ə)l], *s.* **1.** *(masticatory)* bétel *m.* **2.** *Bot: (a)* bétel; *(b)* **b. nut,** (noix *f* d')arec *m*; **b. (nut) palm,** arec, aréquier *m.*

Betelgeuse [bi:tl'(d)ʒə:z], *Pr.n. Astr:* Bételgeuse.

bête noire ['beit'nwa:r, 'bet-], *s.* bête noire.
Bethany ['beθəni], *Pr.n. B.Hist:* Béthanie *f.*
Bethel ['beθəl]. **1.** *Pr.n. B.Hist:* Béthel *m.* **2.** *s. Ecc:* **bethel,** (*a*) *A:* temple *m* (d'une secte dissidente); (*b*) *NAm:* chapelle *f* (à terre ou à flot) pour marins.
Bethesda [be'θezdə]. **1.** *Pr.n. B.Hist:* Béthesda; **the pool of B.,** le lavoir, la piscine, de Béthesda. **2.** *s.* **bethesda,** temple *m* (d'une secte dissidente).
bethink [bi'θiŋk], *v.pr.* (*p.t. & p.p.* **bethought** [bi'θɔ:t]) *A:* **1. to b. oneself,** réfléchir, considérer; **b. yourself!** y pensez-vous! **to b. oneself of sth., to do sth., that . . .,** s'aviser de qch., de faire qch., que . . .; **b. yourself how they would grieve,** songez combien ils s'affligeraient; *A:* **I bethought me, he bethought him, of . . .,** je me suis avisé, il s'est avisé, de . . .. **2.** se rappeler (qch., que . . .).
Bethlehem ['beθlihem, -liəm], *Pr.n. B.Hist:* Bethléem *m*; *Bot:* **star of B.,** ornithogale *m* (à ombelle); *F:* dame *f*, belle *f*, d'onze-heures.
Betic ['bi:tik], *a. Geog:* **the B. Cordillera,** la chaîne Bétique.
betide [bi'taid], *v.* (*used only in 3rd sing. pres. sub.*) *A: & Lit:* **1.** *v.i.* **whate'er b.,** quoi qu'il arrive, quoi qu'il advienne; advienne que pourra. **2.** *v.tr.* **woe b. him if ever . . .,** malheur à lui, gare à lui, si jamais . . ..
betille ['betil], *s. Tex:* bétille *f.*
betimes [bi'taimz], *adv.* **1.** *Lit:* de bonne heure; *esp.* **to be up b.,** être levé de bonne heure; se lever tôt. **2.** *A:* bientôt.
betoken [bi'touk(ə)n], *v.tr. Lit:* **1.** (*of thg*) être signe de (qch.); être l'indice de (qch.); accuser, dénoter, révéler; **complexion that betokens ill-health,** teint *m* qui indique, accuse, un manque de santé; **here everything betokens peace,** ici tout respire la paix. **2.** présager, annoncer (le beau temps, etc.).
betonica [bi'tɔnikə], *s. Bot:* betonica *f.*
betony ['betəni], *s. Bot:* **1. wood b.,** (i) bétoine *f*; (ii) *U.S:* pédiculaire *f* des bois. **2. water b.,** scrofulaire *f* aquatique, bétoine d'eau; *F:* herbe carrée, herbe du siège.
betray [bi'trei], *v.tr.* **1.** (*a*) trahir (qn, sa patrie, sa foi, la confiance de qn); vendre (qn); **I was betrayed by the barking of the dog,** je fus trahi par les aboiements du chien; **at the first step his legs betrayed him,** au premier pas ses jambes le trahirent; (*b*) *A:* **to b. a woman,** tromper, séduire, une femme; abuser d'une femme; (*c*) **to b. s.o. into s.o.'s hands,** livrer qn aux mains de qn (par trahison). **2.** (*a*) révéler, montrer, laisser voir, laisser deviner, trahir (son ignorance, son émotion); **words that b. great ignorance,** paroles *f* qui accusent une grande ignorance; (*b*) **to b. a secret,** trahir, livrer, révéler, vendre, un secret.
betrayal [bi'treiəl], *s.* **1.** action *f* de trahir; trahison *f.* **2.** révélation *f* (de son ignorance, etc.).
betrayer [bi'treiər], *s.* **1.** (*a*) traître, -esse; **b. of his country,** traître envers sa patrie; **betrayers of honour,** traîtres à l'honneur; (*b*) révélateur, -trice (d'un secret). **2.** *A:* trompeur *m* (d'une femme); séducteur *m.*
betraying [bi'treiiŋ], *s.* = BETRAYAL.
betroth [bi'trouð], *v.tr. Lit:* promettre (sa fille) en mariage (to, à); fiancer (to, à, avec).
betrothal [bi'trouðəl], *s. Lit:* fiançailles *fpl* (to, avec).
betrothed [bi'trouðd], *a. & s. Lit:* fiancé(e); *pl.* **the b.,** les fiancés.
better[1] ['betər]. **1.** *a. & s.* meilleur; **b. days,** des jours meilleurs; **the b. the day the b. the deed,** bon jour, bonne œuvre; **they have seen b. days,** ils ont eu des malheurs; ils ont connu des jours meilleurs; **what do you think of this coffee?—I've had b.,** que penses-tu de ce café?—j'en ai bu d'autre; **you will find no b. hotel,** vous ne trouverez pas mieux comme hôtel; **he's a b. man than you,** il est votre supérieur; il vaut plus que vous; **you look so much b. in that hat!** ce chapeau vous embellit; (*at games, etc.*) **you are b. than I am,** vous êtes plus fort que moi; **he is no b. than his brother,** il ne vaut pas mieux que son frère; *F: O:* **she is no b. than she ought to be, than she should be,** elle ne vaut pas grand-chose; ce n'est pas une vertu; **to appeal to s.o.'s b. feelings,** faire appel aux bons sentiments de qn; **the respect due to one's betters,** le respect dû à ses supérieurs; *A:* **the b. classes,** les hautes classes (la bonne bourgeoisie, etc.); **the b. working class,** l'élite ouvrière; **a street of b.-class houses,** une rue de maisons de bonne apparence, de maisons cossues; **I had hoped for b. things,** j'avais espéré mieux; **for the b. part of the day,** pendant la plus grande partie du jour; *P:* **my b. half,** ma (chère) moitié, mon épouse, ma légitime; *Lit:* **to go to a b. world,** mourir, partir pour l'autre monde. **2.** *adv. & a.* mieux; (*a*) **that's b.,** voilà qui est mieux; à la bonne heure! **nothing could be b., it couldn't be b.,** c'est on ne peut mieux; **so much the b.,** tant mieux; **to do sth. for b. or (for) worse,** faire qch. vaille que vaille; **for b. or for worse I am going to emigrate,** pour le meilleur ou pour le pire, je vais émigrer; (*in marriage ceremony*) **to take s.o. for b. or worse,** prendre qn pour les bons comme pour les mauvais jours; **to get b.,** (i) (*of thgs*) s'améliorer, s'amender; (*of wine, etc.*) rabonnir; se bonifier; (ii) (*of pers.*) guérir, se remettre, se rétablir; **the weather is b.,** il fait meilleur; **to be b. (in health),** aller, se porter, mieux; **I hope you will soon be b.,** j'espère que vous serez bientôt rétabli; **he is a little b.,** il va un peu mieux, il y a un léger mieux; **change for the b.,** amélioration *f*; changement *m* en bien; **there is a change for the b.,** il y a un léger mieux; **he has changed for the b.,** il a changé à son avantage; **things are taking a turn for the b.,** les choses prennent meilleure tournure; **to get the b. of s.o.,** (i) l'emporter sur qn, remporter un avantage sur qn, prendre le dessus sur qn, avoir raison de qn; *F:* enfoncer qn; (ii) (*cheat*) refaire qn, mettre qn dedans; rouler, empaumer, qn; **they'd got the b. of him,** il avait été refait; **to get the b. of an obstacle, of one's grief, of one's anger,** vaincre, surmonter, un obstacle, sa douleur; maîtriser sa colère; **his shyness got the b. of him,** sa timidité l'a repris; **to be (all) the b. for doing sth.,** se trouver bien d'avoir fait qch.; **how are you any the b. for it?** à quoi cela vous avance-t-il? **I think all the b. of you for it,** je vous en estime d'autant plus; **you will be all the b. for it,** vous vous en trouverez (d'autant) mieux; **all the b. (for me)!** tant mieux pour moi! **I love him all the b. for his faults,** ses défauts me le rendent d'autant plus cher; **(all) the b. to . . .,** afin de mieux . . .; **to go one b. than s.o.,** (r)enchérir, surenchérir, faire une surenchère, sur qn; damer le pion à qn; **can you go one b.?** pouvez-vous faire mieux que cela? **I'll go one b. on you,** je vais damer votre pion; **he was b. than his word,** il a tenu, donné, accompli, plus qu'il n'avait promis; il est allé au delà de ses promesses; (*b*) **it is b. that it should be so; b. so,** il vaut mieux qu'il en soit ainsi; **b. lose one's fortune than one's honour,** mieux vaut perdre sa fortune que son honneur; **it is b. to go away than stay,** il vaut mieux, mieux vaut, partir que de rester; **it is b. to suffer than to lie,** plutôt souffrir que mentir; **it is b. to do without it,** il vaut mieux s'en passer; mieux vaut s'en passer; **it would be b. to see him again,** il serait préférable de le revoir; **it would be b. for you to go,** ce serait mieux, il convient, que vous y alliez; **that's b. than being faced with a lawsuit,** cela vaut mieux que si je me voyais menacé d'un procès. **3.** *adv.* (*a*) mieux; **b. and b.,** de mieux en mieux; **I know that b. than you,** je sais cela mieux que vous; **to know s.o. b.,** mieux connaître qn; **do I know Teissier? why, there's no man I know b.!** si je connais Teissier? mais je ne connais que lui! **the more I know him the b. I like him,** plus je le connais plus je l'aime; **if he has the courage of his convictions I like him the b. for it,** s'il a le courage de ses convictions je l'en aime d'autant plus; **I can understand it all the b. because . . .,** je le conçois d'autant mieux que . . .; **you had b. stay,** il vaut mieux que vous restiez; vous ferez, feriez, bien de rester; **I had b. begin by . . .,** je ferai bien de commencer par . . .; **we'd b. be going back,** il est temps de rebrousser chemin; **you had b. not have said anything,** vous auriez mieux fait de ne rien dire; **you had b. not,** ne vous en avisez pas; *F:* **(you'd) b. mind your own business!** occupe-toi de tes affaires! mêlez-vous de ce qui vous regarde! **to think b. of it,** changer d'opinion, se raviser; revenir sur son idée, sur sa première décision, sur sa résolution; **you'll think b. of it,** vous en reviendrez; **to think b. of s.o. for doing sth.,** estimer qn davantage d'avoir, pour avoir, fait qch.; **b. still . . .,** (i) mieux encore . . .; (ii) qui mieux est . . .; (iii) ce qui serait mieux . . .; (*b*) **b. dressed,** mieux habillé; **b. known,** plus connu; **b. looking,** de meilleure mine, *f* plus jolie; **you are like him but b. looking,** vous lui ressemblez mais en mieux; **b. tempered,** d'une humeur plus égale; **to be b. off,** (i) être plus à son aise matériellement; (ii) se trouver dans de meilleures conditions; **he is b. off where he is,** il est bien mieux, dans une meilleure situation, où il est; **the children of b.-off, b.-to-do, parents,** les enfants de parents aisés.
better[2]. **1.** *v.tr.* (*a*) améliorer (qch.); rendre (qch.) meilleur; rabonnir (le vin, etc.); **to b. oneself, one's circumstances,** améliorer sa position, sa condition, sa situation pécuniaire; (*b*) surpasser (un exploit, un ouvrage); **can you b. that?** pouvez-vous faire mieux que cela? **we can never b. that; we cannot b. his performance,** *F:* après lui il faut tirer l'échelle. **2.** *v.i.* (*of thg*) s'améliorer, devenir meilleur; (*of wine, etc.*) se bonifier, (se) rabonnir.
better[3], **bettor** ['betər], *s.* parieur, -euse.
betterment ['betəmənt], *s.* **1.** amélioration *f.* **2.** plus-value foncière, *pl.* plus-values; **b. tax, b. levy,** impôt *m* sur les plus-values.
betting ['betiŋ], *s.* (*a*) **ruined by b.,** ruiné par les paris; **the b. ran high,** on a parié gros; **the art of b.,** la technique de la mise; (*b*) cote *f*; **the b. is twenty to one,** la cote est à vingt contre un; **the b. is that . . .,** il y a fort à parier que . . .; **what is the b. on his horse?** quelle cote fait son cheval? (*c*) *attrib.* **b. book,** carnet *m* de paris; **b. news,** (i) rubrique *f* des courses; (ii) résultat *m* des courses; compte rendu des courses (dans les journaux); **b. shop,** (i) bureau *m*, agence *f*, de bookmaker; (ii) = bureau du pari mutuel.
Betty ['beti], *Pr.n.f. F:* (*dim. of Elizabeth*) Babette, Babet; *F:* **that's all my eye and B. Martin,** tout ça c'est de la blague, c'est de la poudre aux yeux; tout ça c'est des histoires; tout ça c'est des excuses à la noix (de coco).
betula ['betjulə], *s. Bot:* bétula *f.*
Betulaceae [betju'leisii:], *s.pl. Bot:* bétulacées *f.*
betulin(ol) ['betjulin(ɔl)], *s. Ch:* bétuline *f.*
between [bi'twi:n]. **1.** *prep.* entre; (*a*) **b. the two hedges,** entre les deux haies; **space b. two lines of writing,** entreligne *m*, interligne *m*; *Veh:* **space b. the axles,** entre-axe *m* des essieux; **a table stood b. him and the door,** une table le séparait de la porte; **to stand b. two opponents,** s'interposer, intervenir, entre deux adversaires; **I don't want to come, stand, b. them,** je ne veux pas m'interposer; **no one can come b. us,** personne ne peut nous séparer; **to be b. life and death,** être entre la vie et la mort; **the truth is b. the two,** la vérité est entre les deux, dans l'entre-deux; **to be something b. . . . and . . .,** tenir le milieu entre . . . et . . .; *Phot:* **b.-lens shutter,** obturateur *m* entre lentilles; (*b*) **b. eight and nine o'clock,** entre huit et neuf heures; **b. now and Monday,** d'ici à lundi; **you shall have it b. now and this evening,** vous l'aurez d'ici ce soir; **some date b. . . . and . . .,** une date intermédiaire entre . . . et . . .; **b. twenty and thirty,** de vingt à trente; **we went out b. the acts,** nous sommes sortis pendant l'entr'acte, pendant les entr'actes; **I got a snack b. trains,** j'ai pu manger un morceau entre deux trains; **there are two thousand years b. us and the Romans,** deux mille ans nous séparent des Romains; **the period b. the wars,** les années *fpl* entre les deux guerres; l'entre-deux-guerres *m or f. inv.*; (*c*) **you must choose b. them,** il faut choisir entre les deux; **to distinguish b. A, B, and C,** distinguer entre A, B, et C; (*d*) **we bought it b. us,** nous l'avons acheté à nous deux, à nous trois, etc.; **b. them, b. the three of them, they will soon have it done,** elles auront bientôt fait à elles deux, à elles trois; **they scored 1500 b. them,** ils ont marqué 1500 à eux deux; (*e*) **they shared the loot b. them,** ils se sont partagé le butin; **b. ourselves . . .,** entre nous; de vous à moi; **this is strictly b. ourselves, b. you and me,** que cela reste entre nous; *F:* **b. you (and) me and the bedpost, gatepost,** soit dit entre nous; **there is no love lost b. them,** ils ne peuvent pas se souffrir, se sentir. **2.** *adv.* **(in) b.: he separated them by rushing (in) b.,** il les a séparés en se jetant entre eux; **we attended two meetings and had lunch (in) b.,** nous avons assisté à deux séances et avons déjeuné dans l'intervalle; **he is neither conservative nor socialist but something (in) b.,** il n'est ni conservateur ni socialiste mais entre les deux.
between-brain [bi'twi:n'brein], *s. Anat:* diencéphale *m.*
between-decks [bi'twi:n'deks]; *Nau:* **1.** *adv.* dans l'entrepont; sous barrots; **baggage room b.-d.,** soute *f* à bagages dans le faux-pont. **2.** *s.* l'entrepont *m.*
between(-)maid [bi'twi:nmeid], *s.f.* bonne qui aide la cuisinière et la femme de chambre.
between-season [bi'twi:n'si:zn], *s.* demi-saison *f*, *pl.* demi-saisons; **b.-s. prices,** prix (réduits) de demi-saison.
betweentime(s), betweenwhile(s) [bi'twi:ntaim(z), -(h)wail(z)], *adv.* **1.** dans l'intervalle *m*, dans les intervalles; entre-temps. **2.** de temps en temps.
betwixt [bi'twikst]. **1.** *prep. A: Lit: Dial:* = BETWEEN 1. **2.** *adv. F:* **it's b. and between,** c'est entre les deux; **the truth lies b. and between,** il y a une part de vrai dans chacun des deux (récits, etc.).
beudantine [bju'dæntain], **beudantite** [bju'dæntait], *s. Miner:* beudantine *f*, beudantite *f.*
bevatron ['bevətrɔn], *s. Atom.Ph:* bévatron *m.*
bevel[1] ['bev(ə)l], *s.* **1.** angle *m* oblique; (*a*) biseau *m*, biais *m*; **standing b.,** équerrage *m* en gras; **b. edge,** bord biseauté, en chanfrein; **b. cut,** fausse coupe; **b. joint,** assemblage *m* en fausse coupe; *Typ:* **b. of a rule,** onglet *m* d'un filet; *Geol:* **stratigraphic b.,** biseau stratigraphique; (*b*) conicité *f* (d'un engrenage, etc.); **b. gear,** engrenage à biseau; engrenage conique, d'angle; renvoi *m* d'angle; *Aut:* **axle-drive b. gear,** pignon *m* du centre du différentiel; **b. wheel, b. pinion,** roue dentée

conique; roue d'angle; pignon conique, d'angle, d'échange, engrenage conique; **b. drive,** transmission *f* par pignons; (*c*) **b. coupling,** embrayage *m* à cône. **2. b. rule, b. square,** fausse équerre; biveau *m*; télégraphe *m*; sauterelle *f*; angloir *m*; angle oblique; **b. protractor,** fausse équerre à rapporteur.

bevel[2], *v.* (**bevelled**) **1.** *v.tr.* biseauter, équerrer, ébiseler, chanfreiner; tailler (qch.) en biseau; couper (qch.) obliquement; couper (qch.) en sifflet; **to b. off a corner,** dégraisser un coin. **2.** *v.i.* (*of thg*) biaiser; aller de biais; aller en biseau.

bevelled [bev(ə)ld], *a.* (bord) biseauté, en biseau, ébiselé, en chanfrein, en biais.

beveller ['bevələr], *s. Glassm: etc:* biseauteur, -euse.

bevelling ['bev(ə)liŋ], *s.* **1.** biseautage *m*, équerrage *m*, ébisèlement *m*, chanfreinage *m*; **b. machine,** biseautoir *m* mécanique; biseauteuse *f*. **2.** = BEVEL[1] 1; **standing b.,** équerrage en gras.

beverage[1] ['bevəridʒ], *s.* breuvage *m*, boisson *f*; **alcoholic b.,** boisson alcoolisée; **b. wine,** vin *m* ordinaire; *Can:* **b. room,** bar *m*; café-brasserie *f*, *pl.* cafés-brasseries (pour la vente de la bière).

beverage[2], *s. W.Tel:* **b. antenna,** béverage *m*.

Bevin ['bevin], *Pr.n. Hist:* (1939–1945) **B. boy,** conscrit choisi au sort pour le travail dans une houillère.

bevvy[1] [bevi], *s. P:* boisson *f*; **this calls for a b.,** allons boire un coup.

bevvy[2], *v.i. & tr.* (**bevvied**) *P:* boire; **to be bevvied,** être ivre, soûl.

bevy ['bevi], *s.* **1.** bande *f*, troupe *f*, compagnie *f*; **b. of girls,** bande, essaim *m*, de jeunes filles. **2.** *Ven:* volée *f* (d'alouettes, de cailles); harde *f*, troupe (de chevreuils).

bewail [bi'weil], *v.tr.* pleurer (qch.); **to b. one's lot,** se lamenter sur son sort; déplorer son destin.

bewailing [bi'weiliŋ], *s.* lamentation *f* (**of,** sur).

beware [bi'wɛər], *v.ind.tr., & Poet: v.tr.* (*used only in inf. and imp.*) **to b. of s.o.,** se méfier, se défier, de qn; **to b. of sth.,** se garder de qch.; prendre garde à qch.; **b.!** prenez garde! ne vous y fiez pas! **b. of the train,** attention au train; **b. of pickpockets,** méfiez-vous des voleurs; attention aux pickpockets; **b. of the dog,** prenez garde au chien; chien méchant; **to b. of doing sth.,** prendre garde, se garder, de faire qch.; **b. how you tread,** veillez à vos pas; *A:* **b. lest you fall,** prenez garde de tomber; **b. lest he deceive you,** prenez garde qu'il ne vous trompe.

bewhiskered [bi'(h)wiskəd], *a.* aux favoris abondants; barbu.

bewigged [bi'wigd], *a.* portant (une) perruque.

bewilder [bi'wildər], *v.tr.* (*a*) désorienter, égarer, dérouter (qn); troubler, embrouiller (qn); ahurir (qn); **to b. a candidate,** faire perdre la tête à un candidat; ahurir un candidat; **to b. s.o. with questions,** dérouter qn à force de questions; (*b*) abasourdir (qn).

bewildered [bi'wildəd], *a.* (*a*) désorienté; ahuri, **b. air,** air hébété, perdu; **to be b.,** ne savoir plus que penser; avoir la tête à l'envers; avoir la tête perdue; *F:* être réduit à quia; être tout désorienté; **I'm b.,** j'y perds la tête; ma tête s'y perd; je m'y perds; **to get b.,** perdre la tête; s'embrouiller; (*b*) abasourdi, confondu.

bewildering [bi'wild(ə)riŋ], *a.* déroutant; ahurissant, ébouriffant; **it was b.,** c'était à perdre la tête, à y perdre son latin.

bewilderment [bi'wildəmənt], *s.* (*a*) désorientation *f*; trouble *m*, confusion *f*; ahurissement *m*; **he gazed at them in open-mouthed b.,** il les regarda interdit et bouche bée; (*b*) abasourdissement *m*.

bewitch [bi'witʃ], *v.tr.* ensorceler; (*a*) jeter un sort sur (qn); (*b*) charmer, enchanter (qn); **she had bewitched him into marrying her,** elle l'avait ensorcelé au point de se faire épouser.

bewitching [bi'witʃiŋ], *a.* ensorcelant, ravissant; enchanteur, -eresse; **b. glance,** œillade assassine; **b. grace,** grâce charmeuse, enchanteresse.

bewitchingly [bi'witʃiŋli], *adv.* à ravir; **she smiled at him b.,** elle lui adressa un sourire ensorcelant.

bewitchment [bi'witʃmənt], *s.* ensorcellement *m*, charme *m*.

bewray [bi'rei], *v.tr. A:* trahir (involontairement); *B:* **thy speech bewrayeth thee,** ton langage te donne à connaître; **he heareth cursing and bewrayeth it not,** il entend le serment d'exécration, et il ne le décèle point.

bey [bei], *s.* bey *m*.

beylic ['beilik], *s.* beylik *m*; beylicat *m*.

beylical ['beilikl], *a.* beylical, -aux.

beyond [bi'jɔnd]. **1.** *adv.* au-delà, par-delà, plus loin; **the ocean and the lands b.,** l'océan *m* et les terres au-delà, et les terres lointaines. **2.** *prep.* au-delà de, par-delà; (*a*) (*place*) **the house is b. the church,** la maison est au delà de, plus loin que, l'église; **the countries b. the Rhine, b. the Alps, b. the seas,** les pays d'outre-Rhin, d'outre-monts, d'outre-mer; **we could see peak b. peak,** nous apercevions une succession de cimes; **b. the seas,** par-delà les mers; au-delà des mers; **to come from b. the seas,** venir de delà les mers, d'outre-mer; **b. this country,** au dehors de ce pays; **b. the trenches there is no shelter,** passé (*sometimes* passées) les tranchées, pas un abri; **he heard a voice calling from b. the grave,** il entendit une voix qui l'appelait de l'au-delà, d'outre-tombe; **to be b. the pale,** être au ban de la société; (*b*) (*time*) **to stay b. one's time,** rester trop longtemps; **b. a certain date,** passé une certaine date; **to go back b. the Flood,** remonter avant le Déluge; **b. the usual hour,** plus tard que d'ordinaire; (*c*) (*surpassing*) **b. all praise,** au-dessus de tout éloge; **beautiful b. all others,** belle entre toutes; **to succeed b. one's hopes,** réussir au-delà de ses espérances; **to live b. one's income, one's means,** vivre au-delà, au-dessus, de ses moyens; dépenser plus que son revenu; **this car is b. my means, is b. me,** cette voiture est hors de ma portée, est trop chère pour moi; **to go b. one's authority,** outrepasser ses pouvoirs; **to go b. one's rights,** sortir des limites de son droit; **to go b. the law,** donner une entorse au code; **to go b. one's duties,** sortir du cadre de ses fonctions; **this work is b. me,** ce travail est au-dessus de, dépasse, mes forces, mes moyens; **difficulties b. my understanding,** difficultés *f* au-dessus de, qui dépassent, mon entendement, mes lumières; **it's b. me,** cela me dépasse; je n'y comprends rien; **circumstances b. our control,** circonstances indépendantes de notre volonté, qui échappent à, sont en dehors de, notre action, qui ne dépendent pas de nous; **these things are b. our control,** ces choses-là ne se commandent pas; **it's b. my power,** cela passe ma capacité, ne m'est pas possible; **it's b. my power to save him,** je suis impuissant à le sauver; **I will not go b. what I said,** je m'en tiens à ce que j'ai dit; **b. doubt, b. question,** hors de doute, sans le moindre doute, à n'en pas douter, indiscutablement; incontestable, incontestablement; à coup sûr; **fact b. doubt, question,** fait avéré; **reputation b. question,** réputation indiscutée, indiscutable, au-dessus de toute discussion; **b. belief,** incroyable(ment); à ne pas y croire; **b. measure,** outre mesure, sans mesure; à l'excès; démesurément; **exasperated b. measure,** à la dernière limite de l'exaspération; **that's (going) b. a joke, b. all bounds,** cela dépasse les bornes (de la plaisanterie); c'est par trop violent; **they are b. recovery,** il n'est plus possible de les ravoir; (*of sick pers.*) **he is b. recovery,** il n'est plus possible de le sauver; (*d*) (*except*) **he has nothing b. his wages,** il n'a rien que son salaire. **3.** *s.* **the b.,** l'eau-delà *m*; **she heard voices from b.,** elle entendait des voix de l'autre monde, de l'au-delà; *F:* **at the back of b.,** tout au bout du monde; dans une région inaccessible; **he lives at the back of b.,** il habite un trou perdu; il habite au diable.

bezant ['bez(ə)nt], *s.* **1.** *Num:* besant *m* (d'or, d'argent); **white b.,** besant d'argent. **2.** *Her:* besant d'or. **3.** *Arch:* besant.

bezel[1] ['bezl], *s.* **1.** biseau *m*, bezel *m* (d'une pierre taillée). **2.** chaton *m*, portée *f* (de bague); *Clockm:* drageoir *m*, biseau (de boîtier de montre).

bezel[2], *v.tr.* (**bezelled**) biseauter (une pierre précieuse).

bezelling ['bezəliŋ], *s. Lap: etc:* biseautage *m*.

bezique [bi'zi:k], *s. Cards:* bésigue *m*.

bezoar ['bezouər], *s.* **b. (stone),** bézoard *m*; **b. goat,** chèvre *f* à bézoard; pasang *m*; paseng *m*.

B-girl ['bi:gə:l], *s.f. U.S: P:* (*a*) entraîneuse (dans un bar); (*b*) prostituée (qui récolte ses clients dans les bars).

bhakti ['bɑ:kti], *s. Hindu Rel:* bhakti *f*.

bhang [bæŋ], *s.* bang *m*; ha(s)chisch (indien).

bhar(h)al ['bɑ:rəl], *s. Z:* bharal *m*, nahor *m*.

bher [bɛər], *s. Bot:* **b. (fruit),** jujube *m*; **b. (-fruit) tree,** jujubier *m*.

Bhil [bil], *s. Ethn:* Bhil *m*.

bhokra ['boukrə], *s. Z:* tétracère *m*.

Bhotia ['boutiə], **Bhutia** ['bu:tiə], **Bhutanese** [bu:tə'ni:z], *Geog:* **1.** *a.* du Bhoutan. **2.** *s.* Bhotia *m*.

Bhutan ['bu:tɑ:n], *s. Geog:* B(h)outan *m*.

bi- [bai], *pref.* bi-; di-; semi-.

biacid [bai'æsid], *s. Ch:* biacide *m*.

biacromial [baiə'kroumiəl], *a. Anat:* biacromial, -aux.

biacuminate [baiə'kju:mineit], *a. Bot:* biacuminé.

Biafra [bi:'æfrə], *Pr.n. Geog:* Biafra *m*.

Biafran [bi:'æfrən], *Geog:* (*a*) *a.* biafrais; (*b*) *s.* Biafrais, -aise.

bi-angular [bai'æŋgjulər], *a. Geom:* biangulé.

bi-annual [bai'ænjuəl]. **1.** *a.* (*a*) (*occurring every two years*) bisannuel; biennal, -aux; (*lasting two years*) biennal; (*b*) (*half-yearly*) semestriel. **2.** *s. Bot:* plante bisannuelle.

bi-annually [bai'ænju(ə)li], *adv.* (*a*) tous les deux ans; (*b*) deux fois par an; semestriellement.

bias[1] ['baiəs], *s.* **1.** *Dressm:* biais *m*; **material cut on the b.,** *adv.* **cut b.,** étoffe coupée en biais, de biais; **b. band,** bande coupée en, de, biais; biais; **b. binding,** ruban *m* en biais. **2.** *Sp:* (*bowls*) (*a*) décentrement *m*, (*b*) déviation (due au décentrement). **3.** (*a*) prévention *f* (**towards,** en faveur de; **against,** contre); **to have a b. towards s.o., sth.,** avoir un parti pris pour qn, pour qch.; **to have a b. against s.o.,** avoir une prévention contre qn; **to speak without b.,** parler sans prévention; **to be without b.,** n'avoir aucun parti pris; (*b*) penchant *m*; **to have a b. towards sth.,** avoir un penchant pour qch.; pencher vers (une opinion, etc.); **professional, vocational, b.,** déformation professionnelle. **4.** (*a*) *Artil:* **aim b.,** erreur *f* systématique de visée; (*b*) *Cmptr:* **b. distortion,** distorsion *f* dissymétrique; **b. test,** test *m* de marges. **5.** *Elcs:* **grid b.,** polarisation *f* de la grille; tension *f* de polarisation; **fixed b.,** tension de polarisation fixe, invariable; **b. cell,** pile *f* de polarisation; **b. detection,** détection *f* grille; **b. winding,** enroulement *m* de polarisation.

bias[2], *v.tr.* (*p.p. & p.t.* **bias(s)ed**) **1.** *Sp:* (*bowls*) altérer le centre de gravité de (la boule). **2.** rendre (qn) partial; prédisposer, prévenir (qn) (**towards,** en faveur de; **against,** contre); influencer (qn). **3.** *Elcs:* polariser (la grille).

bias(s)ed ['baiəst], *a.* **1.** *Sp:* (*bowls*) (boule) décentrée. **2.** *Tex:* (tissu *m*) en fil biais. **3.** partial, -aux; **b. opinion,** opinion préconçue. **4.** *Stat:* **b. sample,** échantillon biaisé, avec erreur systématique; **b. error,** erreur *f* systématique.

biathlon [bai'æθlən], *s. Sp:* biathlon *m*.

biaural [bai'ɔ:r(ə)l], *a.* = BINAURAL.

biauricular [baiɔ'rikjulər], *a.* **1.** binauriculaire, des deux oreilles. **2.** = BIAURICULATE.

biauriculate [baiɔ'rikjuleit], *a. Z:* (cœur *m*, etc.) à deux auricules *f*, oreillettes *f*.

biaxal [bai'æksl], **biaxial** [bai'æksiəl], **biaxiate** [bai'æksieit], *a. Ch: Ph:* (polarisation *f*) biaxe; **b. crystal,** cristal *m* biaxe, à deux axes.

bib[1] [bib], *s.* **1.** bavette *f*, bavoir *m* (d'enfant). **2.** bavette (de tablier); **b.-and-brace overalls,** cotte américaine; *F: O:* (*of woman*) **to put on one's best b. and tucker,** se mettre sur son trente et un. **3.** *Orn:* gorge *f* (d'oiseau).

bib[2], *v.i.* (**bibbing**) *O:* boire (intempéramment); *F:* biberonner.

bib[3], *s. Ich:* tacaud *m*.

bibasic [bai'beisik], *a. Ch:* bibasique, dibasique.

bibb [bib], *s. Nau:* jottereau *m*.

bibber ['bibər], *s.* buveur, -euse; biberon, -onne; *P:* sac *m* à vin.

bibcock ['bibkɔk], *s.* robinet (coudé); robinet à bec courbe.

bibelot ['bi:blou], *s.* **1.** bibelot *m*. **2.** livre miniature (très soigné).

bibenzyl [bai'benzil], *s. Ch:* dibenzyle *m*.

bibio ['bibiou], *s. Ent:* bibion *m*; mouche *f* de la Saint-Jean, de la Saint-Marc.

Bibionidae [bibi'ɔnidi:], *s.pl. Ent:* bibionidés *m*.

bible ['baibl], *s.* **1. the B.,** la Bible; **a B.,** une Bible; **family B.,** Bible de grand format pour les dévotions de famille (et sur les feuillets de garde de laquelle sont consignés les naissances, mariages et décès intéressant la famille); *F:* **it's in the B.,** c'est dans l'histoire sainte; **I promise you on my B. oath that . . .,** je vous jure que . . .; **B. class,** (i) classe *f* d'histoire sainte; (ii) (classe du) catéchisme; **B. history,** histoire sainte; **B. paper,** papier *m* Bible, indien; *A:* **B. reader, B. woman,** évangéliste *mf* qui faisait la lecture de la Bible chez les malades et les indigents; **B. Society,** société *f* biblique; *U.S:* **B. belt,** région *f* des États-Unis méridionaux où le fondamentalisme est solidement établi; *F:* **B. thumper, puncher,** *Austr: N.Z:* **B. banger, basher,** évangéliste de carrefour; **this dictionary is his b.,** il a fait de ce dictionnaire sa bible, son évangile *m*. **2.** *Z:* feuillet *m* (de ruminant).

biblical ['biblik(ə)l], *a.* biblique; **b. scholar,** bibliste *mf*.

biblically ['biblikəli], *adv.* bibliquement.

biblicism ['biblisizm], *s.* biblicisme *m*.

biblicist ['biblisist], *s.* bibliciste *mf*.

biblio- ['bibliou-, bibliə-, bibli'ɔ], *comb.fm.* biblio-.

bibliofilm ['biblioufilm], *s.* microfilm *m*.

bibliographer [bibli'ɔgrəfər], *s.* bibliographe *mf*.

bibliographic(al) [bibliə'græfik(ə)l], *s.* bibliographique; (*at end of book*) **b. note,** souscription *f*.

bibliography [bibli'ɔgrəfi], *s.* **1.** (*as a study*) bibliographie *f*. **2.** liste *f* bibliographique; bibliographie *f*; **short b.,** bibliographie sommaire.

bibliolater [bibli'ɔlətər], *s.* bibliolâtre *mf*.

bibliolatrous [bibli'ɔlətrəs], *a.* bibliolâtre.

bibliolatry [bibli'ɔlətri], *s.* bibliolâtrie *f*.

bibliological [bibliə'lɔdʒik(ə)l], *a.* bibliologique.

bibliology [bibli'ɔlədʒi], *s.* bibliologie *f.*
bibliomancy [bibliou'mænsi], *s.* bibliomancie *f.*
bibliomania [bibliou'meinjə], *s.* bibliomanie *f.*
bibliomaniac [bibliou'meiniæk], *a. & s.* bibliomane *mf.*
bibliomaniacal [biblioumæ'naiək(ə)l], *a.* bibliomaniaque, bibliomane.
bibliophagous [bibli'ɔfəgəs], *a.* bibliophage.
bibliophile ['bibliəfail], *s.* bibliophile *mf.*
bibliophilism [bibli'ɔfilizm], **bibliophily** [bibli'ɔfili], *s.* bibliophilie *f.*
bibliopole ['bibliəpoul], **bibliopolist** [bibli'ɔpəlist], *s.* libraire *m*; *esp.* bouquiniste *m.*
bibliopoly [bibli'ɔpəli], *s.* (commerce *m* de) librairie *f*; *esp.* bouquinerie *f.*
biblist ['biblist, 'bai-], *s.* bibliste *mf.*
bibulosity [bibju'lɔsiti], *s.* **1.** penchant *m* à la boisson. **2.** légère ivresse.
bibulous ['bibjuləs], *a.* **1.** spongieux, absorbant; *Tchn:* **b. paper,** papier buvard. **2.** adonné à la boisson; buveur, -euse; **b. nose,** nez vineux; nez d'ivrogne.
bibulously ['bibjuləsli], *adv.* d'une voix avinée; entre deux vins.
bibulousness ['bibjuləsnis], *s.* = BIBULOSITY.
bi-cable ['bai'keibl], *a. Civ.E:* **b.-c. ropeway,** téléferique *m* bicâble.
bicameral [bai'kæmər(ə)l], *a.* (gouvernement, etc.) bicaméral, -aux; **b. system,** bicamér(al)isme *m.*
bicameralism [bai'kæmərəlizm], *s. Pol:* bicamér(al)isme *m.*
bicapsular [bai'kæpsjulər], *a. Bot:* bicapsulaire.
bicarb [bai'kɑ:b], *s. F:* bicarbonate *m* de soude.
bicarbonate [bai'kɑ:bəneit], *s.* bicarbonate *m* (de soude, etc.).
bice [bais], *s. Ind:* bleu *m* de cobalt; **green b.,** vert *m* de cobalt.
bicentenary ['baisen'ti:nəri], **bicentennial** ['baisen'teniəl], *a. & s.* bicentenaire *(m).*
bicentral ['bai'sentrəl], *a. Mth:* à deux centres.
bicephalous ['bai'sefələs], *a.* bicéphale.
biceps ['baiseps], *s. Anat:* biceps *m.*
bichir ['bitʃər], *s. Ich:* bichir *m,* polyptère *m.*
bichloride [bai'klɔ:raid], *s. Ch:* bichlorure *m.*
bichon ['bi:ʃɔn], *s. Z:* bichon *m*; chien maltais.
bichromate [bai'kroumeit], *s. Ch:* bichromate *m*; *Phot:* **gum b.,** gomme bichromatée; *El:* **b. cell,** pile *f* au bichromate (de potasse).
bichromatic [baikrou'mætik], **bichrome** ['baikroum], *a.* bicolore.
bicipital [bai'sipit(ə)l], *a. Anat:* bicipital, -aux.
bicker ['bikər], *v.i.* **1.** se quereller, s'entre-quereller, se chamailler; être toujours en zizanie, en bisbille. **2.** *Lit:* *(of stream)* murmurer.
bickerer ['bikərər], *s. F:* querelleur, -euse, chamailleur, -euse.
bickering[1] ['bik(ə)riŋ], *a.* **1.** querelleur, -euse. **2.** *(a)* *(of stream)* murmurant; *(b)* *(of light)* tremblotant, scintillant.
bickering[2], *s.* querelles *fpl*; bisbille *f*; chamailleries *fpl.*
bick(iron) ['bikaiən], **bickern** ['bikɔ:n], *s.* bec *m* (d'enclume); bigorne *f.*
Bickford ['bikfəd], *Pr.n. Exp:* **B. fuse, match,** (cordeau *m*) Bickford *m.*
bicolour(ed) ['bai'kʌlər, -'kʌləd], *a. Bot: etc:* bicolore.
biconcave ['bai'kɔŋkeiv], *a.* biconcave.
biconditional ['baikən'diʃ(ə)n(ə)l], *a. Cmptr:* **b. operation,** opération *f* d'équivalence.
biconical ['bai'kɔnik(ə)l], *a.* biconique.
biconjugate ['bai'kɔndʒugeit], *a. Bot:* biconjugué.
biconvex ['bai'kɔnveks], *a.* biconvexe.
bicorn(ed) ['baikɔ:n(d)], *a.* à deux cornes; bicorne.
bicornate [bai'kɔ:neit], **bicornuate** [bai'kɔ:njueit], **bicornute** [bai'kɔ:njut], *a. Nat.Hist: Anat:* bicorne.
bicorne ['baikɔ:n], *s.* (chapeau) bicorne *m.*
bicrural ['bai'kruərəl], *a.* à deux jambes.
bicultural ['bai'kʌltjərəl], *a. Can:* (province *f*) qui a deux cultures.
biculturalism ['bai'kʌltjərəlizm], *s.* biculturalisme *m.*
bicuspid(ate) ['bai'kʌspid(eit)]. **1.** *a. Nat.Hist: etc:* bicuspide; bicuspidé; *Anat:* **bicuspid valve,** valvule *f* bicuspide. **2.** *s.* **bicuspid,** (dent) prémolaire *f.*
bicycle[1] ['baisikl], *s.* **1.** bicyclette *f*; vélo *m*; *O:* bécane *f*; **carrier b.,** bicyclette de livreur (de maison de commerce); **motorized b.,** bicyclette à moteur; **motor-assisted b.,** bicyclette à moteur auxiliaire; **water b.,** pédalo *m*; **I can ride a b.,** je sais aller à, en, bicyclette; **b. rickshaw,** vélotaxi *m,* vélo-pousse *m, pl.* vélo-pousses; **b. stand,** support *m,* pied *m,* de bicyclette; soutien-vélo *m, pl.* soutien-vélos; **b. track,** piste *f* cyclable. **2.** *Av:* **b. (landing) gear,** train *m* (d'atterrissage) monotrace.
bicycle[2], *v.i.* **1.** faire de la bicyclette; aller à bicyclette. **2.** **to b. to Bristol,** aller à bicyclette à Bristol, jusqu'à Bristol.
bicyclic ['bai'saiklik], *a. Ch:* bicyclique.
bicycling ['baisikliŋ], *s. O:* cyclisme *m.*
bicyclist ['baisiklist], *s. O:* cycliste *mf*; *A:* bicycliste *mf*; *F:* pédaleur, -euse.
bid[1] [bid], *s.* **1.** *(a)* enchère *f,* offre *f,* mise *f*; **to make a b. for a property,** (i) faire une offre pour un immeuble; (ii) mettre (une) enchère sur un immeuble; **to make a higher, further, b.,** couvrir l'enchère; surenchérir; **higher, further, b.,** offre supérieure; surenchère *f*; **closing, last, b.,** dernière mise, dernière enchère; **takeover b.,** offre publique d'achat; *(b)* **to make a b. for a directorship,** tâcher d'avoir un poste d'administrateur; **to make a b. for power,** (i) viser au pouvoir; (ii) tenter un coup d'état; **to make a b. to escape, an escape b.,** faire une tentative d'évasion; **he made a good b. for the championship,** il fut à deux doigts du championnat; *(c)* *Cards: (bridge)* appel *m*; *(solo whist, boston)* demande *f*; **b. of two diamonds,** appel de deux carreaux; **no b.!** parole! passe! *(bridge)* **to raise the b.,** relancer. **2.** *U.S:* soumission *f* (dans une adjudication). **3.** *NAm: F:* invitation *f.*
bid[2], *v.tr. & i.* *(p.t.* **bade** [bæd, beid], **bid**; *p.p.* **bidden** [bidn], **bid**) **1.** *O:* *(command)* commander, ordonner **(s.o. (to) do sth.,** à qn de faire qch.); **to b. s.o. (to) be silent,** ordonner à qn de se taire; commander le silence à qn; **they were bidden to attend,** ils reçurent l'ordre de comparaître; **b. him come in,** dites-lui, priez-le, d'entrer; **do as you are b.,** faites ce qu'on vous dit; **Madam bids me say that she is ready,** Madame fait dire qu'elle est prête. **2.** *(a)* *O:* *(invite)* **to b. s.o. to dinner,** inviter qn à dîner; **the bidden guests,** les invités; *(b)* **to b. s.o. welcome,** souhaiter la bienvenue à qn; **to b. s.o. good-day,** souhaiter, donner, le bonjour à qn; **to b. s.o. farewell,** dire adieu, faire ses adieux, à qn; **to b. defiance to s.o.,** lancer, porter, jeter, un défi à qn; lancer des provocations à qn; *(c)* **the weather bids fair to be fine, to improve,** le temps s'annonce beau, promet de s'améliorer; il y a toute apparence de beau temps; **he bids fair to succeed,** il est en passe de réussir; il est en bonne voie de réussir; **the expedition bade fair to be successful,** l'expédition s'annonçait bien, promettait de réussir. **3.** *(p.t. & p.p.* **bid)** *(offer)* *(a)* *(at auction sale)* **to b. for sth.,** (i) faire une offre pour qch.; (ii) mettre une enchère sur qch.; **to b. a fair price,** offrir un juste prix; **to b. ten pounds,** faire une offre de dix livres; miser dix livres; **to b. another pound,** faire une enchère d'une livre; **to b. over s.o., more than s.o.,** enchérir sur qn; **to b. in (a lot),** racheter un lot (pour le compte du vendeur); **the buyers were bidding (up) well,** les enchères montaient vite; *(b)* *Cards:* **to b. three diamonds,** demander, appeler, trois carreaux; **little slam b. and made,** petit chelem demandé et réussi.
biddability [bidə'biliti], *s.* docilité *f*; promptitude *f* à obéir (d'un chien dressé).
biddable ['bidəbl], *a.* traitable, obéissant, docile, soumis; doux, *f* douce.
bidder ['bidər], *s.* **1.** *(at sale)* enchérisseur *m,* amateur *m*; **there were no bidders,** il n'y a pas eu de preneurs *m*; **the lowest b.,** le moins disant; **the highest b.,** le plus offrant; le dernier enchérisseur; l'adjudicataire *m*; **knocked down to the highest b.,** alloué, adjugé, au plus offrant et dernier enchérisseur; **allocation to the highest b.,** adjudication *f* à la surenchère. **2.** *Cards:* demandeur, -euse; déclarant, -ante.
bidding ['bidiŋ], *s.* **1.** *(a)* commandement *m,* ordre *m*; **to be at s.o.'s b.,** être aux ordres de qn; **to do s.o.'s b.,** exécuter, remplir, les ordres de qn; **I did his b.,** j'ai fait ce qu'il m'a dit; *(b)* *NAm:* invitation *f.* **2.** *(a)* enchères *fpl,* mises *fpl*; **the b. was very brisk,** les surenchères abondaient; la vente a été bonne, a bien marché; **to start the b. for a picture at £5000,** mettre un tableau à prix £5000; *(b)* *Cards: etc:* **the b. is closed,** l'enchère est faite.
Biddy[1] ['bidi]. **1.** *Pr.n.f.* *(dim. of Bridget)* Brigitte. **2.** *s.f.* *F:* **biddy,** *(a)* femme de ménage, domestique, irlandaise; *(b)* femme, fille; *P:* jupon *m.*
biddy[2], *s.* poussin *m,* poulet *m.*
biddy[3], *s. F:* **(red) b.,** vin rouge corsé d'alcool dénaturé.
bide [baid], *v.tr. & i.* **(bided)** *A. Lit. & Dial:* = ABIDE; *still used in:* **to b. one's time,** attendre l'heure, son heure; attendre le bon moment, l'heure d'agir; se réserver.
bidentate [bai'denteit], *a. Nat.Hist:* bidenté.
bidet ['bi:dei], *s. Hyg:* bidet *m* (de toilette).
bidirectional [baidi'rekʃən(ə)l], *a. W.Tel: Cmptr: etc:* bidirectionnel.
bieberite ['bi:bərait], *s. Miner:* biebérite *f.*
Bielids ['bi:lidz], *Pr.n. pl. Astr:* Biélides *f.*
biennale [bi:ə'nɑ:lei], *s.* *(exhibition)* biennale *f.*
biennial [bai'enjəl]. **1.** *a.* biennal, -aux. **2.** *a. & s. Bot:* **b. (plant),** plante bisannuelle.
biennially [bai'enjəli], *adv.* tous les deux ans.
biennium [bai'eniəm], *s.* période *f* de deux ans.
bier [biər], *s.* **1.** *(a)* civière *f* (pour un cercueil, pour porter un mort); *(b)* *(hearse)* corbillard *m.* **2.** *A:* **(hand-)b.,** brancard *m.*
Biermer ['biəmər], *Pr.n. Med:* **Biermer's anaemia, disease,** maladie *f* de Biermer; anémie pernicieuse.
biface ['baifeis], *s. Prehist:* biface *m*; coup-de-poing *m, pl.* coups-de-poing.
bifacial [bai'feiʃ(ə)l], *a.* à deux faces *f*; *Bot:* *(of leaf)* bifacial, -aux.
bifarious [bai'fɛəriəs], *a. Bot:* *(of leaves)* distique.
bifer ['baifər], *s. Bot:* plante *f* bifère.
biferous ['baifərəs], *a. Bot:* bifère.
bif[1] [bif]. **1.** *s. P:* gnon *m,* beigne *f,* torgnole *f.* **2.** *int.* v'lan! pan!
bif[2], *v.tr. P:* flanquer un gnon, une beigne, à (qn).
biffin ['bifin], *s.* **1.** pomme *f* à cuire (du pommier de Norfolk). **2.** *Cu:* pomme cuite au four et tapée.
bifid ['baifid], *a. Nat.Hist:* bifide.
bifilar [bai'failər], *a.* (magnétomètre *m*) bifilaire; **b. winding,** enroulement anti-inductif.
biflagellate [bai'flædʒəleit], *a.* (zoospore *f*) à deux flagelles.
biflorate [bai'flɔ:reit], **biflorous** [bai'flɔ:rəs], *a. Bot:* biflore.
bifocal [bai'fouk(ə)l], *a. Opt:* bifocal, aux; **b. glasses,** *s.* **bifocals,** verres bifocaux, à double foyer.
bifoliate [bai'foulieit], *a. Bot:* bifolié.
bifoliolate [bai'fouliouleit], *a. Bot:* bifoliolé.
biform ['baifɔ:m], *a.* biforme.
bifurcate[1] ['baifə:keit]. **1.** *v.tr.* bifurquer. **2.** *v.i.* (se) bifurquer.
bifurcate[2] ['baifə:kət], *a. Bot: etc:* bifurqué.
bifurcation [baifə:'keiʃ(ə)n], *s.* bifurcation *f,* embranchement *m.*
big [big], *a.* **(bigger** ['bigər]; **biggest** ['bigist]) **1.** *(a)* *(large)* grand; *(bulky)* gros; **b. hotel,** grand, vaste, hôtel; **take a piece of butter as b. as a walnut,** prenez gros comme une noix de beurre; **b. man,** (i) homme de grande taille; (ii) gros homme; (iii) homme marquant; (iv) homme à l'esprit large, aux idées larges; *F:* **it's Mr X. who's the b. man here,** c'est M. X. qui tient le haut du pavé; *P:* **Mr B.,** le chef, le singe; **b. girl,** grande jeune fille; **b. enough to defend oneself,** de taille à se défendre; **b. fortune,** grosse fortune; **to earn b. money,** gagner gros; **there's b. money in it,** cela rapporte, rapportera, gros; **b. drop in prices,** forte baisse de prix; **to be doing a b. trade,** faire un commerce actif; faire de grosses affaires; **he had b. ideas,** il voyait grand; **to do, see, things in a b. way,** faire, voir, grand; **that's b. of you,** (i) c'est généreux, magnanime, de votre part; (ii) *Iron:* grand merci! **the b. people in the theatre world,** les gens importants du théâtre; *F:* **b. pot, shot, noise, gun, bug,** gros bonnet, *P:* grosse légume; **the b. noise of a party,** la grosse corde d'un parti; **he's the b. noise round here,** c'est lui qui fait la pluie et le beau temps ici; **the b. three, four,** les chefs, les patrons (de l'entreprise); *Pol:* **the B. Four,** les Quatre Grands; *Hist:* *(League of Nations)* **the B. Five,** les cinq grandes Puissances: les États-Unis, la France, l'Angleterre, l'Italie et le Japon; *Th:* **the b. scene,** la grande scène; la scène à faire; *Sp:* **b. field (of starters),** champ fourni; **to grow big(ger),** (i) grandir; (ii) grossir; *F:* **he's getting too b. for his boots, shoes,** il prend des airs qui ne lui conviennent pas; il se croit; **you're a b. liar!** vous êtes un fameux menteur! **you're the biggest fool of the lot!** c'est vous le plus bête de tous! **he's not a b. eater,** il n'est pas gros mangeur; il ne mange pas beaucoup; **the b. toe,** le gros orteil; **b. drum,** grosse caisse; **a b. A,** un A majuscule; **b. brother,** frère aîné; **B. Brother,** (i) chef *m* d'un état autoritaire; (ii) état qui exerce un paternalisme autoritaire; **B. Brotherism,** paternalisme autoritaire; *Vet:* **b. jaw,** actinomycose *f*; *NAm: Sp:* **b. league,** équipes *f* vedettes du baseball professionnel; **b. leaguer,** membre *m* d'une équipe vedette du baseball; **to be in the b. time,** (i) être dans les hautes sphères, en haut de l'échelle; (ii) être le dessus du panier; **to hit the b. time,** s'élever au premier plan; **b.-time actor, play,** acteur, pièce *f,* de premier rang; **b.-time undertaking,** entreprise *f* de grande envergure; **b. top (of circus),** chapiteau *m*; *I.C.E:* **b. end,** tête *f* de bielle; *Ven:* **b. game,** (i) gros gibier; (ii) les grands fauves; *Bot:* **b. tree (of California),** séquoia géant; *(b)* **b. with child,** grosse (d'enfant); enceinte; **b. with consequences,** gros, lourd, de conséquences. **2.** *adv.* **to talk b.,** (i) se vanter; faire l'important; fanfaronner; faire le hâbleur; hâbler; *P:* faire le mariol; (ii) le prendre de haut; **to think b.,** avoir des idées larges, voir grand; *F:* **to go over b.,** décrocher le grand succès.
biga, *pl.* **-ae** ['bi:gə, -i:], *s. Rom.Ant:* bige *m.*

bigamist ['bigəmist], *s.* bigame *mf.*
bigamous ['bigəməs], *a.* bigame.
bigamy ['bigəmi], *s.* bigamie *f.*
bigarade ['bigərɑ:d], *s. Hort:* bigarade *f.*
bigaroon [bigə'ru:n], **bigarreau** ['bigərou], *s. Hort:* bigarreau *m.*
big-bellied ['big'belid], *a.* ventru, pansu.
big-boned ['big'bound], *a.* ossu; fortement charpenté.
big-eared ['big'iəd], *a.* aux grandes oreilles; *Z:* **b.-e. bat,** mégaderme *m.*
bigeminal [bai'dʒemin(ə)l], *a. Nat.Hist:* bigéminé.
bigeminate [bai'dʒeminət], *a. Bot:* bigéminé.
bigeminy [bai'dʒemini], *s. Med:* bigéminisme *m.*
bigeneric [baidʒə'nerik], *a. Nat.Hist:* bigénérique.
bigeye ['bigai], *s. Ich:* priacanthe *m.*
bigg [big], *s. Agr:* orge carrée.
biggish ['bigiʃ], *a.* assez grand; assez gros.
bighead ['bighed], *s.* **1.** *esp. NAm: F:* (*a*) prétentieux, -euse; **he's a b.,** *P:* il ne se prend pas pour de la merde; (*b*) **his trouble's b.,** son grand défaut est la suffisance, la prétention. **2.** *Vet:* ostéoporose *f* (des chevaux).
bigheaded ['big'hedid], *a. esp. NAm: F:* suffisant, vaniteux, prétentieux.
bigheadedness ['big'hedidnis], *s. esp. NAm: F:* suffisance *f.*
big-hearted ['big'hɑ:tid], *a.* **to be b.-h.,** avoir du cœur.
bighorn ['bighɔ:n], *s. Z:* **b. (sheep),** mouflon *m* des Rocheuses; bighorn *m.*
bight [bait], *s.* **1.** *Nau:* double *m,* bal(l)ant *m,* anse *f* (d'un cordage). **2.** *Geog:* enfoncement *m* (d'une côte); crique *f,* anse (peu profonde et assez étendue); **the Great Australian B.,** la Grande Baie Australienne; le Grand Golfe Australien, de l'Australie; **the B. of Benin,** le Golfe de Bénin.
bigmouth ['bigmauθ], *s. P:* gueulard, -arde; **he's a b.,** il a une grande gueule.
big-mouthed ['big'mauðd], *a.* **1.** (*a*) (*of pers.*) à large bouche; (*b*) *P:* gueulard. **2.** (*of receptacle*) évasé.
bigness ['bignis], *s.* **1.** grandeur *f.* **2.** grosseur *f.*
bignonia [big'nouniə], *s. Bot:* bignone *f.*
Bignoniaceae [bignouni'eisii:], *s.pl.* bignoniacées *f.*
bigot ['bigət], *s.* **1.** fanatique *mf* (en politique, etc.); sectaire *mf.* **2.** (*religious*) bigot, -e.
bigoted ['bigətid], *a.* **1.** fanatique; au zèle, à l'esprit, étroit, sectaire. **2.** (*religious*) bigot.
bigotry ['bigətri], *s.* **1.** fanatisme *m;* sectarisme *m;* étroitesse *f* d'esprit. **2.** (*in religion*) bigotisme *m,* bigoterie *f;* cagoterie *f.*
bigrid ['baigrid], *a. W.Tel:* (lampe *f*) bigrille.
big-ticket ['big'tikit], *a. U.S:* de prix élevé; cher.
biguanide ['bigwənaid], *s. Ch:* biguanide *f.*
bigwig ['bigwig], *s. F:* personnage important; gros bonnet; *P:* grosse légume; **the bigwigs of high finance,** les (hauts) barons de la finance.
bijou ['bi:ʒu:], *s.* bijou, -oux *m;* objet *m* d'art de facture délicate; *attrib.* **b. flat to let,** petit appartement coquet à louer.
bijugate [bai'dʒu:geit], *a. Bot:* bijugué.
bike[1] [baik], *s.* **1.** *F:* (= BICYCLE) vélo *m,* bécane *f;* **motor b.,** moto (cyclette) *f.* **2.** *P: Austr:* fille *f,* grue *f,* poule *f.*
bike[2], *v.i. F:* **1.** faire de la bicyclette; *F:* pédaler. **2.** aller à bicyclette, à, en, vélo (to, jusqu'à).
bikini [bi'ki:ni], *s. Cost:* bikini *m.*
bilabial [bai'leibiəl], *a. & s. Ling:* (consonne) bilabiale (*f*).
bilabiate [bai'leibieit], *a. Bot:* (*of flower*) bilabié.
bilander ['biləndər], *s. Nau:* bélandre *f.*
bilateral [bai'læt(ə)r(ə)l], *a.* bilatéral, -aux; *Jur:* **b. contract, agreement,** contrat *m* synallagmatique; accord bilatéral; *Med:* **b. paralysis,** diplégie *f.*
bilateralism [bai'læt(ə)rəlizm], *s.* convention *f* réciproque; balance commerciale (entre deux pays).
bilaterally [bai'lætər(ə)li], *adv.* bilatéralement.
bilberry ['bilbəri], *s. Bot:* airelle *f* (myrtille); myrtille *f;* *F:* vaciet *m,* coussinet *m* (des marais).
bilbo, *pl.* -os ['bilbou, -ouz], *s. A:* épée *f,* rapière *f.*
bilboes ['bilbouz], *s.pl. A:* (*esp. Nau:*) fers *m* d'attache (d'un prisonnier).
bile [bail], *s. Physiol:* bile *f;* **b. duct,** canal *m* biliaire; **b. vessels,** conduits *m* biliaires; **b. pigments,** pigments *m* biliaires; **b. salts,** sels *m* biliaires; **b. calculus stones,** calculs *m* biliaires; *F: O:* **to stir, rouse, s.o.'s b.,** échauffer la bile à qn.
bilge[1] [bildʒ], *s.* **1.** *Nau:* (*a*) fond *m* de cale; bouchain *m,* sentine *f,* petits fonds; **hard, sharp, b.,** bouchain vif; **b. block,** ventrière *f;* (*in bottom of boat*) **b. channel,** lousse *f,* lousseau *m,* loussec *m,* lousset *m;* **b. keel,** quille *f* de bouchain; quille latérale; quille de roulis; aileron *m* (de sous-marin); **b. planks,** bordages *m* des fleurs; fleurs *f;* **b. pump,** pompe *f* de drain, de cale; pompe *f* d'assèchement; **b. shores,** accores *m* de bouchain; (*b*) **b. (water),** eau *f* de cale; *F:* **to talk a lot of b.,** dire des bêtises *f;* bafouiller; **get rid of all that b.,** débarrassez-vous de tout ce fatras. **2.** bouge *m* (d'une barrique).
bilge[2], *v.* **1.** *Nau:* (*a*) *v.tr.* crever, défoncer (un navire); (*b*) *v.i.* (*of ship*) crever, faire eau. **2.** *v.tr. & i.* (faire) bomber.
bilharzia [bil'hɑ:ziə], *s. Med:* **1.** bilharzia *f* (haematobia); schistosoma *m.* **2.** bilharziose *f.*
bilharziasis, *pl.* **-ases** [bilhɑ:'zi:əsis, -əsi:z], **bilharziosis,** *pl.* **-oses** [bilhɑ:zi'ousis, -'ousi:z], *s. Med:* bilharziose *f.*
bilian ['biliən], *s.* bois *m* de fer de Bornéo.
biliary ['biljəri], *a. Physiol:* biliaire; **b. colic,** colique *f* hépatique; **b. calculus,** calcul *m* biliaire; **b. passages,** voies *f* biliaires; *Vet:* **b. fever,** piroplasmose *f* (des chiens, des chevaux).
bilicyanin [bili'saiənin], *s. Physiol:* bilicyanine *f.*
bilifaction [bili'fækʃ(ə)n], **biligenesis** [bili'dʒenisis], *s. Physiol:* biligénèse *f,* biligénie *f,* fonction *f* biligénique.
bilimbi [bi'limbi], *s. Bot:* bilimbi *m.*
bilinear [bai'liniər], *a. Mth:* bilinéaire.
bilingual [bai'liŋgw(ə)l], *a.* bilingue; *Publ:* **b. series,** collection *f* bilingue, de textes jumelés.
bilingualism [bai'liŋgwəlizm], *s.* bilinguisme *m.*
bilinguist [bai'liŋgwist], *s.* bilingue *mf.*
bilinite ['bilinait], *s. Miner:* bilinite *f.*
bilious ['biliəs], *a.* **1.** bilieux; (tempérament *m*) cholérique; **b. attack,** débordement *m* de bile, accès *m* de bile; (*caused by overeating*) embarras *m* gastrique; **I feel b. today,** j'ai de la bile aujourd'hui; *F:* j'ai l'estomac barbouillé. **2.** *F:* bilieux, colérique.
biliousness ['biliəsnis], *s.* état bilieux, affection bilieuse; crise *f* du foie; attaque *f* de bile; crise hépatique.
bilirubin [bili'ru:bin], *s. Physiol:* bilirubine *f.*
bilirubinaemia [biliru:bi'ni:miə], *s. Med:* bilirubinémie *f.*
biliteral [bai'lit(ə)r(ə)l], *a. Ling:* **1.** (mot *m,* racine *f*) bilitère. **2.** (inscription) écrite en deux écritures.
biliverdin [bili'və:din], *s. Physiol:* biliverdine *f.*
bilk[1] [bilk], *s.* **1.** (*pers.*) escroc *m.* **2.** (*act*) escroquerie *f.*
bilk[2], *v.tr.* **1.** tromper, attraper (qn); payer (qn) en monnaie de singe; **to b. s.o. out of his money,** soutirer son argent à qn; escroquer qn. **2.** laisser (qn) en plan; fausser compagnie à (qn); filouter (un conducteur de taxi, etc.); **he bilked us,** il s'est esquivé; *F:* il nous a plaqués.
bilker ['bilkər], *s.* escroc *m* (*esp.* qui s'enfuit sans payer un conducteur de taxi).
bill[1] [bil], *s.* **1.** *A.Arms:* hallebarde *f.* **2.** = BILLHOOK.
bill[2], *s.* **1.** bec *m* (d'oiseau, d'ancre). **2.** *Geog:* bec, promontoire *m;* **Portland B.,** le Bec de Portland.
bill[3], *v.i.* (*of birds*) se becqueter; *F:* (*of pers.*) **to b. and coo,** faire les tourtereaux; s'aimer comme deux tourtereaux; se faire des mamours, se becqueter, se bécoter.
bill[4], *s.* **1.** *Com:* note *f,* facture *f,* mémoire *m;* (*in restaurant*) addition *f;* **exorbitant b.,** mémoire, compte *m,* d'apothicaire; **to make out a b.,** rédiger une facture; **shall I charge it on the b.?** faut-il le porter sur la note? *Jur:* **b. of costs,** état *m* de frais. **2.** *Com: Fin:* (*a*) effet *m* (de commerce); billet *m;* *pl.* valeurs *f,* papier *m* (bancable); **b. of debt,** reconnaissance *f* de dette; **long(-dated), short(-dated) bills,** papier, effets, à longue, courte, échéance; **b. payable at sight, sight b.,** effet payable à vue, à présentation, sur demande; effet à vue; **day b.,** effet à date fixe; **bills payable,** effets à payer; **bills in hand,** effets en portefeuille, portefeuille *m* effets; **b. of exchange,** lettre *f* de change; traite *f;* (*for small amounts*) broche *f;* **accommodation b.,** billet de complaisance; **b. book,** carnet *m* d'échéances; *F:* échéancier *m;* **b. broker, discounter,** courtier *m* de change, agent *m* de change; (*b*) *NAm:* billet de banque; **five-dollar b.,** billet de cinq dollars; (*c*) *Adm:* bon *m* (de l'Amirauté, etc.); **exchequer b.,** bon du Trésor britannique. **3.** affiche *f;* placard *m,* écriteau *m;* **to stick a b. on a wall,** placarder, coller, apposer, une affiche sur un mur; **to stick bills on a wall,** placarder un mur; **stick no bills!** défense d'afficher; *Th:* **(play)b.,** affiche; programme *m* du spectacle; **to change the b.,** renouveler l'affiche, changer de programme; (*of actor*) **to head, top, the b.,** éclipser tout le monde sur l'affiche; être en vedette sur l'affiche; faire tête d'affiche; (*of play*) **to fill the b.,** tenir l'affiche; *F:* **that will fill the b.,** cela fera l'affaire; **it tops the b.!** c'est le comble! **double, triple, b.,** programme de deux, trois, pièces de théâtre. **4.** (*a*) **b. of fare,** carte *f* du jour, menu *m;* **the daily b. of fare,** l'ordinaire *m;* (*b*) *Nau:* **(clean, foul) b. of health,** patente *f* de santé (nette, suspecte, brute); **b. of lading,** (i) connaissement *m;* police *f* de chargement; (ii) *Rail: U.S:* feuille *f* d'expédition; **through b. of lading (with transhipment),** connaissement *m* direct (avec rupture de charge); *Cust:* **b. of entry,** déclaration *f* d'entrée (en douane); **b. of sight,** déclaration provisoire; **transit b.,** passavant *m;* **victualling b.,** autorisation *f* d'embarquer des provisions soumises aux droits; *Av:* **airway b.,** lettre *f* de transport aérien; (*c*) **b. of sale,** acte *m,* contrat *m,* de vente; facture; (*d*) **wages b.,** masse globale des salaires; masse salariale; *Civ.E:* **b. of quantities,** devis *m;* *Typ:* **b. of type, of fount,** police *f;* (*e*) *Navy:* **quarter b.,** rôle *m* de combat; **station b.,** rôle de manœuvre; (*f*) *Sch:* (*at Harrow*) (i) liste *f* des élèves; (ii) appel nominal. **5.** *Pol:* (*a*) projet *m* de loi (émanant du gouvernement); proposition *f* de loi (émanant de l'initiative d'un membre du Parlement); **private b.,** projet de loi présenté par un député qui n'engage pas l'initiative du gouvernement; **b. of supply,** projet de crédit supplémentaire; collectif *m* budgétaire; **money b.,** projet de loi de finances; **to pass, to reject, a b.,** adopter, repousser, un projet de loi; (*b*) *Hist;* **b. of rights,** (i) la Loi de 1689 déterminant les droits du citoyen anglais; (ii) *U.S:* les amendements de 1791 à la Constitution de 1787. **6.** *Jur:* résumé des chefs d'accusation (présenté au jury); *U.S:* (*of Grand Jury*) **to find a true b. against s.o.,** déclarer fondés les chefs d'accusation; **to ignore the b.,** refuser la mise en accusation.
bill[5], *v.tr.* **1.** (*a*) facturer (des marchandises); (*b*) **to b. s.o. for sth.,** envoyer une facture à qn pour qch. **2.** afficher; mettre (qch.) à qn pour qch. **2.** afficher; mettre (qch.) à l'affiche; annoncer (une vente, etc.) par voie d'affiches; *Th:* mettre (une pièce) au programme, à l'affiche. **3.** couvrir (une surface) d'affiches.
Bill[6], *Pr.n.m.* (*dim. of William*) Guillaume.
billabong ['biləbɔŋ], *s. Austr:* bras mort (d'une rivière).
bill-board ['bilbɔ:d], *s. Nau:* renfort *m* d'ancre; soufflage *m.*
billboard ['bilbɔ:d], *s.* panneau *m* d'affichage.
billbug ['bilbʌg], *s. Ent: U.S:* charançon *m* du blé.
-billed [bild], *a.* (*with adj. prefixed*) **yellow-b.,** au, à, bec jaune.
biller ['bilər], *s. U.S:* **1.** (*pers.*) facturier, -ière. **2.** (*machine*) facturière; machine *f* à facturer.
billet[1] ['bilit], *s.* **1.** *Mil:* (*a*) *O:* billet *m* de logement; (*b*) logement *m* (chez l'habitant); **b. ticket,** billet de logement; (*c*) cantonnement *m;* *F:* **every bullet has its b.,** toute balle a sa destination; on ne lutte pas contre le sort; (*d*) *pl.* **billets,** cantonnement(s); **close, emergency, stand-by, billets,** cantonnement d'alerte; *O:* cantonnement-bivouac *m, pl.* cantonnements-bivouacs; **rest billets,** cantonnement de repos; **billets with, without, subsistence,** logement (chez l'habitant) avec, sans, subsistance; **to allot billets,** répartir le cantonnement; **to go into billets,** occuper le cantonnement, occuper les logements (chez l'habitant). **2.** logement *m* (d'un évacué). **3.** *F:* place *f,* situation *f,* emploi *m;* **he's got a good b.,** il a une bonne place, il est bien casé.
billet[2], *v.* (**billeted**) **1.** *v.tr.* (*a*) *Mil:* **to b. troops on s.o., on, in, a town,** loger des troupes chez qn; cantonner des troupes dans une ville, loger des troupes chez l'habitant par billets de logement; (*b*) loger (un évacué; **on,** chez). **2.** *v.i.* loger (**with,** chez).
billet[3], *s.* **1.** bûche *f;* rondin *m,* bille *f,* billette *f* (de bois de chauffage, etc.); **b. wood,** bois *m* de quartier; **round b. wood,** rondins *mpl.* **2.** *Metall:* billette, larget *m* (d'acier); lopin *m;* **b. mills,** (train) ébaucheur *m.* **3.** *Arch: Her:* billette; **b. moulding,** billettes.
billet doux ['bilei'du:], *pl.* **billet(s) doux** ['bilei'du:z], *s.* billet doux.
billeting ['bilitiŋ], *s.* cantonnement *m;* logement *m* chez l'habitant; **b. area,** zone *f* de cantonnement; **b. distribution list,** état *m* de cantonnement; **b. officer,** officier de cantonnement; **advance b. party,** détachement, cadre, précurseur; campement *m;* **b. paper,** billet *m* de logement; **b. with, without, subsistence,** logement (chez l'habitant) avec, sans, subsistance.
billeting-roll ['bilitiŋroul], *s. Metall:* (train) ébaucheur (*m*).
billfish ['bilfiʃ], *s. Ich:* (i) scombrésoce *m;* (ii) aiguille *f* de mer; (iii) (requin) pèlerin *m.*
billfold ['bilfould], *s. NAm:* portefeuille *m.*
billful ['bilful], *s.* becquée *f.*
billhead ['bilhed], *s.* en-tête *m* de facture, *pl.* en-têtes.
billhook ['bilhuk], *s. Tls:* vouge *m;* serpe *f;* croissant *m* (à élaguer); serpette *f;* courbet *m.*
billian ['biliən], *s.* bois *m* de fer de Bornéo.
billiard ['biliəd], *s.* **1.** (*a*) *pl.* (*usu. with sg. const.*) **billiards,** (jeu *m* de) billard *m;* **bar billiards,** billard russe; **to play, have a game of, billiards,** jouer au billard; faire une partie de billard; (*b*) *attrib.* **b. ball,** bille *f* de billard; **b. cue,** queue *f* de billard; **b. room,** (salle *f* de) billard; **b. table,** billard; **b.-table top,** billard de table; **b. cloth,** tapis *m* de billard; **b. player,** joueur,

-euse, de billard; **b. marker,** garçon *m* de billard. **2.** *NAm:* carambolage *m.*

billing[1] ['biliŋ], *s. F:* **b. and cooing,** mamours *mpl.*

billing[2], *s.* **1.** facturation *f* (de marchandises); **b. machine,** machine *f* à facturer; facturière *f.* **2.** affichage *m*; *Cin:* **double b., twin b.,** programme *m* double, à deux longs métrages; **to get the top of the b.,** faire tête d'affiche.

Billingsgate ['biliŋzgeit]. **1.** *Pr.n.* marché *m* au poisson (à Londres). **2.** *s. F:* **billingsgate,** langage *m* des halles, des poissardes; **to talk b.,** parler comme une poissarde.

billion ['biliən], *s.* **1.** billion *m* (10^{12}). **2.** *NAm:* milliard *m* (10^9).

billionaire [biliə'nɛər], *s.* (*a*) billionnaire *mf*; (*b*) *NAm:* milliardaire *mf*; (*c*) milliardaire, richissime *m.*

billionth ['biliənθ], *a. & s.* **1.** billionième (*m*). **2.** *NAm:* milliardième (*m*).

billon ['bilən], *s.* (*alloy*) billon *m.*

billow[1] ['bilou], *s.* grande vague; lame *f* (de mer); *Lit:* **the billows,** les flots *m*; **afloat on the billows,** voguant sur la vague, sur les flots.

billow[2], *v.i.* (*of the sea*) se soulever en vagues; (*of crowds, flames, etc.*) ondoyer.

billowy ['biloui], *a.* (flot) houleux, (mer) houleuse.

billposter ['bilpoustər], **billsticker** ['bilstikər], *s.* afficheur *m*; colleur *m* d'affiches; placardeur *m.*

billposting ['bilpoustiŋ], **billsticking** ['bilstikiŋ], *s.* affichage *m*, placardage *m.*

Billy ['bili]. **1.** *Pr.n.m.* (*dim. of William*) Guillaume. **2.** *s.* **billy,** *pl.* **billies** ['biliz]; (*a*) *Nau:* **handy b.,** palan *m* de, du, dimanche; (*b*) *Austr: N.Z:* gamelle *f*; bouilloire *f* (à thé); (*c*) *Tex:* boudineuse *f*; (*d*) *P:* gourdin *m*; (*e*) *NAm:* bâton *m* (d'agent de police).

billyboy ['biliboi], *s. Nau:* barge *f.*

billycan ['bilikæn], *s.* = BILLY 2 (*b*).

billycock ['bilikɔk], *s. F: O:* **b. (hat),** (chapeau *m*) melon *m.*

billy-goat ['biligout], *s.* bouc *m.*

billy-o(h) ['biliou], *adv.phr. F: O:* **like b.-o.: it's raining like b.-o.,** il pleut à verse; **they fought like b.-o.,** ils se sont battus avec acharnement.

bilobar [bai'loubər], **bilobate** ['bailoubeit], **bilobed** ['bailoubd], *a.* bilobé.

bilocation [bailou'keiʃ(ə)n], *s. Psy:* bilocation *f.*

bilocular [bai'lɔkjulər], *a. Bot:* biloculaire.

biltong ['biltɔŋ], *s.* (*in S. Africa*) lanières *fpl* de viande desséchée.

Bim(m) [bim], *s. F:* habitant, -ante, de la Barbade.

bimanal ['bai'meinl, 'baimənl], *a. Z:* bimane.

bimane, *pl.* **-s, bimana** ['baimein, -z, 'baimənə], *s. Z:* bimane *m.*

bimanous ['baimənəs], *a. Z:* bimane.

bimanual [bai'mænjuəl], *a. Med:* (examen) fait avec les deux mains.

bimarginate [bai'mɑːdʒineit], *a. Nat.Hist:* bimarginé.

bimastic [bai'mæstik], *a. Z:* à deux mamelles.

bimastoid [bai'mæstɔid], *a. Anat:* bimastoïdien.

bimester ['baimestər], *s.* bimestre *m.*

bimestrial [bai'mestriəl], *a.* bimestriel.

bimetal ['baimet(ə)l], *a.* (fusible *m*) en deux métaux.

bimetallic [baimi'tælik], *a.* **1.** *Pol.Ec:* (système *m*) bimétallique. **2.** *Tchn:* **b. strip,** bilame *f.*

bimetallism [bai'metəlizm], *s. Pol.Ec:* bimétallisme *m.*

bimetallist [bai'metəlist], *s. Pol.Ec:* bimétalliste *m.*

bimillenary ['baimi'lenəri], *s.* bimillénaire *m.*

bimodal [bai'moud(ə)l], *a. Stat:* (*of distribution, etc.*) bimodal, -aux.

bimolecular [baimə'lekjulər], *a. Ch:* bimoléculaire.

bimonthly [bai'mʌnθli]. **1.** *a. & s.* (*a*) bimensuel (*m*); semi-mestriel; (*b*) bimestriel; *s.* revue, publication, bimestrielle. **2.** *adv.* (*a*) bimensuellement, deux fois par mois; (*b*) tous les deux mois.

bimorph ['baimɔːf], *a. Elcs:* **b. cell,** cristal *m* bimorphe.

bimorphemic [baimɔː'fiːmik], *a. Ling:* (mot *m*) à deux morphèmes.

bin[1] [bin], *s.* **1.** (*a*) coffre *m*, huche *f*, bac *m*; (*in stable*) **corn b.,** coffre à avoine; **orderly b.,** poubelle *f*; (*b*) compartiment *m*, casier *m*; **wine b.,** casier à bouteilles; porte-bouteilles *m inv.*; (*c*) *Cmptr:* puits *m*; récipient *m*; (*d*) **cement b.,** silo *m* à ciment; *Min:* **ore b.,** réservoir *m*, caisson *m*, à minerai. **2.** *P:* **(loony) b.,** maison *f* de fous.

bin[2], *v.tr.* **(binned)** ranger, mettre, (qch.) dans (i) une huche, un coffre, (ii) un casier.

binant ['bainənt], *s.* demi-cercle *m*, *pl.* demi-cercles.

binary ['bainəri]. **1.** *a. Mth: Ch: etc:* binaire; *Cmptr:* **b. numeration,** numération *f* binaire; **b. number system,** système *m* binaire, de nombres binaires; *Mus:* **b. measure,** mesure *f* binaire; *Sch:* **b. system,** système d'études supérieures qui sépare les universités des instituts polytechniques. **2.** *a. & s. Astr:* **b. (star),** binaire *f*; **eclipsing b.,** binaire à éclipses; **visual b.,** binaire visuelle; **spectroscopic b.,** binaire spectroscopique.

binate[1] ['baineit], *a. Bot:* biné; rangé par paires.

binate[2], *v.i. Ecc:* biner.

binaural [bi'nɔːr(ə)l], *a.* bi(n)aural, -aux; bi(n)auriculaire; *Med:* **b. stethoscope,** stéthoscope *m* bi(n)auriculaire; **test for b. hearing,** test *m* de binauralité; *Artil:* (*sound ranging*) **b. trainer,** appareil *m* d'entraînement à l'écoute bi(n)auriculaire; *Elcs:* **b. recording,** enregistrement *m* par deux microphones, stéréophonique; **b. effect,** effet *m* stéréophonique.

bind[1] [baind], *s.* **1.** *Mus:* ligature *f*, liaison *f.* **2.** *Hort:* sarment *m*, tige *f*, liane *f* (de houblon, etc.). **3.** *Mec.E: etc:* (*a*) coincement *m*, grippage *m*, blocage *m*; (*b*) gommage *m*, collage *m.* **4.** *Min:* couche *f* d'argile dure (entre deux couches de houille). **5.** *P:* (*a*) (*thg*) scie *f*; (*pers.*) crampon *m*; casse-pieds *m inv.*, **it's an awful b.,** c'est casse-pieds; (*b*) *U.S:* **to be in a b.,** être en mauvaise passe; ne pas en mener large.

bind[2], *v.* **(bound [baund]; bound)**

I. *v.tr. & i.* **1.** *v.tr.* attacher, lier; (*tie fast*) (*a*) **to b. a prisoner, s.o.'s hands,** lier, attacher, ligoter, un prisonnier; lier les mains à qn; **to b. s.o. hand and foot,** lier pieds et poings à qn; garrotter, ligoter, qn solidement; **bound hand and foot,** pieds et poings liés; **bound by a spell,** retenu par un charme; **to be bound to s.o. by gratitude,** être attaché à qn par la reconnaissance; **the ties that b. one to the family,** les liens *m* qui vous rattachent à la famille; **they are bound together by a close friendship,** ils sont liés d'une étroite amitié; (*b*) **they are very much bound up in each other,** ils sont très attachés l'un à l'autre; **the virtues bound up in the soil,** les vertus *f* qui s'attachent à la terre; **the present is bound up with the past,** le présent se relie, est lié, au passé; **question closely bound up with another,** question qui se lie, se rattache, se rapporte, étroitement à une autre; **facts closely bound up with one another,** faits reliés par une relation directe; **chemistry is bound up with physics,** la chimie est liée à la physique; **his interests were bound up with ours,** ses intérêts étaient solidaires des nôtres; **my happiness is bound up with yours,** mon bonheur est attaché au vôtre; **facts closely bound together,** faits étroitement solidaires les uns des autres; (*c*) **to b. sth. (down) to, on, sth.,** attacher qch. à qch.; serrer (une pièce sur l'établi); fixer (un fil à un accu, etc.); **to b. (on) one's skis,** fixer ses skis; (*d*) **to b. a bargain,** ratifier, confirmer, un marché; *F:* toper; (*e*) **food that binds the bowels,** nourriture constipante, échauffante, qui constipe, qui échauffe. **2.** *v.tr.* (*tie round*) (*a*) **to b. (up) a wound,** bander, panser, une blessure; **to b. an artery,** ligaturer une artère; **his head was bound up in a handkerchief,** il avait la tête bandée d'un mouchoir; (*b*) *Fenc:* **to b. one's blade round the adversary's,** lier le fer; (*c*) border (un manteau, un chapeau); brider (une boutonnière); (*d*) fretter (une roue, une poutre, etc.). **3.** *v.tr.* (*tie together*) (*a*) **to b. (up) a sheaf,** lier une gerbe; mettre un lien à une gerbe; **to b. (up) one's hair,** se faire un chignon; **to b. asparagus into bundles,** lier des asperges en bottes; (*b*) relier (un livre); **bound in paper, paper-bound,** broché; **bound in boards,** cartonné; **bound in cloth, cloth-bound,** relié toile; **full-bound in morocco,** relié en plein maroquin; **half-bound in morocco,** relié en demi-maroquin à coins; **quarter-bound in morocco,** relié en demi-maroquin; (*with passive force*) **your book is binding,** votre livre est à la reliure; **to b. up two volumes in one,** relier deux volumes en un seul; (*c*) (i) lier, agglutiner (du sable, etc.); cohérer, fixer (la poussière d'une route); **stones bound together with cement,** pierres liées avec du ciment; (ii) *v.i.* (*of gravel, etc.*) se lier, s'agglomérer; s'agglutiner; s'agréger; (*of cement*) durcir, prendre; (*d*) *v.i.* (*of machine parts, etc.*) (se) coincer; (*of bearings*) gripper; (*of cylinders, etc.*) coller, gommer. **4.** *v.tr.* (*a*) (*of pers., obligation, promise, etc.*) lier, engager (qn); **to b. s.o. to obedience,** astreindre qn à l'obéissance; **to b. s.o. to pay a debt,** astreindre, obliger, qn à payer une dette; **to b. s.o. to obey,** obliger qn à obéir; **to b. oneself to do sth.,** s'engager à faire qch.; **to b. s.o. (over) as an apprentice to s.o.,** mettre qn en apprentissage chez qn; *Theol:* **the power to b. and to loose,** le pouvoir de lier et de délier; (*b*) **to be bound to do sth.,** être obligé, tenu, de faire qch.; devoir faire qch.; **you are in duty bound to do it,** votre devoir vous y oblige; **to be in honour bound to do sth.,** être engagé d'honneur à faire qch.; mettre son honneur à faire qch.; **bound in honour to do sth.,** moralement obligé de faire qch.; **to consider oneself, feel, in honour bound to do sth.,** estimer de son devoir de faire qch.; tenir à honneur de faire qch.; se piquer d'honneur; **to be bound by an oath,** être engagé sous serment, lié par un serment; **to be bound by strict rules,** être soumis à des règles strictes; (*c*) **he's bound to come,** il ne peut pas manquer de venir; **it's bound to rain tomorrow,** il pleuvra sûrement demain; **it's bound to happen,** cela arrivera comme mars en carême; c'est fatal; **we are bound to be successful,** nous réussirons à coup sûr; **you are bound to have a lawsuit over it,** il est inévitable qu'on vous fasse un procès; **it's bound to leak out,** cela se saura forcément; (*d*) *F:* **he'll come, I'll be bound,** il viendra, j'en suis sûr, je vous le promets; (*e*) *NAm:* **he's bound to come and hear you,** il veut absolument venir vous entendre. **5.** *v.i.* ronchonner.

II. (*compound verbs*) **1. bind down,** *v.tr.* **to b. s.o. down to do sth.,** astreindre, contraindre, qn à faire qch. **2. bind over,** *v.tr. Jur:* **to b. s.o. over to appear when called upon,** obliger qn à se tenir à la disposition de la justice; **to b. s.o. over to keep the peace,** exiger de qn sous caution qu'il ne se livrera à aucune voie de fait; **to be bound over,** être sommé par un magistrat d'observer une bonne conduite.

bind-beam ['baindbiːm], *s. Civ.E:* (*on heads of piles*) raineau *m.*

binder ['baindər], *s.* **1.** (*pers.*) (*a*) *Agr:* lieur, -euse; (*b*) (*bookbinder*) relieur, -euse. **2.** (*a*) *Agr:* (*machine*) lieuse *f* (de gerbes); (*for hay*) botteloir *m*, botteleuse *f*; **b. twine,** ficelle *f* à lier; (*b*) *Needlew:* ourleur *m*, bordeur *m* (d'une machine à coudre). **3.** (*a*) lien *m* (de gerbe, fagot); hart *f* (de fagot); (*b*) *Med:* bande *f*, ceinture *f* (de flanelle); bandage *m* de corps. **4.** sous-cape *f*, *pl.* sous-capes (de cigare). **5.** **(spring-back) b.,** biblorhapte *m* (pour papiers); auto-relieur *m*, *pl.* auto-relieurs; relieur *m*; reliure *f* électrique. **6.** (*a*) *Cu:* liant *m* (d'une sauce); (*b*) *Rec:* liant (de disque); (*c*) *Civ.E:* liant; agglomérant *m*; matériau *m* d'agrégation. **7.** (*a*) *Carp:* entrait *m*; sommier *m* (de plancher); (*b*) *Const:* parpaing *m.* **8.** (*binding clip*) étrier *m* de serrage, de pression. **9.** *Com:* convention *f* liant le vendeur.

bindery ['baind(ə)ri], *s.* atelier *m* de reliure.

binding[1] ['baindiŋ], *a.* **1.** (agent) agglomérant, agglutinant; *Ph:* **b. energy,** énergie *f* de liaison. **2.** obligatoire (**upon s.o.,** pour qn); **b. agreement,** obligation *f* irrévocable; **agreement b. (up)on s.o.,** contrat *m* qui lie qn; **this promise is b. on them,** cette promesse les engage; **decision b. on all parties,** décision *f* obligatoire pour tous; **obligation b. on all parties,** obligation solidaire; **to make it b. on s.o. to do sth.,** imposer à qn l'obligation de faire qch. **3.** *Med:* astringent, constipant, échauffant; **quince jelly is b.,** la gelée de coings constipe.

binding[2], *s.* **1.** (*a*) agglutination *f*; agrégation *f*; **b. material,** matière agglomérante, d'agrégation; liant *m*, agglomérant *m* (d'une route); **b. of the dust,** fixation *f* de la poussière; *Ac:* **b. agent,** liant *m* (de disques phonographiques); (*b*) fixation; serrage *m*; frettage *m*; cerclage *m* (d'une roue); *Const: etc:* **b. iron,** patte *f* d'attache; **b. piece,** moise *f*, amoise *f*; **b. wire,** fil *m* d'amarrage, de ligature; fil d'archal; **b. screw,** (i) vis *f* de pression; (ii) *El:* also **b. post,** (borne *f*) serre-fils *m inv.*; **b. clip,** étrier *m* de pression, de serrage; (*c*) *Mec.E: etc:* (i) coincement *m*, grippage *m*, blocage *m*; (ii) gommage *m*, collage *m* (d'un arbre, etc.). **2.** (*a*) lien *m*, ligature *f*; bandage *m* (d'une poutre, etc.); frette *f*; *El:* **armature b.,** frette d'induit; (*b*) *Sp:* fixation (de ski); **release bindings,** fixations de sécurité; (*c*) reliure *f* (d'un livre); **quarter b.,** demi-reliure *f*; **half b.,** demi-reliure à petits coins; **three-quarter b.,** demi-reliure amateur; **b. with leather corners,** reliure avec coins; **cloth b.,** reliure en toile; reliure bradel; reliure anglaise; **limp b.,** cartonnage *m* souple, à l'anglaise; **library b.,** reliure (d')amateur; **plain b.,** reliure janséniste; **perfect b.,** reliure arraphique, sans couture; **spring b.** (*for holding papers*), reliure électrique; relieur *m*; (*d*) bordure *f*, liséré *m* (d'une robe, etc.); *Dressm:* **bias b.,** ruban *m* en biais; *Furn:* **upholstery b.,** galon *m* de finition; (*e*) *Phot:* (*for slides etc.*) **gummed b.,** bande gommée; (*f*) *Arch: N.Arch:* liaison *f.*

bindweed ['baindwiːd], *s. Bot:* liseron *m*; *F:* vrillée *f*; vroncelle *f*; **black b.,** vrillée bâtarde; **small b., field b.,** liseron des champs.

bine [bain], *s.* sarment *m*; tige *f* (de houblon).

binervate [bai'nəːveit], *a. Nat.Hist:* binervé.

Binet-Simon ['biːnei'siːmɔ̃], *Pr.n. Psy:* **B.-S. test,** le (test de) Binet-Simon.

bing [biŋ], *s. Dial: Min:* terril *m.*

binge [bin(d)ʒ], *s. F:* ribote *f*, bombe *f*; **to have, go on, a b.,** faire la bombe, la noce; riboter, nocer; **to be on the b.,** être en bombe, en bordée.

bingle ['biŋgl], *s. Hairdr: A:* coiffure *f* intermédiaire entre à la Ninon et à la garçonne.

bingo ['biŋgou], *s.* (sorte de) loto (joué collectivement).

Bini [bi'niː], *a. & s. Ethn:* (indigène *mf*) du Bénin; *Art:* **B. bronze,** bronze *m* du Bénin.

binnacle ['binəkl], *s. Nau:* habitacle *m*; **compensating b.,**

habitacle à compensateurs; **b. cover,** capot *m* d'habitacle; **b. pillar, stand,** colonne *f* de l'habitacle; pied *m* d'habitacle.

binocle ['binɔkl], *s. Opt:* télescope *m* double; *A:* binocle *m*.

binocular [bi'nɔkjulər, bai-]. **1.** *a.* (vision *f*, etc.) binoculaire; *Phot:* **b. camera,** appareil *m* stéréoscopique. **2.** *s.pl.* **binoculars,** jumelles *f*.

binodal [bai'noudl], *a.* **1.** *Bot:* (cyme *f*, etc.) à deux nœuds. **2.** *Mth:* (quartique) binodale.

binode ['bainoud], *s. Elcs:* diode *f* bianodique.

binomial [bai'noumiəl]. **1.** *a.* (*a*) *Mth:* (facteur *m* etc.) binôme; **the b. theorem,** le binôme de Newton; le théorème de Newton; (*b*) *Stat:* binomial, -aux; **b. distribution,** distribution binomiale; (*c*) *Nat.Hist:* binominal, -aux; **b. nomenclature,** nomenclature binominale. **2.** *s.* binôme *m*.

binominal [bai'nɔminəl], *a.* = BINOMIAL 1 (*c*).

binovular [bin'ouvjulər], *a. Med:* **b. twins,** jumeaux *m* biovulaires.

bint [bint], *s.f. P:* gonzesse.

binturong ['bintjurɔŋ], *s. Z:* binturong *m*.

binuclear [bai'nju:kliər], **binucleate** [bai'nju:klieit], *a. Ph:* binucléaire.

binucleolate ['bai'nju:klioulelt], *a. Bot:* (*of ascospore*) binucléolé.

bio- ['baiou, bai'ɔ, 'baiə], *comb.fm.* bio-.

bioacoustics ['baiouə'ku:stiks], *s.pl.* (*usu with sg. const.*) bioacoustique *f*.

bio-assay ['baiouæ'sei], *s. Pharm:* essai *m* biologique, titrage *m* biologique.

bioastronautics ['baiouæstrou'nɔ:tiks], *s.pl.* (*usu. with sg. const.*) bioastronautique *f*.

biobibliographical ['baioubibliə'græfik(ə)l], *a.* biobibliographique.

biobibliography ['baioubibli'ɔgrəfi], *s.* biobibliographie *f*.

bioblast ['baiəblæst], *s. Bot:* bioblaste *m*.

biocatalyst ['baiou'kætəlist], *s. Biol:* biocatalyseur *m*.

biocenose ['baiou'si:nous], **biocenosis,** *pl.* **-oses** ['baiousi'nousis, -ousi:z], *s. Nat.Hist:* biocénose *f*, biocœnose *f*.

biochemic(al) ['baiou'kemik(əl)], *a.* biochimique.

biochemist ['baiou'kemist], *s.* biochimiste *mf*.

biochemistry ['baiou'kemistri], *s.* biochimie *f*.

biocide ['baiousaid], *s.* pesticide *m*.

bioclimatics ['baiouklai'mætiks], *s.pl.* (*usu. with sg. const.*) bioclimatologie *f*.

bioclimatology ['baiouklaimə'tɔlədʒi], *s.* bioclimatologie *f*.

biocoenose ['baiou'si:nous], **biocoenosis,** *pl.* **-oses** ['baiousi'nousis, -ousi:z], *s. Nat.Hist:* biocénose *f*, biocœnose *f*.

biodynamics ['baioudai'næmiks], *s.pl.* (*usu. with sg. const.*) biodynamique *f*.

bioecology ['baioui'kɔlədʒi], *s.* synécologie *f*.

bioelectrical ['baioui'lektrik(ə)l], *a.* bioélectrique.

bioelectricity ['baiouilek'trisiti], *s. Biol:* bioélectricité *f*.

bioenergetics ['baiouenə'dʒetiks], *s.pl.* (*usu with sg.const.*) *Physiol:* bioénergétique *f*.

bioflavonoid ['baiou'fleivənɔid], *s. Biol:* vitamine P *f*.

biogen ['baiədʒen], *s. Biol:* biogène *m*.

biogenesis ['baiou'dʒenisis], *s. Biol:* biogénèse *f*.

biogenetic ['baiou'dʒi'netik], *a.* biogénétique; **b. law,** loi *f* biogénétique, de récapitulation.

biogenic ['baiou'dʒenik], *a.* biogène, biogénique.

biogenous [bai'ɔdʒənəs], *a.* **1.** *Biol:* biogène, biogénique. **2.** *Bot:* parasite.

biogeny [bai'ɔdʒəni], *s.* biogénèse *f*.

biogeographer ['baioudʒi'ɔgrəfər], *s.* biogéographe *mf*.

biogeographic(al) ['baioudʒiə'græfik(l)], *a.* biogéographique.

biogeography ['baioudʒi'ɔgrəfi], *s.* biogéographie *f*.

biograph ['baiəgræf], *s. A:* biographe *m* (forme primitive du cinématographe).

biographer [bai'ɔgrəfər], *s.* biographe *m* (auteur d'une biographie).

biographic(al) [baiə'græfik(l)], *a.* biographique; **b. novel,** vie romancée, biographie romancée.

biography [bai'ɔgrəfi], *s.* biographie *f*.

biolite ['baiəlait], **biolith** ['baiəliθ], *s. Miner:* biolite *m*, biolithe *f*.

biologic(al) [baiə'lɔdʒik(l)], *a.* biologique; **b. warfare,** guerre *f* bactériologique; **b. control of a noxious plant,** lutte *f* biologique contre une plante nuisible; *Bot:* **b. spectrum,** spectre *m* biologique; *Hyg:* **b. filter,** filtre *m* biologique; lit bactérien.

biologically [baiə'lɔdʒik(ə)li], biologiquement.

biologism [bai'ɔlədʒizm], *s.* biologisme *m*.

biologist [bai'ɔlədʒist], *s.* biologiste *mf*.

biology [bai'ɔlədʒi], *s.* biologie *f*; **plant b.,** phytobiologie *f*.

bioluminescence ['baioul(j)umi'nes(ə)ns], *s.* bioluminescence *f*.

bioluminescent ['baioul(j)umi'nes(ə)nt], *a.* bioluminescent.

biomass ['baiəmæs], *s. Biol:* biomasse *f*.

biome ['baioum], *s. Biol:* biome *m*.

biomechanics ['baioumi'kæniks], *s.pl.* (*usu. with sg. const.*) biomécanique *f*.

biomedical ['baiou'medikl], *a.* **b. engineering,** fabrication *f* et ajustage *m* des appareils prothétiques, de prothèse; **b. engineer,** prothésiste *mf*.

biometer [bai'ɔmitər], *s. Biol:* biomètre *m*.

biometric(al) [baiə'metrik(l)], *a.* biométrique.

biometricien ['baioume'triʃ(ə)n], *s.* biométricien, -ienne.

biometrics [baiə'metriks], *s.pl.* (*usu. with sg. const.*)

biometry [bai'ɔmitri], *s.* biométrie *f*.

biomicroscope ['baiou'maikrəskoup], *s. Opt:* biomicroscope *m*.

bion ['baiən], **biont** ['baiɔnt], *s. Biol:* organisme *m*.

bionics [bai'ɔniks], *s.pl.* (*usu. with sg. const.*) bionique *f*.

bionomic(al) [baiə'nɔmik(l)], *a. Biol:* bionomique; **bionomic levels,** niveaux *m* bionomiques.

bionomics [baiə'nɔmiks], *s.pl.* (*usu. with sg. const.*);

bionomy [bai'ɔnəmi], *s.* bionomie *f*.

biophore ['baiəfɔ:r], *s. Biol:* biophore *m*.

biophysicist ['baiou'fizisist], *s.* biophysicien, ienne.

biophysics ['baiou'fiziks], *s.* (*usu. with sg. const.*) biophysique *f*.

bioplasm ['baiouplæzm], *s. Biol:* bioplasme *m*.

bioplasmic [baiou'plæzmik], *a. Biol:* bioplasmique.

bioplast ['baiouplæst], *s. Biol:* bioplasme *m*.

biopsy ['baiɔpsi, bai'ɔpsi], *s. Surg:* biopsie *f*.

bios ['baiɔs], *s. Bio-Ch:* bios *m*.

biosatellite ['baiou'sætəlait], *s.* satellite habité; biosatellite *m*.

bioscope ['baiəskoup], *s.* **1.** bioscope *m*. **2.** *A:* biographe *m*. **3.** (*in S. Africa*) cinéma *m*.

biosensors ['baiou'sensɔ:z], *s.pl. Space:* harnais *m* biologique.

biosphere ['baiəsfiər], *s.* biosphère *f*.

biostatics ['baiou'stætiks], *s.pl.* (*usu. with sg. const.*) biostatique *f*; biologie *f* statique.

biosynthesis ['baiou'sinθəsis], *s.* biosynthèse *f*.

biosynthetic ['baiousin'θetik], *a. Biol:* biosynthétique.

biota [bai'outə], *s.* flore *f* et faune *f* (d'une région).

biotechnics ['baiou'tekniks], *spl.* (*usu. with sg. const.*) biotechnique *f*.

biotechnology ['baioutek'nɔlədʒi], *s.* ergonomie *f*.

biotherapy ['baiou'θerəpi], *s.* biothérapie *f*.

biotic(al) [bai'ɔtik(l)], *a. Biol:* biotique.

biotin ['baiətin], *s. Bio-Ch:* biotine *f*.

biotite ['baiətait], *s. Miner:* biotite *f*.

biotope ['baiətoup], *s. Nat.Hist:* biotope *m*, habitat *m*.

biotropism ['baiou'trɔpizm], *s. Med:* biotropisme *m*.

biotype ['baiətaip], *s.* biotype *m*.

biotypology ['baioutai'pɔlədʒi], *s.* biotypologie *f*.

biovulate [bai'ouvjuleit], *a.* biovulé.

bioxide [bai'ɔksaid], *s. Ch: A:* bioxyde *m*.

bipack ['baipæk], *s. Phot:* bipack *m*.

biparental ['baipə'rent(ə)l], *a.* (*of heredity, etc.*) biparental, -aux.

biparietal ['baipə'raiət(ə)l], *a. Anthr:* bipariétal, -aux.

biparous ['bipərəs], *a. Z:* bipare.

bipartisan ['baipɑ:ti'zæn], *a. Pol: etc:* biparti; bipartite.

bipartisanism [bai'pɑ:tizənizm], *s. Pol:* bipartisme *m*.

bipartisanship [bai'pɑ:tizənʃip], *s.* bipartisme *m*.

bipartite [bai'pɑ:tait], *a.* **1.** *Nat.Hist:* biparti; bipartite. **2.** *Jur:* (document) rédigé en double.

bipartition ['baipɑ:'tiʃ(ə)n], *s. Nat.Hist:* bipartition *f*.

bi-party ['bai'pɑ:ti], *a. Pol:* **b.-p. system,** système politique fondé sur l'opposition de deux partis.

biped ['baiped], *a.* & *s.* bipède (*m*).

bipedal ['baipedl], *a.* bipède.

bipedalism [bai'pedəlizm], *s.* bipédie *f*.

bipennate [bai'peneit], *a. Nat.Hist:* bipenne, bipenné.

bipetalous ['bai'petələs], *a. Bot:* bipétalé.

biphase ['baifeiz], *a. El:* (courant) biphasé, diphasé.

biphenyl [bai'fenil], *s. Ch:* diphényle *m*.

bipinnaria ['baipi'nɛəriə], *s. Echin:* bipinnaria *f*.

bipinnate ['bai'pineit], *a. Bot:* bipinné.

bipinnatifid ['baipi'nætifid], *a. Bot:* bipennatifide, bipinnatifide.

biplanar [bai'pleinər], *a. Mth:* (point *m*) biplanaire.

biplane ['baiplein], *s.* **1.** *Av:* (avion *m*) biplan *m*. **2.** *attrib.* **b. incandescent lamp,** lampe *f* à filament biplanaire.

bipod ['baipɔd], *s. Mil:* (i) biflèche *m* (de canon); (ii) bipied *m* (de fusil-mitrailleur); **b. mounting,** support *m* bipied; **b. shoe,** semelle *f* de bipied.

bipolar ['bai'poulər], *a. El: Physiol: etc:* bipolaire.

bipolarity [baipou'læriti], *s.* bipolarité *f*.

bipont ['baipɔnt], **bipontine** [bai'pɔntin], *a. Typ.Hist:* **b. editions (of the classics),** éditions bipontines (imprimées à Deux-Ponts).

bipp [bip], *s. Pharm:* onguent composé de bismuth sous-nitrate, d'iodoforme et de paraffine.

biprism ['baiprizm], *s. Opt:* biprisme *m*.

bipropellant ['baiprə'pelənt], *s.* diergol *m*.

bipyramid ['bai'pirəmid], *s. Cryst:* cristal bipyramidal.

bipyramidal ['baipi'ræmid(ə)l], *a. Cryst:* bipyramidal, -aux.

biquadratic ['baikwɔ'drætik], *a.* & *s. Mth:* (nombre) bicarré; **b. root,** racine *f* quatrième; **b. (equation),** équation *f* biquadratique.

biquartz ['baikwɔ:ts], *s. Opt:* biquartz *m*.

biquinary [bai'kwainəri], *a. Cmptr:* (code *m*, notation *f*, nombre *m*, etc.) biquinaire.

biquintile [bai'kwint(a)il], *a. Astr:* **b. aspect,** aspect *m* de deux planètes à 144°.

bir ['biər], *s. Bot:* **b. (fruit),** jujube *m*; **b. (fruit) tree,** jujubier *m*.

biracial [bai'reiʃ(ə)l], *a.* (peuple *m*, etc.) de deux races.

biramose [bai'reimous], **biramous** [bai'reiməs], *a. Ent: Crust:* biramé.

birch[1] [bə:tʃ], *s.* **1.** *Bot:* (*a*) bouleau *m*; **lady b., silver b., white b., common b.,** bouleau blanc; *F:* arbre *m* de sagesse; **pubescent b.,** bouleau pubescent; **weeping b., drooping b.,** bouleau pleureur; **dwarf b.,** bouleau nain; *NAm:* **paper b.,** bouleau à papier; **b. bark (canoe),** canoë *m* d'écorce de bouleau; **b. broom,** balai *m* de bouleau; **b. oil,** essence *f* d'écorce de bouleau; (*b*) **b. (wood),** (bois *m* de) bouleau. **2. b. (rod),** verge *f*, poignée *f* de verges (pour fouetter); **to give s.o. the b.,** donner les verges, le fouet, à qn; fouetter qn.

birch[2], *v.tr.* donner les verges, le fouet, à (qn); fouetter (qn).

birchen ['bə:tʃ(ə)n], *a. Lit: Dial: NAm:* de, en, bouleau.

birching ['bə'tʃiŋ], *s.* fouettée *f*, rossée *f*.

bird[1] [bə:d], *s.* **1.** (*a*) oiseau *m*; **hen b.,** oiseau femelle; **song b.,** oiseau chanteur; **cage b.,** oiseau de volière, d'appartement; **little b., young b.,** oiselet *m*, oisillon *m*; *F:* **a little bird told me,** mon petit doigt me l'a dit; **night b.,** (i) oiseau de nuit, nocturne; (ii) (*pers.*) coureur, -euse, de nuit; noctambule *mf*; oiseau de nuit; **b. of passage,** oiseau de passage, passager; **I'm just a b. of passage,** je ne suis que de passage; **b. of prey,** oiseau de proie; rapace *m*; **b. of paradise,** (i) oiseau de paradis; paradisier *m*; (ii) *Bot:* strelitzia *f*; *F:* **he's a rare b.,** c'est un oiseau rare, un mouton à cinq pattes; **to eat like a b.,** avoir un appétit d'oiseau; manger comme une mauviette; *F: O:* **he accepted like a b.,** il accepta avec empressement; **to give s.o. the (big) b.,** (i) envoyer promener qn; (ii) *Th: etc:* huer, siffler, qn, conspuer (un orateur); *F:* chahuter qn; **to get the (big) b.,** (i) être renvoyé, mis à pied; (ii) *Th: etc:* être sifflé, *F:* ramasser une tape; *P:* boire un bouillon; *Prov:* **the early b. catches the worm,** à qui se lève matin Dieu aide et prête la main; heure du matin, heure du gain; *F:* **to be an early b.,** être (un) matinal; se lever de bon matin; *Prov:* **a b. in the hand is worth two in the bush,** un 'tiens' vaut mieux que deux 'tu l'auras'; mieux vaut tenir que courir; **it's an ill b. that fouls its own nest,** c'est un vilain oiseau que celui qui salit son nid; *F:* **to know all about the birds and the bees,** savoir que les enfants ne se font pas par l'oreille; *U.S: F:* **it's (strictly) for the birds,** c'est de la roupie de sansonnet; *attrib.* **b. shot,** cendrée *f*; **b. dog,** (i) chien *m* d'arrêt; (ii) *NAm: F:* dénicheur *m* (d'occasions, de curiosités, de vedettes, etc.); **b. house,** volière *f*; **b. trade,** oisellerie *f*; **b. fancying,** (i) aviculture *f*; (ii) oisellerie; **b. fancier,** (i) oiselier *m*; aviculteur *m*; marchand *m* d'oiseaux; (ii) connaisseur *m* en oiseaux; **b. (fancier's) shop,** oisellerie; **b. table,** mangeoire *f* pour les oiseaux (dans un jardin); *F:* **b. brain,** étourdi, -ie; homme, femme, qui a une cervelle de moineau; **b.-witted,** étourdi; écervelé; qui a une cervelle de moineau; *Arach:* **b.(-catching) spider,** mygale *f* aviculaire; *Av:* **b. strike,** impact *m* oiseau; *Bot:* **b. cherry,** cerisier *m* des oiseaux, des bois; merisier *m* à grappes; **b. pepper,** piment *m* bec d'oiseau, doux; *Ent:* **b. louse, b. mite,** pou *m*, -x, d'oiseau; *Vet:* **b. fever,** choléra *m* des poules; **b. pest,** peste *f* aviaire, des poules; *U.S: F:* **b. colonel,** colonel *m*; *Carp:* **bird's mouth,** grain *m* d'orge; (*b*) **(farmyard) b.,** volaille *f*; **I'll order a b. for dinner,** je vais commander une volaille pour le dîner; (*c*) *Ven:* **the birds are shy this year,** le gibier est timide cette année. **2.** (*a*) *F:* type *m*, individu *m*; **who's that old b.?** qu'est ce que c'est que ce vieux type là? **he's a queer b.,** c'est un drôle d'individu, un drôle de type; *O:* **he's a rum b.,** c'est un drôle de pierrot; **cunning old b.,** fin merle; **he's a knowing, downy, old b.,** il la connaît (dans les coins); **a home b.,** un casanier, une casanière; (*b*) *U.S: F:* personne *f*, chose *f*, animal *m*, remarquable, admirable, *F:* formidable. **3.** *P:* (*a*) femme (volage), poule *f*, nana *f*; (*b*) prostituée *f*; pépée *f*. **4.** (i) volant *m* (de jeu de badminton); (ii) *Sp:* pigeon artificiel. **5.** *Mil: F:* engin téléguidé. **6.** *NAm: F:* aviateur, -trice. **7.** *P:* prison *m*; **to do b.,** faire de la taule.

bird[2], *v.i.* **1.** chasser les oiseaux. **2.** *NAm:* observer les oiseaux.

birdbath [ˈbəːdbɑːθ], *s.* bain *m* (en ciment) pour les oiseaux.

birdcage [ˈbəːdkeidʒ], *s.* **1.** cage *f* (d'oiseau); (*if large*) volière *f*. **2.** *N.Z: Rac:* paddock *m*.

birdcall [ˈbəːdkɔːl], *s.* **1.** cri *m* d'oiseau. **2.** appeau *m*, pipeau *m*, chanterelle *f*.

birdcatcher [ˈbəːdkætʃər], *s.* oiseleur *m*.

birdcatching [ˈbəːdkætʃiŋ], *s.* piégeage *m* des oiseaux; oisellerie *f*.

birder [ˈbəːdər], *s.* **1.** oiseleur *m*. **2.** observateur, -trice, d'oiseaux.

birdie [ˈbəːdi], *s. F:* **1.** gentil petit oiseau. **2.** *Golf:* trou joué en un coup sous la normale; oiseau *m*.

birding [ˈbəːdiŋ], *s.* chasse *f* aux oiseaux.

birdlike [ˈbəːdlaik], *a.* avien.

birdlime [ˈbəːdlaim], *s.* glu *f*.

birdlore [ˈbəːdlɔər], *s.* ornithologie *f*.

birdman, *pl.* **-men** [ˈbəːdmən], *s.m. F:* **1.** ornithologiste. **2.** *A:* aviateur *m*.

bird organ [ˈbəːdɔːgən], *s.* serinette *f*.

birdseed [ˈbəːdsiːd], *s.* millet *m*; graines *fpl* pour oiseaux.

bird's(-)eye [ˈbəːdzai], *s.* **1.** (*a*) *Bot:* véronique *f*; **b.-e. primrose,** primevère farineuse; (*b*) (*in mahogany*) **bird's eyes,** tourbillons *m*; **b.-e. mahogany,** acajou moucheté; **b.-e. maple,** érable madré, à broussin; (*c*) tabac cordé et haché; (*d*) *Tex:* œil-de-perdrix *m*, *pl.* œils-de-perdrix. **2.** *attrib.* (*a*) **b.-e. view, perspective,** vue *f*, perspective *f*, à vol d'oiseau; perspective à vue d'oiseau; plan cavalier; *Cin:* prise *f* de vues en plongeon; (*photogrammetry*) photographie aérienne oblique; *Fig:* **b.-e. view of the situation,** résumé *m*, relevé *m*, de la situation; (*b*) *Const:* **b.-e. dormer,** lucarne *f* à la capucine.

bird's foot [ˈbəːdzfut], *s. Bot:* pied-d'oiseau *m*, *pl.* pieds-d'oiseau; **b.-f. trefoil,** lotier *m*, corne *f* du diable.

bird-ski [ˈbəːdskiː], *v.i. Sp:* faire du ski nautique plané.

bird-skiing [ˈbəːdskiːiŋ], *s. Sp:* ski nautique plané.

bird's nest [ˈbəːdznest], *s.* **1.** (*a*) nid *m* d'oiseau; (*b*) *Cu:* nid d'hirondelle. **2.** *Bot:* (*a*) faux chervis; (*b*) **b.-n. orchid,** nid d'oiseau; (*c*) **b.-n. fungus,** nidularia *f*. **3.** *Fish:* perruque *f*; **to make a b. n. in one's line,** perruquer sa ligne.

bird's-nest, *v.i.* dénicher des oiseaux; **to go bird's-nesting,** aller dénicher des oiseaux.

bird's nester [ˈbəːdznestər], *s.* dénicheur, -euse, de nids.

birdwatch [ˈbəːdwɔtʃ], *v.i.* observer les oiseaux.

birdwatcher [ˈbəːdwɔtʃər], *s.* observateur, -trice, d'oiseaux.

birdwatching [ˈbəːdwɔtʃiŋ], *s.* observation *f* des oiseaux (dans leur milieu naturel).

birefractive [bairiˈfræktiv], *a. Opt:* biréfringent.

birefringence [bairiˈfrin(d)ʒ(ə)ns], *s. Opt:* biréfringence *f*.

birefringent [bairiˈfrin(d)ʒ(ə)nt], *a. Opt:* biréfringent.

bireme [ˈbairiːm], *s. A.Nau:* birème *f*.

biretta [biˈretə], *s. Ecc.Cost:* barrette *f*.

birgus [ˈbəːgəs], *s. Crust:* birgue *m*; *F:* crabe *m* des cocotiers.

birkenia [bəˈkiːniə], *s. Paleont:* birkenia *m*.

Birmingham [ˈbəːmiŋəm], *Pr.n. Tchn:* **B. wire gauge,** jauge *f* Birmingham.

Biro [ˈbairou], *s. R.t.m:* (marque *f* de) stylo *m* (à) bille.

birth [bəːθ], *s.* **1.** (*a*) naissance *f*; **to give b. to a child,** donner naissance, donner le jour, à un enfant; mettre au jour, mettre au monde, un enfant; **to give b. to a poem,** enfanter, faire naître, un poème; **to give b. to new disputes,** donner naissance à de nouvelles disputes; **Irish by b.,** Irlandais de naissance; **of high b.,** de haute naissance; de haute condition; *A:* de haut lignage; **by right of b.,** par droit de naissance; **since my b.,** depuis que je suis au monde; **delicate from b.,** délicat dès, depuis, sa naissance; **b. certificate,** (i) acte *m*, (ii) extrait *m*, de naissance; **b. control,** régulation *f*, contrôle *m*, limitation *f*, des naissances; *F:* néo-malthusianisme *m*; **b. rate,** (taux *m* de) natalité *f*; **fall in the b. rate,** baisse *f* de la natalité; dénatalité *f*; **rise in the b. rate,** relèvement *m* du taux de natalité; (*b*) **the b. of an idea,** la genèse d'une idée; **to crush a revolt at b.,** écraser une révolte au nid; **the colony owed its b. to . . .,** la colonie devait son origine à . . ., tirait son origine de . . .; **the b. of a new industry,** la naissance d'une nouvelle industrie; (*c*) enfantement *m*, couches *fpl*, accouchement *m*; **premature b.,** accouchement prématuré, avant terme; **b. pangs,** douleurs *f* d'accouchement; *Fig:* **the b. pangs of (a new system of government),** l'accouchement difficile d'(un nouveau système de gouvernement); **three children at a b.,** trois enfants d'une même couche. **2.** mise *f* bas (d'un animal); **to give b. to a litter,** mettre bas une portée.

birthday [ˈbəːθdei], *s.* anniversaire *m* (de naissance); *F:* jour *m* de naissance; date *f* de naissance; **twenty-first b.,** vingt et unième anniversaire; **b. book,** agenda *m* d'anniversaires; **b. party,** réunion *f* d'anniversaire; **b. present,** cadeau *m* d'anniversaire; **B. Honours,** distinctions honorifiques accordées à l'occasion de l'anniversaire du Roi, de la Reine; *F:* **to be in one's b. suit,** être dans le, en, costume d'Adam.

birthmark [ˈbəːθmɑːk], *s.* envie *f*, tache *f* de naissance, nævus *m*, macule *f*.

birthplace [ˈbəːθpleis], *s.* (*a*) lieu *m* de naissance; (i) pays natal; (ii) maison natale; **Rousseau's b. is Geneva,** la patrie de Rousseau est Genève; (*b*) berceau *m* (d'une religion, etc.).

birthright [ˈbəːθrait], *s.* **1.** droit *m* d'aînesse. **2.** droit de naissance, droit du sang; patrimoine *m*.

birthroot [ˈbəːθruːt], *s. Bot:* trillium *m*.

birthstone [ˈbəːθstoun], *s. Astrol: etc:* pierre *f* bénéfique, *F:* de bonheur.

birthwort [ˈbəːθwəːt], *s. Bot:* aristoloche *f*.

bis [bis], *adv. Mus: etc:* bis.

bis-azo [bisˈæzou], *attrib. Ch:* **b.-a. dye,** (colorant *m*) diazoïque (*m*).

Biscay [ˈbiskei], *Pr.n. Geog:* (*a*) *A:* Biscaye *f* (en Espagne); (*b*) **the Bay of B.,** le golfe de Gascogne.

Biscayan [ˈbiskeiən]. **1.** *Geog:* (*a*) *a.* biscaïen; (*b*) *s.* Biscaïen, -ïenne. **2.** *s. Ling:* biscaïen *m*. **3.** *s. Sm.a: A:* **biscayan,** biscaïen.

biscuit [ˈbiskit], *s.* **1.** (*a*) biscuit *m*; **(sweet) biscuits,** gâteaux secs; **finger b.,** biscuit à la cuiller; (*wafer*) langue-de-chat *f*, *pl.* langues-de-chat; **ship's b., sea b.,** biscuits de mer; *F:* cassant *m*, biscotin *m*; *Mil:* **(service) b.,** pain *m* de guerre; biscuit de munition; **dog b.,** (i) biscuit, gâteau, de chien; (ii) pain de cretons; **b. factory,** biscuiterie *f*; **b. trade,** biscuiterie; *F:* **he takes the b.!** à lui le pompon! **that takes the b.!** ça, c'est le bouquet! (*b*) *NAm:* peut gâteau (feuilleté); (*c*) *a.* & *s.* (*colour*) biscuit *inv*, isabelle *inv*.; (*d*) *Mil: P:* galette *f* (de paillasse; trois pour chaque lit); (*e*) *Com: A:* pain circulaire de caoutchouc. **2.** *Cer:* **b. ware,** biscuit; **b.-baked porcelain,** porcelaine dégourdie; dégourdi *m*; **b. oven,** dégourdi.

biscuity [ˈbiskiti], *a.* (*a*) (*in colour*) biscuit *inv*; (*b*) (*crisp*) cassant.

bisect [baiˈsekt]. **1.** *v.tr.* (*a*) *Mth: etc:* couper, diviser, (une ligne, un angle) en deux parties égales; bissecter (un angle, etc.); (*b*) couper, diviser, en deux. **2.** *v.i.* (*of road, etc.*) bifurquer.

bisecting [baiˈsektiŋ], *a.* bissecteur, -trice.

bisection [baiˈsekʃ(ə)n], *s.* bissection *f*; division *f* en deux parties égales.

bisectional [baiˈsekʃ(ə)nəl], *a. Mth:* de bissection; bissecteur, -trice.

bisector [baiˈsektər], *s.* ligne *f* de bissection, bissectrice *f*.

bisectrix [baiˈsektriks], *s. Mth: Opt:* bissectrice *f*.

bisegment [baiˈsegmənt], *s. Mth:* segment *m* d'une bissection.

bisegmentation [baisegmənˈteiʃ(ə)n], *s.* bisegmentation *f*.

biserial [baiˈsiəriəl], **biseriate** [baiˈsiəriət], *a.* bisérié.

biserrate [baiˈsereit], *a. Bot:* doublement dentelé.

bisexual [ˈbaiˈseksjuəl], *a. Bot: Psy:* bis(s)exué, bis(s)exuel.

bisexualism [ˈbaiˈseksjuəlizm], **bisexuality** [ˈbaiseksjuˈæliti], *s. Bot: Psy:* bis(s)exualité *f*.

bishop[1] [ˈbiʃəp], *s.* **1.** *Ecc:* évêque *m*; **B. Stubbs,** l'évêque Stubbs; **bishop's palace,** palais épiscopal; évêché *m*. **2.** *Chess:* fou *m*. **3.** (*mulled wine*) bi(s)chof *m*. **4.** *Bot:* **bishop's cap,** mitelle *f*; **bishop's weed,** (i) égopode *m* des goutteux; petite angélique; (ii) visnage *m*, visnague *m*; (iii) menthe *f* aquatique, herbe *f* aux goutteux; **bishop's wort,** barbiche *f*. **5.** *Ent:* coccinelle *f*. **6.** *Orn:* **b. bird,** euplecte *m*; **red b. bird,** onyx *m*, grenadier *m*; **yellow b. bird,** tisserin *m* à dos jaune.

bishop[2], *v.tr. Farr:* contremarquer, maquignonner (un cheval); **to b. a horse's teeth, a horse,** buriner les dents d'un cheval.

bishoping [ˈbiʃəpiŋ], *s.* contremarque *f*; burinage *m* (d'un cheval).

bishopric [ˈbiʃəprik], *s.* évêché *m*.

bisk [bisk], *s. Cu:* **1.** (*a*) (*shellfish soup*) bisque *f* d'écrevisses; (*b*) (*chicken soup*) bisque à la reine. **2.** *NAm:* glace *f* (i) aux noix, (ii) aux macarons.

Bismarck [ˈbizmɑːk], *Pr.n.* Bismarck; *Ch:* **B. brown,** brun *m* Bismarck; vésuvine *f*; *Cu:* **B. herring,** hareng mariné.

bismite [ˈbizmait], *s. Miner:* bismite *f*.

bismuth [ˈbizməθ], *s. Miner:* bismuth *m*; **b. glance,** bismuthine *f*; **b. ochre,** bismite *f*, bismuthocre *m*; *Ch:* **b. oxychloride,** oxychlorure *m* de bismuth; **b. hydride,** bismuthine *f*; **b. subnitrate, basic b. nitrate,** sous-nitrate *m* de bismuth; oxynitrate *m*, nitrate *m*, de bismuthyle; *El:* **b. spiral,** sonde *f* bismuthique; *Med:* **b. poisoning,** bismuthisme *m*.

bismuthine [ˈbizməθiːn], *s. Miner:* **1.** bismuthine *f*. **2.** hydrure *m* de bismuth.

bismuthinite [ˈbizməθinait], *s. Miner:* bismuthine *f*.

bismuthite [ˈbizməθait], *s. Miner:* nitrate *m* de bismuth.

bismutite [ˈbizmətait], *s. Miner:* bismuthite *f*.

bison [ˈbaisn], *s.* bison *m* (de l'Amérique septentrionale); taureau *m* du Canada: taureau à bosse.

bisque[1] [bisk], *s. Ten:* bisque *f*; *Golf: Croquet:* coup *m* en sus (accordé à un joueur inférieur).

bisque[2], *s. Cer:* (*a*) biscuit *m*; (*b*) porcelaine blanche sans couverte; **b. oven,** dégourdi *m*.

bisque[3], *s.* = BISK.

bisse [bis], *s. Her:* bisse *f*.

bissextile [biˈsekstail], *a.* bissextile.

bistable [ˈbaiˈsteibl], *a. Elcs:* (circuit *m*, etc.) bistable.

bistort [ˈbistɔːt], *s. Bot:* bistorte *f*, *F:* liane *f* à serpents; **amphibious b.,** renouée *f* amphibie.

bistournage [bisˈtəːnidʒ], *s. Vet:* bistournage *m*.

bistoury [ˈbisturi], *s. Surg:* bistouri *m*, feuille-de-sauge *f*, *pl.* feuilles-de-sauge.

bistre [ˈbistər], *s.* & *a.* bistre (*m*).

bisulcate [baiˈsʌlkət], *a. Nat.Hist:* bisulce, bisulque.

bisulphate [baiˈsʌlfeit], *s. Ch:* bisulfate *m*.

bisulphite [baiˈsʌlfait], *s. Ch:* bisulfite *m*; **sodium b.,** sulfite *m* acide de sodium, de soude.

bit[1] [bit], *s.* **1.** *Harn:* mors *m* (d'une bride); **jointed b.,** mors à canon brisé; **oval b.,** escache *f*; **bridle b.,** mors de bride; **curb b.,** mors de bride, mors à gourmette; **Turkish b.,** genette *f*; **b. reins,** rênes *f* de bride; **b. ring,** anneau *m* porte-mors; **to champ the b.,** (i) (*of horse*) mâcher son mors; (ii) (*of pers.*) ronger son frein; **horse (that hangs) on the b.,** cheval *m* qui tire, qui appuie, sur le mors; (*of horse, pers.*) **to take the b. between its, one's, teeth,** prendre le mors aux dents; s'emballer. **2.** *Tls:* (*a*) mèche *f* (de vilebrequin); **square b.,** perçoir *m* à couronne; **shell b., gouge b., spoon b.,** mèche-cuiller *f*, *pl.* mèches-cuillers; foret *m* à cuiller; mèche à cuiller, à louche; **opening b., finishing b.,** alésoir *m*; **centre b.,** mèche anglaise, à trois pointes; foret centré, à centre, à téton; **expanding centre b.,** mèche à trois pointes universelle; **twist b.,** mèche hélicoïdale, américaine; amorçoir *m*; torse *f*; (*for plugging*) **wall b.,** tamponnoir *m*; **plough b.,** bec-d'âne *m*, *pl.* becs-d'âne (de rabot); **b. stock,** tourne-à-gauche *m inv.*, manche *m* de manœuvre; **b. holder,** porte-foret *m*, *pl.* porte-forets; **boring b.,** mèche de foret; *Civ.E:* fleuret *m*, trépan *m*; *Min:* trépan, taillant *m*; **b. gauge,** jauge *f* à trépan; **star b.,** trépan à tranchant en croix; (*b*) mors (d'une tenaille, d'un étau); (*c*) **copper b., soldering b.,** fer *m* à souder, soudoir *m*. **3.** panneton *m* (d'une clef).

bit[2], *v.tr.* **(bitted)** mettre le mors à (un cheval); emboucher, brider (un cheval).

bit[3], *s.* **1.** (*a*) morceau *m* (de pain, etc); *F:* casse-croûte *m*; *F:* **to have a b. of something,** manger un morceau; **after eating my b. of supper,** après avoir mangé mon maigre souper; **he has eaten every b.,** il a tout mangé, il n'en a pas laissé une miette; **a nice b. of architecture,** un beau morceau d'architecture; **a. b. of blood,** un cheval vif, fringant; *F:* **she's a nice little b.,** c'est une jolie fille; *P: A:* **she's a saucy b.,** c'est une effrontée, une délurée; elle n'a pas froid aux yeux; **made of bits and pieces,** *F:* **bits and bobs,** fait de pièces et de morceaux, *F:* de bric et de broc; *F:* **my bits and pieces,** mes affaires *f*; *attrib. Th:* **a b. part,** un rôle de figurant; (*b*) bout *m*, brin *m*; **b. of paper, of string,** bout de papier, de ficelle; **we have a b. of garden,** nous avons un bout de jardin; **we had a b. of dinner together,** nous avons pris un bout de repas ensemble; **b. of straw,** brin de paille; **a (little) b. of hope,** un peu, un petit brin, d'espoir; **a little b. of a fellow,** un (petit) bout d'homme; **to do one's b.,** y aller de sa personne, payer de sa personne, y mettre du sien; **I did my b.,** j'ai servi pendant la guerre; *F: O:* **Devil a b. I got!** moi je n'ai rien eu du tout! *F:* je me suis brossé; *F:* **to make a b.,** faire sa pelote; **to make a b. on the side,** faire de la gratte; **and a b. over,** et le pouce; (*c*) *F:* (*coin*) pièce *f*; *A:* **threepenny b.,** pièce de trois pence (de l'ancienne monnaie); *NAm:* **two bits,** vingt-cinq cents. **2.** (*a*) **a b. (of),** un peu (de); **a tiny, little, b.,** un tout petit peu; **if you loved me just a b.,** si tu m'aimais un tout petit peu, un tant soit peu; **I'm a b. late,** je suis un peu en retard; **he's a b. jealous,** il est quelque peu jaloux; **it's a b. after twelve,** il est midi passé; **he's a b. of an artist,** il est un peu artiste; **he's a b. of a miser, of a liar,** il est tant soit peu avare, tant soit peu menteur; *F:* **he's a b. of a lad,** il aime (i) faire la bombe, (ii) courir les jupes; **wait a b.!** attendez un peu! attendez un instant! attendez un moment! **I'd like to be quiet for a b., I'd like a b. of peace and quiet,** j'aimerais qu'on me laisse tranquille un petit moment; **that takes a b. of doing,** ça c'est bien compliqué; **a good b. older,** sensiblement plus âgé; *F:* **it's a b. much!** ça c'est vraiment trop fort! **b. by b.,** peu à peu, petit à petit; brin à brin; de fil en aiguille; **I heard the story b. by b.,** j'ai appris cette histoire par fragments; **to collect information b. by b.,** amasser des renseignements par bribes et morceaux; **not a b. (of it)!** pas du tout! pas le moins du monde! n'en croyez rien! **I'm not a b. the wiser,** je n'en suis pas plus avancé; **I don't care a b.,** cela m'est bien égal; **it's not a b. of use,** cela ne sert absolument à rien; (*b*) (= PIECE) **a b. of news,** une nouvelle; **a b. of advice,** un conseil; **a b. of luck,** une chance; une aubaine; (*c*) **to tear sth. to bits,** déchirer qch. en morceaux; **smashed to bits,** brisé (en mille morceaux); réduit en miettes; **in bits,** en morceaux; *F:* **after the accident he was picked up in bits,** après l'accident on l'a ramassé en pièces détachées, à la petite cuillère; **to come, fall, to bits,** tomber en morceaux; s'écrouler; *F:* **to go to bits,** s'effondrer; **in the second half our team went all to bits,** dans la deuxième mi-temps notre équipe s'est effondrée, a perdu toute cohésion, était entièrement à bout de souffle, *F:* était dégonflée.

bit[4], *s. Cmptr:* bit *m,* chiffre *m* binaire; **check b.,** bit de contrôle; **sign b.,** bit de signe; **information b.,** bit d'information; **overhead b.,** bit supplémentaire; **parity b.,** bit de parité; **service b.,** bit de service; **zone b.,** bit (d'information) complémentaire; **erroneous b.,** bit erroné; **stop b.,** élément *m* d'arrêt; **b. density,** densité *f* en bits; **b. location,** emplacement *m* (de stockage) d'un bit; **b. position,** emplacement de chiffre; **b. pattern,** profil *m* binaire; **b. rate,** débit *m* binaire, vitesse *f* de transmission de bits; **b. string,** chaîne *f* (d'éléments) binaire(s).

bitangent[1] ['bai'tændʒ(ə)nt], *s. Mth:* droite bitangente; plan bitangent.

bitangent[2], **bitangential** [baitæn'dʒenʃl], *a. Mth:* bitangent (**to,** à).

bitartrate [bai'tɑ:treit], *s. Ch:* bitartrate *m.*

bitch[1] [bitʃ], *s.f.* **1.** (*a*) chienne; **terrier b.,** terrier *m* femelle; (*b*) femelle (de renard, etc.); **wolf b., b. wolf,** louve. **2.** *P:* garce; (vieille) chipie; **she's a little b.,** c'est une petite rosse.

bitch[2]. *P:* **1.** *v.tr.* gâcher, saboter, bousiller (un travail); **he bitched up the whole business for us,** il nous a tout gâché, bousillé. **2.** *v.i.* ronchonner, râler, rouspéter.

bitchy ['bitʃi], *a. P:* garce; vache; **she's in a b. mood,** elle est d'une humeur de chien; **that was a b. thing to do!** quel tour de vache! **she's the bitchiest woman I know,** comme garce elle n'a pas d'égale.

bite[1] [bait], *s.* **1.** (*a*) coup *m* de dent; *Dent:* articulé *m* dentaire; **to eat sth. up at one b.,** manger qch. d'un coup de dent; ne faire qu'une bouchée de qch.; (*b*) *Fish:* touche *f;* **I haven't had a b. all day,** je n'ai pas eu une seule touche de toute la journée; *F:* **got a b.?** ça mord? (*c*) *esp. U.S:* **to put the b. on s.o.,** toucher qn (pour 100 dollars, etc.). **2.** (*a*) (*wound*) morsure *f;* (*b*) piqûre *f,* morsure (d'un insecte). **3.** *F:* (*mouthful*) bouchée *f,* morceau *m;* **would you like a b.?** voulez-vous manger quelque chose, manger un morceau? **to have another b. at sth.,** remordre à qch.; **I haven't had a b. all day,** je n'ai rien mangé de la journée; **I haven't had a b. since . . .,** je n'ai rien eu à me mettre sous la dent depuis . . .; **take a b.,** mangez-en une bouchée; **to take a big b. out of sth.,** mordre dans qch. à pleine bouche; *A:* **without b. or sup,** sans boire ni manger. **4.** (*a*) *Tchn:* mordant *m* (de lime, etc.); **file with plenty of b.,** lime bien mordante; **screw with a good b.,** vis *f* qui mord (bien); *Fig:* **his style has no b.,** son style n'a pas de mordant; (*b*) piquant *m* (d'une sauce, d'un vin); (*c*) adhérence *f* (des roues à la surface, etc.); (*d*) *Engr:* corrosion *f* (d'une plaque par l'acide). **5.** *Typ:* larron *m.*

bite[2], *v.*

I. *v.tr.* (*p.t.* **bit;** *p.p.* **bitten,** *A:* **bit**) **1.** (*a*) mordre; donner un coup de dent à (qn, qch.); (*of insect*) piquer; **to b. again,** remordre (qn, qch.); **the dog bit him in the leg,** le chien le mordit à la jambe; **to b. one's lips, one's nails,** se mordre les lèvres, se ronger les ongles; **to b. through a rope, to b. a rope through,** couper une corde avec les dents; **to b. the dust,** mordre la poussière; **the fish is biting,** le poisson mord (à l'hameçon); *F:* **although I've offered him it cheap he still won't b.,** j'ai beau le lui offrir bon marché, il ne s'y intéresse pas, ne mord pas; **does the dog b.?** le chien est-il méchant? *Prov:* **once bitten twice shy,** chat échaudé craint l'eau froide; **to get bitten,** (i) se faire mordre; se faire piquer; (ii) *F:* se faire attraper; *F:* **what's bitten him?** quel chien l'a mordu? quelle mouche le pique? **once the bug bites you have to go on collecting,** une fois mordu vous continuez à collectionner; **to be bitten with a desire to do sth.,** avoir un vif désir de faire qch.; brûler de faire qch.; **he's got badly bitten over an actress,** il s'est entiché d'une actrice; **I've been badly bitten,** on m'a mis dedans; **there is plenty to b. on,** il y a de quoi mordre; (*b*) *F: Austr:* **to b. s.o.,** toucher qn (pour 10 dollars, etc.). **2.** (*a*) **the wind bites the face,** le vent coupe le visage; **frost bites the leaves,** la gelée brûle les feuilles; **acid bites (into) metal,** l'acide mord, attaque, le métal; **pepper bites the tongue,** le poivre pique la langue; (*b*) *v.i.* (*of screw, file*) mordre (**on,** sur); (*of tool*) mordre, s'engager; (*of anchor*) mordre, prendre fond, crocher, être en prise; **screw that won't b.,** vis *f* qui foire; **the wheels don't b. (on the road),** les roues n'adhèrent pas.

II. (*compound verbs*) **1. bite back,** *v.tr.* **to b. b. an answer,** ravaler une réplique; se mordre les lèvres pour ne pas répondre.

2. bite off, *v.tr.* enlever, détacher, (qch.) avec les dents, d'un coup de dent(s); *F:* **to b. s.o.'s head off,** rembarrer qn; faire, faire essuyer, une algarade à qn; **to b. off more than one can chew,** (i) détacher un trop gros morceau (de tabac à chiquer); (ii) *F:* entreprendre une trop forte tâche; tenter qch. au-dessus de ses forces.

bitemporal ['bai'tempərl], *a. Anat:* bitemporal, -aux.

biter ['baitər], *s.* (*a*) animal *m* qui mord; (*b*) *Fig:* **the b. bit,** le trompeur trompé; **it's a case of the b. bit,** tel est pris qui croyait prendre.

biternate ['bai'tə:neit], *a. Bot:* biterné.

Bithynia [bi'θiniə], *Pr.n. Geog:* Bithynie *f.*

biting ['baitiŋ], *a.* **1.** mordant; (*of cold*) cuisant, âpre, perçant; (*of wind*) cinglant, piquant; (*of style, wit, epigram*) mordant, caustique, satirique; **b. irony,** ironie amère; **b. words,** mots *m* à l'emporte-pièce. **2.** (cheval, etc.) mordeur.

bitingly ['baitiŋli], *adv.* d'un ton mordant; âprement; âcrement.

bitingness ['baitiŋnis], *s.* âpreté *f* (du froid, du vent, d'une critique).

Bitis ['baitis], *s. Rept:* bitis *m.*

bitonal ['bai'tounl], *a. Mus:* bitonal, -als.

bitsy ['bitsi], *a. F:* minuscule (et charmant).

bitt[1] [bit], *s. usu. pl. Nau:* bitte *f* (de tournage, d'amarrage); **small b.,** bitton *m;* **towing bitts,** bittes de remorque; **cruciform bitts,** bittes en croix; **gallows bitts,** potence *f* de drome; **pawl b.,** saucier *m* (de cabestan, de treuil); **b. pin,** paille *f* de bitte.

bitt[2], *v.tr. Nau:* bitter (un câble).

Bittacidae [bi'tæsidi:], *s.pl. Ent:* bittacidés *m.*

bitter ['bitər]. **1.** *a.* (*a*) (goût) amer; (vin *m*) acerbe; (vent) aigre, piquant; (ennemi) implacable; (conflit) aigu; (temps) rigoureux; (ton *m*) aigre, âpre; **b. cold, wind,** froid, vent, glacial, cinglant; **b. beer,** bière piquante, amère, fortement houblonnée; **b. as gall, as wormwood, as aloes,** amer comme chicotin; **b. enemies,** ennemis *m* à mort; **b. reproach,** reproche amer; **b. hatred,** haine acharnée; **b. tears,** larmes amères; **b. disappointment,** cruelle déception; **b. remorse,** remords cuisants; **b. experience,** amère déception; expérience cruelle; **to be a b. opponent of a project,** critiquer un projet avec âpreté; **at five in the morning it's b. driving,** à cinq heures du matin on a rudement froid en voiture; *Nau:* **the b. end,** l'étalingure *f* du puits; *Fig:* **to the b. end,** à outrance; **to go on, to resist, to the b. end,** aller, résister, jusqu'au bout; (*b*) *Bot:* **b. apple, cucumber, gourd,** coloquinte *f;* **b. wood,** quassier *m* de la Jamaïque. **2.** *s.* (*a*) = **bitter beer;** (*b*) *pl.* **bitters,** (i) bitter(s) *m,* amer(s) *m;* (ii) (*with sg. const.*) *O:* **to have a bitters,** prendre un amer; prendre l'apéritif; (*c*) *Lit:* **we must take the b. with the sweet,** il n'y a pas de rose sans épines.

bitterling ['bitəliŋ], *s. Ich:* bouvière *f,* péteuse *f,* rosière *f.*

bitterly ['bitəli], *adv.* amèrement, avec amertume, avec aigreur; **it was b. cold,** il faisait un froid de loup; **b. disappointed,** cruellement déçu; **to feel sth. b.,** ressentir beaucoup d'amertume de qch.

bittern[1] ['bitə(:)n], *s. Orn:* butor *m;* (*Botaurus stellaris*) butor étoilé, grand butor; **American b.,** butor d'Amérique, *Fr.C:* butor américain; **little b.,** butor blongios, blongios *m* nain; **least b.,** *Fr.C:* petit butor.

bittern[2], *s.* (*in salt industry*) eau *f* mère.

bitterness ['bitənis], *s.* **1.** (*a*) amertume *f* (d'une boisson, etc.); (*b*) rigueur *f,* âpreté *f* (du temps); amertume (de la douleur); aigreur *f,* acrimonie *f* (de paroles, d'une querelle); **the b. of his reproaches,** l'âpreté de ses reproches; **memories without b.,** souvenirs *m* sans amertume. **2.** rancune *f,* rancœur *f;* **to act without b.,** agir sans rancœur.

bitter(-)sweet ['bitəswi:t]. **1.** *a.* aigre-doux, -douce; *s. Lit:* **the bitter-sweets of daily life,** les douceurs mêlées d'amertume de la vie quotidienne. **2.** *s. Bot:* (*in one word*) (*a*) douce-amère *f, pl.* douces-amères; morelle grimpante, vigne *f* de Judée; *F:* loque *f;* (*b*) **climbing b.,** célastre grimpant; bourreau *m* des bois.

bittiness ['bitinis], *s. F:* style décousu (d'un livre, etc.).

bittock ['bitək], *s. Scot:* (un) petit peu; (un) bout; **and a b.,** et le pouce; **it's a mile and a b.,** c'est un peu plus d'un mille.

bitty ['biti], *a. F:* (livre, etc.) d'un style décousu; **badly dressed woman, terribly b.,** femme habillée de vêtements disparates.

Bitumastic [bitju'mæstik], *s. Tchn: R.t.m:* Bitumastic *m.*

bitumen ['bitjumin], *s.* (*a*) *Ch: Miner:* bitume *m;* goudron minéral; asphalte minéral; *Miner:* **elastic b.,** élatérite *f;* caoutchouc minéral; **compact b.,** spalt *m;* (*b*) *Austr: F:* route goudronnée; (*drink*) **one for the b.!** encore un coup avant de partir!

bituminiferous [bitjumi'nifərəs], *a. Miner:* bituminifère.

bituminization [bitjuminai'zeiʃ(ə)n], *s.* **1.** *Civ.E:* bitumage *m;* asphaltage *m.* **2.** *Geol: etc:* bituminisation *f.*

bituminize [bi'tju:minaiz], *v.tr.* bituminer, bitumer, bituminiser.

bituminous [bi'tju:minəs], *a.* bitumineux; **b. coal,** houille grasse, collante.

biunivocal ['baijuni'voukl], *a. Mth:* biunivoque.

biuret ['baijuret], *s. Ch:* biuret *m; Med:* **b. reaction,** réaction *f* du biuret.

bivalence ['bai'veiləns], **bivalency** ['bai'veilənsi], *s. Ch:* bivalence *f.*

bivalent ['bai'veilənt], *a. Ch:* bivalent, divalent; *Biol:* **b. chromosome,** *s.* **bivalent,** bivalent *m.*

bivalve ['baivælv], *a. & s. Moll:* bivalve (*m*).

bivalved ['baivælvd], **bivalvular** [bai'vælvjulər], *a.* bivalvulaire; bivalve.

bivium ['biviəm], *s. Echin:* bivium *m.*

bivoltin(e) [bai'vɔltin, -tain], *a. Ent:* bivoltin.

bivouac[1] ['bivuæk], *s. Mil: etc:* bivouac *m.*

bivouac[2], *v.i.* (**bivouacked; bivouacking**) bivouaquer.

bivvy ['bivi], *s.* (= BIVOUAC) *F:* endroit *m* pour dormir; baraque *f,* abri *m,* campement *m;* tente individuelle.

bi-weekly ['bai'wi:kli]. **1.** (*a*) *a.* de tous les quinze jours; (*b*) *adv.* tous les quinze jours. **2.** (*a*) *a.* semi-hebdomadaire; (*b*) *adv.* deux fois par semaine.

Bixaceae [biks'eisii:], *s.pl. Bot:* bixacées *f.*

bixbyite ['biksbiait], *s. Miner:* bixbyite *f.*

biz [biz], *s.* (= BUSINESS) (*a*) *P: O:* **good b.!** à la bonne heure! chouette, papa! (*b*) *F:* **show b.,** le monde des spectacles, du théâtre.

bizarre [bi'zɑ:r], *a.* bizarre.

bizarrely [bi'zɑ:li], *adv.* bizarrement.

bizarreness [bi'zɑ:nis], **bizarrerie** [bi'zɑ:rəri], *s.* bizarrerie *f.*

Bizerta [bi'zə:tə], *Pr.n. Geog:* Bizerte *f.*

bizonal ['bai'zounl], *a.* bizonal, -aux.

bizone ['bai'zoun], *s.* bizone *f.*

blaa(-blaa) ['blɑ:(blɑ:)], *s.* = BLAH(-BLAH).

blaasop ['blɑ:sɔp], *Ich: S. Africa:* tétrodon *m.*

blab[1] [blæb], **blabber** ['blæbər], *esp. U.S:* **blabbermouth** ['blæbəmauθ], *s. F:* jaseur, -euse; indiscret, -ète; bavard, -e; causeur, -euse.

blab[2], *v.* (**blabbed; blabbing**) *F:* **1.** *v.i.* jaser, bavarder; causer (indiscrètement); *F:* vendre la mèche. **2.** *v.tr.* **to b. out a secret,** divulguer, laisser échapper, un secret.

blabbing ['blæbiŋ], *s. F:* jaserie *f,* indiscrétion *f.*

black[1] [blæk], *a. & s.*

I. *a.* **1.** noir; (*a*) **b. dress,** robe noire; **b. hair,** cheveux noirs; *Lit:* **hair as b. as a raven's wing,** cheveux (d'un) noir de corbeau; (**jet-**)**b. horse, mare,** cheval moreau, jument morelle; **b. spot,** (i) (*on furniture, etc.*) noircissure *f;* (ii) *Aut: etc:* point noir; endroit *m* à accidents; **b. hole,** (i) cachot *m;* (ii) *Mil: F:* les cellules *f; Hist:* **the B. Hole of Calcutta,** le Cachot de Calcutta, de Fort William; *Hist:* **the B. Death,** la Peste Noire; *Jur:* **the B. cap,** le bonnet noir (que coiffe le juge en prononçant une condamnation à mort); **b. book,** (i) *Sch: A:* livre *m* des punitions; (ii) *Nau:* cahier *m,* registre *m,* des punitions; **to be in s.o.'s b. books,** être mal vu de qn; *Meteor:* **b. ice,** verglas *m; Can:* **b. blizzard,** tourbillon *m* de poussière; *Metalw:* **b. work,** grosse serrurerie non meulée; *Petr:* **b. oil,** produit noir; *Typ:* **b. letter,** caractères *m* gothiques; *Geog:* **the B. Sea,** la Mer noire; **the B. Forest,** la Forêt noire; *Cu:* **b. pudding,** boudin *m;* **b. velvet,** mélange *m* de champagne et de stout; (*in balloting*) **b. ball,** noire *f;* **b. with age,** noirci par le temps; **picture b. with age,** tableau qui tire au noir; **it, the night, was pitch b., as b. as pitch, as the grave, as hell,** il faisait noir comme dans un four; **b. as sin, as a crow, as ebony,** noir comme une taupe, comme un corbeau; d'un noir d'ébène; **b. as night,** noir comme poix; **to be b. in the face,** avoir le visage tout congestionné; **to be b. in the face with rage,** être violet, pourpre, de fureur; **to look as b. as thunder,** avoir l'air furieux; **to give s.o. a b. look,** regarder qn d'un air furieux, regarder qn de travers; **things are looking b.,** les affaires prennent une mauvaise tournure; **to paint things blacker than they are,** noircir la situation, *F:* le tableau; **to beat s.o. b. and blue,** meurtrir, rosser, qn de coups; battre qn tout bleu; **to be b. and blue all over,** être tout meurtri (de coups), être tout noir de coups; être couvert de bleus; **b. eye,** œil poché, *F:* pruneau *m,* œil au beurre noir; (*b*) **the b. races,** les races noires; **a b. man, woman,** un noir, une noire; **b. servant,** domestique noir(e); *U.S:* **the b. belt,** la région habitée principalement par les noirs; **b. bottom,** (genre *m* de) danse *f* nègre; (*c*) **his hands were b.,** il avait les mains sales, les mains toutes noires; *Geog:* **the B. Country,** le Pays Noir (de l'Angleterre). **2.** (*a*) **b. despair,** sombre désespoir *m;* **he's in one of his b. moods,** il est dans ses mauvais jours; (*b*) **a b. deed, a deed of the blackest dye,** une vilenie; un crime odieux; un crime de la dernière noirceur; **the b. art,** la magie noire; **b. mass,** messe noire; (*c*) **b. humour,** humour *m* macabre.

II. *s.* noir *m.* **1. ivory b.,** noir d'ivoire, noir de velours; **bone b., animal b.,** noir animal; **lamp b.,** noir de fumée, de lampe; **carbon b.,** noir de fumée, de pétrole; **Brunswick b.,** laque *f* à l'asphalte; vernis *m* à l'asphalte; *Art:* **Frankfort b.,** noir d'Allemagne. **2.** (*a*) **she always wears b.,** elle porte toujours le noir; elle est toujours en noir; (*b*) *F:* **in the b.,** solvable; sans dettes; (*c*) **to work in b. and white,** faire du dessin à l'encre, au crayon noir; **b.-and-white artist,** dessinateur *m* à l'encre; **b.-and-white postcard,** carte *f* en noir; **to set sth. down in b. and white,** coucher qch. par écrit; **I have his consent in b. and white,** j'ai son consentement par écrit; **I should like to have it in b. and white,** je voudrais avoir cela dans les formes; je voudrais que cela se fasse par-devant notaire; **he would make you believe that b. was white,** il vous ferait croire à quelque chose contre toute évidence; il vous ferait prendre des vessies pour des lanternes; **to swear that b. is white,** (i) se refuser à l'évidence; (ii) mentir effrontément; se parjurer. **3.** (*a*) (*pers.*) noir, -e; (*b*) cheval noir; (*c*) *Ind: etc:* renard *m,* jaune *m.* **4.** (*smut*) (*a*) noiré *m,* flocon *m* de suie; (*b*) *Agr:* charbon *m,* suie *f,* brûlure *f,* nielle *f* (des céréales). **5.** *F:* **he put up a b.,** il a fait une gaffe.

black[2], *v.*

I. 1. *v.tr.* noircir (qch.); **to b. one's face,** se charbonner le visage; *O:* **to b. boots,** cirer des bottes; **to b. s.o.'s eye,** pocher l'œil à qn; donner à qn un œil au beurre noir. **2.** *v.tr. Ind: etc:* refuser de travailler avec (une compagnie, un homme non syndiqué); **to b. a ship, a firm,** mettre un navire, une entreprise, à l'index. **3.** *v.i. Nau:* **to b. down,** galipoter.

II. (*compound verb*) **black out. 1.** *v.i.* (*a*) devenir obscur; s'estomper; s'éteindre; (*b*) occulter, voiler, masquer, les lumières; faire le black-out; *Th:* éteindre la rampe, couper la lumière; *Cin:* fermer en fondu; (*c*) (i) perdre connaissance, s'évanouir, tomber en syncope; (ii) avoir un trou de mémoire. **2.** *v.tr.* (*a*) effacer, rayer (qch.) (d'un gros trait noir); **these considerations must not b.o. the essential problem,** ces considérations ne doivent pas nous faire oublier le problème essentiel; (*b*) (i) éteindre, (ii) voiler, masquer, les lumières dans (une maison, etc.); faire le black-out dans (une maison); **the stage became blacked out,** la scène disparaissait dans l'obscurité; (*c*) supprimer (des nouvelles, etc.); *Pol:* fermer (un pays) à l'influence extérieure; *W.Tel: T.V:* décrocher (une station de transmission); interdire la retransmission d'(une émission).

blackamoor ['blækəmɔər], *s. O: Pej:* noir, -e; nègre, négresse.

black and tan ['blækənd'tæn]. **1.** *a. & s.* (chien) noir et feu *inv.* **2.** *s.pl. Hist:* **the B. and Tans,** la police militarisée (employée en Irlande en 1921).

black arm ['blæk'ɑ:m], *s. Bot:* black arm *m* (du cotonnier).

black-avised ['blækə'vaizd], *a. Scot: Pej:* noiraud; (mine *f*) patibulaire; (homme *m*) de mauvaise mine.

blackball ['blækbɔ:l], *v.tr.* blackbouler (qn).

blackballing ['blækbɔ:liŋ], *s.* blackboulage *m.*

black bass ['blæk'bæs], *s. Ich:* black-bass *m inv;* **large-mouthed b.b.,** perche-truite *f, pl.* perches-truites; **small-mouthed b.b.,** perche noire.

blackbeetle ['blækbi:tl], *s. Ent: F:* (*a*) blatte *f,* cafard *m,* cancrelat *m;* (*b*) escarbot *m.*

blackberry ['blækb(ə)ri], *s.* mûre *f* (de ronce); mûre sauvage; mûron *m;* **b. bush,** ronce *f,* mûrier *m,* des haies.

blackberrying ['blækberiiŋ], *s.* **to go b.,** aller cueillir des mûres; aller à la cueillette des mûres.

blackbird ['blækbə:d], *s.* **1.** *Orn:* (*a*) merle (noir); **young b.,** merleau *m;* (*b*) *NAm:* (variété d')étourneau *m;* **Brewer's b.,** *Fr.C:* mainate *m* à tête pourprée; **rusty b.,** *Fr.C:* mainate rouilleux; **yellow-headed b.,** *Fr.C:* carouge *m* à tête jaune; **red-winged b.,** carouge à épaulettes rouges, *Fr.C:* carouge à épaulettes. **2.** *A:* nègre (transporté sur un bâtiment négrier).

blackbirder ['blækbə:dər], *s. A:* **1.** marchand *m* d'esclaves; négrier *m.* **2.** bâtiment négrier.

blackbirding ['blækbə:diŋ], *s. A:* traite *f* des noirs.

blackboard ['blækbɔ:d], *s.* tableau noir.

blackbody ['blækbɔdi], *s. Atom.Ph:* corps noir.

black-bordered ['blæk'bɔ:dəd], *a.* à bordure noire; atromargine; **b.-b. notepaper,** papier *m* deuil.

blackbuck ['blækbʌk], *s. Z:* antilope *f* cervicapre, cervicapre *m.*

blackcap ['blækkæp], *s. Orn:* fauvette *f* à tête noire.

black-coated ['blæk'koutid], *a.* vêtu de noir; à jaquette noire, à veston noir; **b.-c. worker,** employé *m* de bureau.

blackcock ['blækkɔk], *s. Orn:* tétras *m* lyre; petit coq de bruyère; coq des bouleaux.

blackcurrant ['blæk'kʌrənt], *s.* cassis *m.*

blacken ['blæk(ə)n]. **1.** *v.tr.* noircir (un mur, la réputation de qn); obscurcir (le ciel); (*with smoke*) enfumer (du papier, du verre); **to b. s.o.'s character,** raconter des vilenies sur le compte de qn; calomnier qn; **his failings have been blackened into vices,** on a travesti ses défauts en vices. **2.** *v.i.* (se) noircir; devenir noir; s'assombrir; (*of painting, portrait*) **to b. with age,** pousser, tirer, au noir.

blackening ['blæk(ə)niŋ], *s.* noircissement *m.*

blackface ['blækfeis], *s.* **1.** mouton *m* à la figure noire. **2.** *Typ:* caractère(s) gras. **3.** *F:* comédien déguisé en nègre.

black-faced ['blækfeist], *a.* **1.** à la figure noire. **2.** *Typ:* (caractère) gras.

blackfellow ['blækfelə], *s. Austr:* aborigène *m* (d'Australie).

blackfish ['blækfiʃ], *s. Ich:* **Alaskan b.,** poisson noir de l'Alaska.

blackfly ['blækflai], *s. Ent: F:* mouche noire.

blackguard[1] ['blægɑ:d], *s.* sale individu *m;* ignoble personnage *m;* canaille *f,* gouape *f,* vaurien *m.*

blackguard[2], *v.tr.* lancer des injures à (qn); apostropher (qn d'injures); agonir (qn) d'injures.

blackguardism ['blægɑ:dizm], *s.* canaillerie *f.*

blackguardly ['blægɑ:dli], *a.* sale, ignoble, canaille; **a b. trick,** un sale coup.

blackhead ['blækhed], *s.* **1.** comédon *m;* tanne *f;* point noir (sur le visage). **2.** *Vet:* crise *f* du rouge, entéro-hépatite *f,* tête noire.

blackheart ['blækhɑ:t], *a. & s.* **b. (cherry),** guigne noire.

blacking ['blækiŋ], *s.* **1.** *O:* cirage *m* (de chaussures); **b. brush,** brosse *f* à cirer. **2.** (*a*) *Nau:* galipot *m;* (*b*) *O:* cirage (à chaussures).

blackish ['blækiʃ], *a.* noirâtre, tirant sur le noir.

blackjack ['blækdʒæk], *s.* **1.** *Min:* spalérite *f,* blende *f.* **2.** *U.S:* nerf *m* de bœuf. **3.** outre *f* en cuir vernie de noir.

blacklead[1] ['blæk'led]. **1.** *s.* mine *f* de plomb; plombagine *f,* graphite *m.* **2.** *a.* (crayon *m*) de mine de plomb.

blacklead[2], *v.tr.* passer (un poêle, etc.) à la mine de plomb.

blackleg[1] ['blækleg], *s.* **1.** *Turf: A:* escroc *m.* **2.** *Ind: F:* renard *m;* jaune *m;* faux frère, traître *mf.*

blackleg[2] (**blacklegged; blacklegging**) *Ind:* (*a*) *v.tr.* prendre la place (des grévistes, etc.); (*b*) *v.i.* trahir ses camarades.

blacklist[1] ['blæklist], *s.* liste noire, liste des suspects; **to be on the b.,** être noté, suspect.

blacklist[2], *v.tr.* inscrire, mettre (qn, une entreprise, etc.) sur la liste noire, la liste des suspects.

blackmail[1] ['blækmeil], *s.* **1.** argent extorqué par chantage. **2.** chantage *m;* extorsion *f* (sous menace de scandale).

blackmail[2], (*a*) *v.tr.* soumettre (qn) à un chantage; *F:* faire chanter (qn); **to be blackmailed,** être victime d'un chantage; (*b*) *v.i.* faire du chantage.

blackmailer ['blækmeilər], *s.* maître-chanteur *m, pl.* maîtres-chanteurs.

blackmailing ['blækmeiliŋ], *s.* chantage *m.*

black market ['blæk'mɑ:kit], *s.* marché noir.

black marketeer ['blæk'mɑ:ki'tiər], *s.* profiteur *m* du marché noir.

blackneb ['blækneb], *s. Ich:* (jeune) truite saumonée.

blackness ['blæknis], *s.* **1.** noirceur *f.* **2.** obscurité *f* (de la nuit).

blackout ['blækaut], *s.* **1.** (*a*) occultation *f;* black-out *m;* (i) extinction *f;* (ii) camouflage *m,* des lumières; (*b*) panne *f* d'électricité; (*c*) *Cin:* fermeture *f* en fondu. **2.** (*a*) *W.Tel: T.V:* décrochage *m* (d'une émission); (*b*) suppression *f* (des nouvelles, etc.). **3.** *Physiol: F:* voile noir; **to have a b.,** (i) tomber faible; (ii) tomber en syncope.

Black Rod ['blæk'rɔd], *s.* (**gentleman Usher of the**) **B. R.,** Huissier de la Verge noire (attaché au Lord Chambellan, à la Chambre des Lords, au chapitre de l'Ordre de la Jarretière, au Sénat canadien).

black rot ['blæk'rɔt], *s. Vit:* black-rot *m.*

Blackshirt ['blækʃə:t], *s. Pol:* fasciste *m;* chemise noire.

blacksmith ['blæksmiθ], *s.* forgeron *m;* maréchal ferrant; **blacksmith's shop,** atelier *m* de maréchalerie; forge (maréchale); **b. welding,** soudage *m* à la forge.

blacksmithery ['blæksmiðəri], *s. U.S:* grosse serrurerie.

blackthorn ['blækθɔ:n], *s.* **1.** *Bot:* épine noire, prunier épineux, prunellier *m.* **2.** gourdin *m* (d'épine).

black-veined ['blækveind], *a.* à veines noires; *Ent:* **b.-v. white** (**butterfly**), gazé *m,* piéride gazée.

blackwash ['blækwɔʃ], *s. Metalw:* enduit *m* de noir.

blackwater ['blækwɔ:tər], *a. Med:* **b. fever,** hématurie *f.*

black widow ['blæk'widou], *s. Arach:* latrodecte *m,* latrodectus *m.*

blackwood ['blækwud], *s. Bot:* trac *m.*

blad [blæd], *s. Publ:* maquette *f.*

bladder ['blædər], *s.* (*a*) *Anat:* vessie *f;* *Cu:* **b. lard,** saindoux *m* en vessie; saindoux de première qualité; *P:* **b. of lard,** caillou déplumé; homme *m* chauve comme un genou; (*b*) *Anat: Bot:* vésicule *f;* **gall b.,** vésicule biliaire; **air b.,** (i) *Ich:* vésicule aérienne; vessie *f* natatoire; (ii) *Algae:* vésicule, aérocyste *f;* (*c*) outre remplie d'air; vessie (de ballon).

bladder herb ['blædəhə:b], *s. Bot:* coquerelle *f,* coqueret *m.*

bladdernut ['blædənʌt], **bladder senna** ['blædə'senə], *s. Bot:* **1.** (*tree*) baguenaudier *m.* **2.** baguenaude *f.*

bladder worm ['blædəwə:m], *s. Z:* ver *m* cystique; cysticerque *m;* *Vet:* **many-headed b. w.,** cénure *m.*

bladderwort ['blædəwə:t], *s. Bot:* utriculaire *f.*

bladder wrack ['blædəræk], *s. Algae:* raisin *m* de mer.

blade [bleid], *s.* **1.** brin *m* (d'herbe); pampe *f* (de blé); *Bot:* limbe *m;* **corn in the b.,** blé *m* en herbe. **2.** (*a*) lame *f* (de couteau, d'épée, *Bot:* de feuille); couperet *m* (de la guillotine); feuille *f,* lame (d'une scie); **razor b.,** lame de rasoir; (*b*) sabre *m* ou épée *f;* *F: A:* **he's a (young, regular, jolly) b.,** c'est un gaillard, un luron. **3.** pelle *f,* plat *m,* pale *f,* palette *f* (d'aviron); aile *f,* pale, branche *f* (d'hélice) ailette *f* (de ventilateur, de souffleur); ailette aube *f* (de turbine); fer *m* (de bêche); pélastre *m* (d'une pelle); *Nau: Hyd.E:* aube, ailette (d'une roue); *Rail:* aiguille *f* (de croisement); *Artil:* **b. portion (of trail-spade),** soc *m* (d'une bêche de crosse); *Aut:* balai *m* (d'un essuie-glace); **twin blades,** double balai; *Cin:* **blades of a shutter,** pales, secteurs *m,* d'un obturateur; **notched-b. shutter,** obturateur à pales échancrées; *Nau: Av: etc:* **adjustable b.,** pale réglable; **feathering b.,** pale mobile, orientable; **b. face,** intrados *m,* face *f* avant, de la pale; **b. back,** extrados *m,* face arrière, de la pale, dos *m* de pale; **b. shank,** pied *m,* corps *m,* de la pale; **b. beam,** bras *m* de la pale; **b. angle,** angle *m* de pale; **b. curvature,** courbure *f* de la pale; **b. root,** emplanture *f* de la pale; *Nau:* **rudder b.,** safran *m* de gouvernail; **b. wheel,** roue *f* à palettes. **4. shoulder b.,** omoplate *f;* **b. of the tongue,** plat *m* de la langue; *Ling:* **b.-point consonant,** consonne prépalatale.

bladebone ['bleidboun], *s.* **1.** *Anat:* omoplate *f.* **2.** *Cu:* paleron *m;* macreuse *f.*

bladed ['bleidid], *a.* à lame(s), à aile(s), à pales, à ailettes; **three-b. propeller,** hélice *f* à trois ailes; *Nau:* **four-b. screw,** hélice à quatre pales.

bladeless ['bleidlis], *a.* sans lame.

blader ['bleidər], *s.* **1.** instrument *m,* machine *f,* à pales, à aubes. **2.** ajusteur *m* de pales, d'aubes.

bladesmith ['bleidsmiθ], *s.* fabricant *m* de lames, de pales, d'aubes.

blading ['bleidiŋ], *s. Mch:* aubage *m,* ailetage *m.*

blaeberry ['bleibəri], *s. Bot: esp. Scot:* airelle *f* myrtille.

blah [blɑ:], *a. U.S: F:* insipide, fade.

blah(-blah) ['blɑ:(blɑ:)], *s. F:* bêtises *fpl,* bla-bla-bla *m,* baratin *m;* **it's all b. (-b.),** tout ça c'est de la blague.

blain [blein], *s.* pustule *f.*

blakeite ['bleikait], *s. Miner:* blakéite *f.*

blamable ['bleiməbl], *a.* = BLAMEWORTHY.

blame[1] [bleim], *s.* **1.** reproches *mpl;* condamnation *f;* **to deserve b.,** mériter des reproches; **to be free from b.,** être inattaquable, au-dessus de tout reproche. **2.** responsabilité *f;* faute *f;* **the b. is mine, lies with me,** la faute en est à moi; **the b. is partly mine,** c'est un peu de ma faute; je suis en partie responsable; **to lay, put, the b. (for sth.) on s.o., to lay the b. (for sth.) at s.o.'s door,** rejeter, faire retomber, le blâme, la faute, (de qch.) sur qn; en rejeter la faute sur qn; incriminer qn; s'en prendre à qn; imputer qch. à blâme à qn; donner tort à qn;

to bear the b., supporter le blâme; endosser la faute; **to shift the b. on to s.o. else,** s'excuser sur qn; se décharger d'une faute sur qn; **it is always I who get the b.,** c'est toujours moi qu'on incrimine; *F:* c'est toujours moi qui paye les pots cassés.

blame², *v.tr.* **1.** blâmer, condamner (qn); **to b. s.o. for sth.,** blâmer qn de qch.; imputer qch. à blâme à qn; reprocher qch. à qn; s'en prendre à qn de qch.; attribuer (un malheur, etc.) à qn; **to b. s.o. for doing sth.,** blâmer qn d'avoir fait qch.; reprocher à qn de faire, d'avoir fait, qch.; **to b. s.o. for a misfortune,** mettre un malheur sur le compte de qn; rendre qn responsable d'un malheur; **he cannot be blamed for it,** on ne peut pas l'en blâmer; **they b. each other,** ils s'en prennent l'un à l'autre; **she blamed herself for having been a dull companion,** elle s'en voulait, s'accusait, de s'être montrée une compagne peu intéressante; **I have nothing to b. myself for,** je n'ai rien à me reprocher; **I am not blaming you,** ce n'est pas à vous que j'en ai; **to have only oneself to b., to have nobody to b. but oneself,** n'avoir à s'en prendre qu'à soi-même; **you have only yourself to b.!** vous l'avez voulu! **he is to b.,** il y a de sa faute; **I am in no way to b.,** il n'y a pas de faute de ma part; on ne peut rien me reprocher; je n'ai rien à me reprocher; **to be much to b.,** avoir de grands torts; **he is entirely to b.,** il a tous les torts. **2.** *(a)* **to b. sth. for an accident, etc.,** attribuer un accident, etc., à qch.; *(b)* **to b. sth. on s.o.,** imputer (la faute de) qch. à qn; rejeter la faute, la responsabilité, de qch. sur qn.

blame(d) ['bleim(d)], *F: O:* **1.** *a.* sacré, maudit; **b. liar,** sacré menteur; **this b. weather,** ce temps de tous les diables. **2.** *adv.* **b. dangerous,** rudement dangereux; **I'll do what I b. well like,** je ferai absolument ce que je veux.

blameful ['bleimful], *a.* = BLAMEWORTHY.

blameless ['bleimlis], *a.* innocent, irréprochable, irrépréhensible, sans tache; **I am b. (in this matter),** je n'ai rien à me reprocher; **after leading a b. life for two years,** après avoir vécu sans reproche pendant deux ans.

blamelessly ['bleimlisli], *adv.* irréprochablement; sans mériter de reproches.

blamelessness ['bleimlisnis], *s.* innocence *f,* irréprochabilité *f.*

blameworthiness ['bleimwəːðinis], *s.* le fait d'être digne de blâme, de reproches; **blame I can bear, though not b.,** je peux supporter le blâme pourvu que je n'aie rien à me reprocher.

blameworthy ['bleimwəːði], *a.* **1.** blâmable, digne de blâme, de reproches. **2.** *(of conduct)* condamnable, répréhensible.

blanc de chine ['blɑ̃dəʃiːn], *s. Cer:* blanc *m* de Chine.

blanch [blɑːn(t)ʃ]. **1.** *v.tr. (a)* blanchir (des légumes, un métal); **to b. almonds,** monder, dérober, des amandes; *(b) Poet. (of illness, etc.)* pâlir, rendre pâle (qn, le teint de qn); blanchir (les cheveux); *(of fear, etc.)* blêmir (le visage). **2.** *v.i. (a) (of hair, etc.)* blanchir; *(b) (of pers.)* blêmir, pâlir.

blancmange [blə'mɔnʒ], *s. Cu:* = blanc-manger *m, pl.* blancs-mangers.

bland [blænd], *a.* **1.** *(of pers., speech) (a)* doux, *f* douce; aimable; affable; caressant; débonnaire; *Iron:* doucereux, mielleux; *(b)* (sourire) narquois. **2.** *(of air, food, drink)* doux, suave.

blandish ['blændiʃ], *v.tr.* cajoler, caresser, flatter.

blandishments ['blændiʃmənts], *s.pl.* **1.** cajoleries *fpl,* câlineries *fpl,* flatterie *f.* **2.** *A:* attrait *m,* charme *m* (du passé, etc.).

blandly ['blændli], *adv.* *(a)* avec affabilité; *Iron:* mielleusement; **to answer b.,** répondre sans se fâcher; *(b)* d'un air un peu narquois.

blandness ['blændnis], *s.* **1.** *(a)* douceur *f,* suavité *f,* affabilité *f;* *(b)* affabilité un peu narquoise. **2.** douceur (du climat, etc.).

blank¹ [blæŋk], *a. & s.*

I. *a.* **1.** *(a)* **b. paper,** papier blanc; **b. page,** page vierge, blanche; **b. voting paper,** bulletin blanc; **to return a b. voting paper,** voter blanc; *(b) Com: Fin:* **b. credit,** crédit *m* en blanc; lettre *f* de crédit dont le montant n'est pas spécifié; **b. cheque,** (i) formule *f* de chèque; (ii) chèque *m* en blanc; (iii) *Fig:* carte blanche; **the government cannot ask for a b. cheque,** le gouvernement ne peut pas demander qu'on lui accorde carte blanche; **to sign a b. document,** signer un document en blanc; **b. acceptance,** acceptation *f* en blanc; *(c)* **b. space,** espace *m* vide; espace en blanc; **b. wall,** mur nu; **to be, come, up against a b. wall,** se trouver devant l'impossible; se trouver coincé; **b. map,** carte muette; *(d)* **b. verse,** vers blancs, non rimés; *(e)* **b. door, window,** fausse porte, fenêtre; porte, fenêtre, feinte, aveugle; *Tchn:* **b. flange,** obturateur *m;* **to fire b. cartridge,** tirer à blanc; *I.C.E:* **b. jet,** gicleur non alésé; *(f) Cards:* **to be b. in clubs,** ne pas avoir de trèfles dans son jeu; *(g) P:* **it's your b. dog that did it,** c'est votre sacré chien qui l'a fait. **2.** *(a)* **b. existence,** existence *f* vide; **b. look,** regard *m* sans expression; **he gave me a b. look,** il m'a regardé d'un air incompréhensif; **b. future,** avenir *m* vide et morne; avenir sans espoir; *(b)* **to look b.,** avoir l'air confondu, déconcerté, ahuri; rester bouche bée; être tout décontenancé; **a look of b. astonishment,** un air ébahi, confondu; *(c)* **b. despair,** profond découragement; **b. impossibility,** impossibilité absolue; **b. refusal,** refus absolu; **b. stupidity,** stupidité *f* sans bornes; crasse, grosse, pure, stupidité.

II. *s.* **1.** *(a) (in document, etc.)* blanc *m,* vide *m;* *(in one's memory)* trou *m,* lacune *f,* vide; *Com: Jur:* **paper signed in b.,** blanc-seing *m, pl.* blancs-seings; **cheque signed in b.,** chèque signé en blanc; **to draw in b.,** tirer une lettre de change en laissant en blanc le nom du bénéficiaire; **to leave blanks,** laisser des blancs; **his death leaves a b.,** sa mort laisse un vide; **his mind is a b.,** (i) sa mémoire est une table rase; (ii) il a, se sent, la tête vide; **the next ten years are a b.,** on ne sait rien des dix années suivantes; **to fill in the blanks in one's education,** combler les lacunes de son éducation; *Cards:* **to have a b. in clubs,** ne pas avoir de trèfles dans son jeu; *(b) NAm:* formulaire *m,* formule *f;* **telegraph b.,** formule de télégramme; imprimé *m* à télégramme; **to fill out a b.,** remplir, compléter, une formule, une feuille, un imprimé; *(c)* **to fire blanks,** tirer à blanc; *(d)* blanc (de cible); *(e) (domino)* blanc; **double b.,** double blanc; *(f) (in lottery)* billet blanc, billet perdant; **to draw a b.,** (i) tirer un numéro blanc; (ii) échouer; éprouver une déception. **2.** *(a) (in minting coins)* flan *m* (de métal); *(b) Metalw: Mec.E:* flan; masselotte *f;* galette *f;* **milling-cutter b.,** flan de fraise; **wheel b.,** galette de roue; **nut b., cam b.,** écrou brut, came brute; **file b.,** semelle *f.* **3.** *(a) Typ:* tiret *m* (remplaçant un mot malsonnant, etc.); *(b) Typ:* blocage *m;* *(c)* **Mr, Mrs, B.,** M., Mme, Trois-Etoiles, M. X, Mme X.

blank², *NAm:* **1.** *v.tr.* *(a)* **to b. (out),** cacher; obscurcir; *(b)* **to b. (off),** obturer (un orifice, un tuyau); **blanked-off T junction,** raccord *m* en T obturé; *(c) Metalw:* **to b. (out),** couper (un dessin dans une feuille de métal, etc.); *(d) Tchn:* polir à blanc; *(e) Typ:* **to b. (out),** faire le blocage; *(f) Sp:* battre (une équipe, etc.) à plates coutures. **2.** *v.i.* **to b. (out),** (i) *(of sound)* s'éteindre; (ii) avoir un trou de mémoire.

blanket¹ ['blæŋkit], *s.* **1.** *(a)* couverture *f* (de lit, de cheval), **electric b.,** couverture chauffante (électrique); **to toss s.o. in a b.,** berner qn, faire sauter qn (à la couverture); **b. of fog, of smoke,** manteau *m* de brouillard, de fumée; **hills under a b. of snow,** collines molletonnées de neige; *Needlew:* **b. stitch,** point *m* de languette; *F: (pers.)* **wet b.,** rabat-joie *m inv,* *(b)* couverture, pagne *m* (d'indigène); *U.S:* **b. Indian,** Indien, -ienne (d'Amérique) qui vit selon les traditions de sa tribu. **2.** *Typ:* **(press) b.,** blanchet *m;* **offset b.,** décharge *f.* **3.** *attrib. Com: etc:* général, applicable à tous les cas; **b. order,** ordre *m* d'une portée générale; **b. mortgage,** hypothèque générale; *Rail: etc:* **b. rate,** tarif *m* applicable à un groupe, à une grande quantité de marchandises.

blanket², *v.tr.* **1.** *(a)* mettre une couverture à (qch.); fournir (un lit) de couvertures; **the mountain was blanketed in fog,** la montagne était couverte d'un manteau de brouillard; *(b) A:* étouffer (un scandale); *(c)* **to b. (out) (a fire, flames),** étouffer (un incendie, des flammes); *(d) W.Tel: T.V:* empêcher la réception d'(une émission). **2.** *F: A:* berner, faire sauter (qn) (à la couverture). **3.** *(a) Nau: esp. Y.* déventer, abriter (un navire, un yacht); manger le vent à (un autre navire); *(b) Navy:* se mettre en travers du feu de (ses propres navires); gêner le tir de (ses propres navires). **4.** appliquer à tous les cas; **additional millions will be blanketed into the pension scheme,** des millions d'autres personnes seront inclus dans le système des retraites.

blanketed ['blæŋkitid], *a.* **1.** *Nau:* sous-venté. **2.** *Navy:* gêné dans son tir (par un autre navire). **3. streets b. with snow,** des rues feutrées de neige.

blanketflower ['blæŋkitflauər], *s. Bot:* gaillarde *f.*

blanketing ['blæŋkitiŋ], *s.* **1.** *coll.* couvertures *fpl.* **2.** *Tex: Com:* lainages *mpl* pour couvertures. **3.** *F: A:* berne *f,* bernement *m* (à la couverture); passage *m* à la couverture. **4.** *Av:* **b. effect,** effet *m* de masque.

blanket weed ['blæŋkitwiːd], *s. Algae:* conferve *f.*

blankety-blank ['blæŋkiti'blæŋk], *a. & s. P:* **you b.-b. fool!** sacré idiot! **and then the b.-b. told me . . .,** et puis le saligaud m'a dit . . . **what the b.-b. d'you think you're doing here?** que diable fais-tu ici?

blankly ['blæŋkli], *adv.* **1. to look b. at s.o.,** regarder qn (i) d'un air confondu, déconcerté, (ii) sans expression, d'un air incompréhensif. **2. to deny sth. b.,** nier qch. absolument, carrément; **to refuse b.,** refuser (tout) net, sans ambages.

blankness ['blæŋknis], *s.* **1.** air confus, décontenancé. **2.** vide *m,* néant *m* (de la pensée, d'une période historique, etc.); vacuité *f* (d'un regard).

blanquette [blɑ̃(n)'ket], *s. Cu:* blanquette *f* (de veau).

blare¹ ['blɛər], *s.* **1.** sonnerie *f,* son *m,* accents cuivrés (de la trompette); **the b. of the brass band,** le son éclatant de la fanfare; les accents retentissants, cuivrés, de la fanfare. **2.** *NAm: (of colour, light)* éclat *m.*

blare². **1.** *v.i. (of trumpet)* sonner; *Mus:* cuivrer le son; **the band blared (out, forth),** la fanfare éclata; **the radio was blaring away,** la radio marchait à fond, à casser les oreilles. **2.** *v.tr.* **the band blared (out) a march,** la fanfare fit retentir une marche; **to b. (out) the news,** proclamer, annoncer, la nouvelle à son de trompe.

blarina [blə'rainə], *s. Z:* **b. (shrew),** blarine *f.*

Blarney¹ ['blɑːni]. **1.** *Pr.n.* **B. Castle,** le château de Blarney (en Irlande); **the B. Stone,** pierre située en contre-bas (et difficile à atteindre) dans la muraille du château; *F:* **to have kissed the B. Stone,** avoir le don de la flatterie, de la cajolerie. **2.** *s. (no cap)* cajolerie *f,* boniments *mpl,* flatterie séduisante.

blarney², *v.tr.* cajoler (qn); séduire (qn) par des propos flatteurs.

blasé ['blɑːzei], *a.* blasé.

blaspheme [blæs'fiːm]. **1.** *v.i.* blasphémer; proférer des blasphèmes. **2.** *v.tr.* **to b. the name of God,** blasphémer le saint nom de Dieu.

blasphemer [blæs'fiːmər], *s.* blasphémateur, -trice.

blasphemous ['blæsfəməs], *a.* *(of pers.)* blasphémateur, -trice; *(of words, etc.)* blasphématoire, impie.

blasphemously ['blæsfəməsli], *adv.* avec blasphème; avec impiété; **to speak b.,** blasphémer; outrager Dieu.

blasphemy ['blæsfəmi], *s.* blasphème *m;* **to utter blasphemies against God,** tenir des propos blasphématoires; outrager Dieu.

blast¹ [blɑːst], *s.* **1.** *(a)* bouffée *f* de vent, coup *m* de vent; rafale *f* (de vent); **b. of steam,** jet *m* de vapeur; *(b)* souffle *m* (du vent). **2.** *Nau: etc:* **b. on the whistle, on the siren,** coup *m* de sifflet, de sirène; *Mil:* **whistle b.,** commandement *m* au sifflet; **b. on the trumpet,** sonnerie *f* de trompette; *Nau:* **to sound a b.,** faire entendre un coup de sifflet, de sirène; **prolonged b.,** son prolongé; **short b.,** son bref; *Aut:* **b. on the horn,** coup d'avertisseur. **3.** *(a) Metall:* air *m,* vent *m* (de la soufflerie); soufflerie *f,* soufflage *m* (d'un haut fourneau); **cold blast,** air froid; vent froid; **hot b.,** air chaud; **hot-b. stove,** récupérateur *m;* **cold-b., hot-b., valve,** valve *f* à vent froid, à vent chaud; **to apply the b.,** faire agir la soufflerie; *(of furnace)* **to be in b.,** être allumé, en marche; **furnace out of b.,** fourneau *m* hors feu; **to be in full b.,** être en pleine activité, travailler à plein rendement; *F:* **to turn, have, the radio on full b.,** faire gueuler, brailler, la radio; *(b) Ind:* **b. engine,** (machine) soufflante *(f),* soufflerie *f;* *Metall:* **b. main,** porte-vent *m inv,* arrivée *f* d'air chaud; **b. plate,** plaque *f* contrevent; **b. pipe,** canalisation *f* de vent; *Metall:* tuyère *f,* buse *f,* porte-vent; *Av:* tuyère (d'un moteur à réaction). **4.** *(a)* souffle (d'une bombe (atomique), etc.); **b. effects,** effets *mpl* de souffle; *Artil:* **muzzle b., breech b.,** souffle de bouche, de culasse; **(anti)b. wall, parapet, bank,** mur *m,* parapet *m,* pare-souffle; *(b) Min:* (i) explosion *f,* coup de mine; (ii) charge *f* d'explosif; **to fire a b.,** faire jouer une mine, faire partir un pétard; **b. hole,** (i) *Min:* pétard, trou *m* de mine; (ii) *Mil:* fourneau de mine. **5.** *(a) A:* coup, influence *f,* néfaste; *(b) Vet:* météorisation *f,* météorisme *m,* ballonnement *m,* empansement *m.*

blast², *v.*

I. *v.tr. & i.* **1.** *v.tr.* *(a) Min:* faire sauter (à la dynamite, etc.); pétarder (des roches); ouvrir (la roche) à coups de mine; tirer (la pierre) à la poudre; *Golf: F:* **to b. the ball** *(from a bunker),* faire sauter la balle d'un coup violent; *(b)* brûler, flétrir (une plante); ruiner, briser (l'avenir de qn); détruire, anéantir (des espérances); détruire (le bonheur); flétrir, ruiner (une réputation); *(c) (of lightning)* foudroyer (un arbre, etc.); *(d) F:* envoyer (qn) au diable; *int.* **b. (it, you, etc.)!** zut! **2.** *v.i.* *(a) (of brass instrument)* sonner; *(b) (of radio, etc.)* **to b. (away),** hurler, brailler.

II. *(compound verb)* **blast off,** *v.i. (of rocket, missile)* décoller; **to make ready to b.o.,** effectuer les opérations préalables au décollage.

blasted ['blɑːstid]. **1.** *a.* **b. hopes,** espérances anéanties; **b. heath,** lande désolée; **b. oak,** chêne foudroyé. **2.** *a. F:* sacré; **you b. idiot!** espèce d'idiot! **3.** *adv. P: (intensive)* **I'm b. well hungry,** j'ai rudement, bigrement, faim; **I b. well will (do it),** je vais le faire, et tu n'as rien à dire là-dessus!

blastema [blæs'tiːmə], *s. Biol:* blastème *m.*

blastemal [blæs'tiːm(ə)l], **blastematic** [blæsti'mætik], *a. Biol:* blastématique.

blast furnace ['blɑ:st'fə:nis], *s. Metall:* haut fourneau.

blasting ['blɑ:stiŋ], *s.* **1.** (*a*) travail *m* aux explosifs; exploitation *f* à la mine; tirage *m* de la pierre à la poudre, abattage *m* à la poudre; tir *m*, tirage; sautage *m*; **beware of b.!** attention aux coups de mine! **b. agent,** explosif *m*; **b. powder,** poudre *f* de mine, de démolition; **b. cartridge,** cartouche *f* de mine; **b. cap,** amorce *f*, capsule *f*, détonateur *m*; **b. machine,** exploseur *m*; (*b*) destruction *f*, anéantissement *m* (d'un espoir, etc.); ruine *f* (d'une carrière); (*c*) foudroiement *m* (d'un arbre). **2.** *F:* braillement *m* (d'une radio, etc.).

blasto- ['blæstou, blæs'tɔ], *pref. Biol:* blasto-.

blastocarpous ['blæstou'kɑ:pəs], *a. Bot:* blastocarpe.

blastocoele ['blæstousi:l], *s. Biol:* blastocoele *m*.

blastocolla [blæstou'kɔlə], *s. Bot:* blastocolle *f*.

blastoderm ['blæstoudə:m], *s. Biol:* blastoderme *m*.

blastodermic ['blæstou'də:mik], *a. Biol:* blastodermique.

blastodisc ['blæstoudisk], *s. Biol:* blastodisque *m*.

blast-off ['blɑ:stɔf], *s.* décollage *m*, mise *f* à feu (d'une fusée, etc.).

blastogenesis ['blæstou'dʒenisis], *s.* blastogénèse *f*.

blastoid ['blæstɔid], *s. Paleont:* blastoïde *m*.

Blastoidea [blæs'tɔidiə], *s.pl. Paleont:* blastoïdes *m*.

blastomere ['blæstoumiər], *s. Biol:* blastomère *m*.

Blastomycetes ['blæstoumai'si:ti:z], *s.pl. Fung:* blastomycètes *m*.

blastomycosis ['blæstoumai'kousis], *s. Med:* blastomycose *f*.

blastophaga [blæs'tɔfədʒə], *s. Ent:* blastophage *m*.

blastophthoria ['blæstou'fθɔ:riə], *s. Biol:* blastophtorie *f*.

blastopore ['blæstoupɔ:r], *s. Biol:* blastopore *m*.

blastosphere ['blæstousfiər], *s. Biol:* blastosphère *m*.

blastospore ['blæstouspɔ:r], *s. Bot:* blastospore *f*.

blastozoite ['blæstou'zouait], **blastozooid** ['blæstou'zouɔid], *s. Biol:* blastozoïde *m*.

blastula ['blæstjulə], **blastule** ['blæstjul], *s. Biol:* blastula *f*, blastule *f*.

blastus ['blæstəs], *s. Bot:* blaste *m*.

blat[1] [blæt], *s. NAm:* (*a*) bêlement *m*; (*b*) *F:* jacassement *m*.

blat[2], *NAm:* **1.** *v.i.* (*a*) bêler; (*b*) *F:* jacasser, jaser. **2.** *v.tr. F:* laisser échapper (un secret, une remarque).

blatancy ['bleitənsi], *s.* vulgarité criarde.

blatant ['bleit(ə)nt], *a.* **1.** (*of pers., manners*) qui s'impose désagréablement à l'oreille, à la vue; d'une vulgarité criarde; braillard. **2.** (injustice) criante; (mensonge) flagrant; **b. lack of interest,** (i) désintéressement flagrant; (ii) manque absolu, total, d'intérêt.

blatantly ['bleit(ə)ntli], *adv.* **1.** avec une vulgarité criarde. **2. motorists who b. ignore the rules of the road,** des automobilistes qui désobéissent d'une manière flagrante le code de la route.

blather[1] ['blæðər], *s. F:* paroles *fpl* en l'air, bêtises *fpl*.

blather[2], *v.i. F:* parler à tort et à travers; dire des bêtises.

blatherskite ['blæðəskait], *s. NAm: F:* grand parleur (qui parle pour ne rien dire); orateur verbeux.

Blattaria [blæ'teəriə], *s.pl. Ent:* blattaires *m*.

blatter[1] ['blætər], *s. Dial:* **1.** jacasserie *f*, bavardage *m*. **2.** crépitement *m*, grésillement *m* (de la grêle, etc.).

blatter[2], *v.i. Dial:* **1.** jacasser, bavarder. **2.** (*of hail, etc.*) crépiter, grésiller.

Blattidae ['blætidi:], *s.pl. Ent:* blattidés *m*, blattides *m*.

blatting ['blætiŋ], *s. NAm:* (*a*) bêlement *m*; (*b*) *F:* jacassement *m*.

Blattopteroidea [blætɔptə'rɔidiə], *s.pl. Ent:* blattoptéroïdes *m*.

blaubok ['blaubɔk], *s. Z:* céphalophe bleu.

blaze[1] [bleiz], *s.* **1.** (*a*) flamme(s) *f*, feu *m*, conflagration *f*, flambée *f*; **in a b.,** en feu, en flammes; **to set sth. in a b.,** enflammer, embraser, qch.; **the whole of Europe was in a b.,** toute l'Europe était en feu; **to burst (out) into a b.,** se mettre à flamber; s'enflammer; **to stir the fire into a b.,** faire flamber le feu; tisonner le feu pour le faire flamber; **in the b. of day,** en plein midi; (*b*) **b. of anger,** éclat *m* de colère; **in a b. of anger,** enflammé de colère; dans une explosion de colère. **2.** flamboiement *m* (du soleil); éclat (des couleurs, des diamants, etc.); **in the full b. of her beauty,** dans tout l'éclat de sa beauté; **in the full b. of publicity,** sous les feux de la rampe; **to end in a b. of glory,** finir, terminer, en beauté. **3.** *pl. F:* (= HELL) (*a*) **go to blazes!** allez au diable! va t'asseoir! va te faire fiche! **to send s.o. to blazes,** envoyer promener qn; *P:* envoyer qn au bain; **it's so much money gone to blazes,** c'est de l'argent flambé, fichu; (*b*) (*intensive*) **what the blazes . . .,** que diable (me veut-il, etc.); **how the blazes can you stand him?** comment diable peux-tu le supporter? **to work like blazes,** travailler furieusement; **to run like blazes,** courir à toute vitesse; brûler le terrain; courir comme un dératé.

blaze[2], *v.*

I. *v.i.* (*a*) (*of fire, etc.*) flamber; (*of sun, colours*) flamboyer; (*of jewels, metals*) étinceler; **the fire was blazing (away) in the grate,** un feu flambait (vigoureusement) au foyer; **when the firemen arrived the fire was blazing (away),** lorsque les pompiers sont arrivés l'incendie faisait rage; **the sun was blazing down on the beach,** le soleil dardait, déversait, ses rayons sur la plage; **the sun blazed out from behind the clouds,** le soleil a apparu tout à coup parmi les nuages; **uniform blazing with gold lace,** uniforme resplendissant de galons d'or; (*b*) (*of pers.*) **to b. with anger,** être enflammé de colère; être furieux; **his eyes were blazing with anger,** ses yeux lançaient des flammes de colère.

II. (*compound verbs*) **1. blaze away,** *v.i.* (*a*) **to b. a. at the enemy,** maintenir un feu nourri, roulant, contre l'ennemi; **to b. a. at the pheasants,** tirer sans désemparer sur les faisans; (*b*) *F: A:* **to b. a. at sth.,** travailler ferme, sans relâche, à qch.; **b. a.!** je t'écoute; vas-y!

2. blaze off, *v.tr. Metall:* recuire (l'acier) par le flambage; faire flamber (la graisse).

3. blaze out, *v.i.* éclater en reproches, en injures; **to b.o. at s.o.,** s'en prendre violemment à qn.

4. blaze up, *v.i.* (*a*) (*of thg*) s'embraser, s'enflammer; (*b*) (*of pers.*) s'emporter, *F:* monter comme une soupe au lait; **to b. up at a proposal,** s'insurger contre une proposition.

blaze[3], *s.* **1.** (*on face of horse, ox*) étoile *f*, pelote *f*, marque *f*, blanche. **2.** (*on tree*) **blaze (mark),** blanchis *m*, griffe *f*, miroir *m*, martelage *m*, encoche *f*, flache *f*.

blaze[4], *v.tr.* griffer, blanchir, marquer, marteler (un arbre); **to b. a trail,** tracer un chemin, frayer le chemin, faire œuvre de pionnier; poser des jalons (dans une science, etc.); ouvrir les voies (au progrès, etc.); (*through forest*) layer une forêt; **they have blazed the trail for their successors,** ils ont jalonné la route à ceux qui suivront.

blaze[5], *v.tr.* **to b. a rumour abroad,** répandre un bruit partout; **it isn't the sort of thing to be blazed abroad,** ce n'est pas une chose à crier sur les toits.

blazer ['bleizər], *s.* **1.** *Cost:* blazer *m*; veston *m* de sport en flanelle (aux couleurs d'une école ou d'un club). **2.** *F: A:* mensonge *m* énorme. **3.** *U.S: F: O:* grosse indiscrétion; gaffe *f*.

blaze-up ['bleizʌp], *s. F:* prise *f* de bec, altercation *f*; **you'll go on until you can't bear it any longer, and then there will be a b.-up,** ça continuera jusqu'au moment où vous ne pourrez plus y tenir et alors ça éclatera.

blazing[1] ['bleiziŋ], *a.* **1.** (*a*) en feu, enflammé; (navire) embrasé; (*b*) (feu, soleil) flambant, ardent; (*c*) *Ven:* **b. scent,** fumet tout récent; piste toute fraîche. **2.** (*a*) *F: A:* **to commit a b. indiscretion,** commettre une indiscrétion formidable, effroyable, insigne; **b. lie,** mensonge éclatant, insigne; (*b*) *F: O:* (*intensive*) **what's the b. hurry?** est-ce que ça presse tant que ça? **he had the b. cheek to tell me that . . .,** il a eu le toupet infernal de me dire que . . .; *Her:* **b. star,** comète *f*; *Bot:* **b. star,** alétris *m*; **blue b. star,** liatris *m*.

blazing[2], *s.* martelage *m*, griffage *m* (des arbres).

blazon[1] [bleizn], *s.* **1.** *Her:* (*a*) blason *m* (composant un écu); (*b*) armoiries *fpl*; (*c*) étendard armorié. **2.** *A:* proclamation *f*, divulgation *f* (de qch.).

blazon[2], *v.tr.* **1.** *Her:* blasonner; marquer (qch.) aux armoiries de qn. **2.** embellir, orner (de dessins héraldiques). **3.** célébrer, exalter (les vertus de qn). **4.** to **b. forth, out, sth.,** publier, proclamer, qch.; **to b. forth vices,** afficher des vices; **to b. news abroad,** publier une nouvelle à son de trompe; trompeter une nouvelle.

blazoner ['bleizənər], *s. Her:* blasonneur *m*.

blazonry ['bleiz(ə)nri], *s. Her:* **1.** blasonnement *m*. **2.** blason *m*, science *f* héraldique. **3.** *Lit:* ornementation *f* magnifique.

bleach[1] [bli:tʃ], *s.* **1.** (*a*) = BLEACHING; (*b*) décoloration *f*, blancheur *f*; (*c*) *Hairdr:* *F:* oxygénée *f*. **2.** agent *m* de blanchiment, de décoloration; décolorant *m*; chlorure décolorant; lessive *f*; blanc *m* de lessive.

bleach[2], *v.tr. & i.* blanchir; *Ch: etc:* (se) décolorer; *Tex:* débouillir; *Hairdr:* oxygéner; *Tex:* **to b. linen,** blanchir la toile; **half-bleached,** demi-blanc, -blanche; mis-bis; **bones bleaching on the battlefield,** ossements *m* qui blanchissent sur le champ de bataille; *Phot:* **to b. out the image,** blanchir l'image.

bleacher ['bli:tʃər], *s. Tex:* blanchisseur, -euse, buandier, -ière.

bleachers ['bli:tʃəz], *s.pl. Sp: NAm:* places découvertes (pour les spectateurs) d'un terrain de baseball, de football, etc.

bleachery ['bli:tʃəri], *s. Tex:* blanchisserie *f*.

bleaching ['bli:tʃiŋ], *s.* blanchiment *m*; *Ch:* décoloration *f*; *Tex:* débouilli *m*; *Hairdr:* traitement *m* à l'oxygène; **b. agent,** produit blanchissant; **b. powder,** poudre *f* à blanchir; chlorure *m* de chaux; *Tex:* **b. house,** blanchisserie *f*; *A:* **b. field, green, ground,** blanchisserie; pré *m* de blanchiment; *Phot:* **b. bath,** bain *m* de blanchiment, de blanchissement.

bleak[1] [bli:k], *s. Ich:* ablette *f*.

bleak[2], *a.* **1.** (terrain) désert, sans abri, exposé au vent, balayé par le vent. **2.** (temps) triste; (vent) froid. **3. b. prospects,** avenir *m* morne; **the outlook is b.,** les perspectives sont peu encourageantes; **b. smile,** sourire *m* pâle.

bleakly ['bli:kli], *adv.* (*a*) froidement, tristement; (*b*) d'un air morne.

bleakness ['bli:knis], *s.* (*a*) tristesse *f*, froidure *f*; (*b*) aspect *m* morne.

blear[1] [bliər], *a.* **1.** (*of eyes*) trouble, larmoyant; chassieux; **b.-eyed,** aux yeux larmoyants. **2.** (*of outline*) vague, indécis, imprécis.

blear[2], *v.tr.* **1.** rendre (les yeux) troubles. **2.** obscurcir, embrumer, estomper (des contours).

bleary ['bliəri], *a.* **1.** (*of eyes*) trouble, larmoyant; chassieux; **b.-eyed,** aux yeux troubles, larmoyants. **2.** (*of outline*) vague, indécis, imprécis. **3.** (*of pers.*) rompu de fatigue.

bleat[1] [bli:t], *s.* (*a*) bêlement *m*; (*b*) *F:* (i) propos plaintifs, stupides; plainte *f*; (ii) **we couldn't get a b. out of him,** il s'obstinait à ne rien dire.

bleat[2]. **1.** *v.i.* bêler; (*of ram*) blatérer; (*of goat, old man, etc.*) chevroter; *F:* **what's he bleating about?** de quoi se plaint-il? **2.** *v.tr. F:* (*of pers.*) **to b. out a protest,** protester d'une voix chevrotante.

bleating[1] ['bli:tiŋ], *a.* (*a*) bêlant; (*b*) **b. voice,** voix chevrotante.

bleating[2], *s.* (*a*) bêlement *m*; (*b*) *F:* **that's enough of your b.!** assez de vos plaintes!

bleb [bleb], *s.* **1.** bouillon *m*, soufflure *f*, bulle *f*, cloche *f* (dans le verre, etc.). **2.** bouton *m*, petite ampoule (sur la peau); *Med:* phlyctène *f*.

blechnum ['bleknəm], *s. Ferns:* blechne *m*, blechnum *m*.

bled [bled], *a. Carp: etc:* **b. timber,** bois essévé; *Typ:* **b.(-off) illustrations,** illustrations *f* à marges perdues, à fond perdu.

bleed[1] [bli:d], *v.* (**bled; bled**) **1.** *v.tr.* (*a*) saigner; **to b. s.o. in the arm,** saigner qn au bras; **to b. s.o. (for money),** saigner, gruger, qn; extorquer de l'argent à qn; *P:* faire casquer qn; faire cracher qn; **they bled him for a cool ten thousand,** on lui extorqua dix mille livres, rien de moins; **to b. s.o. white,** sucer qn jusqu'à la moelle des os; extorquer à qn tout son argent; saigner qn à blanc; sucer qn jusqu'au dernier sou; **to b. oneself white to pay, for one's children,** se saigner aux quatre veines pour payer, pour ses enfants; (*b*) *Mec.E:* purger. **2.** *v.i.* (*a*) saigner; perdre du sang; *P:* (*pay large sums of money*) casquer, cracher; **he is bleeding at the nose, his nose is bleeding,** il saigne du nez; *Box:* **to b. at the nose,** saigner du nez, *P:* pavoiser; **to b. for one's country,** verser son sang pour sa patrie; **to b. to death,** mourir d'effusion de sang; **my heart bleeds at the thought, bleeds for them,** le cœur me saigne rien que d'y penser, quand je pense à eux; (*b*) (*of haemorrhoids*) fluer; (*of tree, etc.*) pleurer, perdre sa sève; (*c*) *Civ.E: etc:* (*of riveted joints; of water, gas, etc.*) fuir; (*d*) (*of dye, of dyed material*) s'étendre, couler (au lavage); déteindre. **3.** *v.tr. Bookb:* trop rogner (un livre).

bleed[2], *s. Mec.E:* purge *f*; dispositif *m* de drainage; **b. screw,** vis *f* de purge.

bleeder ['bli:dər], *s.* **1.** *Med: F:* (*a*) (*pers.*) hémophilique *mf*; (*b*) artère *f* qui gicle (au cours d'une opération). **2.** (*pers.*) (*a*) *F:* parasite *m*; (*b*) *P:* salaud *m*; **poor b.,** pauvre type *m*; (*used semi-affectionately*) **you old b., you!** sacré type, va! **3.** *Tchn:* dispositif *m* de drainage.

bleeding[1] ['bli:diŋ], *a.* **1.** (*a*) saignant; (i) en train de saigner; (ii) ensanglanté; **with a b. heart,** le cœur navré de douleur; *Med:* **b. piles,** hémorroïdes fluentes; (*b*) *Bot:* **b. heart,** (i) giroflée *f* des murailles; (ii) cœur-de-Marie *m*, *pl.* cœurs-de-Marie; cœur-de-Jeannette *m*, *pl.* cœurs-de-Jeannette; (*c*) *Moll:* **b. tooth,** nérite *f*. **2.** *P:* sacré; **you b. liar!** sacré menteur!

bleeding[2], *s.* **1.** (*a*) écoulement *m* de sang; (*of plants*) écoulement de sève; (*of vine, etc.*) pleurs *mpl*; **b. at the nose,** saignement *m* de nez; *Med:* **b. of piles,** flux hémorroïdal; **I can't stop the b.,** je n'arrive pas à arrêter le sang; (*b*) *Surg:* saignée *f*. **2.** *Civ.E: etc:* fuite *f* (d'eau, de gaz, etc., dans une canalisation).

bleep [bli:p], *v.i.* (*of satellite, radio signal*) faire bip-bip.

bleep(-bleep) ['bli:p('bli:p)], **bleeping** ['bli:piŋ], *s.* bip-bip *m* (d'un satellite, etc.).

bleeper ['bli:pər], *s.* récepteur *m* d'appel, récepteur de poche.

blemish[1] ['blemiʃ], *s.* **1.** défaut *m*; défectuosité *f*, imperfection *f* (physique ou morale); **to find a b. in sth.,** trouver à redire à qch. **2.** souillure *f*, tache *f*, flétrissure *f*, tare *f*; **name without b.,** nom *m* sans tache.

blemish², *v.tr.* **1.** tacher, entacher, souiller, ternir (une réputation, etc.). **2.** abîmer, gâter (un travail).

blench¹ [blen(t)ʃ]. **1.** *v.i.* sourciller, broncher; **without blenching,** sans sourciller. **2.** *v.tr.* **to b. the facts,** refuser de voir les faits; se refuser à l'évidence.

blench², *v.i.* pâlir, blêmir; **to b. with terror,** pâlir de terreur.

blend¹ [blend], *s.* mélange *m* (de thés, de whiskys, de tabacs; *F:* de races, etc.); *Com:* **excellent b. of tea,** thé *m* d'excellente qualité.

blend², *v.* (*p.t. & p.p.* **blended,** *Lit:* **blent**) **1.** *v.tr.* (*a*) **to b. sth. with sth.,** mêler qch. à, avec, qch.; joindre, unir, qch. à qch.; **to b. nations, parties,** amalgamer des nations, des partis; **to b. one colour with another,** (i) mélanger une couleur avec une autre; (ii) fondre deux couleurs; faire une dégradation entre deux couleurs; (iii) allier, marier, deux couleurs; *Lit:* **pain blent with joy,** douleur mêlée de joie; *Psy:* **to b. ideas,** fusionner des idées; (*b*) assembler, (re)couper (des vins, des whiskys); mettre (des vins) en cuvée; (*c*) mêler, mélanger (des thés, des cafés; *F:* des races); fusionner (des races); **our teas are carefully blended,** nos thés sont mélangés avec soin. **2.** *v.i.* se mêler, se mélanger, se confondre (**into,** en); (*of voices, etc.*) se marier harmonieusement; (*of colours*) s'allier, se marier; se fondre; se raccorder; (*of parties, etc.*) fusionner, s'amalgamer; (*of ideas*) fusionner; **teas that do not b.,** thés que l'on ne peut pas mélanger; **the colours b. well,** les couleurs sont bien agencées, vont bien ensemble.

blende [blend], *s. Min:* blende *f*, sphalérite *f*.

blender ['blendər], *s.* **1.** mélangeur, -euse. **2.** *Art:* (*brush*) blaireau *m*. **3.** *Dom.Ec:* mixer *m*.

blending ['blendiŋ], *s.* mélange *m* (de thés, de tabacs, etc.); alliance *f* (de deux qualités); *Winem:* assemblage *m*, coupage *m*, mise *f* en cuvée; *Ch: Metall:* alliage *m* (de métaux); *Mus:* union *f*, jonction *f* (des registres de la voix); **b. of ideas,** fusion *f*, coalescence *f*, condensation *f*, des idées; **b. of races,** fusion de races.

Blenheim ['blenim], *Pr.n. Geog: etc:* Blenheim *m*; **a B. spaniel,** un blenheim.

Blenniidae [ble'niidi:], *s.pl. Ich:* blenniidés *m*.

blennorrhagia [blenə'reidʒiə], *s. Med:* blennor-r(h)agie *f*.

blennorrhagic [blenə'reidʒik], *a. Med:* blennorr(h)agique.

blennorrhoea [blenə'riə], *s. Med:* blennorr(h)ée *f*; *occ.* urétrite *f* chronique; **acute b.,** blennophtalmie *f*, ophtalmie purulente.

blenny ['bleni], *s. Ich:* blennie *m or f*; **butterfly b.,** gonelle *f*, papillon *m* de mer; **ocellated b.,** blennie ocellé(e); **viviparous b.,** zoarcès *m* vivipare.

blepharadenitis ['blefɑ:rəde'naitis], *s. Med:* blépharadénite *f*.

blepharal ['blefərəl], *a. Anat:* blépharique.

blepharism ['blefərizm], *s. Med:* blépharospasme *m*.

blepharitis [blefə'raitis], *s. Med:* blépharite *f*; **ciliary, marginal, b.,** blépharite ciliaire.

blepharoblennorrhoea ['blefəroublenə'riə], *s. Med:* blépharo-blennorr(h)ée *f*.

blepharochalasis ['blefəroukə'leisis], *s. Med:* blépharochalasis *f*.

blepharoconjunctivitis ['blefəroukəndʒʌŋkti'vaitis], *s. Med:* blépharo-conjonctivite *f*.

blepharophimosis ['blefəroufi'mousis], *s. Med:* blépharophimosis *m*.

blepharoplast ['blefərouplɑ:st], *s. Prot:* blépharoplaste *m*.

blepharoplasty ['blefərou'plæsti], *s. Surg:* bléfaroplastie *f*.

blepharoplegia ['blefərou'pli:dʒiə], *s. Med:* blépharoplégie *f*.

blepharoptosis ['blefərəp'tousis], *s. Med:* blépharoptose *f*.

blepharospasm ['blefərouspæzm], *s. Med:* blépharospasme *m*.

blepharostat ['blefəroustæt], *s. Med:* blépharostat *m*.

blesbok ['blesbɔk], **blesbuck** ['blesbʌk], *s. Z:* damalisque *m*.

bless [bles], *v.tr.* (*p.t. & p.p.* **blessed** [blest], *p.p. occ.* **blest** [blest]) bénir. **1. to b. God,** bénir, adorer, Dieu. **2.** (*of God, of the priest*) **to b. the people,** bénir le peuple; **to b. a bell,** consacrer, baptiser, une cloche; **bread blessed at the altar,** pain bénit; **God b. (you)!** que (le bon) Dieu vous bénisse! *F:* (*when s.o. sneezes*) **(God) b. you!** à vos souhaits! que Dieu vous bénisse! **3. to be blessed, blest, with sth.,** jouir de qch.; avoir le bonheur de posséder qch.; **to be blessed with a cheerful disposition,** être doué d'un heureux caractère; **he was not greatly blessed with worldly goods,** il avait peu de fortune; *F:* **he hasn't a penny to b. himself with,** il n'a pas le sou; **we were blessed with many years of happiness,** nous avons joui de nombreuses années de bonheur; *Lit:* **their union was blessed with many children,** ils ont eu le bonheur d'engendrer de nombreux enfants; **I b. my good fortune, my stars, that . . .,** je me félicite, je bénis mon étoile, de ce que . . .; *F:* **he'll b. you if you lose his keys,** il vous bénira si vous perdez ses clefs; **b. me! b. my soul!** *O:* **b. my heart!** mon Dieu! tiens, tiens! *F:* **b. me if he didn't sell the lot!** et lui de vendre tout le bataclan! **well, I'm blest!** par exemple! **I'm blest if I know,** que le diable m'emporte si je le sais; **I'm blest if he doesn't want to come with me!** et voilà qu'il veut m'accompagner!

blessed ['blesid], *a.* (*a*) **the B. Virgin,** la Sainte Vierge; **the B. Trinity,** la sainte Trinité; (*b*) *R.C.Ch: etc:* bienheureux; **the B. Urban II,** le bienheureux Urbain II; **the late king, of b. memory,** le feu roi, d'heureuse mémoire; **b. are the poor in spirit,** heureux les pauvres en esprit; *Iron:* **thank heaven for the b. word confrontation!** Dieu merci le mot confrontation existe! (*c*) *F:* (*intensive*) **every b. day,** tous les jours que Dieu fait; **the whole b. day,** toute la sainte journée; **what a b. bind!** quelle corvée! **the whole b. lot,** tout le bazar, tout le bataclan; **not a b. one,** pas la queue d'un, d'une.

blessedness ['blesidnis], *s.* béatitude *f*; félicité *f*.

blessing ['blesiŋ], *s.* bénédiction *f*; **to give, pronounce, the b.,** donner la bénédiction; (*at a meal*) **to ask, say, a b.,** dire le bénédicité; **the blessings of God,** les grâces *f* de Dieu; **papal b.,** bénédiction apostolique; **the blessings of civilization, etc.,** les avantages *m*, bienfaits *m*, dons *m*, de la civilisation, etc.; **b. in disguise,** bienfait insoupçonné; **it is perhaps a b. in disguise,** c'est peut-être un bien pour un mal; **it turned out to be a b. in disguise,** à la longue nous avons pu nous en féliciter; **to count one's blessings,** s'estimer heureux avec ce qu'on a; **b. of a bell,** baptême *m* d'une cloche; **blessings on you!** Dieu vous bénisse! **he gave the plan his b.,** il a donné sa bénédiction au projet; **what a b.!** quel bonheur! quelle chance!

blest [blest]. **1.** *a.* bienheureux. **2.** *s.pl.* **the B.,** les Bienheureux *m*; les Saints *m* au Paradis; *Myth:* **the Islands of the B.,** les Iles Fortunées.

blether¹ ['bleðər], *s. F:* paroles *fpl*, discours *mpl*, en l'air; sottises *fpl*, bêtises *fpl*.

blether², *v.i. F:* parler à tort et à travers; parler pour ne rien dire; débiter, dire, des inepties, des bêtises.

blethering ['bleðəriŋ], *a. F:* **b. idiot,** espèce *f* d'idiot.

bletherskate ['bleðəskeit], *s. F: esp. Scot:* débiteur *m* de sottises; grand parleur.

blewit ['blu:it], *s. Fung:* **wood b.,** pied-bleu *m*, *pl.* pieds-bleus.

blight¹ [blait], *s.* **1.** (*a*) rouille *f*, brûlure *f*; charbon *m*, nielle *f* (des céréales); brunissure *f* (des pommes de terre); cloque *f* (des pêches, etc.); (*b*) (*by the sun*) brouissure *f* (après la gelée). **2.** *Ent:* (*plant louse*) puceron *m*; **covered in b.,** couvert de pucerons. **3.** (*a*) influence *f* néfaste; fléau *m*; (*b*) **his arrival cast a b. over the company,** son arrivée a jeté un froid sur la compagnie.

blight², *v.tr.* rouiller, nieller (le blé); (*of the sun*) brouir; (*of the wind*) flétrir; **blighted leaf,** feuille cloquée; **to b. s.o.'s hopes,** flétrir les espérances de qn; **seeing his hopes blighted he retired from the world,** déchu de ses espérances il se retira du monde; **blighted prospects,** avenir brisé.

blighter ['blaitər], *s. P:* (*a*) salaud *m*; (you) **stinking b.!** espèce de chameau, de salaud! (*b*) individu *m*, type *m*; **poor b.,** pauvre type; **(you) lucky b.!** veinard!

blighting¹ ['blaitiŋ], *a.* flétrissant; **b. influence,** influence *f* funeste.

blighting², *s.* flétrissure *f*.

blighty ['blaiti], *s. Mil: P: A:* **1.** l'Angleterre *f*; (le) retour dans les foyers. **2. a b.,** (*also* **a b. one**) (i) la bonne blessure; (ii) une perme.

blimey ['blaimi], *int. P:* (*attenuated form of* **God blind me**) le diable m'emporte! mon Dieu!

blimp [blimp], *s.* **1.** (*a*) *Aer:* (petit) dirigeable de reconnaissance, d'observation; éclaireur *m*; patrouilleur *m* (contre sous-marins); vedette aérienne; (*b*) *U.S: F:* (*pers.*) rondouillard, -arde. **2.** *Cin:* blindage *m* insonore (de la camera). **3.** conservateur *m* à outrance; réactionnaire endurci; **he's a real Colonel B.,** c'est une vraie culotte de peau, un scro(n)gneugneu.

blind¹ [blaind], *a.* **1.** (*a*) aveugle; **b. from birth,** aveugle-né(e), *pl.* aveugles-né(e)s; **stone b.,** complètement aveugle; **b. in one eye,** borgne; **he was b. in one eye and now he has lost the other eye too,** il était aveugle d'un œil et maintenant il a aussi perdu l'autre; **a b. man, woman,** un, une, aveugle; *s.* **the b.,** les aveugles; **in the country of the b. the one-eyed man is king,** au royaume des aveugles les borgnes sont rois; **it is a case of the b. leading the b.,** c'est un aveugle qui en conduit un autre; **to be struck b.,** être frappé de cécité; *F:* **to drink oneself b.,** se flanquer une bonne cuite; **b. with anger,** aveuglé par la colère; **to go b. with rage,** se mettre dans une colère bleue; **he's as b. as a bat,** *O:* **as a beetle, a mole,** il est myope comme une taupe; **b. obedience,** soumission *f* aveugle; *F:* **to turn a b. eye on, to, sth.,** fermer les yeux sur qch., refuser de voir qch.; **the b. side of s.o.,** le côté faible de qn; **try to get on his b. side,** tâchez de le prendre par son côté faible; *Lit:* **b. man's holiday,** entre chien et loup; *Av:* **b. flying,** vol *m* sans visibilité, vol en P.S.V. (pilotage sans visibilité); (*b*) **to be b. to one's own interests, to s.o.'s faults,** ne pas voir ses propres intérêts, les défauts de qn; être aveugle aux défauts de qn; **to be b. to the obvious,** ne pas voir ce qui est évident; être incapable de voir ce qui s'impose; ne pas voir clair en plein midi; **to be b. to the future,** ne tenir aucun compte de l'avenir; **I am not b. to the drawbacks of the situation,** je n'ignore pas les inconvénients de la situation; **to be b. to an abuse,** fermer les yeux sur un abus; **b. to beauty,** fermé au sentiment du beau; **in a b. stupor,** *F:* **b. to the world,** soûl perdu; (*c*) *Moll:* **b. shell,** caecidé *m*. **2.** (*a*) (*hidden*) **b. ditch,** saut *m* de loup; **b. curve, corner,** virage masqué, sans visibilité; **b. crossroads,** carrefour *m* sans visibilité; **b. spot,** (i) angle mort; (ii) côté faible (de qn); (iii) *Anat:* papille *f* optique; **that's your b. spot,** c'est là où vous refusez de voir clair, où vous montrez des préjugés; **there is a b. spot where the road dips suddenly in a sharp bend,** il n'y a aucune visibilité à l'endroit où la route descend brusquement dans un virage prononcé; *Golf:* **b. hole,** trou dérobé à la vue; *Needlew:* **b. hemming,** point *m* d'ourlet invisible; **b. stitch,** point perdu; (*b*) *Med:* **double b. test,** épreuve pratiquée à l'insu du malade et du médecin; *Com:* **to make a b. purchase,** acheter quelque chose sans l'avoir vu; *F:* **b. date,** (i) rendez-vous fixé par une troisième personne (entre un jeune homme et une jeune fille); (ii) le jeune homme ou la jeune fille qui se rencontrent ainsi. **3.** (*without exit*) **b. hole,** trou *m* borgne; **b. path,** chemin *m* sans issue; **b. alley,** impasse *f*; cul-de-sac *m*, *pl.* culs-de-sac; *Fig:* **he found himself in a b. alley,** il se trouvait dans une impasse; **b. alley occupation,** occupation *f*, situation *f*, sans avenir; cul-de-sac; *Rail:* **b. siding,** cul-de-sac; *Geol:* **b. lode,** filon *m* sans affleurement; **b. valley,** reculée *f*, cul-de-sac; *Med:* **b. fistula,** fistule *f* borgne; *Arch:* **b. door,** fausse porte; **b. wall,** mur *m* aveugle, **b. window,** fenêtre feinte, aveugle; *Mec.E:* **b. nut,** écrou plein, aveugle. **4.** (*a*) (*defective*) *Post:* **b. letter, blind,** *s.*, (i) lettre *f* dont l'adresse est défectueuse, illisible; (ii) lettre refusée; **b. duty,** service *m* des lettres aux adresses défectueuses; **head of the b. duty,** homme-canon *m*, *pl.* hommes-canons; **b. reader,** employé chargé de déchiffrer les adresses défectueuses; (*in handwriting*) **b. e,** e poché; **b. shell,** obus *m* qui n'éclate pas; *Bot:* **b. shoot,** rejet *m* sans bourgeons; (*b*) *U.S: P:* **b. pig, b. tiger,** débit de boisson clandestin. **5.** *F:* **he didn't take a b. bit of notice,** il n'a pas fait la moindre attention. **6.** *adv.* **to fire b.,** tirer au jugé; *Av:* **to fly b.,** voler à l'aveuglette; *F:* **to go at a thing b.,** se lancer à l'aveugle dans une entreprise; **b. drunk,** complètement ivre, soûl.

blind², *v.tr.* **1.** aveugler (qn); (*a*) rendre (qn) aveugle, frapper (qn) de cécité; **the gun went off and blinded him,** le coup partit et lui creva les yeux; **since he was blinded,** depuis qu'il est aveugle; **blinded ex-service men,** aveugles *m* de guerre; (*b*) éblouir (qn); **the sun is blinding him,** le soleil l'aveugle, l'éblouit; **blinded by passion,** aveuglé par la passion; **to b. s.o. to facts,** aveugler qn sur les faits; jeter de la poudre aux yeux de qn; **he was blinded by her beauty,** il fut ébloui de sa beauté. **2.** (*a*) *Civ.E:* ensabler (une chaussée, une voie ferrée); (*b*) *Mil: Min:* blinder (une galerie, etc.). **3.** *v.i. Aut: F: O:* **to b. along,** conduire comme un fou; rouler à tombeau ouvert. **4.** *v.i. F: O:* jurer, sacrer; **blinding and swearing,** jurant et sacrant.

blind³, *s. P:* **to go on a b.,** faire une bombe à tout casser.

blind⁴, *s.* **1.** store *m* (à l'italienne); abat-jour *m inv*; **roller b.,** store à, sur, rouleau; **Venetian b., shutter b.,** jalousie *f* (à lames mobiles); (*over pavement*) **shop b.,** banne *f*. **2.** (*a*) *Mil: Fort:* blinde *f*; (*b*) *NAm:* œillère *f* (de cheval). **3.** (*a*) prétexte *m*, masque *m*; **his attitude was only a b.,** son attitude n'était qu'un prétexte; (*b*) organisation camouflée.

blindage ['blaindidʒ], *s. Mil: Min:* blindage *m*, blindes *fpl*.

blinder ['blaindər], *s. F:* (*a*) *Sp:* coup *m* sensas(s); (*b*) *P:* **to go on a b.,** faire une bombe à tout casser.

blinders ['blaindəz], *s.pl. Harn: NAm:* œillères *f*.

blindfish ['blaindfiʃ], *s. Ich:* amblyopsis *m*, poisson *m* aveugle; **Rocky Mountains b.,** poisson aveugle des Rocheuses.

blindfold[1] ['blaindfould]. **1.** *a.* les yeux bandés; *Chess:* **b. player,** joueur *m* qui joue sans voir l'échiquier. **2.** *adv.* (*recklessly*) aveuglément. **3.** *s.* **he put a b. on the horse to lead him from the burning stable,** il a bandé les yeux du cheval pour le sortir de l'écurie en flammes.
blindfold[2], *v.tr.* bander les yeux à, de (qn); couvrir les yeux de (qn) avec un bandeau; mettre un bandeau à (qn).
blindfolding ['blaindfouldiŋ], *s.* bandage *m* des yeux (de qn).
blinding[1] ['blaindiŋ], *a.* **1.** aveuglant; **her eyes filled with b. tears,** les larmes lui embuèrent les yeux; (*intensive*) **b. headache,** mal de tête fou. **2.** éblouissant; **b. headlights,** phares éblouissants, aveuglants.
blinding[2], *s.* **1.** (*a*) *Jur: A:* aveuglement *m*; (*b*) **b. by headlights, etc.,** éblouissement *m* par les phares, etc. **2.** (*a*) *Civ.E:* ensablement *m*; *Mil:* blindage *m*; (*b*) *Civ.E:* couche *f* de sable (sur une route).
blindman's buff ['blaindmænz'bʌf], *s. Games:* colin-maillard *m.*
blindness ['blaindnis], *s.* **1.** cécité *f*; **b. in one eye,** cécité monoculaire. **2.** (*ignorance, folly*) aveuglement *m*; **b. to the facts,** refus *m* d'envisager les faits.
blind snake ['blaindsneik], *s. Rept:* typhlops *m.*
blindstitch[1] ['blaindstitʃ], *s. Needlew:* point perdu.
blindstitch[2], *v.tr. Needlew:* coudre (qch.) à points perdus.
blind(-)stor(e)y ['blaindstɔ:ri], *s. Arch: A: & U.S:* triforium *m.*
blindworm ['blaindwə:m], *s. Rept:* orvet *m.*
blink[1] [bliŋk], *s.* **1.** battement *m,* clignotement *m,* clignement *m,* de paupières. **2.** (*gleam*) lueur (momentanée); (*glimpse*) vision momentanée. **3.** *F:* (*of television set, etc.*) **on the b.,** en panne, qui cafouille.
blink[2]. **1.** *v.i.* (*a*) battre des paupières, cligner des paupières; clignoter; ciller (les paupières); **to b. at s.o.,** regarder qn avec un clignement d'yeux, de paupières, en clignant des yeux; *v.tr.* **to b. away a tear,** refouler une larme d'un battement de paupières; (*b*) (*of light*) papilloter; vaciller. **2.** fermer les yeux à demi; (*a*) *v.tr.* **to b. the facts,** fermer les yeux sur la vérité; méconnaître les faits; ne pas voir clair en plein midi; **to b. the question,** esquiver, éluder, la question; **there is no blinking the fact that . . .,** il n'y a pas à dissimuler que . . .; (*b*) *v.i.* **to b. at a fault,** fermer les yeux sur un défaut. **3.** *v.tr.* (*a*) *Ven:* (*of hare*) **to b. the dogs,** donner le change aux lévriers; (*b*) *Dial:* (*in Scot. & Ireland*) jeter un sort sur (une vache, etc.).
blinker ['bliŋkər], *s.* **1.** (*a*) *Harn:* œillère *f*; (*b*) *F:* (*of pers.*) **he goes about in blinkers,** il a, il porte, des œillères. **2.** phare *m* à éclats (sur un aérodrome); **morse b. light,** fanal *m* morse; *Aut:* **blinkers,** clignotants *mpl.*
blinkered ['bliŋkəd], *a.* (*a*) (*of horse*) qui porte des œillères; (*b*) *F: O:* (*of pers.*) aux vues étroites.
blinking[1] ['bliŋkiŋ], *a.* **1.** (*a*) clignotant; (*b*) (feu) papillotant; **b. light,** feu clignotant. **2.** *F: O:* **it's a b. nuisance!** ça, c'est un peu fort! *adv.* **he b. well did (do it)!** et je te dis qu'il l'a fait!
blinking[2], *s.* **1.** (*a*) clignotement *m,* cillement *m*; (*b*) papillotage *m.* **2. b. of a fact,** refus *m* d'envisager un fait; méconnaissance *f* d'un fait.
blinks [bliŋks], *s. Bot:* **(water) b.,** mouron *m* des fontaines.
blip [blip], *s. Rad:* spot *m* (sur l'écran); top *m* d'écho.
bliss [blis], *s.* béatitude *f,* félicité *f,* bonheur *m* extrême.
blissful ['blisful], *a.* (bien)heureux; **b. days,** jours sereins.
blissfully ['blisfuli], *adv.* heureusement; **b. happy,** au comble du bonheur; **to look b. happy,** avoir l'air bien content, bien heureux; **to be b. unaware that . . .,** n'avoir aucun soupçon que . . .
blissfulness ['blisfulnis], *s.* = BLISS.
blister[1] ['blistər], *s.* **1.** (*a*) (*on skin*) ampoule *f,* bulle *f*; **water b.,** cloque *f,* phlyctène *f*; (*b*) cloque, boursouflure *f* (de la peinture); *Glassm:* bulle, cloche *f*; *Phot:* ampoule (sur le cliché); *Metall:* soufflure *f,* paille *f,* boursouflure, ampoule, moine *m*; (*in casting*) goutte froide; **b. steel,** acier *m* poule; acier boursouflé, ampoulé; acier de cémentation; **blisters on bread,** coquilles *f* du pain; (*c*) *Med:* vésicatoire *m*; **b. gas,** gaz vésicant; (*d*) *Bot:* **larch b.,** chancre *m* du mélèze; (*e*) *attrib. Ent:* **b. beetle, fly,** cantharide *f,* mouche *f* d'Espagne; *Arch:* **b. mite,** phytopte *m.* **2.** (*a*) *N.Arch:* caisson *m* pare-torpilles; (*b*) *Av:* tourelle *f* (en dessous).
blister[2]. **1.** *v.tr.* (*a*) couvrir d'ampoules; faire venir les ampoules à(la main, etc.); **to b. the tongue,** brûler la langue; **blistered heel,** ampoule *f* au talon; (*b*) *Med:* appliquer un vésicatoire sur (la peau); (*c*) *P: A:* ennuyer, assommer, raser (qn). **2.** *v.i.* se couvrir d'ampoules; se former en vessie; (*of paint*) (se) cloquer; se boursoufler, gondoler; (*of bread*) coquiller (*of chromium plate*); **to b. off,** lever; **I b. easily,** il me vient facilement des ampoules; *Metall:* **blistered casting,** pièce venteuse.
blistering[1] ['blist(ə)riŋ], *a.* **1.** *Med: Pharm:* (emplâtre) vésicant. **2. b. sun,** soleil brûlant, ardent. **3.** (*a*) (*of remark, sarcasm, etc.*) cinglant, mordant, caustique; (*b*) **b. attack, assault,** attaque foudroyante; **at a b. pace,** à une très grande vitesse. **4.** *F: O:* sacré.
blistering[2], *s.* **1.** *Med:* vésication *f.* **2.** formation *f* d'ampoules (à la peau). **3.** cloquage *m,* gondolage *m* (de la peinture); **b. off (of chromium plate),** levage *m* (du chromage).
blite [blait], *s. Bot:* épinard *m* sauvage, blette *f*; **strawberry b.,** épinard fraise, blette à tête.
blithe(some) ['blaið(səm)], *a.* joyeux, folâtre, d'humeur gaie; **blithe as a lark,** gai comme un pinson.
blithely ['blaiðli], *adv.* joyeusement, allègrement; avec entrain.
blithering ['bliðəriŋ], *a. F:* sacré; **what a b. nuisance!** que c'est embêtant! **(you) b. idiot!** espèce d'idiot!
blitz[1] [blits], *s.* (*a*) blitz *m*; bombardement aérien; (*b*) *F:* **I must have a b. on all these papers,** il me faut mettre de l'ordre dans tous ces documents (et en détruire!).
blitz[2], *v.tr.* bombarder; **the house was blitzed,** la maison a été endommagée, détruite, par un bombardement.
blitzkrieg ['blitskri:g], *s.* guerre *f* éclair.
blizzard ['blizəd], *s.* blizzard *m,* tempête *f* de neige, rafale *f* de neige, tourmente *f* de neige.
bloat[1] [blout], *s. Vet:* météorisation *f,* ballonnement *m.*
bloat[2]. **1.** *v.tr.* boursoufler; gonfler; bouffir. **2.** *v.i.* se gonfler; se bouffir. **3.** *v.tr. Vet:* météoriser.
bloat[3], *v.tr.* saurer (des harengs) très légèrement; bouffir (des harengs); **bloated herring** = BLOATER.
bloated ['bloutid], *a.* (*a*) boursouflé, gonflé, bouffi; **b. with pride,** bouffi d'orgueil; (*b*) **b. face,** visage congestionné, vultueux; (*c*) *Vet:* météorisé.
bloater ['bloutər], *s. Com:* hareng bouffi; craquelot *m.*
blob[1] [blɔb], *s.* **1.** (*a*) tache *f* (de couleur); pâté *m* (d'encre); (*b*) goutte *f* d'eau (sur la table, etc.); (*c*) **she had a b. of a nose,** elle avait un petit nez en boule; **a b. of wool,** une petite touffe de laine. **2.** *Cr: F:* zéro *m*; **to make a b.,** remporter une veste. **3.** bourde *f.*
blob[2], *v.i.* **my pen is blobbing,** mon stylo coule, bave; mon stylo fait des pâtés.
bloc [blɔk], *s. Pol: etc:* bloc *m.*
block[1] [blɔk], *s.* **1.** (*a*) bloc *m* (de marbre, de fer, etc.); motte *f* (de beurre); tronçon *m* (de bois); quartier *m* (de roche); carreau *m* (de pierre taillée); brique *f* (de verre); tête *f* à perruque (de coiffeur); poupée *f* (de modiste); forme *f* (pour chapeaux); sellette *f* (de décrotteur); nave b., selle *f* (de chausson); **small b.,** blochet *m*; **b. of soap,** love *f*; **cement-b. foundation,** blocage *m*; *Metall:* **b. tin,** étain *m* en saumons; *Metalw:* **pitch b.,** bloc de mastic (pour travail en repoussé); *I.C.E:* **four-cylinder b.,** bloc de quatre cylindres; *Geol:* **b. mountain,** horst *m*; *Toys:* **building blocks,** cubes *m*; jeu *m* de construction; (*of pers.*) **like a b. of stone,** (i) immobile; (ii) dur; (iii) silencieux, muet; (*b*) **(chopping, anvil) b.,** billot *m*; **butcher's b.,** ais *m* de boucher; hachoir *m*; **cooper's b.,** tronchet *m,* trochet *m*; *Hist:* **to perish on the b.,** périr sur le billot; (*c*) *Equit:* **(mounting) b.,** montoir *m*; (*d*) (*chock*) tin *m,* hausse *f,* cale *f*; **angle blocks,** coins *m*; *Civ.E: etc:* **stay b.,** semelle *f* d'ancrage; *Mec:* **plummer b.,** palier *m,* empoise *f*; **self-lubricating plummer b.,** palier graisseur; *Mec.E:* **pillow b.,** palier (d'arbre); palier-support *m, pl.* paliers-supports; **to put a car up on blocks,** mettre une voiture sur cales; caler une voiture; (*e*) sabot *m* (de frein); (*f*) *P:* tête *f,* caboche *f*; **I'll knock your b. off!** je vais t'amocher la figure! *Austr:* **to do one's b.,** se fâcher (tout rouge). **2.** (*a*) bloc, pâté *m,* îlot *m,* de maisons (entre quatre rues); ensemble *m* de bâtiments; **b. of flats,** immeuble (divisé en appartements); **office b.,** immeuble (divisé en bureaux); **the south wing of the house has been turned into an office b.,** l'aile sud de la maison a été transformée en bureaux; *esp. NAm:* **he lives two blocks from us,** il habite à deux rues de nous; **to walk round the b.,** faire un tour des maisons; (*b*) *Austr:* (i) quartier *m* (d'une ville); (ii) boulevard *m*; *F:* **to do the b.,** se promener sur le boulevard; (*c*) *esp. Austr:* lot *m* (de terrains); *For:* **periodic b.,** affectation *f* périodique; (*d*) *Fin:* **b. of shares,** tranche *f* d'actions; *Com:* **b. booking,** location *f* (de places de théâtre, etc., *Cin:* de films) en bloc. **3.** (*a*) **traffic b.,** embouteillage *m,* encombrement *m* (de voitures); (*b*) *Nau:* **b. ship,** bateau *m* d'embouteillage; (*c*) *Parl:* avis *m* préalable d'opposition (à un projet de loi); obstruction *f* (à un projet de loi); (*d*) *Cr:* **b. (hole),** point *m* en avant du guichet (où le batteur appuie sa batte). **4.** *Rail:* (*a*) canton *m,* tronçon *m* (de ligne); **b. system,** cantonnement *m,* bloc-système *m*; **b. section,** cantonnement; **b. signal,** disque *m* de fermeture; (*b*) rame *f* (de wagons); **b. train,** rame indépendante. **5.** (*a*) *Engr:* (*wood*) planche *f*; bois *m*; *Typ:* (*metal*) cliché *m*; (*b*) *Phot.Engr:* **b. process,** phototypographie *f*; (*c*) *Typ:* **b. letter,** lettre moulée; caractère gras, capitale *f* bâton; **b. letters,** le moulé; **b. capitals,** majuscules *f,* capitales, d'imprimerie; **to write sth. in b. capitals,** écrire qch. en majuscules, en capitales (d'imprimerie); (*d*) *Carp:* **sandpaper b.,** cale; **mitre b.,** boîte *f* à onglet(s); **6.** (*a*) *Nau: etc:* bloc, poulie *f*; **single, double, b.,** poulie simple, double; **leading b.,** poulie de retour, de renvoi; **hook b.,** poulie à croc; moufle à crochet; **tail b.,** poulie à fouet; **fiddle b., thick-and-thin b.,** (poulie à) violon *m*; **snatch b.,** poulie coupée, galoche *f*; *Civ.E:* (*of aerial ropeway*) **carrying b.,** chariot *m,* châssis *m,* de suspension; (*b*) *Mch:* **link b.,** coulisseau *m*; **slide b.,** coulisseau, glissoir *m,* glisseur *m*; tasseau *m* (de crosse de piston); **slipper b., guide b.,** coulisseau (de crosse); patin *m* (de glissière); (*c*) **b. chain,** (i) *Mec.E:* chaîne *f* d'articulation, chaîne à maillons pleins, à galets; (ii) *F:* chaîne de bicyclette. **7.** carcasse dépouillée (de bête de boucherie).
block[2], *v.*
I. *v.tr.* **1.** bloquer, obstruer; **to b. the traffic,** entraver, gêner, la circulation; **to b. s.o.'s way,** barrer le passage à qn; bloquer le chemin à qn; **harbour blocked by ice,** port bloqué, bouché, obstrué, par les glaces; **road blocked,** rue barrée; **don't b. (up) the gangway!** dégagez (le passage) s'il vous plaît! **to b. progress,** arrêter le progrès; *Parl:* **to b. a bill,** donner avis d'opposition à un projet de loi; faire de l'obstruction à un projet de loi; **to b. a wheel,** bloquer, enrayer, une roue; (*with passive force*) **the wheel blocks,** la roue se bloque; *Mec.E:* **to b. the saddle,** verrouiller le chariot (d'un tour) sur la coulisse; *Rail:* **to b. the line,** (i) fermer, (ii) bloquer, la voie. **2.** *Games:* (*a*) *Cr:* **to b. the ball,** arrêter la balle sans la relancer; bloquer la balle; (*b*) (*dominoes*) **to b. the game,** fermer le jeu; (*c*) *Fb: etc:* gêner (un adversaire); (*d*) *Cards:* **to b. (a suit),** faire une impasse. **3.** (*a*) *Bookb:* gaufrer, frapper (la couverture d'un livre); (*b*) *Hatm:* enformer (un chapeau); mettre (un chapeau) en forme; (*c*) *Bootm:* **to b. a shoe,** cambrer la forme d'un soulier; (*d*) **to b. in, out,** ébaucher, esquisser (un projet, etc.). **4.** *v.ind.tr.* (*a*) **to b. (out) the view,** cacher le panorama, la vue; (*b*) (*of censor*) caviarder (un passage); **blocked-out passage,** caviar *m.*
II. (*compound verb*) **block up,** *v.tr.* **1.** (*a*) boucher, bloquer, fermer (un trou); boucher, condamner, murer (une porte, une fenêtre); *Nau:* bâcler (un port); (*b*) obstruer, engorger (un tuyau, etc.). **2. to b. up the car,** caler la voiture sous les essieux.
blockade[1] [blɔ'keid], *s.* **1.** *Mil: Nau:* blocus *m*; **effective b.,** blocus effectif; **paper b.,** blocus fictif; **close b.,** blocus rigoureux; **to run the b.,** forcer le blocus; **b. runner,** forceur *m* de blocus; **b. running,** forcement *m* de blocus; **to raise the b. of a place,** (i) lever le blocus d'une place; (ii) débloquer une place; **raising of the b.,** déblocement *m,* déblocus *m* (d'une place). **2.** *NAm:* arrêt de circulation des trains (dû aux neiges); encombrement *m,* embouteillage *m* (de la voie publique).
blockade[2], *v.tr.* **1.** bloquer (une ville, un port); faire le blocus d'(une place forte). **2.** *NAm:* bloquer (la circulation); encombrer (une rue).
blockader [blɔ'keidər], *s. Mil: Navy:* bloqueur *m.*
blockage ['blɔkidʒ], *s.* obstruction *f* (d'un tuyau, d'une artère, etc.); **the heavy traffic caused a complete b. in the street,** la circulation intense a causé un embouteillage inextricable dans la rue; **he has a complete mental b. on the subject,** il s'obstine à n'y rien comprendre.
blockbuster ['blɔkbʌstər], *s.* (*a*) *Mil:* bombe *f* de très grosse calibre; (*b*) *F:* **his speech was a real b.,** son discours (i) a eu une très grande portée, (ii) a causé beaucoup de consternation; **this show will be a b.,** ce spectacle aura un succès fou.
blocker ['blɔkər], *s.* dresseur, -euse (de chapeaux).
blockhead ['blɔkhed], *s. F:* lourdaud *m*; gros bêta; sot *m*; cruche *f*; bûche *f*; souche *f*; **he's a b.,** c'est une tête de bois.
blockhouse ['blɔkhaus], *s. Mil:* blockhaus *m*; cassine *f.*
blocking ['blɔkiŋ], *s.* **1.** (*a*) encombrement *m*; embouteillage *m* (d'une rue); **b. (up),** (i) obstruction *f*; (ii) murage *m*; (iii) bâclage *m* (d'un port); **b. out,** oblitération *f*; (*by censor*) caviardage *m*; (*b*) *Rail:* **b. device,** dispositif bloqueur; (*c*) *El:* blocage *m* (du courant). **2.** *Bookb:* gaufrage *m,* frappe *f*; **blind b.,** dorure *f* à froid.
blockish ['blɔkiʃ], *a. F: O:* lourdaud, stupide; (esprit) épais.
blockmaker ['blɔmeikər], *s.* **1.** (*a*) photograveur *m*; (*b*) *Typ:* clicheur *m.* **2.** (*pulley maker*) poulieur *m.*
blockship ['blɔkʃip], *s. Nau:* blockship *m.*
blocky ['blɔki], *a.* **1.** (*of pers., animal*) trapu. **2.** (*of soil*) rempli de grosses pierres.
blœ(e)dite ['bloudait], *s. Miner:* blœdite *f.*
bloke [blouk], *s. F:* (*man*) type *m.*

blond, *f;* **blonde** [blɔnd], *a. & s.* **1.** blond, blonde. **2.** **blond(e) (lace),** blonde *f.*

blood[1] [blʌd], *s.* **1.** sang *m;* (*a*) *Physiol:* **b. circulation,** circulation *f* du sang; **b. vessel,** vaisseau sanguin; **red b. disc,** plaquette sanguine, plaque sanguine; **b. heat,** température *f* du sang; **b. group,** groupe sanguin; **b. grouping, typing,** recherche *f* du groupe sanguin; groupage sanguin; **b. count,** dénombrement *m* des hématies; *Med:* **b. transfusion,** transfusion *f* de sang; **b. donor,** donneur, -euse, de sang; **b. donor set,** appareil *m* de prise de sang; **b. donor recipient,** appareil complet de prise et transfusion sanguines; **b. bank,** banque *f* du sang; **b. storage room,** hémothèque *f*; **b. culture,** hémoculture *f*; **b. poisoning,** empoisonnement *m* du sang; septicémie *f*; toxémie *f*; *F:* **b. blister,** pinçon *m*; *A.Med:* **to let b.,** saigner (qn); **b. letting,** saignée *f*; **to spit b.,** (i) cracher du, le, sang; (ii) *F:* voir rouge; *Fig:* **to sweat b.,** suer sang et eau; (*b*) **he has no b. in his veins,** il n'a pas de sang dans les veines, *F:* il a du sang de navet; **the b. rushed to his head,** le sang lui est monté à la tête; **it makes my b. boil,** cela me fait bouillir le sang; cela m'indigne, me met en fureur; **his b. ran cold,** son sang s'est glacé, s'est figé (dans ses veines); **it makes my b. run cold,** cela me glace le sang; **to commit a crime in cold b.,** commettre un crime de sang-froid; **crime committed in cold b.,** crime prémédité, commis de propos délibéré; **he would never have struck her in cold b.,** jamais il ne l'aurait frappée s'il n'avait pas vu rouge, s'il avait gardé son sang-froid; **there is bad b. between them,** il y a de vieilles rancunes entre eux; **to make bad b. between two people,** jeter la discorde entre deux personnes; *Ind: etc:* **new b.,** apport *m* en sang frais; **the committee needs new b., fresh b.,** le comité a besoin d'être rajeuni, de se rajeunir; **these immigrants are bringing new b. into the country,** ces immigrants constituent un apport de sang frais; (*c*) **to shed, spill, b.,** répandre, verser, le sang; **no b. was shed,** il n'y eut point d'effusion de sang; **without shedding b.,** sans effusion de sang; **to stain one's hands with b.,** rougir ses mains de sang; **b. money,** prix *m* du sang; **to draw b.,** faire saigner qn; **to flog s.o. until one draws b.,** fouetter qn jusqu'au sang; **covered with, in, b.,** couvert de sang, ensanglanté; tout en sang; **b. sports,** la chasse; *F:* **he's out for b.,** il cherche à se venger; **his blood's up,** il est furieux; **it's all b. and thunder,** c'est du mélodrame; **his b. be on his own head,** son sang soit sur lui; **his b. shall be on our head,** son sang retombera sur nous, sur nos têtes; **I would give my life's b. to . . .,** je donnerais le plus pur de mon sang pour . . .; *Prov:* **one cannot get b. out of a stone,** on ne saurait tirer de l'huile d'un mur; on ne peut peigner un diable qui n'a pas de cheveux. **2.** (*a*) (*kindred*) **b. relation,** parent(e) par le sang; parent(e) naturel(le); **they are near in b.,** ce sont de proches parents; **it runs in the b.,** cela tient de la famille; c'est dans le sang; **it runs in his b.,** il chasse de race; **the call of b.,** la voix du sang; **it was the call of the b. that drew them together,** c'était la force du sang qui les rapprochait; **b. is thicker than water,** le sang a beaucoup de pouvoir; nous sommes unis par la voix, la force, du sang; **b. brother,** compagnon par le cœur; (*b*) (*birth, race*) **prince of the b.,** prince *m* du sang; **blue b.,** sang royal; sang illustre, aristocratique; *Prov:* **b. will tell,** bon sang ne peut mentir; **of French b., French by b.,** français de souche; **immigrants of Latin b.,** immigrants *m* de race latine; **b. horse,** cheval *m* de sang, de race; (cheval) pur-sang *m inv.* **3.** (*a*) *A:* petit-maître *m, pl.* petits-maîtres; dandy *m*; **the bloods,** la jeunesse dorée; (*b*) **young b.,** les jeunes du parti (politique, etc.).

blood[2], *v.tr.* **1.** *A:* (= BLEED) saigner (qn). **2.** (*a*) *Ven:* acharner (les chiens), leur donner le goût du sang; initier (un chasseur débutant, en l'aspergeant du sang de la bête morte); (*b*) *Mil:* **to b. the troops,** mener les troupes au feu pour la première fois; donner aux troupes le baptême du feu.

blood-and-thunder [ˈblʌdən(d)ˈθʌndər], *attrib. a.* sensationnel, mélodramatique.

bloodbath [ˈblʌdbɑːθ], *s.* carnage *m,* massacre *m.*

bloodcurdler [ˈblʌdkəːdlər], *s. F:* histoire *f,* roman *m,* à sensation.

bloodcurdling [ˈblʌdkəːdliŋ], *a.* figeant; à vous tourner les sangs; qui (vous) fige, à (vous) figer, le sang.

blooded [ˈblʌdid], *a.* **1.** (*of horse, etc.*) **to be b.,** avoir du sang, de la race. **2.** (*with adj. prefixed, e.g.*) **warm-, cold-b. animals,** animaux à sang chaud, à sang froid.

bloodhound [ˈblʌdhaund], *s.* **1.** limier *m*; chien *m* de Saint-Hubert. **2.** *F:* (*of pers.*) limier.

bloodily [ˈblʌdili], *adv.* d'une manière sanglante.

bloodiness [ˈblʌdinis], *s.* état sanglant.

bloodless [ˈblʌdlis], *a.* **1.** (*a*) exsangue, pâle, anémié; *Med:* **b. surgery,** réduction *f* de luxations; (*b*) insensible, froid; (*c*) sans vitalité; (personne) qui n'a pas de sang dans les veines; (*d*) (style, etc.) insipide, dépourvu d'originalité. **2. b. victory,** victoire *f* sans effusion de sang; victoire pacifique.

bloodlessly [ˈblʌdlisli], *adv.* sans effusion de sang.

bloodlessness [ˈblʌdlisnis], *s.* manque *m* de sang; anémie *f.*

bloodmark [ˈblʌdmɑːk], *s.* tache *f,* trace *f,* de sang.

bloodmobile [ˈblʌdməbiːl], *s. NAm:* laboratoire *m* mobile au service des donneurs de sang.

blood orange [ˈblʌdɔrindʒ], *s.* (orange) sanguine *f.*

blood pheasant [ˈblʌdfez(ə)nt], *s. Orn:* ithagine *m or f.*

blood-red [ˈblʌdˈred], *a.* rouge comme du sang; rouge sang; sanglant; *Nat.Hist:* sanguinolent.

bloodroot [ˈblʌdruːt], *s. Bot:* sanguinaire *f.*

bloodshed [ˈblʌdʃed], *s.* **1.** effusion *f* de sang; **the revolution was carried through without b.,** la révolution fut accomplie sans verser de sang. **2.** carnage *m.*

bloodshot [ˈblʌdʃɔt], *a.* **b. eye,** œil injecté de sang; œil éraillé; (*of eye*) **to become b.,** s'injecter; **to have an eye b.,** avoir un épanchement sanguin du globe oculaire.

bloodstain [ˈblʌdstein], *s.* tache *f* de sang.

bloodstained [ˈblʌdsteind], *a.* (*a*) taché de sang, souillé de sang, ensanglanté; **b. handkerchief,** mouchoir taché de sang; (*b*) **b. hands,** mains souillées de sang.

bloodstock [ˈblʌdstɔk], *s.* chevaux *mpl* de race pure, de pur sang.

bloodstone [ˈblʌdstoun], *s. Miner:* (*a*) jaspe sanguin; (*b*) hématite *f,* sanguine *f.*

bloodstream [ˈblʌdstriːm], *s.* (*a*) *Physiol:* le sang; **nitrogen in the b.,** de l'azote *m* dans le sang; (*b*) **the influence of communism had penetrated into the b. of national politics,** l'influence du communisme avait pénétré jusqu'au cœur de la politique nationale.

bloodsucker [ˈblʌdsʌkər], *s.* **1.** *Ann:* sangsue *f.* **2.** *F:* sangsue, vampire *m.*

bloodsucking[1] [ˈblʌdsʌkiŋ], *a.* (*a*) (*of insect*) hématophage; (*b*) vampirique.

bloodsucking[2], *s.* vampirisme *m.*

bloodthirstiness [ˈblʌdθəːstinis], *s.* soif *f* de sang.

bloodthirsty [ˈblʌdθəːsti], *a.* sanguinaire; altéré de sang, assoiffé de sang, avide de sang.

bloodwite [ˈblʌdwait], *s. A.Jur:* prix *m* du sang.

bloodwort [ˈblʌdwəːt], *s. Bot:* **1.** patience *f* rouge, sang (de) dragon *m,* herbe *f* aux charpentiers. **2.** sureau *m* hièble; petit sureau. **3.** grande pimprenelle; pimprenelle commune, des prés.

bloody[1] [ˈblʌdi], *a.* **1.** (*a*) sanglant, ensanglanté, taché de sang; (combat) sanglant, sanguinaire; (tyran) sanguinaire, cruel; *Hist:* **the B. Assizes,** les Assises sanglantes (du juge Jeffreys); *U.S: Hist:* **to wave the b. shirt,** entretenir la discorde entre le Nord et le Sud; *Her:* **the B. Hand,** la main rouge (des armoiries d'un baronnet); **the B. Hand of Ulster,** la main rouge de l'Ulster; *F:* **B. Mary,** (i) la reine Mary I (d'Angleterre); (ii) mélange *m* de vodka et de jus de tomate; (*b*) *NAm:* **maples b. at the first touch of frost,** érables rouge sang, couleur de sang, dès la première gelée. **2.** *P:* (*a*) *a.* sacré; **the weather's been perfectly b. all this month,** il a fait un sacré temps depuis un mois; **a b. liar,** un sacré menteur; **stop that b. row!** taisez-vous, nom de Dieu! **(you) b. fool!** bougre d'idiot! sacré imbécile! (*meaningless vulgarism*) **pass me the b. salt,** donne-moi le sacré sel; (*b*) *adv.* **it's b. hot!** il fait bigrement chaud! quelle sacrée chaleur! **he can b. well do it himself!** il n'a qu'à se démerder tout seul! **not b. likely!** merde! vous pouvez repasser!

bloody[2], *v.tr.* (**bloodied**) (*a*) ensanglanter; souiller (ses mains, etc.) de sang; **battles that have bloodied French soil,** batailles *f* qui ont ensanglanté le sol français; (*b*) *NAm:* **autumn already bloodying the leaves,** l'automne qui fait déjà rougir les feuilles.

bloody-minded [ˈblʌdiˈmaindid], *a. P:* pas commode; **he's just b.-m.,** c'est un mauvais coucheur; **he doesn't have to do it, he's just being b.-m.,** il le fait rien que pour nous emmerder.

bloody-mindedness [ˈblʌdiˈmaindidnis], *s. P:* disposition *f* peu commode; **I'm sick of you and your b.-m.,** j'en ai marre de vous et de votre sacré caractère.

bloom[1] [bluːm], *s.* **1.** (i) fleur *f*; (ii) floraison *f,* épanouissement *m*; **to burst into b.,** fleurir; **all nature is in b. again,** toute la nature est refleurie; **flower in b.,** fleur éclose; **in full b.,** épanoui, en pleine fleur, en pleine floraison; **carnation, rose, in its first b.,** œillet frais épanoui, rose fraîche épanouie; **gardens where thousands of flowers are in b.,** jardins où s'épanouissent des milliers de fleurs; **Mr X exhibited some beautiful blooms,** M. X a exposé plusieurs échantillons *m* magnifiques (de ses roses, de ses chrysanthèmes, etc.); **the b. of youth,** l'incarnat *m* de la jeunesse; **in the b. of youth,** à, dans, la fleur de l'âge, de la jeunesse; en pleine jeunesse; **in the full b. of her loveliness,** dans le plein épanouissement, dans tout l'éclat, de sa beauté; **beauty that has lost its b.,** beauté défraîchie. **2.** (*a*) velouté *m,* pruine *f,* duvet *m* (du raisin, d'une pêche); **to take the b. off (a bunch of grapes, etc.),** déflorer (une grappe de raisin, etc.); *Bot:* **covered with b.,** pruiné, pruineux; (*b*) efflorescence *f,* fleur (du soufre sur le caoutchouc, etc.); (*c*) bouquet *m* (du vin). **3.** *Ch:* **cobalt, zinc, b.,** fleur de cobalt, de zinc.

bloom[2], *v.i.* **1.** fleurir; être en fleur; **to b. into sth.,** devenir qch. (de beau). **2.** *A:* resplendir; être resplendissant.

bloom[3], *s. Metall:* masse *f* de fer cinglé, brame *f*; bloom *m,* renard *m,* lopin *m,* loupe *f,* masseau *m*; **half b.,** massoque *f*; **double b.,** doublon *m*; **b. plate,** tôle forte; **b. pass,** cannelure *f* de blooming.

bloom[4], *v.tr. Metall:* cingler, dégrossir (une masse de fer).

bloomer [ˈbluːmər], *s.* **1.** *Typ:* majuscule ornée. **2.** *F:* bévue *f,* gaffe *f,* boulette *f*; **to make a b.,** mettre les pieds dans le plat; gaffer.

bloomers [ˈbluːməz], *s.pl. Cost: A:* culotte bouffante (de femme).

bloomery [ˈbluːməri], *s. Metall:* bloomerie *f,* affinerie *f*; **b. furnace,** four *m* à loupes; **b. fire,** feu catalan.

blooming[1] [ˈbluːmiŋ]. **1.** *a.* (*a*) (*flowering*) fleurissant; en fleur; (*b*) (*flourishing*) florissant; **a handsome girl, tall and b.,** une belle fille, grande et fraîche. **2.** *F: O:* (*meaningless intensive*) (*a*) *a.* **you b. idiot!** sacré idiot! **it's a b. lie!** ça, pour un mensonge! **no b. fear!** t'en fais pas! (*b*) *adv.* **yes, you b. well will (do it)!** et moi je te dis que oui! je te fiche mon billet que tu le feras!

blooming[2], *s.* floraison *f,* fleuraison *f.*

blooming[3], *s. Metall:* bloomage *m,* dégrossissage *m,* dégrossissement *m* (du fer); **b. mill,** blooming *m,* train *m* à blooms; **b. roll,** cylindre *m* du blooming.

bloomless [ˈbluːmlis], *a. Tchn:* **b. oil,** huile neutre (filtrée et blanchie au soleil).

bloop [bluːp], *s. Cin:* **1.** bruit *m* de collure, claque *f* de collage. **2.** voile *m,* encoche *f,* sonore, éliminateur *m* de bruit de collage.

blooper [ˈbluːpər], *s.* **1.** appareil récepteur rayonnant un signal. **2.** *NAm: F:* (*a*) gaffe *f,* (*b*) *Sp:* (*baseball*) balle lente.

blooping [ˈbluːpiŋ], *s. attrib. Cin:* **b. patch,** cache-collure *m, pl.* cache-collures; voile *m,* encoche *f,* sonore, éliminateur *m* de bruit de collage; **b. notch,** raccord sonore défectueux.

blossom[1] [ˈblɔsəm], *s.* **1.** fleur *f* (des arbres); **tree in b.,** arbre *m* en fleur(s); **orange b.,** fleur d'oranger; **spray of b.,** petite branche fleurie; *P: A:* **b. nose,** nez bourgeonné; nez fleuri; **b.-nosed,** au nez fleuri. **2.** *Geol:* affleurement oxydé.

blossom[2], *v.*

I. *v.i.* (*of tree*) fleurir; **to b. again,** refleurir; (*in same season*) surfleurir; **she had blossomed (out) into a charming young woman,** elle était devenue une charmante jeune femme.

II. (*compound verb*) **blossom out,** *v.i.* s'épanouir.

blossoming [ˈblɔsəmiŋ], *s.* fleuraison *f,* floraison *f*; épanouissement *m.*

blot[1] [blɔt], *s.* (*a*) tache *f*; (*of ink*) pâté *m*; (*b*) **a b. on s.o.'s honour,** une tache, une souillure, à l'honneur de qn; **b. on the escutcheon,** tache au blason; **this factory is a b. on the landscape,** cette usine gâte, gâche, le paysage.

blot[2], *v.*

I. *v.tr. & i.* (**blotted; blotting**) **1.** *v.tr.* (*a*) tacher, souiller, ternir; *F:* **to b. one's copybook,** ternir sa réputation; (*b*) (*of ink*) faire des pâtés sur (qch.). **2.** *v.tr.* sécher l'encre (d'une lettre, etc.); passer le buvard sur (l'encre). **3.** *v.i.* (*of blotting paper*) boire l'encre; **blotting paper that won't b.,** (papier) buvard qui macule.

II. (*compound verbs*) **1. blot off,** *v.tr. Phot:* essorer (un cliché).

2. blot out, *v.tr.* (*a*) effacer (un souvenir, etc.); (*b*) (*of fog, etc.*) cacher, masquer (l'horizon, etc.); (*c*) *Lit:* exterminer (une race, etc.).

3. blot up, *v.tr.* essuyer (de l'encre renversée avec un buvard); *U.S:* éponger, essuyer (du lait, etc., renversé).

blot[3], *s.* **1.** *Games:* (*backgammon*) dame découverte; **to hit a b.,** battre une dame (découverte). **2.** *A:* point *m* faible (dans une position).

blotch[1] [blɔtʃ], *s.* **1.** tache *f,* éclaboussure *f* (d'encre, de couleur). **2.** (*a*) tache rouge (sur la peau); **blotches due to indigestion,** rougeurs dues à l'indigestion; (*b*) pustule *f.* **3.** *Arb: Fung:* blotch *m.*

blotch[2], *v.tr.* couvrir (la peau) de taches, de rougeurs; **cold blotches the skin,** le froid marbre la peau.

blotched [blɔtʃt], *a.* = BLOTCHY.

blotchiness [ˈblɔtʃinis], *s.* couperose *f.*

blotchy [ˈblɔtʃi], *a.* **1.** (teint) brouillé, couperosé; (peau) couverte de rougeurs. **2.** tacheté.

blotter [ˈblɔtər], *s.* **1.** buvard *m*; bloc *m* buvard; cartable *m*; **hand b.,** tampon *m* buvard. **2.** *(a) Com:* brouillard *m*, main courante; *(b) Adm: NAm:* registre *m* (d'arrestations, etc.); livre *m* d'écrou. **3.** *NAm: P:* ivrogne, ivrognesse.

blotting ['blɔtiŋ], *s.* **1.** *(a)* séchage *m* (au papier buvard); *(b)* maculage *m* (du papier). **2. b. (paper),** (papier *m*) buvard *m*; **b. pad,** (bloc *m*) buvard, sous-main *m inv.*

blotting off ['blɔtiŋ 'ɔf], *s. Phot:* essorage *m.*

blotto ['blɔtou], *a. P:* complètement ivre; bourré; blindé.

blouse [blauz], *s.* **1.** blouse *f* (de paysan, etc.). **2.** corsage *m*, chemisier *m* (de femme). **3.** *NAm:* vareuse *f* (de marin, etc.).

blow[1] [blou], *s.* **1.** coup *m* de vent; **to go for a b.,** sortir prendre l'air, (aller) se promener au grand air. **2.** *(a)* souffle *m*; **every morning he has a b. at his trombone,** tous les matins il souffle dans son trombone; **give your nose one good b. and be done with it,** mouche-toi une bonne fois pour toutes; *(b) P: A:* renseignement secret; tuyau *m*. **3.** *Metall:* (charge *f* de) soufflage *m.*

blow[2], *v.*

I. *v.i. & tr.* (*p.t.* **blew** [blu:], *p.p.* **blown** [bloun]) **1.** *v.i.* *(a)* (*of wind*) souffler; **it's blowing, the wind is blowing,** il fait du vent; il vente; **it's blowing hard,** le vent souffle fort, il fait grand vent; **it was blowing a gale,** le vent soufflait en tempête, faisait rage; il faisait un vent à décorner les bœufs; **it's blowing up for rain,** le vent annonce de la pluie; **the wind was blowing down the chimney,** le vent s'engouffrait dans la cheminée; **the leaves were blowing to and fro in the wind,** le vent faisait danser les feuilles; **my papers blew out of the window,** mes papiers se sont envolés par la fenêtre; **the wind's blowing from the west,** le vent souffle de l'ouest; *Nau:* (*of wind*) **to b. from a quarter,** dépendre d'un bord; **wind blowing on the quarter,** vent qui donne sur la hanche; **the door blew open,** le vent a ouvert la porte; *Lit:* **b. high, b. low,** quoi qu'il advienne; *(b)* (*of pers., animal*) souffler; (*of whale*) rejeter l'eau par les évents; **to b. on one's fingers,** souffler dans ses doigts; **to let the horses b.,** laisser souffler les chevaux; *F:* (*of pers.*) **to b. like a grampus,** souffler comme une baleine, comme un phoque, comme un bœuf; *(c) esp. NAm: F:* se vanter; *(d) Lit:* **to b. (up)on s.o.'s reputation,** ternir une réputation; *(e)* (*of fuse*) sauter. **2.** *v.tr.* *(a)* **the wind is blowing the rain against the windows,** le vent chasse la pluie contre les vitres; (*of wind*) **to b. a ship ashore,** pousser un navire à la côte; **to be blown out to sea,** être poussé au large; **we were being blown off our course,** nous tombions sous le vent; **sail blown over a yard,** voile capelée sur une vergue; **it's an ill wind that blows nobody any good,** à quelque chose malheur est bon; *(b)* (*of pers.*) **to b. the dust off sth.,** souffler sur qch. pour enlever la poussière; **to b. s.o. a kiss,** envoyer un baiser à qn; **to b. one's nose,** se moucher; *(c)* **to b. the organ,** souffler l'orgue; **to b. the horn,** sonner du cor; **to b. a trumpet,** souffler dans une trompette; **to b. the trumpet,** jouer de la trompette; (*with passive force*) **the trumpets were blowing,** on sonnait de la trompette; *F:* (*of pers.*) **to b. one's own trumpet,** chanter ses propres louanges; *(d)* **to b. air into sth.,** insuffler de l'air dans qch.; **to b. an egg,** vider un œuf; *Mch:* **to b. a boiler,** évacuer une chaudière; *Nau:* **to b. the tanks** (*of a submarine*), chasser aux ballasts; **to b. bubbles,** faire des bulles de savon; **to b. glass,** souffler le verre; *(e)* essouffler (un cheval, etc.); *Vet:* (*of food*) empanser (un animal); *(f) El:* faire sauter (les plombs); *Aut: etc:* **to b. a gasket,** faire sauter un joint; *F:* (*of pers.*) **to b. one's top,** sortir de ses gonds; *F:* **to b. the gaff,** vendre la mèche, manger le morceau; *(g) P:* (s)chnouffer, prendre une reniflette; **to b. hay, a stack,** fumer de la marijuana; *F:* **this'll b. your mind,** (i) (*of drug, etc.*) ça va vous secouer; (ii) (*of book, etc.*) ça va vous donner toutes sortes d'idées nouvelles; *(h)* (*of fly*) pondre ses œufs dans (la viande, etc.); *(i) F: O:* **b. the expense! expense be blowed!** je me moque de la dépense! **be blowed to you!** zut pour vous! **I'll be blowed if . . .,** que le diable m'emporte si . . .; **well I'm blowed!** non, mais des fois!

II. (*compound verbs*) **1. blow about;** *(a) v.i.* (*of leaves, etc.*) voler çà et là; *(b) v.tr.* agiter, faire voler (qch.); disperser (des feuilles, etc.).

2. blow away; *(a) v.tr.* (*of wind, etc.*) emporter (qch.); **the sails were blown away,** les voiles ont été emportées par le vent; **the wind blew away the fog,** le vent a dissipé le brouillard; *(b) v.i.* (*of papers, etc.*) s'envoler.

3. blow down, *v.tr.* *(a)* (*of wind*) abattre, renverser (un arbre, etc.); *(b) Mch:* **to b. d. the boiler,** vider, évacuer, la chaudière.

4. blow in; *(a) v.tr.* (*of wind, etc.*) enfoncer (un carreau, une porte); *Metall:* mettre (un haut fourneau) en feu; *(b) v.i.* (*of windows, etc.*) s'enfoncer; *F:* (*of pers.*) entrer en passant, s'amener, arriver à l'improviste.

5. blow off; *(a) v.tr.* (*of wind*) emporter (un chapeau, etc.); (*of pers.*) souffler (la poussière); *Mch: etc:* **to b. o. steam,** purger, laisser échapper, lâcher, larguer, de la vapeur; **to b. o. the boiler,** vider, évacuer, vidanger, la chaudière; *(b) v.i.* (*of hat, etc.*) s'envoler.

6. blow on, *v.tr. Metall:* braser, souder, au chalumeau.

7. blow out; *(a) v.tr.* souffler, éteindre (une bougie); chasser, expulser (de l'air); gonfler, enfler (ses joues); **the candle was blown out,** (i) le vent a éteint la bougie; (ii) on a soufflé la bougie; *Mch:* **to b. o. a cylinder,** purger un cylindre; **to b. o. a boiler,** évacuer l'eau d'une chaudière; (*of steam engine*) **to b. o. the packing,** cracher, expulser, l'étoupe; **to b. o. a blast furnace,** mettre un haut fourneau hors feu; **to b. o. one's brains,** se faire sauter, se brûler, la cervelle; *(b) v.i.* (*of candle, etc.*) s'éteindre; *Min:* (*of shot*) faire canon; *Aut: etc:* (*of gasket*) sauter; (*of tyre*) éclater; *El:* (*of fuse*) sauter.

8. blow over; *(a) v.tr.* (*of wind*) renverser (une table, etc.); *(b) v.i.* **the storm has blown over,** la tempête s'est calmée, s'est dissipée; **the scandal soon blew over,** le scandale a été vite oublié.

9. blow through, *v.tr. Mch:* purger (les cylindres); *Plumb: etc:* faire une chasse d'air dans (les canalisations).

10. blow up; *(a) v.i.* (*of mine, etc.*) éclater, sauter; (*of boiler, etc.*) crever, exploser; *Sp: F:* (*of player*) s'effondrer; *Cmptr:* (*of programme*) se planter; **there's a gale blowing up,** il se prépare une tempête; **to b. up into a crisis,** prendre les proportions d'une crise (internationale, etc.); *(b) v.tr.* faire sauter (une mine, un pont, etc.); (faire) exploser (une mine, une poudrière); gonfler (un pneu); souffler (un ballon); agrandir (une photo); **blown up with pride,** bouffi d'orgueil; *F:* **to b. s.o. up,** semoncer, savonner, qn; *Sp: F:* **the referee blew him up,** l'arbitre l'a sifflé.

blow[3], *s. O:* fleuraison *f*; *used in the phr.* **in full b.,** en pleine fleuraison, en plein épanouissement.

blow[4], *v.i.* **(blew; blown)** (*of flower*) s'épanouir, fleurir, s'ouvrir; **fresh-blown poppies, roses,** pavots frais éclos, roses fraîches écloses.

blow[5], *s.* **1.** coup *m*; (*with fist*) coup de poing; (*with stick, etc.*) coup de bâton; **death b.,** coup mortel, fatal; **I knocked him down at the first b.,** je l'ai renversé du premier coup; **at a (single) b.,** d'un (seul) coup; **to strike a b.,** porter, asséner, donner, un coup; **without striking a b.,** sans coup férir; **to miss one's b.,** manquer son coup; **to deal s.o. a b.,** porter un coup à qn; **he dealt him b. after b.,** il lui a porté coup sur coup; **to receive a b.,** recevoir un coup; **to come, get, to blows, to exchange blows,** en venir aux coups, aux mains; *Jur:* en arriver aux voies de fait; **to come to blows with s.o.,** faire le coup de poing avec qn; **blows fell thick and fast,** il pleuvait des coups; **to return b. for b.,** rendre coup pour coup; **slight b. on the arm,** légère atteinte au bras; **lightning b., stinging b.,** coup foudroyant, raide comme balle; **knockout b.,** (i) coup d'assommoir; (ii) *Box:* knock-out *m*; *Prov:* **the first b. is half the battle,** le premier coup en vaut deux; **b. to s.o.'s credit,** atteinte *f* au crédit de qn; **to aim a b. at s.o.'s authority, to deal s.o.'s authority a b.,** porter atteinte à l'autorité de qn; entamer l'autorité de qn. **2.** coup (du sort); **it came as a crushing b. to us,** ce fut un coup d'assommoir pour nous; **it was a b. to me to hear that . . .,** cela m'a porté un coup d'apprendre que . . .; **his death will be a sad b. to his family,** sa mort est un rude coup pour sa famille. **3.** (*impact*) choc *m.*

blowback ['bloubæk], *s. Arms: etc:* retour *m* de souffle.

blowball ['bloubɔ:l], *s. Bot: F:* chandelle *f* (de pissenlit).

blow-by-blow ['bloubai'blou], *a. U.S:* (compte-rendu) minutieux, détaillé.

blowcock ['bloukɔk], *s. Mch:* robinet *m* d'extraction, de vidange.

blow-down ['bloudaun], *s. Mec.E:* purge *f*, chasse *f* (de réservoir, etc.); **b.-d. cock,** robinet *m* d'extraction, de purge; **b.-d. piping, tank,** tuyauterie *f*, réservoir *m*, de vide-vite.

blower ['blouər], *s.* **1.** *(a)* souffleur, -euse (de verre, etc.); *(b)* **horn b.,** sonneur *m* de cor; corneur, -euse. **2.** *(a)* écran *m* à tirage; tablier *m*, rideau *m*, trappe *f* (de cheminée); *(b) Ind: etc:* ventilateur soufflant; souffleur *m*; soufflante *f*, souffleuse *f*; soufflerie *f*; *Navy:* **blowers,** turbo-soufflante *f*, turbo-souffleuse *f* (de sous-marin); **damp air b.,** humidificateur *m*; **b. fuse,** fusible fondu; **b. wheel,** roue soufflante; *(c) Cmptr:* soufflerie, ventilateur; *(d) Agr:* ensileuse *f*; *(e)* insufflateur *m*, soufflet *m* (à poudre insecticide); *(f) F:* téléphone *m*, bigophone *m*, bigorneau *m*. **3.** *Min:* échappement *m* de gaz; soufflard *m* (de grisou). **4.** *Z:* **b. (dolphin),** souffleur.

blowfly, *pl.* **-flies** ['blouflai, -flaiz], *s.* mouche *f* à viande, de la viande; lucilie *f.*

blowgun ['blougʌn], *s.* sarbacane *f.*

blowhard ['blouhɑ:d], *s. U.S: P:* vantard *m*, esbroufeur *m.*

blowhole ['blouhoul], *s.* **1.** évent *m* (d'une baleine). **2.** ventilateur *m* (d'un tunnel). **3.** *Metall:* soufflure *f* (dans la fonte); bouillon *m.*

blowing ['blouiŋ], *s.* **1.** soufflement *m* (du vent). **2.** *(a)* soufflage *m* (d'un fourneau, du verre, etc.); **b. machine,** soufflet *m*; *Glassm:* **b. iron,** canne *f* (de souffleur); *(b) Med:* **b. murmur,** bruit *m* de soufflet.

blowing off ['blouiŋ'ɔf], *s. Mch:* évacuation *f* (d'une chaudière).

blowing out ['blouiŋ'aut], *s.* **1.** extinction *f* (d'une chandelle). **2.** gonflement *m* (des joues). **3.** expulsion *f* (de l'air des conduites de gaz); crachement *m* (de l'étoupe, etc.); *Mch:* purge *f* (d'un cylindre).

blowing up ['blouiŋ'ʌp], *s.* **1.** explosion *f.* **2.** *(a)* gonflement *m* (d'un pneu); *(b) Phot: F:* agrandissement *m*. **3.** *F:* semonce *f*, engueulade *f*; **to give s.o. a good b. up,** passer un savon à qn, engueuler qn.

blowlamp ['bloulæmp], *s.* **1.** chalumeau *m*, lampe *f* à souder, à braser. **2.** brûloir *m* (de peintre en bâtiments).

blown [bloun], *a.* **1.** essoufflé, hors d'haleine; **the team was b.,** l'équipe était à bout de souffle. **2.** (*of food*) gâté (par les mouches). **3.** (*of casting*) qui présente des soufflures. **4.** *El:* **b. fuse,** fusible fondu; plomb sauté.

blow-off ['blouɔf], *s. Tchn:* extraction *f*, vidange *m*; **bottom b.-o., surface b.-o., continuous b.o.,** extraction de fond, de surface, continue; *attrib.* **b.-o. cock,** robinet *m*, bouchon *m*, de vidange; purgeur *m* de vapeur; **b.-o. gear,** appareil *m*, dispositif *m*, de vidange; purgeur de vapeur; **b.-o. pipe,** ventilateur *m*, tuyau *m* d'évent (de fosse d'aisance); tuyau d'extraction; **b.-o. valve,** clapet *m*, soupape *f*, de décharge, de purge, de vidange.

blowout ['blouaut], *s.* **1.** *Metall:* mise *f* hors feu (d'un haut fourneau). **2.** *Min: etc:* éruption *f* (de gaz, de pétrole, etc.) au cours d'un sondage; **b. prevention,** vanne *f* d'éruption. **3.** *El:* *(a)* soufflage *m* d'étincelles; *(b)* **magnetic b.,** souffleur *m* magnétique; **lightning arrester with magnetic b.,** parafoudre *m* à soufflage magnétique. **4.** *Aut: etc:* éclatement *m*, rupture *f* (de pneu, de chambre à air). **5.** *P:* gueuleton *m*, ripaille *f*, régal *m*; **we had a good b.,** on s'est régalés; on s'en est donné plein la ceinture.

blowpipe ['bloupaip], *s.* **1.** sarbacane *f.* **2.** *(a) Ch: Metall:* chalumeau *m*; **electric b.,** chalumeau électrique; **b. flame,** jet *m* de flamme; *(b) Glassm:* canne *f*, fêle *f* (de souffleur). **3.** *Mus:* porte-vent *m inv* (de cornemuse, de biniou).

blow-through ['blouθru:], *s. Mch:* purge *f* (des cylindres); *Plumb: etc:* chasse *f* d'air; **b.-t. pipe, cock,** tuyau *m*, robinet *m*, de purge.

blowtorch ['bloutɔ:tʃ], *s.* = BLOWLAMP.

blow-tube ['bloutju:b], *s.* sarbacane *f.*

blowup ['blouʌp], *s. F:* **1.** *(a)* dispute *f*, querelle *f*; *(b)* explosion *f*, accès *m* de fureur; *(c)* esclandre *m*. **2.** *Phot:* agrandissement *m.*

blow-valve ['blouvælv], *s. Mch:* reniflard *m* (de chaudière à vapeur).

blowy ['bloui], *a.* venteux; tempétueux.

blowzed ['blauzd], *a.* = BLOWZY.

blowziness ['blauzinis], *s.* air mal peigné; air peu ragoûtant (d'une femme).

blowzy ['blauzi], *a.* (*of woman*) *(a)* rougeaude; *(b)* ébouriffée, mal peignée; *(c)* empâtée, avachie.

blub[1] [blʌb], *s. F:* crise *f* de larmes.

blub[2], *v.i.* **(blubbed; blubbing)** *F:* = BLUBBER[3] 1.

blubber[1] ['blʌbər], *s.* **1.** graisse *f*, lard *m*, de baleine. **2.** *F:* (*jellyfish*) méduse *f.*

blubber[2], *a.* **b. lip,** lippe *f*; **b.-lipped,** lippu.

blubber[3], *F:* **1.** *v.i.* *(a)* pleurer bruyamment, pleurer comme un veau **(over,** sur); chialer; *(b)* pleurnicher. **2.** *v.tr.* **to b. out sth.,** dire qch. en pleurant comme un veau.

blubberer ['blʌbərər], *s. F:* pleurnicheur, -euse.

blubbering ['blʌbəriŋ], *a. F:* pleurard, pleurnicheur, -euse.

blubbery[1] ['blʌbəri], *a.* graisseux, pareil à la graisse de baleine.

blubbery[2], *a. F:* bouffi.

bluchers ['blu:tʃəz, 'blu:kəz], *s.pl. A.Cost:* demi-bottes *f.*

bludge [blʌdʒ], *v.i. Austr: P:* *(a)* fainéanter, flémarder; *(b)* faire de l'escroquerie.

bludgeon[1] ['blʌdʒən], *s.* gourdin *m*, matraque *f*; trique *f*, casse-tête *m inv.*

bludgeon[2], *v.tr.* asséner un coup de gourdin, de matraque, à (qn), sur la tête de (qn); matraquer (qn); **to b. s.o. into doing sth.,** (i) faire faire qch. à qn à coups de gourdin, à coups de trique; (ii) forcer qn à faire qch. par des méthodes brutales.

bludger ['blʌdʒər], *s. Austr: P:* *(a)* fainéant *m*; *(b)* escroc *m*, filou *m*.

blue[1] [blu:], *a. & s.* **1.** (*a*) *a. & s.* bleu (*m*); *a.* azuré; *s.* azur *m*; **dark b., Oxford b.,** bleu foncé *inv*; **dark b. socks,** des chaussettes *f* bleu foncé; **light b., Cambridge b.,** bleu clair *inv*; **a light b. dress,** une robe bleu clair; **sky b.,** bleu céleste *inv*, bleu (de) ciel *inv*, (bleu d')azur *inv*; **navy b.,** bleu marine *inv*; **slate b.,** bleu ardoise *inv*, bleu turquin *inv*; **dressed in b.,** vêtu de bleu, habillé en bleu; **b. spectacles,** lunettes bleutées; **b. ribbon,** (i) ruban bleu (de l'Ordre de la Jarretière, des buveurs d'eau, de la traversée de l'Atlantique, etc.); (ii) prix principal (d'une réunion de courses, etc.); **to go b.,** (i) (*of pers.*) prendre un teint violacé; (ii) (*of thg*) virer au bleu; **the baby cried until he was b. in the face,** le bébé a tant pleuré qu'il s'est congestionné le visage; **face b. with cold,** visage violacé par le froid; *F:* **you can talk until you're b. in the face,** vous avez beau parler; **I've told you so until I'm b. in the face,** je m'épuise, m'évertue, à vous le dire; (*b*) *a. Fig:* **b. blood,** sang royal, illustre, aristocratique; *F:* **once in a b. moon,** en de rares occasions; une fois par extraordinaire, en passant; (*c*) *s.* **the b.,** (i) le ciel, le firmament; (ii) la haute mer, le large; **a bolt from the b.,** un événement imprévu, un coup de foudre; **to disappear into the b.,** se perdre dans le lointain; disparaître sans laisser de traces; (*d*) *a. Bot:* **b. gum,** eucalyptus bleu; **b. joint,** calamagrostis *m*; **Kentucky b.,** paturin *m* des prés; (*e*) *a. Z:* **b. duiker,** céphalophe bleu; *a. & s.* **British b. (cat),** chartreux *m*; (*f*) *s. Ent:* lycène *f*; (*g*) *a. Miner:* **b. asbestos,** crocidolite *f*; **b. earth, b. ground,** kimberlite *f*, blueground *m*; *Ch:* **b. vitriol,** vitriol bleu, sulfate *m* de cuivre; *Tchn:* **b. annealing,** recuit bleu; (*h*) *a. Med:* **b. disease,** (i) maladie bleue, cyanose *f*; (ii) rickettsiose *f* (des Montagnes Rocheuses); **b. baby,** enfant bleu; *Vet:* **b. tongue,** langue bleue. **2.** (*a*) *a.* **to look b.,** avoir l'air (i) triste, sombre; (ii) déconcerté; **to feel b.,** avoir le cafard; (*b*) *s.pl.* **to have the blues,** avoir des idées noires, un accès d'humeur noire, broyer du noir; avoir le cafard; (*c*) *a. F:* **to tell b. stories, jokes,** en raconter des vertes (et des pas mûres); **to turn the air b.,** jurer comme un charretier; **b. movie,** film *m* porno; (*d*) *a. U.S:* **b. laws,** lois inspirées par le puritanisme; (*e*) *Mus: Danc:* **the blues,** le blues. **3.** *a. & s. Pol:* conservateur, -trice; **he's a true b.,** c'est (i) un patriote; (ii) un conservateur, un vieux de la vieille. **4.** *s.* (*a*) *Sp:* **the Dark Blues,** les équipes (i) de l'université d'Oxford; (ii) de l'école de Harrow; **the Light Blues,** les équipes (i) de l'université de Cambridge; (ii) du collège d'Eton; **he's a Cambridge b.,** c'est un sportif chevronné de l'université de Cambridge; (*b*) *Mil:* **the Blues,** (i) *Eng:* la Cavalerie de la Maison du Souverain; (ii) *U.S: Hist:* l'armée *f* du Nord. **5.** *s. Laund:* bleu (d'empois); indigo *m*, azur. **6.** *s. Austr:* (*a*) *F:* contravention *f*, (*b*) *F.* erreur *f*; (*c*) *P:* **to bung on a b.,** commencer une querelle; flanquer un coup à qn.

blue[2], *v.tr.* **1.** (*a*) bleuir; teindre (qch.) en bleu; *Laund:* azurer (le linge); mettre, passer, (le linge) au bleu; *Metalw:* bronzer (un canon); (*b*) bleuter. **2.** *F:* **to b. one's money,** gaspiller, manger, son argent; **to b. the pool,** manger la cagnotte.

bluebag ['blu:bæg], *s. Laund:* sachet *m* à bleu, de bleu.

Bluebeard ['blu:biəd], *Pr.n.m.* Barbe-bleue *m*.

bluebell ['blu:bel], *s. Bot:* **1.** jacinthe *f* sauvage, des bois. **2.** *Scot:* campanule *f*.

blueberry ['blu:b(ə)ri], *s. Bot:* (airelle *f*) myrtille *f*; **(Canada) b.,** bluet *m*, bleuet *m*, (du Canada).

blue-bill ['blu:bil], *s. Orn:* tisserin *m* à bec bleu.

bluebird ['blu:bə:d], *s. Orn: NAm:* rouge-gorge bleu; *Austr:* langrayen *m* à face noire; **fairy b.,** irène *f*, oiseau bleu des fées; **eastern b.,** rouge-gorge bleu d'Amérique, *Fr.C:* merle *m* bleu à poitrine rouge; **mountain b.,** *Fr.C:* merle bleu des montagnes; **western b.,** merle bleu à dos marron.

blue-black ['blu:'blæk], *a.* **1.** noir tirant sur le bleu. **2.** (encre) bleue-noire.

blueblossom ['blu:blɔs(ə)m], *s. Bot:* céanothe *m*.

bluebottle ['blu:bɔtl], *s.* **1.** *Bot:* bluet *m*, bleuet *m*. **2.** *Ent:* mouche *f* à viande, mouche bleue (de la viande). **3.** *F:* (*policeman*) flic *m*.

bluebuck ['blu:bʌk], *s. Z:* céphalophe bleu.

blue bull ['blu:'bul], *s. Z:* nilgau(t) *m*.

blue-chip ['blu:tʃip], *a. St.Exch:* **b.-c. stocks,** actions triées sur le volet.

bluecoat ['blu:kout]. **1.** *a.* **b. boy,** élève *m* des écoles de Christ's Hospital (à uniforme bleu). **2.** *s. NAm: F:* agent *m* de police.

blue-collar ['blu:'kɔlər], *a. NAm:* **b. c. worker,** ouvrier *m*, travailleur manuel, *Fr.C:* col bleu.

blue-eyed ['blu:aid], *a.* **1.** aux yeux bleus. **2.** *F:* innocent, candide; **b.-e. boy,** (i) le chouchou de sa maman; (ii) le favori du patron.

bluefin ['blu:fin], *a. & s. Ich:* **b. (tunny),** thon *m* rouge, thonine *f*.

bluegrass ['blu:grɑ:s], *s. Bot: N.Z:* agropyre *m*; *Austr:* andropogon *m*; *U.S:* **(Kentucky) b.,** pâturin *m* des prés.

blue-grey ['blu:grei], *a. & s.* gris bleuté; (cheval *m*) porcelaine *inv*.

blueing ['blu:iŋ], *s.* **1.** bleutage *m*, azurage *m* (du linge); *Metalw:* bleuissage *m*, bronzage *m*. **2.** *NAm:* bleu *m* (d'empois).

bluejacket ['blu:dʒækit], *s.* marin *m*, matelot *m*, de l'État; col-bleu *m*, *pl.* cols-bleus.

bluejohn ['blu:dʒɔn], *s. Miner:* fluorine bleue ou violette (du Derbyshire).

blueness ['blu:nis], *s.* couleur bleue, coloration bleue.

Bluenose ['blu:nouzə], *s. F:* habitant, -ante, de la Nouvelle-Écosse; Nouvel(le)-Écossais(e).

blue-pencil ['blu:'pensl], *v.tr.* marquer au crayon bleu; **to b. p. an article,** censurer un article.

bluepoint ['blu:pɔint], *s. NAm:* huître *f* de Long Island (New York).

blue-point ['blu:pɔint], *a. Z:* **b.-p. Siamese,** (chat) siamois bleu.

blueprint[1] ['blu:print], *s.* (*a*) dessin négatif, photocalque *m*, contre-calque *m*, *pl.* contre-calques, *F:* bleu *m*; (*b*) plan (détaillé), projet *m*, épure *f*.

blueprint[2], *v.tr.* (*a*) faire un dessin négatif, un photocalque, de (qch.); (*b*) élaborer un projet pour (qch.).

blue rot ['blu:rɔt], *s. Arb:* bleuissement *m*.

blue spar ['blu:spɑ:r], *s. Miner:* lazulite *m*, faux lapis, *F:* pierre *f* d'azur.

bluestocking ['blu:stɔkiŋ], *s.* (*of woman*) bas-bleu *m*, *pl.* bas-bleus; *F:* doctoresse *f*.

bluestone ['blu:stoun], *s.* **1.** sulfate *m* de cuivre; vitriol bleu. **2.** *Geol:* trapp *m* (d'Australie).

bluet ['blu:it], *s. Bot: NAm:* houstonia *f*.

bluetail ['blu:teil], *s. Orn:* **red-flanked b.,** rossignol *m* à flancs roux.

bluethroat ['blu:θrout], *s. Orn:* gorge-bleue *f*, *pl.* gorges-bleues; **red-spotted b.,** gorge-bleue à miroir roux; **white-spotted b.,** gorge-bleue à miroir blanc.

bluey-grey ['blu:i'grei], *a.* glauque.

bluff[1] [blʌf]. **1.** *a.* (*a*) (*of cliff, coast*) accore, escarpé, à pic; *Nau:* **b.(-bowed),** (navire) à proue renflée, renflé de l'avant; à grosses formes à l'avant; **b.-headed,** camard; (*b*) (*of pers.*) brusque; un peu bourru; **a straightforward, b., man,** un homme tout rond, *F:* un homme entier. **2.** *s.* cap *m*, falaise *f*, à pic; à-pic *m*, *pl.* à-pics.

bluff[2], *s.* (*a*) *Cards:* (*at poker*) bluff *m*, cassade *f*; (*b*) bluff, battage *m*; **piece of b.,** coup *m* de bluff; **bill that is only a piece of b.,** projet *m* de loi qui n'est qu'un trompe-l'œil; (*c*) menaces exagérées; **to call s.o.'s b.,** (i) (*at poker*) inviter l'adversaire à mettre cartes sur table; (ii) prendre qn au mot; relever le défi de qn.

bluff[3], *Cards: etc.* **1.** *v.tr.* bluffer (qn); *F:* jeter de la poudre aux yeux de (qn). **2.** *v.i.* faire du bluff, de l'épate; *Cards:* faire cassade.

bluffer ['blʌfər], *s.* épateur *m*; faiseur, -euse; bluffeur, -euse.

bluffness ['blʌfnis], *s.* brusquerie (amicale); franc-parler *m*.

bluing ['blu:iŋ], *s. esp. NAm:* = BLUEING.

bluish ['blu:iʃ], *a.* bleuâtre; bleuté; azurescent; **b.-grey,** ardoisé; (marbre) turquin.

blunder[1] ['blʌndər], *s.* bévue *f*, maladresse *f*, erreur *f*; gaffe *f*; **gross b.,** grosse maladresse; **that was a stupid b.!** voilà une sottise!

blunder[2], *v.i. & tr.* **1.** faire une bévue, une gaffe, une maladresse, un faux pas; *F:* gaffer; mettre les pieds dans le plat; **he lost the contract by blundering,** il a manqué le contrat à cause de sa maladresse. **2.** **to b. against, into, s.o., sth.,** se heurter contre qn, qch.; heurter qn, qch.; **to b. one's way along,** avancer à l'aveuglette; **to b. through one's work,** travailler à l'aveuglette; **to b. upon the truth,** découvrir la vérité par hasard; **he managed to b. through,** il s'en est tiré tant bien que mal.

blunderbuss ['blʌndəbʌs], *s.* **1.** (*gun*) tromblon *m*, espingole *f*. **2.** (*pers.*) maladroit, -e, lourdaud, -e.

blunderer ['blʌndərər], *s.* brouillon, -onne; maladroit, -e; malavisé, -ée; étourdi, -ie; gaffeur, -euse.

blundering[1] ['blʌnd(ə)riŋ], *a.* brouillon, malavisé; maladroit.

blundering[2], *s.* maladresse *f*; cafouillage *m*.

blunderingly ['blʌnd(ə)riŋli], *adv.* avec maladresse; à l'aveuglette, au petit bonheur.

blunge [blʌndʒ], *v.tr. Cer: etc:* mélanger (de la glaise) à l'eau.

blunger ['blʌndʒər], *s. Cer: etc:* malaxeur *m*.

blunt[1] [blʌnt]. **1.** *a.* (*a*) (*not sharpened*) mousse; (*having lost its edge*) émoussé; (*having lost its point*) épointé; (instrument) contondant; (angle) obtus; **b. needle, b. pencil,** aiguille épointée, crayon épointé; **scissors with b. ends,** ciseaux à bouts ronds; (*b*) (*of pers.*) brusque, carré; **a b. man,** un homme tout d'une pièce; **the b. fact,** le fait brutal; **b. refusal,** refus tranché; **he's a John B.,** c'est un bourru; (*c*) *A:* (sens) obtus; (homme *m*) à l'esprit obtus. **2.** *s.* aiguille courte et solide.

blunt[2], *v.tr.* **1.** émousser (un couteau); épointer (un crayon); *A:* **blunted tilting-lance,** lance de joute mornée, à morne; **to b. the feelings,** émousser les sentiments; **to b. s.o.'s anger,** émousser la colère de qn; **to b. the palate,** blaser le palais; **to b. the edge of the pain,** émousser la douleur. **2.** aplatir, abattre (un angle).

blunt[3], *s. P: A:* argent comptant; de la pépète.

bluntly ['blʌntli], *adv.* brusquement, carrément, brutalement; de but en blanc; sans ménagements; **to speak b.,** parler net, carrément.

bluntness ['blʌntnis], *s.* **1.** état émoussé, épointé; manque *m* de tranchant. **2.** brusquerie *f*, rudesse *f*; franchise *f*, sans-façon *m*; **b. of speech,** franc-parler *m*.

blur[1] [blə:r], *s.* **1.** tache *f*, macule *f*, barbouillage *m* (d'encre, etc.); *Typ:* frison *m*; (*offset*) graissage *m*. **2.** (*a*) apparence confuse; brouillard *m*; **b. of tears,** voile *m* de larmes; (*b*) buée *f* (sur un miroir, etc.); (*c*) *Phot:* flou *m*. **3.** ternissure *f*.

blur[2], *v.tr.* **(blurred; blurring) 1.** barbouiller (d'encre, etc.); *Typ:* maculer, mâchurer, friser; (*offset*) graisser. **2.** brouiller, troubler; **the rain is blurring the windows,** la pluie brouille les vitres; **eyes blurred with tears,** yeux voilés de larmes; **the haze has blurred the outline of the mountains,** la brume a estompé les contours de la montagne; **the distant hills are becoming blurred,** les collines lointaines s'estompent; **the valley is blurred by a thick mist,** une brume épaisse ouate la vallée; *v.ind.tr.* **everything was blurred out by the fog,** tout était caché par le brouillard, s'effaçait dans le brouillard.

blurb [blə:b], *s. F:* (*a*) annonce avantageuse d'une marchandise sur le point d'être mise en vente; *esp.* **(publisher's) b.,** prière d'insérer, *F:* jus *m*; (*b*) annonce sur le couvre-livre, sur la bande de nouveauté.

blurred [blə:d], *a.* **b. photograph,** photographie mal venue, mal réussie, floue; **b. outlines,** contours noyés, indécis, flous; **b. memories,** souvenirs confus, estompés; **to have a b. vision of sth.,** voir qch. confusément; avoir une vue confuse, trouble, de qch.

blurring ['blə:riŋ], *s.* **1.** maculage *m*, barbouillage *m*. **2.** *Opt:* halo *m*, flou *m*.

blurry ['blə:ri], *a.* = BLURRED.

blurt out ['blə:t'aut], *v.tr.* **to b. o. a secret,** lâcher (à l'étourdie), laisser échapper, trahir maladroitement, un secret; **he blurted out the truth,** (i) il a dit tout bonnement la vérité; (ii) il a révélé, trahi, maladroitement la vérité; la vérité lui échappa; **he blurted out the whole story,** il a raconté l'affaire de but en blanc; **he blurted it out to us,** il nous a lâché cela à la volée.

blush[1] [blʌʃ], *s.* **1.** aspect *m*; **at (the) first b.,** à l'abord, au premier abord, au premier aspect, de prime abord, à première vue; **in the first b. of youth,** aux prémices *f* de la jeunesse; **in the first b. of its novelty,** en sa prime fleur de nouveauté. **2.** (*a*) rougeur *f* (de modestie, de honte); *A:* **to put s.o. to the b.,** (i) faire rougir qn; embarrasser qn; (ii) faire honte à qn; faire rougir qn de honte; **to bring blushes to s.o.'s cheeks,** faire monter le rouge au visage de qn; **a b. rose to her cheeks,** un flux de sang lui est monté au visage; **to hide one's blushes,** baisser le nez; (*b*) incarnat *m* (des roses); **roses of the deepest b.,** roses *f* du plus vif incarnat; **the first b. of dawn,** les premières rougeurs de l'aube.

blush[2], *v.i.* **1.** (*of pers.*) rougir; **to b. for shame,** rougir de honte; **I b. for you,** vous me faites rougir; **she blushed at the mere thought,** rien que d'y penser la faisait rougir, lui faisait venir le rouge au visage; **to b. at a remark,** s'effaroucher d'une remarque; **to b. crimson,** devenir tout rouge; devenir cramoisi; **to b. purple,** devenir pourpre; **to b. pink,** devenir tout(e) rouge; **to b. to the roots of one's hair,** rougir jusqu'au blanc des yeux, jusqu'au bout des oreilles, jusqu'aux oreilles. **2.** *Lit:* (*of flower, dawn, etc.*) rougir.

blusher ['blʌʃər], *s.* **1.** *Toil:* fard *m* à joues. **2.** *Fung:* Amanita rubescens.

blushing ['blʌʃiŋ], *a.* **1.** (*of pers.*) rougissant, timide; **the b. bride,** la mariée toute confuse, toute rose. **2.** *Lit:* (*of flower, etc.*) rouge, rougissant.

blushingly ['blʌʃiŋli], *adv.* en rougissant; timidement.

bluster[1] ['blʌstər], *s.* (*a*) fureur *f*, fracas *m* (de l'orage); (*b*) (*of pers.*) rodomontades *fpl*.

bluster[2], *v.i.* (*a*) (*of wind*) souffler en rafales; (*b*) (*of pers.*) faire du fracas; parler haut; faire des rodomontades; faire le fanfaron; fanfaronner; **to b. at s.o.,** essayer d'intimider qn; **he blusters to cover up his ignorance,** il parle haut pour cacher son ignorance.

blusterer ['blʌstərər], *s.* bravache *m*, fanfaron *m*; *F:* casseur *m* d'assiettes.

blustering[1] ['blʌst(ə)riŋ], *a.* (*a*) (vent) violent; (*b*) bravache, tonitruant.

blustering[2], *s.* = BLUSTER[1].

blusterous ['blʌst(ə)rəs], **blustery** ['blʌst(ə)ri], *a.* (vent) violent.

bo [bou]; *U.S: P:* (= HOBO?) (*meaningless form of address*) **say, bo, can you lend me . . .?** dis donc, toi, peux-tu me prêter . . .?

bo(h) [bou], *int.* hou!

boa ['bouə], *s.* **1.** *Rept:* boa *m*; **b. constrictor,** boa constricteur, boa constrictor, boa royal; **emperor b.,** boa imperator; **water b.,** boa d'eau, anaconda *m*. **2.** *Cost:* **feather b.,** boa.

Boadicea [bouədi'siə], *Pr.n.f. Hist:* Boadicée, Bodicia.

Boanerges [bouə'nə:dʒi:z], *Pr.n.m.* Boanergès.

boar ['bɔ:r], *s. Z:* verrat *m*; **wild b.,** sanglier *m*, *Ven:* bête noire; **young wild b.,** marcassin *m*; *Ven:* **old b.,** solitaire *m*; **b. hunting,** la chasse au sanglier; **b. spear,** épieu *m*; **boar's head,** *Cu:* hure *f* de sanglier; (ii) *Her:* hure.

board[1] [bɔ:d], *s.* **1.** (*a*) planche *f*, ais *m*; (*thick*) madrier *m*; **thin b.,** feuille *f* de bois; *attrib. U.S:* **b. fence,** palissade *f* en planches; *Dom.Ec:* **bread b.,** planche à couper le pain; **ironing b.,** planche à repasser; **sleeve b.,** pied *m* à manches, à repasser; *Swim:* **diving b.,** plongeoir *m*; *Aut: etc:* **toe b.,** plancher *m* oblique; *Nau:* **shifting boards,** bardis *m*; *Mus:* **finger b.,** touche *f* (de violon); clavier *m* (de piano); (*b*) (**notice**) **b.,** tableau *m* de publicité, d'annonces, d'affichage; planche aux affiches; écriteau *m*; **sandwichman's b.,** panneau *m*; *Aut: etc:* **fascia b., instrument b.,** tableau de bord; *Sp:* **telegraph b.,** tableau d'affichage (des résultats); *Sch:* **to write sth. on the b.,** écrire qch. au tableau noir; (*c*) *Cmptr:* **control b.,** tableau de commande; **patch b., problem b., programme b., wiring b.,** tableau de connexions; **pin b.,** tableau à aiguilles; **plotting b.,** table traçante; (*d*) *Th:* **the boards,** la scène, le théâtre, les planches; **to go on the boards, to walk, tread, the boards,** être acteur, actrice; monter, être, sur les planches; aborder la scène; (*e*) (*cardboard*) carton *m*; **Bristol b.,** carton Bristol, bristol *m*; *Bookb:* **the boards,** les plats *m* (d'un livre); **cloth boards,** plats toile; **paper boards,** plats papier; **front b.,** recto *m*; plat supérieur; **off b.,** verso *m*, plat inférieur; **binding in paper boards,** cartonnage *m*, emboîtage *m*; **in paper boards,** cartonné; **binding in cloth boards,** cartonnage pleine toile; emboîtage pleine toile; **limp boards,** cartonnage souple. **2.** (*a*) table *f*; **the festive b.,** la table du festin; **groaning b.,** table surchargée de mets; (*b*) table, nourriture *f*; pension *f*; **b. and lodging, full b.,** pension (complète); **partial, -half, b.,** demi-pension *f*; **with b. and lodging,** nourri et logé; **b. wages,** (i) salaire *m* en nature; (ii) (*of domestic employee*) indemnité *f* de nourriture (et de logement); **to be on b. wages,** toucher pour sa nourriture; (*c*) (**gaming**) **b.,** table de jeu; **to sweep the b.,** faire table rase; nettoyer le tapis; (*d*) *Chess:* tablier *m* (de l'échiquier). **3.** (*a*) *Pol.Ec: Com: Adm: etc:* conseil *m*; comité *m*; **b. of enquiry,** commission *f* d'enquête; **disciplinary b.,** conseil de discipline; **advisory b.,** comité consultatif; **b. of referees,** commission arbitrale; **b. of trustees,** conseil de gestion (d'un musée, etc.); **marketing b.,** office *m* de régularisation de vente; fonds *m* de stabilisation du marché; **b. of examiners,** jury *m*, commission, d'examen; **medical b.,** conseil de santé; **b. of directors,** conseil *m* d'administration (d'une société); **the bank is represented on the b.,** la banque fait partie du conseil; **b. meeting,** réunion *f* du conseil d'administration; (*b*) *Adm:* **B. of Trade,** (i) *Eng: A:* = Ministère *m* du Commerce; (ii) *U.S:* = chambre *f* de commerce; *A:* **B. of Education** = Ministère de l'Éducation nationale; *A:* **B. of Works** = Ministère des Travaux publics; *A:* **National Wheat B.** = Office *m* du blé; **National Coal B.,** = administration *f* des charbonnages. **4.** *Nau:* (*a*) bord *m*; **on b.,** à bord; **on b. my ship,** à mon bord; **to come on b.,** accoster; **to take goods on b.,** embarquer des marchandises; **free on b.,** franco bord; **to go on b.,** monter à bord; s'embarquer; **to go on b. again,** rentrer à bord; se rembarquer; **to go by the b.,** s'en aller par-dessus bord; tomber à la mer; **a mast went by the b.,** un mât a été emporté par la lame; *Fig:* **to let sth. go by the b.,** négliger, abandonner, qch.; **his reputation has gone by the b.,** il est perdu de réputation; (*b*) bordée *f*, bord; **to make a b.,** courir une bordée, un bord; *adv.phr.* **b. and b.,** en louvoyant.

board[2], *v.*

I. *v.tr. & i.* **1.** *v.tr.* (*a*) **to b.,** *v.ind.tr.* **to b. over, the floor of a room,** planchéier, faire un plancher dans, une pièce; (*b*) *Bookb:* cartonner (un livre); (*c*) *Leath:* rebrousser (le cuir). **2.** (*a*) *v.i.* être en pension; **I b. at Mrs B.'s,** je suis en pension chez Mme B.; **to b. at school,** être en pension à l'école; (*b*) *v.tr.* nourrir (des élèves, etc.); avoir (qn) en pension chez soi. **3.** *v.tr.* (*a*) *Nau:* aborder, accoster, *Adm:* arraisonner (un navire); (*b*) aller, monter, à bord d'(un navire, un avion); **to b. a train,** monter dans un train; (*c*) *Navy:* aborder (un navire); prendre (un navire) à l'abordage.

II. (*compound verbs*) **1. board out,** *v.tr.* mettre (des enfants) en pension; placer (des enfants) dans une famille.

2. board up, *v.tr.* (*a*) boucher (une fenêtre); condamner (une porte); (*b*) entourer (un terrain, etc.) de planches.

boarder ['bɔ:dər], *s.* **1.** pensionnaire *mf*; (*in schools*) interne *mf*; **weekly b.,** pensionnaire à la semaine; *Sch:* **the boarders,** l'internat *m*; **to take in boarders,** prendre, recevoir, des pensionnaires. **2.** *Nau:* abordeur *m*. **3.** *Bookb:* cartonneur, -euse (de livres).

boarding ['bɔ:diŋ], *s.* **1.** (*a*) *Const:* planchéiage *m*; (*b*) *Bookb:* cartonnage *m* (d'un livre); (*c*) *Leath:* rebroussement *m* (du cuir). **2.** (*a*) pension *f*; nourriture *f*; (*b*) *attrib.* **b. house,** (i) pension de famille; (ii) *Sch:* maison *f* où logent les internes; **to live in a b. house,** vivre en pension; **b. school,** pensionnat *m*, internat *m*; **to send a child to b. school,** mettre un enfant en pension, dans un pensionnat. **3.** (*a*) *Nau:* accostage *m*; abordage *m*; (*b*) *Nau: esp. Navy:* arraisonnement *m*; **b. officer,** officier chargé de l'arraisonnement; **b. party,** (i) détachement *m* de visite; (ii) détachement d'abordage. **4.** *coll.* planches *fpl*; *Const:* bardage *m*.

boardroom ['bɔ:dru:m], *s. Ind: etc:* salle *f* de réunion du conseil d'administration.

boardwalk ['bɔ:dwɔ:k], *s. NAm:* **1.** trottoir *m* en planches; caillebotis *m*. **2.** (*on the beach*) les planches *f*.

boarfish ['bɔ:fiʃ], *s. Ich:* sanglier *m* de mer, poisson *m* sanglier, capros *m*.

boarhound ['bɔ:haund], *s.* vautre *m*.

boarmia [bou'ɑ:miə], *s. Ent:* boarmie *f*, boarmia *f*.

boar's foot ['bɔ:zfut], *s. Bot:* ellébore vert.

boart [bɔ:t], *s. Lap:* boort *m*, diamant industriel.

boast[1] [boust], *s.* vanterie *f*; **it is their b. that . . .,** ils se vantent que . . .; ils s'enorgueillissent de ce que . . ..

boast[2]. **1.** *v.i.* se vanter; hâbler; **to b. that one can do, has done, sth.,** se vanter de pouvoir faire, d'avoir fait, qch.; **to b. of, about, sth.,** se vanter, se faire gloire, se glorifier, de qch.; **that's nothing to b. of,** ce n'est rien dont on puisse se vanter; il n'y a pas là de quoi être fier; **to b. of one's exploits,** s'enorgueillir à raconter ses exploits; **without wishing to b.,** sans vanité; sans forfanterie. **2.** *v.tr.* revendiquer (qch.); **the school boasts a fine library,** l'école est fière de posséder une belle bibliothèque; l'école possède une belle bibliothèque.

boast[3], *v.tr. Sculp:* ébaucher (une statue).

boaster[1] ['boustər], *s.* vantard *m*, fanfaron *m*; hâbleur *m*.

boaster[2], *s. Tls: Sculp:* ébauchoir *m*.

boastful ['boustful], *a.* vantard.

boastfully ['boustfuli], *adv.* avec vantardise.

boastfulness ['boustfulnis], *s.* vantardise *f*.

boasting ['boustiŋ], *s.* vantardise *f*; fanfaronnade *f*.

boastingly ['boustiŋli], *adv.* avec vantardise.

boat[1] [bout], *s.* **1.** bateau *m*; canot *m*; embarcation *f*; **cargo b.,** cargo *m*; **passenger b.,** paquebot *m*; **sailing b.,** canot, bateau, à voiles; **pleasure b.,** bateau de plaisance; **fishing b.,** bateau de pêche; barque *f* de pêcheur; **canal b.,** péniche *f*; **rubber b.,** bateau pneumatique; **collapsible b.,** bateau pliant; **rescue b.,** bateau de sauvetage; *Navy:* **seaward defence b.,** vedette *f* de défense côtière, de défense vers le large; **ship's b.,** embarcation de bord; chaloupe *f*; **b. deck,** pont *m* des embarcations; **to lower the boats,** amener les embarcations; mettre les embarcations à la mer; **b. stations!** chacun à son poste d'abandon! **b. rope,** bosse *f*; **b. song,** barcarolle *f*; **the b. train leaves Paris at 8.10,** le train du bateau quitte Paris à 8h10; **we took the b. at Calais,** nous nous sommes embarqués, nous avons pris le bateau, à Calais; **we took the b. for Dover,** nous nous sommes embarqués pour Douvres; **I came by b.,** je suis venu sur, par, le bateau; **I'd rather cross the Channel by b. than by hovercraft,** je préfère traverser la Manche par le bateau plutôt que par l'aéroglisseur; **we put the car on the b. at Dover,** nous avons embarqué la voiture à Douvres; **to send goods by b.,** envoyer des marchandises par eau, par bateau; *F:* **we're all in the same b.,** nous sommes tous dans le même cas, tous logés à la même enseigne; **to burn one's boats,** brûler ses vaisseaux, brûler les ponts; **to miss the b.,** manquer le coche. **2.** (*a*) *Ecc:* **incense b.,** navette *f* (liturgique); **b. bearer,** thuriféraire *m*; (*b*) *Dom.Ec:* **sauce b.,** saucière *f*.

boat[2]. **1.** *v.i.* se promener en bateau; canoter; faire du canotage; **we boated up the river,** nous avons remonté la rivière en bateau. **2.** (*a*) *v.tr. Com: A:* transporter (des marchandises) par eau; (*b*) **to b. oars,** border, rentrer, les avirons.

boatbill ['boutbil], *s. Orn:* savacou *m*, *F:* bec-en-cuiller *m*, *pl.* becs-en-cuiller.

boat bug ['boutbʌg], *s. Ent: U.S:* corise *f*.

boatbuilder ['boutbildər], *s.* constructeur *m* de canots, de bateaux de plaisance, etc.

boatbuilding ['boutbildiŋ], *s.* construction *f* de canots, de bateaux de plaisance, etc.

boater ['boutər], *s.* **1.** (*pers.*) canoteur *m*; canotier *m*. **2.** *Cost:* canotier *m*; (**straw**) **b.,** chapeau *m* (en paille) régate.

boat fly ['boutflai], *s. Ent:* corise *f*, *F:* cordonnier *m*.

boatful ['boutful], *s.* = BOATLOAD.

boathook ['bouthuk], *s. Nau:* gaffe *f*; croc *m* de marinier.

boathouse ['bouthaus], *s.* hangar *m*, abri *m*, à bateaux, pour canots; garage *m* (pour canots).

boating ['boutiŋ], *s.* **1.** canotage *m*; **to go b.,** faire du canotage; se promener en bateau; **b. club,** cercle *m* de canotage, d'aviron; **b. song,** barcarolle *f*. **2.** *Com: A:* transport *m* par eau; batelage *m*.

boatkeeper ['boutki:pər], *s.* **1.** *Navy:* homme *m* de garde (d'une embarcation). **2.** (i) propriétaire *m*, (ii) employé *m*, d'un hangar pour canots. **3.** loueur *m* d'embarcations.

boatload ['boutloud], *s.* (*a*) batelée *f* (de bois, etc.); (*b*) plein bateau (de personnes).

boatman, *pl.* **-men** ['boutmən], *s.m.* **1.** batelier. **2.** (*a*) gardien de canots; (*b*) loueur de canots. **3.** *s. Ent:* (**water**) **b.,** corise *f*.

boat race ['boutreis], *s.* course *f* de bateaux, *esp.* course à l'aviron; régate *f*; **the B.R.,** la course (annuelle) à l'aviron entre les universités d'Oxford et de Cambridge.

boatswain ['bousn], *s. Nau:* maître *m* d'équipage, maître principal de manœuvre, *F:* bosco *m*; **boatswain's mate,** (i) (*first class*) second maître d'équipage, de manœuvre; *F:* bosco; (ii) (*second class*) quartier-maître *m* (d'équipage, de manœuvre), *pl.* quartier(s)-maîtres; **boatswain's call,** sifflet *m* du maître.

boatyard ['boutjɑ:d], *s.* chantier *m* de construction pour canots et bateaux de plaisance.

Boaz ['bouæz], *Pr.n.m. B.Hist:* Booz.

bob[1] [bɔb], *s.* **1.** (*a*) *Mec:* lentille *f* (d'un pendule); plomb *m* (d'un fil à plomb); queue *f* (d'un cerf-volant); balancier *m* (d'une machine à vapeur); (*b*) *Fish:* (i) bouchon *m* (de ligne); (ii) paquet *m* de vers (pour la pêche à l'anguille); (*c*) *A:* pendant *m* d'oreille. **2.** (*a*) **b. of hair,** chignon *m*; **b. of ribbons, etc.,** gland *m*; **b. of silk,** houppe *f*; (*b*) coiffure *f* à la Ninon, à la Jeanne d'Arc; (*c*) queue écourtée (d'un cheval). **3.** *A:* refrain *m*; **to bear a b.,** faire chœur au refrain. **4.** *U.S:* (*a*) patin *m* (de traîneau); (*b*) = BOBSLEIGH.

bob[2], *v.tr.* (**bobbed; bobbing**) **1. to have one's hair bobbed,** se faire couper les cheveux à la nuque; porter les cheveux à la Ninon, à la Jeanne d'Arc. **2. to b. a horse's tail,** écourter la queue d'un cheval.

bob[3], *v.i. Fish:* **to b. for eels,** pêcher les anguilles avec un paquet de vers (au bout de la ligne).

bob[4], *v.*

I. *v.i.* **1. something was bobbing on the water,** quelque chose s'agitait sur l'eau; **to b. up and down in the water,** danser sur l'eau; **to bob up and down (in the air),** pendiller; **to b. against s.o.,** se heurter contre qn. **2. to b. to s.o.,** (*with cogn.acc.*) **to b. a curtsey,** faire une petite révérence (à qn); **the old servant came bobbing into the room,** la vieille servante entra avec force petites révérences. **3. to b. for apples,** chercher à saisir avec les dents des pommes suspendues à un fil ou flottant dans un baquet.

II. (*compound verbs*) **1. bob down,** *v.i.* baisser vivement, subitement, brusquement, la tête, se baisser subitement.

2. bob under, *v.i.* (*of fisherman's float*) plonger.

3. bob up, *v.i.* surgir brusquement; **to b. up again,** revenir à la surface; revenir sur l'eau; *F:* (*of pers.*) réapparaître d'une façon inattendue.

bob[5], *s.* **1.** petite secousse; petit coup. **2.** (*curtsey*) petite révérence. **3.** (*a*) carillon *m*; (*b*) chacune des variations du carillon.

Bob[6]. **1.** *Pr.n.m. F:* (*dim*) Robert; **you've only to do that and—Bob's your uncle!** tu n'as qu'à faire cela–et ça y est! **2.** *s.m. F:* (*a*) (*at Eton College*) **dry b.,** joueur *m* de cricket; **wet b.,** canotier *m*; (*b*) *Mil:* **light b.,** soldat *m* de l'infanterie légère.

bob[7], *s.inv. F: A:* shilling *m*; **five b.,** cinq balles; **b.-a-job week,** semaine pendant laquelle les scouts font de petites besognes pour un shilling (maintenant pour cinq pence); *P:* **b. a nob,** un shilling par tête de pipe.

bobac, boba(c)k ['bɔbæk], *s. Z:* bobak *m,* murmel *m.*

bobbed ['bɔbd], *a.* **1. b. hair,** cheveux *mpl* à la Ninon, (*with fringe in front*) à la Jeanne d'Arc. **2. b. tail,** queue écourtée (d'un cheval).

bobbery ['bɔbəri], *O:* **1.** *a.* (*a*) hétérogène, mal assorti, disparate; (*b*) *F:* tapageur; tumultueux. **2.** *s. F:* tapage *m,* vacarme *m.*

bobbin ['bɔbin], *s.* **1.** (*a*) *Tex:* bobine *f,* volue *f* (de la navette); (*for reeling silk*) échignole *f,* espolin *m;* **b. board,** râtelier *m* à bobines; **b. frame,** bobinoir *m;* **b. winder,** bobineuse *f,* machine *f* à bobiner; (*b*) **lace b.,** bloquet *m,* fuseau *m,* pour dentelles. **2.** *El:* corps *m* de bobine. **3.** *A:* **b.(-latch),** bobinette *f.*

bobbinet [bɔbi'net], *s.* dentelle *f* au fuseau.

bobbing ['bɔbiŋ], *s.* pêche *f* aux anguilles.

bobbish ['bɔbiʃ], *a. F: O:* guilleret; bien en train; **how do you feel?–pretty b.!** comment ça va?–ça boulotte!

bobble ['bɔbl], *s. F:* pompon *m.*

Bobby ['bɔbi]. **1.** *Pr.n.m.* (*dim*) Robert. **2.** *s. F:* (*policeman*) flic *m.*

bobby-dazzler ['bɔbidæzlər], *s. F: O:* personnage, objet, épatant.

bobby pin ['bɔbipin], *s. esp. NAm:* pince *f* (à cheveux).

bobbysocks ['bɔbisɔks], *s.pl.esp. NAm: F:* socquettes *f.*

bobbysoxer ['bɔbisɔksər], *s. esp. NAm: F:* adolescente (à la page).

bobcat ['bɔbkæt], *s. Z: NAm: F:* lynx *m* rufus.

bob cherry ['bɔbtʃeri], *s.* cerises jumelles; grappe *f* de deux ou trois cerises; *F:* boucle *f* d'oreille, pendant *m* d'oreille; *Games:* **to play b.c.,** essayer d'attraper (avec les dents) une cerise suspendue à une ficelle.

bobolink ['bɔbəliŋk], *s. Orn:* dolichonyx *m,* bobolink *m, Fr.C:* goglu *m.*

bobsled[1] ['bɔbsled], **bobsleigh**[1] ['bɔbslei], *s.* bobsleigh *m;* bob *m;* **b. race,** course *f* de bob.

bobsled[2], **bobsleigh**[2], *v.i.* (**bobsledded**) faire du bob(sleigh).

bobsleighing ['bɔbsleiiŋ], *s.* le (sport du) bobsleigh; glissades *fpl* en bob.

bobstay ['bɔbstei], *s. Nau:* sous-barbe *f inv,* soubarbe *f* (de beaupré); **b. piece,** taille-mer *m inv.*

bobtail[1] ['bɔbteil], *v.tr.* écourter la queue à (un cheval, un chien).

bobtail[2], *a. & s.* **bobtailed** ['bɔbteild], *a.* **1.** (cheval, chien) à queue écourtée. **2.** *s.* (*dog*) anglais *m* sans queue, bobtail *m.*

bobwhite ['bɔb(h)wait], *s. Orn:* colin *m* de Virginie.

bobwire ['bɔwaiər], *s. NAm:* (fil *m* de fer) barbelé *m.*

bocage ['bɔkɑːʒ], *s. Geog:* bocage *m.*

Boccaccio [bə'kætʃiou], *Pr.n.m.* Boccace.

Boche [bɔʃ], *s. Pej: F: O:* Allemand *m,* Boche *m.*

bock [bɔk], *s.* bière (brune allemande).

bod [bɔd], *s. F:* type *m;* **the area's full of all sorts of Army bods,** il y a je ne sais combien de militaires de toutes sortes dans la région; **any old b.,** n'importe qui, **I'll have to show it to all sorts of odd bods,** j'aurai à le montrer à je ne sais combien de types.

bode [boud], *v.tr. & i. A: & Lit:* présager; **it bodes no good,** cela ne présage, n'annonce, rien de bon; **agitation that bodes no good,** agitation *f* de mauvais augure; **to b. well, ill,** être de bon, de mauvais, augure; **it bodes well for him,** cela est d'un heureux présage pour lui.

bodeful ['boudful], *a. A: & Lit:* de mauvais augure; sinistre.

bodge[1] [bɔdʒ], *s. F:* travail mal fait, bousillé.

bodge[2], *v.tr. F:* bousiller (un travail, etc.).

bodger ['bɔdʒər], *s. F:* bousilleur *m.*

bodgie ['bɔdʒi], *s. Austr: F:* jeune voyou *m.*

bodice ['bɔdis], *s. Cost: O:* (*a*) corsage *m;* **under b.,** cache-corset *m inv;* (*b*) corselet *m.*

bodiless ['bɔdilis], *a.* sans corps.

bodily ['bɔdili]. **1.** *a.* corporel, physique; **b. and mental diseases,** maladies *f* du corps et de l'esprit; **to supply one's b. wants,** pourvoir à ses besoins matériels; **b. fear,** peur *f* physique; **b. harm,** lésion corporelle; **b. pain,** douleur *f* physique; **to go about in b. fear,** craindre pour sa sûreté personnelle, pour sa vie; **to be in b. fear of s.o.,** redouter qn; craindre d'être attaqué par qn. **2.** *adv.* (*a*) *A:* en chair et en os; (*b*) corporellement; **he was carried b. to the door and thrown out,** on l'a saisi (par le corps), l'a transporté jusqu'à la porte et jeté dehors; (*c*) entièrement; en masse; **they resigned b.,** ils ont donné leur démission en corps.

bodkin ['bɔdkin], *s.* **1.** (*a*) passe-lacet *m, pl.* passe-lacets, passe-cordon *m, pl.* passe-cordons, aiguille *f* à passer; (*b*) *Needlew:* poinçon *m;* (*c*) (grande) épingle; (*d*) *Typ:* pointe *f.* **2.** *A:* (*in carriage*) **to ride, sit, b.,** aller, être, en lapin.

bodo ['boudou], *s. Prot:* bodo *m.*

body ['bɔdi], *s.* **1.** (*a*) corps *m* (d'une personne, d'un animal); **basal b.,** corpuscule basal, blépharoblaste *m;* **b. cell,** somatocyte *m;* **the human b.,** le corps humain; **to belong to s.o. b. and soul,** appartenir, être, à qn corps et âme; **to throw oneself b. and soul into sth.,** se jeter à corps perdu dans qch.; **to have just enough to keep b. and soul together,** avoir tout juste de quoi vivre; **they can hardly keep b. and soul together,** ils sont dans une grande gêne; **to work in order to keep b. and soul together,** travailler pour ne pas mourir de faim; **b. linen,** linge *m* de corps; **b. cloth,** housse *f* (de cheval); *A:* **b. servant,** valet, domestique, attaché à la personne de qn; *Art:* **b. colour,** gouache *f;* *Z:* **b. ring,** anneau *m;* (*b*) **(dead) b.,** cadavre *m,* corps (mort); **the resurrection of the b.,** la résurrection de la chair; **over my dead b.!** à mon corps défendant! (*c*) sève *f,* générosité *f* (d'un vin); **wine with b.,** vin généreux, corsé, qui a du corps; (*of wine*) **to get b.,** s'enforcir; **to give b. to a sauce,** (i) corser, (ii) lier, une sauce; **to give b. to wine,** corser le vin; (*d*) corps, consistance *f;* **to give b. to paint,** donner de la consistance à la peinture; **paper without enough b.,** papier qui manque de consistance, de corps; (*e*) *Mus:* **to give b. to the tone,** nourrir le son. **2.** (*a*) **legislative b.,** corps législatif; **public b.,** corporation *f;* **public international bodies,** institutions publiques internationales; **b. politic,** corps politique, corps social; **learned b.,** corps savant; **governing b.,** conseil *m* de direction; **examining b.,** jury *m* d'examen; **electoral b.,** collège électoral; **a b. such as UNO,** un organisme comme l'ONU; (*b*) **large b. of people,** foule nombreuse; assistance nombreuse; **a little b. of disciples,** une petite bande de disciples; **the main b. of the citizens,** la plupart, la masse, des citoyens; **general b. of creditors,** masse des créanciers; **b. of troops,** troupe armée; **the main b. of the army,** le gros de l'armée; **to come in a b.,** venir en masse, en corps; **to do sth. as a b.,** faire qch. d'ensemble; **the judges as a b. were honest,** les juges, pris dans leur ensemble, étaient intègres; (*c*) **strong b. of evidence,** forte accumulation de preuves; faisceau *m* de preuves; **b. of laws,** recueil *m* de lois; **b. of economic laws,** ensemble *m* de lois économiques. **3.** *F:* (*pers.*) **a nice (little) old b.,** une gentille petite vieille; **a queer sort of b.,** un drôle de type. **4.** (*main part*) (*a*) corps (de document, d'un acte, de bâtiment); vaisseau *m,* nef *f* (d'église); tronc *m* (d'arbre); calotte *f,* fond *m* (de chapeau); bombe *f* (de casque); coffre *m* (d'un instrument de musique); fuselage *m* (d'avion); corps (d'un navire); nacelle *f* (d'une voiture d'enfant), ventre *m* (de haut fourneau); estomac *m* (de l'enclume); coque *f* (de chaudière, d'un char d'assaut); fût *m* (d'un cric, d'un tambour); écharpe *f* (d'une poulie mouflée); corps (d'un piston); *Typ:* panse *f* (d'un a, d'un d); *I.C.E:* culot *m* (de bougie); **b. of an abutment,** massif *m* d'une culée; *Jur:* **b. of a ship,** corps et quille *f;* *N.Arch:* **b. plan,** plan latitudinal; projection transversale; *Typ:* **b. type,** caractères *mpl* de texte; **the b. of a speech,** le fond, la substance, d'un discours; (*b*) *Aut: etc:* bâti *m,* corps, caisse *f;* carrosserie *f;* **standard b.,** carrosserie de série; **low b.,** carrosserie surbaissée; **panel b.,** carrosserie à panneaux; **integral all-steel welded b.,** carrosserie (mono)coque, coque auto-porteuse. **5.** (*a*) *Astr: Ch:* corps; **heavenly b.,** astre *m,* corps céleste; (*b*) *Mec:* **b. in motion,** mobile *m;* (*c*) *Atom.Ph: etc:* **black b.,** corps noir.

body-builder ['bɔdibildər], *s.* **1.** *Aut: etc:* (*pers.*) carrossier *m.* **2.** (*a*) aliment reconstituant; (*b*) (*pers.*) culturiste *m.*

body-building[1] ['bɔdibildiŋ], *a.* (*of food*) reconstituant.

body-building[2], *s.* **1.** *Aut: etc:* fabrication *f* de carrosserie. **2.** culture *f* physique, culturisme *m.*

bodyguard ['bɔdigɑːd], *s.* **1.** (*a*) garde *f* du corps; sauvegarde *f;* (*b*) cortège *m* (à la suite de qn). **2.** garde *m* du corps; *F:* gorille *m.*

body-snatcher ['bɔdisnætʃər], *s. Hist:* déterreur *m* (de cadavres); résurrectionniste *m, P:* corbeau *m.*

bodywork ['bɔdiwəːk], *s. Aut: etc:* carrosserie *f.*

Bœotia [bi'ouʃə], *Pr.n. Geog:* la Béotie.

Bœotian [bi'ouʃn]. **1.** *a. Geog:* béotien. **2.** *s.* (*a*) *Geog:* Béotien, -ienne; (*b*) *F: A:* (*stupid person*) béotien, -ienne; lourdaud, -de; esprit épais. **3.** *s. Ling:* béotien *m.*

Boer ['buər, 'bouər]. **1.** *a.* boer; **the B. War,** la guerre des Boers. **2.** *s.* Boer *mf.*

Boethius [bou'iːθiəs], *Pr.n.m.* Boèce.

boffin ['bɔfin], *s. F:* savant *m.*

bog[1] [bɔg], *s.* fondrière *f;* marécage *m;* **peat b.,** tourbière *f,* **b. butter,** beurre *m* des tourbières; **b. oak,** chêne *m* de tourbière; *Bot:* **b. berry,** baie *f* des marais; **b. bean, b. trefoil,** trèfle *m* d'eau; *Miner:* **b. iron, b. ore,** fer *m* des lacs, des marais; *Vet:* **b. spavin,** jarde *f;* *F:* **b. trotter,** (i) habitant, -ante, d'une région marécageuse; (ii) *Pej: A:* Irlandais, -aise.

bog[2], *v.* (**bogged**) **1.** *v.tr.* embourber, enliser (une charrette, etc.); *usu. pass.* **to get bogged,** s'embourber, s'enliser. **2.** *v.i.* (*of horse, etc.*) **to b. down,** s'enfoncer dans une fondrière; s'embourber; *F:* (*of pers.*) **to get bogged down,** se trouver dans une impasse; être submergé (par le travail).

bog[3], *s. P:* latrines *fpl,* cabinets *mpl;* *P:* goguenots *mpl,* chiottes *fpl.*

bog[4], *v.i. P:* se soulager; *P:* chier.

bogan ['boug(ə)n], *s. Geog: Can:* bras *m* de décharge (d'une rivière).

bog-bird ['bɔgbəːd], *s. Orn:* baléniceps *m,* balaeniceps *m.*

bogey ['bougi], *s.* **1.** (*a*) *A:* diable *m;* (*b*) épouvantail *m;* **to scare people with the b. of fascism,** épouvanter les masses en évoquant le spectre du fascisme; (*c*) fantôme *m,* spectre *m;* (*d*) *P: O:* détective *m;* flic *m;* (*e*) *NAm: F:* avion non identifié. **2.** *Golf:* (*a*) *A:* **(Colonel) B.,** la normale du parcours; **the b. for this hole is 5,** ce trou se fait normalement en 5; **to play against b.,** jouer contre la normale; (*b*) (*modern use*) **b.,** un coup au-dessus de la normale.

bogeyman, *pl.* **-men** ['bougimæn, -men], *s.* **the b.,** croque-mitaine *m;* le Père Fouettard (des enfants).

bogginess ['bɔginis], *s.* état marécageux (du terrain).

boggle [bɔgl], *v.i.* (*a*) reculer, rechigner (**at, over, sth.,** devant qch.); **to b. at, about, doing sth.,** rechigner, marchander, à faire qch.; **it makes the mind b., the mind boggles,** cela confond l'imagination; (*b*) (*bungle*) **to b. over an exercise, over the adverbs,** patauger dans un devoir, parmi les adverbes.

boggler ['bɔglər], *s.* (individu) indécis; faiseur, -euse, de difficultés.

boggy ['bɔgi], *a.* marécageux, tourbeux; (terrain) effondré, plein de fondrières.

Boghead ['bɔghed], *Pr.n. Miner:* **B. (coal),** boghead *m,* schiste bitumineux.

bogie ['bougi], *s.* **1.** *Rail:* bog(g)ie *m;* chariot porteur; traverse *f* mobile; **leading b.,** bog(g)ie directeur, avant; **trailing b.,** bog(g)ie remorqué, arrière. **2.** *Mil:* (*of tank*) train *m* de roulement; bog(g)ie; **b. wheel, galet** *m* de roulement; **b. wheel spindle,** fusée *f* de galet (de roulement); **b. wheel gudgeon,** axe *m* de galet (de roulement); **b. bracket,** chariot de galet (de roulement); **b. frame,** bâti *m* de train de roulement; **b. guide slide,** glissière *f* guide du train de roulement.

bogle ['bougl], *s. esp. Scot:* = BOGEY, **1.** (*b*), (*c*).

bogus ['bougəs], *a.* faux, *f* fausse; feint, simulé; *F:* bidon; *Com:* **b. company,** (i) société *f* qui n'existe pas; société fantôme; (ii) société véreuse; **b. concern,** attrape-niais *m inv,* attrape-nigaud *m, pl.* attrape-nigauds; **b. signature,** signature *f* de complaisance; **b. press,** presse *f* qui imprime de faux billets de banque; **a b. baron,** un prétendu, faux, baron; *St.Exch:* **b. transactions (intended to make a market),** transactions véreuses, à la gomme; *F:* **he's completely b.,** c'est une façade.

bogy ['bougi], *s.* = BOGEY 1.

Bohea [bou'hiə]. **1.** *Pr.n.* Bohé *m.* **2.** *s.* (*a*) *A:* thé noir de première qualité; (*b*) *Com:* thé noir de basse qualité.

Bohemia [bou'hiːmiə]. **1.** *Pr.n. Geog:* Bohême *f.* **2.** *s.* (*unconventional life*) bohème *f.*

Bohemian [bou'hiːmiən]. **1.** *Geog:* (*a*) *a.* bohémien; **B. topaz,** fausse topaze; **B. garnet,** pyrope *m,* grenat *m* de Bohême; **B. ruby,** rubis *m* de Bohême, quartz *m* rose; (*b*) *s.* Bohémien, -ienne. **2.** (*a*) *a.* **b. life,** vie *f* de bohème; (*b*) *s.* (i) (*gipsy*) bohémien, -ienne; (ii) bohème *mf.*

bohemianism [bou'hiːmiənizm], *s.* mœurs *fpl* de bohème, vie *f* de bohème; bohémianisme *m.*

bohor ['bouhɔːr], *s. Z:* bohor *f.*

Bohr [bɔːr], *Pr.n. Ph:* **B. atom,** atome *m* de Bohr; **B. magneton,** magnéton *m* de Bohr.

Bohunk ['bouhʌŋk], *s.m. NAm: P: Pej:* (*a*) immigré qui vient de l'Europe centrale; (*b*) homme de peine; (*c*) lourdaud; voyou.

Boidae ['bouidiː], *s.pl. Rept:* boïdés *mpl.*

boiga ['bɔigə], *s. Rept:* boiga *m.*

Boigidae ['bɔidʒidiː], *s.pl. Rept:* boïgidés *m.*

boil[1] [bɔil], *s. Med:* furoncle *m.*

boil[2], *s.* **1.** (*of water, etc.*) **to come to the b.,** commencer à bouillir; entrer en ébullition; **the water, the kettle, is on the b.,** l'eau bout; **to go off the b.,** (i) cesser de bouillir; (ii) *F:* perdre son entrain; **to bring the water to the b.,** amener, porter, l'eau à l'ébullition; faire bouillir l'eau. **2.** (*a*) tourbillon *m* (dans un cours d'eau); remous *m;* (*b*) *Fish:* saut *m* hors de l'eau (du poisson qui happe l'appât).

boil[3], *v.*

I. *v.tr. & tr.* **1.** *v.i.* (*a*) (*of water, etc.*) bouillir; (*violently*) bouillonner; **to begin to b.,** entrer en ébullition; **to b. fast, gently,** bouillir à grand feu, à petit feu; *Cu:* **allow to b. gently, slowly,** faites, laissez, mijoter; **to let the kettle b. dry,** laisser évaporer complètement l'eau de la bouilloire; laisser la bouilloire sans eau; **to keep the pot boiling,** (i) faire bouillir la marmite; entretenir le feu sous la marmite; (ii) *F:* pourvoir aux besoins du ménage; faire marcher la maison; (iii) *F:* maintenir l'entrain (dans une réunion, etc.); faire aller rondement le jeu; *F:* **it makes my blood b.!** ça me fait bouillir le sang! **to b. with rage,** bouillonner, bouillir, de colère; être transporté de fureur; *F:* **I'm boiling!** (i) je crève de chaleur! (ii) je suis furieux! (*b*) *Fish:* (*of trout, salmon*) sauter (pour prendre l'appât). **2.** *v.tr.* (*a*) faire bouillir (de l'eau, etc.); *Cu:* faire cuire (qch.) à l'eau; cuire (du sucre); **to b. an egg,** faire cuire un œuf à la coque; *P:* **go and b. your head!** va te faire cuire un œuf! (*b*) *Laund:* lessiver (le linge); *F:* **to feel like a boiled rag,** se sentir mou comme une chiffe; (*c*) *Paperm:* décreuser (des fibres végétales).

II. (*compound verbs*) **1. boil away,** *v.i.* ébouillir; (*of sauce, etc.*) se réduire.

2. boil down, (*a*) *v.tr.* réduire (une solution); (faire) réduire (un sirop, etc.); *F:* **this article has been boiled down,** cet article a été condensé, amputé; (*b*) *v.ind.tr. F:* se ramener, se borner, se résumer, revenir (to, à); **this is what it all boils down to,** voilà à quoi cela se ramène, se borne, se résume, cela revient.

3. boil off, *v.tr. Tex:* dégommer (la soie grège).

4. boil over, *v.i.* (*of liquid*) s'en aller, se sauver; *F:* **he was boiling over with rage,** il était furieux; il bouillait de colère; il était en ébullition.

boiled [bɔild], *a.* **1.** cuit à l'eau; bouilli; **b. egg,** œuf *m* à la coque; **lightly b. egg, soft b. egg,** œuf mollet; **freshly b. lobster,** homard fraîchement cuit. **2.** *Paint:* **b. oil,** huile cuite. **3.** *P:* ivre soûl.

boiler ['bɔilər], *s.* **1.** (*pers.*) fabricant *m,* raffineur *m* (de sucre, etc.). **2.** (*a*) chaudière *f*; *Sug.-R:* claire *f*; *Mch:* générateur *m*; **cylindrical b.,** chaudière cylindrique; **(multi-)tubular b.,** chaudière (multi-)tubulaire; **direct-draught b.,** chaudière à flamme directe; **return-tube b.,** chaudière à retour de flamme; **French b.,** chaudière à bouilleurs; **exhaust-heat b.,** chaudière à chaleur perdue, à réchauffage; **tube-plate b.,** chaudière cloisonnée; **fuel oil, oil-fired b.,** chaudière à mazout; **externally-, outside-, fired b.,** chaudière à foyer, à chauffage, extérieur; **internally-, inside-, fired b.,** chaudière à foyer, à chauffage, intérieur; **water-tube b.,** chaudière aquatubulaire; **fire-tube b.,** chaudière ignitubulaire; **flash(-steam) b.,** chaudière à vaporisation instantanée; **wag(g)on b.,** chaudière à tombeau; **marine b.,** chaudière (de) marine; **land b.,** chaudière terrestre; *Nau:* **the main boilers,** les grandes chaudières; **donkey b.,** petite chaudière; chaudière auxiliaire; **central-heating b.,** chaudière de chauffage central; **solid-fuel b.,** chaudière à anthracite, à coke; *Brew:* **wort b.,** cuve *f* à moût, chaudière à houblon; (*b*) *Dom.Ec:* **double b.,** bainmarie *m, pl.* bains-marie; (*c*) *attrib.* **b. maker,** chaudronnier *m*; **b. making,** chaudronnerie *f*; **b. works,** atelier *m* de chaudronnerie; **b. plate,** tôle *f* à chaudières; fer *m* en plaques; **b. house, b. room,** salle *f,* bâtiment *m,* des chaudières; *Nau:* **b. room,** chambre *f* de chauffe; **the b. rooms,** la chaufferie; *Nau:* **b. deck,** pont inférieur; *Mch:* **b. float,** flotteur *m* d'alarme; **b. composition, b. compound,** anti-incrustant *m, pl.* anti-incrustants; tartrifuge *m*; **b. graphite,** graphite anti-incrustant; **b. tube,** (i) (*fire tube*) tube *m* de chaudière, de fumée; (ii) (*water tube*) bouilleur *m*; tube d'eau; *Cost:* **b. suit,** bleu *m* de chauffe. **3.** *Cu: F:* poule *f* (à la casserole).

boilerman, *pl.* **-men** ['bɔilәmәn], *s.m. Mch:* chauffeur.

boiling[1] ['bɔiliŋ]. **1.** *a.* bouillant; bouillonnant; **b. water,** eau bouillante. **2.** *adv.* **b. hot,** tout bouillant; *F:* **I'm b. hot,** je crève de chaleur.

boiling[2], *s.* **1.** (*a*) bouillonnement *m,* ébullition *f*; **b. point,** point *m* d'ébullition; (*b*) **sugar b.,** cuisson *f* du sucre; cuite *f*; (*c*) *Paperm:* décreusage *m* (des fibres végétales); lessivage *m*; (*d*) *Soapm:* coction *f.* **2.** *F:* **the whole b.,** toute la bande; tout le bazar; tout le tremblement; toute la boutique; tout le bataclan; toute la ribambelle; et tout ce qui s'ensuit.

boiling off ['bɔiliŋ'ɔf], *s. Tex:* dégommage *m* (de la soie grège).

boisterous ['bɔist(ә)rәs], *a.* (*of pers.*) bruyant, turbulent; tapageur; (*of wind*) violent; (*of sea*) rude, fort, tumultueux; (*of weather*) tempétueux; **b. spirits,** gaieté débordante, tapageuse, bruyante; **to be in b. health,** éclater de santé.

boisterously ['bɔist(ә)rәsli], *adv.* (*a*) bruyamment, tumultueusement; avec une gaieté bruyante, débordante; (*b*) tempétueusement.

boisterousness ['bɔist(ә)rәsnis], *s.* turbulence *f* (de la mer, d'un enfant); violence *f* (du vent); agitation *f* (de la mer).

Bokhara [bә'kɑ:rә], *Pr.n. Geog:* **1.** Boukharie *f.* **2.** (*city*) Boukhara.

Bokharian [bә'kɑ:riәn], *Geog:* **1.** *a.* boukhare, boukharien. **2.** *s.* Boukharien, -ienne.

boko ['boukou], *s. P:* nez *m,* pif *m.*

bola ['boulә], **bolas** ['boulәs], *s.* lacet *m* (de gaucho).

bold [bould], *a.* **1.** hardi; (i) peu timide; courageux; (ii) audacieux, téméraire; (ton, regard) assuré, confiant; **b. stroke,** (i) coup hardi; (ii) coup d'audace; **b. enterprise,** entreprise audacieuse; **grown b. in crime,** enhardi au crime; **b. act,** action courageuse; **b. in action,** hardi à agir; **as b. as a lion,** hardi comme un lion; *O:* **to make b. with s.o.,** prendre des libertés avec qn; **to make b. to do sth.,** oser, se permettre de, prendre la liberté de, avoir la hardiesse de, faire qch.; s'enhardir à faire qch.; **to make so b. as to do sth.,** s'enhardir jusqu'à faire qch.; oser faire qch.; se permettre de faire qch.; **if I may be so b.,** si je puis prendre une telle liberté; **to put a b. face, front, on the matter,** payer d'audace. **2.** impudent, effronté; **as b. as brass,** effronté, hardi, comme un page; **to answer as b. as brass,** (i) répondre effrontément; (ii) répondre sans sourciller. **3.** (*prominent*) (*a*) **b. headland,** promontoire *m* à pic, accore; **b. cliff,** falaise escarpée; *Nau:* **b. coast,** côte accore, sûre; **b. features,** traits accusés; *Typ:* **b. type,** caractères *mpl* gras; *s.* **in b.,** en gras; (*b*) *Art:* **b. style,** style hardi, net, franc; **b. strokes,** traits, coups de pinceau, hardis; **b. brush, pencil,** pinceau *m,* crayon *m,* libre; (*of artist*) **to wield a b. brush,** avoir le pinceau hardi; **in b. relief,** en puissant relief.

boldface ['bouldfeis], *s. Typ:* caractères *mpl* gras.

bold-faced ['bould'feist], *a.* **1.** effronté, impudent. **2.** *Typ:* **b.-f. type,** caractères *mpl* gras.

boldine ['bouldi:n, -ain], *s. Pharm:* boldine *f.*

boldly ['bouldli], *adv.* **1.** hardiment; audacieusement; avec audace; **to state sth. b.,** affirmer qch. carrément, avec confiance; **to treat a subject b.,** traiter un sujet hardiment; **to paint, draw, b.,** avoir la main libre; **b. painted picture,** tableau brossé vigoureusement, hardiment; **to go b. at it,** y aller hardiment, carrément, franchement. **2.** effrontément. **3. the coast rises b.,** la côte s'élève à pic.

boldness ['bouldnis], *s.* **1.** hardiesse *f* (de conduite, etc.); courage *m* (à agir); **b. in crime,** enhardissement *m* au crime; **his b. in attack,** son audace, son intrépidité, *F:* sa crânerie, à attaquer. **2.** effronterie *f,* impudence *f.* **3.** (*a*) escarpement *m* (d'une falaise); (*b*) *Art: Lit:* hardiesse, netteté *f,* liberté *f* (de style, de pinceau).

boldo ['bɔldou], *s. Bot:* boldo *m.*

bole[1] [boul], *s.* fût *m,* tronc *m,* tige *f* (d'un arbre).

bole[2], *s. Miner:* (*clay*) bol *m,* terre *f* bolaire; *Pharm: A:* **b. (Armeniac),** bol d'Arménie.

bolection [bә'lekʃ(ә)n], *s. Join:* moulure *f* en relief (de panneau de porte).

boleite [bou'leiait], *s. Miner:* boléite *f.*

bolero, *s.* **1.** *Danc: Mus:* [bә'lɛәrou], boléro *m.* **2.** *Cost:* ['bɔlәrou], boléro.

boletus [bә'li:tәs], *s. Fung:* bolet *m*; **edible b.,** cèpe *m* (de Bordeaux).

bolide ['boulaid], *s. Meteor:* bolide *m.*

bolivar ['bɔlivәr, bɔ'li:vɑ:r], *s. Num:* bolivar *m.*

Bolivia [bә'liviә], *Pr.n. Geog:* Bolivie *f.*

Bolivian [bә'liviәn], *Geog:* **1.** *a.* bolivien. **2.** *s.* Bolivien, -ienne.

boll[1] [boul], *s.* **1.** *Bot:* capsule *f* (du cotonnier, du lin). **2.** *attrib. Ent:* **b. weevil,** anthonome *m* (du cotonnier).

boll[2]. **1.** *v.i.* (*of flax*) monter en graine. **2.** *v.tr.* égrener (le coton, le lin).

Bollandist ['bɔlәndist], *s. Ecc.Hist:* bollandiste *m.*

bollard ['bɔlәd], *s.* **1.** *Nau:* (*a*) (*on wharf*) pieu *m,* canon *m,* poteau *m,* d'amarrage; borne *f* d'amarrage; *F:* poupée *f* d'amarrage; (*b*) (*on ship*) bitte *f* (de tournage); **small b.,** bitton *m.* **2.** (*on road*) borne *f.*

bolled [bɔld], *a.* **1.** (*of flax*) monté en graine. **2.** (*of cotton, flax*) égrené.

boller ['bɔlәr], *s.* (*machine*) égreneuse *f* (de coton).

Bologna [bә'lounjә], *Pr.n. Geog:* Bologne *f*; *Comest:* **B. sausage,** mortadelle *f* (de Bologne).

Bolognese [bɔlә'nji:z], **Bolognian** [bә'louniәn], *Geog:* **1.** *a.* bolonais. **2.** *s.* Bolonais, -aise.

bolograph ['boulәgræf], *s. Ph:* tracé *m* du bolomètre.

bolometer [bә'lɔmitәr], *s. Ph:* bolomètre *m.*

boloney [bә'louni], *s. F:* **it's all b.,** (i) c'est des histoires, de la foutaise; (ii) c'est du chiqué, du boniment.

Bolshevik ['bɔlʃivik], **Bolshevist** ['bɔlʃivist], *a.* & *s.* bolchevik (*mf*), bolcheviste (*mf*).

Bolshevism ['bɔlʃәvizm], *s.* bolchevisme *m.*

Bolshevization [bɔlʃivai'zeiʃ(ә)n], *s.* bolchevisation *f.*

Bolshevize ['bɔlʃivaiz], *v.tr.* bolcheviser.

Bolshie, Bolshy ['bɔlʃi], *a.* & *s. F:* **1.** moscoutaire (*mf*). **2. he's just (a) b.,** c'est (i) un entêté, (ii) un contestataire, (iii) un communiste.

bolson ['bɔls(ә)n], *s. Geog:* bolson *m.*

bolster[1] ['boulstәr], *s.* **1.** traversin *m,* chevet *m* (de lit); coussin *m* (de canapé, etc.). **2.** embase *f,* épaulement *m,* mitre *f* (de couteau, etc.). **3.** (*a*) *Mec.E:* coussinet *m*; collet *m* (d'un laminoir); (*b*) *Metalw:* matrice *f*; étampe inférieure; contre-poinçon *m, pl.* contre-poinçons. **4.** *Const:* racinal, -aux *m,* sous-poutre *f, pl.* sous-poutres; *Civ.E: Const:* chapeau *m* (de poteau). **5.** *Nau:* coussin (de capelage, de ferrure); **the bolsters of the mast,** les épaulettes *f* du mât. **6.** (*a*) *Veh:* lisoir *m,* traverse *f,* sommier *m*; **lower b., axle-tree b.,** sellette *f* (de wagon); **b. of a gun carriage,** sellette d'un affût; (*b*) *Av:* **wing b. beam,** quille *f* de voilure.

bolster[2], *v.tr.* **1. to b. s.o. up,** (i) soutenir, relever, la tête de qn avec des oreillers; (ii) *F:* appuyer, soutenir, qn (qui a peur, etc.); (iii) **to b. up a theory,** étayer une théorie. **2.** rembourrer.

bolt[1] [boult], *s.* **1.** carreau *m* (d'arbalète); *U.S:* **captive b.,** pistolet *m* d'abattage; **he has shot his last b.,** (i) il a tiré ses dernières cartouches; il a vidé son carquois; (ii) il a fourni son effort maximum; il ne peut plus rien donner; (iii) il a dit son dernier mot. **2.** éclair *m*; coup *m* de foudre; **b. from the blue,** événement imprévu; **it's like a b. from the blue,** c'est comme un coup de foudre; cela nous tombe du ciel. **3.** (*a*) **(sliding) b.,** verrou *m* (de porte); pêne *m* (de serrure); **bevelled b.,** pêne biseauté; **flat b.,** targette *f*; **sash b. (of window),** loqueteau *m*; **top and bottom b. (of French window),** espagnolette *f*; **barrel b.,** verrou à coquille; **to shoot, fasten, the bolts,** pousser, mettre, les verrous; (*b*) *Sm.a:* culasse *f* mobile; **b. assembly,** ensemble *m* (de la) culasse mobile; **b. mechanism,** mécanisme *m* de culasse mobile; **b. cylinder,** cylindre *m* de culasse mobile; **b. head,** tête *f* de culasse mobile; **b. head rim,** feuillure *f*; **b. stop,** arrêtoir *m* de culasse mobile; **b. handle, lever, knob,** levier *m* d'armement, de culasse mobile; *Artil:* **locking b.,** verrou de fermeture de culasse. **4.** *Mec.E:* boulon *m*; cheville *f*; goupille *f*; **long b.,** tire-fond *m inv*; **main b.,** cheville ouvrière; *Const:* **barb b.,** boulon barbelé; **expansion b., toggle b.,** boulon de scellement; **bracket b.,** boulon à tête ronde; **square b.,** boulon à tête carrée; **cap b.,** boulon à chapeau; **carriage b.,** boulon Japy; **spring b.,** boulon à ressort; **machine b.,** boulon décolleté; **clinch b.,** cheville clavetée; **key b.,** goupille clavette; **hold-down b.,** boulon de fixation; **pole b.,** boulon d'assemblage, chevillette *f*; **tie b.,** boulon d'accouplement; **b. circle,** cercle *m* de perçage; **nuts and bolts,** visserie *f,* **b. clipper, cropper, cutter,** coupe-boulons *m inv*; **b. staple,** auberon *m* (de la serrure d'une malle, etc.). **5.** (*a*) pièce *f* (de toile); **a b. of cloth,** une coupe de drap; (*b*) botte *f* (d'osier). **6.** *pl. Bookb:* **bolts,** témoins *m*; **to bind (a book) with bolts out,** laisser les témoins. **7.** *F:* fuite *f*; **to make a b. for sth.,** s'élancer sur, vers, qch.; **to make a b. for it,** décamper, déguerpir, filer.

bolt[2]. **1.** *v.tr.* (*a*) verrouiller; fermer (une porte) à, au, verrou; bâcler (une porte); **to b. the door,** mettre les verrous; **to b. oneself in,** s'enfermer au verrou; se barricader chez soi; **to b. s.o. out,** mettre les verrous contre qn; (*b*) *Mec.E:* boulonner, cheviller. **2.** *v.i.* (*a*) (*of horse*) s'emballer, s'emporter; forcer la main; prendre le mors aux dents; **to b. at a jump,** bourrer sur l'obstacle; (*of game*) **to b. from cover,** débouler; (*of pers.*) **to b. out of the room,** sortir précipitamment, brusquement, de la pièce; (*b*) *F:* (*of pers.*) décamper, déguerpir; lever le pied; prendre la poudre d'escampette; **he bolted to America,** il a filé sur l'Amérique; (*c*) *Pol: NAm:* tourner casaque. **3.** *v.i.* (*of plant*) monter en graine. **4.** *v.tr.* gober; avaler à grosses bouchées, sans mâcher; **to b. one's dinner,** avaler avidement, engloutir, *F:* bouffer, son dîner; expédier son dîner à la galopade.

bolt[3], *adv.* **b. upright,** tout droit, droit comme un piquet, droit comme un I.

bolt[4], *v.tr.* **1.** *Mill:* (*a*) bluter, tamiser, sasser (la farine); (*b*) **to b. the bran from the flour,** séparer le son de la farine. **2.** *F: A:* passer au crible (la conduite de qn, etc.).

bolter[1] ['boultәr], *s.* **1.** cheval porté à s'emballer. **2.** *Pol: NAm:* tourne-casaque *m inv*; déserteur *m* (de son parti).

bolter[2], *s. Mill:* **1.** (*pers.*) bluteur *m.* **2.** (*a*) bluteau *m,* blutoir *m,* sasse *f*; (*b*) **b. (sieve),** tamis *m,* bluteau, sas *m.*

bolt head ['boulthed], *s.* **1.** tête *f* de boulon. **2.** *Sm.a:* tête mobile (de fusil). **3.** *Ch:* matras *m.*

bolt hole ['boulthoul], *s.* **1.** trou *m* ou terrier *m* de refuge (d'un animal); *Mil:* abri *m* de bombardement. **2.** échappée *f*; *F:* **to arrange a b. h. for oneself,** se ménager une porte de sortie.

bolting[1] ['boultiŋ], *s.* **1.** verrouillage *m.* **2.** boulonnage *m,* chevillage *m.*

bolting[2], *s.* blutage *m,* tamisage *m,* sassage *m*; **b. cloth,** solamire *f,* étamine *f*; toile *f* à tamis, bluteau *m*; blutoir *m*; **b. machine,** bluteau *m*, blutoir *m*; **b. mill,** bluterie *f*, bluteau *m*; **b. reel, room, house,** bluterie *f*.

boltonia [bəl'touniə], *s. Bot:* boltonia *f*.

boltonite ['boultənait], *s. Miner:* boltonite *f*.

bolt rope ['boultroup], *s. Nau:* ralingue *f*; **head b. r.,** ralingue d'envergure, de têtière; faix *m*.

bolus ['bouləs], *s.* (*a*) *Pharm: Vet:* bol *m*; grosse pilule; (*b*) (**alimentary**) **b.,** bol alimentaire.

bomarea [bou'mæriə], *s. Bot:* bomarea *f*.

bomb[1] [bɔm], *s.* **1.** (*a*) *Mil: etc:* bombe *f*; **incendiary b.,** bombe incendiaire; **atom b.,** bombe atomique; **hydrogen b.,** bombe à (l')hydrogène; **uranium b.,** bombe à uranium; **cobalt b.,** bombe au cobalt; **nuclear b.,** bombe nucléaire; **glider b., glide b.,** bombe dirigée, planante; **flying b.,** bombe volante; **delayed action b., time b.,** bombe à retardement; **fragmentation b., scatter b.,** bombe à fragmentation; **earthquake b.,** bombe à pénétration; **demolition b.,** bombe de destruction; **armour-piercing b.,** bombe de rupture; **depth b.,** bombe sous-marine; **napalm b.,** bombe au napalm; **plastic b.,** (bombe au) plastic; **smoke b.,** bombe fumigène; **chemical b.,** bombe chimique; **flash b., illuminating b.,** bombe éclairante; **photo-flash b.,** bombe (aérienne) photographique; **winged b.,** bombe empennée, à empennage; **Mills b.,** grenade *f* de Mills; **to release, drop, a b.,** jeter, lâcher, larguer, une bombe; **b. release line, point, circle,** ligne *f*, point *m*, cercle *m*, de largage des bombes; **b. line, b. safety line,** ligne de sécurité de bombardement; **b. disposal, clearance,** déminage *m*; désobusage *m*; **to clear a battlefield of bombs,** désobuser un champ de bataille; **b. crater,** entonnoir *m*, cratère *m*; **b. site,** zone dévastée par les bombardements; *attrib. Av:* **b. aimer,** bombardier *m*; **b. carrier,** dispositif *m* porte-bombes; **b. bay,** soute *f* à bombes; **b. rack,** casier *m*, râtelier *m*, à bombes; **b. load,** charge *f* de bombes; *Fig:* **it came on us like a b.,** ce fut un véritable coup de foudre; *F:* **it goes, it is going, like a b.,** ça marche à merveille; *F:* **it must have cost a b.,** cela a dû coûter les yeux de la tête; (*b*) *Med:* **cobalt b.,** bombe au cobalt; (*c*) *esp. NAm: F:* événement imprévu, coup *m* de foudre; (*d*) *Austr: F:* vieux tacot. **2.** *Geol:* **volcanic b.,** bombe, noyau *m* volcanique; **bread-crust b.,** bombe en croûte de pain; **cracked b.,** bombe craquelée; **spindle(-shaped) b.,** bombe spiralée, fusiforme, en fuseau. **3.** *esp. NAm:* (*aerosol*) bombe.

bomb[2], *v.*

I. *v.tr.* bombarder, lancer des bombes sur (une ville, etc.); **to b. out the enemy,** faire déloger l'ennemi, (i) sous une pluie de bombes; (ii) sous une rafale d'obus; (iii) à coups de grenades; **to b. (out) a factory,** détruire une usine par bombardements; (*of family*) **to be bombed out,** perdre sa maison (dans un bombardement); **bombed out,** (i) sinistré (dans un bombardement); (ii) stupéfié (par des drogues, par l'alcool).

II. **bomb up,** (*a*) **to b. up an aircraft,** charger les bombes dans un avion; (*b*) *v.i.* (*of aircraft*) prendre sa charge de bombes.

Bombacaceae [bɔmbə'keisii:], *s.pl. Bot:* bombaçacées *f*, bombacées *f*.

bombard[1] ['bɔmbɑ:d, 'bʌm-], *s. A.Mil:* bombarde *f*.

bombard[2] [bɔm'bɑ:d], *v.tr.* (*a*) *Mil: etc:* bombarder (une ville, un port); gerber (un fort); *Fig:* **to b. s.o. with questions,** assaillir, bombarder, qn de questions; (*b*) *Atom.Ph:* bombarder.

bombardier [bɔmbə'diər, bʌm-], *s.* **1.** *Mil: A:* bombardier *m*. **2.** *Artil:* brigadier *m*. **3.** *Av: U.S:* bombardier. **4.** *Ent:* **b. beetle,** bombardier.

bombardment [bɔm'bɑ:dmənt], (*a*) bombardement *m*; (*b*) *Atom.Ph:* **b. of the electrons,** bombardement électronique; **radiation b.,** pilonnage *m* des radiations.

bombardon [bɔm'bɑ:d(ə)n], *s. Mus:* **1.** (*a*) bombardon *m*; contrebasse *f* (à vent); (*b*) (*wound round the body*) hélicon *m*. **2.** (*pedal reed stop of organ*) bombarde *f*.

bombasine, bombazine ['bɔmbəzi:n], *s. Tex:* bombasin *m*, alépine *f*.

bombast ['bɔmbæst], *s.* emphase *f*, enflure *f*, pathos *m*, boursouflure *f* (de style); grandiloquence *f*.

bombastic [bɔm'bæstik], *a.* (style) ampoulé, enflé, boursouflé, emphatique.

bombastically [bɔm'bæstik(ə)li], *adv.* d'un style ampoulé, enflé, emphatique; emphatiquement; avec emphase.

bombax ['bɔmbæks], *s. Bot:* bombax *m*, fromager *m*; bombace *m*.

bombe [bɔmb], *s. Cu:* bombe *f*.

bomber ['bɔmər], *s.* **1.** (*pers.*) (*a*) *Mil:* grenadier *m*; (*b*) *Av:* bombardier *m*; (*c*) terroriste *mf* qui se sert de bombes. **2.** *Av:* (*aircraft*) bombardier, avion *m* de bombardement; **heavy, medium, light, b.,** bombardier lourd, moyen, léger; **day, night, b.,** bombardier de jour, de nuit; **b. command, b. forces,** l'aviation *f* de bombardement.

Bombidae ['bɔmbidi:], *s.pl. Ent:* bombidés *m*.

bombinator ['bɔmbineitər], *s. Amph:* bombinator *m*, bombinateur *m*, sonneur *m* (à ventre de feu).

bombing ['bɔmiŋ], *s.* **1.** *Av:* bombardement *m*; **dive b.,** bombardement en piqué; **glide b.,** bombardement (i) en plané, (ii) avec bombes planantes; **trail b.,** bombardement en traînée; **carpet b.,** bombardement par vagues (d'avions) successives; **pattern b.,** bombardement systématique; **skip b.,** bombardement par ricochet en vol rasant; **area b.,** bombardement sur zone; **pinpoint b.,** bombardement, (i) sur objectif ponctuel; (ii) de précision; **b. run,** course *f* de visée (de l'avion de bombardement). **2.** attaque *f* à la grenade.

bombproof ['bɔmpru:f], *a.* à l'épreuve des bombes; **b. shelter,** abri blindé; **b. vault,** abri-voûte *m*, *pl.* abris-voûtes.

bombshell ['bɔmʃel], *s.* (*a*) obus *m*; (*b*) événement imprévu, coup *m* de foudre; **this news came as a b. to us,** cette nouvelle nous a atterrés.

bombsight ['bɔmsait], *s. Av:* viseur *m*, collimateur *m*, de bombardement.

bomb-thrower ['bɔmθrouər], *s.* **1.** (*pers.*) lanceur *m* de bombes, de machine infernale. **2.** (appareil *m*) lance-bombes *m inv*.

Bombycidae [bɔm'bisidi:], *s.pl. Ent:* bombycidés *m*.

Bombyliidae [bɔmbi'laiidi:], *s.pl. Ent:* bombylides *m*, bombylidés *m*.

bombyx ['bɔmbiks], *s. Ent:* bombyx *m*.

bona fide ['bounə'faidi], (*a*) *a. & adv.* de bonne foi; sérieux; **b. f. purchaser,** acheteur *m* de bonne foi; **b. f. offer,** offre sérieuse; *Jur: A:* **b. f. traveller,** voyageur authentique (autorisé à se faire servir des spiritueux à toute heure); (*b*) *s.* **one's bona fides,** sa bonne foi, sa sincérité.

bonanza [bə'nænzə]. **1.** *s.* bonanza *f*, filon *m* riche; **to strike a b.,** rencontrer un filon riche; **mine in b., b. mine,** mine *f* bonanza; **the new store proved a b.,** le nouveau magasin est devenu une vraie mine d'or. **2.** *a.* prospère, favorable; **b. year,** année *f* de prospérité, d'abondance.

Bonapartism ['bounəpɑ:tizm], *s.* bonapartisme *m*.

Bonapartist ['bounəpɑ:tist], *s. & a.* bonapartiste (*mf*).

bonbon ['bɔnbɔn], *s.* bonbon *m*.

bonbonnière [bɔnbɔ'niɛər], *s.* bonbonnière *f*.

bonce [bɔns], *s. P:* tête *f*, cigare *m*.

bon chrétien ['bɔnkrei'tjɛ̃], *s. Hort:* **b. c.** (**pear**), bon-chrétien *m*, *pl.* bons-chrétiens.

bond[1] [bɔnd], *s.* **1.** lien *m*; attache *f*; *pl.* fers *m*, liens, chaînes *f*; *Lit:* **to break one's bonds asunder, to burst one's bonds, to break from one's bonds,** rompre, briser, ses liens, ses fers. **2.** (*a*) lien (d'osier, pour fagots, etc.); *Civ.E: etc:* attache; **bonds of friendship,** liens d'amitié; les attaches, les nœuds *m*, de l'amitié; (*b*) *Rail:* éclisse *f* (de rail conducteur); (*c*) *Const:* (**system of**) **b.,** appareil *m* (en liaison); **Old English b.,** appareil anglais; **Flemish b.,** appareil en carreaux et boutisses; appareil flamand; **double Flemish b.,** appareil polonais; **cross b.,** appareil croisé; **heading b.,** appareil en, de, boutisses; (*d*) *Carp:* assemblage *m*; **b. timber,** pièce *f* d'assemblage; *Metalw:* assemblage; joint *m*; accrochage *m* (en soudure); **b. holes,** trous *m* d'assemblage (pour rivets); **thermite b.,** joint à la thermite; (*f*) *Geol:* agglutinant *m*, liant *m* (de conglomérats); (*g*) *Ch:* liaison *f*; **simple, multiple, b.,** liaison simple, multiple; **coordinate, semi-polar, b.,** liaison de coordination, semi-polaire; **covalent b.,** liaison de covalence; **metallic b.,** liaison métallique; **ionic b.,** liaison électrovalente. **3.** (*a*) engagement *m*, contrat *m*; (*b*) *Jur:* obligation *f*; engagement; **mortgage b.,** titre *m* hypothécaire; lettre *f* de gage; **contract b., performance b.,** garantie *f* d'exécution (d'un contrat); (*c*) *Fin:* bon *m*; *U.S:* obligation; **Treasury bonds,** bons du Trésor; **bearer b.,** bon au porteur; **registered b.,** bon nominatif; **government bonds,** (i) rentes *f* sur l'État; (ii) titres de rente; **public bonds,** effets publics; **prize bonds, lottery bonds,** valeurs *f*, obligations, bons, à lots; **premium bonds,** (i) obligations à primes; (ii) bons à lots; *A:* **national war bonds,** bons de la défense nationale; (*d*) *Jur:* caution *f*; **Admiralty b.,** caution en garantie de dommages-intérêts (dans un procès devant le tribunal maritime). **4.** *Com: Cust:* dépôt *m*, entrepôt *m*; (*of goods*) **to be in b.,** être à l'entrepôt, en dépôt; être entreposé; **tobacco in b.,** tabac *m* en garenne; **goods out of b.,** marchandises sorties de l'entrepôt; **to take goods out of b.,** dédouaner des marchandises; **taking out of b.,** dédouanage *m*; **b. note,** acquit-à-caution *m*, *pl.* acquits-à-caution.

bond[2], *v.tr.* **1.** *Const:* (*a*) enlier, lier, liaisonner (des pierres); (*b*) appareiller (un mur, des moellons). **2.** *Com:* entreposer, mettre en dépôt, à l'entrepôt (des marchandises).

bond[3], *a. A:* en esclavage.

bondage ['bɔndidʒ], *s.* **1.** *esp. Lit:* esclavage *m*, servitude *f*, asservissement *m*; **to be in hopeless b.,** être rivé à la chaîne; **to be in b. to s.o.,** être sous la coupe, sous la férule, de qn; **to escape from b.,** rompre sa chaîne, ses chaînes. **2.** *Hist:* servage *m*. **3.** *Poet:* captivité *f*.

bonded ['bɔndid], *a.* **1.** (*a*) *Const:* (*of masonry*) en liaison; (*b*) *Rail:* **b. joint,** joint *m* à éclisse. **2.** *Com:* (*of goods*) entreposé, en dépôt, en entrepôt, en douane. **3.** *Fin:* (dette) garantie par obligations.

bonder ['bɔndər], *s.* **1.** *Const:* parpaing *m*, boutisse *f*. **2.** *Com:* (*pers.*) entrepositaire *m*.

bonderization [bɔ dərai'zeiʃ(ə)n], *s. Metall:* bondérisation *f*.

bonderize ['bɔndəraiz], *v.tr. Metall:* bondériser.

bondholder ['bɔndhouldər], *s. Fin:* obligataire *m*; détenteur *m*, porteur *m*, de bons, d'obligations.

bonding ['bɔndiŋ], *s.* **1.** *Const:* (*a*) liaison *f* (de pierres); *Hyd.E:* soudage *m*; (*b*) appareillage *m*. **2.** *Metalw:* (*a*) collage *m* (des métaux); (*b*) métallisation *f*; liaison électrique de toutes les parties d'un appareil. **3.** *Com:* entreposage *m* (de marchandises).

bondmaid(en) ['bɔndmeid(n)], *s.f. A:* jeune esclave.

bondman, *pl.* **-men** ['bɔndmən], *s.m.* **1.** (*a*) *Hist:* serf; (*b*) *A:* esclave. **2.** *Const:* **master b.,** maître appareilleur.

bondservant ['bɔndsə:vənt], *s.* (*a*) *Hist:* serf, *f* serve; (*b*) *A:* esclave *mf*.

bondservice ['bɔndsə:vis], *s.* (*a*) *Hist:* servage *m*; (*b*) *A:* esclavage *m*, servitude *f*.

bondslave ['bɔndsleiv], *s. A:* esclave *mf*.

bondsman, *pl.* **-men** ['bɔndzmən], *s.m.* **1.** (*a*) *Hist:* serf; (*b*) *A:* esclave. **2.** *Com:* **to be b. for s.o.,** être la caution de qn, le garant de qn; s'être porté caution pour qn.

bondstone ['bɔndstoun], *s. Const:* parpaing *m*, boutisse *f*.

bond(s)woman, *pl.* **-women** ['bɔnd(z)wumən, -wimin], *s.f.* (*a*) *Hist:* serve; (*b*) *A:* esclave.

bonduc ['bɔndʌk], *s. Bot:* (*a*) guilandine *f* bonduc; bonduc *m*; *F:* chicot *m*; (*b*) bonduc jaune; **b. seed,** œil-de-chat *m*.

bone[1] [boun], *s.* **1.** (*a*) os *m*; (*of fish*) arête *f*; **horse with plenty of b.,** cheval fortement membré; cheval solide; *Prov:* **hard words break no bones,** une parole rude ne casse rien; du dire au fait il y a grand trait; *F:* **he's (nothing but) a bag of bones, nothing but skin and bones,** il est maigre comme un clou; on lui voit les os; c'est une vraie momie; il n'a que la peau et les os; **he won't make old bones,** il ne fera pas de vieux os; **he went to Africa and left his bones there,** il est parti en Afrique et il y laissa sa peau; **chilled to the b.,** gelé jusqu'aux os; transi de froid, **to work one's fingers to the b.,** se tuer à travailler, au travail; **b. of contention,** sujet *m* de dispute; pomme *f* de discorde; **I feel it in my bones,** j'en ai le pressentiment; *F:* **to have a b. in one's leg,** avoir un poil dans la main; *F:* **to make no bones about doing sth.,** ne pas se gêner pour faire qch.; ne pas hésiter à faire qch.; ne pas se faire scrupule de faire qch.; faire qch. sans marchander; **they turned him out and made no bones about it,** on l'a mis bel et bien à la porte; **he makes no bones about it,** (i) il n'y va pas avec le dos de la cuiller; (ii) il ne s'en cache pas; **he made no bones about it,** il y est allé carrément; il n'y a pas été par quatre chemins; **don't make so many bones about it!** ne faites pas tant de difficultés! *Austr: F:* **to point a b. at s.o.,** porter malheur à qn; *F:* (*of joke, etc.*) **near the b.,** risqué; d'un goût douteux; **that's a bit near the b.!** ça, c'est un peu osé! (*b*) *attrib.* **b. ash, b. earth,** cendre *f*, poudre *f*, terre *f*, d'os; *Ch:* claire *f* de coupelle; **b. dust, b. manure, b. meal,** engrais *m* d'os (broyés); **b. black, b. char,** noir animal; *Vet:* **b. spavin,** éparvin calleux; *Cer:* **b. china,** porcelaine *f* phosphatique; porcelaine tendre anglaise; *Lacem:* **b. lace,** dentelle *f* au fuseau; (*c*) *Min:* veine calcaire ou schisteuse (dans une couche de charbon). **2.** *pl.* (*a*) (*of the dead*) ossements *m*; (*b*) *Cost:* armature *f* (d'un bustier, etc.); (*c*) fuseaux *m* (de dentellière); (*d*) *F:* (i) dés *m* à jouer; (ii) dominos *m*; (*e*) *Mus:* (i) cliquettes *f*; (ii) joueur, -euse, de cliquettes. **3.** *U.S: P:* dollar *m*.

bone[2], *v.tr.* **1.** désosser (la viande); ôter les arêtes (du poisson). **2.** garnir (un corset) de baleines. **3.** *P:* chiper, escamoter, voler, chaparder (qch.). **4.** *v.ind.tr. NAm: P:* **to b. up on sth.,** potasser qch.

bone[3], *v.tr. Surv:* niveler.

bonecrusher ['bounkrʌʃər], *s.* casse-os *m inv*.

boned [bound], *a.* **1.** (*with adj. prefixed, e.g.*) **big-b.,** à, aux, gros os; **strong b.,** qui a les os solides; (homme *m*) solide. **2.** (*of meat*) désossé; (*of fish*) sans arêtes. **3.** (corset) baleiné, garni de baleines.

bone-dry ['boun'drai], *a.* absolument, complètement, sec, *f* sèche; *F:* archi-sec, *pl.* archi-secs.

bonefish ['bounfiʃ], *s. Ich:* albula *m*.

bonehead ['bounhed], *s. F:* idiot, -ote; tête *f* de bois.
boneheaded ['boun'hedid], *a. F:* idiot, stupide.
bone-idle ['boun'aidl], **bone-lazy** ['boun'leizi], *a.* paresseux comme une couleuvre.
boneless ['bounlis], *a.* **1.** désossé; sans os; sans arêtes; *F:* **b. wonder,** gymnaste désossé. **2.** *F:* mou; sans énergie; sans caractère.
bonemeal ['bounmi:l], *s.* engrais *m* d'os (broyés).
boner ['bounər], *s. NAm: P:* bourde *f.*
boneset ['bounset], *s. Bot:* eupatoire *f.*
bonesetter ['bounsetər], *s.* rebouteur *m,* rhabilleur *m; F:* renoueur *m.*
bonesetting ['bounsetiŋ], *s.* reboutement *m.*
boneshaker ['bounʃeikər], *s. F:* **1.** *Cy: A:* vélocipède *m* à bandages de fer. **2.** (*car*) vieux clou, vieille guimbarde.
Boney ['bouni], *Pr.n.m. F: A:* = Bonaparte.
boneyard ['bounja:d], *s.* (*a*) ossuaire *m;* (*b*) chantier *m* d'équarrissage; (*c*) *F:* cimetière *m* d'autos, de vieilles machines.
bonfire ['bɔnfaiər], *s.* (*a*) feu *m* de joie; (*b*) feu (de jardin).
bongar ['bɔŋgər], *s. Rept:* bongare *m,* bungare *m.*
bongo ['bɔŋgou], *s. Z:* (antilope *f*) bongo *m.*
bonhomie ['bɔnɔmi], *s.* bonhomie *f,* bonne humeur, jovialité *f.*
boniness ['bouninis], *s.* **1.** (*a*) forte proportion d'os (dans la viande); (*b*) abondance *f* d'arêtes (dans le poisson). **2.** angularité *f,* décharnement *m* (du visage, etc.).
boning[1] ['bouniŋ], *s.* **1.** (*a*) désossement *m;* (*b*) *Cost:* baleinage *m* (d'un corset, etc.). **2.** *P:* vol *m;* chapardage *m.*
boning[2], *s. Surv:* nivellement *m;* **b. rod,** nivelette *f,* voyant *m.*
bonito [bɔ'ni:tou], *s. Ich:* bonite *f.*
bonk ['bɔŋk], *v.tr. P:* flanquer un coup à (qn) (sur la tête).
bonkers ['bɔŋkəz], *a. P:* cinglé.
bonnet[1] ['bɔnit], *s.* **1.** *Cost:* (*a*) (*men*) bonnet (écossais); béret (écossais); (*b*) *A:* (*women*) chapeau *m* à brides; capote *f,* bonnet (de femme, d'enfant); béguin *m* (d'enfant); (*c*) *Her:* bonnet, calotte *f,* coiffe *f* (d'une couronne). **2.** (*a*) *Aut: Av:* capot *m; Aut:* **b. to tail,** parechoc *m* contre pare-choc; (*b*) *Nau:* **funnel b.,** couvercle *m,* chapeau, de cheminée; (*c*) chapeau, capot, couvercle (de soupape, de vanne). **3.** *Nau:* bonnette maillée (de voile). **4.** compère *m* (d'un escamoteur, etc.). **5.** bonnet (de la baleine de Biscaye).
bonnet[2], *v.tr. A:* **1.** mettre un béret, un chapeau, à (qn). **2.** *F:* enfoncer le chapeau sur la tête à (qn); houspiller (qn).
bonneted ['bɔnitid], *a.* coiffé d'un bonnet, d'un chapeau.
bonnet(te) ['bɔnit], *s. Fort:* bonnette *f.*
bonny ['bɔni], *a. esp. Scot:* joli; gentil, *f* gentille; **a b. baby,** un bébé magnifique.
bonspiel ['bɔnspi:l], *s.* match *m,* tournoi *m,* de curling.
bont [bɔnt], *s. Min:* partie dure d'une veine.
bonus, *pl.* **-uses** ['bounəs, -əsiz], *s.* gratification *f,* sursalaire *m,* surpaye *f,* boni *m,* bonification *f,* prime *f;* part *f* de bénéfice; **work on a b. system,** travail *m* à la prime; **cost-of-living b.,** indemnité *f* de vie chère, de cherté de vie; **b. share,** action gratuite, action d'attribution, action donnée en prime; **b. on shares,** dividende *m* supplémentaire; bonification sur les actions; *Ins:* **b. to policy holder,** bénéfice additionnel alloué aux assurés; **no-claim b.,** bonification pour non-sinistre; *Com: etc:* **Christmas b.,** gratification du jour de l'an, de fin d'année; **output b.,** *U.S:* **merit b.,** prime de rendement; *Cards:* **b. for winning the rubber,** queue *f.*
bon viveur ['bɔ̃vi'vœ:r], *s.* bon vivant.
bonxie ['bɔŋksi], *s. Orn:* grand labbe *m.*
bony ['bouni], *a.* **1.** osseux. **2.** (*a*) (personne *f*) à, aux, gros os; (corps, contours) anguleux; (*b*) (doigt, visage) décharné. **3.** (*of meat*) plein d'os; (*of fish*) plein d'arêtes.
bonza ['bɔnzə], *a. U.S: Austr: P:* chic, épatant, fameux.
bonze [bɔnz], *s.* bonze *m.*
bonzer ['bɔnzər], *a. Austr: P:* = BONZA.
boo[1] [bu:]. **1.** *int.* hou! (d'aversion ou de mépris); *F:* **he can't say b. to a goose,** c'est un timide; il a du sang de navet. **2.** *s.* huée *f.*
boo[2], *v.tr. & i.* **to b. (at) s.o.,** huer, conspuer, chahuter, qn; **to be booed off the stage,** quitter la scène au milieu des huées; **the whole audience booed,** toute l'assistance a poussé des huées, des cris de dérision.
boob[1] [bu:b], *s. P:* **1.** (*a*) idiot, -ote, crétin *m,* nouille *f;* (*b*) gaffe *f,* bêtise *f,* boulette *f.* **2.** (*not in polite use*) **the boobs,** les nénés *m.*
boob[2], *v.i. P:* faire une gaffe, une boulette.
booby ['bu:bi], *s.* **1.** (*a*) idiot, -ote, crétin *m,* nouille *f;* **b. trap,** (i) attrape-nigaud *m, pl.* attrape-nigauds; (ii) *Mil:* piège *m;* mine-piège *f, pl.* mines-pièges; *A:* **to beat the b.,** battre des bras (pour se réchauffer); (*b*) le dernier (dans un concours, etc.); **b. prize,** prix décerné par plaisanterie à celui qui vient en dernier. **2.** *Orn:* fou *m;* **blue-faced b.,** fou masqué; **brown b.,** fou brun.
booby hatch ['bu:bihætʃ], *s.* **1.** *Nau:* écoutillon *m,* capot *m* en bois. **2.** *NAm: P:* maison *f* de fous.
booby-trap ['bu:bitræp], *v.tr. Mil: etc:* piéger.
boodle[1] ['bu:dl], *s.* **1.** *esp. NAm: F:* tas *m,* grande quantité; foule *f;* **a big b. of kids,** une foule de gamins; **the whole kit and b.,** tout le bataclan. **2.** *P:* (*a*) argent *m,* fric *m;* (*b*) fausse monnaie; (*c*) gratte *f,* pots-de-vin *mpl; U.S:* caisse noire, fonds secrets (pour les élections); (*d*) *esp. U.S:* butin *m.*
boodle[2], *v.tr. U.S: P:* rouler (qn).
boodler ['bu:dlər], *s. U.S: P:* trafiqueur *m.*
booer ['bu:ər], *F:* hueur *m.*
boofhead ['bu:fhed], *s. Austr: P:* idiot *m,* con *m.*
boogie-woogie ['bu:gi'wu:gi], *s. Mus:* boogie-woogie *m.*
boohoo[1] ['bu:'hu:], *F:* **1.** *int.* heu, heu, heu! **2.** *s.* pleurnichement *m.*
boohoo[2], *v.i. F:* pleurer bruyamment; braire; pleurnicher.
booing ['bu:iŋ], *s.* huées *fpl,* chahutage *m.*
book[1] [buk], *s.* **1.** (*a*) livre *m;* **old books,** (i) vieux bouquins; (ii) vieilles éditions; **the b. trade,** l'industrie *f* du livre; la librairie; **b. publishing,** l'édition *f;* **school b.,** livre scolaire; livre classique; livre de classe; **not published in b. form,** inédit en librairie; **the b.-minded, b.-reading, public,** le public qui lit; **b. club,** club *m* du livre; **b. learning, knowledge,** érudition *f;* savoir acquis dans les livres; connaissances *f* livresques; **b. canvasser,** courtier *m* en librairie; **to be a great b. lover, to have a great love of books,** (i) aimer beaucoup les livres; aimer beaucoup lire; (ii) être bibliophile; **b. hunter,** bibliophile *m,* bouquineur *m;* **he's a confirmed b. hunter, he's always b. hunting,** il est toujours à bouquiner; c'est un bouquineur acharné; **b. plate,** exlibris *m inv;* **b. post,** service postal des imprimés; **b. trough,** repose-livres *m inv; Bookb:* (*pers.*) **b. folder,** plieur, -euse; *Tex:* **b. muslin,** organdi *m; Ent:* **b. louse,** psoque *m,* pou *m* de bois; *Arach:* **b. scorpion,** chélifère *m* cancroïde, scorpion *m* des livres; *F:* **to speak like a b.,** parler comme un livre; compasser tous ses discours; **to speak by the b.,** citer ses autorités; **to speak without the b.,** (i) parler de mémoire; (ii) parler sans autorité; **in accordance with the b.,** conforme à la théorie; **by the b.,** selon les règles; **in my b.,** selon moi; (*of subject*) **to be a closed, sealed, b. to s.o.,** être lettre close pour qn; *F: A:* **the Devil's books,** les cartes à jouer; (*b*) (*libretto*) livret *m,* libretto *m* (d'un opéra); (*c*) *O:* **to swear on the B.,** prêter serment sur la Bible; (*d*) **blue b.,** (i) *Adm:* = livre jaune; (ii) *U.S:* registre *m* (des employés de l'État, etc.); (iii) *U.S:* = Bottin mondain; (iv) *U.S: Sch:* cahier bleu (dans lequel les candidats écrivent leurs copies d'examen); *F:* **to do a blue b.,** passer un examen; (*e*) recueil *m* (de chansons, de prières, etc.); (*f*) **telephone b.,** annuaire *m* du téléphone; (*g*) *P:* revue *f,* magazine *m.* **2.** (*a*) *Com: Fin: etc:* registre; **account b.,** livre de comptes; registre de comptabilité; papier-journal *m, pl.* papiers-journaux; **purchase b., bought b.,** journal *m* des achats; **sales b.,** journal des ventes; **b. of original entry,** journal originaire; **b. credit,** crédit *m* compte; **b. debit,** dette *f* compte; **b. value,** valeur *f* comptable; **cash b.,** livre de caisse; **bank b.,** livret, carnet *m,* de banque; **savings bank b.,** livret de caisse d'épargne; **cheque b.,** carnet de chèques, chéquier *m;* **to keep the books of a firm,** tenir les livres, les écritures, d'une maison; **to put on the books,** faire passer aux écritures; **to be in s.o.'s good books,** être en faveur auprès de qn; être dans les petits papiers de qn; être bien vu de qn; **to be in s.o.'s bad, black, books,** être mal vu, mal noté, de, par, qn; **to get into s.o.'s good books,** se faire bien voir de qn; se mettre dans, entrer dans, les bonnes grâces de qn; **to bring s.o. to b. for sth.,** forcer qn à rendre compte de qch.; demander compte à qn de qch.; forcer qn à s'expliquer; *F:* **to throw the b. at s.o.,** accabler qn d'accusations; (*b*) *Nau:* **ship's books,** livres de bord; **to enter (up) a man on the ship's books,** porter un homme au rôle de l'équipage; **signal b.,** tome *m* des signaux; **victualling b.,** cahier *m* de rations; (*c*) *Sch: etc:* **exercise b.,** cahier; **rough b.,** brouillon *m;* (*d*) *Turf:* **betting b.,** livre de paris; **to make a b.,** faire un livre; *F:* **that suits my b.,** ça fait mon beurre; **that doesn't suit my b.,** ça ne me va pas; ça ne rentre pas dans mes calculs; ça dérange mes combinaisons; ça ne fait pas mon affaire; (*e*) **b. of stamps,** carnet de timbres; **b. of tickets,** carnet de billets; (*f*) **b. of needles,** sachet *m,* jeu *m,* d'aiguilles; **b. of matches,** pochette *f* d'allumettes; **b. matches,** allumettes plates. **3.** (*at whist, bridge*) **the b.,** le devoir.
book[2], *v.tr.* **1.** (*a*) inscrire, enregistrer (une commande, etc.); prendre note (d'une commande); inscrire (un voyageur à l'hôtel); (*in shop*) **would you b. it for me, please,** mettez cela à mon compte, s'il vous plaît; (*b*) *Ind:* **we are heavily booked,** nous avons beaucoup de commandes à exécuter. **2.** retenir, réserver (une chambre, une place); louer (une place) d'avance; *Th:* **seats can be booked from ten to eight,** la location est ouverte de dix heures à huit heures; **all the seats are booked,** tout est loué; **I'm booked (up) for this evening,** je suis déjà invité, on m'a retenu, pour ce soir; ce soir je suis pris. **3.** *Rail:* délivrer un billet à (un voyageur); *v.i.* (*of passenger*) **to b.,** prendre son billet; **to b. through to Marseilles,** prendre un billet direct pour Marseille. **4.** *F:* dresser une contravention à (qn); *U.S:* **to b. s.o.,** arrêter qn.
bookable ['bukəbl], *a.* qui peut être loué, retenu, réservé.
bookbinder ['bukbaindər], *s.* relieur, -euse.
bookbindery ['bukbaind(ə)ri], *s.* atelier *m* de reliure; maison *f* de reliure.
bookbinding ['bukbaindiŋ], *s.* reliure *f.*
bookcase ['bukkeis], *s. Furn:* bibliothèque *f;* **dwarf b.,** bibliothèque d'appui; **revolving b.,** bibliothèque tournante.
bookends ['bukendz], *s.pl.* serre-livres *m inv.*
bookie ['buki], *s. Turf: F:* book *m.*
booking ['bukiŋ], *s.* enregistrement *m,* inscription *f;* réservation *f* (d'une chambre); *Th:* engagement *m* (d'un artiste); *Th:* **b. of tickets,** location *f* de billets; *Rail:* **b. of seats,** réservation *f* des places; *Cin:* **blind b.,** location de films à boîte fermée; **block b.,** location, réservation, en bloc; **b. clerk,** préposé *m* à la distribution, à la délivrance, des billets; employé(e) du guichet; **b. office,** guichet *m* (de délivrance des billets).
bookish ['bukiʃ], *a.* **1.** (*of pers.*) adonné à la lecture; studieux. **2.** (*of pers., of style*) pédantesque, livresque.
book-keeper ['bukki:pər], *s. Com:* teneur *m* de livres; comptable *m.*
book-keeping ['bukki:piŋ], *s. Com:* tenue *f* des livres; comptabilité *f;* **single-entry b.-k.,** unigraphie *f;* **double-entry b.-k.,** tenue des livres en partie double; digraphie *f.*
booklet ['buklit], *s.* livret *m;* opuscule *m;* brochure *f; Com:* **descriptive b.,** notice descriptive (d'une machine, etc.); *U.S:* **(stamp) b.,** carnet *m* de timbres.
booklover ['buklʌvər], *s.* bibliophile *m;* bouquineur *m.*
bookmaker ['bukmeikər], *s.* **1.** faiseur *m* de livres. **2.** *Turf:* bookmaker *m.*
bookmaking ['bukmeikiŋ], *s.* **1.** l'industrie *f* du livre; bibliotechnie *f.* **2.** *Turf:* profession *f* de bookmaker.
bookman, *pl.* **-men** ['bukmən], *s.m.* **1.** savant, lettré; homme d'étude. **2.** *NAm:* (i) éditeur; (ii) libraire.
bookmark(er) ['bukma:k(ər)], *s.* signet *m;* **b. and paper-knife combined,** liseuse *f.*
bookmobile ['bukmoubi:l], *s. NAm:* bibliobus *m.*
bookrest ['bukrest], *s.* pupitre *m,* appui-livre(s) *m inv,* liseuse *f,* porte-livres *m inv.*
bookroom ['bukru:m], *s.* (*a*) cabinet *m* de lecture (d'une librairie); (*b*) (*in house*) (petite) bibliothèque.
bookseller ['bukselər], *s.* libraire *m;* **secondhand b.,** bouquiniste *m;* **new and secondhand b.,** librairie de neuf et d'occasion; **b. and publisher,** libraire-éditeur *m, pl.* libraires-éditeurs.
bookselling ['bukseliŋ], *s.* (commerce *m* de) librairie *f.*
bookshelf, *pl.* **-shelves** ['bukʃelf, -ʃelvz], *s.* rayon *m;* planche réservée aux livres.
bookshop ['bukʃɔp], *s.* librairie *f.*
bookstall ['buksto:l], *s.* **1.** étalage *m* de livres; **secondhand b.,** étalage de bouquiniste. **2.** *Trans:* bibliothèque *f* (de gare); **b. attendant,** libraire *mf.*
bookstore ['buksto:r], *s. NAm:* librairie *f.*
bookwork ['bukwə:k], *s.* **1.** *Com:* tenue *f* des livres, des écritures. **2.** *Sch: etc:* étude *f* des livres; **he's much better at sport than at b.,** il réussit mieux au terrain de jeu qu'à ses études. **3.** *Typ:* labeur *m;* travail *m* de librairie.
bookworm ['bukwə:m], *s.* **1.** *Ent:* anobion *m,* ptine *m.* **2.** *F:* (*pers.*) dévoreur, -euse, de livres; bouquineur acharné.
Boolean ['bu:liən], *a. Mth:* **B. algebra,** algèbre *f* de Boole, algèbre booléenne; **B. connective,** opérateur booléen; **B. rings,** anneaux booléens.
boom[1] [bu:m], *s.* **1.** (*at harbour mouth*) (pannes *fpl* de) barrage *m;* chaîne *f* (de fermeture); barre *f;* estacade flottante; **b. defence,** obstruction littorale. **2.** *Nau:* (*a*) bout-dehors *m* (de foc), *pl.* bouts-dehors; gui *m;* **fore b.,** gui de misaine; **spinnaker b.,** tangon *m,* bout-dehors, de spinnaker; **b. iron,** blin *m* (de bout-dehors); **b. crutch,** croissant *m,* support *m,* de gui; (*b*) **swinging b.,** tangon; **to cast off from the b.,** larguer le tangon; (*c*) **derrick b.,** mât *m* de charge; **cargo b.,** corne *f* de charge; **to rig the booms,** mâter les mâts de charge; **to take the booms down,** amener les mâts de charge; (*d*) **hose b.,** potence *f* de flexibles; (*e*) flèche *f* (d'une grue);

(*f*) *Cin: T.V:* perche *f* (de microphone), *F:* girafe *f*; **b. shot,** coup *m* de la girafe. **3.** *Av:* longeron *m*. **4.** *Civ.E:* (*of web girder*) membrure *f*; (*of built-up girder*) semelle *f*.

boom[2], *v.tr.* **1.** *Nau:* **to b. (out) the sails,** mettre les voiles en ciseaux. **2.** (*a*) **to b. (off) part of a river,** établir un barrage flottant dans une rivière (pour y réserver une piste de course); (*b*) *Nau:* **to b. off a boat,** écarter, déborder, une embarcation.

boom[3], *s.* grondement *m*, retentissement *m*, bruit *m* (du canon, du tonnerre, des vagues); mugissement *m* (du vent); cri *m* (du butor); tons *m* sonores (de la voix); ronflement *m* (de l'orgue); bourdonnement *m* (de cloches, d'insectes); **the b. of the sea,** le bruit de tonnerre de la mer; *Av:* **sonic b.,** bang *m* (supersonique).

boom[4], *v.i.* **1.** (*of wind, etc.*) retentir, gronder, mugir (sourdement); (*of guns*) gronder, tonner; (*of organ*) ronfler; (*of bittern*) crier; (*of insects*) bourdonner; **his voice boomed out above the noise of the crowd,** sa voix retentissait au-dessus du bruit de la foule. **2.** *A:* (*of ship*) marcher à toutes voiles.

boom[5], *s. Com: Fin: etc:* boom *m*, période *f* d'essor; vague *f* de prospérité; **b. town,** ville *f* champignon.

boom[6]. **1.** *v.tr.* (*a*) *O:* faire une grosse publicité en faveur de (qch.); faire valoir (qn, qch.); faire du battage autour de (qn, qch.); faire l'article pour (qch.); (*b*) *NAm:* **they are booming him for senator,** ils donnent tout leur appui à sa candidature pour le sénat. **2.** *v.i.* être en hausse; faire de la hausse; **trade, business, is booming,** les affaires marchent bien, sont en plein essor.

boomer ['bu:mər], *s. Austr:* **1.** kangourou *m* mâle; (*species*) kangourou géant. **2.** *F:* (*a*) chose *f* énorme; (*b*) gros mensonge; **what a b.!** en voilà une forte!

boomerang[1] ['bu:məræŋ], *s.* (*a*) boomerang *m*; (*b*) boomerang, mauvais tour qui retombe sur son auteur.

boomerang[2], *v.i.* revenir comme un boomerang; **his policy boomeranged,** sa politique s'est retournée contre lui.

booming[1] ['bu:miŋ], *a.* (vent) mugissant; (tonnerre) retentissant; **b. voice,** voix ronflante, retentissante, tonitruante.

booming[2], *s.* essor *m* (économique, etc.).

booming[3], *s. Min:* lavage *m* (des terrains aurifères au moyen d'un violent cours d'eau).

boon[1] [bu:n], *s. Lit:* **1.** *A:* requête *f*; demande *f* (d'une faveur). **2.** don *m*, faveur *f*; **to grant a b.,** accorder une faveur. **3.** bienfait *m*, avantage *m*; **I found it a great b.,** cela m'a rendu grand service.

boon[2], *a.* **b. companion,** gai, bon, compagnon; bon vivant, vive-la-joie *m inv*.

boon[3], *s.* chènevotte *f*, tige ligneuse (du chanvre).

boondocks ['bu:ndɔks], *s.pl. NAm: F:* **the b.,** les forêts de l'intérieur; la brousse.

boondoggle[1] ['bu:ndɔgl], *s. U.S: F:* (i) objet *m*, (ii) travail *m*, sans valeur (surtout aux frais de l'État).

boondoggle[2], *v.i. U.S: F:* flâner, perdre son temps (à faire des choses inutiles); peigner la girafe.

boong [bu:ŋ], *s. Austr: F:* aborigène *mf* (d'Australie).

boongary ['bu:ngeəri], *s. Z:* dendrolague *m*.

boor ['buər], *s.* rustre *m*, rustaud *m*; homme malappris.

boorish ['buəriʃ], *a.* rustre, rustaud, grossier; malappris.

boorishly ['buəriʃli], *adv.* grossièrement; en rustre.

boorishness ['buəriʃnis], *s.* grossièreté *f*; manque *m* de savoir-vivre.

boost[1] [bu:st], *s.* **1.** (*a*) **to give s.o. a b.,** (i) soulever qn par derrière; faire la courte échelle à qn; (ii) faire de la réclame, du battage, pour qn; (iii) *F:* pistonner qn; **this product got a good b. from the start,** on a bien lancé ce produit; **to give a b. to an industry,** relancer une industrie; (*b*) *Cards:* relance *f*. **2.** *El:* survoltage *m*; **bass b.,** amplification *f* des basses fréquences; **b. pressure,** pression *f* (d'admission de) suralimentation (d'un moteur); *Av:* surpression *f*.

boost[2], *v.tr.* (*a*) **to b. s.o. (up),** soulever qn par derrière; faire la courte échelle à qn; (*b*) faire de la réclame, du battage, pour, en faveur de (qn, qch.); vanter, faire valoir (sa marchandise); *F:* pistonner (qn); **to b. sth.,** faire l'article de qch.; (*c*) **to b. production,** relancer, augmenter, la production; (*d*) *Cards:* (*poker*) relancer. **2.** *El:* survolter; **to b. up the potential to a hundred volts,** surélever le potentiel jusqu'à cent volts.

booster ['bu:stər], *s.* **1.** prôneur *m*, réclamiste *m*. **2.** (*a*) *El:* survolteur *m*; **feeder b.,** survolteur d'artère; **reversible b.,** survolteur-dévolteur *m*, *pl.* survolteurs-dévolteurs; **negative b.,** dévolteur *m*, sous-volteur *m*, *pl.* sous-volteurs; **b. battery,** batterie survoltrice, batterie de renfort; **b. switch,** commutateur *m* d'appoint; (*b*) (*of missile*) propulseur *m* auxiliaire de départ; fusée *f* auxiliaire, d'appoint, de décollage; **b. rocket,** fusée de démarrage; (*c*) *Av:* démarreur *m* auxiliaire; propulseur auxiliaire de décollage; accélérateur *m* (de décollage); (*d*) *Tchn:* surpresseur *m*; **b. pump,** pompe *f* de surpression; pompe auxiliaire; gaveuse *f*; **b. station,** station *f* auxiliaire de pompage; station relais; (*e*) *Elcs:* préamplificateur *m* d'antenne; (*f*) *Ch:* renforçateur *m*; (*g*) *Med:* **b. dose,** dose *f* de rappel; **b. injection,** *F:* **b. shot,** injection *f*, piqûre *f*, de rappel.

boost-glide ['bu:stglaid], *a.* **b.-g. vehicle,** véhicule *m* mi-balistique-mi-planeur.

boosting ['bu:stiŋ], *s.* **1.** (*a*) réclame *f*, battage *m*; (*b*) *F:* pistonnage *m* (de qn). **2.** (*a*) *El:* survoltage *m*; (*b*) *Hyd:* surpression *f*.

boot[1] [bu:t], *s.* **1.** (*a*) botte *f*, bottine *f*, chaussure montante; (**heavy, laced b.**) brodequin *m*; (*comfortable,* (*fur-*)*lined*) bottillon *m*; **elastic-sided boots,** bottines, bottillons, à élastiques; **riding boots,** bottes à l'écuyère; **b. and shoe manufacturer,** fabricant *m* de chaussures; **b. strap, tag,** tirant *m* de botte; **to put on one's boots,** se chausser; se botter; **to take off one's boots,** se déchausser; se débotter; tirer, quitter, ses bottes; **you're not fit to black his boots,** vous n'êtes pas digne de le déchausser, de dénouer ses lacets; *Mil: A:* **to sound the b. and saddle,** sonner le boute-selle; **to charge b. to b.,** charger botte à botte; *Hist:* (**torture of**) **the b.,** les brodequins; *Geog:* **the b. of Italy,** la botte de l'Italie; *F:* **the boot's on the other foot, leg,** (i) c'est tout (juste) le contraire; (ii) les rôles sont renversés; *F:* **you can bet your boots that . . .,** je te garantis que . . .; *P:* **to give s.o. (the order of) the b.,** mettre, flanquer, qn à la porte; saquer qn; **to get the b.,** être saqué, mis à la porte; *F:* **as tough as old boots,** dur comme tout; *F: O:* (*intensive*) **he was working like old boots,** il travaillait furieusement; (*b*) *pl.* pattes emplumées (d'un pigeon pattu, d'une poule pattue). **2.** *Ind:* hotte *f*, trémie *f* (pour alimenter une machine, etc.); **charging b.,** entonnoir *m*. **3.** *Aut:* coffre *m*; malle *f*; [*V.Veh:* caisson *m*; rotonde *f* (de diligence). **4.** *U.S: FP[* (*a*) recrue *f* (dans les fusiliers marins et la marine); (*b*) apprenti *m*.

boot[2], *v.tr.* **1.** chausser (qn); **to b. (oneself),** se chausser; se botter. **2.** *F:* flanquer des coups de pied à (qn); **to b. s.o. out,** flanquer qn à la porte (à coups de pied dans le derrière). **3.** *Hist:* faire subir le supplice des brodequins à (qn).

boot[3], *s.* (*only in the phrase*) **to b.,** par surcroît, en sus, de plus; par-dessus le marché.

boot[4], *v.tr.impers. A: & Lit:* **what boots it to . . .?** à quoi sert-il de . . .? **it boots not to . . .,** rien ne sert de . . ..

bootblack ['buθtblæk], *s.* décrotteur *m*, cireur *m* (de chaussures).

booted ['bu:tid], *a.* portant des chaussures, de bottines; chaussé; **b. and spurred,** (i) chaussé de ses bottes et de ses éperons; (ii) prêt à partir.

bootee [bu:'ti:], *s.* (*a*) (*occ.*) bottillon *m*; (*b*) bottine *f* d'enfant; chausson tr coté (de bébé).

Boötes [bou'outi:z], *Pr.n. Astr:* le Bouvier; Bootès *m*.

booth [bu:ð], *s.* **1.** baraque *f*, tente *f* (de marché, de forains); loge *f* (de foire); **telephone b.,** cabine *f* téléphonique; **listening b.,** cabine d'audition, d'écoute; **polling b.,** isoloir *m*; bureau *m* de scrutin. **2.** *Cin:* **projection b.,** cabine *f* de projection; **camera b.,** cabine d'enregistrement.

boothook ['bu:thuk], *s.* tire-botte *m* (pour se botter), *pl.* tire-bottes.

bootjack ['bu:tdʒæk], *s.* **1.** arrache-chaussures *m inv*, tire-botte *m* (pour se débotter), *pl.* tire-bottes. **2.** *Th: F: A:* (= *utility man*) utilité *f*.

bootlace ['bu:tleis], *s.* lacet *m* (de chaussure).

bootleg[1] ['bu:tleg], *s.* **1.** tige *f* (d'une botte). **2.** produit *m* (*esp.* boisson *f* alcoolique), (i) vendu, transporté, etc., illégalement, (ii) passé en fraude.

bootleg[2], *a.* (*esp. of alcohol*) vendu, transporté, produit, illégalement; passé en fraude; clandestin.

bootleg[3], *v.* (**bootlegged**) **1.** *v.tr.* (*a*) transporter (de l'alcool) illégalement; (*b*) produire, vendre (des boissons alcooliques, etc.) illégalement. **2.** *v.i.* trafiquer (surtout en boissons alcooliques); faire de la contrebande.

bootlegging ['bu:tlegiŋ], *s.* contrebande *f* (*esp.* de l'alcool); trafic *m*.

bootless[1] ['bu:tlis], *a.* sans chaussures.

bootless[2], *a. A: & Lit:* inutile, infructueux, vain.

bootlick ['bu:tlik], *v.tr. F:* lécher les bottes à (qn).

bootlicker ['bu:tlikər], *s. F:* lèche-bottes *m inv*; chien couchant.

bootmaker ['bu:tmeikər], *s.* bottier *m*; cordonnier *m*.

boots [bu:ts], *s.* **1.** garçon *m* d'étage (dans un hôtel); cireur *m* de chaussures. **2.** *F: A:* le moins ancien (des membres d'un club, d'un cercle d'officiers, etc.).

boot topping ['bu:ttɔpiŋ], *s. Nau:* flottaison *f*.

booty ['bu:ti], *s.* **1.** butin *m*; **to share the b.,** partager le gâteau. **2.** *A:* (*a*) **to play b.,** faire exprès de perdre au début de la partie pour allécher la victime; (*b*) **to play b. with s.o.,** aider au jeu de qn, être de connivence avec qn.

booze[1] [bu:z], *v.i. P:* boire (sec, raide, comme un trou); être adonné à la boisson; lever le coude; picoler; **to get boozed (up),** se poivrer.

booze[2], *s. P:* **1.** la boisson; **I must buy some more b.** = il faut que je repasse chez le marchand de vin. **2. to be on the b.,** être en ribote; **to go on the b.,** se mettre à boire; **we had a good (old) b.(-up),** on s'est payé une bonne cuite; *Austr: P:* **b. artist,** ivrogne *m*, poivrot *m*.

boozer ['bu:zər], *s. P:* **1.** ivrogne *m*, poivrot *m*; pochard, -arde. **2.** bistrot *m*.

boozeroo ['bu:zəru:], *s. N.Z: P:* = BOOZE-UP.

booze-up ['bu:zʌp], *s. P:* beuverie *f*; soûlerie *f*.

boozy ['bu:zi], *a. F: P:* **1.** ivrogne. **2.** un peu gris; pompette; **a b. evening,** une soirée passée à boire.

bop [bɔp], *s. Mus:* bop *m*.

bo-peep [bou'pi:p], *s. F:* **to play (at) bo-p.,** jouer à cache-cache (avec un enfant); faire coucou.

Bopyridae [bou'piridi:], *s.pl. Crust:* bopyridés *m*.

bopyrus [bou'pairəs], *s. Crust:* bopyre *m*.

bora ['bɔ:rə], *s. Meteor:* bora *f*.

boracic [bə'ræsik], *a. Ch:* borique; *Pharm:* **b. ointment,** pommade *f* à l'acide borique; **b. powder,** poudre boriquée; acide *m* borique en poudre.

boracite ['bɔrəsait], *s. Miner:* boracite *f*.

borage ['bɔridʒ], *s. Bot: Pharm:* bourrache *f*.

Boraginaceae [bɔrædʒi'neisii:], *s.pl. Bot:* borraginacées *f*, *A:* borraginées *f*.

boraginaceous [bɔrædʒi'neiʃəs], *a. Bot:* borraginacé.

borak ['bɔræk], *s. Austr: F:* **to poke b. at s.o.,** se moquer de qn.

borane ['bɔrein], *s. Ch:* borane *m*.

borassus [bɔ'ræsəs], *s. Bot:* borasse *m*, borassus *m*.

borate ['bɔ:reit], *s. Ch:* borate *m*.

borated [bɔ'reitid], *a.* boraté.

borax ['bɔ:ræks], *s. Ch: etc:* (*a*) borax *m*; (*b*) (*unrefined*) tincal *m*, tinkal *m*; **b. honey,** mellite *m* de borax; *Metalw:* **b. box,** rochoir *m*.

borazon ['bɔrəzən], *s. Ch:* borazon *m*.

bordeaux [bɔ:'dou], *s.* **1.** vin *m* de Bordeaux; bordeaux *m*. **2.** *Vit: etc:* **b. mixture,** bouillie bordelaise; bouillie cuprique, cuprocalcique.

border[1] ['bɔ:dər], *s.* **1.** bord *m*; lisière *f*, bordure *f*; cadre *m*; marge *f* frontière *f* (entre deux pays); confins *mpl* (d'un pays); **northern b. of a country,** frontière nord d'un pays; **to escape over the b.,** passer la frontière; **b. town,** ville *f* frontière; **the B.,** (i) la frontière écossaise (et les comtés limitrophes); (ii) la frontière entre les États-Unis et le Mexique; *A:* **B. marriage,** mariage en fugue célébré aussitôt passé la frontière d'Écosse (le plus souvent à Gretna Green); *Hist:* **B. riders, B. prickers,** bandes montées et armées qui faisaient des incursions d'Écosse en Angleterre; *For:* **b. tree,** (arbre *m* de) paroi *f*; **b. stone,** (i) borne *f*; (ii) bordure (d'une route). **2.** (*a*) (*edging*) galon *m*, bordé *m* (d'un habit); bordure (d'un tableau, d'un tapis, etc.); encadrement *m* (d'un panneau); carnèle *f* (d'une pièce de monnaie); rive *f* (de fer à cheval); (*on letter paper*) **black b.,** baguette *f*; *Typ:* (**ornamental**) **b.,** (i) dentelle *f*, (ii) vignette *f* (d'une page); **ruled b.,** encadrement en filets; *Cmptr:* **b. punched card,** carte *f* à perforations marginales; *Th:* **the borders,** (i) les coulisses *f*; (ii) les frises *f*; **b. lights,** rampe *f* d'illumination des frises; (*b*) **grass b., turf b.,** plate-bande *f*, *pl.* plates-bandes; cordon *m* de gazon. **3.** *Her:* bordure.

border[2]. **1.** *v.tr.* (*a*) border (un habit, un chemin, etc.); lisérer (un mouchoir); encadrer; **path bordered with box,** allée bordée de buis; (*b*) border; confiner à (un pays, etc.); **the lands that b. the Mediterranean,** les pays qui bordent la Méditerranée. **2.** *v.i.* **to b. on (sth.),** (*a*) (*of territory*) toucher, confiner, à (un autre pays); être limitrophe (d'un autre pays); **the two countries b. on one another,** les deux pays se touchent; **his estate borders on mine,** sa terre tient à la mienne; (*b*) **to b. on insanity,** approcher, être voisin, de la folie; **it borders on fanaticism,** cela touche au fanatisme; **he was bordering on sixty,** il frisait la soixantaine.

bordered ['bɔ:dəd], *a. Her:* bordé, liseré.

borderer ['bɔ:dərər], *s.* **1.** habitant, -ante, de la frontière, *esp.* de la frontière d'Écosse; frontalier, -ière. **2.** *A:* voisin, -ine (on, de).

bordering[1] ['bɔ:d(ə)riŋ], *a.* (*a*) contigu, -uë, touchant, aboutissant (on, à); frontalier; voisin (**on,** de); limitrophe (on, de); **gardens b. on the river,** jardins aboutissant à la rivière, qui côtoient la rivière; **lands b. an estate,** tenants *mpl* d'une propriété; **estates b. the Thames,** propriétés riveraines de la Tamise; **countries b. the Mediterranean,** pays *m* en bordure de la Méditerranée; (*b*) **colour b. on red,** couleur *f* qui tire au rouge, sur le rouge; **statement b. on truth, on falsehood,** déclaration *f* qui côtoie la vérité, qui frise le mensonge; **emotion b. on terror,** émotion voisine de la terreur.

bordering[2], *s.* bordure *f*; rebord *m*.

borderland ['bɔːdəlænd], *s.* (*a*) pays *m* frontière, limitrophe; marche *f*; (*b*) **the b. between sleeping and waking,** la limite entre le sommeil et le réveil.

borderline ['bɔːdəlain], *s.* (*a*) ligne *f*, limites *fpl*, de séparation (entre deux catégories, etc.); bornes *fpl* (d'une catégorie, etc.); frontière *f* (entre deux états); **the b. between sanity and insanity,** la limite entre le bon sens et la folie; (*b*) **b. case,** (i) cas *m* limite; (ii) cas indéterminé; **that's a bit near the b.,** ça frise l'indécence.

bordure ['bɔdjər], *s. Her:* bordure *f*.

bore[1] ['bɔːr], *s.* **1.** (*a*) calibre *m*, alésage *m* (d'un tuyau, etc.); calibre (d'une arme à feu); *Mec.E:* **straight b.,** alésage cylindrique; (*b*) âme *f* (d'une arme à feu); **smooth b.,** âme lisse; **rifled b.,** âme rayée; **b. gauge,** vérificateur *m* d'âme; (*c*) *attrib.* **b. dust,** (i) poussière *f* de foret; farine *f* de forage; alésures *fpl*; (ii) poudre *f* de bois (piqué des vers). **2.** *Min:* trou *m* de sonde; sondage *m*, forage *m*.

bore[2], *v.tr. & i.* **1.** (*a*) **to b. (out),** creuser, (i) forer; (ii) foncer (un puits); forer, percer (un trou); tortiller (une mortaise); aléser (un cylindre); **to b. out a part,** travailler une pièce à la fraise; **to b. into wood, etc.,** forer, vriller, le bois, etc.; **to b. through sth.,** percer, perforer, qch.; *Min:* **to b. for water, minerals, etc.,** faire un sondage, sonder, pour trouver de l'eau, des minéraux, etc.; (*b*) (*with passive force*) **timber that does not b. well,** bois difficile à percer. **2.** *Equit:* (*of horse*) bourrer, encenser; **to b. on the bit,** se braquer sur le mors. **3.** (*a*) *Turf:* couper un concurrent, couper la ligne; pousser son cheval contre un concurrent; (*b*) (*of pers.*) **to b. (one's way) through the crowd,** se frayer (brutalement) un chemin à travers la foule; traverser la foule en bolide.

bore[3], *s.* (*a*) (*pers.*) fâcheux, -euse; importun *m*; *F:* raseur, -euse, casse-pieds *m inv*; **what a b. (he is)!** ce qu'il est barbe, barbant, rasoir, casse-pieds! (*b*) (*thg*) corvée *f*, *F:* scie *f*; **what a b.!** quelle corvée! **it was no end of a b., a, the, hell of a b.,** c'était la barbe et les cheveux.

bore[4], *v.tr.* ennuyer, *F:* raser, empoisonner, enquiquiner, barber (qn); **I hope I'm not boring you,** j'espère que je ne vous ennuie pas; **I'm never bored,** je ne m'ennuie jamais; **cards b. me,** je ne peux pas supporter les jeux de cartes; *F:* **it bores me stiff, bores me to death, to tears,** ça me fait mourir, crever, d'ennui, me donne un de ces cafards; *F:* **I'm bored to death with him and all his complaints,** j'en ai marre de lui et de tous ses griefs; *F:* **he bores me stiff,** ce qu'il est rasoir, enquiquinant, casse-pieds!

bore[5], *s.* mascaret *m*; raz *m* de marée; barre *f* d'eau.

boreal ['bɔːriəl], *a. Lit:* boréal, -aux.

Boreas ['bɔriæs], *Pr.n.m. Myth:* Borée.

borecole ['bɔːkoul], *s. Hort:* chou vert, chou frisé.

boredom ['bɔːdəm], *s.* ennui *m*.

borehole ['bɔːhoul], *s. Min:* **1.** trou *m* de sonde; sondage *m*. **2.** trou de mine. **3.** bure *f*.

Borel [bɔ'rel], *Pr.n. Math:* **B. subset,** partie borélienne.

borer ['bɔːrər], *s.* **1.** (*pers.*) foreur *m*, perceur *m*; sondeur *m* (de puits); *Sm.a: Artil:* **finishing b.,** adoucisseur, -euse. **2.** appareil *m*, outil *m*, de perforation; (*a*) foret *m*, tarière *f*; perçoir *m*, perce *f*, vrille *f*; **long b.,** esseret *m*; (*b*) (*of cylinder*) alésoir *m*; (*c*) *Civ.E:* perforatrice *f*; *Min:* fleuret *m*, sonde *f*, pistolet *m*; **short b.,** fleuret d'amorçage; **cross-mouthed b.,** pistolet à tête carrée. **3.** *Equit:* cheval *m* qui se braque. **4.** (*a*) *Moll:* taret *m*; (*b*) *Ent:* insecte perforant, (insecte) térébrant *m*.

boresome ['bɔːsəm], *a.* ennuyeux; qui manque d'intérêt; *F:* rasoir, enquiquinant.

boric ['bɔrik], *a. Ch:* borique; **b. oxide, anhydride,** oxyde *m*, anhydride *m*, borique.

boride ['bɔːraid], *s. Ch:* borure *m*.

boring[1] ['bɔːriŋ], *a. Ent:* térébrant; *Med:* **b. pain,** douleur térébrante.

boring[2], *s.* **1.** percement *m* (d'un trou, d'un passage); *Mec.E:* forage *m*, perçage *m*; (*of cylinder*) alésage *m*; *Min:* sondage *m*, forage; **rope b.,** sondage à la corde; sondage chinois; **to make borings,** faire des sondages; *Mec.E:* **b. bar,** arbre *m*, tige *f*, de foret; arbre, barre *f*, d'alésage; **b. cutter,** lame *f* à aléser, lame d'aléseuse; **b. mill,** aléseuse fraiseuse *f*; **b. machine,** (i) *Mec.E:* foreuse *f*, perceuse *f*; (*for cylinders*) alésoir *m*, aléseuse *f*, machine *f* à aléser; (ii) *Min: etc:* sondeuse *f*, sonde *f*, foreuse; perforatrice *f*; **b. tool,** (i) *Mec.E:* outil *m* à aléser; outil de perçage; alésoir *m*; (ii) *Min: etc:* outil de forage, de sondage; sonde *f*. **2.** *pl.* **borings,** alésures *f*; copeaux *m* (d'alésage); poussière *f* de foret.

boring[3], *a.* ennuyeux, ennuyant, *F:* barbant, enquiquinant, rasoir; **a thoroughly b. evening,** une soirée des plus ennuyeuses, *F:* à vous donner le cafard.

born [bɔːn]. **1.** *p.p.* (*a*) **to be b.,** naître; **to be b. again,** renaître; **to have been b.,** être né; **I am London b.,** je suis natif de Londres; je suis né à Londres; **the house where I was b.,** ma maison natale; **he is French b.,** il est Français de naissance; **when I was b.,** lors de ma naissance; **he was b. in 1930,** il naquit, il est né, en 1930; **in this town hundreds of children are b. every month,** chaque mois il naît dans cette ville des centaines d'enfants; **to be b. deaf, blind,** être sourd, aveugle, de naissance; **to be b. lucky,** être né coiffé; **b. to trouble,** né pour souffrir; **three sons b. to her,** trois fils mis au monde par elle, nés d'elle; **b. on the wrong side of the blanket,** né en dehors du mariage; de descendance illégitime; *F:* **do you think I was b. yesterday?** croyez-vous que je suis né d'hier? **misfortunes b. of the war,** infortunes nées de la guerre; **confidence is b. of knowledge,** la confiance vient du savoir; **the France b. of the events of 1789,** la France issue des événements de 1789; **philosophy b. of discouragement,** philosophie issue du découragement; **one must be b. a cook,** on naît cuisinier; (*b*) *Theol:* **b. again,** régénéré. **2.** *a.* **he is a b. poet, a poet b.,** il est né poète; **he's a b. storyteller,** c'est un conteur né; **a gentleman b.,** un gentilhomme de naissance; **a Parisian, a Londoner, b. and bred,** un vrai Parisien de Paris, un vrai Londonien de Londres; **he was b. and bred a conservative,** il avait été élevé, nourri, dans le conservatisme; *F:* **b. fool,** parfait idiot; **in all my b. days,** de toute ma vie; depuis que je suis au monde. **3.** *s.* **her latest b.,** son dernier né, sa dernière née.

bornean ['bɔːniən], *Geog:* (*a*) *a.* bornéen; (*b*) *s.* Bornéen -enne.

Borneo ['bɔːniou], *Pr.n. Geog:* Bornéo *m*.

borneol ['bɔːniɔl], *s. Ch:* bornéol *m*.

Bornholm ['bɔːnhɔːm], *Pr.n. Geog:* Bornholm; *Med:* **B. disease,** pleurodynie *f*, myalgie *f*, épidémique.

bornite ['bɔːnait], *s. Miner:* bornite *f*, érubescite *f*, philippsite *f*.

bornyl ['bɔːnil], *s. Ch:* bornyle *m*; **b. acetate,** acétate *m* de bornyle; **b. alcohol,** bornéol *m*.

Borodino [bɔrou'diːnou], *Pr.n. Geog:* Borodino; *Hist:* **the Battle of B.,** la bataille de la Moskova.

borofluoride [bɔrou'fljuːəraid], *s. Ch:* borofluorure *m*.

boron ['bɔːrɔn], *s. Ch:* bore *m*; **b. nitride,** nitrure *m* de bore; *Metall:* **b. steel,** acier *m* au bore.

borosilicate [bɔrou'silikeit], *s. Ch:* borosilicate *m*.

borough ['bʌrə]. **1.** *s.* (*a*) ville *f* (avec municipalité); **b. council,** conseil municipal; **b. rates,** taxes municipales; *Hist:* **county b.,** grande commune dont le système administratif était semblable à celui d'un comté; (*b*) circonscription électorale (urbaine); *Pol.Hist:* **close b., pocket b.,** circonscription électorale qui était dans la poche, sous la coupe, d'un particulier; **rotten b.,** bourg pourri. **2.** *Pr.n.* **the B.,** quartier *m* de Londres (dans Southwark).

Borromean [bɔrou'miːən], *a. Geog:* **the B. Islands,** les îles *f* Borromées.

Borromeo [bɔrou'meiou], *Pr.n.* **St. Charles B.,** Saint Charles Borromée.

borrow[1] ['bɔrou]. **1.** *v.tr. & i.* emprunter (**from,** à); (*a*) *Fin: etc:* **to b. (money) from s.o.,** faire un emprunt à qn; emprunter à qn; **to b. money on the security of an estate,** emprunter de l'argent sur une terre; **to b. on mortgage,** emprunter sur hypothèque; **to b. at interest,** emprunter à intérêt; **to b. long,** emprunter à long terme, à longue échéance; **to b. short,** emprunter à court terme; **general agreement to b.,** accord général de prêt; *St.Exch:* **to b. stock,** (faire) reporter des titres; (*b*) **to b. an idea from s.o.,** emprunter une idée à qn; **to b. a phrase from Kipling,** pour emprunter une expression à Kipling; **this word was borrowed from Latin,** ce mot est un emprunt au latin; **to b. trouble,** aller au-devant du malheur. **2.** *v.i. Golf:* tenir compte du vent, de l'inclinaison du sol, etc.

borrow[2], *s.* **1.** *Civ.E:* emprunt *m* de terre; **b. pit,** ballastière *f*. **2.** *Cmptr:* retenue *f*.

borrowed ['bɔroud], *a.* emprunté; d'emprunt; *Fin:* **b. capital,** capitaux empruntés, d'emprunt; **I don't like having to use b. books,** je n'aime pas être obligé à me servir de livres empruntés; **he's living on b. time,** (i) il a déjà dépassé l'âge où la plupart des gens meurent; (ii) il a survécu à une maladie qui tue la plupart des gens; (iii) il ne lui reste que peu de temps à vivre.

borrower ['bɔrouər], *s.* emprunteur, -euse; **he's a confirmed b.,** il est toujours à emprunter quelque chose; *Fin:* **borrowers' credit,** crédit *m* de l'emprunteur.

borrowing ['bɔrouiŋ], *s.* (*a*) emprunts *mpl*; **to live by b.,** vivre d'emprunts; **financed by b.,** financé par des emprunts; **b. power,** capacité *f* d'emprunter; (*b*) **this word is a b. from Latin,** ce mot est un emprunt au latin.

bor(t)sch [bɔːtʃ], *s. Cu:* bortsch *m*.

Borstal ['bɔːst(ə)l], *Pr.n. Geog:* Borstal (ville du comté de Kent); *Adm:* **b. institution,** *s.* **borstal,** école *f* de redressement pour jeunes gens âgés de plus de 16 ans.

bort [bɔːt], *s. Lap:* égrisée *f*; boort *m*.

borzoi ['bɔːzɔi], *s.* lévrier *m* russe; borzoï *m*.

boscage ['bɔskidʒ], *s. NAm: Lit:* bosquet *m*.

boselaphus [bɔ'zeləfəs], *s. Z:* bosélaphe *m*, cerf-bœuf *m*, *pl.* cerfs-bœufs.

bosh [bɔʃ], *s. & int. F:* bêtises *fpl*, blague *f*; propos idiots; **that's all b.,** tout ça c'est de la blague, ça ne rime à rien; **b.!** pas possible! quelle blague!

boshes ['bɔʃiz], *s.pl. Metall:* étalages *m* (d'un haut-fourneau).

bosk(et) ['bɔsk(it)], *s. NAm: & Lit:* bosquet *m*; fourré *m*.

bosker ['bɔskər], *a. Austr: P:* chic, sensass.

Boskop ['bɔskɔp], *Pr.n. Anthr:* **B. man,** homme *m* de Boskop.

boskopoid ['bɔskɔpɔid], *a. Anthr:* boskopoïde.

bosky[1] ['bɔski], *a. NAm: & Lit:* boisé; broussailleux.

bosky[2], *a. P: A:* ivre, soûl.

bosmina [bɔz'miːnə], *s. Crust:* bosmine *f*.

bos'n ['bousn], *s.* = BOATSWAIN.

Bosnia ['bɔzniə], *Pr.n. Hist:* Bosnie *f*.

Bosnian ['bɔzniən]. **1.** *Hist: Geog:* (*a*) *a.* bosnien; (*b*) *s.* Bosnien, -ienne. **2.** *s. Ling:* bosnien *m*.

bosom[1] ['buz(ə)m]. **1.** *s.* (*a*) (i) poitrine *f* (d'une personne); (ii) seins *mpl* (d'une femme); *A:* **the wife of his b.,** sa femme bien-aimée; *B:* **Abraham's b.,** le sein d'Abraham; (*b*) **in the b. of one's family,** au sein de sa famille; dans son intimité; **in the b. of the Church,** dans le giron de l'Église; **in the b. of the earth,** au sein de la terre; (*c*) *Cost: NAm:* devant *m* du corsage (d'une robe); plastron *m* (d'une chemise). **2.** *a.* **b. friend,** ami(e) intime.

bosom[2], *v.i. esp. NAm:* **to b. (out),** s'enfler (au vent, etc.).

boson ['bousən], *s. Atom.Ph:* boson *m*.

Bosphorus (the) [ðə'bɔsfərəs], (*U.S: also* **Bosporus** ['bɔspərəs]), *Pr.n. Geog:* le Bosphore.

bosqu(et) ['bɔsk(it)], *s.* = BOSK(ET).

boss[1] [bɔs], *s.* protubérance *f*, renflement *m*. **1.** (*a*) *Arch: Metall: Z: etc:* bosse *f*; (*b*) *Arm:* ombon *m* (de bouclier); (*c*) *Furn:* capiton *m*. **2.** *Harn:* bossette *f* (du mors). **3.** *Geol:* (petit) batholit(h)e; mamelon *m* (dénudé). **4.** (*a*) *Mec.E:* mamelon, portée *f*; (*of wheel, crank*) **centre b.,** tourteau *m*; **crank b.,** tourteau de manivelle; *I.C.E:* **(gudgeon-pin) bosses (within the piston),** bossages *m* du piston; (*b*) *Av: Nau:* **propeller b.,** moveu *m* de l'hélice; **continuous b., solid b.,** moyeu traversant.

boss[2], *v.tr.* bosseler (la vaisselle, etc.); orner de bosses *fpl*.

boss[3], *F:* **1.** *s.* (*a*) **the b.,** (i) le patron, *P:* le singe; (ii) (= CONTREMAÎTRE) le chef, *P:* le singe; **the trade-union bosses,** les grands chefs du syndicat; **she's the b. here,** c'est elle qui porte la culotte; **I'll show you who's b. here!** vous ferez ce que je dis, sinon . . .! (*b*) *Pol: NAm:* chef, grand manitou, d'un parti. **2.** *a. esp. NAm:* épatant; **we had a b. time,** on s'est rudement (bien) amusé(s)!

boss[4], *v.tr. F:* mener, diriger (qn, qch.); **to b. the show,** contrôler tout; s'imposer; faire la loi; **it's his wife who bosses the show,** c'est bien sa femme qui porte la culotte; **stop bossing me about!** j'en ai assez de vous et de vos ordres!

boss[5], *a. F:* **to make a b. shot,** rater, manquer, son coup.

boss[6], *v.tr. & i. F:* louper (un travail, etc.); rater (son coup).

boss[7], *s. Z: NAm: F:* vache *f*; veau *m*; (*calling animal*) **b., b.!** viens, viens!

bossage ['bɔsidʒ], *s. Const:* bossage *m*.

bossed [bɔst], *a.* en bosse; en relief.

boss-eyed ['bɔsaid], *a. F:* qui louche.

bossie ['bɔsi], *s.* = BOSSY[2].

bossiness ['bɔsinis], *s. F:* autoritarisme *m*; façons *f* autoritaires; **that's enough of your b.!** cesse de faire la loi!

bossing[1] ['bɔsiŋ], *s. Min:* havage *m*.

bossing[2], *s. F:* façons *f* autoritaires; **I've had enough of you and your b.,** j'en ai marre de vous et de vos ordres.

bossy[1] ['bɔsi], *a. F:* autoritaire; **he's too damn b. (for words),** il veut toujours faire la loi, faire le grand manitou.

bossy[2], *s. Z: NAm: F:* vache *f*; veau *m*.

boston ['bɔstən], *s.* **1.** *A: Cards:* (jeu *m* de) boston *m*. **2.** *Danc:* **b. (two-step),** boston.

Bostrychidae [bɔs'trikidiː], *s.pl. Ent:* bostrychidés *m*.

bostryx ['bɔstriks], *s. Bot:* bostryx *m*, cyme *f* unipare hélicoïde.

bosun ['bousn], *s.* = BOATSWAIN.

bo'sun bird ['bousnbɔːd], *s. Orn:* phaéton *m*, *F: & Fr.C:* paille-en-queue *m*, *pl.* pailles-en-queue, paille-en-cul, *m*, *pl.* pailles-en-cul.

Boswellian [bɔz'weliən], *a. Lit:* qui a rapport à, qui rappelle, Boswell; **B. admiration,** admiration *f* sans réserve.

bot[1] [bɔt], *s.* **1.** *Ent:* (*sheep*) **b.,** larve *f* d'œstre (du mouton). **2.** *P: Austr:* (*pers.*) parasite *m*, tapeur *m*.

bot[2], *v.i.* (**botted**) *P: Austr:* vivre aux dépens de qn; écumer la marmite.

botanic(al) [bə'tænik(l)], *a.* botanique; **b. garden(s),** jardin *m* botanique.

botanist ['bɔtənist], *s.* botaniste *mf.*

botanize ['bɔtənaiz], *v.i.* herboriser, botaniser.

botanizer ['bɔtənaizər], *s.* botaniseur, -euse; herborisateur, -trice.

botanizing ['bɔtənaiziŋ], *s.* herborisation *f.*

botany ['bɔtəni], *s.* botanique *f*; **descriptive b.,** phytographie *f*; **b. wool,** laine très fine importée d'Australie.

botargo [bɔ'tɑːgou], *s. Cu:* bo(u)targue *f.*

botch[1] [bɔtʃ], *s.* **1.** *A:* pustule *f*; ulcère *m*. **2.** *F:* travail mal fait, bousillé, loupé; **you've made an awful b. of it,** tu l'as bien bousillé, loupé, saboté.

botch[2], *v.tr. F:* (*a*) bousiller, saboter, saloper, louper (un travail, etc.); **botched-up work,** travail mal torché, travail loupé; (*b*) **to b. (sth.) up,** rafistoler (qch.); réparer (qch.) grossièrement.

botcher ['bɔtʃər], *s. F:* bousilleur *m*, savetier *m*; gâte-pâte *m inv*; ravaudeur *m*; loupeur, -euse.

botchy ['bɔtʃi], *a. F:* (travail) loupé, bousillé, saboté.

botfly ['bɔtflai], *s. Ent:* œstre *m*; mouche *f* des chevaux; **sheep b.,** œstre du mouton.

both [bouθ]. **1.** *a. & pron.* tous (les) deux, toutes (les) deux; l'un(e) et l'autre; **b. (of) (the) brothers,** les deux frères; l'un et l'autre frère; **b. (of them) are dead,** ils sont morts tous (les) deux; **b. of these possibilities must be taken into account,** il faut tenir compte de l'une et l'autre de ces possibilités; **he has two houses, b. of which are vacant,** il a deux maisons, qui sont vides toutes les deux; **she kissed him on b. cheeks,** elle l'a embrassé sur les deux joues; **b. were punished,** l'un et l'autre a été puni, ont été punis; **to hold sth. in b. hands,** tenir qch. à deux mains; **on b. sides,** des deux côtés; **b. alike,** l'un comme l'autre; **b. of us saw it,** nous deux l'avons vu; nous l'avons vu tous (les) deux; **we wrote to them b.,** nous leur avons écrit à tous les deux; **riches and glory b. vanish,** et les richesses et la gloire s'évanouissent; **it is better to be good than beautiful—but one may be b. at the same time!** il vaut mieux être sage que belle—mais on peut être les deux en même temps! **you can't have it b. ways,** on ne peut pas avoir le drap et l'argent; *Nau:* (*to engine room*) **stop b. engines,** stoppez partout. **2.** *adv.* **b. you and I,** (et) vous et moi; **b. John and I came, John and I b. came,** Jean et moi sommes venus tous les deux; **God will judge b. the righteous and the wicked,** Dieu jugera les bons aussi bien que les méchants; **she b. attracts and repels me,** elle m'attire et me repousse à la fois; elle m'attire autant qu'elle me repousse; **she is remarkable for b. her intelligence and her beauty,** elle est remarquable par son intelligence autant que par sa beauté, tant par son intelligence que par sa beauté; elle est aussi intelligente que belle; **I am fond of music b. ancient and modern,** j'aime la musique tant ancienne que moderne.

bother[1] ['bɔðər], *s.* ennui *m*; anxiété *f*; tracas *m*; *F:* embêtement *m*; **I'm afraid I'm giving you a lot of b.,** je vous dérange beaucoup, je vous donne beaucoup de tracas; **what a b.!** quel embêtement! quelle corvée! **what a b. you are!** ce que vous êtes embêtant!

bother[2]. **1.** *v.tr.* gêner, ennuyer, tracasser, tourmenter (qn); *F:* embêter (qn); **to b. s.o. about sth.,** importuner qn au sujet de qch.; **don't b. me!** laissez-moi tranquille! vous m'ennuyez! **don't b. your head about me!** ne vous inquiétez pas de moi! ne vous faites pas de mauvais sang à mon sujet! ne vous tracassez pas pour moi! **he's always bothering me,** il est toujours à me tracasser; il est toujours à mes trousses; **I can't be bothered to do it,** ça m'embête, j'ai la flemme, de le faire; **don't b. to ring me up,** ce n'est pas la peine de me téléphoner; **he seems very bothered about it,** il s'en fait du mauvais sang; **b. (it)!** zut! **b. the man!** qu'il est embetant! qu'il aille au diable! **2.** *v.i.* **he doesn't b. about anything,** il ne s'inquiète de rien; **without bothering any further,** sans plus s'inquiéter, se tracasser.

botheration [bɔðə'reiʃ(ə)n], *F: O:* **1.** *s.* ennui *m*, vexation *f*. **2.** *int.* zut!

bothered ['bɔðəd], *a.* (*a*) inquiet, embarrassé; (*b*) *F:* **I'm not b.,** je m'en fiche.

bothersome ['bɔðəsəm], *a.* importun, gênant; embarrassant.

bothie, bothy ['bɔθi], *s. Scot:* hutte *f*, cabane *f* (de cantonnier, etc.).

Bothnia ['bɔθniə], *Pr.n. Hist:* Bothnie *f.*

bothridium [bɔ'θridiəm], *s. Ann:* bothridie *f.*

bothriocephalus ['bɔθriou'sefələs], *s. Ann:* bothriocéphale *m*.

bothrops ['bɔθrɔps], *s. Rept:* bothrops *m*.

botonny ['bɔtəni], *a. Her:* (*of cross*) tréflé.

bo tree ['bouːtriː], *s. Bot:* arbre *m* des conseils.

botrychium [bɔ'trikiəm], *s. Bot:* botrychium *m*.

botryllus [bɔ'triləs], *s. Z:* botrylle *m*.

botryogen ['bɔtrioudʒen], *s. Miner:* botryogène *m*.

botryoidal [bɔtri'ɔidl], *a. Miner:* botryoïde.

botryomycoma ['bɔtrioumai'koumə], *s. Med: Vet:* botryomycome *m*.

botryomycosis ['bɔtrioumai'kousis], *s. Med: Vet:* botryomycose *f.*

botrytis [bɔ'traitis], *s. Fung:* botrytis *m*.

Botswana [bɔt'swɑːnə], *Pr.n. Geog:* Botswana *m*.

bott [bɔt], *s. Ent:* = BOT[1], 1.

bott hammer ['bɔthæmər], *s. Tls:* marteau *m* à face cannelée (pour briser le lin).

bottle[1] [bɔtl], *s.* (*a*) bouteille *f*; (*small*) flacon *m*; fiole *f*; (*wide-mouthed*) bocal *m*; **wicker b.,** bouteille clissée; **stone b.,** cruchon *m*; **b. of water,** bouteille, carafe *f*, d'eau; **beer b.,** cannette *f*; **wine b.,** bouteille à vin; **b. of wine,** bouteille de vin; **wine that has been ten years in b.,** vin *m* qui a dix ans de bouteille; **to sit over a b. with s.o.,** vider une bouteille ensemble, avec qn; **they spent the evening passing round the b.,** ils ont passé la soirée à boire, à faire circuler la bouteille; *F:* **to be fond of the b.,** s'adonner à la boisson; *F:* **to hit the b.,** boire (trop); *attrib.* **b. brush,** goupillon *m*; hérisson *m*; **b. drainer,** égouttoir *m* à bouteilles; **b. glass,** verre *m* à bouteilles; verre vert; **b. opener,** ouvre-bouteille(s) *m inv*; décapsuleur *m*; **b. party,** réunion à laquelle chacun apporte à boire; **b. rack,** porte-bouteilles *m inv*; casier *m* à bouteilles; *Wine-m:* pupitre *m*; **b. stand,** (i) jardinière *f* (de café); (ii) porte-bouteille *m*, *pl.* porte-bouteilles; *Glassm:* **b. pincers,** ferre *f*; (*b*) flacon (de parfum, etc.); (*c*) (**feeding, baby's**) **b.,** biberon *m*; **brought up on the b., b.-fed,** élevé, allaité, au biberon; **b. feeding,** allaitement *m* au biberon; (*d*) **hot-water b.,** bouillotte *f*; demoiselle *f*; (*stone*) cruchon *m*; moine *m*; **have you put the bottles in the beds?** est-ce que vous avez mis les bouillottes dans les lits? (*e*) *Med: F:* urinal *m* de lit, *F:* pistolet *m*; (*f*) *Box:* **b. holder,** soigneur *m*, second *m*; (*g*) **b. imp.,** (i) *Ph:* ludion *m*; (ii) *Myth:* génie enfermé dans une bouteille; (*h*) *Bot:* **b. tree,** arbre-bouteille *m*, *pl.* arbres-bouteille(s); **b. gourd,** bouteille.

bottle[2], *v.*

I. *v.tr.* mettre (du vin) en bouteilles; conserver (des fruits, etc.) en bocal.

II. (*compound verbs*) **1. bottle off,** *v.tr.* mettre (du vin, etc.) en bouteilles.

2. bottle up, *v.tr.* (*a*) embouteiller (une flotte, la circulation); (*b*) étouffer (ses sentiments), comprimer, ravaler (sa colère).

bottle[3], *s. Agr:* botte *f* (de foin, etc.).

bottle[4], *v.tr. Agr:* botteler (du foin, etc.).

bottle[5], *s. Bot:* **white b.,** silène renflé, enflé; **yellow b.,** marguerite dorée; **b. of all sorts,** pulmonaire commune.

bottlebrush ['bɔtlbrʌʃ], *s. Bot: Austr:* callistemon *m*.

bottled ['bɔtld], *a.* (*a*) **b. wine, beer,** vin *m*, bière *f*, en bouteille(s); **b. food(s),** conserves *f* en bocaux; (*b*) *F:* ivre, éméché, rond.

bottle-green ['bɔtl'griːn], *a. & s.* vert bouteille (*m*) *inv*, cul-de-bouteille (*m*) *inv*.

bottleneck ['bɔtlnek], *s.* **1.** goulot *m* (de bouteille). **2.** (*a*) (goulot d') étranglement *m*; (*b*) embouteillage *m* (dans une rue); *Rail:* col *m* de bouteille; *Nau:* goulet *m* (d'un port).

bottlenose ['bɔtlnouz], *s.* **1.** gros nez sans distinction; *F:* nez en pied de marmite; truffe *f*, piton *m*. **2.** *Z:* (*a*) hyperoodon *m*; (*b*) **b. (dolphin),** tursiops *m*, souffleur *m*.

bottlenosed ['bɔtlnouzd], *a.* **1.** à gros nez. **2.** *Z:* (*a*) **b. whale,** hyperoodon *m*; (*b*) **b. dolphin,** tursiops *m*, souffleur *m*.

bottler ['bɔtlər], *s.* embouteilleur *m*.

bottlewasher ['bɔtlwɔʃər], *s.* **1.** (*pers.*) laveur, -euse, de bouteilles; plongeur *m*; *F:* **head cook and b.,** (i) factotum *m*; (ii) homme qui mène toute l'affaire. **2.** (*machine*) rince-bouteilles *m inv*, nettoie-bouteilles *m inv*.

bottling ['bɔtliŋ], *s.* mise *f* en bouteille(s), en bocal.

bottom[1] ['bɔtəm], *s.* **1.** (*a*) bas *m* (d'une colline, d'un escalier, d'une robe, d'une page); (*b*) fond *m* (d'un puits, d'une boîte, de la mer); plafond *m* (d'un canal, d'un réservoir); ballast *m*, assiette *f* (d'une chaussée, etc.); **at the b. of the garden,** au fond du jardin; **at the b. of the street,** au bout de la rue; **at the b. of the table, of the class,** au (bas) bout de la table, à la queue de la classe; **at the very b. of the cask,** au fin fond du baril; *Oc: etc:* **gravel b.,** fond de gravier; **rocky b.,** fond de roche; **sandy b.,** fond de sable; **muddy b.,** fond de vase; *Nau:* **loose b.,** fond de mauvaise tenue (pour l'ancre); *Fish:* **b. line,** traînée *f*; **b. fishing,** pêche *f* à la ligne de fond; **b.(-dwelling) fauna,** faune *f* benthique; (*of swimmer*) **to find b. (again),** reprendre fond, pied; **to send a ship to the b.,** envoyer un bâtiment au fond, par le fond; (*of ship*) **to go to the b.,** couler à fond; (*of ship*) **to strike, touch, b.,** donner un coup de talon; talonner; être sur les brasses; **to touch b.,** ((i) *in boring;* (ii) *of prices*), toucher le tuf; *Civ.E:* **the pile has reached hard b.,** le pieu refuse le mouton; **prices have reached rock b.,** les prix sont au plus bas; **to get to the b. of sth., of things,** découvrir la cause, l'origine, de qch.; aller au fond des choses; **I must get to the b. of it,** il faut que j'en sache le fin mot, que j'en aie le cœur net; **at b. he's not bad,** au fond ce n'est pas un mauvais garçon; **from the very b. of the heart,** du (fin) fond du cœur; **feeling that comes from the b. of one's heart,** sentiment *m* qui coule de source; **to be at the b. of sth.,** (i) (*of pers.*) être derrière qch., au fond de qch.; être l'instigateur de qch.; (ii) être la cause de qch.; (*c*) *Petr:* **bottoms,** déchets *m* de raffinage; (*d*) résistance *f*, fond; **horse with a good b.,** cheval *m* qui a du fond. **2.** bas-fond *m*, *pl.* bas-fonds (de terrain); creux *m*; vallée *f*; *NAm:* **b. lands,** plaine alluviale. **3.** (*a*) (i) fond, (ii) dessous *m* (d'assiette, de verre, etc.); siège *m* (d'une chaise); socle *m* (de statue, de colonne); **to put sth. b. up(wards),** mettre qch. sens dessus dessous; **box with a false b.,** boîte *f* à fond intermédiaire, à double fond; **to knock the b. out of a box,** défoncer une boîte; *F:* **to knock the b. out of an argument,** démolir un argument; **the b. has fallen out of the market,** le marché s'est effondré; **the b. seemed to have dropped out of everything,** tout sombrait; *Metall:* **b. of a crucible,** culot *m* d'un creuset; *F:* **bottoms up!** videz vos verres! cul sec! (*b*) *Cmptr:* bas *m* (d'une gamme); **b. of the line, of the range,** bas de gamme; **b. plate,** embase *f* (de chargeur de disques); (*c*) *Bill:* **to put b. on a ball,** faire de l'effet à revenir, de l'effet rétrograde; faire un rétro. **4.** *F:* derrière *m*, postérieur *m*, fondement *m* (d'une personne); **to kick s.o.'s b.,** botter le derrière à qn. **5.** *Nau:* (*a*) carène *f*, fond (d'un navire); **double b.,** double fond; **flat b.,** sole *f*; **copper b.,** doublage *m* d'un navire; **b. boards,** vaigres *f* (d'une embarcation); **ship b. up,** navire la quille en l'air; **boat b. up,** embarcation chavirée; (*b*) navire *m*; **in British bottoms,** sous pavillon anglais; **in neutral bottoms,** sous pavillon neutre. **6.** *attrib.* **b. half,** partie inférieure; **b. book (of a pile),** livre qui est en bas, tout en dessous; **b. end of the table,** bas de la table; **b. stair,** marche *f* du bas, première marche (de l'escalier), dernière marche (en descendant); **b. boy of the class,** dernier élève de la classe; **b. price,** prix plancher; **at b. prices,** aux plus bas prix; *Metalw:* **b. tool,** matrice *f*; *Aut:* **in b. gear,** *F:* **in b.,** en première *f* (vitesse); *F:* **I bet my b. dollar that . . .,** je parie jusqu'à mon dernier sou que . . ..

bottom[2], **1.** *v.tr.* (*a*) mettre ou remettre un fond à (une boîte), un siège à (une chaise); *Coop:* (en)foncer, enjabler (un tonneau); mettre un fond à (un tonneau); (*b*) *A:* **to b. an argument upon sth.,** baser, fonder, asseoir, un argument sur qch.; (*c*) *A:* examiner (un sujet) à fond; (*d*) *Civ.E:* empierrer (une route). **2.** *v.i.* (*a*) (*of ship, etc.*) toucher le fond; (*of piston*) buter au fond (du cylindre); (*b*) *A:* **to b. (up)on sth.,** être basé, fondé, établi, sur qch.; avoir son assiette sur qch.; (*c*) *P: Austr:* **to b. on the gold,** trouver le filon; tenir le filon.

bottoming ['bɔtəmiŋ], *s.* **1.** mise *f* d'un fond (à une boîte, etc.); *Coop:* fonçage *m*, enjablure *f* (d'un tonneau). **2.** *Civ.E:* empierrement *m* (d'une route). **3.** *Mch:* butée *f* (du piston).

bottomless ['bɔtəmlis], *a.* sans fond. **1.** (chaise *f*) sans siège. **2.** insondable; *B:* **the b. pit,** le puits de l'abîme; l'abîme *m*.

bottommost ['bɔtəmmoust], *a.* le plus bas.

bottomry ['bɔtəmri], *s. Nau:* hypothèque consentie sur un navire (pour fournir les fonds nécessaires à son voyage); (emprunt *m* à la) grosse aventure; **b. loan,** prêt *m* à la grosse; bômerie *f*; **b. bond,** contrat *m* à la grosse aventure; contrat en gros; **b. interest,** profit *m* maritime.

botulin ['bɔtjulin], *s. Med:* toxine *f* botulique.

botulinic [bɔtju'linik], *a. Med:* botulinique, botulique.

botulism ['bɔtjulizm], *s. Med:* botulisme *m*.

bouclé ['buːklei], *a. & s. Tex:* bouclé (*m*); **b. wool,** bouclette *f*.

boudoir ['buːdwɑːr], *s.* boudoir *m*.

bouffant ['buːfɑ̃(ɪt)], *a.* (*of skirt, sleeves*) bouffant; (*of hairstyle*) gonflant.

bougainvillea [buːgən'viliə], *s. Bot:* bougainvillée *f*, bougainvillier *m*; bougainvillea *m*.

bougainvillia [buːgə'viliə], *s. Z:* bougainvillée *f*.

bough [bau], *s.* branche *f*, rameau *m* (d'arbre).

boughten ['bɔːtn], *a. esp. NAm: Dial:* acheté (en

magasin); **b. cake,** gâteau *m* de pâtissier; **is that a b. dress?** est-ce que vous avez acheté cette robe toute faite?

bougie ['bu:ʒi:], *s. Med:* bougie *f.*

bouillon ['bu:jɔ̃], *s.* **1.** *Cu:* bouillon *m*; consommé *m.* **2.** *Bac:* bouillon (de culture).

boulangerite [bu:'lɔndʒərait], *s. Miner:* boulangérite *f.*

boulder ['bouldər], *s.* (gros) galet; gros caillou; (gros) bloc de pierre roulé; pierre roulée; bloc erratique; *Geol:* **b. clay,** argile *f* à blocaux.

boule [bu:l], *s.* (*gaming*) (jeu *m* de) boule *f.*

boulevard ['bu:ləvɑ:d], *s. NAm:* **1.** boulevard *m*; grande voie de communication; **entrance b.,** boulevard d'accès, d'entrée; *Aut:* **b. stop,** stop *m* (à l'artère principale). **2.** terre-plein (central), *pl.* terre-pleins.

boulimia [bu:'li:miə], *s. Med:* boulimie *f.*

boulle [bu:l], *s. Furn:* = BUHL.

boulter ['boultər], *s. Fish:* longue ligne munie de plusieurs hameçons.

bounce[1] [bauns], *s.* **1.** (*a*) (*of ball*) rebond *m,* rebondissement *m*; bond *m*; **to take, catch, the ball on the b.,** prendre la balle au bond; *Ten:* faire une demi-volée; (*b*) *NAm:* **b. back,** (i) écho *m*; (ii) *Th: etc:* retour *m,* rentrée *f* (d'un artiste, etc.). **2.** *F:* (*of pers.*) jactance *f,* vantardise *f,* bluff *m,* épate *f*; **in spite of his accident he's as full of b. as ever,** en dépit de son accident il est toujours plein d'élan, d'énergie. **3.** *NAm: F:* **to get the b.,** être renvoyé, saqué, mis à la porte.

bounce[2]. **1.** *v.i.* (*a*) (*of ball, etc.*) rebondir; **the telephone conversation is bounced off a satellite,** la conversation téléphonique rebondit sur un satellite; (*b*) (*of pers.*) **to b. in, out; to b. into, out of, a room,** entrer (dans une pièce), sortir (d'une pièce), en coup de vent, en trombe; entrer, sortir, à l'improviste; (*c*) *F:* (*of pers.*) faire l'important, bluffer, faire de l'esbrouffe, de l'épate; se vanter; (*d*) **I hope this cheque won't b.,** j'espère que ce n'est pas un chèque sans provision. **2.** *v.tr.* (*a*) faire rebondir (une balle); (*b*) *F: O:* ne pas laisser à (qn) le temps de réfléchir; **to b. s.o. into doing sth.,** arriver (i) à force d'esbrouffe, (ii) par le bluff, à faire faire qch. à qn; **to b. sth. out of s.o.,** obtenir qch. de qn à force d'intimidation ou à force de bluff; (*c*) *NAm: F:* donner son congé à (qn); flanquer (qn) à la porte (du cabaret, etc.); (*d*) *A:* **to b. out an oath,** lâcher un juron; (*e*) *A:* semoncer; **he was bounced for his carelessness,** il a reçu un savon pour sa négligence.

bounce[3], *adv.* en bondissant, en se heurtant; **the apple fell b. on my head,** la pomme est tombée en rebondissant sur ma tête; **something came b. against the door,** quelque chose a frappé rudement la porte.

bouncer ['baunsər], *s. F:* **1.** *O:* esbrouffeur *m,* épateur *m,* vantard *m,* hâbleur *m.* **2.** *A:* mensonge effronté. **3.** videur *m.* **4.** chèque *m* sans provision.

bounciness ['baunsinis], *s.* (*a*) élasticité *f*; (*b*) (*of pers.*) élasticité de tempérament; caractère guilleret.

bouncing[1] ['baunsiŋ], *a.* **1.** rebondissant. **2. b. baby,** bébé plein de vie et de santé. **3.** *F:* **b. cheque,** chèque *m* sans provision. **4.** *NAm: Bot: F:* **b. Bet, Bess,** saponaire *f.*

bouncing[2], *s.* rebondissement *m.*

bouncy ['baunsi], *a.* (*a*) rebondissant; élastique; (*b*) *F:* (*of pers.*) réjoui, guilleret.

bound[1] [baund], *s.* **1.** (*usu. pl.*) limite(s) *f,* bornes *fpl*; **to beat the bounds,** constater solennellement (en procession) les limites d'une paroisse; faire le tour de la paroisse en frappant le sol de baguettes, pour en affirmer la délimitation; *Mil: etc:* **to put a public house out of bounds,** consigner (à la troupe) un débit de boissons; *Sch:* **the village is out of bounds,** l'accès du village est défendu aux élèves; *Golf: Fb: etc:* **out of bounds,** hors des limites, hors du jeu; **the ultimate bounds of space,** les dernières limites de l'espace; **human vanity has no bounds,** la vanité humaine n'a pas de limites; **to set bounds to one's ambition,** mettre des bornes, fixer une limite, à son ambition; borner son ambition; **to go beyond the bounds of reason,** dépasser les bornes de la raison; **to go beyond all bounds, to pass all bounds, to know no bounds,** dépasser toutes les bornes, n'avoir pas de bornes; franchir, dépasser, les limites; oublier toute mesure; **my fury knew no bounds,** je n'ai pu contenir ma fureur; **curiosity beyond all bounds,** curiosité *f* qui dépasse les bornes; **this passes all bounds!** c'en est trop! **to keep within bounds,** rester dans la juste mesure; user de modération; **to keep s.o. within bounds,** contenir qn; **within bounds,** avec modération; **within the bounds of probability,** dans les limites du probable; probable; **within the bounds of possibility,** dans l'ordre des choses possibles; dans la limite du possible; bien possible. **2.** *Mth:* **lower b.,** minorant *m*; **upper b.,** majorant *m.*

bound[2], *v.tr.* borner, limiter (un pays, ses désirs).

bound[3], *a.* **1.** restreint, confiné; retenu. **2.** *El:* **b. charge,** charge latente, dissimulée.

bound[4], *s.* bond *m,* saut *m*; (*of horse*) soubresaut *m*; **at a b.,** d'un (seul) bond, d'un saut, d'un seul élan; **he made a b. before he was aware of the water,** il s'élança avant de voir l'eau; **to advance by (leaps and) bounds,** progresser par bonds.

bound[5], *v.i.* bondir, sauter; (*of ball, etc.*) rebondir; (*of horse*) soubresauter; **to b. away,** s'en aller en bondissant; (*of ball*) (re)bondir au loin; **to b. forward,** bondir en avant.

bound[6], *a. Nau:* **ship b. for a country,** navire *m* en partance pour, en route pour, allant à, un pays; **ship b. for foreign parts, for Bordeaux,** navire à destination de l'étranger, de Bordeaux; **the ship was b. for South America,** le navire (i) partait pour, (ii) faisait route vers, l'Amérique du Sud; **homeward b.,** (i) (navire) retournant au port, au pays; (ii) (cargaison *f*) de retour; **outward b.,** (navire) (i) sur son départ, en partance, (ii) en route pour l'étranger, etc.; **where is the ship b. for?** quelle est la destination du navire? **where are you b. for?** où allez-vous?

boundary ['baundri], *s.* **1.** limite *f,* bornes *fpl,* frontière *f*; bornage *m* (d'une concession, etc.); *Mil:* (i) limite de zone d'action, de secteur; (ii) ligne *f* de démarcation (entre un territoire occupé et un territoire non occupé par l'ennemi); *Mil:* **the corps boundaries,** les limites de zone d'action du corps d'armée; **state b.,** frontière d'État; **determination of b.,** délimitation *f* de la frontière; **b. adjustment,** rectification *f* de frontière; **b. commission,** commission *f* de délimitation des frontières; **b. line,** ligne frontière, ligne de démarcation; *Sp:* ligne du jeu; (*at bowls*) noyon *m*; **b. post,** poteau *m* de bornage, de délimitation; **b. stone, mark,** borne, pierre *f* de bornage; *Ph:* **diffuse b.,** frontière diffuse; *Av:* **b. layer,** couche *f* limite; **b. lights,** feux *m* de balisage (d'un aéroport). **2.** *Cr:* **to hit, score, a b.,** envoyer la balle jusqu'aux limites du terrain; **to hit a full pitch b.,** envoyer la balle au delà des limites du terrain.

bounden ['baundən], *a. Lit:* (devoir) impérieux, sacré; **it is my b. duty to . . .,** je ne puis échapper à l'obligation de . . ., je suis dans l'obligation de . . ., c'est mon devoir impérieux de . . ..

bounder ['baundər], *s. F: O:* épateur *m,* plastronneur *m*; goujat *m.*

boundless ['baundlis], *a,* sans bornes, illimité, infini.

boundlessly ['baundlisli], *adv.* infiniment.

boundlessness ['baundlisnis], *s.* infinité *f,* immensité *f.*

bounteous ['bauntiəs], *a. esp. Lit:* **1.** (*of pers.*) libéral, généreux, munificent, bienfaisant. **2. b. harvest,** moisson abondante.

bounteously ['bauntiəsli], *adv. esp. Lit:* libéralement, généreusement, avec munificence; abondamment.

bounteousness ['bauntiəsnis], *s. esp. Lit:* **1.** bonté *f,* libéralité *f,* générosité *f,* munificence *f.* **2.** (*of crops, etc.*) abondance *f.*

bountiful ['bauntiful], *a. esp. Lit:* **1.** bienfaisant; **b. rains,** pluies fécondes. **2.** généreux, libéral; **she has set herself up as the Lady B. of the village,** elle s'est érigée en patronne du village.

bountifully ['bauntifuli], *adv. esp. Lit:* = BOUNTEOUSLY.

bountifulness ['bauntifulnis], *s. esp. Lit:* = BOUNTEOUSNESS.

bounty ['baunti], *s.* **1.** *Lit:* bonté *f,* générosité *f,* libéralité *f,* munificence *f.* **2.** (*a*) don *m,* gratification *f* (à un employé, etc.); **the King's, Queen's, b.,** don fait par le roi, la reine, à chaque mère de trijumeaux; (*b*) *Adm: Ind:* indemnité *f*; prime *f* (à l'exportation, etc.); subvention *f*; **system of bounties,** système *m* de primes; **child b.,** (i) indemnité de charges de famille (à un fonctionnaire); (ii) majoration *f* pour enfants (à un pensionné de guerre); (*c*) *Mil: Nau:* prime (d'engagement).

bouquet, *s.* **1.** [bu'kei] bouquet *m* (de fleurs, de feu d'artifice); **to throw bouquets,** faire des compliments, des éloges (**at,** à). **2.** ['bukei] bouquet (du vin).

Bourbon ['buəbən], *s.* **1.** *Hist:* Bourbon; **the B. nose,** le nez bourbonien. **2.** *Pol: U.S:* **a bourbon,** un réactionnaire. **3.** *NAm:* ['bə:b(ə)n], whisky *m* de maïs.

bourdon[1] ['buəd(ə)n], *s. Mus:* **1.** (*organ stop*) bourdon *m.* **2.** (*of bagpipe*) bourdon.

bourdon[2], *s. Hist:* bourdon *m,* bâton *m* de pèlerin.

Bourdon[3], *Pr.n.m.* **B. tube,** manomètre *m* de Bourdon; **B. barometer,** baromètre *m* de Bourdon.

bourdonasse ['buədə'næs], *s. A.Arms:* lance *f* de tournoi; bourdon *m,* bourdonnasse *f.*

bourdonné [buə'dɔnei], *a. Her:* bourdonné; pommeté.

bourgeois[1] ['buəʒwɑ:], *a. & s. usu. Pej:* bourgeois, -oise.

bourgeois[2] [bə:'dʒɔis], *s. Typ:* petit romain, corps 8.

bourgeoisie [buəʒwɑ:'zi:], *s.* bourgeoisie *f.*

bourn[1] ['buən], *s. A:* ruisseau *m.*

bourn(e)[2], *s. Poet:* **1.** borne *f,* terme *m,* but *m.* **2.** frontière *f*; **the b. from which no traveller returns,** l'au-delà *m* dont on ne revient pas.

bouse [baus], *v.tr. Nau:* palanquer (les colis); **to b. a rope,** peser sur une manœuvre.

boussingaultia [bu:sin'gɔltiə], *s. Bot:* boussingaultia *f.*

boussingaultite [bu:sin'gɔltait], *s. Miner:* boussingaultite *f.*

boustrophedon [bu:strɔ'fi:dɔn], *s. Pal:* boustrophédon *m.*

bout[1] [baut], *s.* **1.** (*at games, etc.*) tour *m,* reprise *f*; **fencing b.,** passe *f* d'armes; assaut *m* d'armes; **wrestling b.,** assaut de lutte; *Box:* **to have a b. with s.o.,** *F:* les mettre avec qn; *F: A:* **not this b.!** pas à cette occasion! pas cette fois-ci! pas ce coup-ci! **2.** (*a*) accès *m* (de fièvre); attaque *f* (de fièvre, d'influenza; etc.) crise *f* (de rhumatisme, etc.); **he has had another b. of fever,** la fièvre lui a repris, l'a repris; **fresh b. of fever,** reprise *f* de (la) fièvre; (*b*) **drinking b.,** soûlerie *f,* soûlographie *f.*

'bout[2], *adv.* (= ABOUT) *Nau:* **'b. ship!** envoyez!

boutique [bu:'ti:k], *s.* (*a*) petit magasin de modes; (*b*) (*in department store*) boutique *f*; **teenage b.,** le coin, la boutique, des jeunes.

Bovidae ['bɔvidi:], *s.pl. Z:* bovidés *m.*

bovine ['bouvain]. **1.** *a.* (*a*) *Z:* bovin, -ine; (*b*) (esprit) lourd, inerte. **2.** *s. Z:* bovin *m.*

bovinely ['bouvainli], *adv.* d'une façon bovine, lourde; stupidement; **he was staring b. into space,** il regardait devant lui d'un air hébété, incompréhensif.

bovista [bou'vistə], *s. Fung:* bovista *m.*

bow[1] [bou], *s.* **1.** arc *m*; **to draw a b.,** bander, tendre, un arc; **to draw the b.,** tirer de l'arc; **b. hand,** la main gauche (qui tient l'arc); **to have two strings, more than one string, to one's b.,** avoir deux cordes, plus d'une corde, à son arc; avoir un pied dans deux chaussures; manger à deux râteliers; **I have still one string to my b.,** il me reste encore une ressource; *Prov:* **one must have more than one string to one's b.,** souris qui n'a qu'un trou est bientôt prise. **2.** (*a*) *Mus:* archet *m* (de violon, etc.); **b. instrument,** instrument *m* à archet; **b. hand,** la main droite (qui tient l'archet); (*b*) *Mus:* coup *m* d'archet; **up b.!** poussez! **down b.!** tirez! **with the down b.,** en tirant; (*c*) *Tls:* arçon *m* (de feutrier, etc.); **b. drill,** foret *m,* drille *f,* à arçon, à archet; touret *m*; **b. saw,** scie *f* à chantourner, à châssis, à archet, à arc; *Mec.E:* **b. spring,** ressort *m* à arc; **b. piece,** cintre *m* (de cintreuse); (*d*) *El:* **b. trolley,** archet *m* de prise de courant (d'un trolley). **3.** *Const:* **b. window,** (i) fenêtre *f* en saillie (courbe), en rotonde; (ii) *F: A:* bedaine *f,* bedon *m*; **b.-windowed,** à fenêtres en saillie. **4.** nœud *m* (de ruban); **b. tie, butterfly b.,** nœud (de) papillon. **5.** *Harn:* **(saddle) b.,** arçon, pontet *m* (de selle). **6.** *Tchn:* (*a*) arceau *m,* anse *f,* branche *f* (de cadenas); anneau *m* (de clef); collier *m* (d'éperon); (*b*) **bow's, b. compass,** compas *m* à balustre; (*c*) *Fish:* **b. net,** (i) caudrette *f*; (ii) casier *m* (à langoustes). **7.** *Poet:* arc-en-ciel *m, pl.* arcs-en-ciel.

bow[2] [bou], *v.tr.* **1.** courber (qch.); *Nau:* **to b. a mast,** arquer un mât. **2.** *Mus:* **to b. a passage,** gouverner l'archet dans un passage; **how do you b. that passage?** quels coups d'archet faites-vous dans ce passage? **3.** *Tchn:* (*felt making*) **to b. the fur,** faire voguer l'étoffe.

bow[3] [bau], *s.* salut *m*; (i) révérence *f*; (ii) inclination *f* de tête; **to make one's b. to the company,** se présenter; débuter; **to make one's b. to the company (and depart),** tirer sa révérence à la compagnie; *Th:* **to make one's b.,** prendre sa retraite; **with a b.,** en saluant, en s'inclinant; **to make a deep, low, b. to s.o.,** saluer qn profondément.

bow[4] [bau], *v.*

I. *v.i. & tr.* **1.** *v.i.* (*a*) (i) s'incliner; baisser la tête; (ii) faire une génuflexion; **to b. to s.o.,** adresser un salut à qn; saluer qn; **to b. low to s.o.,** faire un grand salut à qn; **to b. and scrape to s.o.,** faire force révérences à qn; faire des salamalecs, des courbettes, à qn; **he went out bowing and scraping,** il sortit avec force révérences; **to b. back to s.o.,** rendre son salut à qn; **to b. (down) to, before, s.o.,** (i) se prosterner devant qn; (ii) faire des courbettes devant qn; (*b*) *O: with cogn.acc.* **to b. one's assent,** signifier son consentement d'une inclination de tête; **to b. one's thanks to s.o.,** remercier qn d'un salut; (*c*) **to b. to s.o.,** s'incliner devant qn; **to b. to a decision,** se soumettre à, s'incliner devant, une décision; **to b. to s.o.'s whims,** se plier aux caprices de qn; **to b. to the inevitable,** s'incliner devant les faits. **2.** *v.tr.* (*a*) incliner, baisser (la tête); fléchir (le genou); **I b. my head in admiration before what he has accomplished,** je m'incline devant ce qu'il a accompli; *A:* **to b. the ear to s.o.'s prayer,** prêter l'oreille aux prières de qn; (*b*) courber, voûter (le dos, les épaules, de qn); **to become bowed,** se voûter; **to be bowed (down) by suffering,** être courbé, accablé, par la souffrance; **to become bowed (down)**

by age, s'affaisser.

II. (*compound verbs*) **1. bow in,** *v.tr.* **to b. s.o. in,** faire entrer qn (avec force saluts).

2. bow out, *v.tr.* **to b. s.o. out,** (i) prendre congé de qn (à la porte) avec force saluts; (ii) congédier qn avec un salut.

bow[5] [bau], *s.* **1.** *Nau:* (*often pl.*) avant *m*, étrave *f*, bossoir *m*; cap *m*; nez *m*; **clipper b.,** avant à guibre; **lean b.,** avant fin; **bulbous b.,** avant à bulbe; **bluff b.,** avant renflé; **b. rope,** amarre *f* de bout, de l'avant; **on the b.,** par l'avant, par le bossoir; **on the port, starboard, b.,** par le bossoir bâbord, tribord; **to cross the bows of a ship,** couper la route d'un navire; **bows on to the sea,** debout à la mer, à la lame; **b. wave,** lame d'étrave; *Navy:* **ships in b. and quarter line,** ligne *f* en échiquier; **b. chaser,** pièce *f* de chasse. **2.** *Row:* (*also* **bow oar**) nageur *m* de tête, de l'avant; le brigadier; **b. oar,** aviron *m* de l'avant, du brigadier; **b. side,** tribord *m*; **b.-side oar,** aviron de tribord.

Bowden ['boud(ə)n], *s. Mec.E:* **B. wire,** commande *f* Bowden; bowden *m*.

bowdlerization [baudlərai'zeiʃ(ə)n], *s.* expurgation *f*, émasculation *f* (d'une œuvre littéraire).

bowdlerize ['baudləraiz], *v.tr.* expurger, émasculer, châtrer (une œuvre littéraire).

bowed [baud], *a.* **with b. head,** la tête inclinée; **b. with age,** courbé par le fardeau des ans; **b. (down) with grief,** accablé de douleur.

bowel ['bauəl], *s.* (*a*) *Anat:* intestin *m*; **the bowels,** les intestins; **b. complaint,** affection intestinale; **to keep one's bowels open,** avoir le ventre libre; **to have one's bowels opened,** aller à la selle; (*b*) **the bowels of the earth,** les entrailles *f*, le sein, de la terre; (*c*) *A:* & *Lit:* **bowels of compassion,** sentiment *m* de compassion; **he has no bowels of compassion,** il n'a pas d'entrailles; il a un cœur de pierre.

Bowen ['bouin], *Pr.n.* **Bowen's disease,** maladie *f* de Bowen, dyskératose cutanée.

bower[1] ['bauər], *s.* **1.** berceau *m* de verdure; charmille *f*, tonnelle *f*. **2.** *Poet:* *A:* (*a*) séjour *m*, demeure *f*; (*b*) appartement *m* (d'une dame); boudoir *m*; **the lady withdrew to her b.,** la châtelaine se retira chez elle, dans ses appartements.

bower[2], *s. Nau:* **b. (anchor),** ancre *f* de bossoir; **best b., second b.,** grosse ancre, petite ancre, de bossoir; **small b. anchor,** ancre d'affourche; **b. cable,** chaîne *f* de bossoir.

bower[3], *s.* (*at euchre, etc.*) nom du valet d'atout (**right bower**), et de l'autre valet de la même couleur (**left bower**).

bowerbird ['bauəbə:d], *s. Orn:* ptilorhynque *m*, oiseau *m* à berceau; **satin b.,** oiseau à berceau satiné; **regent b.,** prince-régent *m*; **crestless gardener b.,** amblyornis *m*.

bowery[1] ['bauəri], *a. Lit:* ombragé, touffu; ombreux.

bowery[2], *s.* **1.** *Hist:* ferme coloniale hollandaise. **2.** *U.S:* (*from* **the B.,** *street in New York*) bas quartier (d'une ville); rue mal fréquentée.

bowfin ['boufin], *s. Ich:* amie *f*.

bowfronted ['bou'frʌntid], *a. Furn:* à devant bombé; *Const:* (*of house*) à fenêtres en saillie.

bowhead ['bouhed], *s. Z:* baleine franche.

bowie (knife, *pl.* **knives)** ['bu:i(naif, -naivz); 'boui-], *s. NAm:* (grand) couteau-poignard, *pl.* couteaux-poignards; couteau *m* de chasse.

bowing[1] ['bouiŋ], *s.* **1.** courbage *m* (de qch.). **2.** *Mus:* manière *f* de gouverner l'archet; **the art of b.,** l'art *m* de l'archet; **to indicate the b.,** indiquer les coups d'archet; **his b. is perfect,** il a un coup d'archet parfait.

bowing[2] ['bauiŋ], *s.* saluts *mpl*, salutation *f*; **to have a b. acquaintance with s.o.,** connaître qn pour le saluer, pour lui dire bonjour; **I have a b. acquaintance with him,** nous nous saluons.

bowl[1] [boul], *s.* **1.** (*a*) bol *m*; jatte *f*; coupe *f* (de cristal, etc.); (*larger*) cuvette *f*; bassin *m*; bassine *f*; plonge *f* (d'évier); cuvette (de W.C.); **finger b.,** rince-doigts *m inv*; *Cu:* **mixing b.,** bol à mélanger; **salad b.,** saladier *m*; **washing-up b.,** bassine à vaisselle; **goldfish b.,** bocal *m* à poissons rouges; *A:* **(beggar's) wooden b.,** sébile *f* (de mendiant); *Mil: etc: A:* **mess b.,** gamelle *f*; *Gr.Ant:* **(wine) b.,** cratère *m*; (*b*) (*contents*) **a b. of milk,** un bol, une jatte, une jattée, de lait; **I upset a whole b. of washing-up water down my dress,** j'ai renversé toute une bassine d'eau de vaisselle sur ma robe. **2.** fourneau *m*, godet *m* (de pipe à tabac); cuilleron *m* (de cuiller); coupe *f* (de verre à pied); culot *m* (de lampe); plat *m*, plateau *m* (de balance); *Nau:* cuvette (du compas); **alabaster electric light b.,** vasque lumineuse en albâtre; **(electric) b. fire,** radiateur *m* parabolique; *Ind:* **centrifugal b.,** bol de centrifugation. **3.** *NAm:* (*a*) *Geog:* cuvette, bassin; **the Dust B.,** le Dust-Bowl; (*b*) amphithéâtre *m*.

bowl[2], *s.* boule *f*; **(game of) bowls,** (i) (jeu *m* de) boules; (ii) *U.S:* (jeu de) quilles *f*; **to play (at) bowls,** (i) jouer aux boules; (ii) *U.S:* jouer aux quilles.

bowl[3], *v.*

I. **1.** *v.tr.* rouler, faire courir (un cerceau). **2.** (*at bowls*) (*a*) *v.tr.* lancer, rouler (la boule); (*b*) *v.i.* jouer aux boules. **3.** *Cr:* (*a*) *v.tr.* & *i.* lancer (la balle); bôler, servir (la balle); (*b*) *v.tr.* **to b. s.o. (out),** renverser le guichet à qn; mettre qn hors jeu (à balle servie); **clean bowled,** mis franchement hors jeu à guichet renversé (par le bôleur).

II. (*compound verbs*) **1. bowl along,** *v.i.* rouler rapidement; filer.

2. bowl over, *v.tr.* (*a*) renverser (des quilles); (*b*) *F:* déconcerter, renverser (qn); **the news bowled him over,** la nouvelle lui a cassé bras et jambes.

bow-legged ['bou'leg(i)d], *a.* bancal, -als; aux jambes arquées, torses.

bow legs ['bou'legz], *s.pl.* jambes bancales, arquées, torses; *F:* jambes en manches de veste.

bowler[1] ['boulər], *s.* **1.** joueur *m* de boules; bouliste *m*. **2.** *Cr:* bôleur *m*, lanceur *m*, serveur *m*.

bowler[2], *s.* **b. (hat),** chapeau rond, (chapeau) melon *m*, (chapeau) cape *f*; *Mil: P: A:* **battle b.,** casque *m*, bourguignotte *f*; *Mil: Av: F:* **to give s.o. his b. hat,** renvoyer qn à la vie civile; limoger qn; **golden b.,** compensation en argent donnée à un officier mis prématurément à la retraite.

bowlerhat [boulə'hæt], *v.tr. Mil: Av: F:* **to be bowlerhatted,** être renvoyé à la vie civile, mis à la retraite.

bowlful ['boulful], *s.* plein bol (de qch.); jatte *f*, jattée *f* (de lait, etc.); cuvette *f*, bassinée *f* (d'eau, etc.).

bowline ['boulin], *s. Nau:* bouline *f*; **b.-knot, -hitch,** nœud *m* de chaise, nœud de cabestan, nœud de bouline; (nœud d')agui *m*; **b. on the bight,** nœud de chaise double, nœud d'agui à élingue double; **running b.,** nœud coulant; laguis *m*; **to sail on a b.,** courir près du vent.

bow line ['boulain], *s. Navy:* **order in two bow lines,** ordre *m* en angle de retraite.

bowling ['bouliŋ], *s.* (*a*) jeu *m* de boules; **b. match,** match *m* de boules; **b. green,** (terrain *m* pour) jeu de boules; boulodrome *m*; (*b*) **(tenpin) b.,** bowling *m*; **b. alley,** bowling; (*c*) service *m*, lancement *m*, de la boule, *Cr:* de la balle; *Cr:* **b. crease,** ligne *f* du bôleur; ligne de service.

bowl-shaped ['boulʃeipt], *a.* cratériforme; *Aut:* **b.-s. steering wheel,** volant *m* en tulipe.

bowman[1], *pl.* **-men** ['boumən], *s.m.* archer.

bowman[2], *pl.* **-men** ['baumən], *s.m. Row:* brigadier (d'un canot).

bowmanship ['boumənʃip], *s.* technique *f* du tir à l'arc.

bowse [baus], *v.* = BOUSE.

bowser ['bauzər], *s. Petr:* camion-citerne *m*, *pl.* camions-citernes.

bowshot ['bouʃɔt], *s.* portée *f* de trait, archée *f*; **within b.,** à portée d'arc, de trait.

bowsprit ['bousprit], *s. Nau:* beaupré *m*; **running b.,** beaupré rentrant; **standing b.,** beaupré fixe; **angle of the b.,** apiquage *m* du beaupré.

bowstring[1] ['boustriŋ], *s.* **1.** corde *f* d'arc. **2.** (*as mode of execution*) lacet *m*, cordon *m*. **3.** *Civ.E:* **b. beam, girder,** bowstring *m*.

bowstring[2], *v.tr.* **to b. s.o.,** faire périr qn par le cordon; étrangler qn avec un lacet.

bow-wow[1] ['bau'wau]. **1.** *int.* ouâ-ouâ! **2.** *s. F:* (*child's word*) toutou *m*.

bow-wow[2], *v.i. F:* (*child's word*) aboyer; faire ouâ-ouâ.

bowyer ['boujər], *s.* fabricant *m* d'arcs.

box[1] [bɔks], *s.* (*a*) *Bot:* **b. (tree),** buis *m*; **dwarf b., ground b.,** buis nain, commun, des forêts; **tree b.,** buis arborescent; **b. edging,** bordure *f* de buis; **b. plantation,** buissaie *f*, buissière *f*; (*b*) **b. (wood),** buis.

box[2], *s.* **1.** (*a*) boîte *f*; (*small*) coffret *m*; (*large, wooden*) coffre *m*; caisse *f*; layette *f*; (*for food, etc.*) bac *m*; (*cardboard*) (caisse en) carton *m*; (*for dicing*) cornet *m*; **slotted b.,** caisse à rabats; **glove b.,** boîte à gants; **jewel, jewellery, b.,** coffret à bijoux; **window b.,** caisse, bac, à fleurs (pour fenêtres, balcons); **post b., letter b.,** boîte à, aux, lettres; **slide b.,** (i) boîte à diapositives; (ii) *Com:* boîte à tirette; *Gym:* **(vaulting) b.,** cheval *m* de bois; *Mil:* **ammunition b.,** coffre à munitions; *Av: etc:* **black b.,** boîte noire; *F: A:* **to be, find oneself, in the wrong b.,** s'être trompé (d'endroit, dans ses calculs, etc.), s'être blousé; s'être fourvoyé; *O:* **to be in the same b.,** se trouver dans le même cas; *O:* **to be in a (tight) b.,** se trouver dans une situation critique; (*b*) **strong b., safe-deposit b.,** coffre-fort *m*, *pl.* coffres-forts; **deed b.,** coffret à documents; **cash b.,** caisse; (*c*) *Ecc: etc:* (*for alms, etc.*) tronc *m*; (*d*) *attrib.* **b. maker,** fabricant *m* de boîtes, de coffres, de caisses; layetier *m*; **b. bed,** lit clos, lit en armoire, lit-armoire *m*, *pl.* lits-armoires; **b. ottoman,** divan-coffre *m*, *pl.* divans-coffres; **b. camera,** boîte, appareil *m*, rigide (à chambre de forme rectangulaire); **b. kite,** cerf-volant *m* cellulaire (*pl.* cerfs-volants); *Veh:* **b. tricycle,** triporteur *m*; *Const:* **b. shutter,** volet *m* se repliant à l'intérieur; *Tls:* **b. spanner, b. wrench,** clef *f*, dé *m*, en douille, en tube; **b.-ended spanner,** clef fermée; **b. staple,** gâche *f* (de verrou); *Dressm:* **b. pleat,** pli creux, double pli; **b. front,** devant uni (d'une robe); *Cost:* **b. jacket,** veste vague; *Tchn:* **b. annealing,** recuit *m* en vase clos; (*e*) (*contents*) boîte (de chocolats, etc.); caisse (de marchandises, etc.); (*f*) *F:* **the b.,** la télé; **I saw it on the b.,** je l'ai vu à la télé. **2.** *A.Veh:* siège *m* (du cocher); **b. seat,** place *f* à côté du siège du cocher; *A.Cost:* **b. coat,** houppelande *f*, manteau *m* (de cocher de diligence, etc.); carrick *m*. **3.** (*a*) *Th:* loge *f*; (*on ground floor*) baignoire *f*; **stage b.,** loge d'avant-scène; **b. attendant, opener,** ouvreuse *f*; **prompt b.,** trou *m* du souffleur; (*b*) (i) stalle *f* (d'écurie); **(loose) b.,** box *m*, *pl.* boxes; (ii) **horse b.,** (*a*) *Aut:* van *m*; (*β*) *Rail:* wagon *m* à chevaux; wagon-écurie *m*, *pl.* wagons-écuries; (*c*) *Jur:* **jury b.,** banc(s) *m(pl)* du jury; **witness b.,** = barre *f* des témoins; (*d*) **sentry b.,** guérite *f*; *Rail:* **signal b.,** cabine *f*, poste *m*, d'aiguillage; *Tp:* **call b., telephone b.,** cabine téléphonique; (*e*) (*in restaurant*) *O:* compartiment séparé. **4.** *Tchn:* boîte (d'essieu, de frein); corps *m* (de pompe); moyeu *m* (de roue); palâtre *m*, palastre *m* (d'une serrure); écrou *m* (de vis); *Typ:* cassetin *m*; *Aut:* **gear b.,** boîte de vitesses; carter *m* de transmission; *Mec.E:* **coupling b.,** manchon *m* d'accouplement, d'assemblage; **b. coupling,** accouplement *m* à manchon; **lower b. (of pump),** chopine *f* (de pompe); *Metall:* **moulding b.,** châssis *m* à mouler; **case-hardening b.,** pot *m* de cémentation; *El:* **accumulator b.,** bac d'accumulateur; **cable b.,** boîte de jonction des câbles; *Ph:* **(vacuum) b. (of aneroid barometer),** tambour *m* (de baromètre anéroïde). **5.** (*a*) case *f* (à remplir sur une formule, etc.); encadré *m* (dans un journal); **b. head,** sous-titre *m* (en retrait), *pl.* sous-titres; **b. diagram,** diagramme emboîté; (*b*) *Aut:* **b. junction,** zone quadrillée. **6.** *Cmptr:* case, pavé *m* (d'organigramme); **connection b.,** (i) boîtier *m* de connection; (ii) symbole *m* de renvoi (dans un organigramme); **decision b.,** symbole de décision (logique); **stunt b.,** coffret de commande. **7. Christmas b.** = étrennes *fpl*.

box[3], *v.*

I. *v.tr.* & *i.* **1.** *v.tr.* (*a*) emboîter, encaisser, encartonner (qch.); mettre (qch.) en boîte; coffrer; **to b. an orange tree,** encaisser un oranger; *Com:* **to b. an article for sale,** habiller un article pour la vente; **to b. a horse,** mettre un cheval dans une stalle à part, dans un box; *Typ:* **to b. (in) the text,** encadrer le texte; (*b*) *Civ.E:* *Rail:* ensabler (les traverses, etc.); (*c*) *Jur:* déposer (un document) auprès du tribunal; porter (une plainte); (*d*) **to b. the compass,** (i) *Nau:* réciter, dire, la rose des vents; répéter le compas; (ii) *F: O:* revenir à son point de départ (dans ses opinions); (*e*) *Nau:* masquer (une voile); (*f*) **to b. a tree (for resin, etc.),** saigner un arbre. **2.** *v.i. Nau:* **to b. about,** voguer de çà et de là; errer de droite et de gauche.

II. (*compound verbs*) **1. box in,** *v.tr.* encaisser, enfermer; *Mil:* **to b. in a target (by fire),** encager un objectif (par le feu).

2. box up, *v.tr.* renfermer (qn, qch.); enfermer, emprisonner (qn).

box[4], *s.* **b. (on the ear),** gifle *f*, claque *f*, calotte *f*; *F:* taloche *f*.

box[5], *v.tr.* **to b. s.o.'s ears,** gifler, *F:* talocher, qn; flanquer une claque, une taloche, à qn; frotter les oreilles à qn. **2.** *v.i.* (*a*) *Sp:* boxer; (*of two opponents*) se boxer; **do you b.?** est-ce que vous faites de la boxe? (*b*) *P:* **to b. clever,** se faire travailler les méninges.

Box[6], *Pr.n.* **B. and Cox,** personnes qu'on ne voit jamais ensemble, dont l'une sort quand l'autre rentre; **to play B. and Cox with s.o.,** chercher qn sans jamais le retrouver.

box calf ['bɔks'kɑ:f], *s. Leath:* veau chromé; box-calf *m*; *F:* box *m*.

boxcar ['bɔkskɑ:r], *NAm:* **1.** *s. Rail:* wagon (couvert); fourgon *m*; fourgon à bestiaux. **2.** *s. Aut:* semi-remorque *f*, *pl.* semi-remorques. **3.** *s.pl.* (*dominoes, dice*) **boxcars,** double six *m*. **4.** *a.* énorme, géant.

boxed [bɔkst], *a.* (*a*) *Com:* *Ind:* en boîte, en étui; (*b*) **b. in,** encaissé; enfermé; **b. up,** enfermé; à l'étroit.

boxer[1] ['bɔksər], *s.* **1.** *Ind:* metteur, -euse, en boîtes, en caisses, en étuis. **2.** *Austr:* *F:* chapeau *m* melon. **3.** *Cost:* *U.S:* **b. shorts,** caleçon *m*.

boxer[2], *s.* boxeur *m*, pugiliste *m*.

boxer[3], *s.* (*dog*) boxer *m.*

Boxer[4], *s. Hist:* Boxer *m,* Boxeur *m* (chinois).

boxfish ['bɔksfiʃ], *s. Ich:* **triangular b.,** coffre *m* triangulaire; **horned b.,** coffre cornu, vache *f* de mer.

boxful ['bɔksful], *s.* pleine boîte, plein coffre, pleine caisse (de qch.).

boxhaul ['bɔkshɔ:l], *v.tr. A: Nau:* virer (un navire) lof pour lof en culant.

boxing[1] ['bɔksiŋ], *s.* (*a*) emboîtage *m*; encaissement *m* (d'un oranger, etc.); (*b*) *Civ.E: Rail:* ensablement *m* (des traverses); (*c*) *Const:* lit *m* de charge; ballastage *m.*

boxing[2], *s.* la boxe, le pugilat; **foot b., French b.,** la boxe française, la savate, le chausson; **b. shoe,** chausson *m*; **b. gloves,** gants bourrés, gants de boxe; **b. match,** match *m* de boxe.

Boxing Day ['bɔksiŋdei], *s.* la Saint-Étienne, le lendemain de Noël (fête légale en Angleterre, etc.).

box office ['bɔksɔfis], *s. Th:* bureau *m* de location; caisse *f,* guichet *m.*

boxroom ['bɔksru:m], *s.* (chambre *f* de) débarras *m.*

boxthorn ['bɔksθɔ:n], *s. Bot:* lycium *m, F:* olinet *m.*

boxwood ['bɔkswud], *s.* (bois *m* de) buis *m.*

boxy ['bɔksi], *a.* (*a*) *usu. Pej:* (*of building, design*) trop carré; qui manque d'élégance; (*b*) *Cost:* **b. jacket,** veste *f* vague.

boy [bɔi], *s.m.* **1.** (*a*) garçon; **little b.,** garçonnet; *O:* **b. child,** enfant mâle; **an English b.,** un jeune Anglais; **a blind b.,** un jeune aveugle; **I'm sure it was the b. Martin (who did it)!** c'est bien le jeune Martin qui l'a fait! **when I was a b.,** quand j'étais petit; quand j'étais enfant; **I knew them as a b.,** je les ai connus quand j'étais petit, dans ma jeunesse; **I have known him from a b.,** je le connais (i) depuis sa jeunesse, (ii) depuis ma jeunesse; **boys will be boys,** on ne peut pas empêcher les garçons de se conduire en garçons; les enfants sont toujours les enfants; il faut que jeunesse se passe; **we were b. and girl together,** elle et moi nous avons joué ensemble; **she ought to have been a b.,** c'est un garçon manqué; (*b*) **he has two boys and a girl,** il a deux garçons, deux fils, et une fille; **his little b. of ten,** son fils, son gamin, de dix ans; (*c*) *Sch:* élève *m*; **day b.,** externe; **an old b.,** un ancien élève; *F:* **the old b. net(work),** le réseau des relations entre anciens camarades d'école, de collège; *F:* **there was a rush to find jobs for the boys,** ce fut une ruée pour la distribution des planques, vers l'assiette au beurre; (*d*) *F:* **her b. friend,** son amoureux, son flirt; *P:* **his b. friend,** sa tante; *F:* **b. meets girl (story, etc.),** roman d'amour (conventionnel); (*e*) *F:* **a nice old b.,** un vieillard sympathique; **the old b.,** (i) le paternel; (ii) le patron; **one of the boys,** un joyeux vivant; **what a b.!** ça c'est un type! **come on boys!** allons-y les gars! *esp. NAm:* **oh b.!** ben alors! dis donc! *O:* **my dear b.!** mon cher (ami)! *O:* **I say old b.!** dis, mon vieux! (*f*) *P:* **the big boys,** les grosses légumes; *Pej:* **come on big b.!** allons mon vieux! **2.** (*a*) (*in Africa, etc.*) **(house) b.,** domestique *m,* boy *m*; **to hire boys for a safari,** engager des porteurs *m* pour un safari; (*b*) **stable b.,** garçon d'écurie; **telegraph b.,** porteur de télégrammes; **ship's b.,** mousse *m*; **the grocer's b.,** le garçon épicier; **errand b.,** (i) garçon de courses; (ii) garçon livreur; **office b.,** garçon de bureau; **I don't like being treated like an office b.,** je n'aime pas qu'on me donne tous les travaux sans importance; (*c*) *F:* **the boys, our boys,** les militaires; **the boys in blue,** (i) les marins; (ii) les agents de police, les flics. **3.** *P:* (*a*) *A:* **a bottle of the b.,** une bouteille de champagne; (*b*) *A:* **a yellow b.,** une guinée, un jaunet; (*c*) héroïne *f.*

boyar(d) ['bɔiɑ:r], *s. Hist:* boyard *m,* boïar(d) *m.*

boycott[1] ['bɔikɔt], *s.* mise *f* en interdit; boycottage *m*; **to put s.o., a shop, under a b.,** boycotter qn; interdire un magasin.

boycott[2], *v.tr.* boycotter (qn).

boycotter ['bɔikɔtər], *s.* boycotteur, -euse.

boycotting ['bɔikɔtiŋ], *s.* boycottage *m.*

boyhood ['bɔihud], *s.* (i) enfance *f,* première jeunesse, (ii) adolescence *f* (d'un garçon).

boyish ['bɔiiʃ], *a.* **1.** puéril, enfantin, d'enfant. **2.** (nature *f,* apparence *f*) jeune. **3.** (manières *fpl*) de garçon.

boyishly ['bɔiiʃli], *adv.* (*a*) en petit garçon; (*b*) comme un petit garçon.

boyishness ['bɔiiʃnis], *s.* manières, air, de petit garçon, de jeune homme.

Boyle [bɔil], *Pr.n. Ph:* **Boyle's law,** la loi de Mariotte.

boylike ['bɔilaik]. **1.** *a.* de gamin. **2.** *adv.* en vrai enfant; en vrai gamin qu'il était; en vrai(s) garçon(s).

boy's love ['bɔiz'lʌv], *s. Bot:* aurone *f* (mâle); citronelle *f.*

bra [brɑ:], *s. F:* soutien-gorge *m, pl.* soutiens-gorge.

Brabant [brə'bænt], *Pr.n. Geog:* Brabant *m.*

braccate ['brækeit], *a. Orn:* pattu.

brace[1] [breis], *s.* **1.** (*a*) *Const: etc:* (*in tension*) attache *f,* lien *m,* tirant *m,* armature *f,* entretoise *f,* étrésillon *m*; croisillon *m*; (*in compression*) contrefiche *f,* moise *f,* amoise *f*; bracon *m* (d'un mur en réparation); nervure *f* (de renfort); jambe *f* de force; (*of iron roof*) bielle *f*; **(anchor) b.,** ancre *f,* ancrure *f*; **cross b., diagonal b.,** écharpe *f,* diagonale *f,* moise en écharpe; *Aut:* croisillon (du châssis); **(angle) b.,** aisselier *m*; *Hyd.E:* **diagonal b. (of lockgate),** bracon; *N.Arch:* **braces of the sternpost,** armature de l'étambot; **rudder braces,** pentures *f,* ferrures *f,* du gouvernail; **sway b.,** (i) *Civ.E:* entretoise de contreventement; (ii) cornière *f* de renforcement; **wind b.,** contrevent *m*; entretoise de contreventement; **b. bracket,** support *m* d'entretoise; **b. rod,** tringle *f* de renforcement; tirant *m*; tendeur *m*; **b. strut,** contrefiche *m*; membrure *f* de triangulation; **b. cable,** câble *m* de traille; **rail b.,** pièce *f* de butée latérale; contrefiche de butée; **b. lath,** tasseau *m*; (*b*) *Dent:* appareil *m* dentaire; (*c*) *Med:* **(surgical) b.,** armature *f* orthopédique. **2.** (*a*) *pl. Cost:* bretelles *f* (de pantalon); (*b*) tirant, (de tambour); (*c*) *pl. Veh:* *A:* soupente *f* (de corps de voiture); (*d*) *Aut: A:* **trunk b.,** amarreur *m* (pour malle). **3.** (*archery*) manique *f.* **4.** *inv.* couple *f* (de perdrix); laisse *f* (de lévriers); paire *f* (de pistolets, etc.); **two b. of partridges,** deux couples de perdrix; *F:* **in a b. of shakes,** en un rien de temps; en moins de rien. **5.** *Tls:* **b. (and bit),** vilebrequin *m* (à main); **b. chuck,** porte-outil(s) *m inv*; **angle b.,** foret *m* à angle; **ratchet b.,** (i) *Mec.E:* perçoir *m,* foret, à rochet; fût *m* à rochet; cliquet *m* à percer; (ii) *Carp:* vilebrequin à cliquet, à rochet; *Aut:* **wheel b.,** vilebrequin (à roues). **6.** *Nau:* bras *m* (de vergue); **main b.,** grand bras. **7.** *Mus: Typ:* accolade *f.*

brace[2], *v.tr.* **1.** *Const: etc:* ancrer, amarrer (une construction); armer (une poutre); entretoiser, étrésillonner (une charpente); moiser (des étais); hauban(n)er (un mât, un poteau); **to b. a wall,** affermir un mur par des ancres; consolider, renforcer, un mur; **to b. a steel bridge,** contreventer un pont métallique; *Av:* **to b. a wing,** croisillonner une aile; **centre braced,** entretoisé au centre; **cross braced,** croisillonné. **2.** fortifier (le corps); tonifier (les nerfs); **to b. s.o. up,** retremper qn; (re)donner de la vigueur, du courage, à qn; remonter, *F:* ravigoter, qn; **b. up!** (i) secoue-toi; (ii) *F:* grouille-toi! **sea air braces you up,** l'air de la mer vous donne du ton, vous remonte; **to b. oneself (up) to do sth.,** raidir ses forces, se raidir, pour faire qch.; s'armer de (tout son) courage pour faire qch. **3.** (*a*) **to b. (the skin of) a drum,** tendre la peau d'un tambour; bander un tambour; (*b*) **to b. the knees,** tendre les jarrets; (*c*) **to b. the bow,** tendre, bander, l'arc. **4.** *Typ:* accolader, accoler (des mots); *Mus:* accolader (les portées). **5.** *Nau:* brasser (les vergues); **to b. up the sails,** ouvrir la voilure; brasser en pointe; **to b. sharp up,** orienter (les voiles) au plus près; **to b. in the sails,** fermer la voilure; **to b. round,** contrebrasser.

braced [breist], *a. Av:* **b. rib,** nervure triangulée; **b. spar,** âme *f* de longeron en biellette.

bracelet ['breislit], *s.* **1.** bracelet *m*; **chain b.,** gourmette *f*; **b. watch,** montre-bracelet *f, pl.* montres-bracelets. **2.** *P:* **bracelets,** menottes *f*; bracelets.

bracer ['breisər], *s.* **1.** = BRACE[1] (*a*). **2.** *F:* (*a*) petit verre (de spiritueux); (*b*) **to go out for a b.,** sortir prendre un peu d'air.

brach [brætʃ], *s. A:* chienne *f* de chasse; braque *m.*

brachial ['brækiəl, 'breik-], *a. Anat:* brachial, -aux.

brachialgia [bræki'ældʒiə, breik-], *s. Med:* brachialgie *f.*

brachiate[1] ['brækiət, 'brei-], *a. Nat.Hist:* brachié.

brachiate[2] ['brækieit, 'brei-], *v.i. Z:* pratiquer la brachiation.

brachiation [bræki'eiʃ(ə)n, brei-], *s. Z:* brachiation *f.*

brachiator ['brækieitər, 'brei-], *s. Z:* brachiateur *m.*

brachinus ['brækinəs], *s. Ent:* brachine *m,* brachyne *m.*

branchiocephalic [brækiouse'fælik], *a. Anat:* brachiocéphalique.

brachionalgia [brækiə'nældʒiə], *s. Med:* brachialgie *f.*

brachiopod ['brækiəpɔd], *s. Moll:* brachiopode *m.*

brachiosaur ['brækiəsɔ:r], **brachiosaurus** ['brækiəsɔ:rəs], *s. Paleont:* brachiosaure *m.*

brachistochrone [bræ'kistəkroun], *s. Mth:* brachistochrone *f.*

brachistochronic [brækistə'krɔnik], *a.* brachistochrone.

brachy- ['bræki], *pref.* brachy-.

brachyblast ['brækiblæ:st], *s. Bot:* brachyblaste *m.*

brachycephalic ['brækise'fælik], *a.* brachycéphale.

Brachycephalidae ['brækise'fælidi:], *s.pl. Amph:* brachycéphalidés *m.*

brachycephalism ['bræki'sefəlizm], **brachycephaly** ['bræki'sefəli], *s.* brachycéphalie *f.*

Brachycera [bræ'kisərə], *s.pl. Ent:* brachycères *m.*

brachycerous [bræ'kisərəs], *a. Ent:* brachycère.

brachydactylous ['bræki'dæktiləs], *a. Z: Ter:* brachydactyle.

brachylogy [bræ'kilədʒi], *s.* brachylogie *f.*

brachypterous [bræ'kiptərəs], *a. Ent: Orn:* brachyptère.

brachyteles [bræ'kitəli:z], *s. Z:* brachytèle *m,* singe *m* araignée du Brésil.

Brachyura [bræki'ju:rə], *s.pl. Crust:* brachyoures *m,* brachyures *m.*

bracing[1] ['breisiŋ], *a.* (air, climat, etc.) fortifiant, vivifiant, tonifiant, tonique.

bracing[2], *s.* **1.** ancrage *m,* consolidation *f*; entretoisement *m,* étrésillonnement *m*; armaturage *m,* armement *m* (d'une poutre); consolidation, renforcement *m* (d'un mur); contreventement *m* (d'un pont); *Av:* croisillonnage *m*; **b. wire,** fil tenseur, de hauban, de rappel; *Av:* hauban *m* de croisillonnage; **b. truss,** bielle *f* de triangulation; *Aut: etc:* **centre b.,** croisillons *mpl*; **b. strut,** jambe *f* de force; **strut b.,** poutre *f* en U; **wire b.,** haubannage *m* en fil d'acier. **2.** retrempe *f* (du corps); tonification *f* (des nerfs). **3.** *Nau:* brassage *m* (des vergues).

bracken ['bræk(ə)n], *s. Bot:* fougère (arborescente); fougère impériale, fougère à l'aigle.

bracket[1] ['brækit], *s.* **1.** support *m*; (*a*) *Const: etc:* console *f*; potence *f*; *Arch:* corbeau *m*; **angle b.,** console à équerre; équerre *f* de renforcement; **corner b., triangular b., shoulder b.,** gousset *m* de coin; mouchoir *m*; **brackets of a balcony,** arcs-boutants *m* d'un balcon; (*b*) *Const: Mec.E:* tasseau *m,* taquet *m* de soutien, patte *f* (de fixation, de sustentation), support, (é)chantignole *f*; **bearing b.,** chaise (suspendue, pendante); **b. hanger,** palier *m* à potence; chaise *f* console; (*c*) *N.Arch:* (i) courbaton *m*; (ii) **stern b. of the propeller shaft,** support d'arbre porte-hélice; **the 'A' b.,** la chaise d'hélice; (*d*) *Artil:* flasque *m* (d'affût); (*e*) **(lamp) b.,** applique *f* (pour lampe); **b. lamp,** (lampe *f* d')applique; **wall b.,** console murale; *Cy:* **lamp b.,** porte-lampe *m, pl.* porte-lampes. **2.** (*a*) *Typ: etc:* **square b.,** crochet *m*; **round b.,** parenthèse *f*; **between, in, brackets,** entre parenthèses; entre crochets; (*b*) (*brace*) accolade *f*; (*c*) *Adm:* tranche *f* (de revenus); fourchette *f* (de salaires); **the middle income b.,** la tranche des revenus moyens; **tax b.,** cédule *f* d'impôts; **the 15 to 20 age b.,** le groupe, la classe, des 15 à 20 ans; (*d*) *Artil:* fourchette; **b. fire,** tir *m* à la fourchette, de l'encadrement; **to get the b.,** obtenir l'encadrement; **to reduce the b.,** resserrer la fourchette; **b. ranging,** ajustement *m,* réglage *m* (du tir) à la fourchette; **axial, lateral, b. ranging,** ajustement, réglage, par encadrement, par fourchette latérale.

bracket[2], *v.tr.* **(bracketed) 1.** mettre (des mots) (i) entre crochets; (ii) entre parenthèses. **2.** réunir (des mots) par une accolade; accolader, accoler (deux mots, etc.); accoupler les noms de (deux personnes); associer (deux idées); placer (deux candidats) ex æquo; **bracketed together,** classés ex æquo. **3.** *Artil:* encadrer (un but); prendre (un but) en fourchette; *v.i.* tirer à la fourchette.

bracketing ['brækitiŋ], *s.* **1.** (*a*) mise *f* entre parenthèses; (*b*) accolement *m.* **2.** (*a*) *Artil:* encadrement *m*; tir *m* à la fourchette; **b. method,** méthode *f* de réglage (du tir) à la fourchette, par encadrement; **b. correction,** correction *f* du tir à la fourchette, par encadrement; **b. salvo,** salve encadrante, efficace; (*b*) **b. of a beam,** fourchettage *m* d'un faisceau.

brackish ['brækiʃ], *a.* saumâtre.

brackishness ['brækiʃnis], *s.* nature *f* saumâtre, goût *m* désagréable (d'une eau stagnante).

bracon ['brækən], *s. Ent:* bracon *m.*

Braconidae [bræ'kɔnidi:], *s.pl. Ent:* braconides *m,* braconidés *m.*

bract [brækt], *s. Bot:* bractée *f.*

bracteal ['bræktiəl], *a. Bot:* bractéal, -aux; bractéaire.

bracteate[1] ['bræktieit], *a. & s. Num:* bractéate (*f*).

bracteate[2], **bracted** ['bræktid], *a. Bot:* bractété.

bracteiferous [brækti'ifərəs], *a. Bot:* bractéifère.

bracteiform [bræk'ti:ifɔ:m], *a. Bot:* bractéiforme.

bracteolate ['bræktiəleit], *a. Bot:* bractéolé.

bracteole ['bræktioul], **bractlet** ['bræktlit], *s. Bot:* bractéole *f.*

brad [bræd], *s.* pointe *f,* clou *m* à tête perdue, clou étêté; **flooring b.,** clou à parquet; pointe à tête conique; **b. punch,** chasse-pointe(s) *m inv.*

bradawl ['brædɔ:l], *s. Tls:* alêne plate; poinçon *m*; pointe carrée.

bradbury ['brædbəri], *s. F: A:* billet *m,* coupure *f,* d'une livre.

bradded ['brædid], *a.* (soulier, etc.) clouté.

bradoon [brə'du:n], *s. Harn:* bridon *m.*

Bradshaw ['brædʃɔ:], *s. A:* indicateur *m* des chemins de fer britanniques (dont la première édition fut publiée par G. Bradshaw en 1839).

brady- ['brædi], *comb.fm.* brady-.
bradyarthria [brædi'ɑːθriə], *s. Med:* bradyarthrie *f.*
bradycardia [brædi'kɑːdiə], *s. Med:* bradycardie *f.*
bradylalia [brædi'leiliə], *s. Med:* bradylalie *f.*
bradypepsia [brædi'pepsiə], *s. Med:* bradypepsie *f.*
bradyphagia [brædi'feidʒiə], *s. Med:* bradyphagie *f.*
bradyphasia [brædi'feizlə], *s. Med:* bradyphasie *f.*
bradyphrenia [brædi'friːniə], *s. Med:* bradypsychie *f.*
bradypnea, bradypnoea [brædi'(p)niːə], *s. Med:* bradypnée *f,* brachypnée *f.*
bradypod ['brædipɔd], *s. Z:* bradype *m*; paresseux *m.*
Bradypodidae [brædi'pɔdidiː], *s.pl. Z:* bradypodidés *m.*
bradysphygmia [brædi'sfigmiə], *s. Med:* bradysphygmie *f.*
bradyuria [brædi'juːriə], *s. Med:* bradyurie *f.*
brae [brei], *s. Scot:* pente *f,* côte *f,* colline *f.*
brag[1] [bræg], *s.* vanterie *f,* vantardise *f,* hâblerie *f,* forfanterie *f,* fanfaronnade *f.*
brag[2], *v.i.* (**bragged** [bragd]) hâbler, se vanter; faire le Gascon, le fanfaron; fanfaronner, se faire valoir; faire le glorieux; **to b. of, about, sth.,** vanter qch.; se vanter de qch.
Braganza [brə'gænzə], *Pr.n. Hist: Geog:* Bragance *f.*
braggadocio [brægə'doutʃiou], *s.* **1.** *A:* (*pers.*) bravache *m,* matamore *m,* fanfaron *m,* hâbleur *m,* vantard *m*; *A:* capitan *m.* **2.** *O:* fanfaronnade *f,* forfanterie *f,* hâblerie *f.*
braggart ['brægət], *a.* & *s.* fanfaron (*m*), vantard (*m*); tranche-montagne *m, pl.* tranche-montagnes; *F:* coupeur *m* d'oreilles; avaleur *m* de gens; **great b.,** grand abatteur de bois, de quilles.
bragging[1] ['brægiŋ], *a.* vantard.
bragging[2], *s.* vantardise *f.*
brahma(pootra) ['brɑːmə('puːtrə)], *s. Husb:* coq *m* brahma, poule *f* brahma; brahma(poutre) *m.*
brahman ['brɑːmən], *s.m.* brahmane.
brahmanee, brahmani ['brɑːməniː], *s.f.* brahmine; femme brahmane.
brahmanic(al) [brɑː'mænik(l)], *a.* brahmanique.
brahmanism ['brɑːmənizm], *s.* brahmanisme *m.*
Brahmaputra (the) [ðəbrɑːmə'puːtrə], *Pr.n. Geog:* le Brahmapoutre.
brahmin ['brɑːmin]. **1.** *s.m.* brahmane. **2.** *s. U.S: F:* intellectuel, -elle; **one of the Boston brahmins,** membre *m* d'une des vieilles familles de Boston.
brahminic(al) [brɑː'minik(əl)], *a. NAm: F:* intellectuel.
braid[1] [breid], *s.* **1.** (*a*) tresse *f* (de cheveux); (*b*) *Poet:* bandeau *m*; (pour les cheveux). **2.** (*a*) *Cost: Dressm: Furn:* galon *m,* ganse *f,* bordé *m,* tresse; cordonnet *m,* lacet *m* (de bordure); passepoil *m,* soutache *f,* passement *m*; **flat b.,** tresse plate; **upholstery b.,** galon de finition pour meubles; **gold b. (of officers),** galon; **velvet b.,** velouté *m,* galon en velours, (*b*) *El:* gulpage *m* (de fils conducteurs). **3.** paille tressée.
braid[2], *v.tr.* **1.** (*a*) tresser, natter (ses cheveux, de la paille); tresser (des fleurs), (*b*) *Poet:* mettre un bandeau sur (ses cheveux). **2.** galonner, soutacher, passepoiler; attacher des galons à (un vêtement); passementer (le bord d'une chaise, etc.). **3.** *El:* tresser, guiper (un câble).
braided ['breidid], *a.* **1. b. garment,** vêtement brodé en soutache, soutaché. **2.** *El:* **b. conductor wire,** fil conducteur sous tresse; fil guipé. **3.** *Geog:* (*of stream*) anastomosé.
braiding ['breidiŋ], *s.* **1.** tressage *m*; **b. machine,** métier *m* à tresser; tresseuse *f.* **2.** (garniture *f* de) galon *m*; soutache *f*; nervure *f*; passement *m.* **3.** *El:* guipage *m* (de fils conducteurs).
brail[1] [breil], *s. Nau:* cargue *f*; **throat b.,** étrangloir *m*; **foot b.,** cargue basse.
brail[2], *v.tr. Nau:* **to b. (up) a sail,** carguer une voile.
Braille[1] [breil], *s.* Braille *m*; **B. alphabet,** alphabet *m* Braille; **B. type,** caractères *mpl* Braille; **B. printer,** imprimante *f* en Braille.
Braille[2], *v.tr.* écrire (qch.) en Braille.
brain[1] [brein], *s.* **1.** cerveau *m*; **electronic b.,** cerveau électronique; *Anat:* **b. sand,** acervule *m,* acervulus *m*; **b. exhaustion,** *F:* **b. fag,** épuisement cérébral, fatigue cérébrale, surmenage intellectuel; **b. disorders,** troubles cérébraux; **b. fever,** (i) fièvre cérébrale; (ii) fièvre chaude; **b. diseases,** maladies cérébrales; **to have a tumour on the b.,** avoir une tumeur au cerveau; **to turn s.o.'s b.,** tourner la tête à qn; **to have a subject on the b.,** être monomane, avoir la monomanie, l'obsession, d'un sujet; **to get sth. on the b.,** être hanté par l'image, par la pensée, de qch.; **he has money on the b.,** il est obsédé par l'argent; **to have a tune on the b.,** être hanté, obsédé, par un air. **2.** *pl.* **brains,** cervelle *f*; (*a*) matière cérébrale; *Cu:* **calves' brains,** cervelle de veau; **brains with melted-butter sauce,** cervelle au beurre noir; **to blow s.o.'s brains out,** brûler, faire sauter, la cervelle à qn; **to blow one's brains out,** se faire sauter, se brûler, la cervelle; *F:* se faire sauter le caisson; (*b*) **to puzzle, beat, rack, cudgel, one's brains,** se creuser la cervelle, le cerveau, l'esprit; se torturer l'esprit; se mettre l'esprit à la torture; se rompre la tête; se casser la tête; *F:* s'abîmer les méninges; **to rack one's brains for sth., to remember sth.,** faire des efforts de mémoire, se creuser la tête, pour retrouver qch.; **to rack one's brains for an explanation,** se casser la tête à chercher une explication; **she has the brains of a canary,** elle a une cervelle de moineau, une tête de linotte; **man of brains,** homme *m* de tête; **he has brains,** il est intelligent. **2.** personne qui fait partie d'un brain-trust; *Pol: etc:* **to call in the best brains** (*irrespective of party*), faire appel à tous les talents; **he's a b.,** c'est un cerveau.
brain[2], *v.tr.* défoncer le crâne à (qn); casser la tête à (qn); assommer (qn).
braincap ['breinkæp], *s.* calotte *f* du crâne.
braincase ['breinkeis], *s.* crâne *m*; boîte crânienne, du crâne.
brainchild ['breintʃaild], *s.* idée originale (de qn).
brain drain ['brein'drein], *s.* fuite *f,* exode *m,* drainage *m,* des cerveaux.
brainfever bird ['breinfiːvəbəːd], *s. Orn:* coucou-épervier *m*; *pl.* coucous-éperviers.
braininess ['breininis], *s. F:* intelligence *f*; habileté *f.*
brainless ['breinlis], *a.* sans cervelle; stupide; *F:* **you b. idiot!** (espèce d')imbécile!
brainpan ['breinpæn], *s.* crâne *m*; boîte crânienne, du crâne.
brainpower ['breinpauər], *s.* intelligence *f.*
brainsick ['breinsik], *a.* malade du cerveau; atteint au cerveau.
brainstorm[1] ['breinstɔːm], *s.* **1.** transport *m* au cerveau. **2.** *NAm: F:* (*a*) idée *f* de génie; (*b*) idée insensée.
brainstorm[2], *v.i.* pratiquer le brainstorming.
brainstorming ['breinstɔːmiŋ], *s.* brainstorming *m.*
brains (*NAm:* **brain**) **trust** ['brein(z)trʌst], *s.* brain-trust *m, pl.* brain-trusts; groupe *m* d'experts; équipe *f* de savants.
brainwash ['breinwɔʃ], *v.tr.* soumettre (qn) à un lavage de cerveau.
brainwashing ['breinwɔʃiŋ], *s.* lavage *m,* lessivage *m,* de cerveau, de crâne; décervelage *m.*
brainwave ['breinweiv], *s.* **1.** *Med:* **recording of brainwaves,** enregistrement *m* des différences de potentiel existant entre les cellules cérébrales. **2.** *Psychics:* onde *f* télépathique; communication intermentale. **3.** *F:* inspiration *f*; idée *f,* trait *m,* de génie; trouvaille *f*; idée lumineuse.
brainwork ['breinwəːk], *s.* travail intellectuel, cérébral; travail de tête.
brainworker ['breinwəːkər], *s.* intellectuel, -elle, cérébral, -ale; travailleur intellectuel.
brainy ['breini], *a. F:* intelligent, débrouillard; **how b. of you!** vous avez là une excellente idée! **he's not exactly b.,** ce n'est pas un fort en thème, il n'a pas inventé le fil à couper le beurre.
braird[1] [brɛəd], *s. Scot:* pousses *fpl* (d'herbe, de blé).
braird[2], *v.i. Scot:* (*of grass, wheat*) commencer à pousser, à verdir.
braise [breiz], *v.tr. Cu:* braiser; cuire (qch.) à l'étouffée; **braised beef,** bœuf *m* en, à la, daube; **braised chicken,** poulet *m* en, à la, casserole, à la cocotte.
brake[1] [breik], *s.* = BRACKEN.
brake[2], *s.* fourré *m,* hallier *m*; broussailles *fpl.*; *Ven:* breuil *m.*
brake[3], *s. Nau:* brimbale *f,* levier *m* (de pompe).
brake[4], *s. Tex:* (*for flax, hemp*) brisoir *m,* broie *f,* macque *f.*
brake[5], *v.tr. Tex:* briser, broyer, macquer, mailler (du lin, du chanvre); effilocher (des chiffons).
brake[6], *s. Veh: etc:* frein *m*; (*a*) **rim b.,** frein sur jante; **band b.,** frein à ruban, à collier, à bande; **shoe b.,** frein à sabots; **electro-magnetic b.,** frein à patin électromagnétique; **hand b.,** frein à main; frein à levier; frein de stationnement; **foot b.,** frein à pédale, au pied; **clutch b.,** frein sur l'embrayage; **transmission b.,** frein sur la transmission; **vacuum b.,** frein à vide; **air b.,** frein à air comprimé; *Mec.E: etc:* amortisseur *m* à moulinet; **screw b.,** frein à vis; **mechanical b.,** frein mécanique; **hydraulic b.,** frein hydraulique; **double-acting b.,** frein à double effet; **emergency b.,** frein de secours, de détresse; **b. connections,** tringlerie *f* (de freins mécaniques); tuyauterie *f* (de freins hydrauliques); *Aut:* **four-wheel brakes,** freins, freinage *m,* sur quatre roues; freinage intégral; **front-wheel brakes,** freinage sur roues avant; **drum b.,** frein à tambour; **disc b.,** frein à disque; **servo(-assisted) b.,** servofrein *m*; **b. horsepower,** puissance *f* au frein; *Cy:* **back-pedalling b.,** frein dans le moyeu, à rétropédalage; **b. wire,** câble *m* de frein; (*b*) **b. gear,** (i) dispositif *m,* organe(s) *m*(*pl*), de freinage; (ii) équipage *m* de frein, timonerie *f* (des freins); **b. block,** sabot *m* de frein; patin *m*; **b. band, lock, hoop,** bandage *m,* collier *m,* ruban *m,* de frein; frette *f* de friction; **b. drum,** tambour *m* de frein; couronne *f* de frein; **b. screw,** tige *f* à vis du frein; **b. lining,** garniture *f* de frein; **b. torque,** couple *m* de freinage; **b. rod,** tringle *f* de frein; **b. shoes,** mâchoires *f,* sabots *m,* segments *m,* de frein; **b.-shoe actuator,** poussoir *m* des segments du frein; **b. pads,** plaquettes *f* de frein; **b. fluid,** liquide *m* pour freins (hydrauliques); (*c*) *Rail:* **b. van,** wagon-frein *m, pl.* wagons-freins; fourgon *m*; **b. cabin,** vigie *f* de frein; **b. wheel,** volant *m* (de manœuvre) de frein; (*d*) *Av:* **air b.,** aérofrein *m*; frein aérodynamique; **propeller b.,** frein de l'hélice; **dive b.,** frein de piqué; (*e*) *Artil:* **recoil, buffer, b.,** frein de recul, de tir; **muzzle b.,** frein de bouche; (*f*) **to apply, put on, the brake(s),** freiner; mettre, serrer, le frein; **to slam on the brakes,** donner un brusque coup de frein; **to release the brake(s),** desserrer le frein; **b. reaction time,** durée *f* de la mise en action du frein; **b. lag distance,** distance parcourue pendant le temps mort du freinage; **to put a b. on a project,** donner un coup de frein à un projet; **to act as a b. on s.o.'s activities,** servir de frein aux activités de qn.
brake[7], *v.i.* freiner; serrer, mettre, le frein; **to b. hard,** freiner brusquement.
brake[8], *s.* = BREAK[3], **1.**
brake harrow ['breikhærou], *s. Agr:* grosse herse; brise-mottes *m inv*; broie *f.*
brakesman, *pl.* **-men,** *NAm:* **brakeman,** *pl.* **-men** ['breik(s)mən], *s.m.* **1.** *Rail: etc:* freineur *m*; serre-frein(s), *pl.* serre-freins; garde-frein(s), *pl.* gardes-frein(s). **2.** *Min:* machiniste ou mécanicien d'extraction.
braking[1] ['breikiŋ], *s.* broyage *m,* macquage *m,* maillage *m*; effilochage *m* (des chiffons).
braking[2], *s.* freinage *m*; serrage *m* des freins; coup *m* de frein; **regenerative b.,** freinage à récupération; freinage rétroactif; **aerodynamic b.,** freinage aérodynamique; *Aut:* **engine b.,** freinage par le moteur; **four-wheel b. system,** freinage intégral, sur quatre roues; **b. distance,** distance *f* d'arrêt, de freinage; **b. pull,** effort *m* de freinage; **b. effect,** puissance *f* de freinage; **b. test,** essai *m* de freinage; **b. gear,** (i) dispositif *m,* organe(s) *m* (*pl*), de freinage; (ii) équipage *m* de frein, timonerie *f* des freins.
Bramah ['brɑːmə], *Pr.n.m.* **B. lock,** serrure *f* (de) Bramah; serrure à pompe; **B.-press,** presse *f* de Bramah; presse hydraulique.
bramapithecus [brɑmapi'θiːkəs, -'piθikəs], *s. Paleont:* bramapithecus *m,* bramapithèque *m.*
bramble ['bræmbl], *s. Bot:* **1.** ronce sauvage, commune; ronce des haies, mûrier *m* des haies; mûrier sauvage, *F:* catherinette *f.* **2. brambles,** ronces. **3. b. rose,** (i) (*flower*) églantine *f*; (ii) (*bush*) églantier *m.*
brambleberry ['bræmblberi], *s. O:* mûre *f.*
brambling ['bræmbliŋ], *s. Orn:* pinson *m* du Nord, des Ardennes.
brambly ['bræmbli], *a.* plein, couvert, de ronces; ronceux, broussailleux.
bran[1] [bræn], *s. Mill:* son *m*; remoulage *m*; **b. and offal,** issues *fpl*; **b. water,** eau *f* de son; *Husb:* **b. mash,** son mouillé; confit *m*; eau blanche (pour les chevaux, etc.); mash *m,* mâche *f*; **b. tub,** baquet rempli de son où l'on plonge la main pour en retirer une surprise (à une vente de charité, à une soirée enfantine).
bran[2], *v.tr.* (**branned**) ébrouer (la laine).
brancard ['bræŋkɑːd], *s. A:* litière *f* (à deux chevaux).
branch[1] [brɑːn(t)ʃ], *s.* **1.** branche *f,* rameau *m* (d'un arbre); **the branches,** le branchage, les branches. **2.** (*a*) ramification *f*; *Min:* rameau (d'une galerie); branche, embranchement *m* (d'une route, d'un chemin de fer); branche, bras *m* (d'un fleuve); *Geog: U.S:* affluent *m*; *Rail:* **b. line,** (ligne *f* d')embranchement; antenne *f*; ligne d'intérêt local; *El:* **b. switch,** interrupteur *m* de branchement, de dérivation; (*b*) *Anat:* branche (collatérale, terminale); *Mth:* branche (d'une courbe); (*c*) branche (d'une famille, d'une science, d'une industrie, etc.); **our b. of the family,** notre branche de la famille; **the different branches of industry,** les différentes branches de l'industrie; (*d*) *Adm: Com:* branche, succursale *f,* filiale *f* (d'une société, d'une maison de commerce); succursale (d'une banque); (*of a business*) **main b.,** établissement principal; maison mère; **b. office,** (i) agence *f*; (ii) bureau *m* de quartier; **b. post office,** bureau auxiliaire (des postes); recette *f* auxiliaire; **this shop has branches in fifty different towns,** ce magasin a des succursales dans cinquante villes différentes; (*e*) *Mil:* arme *f* (du service); service *m,* direction *f* (de l'administration); bureau (d'état-major); **the branches of the service(s),** les armes et services; **A**

Branch, Premier Bureau; **I Branch,** Deuxième Bureau; **G Branch,** Troisième Bureau; **Q Branch,** Quatrième Bureau; (*f*) *Cmptr:* branchement *m*; **b. address,** adresse *f* de branchement; **to take a b.,** exécuter un branchement; **conditional, unconditional, b.,** branchement conditionnel, inconditionnel. **3.** *Tchn:* branche (d'une voûte gothique, d'un compas, de la bride); lance *f* (d'un tuyau d'arrosage, etc.); ente *f* (d'une pince). **4.** *Nau:* patente *f* de pilote lamaneur; **b. pilot,** (pilote *m*) lamaneur *m*.

branch[2]. **1.** *v.i.* (*of plants*) pousser des branches; **to b. (out),** se ramifier; (*of an organization, etc.*) étendre au loin ses ramifications; (*of pers.*) **to b. out into . . .,** étendre ses activités, son commerce, à. . .; **to b. out in every direction,** étendre de toutes parts ses ramifications. **2.** *v.i.* (*of road(s), etc.*) **to b. (off, away),** (se) bifurquer, s'embrancher (**from,** sur); **at the point where the road branches,** à la bifurcation des routes. **3.** *v.tr. El:* brancher (un circuit); dériver (le courant). **4.** *v.i. Cmptr:* **to b. to,** se brancher sur (une séquence); **to b. back to,** renvoyer à; **to b. out of a loop,** sortir d'une boucle.

branched ['brɑːn(t)ʃt], *a.* **1.** *Bot:* branchu, rameux. **2. b. candlestick,** chandelier *m* à (plusieurs) branches. **3.** *Ch:* ramifié, à chaîne ramifiée.

branchellion [bræŋ'keliən], *s. Ann:* branchellion *m*.

branchful ['brɑːn(t)ʃful], *s.* branchée *f*.

branchia ['bræŋkiə], *s.pl.,* **branchiae** ['bræŋkiiː], *s.pl. Biol: Ich:* branchies *f*; ouïes *f*.

branchial ['bræŋkiəl], *a. Biol: Ich:* branchial, -aux.

Branchiata [bræŋ'kiɑːtə], *s.pl. Nat.Hist:* branchiates *m*.

branchiate ['bræŋkiət], *a. Biol:* branchié.

branchiform ['bræŋkifɔːm], *a. Biol:* branchiforme.

branching[1] ['brɑːn(t)ʃiŋ], *a.* (*of tree*) branchu, rameux.

branching[2], *s.* **1.** bifurcation *f*, branchement *m*, dérivation *f*; partage *m* du courant (d'une rivière). **2.** *Cmptr:* branchement.

branchiobdella [bræŋkiəb'delə], **branchiobdellid** [bræŋkiəb'delid], *s. Ann:* branchiobdelle *f*.

branchiopod, *pl.* **-s** ['bræŋkiəpɔd, -z], *s. Crust:* branchiopode *m*.

Branchiopoda [bræŋki'ɔpədə], *s.pl. Crust:* branchiopodes *m*.

branchiosaur ['bræŋkiousɔːr], **branchiosaurus** ['bræŋkiou'sɔːrəs], *s. Paleont:* branchiosaure *m*, branchiosaurus *m*.

branchiostegal ['bræŋki'ɔstəgəl], *a. Ich:* branchiostège.

branchiostomidae ['bræŋkiou'stɔmidiː], *s.pl. Ich:* branchiostomes *m*, acraniens *m*.

branchipus ['bræŋkipəs], *s. Crust:* branchipe *m*.

branchless ['brɑːn(t)ʃlis], *a.* sans branches; dépourvu de branches.

branchlet ['brɑːn(t)ʃlit], *s.* petite branche; branchette *f*; branchillon *m*; rameau *m*; ramule *m*.

branchy ['brɑːn(t)ʃi], *a.* branchu; rameux.

brand[1] [brænd], *s.* **1.** brandon *m*, tison *m*; *Lit:* **a b. from the burning,** un tison arraché au feu; un nouveau converti; une âme sauvée. **2.** *Poet:* flambeau *m*. **3.** (*a*) fer chaud; (*b*) marque (faite avec un fer chaud); flétrissure *f*, stigmate *m* (imprimé(e) sur l'épaule). **4.** *Com:* (*a*) marque (de fabrique); **b. image,** image *f* de marque; **a good b. of cigars,** une bonne marque de cigares; (*b*) sorte *f*, qualité *f* (d'une marchandise). **5.** *Agr:* brûlure *f*, brouissure *f*; rouille *f* (des plantes); **b. fungi,** ustilaginales *fpl*. **6.** *Poet:* glaive *m*, épée *f*.

brand[2], *v.tr.* **1. to b. with a hot iron,** marquer (qn, un animal, une marchandise) au fer chaud; flétrir (qn); *A:* **to b. a slave,** estamper un esclave. **2. to be branded on s.o.'s memory,** être gravé dans la mémoire de qn. **3. to b. s.o. with infamy,** flétrir, stigmatiser, qn; marquer qn du sceau de l'infamie; noter qn d'infamie; **to be branded as a swindler,** être noté (d'infamie) comme escroc.

branded ['brændid], *a.* **1.** marqué à chaud; **to be b.,** porter la marque. **2. b. goods,** produits *mpl* de marque; **b. petrol** = supercarburant *m*. *F:* super *m*.

Brandenburg ['brændənbəːg]. **1.** *Pr.n. Geog:* Brandebourg *m*. **2.** *s.pl. A.Cost:* brandebourgs *m*.

brander[1] ['brændər], *s. Dial: Scot: Cu:* gril *m*.

brander[2], *v.tr. Dial: Scot: Cu:* griller.

brandied ['brændid], *a.* **1.** (cerises) à l'eau-de-vie. **2.** (vin) alcoolisé.

branding ['brændiŋ], *s.* impression *f* au fer chaud; **b. iron,** fer *m* à marquer; marque *f* à brûler.

brandish[1] ['brændiʃ], *s. A:* brandissement *m*.

brandish[2], *v.tr.* brandir (une arme, etc.).

brandishing ['brændiʃiŋ], *s.* brandissement *m*.

brandisite ['brændisait], *s. Miner:* brandisite *f*.

brandling ['brændliŋ], *s.* **1.** *Fish:* vérotis *m*; ver *m* rouge. **2.** *Dial: Ich:* saumoneau *m*, parr *m*.

brand-new ['bræn(d)'njuː], *a.* tout (battant) neuf, tout flambant neuf; **his b.-new coat,** son bel habit tout neuf.

brandreth ['brændriθ], *s.* chantier *m* (de tonneau).

brandtite ['bræn(d)tait], *s. Miner:* brandtite *f*.

brandy[1] ['brændi], *s.* (*a*) cognac *m*; **Armagnac b.,** armagnac *m*; **liqueur b.,** fine *f*; **b. and soda,** fine à l'eau; **b. distilling,** distillation *f* du vin; **b. flask,** flacon *m* à cognac; (*b*) **cherry b.,** cherry(-brandy) *m*; **plum b.,** eau-de-vie *f* de prunes; **b. plums,** prunes *fpl* à l'eau-de-vie; (*c*) **b. snap,** galette *f* au gingembre.

brandy[2], *v.tr.* confire (des cerises, etc.) à l'eau-de-vie.

brandyball ['brændibɔːl], *s.* bonbon parfumé à l'eau-de-vie.

brandy bottle [brændibɔtl], *s. Bot: F:* nénuphar *m* jaune.

brandy-pawnee ['brændipɔː'niː], *s. O:* (*Anglo-Indian*) fine *f* à l'eau.

brankursine ['bræŋk'əːsain], *s. Bot:* branche-ursine *f*; acanthe *f*.

bran-new ['bræn'njuː], *a.* = BRAND-NEW.

brant [brænt], *s. Orn:* **(American) b., b. goose,** bernache *f* cravant; **black b.,** bernache noire.

brash[1] [bræʃ], *s. Med:* **1. teething, weaning, brash,** troubles *mpl* de la dentition, du sevrage. **2.** aigreurs *fpl* (d'estomac).

brash[2], *s.* **1.** (*a*) éboulis *m* (de roches); amas *m* de décombres; (*b*) bois cassant. **2. b. (ice),** glace *f* en débâcle, *Nau:* sarrasins *mpl*.

brash[3], *a.* **1.** (*of wood*) cassant. **2.** effronté, présomptueux, impudent; braillard; exubérant; impétueux; sans tact; (*of colour*) cru.

brash[4], *v.tr. For:* **to b. a tree,** émonder les basses branches d'un arbre.

brashly ['bræʃli], *adv.* effrontément.

brashness ['bræʃnis], *s.* **1.** *Tchn:* fragilité *f*. **2.** effronterie *f*, impudence *f*; exubérance *f*; impétuosité *f*.

brashy ['bræʃi], *a.* cassant.

brasque[1] [brɑːsk], *s. Metall:* brasque *f*.

brasque[2], *v.tr.* brasquer (un creuset).

brass[1] [brɑːs], *s.* **1.** (*a*) cuivre *m* jaune; laiton *m*; **b. rod,** baguette *f* de laiton; **b. foundry,** fonderie *f* de cuivre; robinetterie *f*; **b. plate,** plaque *f* de cuivre; plaque à la porte d'un commerçant, d'un médecin, etc.; **latten b.,** laiton en feuilles, laminé; **b. wire,** fil *m* d'archal; **b. plating,** laitonnage *m*; **as bold as b.,** effronté comme un page; **to get down to b. tacks,** en venir au fait; *F:* **b. hat,** officier *m* d'état-major, *P:* grand-calot *m*, *pl.* grands-calots; *F:* **top b.,** *U.S:* **high b.,** les gros bonnets, *P:* les grosses légumes; (*b*) *Bookb:* fer *m*. **2.** (*a*) les cuivres, robinets, etc. (du ménage, à bord, etc.); **to do the b., the brasses,** faire les cuivres; **b. rags,** chiffons *m* à astiquer les cuivres; *F:* **to part b. rags,** se brouiller (ensemble); rompre; **b. smith,** robinetier *m*; **brassware,** dinanderie *f*; (*b*) *usu. pl. Mec.E:* coussinet *m* de bielle, de palier; coquille *f* (de coussinets); (*c*) *Mus:* **the b.** (*in band, orchestra*), les cuivres; **b. band,** fanfare *f*; (*d*) (*in a church*) plaque tombale en cuivre; **b. rubbing,** frottis *m* d'une plaque tombale en cuivre; (*e*) *P:* **b. (nail),** prostituée *f*, poule *f*. **3.** *F:* argent *m*, pépètes *f*, galette *f*; **if I had your b.,** si j'étais aussi riche que vous. **4.** *P: O:* toupet *m*, culot *m*; **if I had your b.,** si j'avais autant de toupet que vous.

brass[2].

I. *v.tr.* **brassed instead of gilded,** laitonné au lieu d'être doré.

II. (*compound verbs*) **1. brass off,** *v.tr. F:* **to be brassed off,** avoir le cafard, en avoir marre.

2. brass up, *v.i. P:* casquer.

brassage ['bræsidʒ], *s.* droit *m* de monnayage.

brassard ['bræsɑːd], *s.* brassard *m*.

brassavola [bræsə'voulə, bræ'sævələ], *s. Bot:* brassavola *f*.

brassed-off ['brɑːst'ɔf], *a. F:* cafardeux.

brasserie ['bræs(ə)riː], *s.* brasserie *f*; restaurant *m*.

brassica ['bræsikə], *s. Bot:* brassica *m*.

brassie ['brɑːsi], *s.* = BRASSY[1].

brassière ['bræsiɛər], *s. Cost:* soutien-gorge *m*, *pl.* soutiens-gorge; **strapless b.,** bustier *m*; **half-cup b.,** balconnet *m* (*R.t.m.*); **uplift b.,** soutien-gorge pigeonnant; **padded b.,** soutien-gorge ampliforme; **sling, cradle, platform, b.,** soutien-gorge corbeille; **preformed b.,** soutien-gorge préformé.

brassily ['brɑːsili], *adv.* **1.** avec des sons cuivrés. **2.** *F:* effrontément.

brassiness ['brɑːsinis], *s.* **1.** apparence 'toc' (d'un bijou censé être en or, etc.). **2.** sons cuivrés (d'une musique). **3.** *F:* effronterie *f*.

brasswork ['brɑːswəːk], *s.* **1.** les cuivres *m*. **2.** *Ind:* (i) cuivrerie *f*; (ii) cuivreries.

brassy[1] ['brɑːsi], *s. Golf:* **1.** brassie *m*. **2.** coup *m* de brassie.

brassy[2], *a.* **1.** (*a*) (*of colour, etc.*) qui ressemble au cuivre; tapageur; (*b*) (son) cuivré, claironnant. **2.** *F:* (*of pers.*) effronté.

brat [bræt], *s. usu. Pej:* (*a*) marmot *m*, gosse *mf*, mioche *mf*, môme *mf*, moutard *m*, bambin, -ine; loupiot, -iotte; **she arrived with all her brats,** elle est venue avec toute sa marmaille; (*b*) petit morveux.

brattice[1] ['brætis], *s.* **1.** *A.Fort: Arch:* bretèche *f*. **2.** *Min:* cloison *f* d'aérage.

brattice[2], *v.tr.* cloisonner.

bratticing ['brætisiŋ], *s. Min:* **1.** cloisonnage *m*. **2.** cloison *f* d'aérage.

braula ['brɔːlə, 'brau-], *s. Ent:* braule *f*.

braunite ['braunait], *s. Miner:* braunite *f*.

bravado [brə'vɑːdou], *s.* bravade *f*; **out of b.,** par bravade.

brave[1] [breiv]. **1.** *a.* (*a*) courageux, brave, vaillant; **as b. as a lion,** brave comme un lion, *Prov:* **none but the b. deserve the fair,** jamais honteux n'eut belle amie; **to put a b. face on sth.,** faire bonne contenance; (*b*) *A: & Lit:* (i) beau, élégant, pimpant; (ii) excellent, parfait. **2.** *s.* brave *m* (guerrier Peau-rouge).

brave[2], *v.tr.* braver, défier (qn); braver, affronter (un danger, etc.); **to b. it out,** ne pas se laisser démonter.

bravely [breivli], *adv.* **1.** courageusement, bravement, vaillamment. **2.** *A: & Lit:* (*a*) élégamment, splendidement; (*b*) **b. done!** excellent!

bravery ['breivəri], *s.* **1.** bravoure *f*, courage *m*; vaillance *f*. **2.** *A:* (*a*) splendeur *f*, magnificence *f*; (*b*) beaux habits; *A:* braverie *f*; **he, she, was decked out in all his (her) b.,** il s'était mis en grand costume; elle était parée de tous ses atours.

bravo[1], *pl.* **-os, -oes** ['brɑːvou, -ouz], *s.* bravo *m*, *pl.* bravi; spadassin *m*, sicaire *m*.

bravo[2], *int.* bravo!

bravura [bræ'v(j)uːrə], *s. Mus:* **b. (air),** air *m* de bravoure.

brawl[1] [brɔːl], *s.* **1.** rixe *f*, bagarre *f*, querelle *f*; **public-house b.,** rixe de cabaret; **drunken b.,** querelle d'ivrognes. **2.** *Lit:* murmure *m* (d'un ruisseau).

brawl[2], *v.i.* **1.** (*of pers.*) (*a*) brailler, clabauder; se chamailler; (*b*) *Jur:* **to b. in church,** troubler l'ordre dans un édifice religieux. **2.** *Lit:* (*of streams*) murmurer, bruire; **the stream brawls over the stones,** le ruisseau coule en murmurant sur les cailloux.

brawl[3], *s. A.Danc:* branle *m*.

brawler ['brɔːlər], *s.* braillard, -arde; tapageur, -euse; *F:* bagarreur, -euse.

brawling[1] ['brɔːliŋ], *a.* **1.** (*of pers.*) braillard, tapageur, -euse. **2.** *Lit:* (*of stream*) murmurant, bruissant.

brawling[2], *s.* **1.** (*a*) braillement *m*, clabauderie *f*; tapage *m*; (*b*) *Jur:* délit *m* de trouble ou de tapage dans un édifice religieux. **2.** *Lit:* murmure *m*, bruissement *m* (d'un ruisseau, etc.).

brawn [brɔːn], *s.* **1.** muscles *mpl*; partie charnue (des membres); *F:* **to have plenty of b.,** être bien musclé; *F:* avoir du biceps. **2.** *Cu:* fromage *m* de tête.

brawniness ['brɔːninis], *s.* carrure musclée, forte carrure; force *f* (de corps).

brawny ['brɔːni], *a.* charnu, musculeux; (*of pers.*) musclé, bien bâti.

bray[1] [brei], *s.* **1.** braiment *m* (d'un âne). **2.** *Pej:* braillement *m*.

bray[2], *v.i.* **1.** (*of donkey*) braire. **2.** *F: Pej:* braire, brailler.

bray[3], *v.tr.* **1.** broyer, piler, concasser (des couleurs, etc.). **2.** *Typ:* (*hard work*) étaler (l'encre).

bray[4], *v.tr. Leath:* (*in S. Africa*) préparer, apprêter (des peaux).

brayer ['breiər], *s. Typ:* rouleau *m* (à étaler l'encre).

braying ['breiiŋ], *s.* = BRAY[1].

brazant ['breiz(ə)nt], *s. Metall:* brasure *f*.

braze[1] [breiz], *v.tr. Tchn:* bronzer.

braze[2], *v.tr. Tchn:* braser; souder (qch.) au laiton.

braze[3], *s. Metalw:* soudure *f* au laiton.

brazeless ['breizlis], *a. Metalw:* sans soudure.

brazen[1] ['breizn], *a.* **1.** (*a*) *Lit:* d'airain; **b. vessel,** vase *m* d'airain; *Pol.Ec:* **(Lassalle's) b. law of wages,** la loi d'airain; (*b*) **the b. notes of the trumpet,** les sons d'airain de la trompette. **2.** effronté, impudent, cynique; **b. denial,** refus impudent; **b. lie,** mensonge audacieux, effronté; **b.-faced,** effronté, impudent.

brazen[2], *v.tr.* **to b. it out,** payer d'effronterie, payer de toupet; crâner; **to b. out a crime,** se vanter cyniquement d'un crime.

brazenly ['breiz(ə)nli], *adv.* effrontément, impudemment; cyniquement; audacieusement; sans honte.

brazenness ['breiz(ə)nnis], *s.* cynisme *m* (dans le mensonge, dans le crime).

brazier[1] ['breiziər], *s. Metalw:* chaudronnier *m*, dinandier *m*.

brazier[2], *s.* brasero *m* (à charbon de bois); **perfume b.,**

brûle-parfums *m inv*.

braziery ['breiziəri], *s. Metalw:* chaudronnerie *f*, dinanderie *f*.

Brazil [brə'zil]. **1.** *Pr.n. Geog:* Brésil *m*. **2.** (*a*) **B. nut,** (i) noix *f* d'Amérique, du Brésil; (ii) (*tree*) berthollétie *f*; (*b*) *Com: Dy:* **B. wood,** bois *m* de, du, Brésil.

brazilein [bræ'ziliən], *s. Ch:* brésiléine *f*.

braziletto [bræzi'letou], *s. Com: Dy:* brésillet *m*.

Brazilian [brə'ziljən], *Geog:* **1.** *a.* brésilien. **2.** *s.* Brésilien, -ienne.

brazilin ['bræzilin], *s. Ch:* brésiline *f*.

brazing ['breiziŋ], *s.* brasage *m*, brasement *m*, brasure *f*; soudure *f* (au laiton); soudure forte; **b.- lamp,** lampe *f* à braser, à souder.

breach[1] [bri:tʃ], *s.* **1.** infraction *f*; **b. of rules,** infraction, contravention *f*, aux règles; **b. of the law,** violation *f* de la loi; **b. of duty, of honour,** infraction, manquement *m*, forfaiture *f*, au devoir, à l'honneur; **b. of discipline,** manquement à la discipline; **b. of friendship,** manquement à l'amitié; **b. of faith,** manque *m* de foi, violation de foi; manque de parole; infidélité *f*; **I cannot, without a definite b. of faith, shirk this obligation,** je ne saurais, sans une véritable forfaiture, me dérober à cette obligation; **b. of trust,** (i) abus *m* de confiance; malversation *f*; (*of official*) fait *m* de charge; prévarication *f*; (ii) violation d'un des devoirs d'un mandataire; **b. of good manners,** manque de savoir-vivre, manquement au savoir-vivre; manquement aux convenances; inconvenance *f*, impolitesse *f*; **to commit a b. of etiquette,** manquer à l'étiquette, au protocole; **b. of secrecy,** indiscrétion *f*; **b. of professional secrecy,** violation du secret professionnel; **b. of privilege,** atteinte portée aux privilèges; **b. of police regulations,** contravention de simple police; **b. of the peace,** attentat *m*, délit *m*, contre l'ordre public; **there was no b. of the peace,** l'ordre public n'a été nullement troublé; **b. of contract,** rupture *f* de contrat; **b. of promise,** (i) manque de parole; (ii) *Jur:* non-accomplissement *m*, violation, de promesse de mariage; rupture de promesse de mariage; **action for b. of promise,** action *f* en dommages-intérêts pour non-accomplissement de promesse de mariage; **b. of close,** effraction *f*; bris *m* de clôture; violation de clôture; **b. of domicile,** (i) violation de domicile; (ii) effraction; **b. of neutrality,** violation de neutralité. **2.** brouille *f*, rupture (entre deux amis, etc.). **3.** trou *m*, brèche *f* (dans un mur, etc.); *Mil:* **to stand in the b.,** monter sur la brèche; **to make a b. in the enemy's lines,** trouer, percer, les lignes de l'ennemi; faire une trouée dans, à travers, les lignes de l'ennemi. **4.** *Nau: Lit:* (*of waves*) **to make a b.,** déferler. **5.** saut *m* (d'une baleine).

breach[2]. **1.** *v.tr.* ouvrir une brèche dans (une digue, un mur); battre (un mur) en brèche; *Geol:* **breached cone,** cratère ébréché, égueulé. **2.** *v.i.* (*a*) (*of embankment, etc.*) se rompre, se disjoindre; (*b*) (*of whale*) sauter, émerger.

breaching ['bri:tʃiŋ], *s.* mise *f* en brèche (d'un mur, etc.); *Mil: etc:* **b. battery,** batterie *f* de brèche; **b. fire,** tir *m* en brèche.

bread[1] [bred], *s.* (*a*) pain *m*; **b. making,** boulange(rie) *f*; **white b.,** pain blanc; **brown b.,** pain bis; **rye b.,** pain de seigle; **black b.,** pain de seigle (de campagne); **French b.,** pain croustillant (à la française); **a loaf of French b.,** une flûte; une baguette; une ficelle; **ship's b.,** biscuit *m* (de mer); **canary b.,** (pain) échaudé *m*; **a loaf of b.,** un pain; une miche; **b. and butter,** pain beurré; **a slice of b. and butter,** une tartine de beurre, une tartine beurrée; *F:* **b. and scrape,** tartines à peine beurrées; **b. and milk,** panade *f* au lait; soupe *f* au lait; **to be on b. and water,** être au pain (sec) et à l'eau; **to live on (nothing but) b. and cheese,** vivre chichement, frugalement; avoir tout juste de quoi vivre; **to take the b. out of s.o.'s mouth,** prendre le pain dans la bouche de qn; **to earn one's daily b., one's b. and butter,** gagner sa vie, son pain, sa croûte; **poetry doesn't earn one one's b. and butter,** la poésie ne nourrit pas son homme; **to look after one's own b. and butter,** défendre ses intérêts, *F:* son bifteck; **to quarrel with one's b. and butter,** casser la marmite; se faire renvoyer; *Publ:* **b.-and-butter books,** livres *m* de fonds, de vente assurée; *Cmptr:* **b.-and-butter programmes,** programmes courants; **b.-and-butter letter,** lettre *f* de remerciements (après avoir séjourné chez qn); lettre de digestion, de château; *O:* **b.-and-butter miss,** jeune fille qui sort de pension, de couvent; **he knows on which side his b. is buttered,** il sait où est son avantage, son intérêt; *Ecc:* **give us this day our daily b.,** donne-nous aujourd'hui notre pain de ce jour; **He took the bread, brake it . . .,** il prit le pain, le rompit . . .; **the b. and wine,** les espèces *f*; *B:* **I am the b. of life,** je suis le pain de la Vie; (*b*) *attrib.* **b. bin,** (i) boîte *f* à pain; (ii) huche *f* à pain; (iii) maie *f*; **b. knife,** couteau *m* à pain; **b. saw,** scie *f* à pain; **b. slicer, cutter,** tranche-pain *m inv*; taille-pain *m inv*; *Cu:* **b. pudding,** gâteau *m* de pain; **b. sauce,** sauce *f* à la mie de pain; *Nau:* **b. locker,** boulangerie *f*; **b. room,** soute *f* au pain, à biscuits; *Adm: A:* **b. card, coupon,** carte *f*, coupon *m*, ticket *m*, de pain; *Med:* **b. poultice,** cataplasme *m* à la mie de pain; (*c*) *Bot:* **monkey b.,** pain de singe; (*d*) *P:* argent *m*, oseille *f*.

bread[2], *v.tr. Cu:* paner.

breadbasket ['bredbɑ:skit], *s.* **1.** (*a*) corbeille *f* à pain; la corbeille au pain; (*b*) *Bak:* banneton *m*; (*c*) *NAm:* région productrice de céréales panifiables. **2.** *P:* estomac *m*, bedaine *f*; **to get one in the b.,** recevoir un coup dans le gésier; **nothing to put in one's b.,** rien à se mettre dans le buffet.

breadboard ['bredbɔ:d], *s.* **1.** planche *f* à pain. **2.** *Elcs: etc:* (*also* **breadboarding**) montage expérimental.

breadcrumb[1] ['bredkrʌm], *s.* (*a*) mie *f* (du pain); mie de pain; (*b*) miette *f* (de pain); *Cu:* **breadcrumbs,** chapelure *f*; **fried in breadcrumbs,** pané.

breadcrumb[2], *v.tr. Cu:* paner (des côtelettes, etc.).

breadcrust ['bredkrʌst], *s.* **1.** croûte *f* de pain. **2.** *Geol:* **b. bomb,** bombe *f* en croûte de pain.

breadfruit ['bredfru:t], *s. Bot:* fruit *m* à pain; **b. tree,** artocarpe *m*; arbre *m* à pain; jaquier *m*.

breadline ['bredlain], *s.* (*a*) *Hist: NAm:* queue *f* (du public) pour toucher les bons de pain, pour recevoir de la nourriture gratuite; (*b*) **on the b.,** indigent; sans ressources.

breadstick ['bredstik], *s. Comest:* gressin *m*.

breadstuff(s) ['bredstʌf(s)], *s.* (*pl.*) **1.** farine *f*. **2.** céréales *f* panifiables.

breadth [bredθ], *s.* **1.** largeur *f*; (*of material*) lé *m*, laize *f*; **finger's b.,** travers *m* de doigt; *Nau:* **extreme b.,** largeur au fort (d'un navire); **tonnage b.,** largeur hors membrures; (*of bird, aircraft*) **b. of wings,** envergure *f*; **the carpet is two metres in b.,** le tapis a deux mètres de large. **2.** largeur, carrure *f* (d'expression, de pensée); largeur (d'esprit, de vues); facture *f* large (d'un tableau); ampleur *f* (de style); **the orchestra plays with b.,** l'orchestre *m* a une belle ampleur de son; **his acting has taken on b.,** il a élargi son jeu; *Art:* **to give b. to the line, to the stroke,** nourrir le trait; **to lack b. of brush,** peindre, dessiner, maigre.

breadthways ['bredθweiz], **breadthwise** ['bredθwaiz], *adv.* en largeur, dans le sens de la largeur.

bread tree ['bred tri:], *s. Bot:* (**African**) **b. t.,** manguier *m* du Gabon.

breadwinner ['bredwinər], *s.* gagne-pain *m inv* ((i) soutien *m* de famille, chef *m* de famille; (ii) instrument *m* de travail).

break[1] [breik], *s.* **1.** rupture *f*; (*a*) brisure *f*, cassure *f*, fracture *f* (dans une assiette, etc.); trouée *f*, percée *f*, brèche *f*, ouverture *f* (dans une haie); éclaircie *f* (à travers les nuages); *Geol:* faille *f* (d'une couche); lacune *f* (dans une succession); *Nau:* coupée *f*, ravalement *m* (du pont); *W.Tel: T.V:* (i) coupure *f* (dans un programme, pour y introduire une publicité); (ii) interruption *f* (en cas de panne); **b. in the voice,** (i) altération *f* de la voix (par l'émotion); (ii) mue *f*, altération de la voix (à la puberté); (iii) *Mus:* passage *m* d'un registre à l'autre; **b. of continuity,** solution *f* de continuité; **b. of slope,** changement *m* de pente; **b. in the skin,** fendillement *m*; **b. in a journey,** arrêt *m* (en cours de route); *Nau:* **b. of bulk,** rupture de charge; **to talk for hours without a b.,** parler pendant des heures sans discontinuer; **there has been a long b. in our correspondence,** notre correspondance a subi une longue interruption; **to write to s.o. after a b. of two years,** écrire à qn après un silence de deux ans; *El:* **b.,** (i) rupture *f* du circuit; (ii) disjoncteur *m*, disrupteur *m*, éclateur *m*; **b. spark,** étincelle *f* d'extra-courant de rupture; *Tg:* **b. signal,** repos *m*; **b. key,** touche *f* d'interruption; *Typ:* **b. line,** dernière ligne (d'un alinéa); (*b*) **b. in the weather,** changement de temps; **b. in the heatwave,** fin *f* de la vague de chaleur; (*c*) *Biol: Breed:* variation sportive; mutation *f*; (*d*) *St.Exch:* **b. in prices, in stocks,** effondrement *m* des prix; (*e*) **b. between two friends,** rupture, brouille *f*, entre deux amis; (*f*) *F:* **to make a (bad) b.,** faire une bourde, une gaffe, un impair; commettre un faux pas, une lourde méprise; (*g*) *F:* **to make a b. for it,** s'évader; (*h*) brisure (d'une ligne); *Const:* brisis *m* (d'un comble); angle *m*, coude *m* (d'un mur); (*i*) déviation *f*; *Games:* effet *m* (de la balle); **to put a b. on the ball,** donner de l'effet à la balle; (*j*) *F:* **we had a lucky b.,** nous avons eu de la veine; **he had a bad b.,** il n'a pas eu de chance; **give me a b.,** (i) laissez moi essayer; (ii) ne soyez pas si dur pour moi. **2.** (*a*) (moment *m* de) repos *m*, répit *m*; pause *f*; **with an hour's b. for lunch,** avec une heure de battement pour le déjeuner; **the coffee b., the tea b.,** la pause-café; **a weekend in the country makes a pleasant b.,** un week-end à la campagne offre un repos agréable; (*b*) *Sch:* intervalle *m* (entre les classes); récréation *f* (d'interclasse); **it happened during b.,** c'est arrivé pendant la récréation; (*c*) *Mus:* pause; (*in jazz*) break *m*. **3. b. of day,** point *m* du jour; aube *f*, aurore *f*; **at b. of day,** à l'aube. **4.** série *f*; *Bill:* série, suite *f* (de carambolages). **5.** *Agr:* sole *f*.

break[2], *v.*

I. *v.tr. & i.* (**broke** [brouk], *A:* **brake** [breik]; *p.p.* **broken** ['broukn]).

1. *v.tr.* (*a*) casser, briser, rompre, (i) casser, briser (un verre); casser, rompre (un bâton); casser (une corde); briser, rompre (ses chaînes); rompre (les rangs); **to b. a pound note,** entamer un billet d'une livre; faire la monnaie d'un billet d'une livre; **to b. one's arm, one's neck,** se casser le bras, se rompre le cou; **to b. sth. in(to) pieces,** mettre, briser, qch. en morceaux; *Tex:* **to b. flax,** battre, teiller, le lin; **to b. wool,** louveter la laine; *Min: etc:* **to b. the ore,** concasser le minerai; *Cr:* **to b. the wicket,** démolir le guichet; **to b. a window pane,** casser, briser, enfoncer, un carreau; **he's, she's, always breaking things,** il, elle, fait toujours de la casse; *A:* **to b. bread with s.o.,** rompre le pain avec qn; *B:* **He brake bread,** il rompit le pain; **to b. the enemy's lines,** enfoncer, rompre, les lignes ennemies; **to b. the ties of friendship,** briser les liens de l'amitié; **to b. an abscess,** crever un abcès; **to b. the skin,** entamer la peau; **to b. ground,** (*α*) *Agr:* commencer à labourer; (*β*) *Civ.E: etc:* donner les premiers coups de pioche; (*γ*) entamer le travail; (*δ*) *Nau:* déraper; **to b. new, fresh, ground,** (*α*) *Agr:* mettre un terrain vierge, une lande, en culture; défricher, déchaumer, une terre; frayer un sentier vierge; (*β*) faire œuvre de pionnier; innover; *Av:* **to b. the sound barrier,** franchir le mur du son; (ii) **to b. a set (of china, etc.),** dépareiller un service (de table); (iii) *El:* interrompre (le courant); rompre, couper, ouvrir (un circuit); (iv) **to b. step,** rompre le pas; **to b. a charm, (the) silence, one's fast,** rompre un charme, le silence, le jeûne; **the silence was broken by a cry,** un cri traversa le silence; **to b. the thread of a story,** interrompre, couper, le fil d'une narration; **to b. one's journey at . . .,** s'arrêter en route, interrompre son voyage, à . . .; faire étape à . . .; *Nau:* faire escale à . . .; *Ten:* **to b. one's opponent's service,** gagner le service de son adversaire; (v) **to b. joint,** (*α*) *Metalw:* alterner les joints; croiser, contrarier, les joints; (*β*) *Const:* (*of wall*) perdre la liaison; (*b*) **to b. a branch from a tree,** détacher une branche d'un arbre; (*c*) **to b. s.o. of a bad habit,** faire perdre à qn une mauvaise habitude; corriger, guérir, qn d'une mauvaise habitude; **to b. oneself of a habit,** se défaire, se corriger, d'une habitude; (*d*) (i) **to b. a way,** se frayer, s'ouvrir, un chemin; (ii) **to b. gaol,** forcer sa prison; s'évader de prison; *Mil: Sch:* **to b. bounds,** violer la consigne; aller dans un endroit défendu; **insolence that has broken all bounds,** insolence qui ne connaît plus de bornes; (*e*) (i) **to b. s.o.'s heart,** briser le cœur à qn; **to b. s.o.'s spirit,** rompre le caractère, abattre les forces, briser le courage, de qn; **to b. s.o.'s pride,** abattre, dompter, l'orgueil de qn; **to b. (down) s.o.'s resistance,** briser la résistance de qn; **to b. s.o. into the work,** rompre qn à un travail; *Equit:* **to b. a horse,** rompre, plier, réduire, un cheval; gagner la volonté d'un cheval; (ii) **to b. a strike,** briser une grève; faire avorter une grève; (*f*) (i) **to b. a fall,** amortir, atténuer, une chute; **to b. the force of a blow,** amortir, rompre, un coup; **to b. (the force of) the wind, the current,** arrêter le vent; rompre le courant; (ii) **to b. the news gently to s.o.,** apprendre une (mauvaise) nouvelle doucement à qn; faire part d'une nouvelle à qn avec tous les ménagements possibles; (*g*) (i) **to b. s.o.** (*of losses, etc.*) ruiner qn; (*of grief*) briser qn; (*of age, illness*) casser qn; **to b. the bank,** faire sauter la banque; (ii) *Mil:* **to b. an officer,** casser un officier; (*h*) (i) violer, enfreindre, ne pas observer (la loi); rompre, enfreindre, violer (une trêve) **to b. the peace,** troubler, violer, l'ordre public; **to b. the Sabbath,** violer le repos dominical; ne pas observer le dimanche; **to b. one's word, one's promise; to b. faith with s.o.,** manquer de parole (à qn); fausser parole (à qn); violer sa promesse; manquer à sa promesse; **to b. an appointment,** manquer à un rendez-vous; *Nau:* **to b. the quarantine regulations,** violer la quarantaine; **my sleep was broken by the noise of the traffic,** le bruit de la circulation a interrompu mon sommeil; (ii) résilier (un contrat); (iii) *Nau:* **to b. a flag, a signal,** déferler un drapeau, un signal. **2.** *v.i.* (*a*) (i) se casser, se rompre, se fracturer, se briser; (*of limbs*) se fracturer; (*of wave*) se briser, déferler, s'écraser; (*of bubble, abscess*) crever; (*of abscess*) percer; **the branch broke,** la branche s'est cassée, s'est rompue; **the sea was breaking against the rocks,** la mer battait les rochers; **the clouds are breaking,** les nuages se dissipent, se dispersent; (ii) (*of troops, etc.*) se débander; **the troops broke and fled,** les troupes lâchèrent pied, les troupes rompirent devant l'ennemi, et prirent la fuite; (iii) *Fenc:* rompre la mesure; rompre; (*b*) (i) (*of heart*) se briser; se fendre, crever; (*of health*) s'altérer, se détraquer, se délabrer, se ruiner; (*of weather*) changer, se gâter; (*of frost*) s'adoucir; (*of heatwave*) passer, prendre fin; **the frost has broken,** le temps est, se met, au dégel; **the frost was breaking,** c'était le dégel; (ii) **their spirit did not b.,** ils ne se laissèrent pas abattre; **his voice is beginning to b.,** sa voix commence à muer; **his voice broke with emotion,** sa voix s'altéra, se troubla, s'étrangla, sous le coup de l'émotion; (*c*) *O:* (*of business, etc.*) faire faillite; (*of bank*) sauter; (*d*) **to b. with s.o., with the traditional ways of life,** rompre, briser, avec qn, avec la vie traditionnelle; rompre toutes relations avec qn; **to b. with one's colleagues,** se désolidariser de, d'avec, ses collègues; *Box: Wr:* **b.!** break! (*e*) (i) **to b. into a house,** entrer de force, s'introduire par effraction, pénétrer, dans une maison; (*of burglar*) cambrioler une maison; **to b. into a room,** entrer en trombe, faire irruption, dans une pièce; envahir une salle; **to b. into the till,** forcer la caisse; **to b. into a pot of jam, a cake,** entamer un pot de confiture, un gâteau; (ii) **to b. into laughter, into sobs,** éclater de rire; partir d'un éclat de rire; éclater en sanglots; **to b. into a tune,** entonner un air; **to b. into explanations,** se répandre en explications; **to b. into a trot,** prendre le trot, se mettre au trot, passer au trot, partir au trot; **her face broke into a radiant smile,** son visage s'épanouit en un sourire radieux; (*f*) (i) **to b. out of prison,** s'échapper, s'évader, de prison; *Lit:* **to b. from one's bonds,** briser ses liens, ses fers; (ii) **a cry broke from his lips,** un cri s'échappa de ses lèvres; (iii) **day was beginning to b.,** le jour commençait à poindre, à paraître, à se lever; (iv) **the storm broke,** la tempête éclata, se déchaîna; (*g*) (i) **the ball breaks,** la balle a de l'effet; la balle dévie en touchant terre; la balle fait faux bond; (ii) *Bill:* **to b.,** donner l'acquit.

II. (*compound verbs*) **1. break away,** (*a*) *v.tr.* détacher (qch.) (**from,** de); (*b*) *v.i.* (i) (*of thg*) se détacher (**from,** de); (*of railway carriages*) partir en dérive; (*of pers.*) se dégager, se détacher (**from,** de); s'échapper, s'évader; **to b. away from a party,** lâcher, abandonner, un parti; *Box:* **to make the opponents b. away,** briser un corps-à-corps; **b. away!** séparez! (ii) *Mil: O:* (*of troops*) rompre les rangs; (iii) *St.Exch:* (*of prices*) s'effondrer.

2. break back, *v.i.* rebrousser chemin.

3. break down, (*a*) *v.tr.* (i) abattre (un mur, *Min:* le charbon); démolir, renverser (un mur, etc.); rompre (un pont); **to b. down all opposition,** vaincre toute opposition; avoir raison de toute opposition; forcer toutes les barricades; **to b. down all resistance,** briser toute résistance; (ii) **to b. down a substance,** concasser, broyer; *Ch:* décomposer, une substance; (iii) *Ch:* dissocier (des molécules); (iv) *Com:* **to b. d. an account,** décomposer un compte; (*b*) *v.i.* (i) (*of health*) s'altérer, se détraquer, s'ébranler, décliner; (*of the mind*) s'ébranler, sombrer; (*of plan*) échouer, s'effondrer; (*of bridge, etc.*) s'effondrer; **the negotiations broke down,** les négociations furent rompues; **the argument breaks down,** l'argument s'effondre; **his mind broke down,** sa raison sombra; **his resistance will b. down in due course,** sa résistance s'usera à la fin; (ii) (*of pers.*) s'arrêter tout court, demeurer court (dans un discours); éclater en sanglots, fondre en larmes; tomber malade (de fatigue); (iii) (*of car, machinery, etc.*) tomber, rester, en panne; (*of ship, etc.*) subir une avarie.

4. break in, (*a*) *v.tr.* (i) enfoncer (une porte, etc.); défoncer (un tonneau); (ii) rompre, mater, dresser, arrondir, assouplir (un cheval); **to b. oneself in to sth.,** se rompre à qch.; **to be broken in,** être plié au métier; (iii) culotter (une pipe); **to b. in a pair of shoes,** briser des souliers neufs; faire des chaussures à son pied; (*b*) *v.i.* (i) **to b. in (on s.o.),** faire irruption (chez qn); intervenir; s'interposer; **to b. in on a conversation,** interrompre une conversation; **to b. in on the enemy,** enfoncer l'ennemi; (ii) (*of burglar*) s'introduire par effraction.

5. break loose, *v.i.* (*a*) se dégager de ses liens; s'évader, s'échapper, s'affranchir (**from,** de); **all hell has broken loose,** les diables sont déchaînés; (*b*) **his fury broke loose,** sa fureur se déchaîna; (*c*) (*of ship*) partir à la dérive.

6. break off, (*a*) *v.tr.* (i) casser, rompre (qch.); détacher (qch.) (**from,** de); **our mast was broken off short,** notre mât se cassa au ras du pont; (ii) interrompre, abandonner (son travail, une discussion); cesser (des relations d'affaires, etc.); rompre (des négociations); **the engagement is broken off,** le mariage est rompu; (*b*) *v.i.* (i) se détacher, se dégager (**from, sth.,** de qch.); se détacher (net); se casser (net); (ii) discontinuer; **to b. off in the middle of a speech,** s'arrêter dans un discours; **to b. off for ten minutes,** interrompre le travail pendant dix minutes; prendre dix minutes de repos; **it's time to b. off,** il est l'heure de cesser le travail.

7. break open, *v.tr.* enfoncer, forcer (une porte); forcer, fracturer (une serrure, un coffre-fort); enfoncer, éventrer (une caisse); faire sauter (une serrure); *v.i.* **the packing case broke open in transit,** la caisse s'est cassée en cours de route.

8. break out, (*a*) *v.i.* (i) (*of war, fire, disease*) éclater, se déclarer; **if a fire should b. out,** si le feu venait à se déclarer; s'il y avait un incendie; **to b. out again,** (*of conflagration, quarrel*) se raviver; (*of wound*) se rouvrir; (*of war*) se rallumer; (ii) (*of the face, etc.*) **to b. out in spots,** se couvrir de boutons; **to b. out into a sweat,** se mettre à transpirer; être pris d'une sueur; entrer en moiteur; (*b*) *v.i.* (i) s'échapper, s'évader (de prison, etc.); (ii) faire une fugue; (iii) *Cmptr:* **to b. out of a loop,** sortir d'une boucle; (*c*) *v.i.* (*of flag*) se déferler; (*d*) *v.tr.* (i) *Min:* brancher (une nouvelle galerie); (ii) *U.S:* ouvrir (une boîte, une bouteille, etc.); sortir (qch.) de sa cachette; (iii) *U.S:* déferler (un drapeau).

9. break through, *v.tr.* **to b. through a barrier,** *v.i.* **to b. through,** enfoncer une barrière; se frayer un passage; **to b. a wall,** faire une brèche dans, à, un mur; **the sun is breaking through (the clouds),** le soleil perce les nuages; **he broke through the crowd,** il s'est frayé (violemment) un chemin à travers la foule; il a percé la foule; **he breaks through all obstacles,** il enfonce tous les obstacles; **the rock breaks through (the surface) in places,** le roc affleure par endroits; *Mil:* **to b. (the enemy lines),** faire une percée; se faire jour à travers les lignes ennemies; *Av:* **to b. through the sound barrier,** franchir le mur du son.

10. break up, (*a*) *v.tr.* mettre (qch.) en morceaux; démolir (un bâtiment, etc.); dépecer, démembrer (une volaille, etc.); démolir, détruire, déborder (un navire); défoncer, *Agr:* ameublir (un terrain); défoncer (une route); *Ch:* résoudre (un composé); morceler (une propriété); démembrer, fragmenter (un empire); disperser (la foule, une famille); dissoudre (une assemblée); rompre, interrompre (une conférence); rompre (une coalition, l'unité nationale); **to b. up a word into syllables,** décomposer un mot en syllabes; **the country was broken up into factions,** le pays était divisé en factions; **to b. up the work,** répartir, fragmenter, le travail; *Typ:* **to b. up copy,** multiplier les alinéas; *Ten:* **to b. up an opponent's game,** casser la cadence d'un adversaire; **to b. up a fight,** séparer des combattants; *F:* **b. it up!** la paix! **their household has been broken up,** toute la famille s'est dispersée; **he broke up his marriage,** il a laissé sa femme; il a détruit son foyer; **he broke up their marriage,** il a causé leur séparation; *P:* **that's all right, b. up the happy home!** faites chauffer la colle! (*b*) *v.i.* (i) (*of empire, ship, etc.*) se démembrer; (*of crowd, etc.*) se disperser; (*of road surface, etc.*) se désagréger; (*of road*) se défoncer; (*of ice*) débâcler; **ship breaking up,** navire *m* en perdition; *F:* **he is beginning to b. up,** il commence à se casser, à décliner; (ii) (*of company, meeting*) se séparer; (*of groups*) se disjoindre; **when the meeting broke up,** à l'issue de la réunion; **the meeting broke up in confusion,** la séance fut levée dans le tumulte; **their marriage has broken up,** ils ont cessé de vivre ensemble; **the clouds are breaking up,** les nuages se dissipent, se dispersent; (iii) *Sch:* entrer en vacances; **we b. up on the fourth,** nos vacances commencent le quatre; **we broke up for the day,** on nous a congédiés pour le reste de la journée; (iv) (*of weather*) se gâter, se brouiller.

break[3], *s.* **1.** (*a*) *A.Veh:* break *m*; (*b*) voiture *f* de dressage (des chevaux). **2.** *Aut:* **(shooting) b.,** break (de chasse); voiture utilitaire.

break[4], *v.tr. Tex:* = BRAKE[5].

breakable ['breikəbl]. **1.** *a.* cassable; cassant, fragile. **2.** *s.pl.* **breakables,** objets *m* fragiles.

breakage ['breikidʒ], *s.* **1.** rupture *f* (d'une chaîne, d'un arbre d'hélice, etc.); bris *m*, fracture *f* (de verre, etc.). **2.** (i) casse *f*; (ii) colis démolis; **to pay for breakages,** payer la casse.

breakaway ['breikəwei], *s.* **1.** sécession *f*, désertion *f* (**from,** de). **2.** *Sp:* (*a*) *Box:* séparation *f* (de deux boxeurs); (*b*) *Fb:* échappée *f* (de l'ailier, etc.). **3.** (*a*) *Rail:* dérive *f* (de wagons); (*b*) *Austr:* ruée *f*, débandade *f* (d'un troupeau); (*c*) *F:* (*of pers.*) **he's a proper b.,** c'est un rebelle; (*d*) *attrib.* **b. union,** syndicat dissident. **4.** *Th: Cin:* décor *m* de scène qui doit s'effondrer (tremblement de terre, etc.).

breakback ['breikbæk], *a.* (*a*) qui brise les reins; **b. trap,** (piège *m*) assommoir *m*; (*b*) *F:* accablant; (travail) éreintant.

breakbone ['breikboun], *a. Med: F:* **b. fever,** dengue *f*.

breakdown ['breikdaun], *s.* **1.** (*a*) insuccès *m* (d'une tentative); débâcle *f* (d'une maison commerciale, d'un gouvernement); rupture *f* (des négociations); écroulement *m* (d'un système); arrêt complet, perturbation *f* (dans un service); **complete b. of all means of transport,** paralysie générale des moyens de transport; (*b*) débâcle, écroulement (de la santé); **nervous b.,** épuisement nerveux; dépression, prostration, nerveuse; **mental b.,** effondrement *m* de la raison; (*c*) panne *f*; *Trans:* avarie *f* de route; **b. service,** service *m* de dépannage; **b. mechanic,** dépanneur *m*; **b. gang,** (i) *Aut:* équipe *f* de dépannage; (ii) *Rail:* corvée *f* de secours; **b. van, lorry, vehicle,** *NAm:* **truck,** camion *m* de dépannage; dépanneuse *f*; camion-grue *m, pl.* camions-grues; **we had a b. on the way home,** en rentrant, nous sommes tombés, restés, en panne. **2.** *El:* claquage *m*; **b. test,** essai *m* de claquage; **b. voltage,** tension *f* claque; **b. of a condenser,** claque *f* d'un condensateur. **3.** *Ch:* dissociation *f*. **4.** analyse *f*; décomposition *f*; **statistical b.,** analyse statistique; **b. of population,** répartition *f*, classement *m*, de la population (par classes, âges, etc.); *Com:* **b. of expenses,** décomposition des dépenses.

breaker[1] ['breikər], *s.* **1.** (*pers.*) (*a*) casseur, -euse; briseur, -euse; **stone b.,** casseur de pierres; **car b.,** casseur de voitures; **breaker's yard,** chantier de démolition (de voitures, navires, etc.); **strike b.,** casseur de grèves; (*b*) dresseur, -euse, entraîneur *m* (de chevaux, etc.); (*c*) violateur, -trice, infracteur, -trice (d'une loi, etc.); **b. of the Sabbath,** violateur, -trice, du repos dominical. **2.** (*apparatus*) (*a*) brisoir *m*, appareil casseur; concasseur *m*; *Paperm:* pilon *m*; **b. (engine),** défilateur *m*, défileur *m*; (pile) défileuse (*f*), effilocheuse (*f*); *Agr:* **clod b.,** brise-mottes *m inv*; rouleur *m* brise-mottes; émotteuse *f*; casse-mottes *m inv*; *Nau:* **ice b.,** brise-glace(s) *m inv*; *Civ.E:* concasseur *m*, broyeur *m*; casse-pierre(s) *m inv*; dérocheuse *f*; **underwater rock b.,** brise-roc *m inv* sous-marin; **stone b.,** casse-pierre(s) *m inv*; concasseur *m*; (*b*) *El:* **circuit b.,** coupe-circuit *m inv*, disjoncteur *m*, interrupteur *m*, rupteur *m*; **minimum circuit b.,** disjoncteur à minimum; **self-closing circuit b.,** conjoncteur-disjoncteur *m, pl.* conjoncteurs-disjoncteurs; **zero circuit b.,** commutateur *m* à zéro. **3.** *Nau:* vague déferlante; **a b. swept over the beach,** une vague a déferlé sur la plage; **breakers ahead!** des brisants *m* devant!

breaker[2], *s. Nau:* baril *m* de galère.

break even ['breik'i:vn], *v.i.* équilibrer son budget; ne faire ni pertes ni profits, rentrer dans ses frais, *F:* dans son argent; *Cards:* cesser la partie à jeu égal.

break-even ['breik'i:vn], *a.* à budget équilibré; **b.-e. deal,** affaire blanche; **b.-e. point,** seuil *m* de rentabilité.

breakfast[1] ['brekfəst], *s.* petit déjeuner; **to have (one's) b. at 7 o'clock,** déjeuner, prendre le, son, déjeuner, à 7 heures; **b. time,** l'heure *f* du (petit) déjeuner; **b. cup (and saucer),** déjeuner; **b. set, service,** service *m* à déjeuner; **b. cereals,** céréales *fpl* (en flocons); **wedding b.,** repas *m* de noces; **there were six of us round the b. table, to b.,** nous étions six à déjeuner; **a working b.,** un petit déjeuner d'affaires.

breakfast[2], *v.i.* déjeuner (le matin); **to b. off a piece of bread,** déjeuner d'un morceau de pain.

breakfaster ['brekfəstər], *s.* déjeuneur, -euse.

breakfront ['breikfrʌnt], *a. & s.* (meuble *m*) à contour brisé.

break-in ['breikin]. **1.** *s.* (*a*) (*by burglars, etc.*) effraction *f*; *Mil:* pénétration *f* (du dispositif ennemi); irruption *f* (dans les lignes adverses); (*b*) *Mec.E: NAm:* rodage *m*. **2.** *attrib. Cmptr: etc:* **b.-in period,** période *f* de rodage.

breaking[1] ['breikiŋ], *a.* (*a*) (*with noun prefixed*) qui brise, rompt, enfreint; **back-b. work,** travail éreintant; (*b*) en train de se briser; à bout de résistance; **with a b. heart,** le cœur brisé; (*c*) **b. point,** (i) *Mec.E: etc:* limite *f* critique (de résistance); point *m* de rupture; (ii) **to try s.o.'s patience to b. point,** pousser à bout la patience de qn; **everything has its b. point,** quand la corde est trop tendue elle se casse.

breaking[2], *s.* **1.** (*a*) rupture *f* (d'un tendon, d'un pont, d'un traité); brisement *m* (d'une statue); concassage *m* (du minerai); *Jur:* (i) bris *m* (d'une vitre, de scellés); (ii) levée *f* (de scellés); *Ling:* fracture *f* (d'une voyelle); *I.C.E:* **b. of a ring,** bris d'un segment; *Mec.E:* **b. load,** charge *f* de rupture; **b. strain,** tension *f* de rupture; *El:* **b. of the circuit,** rupture du circuit, interruption *f* du courant; **sparkless b.,** interruption sans étincelles; (*b*) **b. and entering,** entrée *f* par effraction dans une maison; (*c*) **b. of the law,** violation *f* de la loi, infraction *f* à la loi; **b. of the Sabbath,** violation du repos dominical; **b. of one's word,** manque *m* de parole; (*d*) amortissement *m*, atténuation *f* (d'une chute). **2.** (*a*) brisement (des flots); (*b*) *Med:* aboutissement *m* (d'un abcès); (*c*) **b. of the voice,** (i) (*at manhood*) muance *f*, mue *f*, altération *f*; (ii) (*with emotion*) altération de la voix. **3. b. of new ground,** (i) défrichage *m*, (ii) œuvre *f* de pionnier; **the b. of the German power,** la destruction de la puissance allemande.

breaking down ['breikiŋ'daun], *s.* **1.** (*a*) abattage *m* (d'un mur, etc.); rupture *f* (d'un pont); (*b*) (i) concassage *m*; broiement *m*; (ii) *Ch:* décomposition *f* (d'une substance). **2.** altération *f* (de la santé). **3.** panne *f* (d'une auto, etc.).

breaking in ['breikiŋ'in], *s.* **1.** enfoncement *m* (d'une porte, etc.); défonçage *m*, défoncement *m* (d'un tonneau); effraction *f*. **2.** (*a*) dressage *m*, assouplissement *m* (d'un cheval); manège *m*; adaptation *f*, formation *f*; assouplissement du caractère (d'un enfant); (*b*) culottage *m* (d'une pipe). **3.** irruption *f* (dans une compagnie); interruption *f* (d'une conversation).

breaking off ['breikiŋ'ɔf], *s.* **1.** rupture *f* (d'un mariage, des négociations); interruption *f*, abandon *m* (d'un travail). **2.** pause *f*, arrêt *m* (dans un discours).

breaking open ['breikiŋ'oupn], *s.* fracture *f* (d'une porte, etc.).

breaking out ['breikiŋ'aut], *s.* **1.** éruption *f* (de boutons). **2.** (*a*) évasion *f* (d'un prisonnier); (*b*) fugues *fpl*, bordées *fpl*. **3.** *Min:* branchement *m*.

breaking up ['breikiŋ'ʌp], *s.* **1.** démolition *f* (d'un édifice); défoncement *m*, premier labourage (d'un terrain); broyage *m*, décomposition *f* (d'une substance); dissolution *f* (d'une assemblée); dispersion *f* (d'une foule); morcellement *m* (d'un pays, d'une propriété); dépècement *m*, démembrement *m* (d'un navire); démembrement, fragmentation *f* (d'un empire); **b. up of the work between several collaborators,** fragmentation, répartition *f*, du travail entre plusieurs collaborateurs. **2.** (*a*) séparation *f* (d'une assemblée, d'une famille); désagrégation *f* (d'une famille); **on the b. up of the meeting,** au sortir, à l'issue, de la réunion; (*b*) *Sch:* entrée *f* en vacances; **b.-up party,** soirée *f* de fin de trimestre; (*c*) débâcle *f* (des glaces).

break iron ['breikaiən], *s. Tls:* contre-fer *m* (de rabot), *pl.* contre-fers.

breakneck ['breiknek], *a.* **it was a b. path,** le sentier était un véritable casse-cou; **to go at a b. speed, at a b. pace,** filer à une vitesse, à une allure, folle, vertigineuse; galoper, conduire, à fond de train, à tombeau ouvert.

breakpoint ['breikpɔint], *s.* point *m* d'arrêt, d'interruption; *Cmptr:* **b. instruction,** instruction *f* de renvoi (en cas d'interruption); **b. switch,** bouton *m* de commande d'aiguillage; **b. symbol,** symbole *m* de renvoi.

breakthrough ['breikθru:], *s.* (*a*) *Geol:* affleurement *m*; (*b*) *Mil:* percée *f* (des lignes ennemies); (*c*) poussée *f*, hausse soudaine (des prix); (*d*) percée (technologique), bond *m* en avant; solution soudaine (à un problème scientifique); découverte (sensationnelle); invention *f* révolutionnaire.

breakup ['breikʌp], *s.* **1.** (*a*) dissolution *f*, fin *f*, éclatement *m* (d'un empire, d'une assemblée); affaissement *m* (des forces physiques); bris *m* (d'un navire, etc.); (*b*) *attrib. Com:* **b. price,** prix *m* de liquidation. **2.** changement *m* (du temps); **the b. of the frost,** le dégel; **the b. of the ice,** la débâcle (des glaces).

breakwater ['breikwɔ:tər], *s.* **1.** brise-lames *m inv*; môle *m*; jetée *f*; estacade *f*. **2.** éperon *m* (d'un pont).

break-wind ['breikwind], *s. esp. U.S:* brise-vent *m inv*.

bream[1] [bri:m], *s. Ich:* brème *f*; **sea b.,** (i) pagel *m*, pagelle *f*; (ii) castagnole *f*; (iii) brème de mer, brème des rochers, canthère *m*; **Ray's b.,** brème des mer; **gilthead b.,** dorade (méditerranéenne); **Mediterranean b.,** saupe *f*; *Aust:* **black b.,** girelle *f*.

bream[2], *v.tr. Nau:* flamber (un navire).

breast[1] [brest], *s.* **1.** sein *m*, mamelle *f*; **to give a child the b.,** donner le sein à un enfant; **child at the b.,** enfant au sein; *Med:* **b. exhauster, b. reliever,** téterelle *f*, tire-lait *m inv*; **b. pump,** pompe *f* à sein; tire-lait, téterelle. **2.** (*a*) poitrine *f* (de personne, d'animal); poitrail *m* (de cheval); devant *m* (d'une chemise, etc.); **to press s.o. to one's b.,** serrer qn sur son cœur; **shot under the left b.,** atteint d'une balle au-dessous du sein gauche; **to make a clean b. of it,** tout avouer; faire des aveux complets; *Box:* **b.-to-b. struggle,** corps-à-corps *m*; **b. high, b. deep,** jusqu'à la poitrine; **we were b. deep in water,** nous avions de l'eau jusqu'à la poitrine; **b. high,** à hauteur d'appui; **the grass was b. high,** l'herbe nous montait jusqu' à la poitrine; *Cost:* **b. pocket,** poche *f* de poitrine; **inside b. pocket,** poche intérieure, (à) portefeuille; *NAm:* **b. pin,** (i) broche *f* (de femme); (ii) épingle *f* de cravate; *Swim:* **b. stroke,** brasse *f*; **to swim b. stroke,** nager (à) la brasse; *Harn:* **b. strap,** poitrail *m*; **b. band,** tablier *m*; **b. harness,** bricole *f* (pour cheval); (*b*) *Cu:* blanc *m* (de volaille); avant-cœur *m* (de bœuf). **3.** (*a*) *Metall:* ventre *m* (de haut fourneau); (*b*) *Const:* **chimney b.,** revêtement *m* du conduit de fumée avançant dans la pièce; **b. wall,** (i) mur *m* de soutènement; (ii) allège *f* de fenêtre; mur à hauteur d'appui; (*c*) *Nau: N.Arch:* **b. hook,** guirlande *f*; **b. rail,** lisse *f* d'appui; lisse de fronteau; **b. rope,** sangle *f*; amarre *f* de travers; *Mil.E:* **b. line,** traversière *f*, amarre (d'un pont de bateaux); (*d*) *Hyd.E:* **b. wheel,** roue *f* de côté. **4.** *Min:* front *m* de taille, d'abattage.

breast[2], *v.tr.* **1.** *Lit:* affronter, faire front à, lutter contre (une tempête, un danger); **to b. a hill,** affronter, gravir, une montagne; (*of swimmer*) **to b. the waves,** fendre la lame. **2.** *Sp:* **to b. the tape,** arriver le premier.

breastbone ['brestboun], *s. Anat:* sternum *m* (d'une personne, d'un animal); bréchet *m*, brechet *m* (d'un oiseau).

-breasted ['brestid], *a.* (*with adj. prefixed, e.g.*) **wide-, narrow-b.,** à poitrine large, étroite; **to be high-b., low-b.,** avoir la poitrine haute, basse.

breast-fed ['brestfed], *a.* (enfant) élevé au sein.

breast-feed ['brestfi:d], *v.tr.* (*p.t.* **-fed** [fed]; *p.p.* **-fed**) élever (un enfant) au sein.

breast-feeding ['brestfi:diŋ], *s.* allaitement (naturel).

breastplate ['brestpleit], *s.* **1.** (*a*) *Arm:* plastron *m*; cuirasse *f*; (*b*) *Ecc:* pectoral *m* (d'un grand-prêtre juif). **2.** *Tls:* plastron, conscience *f*, estomac *m* (de vilebrequin, etc.).

breastsummer ['brestsʌmər], *s. Const:* poitrail *m*, sommier *m*; linteau *m* de baie.

breastwork ['brestwə:k], *s.* parapet *m*, garde-corps *m inv*; *Nau:* fronteau *m* (de dunette).

breath [breθ], *s.* (*a*) haleine *f*, souffle *m*; **to draw b.,** respirer; **give me time to take b.,** donnez-moi le temps de souffler; **to draw, take, a deep, long, b.,** respirer profondément, longuement, à pleins poumons; **to draw one's last b.,** exhaler son dernier souffle; rendre le dernier soupir; **I will resist to my last b.,** je résisterai jusqu'à mon dernier souffle, jusqu'à mon dernier soupir; **with his dying b. he made me promise . . .,** de sa voix agonisante il me fit promettre . . .; **to have sweet b.,** avoir l'haleine douce; **to have bad b.,** avoir mauvaise haleine; sentir de la bouche; *F:* tuer les mouches à quinze pas; **offensive b.,** haleine fétide; **his b. was dreadful,** il nous infectait, nous empestait, de son haleine; **the b. of life,** le souffle vital; le souffle de la vie; *Adm:* **b. test,** alcotest *m*; **it is the very b. of life to me,** cela m'est aussi précieux que la vie même; **music is the b. of life to me,** la musique est une nécessité de mon existence; **all in the same b., in one and the same b., at a b.,** tout d'une haleine; **they are not to be mentioned in the same b.,** on ne saurait les comparer; **to hold one's b.,** retenir son souffle; **to gasp for b.,** haleter; **he caught his b.,** il eut un hoquet d'étouffement, de surprise; il eut un sursaut; la respiration lui manqua; **to lose one's b.,** perdre haleine, **to get one's second b.,** reprendre haleine, retrouver son souffle; **to lose one's b. in dragging sth.,** s'essouffler à traîner qch.; **to waste one's b.,** perdre son temps en discours inutiles; perdre ses paroles; *F:* perdre sa salive; **I am wasting my b.,** c'est comme si je chantais; **it's a waste of b.,** c'est peine perdue; *F:* **you're damn well wasting your b.,** c'est comme si on pissait dans un violon; **keep your b. to cool your porridge,** mêlez-vous de ce qui vous regarde; **to be short of b.,** être essoufflé; avoir la respiration coupée; **shortness of b.,** peine *f* à respirer; essoufflement *m*, manque *m* d'haleine; **I find it very hard to get my b.,** j'ai de la difficulté à respirer; **our b. was beginning to fail,** la respiration commençait à nous manquer; **out of b.,** hors d'haleine, à bout de souffle; essoufflé; **to get out of b.,** perdre haleine; **to make s.o. out of b.,** faire perdre haleine à qn; **to run till one is out of b., to run oneself out of b.,** courir à perdre haleine; **to talk oneself out of b.,** s'essouffler à force de parler; **I shook the b. out of him,** je l'ai secoué à lui faire perdre haleine; **to take s.o.'s b. away,** couper la respiration, le souffle, à qn; ébahir, interloquer, qn; *F:* couper le sifflet à qn; **it quite takes my b. away,** cela me coupe la respiration; je n'en reviens pas; j'en ai le souffle coupé; **to take b.; to get, recover, one's b.,** souffler; reprendre haleine; **when I had got my b. back . . .,** quand je fus remis (de cette surprise, etc.) . . .; **to speak, say, sth. under one's b.,** parler d'une voix très basse, à (de)mi-voix, à voix basse; **to swear under one's b.,** jurer en sourdine; **the first b. of spring,** les premiers effluves du printemps; **there is not a b. of wind, of air,** il n'y a pas un souffle de vent, d'air; **b. of stale tobacco,** relent *m* de tabac; **not a b. of suspicion attaches to him,** (i) il est au-dessus de tout soupçon; (ii) personne ne le soupçonne; (*b*) *attrib. Ling:* **b. consonant,** consonne soufflante.

breathable ['bri:ðəbl], *a.* respirable.

breathableness ['bri:ðəblnis], *s.* respirabilité *f*.

breathalyse ['breθəlaiz], *v.tr.* donner l'alcotest *m* à (qn).

breathalyser ['breθəlaizər], *s. Adm:* **b. test,** alcotest *m*.

breathe [bri:ð].

I. *v.i.* (*a*) respirer, souffler; **to b. hard,** (i) souffler, haleter; respirer avec peine; (ii) souffler fort, souffler à pleins poumons; **to b. heavily,** (i) respirer bruyamment; (ii) respirer péniblement, (*with exertion*) ahaner; **to b. with difficulty,** avoir la respiration difficile; avoir (de la) peine à respirer; **to b. again, freely,** respirer de nouveau, librement; **is that all? I breathed again,** n'est-ce que cela? je respirai; **all that breathes,** tout ce qui respire; **the best man that ever breathed,** le meilleur homme qui ait jamais vécu; **to b. on one's fingers,** souffler dans ses doigts; **to b. upon a mirror,** souffler sur une glace; *F:* **to b. down s.o.'s neck,** talonner qn; **to b. (into) a wind instrument,** souffler dans un instrument à vent; (*b*) (*of voice, instrument, wind*) soupirer, souffler doucement; (*c*) **the spirit that breathes through his work,** l'esprit qui anime ses œuvres.

II. *v.tr. or ind.tr.* **1.** respirer (l'air); **to b. in, b. out, the air,** aspirer, exhaler, l'air; **to b. in the pure air,** humer, aspirer, l'air pur; **to b. air into sth.,** insuffler de l'air dans qch. **2. to b. courage into s.o.,** inspirer du courage à qn; **to b. new life into s.o., into a conversation,** ranimer qn, une conversation. **3.** (*a*) **to b. a sigh,** exhaler, laisser échapper, un soupir; **he breathed a sigh of relief,** il poussa un soupir de soulagement; **to b. a prayer,** murmurer une prière; *Lit:* **to b. one's last,** exhaler son dernier souffle; rendre le dernier soupir; rendre l'âme; **I was with him when he breathed his last,** c'est moi qui ai reçu son dernier soupir; **he was already breathing his last,** il était déjà agonisant; **don't b. a word (of it)!** n'en soufflez (pas un) mot! (*b*) **to b. simplicity, health, etc.,** respirer la simplicité, la santé, etc.; (*c*) *Ling:* aspirer (un son); **the h is breathed in German,** l'h est aspirée en allemand. **4.** laisser souffler (un cheval). **5.** *A:* mettre (qn) hors d'haleine.

breathed [bri:ðd], *a. Ling:* **1.** (consonne) sourde, forte. **2.** (voyelle) aspirée.

breather ['bri:ðər], *s.* **1.** *F:* moment *m* de repos (pour souffler); **to give s.o. a b.,** laisser souffler qn; laisser un moment de répit à qn; **to give a horse a b.,** faire souffler un cheval; **to go for a b.,** aller respirer un peu d'air; sortir prendre l'air, un brin d'air. **2.** *I.C.E:* **b. (pipe)** (*of crank case*), renifleur *m*, reniflard *m*, évent *m*; tuyau *m* d'aspiration. **3. mouth b.,** personne *f* qui respire par la bouche.

breathiness ['breθinis], *s.* (*a*) respiration bruyante; (*b*) *Mus:* manque *m* d'attaque (d'une voix.).

breathing[1] ['bri:ðiŋ], *a.* (*of picture, statue*) vivant, qui respire.

breathing[2], *s.* **1.** (*a*) (*of pers.*) respiration *f*; souffle *m*; (*of wind*) souffle; **heavy b.,** (i) respiration bruyante; (ii) respiration pénible; oppression *f*; **mouth b.,** respiration par la bouche; **b. helmet,** casque *m* respiratoire (de pompier, etc.); *Min: etc:* **b. apparatus,** appareil *m* respiratoire, masque *m* de protection; **oxygen b. apparatus,** inhalateur *m* d'oxygène; **b. space,** (i) (*also* **b. time**) le temps de souffler, de respirer; répit *m*, relâche *f*; intervalle *m* de repos; (ii) place *f*, espace *m*, pour respirer; (*b*) **b. hole,** (i) soupirail *m*; (ii) trou *m* de fausset (d'un fût); (*c*) *Bot:* **b. stem,** racine-asperge *f*, *pl.* racines-asperges. **2.** *Ling:* (*a*) aspiration *f* (d'un son); (*b*) *Gr.Gram:* **rough, smooth, b.,** esprit rude, doux.

breathless ['breθlis], *a.* **1.** (*after exertion*) hors d'haleine, essoufflé, haletant, époumoné; **b. with running,** hors d'haleine, essoufflé, d'avoir couru; **b. chase,** poursuite *f* à perte d'haleine; **in b. haste,** en toute hâte; **b. style,** style échevelé. **2. b. suspense,** attente fiévreuse; **to wait in b. suspense,** attendre en retenant son haleine; **a few b. minutes,** quelques minutes angoissantes; (*of book, etc.*) **to hold s.o. b.,** tenir qn en haleine, en suspens. **3.** (*a*) **b. evening,** soirée *f* sans un souffle de vent; (*b*) *A. & Lit:* (*of pers.*) inanimé; mort.

breathlessly ['breθlisli], *adv.* **1.** en haletant; **to run b. after s.o.,** courir à perte d'haleine après qn. **2.** (attendre, écouter) en retenant son haleine.

breathlessness ['breθlisnis], *s.* essoufflement *m*; respiration essoufflée; (*of patient*) manque *m* de souffle; oppression *f*.

breathtaking ['breθteikiŋ], *a. F:* ahurissant; **it's b.,** c'est à vous couper le souffle.

breath-test ['breθtest], *v.tr. F:* donner l'alcotest à (qn).

breathy ['breθi], *a.* (*a*) **to talk in a b. voice,** respirer bruyamment en parlant; (*b*) *Mus:* (voix) qui manque d'attaque.

breccia ['bretʃ(i)ə], *Geol:* (*rock*) brèche *f*; **b. marble,** marbre *m* brèche.

brecciated ['bretʃieitid], *a. Geol:* bréchiforme.

brecciation [bretʃi'eiʃ(ə)n], *s. Geol:* structure anguleuse (du roc).

brecciola [bretʃi'oulə], *s. Geol:* brecciole *f.*

bred [bred], *a.* élevé; **country-b.,** élevé à la campagne, **town-b.,** élevé à la ville.

bredbergite ['bredbə:gait], *s. Miner:* bredbergite *f.*

breech[1] [bri:tʃ], *s.* **1.** (*a*) *A:* le derrière; *Anthr:* **b. cloth, clout,** bande-culotte *f, pl.* bandes-culottes; (*b*) *Obst;* **b. presentation, delivery,** présentation *f,* accouchement *m,* par le siège; (*c*) *Husb:* **b. wool,** laine *f* cuisse; (*d*) *Harn:* **b. band,** avaloire *f*; (courroie *f* de) reculement *m.* **2.** (*a*) **(pair of) breeches** ['britʃiz], culotte *f*; *A:* **to put a child into breeches,** mettre un enfant en culotte; **knee breeches,** culotte; **riding breeches,** culotte de cheval; (*b*) *F:* pantalon *m,* culotte; *F:* (*of wife*) **to wear the breeches,** porter la culotte; *Th: A:* **breeches part,** rôle d'homme (joué par une femme); (rôle) travesti *m.* **3.** *Artil: Sm.a:* culasse *f,* tonnerre *m*; **b. action, mechanism,** mécanisme *m* de culasse; **b. loader,** fusil *m,* pièce *f,* se chargeant par la culasse; **hinged b. loader,** fusil à bascule; **b. loading,** chargement *m* par la culasse; **b.-loading rifle,** fusil se chargeant par la culasse; *Artil:* **b. block,** bloc *m* de culasse; **b. plug,** obturateur *m*; **b. screw,** vis *f* (de) culasse; *Sm.a:* **b. bolt,** verrou *m* (de fusil).

breech[2], *v.tr.* **1.** *F: A:* mettre (un enfant) en culotte. **2. to b. a gun, a rifle,** enculasser un canon, un fusil.

breeches buoy ['bri:tʃizbɔi], *s. Nau:* bouée *f* culotte.

breeches pipe ['bri:tʃizpaip], *s. Hyd.E: etc:* raccord *m* en Y; culotte *f.*

breeching ['bri:tʃiŋ], *s.* **1.** (*a*) *Harn:* avaloire *f*; (courroie *f* de) reculement *m*; *Veh:* **b. hook,** ragot *m*; (*b*) *Artil:* accul *m* (de canon). **2.** *Nau:* brague *f* (de canon). **3.** *Tex:* (*of wool*) écouailles *fpl.*

breechless ['bri:tʃlis], *a.* sans culotte.

breed[1] [bri:d], *s.* race *f* (d'hommes, d'animaux); *Prov:* **b. will tell,** bon sang ne peut mentir; *Pej:* **people of your b.,** des gens de votre sorte, de votre espèce.

breed[2], *v.* **(bred; bred).**

I. *v.tr.* **1.** (*a*) produire, engendrer, procréer (des enfants, des petits); (*b*) faire naître; **dirt breeds disease,** la malpropreté donne naissance aux maladies, engendre, occasionne, des maladies; **misunderstandings that b. war,** malentendus semence *f* de guerre; **environment that breeds crime,** ambiance génératrice de crime; (*c*) *Atom.Ph:* (sur)régénérer (une matière fissile). **2.** (*a*) élever (du bétail, des lapins, etc.); *v.i.* faire de l'élevage; (*b*) *Breed:* **to b. in (stock),** faire des accouplements consanguins; **to b. out (an undesirable characteristic),** éliminer par accouplements contrôlés (une caractéristique indésirable); (*c*) **in his case it was bred in the bone,** chez lui cela tient de famille; *Prov:* **what's bred in the bone will come out in the flesh,** (i) bon chien chasse de race; (ii) chassez le naturel, il revient au galop; la caque sent toujours le hareng; (*d*) **he was bred to the law,** il fut destiné au barreau; **he had been bred a sailor, to the sea,** il avait été élevé pour faire un marin; il avait reçu une éducation de marin. **3. to b. a ram to a ewe,** accoupler un bélier à une brebis.

II. *v.i.* (*a*) (*of animals people*) multiplier; se reproduire; **to b. in,** se reproduire par mariages ou accouplements consanguins; (*b*) (*of opinions, etc.*) se propager.

breeder ['bri:dər], *s.* **1.** reproducteur, -trice; générateur, -trice; **good b.,** (poule) bonne pondeuse; (jument) bonne poulinière. **2.** éleveur, -euse (d'animaux); **poultry b.,** aviculteur, -trice; **silkworm b.,** sériciculteur *m.* **3.** *Atom.Ph:* **b. (reactor),** (réacteur *m*) (sur)régénérateur *m*; **fast b.,** surrégénérateur rapide, réacteur (régénérateur) à neutrons rapides.

breeding ['bri:diŋ], *s.* **1.** (*a*) reproduction *f,* multiplication *f* (des êtres); **b. in,** (i) mariages consanguins; endogamie *f*; (ii) *Husb:* accouplements consanguins; **b. out,** exogamie *f*; **b. season,** (i) (*of birds*) couvaison *f*; (ii) (*of domestic animals*) monte *f*; **b. ground,** endroit fréquenté par certains animaux, etc., à l'époque de la reproduction; *Fig:* **b. ground of anarchists,** pépinière *f* d'anarchistes; *Pisc;* **b. pond, pool,** alevinier *m,* forcière *f*; (*for hens, etc.*) **b. coop,** nichoir *m*; (*b*) élevage *m* (d'animaux domestiques, etc.); **animal kept for b. purposes,** (animal) reproducteur *m*; **b. stock,** animaux élevés en vue de la reproduction; **he goes in for b.,** il fait de l'élevage; **sheep b.,** élevage des moutons; **silkworm b.,** sériciculture *f*; élevage, éducation *f,* des vers à soie; (*c*) *Atom.Ph:* (sur)régénération *f*; **b. gain,** gain *m* de surrégénération; **b. ratio,** rapport *m* de (sur)régénération. **2.** (*a*) éducation (d'un enfant, etc.); (*b*) **(good) b.,** bonne éducation, bonnes manières; savoir-vivre *m*; l'usage du monde; **to lack b.,** manquer d'usage; manquer aux bienséances, aux convenances; **ill b.,** manque *m* d'éducation; mauvais ton, mauvais genre, mauvaises manières; manque de politesse; manque de savoir-vivre, d'usage.

breeks [bri:ks], *s.pl. Scot: F:* pantalon *m,* culotte *f*; *Prov:* **you can't take the b. off a Highlander,** on ne peut pas peigner un diable qui n'a pas de cheveux; où il n'y a rien le roi perd ses droits.

breeze[1] [bri:z], *s. Ent:* **b. (fly),** taon *m.*

breeze[2], *s.* **1.** (assez forte) brise; **gentle, light, b.,** petite, légère, brise; **land b.,** brise de terre; terral *m*; vent *m* d'amont; **sea b.,** brise de mer, du large; **mountain b.,** brise de montagne; *Nau:* **strong, stiff, b.,** vent frais, grosse brise; **commanding b.,** brise maniable; **moderate b.,** jolie brise; **fresh b.,** bonne brise; **the slightest b.,** le moindre souffle (de vent). **2.** (*a*) *F: A:* scène *f* (de ménage), fracas *m,* altercation *f,* querelle *f*; (*b*) *F: O:* **to get the b. up,** avoir le trac, la frousse, la trouille. **3.** *NAm: F:* **it's a b.,** c'est du gâteau, c'est un jeu d'enfant. **4.** *NAm: F:* **to shoot the b.,** bavarder.

breeze[3], *v.i.* (*a*) *O:* souffler (comme une brise); (*b*) *Nau:* (*of wind*) **to b. up,** fraîchir; (*c*) *F:* **to b. in, out,** entrer, sortir (i) en coup de vent, (ii) d'une façon désinvolte; (*d*) *U.S: F: Rac:* **to b. in,** arriver dans un fauteuil; (*e*) *F:* **to b. along,** passer vite.

breeze[4], *s.* (*a*) (*coal cinders*) braise *f* de houille; charbonnaille *f*; fraisil *m,* poussier *m*; menu, petit, coke; poussière *f* de laitier; **coke b.,** grésillon *m* de coke, poussier de coke; (*b*) **b. concrete,** ciment *m* de laitier; **b. block, brick,** parpaing *m.*

breezeway ['bri:zwei], *s. U.S:* passage couvert.

breezily ['bri:zili], *adv. F:* avec jovialité; avec une cordialité bruyante; avec désinvolture.

breeziness ['bri:zinis], *s. F:* cordialité bruyante; jovialité *f* (d'une personne, de manières); qualité *f* leste (du style); verve *f* (d'un discours).

breezy ['bri:zi], *a.* **1.** (*a*) venteux; **b. downs,** dunes exposées au vent, balayées par le vent; (*b*) *F:* **b. meeting,** réunion houleuse. **2.** *F:* (*a*) (*of pers., manners*) jovial; franc, *f* franche; enjoué; dégagé; désinvolte; (*of speech*) plein de verve; **b. welcome,** accueil cordial (et bruyant); (*b*) *A:* (*of pers.*) colérique.

breagma, *pl.* **bregmata** ['bregmə(tə)], *s. Anat:* bregma *m.*

bregmatic [breg'mætik], *a. Anat:* bregmatique.

breithauptite ['braithauptait], *s. Miner:* breithauptite *f.*

brekker ['brekər], *s. F: O:* (= *breakfast*) petit déjeuner.

Bremen ['breimən], *Pr.n. Geog:* Brême.

bremia ['bri:miə], *s. Fung:* bremia *f.*

bremsstrahlung ['bremʃtra:ləŋ], *s. Atom.Ph:* (rayonnement *m* de) freinage *m.*

Bren (gun) ['bren(gʌn)], *s. Mil:* fusil-mitrailleur; **B.-g. carrier,** chenillette *f* porte-fusil-mitrailleur, *pl.* chenillettes porte-fusil(s)-mitrailleur(s).

brent (goose) ['brent(gu:s)], *s. Orn:* bernache *f* cravant.

Brent(h)idae ['brentidi:], *s.pl. Ent:* brenthides *m,* brenthidés *m.*

brentid ['brentid], *s. Ent:* brent(h)e *m.*

brer ['brɛər], *s. U.S:* (*chiefly Southern*) frère *m*; *Lit:* **B. Fox,** compère le Renard; **B. Rabbit,** Jeannot Lapin; **B. Terrapin,** frère Terrapin.

bressummer ['bresʌmər]. = BREASTSUMMER.

brethren ['breðrin], *s.pl. see* BROTHER.

Breton ['bretɔn]. **1.** (*a*) *a. Geog:* breton; *Lit:* **the B. cycle,** le Cycle breton, amororicain; *Wr:* **B. fall,** saut *m* de Breton; (*b*) *s.* Breton, -onne. **2.** *s. Ling:* breton *m.* **3.** *Cost:* chapeau *m* à bords relevés, (chapeau) breton (*m*).

Breughel ['brɔigl, 'brœgl], *Pr.n. Hist. of Art:* Bruegel.

breunnerite ['brɔinərait], *s. Miner:* breunérite *f.*

breve [bri:v], *s.* **1.** *Hist:* bref *m* (du pape). **2.** *Pros:* brève *f.* **3.** *Mus:* (*a*) *A:* (*in plainsong*) brève, carrée *f*; (*b*) **b. rest,** demi-bâton *m, pl.* demi-bâtons.

brevet[1] ['brevit, *esp. NAm:* brə'vet], *s. Mil:* brevet *m* d'honorariat; honorariat *m*; **b. major,** commandant *m* honoraire (avec la solde de capitaine); **b. rank,** grade *m* honoraire; honorariat; **b. promotion,** avancement *m* à titre honoraire; **b. commission,** brevet d'officier honoraire.

brevet[2], *v.tr.* (i) conférer l'honorariat à (un militaire); (ii) promouvoir à titre honoraire, donner (à un militaire) un avancement à titre honoraire.

brevi- ['brevi], *comb.fm.* brévi-.

breviary ['bri:viəri], *s. Ecc:* bréviaire *m.*

brevicaudate ['brevi'kɔ:deit], *a. Z:* brévicaude.

Brevicipitidae ['brevisi'pitidi:], *s.pl. Amph:* brévicipitidés.

brevicite ['brevisait], *s. Miner:* brévicite *f.*

brevier [brə'viər], *s. Typ:* gaillarde *f*; corps 8 *m.*

brevifoliate ['brevi'fouliət], *a. Bot:* brévifolié.

brevilingual ['brevi'liŋgwəl], *a.* brévilingue.

breviped ['breviped], *a. Z:* brévipède.

brevipennate ['brevi'peneit], *a. Orn:* brévipenne.

brevirostrate ['brevi'rɔstreit], *a. Orn:* brévirostre.

brevity ['breviti], *s.* brièveté *f.* **1.** concision *f* (de style); laconisme *m* (d'expression); **for b.'s sake,** pour abréger; pour plus de brièveté; *Prov:* **b. is the soul of wit,** l'esprit réside dans la concision. **2.** courte durée (de la vie, etc.).

brew[1] [bru:], *s.* **1.** (*a*) brassage *m* (de la bière); (*b*) brassin *m,* cuvée *f.* **2.** infusion *f* (de thé); tisane *f* (de plantes). **3. home b.,** bière, cidre, de ménage, bière faite à la maison; vin fait à la maison.

brew[2], *v.*

I. *v.tr. & i.* **1.** *v.tr.* (*a*) brasser (de la bière); **home brewed,** (bière) brassée à la maison, (cidre) de ménage; (*b*) *v.i.* brasser; faire de la bière; (*c*) **to b. tea,** faire infuser du thé; préparer du thé; **to b. a bowl of punch,** mêler, préparer, un bol de punch; (*d*) *F:* **to b. mischief,** tramer une méchanceté, un méfait; fomenter la discorde. **2.** *v.i.* (*a*) (*of tea, etc.*) s'infuser; (*b*) *F:* **there's a storm brewing, a storm is brewing,** (i) un orage couve, s'amoncelle, s'amasse, se prépare, s'apprête; il va faire de l'orage; la tempête menace; (ii) *F:* c'est un bain, un bouillon, qui chauffe; **there's a plot brewing,** un complot se trame; **there's something brewing,** il y a quelque chose dans l'air; il se mijote quelque chose; **there's trouble brewing between them,** les cartes se brouillent.

II. (*compound verb*) **brew up,** *v.i. F:* faire infuser le thé; = faire le jus.

brewer ['bru(:)ər], *s.* brasseur *m.*

brewery ['bru(:)əri], *s.* brasserie *f.*

brewing, *s.* = BREW[1] 1 (*a*) & (*b*).

brewster[1] ['bru:stər], *s.* **1.** *A:* = BREWER. **2.** *Jur:* **B. Sessions,** session *f* judiciaire pour l'octroi des licences de cabaretier.

Brewster[2], *Pr.n. Opt:* **Brewster's law, bands,** loi *f,* franges *fpl,* de Brewster.

brewsterite ['bru:stərait], *s. Miner:* brewstérite *f.*

briar[1] ['braiər], *s.* (*a*) *Bot:* **wild b.,** églantier commun, buisson épineux; rosier *m* sauvage; **sweet b.,** églantier odorant; **b. rose,** églantine *f*; (*b*) **briars,** ronces *f*; (*c*) *Lit:* **briars,** difficultés *f,* ennuis *m.*

briar[2], *.* = BRIER[1].

Briareus [brai'ɛəriəs], *Pr.n.m. Gr.Myth:* Briarée.

bribable ['braibəbl], *a.* corruptible; qui se laisse corrompre.

bribe[1] [braib], *s.* paiement *m* illicite; présent (destiné à corrompre), prébende *f, F:* pot-de-vin *m, pl.* pots-de-vin; **to take a b., bribes,** se laisser corrompre.

bribe[2], *v.tr.* corrompre, acheter, gagner, soudoyer; *F:* graisser la patte à (qn); **to b. a witness,** suborner, séduire, un témoin; **to b. s.o. to silence,** acheter le silence de qn.

briber ['braibər], *s.* corrupteur, -trice; suborneur *m.*

bribery ['braibəri], *s.* corruption *f*; **open to b.,** corruptible; **not open to b.,** incorruptible.

bribing ['braibiŋ], *s.* corruption *f*; subornation *f* (de témoins); *F:* arrosage *m,* graissage *m* de patte.

bric-a-brac ['brikəbræk], *s.* (*no pl.*) bric-à-brac *m.*

brick[1] [brik], *s.* **1.** (*a*) brique *f*; **hollow b., perforated b.,** brique creuse; **air b.,** brique perforée; **air-dried b.,** brique crue; **solid b.,** brique pleine; **paving b.,** brique de pavement; **flue lining b.,** brique de hourdis; **burnt b.,** brique cuite; **glazed b.,** brique vernissée; **fire b.,** brique réfractaire; **b.-on-end course,** assise *f* de bout, assise debout; **b.-on-edge coping,** (assise de) bahut *m*; rouleau-brique *m*; assise de champ; rang *m* de briques posées verticalement; **b. clay, earth,** argile *f,* terre *f,* à briques; **b. kiln,** four *m* à briques; **b. clamp,** four de campagne; **clamp firing of bricks,** cuisson *f* à la volée; **b. dust,** poussière *f* de brique; **one cannot make bricks without straw,** on ne peut pas faire un miracle; *F:* **to be like a cat on hot bricks,** être sur des épines, être comme chat sur braise; *F:* **to come down on s.o. like a ton of bricks,** tomber sur le dos à qn; *F:* **to drop a b.,** faire une bourde, une gaffe; commettre un impair; gaffer lourdement; (*b*) (*toy*) **box of bricks,** jeu *m* de cubes, de construction; (*c*) *attrib.* construit de briques; **b. wall,** mur *m* en briques; *F:* **you might as well talk to a b. wall,** autant (vaut) parler à un sourd; **to run one's head against a b. wall,** donner de la tête contre un mur; se buter à l'impossible; **he can see through a b. wall,** plus fin que lui n'est pas bête; **b. and a half wall,** mur d'une brique et demie d'épaisseur; **b. partition,** cloison *f* de briques; **b. nogging,** hourdis *m,* hourdage *m*; (*d*) *a.* **b.(-red),** rouge brique *inv*; *U.S: F:* **b. top,** rouquin, -ine. **2.** *F:* **he's a b.,** c'est un chic type; **be a b.!** soyez chic! **3.** bloc *m* (de thé, etc.); pain *m* (de savon, etc.); **b. tea,** thé *m* en bloc.

brick[2], *v.tr.* briqueter; garnir (qch.) en briques; **to b. over a gateway,** voûter une porte en briques; **to b. up a window,** murer, maçonner, une fenêtre.

brickbat ['brikbæt], *s.* (i) fragment *m* de brique; briquaillon *m*; briqueton *m*; (ii) *F:* insulte *f*; **to throw brickbats at s.o.,** (i) lancer des morceaux de brique à qn; (ii) *F:* décocher des traits à (l'adresse de) qn; lapider qn (dans la presse, etc.).

bricket(te) [bri'ket], *s. Comest:* (*ice cream*) pavé *m.*

brickfield ['brikfi:ld], *s.* briqueterie *f.*

brick-fielder ['brikfi:ldər], *s. Meteor:* vent chargé de poussière (semblable au sirocco, en Australie).

bricking ['brikiŋ], *s.* briquetage *m*; maçonnerie *f* de briques.

bricklayer ['brikleiər], *s.* maçon *m* en briques; briqueteur *m*; **bricklayer's hammer,** marteau *m* de maçon; **bricklayer's scaffold,** échafaud *m* simple.

bricklaying ['brikleiiŋ], *s.* maçonnerie *f* en briques; briquetage *m.*

brickmaker ['brikmeikər], *s.* briquetier *m.*

bricksetter ['briksetər], *s.* = BRICKLAYER.

brickwork ['brikwə:k], *s.* briquetage *m*; maçonnerie *f* de brique; **cavity b.,** murs *mpl* à parois multiples.

brickyard ['brikjɑ:d], *s.* briqueterie *f.*

bricole ['brik(ə)l, bri'koul], *s.* **1.** *Ten: Bill:* bricole *f.* **2.** *A:* (*man harness*) bricole. **3.** *A.Mil:* (*catapult*) bricole.

bridal ['braid(ə)l]. **1.** *s. Poet:* noce(s)*f*; fête nuptiale. **2.** *a.* nuptial, de noce(s); **b. veil,** voile *m* de mariée; (*in hotel*) **b. suite,** appartement *m* pour jeunes mariés.

bride[1] [braid], *s.f.* **1.** fiancée (sur le point de se marier). **2.** (nouvelle) mariée; **the b. and bridegroom,** (i) les futurs conjoints; (ii) les nouveaux mariés; (*on entering church for a wedding the ushers ask:*) **b. or bridegroom?** êtes-vous ami(s), amie(s), de la mariée ou du marié? **the b. of Christ,** l'épouse de Jésus-Christ.

bride[2], *s. Needlew: etc:* bride *f.*

Bride[3], *Pr.n.f. A:* Brigitte; (*b*) **St. Bride's Church,** l'église Sainte-Brigitte.

bridecake ['braidkeik], *s. A: & U.S:* gâteau *m* de mariage; pièce montée (de mariage).

bridegroom ['braidgrum], *s.m.* **1.** fiancé (sur le point de se marier). **2.** (nouveau) marié.

bridesmaid ['braidzmeid], *s.f.* demoiselle *f* d'honneur (de la mariée).

bridesman, *pl.* **-men** ['braidzmən], *s.m. A: & U.S:* garçon d'honneur (à une noce).

bridewell ['braidwel], *s. A:* maison *f* d'arrêt, de correction; maison de force; (en premier lieu hospice de St Bride's Well à Londres).

bridg(e)able ['bridʒəbl], *a.* (cours d'eau) sur lequel on peut construire, établir, un pont.

bridge[1] [bridʒ], *s.* **1.** (*a*) pont *m*; **stone b.,** pont en pierre; **box (girder) b.,** pont à poutres en caisson, pont tubulaire; **swing b., swivel b., pivot b.,** pont tournant, pivotant; **balance b.,** pont basculant; **suspension b.,** pont suspendu; **cantilever b.,** pont cantilever; **counterpoise b., bascule b.,** pont à bascule; **pontoon b., b. of boats,** pont de bateaux; **Bailey b.,** pont Bailey; **travelling b.,** pont roulant; **crane b.,** pont tournant à un bras, **loading b.,** pont de chargement; **opening b.,** pont mobile; **road, railway, b.,** pont routier; pont de chemin-de-fer; **one-lane b.,** pont à voie unique, à voie simple, à une voie; **b. over,** passage *m* en dessus; **b. under,** passage en dessous; **b. intersection,** croisement *m* à saute-mouton; **to lay, to throw, a b. over, across, a river,** construire, établir, lancer, jeter, un pont sur un cours d'eau; **to dismantle, break up, a b.,** démonter un pont; **b. building,** construction *f* de ponts; pontage *m*; *Mil:* **b. train,** (i) train *m* de pontons; (ii) corps *m* des pontonniers; **to cross a b.,** traverser un pont; *Fig:* **that's a b. we'll cross when we get, come, to it,** chaque chose en son temps; (*b*) *Wr:* pont; **to make a b.,** ponter. **2.** *Nau:* (*a*) passerelle *f*; **fore b.,** passerelle de commandement; **after b.,** passerelle arrière; **fore-and-aft b.,** passerelle volante; **docking b.,** passerelle de manœuvre; **Admiral's b.,** passerelle de majorité, de l'amiral; (*b*) **b. house,** rouf-passerelle *m.* **3.** *El: etc:* (*a*) **measuring b.,** pont de mesure; **slide-wire measuring b.,** pont de mesure à fil; **Wheatstone('s) b.,** pont, parallélogramme *m*, de Wheatstone; **Maxwell b., Campbell b.,** pont de Maxwell, de Campbell; **induction b.,** balance *f* d'induction; **b. network,** réseau maillé, en pont; **b. fuse,** fusible *m* à pont; **b. rectifier,** redresseur *m* en pont; **b. transformer,** transformateur différentiel; **b. transition,** transition *f* série-parallèle (par la méthode du pont); (*b*) **b. piece,** pont polaire (d'accus); **b. connection,** couplage *m*, montage *m*, en pont; (*c*) *Tg: & Elcs:* **b. duplex,** duplex *m* à pont, installation *f* en pont de duplication; **b. duplex system,** système *m* duplex à pont; (*d*) *T.V:* enchaînement *m.* **4.** (*a*) dos *m*, arête *f* (du nez); chevalet *m* (d'un violon); arcade *f* (d'une paire de lunettes); autel *m* (d'une chaudière); *Hor:* pont; *Mus:* **to play near the b. (of violin),** jouer près du chevalet; (*b*) *Dent:* bridge *m*; (*c*) *Bill:* chevalet.

bridge[2], *v.tr.* construire, établir, lancer, jeter, un pont sur (un cours d'eau); **the stream is bridged by a plank,** une planche sert à passer le ruisseau; **to b. a gap,** relier les bords d'une brèche; combler une lacune; (*esp. for supplies*) faire la soudure; **that will b. (over) the difficulty,** cela nous aidera à surmonter la difficulté.

bridge[3], *s. Cards:* bridge *m*; **game of b.,** (partie *f* de) bridge; *O:* **auction b.,** bridge aux enchères; **contract b.,** bridge contrat; **to play b.,** jouer au bridge; *F:* bridger; **what about a game of b.?** si on faisait un bridge? **b. player,** bridgeur, -euse; **b. fiend,** fanatique *mf* du bridge; **b. marker,** carnet-bloc *m* (de bridge), *pl.* carnets-blocs; **b. party,** soirée *f*, réunion *f*, de bridge; **b. drive,** tournoi *m* de bridge; *Cu:* **b. roll,** petit pain (au lait) (dont on fait des sandwichs pour une réunion de bridge, etc.).

bridged [bridʒd], *a.* **1.** (*a*) muni, pourvu, d'un pont, de ponts; (*b*) *Nau:* pourvu d'une passerelle. **2.** *El:* **b. T network,** réseau *m* en T. **3.** (*with adj. or adv. prefixed, e.g.*) **high-b. nose,** nez arqué, busqué.

bridgehead ['bridʒhed], *s. Mil:* tête *f* de pont.

bridgeless ['bridʒlis], *a.* (*a*) (fleuve *m*) sans pont; (*b*) (abîme *m*) infranchissable.

bridge-over ['bridʒouvər], *s.* **1.** *Const:* **b.-o. joist,** lambourde *f.* **2.** *Fin:* crédit *m* provisoire.

Bridget ['bridʒit], *Pr.n.f.* Brigitte.

Bridgettine, Bridgittine ['bridʒitain], *a. & s.* **B. (friar, nun),** brigittin, -ine.

bridgework ['bridʒwə:k], *s.* **1.** construction *f* de ponts. **2.** *Dent:* bridge *m.*

bridging ['bridʒiŋ], *s.* **1.** construction *f* d'un pont (sur un fleuve); pontage *m*; **b. party,** équipe *f* de pontonniers. **2.** liaison *f*; (*a*) comblement *m* (d'une lacune); soudure *f*; **b. loan, finance,** crédit *m* provisoire; (*b*) *Cin:* **b. title,** titre *m* de liaison; (*c*) *Const: Carp:* **b. piece,** traversière *f*; lierne *f*; étrésillon *m*; entretoise *f*; **b. joist,** lambourde; (*d*) *El: Elcs:* **b. connection,** montage *m* en pont; **b. amplifier,** amplificateur *m* de contrôle.

bridle[1] ['braidl], *s.* **1.** (*a*) *Harn:* bride *f*; **snaffle b.,** filet *m*; **to give a horse the b.,** lâcher, rendre; la bride à un cheval; **b. bit,** mors *m* de bride; **b. rein,** rênes *fpl* de bride; **b. butts, backs,** croupons *mpl* de bride; **b. hand,** la main gauche (qui tient la bride); **b. path, b. road, b. trail, b. way,** chemin *m* pour cavaliers; chemin muletier; route cavalière; (*in forest, etc.*) piste cavalière; (*b*) frein *m*; **to put a b. on one's passions, one's tongue,** mettre un frein à ses passions, à sa langue. **2.** *Nau:* branche *f*; **mooring b.,** branche, patte *f* d'oie, de corps mort. **3.** (*a*) *Physiol:* frein, filet *m* (de la langue, etc.); (*b*) *Med:* bride. **4.** (*a*) *Mec.E:* bride (de ressort); (*b*) *Carp:* **b. joint,** joint anglais; embrèvements anglais (séparés par un plat joint); chevronnage *m* à tenon; (*c*) *Paint:* bride (qu'on met sur un pinceau neuf); (*d*) *El:* **b. rod,** tringle *f* de suspente.

bridle[2]. **1.** *v.tr.* (*a*) brider, rêner (un cheval); (*b*) maîtriser, brider, mettre un frein à (ses passions, sa langue). **2.** *v.i.* **to b. (up),** (i) redresser la tête; se rengorger; (ii) se rebiffer; prendre la mouche.

bridled ['braid(ə)ld], *a. Orn:* **b. tern,** sterne bridée.

bridlewise ['braidlwaiz], *a. U.S:* (cheval *m*) sensible aux rênes.

bridoon [bri'du:n], *s. Harn:* bridon *m*; **b. bit,** mors *m* de bridon, de filet.

brief[1] [bri:f], **1.** *a.* bref, *f.* brève; court; **b. speech,** discours bref, succinct, concis, de courte durée; **b. account,** exposé *m* sommaire; **for a b. period,** pendant quelque temps; **b. interval,** court intervalle; **b. stay, visit,** séjour passager, de peu de durée; **in b.,** en raccourci, en résumé; **to be b.,** pour vous dire la chose en deux mots; bref. **2.** *s. Cost:* **briefs,** *Com: occ.* **brief,** slip *m*; **bikini briefs,** slip bikini.

brief[2], *s.* **1.** *Ecc:* bref *m*; **apostolic b.,** bref apostolique, bref du pape. **2.** abrégé *m*, résumé *m*, exposé *m*; (*a*) *Jur:* dossier *m* (d'une procédure); **to take a b.,** accepter un dossier; **to hold a b.,** être chargé d'une cause; **to hold a b. for s.o.,** représenter qn en justice; **to hold a watching b. for s.o.,** veiller (en justice) aux intérêts de qn; *F:* **I wouldn't accept a b. on his behalf,** je ne voudrais pas me porter garant de son intégrité, de son innocence; **I don't hold any b. for him,** ce n'est pas mon affaire de plaider sa cause, de le défendre; je n'ai guère confiance en lui; (*b*) *Jur: U.S:* **b. (of argument),** conclusions (présentées à la cour avant l'audience); (*c*) *attrib.* **b. paper,** papier *m* ministre, papier tellière.

brief[3], *v.tr.* **1. to b. a case,** faire le résumé, l'exposé, d'une affaire; rédiger, établir, le dossier d'une affaire. **2. to b. a barrister,** confier une cause à un avocat; constituer un avoué. **3.** donner une mission à (qn), munir (qn) d'instructions, fournir des directives à (qn), *F:* briefer (qn).

brief bag ['bri:fbæg], **briefcase** ['bri:fkeis], *s.* serviette *f* (en cuir); porte-documents *m inv.*

briefing ['bri:fiŋ], *s.* **1. b. of a case,** constitution *f* du dossier d'une affaire. **2. b. of a barrister,** constitution d'avoué. **3.** instructions *fpl*, directives *fpl*, exposé verbal (de mission); séance *f* d'information, réunion *f* préparatoire; *Av: F:* breffage *m*, briefing *m.*

briefless ['bri:flis], *a.* (avocat *m*) sans cause.

briefly ['bri:fli], *adv.* brièvement; en peu de mots, en quelques mots; en raccourci.

briefness ['bri:fnis], *s.* brièveté *f*; concision *f.*

brier[1] ['braiər], *s.* **1.** *Bot:* (*white heath*) bruyère (arborescente). **2. b. root, b. wood,** racine *f* de bruyère; **b. (pipe),** pipe *f* de, en, bruyère.

brier[2], *s.* = BRIAR[1].

briery ['braiəri], *a.* épineux.

brig[1] [brig], *s.* **1.** *Nau:* brick *m.* **2.** *esp. NAm:* prison *f*, cellule *f* (à bord d'un navire).

brig[2], *s. Scot:* (= *bridge*) pont *m.*

brigade[1] [bri'geid], *s.* **1.** *Mil:* (*a*) brigade *f* (toutes armes); **b. group,** groupement tactique (à l'échelon brigade); **infantry-heavy b.,** brigade à prépondérance d'infanterie; **armour-heavy b.,** brigade à prépondérance de blindés; **b. major,** chef d'État-major d'une brigade; (*b*) *O:* **(infantry) brigade,** régiment d'infanterie; (*c*) *A:* **(artillery) brigade,** groupe *m* d'artillerie; (*d*) *U.S:* **artillery b.,** brigade d'artillerie (4 régiments de 4 groupes chacun); (*e*) *F:* **one of the old b.,** un vieux de la vieille. **2.** corps organisé (pour un service public, etc.); **the Boys' B.,** œuvre *f* de patronage scolaire (fondée à Glasgow en 1883).

brigade[2], *v.tr. Mil:* embrigader (des régiments); verser (une batterie, etc.) dans une brigade; **to be brigaded with s.o.,** être en brigade avec qn.

brigadier [brigə'diər], *s.* **1.** *Mil:* général *m* de brigade. **2. b.-general,** (i) *Eng: A:* général de brigade; (ii) *U.S:* général de brigade; (iii) *U.S:* général de brigade aérienne.

brigalow ['brigəlou], *s. Bot: Austr:* (plusieurs espèces du genre) acacia *m.*

brigand ['brigənd], *s.* brigand *m*, bandit *m.*

brigandage ['brigəndidʒ], **brigandism** ['brigəndizm], *s.* brigandage *m*; **act of b.,** briganderie *f.*

brigandine ['brigəndi:n], *s. A.Arm:* brigandine *f.*

brigantine[1] [brigən'ti:n], *s. Nau:* brigantin *m.*

brigantine[2], *s. A.Arm:* brigandine *f.*

Brighamite ['brigəmait], *s. Rel.H:* sectateur, -trice, de Brigham Young; mormon *m.*

bright[1] [brait], *a.* **1.** lumineux; (*a*) (*of star, metal, gem, etc.*) brillant; (*of sun*) éclatant; **b. fire,** feu clair, vif; **b. light,** lumière vive; **b. eyes,** yeux brillants, lumineux; **b. steel,** acier poli; **b. parts, works** (*of machine, etc.*), parties polies, usinées, blanchies; *s. Com:* **brights,** houille brillante; *Metall:* **b. annealing,** recuit blanc; *Elcs:* **b. emitter,** cathode *f* à filament chauffé visible; *Needlew:* **b. silk thread,** fil brillanté; **as b. as a button, as a sixpence,** brillant comme un sou neuf; (*b*) (*of day, weather, etc.*) clair; **rainy weather with b. intervals,** temps pluvieux avec éclaircies; **to become brighter,** s'éclaircir; **the room was b. with firelight,** un feu clair égayait la pièce; (*c*) (*of colour*) vif, *f* vive; éclatant; **b. red,** rouge vif; (*d*) (*of sound*) clair; éclatant; aigu, -uë; (*e*) **b. future,** avenir brillant; avenir qui promet; **brighter days,** des jours plus heureux; **to look on the b. side of things,** voir tout en beau, en rose; prendre les choses par le bon côté; voir tout du beau côté; (*f*) *Petr:* **b. stock,** bright stock *m.* **2.** (*a*) (*vivacious*) vif, animé, sémillant; **to be witty, or at any rate b.,** avoir de l'esprit, ou tout au moins de l'allant; *A:* **the b. young people, young things,** la jeunesse qui s'amuse; les jeunes gens à la page, modernes; (*b*) *F:* (*quick-witted*) éveillé, intelligent, bien doué; **he is the brightest boy in the class,** il est le plus brillant de la classe; **he's not very b.,** ce n'est pas un as; **a b. idea,** une idée lumineuse.

Bright[2], *Pr.n.m. Med:* **Bright's disease,** maladie *f*, mal *m*, de Bright; brightisme *m*; néphrite *f* chronique; **the doctor had never had a case of Bright's disease before,** le médecin n'avait jamais soigné un brightique.

brighten ['brait(ə)n]. **1.** *v.tr.* **to b. sth. (up),** faire briller, faire reluire, qch.; fourbir (le métal); **to b. (up) a colour,** aviver une couleur; **to b. s.o. up, to b. up a conversation,** égayer qn, une conversation; **news that brightens (up) the situation, the future,** nouvelle *f* qui fait paraître la situation, l'avenir, sous un meilleur jour. **2.** *v.i.* **to b. (up),** (*of pers., face*) s'épanouir, s'éclaircir, s'animer, se dérider, se rasséréner; (*of weather*) s'éclaircir; (*of the future*) s'éclaircir, devenir moins sombre; **his eyes brightened,** ses yeux s'allumèrent, brillèrent; **he began to b. up,** il commença (i) à se ranimer, à se dégourdir, (ii) à se dérider.

brightener ['braitnər], *s.* **1.** (produit) aviveur *m* (de couleurs, etc.). **2.** *Metalw:* (agent) brillanteur *m.*

brightening[1] ['braitniŋ], *a.* **b. sky,** ciel *m* qui s'éclaircit; **b. prospects,** avenir *m* qui commence à promettre; **the b. dawn,** l'aube blanchissante.

brightening[2], *s.* avivage *m* (de couleurs).
brightish ['braitiʃ], *a.* **1.** assez brillant, assez vif. **2.** assez intelligent.
brightly ['braitli], *adv.* **1.** brillamment, avec éclat; **the sun was shining b.,** le soleil brillait avec éclat; **b. polished,** reluisant d'éclat. **2.** *(a)* d'un ton vif; gaiement; **b. written article,** article d'un style facile, aisé; *(b)* avec intelligence; intelligemment.
brightness ['braitnis], *s.* éclat *m* (du soleil, d'une lampe, du teint, d'un son); intensité *f* d'éclairage; luminosité *f* (d'une surface); brillant *m* (de l'acier); clarté *f* (du jour, d'un son); vivacité *f* (de l'intelligence, d'une couleur); intelligence *f* (d'un enfant, etc.); (du regard); *Opt:* brillance *f,* luminance *f; T.V: **b. of image,*** brillance (de l'image); **b. control,** dispositif *m* de réglage de la luminosité.
brightwork ['braitwəːk], *s. Nau:* les cuivres *mpl* (d'un bateau).
Brigittine ['bridʒitiːn], *a. & s.* = BRIDGETTINE.
brill[1] [bril], *s. Ich:* barbue *f.*
Brill[2], *Pr.n. Med:* **Brill's disease,** maladie *f* de Brill.
brilliance ['briljəns], **brilliancy** ['briliənsi], *s.* **1.** *(a)* éclat *m,* brillant *m,* lustre *m;* *(b) Ac:* netteté *f* (du son); qualité acoustique; *(c) Opt: etc:* brillance *f,* luminance *f.* **2. brilliance:** *(a)* intelligence *f* remarquable; *(b)* brillance (du style).
brilliant[1] ['briliənt], *a.* *(a)* brillant, éclatant; **b. illumination,** éclairage intense, brillant; **b. sunshine,** soleil brillant, éclatant; *(b)* *(of pers.)* très intelligent, très doué; **he's not b.,** il n'est pas brillant; ce n'est pas un aigle, une lumière; **b. idea,** idée lumineuse; **b. success,** succès éclatant; *(c) F:* **I'm not feeling very b.,** je ne suis pas dans mon assiette.
brilliant[2], *s.* **1.** *Lap:* brillant *m.* **2.** *Typ:* corps *m* 3½.
brilliantine[1] ['briliəntiːn], *s.* **1.** *Toil:* brillantine *f.* **2.** *Tex:* brillantine.
brilliantine[2], *v.tr. Toil:* brillantiner (les cheveux).
brilliantly ['briliəntli], *adv.* *(a)* brillamment, avec éclat; **the sun was shining b.,** le soleil brillait avec éclat; **b. lighted, lit,** vivement éclairé; *(b)* **b. intelligent,** d'une intelligence brillante; **to pass an examination b.,** être reçu brillamment à un examen; *Mus:* **to play b.,** jouer avec brio.
brim[1] [brim], *s.* bord *m* (de verre, de chapeau, etc.); **to fill s.o.'s glass to the b.,** verser du vin à qn à ras bord; remplir le verre de qn à ras bord.
brim[2], *v.* **(brimmed) 1.** *v.tr.* **to b. the bowl,** remplir la coupe jusqu'au bord. **2.** *v.i.* *(of vessel)* être plein jusqu'au bord; **to b. over (with sth.),** déborder, regorger (de qch.); **brimming over with health,** débordant de santé; **her eyes were brimming with tears,** ses yeux étaient noyés de larmes.
brimful ['brim'ful], *a.* *(a)* *(of glass, etc.)* plein jusqu'au bord; plein à déborder; débordant; **to fill s.o.'s glass b.,** verser du vin (etc.) à ras bord à qn; *(b)* **b. of health, of life, of hope,** débordant de santé, de vie, d'espoir.
brimless ['brimlis], *a.* (chapeau *m*) sans bord(s).
brimmed [brimd], *a.* à bords; **broad-b. hat,** chapeau *m* à larges bords.
brimmer ['brimər], *s. F: O:* rasade *f;* plein verre.
brimstone ['brimstən], *s.* **1.** soufre (brut); *A:* **b. match,** allumette soufrée. **2. vegetable b.,** poudre *f* de lycopode. **3.** *Ent:* **b. (butterfly),** citron *m.*
brindle(d) ['brindl(d)], *a.* (chat) tacheté, tavelé, bringé; (taureau) bringé.
brindling ['brindliŋ], *s. Z:* tavelure *f;* bringeure *f.*
brine[1] [brain], *s.* **1.** eau salée; saumure *f;* **b. gauge,** salinomètre *m,* saturomètre *m;* **b. pit,** saline *f; Nau:* **b. pump,** pompe *f* d'extraction, d'exhaustion, d'épuisement. **2.** *Poet:* mer *f;* océan *m.* **3.** *(a) Ent:* **b. fly,** éphydride *m;* *(b) Crust:* **b. shrimp,** artémia *f.*
brine[2], *v.tr.* saumurer; mettre (qch.) dans la saumure.
Brinell [bri'nel], *Pr.n. Metall:* **B. machine,** machine *f* de Brinell.
bring [briŋ], *v.* **(brought** [brɔːt]; **brought)**
I. *v.tr.* *(a)* amener (qn, un des nouvelles); **b. your friend, your dog (along, round, over),** amenez, votre ami, votre chien; **he brought a large retinue with him,** il amena avec lui une suite nombreuse; **she brought a lot of luggage (with her),** elle a apporté beaucoup de bagages; **did you b. your car?** est-ce que vous avez amené votre voiture? **he brought his car through, down, along, the flooded street without too much difficulty,** il a descendu en voiture la rue inondée sans trop de difficultés; **the doctor brought him through a serious illness,** le médecin l'a guéri d'une maladie sérieuse; **I've brought the key of my hotel room away (with me),** j'ai emporté la clef de ma chambre d'hôtel; **what brings you to London?** qu'est-ce qui vous amène à Londres? **to b. a question to the attention of the public,** attirer l'attention du public sur une question; **he was brought (up) before the magistrate,** on l'amena, on le fit comparaître, devant le tribunal; **to be brought before the assizes,** être traduit en cour d'assises; *Nau:* **to b. a chain to the capstan,** amarrer une chaîne au cabestan; *(b)* **to b. tears to s.o.'s eyes,** faire venir, faire monter, les larmes aux yeux de qn; **to b. s.o. luck, bad luck,** porter bonheur, malheur, à qn; **to b. misfortune on s.o.,** attirer un malheur sur qn; **to b. misfortunes on oneself,** assembler des malheurs sur sa tête; s'attirer des malheurs, des ennuis; **it is you who have brought this trouble on us,** c'est vous qui êtes la cause de ces ennuis; **you've brought it on yourself,** vous l'avez voulu; **to b. discord into a family,** semer la discorde dans une famille; **wealth brings with it many anxieties,** la richesse apporte beaucoup de soucis, ne va pas sans bien des soucis; *(c)* **to b. an action against s.o.,** intenter un procès contre, à, qn; **to b. a dispute before a court,** soumettre, déférer, un litige à un tribunal; porter un différend devant un tribunal; saisir un tribunal d'un différend; *(d)* **to b. s.o. into difficulties, into danger,** mettre qn dans l'embarras, dans le danger; **to b. s.o. into the conversation, into a matter,** mêler qn à la conversation, à une affaire; **to b. a child into the world,** mettre au monde un enfant; **to b. sth. into question,** mettre qch. en question; **to b. sth. into action, into play,** mettre qch. en œuvre; *(e)* **to b. sth. to perfection,** porter qch. à la perfection; **to b. sth. to a successful conclusion,** faire aboutir qch.; **to b. sth. to s.o.'s knowledge,** porter qch. à la connaissance de qn; révéler qch.; **to b. a difficulty under control,** résoudre une difficulté; **to b. sth. to light,** mettre (qch.) en lumière; révéler, découvrir (un crime); mettre à jour (un crime, un secret); déterrer, exhumer (des objets anciens, des manuscrits); **my second attempt brought home to me the difficulties of the task,** mon second essai m'a montré toutes les difficultés de la tâche; **seeing her again brought home to him his loss,** c'est en la revoyant qu'il s'est vraiment rendu compte de sa perte; **this action brought him into the public eye,** cette action a attiré l'attention sur lui; *(f) A: & Lit:* **to b. sth. to pass,** amener, faire arriver, qch.; *(g)* **I don't know what brought him to do it,** je ne sais pas ce qui l'a amené à le faire; **this brings me to observe that. . .,** cela m'amène à remarquer que. . .; **to b. oneself to do sth.,** se résoudre, se décider, à faire qch.; **he cannot b. himself to speak about it,** il lui est trop pénible d'en parler.
II. *(compound verbs)* **1. bring about,** *v.tr.* *(a)* *(cause)* amener, causer, déterminer, occasionner (qch.); **to b. a. a reconciliation,** amener, ménager, une réconciliation; **to b. a. s.o.'s ruin,** entraîner la ruine de qn; **to b. a. an accident, a reform,** provoquer un accident, une réforme; **to b. a. a war,** fomenter, provoquer, une guerre; *(b)* *(accomplish)* effectuer, accomplir, opérer, venir à bout de, qch.; **to b. a. a change,** opérer un changement; **to b. a. s.o.'s ruin,** consommer la perte de qn; *(c) Nau:* retourner, faire virer (un navire).
2. bring back, *v.tr.* rapporter (qch.); ramener (qn); **when you go to town, b. me back two barrels of cider,** quand vous irez à la ville, vous me ramènerez deux fûts de cidre; **to b. b. a borrowed book,** rapporter un livre emprunté; **to b. s.o. back to health,** rétablir la santé de qn; **Jesus brought Lazarus back to life,** Jésus ranima Lazare; **the doctor brought him back to life,** le docteur l'a ramené à la vie; **this brings my childhood back to me,** cela me rappelle mon enfance; **his letter brings back many memories,** sa lettre rappelle bien des souvenirs; **to b. b. a case back before the court,** ressaisir le tribunal d'un différend.
3. bring down, *v.tr.* *(a)* abattre (un arbre, du gibier, un avion); *F:* descendre (une perdrix, un avion); faire tomber (le fruit d'un arbre); mettre à bas, faire crouler, faire effondrer (un mur, une maison); terrasser (un adversaire); faire tomber (un gouvernement); **to b. d. one's man,** coucher son homme par terre, *F:* sur le carreau; *Fb:* faucher son homme; *Th: F:* **to b. d. the house,** faire crouler la salle (sous les applaudissements); se faire applaudir à tout casser, à tout rompre; *Book-k:* **balance brought down,** solde *m* à nouveau; *(b)* faire descendre (qn); descendre (un objet du grenier, etc.); **to b. sth. down again,** redescendre qch.; *(of river)* **to b. d. ice, etc.,** charrier de la glace, etc.; *(c) O:* abattre, abaisser, mater (l'orgueil de qn); *(d)* abaisser, faire baisser (le prix); avilir (la monnaie, les prix); **to b. d. the price of an article to . . .,** ramener le prix d'un article à . . .; **to b. d. the birthrate,** abaisser, réduire, la natalité; *(e)* réduire (une enflure); *(f)* **to b. d. a patient's temperature,** faire baisser la fièvre d'un malade; **the storm has brought down the temperature,** l'orage a rafraîchi le temps.
4. bring forth, *v.tr. A: & Lit:* *(a)* mettre au monde (des enfants); *(of animals)* mettre bas (des petits); *(of plants)* produire (des fruits); accoucher (d'une œuvre); produire (une œuvre); **what the future will b. f.,** ce que l'avenir produira, apportera; *(b)* **to b. f. protests,** provoquer des protestations.
5. bring forward, *v.tr.* *(a)* avancer (une chaise, etc.); amener, faire avancer, faire approcher (qn); produire (un témoin); avancer, présenter, produire (un argument); alléguer (une preuve); **the matter was brought forward at the last meeting,** la question a été mise sur le tapis à la dernière réunion; *(b)* avancer (une réunion, etc.); **the meeting has been brought forward from the 14th to the 7th,** la séance a été avancée du 14 au 7; *(c) Com:* **to b. f. an amount,** reporter une somme; **brought forward,** à reporter; report *m.*
6. bring in, *v.tr.* *(a)* introduire, faire entrer (qn); apporter, rentrer (qch.); introduire, lancer (une mode, etc.); faire intervenir (qn); *Cmptr:* alimenter (un programme); **b. him in,** faites-le entrer; **to b. in the harvest,** rentrer la moisson; **dinner was brought in,** on a servi le dîner; *Jur:* *(marriage settlement)* **estate brought in,** biens *mpl* d'apport; *(b)* *(of capital, investment)* **to b. in interest,** rapporter; porter intérêt; **investment that brings in 6%,** placement *m* qui rend 6%; **this land brings him in an income of ten thousand francs,** cette terre lui vaut dix mille francs de rente; **these little jobs b. me in two or three pounds a week,** ces petits à-côtés me rapportent deux ou trois livres par semaine; *(c)* déposer, présenter (un projet de loi); *(d) Jur:* *(of jury)* **to b. in a verdict,** rendre un verdict; **to b. s.o. in guilty,** déclarer qn coupable; *(e)* *(at auction sale)* **the diamonds were brought in at £65,000,** les diamants ont été retirés de la vente à £65.000; *(f) Petr:* **to b. in a well,** mettre un puits en production.
7. bring off, *v.tr.* réussir (un coup, etc.).
8. bring on, *v.tr.* *(a)* produire, occasionner (une maladie, etc.); **his anger brought on another bout of fever,** sa colère provoqua, détermina, un nouvel accès de fièvre; *(b)* **the sun is bringing on the plants,** le soleil fait pousser les plantes; **to b. s.o. on for an examination,** acheminer qn vers un examen; **he is bringing on his team at a great rate,** il fait faire à son équipe des progrès rapides; *(c) Th:* amener, apporter, sur la scène; **in the second act an elephant is brought on,** au second acte on fait paraître en scène un éléphant; **two waiters b. on a table set for dinner,** deux garçons apportent une table toute dressée.
9. bring out, *v.tr.* *(a)* sortir (qch.); faire sortir (qn); **b. us out a few chairs,** sortez-nous quelques chaises; **he's bringing out his family to join him in Africa,** il fait venir sa famille pour le rejoindre en Afrique; *(b)* prononcer, proférer (un juron, etc.); *(c)* révéler, faire ressortir, mettre en relief, faire valoir, mettre en évidence, dégager (le sens de qch.); faire valoir (une couleur, un détail dans une peinture, etc.); *Mus:* faire sentir (la mélodie); **sketch that brings out every muscle,** esquisse *f* qui accuse tous les muscles; *(d)* publier, sortir (un livre); *Fin:* introduire (des valeurs sur le marché); **to b. o. one's daughter,** présenter sa fille dans le monde; *(e)* **the sun has brought out the roses,** le soleil a fait épanouir les roses.
10. bring over, *v.tr.* convertir, attirer, gagner (qn à une cause, etc.).
11. bring round, *v.tr.* *(a)* rappeler, ramener, (qn) à la vie; faire reprendre connaissance à (qn); remettre (qn) sur pied; **they brought him round with a glass of spirits,** on le ranima avec un verre d'eau-de-vie; *(b)* remettre (qn) de bonne humeur; *(c)* rallier (qn à un parti); **to b. s.o. round to an opinion,** convertir qn à une opinion; *(d)* **to b. the conversation round to a subject,** (r)amener la conversation sur un sujet.
12. bring to, *v.tr.* *(a) Nau:* mettre (un navire) en panne, en travers; couper l'erre à (un navire); *v.i.* *(of ship)* mettre en panne, prendre la panne; *(b)* **to b. s.o. to,** faire reprendre connaissance à qn; **the doctor managed to b. her to,** le médecin a réussi à la ranimer.
13. bring together, *v.tr.* réunir; mettre (des personnes) en contact; affronter (des plaques de métal); rassembler (des documents); **to b. persons together again,** raccommoder, réconcilier, remettre bien ensemble, des personnes; **I brought them together,** je leur fis faire connaissance; **chance brought us together,** le hasard m'a fait la rencontrer; *Jur:* **to b. the parties together,** mettre les parties en présence.
14. bring up, *v.tr.* *(a)* monter (qch.); faire monter (qn); *(b)* **to b. up one's food,** vomir; **he brought up everything he had eaten,** il a rejeté, rendu, tout ce qu'il avait mangé; *(c)* apporter, approcher, avancer (qch.); amener, faire approcher (qn); faire avancer (des troupes); amener (des renforts); **b. your chair up to the fire,** approchez votre fauteuil du feu; *(d)* élever (des enfants); **I was brought up by an aunt,** j'ai été élevé par

une tante; **I was brought up to be polite,** j'ai été élevé dans la politesse; (*e*) *Nau:* mouiller, arrêter (un navire); *v.i.* (*of ship*) mouiller; casser sur son erre; accoster (**along,** le long de); **ship brought up by her anchor,** navire *m* qui fait tête sur son ancre; (*of pers.*) **to be brought up short by sth.,** buter contre qch.; se heurter à qch.; (*f*) soulever (une question); mettre (une question) sur le tapis; évoquer (un souvenir); **to b. up a subject again,** revenir sur un sujet; **to b. sth. up (against s.o.),** objecter qch. (à qn); *Jur:* faire état de qch. (contre un accusé); (*g*) **to be brought up before the magistrate,** comparaître devant le tribunal.

bring-and-buy ['briŋnd'bai], *a.* **b.-a.-b. sale,** vente *f* de charité (où tout le monde est censé d'apporter quelque chose et d'acheter quelque chose).

bringer ['briŋər], *s.* porteur, -euse (d'une lettre, d'une nouvelle, etc.).

bringing up ['briŋiŋʌp], *s.* éducation *f* (d'un enfant); **b. up six children is no easy matter,** il n'est pas facile d'élever six enfants.

brininess ['braininis], *s.* salinité *f.*

brinjal ['brindʒəl], *s. Bot:* aubergine *f.*

brink [briŋk], *s.* bord *m* (d'un précipice, d'un fleuve); **to stand shivering on the b.,** hésiter à plonger, à faire le plongeon; *F:* **on the b. of . . .,** tout près de . . .; **to be on the b. of ruin,** être à deux doigts, à la veille, de la ruine; pencher vers la ruine; être sur le bord de l'abîme; **to be on the b. of tears,** être au bord des larmes; **to be on the b. of a discovery,** ne pas être loin d'une découverte; être à la veille d'une découverte.

brinkmanship ['briŋkmənʃip], *s.* acrobatie *f* politique, politique *f* du bord de l'abîme, de la corde raide; diplomatie *f* du bord du gouffre.

briny ['braini]. **1.** *a.* saumâtre, salé; *Poet:* **the b. deep,** l'onde amère. **2.** *s. F:* **the b.,** la mer, la grande tasse.

brio ['bri(:)ou], *s. Mus:* brio *m.*

brioche [bri(:)'ɔʃ], *s. Bak:* brioche *f.*

briolet(te) ['bri:əlet], *s. Lap:* brillolette *f,* briolette *f.*

briony ['braiəni], *s.* = BRYONY.

briquette[1] [bri'ket], *s.* (*a*) *Fuel:* briquette *f;* aggloméré *m, pl.* **briquettes,** charbon *m* de Paris; (*b*) *Metall:* pellet *m;* (*c*) **(ice-cream) b.,** pavé *m* de glace.

briquette[2], *v.tr.* briqueter; **sawdust can be briquetted easily,** la sciure de bois se transforme facilement en briquettes; **briquetted fuel,** combustible *m* en briquettes.

brisance [bri:zɑ̃s], *s. Exp:* brisance *f.*

brisé[1] ['bri:zei], *a. Her:* brisé.

brisé[2], *s. Danc:* brisé *m.*

brise-bise ['bri:zbi:z], *s. Furn: A:* brise-bise *m inv.*

brise-soleil ['bri:zsɔ'lei], *s. Const:* brise-soleil *m inv.*

brisk[1] [brisk], *a.* **1.** (*of pers., movement*) vif, actif, alerte, animé, plein d'entrain; **b. old man,** vieillard *m* ingambe, alerte, guilleret; **at a b. pace,** à vive allure; **to take a b. walk,** se promener à bon pas; *Com:* **b. trade,** commerce actif; **b. market,** marché animé; **b. demand,** demande animée; **the demand is b.,** la demande présente de l'animation; **business is b.,** les affaires marchent, vont; **b. fire,** (i) feu vif; (ii) *Mil:* feu nourri; *Nau:* **b. wind,** vent rond. **2.** (*a*) (air) vivifiant; (*b*) (champagne) pétillant; (bière *f*) qui mousse bien; (eau de Seltz) bien gazeuse.

brisk[2], *A:* **brisken** ['briskən]. **1.** *v.tr.* **to b. s.o. up,** animer, activer, émoustiller, qn; **to b. up a horse,** animer un cheval; **to b. up a fire,** activer le feu; **to b. (up) one's pace,** presser le pas. **2.** *v.i.* **to b. up,** s'animer, s'émoustiller, se ragaillardir; s'activer; **to b. up again,** se ranimer.

brisket ['briskit], *s.* (*a*) *A:* poitrine *f,* bréchet *m; Box: & P:* **one in the b.,** coup *m* en pleine poitrine; (*b*) *Cu:* poitrine, avant-cœur *m* (de bœuf); **hind b.,** contre-filet *m, pl.* contre-filets.

briskly ['briskli], *adv.* vivement, activement; avec entrain; sans mollesse; **to step out b.,** marcher d'un pas accéléré; **to return home b.,** rentrer d'un pas alerte.

briskness ['brisknis], *s.* **1.** (*a*) vivacité *f,* activité *f,* animation *f,* entrain *m;* (*b*) activité (des affaires, du marché). **2.** (*a*) fraîcheur *f* (de l'air); (*b*) pétillement *m* (du champagne).

brisky ['briski], *a. A:* **1.** (*of pers.*) éméché; légèrement pris de boisson. **2.** (*of lamb, etc.*) folâtre.

brisling ['brizliŋ], *s. Ich:* sprat *m,* anchois *m* de Norvège.

brisque [bri(:)sk], *s. Cards:* (*bezique*) brisque *f.*

bristle[1] ['brisl], *s.* **1.** soie *f* (de porc, de sanglier, de chenille); soie, poil *m* (de brosse); poil raide (de la barbe); *F:* **to stick up one's bristles,** se hérisser, se rebiffer. **2.** (*a*) *Bot:* soie, poil, **b. shaped,** sétiforme; **b. fern,** trichomane *m;* **b. grass,** sétaire *f,* setaria *m;* (*b*) *Ann:* **b. worm,** chétopode *m;* **marine b. worm,** polychète *m.*

bristle[2]. **1.** *v.tr.* (*of animal*) hérisser (ses poils, ses soies). **2.** *v.i.* (*a*) (*of animal, hair, etc.*) **to b. (up),** se hérisser; *F:* (*of pers.*) se rebiffer, se hérisser; *F:* faire le gros dos; (*b*) **to b. with bayonets,** être hérissé de baïonnettes; **to b. with difficulties,** être hérissé de difficultés. **3.** *v.tr.* **this brush is not bristled for cleaning the floor,** les poils de cette brosse ne sont pas suffisamment durs pour nettoyer le plancher.

bristled ['brisld], *a.* couvert, garni, de poils raides; poilu.

bristletail ['brislteil], *s. Ent:* lépisme *m; F:* poisson *m* d'argent, petit poisson d'or; **myrmecophilous b.,** lépisme myrmécophile.

bristling[1] [brisliŋ], *a.* hérissé (**with,** de); **b. moustache,** moustache *f* en bataille.

bristling[2], *s.* = BRISLING.

bristly ['brisli], *a.* (*a*) couvert, garni, de soies, de poils raides; poilu; **b. moustache,** moustache hérissée, raide; **b. beard,** barbe *f* raide, rude; (*b*) *Bot:* poilu; garni de soies; sétacé, sétifère; **b. foxtail,** sétaire *f;* **b. oxtongue,** picride *f,* **b. palmetto,** palmier nain sétigère.

Bristol ['brist(ə)l], *Pr.n. Geog:* Bristol; **the B. Channel,** le Canal de Bristol; **B. board,** carton *m* Bristol; bristol *m;* **B. milk,** (vin *m* de) xérès doux; **B. diamond, B. stone,** cristal *m* de roche; **B. brick,** brique anglaise; *Nau:* **B. fashion,** bien arrangé.

brisure ['bri:ʒu:ər], *s. Her:* brisure *f.*

Britain ['brit(ə)n], *Pr.n.* **1.** *Hist:* la Bretagne (plus tard l'Angleterre). **2.** *Geog:* **Great B.,** la Grande-Bretagne; **North B.,** l'Écosse *f.*

Britannia [bri'tæniə], *Pr.n.* (nom symbolique de) la Grande-Bretagne; *Com:* **B. metal,** métal anglais, britannia *m.*

Britannic [bri'tænik], *a.* **His, Her, B. Majesty,** Sa Majesté britannique.

britannicize [bri'tænisaiz], *v.tr.* angliciser.

britch [britʃ], *s. Tex:* laine *f* cuisse; loquet *m.*

Briticism ['britisizm], *s. Ling: NAm:* anglicisme *m.*

British ['britiʃ], *a.* **1.** britannique, de la Grande-Bretagne; (*in Fr. usu.*) anglais, d'Angleterre; **the B. Isles,** les Iles Britanniques; *Hist:* **B. India,** l'Inde anglais; **the B. consul,** le consul d'Angleterre; **B. goods,** produits anglais, marchandises anglaises; **B. flora,** flore *f* de la Grande-Bretagne; **B. gum,** dextrine *f; NAm:* **B. English,** l'anglais britannique; *Mil: A:* **B. warm,** pardessus *m* d'officier, *s.pl.* **the B.,** les Britanniques, *F:* les Anglais. **2.** *Hist:* breton, -onne (de la Grande-Bretagne); **the B. cycle (of romance),** le cycle breton.

Britisher ['britiʃər], *s. NAm:* natif, -ive, de (la) Grande Bretagne; Britannique *mf, F:* Anglais, -aise.

Britishism ['britiʃizm], *s. NAm:* anglicisme *m.*

Briton ['brit(ə)n], *s.* **1.** *Hist:* Breton, -onne (de la Grande-Bretagne). **2.** Britannique, *F:* Anglais, -aise; **North B.,** Écossais, -aise; **a true B.,** un véritable Anglais; un patriote.

britska ['britʃkə, -skə], *s. Veh:* briska *m.*

Brittany ['britəni], *Pr.n. Geog:* Bretagne *f.*

brittle ['britl], *a.* fragile, cassant; *Metalw.* aigre, sec, rouverin, revêche; (acier) cendreux; *Glassm:* casilleux; **to be as b. as glass,** être fragile comme le cristal; se briser comme du verre; *Miner:* **b. mica,** clintonite *f;* **b. silver ore,** stéphanite *f; Echin:* **b. star,** ophiure *f; Rept:* **b. snake,** ophisaure *m.*

brittleness ['britlnis], *s.* fragilité *f; Metalw:* frangibilité *f.*

Brittonic [bri'tɔnik], *a. & s. Ling:* brittonique (*m*).

britzka ['britʃkə, -tskə], *s. Veh:* briska *m.*

briza ['braizə], *s. Bot:* briza *f,* brize *f.*

brize [bri:z], *s. Ent:* taon *m.*

broach [1] [broutʃ], *s.* **1.** *Cu:* broche *f* (à rôtir). **2.** *Arch:* flèche *f,* aiguille *f* (d'église). **3.** *Tls:* (*a*) équarrissoir *m;* broche (à mandriner); alésoir *m;* louche *f;* alêne *f;* poinçon *m;* mèche *f* de foret; **six-square b.,** alésoir à six pans; **roughing b.,** broche dégrossisseuse; **finishing b.,** broche finisseuse; (*b*) *Coop:* perçoir *m;* (*c*) pivot *m,* broche (d'une serrure). **4.** *Tex:* navette *f* à tapisserie.

broach[2], *v.tr.* **1.** *Cu:* embrocher. **2.** (*a*) *Metalw:* aléser (un trou, un tube); mandriner, équarrir, brocher; (*b*) *Coop:* percer (un fût); mettre (un fût, du vin) en perce; entamer (un fût); **broached cask, wine,** tonneau *m,* vin, en vidange, en perce. **3.** entamer, aborder (une question, etc.); **to b. the subject,** entrer en matière; **if I see him I shall try to b. the subject,** si je le vois je tâcherai de lui en toucher un mot.

broach[3], *v. Nau:* **1.** *v.i.* (*of ship*) **to b. (to),** venir en travers; tomber en travers; embarder au vent; recevoir la lame par le travers; faire chapelle; lancer dans le vent. **2.** *v.tr.* **to b. a ship to,** lancer un vaisseau dans le vent.

broaching ['broutʃiŋ], *s.* **1.** alésage *m* (d'un trou); mandrinage *m;* brochage *m;* **b. machine,** aléseuse équarrisseuse; machine *f* à brocher, à mandriner (à la broche); brocheuse *f.* **2.** mise *f* en perce (d'un fût); perçage *m.* **3.** *Min:* battage *m* au large; entaillage *m* (des épontes).

broad [brɔ:d]. **1.** *a.* (*a*) large; **the road is 15 metres b.,** la route a 15 mètres de large; **the estuary becomes broader below the port,** en aval du port l'estuaire s'élargit; **a b. expanse of wheat,** une vaste étendue de blé; **the b. sea(s),** le baste océan; *Sp: NAm:* **b. jump,** saut *m* en longueur; *Lit:* **the (land of the) b. acres** = le Yorkshire; **to have a b. back,** (i) avoir une forte carrure; (ii) *Fig:* avoir bon dos; **b. grin,** sourire épanoui; **in b. daylight,** (i) dans la lumière crue; (ii) en plein jour; au grand jour; en plein midi; (iii) *Fig:* à la lumière du grand jour; devant tout le monde; **it is b. daylight,** il fait grand jour; *Cin:* **b. lighting,** éclairage frontal; *Ling:* **b. vowel,** voyelle large; **it's as b. as it is long,** cela revient au même; c'est du pareil au même; c'est tout un; c'est la même chose; c'est bonnet blanc et blanc bonnet; (*b*) *Fig:* **b. rule,** règle générale; règle de principe; **b. distinction,** distinction *f* sommaire; **term used in a b. sense, in its broadest sense,** terme employé dans un sens (très) large; (*c*) **b. accent,** accent *m* de la région, du terroir; **he's got a b. accent,** il a un accent prononcé; **to speak b. Scots, Scotch,** parler l'anglais d'Écosse avec un accent prononcé; (*d*) hardi, risqué, cru, *F:* salé, corsé; **b. humour,** (i) humour de mauvais goût, peu délicat, hardi; (ii) grosse farce; **b. laugh,** gros rire; **b. joke,** grosse plaisanterie; plaisanterie risquée; (*e*) **b. views, ideas, outlook,** idées larges, tolérantes. **2.** *s.* (*a*) **the b. of the back,** toute la largeur du dos; le milieu du dos; (*b*) *Geog:* plan d'eau formé par une rivière; **the Norfolk Broads,** la région de lacs et de marécages du Norfolk; (*c*) *esp. U.S: P:* femme *f,* fille *f, P:* gonzesse *f;* (*d*) *Tls:* biseau *m;* gouge *f.* **3.** *adv.* **b. awake,** tout réveillé; complètement réveillé.

broadaxe (*NAm: also* **broadax**) ['brɔ:dæks], *s. Tls:* doloire *f.*

broad-backed ['brɔ:d'bækt], *a.* à large dos; qui a le dos large.

broadband ['brɔ:dbænd], *s. Cmptr:* bande *f* large.

broadbill ['brɔ:dbil], *s. Orn:* eurylaime *m.*

broad-bottomed ['brɔ:d'bɔtəmd], *a.* (*a*) (bateau) à fond plat; (*b*) *F:* (*of pers.*) fessu.

broadbrim ['brɔ:dbrim], *s. NAm:* chapeau *m* à larges bords.

broad-brimmed ['brɔ:d'brimd], *a.* (chapeau *m*) à larges bords.

broadcast[1] ['brɔ:dkɑ:st]. **1.** *adv. Agr:* à la volée; **to sow b.,** semer à la volée, à tout vent; **b. sowing,** semis *m* à la volée; **b. sower,** semoir *m* à la volée; **to scatter money b.,** semer l'argent à pleines mains; **scattered b.,** répandu à profusion. **2.** *a.* (*a*) *Agr:* semé à la volée; (*b*) *W.Tel: T.V:* (radio)diffusé; **b. announcement,** annonce *f* par radio; radio émission *f, pl.* radio-émissions; **b. account of a match,** radioreportage *m* d'un match.

broadcast[2], *v.* (**broadcast; broadcast**) **1.** *v.tr.* (*a*) *Agr:* semer (du grain) à la volée; (*b*) répandre (une nouvelle). **2.** *W.Tel: T.V:* (*p.t. occ.* **broadcasted**) (*a*) *v.tr.* radiodiffuser, transmettre, diffuser (un programme); **running commentary on the Grand Prix b. from Longchamp,** radioreportage *m* du Grand Prix depuis Longchamp; (*b*) *v.i.* chanter, parler, jouer, etc., à la radio; paraître à la télévision. **3.** *v.tr. Cmptr:* diffuser.

broadcast[3], *s.* **1.** *W.Tel: T.V:* émission *f;* programme radiodiffusé, télévisé; **simultaneous b.,** émission simultanée; **live b.,** (i) *W.Tel:* émission en direct; (ii) *T.V:* prise de vue directe; **recorded b.,** émission en différé. **2.** *Cmptr:* diffusion *f.*

broadcaster ['brɔ:dkɑ:stər], *s. W.Tel:* **1.** *O:* (appareil) émetteur *m,* diffuseur *m.* **2.** personne *f* qui parle, qui chante, etc. à la radio, qui paraît à la télévision; radioreporter *m;* chroniqueur, -euse; speaker, speakerine.

broadcasting ['brɔ:dkɑ:stiŋ], *s.* **1.** *Agr:* semaille *f* à la volée. **2.** *W.Tel: T.V:* radio-émission *f,* radiodiffusion *f,* radiophonie *f;* **b. of news,** radioreportage *m;* **b. station,** station *f* de radiodiffusion; poste émetteur; poste d'émission radiophonique; **the British B. Corporation, the B.B.C.** [bi:bi:'si:], la Corporation britannique de radiodiffusion; **a good b. voice,** une voix radiogénique; **this is the end of today's b.,** voici la fin de nos émissions pour aujourd'hui.

broadcloth ['brɔ:dklɔθ], *s. Tex:* **1.** drap noir fin, de première qualité (*A:* de grande largeur), pour vêtements d'hommes. **2.** *NAm:* popeline *f.*

broaden ['brɔ:d(ə)n], **1.** *v.tr.* élargir; **actor who has broadened his style,** acteur *m* qui a élargi son jeu; *Mus:* **to b. the time,** élargir la mesure; **to b. s.o.'s outlook,** élargir l'horizon de qn. **2.** *v.i.* s'élargir; **his face broadened (out) into a grin,** un large sourire lui épanouit le visage; **broadening channel,** chenal *m* qui s'évase.

broad-flanged ['brɔ:d'flændʒd], *a. Const:* **b.-f. beam,** poutre *f* à larges ailes.

broad-headed ['brɔːd'hedid], *a. Anthr:* brachycéphale.

broad-headedness ['brɔːd'hedidnis], *s. Anthr:* brachycéphalie *f.*

broad-leaved ['brɔːd'liːvd], *a.* à larges feuilles; *Bot:* latifolié; **b.-l. forest,** forêt feuillue.

broadloom ['brɔːdluːm], *a.* **b. carpet,** tapis uni grande largeur.

broadly ['brɔːdli], *adv.* **1.** largement; **b. speaking,** généralement parlant; d'une façon générale; grosso modo. **2.** (parler) (i) avec un accent prononcé, (ii) grossièrement.

broad-minded ['brɔːd'maindid], *a.* **to be b.-m.,** (i) avoir l'esprit large, les idées larges; être tolérant, large d'esprit; (ii) *Pej:* avoir la conscience large, élastique.

broad-mindedness ['brɔːd'maindidnis], *s.* (*a*) largeur *f* d'esprit; tolérance *f*; (*b*) *Pej:* élasticité *f* de conscience.

broadness ['brɔːdnis], *s.* **1.** largeur *f.* **2.** (*a*) grossièreté *f,* vulgarité *f* (d'une plaisanterie, etc.); (*b*) **the b. of his speech,** son accent prononcé.

broad-nibbed ['brɔːnibd], *a.* **b.-n. pen,** stylo *m* à grosse plume.

broad-nosed ['brɔːd'nouzd], *a.* (personne *f*) au nez épaté; (outil) camard, camus.

broadsheet ['brɔːdʃiːt], *s.* **1.** *Typ:* in-plano *m inv.* **2.** *Lit.Hist:* canard *m*; feuille imprimée (relatant ou satirisant un fait du jour).

broad-shouldered ['brɔːd'ʃouldəd], *a.* large d'épaules, aux larges épaules; trapu; carré.

broadside ['brɔːdsaid], *s.* **1.** *Nau:* (*a*) flanc *m,* travers *m* (du navire); **on the b.,** par le travers; (*of ship*) **to be b. on to sth.,** présenter le côté, le flanc, le travers, à qch.; se présenter de flanc; **to keep b. on to the sea,** prendre, recevoir, la lame par le travers; **collision b. on,** abordage *m* par le travers; **to ram a ship b. on,** aborder un navire de bout en plein, par le travers; (*b*) **to fire a b.,** (i) tirer une bordée; (ii) *Fig:* assaillir (qn) d'une tempête d'injures; **to exchange broadsides,** se canonner par le travers; **b. fire,** feu *m* de batterie, feu de travers. **2.** (*a*) *A:* BROADSHEET 2; (*b*) *NAm: Com:* dépliant *m.* **3.** *Cin:* projecteur *m* grand angle.

broadstone ['brɔːdstoun], *s.* pierre *f* de parement.

broadsword ['brɔːdsɔːd], *s.* sabre *m*; latte *f.*

broadtail ['brɔːdteil], *s.* **1.** *Z:* (*also* **broadtailed sheep**) caracul *m.* **2.** *Com:* breitschwanz *m.*

broadwalk ['brɔːdwɔːk], *s. A:* (*at the seaside*) les planches *f.*

broadways, broadwise ['brɔːdweiz, -waiz], *adv.* en large; dans le sens de la largeur.

Brobdingnagian [brɔbdiŋ'nægiən], *a.* de Brobdingnag (pays de géants dans les "Voyages de Gulliver" de Swift); pantagruélique.

brocade[1] [brə'keid], *s. Tex:* brocart *m*; **gold, silver, b.,** brocart, drap *m,* d'or, d'argent; **velvet b.,** brocart velours.

brocade[2], *v.tr. Tex:* brocher.

brocaded [brə'keidid], *a. Tex:* broché; **b. gown,** robe *f* de brocart; **b. in gold,** broché d'or.

brocatelle [brɔkə'tel], *s.* **1.** *Tex:* brocatelle *f.* **2.** *Miner:* brocatelle.

brocatello [brɔkə'telou], *s. Miner:* brocatelle *f.*

broc(c)oli ['brɔkəli], *s. Hort: Cu:* brocoli *m.*

broch [brɔχ], *s.* **1.** *Archeol:* tour ronde picte. **2.** halo *m* (de la lune).

brochantite [brɔ'ʃæntait], *s. Miner:* brochantite *f.*

broché ['brɔʃei], *Tex:* **1.** *a.* broché. **2.** *s.* brocart *m.*

brochette [brɔ'ʃet], *s.* (*a*) brochette *f* (à médailles); (*b*) *Cu:* brochette.

brochure [brou'ʃjuər, 'brouʃəːr], *s.* brochure *f,* dépliant *m*; prospectus *m* publicitaire.

brock [brɔk], *s. A: & Dial:* blaireau *m.*

Brocken ['brɔk(ə)n], *Pr.n. Meteor:* **B. spectre,** spectre *m* du Brocken.

brocket ['brɔkit], *s. Ven:* daguet *m.*

brodekin, brodequin, brodkin ['brɔdkin], *s.* brodequin *m.*

broderie Anglaise ['brɔdri ɑːŋ'gleiz], *s.* broderie anglaise.

bröggerite ['brœgərait], *s. Miner:* bröggerite *f.*

brogue[1] [broug], *s.* **1.** *A:* brogue *f*; chaussure *f* en cuir cru (des Irlandais et des Écossais). **2.** soulier *m* de golf; **b. heel,** talon bas (de soulier de dame). **3. fishing brogues,** brodequins *m* de pêche; *f* brogues.

brogue[2], *s.* (*a*) accent *m* de terroir; (*b*) accent irlandais.

broigne [brɔin], *s. A.Arms:* broigne *f.*

broil[1] [brɔil], *s.* querelle *f*; bagarre *f,* échauffourée *f*; (*between two persons*) rixe *f.*

broil[2], *s. NAm:* viande grillée, cuite sur le gril; grillade *f.*

broil[3], *v.tr. & i.* (*a*) *NAm: Cu:* griller; (faire) cuire sur le gril; (*b*) *F:* **we were broiling in the sun,** on grillait au soleil.

broiler[1] ['brɔilər], *s. O:* querelleur, -euse.

broiler[2], *s.* **1.** (*a*) (*pers.*) *NAm:* grilleur *m*; (*b*) *F:* **it's really a b.,** il fait une chaleur torride. **2.** *NAm:* gril *m,* rôtissoire *f.* **3.** *F:* **b. (fowl),** poulet *m* de chair (à rôtir); **b. house,** batterie *f* (pour l'élevage des poulets de chair).

broiling[1] ['brɔiliŋ], *a. F:* (*of the sun*) ardent, brûlant; **b. atmosphere,** atmosphère embrassée; **b. weather,** atmosphère embrasée; **b. weather,** chaleur *f* torride; *adv.* **it's b. hot in this room,** on cuit dans cette pièce.

broiling[2], *s. NAm:* cuisson *f* sur le gril.

broke [brouk], *a. F:* (*a*) **to be b., stony b., dead b., b. to the wide,** être sans le sou, dans la dèche, dans la débine; être fauché; (*b*) *Austr:* **to be b. for a feed,** avoir faim.

broken ['broukn], *a.* (*a*) cassé; brisé; rompu; *O:* **b. meats,** rogatons *mpl,* desserte *f,* restes *mpl*; **b. biscuits,** biscuits cassés; miettes *fpl* de biscuits; *Typ:* **b. line,** tireté *m*; **a table with b. legs,** une table aux pieds cassés; **I don't want to get a b. head,** je ne veux pas me faire casser la tête; **b. ribs,** côtes enfoncées; **he is b. in health,** sa santé est délabrée, détraquée, ruinée; **people b. (in) to servitude,** peuple assoupli à la servitude; **his spirit is b.,** il est abattu, découragé; **a b. man,** (i) un homme ruiné; (ii) un homme au cœur brisé; **b. home,** ménage désuni; foyer détruit; **b. promise,** promesse violée, manquée; (*b*) (terrain) accidenté; (chemin) raboteux, défoncé; (sommeil) interrompu, irrégulier, (entre) coupé, agité; (temps) incertain, variable; **forest b. by wide clearings,** forêt trouée de larges clairières; **b. coast,** rivage tourmenté; **b. outline,** contour anfractueux; **b. sea,** mer battue; **b. water,** brisants *mpl*; **voice b. with sobs,** voix entrecoupée de sanglots; **b. words,** paroles entrecoupées; **in a b. voice,** d'une voix entrecoupée, altérée; **to speak in b. English,** écorcher, estropier, l'anglais; (*c*) *Tchn:* **boiler with b. joints,** chaudière *f* à joints contrariés; **b. coke,** coke cancasse; **b. slag,** laitier concassé; **b. brick(s),** briquaillons *mpl*; pierraille *f*; débris *m* de briques; concassé *m*; **b. gravel,** gravier concassé; gravillons *mpl*; **b. rock, stone,** pierres (con)cassées; **b. concrete,** débris *m* de béton; *Tex:* **b. ends,** casses *fpl*; **b. picks,** fausse duite; (*d*) *Com:* **b. lots,** articles dépareillés; occasions *f,* soldes *m.*

broken-backed ['broukn'bækt], *a.* (*a*) aux reins cassés, brisés; (*b*) *Nau:* (navire) arqué, cassé.

broken down ['broukn'daun], *a.* (*of pers.*) cassé; brisé (par la douleur); (*of horse*) usé, ruiné, fourbu; (*of health, furniture, etc.*) délabré; (*of car, etc.*) (i) en panne; (ii) en mauvais état; (*of any mechanism*) (i) détraqué; (ii) détérioré, qui tombe en morceaux; **b. d. with age,** cassé de vieillesse; **to be b. d. in health,** avoir la santé détraquée, ruinée; **b.-d. firm,** entreprise *f* qui ne bat que d'une aile, qui bat de l'aile.

broken-feathered ['broukn'feðəːd], *a. Ven:* (faucon) halbrené.

broken-gaited ['broukn'geitid], *a. Vet:* (cheval) détraqué.

brokenhearted ['broukn'hɑːtid], *a.* navré de douleur; au cœur brisé; **to die b.-h.,** mourir de douleur, de chagrin.

brokenheartedly ['broukn'hɑːtidli], *adv.* le cœur navré.

brokenheartedness ['broukn'hɑːtidnis], *s.* douleur *f,* chagrin profond.

broken-kneed ['broukn'niːd], *a. Vet:* (cheval) couronné.

brokenly ['brouknli], *adv.* sans suite, par saccades, par à-coups; (parler) à mots entrecoupés.

broken wind ['broukn'wind], *s. Vet:* pousse *f.*

broken-winded ['broukn'windid], *a. Vet:* (cheval) poussif.

broker ['broukər], *s.* **1.** (*a*) *Com:* courtier *m* (de commerce); **bill b.,** courtier de change; **cotton b.,** courtier en coton; **he is a sugar b.,** il est courtier en sucre; il fait le courtage des sucres; **insurance b.,** courtier d'assurances; (*b*) *St.Exch:* **(stock) b.,** agent *m* de change; courtier de bourse; **intermediate b.,** remisier *m*; **outside b.,** coulissier *m*; courtier marron, libre. **2.** (*second-hand*) brocanteur, -euse. **3.** *Jur:* (i) = *approx.* commissaire-priseur *m* (*licensed to appraise and sell goods*); (ii) = *approx.* huissier *m* (*authorized to distrain on a tenant*).

brokerage ['broukəridʒ], *s. Fin:* **1.** (*profession of broker*) courtage *m*; **outside b.,** affaires *fpl* de banque. **2.** (*commission*) (frais *mpl* de) courtage.

broking ['broukiŋ], *s.* = BROKERAGE 1.

brolga ['brɔlgə], *s. Orn:* grue *f* d'Australie.

brolly ['brɔli], *s. F:* (*a*) parapluie *m,* pépin *m,* riflard *m*; (*b*) parachute *m*; pépin.

bromacetic [broumə'setik, -'siːtik], *a. Ch:* bromacétique.

bromacetone [brou'mæsetoun], *s. Ch:* bromacétone *f.*

bromal ['broum(ə)l], *s. Ch: Pharm:* bromal *m.*

bromargyrite [brou'mɑːdʒirait], *s. Miner:* bromargyrite *f,* bromargyre *f,* bromyrite *f,* bromite *f.*

bromate ['broumeit], *s. Ch:* bromate *m.*

bromatology [broumə'tɔlədʒi], *s. Med:* bromatologie *f.*

brome [broum], *s. Bot:* **b. (grass),** brome *f*; **field b. grass,** brome des prés.

bromel ['brouməl], *s. Bot:* broméliacée *f.*

bromelia [brou'miːliə], *s. Bot:* bromélie *f*; bromélia *m.*

Bromeliaceae [broumiːli'eisiiː], *s.pl. Bot:* broméliacées *f.*

bromeliad [brou'miːliæd], *s. Bot:* broméliacée *f.*

bromhidrosis [broumhi'drousis], *s. Med:* bromidrose *f.*

bromic ['broumik], *a. Ch:* bromique; **b. acid,** acide *m* bromique.

bromide ['broumaid], *s.* **1.** *Ch:* bromure *m*; *Phot:* **b. paper,** papier *m* au gélatinobromure; papier au bromure (d'argent); **rough b. print,** bromure *m*; **to add b. to the developer,** bromurer le révélateur. **2.** *P:* (*a*) homme ennuyeux; raseur *m*; (*b*) banalité *f*; lieu commun.

bromidic [brou'midik], *a. P:* (*a*) ennuyeux; rasant, barbant; (*b*) banal.

bromidism ['broumidizm, -maid-], *s. Med:* bromisme *m.*

bromidrosis [broumi'drousis], *s. Med:* bromidrose *f.*

brominate ['broumineit], *v.tr. Ch:* bromer.

bromination [broumi'neiʃ(ə)n], *s. Ch:* bromation *f.*

bromine ['broumi(ː)n, -ain], *s. Ch:* brome *m*; **b. water,** eau bromée.

brom(in)ism ['broum(in)izm], *s. Med:* bromisme *m.*

bromize ['broumaiz], *v.tr. Ch:* bromurer.

bromlite ['brɔmlait], *s. Miner:* bromlite *f.*

bromoacetic ['broumouə'siːtik, -'setik], *a. Ch:* bromacétique.

bromoacetone ['broumou'æsitoun], *s. Ch:* bromacétone *f.*

bromobenzene ['broumouben'ziːn], *s. Ch:* bromobenzène *m.*

bromoform ['broumoufɔːm], *s. Ch:* bromoforme *m.*

bromoil ['broumɔil], *s. A.Phot:* (procédé *m,* épreuve *f*) bromoïl *m*; oléobromie *f.*

bromophenol [broumou'fiːnɔl, -'fenɔl], *s. Ch:* bromophénol *m.*

bromyrite ['broumirait], *s. Miner:* bromyrite *f,* bromargyrite *f,* bromargyre *f,* bromite *f.*

bronchia ['brɔŋkiə], *s.pl. Anat:* bronches *f.*

bronchial ['brɔŋkiəl], *a. Anat:* bronchial, -aux; bronchique; des bronches; **the b. tubes,** les bronches *f*; **b. artery,** artère *f* bronchique; *Med:* **b. asthma,** asthme *m* bronchique; **b. pneumonia,** broncho-pneumonie *f.*

bronchiectasia [brɔŋkiek'teiziə], **bronchiectasis,** *pl.* **-es** [brɔŋki'ektəsis, -iːz], *s. Med:* bronch(i)ectasie *f.*

bronchiole ['brɔŋkioul], *s. Anat:* bronchiole *f,* bronche *f* intralobulaire.

bronchiolitis [brɔŋkiou'laitis], *s. Med:* bronchiolite *f.*

bronchitic [brɔŋ'kitik], *a. & s. Med:* bronchitique (*mf*).

bronchitis [brɔŋ'kaitis], *s. Med:* bronchite *f*; **capillary b.,** bronchite capillaire.

bronchium, *pl.* **-ia** ['brɔŋkiəm, -iə], *s. Anat:* bronche *f* extralobulaire.

bronchocele ['brɔŋkousiːl], *s. Med:* bronchocèle *f.*

bronchogram ['brɔŋkougræm], *s. Med:* bronchographie *f.*

bronchography [brɔŋ'kɔgrəfi], *s. Med:* bronchographie *f.*

broncholith ['brɔŋkouliθ], *s. Med:* broncholithe *f.*

bronchophony [brɔŋ'kɔfəni], *s. Med:* bronchophonie *f.*

bronchopleurisy ['brɔŋkou'pluərisi], *s. Med:* bronchopleurésie *f.*

bronchopneumonia ['brɔŋkounjuː'mouniə], *s. Med:* broncho-pneumonie *f.*

bronchorrhea [brɔŋkou'riːə], *s. Med:* bronchorrhée *f.*

bronchoscope ['brɔŋkəskoup], *s. Med:* bronchoscope *m.*

bronchoscopy [brɔŋ'kɔskəpi], *s. Med:* bronchoscopie *f.*

bronchospasm ['brɔŋkouspæzm], *s. Med:* bronchospasme *m.*

bronchospirometry ['brɔŋkouspai'rɔmitri], *s.* bronchospirométrie *f.*

bronchostenosis ['brɔŋkouste'nousis], *s.* bronchosténose *f.*

bronchotome ['brɔŋkoutoum], *s. Surg:* bronchotome *m.*

bronchotomy [brɔŋ'kɔtəmi], *s. Surg:* bronchotomie *f.*

bronchus, *pl.* **-i** ['brɔŋkəs; -iː, -ai], *s. Anat:* bronche *f* souche.

bronco ['brɔŋkou], *s.* (*a*) cheval sauvage, non dressé, de l'Amérique; (*b*) *U.S: F:* cheval; (*c*) *F:* **b. buster,** dresseur *m* de chevaux; cowboy *m* qui dresse des chevaux sauvages.

brontolite ['brɔntəlait], **brontolith** ['brɔntəliθ], *s. Miner:* brontolithe *m.*

brontometer [brɔn'tɔmitər], *s. Meteor:* brontomètre *m.*

brontosaur ['brɔntəsɔːr], **brontosaurus**

[brɔntə'sɔ:rəs], *s. Paleont:* brontosaure *m*, brontosaurus *m*.
brontothere ['brɔntəθiər], **brontotherium** [brɔntə'θiəriəm], *s. Paleont:* brontothérium *m*.
Brontotheriidae ['brɔntouθə'riidi:], *s.pl. Paleont:* brontothéridés *m*.
bronze[1] [brɔnz]. **1.** *s.* (*a*) *Metall:* bronze *m*; **aluminium b.,** bronze d'aluminium; *Mec.E:* **bearing b.,** bronze pour coussinets; **b. weld(ing),** soudo-brasure *f*; **b. founder,** fondeur *m* en bronze; bronzier *m*; (*b*) *Art:* (objet *m* en) bronze; **imitation b.,** similibronze *m*; **a collection of bronzes and ivories,** une collection de bronzes et d'ivoires. **2.** *attrib.* (*a*) de bronze; **b. statue,** statue *f* de, en, bronze; (*b*) (cuir) bronzé, mordoré; **b. paint,** peinture bronzée; **b. shoes,** souliers mordorés.
bronze[2]. **1.** *v.tr.* (*a*) bronzer (le fer, etc.); *F:* **bronzed skin,** peau bronzée, basanée, cuivrée; (*b*) mordorer (le cuir, des souliers). **2.** *v.i.* se bronzer; brunir; *Phot:* se métalliser.
bronzesmith ['brɔnzsmiθ], *s.* bronzier *m*.
bronzewing ['brɔnzwiŋ], *s. Orn:* **crested b.,** ocyphaps *m*, lophote *m*.
bronzing ['brɔnziŋ], *s.* **1.** bronzage *m*. **2.** *Phot:* métallisation *f*; *Typ:* **b. machine,** bronzeuse *f*.
bronzite ['brɔnzait], *s. Miner:* bronzite *f*.
brooch [broutʃ], *s. Cost:* broche *f*, épingle *f*; **b. pin,** queue *f* de broche; **diamond b.,** broche de diamants.
brood[1] [bru:d], *s.* **1.** (*a*) couvée *f* (de poussins); volée *f* (de pigeons); naissain *m* (d'huîtres, de moules); (*b*) *Breed:* **b. mare,** (jument) poulinière *f*; (*c*) *Ap:* **b. comb,** couvain *m*; **b. cell,** cellule *f* d'incubation. **2.** *F:* (*a*) enfants *mpl*; progéniture *f*; *F:* marmaille *f*; **with all his b. around him,** accompagné de toute sa smala; (*b*) *Pej:* **b. of scoundrels,** race *f* de scélérats.
brood[2], *v.i.* **1.** (*of hen*) couver, accouver. **2.** *Fig:* (*a*) broyer du noir; **to b. on, over, sth.,** remâcher, ressasser (le passé); rêver à qch.; ruminer (une idée); **to b. over things,** remuer, repasser, des idées dans sa tête; **to b. over the fire,** couver le feu; **old woman brooding over the fire,** vieille accouvée au coin du feu; **to b. over plans for revenge,** ruminer des projets de vengeance; (*b*) **night, silence, broods over the scene,** la nuit, le silence, plane sur la scène; **a deathly silence broods over the whole of nature,** un silence de mort pèse sur toute la nature; **the storm brooding over us,** l'orage *m* qui plane, qui couve, sur nos têtes.
brooder ['bru:dər], *s.* **1.** (poule) couveuse *f*. **2.** couveuse (artificielle).
broodiness ['bru:dinis], *s.* humeur songeuse.
brooding ['bru:diŋ], *a.* **1.** *Lit:* **b. darkness,** obscurité *f* qui enveloppe, recouvre, tout. **2. b. thoughts,** idées rêveuses.
broody ['bru:di]. **1.** *a.* (*a*) **b. hen,** poule couveuse, qui veut couver, qui demande à couver; (*of hen*) **to go b.,** demander à couver; (*b*) *F:* (*of pers.*) distrait, rêveur. **2.** *s.* poule couveuse.
brook[1] [bruk], *s.* **1.** ruisseau *m*. **2.** *Ich:* **b. trout,** saumon *m* de fontaine.
brook[2], *v.tr.* (*used only in neg. sentences*) *Lit:* (ne pas) souffrir; (ne pas) endurer; **the matter brooks no delay,** l'affaire *f* ne souffre pas de retard, n'admet aucun retard; **he will b. no insolence,** il ne souffre, n'endure, ne supporte, pas d'impertinence; **nature that will b. no restraint,** caractère *m* indocile (au joug).
brookite ['brukait], *s. Miner:* brookite *f*.
brooklet ['bruklit], *s. Lit:* ruisselet *m*; petit ruisseau.
brooklime ['bruklaim], *s. Bot:* véronique cressonnée; *F:* cresson *m* de cheval, de chien.
brookweed ['brukwi:d], *s. Bot:* samole *m* aquatique; pimprenelle *f* aquatique; mouron *m* d'eau.
broom [bru:m], *s.* **1.** *Bot:* genêt *m* (à balai); **dyer's b.,** genêt des teinturiers; genette *f*. **2.** balai *m*; **small b.,** balayette *f*; **wall b.,** tête-de-loup, *pl.* têtes-de-loup; *Prov:* **a new b. sweeps clean,** tout nouveau tout beau; il n'est ferveur que de novice; il fait balai neuf; **oh, he's a new b.!** il a tout l'enthousiasme du débutant, du novice!
broomrape ['bru:mreip], *s. Bot:* orobanche *f*.
broomstick ['bru(:)mstik], *s.* **1.** manche *m* à balai; *F: A:* **to marry over the b., to jump (over) the b.,** avoir une fausse cérémonie de mariage. **2.** *pl. F:* jambes *f* (ou bras *m*) comme des allumettes.
brose [brouz], *s. Cu: Scot:* farine *f* d'avoine sur laquelle on verse du lait bouillant; bouillie *f*; **pease b.,** purée *f* de pois.
brosimum ['brɔzimәm], *s. Bot:* brosimum *m*.
broth [brɔθ], *s. Cu:* (*a*) bouillon *m*, potage *m*; *F: A: & Dial:* **a b. of a boy,** un excellent garçon; un gaillard; (*b*) **Scotch b.,** soupe *f* (de mouton) avec orge et légumes; (*c*) *Bac:* bouillon de culture.
brothel ['brɔθl], *s.* maison *f* de prostitution, bordel *m*; *Jur:* maison de débauche.
brother ['brʌðər], *s.m.* **1.** frère; **own b., full b.,** *Jur:* **b. german,** frère germain, frère de père et mère; **half b.,** demi-frère; **half b. (on mother's side),** *Jur:* **uterine b.,** frère utérin; **half b. (on father's side),** frère consanguin; **older b.,** frère aîné; **younger b.,** (frère) cadet; **the brothers Martin, the Martin brothers,** les frères Martin; *Com:* **Thomas Brothers, Thomas Bros.,** maison *f* Thomas frères. **2.** (*a*) *Ecc:* frère (d'une communauté); **lay b.,** frère lai; **B. of the Christian Schools, Christian B.,** frère des écoles chrétiennes; (*b*) (*fellow member of religious, etc., society, pl. usu.* **brethren** ['breðrin]) frère; *Ecc:* **dearly beloved brethren,** mes très chers frères, mes bien chers frères; (*c*) (*pl.* **brethren**) confrère (d'un corps de métier); (*d*) *Adm:* **The Elder Brethren of Trinity House,** les maîtres de la Corporation de Trinity House; (*e*) *Hist:* **Brethren of the Coast,** frères de la côte; (*f*) **brothers in arms,** frères d'armes.
brotherhood ['brʌðəhud], *s.* **1.** fraternité *f*. **2.** (*a*) confraternité *f*, société *f*; (*religious*) confrérie *f*; (*b*) **literary b.,** cénacle *m* littéraire; (*c*) *esp. U.S:* syndicat ouvrier.
brother-in-law ['brʌðərinlɔ:], *s.m.* (*pl.* **brothers-in-law**) (*a*) beau-frère, *pl.* beaux-frères; (*b*) *A:* (*stepbrother*) demi-frère, *pl.* demi-frères, *A:* beau-frère.
brotherlike ['brʌðəlaik], *a.* de frère, fraternel.
brotherliness ['brʌðəlinis], *s.* **1.** amour fraternel. **2.** confraternité *f*.
brotherly ['brʌðəli]. **1.** *a.* fraternel. **2.** *adv. A:* fraternellement.
brotulid ['brɔtjulid], *a. & s. Ich:* (poisson *m*) brotulide *m*.
Brotulidae [brɔ'tju:lidi:], *s.pl. Ich:* brotulidés *m*, brotulides *m*.
brouchant ['broutʃənt], *a. Her:* brochant (**over,** sur).
brougham ['bru:əm, bru:m], *s. A.Veh:* brougham *m*, coupé *m*; *Aut: A:* coupé (de ville).
brouhaha [bru:'hɑ:hɑ:], *s.* brouhaha *m*.
broussonetia [bru:sə'ni:ʃiə], *s. Bot:* broussonétie *f*, broussonetia *f*, mûrier *m* à papier, mûrier d'Espagne.
brow[1] [brau], *s.* **1.** (*a*) arcade sourcilière; (*b*) sourcil *m*; **to knit, pucker, one's brows,** froncer les sourcils. **2.** (*a*) (*forehead*) front *m*; (*b*) *Harn:* **b. band,** frontal *m*, -aux; frontail *m*, fronteau *m*. **3.** (*a*) front, croupe *f* (de colline); bord *m* (de précipice, etc.); (*on road*) **the b. of a hill,** le haut d'une côte; (*b*) galerie *f* (de mine).
brow[2], *s. Nau:* échafaudage *m* à transbordement; planche(s) *f* (*pl*) de débarquement, d'embarquement.
browbeat ['braubi:t], *v.tr.* intimider, brusquer, rudoyer (qn); **to b. s.o. into doing sth.,** rabrouer, violenter, qn pour lui faire faire qch., jusqu'à ce qu'il fasse qch.
browbeater ['braubi:tər], *s.* brutal *m*, brute *f*.
browbeating[1] ['braubi:tiŋ], *a.* brutal, arrogant.
browbeating[2], *s.* intimidation *f*; rudoiement *m*.
browed [braud], *a.* (*with adj. prefixed*) au front . . .; **high-b.,** au front haut; **black-b.,** (i) sourcilleux; au visage sombre; à l'air courroucé; (ii) *occ.* aux sourcils noirs.
brown[1] [braun]. **1.** *a.* (*a*) brun; marron *inv*; **b. hair,** cheveux bruns, châtains; **light b. hair,** cheveux châtain clair; **b. shoes,** chaussures marron, brunes; **b. paper,** papier *m* d'emballage, papier gris; **b. leather,** cuir *m* havane; **b. bread,** pain bis; **b. sugar,** cassonade *f*; **b. ale** = bière brune; *Tex:* **b. holland,** toile écrue; *Cu:* **b. butter,** beurre roux, beurre noisette; (*of pers.*) **to be as b. as a berry,** être hâlé, bruni, bronzé (comme un romanichel); **the b. tints of autumn,** les teintes *f* de rouille de l'automne; *P: O:* **to do s.o. b.,** refaire, rouler, qn; **to have been done b.,** être chocolat; (*b*) *Z:* **b. rat,** surmulot *m*; **b. bear,** ours brun; **b. body,** corps brun; *Ich:* **b. trout,** truite saumonée; *Bot:* **b. algae,** algues brunes; *Fung:* **b. rot,** moniliose *f*, brown rot *m*. **2.** *s.* (*a*) brun *m*; marron *m*; *Art:* **Vandyke b.,** brun Van Dyck; *Ven: etc:* **to fire into the b.,** tirer dans le tas; (*b*) *P: A:* (*halfpenny*) = sou *m*.
brown[2], *v.*
I. *v.tr. & i.* (*a*) *v.tr.* (i) brunir; **face browned by the sun,** teint bruni, hâlé, au soleil; (ii) *Cu:* rissoler (la viande); faire dorer (le poisson); faire roussir (du beurre, une sauce); praliner (des amandes); *Metall:* bronzer, brunir (des armes, etc.); (*b*) *v.i.* (i) (se) brunir; **his skin browns easily in the sun,** son visage (se) brunit facilement au soleil; (ii) *Cu:* prendre couleur; se rissoler; roussir; (*c*) *v.tr. Ven: etc:* **to b. a covey,** *F: O:* **a troop of men,** tirer dans le tas.
II. (*compound verb*) **brown off,** *v.tr. F:* décourager (qn); **to be browned off,** avoir le cafard, être découragé.
brown eyed ['braunaid], *a.* (*a*) aux yeux bruns; (*b*) *Bot: N.Am:* **b.-e. Susan,** (i) rudbeckie *f*; (ii) gaillarde *f*.
brown-haired ['braun'hɛəd], *a.* châtain, aux cheveux châtains.
Brownian ['brauniən], *a. Ph:* (mouvement) brownien.
brownie ['brauni], *s.* **1.** lutin *m* (bienfaisant); farfadet *m*. **2.** *Scout:* jeannette *f*. **3.** *Phot: A:* (*R.t.m.*) appareil *m*, kodak *m*, Brownie. **3.** *Cu: N.Am:* gâteau *m* au chocolat et aux noisettes.
browning[1] ['brauniŋ], *s.* **1.** brunissement *m*; bronzage *m*; rissolement *m* (des viandes, etc.); pralinage *m* (des amandes). **2.** *Cu:* colorant brun (pour les sauces).
Browning[2], *s. Sm.a:* Browning *m*; pistolet *m* automatique.
brownish ['brauniʃ], *a.* brunâtre, brunet.
brownness ['braunnis], *s.* couleur brune (**of,** de).
brownout ['braunaut], *s. U.S:* blackout partiel.
brownshirt ['braunʃə:t], *s. Pol.Hist: F:* chemise brune.
brownstone ['braunstoun], *s. U.S:* grès *m* de construction; *F:* **the b. vote,** les suffrages *m* des classes aisées.
browntail ['braunteil], *a. & s. Ent:* **b. (moth),** liparis *m* cul-doré; cul-doré *m*, *pl.* culs-dorés; cul-brun *m*, *pl.* culs-bruns.
browse[1] [brauz], *s.* **1. b. (wood),** brout *m*; jeunes pousses *f*. **2. goats enjoying a b.,** chèvres *f* en train de brouter.
browse[2], *v.tr. & i.* (*a*) **to b. (on) leaves,** brouter des feuilles; *Ven:* (*of deer*) gagner; (*b*) (= GRAZE) **to b. the grass,** brouter l'herbe; paître; **to b. in a meadow,** brouter dans un pré; (*c*) **to b. (among books),** feuilleter des livres; butiner dans les livres; bouquiner; (*d*) *Cmptr:* passer en revue; balayer.
browsing ['brauziŋ], *s.* **1.** (*a*) abroutissement *m* (des arbres par le gibier); *Ven:* **b. ground, land,** gagnage *m*; (*b*) broutement *m* (des animaux). **2.** flânerie *f* (*esp.* parmi les livres).
bruang ['bru:æŋ], *s. Z:* bruan *m*, ours *m* des cocotiers, ours malais.
brucella [bru'selə], *s. Bac:* brucella *f*.
brucellosis [bru:si'lousis], *s. Med: Vet:* brucellose *f*.
bruchid ['bru:kid], *s. Ent:* bruche *f*, bruchidé *m*; **b. larva,** cosson *m*, cuceron *m*, cus(s)eron *m*.
Bruchidae ['bru:kidi:], *s.pl. Ent:* bruchidés *m*.
bruchus ['bru:kəs], *s. Ent:* bruche *f*.
brucine ['bru:si(:)n], *s. Ch:* brucine *f*.
brucite ['bru:sait], *s. Miner:* brucite *f*.
Bruin ['bru(:)in], *Pr.n.* (*a*) *Lit:* Brun *m*; l'Ours *m*; (*b*) (l'ours) Martin.
bruise[1] [bru:z], *s.* meurtrissure *f*; contusion *f*; bleu *m*; (*on fruit*) talure *f*, cotissure *f*; (*on metal*) bosse *f*, renfoncement *m*; mâchure *f* (faite par l'étau); *Surg:* coup *m* orbe; **body covered with bruises,** corps couvert de coups.
bruise[2], *v.tr.* **1.** (*a*) meurtrir, contusionner, froisser (une partie du corps); écraser (un fruit, un doigt); taler (un fruit); **bruised fruit,** fruit taché, coti (par la grêle); *Vet:* **bruised hoof,** sole battue; **bruised in the hoof,** solbatu; **to b. one's arm,** se meurtrir au bras, se meurtrir le bras; *Nau:* (*of paddle boat*) **to b. water,** pagayer; (*b*) (*with passive force*) (*of fruit*) se meurtrir, se tacher, s'abîmer (au moindre coup). **2.** bosseler, bossuer (le métal); *Mec.E:* mater, matir; mâchurer (dans l'étau). **3.** broyer, écraser, concasser (une substance); égruger (le blé).
bruiser ['bru:zər], *s.* **1.** *Box: F:* boxeur *m* (brutal); cogneur *m*. **2.** *Ind:* appareil *m* de broyage; broyeur *m*.
bruisewater ['bru:zwɔ:tər], *s. Nau: F:* (navire) tangueur *m*; canardeur *m*.
bruising ['bru:ziŋ], *s.* **1.** écrasement *m* (des chairs); contusion *f*, froissement *m*. **2.** broyage *m*, écrasement, concassage *m*; égrugeage *m*. **3.** *Mec.E:* matage *m*; mâchure *f*.
bruit[1] [bru:t], *s.* **1.** *A: & Lit:* bruit *m* (qui se répand); rumeur *f* (publique). **2.** *Med:* bruit, murmure (anormal).
bruit[2], *v.tr. A: & Lit:* **to b. sth. abroad, about,** faire courir le bruit de qch.; ébruiter qch.; **it was bruited that . . .,** le bruit courait que . . ..
brulé ['bru:lei], *s. Can:* **1.** (*a*) forêt détruite par un incendie, *Fr.C:* brûlé *m*; (*b*) terrain *m* incultivable. **2.** métis, -isse.
Brum [brʌm], *Pr.n. F:* = BIRMINGHAM.
brumal ['bru:ml], *a. A: & Lit:* brumal, d'hiver; hivernal, -aux; hiémal, -aux.
brumbie, brumby ['brʌmbi], *s. F: Austr:* cheval sauvage, non dressé.
Brummagem ['brʌmədʒəm], *s. F:* (= *Birmingham*) **B. ware,** joaillerie *f*, etc., de camelote, de pacotille, en toc; clinquant *m*; **B. clock,** pendule *f* en toc.
brumous ['bru:məs], *a. A: & Lit:* brumal, d'hiver.
brunch [brʌnʃ], *s. F:* repas *m* tenant lieu de *breakfast* et de *lunch*.
brunette (*m occ.* **brunet,** *esp. Anthr: N.Am:*) [bru:'net], *a. & s.* brune (*f*), brunette (*f*); brunet (*m*).
brunsvigite ['brʌnzvigait], *s. Miner:* brunsvigite *f*.
brunt [brʌnt], *s.* choc *m*; **to bear the b. of the attack,** soutenir le plus fort, le choc, la violence, de l'attaque; **the b. of the battle,** le plus fort de la bataille; **to bear the b. of s.o.'s displeasure,** soutenir le poids de la colère de

qn; **to bear the b. (of the work, fight),** payer de sa personne; **to bear the b. of the expense,** faire tous les frais; **to bear the b. of the storm,** essuyer, subir, l'orage; *F:* **you will have to bear the b. of it,** c'est sur vous que la tempête se déchaînera.

brush[1] [brʌʃ], *s.* **1.** (*a*) broussailles *fpl*; **b. harrow,** herse *f* d'épines; (*b*) *U.S: Austr: etc:* brousse *f*; **b. fire,** incendie *m* de forêt; *Orn:* **b. turkey,** mégapode *m*. **2.** (*a*) brosse *f*; balai *m*; **(small household) b.,** balayette *f*; **b. (of broom),** brosse-balai *f, pl.* brosses-balais; **hard b.,** (i) (*for shoes, etc.*) brosse à décrotter; (ii) (*for pans, etc.*) brosse à récurer; **scrubbing b.,** brosse (à main) en chiendent, brosse dure, brosse de cuisine; **ceiling b., long-handled b.,** *O:* **Turk's head, Pope's head, b.,** tête-de-loup, *pl.* têtes-de-loup; **hearth b., banister b.,** balayette, époussette *f*; **dustpan and b.,** balayette et ramasse-poussière *m inv*; **radiator b.,** balayette de radiateur; **bottle b.,** goupillon *m*; **saucepan b., washing-up b.,** lavette *f*; **b. hanger,** accroche-balai *m, pl.* accroche-balais; *Mch:* **scaling b.,** brosse à tubes; **b. maker,** brossier *m*; fabricant *m* de brosses; **b. making, b. manufacture,** brosserie *f*; (*b*) **clothes b.,** brosse à habits; **hat b.,** brosse à chapeau; **shaving b.,** blaireau *m*; **back b.,** lave-dos *m inv*, gratte-dos *m inv*; *Hairdr:* **b. cut,** cheveux (taillés) en brosse; (*c*) **(paint) b.,** pinceau *m*, brosse; **flat b.,** queue-de-morue *f, pl.* queues-de-morue; **paste b.,** pinceau à colle; **whitewash b., distemper(ing) b.,** badigeon *m*; **air b.,** aérographe *m*, pinceau à air, pinceau vaporisateur, pistolet *m* vaporisateur, pistolet pulvérisateur; **b. washer,** lave-pinceaux *m inv*; (*d*) *Art:* touche *f* (de peintre); **to paint with a full b.,** peindre dans la pâte; peindre en pleine pâte; **she is worthy of an artist's b.,** elle est à peindre; (*e*) *Typ:* **b. proof,** épreuve *f* à la brosse; morasse *f*; (*f*) *Ven:* queue *f* (de renard); *F: A:* **to show one's b.,** se sauver, s'enfuir. **3.** (*a*) *El: etc:* balai (de commutateur, de génératrice); **(contact) b.,** frotteur *m*; **third b.,** balai auxiliaire, de réglage; **current-collecting b.,** balai de prise de courant; **carbon b.,** balai en charbon; **slip-ring b.,** balai collecteur; **b. carrier, b. gear, b. holder,** porte-balai(s) *m inv*; **b. lead, b. shift,** decalage *m* des balais; **b. rocker,** couronne *f* porte-balais; **b. setting,** ajustage *m* des balais; **b. yoke,** armature *f* de porte-balai(s); (*b*) *Cmptr:* **(read(ing)) b.,** balai de lecture; **b. station,** poste *m* de lecture; **b. assembly,** ensemble *m* porte-balais; **b. compare check,** contrôle *m* de balai. **4.** (*a*) faisceau *m* de rayons électriques; **b. discharge,** décharge *f* en aigrette *f*; (*b*) *Opt: Cryst:* **Haidinger's brushes,** houppes *f* d'Haidinger. **5.** (*a*) coup *m* de brosse (à des vêtements, etc.); (*b*) rencontre *f*, échauffourée *f*, escarmouche *f* (avec l'ennemi); **at the first b.,** au premier abord; **after the first b.,** après le premier abord; (*c*) *Sp: U.S:* petite partie; défi *m*; (*d*) *Farr:* éraflure *f* (à la jambe du cheval); (*e*) *F:* **to have a b. with s.o.,** avoir une prise de bec avec qn; (*f*) *F:* = BRUSHOFF.

brush[2], *v.*

I. *v.tr. & i.* **1.** *v.tr.* (*a*) brosser (un habit, les cheveux); balayer (un tapis); **to b. one's hair,** se brosser les cheveux; **to b. out one's hair,** (i) se démêler les cheveux; (ii) se défaire la coiffure (à la brosse); **hair brushed back,** cheveux rejetés en arrière; **to b. out sth.,** nettoyer qch. (avec un balai, une balayette); (*b*) effleurer, raser, frôler, érafler (une surface); (*c*) gratter (la laine, le nylon); (*d*) **to b. the dust off sth.,** enlever la poussière de qch. (à la brosse, en brossant); **to b. sth. clean,** nettoyer qch. avec une brosse, à la brosse; (*e*) *Art:* **to b. out a detail,** supprimer un détail (avec le pinceau); **to b. in,** brosser (le fond, les draperies). **2.** *v.i.* (*a*) **to b. against, by, past, s.o.,** frôler, friser, qn en passant; passer rapidement auprès de qn; **to b. against sth.,** frôler, érafler, qch.; (*b*) *Farr:* (*of horse*) se friser (en marchant, en trottant).

II. (*compound verbs*) **1. brush aside,** *v.tr.* écarter (qn, une pensée, un avis, une difficulté); (*at meeting*) **to b. a. an objection,** passer à l'ordre du jour sur une objection.

2. brush away, *v.tr.* enlever (de la boue, etc.) d'un coup de brosse, de balai; essuyer furtivement (une larme); écarter (une difficulté, etc.).

3. brush down, *v.tr.* donner un coup de brosse à (qn); brosser, panser (un cheval); coucher (le poil d'un chapeau, etc.).

4. brush over, *v.tr.* enduire (une surface) à la brosse; badigeonner (une surface) **(with,** de).

5. brush up, *v.tr.* (*a*) brosser, donner un coup de brosse à (un chapeau, etc.); *F:* **to b. up a subject,** se remettre à un sujet; repasser, rafraîchir, un sujet; **to b. up one's French,** dérouiller son français; se remettre au français; *F:* **to b. s.o. up,** dégauchir, dégourdir, qn; (*b*) **to b. one's hair up, to b. up one's hair,** rejeter ses cheveux en arrière; **to b. up wool,** gratter la laine; **to b. up the hair of a fur,** éveiller le poil d'une fourrure; (*c*) **to b. up the crumbs,** ramasser les miettes (avec la brosse).

brushdown ['brʌʃdaun], *s.* **to give s.o. a b.,** donner un coup de brosse à qn; **to give a horse a b.,** brosser, panser, un cheval; **to have a b.,** se (faire) donner un coup de brosse.

brushed [brʌʃt], *a. Tex:* **b. wool, b. nylon,** laine grattée, nylon gratté.

brusheroo [brʌʃə'ru:], *s. Austr: F:* = BRUSHOFF.

brushing ['brʌʃiŋ], *s.* coup *m* de brosse, brossage *m*, balayage *m*; *Tex:* **b. mill, b. machine,** brosseuse *f*.

brushoff ['brʌʃɔf], *s. F:* **to give s.o. the b.,** envoyer promener, *F:* balader, qn.

brush-tailed ['brʌʃteild], *a. Z:* **b.-t. porcupine,** athérure *m*.

brush-tongued ['brʌʃ'tʌŋd], *a. Orn:* **b.-t. parrot,** trichoglosse *m*.

brush up ['brʌʃʌp], *s.* **1.** coup *m* de brosse; **to have a wash and b. up,** faire un brin, un bout, de toilette. **2. to give one's French a b. up,** dérouiller son français.

brushware ['brʌʃwεər], *s.* brosserie *f*.

brush wheel ['brʌʃ(h)wi:l], *s. Ind:* brosse tournante.

brushwood ['brʌʃwud], *s.* (*a*) broussailles *fpl*, brosses *fpl* (sur la lisière d'une forêt); bois taillis; fourré *m*; hallier *m*; **b. killer,** débroussaillant *m*; (*b*) mort-bois *m*; menu bois; brindilles *fpl*; (*c*) *Civ.E: etc:* fascines *fpl*.

brushwork ['brʌʃwə:k], *s.* **1.** travail *m* au pinceau. **2.** *Art:* touche *f* (du peintre); facture *f*.

brushy ['brʌʃi], *a.* **1.** en brosse; hérissé; velu. **2. b. tail,** queue bien fournie. **3.** couvert de broussailles ou de brousse; broussailleux.

brusque [bru:sk], *a.* brusque; (ton) rude, bourru.

brusquely ['bru:skli], *adv.* brusquement.

brusqueness ['bru:sknis], *s.* brusquerie *f*, rudesse *f*.

Brussels ['brʌslz], *Pr.n. Geog:* Bruxelles; **B. lace,** point *m*, dentelle *f*, de Bruxelles; **B. sprouts,** choux *m* de Bruxelles.

brutal ['bru:tl], *a.* brutal, -aux; (instinct) animal, de brute; **to say b. things to s.o.,** dire des brutalités à qn; **the b. truth,** la vérité brutale; **you're being absolutely b.!** tu es une vraie brute!

brutality [bru:'tæliti]. **1.** brutalité *f* **(to,** envers). **2.** *Jur:* sévices *mpl* **(to,** envers).

brutalization [bru:təlai'zeiʃ(ə)n], *s.* abrutissement *m*.

brutalize ['bru:təlaiz], *v.tr.* abrutir, animaliser (qn); **to become brutalized,** s'animaliser, s'abrutir.

brutalizing ['bru:təlaiziŋ], *a.* qui abrutit; digne des brutes.

brutally ['bru:təli], *adv.* brutalement; en brute; comme une brute.

brute [bru:t]. **1.** *s.* (*a*) brute *f*; bête *f* brute; **alcohol turns men into brutes,** l'alcool *m* abrutit les hommes; *F:* **mosquitoes and midges and other little brutes,** moustiques et cousins et autres sacrées petites bestioles; (*b*) *F:* (*of pers.*) brute; brutal, -aux *m*; **you b.!** espèce d'animal! **what a b.!** quel animal! (*c*) *F:* **it was a b. of a job,** c'était un métier, un travail, de chien; **what a b. of a day!** quel chien de temps! (*d*) *Rail:* chariot *m* à bagages. **2.** *a.* (*a*) **b. beast,** bête brute; (*b*) **b. force,** la force brutale; **by b. force,** de vive force; (*c*) **b. matter,** matière *f* brute; (*d*) **b. fidelity,** fidélité *f* de chien.

brutify ['bru:tifai], *v.tr.* abrutir.

brutish ['bru:tiʃ], *a.* **1.** de brute; bestial, -aux; **b. appetites,** appétits bestiaux. **2.** abruti, brutal, -aux.

brutishly ['bru:tiʃli], *adv.* en brute, comme une brute.

brutishness ['bru:tiʃnis], *s.* brutalité *f*. **1.** bestialité *f*. **2.** abrutissement *m*.

bruxism ['brʌksizm], **bruxomania** [brʌksou'meiniə], *s. Med:* brycomanie *f*.

Bryaceae [brai'eisii:], *s.pl. Bot:* bryacées *f*.

bryologist [brai'ɔlədʒist], *s.* bryologiste *mf*.

bryology [brai'ɔlədʒi], *s.* bryologie *f*.

bryony ['braiəni], *s. Bot:* **1. white b.,** bryone *f*, couleuvrée *f*. **2. black b.,** taminier *m*, sceau *m* de la Vierge, de Notre-Dame.

Bryophyta [brai'ɔfitə], *s.pl. Bot:* bryophytes *f*.

bryophyte ['braioufait], *s. Bot:* bryophyte *f*.

Bryozoa [braiou'zouə], *s.pl. Biol:* bryozoaires *m*.

bryozoan, -zoon [braiou'zouən, -zouɔn], *s. Biol:* bryozoaire *m*.

Brythonic [bri'θɔnik], *a. & s. Ling:* brittonique (*m*).

bryum ['braiəm], *s. Bot:* bryon *m*, bryum *m*.

bub [bʌb], *s. P:* (*not in polite use*) **1.** *pl.* **bubs,** nichons *m*, nénés *m*. **2.** *U.S:* (*form of address*) **come on, b.!** ramène-toi ici, mon vieux!

bubal(e) ['bju:bl], **bubalis** ['bju:bəlis], *s. Z:* bubale *m*, bubalis *m*.

bubble[1] ['bʌbl], *s.* **1.** (*a*) bulle *f* (d'air, de savon); (*in boiling liquid*) bouillon *m*; **b. bath,** bain *m* de mousse; *Aut: F: A:* **b. car,** pot *m* de yaourt; *Ph:* **b. chamber,** chambre *f* à bulles; (*b*) *Glassm:* soufflure *f*; *Cer:* cloche *f*; *Metall:* soufflure, boursouflement *m*; poche *f* d'air; (*c*) bouillonnement *m*; *Ch: etc:* barbotage *m*; **b. scrubber,** laveur *m* à barbotage (du gaz); *Petr:* **b. tower,** tour *f* de fractionnement; *Atom.Ph: etc:* **b. cap,** calotte *f* de barbotage, coupelle *f*; **b. plate, b. tray,** plateau *m* de barbotage, plateau à coupelles; (*d*) *Surv:* **b. sextant,** sextant *m* à niveau; **b. tube,** tube *m* à bulle; (*e*) *Moll:* **b. shell, b. snail,** bulle. **2.** projet *m* chimérique; chimère *f*, illusion *f*; tromperie *f*; *Lit:* **the b. Reputation,** cette chose vaine qu'on appelle Renommée; **to prick the b. of s.o.'s expectations,** réduire à néant les espérances de qn; **the b. was pricked,** ce fut une désillusion; *attrib. Fin:* **b. scheme,** entreprise véreuse; duperie *f*; **b. company,** (i) société *f* fantôme; (ii) société de filous; *Hist:* **the South Sea B.,** l'Affaire des mers du Sud (1720).

bubble[2], *v.*

I. *v.i. & tr.* **1.** *v.i.* (*a*) (*of boiling liquid, of stream*) bouillonner; dégager des bulles; (*of wine*) pétiller; *Ch: Ind:* (*of gas through liquid*) barboter; (*b*) (*of liquid poured*) faire glouglou, glouglouter. **2.** *v.tr.* **to b. a gas through a liquid,** faire barboter un gaz dans un liquide.

II. (*compound verbs*) **1. bubble over,** *v.i.* déborder (en bouillonnant, en moussant); **to b. over with vitality, with high spirits,** déborder de vie, de gaîté; **children bubbling over with life,** enfants bouillonnants de vie; **to b. over with joy,** pétiller de joie; **he was bubbling over with laughter,** il ne se tenait pas de rire; il pouffait de rire.

2. bubble up, *v.i.* (*of spring*) sortir à gros bouillons.

bubble and squeak ['bʌblnd'skwi:k], *s. Cu: F:* (*a*) réchauffé *m* en friture de pommes de terre et de choux; (*b*) *A:* rata *m* aux choux.

bubbler ['bʌblər], *s. Ind:* barboteur *m* (pour gaz).

bubbling[1] ['bʌbliŋ], *a.* (*a*) bouillonnant; (*of wine*) pétillant; (*b*) **the b. song of the curlew,** le chant perlé, roulé, du courlis; *Med:* **b. râle,** râle bulleux.

bubbling[2], *s.* **1.** bouillonnement *m*, pétillement *m*. **2.** *Ch: etc:* barbotage *m*.

bubbly ['bʌbli]. **1.** *a.* plein de bulles; pétillant. **2.** *s. F:* (vin de) champagne *m*; vin mousseux.

bubinga [bju:'biŋgə], *s. Bot:* bubinga *m*.

bubo, *pl.* **-oes** ['bju:bou, -ouz], *s. Med:* bubon *m*.

bubonic [bju(:)'bɔnik], *a. Med:* bubonique; **b. plague,** peste *f* bubonique, peste noire.

bubonocele [bju(:)'bɔnəsi:l], *s. Med:* bubonocèle *f*, hernie inguino-pubienne.

buccal ['bʌkl], *a. Anat:* buccal, -aux; **b. cavity,** cavité buccale.

buc(c)an ['bʌkən], *s.* boucan *m* (des Caraïbes).

buccaneer[1] [bʌkə'niər], *s.* (*a*) *Hist:* flibustier *m*; (*b*) boucanier *m*, flibustier; pirate *m*.

buccaneer[2], *v.i.* faire le boucanier; faire le métier de pirate; flibuster.

buccaneering[1] [bʌkə'niəriŋ], *a.* (*of habits, people, etc.*) boucanier, -ière.

buccaneering[2], *s.* métier *m* de boucanier, de pirate, de flibustier; flibusterie *f*.

buccina [bu:'si:nə], *s. Cl.Ant:* buccin *m*, buccine *f*.

buccinal [bu:'si:nl], *a.* buccinal, -aux.

buccinator ['bʌksineitər], *s. Anat:* (muscle) buccinateur *m*.

Buccinidae [bʌk'sinidi:], *s.pl. Moll:* buccinidés *m*.

bucco-labial ['bʌkou'leibiəl], *a. Anat:* bucco-labial, -aux.

Bucconidae [bʌ'kɔnidi:], *s.pl. Orn:* bucconidés *m*.

bucentaur [bju'sentɔ:r], *s. Myth:* bucentaure *m*.

Bucephalus [bju(:)'sefələs], *Pr.n.* Bucéphale *m*.

Bucerotidae [bjusə'rɔtidi:], *s.pl. Orn:* bucérotidés *m*, les calaos *m*.

bucholzite ['bju:kɔlzait], *s. Miner:* bucholzite *f*.

buchu ['bu:χu:], *s. Bot:* buchu *m*, bukku *m*.

buck[1] [bʌk], *s.* **1.** (*a*) daim *m*, chevreuil *m* (mâle); **b. horn,** corne *f* de cerf; (*esp. U.S:* (*of inexperienced shot*) **to have b. fever,** avoir la gâchette facile; (*b*) mâle *m* (du renne, du chamois, de l'antilope, du furet, du lapin, du lièvre); **b. rabbit,** lapin *m* (mâle); (*of doe*) **to go to b.,** s'accoupler; (*c*) *U.S:* bélier *m*; (*d*) = BUCKSKIN; (*e*) *U.S:* = BUCKSHOT. **2.** (*a*) *A: & Hist:* dandy *m*, élégant *m*; **old b.,** vieux marcheur; (*b*) *NAm: usu. Pej:* (i) Indien *m* (d'Amérique); (ii) noir *m*; *A: & Pej:* **an old b. nigger,** un vieux nègre; (*c*) *NAm: F:* homme, type *m*; (*d*) *U.S: F:* **b. (private),** simple soldat *m*, troufion *m*. **3.** *Equit:* **b. (jump),** saut *m* de mouton; **b. jumper,** cheval *m* qui fait le saut de mouton; cheval méchant. **4.** *NAm: F:* dollar *m*.

buck[2], *v.*

I. *v.tr. & i.* **1.** *v.tr.* (*of rabbit, hare*) bouquiner, couvrir (la femelle). **2.** (*a*) *v.i.* (*of horse*) faire le gros dos; faire un haut-de-corps; **to b. (jump),** faire le saut de mouton; (*b*) *v.tr.* (*of horse*) **to b. s.o. off,** désarçonner qn; jeter

bas le cavalier; *U.S:* **to b. the question,** renvoyer la balle; (*c*) *v.i. Av:* (*of aircraft*) se cabrer; (*d*) *v.i. esp. U.S:* résister; se regimber; s'opposer (**against,** à); (*e*) *U.S:* faire tout pour arriver; **he's bucking for promotion,** il fait tout pour avoir de l'avancement.
II. (*compound verb*) **buck up;** *F:* (*a*) *v.tr.* **to b. s.o. up,** encourager qn (à continuer); remonter le courage de qn; stimuler, ragaillardir, ravigoter, qn; donner du cœur à qn; **that will b. you up,** ça vous remontera, vous retapera; ça vous remettra du cœur au ventre; ça vous remettra d'aplomb; (*b*) *v.i.,* (i) reprendre courage, se ragaillardir, se ravigoter, se ressaisir; *F:* se retaper le moral; (ii) se hâter, se remuer; **b. up!** (i) courage! (ii) remue-toi! dépêche-toi! presse-toi! *F:* (dé)grouille-toi!

buck[3], *s. NAm:* (*a*) chevalet *m,* chèvre *f* (à scier le bois); (*b*) *Gym:* mouton *m.*

buck[4], *s. Fish:* nasse *f* à prendre les anguilles.

buck[5], *s.* (*a*) *U.S: Cards:* couteau *m,* etc., que l'on place devant un joueur pour marquer que c'est à lui de donner; (*b*) *F:* **to pass the b. to s.o.,** (i) (*at poker*) passer la parole au suivant; (ii) *Fig:* mettre l'affaire sur le dos de qn; passer la décision à qn; (iii) *Fig:* mettre qn dedans, refaire qn.

buck[6], *s.* (*a*) *A:* lessive *f*; (*b*) *Agr: Glassm:* **b. ashes,** charrée *f.*

buck[7], *v.tr. A:* lessiver (le linge).

buck[8], *v.tr. Min:* concasser (le minerai).

buck[9], *adv. F: Dial:* **b. naked,** complètement nu, nu comme un ver.

buckaroo [bʌkə'ru:], *s. NAm: F:* cow-boy *m, pl.* cow-boys.

buckbean ['bʌkbi:n], *s. Bot:* trèfle *m* d'eau; ményanthe *m.*

buckboard ['bʌkbɔ:d], *s. A.Veh: U.S:* chariot composé d'une longue planche montée sur quatre roues.

bucked [bʌkt], *a. F: O:* ragaillardi; enchanté; **I was tremendously b. to hear the news,** j'ai été enchanté d'apprendre la nouvelle; ça m'a remonté le cœur d'apprendre ça!

bucker ['bʌkər], *s.* cheval *m* qui fait le saut de mouton; cheval méchant.

bucket[1] ['bʌkit], *s.* **1.** (*a*) seau *m*; **canvas b.,** seau en toile; *F:* **it's coming down in buckets,** il pleut à verse; *P:* **to kick the b.,** mourir, casser sa pipe; *P:* **to give s.o. the b.,** renvoyer, saquer, qn; (*b*) *Min: Ind:* baluchon *m,* baquet *m*; benne *f* (d'une grue); *Nau:* **tar b.,** baille *f* à goudron; (*c*) piston *m* (à clapet) (d'une pompe); **b. pump,** pompe élévatoire, soulevante; (*d*) auget *m,* auge *f* (d'une roue hydraulique); **b. wheel,** roue *f* à augets; **chain of buckets,** (pompe à) chapelet *m*; **b. chain,** chaîne *f* de personnes qui se passent des seaux d'eau (en cas d'incendie); patenôtre *f*; **b. conveyor,** transporteur *m* à godets, à augets; **b. elevator,** élévateur *m* à godets, à augets; (*e*) godet *m,* benne (d'une drague, etc.); louchet *m* (d'une drague); **dredging b.,** godet, hotte *f,* à draguer; baluchon; **b. dredger,** drague à godets; (*f*) bassicot *m* (de téléphérage); (*g*) *Aut:* **b. seat,** baquet; (*h*) *Cmptr:* compartiment *m* (en mémoire). **2.** (*a*) cuissard *m* (d'une jambe artificielle); (*b*) *Mil:* **rifle b.,** botte *f* de fusil, de carabine; étui *m* de crosse; (*c*) *Veh:* porte-fouet *m inv.* **3.** *Fin: F:* **b. shop,** bureau *m* d'un courtier marron.

bucket[2]. **1.** *v.tr.* tirer (de l'eau) avec un seau; transporter (de l'eau) dans un seau. **2.** *v.tr. Equit:* surmener (un cheval); *Aut: F:* conduire (une voiture) brutalement; *v.i.* **the car was bucketing along the road,** la voiture cahotait sur la route. **3.** *v.i. & tr. Row:* **to b. (the recovery),** dégager, revenir, sur l'avant, en s'appuyant sur l'aviron; trop presser le retour sur l'avant. **4.** *v.i.* **it's bucketing down,** il pleut à verse.

bucket[3], *s. Row:* retour *m* sur l'avant en s'appuyant sur l'aviron; retour sur l'avant précipité.

bucketful ['bʌkitful], *s.* (*pl.* **bucketsful, bucketfuls**) plein seau; *F:* **it's raining (in) bucketfuls,** il pleut à seaux.

buckeye ['bʌkai], *s. Bot: U.S: F:* pavier *m*; marronnier *m* à fleurs rouges.

buckhorn ['bʌkhɔ:n], *s. Z:* corne *f* de cerf; *Bot:* **b. (plantain),** plantain lancéolé; **b. brake, b. fern,** osmonde royale.

buckhound ['bʌkhaund], *s.* (chien courant dénommé) buck-hound *m.*

bucking[1] ['bʌkiŋ], *s.* sauts *mpl* de mouton (d'un cheval, d'un mulet).

bucking[2], *s. A:* lessivage *m*; **b. cloth,** charrier *m.*

bucking[3], *s. Min: etc:* concassage *m* (du minerai).

bucklandite ['bʌklændait], *s. Miner:* bucklandite *f.*

buckle[1] ['bʌkl], *s.* **1.** boucle *f,* agrafe *f* (d'une courroie); **b. loop,** enchapure *f*; *NAm: F:* **to make b. and tongue meet,** arriver à joindre les deux bouts. **2.** *Tchn:* flambement *m,* gauchissement *m* (d'une tige, d'une surface, d'une roue, etc.); voile *m* (d'une roue, etc.); flambage *m*; foisonnement *m*; **minor buckles,** flambements secondaires.

buckle[2]. **1.** *v.tr.* (*a*) boucler (une valise, un soulier, etc.); agrafer, serrer, attacher (une ceinture, etc.); **to b. on one's armour, one's sword,** revêtir, endosser, son armure; ceindre son épée; (*b*) *Tchn:* déjeter; gauchir; voiler (une roue); faire flamber (une tige de métal, etc.); tordre (une plaque d'accumulateur, etc.). **2.** *v.i.* (*a*) (*of shoe, belt*) se boucler (de telle ou telle façon); (*b*) *F:* (*of pers.*) **to b. to a task,** s'appliquer, s'atteler, à un travail; **to b. to,** s'y atteler; s'y mettre; s'atteler au travail. **3.** *v.i.* (*a*) **to b. (up),** (*of metal, etc.*) se déformer, se déjeter, (se) gondoler, gauchir, foisonner, flamber, arquer; (*of wheel, sheet iron*) se voiler; (*b*) *F:* (*of pers.*) **to b. up,** flancher, s'effondrer.

buckled ['bʌkld], *a.* **1.** bouclé; agrafé. **2.** déjeté; gauchi; voilé; tordu.

buckler ['bʌklər], *s.* **1.** (*a*) *Arm:* écu *m,* bouclier *m*; targe *f*; (*b*) *Fig:* bouclier. **2.** *Nau:* tampon *m,* tape *f* (d'écubier).

Buckley ['bʌkli], *Pr.n. Austr: P:* **he hasn't Buckley's chance,** il n'a pas l'ombre d'une chance.

buckling[1] ['bʌkliŋ], *s.* **1.** agrafage *m.* **2.** (*of metal, etc.*) déformation *f,* flambement *m,* flambage *m,* gauchissement *m,* gaufrage *m,* flexion *f,* déjettement *m,* voilure *f,* arcure *f*; foisonnement *m,* gondolage *m,* gondolement *m* (d'une tôle, de plaques d'accu, etc.); *Mec.E:* **b. load, stress,** charge *f* au flambage; *Phot:* gondolage (d'un film). **3.** *F:* **b. to,** (i) application assidue au travail; (ii) commencement *m* du travail.

buckling[2], *s.* hareng cuit et fumé.

bucko, *pl.* **-oes** ['bʌkou, -ouz], *s. P:* **1.** *esp. Nau:* (*a*) *a.* tyrannique, autoritaire; brutal; (*b*) *s.* officier autoritaire, tyrannique. **2.** *s.* (*esp. Irish*) jeune homme; (*as term of address*) **(me) b.!** mon vieux!

buckra ['bʌkrə], *s. U.S: P: usu. Pej:* blanc *m*; patron *m.*

buck rake ['bʌkreik], *s. Agr:* buck-rake *m,* râteau-ameulonneur *m.*

buckram[1] ['bʌkrəm], *s.* **1.** *Tex:* bougran *m*; (*for hat shapes*) linon *m.* **2.** (*a*) raideur *f,* empesé *m* (du style, etc.); (*b*) *A:* fausse apparence de solidité (d'une toile gommée).

buckram[2], *v.tr.* **1.** *Tail: etc:* bougraner, renforcer (un revers, etc.). **2.** *F: A:* empeser (son style).

bucksaw ['bʌksɔ:], *s. Tls:* scie *f* de long; scie à bûches.

buckshee ['bʌk'ʃi:]. **1.** *a. & adv. F:* gratis (*inv.*), à l'œil; **two b. tickets,** deux billets gratis; **we got in b.,** on est entré gratis, sans payer. **2.** *s. esp. Mil: P: O:* **a bit of b.,** du rabiot.

buckshot ['bʌkʃɔt], *s. Ven:* chevrotines *fpl.*; gros plomb.

buckskin ['bʌkskin], *s.* peau *f* de daim; **b. breeches,** *s.pl.* **buckskins,** culotte *f* de peau (de daim); **white b. shoes,** souliers *m* en daim blanc.

buckthorn ['bʌkθɔ:n], *s. Bot:* nerprun *m*; **alder b.,** bourdaine *f*; **sea b.,** argousier *m*; faux nerprun; **common b. seed,** graine *f* de Perse.

buckwheat ['bʌk(h)wi:t], *s.* (*a*) *Agr:* sarrasin *m*; blé noir; **b. flour,** bandine *f*; **b. cake,** galette *f* de blé noir; (*b*) *Husb:* dragée *f* de cheval; *Vet:* **b. rash,** fagopyrisme *m.*

bucolic [bju(:)'kɔlik], *a. & s.* bucolique (*f*); *a.* pastoral, -aux; **b. poet,** poète *m* bucolique, bucoliaste *m.*

bucrane [bju'krein], **bucranium** [bju'kreiniəm], *s. Arch:* bucrane *m.*

bud[1] [bʌd], *s.* (*a*) *Bot:* bourgeon *m*; œil *m* (d'une plante); maille *f* (de vigne); *Hort:* (*of tree*) **to be in b.,** bourgeonner; *Fig:* **sedition in the b.,** sédition *f* en germe; germes *m* de sédition; **poets in the b.,** poètes *m* en herbe; (*b*) *Bot:* bouton *m* (de fleur); **the roses are in b.,** les roses sont en bouton; (*c*) *Z:* bourgeon, gemme *f*; *Moss:* **brood b.,** sorédie *f*; (*d*) *Anat:* **taste b., gustatory b.,** papille gustative, bourgeon gustatif; (*e*) (i) *F: Dial: O:* débutante *f,* jeune fille *f*; (ii) *NAm: P:* copain *m*; **say, b.!** dis, mon vieux!

bud[2], *v.* (**budded**) **1.** *v.i.* (*a*) (*of tree, plant*) bourgeonner; se couvrir de bourgeons; (*of vine*) mailler; (*b*) (*of flower*) boutonner; commencer à éclore; (*c*) (*of talent, etc.*) commencer à éclore, à se révéler, à se manifester. **2.** *v.tr. Hort:* greffer (un arbre fruitier) par œil détaché; écussonner (un arbre).

Buda ['b(j)u:də], *Pr.n. Geog:* Bude *f.*

budded ['bʌdid], *a.* **1.** (arbre) couvert de bourgeons; (rose *f*) en bouton. **2.** *Hort:* (arbre) greffé en écusson.

budder ['bʌdər], *s. Hort:* greffeur *m.*

Buddha ['budə], *s.* (le) Bouddha.

Buddhic ['budik], *a.* = BUDDHIST 2.

Buddhism ['budizm], *s.* bouddhisme *m.*

Buddhist ['budist]. **1.** *s.* bouddhiste *mf.* **2.** *a.* bouddhique, bouddhiste.

Buddhistic(al) [bu'distik(l)], *a.* bouddhique.

budding[1] ['bʌdiŋ], *a.* (*a*) (plante *f,* arbre *m,* fleur *f*) qui bourgeonne ou qui boutonne; **a b. rose,** un bouton de rose; une rose en bouton; (*b*) **b. artist,** artiste *mf* en herbe; **b. beauty,** beauté *f* à son aurore; **b. passion,** passion naissante; **b. genius,** génie *m* près d'éclore.

budding[2], *s.* **1.** (*a*) bourgeonnement *m* (des plantes); débourrement *m* (d'un arbre); (*b*) poussée *f* des boutons. **2.** *Hort:* écussonnage *m*; greffe *f* par œil détaché; **b. knife,** écussonnoir *m.* **3.** *Biol:* gemmation *f.*

buddle[1] ['bʌdl], *s. Min:* augette *f,* auge *f* à laver, lavoir *m.*

buddle[2], *v.tr.* laver (le minerai) à l'auge, à l'augette.

buddleia ['bʌdliə], *s. Bot:* buddleia *f.*

buddy ['bʌdi], *s. F:* ami *m,* copain *m*; **they're real buddies now,** ils sont à tu et à toi maintenant.

buddy-buddy ['bʌdi'bʌdi], *a. F:* **to be b.-b. with s.o.,** être à tu et à toi avec qn.

budge [bʌdʒ]. **1.** *v.i.* (*a*) bouger, céder; reculer; **to refuse to b.,** refuser de bouger; **I won't b. an inch,** je ne reculerai pas d'un centimètre; **he doesn't b.** il ne décolle pas; (*b*) bouger, remuer; **they dare not b.,** ils n'osent pas broncher; **if you (so much as) b.,** si vous faites le moindre mouvement. **2.** *v.tr.* (*in neg. sentences*) **I couldn't b. him,** il est resté inébranlable; **he couldn't b. it,** il ne pouvait pas le bouger.

budgeree [bʌdʒə'ri:], *a. Austr: P:* bon, excellent, fameux, chouette, bath.

budgerigar ['bʌdʒərigɑ:r], *s. Orn:* perruche *f* ondulée.

budget[1] ['bʌdʒit], *s.* **1.** *A:* (*a*) sac *m*; (*b*) tas *m,* collection *f* (de papiers, etc.); recueil *m* (d'anecdotes); **b. of letters,** paquet *m* de lettres. **2.** (*a*) *Fin: etc:* budget *m*; **balanced b.,** budget équilibré; **flexible b.,** budget adaptable; **to fix the b.,** établir le budget; **to balance the b.,** équilibrer le budget; **family, household, b.,** budget familial; budget du ménage; **this doesn't come within my b.,** cela n'est pas dans mes prix; je ne peux pas me payer cela; *Pol.Ec: etc:* **time b.,** budget temps; *Parl:* **to introduce, open, the b.,** présenter le budget; **to pass the b.,** voter le budget; **b. statement for the year,** situation *f* budgétaire de l'année; (*b*) *attrib. Com:* **b. prices,** prix raisonnables, avantageux; **several attractive b. dresses,** plusieurs jolies robes à des prix avantageux; **b. account** = compte permanent.

budget[2], *v.i. Fin: Parl:* **to b. for (a certain expenditure),** porter, inscrire, (certaines dépenses) au budget; budgétiser (certaines dépenses); **to b. one's time,** bien organiser son temps; **we had not budgeted for that difficulty,** nous n'avions pas prévu cette difficulté.

budgetary ['bʌdʒitri], *a. Fin: Parl: etc:* budgétaire; **b. policy,** politique *f* budgétaire; **b. control,** contrôle *m* budgétaire.

budgeting ['bʌdʒitiŋ], *s.* budgétisation *f*; **she has only just enough to live on, and budgeting for things such as illness has become impossible for her,** elle a juste de quoi vivre et il lui est impossible de faire des prévisions contre des imprévus tels que la maladie.

budgie ['bʌdʒi], *s. Orn: F:* perruche ondulée.

budless ['bʌdlis], *a. Bot:* **1.** sans bourgeons. **2.** sans boutons.

budlet ['bʌdlit], *s.* **1.** petit bourgeon. **2.** petit bouton (de fleur).

budorcas [bju'dɔ:kəs], *s. Z:* budorcas *m,* takin *m,* takang *m.*

bud-shaped ['bʌdʃeipt], *a. Bot:* gemmiforme.

Buenos-Ayrean ['bwenəs'aiəriən, 'bju:nəs'ɛəriən], *s. Geog:* Buénos-ayrien, -ienne.

Buerger ['bə:gər], *Pr.n. Med:* **Buerger's disease,** maladie de Buerger, thrombo-angéite oblitérante.

buff[1] [bʌf], *s.* **1.** peau *f* de buffle; cuir épais; **b. leather,** buffle *m*; *A.Mil:* **b. coat, b. jerkin,** (pourpoint *m* de) buffle; pourpoint de cuir épais; *Metalw:* **b. (stick),** buffle, polissoir *m,* carbon *m*; **b. (wheel),** meule *f* à polir, à buffler; polissoir; disque *m* en buffle. **2.** (*a*) couleur *f* chamois; jaune clair *inv*; *a.* de couleur chamois; jaune clair; **b.(-coloured) gloves,** gants *m* chamois; (*b*) *pl. Mil:* **the Buffs,** sobriquet officiel de l''East Kent Regiment'; (*c*) *Ent:* **b. tip, b.-tipped moth,** (phalène *f*) bucéphale *m*; *Husb:* **b. Orpington,** Orpington *mf* fauve. **3.** *F:* **in the b.,** tout nu; **to strip to the b.,** se mettre dans le costume d'Adam, *P:* se mettre à poil; **stripped to the b.,** nu comme un ver; nu comme la main. **4.** *Med:* **b. (of clotted blood),** couenne *f* inflammatoire. **5.** enthousiaste *mf*; **film, cinema, b.,** mordu, -ue, du cinéma.

buff[2], *v.tr.* **1.** *Metalw: etc:* polir, émeuler (un métal, etc.) (au buffle); **to b. one's nails,** se polir les ongles. **2.** *Leath:* effleurer (les peaux).

buff[3], *s. A:* = BUFFET[1]; *still found in* BLIND-MAN'S-BUFF.

buffalo[1], *pl.* **-oes** ['bʌfəlou, -ouz], *s.* **1.** *Z:* (*a*) buffle *m*; **Indian b., Asiatic b.,** buffle commun, d'Asie; **pygmy b. of the Celebes,** buffle pygmée des Célèbes, anoa *m* tamarou; **Cape b.,** buffle de Cafrerie, buffle du Cap; **water b.,** karbau *m*; **a herd of fifty buffalo(es),** un troupeau de cinquante buffles; **young b.,** bufflon *m*; **b.**

calf, buffletin *m*; **cow b.,** bufflesse *f*, bufflonne *f*; (*b*) *U.S:* bison *m*; **b. robe,** peau *m* de bison; (*c*) *Bot:* **b. berry, b. bush,** shepherdia *m*; **b. grass,** bouteloue *m*; *Ent:* **b. bug, b. carpet beetle,** anthrène *m*, amourette *f*; *Ich:* **b. fish,** catostome *m*; (*d*) *U.S: Hist:* **b. soldier,** soldat noir (dans l'Ouest de l'Amérique); (*e*) *Mil:* char *m* amphibie.

buffalo², *v.tr. U.S:* (*a*) intimider, terroriser; (*b*) dérouter; déconcerter; embrouiller; ahurir.

buffer¹ ['bʌfər], appareil *m* de choc; amortisseur *m*; (*a*) *Rail:* tampon *m* (de choc); **coupling b.,** tampon d'attelage; **spring b.,** tampon à ressort; ressort amortisseur; **hydraulic b.,** tampon hydraulique; **pneumatic b., air b.,** tampon pneumatique, à air; **b. (stop),** (*at end of line*) butoir *m*, heurtoir *m*; (*on rolling stock*) tampon d'arrêt; **b. bar, b. beam,** traverse *f* avant, traverse frontale (de la machine); **b. box,** faux-tampon *m*, *pl.* faux-tampons; **b. spring,** ressort *m*, amortisseur, de choc; (*b*) *Nau:* défense *f*; (*c*) *El: Elcs:* (circuit *m*) tampon; circuit intermédiaire; circuit de séparation; **b. battery,** batterie *f* tampon; **b. capacitator,** condensateur *m* shunt; **b. tube,** tube *m* intermédiaire; *W.Tel:* **b. stage,** étage *m* tampon, intermédiaire; *Cmptr:* **b. amplifier,** amplificateur *m* tampon; **b. store,** mémoire *f* tampon, mémoire intermédiaire; (*d*) *Artil:* **recoil b.,** frein *m*, amortisseur de recul; **counter-recoil b.,** frein, amortisseur, de retour en batterie; (*e*) *Ch:* **b. solution,** solution *f* tampon; (*f*) *Pol:* **b. (state),** état *m* tampon; *Pol.Ec:* **b. stocks,** stocks régulateurs, stocks tampon, stocks de régularisation; (*of pers.*) **to act as a b.,** servir de tampon; **she stood as a b. between her son and his exacting father,** elle protégeait son fils contre les exigeances de son père; (*g*) *Aut: U.S:* pare-choc(s) *m inv*.

buffer², *v.tr.* tamponner; amortir; *Ch:* ajuster à un pH donné.

buffer³, *s.* **1.** *Nau:* second maître *m* d'équipage. **2.** *F:* **old b.,** (i) vieux copain; (ii) vieille ganache, vieux bonze.

buffer⁴, *s.* **1.** meule *f* à polir, à buffler; polissoir *m*; disque *m* en buffle. **2.** (*pers.*) polisseur, -euse.

buffered ['bʌfəd], *a. Cmptr:* **b. computer,** calculateur *m* à mémoire(s) tampon(s); **b. peripheral,** périphérique *m* à mémoire tampon.

buffering ['bʌfəriŋ], *s. Cmptr:* **exchange b.,** assignation *f* de tampons par méthode d'échange; **simple b.,** assignation unique de tampons.

buffet¹ ['bʌfit], *s.* coup *m* (de poing); *Lit:* soufflet *m*; *F:* torgn(i)ole *f*; **the buffets of fortune,** les coups de la fortune; les vicissitudes *f* du sort; **b. of wind,** coup de vent.

buffet², *v.tr. & i.* (*a*) flanquer une torgn(i)ole à (qn); bourrer (qn) de coups; tomber sur (qn) à coups de poing; *Lit:* **they spat upon Him and buffeted Him,** ils ont craché sur lui et l'ont souffleté; (*b*) **to b. (with) the waves,** lutter contre les vagues; (*of ship*) **buffeted by the waves, by the wind,** battu, ballotté, par les vagues; secoué par le vent; **buffeting wind,** vent violent; **to be buffeted by the crowd,** être bousculé par la foule; **buffeted by fortune,** cahoté par la fortune; **he has been buffeted by fate,** il en a vu de dures.

buffet³, *s.* **1.** ['bʌfit] (*sideboard*) buffet *m*. **2.** ['bufei] (*a*) (*refreshment bar*) buffet; *Rail:* **b. car,** voiture-buffet, *pl.* voitures-buffets; (*b*) (*on menu*) **cold b.,** viandes froides; assiette anglaise; (*c*) **b. lunch, fork b., b. meal,** lunch *m*; repas *m* à la fourchette; **cold b.,** buffet froid.

buffet⁴ ['bʌfit], *s. Dial:* tabouret *m*; petit pouf; coussin *m* pour les pieds.

buffeting ['bʌfitiŋ], *s.* (*a*) succession *f* de coups, de chocs; **we got a b. in the Bay of Biscay,** nous avons été fortement secoués dans le golfe de Gascogne; **flowers that stand up to the b. of rain and wind,** fleurs *f* qui résistent aux assauts de la pluie et du vent; (*b*) *Aer:* buffeting *m*.

buffing ['bʌfiŋ], *s.* **1.** polissage *m*, émeulage *m*. **2.** effleurage *m*. **3.** *E: Metalw:* bufflage *m*; **b. wheel,** meule *f* à polir, à buffler; polissoir *m*; disque *m* en buffle. **4.** *Civ.E:* **b. machine,** polisseuse *f*.

bufflehead ['bʌflhed], *s.* **1.** *Orn:* garrot *m* albéole, *Fr.C:* petit garrot. **2.** *NAm: F:* imbécile *m*, idiot *m*.

buffo ['bufou], *s.m. Mus: Th:* buffo.

buffoon¹ [bə'fu:n], *s.* bouffon *m*, paillasse *m*, clown *m*; baladin, -ine; *A:* trivelin *m*; **to act, play, the b.,** faire le bouffon.

buffoon², *v.i.* faire le bouffon.

buffoonery [bə'fu:nəri], *s.* bouffonneries *fpl*; baladinage *m*.

buffy¹ ['bʌfi], *a. Med:* couenneux; **b. coat,** couenne *f* inflammatoire.

buffy², *a. P:* ivre, gris.

Bufo ['b(j)ufou], *s. Amph:* bufo *m*.

Bufonidae [bju:'fɔnidi:], *s.pl. Amph:* bufonidés *m*.

bufotalin [bjufou'teili(:)n], *s. Bio-Ch:* bufotaline *f*.

bufotenin(e) [bjufou'teni(:)n], *s. Bio-Ch:* bufoténine *f*.

bug¹ [bʌg], *s.* **1.** (*a*) (**bed**) **b.,** punaise *f*; (*b*) *esp. U.S:* insecte *m*; *Ent:* **mealy b.,** aleurode *m*; *U.S:* **potato b.,** doryphore *m*; *Arach:* **harvest b.,** lepte automnal; *F:* **b. hunter,** entomologiste *mf*; **b. hunting,** entomologie *f*; *F:* **b. killer,** tue-punaises *m inv*; insecticide *m*; (*c*) *F:* virus *m*, microbe *m*; **to catch a b.,** attraper un microbe; (*d*) *F:* **to have the skiing b.,** avoir la passion du ski. **2.** *F:* **big b.,** gros bonnet, *P:* grosse légume, huile *f*; (*b*) *U.S:* (i) cinglé, -ée; (ii) fanatique *mf*; **a skiing b.,** un mordu du ski. **3.** *esp. U.S:* erreur *f*, mauvais fonctionnement; **there are still a few bugs to be ironed out,** il y a encore quelques petits trucs qui clochent; *Cmptr:* **programme b.,** erreur dans un programme. **4.** (*a*) microphone clandestin; (*b*) *Rad:* indicateur *m* de position; (*c*) *Tg:* manipulateur *m* semi-automatique. **5.** *Space:* lem *m*, module *m* lunaire. **6.** *U.S: Turf:* décharge *f*; **b. boy,** apprenti ayant droit à une décharge.

bug², **1.** *v.tr.* (*a*) *U.S:* désinsectiser (des plantes, etc.); (*b*) **to b. a room,** camoufler des microphones clandestins dans une pièce; (*c*) *U.S:* taper sur les nerfs à (qn); emmerder (qn). **2.** *v.i. U.S:* collectionner les insectes; faire de l'entomologie. **3.** *v.i. NAm:* **to b. out,** déguerpir, décamper, se sauver; *esp. Mil:* déserter en présence de l'ennemi.

bug³, *v.i. NAm:* bomber; ballonner; faire saillie.

bugaboo ['bʌgəbu:], *s. F:* (*a*) croquemitaine *m*, loup-garou *m*, *pl.* loups-garous; (*b*) (*causing anxiety*) cauchemar *m*.

bugbane ['bʌgbein], *s. Bot: F:* (*a*) cimicaire *f*, cimicifuge *m*; chasse-punaise *m*, *pl.* chasse-punaise(s); (*b*) vératre *m*.

bugbear ['bʌgbɛər], *s. F:* (*a*) croquemitaine *m*, loup-garou *m*, *pl.* loups-garous; (*b*) cauchemar *m*; **maths is my b.,** j'ai horreur des math; les math, c'est mon cauchemar, ma bête noire; (*c*) (*snag*) problème *m*, obstacle *m*; inconvénient *m*; **this old fashioned stove is really a b.,** je ne sais que faire avec cette cuisinière démodée.

bugeater ['bʌgi:tər], *s. U.S:* **1.** *Orn:* (espèce de) caprimulgidé *m*. **2.** *F:* habitant *m* du Nébraska.

bug-eyed ['bʌg'aid], *a. U.S:* (*a*) aux yeux exorbités, aux yeux en boules de loto; (*b*) qui ouvre de grands yeux; (*c*) **b.-e. monster,** monstre *m* aux yeux menaçants (dans un roman de science-fiction).

bugger¹ ['bʌgər], *s.* **1.** *Jur:* pédéraste *m*. **2.** *P:* (*not in polite use*) (*a*) bougre *m*, salaud *m*, salopard *m*; **silly b.!** espèce d'idiot! **listen to that little b.!** écoutez-moi ce petit bougre-là; (*b*) **a b. of a job,** un travail infernal; (*c*) (*attenuated, friendly sense*) **he's a nice little b.,** c'est un bon petit bougre.

bugger², **1.** *v.tr.* sodomiser. **2.** *P:* (*not in polite use*) (*a*) *v.i.* **to b. about,** lambiner; **to b. off,** foutre le camp; **b. off!** (i) fous le camp! (ii) fous-moi la paix! (*b*) *v.tr.* **b. it! I'll be buggered!** merde! (*c*) *v.tr.* **to be completely buggered,** être éreinté; (*d*) *v.tr.* **to b. sth. up,** mettre le bordel dans qch., faire un gâchis de qch., bousiller qch.

buggery ['bʌgəri], *s.* sodomie *f*.

buggy¹ ['bʌgi]. **1.** *a.* (*a*) infesté (i) de punaises, (ii) *U.S:* d'insectes; (*b*) **b. about skiing,** mordu du ski; (*c*) fou, cinglé, toqué. **2.** *s. Tail:* doublure *f* entre les épaules.

buggy², *s. Veh:* (*a*) boghei *m*, buggy *m*, boguet *m*; araignée *f*; **high b.,** stanhope *m*; (*b*) *A:* (*four-wheeled*) (**American**) **b.,** américaine *f*.

buggy³, *a. U.S:* (yeux) exorbités, qui font saillie.

bughouse ['bʌghaus], **1.** *s. U.S: F:* maison *f* de fous; cabanon *m*. **2.** *a.* fou, cinglé, toqué.

bugle¹ ['bju:gl], *s.* **1.** *A:* cor *m* de chasse. **2.** *Mil:* clairon *m*; **key(ed) b.,** bugle *m*; **b. call,** coup *m*, sonnerie *f*, de clairon; **B.-major,** chef *m* de musique; (*in Chasseurs à pied*) chef de fanfare.

bugle², *v.i.* sonner du clairon.

bugle³, *s. Bot:* bugle *f*; **common b.,** bugle rampante.

bugler ['bju:glər], *s.* clairon *m*; sonneur *m* de clairon.

bugles ['bju:glz], *s.pl. Dressm: A:* tubes *m* (de verre); verroterie noire.

bugleweed ['bju:glwi:d], **buglewort** ['bju:glwə:t], *s. Bot:* lycopus *m*.

bugling ['bju:gliŋ], *s.* sonneries *fpl* de clairon.

bugloss ['bju:glɔs], *s. Bot:* (*a*) **corn, field, b.,** buglosse *f*, lycopside *f* des champs; (*b*) **viper's b.,** vipérine *f*, herbe *f* aux vipères; (*c*) **dyer's b.,** orcanette *f*; (*d*) picride *f*; (*e*) asperugo *m*; (*f*) **b. cowslip,** pulmonaire *f*.

bugout ['bʌgaut], *s. NAm:* (*a*) désertion *f* (en présence de l'ennemi); (*b*) déserteur *m*.

bugs [bʌgz], *a. F:* fou, cinglé, toqué.

bugseed ['bʌgsi:d], *s. Bot:* corispermum *m*.

bugula ['bju:gju:lə], *s. Biol:* bugule *f*.

Bugulidae [bʌ'gju:lidi:], *s.pl. Biol:* bugulidés *m*.

bugweed ['bʌgwi:d], *s. Bot:* corispermum *m*.

bugwort ['bʌgwə:t], *s.* = BUGBANE (*a*).

buhl [bu:l], *s. Furn:* (marqueterie *f* de) boul(l)e *m*; **b. cabinet,** cabinet *m* de boul(l)e.

buhrstone ['bə:stoun], *s. Geol:* (pierre) meulière *f*.

build¹ [bild], *s.* **1.** construction *f*; façons *fpl* (d'un navire, etc.); style *m* (d'un édifice). **2.** carrure *f*, taille *f*, conformation *f* (d'une personne); **man of powerful b.,** homme d'une ossature puissante, à forte membrure; **man of slight b.,** homme fluet, de faible corpulence; **a man of my b.,** un homme bâti comme moi; un homme de ma taille; **to be spare of b.,** avoir une charnure sèche; **I know him by his b.,** je le reconnais à sa taille, *F:* à son encolure.

build², *v.* (**built** [bilt]; **built**)

I. *v.tr.* **1.** (*a*) (faire) construire, bâtir, une maison, construire (un navire, un pont, une route, etc.); édifier (un temple); faire (son nid, etc.) (**with,** avec); **birds use hay to b. their nests (with),** l'oiseau se sert de foin pour bâtir son nid; **the walls were built of granite,** les murs étaient (bâtis) en granit; **to b. a new wing to a hotel,** ajouter une aile à un hôtel; **to b. beams into a wall,** encastrer des poutres dans un mur; **to b. over, on, a piece of land,** bâtir un terrain; **church built on to the city walls,** église accolée aux murs de la ville; **the stables are built on to the house,** les écuries tiennent à la maison; **we built on, out, a studio,** nous avons ajouté un studio (à la maison); **to b. on sand,** bâtir sur le sable; **foundations built on a rock,** fondations *f* qui reposent sur le roc; *F:* **I'm built that way,** je suis fait comme ça; je suis comme ça; **I'm not built that way,** cela ne s'accorde pas avec mes principes; cela ne rentre pas dans mes goûts; (*b*) **the house is being built,** la maison est en construction. **2.** (*a*) **to b. one's hopes on sth.,** fonder, baser, mettre, ses espoirs sur qch.; **to b. on a promise,** miser, faire fond, sur une promesse; **I'm building my hopes on you,** je compte sur vous; (*b*) *esp. NAm: Com:* **to b. (certain characteristics) into a product,** incorporer (certaines caractéristiques) dans un produit; (*c*) *Med: etc:* **to b. in an immunity,** créer une immunité.

II. (*compound verb*) **build up,** *v.tr. & i.* (*a*) *v.tr.* affermir (la santé); (*b*) *v.tr.* bâtir, échafauder, construire (une théorie, etc.); **he has built up a fine reputation,** il s'est fait une belle réputation; **to b. up one's business,** développer son affaire, son commerce; *v.i.* **pressure is building up,** la pression s'accumule, s'accroît; **the traffic is building up,** la circulation devient très dense; *v.tr.* **to b. up a story,** structurer une histoire; (*c*) *v.tr.* **this area has been very much built up,** on a beaucoup construit par ici; **to b. up a wall,** (i) rehausser; (ii) réparer, un mur; *v.i.* **the snow is building up against the wall,** la neige s'amoncelle contre le mur; (*d*) *v.tr. Mil: etc:* (i) mettre sur pied (des unités, des renforts, etc.); (ii) constituer (des stocks, etc.); (iii) rassembler à pied d'œuvre (des troupes, du matériel, etc.); (*e*) *v.tr. Com:* faire de la publicité pour (un produit); (*f*) *El: v.tr.* amorcer (un champ magnétique); *v.i.* (*of magnetic field*) s'amorcer.

builder ['bildər], *s.* entrepreneur *m* (en bâtiments); constructeur *m* (de navires, de machines); facteur *m* (d'orgues); créateur, -trice, fondateur, -trice (d'un empire, etc.); *Veh:* **body b.,** carrossier *m*.

building ['bildiŋ], *s.* **1.** construction *f*; **b. land,** terrains *mpl* bâtissables, à bâtir; terrains non bâtis; **b. plot,** terrain à bâtir; **b. estate,** lotissement *m*; **b. line,** alignement *m* (d'une rue); **b. lease,** bail *m* emphytéotique; **b. materials,** matériaux *m* de construction; **b. stone,** pierre *f* à bâtir; **b. timber,** bois *m* de charpente, de construction; *For:* maisonnage *m*; **b. contractor,** entrepreneur *m* en bâtiment, de bâtiment; **b. society** = coopérative, société, immobilière; **the b. trade,** le bâtiment; **the b. trades,** les industries du bâtiment; *N.Arch:* **b. slip,** cale *f* de construction. **2.** bâtiment; immeuble *m*; maison *f*; local *m*, -aux; édifice *m*; **portable b.,** construction démontable; **public b.,** (i) édifice public; (ii) monument *m*; **municipal buildings** = mairie *f*, hôtel *m* de ville; *Const:* **frame b.,** bâtisse *f* de bois; **farm buildings,** bâtiments, dépendances *f*, d'une ferme.

building up ['bildiŋ'ʌp], *s.* **1.** affermissement *m* (de la santé, etc.); *Med:* **b.-up food,** (aliment) analeptique *m*, reconstituant *m*. **2. b. up of a map, etc.,** élaboration *f*, rédaction *f*, d'une carte, etc.; **the gradual b. up of a new social structure,** le lent échafaudage d'un nouvel édifice social. **3.** *El:* amorçage *m* (du champ, d'une dynamo).

build-up ['bildʌp], *s.* **1.** consolidation *f*; élaboration *f*, développement *m* (d'un système, etc.). **2.** *Mil:* (i) mise *f* sur pied (d'unités, de renforts, etc.); (ii) constitution *f* (de réserves en hommes, de matériel, etc.); (iii) rassemblement *m* à pied d'œuvre (de troupes, de matériel); **the NATO military b.-up,** la mise sur pied des forces militaires, du système militaire, de l'OTAN. **3.** *Ph:* manifestation croissante (d'un phénomène); *Mec:* montée *f* en accélération **4.** publicité *f*; campagne *f* publicitaire. **5. traffic b.-up,** bouchon *m* de circulation.

built ['bilt], *a.* bâti; **British-b. ships,** navires *m* de construction anglaise; **to be solidly, powerfully, b.,** avoir la charpente solide; être puissamment charpenté; **well-b. man,** homme bien bâti, solidement charpenté, d'une belle carrure.

built-in ['biltin], *a.* (*a*) incorporé; **b.-in beam,** poutre encastrée; **b.-in cupboard,** placard incorporé; **b.-in check,** contrôle *m* automatique; *F:* **b.-in resistance,** opposition congénitale; (*b*) **the b.-in energy of the atom,** l'énergie inhérente à l'atome.

built-up ['biltʌp], *a.* **1. b.-up area,** agglomération (urbaine); **b.-up land,** terrain bâti. **2. b.-up beam,** poutre composée, rapportée. **3.** *Cost:* **b.-up neckline,** col remonté; **b.-up shoulders,** épaules surhaussées; **b.-up heels,** talons compensés.

buisson ['bwi:sɔ̃], *s. Cu:* buisson *m* (d'écrevisses).

bulb[1] [bʌlb], *s.* **1.** *Bot:* bulbe feuillé, oignon *m* (de tulipe, etc.); **offset b.,** caïeu *m*; **back b.,** pseudo-bulbe *m* d'orchidée; **b. of garlic,** tête *f* d'ail; **b. grower,** bulbiculteur *m*; **b. growing,** bulbiculture *f*; culture *f* des oignons à fleurs. **2.** *Anat:* bulbe; **hair b.,** bulbe pileux. **3.** *El:* ampoule *f*, lampe *f*; **gas-filled b.,** lampe à atmosphère gazeuse; **vacuum b.,** ampoule à vide; *U.S: P:* **he's a dim b.,** il n'est pas très intelligent. **4.** (*a*) *Ph:* boule *f*, cuvette *f*, ampoule, réservoir *m* (de thermomètre); (*b*) *Ch:* (*flask*) ballon *m*; (*c*) poire *f* (en caoutchouc); *Aut: A:* **b. horn,** trompe *f* à poire; (*d*) **b. angle,** cornière *f* à boudin; **b. iron,** fer *m* à boudin; (*e*) *Nau:* **b. keel,** étrave *f* en bulbe; *Y:* bulb-keel *m*.

bulb[2], *v.i.* (*a*) *Bot: Hort:* se former en bulbe; (*b*) se renfler.

bulbaceous [bʌl'beiʃəs], *a.* bulbeux; **b. plant,** plante bulbeuse.

bulbar ['bʌlbər], *a.* bulbaire.

bulbed ['bʌlbd], *a.* bulbeux.

bulberry ['bʌlb(ə)ri], *s. Bot:* shepheardia *m*.

bulbiferous [bʌl'bifərəs], *a.* bulbifère.

bulbiform ['bʌlbifɔ:m], *a.* bulbiforme.

bulbil ['bʌlbil], **bulblet** ['bʌlblit], *s. Bot:* bulbille *f*.

bulblike ['bʌlblaik], *a.* bulbeux, en forme de bulbe.

bulbocavernous ['bʌlbou'kævənəs], *a. Anat:* bulbocaverneux.

bulbocodium ['bʌlbou'koudiəm], *s. Bot:* bulbocodium *m*.

bulbonuclear ['bʌlbou'nju:kliər], *a. Z:* bulbonucléaire.

bulbourethral ['bʌlbouju'ri:θrl], *a. Anat:* bulbo-urétral, -aux.

bulbous ['bʌlbəs], *a.* bulbeux; *Bot:* **b. root,** racine bulbeuse; (*of pers.*) **b. nose,** gros nez.

bulbul ['bulbul], *s. Orn:* bulbul *m*.

bulbus ['bʌlbəs], *s. Anat:* **b. aortae, b. arteriosus,** bulbe *m* aortique; **b. oculi,** globe *m* de l'œil.

bulean ['bju:liən], *s. Bot:* bois *m* de fer de Bornéo.

Bulgar ['bʌlgɑ:r], *s.* = BULGARIAN 1.

Bulgaria [bʌl'gεəriə], *Pr.n. Geog:* Bulgarie *f*.

Bulgarian [bʌl'gεəriən]. **1.** *Geog:* (*a*) *a.* bulgare; (*b*) *s.* Bulgare *mf*. **2.** *s. Ling:* bulgare *m*.

bulge[1] [bʌldʒ], *s.* (*a*) bombement *m*, ventre *m*, renflement *m*; protubérance *f*; saillie *f*; (*of bottle, vase*) panse *f*; *Arch:* jarret *m*; (*in tyre*) soufflure *f*, hernie *f*; *Pol.Ec: F:* **the b.,** le ventre (de la courbe), la poussée; *Hist: F:* **the Battle of the B.,** la Bataille des Ardennes; (*b*) *N.Arch:* (i) caisson *m* pare-torpilles; bulge *m*; (ii) bulb *m*; (*c*) *U.S: F:* **to have, get, the b. on s.o.,** avoir, remporter, l'avantage sur qn; dégotter qn; mettre qn dedans; (*d*) *St.Exch: U.S:* hausse *f*.

bulge[2], *v.tr. & i.* **1. to b. (out),** bomber, ballonner; faire ventre; faire saillie; faire une bosse; (*of wall, etc.*) se déjeter; *Arch:* jarreter; **to b. one's cheeks,** gonfler les joues; **to b. one's pockets,** bourrer ses poches **(with,** de); **sack bulging with potatoes,** sac bourré, plein à craquer, de pommes de terre; *F:* **this dress is too tight and makes me b.,** cette robe me boudine car elle est trop juste. **2.** *U.S: F:* **to b. in,** faire irruption; **to b. off,** partir à toute vitesse; **to b. for the door,** s'élancer vers la porte.

bulged ['bʌldʒd], *a.* déjeté; *Nau: etc:* **b. plates,** tôles faussées.

bulginess ['bʌldʒinis], *s.* excès *m* de volume.

bulging[1] ['bʌldʒiŋ], *a.* (front, etc.) bombé; (ventre) ballonnant; **b. eyes,** yeux protubérants, qui sortent de la tête; **man with b. cheeks,** homme joufflu, aux joues bouffies; **b. wall,** mur *m* qui fait ventre.

bulging[2], *s.* bombement *m*, renflement *m* (d'un mur, etc.); ballonnement *m*.

bulgy ['bʌldʒi], *a.* bombé, ballonnant; **b.-cheeked,** joufflu.

bulimia [bju:'limiə], **bulimy** ['bju:limi], *s. Med:* boulimie *f*.

bulimus, -mi [bju:'laiməs, -mai], *s. Moll:* bulime *m*.

bulk[1] [bʌlk], *s.* **1.** (*a*) *Nau:* charge *f*; chargement arrimé; **to break b.,** (i) désarrimer; rompre charge; commencer le déchargement; entrer en déchargement; (ii) disposer d'une partie des marchandises; **breaking b.,** (i) changement *m* d'arrimage, désarrimage *m*; (ii) commencement *m* du déchargement; **to sell sth. without breaking b.,** vendre qch. sous corde; **to load (a ship) in b.,** charger un navire en volume, (*with grain*) en grenier; (*b*) *Com: etc:* **in b.,** en bloc, globalement; en gros, en quantité; **to buy in b.,** acheter par grosses quantités, en gros; **b. buying,** achat massif, en gros; **to sell in b.,** vendre en vrac, en gros; **b. concrete,** béton *m* en masse; **b. spreader,** épandeur *m*; épandeuse *f*; *Post:* **b. rate,** affranchissement *m* à forfait; **per b. post,** par sacs postaux; (*c*) *Cmptr:* volume *m*, masse *f* (d'informations); **b. memory, b. storage,** mémoire *f* de masse; **b. storage,** archivage *m*. **2.** (*a*) grandeur *f*, grosseur *f*, masse, volume *m*; encombrement *m* (d'un colis); **gold represents great value in small b.,** l'or représente une grande valeur sous peu de volume; **ship of great b.,** vaisseau *m* de grandes dimensions, d'un port considérable; *Bookb:* **b. in millimetres,** millième *m* (du dos de l'emboîtage); (*b*) *Paperm:* bouffant *m* (du papier). **3. the b.,** l'ensemble *m*; **the b. of mankind,** la masse, la plupart, le commun, des hommes; **to lose the b. of one's goods,** perdre le plus gros de ses biens, la majeure partie de ses biens; **the b. of the army,** le gros de l'armée; **the b. of their business is with France,** c'est avec la France qu'ils font la plus grosse partie de leurs affaires.

bulk[2]. **1.** *v.i.* (*a*) **to b. large,** occuper une place importante, faire figure importante **(in s.o.'s eyes,** aux yeux de qn); (*b*) **to b. up,** s'amasser; **to b. up to . . .,** s'élever au total de . . .. **2.** *v.tr.* (*a*) entasser (des poissons, etc.); (*b*) réunir, grouper, (plusieurs colis) en un seul; entasser (des marchandises) en vrac; (*c*) *Cust:* **to b. a chest of tea,** mesurer, estimer, le contenu d'une caisse de thé; (*d*) *v.ind.tr. Publ:* **to b. up a book,** imprimer un livre sur du papier bouffant.

bulkhead[1] ['bʌlked], *s. N.Arch:* cloison *f*; **armoured b.,** cloison blindée; **watertight b.,** cloison étanche; **fireproof, fire-retarding, b.,** cloison coupe-feu; **oil-tight, gas-tight, b.,** cloison étanche au pétrole, aux gaz; **collision b.,** cloison de choc, d'arbordage; **fore-and-aft b.,** cloison longitudinale; **athwartship b.,** cloison transversale; **b. deck,** pont *m* de cloisonnement; **break b.,** fronteau *m*; **fire b.,** cloison pare-feu.

bulkhead[2], *v.tr. N.Arch:* **to b. (off),** cloisonner.

bulkheading ['bʌlkhediŋ], *s. N.Arch:* cloisonnement *m*.

bulkiness ['bʌlkinis], *s.* **1.** volume excessif; encombrement *m*. **2.** grosseur *f*.

bulking[1] ['bʌlkiŋ], *a. Com:* **b. paper,** papier bouffant.

bulking[2], *s.* groupage *m* (de colis).

bulky ['bʌlki], *a.* **1.** volumineux, encombrant; **b. book,** livre épais; *Nau:* **b. cargo,** chargement volumineux. **2.** gros, grosse.

bull[1] [bul], *s.* **1.** (*a*) taureau *m*; **b. calf,** jeune taureau, taurillon *m*; **b. for service,** taureau reproducteur; **b. pen,** parc *m* à taureaux; toril *m*; **to have a neck like a b.,** avoir un cou de taureau; **to take the b. by the horns,** prendre le taureau par les cornes; prendre le tison par où il brûle; **like a b. in a china shop,** comme un taureau en rupture d'étable; comme un éléphant dans un magasin de porcelaine; **to charge like a b. at a (five-barred) gate,** y aller la tête baissée; **b.-at-a-gate tactics,** tactique *f* de choc; (*b*) **b. elephant, whale, seal,** éléphant *m* mâle, baleine *f* mâle, phoque *m* mâle; **the rhinoceros was a b.,** le rhinocéros était un mâle; (*c*) *Astr:* **the B.,** le Taureau; (*d*) *P:* agent *m* de police, flic *m*; (*e*) *Mil: P:* fourbissage *m*, astiquage exagéré et inutile. **2.** *St.Exch:* spéculateur *m* à la hausse; haussier *m*; **b. transaction,** opération *f* à la hausse; **to go a b.,** spéculer à la hausse; **the market is all bulls,** le marché est à la hausse. **3.** noir *m*, centre *m*, blanc *m*, mouche *f* (d'une cible); **he made six bulls,** il a fait mouche six fois. **4.** (*a*) = BULLDOG 1, 2; **b. bitch,** chienne *f* de bouledogue; **b. pup,** petit chien bouledogue, chiot *m* de bouledogue; (*b*) **b. terrier,** (chien) bull-terrier *m*, *pl.* bull-terriers; (*c*) **b. mastiff,** molosse *m*. **5.** *Orn: F:* **b. of the bog,** butor *m*. **6.** *Bot: U.S:* **b. bay,** laurier-tulipier *m*, *pl.* lauriers-tulipiers; magnolia *m*, magnolier *m*, à grandes fleurs. **7.** *Ent: NAm:* **b. fly,** taon *m*.

bull[2]. **1.** (*a*) *v.i.* (*of cow*) être en rut, en chaleur; (*b*) *v.tr.* (*of bull*) servir (la vache). **2.** *St.Exch:* (*a*) *v.tr.* **to b. the market,** chercher à faire hausser les cours; (*b*) *v.i.* spéculer à la hausse; (*c*) *v.i.* (*of stocks, etc.*) être en hausse. **3.** *v.tr. U.S:* **to b. through,** forcer (une décision, etc.); **to b. one's way (through),** se frayer un chemin.

bull[3], *s. Ec:* bulle *f*; **Papal b.,** bulle du Pape; bulle papale; **the Golden B.,** la Bulle d'or.

bull[4], *s.* **1. (Irish) b.,** inconséquence *f*; coq-à-l'âne *m inv*; naïveté *f*. **2.** bévue *f* (comique); naïveté; gaffe *f*.

bull[5], *s. U.S: P:* foutaise *f*.

bull[6], *v.i. U.S: P:* (*a*) dire des foutaises; (*b*) faire des gaffes.

bulla ['bulə], *s. Moll:* bulle *f*.

bullace ['buləs], *s. Bot:* béloce *f*; prune *f* sauvage; **b. tree,** bélocier *m*.

bullate ['buleit], *a. Bot:* bullé.

bullberry ['bulb(ə)ri], *s. Bot:* shepherdia *m*.

bulldog ['buldɔg], *s.* **1.** bouledogue *m*. **2.** *F:* (i) personne d'un courage obstiné; (ii) appariteur *m* du censeur (aux universités d'Oxford et de Cambridge); *F:* **he's one of the b. breed,** c'est un homme qui a du cran. **3.** *F:* gros revolver. **4. b. clip,** pince *f* à dessin. **5.** (*a*) *Z:* **b. bat,** molosse *m*, molossidé *m*; (*b*) *Ent: NAm:* **b. (fly),** taon *m*.

bulldoze ['buldouz]. **1.** *v.tr.* (*a*) dégager, déblayer (un terrain) (avec un bulldozer); (*b*) *F:* menacer, intimider, brutaliser (qn). **2.** *v.i.* manœuvrer un bulldozer.

bulldozer ['buldouzər], *s.* **1.** *F:* (*pers.*) brutal *m*, -aux. **2.** *Metalw:* machine *f* à refouler, à cintrer. **3.** *Civ.E:* bulldozer *m*; tracteur-niveleur *m*, *pl.* tracteurs-niveleurs; *esp. Fr.C:* bélier *m* mécanique.

bullen (nail) ['bulən(neil)], *s. Arch: Furn:* bulle *f*; clou *m* de tapissier.

bullet ['bulit], *s.* **1.** (*a*) *A:* boulet *m*; (*b*) plomb *m*, balle *f* (d'une ligne de pêche). **2.** *Sm.a:* balle (de fusil, de revolver); **jacketed b.,** balle blindée, à enveloppe; **shrapnel b.,** balle d'obus; **solid b.,** balle pleine; **b. nose,** ogive *f* de balle; **b. hole,** trou *m* de balle; **riddled with bullets,** criblé de balles; *Surg:* **b. extractor,** tire-balle *m*, *pl.* tire-balles; sonde *f*; *F:* **to stop a b.,** être blessé; recevoir une balle; *P: O:* **to get the b.,** recevoir son congé; être saqué.

bullethead ['bulithed], *s.* **1.** tête ronde. **2.** *esp. U.S: F:* personne entêtée.

bullet-headed ['bulit'hedid], *a.* **1.** à tête ronde. **2.** *esp. U.S: F:* entêté.

bulletin ['bulitin], *s. Mil: etc:* bulletin *m*, communiqué *m*; **news b.,** bulletin d'actualités; *W.Tel: etc:* radio journal *m*; informations *fpl*. *U.S:* **b. board,** tableau *m* d'affichage (des nouvelles du jour); *U.S: Mil:* **daily b.,** décision journalière.

bulletproof ['bulitpru:f], *a.* à l'épreuve des balles; (gilet, etc.) antiballes, pare-balles *inv*.

bullet tree ['bulit tri:], *s. Bot:* balata *m*.

bull-faced ['bulfeist], *a.* à la face tauresque, à (la) face de taureau.

bullfight ['bulfait], *s.* course *f*, combat *m*, de taureaux; corrida *f*.

bullfighter ['bulfaitər], *s.* toréador *m*.

bullfighting ['bulfaitiŋ], *s.* combats *mpl* de taureaux, courses *fpl* de taureaux; tauromachie *f*.

bullfinch ['bulfintʃ], *s.* **1.** *Orn:* bouvreuil *m* (pivoine); **northern b.,** bouvreuil ponceau; **trumpeter b.,** bouvreuil githagine. **2.** *Equit:* (obstacle *m* en) bullfinch *m*; haie *f* avec fossé.

bullfrog ['bulfrɔg], *s. Amph:* grenouille mugissante; grenouille taureau, grenouille bœuf.

bullhead ['bulhed], *s.* **1.** (*a*) *Ich:* chabot *m* de rivière; cabot *m*; tête *f* d'âne; cotte *m*; (*b*) *Dial:* têtard *m*. **2.** *Rail:* **b. rail,** rail *m* à double champignon. **3.** *Bot:* **b. lily,** nuphar *m*.

bullheaded ['bul'hedid], *a.* **1.** au front de taureau. **2.** d'une impétuosité de taureau.

Bullidae ['bulidi:], *s.pl. Moll:* bullidés *m*.

bulliform ['bulifɔ:m], *a. Bot:* bullé.

bulling ['buliŋ], *s. Min:* bourrage *m* (d'un trou de mine).

bullion[1] ['buliən], *s.* or *m* en barres; or, argent *m*, en lingot(s); matières *fpl* d'or ou d'argent; valeurs *fpl* en espèces; *Fin:* métal *m*; **b. office,** bureau *m* pour l'achat des lingots d'or et d'argent; **b. reserve,** réserve *f* métallique; *Nau:* **b. room,** soute *f* à valeurs; *Veh:* **b. van,** fourgon *m* bancaire; *Metalw:* **base b.,** plomb *m* d'œuvre.

bullion[2], *s. Tex:* (*a*) cannetille *f*; (*b*) *Mil: Navy:* **thick b.,** torsades *fpl*; **thin b.,** franges *fpl*.

bullionism ['buliənizm], *s. Pol.Ec:* bullionisme *m*.

bullish ['buliʃ], *a. St.Exch:* **b. tendency,** tendance *f* à la hausse.

bullishness ['buliʃnis], *s. St.Exch:* tendance *f* à la hausse.

bull-like ['bullaik], *a.* tauresque.

bull-necked ['bul'nekt], *a.* au col de taureau; au col court.

bullock ['bulək], *s.* (*a*) *Husb:* bœuf *m*; **young b.,** bouvillon *m*; **b. cart,** char *m* à bœufs; (*b*) *Bot: F:* **bullock's heart,** cœur-de-bœuf *m*, *pl.* cœurs-de-bœuf; cachiman *m*; anone réticulée.

bullring ['bulriŋ], *s.* arène *f* (pour les courses de taureaux).

bull's eye ['bulzai], *s.* **1.** *Glassm:* boudine *f*; **b.-e. panes,** carreaux *m* à boudines, en culs-de-bouteille. **2.** (*a*)

Nau: verre mort; lentille *f*; (*b*) (*sheaveless block*) moque *f*. **3. b.-e. (window),** œil-de-bœuf *m*, *pl.* œils-de-bœuf; oculus *m*; **b.-e. lens,** lentille plan-convexe (à court foyer); **b.-e. lantern,** lanterne sourde. **4.** noir *m*; centre *m*, blanc *m*, mouche *f*, visuel *m* (d'une cible); **to hit the b.-e., make a b.-e.,** faire mouche; mettre dans le noir, dans le blanc, (*at darts*) dans le mille. **5.** *Comest:* gros bonbon (en boule) à la menthe.

bullshit[1] ['bulʃit], *s. P:* (*not in polite use*) foutaise *f*.

bullshit[2], *v.i. P:* (*not in polite use*) dire des foutaises.

bullsucker ['bulsʌkər], *s. Bot:* opuntia *m*.

bullswool ['bulzwul], *s. Bot: Austr:* (espèce d')eucalyptus *m*.

bully[1] ['buli], *s.* **1.** (*a*) *A:* bravache *m*; *F:* coupeur *m* d'oreilles; **to play the b.,** faire le fendant; (*b*) brute *f*, tyran *m*, brutal *m*; *Sch:* brimeur *m*; (*c*) homme *m* de main (d'un aventurier politique, etc.). **2.** (*pimp*) souteneur *m*.

bully[2], *v.tr.* intimider, malmener, brutaliser, rudoyer, houspiller, maltraiter (qn); **to b. s.o. into doing sth.,** faire faire qch. à qn à force de menaces; **he's got to be bullied into working,** il faut le rudoyer pour qu'il travaille; **to b. sth. out of s.o.,** arracher qch. à qn par des menaces, en le rudoyant; **he bullies his wife,** il brutalise sa femme.

bully[3], *a. & int. P: O:* fameux, épatant, chouette; **b. for you!** (i) vous avez de la chance! (ii) bravo pour vous!

bully[4], *s. Sp:* **1.** *Fb: A:* mêlée *f*. **2.** (*hockey*) engagement *m* (du jeu).

bully[5], *Sp:* (*hockey*) **1.** *v.tr.* mettre (la balle) en jeu. **2.** *v.i.* **to b.** (**off**), engager (le jeu); mettre la balle en jeu.

bully[6], *a. F:* **b. beef,** bœuf *m* de conserve, *F:* singe *m*.

bully boy ['buli bɔi], *s. F:* voyou *m*, dur *m*.

bullying[1] ['buliiŋ], *a.* brutal, -aux.

bullying[2], *s.* **1.** intimidation *f*, brutalité *f*, rudoiement *m*. **2.** *Sch:* brimades *fpl*.

bullyrag ['bulirӕg], *v.i. & tr.* chahuter; faire du chahut.

bully tree ['bulitri:], *s. Bot:* balata *m*.

bulrush ['bulrʌʃ], *s. Bot:* **1.** scirpe *m*; *F:* jonc *m* des marais; jonc des chaisiers. **2.** (*cat's tail*) typha *m*; *F:* massette *f*, quenouille *f*.

bulwark ['bulwə:k], *s.* **1.** (*a*) *A.Fort:* rempart *m*, boulevard *m*; *Lit:* **England, the b. of liberty,** l'Angleterre gardienne de la liberté; **the b. of our liberties,** le rempart de nos libertés; (*b*) *A:* digue *f*; brise-lames *m inv.* **2.** *pl. Nau:* pavois *m*, bastingage *m*.

bum[1] [bʌm], *s. F:* **1.** derrière *m*, *P:* cul *m*. **2.** = BUMBAILIFF.

bum[2], *NAm: P:* **1.** *a.* (*a*) sans valeur, moche; **b. check,** chèque *m* sans provision; (*b*) (*of pers.*) patraque; cafardeux. **2.** *s.* (*pers.*) fainéant *m*; clochard *m*; trimardeur *m*. **3.** *s.* (*a*) bordée *f*; (*b*) **to be on the b.,** (i) (*of pers.*) (essayer de) vivre aux dépens des autres; faire du tapage; trimarder; lambiner; (ii) (*of thg*) être en panne; (*c*) **to give s.o. the bum's rush,** flanquer qn à la porte; balancer qn; **to get the bum's rush,** être flanqué à la porte.

bum[3], *v.* (**bummed**) *NAm: P:* **1.** *v.i.* (*a*) flâner; fainéanter; (*b*) lever le coude; (*c*) faire du tapage. **2.** *v.tr.* **to b. a cigarette from, off, s.o.,** taper qn d'une cigarette; **to b. a ride,** faire de l'auto-stop.

bumbailiff ['bʌmbeilif], *s. F: A:* pousse-cul *m inv.*

bumbershoot ['bʌmbəʃu:t], *s. U.S: F:* parapluie *m*, pépin *m*.

bumble[1] ['bʌmbl], *s.* **1.** *A: Pej:* petit fonctionnaire rempli de sa propre importance; (personnage d'*Oliver Twist*, roman de Dickens.) **2.** *NAm:* bévue *f*, gaffe *f*.

bumble[2], *v.i.* **1.** (*of bee*) bourdonner. **2.** (*a*) *esp. NAm:* gaffer; être gauche, maladroit; (*b*) **to b. along,** aller de son petit train-train.

bumblebee ['bʌmblbi:], *s. Ent: F:* bourdon *m*.

bumbledom ['bʌmbldəm], *s. Pej:* étalage pompeux de son incompétence en matière administrative; fonctionnarisme *m*.

bumble-puppy ['bʌmblpʌpi], *s. Games:* **1.** *A:* forme enfantine de certains jeux (whist, etc.); jeu peu scientifique. **2.** spira-pole *m*.

bumbo ['bʌmbou], *s.* punch au rhum (bu froid).

bumboat ['bʌmbout], *s. Nau:* bateau *m* à provisions.

bumf [bʌmf], *s. P:* **1.** papier *m* hygiénique, papier torchecul, papier cul. **2.** paperasserie *f*.

bumfodder ['bʌmfɔdər], *s. P:* = BUMF 1.

bumfreezer ['bʌmfri:zər], *s. Cost: P:* veston *m* rase-pet, pet-en-l'air *m*.

bumkin ['bʌmkin], *s. Nau:* minot *m*, pistolet *m* d'amure (de la misaine); bout-dehors *m* (de tapecul), *pl.* bouts-dehors.

bummaree [bʌmə'ri:], *s.* (*a*) courtier *m* en poisson (au marché de Billingsgate); (*b*) courtier en viande (au marché de Smithfield).

bummer ['bʌmər], *s.* (*a*) *NAm: P:* fainéant *m*; clochard *m*; trimardeur *m*; (*b*) *U.S: Hist:* maraudeur *m*, pillard *m* (pendant la Guerre de Sécession).

bump[1] [bʌmp], *s.* **1.** (*a*) choc (sourd); secousse *f*, heurt *m*, coup *m*; cahot *m* (d'une voiture); *Aut:* coup de raquette (des ressorts); **I felt a b.,** j'ai senti une secousse; **to sit down with a b.,** faire un casse-cul; (*b*) *Row:* heurt d'un canot par le poursuivant (dans une *bumping race*). **2.** (*swelling*) bosse *f*; (*in phrenology*) protubérance *f*, bosse; **bumps in a road,** bosses, inégalités *f*, rugosités *f*, cahots, d'un chemin; **to have the b. of invention, of locality,** avoir la bosse de l'invention, de l'orientation; **to feel s.o.'s bumps,** passer la main sur le crâne à qn, tâter, palper, les bosses de qn (pour découvrir ce dont il est capable); **heat b.,** élevure *f* due à l'urticaire. **3.** *Av:* trou *m* d'air. **4.** *Cmptr:* mémoire *f* annexe.

bump[2], *v.*

I. *v.tr. & i.* **1.** *v.tr.* (*a*) cogner, frapper; **to b. one's head on, against, sth.,** se cogner la tête contre qch.; *F:* **I bumped into him in the street,** je l'ai rencontré par hasard, je suis tombé sur lui, dans la rue; (*b*) *Sch: F:* culer (qn); (*c*) faire exploser (une mine); (*d*) *U.S: F:* mettre, flanquer (qn) à la porte; (*e*) *F:* annuler un voyage; (*f*) *Row:* heurter (le canot qu'on poursuit, dans une *bumping race*); (*g*) *Cmptr:* éjecter; **to b. from core,** expulser de la mémoire. **2.** *v.i.* (*a*) se cogner, se heurter, buter (**into, against, sth.,** contre qch.); entrer en collision (avec qch.); **to b. along** (*in cart, etc.*), avancer avec force cahots; cahoter; (*of train, car*) **to b. into another train, car,** tamponner un autre train, une autre voiture; (*of car*) **to b. against the kerb,** donner, buter, contre le trottoir; **b. 'em cars,** autos tamponneuses; (*b*) *Nau:* (*of ship, boat*) talonner; toucher (le fond); donner un coup de talon; (*c*) *Cr:* (*of ball*) rebondir en hauteur.

II. (*compound verbs*) **1. bump off,** *v.tr. P:* assassiner, supprimer (qn).

2. bump up, *v.tr. F:* **to b. up the prices,** faire monter les prix (d'une façon exagérée).

bump[3], *adv. & int.* pan! boum! **the car ran b. into the wall,** la voiture donna en plein contre le mur; *F:* **things that go b. in the night,** des bruits étranges qui se font entendre pendant la nuit.

bump[4], *s.* cri *m* du butor.

bump[5], *v.i.* (*of the bittern*) crier.

bumper ['bʌmpər], *s.* **1.** rasade *f* (de champagne, etc.); rouge-bord *m* (de vin); *attrib.* **b. crop,** récolte *f* magnifique, exceptionnelle; *Th:* **b. house,** salle bondée; salle comble. **2.** (*a*) *Rail: U.S:* tampon *m*; **b. (beam),** traverse *f* avant (de locomotive); (*b*) *Aut:* pare-choc(s) *m*; **front b.,** pare-choc(s) avant; **rear bumpers,** pare-choc(s) arrière; **double-bar b.,** pare-choc(s) jumelé; **wrap-round b.,** pare-choc(s) enveloppant; **the cars were b. to b.,** les voitures se suivaient pare-choc(s) contre pare-choc(s); (*c*) *Aer:* tampon de nacelle; (*d*) *Rail:* butoir *m* (de portière, etc.); (*e*) *Mec.E:* tampon amortisseur (de pédale, etc.). **3.** *Cr:* balle *f* qui rebondit en hauteur.

bumpety-bump ['bʌmpiti'bʌmp], *adv. F:* en cahotant; en rebondissant; **my heart went b.-b.,** mon cœur battait la chamade.

bumpiness ['bʌmpinis], *s.* état cahoteux, inégalités *fpl* (d'un chemin).

bumping ['bʌmpiŋ], *s.* heurtement *m*, cahotement *m*; *Aut:* coups *mpl* de raquette (des ressorts); *Nau:* talonnement *m*; *Rail: U.S:* **b. post,** heurtoir *m*, butoir *m*; *Tls:* **b. hammer,** marteau *m* à débosseler; *Row:* (*à Oxford la rivière étant de médiocre largeur, les bateaux ne courent pas côte à côte, mais en procession; chacun doit rattraper, s'il le peut, celui qui le précède, et de son avant en heurter l'arrière; dans ce cas il gagne un place.*) **b. race,** course-poursuite *f*.

bumpkin ['bʌm(p)kin], *s.* **1.** rustre *m*, rustaud *m*, lourdaud *m*. **2.** *Nau:* = BUMKIN.

bump-off ['bʌmpɔf], *s. U.S: P:* assassinat *m*.

bumpology [bʌm'pɔlədʒi], *s. F: A:* phrénologie *f*.

bumptious ['bʌm(p)ʃəs], *a.* présomptueux, orgueilleux, avantageux, suffisant, outrecuidant; **to be b.,** faire l'important, le capable.

bumptiously ['bʌm(p)ʃəsli], *adv.* d'un air suffisant; avec suffisance.

bumptiousness ['bʌm(p)ʃəsnis], *s.* suffisance *f*, orgueil *m*, outrecuidance *f*, air important.

bumpy ['bʌmpi], *a.* **1.** (chemin, etc.) cahoteux, défoncé, inégal; *Av:* **b. flight,** vol chahuté. **2.** (*of forehead, etc.*) couvert de bosses.

bumsucker ['bʌmsʌkər], *s. P:* (*not in polite use*) lèche-cul *m inv.*

bun [bʌn], *s.* **1.** *Cu:* petit pain au lait (avec ou sans raisins); **Bath b.,** *bun* saupoudré de sucre; **hot cross b.,** *bun* à la cannelle (qu'on mange le vendredi saint); *F: O:* **that takes the b.!** ça, c'est le comble! *P:* **to have a b. in the oven,** être enceinte, avoir le ballon; *U.S: P:* **to have a b. on,** être soûl. **2.** *Hairdr:* chignon *m*.

Buna ['bu:nə], *s. R.t.m:* Buna *m*.

bunce [bʌns], *s. P: A:* un boni; de l'extra.

bunch[1] [bʌn(t)ʃ], *s.* (*a*) botte *f* (de radis, etc.); bouquet *m* (de fleurs); grappe *f* (de raisin); touffe *f* (d'herbes, de rubans); houppe *f* (de plumes); trousseau *m* (de clefs); flot *m* (de rubans); régime *m* (de dattes, de bananes); poignée *f* (de brindilles, etc.); *Pharm:* fascicule *m* (d'herbes); **she wears her hair in bunches,** elle porte des couettes; (*b*) groupe *m* (de personnes); *U.S:* troupeau *m* (de bestiaux); **he's the best, the pick, of the b.,** c'est lui le meilleur (de la bande); *Rac:* **the b.,** le peloton; *Box: P:* **b. of fives,** (i) le poing (fermé); (ii) la main.

bunch[2]. **1.** *v.tr.* grouper; botteler (des radis, etc.); lier (des fleurs, etc.) en bouquet; **to b. up one's skirt,** retrousser sa jupe; **to sit all bunched up,** être entassés. **2.** *v.i.* **to b. (together),** se presser en foule, se serrer, se grouper, se tasser, se mettre en tas, se pelotonner.

bunchberry ['bʌn(t)ʃb(ə)ri], *s. Bot:* cornouiller *m* du Canada.

bunched ['bʌn(t)ʃt], *a. Bot:* **1.** gibbeux. **2.** qui pousse en touffes, en grappes.

bunchy ['bʌn(t)ʃi], *a.* ramassé; pelotonné; gibbeux.

bunco ['bʌŋkou], *s. & v.tr.* = BUNKO.

bund[1] [bʌnd], *s.* (*in India, etc.*) (*a*) digue *f*; (*in paddy fields*) diguette *f*; (*b*) promenade *f*, boulevard *m* (au bord de la mer, le long d'une rivière).

bund[2], *v.tr.* (*in India, etc.*) endiguer (une rivière, etc.).

bundle[1] ['bʌndl], *s.* **1.** (*a*) paquet *m* (de linge, etc.); ballot *m* (de marchandises, d'effets); baluchon *m* (d'effets); botte *f* (d'asperges, de violettes, etc.); faisceau *m* (de cannes, de nerfs, de fils, etc.); liasse *f* (de billets de banque, de papiers); fagot *m* (de bois); tas *m* (de choses diverses); *Pharm:* fascicule *m* (d'herbes); *Mil: F: O:* **b. of ten,** (i) paquet de dix cigarettes; (ii) rouleau *m* de dix couvertures; *P:* **to go a b. on sth.,** en pincer pour qch.; (*b*) *Nat.Hist:* **vascular b.,** faisceau vasculaire; *F:* **she's a b. of nerves,** c'est un paquet de nerfs; (*c*) *U.S: F:* **to make a b.,** faire un paquet, faire sa pelote; **to drop a b.,** perdre beaucoup d'argent, être lessivé; (*d*) *F:* **to drop one's b.,** y renoncer (en désespoir). **2.** *Meas:* deux rames *f* (de papier).

bundle[2]. **1.** *v.tr.* (*a*) **to b. (sth.) (up),** empaqueter (qch.); mettre, lier, (qch.) en paquet; botteler (du foin); mettre (du blé) en javelles; mettre (des documents) en liasse; **he bundled all the papers into the drawer,** il a fourré pêle-mêle tous les papiers dans le tiroir; (*of pers.*) **to be (all) bundled up,** être habillé chaudement; *F:* être boudiné; *Nau:* **bundled sail,** voile *f* en paquet; (*b*) *F:* **to b. s.o. out (of the house),** (i) faire sortir (qn) à la hâte; (ii) jeter, flanquer, qn à la porte; **to b. s.o. off,** se débarrasser de qn (sans cérémonie); **he was bundled off to Australia,** on l'a expédié en Australie; **he was bundled off quickly to hospital,** on l'a expédié, l'a envoyé, sans plus attendre à l'hôpital; **to b. sth. into a corner,** fourrer qch. dans un coin. **2.** *v.i. F:* **to b. off, away, out,** s'en aller (sans cérémonie); **to b. into s.o.,** heurter qn; entrer en collision avec qn.

bundook ['bʌndu:k], *s. A: Mil: P:* fusil *m*.

bunfight ['bʌnfait], *s. F:* thé *m* (où le monde s'écrase).

bung[1] [bʌŋ], *s.* (*a*) bondon *m* (de fût); tampon *m* de liège; tape *f* (de bouche à feu); (*b*) bonde *f* (de fût); *Tls:* **b. drawer,** tire-bonde *m*, *pl.* tire-bondes; *U.S:* **b. starter,** maillet *m* (pour enfoncer la bonde); (*c*) *A: F:* brasseur *m*; les brasseurs; (*d*) *NAm: P:* contusion *f*, bleu *m*.

bung[2], *v.tr.* **1. to b. (up),** bondonner (un fût); mettre un bondon à (un fût); boucher (un orifice); *F:* **to b. up s.o.'s eye,** pocher un œil à qn; **bunged up eyes,** yeux pochés, gonflés; **to be bunged up,** (i) (*of nose, pipe, etc.*) être bouché; (ii) *P: O:* (*of pers.*) être constipé. **2.** *F:* lancer, jeter; enfoncer; mettre; **I bunged a lump of earth at him,** je lui lançai une motte de terre; **b. it in a drawer,** fourre-le dans un tiroir; **we must b. in a love scene,** il faut y fourrer une scène d'amour.

bung[3], *P: Austr:* **to go b.,** faire faillite; **my watch has gone b.,** ma montre est détraquée, ne marche plus.

bung[4], *s. F: A:* mensonge *m*, craque *f*.

bung[5], *adv. F:* **she sank b. in the middle of the channel,** le navire a coulé en plein milieu de la passe.

bungaloid ['bʌŋgəlɔid], *a. Pej:* **a horrid b. growth,** une éruption de petits bungalows, de baraquements, affreux (et mal bâtis).

bungalow ['bʌŋgəlou], *s.* (*a*) (*in India, etc.*) bungalow *m*; villa *f* à véranda; (*b*) bungalow, maison *f* de plain-pied.

bungarus [bʌŋ'gɑ:rəs], *s. Rept:* bungare *m*.

bungee ['bʌndʒi], *s.* **b. cord,** Sandow (*R.t.m.*).

bunghole ['bʌŋhoul], *s.* bonde *f*.

bungle[1] ['bʌŋgl], *s.* gâchis *m*, maladresse *f*, bousillage *m*; **to make a b. of sth.,** bousiller, gâcher, qch.; mettre les pieds dans le plat; **he made a b. of it,** il y est allé maladroitement.

bungle². 1. *v.tr.* bousiller, gâcher, saboter, saveter, fagoter, *F:* louper (un travail); barbouiller (une affaire); *Av:* **bungled landing,** atterrissage raté, loupé. 2. *v.i.* (*a*) patauger, se fourvoyer (dans une discussion, etc.); (*b*) s'y prendre maladroitement, manquer de doigté.

bungler ['bʌŋglər], *s.* (*a*) bousilleur, -euse (de travail); gâcheur, -euse; *F:* savetier *m,* sabot *m,* maçon *m;* loupeur, -euse; (*b*) maladroit, -e.

bungling¹ ['bʌŋgliŋ], *a.* maladroit, dénué d'adresse; **b. attempt,** essai gauche, maladroit.

bungling², *s.* bousillage *m,* gâchis *m,* mauvaise besogne, barbouillage *m.*

bunion ['bʌnjən], *s. Med:* inflammation *f* de la base du gros orteil (qui accompagne l'hallux valgus); *F:* oignon *m.*

bunk¹ [bʌŋk], *s.* 1. (*a*) lit-placard *m;* (*b*) *Nau: Rail: etc:* couchette *f; Furn:* **b. beds, twin bunks,** lits superposés; (*c*) *NAm: F:* logement *m.*

bunk², *v.i.* (*a*) *Nau:* **the crew b. forward,** l'équipage a son logement à l'avant; (*b*) *F:* **to b. down,** (aller) se coucher; (*c*) *NAm: F:* **he bunked at our house,** il a passé la nuit chez nous.

bunk³, *v.i. & s. F:* **to b. (off), to do a b.,** déguerpir, filer, décamper; se cavaler; mettre les bouts de bois.

bunk⁴, *s. F:* bêtises *fpl, P:* foutaise *f.*

bunker¹ ['bʌŋkər], *s.* 1. *Nau:* soute *f* (à, au, charbon, mazout, etc.); réservoir *m,* caisse *f,* à huile; **to take bunkers,** embarquer le charbon; faire le charbon; faire le mazout; *Min:* **ore b.,** réservoir *m* à minerai; caisson *m* à minerai; **b. coal,** charbon *m* de soute; **b. hand,** soutier *m;* (*b*) *Dom.Ec:* **coal b.,** coffre *m* à charbon. 2. (*a*) *Scot:* coffre (servant de banc); banc *m;* (*b*) *Scot:* talus *m* (où l'on peut s'asseoir); (*c*) *Golf:* banquette *f,* bunker *m;* (*d*) *Mil:* blockhaus *m;* abri bétonné; bunker; **spotting b.,** casemate *f* d'observation.

bunker², *v.tr.* 1. *Nau:* (*a*) mettre (du combustible) en soute; (*b*) *v.i.* charbonner. 2. *Golf:* **to be bunkered,** se trouver derrière une banquette, dans le sable d'une banquette; *F:* **I'm bunkered,** je suis dans une impasse.

bunkering ['bʌŋk(ə)riŋ], *s. Nau:* charbonnement *m.*

bunkhouse ['bʌŋkhaus], *s. NAm:* baraquement pourvu de couchettes (pour bûcherons, cow-boys, moissonneurs, etc.).

bunkie ['bʌŋki], **bunkmate** ['bʌŋkmeit], *s. F: U.S:* compagnon *m* de chambre; *Nau:* **my b.,** mon matelot.

bunko¹ ['bʌŋkou], *s. NAm: P:* tricherie *f;* escroquerie *f;* **b. game,** jeu de cartes déloyal; jeu de filous; **b. man, b. steerer,** escroc *m,* filou *m.*

bunko², *v.tr. NAm: P:* filouter; mettre (qn) dedans; refaire, rouler (qn).

bunkum ['bʌŋkəm], *s. F:* 1. discours oiseux; paroles *f* vides. 2. blague *f,* bêtises *fpl;* **that's all b.!** tout ça c'est des histoires! c'est de la blague! c'est de la frime! ce sont des balivernes, des sornettes.

bunny ['bʌni], *s. F:* 1. Jeannot lapin *m;* petit lapin. 2. **b. (girl),** employée de boîte de nuit (travestie en lapin).

bunodont ['bju:noudɔnt], *a. Z:* bunodonte.

bunoselenodont ['bju:nousi'li:noudɔnt], *a. Z:* bunosélénodonte.

Bunsen ['bʌns(ə)n], *Pr.n. Ch: etc:* **B. burner,** bec *m* Bunsen; *F:* **a B.** un Bunsen.

bunsenite ['bʌnsənait], *s. Miner:* bunsénite *f.*

bunt¹ [bʌnt], *s. Nau:* fond *m,* chapeau *m* (d'une voile).

bunt², *Nau:* (*a*) *v.i.* (*of sail*) faire le sac; (*b*) *v.ind.tr.* **to b. up the sails,** hisser les voiles.

bunt³, *s.* 1. (*a*) petit coup (de la tête, du coude); (*b*) *Sp:* (*baseball*) coup retenu. 2. *Av:* looping *m* à l'envers, demi-boucle inversée.

bunt⁴, *v.tr.* (*a*) donner un petit coup (de tête, etc.) à (qn); (*b*) *Sp:* (*baseball*) frapper doucement.

bunt⁵, *s.* 1. *Agr:* carie *f* du froment; bruine *f.* 2. *Fung:* tilletia *m.*

Bunter ['bʌntər], *a. & s. Geol:* **B. (sandstone),** grès bigarré.

bunting¹ ['bʌntiŋ], *s.* 1. *Orn:* bruant *m;* **corn b.,** bruant proyer, *F:* toute-vive *f,* tritri *m;* **ortolan b.,** (bruant) ortolan *m;* **reed b.,** bruant des roseaux; **black-headed b.,** bruant crocote, mélanocéphale, à tête noire; **little b.,** bruant nain; **yellow-breasted b.,** bruant auréole; **cinereous, grey-bearded, b.,** bruant cendré; **cirl b.,** bruant zizi; **Cretzchmar's b.,** bruant cendrillard; **Lapland b.,** bruant lapon; **masked b.,** bruant masqué; **pine b.,** bruant à calotte blanche; **red-headed b.,** bruant à tête rousse; **rock b.,** bruant fou; **rufous b.,** bruant roux; **rustic b.,** bruant rustique; **Siberian meadow b.,** bruant des prés; **yellow-browed b.,** bruant à sourcils jaunes; **indigo b.,** ministre *m, Fr.C:* bruant indigo; **lark b.,** *Fr.C:* pinson noir et blanc: **lazuli b.,** pape *m* lazuli, *Fr.C:* bruant azuré; **snow b.,** bruant des neiges, *Fr.C:* plectrophane *m* des neiges; **nonpareil b., painted b.,** pape de la Louisiane. 2. *Crust:* crangon *m,* crevette *f.*

bunting², *s.* 1. *Tex:* étamine *f* (à pavillon); molleton *m* à drapeaux; draperie *f.* 2. *Coll: F:* drapeaux *m,* pavillons *m,* pavoisement *m;* **to put out b.,** pavoiser; **street gay with b.,** rue (toute) pavoisée. 3. *U.S: Cost:* nid *m* d'ange.

buntline ['bʌntlain], *s. Nau:* cargue-fond *m, pl.* cargues-fonds; contre-fanon *m, pl.* contre-fanons.

bunyip ['bʌnjip], *s. F: Austr:* (*a*) loup-garou *m, pl.* loups-garous; (*b*) imposteur *m,* charlatan *m.*

buoy¹ [bɔi], *s. Nau:* bouée *f;* balise flottante; **fairway b.,** bouée de chenal; **leading b.,** bouée d'atterrissage; **wreck b.,** bouée d'épave; **mooring b., anchor b.,** (bouée de) corps-mort *m, pl.* corps-morts; bouée d'ancre, d'orin; coffre *m* d'amarrage; **bell b.,** bouée à cloche; **breeches b.,** bouée culotte; **leading b.,** bouée-balise *f, pl.* bouées-balises; **light b.,** bouée lumineuse; **dan b.,** bouée de jalonnement, de pêcheur; **spar b.,** balise (à espars); **whistle b.,** bouée à sifflet; bouée sonore; **can b.,** bouée conique; **flag b.,** bouée à pavillon; **barrel b., cask b.,** bouée-tonne *f, pl.* bouées-tonnes; bouée barrique; **danger b.,** vigie *f,* interdiction *f;* **secured to a b.,** amarré à un corps-mort; **to put down a b.,** mouiller une bouée; **to pick up one's b.,** prendre son coffre (d'amarrage); **the b. watches,** la bouée est à poste, veille; **b. rope,** orin *m;* (*pers.*) **b. keeper,** baliseur *m.*

buoy², *v.tr.* 1. (*a*) *Nau:* **to b. up an object,** faire flotter un objet; soutenir un objet sur l'eau; **to b. a net,** liéger un filet; (*b*) **to b. s.o. up,** soutenir, appuyer, encourager, qn; **buoyed up with new hope,** animé, soutenu, par un nouvel espoir. 2. **to b. (out) a channel,** baliser un chenal.

buoyage ['bɔiidʒ], *s. Nau:* balisage *m;* **b. system of a channel,** règlements de balisage d'un chenal; **b. vessel,** baliseur *m.*

buoyancy ['bɔiənsi], *s.* 1. (*a*) *Nau: Aer:* flottabilité *f* (d'un objet); légèreté *f* sur l'eau; *Aer:* **reserve b.,** surplus *m* de force ascensionnelle; **b. bag,** ballonnet *m* de flottabilité; **b. chamber, compartment,** chambre *f* de flottabilité; **b. tank,** réservoir *m* de flottabilité; (*b*) poussée *f* (d'un liquide); **centre of b.,** centre *m* de poussée; *NArch:* centre de carène; **b. chamber** (of **torpedo),** flotteur *m* (d'une torpille). 2. (*a*) entrain *m,* allant *m,* optimisme *m;* élasticité *f* de caractère; **man full of b.,** homme *m* qui a du ressort, de l'allant, qui ne se laisse pas démonter; (*b*) *Com:* **the b. of the market,** la fermeté du marché.

buoyant ['bɔiənt], *a.* 1. (*a*) flottable; léger, -ère; (*b*) **salt water is more b. than fresh,** l'eau salée porte mieux que l'eau douce; (*c*) *Civ.E:* **b. foundation,** radier *m* en béton. 2. (*of pers.*) optimiste, plein d'entrain, allègre; qui a du ressort; **to be of a b. disposition,** être porté à l'optimisme; **b. step,** pas *m* élastique; *Com:* **b. market,** marché soutenu; **the market is b.,** le marché a du ressort; le marché se soutient.

buoyantly ['bɔiəntli], *adv.* avec entrain; avec optimisme.

buphagus ['bju:fəgəs], *s. Orn:* buphagus *m,* pique-bœuf *m, pl.* pique-bœufs.

buphthalmia [b(j)uf'θælmiə], **buphthalmos** [b(j)uf'θælmɔs], *s. Med:* bupht(h)almie *f.*

buphthalmum [bju(j)uf'θælməm], *s. Bot:* buphthalme *m.*

bupleurum [bju'plə:rəm], **buplever** [bju'plevər], *s. Bot:* buplèvre *m.*

buprestid [bju'prestid], *s. Ent:* bupreste *m; attrib.* **b. beetles,** buprestidés *mpl.*

Buprestidae [bju'prestidi:], *s.pl. Ent:* buprestidés *m,* buprestides *m.*

buprestis [bju'prestis], *s. Ent:* bupreste *m.*

bur [bə:r], *s. & v.* = BURR.

Burberry ['bə:bəri], *s. R.t.m:* imperméable *m* (de la marque Burberry).

burble¹ ['bə:bl], *s.* 1. murmure *m* (de paroles); sons inarticulés. 2. *Av:* remous *m;* **b. point,** vitesse *f* critique; angle *m* critique.

burble², *v.i.* 1. (*a*) murmurer (des sons inarticulés); (*b*) *F:* débiter des inepties. 2. **to b. with laughter,** glousser de rire.

burbling ['bə:bliŋ], *s.* = BURBLE¹.

burbot ['bə:bət], *s. Ich:* lotte *f,* barbot *m,* barbot(t)e *f.*

burden¹ ['bə:dn], *s.* 1. (*a*) fardeau *m,* charge *f; Lit:* **to bend beneath the b.,** plier sous le faix; **the b. of (the) years,** le poids des années; **to bear the b. and heat of the day,** porter le poids du jour et de la chaleur; **the white man's b.,** le fardeau de l'homme blanc; *Fin:* **tax b., b. of taxation,** poids de la fiscalité, des impôts; *Jur:* **b. of proof,** charge, fardeau, de la preuve; obligation *f* de faire la preuve; **the b. of proof rests with him,** c'est à lui que la preuve incombe; **to be a b. to s.o.,** être à charge à qn; **to become a b. on s.o.,** tomber à la charge de qn; **his family is a b. to him,** sa famille lui pèse sur les bras; **to make s.o.'s life a b.,** rendre la vie impossible, intenable, dure, à qn; **beast of b.,** bête *f* de somme, de charge; bête à dos; (*b*) *Nau:* **b. of a ship,** charge, contenance *f,* d'un navire; **ship of five thousand tons b.,** navire (du port) de cinq mille tonneaux, qui jauge cinq mille tonneaux; (*c*) *Metall:* lit *m* de fusion. 2. (*a*) refrain *m* (d'une chanson); (*b*) substance *f,* fond *m* (d'un discours, d'une plainte).

burden², *v.tr.* (*a*) charger, alourdir (**s.o. with sth.,** qn de qch.); **to b. one's memory with useless facts,** se charger la mémoire de faits inutiles; **I'm not going to b. myself with all that,** je ne vais pas me charger de tout cela; **to b. the people with taxes,** accabler le peuple d'impôts; **burdened estate,** domaine grevé, affecté, d'hypothèques; domaine hypothéqué; (*of heritage, etc.*) **burdened with debt,** grevé de dettes; **burdened forest,** forêt grevée d'usages; (*b*) être un fardeau pour (qn).

burdensome ['bə:dnsəm], *a.* onéreux (**to, à**); fâcheux, incommode; ennuyeux; vexatoire; *Jur:* **b. contract,** contrat *m* où il y a lésion.

Burdigalian [bə:di'geiliən], *a. & s. Geol:* burdigalien (*m*).

burdock ['bə:dɔk], *s. Bot:* bardane *f,* glouteron *m; F:* herbe *f* aux teigneux.

bureau, *pl.* **-eaux** ['bjuərou, -ouz], *s.* 1. *Furn:* (*a*) bureau *m;* secrétaire *m;* commode-bureau *f, pl.* commodes-bureaux; (*b*) *U.S:* commode *f.* 2. (*a*) (*office*) bureau; **employment b.,** bureau de placement; **information b.,** (i) office *m* de renseignements; (ii) syndicat *m* d'initiative; (*b*) *U.S:* (*government department*) bureau; service *m;* **Census B.,** Bureau des statistiques; **National B. of Economic Research,** Bureau national de recherches économiques; (*c*) *Cmptr:* (**service**) **b.,** centre *m,* service, de travail à façon, façonnier.

bureaucracy [bjuə'rɔkrəsi], *s.* bureaucratie *f.*

bureaucrat ['bjuərəkræt], *s.* bureaucrate *m.*

bureaucratic [bjuərə'krætik], *a.* bureaucratique.

bureaucratically [bjuərə'krætik(ə)li], *adv.* bureaucratiquement.

bureaucratization [bju'rɔkrətai'zeiʃ(ə)n], *s.* bureaucratisation *f.*

bureaucratize [bju'rɔkrətaiz], *v.tr.* bureaucratiser.

burelé ['bjuərəlei], *s.* (*philately*) burelage *m.*

burette [bjuə'ret], *s.* 1. *Ecc:* burette *f.* 2. *Ch:* éprouvette graduée, burette.

burg [bə:g], *s. NAm: F:* bourg *m;* municipalité *f,* ville *f.*

burgao, burgau [bə:'gau], **burgo** [bə:'gou], *s. Moll:* burgau *m,* burgo *m; Com:* **b. shell,** burgaudine *f.*

burgee [bə:'dʒi:], *s. Nau:* guidon *m,* cornette *f* (d'un yacht, etc.).

burgeon¹ ['bə:dʒ(ə)n], *s.* 1. *Lit:* bourgeon *m.* 2. *Z:* bourgeon (d'un zoophyte).

burgeon², *v.i. Lit:* bourgeonner.

burgess ['bə:dʒis], *s. Hist:* 1. citoyen *m;* électeur *m* (dans une ville). 2. (*a*) député *m* (représentant une ville); (*b*) *Hist: & U.S:* = conseiller municipal.

burgh ['bʌrə], *s. Scot:* municipalité *f,* ville *f.*

burgher ['bə:gər], *s.* 1. *Hist:* bourgeois *m,* citoyen *m;* **the Burghers of Calais,** les bourgeois de Calais. 2. *S. African Hist:* Burgher *m.*

burglar ['bə:glər], *s.* cambrioleur *m;* voleur *m* de nuit; **cat b.,** cambrioleur par escalade; cambrioleur acrobate, *F:* monte-en-l'air *minv;* **b. alarm,** signalisateur *m* anti-vol, protection *f* électrique contre le vol.

burglarious [bə:'glɛəriəs], *a.* **b. attempt,** tentative *f* de cambriolage, de vol (de nuit) avec effraction.

burglarize ['bə:gləraiz], *v.tr. & i. F:* cambrioler.

burglarproof ['bə:gləpru:f], *a.* (serrure *f,* coffre-fort *m*) incrochetable, inviolable, à l'épreuve de l'effraction.

burglary ['bə:gləri], *s.* (*a*) *Jur:* vol *m* de nuit avec effraction; vol qualifié; (*b*) *F:* vol avec effraction (nocturne ou en plein jour); cambriolage *m.*

burgle ['bə:gl], *v.tr. & i. F:* cambrioler, dévaliser (une maison); faire du cambriolage.

burgling ['bə:gliŋ], *s.* cambriolage *m.*

burgomaster ['bə:gəmɑ:stər], *s.* bourgmestre *m,* = maire *m.*

burgonet ['bə:gənet], *s. A.Arm:* bourguignotte *f.*

burgrave ['bə:greiv], *s. Hist:* burgrave *m.*

burgraviate [bə'greivieit], *s. Hist:* burgraviat *m.*

Burgundian [bə:'gʌndiən], (*a*) *a.* bourguignon; (*b*) *s.* Bourguignon, -onne.

Burgundy ['bə:gəndi]. 1. *Pr.n. Geog:* Bourgogne *f; Agr: A:* **B. hay,** sainfoin *m; Vit: etc:* **B. mixture,** bouillie (cuprique) bourguignonne. 2. *s.* **a glass of b.,** un verre de bourgogne *m,* de vin *m* de Bourgogne.

burhel ['bʌr(ə)l], *s. Z:* nahor *m.*

Burhinidae [bju'rinidi:], *s.pl. Orn:* burhinidés *m,* œdicnèmes *m.*

burial ['beriəl], *s.* (*a*) enterrement *m,* inhumation *f;* **Christian b.,** sépulture *f* en terre sainte; sépulture

ecclésiastique; **to refuse Christian b. to s.o.,** refuser la sépulture à qn; (*b*) *attrib.* **b. ground,** cimetière *m*; **b. place,** lieu *m* de sépulture; tombeau *m*, tombe *f*; **b. service,** office *m* des morts; *Prehist:* **b. mound,** tumulus *m*.
Buriat ['buriæt], *Ethn:* (*a*) *a.* bouriate; (*b*) *s.* Bouriate *mf*.
buried ['berid], *a.* (*a*) enterré; enseveli; (*b*) **b. cable,** câble souterrain; (*c*) *Geol:* **b. outcrop,** affleurement masqué.
burin ['bjuərin], *s. Tls: Prehist:* burin *m*.
burinist ['bjuərinist], *s.* burineur *m*.
burk [bəːk], *s. P:* **you b.!** espèce d'idiot!
burke [bəːk], *v.tr.* **1.** *A:* étouffer ou étrangler (qn) pour vendre le cadavre aux fins de dissection (comme le fit Burke à Édimbourg). **2.** étouffer, étrangler (un scandale); éviter, étrangler (une discussion); supprimer (un fait); **to b. the question,** escamoter la vraie question.
burl[1] [bəːl], *s.* **1.** *Tex:* nope *f*, nœud *m*, époutí *m*. **2. walnut b.,** (plaqué *m* de) ronce *f* de noyer. **3.** *F: Austr:* **to give it a b.,** essayer le coup.
burl[2], *v.tr. Tex:* noper, énouer, époutier, épinceter, épincer (le drap).
burlap[1] ['bəːlæp], *s. Tex:* gros canevas; toile *f* d'emballage.
burlap[2], *v.tr.* envelopper (une racine, etc.) dans du canevas.
burler ['bəːlər], *s. Tex:* (*pers.*) nopeuse *f*; énoueur, -euse.
burlesque[1] [bəː'lesk]. **1.** *a.* burlesque. **2.** *s.* (*a*) burlesque *m*; (*b*) parodie *f*; poème *m* héroï-comique; (*c*) *U.S:* (*also* **burlesk**) revue *f* vulgaire, *esp.* striptease *m*.
burlesque[2], *v.tr.* travestir, parodier; tourner (qn, qch.) en ridicule; se moquer de (qn, qch.).
burliness ['bəːlinis], *s.* corpulence *f*; forte carrure.
burling ['bəːliŋ], *s. Tex:* époutiage *m*, épinçage *m*, épincetage *m*; **b. iron, tweezers,** épincette *f*.
burly ['bəːli], *a.* (*of pers.*) (*a*) fort; solidement bâti; robuste; de forte carrure; (*b*) *NAm:* brusque; bourru.
Burma ['bəːmə], *Pr.n. Geog:* Birmanie *f*.
Burman ['bəːmən], **Burmese** [bəː'miːz], (*a*) *a. Geog:* birman; *Z:* **Burmese cat,** (i) chat burmese; (ii) chat birman ganté; (*b*) *s. Geog:* Birman, -ane.
bur marigold ['bəː'mærigould], *s. Bot:* bidens *m*, bident *m*.
burmite ['bəːmait], *s. Miner:* burmite *f*, résine *f* fossile.
burn[1] [bəːn], *s.* **1.** (*a*) brûlure *f*; (*b*) *Med:* (*resulting from X rays, electricity, etc.*) lucite *f*. **2.** *U.S:* (*a*) région (dans une forêt) détruite par le feu; (*b*) *Agr:* brûlis *m*. **3.** *Space:* allumage *m*; poussée *f* (d'une fusée).
burn[2], *v.* (**burnt; burnt;** *occ.* **burned, burned**).
I. *v.tr. & i.* **1.** *v.tr.* (*a*) brûler; (*of boiler*) **to b. coal, oil, gas,** chauffer au charbon, au mazout, au gaz; **our boiler burns too much oil,** notre chaudière consomme trop de mazout; **we b. wood in our fireplace,** nous nous servons de bois pour notre feu de cheminée; *Fig:* **to b. the candle at both ends,** brûler la chandelle par les deux bouts; **to b. the midnight oil,** travailler, veiller, fort avant dans la nuit; **to b. a house to the ground,** brûler une maison de fond en comble; **to b. sth. to ashes, to b. sth. (completely) away,** réduire qch. en cendres, brûler, consumer, qch. (complètement); **to be burnt alive,** être brûlé vif; **to be burnt to death,** être brûlé vif; être calciné, carbonisé; périr carbonisé; **to b. one's fingers,** se brûler les doigts; *Fig:* **he burnt his fingers over it,** il lui en a cuit; il s'est fait échauder (dans cette affaire); **money burns his fingers, burns a hole in his pocket,** l'argent lui brûle les doigts, lui fond dans les mains, lui brûle la poche; c'est un panier percé; **your cigarette has burnt a hole in the tablecloth,** votre cigarette a fait un trou dans la nappe; **to have money to b.,** avoir de l'argent à n'en savoir que faire; **acids b. the skin, b. into metal,** les acides *m* brûlent la peau, rongent le métal; **mustard burns the tongue,** la moutarde brûle la langue; **this coffee has burnt my throat,** ce café m'a brûlé, m'a écorché, le gosier; *A: & Lit:* **to b. daylight,** perdre son temps; s'attarder à des vétilles; *Fish:* **to b. the water,** tuer un saumon à la lueur des flambeaux; (*b*) *Ind:* cuire (des briques, du charbon de bois); vulcaniser, cuire (le caoutchouc); (*c*) *Cu:* **to b. the roast,** brûler le rôti; donner un coup de feu au rôti; **I've burnt the saucepan,** j'ai brûlé la casserole; *Metalw:* **to b. the iron,** surchauffer le fer; (*d*) marquer (un criminel) au fer rouge; *Surg:* cautériser (une plaie, une morsure); **the memory of this has burnt itself into my mind,** ce souvenir s'est gravé, reste gravé, dans ma mémoire; (*e*) *U.S: F:* électrocuter (qn). **2.** *v.i.* (*a*) brûler; **to b. like matchwood,** flamber comme une allumette; **to b. like tinder,** brûler comme de l'amadou; brûler sec; **the whole village was burning,** tout le village était en feu; tout le village flambait; **the fire is burning low,** le feu baisse; **to b. clear,** jeter une flamme claire; **to make the fire b.,** activer le feu; faire flamber, faire marcher, le feu; **the fire, this coal, won't b.,** le feu ne prend pas; ce charbon refuse de brûler; **my head's burning,** la tête me brûle; **his cheeks were burning with shame,** il avait les joues rouges de honte; **my wound was burning,** ma blessure cuisait; **he was burning with enthusiasm, burning to do it,** il brûlait d'enthousiasme, de le faire; **to b. with impatience,** griller d'impatience; **burning with revenge,** brûlant de se venger; (*in games, riddles, etc.*) **you're burning!** vous brûlez! vous y êtes presque! **magnesium burns white,** le magnésium brûle avec une flamme blanche; (*b*) *I.C.E:* (*of mixture*) exploser; (*c*) *Cu:* **the meat is burning,** la viande brûle; **the sauce, the milk, has burnt,** la sauce, le lait, a attaché.
II. (*compound verbs*) **1. burn down,** (*a*) *v.tr.* brûler, incendier (une ville, etc.); détruire (une maison) par le feu, par un incendie; (*b*) *v.i.* **the fire had burned down,** le feu était bas.
2. burn in, *v.tr.* graver (qch.) par le feu.
3. burn off, *v.tr.* brûler (la peinture, etc.); décaper (la peinture) à la lampe à brûler; enlever (de la rouille, etc.) au feu; *I.C.E:* **to b. off the carbon,** flamber l'encrassement.
4. burn out, (*a*) *v.tr.* (i) **to b. s.o.'s eyes out,** brûler les yeux à qn; **the building was completely burnt out,** le feu a complètement détruit l'intérieur du bâtiment; **the house is burning itself out,** la maison achève de brûler; *Aut: etc:* **to b. out the brake linings,** brûler la garniture des freins, brûler ses freins; *Mec.E:* **to b. out the babbit,** fondre l'antifriction; (ii) **to b. s.o. out,** chasser qn par le feu; **they were burnt out of house and home,** leur maison fut réduite en cendres; (iii) **the candle has burnt itself out,** la chandelle est brûlée jusqu'au bout, s'est consumée entièrement; (iv) *El:* **to b. out a coil,** brûler, court-circuiter, une bobine; **to b. out a lamp,** griller une lampe; (v) *Med:* cautériser; (*b*) *v.i.* se consumer; brûler; griller; (*of electric lamp*) claquer, griller; (*of fire*) **to b. out for lack of fuel,** s'éteindre faute de combustible.
5. burn up, (*a*) *v.tr.* (i) brûler (entièrement); consumer; (ii) **the hot sun has burnt up the countryside,** la chaleur du soleil a brûlé, a grillé, tout le paysage; **leaves burnt up by a hot wind,** feuilles grillées, roussies, flétries, par un vent chaud; (iii) *F:* **to b. up the kilometres, the miles,** aller à toute vitesse; brûler les étapes; (*b*) *v.i.* (i) (*of fire*) se ranimer; flamber; (ii) *F:* (*of pers.*) s'emporter, s'enflammer de colère.
burn[3], *s. Scot:* ruisseau *m*.
burnable ['bəːnəbl], *a.* brûlable.
burnbeat ['bəːnbiːt], *v.tr. Agr:* écobuer (un champ).
burnbeating ['bəːnbiːtiŋ], *s. Agr:* écobuage *m*.
burner ['bəːnər], *s.* **1.** (*pers.*) brûleur, -euse; **brick b.,** cuiseur *m*; **charcoal b.,** charbonnier *m*; **lime b.,** chaufournier *m*, chaulier *m*. **2.** (*a*) (*of gas cooker*) brûleur; feu *m*; (*b*) bec *m* (de gaz, pour acétylène, etc.); brûleur (à gaz); **incandescent b.,** bec Auer; **bat's wing b.,** bec (de gaz) en ailes de chauve-souris, (bec) papillon (*m*); **oxyacetylene b.,** chalumeau *m*; (*c*) *Av:* (*of ramjet*) **spill b.,** brûleur en retour.
burnet ['bəːnit], *s.* **1.** *Bot:* (*a*) **b. (bloodwort), salad b.,** pimprenelle commune, petite pimprenelle; **great b.,** grande pimprenelle, pimprenelle des prés; (*b*) **b. (saxifrage),** pied-de-chèvre *m*, *pl.* pieds-de-chèvre. **2.** *Ent:* **b. moth,** sphinx *m* bélier, zygène *f*.
burning[1] ['bəːniŋ], *a.* **1.** (*a*) (*of fever, thirst, desire, etc.*) brûlant, ardent; **b. question,** question brûlante; (*b*) *Ven:* **b. scent,** fumet récent, fort; (*c*) *F:* (*intensive*) **it's a b. shame,** c'est vraiment honteux. **2.** (*a*) en ignition; **b. coals,** du charbon embrasé, allumé; **b. town,** ville incendiée, enflammée, en feu; (*b*) **b. heat,** chaleur brûlante, torride; *F:* **I'm b. (hot),** je suis en train de rôtir; (*c*) **b. bush,** (i) *B:* buisson ardent; (ii) *Bot:* (*α*) fraxinelle *f*; (*β*) pillée *f*, pilea *m*, herbe *f* à feu d'artifice; (*γ*) belvédère *m*, belle-à-voir *f*, *pl.* belles-à-voir, ansérine *f* à balais; (*δ*) évonyme *m*, fusain *m*. **3.** (bois *m*, etc.) à brûler.
burning[2], *s.* **1.** (*a*) brûlage *m*; incendie *m* (d'une maison, etc.); *Hist:* **b. (at the stake),** supplice *m* du bûcher; **there's a smell of b.,** on sent une odeur de brûlé; cela sent le brûlé, le roussi; **b. sensation,** (i) sensation *f* de chaleur (excessive); (ii) douleur cuisante; (*b*) *Ch: etc:* combustion *f*; **b. point,** point *m* de combustion, d'ignition; **b. glass,** verre ardent; (*c*) *Cu:* coup *m* de feu; *Metalw:* brûlure *f* (de l'acier). **2.** (*a*) cuite *f*, cuisson *f* (de briques, de tuiles, etc.); (*of metal*) bleuissement *m* par l'échauffement; **lime b.,** chaufournerie *f*, cuisson de la chaux; (*b*) fournée *f* (de briques, etc.).
burnish[1] ['bəːniʃ], *s.* (*a*) éclat *m*; lustre *m*; poli *m*, brillant *m*; bruni *m*, brunissure *f*; (*b*) *Phot:* satiné *m*.
burnish[2]. **1.** *v.tr.* (*a*) brunir; polir, aviver, lisser; roder (un métal); éclaircir (des épingles); (*b*) *Phot:* satiner (une épreuve). **2.** *v.i.* se polir; prendre de l'éclat, du brillant, du poli.
burnisher ['bəːniʃər], *s.* **1.** (*pers.*) (*a*) brunisseur, -euse; (*b*) satineur, -euse. **2.** (*a*) *Tls:* brunissoir *m*; polissoir *m*, avivoir *m*, dent-de-loup *f*, *pl.* dents-de-loup; (*b*) *Phot:* presse *f* à satiner.
burnishing ['bəːniʃiŋ], *s.* (*a*) brunissage *m*; polissage *m*, lissage *m*; éclaircissage *m*; *Leath:* noircissage *m*; *Metalw:* **b. brush,** boësse *f*; *Bootm:* **b. iron,** bizé *m*; (*b*) *Phot:* satinage *m*.
burnous(e) [bəː'nuːs], *s.* burnous *m* (d'Arabe).
burnout ['bəːnaut], *s. Ball:* (*of rocket, missile*) arrêt *m* par épuisement (du combustible).
burnside ['bəːnsaid], *s. Scot:* bord *m* d'un ruisseau; **b. village,** village *m* au bord d'un ruisseau.
burnsides ['bəːnsaidz], *s.pl. NAm:* favoris *m*, *F:* pattes *f* de lapin.
burnt [bəːnt], *a.* **1.** (*a*) (*of pers., thg*) brûlé; (*of pers.*) **to be b. beyond recognition,** être carbonisé; **a b. child dreads the fire,** expérience passe science; chat échaudé craint l'eau froide; *Cu:* **b. almonds,** amandes grillées; **b. sugar,** caramel *m*; *Lap:* **b. topaz,** rubis *m* du Brésil; (*b*) **b. smell, taste,** odeur *f*, goût *m*, de brûlé, de roussi. **2.** (*of earth, clay*) cuit.
burnt out ['bəːnt'aut], *a.* **1.** (*a*) (volcan) éteint; (*b*) **b.-o. case,** (i) *Med:* lépreux *m* dont la maladie a été arrêtée; (ii) homme, femme, qui a épuisé son talent; (iii) désillusionné(e). **2.** *Mch: etc:* (tube) brûlé; **b. o. bearing,** roulement grippé. **3.** *El:* **b.-o. coil,** bobine brûlée, grillée, court-circuitée.
burnup ['bəːnʌp], *s. Atom.Ph: etc:* volatilisation *f*.
burnut ['bəːnʌt], *s. Bot:* croix *f* de Malte, tribulus *m*.
burp[1] [bəːp], *s.* éructation *f*, *F:* rot *m*.
burp[2]. **1.** *v.i.* éructer, *F:* roter. **2.** *v.tr.* **to b. a baby,** faire roter un bébé.
burr[1] [bəːr], *s.* **1.** *Bot:* (*a*) capsule épineuse (du fruit de certaines plantes); teigne *f*, bouton *m* de pompier (de bardane); **chestnut b.,** bogue *f*; **teasel b.,** carde *f*; *Tex:* **to remove the burrs from wool,** enlever les gratterons *m* de la laine; **b.-picking machine,** échardonneuse *f*; (*b*) **b. marigold,** bidens *m*, bident *m*; **b. reed,** chou *m* de Dieu, ruban *m* d'eau; **branched b. reed,** rubanier *m*; **b. thistle,** chardon *m* d'âne, chardon commun; (*c*) *F:* (*pers.*) crampon *m*; **to stick to s.o. like a b.,** se cramponner, s'accrocher, à qn. **2.** (*a*) (*on tree*) broussin *m*; (*b*) **b. walnut,** (plaqué *m* en) ronce *f* de noyer; **elm b.,** loupe *f* d'orme; (*c*) *Ven:* meule *f* (du bois d'un cerf). **3.** *Engr: Metalw:* (*a*) barbe *f*, bavure *f*, barbure *f*, balèvre *f*; **to take the burrs off metal,** ébarber le métal; **b.-removing press,** presse *f* à ébarber; (*b*) (*when removed*) ébarbure *f*; (*c*) **(rivetting) b.,** contre-rivure *f*, *pl.* contre-rivures. **4.** *Tls:* (*a*) **b. (cutter),** ébarboir *m*; (*b*) burin *m* triangulaire; (*c*) *Dent: Surg:* fraise *f*; **b. (drill),** burin; **surgical, bone, b.,** fraise chirurgicale; **fissure b.,** fraise à fissure; **cross-cut b.,** fraise (à) double taille; **non-end-cutting b.,** fraise à extrémité mousse. **5.** *Geol:* (pierre) meulière *f*.
burr[2], *v.tr.* **(burred) 1.** *Tex:* chardonner (le drap). **2.** (*a*) mater (l'extrémité d'un boulon, etc.); rabattre (un clou); (*b*) ébarber (une pièce emboutie, etc.); (*c*) *Dent:* buriner (une dent).
burr[3], *s.* (*a*) *Ling:* r de la gorge (fricative postpalatale); r uvulaire (plutôt sourd); **to speak with a b.,** prononcer l'r de la gorge; (*b*) bruissement *m* (d'une roue, d'une machine).
burr[4], *v.* **(burred) 1.** *v.tr. & i.* **to b. (one's r's),** prononcer r de la gorge; rouler ses r. **2.** *v.i.* (*of wheel, machine, etc.*) ronfler.
burrawang ['bʌrəwæŋ], *s. Bot:* macrozamia *m*.
burring[1] ['bəːriŋ], *s.* (*a*) *Metalw:* ébarbage *m*; **b. machine,** machine *f* à ébarber; (*b*) *Dent:* burinage *m*; **b. engine,** machine dentaire.
burring[2], *s. Ling:* prononciation sourde de l'r uvulaire.
burro ['bʌrou], *s. Z: U.S:* âne *m*, *esp.* âne sauvage du sud-ouest des États-Unis; **b. deer,** cerf *m* à queue noire.
burrow[1] ['bʌrou], *s.* terrier *m*, renardière *f* (de renard); terrier, trou *m*, clapier *m*, accul *m*, halot *m* (de lapin); **nursery b.,** rabouillère *f* (de lapin); **otter's b.,** cattiche *f*.
burrow[2]. **1.** *v.i.* (*of rabbits, etc.*) (i) fouir la terre; (ii) (se) terrer; (*of moles*) tracer; **inhabitants burrowing among the ruins of the village,** habitants terrés dans les ruines du village; **to b. into the archives,** fouiller, fouiner, dans les archives; **to b. into a mystery,** creuser un mystère. **2.** *v.tr.* (*a*) **to b. a hole,** creuser, pratiquer, un trou, un terrier; **to b. one's way underground,** creuser (un chemin) sous terre; (*b*) (*of rabbits*) **to b. the ground,** percer la terre de terriers.
burrow[3], *s. Min:* halde *f* (de déchets).
burrower ['bʌrouər], *s.* (animal) fouisseur *m*.
burrowing ['bʌrouiŋ], *a.* (*of animals*) fouisseur, -euse; *Ent:* fossoyeur, -euse; mineur, -euse.
burrstone ['bəːstoun], *s. Geol:* (pierre) meulière *f*.
bursa, *pl.* **-ae** ['bəːsə, -iː], *s. Anat:* bourse *f*, poche *f*, sac *m*; **synovial bursae,** bourses synoviales.
bursar ['bəːsər], *s.* **1.** (*a*) *Sch:* économe *mf*, intendant *m*;

(*b*) *Ecc:* procureur *m,* dépensier *m* (de certains ordres monastiques). 2. *Sch: esp. Scot:* boursier, -ière.

bursarship [ˈbəːsəʃip], *s.* **1.** économat *m.* **2.** *Sch: esp. Scot:* bourse *f* (d'études).

bursary [ˈbəːsəri], *s.* **1.** bureau *m* de l'économe; économat *m;* intendance *f.* **2.** *Sch: esp. Scot:* bourse *f* (d'études).

burse [bəːs], *s. Ecc:* bourse *f* (des corporaux).

burseed [ˈbəːsiːd], *s. Bot:* lappula *m,* bardanette *f,* faux myosotis.

bursera [ˈbəːsərə], *s. Bot:* burséra *f.*

Burseraceae [bəːsəˈreisiiː], *s.pl. Bot:* burséracées *f.*

bursicle [ˈbəːsikl], *s. Bot:* bursicule *f.*

bursitis [bəˈsaitis], *s. Med:* bursite *f;* hygroma *m* (des bourses).

burst¹ [bəːst], *s.* **1.** éclatement *m,* explosion *f* (d'une bombe, etc.); *Artil:* **high b.,** éclatement haut, coup (fusant) haut; **low b.,** éclatement bas, coup (fusant) bas; **surface b.,** éclatement en surface; **height of b.,** hauteur *f* d'éclatement; **b. centre,** point moyen d'éclatement; (*of atom bomb*) **air b.,** explosion en altitude; **surface b.,** explosion en surface; **sub-surface b.,** explosion en sous-sol; *Av:* (*aerobatics*) **bomb b.,** éclatement d'une formation. **2.** (*a*) jaillissement *m,* jet *m* (de flamme); coup *m* (de tonnerre); (*of gunfire*) rafale *f;* (*of machine gun*) giclée *f; I.C.E:* **to give the engine a b.,** emballer le moteur; **b. of laughter,** éclat *m* de rire; **there was a b. of laughter,** il y eut une explosion de rires; **b. of tears,** crise *f* de larmes; **b. of anger,** explosion, bouffée *f,* mouvement *m,* de colère; **b. of fury,** transport *m,* explosion, de fureur; **b. of eloquence,** élan *m,* mouvement, d'éloquence; **b. of applause,** salve *f* d'applaudissements; **b. of activity, of energy,** emballement *m;* poussée *f* d'activité; **b. of enthusiasm,** accès *m* d'enthousiasme; *Sp:* **b. of speed,** emballage *m;* **final b.,** finish *m;* (*b*) *Cmptr:* (i) rafale (d'impression); (ii) giclée de signaux (comptant pour une unité); **error b.,** paquet *m,* groupe *m,* d'erreurs; **b. forms,** imprimés détachés; **b. mode,** mode continu. **3.** *P:* **to go on the b.,** faire la bombe.

burst², *v.* (**burst; burst**)

I. *v.i. & tr.* **1.** *v.i.* (*a*) (*of boiler, bomb, etc.*) éclater, exploser, faire explosion; (*of boiler*) sauter; (*of abscess*) crever, percer, aboutir; (*of bubble, cloud*) crever; (*of bud*) éclore; *F:* **he ate till he was fit to b.,** il mangeait à éclater; **one of my buttons has burst,** un de mes boutons a sauté; **to b. in pieces,** voler en éclats, **to b. apart,** *Lit:* **asunder,** éclater; se rompre; **her heart was ready to b.,** son cœur se brisait; (*b*) **sack bursting with corn,** sac tout plein, bourré, regorgeant, de blé; **the sacks were bursting,** les sacs étaient pleins à crever; les sacs regorgeaient; **to be bursting, ready to b., with laughter, envy, pride,** crever de rire, de jalousie, d'orgueil; pouffer de rire; **to be bursting with health,** déborder, crever, regorger, de santé; être éclatant de santé; **I was bursting to tell him so,** je mourais d'envie de le lui dire; (*c*) **a cry b. from his lips,** un cri s'échappa de ses lèvres; (*d*) (*of flower*) **to b. into bloom,** fleurir, s'épanouir; (*of tree*) **to b. into blossom,** fleurir, commencer à fleurir; **to be bursting with self-satisfaction,** déborder de contentement de soi; **to be bursting with impatience,** bouillir d'impatience; **to be bursting at the seams,** (i) (*of dress, etc.*) se découdre; (ii) *F:* (*of building, etc.*) être plein à éclater; **the horses b. into a gallop,** les chevaux prirent le galop; **to b. into (loud) laughter, into tears, to b. out laughing, crying,** éclater de rire; fondre en larmes, avoir une crise de larmes; partir d'un grand éclat de rire; (*e*) **to b. into a room,** entrer dans une pièce en coup de vent, en trombe, en ouragan; **to b. through the crowd,** percer, fendre, la foule; **the crowd b. t. the police cordon,** la foule a enfoncé le cordon de police; (*of sun*) **to b. through a cloud,** percer un nuage; (*f*) **to b. upon s.o.'s sight,** se présenter, s'offrir, surgir, se découvrir, à la vue de qn, aux yeux de qn; (*of sound*) **to b. upon s.o.'s ears,** venir (subitement) frapper les oreilles de qn; **the truth b. (in) upon me,** soudain la vérité m'apparut; j'eus soudain l'intuition de la vérité. **2.** *v.tr.* faire éclater (qch.); crever, claquer, éclater (un ballon, un pneu); faire sauter (une chaudière); rompre (ses liens); *F:* **to b. s.o.'s balloon,** clore le bec à qn; **to b. a blood vessel,** se rompre un vaisseau sanguin; *F:* **he nearly b. a blood vessel,** il a failli crever d'un coup de sang; **to b. one's buttons,** faire sauter ses boutons; (*of river*) **to b. its banks,** crever, rompre, ses berges; *Bac:* **bursting factor,** facteur déchaînant; (*b*) *Cmptr:* séparer les feuillets (d'un document en continu).

II. (*compound verbs*) **1. burst in,** (*a*) *v.tr.* enfoncer (une porte); (*b*) *v.i.* faire irruption; (*of pers.*) entrer en coup de vent; **to b. in on a conversation,** interrompre brusquement une conversation; **he'll be bursting in on us at any moment,** il va nous tomber sur le dos d'un moment à l'autre.

2. burst open, (*a*) *v.tr.* ouvrir (une porte) subitement; enfoncer, briser (une porte, etc.); faire sauter (le couvercle, la serrure); (*b*) *v.i.* (*of door, etc.*) s'ouvrir tout d'un coup.

3. burst out, (*a*) *v.i.* (*of pers.*) s'écrier, s'exclamer; **to b.o. laughing,** éclater, pouffer, de rire; **to b.o. of the gates,** sortir précipitamment par la porte; (*b*) *v.tr.* **to b.o. the rivets,** faire sauter les rivets.

burstable [ˈbəːstəbl], *a. Cmptr:* (papier en continu) séparable en feuillets.

burster [ˈbəːstər], *s. Cmptr:* rupteuse *f,* rupteur *m,* éclateur *m;* **b. imprinter,** rupteuse imprimante.

bursting¹ [ˈbəːstiŋ], *a.* sur le point de crever, d'éclater, d'éclore; **b. heart,** cœur gonflé; cœur prêt à éclater; cœur près d'éclater.

bursting², *s.* éclatement *m,* explosion *f* (d'une bombe, d'une chaudière, etc.); crevaison *f* (de pneu); rupture *f* (de liens, *Hyd.E:* de barrage); déchaînement *m* (d'une tempête); **b. strength,** résistance *f* à l'éclatement; *Exp:* **b. charge,** charge explosive; *Cmptr:* **b. machine,** rupteuse *f,* rupteur *m,* éclateur *m.*

burstone [ˈbəːstoun], *s. Geol:* (pierre) meulière *f.*

burst-up [ˈbəːstʌp], *s. P:* = BUST-UP.

burstwort [ˈbəːstwəːt], *s. Bot:* turquette *f;* herniaire *f* glabre.

burthen [ˈbəːð(ə)n], *s. & v.tr. Lit:* = BURDEN[1,2].

Burton [ˈbəːtn]. **1.** *Pr.n. Geog:* Burton (sur le Trent). **2.** *s.* (*a*) **B. (ale),** bière *f* de Burton; (*b*) *P:* **he's gone for a B.,** il est mort manquant; *Av:* il a fait un trou dans l'eau; **the plate went for a B.,** l'assiette s'est cassée; **the ball's gone for a B.,** la balle s'est perdue pour de bon.

burweed [ˈbəːwiːd], *s. Bot:* petite bardane, glouteron épineux; lampourde *f; F:* herbe *f* aux écrouelles.

bury [ˈberi], *v.tr.* (*p.p. & p.t.* **buried**) enterrer, inhumer, ensevelir (un mort); (*at sea*) immerger (un mort); porter (qn) en terre; enfouir (un animal); **buried treasure,** trésor enterré, enseveli, enfoui; **to b. s.o. alive,** enterrer qn vif; **to b. oneself (alive),** s'enterrer vivant; se terrer (dans un endroit retiré); **buried in the ruins,** enseveli sous les décombres; **to b. one's face in one's hands,** se cacher la figure dans les mains; se couvrir la figure de ses mains; **to b. one's hands in one's pockets,** fourrer les, ses, mains dans ses poches; **to b. oneself in sth.,** s'abstraire dans, en, qch.; **to b. oneself in the country,** s'enterrer, s'enfouir, dans la campagne; se blottir dans le fond d'une campagne; **to b. oneself in one's studies,** s'ensevelir, s'enfermer, dans ses études; **I found it buried under my papers,** je l'ai trouvé enfoui sous mes papiers; **buried in one's work,** plongé, enfoncé, absorbé, dans son travail; **she wants the whole thing buried and forgotten,** elle veut enterrer toute l'histoire; **to b. the hatchet,** enterrer la hache de guerre; faire la paix; se réconcilier; *P:* **go and b. yourself!,** fiche le camp!

Buryat [ˈburiæt], *s. Ethn:* Bouriate *mf.*

burying¹ [ˈberiiŋ], *a.* (insecte) enfouisseur; **b. beetle,** nécrophore *m.*

burying², *s.* **1.** enterrement *m;* ensevelissement *m;* **b. ground,** cimetière *m;* **b. place,** sépulture *f.* **2.** enfouissement *m.*

bus¹, *pl.* **buses,** *U.S:* **busses** [bʌs, ˈbʌsiz], *s.* **1.** autobus *m;* (*on country services*) car *m;* **double-decker b.,** autobus à impériale; **we went there by b.,** nous y sommes allés en autobus; **to miss the b.,** (i) manquer, rater, l'autobus; (ii) *F:* laisser échapper l'occasion, manquer le coche; (iii) *F:* n'arriver à rien, rater; *P.N:* **all buses stop here,** arrêt *m* obligatoire (de l'autobus); **school b. service,** service *m* de ramassage des écoliers; **b. station,** gare routière; **b. route,** itinéraire *m,* ligne *f,* parcours *m,* d'autobus. **2.** *F:* (*a*) *Aut: O:* **my old b.,** ma vieille bagnole; (*b*) *Av:* coucou *m.* **3.** (*a*) *El:* = BUSBAR; (*b*) *Cmptr:* (i) câblage *m;* (ii) circuit *m* d'alimentation. **4.** *esp. NAm:* (*a*) table desserte roulante (dans un restaurant); (*b*) *F:* **b. (boy, girl),** aide-serveur, -serveuse, *pl.* aides-serveurs, -serveuses.

bus², **1.** (*a*) voyager par autobus, en car; (*b*) *esp. NAm:* travailler comme aide-serveur, aide-serveuse. **2.** *v.tr.* transporter (qch., qn) par autobus, en car.

busbar [ˈbʌsbaːr], *s. El:* barre *f* omnibus.

busboy [ˈbʌsbɔi], *s. esp. NAm:* (*in restaurant*) aide-serveur *m, pl.* aides-serveurs; commis-débarrasseur *m, pl.* commis-débarrasseurs.

busby [ˈbʌzbi], *s. Mil:* bonnet *m* de hussard; colback *m,* talpack *m.*

bush¹ [buʃ], *s.* **1.** (*a*) buisson *m;* arbre *m* en buisson; (*of lilac, etc.*) arbrisseau *m;* (*small*) arbuste *m,* buissonnet *m;* **rose b.,** rosier *m;* **redcurrant b., gooseberry b.,** groseillier *m;* (*b*) (*clump of bushes*) fourré *m,* taillis *m; NAm:* **sugar b.,** bosquet *m,* plantation *f,* d'érables à sucre; *Can:* **b. lot,** plantation d'arbres (dont le bois sert aux besoins de la ferme); (*c*) queue *f* (du renard). **2.** (*vintner's*) bouchon *m; Prov:* **good wine needs no b.,** à bon vin point d'enseigne. **3.** (*a*) (*esp. in Africa, Austr.*) **the b.,** la brousse; **to take to the b.,** *Austr:* **to go b.,** prendre la brousse; **b. shirt, b. jacket** = saharienne *f;* **b. hat,** chapeau *m* de brousse; *F:* **b. telegraph,** téléphone *m* arabe, radio *f* cocotier; **I heard on the b. telegraph that . . .,** on m'a dit que . . .; (*b*) *Austr:* **to live in the b.,** habiter (i) à la campagne, (ii) en banlieue; (*c*) *Av:* **b. pilot,** pilote *m* de ligne opérant sur une région peu habitée, sur la brousse, *Can:* le Grand Nord; *Can:* **b. line,** ligne *f* desservant le Grand Nord.

bush², *v.tr. Agr:* herser (un champ) à la herse d'épines.

bush³, *s.* (*a*) *Mec.E:* fourrure *f* métallique; bague *f;* buselure *f;* coussinet *m,* grain *m* (de palier); douille *f* (de réa); manchon *m; I.C.E:* **bronze b. (of small end of connecting-rod),** bague en bronze (de pied de bielle); (*b*) *N.Arch:* alumelle *f* (de la mortaise du gouvernail).

bush⁴, *v.tr. Mec.E:* baguer, manchonner; mettre un coussinet à (un palier, etc.); **bushed pulley,** poulie guillochée; **bushed with bronze,** bagué en bronze.

bush baby [ˈbuʃbeibi], *s. Z:* galago *m.*

bushbuck [ˈbuʃbʌk], *s. Z:* guib *m.*

bush cat [ˈbuʃkæt], *s. Z:* serval, -als *m,* chat *m* des savanes.

bushcraft [ˈbuʃkraːft], *s.* connaissance *f* de la brousse.

bushdog [ˈbuʃdɔg], *s. Z:* icticyon *m,* chien *m* des buissons.

bushed [buʃt], *a. Austr:* (*a*) perdu, égaré, dans la brousse; (*b*) *F:* désorienté, interdit, fatigué.

bushel¹ [ˈbuʃl], *s.* boisseau *m* (= 8 *gallons* = *approx.* 36 litres); *F:* **there are bushels of it,** il y en a des quantités, des tas.

bushel², *v.i.* (**bushel(l)ed**) *NAm:* faire un travail sans importance; *Tail:* retoucher, remettre à neuf, un vêtement.

bushel(l)er [ˈbuʃələr], **bushelman,** *pl.* **-men, -woman,** *pl.* **-women** [ˈbuʃəlmən, -wumən, -wimin], *s. Tail: NAm:* prompier, -ière.

bushfighter [ˈbuʃfaitər], *s.* franc-tireur *m, pl.* francs-tireurs; guérillero *m.*

bushfighting [ˈbuʃfaitiŋ], *s.* guerre *f* de buissons, d'embuscades.

bushfire [ˈbuʃfaiər], *s.* feu *m* de brousse.

bush hammer [ˈbuʃhæmər], *s. Tls:* laie *f;* boucharde *f;* marteau *m* rustique; rustique *m.*

bush hammering [ˈbuʃhæməriŋ], *s. Civ.E: etc:* bouchardage *m.*

bush harrow [ˈbuʃhærou], *s. Agr:* herse *f* d'épines; balayeuse *f,* traînoir *m.*

bush hook [ˈbuʃhuk], *s. U.S:* serpe *f.*

bushiness [ˈbuʃinis], *s.* épaisseur *f;* **the b. of his hair,** ses cheveux touffus, embroussaillés, en broussaille.

bushing [ˈbuʃiŋ], *s.* **1.** manchonnage *m.* **2.** manchon *m;* coussinet *m* métallique; douille *f,* bague *f;* **blind b.,** bague borgne; **conical b.,** coquille *f* de coussinet; **antifriction b.,** fourrure *f* d'antifriction; *Artil:* **breech b.,** écrou *m* de culasse.

Bushire [bju(ː)ˈʃaiər], *Pr.n. Geog:* Bouchir *m,* Bouchaïr *m.*

bushman, *pl.* **-men** [ˈbuʃmən], *s.* **1.** *Ethn:* **Bushman** (*a*) *a.* boschiman; (*b*) *s.* Boschiman, -ane; (*c*) *Ling:* boschiman *m.* **2.** (*a*) colon *m* (de la brousse australienne); (*b*) personne *f* qui connaît la brousse; broussard *m.*

bushranger [ˈbuʃreindʒər], *s.* (*a*) broussard *m;* (*b*) *Austr:* réfugié *m* dans la brousse; brigand *m.*

bushrope [ˈbuʃroup], *s. Bot:* cissampélos *m.*

bush shrike [ˈbuʃˈʃraik], *s. Orn:* gonolek *m.*

bushtit [ˈbuʃtit], *s. Orn:* **common b., coast b.,** *Fr.C:* mésange buissonnière.

bushveld [ˈbuʃfelt], *s.* bushveldt *m.*

bushw(h)ack [ˈbuʃ(h)wæk], *esp. NAm:* **1.** *v.i.* (*a*) se frayer un chemin à travers la brousse; (*b*) habiter, travailler dans, la brousse. **2.** *v.tr.* attirer (qn) dans une embuscade, un guet-apens; **to be bushw(h)acked,** être victime d'un guet-apens.

bushw(h)acker [ˈbuʃ(h)wækər], *s. esp. NAm:* **1.** (*a*) (i) colon *m,* habitant, -ante, de la brousse; (ii) bûcheron *m;* (*b*) franc-tireur *m, pl.* francs-tireurs, bandit *m* (de la brousse). **2.** *Tls:* serpe *f.*

bushw(h)acking [ˈbuʃ(h)wækiŋ], *s. esp. NAm:* **1.** (i) la vie, (ii) le travail, dans la brousse. **2.** guerre *f* d'embuscades.

bushworker [ˈbuʃwəːkər], *s. Can:* bûcheron *m.*

bushy [ˈbuʃi], *a.* **1.** touffu, épais, -aisse; buissonneux, broussailleux; **b. ground, eyebrows,** terrain, sourcils, broussailleux; **b. beard,** barbe fournie; **b. hair,** cheveux épais, touffus, embroussaillés. **2.** (*of shrub*) buissonnant.

busily ['bizili], *adv.* activement; avec empressement; d'un air affairé.

business ['biznis], *s.* **1.** (*a*) (*task, duty*) affaire *f*, besogne *f*, occupation *f*, devoir *m*; **we've got through a lot of b.,** nous avons abattu de la besogne, nous avons fait beaucoup de travail; **this b. of preparing for their arrival,** ce remue-ménage de préparatifs pour leur arrivée; **to make it one's b. to do sth.,** se faire un devoir, se mettre en devoir, de faire qch.; prendre à tâche de faire qch.; prendre sur soi de faire qch.; **to have b. with s.o.,** avoir affaire avec qn; **what's your b. with him?** que lui voulez-vous? **please state your b. to the secretary,** veuillez bien indiquer au secrétaire l'objet de votre visite; **what is your b. here?** que venez-vous faire ici? **that's the manager's b.,** ça c'est l'affaire du gérant; **it is my b. to . . .,** c'est à moi de . . .; **it is not my b. to warn them,** ce n'est pas à moi, ce n'est pas mon rôle, de les avertir; **it's not your b., it's none of your b.,** ce n'est pas votre affaire; cela ne vous regarde pas; **it's no b. of his,** il n'a rien à voir là-dedans; **what b. is it of yours?** est-ce que cela vous regarde? **what b. had you to tell him?** était-ce à vous de le lui dire? *F:* **to send s.o. about his b.,** envoyer promener qn; envoyer paître qn; **you'd better go, get, about your b.,** vous n'avez qu'à aller vous promener; **you've no b. to do that,** vous n'avez pas le droit de faire cela; ce n'est pas à vous de le faire; **it's a bad b.,** c'est une malheureuse, une triste, affaire; **it's a funny, dirty, b.,** c'est une affaire louche; **the best of the b. is that . . .,** le plus beau de l'histoire c'est que . . .; **now to b.!** maintenant, allons-y! *Prov:* **what is everybody's b. is nobody's b.,** il n'y a point d'âne plus mal bâté que celui du commun; affaire à tout le monde, affaire à personne; (*b*) **b. meeting,** séance *f* de travail (d'une société, etc.); **the b. before the meeting,** l'agenda *m*; l'ordre *m* du jour; **to proceed with the b. of the day,** passer à l'ordre du jour. **2.** (*a*) les affaires; **b. is b.,** les affaires sont les affaires; **profitable b.,** entreprise rémunératrice; **to carry on a b.,** exercer un métier, un commerce; **to set up in b. as a grocer,** s'établir épicier; **what's his line of b.?** qu'est-ce qu'il fait (comme métier)? **this is too expensive for my line, class, of b.,** c'est trop cher pour ma clientèle; **to do b. with s.o.,** faire des affaires avec qn; **to lose b.,** perdre de la clientèle; **shop that does a thriving b.,** commerce qui marche bien; **to be in, give up, b.,** être dans les, se retirer des, affaires; **I'm going to London on b.,** je vais à Londres pour affaires; **piece of b.,** affaire, opération (commerciale); **how's b.?** comment vont les affaires? **b. is slow,** les affaires ne vont pas; la vente ne va pas; **to talk b.,** parler affaires; **to mean b.,** avoir des intentions sérieuses; ne pas plaisanter; **d'you mean b.?** êtes-vous sérieux? **big b.,** (i) les grosses affaires; les consortiums *m*, les trusts *m*; (ii) *F:* les gros bonnets, les grosses légumes; **big b. has got a bad name,** le public se méfie des grosses affaires; **the tourist trade is big b. today,** le tourisme est une affaire de grande importance aujourd'hui; **he worked up a small firm into a big b.,** à partir d'une petite maison il a créé une grosse entreprise; (*b*) entreprise; maison *f*; firme *f*; établissement *m*; fonds *m* de commerce; **he is the owner of a small b.,** il est propriétaire (i) d'une petite entreprise, (ii) d'un petit commerce, d'un petit magasin; **his b. is near the station,** son établissement, son atelier *m*, son usine *f*, etc., est près de la gare; (*c*) *attrib.* **b. career,** carrière *f* dans les affaires; **b. manager,** directeur commercial; **b. trip,** voyage *m* d'affaires; **b. lunch,** déjeuner *m* d'affaires; **b. call,** visite *f* d'affaires; **b. hours,** heures *fpl* de bureau, de travail, d'ouverture; **b. suit,** complet *m* de bureau; **b. card,** carte *f* (de visite) d'affaires; **b. language,** langage (i) d'affaires, (ii) *Cmptr:* de gestion; **b. computing, data processing,** informatique *f* de gestion; *NAm:* **b. machine,** machine *f* comptable, machine de gestion; **b. college,** école *f* d'études commerciales; *F:* **the b. end of a chisel,** le tranchant d'un ciseau. **3.** *Th:* (*a*) jeux *mpl* de scène; (*b*) emploi *m*, rôle *m*.

businesslike ['biznislaik], *a.* **1.** (*of pers.*) capable; pratique; méthodique; (*of transaction*) régulier, sérieux; (*of thg*) pratique. **2.** (*of style*) net, précis; (*of manner*) sérieux, avisé.

businessman, *pl.* **-men** ['biznismæn, -men], *s.m.*, **businesswoman,** *pl.* **women** ['bizniswumən, -wimin], *s.f.* (i) homme, femme, d'affaires; (ii) commerçant, -ante; **to be a good b.,** s'entendre aux affaires; **big businessman,** brasseur *m* d'affaires.

busk[1] [bʌsk], *s.* **1.** busc *m* (de corset). **2.** *Dial:* corset *m*.

busk[2], *v.tr.* busquer (un corset).

busk[3], *v.i. F:* (*of actor, etc.*) faire les plages en été; cabotiner; chanter, etc., dans les bars, dans les rues.

busker ['bʌskər], *s. F:* cabotin *m*; chanteur *m*, etc., de bars, des rues.

buskin ['bʌskin], *s. Ant: Th:* cothurne *m*; *Lit:* **to put on, to don, the b.,** chausser le cothurne.

busman, *pl.* **-men** ['bʌsmən], *s.m.* (i) conducteur, (ii) receveur, d'autobus; *F:* **to take a busman's holiday,** faire du métier en guise de congé ou de loisirs.

buss[1] [bʌs], *s. A: & Dial:* baiser *m*.

buss[2], *v.tr. A: & Dial:* embrasser, *F:* bécoter.

bussu [bə'su:], *s. Bot:* manicaria *m*.

bust[1] [bʌst], *s.* **1.** *Sculp:* buste *m*. **2.** buste, gorge *f*, poitrine *f* (de femme); *Cost: A:* **b. bodice,** cache-corset *m inv*; *Dressm: A:* **b. improver,** fausse gorge.

bust[2], *s. P:* **1.** explosion *f*; crevaison *f*. **2.** (*a*) fiasco *m*, four *m*; (*b*) faillite *f*. **3. to go on the b.,** faire la bombe; **to go a b.,** faire une grosse dépense.

bust[3], *a. F:* criblé de dettes; fauché; **to go b.,** faire faillite.

bust[4]. **1.** *v.i.* (*a*) *F:* éclater, casser, crever; (*b*) *P:* **to be (up),** faire faillite. **2.** *v.tr.* (*a*) diviser (un trust, un consortium) en entreprises moins importantes; (*b*) dresser (des chevaux sauvages); (*c*) *Mil: P:* **to b. (a sergeant),** rétrograder, casser (un sergent).

bustard ['bʌstəd], *s. Orn:* outarde *f*; **great b.,** outarde barbue; **houbara b.,** outarde houbara; **little b.,** outarde canepetière; **b. quail,** turnix *m*.

buster ['bʌstər], *s.* **1.** *NAm: F:* (i) (petit) garçon; (ii) homme *m*, type *m*; (*as form of address*) **hi, b.!** *P:* alors, mon pote! **2.** *NAm:* **(bronco) b.,** dresseur *m* de chevaux. **3.** *F:* (*a*) chose *f* remarquable, étonnante; (*b*) chute violente; (*c*) bombe *f* de très gros calibre. **4.** *Meteor:* (*in Austr:*) **northerly b.,** vent (violent) du nord; **southerly b.** burster *m*, vent (violent) du sud.

bustle[1] ['bʌsl], *s.* mouvement *m*, confusion *f*, remue-ménage *m*, branle-bas *m*, affairement *m*; **the b. in the streets,** l'animation *f* des rues; **we are all in a b.,** nous sommes en remue-ménage.

bustle[2]. **1.** *v.i.* **to b. (about),** se remuer, s'activer, s'affairer; déployer de l'activité; se donner du mouvement; aller et venir d'un air affairé; faire l'empressé; **we must b. a bit,** il faut nous remuer; **to b. off,** partir d'un air affairé, important; **they b. in and out,** ils entrent et sortent d'un air affairé; **to b. forward,** s'avancer d'un air empressé. **2.** *v.tr.* faire dépêcher (qn); **don't b. him!** ne le bousculez pas! donnez-lui le temps! **to b. s.o. out of the house,** pousser qn dehors.

bustle[3], *s. A. Cost:* tournure *f* (de derrière de jupe).

bustling ['bʌsliŋ], *a.* affairé, agissant, allant; empressé; **busy and b. street,** rue affairée et trépidante.

bust-up ['bʌstʌp], *s. P:* **1.** débâcle *f* (d'un système); faillite *f* (d'une maison de commerce). **2. to have a b.-up with s.o.,** avoir une prise de bec avec qn; rompre avec qn; **there's been a b.-up,** ils sont brouillés (à la suite d'une violente querelle).

busy[1] ['bizi]. **1.** *a.* **(busier, busiest)** (*a*) affairé; occupé; actif, allant; **a b. man,** un homme (i) occupé, (ii) actif; **the b. bee,** l'abeille diligente; **b. day,** jour chargé; **to spend a b. morning,** avoir une matinée très occupée; **my work keeps me b. all the morning,** mon travail m'occupe toute la matinée; **though he has retired he knows how to keep himself b.,** quoiqu'il ait sa retraite il sait bien employer son temps; **I'm too b. to do it now,** je suis trop occupé pour le faire maintenant; **b. (railway) line,** ligne *f* à grand trafic; **b. road,** route *f* à grande circulation; **b. street,** rue (i) mouvementée, animée, passante, (ii) très affairée, très commerçante; **the hotel industry is at its busiest in August,** l'industrie hôtelière est au plus haut de son activité au mois d'août; **shops are very b. at Christmas time,** il y a beaucoup de monde dans les magasins au moment de Noël; (*of business, etc.*) **we're not at all b. at the moment,** nous travaillons au ralenti en ce moment; **b. brain,** esprit actif; **his brain was b. with all sorts of ideas,** des idées de toutes sortes roulaient dans sa tête; **to be b. at, with, about, sth., b. doing sth.,** être occupé à, de, qch., à faire qch.; être en train de faire qch.; **they're always b. with, about, trifles,** ils sont toujours affairés de riens; **I can't come now, I'm b. putting the children to bed,** je ne puis pas venir tout de suite, je suis en train de coucher les enfants; **we must get b.,** il faut nous y mettre, nous mettre à la tâche; *F:* **get b.!** grouille-toi! **then the police got b.,** puis la police s'en mit; *Tp: NAm:* **line b.,** ligne occupée; **b. tone,** tonalité *f* d'occupation; *Cmptr:* **b. test,** test *m* d'occupation; (*b*) *Pej:* empressé; empêché; curieux; **to be b.,** faire l'empêché. **2.** *s. P:* agent *m*, inspecteur *m* de la Sûreté; détective *m*.

busy[2], *v.tr. & pr.* **to b. oneself with, about, sth.,** s'occuper à, se mêler de, qch.; occuper ses mains à qch.; **to b. oneself (with) doing sth.,** s'occuper à, de, faire qch.; s'activer à (faire) qch.; **to b. oneself tidying things (up),** s'affairer à tout remettre en place.

busybody ['bizibɔdi], *s.* **1.** officieux, -euse; important *m*; indiscret, -ète; mouche *f* du coche; touche-à-tout *m inv*; réparateur *m* de torts; **to play the b.,** faire l'empressé; faire le, la, nécessaire. **2.** (*window mirror*) espion *m*.

busyness ['bizinis], *s.* affairement *m*.

but[1] [bʌt]. **1.** *conj.* (*a*) (*coordinating*) mais; **he pretended to listen b. his thoughts were elsewhere,** il feignait d'écouter mais sa pensée était ailleurs; **she is not dead b. asleep,** elle n'est pas morte mais elle dort; **he is small b. strong,** il est petit mais fort; **a clever b. lazy pupil,** un élève doué mais paresseux; **b. I tell you I saw it!** (mais) puisque je vous dis que je l'ai vu! **b. yet . . .,** néanmoins . . ., toutefois . . .; (*b*) (*subordinating*) *A: & Lit:* **there is no one b. understands this,** il n'y a personne qui ne comprenne cela; **I never pass there b. I think of you,** je ne passe jamais par là sans penser à vous; **never a year passes b. he writes to us,** il ne se passe jamais une année qu'il ne nous écrive; **I cannot b. believe that . . .,** il m'est impossible de ne pas croire que . . .; **who among you b. remembers . . .?** lequel d'entre vous ne se souvient de . . .? **I do not doubt b. that he will consent,** je ne doute pas qu'il (ne) consente; **not b. that I pity you,** non que je ne vous plaigne; **b. that I saw it myself . . .,** si ce n'était que je l'ai vu moi-même . . .; **he would have done it b. that he lacked the courage,** il l'aurait fait s'il n'eût manqué de courage; (*c*) (*intensive*) **not merely once, b. twice,** par deux fois; **nobody, b. nobody . . .,** personne, mais absolument personne . . .. **2.** *adv.* ne . . . que; seulement; **she is b. a child,** ce n'est qu'une enfant; **he's nothing b. a student,** ce n'est qu'un étudiant; **it's nothing b. laziness,** c'est de la pure paresse; **had I b. known!** si j'avais su! **one can b. try,** on peut toujours essayer; *esp. Lit:* **the journey had b. begun,** le voyage ne faisait que commencer; **b. a moment ago,** il n'y a qu'un instant; **it seems b. yesterday,** cela me semble pas plus tard qu'hier; **you have b. to tell me,** vous n'avez qu'à me le dire; **if I could b. see him!** si je pouvais seulement le voir! **3.** *conj. or prep.* (*except*) (*a*) **come any day b. tomorrow,** venez n'importe quel jour excepté demain; **who will do it b. me?** qui le fera si ce n'est moi? sinon moi? **all b. he, b. him,** tous excepté lui; tous sauf lui; **there is a cure for everything b. death,** il y a remède à tout, sauf à la mort; **none b. he,** personne d'autre que lui; **anyone b. me,** tout autre que moi; **I don't know anyone b. you fit to undertake it,** je ne sais que vous capable de l'entreprendre; **give me anything b. that,** donnez-moi ce que vous voudrez, mais pas cela; tout plutôt que cela; **at any time b. the present,** n'importe quand sauf à présent; **it never rains b. it pours,** un malheur ne vient jamais seul; **he is anything b. a hero,** il n'est rien moins qu'un héros; **I am anything b. proud of my juvenile productions,** je ne tire aucune vanité de mes œuvres de jeunesse; **there is nothing for it b. to obey,** il n'y a qu'à obéir; **there remains no more b. to thank you,** il ne me reste plus qu'à vous remercier; **I have no choice b. to marry her,** je n'ai d'autre choix que de l'épouser; **what is all that b. a warning?** qu'est-ce que tout cela sinon un avertissement? **what could I do b. invite him?** que pouvais-je faire d'autre que de l'inviter? **if we are aiming at anything b. a superficial knowledge,** si nous visons à autre chose que des connaissances superficielles; **I do not suppose that his life was anything b. happy,** je ne suppose pas que sa vie ait été autre qu'heureuse; **what could I do b. laugh?** comment pouvais-je m'empêcher de rire? (*b*) **b. for,** sans; **b. for the rain I should have gone out,** sans la pluie je serais sorti; **b. for you I was done for,** sans vous j'étais perdu; **b. for that,** à part cela, excepté cela; **b. for his shyness . . .,** n'était sa timidité . . .. **4.** (*a*) *s.* **there is a b.,** il y a un mais; (*b*) *v.tr. A: & Hum:* **b. me no buts,** ne m'objectez pas de mais.

but[2], *Scot:* **1.** *adv.* (i) dehors; (ii) dans la pièce d'entrée (de la maison), dans la salle commune; **go b. and wait,** allez attendre (i) dehors, (ii) à la cuisine; *s.* **a b. and a ben,** une maison à deux pièces. **2.** *prep.* **b. the house,** (i) dehors, (ii) dans la salle commune.

butadiene [bju:tædi'i:n], *s. Ch:* butadiène *m*.

butane ['bju:tein], *s. Ch:* butane *m*.

butanol ['bju:tənɔl], *s. Ch:* butanol *m*.

butch [butʃ], (*a*) *a. & s. P:* (*man*) dur (*m*); (*b*) *s. P:* lesbienne *f* (d'apparence masculine); (*c*) *s. F:* coupe *f* (de cheveux) en brosse.

butcher[1] ['butʃər], *s.* **1.** (*a*) boucher *m*; **the butcher's wife,** la bouchère; **butcher's boy,** garçon boucher; **wholesale b.,** boucher en gros; **pork b.** = charcutier *m*; **butcher's meat,** viande *f* de boucherie, grosse viande; **butcher's shop, trade,** boucherie *f*; **the butcher's will be closed,** la boucherie sera fermée; **butcher's stall,** étal *m*; (*b*) *F:* boucher, massacreur *m*; *Hist:* **the Bloody B.,** le duc de Cumberland; (*c*) *F:* (i) saboteur *m* (de travail); (ii) chirurgien incompétent, charcutier *m*. **2.** *Rail: U.S: F:* vendeur *m* (de fruits, de cigarettes, etc.).

butcher[2], *v.tr.* **1.** (*a*) égorger, massacrer; (*b*) envoyer (des troupes) à la boucherie. **2.** *F:* massacrer, saboter (un travail, une symphonie, etc.); (*of surgeon*) **to b. a patient,** charcuter un patient. **3.** *U.S:* dépecer (une bête); couper (un morceau de chair).

butcher bird ['butʃəbə:d], *s. Orn:* écorcheur *m*, pie-grièche *f* écorcheur; *Austr:* **pied b. b.,** cassican *m* à gorge noire.

butchering ['butʃəriŋ], *s.* **1.** tuerie *f*, massacre *m* (**of,** de). **2.** *F:* **the b. trade,** la boucherie; **he has taken to b.,** il s'est fait boucher.

butcher's broom ['butʃəz'bru:m], *s. Bot:* petit houx, buis piquant, faux buis; myrte épineux, fragon épineux; housson *m*; épine *f* de rat.

butchery ['butʃəri], *s.* **1.** (*trade*) boucherie *f*; **wholesale b. trade,** vente *f* à la cheville, **2.** tuerie *f*, boucherie, massacre *m*.

butea ['bju:tiə], *s. Bot:* butéa *f*; **b. gum,** kino *m* du Bengale.

butene ['bju:ti:n], *s. Ch:* butène *m*, butylène *m*.

butic ['bju:tik], *a. Ch:* (acide *m*) butique, arachique.

butler ['bʌtlər], *s.* (*a*) maître *m* d'hôtel (d'une maison privée); **when I was b. to Sir James,** du temps où j'étais le maître d'hôtel de Sir James, où j'étais maître d'hôtel chez Sir James . . .; **Butler's tray,** desserte *f*, servante *f*; **butler's pantry,** office *f*; (*b*) *B.Lit:* échanson *m* (du pharaon).

butlership ['bʌtləʃip], *s.* (*a*) charge *f* de maître d'hôtel; (*b*) *B:* charge d'échanson.

Butomaceae [bjuto'meisii:], *s.pl. Bot:* butomacées *f*.

butt[1] [bʌt], *s.* (*a*) barrique *f*, futaille *f*, gros tonneau; **to fill a b. with water,** embarriquer de l'eau; (*b*) tonneau *m* (pour l'eau de pluie, etc.); tine *f* (pour transporter l'eau).

butt[2], *s.* **1.** (*a*) bout *m*; souche *f* (d'arbre, de chèque); billot *m* (d'arbre); bout (de cigare); **b. of a plank,** tête *f* d'un bordage; *Join: etc:* **b. and b.,** bout à bout; (*b*) *Bookb:* onglet *m* (d'une feuille isolée); (*c*) *NAm: F:* (*of pers.*) derrière *m*. **2.** (*a*) gros bout, talon *m*, pommeau *m* (d'une canne à pêche); (*b*) gros brin (d'une canne à pêche). **3.** *Bill:* (*a*) masse *f*, talon (de la queue); (*b*) **long b.,** grande queue; **half b.,** cadette *f*. **4.** crosse *f* (de fusil); poignée *f* (de pistolet, de revolver); **b. handle,** poignée de crosse; **b. toe,** bec *m* de crosse; **b. swivel,** anneau *m*, battant *m*, de crosse. **5.** *Carp:* about *m*; **b. hinge,** charnière *f*. **6.** *Leath:* croupon *m*. **7.** *Ich: Com:* poisson plat.

butt[3], *v.tr. & i.* **1.** (*a*) *Carp: etc:* abutter, abouter, rabouter, raboutir (deux pièces); **to b. two timbers,** faire abutter deux pièces; (*b*) étayer, buter (une poutre, etc.) (**against,** contre); (*c*) *v.i.* (*of prop, etc.*) s'étayer, buter (contre). **2.** *Nau:* mettre (des colis) à toucher (dans l'arrimage).

butt[4], *s.* **1.** (*a*) *Mil:* butte *f*, **the butts,** le champ de tir; (*b*) *Ven:* butte (d'où l'on tire au passage le coq de bruyère). **2.** (*thing aimed at*) but *m*; (*of pers.*) souffre-douleur *m inv*; **to be a b. for s.o.'s jokes,** servir de plastron à qn; **to be a b. for ridicule,** être en butte au ridicule; **he is the b. of the whole place,** c'est la tête de Turc du quartier.

butt[5], *s.* (*a*) coup *m* de (la) tête; coup de corne (d'un bélier, etc.); **the two goats came full b. at each other,** les deux chèvres se heurtèrent de front; (*b*) *Wr:* **head b.,** coup de tête; **flying head b.,** coup de bélier.

butt[6]. **1.** *v.i.* **to b. into, against, s.o., sth.,** donner du front, buter, contre qn, qch.; foncer sur qn; (*of ram, etc.*) **to b. at s.o.,** donner un coup de corne à qn; **to b. into the conversation, to b. in,** intervenir sans façon dans la conversation; se mêler à la conversation, à la discussion; placer son mot. **2.** *v.tr.* donner contre (qn, qch.) de la tête; (*of ram*) cosser contre (qn); donner un coup de corne à (qn).

butte [bju:t], *s. Geog:* butte *f*.

butt end ['bʌt'end], *s.* **1.** extrémité inférieure; pied *m*, bout *m*; gros bout; talon *m* (de canne à pêche). **2.** crosse *f* (de fusil); poignée *f* (de revolver). **3.** barbe *f* (d'une planche).

butter[1] ['bʌtər], *s.* (*a*) beurre *m*; **fresh, unsalted, b.,** beurre frais; **salt(ed) b.,** beurre salé; **dairy b.,** beurre laitier; *Cu:* **melted b.,** (i) beurre fondu; (ii) *O:* = béchamel *m*; **clarified b.,** beurre clarifié; **(served) with melted b.,** au beurre; **with brown(ed) b.,** au beurre noir; *F:* **b. wouldn't melt in her mouth,** elle fait la sainte nitouche; on lui donnerait le bon Dieu sans confession; *attrib.* **b. industry,** industrie beurrière; **b. dish,** beurrier *m*; **b. knife,** couteau *m* à beurre; **b. cooler,** beurrier rafraîchisseur; **b. pat, b. spade,** palette *f*, spatule *f*, à beurre; **b. pat, pat of b.,** pain *m*, pelote *f*, médaillon *m*, de beurre; **b. shaper,** frise-beurre *m inv*; **b. stamp,** moule *f* à beurre, moule-beurre *m inv*; **b. paper,** papier sulfurisé, parcheminé; papier beurre; *Comest:* **b. almonds,** amandes enrobées de caramel; (*b*) **vegetable b.,** beurre végétal; végétaline *f*; **bog b.,** butyrite *f*, beurre des tourbières; **shea b., karite b.,** beurre de karité; **shea b. tree,** butyrospermum *m*, karité *m*; **b. tree,** bassie butyracée; *Bot: F:* **b. and eggs,** linaire *f*, *F:* muflier bâtard; *U.S: F:* **b. and egg man,** homme d'affaires provincial et naïf qui veut faire figure dans les milieux métropolitains; (*c*) *Ch:* **b. of antimony,** beurre d'antimoine; **b. of tin,** beurre d'étain; **b. of zinc,** beurre de zinc.

butter[2], *v.tr.* (*a*) beurrer (du pain); *see also* BREAD; *F:* **to b. s.o. up,** flatter, louanger, pateliner, qn; coucher le poil à qn; lui passer la main dans le dos; *P:* passer de la pommade à qn; (*b*) *Cu:* accommoder (des légumes, etc.) au beurre; **buttered eggs,** œufs brouillés au beurre; (*c*) **to b. (bricks, etc.),** étendre du mortier sur (des briques, etc.).

butterball ['bʌtəbɔ:l], *s. NAm: F:* **1.** *Orn:* (*a*) garrot *m* albéole; (*b*) érismature roux. **2.** (*pers.*) boulot, -otte; pot *m* à tabac.

butterbur ['bʌtəbə:r], **butterdock** ['bʌtədɔk], *s. Bot:* pétasite commun.

buttercloth ['bʌtəklɔθ], *s.* gaze *f* à envelopper le beurre; étamine *f*.

buttercup ['bʌtəkʌp], *s. Bot:* **1.** renoncule *f* des champs; *F:* bouton *m* d'or, bassinet *m* des champs. **2.** *occ:* (i) renoncule âcre; (ii) renoncule bulbeuse; (iii) renoncule rampante.

butterfat ['bʌtəfæt], *s.* matière grasse; **the b. content of milk,** la teneur du lait en matière grasse.

butterfingered ['bʌtəfiŋgəd], *a. F:* maladroit, empoté; **he's b.,** tout lui glisse dans les mains; tout lui glisse des doigts.

butterfingers ['bʌtəfiŋgəz], *s. F:* maladroit, -e; empoté, -ée; brise-tout *m inv*; **he's a b.,** il a des mains de beurre.

butterfish ['bʌtəfiʃ], *s. Ich:* blennie *f*, gon(n)elle *f*, papillon *m* de mer.

butterfly ['bʌtəflai], *s.* **1.** *Ent:* papillon *m* (diurne); **leaf b.,** papillon feuille; **common blue b.,** lycène *f*; **bird-wing(ed) b.,** ornithoptère *m*; **b. net,** filet *m* à papillons; freloche *f*; *F:* **b. kiss,** baiser *m* papillon; *F:* **to have butterflies,** avoir l'estomac serré. **2.** (*a*) *Cost:* **b. bow,** nœud *m* (de) papillon; (*b*) *Tchn:* **b. nut,** écrou *m* à oreilles, à ailettes; écrou ailé; (écrou) papillon; **b. valve,** (soupape *f* à) papillon; vanne *f*; *Elcs:* **b. resonator, circuit,** circuit *m* papillon; (*c*) *Swim:* **b. (stroke),** (nage *f*, brasse *f*) papillon; (*d*) *Bot:* **b. orchis,** orchis *m* à deux feuilles; orchis papilionacé; *F:* **b. flower,** schizante *m*; (*e*) **b. fish,** (i) dactyloptère *m*; exocet *m*; poisson papillon *m*; poisson volant d'eau douce; dragon *m* de mer; blennie ocellée; (ii) *Moll:* chiton *m*. **3.** *F:* personne *f* frivole, papillon.

butteris ['bʌtəris], *s. Tls: Farr:* boutoir *m*.

buttermilk ['bʌtəmilk], *s.* lait battu; babeurre *m*.

butter muslin ['bʌtə'mʌzlin], *s.* gaze *f* à envelopper le beurre; étamine *f*; beurrière *f*.

butternut ['bʌtənʌt], *s. Bot:* **1.** noyer cendré. **2.** noix cendrée.

butter-producing ['bʌtəprə'dju:siŋ], *a.* (pays, etc.) beurrier.

butter quail ['bʌtə'kweil], *s. Orn:* tridactyle *m*.

butterscotch ['bʌtəskɔtʃ], *s.* caramel *m* au beurre.

butterweed ['bʌtəwi:d], *s. Bot:* (i) érigeron *m* du Canada; (ii) abutilon *m*.

butterwort ['bʌtəwə:t], *s. Bot:* pinguicule *f*, pinguicula *f*, grassette *f*.

buttery[1] ['bʌtəri], *s.* (*a*) dépense *f*, office *f* (*esp.* dans les universités anglaises); **b. hatch,** passe-plats *m inv*; (*b*) buffet *m* (où l'on sert des repas légers).

buttery[2], *a.* (*a*) de beurre; (*b*) (*like butter*) butyreux; (*c*) graisseux, onctueux.

butting[1] ['bʌtiŋ], *s. Tchn:* aboutement *m*.

butting[2], *s.* coup *m* de cornes, de tête.

buttinsky [bʌ'tinski], *s. F:* mêle-tout *mf inv*.

butt joining ['bʌtdʒɔiniŋ], *s. Tchn:* (*a*) assemblage *m* à plat; (*b*) abouchement *m*, aboutement *m* (de deux tuyaux).

butt joint ['bʌtdʒɔint], *s. Carp: Mec.E: etc:* assemblage *m* à plat; joint *m* d'about; assemblage ou joint bout à bout; joint abouté, en about; joint carré, plat; *Metalw:* soudure *f* bout à bout; *Plumb:* nœud *m* de jonction.

butt-joint, *v.tr. Carp:* assembler (deux morceaux) à plat; *Mec.E: etc:* joindre (deux tôles) bout à bout; abouter (deux tôles); *Metalw:* souder bout à bout.

buttock[1] ['bʌtək], *s.* **1.** (*a*) fesse *f*; (*b*) *pl.* **the buttocks,** le derrière, le postérieur, les fesses; la région fessière; **shot through the buttocks,** atteint d'une balle dans les parties charnues; *Wr:* **cross b.,** ceinture *f* arrière, à rebours; tour *m* de hanche; (*c*) *Cu:* **the b.,** la culotte (de bœuf). **2.** *pl.* croupe *f* (de bœuf). **3.** *pl. N.Arch:* fesse, arcasse *f*.

buttock[2], *v.tr. Wr:* terrasser (son adversaire) par une ceinture à rebours.

button[1] ['bʌtn], *s.* **1.** (*a*) bouton *m*; **plain b.,** bouton uni; **shank b.,** bouton à queue; **shankless b.,** bouton sans queue; **bachelor's b.,** bouton mobile, automatique (pour vêtements); **ball b.,** bouton boule; **tufted b.,** bouton à freluche; **cloth b., self b.,** bouton d'étoffe; **shoe, boot, b.,** bouton à chaussures, à bottines; **upholstery b.,** bouton de garniture (de meuble, etc.); *F: O:* **I don't care a b.,** ça m'est égal; *Mil: etc:* **b. stick,** patience *f*; (*b*) **buttons,** chasseur *m* (d'hôtel, de club, etc.); groom *m*. **2.** (*a*) bouton, pressoir *m*, bouton-poussoir *m* (*pl.* boutons-poussoirs) (de sonnerie électrique, etc.); poussoir *m* (d'une montre à répétition); *F:* **you've only to press the b.,** vous n'avez qu'à appuyer sur le bouton; ça se fait tout seul; c'est automatique; (*b*) bouton (de fleuret, de queue de violon); mouche *f* (de fleuret); **to put a b. on a sword,** moucheter une épée; **to take the b. off a foil,** démoucheter un fleuret; *Harn:* **running, sliding, b.,** bouton mobile, coulant; (*c*) *Row:* taquet *m* (d'aviron); (*d*) bouton (pour tourner); **knurled b.,** bouton moleté; (*e*) **chocolate buttons,** pastilles *fpl* de chocolat; (*f*) *Med:* **Bagdad b., Biskra b., Aleppo b.,** bouton d'Alep; ulcère *m* d'Orient; (*g*) *Ch:* culot *m* (au fond du creuset); bouton (de fin, d'essai); grain *m* (d'essai); **lead b.,** culot de plomb; (*h*) *Bot:* bouton (de rose, de champignon); (*i*) *NAm: P:* menton *m*.

button[2]. **1.** *v.tr.* (*a*) **to b. sth. (up),** boutonner qch.; (*of pers.*) **to be all buttoned up,** (i) être boutonné jusqu'au menton; (ii) *F:* être silencieux, renfermé; *F:* **it's all buttoned up,** c'est du tout cuit; (*b*) (*with passive force*) (*of garment*) se boutonner; **dress that buttons behind,** robe *f* qui se boutonne par derrière. **2.** *v.tr.* (*a*) *Fenc:* **to b. a sword,** moucheter une épée; **to b. one's adversary,** toucher son adversaire; (*b*) *Tail:* mettre les boutons à (un vêtement). **3.** *v.i.* (*of flower, plant*) boutonner; bourgeonner.

buttonball ['bʌtnbɔ:l], *s. Bot:* **b. (tree),** (i) platane *m*; (ii) céphalanthe *m*.

buttonbush ['bʌtnbuʃ], *s. Bot:* céphalanthe *m*.

buttonhead ['bʌtnhed], *a. & s. Mec.E:* **b. (rivet),** rivet *m* à tête en goutte de suif; **b. (screw),** vis *f* à tête ronde.

buttonhole[1] ['bʌtnhoul], *s.* **1.** boutonnière *f*; *Needlew:* **b. stitch,** point *m* de feston, de languette; point de boutonnière. **2.** *Surg:* boutonnière; petite incision. **3.** (fleur portée à la) boutonnière.

buttonhole[2], *v.tr.* **1.** *F:* **to b. s.o.,** attraper, retenir, qn par le revers de l'habit; cramponner, accrocher, agrafer, cueillir, qn (au passage). **2.** *Needlew:* festonner; *v.i.* faire une boutonnière. **3.** *Surg:* inciser.

buttonhook ['bʌtnhuk], *s.* crochet *m* à boutons; tire-bouton *m*, *pl.* tire-boutons.

buttoning ['bʌtniŋ], *s.* boutonnage *m*; *Bot: Hort:* boutonnement *m*, bourgeonnement *m*.

button-through ['bʌtnθru:], *a.* **b.-t. dress,** robe *f* qui s'ouvre entièrement devant, qui boutonne entièrement devant; robe entièrement ouverte devant.

button tree ['bʌtntri:], *s. Bot:* (i) platane *m*; (ii) conocarpe *m*.

buttonwood ['bʌtnwud], *s. Bot:* (i) platane *m*; (ii) conocarpe *m*; (iii) céphalanthe *m*.

buttress[1] ['bʌtris], *s. Const: Arch:* (*a*) contrefort *m*, contre-boutant *m*, *pl.* contre-boutants; éperon *m*; **flying b.,** arc-boutant *m*, *pl.* arcs-boutants; (*b*) pilier *m* (d'arc-boutant); ressaut *m* (de pilier); dosseret *m*; **b. retaining wall,** mur *m* de soutènement à contreforts; **b. dam,** barrage *m* à contreforts.

buttress[2], *v.tr. Const:* arc-bouter; étayer; *Fig:* **to b. (up) an argument,** étayer une thèse.

buttressing ['bʌtrisiŋ], *s.* arc boutement *m*, étayage *m*.

butt-rivetted ['bʌt'rivitid], *a.* rivé à couvre-joint.

butt weld[1], *s.* ['bʌtweld], *s. Metalw:* soudure *f* en bout, par rapprochement.

butt weld[2], *v.tr. Metalw:* souder par bouts, par rapprochement; souder bout à bout; **butt-welded tube,** tube soudé par rapprochement.

butt welding ['bʌt'weldiŋ], *s.* soudure *f* bout à bout, au point; soudure par rapprochement.

butty ['bʌti], *s.* **1.** *Min: F:* (*a*) copain *m*, porion *m*; (*b*) = casse-croûte *m inv*. **2.** balandre *f* en remorque.

butyl ['bju:til], *s. Ch:* butyle *m*; **b. alcohol,** alcool *m* butylique; **b. rubber,** caoutchouc *m* butyle, butylcaoutchouc *m*.

butylene ['bju:tili:n], *s. Ch:* butylène *m*, butène *m*.

butylic [bju(:)'tilik], *a. Ch:* butylique.

butyraceous [bju:ti'reiʃəs], *a.* butyracé; butyreux.

butyraldehyde [bju:ti'rældihaid], *s. Ch:* aldéhyde *m* butyrique.

butyrate ['bju:tireit], *s. Ch:* butyrate *m*.

butyric [bju(:)'tirik], *a. Ch:* butyrique.

butyrin(e) ['bju:tirin, -ri:n], *s. Ch:* butyrine *f*; tributyrine *f*.

butyrometer [bju:ti'rɔmitər], *s.* butyromètre *m*.

butyrospermum [bju:tirou'spə:məm], *s. Bot:* butyrospermum *m,* karité *m.*

butyrous ['bju:tirəs], *a.* butyreux.

Buxaceae [bʌk'seisii:], *s.pl. Bot:* buxacées *f.*

buxom ['bʌksəm], *a.* (femme) à la forte poitrine; (femme) grassouillette, bien en chair, aux formes plastiques, rebondies, plantureuses; (femme) fraîche et rondelette.

buxomness ['bʌksəmnis], *s.* ampleur *f* de formes; fraîcheur *f* robuste (d'une femme).

buy[1] [bai], *v.* (**bought** [bɔ:t]; **bought**)

I. *v.tr.* **1.** (*a*) acheter (**sth. from s.o.,** qch. à qn); **I bought this horse cheap,** j'ai acheté ce cheval (à) bon marché; **I bought it from a farmer,** je l'ai acheté à un cultivateur; **to b. for cash,** acheter comptant; **to b. firm,** acheter ferme; **to b. in bulk, wholesale,** acheter en gros, par grosses quantités; **to b. on credit,** acheter à crédit, à terme; **it's not worth buying,** cela ne vaut pas le prix; ce n'est pas la peine de l'acheter; *B:* **those that bought and sold in the temple,** les marchands dans le temple; **these things are not to be bought,** ces choses-là ne s'achètent pas, ne se vendent pas; **money cannot b. it,** cela ne se paie pas; **a dearly bought advantage,** un avantage chèrement payé; *Com:* **bought of David Thomas & Co.,** doit M. X à David Thomas et Cie; *Turf: F:* **to b. money,** parier à une cote désavantageuse; (*b*) **to b. s.o. sth.,** acheter qch. à qn; **my father had bought me a bicycle,** mon père m'avait acheté une bicyclette. **2.** (*a*) **to b. a witness,** corrompre, suborner, acheter, un témoin; (*b*) *F:* croire; gober; **I won't b. that!** tu ne me feras pas gober ça! parle toujours! **I'll b. it!** (i) je ne sais pas; je donne ma langue au chat; (ii) je te crois, (*c*) *P:* **he's bought it,** (i) il est foutu; (ii) il a passé l'arme à gauche; il s'est fait rectifier.

II. (*compound verbs*) **1. buy back,** *v.tr.* racheter.

2. buy in, *v.tr.* (*a*) (*at auction sales*) racheter (pour le compte du vendeur); (*b*) s'approvisionner de (denrées, etc.) (*c*) *St.Exch:* **to b. in against a client,** exécuter un client.

3. buy off, *v.tr.* se débarrasser de (qn) en lui payant une somme d'argent; *F:* acheter (qn).

4. buy out, *v.tr.* (*a*) *Com:* désintéresser (un associé, etc.); **he was bought out for £50,000,** on lui a acheté sa part, son intérêt, dans l'affaire, pour £50,000; (*b*) *Mil:* racheter (qn); **to b. oneself out,** se racheter.

5. buy over, *v.tr.* corrompre, acheter (qn).

6. buy up, *v.tr. Com:* acheter (qch.) en masse; rafler, accaparer (des denrées, etc.).

buy[2], *s.* achat *m;* affaire *f;* **it's a good b.,** c'est un bon placement; c'est une occasion, une affaire; **to make a bad b.,** faire une mauvaise emplette, une mauvaise affaire, un mauvais placement.

buyable ['baiəbl], *a.* qui peut être acheté; qui est à vendre.

buyer ['baiər], *s.* **1.** acheteur, -euse; acquéreur *m;* preneur, -euse; **potentiel, prospective, b.,** acheteur potentiel, éventuel; **there are few buyers,** il y a peu d'acheteurs; *Fin:* **buyers' market,** marché demandeur; marché orienté à la hausse; **buyer's option,** prime acheteur; **we are not buyers of . . .,** nous ne sommes pas preneurs de . . ., nous n'achetons pas . . . . **2.** *Com:* (*for firm*) acheteur; commissionnaire *m* d'achat; (*for a department*) chef *m* de rayon; **head b.,** acheteur principal.

buying ['baiiŋ], *s.* achat(s) *m* (*pl.*); **speculative b.,** achats spéculatifs; **shop b.,** achats professionnels (à la Bourse); **b. back,** rachat *m;* **b. in,** rachat; approvisionnement *m; St.Exch:* exécution *f* (d'un client); **b. out,** (i) désintéressement *m* (d'un associé); *Fin:* exclusion *f* (d'un actionnaire) par voie d'achat; (ii) rachat (de qn); **b. up,** accaparement *m* (des denrées).

buzz[1] [bʌz], *s.* (*a*) bourdonnement *m,* vrombissement *m* (d'un insecte); bruissement *m* (d'abeilles); bruit confus, brouhaha *m* (de conversations); vrombissement (d'un avion); *W.Tel:* ronflement *m,* (bruits *mpl* de) friture *f; Tp:* bourdonnement; *F:* **to give s.o. a b.,** donner un coup de fil à qn; (*b*) *Ling:* fricative *f* sonore; (*c*) *U.S: F:* conversation générale; bavardage *m;* (*d*) *Cin: F:* **b. track,** piste *f* d'essai de bruit.

buzz[2].

I. *v.i. & tr.* **1.** *v.i.* (*a*) (*of insects, etc.*) bourdonner, vrombir; murmurer; **cars buzzing along the roads,** des voitures qui vrombissent sur la route; **my ears were buzzing,** les oreilles me tintaient; (*b*) *U.S: F:* bavarder; (*c*) **to b. about, around,** s'activer. **2.** *v.tr.* (*a*) *A:* répandre (des nouvelles) à petit bruit; (*b*) *Tp: F: NAm:* donner un coup de téléphone à (qn); (*c*) *Av: etc: F:* **to b.** (**an aircraft, etc.**), frôler, harceler (un avion, etc.); (*d*) *P:* lancer (une pierre, etc.); (*e*) *P:* **let's b. the bottle,** vidons la bouteille.

II. (*compound verb*) **buzz off,** *v.i. F:* s'en aller, décamper, filer, se tailler; **b. off!** va-t-en! barre-toi!

buzzard ['bʌzəd], *s.* **1.** *Orn:* (*a*) buse *f;* **common b.,** buse variable; **long-legged b.,** buse féroce; **rough-legged b.,** buse pattue; **desert b.,** buse des déserts; **bat-eating b.,** buse des chauves-souris; (*b*) **bald b.,** balbuzard pêcheur, fluviatile; **honey b.,** bondrée *f* apivore. **2.** *P:* **that old b.,** ce sacré type; ce vieux fossile; cette espèce d'idiot.

buzz bomb ['bʌzbɔm], *s. F: O:* bombe volante.

buzzer ['bʌzər], *s.* (*a*) *Nau: Ind:* sirène *f;* (*b*) *El: Tp: etc:* appel *m* phonique, appel vibré; sonnerie ronflante; ronfleur *m;* vibreur *m,* vibrateur *m,* trembleur *m,* autotrembleur *m;* trompe *f* électrique; trompette *f* électrique; trompette d'appel; couineur *m;* **rhythmic b.,** ronfleur à interruption; **b. call,** appel vibré; **b. coil,** bobine *f* à trembleur, à rupteur.

buzzing ['bʌziŋ], *s.* bourdonnement *m;* **b. in the ears,** tintement *m* des oreilles, *Med:* bourdonnement *m.*

buzz saw ['bʌzsɔ:], *s. NAm:* scie *f* circulaire; *F:* **don't monkey with the b.s.!** n'y touchez pas!

by [bai], *prep. & adv.*

I. *prep.* **1.** (*near*) (*a*) (au)près de, à côté de (qn, qch.); **sitting by the fire,** assis près du feu; assis contre le poêle; **a house by the church,** une maison à proximité de l'église, voisine, près, de l'église; **by the sea,** au bord de la mer; *Post: A: & Scot:* **by Galashiels,** par Galashiels; (*in place names*) **X-by-Y,** X-lès-Y, X-lez-Y; **X-by-Sea,** X-sur-Mer; **by oneself,** seul, à l'écart; **he kept by himself,** il se tenait à l'écart; **I have no money by me,** (i) je n'ai pas d'argent sous la main; (ii) je n'ai pas d'argent disponible; (*b*) (*in naming the cardinal points*) quart *m;* **North by East,** Nord quart nord-est; **North-East by North,** Nord-est quart-nord; **North-east by East,** Nord-est quart-est; **East by North,** Est quart nord-est; (*c*) *Nau:* **by the head, by the stern,** sur nez, sur cul. **2.** (*along, via*) par; **to go by the same road,** aller par la même route; **by land and sea,** par terre et par mer; **to travel by (way of) Basle,** passer par Bâle. **3.** (*agency, means*) (*a*) par, de; **to be punished by s.o.,** être puni par qn; **to be loved by s.o.,** être aimé, se faire aimer, de qn; **I was summoned home by my father's illness.** je fus rappelé à la maison par une maladie de mon père; **to have a child by s.o.,** avoir un enfant de qn, des œuvres de qn; **to die by one's own hand,** mourir de ses propres mains; **to lead s.o. by the hand,** conduire qn par la main; **he took me by the arm,** il me prit par le bras; **made by hand,** fait à la main; **to call s.o. by his name,** appeler qn par son nom; **to be known by, to go by, the name of X,** être connu sous le nom d'X; **to read by candlelight,** lire à la chandelle; **to live by one's work,** vivre de son travail; **what do you mean by that?** qu'entendez-vous par là? **by force,** de force; **by way of a joke,** par plaisanterie; **by (an) error,** par suite d'une erreur; **by chance,** par hasard; **by good fortune,** par bonheur; **cheerful by nature,** gai de caractère; gai par nature; **to do sth. (all) by oneself,** faire qch. (tout) seul; **I did it by myself,** je l'ai fait à moi seul; **by heart,** par cœur; **to divide by three,** diviser par trois; **three metres by two,** trois mètres sur deux; **by land, by sea,** par (voie de) terre, mer; **to travel by rail,** voyager par le, *F:* en, chemin de fer; **to come by tram, by car, by motorcycle, by mule,** venir en tramway, en voiture, à motocyclette, à dos de mulet; (*b*) (*with gerund*) **to earn one's living by teaching,** gagner sa vie en enseignant; **to win respect by compelling obedience,** se faire respecter en se faisant obéir; **by doing that you will offend him,** en faisant cela vous l'offenserez; **what do you gain by doing that?** que gagnez-vous à faire cela? **I shall gain, lose, by it,** j'y gagnerai, j'y perdrai; **by sharing the same perils we learn to know each other,** à partager les mêmes périls on apprend à se connaître; **to begin, end, by laughing,** commencer, finir, par rire; **we shall lose nothing by waiting,** nous ne perdrons rien pour attendre. **4.** (*according to*) **by rote,** par routine; **by my watch,** à ma montre; **by the clock it is three,** d'après l'horloge il est trois heures; **to set one's watch by the time signal,** régler sa montre sur le signal horaire; **to judge by appearances,** juger sur l'apparence; **I can tell it by your face,** on le voit à votre visage; **by what he said, I believed . . .,** d'après ce qu'il a dit j'ai cru . . .; **by the stipulations of the treaty,** de par les stipulations du traité; **by (the terms of) article 5,** aux termes, selon les termes, de l'article 5; **I know him by his walk,** je le reconnais à sa démarche; **by my father's wish,** sur, selon, le désir de mon père; **to sell sth. by the pound, by the dozen,** vendre qch. à la livre, à la douzaine; **to rent a house by the year,** louer une maison à l'année; **they are to be had by the dozen, by the score,** on les a par douzaines, par vingtaines. **5. by degrees,** par degrés; **by turn(s),** tour à tour; **one by one,** un à un; **to come in two by two, to come in by twos,** entrer deux par deux; **by twos and threes,** par deux ou trois; **little by little,** peu à peu, petit à petit; **day by day,** jour par jour, de jour en jour. **6.** (*during*) **by day,** de jour, le jour; **by night,** de nuit, la nuit; **by daylight,** au jour. **7.** (*of point in time*) **he will be here by three o'clock,** il sera ici avant, pour, trois heures; **you will hear from us by Monday,** vous aurez de nos nouvelles d'ici lundi; **he ought to be here by now, by this time,** il doit, il devrait, être déjà ici; **they have gone to bed by this time,** ils sont couchés à cette heure; **he must have gone by now,** à l'heure qu'il est il doit être parti; **by that time they had gone,** ils étaient déjà partis; ils étaient partis dans l'intervalle; **by the time (that) you have finished, I shall be gone,** quand vous aurez fini, avant que vous ayez fini, je serai parti; **you shall have it by tomorrow,** vous l'aurez pour demain, demain au plus tard; **they were tired by the end of the day,** ils étaient fatigués à la fin de la journée; **by 1970 they had already achieved their aim,** dès 1970 ils avaient déjà atteint leur but. **8.** (*to the extent of*) **longer by two metres,** plus long de deux mètres; **by far,** de beaucoup. **9.** (*in respect of*) **I know him by name, by sight,** je le connais de nom, de vue; **he is a grocer by trade,** il est épicier de son métier; **to do one's duty by s.o.,** faire son devoir envers qn; *F:* **it's all right by me!** ça va! d'accord! **is it all right by you?** ça vous va-t-il? **10.** (*in oaths*) **by God,** au nom de Dieu; **to swear by all one holds sacred,** jurer par tout ce qu'on a de plus sacré. **11.** *Mil:* **by the right!** guide à droite!

II. *adv.* **1.** (*near*) près; **close by, hard by,** tout près, ici près, tout à côté, tout contre; **he lives close by,** il demeure tout près; **was there no one by?** est-ce que personne n'était présent? *Nau:* **by and large!** près et plein! **taking it by and large . . .,** à tout prendre . . .; généralement . . .. **2.** (*aside*) **to lay, set, put, sth. by,** mettre qch. de côté; **to put, lay, money by,** mettre de l'argent de côté; faire des économies. **3.** (*past*) **to go, pass, by,** passer; **the time is gone by when . . .,** le temps est passé où . . .; *Scot:* **to be by with it,** (i) avoir achevé, fini; (ii) être un homme achevé, fini, ruiné; (iii) être mort. **4.** *adv.phrs.* **by and by,** tout à l'heure, bientôt, tantôt; **he will do better by and by,** il fera par la suite; **by the by(e) . . ., by the way . . .,** à propos . . .. **5.** *Scot: NAm: F:* chez (qn); **come by and eat with me,** venez manger chez moi.

byblow ['baiblou], *s.* **1.** coup *m* oblique. **2.** *F:* enfant bâtard.

by(e)[1] [bai], *a.* **by(e) effect,** effet secondaire, indirect; contrecoup *m;* **by(e) consideration,** considération *f* secondaire; considération d'ordre privé; **bye interest,** intérêt privé.

bye[2] [bai], *s.* **1.** *Cr:* balle passée; *Artil:* coup trop allongé. **2.** *Sp:* (*of player*) **to have a b.,** être exempt (d'une épreuve, d'un match dans un tournoi).

bye-bye ['bai 'bai], *F:* (*child's language*) **1.** *int.* adieu! au revoir! **2.** *s.* **to go to b.-b.,** aller faire dodo; aller au dodo.

by(e)-law, by(e)law ['bailɔ:], *s.* arrêté *m* émanant d'une autorité locale; statut *m,* règlement administratif, émanant d'une autorité locale; arrêté municipal.

by-election ['baiilekʃən], *s. Pol:* élection partielle.

Byelorussia [bi(:)elou'rʌʃə], *Pr.n. Geog:* Biélorussie *f,* Russie Blanche.

Byelorussian [bi(:)elou'rʌʃ(ə)n]. **1.** *Geog:* (*a*) *a.* biélorusse; (*b*) *s.* Biélorusse *mf.* **2.** *s. Ling:* biélorusse *m.*

bygone ['baigɔn]. **1.** *a.* passé, écoulé, ancien, d'autrefois; **in b. days,** dans l'ancien temps. **2.** *s.pl.* (*a*) le passé; **let bygones be bygones,** oublions le passé; ne revenons plus sur le passé; passons l'éponge (là-dessus); (c'est) sans rancune! (*b*) **he had a collection of wooden bygones,** il avait une collection d'anciens outils en bois.

by-issue ['baiisju:, -iʃu:], *s.* question *f* d'intérêt secondaire.

bylander ['bailændər], *s. Nau:* bélandre *f.*

bylina [bi'li:nə], *s.* byline *f.*

byline ['bailain], *s. Journ:* ligne *f* qui porte le titre de l'auteur (d'un article).

byname ['baineim], *s. A:* surnom *m.*

bypass, by-pass[1] ['baipɑ:s], *s.* **1.** *Mec.E:* (*a*) *Mch: etc:* (conduit *m* de) dérivation *f;* bipasse *m;* (*of valve*) tube *m* de dégagement; **b. valve,** soupape *f* de dérivation; *I.C.E:* **b. engine,** réacteur *m* à double flux; (*b*) *Av:* **b. ratio,** taux *m* de dilution; **high b. turbofan engine,** turboréacteur *m* à double flux, à taux de dilution élevé; **this engine is designed for a b. ratio of 5 : 1 at cruising speed,** ce réacteur est conçu pour un taux de dilution de 5/1 au régime de croisière. **2.** *El:* dérivation; **b. condenser,** condensateur *m* de découplage, de dérivation; **b. transformer,** transformateur *m* de dérivation. **3.** (*of gas burner*) veilleuse *f;* bec allumeur. **4.** *Civ.E:* **b. (road),** (i) route *f* de contournement, d'évitement; (ii) voie détournée, route d'emprunt; (iii) rocade *f*.

bypass, by-pass[2], *v.tr.* **1.** *Mch:* amener (la vapeur, etc.) en dérivation; *I.C.E:* **to b. a jet,** placer un gicleur en dérivation. **2.** *El:* mettre hors circuit. **3.** (*a*) (*of road, pers.*) contourner, éviter (une ville, etc.); (*b*) **to b. the traffic,** dévier la circulation; (*c*) laisser (qn) de côté; ne tenir aucun compte de (qch.); passer (qch.) sous silence; court-circuiter (qch.).

bypath ['baipɑːθ], *s.* **1.** sentier écarté, détourné. **2.** *Pej: A:* voie détournée.

by-play ['baiplei], *s. Th: etc:* jeu *m* accessoire; jeu de scène; jeu de second plan; aparté mimé; jeu muet.

by-plot ['baiplɔt], *s. Th: etc:* intrigue *f* secondaire.

by-product ['baiprɔdʌkt], *s.* (*a*) *Ind:* sous-produit *m, pl.* sous-produits; produit secondaire, accessoire; produit dérivé; dérive *m*; **by-products (of butchery),** issues *fpl* (de boucherie); (*b*) *Cmptr:* **b.-p. circuit,** circuit *m* superposé; **b.-p. tape,** bande perforée en sous-produit.

byre ['baiər], *s. esp. Scot:* vacherie *f*; bouverie *f*; étable *f* à vaches.

byrnic ['bəːni], *s. A.Arm:* broigne *f*.

byroad ['bairoud], *s.* (*a*) chemin détourné, *F:* chemin des écoliers; embranchement *m*; (*b*) chemin vicinal; route vicinale, cantonale; chemin auxiliaire.

Byronic [bai'rɔnik], *a.* byronien.

byssinosis [bisi'nousis], *s. Med:* byssinose *f*, byssinosis *f*.

byssogenous [bi'sɔdʒinəs], *a. Moll:* byssogène.

byssus ['bisəs], *s. Archeol: Moll:* bysse *m*, byssus *m*, bissus *m*.

bystander ['baistændər], *s.* assistant *m*; spectateur, -trice; **a few of the bystanders,** quelques-unes des personnes présentes.

byte [bait], *s. Cmptr:* multiplet *m*, groupe *m* de positions binaires, de bits consécutifs; **four-bit b.,** quartet *m*; **six-bit b.,** hexet *m*; **eight-bit b.,** octet *m*; **b. mode,** mode discontinu.

bytownite ['baitaunait], *s. Miner:* bytownite *f*.

byway ['baiwei], *s.* chemin détourné, voie indirecte; **to take a b.,** faire un détour; prendre le chemin des écoliers; **byways of history,** à-côtés *m* de l'histoire.

byword ['baiwəːd], *s.* **1.** *A:* proverbe *m*, dicton *m*; **to have become a b.,** être passé en proverbe. **2.** (*of pers.*) **to be the b. of the village,** être la fable, la risée, du village; **to become a b. for lying,** se faire connaître comme menteur insigne.

Byzantine ['bizəntain, bai'zæntain], *Hist:* **1.** *a.* byzantin; **the B. Empire,** l'Empire byzantin, l'Empire romain d'Orient; **B. architecture,** architecture byzantine. **2.** *s.* Byzantin, -ine.

Byzantinism [bi'zæntinizm], *s.* byzantinisme *m*.

Byzantinist [bi'zæntinist], *s.* byzantiniste *mf*.

Byzantium [bi'zæntiəm, bai'zæntiəm], *Pr.n. A.Geog:* Byzance *f*.

C

C, c [si:], *s.* **1.** (*a*) (la lettre) C, c *m*; *Tp:* **C for Charlie,** C comme Célestin; (*b*) **C-shaped iron bar,** fer *m* en C; **C spring,** ressort *m* en C; *El: Elcs:* **C battery,** batterie *f* (de polarisation) de grille; **C bias,** polarisation *f* de grille; **C meter,** capacimètre *m*; **C network,** réseau *m* en C; **C band,** bande *f* C; **C scan, scanner,** explorateur *m* de type C; **C minus, negative,** pôle négatif; **C plus, positive,** pôle positif. **2.** *Mus:* ut *m*, do *m*. **3.** (*a*) *Geol:* **C horizon,** horizon *m* C; (*b*) *Sch:* **to get a C (for an exercise),** avoir une note médiocre (pour un devoir); (*c*) **a C3 man,** homme classé dans la dernière catégorie par le conseil de révision.

Caaba [ˈkɑːbə], *s. Rel.H:* Caaba *f*, Kaaba *f*.

caa'ing [ˈkɑːiŋ], *a. Z:* **c. whale,** globicéphale *m*.

caama [ˈkɑːmə], *s. Z:* caama *m*.

caatinga [kɑːˈtiŋgə], *s. Geog:* caatinga *f*.

cab [kæb], *s.* **1.** (*a*) *A:* voiture *f* de place; fiacre *m*; **hansom c.,** cab *m*; **c. horse,** cheval *m* de fiacre; **c. runner, tout,** bagotier *m*; (*b*) taxi *m*; **to call, hail, a c.,** appeler, héler, un taxi; faire avancer un taxi; **c. driver,** chauffeur *m* de taxi; **c. rank, c. stand,** station *f*, stationnement *m*, de taxis. **2.** (*a*) *Rail:* abri *m*, cabine *f*, poste *m* de conduite (du mécanicien); **c. window,** lunette *f* (de locomotive); (*b*) cabine (de grue); (*c*) cabine, guérite *f* (d'un autobus, d'un camion); **c. over engine,** cabine avancée; **chassis with forward control c.,** châssis avancé.

caba [ˈkæbə], *s. NAm:* cabas *m* (d'ouvrier).

cabal[1] [kəˈbæl], *s.* **1.** cabale *f*, brigue *f*. **2.** coterie *f*. **3.** *Eng.Hist:* **the C.,** le ministère de la Cabal(e), le Comité des affaires étrangères de Charles II.

cabal[2], *v.i.* **(caballed)** cabaler, comploter.

cabala [ˈkæbələ], *s. Rel.H:* cabale *f*.

cabalism [ˈkæbəlizm], *s. Rel.H:* cabalisme *m*.

cabalist [ˈkæbəlist], *s. Rel.H:* cabaliste *mf*.

cabalistic [kæbəˈlistik], *a.* cabalistique.

caballer [kəˈbælər], *s.* cabaleur, -euse.

caballine [ˈkæbəlain], *a.* **1.** *Myth:* **the C. Fountain,** la Fontaine caballine. **2.** *Bot:* **c. aloes,** aloès caballin.

cabana [kəˈbɑːnə], *s. U.S:* cabine *f* (de bain).

cabane [kəˈbɑːn], *s. Av: A:* cabane *f*.

cabaret [ˈkæbərei], *s.* **1.** cabaret *m* (genre montmartrois). **2. c. (show),** concert *m* genre music-hall (donné dans un restaurant, à une vente de charité, etc.); attractions *fpl*; **c. singer,** chanteuse réaliste. **3.** (*tea, coffee, service*) cabaret (de porcelaine).

cabas [ˈkæbəs], *s.* cabas *m*.

cabassou [kæˈbæsuː, ˈkæbæsuː], *s. Z:* cabassou *m*, armadillo *m* à onze bandes.

cabbage[1] [ˈkæbidʒ], *s.* **1.** (*a*) chou *m*, *pl.* choux; **Savoy c.,** chou frisé de Milan; **red c.,** chou rouge, chou roquette; **c. patch, bed,** carré *m*, plant *m*, de choux; **to lead a c.-like existence,** mener une vie de ruminant; (*b*) **dog c.,** cynocrambe *m*; **turnip c.,** chou-rave *m*, *pl.* choux-raves; turnep(s) *m*; **sea c.,** chou marin; **c. lettuce,** laitue pommée; **c. palm, c. palmetto, c. tree,** (i) (chou)(-)palmiste *m*; palmier *m* Pinot (de l'Amazonie); (ii) *Austr:* livistona *m*; *N.Z:* cordyline *f*; (iii) euterpe *f*; (iv) arec *m*, areca *m*; *Austr:* **c. tree hat,** chapeau *m* de paille; (*c*) **c. rose,** rose *f* chou, *pl.* roses chou; (*d*) *Ent:* **c. butterfly, c. white (butterfly),** piéride *f* du chou, piéride brassicaire, papillon blanc du chou; **c. moth,** plutelle *f*, teigne *f* des crucifères; **c.-root fly,** hylémyie *f*; **c. maggot,** larve *f* de hylémyie; **c. worm,** larve (i) de piéride du chou, (ii) de noctuelle *f*; (*e*) *Cost:* **c. bow, c. knot,** chou. **2.** *P:* billets *mpl* de banque.

cabbage[2], *v.i.* (*of lettuce, etc.*) pommer.

cabbage[3], *s.* **1.** *Tail: F:* retailles *fpl*; gratte *f*. **2.** *Ind:* ferraille *f*. **3.** *Sch: A:* traduction *f* illicite.

cabbage[4], *v.i. F:* **1.** *Tail: etc:* rabioter; faire de la gratte. **2.** *Ind:* comprimer (de la ferraille) à la presse hydraulique. **3.** *Sch: A:* se servir d'une traduction illicite.

cabbagehead [ˈkæbidʒhed], *s.* **1.** tête *f* de chou. **2.** *P:* sot *m*; tête de bois.

cabbaging press [ˈkæbidʒiŋpres], *s. Ind: F:* presse *f* à ferrailles.

cabbala, cabbalism, etc: = CABALA, CABALISM, *etc.*

cabby [ˈkæbi], *s. F:* (*a*) *A:* cocher *m* (de fiacre); (*b*) chauffeur *m* de taxi.

caber [ˈkeibər], *s. Sp:* tronc *m* de mélèze, de pin, ou de sapin; **tossing the c.,** sport écossais qui consiste à lancer le tronc d'un jeune mélèze (tenu verticalement par le petit bout) de manière à le faire retomber aussi loin que possible sur le gros bout et à lui faire accomplir trois quarts de tour.

cabera [ˈkeibərə], *s. Ent:* cabère *f*.

cabin[1] [ˈkæbin], *s.* **1.** (*a*) cabane *f*, case *f*; *Lit:* **Uncle Tom's Cabin,** la Case de l'oncle Tom: (*b*) *Rail:* poste *m*, cabine *f*, d'aiguillage; **driver's c.,** loge *f*; poste de conduite; (*c*) (*on barge, etc.*) cabane. **2.** (*a*) *Nau:* cabine; *Navy:* chambre *f*; **fore, after, c.,** cabine de l'avant, de l'arrière; *O:* **c. class,** classe *f* cabine; **c. boy,** mousse *m*; **c. trunk,** malle *f* de cabine, de paquebot; (*b*) *Nau:* **c. cruiser,** bateau *m* de plaisance (avec cabines); (*c*) *Av:* cabine; habitacle *m*; **pilot's c.,** cabine de pilotage.

cabin[2]. **1.** *v.tr. A:* enfermer (qn à l'étroit). **2.** *v.i. esp. NAm:* habiter une cabane.

cabinet [ˈkæbinit], *s.* **1.** *Furn:* (*a*) meuble *m* à tiroirs; (*antique*) cabinet *m*; **medal c.,** cabinet de médailles, médaillier *m*; **music c.,** casier *m* à musique; **filing c.,** fichier *m*, classeur *m*; **writing c.,** bureau *m*, secrétaire *m*; **roll-top c., roll-shutter c.,** classeur à rideau; (*b*) coffret *m*, ébénisterie *f* (de poste de radio, etc.); (*c*) **bathroom, medicine, c.,** armoire *f* à toilette, à pharmacie; **kitchen c.,** rangement *m* de cuisine; (*d*) vitrine *f*; **c. of butterflies,** collection *f* de papillons (sous vitrine); (*e*) armoire (de magasinage); (*f*) **testing c.,** armoire à analyses; (*g*) **c. maker,** ébéniste *m*; menuisier *m* en meubles; **c. making,** ébénisterie *f*. **2.** (*a*) petite chambre, cabinet; (*b*) *Pol:* cabinet, ministère *m*; **shadow c.,** conseil *m* de ministres fantôme; **a c. was held,** les membres *m* du gouvernement se sont réunis; **c. council,** conseil du cabinet, des ministres; **C. minister,** ministre *m* (d'Etat), membre du cabinet (ministériel); **C. crisis,** crise ministérielle; **to form a c.,** former un ministère. **3.** *Phot:* **c. size,** format *m* album; **c. photograph,** photographie *f* format album. **4.** *Cu:* **c. pudding,** pouding *m* qui contient des raisins secs, etc.

cable[1] [ˈkeibl], *s.* **1.** *Nau: etc:* câble *m*; **cable's length,** encâblure *f*; **steel-wire c.,** câble d'acier; câble métallique; *Av: etc:* **c. guide,** glissière *f*. **2.** *Nau:* **anchor, bower, sheet, c.,** câble d'ancre, de bossoir, de veille; **c. (chain),** câble-chaîne *m*, *pl.* câbles-chaînes; **c. ship,** câblier *m*; **c. locker,** puits *m* aux chaînes; **to pay out the c.,** filer le câble; **to slip one's c.,** filer son câble par le bout; **range of c.,** bitture *f*. **3.** *El: etc:* (*a*) câble, fil *m*, canalisation *f*; (fil) conducteur *m*; **overhead c.,** câble aérien; **underground c.,** câble enterré, souterrain; **submarine c.,** câble sous-marin; conduite sous-marine; **deep-sea c.,** câble des grandes profondeurs; **transatlantic c.,** câble transatlantique; **armoured c.,** câble armé, câble blindé, câble sous gaine; **lead-covered c.,** câble sous plomb; **rubber c., rubber-covered, -sheathed, -insulated, c.,** câble isolé au caoutchouc, sous caoutchouc; **oil-filled, gas-filled, c.,** câble à huile, à gaz; **twin c.,** câble à deux conducteurs; **quad(ded) c., quad pair c.,** câble à paires câblées en étoile; **paired, non-quadded, c.,** câble à paires; **coaxial c.,** câble coaxial; **five-wire c.,** câble à cinq conducteurs; **feeding c.,** artère *f* alimentaire; **bearer c.,** câble horizontal de suspension; **distribution c.,** câble de répartition, de distribution; **inlet, outlet, c.,** câble d'arrivée, de sortie; **ring c.,** câble de ceinture, de rocade; **by-pass c.,** câble d'évitement, de contournement; **remote-control c.,** câble de commande à distance; **current-supply c.,** câble d'amenée de courant; **telegraph c.,** câble télégraphique; **keying c.,** câble de télécommande, de télémanipulation; **to lay a c.,** poser un câble; **c. laying,** pose *f* de câbles; **c. layer,** poseur *m* de câbles; **c. conduit,** tube *m* guide-fil(s); **c. maker, manufacturer,** câblier *m*; **c. making, manufacturing,** câblerie *f*; (*b*) *Telecom:* câble, câblogramme *m*; **c. address,** adresse *f* télégraphique; (*c*) **c. railway,** (chemin *m* de fer) funiculaire *m*; **c. car,** (i) funiculaire; (ii) (cabine *f* de) téléphérique *m*; **c. seat,** siège *m* téléphérique; (*d*) *Phot:* **c. release,** déclencheur *m*; (*e*) *Tex:* **c. cord,** câblé *m*; **c. cord fabric,** tissu *m* en toile câblée; *Knit:* **c. stitch,** point natté. **4.** *Arch: etc:* **c. moulding,** câble, rudenture *f*, cordelière *f*, torsade *f*. **5.** *Her:* gumène *f*.

cable[2], *v.tr.* **1.** attacher (qch.) avec un câble. **2.** câbler (un message); *v.i.* **to c. (to) s.o.,** câbler à qn; aviser qn par câble. **3.** *Arch:* rudenter (une colonne).

cablegram [ˈkeiblgræm], *s.* câblogramme *m*; câblegramme *m*; télégramme sous-marin.

cable-laid [ˈkeiblleid], *a. Nau:* (cordage) commis en grelin, en aussière.

cablese [ˈkeibliːz], *s. F:* abréviations utilisées dans les câblogrammes.

cablet [ˈkeiblit], *s. Nau:* câblot *m*.

cableway [ˈkeiblwei], *s.* transporteur aérien à câbles; blondin *m*; aérocâble *m*.

cabling [ˈkeibliŋ], *s.* **1.** câblage *m* (des brins d'un câble). **2.** envoi *m* d'un câblogramme. **3.** *coll.* câbles *mpl*; **a hundred metres of c.,** cent mètres de câble.

cabman, *pl.* **-men** [ˈkæbmən], *s.* (*a*) *A:* cocher *m* de fiacre; (*b*) chauffeur *m* de taxi.

caboceer [kæbouˈsiər], *s.* (*in W. Africa*) cabécère *m*.

caboched [kəˈbɔʃt], *a. Her:* caboché; **beast's head c.,** rencontre *f*.

cabochon [ˈkæbəʃɔn], *s. Lap:* cabochon *m*.

cabomba [kəˈbɔmbə], *s. Bot:* cabomba *m*.

caboodle [kəˈbuːdl], *s. F:* **the whole (kit and) c.,** tout le bazar; tout le tremblement; tout le bataclan.

caboose [kəˈbuːs], *s.* **1.** *Nau:* cuisine *f*, coquerie *f*. **2.** (*a*)

NAm: Rail: fourgon *m* du personnel (d'un train de marchandises); (*b*) *Can:* baraquement mobile pourvu de couchettes (pour bûcherons, moissonneurs, etc.); (*c*) *Can:* hutte, cabane, montée sur un traîneau.
caboshed [kə'bɔʃt], **cabossed** [kə'bɔst], *a.* = CABOCHED.
cabotage ['kæbətidʒ], *s. Nau:* cabotage *m.*
caboteur ['kæbətər], *s. Nau: Can:* caboteur *m* (du Saint-Laurent).
cabré ['kɑːbrei], *a.* **1.** *Her:* (cheval) acculé. **2.** *Av:* cabré.
cabriole ['kæbrioul], *s.* **1.** *Furn:* pied *m* de biche (d'un meuble). **2.** *Danc:* cabriole *f.*
cabriolet ['kæbrioulei], *s.* (*a*) *Veh:* (*one-horse carriage*) cabriolet *m*; (*b*) *Aut: NAm:* cabriolet; (*c*) *A.Furn:* cabriolet.
ca'canny ['kɑː'kæni]. **1.** *v.i.* y aller doucement; *Ind:* faire la grève perlée. **2.** *a. & s. Ind:* **c. (policy),** ralentissement (voulu) du rythme du travail; **c. strike,** grève perlée.
cacao [kə'kɑːou, kə'keiou], *s.* **1. c. (bean),** cacao *m*; **c. nut, pod,** cabosse *f*; **c. butter,** beurre *m* de cacao; **c. mill,** moulin *m* à cacao. **2. c. (tree),** cacaotier *m*, cacaoyer *m*; **c. plantation,** cacaotière *f*, cacaoyère *f.*
cachalot ['kæʃəlɔt], *s. Z:* cachalot *m.*
cache[1] [kæʃ], *s.* **1.** cache *f*, cachette *f* (d'explorateur); **to make a c. of one's stores,** mettre ses vivres à l'abri. **2.** vivres déposés en cache.
cache[2], *v.tr.* mettre (des provisions, etc.) dans une cache.
cachectic [kə'kektik], *a. & s. Med:* cachectique (*mf*).
cache-sexe ['kæʃseks], *s.* cache-sexe *m inv.*
cachet ['kæʃei], *s.* **1.** (*of a work, etc.*) **to have a certain c.,** avoir un certain cachet. **2.** *Pharm:* cachet (d'aspirine, etc.). **2.** *Post:* cachet (commémoratif, etc.).
cachexia [kæ'keksiə], **cachexy** [kæ'keksi], *s. Med:* cachexie *f.*
cachinnate ['kækineit], *v.i.* rire aux éclats.
cachinnation [kæki'neiʃ(ə)n], *s.* gros rire; fou rire.
cacholong ['kætʃəlɔŋ], *s. Miner:* cacholong *m.*
cachou [kæ'ʃuː], *s.* cachou *m.*
cacique [kə'siːk], *s.* cacique *m.*
cack-handed [kæk'hændid], *a. F:* (*a*) gaucher; (*b*) gauche; maladroit.
cackle[1] ['kækl], *s.* **1.** (*of hen*) caquet *m.* **2.** *F:* (*of pers.*) (*a*) caquet, caquetage *m*, cailletage *m*; **cut your, the, c.!** en voilà assez! (*b*) ricanement *m*; rire saccadé.
cackle[2]. **1.** *v.i.* (*a*) (*of hen*) caqueter; (*of goose*) cacarder; (*b*) (*of pers.*) (i) caqueter, cailleter; (ii) ricaner; faire entendre un rire saccadé, un petit rire sec. **2.** *v.tr.* **to c. (out) sth.,** dire qch. en ricanant.
cackler ['kæklər], *s.* **1.** poule *f* qui caquette. **2.** *F:* (*pers.*) (*a*) caqueteur, -euse; (*b*) ricaneur, -euse.
cackling[1] ['kækliŋ], *a.* **1.** (poule) qui caquette. **2.** *F:* (rire) saccadé.
cackling[2], *s.* **1.** caquetage *m* (d'une poule). **2.** *F:* (*of pers.*) caquetage; ricanement *m*; rires saccadés.
caco- ['kækou, kæ'kɔ], *pref.* caco-.
cacochymia ['kækou'kaimiə], **cacochymy** ['kækou'kaimi], *s. Med:* cacochymie *f.*
cacodemon ['kækou'diːmən], *s.* cacodémon *m.*
cacodyl ['kækoudil], *s. Ch:* cacodyle *m*; **c. oxide,** oxyde *m* de cacodyle.
cacodylate ['kækou'dileit], *s. Ch:* cacodylate *m*; **sodium c.,** cacodylate de soude.
cacodylic ['kækou'dilik], *a. Ch:* cacodylique; **c. acid,** acide *m* cacodylique.
cacoepy ['kækouepi], *s.* mauvaise prononciation.
cacoethes ['kækou'iːθiːz], *s. Lit:* mauvaise habitude; **c. scribendi,** démangeaison *f*, manie *f*, d'écrire; graphomanie *f*; **c. loquendi,** manie de parler.
cacographer [kæ'kɔgrəfər], *s.* cacographe *m.*
cacographic(al) ['kækou'græfik(l)], *a.* cacographique.
cacography [kæ'kɔgrəfi], *s.* cacographie *f.*
cacological ['kækou'lɔdʒikl], *a.* cacologique.
cacology [kæ'kɔlədʒi], *s.* cacologie *f.*
cacoon [kæ'kuːn], *s. Bot:* févillée cordifoliée; **c. (seed),** noix *f* de serpent.
cacophonous [kæ'kɔfənəs], *a.* cacophonique.
cacophony [kæ'kɔfəni], *s.* cacophonie *f.*
cacosmia [kæ'kɔzmiə], *s. Med:* cacosmie *f.*
cacotheline [kæ'kɔθəliːn], *s. Ch:* cacothéline *f.*
cacotrophy [kæ'kɔtrəfi], *s.* cacotrophie *f.*
cacoxene [kæ'kɔksiːn], **cacoxenite** [kæ'kɔksinait], *s. Miner:* cacoxène *m.*
Cactaceae [kæk'teisiiː], *s.pl. Bot:* cactacées *f*, *A:* cactées *f.*
cactaceous [kæk'teiʃəs], **cactiform** ['kæktifɔːm], *a.* cactiforme, cactoïde.
cactus, *pl.* **-ti** ['kæktəs; -tiː, -tai], *s. Bot:* cactus *m*; **cochineal c.,** nopal *m*; **giant c.,** cierge géant; **hedge c.,** grand cierge; **hedgehog c.,** échinocactus *m*; **melon c.,** mélocacte *m*, mélocactus *m*; **mistletoe c.,** rhipsalide *f*, rhipsalis *m.*
cad [kæd], *s.m.* goujat; canaille *f.*
cadastral [kə'dæstrəl], *a. Surv:* cadastral, -aux; **c. survey,** cadastre *m.*
cadastre [kə'dæstər], *s. Surv:* cadastre *m.*
cadaver [kə'dævər], *s. esp. NAm:* cadavre *m.*
cadaveric [kə'dævərik], *a.* (rigidité *f*) cadavérique.
cadaverine [kə'dævəriːn], *s. Bio-Ch:* cadavérine *f.*
cadaverous [kə'dævərəs], *a.* (*a*) cadavéreux; **c. face,** figure cadavéreuse, blême, exsangue; (*b*) émacié, décharné.
cadaverousness [kə'dævərəsnis], *s.* pâleur cadavéreuse (du visage, etc.).
caddice ['kædis], *s.* = CADDIS.
caddie[1] ['kædi], *s. Golf:* caddie *m*; **c. car(t),** poussette *f* (pour crosses de golf).
caddie[2], *v.i. Golf:* **to c. for s.o.,** servir de caddie à qn.
caddis ['kædis], *s.* **c. (fly),** phrygane *f*; **c. (worm),** *Fish:* **c. (bait),** larve *f* de phrygane, (ver) caset *m*; cherfaix *m*, chairfaix *m*; *F:* ver *m* d'eau; porte-faix *m inv*; porte-bois *m inv*; porte-bûche *m inv.*
caddish ['kædiʃ], *a.* voyou; digne d'un goujat.
caddishness ['kædiʃnis], *s.* goujaterie *f.*
caddy[1] ['kædi], *s.* **(tea) c.,** boîte *f* à thé.
caddy[2], *s. & v.i.* = CADDIE[1,2].
cade[1] [keid], *s. Bot:* cade *m*; genévrier *m* oxycèdre; **c. fruit,** cadenelle *f*; **c. oil,** huile *f* de cade.
cade[2], *s.* cade *m*, baril *m*, caque *f.*
cade[3], *s.* agneau élevé au biberon.
cadelle [kə'del], *s. Ent:* cadelle *f.*
cadence ['keid(ə)ns], *s.* **1.** cadence *f*, rythme *m*, battement *m.* **2.** *Mus:* cadence; **perfect c.,** cadence parfaite; **interrupted c.,** cadence rompue, interrompue; **avoided c.,** cadence évitée; **trilled c.,** cadence brisée; **half c.,** demi-cadence *f*, *pl.* demi-cadences; **imperfect, half close, c.,** cadence imparfaite; **plagal c.,** cadence plagale. **3.** (i) chute *f*, (ii) intonation *f*, cadence, modulation *f* (de la voix).
cadenced ['keid(ə)nst], *a.* cadencé.
cadency ['keid(ə)nsi], *s.* descendance *f* de la branche cadette; *Her:* **mark of c., c. mark,** brisure *f.*
cadenza [kə'denzə], *s. Mus:* cadence *f*; cadenza *f.*
cadet [kə'det], *s.* **1.** *A:* (*younger son*) cadet *m.* **2.** *Mil: etc:* (*a*) élève *m* d'une école militaire; élève officier; (*b*) *Sch:* élève de la préparation militaire; **c. corps,** peloton *m* de préparation militaire; (*c*) *Austr:* jeune homme qui fait son apprentissage chez un grand éleveur, un grand cultivateur. **3.** *U.S: P:* souteneur *m.*
cadge[1] [kædʒ]. **1.** *v.i. A:* faire le petit commerce (dans les campagnes); colporter. **2.** *v.tr.* mendier, quémander; *v.i.* faire du tapage; **to c. sth. from s.o.,** taper qn de qch.
cadge[2], *s. F:* **he's always on the c.,** c'est un tapeur chronique.
cadger ['kædʒər], *s.* **1.** *A:* marchand ambulant (dans les campagnes); colporteur *m*, camelot *m.* **2.** mendiant, -ante, quémandeur, -euse; tapeur, -euse.
cadging ['kædʒiŋ], *s.* quémanderie *f*; tapage *m.*
cadi ['kɑːdi, 'keidi], *s.* cadi *m.*
Cadiz [kə'diz], *Pr.n. Geog:* Cadix.
Cadmean [kæd'miːən], *a. Gr.Myth:* cadméen; **C. victory,** victoire cadméenne.
cadmia ['kædmiə], *s. Metall: A:* cadmie *f.*
cadmiated ['kædmieitid], *a.* cadmié.
cadmic ['kædmik], *a. Ch:* cadmique.
cadmiferous [kæd'mifərəs], *a. Miner:* cadmifère.
cadmium ['kædmiəm], *s. Miner:* cadmium *m*; **c. blende, sulphide,** cadmium sulfuré, sulfure (naturel) de cadmium; greenockite *f*; **c. sulphate,** sulfate *m* de cadmium; **c. lithopone,** cadmopone *m*; **c. yellow,** jaune *m* de cadmium; **to coat with c.,** cadmier; **c. coating,** cadmiage *m.*
cadmium-coated ['kædmiəm'koutid], **cadmium-plated** ['kædmiəm'pleitid], *a.* cadmié.
cadmopone ['kædməpoun], *s. Ch:* cadmopone *m.*
cadogan [kə'dʌg(ə)n], *s. A.Hairdr:* catogan *m*, cadogan *m.*
cadrans ['kædrənz], *s. Lap:* cadrant *m.*
cadre ['kædr, 'kædər, 'kɑːdər], *s.* **1.** plan *m*, canevas *m* (d'un ouvrage); cadre *m.* **2.** (*a*) *Mil:* cadre; (*b*) *Pol:* (i) cadre, cellule *f*; (ii) cadre, membre *m* d'une cellule.
caduceus, *pl.* **-cei** [kə'djuːsiəs, -siai], *s. Gr.Ant:* caducée *m.*
caducity [kə'djuːsiti], *s.* **1.** (*a*) caducité *f*, sénilité *f*; (*b*) *Bot:* caducité. **2.** nature passagère, fugacité *f* (d'une mode, etc.).
caducous [kə'djuːkəs], *a.* **1.** caduc, *f* caduque. **2.** passager, fugace.
caecal ['siːk(ə)l], *a. Anat:* cæcal, -aux.
Caecidae ['siːsidiː, 'siːk-], *s.pl. Moll:* cæcidés *m.*
caeciform ['siːsifɔːm], *a. Anat:* cæciforme.
caecilian [siː'siliən], *s. Amph:* typhlonecte *m*, cécilie *f.*
Caeciliidae [siːsi'liːidiː], *s.pl. Amph:* cæciliides *m*, céciliides *m.*
caecotomy [siː'kɔtəmi], *s. Surg:* cæcotomie *f.*
caecum, *pl.* **-a** ['siːkəm, -ə], *s. Anat:* cæcum *m.*
Caen [kɑ̃], *Pr.n. Geog:* Caen; *Const:* **C. stone,** pierre *f* de Caen.
caenogenesis [siːnou'dʒenisis], *s. Biol:* cænogénèse *f*, cénogénèse *f.*
caenogenetic [siːnoudʒə'netik], *a. Biol:* cænogénétique.
Caesalpiniaceae [siːzælpiniː'eisiiː], *s.pl. Bot:* césalpiniacées *f*, césalpin(i)ées *f.*
Caesar ['siːzər], *Pr.n.m.* César; **Julius C.,** Jules César; **a man in your position must be like Caesar's wife,** un homme dans votre situation doit être à l'abri de tout soupçon; **to appeal to C.,** en appeler à l'autorité suprême.
Caesarea [siːzə'riə], *Pr.n. Geog: Hist:* Césarée *f*; **C. Philippi,** Césarée de Philippe.
Caesarean, Caesarian [si(ː)'zɛəriən], *a. & s.* **1.** *Hist: Pol:* Césarien, -ienne. **2.** *Obst:* **C. (operation, section),** (opération) césarienne *f*; hystérotomie abdominale.
Caesarism ['siːzərizm], *s. Hist: Pol:* césarisme *m.*
Caesarist ['siːzərist], *s. Hist: Pol:* césariste *m.*
caesaropapism ['siːzərou'peipizm], *s. Hist:* césaropapisme *m.*
caesious ['siːziəs], *a.* bleu *inv.* verdâtre, grisâtre.
caesium ['siːziəm], *s. Ch:* cæsium *m*, césium *m*; *Elcs:* **c. cell,** cellule *f* au cæsium; *Med:* **c. bomb,** bombe *f* au cæsium.
caespitose ['siːspitous], *a. Bot:* cespiteux.
caestus ['sestəs], *s.* = CESTUS.
caesura [si'zjuərə], *s. Pros:* césure *f.*
café ['kæfei, *P:* keif], *s.* = café-restaurant *m*, *pl.* cafés-restaurants; **transport c.** = restaurant *m* de routiers.
café-au-lait ['kæfiou'lei], *a.* (*colour*) café au lait *inv.*
cafeteria [kæfi'tiəriə], *s.* (*a*) cafétéria *f*, (restaurant *m*) libre-service *m*, *pl.* libres-services; (*b*) *Rail: U.S:* **c. car,** cafétéria, voiture-buffet *f*, *pl.* voitures-buffets.
caff [kæf], *s. P:* = CAFÉ.
caffeic [kæ'fiːik], *a. Ch:* caféique.
caffeine [kæ'fiːn, 'kæfiiːn], *s.* caféine *f*; **c.-free,** décaféiné.
caffeinism ['kæfiinizm], **caffeism** ['kæfiizm], *s. Med:* caféisme *m.*
caffeol ['kæfiəl], **caffeone** ['kæfioun], *s. Ch:* caféone *f.*
caffetannic ['kæfitænik], *a. Ch:* cafétannique.
caffetannin ['kæfitænin], *s. Ch:* acide *m* cafétannique.
caftan ['kæftæn], *s. Cost:* caf(e)tan *m.*
cafuso [kæ'fuːzou], *s. Anthr:* cafuso *m.*
cage[1] [keidʒ], *s.* **1.** cage *f* (à oiseaux, etc.); **c. bird,** oiseau *m* de volière, d'appartement; *Mil:* **prisoners' c.,** parc *m*, cage, à prisonniers (de guerre). **2.** (*a*) **(lift) c.,** (i) cage; (ii) cabine *f* (d'ascenseur); (*b*) *Min:* cage, benne *f*, d'extraction; **(shaft) c.,** cage (de puits). **3.** (*a*) *Anat:* **rib c.,** cage thoracique; (*b*) cage, ossature *f* (d'un bâtiment). **4.** *Mec.E:* cage, lanterne *f* (de roulement à billes); **valve c.,** corbeille *f* de soupape; *El:* **Faraday c.,** cage de Faraday; *W.Tel: etc:* **c. aerial, c. antenna,** antenne *f* en cage. **5.** *Sp: NAm:* (*a*) (*ice hockey, etc.*) but *m*; (*b*) (*basketball*) panier *m.*
cage[2], *v.tr.* (*a*) encager; mettre (un oiseau, etc.) en cage; (*b*) emprisonner, encager (qn); (*c*) *Min:* **to c. the trucks,** encager, clicher, les wagons; (*d*) *Sp: NAm:* (i) (*ice hockey, etc.*) marquer (un but); (ii) (*basketball*) faire (un panier).
cageful ['keidʒful], *s.* cagée *f.*
cageling [keidʒliŋ], *s.* oiseau *m* de volière, d'appartement.
cager ['keidʒər], *s. Min:* clicheur *m*; (*man or machine*) encageur *m*; moulineur *m.*
cagework ['keidʒwəːk], *s.* grillage *m*, grille *f.*
cagey ['keidʒi], *a. F:* prudent, circonspect, défiant; cauteleux, précautionneux; cachottier; **my father was c. about his age,** mon père cachait astucieusement son âge, ne voulait pas avouer son âge.
cagily ['keidʒili], *adv. F:* prudemment, avec circonspection; avec précaution; d'une manière cachottière.
caginess ['keidʒinis], *s. F:* prudence *f*, circonspection *f*; précaution(s) *f*(*pl*); cachotterie *f.*
cahinca [kə'hiŋkə], *s. Bot:* caïnça *m.*
cahoot [kə'huːt], *s. F:* **to be in cahoot(s) with s.o.,** être associé, être d'intelligence avec, qn; être de mèche, en cheville, avec qn; **to go cahoots with s.o.,** partager avec qn.
cahot [kə'hou], *s. Can:* traînée *f* de neige dure (sur une route); inégalités *fpl* (d'une route); *Aut:* **the cahots made the drive very bumpy,** on a été bien cahoté, secoué, à cause des inégalités de la route.
Caiaphas ['kaiəfæs], *Pr.n.m. B:* Caïphe.
cailcedra [kail'siːdrə], *s. Bot:* caïl-cédra *m*, cailcédrat *m.*
caiman ['keimən], *s. Rept:* caïman *m.*
Cain [kein], *Pr.n.m. B:* Caïn; *F:* **to raise C.,** (i) faire un

bruit, un fracas, de tous les diables; (ii) faire une scène monumentale.

cainca [kə'iŋkə], *s. Bot:* caïnça *m.*

ca'ing ['kɑːiŋ], *s. Z:* **c. whale,** globicéphale *m.*

cainozoic [kainou'zouik, kei-], *a. Geol:* cænozoïque.

caïque [kai'iːk], *s. Nau:* caïque *m.*

Cairene [kai'riːn], *Geog: (a) a.* cair(i)ote; *(b) s.* Cair(i)ote *mf.*

cairn ['kɛən], *s.* **1.** cairn *m,* tumulus *m,* de pierres; mont-joie *m, pl.* monts-joie; galgal *m, pl.* galgals; *A:* **to add a stone to s.o.'s c.,** apporter son tribut à la mémoire de qn. **2.** *(dog)* **c. (terrier),** terrier *m* cairn.

cairngorm [kɛən'gɔːm], *s. Lap:* pierre *f* de cairngorm; **smoky c.,** quartz enfumé.

Cairo ['kaiərou], *Pr.n. Geog:* le Caire.

caisson ['keis(ə)n], *s.* **1.** *Hyd.E:* caisson *m,* bâtardeau *m; Civ.E:* **Gow c., Boston c., c. pile,** pieu *m* caisson; puits *m;* **open c., cylinder c.,** tour *f* de cuvelage, tour à trousse coupante; *Med:* **c. disease,** mal *m* des caissons. **2.** *Nau:* bateau-porte *m* (de bassin de radoub), *pl.* bateaux-portes. **3.** *Arch:* caisson. **4.** *A.Mil:* caisson (à munitions).

caitiff ['keitif], *a. & s. A: & Poet:* misérable *(m);* lâche *(m).*

cajeput ['kædʒpʌt], *s. Bot:* cajeput *m; (tree)* cajeputier *m;* **oil of c.,** goménol *m,* cajeput.

cajole [kə'dʒoul], *v.tr.* cajoler; enjôler; *F:* embobiner, embobeliner; **to c. s.o. from, out of, a course of action,** faire changer d'avis à qn à force de cajoleries; **to c. s.o. into doing sth.,** persuader à qn de faire qch.; **to c. sth. out of s.o.,** obtenir qch. de qn à force de cajoleries; soutirer (de l'argent) à qn.

cajolement [kə'dʒoulmənt], *s.* = CAJOLERY.

cajoler [kə'dʒoulər], *s.* cajoleur, -euse.

cajolery [kə'dʒouləri], *s.* cajolerie(s) *f(pl);* enjôlement *m.*

cajoling[1] [kə'dʒouliŋ], *a.* cajoleur, -euse.

cajoling[2], *s.* = CAJOLERY.

cajolingly [kə'dʒouliŋli], *adv.* d'un ton cajoleur; d'une manière cajoleuse.

cake[1] [keik], *s.* **1.** *(a)* gâteau *m;* pâtisserie *f;* **(small) cakes,** pâtisserie légère, (petits) gâteaux, pâtisseries; **fruit c.,** gâteau aux fruits, cake *m;* **sponge c.,** (i) = gâteau de Savoie, gâteau mousseline; (ii) *(small)* = biscuit *m* de Savoie; madeleine *f;* **wedding c.,** grand gâteau de noce(s), de mariage (en pièce montée); *Lit:* **cakes and ale,** réjouissances *fpl; F:* **to take the c.,** remporter la palme; **to take the c. for sth.,** primer par qch.; *Iron:* **that takes the c.!** ça c'est le comble, le bouquet, le pompon! **it's a piece of c.,** c'est en or, c'est du gâteau, c'est donné; **to have one's slice of the c.,** partager le gâteau, avoir part au gâteau; **they're going, selling, like hot cakes,** ça se vend comme des petits pains; *Prov:* **you can't have your c. and eat it, eat your c. and have it,** on ne peut pas manger le gâteau à midi tout en le gardant pour le dîner; on ne peut pas avoir le drap et l'argent; *(b)* croquette *f;* boulette *f.* **2.** *(a)* pain *m* (de savon, etc.); tablette *f* (de chocolat, de couleur); **c. of salt,** salignon *m; (b) Husb:* **cattle c., cow c., press c.,** tourteau *m;* **oil c., linseed c.,** (i) tourteau de lin; (ii) tourte *f* (pour engrais); **c. of oats, peas, etc.,** biscuit *m* de fourrage; **bird c.,** colifichet *m.* **3.** masse *f,* croûte *f* (de glace, de sang coagulé); motte *f* (de terre, etc.); agglutination *f* (de houille, etc.); *El:* pastille *f* (d'accu); **c. of carbon,** aggloméré *m* de charbon.

cake[2]. **1.** *v.i. (a)* former une croûte; faire croûte; *(b) (of coal, etc.)* (se) coller; (se) prendre; s'agglutiner; s'agglomérer; *(of blood, etc.)* se cailler; *(of paste)* se concrétionner. **2.** *v.tr.* concréter (une poudre).

caked [keikt], *a.* **1.** *(a)* qui forme une croûte; *(b)* agglutiné. **2. c. with mud, with blood,** plaqué de boue, de sang. **3.** *Vet:* **c. udder,** mammite contagieuse (des vaches laitières).

cakehole ['keikhoul], *s. P:* bouche *f,* gueule *f;* **shut your c.!** ta gueule!

cakelet ['keiklit], *s.* petit gâteau.

cakeshop ['keikʃɔp], *s.* pâtisserie *f.*

cakewalk[1] ['keikwɔːk], *s. Danc: A:* cake-walk *m inv.*

cakewalk[2], *v.i. A:* danser le cake-walk.

cakewalker ['keikwɔːkər], *s. A:* danseur, -euse, de cake-walk.

cakile ['kækiliː], *s. Bot:* cakile *m,* caquillier *m.*

caking[1] ['keikiŋ], *a.* collant, agglutinant; **c. coal,** houille collante.

caking[2], *s.* **1.** agglomération *f,* agglutination *f* (de la houille); coagulation *f* (du sang); concrétion *f* (d'une pâte). **2.** couche *f* (de boue sèche, etc.); croûte *f* (de sang, etc.).

caky ['keiki], *a.* **c. substance,** substance agglutinante, collante, encroûtante.

cal [kæl], *s. Miner: Dial: (in Cornwall)* wolframite *f.*

calaba [kə'lɑːbə], *s. Bot:* **c. (tree),** calaba *m,* calophyllum *m;* **c. balsam,** baume *m* Marie, baume vert des Antilles.

calabar[1] ['kæləbɑːr], *s. Com: (fur)* petit-gris *m, pl.* petits-gris.

Calabar[2] [kælə'bɑːr], *Pr.n. Geog:* (la côte de) Calabar *m; Bot:* **c. bean,** fève *f* de Calabar; *(plant)* physostigma *m.*

calabash ['kæləbæʃ], *s.* **1. c. (gourd),** calebasse *f,* gourde *f;* **c. tree,** calebassier *m.* **2. c. (bottle),** calebasse, (cou)gourde *f.* **3. c. (pipe),** pipe *f* en calebasse, en forme de calebasse.

calaber ['kæləbər], *s.* = CALABAR[1].

calaboose [kælə'buːs], *s. F:* prison *f,* boîte *f,* cage *f.*

Calabria [kə'lɑːbriə], *Pr.n. Geog:* Calabre *f.*

Calabrian [kə'lɑːbriən], *Geog: (a) a.* calabrais; *(b) s.* Calabrais, -aise.

calade [kæ'lɑːd], *s. Equit:* calade *f.*

caladium [kə'leidiəm], *s. Bot:* caladium *m.*

calalu ['kæləluː], *s. Bot:* calalou *m.*

calamagrostis [kæləmæ'grɔstis], *s. Bot:* calamagrostis *m.*

calamanco [kælə'mæŋkou], *s. Tex: A:* calmande *f;* satin *m* de laine.

calamander [kælə'mændər], *s.* **c. (wood),** bois *m* de Coromandel; Calamandre *m.*

calamar ['kæləmɑːr], *s. Moll:* calmar *m;* encornet *m.*

Calamariaceae [kæləmæri'eisiiː], *s.pl. Paleont:* calamariées *f.*

calambac ['kæləmbæk], **calambour** ['kæləmbuər], *s.* calambar *m,* calambac *m,* calambour *m.*

calamiferous [kælə'mifərəs], *a. Bot:* calamifère.

calamine[1] ['kæləmain], *s. Miner:* calamine *f.*

calamine[2], *v.tr.* calaminer.

calamint ['kæləmint], *s. Bot:* calament *m,* calamintha *f.*

calamistrum, *pl.* **-tra** [kælə'mistrəm, -trə], *s. Arach:* calamistrum *m.*

Calamitaceae [kæləmai'teisiiː], *s.pl. Paleont:* calamariées *f.*

calamite[1] ['kæləmait], *s. Miner:* calamite *f.*

calamite[2], **calamites** [kælə'maitiz], *s. Paleont:* calamite *f,* calamites *f.*

calamitous [kə'læmitəs], *a.* calamiteux; désastreux.

calamitously [kə'læmitəsli], *adv.* calamiteusement, désastreusement.

calamity [kə'læmiti], *s.* **1.** calamité *f,* infortune *f,* malheur *m; U.S: F:* **a c. howler,** *f;* **a c. Jane,** un(e) pessimiste; un prophète de malheur; un(e) rabat-joie *inv.* **2.** désastre *m;* sinistre *m.*

calamondin [kælə'mɔndin], *s. Bot:* calamondin *m.*

calamus ['kæləməs], *s.* **1.** *(a) Bot:* calamus *m,* rotin *m,* rotang *m; (b) (reed pen)* calame *m.* **2.** *Bot:* **sweet c.,** jonc odorant ((i) lis *m* des marais; roseau *m* aromatique; (ii) schénanthe *m*). **3.** *Anat:* calamus.

calander [kə'lændər], *s. Orn:* calandre *f.*

calandra[1] [kə'lændrə], *s. Ent:* calandre *f.*

calandra[2], *s. Orn:* calandre *f.*

calandria [kæ'lændriə], *s. Atom.Ph:* vaisseau *m* à serpentin.

calandrinia [kælæn'driniə], *s. Bot:* calandrinia *f.*

calanque [kæ'læŋk], *s. Geog:* calanque *f,* calanche *f.*

calanthe [kə'lænθiː], *s. Bot:* calanthe *m.*

calanus ['kælənəs], *s. Crust:* calane *m,* calanus *m.*

calao [kə'lau], *s. Orn:* calao *m.*

calappa [kə'læpə], *s. Crust:* calappe *m.*

calash [kə'læʃ], *s.* **1.** *Veh: (a)* calèche *f; (b) (in Can:)* sorte de charrette anglaise. **2.** *(a) A:* capote *f* (de voiture); *(b) A.Cost: (woman's bonnet)* calèche, cabriolet *m.*

calathea [kælə'θiːə], *s. Bot:* calathea *m.*

calathos, calathus ['kæləθəs], *s. Gr.Ant:* calathos *m.*

calaverite [kælə'verait, kæ'lævərait], *s. Miner:* calavérite *f.*

calc- [kælk], *comb.fm.* calc-; calcaire.

calcaemia [kæl'siːmiə], *s. Med:* calcémie *f.*

calcaneal [kæl'keiniəl], **calcanean** [kæl'keiniən], *a. Anat:* calcanéen.

calcaneum [kæl'keiniəm], **calcaneus** [kæl'keiniəs], *s. Anat:* calcanéum *m.*

calcar[1] ['kælkɑːr], *s.* **1.** *Cer:* arche *f.* **2.** *Metall:* four *m* à recuire.

calcar[2], *s. Nat.Hist:* éperon *m; Ent:* calcar *m.*

calcarate(d) ['kælkəreit(id)], *a. Nat.Hist:* calcarifère.

calcareo-argillaceous [kæl'kɛəriouɑːdʒi'leiʃəs], *a. Miner:* calcaréo-argileux, -euse.

calcareous [kæl'kɛəriəs], *a. Geol: etc:* calcaire; **c. sinter,** travertin *m;* **c. spar,** calcite *f.*

calcariform [kæl'kærifɔːm], *a. Nat.Hist:* calcariforme; en forme d'éperon.

calcarine ['kælkərain], *a. Anat:* calcarin, calcarinien; **c. fissure,** scissure calcarine.

calced [kælst], *a. Ecc:* chaussé; (carmes) mitigés.

calceiform ['kælsiifɔːm], *a. Bot:* calcéiforme, calcéoliforme.

calceolaria [kælsiə'lɛəriə], *s. Bot:* calcéolaire *f.*

calceolate ['kælsiəleit], *a. Bot:* calcéiforme, calcéoliforme.

calcic ['kælsik], *a. Ch:* calcique.

calcicole ['kælsikoul], **calcicolous** [kælsi'kouləs], *a. Bot:* calcicole.

calcicosis [kælsi'kousis], *s. Med:* chalicose *f,* chalicosis *m.*

calciferol [kæl'sifərɔl], *s. Bio-Ch:* calciférol *m.*

calciferous [kæl'sifərəs], *a. Geol: etc:* calcifère.

calcific [kæl'sifik], *a.* calcifié.

calcification [kælsifi'keiʃ(ə)n], *s.* calcification *f* (des tissus organiques).

calcified ['kælsifaid], *a.* calcifié.

calcifuge ['kælsifjuːdʒ], **calcifugous** [kæl'sifjuːgəs], *a. Bot:* calcifuge.

calcify ['kælsifai], *Ch: etc:* **1.** *v.tr.* calcifier; *(a)* convertir en carbonate de chaux; *(b)* pétrifier (le bois, etc.). **2.** *v.i.* se calcifier.

calcimeter [kæl'simitər], *s. Ch:* calcimètre *m.*

calcimine[1] ['kælsimain], *s.* badigeon *m.*

calcimine[2], *v.tr. NAm:* badigeonner (un mur, etc.).

calcinable [kæl'sainəbl], *a.* calcinable; **not c.,** incalcinable.

calcination [kælsi'neiʃ(ə)n], *s. Ch: Ind:* calcination *f;* frittage *m;* cuisson *f;* grillage *m.*

calcine ['kælsain]. **1.** *v.tr. Ch: Ind:* calciner; fritter (des carbonates, etc.); cuire (le gypse, etc.); *Metall:* griller (le minerai). **2.** *v.i.* se calciner.

calciner [kæl'sainər], *s. Ind:* **1.** *(pers.)* calcinateur *m,* calcineur *m.* **2.** four *m* de, à, calcination; four à calciner.

calcining [kæl'sainiŋ], *s.* calcination *f;* **c. furnace,** four *m* de calcination, de grillage; four à fritter.

calcino [kæl'tʃiːnou], *s. Ser:* muscardine *f.*

calcinosis [kælsi'nousis], *s. Med:* calcinose *f.*

calcioferrite ['kælsiou'ferait], *s. Miner:* calcioferrite *f,* calcoferrite *f.*

calcipexy ['kælsi'peksi], *s. Med:* calcipexie *f.*

calciphile ['kælsifail], **calciphilous** [kæl'sifiləs], *a. Bot:* calciphile, calcicole.

calciphobe ['kælsifoub], **calciphobic** [ælsi'foubik], **calciphobous** [kæl'sifəbəs], *a. Bot:* calciphobe.

calcisponge ['kælsispʌnʒ], *s. Spong:* calcispongiaire *m.*

Calcispongiae [kælsi'spʌnʒiiː], *s.pl. Spong:* calcispongiaires *m.*

calcite ['kælsait], *s. Miner:* calcite *f;* spath *m* calcaire.

calcium ['kælsiəm], *s. Ch:* calcium *m;* **c. carbide,** **c. chloride,** carbure *m,* chlorure *m,* de calcium; **c. carbonate,** carbonate *m* de calcium; **c. oxide,** oxyde *m* de calcium; **c. fluoride,** fluorure *m* de calcium; **c. cyanamide,** cyanamide *f* calcique; **c. phosphate,** phosphate *m* de chaux.

calcosph(a)erite [kælkou'sfiərait], *s. Biol:* calcosphérite *f.*

calco-uranite [kælkou'juːrənait], *s. Miner:* calco-uranite *f.*

calc-schist ['kælk'ʃist], *s. Miner:* calcschiste *m.*

calc-sinter ['kælk'sintər], *s. Miner:* travertin *m* calcaire.

calc-spar ['kælk'spɑːr], *s. Miner:* calcite *f,* spath *m,* calcaire.

calc-tufa ['kælk'tuːfə], **calc-tuff** ['kælk'tuːf], *s. Miner:* tuf(f)eau *m,* tuf *m* calcaire.

calculability ['kælkjulə'biliti], *s.* calculabilité *f.*

calculable ['kælkjuləbl], *a.* calculable; chiffrable.

calculableness ['kælkjuləblnis], *s.* calculabilité *f.*

calculably ['kælkjuləbli], *adv.* à ce qu'on peut estimer.

calculagraph ['kælkjuləgræf], *s. Tp:* calculagraphe *f.*

calculate ['kælkjuleit], *v.tr. & i.* **1.** *(a)* calculer, évaluer; estimer (une distance); calculer, mesurer (ses paroles); faire le compte de (sa fortune); supputer (sa fortune); *abs.* faire un calcul, compter; *(b) esp. NAm:* **to c. on sth., on doing sth., on sth. happening,** compter sur qch., compter faire qch., compter que qch. arrivera; **to c. to do sth.,** compter faire qch. **2.** *NAm: F:* croire, supposer **(that,** que).

calculated ['kælkjuleitid], *a. (a)* **c. insolence,** insolence délibérée, calculée; **to arrive at a well c. moment,** arriver à un moment bien calculé; **c. risk,** risque calculé; *(b)* **c. to do sth.,** fait pour, propre à, faire qch.; **news c. to astonish him,** nouvelle *f* de nature à l'étonner, faite pour l'étonner; **words c. to reassure us,** paroles *f* propres à nous rassurer.

calculatedly ['kælkjuleitidli], *adv.* délibérément; d'une manière calculée.

calculating[1] ['kælkjuleitiŋ], *a. (a) (of pers.)* calculateur, -trice; réfléchi; égoïste; *(b)* **c. policy,** politique de calcul, intéressée.

calculating[2], *s.* calcul *m;* estimation *f;* **c. machine,** machine *f* à calculer.

calculation [kælkju'leiʃ(ə)n], *s.* calcul *m*; **to make a c.,** effectuer un calcul; **to upset s.o.'s calculations,** déjouer les calculs de qn; **to be out in one's calculations,** être loin de son compte.

calculative ['kælkjulətiv], *a.* = CALCULATING[1].

calculator ['kælkjuleitər], *s.* **1.** (*pers.*) calculateur, -trice; chiffreur, -euse. **2.** (*a*) machine *f* à calculer; calculatrice *f*; (*b*) *Mec.E: etc:* **speed c.,** calculateur de vitesse. **3.** barème *m*.

calculiform [kæl'kju:lifɔ:m], *a.* calculiforme.

calculous ['kælkjuləs], *a. Med:* calculeux.

calculus ['kælkjuləs], *s.* **1.** *Med:* (*pl.* **calculi** ['kælkjulai]) calcul (vésical, etc.); **urinary c.,** urolithe *m*. **2.** *Mth:* (*a*) **(infinitesimal) c.,** calcul infinitésimal; **differential c.,** calcul différentiel; **integral c.,** calcul intégral; **vector c.,** calcul vectoriel; **c. of variations,** calcul des variations; **c. of probability, probability c.,** calcul des probabilités; (*b*) manuel *m* de calcul infinitésimal.

Calcutta [kæl'kʌtə], *Pr.n. Geog:* Calcutta; **the C. Cup,** coupe *f* du championnat annuel de rugby entre l'Angleterre et l'Écosse; *A:* **C. sweepstake,** grand sweepstake sur la course du Derby à Epsom, organisé sous les auspices du *Calcutta Turf Club*.

caldera [kæl'deərə], *s. Geol:* caldeira *f*, caldère *f*.

caldron ['kɔ:ldrən], *s.* = CAULDRON.

calèche, caleche [kæ'leʃ], *s. Veh:* calèche *f*.

Caledonia [kæli'douniə], *Pr.n. Lit:* Calédonie *f*, Écosse *f*.

Caledonian [kæli'douniən]. **1.** *Lit:* (*a*) *a.* calédonien, écossais; (*b*) *s.* Calédonien, -ienne; Écossais, -aise. **2.** *Geog:* **the C. Canal,** le canal calédonien.

caledonite [kæ'ledənait], *s. Miner:* calédonite *f*.

calefacient [kæli'feiʃ(ə)nt], *a.* & *s. Med:* (agent) réchauffant (*m*).

calefaction [kæli'fækʃ(ə)n], *s.* caléfaction *f*.

calefactive [kæli'fæktiv], *a.* chauffant, qui chauffe; calorifiant, calorifique.

calefactor [kæli'fæktər], *a.* & *s.* calorifère (*m*).

calefactory [kæli'fækt(ə)ri]. **1.** *a.* calorifiant, calorifique. **2.** *s.* chauffoir *m* (de monastère).

calefy ['kælifai], *v.tr.* & *i.* chauffer; échauffer; s'échauffer.

calendar[1] ['kælindər], *s.* **1.** calendrier *m*; (*a*) **Julian, old-style, c.,** calendrier julien; le vieux calendrier; **Gregorian, new-style, c.,** calendrier grégorien; le nouveau calendrier; (*b*) **tear-off c., block c.,** calendrier bloc; calendrier éphéméride, à effeuiller; **perpetual c.,** calendrier perpétuel; **c. watch,** montre *f* à quantièmes. **2.** (*a*) *Ecc:* calendrier (des saints); (*b*) annuaire *m* (d'une université, d'une institution, etc.); (*c*) *Jur:* liste *f* des accusés, des causes au criminel; rôle *m* des causes; rôle des assises; (*d*) *U.S:* ordre *m* du jour (du Congrès).

calendar[2], *v.tr.* **1.** inscrire (un nom, etc.) sur un calendrier, sur une liste. **2.** classer, cataloguer, mettre sur fiches (des documents, etc.).

calender[1] ['kælindər], *s.* **1.** *Tex: etc:* calandre *f*. **2.** *Ind:* laminoir *m*.

calender[2], *v.tr.* **1.** calandrer, cylindrer (des étoffes, le papier). **2.** laminer.

calend(e)rer ['kælind(ə)rər], *s.* (*pers.*) calandreur, -euse; lamineur *m*.

calendering ['kælindriŋ], *s.* calandrage *m*; laminage *m*; **c. machine,** calandre *f*; laminoir *m*.

calendra [kə'lendrə], *s. Ent:* calandre *f*.

calends ['kælindz, 'kei-], *s.pl. Rom.Ant:* calendes *f*; **on, at, the Greek c.,** aux calendes grecques; jamais.

calendula [kæ'lendjulə], *s. Bot:* calendule *f*.

calenture ['kæləntjuər], *s. Med:* *A:* calenture *f*; fièvre *f*.

calf[1], *pl.* **calves** [kɑ:f, kɑ:vz], *s.* **1.** (*a*) veau *m*; **cow in, with c.,** vache pleine; *Cu:* **calf's head,** tête *f* de veau; *Cu:* **calf's, calves', foot jelly,** gelée *f* de pied de veau; *Anat:* **calf's teeth,** dents *f* de lait; *attrib.* **c. love,** amours enfantines; les premières amours; (*b*) *Leath:* veau; vachette *f*; *Bookb:* **c. binding,** reliure *f* en veau; **c.-bound,** relié en veau; **c. shoes,** chaussures *f* en veau mégis; **tobacco pouch in c.,** blague *f* en vachette. **2.** (*a*) petit *m* de certains animaux; **buffalo c.,** bufflctin *m*; **whale c.,** baleineau *m*; **elephant c.,** éléphanteau *m*; **seal c.,** petit du phoque; **roe c.,** faon *m* (de chevreuil); **hind c.,** faon *m* femelle; (*b*) **sea c.,** phoque commun; veau marin; (*c*) glaçon (détaché d'un iceberg); veau. **3.** *F:* (*a*) sot *m*, lourdaud *m*, veau; (*b*) blanc-bec *m*, *pl.* blancs-becs.

calf[2], *pl.* **calves,** *s.* mollet *m* (de la jambe); gras *m* de la jambe; **c.-length boots,** demi-bottes *f*; **c.-length trousers,** (pantalon *m*) corsaire (*m*).

calfdozer ['kɑ:fdouzər], *s. F:* petit bulldozer.

calfskin ['kɑ:fskin], *s.* (cuir *m* de) veau *m*.

calibrate ['kælibreit], *v.tr.* étalonner (un compteur, etc.); calibrer (un tube); graduer (un thermomètre); tarer (un ressort), faire la tare d'(un ressort); **to c. a gun,** vérifier le calibre d'un canon.

calibrating ['kælibreitiŋ], *s.* = CALIBRATION; *attrib.* **c. device,** appareil *m* d'étalonnage; **c. electrometer,** électromètre *m* étalon; *Cmptr:* **c. tape,** bande *f* d'étalonnage.

calibration [kæli'breiʃ(ə)n], *s.* étalonnage *m*; calibrage *m* (d'un tube); tarage *m* (d'un ressort); *El:* **c. condenser,** condensateur *m* étalon; *Mil:* **c. firing,** tir *m* d'accord.

calibrator ['kælibreitər], *s.* appareil *m* étalon, calibreur *m*.

calibre ['kælibər], *s.* (*a*) calibre *m*, alésage *m* (d'un canon, d'un tube); *Artil:* **gun of large c.,** pièce *f* de gros calibre; **small, light, c.,** petit calibre; (*b*) calibre (d'une personne, de l'entendement); **if we could get a man of your c.,** si nous pouvions trouver un homme de votre calibre, de votre envergure.

-calibred ['kælibəd], *a.* **small-c., large-c.,** de petit, gros, calibre.

caliceal [kæli'si:l], *a.* = CALYCEAL.

caliche [kə'li:tʃi:], *s.* (*a*) *Miner:* caliche *m*; (*b*) *Geol:* caliche, croûte *f* calcaire.

caliciform [kə'lisifɔ:m], *a.* caliciforme.

calicle ['kælikl], *s. Bot:* calicule *m*.

calico ['kælikou]. **1.** *s. Tex:* (*a*) calicot *m*; *Com:* blanc *m* de coton; **fine c.,** madapolam *m*; **glazed c.,** treillis *m*; **printed c.,** calicot imprimé; indienne *f*; **c. printer,** imprimeur *m* sur calicot; imprimeur d'indienne; rouennier *m*; **c. printing,** (i) (*trade*) indiennerie *f*; (ii) (*process*) indiennage *m*; (*b*) *NAm:* calicot imprimé; indienne; (*c*) *Dressm:* percaline *f* (pour doublures). **2.** *a.* (*a*) de calicot; **c. weave,** armure *f* toile; (*b*) *NAm:* varié, bigarré; (*of material*) à pois; (*c*) *Bot:* **c. bush, c. flower, c. tree,** kalmie *f* à larges feuilles; **c. wood,** halesia *m*, halésie *f*.

calicular [kə'likjulər], *a. Bot:* caliculaire.

caliculate [kə'likjuleit], *a.* caliculé.

caliculus, *pl.* **-i** [kə'likjuləs, -ai], *s. Bot:* calicule *m*.

California [kæli'fɔ:niə], *Pr.n.* (*a*) *Geog:* Californie *f*; (*b*) *attrib. Bot:* **C. lilac,** céanothe *m*, céanothus *m*; **C. poppy,** (i) eschscholtzie *f*; (ii) platystémon *m*.

Californian [kæli'fɔ:niən]. **1.** *a.* californien; **C. poppy,** (i) eschscholtzie *f*; (ii) platystémon *m*. **2.** *s.* Californien, -ienne.

californium [kæli'fɔ:niəm], *s. Ch:* californium *m*.

caliginous [kə'lidʒinəs], *a.* caligineux; ténébreux.

caligo [kə'li:gou, -'laigou], *s. Ent:* caligo *m*.

calin [kalɛ̃], *s. Metall:* calin *m*.

calipash ['kælipæʃ], *s. Cu:* partie gélatineuse de la tortue au-dessous de la carapace.

calipee ['kælipi:], *s. Cu:* partie gélatineuse du ventre de la tortue.

caliper[1,2] ['kælipər], *s.* & *v.* = CALLIPER[1,2].

caliph ['keilif], *s.* calife *m*.

caliphate ['keilifeit], *s.* califat *m*.

calippic [kæ'lipik], *a. Astr:* callipique.

calisthenics [kælis'θeniks], *s.pl.* (*usu. with sg. const.*) callisthénie *f*.

calix, *pl.* **-ices** ['keiliks, -isi:z], *s.* (*a*) *Anat:* calice *m* (coiffant chaque lobe de rein); (*b*) *Ecc:* calice.

Calixtus [kə'likstəs], *Pr.n.m.* Calixte.

calk[1] [kɔ:k], *s.* **1.** *Farr:* crampon *m* (de fer à cheval). **2.** *Bootm:* crampon à glace.

calk[2], *v.tr.* **1.** *Farr:* ferrer (un cheval) à glace. **2.** *Bootm:* garnir (les talons, etc.) de crampons à glace.

calk[3] [kælk, kɔ:k], *v.tr. Art: etc:* décalquer.

calk[4] [kɔ:k], *v.* **calker** ['kɔ:kər], *s.* = CAULK, CAULKER.

calkin ['kælkin, 'kɔ:kin], *s. Farr:* **1.** crampon *m*, éponge *f* (de fer à cheval). **2.** clou *m* à glace; grappe *f*.

calking[1] ['kælkiŋ, 'kɔ:kiŋ], *s.* ferrage *m* à glace.

calking[2], *s.* décalque *m*, décalquage *m*.

call[1] [kɔ:l], *s.* **1.** (*a*) (*shout*) appel *m*, cri *m*; cri d'appel; (*b*) (i) cri (d'un oiseau); (ii) (*instrument*) **(bird) c.,** pipeau *m*, appeau *m*. **2.** (*summons*) (*a*) appel; **to come at, answer, s.o.'s c.,** venir, répondre, à l'appel de qn; (*of doctor*) **on c.,** de garde; **to be within c.,** être à portée de voix; **to give s.o. a c.,** (i) appeler qn; (ii) *Tp:* see 2(*e*); (iii) réveiller qn; **to answer the c. of duty,** se rendre à son devoir; **the c. of nature, of conscience,** la voix de la nature, de la conscience; **the c. of spring,** l'appel du printemps; **the c. of justice,** la voix impérieuse de la justice; **the c. of ambition,** l'appel de l'ambition; **the c. of hunger,** les sollicitations *f* de la faim; **you have no c. to do so,** vous n'avez aucune raison de le faire, rien ne vous oblige à le faire; **there's no c. to be afraid,** il n'y a aucune raison pour avoir peur; *F:* **to have a close c.,** l'échapper belle; **it was a close c.,** il était moins cinq; *attrib.* **c. button,** bouton *m*, clef *f*, d'appel; *U.S:* **c. number, c. slip,** fiche *f* de bibliothèque; *Cin: T.V:* **c. sheet,** fiche de tournage; (*b*) sonnerie *f* (de clairon); batterie *f* (de tambour); *Nau:* coup *m* de sifflet; **bugle c., trumpet c.,** coup, appel, de clairon, de trompette; **the regimental c.,** le refrain du régiment; (*c*) **(roll) c.,** appel nominal; (*d*) **he felt a c. (to the ministry),** il se sentait la vocation; il voulait entrer dans l'Église; (*e*) *Tp:* **telephone c.,** (i) appel téléphonique; coup de téléphone; (ii) (*apparatus*) appel phonique; **local c.,** communication urbaine, locale; **to give s.o. a c.,** téléphoner à qn; **I have a c. for you,** on vous parle; **personal c.,** *esp. U.S:* **person to person c.,** appel avec préavis, de personne à personne; **advise duration and charge c., A.D.C. c.,** appel avec indication de durée, avec I.D.; *U.S:* **to make a collect c.,** demander une communication en, avec, P.C.V.; **who answered, took, the c.?** qui a répondu au téléphone? **to give in a c.,** demander une communication; **to put a c. through,** donner la communication; **to pay for the c.,** payer la communication; *attrib.* **c. office,** bureau *m* téléphonique; *W.Tel: Navy:* **c. letters, c. sign,** lettres *fpl*, indicatif *m*, d'appel; *Tg:* **c. key,** touche *f* d'appel; (*f*) invitation *f*; *Ecc:* **c. to a church,** invitation à remplir le pastorat d'une église (protestante); (*g*) *Cards:* (*at bridge*) appel; (*at solo whist, boston*) demande *f*; **c. for trumps,** invite *f* d'atout; **a c. of three diamonds,** une annonce de trois carreaux; **to leave the c. to one's partner,** passer parole; (*h*) *Th:* **(curtain) c.,** rappel *m* (d'un acteur); **she was presented with a bouquet when she took her c.,** on lui offrit un bouquet lorsqu'elle parut devant le rideau. **3.** (*visit*) visite *f*; **to pay, make, a c. on s.o.,** faire (une) visite à qn; **to pay a formal c. on s.o.,** aller présenter ses devoirs à qn; **official c.,** visite officielle; **to pay calls,** faire des visites; **to return s.o.'s c.,** rendre la visite de qn; *F:* **to pay a c.,** aller faire pipi, aller faire une petite commission; *Com:* **c. of a traveller,** passage *m* d'un représentant; *Nau:* **port of c., place of c.,** port *m* d'escale, de relâche. **4.** (*a*) (*claim*) demande *f* (d'argent); *Fin:* appel de fonds, de versement; **c. letter,** avis *m* d'appel de fonds; **payable at c.,** remboursable sur demande, à présentation, à vue; **money at, on, c., c. money,** prêts *mpl* au jour le jour; argent *m* à court terme; **yet another c. on my purse!** encore de l'argent à trouver! **I have too many calls on my time,** trop de choses accaparent mon temps; (*b*) *St.Exch:* option *f* d'achat; prime *f*; marché *m* à prime; **c. on a hundred shares,** option de cent actions; **c. of more,** faculté *f* du double; achat *m* d'encore autant à prime; **c. of twice more,** achat du double à prime.

call[2], *v.*

I. *v.tr.* & *i.* **1.** *v.tr.* (*a*) (i) appeler (qn); crier (qch.); *abs.* **who is calling?** qui est-ce qui appelle? **he called (out),** il a appelé; *A:* **the watch called the hour,** la ronde de nuit cria l'heure, annonça l'heure; **to c. (out) "fire,"** crier au feu; **to c. the banns,** publier les bans; **to c. (over) (the names),** faire l'appel; **to c. a halt,** (*α*) crier halte; (*β*) faire halte; **it is time to c. a halt,** il est temps de s'arrêter; **to c. the roll,** faire l'appel; *W.Tel:* **London calling,** ici Londres; *Nau:* **to c. the soundings,** crier, chanter, le fond; (ii) **I called (out) to him to stop,** je lui ai crié de s'arrêter; (*b*) (i) (*summon*) appeler (qn); héler (un taxi); convoquer (une assemblée); appeler (les pompiers, un ascenseur); *Jur:* appeler (une cause); *Th:* rappeler (un acteur); **to c. a cab from the rank,** faire avancer un taxi; **to c. (in) the doctor,** faire venir, appeler, le médecin; **c. him over,** demandez-lui de venir; **he called us all together,** il nous a rassemblés tous; **to be called to the throne,** être appelé au trône; *B:* **many are called but few are chosen,** il y a beaucoup d'appelés mais peu d'élus; **duty calls (me),** le devoir m'appelle; **to c. s.o. to order,** rappeler qn (*α*) à l'ordre, (*β*) à la question; *Mil:* **to c. to arms,** battre la générale; **to c. into play all one's powers,** faire appel à, exercer, toutes ses facultés; **to c. s.o.'s attention to sth.,** attirer l'attention de qn sur qch.; **to c. s.o.'s attention away from sth.,** distraire l'attention de qn; **to c. s.o. aside,** prendre, tirer, qn à part; **to be called away,** être appelé dehors; **I am called away on business,** je suis obligé de m'absenter pour affaires; (ii) *Tp:* téléphoner à (qn), appeler (qn); **the called party, person,** le demandé; **who's calling, please?** c'est de la part de qui? *NAm:* **to c. collect,** demander une communication en, avec, P.C.V.; (iii) *Ven:* frouer; (iv) **c. me at six o'clock,** réveillez-moi à six heures; (v) *Jur:* **to c. the jury,** tirer le jury au sort; (*c*) (*name*) appeler; **he is called Martin,** il s'appelle Martin; on l'appelle Martin; **to c. s.o. after s.o.,** donner le nom de qn à qn; **he is called after his uncle,** il porte le nom de son oncle; **to c. oneself a colonel,** se qualifier de colonel; s'attribuer le titre de colonel; **he calls himself a philosopher,** il se croit philosophe; **I am too young to be called "mademoiselle,"** je suis trop jeune pour qu'on me donne du "mademoiselle"; **c. me Sophie, c. me by my Christian, first, name,** appelez-moi Sophie, appelez-moi par mon prénom; **to c. s.o. names,** injurier, invectiver, qn; **to c. s.o. a liar, a child,** traiter, qualifier, qn de menteur, d'enfant; *F:* **to c. s.o. everything under the sun,** adjectiver qn de la belle façon, traiter qn de tous les noms; **we'll c. it three francs,** (i) mettons trois francs; (ii) va pour trois francs; **I c. that a dirty trick,** voilà ce que j'appelle un sale tour; **that's what I c. a real meal, that's what I c. a meal,** ça, c'est un vrai repas; **you c. that dancing?** vous appelez cela danser? *F:* **(you) c. yourself a soldier!** tu te crois soldat! (*d*) *Cards:* appeler, déclarer (deux carreaux, etc.); **to c. spades,** déclarer pique; *abs.* **to c.,** (i) appeler (l'atout); (ii) (*at poker*) forcer l'adversaire à déclarer son jeu; (*e*) **to c. a strike,** décréter, ordonner, une grève; (*f*) *NAm:* arrêter (un match à cause de la pluie, etc.). **2.** *v.i.* (*a*) **to c. (at s.o.'s house, on s.o.),** (i) faire une visite (chez qn); (ii) passer, se rendre, se présenter (chez qn); **has anyone called?** est-il venu quelqu'un? **to be asked to c.,** recevoir une invitation à passer chez qn, à faire visite à qn; *Adm:* recevoir une convocation; **I called to see you,** (*α*) je viens pour vous voir; (*β*) j'étais venu dans l'espoir de vous voir; **I only called to see how you were,** je ne fais que passer pour demander de vos nouvelles; **I must c. at Johnson's, at the grocer's,** il faut que je passe chez Johnson, chez l'épicier; **to c. again,** repasser (**on,** chez); **the gas man said he would c. again on Thursday,** l'employé du gaz a dit qu'il repasserait, reviendrait, jeudi; (*b*) **the train calls at every station,** le train s'arrête, fait halte, à toutes les gares; *Nau:* (*of ship*) **to c. at a port,** faire escale, relâcher, toucher, à un port; **places not called at by a shipping line,** points *m* qu'une compagnie ne dessert pas.

II. (*compound verbs*) **1. call back;** (*a*) *v.tr.* rappeler (qn); (*b*) rappeler (un produit déjà vendu pour mise au point); (*c*) *Tp:* **c. me back later,** rappelez-moi plus tard; (*d*) *v.i.* **I shall c. back for it,** je repasserai le prendre.

2. call down, *v.tr.* (*a*) faire descendre (qn); inviter (qn) à descendre; (*b*) **to c. down curses on s.o.'s head,** appeler des malédictions sur la tête de qn; (*c*) *NAm: F:* (i) injurier, dire des injures à (qn); (ii) reprendre (qn); laver la tête à (qn).

3. call for, *v.ind.tr.* (*a*) appeler, faire venir (qn); faire apporter (qch.); commander (une consommation, etc.); **to c. loudly for s.o.,** appeler qn à grands cris; **to c. for help,** crier au secours; appeler à l'aide; (*b*) venir prendre, venir chercher (qn, qch.); **I will c. for you at nine,** je viendrai vous chercher, je passerai vous prendre, à neuf heures; **to c. for sth. (at s.o.'s house),** passer prendre qch. (chez qn); **to be (left till) called for,** à remettre au messager; à laisser jusqu'à ce qu'on vienne le chercher; *Post:* pour attendre l'arrivée; (*on envelope*) poste restante; colis restant; *Rail:* en gare; (*c*) **to c. for an explanation, for an apology,** demander, exiger, une explication, des excuses; **to c. for volunteers,** demander des hommes de bonne volonté; **the audience called for the author,** le public réclama l'auteur; *Cards:* **to c. for trumps,** inviter l'atout; (*d*) demander, comporter, réclamer, exiger (l'attention, des réformes); **expansion that calls for extra staff,** expansion *f* qui exige du personnel supplémentaire; **plant that calls for continual care,** plante *f* qui réclame, requiert, des soins continuels; **situation that calls for tactful handling,** situation qui demande à être maniée avec tact; **this problem calls for an immediate solution,** ce problème appelle une solution immédiate; **process that calls for very high temperatures,** procédé *m* qui impose des températures très élevées; *F:* **this calls for a celebration, a drink!** il faut fêter, arroser, ça!

4. call forth, *v.tr.esp. Lit:* (*a*) (i) produire, faire naître (des protestations, etc.); évoquer, faire surgir (un souvenir); exciter (l'admiration); (ii) faire appel à (tout son courage); mettre en jeu (tous ses talents); (iii) évoquer (un esprit); (*b*) appeler, faire sortir (qn).

5. call in, *v.tr.* (*a*) faire entrer (qn); demander à (qn) d'entrer; **to c. the children in,** faire rentrer les enfants; (*b*) (i) retirer (une monnaie, un livre) de la circulation; (ii) **to c. in one's money,** faire rentrer ses fonds; (*c*) **to c. in a specialist,** faire appel, avoir recours, à un spécialiste.

6. call off; (*a*) *v.tr.* (i) rappeler (un chien); *Ven:* rompre (les chiens); (ii) **to c. off a strike,** décommander une grève; rapporter, révoquer, annuler, un ordre de grève; **to c. off a deal,** rompre, annuler, un marché; **to c. off an engagement,** (*α*) s'excuser de ne pouvoir tenir une promesse; (*β*) rompre ses fiançailles; (*b*) *v.i.* se dédire; revenir sur sa parole.

7. call on, *v.tr.* (*a*) invoquer (le nom de Dieu); **to c. on the Lord,** en appeler au Seigneur; (*b*) **to c. on s.o. for sth.,** demander qch. à qn; réclamer qch. à qn; (*c*) **to c. on s.o. to do sth.,** sommer, requérir, qn de faire qch., mettre qn en demeure de faire qch.; appeler qn à faire qch.; **to c. on s.o.'s help,** faire appel à qn, à l'aide de qn; **to c. on s.o. to give assistance,** requérir qn (de venir en aide); **to c. on s.o. to keep his promise,** mettre qn en demeure de tenir sa promesse; **to c. on s.o. to apologize,** exiger de qn qu'il fasse des excuses; **to c. on s.o. to tell the truth,** sommer qn de dire la vérité; **I had to c. on all my strength,** j'ai dû faire appel à toute ma force; **I feel called on to warn you that . . .,** je me sens dans l'obligation de vous avertir que . . .; **I now c. on Mr S.,** la parole est à M. S.; **I will c. on Mr S. to say grace,** je demanderai à M. S. de dire le bénédicité; (*d*) faire visite chez (qn); rendre visite à (qn); aller, passer, se rendre, chez (qn); aller voir (qn); **to c. on s.o. again,** repasser chez qn.

8. call out; (*a*) *v.tr.* (i) faire sortir (qn); prier (qn) de sortir; **to c. out the army,** faire intervenir la force armée; **to c. out the firemen,** appeler les pompiers; **to c. out workers,** faire mettre en grève, donner l'ordre de grève à, des ouvriers; (ii) provoquer (qn) en duel; appeler (qn) sur le terrain; (iii) = CALL UP (*d*) (i); (*b*) *v.i.* (i) appeler; appeler au secours; (ii) **to c. out for sth.,** appeler pour demander qch.

9. call up, *v.tr.* (*a*) faire monter (qn); (*b*) (i) évoquer (une idée, un souvenir); (ii) **to c. up a spirit, the souls of the dead,** évoquer un esprit, les âmes des morts; (*c*) appeler (qn) au téléphone; attaquer (le central); (*d*) (i) *Mil: Navy:* mobiliser (un réserviste); appeler (un réserviste) sous les drapeaux, sous les armes; **to be called up,** être appelé au service; (ii) *Fin:* **called-up capital,** capital appelé.

10. call upon, *v.i. usu. Lit: or O:* = CALL ON.

calla ['kælə], *s. Bot:* (*a*) calla *f*, calle *f*; (*b*) **c. lily, golden c., pink c.,** (espèces de) zantedeschia *m*.

call box ['kɔ:lbɔks], *s.* cabine *f* (téléphonique).

callboy ['kɔ:lbɔi], *s. Th: etc:* avertisseur *m*.

call day ['kɔ:l'dei], *s.* jour *m* de réception des nouveaux étudiants aux *Inns of Court* (à Londres).

calldown ['kɔ:ldaun], *s. U.S: F:* semonce *f*.

caller[1] ['kɔ:lər], *s.* **1.** (*a*) personne *f* qui appelle; (*b*) visiteur, -euse; **to be a frequent c. at s.o.'s house,** fréquenter chez qn; **the c. who has just left is the editor,** la visite qui vient de sortir est le rédacteur. **2. c. (-up),** (*a*) éveilleur, -euse; (*b*) *Tp:* demandeur, -euse (de la communication).

caller[2] ['kælər], *a. Scot:* (air, etc.) frais, *f* fraîche; pur; (hareng) frais.

call girl ['kɔ:lgə:l], *s.* prostituée *f* (sur rendez-vous téléphonique), call-girl *f*.

calli- ['kæli], *pref.* calli-.

calliactis [kæli'æktis], *s. Cœl:* sagartia *f*, sagartiade *f*.

callianassa [kæliə'næsə], *s. Crust:* callianasse *f*.

callicarpa [kæli'kɑ:pə], *s. Bot:* callicarpa *m*.

callicebus [kæli'si:bəs], *s. Z:* callicèbe *m*.

Callicrates [kə'likrəti:z], *Pr.n.m. Gr.Hist:* Callicrate.

Callidulidae [kæli'dju:lidi:], *s.pl. Ent:* callidulides *m*.

calligram, -me ['kæligræm], *s.* calligramme *m*.

calligraph[1] ['kæligræf], *s.* beau spécimen de calligraphie; modèle *m* d'écriture.

calligraph[2], *v.tr.* calligraphier (une lettre, etc.).

calligrapher [kə'ligrəfər], *s.* calligraphe *m*.

calligraphic [kæli'græfik], *a.* calligraphique.

calligraphist [kə'ligrəfist], *s.* calligraphe *m*.

calligraphy [kə'ligrəfi], *s.* calligraphie *f*.

Callimorphidae [kæli'mɔ:fidi:], *s.pl. Ent:* callimorphides *m*.

calling ['kɔ:liŋ], *s.* **1.** (*a*) appel *m*, cri(s) *m(pl)*; (*b*) **c. (together),** convocation *f* (d'une assemblée, etc.); (*c*) *Jur:* **c. of the jury,** tirage *m* au sort du jury. **2.** visite *f* (**on,** à); **c. hours,** heures *f* de visite. **3.** (*a*) vocation *f*; **I feel no c. for the Church,** je ne me sens pas la vocation de la prêtrise; (*b*) vocation, profession *f*, métier *m*. **4. c. in,** retrait *m* (de monnaies).

calling off ['kɔ:liŋ'ɔf], *s.* **1.** rappel *m* (des chiens). **2. c. off of a strike,** retrait *m* d'un ordre de grève; **c. off of a deal,** rupture *f* d'un marché.

calling up ['kɔ:liŋ'ʌp], *s.* **1.** (*a*) évocation *f* (d'une idée, d'un souvenir); (*b*) évocation (d'un esprit, des âmes des morts). **2.** appel *m* (de qn) au téléphone. **3.** appel sous les drapeaux, sous les armes.

callionymus [kæli'ɔniməs], *s. Ich:* callionyme *m*, dragonnet *m*.

Calliope [kə'laiəpi], *Pr.n.f. Astr: Gr.Myth:* Calliope.

calliopsis [kæli'ɔpsis], *s. Bot:* coréopsis *m*.

calliper[1] ['kælipər], *s.* **1. c. compasses, (pair of) callipers,** compas *m* de calibre, à calibrer; maître-à-danser *m, pl.* maîtres-à-danser; **inside callipers,** compas d'intérieur; compas à calibrer; **outside callipers,** compas d'épaisseur; **figure-of-eight c., hour-glass c., double c.,** huit-de-chiffre(s) *m, pl.* huits-de-chiffres; **callipers with regulating screw,** compas de précision; **micrometer callipers,** calibre *m* à vis micrométrique; palmer *m*; **vernier c.,** jauge *f* micrométrique; **c. square,** pied *m* à coulisse, compas à coulisse; **c. gauge,** calibre de précision; calibre mâchoire; calibre, jauge, à coulisse; **sliding c., slide c.,** calibre à coulisse. **2.** *Med:* armature *f* orthopédique; *Surg:* **c. (splint),** attelle-étrier *f, pl.* attelles-étriers.

calliper[2], *v.tr.* calibrer (un tube); mesurer (au compas à coulisse) le diamètre (d'un arbre, etc.).

calliphora [kæ'lifərə], *s. Ent:* calliphore *m*.

Calliphoridae [kæli'fɔ:ridi:], *s.pl. Ent:* calliphoridés *m*.

callippic [kæ'lipik], *a. Astr:* callipique.

Callipygean, -gian [kæli'pidʒiən], *a.* **the C. Venus,** la Vénus Callipyge.

callistemon [kæli'sti:mən], *s. Bot:* callistémon *m*.

Callisthenes [kæ'lisθəni:z], *Pr.n.m. Gr.Hist:* Callisthène.

callisthenic [kælis'θenik], *a.* callisthénique.

callisthenics [kælis'θeniks], *s.pl.* (*usu. with sg. const.*) callisthénie *f*.

Callithricidae [kæli'θrisidi:], *s.pl. Z:* callithricidés *m*.

callithrix ['kæliθriks], *s. Z:* callithrix *m*, callithrique *m*.

Callitrichaceae [kælitri'keisii:], *s.pl. Bot:* callitrich(ac)ées *f*, callitrichinées *f*.

callitriche [kə'litriki(:)], *s. Bot:* callitriche *m*.

callitris ['kælitris], *s. Bot:* callitris *m*.

callor(h)ynchus [kælou'riŋkəs], *s. Ich:* callorhynque *m*.

callose[1] [kæ'lous], *a. Nat.Hist:* calleux.

callose[2], *s. Bot:* callose *f*.

callosity [kæ'lɔsiti], *s.* callosité *f*, durillon *m*; cal *m, pl.* cals; cornes cutanées.

callosum [kæ'lousəm], *a. & s. Anat:* **(corpus) c.,** corps calleux.

callous ['kæləs], *a.* **1.** (*of skin, feet, hands*) calleux. **2.** (homme, cœur) insensible, peu sensible, endurci; (homme) dur, sans cœur; **to grow c.,** se racornir; **to become c. to the sufferings of others,** devenir insensible, s'endurcir, aux souffrances d'autrui.

calloused ['kæləst, kæ'louzd], *a.* **c. hands,** mains calleuses.

callously ['kæləsli], *adv.* d'une manière insensible; sans pitié, sans cœur.

callousness ['kæləsnis], *s.* insensibilité *f* (**to,** à); dureté *f*; manque *m* de cœur, de pitié.

Callovian [kə'louviən], *a. & s. Geol:* callovien (*m*).

callow ['kælou]. **1.** *a.* (*a*) (*of fledgling*) sans plumes; **c. youth,** la verte jeunesse; (*b*) **a c. youth,** un jeune homme imberbe, sans expérience; un blanc-bec, *pl.* blancs-becs. **2.** *s.* (*in Ireland*) bas-fond *m, pl.* bas-fonds; fondrière *f*.

callowness ['kælounis], *s.* jeunesse *f*; manque *m* de maturité.

calluna [kæ'lju:nə], *s. Bot:* calluna *f or m*, callune *f*.

call-up ['kɔ:lʌp], *s. Mil: etc:* appel *m* sous les drapeaux; **longer c.-up,** augmentation *f* du temps de service; **c.-up papers,** fascicule *m* de mobilisation.

callus ['kæləs], *s.* **1.** calus *m*, callosité *f*. **2.** *Bot: Surg:* cal *m, pl.* cals; calus.

calm[1] [kɑ:m], *s.* calme *m*; tranquillité *f*, sérénité *f* (d'esprit); **the c. of the woods,** la paix des bois; **period of c.,** accalmie *f*; *Nau:* **c. before a storm,** bonace *f*; **the calms of the tropics,** les calmes des tropiques; **dead, flat, c.,** calme plat; *Prov:* **after a storm comes a c.,** après la pluie, le beau temps.

calm[2], *a.* calme, tranquille; **c. disposition,** esprit rassis, posé; **c. retreat,** retraite *f* paisible; **on a c. day,** par une journée sans vent; *Nau:* (*of wind*) **to fall c.,** calmir; **c. sea,** mer calme, molle; **the sea was as c. as a millpond,** nous avions une mer d'huile; **to remain c. and collected,** rester serein, impassible; ne pas perdre la tête; **to keep c.,** rester calme, se modérer; **to grow calmer,** se calmer; *F:* **he had the c. audacity to . . .,** il fut assez cynique pour . . . .

calm[3]. **1.** *v.tr.* calmer, apaiser (la tempête, la colère); remettre, détendre, tranquilliser (l'esprit); atténuer, adoucir (la douleur); **c. yourself,** remettez-vous! **to c. s.o.'s fears,** remettre qn de sa frayeur; **to c. s.o. down,** pacifier qn. **2.** *v.i.* **to c. down,** (i) (*of storm, grief, etc.*) se calmer, s'apaiser, se modérer; se pacifier; (ii) (*of grief*) s'adoucir; (iii) (*of the mind*) se tranquilliser; (iv) *Nau:* (*of sea*) calmir.

calm[4], *s.* plomb *m* (de vitrail).

calmative ['kɑ:mətiv], *a. & s. Med:* calmant (*m*).

calming[1] ['kɑ:miŋ], *a.* tranquillisant, adoucissant, calmant; **she has a c. influence on him,** elle sait le calmer, le tranquilliser.

calming[2], *s.* apaisement *m* (des flots, de la colère); adoucissement *m* (de la douleur).

calmly ['kɑ:mli], *adv.* avec calme, tranquillement; de sens rassis; **to take things c.,** prendre les choses tranquillement, en douceur; **everything went off c.,** tout s'est passé dans le calme; **he received the news c.,** il a appris la nouvelle sans s'émouvoir.

calmness ['kɑ:mnis], *s.* tranquillité *f*, calme *m*.

calomel ['kæləməl], *s. Pharm:* calomel *m*; mercure doux.
calophyllum ['kælou'filəm], *s. Bot:* calophyllum *m*.
calorescence [kælə'resəns], *s. Ph:* calorescence *f*.
caloric [kə'lɔrik], *s. Ph:* calorique *m*; *Mec.E:* **c. engine,** machine *f* à air chaud; **c. energy,** énergie *f* thermique.
caloricity [kælə'risiti], *s.* caloricité *f*.
calorie ['kæləri], *s. Ph:* calorie *f*; **large, great, major, kilogram, c.,** grande calorie, millithermie *f*, kilocalorie *f*; **small, lesser, gramme, c.,** petite calorie, calorie-gramme *f*, *pl.* calories-grammes, microthermie *f*; **mean c.,** moyenne calorie.
calorifacient [kələri'feiʃənt], *a. Ph:* calorifiant.
calorific [kælə'rifik], *a. Ph:* calorifique, calorifiant; **c. power,** puissance *f* calorifique; **c. value,** valeur *f* calorifique.
calorification [kælɔrifi'keiʃ(ə)n], *s. Ph:* calorification *f*.
calorimeter [kælə'rimitər], *s. Ph:* calorimètre *m*; **electric resistance c.,** calorimètre électrique; **bomb c.,** bombe *f* calorimétrique.
calorimetric(al) [kælɔri'metrik(l)], *a. Ph:* calorimétrique.
calorimetry [kælə'rimitri], *s.* calorimétrie *f*.
calorization [kælərai'zeiʃ(ə)n], *s. Metalw:* calorisation *f*.
calorize ['kæləraiz], *v.tr. Metalw:* caloriser (à l'aluminium).
calorizing ['kæləraiziŋ], *s.* calorisation *f*.
calory ['kæləri], *s.* = CALORIE.
calosoma [kælou'soumə], *s. Ent:* (coléoptère) calosome *m*.
calotropis [kælou'troupis], *s. Bot:* calotropis *m*.
calotte [kə'lɔt], *s.* **1.** (*skull cap*) calotte *f*. **2.** *Geol:* calotte glaciaire. **3.** *Arch:* calotte.
calotype ['kæloutaip], *s. Phot: A:* calotype *m*.
caloyer ['kælɔiər], *s. Ecc:* moine grec de l'ordre de Saint Basile; caloyer *m*.
calp [kælp], *s. Geol:* calp *m*.
calque [kælk], *s. Ling:* calque *m*.
caltha ['kælθə], *s. Bot:* caltha *m*.
caltrop ['kæltrɔp], *s.* **1.** *Mil: A:* chausse-trape *f*, *pl.* chausse-trapes. **2.** *Spong:* spicule *f* à quatre pointes. **3.** *pl. Bot:* chardon étoilé; chausse-trape (étoilée); **water caltrops,** (i) macle *f*, macre *f*, cornue *f*; châtaigne *f* d'eau; truffe *f* d'eau; écharbot *m*, marron *m* d'eau, trapa *m*; (ii) potamogeton *m*, potamot *m*; **land caltrops,** croix-de-Malte *f*.
calumba ['kæləmbə], *s. Bot:* colombo *m*.
calumet ['kæljumet], *s.* calumet *m*.
calumniate [kə'lʌmnieit], *v.tr.* calomnier.
calumniation [kəlʌmni'eiʃ(ə)n], *s.* calomnie *f*.
calumniator [kə'lʌmnieitər], *s.* calomniateur, -trice.
calumniatory [kə'lʌmniət(ə)ri], *a.* calomniateur, -trice; calomnieux.
calumnious [kə'lʌmniəs], *a.* calomnieux.
calumniously [kə'lʌmniəsli], *adv.* calomnieusement.
calumny ['kæləmni], *s.* calomnie *f*.
calutron [kæ'lju:trɔn], *s. Atom.Ph:* calutron *m*.
calvarium [kæl'veəriəm], *s. Anat:* sinciput *m*.
Calvary ['kælvəri]. **1.** *Pr.n.* **(Mount) C.,** le Calvaire. **2.** *s.* (*a*) (*monument or cross*) calvaire *m*; (*b*) (*in churches*) chemin *m* de la Croix; calvaire; (*c*) *Fig:* calvaire.
calve [kɑ:v]. **1.** *v.i.* (*of cow, iceberg, etc.*) vêler. **2.** *v.tr.* (*of cow*) mettre bas (un veau); (*of iceberg*) vêler (un glaçon).
calving ['kɑ:viŋ], *s.* vêlage *m*, vêlement *m*; *Vet:* **c. fever,** fièvre *f* vitulaire.
Calvinism ['kælvinizm], *s. Rel.H:* calvinisme *m*.
Calvinist ['kælvinist], *s.* & *a. Rel.H:* calviniste (*mf*).
Calvinistic(al) [kælvi'nistik(l)], *a.* calviniste.
calvities [kæl'viʃii:z], *s.* calvitie *f*.
calx, *pl.* **calces** [kælks, 'kælsi:z], *s.* **1.** résidu *m* de calcination; cendres *f* métalliques. **2.** *Anat:* calcanéum *m*.
calycal ['kælikl], *a.* = CALYCEAL.
Calycanthaceae [kælikæn'θeisii:], *s.pl. Bot:* calycanthacées *f*.
calycanthus [kæli'kænθəs], *s. Bot:* calycanthe *m*, calycanthus *m*.
calyceal [kæli'si:əl], *a. Bot:* calicinal, -aux, calicinaire, calicinien; calicin.
calycifloral [kælisi'flɔ:rəl], **calycifloraté** [kælisi'flɔ:reit], **calyciflorous** [kælisi'flɔ:rəs], *a. Bot:* caliciflore.
calyciform ['kælisifɔ:m], *a.* caliciforme.
calycinal [kæ'lisinl], **calycine** ['kælisain], *a. Bot:* calicinal, -aux; calicin; calicinaire.
calycle ['kælikl], *s. Bot:* calicule *m*.
calycled ['kælikld], *a. Bot:* caliculé.
Calycophora [keili'kɔfərə], *s.pl. Coel:* calycophores *m*.
calycular [kə'likjulər], *a. Bot:* caliculaire.
calyculate [kə'likjuleit], *a. Bot:* caliculé.
calyculus [kæ'likjuləs], *s. Bot:* calicule *m*.
calymene [kæ'limənі:], *s. Paleont:* calymène *f*.
Calypso[1] [kə'lipsou], *Pr.n. Gr.Lit: Astr:* Calypso *f*.
calypso[2], *s. Poet: Danc: Mus:* (*West Indies*) calypso *m*.
Calyptoblastea [kæliptou'blɑ:stiə], *s.pl. Coel:* calyptoblastides *m*, calyptoblastiques *m*.
calyptoblastic [kæliptou'blɑ:stik], *s. Coel:* calyptoblastique.
calyptop(s)is [kælip'tɔp(s)is], *s. Crust:* calyptopis *m*.
calyptra [kə'liptrə], *s. Bot:* calyptre *f*, coiffe *f*.
calyptraea [kælip'treiə], *s. Moll:* calyptrée *f*.
calyptrate [kə'liptreit], *a. Bot:* calyptré; **not c.,** écalyptré.
calyptriform [kə'liptrifɔ:m], *a. Bot:* calyptriforme.
calyptrogen [kæ'liptrədʒen], *a.* & *s. Bot:* calyptrogène (*f*).
calyx, *pl.* **-yxes, -yces** ['keiliks, -iksi:z, -isi:z], *s.* **1.** *Bot: Z:* calice *m*. **2.** *Mch: etc:* couronne dentée; **c. drill,** sondeuse *f* à couronne dentée.
cam [kæm], *s. Mec.E: etc:* came *f*; excentrique *m*; levée *f*; lève *f*; mentonnet *m*; alluchon *m*; doigt *m* d'entraînement; **c. lift,** levée de la came; **actuating c.,** came de poussée, de commande; **compound c.,** came à plusieurs échelons; **quick-action c.,** came à profil brusque; **heart c.,** came, excentrique, en forme de cœur; **c. engine,** moteur *m* à came(s); **c. profile,** profil *m*, tracé *m*, de la came; **top of a c.,** palier *m* de came; **c. box,** boîte *f* à cames; **c. circle,** cercle primitif de la came; **c. follower,** commande *f*, galet *m*, de came; basculeur *m*, poussoir *m*, taquet *m*; **c. gear,** distribution *f* à came(s); **c. head,** rebord saillant (d'une came); **c. wheel,** roue *f*, bague *f*, à cames.
camaieu ['kæmaijə, kæ'maijə], *s. Art:* (peinture *f* en) camaïeu *m*; **yellow c.,** tableau *m* de cirage.
camaraderie [kæmə'rɑ:dəri], *s.* camaraderie *f*.
Camargue (the) [ðəkæ'mɑ:g], *Pr.n. Geog:* la Camargue.
camarilla [kæmə'rilə], *s. Pol:* camarilla *f*; coterie *f*.
camaron [kæmə'roun, 'kæmərən], *s. Crust:* crevette *f* d'eau douce.
camber[1] ['kæmbər], *s.* **1.** (*a*) cambrure *f* (d'une poutre, etc.); courbure *f*, bombement *m* (d'une chaussée); *N.Arch:* tonture *f*, bouge *m* (du pont); *Hyd.E:* enclave *f* (d'une écluse); *Av:* **airfoil c.,** flèche *f* de profil d'aile; courbure d'aile; **(rise of) c.,** flèche, contre flèche *f*, *pl.* contre-flèches (d'une poutre, etc.); (*b*) *Veh:* carrossage *m*, devers *m*, écuanteur *f* (des roues); (*c*) **c. (beam),** poutre cambrée. **2.** *Nau:* darse *f* au bois; bassin *m*, chantier *m*, au bois.
camber[2]. **1.** *v.tr.* bomber (une chaussée); cambrer (une poutre); donner de la flèche, de la cambrure, à (une poutre, etc.); cintrer (un ressort, etc.); donner de l'écuanteur à (une roue). **2.** *v.i.* (*a*) se bomber, se cambrer, arquer; faire flèche; (*b*) avoir de la cambrure; bomber.
cambered ['kæmbə:d], *a.* arqué, courbé, cambré; *Aut:* **c. chassis,** châssis *m* à avant rétréci; châssis étranglé, cintré; *N.Arch:* **c. ship,** navire arqué, qui a de l'arc; **c. deck,** pont *m* en pente; *Civ.E:* **c. road,** chaussée bombée.
cambering ['kæmb(ə)riŋ], *s.* bombement *m*, cambrage *m*; cintrement *m*.
Camberwell ['kæmbəwel], *Pr.n. Ent:* **C. beauty,** morio *m*.
cambial ['kæmbiəl], *a. Bot:* cambial, -aux.
cambism ['kæmbizm], *s.* cambisme *m*.
cambist ['kæmbist], *s. Fin:* cambiste *m*; agent *m* de change.
cambium ['kæmbiəm], *s. Bot:* cambium *m*.
Cambodia [kæm'boudiə], *Pr.n. Geog:* Cambodge *m*.
Cambodian [kæm'boudiən]. **1.** *Geog:* (*a*) *a.* cambodgien; (*b*) *s.* Cambodgien, -ienne. **2.** *s. Ling:* cambodgien *m*.
Cambrian ['kæmbriən]. **1.** *Geog:* (*a*) *a.* gallois; (*b*) *s.* Gallois, -oise. **2.** *a.* & *s. Geol:* cambrien (*m*); *Geog:* **C. Mountains,** montagnes *fpl* du Pays de Galles.
cambric ['kæmbrik, 'keim-], *s. Tex:* batiste *f* (de lin); **cotton c.,** batiste, mousseline *f*, de coton; percale *f*; *attrib.* **c. handkerchief,** mouchoir *m* de batiste, mouchoir fin; **c. paper,** papier *m* (à lettres) toile; *U.S:* **c. tea,** thé clair, faible, thé au lait.
Cambridge ['keimbridʒ], *Pr.n. Geog:* Cambridge; **to go to C.,** (i) see rendre à Cambridge; (ii) entrer à l'université de Cambridge; **a C. man,** (i) un étudiant (ii) = un licencié, de l'université de Cambridge; **the C. economists,** les économistes *m* de l'école de Cambridge; **C. blue,** bleu clair.
Cambyses [kæm'baisi:z], *Pr.n.m. A.Hist:* Cambyse.
came [keim], *s.* plombure *f*, aile *f* (d'un vitrail); plomb *m* (pour vitraux); **the cames,** la résille.
camel ['kæml], *s.* **1.** (*a*) *Z:* chameau *m*; **she c.,** chamelle *f*; **young c., c. colt,** chamelot *m*, chamelon *m*; **Bactrian c., two-humped c.,** chameau (bactrien); **Arabian c., one-humped c.,** dromadaire *m*; **c. driver,** chamelier *m*; **c. load,** chamelée *f*; **c. (pack) transport,** transport *m* à dos de chameau; *Mil:* **c. corps,** (i) compagnies *fpl* de méharistes; (ii) *Austr: F:* l'infanterie *f*, les biffins *m* (portant le sac); (*b*) (*colour*) chameau *inv.* **2.** *Mil.Av: A:* avion *m* de chasse (de fabrication Sopwith). **3.** *Nau:* chameau (de renflouage). **4.** *Bot:* **camel's hay, c. grass,** jonc odorant; schénanthe *m*; **camel's thorn,** épine *f* de chameau, alhagi *m*.
camelback ['kæmlbæk], *s.* **on c.,** à dos de chameau.
cameleer [kæmi'liər], *s.* chamelier *m*.
camelhair ['kæmlhɛər], *s.* poil *m* de chameau; **c. brush,** pinceau *m* enn petit-gris (pour l'aquarelle); **c. coat,** manteau *m* en poil de chameau.
Camelidae [kæ'melidi:], *s.pl. Z:* camélidés *m*.
camelina [kæmə'li:nə], *s. Bot:* cameline *f*, caméline *f*.
cameline[1] ['kæməli:n], *a. Bot:* **c. oil,** huile *f* de caméline.
cameline[2], *s. Tex:* camelin *m*.
camellia [kə'mi:liə], *s. Bot:* camélia *m*, camellia *m*; **c. red,** rouge *m* camélia *inv*.
camelopard [kæ'meləpɑ:d], *s. Z: A:* caméléopard *m*, girafe *f*.
camelry ['kæmlri], *s. Mil:* compagnies *f* méharistes.
cameo ['kæmiou], (*a*) *s.* camée *m*; **c. ware,** poterie *f* avec décors en camée; *Moll:* **c. shell, c. conch,** cassis *m*, casque *m*; (*b*) *a.* miniature.
camera ['kæm(ə)rə], *s.* **1.** (*a*) *Phot:* appareil *m* (photographique); appareil-photo *m*; **the c. (body),** la chambre noire; **plate, film, c.,** appareil à plaques, à pellicules; **field c., stand c.,** appareil à pied; **hand c.,** appareil à main; **pocket c.,** appareil de poche, à main; **box c.,** appareil rigide, à chambre de forme rectangulaire; **folding c.,** appareil à soufflet; **studio c.,** appareil d'atelier, de studio; **automatic, Polaroid, c.,** appareil automatique, Polaroïd (*R.t.m.*); **camera-ready copy,** texte prêt à être photographié; **reflex c.,** appareil reflex; **stereoscopic c.,** appareil stéréoscopique; **air c., aerial c.,** appareil pour photographie aérienne, de prises de vue aériennes; **film,** *NAm:* **movie, c.,** camera *f*, caméra *f*; **television c.,** caméra de télévision; **motor(-driven) c.,** caméra à moteur; **on c.,** en champ, à l'écran; **off c.,** hors champ; **c. stand,** pied *m* photographique; *Cin:* **c. booth,** chambre insonorisée de prise de vues; *Mil:* **c. gun,** photomitrailleuse *f*; *U.S: P:* **c. eye,** agent *m* de police qui n'oublie jamais un visage; (*b*) *Opt:* **c. obscura,** chambre noire; **c. lucida,** chambre claire. **2.** *Jur:* **in c.,** à huis clos.
cameraman, *pl.* **-men** ['kæm(ə)rəmæn, -men], *s.m.* **1.** photographe de la presse. **2.** *Cin:* cadreur, cameraman, opérateur; preneur de vues.
Camerata [kæmə'rɑ:tə, -'reitə], *s.pl. Echin: Paleont:* camerata *m*.
camerlengo [kæmə'leŋgou], **camerlingo** [kæmə'lingou], *s. R.C.Ch:* camerlingue *m*.
Cameronian [kæmə'rouniən], *a.* & *s. Rel.H:* caméronien, -ienne.
Cameroons (the) [ðəkæmə'ru:nz], *Pr.n.pl. Hist: Geog:* le Cameroun.
Cameroun [kæmə'ru:n], *Pr.n.* **the Republic of C.,** la République fédérale du Cameroun.
cami-knickers ['kæmi'nikəz], *s.pl. Cost: O:* combinaison-culotte *f*, *pl.* combinaisons-culottes; chemise-culotte *f*, *pl.* chemises-culottes.
Camilla [kə'milə], *Pr.n.f.* Camille.
Camillus [kə'miləs], *Pr.n.m.* Camille.
cami-petticoat ['kæmi'petikout], *s. Cost: A:* combinaison *f* à trois pièces; tout-en-un *m inv.*
Camisard ['kæmisɑ:d]. *Rel.H:* **1.** *s.* Camisard, -arde. **2.** *a.* **the C. Rebellion,** l'insurrection *f* des Camisards.
camisole ['kæmisoul], *s. Cost: A:* **1.** cache-corset *m inv.* **2.** camisole *f*.
camlet ['kæmlit], *s. Tex: O:* camelot *m*.
cammock ['kæmək], *s. Bot:* bugrane *f* des champs; arrête-bœuf *m inv.*
camomile ['kæməmail], *s. Bot:* **1.** camomille *f*; **c. tea,** (tisane *f* de) camomille. **2. stinking c.,** camomille puante; maroute *f*; **wild c.,** matricaire *f* camomille. **3. c. oil,** huile *f* de camomille.
camorra [kə'mɔ:rə], *s.* camorra *f*.
camorrist(a) ['kæmərist, 'kæmə'ristə], *s.* camorriste *m*.
camouflage[1] ['kæmuflɑ:ʒ], *s.* camouflage *m* (d'un vaisseau, etc.; *F:* de la vérité); *F:* fardage *m* (de marchandises, etc.); *Mil:* **c. painting,** peinture *f* de camouflage; **c. net(ting),** filet *m* de camouflage; **c. helmet net,** filet de camouflage de casque (métallique); **it's only a piece of c.,** ce n'est que du camouflage, qu'un trompe-l'œil; **his attitude is sheer c.,** son attitude *f* ne fait que camoufler ses intentions.

camouflage[2], *v.tr.* camoufler.
camouflager [ˈkæmuflɑːʒər], *s.* camoufleur *m.*
camouflet [ˈkæmuflei], *s. Mil: Min: etc:* camouflet *m.*
camp[1] [kæmp], *s.* **1.** (*a*) camp *m*; campement *m*; **holiday c.**, camp de vacances; camping *m*; **children's holiday c.** = colonie *f* de vacances; **work c., agricultural c.**, chantier *m* (de travail); **gipsy c.**, camp de bohémiens; *Pol:* **concentration c.**, camp de concentration; **internment, detention, c.**, camp d'internement; *Mil:* **entrenched c.**, camp retranché; **training c.**, camp d'instruction; **transit c.**, camp de passage; *U.S:* **practice c.**, champ *m* de tir, polygone *m* d'artillerie; camp d'instruction; **c. under canvas**, camp de tentes, de toile; **hut(ment), hutted, c.**, camp de baraques, de baraquements; **to pitch c.**, établir un camp; **to strike, break (up), c.**, lever le camp; **to be in c.**, être dans un campement; faire du camping; (*of reservist, etc.*) **to go to c.**, faire une période, un stage, dans un camp; *attrib.* **c. equipment**, matériel *m* de campement, de camping; **c. bed**, lit *m* de camp; **c. stool, chair**, pliant *m*; chaise pliante; **c. site**, emplacement *m*, assiette *f*, du camp; camping; *Mil:* **c. commandant**, commandant *m* d'armes du camp; **c. colour**, fanon *m*, guidon *m*; *O:* **c. fever**, (i) maladie *f* des camps; (ii) typhus *m*; *A:* **c. followers**, (i) mercantis *m* et prostituées *f*; (ii) non-combattants *m*, à la suite de l'armée; *U.S:* **c. meeting**, assemblée religieuse en plein air; (*b*) **the opposition c.**, le camp opposé; le parti adversaire; **to go over to the other c.**, passer dans l'autre camp; passer, se joindre, à l'ennemi; **to have a foot in both camps**, manger à deux râteliers. **2.** (*troops on campaign*) **flying c.**, camp volant.
camp[2]. **1.** *v.i.* (*a*) **to c. (out)**, camper; vivre sous la tente; **to c. under canvas**, camper sous la tente, sous la toile; **to c. in huts, in hutments**, camper dans des baraques, dans des baraquements; (*b*) (*of camel*) s'accroupir. **2.** *v.tr.* (*a*) camper (une armée); (*b*) **land that can c. forty**, terrain *m* pouvant servir de camping à quarante personnes. **3.** (*a*) *v.tr. & i. Th: F:* **to c. (it up)**, outrer (le mauvais goût); (*b*) *v.i. P:* être (i) pédéraste, (ii) lesbienne.
camp[3], *a.* **1.** *esp. Th: F:* d'un goût douteux; affecté, poseur; chichiteux. **2.** *P:* homosexuel; lesbien.
Campagna (the) [ðəkæmˈpænjə], *Pr.n. Geog:* la Campagne de Rome.
campaign[1] [kæmˈpein], *s.* (*a*) campagne *f* (militaire); **c. medal**, médaille commémorative; **to begin a c., to enter on a c.**, se mettre en campagne, entrer en campagne; **to go through one's first c. under s.o.**, faire ses premières armes sous qn; (*b*) **electoral c.**, campagne électorale; **to lead, conduct, a c. against s.o.**, mener (une) campagne contre qn; (*c*) *Com:* **sales c.**, campagne de vente; **advertising c.**, campagne publicitaire, de publicité; **press c.**, campagne de presse; (*d*) *Metall: etc:* campagne (d'un haut fourneau, etc.).
campaign[2], *v.i.* faire (une) campagne; faire des campagnes.
campaigner [kæmˈpeinər], *s.* **1.** soldat *m* en campagne. **2. old c.**, vieux soldat; vieux troupier; vieux routier; vétéran *m*; vieux briscard.
campanero [kæmpæˈnɛərou], *s. Orn:* araponga *m*, oiseau-cloche *m*, *pl.* oiseaux-cloches.
Campania [kæmˈpeiniə], *Pr.n. Geog:* Campanie *f.*
campaniform [kæmˈpænifɔːm], *a.* campaniforme.
campanile [kæmpəˈniːle], *s. Arch:* campanile *m.*
campanological [kæmpənəˈlɔdʒikl], *a.* campanaire.
campanist [ˈkæmpənist], **campanologist** [kæmpəˈnɔlədʒist], *s.* spécialiste *mf* de l'art campanaire; carillonneur *m.*
campanology [kæmpəˈnɔlədʒi], *s.* **1.** science *f* de la fonte des cloches. **2.** art *m* campanaire; art du carillon.
campanula [kəmˈpænjulə], *s. Bot:* campanule *f.*
Campanulaceae [kæmpænjuˈleisiiː], *s.pl. Bot:* campanulacées *f*, campanulées *f.*
campanulaceous [kæmpænjuˈleiʃəs], *a. Bot:* campanulacé.
Campanulales [kæmpænjuˈleiliːz], *s.pl. Bot:* campanulales *f.*
campanular [kæmˈpænjulər], *a. Bot:* campanulé; campanuliforme; campanuliflore.
campanularia [kæmpænjuˈlɛəriə], *s. Coel:* campanularia *f.*
Campanulariidae [kæmpænjuləˈriːidiː], *s.pl. Coel:* campanulariidés *m.*
campanulate [kəmˈpænjuleit], *a. Bot:* campanulé, campanuliflore, campanuliforme.
campcraft [ˈkæmpkrɑːft], *s.* l'art *m* du camping.
Campeachy [kæmˈpiːtʃi], *Pr.n.* **C. wood**, bois *m* de Campêche.
Campeche [kæmˈpiːtʃi], *Pr.n. Geog:* Campêche *m.*
campephilus [kæmˈpefiləs], *s. Orn:* campéphile *m.*
camper [ˈkæmpər], *s.* **1.** campeur, -euse. **2.** *U.S:* chalet *m* mobile (pour vacances).
campfire [ˈkæmpˈfaiər], *s.* feu *m* de camp.
camphene [ˈkæmfiːn], *s. Ch:* camphène *m.*
camphol [ˈkæmfɔl], *s. Ch:* camphol *m.*
campholic [kæmˈfɔlik], *a.* (acide) campholique.
campholide [ˈkæmfoulaid], *s. Ch:* campholide *f.*
camphor [ˈkæmfər], *s.* camphre *m*; **c. oil**, essence *f* de camphre; **peppermint c.**, menthol *m*; **c. tree**, camphrier *m.*
camphorate[1] [ˈkæmfəreit], *s. Ch:* camphorate *m.*
camphorate[2], *v.tr. Pharm: etc:* camphrer.
camphorated [ˈkæmfəreitid], *a.* camphré; **c. oil**, huile camphrée.
camphoric [kæmˈfɔrik], *a. Ch:* camphorique.
Campignian [kæmˈpigniən], *a. & s. Prehist:* campignien (*m*).
campimeter [kæmˈpimitər], *s. Opt:* campimètre *m.*
Campine [ˈkæmpain], *Pr.n.* (*a*) *Geog:* **the C.**, la Campine; (*b*) *Husb:* **silver C. fowl**, coq *m*, poule *f*, de la Campine; campine *f.*
camping [ˈkæmpiŋ], *s.* camping *m*; *esp. Mil:* campement *m*; **c. site, c. ground**, (terrain *m* de) camping; campement (de bohémiens, etc.); village *m* de toile.
campion [ˈkæmpiən], *s. Bot:* lychnide *f*, lychnis *m*; **red c.**, lychnide diurne, compagnon *m* rouge; **white c.**, compagnon blanc; **bladder c.**, silène enflé, béhen blanc; **sea c.**, silène maritime; **night-flowering c.**, silène nocturne; **moss c.**, silène acaule; **rose c.**, agrostemme *f* en couronne; coquelourde *f*; jalousie *f* des jardins; passe-fleur *f*, *pl.* passe-fleurs.
campo [ˈkæmpou], *s. Geog:* campo *m.*
campodea [kæmˈpoudiə], *s. Ent:* campode *m.*
Campodeidae [kæmpoudiːˈidiː], *s.pl. Ent:* campodéidés *m.*
campodeiform [kæmpouˈdiːifɔːm], *a. Ent:* campodéiforme.
camp-on [ˈkæmpɔn], *s. Cmptr:* mise *f* en attente, mise en garde.
camponotus [kæmpouˈnoutəs], *s. Ent:* camponote *m.*
camp-shed [ˈkæmpʃed], *v.tr.* border (une rive) de pieux, d'un épi.
camp sheathing, shedding, sheeting [ˈkæmpʃiːðiŋ, -ʃediŋ, -ʃiːtiŋ], *s. Civ.E:* épi *m* de bordage (d'un fleuve); rideau *m* de palplanches.
campsis [ˈkæmpsis], *s. Bot:* campsis *m.*
camptonite [ˈkæmptənait], *s. Miner:* camptonite *f.*
camptosaur [ˈkæmptousɔːr], **camptosaurus** [kæmptouˈsɔːrəs], *s. Paleont:* camptosaure *m.*
campus [ˈkæmpəs], *s.* campus *m* (universitaire).
campylometer [kæmpiˈlɔmitər], *s. Surv:* campylomètre *m.*
campylotropal [kæmpiˈlɔtrəpəl], **campylotropous** [kæmpiˈlɔtrəpəs], *a. Bot:* campylotrope.
camshaft [ˈkæmʃɑːft], *s. Mec.E:* arbre *m* à came(s), à excentrique; arbre porte-came(s); *I.C.E:* arbre de distribution; **overhead c. engine**, moteur *m* avec arbre à cames en tête, en dessus; **ignition c.**, arbre de distribution d'allumage.
camwood [ˈkæmwud], *s. Bot:* bois *m* de cam; camwood *m.*
can[1] [kæn], *s.* **1.** (*a*) bidon *m*, broc *m*, pot *m* (pour liquides); boîte *f* (à lait, d'un film); **watering c.**, arrosoir *m*; *Aut:* **spare c. (of petrol)**, bidon de secours; nourrice *f*; *U.S: P:* **c. of worms**, problème *m* difficile à résoudre; (*b*) *Ind:* burette *f* (à huile, etc.); (*c*) *Atom.Ph:* chemise *f*, gaine *f*; (*d*) *Cin: T.V: F:* (*of film*) **in the c.**, prêt à montrer, à téléviser; (*e*) *F:* **to carry the c.**, payer les pots cassés; **I'll have to carry the c.**, tout ça me retombera sur le nez. **2.** cannette *f* (en métal); boîte (de viande conservée, etc.); **c. opener**, ouvre-boîte(s) *m*, *pl.* ouvre-boîtes. **3.** *Tex:* **spinning c.**, pot de filature. **4.** (*a*) *U.S: F: A:* avion *m*; (*b*) *F: A:* **an old tin c.**, une vieille bagnole; (*c*) *U.S: P:* prison *f*; (*d*) *NAm: F:* (i) grenade sous-marine; (ii) (contre-)torpilleur *m*, *pl.* (contre-)torpilleurs. **5.** *U.S: P:* chiottes *fpl.*
can[2], *v.tr.* **(canned) 1.** mettre, conserver (de la viande, etc.) en boîte. **2.** *NAm:* (*a*) congédier, renvoyer (qn); (*b*) supprimer, caviarder (un passage, etc.). **3.** *W.Tel: T.V:* enregistrer; transcrire; *F:* **canned music**, musique enregistrée, *F:* de conserve; *F:* **c. it!** tais-toi! assez de ces bêtises! **4.** *F:* **to get canned**, se soûler.
can[3] [*stressed form* kæn; *unstressed* k(ə)n], *modal aux. v.* (*pr.* **can, canst, can,** *pl.* **can**; *neg.* **cannot** [ˈkænɔt] (*U.S:* **can not** [ˈkænˈnɔt]), **canst not**; *p.t. & condit.* **could** [kud], **could(e)st**; *inf., pr.p. & p.p. wanting; defective parts are supplied from "to be able to"; "cannot" and "could not" are often contracted into can't* [kɑːnt], *couldn't* [ˈkudnt]) **1.** (*a*) (*ability*) pouvoir; **I c. do it**, je peux, je puis, le faire; **we cannot**, *U.S:* **c. not, possibly do it**, nous ne pouvons absolument pas le faire; **I cannot allow that**, je ne saurais permettre cela; **you know how it is when you, one, c. do nothing**, vous savez ce que c'est que d'être impuissant à rien faire; **I will come as soon as I c.**, je viendrai aussitôt que possible, aussitôt que je pourrai; **you c. never understand . . .**, jamais vous ne pourrez comprendre . . .; **I come as often as I possibly c.**, je viens aussi souvent que je peux; **I reassured her as well as I could, as best I could**, je l'ai rassurée comme j'ai pu, de mon mieux; **I took every step that I possibly could**, j'ai fait toutes les démarches que j'ai pu, toutes les démarches possibles; **he will do what he c.**, il fera ce qu'il pourra, il fera son possible; **I will help you all I c.**, je vous aiderai de tout mon pouvoir, de mon mieux; **I think I c. help you**, je pense, j'espère, pouvoir vous aider; **I do not see how I c. help you, c. have helped you, could have helped you**, je ne vois pas en quoi je peux, j'ai pu, j'aurais pu, vous aider; **help him if you c.**, aidez-le si vous pouvez; **I can't very well accept**, il m'est difficile d'accepter; **I could not have remained**, il m'aurait été impossible de rester; je n'aurais pas pu rester; **I tried to lift the sack, but I could not**, j'essayai de soulever le sac, mais c'était impossible; *F:* **c. do?** ça va? tu peux le faire? **c. do!** ça va! bien sûr! **(it) can't be helped!** rien à faire! (*b*) (*possibility*) **it cannot be done**, cela ne peut pas se faire; c'est impossible (à faire); cela n'est pas possible (à faire); il n'y a pas moyen; **twenty-five people c. be accommodated for tea**, la maison est en mesure de servir le thé à vingt-cinq personnes; **how could he say that?** comment a-t-il pu dire cela? **that cannot be**, cela ne se peut pas; **what c. it be?** qu'est-ce que cela peut bien être? **c. it be that . . .?** se peut-il, est-il possible, que + *sub.*? **c. it be true?** serait-ce vrai? (*c*) (*emphatic*) **I never *could* understand music**, je n'ai jamais été capable de comprendre la musique; **the neighbours were as generous as they *could* be**, les voisins se montrèrent aussi généreux que leurs moyens le leur permettaient; **Mr X? what *can* he want?** M. X? qu'est-ce qu'il peut bien me vouloir? **where *could* he be at this time?** où pouvait-il bien être à cette heure? (*d*) (*intensive*) **how *could* you!** vous! faire ça! dire ça! à quoi pensez-vous? **the neighbours were as generous as could be**, les voisins firent preuve d'une grande générosité; **she is as pleased as c. *be***, elle est on ne peut plus contente, *F:* elle est aux anges; **he was as rude as could *be***, il s'est montré on ne peut plus grossier; **it's as ugly as could *be***, rien ne saurait être plus laid; **he could not have been kinder**, il s'est montré aimable au possible. **2.** (*know how to*) savoir; **I c. swim**, je sais nager; **wanted: a man who c. cook**, on demande un homme sachant faire la cuisine; **he c. play the violin**, il joue du violon; **I c. never thank you enough**, je ne saurais jamais vous exprimer ma reconnaissance. **3.** (*a*) (*of occasional occurrence*) **you don't know how silly a girl c. be**, vous ne savez pas à quel point les jeunes filles sont parfois sottes; **Jane Austen c. be tart**, il arrive à Jane Austen de montrer une certaine acerbité; **the crossing c. be rough in February**, il arrive que la traversée soit mauvaise au mois de février; (*b*) (*permission*) **when c. I move in?** quand pourrai-je emménager? (*to servant*) **you c. go**, vous pouvez vous retirer. **4.** (*often not translated*) **I c. understand your doing it**, je comprends que vous le fassiez; **I c. see nothing**, je ne vois rien; **I don't see what he c. gain by it**, je ne vois pas ce qu'il y gagnera; **I could hear them talking**, je les entendais parler; **I c. see you don't believe me**, je vois bien que vous ne me croyez pas; **how c. you tell?** comment le savez-vous? **5.** (*a*) (*conditional*) **he could have done it if he had wanted to**, il aurait pu le faire s'il avait voulu; (*b*) **I could have wished it otherwise**, j'aurais préféré qu'il en fût autrement; **I could not have wished it otherwise**, je n'aurais pas désiré qu'il en fût autrement; je n'aurais pas désiré mieux; (*c*) **I could weep, could have wept**, je me sens, sentais, près de pleurer; j'ai, j'ai eu, peine à ne pas pleurer; j'ai envie, j'avais envie, de pleurer; j'en aurais pleuré! **he could have sung for joy**, il aurait chanté de joie; **I could have smacked his face!** je l'aurais giflé! **6.** (*elliptically*) **I cannot but believe him**, je suis bien forcé de le croire; **you cannot but succeed**, vous ne pouvez pas ne pas réussir; **you cannot but know him**, vous n'êtes pas sans le connaître; *A:* **she could no more**, elle n'en pouvait plus; **you c. but try**, vous pouvez toujours essayer.
Canaan [ˈkeinən], *Pr.n. B:* (la Terre de) C(h)anaan *m.*
Canaanite [ˈkeinənait, -njənait], *s.* C(h)ananéen, -éenne.
Canaanitish [ˈkeinənaitiʃ, -njənaitiʃ], *a.* c(h)ananéen, -éenne.
Canada [ˈkænədə], *Pr.n. Geog:* (*a*) Canada *m*; **in C.**, au Canada; (*b*) *attrib. Z:* **C. lynx**, chat *m* du Canada; *Orn:* **C. goose, C.**, bernache *f* du Canada; *Bot:* **C. fleabane**, érigéron *m* du Canada; **C. hemp**, apocyn chanvrin, chanvre *m* du Canada; **C. birch**, bouleau *m*

du Canada; **C. thistle,** cirsium *m,* chardon *m* des champs; **C. balsam, C. turpentine,** baume *m* de, du, Canada; **C. balsam fir,** sapin baumier; **C. pitch,** exsudat *m,* résine *f,* du tsuga.

Canadian [kə'neidiən]. **1.** *a.* canadien; *Ling:* **C. French,** le français canadien, du Canada; **C. English,** l'anglais du Canada; *Geog:* **C. shield,** bouclier canadien; *Bot:* **C. waterleaf,** hydrophylle *f*; **C. waterweed,** élodée *f* du Canada. **2.** *s.* Canadien, -ienne.

Canadiana [kəneidi'ɑːnə], *s.pl.* objets *mpl,* livres *mpl,* etc., qui se rattachent à l'histoire, à la civilisation, canadienne.

Canadianism [kə'neidiənizm], *s.* (*a*) mot canadien, expression canadienne; (*b*) coutume canadienne.

canadite ['kænədait], *s. Miner:* canadite *f.*

canaigre [kə'naigri], *s. Bot:* canaigre *f.*

canal[1] [kə'næl], *s.* **1.** *Hyd.E:* canal, -aux; **summit c.,** canal à point de partage; **branch c.,** canal de dérivation; **junction c.,** canal de jonction; **ship c.,** canal maritime, de navigation; **c. lift,** ascenseur *m* à sas, élévateur *m* de bateaux; *Geog:* **C. Zone,** zone *f* du Canal de Panama; **c. boat, barge,** balandre *f*; péniche *f*; **c. builder,** canalisateur *m.* **2.** *Anat: etc:* canal; aqueduc *m* (de Fallope, etc.); **alimentary c.,** canal alimentaire; **auditory c.,** conduit auditif. **3.** *Astr:* **the Martian canals,** les canaux de Mars. **4.** *Rad.-A:* **c. rays,** rayons positifs (d'un tube à vide).

canal[2], *v.tr.* **(canalled)** canaliser (une région).

canalicular [kænə'likjulər], *a.* canaliculaire.

canaliculate(d) [kænə'likjuleit(id)], *a. Biol:* canaliculé, strié.

canaliculus [kænə'likjuləs], *s. Anat: Arch: Bot:* canalicule *m.*

canaliferous [kænə'lifərəs], *a. Anat:* canalifère.

canalizable [kænə'laizəbl], *a.* (cours *m* d'eau) canalisable.

canalization [kænəlai'zeiʃ(ə)n], *s.* canalisation *f*; (*for water supply*) adduction *f.*

canalize ['kænəlaiz]. **1.** *v.tr.* (*a*) canaliser (une rivière, etc.); (*b*) canaliser (une ville); poser les conduites *f,* la canalisation, dans (une ville). **2.** *v.i.* (*of public opinion, etc.*) se canaliser.

cananga [kə'næŋgə], **canangium** [kə'nændʒiəm], *s. Bot:* cananga *f.*

canape ['kænəpei], *s. Cu:* canapé *m.*

canard ['kænɑːd], *s.* **1.** *Av.Hist:* avion-canard *m, pl.* avions-canards. **2.** canard *m,* fausse nouvelle.

Canarian [kə'nɛərlən], *Geog:* (*a*) *a.* canarien; (*b*) *s.* Canarien, -ienne.

canarium [kə'nɛəriəm], *s. Bot:* canarium *m.*

Canary [kə'nɛəri]. **1.** *Pr.n. Geog:* **the C. Islands, the Canaries,** les îles Canaries; **C. banana,** banane *f* des Canaries, de Chine; *A:* **C. (wine),** vin *m* des Canaries. **2.** *s.* (*a*) *Orn:* serin *m,* canari *m*; **yellow-fronted c.,** serin de Mozambique; (*b*) *Bot:* **c. creeper, c. bird plant,** capucine *f* jaune canari; **c. grass, c. seed,** phalaris *m,* alpiste *m,* millet long; *Com:* **c. seed,** (grains *mpl* de) millet; **c. wood,** (bois *m* de) tulipier *m*; (*c*) *Austr: P: A:* forçat *m*; (*d*) *U.S: P:* mouchard *m*; (*e*) **c.(-coloured), c. yellow,** jaune serin; jaune canari; **bright c. yellow,** jaune queue de serin.

canasta [kə'næstə], *s. Cards:* canasta *f.*

canaster [kə'næstər], *s.* **1.** canasse *f,* kanaster *m* (pour l'importation du tabac). **2. c. (tobacco),** canasse.

cancan ['kænkæn], *s. Danc:* **French c.,** French can can *m.*

cancel[1] ['kænsl], *s.* **1.** = CANCELLATION. **2.** *Typ:* (*a*) **c. (page, leaf),** onglet *m*; **c. of four pages,** carton *m*; **8-page c.,** carton de 8 pages; **to put in the cancels,** cartonner les feuilles; (*b*) **c. matter,** suppression *f.* **3.** (*a*) oblitérateur *m*; *Rail: etc:* **(pair of) cancels,** poinçon *m,* poinçonneuse *f*; (*b*) **c. (key),** (i) *Tp:* bouton *m* d'annulation; (ii) *Cmptr:* touche *f* d'annulation; *Cmptr:* **c. character,** caractère *m* (d')annulation.

cancel[2], *v.* **(cancelled).**

I. *v.tr.* **1.** (*a*) annuler (un chèque, une dette, une commande); faire remise d'(une dette); annuler, résilier, résoudre, *Jur:* rescinder (un marché, un contrat); révoquer, annihiler (un acte, un testament); rappeler (un message); révoquer, contremander (un ordre); rapporter (une loi, une décision); supprimer (un train); décommander (une réunion, un dîner); infirmer (une lettre); oblitérer (un timbre); rayer, biffer (un mot, etc.); *Mil:* lever (une consigne); **to c. a mortgage,** radier une hypothèque; **to consider a letter as cancelled,** considérer une lettre comme nulle et non avenue; **our journey is cancelled,** notre voyage est supprimé; **to c. one's booking** (*for a journey, etc.*), décommander sa place; **we had to c. the invitations,** il nous a fallu décommander les invités; *Com:* **to c. and strip files,** purger les dossiers; (*b*) *Typ:* supprimer une page imprimée (en la remplaçant par un onglet); (*c*) *Cmptr:* (i) remettre à zéro; (ii) annuler. **2.** *Mth:* (*a*) *v.i.* simplifier une fraction; (*b*) *v.tr.* **by cancelling** *y* **from both sides of the equation one obtains the solution** $x = 2$, en éliminant *y* de l'équation on obtient le résultat $x = 2$; *Book-k:* (*of two entries*) **to c. each other,** s'annuler, se contre-passer.

II. (*compound verb*) **cancel out,** *v.i. Mth:* (*of terms*) s'annuler, se détruire, s'éliminer; **criticisms that c. out,** critiques *f* qui se détruisent mutuellement.

cancellable ['kæns(ə)ləbl], *a.* annulable; révocable; *Jur:* résoluble; résiliable.

cancellans ['kænsəlænz], *s. Typ:* onglet *m.*

cancellate(d) ['kæns(ə)leit(id)], *a. Nat.Hist:* réticulé; cancellé.

cancellation [kænsə'leiʃ(ə)n], *s.* annulation *f*; résiliation *f* (d'une commande, d'une vente, d'un contrat); résolution *f* (d'une vente); *Post:* oblitération *f*; **c. of a debt,** radiation *f* d'une dette; **c. of an order,** révocation *f* d'un ordre; contrordre *m*; *Jur:* **c. of garnishee order,** mainlevée *f* de saisie; **c. of a licence,** retrait (définitif) d'une patente; annulation d'un permis.

cancelled ['kæns(ə)ld], *a.* annulé; décommandé; révoqué; supprimé; (contrat) nul et non avenu, rescindé; (timbre) oblitéré.

cancelling ['kæns(ə)liŋ], *s.* **1.** = CANCELLATION. **2. c. stroke,** biffure *f.*

cancer ['kænsər]. **1.** *s.* (*a*) *Med:* cancer *m*; **c. of the stomach,** cancer à, de, l'estomac; **c. of the lung,** cancer du poumon; **soot c.,** cancer des ramoneurs; **scirrhous c.,** cancer en cuirasse; **c. hospital,** centre anticancéreux; **c. serum,** sérum anticancéreux; **c. patient,** cancéreux, -euse; **c. specialist,** cancérologue *mf*; (*b*) *Bot:* **c. root,** orobanche *f* de Virginie; (*c*) *Lit:* influence corruptrice; plaie *f*; fléau *m.* **2.** *Pr.n. Astr:* le Cancer; *Geog:* **the Tropic of C.,** le tropique du Cancer.

cancerate ['kænsəreit], *v.tr. & i.* cancériser.

canceration [kænsə'reiʃ(ə)n], *s. Med:* cancérisation *f.*

cancered ['kænsəd], *a. Med:* cancéré, cancéreux.

cancerigenic [kænsəri'dʒenik], **cancerogenic** [kænsərou'dʒenik], *a.* cancérigène, cancérogène, carcinogène.

cancerologist [kænsə'rɔlədʒist], *s.* cancérologue *mf.*

cancerology [kænsə'rɔlədʒi], *s.* cancérologie *f.*

cancerophobia [kænsərou'foubiə], *s.* cancérophobie *f.*

cancerous ['kæns(ə)rəs], *a. Med:* cancéreux; **c. tumour,** tumeur cancéreuse.

cancer prone ['kænsəproun], *a. Med:* cancérisable.

cancriform ['kæŋkrifɔːm], *a.* cancériforme.

cancrinite ['kænkrinait], *s. Miner:* cancrinite *f.*

cancroid ['kæŋkrɔid]. **1.** *a.* (*a*) *Z:* cancériforme; (*b*) *Med:* (ulcère) cancroïde, cancéreux. **2.** *s. Crust: Med:* cancroïde *m.*

candela ['kændilə], *s. Ph.Meas:* candéla *f,* bougie nouvelle.

candelabra, *pl.* **-as** [kændi'lɑːbrə, -əz; -'læb-], **candelabrum,** *pl.* **-a** [kændi'lɑːbrəm, -ə; -'læb-], *s.* (*a*) candélabre *m*; torchère *f*; lampadaire *m*; (*b*) *Bot:* **candelabrum tree,** euphorbe arborescente.

candelilla [kændi'lilə], *s. Ch:* **c. wax,** cire *f* de candelilla.

candescence [kæn'des(ə)ns], *s. Metall: etc:* blancheur éblouissante; chauffe *f* à blanc.

candescent [kæn'des(ə)nt], *a.* d'une blancheur éblouissante; chauffé à blanc.

Candia ['kændiə], *Pr.n. A.Geog:* (l'île *f* de) Candie (*f*).

candid ['kændid], *a.* **1.** franc, franche; sincère; **c. camera,** caméra *f* invisible; **c. friend,** (i) *Iron:* ami(e) qui vous dit vos vérités; (ii) *Pej:* ami(e) qui prend plaisir à vous débiner. **2.** impartial, -aux; désintéressé; **c. opinion,** opinion impartiale; **tell us your c. opinion,** de bonne foi dites-nous votre opinion, avis.

candidacy ['kændidəsi], *s. NAm:* candidature *f.*

candidate[1] ['kændideit], *s.* candidat *m,* aspirant *m,* prétendant *m* (**for sth.,** à qch.); **to stand, offer oneself, as c. for sth.,** se porter candidat, se présenter comme candidat, à qch.; poser sa candidature à qch.; se mettre sur les rangs; **to be a c.,** être sur les rangs; **to offer oneself again as a c.,** se représenter; **he has a c. running against him,** il a un concurrent.

candidate[2], *v.i. U.S:* **to c. for sth.,** se présenter comme candidat à qch.; poser sa candidature à qch.

candidature ['kændiditjər], *s.* candidature *f*; **to withdraw one's c.,** retirer sa candidature.

candidly ['kændidli], *adv.* **1.** franchement, sincèrement, de bonne foi. **2.** impartialement, avec impartialité, d'une manière désintéressée; sans parti pris.

candidness ['kændidnis], *s.* **1.** franchise *f,* bonne foi, sincérité *f.* **2.** impartialité *f,* désintéressement *m.*

candied ['kændid], *a.* (*a*) candi; glacé, confit (au sucre); **c. peel,** zeste confit, zeste d'Italie; écorces confites; **c. orange peel,** zeste d'orange confit, orangeat *m*; **c. lemon peel,** zeste de citron confit, citronnat *m*; (*b*) *A: & Lit:* flatteur; (discours) mielleux.

candle[1] ['kændl], *s.* **1.** (*a*) **wax c.,** bougie *f*; **tallow c.,** chandelle *f*; **composite c.,** bougie stéarique; **church c.,** cierge *m*; **Paschal c.,** cierge pascal; *El:* **c. lamp,** ampoule *f* flamme; **c. end,** bout *m* de chandelle, lumignon *m*; **to burn the c. at both ends,** brûler la chandelle par les deux bouts; **c. grease,** suif *m*; **c. wax,** paraffine *f* solide, stéarine *f*; **c. ring,** bobèche *f*; **c. snuffer,** (i) (*instrument*) mouchettes *fpl*; (ii) *A:* (*pers.*) moucheur *m*; **c. shade,** abat-jour *m inv* de bougie; garde-vue *m inv*; **c. works, factory,** chandellerie *f*; *Ecc:* **c. stock,** souche *f* de chandelier; **c. bearer,** céroféraire *m*; **the game's not worth the c.,** le jeu n'en vaut pas la chandelle; **to hold a c. to the devil,** tenir la chandelle; garder les manteaux; **he cannot, is not fit to, hold a c. to you,** il vous est très inférieur; il n'est rien à côté de vous; il ne vous va, vient, monte, pas à la cheville, à la ceinture; il n'est pas digne de dénouer les cordons de vos souliers; **c. auction,** *A:* **sale, auction, by inch of c.,** vente *f* à la chandelle éteinte; (*b*) jet *m* de gaz; (*c*) *Meas:* **standard, decimal, c.,** bougie décimale; *A:* **British standard c.,** bougie anglaise (= 1,02 bougie décimale); **international c.,** bougie internationale; **Hefner c.,** bougie standard; **new c.,** candéla *f,* bougie nouvelle. **2.** *Pyr:* **Roman c.,** chandelle romaine. **3.** *Bot:* **c. tree,** (i) cirier *m,* arbre *m* à cire; (ii) parmentiera *f.*

candle[2], *v.tr.* mirer (des œufs).

candleberry ['kændlberi], *s. Bot:* **1.** (noix *f* de) bancoul *m.* **2.** (*a*) **c. (myrtle, tree),** cirier *m,* arbre *m* à cire; (*b*) **c. (tree),** bancoulier *m.*

candle coal ['kændlkoul], *s. Min:* = CANNEL.

candlefish ['kændlfiʃ], *s. Ich:* hémiramphe *m,* demi-bec *m, pl.* demi-becs.

candle-hour ['kændlauər], *s. Meas:* bougie-heure *f, pl.* bougies-heures.

candlelight ['kændllait], *s.* lumière *f* de chandelle, de bougie; **by c.,** à la chandelle, à la bougie; à la lumière, à la clarté, d'une bougie; **c. dinner,** dîner *m* aux chandelles.

candle-lit ['kændllit], *a.* éclairé à la chandelle, à la bougie.

candlemaker ['kændlmeikər], *s.* fabricant *m* de chandelles, de bougies, de cierges.

Candlemas ['kændlmæs], *s. Ecc:* la Chandeleur.

candle-metre ['kændlmiːtər], *s. Meas:* bougie-mètre *f, pl.* bougies-mètres.

candlenut ['kændlnʌt], *s. Bot:* (noix *f* de) bancoul *m.*

candlepower ['kændlpauər], *s. Ph.Meas:* **1.** (puissance lumineuse d'une) bougie. **2.** puissance lumineuse, intensité *f,* en bougies; **sixty c. lamp,** lampe *f* de soixante bougies.

candler ['kændlər], *s.* **1.** (*pers.*) mireur, -euse (d'œufs). **2.** (*instrument*) mire-œuf(s) *m inv*; ovoscope *m.*

candlestick ['kændlstik], *s.* chandelier *m,* bougeoir *m*; **flat c.,** bougeoir; **cluster c.,** candélabre *m.*

candlewick ['kændlwik], *s.* **1.** mèche *f* de bougie, de chandelle. **2.** *Tex:* candlewick *m,* chenille *f* de coton.

candlewood ['kændlwud], *s. Bot:* bois-chandelle *m.*

candling ['kændliŋ], *s.* mirage *m* (des œufs); **c. apparatus,** mire-œuf(s) *m inv*; ovoscope *m.*

candock ['kændɔk], *s. Bot:* nénuphar *m* jaune.

candour ['kændər], *s.* **1.** franchise *f,* bonne foi, sincérité *f.* **2.** impartialité *f,* désintéressement *m.* **3.** *A:* bonté *f,* douceur *f.*

candy[1] ['kændi], *s.* **1. (sugar) c.,** sucre candi; **stick of sugar c.,** sucre *m* de pomme; sucre d'orge. **2.** *NAm:* bonbon *m*; **c. store,** confiserie *f*; *F:* **it's like taking c. from a baby,** c'est simple comme bonjour.

candy[2]. **1.** *v.tr.* (*a*) faire candir (le sucre); (*b*) glacer (des fruits). **2.** *v.i.* (*of sugar*) se cristalliser; se candir. **3.** *v.tr. NAm: Fig:* adoucir.

candyfloss ['kændiflɔs], *s.* (*a*) *Comest:* barbe *f* à papa; (*b*) *Fig:* **it's just c.,** c'est joli (si vous voulez), mais ça manque de substance, ce n'est pas sérieux.

candy-striped ['kændistraipt], *a. Tex:* pékiné.

candytuft ['kænditʌft], *s. Bot:* ibéride *f,* ibéris *f*; thlaspi *m,* téraspic *m.*

cane[1] [kein], *s.* **1.** *Bot: etc:* (*a*) canne *f,* jonc *m*; (canne de) bambou *m*; rotin *m*; **c. plantation, brake,** cannaie *f,* jonchaie *f*; **c. chair, furniture,** siège *m,* meubles *mpl,* en rotin; **c.-seated, c.-bottomed, chair,** chaise cannée; **c. work,** cannage *m*; **c. worker,** cannier *m*; (*chair-maker*) canneur, -euse; **split c. fishing rod,** canne à pêche en bambou refendu; (*b*) **sugar c.,** canne à sucre; **African, Chinese, sugar c.,** sorgho sucré; **c. sugar,** sucre *m* de canne; *Sug.-R:* **c. juice,** vesou *m*; **c. trash,** bagasse *f*; **c. mill,** (i) sucrerie *f,* raffinerie *f* (de sucre de canne); (ii) moulin *m* à broyer la canne à sucre; (*c*) **raspberry c.,** tige *f* de framboisier; (*d*) **c. grass,** arundinaire *f* macrosperme; (*e*) **c. apple,** arbouse *f*; (*tree*) arbousier *m*. **2.** (*a*) (*walking stick*) canne; **malacca c.,** (canne de) jonc; (*b*) (*switch*) badine *f*; (*c*) (*for punishment*) canne; **to get the c.,** être fouetté. **3.** *Com:* bâton *m* (de soufre, de cire).

cane[2], *v.tr.* **1.** battre, frapper, (qn) à coups de canne; donner des coups de canne à (qn); corriger (un enfant) avec une canne; **to c. Latin into s.o.,** faire entrer le latin dans la tête de qn à coups de férule. **2.** canner (une chaise).

canella [kæ'nelə], *s. Bot:* cannelle *f*.

canephor(e) ['kænifɔər], **canephora,** *pl.* **-ae** [kə'nefərə, -iː], **canephoros,** *pl.* **-ae** [kə'nefərəs, -iː], **canephorus,** *pl.* **-i** [kə'nefərəs; -ai, -iː], *s. Gr.Ant: Arch:* canéphore *f*.

caner ['keinər], *s. Ind:* cannier *m*; canneur, -euse.

cane rat ['kein ræt], *s. Z:* (i) aulacode *m*; (ii) thryonomys *m*; (iii) capromys *m*, hutia *m*.

canescent [kæ'nesənt], *a.* **1.** *Lit:* (*a*) blanchissant; qui tourne au blanc; (*b*) blanchi, chenu. **2.** *Bot:* incanescent.

canfieldite ['kænfiːldait], *s. Miner:* canfieldite *f*.

canful ['kænful], *s.* plein bidon, plein broc; boîte *f* (de petits pois, etc.); *F:* **he's got a c.,** il est soûl comme une bourrique.

cangia ['kændʒiə], *s. Nau:* cange *f*.

cang(ue) [kæŋ], *s.* cangue *f*.

canhook ['kænhuk], *s. Nau:* élingue *f* à pattes, à griffes; patte *f* d'élingue; patte à barriques.

canicular [kə'nikjulər], *a.* caniculaire.

canicule ['kænikjuːl], *s.* canicule *f*.

canid ['kænid], *s. Z:* canidé *m*.

Canidae ['kænidiː], *s.pl. Z:* canidés *m*.

canine ['kænain, *occ.* 'keinain]. **1.** (*a*) *a.* canin; de chien; **c. devotion,** dévotion *f* de chien; (*b*) *s.pl.* **canines,** canidés *m*. **2.** *a. & s. Anat:* **c. fossa,** fosse canine; **c. (tooth),** (dent) canine *f*, (dent) œillère *f*.

caning [keiniŋ], *s.* **1.** (volée *f* de) coups *mpl* de canne; *Sch:* correction *f*; **to get a good, a sound, c.,** recevoir une bonne correction, être fouetté. **2.** cannage *m* (de chaises).

canions ['kæniənz], *s.pl. A.Cost:* canons *m*.

Canis ['kænis], *Pr.n. Astr:* **C. Major,** le Grand Chien; **C. Minor,** le Petit Chien.

canister ['kænistər], *s.* **1.** (*a*) boîte *f* en fer blanc, boîte métallique; **tea c.,** boîte à thé; (*b*) *Cmptr:* boîte de rangement. **2.** *Mil: A:* boîte à mitraille; **c. shot,** mitraille *f*. **3.** *Ecc:* boîte à hosties.

canities [kæ'niʃiiːz], *s. Med:* canitie *f*.

canker[1] ['kæŋkər], *s.* (*a*) *Med:* ulcère rongeur; ulcération buccale; (*b*) *Vet:* (i) crapaud *m* (au sabot); (ii) gale *f* de l'oreille (du chat, du chien, etc.); (*c*) *Bot:* chancre *m*; gangrène *f*; (*in wood*) nécrose *f*; **black c.,** maladie *f* de l'encre; (*d*) = CANKERWORM; (*e*) *Fig: Lit:* influence corruptrice; plaie *f*, fléau *m*.

canker[2]. **1.** *v.tr.* (*a*) ronger (un arbre, une fleur, etc.); nécroser (le bois, etc.); (*b*) *Lit:* corrompre (une âme, une société); ulcérer (le cœur). **2.** *v.i. Lit:* se ronger, se corrompre; (*of heart, etc.*) se remplir d'amertume; s'ulcérer.

cankered ['kæŋkəd], *a.* (*a*) (arbre, etc.) atteint par le chancre; (bois) pouilleux; **c. rose,** rose rongée des vers; (*b*) (*of pers.*) plein d'amertume; amer; *Lit:* **c. heart,** cœur ulcéré, plein d'amertume; **heart c. by grief,** cœur rongé par le chagrin; (*c*) *Lit:* malveillant; acariâtre.

cankerous ['kæŋk(ə)rəs], *a.* chancreux.

cankerworm ['kæŋkəwəːm], *s.* ver rongeur (des plantes); chenille *f*.

canna ['kænə], *s. Bot:* balisier *m*, canna *m*.

cannabic ['kænəbik], *a. Bot:* cannabin.

cannabin ['kænəbin], *s. Bot:* cannabine *f*, cannabène *m*.

Cannabinaceae [kænəbi'neisiiː], *s.pl. Bot:* cannabinacées *f*, cannabinées *f*.

cannabis ['kænəbis], *s.* cannabis *m*; **c. resin,** cannabine *f*.

cannabism ['kænəbizm], *s.* cannabisme *m*.

Cannae ['kæniː], *Pr.n. Rom.Hist:* Cannes *fpl*.

canned [kænd], *a.* (*a*) (*of food*) conservé en boîtes (de fer blanc); (*b*) *F:* **c. music,** musique enregistrée, reproduite, *F:* musique de conserve; (*c*) *Journ: U.S:* (*of article*) publié simultanément dans plusieurs journaux; (*d*) *Cmptr:* **c. routine,** programme prêt à l'emploi; (*e*) *U.S:* banal, stéréotypé; (*f*) *F:* ivre, soûl.

cannel ['kænl], *s. Min:* **c. (coal),** houille grasse; cannel(-coal) *m*.

cannelloni [kæni'louni], *s.pl. Cu:* cannelloni *m*.

cannelure ['kæniljuər], *s.* cannelure *f*.

canner ['kænər], *s.* **1.** *Ind:* conserveur *m* (de viande, etc.). **2.** bétail destiné à la conserverie.

cannery ['kænəri], *s.* conserverie *f*.

canneryman, *pl.* **-men** ['kænərimæn, -men], *s. Ind: U.S:* conserveur *m*.

cannibal ['kænib(ə)l], *s. & a.* **1.** cannibale (*mf*); anthropophage (*mf*). **2.** *Z:* (animal *m*) qui dévore ses semblables.

cannibalism ['kænibəlizm], *s.* cannibalisme *m*; anthropophagie *f*.

cannibalistic [kænibə'listik], *a.* cannibale, anthropophage.

cannibalization [kænibəlai'zeiʃ(ə)n], *s. Mec.E: etc:* cannibalisation *f*.

cannibalize ['kænibəlaiz], *v.tr. Mec.E: etc:* cannibaliser.

cannikin ['kænikin], *s.* petit bidon, petit broc.

cannily ['kænili], *adv.* prudemment, avec circonspection.

canniness ['kæninis], *s.* prudence *f*, circonspection *f*.

canning ['kæniŋ], *s.* mise *f* en conserve, en boîtes (de fer blanc); **c. industry,** industrie *f* des conserves alimentaires; **c. factory,** conserverie *f*.

cannions ['kæniənz], *s.pl. A.Cost:* canons *m*.

cannon[1] ['kænən], *s.* **1.** *Artil:* (*pl. usu.* **cannon**) canon *m*; **six machine-guns and three c.,** six mitrailleuses et trois canons, trois pièces de canon, trois pièces d'artillerie; **c. shot,** (i) boulet *m* de canon; (ii) coup *m* de canon; **within c. shot,** à portée de canon; *F:* **c. fodder,** chair *f* à canon. **2.** (*a*) *Harn:* **c. (bit),** canon (du mors); (*b*) **c. bone,** canon (de la jambe du cheval); (*c*) **c. of a bell,** cerveau *m* d'une cloche. **3.** *Bill:* carambolage *m*; **c. off the cushion,** bricole *f*. **4.** canon (de clef de montre, etc.). **5. c. (curl),** grosse boucle de cheveux horizontale.

cannon[2], *v.* **(cannoned) 1.** *v.tr. & i. esp. NAm:* canonner. **2.** *v.i. Bill:* faire un carambolage; caramboler; **to c. off the red,** caramboler par le rouge; **to c. off the cushion,** jouer la bricole. **3.** *v.i.* **to c. into, against, s.o.,** heurter violemment qn; se heurter contre qn; entrer en collision avec qn; **the car cannoned into a tree,** la voiture s'est heurtée contre un arbre, s'est emboutie contre un arbre.

cannonade[1] [kænə'neid], *s.* canonnade *f*.

cannonade[2], *v.tr. & i.* canonner (l'ennemi).

cannonball[1] ['kænənbɔːl], *s.* **1.** *Artil:* boulet *m* de canon. **2.** *Bot: F:* boulet de canon, calebasse *f* à Colin, abricot *m* de singe. **3.** (*a*) *Rail: U.S: F:* rapide *m*; (*b*) *Ten:* **c. service,** service *m* canon.

cannonball[2], *v.i. U.S: F:* rouler vite; passer comme un éclair.

cannoning ['kænəniŋ], *s. Bill:* carambolage *m*.

cannula ['kænjulə], *s.* **1.** *Surg:* canule *f*. **2.** *Ecc:* burette *f* (d'autel).

cannular ['kænjulər], *a.* tubulaire.

cannulate ['kænjuleit], *v.tr.* insérer une canule dans (une cavité).

cannulated ['kænjuleitid], *a. Surg:* **c. needle,** aiguille tubulée.

cannulation [kænju'leiʃ(ə)n], *s. Surg:* insertion *f* d'une canule (dans une cavité).

canny ['kæni], *a. esp. Scot:* (*a*) prudent, circonspect; avisé; **c. answer,** réponse *f* de Normand; (*b*) économe, ménager; (*c*) **it's not c.,** c'est inquiétant, mystérieux; (*d*) confortable; agréable.

canoe[1] [kə'nuː], *s.* **1.** canoë *m*; **Rob-Roy c.,** périssoire *f*; **(dugout) c.,** pirogue *f*; *Can:* **North c.,** *Fr.C:* canot *m* du nord; **Montreal c.,** *Fr.C:* canot du maître; **to paddle one's own c.,** arriver par soi-même; conduire seul sa barque. **2.** *Moll:* **c. shell,** scaphandre *m*.

canoe[2], *v.i.* **(canoed; canoeing)** faire du canoë, de la périssoire; aller en canoë, en périssoire.

canoeing [kə'nuːiŋ], *s.* canoëisme *m*.

canoeist [kə'nu(ː)ist], *s.* canoëiste *mf*; piroguier *m*.

Canoidea [kə'nɔidiə], *s.pl. Z:* canoïdes *m*.

canon[1] ['kænən], *s.* **1.** (*a*) *Ecc:* canon *m* (d'un ordre religieux, de la messe, etc.); **c. law,** droit *m* canon; (*b*) **the Paschal c.,** le canon pascal; (*c*) *Jur:* **canons of inheritance,** ordre *m* de succession; (*d*) **the Shakespearian c.,** l'œuvre *f* authentique de Shakespeare; (*e*) règle *f*, critère *m*; canon; **the canons of good taste,** les règles, le code, du bon goût. **2. c. of a bell,** cerveau *m* d'une cloche. **3.** *Mus:* canon. **4.** *Typ:* gros canon (de 48 points).

canon[2], *s. Ecc:* chanoine *m*; **resident c., c. residentiary,** chanoine résident; **honorary c.,** chanoine honoraire; **minor c., petty c.,** chanoine qui n'est pas membre du chapitre; **C. Regular,** chanoine régulier.

cañon ['kænjən], *s. Geog:* cañon *m*, canyon *m*.

canoness ['kænənes], *s.f. Ecc:* chanoinesse.

canonical [kə'nɔnikl], *a. Ecc:* **1.** (devoir, etc.) canonial, -aux; (droit, épître, résidence, etc.) canonique; **c. hours,** (i) heures canoniales; (ii) *Jur:* heures pendant lesquelles il est permis de célébrer les mariages. **2. c. dress,** *s.pl.* **canonicals,** vêtements sacerdotaux. **3.** (opinion, etc.) canonique, orthodoxe, catholique. **4.** *Mus:* (passage) en forme de canon. **5.** *Math:* canonique.

canonically [kə'nɔnik(ə)li], *adv.* **1.** (vivre) canonicalement. **2.** canoniquement.

canonicate [kə'nɔnikeit], *s. Ecc:* canonicat *m*.

canonicity [kænə'nisiti], *s.* **1.** canonicité *f*. **2.** orthodoxie *f*, authenticité *f* (d'un passage, etc.).

canonist ['kænənist], *s. Ecc: Jur:* canoniste *m*; spécialiste *m* en droit canon.

canonizable [kænə'naizəbl], *a. Ecc:* canonisable.

canonization [kænənai'zeiʃ(ə)n], *s. Ecc:* canonisation *f*.

canonize ['kænənaiz], *v.tr.* **1.** *Ecc:* canoniser (qn); mettre (qn) au nombre des saints. ûù. sanctionner (un usage).

canonry ['kænənri], *s. Ecc:* canonicat *m*.

canons ['kænənz], *s.pl. A.Cost:* canons (portés au-dessous du genou).

canoodle [kə'nuːdl], *v. P:* **1.** *v.tr.* faire des mamours à (qn); *P:* faire du plat à (qn). **2.** *v.i.* se faire des mamours; *P:* se peloter.

canoodler [kə'nuːdlər], *s. P:* faiseur, -euse, de mamours; amoureux, -euse; **a couple of canoodlers,** une paire de tourtereaux.

canophilist [kə'nɔfilist], *s.* cynophile *mf*.

canopic [kə'noupik], *a. Archeol:* **c. jar,** canope *m*.

canopied ['kænəpid], *a.* recouvert d'un dais, de feuillage, d'une voûte de verdure; *For:* **c. forest,** massif fermé.

Canopus [kə'noupəs]. **1.** *Pr.n. A.Geog:* Canope *m*. **2.** *Pr.n. Astr:* Canope. **3.** *s. Archeol:* canope *m*.

canopy[1] [kænəpi], *s.* **1.** dais *m* (d'un trône); baldaquin *m* (de lit); *Ecc:* ciel *m* (d'autel, etc.); conopée *m* (de tabernacle); hotte *f* (de foyer); (*over doorway*) auvent *m*, marquise *f*; calotte *f* (de parachute); *Av:* **air c.,** protection aérienne; *Av: A:* **pilot's c.,** verrière *f* d'habitacle; **branches that form a c.,** branches *fpl* en voûte; **c. of leaves,** voûte *f* de feuillage; dôme *m* de verdure; *Lit:* **the c. of heaven,** la voûte du ciel, la voûte céleste; la calotte des cieux. **2.** *Arch:* gable *m*, gâble *m* (de comble, de fenêtre).

canopy[2], *v.tr.* couvrir d'un dais, d'un dôme de verdure; *Lit:* **the trees that canopied the lawn,** les arbres *m* qui recouvraient, qui ombrageaient, la pelouse de leur verdure.

cant[1] [kænt], *s.* **1.** (*a*) *Arch: Carp: etc:* pan coupé; chanfrein *m*; biseau *m*; *Mec.E:* arête *f* (de boulon); **c. chisel,** ciseau *m* en biseau; **c. file,** lime *f* à biseau, à barrettes; barrette *f*; **c. hook, dog,** (i) croc *m* à levier; grappin *m*; (ii) patte *f* d'élingue; (*b*) *U.S:* bille de bois équarrie. **2.** (*a*) *Carp: Civ.E: etc:* (*slope*) inclinaison *f*, dévers *m*; relèvement *m* (d'un virage); *Rail:* **c. of the outer rail,** surélévation *f*, dévers, du rail extérieur; **c. frame,** *N.Arch:* **c. timber,** *Nau:* fourcat *m*. (*b*) **to give (sth.) a c.,** incliner (qch.); **to have a c.,** pencher.

cant[2]. **1.** *v.tr.* (*a*) *Carp: etc:* biseauter, écorner; **to c. the edge of a board,** couper obliquement le champ d'une planche; **to c. off an angle,** délarder une arête; (*b*) **to c. a beam, an upright,** dévoyer, incliner, une poutre, un montant; **to c. a cask,** incliner, pencher, un fût; *Nau:* **to c. a ship,** mettre un navire à la bande; *Rail:* **to c. the outer rail,** surhausser le rail extérieur; (*c*) renverser, retourner (qch.); *Nau:* **to c. a boat for repairs,** cabaner, chavirer, un canot pour le réparer; (*d*) jeter, lancer, (qch.) de côté, de biais. **2.** *v.i.* (*a*) *Carp: Civ.E: etc:* s'incliner; (*b*) se trouver incliné, en pente; pencher; (*c*) *Nau:* (*of ship*) éviter.

cant[3], *a.* (*a*) biseauté, écorné; (*b*) incliné, penché; (*c*) renversé, retourné; (*d*) lancé, jeté, de côté, de biais.

cant[4]. **1.** *s.* (*a*) jargon *m*, argot *m* (des voleurs, des mendiants, etc.); argot du milieu; la langue verte; (*b*) langage *m* hypocrite; hypocrisie *f*; cant *m*; (*c*) boniments *mpl* à la graisse d'oie; **that's all c.,** tout ça c'est du boniment. **2.** *a.* **c. phrase,** (i) phrase toute faite, stéréotypée; cliché *m*; (ii) expression *f* argotique.

cant[5], *v.i.* **1.** faire l'hypocrite. **2.** parler en argot.

cant[6], *s.* (*esp. Irish*) encan *m*, enchère *f*.

cant[7], *v.tr.* (*esp. Irish*) vendre (qch.) aux enchères.

cantabile [kæn'tɑːbili], *adv. & s. Mus:* cantabile (*m*).

Cantabri [kæn'tæbri, -'tei-], *s.pl. Hist:* Cantabres *m*.

Cantabrian [kæn'tæbriən]. **1.** *a. Hist:* cantabre; *Geog:* **C. Mountains,** monts *m* cantabriques; chaîne cantabrique. **2.** *s. Hist:* Cantabre *mf*.

Cantabrigian [kæntə'bridʒiən], *a. & s.* **1.** *Eng:* (*a*) (habitant, -ante) de Cambridge; (*b*) (membre *m*) de l'université de Cambridge. **2.** *U.S:* (*a*) (habitant, -ante) de Cambridge (Mass.); (*b*) (membre *m*) de l'université de Harvard.

cantaloup(e) ['kæntəluːp], *s. Hort:* cantaloup *m*.

cantankerous [kæn'tæŋk(ə)rəs], *a.* revêche, acariâtre, bourru; pas commode; d'humeur hargneuse; tracassier; disputailleur, -euse; **to be c.,** avoir mauvais caractère, être mauvais coucheur.

cantankerously [kæn'tæŋk(ə)rəsli], *adv.* d'une manière bourrue, acariâtre; en mauvais coucheur.

cantankerousness [kæn'tæŋk(ə)rəsnis], *s.* humeur *f*

revêche, acariâtre, hargneuse.
cantata [kæn'tɑ:tə], *s. Mus:* cantate *f.*
Cantate [kæn'tɑ:tei], *s. Ecc:* Cantate Domino *m inv.*
cantatrice [kæntə'tri:s], *s.* cantatrice *f*; chanteuse professionnelle (de talent).
cantboard ['kæntbɔ:d], *s.* planche inclinée; volige *m*, planche, de pied; coyau *m.*
canted ['kæntid], *a.* incliné, renversé; *Carp: etc:* biseauté.
canteen [kæn'ti:n], *s.* **1.** cantine *f*; restaurant *m*; (*in shipyard*) cambuse *f*; *NAm:* cantine, magasin *m* à l'usage des soldats; (*in S. Africa*) cabaret *m*, café *m*; **c. keeper, manager,** cantinier, -ière; (*in shipyard*) cambusier *m.* **2.** *Mil:* (*a*) bidon *m*; (*b*) gamelle *f*; (*c*) cantine à vivres. **3. c. of cutlery,** service *m* de table (couteaux et orfèvrerie) en coffre; ménagère *f.*
canter[1] ['kæntər], *s. A:* & *Lit:* **1.** hypocrite *mf*; tartufe *m*; cafard, -arde. **2.** mendiant *m*; vagabond *m.*
canter[2], *s. Equit:* petit galop, galopade *f*; **preliminary c.,** petit galop d'essai; **to have a c.,** faire un petit galop; *Rac:* **trial c.,** canter *m*; **to win in a c.,** gagner la course haut la main, dans un canter; arriver bon premier; *F:* arriver dans un fauteuil.
canter[3]. **1.** *v.i.* aller au petit galop; *F:* **to c. along,** ambler. **2.** *v.tr.* faire aller (un cheval) au petit galop.
Canterbury ['kæntəb(ə)ri]. **1.** *Pr.n. Geog:* Cantorbéry *m*; *Bot:* **C. bell(s),** campanule *f* à grosses fleurs, carillon *m*; *Hort:* **C. hoe,** croc *m* à pommes de terre; *Cu:* **C. lamb,** agneau néo-zélandais. **2.** *s. A.Furn:* (*a*) casier *m* à musique; (*b*) servante *f*, desserte *f.*
cantharid ['kænθərid], *s. Ent:* cantharide *f.*
cantharidin(e) [kæn'θæridin, -ain], *s. Ch: Pharm:* cantharidine *f.*
cantharis, *pl.* **cantharides** ['kænθəris, kæn'θæridi:z], *s.* **1.** *Ent:* cantharide *f.* **2.** *pl. Pharm:* **c.,** poudre *f* de cantharides.
cantharos, cantharus, *pl.* **-i** ['kænθərəs; -i:, -ai], *s. Ant:* canthare *m.*
canthoplasty [kænθou'plæsti], *s. Surg:* canthoplastie *f.*
canthus, *pl.* **-i** ['kænθəs; -ai, -i:], *s. Anat: etc:* commissure *f* des paupières; canthus *m*; **inner c.,** larmier *m*; **greater c., lesser c.,** grand, petit, canthus.
canticle ['kæntikl], *s.* cantique *m*; *B:* **the C. of Canticles,** le Cantique des Cantiques.
cantilena [kænti'leinə, -'li:nə], *s. Mus:* cantilène *f.*
cantilever ['kæntili:vər], *s.* (*a*) *Arch:* encorbellement *m*, modillon *m*; (*b*) *Civ.E:* *Const:* **c. beam,** poutre *f* en console, en porte-à-faux, en encorbellement, en cantilever; travée *f* en porte-à-faux; **c. foundation,** montage *m* en porte-à-faux, en encorbellement; construction *f* par encorbellement; **c. wall,** mur *m* en porte à faux; **c. bridge,** pont *m* en encorbellement, à consoles; cantilever *m*; (*c*) *Aut:* **c. springs,** ressorts *m* cantilever; ressorts en porte-à-faux; *Av:* **c. wing,** aile *f* en porte-à-faux; aile cantilever.
canting[1] ['kæntiŋ], *s.* inclinaison *f*; dévoiement *m* (d'un tuyau, etc.); cabanage *m* (d'un canot); **c. table,** table *f* inclinable, à bascule.
canting[2], *a.* **1.** hypocrite. **2.** *Her:* **c. arms,** armes parlantes.
cantle ['kæntl], *s.* **1.** *O:* morceau *m* (de pain, de fromage); parcelle *f.* **2.** *Harn:* troussequin *m*; arçon *m* de derrière.
canto ['kæntou], *s.* **1.** *Lit:* chant *m* (d'un poème). **2.** *Mus:* (*a*) (*in harmony*) chant; (*b*) *A:* **c. fermo,** cantus firmus.
canton[1] ['kæntɔn, -t(ə)n], *s.* **1.** *Adm:* canton *m.* **2.** *Her:* canton (de l'écusson).
canton[2], *v.tr.* (**cantoned**) **1.** ['kæntɔn, -t(ə)n], diviser (en cantons). **2.** *Mil:* [kən'tu:n], cantonner (des troupes).
Canton[3] ['kæn'tɔn], *Pr.n. Geog:* Canton; *Tex:* **C. crape, crêpe,** crêpe *m* de Chine.
cantonal ['kæntənl], *a. Adm:* cantonal, -aux.
Cantonese [kæntə'ni:z]. **1.** *Geog:* (*a*) *a.* cantonais; (*b*) *s.* Cantonais, -aise. **2.** *s. Ling:* Cantonais *m.*
cantonment [kən'tu:nmənt], *s. Mil:* cantonnement *m.*
cantor ['kæntɔ:r], *s. Ecc:* chantre *m.*
cantorial [kæn'tɔ:riəl], **cantoris** [kæn'tɔ:ris], *a. Ecc:* (côté *m*) du chantre.
Canuck [kə'nʌk], *F:* **1.** *NAm:* (*a*) *a.* canadien; (*b*) *s.* Canadien, -ienne. **2.** *Can: often Pej:* (*a*) *a.* canadien français; (*b*) *s.* Canadien, -ienne, français(e).
canula ['kænjulə], *s.* = CANNULA.
Canute [kə'nju:t], *Pr.n.m. Hist:* (le roi) Canut, Knut.
canvas ['kænvəs], *s.* **1.** (*a*) *Tex:* canevas *m*; (grosse) toile; toile à voiles; toile de tente; **waterproof c.,** toile grasse, imperméable, *Art:* **primed c.,** toile imprimée (pour artistes); **c. bucket,** seau *m* en toile; *Nau:* **c. screen,** rideau *m*, cloison *f*, en toile; *Aut: etc:* **c. of a tyre,** toiles d'un pneu; **tailor's c.,** toile tailleur; **to put a new c. to a painting,** rentoiler un tableau; **under c.,** (i) *Mil: etc:* sous la tente; (ii) *Nau:* sous voile; *Nau:* **with every stitch of c. set, with all her c. spread,** toutes voiles dehors; couvert de toile; à toc de toile; *F:* **c. town,** village *m* de toile; (*b*) *Needlew:* **c. work,** tapisserie *f*, broderie *f*, sur canevas, sur toile; (*c*) *Nau:* pointe *f* de canot. **2.** *Art:* **a fine c.,** un beau tableau, une belle toile. **3.** *Box: Wr:* tapis *m*; **to put one's opponent on the c.,** envoyer son adversaire au tapis.
canvasback ['kænvəsbæk], *s. Orn:* fuligule *f* aux yeux rouges; *Fr.C:* morillon *m* à dos blanc.
canvas-backed ['kænvəs'bækt], *a.* **c.-b. chair,** fauteuil *m* de toile.
canvass[1] ['kænvəs], *s.* **1.** examen minutieux; vérification *f*; *NAm:* dépouillement *m* (des suffrages); pointage *m* (des votes). **2.** *Pol: Com:* sollicitation *f* (de suffrages, de commandes); prospection *f* (de la clientèle); *Pol:* **to make a c.,** faire une tournée, une campagne, électorale.
canvass[2], *v.tr.* & *i.* **1.** discuter (une affaire); débattre, examiner minutieusement (une question); éplucher (une réputation); *NAm: Pol:* pointer, vérifier (des suffrages). **2.** *Pol: Com:* solliciter (des suffrages, des commandes); **to c. s.o.,** solliciter (i) la voix, (ii) la clientèle, de qn; démarcher qn; *Pol:* **to c. (a district),** faire une tournée électorale (dans une région); **to c. for s.o.,** faire des démarches en faveur de la candidature de qn; soutenir la candidature de qn; *Com:* **to c. for customers,** prospecter la clientèle; **to c. from door to door,** faire le porte(-) à (-) porte.
canvasser ['kænvəsər], *s.* solliciteur, -euse; démarcheur, -euse; prospecteur, -trice; *Com:* placier *m* (de marchandises).
canvassing ['kænvəsiŋ], *s.* **1.** discussion *f*; épluchage *m* (de réputations); *NAm:* pointage *m*, vérification *f* (des suffrages). **2.** sollicitation *f* (de suffrages, de commandes); *Pol:* propagande électorale; *Com: Adm:* **no c. allowed,** les visites et démarches des candidats ne sont pas admises.
canyon ['kænjən], *s. Geog:* canyon *m*, cañon *m.*
canzone [kæn'tsouni], *s. Lit: Mus:* canzone *f.*
canzonet [kænzə'net], **canzonetta** [kænzə'netə], *s. Mus:* canzonette *f.*
Caodaism ['kaudaiizm], *s. Rel:* caodaïsme *m.*
caoutchouc ['kautʃu:k], *s.* **1.** caoutchouc *m.* **2. mineral c.,** caoutchouc minéral; élatérite *f.*
cap[1] [kæp], *s.* **1.** (*a*) *Cost:* (*brimless*) bonnet *m*; (*with peak*) casquette *f*; têtière *f* (d'enfant); toque *f* (universitaire, de jockey); képi *m* (de militaire); bonnet, béret *m* (de marin); **paper c.,** coiffure *f* de cotillon, chapeau *m* de papier; **skull c.,** calotte *f*; **bathing c., swimming c.,** bonnet de bain, baigneuse *f*; *A.Cost:* **mob c.,** bonnet (de femme) s'attachant sous le menton; *Sp:* **football c.,** cape *f*; **to win one's c.,** gagner sa cape; **scrum c.,** protège-oreilles *m inv*; *Jur:* **black c.,** bonnet noir (que coiffe le juge en prononçant une condamnation à mort); **c. and bells,** marotte *f* (de bouffon); *Sch:* **in c. and gown,** en costume académique, en toque et en toge; **to come c. in hand,** se présenter chapeau bas, le bonnet à la main; *F:* (*of woman*) **to set her c. at a man,** entreprendre la conquête d'un homme; faire des avances à un homme; **if the c. fits, wear it!** qui se sent morveux se mouche! à bon entendeur salut! **to put on one's thinking c.,** méditer une question; prendre le temps de réfléchir; (*b*) *Orn:* capuchon *m*, chapeau *m* (d'un oiseau); (*c*) quote-part (payée par les invités d'une chasse à courre). **2.** (*a*) chapiteau *m* (de colonne); chapeau (de champignon); comble *m* en dôme, lanterne *f* (de bâtiment); (*b*) *Tchn:* chapeau (de protection); capuchon (d'un stylo); capuchon (de valve à pneu); calotte (d'une pompe); couvre-bec *m* (de clarinette); cuvette *f* (de montre); capsule *f* (de bouteille); chape *f* (d'aiguille aimantée); *El:* culot *m* (de lampe); *Mec.E:* chapeau, couvercle *m* (de palier, de soupape); **c. bearing,** palier *m* (à chapeau); **lubricator c., oil c.,** chapeau graisseur; **end c. of a torpedo tube,** capot *m* d'un tube lance-torpille; *Hyd.E:* **c. sill,** chapeau (d'une vanne); *Phot:* **lens c.,** bouchon *m* d'objectif; *Med: F:* (**Dutch**) **c.,** diaphragme (contraceptif); (*c*) chapeau, coiffe *f* (de pieu); *Nau:* chouque(t) *m* (de mâture); *Artil:* coiffe de rupture; chapeau, coiffe (de fusée); (*d*) *Bookb:* coiffe (de tranchefile). **3.** *Exp:* amorce *f*, capsule; *Sm.a:* **cartridge c., percussion c.,** amorce; **c. chamber,** porte-amorce *m inv*, couvre-amorce *m inv* (de cartouche). **4.** *Min:* **c. lamp,** photophore *m*, lampe frontale; **gas c., blue c.** (**in lamp**), auréole *f.* **5.** *Furn:* capiton *m* (entre boutons).
cap[2], *v.tr.* (**capped** [kæpt]) **1.** (*a*) coiffer (qn) d'un bonnet, d'une casquette; (*b*) *Sch:* (*in Scot.*) **to c. a candidate,** conférer un grade à un candidat; (*c*) *Sp:* donner sa cape à (un joueur). **2.** coiffer, couronner, recouvrir (**sth. with sth.,** qch. de qch.); coiffer (une fusée, un pieu); capsuler (une bouteille); (*over cork*) surboucher (une bouteille); armer (un aimant); amorcer (un obus). **3.** *A:* saluer (qn); se découvrir devant (qn); donner un coup de chapeau à (qn). **4.** (*outdo*) surpasser; **to c. a quotation,** renchérir sur une citation; **that caps everything, the lot!** ça c'est le comble! le bouquet! il ne manquait plus que ça! **5.** *Vet:* **to c. a horse's hocks,** faire naître un capelet au jarret d'un cheval.
cap[3], *s. Typ: F:* majuscule *f.*
cap[4], *s. F:* (*form of address*) (i) capitaine (*m*); (ii) mon vieux.
capability [keipə'biliti], *s.* **1.** (*a*) capacité *f* (**of doing sth.,** pour faire qch.); faculté *f* (**to do sth.,** de faire qch.); (*b*) susceptibilité *f* (d'amélioration, etc.). **2. the plan has capabilities,** le projet présente des possibilités; **the boy has capabilities,** c'est un enfant bien doué, un enfant qui promet; c'est un enfant qui a des moyens.
capable ['keipəbl], *a.* **1.** (*a*) capable (**of sth., of doing sth.,** de qch., de faire qch.); **c. of any crime,** capable de tous les crimes; **to show what one is c. of,** montrer ce dont on est capable; donner sa mesure; (*b*) **very c. doctor, teacher,** médecin, professeur, très capable, très compétent, *F:* tout à fait à la hauteur; **I have left the business in c. hands,** j'ai laissé l'affaire en bonnes mains. **2.** susceptible (d'amélioration, d'explication, etc.).
capably ['keipəbli], *adv.* avec compétence; d'une manière compétente.
capacious [kə'peiʃəs], *a.* vaste, spacieux; (salle *f*) de vastes proportions; **his c. pockets were stuffed with . . .,** ses amples poches étaient bourrées de . . .; **a c. jug,** un pot de dimensions respectables; **a c. memory,** une mémoire bourrée de faits; une mémoire qui retient tout; une vaste mémoire.
capaciousness [kə'peiʃəsnis], *s.* amples proportions *fpl* (d'une salle, etc.).
capacitance [kə'pæsitəns], *s. El: Elcs:* capacitance *f*, réactance *f* capacitaire; **c. bridge,** pont *m* de capacitance; **c. feedback,** réaction capacitive; **c. loading,** charge capacitive; **c. relay,** relai capacitif; **c. meter,** capacimètre *m.*
capacitate [kə'pæsiteit], *v.tr.* **1.** rendre (qn) capable, qualifier (qn) (**for sth., to do sth.,** de qch., de faire qch.). **2.** *Jur:* donner pouvoir, donner qualité, à (qn) (**to act,** pour agir); **to be capacitated to act,** avoir qualité pour agir.
capacitative [kə'pæsitətiv], **capacitive** [kə'pæsitiv], *a. El: Elcs:* capacitif; capacitaire; **c. coupling,** couplage capacitif; **capacitative reactance,** réactance *f* de capacité.
capacitor [kə'pæsitər], *s. El: Elcs:* condensateur *m*; **c. antenna,** antenne *f* condensateur; **antenna c.,** condensateur d'antenne; **c. microphone,** microphone *m* électrostatique; **trimmer, trimming, c.,** condensateur d'appoint, de correction; **blocking, stopping, c.,** condensateur d'arrêt; **coupling c.,** condensateur de couplage; **by-pass c.,** condensateur de découplage, de dérivation; **balancing c.,** condensateur d'équilibrage; **smoothing c.,** condensateur de filtrage; **feedback c.,** condensateur de réaction; **two-cell, three-cell, c.,** condensateur double, triple; **series c.,** condensateur en série; **polarized c.,** condensateur polarisé; *Cmptr:* **c. storage, store,** mémoire *f* à condensateur.
capacity [kə'pæsiti], *s.* **1.** (*a*) capacité *f* (d'un cylindre, etc., *El:* d'un accumulateur, d'un condensateur); contenance *f* (d'un tonneau, etc.); *El:* **installed c.,** puissance installée, **cut-out, load, c.,** capacité limite; *W.Tel: etc:* **c. earth,** contrepoids *m* (d'antenne); **cubic c.,** volume *m*; *Nau:* **bunker c., c. of the bunkers,** volume des soutes; *Mch: I.C.E: etc:* **cubic c. of cylinders,** cylindrée *f*; (*b*) *Trans: Ind: etc:* rendement *m*; débit *m*; **production c.,** capacité de production; **to work at full c.,** travailler à plein rendement; **c. output,** production *f* maximum; **idle c.,** potentiel *m* non utilisé; **profit-earning c.,** rentabilité *f*; *Nau: etc:* **deadweight c.,** portée en lourd; **measurement c.,** portée en volume; (*of vehicle*) **carrying c.,** charge admise, utile; (*of crane*) **lifting c.,** puissance de levage; **light-transmitting c.** (**of field glasses**), intensité lumineuse (d'une jumelle); (*c*) **seating c.,** nombre *m* de places (dans une voiture, un autobus, un théâtre, etc.); (*in bus, etc.*) **seating c., 30,** places assises: 30; *Th: etc:* **house filled to c.,** salle comble, bondée; **to play to c.,** (i) *Th: etc:* jouer à bureaux fermés; (ii) *Sp:* jouer à guichets fermés; **storage c.,** (i) *Ind: etc:* capacité de stockage; (ii) *Cmptr:* capacité de mémoire; *F:* **I'm full to c.,** je ne puis plus rien manger; **he has a remarkable c. for whisky,** il peut absorber des quantités extraordinaires de whisky (sans broncher). **2.** (*talent, ability*) capacité (**for,** pour, de); aptitude *f* (à faire qch.); **c. for work, for love,** capacité de travailler, d'aimer; **business c.,** capacité pour les affaires; **to show one's capacities,** donner sa mesure; **to the utmost of**

my c., de tout mon pouvoir; dans toute la mesure de mes moyens; **a man of great c.,** un homme très capable; un homme doué; **that seems beyond the c. of the average man,** l'homme moyen serait incapable de faire, de comprendre, cela. **3. to have c. to act,** avoir qualité pour agir; **in the c. of. . .,** en qualité de . . .; **in my c. as a priest,** en ma qualité de prêtre; **to act in one's official c.,** agir dans l'exercice de ses fonctions; **to act in one's individual c.,** agir à titre individuel, sur son initiative privée; agir en (qualité de) simple particulier; **to serve in the c. of . . .,** servir en qualité de . . ., en caractère de . . .; remplir les fonctions de . . .; **to have no c. to act,** ne pas avoir qualité, caractère, pour agir.

cap-à-pie [kæpə'pi:], *adv.* (armé) de pied en cap.

caparison[1] [kə'pærisn], *s. A: & Lit:* **1.** caparaçon *m.* **2.** *pl.* équipement somptueux; parure *f.*

caparison[2], *v.tr.* **(caparisoned)** *A: & Lit:* caparaçonner (un cheval).

cape[1] [keip], *s.* **1.** *Cost:* (*a*) pèlerine *f,* cape *f*; (*small*) collet *m*; (*b*) *Ecc:* camail *m, pl.* camails. **2.** *Orn:* collier *m,* camail (du coq).

cape[2], *s.* **1.** cap *m,* promontoire *m*; **C. Finisterre, C. Horn,** le cap Finisterre, le cap Horn; **North C.,** le Cap Nord; *A:* (*of deceived husband*) **to go round C. Horn,** être cocufié. **2.** (*a*) **the C. (of Good Hope),** le Cap (de Bonne-Espérance); *Hist:* **C. Colony,** la colonie du Cap; *Hist:* **the C.-to-Cairo railway,** le chemin de fer du Cap au Caire; le Transafricain; **C. Coloured,** métis *m* (de l'Afrique du Sud); *Veh:* **C. cart,** chariot couvert (généralement à bœufs); *Meteor:* **the C. doctor,** le vent fort du sud-est (de l'Afrique du Sud); **the C. Dutch,** les Afrikanders *m*; *Ling:* **C. Dutch,** afrikander *m*; (*b*) *Orn:* **C. hen,** pétrel équinoxial; **C. pigeon,** pétrel damier, *F:* pigeon *m* du Cap; *Bot:* **C. primrose,** streptocarpus *m*; **C. gooseberry,** coqueret *m* du Pérou; *Z:* **C. hartebeest,** caama *m.*

caped [keipt], *a.* (*a*) (manteau *m*) à pèlerine; (*b*) vêtu d'une pèlerine.

Cape-Horner ['keip'hɔ:nər], *s. A: Nau:* cap-hornier *m.*

capel ['keipl], *s. Miner:* silex corné.

capelin ['kæplin], *s. Ich:* capelan *m* de Terre-Neuve.

capeline ['keiplin], *s. Cost: Med:* capeline *f.*

Capella [kæ'pelə], *s. Astr:* la Chèvre.

capellet ['kæpəlet], *s. Vet:* capelet *m.*

caper[1] ['keipər], *s. Bot:* **1.** câprier *m*; **c. plantation,** câprière *f.* **2.** (*a*) *Cu:* câpre *f*; **c. jar, pot,** câprière; **c. sauce,** sauce *f* aux câpres; (*b*) **bean c.,** fabagelle *f,* fabago *m*; (*c*) **English capers,** câpres capucines.

caper[2], *s.* **1.** entrechat *m,* cabriole *f,* gambade *f*; **to cut a c.,** faire une cabriole, un entrechat; **to cut capers,** (i) faire des entrechats; (ii) *F:* faire des siennes; **that's another of his capers,** c'est encore un de ses tours. **2.** *Equit:* cabrade *f,* escapade *f.*

caper[3], *v.i.* **to c. (about),** faire des entrechats, des cabrioles, *F:* des sauts de cabri; cabrioler; gambader.

caper[4], *s. Hist:* corsaire *m.*

capercailzie, capercailye, capercaillie ['kæpə'keili], *s. Orn:* grand tétras; (grand) coq de bruyère (d'Ecosse); **hybrid c.,** petit tétras.

caperer ['keipərər], *s.* **1.** cabrioleur, -euse; gambadeur, -euse. **2.** *Ent:* phrygane *f.*

Capernaite [kə'pə:nait], *s.* habitant, -ante, de Capharnaüm.

Capernaum [kə'pə:niəm], *Pr.n. B.Hist:* Capharnaüm *m.*

Capetian [kæ'pi:ʃən], *Hist:* **1.** *a.* capétien. **2.** *s.* Capétien *m.*

Cape Town ['keip'taun], *Pr.n. Geog:* le Cap, Capetown *m.*

capful ['kæpful], *s.* pleine casquette; *Nau:* **a c. of wind,** une bouffée de vent.

capias ['keipiæs], *s. Jur:* **writ of c.,** mandat *m* d'arrêt; mandat d'amener.

capibara [kæpii'bɑ:rə], *s. Z:* = CAPYBARA.

capillaceous [kæpi'leiʃəs], *a.* capillacé.

capillarimeter [kæpilə'rimitər], *s. Ph:* capillarimètre *m.*

capillaritis [kæpilə'raitis], *s. Med:* capillarite *f.*

capillarity [kæpi'læriti], *s. Ph:* capillarité *f.*

capillary [kə'piləri], *a.* capillaire; *Ph:* **c. attraction,** attraction *f* capillaire; *Anat:* **the c. vessels,** *s.* **the capillaries,** les vaisseaux capillaires; les capillaires *m*; **c. tube,** tube *m* capillaire; **c. pressure,** pression *f* capillaire; *Med:* **c. bronchitis,** bronchite *f* capillaire.

capilliculture [kə'pilikʌltjər], *s.* capilliculture *f.*

capillifolious [kæpili'fouliəs], *a. Bot:* capillifolié.

capilliform [kæ'pilifɔ:m], *a. Nat.Hist:* capilliforme; criniforme.

capillitium [kæpi'liʃiəm], *s. Bot:* capillitium *m.*

capita, *see* CAPUT.

capital[1] ['kæpitl], *s. Arch:* chapiteau *m.*

capital[2], *a. & s.*

I. *a.* **1.** (*a*) capital, -aux; **c. letter,** (lettre) capitale (*f*), (lettre) majuscule (*f*); **a c. A,** un grand A; **love with a c. L,** l'amour avec un grand A; (*b*) **c. city,** (ville) capitale (*f*). **2.** (*a*) *Jur:* **c. crime, offence,** crime capital, puni de mort; **c. punishment,** peine capitale, peine de mort; **c. case,** procès capital; (*b*) **c. sin,** péché capital; **c. error,** erreur fatale; *Navy:* **c. ship,** bâtiment *m* de ligne; **of c. importance,** d'une importance capitale, de la plus haute importance. **3.** *F:* excellent, de premier ordre; **a c. speech,** un discours admirable; **c.!** excellent! fameux!

II. *s.* **1.** (*a*) *Typ:* capitale *f,* majuscule *f*; **large capitals,** grandes capitales, majuscules; **small capitals,** petites capitales; (*on form*) **(write in) block capitals,** écrire en capitales (d'imprimerie); (*b*) capitale (d'un pays). **2.** *Fin:* capital *m,* capitaux *mpl,* fonds *m*(*pl*); **paid-up, paid-in, called-up, c.,** capital versé, appelé, réel, effectif; mise *f* de fonds; **registered, authorized, c.,** capital social, nominal, déclaré; **working c.,** fonds, capital, de roulement, d'exploitation; fonds roulant; **circulating c.,** capitaux circulants, roulants; **funded c.,** capitaux investis; **subscribed c.,** capital souscrit; **to live on one's c.,** vivre sur son capital; **to make c. out of sth.,** profiter de qch.; exploiter qch.; tirer parti de qch.; **c. accumulation,** accumulation *f* du capital; **c. assets,** actif immobilisé; **c. goods,** moyens *mpl* de production; **c. bonus, c. distribution,** actions données en prime; **c. expenditure,** dépenses *fpl* en capital, en immobilisations; frais *mpl* d'équipement; **c. expenditure account,** compte *m* immobilisations; **c. investment,** investissement *m* de capitaux; **c. movements,** mouvements *m* des capitaux; **c. levy,** prélèvement *m* sur le capital, sur les fortunes; **c. gain,** plus-value *f* (en capital); **c. gains tax,** impôt *m* sur les plus-values en capital.

capitalism ['kæpitəlizm], *s.* capitalisme *m.*

capitalist ['kæpitəlist], *s.* (*a*) capitaliste *mf*; **the great capitalists,** les grands financiers; la haute finance; (*b*) bailleur *m* de fonds.

capitalist(ic) [kæpitə'list(ik)], *a.* capitaliste.

capitalizable [kæpitə'laizəbl], *a.* capitalisable.

capitalization [kæpitəlai'zeiʃ(ə)n], *s.* **1.** capitalisation *f* (des intérêts, etc.); **market c.,** capitalisation par le marché; **c. issue,** attributions *fpl* d'actions gratuites. **2.** emploi *m* des majuscules.

capitalize ['kæpitəlaiz], *v.tr.* **1.** capitaliser (une rente, etc.); **your income, if capitalized, would run to . . .,** votre revenu, en termes de capital, se monterait à . . .; **capitalized value,** valeur capitalisée. **2.** écrire (un mot) avec une majuscule. **3.** *v.tr. & i.* **to c. (on) sth.,** tourner qch. à son avantage.

capitally ['kæpit(ə)li], *adv.* **1.** *Jur:* **c. condemned,** condamné à mort. **2.** admirablement (bien); à merveille.

capitate ['kæpiteit], **capitated** ['kæpiteited], *a.* (*a*) *Bot:* en capitule; capité; (*b*) *Ent:* **c. antennae,** antennes *f* en massue.

capitation [kæpi'teiʃ(ə)n], *s. Pol.Ec:* capitation *f*; *Adm:* **c. grant,** allocation *f* (de tant) par tête; *Sch:* **c. fees,** surcroît *m* de traitement (du directeur) à raison de tant par élève.

capitellate [kæpi'teleit], *a. Bot:* capitellé.

capitellid [kæpi'telid], *s. Ann:* capitellidé *m.*

Capitellidae [kæpi'telidi:], *s.pl. Ann:* capitellidés *m.*

capitellum, *pl.* **-a** [kæpi'teləm, -ə], *s.* **1.** *Anat:* condyle *m.* **2.** *Nat.Hist:* capitule *m.*

Capitol (the) [ðə'kæpitəl], *s.* le Capitole (de Rome, de Washington, etc.).

Capitoline [kə'pitəlain], *a. Rom.Ant: etc:* capitolin; **the C. (Hill),** le (mont) Capitolin; **the C. games,** les jeux capitolins.

Capitonidae [kæpi'tɔnidi:], *s.pl. Orn:* capitonidés *m,* les barbus *m.*

capitulant [kə'pitjulənt], *s.* capitulard *m.*

capitular[1] [kə'pitjulər], *a.* **1.** *Ecc:* capitulaire. **2.** *Nat.Hist:* capitulé.

capitular[2], *s.* **1.** *Jur: Hist:* capitulaire *m.* **2.** *Ecc:* (*a*) capitule *m*; (*b*) acte *m* capitulaire. **3.** *Ecc:* capitulant *m.*

capitulary[1] [kə'pitjuləri], *a. Ecc:* capitulaire.

capitulary[2], *s.* **1.** *Jur: Hist:* capitulaire *m*; **the Capitularies of Charlemagne,** les capitulaires de Charlemagne. **2.** *Ecc:* capitulant *m.*

capitulate[1] [kə'pitjuleit], *a. Bot:* capitellé.

capitulate[2], *v.i.* capituler.

capitulation [kəpitju'leiʃ(ə)n], *s.* **1.** (*a*) énumération *f* des chapitres, des articles (d'un traité, etc.); (*b*) *A:* **the Capitulations,** les Capitulations *f* (réglant les droits des sujets chrétiens en Turquie). **2.** capitulation, reddition *f* (d'une place forte).

capituliform [kæpi'tju:lifɔ:m], *a. Bot:* capituliforme.

capitulum, *pl.* **-a** [kə'pitjuləm, -ə], *s.* **1.** *Anat:* condyle *m.* **2.** *Nat.Hist:* capitule *m.* **3.** *Ecc:* capitule.

capless ['kæplis], *a.* sans bonnet, sans casquette; nu-tête.

caplin ['kæplin], *s. Ich:* capelan *m* de Terre-Neuve.

capnomancy [kæpnou'mænsi], *s.* capnomancie *f.*

capoc ['keipɔk], *s.* capok *m.*

capodastro ['kæpou'dæstrou], *s. Mus:* = CAPOTASTO.

capon ['keipən], *s. Cu:* chapon *m.*

caponier, caponiere [kæpə'niər], *s. Fort:* caponnière *f,* chaponnière *f.*

caponization [keipənai'zeiʃ(ə)n], *s. Husb:* chaponnage *m.*

caponize ['keipənaiz], *v.tr.* chaponner, châtrer (un poulet).

capot[1] [kə'pɔt], *s. Cards:* (*piquet*) capot *m.*

capot[2], *v.tr.* **(capotted)** *Cards:* faire (qn) capot.

capotasto ['kæpou'tæstou], *s. Mus:* capodastre *m,* capotasto *m,* barre *f* (de guitare etc.), *F:* capo *m.*

capote [kə'pout], *s. A:* manteau *m* à capuchon (de soldat, de voyageur).

cappadine ['kæpədi(:)n], *s. Com:* capiton *m*; bourre *f* de soie.

Cappadocia [kæpə'dousiə], *Pr.n. A.Geog:* Cappadoce *f.*

Cappadocian [kæpə'dousiən]. **1.** *A.Geog:* (*a*) *a.* cappadocien; (*b*) *s.* Cappadocien, -ienne. **2.** *s. Ling:* cappadocien *m.*

cap paper ['kæppeipər], *s. Paperm:* **1.** papier gris épais; papier bulle; papier d'emballage. **2.** papier à écrire de format 19 × 30.5 cms.

Capparidaceae [kæpəri'deisii:], *s.pl. Bot:* capparidacées *f.*

capped [kæpt], *a.* (*a*) *Vet:* **c. hock,** campane *f,* capelet *m*; (*b*) *Artil:* **c. shell,** obus *m* à coiffe (de rupture); **armour-piercing c. shell,** obus perforant à coiffe; (*c*) **c. dice,** dés faussés; (*d*) (*with s. or a. prefixed*) couvert de . . .; **snow-c.,** coiffé, couronné, couvert, de neige; **white-c. nurse,** infirmière coiffée de blanc; **screw-c. bottle,** flacon *m* à couvercle vissé.

cappelenite ['kæplənait], *s. Miner:* cappelénite *f.*

capper ['kæpər], *s.* **1.** (*pers.*) (*a*) capsuleur, -euse (de bouteilles); (*b*) (*at auction sale*) enchérisseur *m* complice (qui fait des offres pour faire monter les prix); (*c*) *esp. U.S: P:* compère *m* (d'escroc). **2.** (*machine*) capsulateur *m,* capsuleur *m,* capsuleuse *f* (de bouteilles).

capping ['kæpiŋ], *s.* **1.** (*a*) capsulage *m* (d'un flacon); **bottle-c. machine,** capsulateur *m,* capsuleur *m,* capsuleuse *f*; (*b*) amorçage *m* (d'un obus); (*c*) *Nau:* capelage *m* (de câbles); (*d*) *Sch: Scot: N.Z:* (i) séance *f* académique pour l'octroi des grades; (ii) octroi *m* d'un grade. **2.** (*a*) chapeau *m,* chape *f* (d'une charpente, d'un pieu, etc.); embout *m*; **the cappings of a timber platform,** les chapes d'une plate-forme en charpente; (*b*) *Min:* chapeau (d'un gisement de minerai).

Capreae ['kæprii:], *Pr.n. A.Geog:* Caprée *f.*

caprella [kə'prelə], *s. Crust:* caprelle *f*; (*genus*) caprella *f.*

Caprellidae [kə'prelidi:], *s.pl. Crust:* caprellidés *m.*

capreolar [kæpri'oulər], *a. Anat:* capréolaire.

capreolate ['kæpriəleit], *a. Bot:* capréolé.

Capri ['kæpri], *Pr.n. Geog:* (l'île *f* de) Capri.

capric ['kæprik], *a. Ch:* caprique.

capriccio [kə'pritʃiou], *s. Mus:* caprice *m.*

capriccioso [kə'pritʃiousou], *a. & adv. Mus:* capriccioso.

caprice [kə'pri:s], *s.* **1.** caprice *m,* lubie *f*; **to do sth. out of c.,** faire qch. par fantaisie, par pur caprice; **she makes him give in to all her caprices,** elle lui fait faire ses quatre volontés. **2.** *Mus:* caprice.

capricious [kə'priʃəs], *a.* capricieux.

capriciously [kə'priʃəsli], *adv.* capricieusement.

capriciousness [kə'priʃəsnis], *s.* humeur capricieuse, inégale; **c. of temper,** inégalité *f* d'humeur.

Capricorn ['kæprikɔ:n], *s.* **1.** *Astr:* Capricorne *m*; *Geog:* **the Tropic of C.,** le tropique du Capricorne. **2.** *Ent:* **c. beetle,** capricorne.

Capridae ['kæpridi:], *s.pl. Z:* capridés *m.*

caprification [kæprifi'keiʃ(ə)n], *s. Hort:* caprification *f* (des figues).

caprifig ['kæprifig], *s. Bot:* (*a*) caprifigue *f*; (*b*) caprifiguier *m.*

Caprifoliaceae [kæprifouli'eisii:], *s.pl. Bot:* caprifoliacées *f.*

Caprimulgidae [kæpri'mʌldʒidi:], *s.pl. Orn:* caprimulgidés *m,* les engoulevents *m.*

Caprimulgiformes [kæprimʌldʒi'fɔ:mi:z], *s.pl. Orn:* caprimulgiformes *m.*

Caprinae ['kæprini:], *s.pl. Z:* caprinés *m*; caprins *m.*

caprine ['kæprain], *a. Z:* caprin.

capriole[1] ['kæprioul], *s. Equit:* cabriole *f.*

capriole[2], *v.i.* (*of horse*) cabrioler.

capriped [ˈkæpriped], *a.* capripède.
caprizant [ˈkæpriz(ə)nt], *a. Med:* (pouls) capricant.
caproic [kəˈprouik], *a. Ch:* caproïque.
caproin [ˈkæprɔin], *s. Ch:* caproïne *f.*
caprolactam [kæprouˈlæktəm], *s. Ch:* caprolactame *m.*
Capromyidae [kæprouˈmaiidi:], *s.pl. Z:* capromyidés *m.*
capromys [ˈkæproumis], *s. Z:* capromys *m.*
capros [ˈkæprəs], *s. Ich:* capros *m,* poisson *m* sanglier.
caproyl [ˈkæprɔil], *s. Ch:* caproyle *m.*
capryl [ˈkæpril], *s. Ch:* caprylе *m.*
caprylic [kəˈprilik], *a. Ch:* caprylique.
capsaicin [kæpˈseiisin], *s. Ch:* capsaïcine *f.*
Capsian [ˈkæpsiən], *a. Prehist:* capsien.
capsicin [ˈkæpsisin], *s. Ch:* capsicine *f.*
capsicum [ˈkæpsikəm], *s.* **1.** *Bot:* piment *m.* **2.** *Cu:* piment, poivron *m.*
capsid [ˈkæpsid], *s.* **1.** *Biol:* capside *f.* **2.** *Ent:* capsidé *m.*
Capsidae [ˈkæpsidi:], *s.pl. Ent:* capsidés *m.*
capsizable [kæpˈsaizəbl], *a.* chavirable, renversable.
capsize [kæpˈsaiz]. **1.** *v.i.* (*of boat*) chavirer; cabaner; (*of car*) capoter, faire panache, faire capote; (*of small boat*) to (**broach to and**) **c.,** rouler. **2.** *v.tr.* faire chavirer (une embarcation).
capsizing [kæpˈsaiziŋ], *s.* chavirement *m;* capotage *m.*
capsomere [ˈkæpsoumi:ər], *s. Biol:* capsomère *m.*
capstan [ˈkæpst(ə)n], *s.* **1.** *Nau: etc:* cabestan *m;* poupée *f* de halage; **c. engine,** moteur *m* du cabestan; **hand c.,** cabestan à bras; **to rig the hand c.,** mettre les barres en place; **double-headed c.,** cabestan à double cloche; **horizontal c.,** guindas *m;* vindas *m;* vindau, -aux *m;* **c. bar,** barre *f* de cabestan; **c. swifter,** raban *m* de barres. **2.** *Mec.E:* revolver *m* (de tour); tourelle *f* (de tour); **c. lathe,** tour *f* à revolver; **c. nut,** écrou *m* à tête romaine; **c. headed screw,** vis *f* à œil, à tête romaine. **3.** *Furn:* **c. table,** guéridon *m.*
capstone [ˈkæpstoun], *s.* **1.** *Const:* chaperon *m* (d'un toit); pierre *f* de faîte. **2.** *Prehist:* table *f* (couronnant un dolmen).
capsular [ˈkæpsjulər], *a.* (*a*) *Bot:* (fruit *m*) capsulaire; (*b*) *Anat:* (vaisseau *m*) capsulaire.
capsule[1] [ˈkæpsju:l], *s.* (*a*) *Bot: Anat:* capsule *f; Anat:* **Glisson's c.,** capsule de Glisson; (*b*) *Ent: Moll.* **egg c.,** oothèque *f;* (*c*) *Pharm:* capsule, gélule *f;* (*d*) *Tchn:* **space c.,** cabine spatiale, capsule spatiale; *Av:* **ejection c.,** cabine largable; *W.Tel: etc:* **c. of transmitter,** pastille *f* microphonique.
capsule[2], *v.tr.* capsuler, surboucher (une bouteille).
capsuliferous [kæpsjuˈlifərəs], *a. Bot:* capsulifère.
capsuliform [kæpˈsju:lifɔ:m], *a.* en forme de capsule.
capsuling [ˈkæpsjuliŋ], *s.* capsulage *m.*
capsulitis [kæpsjuˈlaitis], *s. Med:* capsulite *f.*
capsulize [ˈkæpsjulaiz], *v.tr. Journ:* **capsulized account,** reportage *m* en bref.
capsulorraphy [kæpsjuloˈræfi], *s. Surg:* capsulorraphie *f.*
capsulotomy [kæpsjuˈlɔtəmi], *s. Surg:* capsulotomie *f.*
capsus [ˈkæpsəs], *s. Ent:* capsus *m.*
captain[1] [ˈkæptin], *s.* **1.** (*a*) chef *m,* capitaine *m;* **the great captains of industry,** les grands capitaines, les chefs, de l'industrie; (*b*) *Sp:* capitaine, chef, d'équipe; (*c*) *Scout:* chef(e)taine *f* (de guides); (*d*) *Nau:* capitaine, commandant *m* (d'un navire); **c. of the watch,** chef de quart; **c. of the hold,** chef de cale; *Navy:* **c. of the gun, gun c.,** chef de pièce; (*e*) *Av:* commandant de bord; (*f*) capitaine (des pompiers). **2.** (*military rank*) (*a*) *Mil:* capitaine; (*W.R.A.C.*) première classe; (*b*) *Navy:* capitaine de vaisseau; **c. of the fleet,** capitaine de pavillon; (*c*) *Mil.Av:* **group c.,** colonel *m* (d'aviation).
captain[2], *v.tr.* **1.** commander (une compagnie, etc.). **2.** conduire, mener (une expédition, etc.); *Sp:* **to c. a team,** être chef, capitaine, d'une équipe; mener, diriger, une équipe.
Captain Cook(er) [ˈkæptinˈkuk(ər)], *s. N.Z: Z: F:* sanglier *m.*
captaincy [ˈkæptinsi], *s.* **1.** grade *m* de capitaine; capitainat *m;* **to obtain one's c.,** être promu capitaine; passer capitaine. **2.** (*a*) conduite *f* (d'une expédition, etc.); **under the c. of . . .,** sous la conduite de . . .; (*b*) *Sp:* commandement *m* de l'équipe.
captainship [ˈkæptinʃip], *s.* **1.** = CAPTAINCY. **2. to handle one's troops with consummate c.,** diriger ses troupes avec l'art d'un grand capitaine.
captation [kæpˈteiʃ(ə)n], *s. Jur:* captation *f;* **c. of an inheritance,** captation d'héritage.
caption[1] [ˈkæpʃ(ə)n], *s.* **1.** (*a*) (*in newspaper, book*) en-tête *m, pl.* en-têtes; chapeau *m;* (*b*) (*of illustration*) légende *f;* (*c*) *Cin:* sous-titre *m, pl.* sous-titres; **c. writer,** titulateur *m;* (*d*) *Journ:* rubrique *f.* **2.** *Jur:* arrestation *f;* prise *f* de corps. **3.** *Jur:* indication *f* (sur un acte de procédure) du requérant, du lieu et de la date; indication d'origine.
caption[2], *v.tr.* écrire la légende d'(une illustration); sous-titrer (un film).
captious [ˈkæpʃəs], *a.* **1.** (raisonnement) captieux, insidieux, sophistique. **2.** (*of pers.*) difficultueux, pointilleux, chicaneur, vétilleux.
captiously [ˈkæpʃəsli], *adv.* pointilleusement; dans un esprit de chicane.
captiousness [ˈkæpʃəsnis], *s.* **1.** caractère *m* sophistique (d'un argument). **2.** pointillerie *f,* chicanerie *f;* esprit *m* de chicane.
captivate [ˈkæptiveit], *v.tr.* charmer, captiver, subjuguer, séduire (tous les cœurs, etc.).
captivating [ˈkæptiveitiŋ], *a.* séduisant; captivant; enchanteur, -eresse.
captivation [kæptiˈveiʃ(ə)n], *s.* séduction *f;* ensorcellement *m;* charme fascinateur.
captive [ˈkæptiv]. **1.** *a.* (*a*) captif; **he was taken c.,** on l'a fait prisonnier; **c. balloon,** ballon captif; captif *m;* **c. bird,** oiseau captif, en captivité; **the films which the airlines inflict on their c. audiences,** les films imposés par les compagnies aériennes sur une assistance incapable d'y échapper; (*b*) **c. state,** état *m* de captivité. **2.** *s.* captif, -ive; prisonnier, -ière.
captivity [kæpˈtiviti], *s.* captivité *f;* **taken (away) into c.,** emmené en captivité; **animals in c.,** animaux *m* en captivité.
captor [ˈkæptər]. **1.** *s.* (*a*) celui qui fait qn prisonnier; (*b*) ravisseur *m.* **2.** *a.* & *s. Navy:* **c. (ship),** (navire *m*) capteur (*m*).
captorhinomorph [ˈkæptouˈrainoumɔ:f], *s. Rept: Paleont:* captorhinomorphe *m.*
Captorhinomorpha [ˈkæptourainouˈmɔ:fə], *s.pl. Rept: Paleont:* captorhinomorphes *m.*
capture[1] [ˈkæptjər], *s.* **1.** (*action*) (*a*) capture *f,* prise *f* (d'un navire, d'un prisonnier, d'un animal, etc.); **c. at sea,** prise en mer; **the law of Warlike C.,** le code qui régit le droit de prise entre belligérants; (*b*) *Geog:* **(river) c.,** capture (d'un cours d'eau); **c. by regressive erosion,** capture par érosion régressive, par recul de tête; **c. by overflow,** capture par déversement; **elbow of c.,** coude *m* de capture; (*c*) *Cmptr:* **data c.,** saisie *f,* collecte *f,* de données. **2.** (*thg or pers. taken*) prise.
capture[2], *v.tr.* **1.** (*a*) capturer (un navire, un malfaiteur, un animal, etc.); prendre (une ville) **(from,** sur); s'emparer d'(un malfaiteur); *Com:* **to c. the market,** accaparer la vente; **to c. s.o.'s affections,** se faire aimer de qn; attirer l'amitié de qn; (*b*) *Cmptr:* saisir (des données). **2.** *W.Tel: etc:* capter (des ondes, une émission).
capturer [ˈkæptjərər], *s.* = CAPTOR 1.
capturing [ˈkæptjəriŋ], *s.* **1.** capture *f* (d'un navire, d'un malfaiteur), prise *f* (d'une ville). **2.** *W.Tel: etc:* captage *m* (des ondes, d'une émission).
Capua [ˈkæpjuə], *Pr.n. Geog:* Capoue *f.*
Capuan [ˈkæpjuən], *Geog:* (*a*) *a.* capouan, de Capoue; (*b*) *s.* Capouan, -ane.
capuche [kæˈpu:ʃ], *s. Cost:* capuchon *m,* capuce *m.*
capuchin [ˈkæpu(t)ʃin], *s.* **1.** *Ecc:* capucin, -ine; **C. convent, friary,** couvent *m* de capucins. **2.** *Cost:* mante *f* à capuchon; capeline *f.* **3.** *Husb:* pigeon capucin; pigeon nonnain. **4.** *Z:* (*monkey*) saï *m, F:* capucin.
caput, *pl.* **capita** [ˈkæput, ˈkæpitə], *s. used in the phr.* **per capita,** par tête; par habitant.
capybara [kæpiˈbɑ:rə], *s. Z:* capybara *m,* cabiai *m,* cochon *m* d'eau (sud-américain).
car [kɑ:r], *s.* **1.** (*a*) *Lit:* (*chariot*) char *m;* **triumphal c.,** char de triomphe; (*b*) **jaunting c.,** carriole irlandaise à deux roues. **2.** (*a*) **(motor) c.,** automobile *f, F: O:* auto *f* voiture *f; Fr.C: F:* char; **private c.,** voiture de tourisme; **sports c.,** voiture (de) sport; **racing c.,** voiture de course; **radio c.,** voiture radio; **armoured c.,** voiture blindée; blindée *f;* **c. manufacturer,** constructeur *m* (d')automobile(s); **c. licence,** carte grise; **c. park,** parc *m* de stationnement; *F:* parking *m;* **multi-storey c. park,** garage *m* à plusieurs étages; **c. park attendant,** gardien *m* de voitures; **c. carrier,** plate-forme *f* de transport auto; **double-deck c. carrier,** plate-forme double de transport auto; (*b*) *Min: etc:* chariot *m,* berline *f,* wagon *m,* wagonnet *m* (de) mine; **coal c.,** chariot à charbon. **3.** *Rail:* (*a*) *NAm:* voiture, wagon (de chemin de fer); **parlour c.,** voiture-salon *f, pl.* voitures-salons; **freight c.,** wagon à, de, marchandises; **flat c.,** wagon plate-forme; **gondola c.,** wagon découvert, ouvert; **stock, horse, c.,** wagon à bestiaux, à chevaux; **dump c.,** wagon à bascule; (*b*) **dining c., restaurant c.,** wagon-restaurant *m, pl.* wagons-restaurants; **buffet c., refreshment c.,** voiture-buffet *f, pl.* voitures-buffets; voiture-bar *f, pl.* voitures bars; wagon-bar *m, pl.* wagons-bars; **sleeping c.,** wagon-lit *m, pl.* wagons-lits. **4.** (*a*) nacelle *f* (d'un pont transbordeur, *Aer:* d'un ballon); (*b*) *NAm:* cabine *f* (d'un ascenseur).
carabao [kærəˈbeiou], *s. Z:* karbau *m,* kérabau *m.*
carabid [ˈkærəbid], **carabidan** [kəˈræbidən], *s. Ent:* carabidé *m,* carabique *m.*
carabineer [kærəbiˈniər], *s. A.Mil:* carabinier *m;* **the Carabineers,** le 6e régiment des Dragons de la Garde.
caraboid [ˈkærəbɔid], *a. Ent:* caraboïde; **c. beetle,** zabre *m.*
carabus [ˈkærəbəs], *s. Ent:* carabe *m.*
caracal [ˈkærəkæl], *s. Z:* caracal *m, pl.* -als, chat *m* du désert.
caracara [kærəˈkɑ:rə], *s. Orn:* caracara *m;* **Audubon's c.,** *Fr.C:* caracara commun.
caracole[1] [ˈkærəkoul], *s.* **1.** *Equit:* caracole *f.* **2.** *Arch:* escalier *m* en spirale, en colimaçon.
caracole[2], *v.i. Equit:* caracoler.
caracolite [kærəˈkoulait], *s. Miner:* caracolite *f.*
caracore [ˈkærəkɔər], **caracora** [kærəˈkɔ:rə], *s. Nau:* caracore *m.*
caracul [ˈkæriəkʌl], *s. Com:* (fourrure *f* de) caracul *m.*
carafe [kəˈræf, -ˈrɑ:f], *s.* carafe *f;* **c. wine,** vin en carafe.
carambola [kærəmˈboulə], *s. Bot:* (*a*) carambole *f;* (*b*) (*tree*) carambolier *m.*
caramel[1] [ˈkærəmel], *s.* **1.** caramel *m;* **c. flavour,** goût caramélé; **c. cream, cream c.,** crème caramel; **c. custard,** crème (renversée) au caramel. **2.** bonbon *m* au caramel. **3.** (couleur *f*) caramel *inv.*
caramel[2]. **1.** *v.tr.* caraméliser. **2.** *v.i.* se caraméliser.
caramelization [kærəmelaiˈzeiʃ(ə)n], *s.* caramélisation *f.*
caramelize [ˈkærəməlaiz], *v.tr.* caraméliser.
carangid [kəˈrændʒid], *s. Ich:* carangidé *m.*
Carangidae [kəˈrændʒidi:], *s.pl. Ich:* carangidés *m.*
carangus [kəˈræŋgəs], **caranx** [kəˈræŋks], *s. Ich:* carangue *f,* carange *f,* caranx *m.*
carapace [ˈkærəpeis], *s. Crust:* carapace *f;* bouclier *m.*
carat [ˈkærət], *s. Meas:* **1. metric c.** (*for weighing diamonds*), carat *m* (de 200 milligrammes). **2.** (*measure of fineness of gold*) carat (de fin); **twenty-four c. gold,** or *m* au titre 1000; **eighteen-c. gold,** or à dix-huit carats; or au titre 750; **twelve-c. bracelet,** bracelet *m* (en) demi-fin.
carau [kæˈrau], *s. Orn:* courlan *m.*
Caravaggio [kærəˈvædʒiou], *Pr.n.m.* le Caravage.
caravan[1] [ˈkærəvæn], *s.* **1.** caravane *f;* convoi *m* des déserts; **to travel in c.,** voyager en convoi. **2.** *Aut:* roulotte *f* automobile, roulotte remorque (de forains); caravane; **(touring) c.,** remorque *f* camping, *F:* camping *m;* remorque roulotte; **c. site,** camping.
caravan[2], *v.i.* faire du caravan(n)ing; faire du camping (en caravane).
caravaneer [kærəvəˈniər], *s.* caravanier *m* (de l'Orient).
caravan(n)er [kærəˈvænər], **caravanist** [kærəˈvænist], *s.* caravanier *m.*
caravan(n)ing [kærəˈvæniŋ], *s.* camping *m* (en caravane).
caravanserai [kærəˈvænsərai], *s.* caravansérail *m.*
caravel [ˈkærəvel], *s. A.Nau:* caravelle *f.*
caraway [ˈkærəwei], *s. Bot:* carvi *m,* cumin *m* (des prés); chervi(s) *m;* **c. seeds,** graines *f* de carvi.
carbamate [ˈkɑ:bəmeit], *s. Ch:* carbamate *m.*
carbamic [kɑ:ˈbæmik], *a. Ch:* carbamique.
carbamide [ˈkɑ:bəmaid], *s. Ch:* carbamide *f.*
carbamyl(e) [ˈkɑ:bəmil, -mail], *s. Ch:* carbamyle *m.*
carbanil [ˈkɑ:bənil], *s. Ch:* carbanile *m.*
carbanion [kɑ:bænˈaiən], *s. Ch:* carbanion *m.*
carbarn [ˈkɑ:bɑ:n], *s. U.S:* garage *m,* dépôt *m,* de tramways, d'autobus.
carbazide [ˈkɑ:bəzaid], *s. Ch:* carbazide *f.*
carbazol(e) [ˈkɑ:bəzɔl], *s. Ch:* carbazol(e) *m.*
carbide [ˈkɑ:baid], *s. Ch: Ind:* carbure *m;* **calcium c.,** *F:* **c.,** carbure de calcium.
carbine [ˈkɑ:bain], *s.* **1.** (*a*) carabine *f;* (*b*) *Mil:* mousqueton *m.* **2.** *U.S:* mitraillette *f.*
carbineer [kɑ:biˈniər], *s.* = CARABINEER.
carbinol [ˈkɑ:binɔl], *s. Ch:* carbinol *m.*
carbo- [ˈkɑ:bou], *pref.* carbo-.
carbocyclic [ˈkɑ:bouˈsaiklik], *a. Ch:* carbocyclique.
carbodiimide [ˈkɑ:bouˈdaiimaid], *s. Ch:* carbodiimide *m.*
carbogen [ˈkɑ:boudʒen], *s. Petr:* carbogène *m.*
carboh(a)emoglobin [ˈkɑ:bouhi:mouˈgloubin], *s. Bio-Ch:* carbohémoglobine *f.*
carbohydrase [ˈkɑ:bouˈhaidreis], *s. Ch:* carbohydrase *f.*
carbohydrate [ˈkɑ:bouˈhaidreit], *s.* (*a*) *Ch:* hydrate *m* de carbone; (*b*) (*in dieting*) **to avoid carbohydrates,** éviter les aliments glucidiques, les glucides, *F:* le sucre.
carbolated [ˈkɑ:bəleitid], *a. Ch:* phéniqué.
carbolic [kɑ:ˈbɔlik], *a. Ch:* phénique; carbolique; **c.**

acid, acide *m* phénique, carbolique; phénol *m,* carbol *m*; **c. oil,** huile *f* carbolique; *Pharm:* **c. lotion,** eau phéniquée.
carbolize ['kɑ:bəlaiz], *v.tr.* phéniquer; baigner, traiter, (une plaie) à l'acide phénique.
carbomycin [kɑ:bou'maisin], *s. Med:* carbomycine *f.*
carbon ['kɑ:bən], *s.* **1.** *Ch:* carbone *m*; **c. dioxide,** acide *m* carbonique; anhydride *m* carbonique; **c. disulphide,** carbo-sulphure *m*; **c. monoxide,** monoxyde, oxyde *m,* de carbone; *Med:* **c.-monoxide poisoning,** oxycarbonisme *m*; **c. black,** noir *m* de carbone; **c. cycle,** cycle *m* du charbon; *Prehist:* **c. dating, c. 14,** datation *f* par la méthode du carbone 14. **2.** *(a) Metall:* **powdered c.,** charbon *m* en poudre; cément *m*; **gas c.,** charbon de cornue; **c. filter,** filtre *m* à charbon; *El:* **c. filament lamp,** lampe *f* à filament de charbon; **c. electrode,** électrode *f* de charbon; **c. rheostat,** rhéostat *m* à compression de charbon; **c. brush,** baguette *f,* balai *m,* de charbon; crayon *m* (d'une lampe à arc); charbon; **c. holder,** porte-crayon *m,* porte-charbon *m inv* (de lampe à arc, de magnéto, etc.); *(b)* **c. process,** (i) *Phot:* procédé *m* au charbon; (ii) *Typ:* carbonnage *m*; *(c) I.C.E: etc:* **c. deposit,** encrassement *m,* calamine *f*; *(d) Typew:* **c. (paper),** (papier *m*) carbone; **c. (copy),** carbone, double *m.* **3.** *Lap:* carbonado *m.*
carbonaceous [kɑ:bə'neiʃəs], *a.* **1.** *Ch:* carboné. **2.** *Geol:* carbonifère.
carbonado [kɑ:bə'neidou], *s. Miner:* carbonado *m.*
carbonaro, *pl.* **-i** [kɑ:bə'nɑ:rou, -i], *s. Hist:* carbonaro *m, pl.* carbonari.
carbonatation [kɑ:bənei'teiʃ(ə)n], *s. Ch:* carbonatation *f.*
carbonate[1] ['kɑ:bəneit], *s. Ch:* carbonate *m*; **calcium c.,** carbonate de calcium.
carbonate[2], *v.tr. Ch:* carbonater.
carbonation [kɑ:bə'neiʃ(ə)n], *s. Ch:* carbonatation *f.*
carbonic [kɑ:'bɔnik], *a. Ch:* carbonique; **c. acid,** acide *m* carbonique; **c. acid gas, c. anhydride,** gaz *m* carbonique, anhydride *m* carbonique.
carboniferous [kɑ:bə'nifərəs], *a. & s. Geol:* carbonifère *(m).*
carbonite ['kɑ:bənait], *s.* **1.** *Miner:* cokéite *f.* **2.** *Exp:* carbonite *f.*
carbonitride [kɑ:bou'naitraid], *v.tr.* carbonitrurer.
carbonitriding [kɑ:bou'naitridiŋ], *s. Metall:* carbonitruration *f.*
carbonium [kɑ:'bouniəm], *s. Ch:* carbénium *m,* carbonium *m.*
carbonization [kɑ:bənai'zeiʃ(ə)n], *s.* **1.** carbonisation *f* (du bois, etc.); houillification *f* (de matières végétales). **2.** *I.C.E: etc:* encrassement *m,* calaminage *m.* **3.** *Tex:* carbonisage *m.*
carbonize ['kɑ:bənaiz]. **1.** *v.tr.* *(a) Ch:* carboniser, *I.C.E:* carburer; *(b) Ind:* carboniser, charbonner (du bois, etc.); *Geol:* houillifier (des matières végétales). **2.** *v.i.* *(a) I.C.E: etc:* s'encrasser, se calaminer; *(b) Geol:* se houillifier.
carbonizing ['kɑ:bənaiziŋ], *s.* = CARBONIZATION.
carbonyl ['kɑ:bənil], *s.* carbonyle *m*; **c. chloride,** acide *m* chlorocarbonique; phosgène *m,* chlorure *m* de carbonyle.
carborundum [kɑ:bə'rʌndəm], *s.* carborundum *m*; carbure *m* de silicium; **c. wheel,** meule *f* en carborundum.
carbostyril ['kɑ:bou'stiril], *s. Ch:* carbostyryle *m.*
carboxyhaemoglobin [kɑ:'bɔksihi:mou'gloubin], *s. Bio-Ch:* carboxyhémoglobine *f.*
carboxyl [kɑ:'bɔksil], *s. Ch:* carboxyle *m*; *Biol:* carboxylase *f.*
carboxylic [kɑ:bɔk'silik], *a. Ch:* carbonique.
carboy ['kɑ:bɔi], *s.* tourie (clissée); bonbonne *f,* ballon *m* (d'acide).
carbuncle ['kɑ:bʌŋkl], *s.* **1.** *Lap:* escarboucle *f.* **2.** *Med:* *(a)* charbon *m*; pustule maligne; *(b)* furoncle *m,* clou *m,* anthrax *m*; bourgeon *m* (sur le nez).
carbuncled ['kɑ:bʌŋkld], *a.* **1.** orné d'escarboucles. **2.** *(a) Med:* charbonneux; *(b) F:* (nez) couvert de boutons, bourgeonné.
carbuncular [kɑ:'bʌŋkjulər], *a. Med:* charbonneux; rouge et enflammé; **c. tumour,** tumeur charbonneuse; *Vet:* **c. fever,** fièvre charbonneuse; charbon *m.*
carburant ['kɑ:bjurənt], *s. I.C.E:* carburant *m.*
carburate ['kɑ:bjureit], *v.tr.* carburer.
carburated ['kɑ:bjureitid], *a.* carburé.
carburation [kɑ:bju'reiʃ(ə)n], *s.* carburation *f.*
carburet ['kɑ:bjuret], *v.tr.* carburer.
carburettant [kɑ:bju'retənt], *s. I.C.E:* carburant *m.*
carburetted [kɑ:bju'retid], *a. I.C.E:* **c. air,** air carburé; *Ch:* **c. hydrogen,** hydrogène carburé; méthane *m*; gaz *m* des marais.
carburetter, carburettor [kɑ:bju'retər], *s.* carburateur *m*; *I.C.E:* **constant level, float, c.,** carburateur à niveau constant; **dual c.,** carburateur double, jumelé; **jet c.,** carburateur à gicleur, à ajutage; **gravity-fed c.,** carburateur alimenté, par gravité, par différence de niveau; **pressure-fed c.,** carburateur alimenté sous pression; **pump-fed c.,** carburateur alimenté par pompe; **spray c.,** carburateur à pulvérisation; **suction c.,** carburateur à dépression; **two-stage c.,** carburateur à deux phases; **metering pin c.,** carburateur à pointeau de dosage; **flooded c.,** carburateur noyé.
carburetting [kɑ:bju'retiŋ], *s.* carburation *f.*
carburization [kɑ:bjurai'zeiʃ(ə)n], *s.* carburation *f,* cémentation *f.*
carburize ['kɑ:bjurɑ:iz], *v.tr.* **1.** carburer (un gaz, etc.). **2.** *Metall:* carburer, cémenter (l'acier, etc.).
carburizing ['kɑ:bjuraiziŋ], *s.* **1.** carburation *f* (d'un gaz). **2.** *Metall:* carburization.
carbylamine [kɑ:'biləmin], *s. Ch:* carbylamine *f.*
carcajou ['kɑ:kəʒu:], *s. Z:* carcajou *m.*
carcanet ['kɑ:kənet], *s. A:* collier *m* (de diamants, etc.); parure *f.*
carcass[1], *occ.* **carcase** ['kɑ:kəs], *s.* **1.** (i) cadavre *m* (humain); (ii) corps *m*; *F:* **to save one's c.,** sauver sa peau; *P:* **move your c.!** bouge ta viande! **2.** cadavre, carcasse *f* (d'un animal); **c. butcher,** boucher *m* en gros; **c. meat,** viande en carcasse. **3.** *Const: N.Arch:* carcasse, charpente *f,* cage *f* (d'une maison); squelette *m,* carcasse (d'un navire); *Aut: etc:* carcasse, ossature *f* (de carrosserie); carcasse (de pneu); *Tls:* **c. saw,** scie *f* à dos. **4.** *Mil: A:* obus *m* incendiaire, carcasse.
carcass[2], *v.tr. Const:* poser, monter, la charpente d'(une maison, etc.).
carcassing ['kɑ:kəsiŋ], *s.* **1.** *Const:* pose *f,* montage *m,* de la charpente (d'une maison, etc.); **c. timber,** bois *m* de charpente. **2.** *(gas fittings)* **exposed c.,** installation visible, non dissimulée; **concealed c.,** installation encastrée.
carcel ['kɑ:sel], *s. A:* **1. c. lamp,** carcel *m.* **2.** *Ph.Meas:* carcel (9,5 bougies).
carcerulus [kɑ:'serjuləs], *s. Bot:* carcérule *f.*
Carcharhinidae [kɑ:kə'rinidi:], *s.pl. Ich:* carcharhinidés *m.*
carcharias [kɑ:'kɑ:riəs], *s. Ich:* carcharias *m.*
carcharodon [kɑ:'kærədən], *s. Ich:* caracharodon *m.*
carcinogen [kɑ:'sinədʒen], *s. Med:* substance *f* carcinogène, cancérigène.
carcinogenesis ['kɑ:sinou'dʒenisis], *s.* carcinogénèse *f.*
carcinogenic ['kɑ:sinou'dʒenik], *a. Med:* cancérigène, cancérogène, carcinogène.
carcinogenicity ['kɑ:sinoudʒə'nisiti], *s. Med:* qualité *f* cancérigène (d'un tissu,etc.).
carcinoid ['kɑ:sinɔid], *a. & s.* **c.(tumour),** carcinoïde *m.*
carcinological ['kɑ:sinou'lɔdʒikl], *s.* carcinologique.
carcinologist [kɑ:si'nɔlədʒist], *s.* carcinologiste *mf,* carcinologue *mf.*
carcinology [kɑ:si'nɔlədʒi], *s.* carcinologie *f.*
carcinoma [kɑ:si'noumə], *s. Med:* carcinome *m.*
carcinomatosis, *pl.* **-es** [kɑ:sinoumə'tousis, -i:z], *s. Med:* carcinose *f,* carcinomatose *f.*
carcinomatous [kɑ:si'noumətəs], *a. Med:* carcinomateux.
carcinosarcoma ['kɑ:sinousɑ:'koumə], *s. Med:* carcinosarcome *m.*
carcinosis, *pl.* **-es** [kɑ:si'nousis, -i:z], *s. Med:* carcinose *f.*
carcinotron [kɑ:si'noutrən], *s. Elcs:* carcinotron *m.*
card[1] [kɑ:d], *s.* **1. (playing) c.,** carte *f* à jouer; **low, small, c.,** basse carte; **court c.,** *NAm:* **face c.,** figure *f*; **game of cards,** partie *f* de cartes; **pack,** *NAm:* **deck, of cards,** jeu *m* de cartes; **to make a c.** *(in playing),* faire une levée (avec une carte); **to play one's cards well,** (i) bien jouer ses cartes; (ii) *Fig:* bien mener sa barque, bien jouer son jeu; tirer parti de toutes ses ressources; **to play one's last c.,** jouer sa dernière carte, son va-tout; **that's his strongest c.,** c'est la meilleure pièce de son sac; **to hold all the winning cards,** avoir tous les atouts dans son jeu, en main; **to play one's best c.,** jouer son atout; **c. player,** joueur, -euse, de cartes; **c. playing,** jeu; **c. playing was his downfall,** c'est le jeu qui a fait son malheur; **c. table,** table *f* de jeu; **to show one's cards,** (i) montrer, découvrir, son jeu; (ii) jouer cartes sur table; (iii) dévoiler ses batteries; **to hide one's cards, to play, hold, one's cards close to one's chest,** cacher son jeu; **to throw, lay, put, one's cards on the table,** mettre cartes sur table; **with one's cards on the table,** cartes sur table, à jeu découvert; **to throw in one's cards,** abandonner la partie; s'avouer vaincu; y renoncer; **to have a c. up one's sleeve,** avoir encore une ressource; n'être pas à bout de jeu; **it is (quite) on the cards that . . .,** il est bien possible, il se pourrait fort bien, que . . .; **house of cards,** château *m* de cartes; **the scheme collapsed like a house of cards,** le projet est tombé à l'eau, s'est effondré; *P:* **it's a sure c.,** c'est une certitude; *F: O:* **he's a knowing c.,** c'est une fine mouche, c'est un rusé compère, c'est un malin, il est ficelle; **he's a (great) c.,** c'est un original, il n'a pas son pareil. **2.** *(a)* **(visiting) c.,** carte (de visite); **business c.,** carte d'adresse, d'affaires; **to send in one's c. to s.o.,** faire passer sa carte à qn; **to leave a c. (at s.o.'s house),** laisser sa carte (chez qn); **c. case,** porte-cartes *m inv*; *(b)* **invitation c.,** carte d'invitation; **admission c.,** carte, billet *m,* d'entrée; **funeral c.,** carte de remerciements (après un enterrement); *(c)* **correspondence c.,** carte correspondance; **Christmas c.,** carte de Noël; **cigarette c.,** bon *m,* image *f* (offert(e) avec un paquet de cigarettes); *(d)* pancarte *f,* écriteau *m*; **show c.,** (i) étiquette *f* (de vitrine, etc.); (ii) carte d'échantillons; *(e) Nau: A:* **mariner's c.,** rose *f* des vents; *Fig:* **to speak by the c.,** parler d'autorité; *(f) (for card index)* fiche *f*; *Cmptr:* carte; *Adm:* **passport control c.,** fiche de voyageur; **c. catalogue,** catalogue *m* sur fiches; fichier *m* (de bibliothèque); *Cmptr:* **tab(ulating) c., punch c.,** carte mécanographique; **punched c.,** carte perforée; **c. punch,** perforateur *m,* perforatrice *f,* de cartes; **c. sorter,** trieuse *f* (de cartes); **control c.,** carte paramètre; **pilot c.,** carte-pilote *f, pl.* cartes-pilotes; **program(me) c.,** carte (de) programme; **c. bed, track,** chemin *m* de cartes; *(g) Golf:* (carte portant le) compte des points; carte du parcours; *Rac:* programme *m* des courses; **(score) c.,** carton *m*; *P:* **that's the c.!** à la bonne heure! bien combiné! *(h)* mandat donné à un délégué de syndicat à un congrès pour représenter un certain nombre de ses mandants; **c. vote,** vote plural (dans un congrès de syndicats); vote par mandats; *(i)* carte (de sécurité sociale), *F:* **to get one's cards,** être renvoyé; **to give s.o. his cards,** renvoyer, virer, qn; *(j) Mec.E:* **(indicator) c.,** diagramme *m* d'indicateur (d'une machine à vapeur, etc.); *(k)* **dance c.,** carnet *m* de bal; *(l)* **c. of cotton, of wool, of buttons,** carte de coton, de laine, de boutons. **3.** *Games: (dominoes)* dé *m.*
card[2], *v.tr.* **1.** mettre (des notes, etc.) sur fiche. **2. the races carded for the meeting,** les courses inscrites au programme de la réunion. **3.** encarter (des boutons, etc.).
card[3], *s.* **1.** *Tex:* carde *f,* peigne *m*; **c. tender, tenter, winder,** cardeur, -euse. **2.** *Bot:* **c. thistle,** chardon *m* à foulon; chardon bonnetier; **c. teasel,** cardère *f* sauvage.
card[4], *v.tr. Tex:* carder, peigner, chiqueter, écharper (la laine, etc.).
cardamine ['kɑ:dəmain], *s. Bot:* cardamine *f, F:* cressonnette *f.*
cardamom ['kɑ:dəməm], *s.* **1.** *Bot:* cardamome *m.* **2.** *Com:* graine *f* de cardamome.
Cardan, cardan ['kɑ:d(ə)n], *s. Mec.E:* **C. (joint),** joint *m* de Cardan, à la Cardan; joint brisé, articulé; joint universel; **C. shaft,** arbre *m* à Cardan; **cross-pin C. joint,** joint *m* de Cardan à croisillon.
cardboard ['kɑ:dbɔ:d], *s.* carton *m,* cartonnage *m*; **fine c.,** bristol *m*; **corrugated c.,** carton d'emballage, carton ondulé; *Fig:* **c. empire,** empire *m* de carton-pâte.
carder ['kɑ:dər], *s.* **1.** *Tex:* *(a) (pers.)* cardeur, -euse; *(b) (machine)* cardeuse *f.* **2.** *Ent:* bourdon *m* des mousses.
cardful ['kɑ:dful], *s. Tex:* peignée *f* (de laine).
cardia ['kɑ:diə], *s. Anat:* cardia *m* (de l'estomac).
cardiac ['kɑ:diæk], *a.* *(a) Anat:* **c. glands,** glandes cardiales; **c. muscle,** muscle *m* cardiaque; *(b) Med:* cardiaque, cardiaire; **c. aneurysm,** anévrisme *m* du cœur.
cardialgia [kɑ:di'ældʒiə], *s. Med:* cardialgie *f.*
cardialgic [kɑ:di'ældʒik], *a.* cardialgique.
cardiectomy [kɑ:di'ektəmi], *s. Surg:* excision *f* du cardia.
cardiectosis [kɑ:di'ektəsis], *s. Med:* cardiectasie *f.*
cardigan ['kɑ:digən], *s.* cardigan *m*; gilet *m* (de laine).
cardinal [kɑ:dinl], *a. & s.*
I. *a.* **1.** *(a) (pertaining to a hinge) Moll: etc:* **c. region,** région *f* de la charnière (d'une coquille); **c. edge,** bord dorsal; *(b)* cardinal, -aux; principal, -aux; **c. numbers,** nombres cardinaux; **the four c. points,** les quatre points cardinaux; **the c. virtues,** les vertus cardinales; **matter of c. importance,** affaire *f* d'importance capitale; *Anat: etc:* **c. veins,** veines cardinales; *Ecc:* **c. altar,** maître-autel *m, pl.* maîtres-autels. **2.** *(a) (colour)* pourpre, cardinal *inv*; *(b) Bot:* **c. flower,** cardinale *f.*
II. *s.* **1.** *Ecc:* cardinal *m, pl.* cardinaux; **c. bishop,** cardinal-évêque, *pl.* cardinaux-évêques; **c. priest,** cardinal-prêtre, *pl.* cardinaux-prêtres; **c. deacon,** cardinal-diacre, *pl.* cardinaux-diacres; **to be made c.,** être créé cardinal; *F:* recevoir le chapeau. **2.** *Orn:* **c. (bird),** cardinal rouge, *Fr.C:* cardinal; **green c.,** cardinal vert; **pope c.,** paroare dominicain; **red-crested c.,** paroare huppé.
cardinalate ['kɑ:dinəleit], **cardinalship** ['kɑ:dinlʃip], *s. Ecc:* cardinalat *m*; **cardinalate purple,** pourpre cardinalice, pourpre romaine.

card index [ˈkɑːdˈindeks], *s.* fichier *m.*
card-index [ˈkɑːdˈindeks], *v.tr.* mettre (des informations, etc.) sur fiches, classer en fiches.
card-indexing [ˈkɑːdˈindeksiŋ], *s.* mise *f* sur fiches.
carding [ˈkɑːdiŋ], *s. Tex:* **1.** cardage *m,* peignage *m,* écharpage *m*; **c. wool,** laine *f* à carde; **c. machine,** cardeuse *f,* machine *f* à carder. **2.** *pl.* peignons *m.*
cardio- [ˈkɑːdiou], *pref.* cardio-.
cardiocele [ˈkɑːdiousiːl], *s. Med:* cardiocèle *f.*
cardiocentesis [ˈkɑːdiousenˈtiːsis], *s. Med:* ponction *f* cardiaque.
cardiogram [ˈkɑːdiougræm], *s. Med:* cardiogramme *m.*
cardiograph [ˈkɑːdiougræf], *s. Med:* cardiographe *m.*
cardiographer [kɑːdiˈɔgrəfər], *s.* cardiographe *mf.*
cardiographic [ˈkɑːdiouˈgræfik], *a.* cardiographique.
cardiography [kɑːdiˈɔgrəfi], *s. Med:* cardiographie *f.*
cardioid [ˈkɑːdiɔid], *s. Mth:* cardioïde *f.*
cardiological [ˈkɑːdiouˈlɔdʒikl], *a.* cardiologique.
cardiologist [kɑːdiˈɔlədʒist], *s. Med:* cardiologue *mf.*
cardiology [kɑːdiˈɔlədʒi], *s. Med:* cardiologie *f.*
cardiolysis [kɑːdiˈɔlisis], *s. Surg:* cardiolyse *f.*
cardiomegaly [ˈkɑːdiouˈmegəli], *s. Med:* cardiomégalie *f.*
cardiometer [kɑːdiˈɔmitər], *s. Med:* cardiomètre *m.*
cardiopathy [kɑːdiˈɔpəθi], *s. Med:* cardiopathie *f.*
cardiopericarditis [ˈkɑːdiouperikɑːˈdaitis], *s. Med:* cardiopéricardite *f.*
cardioplasty [ˈkɑːdiouˈplæsti], *s. Surg:* cardioplastie *f.*
cardiopneumograph [ˈkɑːdiouˈnjuːməgræf], *s.* cardiopneumographe *m.*
cardiopulmonary [ˈkɑdiouˈpʌlmən(ə)ri], *a.* cardio-pulmonaire.
cardiorenal [ˈkɑːdiouˈriːnl], *a.* cardio-rénal, -aux.
cardiorespiratory [ˈkɑːdioureˈspirət(ɔ)ri], *a. Med:* cardio-respiratoire.
cardiorrhaphy [kɑːdiˈɔrəfi], *s. Surg:* cardiorraphie *f.*
cardiorrhexis [ˈkɑːdiouˈreksis], *s. Med:* cardiorhexie *f.*
cardiosclerosis [ˈkɑːdiouskleˈrousis], *s.* cardiosclérose *f.*
cardioscope [ˈkɑːdiouskoup], *s.* cardioscope *m.*
cardiospasm [ˈkɑːdiouˈspæzm], *s.* cardiospasme *m.*
cardiospermum [ˈkɑːdiouˈspəːməm], *s. Bot:* cardiosperme *m.*
cardiotachometer [ˈkɑːdioutæˈkɔmitər], *s. Elcs:* électrocardiographe *m.*
cardiotomy [kɑːdiˈɔtəmi], *s. Surg:* cardiotomie *f.*
cardiotonic [ˈkɑːdiouˈtɔnik], *s. & a.* cardiotonique *m,* tonicardiaque *m.*
cardiotrophia [ˈkɑːdiouˈtroufiə], *s.* cardiotrophie *f.*
cardiovascular [ˈkɑːdiouˈvæskjulər], *a. Med:* cardio-vasculaire, *pl.* cardio-vasculaires.
carditis [kɑːˈdaitis], *s.* cardite *f.*
Cardium [ˈkɑːdiəm], *s. Moll:* cardium *m.*
cardo, *pl.* **cardines** [ˈkɑːdou, ˈkɑːdiniːz], *s. Ent:* cardo *m.*
cardoon [kɑːˈduːn], *s. Hort:* cardon *m,* chardonnette *f*; **false c.,** faux-chardon *m, pl.* faux-chardons.
cardsharp(er) [ˈkɑːdʃɑːp(ər)], *s.* tricheur *m*; fileur *m* de cartes.
care[1] [ˈkɛər], *s.* **1.** souci *m,* inquiétude *f*; **to be full of cares,** être plein de soucis; **life of c.,** vie pleine de soucis; **my greatest c.,** ma plus grande préoccupation; mon plus grand souci; *Prov:* **c. killed the cat,** il ne faut pas se faire de bile. **2.** soin(s) *m(pl),* attention *f,* précaution(s) *f(pl),* ménagement *m*; **constant c.,** soins continuels, assidus; **to do sth. with great c.,** faire qch. avec beaucoup de soin; **c. for details,** attention aux détails; **to take, show, c. in doing sth.,** apporter du soin à faire qch.; **to drive without due c.,** conduire avec négligence; **to take c. of s.o., of sth.,** (i) prendre, avoir, soin de qn, de qch.; (ii) s'occuper de qn, de qch.; (iii) *U.S: F:* écarter (un obstacle, etc.); **to take c. to do sth.,** avoir (bien) soin, prendre (bien) garde, de faire qch.; **to take c. not to do sth.,** se garder de faire qch.; prendre garde de ne pas faire qch.; **take c.!** faites attention! prenez garde! **take c. of yourself,** (i) soignez-vous bien; (ii) prenez des précautions; ne prenez pas de risques; **to take c. of one's health,** ménager sa santé; **to be old enough to take c. of oneself,** être d'âge à se conduire; **take c. he doesn't see you,** prenez garde qu'il ne vous voie; **that will take c. of itself,** cela s'arrangera tout seul; (*on parcel, etc.*) **glass with c.,** fragile. **3.** soin(s), charge *f,* tenue *f,* conservation *f*; **c. and treatment of animals,** soins et traitement des animaux; **parents are responsible for the c. of their children,** les parents sont responsables des soins à donner à leurs enfants; *Adm:* **children in c.,** enfants assistés, **the c. of the aged, of old people,** les soins des personnes âgées; *Ecc:* **to have c. of souls,** avoir charge d'âmes; **to put s.o., sth., in s.o.'s c.,** confier qn, qch., aux soins de qn; **write to me c. of Mrs X, c/o Mrs X,** *U.S:* **in c. of Mrs X,** écrivez-moi aux bons soins de Mme X, chez Mme X; **to be in, under, s.o.'s c.,** être confié aux soins de qn; être à la charge de qn; être sous la garde, sous la conduite, de qn; **to entrust s.o. with the c. of sth.,** commettre qch. à la garde de qn; **to entrust s.o. with the c. of doing sth.,** confier à qn le soin de faire qch.; **c. of boilers,** entretien *m,* tenue *f,* des chaudières; **c. and maintenance of a car, of a battery,** entretien d'une voiture, d'un accu; **c. of explosives,** conservation des explosifs; **c. of public money,** maniement *m,* gestion *f,* des deniers publics; **lack of c.,** incurie *f,* négligence *f.* **4. cares of State,** responsabilités *f* d'État; **my main c. is their well-being,** je suis soucieux avant tout d'assurer leur bien-être.
care[2], *v.i.* **1.** se soucier, s'inquiéter, s'occuper, se préoccuper (**for, about,** de); **that's all he cares about,** il n'y a que cela qui l'intéresse; **I don't c. what he says,** peu m'importe ce qu'il dit; **what do I c.?** que m'importe? qu'est-ce que cela me fait? **who cares?** qu'est-ce que ça fait? bah! *Lit:* **I c. not,** peu m'en chaut; **I don't c. much about, for, it,** cela ne me plaît guère; je n'y tiens pas; **he doesn't c. for, about, music,** il ne s'intéresse pas à la musique; **I don't really c. for Wagner,** je n'arrive pas à apprécier Wagner; **to c. for nothing,** se désintéresser de tout; ne se soucier de rien; **I don't c. what people say,** je ne m'inquiète pas de ce qu'on dit; **I don't c. whether he likes it or not,** que cela lui plaise ou non, ça m'est parfaitement égal; **not that I c.,** non pas que cela m'inquiète, que ça me fasse quelque chose; **for all I c.,** pour (tout) ce que ça me fait; **I don't c.! as if I cared!** ça m'est égal! que voulez-vous que cela me fasse? je m'en fiche! **I don't c. either way,** cela m'est indifférent; *F:* **I couldn't c. less,** je m'en fiche éperdument; je m'en fous; **couldn't-c.-less attitude,** je-m'en-foutisme *m*; **I don't c. a damn, two hoots,** je m'en moque absolument; ça c'est le dernier, le cadet, de mes soucis; je m'en moque, m'en soucie, comme de l'an quarante, comme de ma première culotte; **he doesn't c. for anything or anybody,** il se moque du tiers comme du quart. **2. to c. for invalids, children,** soigner des malades, des enfants; **to look well cared for,** avoir un air soigné, une apparence soignée. **3.** *(a)* **to c. for s.o.,** aimer qn; avoir un penchant pour qn, **he doesn't c. for her,** elle ne lui plaît pas; *(b)* **he cares little for such a life,** cette vie ne lui plaît guère; **I have ceased to c. for these things,** je me suis désintéressé de tout cela; **I don't c. for my wife to write to the papers,** il me déplaît que ma femme envoie des lettres aux journaux; **I don't c. for this music,** cette musique ne me dit rien; **pictures are the only things he cares about,** les tableaux sont ses seules amours; **he does not c. to go out alone,** il n'aime pas (à) sortir seul; **I was more afraid than I cared to show,** j'étais plus effrayé que je ne voulais le laisser paraître; **would you c. to come with me?** voulez-vous m'accompagner? aimeriez-vous (à) m'accompagner? êtes-vous disposé à m'accompagner? *F: O:* **I don't c. if I do,** je veux bien; je ne dis pas non; je ne demande pas mieux; **if you c. to join us,** si cela vous plaît de venir avec nous, d'être des nôtres; **if you c. to,** si cela vous plaît, si le cœur vous en dit; **I shouldn't c. to be a doctor,** cela ne me dirait rien d'être médecin; **she doesn't c. about going to Paris now,** elle ne tient plus à aller à Paris.
careen [kəˈriːn], *Nau:* **1.** *v.tr.* *(a)* abattre, mettre, (un navire) en carène; *(b)* caréner (un navire); nettoyer la carène d'(un navire). **2.** *v.i.* *(a)* (*of ship*) donner de la bande; se coucher; plier sous le vent; *(b)* *NAm:* (*of car, etc.*) pencher sur le côté; (*of elephant, F: of pers.*) **to c. (along),** avancer en se balançant; *F:* **the waitress careened among the tables, balancing a tray on one hand,** la serveuse se frayait un chemin entre les tables, un plateau à la main.
careenage [kəˈriːnidʒ], *s. Nau:* **1.** = CAREENING 1. **2.** frais *mpl* de carénage. **3.** chantier *m* de carénage.
careening [kəˈriːniŋ], *s.* **1.** carénage *m*; abattage *m* en carène; **c. basin,** bassin *m* de carénage. **2.** *Nau:* carénage; bande dangereuse.
career[1] [kəˈriər], *s.* **1.** course (précipitée); **to be off in full c.,** s'élancer à toute vitesse; **to stop in mid c.,** rester, demeurer, en (beau) chemin; **to stop s.o. in mid c., in full c.,** arrêter qn au milieu de sa course, en pleine course; **nothing could stop Napoleon in his c.,** rien n'arrêtait Napoléon dans sa carrière. **2.** carrière *f*; **to take up a c.,** embrasser une carrière; **to have a successful school c.,** faire de bonnes études; *Sch:* **careers master,** orienteur professionnel; *NAm:* **c. diplomat,** diplomate *m* de carrière; **c. girl, woman,** femme qui se consacre à une profession, un métier.
career[2], *v.i.* courir rapidement, follement; **to c. along,** aller à toute vitesse; **to c. about (the place),** mener une vie mouvementée; sortir beaucoup; aller de côté et d'autre; **the horse careered through the village,** le cheval a traversé le village à une allure vertigineuse.
careerism [kəˈriərizm], *s.* arrivisme *m*; carriérisme *m.*
careerist [kəˈriərist], *s.* arriviste *mf*; carriériste *mf.*
carefree [ˈkɛəfriː], *a.* libre de soucis; exempt de soucis; insouciant; sans souci; **c. childhood,** enfance insouciante.
careful [ˈkɛəf(u)l], *a.* **1.** soigneux (**of,** de); attentif (**of,** à); **to be c. of one's reputation,** être soucieux, jaloux, de sa réputation; tenir à sa réputation; **to be c. of one's money,** regarder à ses sous; **be c. of it!** ayez-en soin! **to be c. to do sth.,** avoir soin de faire qch.; être attentif à faire qch.; veiller à faire qch.; **be c. you don't fall, not to fall,** faites attention à, de, ne pas tomber; **be c. what you say,** faites attention à ce que vous dites; **he is not always c. about his choice of words,** il ne fait pas toujours attention au choix de ses paroles; il ne pèse pas toujours ses paroles; **(be) c.!** prenez garde! faites attention! pas d'imprudence(s)! **c. workman,** ouvrier soigneux, appliqué; **c. English speech,** l'anglais parlé surveillé; **c. consideration of a question,** examen attentif, approfondi, d'une question; **c. copy,** copie soignée. **2.** prudent, circonspect, précautionneux; **a c. answer,** une réponse bien pesée, réfléchie.
carefully [ˈkɛəf(u)li], *adv.* **1.** soigneusement, avec soin, avec minutie; prudemment; attentivement; **to copy sth. c.,** copier qch. à main posée; **question that has been c. examined,** question *f* qui a fait l'objet d'une étude approfondie; **this book is more c. written than the others,** ce livre est plus soigneusement écrit que les autres. **2.** prudemment, avec circonspection; **to live c.,** (i) soigner sa santé; (ii) être frugal; vivre avec économie.
carefulness [ˈkɛəf(u)lnis], *s.* **1.** soin *m,* attention *f.* **2.** prudence *f.*
careless [ˈkɛəlis], *a.* **1.** *(a)* insouciant, peu soucieux (**of, about,** de); nonchalant; étourdi; **a c. person,** un, une, sans-souci *inv*; *(b)* **a c. remark,** une observation inconsidérée, irréfléchie, à la légère; **c. mistake,** faute *f* d'inattention. **2.** négligent, sans soin; **c. in his bookkeeping,** négligent à tenir ses livres; **accused of c. driving,** accusé de négligence au volant; **to be c. about one's appearance,** être négligé de sa personne; **c. copy,** copie faite sans soin; **one should not be c. about details,** il faut faire attention aux petites choses.
carelessly [ˈkɛəlisli], *adv.* avec insouciance, nonchalamment, étourdiment, sans réflexion, négligemment, sans soin, à la légère.
carelessness [ˈkɛəlisnis], *s.* **1.** *(a)* insouciance *f*; nonchalance *f*; *(b)* inattention *f,* étourderie *f*; **piece of c.,** étourderie. **2.** manque *m* de soin; négligence *f,* incurie *f.*
carene [ˈkæriːn], *s. Ch:* carène *m.*
caress[1] [kəˈres], *s.* caresse *f.*
caress[2], *v.tr.* caresser.
caressing [kəˈresiŋ], *a.* caressant; **c. tones,** tons câlins, modulations câlines.
caressingly [kəˈresiŋli], *adv.* d'une manière câline, caressante; **to speak c.,** prendre un ton câlin.
caret [ˈkærət], *s. Typ:* signe *m* d'omission; renvoi *m* de marge.
caretake [ˈkɛəteik], *v.tr.* servir de concierge pour (un immeuble); avoir la charge de (bureaux, etc., alors que le personnel est absent).
caretaker [ˈkɛəteikər], *s.* **1.** concierge *mf* (d'un immeuble, etc.); gardien *m* (d'un musée, etc.). **2.** *attrib. Pol:* **c. cabinet,** cabinet *m* intérimaire.
caretaking [ˈkɛəteikiŋ], *s.* gardiennage *m*; métier *m* de concierge.
careworn [ˈkɛəwɔːn], *a.* rongé, usé, par les soucis; **her face was c.,** son visage portait l'empreinte de ses soucis; elle avait l'air accablée de soucis.
carfare [ˈkɑːfɛər], *s. NAm:* prix *m* du trajet (par tramway, par autobus).
carful [ˈkɑːful], *s.* pleine voiture; **we've got such a c. of luggage that there's scarcely enough room for the passengers,** la voiture est si pleine de bagages qu'il n'y a guère de place pour les voyageurs.
cargo[1], *pl.* **-oes** [ˈkɑːgou, -ouz], *s. Nau: Av:* *(a)* cargaison *f,* chargement *m,* marchandises *fpl*; **to take in, embark, c.,** charger des marchandises; prendre du fret; prendre chargement; **full c.,** plein chargement; **general, mixed, c.,** cargaison mixte, marchandises diverses, divers *mpl*; **laden with general, mixed, c.,** chargé en, à, cueillette; **c. outward,** chargement d'aller; **c. homeward,** chargement de retour; *(b)* *A:* **private c.,** pacotille *f*; *(c)* *attrib.* **c. boat, ship,** cargo *m*; navire *m* de charge; **c. plane,** avion-cargo *m, pl.* avions-cargos; cargo aérien; **c. liner,** (i) navire de charge, cargo; (ii) avion cargo.
cargo[2], *v.tr.* charger (un navire); **ship cargoed with coal,** navire avec une cargaison de houille.
cariama [kæriˈɑːmə], *s. Orn:* cariama *m.*
Carian [ˈkɛəriən], *A.Geog:* **1.** *a.* carien. **2.** *s.* Carien, -ienne.
Carib [ˈkærib]. **1.** *Ethn:* *(a)* *a.* caraïbe; *(b)* *s.* Caraïbe *mf*;

(c) s. *Ling:* caraïbe m. 2. *Orn:* **purple-throated c. (hummingbird),** oiseau-mouche grenat.

Caribbean [kæri'bi(:)ən], a. & s. *Geog:* **the C. (Sea),** la Mer des Caraïbes, des Antilles; **the C. islands,** les Antilles *f*; **a little island in the C.,** une petite île dans la Mer des Antilles.

caribe ['kæribi:], s. *Ich:* cariba *m*, piranha *m*, piraya *m*, serrasalme *m*.

Caribee ['kæribi:], s. *A:* Caraïbe *mf*.

caribou [kæri'bu:], s. 1. *Z:* caribou *m*, *pl.* -ous; renne *m* du Canada. 2. **C. Eskimo,** Esquimau *m*, *pl.* -aux, du *Barren Ground*.

Caricaceae [kæri'keisii:], s.pl. *Bot:* caricacées *f*.

caricaturable [kærikə'tju:rəbl], a. qui se prête à la caricature.

caricatural [kærikə'tju:r(ə)l], a. caricatural, -aux.

caricature[1] ['kærikətjuər], s. caricature *f*; charge *f*; **to turn a portrait into a c.,** tourner un portrait en caricature, en charge; charger un portrait.

caricature[2], v.tr. caricaturer; *Th:* **to c. a part,** charger un rôle; *F:* prendre un rôle à la cascade.

caricaturist [kærikə'tju:rist], s. caricaturiste *m*.

caricous ['kærikəs], a. *Med:* caricoïde, cariqueux; **c. tumour,** tumeur cariqueuse.

Carid(e)a [kæ'rid(i)ə], **Carides** ['kæridi:z], s.pl. *Crust:* caridides *m*.

caries ['kɛərii:z], s. *Med:* carie *f*.

carillon[1] [kə'riljən], s. *Mus:* carillon *m*; **to play on the c.,** carillonner; **c. player,** carillonneur *m*.

carillon[2], v.i. *Mus:* carillonner.

carillon(n)eur [kæriljə'nə:r], s. *Mus:* carillonneur *m*.

carina [kə'rainə], s. 1. *Anat:* carène *f*. 2. *Ent:* *Orn:* carène; *Orn:* bréchet *m*. 3. *Bot:* carène.

carinal [kə'rainl], a. *Bot:* carénal, -aux; carinal, -aux.

carinaria [kæri'nɛəriə], s. *Moll:* carinaire *f*.

Carinatae [kæri'neiti:], s.pl. *Orn:* carinates *m*.

carinate ['kærineit]. 1. a. *Nat.Hist:* caréné. 2. s. *Orn:* carinate *m*.

cariniana [kærini'einə], s. *Bot:* cariniana *m*.

Carinthia [kə'rinθiə], *Pr.n. Geog:* Carinthie *f*.

Carinthian [kə'rinθiən], *Geog:* (a) a. carinthien; (b) s. Carinthien, -ienne.

carious ['kɛəriəs], a. *Med:* (os) carié; **c. tooth,** dent gâtée, malade.

caritive ['kæritiv], s. *Gram:* caritif *m*.

carking ['kɑ:kiŋ], a. *used in* **c. care, anxieties,** soucis rongeurs.

carl(e) [kɑ:l], s. *A:* manant *m*, rustre *m*.

carless ['kɑ:lis], a. sans voiture.

carline[1] ['kɑ:lin], s. *Bot:* **c. thistle,** carline *f* vulgaire, chardon doré.

carline[2], **carling** ['kɑ:liŋ], s. *N.Arch:* entremise *f*, traversin *m* des baux.

Carlism ['kɑ:lizm], s. *Hist:* carlisme *m*.

Carlist ['kɑ:list], a. & s. *Hist:* carliste (*mf*).

carload ['kɑ:loud], s. 1. pleine voiture; voiturée *f*. 2. *NAm:* *Rail:* (a) plein wagon (de marchandises); (b) quantité *f* (de marchandises) nécessaire pour remplir un wagon; **c. rate,** tarif *m* par plein wagon.

Carlovingian [kɑ:lou'vin(d)ʒiən], a. *Hist:* *A:* carolingien.

carmagnole [kɑ:mæ'njoul], s. *Hist:* 1. *Danc:* *Mus:* carmagnole *f*. 2. *Cost:* carmagnole.

carman, *pl.* **-men** ['kɑ:mən], s.m. (a) camionneur; charretier, voiturier; (b) *Com:* livreur; **c. and contractor,** entrepreneur de camionnage.

Carmania [kɑ:'meiniə], *Pr.n. A.Geog:* Carmanie *f*.

Carmelite ['kɑ:məlait], s. 1. *Rel.H:* carme *m*; **C. nun,** carmélite *f*; **the C. order,** l'ordre *m* du Carmel. 2. *Tex:* carmeline *f*.

carminative ['kɑ:minətiv], a. & s. *Med:* carminatif (*m*).

carmine[1] ['kɑ:m(a)in]. 1. s. carmin *m*. 2. a. carminé; carmin *inv*; **c. lips,** des lèvres *f* de carmin; *Paint:* **c. (lake),** laque carminée.

carmine[2], v.tr. carminer (les lèvres, etc.).

carminic [kɑ:'minik], a. *Ch:* (acide) carminique.

carminite ['kɑ:minait], s. *Miner:* carminite *f*, carminspath *m*.

carnac ['kɑ:næk], s. cornac *m*.

carnage ['kɑ:nidʒ], s. carnage *m*.

carnal ['kɑ:nl], a. 1. charnel; (i) sensuel; (ii) sexuel; **c. appetites,** appétits charnels; **c. sins,** péchés *m* de la chair; **c. knowledge,** connaissance charnelle; *Jur:* *U.S:* **c. abuse,** rapports sexuels illicites. 2. mondain.

carnality [kɑ:'næliti], s. sensualité *f*.

carnalize ['kɑ:nəlaiz], v.tr. sensualiser.

carnallite ['kɑ:nəlait], s. *Miner:* carnallite *f*.

carnally ['kɑ:nəli], adv. charnellement; sensuellement.

carnal-minded ['kɑ:nl'maindid], a. 1. charnel, sensuel. 2. mondain.

carnal-mindedness ['kɑ:nl'maindidnis], s. 1. sensualité *f*. 2. mondanité *f*.

carnassial [kɑ:'næsiəl], a. & s. *Z:* (dent) carnassière (*f*).

Carnatic [kɑ:'nætik], *Pr.n.* Carnatic *m*.

carnation[1] [kɑ:'neiʃ(ə)n]. 1. (a) s. carnation *f*, incarnat *m*; (b) a. (teint) incarnat, incarnadin; (ruban) rose clair *inv*. 2. s.pl. *Art:* **picture in which the carnations are a failure,** tableau *m* dont les carnations sont manquées.

carnation[2], s. *Bot:* œillet *m*; **c. rust,** rouille *f* de l'œillet, uromyces *m*.

carnauba [kɑ:'noubə], s. *Bot:* 1. carnauba *m*. 2. **c. (wax),** carnauba.

carnelian [kə'ni:ljən], s. *Miner:* cornéliane *f*.

Carnic ['kɑ:nik], a. *Geog:* **the C. Alps,** les Alpes *f* carniques.

carnification [kɑ:nifi'keiʃ(ə)n], s. *Med:* carnification *f*.

carnify ['kɑ:nifai], v.i. *Med:* (*of tissue*) se carnifier.

Carniola [kɑ:ni'oulə], *Pr.n. Geog:* Carniole *f*.

carnitine ['kɑ:niti:n], s. *Bio-Ch:* carnitine *f*.

carnival ['kɑ:nivl], s. 1. carnaval *m*, *pl.* -als (avant le carême). 2. (a) saturnale *f*; (b) réjouissances *fpl*; fête *f* (avec travestissements); **c. novelties,** accessoires *m* de cotillon.

carnivora [kɑ:'nivərə], s.pl. *Z:* carnivores *m*.

carnivore ['kɑ:nivɔ:r], s. 1. *Z:* carnivore *m*. 2. *Bot:* plante *f* carnivore.

carnivorous [kɑ:'niv(ə)rəs], a. 1. (*of animal*) carnivore, carnassier. 2. (*of pers., plant*) carnivore.

carnosine ['kɑ:nousi:n], s. *Bio-Ch:* carnosine *f*.

carnotite ['kɑ:noutait], s. *Miner:* carnotite *f*.

carob ['kærəb], s. *Bot:* 1. **c. (bean),** caroube *f*, carouge *f*. 2. **c. (tree),** caroubier *m*.

carol[1] ['kærəl], s. (a) chant *m*, chanson *f*; *esp.* **Christmas c.,** noël *m*; **c. singer,** chanteur, -euse, de noëls; (b) tirelire *m* (de l'alouette).

carol[2], v.i. & tr. **(carolled)** *Poet:* (a) chanter (joyeusement); (b) (*of lark*) tire-lirer; **carolling lark,** alouette *f* qui grisolle.

carol(l)er ['kærələr], s. chanteur, -euse, de noëls.

Carolina [kærə'lainə], *Pr.n. Geog:* 1. la Caroline; **South, North, C.,** Caroline du Sud, du Nord. 2. **the Carolinas,** (a) l'archipel *m* des Carolines; (b) *in U.S:* la Caroline du Sud et la Caroline du Nord.

Caroline ['kærəlain, -lin]. 1. *Pr.n.f.* Caroline. 2. a. (a) carolingien; (b) *Eng.Hist:* qui appartient aux rois Charles; du temps des rois Charles; (c) *Geog:* **the C. Islands,** l'archipel *m* des Carolines.

Carolingian [kærou'lin(d)ʒiən], (a) a. carolingien; (b) s. Carolingien *m*.

Carolinian [kærou'liniən], *Geog:* 1. a. & s. (natif, -ive, habitant, -ante) de la Caroline. 2. (a) a. carolinien, de l'archipel des Carolines; (b) s. Carolinien, -ienne.

carolus ['kærələs], s. *A.Num:* carolus *m*.

carom[1] ['kærəm], s. *Bill:* *NAm:* carambolage *m*.

carom[2], v.i. *Bill:* *NAm:* caramboler; faire un carambolage.

carone ['kæroun], s. *Ch:* carone *f*.

carotene ['kærəti:n], s. *Ch:* carotène *m*.

caroten(a)emia [kærəti'ni:miə], s. *Med:* carotinémie *f*.

carotenoid [kæ'rɔtinɔid], a. & s. *Bio-Ch:* caroténoïde (*m*).

carotic [kə'rɔtik], a. carotique.

carotid [kə'rɔtid], a. & s. *Anat:* carotide (*f*); **c. artery,** artère *f* carotide; **c. ganglion,** ganglion carotidien.

carotin(a)emia [kærəti'ni:miə], s. *Med:* carotinémie *f*.

carotinoid [kæ'rɔtinɔid], a. & s. *Bio-Ch:* caroténoïde (*m*).

carousal [kə'rauz(ə)l], **carouse**[1] [kə'rauz], s. b(e)uverie *f*; *F:* noce *f* (à tout casser); bombe *f*; bamboche *f*.

carouse[2], v.i. faire la fête, *F:* la bombe, la noce; festoyer; faire ripaille, faire la bringue.

carousel [kærə'sel], s. carrousel *m*, chevaux *mpl* de bois.

carouser [kə'rauzər], s. fêtard *m*, noceur *m*; bambocheur, -euse.

carousing [kə'rauziŋ], s. festoiement *m*.

carp[1] [kɑ:p], s. 1. *Ich:* (*pl.* **carp** *or* **carps**) carpe *f*; **young c.,** carpeau *m*, *f* carpette; carpillon *m*; **leather c.,** carpe cuir; **mirror c.,** carpe miroir; **beaked c., nose c.,** nase *m*, hotu *m*; **crucian c.,** carassin *m*; **c. breeding,** carpiculture *f*; **c. pond,** carpier *m*, carpière *f*. 2. *Crust:* **c. louse,** argule foliacé.

carp[2], v.i. épiloguer, gloser; **to c. at s.o.,** censurer qn; crier après qn; épiloguer, gloser, sur qn; **to c. at sth.,** trouver à redire à qch.

carpal ['kɑ:pl], *Anat:* 1. a. carpien, -ienne; du carpe; **c. gland,** glande carpienne. 2. s. os carpien.

Carpathian[1] [kɑ:'peiθiən], a. *Geog:* **the C. Mountains,** s.pl. **the Carpathians,** les (Monts) Carpathes, Karpathes *m*.

Carpathian[2], a. *Geog:* Carpathien; **the C. Sea,** la Mer Carpathienne.

carpel ['kɑ:pel], s. *Bot:* carpelle *m*, carpophylle *m*.

carpellary ['kɑ:pələri], a. *Bot:* carpellaire.

Carpentaria [kɑ:pən'tɛəriə], *Pr.n. Geog:* **the Gulf of C.,** le Golfe de Carpentarie.

carpenter[1] ['kɑ:pintər], s. charpentier *m*; appareilleur *m*; menuisier *m* en bâtiments; **ship c.,** charpentier en navires; *Nau:* **ship's c.,** matelot *m* charpentier; **carpenter's shop,** atelier *m* de menuiserie; *Th:* **carpenter('s) scene,** scène jouée à l'avant-scène (pour laisser aux machinistes le temps de préparer une scène à gros effets).

carpenter[2]. 1. v.i. faire de la charpenterie. 2. v.tr. charpenter (qch.); **carpentered play,** pièce charpentée à coups de hache.

carpentering ['kɑ:pint(ə)riŋ], s. charpenterie *f*; menuiserie *f*; métier *m* de charpentier ou de menuisier.

carpentry ['kɑ:pintri], s. 1. (a) charpenterie *f*; (b) grosse menuiserie. 2. charpente *f*; les bois *m* (d'un édifice, etc.).

carper ['kɑ:pər], s. (a) critique malveillant; (b) *F:* aboyeur, -euse; ronchonneur, -euse; ronchon *m*.

carpet[1] ['kɑ:pit], s. 1. (a) tapis *m*; **pile c.,** tapis velouté; **long-pile c.,** tapis de haute laine; **short-pile c.,** tapis de laine rase; **Brussels c.,** moquette *f* de Bruxelles, moquette bouclée; **Turkey c.,** tapis d'Orient, de Smyrne, de Turquie; **fitted c.,** tapis cloué, ajusté; **c. felt,** carton-feutre *m*, *pl.* cartons-feutres; thibaude *f*; **c. broom,** balai *m* de jonc; **c. beater,** battoir *m* de tapis; tapette *f*; **c. sweeper,** balai *m* mécanique; balayeuse *f* automatique, mécanique; **c. tack,** fixe-tapis *m inv*; **c. slippers,** pantoufles *f* en tapisserie; *A:* **c. knight,** héros *m* de salon; **to lay a c.,** poser un tapis; *F:* **to lay down the red c. for s.o., to give s.o. the red-c. treatment,** recevoir qn avec la croix et la bannière, avec tous les égards possibles; *F:* **to sweep (sth.) under the c.,** enterrer (une question); mettre (qch.) sur une voie de garage; *F:* **to be on the c.,** (i) (*of question*) être sur le tapis; (ii) (*of pers.*) être sur la sellette; **to have, put, s.o. on the c.,** réprimander qn, mettre qn sur la sellette; (b) tapis (de verdure, de fleurs, etc.); *Hort:* **c. bed,** parterre *m* de fleurs formant motifs et bordure; **c. path,** chemin gazonné; allée gazonnée; (c) *Mil.Av:* **c. bombing,** bombardement *m* par vagues (d'avions) successives. 2. (a) *Ich:* **c. shark,** requin zébré; requin-tapis *m*, *pl.* requins-tapis; (b) *Moll:* **c. shell,** (i) clovisse *f*; (ii) palourde *f*; (c) *Ent:* **c. beetle,** anthrène *m*, *F:* amourette *f*; (d) *Bot:* **c. pink,** silène *m* acaule. 3. *Civ.E:* revêtement *m* (d'une chaussée).

carpet[2], v.tr. 1. mettre un tapis à (l'escalier); recouvrir (le plancher) d'un tapis. 2. *F:* *A:* mettre (qn) sur la sellette.

carpet(-)bag[1] ['kɑ:pitbæg], s. *A:* sac *m* de voyage, de nuit.

carpet(-)bag[2], v.i. *U.S:* *F:* (a) voyager avec très peu de bagages; (b) mener une vie d'aventurier politique.

carpet(-)bagger ['kɑ:pit'bægər], s. *esp. U.S:* *F:* 1. candidat (au parlement) étranger à la circonscription. 2. aventurier *m* politique.

carpeted ['kɑ:pitid], a. couvert d'un tapis; **ground c. with turf,** terrain recouvert d'un tapis de gazon; **slope c. with flowers,** pente tapissée de fleurs.

carpeting ['kɑ:pitiŋ], s. 1. (a) pose *f* de tapis; **the c. of the stairs took a long time,** la pose du tapis d'escalier a pris beaucoup de temps; (b) *coll.* tapis *mpl* en pièce. 2. *F:* *A:* semonce *f*, réprimande *f*.

carpholite ['kɑ:fəlait], s. *Miner:* carpholite *f*.

carphology [kɑ:'fɔlədʒi], s. *Med:* carphologie *f*.

carphosiderite [kɑ:fou'sidərait], s. *Miner:* carphosidérite *f*.

carpincho [kɑ:'pintʃou], s. *Z:* cabiai *m*, cochon *m* d'eau.

carping[1] ['kɑ:piŋ], a. chicanier; malveillant; **c. criticism,** critique pointilleuse, malveillante; **c. spirit,** esprit censeur, pointilleux, grondeur.

carping[2], s. censure *f*; critique *f* (malveillante); *F:* chinage *m*.

carpingly ['kɑ:piŋli], adv. pointilleusement; avec malveillance; d'un ton censeur, critique, grondeur.

carpo- ['kɑ:pou], *pref.* carpo-.

carpocapsa ['kɑ:pou'kæpsə], s. *Ent:* carpocapse *f*.

carpogonium, *pl.* **-ia** ['kɑ:pou'gouniəm, -iə], s. *Bot:* carpogone *f*.

carpolite ['kɑ:poulait], **carpolith** ['kɑ:pouliθ], s. *Bot:* carpolithe *m*, carpolithus *m*.

carpological [kɑ:pou'lɔdʒikl], a. *Bot:* carpologique.

carpology [kɑ:'pɔlədʒi], s. carpologie *f*.

carpometacarpal ['kɑ:poumetə'kɑ:pl], a. *Anat:* carpo-métacarpien.

Carpophaga [kɑ:'pɔfəgə], s.pl. *Z:* carpophages *m*.

carpophagous [kɑ:'pɔfəgəs], a. carpophage.

carpophore ['kɑ:poufɔ:r], s. *Bot:* carpophore *m*.

carpophyl(l) ['kɑ:poufil], s. *Bot:* carpophylle *m*.

carpopodite ['kɑ:pou'poudait], s. *Crust:* carpopodite *m*.

carport ['kɑːpɔːt], *s. Aut:* abri-garage *m, pl.* abris-garages.
carpospore ['kɑːpouspɔːr], *s. Algae:* carpospore *f.*
carpus ['kɑːpəs], *s.* (*a*) *Anat: Z:* carpe *m*; (*b*) *Crust:* carpopodite *m.*
carrack ['kærək], *s. A.Nau:* car(r)aque *f.*
carrag(h)een ['kærəgiːn, kærə'giːn], *s. Algae:* carragheen *m*; chondrus *m*; mousse perlée, mousse d'Irlande.
Carrara [kə'rɑːrə], *Pr.n. Geog:* Carrare *f*; **C. marble,** marbre *m* de Carrare; carrare *m.*
carreau ['kærou], *s. Med:* carreau *m.*
carrel(l) ['kærəl], *s.* (*in library*) cabinet particulier; alcôve *f.*
carriage ['kæridʒ], *s.* **1.** (*a*) port *m,* transport *m,* charriage *m,* portage *m*; *Com:* **c. free,** franc de port; franco; **c. paid,** (en) port payé; port perçu; franc de port; franco à domicile; **c. forward,** (en) port dû; **c. (expenses),** frais *mpl* de port, de transport; **to pay the c.,** payer le factage; (*b*) exécution *f* (d'un projet, d'un ordre); *Pol:* **c. of a bill,** vote *m,* adoption *f,* d'un projet de loi; (*c*) portage (d'un canoë entre deux rivières, etc.). **2.** port, maintien *m,* démarche *f,* tenue *f* (d'une personne); **free, easy, c.,** allure dégagée. **3.** (*a*) *Veh:* voiture *f*; équipage *m,* attelage *m*; **open c.,** voiture découverte; **closed c.,** voiture fermée; **c. and pair, and four,** voiture à deux, à quatre, chevaux; *A:* **livery(-stable) c.,** voiture de remise, de louage; *A:* **hackney c.,** voiture de place, de louage; **baby c.,** voiture d'enfant; **to keep a c., to ride in one's own c.,** avoir équipage, *A:* rouler carrosse; **c. drive,** avenue *f* pour voitures; allée *f*; grande avenue; **c. entrance,** porte cochère; (*of farm*) porte charretière; *A:* **c. road,** route *f* carrossable; voie routière, charretière; (*b*) *Rail:* voiture, wagon *m* (de chemin de fer); *A:* **slip c.,** voiture remorque. **4.** *Tchn:* (*a*) *Artil:* **(gun) c.,** affût *m*; **slide c.,** affût à châssis; **automatic c.,** affût à mise en batterie automatique; **mobile, wheeled, c.,** affût mobile; **sledge c.,** affût à traîneau; **cradle c.,** affût berceau; **tilting c.,** affût basculant; **field c.,** affût de campagne; **fixed c.,** affût (à poste) fixe; **disappearing gun c.,** affût à éclipse; **trail c.,** affût à crosse, à flèche; **split-trail c.,** affût à flèche ouvrante; **electrically controlled c.,** affût à commande électrique; **self-propelled c.,** affût automoteur, automouvant; **pedestal c., pintle c.,** affût à piédestal, à pivot central; **turret c.,** affût de tourelle; **railway-truck gun c.,** affût-truc(k) *m, pl.* affûts-truc(k)s; *Navy:* **launching c., (of torpedo),** chariot *m* (de torpille); (*b*) *Veh:* train *m* (de la voiture); (*c*) *Mec.E:* chariot (d'un tour, d'une machine à écrire, etc.); traînard *m* (d'un tour); **c. return,** retour *m* de chariot; *Typ:* **press c.,** train; (*d*) roulement *m* (d'un wagon, etc.); (*e*) *Mec.E:* coussinet *m,* dé *m*; (*f*) *Cmptr:* chariot; **c. (control) tape,** bande *f* pilote; **c. length,** largeur *f* de chariot.
carriageable ['kæridʒəbl], *a.* **1.** (objet *m*) charriable. **2.** *A:* (chemin *m*) praticable aux voitures, carrossable, voiturier, charretier.
carriageful ['kæridʒful], *s.* pleine voiture (de personnes); voiturée *f.*
carriageway ['kæridʒwei], *s.* chaussée *f*; voie routière; **dual c.,** route jumelée, à double piste, à deux voies.
carrier ['kæriər], *s.* **1.** (*a*) (*pers. animal, plant*) porteur, -euse (d'une maladie, de germes, de bacilles); (*b*) *Com:* (i) entrepreneur *m* de voitures publiques; commissionnaire *m* de roulage; camionneur *m,* messagiste *m*; (ii) commissionnaire *m* expéditeur; transporteur *m*; (iii) voiturier *m,* roulier *m,* messager *m*; *Jur:* **common c.,** (i) voiturier public; (ii) entrepreneur de messageries maritimes; *Cmptr:* **common (communications) c.,** société exploitante. **2.** (*a*) support *m*; *Cmptr:* **data c.,** support d'information, de données; **data c. store,** mémoire *f* à support amovible; (*b*) bac *m* (d'accumulateurs); **(luggage) c.,** porte-bagages *m inv* (de bicyclette, etc.); **c. bag,** (grand) sac (en papier); (*c*) étui *m* (de capsules pharmaceutiques, etc.); cartouche *f* (pour pigeon voyageur, *O:* pour correspondances pneumatiques); (*d*) *Mec.E:* toc *m,* doguin *m* (de tour); (*heart-shaped*) cœur *m* de tour; (*e*) *Phot:* (cadre) intermédiaire *m* (pour châssis négatifs); châssis *m* passe-vue (de projecteur); (*f*) *Ind:* transporteur; **overhead c.,** transporteur aérien; (*g*) *Hyd.E:* canal *m.* **3.** *Navy:* **(aircraft) c.,** porte-avions *m inv,* porte-aéronefs *m inv*; **helicopter c.,** porte-hélicoptères *m inv*; *Navy: Av:* **c. air forces,** aviation embarquée; *Av:* **troop c. (aircraft),** avion *m* de transport de troupes; *Mil:* **machine-gun, mortar, ammunition, c.,** chenillette *f* porte-mitrailleuse, porte-mortier, porte-munitions; **bren (gun) c.,** chenillette porte-fusil-mitrailleur; **armoured personnel c.,** véhicule blindé de transport de troupe; **full-track, half-track, personnel c.,** véhicule chenillé, semi-chenillé, de transport de troupe; **full-track, half-track, cargo c.,** véhicule chenillé, semi-chenillé, de transport de matériel; véhicule cargo chenillé, semi-chenillé. **4.** *Orn:* **c. (pigeon),** pigeon voyageur. **5.** (*a*) *Ch:* support de réaction; *Agr:* support (pour insecticides et produits agricoles); (*b*) *Atom.Ph:* entraîneur *m*; **holdback c.,** entraîneur de rétention; **c.-free,** sans entraîneur; (*c*) *Art:* véhicule *m* (pour couleurs). **6.** *Nau:* chasse-marée *m inv.* **7.** *attrib. El: Elcs:* **c. current,** courant porteur; **c. frequency,** fréquence porteuse; **c. wave,** onde porteuse; **c. drop,** chute *f* de porteuse; **c. shift, deviation,** décalage *m,* déplacement *m,* de la fréquence (porteuse).
carrier-based ['kæriəbeist], *a. Av: Navy:* embarqué; **c.-b. aircraft, air forces,** l'aviation embarquée.
carrier-borne ['kæriəbɔːn], *a. Av: Navy:* embarqué; **c.-b. aircraft,** l'aviation embarquée.
carriole ['kærioul], *s. Veh:* carriole *f.*
carrion ['kæriən]. **1.** *s.* charogne *f*; *attrib.* **c. (fly, etc.),** (insecte) cadavérin; *Ent:* **c. beetle,** bouclier *m,* silphe *m,* nécrophore *m*; *Orn:* **c. hawk,** caracara *m*; **c. buzzard,** cathartes *m*; **c. crow,** corneille noire, corbine *f*; *Fung:* **c. fungus,** phallus *m* impudique, satyre puant; *Bot:* **c. flower,** stapelia *m.* **2.** *a. A:* (*a*) pourri, répugnant; (*b*) vil, sale.
carrom ['kærəm], *s. & v.i.* = CAROM.
carronade ['kærəneid], *s. Nau: A:* caronade *f.*
carron oil ['kærənɔil], *s. Pharm:* mélange d'huile de lin et d'eau de chaux (employé pour les brûlures); liniment *m* oléo-calcaire.
carrot[1] ['kærət], *s.* **1.** *Hort:* carotte *f*; **to dangle a c. in front of a donkey,** attacher la carotte devant le nez d'un bourricot; *F:* **carrots, c. top,** (i) cheveux *m* rouges; (ii) (*pers.*) rouquin *m*; poil *m* de carotte. **2.** *Bot:* **deadly c.,** thapsie *f* garganique; **wild c.,** faux chervis. **3.** carotte de tabac. **4.** *attrib. Ent:* **c. fly, c. rust fly,** psile *f.*
carrot[2], *v.tr. Tan:* secréter (les peaux).
carroting ['kærətiŋ], *s. Tan:* secrétage *m.*
carroty ['kærəti], *a. F:* (*of pers. hair*) roux, *f* rousse; roussâtre; couleur (de) carotte *inv,* rouge carotte *inv.*
carrousel [kærə'sel], *s. U.S:* carrousel *m,* chevaux *mpl* de bois.
carry[1] ['kæri], *s.* **1.** *Mil:* **sword at the c.,** sabre *m* en main. **2.** (*a*) portée *f* (d'un fusil, etc.); (*b*) *Golf:* trajet *m* (d'une balle). **3.** portage *m* (d'un canoë entre deux cours d'eau, etc.).
carry[2], *v.* **(carried)**
I. *v.tr.* **1.** porter (un enfant, un fardeau, etc.); transporter (des marchandises, etc.); camionner (des marchandises); charrier (du fumier, etc.); **I don't c. much money about, on, me,** je ne porte jamais beaucoup d'argent sur moi; **he carried his case upstairs,** il a porté sa valise à sa chambre; **he carried the luggage, the baby, into the house, in,** il est entré (dans la maison) avec les bagages, en portant le bébé; **the porter carried the trunk across the hall,** le porteur a traversé le vestibule en portant, avec, la malle; **the bus carried us to our destination,** l'autobus nous a conduits, transportés, à notre destination; **the ship was carried on to a reef,** le navire fut mis sur un écueil; **a memory that he will c. with him to the grave,** un souvenir qu'il emportera dans la tombe; **his car can c. seven people,** sa voiture tient sept personnes; **to c. one's life in one's hands,** risquer sa vie; risquer la mort; *Nau:* **we were carrying livestock,** nous avions du bétail à bord. **2.** (*of wires, etc.*) conduire, transmettre (le son, etc.); (*of pipes*) amener (l'eau); **to c. crude oil to the refinery,** acheminer le pétrole brut sur la raffinerie. **3.** **to c. pipes under a street,** faire passer des tuyaux par-dessous une rue; **to c. a wall one foot higher,** élever, surélever, un mur d'un pied; **to c. death and destruction everywhere,** porter partout le carnage; **to c. sth. in one's head,** retenir qch. dans sa tête; **a can of petrol won't c. you very far,** vous n'irez pas loin avec un bidon d'essence; **to c. the war to its conclusion,** mener la guerre jusqu'au bout; **things were carried to such a point that . . .,** les choses en vinrent à ce point, à tel point, au point, que . . .; **he carries scepticism to some length, pretty far,** il aboutit à un scepticisme assez poussé; **modesty will not c. you far,** la modestie ne vous mènera pas loin; **freedom carried to the point of anarchy,** liberté poussée jusqu'à l'anarchie. **4.** enlever (une forteresse); emporter (une position) d'assaut; **to c. the enemy's last positions,** forcer l'ennemi dans ses derniers retranchements; **to c. all before one,** (i) faire brillamment son chemin; remporter tous les prix; (ii) vaincre toutes les résistances; triompher sur toute la ligne; **he carries everything before him,** tout cède, tout plie, devant lui; **to c. one's hearers with one,** entraîner son auditoire; **to c. one's point,** établir la validité d'un argument, d'une réclamation; imposer sa manière de voir; arriver à ses fins; atteindre son but. **5.** (i) adopter, (ii) faire adopter, faire passer (une proposition); (*of a bill, etc.*) **to be carried,** passer, être adopté, être voté. **6.** (*a*) porter (un revolver, une montre) sur soi; **to c. the mark of sth. on one,** porter l'empreinte de qch.; (*of pers., opinion*) **to c. authority,** avoir du poids, de l'autorité; (*of money*) **to c. interest,** porter intérêt; **to c. an interest of 4%,** rapporter un intérêt de 4%; **does your job c. a pension?** est-ce que vous avez droit à une retraite? **paper that carries a financial page,** journal *m* qui a une page financière; **power carries responsibility with it,** le pouvoir ne va pas sans responsabilité; **these abuses c. their own punishment,** ces abus portent en eux leur propre châtiment; (*b*) (*of shop*) avoir (des marchandises) en magasin, en dépôt. **7.** (*of woman*) **to c. a child,** être enceinte; **while she was carrying her third child,** pendant qu'elle était enceinte de son troisième enfant. **8.** *Mil:* **to c. swords,** mettre le sabre en main. **9.** **to c. one's head high,** porter la tête haute; **to c. oneself well, badly,** se tenir bien, mal; **to c. one's liquor well,** bien supporter l'alcool; *F:* **he's had as much as he can c.,** il en a son compte; il est rétamé; **boat that carries her canvas well,** barque *f* qui porte bien sa toile. **10.** *Arch: Const:* porter, supporter (une poutre, une voûte); **girder carried on trestles,** poutre portée sur, supportée par, des tréteaux. **11.** (*a*) (*of district*) nourrir (de nombreux moutons, etc.); **region carrying wheat,** région mise en blé; (*b*) *Com:* tenir (un article). **12.** *Mth:* **to c. a figure,** retenir un chiffre; **c. two and seven are nine,** deux de retenue et sept font neuf. **13.** *v.i.* (*of gun, sound, etc.*) porter; **his voice carries well,** il a une voix qui porte bien; **the ball carried a hundred metres,** la balle fit une trajectoire de cent mètres. **14.** *St.Exch:* (*of broker*) accorder un crédit à (un client); **to c. a customer for everything except small deposit,** supporter les risques des transactions d'un client moyennant une avance minime.
II. (*compound verbs*) **1. carry along,** *v.tr.* emporter, entraîner (qn, qch.); **he was carried along with the wreckage of his boat,** le courant l'entraîna avec les épaves de sa barque; **the mud carried along by the stream,** la vase charriée par le ruisseau.
2. carry away, *v.tr.* (*a*) emporter, enlever (qch.); entraîner, emmener (qn); *Nau:* **to c.a. a mast,** avoir un mât emporté (par une rafale); perdre un mât; (*b*) **carried away by his feelings,** emporté, entraîné, par ses émotions; **the crowd was carried away by these words,** la foule fut enlevée par ces paroles; (*c*) *A: & Lit:* **to be carried away by an illness,** être emporté par une maladie; succomber à une maladie.
3. carry back, *v.tr.* (*a*) rapporter (qch.); ramener (qn); (*b*) reporter (qch.), remmener (qn); (*c*) **that carries me back to my youth,** cela me rappelle ma jeunesse.
4. carry down, *v.tr.* descendre (qch.); (*of rivers*) charrier (de la vase, etc.).
5. carry forward, *v.tr.* (*a*) avancer (qch.); (*b*) *Book-k:* **to c. an item forward,** reporter un article; **carried forward,** report *m*; à reporter.
6. carry off, *v.tr.* (*a*) emporter (qch.); emmener (qn); enlever, emporter (qn); *F: O:* (*of illness, etc.*) tuer (qn); (*b*) remporter (le prix); (*c*) faire passer, faire accepter (qch. d'insolite); *F:* **to c. it off,** (i) faire passer la chose; (ii) réussir le coup.
7. carry on, (*a*) *v.tr.* (i) poursuivre, continuer, pousser (un travail); continuer (une tradition); exercer (un commerce, un métier); entretenir (une correspondance); soutenir (une conversation); **to c. on a conversation (where it was broken off),** continuer une conversation; reprendre le fil d'une conversation; **the war was carried on until the following year,** la guerre se prolongea jusqu'à l'année suivante; (ii) **to c. on a word (to the next stanza),** rejeter un mot; (*b*) *v.i.* (i) **to c. on during s.o.'s absence,** continuer le travail, diriger les affaires, pendant l'absence de qn; *Adm:* assurer l'intérim; **I shall stay behind to c. on the ordinary business,** je vais rester pour assurer l'expédition des affaires courantes; *Mil: Nau:* **c. on!** continuez! (ii) persévérer, persister; **I shall c. on to the end,** j'irai jusqu'au bout; (iii) *F:* se comporter; **I don't like the way she carries on,** je n'aime pas ses façons; **I noticed how they were carrying on,** j'observais leur manège; (iv) *F:* faire des scènes; s'emporter; **she carried on dreadfully,** elle nous a fait une scène terrible; **don't c. on like that!** ne vous emballez pas comme ça! (v) *P:* **to c. on with s.o.,** flirter, folichonner, avec qn; faire des coquetteries à qn; aguicher qn.
8. carry out, *v.tr.* (*a*) porter (qch.) dehors, hors de la salle, etc.; transporter (qn) au grand air; (*b*) mettre à exécution (un projet, une idée, une menace, une décision); *Av:* effectuer (un vol); remplir (les instructions de qn); mettre en pratique (une théorie); exécuter (un programme); exercer (un mandat); donner suite à (une idée, *Com:* une commande); satisfaire à (une

obligation, un désir); se décharger (d'une commission); mener à bien (une mission); mener à bonne fin (un travail); s'acquitter (d'une tâche, d'une fonction); **to c. out the law, a principle,** appliquer la loi, un principe; **to c. out an experiment,** effectuer une expérience; **to c. out a procedure,** suivre un mode de procédure; **to c. out an execution,** exécuter qn; **the night duty will be carried out by X,** la permanence de nuit sera assurée par X.

9. carry over, *v.tr.* (*a*) transporter (qch.) de l'autre côté; (faire) passer (qn) (dans le bac, etc.); (*b*) *Book-k:* reporter (une somme) d'une page à une autre; **to c. over a balance,** transporter un solde; (*c*) *St.Exch:* **to c. over stock,** reporter des titres; prendre des titres en report; **stock carried over,** titres *m* en report; *Typ:* **lines carried over,** report *m.*

10. carry through, *v.tr.* (*a*) mener (une entreprise) à bien, à bonne fin, à bon terme; exécuter (un travail, un calcul); (*b*) **his strong constitution carried him through (his illness),** sa forte santé l'aida à surmonter cette maladie.

11. carry up, *v.tr.* (*a*) monter (qch.); porter (qch.) en haut; **to c. sth. up (again),** remonter qch.; (*b*) enlever, emporter (en l'air).

carryall ['kæriɔ:l], *s.* **1.** *Veh: NAm:* carriole *f.* **2.** (sac *m*) fourre-tout *m inv.*

carrycot ['kærikɔt], *s.* moïse *m* de toile, porte-bébé(s) *m inv,* berceau *m* de voyage.

carrying[1] ['kæriiŋ], *a.* **1. c. party,** équipe *f* de porteurs. **2.** *Mch:* (*of locomotive*) **c. axle,** essieu porteur; **c. wheel,** roue porteuse.

carrying[2], *s.* **1.** (*a*) port *m,* transport *m; attrib.* **c. company,** entreprise *f* de transports, de roulage; **c. trade,** transport de marchandises; messageries *fpl;* (*of vehicle*) **c. capacity,** charge *f* utile; (*b*) **c. of arms,** port d'armes. **2.** enlèvement *m* (d'une forteresse). **3.** adoption *f,* vote *m* (d'un projet de loi, etc.).

carrying(s) on ['kæriiŋ(z)'ɔn], *s.* (*pl.*) **carry-on** ['kæri'ɔn], *s. P:* scandale *m;* **what a carry-on!** quelle histoire!

carrying over ['kæriiŋ'ouvər], **carry-over** ['kæriouvər], *s. St.Exch:* report *m.*

carse [kɑ:s], *s. Geog: Scot:* plaine alluviale.

carshop ['kɑ:ʃɔp], *s. Rail: esp. NAm:* (*usu. pl.*) atelier(s) *m*(*pl.*) de réparation (du matériel roulant).

carsick ['kɑ:sik], *a.* **to be c.,** avoir le mal de voiture, de la route.

carsickness ['kɑ:siknis], *s.* mal *m* de voiture, de la route.

car sleeper ['kɑ:sli:pər], *s.* train *m* (à) autos-couchettes.

cart[1] [kɑ:t], *s.* charrette *f* (à deux roues); (*with springs*) carriole *f,* voiture *f; A.Mil:* fourgon *m;* **bullock, ox, c.,** char *m* à bœufs; **hay c.,** charrette à foin; **coal c.,** banne *f;* **tip c.,** tombereau *m; Fig:* **to put the c. before the horse,** mettre la charrue devant les bœufs; *F:* **we're in the c. (all right),** nous voilà dans le pétrin, dans les choux, dans de beaux draps; **that would land us in the c.,** ça nous coulerait, nous mettrait dans le pétrin; (*b*) *attrib.* **c. ladder,** bers *mpl;* fausse ridelle; **c. prop,** chambrière *f,* béquille *f;* **c. track,** chemin *m* de charroi; route charretière, chemin charretier; charrière *f.*

cart[2], *v.tr.* charrier, charroyer, voiturer (qch.); transporter (qch.) dans une charrette; **I'm tired of carting these huge parcels (around, about),** j'en ai assez de (trans)porter ces gros colis; *F:* **I've got to c. some friends around London,** j'ai à amener des amis à Londres, à trimbaler des amis dans Londres; **they carted the rubbish away, off,** ils ont enlevé, emporté, les ordures; *P:* **oh, c. yourself off!** fiche-moi le camp!

cartage ['kɑ:tidʒ], *s.* charroi *m,* charriage *m;* transport *m* par voiture, par roulage, par camions; camionnage *m.*

Cartagena [kɑ:tə'dʒi:nə], *Pr.n. Geog:* Carthagène *f.*

carte[1] **(à la)** [ælæ'kɑ:t], *Fr.a.phr. & adv.phr.* **à la c. dinner,** dîner *m* à la carte; **to dine à la c.,** manger à la carte.

carte[2], *s. Fenc:* quarte *f.*

carte blanche ['kɑ:t'blɑ̃:ʃ], *s.* carte blanche.

carted ['kɑ:tid], *a. Ven: Pej:* **c. stag,** cerf *m* en boîte.

cartel [kɑ:'tel], *s.* (*a*) *A:* cartel *m,* provocation *f* en duel; (*b*) cartel, convention *f* pour l'échange de prisonniers; **c. (ship),** navire *m* parlementaire; navire qui a mission d'échanger des prisonniers; (*c*) *Ind: etc:* cartel.

cartel(l)ism ['kɑ:telizm], *s. Pol:* cartellisme *m.*

cartel(l)ist ['kɑ:telist], *s. Pol:* cartelliste *m.*

cartel(l)ization [kɑ:telai'zeiʃ(ə)n], *s. Ind:* cartellisation *f.*

cartel(l)ize ['kɑ:telaiz], *v.tr. Ind:* cartelliser.

carter ['kɑ:tər], *s.* (*a*) charretier *m, A:* roulier *m;* (*b*) camionneur *m.*

Cartesian [kɑ:'ti:ziən], (*a*) *a. Phil: Mth:* Cartésien; **C. co-ordinates,** coordonnées cartésiennes; *Ph:* **C. diver, devil, imp,** ludion *m;* (*b*) *s. Phil:* cartésien *m.*

Cartesianism [kɑ:'ti:ziənizm], *s. Phil:* Cartésianisme *m.*

cartful ['kɑ:tful], *s.* charretée *f;* pleine charrette (de qch.).

Carthage ['kɑ:θidʒ], *Pr.n. Geog:* Carthage *f.*

Carthaginian [kɑ:θə'dʒiniən], *Geog:* (*a*) *a.* carthaginois; (*b*) *s.* Carthaginois, -oise.

carthorse ['kɑ:thɔ:s], *s.* cheval *m* de charrette, de roulage; charretier *m.*

Carthusian [kɑ:'θju:ziən], *a. & s.* **1.** chartreux, -euse; des chartreux; **the C. friars,** les chartreux. **2.** (élève ou ancien élève) de l'école de *Charterhouse.*

cartilage ['kɑ:tilidʒ], *s.* cartilage *m;* **temporary c.,** cartilage d'ossification; cartilage temporaire; **hyaline c.,** cartilage hyalin.

cartilagenous, cartilaginous [kɑ:ti'lædʒinəs], *a.* cartilagineux; **c. fish,** poisson cartilagineux.

carting ['kɑ:tiŋ], *s.* = CARTAGE.

cartload ['kɑ:tloud], *s.* charretée *f,* voiturée *f,* enlevée *f* (of, de); **c. of coal, of manure,** tombereau *m* de charbon, de fumier; *F:* **a c. of trouble,** toute une accumulation de malheurs, de soucis; **as artful as a c. of monkeys,** malin comme un singe; **a c. of old rubbish,** une histoire à dormir debout.

cartogram ['kɑ:tougræm], *s.* cartogramme *m.*

cartographer [kɑ:'tɔgrəfər], *s.* cartographe *m.*

cartographic(al) [kɑ:tou'græfik(l)], *a.* cartographique.

cartography [kɑ:'tɔgrəfi], *s.* cartographie *f.*

cartomancy ['kɑ:təmænsi], *s.* cartomancie *f.*

carton ['kɑ:tən], *s.* (*a*) carton *m;* (*b*) petite boîte en carton.

carton pierre ['kɑ:tənpi:'ɛər], *s.* carton-pierre *m.*

cartoon[1] [kɑ:'tu:n], *s.* **1.** *Art:* carton *m.* **2.** (*a*) dessin *m* (humoristique ou satirique); **strip c.,** bande dessinée; (*b*) portrait caricaturé; caricature *f,* charge *f;* (*c*) *Cin:* dessin animé.

cartoon[2], *v.tr. & i.* dessiner un portrait humoristique de (qn); faire la caricature, la charge, de (qn); faire un dessin humoristique, satirique.

cartooning [kɑ:'tu:niŋ], *s.* (l'art *m* de) la caricature.

cartoonist [kɑ:'tu:nist], *s.* caricaturiste *m;* dessinateur *m* (de dessins humoristiques, satiriques).

cartop ['kɑ:tɔp], *a. U.S:* (bateau, etc.) qui peut être transporté sur le toit d'une voiture.

cartouche [kɑ:'tu:ʃ], *s. Arch: etc:* cartouche *m.*

cartridge ['kɑ:tridʒ], *s.* **1.** (*a*) cartouche *f* (d'arme à feu); **sporting c.,** cartouche de chasse; **central-fire c.,** cartouche à percussion centrale; **flanged, rimmed, c.,** cartouche à bourrelet; **grooved, rimless, c.,** cartouche à gorge; **rim-fire c.,** cartouche à percussion périphérique; *A:* **pin-fire c.,** cartouche à broche; **live c.,** cartouche réelle; **blank c., ball c.,** cartouche à blanc, à balle; **dummy c.,** fausse cartouche, cartouche inerte, cartouche d'instruction; **armour-piercing c.,** cartouche à balle perforante; **high-explosive c.,** cartouche à balle explosive; **signal c.,** cartouche de signalisation; **to remove the cartridges from the magazine of a rifle,** désapprovisionner le magasin d'un fusil; (*b*) *Artil:* gargousse *f* (de grosse pièce); **blank c.,** gargousse à blanc; **dummy c.,** gargousse sans poudre; *Exp:* **dynamite c.,** cartouche de dynamite; (*c*) *attrib.* **c. box, c. pouch,** cartouchière *f;* **c.-box sling,** bretelle *f* de cartouchière; *Sm.a:* **c. clip,** chargeur *m;* lame-chargeur *f, pl.* lames-chargeurs; **c. case,** (i) étui *m,* douille *f* (pour cartouche de fusil, etc.); (ii) *Artil:* gargoussier *m;* **c. belt,** (i) ceinture-cartouchière *f, pl.* ceintures-cartouchières; (ii) bande-chargeur souple, articulée (*pl.* bandes-chargeurs) (de mitrailleuse). **2.** *Ind:* **filter c.,** cartouche filtrante, à filtre. **3.** *Phot:* cartouche. **4.** *W.Tel: Rec: etc:* (*a*) robot *m;* (*b*) tête *f* de lecture; phonolecteur *m;* **magnetic c.,** cellule *f* magnétique. **5.** *El:* cartouche (de fusible); **c. fuse,** fusible *m* à cartouche.

cartridge paper ['kɑ:tridʒpeipər], *s. Ind: Art:* papier *m* à cartouches, papier-cartouche *m;* papier de moulage, carte *f* de moulage; papier fort.

cartulary ['kɑ:tjuləri], *s.* cartulaire *m.*

cartwheel[1] ['kɑ:t(h)wi:l], *s.* **1.** (*a*) roue *f* de charrette; (*b*) *F: A:* grosse pièce (d'argent); pièce d'une couronne, d'un dollar; grande pièce d'un penny, de deux pence (du 18e. siècle); (*c*) **c. hat,** chapeau *m* à larges bords. **2.** *Gym:* **to turn cartwheels,** faire la roue.

cartwheel[2], *v.i.* faire tonneau.

cartwright ['kɑ:trait], *s.* charron *m;* **cartwright's wood,** bois *m* de charronnage; **cartwright's workshop,** charronnerie *f.*

carucate ['kæru:keit], *s. Hist:* charruage *m.*

caruncle ['kærəŋkl, kə'rʌŋkl], *s. Anat: Bot:* caroncule *f.*

caruncular [kə'rʌŋkjulər], *a.* caronculeux.

carunculate(d) [kə'rʌŋkjuleit(id)], *a. Nat.Hist:* caronculé.

carvacrol(e) ['kɑ:vəkrɔl], *s. Ch:* carvacrol *m.*

carve [kɑ:v], *v.tr.* **1.** (*a*) sculpter, graver, ciseler (du marbre, etc.); **to c. a statue in, out of, marble,** sculpter une statue dans le marbre; **(piece of) stone carved into the shape of a lion,** pierre taillée en forme de lion; **carved lion,** lion sculpté; *v.i.* **to c. in, on, marble,** sculpter dans le marbre; graver sur le marbre; **to c. out a career for oneself,** se faire une carrière; **to c. one's way,** se tailler, se frayer, un chemin (**through,** à travers); (*b*) (*with pass. force*) **marble, wood, that carves well, badly,** marbre *m,* bois *m,* qui se prête bien, mal, à la sculpture, à la taille. **2.** (*a*) découper (de la viande); dépecer (une volaille); **to c. a slice of meat,** découper une tranche de viande; (*b*) *F:* **to c. up a country,** démembrer, morceler, un pays; **to c. s.o. up,** (i) attaquer qn avec un couteau; charcuter qn; (ii) rouler qn; (iii) critiquer qn brutalement.

carvel ['kɑ:vel], *s.* **1.** *A.Nau:* caravelle *f.* **2.** *N.Arch:* **c. built,** bordé à franc-bord; **c. joint,** joint *m* à franc-bord.

carven ['kɑ:v(ə)n], *a. A:* gravé; sculpté; ciselé.

carvene ['kɑ:vi:n], *s. Ch:* carvène *m.*

carver ['kɑ:vər], *s.* **1.** (*a*) *Art:* sculpteur *m* (sur bois); ciseleur *m;* (*b*) (*at table*) découpeur, -euse; (*at hotel*) serveur, -euse; *Hist:* **c. to the King,** écuyer tranchant. **2.** couteau *m* à découper, *pl.* service *m* à découper. **3.** fauteuil *m* de table (qu'occupe le chef de famille).

carvestrene ['kɑ:vəstri:n], *s. Ch:* carvestrène *m.*

carve-up ['kɑ:vʌp], *s.* **1.** *F:* division *f* (du butin); démembrement *m* (d'un pays). **2.** *P:* escroquerie *f.*

carving ['kɑ:viŋ], *s.* **1.** (*a*) sculptage *m;* (*b*) *Art:* sculpture *f;* gravure *f;* ciselure *f;* **wood c.,** sculpture sur bois. **2.** découpage *m* (de la viande); **c. knife, fork,** couteau *m,* fourchette *f,* à découper.

carvomenthene ['kɑ:vou'menθi:n], *s. Ch:* carvomenthène *m.*

carvomenthol ['kɑ:vou'menθɔl], *s. Ch:* carvomenthol *m.*

carvomenthone ['kɑ:vou'menθoun], *s. Ch:* carvomenthone *f.*

carvone ['kɑ:voun], *s. Ch:* carvone *f.*

caryatid, *pl.* **-ides, -ids** [kæri'ætid, -idi:z, -idz], *s.* caryatide *f,* cariatide *f.*

caryinite ['kæriinait], *s. Miner:* caryinite *f.*

caryocar [kæri'oukər], *s. Bot:* caryocar *m.*

Caryophillaceae, Caryophyllaceae [kæriouf i'leisii:], *s.pl. Bot:* caryophyllacées *f.*

caryophyllaceous, -phylleous [kæriouf i'leiʃəs, -'filiəs], *a. Bot:* caryophyllé.

caryophyllene [kæriouf i'li:n], *s. Ch:* caryophyllène *m.*

caryophyllia ['kæriou'filiə], *s. Coel:* caryophyllie *f,* caryophillia *f.*

caryopsis [kæri'ɔpsis], *s. Bot:* caryopse *m.*

caryota ['kæri'outə], *s. Bot:* caryota *m.*

casaque ['kæsæk], *s. Cost:* casaque *f.*

casbah ['kæzbə], *s.* casbah *f,* kasbah *f.*

cascabel ['kæskəbel], *s. Rept:* cascabelle *f.*

cascade[1] [kæs'keid], *s.* **1.** chute *f* d'eau; cascade *f;* (*small*) cascatelle *f; El:* **c. connection,** couplage *m* en cascade. **2.** *Dressm: etc:* **c. of lace, etc.,** flot *m,* jabot *m,* de dentelle; flot (de rubans). **3.** *Pyr:* cascade.

cascade[2]. **1.** *v.i.* tomber en cascade; cascader. **2.** *v.tr. El:* **to c.(-connect),** monter en cascade.

cascalho [kæs'kælou], *s. Miner:* cascalho *m.*

cascara (sagrada) [kæs'kɑ:rə(sə'grɑ:də)], *s. Pharm:* cascara sagrada *f.*

cascarilla [kæskə'rilə], *s. Bot:* cascarille *f.*

case[1] [keis], *s.* **1.** cas *m;* **the c. in point, the c. before us,** le cas dont il s'agit; la chose en question; le cas qui nous occupe; *Jur:* **a c. in point, a concrete c.,** un cas d'espèce; **law that is inapplicable to the c. in point,** loi *f* qui n'est pas applicable en l'espèce; **to quote a c. in point,** citer un exemple topique; **to state a c.,** formuler un point de droit; **c. of conscience,** cas de conscience; **to put the c. clearly,** exposer clairement le cas, la situation; **I put my c. to him,** je lui ai exposé mon cas; **should the c. occur,** le cas échéant; **this is not the c.,** ce n'est pas le cas; il n'en est rien; **if that is the c.,** s'il en est ainsi; **that is often the c.,** cela arrive souvent; **as the c. stands,** dans l'état (actuel) des choses; **that alters the c.,** c'est une autre affaire; ce n'est plus la même chose; voilà qui change la thèse! *F:* c'est une autre paire de manches! **your c. is different, this is not the c. with you,** votre cas est différent, il n'en est pas ainsi de vous; **my c. is the same,** je suis dans le même cas; **that's a hard c.,** (i) c'est un cas difficile; (ii) c'est un cas bien triste; **that would meet the c.,** cela ferait (bien) l'affaire; **it's a c. of now or never,** il s'agit de saisir l'occasion, de faire vite; **it was a c. of love at first sight,** ils se sont aimés du premier coup, à première vue; *F:* ç'a été le coup de foudre; *F:* **it's a c.,** les voilà épris l'un de l'autre; **that will never be their c.,** cela ne leur arrivera jamais; **in c. of emergency,** en cas d'urgence; **in the c. of children under 14,** dans le cas des enfants au-dessous de 14 ans; **in c. of accident, of need,** en cas d'accident, de besoin;

in c. he isn't there, au cas qu'il n'y soit pas; au cas, dans le cas, pour le cas, où il n'y serait pas; **in any c.,** en tout cas; dans tous les cas; de toute façon; en tout état de cause; **you must have patience; in any c. you are only twenty,** il faut patienter un peu; aussi bien n'avez-vous que vingt ans; **in that c.,** en ce cas; à ce compte; alors; **in such a c., in such cases,** en pareil cas; en pareille circonstance; **in every c.,** en toute hypothèse; **in this particular c.,** en l'espèce; **in his c.,** dans son cas; quant à lui; **we will make an exception in his c.,** nous ferons une exception en ce qui le concerne; **as in Martin's c.,** comme pour Martin; **if that's the c.,** si c'est comme ça; **just in c.,** à titre de précaution; **I don't think he'll come but I'll wait half an hour in c.,** je ne pense pas qu'il vienne, mais je vais attendre encore une demi-heure à tout hasard; **as the c. may be,** selon le cas; selon les circonstances; **in most cases,** dans la plupart des cas; en général. **2.** *(a)* cas (de jaunisse, de scarlatine, etc.); **c. history,** antécédents *mpl*; *Med:* histoire *f* de la maladie, dossier médical; (antécédents) commémoratifs *mpl*; **c. study,** étude individuelle; *(b)* malade *mf*; blessé, -ée; **heart c.,** cardiaque *mf*; *(c) F:* type *m* (bizarre, etc.); **he's a hard c.,** (i) on ne sait par où le prendre; (ii) il est inflexible; (iii) il est incorrigible. **3.** *Jur: etc: (a)* cause *f*; affaire *f*; **civil, criminal, c.,** affaire civile, criminelle; **divorce c.,** procès *m* en divorce; **famous cases,** causes célèbres; **the Dreyfus c.,** l'affaire Dreyfus; **leading c.,** cause qui a établi un précédent; **test c.,** cas dont la solution fait jurisprudence; précédent *m*; **marginal c.,** cas limite; **c. law,** jurisprudence *f*; **to open the c.,** ouvrir l'affaire; **to win one's c.,** gagner sa cause, son affaire, son procès; avoir gain de cause; **to decide a c.,** rendre un jugement; **to state the c.,** faire l'exposé des faits; **the facts of the c.,** les données *f* du problème; *(b)* **to put the c. for the prisoner at the bar,** présenter la défense du prévenu; **that is my c., my Lord,** plaise au tribunal d'adopter mes conclusions; *(in criminal trial)* **the c. for the Crown,** l'accusation *f*; **to get up the c. against s.o.,** instruire contre qn; **there is no c. against you,** vous êtes hors de cause; **you have no c.,** vous serez débouté (de votre demande); **to make out a c.,** établir une réclamation, une accusation; **to make out one's c.,** prouver son cas; prouver, justifier, sa plainte; **the c. for s.o., sth.,** les arguments *m* en faveur de qn, qch.; **to put up a strong c. for s.o.,** (i) prendre le parti de qn, défendre qn; (ii) recommander qn très chaudement. **4.** *Gram:* cas; **c. endings,** flexions casuelles.

case², *s.* **1.** **(packing)** **c.,** caisse *f*, boîte *f* (d'emballage); **c. of goods,** caisse de marchandises; **c. of wine,** caisse (de 12 bouteilles) de vin; **c. opener,** ciseau *m* à déballer; arrache-clou *m*, *pl.* arrache-clous; ouvre-caisse(s) *m*, *pl.* ouvre-caisses; *A: & U.S:* **c. bottle,** bouteille carrée; flacon *m*; **c. maker,** fabricant *m* de caisses (d'emballage); *Mil: A:* **uniform c.,** cantine *f* (d'officier). **2.** *(a)* étui *m*; coffret *m*, écrin *m* (pour bijoux); trousse *f* (d'instruments); boîte *f* (de violon); gaine *f* (de poignard, de pistolet, de momie); fourreau *m* (de parapluie); peau *f* (de saucisse, *Bot:* de péricarpe); **spectacle c.,** étui à lunettes; **c. of surgical instruments,** trousse de chirurgien; **record c.,** mallette *f* porte-disques; **dressing c.,** nécessaire *m*, trousse, de toilette; **cigar, cigarette, c.,** étui à cigares, à cigarettes; **card c.,** porte-cartes *m inv*; **needle c.,** étui à aiguilles, porte-aiguilles *m inv*; **c. knife,** couteau *m* à gaine; *(b)* **(display) c.,** vitrine *f*. **3.** *(a)* coffre *m*, caisse (de piano); buffet *m* (d'orgue); caisse (d'horloge); *(b)* boîtier *m* (de montre, etc.); palastre *m*, coffre (de serrure); *Sm.a:* **cartridge c.,** douille *f*, étui, de cartouche; *Tp:* **diaphragm c.,** capsule *f* (de la membrane vibrante). **4.** *(a)* chemise *f*, enveloppe *f* (de cylindre de moteur); bâche *f* (de turbine); *Aut:* carter *m* (du différentiel, etc.); *I.C.E:* **crank c.,** carter (du moteur); **timing c.,** petit carter de la distribution; *Ball:* **bomb c.,** corps *m* de bombe; *(b)* revêtement *m* de bois; **mine-shaft c.,** cadre coffrant; *Nau:* **c. of a mast,** cornet *m* d'un mât. **5.** *(a) Bookb:* couverture *f*; **c. binding,** emboîtage *m*; reliure *f* Bradel; *(b)* **filling c.,** carton *m*. **6.** *Typ:* casse *f*; **c. rack,** cassier *m*; **half c.,** casseau *m*; **lower c.,** bas *m* de casse; **lower-c. letter,** minuscule *f*; **upper c.,** haut *m* de casse; **upper-c. letter,** majuscule *f*, capitale *f*. **7.** *P:* **c. (house),** bordel *m*.

case³, *v.tr.* **1.** **to c. goods,** encaisser, emballer, des marchandises; mettre des marchandises en caisse(s). **2.** *(a)* envelopper **(with,** de); **to c. (over) a surface with plaster,** revêtir une surface de plâtre; **to c. sth. with iron plates,** ferrer qch.; blinder qch. de plaques de fer; **to c. a boiler, a cylinder,** chemiser une chaudière, un cylindre; **to c. a turbine,** bâcher une turbine; **to c. a bottle with wicker,** clisser une bouteille; **to c. sth. with leather,** gainer qch.; *(b) Bookb:* cartonner (un livre). **3.** **to c. a well,** tuber, cuveler, un puits. **4.** *P:* **to c. a joint,** prospecter, examiner les lieux (avant un cambriolage). **5.** *P:* **to c. up with s.o.,** faire ménage, cohabiter, avec qn.

caseate¹ ['keisiət], *s. Ch:* caséate *m*.

caseate² ['keisieit], *v.i. Med: (of tissue)* devenir caséeux.

caseation [keisi'eiʃ(ə)n], *s. Ch: Med:* caséation *f*.

casebook ['keisbuk], *s.* **1.** recueil *m* de jurisprudence. **2.** dossier médical.

casefy ['keisifai], *v.tr. Ch:* caséifier (le lait).

case-harden ['keishɑ:d(ə)n], *v.tr. Metall:* cémenter, aciérer (le fer); tremper, durcir, (l'acier) à la surface.

case-hardened ['keishɑ:dənd], *a.* **1.** cémenté, aciéré, trempé à la surface; (moulé) en coquille. **2.** *F: (of pers.)* endurci (dans le crime).

case hardening ['keis'hɑ:d(ə)niŋ], *s. Metall:* cémentation *f*, aciérage *m*; trempe *f* de surface; trempe par cémentation.

caseic ['keisiik], *a. Ch:* caséique.

casein ['keisiin], *s. Ch: Ind:* caséine *f*, caséum *m*; **c. factory,** caséinerie *f*.

casemate¹ ['keismeit], *s. Fort:* casemate *f*, coffre *m*; **flanking c.,** coffre flanquant; *N.Arch:* **gun c.,** réduit *m*.

casemate², *v.tr.* casemater.

casemated ['keismeitid], *a.* casematé; **c. battery,** batterie blindée.

casemating ['keismeitiŋ], *s.* casematage *m*.

casement ['keismənt], *s.* **1.** châssis *m* de fenêtre à deux battants; **c. window,** fenêtre *f* à deux battants; croisée *f*; **c. stay,** entrebâillement *m* (d'une fenêtre à battants); **c. cloth,** toile *f* (pour rideaux de fenêtre). **2.** *Poet:* fenêtre.

caseous ['keisiəs], *a.* caséeux.

caser ['keisər], *s. Turf: P: A:* cinq shillings.

case-shot ['keisʃɔt], *s. A:* mitraille *f*; **to fire c.-s.,** tirer à mitraille; **c.-s. fire,** tir *m* à mitraille; **discharge of c.-s.,** mitraillade *f*.

caseum ['keisiəm], *s. Ch:* caséum *m*.

casework ['keiswə:k], *s. Med: etc:* traitement individuel; assistance individuelle.

caseworker ['keiswə:kər], *s.* assistant(e) social(e).

case-worm, *s.* = **caddis-worm**, *q.v. under* CADDIS.

cash¹ [kæʃ], *s. (no pl.)* espèces *fpl*; numéraire *m*; argent comptant; valeurs *fpl* en espèces; **hard c.,** espèces sonnantes (et trébuchantes); argent liquide; numéraire; *Com:* **c. balance,** solde actif, solde de caisse; **c. reserve,** encaisse *f* liquide; *(of bank, etc.)* **c. holdings,** avoirs *mpl* en monnaie fluide; **c. price,** prix *m* au comptant; **to buy for c.,** acheter comptant; **c. purchase,** achat *m* comptant; **to pay c.,** payer comptant; **to pay in c.,** payer en espèces; **c. payment, settlement in c.,** paiement *m* (au) comptant; versement *m*, règlement *m*, en espèces; **to sell for c.,** vendre (au) comptant; **c. transaction, c. sale,** transaction *f*, vente *f*, au comptant; **c. with order,** payable à la commande; **terms c.,** payable au comptant; **discount for c.,** rabais *m* pour paiement comptant; **c. less discount,** comptant avec escompte; **c. on delivery,** paiement à la livraison; (livraison) contre remboursement; **c. account,** compte *m* de caisse; **c. and carry,** libre service *m* de gros; marchandises à emporter contre paiement comptant; **c. store,** magasin *m* qui ne vend pas à crédit; *Jur:* **c. offer,** offre réelle; *Fin:* **c. shares,** actions *f* de numéraire, en numéraire; **shares issued for c.,** actions émises contre espèces; **securities dealt for in c.,** valeurs au comptant; **c. at maturity,** valeur aux échéances; *Book-k:* **c. in hand,** fonds *mpl*, espèces, en caisse; caisse *f*; encaisse disponible; **petty c.,** petite caisse; **to have c. in hand,** avoir de l'argent en caisse; **to keep the c.,** tenir la caisse; **to balance the c.,** faire la caisse; **c. box,** caisse, cassette *f*; **c. desk,** caisse; **c. register,** caisse enregistreuse; caisse automatique; *F:* **how are you off for c.?** est-ce que tu es en fonds? as-tu de l'argent? **I'm short of c.,** (i) je n'ai pas d'argent sur moi; (ii) je n'ai presque pas d'argent; je suis à sec.

cash², *v.*

I. *v.tr.* **1.** toucher (un chèque, un mandat-poste, etc.); encaisser (un effet, un coupon); escompter (un effet); changer (un billet de banque). **2.** **to c. a cheque for s.o.,** verser à qn le montant d'un chèque. **3.** *Austr: N.Z: F:* **to be (well) cashed up,** avoir beaucoup d'argent, avoir de quoi.

II. *(compound verbs)* **1.** **cash in,** *(a) v.i. (of salesman, etc.)* verser sa recette à la caisse; régler ses comptes; *(b) v.i. (after attendance at board meeting, etc.)* toucher ses jetons; *(c) v.i. P:* **to c. in one's chips, checks,** mourir, lâcher la rampe; *(d) v.ind.tr. F:* **to c. in on sth.,** tirer profit de qch.; **to c. in on one's influence,** monnayer son influence.

2. **cash up,** *v.i. F:* payer.

cash³, *s. Num: (China)* cache *m*, cash *m*.

cashable ['kæʃəbl], *a.* encaissable, payable (à vue).

cashbook ['kæʃbuk], *s.* livre *m* de caisse; sommier *m*; **counter c.,** chiffrier *m*; main courante de caisse; **paid c.,** main courante de sorties de caisse.

cashew [kæ'ʃu:], *s.* **1.** *Bot:* **c. (nut tree),** acajou *m* à pommes, anacardier *m*; **c. nut,** noix *f* d'acajou, anacarde *m*. **2.** *Orn:* **c. bird,** pauxi *m*.

cashier¹ [kæ'ʃiər], *s.* caissier, -ière; **cashier's desk, office,** caisse *f*; comptoir *m* de recette.

cahier², *v.tr. Mil: Navy:* casser (un sous-officier); réformer (un officier, par mesure disciplinaire); mettre (un officier) à la réforme.

Cashmere [kæʃ'miər]. **1.** *Pr.n. Geog: A:* Cachemire *m*. **2.** *s. Tex:* cachemire *m*; **c. shawl,** cachemire de l'Inde.

cashmerette [kæʃmiə'ret], *s. Tex: A:* cachemirette *f*.

casing ['keisiŋ], *s.* **1.** *(a)* encaissage *m* (de marchandises); clissage *m* (d'une bouteille); *Bookb:* **casing (in),** cartonnage *m*, finissure *f* (d'un livre); *(b)* coffrage *m*, boisage *m*, tubage *m*, cuvelage *m* (d'un puits de mine, etc.). **2.** enveloppe *f*, garniture *f* (d'une pompe, etc.); blindage *m*, tôle *f* d'enveloppe, chemise *f* (d'un cylindre); parois *fpl* (d'un fourneau); huche *f*, bâche fermée (d'une turbine); cage *f*, entourage *m*, coquille *f* (d'une machine); boisseau *m* (d'un robinet); boîte *f*, caisse *f* (de l'embrayage); capot *m* (d'une lampe à arc, etc.); revêtement *m* (d'une maçonnerie); dormant *m*, bâti *m*, chambranle *m* (d'une porte, d'une fenêtre); *Min:* boisage (d'un puits, d'une galerie, etc.); *N.Arch:* vaigrage plein, entourage plein; cadre *m* (d'une hélice); *Civ.E:* coffrage (pour béton armé); *Mec.E: etc:* gainage *m*; *Atom.Ph:* gainage (du combustible); *Av:* **control c.,** gaine *f* de protection des commandes; *(of machine gun, etc.)* **barrel c., radiator c.,** manchon réfrigérant, de refroidissement; *Metall:* **outer c. (of furnace),** contre-paroi *f* (d'un fourneau), *pl.* contre-parois; *El:* **armature c.,** enveloppe d'induit; *Metall:* **c. (of mould),** manteau *m*; *N.Arch:* **rudder c.,** manchon *m* de gouvernail; *Aut:* **differential c.,** carter *m* du différentiel; **tyre c.,** enveloppe (extérieure) de pneu; **(sausage) c.,** boyau *m*; **c. dog, c. spear,** arrache-tuyau *m*, *pl.* arrache-tuyaux.

casino [kə'si:nou], *s.* casino *m*.

cask¹ [kɑ:sk], *s. (a)* barrique *f*, baril *m*, fût *m*, futaille *f*, tonneau *m*; pièce *f* (de vin); **to put wine into casks,** mettre le vin en fût(s), en tonneau(x); embarriquer du vin; **c. stand,** chantier *m* (pour fûts); *Com:* **wine in the c.,** vin en fût, en cercles; vin en pièce; vin logé; **half c.,** *(of burgundy)* feuillette *f*, *(of claret)* demi-pièce *f*, *pl.* demi-pièces; *(b) (for dry goods)* boucaut *m*; *(c) Atom.Ph:* **(lead) c.,** château *m* (de plomb).

cask², *v.tr.* enfûter, enfutailler (le vin); mettre (le vin) en fût(s), en tonneau(x).

casket ['kɑ:skit], *s.* **1.** coffret *m* (à bijoux); cassette *f* (pour bijoux ou argent). **2.** *NAm:* cercueil *m*. **3.** *(for cremated remains)* urne *f*.

Caspian ['kæspiən], *a. Geog:* caspien; **the C. Sea,** la mer Caspienne.

casque [kæsk], *s.* **1.** *Arm:* casque *m*. **2.** *Nat.Hist:* casque.

Cassander [kə'sændər], *Pr.n.m. Gr.Hist:* Cassandre.

Cassandra [kə'sændrə], *Pr.n.f.* **1.** *Gr.Myth:* Cassandre. **2.** cassandre, prophète *m* de malheur.

cassata [kə'sɑ:tə], *s. Comest:* cassate *f*.

cassation [kæ'seiʃ(ə)n], *s. Jur:* cassation *f*; **Court of C.,** cour *f* de cassation.

cassava [kə'sɑ:və], *s. (a) Bot:* cassave *f*, manioc *m*; *(b)* **c. (flour),** farine *f* de cassave; manioc *m*; *(c) (bread)* cassave.

casse [kæs], *s. Wine-m:* casse *f*.

casse paper ['kæsipeipər], *s. Tchn:* papier cassé.

casserole ['kæsəroul], *s. Cu:* **1.** cocotte *f* (en terre, en verre, etc. allant au feu). **2.** ragoût *m* en cocotte.

cassette [kæ'set], *s. (a) Phot:* chargeur *m*; *(b) Rec: Cmptr: etc:* cassette *f*; **c. recorder,** magnétophone *m* à cassettes; magnétocassette *m*.

cassia ['kæsiə], *s.* **1.** *Bot: (a)* casse *f*, canéfice *f*; *(b)* **c. (tree),** cassier *m*, canéficier *m*. **2.** *Pharm:* casse.

cassida ['kæsidə], *s. Ent:* casside *f*.

Cassididae [kæ'sididi:], *s.pl. Moll:* cassididés *m*.

Cassinese [kæsi'ni:z], *a. Ecc:* **C. congregation,** congrégation cassinaise.

Cassino [kə'si:nou], *Pr.n. Geog:* **Monte C.,** le mont Cassin.

cassiope [kə'saiəpi], *s. Bot:* cassiope *m*.

Cassiopeia [kæsiou'pi(:)ə], *Pr.n.f.* Cassiopée; *Astr:* **Cassiopeia's Chair,** la Chaise; le trône de Cassiopée.

cassique ['kæsik], *s. Orn:* cassique *m*.

cassis ['kæsis], *s. Moll:* cassis *m*.

Cassiterides (the) [ðəkæsi'teridi:z], *Pr.n.pl. A.Geog:* les Cassitérides *f*.

cassiterite [kæ'sitərait], *s. Miner:* cassitérite *f*.

cassock ['kæsək], *s. Ecc:* soutane *f*; **short c.,** soutanelle *f*.

cassocked ['kæsəkt], *a.* (prêtre, etc.) en soutane. *F:* ensoutané.

cassolette [kæsou'let], *s.* cassolette *f.*

cassowary ['kæsəwεəri], *s. Orn:* casoar *m.*

cassweed ['kæswi:d], *s. Bot:* capselle *f*, bourse-à-pasteur *f.*

cast[1] [kɑ:st], *s.* **1.** *(a)* jet *m* (d'une pierre); coup *m* (de dés, de filet); **at a single c.,** (i) d'un seul jet, d'un seul coup; (ii) d'un seul coup de filet; *O:* **within a stone's c.,** à un jet de pierre; **to stake everything on a single c. (of the die),** jouer son va-tout en un seul coup; *Nau:* **c. of the lead,** coup de sonde; *(b) Fish:* (i) lancer *m* (de la ligne, de la mouche, du filet); (ii) bas *m* de ligne; empile *f*; avançon *m*; (iii) endroit *m* propice à la pêche au lancer; **back c.,** lancer arrière; **forward c.,** lancer avant; **underhand c.,** lancer sous la main; **switch c.,** lancer roulé; **to change one's c.,** (i) changer de mouche; (ii) changer d'endroit; *(c)* (*of sheepdog*) **to make a c.,** cerner un troupeau (pour le rassembler). **2.** *(a)* dépouille *f* (d'insecte); *(b)* déjections *fpl* (de lombric, de ver de terre); *(c)* aliments dégorgés (par les hiboux, les faucons); *(d)* agneaux *mpl* mis bas. **3.** *(a)* jet (d'abeilles); rejet *m* (d'essaim); *(b)* **c. of hawks,** couple *m* de faucons; vol *m* de faucons. **4.** *(a) Metall:* coulée *f*; (jet de) fonte *f*; *(b)* (i) pièce moulée; plâtre *m*; (ii) moule *m* en creux; (iii) *Med:* appareil plâtré; **plaster c.,** moulage *m* au plâtre; empreinte *f* en plâtre; **to take a c. of sth.,** mouler qch.; tiner un plâtre de qch.; *(c) Geol:* (*of fossil*) moule interne; *(d) Med:* calcul *m* (épousant la forme de l'organe où il se trouve); *(e) Typ:* cliché *m.* **5.** *usu. O: or Lit:* *(a)* **a man of his c.,** un homme de sa trempe, de son acabit; **c. of mind,** tournure *f* d'esprit; **c. of features,** physionomie *f*; expression *f*; **c. of thought,** tournure *f* de pensée; *(b)* **c. of a sentence,** ordonnance *f*, allure *f*, d'une phrase; **c. of a drapery,** arrangement *m* d'une draperie (dans un tableau, etc.). **6.** *(a)* voilure *f* (d'une poutre, etc.); *(b)* **to have a c. in one's eye,** avoir une tendance à loucher; **he has a c. in his left eye,** il louche légèrement de l'œil gauche. **7.** *O:* addition *f* (de chiffres). **8.** *Th:* distribution *f* (des rôles); la troupe; l'interprétation *f*; **with the following c.,** avec la distribution suivante; avec le concours de . . .; **all-star c.,** interprétation confiée entièrement à des vedettes. **9.** *Sp:* (*bowls*) point (marqué). **10.** *Ven:* (*of hounds*) **to make a c.,** billebauder.

cast[2], *v.* **(cast; cast)**

I. *v.tr. & i.* **1.** *v.tr.* *(a)* (i) jeter, lancer (une pierre, un filet); porter, projeter (une ombre); **the die is c.,** le dé, le sort, en est jeté; *O:* **to c. sth. in s.o.'s teeth,** jeter (un fait passé) à la figure de qn; reprocher qch. à qn; **the ship was c. ashore,** le navire fut jeté à la côte; **to c. the blame on s.o.,** rejeter le blâme sur qn; **to c. an eye, a glance, at s.o.,** jeter un coup d'œil, un regard, porter ses regards, sur qn; **to c. a beam of light on sth.,** projeter un faisceau de lumière sur qch.; **to c. light on sth.,** mettre qch. en lumière; **the trees were casting their shadows on the wall,** les arbres projetaient une ombre sur le mur; **the pillars c. a long shadow,** les piliers allongent de grandes ombres; **to c. one's thoughts, one's mind, back to sth., to the past,** promener sa pensée, son esprit, sur qch.; faire un retour sur le passé; **to c. sth. aside,** se défaire de qch.; mettre qch. de côté, au rancart; **to c. one's lot in with s.o.,** épouser le parti de qn; partager le sort de qn; *Nau:* **to c. the lead,** donner un coup de sonde; (ii) (*of reptile*) jeter bas; **to c. its slough,** jeter sa dépouille; faire peau neuve; (*of bird*) **to c. its feathers,** muer; *A:* (*of pers.*) **to c. (off) a garment,** se dévêtir de, ôter, un vêtement; (*of horse*) **to c. a shoe,** perdre un fer; (iii) *Ap:* (*of hive*) **to c. a swarm,** *v.i.* **to c.,** jeter un essaim; (iv) *Husb:* (*of dam*) **to c. her young,** mettre bas (ses petits, un petit) avant terme; avorter; (v) (*of hawk*) régurgiter, dégorger (des matières indigérées); rendre gorge; *(b) Fish:* (i) **to c. the line,** lancer la ligne; (ii) **to c. a stream,** *v.i.* **to c. for fish,** pêcher au lancer; *(c) Pol: etc:* donner (une voix); **to c. a vote for X,** voter pour X; **number of votes c.,** nombre *m* de voix, de suffrages; *(d) Astrol:* **to c. a horoscope,** tirer, faire, dresser, un horoscope; *(e) O:* **to c. (up) figures,** additionner des chiffres; **to c. (up) the total,** faire l'addition; faire le total; *(f)* (i) *Wr:* terrasser (son adversaire); (ii) (*of horse-tamer, etc.*) **to c. a horse,** jeter un cheval par terre; *(g)* (i) *Jur:* débouter (un défendeur); **to be c. in damages,** être condamné à des dommages-intérêts; (ii) *Mil: etc: O:* réformer (un cheval, etc.); mettre (un cheval) à la réforme; *(h)* (i) *Metall:* fondre (du métal); mouler, couler, (un cylindre, etc.); sabler (une médaille); **to c. a statue in bronze,** couler une statue en bronze; **c. in one piece,** coulé en bloc; **c. in one piece with . . .,** venu de fonte, de coulée, avec . . .; *I.C.E: etc:* **cylinders c. in one piece,** cylindres monobloc; *Typ:* **to c. a page,** clicher une page; (ii) (*with passive force*) **metal that casts well,** métal qui se coule bien; *(i)* **to c. a ship,** virer un navire; *(j) Th:* **to c. a play,** distribuer les rôles d'une pièce; **to c. s.o. for a part,** assigner, attribuer, un rôle à qn; *(k) Agr:* labourer (une terre) en planches. **2.** *v.i.* *(a)* (*of wood, etc.*) se voiler, se déjeter, gauchir; *(b) Nau:* (*of ship*) **to c. to port,** abattre sur bâbord; *(c)* (*of file of dancers*) tourner (à droite, à gauche); *(d)* (*of sheepdog*) cerner un troupeau (pour le rassembler).

II. (*compound verbs*) **1. cast about,** *v.i.* *(a) Ven:* (*of hounds*) billebauder; *(b)* **to c.a. for an excuse,** chercher une excuse; *(c) Nau:* virer.

2. cast away, *v.tr. Nau:* **to be c.a.,** faire naufrage.

3. cast down, *v.tr.* *(a)* baisser (les yeux); *(b) Lit:* **to be c.d.,** être abattu, découragé, déprimé.

4. cast loose, *v.tr. & i. Nau:* larguer (une amarre).

5. cast off, *v.tr. & i.* *(a) v.tr.* (i) rejeter, repousser (qn); **c.o. by his family,** renié par sa famille; (ii) *A:* se dévêtir de (ses vêtements); (iii) **to c.o. one's reserve,** se dépouiller de sa réserve; (iv) se soustraire à (l'oppression, etc.); **to c.o. all sense of shame,** abjurer toute pudeur; (v) *Nau:* **to c.o. the hawsers,** larguer les amarres; démarrer; quitter la jetée, le quai; **to c.o. the painter,** larguer la bosse; **to c.o. the bight of a rope,** décapeler le double d'une amarre; *v.i.* **to c. o. from the buoy,** larguer, filer, le corps-mort; **to c.o. from the jetty,** quitter la jetée; (vi) *Ven:* lâcher (les chiens); (vii) *Knit:* **to c.o. five stitches,** fermer cinq mailles; *v.i.* **to c.o.,** arrêter, rejeter, rabattre, fermer, les mailles; (viii) *Typ:* **to c.o. a manuscript,** évaluer le nombre de pages imprimées auquel se montera un manuscrit; *(b) v.i. Nau:* (*of ship*) abattre sous le vent; **she's casting off,** nous abattons.

6. cast on, *v.tr. & i. Knit:* monter les mailles; **to c. on 20 stitches,** monter 20 mailles.

7. cast out, *v.tr.* chasser, exorciser (des démons); *B:* **perfect love casteth out fear,** la parfaite charité bannit la crainte.

8. cast up, *v.tr.* *(a) Lit:* lever (les yeux) au ciel; *(b) A: & Lit:* **to c. sth. up to, at, s.o.,** reprocher, objecter, qch. à qn; jeter (un fait passé) au nez, à la figure, de qn; *(c)* **flotsam c. up on the shore,** épaves rejetées sur la plage; *Lit:* **the sea c. up its dead,** l'océan rejeta, vomit, ses morts; *A:* **to c. up one's food,** rejeter des aliments; *(d) Mth: A:* additionner (des chiffres).

cast[3], *a.* **1.** *Art:* **c. shadow,** ombre portée. **2.** *O:* **c. horses,** chevaux *m* de réforme. **3.** *(a) Metall:* coulé, fondu; **c. steel,** fonte *f* d'acier, acier fondu; **c. iron,** (fer *m* de) fonte; fonte de fer; **c.-iron stove,** poêle *m* en fonte; **c.-iron discipline, constitution,** discipline *f*, santé *f*, de fer; *F:* **c.-iron throat,** gosier blindé, pavé; *F:* **c.-iron stomach,** estomac *m* d'autruche; **to have a c.-iron belief in . . .,** croire dur comme (le) fer à . . .; **c.-iron case, argument,** cas *m*, argument *m*, irréfutable; *(b) Cer:* **c. ware,** pièces coulées.

Castalia [kæs'teiliə]. **1.** *Pr.n. Gr.Lit:* (la fontaine de) Castalie *f.* **2.** *s. Bot:* nymphée *f.*

Castalian [kæs'teiliən], *a. Gr.Lit:* de Castalie; des Muses.

castanet [kæstə'net], *s.* **1.** *Gr.Ant:* crotale *m.* **2. (pair of) castanets,** castagnettes *fpl*; cliquette *f*; **c. player,** castagnettiste *mf.*

castanopsis [kæstə'nɔpsis], *s. Bot:* castanopsis *m.*

castaway ['kɑ:stəwei]. **1.** *a.* *(a)* rejeté; *(b) F: A:* ivre, soûl. **2.** *s.* *(a)* naufragé, -ée; **c. crew,** équipage naufragé; *(b) A:* proscrit, -ite; paria *m*; déshérité, -ée.

cast-back ['kɑ:stbæk], *s. Ven:* hourvari *m.*

caste [kɑ:st], *s.* caste *f*; **high-c., low-c., Indian,** Indien *m* de haute caste, de basse caste; *Fig:* **to lose c.,** déroger (à son rang); déchoir (de son rang); **he would think he was losing c. if he accepted,** il croirait déroger en acceptant.

casteless ['kɑ:stlis], *a.* sans caste.

castellan ['kæstilən], *s. A:* gouverneur *m* (du château).

castellated ['kæstileitid], *a.* **1.** *(a) Fort:* crénelé; *(b)* (écrou) crénelé, à entailles, à créneaux. **2.** *(a) A: & Lit:* (région) abondante en châteaux forts; *(b)* (château, immeuble) bâti dans le style féodal.

caster[1] ['kɑ:stər], *s.* **1.** (*pers.*) *(a)* jeteur, -euse; **c. of horoscopes,** faiseur *m* d'horoscopes; *(b) Metall:* couleur *m*, fondeur *m*; mouleur, -euse (de plâtre, etc.); *(c) O:* **c.-up,** additionneur, -euse (de chiffres); *(d) Min:* (*coal*) déschisteur, -euse. **2.** (*machine*) fondeuse *f.*

caster[2], *s.* = CASTOR[1].

castigate ['kæstigeit], *v.tr.* *(a)* châtier, corriger (qn); *(b)* critiquer sévèrement (qn, un ouvrage); *(c)* revoir, châtier (une œuvre littéraire).

castigation [kæsti'geiʃ(ə)n], *s.* *(a)* châtiment *m*, correction *f*; *(b)* critique *f* sévère; *F:* abattage *m*; éreintement *m.*

castigator ['kæstigeitər], *s.* châtieur *m*; **a c. of the abuses of his time,** critique *m* sévère des abus de son époque.

castigatory ['kæstigeitəri], *a.* qui châtie, qui corrige.

Castile [kæs'ti:l], *Pr.n.* *(a) Geog:* Castille *f*; **New C.,** Nouvelle-Castille; **Old C.,** Vieille-Castille; *(b) attrib.* **C. soap,** savon blanc.

Castilian [kæs'tiliən]. **1.** *Geog:* *(a) a.* castillan; *(b) s.* Castillan, -ane. **3.** *s. Ling:* castillan *m.*

casting[1] ['kɑ:stiŋ], *a.* **c. vote,** voix prépondérante (accordée au président d'une assemblée, d'un conseil, quand les avis sont également partagés); **the chairman has the c. vote,** la voix du président est prépondérante; **to give the c. vote,** départager les voix, les votes.

casting[2], *s.* **1.** *(a)* jet *m* (d'une pierre, etc.); *Fish:* (pêche *f* au) lancer *m*; **surf c.,** surf-casting *m*; **c. line,** empile *f*; **c. net,** épervier *m*; *(b) Metall: Glassm: etc:* coulée *f*, coulage *m*, moulage *m*, fonte *f*; **c. under cover,** coulée en halle; **loam c.,** moulage en terre; **hollow c.,** moulage à noyau; **top c.,** coulée à la descente; **bottom c.,** coulée en source; **chilled c.,** moulage en coquille; **investment c.,** moulage par enrobage; **permanent-mould c.,** coulée en moule permanent; **sand c.,** coulée en sable; **slip c.,** coulée en barbotine; *Dent:* **c. machine,** fronde *f*; *Glassm:* **c. slab, table,** table *f* de coulée; *(c) Husb:* **c. of young,** avortement *m* (d'une brebis, etc.); *(d) Mil: etc:* réforme *f* (de chevaux, etc.); *(e) Th:* distribution *f* des rôles; *(f) Nau:* abattée *f* (d'un navire); *(g) O:* **c. (up) of figures,** addition *f* de chiffres; *(h)* gauchissement *m* (du bois); *(i)* **castings (of an earthworm),** déjections *fpl* (de ver de terre). **2.** *Metall: Glassm:* pièce coulée, pièce moulée, pièce de fonte; coulé *m*; **heavy castings,** grosses pièces; **fine castings,** petites pièces; **hollow c.,** pièce creuse; **die c.,** pièce moulée sous pression. **3.** *Art:* jet (de draperies).

casting off ['kɑ:stiŋɔf], *s.* **1.** *Knit:* fermeture *f* des mailles. **2.** *Typ:* = CAST-OFF.

casting on ['kɑ:stiŋɔn], *s. Knit:* montage *m* (des mailles).

castle[1] ['kɑ:sl], *s.* **1.** *(a)* château fort; *(b)* château (royal ou seigneurial); **Windsor C.,** le château (royal) de Windsor; **to build castles in the air,** bâtir des châteaux en Espagne; *Prov:* **an Englishman's home is his c.,** charbonnier est maître chez lui, en sa maison. **2.** *Chess:* tour *f.* **3.** *Atom.Ph:* **(lead) c.,** château (de plomb).

castle[2], *v.tr. & i. Chess:* **to c. (the king),** roquer.

castling ['kɑ:sliŋ], *s. Chess:* roque *m*; **c. base,** ligne *f* de rocade; **king-side c.,** petit roque; **queen-side c.,** grand roque.

Castniidae [kæst'ni:idi:], *s.pl. Ent:* castniides *m.*

cast-off[1] ['kɑ:stɔf], *a.* **c.-o. clothing,** *s. F:* **cast-offs,** vêtements *mpl* de rebut; défroque *f*, vieilles frusques; **c.-o. mistress,** ancienne maîtresse, *F:* maîtresse qu'on a plaquée.

cast-off[2], *s. Typ:* évaluation *f* du nombre de pages imprimées que fournira un manuscrit; évaluation du manuscrit.

castor[1] ['kɑ:stər], *s.* **1.** *(a)* poivrière *f*; saupoudoir *m* (à sucre, etc.); **c. sugar,** sucre en poudre; *(b) pl.* **(pair of) castors,** huilier *m.* **2.** *Furn:* roulette *f* (de fauteuil ou meuble); *Aut:* **c. action (of front wheels),** chasse *f* (de l'essieu avant); **c. wheel,** roue pivotante.

castor[2], *s. Vet:* châtaigne *f* (de jambe de cheval).

castor[3], *s.* **1.** *(a) Z: A:* castor *m*; *(b) Pharm:* castoréum *m.* **2.** *P: A:* chapeau *m*, castor. **3.** *Leath:* castor; **c. gloves,** gants *m* de castor.

castor[4], *s. Miner:* castor *m*, castorite *f.*

Castor[5], *Pr.n.m. Myth:* **C. and Pollux,** Castor et Pollux.

castoreum [kæs'tɔ:riəm], *s. Pharm:* castoréum *m.*

Castoridae [kæs'tɔridi:], *s.pl. Z:* castoridés *m.*

castorin ['kɑ:stərin], *s. Ch:* castorine *f.*

castorite ['kæstərait], *s. Miner:* castorite *f*, castor *m.*

castor oil ['kɑ:stər'ɔil], *s. Pharm:* huile *f* de ricin; **cold-drawn c.o.,** huile de ricin exprimée à froid; *Bot:* **c.-o. plant,** ricin commun; grande épurge; palma-christi *m inv*; **c.-o. bean,** graine *f* de ricin.

castrametation [kæstrəme'teiʃ(ə)n], *s. A.Mil:* castramétation *f.*

castrate[1] ['kæstreit], *s. A:* châtré *m*; castrat *m.*

castrate[2] [kæs'treit], *v.tr.* **1.** châtrer (une bête); castrer, évirer (un homme); *Husb:* **castrated by torsion,** bistourné. **2.** *Fig: A:* châtrer, expurger, émasculer (un livre, etc.).

castration [kæs'treiʃ(ə)n], *s.* **1.** castration *f*; (*of a man*) émasculation *f*, éviration *f*; *Psy:* **c. complex,** complexe *m* de castration. **2.** *Fig: A:* expurgation *f*, émasculation *f.*

castrato, *pl.* **-ti** [kæ'strɑ:tou, -ti], *s. Mus:* castrat *m.*

Castroism ['kæstrouizm], *s. Pol:* castrisme *m.*

Castroist ['kæstrouist], *s. Pol:* castriste *mf.*

casual ['kæʒju(ə)l, 'kæz-]. **1.** *a.* *(a)* fortuit, accidentel; (bourgeon *m*, plante *f*, sujet *m*) adventice; **to engage in c. conversation,** parler de choses et d'autres, de choses banales, de la pluie et du beau temps; **piece of c. information,** renseignement ramassé en passant, par hasard; **to throw out a c. suggestion,** suggérer qch. en passant; **c. labour,** main-d'œuvre occasionnelle, temporaire; **c. worker,** travailleur, employé, occasionnel; ouvrier employé par intermittence, à l'heure; *Fin:* **c. profit,** profit casuel; *Golf: etc:* **c. water,** eau fortuite; (*b*) *Cost:* **c. clothes, clothes for c. wear,** costume *m,* tenue *f,* sport; tenue de loisirs; (*c*) **c. person,** personne imprévoyante, insouciante, sans méthode; **he is really too c.,** il en prend trop à son aise; **to give a c. answer,** répondre d'un air détaché, cavalier, désinvolte. **2.** *s.* (*a*) *A:* indigent, -ente, de passage; **c. ward,** asile *m* de nuit (d'un hospice); établissement *m* d'hospitalité de nuit; (*b*) = **casual worker;** (*c*) *Mil:* (homme) isolé *m*; (*d*) *Bootm:* **casuals,** mocassins *mpl.*

casualism ['kæʒuəlizm], *s. Phil:* casualisme *m.*

casualist ['kæʒuəlist], *s. Phil:* casualiste *m.*

casually ['kæʒuli, 'kæz-], *adv.* (*a*) fortuitement, par hasard, en passant; **he added c. that . . .,** il ajouta comme par hasard que . . .; (*b*) **to reply c.,** répondre d'un air indifférent, négligemment, d'un air détaché, avec désinvolture.

casualness ['kæʒuəlnis], *s.* (air *m* d') indifférence *f*; insouciance *f*; désinvolture *f*; manque *m* de méthode.

casualty ['kæʒuəlti], *s.* (*a*) accident *m* (de personne); désastre *m*; **casualties at sea,** désastres en mer; **c. ward,** salle *f* des accidentés (dans un hôpital); *U.S:* **c. insurance,** assurance *f* contre les accidents; (*b*) victime *f* (d'un accident); mort, morte; blessé, -ée; accidenté, -ée; **the earthquake caused many casualties,** le tremblement de terre a fait beaucoup de victimes; **accident with fifteen casualties,** accident où il y a eu (i) quinze morts, (ii) quinze blessés, (iii) quinze morts et blessés; **there were no casualties,** il n'y a pas eu de victimes; personne n'a été ni tué ni blessé; (*c*) *Mil:* **casualties,** pertes *f*; **c. list, return,** état *m* des pertes; état des morts, blessés et disparus; **battle, non-battle, casualties,** pertes au combat, pertes santé; **c. clearing station,** centre *m* d'évacuation (des blessés, malades, etc.); **c. collecting station,** poste *m* de secours; **to make good the casualties,** combler les vides; (*d*) *Pol:* **the party had many casualties in the last election,** le parti a perdu beaucoup de députés aux dernières élections.

Casuariidae [kæʒjuə'raiidi:], *s.pl. Orn:* casuari(i)dés *m.*

casuarina [kæʒjuə'ri:nə], *s. Bot:* casuarina *f.*

Casuarinaceae [kæʒjuəri'neisii:], *s.pl. Bot:* casuarinacées *f.*

casuist ['kæzjuist], *s.* (*a*) *Theol:* casuiste *m*; (*b*) *Pej:* casuiste.

casuistic(al) [kæzju'istik(l)], *a.* de casuiste.

casuistically [kæzju'istik(ə)li], *adv.* en casuiste.

casuistry ['kæzjuistri], *s.* (*a*) *Theol:* casuistique *f*; (*b*) *Pej:* casuistique.

casus belli ['keizəs'belai, 'kɑ:zʊg'beli:], *s. Dipl:* casus belli *m.*

cat[1] [kæt], *s.* **1.** (*a*) chat, *f* chatte; **Abyssinian, Persian, Siamese, c.,** chat abyssin, persan, siamois; **Chartreux c.,** chat des Chartreux; **Birman c., sacred c. of Burma,** chat Birman, chat sacré de Birmanie; (**brown, sable**) **Burmese c.,** chat Burmese (brun, zibeline); **Rex c.,** chat Rex; **British, Russian, blue c.,** chat bleu britannique, russe; **chinchilla c.,** chat chinchilla; **Manx c.,** chat de l'Ile de Man; **longhaired, shorthaired, c.,** chat à poil long, court; **tortoiseshell c.,** chat écaille de tortue; **shell cameo c.,** chat camée nacré; **bicoloured c.,** chat bicolore, chat pie; **tabby c.,** chat marbré, *F:* chat tigré; **spotted c.,** chat (à poil court) tacheté; **tom c.,** matou *m*; *F:* **ginger, marmalade, c.,** chat roux tigré; **he's just an ordinary c., an alley c.,** c'est un chat de gouttière; **c. that has run wild,** chat haret; **c. breeder,** éleveur *m* de chats; **c. breeding,** élevage *m* de chats; **c.-breeding establishment,** chatterie *f*; **c. fancy,** association *f* des amateurs de chats; **c. show,** exposition féline; **c. door,** chattière *f*; *P:* **that looks like something the cat's brought in,** ça, c'est dégoûtant; *F:* **cats' chorus,** sabbat *m,* musique *f,* de chats; **to quarrel like c. and dog, to lead a c.-and-dog life,** s'entendre, s'accorder, vivre, comme chien et chat; faire mauvais ménage; **cat's whiskers,** moustache *f* du chat; *F:* **he's, she's, the cat's whiskers,** c'est un as, une perle; **he thinks he's the cat's whiskers, pyjamas,** il se croit quelqu'un; *W.Tel:* *A:* **cat('s) whisker,** spirale *f* métallique, chercheur *m* (du détecteur); *Hist:* *F:* **C. and mouse Act,** loi *f* ordonnant la mise en liberté provisoire des prisonniers qui font la grève de la faim; (*b*) *Fig:* **to see which way the c. jumps,** voir d'où vient le vent; prendre l'aire du vent; **to watch s.o. like a c. watching a mouse,** guetter qn comme un chat (fait de) la souris; *Prov:* **a c. may look at a king,** un chien regarde bien un évêque; **while the cat's away the mice (will) play,** quand le chat n'est pas là les souris dansent; *F:* **to be like a c. on hot bricks,** être sur des épines; être comme chat sur braise; ne pas pouvoir se tenir en place; **to put the c. among the pigeons,** (i) mettre le loup dans la bergerie; mettre le renard dans les poules; jeter une pierre dans la mare aux grenouilles; (ii) faire une gaffe; **there's not room to swing a c.,** il n'y a pas de place pour se retourner; c'est grand comme un mouchoir de poche; **it's enough to, it would, make a c. laugh,** c'est à mourir de rire, c'est à se tordre; ça ferait rire les pierres; *A:* **to turn c. in pan,** tourner casaque (au moment critique); (*c*) *F:* (*pers.*) (i) (**old**) **c.,** vieille chipie; rosse *f*; **don't be such a c.!** ne sois pas si méchante! (ii) *U.S:* *P:* type *m,* individu *m.* **2.** *Z:* **wild c.,** chat sauvage; chat haret; **African wild c.,** pard *m*; **Australian native c.,** dasyure *m,* chat marsupial australien; **viverine c., fishing c.,** chat viverin; **civet c., musk c.,** civette *f*; **bush c., tiger c.,** serval *m*; chat tigre; **Pallas, Pallas's, c.,** chat de Pallas, chat du désert; **palm c.,** paradoxure *m*; martre *f* des palmiers; **the big cats,** les (grands) félidés; les grands félins. **3.** (*a*) *Nau:* **c. (purchase, tackle),** capon *m*; **c. block,** poulie *f* de capon; (*b*) (*in game of tip cat*) bistoquet *m*; (*c*) trépied double (qui repose toujours sur trois pieds); (*d*) *Nau:* **c. (-o'-nine-tails),** martinet *m* à neuf cordes; garcette *f*; fouet *m,* dague *f*; (*d*) *Bot:* *F:* **cat's ear,** porcelle *f*; **cat's foot,** (i) pied-de-chat *m*; (ii) lierre terrestre, rampant; herbe *f* de Saint-Jean; **cat's cradle,** (i) *Bot:* plantain lancéolé; (ii) (jeu *m* de la) scie; jeu du berceau (joué avec une ficelle); *Bot:* **cat's tail,** (i) (*also* **cat tail**) massette *f,* typha *m,* quenouille *f,* roseau *m* de la Passion, des étangs; (ii) prêle *f* des prés; (iii) fléole *f* des prés; (iv) vipérine *f*; (v) linaigrette *f,* jonc *m* à coton, lin *m* des marais; *Meteor:* **cat's tail,** queue-de-chat *f*; (*f*) **cat's eye,** (i) *Lap:* œil de-chat *m*; (ii) catadioptre *m,* cataphote *m* (*R.t.m:*) (au milieu de la route).

cat[2], *v.* (**catted**) **1.** *v.tr. Nau:* caponner (l'ancre). **2.** *v.i.* *F:* vomir, renarder.

cat[3], *s. Bot:* kat *m,* qat *m.*

cat[4], *a. Petr:* (= **catalytic**) **c. cracking,** craquage *m* catalytique.

cat[5], *s. Phot:* *F:* objectif *m* catadioptrique.

cata- ['kætə, kætə, kæ'tæ], *pref.* cata-.

catabolic [kætə'bɔlik], *a. Biol:* catabolique.

catabolism [kæ'tæbolizm], *s. Biol:* *Physiol:* catabolisme *m.*

catacaustic [kætə'kɔ:stik], *a. Opt:* catacaustique.

catachresis [kætə'kri:sis], *s.* catachrèse *f.*

cataclastic [kætə'klæstik], *a. Geol:* cataclastique.

cataclinal [kætə'klainl], *a. Geog:* cataclinal.

cataclysm ['kætəklizm], *s.* cataclysme *m.*

cataclysmal, -mic [kætə'klizml, -mik], *a.* cataclysmique.

cataclysta [kætə'klistə], *s. Ent:* cataclyste *f.*

catacomb ['kætəkoum], *s.* (*usu.pl.*) catacombe *f*; **the C. of Saint Calixtus,** la catacombe de Saint Calixte.

catacoustics [kætə'ku:stiks], *s.pl.* (*usu. with sg.const.*) *Ph:* catacoustique *f.*

catadioptric(al) ['kætədai'ɔptrik(l)], *a. Ph:* *Phot:* catadioptrique.

catadromous [kə'tædrəməs], *a. Ich:* catadrome.

catafalque ['kætəfælk], *s.* **1.** catafalque *m.* **2.** char *m* funèbre.

catagenesis [kætə'dʒenisis], *s. Biol:* catagenèse *f.*

catagenetic ['kætədʒə'netik], *a. Biol:* catagénétique.

Catalan ['kætə'læn]. **1.** *a.* (*a*) *Geog:* catalan; (*b*) *Metall:* **C. forge, furnace,** feu catalan. **2.** *s. Geog:* Catalan, -ane. **3.** *s. Ling:* catalan *m.*

Catalanism ['kætəlænizm], *s. Ling:* *Pol:* catalanisme *m.*

Catalanist ['kætəlænist], *s. Pol:* catalaniste *mf.*

catalase ['kætəleis], *s.* catalase *f.*

catalectic [kætə'lektik], *a. Pros:* catalectique.

catalepsy ['kætəlepsi], *s. Med:* catalepsie *f.*

cataleptic [kætə'leptik], *a.* & *s. Med:* cataleptique (*mf*).

catalептiform [kætə'leptifɔ:m], *a. Med:* cataleptiforme.

catalexis [kætə'leksis], *s. Pros:* catalexe *f.*

catalogue[1] ['kætəlɔg], *s.* (*NAm:* *also* **catalog**) **1.** catalogue *m,* liste *f,* répertoire *m*; **author c.,** catalogue par noms d'auteurs; **subject c.,** catalogue méthodique, matière; **descriptive c.,** catalogue raisonné. **2.** *Com:* catalogue, prix-courant *m, pl.* prix-courants; **trade c.,** album(tarif) *m,* tarif-album *m.* **3.** *Sch:* *U.S:* (*a*) (*calendar*) annuaire *m*; (*b*) prospectus *m* (d'une école).

catalogue[2], *v.tr.* cataloguer. **1.** faire le catalogue de (qch.). **2.** inscrire (qch.) dans le catalogue.

catalog(u)er ['kætəlɔgər], *s.* catalogueur *m.*

cataloguing ['kætəlɔgiŋ], *s.* cataloguage *m*; classement *m*; établissement *m* d'un catalogue.

Catalonia [kætə'louniə], *Pr.n. Geog:* Catalogne *f.*

Catalonian [kætə'louniən], *a.* & *s.* = CATALAN.

catalpa [kə'tælpə], *s. Bot:* catalpa *m.*

catalyse ['kætəlaiz], *v.tr. Ch:* catalyser.

catalyser ['kætəlaizər], **catalyst** ['kætəlist], *s. Ch:* catalyseur *m.*

catalysis [kə'tælisis], *s. Ch:* catalyse *f.*

catalytic [kætə'litik], *a. Ch:* catalytique, catalyseur.

catalytically [kætə'litik(ə)li], *adv.* catalytiquement.

catalyze ['kætəlaiz], **catalyzer** ['kætəlaizər], = CATALYSE, CATALYSER.

catamaran [kætəmə'ræn], *s.* **1.** *Nau:* catamaran *m*; **c. dredge,** drague *f* en catamaran. **2.** *F:* femme hargneuse; mégère *f.*

catamenia [kætə'mi:niə], *s. Physiol:* menstruation *f.*

catamenial [kætə'mi:niəl], *a. Physiol:* cataménial.

catamite ['kætəmait], *s.* mignon *m,* giton *m.*

catamnesis, *pl.* **-es** [kætəm'ni:sis, -i:z], *s. Med:* catamnèse *f.*

catamorphism [kætə'mɔ:fizm], *s. Geol:* catamorphisme *m.*

catamount(ain) [kætə'maunt(in)], *s. Z:* (*a*) chat *m* sauvage (d'Europe); (*b*) *A:* léopard *m.*

catananche [kætə'næŋki, -'næntʃi], *s. Bot:* catananche *f.*

Catania [kə'teiniə], *Pr.n. Geog:* Catane *f.*

catapetalous [kætə'petələs], *a. Bot:* catapétale.

cataphasia [kætə'feiziə], *s. Med:* cataphasie *f.*

cataphora [kætə'fɔ:rə], *s. Med:* cataphora *f.*

cataphoresis, *pl.* **-es** [kætəfɔ'ri:sis, -i:z], *s. Ch:* *Med:* cataphorèse *f.*

cataphoretic [kætəfɔ'ri:tik], **cataphoric** [kætə'fɔ:rik], *a.* cataphorétique.

cataphract ['kætəfrækt], *s. Ant:* **1.** *Arm:* cataphracte *f.* **2.** (*soldier*) cataphracte *m,* cataphractaire *m.*

cataplasm ['kætəplæzm], *s. Med:* cataplasme *m.*

cataplectic [kætə'plektik], *a. Med:* cataplectique.

catapleiite [kætə'plaiait], *s. Miner:* catapléite *f.*

cataplexy [kætə'pleksi], *s. Med:* cataplexie *f.*

catapult[1] ['kætəpʌlt], *s.* **1.** (*a*) *A.Mil:* catapulte *f*; lance-pierre *m, pl.* lance-pierres; (*b*) fronde *f.* **2.** *Av:* catapulte (de lancement); **c.-launched,** (avion *m*) catapultable.

catapult[2]. **1.** *v.tr.* (*a*) fronder, attaquer avec une fronde; (*b*) *Av:* catapulter (un avion); (*c*) catapulter, projeter (qn, qch., au loin). **2.** *v.i.* (*a*) **stream catapulting down the mountain side,** torrent *m* qui descend la montagne par bonds; (*b*) **he catapulted into the room,** il est entré en trombe dans la pièce.

catapultier [kætəpʌl'tiər], *s. Mil.Hist:* catapultaire *m.*

catapulting ['kætəpʌltiŋ], *s. Av:* catapultage *m.*

cataract ['kætərækt], *s.* **1.** cataracte *f* (d'un fleuve). **2.** *Med:* cataracte (de l'œil); *Vet:* **web c.** (**of horse's eye**), cul *m* de verre (de l'œil d'un cheval). **3.** *Mch:* cataracte; régulateur *m.*

cataractous [kætə'ræktəs], *a. Med:* cataracté.

catarrh [kə'tɑ:r], *s.* **1.** *Med:* catarrhe *m*; **recurrent bronchial c.,** bronchite *f* à répétition; **gastric c.,** catarrhe de l'estomac; pituite *f.* **2.** *Vet:* (*of horse*) **nasal c.,** morfondure *f.*

catarrhal [kə'tɑ:r(ə)l], **catarrhous** [kə'tɑ:rəs], *a.* catarrhal, -aux; catarrheux.

Catarrhina [kætə'rainə], *s.pl. Z:* catarrhiniens *m.*

catarrhine ['kætərain], *a.* & *s. Z:* catarrhinien (*m*).

catasetum [kætə'si:təm], *s. Bot:* catasetum *m.*

catastasis, *pl.* **-es** [kə'tæstəsis, i:z], *s. Lit:* catastase *f.*

catastrophe [kə'tæstrəfi], *s.* **1.** (*a*) catastrophe *f*; désastre *m*; (*fire, shipwreck, explosion, etc.*) sinistre *m*; **the victims of the c.,** les sinistrés *m*; (*b*) *Geol:* cataclysme *m,* catastrophe. **2.** *Lit:* catastrophe, dénouement *m.*

catastrophic [kætə'strɔfik], *a.* catastrophique, désastreux.

catastrophically [kætə'strɔfik(ə)li], *adv.* d'une façon catastrophique, désastreuse.

catastrophism [kə'tæstrəfizm], *s. Geol:* catastrophisme *m.*

catastrophist [kə'tæstrəfist], *s.* catastrophiste *mf.*

catathermometer ['kætəθə'mɔmitər], *s.* catathermomètre *m.*

catathymia [kætə'θaimiə], *s. Psy:* catathymie *f.*

catatonia [kætə'touniə], *s. Med:* catatonie *f.*

catatonic [kætə'tɔnik], *a.* & *s. Med:* catatonique (*mf*); **c. schizophrenia,** catatonie *f.*

catatype ['kætətaip], *s. Phot:* catatypie *f.*

catavothron [kætə'vouθrən], *s. Geol:* catavothre *m,* katavothre *m.*

catawba [kə'tɔ:bə], *s. Bot:* **c. tree,** catalpa *m.*

catbird ['kætbə:d], *s.* (*a*) *Orn:* oiseau-chat *m, Fr.C:* moqueur-chat *m*; (*b*) *U.S:* *F:* **to be in the c. seat,** être bien placé, dans une situation privilégiée.

catboat ['kætbout], *s.* petit bâtiment gréé à taille-vent; cat-boat *m.*

cat burglar ['kæt'bə:glər], *s.* cambrioleur *m* par escalade; cambrioleur acrobate: *F:* monte-en-l'air *m inv.*

cat burglary ['kæt'bə:gləri], *s.* vol *m* de nuit à l'escalade.

catcall[1] ['kætkɔ:l], *s. Th: etc:* (coup *m* de) sifflet *m* (dirigé contre un acteur, etc.); miaulement *m.*

catcall[2], *v.i.* & *tr.* siffler (un acteur); chahuter.

catch[1] [kætʃ], *s.* **1.** (*a*) prise *f* au vol (d'une balle, d'un ballon); *Rugby Fb:* **fair c.,** arrêt *m* de volée; (*of pers.*) **he's a safe c.,** pour attraper la balle au vol il a la main très sûre; (*of children*) **to play c.,** jouer au ballon, à attraper le ballon; (*b*) *Row:* attaque *f* (au commencement du coup de nage); (*c*) **with a c. in one's voice,** (i) d'une voix entrecoupée; (ii) en poussant un *ah* de surprise. **2.** (*a*) *Fish:* prise, pêche *f*; **to have a good c.,** faire (une) bonne pêche; (*b*) *F:* bon parti (à épouser); **he's, she's, no great c.,** c'est un médiocre parti; **he's getting on, but he's a good c. for all that,** il vieillit, mais ce n'est pas un parti à dédaigner; (*c*) *F:* (*esp. in neg.*) avantage *m*, profit *m*; aubaine *f*; **it's no great c.,** ce n'est pas le Pérou; ça ne vaut pas grand-chose. **3.** *O:* fragment *m*, bribe *f* (d'une conversation, d'une chanson, etc.). **4.** (*a*) (*on door, etc.*) loquet *m*, loqueteau *m*; (*of latch*) mentonnet *m*, bec *m*; (*of window*) loqueteau; (*of buckle*) ardillon *m*; (*of clasp knife*) mouche *f*; (*on garment*) agrafe *f*; *Mec.E:* crochet *m* d'arrêt; dispositif *m* d'arrêt; chien *m* (d'arrêt); doigt *m*; talon *m*; arrêt *m*; arrêtoir *m*; heurtoir *m*; (*of pile driver, etc.*) déclic *m*; (*of wheel, winch shaft, etc.*) cliquet *m*; (*on gearing, etc.*) ergot *m*; (*of capstan*) linguet *m*; **bolt c.,** auberon *m*, bonhomme *m*; **spring c.,** bonhomme à ressort; **espagnolette c.,** panneton *m* d'espagnolette; **shutter c.,** battement *m* de persienne; **gate c. with counterpoise,** boule *f* à gibecière; **safety c.,** fermoir *m* de sûreté; cran *m* de sûreté; *Phot:* **infinity c.,** accrochage *m* à l'infini; (*b*) tenon *m* d'accrochage; *Min:* **catches,** taquets *m*, clichages *m* (de puits de mine). **5.** attrape *f*; **there's a c. in it,** c'est une attrape; ce n'est pas si simple que ça; *Sch: etc:* **c. question,** colle *f*. **6.** *Mus:* chant *m*, chanson *f*, à reprises (successives); canon *m*. **7.** *attrib.* (*derived mainly from the verb rather than the noun*) (*a*) *Agr:* **c. crop,** culture dérobée; (*b*) *Hyd.E:* **c. basin, c. pit,** bassin collecteur; **c. drain,** tranchée *f*; rigole *f* de captage, d'écoulement; fossé *m* de captage; **c. feeder,** canal *m* d'irrigation; (*c*) *Mec.E: etc:* **c. pin,** cheville *f* d'embrayage; **c. wheel,** roue *f* à cliquet; **c. plate,** plateau *m* toc (de tour); auberonnière *f* (de serrure, etc.); *Rail:* **c. points,** aiguille prise en pointe; (*d*) *Min:* **c. props,** étais *m*, étançons *m*, provisoires; (*e*) *El:* **c. net,** filet *m* de protection (d'une ligne de haute tension); (*f*) **c. title,** titre abrégé (d'un ouvrage catalogué); **c. line,** (i) *Journ:* titre flamboyant; (ii) *Th: etc:* phrase comique (répétée); **c. phrase,** scie *f*, rengaine *f*; *Th:* phrase comique (répétée); (*g*) *Needlew:* **c. stitch,** point *m* de chausson.

catch[2], *v.* (**caught** [kɔːt]; **caught**)
I. *v.tr. & i.* **1.** *v.tr.* (*a*) (i) attraper, prendre (un poisson, un voleur, etc.); attraper, saisir (une balle, etc.); pêcher (un poisson); saisir (un voleur); attraper, ne pas manquer (un train, etc.); attirer (l'attention de qn); (*when throwing sth. to s.o.*) **c.!** attrape! prends! **to c. s.o. by the scruff of the neck,** empoigner qn par la peau du cou; **to be caught by the police,** se laisser attraper, *F:* se faire pincer, par la police; *Fish:* **to c. nothing,** ne rien attraper; revenir bredouille; **I caught my train all right this morning,** j'ai bien eu mon train ce matin; *Nau:* (*of sail, etc.*) **to c. the wind,** prendre le vent; *Row:* **to c. the stroke,** attaquer; (ii) **I caught him as he fell,** je l'ai retenu, attrapé, au moment où il allait tomber; (iii) **to c. s.o. doing sth., in the act, red-handed,** prendre qn en flagrant délit; **to c. s.o. unprepared,** surprendre qn désarmé, à l'improviste; **I sometimes c. myself smiling,** parfois je me (sur)prends à sourire; *F:* **I caught him at it,** je l'y ai pris; *F:* **c. me!** pas de danger! pas si bête! *F:* **you won't c. me doing that again,** on ne m'y reprendra plus; bien fin qui m'y reprendra; *F:* (*of woman*) **to be caught,** se trouver enceinte; (iv) **to be caught in a fog, in a shower,** être pris dans un brouillard; être surpris par une averse; (*b*) (i) saisir, percevoir (des sons); rencontrer (le regard de qn); (*of thg*) frapper (la vue, l'oreille); **I caught his eye,** mes yeux ont rencontré les siens; (*at meeting, etc.*) **to c. the chairman's eye,** attirer l'attention du président; **the sound of distant barking caught my ears,** j'ai entendu un aboiement au lointain; **a pungent smell caught me in the throat,** une odeur âcre m'a pris à la gorge; *Th: etc:* **to c. the spirit of a part,** saisir un rôle; **the artist has caught the likeness,** l'artiste a bien saisi la ressemblance; **I saw sth. in the (shop) window that caught my eye,** j'ai vu qch. à la devanture qui m'a plu; **I don't quite c. your idea,** je ne saisis pas bien ce que vous avez en tête; (ii) *W.Tel: T.V:* écouter, regarder (un programme); (iii) **I didn't c. what you were saying,** je n'ai pas entendu ce que vous disiez; **I didn't (quite) c. that,** pardon? vous avez dit . . .? **he added something I didn't c.,** il a ajouté quelque chose que je n'ai pas entendu, saisi; (iv) accrocher; happer; **I caught my dress on a nail,** j'ai accroché ma robe à un clou; **he caught his foot on a root and fell,** il s'est pris le pied dans une racine et il est tombé; **to be caught by one's hair,** être retenu, accroché, par les cheveux; **to be caught in a machine,** se trouver pris dans une machine; **the car was caught between two buses,** la voiture s'est trouvée coincée entre deux autobus; (*c*) attraper (une maladie); être atteint d'(une maladie); contracter (une habitude); prendre (l'accent du pays); **to c. (a) cold,** s'enrhumer, attraper un rhume; **to c. fire,** prendre feu; (*d*) *Box:* **he caught him with a left to the chin,** il lui a porté un gauche au menton; *P:* **I caught him one on the nose,** je lui ai flanqué un gnon en plein nez; *F:* **he caught it right in the chest,** il a été atteint en pleine poitrine; *F:* **you'll c. it!** votre affaire est bonne! vous allez vous faire attraper! tu vas étrenner, écoper, prendre, quelque chose! (*e*) (*entrap*) (i) *F:* attraper (qn); mettre (qn) dedans; tromper (qn); **you won't c. me!** ça ne mord pas! ça ne prend pas (avec moi)! (ii) *P:* **she caught her man,** elle a déniché un mari. **2.** *v.i.* (*a*) **to c. at sth.,** essayer de saisir qch.; s'accrocher à qch.; **to c. at an opportunity,** saisir une occasion; **a drowning man catches at a straw,** un homme qui se noie se retient à tout; (*b*) (i) (*of cog wheel*) mordre; (*of gearing*) quotter; (*of door bolt*) s'engager; (ii) (*of fire*) prendre; s'allumer; (*c*) *Cu:* (i) **to c.** (**in the pan**), attacher; **the milk, the stew, has caught,** le lait, le ragoût, a pris, a attaché; (ii) **my cakes have caught,** mes gâteaux ont commencé à brûler.
II. (*compound verbs*) **1. catch on,** *v.i. F:* (*a*) (*of fashion, play, etc.*) prendre, réussir, avoir du succès; (*of tune*) accrocher; (*b*) comprendre, saisir, piger; **I don't c. on,** je n'y suis pas.
2. catch out, *v.tr.* (*a*) *Cr:* **to c. s.o. out,** mettre qn hors (de) jeu à balle attrapée; (*b*) *F:* attraper, coller (qn); prendre (qn) sur le fait, en faute; **to c. s.o. out in a lie,** surprendre qn à mentir.
3. catch up, *v.tr. & i.* (*a*) saisir (qch.); prendre (qch.) brusquement; **we were caught up in this wave of enthusiasm,** nous nous sommes trouvés gagnés par cette vague d'enthousiasme; (*b*) **to c. s.o. up, to c. up with s.o.,** rattraper qn; **he caught us up at the village,** il nous a rattrapés, il nous a rejoints, au village; **to c. up (with) another car,** rattraper une autre voiture; **our rivals are catching up with us,** nos concurrents gagnent le pas sur nous; **to c. up (with) arrears,** se remettre au courant; **if you give him time he'll c. up again,** si vous lui donnez du temps il va se rattraper, se remettre à flot; **to c. up on some sleep,** rattraper du sommeil; *F:* **it will c. up with you (one of these days),** ça va vous retomber sur le nez.

catchall ['kætʃɔːl], *s. F:* fourre-tout *m inv*; (*b*) *U.S:* (pièce *f* de) débarras *m*.

catch-as-catch-can ['kætʃəz'kætʃ'kæn], *s. Wr:* catch *m*, lutte *f* libre.

catchcry ['kætʃkrai], *s.* scie *f* (du jour); rengaine *f*.

catcher ['kætʃər], *s.* **1.** (*a*) attrapeur, -euse; preneur, -euse; **rat c.,** preneur de rats; **mole c.,** taupier *m*, preneur de taupes; (*b*) *Games:* (*baseball*) attrapeur, receveur *m*. **2.** *Mec.E:* garde *f* (d'un clapet); *Min:* évite-molettes *m inv*; *Metall:* **gas c.,** prise *f* de gaz; *Mch:* **cinder c.,** collecteur *m* d'escarbilles.

catchfly ['kætʃflai], *s. Bot:* **1.** silène *m*; **Nottingham c.,** silène penché. **2.** dionée *f* gobe-mouches.

catching[1] ['kætʃiŋ], *a.* (*of disease*) contagieux, -euse; infectieux, -euse; (*of laughter, etc.*) communicatif.

catching[2], *s.* **1.** (*a*) prise *f*; capture *f*; **rat c.,** chasse *f* aux rats; (*b*) accrochage *m*. **2.** (*of toothed wheel*) engrenure *f*; (*of gearing*) quottement *m*.

catchment ['kætʃmənt], *s.* **1.** *Geog: Hyd.E:* (**water**) **c.,** prise *f* d'eau; captation *f*, captage *m* (d'eaux); **c. (area),** surface *f* de captation des eaux (d'un fleuve); bassin *m* (d'un fleuve); **c. basin,** bassin de réception. **2.** *Adm:* **c. area of a school,** réseau *m* de ramassage des écoliers.

catchpenny ['kætʃpeni], *s.* (*thg*) attrape-sou *m*, attrape-nigaud *m*; camelote *f* de réclame; *attrib.* **c. scheme, show,** attrape-nigaud.

catchpole, catchpoll ['kætʃpoul], *s. Jur: A:* agent *m* de poursuites; porteur *m* de contraintes.

catchup ['kætʃʌp], *s. Comest:* sauce piquante (à base de tomates, de champignons).

catch-up ['kætʃʌp], *s. F:* rattrapage *m*; **postwar c.-up in construction work was rapid,** l'industrie du bâtiment a vite repris après la guerre.

catchwater ['kætʃwɔːtər], *s. Hyd.E:* **c. (drains),** fossé *m* de réception, d'irrigation.

catchweed ['kætʃwiːd], *s. Bot:* grat(t)eron *m*; gaillet accrochant.

catchweight ['kætʃweit], *s. Box: Wr: Turf:* poids *m* à volonté.

catchword ['kætʃwəːd], *s.* **1.** (*a*) *Pol: etc:* mot *m* de ralliement; (*b*) scie *f*, rengaine *f*. **2.** *Typ:* (*a*) mot-souche *m*, *pl.* mots-souches; (*b*) *A:* réclame *f* (en bas de page). **3.** *Th:* réplique *f*.

catchwork ['kætʃwəːk], *s. Hyd.E:* = CATCHWATER.

catchy ['kætʃi], *a.* **1.** (*of tune, etc.*) (i) entraînant; (ii) accrochant, facile à retenir. **2. c. question,** question insidieuse, qui renferme un piège; colle *f*. **3.** *Nau:* **c. wind,** vent fou.

catechesis [kætə'kiːsis], *s. Ecc: A:* catéchèse *f*.

catechetic(al) [kætə'ketik(l)], *a. Ecc: A:* (*a*) catéchétique; (*b*) (méthode *f* de discussion) par demandes et réponses.

catechetically [kætə'ketik(ə)li], *adv.* par demandes et réponses.

catechetics [kætə'kiːtiks], *s.pl.* (*usu. with sg.const.*) catéchétique *f*.

catechin ['kætitʃin, -kin], *s. Ch:* catéchine *f*.

catechism ['kætəkizm], *s.* **1.** = CATACHESIS. **2.** catéchisme *m*; **the shorter c.,** le petit catéchisme.

catechist ['kætəkist], *s. Ecc: A:* catéchiste *mf*.

catechistic(al) [kætə'kistik(l)], *a.* catéchistique.

catechize ['kætəkaiz], *v.tr.* **1.** catéchiser. **2.** poser une série de questions à (qn); tenir (qn) sur la sellette; **he was catechized at great length,** on lui a fait subir un long interrogatoire.

catechizer ['kætəkaizər], *s.* **1.** catéchiste *mf*. **2.** interrogateur, -trice.

catechizing ['kætəkaiziŋ], *s.* **1.** catéchisation *f*. **2.** interrogation *f* (de qn).

catechol ['kætitʃɔl, -kɔl], *s. Ch:* catéchine *f*, acide *m* catéchique.

catechu ['kætiʃuː, 'kætitʃuː], *s.* **1.** *Pharm: Dy:* catéchu *m*; cachou *m*; *Bot:* **c. acacia, c. tree,** acacia *m* catéchu, acacia au cachou; *Com:* **pale c.,** gambir *m*. **2.** (*colour*) **c. brown,** cachou *m inv*; tabac *m inv*.

catechumen [kætə'kjuːmən], *s.* catéchumène *mf*.

catechumenate [kætə'kjuːmeneit], *s.* catéchuménat *m*.

catechutannic ['kætiʃu'tænik], *a. Ch:* catéchutannique, cachoutannique.

categorem [kæ'tegərem], *s. Phil:* catégorème *m*.

categorematic ['kætigɔri'mætik], *a. Phil:* catégorématique; **c. word, expression,** catégorème *m*.

categoric(al) [kætə'gɔrik(l)], *a.* catégorique; *Phil:* **the c. imperative,** l'impératif catégorique; **c. answer,** réponse *f* catégorique.

categorically [kætə'gɔrik(ə)li], *adv.* catégoriquement.

categorist [kæ'tegərist], *s.* catégoriseur *m*.

categorize ['kætəgəraiz], *v.tr.* catégoriser; classer.

category ['kætəgəri], *s.* **1.** *Phil:* catégorie *f*, catégorème *m*, prédicament *m*. **2.** catégorie; **these facts fall into another c.,** ces faits se classent dans une autre catégorie.

catelectrotonus ['kætilektrou'tounəs], *s.* catélectrotonus *f*.

catena, *pl.* **-ae, -as** [kə'tiːnə, -iː, -əz], *s.* (*a*) chaîne *f* (de faits, d'écrits); catène *f* (de remarques sur l'Écriture sainte); (*b*) *Geol:* chaîne de sols; (*c*) *Bot:* chaîne de végétation.

catenary [kə'tiːnəri], *a. & s. Mth:* (arc *m*) en chaînette; caténaire (*f*); (ligne *f* de) chaînette *f*; **c. curve,** funiculaire *f*; **c. suspension (of bridge),** suspension *f* caténaire (d'un pont); **c. bridge,** pont *m* à suspension caténaire; *El:* **trolley wire with c. suspension,** caténaire.

catenate ['kætəneit], *v.tr.* enchaîner (des faits).

catenation [kætə'neiʃ(ə)n], *s.* **1.** enchaînement *m* (de faits). **2.** *Biol:* caténation *f*.

catenoid ['kætənɔid], *s. Mth:* caténoïde *f*; alysséide *f*.

cater ['keitər], *v.i.* **to c. for s.o.,** (i) approvisionner qn; pourvoir à la nourriture de qn, aux besoins matériels de qn; (ii) pourvoir aux plaisirs de qn; *P.N:* (*at restaurant*) **parties catered for** = banquets, noces, etc.; **I can't c. for more than ten,** je ne puis pas donner à manger à plus de dix personnes; **hotel that caters particularly for English visitors,** hôtel *m* qui s'adresse surtout à la clientèle anglaise; **this school caters for engineering students,** cette école remplit les exigences des étudiants ingénieurs; **to c. for all tastes,** pourvoir à tous les goûts.

cateran ['kætərən], *s.m. Scot: A:* homme de guerre; maraudeur.

catercorner(ed) ['keitə'kɔːnə(d)], *a. & adv. esp. NAm:* diagonalement opposé(s).

cater-cousin ['keitəkʌzn], *s. A:* **1.** cousin, -ine, au quatrième degré. **2.** ami(e) intime.

caterer ['keitərər], *s.* **1.** *A:* approvisionneur, -euse; pourvoyeur, -euse, fournisseur *m* (**for, to, s.o.,** de qn; **of sth.,** de qch.). **2.** restaurateur *m*; traiteur *m*.

catering ['keitəriŋ], *s.* **1.** (*a*) *O:* approvisionnement *m*; (*b*) *Com:* **c. department,** rayon *m* d'alimentation (d'un grand magasin); (*c*) **c., the c. industry,** restauration *f*; **the c. was in the hands of Messrs X,** la maison X a fourni le repas.

caterpillar ['kætəpilər], *s.* **1.** (*a*) *Ent:* chenille *f*; (*b*) *A:*

the caterpillars of society, les rongeurs *m* du peuple. **2.** (*a*) **c. (tread, chain, track),** chaîne *f* sans fin à patins; chenille; caterpillar *m*; chemin *m* de roulement; (*b*) **c. tractor,** *R.t.m:* **Caterpillar,** tracteur *m* à chenilles; autochenille *f*; (*c*) **c. wheel,** roue *f* à chenille, à patin; roue-chenille *f*, *pl.* roues-chenilles. **3.** *Bot:* chenille, chenillette *f*.

caterwaul[1] ['kætəwɔ:l], *s.* **1.** miaulement *m* (de chat en chaleur). **2.** *pl.* = CATERWAULING.

caterwaul[2], *v.i.* **1.** (*of cat in rut*) miauler. **2.** *F:* crier (comme les chats la nuit); faire du vacarme; faire un vrai sabbat.

caterwauling ['kætəwɔ:liŋ], *s.* **1.** miaulements *mpl* (de chats). **2.** *F:* musique *f* de chats; sabbat *m* de chats; charivari *m*.

cat-eyed ['kætaid], *a.* aux yeux de chat; qui y voit la nuit.

catfall ['kætfɔ:l], *s. Nau:* garant *m* de capon.

catfight ['kætfait], *s.* (*a*) combat *m* de chats; (*b*) *F:* chamaillerie *f*.

catfish ['kætfiʃ], *s. Ich:* **1.** blennie *m or f*. **2.** silure *m*, poisson-chat *m*, *pl.* poissons-chats; **armoured c.,** poisson-chat, silure cuirassé; **electric c.,** malaptérure *m*; silure, poisson-chat, électrique; **fox-snouted c.,** silure à nez de renard.

cat-foot ['kætfut], *v.i. F: esp. U.S:* marcher à pas feutrés.

cat-footed ['kætfutid], *a.* qui marche à pas feutrés.

catgut ['kætgʌt], *s.* (*a*) corde *f* de boyau; **c. strings for violins,** cordes en boyau pour violons; (*b*) *Med:* catgut *m*.

Cathar [kəθɑ:r], **Catharian** [kə'θεəriən], **Catharist** ['kæθərist], *s. Rel.H:* cathare *mf*.

catharpin(g)s [kæt'hɑ:pinz, -iŋz], *s.pl. Nau:* trélingage *m*.

catharsis [kə'θɑ:sis], *s. Med: Gr.Lit:* catharsis *f*; *Med:* purgation *f*.

cathartic [kə'θɑ:tik], *a.* & *s. Med:* cathartique (*m*); purgatif (bénin); légère purge.

cat-haul[1] ['kæthɔ:l], *s. A:* punition qu'on infligeait à un esclave (on excitait un chat furieux à lui lacérer le dos).

cat-haul[2], *v.tr. A:* faire subir le **cat-haul** à un esclave.

Cathay [kə'θei], *Pr.n. Geog: A: & Lit:* Cathay *m*.

Cathayan [kə'θeiən], *a. A:* (natif, originaire) de Cathay; *Hist:* chinois.

cathead[1] ['kæthed], *s.* **1.** *Nau:* bossoir *m* (de capon). **2.** *Petr:* cabestan *m*. **3.** *Geol:* tête-de-chat *f*, *pl.* têtes-de-chat.

cathead[2], *v.tr. Nau:* caponner (l'ancre).

cathedral [kə'θi:drəl]. **1.** *a.* cathédral, -aux; (*a*) *Lit:* **c. utterance,** allocution *f* ex cathedra; (*b*) **c. church,** église cathédrale; **c. glass,** verre *m* cathédrale. **2.** *s.* cathédrale *f*; **Wells C.,** la cathédrale de Wells; **c. town,** ville épiscopale; évêché *m*; **pro c.,** église *f* qui tient lieu de cathédrale.

Catherine ['kæθ(ə)rin], *Pr.n.f.* Catherine; *Hist:* **C. the Great,** la Grande Catherine; **C. wheel,** (i) *Her:* roue hérissée de rayons en pointe (du martyre de sainte Catherine); (ii) *Arch:* rosace rayonnante; rose *f*; (iii) *Pyr:* soleil *m*; roue *f* à feu; tourniquet *m*; *Gym:* **to turn C. wheels,** faire la roue.

catheter ['kæθitər], *s. Med:* sonde creuse; cathéter *m*.

catheterization [kæθitərai'zeiʃ(ə)n], *s. Med:* cathétérisme *m*.

catheterize ['kæθitəraiz], *v.tr. Med:* cathétériser (l'urètre, etc.).

cathetometer [kæθi'tɔmitər], *s. Med:* cathétomètre *m*.

cathexis, *pl.* **-es** [kə'θeksis, -i:z], *s. Psy:* cathexie *f*.

cathode ['kæθoud], *s. El:* cathode *f*; **pool c.,** cathode à bain, à liquide; **mercury-pool c.,** cathode à bain de mercure; **oxide(-coated) c.,** cathode à oxydes; **directly-heated, indirectly-heated, c.,** cathode à chauffage direct, indirect; **photo(electric) c.,** cathode photoélectrique; **unipotential, equipotential, c.,** cathode équipotentielle; **c. follower,** cathode asservie, suiveuse; **c. bias,** polarisation *f* de cathode; **c. coating,** revêtement *m* de cathode; **c. current,** courant *m* cathodique; **c. ray,** rayon *m* cathodique; **c. ray tube,** tube *f* cathodique; **c. ray glowlamp,** lampe *f* à luminescence cathodique; **c.-loaded circuit,** montage *m* à charge cathodique; **c. beam,** faisceau *m* cathodique.

cathodic [kə'θɔdik], *a. El: etc:* cathodique; **c. beam,** faisceau *m* cathodique; **c. protection,** protection *f* cathodique.

cathole ['kæthoul], *s.* **1.** chatière *f*. **2.** *Nau:* écubier *m* arrière.

catholic ['kæθ(ə)lik]. **1.** *a.* (*a*) universel; (*b*) tolérant; à l'esprit large; éclectique; **c. observer,** observateur *m* sans prévention; **c. mind,** esprit *m* large; **c. tastes,** goûts *m* éclectiques. **2.** *a.* & *s. Ecc:* (*a*) orthodoxe (*mf*), catholique (*mf*); **the C. Church,** toute la chrétienté; (*b*) *R.C.Ch:* catholique *mf*; **I believe in one holy, c. and apostolic church,** je crois en l'Église, une, sainte, catholique et apostolique; **old catholics,** (i) *Eng:* les vieilles familles catholiques (qui voulaient se distinguer des convertis); (ii) (*in the Netherlands*) les vieux-catholiques (des Pays-Bas); *Hist:* **His C. Majesty,** sa Majesté très Catholique (le roi d'Espagne).

catholically [kə'θɔlik(ə)li], *adv.* **1.** = CATHOLICLY. **2. c. minded,** aux idées larges; à l'esprit large, impartial, sans prévention.

catholicism [kə'θɔlisizm], *s. Ecc:* catholicisme *m*.

catholicity [kæθə'lisiti], *s.* **1.** (*a*) universalité *f*; (*b*) largeur *f* (d'esprit); tolérance *f*; éclectisme *m*. **2.** *Theol:* (*a*) orthodoxie *f*; (*b*) (*conformity with the R.C. Church*) catholicité *f* (d'une opinion).

catholicize [kə'θɔlisaiz], *v.tr.* catholiciser.

catholicly ['kæθ(ə)likli], *adv.* catholiquement; en bon catholique.

catholicon [kə'θɔlikən], *s. A:* panacée *f*.

catholyte ['kæθəlait], *s. El:* catholyte *m*.

cathouse ['kæthaus], *s. P: esp. U.S:* bordel *m*.

Catiline ['kætilain], *Pr.n.m. Rom.Hist:* Catilina; **the C. orations,** les Catilinaires *f*.

cation ['kætaiən], *s. Ph: Elcs: etc:* cation *m*; **c. exchanger,** résine *f* cationique, résine échangeuse de cations.

cationic [kætai'ɔnik], *a.* cationique.

cativo [kæ'ti:vou], *s. Bot:* cativo *m*.

catkin ['kætkin], *s. Bot:* chaton *m*.

catlap ['kætlæp], *s. F: O:* lavasse *f*; thé *m* trop faible.

catlick ['kætlik], *s. F:* **to have, give oneself, a c.,** se laver le bout du nez.

catlike ['kætlaik], *a.* comme un chat; de chat; félin; **c. grace,** grâce féline; **c. tread,** pas *m* de loup.

catling ['kætliŋ], *s.* **1.** petit chat, chaton *m*. **2.** *A:* corde *f* à boyau. **3.** *Surg:* couteau interosseux (pour amputations).

catmeat ['kætmi:t], *s.* viande *f* pour chats.

catmint ['kætmint], *s. Bot:* cataire *f*, herbe *f* aux chats.

catnap[1] ['kætnæp], *s. F:* sieste *f*, somme *m* (de courte durée).

catnap[2], *v.i. F:* faire la sieste; sommeiller.

catnip ['kætnip], *s. U.S:* = CATMINT.

Cato ['keitou], *Pr.n.m. Rom.Hist:* Caton.

catoblepas [kætou'bli:pəs], *s. Z: Myth:* catoblépas *m*.

catocala [kə'tɔkələ, kætə'kɑ:lə], **catocalid** [kə'tɔkəlid], *s. Ent:* catocala *f*.

catoptric [kæt'ɔptrik], *a. Opt:* catoptrique.

catoptrics [kæt'ɔptriks], *s.pl.* (*usu. with sg. const.*) catoptrique *f*.

catoptromancy [kætɔptrou'mænsi], *s.* catoptromancie *f*.

cat rig ['kætrig], *s. Nau:* gréement *m* à taille-vent.

cat-rigged ['kætrigd], *a. Nau:* gréé à taille-vent.

catsmeat ['kætsmi:t], *s.* viande *f* pour chats; *F:* **to make c. of s.o.,** abîmer le portrait à, de, qn.

catspaw, cat's paw [kætspɔ:], *s.* **1.** *Nau:* petite bouffée de vent; risée *f*, risette *f*, fraîcheur *f*. **2.** *Nau:* (*knot*) gueule *f* de raie. **3. to make a c. of s.o.,** se servir de la patte du chat pour tirer les marrons du feu; faire tirer les marrons du feu par qn; prendre qn pour sa dupe; *F:* faire marcher qn; **to be s.o.'s c., to be made a c. of,** tirer les marrons du feu (pour qn); être la dupe de qn.

catstep ['kætstep], *s. Geog:* rideau *m*.

catsup ['kætsəp], *s. Comest:* sauce piquante (à base de tomates, de champignons).

cattery ['kætəri], *s.* chatterie *f*; pension *f* (i) pour chats, (ii) *F: Iron:* pour vieilles dames.

cattily ['kætili], *adv. F:* méchamment; sournoisement; d'un ton aigre-doux.

cattiness ['kætinis], *s. F:* méchanceté *f*, sournoiserie *f*; rosserie *f*.

cattish ['kætiʃ], *a.* **1.** félin; comme un chat. **2.** *F:* = CATTY 2.

cattishly ['kætiʃli], *adv.* = CATTILY.

cattishness ['kætiʃnis], *s.* = CATTINESS.

cattle ['kætl], *s. Coll.inv.* **1.** bétail *m*; bestiaux *mpl*; **horned c.,** bêtes *fpl* à cornes; bovins *mpl*; **black c.,** bœufs *mpl* de race écossaise ou galloise; **c. breeding,** élevage *m* du bétail; **c. market,** marché *m* aux bestiaux; **c. drover,** bouvier *m*; **c. lifter,** voleur *m* de bétail; **c. lifting, stealing, rustling,** vol *m*, détournement *m*, de bétail; **c. float,** bétaillère *f*; **c. truck,** fourgon *m*, wagon *m*, à bestiaux; **c. pen,** parc *m* à bestiaux; **c. shed,** étable *f*, bouverie *f*; **c. show,** concours *m* d'élevage d'animaux gras; comice *m* agricole; **c. plague,** peste bovine; *P.N:* **c. crossing,** passage *m* de troupeaux. **2.** *F: A:* chevaux *mpl*; **he always had some good c. in his stable,** il avait toujours quelques bons chevaux, quelques belles bêtes, dans son écurie. **3.** *A:* individus *mpl*, gens *mpl*, personnes *fpl*.

cattleman, *pl.* **-men** ['kætlmən], *s.m.* **1.** conducteur de bétail; bouvier. **2.** *U.S:* éleveur de bétail.

cattleya [kæt'li:jə], *s. Bot:* cattleya *m*.

catty ['kæti], *a. F:* **1. there's a c. smell,** ça sent la pisse de chat. **2.** (*esp. of woman*) méchant(e), sournois(e); rosse; **c. answer,** réponse aigre-douce, rosse; **c. remark,** rosserie *f*.

catty-corner(s) ['kæti'kɔ:nə(z)], *a.* & *adv. F:* diagonalement opposé(s).

Catullus [kə'tʌləs], *Pr.n.m. Rom.Lit:* Catulle.

catwalk ['kætwɔ:k], *s.* coursive *f*; passerelle *f* de visite; passavant *m*.

catwort ['kætwə:t], *s.* = CATMINT.

Caucasian [kɔ:'keiʒ(ə)n, -'keiziən]. **1.** *a. Geog: Ethn: Ling:* caucasien; *Geol:* caucasique. **2.** *s. Ethn: Geog:* Caucasien, -ienne. **3.** *s. U.S:* (*also in S. Africa*) membre *m* de la race blanche.

Caucasic [kɔ:'keizik], *a. Ling:* caucasien.

Caucasus (the) [ðə'kɔ:kəsəs], *Pr.n. Geog:* le Caucase.

caucho ['kautʃou], *s.* caoutchouc *m*; (*plant*) **c. rubber,** castilloa *m*.

caucus[1] ['kɔ:kəs], *s. Pol:* **1.** *U.S:* réunion *f* préliminaire (d'un comité électoral). **2.** comité électoral; clique *f* politique; **government by c.,** gouvernement *m* par les comités.

caucus[2]. **1.** *v.tr.* gouverner (un parti) par des comités électoraux. **2.** *v.i.* former des groupes, des cliques.

cauda equina ['kɔ:dəi'kwainə, 'kaudɑ:e'kwi:nɑ:], *s. Anat:* queue-de-cheval *f*, *pl.* queues-de-cheval.

caudal ['kɔ:dl], *a. Z:* caudal, -aux; *Ich:* **c. fin,** caudale *f*.

Caudata [kɔ:'deitə], *s.pl. Nat.Hist:* urodèles *m*.

caudate ['kɔ:deit], *a. Nat.Hist:* caudé, caudifère, caudigère.

caudicle ['kɔ:dikl], *s. Bot:* caudicule *f*.

Caudine ['kɔ:dain], *a. Rom.Hist:* **the C. forks,** les fourches Caudines.

caudle ['kɔ:dl], *s. A:* chaudeau *m*, brouet *m*, lait *m* de poule (pour malades).

caul[1] [kɔ:l], *s.* **1.** coiffe *f* (de nouveau-né); **born with a c.,** né coiffé. **2.** *Cu:* crépine *f*, toilette *f*, coiffe *f*, parement *m* (d'un gigot, etc.). **3.** *Cost: A: & Hist:* (*a*) résille *f*; (*b*) (fond *m* de) coiffe.

caul[2], *s. Carp:* cale *f*, goberge *m*.

cauldron ['kɔ:ldrən], *s.* **1.** (*a*) chaudron *m*; (*b*) *Ind:* chaudière *f*. **2.** *Geol:* gouffre *m* d'effondrement); **c. subsidence,** effondrement *m* (entre deux failles).

caulerpa [kɔ:'lə:pə], *s. Algae:* caulerpe *f*.

caulescent [kɔ:'les(ə)nt], *a. Bot:* caulescent.

caulicle ['kɔ:likl], **caulicule** ['kɔ:likjul], *s. Bot:* caulicule *f*.

caulicoli [kɔ:'likəli], *s.pl. Arch:* caulicoles *f*.

caulicolous [kɔ:'likələs], *a. Nat.Hist:* caulicole.

cauliferous [kɔ:'lifərəs], *a. Bot:* caulifère, caulescent.

cauliflorous [kɔ:li'flɔ:rəs], *a. Bot:* cauliflore.

cauliflory ['kɔ:liflɔ:ri], *s. Bot:* cauliflorie *f*.

cauliflower ['kɔliflauər], *s. Hort:* chou-fleur *m*, *pl.* choux-fleurs; *Cu:* **c. cheese,** chou-fleur au gratin. **2.** *Box: etc:* **c. ear,** oreille *f* en chou-fleur.

cauliform ['kɔ:lifɔ:m], *a. Bot:* cauliforme.

caulinary ['kɔ:linəri], **cauline** ['kɔ:lain], *a. Bot:* caulinaire.

caulis, *pl.* **-es** ['kɔ:lis, -i:z], *s. Bot:* caule *f*.

caulk[1] [kɔ:k], *v.tr.* **1.** (*a*) calfater, étouper (un navire); (*b*) calfeutrer (une fenêtre, etc.). **2.** mater (une tôle de chaudière, un rivet, etc.). **3.** *P:* **to c. (off),** roupiller, piquer un roupillon.

caulk[2], *s. P:* roupillon *m*.

caulker ['kɔ:kər], *s.* **1.** (*pers.*) calfat *m*. **2.** *Tls:* = CAULKING IRON. **3.** *P: A:* gros mensonge. **4.** *P:* petit verre (de gnole).

caulking ['kɔ:kiŋ], *s.* **1.** (*a*) calfatage *m* (d'un navire en bois); (*b*) calfeutrage *m*; calfeutrement *m*. **2.** matage *m* (de tôles). **3.** *attrib.* **c. iron, chisel, tool,** (i) calfait *m*, burin *m*; ciseau *m* de calfat; (ii) *Metalw:* matoir *m*; **pneumatic c. tool,** frappeur *m* pneumatique (à mater); **c. felt,** feutre goudronné.

caulo- ['kɔ:lou], *pref. Nat.Hist:* caulo-.

caulocarpic [kɔ:lou'kɑ:pik], **caulocarpous** [kɔ:lou'kɑ:pəs], *a. Bot:* caulocarpe, caulocarpien, caulocarpique.

caulosarc ['kɔ:lousɑ:k], *s. Bot:* caulosarque *m*.

caurale [kɔ:'reil], *s. Orn:* caurale *m*.

causal ['kɔ:zl], *a.* causal (*no mpl*); causatif; *Gram:* **c. conjunction,** conjonction causative.

causalgia [kɔ:'zældʒiə], *s. Med:* causalgie *f*.

causality [kɔ:'zæliti], *s. Phil:* causalité *f*; rapport *m* de cause à effet.

causation [kɔ:'zeiʃ(ə)n], *s.* **1.** causation *f*. **2.** = CAUSALITY.

causative ['kɔ:zətiv], *a.* causatif; *esp. Gram:* **c. verb,** verbe causatif.

cause[1] [kɔ:z], *s.* **1.** (*a*) cause *f*; **prime, secondary, c.,**

cause première, secondaire; **c. and effect,** la cause et l'effet; **no effect without a c.,** point d'effet sans cause; **to be the c. of an accident,** être (la) cause d'un accident; **he is the c. of my failure, of my ruin,** il est cause que je n'ai pas réussi; il est la cause de mon échec, l'auteur de ma ruine; *Phil:* **efficient c.,** cause efficiente; **material c.,** cause matérielle; **final c.,** cause finale; fin *f*; *Theol:* **the First C.,** la cause première, la cause des causes; Dieu *m*; (*b*) *Jur:* **c. of a valid contract,** cause d'une obligation. **2.** raison *f*, motif *m*, sujet *m*; **c. for litigation,** matière *f* à procès; **to have c. for dissatisfaction,** avoir un sujet, un motif, de mécontentement; avoir sujet à mécontentement; **I have c. to be thankful,** j'ai lieu d'être reconnaissant; j'ai de bonnes raisons pour être reconnaissant; **I have c. for astonishment,** j'ai lieu d'être surpris; j'ai de quoi être surpris; **I have c. to complain of. . .,** j'ai à me plaindre de. . .; **to have good c. for doing sth.,** être justifié à faire qch.; faire qch. à bon droit; avoir de bonnes raisons pour faire qch.; **if I complain, I have good c.,** si je me plains c'est que j'en ai sujet; **to show c.,** exposer ses raisons; **what possible c. have you for taking such an action?** quel motif pouvez-vous invoquer pour une action pareille? **to give serious c. for complaint,** donner de grands sujets de plainte; **the situation gives c. for apprehension,** la situation motive, justifie, des craintes; **and with good c.,** et pour cause. **3.** (*a*) *Jur:* cause; procès *m*; **to plead s.o.'s c.,** plaider la cause de qn; **c. list,** rôle *m*, tableau *m*, feuille *f*, d'audience; (*b*) **to win s.o. over to one's c.,** gagner qn à sa cause; **to take up s.o.'s c.,** embrasser, épouser, la querelle de qn; **to make common c. with s.o.,** faire cause commune, se solidariser, avec qn; **in the c. of justice,** pour (la cause de) la justice; **to labour in the c. of humanity,** travailler pour l'humanité; **to work in a good c.,** travailler pour une bonne cause; **the week's good c.** = appel *m* (hebdomadaire) à la radio pour une œuvre charitable; *F:* **it's all in a good c.,** ce n'est pas du temps perdu. **4.** *Phil:* **treatise on c.,** traité *m* sur la causalité.

cause[2], *v.tr.* **1.** causer, occasionner (un malheur, du retard, etc.); faire arriver (un accident); provoquer (la gaîté, un accident); faire naître (une querelle); susciter (de l'étonnement); **to c. a fire,** provoquer un incendie; *Nau:* **losses caused by bad stowing,** pertes *f* du fait du mauvais arrimage; **to c. s.o. anxiety,** causer de l'anxiété à qn; **to c. a sensation,** faire sensation. **2. to c. s.o. to do sth.,** faire faire qch. à qn; **to c. s.o. to be punished,** faire punir qn; **to c. sth. to be done,** faire faire qch.; **what caused you to be late?** quelle est la cause de votre retard? qu'est-ce qui vous a mis en retard?

causeless ['kɔ:zlis], *a.* **causelessly** ['kɔ:zlisli], *adv.* sans cause, sans raison, sans motif, sans sujet.

causerie ['kouzəri], *s.* causerie *f*; conférence familière.

causeuse ['kɔ:zə:z], *s. A.Furn:* causeuse *f*.

causeway[1] ['kɔ:zwei], *s.* **1.** (*a*) chaussée *f*, levée *f*, digue *f* (coupant à travers des marécages); (*b*) *A: & Hist:* chaussée empierrée; route *f*; *Geog:* **the Giant's C.,** la chaussée des Géants. **2.** *Scot: A:* trottoir *m*.

causeway[2], *v.tr.* **1. to c. a marsh,** construire une chaussée à travers un marais. **2.** empierrer, caillouter, paver (un chemin).

causse [kous], *s. Geog:* causse *m*.

caustic ['kɔ:stik]. **1.** *a.* (*a*) caustique; (i) corrosif, (ii) mordant; **c. soda,** soude *f* caustique; hydrate *m* de soude; **c. wit,** esprit mordant, sarcastique; (*b*) *Bot: Austr:* **c. creeper, c. weed,** (espèce d') euphorbe *f*. **2.** *s.* (*a*) *Ch: Med:* caustique *m*; *Med:* **lunar c.,** caustique lunaire; pierre infernale; **common c.,** pierre *f* à cautère; (*b*) *Opt:* caustique *f*.

caustically ['kɔ:stik(ə)li], *adv.* caustiquement; d'un ton caustique, mordant, sarcastique.

causticity [kɔ:s'tisiti], *s.* causticité *f*; (i) pouvoir corrosif; (ii) caractère mordant (d'une observation).

cauter ['kɔ:tər], *s.* cautère *m*.

cauterization [kɔ:tərai'zeiʃ(ə)n], *s. Med:* cautérisation *f*; **heat c.,** ignipuncture *f*; pointes *fpl* de feu.

cauterize ['kɔ:təraiz], *v.tr. Med:* cautériser; *Lit: A:* endurcir (la conscience).

cautery ['kɔ:təri], *s.* cautère *m*; **actual c.,** cautère actuel.

caution[1] ['kɔ:ʃ(ə)n], *s.* **1.** précaution *f*, prévoyance *f*, prudence *f*, circonspection *f*; **to go to work, to set about sth., with great c.,** s'attaquer à la tâche avec beaucoup de circonspection; **to do sth. with great c.,** faire qch. avec de grands ménagements. **2.** (*a*) *Jur: Scot: & U.S:* caution *f*, garant *m*, répondant *m* (**for s.o.,** de qn); (*b*) **c. money,** cautionnement (versé par les étudiants en droit et par les étudiants de certaines universités). **3.** (*a*) vis *m*, avertissement *m*; **c.! steep gradient,** attention! descente rapide; (*b*) *Mil:* commandement *m* préparatoire; (*c*) réprimande *f*; **he was dismissed,** *F:* **let off, with a c.,** le magistrat s'est contenté de le réprimander, *F:* il s'en est tiré avec une réprimande; **to inflict a punishment as a c. to others,** infliger une punition pour l'exemple, pour encourager les autres; **4.** *F:* **a c.,** un drôle de type, de bonhomme, de numéro; une drôle de femme; un(e) drôle d'enfant; une drôle de chose; **she's a c.,** elle est formidable.

caution[2], *v.tr.* **1.** avertir (qn); mettre (qn) sur ses gardes; **to c. s.o. against sth.,** prémunir, prévenir, précautionner, qn contre qch.; mettre qn en garde contre qch.; *Jur:* **to c. (a suspect),** prévenir (un suspect) que ce qu'il dira peut être utilisé contre lui au cours des poursuites, du procès. **2.** menacer (qn) de poursuites à la prochaine occasion; réprimander (qn).

cautionary ['kɔ:ʃən(ə)ri], *a.* (*a*) d'avertissement, de précaution; **c. signal,** signal *m* d'avertissement; **c. tales,** contes moraux; (*b*) *Mil:* **c. command,** commandement *m* préparatoire.

cautious ['kɔ:ʃəs], *a.* **1.** circonspect, précautionneux, prudent, avisé; **c. judgment,** jugement retenu; **c. of sth.,** en garde, prévenu, contre qch.; **to be c. of doing sth.,** prendre garde, se garder, de faire qch.; **to be c. in doing sth.,** faire qch. avec circonspection; **to play a c. game,** jouer serré. **2.** *Pej:* cauteleux.

cautiously ['kɔ:ʃəsli], *adv.* **1.** avec précaution, avec circonspection, précautionneusement, prudemment; **to do sth. c.,** faire qch. avec ménagement(s). **2.** *Pej:* cauteleusement.

cautiousness ['kɔ:ʃəsnis], *s.* prudence (habituelle); esprit *m* de précaution.

cavalcade[1] [kævl'keid], *s.* cavalcade *f*; cortège *m*.

cavalcade[2], *v.i.* cavalcader.

cavalier [kævə'liər]. **1.** *s.m.* (*a*) *Hist:* cavalier; gentilhomme; (*b*) *Eng.Hist:* royaliste; **the Cavaliers and the Roundheads,** les Cavaliers et les Têtes rondes; *Dressm: A:* **c. cuff,** manche évasée; (*c*) *O:* galant; chevalier servant (d'une dame). **2.** *a.* cavalier, dégagé, désinvolte; libre d'allures; sans ménagements; **with a c. air,** d'un air cavalier; à la hussarde; avec désinvolture.

cavalierly [kævə'liə:li], *adv.* cavalièrement; à la cavalière, à la dragonne.

cavally [kə'væli], *s. Ich: E5S:* caranx *m*, carangue *f*.

cavalry ['kævəlri], *s.* cavalerie *f*; **horse c.,** cavalerie à cheval, montée; **motorized, mechanized, c.,** cavalerie motorisée, mécanisée; **armoured c.,** cavalerie blindée; **c. officer,** officier *m* de cavalerie.

cavalryman, *pl.* **-men** ['kævəlrimən], *s.m. Mil:* cavalier; soldat de cavalerie.

cavatina [kævə'ti:nə], *s. Mus:* cavatine *f*.

cave[1] [keiv], *s.* **1.** (*a*) caverne *f*, antre *m*; grotte *f*; souterrain *m*; **Fingal's c.,** la Grotte de Fingal; **the Cheddar Caves,** les grottes de Cheddar; (*b*) *Mus.Hist:* **c. of harmony,** caveau *m*; (*c*) (*cheesemaking*) cave *f*; (*d*) *Atom.Ph:* cellule *f* d'essais (de réacteur); (*e*) *attrib.* **c. art,** art *m* rupestre; **c. dweller,** troglodyte *mf*; homme *m*, femme *f*, des cavernes; **c. dwelling,** maison *f* troglodyte; *Nat.Hist:* **c.-dwelling (animal, etc.)** (animal, etc.) cavernicole; **c. spider,** araignée *f* cavernicole; *Prehist:* **c. hunter,** homme des cavernes (qui vit de la chasse); **c. hunting,** spéléologie *f*; *Paleont:* **c. bear,** ours *m* des cavernes, ours cavernaire; *Ich:* **c. fish,** amblyopsis *m*. **2.** *Pol. Hist:* (*a*) scission *f*; (*b*) dissidents *mpl*.

cave[2] [keiv], *s.* effondrement *m* (du sol); éboulement *m*.

cave[3] [keiv], *v.*

I. *v.tr. & i.* **1.** *v.tr.* caver, excaver, creuser (la terre); former une caverne, une dépression, dans (le sol); **waters caving the (river) banks,** les eaux qui minent, sapent, les berges (de la rivière). **2.** *v.i.* faire de la spéléologie; explorer des cavernes.

II. (*compound verb*) **cave in;** (*a*) *v.i.* (i) (*of ground, structure, etc.*) céder, s'affaisser, s'effondrer, s'ébouler; (*of structure, beam*) s'infléchir; **I felt my ribs c. in,** j'ai senti mes côtes s'enfoncer; (ii) (*of pers.*) céder, se soumettre, se rendre; (*b*) *v.tr.* **car with its bumper caved in,** voiture *f* dont le pare-choc a été défoncé.

cave[4] ['keivi, 'ka:vei], *int. Sch: F:* attention! pet! vingt-deux! *s.* **to keep c.,** faire le guet, le pet.

caveat[1] ['kæviæt], *s.* **1.** *Jur:* (*a*) opposition *f* (**to,** à); **to enter, put in, a c.,** former, mettre, opposition (**against,** à); **c. against unfair practices,** avertissement *m* contre la concurrence déloyale; (*b*) avis *m* d'opposition (au renouvellement d'un brevet d'invention, etc.); (*c*) *U.S: A:* demande *f* de brevet provisoire. **2.** *A: & Lit:* avertissement; mise *f* en garde (**against,** contre).

caveat[2], *v.i.* **1.** *Jur: etc.* mettre opposition (**against,** à). **2.** *Fenc:* dégager.

caveat emptor ['kæviæt'emtɔr], *Lt.phr. Com:* aux risques de l'acheteur.

caveating ['kæviætiŋ], *s. Fenc:* contre-appel *m*.

caveator ['kævieitər], *s. Jur:* opposant *m*.

cave-in ['keivin], *s. F:* affaissement *m*; effondrement *m*.

caveman, *pl.* **-men** ['keivmæn, -mən], **cave woman,** *pl.* **-women** ['keivwumən, -wimin], *s.* (*a*) *Prehist:* troglodyte *mf*; homme *m*, femme *f* des cavernes; **the age of the c.,** l'âge *m* des cavernes; (*b*) *F:* brute *f*, homme à la manière forte (avec les femmes); **a real cavewoman,** un dragon; **that's (real) c. stuff,** ça c'est des manières brutales (dignes de l'homme des cavernes).

cavendish ['kævəndiʃ], *s.* tabac foncé édulcoré et comprimé.

caver ['keivər], *s. F:* spéléologue *mf*.

cavern[1] ['kævə(:)n], *s.* caverne *f*, antre *m*; souterrain *m*.

cavern[2]. **1.** *v.tr.* creuser une caverne dans (qch.); évider (qch.). **2.** *v.i. A:* vivre dans une caverne, dans un antre.

cavernicole [kə'və:nikoul], *s. Nat.Hist:* cavernicole *mf*.

cavernicolous [kævə'nikələs], *a. Nat.Hist:* (animal, etc.) cavernicole.

cavernous ['kævənəs], *a.* (*of rock, tissue, respiration, etc.*) caverneux.

cavernulous [kə'və:njuləs], *a. Anat:* (tissu) caverneux, plein de cavernules.

cavesson ['kævis(ə)n], *s. Equit:* caveçon *m*.

cavetto, *pl.* **-ti, -tos** [kə'vetou, -ti:, -touz], *s. Arch:* cavet *m*.

caviar(e)[1] ['kævia:r], *s.* **1.** caviar *m*; *F:* **it's c. to the general,** c'est du caviar pour le peuple; c'est trop fin pour la foule; **he doesn't eat c. every day,** il ne mange pas des ortolans tous les jours. **2.** caviar, passage caviardé (d'un journal, etc.).

caviar(e)[2], *v.tr.* caviarder (un passage dans un journal, etc.).

cavicorn ['kæviko:n], *a. Z:* cavicorne.

Cavicornia [kævi'kɔ:niə], *s.pl. Z:* cavicornes *m*.

Caviidae [kei'vi:idi:], *s.pl. Z:* caviidés *m*.

cavil[1] ['kæv(i)l], *s.* argutie *f*; objection oiseuse.

cavil[2], *v.i.* (**cavilled**) **1.** chicaner, ergoter; couper les cheveux en quatre; **he's always cavilling,** il trouve à redire sur tout; il n'a jamais fini de critiquer; **to c. at, about, sth.,** argumenter, chicaner, ergoter, pointiller, épiloguer, sur qch.; mettre qch. en question. **2.** *Jur:* multiplier les incidents.

caviller ['kævilər], *s.* chicaneur, -euse; chicanier, -ière; ergoteur, -euse.

cavilling[1] ['kæviliŋ], *a.* argutieux; chicaneur, -euse; vétilleux.

cavilling[2], *s.* arguties *fpl*, chicanes *fpl*, chicanerie *f*, ergotage *m*, pointillerie *f*.

caving ['keiviŋ], *s.* **1.** spéléologie *f*, exploration *f* des cavernes. **2.** *Min:* **undercut c.,** foudroyage *m* après sous-cavage; **total c.,** foudroyage intégral.

caving in ['keiviŋ'in], *s.* effondrement *m*, éboulement *m*, affaissement *m*, tombée *f*; *Min:* écrasée *f*.

cavitation [kævi'teiʃ(ə)n], *s. Av: Nau:* cavitation *f*.

cavity ['kæviti], *s.* **1.** cavité *f*; creux *m*; alvéole *m*; trou *m*, *pl.* trous; *Metall:* grumelure *f* (dans la fonte); *Const:* **c. wall,** mur *m* double; *Elcs:* **c. resonator,** cavité résonnante; *Anat:* **the nasal c.,** les fosses nasales; **dental c.,** cavité dentaire. **2.** *N.Arch:* déplacement *m*.

cavort [kə'vɔ:t], *v.i.* cabrioler; faire des galopades, des galipettes.

cavy ['keivi], *s. Z:* **1.** cobaye *m*, cochon *m* d'Inde; **southern c.,** cobaye austral; **restless c.,** cobaye du Brésil. **2. water c.,** cabiai *m*.

caw[1] [kɔ:], *s.* croassement *m*.

caw[2], *v.i.* (*of crow, etc.*) croasser.

cawing ['kɔ:iŋ], *s.* croassement *m*.

cay [kei], *s. Geog:* caye *f*; récif *m* de corail (des mers de la Floride).

Cayenne [kei'en]. **1.** *Pr.n. Geog:* Cayenne *f*. **2.** *s.* **c. (pepper),** poivre *m* de Cayenne; cayenne *m*; poivre rouge.

cayman ['keimən], *s. Rept:* caïman *m*; **spectacled c.,** caïman à lunettes. *Geog:* **Cayman Islands,** îles Cayman.

ceanothus [si:ə'nouθəs], *s. Bot:* ceanothus *m*.

cease[1] [si:s], *s. used in the Lit: phr.* **without c.,** sans cesse, sans arrêt, sans discontinuer.

cease[2], *v.tr. & i.* **1.** cesser ((**from**) **doing sth.,** de faire qch.); **he has ceased to see anybody,** il ne voit plus personne; **life has ceased,** il est mort, elle est morte; *Lit:* **they have ceased to be,** ils ne sont plus. **2.** cesser (ses efforts, etc.); **to c. work,** cesser le travail; arrêter les travaux; *Lit:* **to c. from work,** cesser son travail; *Mil:* **to c. fire,** cesser le feu; **when the storm had ceased,** lorsque l'orage fut passé; **he talked without ceasing,** il parlait sans arrêt.

cease-fire ['si:s'faiər], *s.* cessez-le-feu *m inv*; **to agree to a c.-f.,** accepter le, un, cessez-le-feu; convenir d'un cessez-le-feu.

ceaseless ['si:slis], *a.* incessant; sans arrêt; continuel, éternel; sans fin.

ceaslessly ['si:slisli], *adv.* sans cesse, sans arrêt; continuellement, éternellement; sans fin.

ceaselessness ['si:slisnis], *s.* continuité *f*, persistance *f* (d'un bruit, etc.).

ceasing ['si:siŋ], *s.* cessation *f*.

Cebidae ['sebidi:], *s.pl. Z:* cébidés *m*.

Ceboidea [si'bɔidiə], *s.pl. Z:* céboïdes *m*, platyr(r)hiniens *m*.

cebus ['si:bəs], *s. Z:* cebus *m*.

cecal ['si:kl], *a.* = CAECAL.

cecidium [si'sidiəm], *s. Bot:* cécidie *f*.

cecidogenous [sesi'dɔdʒənəs, si:si-], *a. Biol:* cécidogène.

cecidomyia [sesidou'maiə, si:si-], *s. Ent:* cécidomyie *f*.

cecidomyiid [sesidou'maiid, si:si-], *s. Ent:* cécidomyidé *m*.

Cecidomyiidae [sesidou'maiidi:, 'si:si-], *s.pl. Ent:* cécidomyidés *m*.

Cecilia [si'si:liə], *Pr.n.f.* Cécile.

cecity ['si:siti], *s.* cécité *f*.

cecotomy [si:'kɔtəmi], *s.* = CAECOTOMY.

cecropia [si(:)'kroupiə], *s. Bot:* cecropia *m*.

Cecropidae [si(:)'krɔpidi:], *Pr.n.m.pl. Gr.Hist:* Cécropides.

Cecrops ['si:krɔps]. **1.** *Pr.n.m.* Cécrops. **2.** *s. Crust:* cécrops *m*.

cecum ['si:kəm], *s.* = CAECUM.

cedar ['si:dər], *s. Bot:* **c. (tree),** cèdre *m*; **c. of Lebanon,** cèdre du Liban; **red c., pencil c.,** cèdre rouge; cèdre de Virginie; genévrier *m* de Virginie; **atlas c., silver c.,** cèdre de l'Atlas; cèdre argenté; **Barbados bastard c., Spanish c., Honduras c.,** cèdre acajou; cedrela, cédrel, odorant; acajou *m* femelle; **Moulmein c.,** (espèce de) cedrela; **c. (wood),** (bois *m* de) cèdre; **Spanish c., (wood), cigar-box c.,** cedro *m*; **c. resin, pitch,** cédrie *f*; **oil of c.,** cédréléon *m*.

cede [si:d], *v.tr.esp. Jur:* céder (un bien immobilier, une province, une dette) (**to,** à).

cedent ['si:dənt], *s. Jur:* cédant, -ante.

cedilla [si'dilə], *s.* cédille *f*; **to put a c. under a c,** cédiller un c.

cedrela [si:'drelə], *s. Bot:* cédrel *m*, cedrela *m*.

cedrene ['si:dri:n], *s. Ch:* cédrène *m*.

cedrol ['si:drɔl], *s. Ch:* cédrol *m*.

Cedron ['ki:drən], *Pr.n. B.Hist:* **the (brook) C.,** le Cédron.

cee [si:], *s.* (la lettre) c. *Veh:* **c. spring,** ressort *m* en C.

ceil [si:l], *v.tr.* (*a*) plafonner (une pièce); (*b*) *A:* lambrisser (une paroi).

ceiling ['si:liŋ], *s.* **1.** *Const:* **c. (work),** plafonnage *m*. **2.** (*a*) *Const:* plafond *m*; **ribbed c.,** plafond à nervures; **c. beam,** doubleau *m*; **c. light,** plafonnier *m*; **counterpoise c. lamp,** suspension *f* à contrepoids; (*b*) *Aut:* plafond (de voiture); **body c.,** pavillon *m*; (*c*) *F:* **to hit the c.,** entrer dans une colère bleue. **3.** (*a*) *Av:* (i) plafond; (ii) vol *m* en plafond; **absolute c.,** plafond absolu, théorique; **service c.,** plafond pratique; **static c.,** plafond statique; *Mil.Av:* **operational c.,** plafond opérationnel; **to fly at the c.,** plafonner; (*b*) *Meteor:* plafond (nuageux); **c. (and visibility) unlimited,** plafond nul; **c. zero,** visibilité nulle; **c. height indicator,** indicateur *m* de plafond; (*c*) *Pol.Ec: etc:* plafond; **output has reached its c.,** la production plafonne, est en plein plafonnement; **prices have reached the c. of . . .,** les prix *m* plafonnent à . . .; **c. price,** prix plafond; **monetary ceilings,** plafonds monétaires; **to fix a c. to a budget,** fixer un plafond à un budget; (*d*) *F:* **he's hit the c.,** il plafonne, il a atteint son plafond. **4.** *Nau:* vaigres *fpl*, vaigrage *m*; **floor c.,** vaigrage de fond; **c. plate,** vaigre; **to put in the c.,** vaigrer (un navire).

ceilinged ['si:liŋd], *a.* (*with adj. prefixed, e.g.*) **high-, low-c. room,** pièce haute, basse, de plafond.

celadon ['selədən], *a. & s.* (*colour*) céladon *inv*; vert pâle *inv*; *Cer:* céladon *m*.

celadonite ['selədənait], *s. Miner:* céladonite *f*.

celandine ['selәndain], *s. Bot:* (*a*) **greater c.,** chélidoine *f*; grande éclaire; *F:* herbe *f* aux boucs; herbe aux verrues; herbe de l'hirondelle; (*b*) **lesser c.,** ficaire *f*; petite éclaire; *F:* herbe de fic; herbe aux hémorroïdes; jauneau *m*.

celanese [selə'ni:z], *s. R.t.m: Tex:* soie artificielle (à base de cellulose).

Celastraceae [seləs'treisii:], *s.pl. Bot:* célastracées *f*.

celastrus [si'læstrəs], *s. Bot:* célastre *m*.

Celebes ['selibi:z], *Pr.n. Geog:* **(the Island of) C.,** l'île *f* de Célèbes.

Celebesian [seli'bi:zlən], *Geog:* (*a*) *a.* célébéen; (*b*) *s.* Célébéen, -éenne.

celebrant ['selibrənt], *s. Ecc:* célébrant *m*; officiant *m*.

celebrate ['selibreit], *v.tr.* **1.** *Ecc:* (*a*) célébrer (la messe, un mariage, une fête); **the marriage will be celebrated at . . .,** la bénédiction nuptiale sera donnée à . . .; (*b*) *abs.* célébrer la messe; célébrer; officier. **2.** (*a*) célébrer, glorifier (la mémoire de qn); célébrer, commémorer, solenniser (un événement); (*b*) *F:* fêter (qch.).

celebrated ['selibreitid], *a.* célèbre (**for sth.,** par qch.); renommé (**for,** pour).

celebration [seli'breiʃ(ə)n], *s.* **1.** *Ecc:* célébration *f* (de l'office divin, de la communion, d'une fête); **to go to early c.,** communier de bonne heure, à un office du matin; **the Easter celebrations,** les solennités *f* de Pâques. **2.** (*a*) célébration, commémoration *f* (d'un événement, etc.); (*b*) manifestation *f* de sympathie (à l'occasion de l'avancement, de la retraite, de qn, etc.); (*c*) *F:* **this calls for a c.!** il faut fêter ça! ça s'arrose!

celebrity [si'lebriti], *s.* **1.** célébrité *f*, renommée *f*. **2.** (*pers.*) célébrité.

celeriac [si'leriæk], *s. Hort:* céleri-rave *m*, *pl.* céleris-raves.

celeripede [si'leripi:d], *s. A:* célérifère *m*.

celerity [si'leriti], *s.* célérité *f*.

celery ['seləri], *s.* **1.** *Hort:* céleri *m*; **turnip-rooted c.,** céleri-rave *m*; **head of c.,** pied *m* de céleri. **2.** *Bot:* **wild c.,** (i) ache *f*; (ii) vallisnérie *f* spirale.

celesta [si'lestə], *s. Mus:* célesta *m*.

celeste [si'lest]. **1.** *a. & s.* bleu céleste (*m*) *inv*. **2.** *s. Mus:* (*organ stop*) voix *f* céleste.

celestial [si'lestiəl]. **1.** *a.* (*a*) céleste; **c. sphere,** sphère *f* céleste; *Aer:* **c. navigation,** navigation *f* (par visée) astronomique; (*for missiles*) **(radio-)c. guidance,** guidage *m* (radio-)astronomique; (*b*) *A:* **the C. Empire,** le Céleste Empire. **2.** *s.* (*a*) esprit *m* céleste; habitant *m* du ciel; (*b*) *A:* Céleste *mf*; Chinois, -oise.

celestine[1] ['selesti:n], *a. & s. Ecc:* (*monk*) célestin; (*nun*) célestine.

celestine[2] ['selesti:n, sə'lestain], **celestite** ['selestait, sə'lestait], *s. Miner:* célestin *m*, célestine *f*.

celi- ['si:li], *pref.* = COELI-.

celibacy ['selibəsi], *s.* célibat *m*.

celibate ['selibət]. **1.** *a.* (personne *f*) célibataire; (vie *f*) de célibataire. **2.** *s.* célibataire *mf*.

cell [sel], *s.* **1.** (*a*) cellule *f* (de moine, d'ermite); (*b*) (*in prison*) cellule, cachot *m*; cabanon *m*; **the cells,** les locaux *m* disciplinaires (d'un poste de police); *Mil:* **three days' cells,** trois jours de cellule; (*c*) *Arch:* canton *m* (d'une voûte); (*d*) *Ap:* cellule, alvéole *m* (de ruche); (*e*) *Av:* cellule; (*f*) *Bot: etc:* loge *f*; (*g*) *Ent:* cellule (des ailes d'un insecte). **2.** *El: Elcs: etc:* (*a*) élément *m* (de pile); couple *m*; **carbon-zinc c.,** élément charbon-zinc; **cadmium, Weston, c.,** élément, pile *f*, au cadmium; pile (étalon) Weston; **bias c.,** pile de polarisation; **solar c.,** pile solaire; **weak c.,** pile usée; **inert c.,** pile non amorcée; **active c.,** élément chargé; **control c.,** élément témoin; **dry c.,** pile sèche; **wet c.,** pile humide, à liquide; **porous c.,** vase poreux; **c. arrangement,** montage *m* des piles; **three-c. battery,** batterie *f* à trois éléments; **storage c.,** (i) élément d'accumulateur; (ii) *Cmptr:* cellule de mémoire; *Cmptr:* **data c. storage,** mémoire *f* de masse à cellules; **binary c.,** position *f*, élément, binaire; (*b*) **electrolytic c.,** cuve *f* électrolytique; cellule électrolytique, d'électrolyse; (*c*) **photoelectric c.,** cellule photoélectrique; (*d*) *T.V:* **Kerr c.,** cellule de Kerr. **3.** (*a*) *Biol:* cellule; **mother c.,** cellule mère; **granule c.,** cellule granuleuse; **c. membrane,** membrane *f* cellulaire; **c. wall,** paroi *f* cellulaire; **c. sap,** suc *m* cellulaire; **air c.,** (i) *Anat:* vésicule *f*, alvéole, pulmonaire; (ii) *Bot:* vésicule; (iii) vésicule aérienne (des siphonophores); *Bot:* **apical c.,** cellule apicale; *Anat:* **ganglion c.,** ganglion nerveux; **blood c.,** globule *m*; **white blood c.,** globule blanc; **red blood c.,** globule rouge, hématie *f*; (*b*) *Coel:* **thread c.,** nématocyste *m*, cnidoblaste *m*. **4.** *Pol: Ind:* **communist c.,** cellule, noyau *m*, communiste. **5.** *Meteor:* cellule (anticyclonique, de convection).

cella ['selə], *s. Arch: Ant:* cella *f*.

cellar[1] ['selər], *s.* (*a*) cave *f*; (*small*) caveau *m*; (*above ground*) cellier *m*; **wine c.,** cave à vin; **to keep a good c.,** avoir une bonne cave; (*b*) (*cheesemaking*) cave; (*c*) chai *m* (de négociant en vins).

cellar[2], *v.tr.* encaver (du vin); mettre (du vin) en cave, en chai.

cellarage ['selәridʒ], *s.* **1.** emmagasinage *m* (en cave); encavement *m*. **2.** *coll.* caves *fpl*. **3.** cavage *m*.

cellarer ['selərər], *s.m. Ecc:* cellérier, sommelier.

cellaress ['selәres], *s.f. Ecc:* cellérière.

cellaret [selə'ret], *s.* cave *f* à liqueurs (de buffet).

cellaring ['seləriŋ], *s.* mise *f* en cave; avalage *m* (du vin); mise en cellier; rentrage *m* (du bois de chauffage, etc.).

cellarman, *pl.* **-men** ['seləmən], *s.m.* caviste; sommelier.

cellated ['seleitid], **celled** [seld], *a.* **1.** *Biol:* cellulé. **2. celled:** *Biol: etc:* **one-c., two-c.,** à une cellule, à deux cellules; *El:* **two-c. battery,** batterie *f* à deux piles; accumulateur *m* à deux éléments.

cellepora [seli'pɔ:rə], *s. Prot:* cellepora *m*, cellépore *m*.

Celleporidae [seli'pɔridi:], *s.pl. Prot:* celléporidés *m*.

celliform ['selifɔ:m], *a. Biol:* celluliforme.

cellifugal [se'lifjug(ə)l], *a. Physiol:* cellifuge.

'cellist ['tʃelist], *s. Mus:* violoncelliste *mf*.

'cello ['tʃelou], *s. Mus:* violoncelle *m*.

cellobiase [selou'baiæs], *s. Ch:* cellobiase *f*.

cellobiose [selou'baious], *s. Ch:* cellobiose *f*.

celloidin [se'lɔidin], *s. Phot: etc:* celloïdine *f*.

'celloist ['tʃelouist], *s. Mus:* violoncelliste *mf*.

Cellophane ['seləfein], *s. R.t.m:* Cellophane *f*.

cellular ['seljulər], *a.* **1.** *Biol:* cellulaire, celluleux; **c. structure,** structure *f* cellulaire; **c. line,** lignée *f* de cellules. **2.** cellulaire, alvéolaire; alvéolé; à alvéoles; **c. girder,** poutre *f* cellulaire; *I.C.E:* **c. radiator,** radiateur *m* cellulaire, alvéolaire, à nid d'abeilles; *Tex:* **c. linen,** cellular *m* (pour chemises, etc.); **c. blanket,** couverture *f* (de lit) en maille aérée. **3.** *Bot:* **c. plant,** plante *f* cellulaire. **4.** *s. Tex:* cellular *m*.

cellularity [selju'læriti], *s.* cellularisme *m*.

cellulase ['seljuleis], *s. Biol:* cellulase *f*.

cellulate(d) ['seljuleit(id)], *a. Nat.Hist:* cellulé, celluleux.

cellule ['selju:l], *s.* **1.** *Physiol: Nat.Hist:* cellule *f*; (*small*) favéole *f*. **2.** *Av: O:* cellule (de biplan).

cellulifugal [selju'lifjug(ə)l], *a. Physiol:* cellulifuge.

cellulin ['seljulin], *s. Bot:* cellulines *f*.

cellulipetal [selju'lipit(ə)l], *a. Physiol:* cellulipète.

cellulitis [selju'laitis], *s. Med:* cellulite *f*.

celluloid ['seljulɔid], *s.* celluloïd(e) *m*.

cellulose ['seljulous]. **1.** *a.* celluleux. **2.** *s.* cellulose *f*; **starch c.,** amyline *f*; *Tex:* **c. acetate,** acétate *m* de cellulose; cellite *f*; *Ind:* **c. varnish,** vernis *m* cellulosique; **c. finish, c. enamel,** émail *m* cellulosique, à la cellulose; **c. tape,** ruban adhésif, Scotch *m* (*R.t.m:*).

cellulosity [selju'lɔsiti], *s.* cellulosité *f*.

cellulous ['seljuləs], *a.* celluleux.

celosia [si'lousiə, -ʃə], *s. Bot:* célosie *f*.

Celotex ['selouteks], *s. R.t.m:* Célotex *m*.

celsia ['selsiə], *s. Bot:* celsia *m*.

celsian ['selsiən], *s. Miner:* celsiane *f*.

Celsius ['selsiəs], *Pr.n.m. Ph:* **C. thermometer,** thermomètre *m* de Celsius.

Celsus ['selsəs], *Pr.n.m. A.Hist:* Celse.

celt[1] [kelt], *s. Archeol:* celt *m*, éolithe *m*.

Celt[2], *s. Ethn:* Celte *mf*.

Celtiberi [selti'bi:rai], *Pr.n.pl. Hist:* Celtibères *m*.

Celtiberia [selti'bi:riə], *Pr.n. Hist:* Celtibérie *f*.

Celtiberian [selti'bi:riən], *Hist:* (*a*) *a.* celtibérien; (*b*) *s.* Celtibère *mf*, Celtibérien, -ienne.

Celtic ['keltik, *occ.* 'seltik]. **1.** *a. Ethn:* celtique; celte; **the C. fringe,** l'Écosse, l'Irlande, et le Pays de Galles. **2.** *s. Ling:* le celtique; les langues *f* celtiques.

Celticism ['keltisizm], *s.* celticisme *m*.

Celticist ['keltisist], *s.* = CELTIST.

Celtish ['keltiʃ], *a.* celtique.

Celtist ['keltist], *s.* celtiste *m*; celtisant, -ante.

celtium ['seltiəm], *s. Miner:* celtium *m*.

Celto- ['keltou], *comb.fm.* celto-.

Celtologist [kelt'ɔlədʒist], *s.* celtiste *m*, celtisant, -ante.

Celtomania [keltou'meiniə], *s.* celtomanie *f*.

Celtophil ['keltoufil], *s.* celtophile *mf*.

cembra ['sembrə], *s. Bot:* **c. pine,** cembro *m*.

cement[1] [si'ment], *s.* **1.** *Const: Civ.E:* ciment *m*; **Portland c.,** ciment Portland; **bauxite c., (high) alumina c.,** ciment fondu, ciment alumineux; **blast-furnace c.,** ciment de haut fourneau; **slow-setting c.,** ciment à prise lente; **quick-setting c.,** ciment prompt, à prise rapide; **expanding c.,** ciment expansif; **hydraulic c.,** mortier *m* hydraulique; **marble c.,** plâtre aluné; **iron c.,** ciment de fer; **c. manufacturer, c. worker,** cimentier *m*; **c. factory, c. works,** cimenterie *f*; **c. mixer,** bétonnière *f*. **2.** (*binding element*) ciment; mastic *m*; lut *m*; **gasket c.,** enduit *m*, ciment, pour joints; **iron c.,** mastic de fer. **3.** *Anat:* cément *m* (d'une dent). **4.** *Geol:* ciment. **5.** *Metall:* cément. **6.** précipité de sulfure d'or (obtenu dans l'extraction par chloruration).

cement[2], *v.tr.* **1.** (*a*) cimenter (des pierres, des briques); cimenter, consolider (la paix, une amitié); (*b*) cimenter, enduire d'une couche de ciment, mettre en ciment (une paroi, le fond d'un puits, etc.). **2.** lier au ciment; coller. **3.** *Dent:* mastiquer, obturer (une dent). **4.** *Metall:* cémenter (le fer).

cemental [si'mentl], *a. Metall:* cémenteux.

cementation [si:men'teiʃ(ə)n], *s.* **1.** cimentage *m*, cimentation *f*; collage *m*. **2.** *Metall:* cémentation *f*; **c. powder,** cément *m*; poudre *f* à cémenter.

cementatory [si'mentətəri], *a. Metall:* cémentatoire.

cemented [si'mentid], *a.* cimenté, consolidé; *Opt:* **c. lens,** objectif *m* à lentilles collées.

cementing[1] [si'mentiŋ], *a. Const:* cimentaire; *Metall:* cémenteux.

cementing[2], *s.* **1.** = CEMENTATION. **2.** masticage *m,* obturation *f* (d'une dent).
cementite [si'mentait], *s. Metall:* cémentite *f.*
cementoblast [si'mentoublæst], *s. Anat:* cémentoblaste *m.*
cemetery ['semətri], *s.* cimetière *m.*
cenacle ['senəkl], *s.* **1.** *Ant: B:* cénacle *m.* **2.** cénacle littéraire.
ceno- ['senou], *pref. see* COENO-.
cenobite ['senoubait], *s.* = COENOBITE.
cenogenesis [senou'dʒenisis], *s. Biol:* cænogénèse *f,* cénogénèse *f.*
Cenomanian [senou'meiniən], *a. & s. Geol:* cénomanien (*m*).
cenosite ['senəsait], *s. Miner:* cénosite *f.*
cenotaph ['senətæf], *s.* cénotaphe *m;* **the C.,** le cénotaphe de Whitehall.
cenote [se'nouti], *s. Geog:* (*esp. in Central America*) cénoté *m.*
Cenozoic [senou'zouik], *a. & s. Geol:* cénozoïque (*m*).
cense [sens], *v.tr. Ecc:* encenser; **to c. the priest three times,** donner trois coups d'encensoir au prêtre.
censer ['sensər], *s. Ecc:* encensoir *m;* **c. bearer,** encenseur *m,* thuriféraire *m.*
censor[1] ['sensər], *s.* **1.** (*a*) *Rom.Ant:* censeur *m;* (*b*) *Adm: Mil:* censeur; **the Board of Censors, the Censor's office,** la Censure; **the film c.,** la censure cinématographique; *Cin:* **c. print,** copie approuvée par la censure; **play banned by the c.,** pièce interdite par la censure; (*c*) censeur, critiqueur *m* (des actions d'autrui). **2.** *Psy:* **the c.,** la censure.
censor[2], *v.tr.* **1.** (*a*) interdire, censurer (une pièce de théâtre); (*b*) soumettre (une pièce, etc.) à des coupures; caviarder (un article); censurer (un film). **2. to be censored,** (i) (*of article, play, etc.*) passer par la censure; (*of letter*) passer par le contrôle; (ii) être interdit, supprimé, par la censure; (iii) être expurgé; être soumis à des coupures; *Journ:* **censored passage** (*blocked out*), caviar *m.*
censorial [sen'sɔ:riəl], *a.* censorial, -aux.
censoring ['sensəriŋ], *s.* censure *f* (des journaux, etc.).
censorious [sen'sɔ:riəs], *a.* **1.** porté à censurer; sévère (**of, upon,** pour); **c. air,** air *m* de censeur; **it is easy to be c.,** la critique est aisée. **2. c. remark,** observation malveillante.
censoriousness [sen'sɔ:riəsnis], *s.* **1.** penchant *m* à la censure; disposition *f* à critiquer. **2.** malveillance *f.*
censorship ['sensəʃip], *s.* **1.** *Adm:* (*a*) **the c.,** la censure; (*b*) **postal c.,** contrôle postal; *Adm:* **c. of the press,** régime préventif; **papers under c.,** presse soumise à la censure. **2.** *Psy:* = CENSOR[1] 2.
censurable ['senʃərəbl], *a.* censurable, blâmable; digne de censure.
censure[1] ['senʃər], *s.* censure *f,* blâme *m,* condamnation *f; Jur:* réprimande *f;* **to deserve c.,** mériter des reproches; **deserving of c.,** répréhensible; **to incur (a) c.,** s'attirer un blâme; **to incur general c.,** encourir l'animadversion générale; être unanimement critiqué; **to incur the c. of the Church,** encourir les censures de l'Église; **the fear of public c.,** la crainte de la réprobation publique; **vote of c.,** motion *f* de censure.
censure[2], *v.tr.* censurer; (i) blâmer, condamner; (ii) critiquer.
censurer ['senʃərər], *s.* censeur *m* (des actions d'autrui).
census ['sensəs], *s.* recensement *m; Adm:* **to take a c. of the population,** faire le recensement de la population; dénombrer la population; *Mil: A:* **c. of horses,** conscription *f* des chevaux; **c. paper,** bulletin *m,* feuille *f,* de recensement.
cent [sent], *s.* **1.** *Num:* (*a*) cent *m;* (*b*) *F:* (*small coin*) sou *m,* liard *m; U.S:* **red c.,** sou (de bronze); **I haven't a red c.,** je n'ai pas le sou; **to pay to the last c.,** payer jusqu'au dernier sou. **2. per c.,** pour cent; **commission of ten per c.,** commission de dix pour cent; *Fin:* **the three per cents,** le trois pour cent, le 3%; (*of investment*) **to bring in nine per c.,** rapporter neuf pour cent, 9%; *Ch: etc:* **thirty per c. solution,** solution *f* à trente pour cent; **sixty per c. of the candidates passed the examination,** soixante pour cent des candidats ont été reçus à l'examen; **a hundred per c. efficient,** efficace au maximum.
cental ['sent(ə)l], *s. Meas:* (*for cereals*) quintal, -aux *m* (de cent livres anglaises).
centaur ['sentɔ:r], *s.m.* **1.** *Myth:* centaure. **2.** *Astr:* **the C.,** le Centaure.
centaurea [sen'tɔ:riə], *s. Bot:* centaurée *f.*
centauress ['sentɔ:res], *s.f. Myth:* centauresse.
centauromachia [sentərou'mækiə], **centauromachy** [sentə'rɔməki], *s. Myth:* centauromachie *f.*
centaury ['sentɔ:ri], *s. Bot:* centaurée *f.Esp.* (*a*) **great c.,** grande centaurée; (*b*) **lesser c., common c.,** petite centaurée; fiel *m* de terre; érythrée *f;* herbe *f* à mille florins.
centavo [sen'teivou], *s. Num:* centavo *m.*
centenarian [senti'neəriən], *a. & s.* (*pers.*) centenaire (*mf*).
centenary [sen'ti:nəri]. **1.** *a. & s.* (anniversaire) centenaire (*m*). **2.** *s. A:* = CENTURY 1.
centennial [sen'teniəl]. **1.** *a.* centennal, -aux; séculaire. **2.** *s. U.S: N.Z:* = CENTENARY 1.
centering ['sentəriŋ], *s.* = CENTRING.
centesimal [sen'tesim(ə)l], *a.* centésimal, -aux.
centetid [sen'tetid], *s. Z:* centète *m.*
Centetidae [sen'tetidi:], *s.pl. Z:* centétidés *m.*
centi- ['senti], *pref.* centi-.
centiare ['sentiɑ:r], *s. Meas:* centiare *m.*
centibar ['sentibɑ:r], *s. Meteor:* centibar *m.*
centigrade ['sentigreid], *a. Meas:* centigrade; centésimal, -aux; **c. thermometer,** thermomètre *m* centigrade.
centigram(me) ['sentigræm], *s. Meas:* centigramme *m.*
centile ['sentail], *s. Stat:* centile *m,* percentile *m.*
centilitre ['sentili:tər], *s. Meas:* centilitre *m.*
centime ['senti:m, sɑ̃-], *s. Num:* centime *m.*
centimetre ['sentimi:tər], *s. Meas:* centimètre *m;* **square c.,** centimètre carré; **cubic c.,** centimètre cube; millilitre *m; Ph.Meas:* **c.-gramme-second,** centimètre-gramme-seconde *m; pl.* **centimetre-gramme-seconds,** centimètres-grammes-secondes.
centinormal [senti'nɔ:ml], *a. Ch: etc:* centinormal, -aux.
centipede ['sentipi:d], *s. Myr:* scolopendre *f,* myriapode *m, F:* mille-pattes *m inv.*
centipoise ['sentipɔiz], *s. Meas:* centipoise *m.*
centner ['sentnər], *s. Meas:* **1.** (*a*) quintal *m,* -aux (de 50 kilos); (*b*) = CENTAL. **2. metric c.,** mesure *f* de 100 kilos.
cento ['sentou], *s. Mus: Lit:* centon *m;* pastiche *m.*
central ['sentr(ə)l]. **1.** *a.* (*a*) central, -aux; **c. point,** centre *m;* **in a c. position,** situé au centre; **the c. car park,** le parking au centre de la ville; **c. heating,** chauffage central; *Fin:* **c. bank,** banque centrale; **c. monetary institutions,** établissements *m* monétaires de l'État; *Cmptr:* **c. computer,** ordinateur central; **c. data base,** fichier central; **c. processing unit, c. processor,** unité centrale; *Geog:* **C. America,** Amérique Centrale; *Hist:* **the C. Powers,** les Puissances *f* de l'Europe centrale; (*b*) modéré; **c. tendency,** tendance *f* à la moyenne. **2.** *s. U.S:* (*a*) *Tp:* central *m* (téléphonique); (*b*) bureau central.
centralism ['sentrəlizm], *s. Pol:* centralisme *m.*
centralist ['sentrəlist], *s. Pol:* centraliste *mf;* centralisateur, -trice.
centrality [sen'træliti], *s.* centralité *f;* position *f* au centre.
centralization [sentrəlai'zeiʃ(ə)n], *s.* centralisation *f.*
centralize ['sentrəlaiz]. **1.** *v.tr.* centraliser. **2.** *v.i.* se centraliser.
centralized ['sentrəlaizd], *a.* centralisé; **c. planning,** planification centralisée; *Cmptr:* **c. data planning,** traitement centralisé, gestion centralisée, de l'information.
centralizer ['sentrəlaizər], *s.* centralisateur, -trice.
centralizing ['sentrəlaiziŋ], *a.* centralisateur, -trice.
centrally ['sentrəli], *adv.* centralement; **c. located, situated,** central.
centranthus [sen'trænθəs], *s. Bot:* centranthe *m,* centranthus *m;* valériane *f.*
centrarchid [sen'trɑ:kid], *s. Ich:* centrarchidé *m.*
Centrarchidae [sen'trɑ:kidi:], *s.pl. Ich:* centrarchidés *m.*
centre[1] ['sentər], *s.* (*a*) centre *m* (d'un cercle, de la terre, d'une ville, etc.); milieu *m* (d'une table, etc.); corps *m,* centre (d'une roue); **in the c.,** au centre, au milieu; **the great urban centres, the great centres of population,** les grandes agglomérations urbaines; **business c.,** centre des affaires; **commercial c.,** centre commercial; **industrial c.,** centre industriel; **civic, community, c.,** centre civique, social; **infant welfare c.,** consultation *f* de nourrissons; **maternity child welfare c.,** centre de protection maternelle et infantile; **(rural) health c.,** centre médical, d'hygiène (rural); *Med:* **c. of infection,** foyer *m* d'infection; *Geol:* **seismic c.,** centre séismique, d'un séisme; *Meteor:* **storm c.,** centre de dépression; **c. of action,** centre d'action; *Ph:* **c. of gravity,** centre de gravité; **c. of attraction,** (i) *Ph:* centre d'attraction, de gravitation; (ii) *Fig:* clou *m* (d'une fête, etc.); **she was the c. of attraction,** c'était sur elle que portaient tous les regards; **c. of interest,** centre d'intérêt; *N.Arch:* **c. of buoyancy,** centre de carène; *Nau:* **c. of effort of the sails,** point *m* vélique; centre de poussée; **c. board,** (quille *f* de) dérive *f;* dériveur *m;* **c. boarder,** yacht *m* à quille de dérive; *Tls:* **c. square,** équerre *f* à centrer; **c. finder,** centreur *m;* **c. pin,** cheville ouvrière; **c. line,** ligne médiane; axe *m* (d'une voiture, d'une route); **out of c.,** décentré; *Aut: etc:* **c. to c. of bearings,** entre-axe *m* des roulements; *Cmptr:* **data (processing) c.,** centre de calcul, de traitement de l'information; **c. piece,** pièce maîtresse (d'un système); **c. cutting, slitting,** coupe *f* en Y; (*b*) *Const:* cintre *m;* **c. striking,** décintrement *m;* (*c*) *Mec.E:* pointe *f* (d'un tour); **live c.,** pointe mobile (de la poupée); **height of centres,** hauteur *f* des pointes; **c. mark,** coup *m,* trou *m,* de pointeau; *Tls:* **c. punch,** pointeau *m,* amorçoir *m;* **bell, self-centring, c., punch,** pointeau à cloche; (*d*) *Sp:* (i) (*esp. Fb., hockey*) **c. (forward),** avant-centre *m;* **c. half,** demi-centre *m;* (ii) *Fb: etc:* envoi *m* du ballon au centre du terrain; (*e*) *attrib.* central, -aux; du centre; *Pol:* **the c. (party),** les membres *mpl* du Centre; **the c. right, left,** le centre droit, gauche; *Arch:* **c. arch,** arche centrale, du centre; *Rail:* **c. rail,** (i) crémaillère *f* (de chemin de fer de montagne); (ii) rail conducteur (de train électrique); **c. rib,** âme *f* (de rail).
centre[2], *v.tr. & i.* **1.** (*a*) *v.tr.* placer (qch.) au centre; axer (qch.) sur; *v.tr. & i.* **to c., to be centred, on, about, (a)round, s.o., sth.,** se concentrer dans, sur, autour de, qn, qch.; aboutir à qch.; s'appuyer, reposer, sur qn; **to c. one's affections on s.o.,** concentrer, rassembler, toute son affection sur qn; **all his thoughts were centred on . . .,** toutes ses pensées convergeaient vers . . ., gravitaient, tournaient, autour de . . .; **the whole debate centres, is centred, on one idea,** tout le débat se circonscrit autour d'une seule idée; (*b*) *v.tr.* centrer (une roue, une pièce sur le tour, une lentille sur l'axe optique, etc.); amorcer (un trou) au pointeau; (*c*) *v.tr. Cin: Phot:* centrer, cadrer (une photo); (*d*) *v.tr. & i. Fb: etc:* centrer (le ballon, etc.); (*e*) *Const:* cintrer (une voûte); (*f*) *NAm:* être au centre de (qch.). **2.** *v.i. Cmptr:* **to c. slit,** faire une coupe en Y.
centre-dot ['sentədɔt], *v.tr. Metalw:* amorcer (un trou) au pointeau.
centrepiece ['sentəpi:s], *s.* (pièce *f* de) milieu *m;* surtout *m,* girandole *f, A:* dormant *m* (de table).
centric(al) ['sentrik(əl)], *a.* (*a*) du centre; central, -aux; (*b*) *Anat:* qui se rapporte à un centre nerveux.
centricity [sen'trisiti], *s.* centralité *f.*
centrifugal [sentri'fju:gl, sen'trif-], *a.* **1.** centrifuge; (*a*) *Ph:* **c. force,** force *f* centrifuge; (*b*) *Hyd.E:* **c. pump,** pompe *f* centrifuge; *Ind:* **c. machine,** *s.* **centrifugal,** centrifugeur *m;* centrifugeuse *f;* **c. casting,** moulage *m* par centrifugation. **2.** (*of cream, etc.*) centrifugé.
centrifugalize [sentri'fju:gəlaiz], **centrifuge**[1] ['sentrifju:dʒ], *v.tr. Ind:* centrifuger (un liquide).
centrifugally [sentri'fju:gəli], *adv. Tchn:* **to cast c.,** mouler, couler, par centrifugation.
centrifugation [sentrifju'geiʃ(ə)n], *s.* centrifugation *f.*
centrifuge[2], *s.* centrifugeur *m,* centrifugeuse *f.*
centring ['sentriŋ], *s.* **1.** centrage *m,* guidage *m* (d'une pièce sur le tour, etc.); *Cin:* **c. of the film image,** cadrage *m; Mec.E:* **c. machine,** machine *f* à centrer; **c. tool,** centreur *m.* **2.** *Const:* (*a*) cintrage *m* (d'une voûte); (*b*) cintre *m* (échafaudage en arc.); **to strike the c. of an arch,** décintrer une voûte; **striking of the c.,** décintrement *m.*
centriole ['sentrioul], *s. Biol:* centriole *f.*
centripetal [sen'tripətl], *a. Ph: Biol: Bot:* centripète; **c. force, tendency,** force *f* centripète.
Centriscidae [sen'triskidi:], *s.pl. Ich:* centriscidés *m.*
centriscus [sen'triskəs], *s. Ich:* centrisque *m.*
centrist ['sentrist], *Pol:* **1.** *s.* centriste *mf,* membre *m* du parti du centre. **2.** *a.* (*of opinions, etc.*) du centre, centriste.
centro- ['sentrou], *pref.* centro-.
centrocercus [sentrou'sə:kəs], *s. Orn:* centrocerque *m.*
centrolecithal [sentrou'lesiθəl], *a. Biol:* centrolécithe.
centromere ['sentroumiər], *s. Biol:* centromère *m.*
centrosoma [sentrou'soumə], **centrosome** ['sentrousoum], *s. Biol:* centrosome *m.*
centrosphere ['sentrousfiər], *s.* centrosphère *f.*
centrotus [sen'troutəs], *s. Ent:* centrote *m.*
centrum ['sentrəm], *s.* **1.** *Anat: Z:* centrum *m.* **2.** *Meteor:* foyer réel, centre *m* (d'un séisme).
centunculus [sen'tʌŋkjuləs], *s. Bot:* centunculus *m.*
centuple[1] ['sentju:pl], *a. & s.* centuple (*m*).
centuple[2], *v.tr.* centupler.
centuplicate[1] [sen'tju:plikət], *a.* centuplé.
centuplicate[2] [sen'tju:plikeit], *v.tr.* centupler.
centuriate [sen'tju:rieit], *a. Rom.Ant:* centuriate.
centuriation [sentjuri'eiʃ(ə)n], *s. Rom.Ant:* centuriation *f.*
centurion [sen'tjuəriən], *s. Rom.Hist:* centurion *m; B:* centenier *m.*
century ['sentjəri], *s.* **1.** siècle *m;* **in the nineteenth c.,** au dix-neuvième siècle; **trees centuries old,** arbres *m*

séculaires. **2.** *Rom.Hist:* centurie *f.* **3.** *Cr:* centaine, série *f* de cent. **4.** *U.S: F:* cent dollars. **5.** *Bot:* **c. plant,** agave *m* d'Amérique.
cepaceous [si'peiʃəs], *a.* cépacé.
cepe [sep], *s. Fung:* cèpe *m.*
cephalalgia [sefə'lældʒiə], *s. Med:* céphalalgie *f,* céphalée *f.*
cephalanthus [sefə'lænθəs], *s. Bot:* céphalanthe *m.*
cephalaspis [sefə'læspis], *s. Paleont:* céphalaspis *m.*
cephalate ['sefəleit], *a. Ent: Moll:* céphalé.
cephalhaematoma [sefəlhi:mə'toumə], *s. Med:* céphalématome *m.*
cephalic [se'fælik]. **1.** *a.* céphalique; *Anat:* **c. vein,** veine *f* céphalique, céphalique *f*; *Anthr:* **c. index,** indice *m* céphalique. **2.** *s. Pharm: A:* remède *m* céphalique, pour les maux de tête.
cephalin ['sefəlin], *s. Bio-Ch:* céphaline *f.*
cephalization [sefəlai'zeiʃ(ə)n], *s.* céphalisation *f.*
Cephalochorda, -data ['sefəlou'kɔ:də, -deitə], *s.pl. Z:* céphalocordés *m.*
cephalogenesis ['sefəlou'dʒenəsis], *s.* céphalogénèse *f.*
cephalograph [se'fælougræf], *s. Anthr:* céphalographe *m.*
cephaloid ['sefəlɔid], *a. Biol:* céphaloïde.
cephalometer [sefə'lɔmitər], *s. Anthr:* céphalomètre *m.*
cephalometric [sefəlou'metrik], *a. Anthr:* céphalométrique.
cephalometry [sefə'lɔmitri], *s. Anthr:* céphalométrie *f.*
Cephalonia [sefə'louniə], *Pr.n. Geog:* Céphalonie *f.*
cephalopagus [sefəlou'peigəs], *s. Ter:* céphalopage *m.*
cephalopagy [sefə'lɔpədʒi], *s. Ter:* céphalopagie *f.*
cephalopod ['sefəloupɔd], *s. Moll:* céphalopode *m.*
Cephalopoda [sefəlou'poudə], *s.pl. Moll:* céphalopodes *m.*
cephalo-rachidian ['sefəlouræ'kidiən], *a.* céphalo-rachidien, *pl.* céphalo-rachidiens.
cephalo-spinal ['sefəlou'spainl], *a.* céphalo-spinal, -aux.
cephalosporium ['sefəlou'spɔriəm], *s. Fung:* céphalosporium *m.*
cephalotaxus ['sefəlou'tæksəs], *s. Bot:* céphalotaxus *m.*
cephalothorax ['sefəlou'θɔ:ræks], *s. Arach: Crust:* céphalothorax *m.*
cephalotome ['sefəloutoum], *s. Surg:* trépan perforatif.
cephalotribe ['sefəloutraib], *s. Obst:* céphalotribe *m.*
Cephalotus [sefə'loutəs], *s. Bot:* céphalote *m.*
Cepheid ['sefi:d, 'si:-], *a. & s. Astr.* **C. (variable),** céphéide *f.*
cephenomyia [sefi:nou'maiə], *s. Ent:* céphénomyie *m.*
cephid ['sefid], *s. Ent:* cèphe *m.*
Cephidae ['sefidi:], *s.pl. Ent:* céphidés *m.*
Cephisodotus [sefisou'doutəs], *Pr.n.m. Gr.Ant:* Céphisodote.
Cephissus [si'fisəs], *Pr.n. A.Geog:* le (fleuve) Céphise.
cephus ['sefəs], *s. Ent:* cèphe *m.*
ceraceous [sə'reiʃəs], *a.* céracé.
ceramal ['serəmæl], *s.* cermet *m* (matériau mixte céramique-métal).
Cerambycidae [seræm'baisidi:], *s.pl. Ent:* cérambycidés *m.*
cerambycoid [seræm'baikɔid], *s. Ent:* cérambycidé *m.*
ceramic [sə'ræmik], *a.* céramique.
ceramics [sə'ræmiks], *s.pl.* (*usu. with sg.const.*) la céramique.
ceramist ['serəmist], *s.* céramiste *m.*
ceramium [sə'ræmiəm, -'reim-], *s. Algae:* céramium *m.*
ceramographic [serəmou'græfik], *a.* céramographique.
ceramography [serə'mɔgrəfi], *s.* céramographie *f.*
cerargyrite [sə'rɑ:dʒirait], *s. Miner:* cérargyrite *f*; argent corné.
cerasin ['serəsin], *s. Ch:* cérasine *f.*
cerastes [si'ræsti:z], *s. Rept:* céraste *m.*
cerastium [si'ræstiəm], *s. Bot:* céraiste *m.*
cerate[1] ['siəreit], *s. Pharm:* cérat *m.*
cerate[2], *a. Orn:* cérastium.
ceratias [se'rɑ:tiəs], *s. Ich:* cérastium *m.*
Ceratiidae [serə'ti:idi:], *s.pl. Ich:* cérati(i)dés *m,* ceratides *m.*
certian ['serətin], *s. Physiol: Ch:* kératine *f.*
ceratinous [sə'rætinəs], *a.* kératinique.
ceratioid [serə'ti:ɔid], *a. & s. Ich:* cératide (*m*).
ceratite ['serətait], *s. Paleont:* cératite *m.*
Ceratitis [serə'taitis], *s. Ent:* ceratitis *f.*
Ceratium [sə'reiʃiəm], *s. Algae:* ceratium *m,* cération *m.*
cerato- ['serətou-], *pref.* cérato-.
Ceratocampidae ['serətou'kæmpidi:], *s.pl. Ent:* cératocampides *m.*
ceratodus [sə'rætədəs], *s. Ich:* ceratodus *m.*
ceratogenous [serə'tɔdʒənəs], *a.* kératogène.
ceratoglossal ['serətou'glɔsl], *a. Anat:* cératoglosse.
ceratoglossus, *pl.* **-i** ['serətou'glɔsəs, -i], *s. Anat:* cératoglosse *m.*
ceratoid ['serətɔid], *a.* kératoïde.
Ceratophyllaceae ['serətoufi'leisii:], *s.pl.* cératophyll(ac)ées *f.*
Ceratopsidae [serə'tɔpsidi:], *s.pl. Paleont:* cératopsidés *m.*
ceratosaurus ['serətou'sɔ:rəs], *s. Paleont:* cératosaure *m,* ceratosaurus *m.*
Ceratostomella ['serətoustə'melə], *s. Fung:* ceratostomella *m.*
ceratotheca, *pl.* **-ae** ['serətou'θi:kə, -z:], *s. Ent:* cératothèque *f.*
ceratozamia ['serətou'zeimiə], *s. Bot:* ceratozamia *m.*
ceraunograph [sə'raunougræf], *s. Meteor:* céraunographe *m.*
Cerberus ['sə:bərəs], *Pr.n.m. Myth:* Cerbère.
cercaria, *pl.* **-ae** [sə'keəriə, -i:], *s. Ann:* cercaire *f.*
Cercocebus [sə:kou'si:bəs], *s. Z:* cercocèbe *m.*
Cercopidae [sə'kɔpidi:], *s.pl. Ent:* cercopidés *m.*
cercopith ['sə:koupiθ], *s. Z:* cercopithèque *m.*
Cercopithecidae ['sə:koupi'θi:sidi:], *s.pl. Z:* cercopithécidés *m.*
cercopithecoid ['sə:koupiθikɔid], *s. Z:* cercopithèque *m.*
cercopithecus ['sə:koupi'θi:kəs], *s. Z:* cercopithèque *m.*
cercospora [sə'kɔspərə], *s. Fung:* cercospora *m.*
cercosporella [sə:kɔspə'relə], *s. Fung:* cercosporella *m.*
cercosporiosis [sə:kɔspəri'ousis], *s. Bot:* cercosporiose *f.*
cercus ['sə:kəs], *s. Ent:* cerque *m.*
cere ['siər], *s. Orn:* cire *f* (du bec).
cereal ['siəriəl]. **1.** *a. & s.* céréale (*f*); **c. crops,** céréales. **2.** *s.pl.* **(breakfast) cereals,** céréales (en flocons).
cerealin ['siəriəlin], *s. Ch:* céréaline *f.*
cerealist ['siəriəlist], *s.* céréaliste *m.*
cerealose [siəriə'lous], *s. Ch:* céréalose *f.*
cerebellar [seri'belər], *a. Anat:* cérébelleux; **c. arteries,** artères cérébelleuses.
cerebellum [seri'beləm], *s. Anat:* cervelet *m.*
cerebral ['serəbrəl], *a.* **1.** cérébral, -aux. **2.** *Ling:* (consonne) cérébrale, rétroflexe, cacuminale.
cerebration [seri'breiʃ(ə)n], *s.* cérébration *f.*
Cerebratulus [seri'brætjuləs], *s. Ann:* cérébratule *m,* cerebratulus *m.*
cerebriform [sə'rebrifɔ:m], *a.* cérébriforme.
cerebrocardiac ['seribrou'kɑ:diæk], *a. Med:* cérébro-cardiaque, *pl.* cérébro-cardiaques.
cerebroid ['seribrɔid], *a.* cérébroïde.
cerebrology [seri'brɔlədʒi], *s.* cérébrologie *f.*
cerebrorachidian ['seribrouræ'kidiən], *a.* cérébro-rachidien, *pl.* cérébro-rachidiens.
cerebrosclerosis ['seribrouskle'rousis], *s.* cérébrosclérose *f.*
cerebroside ['seribrousaid], *s. Bio-Ch:* cérébroside *m.*
cerebrospinal ['seribrou'spainl], *a.* cérébro-spinal, -aux; **c. meningitis, c. fever,** méningite cérébro-spinale; **c. fluid,** liquide céphalo-rachidien.
cerebrum ['seribrəm], *s. Anat:* cerveau *m.*
cerecloth ['siəklɔθ], *s. A:* toile *f* d'embaumement.
cerement(s) ['siəmənt(s)], *s.* (*usu. pl.*) **1.** toile(s) *f* d'embaumement. **2.** *Lit:* linceul *m,* suaire *m.*
ceremonial [seri'mouniəl]. **1.** *a.* de cérémonie; *occ.* cérémonial, -aux; **c. visit,** visite *f* de cérémonie; *Mil:* **c. parade,** prise *f* d'armes. **2.** *s.* (*a*) cérémonial *m*; **Court c.,** l'étiquette *f* de la Cour; (*b*) (*book*) cérémonial; *R.C.Ch:* rituel *m.*
ceremonialism [seri'mouniəlizm], *s. often Pej:* cérémonialisme, ritualisme *m.*
ceremonialist [seri'mouniəlist], *s. esp. Ecc: often Pej:* ritualiste *mf.*
ceremonially [seri'mouniəli], *adv.* avec tout le cérémonial d'usage; en grande cérémonie.
ceremonious [seri'mouniəs], *a.* cérémonieux.
ceremoniously [seri'mouniəsli], *adv.* cérémonieusement; avec cérémonie; en cérémonie.
ceremoniousness [seri'mouniəsnis], *s.* manières cérémonieuses.
ceremony ['seriməni], *s.* **1.** cérémonie *f*; **with c.,** avec cérémonie; solennellement; **without c.,** sans formalités, sans cérémonie, sans façon; **without further c.,** sans plus de façons; **to stand on c.,** faire des cérémonies, des façons; **he doesn't stand on c. with them,** il les traite sans formalités; **he doesn't stand on c.,** il est simple, il ne tient pas aux formalités; **master of ceremonies,** maître *m* des cérémonies, (*at Court*) introducteur *m* des ambassadeurs, etc. **2.** (*function*) **to attend a c.,** assister à une cérémonie; **the marriage c.,** la cérémonie du mariage.
Ceres ['siəri:z], *Pr.n.f. Myth:* Cérès.
ceresine ['siərəsin,-i:n], *s. Ch:* cérésine *f.*
cereus ['siəriəs], *s. Bot:* cierge *m.*
ceria ['siəriə], *s. Ch:* oxyde *m* de cérium.
cerianthid [siri'ænθid], *s. Coel:* **c. (anemone),** cérianthe *m.*
Cerianthidae [siri'ænθidi:], *s.pl. Coel:* cérianthidés *m.*
cerianthus [siəri'ænθəs], *s. Coel:* cérianthe *m,* cerianthus *m.*
ceric[1] ['siərik], *a. Ch:* cérique, de cérium.
ceric[2], *a. Ch:* (acide *m*) cérique.
ceride ['siər(a)id], *s. Bio-Ch:* céride *f.*
ceriferous [siə'rifərəs], *a. Bot:* cérifère.
cerigerous [siə'ridʒərəs], *a. Orn:* cérigère.
cerin ['siərin], *s.* cérine *f.*
ceriph ['serif], *s. Typ:* (*at top of letter*) obit *m*; (*at foot of letter*) empattement *m.*
cerise [sə'ri:s], *a. & s.* (*colour*) cerise (*m*) *inv.*
cerite ['siərait], *s. Miner:* cérite *f*; silicate hydraté de cérium.
Cerithiidae [siəri'θi:idi:], *s.pl. Moll:* cérithiidés *m.*
cerithium [siə'riθiəm], *s. Moll:* cérithe *m,* cerithium *m.*
cerium ['siəriəm], *s. Ch:* cérium *m*; **c. dioxide,** dioxide *m* de cérium.
cermet ['sə:met], *s.* cermet *m* (matériau mixte céramique-métal).
cernuous ['sə:njuəs], *a. Bot:* (*of plant*) retombant, pendant; penché, incliné.
cerography [siə'rɔgrəfi], *s.* cérographie *f,* gravure *f* à l'encaustique.
cerolite ['siərəlait], *s. Miner:* cérolite *f.*
ceroma [siə'roumə], *s. Orn:* cire *f* (d'un bec d'oiseau).
ceroplastic [siərou'plæstik]. **1.** *a.* céroplastique; (panorama, etc.) modelé en cire. **2.** *s.pl.* **ceroplastics:** (*a*) (*usu. with sg.const.*) céroplastique *f*; (*b*) figures *f* de cire.
ceroplasty ['siərouplæsti], *s.* céroplastique *f.*
cerotic [siə'rɔtik], *a. Ch:* cérotique.
cerous ['siərəs], *a. Ch:* céreux.
cert [sə:t], *s. F:* (= CERTAINTY) **a dead c.,** une certitude (absolue); un coup sûr, une affaire sûre; *Turf:* un gagnant sûr; **it's a c.,** c'est couru.
certain ['sə:t(ə)n], *a.* certain. **1.** (*assured*) (*a*) **a c. cure,** une guérison certaine, assurée; **a c. success,** un succès infaillible, assuré; **this much, one thing, is c., that . . .,** ce qu'il y a de sûr, de certain, c'est que . . .; **it's absolutely c.,** *U.S:* **it's sure and c.,** c'est sûr et certain; **he is c. to come,** il viendra sûrement; il est certain qu'il viendra; **to my c. knowledge, they are . . .,** je sais pertinemment qu'ils sont . . .; (*b*) (*of pers.*) **to be c. of sth.,** être certain, sûr, de qch.; **I am almost c.,** j'en suis presque sûr, j'en ai la presque certitude; **I am c. that he will come,** je suis certain, sûr, qu'il viendra; **I am not c. that he will come,** je ne suis pas certain qu'il vienne; **I want to be c. about it,** je veux en avoir le cœur net; **to make s.o. c. of sth.,** donner à qn la certitude de qch.; (*c*) **to know sth. for c.,** savoir qch. pour certain; être bien sûr de qch.; savoir qch. à n'en pouvoir douter; **he will come for c.,** il viendra certainement, sûrement, à coup sûr; **I cannot say for c.,** je ne saurais dire avec certitude; je n'en suis pas bien certain; **I cannot say for c. when he will start,** je ne puis préciser la date, l'heure, de son départ; **I know for c. that . . .,** je sais à n'en pas douter que . . .; (*d*) **to make c. of sth.,** (i) s'assurer de qch.; constater qch.; (ii) s'assurer qch.; **to make c. of a seat,** s'assurer une place; (*e*) *Fin:* **to quote c.,** donner le certain; (*f*) *F:* **you shall have it tomorrow for c.,** vous l'aurez demain sans faute. **2.** (*a*) (*undetermined*) **there are c. things that . . .,** il y a certaines choses que . . .; **there is a c. pleasure in** + *ger.,* il y a un certain plaisir, une sorte de plaisir, à + *inf.*; **with women of a c. age,** chez les femmes d'un certain âge; *occ. Pej:* **a c. person,** (une) certaine personne; **c. people,** (de) certaines gens; certains *mpl*; **a c. Mr Thomas,** un certain M. Thomas; (*b*) **he used to write to me on a c. day,** il m'écrivait à jour fixe.
certainly ['sə:t(ə)nli], *adv.* (*a*) certainement; certes; assurément; à coup sûr; infailliblement; **most c.,** très certainement; (*b*) (*assent*) assurément; parfaitement; **you shall c. have it tomorrow,** vous l'aurez demain sans faute; (*intensive*) *esp. NAm:* **I am c. pleased you came,** je suis vraiment très content que vous soyez venu; **may I?—c.!** vous permettez?—je vous en prie! **c. not!** bien sûr que non! non, par exemple!
certainty ['sə:t(ə)nti], *s.* (*a*) certitude *f* (d'un fait à venir); (*b*) chose certaine, fait certain; **I know it for a c.,** je le sais à coup sûr; j'en ai la certitude; **it's a dead c.,** c'est une certitude absolue; **to bet on a c.,** parier à coup sûr; (*c*) certitude (morale), conviction *f*; **the c. of punishment,** la certitude du châtiment.
certifiable ['sə:tifaiəbl], *a.* que l'on peut certifier; **c. lunatic,** aliéné interdit; *F:* **he's c.,** il est fou à lier.
certificate[1] [sə'tifikət], *s.* **1.** certificat *m,* attestation *f*; (*a*) **medical c.,** certificat médical; **health c.,** billet *m* de

santé; (*b*) *Fin: etc:* **loan c.,** titre *m* de prêt; **bearer c.,** titre au porteur; **negotiable exchange c.,** certificat d'échange négociable; **share, stock, c.,** certificat d'action(s); **registered share c.,** certificat nominatif d'action(s); **trustee c.,** certificat fiduciaire; **(government) savings c.,** bon *m* d'épargne; **c. of insurance,** attestation d'assurance; *Com:* **c. of compliance,** certificat de conformité; **c. of approval,** certificat d'homologation; **c. of origin,** certificat d'origine; *Nau:* **c. of receipt,** certificat de chargement; **tonnage c.,** certificat de jauge; (*c*) *Av:* **c. of airworthiness,** certificat de navigabilité; *Aut:* **test c.** = certificat d'aptitude à rouler; **international c. for motor vehicles,** certificat international pour automobiles; *Nau:* **gas free c.,** certificat de dégazage; **rat free c.,** certificat de dératisation; (*d*) *Jur:* **(bankrupt's) c.** = (acte *m* de) concordat *m* (entre un failli et ses créanciers). **2.** (*a*) **c. (of competency),** certificat (d'aptitude); diplôme *m,* brevet *m; Nau:* **master's c.,** brevet de capitaine; (*b*) *Sch:* **C. of Secondary Education** = certificat de fin d'études secondaires; **General C. of Education, Ordinary Level,** (*in Eire*) **Intermediate C.,** *A:* **School C.** = certificat de fin d'études du premier cycle; **General C. of Education. Advanced Level,** *Scot:* **C. of Education,** (*in Eire*) **Leaving C.,** *A:* **Higher School C.** = baccalauréat *m, F:* bachot *m,* bac *m.* **3.** *Adm:* acte; **birth c., marriage c.,** acte de naissance, de mariage; (*when making application for passport, etc.*) extrait *m* de naissance, d'actes de l'état civil; **death c.,** (i) acte de (constat de) décès; (ii) extrait mortuaire; **registration c., c. of registration,** (i) matricule *f;* (ii) (*for alien*) permis *m* de séjour; *Mil: etc:* **service c.,** fiche *f,* certificat, de libération, de démobilisation; **last pay c.,** certificat de cessation de paiement.

certificate[2] [sə'tifikeit], *v.tr.* délivrer un certificat, un diplôme, un brevet, à (qn); diplômer, breveter (qn).

certificated [sə'tifikeitid], *a.* **1.** diplômé, titré; **fully c.,** pourvu de tous ses titres, de tous ses diplômes; **c. teacher,** instituteur diplômé, institutrice diplômée. **2.** *Jur:* **c. bankrupt,** concordataire *mf.*

certification [sətifi'keiʃ(ə)n], *s.* certification *f;* **c. of aircraft,** délivrance *f* du certificat de navigabilité; **c. test,** essai *m* d'homologation.

certificatory [sə'tifikeitəri], *a.* certificatif; **letter c.,** certificat *m;* lettre *f* de recommandation.

certifier ['sə:tifaiər], *s.* certificateur *m.*

certify ['sə:tifai], *v.tr.* **1.** (*a*) certifier, déclarer, attester; **to c. that sth. is true,** attester, porter témoignage, que qch. est vrai; **I c. this a true copy,** certifié pour copie conforme; **to c. a death,** constater un décès; *A:* (*of doctor*) **to c. a lunatic,** déclarer qn atteint d'aliénation mentale; *Jur: A:* **certified lunatic,** aliéné interdit; *F:* **you ought to be certified,** tu es complètement fou; *Fin:* **certified transfers,** transferts déclarés; (*b*) authentiquer, homologuer, légaliser (un document); *Com:* **certified cheque,** chèque visé pour provision; *U.S:* **certified letter** = lettre recommandée; (*c*) diplômer, breveter (qn); **certified broker,** courtier attitré; *Sch: U.S:* **certified teacher,** instituteur diplômé. **2.** *v.ind.tr.* **to c. to sth.,** attester qch; (*of doctor*) **to c. to s.o.'s insanity,** déclarer qn atteint d'aliénation mentale.

certifying[1] ['sə:tifaiiŋ], *a.* (document) certificatif.

certifying[2], *s.* **1.** attestation *f; Jur: A:* **c. of a lunatic,** interdiction *f* d'un aliéné. **2.** approbation *f* (d'un document); homologation *f.*

certiorari [sə:tiɔ:'reərai], *s. Jur:* ordonnance délivrée à un tribunal inférieur de soumettre le dossier d'une affaire au tribunal supérieur, aux fins de vérification.

certitude ['sə:titju:d], *s.* certitude *f.*

cerulean [si'ru:liən], *a. Lit: Art:* bleu céleste *inv;* cérulé; céruléen, azuré.

ceruleum [si'ru:liəm], *s. Ch: Paint:* céruleum *m.*

cerumen [si'ru:men], *s. Physiol:* cérumen *m.*

ceruminous [si'ru:minəs], *a. Physiol:* cérumineux; **c. glands,** glandes cérumineuses.

ceruse ['siəru:s, si'ru:s], *s.* céruse *f;* blanc *m* de céruse; blanc de plomb.

cerusite ['siəru:sait], *s. Miner:* cérusite *f;* plomb carbonaté.

cervantite [sə:'væntait], *s. Min:* cervantite *f.*

cervelat ['sə:vəlæt], *s. Cu:* cervelas *m.*

cervelière ['sə:vəljɛər], *s. A.Arm:* cervelière *f.*

cervical ['sə:vikl, sə:'vaikl], *Anat:* **1.** *a.* cervical, -aux; **c. smear,** frottis *m* cervical. **2.** *s.* (*a*) vertèbre cervicale; (*b*) **the cervicals,** les nerfs cervicaux.

cervicitis [sə:vi'saitis], *s. Med:* cervicite *f.*

cervicobrachial ['sə:vikou'breikiəl], *a. Anat:* cervico-brachial, -aux.

cervicobregmatic ['sə:vikoubreg'mætik], *a. Anat:* cervico-bregmatique.

Cervidae ['sə:vidi:], *s.pl. Z:* cervidés *m.*

cervine ['sə:vain], *a.* cervin.

cervix, *pl.* **-vices** ['sə:viks, -visi:z], *s. Anat:* (*a*) cou *m;* (*b*) **c. uteri,** col *m* de l'utérus.

cervulus ['sə:vjuləs], *s. Z:* cervule *m.*

cerylic [si'rilik], *a. Ch:* cérylique.

Cesarean, Cesarian [si'zɛəriən], *a.* = CAESARIAN.

Cesarevitch [si'zɑ:rəvitʃ], *s.* = CZAREVITCH.

cesarolite [tʃei'zɑ:roulait], *s. Min:* césarolite *f.*

cesium ['si:ziəm], *s. Ch:* caesium *m,* césium *m.*

cespitose ['sespitous], *a. Bot:* cespiteux.

cess[1] [ses], *s. A:* **1.** assiette *f* de l'impôt. **2.** impôt *m,* taxe *f.*

cess[2], *s. Dial:* (*Irish*) **bad c. to him!** que le diable l'emporte!

cessation [se'seiʃ(ə)n], *s.* cessation *f,* arrêt *m;* **c. from work,** suspension *f,* interruption *f,* du travail; **c. of arms, from arms,** suspension d'armes; armistice *m.*

cesser ['sesər], *s. Jur:* cessation *f* (de ses engagements).

cession ['seʃ(ə)n], *s.* **1.** cession *f;* abandon *m* (de marchandises, de droits, etc.). **2.** *Jur:* cession de biens (aux créanciers); **c. (of a territory),** cession (d'un territoire).

cessionary ['seʃən(ə)ri]. **1.** *a.* cessionnaire. **2.** *s. Jur:* ayant cause *m, pl.* ayants cause.

cesspit ['sespit], *s.* **1.** *Agr:* fosse *f* à fumier et à purin. **2.** = CESSPOOL.

cesspool ['sespu:l], *s.* **1.** fosse *f* d'aisances, puisard *m* d'aisance; puits absorbant; puits perdu; **leaching c.,** boit-tout *m inv;* **tight c. system,** système diviseur (de vidange); **c. emptier,** (i) vidangeur *m;* (ii) voiture *f* de vidangeur. **2.** fosse de curage (d'un égout); **a c. of iniquity,** une sentine, un cloaque, de vice.

cess-water ['seswɔ:tər], *s. Hyg:* eaux *f* vannes.

Cestoda [ses'toudə], *s.pl. Nat.Hist:* cestodes *m.*

cestoid ['sestɔid]. **1.** *a.* cestoïde. **2.** *s.* ver *m* cestoïde.

cestrum ['sestrəm], *s. Bot:* cestrum *m.*

cestus[1], *pl.* **-ti** ['sestəs, -tai], *s. Rom.Ant:* ceste *m,* ceinture *f* (de Vénus).

cestus[2], *s. inv. Rom.Ant:* ceste *m* (de pugilat).

Cetacea [si'teiʃiə, -'teisiə], *s.pl. Z:* cétacés *m.*

cetacean [si'teiʃən, -'teisiən], *a.* & *s. Z:* cétacé (*m*).

cetaceous [si'teiʃəs], *a. Z:* cétacé.

cetane ['si:tein], *s. Ch:* cétane *m,* hexadécane normal; **c. number, c. rate,** indice *m* de cétane.

ceteosaur(us) ['si:tiousɔ:r, si:tiou'sɔ:rəs], *Paleont:* cétéosaure *m.*

ceterach ['setiræk], *s. Bot:* cétérac(h) *m.*

cetic ['si:tik], *a. Z:* cétacé; de la baleine.

cetin ['si:tin], *s. Ch:* cétine *f.*

cetologist [si'tɔlədʒist], *s.* cétologue *m.*

cetology [si'tɔlədʒi], *s. Z:* cétographie *f.*

cetonia [si'touniə], *s. Ent:* cétoine *f.*

Cetorhinidae [sitou'rinidi:], *s.pl. Ich:* cétorhinidés *m.*

cetorhin(o)id [sitou'ri:n(ɔ)id], *s. Ich:* cétorhinidé *m.*

cetorhinus [sitou'rainəs], *s. Ich:* cetorhinous *m.*

cetraria [si'trɛəriə], *s. Moss:* cetraria *m.*

cetyl ['si:til], *s. Ch:* cétyle *m;* **c. alcohol,** alcool cétylique.

cevadilla [sevə'dilə], *s. Bot:* cévadille *f.*

cevadine ['sevədi:n], *s. Ch:* vératrine *f.*

ceylanite, ceylonite ['silənait], *s. Miner:* ceylanite *f,* ceylonite *f.*

Ceylon [si'lɔn], *Pr.n. Geog: Hist:* Ceylan *m.*

Ceylonese [silə'ni:z], *a.* cing(h)alais; *Min:* **C. ruby,** rubis cing(h)alais; **C. zircon,** zircon *m* cing(h)alais.

ceyssatite ['sesətait], *s. Miner:* ceyssatite *f.*

chabasie ['kæbəsi], **chabasite** ['kæbəsait], **chabazite** ['kæbəzait], *s. Miner:* chabasie *f,* chabacite *f.*

chabot ['ʃæbou], *s. Her:* chabot *m.*

chachalaca ['tʃɑ:tʃə'lɑ:kə], *s. Orn:* ortalide *f.*

chacma ['tʃækmə], *s. Z:* chacma *m.*

chacon(n)e [ʃə'kɔn], *s. Danc: Mus:* chacon(n)e *f.*

chad[1] [tʃæd], *s. Ich:* **1.** dorade (bilunée). **2.** alose *f.*

chad[2], *s. Cmptr:* confetti *m;* **c. box,** boîte *f,* bac *m,* à confetti; **c. tape,** bande *f* à confetti totalement détachés; **c. type perforation,** perforation *f* complète.

Chadburn ['tʃædbən], *Pr.n.m. Nau:* **C. telegraph,** chadburn *m.*

chadded ['tʃædid], *a. Cmptr:* **c. paper tape,** bande *f* à perforations complètes, à confetti détachés.

chadless ['tʃædlis], *a. Cmptr:* **c. perforation,** perforation partielle; **c. tape,** bande semi-perforée (à confetti non détachés).

Chaeronea [kerə'ni(:)ə], *Pr.n. A.Geog:* Chéronée *f.*

chaeta ['ki:tə], *s. Nat.Hist:* poil *m* raide; *Z:* soie *f.*

chaetiferous [ki:'tifərəs], *a.* sétifère, sétigène.

chaetodon ['ki:toudɔn], *s. Ich:* chétodon *m.*

Chaetodontidae [ki:tou'dɔntidi:], *s.pl. Ich:* chætodontidés *m.*

Chaetognatha [ki'tɔgnəθə], *s. Ann:* chétognatis *m.*

chaetopod ['ki:toupɔd], *s. Ann:* chétopode *m.*

Chaetopoda [ki'tɔpədə], *s.pl. Ann:* chétopodes *m.*

chaetopterus [ki'tɔptərəs], *s. Ann:* chétoptère *m,* chétopterus *m.*

chaetotaxy ['ki:toutæksi], *s. Ent:* chétotaxie *f.*

Chaetura ['ki:tjurə, ki'tju:rə], *s. Orn:* chæture *f,* chætura *f.*

chafe[1] [tʃeif], *s.* **1.** = CHAFING. **2.** écorchure *f.* **3.** *F: O:* irritation *f;* **to be in a c.,** se faire de la bile.

chafe[2]. **1.** *v.tr.* (*a*) frictionner, dégourdir, réchauffer (les membres de qn); (*b*) user, échauffer, (qch.) par le frottement; irriter, écorcher (la peau); érailler, raguer, fatiguer (un cordage); (*c*) irriter, énerver (qn). **2.** *v.i.* (*a*) s'user par le frottement; (*of skin*) s'irriter, s'écorcher; (*of rope*) s'érailler, raguer, s'échauffer; **chafed sail,** voile cotonnée; (*b*) (*of pers.*) **to c. at, under, sth.,** s'irriter de, contre, qch.; s'énerver de qch.; **to c. under restraint,** ronger son frein.

chafer ['tʃeifər], *s. Ent:* **1.** hanneton *m;* **garden c.,** hanneton de la Saint-Jean; **c. grub,** larve *f* de hanneton. **2. rose c.,** escarbot doré.

chafery ['tʃeifəri], *s. Metall:* chaufferie *f.*

chafewax ['tʃeifwæks], *s. Hist:* chauffe-cire *m;* cirier *m* de la grande chancellerie.

chaff[1] [tʃæ:f], *s.* **1.** (*a*) balle(s) *f* (du grain); *Bot:* glumelles *fpl,* glumes *fpl;* **c. pillow,** oreiller *m* de balle; *Prov:* **old birds are not to be caught with c.,** on ne prend pas les vieux merles à la pipée; **he is too old a bird to be caught with c.,** c'est un trop vieux poisson pour se laisser prendre; (*b*) *Agr:* (i) menue paille, paille d'avoine; (ii) paille hachée; **poppy c.,** brisures *fpl* de pavot; **c. cutter,** hache-paille *m inv,* coupe-paille *m inv; B:* **he will burn up the c. with unquenchable fire,** il brûlera la paille au feu qui ne s'éteint pas; (*c*) choses *fpl* sans importance; vétilles *fpl.* **2.** raillerie *f,* taquinerie *f,* persiflage *m;* blague *f.* **3.** *Elcs: U.S:* ruban *m* métallique antiradar, de brouillage radar; leurre *m* (antiradar).

chaff[2], *v.tr.* **1.** *Agr:* hacher (la paille). **2.** plaisanter, railler, blaguer, taquiner (qn); persifler (qn); dire des malices à (qn); *F:* chiner (qn); **they chaffed her about his coming so often,** on la plaisantait de ce qu'il venait si souvent.

chaffer[1] ['tʃæ:fər], *s.* railleur, -euse; persifleur, -euse; blagueur, -euse; *F:* chineur, -euse.

chaffer[2] ['tʃæfər], *s. O:* = CHAFFERING.

chaffer[3] ['tʃæfər], *v.i. O:* **1.** marchander, barguigner; **to c. with s.o.,** marchander qn; **to c. with s.o. for sth.,** marchander qch. avec qn; **to c. over the price,** débattre le prix; marchander sur le prix. **2.** parler pour ne rien dire.

chaffering ['tʃæfəriŋ], *s. O:* marchandage *m,* barguignage *m.*

chaffinch ['tʃæfin(t)ʃ], *s. Orn:* pinson *m* (des arbres).

chaffingly ['tʃæfiŋli], *adv.* en taquinant, en badinant, en plaisantant.

chaffwax ['tʃɑ:fwæks], *s. Hist:* chauffe-cire *m.*

chaffweed ['tʃɑ:fwi:d], *s. Bot:* **1.** centenille *f.* **2.** cotonnière *f.*

chaffy ['tʃɑ:fi], *a.* **1.** (*a*) couvert de balle(s); (*b*) semblable à la menue paille; (sujet *m*) aride, stérile; (*c*) *A:* sans valeur; (homme *m*) de paille. **2.** (ton) blagueur, taquin.

chafing ['tʃeifiŋ], *s.* **1.** friction *f* (des membres). **2.** (*a*) irritation *f,* écorchement *m* (de la peau); (*b*) usure *f,* friction, frottement *m,* échauffement *m* (d'une courroie, d'un pneu, etc.); rag(u)age *m* (d'une corde); *Nau:* **c. mat,** sangle *f;* **c. block, gear,** martyr *m; Mec.E:* **c. plate,** plaque *f* de friction, de frottement. **3.** *O:* (*of pers.*) irritation *f,* énervement *m.* **4.** *Dom.Ec:* **c. dish,** réchaud *m* de table.

chagrin[1] ['ʃægrin], *s.* chagrin *m,* dépit *m;* vive contrariété; déplaisir *m;* **to the great c. of. . . ,** au grand chagrin de . . ., à la grande déception de . . ..

chagrin[2], *v.tr. esp. Lit:* chagriner, dépiter (qn); **to be chagrined at sth.,** être mortifié de qch.; être vexé de, par, qch.; se vexer de qch.; **he was greatly chagrined,** il en éprouva une vive contrariété, un grand dépit.

chain[1] [tʃein], *s.* **1.** (*a*) chaîne *f;* (*small*) chaînette *f; Jewel:* chaînette (pour pendentif); **watch c.,** chaîne de montre; **safety c.,** (i) (*for door*) chaîne de sûreté, de porte; (ii) (*for bracelet, etc.*) chaînette de sûreté; **to put a dog on the c.,** mettre un chien à l'attache, à la chaîne; enchaîner un chien; **prisoner in chains,** prisonnier enchaîné; **c. gang,** chaîne, cadène *f,* de forçats; *Fig:* **to break, burst, one's chains,** rompre ses chaînes; briser ses fers; **c. link,** chaînon *m,* maillon *m* de chaîne; **c.-link fence,** clôture *f* à mailles en losanges, à mailles losangées; **c. armour, c. mail,** (i) mailles; (ii) cotte *f* de mailles; **c. bag,** sac *m* (de dame) à maillons de métal; **c. hook,** croc *m* à chaîne; **c. maker,** chaîniste *m;* chaînier *m;* chaînetier *m;* **bicycle c.,** chaîne de bicyclette; **stud c.,** chaîne à fuseaux; **c. wheel,** roue *f* à chaînes, de chaînes; *Cy:* plateau *m;* **front c. wheel,** plateau de pédalier, grand pignon; *Cy: etc:* **c. guard, c. case,** carter *m;* gaine *f* rigide; garde-chaîne *m inv,* couvre-chaîne *m inv;* **c. lock,** chaînette anti-vol; **c. adjuster,**

tendeur *m* de chaîne; patte *f* de tension; *Aut:* **(anti-)skid chains, snow chains,** chaînes antidérapantes, chaînes à neige; **the pass is open, but you'll need chains,** le col est ouvert mais il vous faudra des chaînes; *Tls:* **c. saw,** tronçonneuse *f*; *Agr:* **c. harrow,** herse *f* à chaînons; *Agr: Nau:* **c. towing,** touage *m*; *Civ.E:* **c. bridge,** pont suspendu à chaînes; *Const:* **houses with c. courses,** maisons *f* de briques à chaînes, à chaînages, de pierre; *Glassm: etc:* **c. screen,** écran *m* à chaînes; *Plumb:* **c. tongs,** (clef *f*) serre-tubes *m inv* à chaîne; pince *f* à chaîne; *El:* **c. of insulators,** chapelet *m* d'insulateurs; **c. winding,** enroulement *m* à la chaîne; *Tchn:* **polishing c.,** gourmette *f*; *Harn:* **curb c.,** gourmette; **c. bit,** mors *m* à gourmette; **c. horse,** cheval *m* de renfort, côtier *m*; *Paperm:* **c. line, c. mark,** pontuseau *m*; *Artil: A:* **c. shot,** boulets ramés; (*in W.C.*) **to pull the c.,** tirer la chasse d'eau; (*b*) *Nau: etc:* **the chains,** les porte-haubans *m inv*; **anchor c.,** chaîne d'ancrage; **c. cable,** câble-chaîne, *m, pl.* câble-chaînes; **c. well, c. locker,** puits *m* à chaînes, aux chaînes, aux câbles; **c. pipe,** manchon *m* de puits à chaîne, de chaîne; écubier *m* de pont; **c. messenger,** tournevire *m* (du cabestan) en chaîne; (*c*) *Techn: Mec.E:* **drive, driving, transmission, c.,** chaîne de transmission; **c. drive,** commande *f*, transmission *f*, par chaînes; **c.-driven,** commandé par chaîne(s); avec transmission par chaînes; *A:* (*of motor cycle*) **all-c. transmission,** transmission chaîne-chaîne; **stud-link c.,** chaîne à étais; **pitch(ed) c.,** chaîne calibrée; **block c.,** chaîne à maillons pleins, à blocs; **sprocket c., Gall's c.,** chaîne à barbotins, chaîne de Galle; **roller c.,** chaîne à galets; **ladder c.,** chaîne de, à la, Vaucanson; **endless c.,** chaîne sans fin; **timing c.,** chaîne de distribution; **c. wheel,** roue *f* à chaîne; **c. gear,** engrenage *m* à chaîne; **c. of gears,** suite *f* d'engrenages; **c. conveyor,** transporteur *m* à chaîne; **c. belt,** courroie articulée; **c. pulley,** barbotin *m*; **c. grate,** grille *f* à chaînons; **c. sheave,** rouet *m* à chaîne (d'une poulie); **c. feed,** entraînement (de l'outil) commandé par chaîne; **c. guide,** guide-chaîne *m inv*; **c. stop, c. catch,** arrêt *m* de chaîne, arrête-chaîne *m inv*; **c. slack,** relâchement *m* de la chaîne; *Hyd.E:* **c. pump,** pompe *f* à chapelet, à godets; chapelet *m* hydraulique; **bucket c.,** chaîne à augets, à godets; *Rail:* **c. coupling,** attelage *m* à chaînes; **the c. couplings,** les chaînes d'attelage; (*d*) *Geog:* chaîne (de montagnes); (*small*) chaînon; *Ind:* **c. work,** travail *m* à la chaîne, *Cmptr:* **c. code,** code *m* à enchaînement; **c. printer,** imprimante *f* à la chaîne; *Com:* **c. store,** (i) magasin *m* à succursales (multiples); (ii) succursale *f* (de grand magasin); (*of people*) **to form a c.,** former la chaîne, faire la chaîne (pour passer des seaux, etc.); **c. letter,** chaîne; **don't break the c.,** ne rompez pas la chaîne; **c. of ideas,** enchaînement d'idées; **c. of events,** suite *f*, série *f*, d'événements; *Mil: etc:* **c. of observation posts, of sentries,** cordon *m* de postes d'observation, de sentinelles; *Danc:* **grand c.,** chaîne anglaise; (*e*) *Ph: Ch: etc:* **disintegration, decay, c.,** chaîne de désintégration; **closed c. of atoms,** chaîne fermée d'atomes; **branched c.,** chaîne ramifiée; **side c.,** chaîne latérale; **c. reaction,** réaction *f* en chaîne. **2.** *Surv: Meas:* longueur *f* de 20 m 116; double décamètre *m*; **surveyor's c., land c., measuring c.,** chaîne d'arpenteur, d'arpentage; **band c.,** chaîne à ruban (d'acier); **c. length,** portée *f*; **c. measuring,** chaînage *m*. **3.** *Knit:* maille *f* en l'air; *Tex:* **c. (warp),** chaîne.

chain², *v.tr.* **1. to c. s.o., sth., to sth.,** attacher qn, qch., à qch. par une chaîne, par des chaînes. **2. to c. sth. down,** retenir qch. par une chaîne, par des chaînes; **to c. s.o. (down),** enchaîner qn; **chained to one's desk,** cloué à son bureau; **to c. (up) a dog,** mettre un chien à la chaîne, à l'attache; attacher un chien à la chaîne; renchaîner un chien; **chained up, chained together,** à la chaîne. **3.** fermer (un port, une porte, etc.) avec des chaînes; barrer (une rue) avec une chaîne. **4.** nettoyer (un fût) à la chaîne. **5.** *Surv:* chaîner (un champ, etc.).

chain-dotted ['tʃeindɔtid], *a.* en traits *m* mixtes.

chained ['tʃeind], *a.* (*a*) attaché par une chaîne; (*b*) *Cmptr:* **c. list,** liste *f* d'articles chaînés; **c. sequential file,** fichier *m* en séquentiel enchaîné.

chaining ['tʃeiniŋ], *s.* **1.** enchaînement *m*; chaînage *m*; *Cmptr:* **c. search,** recherche *f* par chaînage. **2.** nettoyage *m* (d'un fût) à la chaîne. **3.** *Surv:* chaînage *m*.

chainless ['tʃeinlis], *a.* sans chaîne(s); *A:* **c. bicycle,** (bicyclette *f*) acatène *f*.

chainlet ['tʃeinlit], *s.* chaînette *f*; petite chaîne.

chainman, *pl.* **-men** ['tʃeinmən], *s.m.* *Surv:* chaîneur; porte-chaîne *inv*; aide (d'arpenteur).

chainsmith ['tʃeinsmiθ], *s.* chaîniste *m*.

chain-smoke ['tʃeinsmouk], *v.i.* fumer cigarette sur cigarette, fumer des cigarettes à la file.

chain-smoker ['tʃeinsmoukər], *s.* fumeur, -euse, de cigarettes à la file.

chainstitch ['tʃeinstitʃ], *s.* *Needlew:* point *m* de chaînette.

chainwale ['tʃeinweil], *s.* *Nau:* porte-haubans *m inv*; **to roll chainwales under,** rouler bord sur bord.

chainwork ['tʃeinwə:k], *s.* travail *m* à la chaîne.

chair¹ [tʃɛər], *s.* **1.** (*a*) chaise *f*; siège *m*; **folding c.,** chaise pliante; pliant *m*; **easy c.,** fauteuil *m*; bergère *f*; **grandfather c.,** fauteuil à oreillettes; bergère à oreilles; **rocking c.,** fauteuil à bascule; **Roorkie c.,** fauteuil saharien; **club c.,** fauteuil club; **deck c.,** transatlantique *m, F:* transat *m*; **high c.,** chaise haute (pour enfants); **Bath c., invalid c.,** voiture *f* de malade; fauteuil roulant; *Games:* **musical chairs,** jeu *m*, polka *f*, des chaises; **please take a c.,** asseyez-vous, s'il vous plaît; *attrib.* **c. maker,** chaisier, -ière; fabricant *m* de chaises; **c. mender,** réparateur *m*, rempailleur, -euse, de chaises; **c. attendant,** chaisier, -ière; loueur, -euse, de chaises (dans un parc, etc.); **c. bed,** chaise-lit *m, pl.* chaises-lits; fauteuil-lit *m, pl.* fauteuils-lits; *Ski:* **c. lift,** télésiège *m*; **double c. lift,** télébenne *f*; *Rail: U.S:* **c. car,** voiture salon; (*b*) *Jur:* chaise électrique; *NAm: F:* **to get the c.,** être condamné à mort; (*c*) *Sch:* chaire *f* (de professeur de faculté); (*d*) siège (de juge); fauteuil (de président); **to be in,** *occ.* **to occupy, the c.,** occuper le fauteuil présidentiel; présider; diriger les débats; **to be voted into the c.,** être élu président; **Mr X was in the c.,** M. X présidait la réunion; la réunion était sous la présidence de M. X; **to speak from the c.,** parler en tant que président; **to leave, vacate, the c.,** lever la séance; **to support the c.,** se ranger à l'avis du président; **to address, to appeal to, the c.,** s'adresser, en appeler, au président; **c.! (c.!),** à l'ordre! (*e*) *Jur: U.S:* banc *m* des témoins. **2.** *Rail:* coussinet *m*, chaise (de rail); **c. foot,** semelle *f* de coussinet.

chair², *v.tr.* **1.** (*a*) nommer (qn) président; élire (qn) au fauteuil présidentiel; porter (qn) à la présidence; (*b*) **to c. a meeting,** présider une réunion. **2.** porter (qn) en triomphe. **3.** *Rail:* **to c. the sleepers,** garnir les traverses de coussinets; saboter les traverses.

chairback ['tʃɛəbæk], *s.* **1.** dossier *m* de chaise. **2.** voilette *f* de chaise; têtière *f*.

chairman, *pl.* **-men** ['tʃɛəmən], *s.* **1.** (*a*) président, -ente; **to act as c.,** présider (la séance); **a committee with Mr X as c.,** un comité sous la présidence de Monsieur X; **Mr C., Madam C., allow me to . . .,** Monsieur le Président, Madame la Présidente, permettez-moi de . . .; (*b*) **he was c. of the firm for ten years,** il a été président, directeur général, de la maison pendant dix ans. **2.** *A:* porteur *m* (de chaise à porteurs).

chairmanship ['tʃɛəmənʃip], *s.* présidence *f*; **under the c. of Mr X,** sous la présidence de M. X.

chairwoman, *pl.* **-women** ['tʃɛəwumən, -wimin], *s.occ.esp. NAm:* présidente *f* (d'une séance, etc.).

chaise [ʃeiz], *s. A.Veh:* **1.** chaise *f*, cabriolet *m*. **2.** chaise de poste.

chaise longue ['ʃeiz'lɔŋ], *s.* chaise-longue *f, pl.* chaise(s)-longues.

chaja [tʃɑ:'hɑ:], *s. Orn:* kamichi *m* à crête.

Chalastogastra [kəlæstou'gæstrə], *s.pl. Ent:* tenthrèdes *f*.

chalaza [kə'leizə], *s. Biol: Bot:* chalaze *f*.

chalazion, -ium [kə'leiziən, -iəm], *s. Med:* chalazie *f*, chalazion *m*, orgelet *m*.

chalazogamic [kælə'zɔgəmik], *a. Bot:* chalazogame.

chalazogamy [kælə'zɔgəmi], *s. Bot:* chalazogamie *f*.

chalcanthite ['tʃælkənθait], *s. Miner:* cyanose *f*, chalcanthite *f*.

Chalcedon ['kælsidɔn], *Pr.n. A.Geog:* Chalcédoine *f*.

Chalcedonian [kælsi'dounian], *A.Geog:* (*a*) *a.* chalcédonien; (*b*) *s.* Chalcédonien, -ienne.

chalcedony [kæl'sedəni], *s. Lap:* calcédoine *f*.

chalcid ['kælsid], *s. Ent:* **c. (fly),** chalcis *m*.

Chalcidian [kæl'sidiən], *a. & s. Geog:* (originaire, natif) de Chalcis, Chalkis.

chalcidic [kæl'sidik], **chalcidicum,** *pl.* **-a** [kæl'sidikəm, -ə], *s. Arch: Ant:* chalcidique *m*.

Chalcidice [kæl'sidike], *Pr.n. A.Geog:* Chalcidique *f*.

Chalcididae [kæl'sididi:], *s.pl. Ent:* chalcididés *m*, chalcidiens *m*.

chalcis ['kælsis], *s. Ent:* **c. (fly),** chalcis *m*.

chalcocite ['kælkousait], *s. Miner:* chalcocite *f*, chalcosine *f*.

chalcographer [kæl'kɔgrəfər], *s.* chalcographe *m*; graveur *m* sur cuivre; graveur en taille douce.

chalcographic [kælkou'græfik], *a.* chalcographique.

chalcography [kæl'kɔgrəfi], *s. Engr:* chalcographie *f*; gravure *f* sur cuivre; gravure en taille douce.

chalcolite ['kælkəlait], *s. Miner:* chalcolite *f*, torbernite *f*.

chalcolithic [kælkou'liθik], *a. Prehist:* chalcolithique.

chalcomenite [kælkou'mi:nait], *s. Miner:* chalcoménite *f*.

chalcone ['kælkoun], *s. Ch:* chalcone *f*.

chalcophanite [kæl'kɔfənait], *s. Miner:* chalcophanite *f*.

chalcophyllite [kælkou'filait], *s. Miner:* chalcophyllite *f*.

chalcopyrite [kælkou'pairait], *s. Miner:* chalcopyrite *f*; cuivre pyriteux; pyrite cuivreuse; pyrite de cuivre.

chalcosiderite [kælkou'sidərait], *s. Miner:* chalcosidérite *f*.

chalcosiid [kælkou'si:id], *a. Ent:* (papillon) chalcosiide.

Chalcosiidae [kælkou'si:idi:], *s.pl. Ent:* chalcosiides *m*.

chalcosine ['kælkousi:n], *s. Miner:* chalcosine *f*, chalsosite *f*.

chalcostibite [kælkou'stibait], *s. Miner:* chalcostibite *f*, wolfsbergite *f*.

chalcotrichite [kælkou'trikait, kæl'kɔtrikait], *s. Miner:* chalcotrichite *f*.

Chaldaic [kæl'deiik], *a. A.Geog:* chaldaïque.

Chaldea [kæl'di(:)ə], *Pr.n. A.Geog:* Chaldée, *f*.

Chaldean [kæl'di(:)ən], **Chaldee** [kæl'di:]. **1.** *A.Geog:* (*a*) *a.* chaldéen; (*b*) *s.* Chaldéen, -éenne. **2.** *s. Ling:* chaldéen *m*.

chalet ['ʃælei], *s.* chalet *m*.

chalice ['tʃælis], *s.* **1.** (*a*) *A: & Lit:* coupe *f* (à boire); (*b*) *Ecc:* calice *m*; **c. cover,** pale *f*, volet *m*; **c. veil,** voile *m* (du calice). **2.** *Bot:* calice.

chaliced ['tʃælist], *a.* (*of flower*) en forme de calice.

chalicosis [kæli'kousis], *s. Med:* chalicose *f*, chalicosis *m*.

chalicothere ['kælikouθiər], *s. Paleont:* chalicotherium *m*.

Chalicotheriidae [kælikouθə'ri:idi:], *s.pl. Paleont:* chalicothéridés *m*.

chalina [kə'lainə, -'li:nə], *s. Spong:* chalina *f*.

chalk¹ [tʃɔ:k], *s.* **1.** (*a*) *Geol:* craie *f*; **c. marl,** craie marneuse; **c. hills, cliffs,** collines, falaises, crayeuses; **there is a great deal of c. in this water,** cette eau est très calcaire; (*b*) (*for writing, etc.*) craie; *Art:* (crayon) pastel *m*; *Bill:* blanc *m*; **black c.,** sauce *f*; **c. drawing,** pastel; **c. line, mark,** (i) trait *m* à la craie; (ii) *Carp: etc:* cordeau (blanchi à la craie); (iii) ligne faite au cordeau; tringle *f*; **written in c.,** écrit à la craie; *F:* **he doesn't know c. from cheese,** il ne sait rien de rien; il prendrait des vessies pour des lanternes; **they are as different as c. and cheese,** c'est le jour et la nuit; (*c*) **French c.,** talc *m*; craie de tailleur, de Meudon; (*d*) *Pharm:* **precipitated c.,** carbonate *m* de chaux précipité; **c. mixture,** craie préparée (contre la diarrhée); (*e*) *Paperm:* **c. overlay,** papier baryté; papier porcelaine. **2.** (*a*) trait *m*, point *m*, à la craie (pour marquer les points dans certains jeux); (*b*) compte *m* des consommations (à l'ardoise); *F: A:* **his c. is up,** son crédit est épuisé; *F:* **not by a long c.,** tant s'en faut, pas du tout; pas à beaucoup près; **the best by a long c.,** de beaucoup le meilleur.

chalk², *v.tr.* **1.** (*a*) marquer (qch.) à la craie; *Carp: etc:* **to c. a line,** tringler une ligne (au cordeau); **to c. the pavement,** écrire à la craie sur le trottoir; (*b*) blanchir (sa figure, etc.) avec de la craie; *Bill:* **to c. one's cue,** mettre du blanc au procédé; frotter sa queue de blanc; (*c*) talquer; saupoudrer de talc. **2. to c. (up) sth. on sth.,** écrire qch. à la craie sur qch.; *F:* **to c. up the drinks,** inscrire les consommations à l'ardoise; **c. it up for me,** mettez ça à mon compte; **c. it up!** on aura tout vu! **3. to c. out a plan,** tracer un plan (de conduite).

Chalkidike [kælki'di:ki], *Pr.n. Geog:* Chalcidique *f*.

chalkiness ['tʃɔ:kinis], *s.* **1.** nature crayeuse (du sol). **2.** extrême pâleur *f* (du teint de qn).

chalking ['tʃɔ:kiŋ], *s. Paint:* farinage *m*, *F:* chalking *m*.

chalkpit ['tʃɔ:kpit], *s.* carrière *f* de craie; crayère *f*.

chalkstone ['tʃɔ:kstoun], *s. Med:* concrétion *f* calcaire, tophus *m* (des arthritiques); *pl.* **chalk-stones,** incrustations *f*.

chalky ['tʃɔ:ki], *a.* **1.** crayeux, crétacé; **c. soil,** terrain crayeux; sol *m* calcaire; **c. water,** eau *f* calcaire; **c. deposit,** dépôt *m* calcique. **2.** (teint) pâle, terreux.

challenge¹ ['tʃælin(d)ʒ], *s.* **1.** (*a*) défi *m*; *A:* provocation *f* (en duel); **to accept, take up, a c.,** relever un défi; **this work is a real c. to me,** ce travail est une vraie gageure pour moi; (*b*) *Sp:* défi, challenge *m*; **to issue a c.,** lancer un challenge; **c. match,** challenge; **c. cup,** coupe-challenge *f, pl.* coupes challenge; (*c*) *Mil:* interpellation *f*, sommation *f* (par une sentinelle); qui vive *m inv.* **2.** *Jur:* récusation *f* (du jury); **c. to the array,** récusation de tout le corps des jurés; **c. to the polls,** récusation de certains jurés; **peremptory c.,** récusation sans qu'une cause soit fournie.

challenge², *v.tr.* **1.** (*a*) **to c. s.o.,** (i) provoquer qn (au combat), jeter le gant à qn; (ii) *Sp:* challenger qn; **to c. s.o. to do sth.,** (i) défier qn de faire qch.; (ii) sommer qn de faire qch.; **to c. s.o. to a game of chess,** défier qn aux échecs; to c. s.o. **to a drinking match,** défier qn à qui boira le plus; **forgery that challenges discovery,** faux *m* qui est un défi porté à la perspicacité des experts; (*b*) *Mil:* (*of sentry*) **to c. s.o.,** interpeller, arrêter qn (en criant qui vive); faire une sommation à qn. **2.** (*a*) protester contre, disputer, relever (une affirmation); mettre en question, en doute (la parole, l'honneur, de qn); **to c. s.o.'s right to do sth.,** contester à qn le droit de faire qch.; **to c. s.o.'s right to sth.,** inquiéter qn dans la possession de qch.; contester les titres de qn; (*b*) récuser (un juré). **3.** *v.i. Ven:* (*of hounds*) donner de la voix, crier (en reconnaissant la voie).

challengeable ['tʃælin(d)ʒəbl], *a.* **1.** qu'on peut disputer, critiquer. **2.** (juré) récusable.

challenger ['tʃælin(d)ʒər], *s.* **1.** (*a*) provocateur, -trice; (*b*) *Sp:* lanceur *m* d'un challenge, challenger *m*; **the challengers,** les invitants *m*; **the holder and the c.,** le détenteur du challenge et le challenger. **2.** *Jur:* récusant, -ante.

challenging ['tʃælin(d)ʒiŋ], *a.* (*a*) (*of look, remark, etc.*) provocateur, -trice; (air *m*) de défi; **the most c. thing,** la chose la plus provocante; (*b*) *Sp:* **the c. team,** les invitants *m,* l'équipe *f* qui a lancé le challenge.

challengingly ['tʃælin(d)ʒiŋli], *adv.* avec un air de défi; d'un air provocant.

chalone ['kæloun], *s. Bio-Ch:* chalone *f.*

chalonic [kə'lounik], *a. Bio-Ch:* chalonique.

chalybeate [kə'libiət], *a. Ch:* **c. water, spring,** eau, source, ferrugineuse.

chalybite ['kælibait], *s. Miner:* chalybite *f.*

cham [kæm], *s.* K(h)an *m*; *F: A:* **great C.,** grand Manitou.

chama ['keimə], *s. Moll:* chame *f,* came *f.*

chamade [ʃə'mɑ:d], *s. A.Mil:* chamade *f.*

chamae- ['kæmi-], *pref.* chamæ-, chamé-.

chamaecephalic ['kæmise'fælik], **chamaecephalous** ['kæmi'sefələs], *a. Anthr:* chamæcéphale, chamécéphale.

chamaecephaly ['kæmi'sefəli], *s. Anthr:* chamæcéphalie *f,* chamécéphalie *f.*

chamaeconch(ic) [kæmi'kɔnʃ(ik)], **chamaeconchous** [kæmi'kɔnʃəs], *a. Anthr:* chamæconque, chaméconque.

chamaecranial [kæmi'kreiniəl], *a. Anthr:* chamæcrâne, chamécrâne.

Chamaecyparis [kæmi'siparis], *s. Bot:* chamæcyparis *m.*

Chamaeleonidae [kæmili'ɔnidi:], *s.pl. Rept:* chamæléonidés *m.*

chamaephyte ['kæmifait], *a. & s. Bot:* chaméphyte (*f*).

chamaerops [kə'mi:rɔps], *s. Bot:* chamærops *m.*

chamber[1] ['tʃeimbər], *s.* **1.** (*a*) *A: & Lit:* (*room*) pièce *f,* salle *f*; (*still so used in*) **audience c.,** salle d'audience; **presence c.,** salle du trône; **council c.,** salle du conseil; **c. music,** musique *f* de chambre; **c. concert,** concert *m* de musique de chambre; (*b*) *Lit:* **(bed-)c.,** chambre *f* (à coucher); **Gentlemen of the Privy C.,** gentilshommes *m* de la Chambre du Roi; (*c*) **c. (pot),** pot *m* de chambre, vase *m* de nuit. **2.** (*a*) **c. of commerce, of trade,** chambre de commerce, de métiers; (*b*) *Pol:* **double c. system,** système bicaméral; **Upper C.,** Chambre haute; *in Eng.* = Chambre des Lords; **Lower C.,** Chambre basse; *in Eng.* = Chambre des Communes. **3.** *pl.* **chambers;** (*a*) *O:* appartement *m* de garçon; (*b*) cabinet *m* de consultation (d'un avocat); étude *f* (d'un avoué); *Jur:* **in chambers,** en chambre du conseil; **c. counsel,** avocat consultant, avocat conseil; **to hear a case in chambers,** juger une cause en référé; **judge in chambers,** juge *m* des référés. **4.** *Tchn:* (*a*) *Ind:* **lead c.,** chambre de plomb; **c. process,** procédé *m* des chambres; (*b*) *Metall:* laboratoire *m* (de fourneau); *Mch:* **steam c.,** (i) boîte *f* à vapeur; (ii) réservoir *m* de vapeur; **fire c.,** chambre à feu; *I.C.E: etc:* **combustion c.,** chambre de combustion; **mixing c.,** chambre de carburation; **compression c.,** chambre de compression; **suction c.,** chambre d'aspiration; (*of carburettor*) **float c.,** chambre à niveau constant; (*c*) chambre, tonnerre *m* (d'une arme à feu); **the chambers of a revolver,** les alvéoles *m* d'un revolver; *Mil:* **fighting c. (of tank),** poste *m* de tir (de char); (*d*) *Min:* fourneau *m* (d'une mine); *Petr:* **surge c.,** chambre d'équilibre, de tranquillisation; (*e*) **air c. (of pump),** chambre à air (d'une pompe); **piston c.,** barillet *m* (de pompe); *Hyd.E:* **(lock) c.,** chambre, sas *m* (d'écluse); **turbine c.,** chambre de mise en charge, chambre d'eau; (*f*) *Ph:* **cloud c., Wilson's expansion c.,** chambre de Wilson; *Atom.Ph:* **ionization c., expansion c.,** chambre d'ionization, à détente; (*g*) *Nat.Hist: etc:* cavité *f*; alvéole; *Conch:* chambre, loge *f*; **first c.,** loge initiale; **body c.,** loge dernière.

chamber[2], *v.tr.* (*a*) *Mec.E: etc:* **to c. (out) a piece,** évider une pièce; (*b*) **to c. a gun,** chambrer une arme à feu.

chambered ['tʃeimbəd], *a.* évidé, chambré; *Conch:* **c. shell,** coquillage *m* à loges, coquille chambrée; **six-c. revolver,** revolver *m* à six coups.

chamberlain ['tʃeimbəlin], *s.* **1.** chambellan *m*; (*a*) **the Lord Great C. of England,** le grand Chambellan (fonction héréditaire); **the Lord C. of the Household,** le Chambellan de la Maison du souverain; (*b*) **Pope's c.,** camérier *m.* **2.** trésorier *m* (d'une grande ville).

chamberlainship ['tʃeimbəlinʃip], *s.* office *m* de chambellan, de camérier, de trésorier.

chambermaid ['tʃeimbəmeid], *s.f.* femme de chambre (d'hôtel).

chame- ['kæmi], *pref.* = CHAMAE-.

chameleon [kə'mi:liən], *s.* (*a*) *Rept:* caméléon *m*; (*b*) *Tex:* **c. silk,** caméléon de soie.

chameleonic [kəmi:li'ɔnik], *a.* inconstant; versatile.

chameleon-like [kə'mi:liənlaik], *a.* versicolore.

chamfer[1] ['tʃæmfər], *s.* **1.** biseau *m,* chanfrein *m*; pan abattu; arête *f* (de moulure); **gear-tooth c.,** entrée *f* de dent (d'un engrenage). **2. hollow c.,** cannelure *f*; arête creuse.

chamfer[2], *v.tr.* **1.** *Carp: etc:* biseauter, chanfreiner, ébiseler, délarder, tailler en biseau (une planche, etc.); abattre les angles, les arêtes (d'un meuble, etc.); abattre (une arête); fraiser (un trou). **2.** canneler (une colonne, etc.).

chamferer ['tʃæmfərər], *s.* tailleur *m* en biseau.

chamfering ['tʃæmfəriŋ], *s.* biseautage *m*; **c. iron,** (fer *m* à) biseau *m*; **c. bit,** fraisoir *m*; **c. machine,** machine *f* à chanfreiner, chanfreineuse *f.*

chamfrain ['tʃæmfrin], **chamfron** ['tʃæmfr(ə)n], *s. A.Harn:* chanfrein *m* (de cheval de guerre).

chamidae ['kæmidi:], *s.pl. Moll:* chamidés *m.*

chamois[1] ['ʃæmwɑ:], *s.* (*a*) *Z:* chamois *m*; (*b*) *c.* **(yellow),** (jaune) chamois *m inv*; (*c*) **c.** (*also* **chammy** ['ʃæmi]) **leather,** peau *f* de chamois.

chamois[2] ['ʃæmi], *v.tr. Leath:* chamoiser (le cuir).

chamo(i)site ['ʃæmizait, -mwə-], *s. Miner:* chamo(i)site *f.*

chamomile ['kæməmi:l, -mail], *s.* = CAMOMILE.

chamotte [ʃə'mɔt], *s. Cer:* chamotte *f.*

champ[1] [tʃæmp], *s.* mâchonnement *m.*

champ[2], *v.tr.* (*of horse, etc.*) mâcher bruyamment (le fourrage); ronger, mâcher, mâchonner (le mors); **horse that champs the bit,** cheval *m* qui badine avec son mors, qui mord, ronge, son frein; *F:* (*of pers.*) **to c. the bit with impatience,** ronger son frein.

champ[3], *s. Sp: F:* champion *m.*

Champagne [ʃæm'pein]. **1.** *Pr.n. Geog:* Champagne *f*; **Dry C.,** Champagne pouilleuse; **Wet C.,** Champagne humide; **a native of C.,** un(e) Champenois(e). **2.** *s.* vin *m* de Champagne; champagne *m*; **still c.,** champagne nature; **sparkling c.,** champagne mousseux; **new c.,** tocane *f*; *A:* **light c.,** tisane *f* de Champagne; **c. cup,** marquise *f*; **c. cider,** cidre champagnisé, mousseux. **3.** *a.* (*colour*) champagne.

champagnization [ʃæmpeinai'zeiʃ(ə)n], *s.* champagnisation *f.*

champagnize [ʃæm'peinaiz], *v.tr.* champagniser.

champaign ['tʃæmpein], *a. & s. A: & Lit:* **c. (land),** plaine *f*; campagne ouverte.

champart [ʃɑ̃pɑ:r], *s. Hist:* champart *m.*

champers ['ʃæmpə:z], *s. F: O:* champagne *m.*

champerty ['tʃæmpə(:)ti], *s. Jur:* pacte *m* (illicite) de quota litis.

champignon [tʃæm'pinjən], *s. Fung:* faux mousseron; **false c.,** clitocybe blanchi.

champing ['tʃæmpiŋ], *s.* mâchonnement *m.*

champion[1] ['tʃæmpiən]. **1.** *s.* (*a*) champion *m*; **the champions of free trade,** les tenants *m* du libre-échange; **the King's, Queen's, C.,** le Champion du Roi, de la Reine (office héréditaire exercé à la cérémonie du sacre); (*b*) *Sp:* champion, -ionne; **world c.,** champion du monde. **2.** (*a*) *attrib.* **a c. tennis player,** un champion du tennis; **c. driver,** champion de vitesse; *F:* **c. cabbage, liar, etc.,** chou *m,* menteur *m,* etc. de première classe; maître chou, maître menteur; (*b*) *a. Dial:* (*in N. of Eng.*) **that's c.!** à la bonne heure! bravo! **isn't that c.!** qu'est-ce que vous dites de ça! (*c*) *adv. P:* **we get on c.,** on est bien ensemble.

champion[2], *v.tr.* soutenir, défendre (une cause); prendre fait et cause pour (qn); se faire le chevalier de (qn); se faire le champion d'(une cause).

championship ['tʃæmpiənʃip], *s.* **1.** *Sp: etc:* championnat *m.* **2. c. of a cause,** défense *f* d'une cause.

champlevé ['ʃæmplə'vei], *s.* **c. (enamel),** champlevé *m.*

chance[1] [tʃɑ:ns], *s.* **1.** (*a*) chance *f,* hasard *m*; fortune *f*; sort *m*; **game of c.,** jeu *m* de hasard; **by (mere) c.,** par hasard; par un coup de hasard; **it was quite by c., by the merest c., that. . .,** c'est par un pur hasard, par le plus grand des hasards, que. . .; **by a happy, lucky, c.,** par un heureux hasard, par un coup de bonheur; **somebody I met by c.,** une connaissance de rencontre; **shall we see you there by any c.?** est-ce qu'on vous y verra par extraordinaire? **do you by any c. know his address?** sauriez-vous son adresse par hasard? *Lit:* **c. so ordained it that. . .,** le hasard voulut, fit, que + *ind. or sub.*; **to act as c. directs,** s'en remettre au hasard; agir au petit bonheur; **to leave nothing to c.,** ne rien laisser au hasard; parer à toute éventualité; **to leave everything to c.,** s'en remettre au hasard; **the chances are against me,** les chances sont contre moi; **I'm not taking any chances,** je ne veux rien laisser au hasard; **the chances are that. . .,** il y a gros à parier que. . .; **to do sth. on the off c.,** faire qch. à tout hasard; **I went there on the off c. of meeting him,** je m'y suis rendu dans le vague espoir de le rencontrer, dans le cas où il y serait; (*b*) **to submit to the chances of war,** se soumettre au sort, à la fortune, de la guerre; **to look, have an eye, to the main c., to keep an eye on the main c.,** songer à ses propres intérêts; ne pas perdre de vue son propre intérêt; songer au solide. **2.** (*a*) occasion *f*; **now's your c.,** vous avez la partie belle, vous avez beau jeu; **it's your last c.,** c'est votre dernière chance (de succès, de vous corriger, etc.); *Sch: etc:* **those who failed in July get a second c. in November,** ceux qui ont échoué au mois de juillet peuvent se repêcher en novembre; **second-c. exam.,** examen *m* de repêchage; **it's a c. in a thousand,** ces chances-là n'arrivent qu'une fois; **I will call to see you the first c. I get,** je passerai chez vous à la première occasion; (*b*) **to have, to stand, a c.,** avoir des chances de succès; **he runs, stands, a good c. of being chosen,** il a des chances d'être choisi; **to stand no c. against s.o.,** n'être pas de taille à lutter contre qn; **he hasn't the slightest c., the ghost of a c., an earthly c., of succeeding,** *F:* **he doesn't stand a snowball's c. in hell,** il n'a pas la moindre chance, l'ombre d'une chance, de réussir; **you haven't a dog's c.,** tout est contre vous; **I wouldn't give much for his chances,** (i) il n'a pas la moindre chance de réussir; (ii) je ne donne pas cher de sa peau; **to have an even, a fifty-fifty, c.,** avoir des chances égales; **to give s.o. a c., a sporting c.,** (i) mettre qn à l'essai; (ii) donner une chance à qn; (iii) entendre qn jusqu'au bout; agir loyalement avec qn; **he never had a fair c.,** il n'a jamais eu l'occasion de montrer ce qu'il savait faire; **the scheme was never given a c.,** on n'a rien fait pour aider la réussite de ce projet; **to take one's c.,** risquer (les chances). **3.** risque *m*; **to take a c.,** encourir un risque; **I'm taking no chances,** je ne veux rien risquer; **don't take too many chances!** ne vous hasardez pas trop! **to take a sporting c.,** essayer le coup. **4.** *attrib.* fortuit, accidentel; **c. event,** événement fortuit; **c. discovery,** découverte accidentelle; **c. meeting,** rencontre de hasard; rencontre fortuite; **c.-met,** rencontré par hasard; **a c. acquaintance,** une connaissance fortuite, de rencontre; **c. visitors,** visiteurs inattendus.

chance[2]. **1.** *v.i.* (*a*) (*happen*) **to c. to do sth.,** faire qch. par hasard; **if I c. to find it,** si par hasard je le trouve; si je viens à le trouver; **it chanced that I. . ., I chanced to . . .,** il arriva par hasard que je. . ., il m'arriva de . . ., il se trouva que je. . .; (*b*) *O: & Lit:* **to c. on s.o., on sth.,** trouver, rencontrer, qn, qch., par hasard; tomber (par hasard) sur qn, sur qch.; **a taxi chanced by,** un taxi passait. **2.** *v.tr.* risquer; **I decided to c. a rebuff,** je décidai de courir la chance d'une rebuffade; **I'll do it and c. the scolding,** je le ferai quitte à être grondé; **to c. it,** risquer le coup; **I'll c. it! let's c. it!** risquons le coup! **to c. one's luck, one's arm,** risquer le coup, tenter sa chance.

chancel ['tʃɑ:nsəl], *s. Ecc.Arch:* chœur *m* (et sanctuaire *m*); **c. screen,** jubé *m.*

chancellor ['tʃɑ:nsələr], *s.* (*a*) chancelier *m* (d'une cathédrale, d'un ordre de chevalerie, d'une université); (*b*) **the Lord (High) C., the C. of England,** le Grand Chancelier (préside la Chambre des Lords, exerce la haute autorité judiciaire, = Ministre *m* de la Justice), (*pl. Lord Chancellors*); **C. of the Exchequer,** Chancelier de l'Échiquier, = Ministre des Finances; **C. of the Duchy of Lancaster,** le Chancelier du duché de Lancastre (membre du Cabinet, le plus souvent sans portefeuille, qui représente le monarque).

chancellery, chancellory ['tʃɑ:nsələri], *s.* chancellerie *f.*

chancellorship ['tʃɑ:nsələʃip], *s.* charge *f,* dignité *f,* de chancelier; chancelariat *m,* cancellariat *m.*

chance-medley ['tʃɑ:ns'medli], *s. Jur:* homicide *m* involontaire (au cours d'une rixe, etc.).

chancery ['tʃɑ:nsəri], *s.* **1.** (*a*) *Jur:* **(Court of) C.,** cour *f* de la chancellerie (une des divisions de la Haute Cour de Justice); (*b*) *Dipl:* chancellerie (d'une ambassade).

2. *Box: Wr:* **hold in c.,** cravate *f*; **to get one's opponent's head in c.,** enfourcher la tête de son adversaire; cravater son adversaire; *Fig:* **in c.,** dans une impasse; à la merci de ses adversaires.

chancre ['ʃæŋkər], *s. Med:* chancre (vénérien); **hard c.,** chancre induré; **soft c.,** chancre mou; chancroïde *m*, chancrelle *f*.

chancroid ['ʃæŋkrɔid], *s. Med:* chancroïde *m*; chancre mou.

chancrous ['ʃæŋkrəs], *a. Med:* chancreux.

chancy ['tʃɑːnsi], *a. F:* **1.** chanceux, incertain; risqué. **2.** *Scot:* propice; qui porte bonheur.

chandelier [ʃændə'liər], *s.* lustre *m* (pour éclairage).

chandler ['tʃɑːndlər], *s.* (*a*) **(tallow) c.,** chandelier, -ière; (i) fabricant *m*, (ii) marchand *m*, de chandelles; (*b*) = épicier-droguiste *m*, *pl.* épiciers-droguistes; marchand *m* de couleurs; **ship('s) c.,** fournisseur *m*, approvisionneur *m*, de navires; entrepreneur *m* de marine; **corn c.,** marchand de blé, de grains; grainetier, -ière.

chandlery ['tʃɑːndləri], *s.* (*a*) épicerie-droguerie *f*; (*b*) (*also pl.* **chandleries**) articles *mpl* d'épicerie-droguerie; (*c*) **ship('s) c.,** fournitures *fpl* de navires.

change[1] [tʃein(d)ʒ], *s.* **1.** changement *m* (d'air, d'occupation, de lieu, dans les affaires, etc.); retour *m* (de la marée); changement, variation *f* (du temps); altération *f* (du visage, de la voix); revirement *m* (d'opinion, de fortune); **c. from fear to hope,** passage *m* de la crainte à l'espoir; **c. in the moon,** changement de lune, *esp.* nouvelle lune; **changes in a frontier line,** modifications *f* de frontière; **c. of address,** changement de domicile; **I'll give you a card with my c. of address,** je vous donnerai une carte avec ma nouvelle adresse; *Mil:* **c. of station,** changement de garnison; *Aut: etc:* **oil c.,** vidange *f*; **c. for the better, for the worse (in health, etc.),** amélioration *f*, altération (de la santé, etc.); changement en mieux, en mal; **the changes of life,** les vicissitudes *f* de la vie; **sudden c. of fortune,** revirement de fortune; **sudden c. in the wind,** saute *f* de vent; **the barometer is at c.,** le baromètre est à, au, variable; **to make, effect, a c.,** effectuer un changement, apporter une modification **(in,** à); **to undergo a c.,** changer; subir un changement; **to undergo a complete c.,** se métamorphoser; **a great c. had come over him,** un grand changement s'était opéré en lui; **there have been many changes on the staff,** il y a eu beaucoup de mutations *f* dans le personnel; **complete c. of staff,** renouvellement *m* du personnel; **there has been a complete c. of staff,** le personnel a été complètement renouvelé; **the changes in the cabinet have been well received,** le remaniement du ministère a été bien accueilli du public; **it is quite a c. to see you smile,** c'est une nouveauté que de vous voir sourire; **there are never any changes here,** on ne change jamais rien ici; **old people hate c.,** les vieillards détestent le changement; la nouveauté répugne aux vieillards; **you need a c.,** il vous faudra un changement d'air, d'occupation; **the country will make a nice c. for me,** la campagne me changera; **this journey will be (a bit of) a c. for you,** ce voyage vous changera un peu; **for a c.,** comme distraction; pour changer; **anything for a c.,** tout nouveau, tout beau; *F:* **it, that, makes a c.,** ça change toujours les idées; *Jur:* **c. of ownership,** mutation *f*; **c. of life,** *F:* **the c.,** retour *m* d'âge; *Rail: etc:* **c. of route,** déviation *f* de parcours; *Artil: etc:* **c. in range,** variation *f* de hausse; *El:* **c. of connection,** commutation *f*; **c. of direction of current,** inversion *f* du courant; *Mth: Opt:* **c. of direction (of curve, ray),** inflexion *f*; **c. of front,** (i) *Mil:* mouvement *m* de conversion; (ii) volte-face *f inv* (politique, etc.); revirement (d'opinions); *Nau:* **c. round,** renverse *f* (du vent). **2.** (*a*) **c. of clothes,** vêtements *mpl* de rechange; **c. of linen,** linge *m* de rechange; linge blanc; (*b*) *A.Trans:* (*in coaching*) **c. of horses,** relais *m*. **3.** (*exchange*) change *m*; **to gain by the c.,** gagner au change. **4.** (*a*) monnaie *f*; **small c.,** petite monnaie; **to get c.,** faire de la monnaie; **to get c. for £5,** faire la monnaie de cinq livres; **to give c. for £5,** donner, rendre, la monnaie de cinq livres; **you may keep the c.,** vous pouvez garder le reste; **no c. given,** on ne rend pas de monnaie; le public est tenu de faire l'appoint; *P: A:* **take your c. out of that!** voilà tout ce que vous aurez de moi! si ça ne vous plaît pas, allez vous promener! *F:* **he won't get much c. out of me,** il perdra ses peines avec moi; (*b*) *F:* la Bourse; **on 'C.,** à la Bourse. **5. to ring the changes,** carillonner avec variation, avec permutations; **to ring the changes on a subject,** ressasser, rabâcher, un sujet; chanter qch. sur tous les tons; broder des variations sur un sujet; *P:* **ringing the changes,** vol *m* au rendez-moi.

change[2], *v.*

I. *v.tr. & i.* **1.** *v.tr.* (*a*) changer, modifier (ses projets, son genre de vie, etc.); **to want to c. everything,** vouloir tout changer; **to c. one thing into another,** changer, transformer, une chose dans une autre; **to c. one's ways, one's habits,** se refaire; **to c. one's mind, one's opinion,** changer d'avis; **to c. the subject,** changer de sujet; parler d'autre chose; passer à autre chose; **to c. the conversation,** changer de conversation; détourner la conversation; **the river has changed its course,** la rivière a changé de cours; **the name of the street has been changed,** la rue a changé de nom; (*b*) **to c. the sheets,** changer les draps; **to c. one's clothes,** *v.i.* **to change,** se changer; **to c. one's dress, one's shoes, one's hairstyle,** changer de robe, de chaussures, de coiffure; **I've nothing to c. into,** je n'ai pas de quoi me changer; *F:* **to c. the baby,** changer le bébé; **to c. the air of a room,** renouveler l'air d'une pièce; (*c*) *Aut: etc:* **to c. a tyre,** remplacer un pneu; **to c. the oil,** faire la vidange; **to c. gear,** changer de vitesse; **the engine has changed its note,** le moteur a changé de régime; (*d*) **to c. one's place,** changer de place; **to c. trains,** changer de train; *v.i.* **do we c. (trains, buses, planes) here?** est-ce qu'on change (de train, de car, d'avion) ici? **all c.!** tout le monde descend! *Pol:* **to c. parties,** changer de parti, tourner casaque; **to c. colour,** changer de couleur, de visage; **to c. front,** (i) *Mil:* changer de front; converser; (ii) faire volte-face; **he's always changing front, changing about, around,** il passe sans cesse d'une idée à l'autre; avec lui on ne sait jamais sur quel pied danser; *Mil:* **to c. arms,** changer son fusil d'épaule; **to c. the guard,** relever la garde; (*e*) (*exchange*) **to c. one thing for another,** changer, troquer, une chose contre une autre; **I changed the gloves for a larger pair,** j'ai changé les gants pour une paire plus grande; **to c. places, seats, with s.o.,** changer de place avec qn; *Fig:* **I wouldn't (like to) c. places with him,** je ne changerais pas avec lui; *Fin:* **to c. one investment for another,** arbitrer une valeur contre une autre; **to c. dollars into francs,** changer des dollars contre des francs, en francs; (*f*) **to c. a note,** (i) changer un billet (de banque); (ii) donner la monnaie d'un billet (de banque). **2.** *v.i.* (*a*) (se) changer, se modifier, varier; (*of moon*) changer de quartier; se renouveler; (*of luck*) tourner; **to c. completely,** se métamorphoser; **to c. for the better,** changer en mieux; s'améliorer; (*of weather*) tourner au beau; **the weather has changed since yesterday,** le temps a changé depuis hier; **to c. for the worse,** s'altérer; **to c. in appearance,** changer d'aspect; **the lights changed from green to amber,** les feux ont passé du vert à l'orange; **to c. (over) from one system to another,** passer d'un système à un autre; **the water changed into steam,** l'eau s'est changée, s'est transformée, en vapeur; **the rain has changed to snow,** la pluie s'est changée en neige; **the wind has changed,** le vent a sauté, a tourné; **the wind has changed to the west,** le vent a tourné à l'ouest; **I wouldn't wish it to be changed,** je ne voudrais pas qu'il en fût autrement; (*b*) (*of sentries, Nau: of watches, Ind: of shifts*) se relever.

II. (*compound verbs*) **1. change down,** *v.i. Aut:* rétrograder, passer à une vitesse inférieure; descendre les vitesses; **to c. d. into third,** passer en troisième. **2. change over,** *v.i. El:* permuter, commuter.

3. change up, *v.i. Aut:* passer à une vitesse supérieure; monter les vitesses.

changeability [tʃein(d)ʒə'biliti], **changeableness** ['tʃein(d)ʒəblnis], *s.* variabilité *f* (du temps, de l'humeur); inconstance *f*, mobilité *f* (de caractère); versatilité *f*.

changeable ['tʃein(d)ʒəbl], *a.* **1.** changeant; variable, inconstant, instable; **c. wind,** vent inégal; **c. character, nature,** caractère changeant, instable. **2.** susceptible d'être changé; modifiable.

changeful ['tʃein(d)ʒful], *a. Poet:* capricieux, changeant, inconstant.

changeless ['tʃein(d)ʒlis], *a.* immuable, inaltérable; constant, fixe.

changeling ['tʃein(d)ʒliŋ], *s.* **1.** enfant de fées, substitué à un enfant qu'elles ont volé. **2.** enfant changé en nourrice.

changeover ['tʃein(d)ʒouvər], *s.* **1.** changement *m*, passage *m*, (d'un système à un autre, etc.); *Mec.E:* **c. mechanism,** appareil *m* de substitution. **2.** changement radical, renversement *m* (politique, etc.). **3.** relève *f* (de factionnaires, *Nau:* du quart, etc.). **4.** *El:* commutation *f*; **c. switch,** commutateur *m*; permutateur *m*.

changer ['tʃein(d)ʒər], *s. Tchn:* changeur *m*; *Rec:* **record c.,** changeur de disques; *W.Tel:* **frequency c.,** changeur de fréquence.

change ringing ['tʃein(d)ʒriŋiŋ], *s.* (*campanology*) sonnerie *f* à permutations.

changing[1] ['tʃein(d)ʒiŋ], *a.* changeant; (expression *f*, etc.) mobile.

changing[2], *s.* (*a*) changement *m*; *Sp: etc:* **c. room,** vestiaire *m*; **the c. of the guard,** la relève de la garde; *Meteor:* **c. of the monsoon,** renversement *m* de (la) mousson; (*b*) *Phot:* escamotage *m* (d'une plaque); **c. bag,** manchon *m* de chargement; **c. box,** châssis-magasin *m*, *pl.* châssis-magasins; (*c*) *Mus:* **c. note,** note *f* d'appoggiature.

channel[1] ['tʃænl], *s.* **1.** lit *m* (d'une rivière). **2.** (*a*) passe *f*, chenal *m* (d'un port); **c. entrance, entrance c.,** chenal d'accès; passe; goulet *m*; (*b*) *Geog:* détroit *m*, canal *m*; **the (English) C.,** la Manche; **the C. Fleet,** la flotte de la Manche; **on the other side of the C.,** outre-Manche; **the Irish C.,** la mer d'Irlande; **St George's C.,** le canal Saint-Georges; **the C. Islands,** les îles Anglo-Normandes; **the C. Tunnel,** le tunnel sous la Manche; *Nau:* **to enter a c.,** emmancher. **3.** canal, conduit *m* (d'un liquide, d'un gaz); goulotte *f*; *Hyd.E:* **discharge, overflow, c.,** canal de fuite; **inlet c.,** canal d'amenée; **diversion, bypass, c.,** canal de dérivation; **spillway c.,** canal d'évacuation; *Mec.E: etc:* **oil c.,** rainure *f* de graissage; chenal à huile; patte *f* d'araignée; *Metall:* **c. from the furnace to mould,** goulée *f* du fourneau pour la fonte. **4.** (*a*) *Arch: etc:* cannelure *f*, glyphe *m* (d'une colonne); rainure; *Mec.E:* **c. guide,** rainure-guide *f*, *pl.* rainures-guides; (*b*) **c. iron,** (i) fer cannelé; barre *f* en U, fer en U; (ii) *Const:* crochet *m* de gouttière; **c. (bar),** profilé *m* en U; *Const:* **c. stone,** culière *f*; (*c*) gorge *f*, goujure *f* (d'une poulie). **5.** (*a*) *Hyd.E:* rigole *f* (d'irrigation); **draining c.,** barbacane *f* (d'un pont); **guide c.,** coursier *m*; (*b*) *Arch: Civ.E:* dalot *m*; (*c*) rigole (de rue, de route). **6.** (*a*) voie *f*; **news that has come to us through various channels,** nouvelles qui nous sont venues par différentes voies; **to go through the official channels,** suivre la filière, la voie hiérarchique, les degrés hiérarchiques; **through the channels of diplomacy, through diplomatic channels,** par voie diplomatique; **channels of communication (of a country),** artères *f* (d'un pays); **to withdraw capital from its natural channels of circulation,** enlever des capitaux à leur circuit naturel; **to open up new channels for trade,** créer de nouveaux débouchés au commerce; (*b*) *El: Elcs: etc:* voie; *T.V: W.Tel:* chaîne *f*; voie, piste *f* (de bande magnétique); canal (de bande perforée); **simplex, duplex, c.,** voie simplex; voie duplex, duplexée; **c. capacity,** capacité *f* de voie; débit *m* d'un canal.

channel[2], *v.tr.* **(channelled) 1.** creuser des rigoles dans (un terrain); (*of rain, etc.*) raviner (un terrain). **2.** (*a*) canaliser; (*b*) *Cmptr:* acheminer, canaliser (des informations). **3.** *Arch: etc:* canneler (une colonne); rainurer. **4.** (*a*) *Tchn:* tailler (une pierre) en caniveau; (*b*) évider (une lame de sabre, etc.); **to c. (out) the table of a machine tool,** échancrer le plateau d'une machine-outil.

channel[3], *s. Nau:* porte haubans *m inv.*; **c. plate,** cadène *f* de haubans.

channel-bill ['tʃænəlbil], *s. Orn:* scythrops géant.

channelize ['tʃænəlaiz], *v.tr. U.S:* canaliser; *Aut: etc:* **channelized intersection,** croisement *m* de routes à chaussée divisée en voies (obligatoires).

chanson [ʃɑ̃:sɔ̃], *s. Lit:* **c. de geste,** chanson *f* de geste.

chant[1] [tʃɑːnt], *s.* chant *m* (monotone), mélopée *f*; *Ecc:* psalmodie *f*; **plain c.,** plain-chant *m*, *pl.* plains-chants; **Gregorian c.,** chant grégorien.

chant[2], *v.tr.* **1.** (*a*) *A:* chanter; **to c. s.o.'s praises,** chanter les louanges de qn; louanger qn; (*b*) *Ecc:* psalmodier. **2.** *A:* maquignonner (un cheval); vanter (un mauvais cheval).

chantefable [ʃɑ̃:nt'feibl], *s. Lit:* chantefable *f*.

chanter ['tʃɑːntər], *s.* **1.** (*pers.*) (*a*) *Ecc:* chantre *m*; (*b*) *Pej: A:* **horse c.,** maquignon *m*. **2.** *Mus:* chalumeau *m*, musette *f* (de la cornemuse, du biniou). **3.** *Orn:* mouchet *m*.

chanterelle[1] [tʃæntə'rel], *s. Fung: Cu:* chanterelle *f*, girolle *f*.

chanterelle[2], *s. Mus:* chanterelle *f*.

chanteuse [ʃɑ̃:'təːz], *s.f.* chanteuse (de cabaret).

chantey ['ʃænti], *s.* = CHANTY.

chanticleer [tʃænti'kliər], *s. Lit:* chantecler *m* (le coq).

Chantilly [ʃɑ̃'tiːji], *Pr.n. Geog:* Chantilly; **c. lace,** dentelle *f* de Chantilly; *Cu:* **crème C.,** crème *f* Chantilly.

chanting[1] ['tʃɑːntiŋ], *a.* (*of voice, intonation*) monotone, traînant; (*of accent*) chantant.

chanting[2], *s.* psalmodie *f*.

chantlate ['tʃɑːtleit], *s. Const:* chanlatte *f*.

chantress ['tʃɑːntres], *s.f. A: Lit:* chanteuse; femme-poète, *pl.* femmes-poètes.

chantry ['tʃɑːntri], *s. Ecc:* (*a*) fondation *f* de messes pour le repos de l'âme du fondateur; (*b*) **c. priest,** prêtre *m* de la fondation; (*c*) **c. (chapel),** chantrerie *f*.

chanty ['ʃænti], *s.* **(sea) c.,** chant *m* de manœuvre (à bord); chanson *f* à hisser, de bord.

chaos [ˈkeiɔs], *s.* chaos *m*; **everything is in a state of c.,** tout est dans le chaos, dans la confusion.

chaotic [keiˈɔtik], *a.* chaotique; complètement désorganisé.

chaotically [keiˈɔtik(ə)li], *adv.* chaotiquement; d'une manière complètement désorganisée.

chap[1] [tʃæp], *s.* gerçure *f*, crevasse *f*, gerce *f* (sur la peau).

chap[2], *v.tr.* **(chapped)** gercer, crevasser (la peau); (*of hands*) **to get chapped,** *v.i.* **to c.,** se gercer, se crevasser; **my hands are chapped,** j'ai des crevasses, des gerçures, des gerces, aux mains.

chap[3], *s.* (*usu. pl.*) **1.** bajoue(s) *f* (d'un cochon, *F:* d'une personne); *Cu:* **Bath c.,** joue *f* de porc fumée. **2.** *Tls:* mors *m*, mâchoire *f* (d'étau).

chap[4], *s.* **1.** (*a*) *A:* = CHAPMAN; (*b*) *A: & Dial:* acheteur *m*, client *m* **2.** *F:* garçon *m*, type *m*, individu *m*; **a good c.,** un bon type; **a poor sort of c.,** un pauvre type; **an odd, a queer, c.,** un drôle de type, de bonhomme; *O:* **I say, old c.!** dis, mon vieux!

chaparral [tʃæpəˈræl], *s. Geog:* chapar(r)al *m* (du Mexique, etc.).

chapbook [ˈtʃæpbuk], *s. A.Publ:* livre *m* de colportage.

chape [tʃeip], *s.* **1.** attache *f* (d'une boucle, etc.). **2.** chape *f*, bouterolle *f*, dard *m* (d'un fourreau de sabre). **3.** *Ven:* bout *m* de la queue (d'un renard).

chapel [ˈtʃæpl], *s.* **1.** (*a*) chapelle *f*; oratoire (particulier); **C. royal,** chapelle d'un palais royal; (*b*) chapelle (d'un collège, etc.); *Sch: A:* **to keep one's chapels,** faire acte de présence à un office; **to miss a c.,** manquer un office; (*c*) **c. of ease,** (i) (chapelle de) secours *m*, (église) succursale *f*; annexe *f*; (ii) *A: Lit:* cabinet *m* d'aisances; **mortuary c., c. of rest** = chapelle ardente; (*d*) chapelle latérale (d'une cathédrale, etc.); **Lady c.,** chapelle de la Vierge; (*e*) temple (protestant); *O:* **are you church or c.?** êtes-vous anglican ou dissident? **2.** (i) *Typ: A:* atelier (syndiqué); (ii) *Typ: Publ:* branche *f* du syndicat (des imprimeurs, des éditeurs); **Father of the C.,** chef *m* de l'atelier.

chapelry [ˈtʃæp(ə)lri], *s.* région desservie par une chapelle.

chaperon[1] [ˈʃæpəroun], *s.* chaperon *m* (d'une jeune fille); **to act as c.,** jouer le rôle de chaperon.

chaperon[2], *v.tr.* **(chaperoned)** chaperonner (une jeune fille).

chaperonage [ˈʃæpərənidʒ], *s.* surveillance *f* (d'une jeune fille).

chapfallen [ˈtʃæpfɔːl(ə)n], *a. A:* **1.** *Lit:* aux joues flasques; (mort) dont la mâchoire retombe. **2.** penaud, décontenancé; l'oreille basse.

chapiter [ˈtʃæpitər], *s. A: B:* chapiteau *m* (de colonne).

chaplain [ˈtʃæplin], *s. Ecc:* aumônier *m*; **army c.,** aumônier militaire; *Mil:* **Chaplains' Branch,** Direction *f* de l'Aumônerie militaire.

chaplaincy [ˈtʃæplinsi], **chaplainship** [ˈtʃæplinʃip], *s.* aumônerie *f*.

chaplet [ˈtʃæplit], *s.* **1.** *Lit:* guirlande *f*, couronne *f* (de fleurs, etc.); bandeau *m*. **2.** *Ecc:* chapelet *m* (d'un tiers du rosaire, de 55 grains). **3.** *Arch:* moulure *f* en perles; chapelet. **4.** *Metall:* support *m* d'âme (d'un moule); **stud c.,** support double. **5.** *Orn:* huppe *f*, aigrette *f*.

chapman, *pl.* **-men** [ˈtʃæpmən], *s.m. A:* colporteur.

chappie, chappy[1] [ˈtʃæpi], *s.m. F: O:* garçon, type; (*to dog*) **there's a good little c.,** t'es un joli chien-chien!

chappy[2], *a.* couvert de gerçures; gercé.

chaps [tʃæps], *s.pl.* pantalon *m* de cuir (de cowboy).

chaptalization [ʃæptəlaiˈzeiʃ(ə)n], *s. Winem:* chaptalisation *f*.

chaptalize [ˈʃæptəlaiz], *v.tr. Winem:* chaptaliser (le moût).

chapter [ˈtʃæptər], *s.* **1.** chapitre *m* (d'un livre, etc.); **to give c. and verse for sth.,** (i) citer le chapitre et le verset (de la Bible); (ii) citer ses autorités, fournir des documents, à l'appui d'une affirmation; **to begin a new c. in one's life,** commencer un nouveau chapitre de sa vie; **to the end of the c.,** jusqu'au bout, jusqu'à la fin; jusqu'à la fin des fins; **a c. of accidents,** une suite de malheurs; une succession de mésaventures; *F:* la série noire. **2.** *Ecc:* chapitre (de chanoines, de moines); **c. house,** (i) *Ecc:* salle *f* capitulaire, (salle du) chapitre; (ii) *NAm:* salle de réunion (d'une confrérie universitaire).

char[1] [tʃɑːr], *s. Ich:* ombre *m* (chevalier), omble *m* (chevalier).

char[2], *s.f. F:* femme de ménage.

char[3], *v.i. F:* faire des ménages.

char[4], *s.* noir animal, charbon animal.

char[5]. **1.** *v.tr.* **(charred)** (*a*) carboniser (superficiellement); flamber; charbonner; (*b*) réduire (du bois, des os) en charbon. **2.** *v.i.* se carboniser, (se) charbonner.

char[6], *s. P:* thé (très fort).

chara [ˈkeirə], *s. Algae:* chara *f*, charagne *f*.

charabanc [ˈʃærəbæŋ], *s. A:* (*a*) **horse c.,** char à bancs; (*b*) autocar *m*.

Characeae [kæˈreisiiː], *s.pl. Algae:* characées *f*.

Characidae [kæˈræsidiː], **Characinidae** [kærəˈsinidiː], *s.pl. Ich:* characinidés *m*, characins *m*.

characin [ˈkærəsin], **characinid** [kəˈræsinid], *s. Ich:* characin *m*, characinidé *m*.

character [ˈkærəktər], *s.* **1.** (*a*) *Typ: etc:* caractère *m*; lettre *f*; **printed in Roman, Greek, characters,** imprimé en caractères romains, grecs; (*b*) *Cmptr:* **special c.,** caractère spécial; **shift-in c.,** caractère de série normale; **shift-out c.,** caractère de série spéciale; **binary c.,** caractère binaire; **binary-coded c.,** caractère codé (en) binaire. **2.** (*a*) (*nature*) caractère, marque distinctive (de qn, d'une race, d'un livre, d'une maladie, etc.); **books of this c.,** les livres de ce genre; *Biol:* **hereditary, acquired, c.,** caractère héréditaire, acquis; **these paintings are not in keeping with the c. of the room,** ces peintures ne s'harmonisent pas avec la pièce; (*b*) **work that lacks c.,** œuvre *f* qui manque de caractère; **face full of c.,** physionomie *f* qui a du caractère; **house of c.,** maison qui a beaucoup de caractère; **region with a c. of its own,** région *f* qui a une physionomie particulière, un caractère particulier. **3.** (*moral strength*) **man of (strong) c.,** homme *m* de caractère, de volonté; **man without c.,** homme dépourvu de caractère; **he lacks (strength of) c.,** il n'a pas de (force de) caractère; **c. building,** formation *f* du caractère. **4.** (*a*) (*reputation*) réputation *f*; **man without a c.,** homme perdu de réputation; **place of a very dubious c.,** endroit mal famé, de mauvaise réputation; (*b*) (*testimonial*) certificat *m* (de moralité, de bonne conduite); **certificate of good c.,** certificat de bonne vie et mœurs; **to give a servant a good, bad, c.,** donner un bon, un mauvais, certificat à un(e) domestique. **5.** (*a*) *Lit: Th: etc:* personnage *m*; *Cin:* rôle *m* de composition; **a c. straight out of a novel,** un vrai personnage de roman; **in c.,** (i) *Th: etc:* dans son rôle, dans le vrai, dans la peau du personnage; (ii) (*of person's action*) qui s'accorde bien avec son caractère; **out of c.,** (i) *Th: etc:* pas dans le rôle; (jeu) déplacé; (rôle) interprété à contre-sens; (ii) (*of person's action*) étonnant de sa part; qui ne s'accorde guère avec son caractère; **c. actor,** acteur *m* de genre; **c. part,** rôle chargé; **characters (in order of appearance),** personnages (*Th:* par ordre d'entrée en scène, *Cin:* par ordre d'apparition (à l'écran)); *W.Tel:* **characters (in order of speaking),** distribution *f* (par ordre d'entrée en ondes); *Danc:* **c. dance,** danse *f* de caractère; *Lit:* **c. study,** étude *f* de caractère; **c. drawing, painting,** peinture *f* de caractères; *Lit.Hist:* **c. comedy,** comédie *f* de caractère; *Gr.Lit:* **the Characters of Theophrastus,** les caractères de Théophraste; (*b*) **a public c.,** une personnalité; **the outstanding characters in history,** les figures *f* remarquables de l'histoire; **a bad c.,** un mauvais sujet, un mauvais garnement; **a suspicious c.,** un individu suspect, louche; **he's a c.!** c'est un type, un original, un numéro!

characterful [ˈkæriktəful], *a.* plein de caractère.

characterial [kærəkˈtiəriəl], *a.* caractériel.

characteristic [kærəktəˈristik]. **1.** *a.* caractéristique; **this attitude is c. of him,** cette attitude le caractérise, lui est particulière; **his c. cynicism,** le cynisme qui le caractérise; **oranges have a c. smell,** les oranges ont une odeur stique, particulière; **symptoms c. of an illness,** symptômes diacritiques, qui caractérisent une maladie; *Adm:* **c. signs,** signalement *m*; signes particuliers; *Bot:* **c. species,** espèce *f* caractéristique; *Mus:* **c. piece,** morceau *m* de genre. **2.** *s.* caractéristique *f*; (*a*) trait *m*, signe *m*, de caractère; trait caractéristique; particularité *f*; caractère *m*, attribut *m*; **a c. of French farmers,** un trait caractéristique, une particularité, de l'agriculteur français; **the Siamese cat has some of the characteristics of a dog,** le chat siamois a certains attributs du chien; **the characteristics of this fashion,** les caractéristiques de cette mode; **this wine has some of the characteristics of burgundy,** ce vin ressemble à certains points de vue au bourgogne; (*b*) *Mth:* caractéristique (d'un logarithme); (point *m*) caractéristique (d'une courbe); *Ph: etc:* **c. (curve),** (courbe) caractéristique; *Av:* **surge characteristics,** caractéristiques de stabilité.

characteristically [kærəktəˈristik(ə)li], *adv.* d'une manière caractéristique; **c., he refused,** il a refusé, ce qui était bien de lui.

characterization [kærəktəraiˈzeiʃ(ə)n], *s.* caractérisation *f*.

characterize [ˈkærəktəraiz], *v.tr.* caractériser (un personnage, un siècle); être caractéristique de (qn); **scheme characterized by a certain idealism,** projet marqué d'un certain idéalisme.

characterless [ˈkærəktəlis], *a.* (*a*) sans caractère, dépourvu de caractère; mou, *f* molle; **he's completely c.,** il est complètement nul; (*b*) insipide, terne, sans intérêt; *Th:* **c. interpretation of Macbeth,** interprétation insipide du rôle de Macbeth.

characterologist [kærəktəˈrɔlədʒist], *s.* caractérologue *mf*.

characterology [kærəktəˈrɔlədʒi], *s.* caractérologie *f*.

charade [ʃəˈrɑːd], *s.* charade *f*; **dumb c.,** charade mimée; **to act a c.,** jouer une charade.

Charadriidae [kæræˈdraiidiː], *s.pl. Orn:* charadriidés *m*.

Charadriiformes [kærədriiˈfɔːmiːz], *s.pl. Orn:* charadriiformes *m*.

Charales [kəˈreiliːz], *s.pl. Algae:* charales *f*.

charas [ˈtʃɑːrəs], *s.* charras *m*, résine *f* provenant du chanvre indien.

charcoal [ˈtʃɑːkoul], *s.* **1.** (*a*) charbon *m* (de bois); **activated c.,** charbon activé; **c. powder,** charbon de bois pulvérulent, en poudre; **c. iron,** fer *m* au (charbon de) bois; **c. block,** aggloméré *m* de charbon de bois; **c. furnace,** carbonisateur *m*; **c. kiln,** meule *f* (de charbon de bois); charbonnière *f*, faulde *f*, place *f* à charbon; *Med:* **c. biscuit,** biscuit *m* au charbon de bois; (*b*) **animal c.,** noir animal, charbon animal. **2.** *Art:* fusain *m*; **drawn in c.,** dessiné au fusain; **c. drawing,** (dessin *m* au) fusain; charbonnée *f*; **sketch in c. and (white) chalk,** dessin à deux crayons.

chard [tʃɑːd], *s. Hort: Cu:* carde *f*; **Swiss c.,** bette, blette, poirée.

charge[1] [tʃɑːdʒ], *s.* **1.** (*a*) charge *f* (d'une cartouche, d'une mine, etc.); **one of the beaters received the c. full in the face,** un des rabatteurs a reçu la décharge en pleine figure; *Exp:* **bursting c.,** charge d'explosion; **hollow, shaped, c.,** charge creuse; *Artil:* **full c.,** charge de combat; **blank c.,** charge de salut; (*b*) (*of kiln, blast furnace, etc.*) fournée *f*; (*c*) *El:* charge; **bound c.,** charge latente; **space c.,** charge spatiale, d'espace; **residual c.,** charge résiduelle; (*d*) *I.C.E:* **c. of fuel and air,** dose *f* de gaz carburés; (*e*) *P:* (i) marijuana *f*; (ii) piquouse *f*; **to go on the c.,** se camer; (iii) plaisir *m*, émotion *f*; **I got a c. out of it,** ça m'a fait quelque chose. **2.** (*a*) frais *mpl*, prix *m*; *Adm:* droits *mpl*; **advertising charges,** frais de publicité, d'insertion; **list of charges,** tarif *m*; **scale of charges,** barème *m* des prix; **inclusive c.,** tarif tout compris; **extra c.,** supplément *m*; **maintenance charges,** frais d'entretien; **customs charges,** frais de douane; *Tp:* **(tariff) c. for calls,** taxe *f* des conversations; *Adm: etc:* **overnight c.,** hébergement *m*; *Bank:* **bank charges,** frais bancaires; **capital c.,** intérêt *m*, service *m*, des capitaux (investis); **c. account,** compte crédit d'achats; (*in taxi*) **minimum c.,** prise *f* en charge; (*in theatre, museum, etc.*) **c. for admittance, admission,** prix des places; (prix d')entrée *f*; **no c. for admission,** entrée gratuite, gratis; **show with c. for admission,** spectacle payant; **to make a c. for sth.,** compter qch.; **no c. is made for packing,** on ne compte pas l'emballage; l'emballage n'est pas facturé, est gratuit; **free of c.,** (i) *Com: Bank:* exempt de frais, sans frais; (ii) gratis, franco; (iii) à titre gratuit, à titre gracieux; **at a c. of. . .,** moyennant. . .; **at a small c.,** moyennant une faible rétribution; *Com:* **charges forward,** frais *m* à percevoir à la livraison; (*b*) *Jur:* privilège *m*, droit; **subject to the c.,** grevé du privilège; **right of c.,** droit de constitution de privilège; **mortgage c.,** privilège d'hypothèque; **to have a c. on sth.,** avoir un privilège sur qch.; **charges on an estate,** charges d'une succession; **to be a c. on s.o.,** être à la charge de qn. **3.** (*a*) commission *f*, devoir *m*; **to lay a c. on s.o.,** charger qn d'une commission; imposer un devoir à qn; (*b*) charge; emploi *m*; fonction *f*; (*of clergy*) cure *f*; **he conscientiously performed the duties of his charge,** il s'acquittait en conscience des devoirs de sa charge. **4.** (*a*) (*responsibility*) garde *f*, soin *m*; **to take c. of s.o., of sth.,** (i) se charger, avoir soin, de qn, de qch.; prendre qn en garde; faire son affaire de qch.; (ii) (*provide for*) prendre qn à sa charge; *Nau: F:* (*of capstan*) **to take c.,** se dévirer; **nurse in c. of a child,** bonne commise à la garde d'un enfant; **child in c. of a nurse,** enfant sous la garde, la conduite, d'une bonne; **men in c. of an officer,** hommes *m* sous les ordres d'un officier; **to place sth. in s.o.'s c.,** confier qch. à qn, à la garde de qn, aux mains de qn; remettre qch. entre les mains de qn; **to have c. of sth.,** avoir qch. en garde; (*of official*) **to have c., be in c., of sth.,** être préposé à la garde de qch.; **she is in c. of the poultry yard,** c'est elle qui s'occupe de la basse-cour; **person in c.,** administrateur *m* (of, de); délégué, préposé (of, à); *Adm:* **official in c.,** gestionnaire *m* (d'un service); *Mil:* **the captain in c.,** le capitaine de service, de semaine; **c. hand, c. man,** chef *m* d'équipe; **c. engineer,** chef de service (de centrale électrique, etc.);

c. nurse, infirmier *m* en chef; *Jur:* **to take s.o. in c.,** arrêter qn; **to give s.o. in c.,** faire arrêter qn; remettre qn entre les mains de la police; *Mil:* **to take sth. on c.,** porter qch. sur les contrôles; **to write sth. off c.,** rayer qch. des contrôles; (*b*) personne, chose, confiée à la garde de qn; **nurse and her c.,** bonne et l'enfant confié à ses soins; (*c*) **the priest and his c.,** le prêtre et ses ouailles *f.* **5.** recommandation *f,* exhortation *f;* allocution *f* (d'un évêque à son clergé, du juge au jury); résumé *m* (du juge après cause entendue); mandement *m* (d'un évêque). **6.** *Jur:* charge; motif *m,* chef *m* d'accusation, acte *m* d'accusation; inculpation *f;* mise *f* en prévention; (*by public prosecutor*) réquisitoire *m;* **to bring, lay, a c. against s.o.,** relever une charge, porter une accusation, porter plainte, contre qn; **to put on a c.,** porter le motif; **c. book,** rôle *m* d'accusations; (*in police station*) **c. sheet,** cahier *m* des délits et écrous; **c. room,** bureau *m* (de poste de police); **to withdraw one's c.,** retirer sa plainte; **to lay sth. to s.o.'s c.,** charger, accuser, qn de qch.; mettre qch. sur le compte de qn; imputer un grief à qn; **to lay a crime to s.o. else's c.,** rejeter un crime sur autrui; **on a c. of having . . .,** sous l'inculpation d'avoir . . .; **he repudiates the c.,** il repousse l'accusation. **7.** (*a*) *Mil:* charge, attaque *f;* **bayonet c.,** charge, assaut *m,* à la baïonnette; **the cavalry returned to the c. with new courage,** la cavalerie redonna avec un nouveau courage; **to return to the c.,** revenir à la charge; (*b*) *Fb:* choc *m,* charge. **8.** *Her:* charge, chargeure *f;* pièce *f,* meuble *m* (de l'écu).

charge², *v.tr.* **1.** (*a*) charger (un fusil, un conducteur d'électricité, un accumulateur, un haut fourneau, un trou de mine, etc.) (**with,** de); **to c. one's memory with trifles,** charger, bourrer, sa mémoire de vétilles; (*for toast*) **be pleased to c. your glasses!** remplissez vos verres! *El:* **charged conductor,** conducteur chargé, sous tension; **air charged with vapour,** air saturé d'humidité; (*b*) *Her:* charger (une pièce de blason d'une autre); (*c*) *P:* **charged (up),** drogué, bourré, camé. **2.** (*a*) **to c. s.o. with a commission,** charger qn d'une commission, donner une commission à qn; *O:* **to c. s.o. with the task of doing sth.,** charger qn de faire qch.; **to c. s.o. to do sth.,** ordonner, recommander, à qn de faire qch., adjurer qn, sommer qn, de faire qch.; (*b*) *Jur:* (*of judge*) **to c. the jury,** faire l'allocution au jury; faire le résumé des débats. **3.** (*a*) **to c. s.o. with a crime, to c. a crime upon s.o.,** charger qn d'un crime; imputer un crime à qn; inculper qn d'un crime; incriminer qn; **to c. s.o. with complicity, with assault and battery,** inculper qn de complicité, de coups et blessures; **to c. s.o. with having done sth.,** accuser qn, reprocher à qn, d'avoir fait qch.; **charged with . . .,** sous la prévention de . . ., prévenu de . . ., inculpé de . . .; **charged with robbing a wayfarer,** inculpé d'avoir dévalisé un voyageur; **he denies the actions with which he is charged,** il nie les faits qui lui sont reprochés; (*b*) *U.S:* **to c. that . . .,** alléguer que . . . **4.** (*a*) *Com: Fin:* charger, imputer; **to c. an account with all the expenses,** charger un compte de tous les frais; **to c. the postage to the customer,** débiter les frais de poste au client; **commission charged by the bank,** commission prélevée par la banque; **to c. an expense on, to, an account,** imputer, passer, mettre, une dépense à un compte; **to c. a sum to the debit (of an account),** passer une somme au débit (d'un compte); **to c. an expense to the public debt,** assigner une charge sur le Trésor public; **pension charged on an income,** pension payée sur un revenu; **c. it on the bill,** portez-le sur la note; (*b*) **property charged as security for a debt,** immeuble affecté à la garantie d'une créance; (*c*) **to c. s.o. a price for sth.,** prendre, compter, demander, un prix à qn pour qch.; **we are charging you the old prices,** nous vous faisons encore les anciens prix; on vous applique encore l'ancien tarif; **to c. ten francs a yard (for sth.),** demander dix francs du mètre; **how much will you c. for the lot?** combien me faites-vous le tout? **how much do you c. for a car by the day?** combien demandez-vous, prenez-vous, pour une voiture à la journée? **how much do you c. an hour?** combien prenez-vous de l'heure? **to c. a fee,** percevoir un droit; *Tp:* **calls charged for,** conversations taxées; **charging area,** zone *f* de taxation *f.* **5.** *v.tr. & i. Mil: etc:* charger (l'ennemi); courir sus à (l'ennemi); faire une charge; *F:* **to c. into sth.,** donner (de la tête) contre qch.; **the crowd charged across the square,** la foule s'élança à travers la place; **to c. down upon s.o.,** foncer sur qn.

chargeable ['tʃɑːdʒəbl], *a.* **1.** (*of pers.*) accusable, inculpable (**with,** de). **2.** (*a*) (*of pers., thg*) à la charge (**to,** de); **repairs c. to, against, the owner,** réparations *f* à la charge du propriétaire; (*b*) *Fin:* **sum c. to a reserve,** somme *f* imputable sur une réserve. **3.** (*of loss, etc.*) imputable (**to,** à). **4.** (*taxable*) imposable; affectable; grevé (d'un impôt).

chargé d'affaires ['ʃɑːʒeidæ'fɛər], *s. Dipl:* chargé *m* d'affaires.

chargee [tʃɑː'dʒiː], *s. Jur:* créancier privilégié.

charger¹ ['tʃɑːdʒər], *s. A:* grand plat.

charger², *s.* **1.** cheval *m* de bataille, cheval d'armes; *A:* destrier *m.* **2.** (*device*) chargeur *m* (de fusil, d'accumulateur); chargeuse *f* mécanique (de haut fourneau, etc.); *El:* **trickle c.,** chargeur à régime lent, par filtrage.

charging ['tʃɑːdʒiŋ], *s.* chargement *m;* remplissage *m;* *Ind:* **c. hopper,** remplisseur *m;* *Gasm: etc:* **c. machine,** chargeur *m* mécanique; chargeuse *f;* *El:* **battery c.,** (re)charge *f* des accus; **trickle c.,** chargement par filtrage; **c. current,** courant *m* de charge; **c. panel,** tableau *m* de charge.

charily ['tʃɛərili], *adv.* **1.** avec précaution; avec circonspection. **2.** parcimonieusement; avec parcimonie.

chariness ['tʃɛərinis], *s.* **1.** circonspection *f,* prudence *f* (**of doing sth.,** à faire qch.). **2.** parcimonie *f* (de paroles, de louanges).

chariot ['tʃæriət], *s.* **1.** *Poet: Hist:* char *m.* **2.** *A:* carrosse *m.* **3.** *Rom.Ant: etc:* **war c.,** char de guerre. **4.** *Tg: Th:* chariot *m.*

charioteer [tʃæriə'tiər], *s.* **1.** conducteur *m* de char. **2.** *Pr.n. Astr:* **the C.,** le Cocher.

chariotry ['tʃæriətri], *s. A.Mil:* les chars *mpl* de guerre (d'une armée).

charism ['kærizm], **charisma,** *pl.* **charismata** [kæ'rizmə, kæ'rizmətə], *s.* charisme *m.*

charismatic [kæriz'mætik], *a.* charismatique.

charitable ['tʃæritəbl], *a.* **1.** (personne *f,* action *f*) charitable. **2.** (œuvre *f,* société *f*) de bienfaisance, de charité; *Jur:* **c. contract,** contrat *m* de bienfaisance; **c. trust,** œuvre de charité; fondation pieuse.

charitably ['tʃæritəbli], *adv.* charitablement.

charity ['tʃæriti], *s.* **1.** charité *f;* **out of c., for charity's sake,** par charité; *Ecc:* **to be in c. with one's neighbour,** vouloir du bien à son prochain; **to be out of c. with one's fellow men,** être rempli de misanthropie *f;* **she judges others with c.,** elle juge ses semblables avec indulgence *f;* *Prov:* **c. begins at home,** charité bien ordonnée commence par soi(-même); *Ecc:* **Sister of C.,** sœur *f* de charité; **the Sisters of C.,** les Filles *f* de la Charité. **2.** (*a*) acte *m* de charité; **it would be a c. on your part to write to me now and again,** vous feriez acte de charité en m'écrivant de temps en temps; (*b*) charité, aumônes *fpl,* bienfaisance *f;* **to live on c.,** vivre d'aumônes; être à la charité; **c. organization,** société *f,* bureau *m,* de bienfaisance; **c. ball,** bal *m* de bienfaisance; **c. bequest,** legs pieux; **c. fund,** caisse *f* de secours; *A:* **c. boy, girl,** (i) enfant élevé(e) dans un orphelinat, pupille *mf* de l'Assistance publique, (ii) élève *mf* d'une école gratuite; **c. school,** (i) orphelinat *m;* (ii) école gratuite. **3.** œuvre *f* de bienfaisance, de charité; fondation pieuse; *Adm:* **the C. Commissioners,** la Commission de surveillance des œuvres de bienfaisance. **4.** *Bot:* polémonie bleue.

charivari [ʃɑːri'vɑːri, *NAm:* ʃivə'riː, ʃarivə'riː], *s.* charivari *m.*

charlady ['tʃɑːleidi], *s.f. O:* femme de ménage.

charlatan ['ʃɑːlət(ə)n], *s.* charlatan *m.*

charlatanic(al) [ʃɑːlə'tænik(l)], *a.* charlatanesque.

charlatanism ['ʃɑːlətənizm], *s.* charlatanisme *m.*

charlatanry ['ʃɑːlətənri], *s.* charlatanerie *f.*

Charles [tʃɑːlz], *Pr.n.m.* Charles; *Fr.Hist:* **C. the Fair,** Charles le Bel; **C. the Bold, the Rash,** Charles le Téméraire.

charleston ['tʃɑːlstən], *s. Danc:* charleston *m.*

Charley, Charlie ['tʃɑːli], *Pr.n.m.* **1.** Charlot; *Cin:* **Charlie Chaplin,** Charlot. **2.** *F:* **Charley's dead,** ton jupon passe; tu cherches une belle-mère? **3.** *P:* **he's a right, proper, C.,** il en a, en tient, une couche; **good-time C.,** viveur *m,* bambocheur *m;* **cheerful C.,** gai luron. **4.** *pl. P:* seins *mpl,* nénés *mpl.* **5.** *U.S: P:* un blanc (terme employé par les Noirs). **6.** *NAm: F:* **c. horse,** crampe *f;* douleur *f* musculaire.

charlock ['tʃɑːlɔk], *s. Bot:* sanve *f;* moutarde *f* des champs; *F:* moutardin *m,* moutardon *m;* **joint-podded c.,** ravenelle *f.*

Charlotte ['ʃɑːlət]. **1.** *Pr.n.f.* Charlotte. **2.** *s. Cu:* **apple c.,** charlotte *f* (aux pommes); **c. russe,** charlotte russe.

charm¹ [tʃɑːm], *s.* **1.** charme *m* (**against,** contre); sortilège *m,* sort *m,* enchantement *m;* **to be under the c.,** se trouver sous le charme; **to break a c.,** rompre un charme, un enchantement; *F:* **it works like a c.,** ça marche à merveille. **2.** (*a*) amulette *f,* fétiche *m;* (*b*) **(lucky) c.,** breloque *f;* porte-bonheur *m inv.* **3.** (*a*) charme, agrément *m,* aménité *f;* attrait *m* (de la jeunesse, etc.); **to be devoid of c.,** manquer de charme; **it adds c. to the landscape,** cela donne du charme au paysage; **to fall a victim to s.o.'s charms,** succomber aux séductions de qn; tomber sous le charme; *F:* **to turn on the c.,** faire du charme; (*b*) (*of woman*) **(physical) charms,** attraits *mpl,* appas *mpl.*

charm², *v.tr.* **1.** (*a*) charmer, enchanter; **to c. s.o. to sleep,** endormir qn au moyen d'un charme; **to c. away s.o.'s cares,** charmer les ennuis de qn; **he bears a charmed life,** sa vie est sous un charme; (*b*) **to c. a snake,** charmer un serpent. **2. music that charms the ear,** musique *f* qui charme, enchante, l'oreille; **we were charmed by their friendly welcome,** leur accueil chaleureux nous a enchantés.

charmer ['tʃɑːmər], *s.* (*a*) charmeur, -euse; **snake c.,** charmeur de serpents; (*b*) **she's a c.,** elle est adorable; **he's a c.,** il est charmant.

charmeuse [ʃɑː'məːz], *s. Tex:* charmeuse *f.*

charming ['tʃɑːmiŋ], *a.* charmant, ravissant, exquis; délicieux, adorable; **Prince C.,** le Prince Charmant; **he has c. manners,** il est d'une politesse exquise; **a c. child,** un enfant adorable; **what a c. house!** quelle maison ravissante!

charmingly ['tʃɑːmiŋli], *adv.* d'une façon charmante, ravissante; à ravir; **she smiles c.,** elle a un sourire ravissant, adorable.

charmless ['tʃɑːmlis], *a.* sans charme; dépourvu(e) de charme.

charmlessness ['tʃɑːmlisnis], *s.* manque *m* de charme.

charnel ['tʃɑːnl], *s.* **c. (house),** charnier *m* (d'un cimetière, etc.); ossuaire *m.*

Charon ['kɛər(ə)n], *Pr.n.m. Gr.Myth:* C(h)aron; **Charon's boat,** la barque de Charon.

Charophyceae [kærou'faisiiː], *s.pl. Algae:* charophycées *f.*

Charophyta [kæ'rɔfitə], *s.pl. Algae:* charophytes *m.*

charophyte ['kæroufait], *s. Algae:* charophyte *m.*

charqui ['tʃɑːkiː], *s.* charqui *f,* charque *f;* lanières de bœuf desséchées au soleil.

charring¹ ['tʃɑːriŋ], *s.* carbonisation *f;* flambage *m.*

charring², *s.* **to do c.,** faire des ménages.

chart¹ [tʃɑːt], *s.* **1.** carte *f* (marine, aéronautique); **track c.,** (i) carte routière; (ii) carte de la route suivie; **large-scale c., coast c.,** carte à grand point; **small-scale c., ocean c.,** carte à petit point; **c. correction,** amélioration *f* de la carte; **wind c.,** carte des vents; **c. house, c. room,** cabine *f,* chambre *f,* des cartes; kiosque *m,* chambre, de veille, de navigation. **2.** (*a*) graphique *m;* diagramme *m;* **pie c.,** graphique à secteurs; **bar c., band c.,** graphique à barres, à bandes; **scatter c.,** diagramme de dispersion; *Med:* **temperature c.,** feuille *f* de température; *Aut: etc:* **lubrication c.,** tableau *m* de graissage; *Artil:* **battery c., gun c.,** carnet *m* de tir de batterie, de pièce; **trajectory c.,** abaque *m* des trajectoires, **lead c.,** abaque des corrections-but, *Elcs:* **operating c., flow c.,** organigramme *m;* **organization c.,** organigramme hiérarchique; (*b*) tableau; *Sch:* **wall c.,** tableau mural; *Com:* **colour c.,** nuancier *m;* (*c*) *Phot: etc:* **(test) c.,** tableau de mise au point.

chart², *v.tr.* **1.** *Nau:* (*a*) porter (un rocher, etc. sur une carte); (*b*) hydrographier, faire l'hydrographie d'(une mer, etc.). **2.** porter (la température d'un malade, etc.) sur la feuille; établir le graphique d'(une série de relèvements, etc.).

charter¹ [tʃɑːtər], *s.* **1.** (*a*) *Hist: Jur:* charte *f* (d'une ville, d'une université, etc.); status *mpl* (d'une société); privilège *m;* **bank c.,** privilège de la banque; *Hist:* **the Great C.,** la Grande Charte (1215); *Pol:* **the Atlantic C.,** la Charte de l'Atlantique; (*b*) *U.S:* **c. member,** membre *m* originaire (d'une société, etc.). **2.** *Nau: Av:* affrètement *m;* **trip c., time c.,** affrètement au voyage, à temps; **c. plane,** avion-taxi *m, pl.* avions-taxis; *F:* (avion) charter *m;* **c. flight,** vol *m* d'affrètement; vol affrété, nolisé; **on c.,** (i) affrété; (ii) loué; (iii) sous contrat. **3.** *Nau:* **c. (party),** charte-partie *f, pl.* chartes-parties; contrat *m* d'affrètement, de nolisement.

charter², *v.tr.* **1.** instituer (une compagnie) par charte; accorder une charte à (une compagnie, etc.). **2.** affréter, noliser (un navire, un avion); prendre (un navire) à fret; **to c. a coach,** affréter un car.

chartered ['tʃɑːtəd], *a.* **1. c. company,** compagnie privilégiée, à charte; **c. bank,** banque privilégiée; **c. accountant** = expert *m* comptable. **2. c. ship, aircraft,** navire, avion, affrété.

charterer ['tʃɑːtərər], *s. Nau:* affréteur *m,* nolis(at)eur *m.*

Charterhouse ['tʃɑːtəhaus], *s. A:* chartreuse *f,* couvent *m* de chartreux.

chartering ['tʃɑːt(ə)riŋ], *s.* affrètement *m,* nolisement *m* (d'un navire, etc.).

charting ['tʃɑːtiŋ], *s.* reconnaissance *f* (du littoral); relèvement *m* (d'un récif, etc.).

Chartism ['tʃɑːtizm], *s. Eng.Hist:* chartisme *m.*

chartist ['tʃɑːtist], *s. Eng.Hist:* chartiste *m.*

chartless ['tʃɑːtlis], *a.* **1.** sans charte, sans privilège. **2.**

(*a*) (littoral, etc.) non hydrographié; (*b*) (navire *m*) sans cartes marines.

chartreuse [ʃɑːˈtrəːz], *s.* **1.** (*liqueur*) Chartreuse *f.* **2.** *Cu:* (*a*) chartreuse (de légumes); (*b*) gelée garnie de fruits.

chartulary [ˈtʃɑːtjuləri], *s.* cartulaire *m.*

charwoman, *pl.* **-women** [ˈtʃɑːwumən, -wimin], *s.f. O:* femme de ménage.

chary [ˈtʃɛəri], *a.* **1.** prudent, circonspect; **to be c. of, in, doing sth.,** hésiter à faire qch. **2. to be c. of praise,** être avare, chiche, de louanges; ménager, ne pas prodiguer, les éloges.

Charybdis [kəˈribdis], *Pr.n.m. Gr.Myth:* Charybde; **to fall from Scylla into C.,** tomber de Charybde en Scylla.

chase[1] [ˈtʃeis], *s.* **1.** (*a*) chasse *f,* poursuite *f;* **to give c. to s.o.,** donner la chasse à qn; **in c. of s.o.,** à la poursuite de qn; **to go on a wild goose c.,** courir après la lune; **he sent me on a wild goose c.,** il m'a fait courir pour rien; **paper c.,** rallye-paper *m, pl.* rallye-papers; *Navy:* **stern c.,** chasse, poursuite, (dans les eaux du navire chassé); **c. gun,** pièce *f* (i) de chasse, (ii) de retraite; **c. port,** sabord *m* de chasse; (*b*) (= STEEPLECHASE) steeple *m;* (*c*) *Sp:* (*jeu de paume*) chasse; **to make a c.,** marquer une chasse; (*d*) *Ven:* **the c.,** la chasse, *esp.* la chasse à courre. **2.** chasse (terrain non enclos réservé à la chasse). **3.** gibier chassé; proie *f;* *Navy:* navire poursuivi, auquel on donne la chasse.

chase[2], *v.tr.* **1.** chasser, pourchasser (le cerf); *Ven:* (*of hawk*) voler (le gibier). **2.** poursuivre; donner la chasse à (un voleur, l'ennemi, etc.); **to c. away a dog,** chasser un chien; **to c. s.o. out of the house,** chasser qn de la maison; **to c. s.o. up the street,** poursuivre qn dans la rue; **to c. (off) after sth.,** partir à la poursuite de qch.; *F:* **the letter had been chasing him for three months,** la lettre le suivait d'adresse en adresse depuis trois mois; *F:* **to c. after women,** courir les jupons; *P:* **go c. yourself,** va te faire fiche.

chase[3], *s.* **1.** volée *f* (d'un canon). **2.** *Tchn:* rainure *f.*

chase[4], *v.tr.* **1.** (*a*) ciseler, bretteler (l'or, l'argent); **to c. a gun,** graver une bouche à feu; (*b*) relever (le métal) en bosse; repousser (le métal); emboutir; **chased silver,** argent repoussé. **2. to c. a diamond in gold,** enchâsser, sertir, un diamant dans de l'or. **3.** *Metalw:* peigner (un filet de vis, etc.); fileter, tarauder (une vis); repasser, raviver (un filet usagé).

chase[5], *s. Typ:* châssis *m* (de mise en pages).

chaser[1] [ˈtʃeisər], *s.* **1.** (*a*) chasseur *m* (du cerf); (*b*) (= STEEPLECHASER) (i) jockey *m* d'obstacles; (ii) (*horse*) steeple-chaser *m;* (*c*) *F:* **skirt c., woman c.,** coureur *m* de jupons. **2.** (*a*) *Navy:* (navire) chasseur; *Av:* avion *m* de chasse; chasseur; **submarine c.,** chasseur de sous-marins; **bow c., stern c.,** pièce *f* de chasse, de retraite. **3.** *F:* (i) verre *m* d'alcool qu'on prend après un verre de bière, etc.; (ii) verre de bière, etc., qu'on prend après un whisky, etc.

chaser[2], *s. Metalw:* **1.** (*pers.*) ciseleur *m.* **2.** peigne *m* à fileter (pour vis).

Chasidim [ˈkæsidim], *s.pl. Jew.Rel:* Chassidiens *m,* Hasidim *m.*

chasing [ˈtʃeisiŋ], *s.* **1.** (*a*) ciselage *m,* ciselure *f,* brettelure *f;* **c. hammer,** marteau *m* à chasser; (*b*) emboutissage *m,* repoussage *m.* **2.** enchâssure *f.* **3.** filetage *m,* peignage *m* (de pas de vis).

chasm [ˈkæz(ə)m], *s.* **1.** gouffre béant; précipice *m;* fissure *f,* solution *f* de continuité (dans la surface de la terre, etc.). **2.** abîme *m* (entre deux personnes, entre deux choses). **3.** vide *m* énorme; immense lacune *f.*

chasmogamic [kæzmouˈgæmik], **chasmogamous** [kæzˈmɔgəməs], *a. Bot:* chasmogame.

chasmogamy [kæzˈmɔgəmi], *s. Bot:* chasmogamie *f.*

chasmophyte [ˈkæzmoufait], *s. Bot:* chasmophyte *f.*

chassé[1] [ˈʃæsei], *s. Danc:* chassé *m;* **a c. to the left,** un déchassé.

chassé[2], *v.i. Danc:* **to c. to the right,** chasser; **to c. to the left,** déchasser.

chassé-croisé [ˈʃæseiˈkrwɑːzei], *s. Danc:* chassé-croisé *m, pl.* chassés-croisés.

chasselas [ˈʃæsəlɑː], *s. Vit:* chasselas *m.*

chassis [ˈʃæsi], *s.* (*a*) *Aut: Av: etc:* châssis *m;* (*b*) *F:* (*of woman*) **she's got a good c.,** elle est bien carrossée.

chaste [tʃeist], *a.* **1.** (*of pers.*) chaste; pudique. **2.** (*of speech, taste, style*) pur, châtié, simple, sévère; sans ornement. **3.** *Bot:* **c. tree,** petit poivre, poivre sauvage; gattilier *m;* agnus-castus *m;* **c. shrub,** itea *m.*

chastely [ˈtʃeistli], *adv.* chastement, pudiquement; purement.

chasten [tʃeisn], *v.tr. esp. Lit:* **1.** (*a*) (*of providence, suffering, etc.*) châtier, éprouver (qn); (*b*) châtier (ses passions); (*c*) rabattre la présomption, l'orgueil, de (qn); assagir (qn). **2.** châtier (son style, etc.).

chastened [ˈtʃeis(ə)nd], *a.* assagi; calmé, radouci; châtié; **he was in a c. mood,** il était plutôt abattu.

chastener [ˈtʃeisənər], *s.* châtieur *m* (des passions, etc.).

chasteness [ˈtʃeistnis], *s.* (*a*) chasteté *f;* (*b*) *Lit: etc:* pureté *f,* simplicité *f* (de style, etc.).

chastening[1] [ˈtʃeisniŋ], *a.* modérateur, -trice; **the war had had a c. effect upon him,** la guerre l'avait assagi.

chastening[2], *s.* mortification *f* (des passions).

chasteweed [ˈtʃeistwiːd], *s. Bot:* pied-de-chat *m, pl.* pieds-de-chat.

chastise [tʃæsˈtaiz], *v.tr.* châtier; infliger une correction à (qn); corriger (un enfant).

chastisement [tʃæsˈtaizmənt, ˈtʃæstiz-], *s.* châtiment *m;* correction *f* (d'un enfant).

chastiser [tʃæsˈtaizər], *s.* châtieur *m.*

chastity [ˈtʃæstiti], *s.* (*a*) chasteté *f;* continence *f;* pudeur *f,* pudicité *f,* pureté *f;* *A:* **c. belt,** ceinture *f* de chasteté; (*b*) célibat *m;* virginité *f.*

chasuble [ˈtʃæzjubl, ˈtʃæzəbl], *s. Ecc:* chasuble *f.*

chat[1] [tʃæt], *s.* causerie *f,* causette *f;* **a little c., a bit of a c.,** un bout, un brin, de causette; **to have a c. with s.o.,** faire la causette, tailler une bavette, des bavettes, avec qn; **we had a long c.,** nous avons taillé une bonne bavette, nous avons bien bavardé; **he was glad of a c.,** il était content de pouvoir bavarder; *F:* **none of your c.!** pas de réplique! ça suffit! à toi de te taire!

chat[2], *v.* **(chatted).**

I. *v.i.* causer, bavarder; **to c. with s.o.,** bavarder avec qn; faire la causette avec qn; **to c. about one thing and another,** parler de choses et d'autres.

II. (*compound verb*) **chat up,** *v.tr. F:* **to c. up (a girl),** baratiner (une fille).

chat[3], *s. Orn:* tarier *m;* **pied c.,** traquet *m* leucomèle; **yellow-breasted c.,** *Fr.C:* fauvette *f* polyglotte; **cliff c.,** traquet *m* de roche; **palm c.,** jaseur *m* des palmes, *F:* oiseau-palmiste *m, pl.* oiseaux-palmistes.

château [ˈʃætou], *s.* château *m;* **c.-bottled wine,** vin mis en bouteille au château, au domaine.

chatelain [ʃætəlein], *s.* châtelain *m.*

chatelaine [ˈʃætəlein], *s.* **1.** (*pers.*) châtelaine *f;* femme *f* du châtelain. **2.** châtelaine (pour clefs).

chathamite [ˈtʃætəmait], *s. Miner:* chathamite *f.*

chati [(t)ʃɑːˈti], *s. Z:* chati *m.*

chaton [ʃæˈtɔn], *s. Lap:* chaton *m.*

chattel [ˈtʃætl], *s. Jur:* (*a*) bien *m* meuble, bien mobilier; (*b*) *pl.* objets mobiliers; meubles *m;* **chattels personal,** biens personnels; **goods and chattels,** biens et effets *m;* (*c*) **chattels real,** biens réels; (*d*) *Hist:* **the serf was the c. of the lord (of the manor),** le serf était la chose du seigneur.

chatter[1] [ˈtʃætər], *s.* **1.** caquet(age) *m,* jacasserie *f,* jacassement *m,* jaserie *f* (d'oiseaux, de commères); bavardage *m* (de personnes); babil *m* (de bébés, de singes); **the debate degenerated into c.,** la discussion dégénérait en parlotte. **2.** broutage *m* (d'un outil); claquement *m* (d'une machine); *Rec: O:* grattement *m* de l'aiguille); *W.Tel:* **monkey c.,** interférence *f* des bandes latérales; **c. mark,** (i) *Mec.E:* trait *m* de broutage; (ii) *Geol:* strie (faite par un glacier).

chatter[2], *v.i.* **1.** (*of birds*) caqueter, jacasser, jaser; (*of pers.*) bavarder, caqueter, causailler, jaser, papoter; (*of monkeys*) babiller; **to c. like a magpie,** jaser comme une pie (borgne). **2.** (*a*) (*of teeth*) claquer; **my teeth were chattering,** je claquais des dents; (*b*) (*of tool*) brouter; (*c*) (*of machinery, engine, etc.*) faire du bruit; cogner; vibrer.

chatterbox [ˈtʃætəbɔks], *s.* (*a*) *F:* babillard, -arde; grand(e) bavard(e); moulin *m* à paroles; **to be a great c.,** avoir la langue bien pendue; avoir une fière tapette; **she's a regular c.,** c'est une crécelle; **what a c.!** quelle langue! (*b*) *Bot:* **c. tree,** albizzia *m* lebbek, bois *m* à feu.

chatterer [ˈtʃætərər], *s.* **1.** bavard, -arde; caqueteur, -euse; jaseur, -euse; *F:* jacasse *f.* **2.** *Orn:* (*a*) *A:* ampélis *m;* (*b*) (*S. America*) piauhau *m;* cotinga *m;* (*c*) (*Africa*) cratérope *m;* (*d*) *NAm:* jaseur *m.*

chattering [ˈtʃæt(ə)riŋ], *s.* **1.** caquetage *m;* bavardage *m.* **2.** (*a*) claquement *m* (des dents); (*b*) *Ind:* broutage *m,* broutement *m* (d'un outil); (*c*) bruit *m* de jeu, cognement *m* (de machines); *Aut:* broutement (de l'embrayage); *El:* **c. of the brushes,** cliquetis *m* des balais.

Chatterton [ˈtʃætətn], *Pr.n.m. El: O:* **Chatterton's compound,** chatterton *m.*

chattily [ˈtʃætili], *adv.* avec loquacité; d'une manière loquace; **to write c.,** écrire comme on parle, d'un style libre.

chattiness [ˈtʃætinis], *s.* loquacité *f;* amour *m* du bavardage.

chatty [ˈtʃæti], *a.* bavard, qui aime à bavarder; **a c. old lady,** une vieille dame bavarde, qui a la langue bien pendue; **the wine made him c.,** le vin l'a lancé; **the article was too c.,** l'article était trop sur le ton de la conversation; **a c.. book on Dickens,** un livre sur Dickens qui ne s'élève pas au-dessus de l'anecdote.

chaudfroid [ˈʃoufrwɑː], *s. Cu:* chaud-froid *m, pl.* chauds-froids.

chauffeur[1] [ˈʃoufər], *s.m. Aut:* chauffeur (employé par un particulier); **c.-driven,** (voiture) conduite par un chauffeur.

chauffeur[2], *Aut: etc:* (*a*) *v.i.* travailler comme chauffeur (pour un particulier); (*b*) *v.tr.* conduire (une voiture); **she chauffeurs the children to school,** elle mène les enfants à l'école (en voiture); **he chauffeurs a plane for a millionaire,** c'est le pilote particulier d'un millionnaire.

chauffeuse[1] [ʃouˈfəːz], *s.f. Aut: O:* chauffeuse (employée par un particulier).

chauffeuse[2], *s. Furn:* chauffeuse *f.*

chaulmoogra, chaulmugra [ʃɔlˈmuːgrə], *s. Ch:* **c. (oil),** chaulmoogra *m.*

chaulmoogric [ʃɔlˈmuːgrik], *a. Ch:* chaulmoogrique.

chautauqua [ʃæˈtɔːkwə], *s. NAm:* cours *m* d'été, de vacances.

chauvinism [ˈʃouvinizm], *s.* chauvinisme *m.*

chauvinist [ˈʃouvinist]. **1.** *s.* chauvin *m.* **2.** *a.* = CHAUVINISTIC.

chauvinistic [ʃouviˈnistik], *a.* chauvin, chauviniste.

chavibetol [tʃæviˈbiːtɔl], *s. Ch:* chavibétol *m.*

chavicol [ˈtʃævikɔl], *s. Ch:* chavicol *m.*

chaw[1] [tʃɔː], *s. Dial:* chique *f* (de tabac).

chaw[2], *v.tr. Dial: F:* (*a*) mâcher; (*b*) chiquer (du tabac); (*c*) *U.S:* **all chawed up,** complètement démoli.

chawbacon [ˈtʃɔːbeik(ə)n], *s. F: O:* rustre *m.*

chayote [tʃɑːˈjoutei], *s. Bot:* chayotte *f.*

cheap [tʃiːp]. **1.** *a.* (*a*) (à) bon marché, (à) bon compte; pas cher; **exceptionally c. article,** article *m* d'un bon marché exceptionnel; **a c. hat,** un chapeau (à) bon marché, peu coûteux; **to buy sth. c.,** acheter qch. (à) bon marché, à bon compte, pour pas cher; **isn't it c.?** n'est-ce pas que c'est bon marché? **cheaper,** (à) meilleur marché, à meilleur compte, moins coûteux, moins cher; **it comes cheaper to take a whole bottle,** on a avantage à, cela revient moins cher de, prendre la bouteille entière; **cheaper and cheaper,** de moins en moins cher; **cheapest,** le meilleur marché, le moins cher; **to travel by the cheapest route,** voyager par la route, la ligne, la plus avantageuse; **dirt c.,** à vil prix; pour rien; **it's dirt c.,** c'est donné, d'un bon marché ridicule; (*in theatre, etc.*) **c. seats,** places *f* populaires, petites places; **c. fare, rate,** tarif, taux, réduit; **c. tickets,** billets *m* à prix réduits; **c. trip,** excursion *f* à prix réduit; *F:* (*of shopkeeper*) **he's very c.,** il n'est pas cher, il ne prend pas cher; *Pol.Ec:* **c. money policy,** politique *f* de facilités d'escompte, de l'argent à bon marché; **to do sth. on the c.,** faire qch. (i) à peu de frais, (ii) chichement; **to buy sth. on the c.,** acheter qch. au rabais, à bas prix; **I got it on the c.,** je l'ai eu pour pas cher; (*b*) de peu de valeur; **I am not out for a c. success,** je ne suis pas en quête d'un succès facile; **c. emotion,** émotion superficielle, peu profonde; **c. flattery,** compliments *mpl* d'occasion; **c. and nasty,** bon marché et de mauvaise qualité; *F:* **to feel c.,** (i) être honteux; (ii) se sentir malade, patraque; ne pas être dans son assiette; **to make oneself c.,** déroger; se déprécier; ne pas tenir son rang (social); **to hold s.o., sth., c.; to have a c. opinion of s.o., sth.,** dédaigner qn; ne pas penser grand bien de qn; faire bon marché, peu de cas, de qch.; faire fi de qch.; **to hold life c.,** ne pas marchander sa vie; **I think that's very c. on his part,** ça me semble bien mesquin de sa part. **2.** *adv. F:* = CHEAPLY.

cheapen [ˈtʃiːp(ə)n]. **1.** *v.tr.* (ra)baisser, faire baisser, le prix de (qch.); diminuer la valeur de (qch.); discréditer (une réputation); **you mustn't c. yourself,** il ne faut pas vous déprécier. **2.** *v.i.* devenir moins cher; diminuer de prix.

cheapish [ˈtʃiːpiʃ], *a.* d'un prix assez bas; relativement bon marché.

cheapjack [ˈtʃiːpdʒæk]. **1.** *s.* camelot *m;* charlatan *m.* **2.** *a.* **c. goods,** pacotille *f,* *F:* camelote *f.*

cheaply [ˈtʃiːpli], *adv.* (à) bon marché; à bas prix; à peu de frais; **they can manufacture more c. than we do,** ils sont à même de fabriquer à meilleur marché que nous; **he got off c.,** il en est quitte, il s'en est tiré, à bon compte, à bon marché.

cheapness [ˈtʃiːpnis], *s.* **1.** bon marché; bas prix (de qch.). **2.** peu *m* de valeur, basse qualité, médiocrité *f* (de qch.).

cheapskate [ˈtʃiːpskeit], *s. F:* radin *m.*

cheat[1] [tʃiːt], *s.* **1.** (*a*) trompeur, -euse (par habitude); escroc *m;* imposteur *m;* fourbe *mf;* (*b*) (*at games*) tricheur, -euse (par habitude). **2.** *A:* tromperie *f,* fourberie *f,* escroquerie *f.* **3.** *Bot:* ivraie *f,* vorge *f.*

cheat[2], *v.tr.* **1.** tromper; frauder (qn); voler (qn); attraper (qn); *v.i.* frauder; **to c. the customs,** frauder la douane; **to c. the gallows,** échapper à la potence; **to c. s.o. out of sth.,** frustrer qn de qch.; escroquer qch. à qn; **you've**

cheated me out of 50 francs, vous m'avez refait (de) 50 francs; **to c. s.o. into doing sth.,** user de tromperie pour faire faire qch. à qn. **2.** (*at games*) tricher (qn); *v.i.* tricher, truquer.

cheater ['tʃiːtər], *s.* **1.** trompeur *m,* tricheur *m* (par occasion). **2.** *pl. U.S: F:* **cheaters,** lunettes *f.*

cheating[1] ['tʃiːtiŋ], *a.* **1.** trompeur, -euse. **2.** tricheur, -euse.

cheating[2], *s.* **1.** tromperie *f*; fourberie *f,* truquage *m*; *Jur:* fraude pénale. **2.** *Cards:* tricherie *f.*

chechia ['ʃeiʃiə], *s. Cost:* chéchia *f.*

check[1] [tʃek], *s.* **1.** (*a*) *Chess:* échec *m*; **c.!** échec au roi! (*b*) revers *m*; obstacle *m*; **checks on economic development,** obstacles au développement économique; *Mil: etc:* **to meet with a c.,** essuyer, éprouver, un échec, un revers; (*c*) *Ven:* (*of pack*) **to come to a c.,** venir à bout de voie; perdre la voie. **2.** (*a*) arrêt *m*; pause *f*; anicroche *f*; **(sudden) c.,** à-coup *m,* aheurtement *m*; **to travel without c.,** voyager sans encombre, sans accident; (*b*) *Sp:* (i) (*ice hockey*) interception *f*; (ii) *Wr:* **body c.,** coup *m* de bélier. **3.** (*a*) (*restraint*) frein *m*; **to keep, hold, the enemy in c.,** tenir l'ennemi en échec; faire échec à l'ennemi; contenir l'ennemi; **to keep a child in c.,** freiner les activités d'un enfant; **to put a c. on sth., to act as a c. on s.o., sth.,** servir de frein, mettre un frein, à qch., à qn; **to keep one's feelings in c.,** se contraindre, se contenir; **to put a c. on production,** freiner la production; **rebound c.,** amortisseur *m* de rebondissement; (*b*) *Harn:* **c. (rein),** fausses rênes. **4.** (*a*) butée *f,* arrêt; **door c.,** arrêt de porte; **c. chain, c. cord,** chaîne *f,* corde *f,* d'arrêt; *Mec.E:* **c. bolt,** boulon *m* d'arrêt; **c. nut,** contre-écrou *m, pl.* contre-écrous; écrou *m* de blocage, d'arrêt, de sûreté; doubles écrous; **c. screw,** contre-vis *f inv*; **c. valve,** (i) *Mch:* soupape *f,* clapet *m,* de retenue; (ii) *Hyd.E: etc:* soupape de retenue; retour *m* d'eau; (*b*) **c. (actions),** attrape-marteau *m, pl.* attrape-marteaux (de piano). **5.** contrôle *m*; (*a*) vérification *f* (d'un compte, etc.); **c. sample,** échantillon *m* témoin; *Ch: Metall:* **c. assay,** essai *m* contradictoire; **cross c.,** recoupement *m*; *Mil: etc:* **c. roll call,** contre-appel *m*; *Aut: etc:* **spot c.,** vérification sur place; **c. point,** contrôle; **radar speed c.,** contrôle de vitesse par radar; **c. list,** liste *f* de contrôle; **c. analysis,** contre-analyse *f*; **c. (counting),** récolement *m*; **c. test,** contre-essai *m*; *Mec.E: etc:* **c. mark,** trait *m* de repère; *Com:* **c. till,** caisse enregistreuse; **to keep a c. on sth.,** contrôler qch.; **there is no possible c. on his administration,** sa gestion échappe à tout contrôle; (*b*) *Cmptr:* **automatic, hardware, c.,** contrôle automatique; **programmed c.,** contrôle programmé, par programme; **summation c.,** contrôle par totalisation; **parity c.,** contrôle de parité; **arithmetic, mathematical, c.,** contrôle arithmétique; **loop c.,** contrôle par retour de l'information; **forbidden combination c.,** contrôle de caractère invalide; (*c*) billet *m*; ticket *m*; (*in restaurant, etc.*) note *f*; *Th:* **pass-out c.,** contremarque *f* de sortie; *Rail: etc:* **luggage c.,** bulletin *m* de bagages, d'enregistrement; **cloakroom c.,** bulletin de consigne; *Ind:* **tool c.,** jeton *m* d'outil(s); (*d*) *U.S:* jeton de présence (à une séance); (*e*) *P:* **to hand in one's checks,** mourir, dévisser son billard. **6.** *NAm:* = CHEQUE. **7.** *int. U.S.:* oui, d'acc!

check[2], *v.*

I. *v.tr. & i.* **1.** *v.tr.* (*a*) *Chess:* mettre (le roi) en échec; faire échec (au roi); (*b*) faire échec à, arrêter net (qn, qch.); mettre obstacle à (qch.); contenir (l'ennemi, la foule); enrayer (une crise, le progrès de l'ennemi, d'une maladie, la hausse des prix); arrêter (une attaque); étancher, capturer (une voie d'eau); *Nau:* choquer, filer (une amarre, les écoutes); **checked in full career,** arrêté en pleine course; *Equit:* **horse easy to c.,** cheval sûr à la parade; (*c*) refouler, comprimer, retenir (ses larmes, sa colère); modérer (sa violence, la vitesse d'une machine); réprimer, refréner (une passion); freiner (la production, *Ch:* une réaction); *I.C.E:* régler (l'allumage, etc.); **checked feeling, laughter,** sentiment, rire, rentré; *Ling:* **checked vowel,** voyelle entravée; (*d*) réprimander, reprendre, freiner (un enfant, etc.); (*e*) vérifier, apurer (un compte); vérifier (la pression, etc.); collationner (des documents), collationner, compulser, (un document) sur l'original; *Jur:* récoler (un inventaire); *Typ:* (i) réviser, (ii) conférer (des épreuves); **all the sales are checked,** toutes les ventes sont contrôlées; **to c. (off) names on a list, etc.,** pointer, *F:* cocher, des noms sur une liste, etc.; **to c. (off, over) goods,** vérifier, recenser, des marchandises; **to c. and sign for goods on delivery,** réceptionner des marchandises; *Com:* **to c. the books,** pointer les écritures; **checked, double checked and cross-checked,** vérifié et revérifié; **to c. (up on) information,** contrôler, vérifier, recouper, des renseignements; *v.i.* **to c. up,** faire la vérification; *Adm: Mil:* **to c. up on s.o.,** (i) effectuer une enquête de sécurité sur qn; enquêter sur qn du point de vue de la sécurité; (ii) contrôler, s'assurer, que qn possède un certificat d'habilitation (au degré de secret voulu); effectuer un contrôle de sécurité sur qn; (*f*) contrôler (une expérience, etc.; *Rail: etc:* les billets); (*g*) (faire) enregistrer (ses bagages); (*at restaurant, etc.*) **to c. one's hat, coat,** mettre son chapeau, son pardessus, au vestiaire. **2.** *v.i.* hésiter, s'arrêter (**at,** devant); (*of horse*) refuser; *Ven:* (*of hounds*) hésiter sur la voie; perdre la voie.

II. (*compound verbs*) **1. check in,** *v.i.* s'inscrire (à un hôtel, etc.); signer à l'arrivée.

2. check out; (*a*) *v.tr.* **to c.o. (luggage, etc),** retirer (des bagages, etc.); (*b*) *v.i.* (i) (*at hotel, etc.*) régler sa note au départ; (ii) *F:* partir, filer; (iii) *P:* mourir, déposer le bilan.

check[3], *s. Tex:* carreau *m,* damier *m*; **broken c. (design),** pied-de-poule *m*; **c. material,** tissu quadrillé, carrelé, à carreaux, en damier.

checked [tʃekt], *a.* à carreaux, quadrillé; *Tex:* **c. material,** tissu *m* à carreaux.

checker[1] ['tʃekər], *s.* (*pers.*) **1.** contrôleur *m,* pointeur *m,* marqueur *m.* **2.** enrayeur *m* (d'une attaque, etc.).

checker[2] = CHEQUER[1,2].

checkerberry ['tʃekəberi], *s. Bot:* gaulthérie *f* du Canada.

checkers ['tʃekəz], *s.pl. NAm:* jeu *m* de dames.

checking ['tʃekiŋ], *s.* **1.** (*a*) répression *f*; enrayage *m*; (*b*) *Equit:* (*of horse*) parade *f.* **2.** (*a*) contrôle *m*; vérification *f*; apurement *m*; pointage *m*; *Jur:* récolement *m* (d'un inventaire); *Ind:* **c. form,** fiche *f* de contrôle; (*b*) enregistrement *m* (de bagages). **3.** *NAm:* (*a*) **c. account,** compte *m* en banque; (*b*) **c. room** = CHECKROOM.

checkmate[1] ['tʃekmeit], *s.* **1.** *Chess:* échec et mat *m.* **2.** échec complet; défaite *f.*

checkmate[2], *v.tr.* **1.** *Chess:* faire (le roi) échec et mat; mater (le roi). **2.** (*a*) faire échec et mat à (qn); donner le mat à (qn); détruire les projets de (qn); (*b*) contrecarrer, déjouer (les projets de qn).

check-out ['tʃekaut], *s.* (*a*) **c.-o. (point, etc.),** caisse *f* (dans un supermarché); (*b*) (*in hotel*) **c.-o. time is at 12 noon,** les clients doivent quitter la chambre avant midi (le jour du départ).

checkroom ['tʃekruːm], *s. NAm:* (*a*) consigne *f,* salle *f* des bagages; (*b*) vestiaire *m.*

checkup ['tʃekʌp], *s.* (*a*) vérification *f*; inspection *f*; (*of machinery*) révision *f*; (*b*) examen médical complet; **to give s.o. a c.,** faire le bilan de santé de qn.

checky ['tʃeki], *a. Her:* échiqueté; **c. of nine pieces, panes, azure and ermine,** cinq points d'azur équipollé à quatre points d'hermine.

cheddar ['tʃedər], *s.* (fromage *m* de) cheddar *m.*

cheddite ['tʃedait], *s. Exp:* cheddite *f.*

cheek[1] [tʃiːk], *s.* **1.** (*a*) *Anat:* joue *f*; **flabby, pendulous, cheeks,** bajoues *f*; **to be c. by jowl with s.o.,** (i) être côte à côte avec qn, tout près de qn, tout contre qn; (ii) être intime avec qn; (*b*) *Harn:* branche *f* (de mors); **c. piece,** porte mors *m inv* (de bride); **c. strap,** montant *m* (de bride). **2.** *F:* effronterie *f,* impudence *f,* impertinence *f,* insolence *f,* toupet *m,* culot *m*; **he had the c. to write to me,** il a eu l'effronterie, le culot, de m'écrire; **he's got a c., plenty of c., the, a, hell of a c.,** il a pas mal de toupet, de culot, un culot monstre; **it's awful c. my talking to you like this,** c'est bien impertinent de ma part de vous parler comme ça; **that's enough of your c.!** (ne) te fiche pas de moi! **3.** (*a*) *Tchn: Carp:* joue (de poignée de scie, de mortaise); *Mec.E:* joue (de poulie, de coussinet); flasque *m,* bras *m* (de manivelle); mâchoire *f* (d'étau); *Const:* montant *m* (de fenêtre); *Artil:* flasque (d'affût); **cheeks of a lathe,** flasques, jumelles *f,* d'un tour; **c. stones,** jumelles *f* (d'une rigole); *Mec.E: Const:* **c. plate,** contre-plaque *f, pl.* contre-plaques; (*b*) *Nau:* jottereau *m* (de mât); safran *m* (de gouvernail).

cheek[2], *v.tr. F:* dire des impertinences à (qn), faire l'insolent avec (qn); se payer la tête de (qn).

cheekbone ['tʃiːkboun], *s.* pommette *f*; os *m* malaire, génal, jugal; zygoma *m*; **high, prominent, cheekbones,** pommettes saillantes.

cheekily ['tʃiːkili], *adv.* d'une manière impertinente; d'un air effronté.

cheekiness ['tʃiːkinis], *s. F:* effronterie *f.*

cheeky ['tʃiːki], *a. F:* effronté, insolent; qui a du toupet, du culot; **he's a c. customer,** il n'a pas froid aux yeux; **as c. as a cock sparrow,** effronté comme un page.

cheep[1] [tʃiːp], *s.* (*a*) piaulement *m,* piaulis *m* (de petits oiseaux); (*b*) *F:* **one never gets a c. out of her,** elle ne dit jamais mot; **there hasn't been a c. out of her since she went,** on n'a pas eu de ses nouvelles depuis son départ.

cheep[2], *v.i.* (*of young birds*) piauler.

cheeping ['tʃiːpiŋ], *s.* = CHEEP[1].

cheer[1] [tʃiər], *s.* **1.** bonne disposition (d'esprit); (*so used esp. in*) **words of c.,** paroles consolatrices, d'encouragement; *Lit:* **be of good c.!** courage! prenez courage! ayez bon espoir! *A:* **what c.?** comment ça va? **2.** *A:* (*fare*) bonne chère; **to make good c.,** faire bonne chère. **3.** (*a*) hourra *m, pl.* acclamations *f,* bravos *m,* vivats *m*; **loud cheers,** vifs applaudissements; **speech greeted with cheers,** discours salué d'acclamations; **to give a c.,** pousser un hourra; **to give three cheers,** pousser trois hourras; accorder un ban à qn; **three cheers for X!** un ban pour X! vive X! *NAm:* **c. leader,** meneur, -euse, de ban; (*b*) *F:* **cheers!** à votre santé! *F:* à la vôtre!

cheer[2]. **1.** *v.tr.* (*a*) **to c. s.o. (up),** égayer, réjouir, ragaillardir, dérider, désassombrir, désattrister, remonter, qn; relever le courage, le moral, de qn; rendre courage à qn; réconforter qn; **that cheers me up,** cela me remet du cœur au ventre; **to c. s.o. on (to do sth.),** encourager qn (à faire qch.); encourager qn à continuer; (*b*) acclamer, applaudir (qn). **2.** *v.i.* (*a*) **to c. up,** reprendre sa gaieté; se ragaillardir; retrouver son entrain; **c. up!** courage! (*b*) pousser des hourras, des vivats, des acclamations, applaudir.

cheerful ['tʃiəf(u)l], *a.* (*of pers.*) gai; de bonne humeur; allègre; (*of face, view, etc.*) riant; (*of room*) gai, d'aspect agréable, riant; (*of fire*) réconfortant, vif, clair, gai; (*of conversation, music, etc.*) égayant; **a c. giver,** celui qui donne de bon cœur; **to look c.,** avoir l'air content, gai, plein d'entrain; **he always keeps c.,** il garde toujours sa bonne humeur; **to become c.,** s'animer; **c. news,** nouvelles encourageantes; **you're not exactly c.,** vous n'êtes pas d'une gaieté folle; **that's a c. thought!** (i) ça c'est encourageant, ça me remonte! (ii) *Iron:* comme vous êtes optimiste!

cheerfully ['tʃiəf(u)li], *adv.* **1.** gaiement, avec entrain; allègrement. **2.** de bon cœur, volontiers.

cheerfulness ['tʃiəf(u)lnis], *s.* (*a*) (*of pers.*) gaieté *f,* bonne humeur; (*b*) aspect riant (du paysage); gaieté, aspect agréable (d'un intérieur); gaieté, belle flambée (du feu).

cheerily ['tʃiərili], *adv.* gaiement, avec gaieté; de bonne humeur.

cheeriness ['tʃiərinis], *s.* joyeux caractère; gaieté communicative.

cheering[1] ['tʃiəriŋ], *a.* encourageant, réjouissant; **c. letter,** lettre réconfortante.

cheering[2], *s.* hourras *mpl,* vivats *mpl,* acclamations *fpl*; applaudissements *mpl.*

cheerio [tʃiəri'ou], *int. F:* **1.** (*at parting*) à bientôt! bon courage! **2.** (*in drinking a toast*) à la vôtre! à la tienne!

cheerless ['tʃiəlis], *a.* morne, triste, sombre, **c. weather,** temps *m* maussade.

cheerlessly ['tʃiəlisli], *adv.* tristement.

cheerlessness ['tʃiəlisnis], *s.* tristesse *f,* mélancolie *f*; aspect *m* morne, sombre, triste.

cheery ['tʃiəri], *a.* **1.** (*of pers.*) joyeux, gai, réjoui, guilleret. **2.** = CHEERING[1].

cheese[1] [tʃiːz], *s.* **1.** (*a*) fromage *m*; **France is the land of c.,** la France est le pays des fromages; **Dutch c.,** fromage de Hollande; *F:* tête *f* de maure, de mort; **blue c.,** (fromage) bleu *m,* fromage à pâte persillée; **cream c.,** fromage blanc; fromage à la crème; **cottage c.,** caillé *m*; **processed c.,** fromage fondu, industriel; crème (de gruyère, etc.); **green c.,** fromage (i) frais, pas encore fait, (ii) fait de petit-lait; (iii) à la pie; **he believes the moon is made of green c.,** il prend des vessies pour des lanternes; *Cu:* **cauliflower c., macaroni c.,** chou-fleur *m,* macaronis *mpl,* au gratin; **toasted c.,** rôtie *f* au fromage; *F: O:* **hard c.!** ça c'est la déveine! pas de chance! *Phot: F:* **say c.!** souriez! (*b*) *attrib.* **the c. industry,** l'industrie fromagère; **cheese maker, manufacturer,** fromager, -ère; **c. rennet,** (i) présure *f*; (ii) *Bot:* caille-lait *m,* gaillet *m*; **c. basket, c. drainer, c. sieve,** cagerotte *f,* fromager *m,* caserel *m,* caserette *f*; faisselle *f*; égouttoir *m*; clisse *f*; **c. press,** presse *f* à fromage; **c. mould, c. tub,** moule *f* à fromage; échinon *m*; *Fung:* **c. mould,** moisissure *f* du fromage; **c. taster,** sonde *f* à fromage; **c. cutter, c. scoop,** pelle *f* à fromage; **c. cover,** cloche *f* à fromage; *Comest:* **c. biscuit,** biscuit sec (pour manger avec le fromage); **c. finger,** biscuit fourré au fromage; **c. straws,** craquelins *m,* allumettes *f,* au fromage; pailles *f* au parmesan; paillettes *f* au fromage; (*c*) *Ent:* **c. fly,** piophile *f*; mouche *f* du fromage; **c. hopper, c. skipper, c. maggot,** ver *m* du fromage, *F:* asticot *m*; *Arach:* **c. mite,** tyroglyphe *m,* mite *f* du fromage. **2.** (*pl.* **cheeses**) (*a*) **a c.,** un fromage (entier); **round c.,** meule *f* de fromage; **a gruyère c.,** une meule de gruyère; **a cream c.,** (i) fromage blanc; (ii) un demi-sel *pl.* demi-sels; *Games: A:* **to make, play at, cheeses,** faire des fromages (avec sa jupe); (*b*) *P:* **big c.,** gros bonnet, grosse légume. **3.** (*a*) marc *m* (de pommes, de raisins); (*b*) gelée *f* (de prunes de Damas, etc.); **quince c.,** pâte *f* de coings.

cheese[2], *s. P: A:* ce qu'il faut ou ce qui est comme il faut; chose à la hauteur; **that's the c.!** ça c'est à la hauteur! ça c'est pépère! à la bonne heure! **he thinks he's quite the c.,** il s'imagine qu'il est tout à fait dans le mouvement, tout à fait à la page; il se croit un type chic.

cheese[3], *v.tr. P:* (*a*) **c. it!** (i) en voilà assez! veux-tu te taire! la ferme! (ii) fiche le camp! (*b*) **c. it, the cops!** vingt-deux, voilà les flics! (*c*) **to be cheesed (off),** avoir le cafard, en avoir marre.

cheeseboard [ˈtʃiːzbɔːd], *s.* planche *f,* plateau *m,* à fromage.

cheeseburger [ˈtʃiːzbəːgər], *s. Comest:* (espèce de) petit pain fourré de biftek haché et de fromage.

cheesecake [ˈtʃiːzkeik], *s.* **1.** *Cu:* tarte *f* au fromage blanc et aux raisins secs. **2.** *NAm: P:* pin-up *f* (où la jeune fille fait valoir ses belles jambes).

cheesecloth [ˈtʃiːzklɔθ], *s.* gaze *f*; étamine *f*; beurrière *f.*

cheese-head(ed) [ˈtʃiːzhed(id)], *a.* **c.-h. screw,** vis *f* à tête cylindrique chanfreinée, à tête ronde plate.

cheesemonger [ˈtʃiːzmʌŋgər], *s.* marchand, -ande, de fromage; fromager, -ère; **bought at the cheesemonger's,** acheté dans une fromagerie.

cheesemongery [ˈtʃiːzmʌŋgəri], *s.* fromagerie *f.*

cheeseparer [ˈtʃiːzpɛərər], *s.* lésineur, -euse.

cheeseparing[1] [ˈtʃiːzpɛəriŋ], *a.* parcimonieux; **c. economy,** économies *fpl* de bouts de chandelle.

cheeseparing[2], *s* parcimonie *f,* lésine *f*; économies *fpl.* de bouts de chandelle.

cheesy [ˈtʃiːzi], *a.* **1.** caséeux, caséiforme. **2.** qui sent le fromage. **3.** *P:* de mauvaise qualité; miteux; moche.

cheeta(h) [ˈtʃiːtə], *s. Z:* guépard *m.*

chef [ʃef], *s.m.* chef de cuisine.

cheil- [kail], *pref.* chéil-; chil-.

cheilalgia [kaiˈlældʒiə], *s. Med:* chéilalgie *f.*

cheilanthes [kaiˈlænθiːz], *s. Ferns:* cheilanthes *m.*

cheilitis [kaiˈlaitis], *s. Med:* chéilite *f.*

cheiloplasty [ˈkailouplæsti], *s. Surg:* chéiloplastie *f.*

cheilopod [ˈkailəpɔd], *s. Myr:* chilopode *m.*

Cheilopoda [kaiˈlɔpədə], *s.pl. Myr:* chilopodes *m.*

cheilopodan [kaiˈlɔpədən], **cheilopodous** [kaiˈlɔpədəs], *a. Myr:* chilopode.

cheilosis [kaiˈlousis], *s. Med:* cheïlose *f.*

cheilostomata [ˈkeilouˈstoumətə], *s.pl. Coel:* chilostomates *m.*

cheir- [kaiər], *pref.* chéir-; chir-.

cheiragra [kaiəˈrægrə], *s. Med:* chiragre *f.*

cheiralgia [kaiəˈrældʒiə], *s. Med:* chiralgie *f.*

Cheirogaleus [kaiərougæˈliːəs], *s. Z:* chéirogale *m.*

cheirognomy [kaiəˈrɔgnəmi], *s.* chirognomonie *f.*

cheirograph [ˈkaiərougræf], *s.* chirographe *m.*

cheirographary [kaiəˈrɔgræfəri], *a. Jur:* (créancier *m,* dette *f*) chirographaire.

cheirographic [kaiərouˈgræfik], *a.* chirographique.

cheirography [kaiəˈrɔgrəfi], *s.* chirographie *f.*

cheirology [kaiəˈrɔlədʒi], *s.* chirologie *f.*

cheiromancer [ˈkaiəroumænsər], *s.* chiromancien, -ienne.

cheiromancy [ˈkaiəroumænsi], *s.* chiromancie *f.*

cheiromegaly [kaiərouˈmegəli], *s. Med:* chiromégalie *f.*

cheirometer [kaiəˈrɔmitər], *s.* chiromètre *m.*

cheiromys [ˈkaiəroumis], *s. Z:* ch(é)iromys *m*; aye-aye *m, pl.* ayes-ayes.

cheiroptera [kaiəˈrɔptərə], *s.pl. Z:* ch(é)iroptères *m,* chauves-souris *f.*

cheiropteran [kaiəˈrɔptərən], *s. Z:* ch(é)iroptère *m,* chauve-souris *f.*

cheiropterophilous [kaiˈrɔptəˈrɔfiləs], *a. Bot:* ch(é)iroptérophile, ch(é)iroptérogame.

cheiropterophily [kaiˈrɔptəˈrɔfili], *s.* ch(é)iroptérogamie *f.*

cheiropterous [kaiəˈrɔptərəs], *a. Z:* ch(é)iroptère.

Cheka [ˈtʃekə], *s. Russian Hist:* **the C.,** la Tchéka.

chekist [ˈtʃekist], *a. & s. Russian Hist:* (membre *m*) de la Tchéka.

chela[1], *pl.* **-ae** [ˈkiːlə, -iː], *s. Crust:* chélate *m.*

chela[2] [ˈtʃeilə], *s. Buddhist Rel:* novice *m.*

chelate[1] [ˈkiːleit], *s. Ch:* chélate *m.*

chelate[2], *v.tr. & i. Ch:* chélater.

chelating [kiˈleitiŋ], *a. Ch:* (agent) chélateur.

chelation [kiˈleiʃ(ə)n], *s. Ch:* chélation *f.*

chelator [kiˈleitər], *s. Ch:* chélateur *m.*

chelicera [kiˈlisərə], *s. Arach:* chélicère *f.*

Chelicerata [kilisəˈrɑːtə], *s.pl. Arach:* chélicérates *m.*

Chelidae [ˈkiːlidiː], *s.pl. Rept:* chélidés *m.*

chelidonic [kiːliˈdɔnik], *a. Ch:* chélidonique.

chelifer [ˈkelifər], *s. Arach:* chélifère *m,* chélifer *m.*

cheliform [ˈkiːlifɔːm], *a. Z:* chéliforme.

chellean [ˈʃeliən], *a. Prehist:* chelléen.

chelodina, -dine [kelouˈdiːnə, ˈkeloudain, -din], *s. Rept:* chélodine *f.*

cheloid [ˈkiːlɔid], **cheloma** [kiˈloumə], *s. Med:* chéloïde *f.*

chelone [kiˈlouni], *s.* **1.** *Rept:* chélonée *f,* chélone *f.* **2.** *Bot:* chélone.

Chelonethida [keləˈniːθidə], *s.pl. Arach:* chélonétidés *m.*

chelonian [kiˈlouniən], *s. Rept:* chélonien *m.*

Cheloni(i)dae [kilouˈniːidiː, kiˈlɔnidiː], *s.pl. Rept:* chélonidés *m.*

Chelsea [ˈtʃelsi], *Pr.n.* Chelsea *m* (quartier de Londres); **C. porcelain, ware,** porcelaine *f* de Chelsea; **C. (Royal) Hospital,** l'Hôtel des Invalides de l'armée; **C. pensioner,** invalide *m* du *Chelsea Royal Hospital.*

Cheltonian [tʃelˈtouniən], *s.* (*a*) habitant, -ante, originaire, de Cheltenham; (*b*) élève *m* ou ancien élève de *Cheltenham College.*

chelydra [ˈkelidrə], *s. Rept:* chélydre *f.*

Chelydridae [keˈlidridiː], *s.pl. Rept:* chélydridés *m.*

chelys [ˈkelis], *s. Rept:* chelys *m,* chélyde *f.*

chemawinite [tʃəˈmɑːwinait], *s. Miner:* chémawinite *f,* cédarite *f,* ambre canadien.

chemical [ˈkemik(ə)l]. **1.** *a.* chimique; **c. constitution,** composition *f* chimique; **c. agent,** agent *m* chimique; **c. balance,** balance *f* de laboratoire; **c. bench,** table *f* de laboratoire, de manipulation; **c. factory,** usine *f* de produits chimiques; **c. engineering,** génie *m* chimique; **c. engineer,** ingénieur *m* chimiste; *Mil:* **c. warfare,** guerre *f* chimique, des gaz; **c. defence,** défense *f* contre les agents chimiques, contre les gaz; **c. weapon,** arme *m* chimique; **c. officer,** officier *m* "Z". **2.** *s.* produit *m* chimique.

chemically [ˈkemik(ə)li], *adv.* chimiquement; *Mec.E:* **c. cooled engine,** moteur *m* à refroidissement chimique.

chemicalization [kemikəlaiˈzeiʃ(ə)n], *s.* **the c. of agriculture,** l'utilisation des produits chimiques en agriculture.

chemicalize [ˈkemikəlaiz], *v.tr.* traiter (qch.) par des procédés chimiques, avec des produits chimiques.

chemico-legal [ˈkemikouˈliːgl], *a.* chimico-légal, -aux.

chemi(co)luminescence [ˈkemi(kou)l(j)umiˈnesəns], *s.* chimi(o)luminescence *f.*

chemico-physical [ˈkemikouˈfizikl], *a.* chimico-physique, *pl.* chimico-physiques.

chemin de fer [ʃəmɛ̃dəfɛər], *s.* (*gaming*) chemin *m* de fer.

chemin de ronde [ʃəmɛ̃dərɔ̃ːd], *s. Fort:* coursière *f,* chemin *m* de ronde.

chemiotaxis [ˈkemiouˈtæksis], **chemiotaxy** [ˈkemiouˈtæksi], *s. Biol:* chimiotaxie *f.*

chemise [ʃəˈmiːz], *s.* **1.** *Cost:* (*a*) *A:* chemise *f* (de femme); (*b*) *NAm:* robe *f* chemisier. **2.** *A.Fort:* chemise, revêtement *m* (de bastion).

chemisette [ʃemiˈzet], *s. A.Cost:* **1.** chemisette *f.* **2.** guimpe *f*; bouffante *f.*

chemism [ˈkemizm], *s. Biol:* chimisme *m.*

chemist [ˈkemist], *s.* **1.** pharmacien, -ienne; **chemist's shop,** pharmacie *f*; **at the chemist's,** chez le pharmacien. **2.** chimiste *m*; **analytical c.,** chimiste (analyste); chimiste expert.

chemistry [ˈkemistri], *s.* (*a*) chimie *f*; **organic c.,** chimie organique; **inorganic c.,** chimie minérale; **applied c.,** chimie appliquée; **physical c.,** chimie physique; **metallurgical c., c. of metals,** métallochimie *f*; **industrial, technical, c.,** chimie industrielle; **nuclear c.,** chimie nucléaire; **radiation c.,** radiochimie *f,* chimie sous radiations; (*b*) *Sch:* (*textbook*) chimie.

chemitype [ˈkemitaip], *s. Phot.Engr:* chimitypie *f.*

chemmy [ˈʃemi], *s. F:* (*gaming*) chemin *m* de fer.

chemosis, *pl.* **-es** [kiˈmousis, -iːz], *s. Med:* chémosis *m.*

chemosphere [ˈkemousfiər], *s.* chimosphère *f.*

chemosterilization [ˈkemousterilaiˈzeiʃ(ə)n], *s. Agr:* stérilisation *f* (des insectes nuisibles, etc.) avec des produits chimiques.

chemosynthesis [kemouˈsinθisis], *s.* chimiosynthèse *f.*

chemotactic [kemouˈtæktik], *a. Biol:* chimiotactique.

chemotactism [kemouˈtæktizm], *s. Biol:* chimiotactisme *m.*

chemotaxis [kemouˈtæksis], **chemotaxy** [kemouˈtæksi], *s. Biol:* chimiotaxie *f.*

chemotherapeutic [ˈkemouθerəˈpjuːtik], *a. Med:* chimiothérapique.

chemotherapist [kemouˈθerəpist], *s. Med:* chimiothérapeute *m.*

chemotherapy [kemouˈθerəpi], *s. Med:* chimiothérapie *f.*

chemotropism [kiˈmɔtrəpizm], *s.* chimiotropisme *m.*

chemurgy [keˈməːdʒi], *s.* chimiurgie *f.*

chenevixite [ʃeniˈviksait], *s. Miner:* chenevixite *f.*

chenille [ʃəˈniːl], *s. Tex:* chenille *f.*

chenopod [ˈkiːnoupɔd, ˈken-], *s. Bot:* chénopode *m.*

Chenopodiaceae [kiːnoupoudiˈeisiiː, ken-], *s.pl. Bot:* chénopodiacées *f.*

Chenopodiales [kiːnoupoudiˈeiliːz], *s.pl. Bot:* chénopodiales *f.*

Chenopodium [kiːnouˈpoudiəm], *s. Bot:* chénopode *m,* chénopodium *m.*

cheptel [ˈtʃeptəl], *s. Jur:* cheptel *m.*

cheque [tʃek], *s.* chèque *m*; **c. for ten pounds,** chèque de dix livres sterling; **c. to order,** chèque à ordre; **c. to bearer,** chèque au porteur; **crossed c.,** chèque barré; **open, uncrossed, c.,** chèque ouvert, non barré; **blank c.,** chèque en blanc; **traveller's c.,** chèque de voyage; **c. without cover, worthless c.,** *F:* **dud c.,** chèque sans provision, sans contre-partie; **c. book,** carnet *m* de chèques; chéquier *m*; **c. imprinter, writer; c. imprinting, personalization, writing, machine,** machine *f* à personnaliser les cheques; **c. paper,** papier *m* de surete; **to make out a c. to . . .,** établir un chèque à l'ordre de . . .; **to cash a c.,** toucher un chèque; **to refer a c. to drawer,** refuser d'honorer un chèque; **to stop a c.,** suspendre le paiement d'un chèque.

chequer[1] [ˈtʃekər], *s.* **1.** (*a*) *A:* échiquier *m*; (*b*) enseigne *f* (d'auberge) en échiquier; (*c*) *Pr.n.* **Chequers,** manoir du Buckinghamshire affecté aux villégiatures du Premier Ministre. **2.** *usu. pl.* quadrillage *m.*

chequer[2], *v.tr.* **1.** quadriller (un tissu, etc.); marquer (qch.) en carreaux; diviser (qch.) en carreaux, en damier; *Metalw:* guillocher. **2.** (*variegate with colour*) diaprer, bigarrer. **3.** diversifier; marquer (l'existence, etc.) de vicissitudes.

chequerboard [ˈtʃekəbɔːd], *s.* damier *m*; *Town P:* **c. layout,** échiquier *m,* damier.

chequered [ˈtʃekəd], *a.* **1.** quadrillé, à carreaux, en damier, en échiquier; **c. pattern,** (i) gaufrage *m*; (ii) étoffe *f,* etc., en damier; (iii) (*on metal*) guillochis *m*; **c. plate,** tôle striée. **2.** diapré, bigarré; *Lit:* **the c. shade under the trees,** la marqueterie de l'ombre sous les arbres. **3. c. career,** vie accidentée, mouvementée, pleine de vicissitudes; *Lit:* **life's c. scene,** le spectacle varié de la vie.

chequering [ˈtʃekəriŋ], *s.* **1.** quadrillage *m* (d'un tissu, etc.); guillochage *m* (d'une montre, etc.); **c. tool,** guilloche *f.* **2.** *Metalw:* gaufrage *m* (de la tôle).

chequerwise [ˈtʃekəwaiz], *adv.* en échiquier.

chequerwork [ˈtʃekəwəːk], *s.* = CHEQUERING; *Cokem:* (*of regenerator*) **fire-brick c.,** empilages *m* réfractaires.

chequy [ˈtʃeki], *a. Her:* = CHECKY.

cherish [ˈtʃeriʃ], *v.tr.* **1.** chérir; soigner tendrement (un enfant); *see also* SNAKE[1]. **2.** bercer, caresser, choyer (un espoir); nourrir, entretenir (une idée, une opinion, du ressentiment); **to c. sth. with a jealous care,** veiller sur qch. avec un soin jaloux; **to c. illusions,** se nourrir, se bercer, d'illusions; **his most cherished hopes,** ses espérances les plus chères.

chernozem [ˈtʃəːnouzem, -zjɔm], *s. Geol:* tchernoziom *m.*

cheroot [ʃəˈruːt], *s.* (*a*) manille *m* (à bouts coupés); (*b*) cigare *m* d'une marque quelconque à bouts coupés.

cherry [ˈtʃeri]. **1.** (*a*) *s. Bot: Hort:* (*fruit*) cerise *f*; **blackheart c.,** guigne noire; **whiteheart c.,** bigarreau *m*; **wild c.,** merise *f*; **choke c.,** merise de Virginie; **winter c.,** (i) cerisette *f,* faux piment; (ii) alkékenge *f*; **Jerusalem c.,** faux piment; **dried c.,** cerisette; **c. bob,** cerises jumelles, grappe *f* de deux ou trois cerises, *F:* boucle *f* d'oreille; **c. brandy,** (i) cherry-brandy *m, F:* cherry *m*; (ii) eau-de-vie *f* de cerises; **brandied cherries, c. bounce,** cerises à l'eau-de-vie; **c. liqueur,** liqueur *f* de cerises; **c. pie,** (i) *Cu:* tourte *f* aux cerises; (ii) *Bot:* héliotrope *m* (du Pérou); *A:* (*street cry*) **c. ripe!** à la douce, à la douce! aux cerises mûres! *Ent:* **c. fruit fly,** rhagoletis *m,* mouche *f* des cerises; *F:* **to take two bites at the c.,** faire deux morceaux d'une cerise; s'y prendre à deux fois, y remordre; **not to take two bites at the c.,** y aller sans hésiter; (*b*) *s.* (*tree*) **c. (tree),** cerisier *m*; **wild c.,** merisier *m*; **bird c.,** cerisier à grappes; **heart c.,** guignier *m*; **Jerusalem c.,** pommier *m* d'amour; oranger *m* des savetiers; **winter c.,** cerisier d'amour; petit cerisier d'hiver; **c. bay, c. laurel,** laurier-cerise *m, pl.* lauriers-cerise(s); laurier *m* amandier; **c. plum,** prunier *m* myrobolan; **c. orchard,** *A:* **c. garden,** cerisaie *f*; (*c*) *a.* (*colour*) (i) **c. (-red),** cerise *inv*; **c. lips,** lèvres *f* vermeilles; (ii) *Metall:* rouge cerise *inv*; **dark c.,** cerise naissant *inv*; **full red c.,** cerise accentué *inv.* **2.** *s.* (*a*) *Tls:* foret globuleux; fraise ronde; (*b*) *Civ.E: etc:* **c. picker,** (petite) grue transportable, roulante. **3.** *s. P:* virginité *f,* pucelage *m,* fleur *f*; **to lose one's c.,** perdre sa fleur.

cherrystone [ˈtʃeristoun], *s.* **1.** noyau *m* de cerise. **2.** *Moll: NAm:* palourde *f.* **3.** *U.S:* **I wouldn't give a c. for it,** je n'en donnerais pas cher.

cherrywood [ˈtʃeriwud], *s.* **1.** (bois *m* de) cerisier *m*; **c.**

pipe, pipe *f* en merisier. **2.** *Bot:* rose *f* de Gueldre.
Chersonese [kəːsə'niːs], *Pr.n. A.Geog:* la Chersonèse.
chert [tʃəːt], *s. Miner:* silex noir, chert *m*; pierre *f* de corne.
cherub, *pl.* **cherubs,** *B:* **cherubim** ['tʃerəb, -z, -əbim, -jubim], *s.* (*a*) *B:* chérubin *m*, angelet *m*; (*b*) *Art:* angelot *m*, ange joufflu; (*c*) (*of child*) **a little c.,** un petit ange, un petit chérubin.
cherubic [tʃi'ruːbik], *a.* (*a*) chérubique; de chérubin; (*b*) **c. smile,** sourire *m* d'ange.
chervil ['tʃəːvil], *s. Bot:* cerfeuil *m*; **great c., sweet c.,** cerfeuil musqué, odorant, d'Espagne; **needle c.,** cerfeuil à aiguillettes.
Cheshire ['tʃeʃər], *Pr.n. Geog:* le comté de Cheshire, de Chester; *Com:* **C. cheese,** fromage *m* de Chester; chester *m*; **to grin like a C. cat,** sourire jusqu'aux oreilles.
chess[1] [tʃes], *s.* jeu *m* d'échecs; **to play (at) c.,** jouer aux échecs; **c. player,** joueur, -euse, d'échecs; **c. club,** cercle *m* de joueurs d'échecs; *Her:* **c. rook,** roc *m* d'échiquier.
chess[2], *s. Mil:* volet *m* de plate-forme; madrier *m* (d'un ponton).
chessboard[1] ['tʃesbɔːd], *s.* échiquier *m*; *Tex:* **in c. pattern,** en damier.
chessboard[2], *v.tr.* disposer (qch.) en échiquier; quadriller (qch.).
chessel ['tʃesl], *s.* moule *m* à fromage.
chessman, *pl.* **men** ['tʃesmən], *s.* pièce *f* (du jeu d'échecs).
chesstree ['tʃestriː], *s. Nau: A:* dogue *m* d'amure.
chessylite ['tʃesilait], *s. Ch:* chessylite *f*, azurite *f*, cuivre carbonaté bleu.
chest [tʃest], *s.* **1.** coffre *m*, caisse *f*, boîte *f*; *Furn:* **c. of drawers,** commode *f*; **sea c.,** coffre de marin; *Min:* **ore c.,** (*of stamp*) calandre *f* (de bocard); *Hist:* **money chests,** coffres d'État; **tea c.,** caisse à thé; *Com:* barse *f*; **medicine c.,** (coffret *m* de) pharmacie *f*; coffre à médicaments; armoire *f* à pharmacie. **2.** *Anat:* poitrine *f* (d'homme, etc.); poitrail *m* (de cheval); corsage *m* (de cheval, de cerf, etc.); **cold on the c., c. cold,** rhume *m* de poitrine; **c. troubles,** maladies *f* de poitrine, des voies respiratoires; **c. protector,** plastron *m* hygiénique; **to have a weak c.,** avoir les bronches délicates; être sujet aux rhumes de poitrine; **syrup to relieve the c.,** sirop calmant la toux; sirop pectoral; **to throw out one's c.,** bomber la poitrine, le torse; **to get sth. off one's c.,** dire ce qu'on a sur le cœur, se déboutonner; *Mus:* **c. register,** registre inférieur (de la voix); **c. note,** note *f* de poitrine; **c. voice,** voix *f* de poitrine.
-chested ['tʃestid], *a.* (*with adj. prefixed, e.g.*) **broad-c.,** à large poitrine; de forte carrure; (*of horse*) au poitrail large; empoitraillé; **big-c.,** à forte poitrine.
chesterfield ['tʃestəfiːld], *s.* **1.** *Furn:* canapé rembourré et capitonné (à deux accoudoirs). **2.** *Cost: A:* pardessus *m* de ville.
chestnut ['tʃes(t)nʌt]. **1.** *s.* (*a*) **(sweet, Spanish) c.,** (i) châtaigne *f* (comestible); (ii) (*if very large owing to the abortion of the other two nuts in the husk*) marron *m*; **horse c.,** marron d'Inde; **water c.,** châtaigne d'eau; **c. man, seller,** marchand *m* de marrons; (*b*) (sweet) **chestnut (tree),** châtaignier commun, marronnier *m*; **c. grove,** châtaigneraie *f*; **horse c. tree,** marronnier *m* d'Inde; (*c*) *F:* plaisanterie usée; vieille histoire; **that's a c., an old c.!** connu! (*d*) *Farr:* châtaigne (des membres du cheval, de l'âne, du zèbre). **2.** *attrib.* (*a*) (*wood*) de châtaignier; **c. bookcase,** bibliothèque *f* de châtaignier; (*b*) (*colour*) châtain, -aine; **a c. (horse),** un (cheval) alezan; **a c. bay,** un bai châtain.
chestnutting ['tʃes(t)nʌtiŋ], *s.* cueillette *f* des châtaignes, des marrons; **to go c.,** aller à la cueillette des châtaignes.
chesty ['tʃesti], *a.* **1.** *U.S: P:* qui aime à plastronner; vaniteux. **2.** *F:* délicat des bronches.
cheval-glass [ʃə'vælglɑːs], *s., Furn:* psyché *f*.
chevalier [ʃevə'liər, ʃə'væliei], *s. A: & Lit:* chevalier *m*; *Hist:* **the C. (de Saint George),** le Chevalier de Saint-Georges; le Prétendant; **the Young C.,** Charles-Édouard.
cheval-trap [ʃə'vælltræp], *s. Her:* chausse-trape *f*, *pl.* chausse-trapes.
chevaux de frise [ʃə'voudə'friːz], *s.pl. Fort:* chevaux *mpl* de frise.
chevet ['ʃəvei], *s. Ecc.Arch:* chevet *m* (d'une église).
chevin ['tʃevin], *s. Ich:* chabot *m* de rivière; chevesne *m*, meunier *m*.
Cheviot ['tʃiːviət, 'tʃev-]. **1.** *Pr.n. Geog:* **the C. Hills, the Cheviots,** les (monts) Cheviots *m*. **2.** *s.* (*a*) *Husb:* **C. sheep,** (mouton *m*) cheviot *m*; (*b*) *Tex:* **C. (cloth),** cheviote *f*; **C. suit,** complet *m* en cheviote.
chevron ['ʃevrən], *s.* (*a*) *Mil:* brisque *f*, chevron *m*; **c. of rank,** chevron de grade; **service c.,** brisque d'ancienneté; **war-service c.,** brisque de campagnes; **wound c.,** brisque de blessure; (*b*) *Her:* chevron; **party per c.,** divisé en chevron; **c. couched,** chevron couché; (*c*) *Arch:* **c. moulding,** chevrons; (*d*) *Anat:* arc hémal.
chevronel ['ʃevrənel], *s. Her:* **three chevronels or,** trois chevronels or, trois chevrons d'or.
chevron(n)y ['ʃevrəni], *a. Her:* chevronné.
chevronwise ['ʃevrənwaiz], *a. & adv. Her:* en chevron.
chevrotain ['ʃevrətein], *s. Z:* chevrotain *m*; **water c.,** chevrotain aquatique; **(Indian) spotted c.,** chevrotain tacheté (de l'Inde).
chevy ['tʃevi], *s. Games:* (jeu *m* de) barres *fpl*.
chew[1] [tʃuː], *s.* **1.** (*mastication*) **to have a c. at sth.,** mâchonner qch. **2.** chique *f* (de tabac).
chew[2], *v.tr.* **1.** mâcher, mastiquer (des aliments, etc.); chiquer (du tabac); mâchonner, mâchiller (un cigare); *F:* **to c. sth. over,** méditer sur qch.; remâcher, ruminer, une idée; **to chew sth. up,** abîmer qch.; mettre qch. en morceaux; *F:* **to c. the rag, the fat,** (i) *A:* ronchonner; (ii) parler; **to c. the cud,** ruminer. **2.** *Nau:* (*of wooden ship*) **to c. oakum,** cracher ses étoupes.
chewer ['tʃuːər], *s.* chiqueur, -euse (de tabac).
chewing ['tʃuːiŋ], *s.* (*a*) mastication *f*, mâchement *m*, mâchonnement *m*; (*b*) **c. gum,** chewing-gum *m*; gomme *f* à mâcher; **c. tobacco,** tabac *m* à chiquer.
chewy ['tʃu(ː)i], *a.* que l'on peut mâchonner; agréable à mâchonner; difficile à mâchonner.
chi [kai], *s. Gr.Alph:* khi *m*.
chianti [ki'ænti], *s.* vin *m* de Chianti; chianti *m*.
chiaroscurist ['kjɑːrou'sk(j)uːrist], *s.* clair-obscuriste *m*, peintre *m* de clair-obscur.
chiaroscuro ['kjɑːrou'sk(j)uːrou], *s. Art:* clair-obscur *m*.
chiasma, *pl.* **-mata** [kai'æzmə, -mətə], *s.* **1.** *Biol:* chiasma *m*. **2.** *Anat:* **(optic) c.,** chiasma, chiasme *m*.
chiasmal [kai'æzml], **chiasmatic** [kai'æzmætik], **chiasmic** [kai'æzmik], *a.* chiasmatique.
chiasmus [ki'æzməs], *s. Rh:* chiasme *m*.
chiasto- [kai'æstou], *pref.* chiasto-.
chiastolite [kai'æstoulait], *s. Miner:* chiastolite *f*, macle *f*.
chiastoneural [kaiæstou'njuːr(ə)l], **chiastoneurous** [kaiæstou'njuːrəs], *a. Moll:* chiastoneure.
chiastoneury [kaiæstou'njuːri], *s. Moll:* chiastoneure *m*.
chic [ʃiːk, ʃik]. **1.** *a.* élégant, chic. **2.** *s. F:* **she's got some c. (about her),** elle a du chic.
chicane[1] [ʃi'kein], *s.* **1.** chicane *f*; avocasserie *f*. **2.** *Cards:* chicane. **3.** *Sp:* chicane.
chicane[2], *Lit:* **1.** *v.i.* chicaner. **2.** *v.tr.* chicaner (qn); **to c. s.o. into doing sth.,** user de chicane pour persuader à qn de faire qch.; **to c. s.o. out of sth.,** frustrer qn de qch. à force de chicanes.
chicanery [ʃi'keinəri], *s.* **1.** chicanerie *f*, chicane *f*, tracasserie *f*. **2.** arguties *fpl*; subtilités *fpl*; sophismes *mpl*.
chichi ['ʃiːʃiː], *F:* **1.** *a.* recherché, prétentieux; précieux; chichiteux. **2.** prétention *f*; affectation *f*; préciosité *f*.
chick [tʃik], *s.* **1.** (*a*) (i) (*unfledged*) poussin *m*; (ii) poulet *m*, poulette *f*; **to have neither c. nor child,** être sans enfant, sans progéniture; n'avoir ni enfants ni suivants; (*b*) *Com:* **c. turbot,** jeune turbot *m*. **2.** *F: esp. U.S:* fille *f*, poupée *f*, nana *f*.
chickabiddy ['tʃikəbidi], *s. F:* cocot(t)e *f* (poule ou enfant).
chickadee [tʃikə'diː], *s. Orn: NAm:* **gray-headed, Alaska, c.,** mésange lapone, *Fr.C:* mésange à plastron; **black-capped c.,** *Fr.C:* mésange à tête noire; **boreal, brown-capped, Columbian, c.,** *Fr.C:* mésange à tête brune; **chestnut-backed c.,** *Fr.C:* mésange à dos marron; **mountain c.,** *Fr.C:* mésange de Gambel.
chickaree ['tʃikəriː], *s. Z: NAm:* écureuil *m* d'Amérique.
chicken[1] ['tʃikin], *s.* **1.** (*a*) (*recently hatched*) poussin *m*; (*fledged*) poulet *m*, poulette *f*; **don't count your chickens before they are hatched,** il ne faut pas vendre la peau de l'ours avant de l'avoir tué; *F:* **she's no c.,** ce n'est plus une enfant, une gamine; elle n'est plus dans sa première jeunesse; elle est déjà d'un certain âge; elle est plutôt mûre; *F:* **that's not my c.,** ça, ce n'est pas mon affaire; (*b*) *Cu:* poulet; **spring c.,** poussin; **corn-fed c.,** poulet de grain; **free-range c.,** poulet fermier; **c. livers,** foie *m* de volaille; (*c*) *coll.* volaille *f*; **c. farm,** élevage *m* avicole; **c. farming,** élevage de volaille; **c. farmer,** aviculteur *m*; **c. run,** enclos, parquet, grillagé (d'un poulailler); cour-volière *f*, *pl.* cours-volières; **to look after the chicken(s),** s'occuper de la basse-cour; (*d*) *U.S: F:* **c. colonel,** colonel *m* (pour le distinguer d'un lieutenant-colonel); (*e*) *Orn: F:* **Mother Car(e)y's c.,** pétrel *m* des tempêtes; *NAm:* **prairie c.,** tétras *m* cupidon, cupidon *m* des prairies; *Fr.C:* poule *f* des prairies; (*f*) *NAm: P:* mineur(e), gamin(e), poulet de grain, poulette *f*; (*g*) *P:* lâche *m*, caneur *m*, froussard *m*, poule mouillée.
chicken[2], *a. NAm:* **1.** jeune; petit; **c. lobster,** jeune homard. **2.** *P:* (*a*) poltron, froussard, capon; (*b*) tatillon.
chicken[3], *v.i. P:* **to c. (out),** caner.
chicken-breasted ['tʃikin'brestid], *a. Med:* qui a la poitrine bombée; rachitique; *F:* à poitrine de canard.
chickenburger ['tʃikinbəːgər], *s. Comest:* (sorte de) petit pain fourré de tranches de poulet.
chickenfeed ['tʃikinfiːd], *s.* **1.** nourriture *f* pour les volailles. **2.** *F:* (*a*) **it's just c.,** c'est de la gnognote; (*b*) petite monnaie.
chickenhearted ['tʃikin'hɑːtid], **chickenlivered** ['tʃikin'livəd], *a. F:* poltron, froussard, capon; **to be c., c.,** manquer de courage, de cran; avoir du sang de poulet, de navet; être une poule mouillée.
chickenpox ['tʃikinpɔks], *s. Med:* varicelle *f*.
chickling ['tʃikliŋ], *s. Bot:* **c. (vetch),** (i) gesse *f*; (ii) gesse chiche, jaro(u)sse *f*.
chick-pea ['tʃikpiː], *s. Bot:* pois *m* chiche.
chickweed ['tʃikwiːd], *s. Bot:* mouron *m* des oiseaux; morgeline *f*, alsine *f*, argentine *f*; **water c.,** mouron des fontaines.
chicle ['tʃikl, 'tʃikliː], *s.* **1. c. (gum),** chiclé *m*. **2.** (*colour*) café au lait *inv*.
chicory ['tʃikəri], *s.* **1.** *Bot:* chicorée *f*; **broad-leaved c.,** endive *f*; **wild c.,** (i) *Bot:* chicorée sauvage; *F:* mignonnette *f*; (ii) *Hort:* barbe-de-capucin *f*, chicorée sauvage. **2.** *Com:* **dry c. roots,** cossettes *fpl*; **(ground) c.,** (poudre *f* de) chicorée; **coffee with c.,** café *m* à la chicorée. **3.** *Com: Cu:* endive.
chicote [ʃi'koutiː], *s.* chicote *f*.
chide [tʃaid], *v.tr. & i.* (*p.t.* **chid,** *occ.* **chided;** *p.p.* **chidden** *or* **chid,** *occ.* **chided).** *A: & Lit:* réprimander, gourmander, gronder, reprendre (qn); **to c. s.o. for sth., for doing sth.,** reprocher qch. à qn; reprocher à qn d'avoir fait qch.; **to c. against fortune,** gronder, murmurer, contre la fortune.
chiding ['tʃaidiŋ], *s. A: & Lit:* réprimandes *fpl*.
chief [tʃiːf], *a. & s.*
I. *s.* (*pl.* **chiefs**) **1.** (*a*) (*pers.*) chef *m* (de tribu, de bande, de service); *F:* **the c.,** le patron; *Mil:* **c. of staff,** chef d'état-major; **service chiefs,** (i) les chefs des trois armées (Terre, Air, Mer); (ii) les chefs, les directeurs *m*, d'armes; (iii) les chefs, les directeurs, des divers services; *U.S:* **c. of section,** chef de pièce (de mitrailleuse); *Navy: F:* **aye, aye, c.!** bien, chef! *F:* **he's the great, big, white c. (around here),** c'est lui le grand patron; (*b*) **in c.,** en chef; *Mil: Navy:* **Commander-in-c.,** commandant *m* en chef; *A: & Lit:* **with this object in c.,** principalement dans cette intention. **2.** *Her:* chef (de l'écu).
II. *a.* principal; premier; (en) chef; **c. guest,** hôte *m* d'honneur; *Com:* **my c. assistant,** mon principal collaborateur; *Jur:* **C. Justice,** premier président, *Jew.Rel:* **C. Rabbi of France,** Grand Rabbin de France; **c. engineer,** (i) *Civ.E:* ingénieur en chef, ingénieur principal; (ii) *Mil:* commandant *m* en chef du génie, commandant du génie (de la division, du corps d'armée); (iii) *Nau: Navy:* officier chef mécanicien; **c. stoker,** chef *m* de chauffe; **he is the c. sinner,** c'est lui le plus grand pécheur; **c. object,** but principal; **c. reason for sth.,** raison majeure de qch.; **the c. motive,** le principal motif; *A:* **the chief(est) good,** le bien suprême.
chiefdom ['tʃiːfdəm], *s.* dignité *f*, rang *m*, de chef; souveraineté *f*.
chiefly ['tʃiːfli], *adv.* **1.** surtout, avant tout. **2.** principalement; **c. composed of. . .,** composé en majeure partie de . . .
chiefship ['tʃiːfʃip], *s.* dignité *f* de chef; autorité *f*.
chieftain ['tʃiːftən], *s.m.* chef (de clan).
chieftainry ['tʃiːft(ə)nri], *s.* chefferie *f*.
chieftainship ['tʃiːftənʃip], *s.* autorité *f*, dignité *f*, rang *m*, de chef (de clan).
chiff-chaff ['tʃiftʃæf], *s. Orn:* pouillot *m* véloce.
chiffon ['ʃifɔn], *s.* **1.** *Tex:* chiffon *m*, gaze *f*, mousseline *f* de soie. **2.** *pl.* chiffons, atours *m* (de toilette).
chiffon(n)ade [ʃifə'neid], *s. Cu:* chiffonnade *f*.
chiffonier [ʃifə'niər], *s. Furn:* chiffonnier *m* (à tiroirs).
chigger ['tʃigər], *s.* (*a*) *Arach:* lepte automnal, *F:* aoûtat *m*, rouget *m*, vendangeon *m*, vendangeron *m*; (*b*) *Ent:* puce pénétrante; *F:* chique *f*.
chignon ['ʃiːnjɔn], *s.* chignon *m*.
chigoe ['tʃigou], *s. Ent:* puce pénétrante; *F:* chique *f*.
chihuahua [tʃi'wɑːwɑː]. **1.** *Pr.n. Geog:* Chihuahua *m*. **2.** *s. Z:* (*dog*) chihuahua.
chil- [kail], *pref. Nat.Hist: Med: etc: see* CHEIL-.
chilalgia [kai'lældʒiə], *s.* = CHEILALGIA.
chilblain ['tʃilblein], *s. Med:* pernion *m*; engelure *f*.
child, *pl.* **children** [tʃaild, 'tʃildrən], *s.m. or f.* (*a*) enfant *mf*; **problem c.,** enfant problème; **difficult c.,** enfant

difficile; **unwanted c.,** enfant non désiré; **we have four children,** nous avons quatre enfants; **two little children,** deux enfants en bas âge; **be a good c.!** sois sage! **to treat s.o. like a c.,** traiter qn en petit garçon, en petite fille; **I'm taking the c. with me,** j'emmène le petit, la petite; **come here, c.!** viens ici, petit(e)! **English children,** les petits Anglais; **the Harrison children,** les petits Harrison; **children's literature,** littérature enfantine; **he has been delicate from a c.,** il a été délicat même dès son enfance; il est délicat depuis son plus jeune âge; **I have known him from a c.,** (i) je l'ai connu enfant; (ii) je le connais depuis mon enfance; **the c. of well-to-do parents, he has never had to earn his living,** fils *m* de parents riches, il n'a jamais été obligé de gagner sa vie; *A: & Lit:* **to be with c.,** être enceinte, grosse; **to get a woman with c.,** faire un enfant à une femme; engrosser une femme; *P: O:* **this c.** (= **I, me),** moi; bibi *m;* mézigue; (*b*) **c. welfare,** protection *f* de l'enfance; **c. welfare centre,** centre *m* de protection infantile; **c. psychiatry,** psychiatrie *f* infantile; **c. murder,** infanticide *m;* **c. marriage,** mariage *m* d'enfants; **c. wife,** (i) mariée *f* qui est toujours enfant; (ii) femme restée enfant (dans le mariage); (*c*) *Lit: B:* descendant; enfant; **the children of Israel,** les enfants d'Israël; **our children's children,** nos arrière-petits-enfants *m;* (*d*) *Lit: A: see* CHILD(E); (*e*) *Lit:* (*result*) **sin is the c. of idleness,** le péché naît de l'oisiveté.

childbearing ['tʃaildbɛəriŋ], *s.* **1.** = CHILDBIRTH. **2.** gestation *f,* grossesse *f;* **woman past c.,** femme trop âgée pour avoir des enfants.

childbed ['tʃaildbed], *s.* couches *fpl;* **to die in c.,** mourir en couches.

childbirth ['tʃaildbəːθ], *s.* enfantement *m;* couches *fpl;* accouchement *m;* **to die in c.,** mourir en couches; **natural, painless, c.,** accouchement naturel, sans douleur.

child(e) [tʃaild], *s.m. Lit: A:* titre donné dans les anciennes *ballads* aux fils de famille noble; **C. Rowland** (dans **King Lear**), le jeune seigneur Roland; **C. Harold's Pilgrimage,** le pèlerinage de Childe Harold.

Childermas ['tʃildəmæs], *s. Ecc:* la fête des (Saints) Innocents (28 décembre).

childhood ['tʃaildhud], *s.* (*a*) enfance *f;* l'âge puéril; *Med:* **later c.,** deuxième, seconde, enfance; (*b*) **to be in one's second c.,** être retombé en enfance.

childish ['tʃaildiʃ], *a.* **1.** enfantin, d'enfant, d'enfance; **c. questions,** questions naïves; **c. games,** jeux enfantins, d'enfant; **his c. recollections of Paris,** les souvenirs *m* d'enfance qu'il gardait de Paris. **2.** *Pej:* (*of grown-up pers.*) enfant, puéril, *F:* bébête; **don't be so c.,** ne faites pas l'enfant; ne soyez pas si enfant(s); **to make c. remarks,** faire des observations enfantines; dire des puérilités. **3.** (*of aged pers.*) **to grow c.,** retomber en enfance.

childishly ['tʃaildiʃli], *adv.* comme un enfant, d'une manière enfantine; puérilement.

childishness ['tʃaildiʃnis], *s. Pej:* enfantillage *m,* puérilité *f;* **that's pure c.!** c'est de la puérilité!

childless ['tʃaildlis], *a.* sans enfant(s); **c. marriage,** mariage *m* stérile, union *f* stérile; **she died c.,** elle mourut sans enfants.

childlessness ['tʃaildlisnis], *s.* le fait de ne pas avoir d'enfants.

childlike ['tʃaildlaik]. **1.** *a.* enfantin; naïf; **his c. smile,** son sourire d'enfant. **2.** *adv.* **he answered, childlike . . .,** il répondit, en enfant qu'il était . . ..

childproof ['tʃaildpruːf], *a.* **c. device,** dispositif *m* de sécurité pour enfants.

child's play ['tʃaildzplei], *s.* jeu *m* d'enfant; travail *m* facile; **it's mere c. p. for him,** cela n'est qu'un amusement pour lui, ce n'est pour lui qu'une amusette; il n'y trouve aucune difficulté; pour lui c'est l'enfance de l'art; **to make c. p. of sth.,** faire qch. en se jouant.

Chile ['tʃili], *Pr.n. Geog:* Chili *m; Bot:* **C. pine,** araucaria *m;* **C. nettle,** loasa *m; Miner:* **C. copper,** mélaconite *f,* oxyde noir de cuivre; **C. saltpetre,** salpêtre *m* du Chili.

Chilean, Chilian ['tʃiliən]. **1.** *a. Geog:* chilien; *Bot:* **C. laurel,** (i) laurier *m* du Chili; (ii) (*timber*) laurelia *m;* **C. glory flower,** eccremocarpus *m.* **2.** *s. Geog:* Chilien, -ienne.

chili ['tʃili], *s.* = CHILLI.

chiliarch ['kiliɑːk], *s. Gr.Mil:* chiliarque *m.*

chiliasm ['kiliæzm], *s. Rel.H:* chiliasme *m,* millénarisme *m.*

chiliast ['kiliæst], *s. Rel.H:* chiliaste *mf,* millénaire *mf.*

chiliastic [kili'æstik], *a. Rel.H:* chiliastique.

chilitis [kai'laitis], *s. Med:* chéilite *f.*

chill¹ [tʃil], *s.* **1.** (*a*) *Med:* coup *m* de froid; **to catch a c.,** prendre froid; attraper un refroidissement, un chaud et froid; (*from a draught*) attraper un coup d'air; se refroidir; **a c. came over me,** je me sentis glacé; je fus pris d'un frisson; (*b*) **c. of fear,** frisson *m* de crainte. **2.** (*a*) froideur *f* (de l'eau, du marbre, etc.); **to take the c. off (sth.),** (faire) dégourdir, (faire) tiédir (l'eau); chambrer (le vin); **I always take the c. off my drink,** je bois toujours tiède; (*b*) **to cast a c. over a conversation, over the company,** jeter du froid, un froid, dans la conversation, sur l'assemblée. **3.** *Metall:* (*a*) **c. (mould),** moule *m* en fonte; coquille *f;* **c. casting,** fonte *f* en coquille; moulage *m* en coquille; (*b*) refroidissement rapide (du métal coulé en coquille). **4.** ternissure *f* (d'une surface vernie, due au froid, etc.).

chill², *a.* froid, glacé; *Lit:* **the wind blows c.,** il souffle un vent glacial; **a c. wind,** un vent frais; (*of blood*) **to run c.,** se glacer.

chill³. **1.** *v.tr.* (*a*) refroidir, glacer (qn, qch.); faire frissonner (qn); donner le frisson à (qn); **he was chilled with fear at the news,** cette nouvelle le transit de peur; *F:* **chilled to the bone,** morfondu; transi de froid; gelé jusqu'aux os; **he is chilled to the marrow (of his bones),** il est glacé jusqu'à la moelle des os; il meurt de froid; **to c. the enthusiasm,** refroidir, glacer, l'enthousiasme; (*b*) réfrigérer (la viande, etc.); **chilled meat,** viande réfrigérée, frigorifiée; (*c*) *Metal:* **to c.(-harden),** tremper, couler, (le fer) en coquille; coquiller (le fer); tremper à l'air; **chilled casting,** moulage *m* en coquille; **chilled steel,** acier coulé en coquille; **chilled (cast) iron,** fer dur; fonte trempée, coulée, en coquille; (*d*) ternir (une surface vernie, par le froid, etc.). **2.** *v.i.* se refroidir, se glacer.

chilli ['tʃili], *s.* **1.** *Cu:* cosse (séchée ou confite) du poivre de Guinée; piment *m;* **red c.,** piment rouge. **2.** *Bot:* piment annuel, poivre de Guinée.

chillily ['tʃilili], *adv.* avec froideur; froidement.

chilliness ['tʃilinis], *s.* **1.** (*a*) froid *m,* froideur *f,* fraîcheur *f;* **the c. of the early morning air,** le frisquet du petit jour; (*b*) froideur (d'un accueil, etc.). **2.** frisson *m,* frissonnement *m;* sensation *f* de froid.

chilling¹ ['tʃiliŋ], *a.* (vent, accueil) glacial (*pl.* -als); **c. tale,** récit *m* qui donne la chair de poule.

chilling², *s.* **1.** (*a*) réfrigération *f* (des aliments); glacement *m* (du corps, du cœur); **c. chamber,** chambre froide; (*b*) *Paint:* détérioration causée par une température trop basse. **2.** *Metall:* trempe *f* en coquille, trempe glacée; coquillage *m.*

chillness ['tʃilnis], *s.* = CHILLINESS.

chillsome ['tʃilsəm], *a.* glacial, -als.

chilly¹ ['tʃili], *a.* **1.** (*of pers.*) (*a*) frileux; **I'm very c.,** (i) je suis très sensible au froid; (ii) j'ai très froid; (*b*) **to feel c.,** avoir froid; se sentir gelé; frissonner; se sentir des frissons. **2.** (*of weather, etc.*) frais, *f.* fraîche; (un peu) froid; **it's c. this morning,** il fait frais ce matin; **it's getting c.,** il commence à faire frais, frisquet. **3.** (*of pers., manner*) froid; (accueil) froid, sans cordialité; **c. politeness,** politesse glaciale.

Chilognatha [kai'lɔgnəθə], *s.pl. Myr:* chilognathes *m.*

chiloplasty ['kailouplæsti], *s. Surg:* chiloplastie *f.*

chilopod ['kailəpɔd], *s. Myr:* chilopode *m.*

Chilopoda [kai'lɔpədə], *s.pl. Myr:* chilopodes *m.*

chilopodan [kai'lɔpədən], **chilopodous** [kai'lɔpədəs], *a. Myr:* chilopode.

Chiltern ['tʃiltən], *a.* (*a*) *Geog:* **the C. Hills,** *s.* **the Chilterns,** l'escarpement *m* des Chilterns; (*b*) **the C. Hundreds,** bailliage royal dans le Buckinghamshire; *Parl:* **to apply for, to accept, the (stewardship of the) C. Hundreds,** se démettre de son siège à la Chambre des Communes.

chimaera [k(a)i'miərə], *s.* **1.** = CHIMERA. **2.** *Ich:* chimère *f.*

chimb [tʃaim], *s.* = CHIME³.

chime¹ [tʃaim], *s.* **1. c., chimes (of bells),** carillon *m;* **chimes,** sonnerie *f* (d'une église); **the full chimes,** la grosse sonnerie; **to ring the chimes,** carillonner; **(front)door chimes,** carillon de porte. **2.** *A:* accord *m* (de sons, d'instruments); harmonie *f;* **to keep c. with sth.,** s'accorder, s'harmoniser, avec qch.; être à l'unisson de qch.

chime². **1.** *v.i.* (*of clock, bells*) carillonner; **to c. iin with s.o.'s ideas,** s'harmoniser, se concilier, s'accorder, tomber d'accord, avec les idées de qn; *F:* **to c. in,** placer son mot, intervenir (dans la conversation, etc.); se mêler à la conversation, à la discussion; se mettre de la partie; **"of course," he chimed in,** "naturellement," interposa-t-il. **2.** *v.tr.* **to c. the bells,** sonner les cloches en carillon; carillonner; (*of clock*) **to c. the hour,** carillonner l'heure; **to c. out a tune,** carillonner un air.

chime³, *s.* jable *m* (d'un tonneau); *Tls:* **c. plane,** colombe *f* (de tonnelier).

chimera [k(a)i'miərə], *s.* **1.** *Gr.Myth:* chimère *f.* **2.** *Fig:* chimère; **to indulge in chimeras,** se bercer de chimères. **3.** *Bot:* chimère.

chimere [tʃi'miər], *s. Ecc.Cost:* simarre *f* (d'évêque).

chimeric(al) [k(a)i'merik(l)], *a.* chimérique; imaginaire.

chimerically [k(a)i'merik(ə)li], *adv.* chimériquement.

chiming¹ ['tʃaimiŋ], *a.* carillonnant; **c. clock,** (horloge *m,* pendule *f* à) carillon *m.*

chiming², *s.* carillonnement *m,* carillon *m,* sonnerie *f.*

chimney ['tʃimni], *s.* **1.** cheminée *f* (de maison, etc.); **c. breast,** revêtement *m* du conduit de fumée avançant dans la pièce; **c. stack, stalk,** (i) (corps *m* de) cheminée; tuyau *m* de cheminée; souche *f;* (ii) cheminée d'usine; **c. pot,** pot *m* de cheminée; *F: O:* **c.-pot hat,** tube *m;* tuyau de poêle; huit-reflets *m inv;* **c. cap, hood,** capote *f,* capuchon *m,* de cheminée; **c. cowl,** mitre *f* (de cheminée); **c. sweep,** ramoneur *m; A:* **c. boy,** petit ramoneur; **c. sweeping,** ramonage *m;* **c. brush,** ramoneuse *f;* **c. on fire,** feu *m* de cheminée; **c. corner,** coin *m* de cheminée, de feu, du foyer, de l'âtre; **to stay in one's c. corner,** garder le coin du feu; *F:* (*of pers.*) **to smoke like a c.,** fumer cigarette sur cigarette. **2.** (*funnel*) cheminée (de bateau); **lamp c.,** verre *m* de lampe. **3.** *Geog:* (*a*) cheminée, corridor étroit; (*b*) **(volcanic) c.,** cheminée volcanique; (*c*) *U.S:* cheminée de fée. **4.** *Orn:* **c. swift,** chæture *f,* chætura *f;* **c. swallow,** (i) chæture, chætura; (ii) hirondelle *f* des cheminées.

chimney², *v.i. Mount:* **to c. up, down,** monter, descendre, une cheminée.

chimneypiece ['tʃimnipiːs], *s. Const:* chambranle *m* de cheminée, manteau *m* de cheminée; *F:* la cheminée.

chimonanthus [kaimou'nænθəs], *s. Bot:* chimonanthe *m.*

chimpanzee [tʃimpæn'ziː], *F:* **chimp** [tʃimp], *s.* chimpanzé *m.*

chin¹ [tʃin], *s.* menton *m;* **double c.,** double menton; **nutcracker c.,** menton de, en, galoche; **receding c.,** menton effacé; **to be up to the c. in water,** avoir de l'eau jusqu'au menton; **with one's c. cupped in one's hand,** le menton dans le creux de la main; **to chuck s.o. under the c.,** relever le menton à qn; *F:* **to keep one's c. up,** tenir bon, tenir le coup; **chins up!** (i) *Mil:* levez la tête! (ii) courage! *F:* **to take it on the c.,** (i) encaisser un sale coup; (ii) ne pas se laisser abattre; *Med:* **c. bandage,** mentonnière *f; Mil: etc:* **c. strap, piece,** jugulaire *f,* mentonnière, sous-mentonnière *f* (de casque, etc.); *Mus:* **c. rest,** mentonnière (de violon).

chin², *v.* **(chinned) 1.** *v.tr. Gym:* **to c. the bar,** faire une traction (des bras) à la barre fixe. **2.** *v.i. U.S: F:* bavarder.

China ['tʃainə]. **1.** *Pr.n. Geog:* Chine *f;* **the C. Sea,** la mer de Chine. **2.** *s.* (*no pl.*) (i) porcelaine *f;* faïence fine; (ii) vaisselle *f* (de porcelaine); **old c.,** vieilles porcelaines; *P:* **my old c.,** mon copain, mon pote; **c. shop,** magasin *m* de porcelaine; **the c. industry,** l'industrie porcelainière; **c. clay,** kaolin *m;* terre *f* à porcelaine; **c. stone,** pétunsé *m,* pétunzé *m;* **c. cupboard, closet,** (i) armoire *f* à porcelaine, à vaisselle; (ii) cabinet *m* de vieilles porcelaines; vitrine *f* à porcelaine; **where do you keep your c.?** où est-ce que vous mettez la vaisselle? **c. doll,** poupée *f* en porcelaine; **c. bowl,** vase *m* (i) de porcelaine, (ii) de faïence. **3.** (*a*) *Bot:* **C. grass,** ortie *f* de Chine, ortie utile; ramie *f* de Chine, ramie blanche; (*b*) *Ent:* **c. mark moth,** hydrocampiné *m.*

china², *s. Pharm: A:* **c. (bark),** écorce *f* de cinchona.

chinaberry ['tʃainəberi], *s. Bot:* **1.** baie *f* de l'arbre à chapelets. **2.** pomme *f* de savon; cerise gommeuse.

Chinaman, *pl.* **-men** ['tʃainəmən], *s.* **1.** Chinois *m; F:* **John C.,** le Chinois; **he hasn't a Chinaman's chance,** il n'a pas l'ombre d'une chance. **2.** *Nau: A:* navire *m* qui fait le commerce avec la Chine.

chinaroot ['tʃainəruːt], *s. Bot:* smilax *m* de Chine; squine *f; Pharm:* squine, china *m.*

Chinatown ['tʃainətaun], *s.* quartier chinois (d'une ville).

chinaware ['tʃainəwɛər], *s.* vaisselle *f* de porcelaine; porcelaine *f.*

chinbone ['tʃinboun], *s. Anat:* mandibule *f.*

chinch [tʃintʃ], *s. Ent: U.S:* (*a*) punaise *f;* (*b*) **c. (bug),** blissus *m.*

chincherinchee [tʃintʃərin'tʃiː], *s. Bot:* ornithogale *m.*

chinchilla [tʃin'tʃilə], *s.* **1.** *Z:* chinchilla *m;* **c. cat, rabbit,** chat *m,* lapin *m,* chinchilla; **c. rat,** abrocome *m.* **2.** (*fur, cloth*) chinchilla.

Chinchillidae [tʃin'tʃilidiː], *s.pl. Z:* chinchillidés *m.*

chin-chin¹ ['tʃin'tʃin]. **1.** *int. P:* (*a*) bonjour! (*b*) au revoir! (*c*) (*as a toast*) santé! à la vôtre! à la tienne! **2.** *s. esp. U.S: F:* (*a*) salutation *f;* (*b*) bavardage *m.*

chin-chin², *v.i.* **(chin-chinned)** *esp. U.S: F:* (*a*) (se) saluer; (*b*) bavarder.

chine¹ [tʃain], *s. Geog:* (*gully*) ravinée *f,* ravin *m.*

chine², *s.* **1.** (*a*) *Anat:* échine *f;* (*b*) *Cu:* échinée *f* (de porc). **2.** *Geog:* arête *f,* crête *f* (d'une montagne). **3.** *N.Arch:* bouchain *m.*

chine³, *v.tr.* (*of butcher*) fendre (une carcasse).

chiné ['ʃi:nei], *a. & s. Tex:* chiné (*m*).
Chinee [tʃai'ni:], *s. P:* Chinois, -oise.
Chinese [tʃai'ni:z]. **1.** *a.* chinois; **the C. People's Republic,** la République populaire de Chine; **the C. Ambassador,** l'ambassadeur *m* de Chine; **C. curio,** chinoiserie *f*; **C. white,** blanc *m* de Chine; **C. lantern,** lanterne vénitienne; *Bot:* **C. orange,** kumquat *m*; **C. artichoke,** crosne *m*; **C. scholartree,** sophora *m* du Japon; *Cmptr:* **C. binary (code),** binaire *m* par colonne. **2.** *s.* Chinois, -oise. **3.** *s. Ling:* chinois *m*.
chinidine ['tʃinidain], *s. Ch:* quinidine *f*.
chink[1] [tʃiŋk], *s.* fente *f*, crevasse *f*, lézarde *f*, interstice *m* (dans un mur, etc.); entrebâillement *m* (de la porte); **there are chinks between the planks,** il y a des jours *m* entre les planches; **I found the c. in his armour,** j'ai trouvé le défaut de sa cuirasse.
chink[2], **1.** *v.i. A:* se fendiller. **2.** *v.tr. esp. U.S:* **to c. up a crack, etc.,** remplir, boucher, une crevasse, etc.
chink[3], *s.* **1.** tintement *m* (du métal, du verre); *F:* tintin *m*; **the c. of gold,** le son de l'or; **I heard a c. of money,** j'ai entendu sonner de la monnaie. **2.** *P: A:* argent *m*, galette *f*, clinquaille *f*.
chink[4]. **1.** *v.tr.* faire sonner (son argent); faire tinter (des verres, etc.). **2.** *v.i.* sonner (sec).
Chink[5], *s. P: Pej:* Chinois, -oise; Chinetoc *m*.
chinking ['tʃinkiŋ], *s.* tintement *m* (du métal, etc.).
chinless ['tʃinlis], *a.* au menton fuyant; *F:* **c. wonder,** jeune homme (de bonne famille) aimable mais mou.
chino ['tʃi:nou, 'ʃi:nou], *s. Tex: U.S:* twill *m* (khaki); **c. pants,** *s.* **chinos,** pantalon *m* en twill.
chinoiserie [ʃi:n'wæz(ə)ri:], *s.* chinoiserie *f*.
Chinook [tʃi'nu:k, ʃi-], *s.* (*a*) *Ethn:* Chinook *mf*; (*b*) *Ling:* chinook *m*; (*c*) *attrib.* **C. salmon,** quinnat *m*.
chinook [ʃi'nu:k], *s. Meteor:* chinouk *m*.
chintz [tʃints], *s. Tex:* chintz *m*, perse *f*, indienne *f*; **c. curtains,** rideaux *m* de perse.
chinwag[1] ['tʃinwæg], *s. F: O:* causette *f*; bavardage *m*; bavette *f*.
chinwag[2], *v.i.* (**chinwagged**) *F: O:* discourir, bavarder, jaboter.
chinwagging ['tʃinwægiŋ], *s. F: O:* bavardage *m*.
chiolite ['kaioulait], *s. Miner:* chiolite *f*.
chionaspis [kaiou'næspis], *s. Ent:* chionaspis *m*.
Chione ['kaiouni:], *s. Moll:* chione *f*.
Chionidae [kai'ɔnidi:], **Chionididae** [kaiou'nididi:], *s.pl. Orn:* chionidés *m*, chionididés *m*.
Chios ['kaiɔs], *Pr.n. Geog:* (l'île de) Chio *m*.
chip[1] [tʃip], *s.* **1.** (*a*) éclat *m*, copeau *m* (de bois); écaille *f*, éclat (de marbre); *Metalw:* paille *f* (de laminage); alésure *f* (de tour); *Nau:* écli *m* (de vergue, etc.); **chips of stone,** éclats, recoupe *f*, de pierre; **quarry chips,** déchets *m*, détritus *m*, de carrière; **cinnamon chips,** déchets de cannelle; **diamond chips,** semence *f* de diamants; **c. breaker,** brise-copeau *m*, *pl.* brise-copeaux; **c. axe, ax,** doloire *f*; **c. carving,** sculpture *f* sur bois (en dessins géométriques en bas-relief); *Golf:* **c. shot,** coup sec joué en dessous de la balle pour lui donner de l'effet arrière; coup coché; **to have a c. on one's shoulder,** (i) chercher noise à tout le monde; (ii) avoir l'amour-propre chatouilleux; *F:* **he's a c. of, off, the old block,** c'est bien le fils de son père; il chasse de race; (*b*) *Nau: F:* **chips,** le charpentier (du bord); (*c*) *Cmptr:* confetti *m*; **chips box,** boîte *f* à confetti. **2.** brisure *f*, écornure *f* (d'assiette); brèche *f* (de lame de couteau). **3.** tranche *f* mince (de légume, etc.); *Cu:* **chips,** (i) pommes (de terre) frites, *F:* frites *fpl*; (ii) *NAm:* chips *mpl*; *Dom.Ec:* **c. cutter,** coupe-frites *m inv*; *Cu:* **game chips,** croustilles *fpl*. **4.** (*a*) *Cards: etc:* jeton *m*; **the chips are down,** les jeux sont faits; (*b*) *Fins:* **blue chips,** valeurs sûres, de père de famille; (*c*) *P:* pièce *f* de monnaie; pièce de cinq pence; **the chips,** l'argent; **to hand out the chips,** abouler le fric; (*d*) *P:* **he's had his chips,** il est cuit, fichu. **5.** *pl.* **chips,** fiente *f*, bouse *f* (pour combustible).
chip[2], *v.* (**chipped**).
I. *v.tr.* **1.** (*a*) tailler par éclats; hacher, doler (le bois); cliver (la pierre); buriner (une inscription); enlever (du marbre) au burin, au ciseau; (*b*) *v.ind.tr.* **to c. at a block of stone,** faire voler des éclats d'un bloc de pierre. **2.** (*a*) ébrécher (un couteau, une assiette); écorner (un engrenage, un meuble); (*of chicken*) briser (la coque de l'œuf); **to c. a piece off sth.,** enlever un morceau à qch.; ébrécher (une tasse, un outil); écailler (de l'émail); (*b*) (*with passive force*) **stone, china, that chips easily,** pierre *f*, porcelaine *f*, qui s'écaille, s'ébrèche, facilement; (*c*) piquer (les incrustations d'une chaudière); *Nau:* **to c. the hull,** piquer la rouille de la coque; (*d*) *F:* **to c. (at) s.o.,** blaguer, railler, qn; se moquer de qn; se ficher de qn; se payer la tête de qn. **3.** *Golf:* **to c. (the ball),** prendre la balle en dessous.
II. (*compound verb*) **chip in,** *v.i.* (*a*) *Cards:* miser; (*b*) *F:* intervenir; placer son mot; se mêler à la conversation; (*c*) *F:* payer sa part.
chip[3], *s. Wr:* croc-en-jambe *m*, *pl.* crocs-en-jambe.
chip[4], *v.tr. Wr:* donner un croc-en-jambe à (l'adversaire).
chipboard ['tʃipbɔ:d], *s. Paperm:* carton gris.
chipmunk ['tʃipmʌŋk], *s. Z:* tamia rayé, chipmunk *m*, écureuil rayé, *Fr.C:* suisse rayé, barré.
chipolata [tʃipə'lɑ:tə], *s. Comest:* **c. (sausage),** chipolata *f*.
chipped [tʃipt], *a.* **1.** (*a*) ébréché, écaillé; (*b*) *Prehist:* **c. stone,** pierre taillée. **2.** *Cu:* **c. potatoes,** pommes de terre frites.
Chippendale ['tʃipəndeil], *Pr.n.* **C. furniture,** meubles Chippendale.
chipper[1] ['tʃipər], *v.i.* **1.** *esp. U.S:* = CHIRP[2]. **2.** *U.S: F:* **to c. up,** se ragaillardir.
chipper[2], *v.tr.* buriner (une pièce de fonte, etc.).
chipper[3], *s.* **1.** (*pers.*) *Metalw: etc:* burineur *m*. **2.** *Tls:* burineur; *Paperm:* coupeuse *f* à bois; déchiqueteur *m*.
chipper[4], *a. NAm: F:* (*of pers.*) (*a*) gai, vif, en train; (*b*) en bonne forme (physique).
chippie ['tʃipi], *s.* = CHIPPY[2].
chipping[1] ['tʃipiŋ], *s.* **1.** (*a*) taille *f* (de qch.) par éclats; écaillement *m* (de pierre, de métal, etc.); clivage *m* (de pierre); burinage *m* (de métal); piquage *m* au marteau (d'une chaudière); **c. hammer,** marteau *m* à piquer; (*b*) *F:* blague *f*, taquinerie *f*. **2.** *pl.* **chippings,** éclats *m*, recoupe *f* (de pierre); graillons *m* (de marbre); éclats, copeaux *m* (de bois); *P.N:* **loose chippings,** gravillons *m*, *Fr.C:* gravelle *f*, *Belg:* pierres errantes.
chipping[2], *a. NAm: Z:* **c. squirrel** = CHIPMUNK; *Orn:* **c. sparrow,** *Fr.C:* pinson familier.
chippy[1] ['tʃipi], *a.* **1.** *F:* (*esp. of food*) sec, *f* sèche. **2.** *F:* fade, sans intérêt, barbant. **3.** *P:* (*a*) patraque, mal fichu; **to feel c.,** avoir la gueule de bois; avoir mal aux cheveux; (*b*) grincheux; mal luné; *Sp: esp. Can:* **c. player,** joueur *m* difficile.
chippy[2], *s.* **1.** *NAm: F:* (*a*) *Z:* = CHIPMUNK; (*b*) *Orn: Fr.C:* pinson familier. **2.** *P:* racoleuse *f*. **3.** *U.S: Rail:* wagon *m* (de ligne de chemin de fer à voie étroite).
chir(o)- [kaiər(ou)], *pref. see* CHEIR(O)-.
chiral ['kaiərəl], *a. Opt:* (solution *f*) possédant le pouvoir rotatoire.
chirality [kaiə'ræliti], *s. Opt:* pouvoir *m* rotatoire (d'une solution, etc.).
Chirocentrus [kaiərou'sentrəs], *s. Ich:* chirocentre *m*.
chironomid [kaiə'rɔnəmid], *a. & s. Ent:* chironomide (*m*).
Chironomidae [kaiərou'nɔmidi:], *s.pl. Ent:* chironomidés *m*.
chiropodist [ki'rɔpədist], *s.* pédicure *mf*.
chiropody [ki'rɔpədi], *s.* chirurgie *f* pédicure.
chiropractic ['kaiəroupræktik], *s.* chiropractie *f*, chiropraxie *f*.
chiropractor ['kaiəroupræktər], *s.* chiropracteur *m*, chiropractor *m*.
chirotony [kaiə'rɔtəni], *s. Ecc:* chirotonie *f*.
chirp[1] [tʃə:p], *s.* **1.** pépiement *m*, gazouillement *m*, gazouillis *m*, ramage *m*, guilleri *m* (d''oiseaux); piaulement *m* (d'un poussin); fringot(t)ement *m* (du pinson); cri *m*, chant, grésillement *m* (du grillon). **2.** *F:* (*of child, etc.*) gazouillement, gazouillis, babillage *m*.
chirp[2], *v.*
I. *v.i.* **1.** (*of bird*) pépier, gazouiller, ramager; (*of chicken*) piauler; (*of chaffinch*) fringot(t)er; (*of grasshopper*) crier, chanter, grésiller. **2.** *F:* (*of pers.*) (*a*) gazouiller, babiller; (*b*) chanter (d'une voix d'oiseau); *v.tr.* **she chirped out a little song,** elle a gazouillé une petite chanson.
II. (*compound verb*) **chirp up,** *F:* (*a*) *v.tr.* ragaillardir (qn); (*b*) *v.i.* (i) faire entendre sa petite voix; (ii) se ragaillardir; reprendre sa gaieté.
chirpily ['tʃə:pili], *adv. F:* gaillardement, gaiement.
chirpiness ['tʃə:pinis], *s. F:* enjouement *m*; humeur gaie; humeur gaillarde.
chirping ['tʃə:piŋ], *s.* = CHIRP[1].
chirpy ['tʃə:pi], *a. F:* d'humeur gaie; bien en train; **you look quite c. this morning,** vous voilà tout gaillard ce matin.
chirr[1] [tʃə:r], *s.* grésillement *m*, stridulation *f* (du grillon).
chirr[2], *v.i.* (*of grasshopper*) grésiller, chanter, striduler.
chirring[1] ['tʃə:riŋ], *a.* stridulant.
chirring[2], *s.* = CHIRR[1].
chirrup[1] ['tʃirəp], *s.* **1.** = CHIRP[1]. **2.** *Equit:* claquement *m* de langue, sifflotement *m* (pour encourager son cheval).
chirrup[2], *v.i.* **1.** = CHIRP[2]. **2.** (*a*) *Equit:* siffloter, faire claquer sa langue (pour encourager son cheval); (*b*) *Th: P: A:* faire la claque.
chisel[1] ['tʃizl], *s.* **1.** ciseau *m* (de menuisier, de maçon, de sculpteur); grain *m* (de maçon); hougnette *f*, ognette *f* (de sculpteur); *Nau:* gratte *f* (de calfat, etc.); **diamond-point c.,** grain-d'orge *m*, *pl.* grains-d'orge; **roughing-out c.,** ébauchoir *m*; **hollow c.,** gouge *f*; **corner c.,** gouge triangulaire; **mortise, heading, c.,** ciseau à mortaiser; bédane *m*; **flat c.,** trépan plat; **paring c.,** (i) *Carp:* ciseau long; (ii) *Const:* riflard *m*; **ripping c.,** ciseau à planches; ciseau fort; **turning c.,** fermoir *m* de tour; plane *f*; *Jewel:* **chasing c.,** bouge *m*; boësse *f*. **2.** *Engr:* burin *m*. **3.** *Metalw:* **anvil c.,** tranche *f*; **cross-cut c.,** bédane; **chipping c.,** burin; ébarboir *m*; **pneumatic hammer c.,** burin pour frappeur *m* pneumatique; **cold c.,** ciseau à froid; burin; langue-de carpe *f*, *pl.* langues-de-carpe; *Min:* **cross-mouthed c.,** pistolet *m* à tête carrée. **4.** *Ich:* **c. jaw,** pantodon *m*. **5.** *P:* filouterie *f*; sale coup *m*.
chisel[2], *v.tr.* **1.** ciseler (le bois, la pierre); buriner, ciseler (le métal); tailleer au ciseau, au burin; **to c. sth. off,** enlever, détacher, qch. au ciseau, au burin; **to c. off a nut,** cisailler un écrou; **boldly chiselled features,** visage *m* aux méplats hardis, accentués; **delicately chiselled features,** visage délicatement ciselé. **2.** *P:* duper, filouter, rouler (qn); mettre (qn) dedans; **to c. s.o. out of a fiver, to c. a fiver out of s.o.,** rouler, taper, qn de cinq livres.
chiseller ['tʃiz(ə)lər], *s.* **1.** ciseleur *m*; burineur *m*. **2.** *P:* filou *m*, escroc *m*, carotteur *m*.
chiselling ['tʃiz(ə)liŋ], *s.* **1.** ciselure *f*; burinage *m*. **2.** *P:* escroquerie *f*, filouterie *f*; resquille *f*.
chit[1] [tʃit], *s. F:* (*a*) mioche *mf*; gosse *mf*; **a mere c. of a child,** un petit bout d'enfant; (*b*) *Pej:* garce *f*.
chit[2], *s.* (*a*) lettre *f*, petit mot; (*b*) mémorandum *m*, note *f*; **give me a c. for what I owe you,** donnez-moi la note de ce que je vous dois.
chit[3], *s. Arb:: Hort: U.S:* pousse *f*; germe *m*.
chital ['tʃi:tæl], *s. Z:* **(Indian) c.,** (cerf *m*) chital *m* (de l'Inde).
chitchat ['tʃittʃæt], *s. F:* **1.** causerie *f*, bavardage *m*. **2.** bavardages, commérages *mpl*, racontages *mpl*, racontars *mpl*.
chitin ['kaitin], *s. Ch: Z:* chitine *f*.
chitinous ['kaitinəs], *a. Ch: Z:* chitineux.
chiton ['kaitən], *s.* **1.** *Gr.Ant:* chiton *m*. **2.** *Moll:* chiton, oscabrion *m*.
Chitonidae [kai'tɔnidi:], *s.pl. Moll:* chitonidés *m*.
chitosamine [kai'tousəmi:n], *s. Ch:* chitosamine *f*.
chitter ['tʃitər], *v.i.* (*of bird*) pépier.
chitter-chatter ['tʃitətʃætər], *s. F:* = CHITCHAT.
chitterlings ['tʃitəliŋz], *s.pl. Cu:* = andouillette *f*.
chivalric [ʃi'vælrik, 'ʃivəlrik], *a. Lit:* = CHIVALROUS.
chivalrous ['ʃivəlrəs], *a.* **1.** chevaleresque; courtois; désintéressé, magnanime. **2.** porté au donquichottisme; exalté.
chivalrously ['ʃivəlrəsli], *adv.* chevaleresquement.
chivalrousness ['ʃivəlrəsnis], *s.* = CHIVALRY 2.
chivalry ['ʃivəlri], *s.* **1.** chevalerie *f*; *Lit:* **the flower of c.,** la fine fleur de la chevalerie. **2.** conduite *f* chevaleresque; courtoisie *f*; désintéressement *m*, magnanimité *f*.
chives [tʃaivz], *s.pl. Bot: Cu:* ciboulette *f*, cive *f*, civette *f*.
chiviattite ['tʃiviətait], *s. Miner:* chiviatite *f*.
chiv(v)y[1] ['tʃivi], *s.* **1.** poursuite *f*, course *f*. **2.** *Games: O:* (jeu *m* de) barres *fpl*.
chiv(v)y[2], *v.tr.* poursuivre, chasser; **to c. s.o. about,** relancer qn; ne laisser aucun repos à qn.
chladnite ['klædnait], *s. Miner:* chladnite *f*.
chlamydate ['klæmideit], **chlamydeous** [klæ'midiəs], *a. Bot:* chlamydé.
Chlamydobacteriales ['klæmidoubæktiəri'eili:z], *s.pl. Bac:* chlamydobactériales *f*.
Chlamydomonadaceae ['klæmidoumɔnə'deisii:], *s.pl. Bac:* chlamydomonadidés *m*.
chlamydomonas [klæmi'dɔmənəs], *s. Bac:* chlamydomonade *f*, chlamydomonas *f*.
chlamydophore [klæ'mi:doufɔ:r], **chlamyphore** ['klæmifɔ:r], *s. Z:* chlamydophore *m*.
chlamydosaurus ['klæmidou'sɔ:rəs], *s. Rept:* chlamydosaure *m*.
chlamydospore ['klæmidouspɔ:r], *s. Fung:* chlamydospore *f*.
chlamys ['klæmis], *s.* **1.** *Gr.Ant:* chlamyde *f*. **2.** *Moll:* chlamys *m*.
chlamyde *f*. **2.** *Moll:* chlamys *m*.
chloanthite [klou'ænθait], *s. Miner:* chloanthite *f*.
chloasma [klou'æzmə], *s. Med:* chloasma *m*, chloasme *m*.
Chloe ['kloui], *Pr.n.f.* (*a*) Chloé; (*b*) *Austr: P:* **as drunk as C.,** complètement ivre, soûl.
chlor- [klɔ:r], *pref.* chlor-.
chloracetate [klɔ:'ræsiteit], *s. Ch:* chloracétate *m*.
chloracetic [klɔ:rə'si:tik], *a. Ch:* chloracétique.

chlor(a)emia [klɔ:ri:miə], *s. Med:* (*a*) chlorémie *f*; (*b*) chloroanémie *f*, chlorose *f*.
chloral ['klɔ:r(ə)l], *s. Ch:* chloral *m*; *Pharm:* **c. hydrate,** *F:* **chloral,** (hydrate *m* de) chloral.
chloralide ['klɔ:rəlaid], *s. Ch:* chloralide *f*.
chloralism ['klɔ:rəlizm], *s. Med:* chloralisme *m*.
chloralose ['klɔ:rəlous], *s. Ch:* chloralose *m*.
Chloramphenicol ['klɔ:ræm'fenikɔl], *s. Pharm: R.t.m:* Chloramphénicol *m* (*R.t.m.*), Chloromycétine *f*.
chloran(a)emia [klɔ:rə'ni:miə], *s. Med:* chloroanémie *f*, chlorose *f*.
chloranthy ['klɔ:rænθi], *s. Bot:* chloranthie *f*.
chlorate ['klɔ:reit], *s. Ch:* chlorate *m*.
chlordan(e) ['klɔ:dən, -dein], *s. Ch:* chlordane *m*.
chlore [klɔ:r], *v.tr. Ind:* chlorer.
chlorella [klɔ:'relə], *s. Algae:* chlorelle *f*.
chlorhydrate [klɔ:r'(h)aidreit], *s. Ch:* chlorhydrate *m*.
chlorhydrin [klɔ:r'(h)aidrin], *s. Ch:* chlorhydrine *f*.
chloric ['klɔ:rik], *a. Ch:* chlorique.
chloride ['klɔ:raid], *s. Ch:* chlorure *m*; **calcium c., c. of lime,** chlorure de calcium, de chaux; **stannous c.,** chlorure stanneux; **mercuric c.,** chlorure mercurique; **arsenious c.,** trichlorure *m* d'arsenic; **ferric c.,** perchlorure *m* de fer; **carbonyl c.,** acide *m* chlorocarbonique; phosgène *m*.
chlorinate ['klɔrineit], *v.tr.* chlorurer.
chlorinating ['klɔrineitiŋ], **chlorination** [klɔri'neiʃ(ə)n], *s.* (*a*) chloruration *f*; (*b*) chloration *f* (de l'eau); (*c*) chlorage *m* (de la laine).
chlorine ['klɔ:ri:n], *s. Ch:* chlore *m*.
chloring ['klɔ:riŋ], *s.* chlorage *m*.
chlorinize ['klɔrinaiz], *v.tr.* = CHLORINATE.
chlorite ['klɔ:rait], *s. Ch:* chlorite *m*.
chloro- ['klɔ:rou, 'klɔrou], *pref.* chloro-.
chloroacetic ['klɔ:rouə'si:tik], *a. Ch:* chloracétique.
chloroan(a)emia ['klɔ:rouə'ni:miə], *s. Med:* chloroanémie *f*, chlorose *f*.
chlorobenzene ['klɔ:rouben'zi:n], *s. Ch:* chlorobenzène *m*.
chlorobromide ['klɔ:rou'broumaid], *s. Ch:* chlorobromure *m*; *Phot:* **c. paper,** papier *m* au chlorobromure.
chlorobutanol ['klɔ:rou'bju:tənɔl], *s. Ch:* chlorbutol *m*.
chlorocalcite ['klɔ:rou'kælsait], *s. Miner:* chlorocalcite *f*.
chlorodyne ['klɔrədain], *s. Pharm:* chlorodyne *f*.
chloroform[1] ['klɔrəfɔ:m], *s. Med:* chloroforme *m*; **he was still under c.,** il était encore sous l'influence du chloroforme; *Pharm:* **c. water,** eau chloroformée.
chloroform[2], *v.tr.* chloroformer, chloroformiser (qn); endormir (qn) au chloroforme.
chloroformate [klɔrə'fɔ:meit], *s. Ch:* chloroformiate *m*.
chloroformic [klɔrə'fɔ:mik], *a.* (inhalation *f*, etc.) chloroformique.
chloroforming ['klɔrəfɔ:miŋ], *s.* chloroformisation *f*.
chlorohydrin ['klɔ:rou'haidrin], *s. Ch:* chlorhydrine *f*.
chloroleucite ['klɔ:rou'lju:sait], *s. Biol:* chloroleucite *m*, chloroplaste *m*.
chloroma [klɔ'roumə], *s. Med:* chlorome *m*, chloroma *m*.
chloromelanite ['klɔ:rou'melənait], *s. Miner:* chloromélanite *f*.
chlorometer [klɔ'rɔmitər], *s.* chloromètre *m*.
chlorometric [klɔrou'metrik], *a.* chlorométrique.
chlorometry [klɔ'rɔmitri], *s.* chlorométrie *f*.
Chloromycetin ['klɔ:roumai'si:tin], *s. R.t.m: Pharm:* chloromycétine *f*.
chlorophaeite ['klɔ:rou'fi:ait], *s. Miner:* chlorophæite *f*, chlorophazite *f*, chlorophænérite *f*.
chlorophane ['klɔ:roufein], *s. Miner:* chlorophane *f*.
chlorophenol ['klɔ:rou'fenɔl, -'fi:-], *s. Ch:* chlorophénol *m*.
Chlorophora [klɔ'rɔfərə], *s. Bot:* chlorophora *m*.
Chlorophyceae ['klɔ:rou'faisii:], *s.pl. Algae:* chlorophycées *f*.
chlorophyll ['klɔrəfil], *s. Ch: Bot:* chlorophylle *f*.
chlorophyllase [klɔrou'fileiz], *s. Bio-Ch:* chlorophyllase *f*.
chlorophyllian [klɔrə'filiən], *a. Biol:* chlorophyllien.
chlorophyllite ['klɔrou'filait], *s. Miner:* chlorophyllite *f*.
chloropicrin ['klɔ:rou'pikrin], *s. Ch:* chloropicrine *f*.
Chloropidae [klɔ'rɔpidi:], *s.pl. Ent:* chloropidés *m*.
chloroplast ['klɔrouplæst], *s. Biol:* chloroplaste *m*.
chloroplatinate ['klɔ:rou'plætineit], *s.* chloroplatinate *m*.
chloroprene ['klɔ:roupri:n], *s. Ch:* chloroprène *m*; chlorobutadiène *f*.
chloropsis [klɔ'rɔpsis], *s. Orn:* verdin *m*; **gold-fronted c.,** verdin à front d'or; **Jerdon's c.,** verdin de Jerdon.
chlorosis [klɔ:'rousis], *s.* **1.** *Med:* chlorose *f*. **2.** *Bot:* chlorose, étiolement *m*.
chlorospinel ['klɔ:rou'spinəl, -spi'nel], *s. Miner:* chlorospinelle *m*.
chlorotic [klɔ:'rɔtik], *a. & s. Med:* chlorotique (*mf*).
chlorous ['klɔ:rəs], *a. Ch:* chloreux.
Chloroxiphite [klɔ:'rɔksifait], *s. Miner:* chloroxiphite *f*.
chloruria [klɔ'ru:riə], *s. Med:* chlorurie *f*.
choana, *pl.* **-ae** ['kouənə, -i:], *s. Anat:* choane *f*, narine *f* interne.
choanocyte ['kouənousait], *s. Spong:* choanocyte *m*.
Choanoflagellata ['kouənouflædʒe'leitə], *s.pl. Prot:* choanoflagellés *m*.
choanoid ['kouənɔid], *a. Anat:* choanoïde.
choc-ice ['tʃɔkais], *s. F:* esquimau *m*, chocolat glacé.
chock[1] [tʃɔk], *s.* cale *f*; accotoir *m*, tin *m*, taquet *m*, coin *m*, cabrion *m*; support *m* (d'ancre, etc.); empoise *f* (de laminoir); *Av: etc:* **to remove the chocks,** enlever les cales; **chocks away!** enlevez les cales! *Nau:* **boat chocks,** chantier *m* d'embarcation; **shell c.,** accotar *m*.
chock[2], *v.tr.* **1. to c. (up),** caler, accorer, accoter (un tonneau, etc.); accoter, caler (une roue). **2.** *Mec.E: etc:* coincer (une pièce). **3.** *F:* **room chocked (up) with furniture,** pièce encombrée de meubles.
chock-a-block, chockablock ['tʃɔkə'blɔk], *a.* **1.** (poulie *f*) à bloc; *Nau:* (vergue *f*) en coche. **2.** *F:* = CHOCK(-)FULL.
chocker ['tʃɔkər], *v.tr. Cards:* bloquer (le jeu, un joueur).
chockful, chock-full ['tʃɔk'ful], *a. F:* plein comme un œuf; **to be c.-f. of sth.,** regorger de qch.; **room c.-f. of spectators,** salle bondée de spectateurrs; *Th:* **the house was c.-f.,** la salle était comble; **work c.-f. of quotations,** ouvrage bourré de citations.
chocking ['tʃɔkiŋ], *s.* **1.** calage *m*. **2.** coinçage *m* (des rails, etc.).
chockstone ['tʃɔkstoun], *s. Mount:* masse *f* de rochers coincée dans une cheminée.
chocolate ['tʃɔklət]. **1.** *s.* chocolat *m*; (*a*) **slab, bar, of c.,** tablette *f* de chocolat; **cup of c.,** tasse *f* de chocolat; **c. cream,** (i) (crotte *f* de) chocolat à la crème, chocolat fourré à la crème; (ii) *Cu:* crème au chocolat, crème chocolatée; **c. drops, buttons,** pastilles *f* de chocolat; **c. biscuit,** biscuit enrobé de chocolat; **cooking c.,** chocolat à cuire; **fondant, plain, c.,** chocolat fondant; **eating c.,** chocolat à croquer; (*b*) **a c.,** un chocolat; (*c*) **c. box,** (i) *s.* boîte *f* à chocolats; (ii) *a. F:* **c.-b., picture,** sujet sucré, trop joli (tel qu'on en voit sur les boîtes de confiserie); **c. factory,** chocolaterie *f*; (*d*) *Bot: F:* **c. nut,** cabosse *f*. **2.** *a.* (de couleur) chocolat *inv*; **c. brown,** brun chocolat *inv*.
Choctaw ['tʃɔktɔ:], *s. Ethn:* Chacta *m*, Choctaw *m*.
choice[1] [tʃɔis], *s.* **1.** choix *m*; (*a*) préférence *f*; **to make, take, one's c.,** faire son choix; choisir; **that is my c.,** voilà ce que je préfère; **for c.,** de préférence; **I don't live here by c.,** je ne vis pas ici par goût; **to do sth. of one's own c.,** faire qch. volontairement, de son propre gré; **the country of my c.,** mon pays d'élection; (*b*) alternative *f*; **to have the c. of two evils,** avoir le choix entre deux maux; **to have the c. of doing sth. or not,** avoir le choix de faire qch. ou non; **to have the c. between doing sth. and doing sth. else,** avoir le choix entre faire qch. et faire qch. d'autre; **to have no c. but to . . .,** ne pas avoir d'autre choix, d'autre ressource, d'autre alternative, que de . . .; **you have no c. in the matter,** vous n'avez pas le choix; **there is no c.,** on n'a pas le choix. **2.** (*variety*) assortiment *m*, choix; **to have a wide c.,** trouver grandement, amplement, de quoi choisir; *Com:* **wide c. of materials,** choix important de tissus. **3.** *A:* **all the c. of the town was there,** toute l'élite, toute la fleur, de la ville s'y trouvait.
choice[2], *a.* **1.** (*a*) bien choisi; **in a few c. sentences,** en quelques phrases bien choisies; (*b*) *F:* **his language isn't very c.,** son langage n'est pas très choisi. **2.** *Com:* choisi, recherché, précieux; **c. article,** article *m* de choix; article surfin; **c. dates,** dattes *f* surchoix; **c. dainties,** friandises raffinées; **c. wine,** vin fin, de première qualité; **c. vintage,** vin de choix; **c. liqueur,** liqueur *f* de marque; **he was served with c. food,** on lui a servi un repas de premier ordre.
choicely ['tʃɔisli], *adv.* avec soin; avec goût.
choiceness ['tʃɔisnis], *s.* excellence *f*, supériorité *f*, valeur particulière.
choir[1] ['kwaiər], *s.* **1.** *Arch:* chœur *m* (d'église); **c. screen,** (i) clôture *f* (du chœur); (ii) jubé *m*. **2.** (*a*) chœur (de chanteurs, d'anges); **male-voice c.,** orphéon *m*; (*b*) *Ecc:* maîtrise *f*; **c. and orchestra,** chapelle *f*; **c. school,** maîtrise; manécanterie *f*; **c. organ,** (i) positif *m* (du grand orgue); (ii) orgue du chœur, de la maîtrise (situé dans le chœur); orgue d'accompagnement.
choir[2], *v.tr. & i. Poet:* chanter en chœur.
choirboy ['kwaiəbɔi], *s.m. Ecc:* jeune choriste.
choirman, *pl.* **-men** ['kwaiəmən], *s.m. Ecc:* chantre.
choirmaster ['kwaiəma:stər], *s.m. Ecc:* maître de chapelle, de chœur.
choke[1] [tʃouk], *s.* **1.** (*a*) étranglement *m* (de canon de fusil); *Sm.a:* **c. bore,** (i) étranglement (du canon); choke-bore *m*; (ii) fusil *m* de chasse à choke-bore; **c.-bored,** (fusil de chasse) à canon étranglé, à choke-bore; (canon) étranglé; (*b*) *I.C.E:* buse *f* (du carburateur); starter *m*; self *f* de filtrage; **to pull out the c.,** tirer sur le starter; (*c*) *Aer:* étouffoir *m*; (*d*) *Mch:* **calibrated c.,** étranglement calibré. **2.** *Bot:* foin *m* (d'artichaut). **3.** *El:* **c. (coil),** bobine *f* d'impédance; self; **air c.,** self protectrice; *T.V:* **iron-cored c.,** rotacteur *m*. **4.** (*a*) étranglement, étouffement *m* (de la voix, de la respiration); **he answered with a c. in his voice,** il a répondu d'une voix étranglée; (*b*) *Min: etc:* **c. damp,** mofette *f*; touffe *f*; gaz étouffant, méphitique.
choke[2], *v.*
I. *v.tr. & i.* **1.** *v.tr.* (*a*) étouffer, suffoquer, étrangler (qn); **the foul air of the room nearly choked us,** l'air empesté de cette pièce nous suffoquait, était suffocant; **voice choked with sobs,** voix suffoquée, entrecoupée, par les sanglots; (*b*) étrangler (une cartouche, etc.); (*c*) **to c. (up) a pipe, etc.,** obstruer, engorger, boucher, un tuyau, etc. (**with,** de); (*of pipe, etc.*) **to get choked up,** s'engorger; super; **choked pump,** pompe engorgée; *I.C.E:* **choked jet (of carburettor),** gicleur bouché; **harbour choked (up) with sand,** port ensablé; **plane choked with shavings,** rabot bourré de copeaux; **rope choked in the block,** manœuvre engagée à la poulie; (*d*) **to c. (up) a filter,** *I.C.E:* **the engine,** colmater un filtre, le moteur; **to c. (up) a file,** empâter une lime; (*e*) (*of weeds*) étouffer (les fleurs, les légumes); (*f*) **to c. the fire,** étouffer le feu (par mégarde). **2.** *v.i.* (*a*) étouffer, étrangler (**with,** de); **he was choking with anger,** il suffoquait de colère; **to c. with laughter,** s'étrangler, suffoquer, de rire; **I feel like choking,** je me sens étouffer; (*b*) s'engorger, s'obstruer, se boucher (**with,** de); (*of pipe*) super; (*of rope*) s'engager; (*of filter, etc.*) se colmater; (*of file*) s'empâter; **to c. with sand,** s'ensabler; (*c*) *Carp:* (*of plane, etc.*) bourrer.
II. (*compound verbs*) **1. choke back,** *v.tr.* refouler, renfoncer, retenir, *F:* ravaler (ses larmes); refouler (ses paroles).
2. choke down, *v.tr.* étouffer, ravaler (un sanglot).
3. choke off, *v.tr.* (*a*) décourager la curiosité, les attentions, de (qn); **to c. s.o. off from doing sth.,** dissuader qn de faire qch.; (*b*) envoyer promener (qn); se débarrasser de (qn); écarter (un importun).
chokeberry ['tʃoukberi], *s. Bot:* aronia *f*.
choker ['tʃoukər], *s. F:* **1.** (*a*) foulard *m*; (*b*) **(ladies' fur) c.,** cravate *f* de fourrure; tour *m* de cou; (*c*) **(bead) c.,** collier (de perles) court; (*d*) *Cost: A:* carcan *m*; **clergyman in a white c.,** pasteur amplement cravaté de blanc. **2.** (*a*) *El: F:* = CHOKING COIL; (*b*) *I.C.E: etc:* étrangleur *m*; obturateur *m* d'air; soupape *f* d'étranglement; **c.-plate,** volet *m* d'air.
chokeweed ['tʃoukwi:d], *s. Bot:* orobanche *f*.
chokey ['tʃouki], *s.* **1.** (*in India*) (*a*) bureau *m* de la douane, de l'octroi; (*b*) péage *m*; relais *m* (de chevaux). **2.** *F:* dépôt *m* (pour prévenus); *F:* violon *m*, bloc *m*.
choking ['tʃoukiŋ], *s.* **1.** étouffement *m*, suffocation *f*, étranglement *m*, strangulation *f*. **2.** engorgement *m*, obstruction *f*; ensablement *m*. **3.** *El:* **c. coil,** bobine *f* d'impédance, de réactance; self *f*.
choky ['tʃouki], *a. F:* **in a c. voice,** d'une voix étranglée; **c. atmosphere,** atmosphère suffocante.
chol(a)emia [kə'li:miə], *s. Med:* cholémie *f*.
cholagogic [kɔlə'gɔdʒik], *a. Med:* cholagogue.
cholagogue ['kɔləgɔg], *s. Med:* (médicament *m*) cholagogue *m*.
cholangiography ['kɔlændʒi'ɔgrəfi], *s. Med:* cholangiographie *f*.
chole- ['kɔli-], *pref. Ch: Med:* cholé-.
cholecyst ['kɔlisist], *s. Anat:* cholécyste *f*.
cholecystectomy [kɔlisis'tektəmi], *s. Surg:* cholécystectomie *f*.
cholecystitis [kɔlisis'taitis], *s. Med:* cholécystite *f*.
cholecystography [kɔlisis'tɔgrəfi], *s. Med:* cholécystographie *f*.
cholecystostomy [kɔlisis'tɔstəmi], *s. Surg:* cholécystostomie *f*.
cholecystotomy [kɔlisis'tɔtəmi], *s. Surg:* cholécystotomie *f*.
choledoch ['kɔlidɔk], **choledochal** [kɔli'dɔkl], *a. Anat:* (canal) cholédoque.
choledochitis ['kɔlidou'kaitis], *s. Med:* cholédocite *f*.
choledochotomy ['kɔlidou'kɔtəmi], *s. Surg:* cholédochotomie *f*.
choledochus, *pl.* **-i** [kə'ledəkəs, -ai], *s. Anat:* (canal *m*) cholédoque *m*.
cholein ['kɔliin, -ii:n], *s. Bio-Ch:* choléine *f*.

choler [ˈkɔlər], *s.* **1.** *Med: A:* bile *f.* **2.** *Lit: & NAm:* (*a*) colère *f*; bile; (*b*) *A:* irascibilité *f.*
cholera [ˈkɔlərə], *s.* **1.** *Med:* choléra *m*; **a c. patient,** un, une, cholérique; **Asiatic c., c. morbus,** choléra asiatique, choléra morbus; **c. nostras,** choléra nostras; **dry c., c. sicca, c. siderans,** choléra sec; *A:* **c. belt,** ceinture *f* de flanelle. **2.** *Vet:* **chicken c.,** choléra des poules, choléra aviaire, peste *f* aviaire, pasteurellose *f* des volailles; **swine, hog, c.,** choléra du porc, peste porcine, typhose *f* porcine.
choleraic [kɔləˈreiik], *a. Med:* cholérique (relatif au choléra, atteint du choléra).
choleretic [kɔləˈretik], *a.* cholérétique.
choleric [ˈkɔlərik, kəˈlerik], *a.* **1.** colérique, irascible; rageur, -euse; **to be c.,** avoir le sang chaud. **2.** *Med:* = CHOLERAIC.
choleriform [ˈkɔlərifɔːm], *a. Med:* cholériforme.
cholerine [ˈkɔlərain, -iːn], *s. Med:* cholérine *f*; choléra *m* nostras.
cholester(a)emia [kɔlestəˈriːmiə], **cholesterol(a)emia** [kɔlestərɔˈliːmiə], *s. Med:* cholestérolémie *f*, cholestérinémie *f.*
cholesterol [kəˈlestərɔl], *s. Ch:* cholestérol *m.*
choliamb [ˈkouliæmb], *s. Pros:* choliambe *m.*
choliambic [kouliˈæmbik], *a. Pros:* choliambique.
cholic [ˈkoulik], *a.* (acide) cholique.
choline [ˈkoulain], *s. Bio-Ch:* choline *f.*
cholinergic [kouliˈnəːdʒik], *a. Ch:* cholinergique.
cholinesterase [kouliˈnestəreis], *s. Ch:* cholinestérase *f.*
choluria [kouˈljuːriə], *s. Med:* cholurie *f.*
chon [tʃoun], *s. Num:* chon *m.*
chondre [ˈkɔndər], *s. Geol:* chondre *m.*
chondrilla [kɔnˈdrilə], *s. Bot:* chondrilla *f.*
chondrin [ˈkɔndrin], *s. Ch:* chondrine *f.*
chondriocont, chondriokont [ˈkɔndrioukɔnt], *s. Biol:* chondrioconte *m.*
chondrioma [kɔndriˈoumə], **chondriome** [kɔndriˈoum], *s. Biol:* chondriome *m.*
chondriomite [ˈkɔndrioumait], *s. Biol:* chondriomite *m.*
chondriosome [ˈkɔndriousoum], *s. Biol:* élément *m* du chondriome, chondriosome *m.*
chondrite [ˈkɔndrait], *s. Miner:* chondrite *f.*
chondritis [kɔnˈdraitis], *s. Med:* chondrite *f.*
chondroblast [ˈkɔndroublɑːst], *s. Anat:* chondroblaste *m.*
chondrocostal [ˈkɔndrouˈkɔstl], *a. Anat:* chondrocostal, -aux.
chondrodite [ˈkɔndroudait], *s. Miner:* chondrodite *f.*
chondromucoid [ˈkɔndrouˈmjuːkɔid], *s. Bio-Ch:* chondrogénèse *f.*
chondroid [ˈkɔndrɔid], *a. Med:* chondroïde.
chondrology [kɔnˈdrɔlədʒi], *s. Anat:* chondrologie *f.*
chondroma [kɔnˈdroumə], *s. Med:* chondrome *m.*
chondromucoid [ˈkɔndrouˈmjuːkɔid], *s. Bio.-Ch:* chondromucoïde *m.*
chondroplast [ˈkɔndrouplæst], *s. Anat:* chondroplaste *m.*
chondrosarcoma [ˈkɔndrousɑːˈkoumə], *s. Med:* chondrosarcome *m.*
chondrostean [kɔnˈdrɔstiən], *s. Ich:* chondrrostéen *m.*
Chondrostei [kɔnˈdrɔstiːai], *s.pl. Ich:* chondrostéens *m.*
chondrule [ˈkɔndruːl], *s. Miner:* chondre *m.*
Chondrus, *pl.* **-dri** [ˈkɔndrəs, -drai], *s. Algae:* chondrus *m*, chondre *m.*
choose [tʃuːz], *v.tr.* (**chose** [tʃouz]; **chosen** [ˈtʃouzn]) **1.** (*a*) choisir; faire choix de (qch.); porter son choix sur (qch.); *Lit:* jeter son dévolu sur (qch.); élire (un roi); **to c. a method,** adopter une méthode; **I have too much to c. from,** j'ai l'embarras du choix; **c. for yourself,** je vous laisse le choix; **to c. s.o. as, for, king,** choisir qn pour roi, comme roi; (*b*) *Lit:* **he cannot c. but obey,** il ne peut faire autrement qu'obéir; il ne peut pas ne pas obéir; **I cannot but c. to do so,** j'y suis bien forcé, je n'ai pas le choix; (*c*) **to c. from, between, several people,** choisir, opter, entre, parmi, plusieurs personnes; **to c. an apple from the basket,** choisir une pomme dans le panier; **he had to c. between a fine and seven days' imprisonment,** il a dû choisir entre une amende et sept jours de prison; **war or peace; they chose war,** la guerre ou la paix; ils optèrent pour la guerre; **there is nothing to c. between them,** l'un vaut l'autre; ils se valent; **to pick and c.,** se montrer difficile, faire le difficile, chipoter; **I pick and c.,** j'en prends et j'en laisse; *B:* **many are called but few are chosen,** il y a beaucoup d'appelés mais peu d'élus; **there isn't anything to c. between them,** il n'y a pas la moindre différence entre eux. **2. I didn't c. to go there,** je n'ai pas choisi d'y aller; **whether he chooses or not,** qu'il le veuille ou non; **as you c.,** comme vous voudrez; **when I c.,** quand je veux; quand je voudrai; quand cela me paraît, me paraîtra, à propos; **to do sth. when one chooses,** faire qch. selon son bon plaisir; **if you c.,** si vous (le) voulez; si cela vous plaît; **I do as I c.,** je fais comme il me plaît, comme je l'entends, comme bon me semble.
chooser [ˈtʃuːzər], *s.* personne *f* qui choisit.
choosing [ˈtʃuːʒiŋ], *s.* choix *m*; **c. (of) a hat,** choix d'un chapeau; **the difficulty of c.,** l'embarras du choix; **it was none of my c.,** (i) ce n'est pas moi qui l'ai choisi; (ii) ce n'est pas de mon propre gré que je l'ai fait.
choosy [ˈtʃuːzi], *a. F:* difficile; **a c. customer,** un client, une personne, difficile.
chop[1] [tʃɔp], *s.* **1.** (*a*) coup *m* de hache, de couperet; *F: A:* **to do sth. at the first c.,** faire qch. du premier coup; (*b*) *F:* **to get the c.,** (i) *Mil.Av:* être abattu; (ii) être mis à la porte; (*c*) *A:* crevasse *f*, gerçure *f* (de la peau). **2.** *Cu:* côtelette *f* (de mouton, de porc); **loin c.,** côtelette de filet; côte première. **3.** *Nau:* clapotage *m*, clapotis *m* (de la mer). **4.** *Husb:* **c. (feed),** paille hachée, foin haché. **5.** *Ten:* **c. (stroke),** volée coupée-arrêtée; *Bill:* **c. (shot),** coup piqué.
chop[2], *v.* **(chopped).**
I. *v.tr. & i.* **1.** *v.tr.* (*a*) couper, fendre (du bois); hacher (de la viande); **to c. sticks,** casser, débiter, du bois; **chopped wood,** petit bois, menu bois; **to c. sth. in pieces,** couper qch. en morceaux, hacher qch.; **to c. sth. (up) small,** hacher qch. menu; **to c. up an eel,** tronçonner une anguille; **to c. one's way through the undergrowth,** se frayer un chemin à coups de hache à travers la broussaille; (*b*) *Ten:* **to c. the ball,** couper la balle. **2.** *v.i.* (*a*) **to c. at sth.,** (i) donner des coups de hache à qch.; (ii) tenter de porter un coup à qch.; (*b*) (*of sea*) clapoter; (*c*) *F:* **c., c.!** vite, vite! dépêche-toi! grouille-toi!
II. (*compound verbs*) **1. chop away,** *v.tr.* couper, détacher (qch. à coups de cognée); trancher (qch.); retrancher (qch.).
2. chop down, *v.tr.* abattre (un arbre) (à coups de cognée).
3. chop off, *v.tr.* trancher, retrancherr, couper, abattre (qch.); **to c. off s.o.'s head,** trancher la tête à qn.
4. chop up, *v.tr.* couper (qch.) en morceaux; hacher (qch.) menu.
chop[3], *s.* **1.** *pl.* **chops,** bajoues *f* (d'un cochon, *F:* d'une personne); **to lick one's chops,** se (pour)lécher les babines; **to lick one's chops over sth.,** s'en lécher les babines; **the chops of the Channel,** l'entrée *f* de la Manche. **2.** *Tls:* mors *m*, mâchoire *f* (d'étau).
chop[4], *v.i. P: A:* manger; déjeuner.
chop[5], *s.* **1.** *A:* troc *m*, échange *m*. **2. c. of the wind,** saute *f* de vent; **chops and changes,** changements *m*, vicissiitudes *f.*
chop[6]. **1.** *v.i.* (*a*) *A:* faire le troc; **to c. and change,** (i) *A:* acheter et vendre; (ii) tergiverser; manquer de suite (dans les idées); **he's always chopping and changing,** avec lui on ne sait pas sur quel pied danser; il change d'opinion à tout bout de champ; c'est une vraie girouette; (*b*) *Nau:* (*of wind*) **to c. (round),** changer, sauter; **the wind keeps chopping about,** le vent varie à chaque instant. **2.** *v.tr. A:* **to c. logic,** ergoter, disputailler (**with s.o.,** avec qn); discuter pour le plaisir.
chop[7], *s. Com:* (*in Far East*) (*a*) marque *f* (de qualité); étiquette *f*; **first c.,** de première qualité; **second-c. actors,** acteurs *m* de deuxième rang; (*b*) certificat *m*; **grand c.,** acquit *m* de douane.
chophouse [ˈtʃɔphaus], *s.* (*a*) restaurant où on sert surtout des côtelettes et des steaks; (*b*) *F:* restaurant (populaire).
chopper [ˈtʃɔpər], *s.* **1.** (*pers.*) (*a*) fendeur, -euse (de bois); (*b*) *U.S: F:* poinçonneur, -euse (de billets). **2.** *Tls:* (*a*) couperet *m*, hachoir *m*; coutre *m*; **meat c.,** (i) feuille *f* de boucher; (ii) *Dom.Ec:* hache-viande *m inv.*; (*b*) *Paperm:* coupeuse *f* à bois; déchiqueteur *m*. **3.** *F:* hélicoptère *m*. **4.** *Rail: F:* locomotive *f* (à commande électronique).
choppiness [ˈtʃɔpinis], *s.* agitation *f* (de la mer).
chopping[1] [ˈtʃɔpiŋ], *s.* **1.** coupe *f* (du bois); hachage *m* (du tabac, etc.); **c. block, board,** hachoir *m*, billot *m*; **c. knife,** couperet *m*; hachoir *m*. **2.** clapotage *m*, clapotis *m* (de la mer).
chopping[2], *s.* (*a*) *A:* troc *m*, échange *m*; (*b*) **c. and changing,** tergiversation(s) *f*; (*c*) *A:* **logic-c.,** ergotage *m*, ergoterie *f.*
choppy[1] [ˈtʃɔpi], *a.* (*a*) *A:* (*of skin, finger*) crevassé; (*b*) *Nau:* clapoteux; **c. sea,** mer agitée, hachée; mer avec clapotis, clapotante; vague courte, lame courte; (*c*) **c. style,** style haché.
choppy[2], *a.* (vent) changeant, variable.
chopsticks [ˈtʃɔpstiks], *s.pl.* baguettes *f* (tenant lieu de fourchette).
chop-suey [ˈtʃɔpˈs(j)uːi], *s.* (*plat style chinois*) chop-souy *m.*
choragic [kɔˈrædʒik], *a. Gr.Ant:* chorégique.
choragus [kɔːˈreigəs], *s. Gr.Ant:* chorège *m.*
choral [ˈkɔːr(ə)l], *a. Mus:* **1.** choral, -als; **c. society,** société chorale; chorale *f*; (*of male voices*) orphéon *m*; **c. singer,** membre *m* d'une chorale; orphéoniste *m*. **2.** chanté en chœur; *Ecc:* chanté par la maîtrise; **c. service,** office *m* avec musique; **c. symphony,** symphonie avec chœur.
choral(e) [kɔˈrɑːl], *s. Mus:* choral *m*, -als; cantique *m.*
choralist [ˈkɔːrəlist], *s.* choriste *mf*; orphéoniste *m.*
chord[1] [kɔːd], *s.* **1.** *Poet:* corde *f* (d'une harpe); **to touch the right c.,** faire vibrer la corde sensible. **2.** (*a*) *Geom:* corde (d'un arc); (*b*) *Av:* corde, profondeur *f* (de l'aile). **3.** *Civ.E:* semelle *f* (de poutre).
chord[2], *s. Mus:* accord *m*; **common c.,** accord parfait; **to break, spread, a c.,** briser, arpéger, figurer, un accord; **broken c., spread c.,** arpège *m*; accord arpégé, brisé, figuré; **(series of) broken chords,** batterie *f*; **c. played on open strings (of violin, etc.),** accord à l'ouvert.
chord[3], *v. Mus: U.S:* **1.** *v.i.* être en harmonie (**with,** avec). **2.** *v.tr.* harmoniser, accorder.
chorda [ˈkɔːdə], *s. Algae:* chorda *m.*
chordal [ˈkɔːdl], *a. Mus:* (accompagnement *m*) en accords.
chordata [kɔːˈdeitə], *s.pl. Z:* c(h)ordés *m.*
chorded [ˈkɔːdid], *a.* (sons *mpl*, voix *f*) en accord.
chordee [kɔːˈdiː, ˈkɔːdiː], *s. Med:* corde dure (dans la blennorragie); **gonorrhea accompanied by c.,** chaude-pisse cordée.
chorditis [kɔːˈdaitis], *s. Med:* chordite *f.*
chordoma [kɔːˈdoumə], *s. Med:* chordome *m.*
chordotomy [kɔːˈdɔtəmi], *s. Surg:* cordotomie *f.*
chordotonal [ˈkɔːdouˈtounəl], *a. Biol: Ent:* **c. organ,** organe chordotonal, scolopidie *f.*
chore [tʃɔːr], *s.* **1.** corvée *f*. **2.** *usu. pl.* travail *m* quotidien (d'une ferme, d'un ménage); train-train *m*, occupations *fpl*, du ménage; **the daily chores,** les corvées quotidiennes; **to do the chores,** faire le ménage.
chorea [kɔˈriə], *s. Med:* chorée *f*; *F:* danse *f* de Saint-Guy.
choregy [ˈkɔːridʒi], *s. Gr.Ant:* chorégie *f.*
choreiform [kɔˈriːifɔːm], *a. Med:* choréiforme.
choreodrama [kɔːriouˈdrɑːmə], *s.* chorédrame *m.*
choreographer [kɔriˈɔgrəfər], *s.* chorégraphe *mf.*
choreographic [kɔriouˈgræfik], *a.* chorégraphique.
choreography [kɔriˈɔgrəfi], *s.* chorégraphie *f.*
choriamb(us) [ˈkɔriæmb, kɔriˈæmbəs], *s. Pros:* choriambe *m.*
choriambic [kɔriˈæmbik], *a. Pros:* choriambique.
choric [ˈkɔːrik], *a.* chorique.
chorine [ˈkɔːriːn], *s. Th: U.S:* girl *f.*
chorion [ˈkɔːriən], *s. Biol:* chorion *m.*
chorionic [kɔriˈɔnik], *a. Biol:* chorionique.
chorio(n)epithelioma [ˈkɔriouepiθiːliˈoumə, ˈkɔriɔn-], *s. Med:* chorio-épithéliome *m.*
chorioretinitis [ˈkɔriouretiˈnaitis], *s. Med:* chorio-rétinite *f.*
Choripetalae [kɔːriˈpetəliː], *s.pl. Bot:* dialypétales *fpl.*
choripetalous [kɔːriˈpetələs], *a. Bot:* choripétale.
chorisis [ˈkɔːrisis], *s. Bot:* duplicature *f.*
chorister [ˈkɔristər], *s.m.* **1.** choriste. **2.** *U.S:* chef de chœur.
chorizo [tʃɔˈriːzou, -θou], *s. Comest:* chorizo *m.*
chorography [kɔˈrɔgrəfi], *s. A:* chorographie *f.*
choroid [ˈkɔrɔid], *s. Anat:* choroïde *f.*
choroid(al) [ˈkɔːrɔid, kɔˈrɔidl], *a. Anat:* choroïde; choroïdien; **c. coat, membrane,** (membrane *f*) choroïde *f*; **c. plexus,** plexus *m* choroïde; **c. artery,** artère choroïdienne.
choroiditis [kɔrɔiˈdaitis], *s. Med:* choroïdite *f.*
chorology [kɔˈrɔlədʒi], *s. Biol:* chorologie *f.*
chortle[1] [ˈtʃɔːtl], *s. F:* gloussement *m* (de rire, de gaieté).
chortle[2], *v.i. F:* glousser (de joie).
chorus[1], *pl.* **-uses** [ˈkɔːrəs, -əsiz], *s.* **1.** chœur *m*; (*a*) **to sing in c.,** chanter en chœur; **to cry out in (a) c.,** s'écrier en chœur; s'écrier tous ensemble; **c. of praise,** concert *m* de louanges; (*b*) (*body of singers*) **she belongs to the c.,** elle fait partie du chœur; *Th:* **c. singer,** choriste *mf*; **c. girl,** (i) choriste *f*; (ii) girl *f* (de music-hall); **c. master,** chef *m* du chant. **2.** refrain *m* (d'une chanson); **to join in the c.,** faire chœur (au refrain); chanter le refrain en chœur; **all join in the c.!** reprenez tous en chœur! (*of jazz musician, etc.*) **to take a c.,** prendre un chorus.
chorus[2], *v.* **(chorused) 1.** *v.i.* faire chorus, faire chœur; reprendre en chœur. **2.** *v.tr.* **to c. sth.,** répéter qch. en chœur; faire chorus à (des souhaits, etc.).
chose [ʃouz], *s. Jur:* chose *f*; **c. in action,** droit incorporel; **assignation of c. in action,** cession-transport *f*, transport *m* de cession.
chosen [ˈtʃouz(ə)n], *a.* choisi; **to address a c. few,** s'adresser à quelques auditeurs choisis; **the c. people,** le peuple élu (de Dieu); les Juifs; *B.Lit:* **c. vessel,** vase *m*

d'élection; *s.* **the c.,** les élus.

chou [ʃu:], *s.* **1.** *Dressm:* chou *m.* **2.** *Cu:* **c. pastry,** pâte *f* à choux.

chough [tʃʌf], *s.* **1.** *Orn:* crave *m* à bec rouge; coracias *m*; **Alpine c.,** chocard *m* à bec jaune, chocard des Alpes; *Austr:* **white-winged c.,** corbeau *m,* crave, à ailes blanches. **2.** *Her:* **Cornish c.,** choucas *m.*

chouse[1] [tʃaus], *s. F: A:* filouterie *f,* duperie *f*; mauvais tour; carotte *f.*

chouse[2], *v.tr. F:* filouter, duper, refaire, carotter (qn); **to c. s.o. (out) of sth.,** soutirer, souffler, qch. à qn.

chousingha ['tʃausiŋə], *s. Z:* antilope *f* tétracère, tétracère indien.

chow[1] [tʃau]. **1.** *a.* & *s.* (chien) chow-chow (*m*). **2.** *s.m. Austr: P: Pej:* Chinois.

chow[2], *s. P:* mangeaille *f,* boustifaille *f*; **c. time,** l'heure *f* du repas.

chow(-)chow ['tʃautʃau], *s.* **1.** *Cu:* (*a*) fruits exotiques conservés dans du sirop; (*b*) conserve chinoise de légumes à la moutarde. **2.** (chien) chow-chow *m.* **3.** *Hort:* chayotte *f.*

chowder ['tʃaudər], *s. Cu: NAm:* soupe *f* aux poissons ou aux fruits de mer.

chrematistic [kremə'tistik], *a.* chrématistique.

chrematistics [kremə'tistiks], *s.pl.* (*usu. with sg.const.*) chrématistique *f.*

chrestomathy [kres'tɔməθi], *s.* chrestomathie *f.*

chrism ['kriz(ə)m], *s. Ecc:* **1.** chrême *m*; saint chrême. **2.** *A:* confirmation *f.*

chrismal ['krizm(ə)l]. **1.** *a.* du chrême. **2.** *s.* (*a*) flacon *m* à huile; burette *f* (aux saintes huiles); *A:* chrismal *m*; (*b*) chrémeau *m.*

chrismation [kriz'meiʃ(ə)n], *s. Gr. Orthodox Ch:* chrismation *f.*

chrismatory ['krizmətɔri], *s. Ecc:* **1.** chrismatoire *m.* **2.** chrismation *f.*

chrisom ['kriz(ə)m], *s.* = CHRISM; **c. child,** enfant (i) âgé de moins d'un mois, (ii) qui meurt dans son premier mois; (iii) *A:* qui meurt sans être baptisé; *A:* **c. cloth, robe,** chrémeau *m.*

Christ [kraist], *Pr.n.m.* **1.** le Christ; Jésus-Christ; **the C. Child,** l'Enfant Jésus. **2.** *Bot:* **Christ's thorn,** pyracanthe *f*; épine *f* du Christ.

Christadelphian [kristə'delfiən], *a.* & *s. Ecc:* christadelphe (*m*).

christen ['krisn], *v.tr.* **1.** baptiser (qn, un navire); **to c. a child George,** baptiser un enfant (sous le nom de) Georges; **to c. a child after s.o.,** donner à un enfant le nom de qn. **2.** étrenner (qch.).

Christendom ['krisndəm], *s.* la chrétienté.

christener ['krisnər], *s.* marraine *f,* parrain *m* (d'un navire, d'une cloche).

christening ['krisniŋ], *s.* baptême *m* (d'une personne, d'un navire).

Christian ['kristjən], *a.* & *s.* chrétien, -ienne; **to become a C.,** se faire chrétien; **the C. era,** l'ère chrétienne; **C. Scientist,** scientiste chrétien; **C. burial,** sépulture *f* en terre sainte; **C. name,** nom *m* de baptême; **if he can't behave like a good C. . . .,** s'il ne sait pas se conduire en homme civilisé, comme un chrétien.

christiania [kristi'ɑ:niə], *s. Ski:* **C. (turn),** christiania *m.*

Christianity [kristi'æniti], *s.* **1.** christianisme *m.* **2.** **to act in a spirit of c.,** se conduire en chrétien; agir chrétiennement. **3.** *Ecc:* **deaneries of C.,** doyennés *m* de certaines villes (Exeter, Lincoln, Leicester, etc.).

christianization [kristjənai'zeiʃ(ə)n], *s.* christianisation *f.*

christianize ['kristjənaiz]. **1.** *v.tr.* convertir (un peuple) au christianisme; christianiser. **2.** *v.i.* devenir chrétien; adopter le christianisme.

Christina [kris'ti:nə], *Pr.n.f.* Christine.

Christlike ['kraistlaik], *a.* ressemblant au Christ.

Christmas ['krisməs], *s.* Noël *m*; **C. Day,** le jour de Noël; la (fête de) Noël; **C. Eve,** (i) la veille, (ii) la nuit, de Noël; **at C.,** à (la) Noël; **we expect him this C.,** nous l'attendons ce Noël; **merry C.!** joyeux Noël! **Father C.,** le père Noël; **to spend C. in the country,** passer la Noël à la campagne; **C. comes but once a year,** ce n'est pas tous les jours fête; **C. present,** cadeau *m* de Noël; **C. box,** (i) *O:* cadeau de Noël; (ii) étrennes (données à un fournisseur, etc.); **C. card,** carte *f* de Noël; **C. stocking** = soulier *m,* sabot *m,* de Noël; **C. party,** réunion *f* de Noël; **C. carol,** chant *m* de Noël, noël *m*; **C. pudding,** pudding *m* de Noël, plum-pudding *m* (que l'on fait flamber au cognac au moment de servir); **C. tree,** (i) arbre *m* de Noël; (ii) colonne *f,* mât *m,* à signaux; (iii) *Min:* arbre de Noël, tête *f* d'éruption; *Bot:* **C. rose,** rose *f* de Noël; ellébore noir.

Christmas(s)y ['krisməsi], *a.* (scène *f*) qui rappelle la fête de Noël; (décoration *f*) en accord avec les fêtes de Noël; **the whole street looks C.,** en descendant la rue on sent que Noël est proche.

Christmastide ['krisməstaid], *s.* époque *f,* saison *f,* de Noël; **at C.,** à la Noël.

Christological ['kristou'lɔdʒikl], *a.* christologique.

Christology [kris'tɔlədʒi], *s.* christologie *f.*

christophany [kris'tɔfəni], *s. Rel:* christophanie *f.*

Christopher ['kristəfər], *Pr.n.m.* Christophe.

chromaffin(e) ['kroumәfin, krou'mæfin], *a. Biol:* chromaffine.

chromate ['kroumeit], *s. Ch:* chromate *m.*

chromatic [krou'mætik], *a.* **1.** chromatique; **c. printing,** impression *f* en couleurs; impression polychrome; *Opt:* **c. aberration,** aberration *f* chromatique; chromatie *f,* chromatisme *m.* **2.** *Mus:* **c. scale, interval,** gamme *f,* intervalle *m,* chromatique.

chromatically [krou'mætik(ə)li], *adv.* chromatiquement.

chromatics [krou'mætiks], *s.pl.* (*usu. with sg.const.*) *Opt: Art:* chromatique *f*; science *f* des couleurs ou de la coloration.

chromatin ['kroumətin], *s. Ch: Biol:* chromatine *f.*

chromatism ['kroumətizm], *s.* chromatisme *m,* chromatie *f.*

chromatocyte [krou'mætousait], *s. Biol:* chromatocyte *m.*

chromatogram [krou'mætougræm], *s.* chromatogramme *m.*

chromatographic [kroumætou'græfik], *a.* chromatographique.

chromatography [kroumə'tɔgrəfi], *s. Ch:* chromatographie *f.*

chromatolysis [kroumə'tɔlisis], *s. Biol:* chromatolyse *f.*

chromatometer [kroumə'tɔmitər], *s.* chromatomètre *m.*

chromatophil(e) [krou'mætoufil, -fail], *a.* & *s. Biol:* chromophile (*mf*).

chromatophore ['kroumətoufɔ:r], *s. Biol:* chrom(at)ophore *m.*

chromatophoric [kroumætou'fɔrik], **chromatophorous** [kroumə'tɔfərəs], *a. Ich:* chromatophore.

chromatoplasm [krou'mætouplæzm], *s. Biol:* chromoplasme *m.*

chromatoscope ['kroumətouskoup], *s. Opt:* chromatoscope *m.*

chrome[1] [kroum], *s.* **1.** *A:* = CHROMIUM. **2.** *Dy: Tan:* bichromate *m* de potasse. **3.** *attrib.* chromé; (*a*) **c. leather,** cuir chromé; **c. tanning,** tannage *m* aux sels de chrome; **c.-tanned,** chromé; (*b*) **c. steel,** acier chromé, au chrome; **c. iron,** ferro-chrome *m,* sidérochrome *m*; **c. nickel,** nickel-chrome *m*; **c.-nickel steel,** acier nickel-chrome; (*c*) **c. yellow,** jaune de chrome.

chrome[2], *v.tr.* chromer.

chromic ['kroumik], *a. Ch:* chromique; *Miner:* **c. signal,** picotite *f.*

chromiferous [krou'mifərəs], *a. Miner:* chromifère.

chromite ['kroumait], *s. Miner:* chromite *f.*

chromium ['kroumiəm], *s. Ch:* chrome *m*; **c. garnet,** grenat *m* chromifère; **treated with c.,** chromé; **c. steel,** acier chromé, au chrome; **c. tungsten,** chrome-tungstène *m*; **c. plating,** chromage *m*; placage *m* au chrome; **c.-plated,** chromé.

chromize ['kroumaiz], *v.tr. Metall:* chromiser.

chromo ['kroumou], *s. F:* (= CHROMOLITHOGRAPH) chromo *m.*

chromo- ['kroumou, 'kroumə-], *pref.* chromo-.

chromoblast ['krouməblæst], *s. Biol:* chromoblaste *m.*

chromocollotypy ['kroumoukɔlə'taipi], *s. Phot.Engr:* photocollotypie *f.*

chromogen ['kroumədʒen], *s. Ch: Biol:* chromogène *m.*

chromogenesis ['kroumou'dʒenisis], *s. Biol:* chromogénèse *f.*

chromogenic ['kroumou'dʒenik], **chromogenous** [krou'mɔdʒinəs], *a. Biol: etc:* chromogène.

chromogram ['krouməgræm], *s. Phot:* négatif *m* monochrome (de la méthode trichrome pour prise de vues).

chromograph[1] ['krouməgræf], *s. Ind:* chromographe *m* (pour polycopie).

chromograph[2], *v.tr.* polycopier (un écrit, etc.) avec le chromographe.

chromolithograph ['kroumou'liθəgræf], *s.* chromolithographie *f.*

chromolithographer ['kroumouli'θɔgrəfər], *s.* chromolithographe *m.*

chromolithographic ['kroumouliθou'græfik], *a.* chromolithographique.

chromolithography ['kroumouli'θɔgrəfi], *s.* (*process*) chromolithographie *f,* oléographie *f.*

chromomere ['kroumoumiər], *s. Biol:* chromomère *m.*

chromometer [krou'mɔmitər], *s.* chromomètre *m.*

chromone ['kroumoun], *s. Bio-Ch:* chromone *f.*

chromonema [kroumə'ni:mə], *s. Biol:* chromonéma *m.*

chromophil(e) ['krouməfil, -fail], *a.* & *s.* chromophile (*mf*).

chromophobe ['krouməfoub], *a. Biol:* chromophobe.

chromophore ['krouməfɔ:r], *s. Biol:* chromophore *m.*

chromophoric ['kroumou'fɔrik], **chromophorous** [krou'mɔfərəs], *a. Biol:* chromophore.

chromoplast ['krouməplæst], *s. Biol:* chromoplaste *m.*

chromoprotein ['kroumou'prouti:n], *s. Biol:* chromoprotéide *f.*

chromoscope ['krouməskoup], *s. Phot:* chromoscope *m.*

chromosomal ['kroumou'soum(ə)l], **chromosomic** ['kroumou'soumik], *a. Biol:* chromosomique.

chromosome ['krouməsoum], *s. Biol:* chromosome *m.*

chromosphere ['krouməsfiər], *s. Astr:* chromosphère *f.*

chromospheric [kroumə'sferik], *a. Astr:* chromosphérique.

chromotherapy ['kroumou'θerəpi], *s. Med:* chromothérapie *f.*

chromotropic ['kroumou'trɔpik], *a. Ch:* chromotropique.

chromotropism ['kroumou'trɔpizm], *s. Ch:* chromotropisme *m.*

chromotype ['kroumətaip], *s.* **1.** (*process*) chromotypie *f,* chromotypographie *f.* **2.** (*print*) chromotype *m,* chromotypie, chromotypographie.

chromotypography ['kroumoutai'pɔgrəfi], *s.* chromotypographie *f,* chromotypie *f.*

chronaxia [krɔ'næksiə], **chronaxie, chronaxy** [krɔ'næksi], *s. Physiol:* chronaxie *f.*

chronaximetry [krɔnæk'simitri], *s. Physiol:* chronaximétrie *f.*

chronic ['krɔnik], *a.* **1.** (*a*) *Med:* chronique; passé à l'état chronique; **c. ill health,** invalidité *f*; **a c. invalid,** un, une, chronique; (*b*) constant, continuel; **c. financial difficulties,** problèmes financiers continuels, chroniques, qui ne donnent pas de répit. **2.** *F:* insupportable; (i) rasant; (ii) tout ce qu'il y a de plus désagréable; **a c. headache,** un mal de tête fou, affreux; **the weather's c.,** il fait un temps de chien.

chronically ['krɔnik(ə)li], *adv.* chroniquement.

chronicity [krɔ'nisiti], *s. Med:* chronicité *f* (d'une maladie).

chronicle[1] ['krɔnikl], *s.* chronique *f*; **the Anglo-Saxon C.,** la Chronique anglo-saxonne; *B.Lit:* **the Chronicles,** les Chroniques.

chronicle[2], *v.tr.* **to c. events,** faire la chronique des événements; enregistrer, raconter, les faits.

chronicler ['krɔniklər], *s.* chroniqueur *m.*

chrono- ['krɔnə, krə'nɔ], *pref.* chrono-.

chronogram ['krɔnəgræm], *s.* chronogramme *m.*

chronograph ['krɔnəgræf], *s.* chronographe *m.*

chronographic [krɔnə'græfik], *a.* chronographique.

chronologer [krə'nɔlədʒər], *s.* = CHRONOLOGIST.

chronological [krɔnə'lɔdʒikl], *a.* chronologique; **in c. order,** par ordre de dates; dans l'ordre chronologique.

chronologically [krɔnə'lɔdʒik(ə)li], *adv.* chronologiquement.

chronologist [krə'nɔlədʒist], *s.* chronologiste *m,* chronologue *m.*

chronology [krə'nɔlədʒi], *s.* chronologie *f.*

chronometer [krə'nɔmitər], *s.* chronomètre *m*; garde-temps *m inv*; *Nau:* **ship's c.,** chronomètre, montre *f,* de bord; montre marine; **standard c.,** chronomètre étalon.

chronometric(al) [krɔnə'metrik(l)], *a.* chronométrique; **c. measurement,** chronométrage *m.*

chronometry [krə'nɔmitri], *s.* chronométrie *f.*

chronopher ['krɔnəfər], *s.* transmetteur *m* automatique de signaux.

chronoscope ['krɔnəskoup], *s.* chronoscope *m.*

chronotropic [krɔnou'trɔpik], *a.* chronotrope.

chrys- [kris], *pref.* chrys-.

chrysalid ['krisəlid], *Ent:* **1.** *s.* chrysalide *f.* **2.** *a.* (*also* **chrysalidian**) de chrysalide.

chrysalis, *pl.* **chrysalides, chrysalises** ['krisəlis, kri'sælidi:z, 'krisəlisiz], *s. Ent:* chrysalide *f.*

chrysaniline [kri'sænilain], *s. Ch:* chrysaniline *f.*

chrysanthemum [kri'sænθəməm], *s.* **1.** *Bot:* chrysanthème *m*; **c. grower,** chrysanthémiste *m.* **2.** *Z:* **c. dog,** griffon *m* du Tibet.

chryselephantine ['kriseli'fæntain], *a.* chryséléphantin.

chrysene ['kraisi:n], *s. Ch:* chrysène *m.*

Chrysididae [kri'si:didi:], *s.pl. Ent:* chrysididés *m.*

chrysin ['kraisin], *s.* chrysine *f,* chrysol *m.*

chrysis ['kraisis, 'kri-], *s. Ent:* chrysis *f.*

chryso- ['krisou], *pref.* chryso-.

chrysoberyl ['krisouberil], *s. Miner:* chrysobéryl *m*; **c. cat's eye,** cymophane *f.*

chrysochlore ['krisouklɔ:r], *s. Z:* chrysochlore *m,* taupe dorée.

Chrysochloridae ['krisouklɔridi:], *s.pl. Z:* chrysochloridés *m.*
chrysocolla [krisou'kɔlə], *s. Miner:* chrysocolle *f. Min:* chrysocolle *f.*
chrysography [kri'sɔgrəfi], *s.* chrysographie *f.*
chrysoidine [kri'sɔidin, -dain], *s. Ch:* chrysoïdine *f.*
chrysolite ['krisəlait], *s. Miner:* chrysolit(h)e *f,* péridot *m.*
chrysomelid [krisou'melid], *s. Ent:* chrysomèle *m.*
Chrysomelidae [krisou'melidi:], *s.pl. Ent:* chrysomélidés *m.*
chrysopa ['krisəpə], *s. Ent:* chrysope *f.*
chrysophrys ['krisoufris], *s. Ich:* daurade *f.*
chrysoprase ['krisoupreiz], *s. Miner:* chrysoprase *f.*
Chrysostom ['krisəstəm], *Pr.n.m.* Chrysostome.
chrysotherapy ['krisou'θerəpi], *s. Med:* chrysothérapie *f;* thérapeutique *f* par les sels d'or.
chrysotile ['krisoutail], *s. Miner:* chrysotile *f.*
chub [tʃʌb], *s. Ich:* chevesne *m,* chevaine *m,* meunier *m,* chabot *m.*
chubbiness ['tʃʌbinis], *s.* (*of pers.*) rondeur *f.*
chubby ['tʃʌbi], *a.* potelé, boulot, dodu, grassouillet; (*of face*) joufflu; **c. cheeks,** joues rebondies; **c. little Cupids,** amours joufflus.
chuck¹ [tʃʌk]. **1.** *s.* gloussement *m* (de la volaille); appel *m* de la poule aux poussins. **2.** (*a*) *int.* (*call to fowls*) **c.! c.!** petit! petit! (*b*) *s.* (*child's word*) **a c.-c.,** une poule, une cocotte.
chuck², *v.i.* (*a*) (*of fowls*) glousser; (*b*) *F:* (*of pers.*) clapper (de la langue).
chuck³, *s. esp. NAm: P:* mangeaille *f,* boustifaille *f;* (*of unemployed cowboy, etc.*) **to ride the c. line,** faire le tour des ranchs (dans l'espoir de trouver un repas gratuit).
chuck⁴, *s.* **1.** petite tape (sous le menton). **2.** action *f* de lancer, de jeter, qch.; *P:* **to give s.o. the c.,** (i) lâcher, plaquer, qn; (ii) congédier, balancer (un employé, etc.); **so she has definitely given you the c.,** alors c'est un plaquage en règle; **to get the c.,** être congédié, remercié, renvoyé, balancé, saqué. **3.** *Games:* **to play at chucks,** jouer à la fossette.
chuck⁵, *v.*
I. *v.tr.* **1. to c. s.o. under the chin,** donner une tape à qn sous le menton; relever le menton à qn. **2.** (*a*) *F:* jeter, lancer (une pierre, etc.); **to c. stones at s.o.,** lancer des pierres à qn; **c. me (over) a cigarette,** lance moi une cigarette; **to c. sth. on the floor,** flanquer qch. par terre; **to c. one's money about, around,** gaspiller son argent, jeter son argent par la fenêtre; **to c. one's weight about, around,** faire l'important; *Games: A:* **c. farthing,** (i) jeu *m* de bouchon; (ii) jeu de la bloquette (joué avec des sous); (*b*) *F:* lâcher, plaquer (qn, son emploi); (*c*) *P:* **c. it!** en voilà assez! la ferme!
II. (*compound verbs*) **1. chuck away,** *vtr. F:* jeter (qch.) (pour s'en défaire); se débarrasser de (qch.); **that's just chucking money away,** ça c'est du gaspillage.
2. chuck in, *v.tr. F:* (*a*) **to c. one's hand in,** (i) jeter ses cartes sur la table; (ii) s'avouer battu; y renoncer, quitter la partie; (*b*) lâcher (son emploi, son boulot).
3. chuck out, *v.tr. F:* (*a*) jeter (qch. dont on n'a plus besoin); (*b*) flanquer (qn) à la porte; balancer, vider (qn); **to get chucked out of meeting,** se faire rider d'une réunion; **chucking-out time,** l'heure *f* de la fermeture (des cafés).
4. chuck up, *v.tr.* (*a*) *F:* abandonner, renoncer à, envoyer balader (un travail); **to c. up one's job,** lâcher son travail; démissionner; **to c. it up,** y renoncer; quitter la partie; (*b*) *P:* lâcher, plaquer (qn); (*c*) *v.i. P:* vomir, dégobiller.
chuck⁶, *s.* **1.** *Mec.E:* mandrin *m;* **c. (plate) (of lathe),** plateau *m* (d'un tour); **auto-centring c.,** plateau à centrage automatique; **pneumatic c.,** mandrin à commande pneumatique; **claw c., dog c.,** mandrin à griffes; **jaw c.,** mandrin à mâchoires, à mordaches, à mors; **three-jaw c.,** mandrin à trois mordaches, à trois mors; **fork c., prong c., spur c.,** mandrin à pointes; **bell c., screw c.,** mandrin à vis; **four-screw bell c.,** mandrin à quatre vis; **clamp c.,** mandrin de serrage; **drill c.,** mandrin porte-foret; **c. drill,** foret *m* (pour tour). **2.** *Cu:* paleron *m* (de bœuf).
chuck⁷, *v.tr.* mandriner; monter (une pièce) dans le mandrin, sur le tour.
chuck⁸, *s. NAm:* grande étendue d'eau; anse *f; F:* **the salt c.,** la mer, l'océan *m.*
chucker¹ ['tʃʌkər], *s. Sp:* (*polo*) = CHUKKER.
chucker², *s. Mec.E:* (*pers.*) mandrineur *m.*
chucker-out ['tʃʌkə'aut], *s. F:* agent *m* du service d'ordre (à une réunion publique, etc.); videur *m* (dans une boîte de nuit, etc.).
chuckhole ['tʃʌkhoul], *s.* **1.** *U.S:* nid *m* de poule (dans une route). **2.** *Games:* (*marbles*) fossette *f.*
chuck-in ['tʃʌkin], *s. F: Austr:* cotisation *f,* écot *m.*
chucking ['tʃʌkiŋ], *s. Mec.E:* mandrinage *m;* montage *m* (d'une pièce) sur le tour.
chuckle¹ ['tʃʌkl], *s.* **1.** rire étouffé; petit rire. **2.** gloussement *m* (d'une poule).
chuckle², *v.i.* **1.** rire tout bas, en soi-même, sous cape (**at, over, sth.,** de qch.). **2.** (*of hen*) glousser.
chuckle³, *a. & s. A:* lourdaud (*m*).
chucklehead ['tʃʌklhed], *s. F:* idiot, -ote; andouille *f.*
chuckleheaded ['tʃʌklhedid], *a. F:* stupide, bête, bas de plafond.
chuckwagon ['tʃʌkwæg(ə)n], *s. NAm: F:* (i) charrette *f,* (ii) camion *m,* qui transporte la nourriture (à des moissonneurs, des cowboys, etc.).
chuck-will's-widow ['tʃʌk'wilz'widou], *s. Orn: Fr.C:* engoulevent *m* de la Caroline.
chuff¹ [tʃʌf], *s.* souffle *m* (d'une machine à vapeur).
chuff², *v.i.* (*of engine, etc.*) souffler; haleter.
chuff-chuff¹ ['tʃʌftʃʌf], *s. F: O:* (*child's word*) train *m,* teuf-teuf *m.*
chuff-chuff², *v.i. F: O:* faire teuf-teuf.
chuffed [tʃʌft], *a. F:* **1.** ravi. **2. to be c.,** en avoir marre.
chug¹ [tʃʌg], *s.* souffle *m* (d'une machine à vapeur).
chug², *v.i.* (**chugged**) (*of engine, etc.*) souffler, haleter; **we were chugging along (in the car),** (i) nous avancions en haletant; (ii) nous roulions doucement, tant bien que mal.
chukka(r), chukker ['tʃʌkə(r)], *s. Sp:* (*polo*) chaque période *f* de huit minutes de jeu.
chuk(k)ar [tʃə'kɑ:r], *s. Orn:* chukar *m.*
chum¹ [tʃʌm], *s. F:* **1.** *A:* compagnon *m* de chambre. **2.** (*a*) camarade *mf;* ami(e) intime; copain *m,* copine *f;* (*b*) *O: Austr:* **new c.,** (i) immigrant, nouveau débarqué; (ii) béjaune *m,* cornichon *m.*
chum², *v.i.* (**chummed**) *F:* **1.** *A:* **to c. with s.o.,** faire chambre commune avec qn. **2. to c. up with s.o.,** se lier d'amitié avec qn.
chummery ['tʃʌməri], *s. F:* appartement (partagé par des célibataires).
chummy ['tʃʌmi], *a. F: O:* familier, amical, bon copain.
chump [tʃʌmp], *s.* **1.** (*a*) tronçon *m* (de bois); gros bout, gros morceau (de qch.); (*b*) *Cu:* **c. (end),** bas *m* de gigot; bout *m* de gigot; **c. chop,** côtelette *f* de gigot. **2.** (*a*) *P:* (*head*) trognon *m,* caboche *f;* **off one's c.,** timbré, maboule, loufoque; (*b*) *F:* (**silly**) **c.,** idiot, -ote; andouille *f;* cruche *f.*
chunk [tʃʌŋk], *s.* gros morceau (de pain, de fromage, etc.); quignon *m* (de pain); tronçon *m* (de bois).
chunky ['tʃʌŋki], *a.* (*a*) (*of pers.*) trapu; (*b*) volumineux; **c. sweater,** gros pullover.
Chunnel ['tʃʌnl], *s. F:* **the C.,** le tunnel sous la Manche.
church¹ [tʃə:tʃ], *s.* **1.** église *f;* (*protestant*) temple *m;* **c. clock,** horloge *f* d'église; **the c. clock,** l'horloge de l'église; **c. hall,** salle paroissiale, salle d'œuvres. **2.** (*a*) **the Established C.,** (i) l'Église établie, l'Église conformiste; (ii) la religion d'État; **the C. of England, the Anglican C.,** l'Église anglicane; **the C. of Scotland,** l'Église d'Écosse; **C. and State,** l'Église et l'État; **C. history,** histoire *f* de l'Église; **the C. Assembly,** l'assemblée nationale de l'Église anglicane; **C. lands,** terres *f,* biens *m,* d'Église; **to go into the C.,** (i) se destiner à l'Église; (ii) entrer dans les ordres; **to be received into the C.,** (i) prendre le voile; (ii) faire sa première communion; (iii) devenir chrétien par le baptême; *Hist:* **the C. party,** (i) le parti de l'Église; (ii) le parti anglican; *O:* **they are c. people,** ils sont anglicans; **High C.,** section *f* de l'Église anglicane qui se rapproche du catholicisme en matière de rituel, etc.; **Low C.,** section de l'Église anglicane qui se distingue par la simplicité du rituel; **the Free Churches,** les Églises non-conformistes, protestantes; **the (Roman) Catholic C.,** l'Église catholique; **I believe in one holy, catholic and apostolic C.,** je crois à l'Église, une, catholique et apostolique; **the Eastern Churches,** la chrétienté de l'Orient; **the Greek Orthodox C.,** l'Église orthodoxe grecque; (*b*) **c. service,** office *m;* **to go to c.,** (i) aller à l'église, à l'office, *R.C.Ch:* à la messe; (ii) pratiquer (sa religion); **I'll see you after c.,** je vous verrai après l'office, après la messe.
church², *v.tr.* (*of woman after childbirth*) **to be churched,** faire ses relevailles.
churchgoer ['tʃə:tʃgouər], *s. Ecc:* pratiquant, -ante; **he's not much of a c.,** il n'est pas très pratiquant; il va rarement aux offices, à la messe.
churchgoing ['tʃə:tʃgouiŋ], *Ecc:* **1.** *a.* pratiquant; dévot. **2.** *s.* pratique *f* (de sa religion); assiduité *f,* assistance *f,* aux offices, à la messe.
churchiness ['tʃə:tʃinis], *s. F: Pej:* bondieuserie *f.*
churching ['tʃə:tʃiŋ], *s.* (*of woman after childbirth*) relevailles *fpl.*
churchman, *pl.* **-men** ['tʃə:tʃmən], *s.* **1.** homme *m* d'église; ecclésiastique *m.* **2.** membre *m* d'une église, *in Eng: esp.* de l'Église anglicane; **he's a good c.,** il est pratiquant.
churchwarden ['tʃə:tʃ'wɔ:d(ə)n], *s.* **1.** *Ecc:* marguillier *m;* fabricien *m.* **2. c. (pipe),** longue pipe (en terre blanche); pipe hollandaise.
churchwoman, *pl.* **-women** ['tʃə:tʃwumən, -wimin], *s.f.* membre *m* d'une église, *in Eng. esp.* de l'Église anglicane; **she's a good c.,** elle est pratiquante.
churchy ['tʃə:tʃi], *a. F: Pej:* bigot; bondieusard; **c. old women,** vieilles punaises de sacristie.
churchyard ['tʃə:tʃjɑ:d], *s.* cimetière *m;* enclos *m* d'église; *F:* **c. cough,** toux *f* qui sent le sapin; *Ent:* **c. beetle,** blaps *m;* bête *f* de la mort.
churl [tʃə:l], *s. A:* (*a*) *Hist:* manant *m;* (*b*) rustre *m;* (*c*) grincheux *m;* (*d*) ladre *m,* avare *m;* grippe-sou *m, pl.* grippe-sou(s).
churlish ['tʃə:liʃ], *a.* (*a*) mal élevé; qui n'a pas de savoir-vivre; grossier; (*b*) hargneux, grincheux; mauvais coucheur.
churlishly ['tʃə:liʃli], *adv.* (*a*) grossièrement, en rustre; (*b*) avec mauvaise grâce.
churlishness ['tʃə:liʃnis], *s.* (*a*) grossièreté *f;* manque *m* de savoir-vivre; (*b*) tempérament hargneux.
churn¹ [tʃə:n], *s.* **1.** baratte *f; occ.* beurrière *f.* **2. milk c.,** bidon *m* à lait. **3.** *Min:* **c. drill,** foreuse *f* à câble.
churn², *v.*
I. *v.tr. & i.* **1.** *v.tr.* (*a*) baratter (la crème); battre (le beurre); (*b*) (*of the screw of a steamer*) **to c. up the foam,** brasser l'écume; (*c*) **to c. a thought (over) in one's mind,** agiter une pensée dans son esprit; ruminer une pensée. **2.** *v.i.* (*of sea*) bouillonner; *F:* **it made my stomach c.,** j'en avais des nausées.
II. (*compound verb*) **churn out,** *v.tr. F:* (*a*) sortir, produire, beaucoup de (qch. sans valeur); (*b*) écrire beaucoup et sans soin; *Journ:* **to c. it out,** pisser de la copie.
churning ['tʃə:niŋ], *s.* **1.** (*a*) barattage *m* (de la crème); (*b*) bouillonnement *m* (de l'eau). **2.** quantité *f* de beurre fabriquée en une fois.
churr¹ [tʃə:r], *s.* **1.** son vibrant du battement d'ailes (d'une perdrix, etc.). **2.** *Dial:* perdrix *f.*
churr², *v.i.* (*of partridge, etc.*) battre rapidement des ailes; faire vibrer l'air.
chute [ʃu:t], *s.* **1.** (*a*) *esp. NAm:* chute *f* d'eau; (*b*) *Sp:* piste *f,* glissière *f* (pour luges, toboggans); (*c*) (*in swimming pool*) toboggan *m.* **2.** couloir *m,* plan incliné, glissière, gouttière *f; NAm: Post:* chute (*Fr.C:*); *Min:* cheminée *f; Hyd.E:* (**overflow**) **c.,** déversoir *m; Artil: Sm.a:* **feed c.,** couloir d'alimentation; **ejection c.,** couloir d'éjection. **3.** *F:* parachute *m.*
chutney ['tʃʌtni], *s. Cu:* chutney *m.*
chylaceous [kai'leiʃəs], *a. Physiol:* chylaire, chyleux.
chyle [kail], *s. Physiol:* chyle *m.*
chyliferous [kai'lifərəs], *a. Physiol:* (canal *m*) chylifère.
chylification [kailifi'keiʃ(ə)n], *s.* chylification *f.*
chyliform ['kailifɔ:m], *a. Physiol:* chyliforme.
chylify ['kailifai], *v.tr.* chylifier.
chylo- ['kailou], *pref. Physiol:* chylo-.
chyloid ['kailɔid], *a. Physiol:* chyliforme.
chylopoiesis ['kailoupɔi'i:sis], *s. Physiol:* chylification *f.*
chylopoietic ['kailoupɔi'i:tik], *a. Physiol:* chylopoiétique.
chylosis [kai'lousis], *s. Physiol:* chylification *f.*
chylous ['kailəs], *a. Physiol:* chylaire, chyleux.
chyluria [kai'ljuəriə], *s. Med:* chylurie *f.*
chyme [kaim], *s. Physiol:* chyme *m.*
chymification ['kaimifi'keiʃ(ə)n], *s. Physiol:* chymification *f.*
chymify ['kaimifai], *v.tr. Physiol:* chymifier.
chymosin ['kaimousin], *s. Biol:* chymosine *f.*
chymotrypsin ['kaimou'tripsin], *s. Bio-Ch:* chymotrypsine *f.*
Chytridiaceae [kaitridi'eisii:], *s.pl. Fung:* chytridiacées *f.*
Chytridiales [kaitridi'eili:z], *s.pl. Fung:* chytridiales *f.*
ciborium, *pl.* **-ia** [si'bɔ:riəm, -iə], *s.* **1.** *Ecc.Arch:* ciborium *m.* **2.** *Ecc:* (*a*) ciboire *m;* (*b*) tabernacle *m* (du ciboire).
cicada [si' kɑ:də, -'keidə], *s. Ent:* cigale *f.*
Cicadellidae [sikə'delidi:], *s.pl. Ent:* cicadelles *f,* cicadellides *m.*
Cicadidae [si'kædidi:], *s.pl. Ent:* cicadidés *m.*
cicala [si'kɑ:lə], *s. Ent:* = CICADA.
cicatrice, cicatrix, *pl.* **-ices** ['sikətris, -triks, sikə'traisi:z], *s.* **1.** (*scar*) cicatrice *f.* **2.** *Bot:* (*a*) cicatrice foliaire; (*b*) hile *m* (de l'ovule). **3.** *Biol:* cicatricule *f.*
cicatricial [sikə'triʃ(ə)l], *a.* (tissu) cicatriciel.
cicatric(u)le ['sikətrik(ju:)l], *s.* **1.** *Biol:* cicatricule *f.* **2.** *Bot:* = CICATRICE 2.

cicatrizant [sikə'traizənt], *s.* cicatrisant *m.*
cicatrization [sikətrai'zeiʃ(ə)n], *s.* cicatrisation *f.*
cicatrize ['sikətraiz]. **1.** *v.tr.* (*a*) cicatriser; (*b*) marquer de cicatrices. **2.** *v.i.* se cicatriser.
cicatrizing ['sikətraiziŋ], *a.* (*of lotion, etc.*) cicatrisant.
Cicely ['sis(i)li]. **1.** *Pr.n.f.* Cécile. **2.** *s. Bot:* (*a*) **sweet c.,** myrrhe, myrrhide odorante; cerfeuil odorant, musqué, d'Espagne; (*b*) **fool's c.,** petite ciguë.
cicer ['sisər], *Bot:* cicérole *f*; pois *m* chiche.
Cicero ['sisərou], *Pr.n.m.* Cicéron.
cicerone, *pl.* **-oni, -ones** [tʃitʃə'rouni, sisə-; -ouni, -ouniz], *s.m.* cicerone, cicérone, guide.
Ciceronian [sisə'rouniən], *a.* cicéronien.
cichlid ['siklid], *s. Ich:* cichlide *m.*
Cichlidae ['siklidi:], *s.pl. Ich:* cichlides *m*; cichlidés *m.*
cicindelid [si'sindəlid], **cicindela** [sisin'di:lə], *s. Ent:* cicindèle *f.*
cicisbeo, *pl.* **-eos, -ei** [tʃitʃiz'beiou, -eiouz, -eii(:)], *s.m.* sigisbée.
Ciconiidae [sikɔ'ni:idi:], *s.pl. Orn:* ciconiidés *m*; cigognes *f.*
Ciconiiformes [sikɔni:i'fɔ:mi:z], *s.pl. Orn:* ciconiiformes *m.*
cicuta [si'kju:tə], *s. Bot:* cicutaire *f,* cicuta *f.*
cicutoxin [sikju'tɔksin], *s. Pharm:* cicutine *f.*
cidarid ['sidərid], *s. Echin:* cidaris *m.*
Cidaridae [si'dæridi:], *s.pl. Echin:* cidaridés *m,* cidarides *m.*
cidaris, *pl.* **-res** ['sidəris, -ri:z], *s.* **1.** *Ant:* cidaris *f.* **2.** *Echin:* cidaris *m.*
cider ['saidər], *s.* cidre *m*; **rough c.,** cidre sec; **champagne c.,** cidre bouché; **water c.,** cidre du deuxième pressurage, rémiage *m*; boisson *f*; **c. apples,** pommes *f* à cidre; **c. cup,** boisson glacée au cidre; **c. house,** cidrerie *f*; **c. making,** cidrerie; **c. press,** pressoir *m* à cidre, à pommes; **c.-producing region,** région *f* cidricole; **c. vinegar,** vinaigre *m* de cidre.
ciderkin ['saidəkin], *s.* cidre *m* du deuxième pressurage; boisson *f.*
cig [sig], *s. P:* cigarette *f*; *P:* sèche *f,* cibiche *f.*
cigar [si'gɑ:r], *s.* cigare *m*; **c. case,** étui *m* à cigares; **c. cutter,** coupe-cigares *m inv*; **c. end,** bout *m* de cigare, *P:* mégot *m*; **c. holder,** fume-cigare, *pl.* fume-cigare(s); porte-cigare, *pl.* porte-cigare(s); **c. lighter,** allume-cigare, *pl.* allume-cigares; **c. rest,** pose-cigare(s) *m inv*; **c. maker,** cigarière *f*; **c.-shaped,** en forme de cigare; *U.S:* **c. store,** bureau *m* de tabac.
cigarette [sigə'ret], *s.* cigarette *f*; **hand-made c.,** cigarette à la main; **ready made, ready rolled, c.,** cigarette toute faite, *F:* roulée *f*; **cork tipped, gold tipped, c.,** cigarette à bout de liège, à bout doré; **c. card,** vignette *f*; **c. case,** étui *m* à cigarettes; porte-cigarettes *m inv*; **c. end,** bout *m* de cigarette, *P:* mégot *m*; *F: O:* **c. heart,** affection cardiaque occasionnée par le tabagisme; **c. holder,** fume-cigarette *m, pl.* fume-cigarette(s); porte-cigarette, *pl.* porte-cigarette(s); **c. lighter,** allume-cigarette *m, pl.* allume-cigarettes; **c. machine,** (i) machine *f,* moule *m,* à cigarettes; rouleuse *f*; (ii) distributeur *m* automatique de cigarettes; **c. maker,** cigarettеuse *f*; **c. paper,** papier *m* à cigarettes; **packet of c. paper,** cahier *m* de papier à cigarettes.
cigarillo [sigə'rilou], *s.* cigarillo *m.*
ciggy ['sigi], *s. P:* cigarette *f*; *P:* sèche *f,* cibiche *f.*
ciliarotomy [siliə'rɔtəmi], *s. Surg:* ciliarotomie *f.*
ciliary ['siliəri], *s. Nat.Hist:* ciliaire; *Anat:* **c. body,** procès *m* ciliaires; **c. muscles,** muscles *m* ciliaires.
Ciliata [sili'eitə], *s.pl. Prot:* ciliates *m*; ciliés *m.*
ciliate ['silieit], **ciliated** ['silieitid], *a. Nat.Hist: Biol:* cilié, cilifère, ciligère.
cilice ['silis], *s. Ecc:* cilice *m.*
Cilicia [s(a)i'liʃ(i)ə], *Pr.n. Geog:* Cilicie *f.*
Cilician [s(a)i'liʃ(iə)n], *Geog:* **1.** *a.* cilicien. **2.** *s.* Cilicien, -ienne.
ciliferous [si'lifərəs], *a. Nat.Hist:* cilifère, ciligère.
ciliform ['silifɔ:m], *a. Nat.Hist:* ciliforme.
ciliolate ['siliəleit], *a. Bot:* à petits cils.
Ciliophora [sili'ɔfərə], *s.pl. Prot:* ciliophores *m.*
cilium, *pl.* **-ia** ['siliəm, -iə], *s. Nat.Hist: Biol:* cil *m.*
ciminite ['siminait], *s. Miner:* ciminite *f.*
cimbalom ['simbələm], *s. Mus:* cymbalum.
Cimbrian ['simbriən], **Cimbric** ['simbrik], *Hist:* **1.** *a.* cimbrien, cimbrique. **2.** *s.* **Cimbrian,** Cimbre *mf.*
Cimicidae [si'misidi:], *s.pl. Ent:* cimicidés *m.*
cimicifuga [simi'sifjugə], *s. Bot:* cimicifuge *m,* cimicaire *f.*
Cimmerian [si'miəriən], *Hist:* **1.** *a.* cimmérien; *Fig:* **C. darkness,** ténèbres cimmériennes. **2.** *s.* Cimmérien, -ienne.
cimolite ['siməlait], *s. Miner:* cimolitee *f.*
cinch[1] [sin(t)ʃ], *s.* **1.** *NAm:* (*a*) *Harn:* sangle *f*; sous-ventrière *f, pl.* sous-ventrières; (*b*) *F:* **to have a c. on** s.o., avoir prise sur qn. **2.** *F:* certitude *f*; **it's a c.,** (i) c'est certain; c'est couru; (ii) c'est facile à faire; c'est tout cuit.
cinch[2], *v.tr. NAm:* **1.** serrer les sangles (d'une selle); sangler (un cheval). **2.** *F:* mettre (qn) au pied du mur; pousser (qn) dans une impasse; *F:* serrer la vis à (qn).
cinchomeronic [siŋkoumə'rɔnik], *a. Ch:* (acide *m*) cinchoméronique.
cinchona [siŋ'kounə], *s. Bot: Med:* quinquina *m.*
cinchonia [siŋ'kouniə], *s. Ch:* cinchonine *f.*
cinchonic [siŋ'kɔnik], *a. Ch:* (acide *m*) cinchonique.
cinchonin(e) ['siŋkənin, -ni:n], *s. Ch:* cinchonine *f.*
cinchonism ['siŋkənizm], *s. Med:* quinquinisme *m.*
cinchophen ['siŋkəfen], *s. Pharm:* cinchophène *m.*
Cincinnatian [sinsi'nætiən], *a. & s. Geog:* (originaire, natif) de Cincinnati.
cincinnus ['sinsinəs], *s. Bot:* cincinnus *m.*
cinclus ['siŋkləs], *s. Orn:* cincle *m.*
cincture[1] ['siŋktjər], *s.* **1.** *Poet:* ceinture *f* (d'homme, de femme); *Ecc:* **alb and c.,** l'aube *f* et la ceinture. **2.** *A: & Lit:* enceinte *f*; **town enclosed in a c. of walls,** ville entourée d'une enceinte, d'une ceinture, de murailles. **3.** *Arch:* ceinture, filet *m* (d'une colonne); moulure *f.*
cincture[2], *v.tr. O:* ceindre, ceinturer (qn, une ville) (**with,** de).
cinder[1] ['sindər], *s.* **1.** (*a*) cendre *f*; *Cu:* **to cook a joint to a c.,** carboniser, calciner, un rôti; **joint done to a c.,** rôti en charbon; *P: A:* **yours to a c.,** ton ami jusqu'à la gauche, à la vie, à la mort; (*b*) *pl.* cendres; **to rake out the cinders,** racler les cendres (du foyer); **c. guard,** garde-cendre(s) *m inv.* (de foyer); **c. sifter,** crible *m,* tamis *m,* à escarbilles, à cendres; seau tamiseur; *Ind:* **c. bank,** crassier *m*; (*c*) *pl.* (*for racing track*) cendrée *f*; **c. path, c. track,** piste cendrée, en cendrée; **c. track race,** course *f* sur cendrée. **2.** *pl. Ind: Mch: etc:* (*a*) (*partly burnt coal*) escarbilles *f*; (*of forge*) fraisil *m*; **c. catcher,** collecteur *m* d'escarbilles; (*b*) *Metall:* laitier *m,* scorie(s) *f*(*pl*), crasse *f*; **c. notch,** sortie *f* du laitier; (*c*) *Geol:* **volcanic cinders,** lapilli *mpl*; **c. cone,** cône *m* de scories.
cinder[2], *v.tr.* cendrer (une piste, une allée).
Cinderella [sində'relə], *Pr.n.f.* Cendrillon; **the minister complained that his department was a C.,** le ministre se plaignait que son département fût traité en parent pauvre; *A:* **C. dance,** sauterie *f* (qui se termine à minuit).
cindery ['sindəri], *a.* cendreux.
cine- ['sini], *comb.fm.* ciné-.
cinecamera ['sini'kæm(ə)rə], *s.* camera *f,* caméra *f.*
cinefilm ['sinifilm], *s.* film *m* cinématographique.
cinema ['sinimə], *s.* cinéma *m*; (*a*) *c.* **fan,** fervent, -e, fanatique *mf, F:* fana *m,* du cinéma; **c. film,** film *m* cinématographique; **c. goer,** amateur *m* du cinéma; habitué, -ée, des salles de cinéma; **c. rights,** droits *m* d'adaptation cinématographique; *O:* **c. star,** vedette *f* de l'écran; (*b*) (salle *f* de) cinéma; **to go to the c.,** aller au cinéma; *O:* **news c.,** ciné-actualité *m, pl.* cinés-actualités.
Cinemascope ['siniməskoup], *s. R.t.m:* Cinémascope *m.*
cinematic [sini'mætik], *a.* du cinéma; cinématographique; (situation *f,* etc.) filmique.
cinematize ['sinimətaiz], *v.tr.* adapter (un roman) à l'écran.
cinematograph[1] [sini'mætəgræf, -grɑ:f], *s.* cinématographe *m*; cinéma *m.*
cinematograph[2], *v.tr. O:* cinématographier; filmer, tourner (une scène).
cinematographer [sinimə'tɔgrəfər], *s.* preneur *m* de vues (cinématographiques).
cinematographic [sinimætə'græfik], *a.* cinématographique.
cinematographically [sinimætə'græfik(ə)li], *adv.* cinématographiquement.
cinematography [sinimə'tɔgrəfi], *s.* cinématographie *f.*
cinemicrography [sinimai'krɔgrəfi], *s.* microcinématographie *f.*
cineol(e) ['siniɔl], *s. Ch:* cinéol *m.*
cineolic [sini'ɔlik], *a. Ch:* cinéolique.
cinephotomicrography ['sini'foutoumai'krɔgrəfi], *s.* microcinématographie *f.*
cineplastics [sini'plæstiks], *s.pl.* (*usu. with sg.const.*), **cineplasty** ['siniplæsti], *s. Surg:* cinématisation *f*; amputation *f* cinématique.
cine projector ['sinipro'dʒektər], *s. O:* projecteur *m* cinématographique, cinéprojecteur *m.*
Cinerama [sini'rɑ:mə], *s. R.t.m:* Cinérama *m.*
cineraria [sinə'reəriə], *s. Bot:* cinéraire *f.*
cinerarium [sinə'reəriəm], *s. Archeol:* cinéraire *m.*
cinerary ['sinərəri], *a.* cinéraire; *esp. Ant:* **c. urn, vase,** urne cinéraire, sépulcrale.
cineration [sinə'reiʃ(ə)n], *s.* incinération *f.*
cinerea [sinə'riə], *s. Anat:* substance grise, cendrée (du cerveau).
cinereous [si'ni:riəs], *a.* **1.** (plumage, etc.) cendré. **2.** *Miner:* cinéritique.
Cingalese [siŋgə'li:z], *Hist:* **1.** (*a*) *a.* cing(h)alais; (*b*) *s.* Cing(h)alais, -aise. **2.** *s. Ling:* cing(h)alais *m.*
cingulum ['siŋgjuləm], *s.* (*a*) *Anat:* ceinture *f*; cingulum *m*; (*b*) *Surg:* ceinture; (*c*) *Ann:* clitellum *m.*
cinnabar ['sinəbɑ:r], *s.* (*a*) *Miner:* cinabre *m*; mercure sulfuré; vermillon naturel; (*b*) *Ind:* vermillon; (*c*) *Ent:* (i) **c. (moth),** (ii) **c. caterpillar,** tyria (jacobeae) *f.*
cinnabaric [sinə'bærik], **cinnabarine** ['sinəbəri:n], *a.* cinabarin; cinabrifère.
cinnamaldehyde [sinə'mældihaid], *s. Ch:* aldéhyde *mf* cinnamique.
cinnamate ['sinəmeit], *s. Ch:* cinnamate *m.*
cinnamic [si'næmik], *a. Ch:* cinnamique.
cinnamomum [sinə'moumәm], *s. Bot:* cinname *m,* cinnamome *m.*
cinnamon ['sinəmən], *s.* **1.** *c.* (**bark**), cannelle *f,* cinnamome *m*; **candied c.,** cannelas *m*; *Cu:* **c. toast,** rôtie *f* au beurre parfumé de cannelle. **2.** *Bot:* **c.** (**tree**), cannelier *m*; **bastard c.,** cannelle fausse, bâtarde; **wild c.,** cannelle blanche, poivrée. **3. c.(-coloured),** cannellé; cannelle *inv*; *Miner:* **c. stone,** grenat *m* jaune; *Z:* **c. bear,** ours *m* d'Amérique (de couleur de châtaigne).
cinnamyl [si'næmil], *s. Ch:* cinnamyle *m.*
cinnoline ['sinəli(:)n], *s. Ch:* cinnoline *f.*
cinquain ['siŋkein], *s. Mil.Hist:* cinquain *m.*
cinque [siŋk], *s. Cards: etc:* cinq *m.*
cinquecentist [tʃiŋkwi'tʃentist], *s. Art: Lit:* cinq(ué)centiste *m.*
cinquecento [tʃiŋkwi'tʃentou], *s.* l'art italien du XVIe siècle.
cinq(ue)foil ['siŋkfɔil], *s.* **1.** *Bot:* potentille rampante; *F:* quintefeuille *f.* **2.** *Her:* quintefeuille *f.* **3.** *Arch:* cinq-feuilles *m inv,* quintefeuille *m.*
Cinque Ports ['siŋk'pɔ:ts], *s.pl. Hist:* les Cinq-Ports *m* (Douvres, Hastings, Hythe, Romney, et Sandwich, auxquels s'ajoutèrent par la suite Rye, Winchelsea, et Seaford; ils jouissaient de certains privilèges).
cionitis [saiə'naitis], *s. Med:* cionite *f.*
cionotome ['saiənətoum], *s. Surg:* cionotome *m.*
cipher[1] ['saifər], *s.* **1.** *Mth:* (*a*) zéro *m*; **he's a mere c.,** il est nul; c'est un homme nul, un zéro, une nullité; (*b*) *occ.* chiffre *m* (arabe). **2.** (*a*) (*secret writing*) chiffre; *Com:* marque *f*; **writing in c.,** écriture *f* en chiffre; **to write a message in c.,** transmettre une dépêche en chiffre, en écriture chiffrée; **c. key,** clef *f* de chiffre; **c. book,** carnet *m* de chiffrement; **c. clerk,** chiffreur, -euse; **c. machine,** (i) machine *f* à chiffrer, cryptographe *m*; (ii) machine à déchiffrer; **c. office,** bureau *m* du chiffre; **c. officer,** officier *m* du chiffre; (*b*) (i) message chiffré; (ii) signal chiffré; (*c*) clef (d'un chiffre). **3.** (*monogram*) chiffre, monogramme *m.* **4.** *Mus:* cornement *m* (d'un tuyau d'orgue).
cipher[2]. **1.** *v.tr.* (*a*) *O:* **to c. (out) a sum,** chiffrer un calcul; calculer une somme; (*b*) chiffrer (une dépêche); transmettre (une dépêche) en chiffre; (*c*) *NAm: F: O:* **to c. out a mystery, the cause of sth.,** approfondir, sonder, un mystère; découvrir les causes de qch. **2.** *v.i.* (*a*) chiffrer, calculer; (*b*) *Mus:* (*of organ pipe*) corner.
cipherer ['saifərər], *s.* chiffreur, -euse; officier *m* du chiffre.
ciphering ['saifəriŋ], *s.* **1.** *A:* chiffrage *m,* calcul *m.* **2.** chiffrage, chiffrement *m* (d'une dépêche); **c. grid, square,** châssis-grille *m, pl.* châssis-grilles; grille *f.* **3.** *Mus:* cornement *m* (d'un tuyau d'orgue).
ciphony ['saifəni], *s.* brouillage *m* radioélectrique (d'une dépêche).
cipolin ['sipəlin], *s. Miner:* cipolin *m.*
cippus, *pl.* **-i** ['sipəs, -ai], *s. Arch: Archeol:* cippe *m.*
circadian [sə:'keidiən], *a. Biol:* (rythme, etc.) circadien.
circaea [sə:'si:ə], *s. Bot:* circée *f.*
circaëtus [sə:'keiətəs], *s. Orn:* circaète *m.*
Circassia [sə:'kæsiə], *Pr.n. Geog:* Circassie *f.*
Circassian [sə:'kæsiən]. **1.** *Geog:* (*a*) *a.* circassien; (*b*) *s.* Circassien, -ienne. **2.** *s. Ling:* circassien *m.* **3.** *s. Tex:* **circassian,** circassienne *f.*
Circe ['sə:si], *Pr.n.f. Gr.Lit:* Circé.
Circean [sə:'si:ən], *a.* de Circé; enchanteur, -eresse.
circinate ['sə:sineit], *a. Nat.Hist:* circinal, -aux; circiné.
circle[1] ['sə:kl], *s.* **1.** (*a*) cercle *m*; **to draw a c.,** tracer un cercle, une circonférence; (*of points*) **to fall, lie, in a c.,** faire, former, cercle; (*of persons*) **to stand in a c.,** se tenir en cercle; faire cercle; *F:* **to go all round the c.,** prendre par le plus long; **to run, rush, round in circles,** tourner en rond; **to have circles round one's eyes,** avoir les yeux cernés, battus; *Aut:* **turning c.,** cercle de

braquage; **radius of turning c.,** rayon *m* de braquage; *Nau:* **swinging c.,** champ *m* d'évitement; *Aer:* **c. of the propeller,** diamètre *m* de l'hélice; *Fb:* **centre c.,** cercle d'envoi; *Mth:* **c. of curvature,** cercle osculateur (d'une courbe); (*b*) **polar c.,** cercle polaire; **Arctic, Antarctic, C.,** cercle (polaire) arctique, antarctique; **great, small, c. (of a sphere),** grand, petit, cercle; *Nav:* **great c. sailing,** navigation *f* par, sur, l'arc de grand cercle; *Astr:* **declination c.,** cercle de déclinaison; (*c*) *Gym:* **to do the grand c. (on the horizontal bar),** faire le grand soleil; (*d*) *Log:* **vicious c.,** argument *m* circulaire; cercle vicieux; **to reason in a c.,** tourner dans un cercle (vicieux); **you are arguing in a c.,** vous êtes dans un cercle; (*e*) *NAm:* **traffic c.,** rond-point *m, pl.* ronds-points; carrefour *m*. **2.** (*a*) révolution *f*, orbite *mf* (d'une planète); **to come full c.,** (i) compléter son orbite; (ii) (*of pers.*) revenir à son point de départ; **the century had not yet come full c.,** le siècle n'était pas encore révolu; **the c. of his activities,** le cercle, l'orbite, de ses activités; (*b*) *Equit:* volte *f*, virevolte *f* (de cheval). **3.** *Rail:* **the Inner C.,** une des lignes du métro de Londres. **4.** *Th:* **family c., upper c.,** seconde galerie; **dress c.,** (premier) balcon, corbeille *f*; **dress-c. seats,** fauteuils *m* de (premier) balcon. **5.** cercle, milieu *m*, coterie *f*; **the family c.,** le sein de la famille; **the guests were drawn from every political c.,** les invités représentaient tous les milieux politiques; **he doesn't belong to our c.,** il n'appartient pas à notre milieu; **a newcomer to our c.,** un nouveau venu dans notre société; **to enlarge the c. of one's acquaintances,** étendre le cercle de ses relations; **in certain circles,** dans certains milieux; dans un certain monde; **in high circles,** dans la haute société; **in theatrical circles,** dans le monde des théâtres; **the inner c.,** le cercle intime (d'amis); le groupe dirigeant (d'un parti politique). **6.** *Astr:* **dip c.,** boussole *f* d'inclinaison; *Artil: Sm.A:* **inner c. of a target,** cercle de visée; **aiming c.,** goniomètre-boussole *m, pl.* goniomètres-boussoles; cercle de visée.

circle². **1.** *v.tr.* (*a*) *Poet:* ceindre, entourer (**with,** de); (*b*) (*go round*) faire le tour de (qch.); (*c*) *Gym:* **to c. the bar,** faire le grand soleil. **2.** *v.i.* (*a*) **to c. round, about, sth.,** tourner, tournoyer, autour de qch.; **the planes are circling overhead,** les avions *m* décrivent des cercles au-dessus de nos têtes; (*b*) *Equit:* (*of horse*) virevolter, volter; (*c*) *Mil:* opérer une conversion; se rabattre (**round, upon,** sur).

circled ['sə:kld], *a.* encerclé, cerclé.

circlet ['sə:klit], *s.* **1.** petit cercle. **2.** (*a*) anneau *m*; (*b*) bandeau *m* (pour les cheveux); *esp.* étroit bandeau d'or.

circlip ['sə:klip], *s. Tchn:* circlip *m*.

circs [sə:ks], *s.pl. F:* (= CIRCUMSTANCES) **under, in, the c.,** dans ces circonstances, en cette circonstance; puisqu'il en est ainsi.

circuit¹ ['sə:kit], *s.* **1.** (*a*) pourtour *m* (d'une ville, d'un fleuve, etc.); enceinte *f* (de murailles); (*b*) *Sp:* circuit *m*, parcours *m* (d'une course d'automobiles, etc.). **2.** (*a*) révolution *f*, marche *f* circulaire (du soleil); (*b*) **to make the c. of the town,** faire le tour de la ville; (*c*) tournée *f*, circuit (de juge d'assises, etc.); *Th:* tournée dramatique; (*of judge*) **to go on c.,** aller en tournée; **to be on c. with the court,** être à la suite du tribunal; *Jur:* **c. court,** cour *f* de circuit; (*d*) circonscription *f* de tournée, ressort *m* (d'un juge d'assises; au nombre de huit); circonscription ecclésiastique (de l'Église méthodiste). **3.** détour *m*; **to make a wide c.,** faire un grand détour; **to make a long c.** (*in order to reach a place*), faire le grand tour. **4.** *El:* circuit; (*a*) **in c.,** en circuit; **out of c.,** hors de circuit; **to close, make, complete, the c.,** fermer le circuit; **c. closer,** conjoncteur *m*; ferme-circuit *m inv*; **closed c., complete c.,** circuit fermé; **to break, open, the c.,** rompre, ouvrir, le circuit; **broken, open, c.,** circuit ouvert; **c. breaker,** coupe-circuit *m inv*, disjoncteur *m*, interrupteur *m*, rupteur *m*; **minimum c. breaker,** disjoncteur à minimum; **self-closing c. breaker,** conjoncteur-disjoncteur *m, pl.* conjoncteurs-disjoncteurs; **zero c. breaker,** commutateur *m* à zéro; **short c.,** court-circuit *m, pl.* courts-circuits; **branch c.,** dérivation *f*, branchement *m*; **earthed c., grounded c.,** circuit mis à la masse; **earth return c., ground return c.,** circuit de retour par terre; **earth c., ground c.,** circuit de la terre; **unearthed c.,** circuit sans retour à la terre; **input c.,** circuit d'entrée; **outgoing c.,** circuit de départ; **return c.,** circuit de retour; **parallel c.,** circuit en parallèle; **series c.,** circuit en série; **live c.,** circuit sous tension; **load c.,** circuit de charge; *Rail:* **track-return c., axle-return c.,** circuit de retour par la voie, par les essieux; (*b*) *Elcs:* **anode c., plate c.,** circuit anodique, de plaque; **grid c.,** circuit de grille; **back-up c.,** circuit de doublage, de secours; **printed c., sprayed c.,** circuit imprimé; **printed foil c.,** circuit métallique imprimé; *Cmptr:* **differentiating c.,** circuit, montage, différentiateur; **integrating c.,** circuit, montage, intégrateur; (*c*) *Tp:* **loop c., metallic c.,** circuit bifilaire; **one-way c., unidirectional c.,** circuit spécialisé; **two-way c.,** circuit exploité dans les deux sens; **order-wire c.,** circuit de service; **superposed c.,** circuit supplémentaire; **through c.,** circuit de transit; **transfer c.,** circuit intermédiaire; **trunk c.,** circuit interurbain, entre centraux; (*d*) *W.Tel: T.V:* **music c.,** circuit pour radiodiffusion musicale; **closed c. television,** télévision *f* à circuit fermé.

circuit², *v.tr.* faire le tour de (qch.).

circuitous [sə:'kju(:)itəs], *a.* (chemin) détourné, indirect, sinueux; (rivage) anfractueux; **to take a c. road,** faire un détour; **by c. means,** par des moyens détournés.

circuitously [sə:'kju(:)itəsli], *adv.* (*a*) (agir) par des moyens indirects; (*b*) (voyager) par des chemins indirects, en faisant un détour.

circuitry ['sə:kitri], *s. El:* (*a*) schéma *m*, ensemble *m*, d'un circuit; montage *m*; (*b*) éléments *mpl* composant un circuit.

circular ['sə:kjulər]. **1.** *a.* circulaire; (*a*) *Geom:* **c. arc,** arc *m* de cercle; *Ind:* **c. bellows,** soufflet *m* cylindrique; (*b*) **c. motion,** mouvement *m* circulaire; **c. letter,** lettre *f* circulaire; circulaire *f*; lettre collective; *Com:* **c. note,** billet *m* ou lettre de crédit circulaire; mandat *m* ou chèque *m* de voyage; *Rail:* **c. railway,** chemin *m* de fer de ceinture; **c. ticket,** billet *m* circulaire; **c. tour,** tour *m* circulaire; (*c*) *Mth:* **c. constant,** pi *m*; rapport *m* de la circonférence au diamètre; **c. functions,** fonctions *f* circulaires; (*d*) *Med:* **c. insanity,** folie *f* circulaire. **2.** *s.* (*a*) (lettre) circulaire; lettre collective; (*b*) prospectus (envoyé à tous les clients); (*c*) *Journ:* **the Court c.,** les éphémérides *f* de la Cour; la Cour au jour le jour; la chronique mondaine.

circularity [sə:kju'læriti], *s.* forme *f* circulaire (**of,** de); circularité *f*.

circularization [sə:kjulərai'zeiʃ(ə)n], *s.* expédition *f*, envoi *m*, de circulaires, de prospectus (**of the public,** au public).

circularize ['sə:kjuləraiz], envoyer, expédier, des circulaires, des prospectus, à (ses clients, etc.); *Com:* prospecter (le public).

circularizing ['sə:kjuləraiziŋ], *s.* = CIRCULARIZATION.

circularly ['sə:kjuləli], *adv.* circulairement; en cercle; en rond.

circulate ['sə:kjuleit]. **1.** *v.i.* (*of thg, of pers.*) circuler; *Fin:* (*of money*) **to c. freely,** circuler librement; rouler. **2.** *v.tr.* (*a*) faire circuler (l'air, le vin, etc.); (*b*) mettre en circulation, émettre (de l'argent, des nouvelles, etc.); propager, répandre, faire circuler (un bruit, etc.); (*c*) = CIRCULARIZE.

circulating¹ ['sə:kjuleitiŋ], *a.* circulant; **c. library,** bibliothèque circulante; *Fin:* **c. capital,** capitaux circulants, roulants; capital disponible; *Cmptr:* **c. store,** mémoire circulante, cyclique; *Mth:* **c. fraction,** fraction *f* périodique.

circulating², *s.* circulation *f*; **c. pump,** pompe *f* de circulation; *Fin:* **c. medium,** agent *m* monétaire; monnaie *f* d'échange.

circulation [sə:kju'leiʃ(ə)n], *s.* (*a*) circulation *f* (de l'air, d'un liquide, de nouvelles, etc.); **the c. of this communiqué will reassure the nation,** la diffusion de ce communiqué rassurera la nation; **the c. of capital,** le roulement de fonds; **to withdraw capital from its natural channels of c.,** enlever des capitaux à leur circuit naturel; **to put a book into c.,** mettre un livre en circulation; **to withdraw a book from c.,** retirer un livre de la circulation; *F:* (*of pers.*) **to be out of c.,** (i) garder la maison (à cause de maladie); (ii) être en retraite; (iii) être en prison, *F:* à l'écart; *Publ:* **for private c.,** hors commerce; **the c. of a newspaper,** la diffusion d'un journal; **newspaper with a large c.,** journal à grand tirage; *I.C.E: etc:* **gravity c.,** circulation (de l'eau) par gravité; **forced-feed c.,** circulation sous pression (de l'eau, de l'huile); **pump c.,** circulation par pompe; (*b*) *Physiol:* **systemic c., pulmonary c.,** circulation générale, pulmonaire; **to restore the c. in one's legs,** se dégourdir les jambes; (*c*) cours *m* (de la monnaie); **to put a coinage into c.,** donner cours à une monnaie; **to put forged notes into c.,** écouler de faux billets; (*of money*) **to be in c.,** circuler; **many false coins are in c.,** il circule beaucoup de fausses pièces; **notes in c.,** billets circulants; **coinage withdrawn from c.,** monnaie qui n'a plus cours; **credit c.,** circulation fiduciaire.

circulative ['sə:kjuleitiv], *a.* qui favorise la circulation.

circulator ['sə:kjuleitər], *s.* propagateur *m* (de nouvelles).

circulatory [sə:kju'leit(ə)ri, 'sə:kjulət(ə)ri], *a.* circulatoire; *Anat:* **the c. system,** l'appareil *m* circulatoire; *Med:* **c. troubles,** troubles *m* de la circulation.

circum- ['sə:kəm], *pref.* circon-; circum-.

circumambiency [sə:kəm'æmbiənsi], *s. Lit:* ambiance *f*.

circumambient [sə:kəm'æmbiənt], *a. Lit:* ambiant.

circumambulate [sə:kəm'æmbjuleit], *Lit. & Hum:* **1.** *v.tr.* faire le tour de (qch.); marcher autour de (qch.). **2.** *v.i.* (*a*) se promener çà et là; (*b*) *F:* tourner autour du pot; barguigner.

circumambulation [sə:kəmæmbju'leiʃ(ə)n], *s. Lit:* (*a*) promenades *fpl* sans but; (*b*) *F:* barguignage *m*.

circumbendibus [sə:kəm'bendibəs], *s. A: Hum:* circonlocutions *fpl*.

circumcircle ['sə:kəmsə:kl], *s. Mth:* cercle circonscrit (à un polygone).

circumcise ['sə:kəmsaiz], *v.tr.* circoncire (un enfant mâle, *Lit:* le cœur, les passions).

circumcised ['sə:kəmsaizd], *a.* circoncis; *s.* **the c.,** les circoncis.

circumcision [sə:kəm'siʒ(ə)n], *s.* **1.** circoncision *f*. **2.** **the C.,** (i) *coll.* les Circoncis, les Juifs; (ii) *Ecc:* la (fête de la) Circoncision.

circumduction [sə:kəm'dʌkʃ(ə)n], *s. Physiol:* circumduction *f*.

circumference [sə'kʌmfərəns], *s.* circonférence *f*; périphérie *f*; pourtour *m* (d'un piston, etc.); **the tower is thirty metres in c.,** la tour a trente mètres de circonférence; **the walls are a mile in c.,** les murs ont un mille de tour, de circuit, d'enceinte; **on the c.,** à la circonférence; à la périphérie.

circumferential [sə:kʌmfə'renʃ(ə)l], *a.* circonférentiel; *Mec:* **c. force,** force appliquée à la circonférence; force tangentielle.

circumferentor [sə'kʌmfərentər], *s. Surv:* graphomètre *m*.

circumflex¹ ['sə:kəmfleks]. **1.** *a. & s. Gram:* **c. (accent),** (accent *m*) circonflexe (*m*). **2.** *a. Anat:* (nerf *m* etc.) circonflexe.

circumflex², *v.tr.* mettre l'accent circonflexe sur (une voyelle).

circumfluent [sə:kəm'fluənt], **circumfluous** [sə:'kʌmfluəs], *a.* qui coule autour (de qch.).

circumfuse [sə:kəm'fju:z], *v.tr. A: & Lit:* **1.** répandre; **to c. sth. with air, light, to c. air, light, about sth.,** répandre de l'air, de la lumière, autour, à l'entour, de qch.; **circumfused with light,** baigné de lumière. **2.** (*of light*) se répandre autour, à l'entour, de (qch.).

circumfusion [sə:kəm'fju:ʒ(ə)n], *s. A: & Lit:* dispersion *f* (de l'air, etc.) à l'entour.

circumjacent [sə:kəm'dʒeis(ə)nt], *a. Lit:* circonjacent, circonvoisin.

circumlocution ['sə:kəmlə'kju:ʃ(ə)n], *s.* circonlocution *f*; **without c.,** sans ambages.

circumlocutory ['sə:kəm'lɔkjut(ə)ri], *a.* (langage, etc.) rempli de circonlocutions; **to talk in a c. style,** user de circonlocutions.

circumlunar [sə:kəm'lu:nər], *a.* circumlunaire.

circummeridian ['sə:kəmmə'ridiən], *a.* circumméridien, -ienne.

circumnavigate ['sə:kəm'nævigeit], *v.tr.* circumnaviguer (une île); faire (par mer) le tour de (qch.); *F:* **to c. a traffic bottleneck,** contourner un embouteillage.

circumnavigation ['sə:kəmnævi'geiʃ(ə)n], *s.* circumnavigation *f*.

circumnavigator ['sə:kəm'nævigeitər], *s.* circumnavigateur *m*.

circumnutation ['sə:kəmnju'teiʃ(ə)n], *s. Bot:* circumnutation *f* (de la tige).

circumpolar ['sə:kəm'poulər]. **1.** *a.* circompolaire. **2.** *s.* étoile *f* circompolaire.

circumscissile [sə:kəm'sis(a)il], *a. Bot:* (fruit) circoncis.

circumscribable ['sə:kəm'skraibəbl], *a.* circonscriptible.

circumscribe ['sə:kəmskraib], *v.tr.* **1.** circonscrire; **to c. a polygon about a circle,** circonscrire un polygone à un cercle. **2.** limiter, restreindre, borner (un champ d'opérations, des pouvoirs). **3.** *A:* signer en rond (une pétition).

circumscribed ['sə:kəmskraibd], *a.* **1.** *Mth:* (cercle, etc.) circonscrit. **2.** restreint, limité; **c. intellect,** esprit *m* de peu d'envergure; esprit borné.

circumscriber ['sə:kəmskraibər], *s. A:* signataire *mf* d'une pétition (signée en rond).

circumscription [sə:kəm'skripʃ(ə)n], *s.* **1.** *Mth:* **c. of a triangle by a circle, c. of a circle about a triangle,** circonscription *f* d'un cercle à un triangle. **2.** restriction *f*, limitation *f* (de l'action de qn, etc.). **3.** périphérie *f*, contours *mpl*, profil *m*. **4.** région *f*, circonscription (administrative). **5.** *Num:* légende *f* circulaire, inscription *f* circulaire.

circumspect ['sə:kəmspekt], *a.* circonspect; (*of pers.*)

avisé; (*of conduct*) prudent; (*of speech*) mesuré.

circumspection [sə:kem'spekʃ(ə)n], *s.* circonspection *f*, ménagement *m*; **to use words with c.,** ménager les mots.

circumspectly ['sə:kəmspektli], *adv.* prudemment; avec circonspection.

circumspectness ['sə:kəmspektnis], *s.* = CIRCUMSPECTION.

circumstance ['sə:kəmstəns], *s.* **1.** *pl.* (*a*) circonstance(s) *f*; **extenuating circumstances,** circonstances atténuantes; **in, under, the circumstances,** dans ces circonstances; en telles circonstances; en cette circonstance; en l'occurrence; puisqu'il en est ainsi; **under any circumstances . . ., whatever the circumstances . . .,** en tout état de cause . . .; **to do sth. under favourable circumstances,** faire qch. sous des auspices favorables; **under such circumstances,** en pareille circonstance; **in no circumstances,** en aucun cas; aucun prétexte; à aucune condition; **as circumstances (may) require,** selon les nécessités; **under similar circumstances,** en pareille occasion; **I am aware of all the circumstances,** je connais tous les détails; **that depends on circumstances,** c'est selon; **we must take the circumstances into account,** il faut faire la part des circonstances; **circumstances alter cases,** les cas changent avec les circonstances; **he was the victim of circumstances,** il a été la victime des circonstances; il n'y a pas eu de sa faute; **by force of circumstances,** par la force des choses; (*b*) conditions *f*, moyens *m*; état *m* de choses; **if his circumstances allowed,** si ses moyens le permettaient; (*of pers.*) **to be in good, bad, circumstances,** être bien, mal, dans ses affaires; faire de bonnes, de mauvaises, affaires; *O:* **what are his circumstances?** (i) de quelle condition est-il? (ii) quelle est sa situation pécuniaire? **in easy circumstances,** dans l'aisance, à l'aise; **people in humble circumstances,** gens *m* de simple condition. **2.** *sg. Lit:* (*a*) circonstance, détail *m*, fait *m*, particularité *f*; **without omitting a single c.,** sans omettre aucun détail; **were it not for the c. that . . .,** n'était le fait que . . .; (*b*) **to relate with much c. that . . .,** raconter avec force détails que . . .. **3.** pompe *f*, appareil *m*; **to receive s.o. with pomp and c.,** recevoir qn en grande cérémonie, en grand apparat, *F:* avec la croix et la bannière; **without c.,** sans cérémonie. **4.** *U.S: A:* **he is not a c. to his father,** il n'est pas comparable à, n'est rien auprès de, son père; **a mere, poor, remote, c.,** une personne, chose, sans importance.

circumstanced ['sə:kəmstənst], *a. O:* **well c.,** dans une bonne situation; dans l'aisance; **poorly c. people,** gens peu fortunés; **as I was c. . . .,** dans la situation où je me trouvais . . ..

circumstantial [sə:kəm'stænʃ(ə)l], *a.* **1.** circonstanciel; **c. evidence,** preuves indirectes; preuve par présomption. **2.** accessoire, secondaire, accidentel; *Gram:* **c. clause,** incidente explicative. **3.** circonstancié, détaillé; **c. account of what happened,** relation circonstanciée de ce qui s'est passé; **to give a c. account of an event,** raconter un événement en détail; entrer dans le détail, dans tous les détails, d'un événement.

circumstantiality [sə:kəmstænʃi'æliti], *s.* **1.** abondance *f* de détails. **2.** *F:* circonstance *f*, détail *m*.

circumstantially [sə:kəm'stænʃ(ə)li], *adv.* **1.** accessoirement, accidentellement. **2.** en détail; **to go c. into the matter,** entrer dans le détail de la question.

circumstantiate [sə:kəm'stænʃieit], *v.tr.* **to c. a report,** donner des détails circonstanciés sur, circonstancier, un rapport.

circumterrestrial ['sə:kəmte'restriəl], *a.* circumterrestre.

circumvallate [sə:kəm'væleit], *v.tr.* entourer (un camp, etc.) de retranchements.

circumvallation ['sə:kəmvæ'leiʃ(ə)n], *s.* circonvallation *f*; retranchements *mpl*.

circumvent [sə:kəm'vent], *v.tr.* (*a*) circonvenir (qn, une manœuvre); **to c. the law,** tourner la loi; se dérober, se soustraire, à (l'atteinte *f* de) la loi; (*b*) *Mil:* tourner (l'ennemi).

circumvention [sə:kəm'venʃ(ə)n], *s.* circonvention *f* (de la loi, etc.).

circumvolution ['sə:kəmvə'l(j)u:ʃ(ə)n], *s.* circonvolution *f*; *Anat:* **the circumvolutions of the brain,** les circonvolutions du cerveau.

circumzenithal ['sə:kəm'zenniθ(ə)l], *a. Astr:* circumzénithal, -aux.

circus, *pl.* **-uses** ['sə:kəs, -əsiz], *s.* **1.** (*a*) *Rom.Ant:* cirque *m*; (*b*) (*of roads, as Pr.n.*) rond-point *m*, *pl.* ronds-points. **2.** (*a*) cirque ((i) spectacle *m* équestre; (ii) enceinte *f* du spectacle); **travelling c.,** cirque forain; *F: O:* **to go off to the seaside with all one's c.,** partir au bord de la mer avec toute sa smala; (*b*) (i) *Mil: F: A:* escadrille *f* (d'avions); (ii) *Av: F:* exercices acrobatiques aériens; (*c*) troupe *f*, équipe *f* (de pilotes d'automobiles de course, etc.); (*d*) *F:* charivari *m* de tous les diables.

cire perdue ['siə:pɛə'dju], *s. Art:* **c.p. casting, process,** fonte *f* à cire perdue; (la) cire-perdue.

cirque [sə:k], *s. Geol:* cirque *m*; **nivation c.,** cirque de nivation.

cirrate ['sirət, -eit], *a. Nat.Hist:* cirrifère; (*of antenna*) cirré; (*of leaf*) cirreux.

cirratulus [si'rætjuləs], *s. Ann:* cirr(h)atule *m*.

cirrhopetalum [sirou'petələm], *s. Bot:* cirrhopetalum *m*.

cirrhose ['sirous], **cirrhous** ['sirəs], *a.* = CIRROSE, CIRROUS.

cirrhosis [si'rousis], *s. Med:* cirrhose *f*; **c. of the liver,** cirrhose du foie, hépatocirrhose *f*; **enlarged c., hypertrophic c.,** cirrhose hypertrophique; **atrophic c.,** cirrhose atrophique.

cirrhotic [si'rɔtik], *a. & s. Med:* cirrhotique (*mf*).

cirri- [siri], *comb.fm.* cirri-.

cirriferous [si'rifərəs], *a. Nat.Hist:* cirrifère; (*of antenna*) cirré.

cirriflorous [siri'flɔrəs], *a.* cirriflore.

cirriform ['sirifɔ:m], *a. Nat.Hist:* cirriforme.

cirrigerous [si'ridʒərəs], *a.* cirrifère.

cirriped ['siriped], *s. Crust:* cirr(h)ipède *m*.

Cirripedia [siri'pi:diə], *s.pl. Crust:* cirr(h)ipèdes *m*.

cirrocumulus [sirou'kju:mjuləs], *s. Meteor:* cirrocumulus *m*.

cirrose [si'rous], **cirrous** ['sirəs], *s. Nat.Hist: Meteor:* cirreux; cirré; *Bot:* cirr(h)al, -aux; (*of leaf, etc.*) cirreux.

cirrostratus [sirou'strɑ:təs, -eitəs], *s.* cirro-stratus *m*.

cirrus, *pl.* **-ri** ['sirəs, -rai], *s.* **1.** *Nat.Hist:* cirr(h)e *m*; *Bot:* vrille *f*. **2.** *Meteor:* cirrus *m*.

cirsium ['sə:siəm], *s. Bot:* cirse *m*, cirsium *m*.

cirsoid ['sə:sɔid], *a. Med:* (anévrisme *m*) cirsoïde.

cis- [sis], *pref.* cis-.

cis [sis], *a. Ch:* (forme *f*) cis (d'un composé).

cisalpine [sis'ælpain], *a. Hist:* cisalpin; **the C. Republic,** la République cisalpine.

cisco ['siskou], **ciscoette** ['siskouwet], *s. Ich: NAm:* espèce *f* de corégone des Grands Lacs.

ciseaux ['si:zou], *s.pl.* (*usu. with sg.const.*) *Danc:* ciseaux *mpl*.

cisjuran [sis'dʒuərən], *a. Hist:* cisjuran; **C. Burgundy,** la Bourgogne cisjurane, la Cisjurane.

cislunar [sis'lu:nər], *a. Space:* cislunaire.

cismontane [sis'mɔntein], *a. Geog: Rel.H:* cismontain.

cispadane ['sispədein], *a. Geog: Hist:* cispadan.

cisrhenan [sis'renən], *a. Hist:* cisrhénan.

cissampelos [si'sæmpələs], *s. Bot:* cissampélos *m*; *F:* vigne bâtarde; herbe *f* Notre-Dame.

cissoid ['sisɔid], *s. Mth:* cissoïde *f*.

cissus ['sisəs], *s. Bot:* cissus *m*.

cissy ['sisi], *F:* **1.** *s.m.* mollasson *m*; poule mouillée. **2.** *a.* **young people think it's c. to wear a safety belt,** porter une ceinture de sécurité est mollasse pour les jeunes gens.

cist [sist], *s.* **1.** *Archeol:* **c. (grave),** sépulture préhistorique revêtue de dalles de pierre, coffre sépulcral. **2.** *Gr. & Rom.Ant:* ciste *f*, corbeille (portée en procession).

Cistaceae [sis'teisii:], *s.pl. Bot:* cistacées *f*.

Cistercian [sis'tə:ʃ(ə)n], *a. & s. Ecc:* cistercien, -ienne; **the C. Order,** l'ordre *m* de Cîteaux.

cistern ['sistən], *s.* **1.** (*a*) réservoir *m* à eau (sous les combles); **W.C. c.,** réservoir de chasse d'eau; (*b*) (*underground*) citerne *f*; **the c. of a pump,** le réservoir d'une pompe; (*c*) *Ind:* bâche *f*, caisse *f*, cuve *f*. **2.** (*of barometer*) cuvette *f*. **3.** *Anat:* **lumbar c.,** citerne lombaire; **c. of Pecquet,** citerne de Pecquet.

cisternae [si'stə:ni:], *s.pl. Biol:* cisternae *f*, saccules aplatis (de l'appareil de Golgi).

cisternal [si'stə:n(ə)l], *a. Anat: Med:* d'une citerne, des citernes.

cistophorus, *pl.* **-ri** [si'stɔfərəs, -rai], *s. Num:* cistophore *m*.

cis-trans ['sis'træns], *a. Biol:* (effet *m*) cis-trans.

cistron ['sistrɔn], *s. Biol:* cistron *m*.

cistudo [si'stju:dou], *s. Rept:* cistude *f*.

cistus ['sistəs], *s. Bot:* ciste *m*.

cit [sit], *s. F: A:* (= CITIZEN) (*a*) bourgeois *m*, citadin *m*; (*b*) parvenu *m*; nouveau riche; (*c*) *U.S: O:* **officer in cits,** officier *m* en civil.

citable ['saitəbl], *a.* citable.

citadel ['sitədl, -del], *s.* **1.** (*a*) citadelle *f*; (*b*) lieu *m* de refuge; **the last c. of a dying sect,** les derniers retranchements d'une secte moribonde; (*c*) temple *m* (de l'Armée de Salut). **2.** *N.Arch:* réduit *m*.

citation [sai'teiʃ(ə)n], *s.* **1.** *Jur:* citation *f* à comparaître. **2.** citation (i) d'un auteur, d'une autorité, (ii) empruntée à un auteur. **3.** *Mil:* citation (à l'ordre du jour).

cite [sait], *v.tr.* **1.** *Jur:* (*a*) *Ecc:* **to c. s.o. before a court,** citer qn devant un tribunal; (*b*) assigner (un témoin). **2.** (*a*) citer (un passage, un auteur); (*b*) alléguer (un auteur, une autorité). **3.** *Mil:* citer (un militaire pour sa bravoure).

citer ['saitər], *s.* citateur, -trice.

cithara ['siθərə], *s. Mus: Gr.Ant:* cithare *f*.

citharexylum [siθə'reksiləm], *s. Bot:* citharexylum *m*.

citharist ['siθərist], *s. A:* cithariste *mf*.

citharoedus [siθə'ri:dəs], *s. Gr.Ant:* citharède *m*; **Apollo C.,** Apollon citharède.

cither(n) ['siθər, -θən], *s. Mus: A:* cistre *m*.

Citheroniidae [siθə:rɔ'ni:idi:], *s.pl. Ent:* cithéroniides *m*.

citied ['sitid], *a. Lit:* **1.** parsemé de cités. **2.** urbanisé.

citified ['sitifaid], *a. F:* (air, etc.) citadin.

citizen ['sitizən], *s.m. & f.*, **citizeness** ['sitizənes], *s.f.* **1.** (*a*) citoyen, -enne, citadin *m*; *A:* bourgeois, -oise; **the citizens raised a strong protest,** les habitants élevèrent des protestations énergiques; **private c.,** simple particulier *m*; **the ordinary c.,** le grand public; **my fellow citizens,** mes concitoyens; (*b*) **c. of the world,** citoyen du monde, de l'univers; *Poet:* **the citizens of the air,** les citoyens des airs; (*c*) *NAm:* civil *m* (par opposition à l'armée, la marine); **c. rights,** droits *m* civiques. **2. Old C.,** ancien élève de la *City of London School*.

citizenhood ['sitizənhud], *s.* **1.** citoyenneté *f*; rang *m*, qualité *f*, de citoyen. **2. all the c. of the town,** tous les citoyens, toute la bourgeoisie, de la ville.

citizenry ['sitiznri], *s.* masse *f* des citoyens; toute la bourgeoisie de la ville.

citizenship ['sitiznʃip], *s.* **1.** droit *m* de cité, de bourgeoisie. **2. good c.,** civisme *m*. **3. to have French c.,** jouir de la citoyenneté française.

citole [si'toul], *s. A.Mus:* citole *f*.

citraconic [sitrə'kɔnik], *a. Ch:* citraconique.

citral ['sitrəl], *s. Ch:* citral *m*.

citrange ['sitrən(d)ʒ], *s. Hort:* citrange *m*.

citrate[1] ['sitreit], *s. Ch:* citrate *m*; **c. of sodium,** citrate de sodium, de soude.

citrate[2], *v.tr. Med:* citrater (du sang).

citrene ['sitri:n], *s. Ch:* citrène *m*.

citric ['sitrik], *a. Ch:* citrique; *Bio-Ch:* **c. acid cycle,** cycle *m* de l'acide citrique; cycle de Krebs.

citrin ['sitrin], *s. Bio-Ch:* citrine *f*; (la) vitamine P.

citrine ['sitrin]. **1.** *a.* (*a*) citrin; jaune verdâtre; (*b*) *Pharm:* **c. ointment,** onguent citrin. **2.** *s. Miner:* citrine *m or f*; prime *f* de topaze; topaze occidentale.

citron ['sitrən], *s.* **1.** (*a*) cédrat *m*; (*b*) **c. (tree),** cédratier *m*; **c. plantation,** cédraterie *f*; (*c*) *Cu:* zeste *m* de cédrat confit. **2.** *NAm:* petite espèce de pastèque (utilisée pour les conserves). **3.** *Com:* **c. wood,** (i) citronnier *m*; (ii) bois *m* de thuya. **4.** *Dist:* **c. water,** citronnelle *f*; eau *f* des Barbades. **5.** *a.* (jaune) citron *inv*.

citronella [sitrə'nelə], *s. Bot:* citronnelle *f*.

citronellal [sitrə'nellæl], *s. Ch:* citronellal *m*.

citronellol [sitrə'nelɔl], *s. Ch:* citronellol *m*.

citronyl ['sitrənil], *s. Ch:* citronyle *f*.

citrus ['sitrəs], *s.* citron *m*; **c. fruit(s),** agrumes *mpl*; **c. tree,** citronnier *m*; **c. wood,** bois *m* de citron.

cittern ['sitən], *s.* = CITHERN.

city ['siti], *s.* **1.** grande ville; (*a*) *Gr.Hist: Poet:* cité *f*; **the Holy C.,** la Cité sainte; **the Celestial C.,** la Cité céleste; **the Eternal C.,** la Ville éternelle; **the Cities of the Plain,** Sodom et Gomorrhe; *Gr.Hist:* **c. state,** état-cité *m*, *pl.* états-cités; (*b*) **(cathedral) c.,** ville épiscopale; **the c. of Manchester, Birmingham,** la ville de Manchester, Birmingham; **c. council,** conseil municipal; **c. hall,** hôtel *m* de ville; **c. dwellers,** la population urbaine; **the life, civilisation, of the cities,** la vie, civilisation, citadine; (*c*) *NAm:* ville. **2.** cité; agglomération *f*; **garden c.,** cité-jardin *f*, *pl.* cités-jardins. **3.** (*a*) centre *m* (d'une grande ville); (*b*) **the C.,** la Cité de Londres (centre des affaires distinct de la *Metropolitan Area*); **C. man,** homme d'affaires de la Cité, de Londres; **he's in the C.,** il est dans la finance (dans la Cité de Londres); *Journ:* **C. article,** bulletin financier; compte rendu de la Bourse et du commerce; **the City,** Bourse, finance, commerce; **C. editor,** (i) rédacteur *m* de la rubrique financière; (ii) *U.S:* rédacteur de la chronique du jour; *Fr.C:* chef *m* des nouvelles.

cityward(s) ['sitiwəd(z)], *adv.* vers la ville, vers la cité.

civet ['sivit], *s.* **1.** *Z:* **c. (cat),** civette *f*; **Indian c.,** civette orientale grise; zibeth *m*; **Malagasy c.,** genette *f* de Madagascar: **Celebes palm c.,** civette des palmiers; **small-toothed palm c.,** civette arboricole malaise; **small c. (cat),** viverricule *f*, viverricula *f*; civette rasse. **2.** (*perfume*) civette.

civetone ['sivitoun], *s. Ch:* civettone *f*.

civic ['sivik], *a.* civique; **the c. authorities,** les autorités municipales; **c. guard,** garde civique, nationale; **c. rights, position,** droits civils, droits de citoyen; état

civil; **c. virtues,** vertus *f* civiques; civisme *m*; **c.-minded,** enclin, dévoué, au civisme; doué des vertus civiques; **c. mindedness,** civisme; *Town P:* **c. centre,** centre civique, social.
civically ['sivik(ə)li], *adv.* **1.** du point de vue civique. **2.** (se conduire) en citoyen.
civics ['siviks], *s.pl.* (*usu. with sg.const.*) *Sch:* instruction *f* civique.
civies ['siviz], *s.pl. see* CIVVY 2.
civil ['siv(i)l], *a.* **1.** (*a*) (*of society, law, institution, day, year, etc.*) civil; **c. war,** guerre civile; *Mil:* **c. affairs,** (service *m*, bureau *m*, des) affaires civiles; **c. defence,** protection civile; **c. rights,** (i) droits *m* civiques; (ii) *Jur:* droits civils; **c. liberty,** liberté civile; *Jur:* **c. death,** mort civile; **c. fruits,** fruits civils; **c. marriage,** mariage civil; **to contract a c. marriage,** se marier civilement; **c. law,** (i) droit romain; (ii) droit civil, = le code civil; **c. action, proceedings,** action civile; **to bring a c. action against s.o.,** poursuivre qn civilement; **c. servant,** fonctionnaire *m* (de l'État); **to become a c. servant,** entrer dans l'Administration; **the military and c. services,** les emplois militaires et civils de l'État; **to be in the c. service,** être fonctionnaire (de l'État); être dans l'Administration (civile); *Hist:* **the Indian C. Service,** le Service d'administration de l'Inde anglaise; (*b*) **in c. life,** dans le civil; (*c*) *Adm:* **the C. List,** la liste civile (du roi, de la reine); **C. List pension,** pension *f* sur les fonds de la Couronne; (*d*) **c. engineer,** ingénieur constructeur; ingénieur des travaux publics. **2.** poli, honnête, civil; **he was very c. to me,** il s'est montré très aimable; *O:* **c.-spoken,** courtois; **keep a c. tongue in your head!** soyez plus poli (dans vos propos)! *F:* **to do the c. (thing),** se mettre en frais de politesse, de civilité, de courtoisie.
civilian [si'viljən]. **1.** *s. Jur:* civiliste *mf.* **2.** *s.* civil *m* (par opposition à l'armée et la marine). **3.** *a.* civil; **c. clothes,** tenue civile; **in c. life,** dans le civil.
civilianize [si'viljənaiz], *v.tr.* **to c. a military establishment,** remplacer le personnel d'un établissement militaire par des civils.
civilist ['sivilist], *s. Jur:* civiliste *mf.*
civility [si'viliti], *s.* civilité *f*; courtoisie *f*, politesse *f*; **to show s.o. c.,** faire des politesses, des amabilités, à qn; **common c. requires . . .,** la politesse élémentaire veut . . .; **exchange of civilities,** échange *m* d'amabilités, de bons procédés.
civilizable ['sivilaizəbl], *a.* civilisable.
civilization [sivilai'zeiʃ(ə)n], *s.* civilisation *f.*
civilize ['sivilaiz], *v.tr.* **1.** civiliser (un peuple sauvage). **2.** civiliser, dégrossir (un ignorant).
civilized ['sivilaizd], *a.* **1.** (*of tribe*) civilisé. **2.** (homme) civilisé, bien élevé, cultivé.
civilizer ['sivilaizər], *s.* civilisateur, -trice.
civilizing ['sivilaiziŋ], *a.* civilisant; civilisateur, -trice; **music has a c. effect,** la musique adoucit les mœurs.
civilly ['sivili], *adv.* civilement, poliment.
civism ['sivizm], *s.* civisme *m.*
civvy, *pl.* **-ies** ['sivi, -iz], *P:* **1.** *a.* civil; **to get back to c. street,** rentrer dans le civil, *O:* reprendre la vie de pékin. **2.** *s.* (*a*) bourgeois *m*; *Mil: P: O:* pékin *m*; (*b*) *pl.* **civ(v)ies,** vêtements civils; **in civvies,** en bourgeois; *P: O:* en pékin.
clachan ['klaːχən], *s. Scot:* bourg *m*, village *m.*
clack[1] ['klæk], *s.* **1.** bruit sec; claquement *m*; **click-c.,** clic-clac *m.* **2.** *Tchn:* (*a*) **c. (valve),** (i) (soupape *f* à) clapet *m*; soupape à charnière; (ii) *Mch:* soupape à boulet; *Hyd.E:* **c. box,** chapelle *f* de soupape; (*b*) **(mill) c.,** traquet *m.* **3.** *F:* (*a*) (*of pers.*) caquet *m*, jacasserie *f*, tapette *f*, bavardage *m*; **stop your c.! cut your c.!** assez jacassé! *P:* la ferme! ferme ça! (*b*) racontar *m*, bavardage.
clack[2], *v.i.* **1.** (*of thg*) claquer, faire clic-clac. **2.** *F:* (*of pers.*) caqueter, bavarder, jacasser.
clacking ['klækiŋ], *s.* **1.** claquement *m* (d'un fouet, d'une trémie de moulin). **2.** *F:* caquetage *m.*
Clactonian [klæk'tounjən], *a.* & *s. Geol: Prehist:* clactonien (*m*).
clad[1] [klæd], *a.* **1.** **warmly, lightly, c.,** chaudement, légèrement, vêtu. **2.** *Tchn:* (métal, etc.) revêtu (**with,** de).
clad[2], *v.tr.* **(cladded)** revêtir (un pan de mur, une tôle, etc.) (**with,** de).
cladding ['klædiŋ], *s. Tchn:* revêtement *m*; *Atom.Ph:* **fuel c.,** gaine *f* de combustible.
clade [kleid], *s. Biol:* clade *m.*
cladocarpous [klædou'kaːpəs], *a. Bot:* cladocarpe.
Cladocera [klæ'dɔsərə], *s.pl. Crust:* cladocères *m.*
cladoceran [klæ'dɔsərən], *s. Crust:* cladocère *m.*
cladode ['klædoud], *s. Bot:* cladode *m*; phylloclade *m.*
cladome ['klædoum], *s. Bot:* cladome *m.*
cladonia [klæ'douniə], *s. Moss:* cladonie *f.*
cladosporium [klædou'spɔːriəm], *s. Fung:* cladosporium *m.*
claim[1] [kleim], *s.* **1.** demande *f* (de secours, etc.); revendication *f*, réclamation *f*; **the papal claims,** les revendications de la papauté; **pensions c.,** demande de pension; **wage claims,** revendications de salaire; **wage claims dispute,** lutte revendicative; *Adm:* **fares c.,** demande de remboursement de voyage. **2.** droit *m*, titre *m*, prétention *f* (**to sth.,** à qch.); **to have a c. to sth.,** avoir droit à qch.; avoir des prétentions sur qch.; **to renounce one's claims,** renoncer à ses prétentions; **to lay c. to sth.,** (i) prétendre à qch.; revendiquer son droit à qch.; jeter son dévolu sur qch.; (ii) s'attribuer qch.; **I do not lay c. to learning,** je ne pose pas au savant: je n'ai pas de prétentions à l'érudition; **legal c. to sth.,** titre juridique à qch.; **c. of ownership,** action *f* pétitoire; **to put in a c.,** faire valoir ses droits; **to set up a c.,** émettre une revendication. **3.** *Jur:* (*debt*) créance *f*; **claims and liabilities,** créances et engagements *m*; **contractual c.,** créance contractuelle; **preferential c.,** créance privilégiée; privilège *m* du créancier. **4.** (*a*) *Jur:* réclamation; **to set up a c.,** faire une réclamation; **statement of c.,** exposé détaillé des prétentions du demandeur; conclusions *fpl* de l'avocat (en dommages-intérêts); **to lodge a c. against s.o.,** actionner qn en revendication; **to make, put in, a c. for damages,** demander une indemnité; réclamer des dommages-intérêts; **to have no c. whatever on s.o.,** n'avoir aucun recours contre qn; *Ins:* **to put in a c.** (*after an accident*), réclamer l'indemnité (d'assurance); s'adresser à l'assurance; *Adm:* **disputed claims office,** le contentieux; *Mil:* **c. officer,** officier du contentieux; (*b*) **to have a c. on s.o.,** avoir prise sur qn; **I have some claims on his friendship,** j'ai des titres à son amitié; j'ai le droit de me réclamer de son amitié; **I have no c. on you,** vous ne m'êtes redevable de rien; vous n'êtes aucunement tenu de me servir; **I have many claims on my time,** mon temps est entièrement pris. **5.** *esp. NAm: Austr:* concession (minière); **c. holder,** concessionnaire *m*; *F:* **c. jumper,** individu *m* (i) qui empiète sur les concessions minières d'autrui, (ii) qui prétend à tort à un droit, a un titre. **6.** *NAm:* affirmation *f*, prétention.
claim[2], *v.tr.* (*a*) réclamer (un droit, les soins de qn); revendiquer (un droit, un honneur); exiger, demander (du respect, de l'attention); *Jur:* requérir; **to c. sth. from s.o.,** réclamer qch. à qn; **to c. one's luggage at the left luggage office,** reprendre ses bagages à la consigne; **does anybody c. this umbrella?** est-ce que ce parapluie appartient à quelqu'un? **to c. s.o.'s attention,** (i) demander, réclamer, (ii) attirer, appeler, l'attention de qn; **to c. a privilege,** prétendre à un privilège; se targuer d'un privilège; **to c. the right to do sth.,** (i) revendiquer le droit de faire qch.; (ii) prétendre avoir le droit de faire qch.; **to c. one's due,** réclamer son dû; faire valoir ses droits; **the sea claims many victims,** la mer fait de nombreuses victimes; **to c. sth. back from s.o.,** demander à qn la restitution de qch.; *Jur:* répéter qch. contre qn; (*b*) **to c. that . . .,** prétendre, avancer, affirmer, soutenir, que . . .; **the witness claimed to have seen the accused,** le témoin déposa qu'il avait vu l'accusé, affirma avoir vu l'accusé; **to c. to be an expert,** se prétendre, se faire passer pour, expert; **to c. to be an honest man,** se donner pour un honnête homme; **to c. to be a gentleman,** se piquer d'être un gentleman; **to c. a virtue,** s'attribuer une vertu; **he has a quality that few of us can c.,** il possède une qualité que peu d'entre nous peuvent revendiquer; **to c. acquaintance with s.o.,** prétendre connaître qn; **to c. kinship with s.o.,** se dire, se prétendre, parent de qn; **family that claims to descend from . . .,** famille *f* qui rapporte son origine à . . . .
claimable ['kleiməbl], *a.* revendicable, exigible, demandable.
claimant ['kleimənt], **claimer** ['kleimər], *s.* prétendant, -ante; revendicateur, -trice; *Jur:* réclamant, -ante; demandeur, -eresse; partie requérante; **rightful c.,** ayant droit *m*, *pl.* ayants droit; **c. for a patent,** demandeur d'un brevet; **estate without a c.,** succession vacante.
claiming ['kleimiŋ], *s.* réclamation *f*, revendication *f* (d'un droit, etc.); *Turf:* **c. race,** course *f* à réclamer; **c. jockey,** jockey *m* ayant droit à une décharge.
claiming back ['kleimiŋ'bæk], *s. Jur:* répétition *f*; action *f* en restitution.
clairce [klɛəs], *s. Sug.-R:* clairce *f.*
claircolle ['klɛəkɔl], *s.* = CLEARCOLLE.
claire [klɛər], *s. Ost:* claire *f.*
clairvoyance [klɛə'vɔiəns], *s.* **1.** voyance *f*; lucidité *f* (somnambulique); don *m* de seconde vue. **2.** (*shrewdness*) clairvoyance *f.*
clairvoyant [klɛə'vɔiənt]. **1.** *a.* (*a*) doué de seconde vue; (*b*) (*shrewd*) clairvoyant. **2.** *s.* (*f.occ.* **clairvoyante**) voyant, -ante; somnambule *mf* (extra-)lucide.
Claisen ['kleisən], *Pr.n. Ch:* **C. condensation,** condensation *f* de Claisen.
clam[1] [klæm], *s.* **1.** *Moll:* clam *m*; palourde *f*; **giant c.,** bénitier *m*; **soft c., long c.,** mye *f*; bec-de-jar *m*, *pl.* becs-de-jar; clanque *f*; **razor c.,** solen *m*; manche *m* de couteau. **2.** *F:* homme, femme, taciturne.
clam[2], *v.i.* **(clammed)** *NAm:* **1.** ramasser des clams; aller à la recherche de clams. **2.** *P:* **to c. (up),** se taire; **just you c. up!** la ferme!
clam[3], *s.* = CLAMP[1]; *Vet:* **clams,** casseaux *m.*
clamant ['klæmənt], *a. Lit:* **1.** criard; **c. crowd,** foule vociférante. **2.** (*a*) **c. injustice,** injustice criante; (*b*) **c. need,** besoin urgent.
Clamatores [klæmə'tɔːriːz], *s.pl. Orn:* clamatores *m.*
clambake ['klæmbeik], *s. NAm:* **1.** pique-nique *m*, *pl.* pique-niques, au bord de la mer (où l'on mange des fruits de mer). **2.** *F:* (*a*) grande réunion tapageuse; (*b*) grand rassemblement politique. **3.** *W.Tel: T.V: F:* four *m*, fiasco *m.*
clamber[1] ['klæmbər], *s.* ascension *f* raide; escalade *f.*
clamber[2], *v.i.* grimper (des pieds et des mains); **to c. up a ladder,** grimper à l'échelle; **to c. up a wall,** (i) (*of pers.*) escalader un mur; (ii) (*of ivy, etc.*) grimper sur un mur.
clamlike ['klæmlaik], *a. F:* (*of pers.*) muet comme une huître.
clamminess ['klæminis], *s.* **1.** moiteur froide (de la peau); humidité froide (de l'air). **2.** état collant, gluant (d'une surface).
clammy ['klæmi], *a.* **1.** (*a*) (*of hands, skin*) (froid et) moite; (*of atmosphere*) (froid et) humide; (*b*) *Med:* **c. skin,** peau halitueuse; **c. mouth,** bouche pâteuse. **2.** gluant, collant; mal essuyé.
clamorous ['klæmərəs], *a.* bruyant, braillard; **c. crowd,** foule vociférante.
clamorously ['klæmərəsli], *adv.* bruyamment, à grands cris.
clamour[1] ['klæmər], *s.* (*a*) clameur *f*; cris *mpl*; vociférations *fpl*; **this action raised a general c.,** cette action souleva un tollé général; (*b*) **the c. of the storm,** la clameur, les hurlements *m*, de la tempête; (*c*) **there was a c. for war,** on réclamait à grands cris la guerre.
clamour[2]. **1.** *v.i.* vociférer, crier; pousser des clameurs *f*; **the troops were clamouring to go home,** les hommes demandaient bruyamment à rentrer dans leurs foyers; **to c. for sth.,** réclamer, demander, qch. à grands cris, à cor et à cri; **to c. against sth.,** élever des clameurs contre qch.; aboyer après qch. **2.** *v.tr. O:* **to c. s.o. down,** faire taire qn à force de clameurs.
clamp[1] [klæmp], *s.* (*a*) crampon *m*, presse *f*; main *f* de fer; **eccentric c.,** levier *m* de coincement; **tailstock-spindle c.,** serrage *m* de contre-pointe (d'un tour); **c. screw,** vis *f* d'arrêt, de blocage; (*b*) *Const:* agrafe *f*, happe *f*, clameau *m*, moufle *f* (de pierres de taille); **(series of) clamps,** chaînage *m*; (*c*) bride *f* de serrage; patte *f* d'attache; anneau *m* de retenue; étrier *m*, collier *m* (de tuyau); *I.C.E:* étrier de soupape; *Nau:* blin *m* (de bout-dehors); clamp *m*; (*d*) *Carp: etc:* (i) serre-joint *m*, *pl.* serre-joints; sergent *m*; étreignoir *m*; (ii) valet *m* (d'établi); mâchoire *f* de serrage; (*e*) mordache *f* (d'étau); (*f*) pince *f*; **brazing c.,** pince à braser; **paper c.,** pince-notes *m inv*, pince-feuilles *m inv*; **tablecloth c.,** pince-nappe *m*, *pl.* pince-nappes; (*g*) pince (pour fils); *El:* (i) **c. (screw),** attache-fil(s) *m inv.*; serre-fil(s) *m inv.*; borne *f*; (ii) **brush c.,** sabot *m* de balai; (*h*) *Surg:* clamp; (*i*) *Phot:* **tripod c.,** entretoise *f* du pied.
clamp[2], *v.*
I. *v.tr.* **1.** cramponner, serrer; mettre (qch.) sous presse. **2.** (*a*) *Const: etc:* agrafer (deux pierres); brider (un tuyau); *Nau:* bliner (un bout-dehors); **to c. a piece between two others,** emprisonner une pièce entre deux autres; **to c. a piece on,** fixer une pièce par une pince, avec une agrafe; (*b*) bloquer, immobiliser (un instrument de précision); caler (un télescope); (*c*) *Ch:* pincer (un tube).
II. (*compound verb*) **clamp down. 1.** *v.tr.* **to c. sth. down,** fixer qch. par une mâchoire, un crampon. **2.** *v.i.* (*a*) (*of clouds*) descendre; (*of weather*) s'assombrir; (*b*) *F:* **to c. down on s.o.,** serrer les pouces, la vis, à qn; **to c. down on an abuse,** mettre le holà à un abus; **to c. down on overdrafts,** réduire les, mettre fin aux, facilités de caisse.
clamp[3], *s.* (*a*) silo *m* (temporaire) (de pommes de terre); (*b*) tas *m* (de rebuts, etc.); (*c*) meule *f* (de briques en cuisson); four *m* de campagne; **c. firing (of bricks),** cuisson *f* à la volée.
clamp[4], *v.tr.* (*a*) mettre (des pommes de terre) en silo; (*b*) entasser (des rebuts, etc.); (*c*) mettre (des briques) en meule.
clamp[5], *s. Dial:* pas lourd.
clamp[6], *v.i. Dial:* marcher lourdement, d'un pas lourd.

clamp-down ['klæmp'daun], *s. F:* **to have a c.-d. on sth.,** mettre le holà à (un abus); mettre fin (aux facilités de caisse); **there will be a c.-d. on credit,** il y aura un resserrement du crédit.

clamping ['klæmpiŋ], *s.* (*a*) agrafage *m*, bridage *m*, calage *m*, blocage *m*, serrage *m*; chaînage *m* (d'un mur); **c. of a tool,** fixation *f* d'un outil; **c. band, ring,** collier *m* de serrage; **c. plate,** plateau *m* de serrage; **c. surface,** surface *f* de joint, d'appui; **c. screw,** (i) (*locking screw*) vis *f* d'arrêt, de blocage; (ii) *El:* vis de serrage; serre-fils *m inv*; attache-fil(s) *m inv*; *Elcs:* **c. circuit,** circuit *m* limiteur (de demi-ondes); (*b*) *Surg:* clampage *m*.

clamp-on ['klæmp'ɔn], *s.* mise *f* en garde (d'un appel téléphonique).

clamshell ['klæmʃel], *s.* **1.** coquille *f* de clam. **2.** *Civ.E:* **c. bucket,** benne preneuse.

clan[1] [klæn], *s.* **1.** *Scot:* clan *m*; **the head of the c.,** le chef de clan. **2.** *Anthr:* clan (d'une tribu); **c. name,** nom clanique. **3.** *F:* coterie *f*, clique *f*; **gathering of the clans,** assemblée *f*, réunion *f*, d'adhérents, de partisans.

clan[2], *v.i. F:* (**clanned**) **to c. together,** se soutenir mutuellement; faire preuve d'esprit de corps.

clandestina [klændes'tainə], *s. Bot:* clandestine *f*; herbe cachée.

clandestine [klæn'destin], *a.* clandestin, subreptice; **c. printing,** marronnage *m*.

clandestinely [klæn'destinli], *adv.* clandestinement, subrepticement; à la dérobée, en cachette; *F:* sous le manteau (de la cheminée); **book printed c.,** marron *m*.

clandestineness [klæn'destinnis], **clandestinity** [klændes'tiniti], *s.* clandestinité *f*.

clang[1] [klæŋ], *s.* son *m*, bruit *m*, métallique; bruit strident, retentissant; résonnement *m* (de cloches, etc.); **the forge rings with the c. of the hammer,** la forge retentit du son du marteau; *attrib. Psy:* **c. associations,** associations *f* sonores.

clang[2]. **1.** *v.i.* retentir, résonner; rendre un son métallique. **2.** *v.tr.* faire résonner (une cloche, un timbre, etc.).

clanger ['klæŋər], *s. F:* **to drop a c.,** faire une gaffe, une boulette; gaffer.

clanging[1] [klæŋiŋ], *a.* retentissant, résonnant.

clanging[2], *s.* = CLANG[1].

clangorous ['klæŋgərəs], *a.* retentissant, strident.

clangour ['klæŋgər], *s.* = CLANG[1].

clanism ['klænizm], *s.* = CLANNISHNESS.

clank[1] ['klæŋk], *s.* bruit sec (de chaînes, de fers); cliquetis *m*.

clank[2]. **1.** *v.i.* rendre un bruit métallique (sans résonance), un bruit de chaînes; **the old bell clangs, or rather clanks,** la vieille cloche résonne, ou plutôt rend un son fêlé. **2.** *v.tr.* **the prisoners c. their chains,** les prisonniers font sonner leurs chaînes, leurs fers.

clankety-clank ['klæŋkəti'klæŋk], *s. F:* clic-clac *m*.

clanking ['klæŋkiŋ], *s.* = CLANK[1].

clannish ['klæniʃ], *a.* **1.** attaché, dévoué, au clan. **2.** *Pej:* attaché aux intérêts (i) de son clan, (ii) de sa coterie; plein des préjugés de sa coterie.

clannishness ['klæniʃnis], *s. usu. Pej:* esprit *m* de corps (des membres du clan, de la tribu, d'une coterie); esprit étroit de famille, d'exclusivisme; esprit de coterie.

clanship ['klænʃip], *s.* système *m* du clan.

clansman, *pl.* **-men, clanswoman,** *pl.* **-women** ['klænzmən, -mən, -wumən, -wimin], *s.* membre *m* d'un clan.

clap[1] [klæp], *s.* **1.** (*a*) battement *m* (de mains); applaudissements *mpl*; **to give s.o. a c.,** applaudir qn; (*b*) coup *m*, tape *f* (de la main); **he gave me a friendly c. on the shoulder,** il me frappa amicalement sur l'épaule. **2. c. of thunder,** coup *m* de tonnerre.

clap[2], *v.* (**clapped**).

I. *v.tr.* & **I.** *v.tr.* (*a*) **to c. one's hands,** battre, claquer, des mains; **to c. s.o. on the back,** donner à qn une tape sur le dos; frapper sur l'épaule de qn; **to c. a performer,** applaudir un artiste; (*b*) (*of bird*) **to c. its wings,** battre des ailes; (*c*) mettre, *F:* coller; **to c. s.o. in prison,** fourrer qn en prison; mettre qn au bloc; **to c. s.o. under lock and key,** enfermer qn à double tour; **to c. s.o. in irons,** mettre qn aux fers; **to c. a pistol to s.o.'s head,** appuyer brusquement un pistolet sur la tempe de qn; *F:* **to c. eyes on s.o.,** voir qn (tout à coup); apercevoir qn; **I hadn't clapped eyes on him since the war,** je ne l'avais jamais rencontré, jamais aperçu, depuis la Guerre. **2.** *v.i.* (*a*) battre des mains; frapper des, dans ses, mains; applaudir; (*b*) (*of wings*) battre.

II. (*compound verbs*) **1. clap on,** *v.tr.* **to c. on one's hat, to c. one's hat on (one's head),** camper, enfoncer brusquement, son chapeau sur sa tête; **to c. on the brakes,** donner un brusque coup de frein; *Nau:* **to c. on more sail,** augmenter de toile; *F:* **to c. on another fiver,** surenchérir de cinq livres.

2. clap to, (*a*) *v.tr.* fermer (avec un bruit sec); **he clapped the lid to,** il ferma sec le couvercle; (*b*) *v.i.* se refermer (avec un bruit sec); se refermer brusquement.

clap[3], *s. P:* (*not in polite use*) blennorragie *f*, gonorrhée *f*; échauffement *m*; *P:* chaude-pisse *f*.

clapboard[1] ['klæpbɔ:d], *s. NAm: Const:* planche *f* à clin.

clapboard[2], *v.tr. NAm:* revêtir (un mur) de planches (à clin).

clapboarding ['klæpbɔ:diŋ], *s. NAm: Const:* revêtement *m* de planches (à clin).

clapnet ['klæpnet], *s. Ven:* tirasse *f*; **to catch quails with a c.,** tirasser des cailles.

clapometer [klæ'pɔmitər], *s. T.V: etc:* applaudimètre *m*.

clapotage [klæpɔ'tɑ:ʒ], **clapotement** [klæ'pɔtmənt], *s. Med:* clapotage *m*.

clapped [klæpt], *a. P:* **c. (out),** à bout de forces; éreinté, fourbu; **he was c. out,** il était claqué.

clapper[1] ['klæpər], *s.* **1.** (*a*) battant *m* (de cloche, de moulin à blé); claquet *m*, traquet *m* (de moulin); clapet *m* (de pompe); **c. ring,** bélière *f* (de cloche); *Mec.E:* **c. valve,** (soupape *f* à) clapet; (*b*) *P: A:* langue *f*; **he likes to hear his own c. going,** il aime à s'entendre parler. **2.** (*a*) claquette *f*, claquoir *m*; *Cin:* **c. board, clappers,** claquette; *Orn:* **c. bill,** bec-ouvert *m*, *pl.* becs-ouverts; (*b*) crécelle *f* (de crieur public); (*c*) *Agr:* moulin *m* à claquet (pour effrayer les oiseaux). **3.** (*pers.*) applaudisseur, -euse; (*hired*) claqueur *m*; **the (hired) clappers,** la claque. **4.** *adv.phr. P:* **(to go) like the clappers,** (travailler) comme un enragé; follement; (courir) comme un dératé; **it was raining like the clappers,** il pleuvait à torrents, à seaux.

clapper[2]. **1.** *v.i.* (*of stork*) claqueter. **2.** *v.tr.* tinter (une cloche) en tirant sur le battant.

clapper-bridge ['klæpə'bridʒ], *s. Dial:* pont primitif (fait de planches ou de dalles).

clappering ['klæpəriŋ], *s.* claquètement *m* (de cigogne).

clapping ['klæpiŋ], *s.* (*a*) claquement *m*, battement *m* (des mains); (*b*) battement des mains; applaudissements *mpl*.

clapstick ['klæpstik], *s. Cin:* claquoir *m*, claquette *f* (de synchronisation); **c. signal,** repère *m*.

claptrap ['klæptræp]. **1.** *s.* (i) phrases *fpl* à effet; boniment *m*; *P:* bobards *mpl*; (ii) verbiage *m*; phrases vides; bla-bla-bla *m*; **to talk c.,** (i) parler pour se faire applaudir; parler pour la galerie; (ii) parler pour ne rien dire; débiter des discours qui ne supportent pas l'examen. **2.** *a.* (discours) creux, sans sincérité.

Clara ['kleərə], *Pr.n.f.* Clara, Claire.

clarain ['klærein], *s. Min:* clarain *m*.

Clare [kleər]. **1.** *Pr.n.f.* Claire. **2.** *s. Ecc:* **the Poor Clares,** les pauvres clarisses *f*.

Clarence ['klærəns]. **1.** *Pr.n.m.* Clarence. **2.** *s. A.Veh:* coupé *m* à quatre places.

Clarenceux ['klærənsju:], *s. Her:* second roi d'armes.

clarendon ['klærəndən], *s. Typ:* normande *f*; caractère gras.

claret ['klærət]. **1.** *s.* (*a*) vin *m* de Bordeaux (rouge); bordeaux *m* rouge; **c. cup,** boisson sucrée au citron et au vin rouge; (*b*) *Box: P:* sang *m*; *A:* **to tap s.o.'s c.,** faire saigner qn du nez. **2.** *a.* **c. (-coloured),** vineux, bordeaux *inv*.

clarification [klærifi'keiʃ(ə)n], *s.* **1.** clarification *f* (d'un liquide); soutirage *m*, collage *m* (du vin); *Sug.-R:* clairçage *m*. **2.** clarification (de son esprit, etc.); **c. of political opinion,** mise *f* au point de l'opinion politique.

clarifier ['klærifaiər], *s.* clarificateur *m*; *Sug.-R:* claire *f*; *Winem:* colle *f*; *Agr:* **(centrifugal) c.,** épurateur *m* centrifuge.

clarify ['klærifai]. **1.** *v.tr.* (*a*) clarifier (le beurre, un sirop); déféquer (un sirop, etc.); coller (le vin); claircer (le sucre); (*b*) clarifier (sa pensée, etc.); éclaircir (l'esprit, la vision, etc.); **to c. a question,** faire la lumière sur, élucider, une question. **2.** *v.i.* (*of liquid, one's thoughts*) se clarifier, s'éclaircir.

clarifying[1] ['klærifaiiŋ], *a.* clarificateur, -trice.

clarifying[2], *s.* = CLARIFICATION.

clariné [klæri'nei], *a. Her:* clariné.

clarinet [klæri'net], *s. Mus:* **1.** (*a*) clarinette *f*; **tenor c. in F,** clarinette-alto *f*; **to play the c.,** jouer de la clarinette; (*b*) **c. stop** (*of organ*), clarinette, cromorne *m*. **2.** (*player*) clarinette *f*.

clarinettist [klæri'netist], *s.* clarinettiste *mf*.

clarion[1] ['klæriən], *s.* **1.** *Poet:* clairon *m*; **c.-voiced,** à la voix claironnante. **2.** (*organ stop*) clairon.

clarion[2], *v.tr. Lit:* **to c. (forth) the news, s.o.'s praises,** proclamer à son de trompe la nouvelle; entonner les louanges de qn.

clarionet [klæriə'net], *s.* = CLARINET.

Clarissa [klə'risə], *Pr.n.f.* Clarisse.

Clarisse [klæ'ri:s], *s.f. Ecc:* (sœur) clarisse.

clarity ['klæriti], *s.* clarté *f*.

Clark [klɑ:k], *Pr.n. El:* **C. cell,** pile *f* étalon au mercure et zinc avec f.é.m. de 14,328 v. à 15°c.

clarkeite ['klɑ:kait], *s. Miner:* clarkéite *f*.

clarkia ['klɑ:kiə], *s. Bot:* clarkie *f*, clarkia *f*.

claro, *pl.* **-oes** ['klɑ:rou, -ouz], *s. U.S:* cigare blond et doux.

Claros, Clarus ['kleərɔs, -rəs], *Pr.n. A.Geog:* Claros.

clary ['kleəri], *s. Bot:* (sauge *f*) sclarée *f*; toute-bonne *f*, *pl.* toutes-bonnes; orvale *f*.

clash[1] [klæʃ], *s.* **1.** fracas *m*; résonnement *m* (de cloches, etc.); choc *m* (de verres, etc.); cliquetis *m* (d'épées, etc.); **the keys fell with a c.,** les clefs tombèrent avec fracas; **the c. of cymbals,** le son strident des cymbales; **the c. of arms,** le tumulte des armes. **2.** (*a*) conflit *m*, choc (d'opinions); choc (d'armées); (*between mobs*) échauffourée *f*; désaccord *m*, opposition *f*, collision *f*, combat *m*, frottement *m* (d'intérêts, de doctrines); **parliamentary c.,** lutte *f* parlementaire; (*b*) disparate *f*, discordance *f*, contrariété *f* (de couleurs). **3.** *Dial:* (*a*) querelle *f*; (*b*) *Scot:* bavardage *m*; cancan *m*, potin *m*, racontar *m*; **it's common c.,** c'est un bruit qui court partout.

clash[2]. **1.** *v.i.* (*a*) (*of cymbals, bells, etc.*) résonner (bruyamment); (*of arms*) s'entrechoquer; **to c. together,** se choquer (bruyamment); s'entrechoquer; **the two engines clashed together,** les deux locomotives se heurtèrent avec fracas; (*b*) (*conflict*) (i) (*of colours*) jurer; faire disparate; discorder, détonner (**with,** avec); (ii) (*of opinions, etc.*) s'opposer; **his opinions c. with mine,** ses opinions sont en conflit, en désaccord, avec les miennes, sont opposées, se heurtent, aux miennes, ne s'accordent pas avec les miennes; **here our interests c.,** ici nos intérêts se heurtent; **the two dates c.,** les deux réunions, dîners, etc., tombent le même jour. **2.** *v.tr.* (*a*) faire résonner (des cymbales, etc.); sonner ensemble (les cloches); **they clashed their shields,** ils heurtaient leurs boucliers l'un contre l'autre; (*b*) *Dial:* (*esp. Scot.*) **to c. the door,** fermer la porte avec fracas.

clashing[1] ['klæʃiŋ], *a.* **1.** bruyant, retentissant. **2. c. colours,** couleurs disparates, discordantes, ennemies, qui jurent ensemble. **3. c. opinions,** opinions opposées.

clashing[2], *s.* = CLASH[1].

clasmatocyte [klæz'mætəsait], *s. Biol:* histiocyte *m*.

clasp[1] [klɑ:sp], *s.* **1.** agrafe *f* (de broche, de médaille, d'album, etc.); fermeture *f* (de collier, etc.); fermoir *m*, fermail *m* (de livre, d'album, de porte-monnaie); **hair-c.,** barrette *f*; **diamond c.,** agrafe de diamants; **(staple) c.** (*for padlock*), moraillon *m*; **bolt c.,** gâche *f* de verrou; **c. hook,** croc *m* à ciseaux. **2.** étreinte *f*; enlacement *m*; **hand c.,** serrement *m* de mains.

clasp[2], *v.tr.* **1.** agrafer, cadenasser (un bracelet, etc.); *v.i.* **this bracelet won't c.,** ce bracelet ne veut pas s'agrafer. **2.** (*a*) serrer, étreindre, enlacer (qn); embrasser (qch., les genoux de qn); prendre (qch.) dans ses bras; **to c. one's arms round sth.,** étreindre, embrasser, qch. des deux bras; **to c. s.o. to one's breast, to one's heart,** serrer qn contre sa poitrine, contre son cœur, sur son cœur; **to be clasped in each other's arms,** se tenir étroitement embrassés; (*b*) **to c. s.o.'s hand,** serrer la main à qn; **they clasped hands,** ils se serrèrent la main; **they clasped hands to ford the stream,** ils se prirent par la main pour traverser la rivière; **to c. one's hands,** joindre les mains.

clasper ['klɑ:spər], *s.* **1.** *Bot:* vrille *f*. **2.** *Ich:* ptérogopode *m*.

clasp(-)knife, *pl.* **-knives** ['klɑ:spnaif, -naivz], *s.* couteau pliant, fermant, de poche; **c.-k. with lock-back,** couteau à cran d'arrêt, à mouche; couteau à loquet.

class[1] [klɑ:s], *s.* classe *f*. **1.** (*order*) (*a*) **the classes of society,** les classes de la société; **the upper classes,** les hautes classes; les gens *m* du monde; la haute société; *F:* la haute; **the middle class(es),** la classe moyenne; la bourgeoisie; **the lower classes,** le prolétariat, le bas peuple, le petit monde; **the working classes,** la classe ouvrière, les classes laborieuses; le prolétariat; **working-c. family,** famille ouvrière; **the better classes,** la haute classe, la bonne bourgeoisie; **the classes and the masses,** les possédants et les prolétaires; **c.-consciousness,** (i) esprit *m* de caste; (ii) conscience *f* de classe; **I am not c. conscious,** je n'ai pas de conscience de classe; **c. war,** lutte *f* de classes; guerre sociale; **good.-c. people,** gens de bonne société, de bonne famille; **what c. does he belong to?** de quel monde est-il? **to marry a girl of one's own c.,** épouser une jeune fille de sa condition; **I don't belong to their c.,** je n'appartiens pas à leur milieu; **to have c.,** avoir de la classe; *F:* **she's no c.,** elle n'est pas de notre monde; elle est d'une vulgarité qui saute aux yeux; (*b*) *Sp: etc:* **first-c. player,** joueur, -euse, de premier ordre; **there's a lot of c. about him,** il est très bien dressé, il a un jeu très classique; **in the Olympic c.,** digne de participer aux

Jeux olympiques; **the actors were adequate but without real c.,** les acteurs étaient capables mais en aucune façon remarkquables; *F:* **this hotel certainly has c.,** cet hôtel est certainement de premier ordre; (*c*) **first-c. road, ticket, etc.,** route *f*, billet *m*, etc., de première classe; *Nau: etc:* **tourist c., cabin c., economy c.,** classe touriste, cabine, économique. **2.** *Sch:* (*a*) **the French c.,** la classe de français; **evening classes,** cours *m* du soir, cours d'adultes; **day release classes,** la scolarité à temps partiel; **dancing classes,** cours de danse; **to hold classes for discussion,** organiser des séances de discussion; **to attend classes at . . .,** suivre des cours à . . .; **in c.,** en classe; **c. book,** (i) livre *m* de classe, livre scolaire; (ii) *Can:* annuaire rédigé par les élèves d'une promotion; **c. list,** (i) état nominatif d'une classe; (ii) liste *f* par ordre de mérite; **c. prize,** prix *m* d'excellence; (*b*) *NAm:* promotion. **3.** (*a*) catégorie *f*, sorte *f*, genre *m*; **to arrange articles in classes,** classifier des objets; **arrangement in classes,** classification *f*; **article which stands in a c. by itself,** article *m* qui est unique; **good-c. article,** article de choix; **classes of ships,** types *m* de vaisseaux; *Aut:* **race for the four-cylinder c.,** course *f* pour la catégorie des quatre cylindres; (*b*) *Nat.Hist:* **the classes of a kingdom,** les classes d'un règne; (*c*) *Ins:* **c. of a ship,** cote *f* d'un navire (au Lloyd); (*d*) *Sch:* **first c., second c., degree** — licence *f* avec mention bien, avec mention; (*e*) *Mil: U.S:* **private first c.,** soldat *m* de première classe.

class[2], *v.tr.* (*a*) classer; ranger (des candidats, etc.) par classes; **you can't c. the labourer with the skilled tradesman,** on ne peut assimiler le manœuvre à l'ouvrier qualifié; **classed wine,** cru classé; **classed first,** classé premier; **not classed,** (i) non classé; (ii) (*at exhibitions*) hors concours; (*b*) *Ins:* coter (un navire); **ship classed A1,** navire classé suivant cote A1.

classable ['klɑːsəbl], *a.* que l'on peut (i) classer, (ii) coter.

classic ['klæsik]. **1.** *a.* (*a*) (auteur *m*, littérature *f*, beauté *f*) classique; *Turf:* **c. (race),** course *f* classique; *U.S:* **the C. City,** Boston; (*b*) *F:* **a c. example of the jealous wife,** un exemple classique, typique, de la femme jalouse. **2.** *s.* (*a*) classique (grec, français); **author who is now a c.,** auteur qui est maintenant un classique; (*b*) humaniste *m*; (*c*) *pl.* (*usu. with sg.const.*) **classics,** études *f* classiques; humanités *f*; **to study classics,** étudier le latin et le grec.

classical ['klæsik(ə)l], *a.* (*a*) classique; **the c. islands of the Aegean,** les îles *f* de la mer Égée célèbres dans l'antiquité; **c. languages, studies,** langues *f*, études *f*, classiques; **to receive a good c. education,** faire ses humanités; **c. scholar,** humaniste *m*; **the c. side of the school,** les classes d'humanités; (*b*) **c. music,** musique *f* classique; **she plays only c. music,** elle ne joue que du classique; (*c*) traditionnel; *Ph:* **c. physics,** la physique avant la théorie (i) des quantas, (ii) de la relativité; *Pol.Ec:* **c. economics,** économie *f* classique; *Cost:* **c. cut,** coupe *f* classique.

classicality [klæsi'kæliti], *s.* **1.** qualité *f* classique. **2.** trait *m* classique.

classically ['klæsik(ə)li], *adv.* classiquement; à la manière des (auteurs) classiques; en érudit.

classicism ['klæsisizm]. **1.** *Lit: Art:* classicisme *m*. **2.** connaissance *f* des classiques. **3.** humanisme *m*. **4.** tour *m* ou locution *f* emprunté(e) au latin ou au grec.

classicist ['klæsisist], *s.* **1.** *Lit:* classique *m*; **the classicists and the romanticists,** les classiques et les romantiques. **2.** *Sch:* humaniste *m*. **3.** partisan *m* des études classiques.

classifiable ['klæsifaiəbl], *a.* que l'on peut classifier, classer.

classification [klæsifi'keiʃ(ə)n], *s.* **1.** classification *f* (des plantes, des animaux); classement *m* (de papiers, de concurrents, etc.); codification *f* (des lois); *Rail: U.S:* **c. yard,** gare *f* de triage. **2.** classification; classe *f*; *Ins:* cote *f* (d'un navire); *Mil:* hiérarchie *f* (de grades).

classified ['klæsifaid], *a.* classifié; *Adm:* **c. roads,** routes classifiées (selon la loi de 1919); **c. document,** document classifié; **c. information,** informations secrètes; *U.S:* **the c. service,** les fonctionnaires et employés de l'État (divisés en quatre classes); *Journ:* **c. advertisements,** petites annonces; **c. results,** résultats *m* et classements *m*; *Sch:* **c. vocabulary,** vocabulaire arrangé par centres d'intérêt; **c. data,** données groupées, classées.

classifier ['klæsifaiər], *s.* **1.** (*pers.*) classificateur, -trice. **2.** *Min:* classificateur; classeur(-trieur) *m*, *pl.* classeurs(-trieurs).

classify ['klæsifai], *v.tr.* classifier, classer, ranger par classes; distribuer (des animaux, des fleurs).

classifying ['klæsifaiiŋ], *a.* classificatoire.

classless ['klɑːslis], *a.* (société *f*) sans classes.

classman, *pl.* **-men** ['klɑːsmən], *s. Sch: A:* (*at university*) = candidat *m* qui a obtenu une mention.

classmate ['klɑːsmeit], *s.* **1.** camarade *mf* de classe; condisciple *m*. **2.** *NAm:* camarade de promotion.

classroom ['klɑːsruːm], *s. Sch:* (salle *f* de) classe *f*.

classy ['klɑːsi], *a. F:* bon genre; (restaurant, etc.) chic; **you must have some furs, they look c.,** il te faudra des fourrures, ça fait riche, ça fait chic.

clastic ['klæstik], *a. Geol:* clastique; **c. rocks,** roches clastiques, agrégées.

clathrate ['klæθrət, -eit], *a.* **1.** *Bot:* cancellé. **2.** *Ch:* **c. compounds,** *s.pl.* **clathrates** [-eits], composés *m* d'insertion.

clathrus ['klæθrəs], *s. Fung:* clathre *m*.

clatter[1] ['klætər], *s.* **1.** bruit *m*, vacarme *m*, fracas *m*; battue *f* (de sabots de cheval); bruit (de vaisselle); clic-clac *m* (de sabots); ferraillement *m* (d'une machine). **2.** brouhaha *m* (de conversation). **3.** *Dial:* (*esp. Scot:*) bavardage *m*; cancan *m*, potin *m*, racontar *m*.

clatter[2]. **1.** *v.i.* (*a*) faire du bruit; se choquer avec fracas; **to c. about,** marcher en faisant claquer ses souliers; **to c. down,** tomber, descendre, avec bruit, avec fracas; **to c. along, by,** passer avec bruit; **to c. downstairs,** descendre bruyamment l'escalier; **to come clattering down,** dégringoler; faire un bruit de dégringolade; (*b*) (*of stork*) craqueter; (*c*) *Dial:* (*esp. Scot:*) (*of pers.*) bavarder; cancaner, potiner. **2.** *v.tr.* faire résonner; **don't c. your spoons!** ne faites pas de bruit avec vos cuillers!

clattering[1] ['klætəriŋ], *a.* bruyant, retentissant.

clattering[2], *s.* **1.** = CLATTER[1]. **2.** craquètement *m* (de la cigogne).

Claud(e) [klɔːd], *Pr.n.m.* Claude.

claudetite ['klɔːditait], *s. Miner:* claudétite *f*.

Claudia ['klɔːdiə], *Pr.n.f.* Claude.

Claudian ['klɔːdiən]. **1.** *a. Rom.Hist:* (*of letters, aqueduct, etc.*) claudien. **2.** *Pr.n.m.* Claudien.

Claudianus [klɔːdi'einəs], *Pr.n.m. Lt.Lit:* Claudien.

claudication [klɔːdi'keiʃ(ə)n], *s. Med:* claudication *f*; **intermittent c.,** claudication intermittente.

Claudius ['klɔːdiəs], *Pr.n.m. Rom.Hist:* Claude.

clause [klɔːz], *s.* **1.** clause *f*, article *m* (d'un traité); **clauses of a law,** dispositions *f* d'une loi; **additional c.,** clause additionnelle; *Ins:* avenant *m* (d'une police); **clauses governing a sale,** conditions *f* d'une vente; **c. of a will,** disposition *f* testamentaire; **customary c.,** clause d'usage; **formal c.,** clause de style; **penalty c.,** clause pénale; **arbitration c.,** clause compromissoire; **saving c.,** clause de sauvegarde, restrictive; réservation *f*; (**restrictive**) **clauses,** modalités *f*. **2.** *Gram:* membre *m* de phrase; **main c.,** proposition principale.

clausthalite ['klaustəlait], *s. Miner:* clausthalite *f*.

claustral ['klɔːstr(ə)l], *a.* claustral, -aux.

claustration [klɔː'streiʃ(ə)n], *s.* claustration *f*.

claustrophilia [klɔːstrə'filiə], *s. Med:* claustromanie *f*.

claustrophobia [klɔːstrə'foubiə], *s. Med:* claustrophobie *f*.

claustrophobic [klɔːstrə'foubik], *a.* & *s. Med:* claustrophobe (*mf*).

claustrum, *pl.* **-tra** ['klɔːstrəm, -trə], *s.* **1.** *Anat:* avant mur *m*, *pl.* avant-murs (du cerveau).

clavaria [klæ'veəriə], *s. Fung:* clavaire *f*, digital, -aux *m*.

clavate ['klæveit, 'klei-], *a. Nat.Hist:* clavé, claviforme; en forme de bâton.

claviceps ['klæviseps], *s. Fung:* claviceps *m*.

clavichord ['klævikɔːd], *s. A.Mus:* clavicorde *m*.

clavicle ['klævikl], *s. Anat:* clavicule *f*.

Clavicornes [klævi'kɔːniːz], *s. pl. Ent:* clavicornes *m*.

clavicular [klə'vikjulər], *a. Anat:* claviculaire.

claviculate [klə'vikjulət, -eit], *a. Nat.Hist:* (*of shell, leaf*) claviculé.

claviform ['klævifɔːm], *a. Nat.Hist:* claviforme; en forme de bâton.

clavus ['kleivəs], *s.* **1.** *Ent:* clavus *m*. **2.** *Med:* **c. hystericus,** clou *m* hystérique.

claw[1] [klɔː], *s.* **1.** (*a*) griffe *f* (de félin); serre *f* (d'oiseau de proie); *Ven:* harpe *f* (de chien courant); *A:* ongle *m* (de sabot d'ongulé); *occ.* ongle (d'un vautour, d'un lion); pince *f* (d'une écrevisse); (*of cat*) **to sharpen its claws,** se faire les griffes; **to draw in its claws,** faire patte de velours; *F:* **to have sharp claws,** avoir la serre bonne; **to fall under s.o.'s claws,** tomber sous les griffes de qn; **to pare, cut, s.o.'s claws,** rogner les ongles à qn; *Nat.Hist:* **c.-shaped,** onguiforme; *Furn:* **c.-footed,** (table, etc.) à pied de griffon; *Med:* **c. foot,** pied creux; **c. hand,** griffe cubitale; (*b*) *P:* (*hand*) pince, patte *f*. **2.** coup *m* de griffe, d'ongle, de patte. **3.** *Tchn:* (*a*) (*of bench*) valet *m*; (*of vice*) mordache *f*; (*of winch shaft, etc.*) cliquet *m*; **clamping c.,** griffe de fixation; *Cin:* **c. movement,** entraînement *m* par griffes; **feeding claws,** griffes de transport du film; *Mec.E:* **coupling-c.,** noix *f* d'entraînement; griffe de commande; **c. coupling,** embrayage *m* à griffe(s), à dents; dent-de-loup *f*, *pl.* dents-de-loup; (*b*) **c. of a grapnel,** patte d'un grappin; (*c*) **nail c.,** arrache-clou(s) *m inv*; arrache-pointe(s) *m inv*; tire-clou(s) *m inv*; pince *f*; loup *m*; pied-de-biche *m*, *pl.* pieds-de-biche; pied-de-chèvre *m*, *pl.* pieds-de-chèvre; bec-de-corbin *m*, *pl.* becs-de-corbin; (*d*) panne fendue (de marteau).

claw[2]. **1.** *v.tr.* (*a*) griffer, égratigner; donner un coup de griffe à (qn); déchirer (qch.) avec ses griffes; *F:* agriffer (qch.); (*b*) saisir (qch.) avec ses griffes, dans ses griffes; (*c*) gratter, chatouiller, racler, légèrement (la peau) du bout des ongles; *F: A:* **c. me and I'll c. thee,** grattez-moi l'épaule et je t'en ferai autant; *F:* passez-moi la rhubarbe et je vous passerai le séné; un barbier rase l'autre; (*d*) *F:* **to c. back sth.,** regagner qch. péniblement; **to c. back an expense,** récupérer une dépense. **2.** *v.i.* (*a*) **to c. at sth.,** s'accrocher à qch.; saisir qch. avec ses griffes; agriffer, agripper, qch.; (*b*) *Nau:* **to c. off (a coast),** gagner le large; se déhaler; s'élever au vent d'une côte; *v.tr.* (*of ship*) **to c. her way to windward,** gagner dans le vent.

claw-back ['klɔːbæk], *s. F:* récupération *f* (d'une dépense).

clawed [klɔːd], *a.* armé de griffes, d'ongles; *Z:* unguifère; **sharp-c.,** à griffes aiguës.

claw hammer ['klɔːhæmər], *s.* **1.** *Tls:* marteau *m* à panne fendue, à dent. **2.** *F: esp. U.S:* **c.-h. (coat),** habit *m* à queue de morue, à queue de pie; *F:* queue *f* de morue.

clay[1] [klei], *s.* **1.** (*a*) argile *f*, (terre-)glaise *f*; (*in coalmine*) gore *f* (*in centre of France*), gord *m* (*in N. of France*); **rich c., greasy c.,** argile grasse; **boulder c.,** argile à blocaux; **slate c., c. slate,** schiste argileux, ardoisier; argile schisteuse; **c.-with-flints,** argile à silex; *Cer: etc:* **ball c.,** argile figuline; **china c., porcelain c.,** terre *f* à porcelaine, kaolin *m*; **modelling c.,** pâte *f* à modeler; **potter's c.,** terre à, de, potier, (terre-)glaise, argile plastique; **tile c.,** argile téguline; *Lit:* **idol with feet of c.,** idole *f* aux pieds d'argile; *F:* **to be under, beneath, the c.,** être enterré, sous (la) terre; *attrib. Geol:* **c. bearing,** argilifère; *Sp:* **c. bird, c. pigeon,** pigeon artificiel; **c. bottom,** fond *m* d'argile; **c. field,** argilière *f*; *Brickm: etc:* **c. mill,** broyeur *m*, malaxeur *m*; **c. modelling,** modelage *m* en glaise; **c. pit,** argilière, glaisière *f*, carrière *f* d'argile; **c. soil,** sol argileux, glaiseux; **c.-stone,** argilolit(h)e *m*; (*b*) *Lit:* **mortal c.,** le corps humain; **he thinks he's formed of another c.,** il se croit d'un autre limon, d'une autre pâte, que les autres; (*c*) *P: O:* **to wet, moisten, one's c.,** se rincer la dalle; s'humecter le gosier. **2.** **c. (pipe),** pipe *f* de, en, terre; **short c.,** brûle-gueule *m inv*; **long c.,** pipe longue (en terre blanche); pipe hollandaise.

clay[2], *v.tr.* **1.** recouvrir, revêtir, d'argile. **2.** *Sug.-R: A:* terrer (le sucre).

claybank ['kleibæŋk], *a. U.S:* **c. horse,** cheval *m* isabelle; cheval louvet.

clayey ['kleii], *a.* argileux, glaiseux.

claying ['kleiiŋ], *s.* **1.** revêtement *m* (de qch.) avec de l'argile. **2.** *Sug.-R: A:* terrage *m* (du sucre).

claymore [klei'mɔːr], *s.* **1.** *Hist:* claymore *f*; grand sabre à deux tranchants (des Écossais). **2.** *Mil:* **c. mine,** (type *m* de) mine antipersonnel.

claytonia [klei'touniə], *s. Bot:* claytonia *f*.

cleading ['kliːdiŋ], *s. Mch:* enveloppe *f* calorifuge, garniture *f*, chemise *f* (de cylindre, de tuyautage).

clean[1] [kliːn], *a.* & *adv.*

I. *a.* **1.** (*a*) propre, pur, net; **as c. as a new pin,** propre comme un sou neuf; **to make sth. c.,** nettoyer qch.; **to keep sth. c.,** tenir qch. propre; **to wash sth. c.,** nettoyer qch. à grande eau; **c. plate,** assiette nette; *F:* **to lick the platter c.,** torcher le plat; faire les plats nets; **c. paper,** papier blanc; *Typ:* **c. proof,** (i) épreuve non chargée, peu chargée; (ii) épreuve corrigée (par l'imprimeur); épreuve pour bon à tirer; **c. linen,** linge propre, blanc; **c. shoes,** souliers propres, cirés; **c. road,** chemin net; **c. land,** terrain nettoyé, sans herbes; *Nau:* **c. anchorage,** mouillage sain; **c. water,** eau pure, claire; **wine c. to the taste,** vin franc de goût; **c. timber,** bois uni, net, sans malandres; **c. jump,** saut franc; **horse that is a c. jumper,** cheval *m* qui saute franchement; **c. break,** cassure nette, franche; **c. sheet,** casier *m* judiciaire vierge; **he's had a c. sheet since he served his time,** depuis qu'il a purgé sa condamnation, sa conduite a été impeccable, il n'y a rien eu à ajouter à son dossier; **c. driving licence,** permis *m* de conduire vierge; *Nau:* **c. bill of health,** patente nette; *F:* **the doctor gave me a c. bill of health,** le docteur m'a trouvé en pleine forme; *Fin:* **c. bill,** effet *m* libre; **c. receipt,** reçu *m* sans réserve; **c. hands,** (i) mains *f* propres; (ii) (*clean from crime*) mains nettes; **in spite of many temptations, he always managed to keep his hands c.,** malgré toutes les tentations, il a gardé ses mains nettes, il n'a jamais failli à l'honneur; *U.S:* **a c. man,** un homme loyal; **the c. thing would be to . . .,** pour agir loyalement il faudrait . . .; **c. tongue,** (i) *Med:* langue nette; (ii) langage honnête, décent; **c. conscience,** conscience nette, pure; **c. living,** vie, conduite, réglée; **c. literature,** littérature *f* propre; **good c. fun,** amusement innocent; *F:* **keep the party, it, c.!** pas de grossièretés! **we had better tell him, just to keep the party c.,** il vaut mieux le lui dire pour jouer franc jeu; *Atom.Ph:* **c. bomb,** bombe *f* propre; (*b*) **c. cat,** chat *m* propre, aux habitudes propres. **2. c. (out)lines,** contours nets; formes fines, dégagées; **car with c. lines,** voiture *f* qui a de la ligne; *Nau:* **c. ship,** navire fin; **c. run,** arrière évidé; *Farr:* **c. hocks** (*of horse*), jarrets vidés; **c. ankles,** chevilles fines; attaches fines. **3. c. player, boxer,** joueur *m*, boxeur *m*, impeccable. **4.** *B:* **c. and unclean animals,** les animaux *m* mondes et immondes.

II. *adv.* **1.** *F:* absolument, tout à fait; **I c. forgot,** j'ai absolument oublié; **c. mad,** absolument fou; complètement fou; **they got c. away,** ils se sont échappés sans laisser de traces. **2.** (*a*) **to cut c. through sth.,** couper, traverser, qch. de part en part; **cut c. through,** coupé net; **to break off c.,** casser net; (*b*) **to jump c.,** sauter franchement. **3.** *P:* **to come c.,** faire des aveux; *P:* se mettre à table.

clean², *s.* nettoyage *m*; **to give sth. a c.,** nettoyer qch.; donner un coup de balai, torchon, brosse, à qch.; **c.-in-service strainer,** filtre *m* nettoyable en marche.

clean³, *v.*

I. *v.tr.* **1.** *v.tr.* nettoyer (qch.); nettoyer, dégraisser, décrasser (des vêtements); récurer (les casseroles); balayer (les rues); curer (un puits); nettoyer, faire (une chambre); nettoyer, décrotter, cirer (les souliers); vider, habiller (le poisson); éplucher (les légumes); sarcler, désherber (un champ); défricher (un terrain); *Ind:* épurer (un gaz); décrasser (le feu); *Metall:* épailler (l'or en fusion); *Min:* débourber, égrapper (le minerai); *Mch:* lessiver, décrasser (une chaudière); ramoner (les tubes); purifier (l'huile); *Surg:* déterger, mondifier (une plaie, un ulcère); *Tex:* épinceter, époutier (les étoffes); **to c. one's teeth, one's nails,** se laver les dents; se curer les ongles; *F:* **to c. oneself (up),** se débarbouiller; *F:* **to c. one's plate,** faire assiette nette; *Tchn:* **to c. a casting,** nettoyer, dessabler, une pièce coulée; **to c. a surface** (*before soldering, repainting*), décaper la surface; **to c. sth. with emery paper,** frotter qch. à l'émeri; *Nau: etc:* **to c. the brasswork,** faire le fourbissage; **2.** *v.i.* faire le nettoyage; **to go out cleaning,** faire des ménages. **3.** *v.tr. P:* = CLEAN OUT (*b*).

II. (*compound verbs*) **1. clean down,** *v.tr.* (*a*) panser (un cheval); (*b*) ragréer (du briquetage).

2. clean off, *v.tr.* enlever, ôter (des saletés).

3. clean out, *v.tr.* (*a*) ranger, nettoyer (une armoire, etc.); curer, décrasser (un fourneau); vidanger, décomber (une fosse, etc.); ébouer (une chaudière); déboucher (un tuyau); désenvaser (un égout, etc.); *I.C.E:* **to c. out the jet,** déboucher le gicleur; (*b*) *F:* **to c. s.o. out,** nettoyer, plumer, dépouiller, ratiboiser, qn; mettre qn à sec; saigner qn à blanc; **cleaned out,** nettoyé (à sec); décavé, fauché; *P:* dans la purée, dans la mouise; (*c*) *U.S: P:* nettoyer (un endroit de gangsters, etc.).

4. clean up, *v.tr.* (*a*) enlever, ramasser (des saletés, etc.); nettoyer (un champ, etc.); *Art:* **to c. up the lines,** nettoyer les contours; *Carp:* **to c. up a board,** blanchir une planche; **to c. up a joint,** ragréer un assemblage; *Metalw:* **to c. up a surface** (*before soldering*), aviver une surface; **to c. up a piece to size,** mettre une pièce à ses dimensions; (*b*) **to c. up the enemy,** balayer l'ennemi; **to c. up a town,** nettoyer une ville (d'ennemis, de gangsters, etc.); (*c*) *P:* **to c. s.o. up,** nettoyer qn (au jeu, etc.); (*d*) *U.S: P:* **to c. up a thousand dollars,** gagner, ramasser, mille dollars; (*e*) *v.i.* (i) faire le nettoyage; (ii) se nettoyer, se laver, se débarbouiller; (iii) mettre tout en ordre; réparer le désordre; (iv) *Min:* récolter l'or; (v) *U.S: P:* taper dans le mille; faire sa pelote.

cleanable ['kli:nəbl], *a.* nettoyable.

clean-bred ['kli:n'bred], *a.* pur de race; (animal) pur-sang *m inv.*

clean-built ['kli:n'bilt], *a.* (cheval) déchargé.

clean-burning ['kli:n'bə:niŋ], *a.* (*of oil, etc.*) brûlant sans résidu de combustible.

clean-cut ['kli:n'kʌt], *a.* (*a*) (contours *mpl*) d'une grande netteté; (*b*) (*of opinion*) net, bien défini; (*of order*) précis; (*c*) (*of division*) net; brutal, -aux.

cleaner ['kli:nər], *s.* **1.** (*pers.*) nettoyeur, -euse; décrotteur, -euse; dégraisseur, -euse (de vêtements, etc.); cureur *m*, écureur *m* (de puits); **French, dry, cleaners,** nettoyeur à sec; *U.S: P:* **to take s.o. to the cleaners,** (i) nettoyer, plumer, qn; mettre qn à sec; (ii) démolir, éreinter (un adversaire); **to go to the cleaners,** perdre tout son argent; se faire nettoyer; **window c.,** laveur *m* de carreaux, de vitres. **2.** (*a*) appareil *m* à nettoyer; nettoyeuse *f*; **air c.,** épurateur *m* d'air; **window c.,** lave-vitres *m inv*; nettoie-glaces *m*; **knife c.,** (machine *f*, tampon *m*) nettoie-couteaux *m inv*; **pipe c.,** cure-pipe *m*, *pl.* cure-pipes; goupillon *m* nettoie-pipes; furet *m*; (*b*) (i) pâte *f*; (ii) liquide *m*, à nettoyer; (*for clothes*) détachant *m*; *Rec:* **tape c.,** (i) nettoyeur; (ii) dépoussiéreur *m* de bande; (iii) produit *m* de nettoyage.

clean-fell ['kli:n'fel], *v.tr.* couper (une forêt) à blanc.

clean-fingered ['kli:n'fiŋgə:d], *a.* **1.** adroit de ses mains. **2.** non corrompu; honnête; loyal, -aux.

clean-handed ['kli:n'hændid], *a.* aux mains nettes; intègre.

clean-handedness ['kli:n'hændidnis], *s.* intégrité *f*.

cleaning¹ ['kli:niŋ], *a.* qui nettoie; *Agr:* **c. crop,** culture nettoyante.

cleaning², *s.* nettoyage *m*, nettoiement *m*; décrottage *m*, dégraissage *m*, purification *f*; lessivage *m*; curage *m* (d'un puits); décrassage *m* (des chaudières); ramonage *m* (des tubes); décapage *m* (d'une surface à repeindre); *Cu:* vidage *m*, habillage *m* (du poisson); *Agr:* sarclage *m*, désherbage *m* (d'un champ); **c. woman,** femme de ménage; **(household) c. materials,** produits *m* d'entretien; *Navy:* **c. stations,** postes *m* de propreté (pour le fourbissage, etc.); *Sm.a:* **c. rod,** baguette *f* (de fusil); ramasse *f* (de fusil de chasse).

cleaning out ['kli:niŋ'aut], *s.* curage *m*, écurage *m*, débourbage *m* (d'un fossé, etc.).

cleaning up ['kli:niŋ'ʌp], *s.* nettoyage *m* (d'une salle, d'un quartier criminel, *P:* d'un nigaud, etc.).

clean-limbed ['kli:n'limd], *a.* (*of pers.*) bien pris, bien découplé.

cleanliness ['klenlinis], *s.* propreté *f*; netteté *f*; **c. of habit,** habitudes *fpl* de propreté; **sanitary c.,** propreté hygiénique.

cleanly¹ ['klenli], *a.* (*of pers.*) propre (par habitude); **c. habits,** habitudes *fpl* de propreté; **in a c. manner,** proprement.

cleanly² ['kli:nli], *adv.* proprement, nettement.

cleanness ['kli:nnis], *s.* **1.** propreté *f* (des habits, de langage, d'un appartement, etc.); pureté *f* (de l'eau). **2. c. of outlines,** netteté *f*, pureté, de lignes.

clean-out ['kli:naut], *s.* **to give a room a c.-o.,** nettoyer une chambre; *F:* **that's a proper c.-o.!** la maison a été complètement nettoyée (par les cambrioleurs); **to give a drain a c.-o.,** curer, écurer, débourber, un fossé.

clean-run ['kli:n'rʌn], *a.* (saumon *m*) qui vient de remonter de la mer; en condition.

cleanse [klenz], *v.tr.* **1.** assainir, curer, débourber (un égout, une rivière, etc.). **2.** purifier, dépurer (le sang); épurer (l'air, le pétrole, etc.); *Surg:* déterger, mondifier (une plaie, un ulcère); désenvenimer (une plaie); *A: & Lit:* **to c. the heart from sinful affections,** purifier le cœur des affections impures; **soul cleansed of all stains,** âme purifiée de toute souillure. **3.** *B:* guérir (un lépreux). **4.** *U.S:* **to c. a city of gangsters,** nettoyer une cité de gangsters.

cleanser ['klenzər], *s.* pâte *f*, poudre *f*, liquide, *m* à nettoyer (la vaisselle, etc.); *Toil:* **face c.,** crème *f*, lait *m*, de démaquillage; cleaner *m*; démaquillant *m*.

cleanshaven ['kli:n'ʃeivn], *a.* (*a*) qui ne porte ni barbe ni moustache; sans barbe ni moustache; **c. face,** visage entièrement rasé; visage glabre; (*b*) rasé de frais.

cleansing¹ ['klenziŋ], *a.* assainissant, purifiant; purificateur, -trice.

cleansing², *s.* **1.** assainissement *m*, curage *m* (d'un chenal, d'un égout). **2.** purification *f* (du sang, de l'âme); dépuration *f* (du sang); épuration *f* (d'un gaz); mondification *f*, détersion *f* (d'une plaie); *Toil:* **c. cream, milk, lotion,** crème *f*, lait *m*, de démaquillage; démaquillant *m*; **c. pads,** disques-lotion *mpl*. **3.** *Obst:* **cleansing(s),** lochies *fpl*, suites *f* de couche.

cleanskins ['kli:nskinz], *s.pl. Austr:* bétail non marqué au fer chaud.

Cleanthes [kli'ænθi:z], *Pr.n.m. Gr.Phil:* Cléanthe.

clean-tongued ['kli:n'tʌŋd], *a.* au langage honnête.

clean-up ['kli:nʌp], *s.* **1.** (*a*) nettoyage *m*; **the weekly c.-u.,** le grand nettoyage hebdomadaire; **to give sth. a c.-u.,** nettoyer qch.; donner un coup de balai, torchon, brosse, à qch.; (*b*) nettoyage (d'une ville capturée); **c.-u. of the slums,** abolissement *m* des taudis. **2.** *F:* **the lines of the new cars show a general c.-u.,** les nouvelles voitures se distinguent par une plus grande netteté de lignes, par la simplification des contours. **3.** *Min:* (*a*) récolte *f* de l'or; (*b*) l'or récolté. **4.** *P:* (i) profit *m*, gains *mpl* (d'un coup de Bourse, etc.); (ii) butin *m* (d'un cambriolage); (*of speculator, gambler, etc.*) **to make a c.-u.,** tout gagner.

clear¹ [kliər], *a., adv., & s.*

I. *a.* **1.** (*a*) (*unclouded*) clair, limpide; net, *f* nette; **c. atmosphere,** atmosphère claire, pure; *Aer:* **c.-air turbulence,** turbulence *f* en ciel clair; **c. water,** eau claire, limpide, transparente; **c. fire, complexion, eye, weather,** feu clair; teint clair, net; œil clair; temps clair, dégagé; **on a c. day,** par temps clair; **wonderfully c.,** d'une netteté admirable; **as c. as day, daylight, crystal,** clair comme le jour, comme de l'eau de roche, comme deux et deux font quatre; *F:* **as c. as mud,** pas clair du tout; (*b*) **c. conscience,** conscience nette, pure; (*c*) **c. voice,** voix claire, nette; **the bell has a c. tone,** la cloche rend un son clair, a un ton pur; (*d*) *Dist:* blanc; **c. lavender water,** eau de lavande blanche. **2.** (*manifest*) clair, net, évident; **c. image, line,** image, ligne, nette; **expressed in c. terms,** exprimé en termes clairs; **c. indication,** signe certain, évident; **c. position,** situation franche; **c. case of bribery,** cas *m* de corruption manifeste; **to write a c. hand,** écrire distinctement; avoir une écriture nette; **to make one's meaning, oneself, c.,** se faire comprendre; **to make it c. to s.o. that . . .,** faire bien, clairement, comprendre à qn que . . .; **I wish to make it c. that . . .,** je tiens à préciser que . . .; **to make it c. as daylight that . . .,** prouver clair comme le jour que . . .; **it is c. that . . .,** il est clair, patent, évident, de toute évidence, que . . .; **that's c. (enough)!** voilà qui est clair! **3.** (*discerning*) **c. idea,** idée claire, nette; **c. perception,** perception claire, distincte; **c. style,** style clair; **c. thinker, c. mind,** esprit *m* lucide; **c. sight,** vision nette; **to have a c. vision of the future,** avoir une vision nette, distincte, de l'avenir. **4.** (*certain*) **to be c. as to, about, sth.,** être convaincu, certain, de qch.; **I am not c. about . . .,** je ne suis pas certain de . . ., j'ai des doutes sur . . .; **I could not see his face, but I was c. about the voice,** je ne pouvais pas voir son visage, mais je reconnaissais parfaitement sa voix; **I am c. that . . .,** il me paraît évident que . . .; **I want to be quite c. on this point,** je tiens à ce qu'il n'y ait aucun malentendu sur ce point; (i) je voudrais en être certain; (ii) je tiens à me faire bien comprendre; **if I could be c. what she means,** si je pouvais bien pénétrer le sens de ses paroles, ses intentions. **5.** (*a*) **c. profit,** bénéfice clair et net; **c. loss,** perte sèche; **a c. five thousand a year,** un revenu (clair et) net de cinq mille livres; **I lost a c. thousand,** j'en ai été de mille livres; **c. majority,** majorité absolue (of, de); *Sp:* **c. winner,** vainqueur détaché; (*b*) *Jur:* **three c. days,** trois jours francs. **6.** libre, non embarrassé, dégagé (of, de); **from the attic one has a c. view of the sea,** de la mansarde la vue est dégagée sur la mer; **my conscience is c. of all reproach,** ma conscience est nette de tout reproche; **c. accounts,** comptes *m* en règle; **c. estate,** bien non hypothéqué; bien franc, libre, d'hypothèque; **c. space,** espace *m* libre; **c. road,** chemin *m* libre; route bien dégagée; **ship with c. holds,** navire *m* avec ses cales libres; (*of pers.*) **to be c. of sth., of s.o.,** être débarrassé de qch., de qn; **the train was c. of the station,** le train était sorti de la gare; **the station was c. of trains,** il n'y avait pas de train(s) en gare; **horizon c. of haze,** horizon dégagé de brume; **the sea is c. of ice,** la mer est libre; **we are c. of the shoals,** (i) *Nau:* nous avons paré les hauts-fonds; (ii) *Fig:* nous sommes hors de danger; **it's all c. sailing,** cela n'offre aucune difficulté; on a paré à toutes les difficultés; *Av:* **you are c. to take off,** vous êtes autorisé à, vous pouvez, décoller; **all this region is c. of the enemy,** toute cette région est sûre; **the town was c. of the enemy,** la ville avait été évacuée par l'ennemi; **the roads are c.,** les routes sont débloquées, sont libres d'obstacles; *Rail:* **c. road, road c., line c.,** voie libre, signal effacé; **all c.!** vous pouvez y aller, c'est libre; *Mil:* fin *f* d'alerte; *Nau:* paré! *Sch: F:* pas de pet, pas de paix! *Mil:* **to signal "all c.", to sound the "all c.",** battre ou sonner la breloque (après un bombardement aérien, etc.); *Nau:* **c. hawse,** chaînes claires; **c. coast,** côte saine, accore; *F:* **the coast is c.,** le champ est libre, (i) il n'y a plus de danger; (ii) les w.c. sont libres; *For:* **c. bole,** portion du fût (d'un arbre) dépourvue de branches; *Carp:* **c. timber,** bois *m* sans nœuds; *Cmptr:* **c. band,** bande *f* de sécurité (sur un document magnétique).

II. *adv.* **1.** (parler, voir) clair. **2.** (*of sun, star*) **to shine c.,** briller de tout son éclat. **3.** *F: U.S:* (*intensive*) **we went c. on to the end,** nous sommes allés jusqu'à l'extrême bout; **to go c. round the globe,** faire tout le tour du globe.

III. *a. or adv.* **to jump five centimetres c. of the bar,** franchir la barre avec cinq centimètres de reste; **to hang c. of the ground,** être suspendu de manière à ne pas toucher le sol; *Nau:* **to get, pass, c. of a ship,** parer, éviter, un navire; **to keep c. of another ship,** s'écarter de la route d'un autre navire; **the two ships passed c. of each other,** les deux navires se croisèrent sans se toucher; **to steer c. of a rock,** passer au large d'un écueil; **to stand c.,** s'écarter, se garer (pour éviter un danger); **to keep, steer, stand, c. of sth.,** rester, se tenir, à distance de qch., éloigné de qch.; éviter qch.; se garer de qch.; **stand c. of the doorway!** dégagez la porte! **stand c. of the doors!** tenez-vous à distance des portes! attention aux portes! *Rail:* = attention au départ! **stand c. of the gangway,** n'encombrez pas le passavant; **to pull s.o. c.,** dégager qn (of, de); **I keep c. of him as far as possible,** je l'évite le plus possible; **in hot climates steer c. of strong drink,** sous les climats chauds abstenez-vous, méfiez-vous, des boissons alcooliques; **to get c. of s.o.,** échapper à qn; **to get c. of debt,** se débarrasser de ses dettes; **to get c.,** se tirer d'embarras; se tirer d'affaire.

IV. *s.* **1.** espace *m* libre. **2.** (*of pers.*) **to be in the c.,** (i) être désinculpé, libre de tout soupçon; (ii) n'avoir pas de dettes; être hors d'embarras. **3. despatch sent in c.,** dépêche *f* en clair. **4.** *Sp:* (*badminton*) lob *m*.

clear[2], *v.*

I. *v.tr.* **1.** (*a*) éclaircir; **the wind has cleared the weather,** le vent a éclairci le temps; **to c. the air,** (i) (*of thunderstorm*) rafraîchir l'air; (ii) *F:* (*of discussion, etc.*) mettre les choses au point; **to c. a doubt,** éclaircir un doute; **to c. one's throat,** s'éclaircir le gosier, la voix; se racler la gorge; tousser un coup; (*b*) clarifier (un liquide); purifier, dépurer (le sang). **2.** (*declare innocent*) **to c. s.o. of a charge,** justifier, innocenter, qn d'une accusation; **to c. s.o. of a suspicion,** disculper qn d'un soupçon; **to c. s.o. from blame,** absoudre qn de tout blâme; innocenter, disculper, désinculper, qn; **to c. oneself of an accusation,** se laver, se purger, se justifier, d'une accusation; se disculper; **to c. one's character, oneself,** se disculper, se justifier, se blanchir; faire reconnaître son innocence. **3.** (*a*) (*free from obstacles*) dégager (une route, un terrain, une entrée); désencombrer (une salle, etc.); défricher, essarter (un terrain); (*from rubbish*) décombrer, faire évacuer (les rues, une salle); vider (une prison); *Mch:* évacuer (les cylindres); ramoner (les tubes de fumée); *W.Tel: etc:* relever (un dérangement), éliminer (l'interférence); *Tex:* débourrer (les cardes); *Jur:* **to c. the court,** faire évacuer la salle; ordonner le huis clos; **to c. one's conscience,** décharger sa conscience; *Cards:* **to c. one's hand of hearts,** se défausser à cœur; **to c. a way, a passage, for s.o.,** ouvrir un passage à qn; **to c. the way for s.o.,** faire place à qn; **c. the way!** faites place! **to c. a way for oneself,** se frayer un passage; **to c. the ground** (*for negotiations*), déblayer le terrain; **to c. an affair of difficulties,** désentraver une affaire; **to c. the table,** (i) débarrasser la table; (ii) défaire, enlever, le couvert; desservir; *Navy:* **to c. (the decks) for action,** faire (le) branle-bas de combat; *F:* **to c. the decks,** (i) déblayer le terrain; (ii) (*at meal*) ne pas laisser une miette; (iii) ranger; *Navy:* **c. lower deck!** l'équipage à l'appel! tout le monde sur le pont! *v.i.* **to c. for anchoring,** faire péneau; parer, dégager, l'ancre; **the rain had cleared the streets,** la pluie avait dépeuplé les rues; **to c. the room for dancing,** enlever les meubles (gênants), faire de la place, pour qu'on puisse danser; dégager le parquet; **to c. ground,** déblayer, débroussailler, défricher, du terrain; **to c. a field (of all its produce),** fourrager un champ; **to c. a path, river, of sand,** dessabler, désensabler, une allée, une rivière; **to c. a room of smoke, the smoke out of a room,** chasser la fumée d'une salle; **to c. a country of robbers,** purger, débarrasser, un pays des bandes de brigands; **to c. the slums,** supprimer les taudis; *Mil:* **to c. the trenches** (*after an attack*), nettoyer les tranchées; **to c. the field of fire,** dégager le champ de tir (d'une arme à feu); **to c. an area of mines,** déminer un terrain; **text cleared of all difficulties,** texte dégagé de toutes ses difficultés; **a cup of coffee clears the head,** une tasse de café dégage le cerveau, vous éclaircit les idées; *Com:* **to c. goods,** (i) solder, liquider, des marchandises; (ii) (*of customers*) enlever toute la marchandise; **to c.,** en solde, solde; **must be cleared,** vente à tout prix; *Rail:* **to c. the line,** (i) dégager la voie; (ii) (*after an accident*) déblayer la voie; *Tchn:* **to c. a drill, a tap,** dépouiller, dégager, un foret, un taraud; **to c. a choked pipe,** déboucher, dégorger, désobstruer, un tuyau; **to c. a filter,** décolmater un filtre; *Typew:* **to c. the tabulator,** supprimer les tabulations; *Cmptr:* **to c. a memory,** remettre une mémoire à zéro; **to c. a card track,** vider une piste de cartes; **cleared condition,** état initial; (*b*) *v.i. Fb:* dégager (le ballon); (*c*) **to c. boxes, furniture, out of the way,** enlever des caisses, des meubles, qui encombrent; **c. all this out of here,** débarrassez-moi de tout cela. **4.** (*empty*) **to c. one's plate,** faire assiette nette; **to c. the letters, the letterbox,** lever les lettres, la boîte aux lettres; **to c. the bowels,** nettoyer, purger, dégager, les intestins; **to c. one's bowels,** se décharger le ventre. **5.** (*a*) **to c. a barrier (by 10 centimetres),** franchir une barrière (avec 10 centimètres de reste); **to c. a ditch,** sauter un fossé; **to c. a ditch with one jump,** franchir le fossé d'un bond; (*of curtain*) **to c. the ground, to c. the ground by a few centimetres,** être disposé de façon à ne pas balayer le sol; pendre à (une distance de) quelques centimètres du sol; **to jack up a wheel till it clears the ground,** soulever une roue jusqu'à ce qu'elle soit libérée du sol, jusqu'à ce qu'elle ne touche plus le sol; (*b*) *Nau:* **to c. the harbour,** sortir du port; quitter le port; **ship cleared,** navire sorti; **to c. the land,** parer la terre; **to c. the channel,** démancher. **6.** (*a*) acquitter (une dette); affranchir (une propriété); purger (une hypothèque); solder, liquider, arrêter (un compte); **to c. one's property of debt,** purger son bien de dettes; **to c. a hospital of debts,** libérer un hôpital de ses dettes; (*b*) *Nau:* (*of ship*) **to c. its quarantine,** purger la quarantaine; **to c. a ship,** expédier un navire; faire la déclaration à la sortie; **to c. goods,** passer, expédier, des marchandises *f* en douane; dédouaner des marchandises; retirer des marchandises de la douane; (*c*) (i) **to c. a project with the authorities,** obtenir l'approbation, le consentement, des autorités pour un projet; (ii) **to c. an article for publication,** (α) demander l'autorisation de publier un article; (β) autoriser la publication d'un article; (iii) *Adm: Mil:* **to c. s.o. for security,** attribuer à qn, un certificat d'habilitation; soumettre qn aux formalités nécessaires à l'attribution d'un certificat d'habilitation. **7. to c. ten per cent,** gagner, réaliser, dix pour cent tous frais payés; faire un bénéfice net de dix pour cent; **not to c. one's expenses,** ne pas faire ses frais; **I cleared a hundred pounds,** j'ai touché, cela m'a rapporté, cent livres net. **8.** *Fin:* compenser, virer (un chèque).

II. *v.i.* **1.** (*a*) (*of the weather*) **to c. (up),** s'éclaircir, se découvrir, se rasséréner, se lever, se mettre au beau; *F:* se débarbouiller; **the weather is clearing up (again),** le temps se remet; (*of mist*) **to c. (away),** se dissiper; **the weather is clearing,** le temps se hausse; **the sky is clearing,** le ciel se dégage; **his brow cleared,** son front s'éclaircit, se dérida, se rasséréna; il défronça les sourcils; (*b*) (*of liquid*) se clarifier. **2.** (*of ship*) prendre la mer; **to c. at, for, a port,** quitter, partir pour, un port.

III. (*compound verbs*) **1. clear away,** *v.tr. & i.* enlever, ôter, faire disparaître (qch.); écarter (un obstacle); **to c. one's things away,** ranger ses affaires; **to c. away (a meal),** enlever, ôter, le couvert, la nappe; desservir.

2. clear off; (*a*) *v.tr.* purger (une hypothèque); s'acquitter (de ses dettes); *Com:* solder (des marchandises); **to c. off arrears of work,** rattraper l'arriéré de besogne; se remettre à jour, au courant; (*b*) *v.i.* (i) (*of rain*) cesser; (ii) *F:* s'en aller, filer, décamper, *P:* fiche(r) le camp.

3. clear out; (*a*) *v.tr.* nettoyer (une chambre); vider (une armoire), débarrasser (un grenier); désencombrer, déblayer (un couloir); décombler (un puits); déblayer, évacuer (des débris); liquider, placer (des stocks); évacuer (des locataires); balayer (tout le personnel); *F:* **these expenses have completely cleared me out,** ces dépenses m'ont complètement désargenté; (*b*) *v.i. F:* filer, déguerpir, se sauver; vider les lieux; débarrasser le plancher; *P:* fiche(r) le camp; **he had to c. out of the country,** il fut obligé de passer la frontière; **c. out!** filez! hors d'ici! débarrassez le plancher! *P:* va-t'en voir si j'y suis!

4. clear up, *v.tr.* (*a*) (re)mettre (une pièce) en ordre; ranger (ses affaires); (*b*) éclaircir, dissiper (un malentendu); éclaircir, élucider (un mystère); dénouer, démêler (une situation, intrigue); résoudre (une difficulté); **to c. up a matter,** tirer une affaire au clair; mettre une affaire au point; faire la lumière sur une affaire; en avoir le cœur net; *s.a.* CLEAR[2] II.1(*a*).

clearance ['kliərəns], *s.* **1.** (*a*) = CLEARING 3; **slum c.,** élimination *f* des taudis; **c. area,** quartier *m* (insalubre) à démolir; *Nau:* **port c., beach c.,** (i) dégagement *m*, évacuation *f*, du frêt, débarqué dans un port, sur une plage; (ii) moyens *mpl*, facilités *fpl*, de dégagement, d'évacuation, du frêt dans un port, sur une plage; *Com:* **c. (sale),** vente *f* de soldes; liquidation *f*; réalisation *f* du stock; *For:* **c. of the felling area,** vidange *f* de la coupe; *F:* **to have a good c.,** se décharger, se débarrasser, le ventre; *Physiol:* **renal c.,** (i) temps *m* d'épuration; clearance *f*; (ii) épreuve *f* d'épuration; (*b*) *For:* défrichement *m*. **2.** (*a*) *Cust: Nau:* acquit(tement) *m* (de marchandises); expédition *f* en douane; déclaration *f* en douane à la sortie; dédouanage *m*, dédouanement *m*, congé *m*; **c. inwards,** (i) déclaration; (ii) permis *m*, d'entrée; **c. outwards,** (i) déclaration; (ii) permis *m*, de sortie; congé des douanes; **c. certificate,** lettre *f* de mer; **to effect customs c.,** procéder aux formalités de la douane; (*b*) affranchissement *m* (d'un domaine grevé); (*c*) *Mil: etc:* congé, libération *f* (d'un officier, d'un fonctionnaire); (*d*) *Nau:* départ *m* (du port); (*e*) *Av:* **flight c.,** autorisation *f* de vol, de décoller; (*f*) *Adm: Mil:* **security c.,** certificat *m* d'habilitation (à un degré de secret). **3.** *Bank:* (i) compensation *f*; (ii) présentation *f* à l'encaissement (d'un chèque). **4.** *Tchn:* espace *m* libre; jeu *m*, liberté *f*, chasse *f* (d'un piston, etc.); voie *f* (d'une scie); claire-voie *f*, *pl.* claires-voies, jour *m*, écartement *m* (entre barreaux); entrefer *m* (entre tôles, etc.); affranchissement, dépouille *f*, dégagement *m* (d'un outil tranchant); creux *m* (d'une roue dentée); débattement *m* (de parties qui pourraient se heurter); *Tls:* **c. angle,** angle *m* de dépouille, d'incidence; **to give c. to a cutting tool,** affranchir un outil tranchant; *Mec.E:* **bearing c.,** jeu de palier; **side c.,** jeu latéral; **bottom c.,** jeu à fond de course, à fond de dents, à fond de filet; **running c.,** jeu de fonctionnement; **permissible c.,** jeu tolérable; *Av:* **propeller c.,** angle de garde; **c. (space),** (i) *Mch:* espace nuisible (du cylindre); (ii) *El:* (*in dynamo, etc.*) intervalle *m*; (iii) *Civ.E:* hauteur libre, maximale; tirant *m* d'air; *Civ.E:* **limited c.,** hauteur limitée; *I.C.E:* **valve c.,** jeu aux queues de soupapes; **c. losses,** (i) pertes dues au jeu du piston, au dégagement; (ii) (*at cylinder end*) pertes de l'espace mort; (iii) (*turbine*) pertes par interstices; **there is not enough c. for the barges under the bridge,** le pont manque de hauteur pour laisser passer les péniches.

Clearchus [kli'ɑːkəs], *Pr.n.m. Gr.Hist:* Cléarque.

clearcole ['kliəkoul], *s.* **1.** *Paint:* encollage blanc; couche *f* d'encollage; première couche. **2.** *Gilding:* encollage.

clear-cut[1] ['kliə'kʌt], *a.* (*a*) (contours *mpl*) d'une grande netteté; **c.-c. features,** traits nettement dessinés; (*b*) **c.-c. opinion,** opinion nette, bien définie, tranchée; **c.-c. orders,** ordres précis; (*c*) **c.-c. division,** division nette, brutale.

clear-cut[2], *v.tr. For:* couper à blanc.

clearer ['kliərər], *s.* **1.** *Fin:* (*a*) membre *m* d'une banque de virement; (*b*) banque de virement, *F:* de clearing. **2.** *Dy:* aviveur *m*. **3.** (*a*) débouchoir *m*; (*b*) **track c.,** (i) *Rail:* chasse-pierres *m inv*; (ii) *Agr:* sabot séparateur (de moissonneuse). **4.** *Tex:* débourreur *m*.

clear-eyed ['kliəraid], *a.* **1.** aux yeux clairs. **2.** = CLEAR-SIGHTED.

clear-fell ['kliəfel], *v.tr. For:* couper à blanc.

clear-felling [kliə'feliŋ], *s. For:* coupe blanche.

clear-headed ['kliə'hedid], *a.* **1.** (*a*) qui voit juste; (*b*) perspicace; à l'esprit net, qui voit net. **2. I was quite c.-h.,** j'avais toute ma tête; je n'étais pas du tout gris; j'avais toute ma lucidité d'esprit.

clear-headedness [kliə'hedidnis], *s.* **1.** perspicacité *f*. **2.** lucidité *f*.

clearing ['kliəriŋ], *s.* **1.** (*a*) **to wait for the c. of the weather,** attendre que le temps se remette au beau; attendre une éclaircie, *Nau:* une embellie; (*b*) clarification *f* (d'un liquide); *Phot:* **c. bath,** bain clarificateur, clarifiant; *Sug.-R:* **c. pan,** claire *f*. **2. c. of s.o. (from a charge),** justification *f*, désinculpation, de qn. **3.** (*a*) dégagement *m*, déblaiement *m* (d'une voie); enlèvement *m* (de débris); défrichement *m*, essartage *m* (d'un terrain); curage *m* (des fossés); éclaircissement *m* (d'une forêt); dépuration *f* (d'un liquide); **c. plough,** déboiseuse *f*, défricheuse *f*; *Lap:* **c. iron,** débouchoir *m*; **you do the c. and I'll wash up,** tu vas débarrasser (la table) et moi je ferai la vaisselle; (*b*) évacuation *f* (d'une salle); *Mil:* **c. station, c. hospital,** centre *m*, hôpital, -aux *m*, de triage, d'évacuation (de blessés); **c. of the letter box, of the mail,** levée *f* des lettres, de la boîte aux lettres; *Cmptr:* **c. signal,** signal, -aux *m* de libération; *Physiol:* **c. of the bowels,** décharge *f* du ventre; (*c*) **c. of goods, merchandise,** liquidation *f*, solde *m*. **4.** franchissement *m* (d'une barrière). **5.** (*a*) expédition *f* (d'un navire); acquittement *m* des droits (sur des marchandises); dédouanement *m*; (*b*) acquittement (de dettes); liquidation (d'un compte); affranchissement *m* (d'un bien); (*c*) *Fin:* compensation *f* (de chèques); **country c.,** virement *m*; **under the c. procedure,** par voie de compensation; **c. agreement,** accord *m* de compensation, de clearing; **c. bank,** banque *f* de virement, de clearing; **c. house,** (i) *Fin:* chambre *f* de liquidation, de compensation; comptoir général de virement; comptoir de règlement; clearing *m*; (ii) *Rail: etc:* bureau central; **to pass a cheque through the c. house,** compenser un chèque. **6.** (*in forest*) éclaircie, clairière *f*, clair *m*; recepée *f*, recépée *f*; arrachis *m* de bois; sommière *f*; **c. in the sky,** éclaircie, *Nau:* embellie, dans le ciel. **7.** = CLEARANCE 4.

clearing away ['kliəriŋə'wei], *s.* enlèvement *m* (de débris, des couverts, etc.).

clearing off ['kliəriŋ'ɔf], *s.* acquittement *m* (d'une dette); solde *m*, liquidation *f* (de marchandises).

clearing out ['kliəriŋ'aut], *s.* **1.** nettoiement *m*, nettoyage *m* (d'une chambre). **2.** évacuation *f* (de locataires); balayage *m* (du personnel).

clearing up ['kliəriŋ'ʌp], *s.* **1.** remise *f* en ordre (de la maison, etc.). **2.** éclaircissement *m* (d'un mystère).

clearly [kliəli], *adv.* **1.** clair, clairement, nettement; **to see, speak, c.,** voir, parler, clair; **it was too dark to see c.,** il faisait trop noir pour bien distinguer; **he has seen c. into the past,** il a pénétré le passé; **to distinguish c.,** distinguer clairement, nettement; **to explain c.,** expliquer clairement, d'une manière claire; **you must c. understand that. . .,** il vous faut bien comprendre que . . .. **2.** évidemment; (*a*) **he is c. wrong,** il est clair qu'il a tort; (*b*) **I was wrong?—c.,** j'ai eu tort?—évidemment; sans aucun doute.

clearness ['kliənis], *s.* **1.** clarté *f*, transparence *f*, limpidité *f* (de l'eau, de l'atmosphère, etc.). **2.** netteté *f* (d'une image, de l'esprit, des idées); **c. of vision,** (i) lucidité *f* de vue; (ii) intelligence *f* lucide. **3.** liberté *f*, dégagement *m* (des routes).

clear(-)out ['kliəraut], *s.* **1.** = CLEARING OUT. **2.** *F:* **to have a c.-o.,** aller à la selle.

clear-sighted ['kliə'saitid], *a.* **1.** à la vue nette. **2.** clairvoyant; qui voit juste.

clear-sightedness [kliə'saitidnis], *s.* **1.** netteté *f* de vision. **2.** clairvoyance *f*.

clearskins ['kliəskinz], *s.pl. Austr:* bétail non marqué au fer chaud.

clear-starch ['kliəstɑ:tʃ], *v.tr. A:* blanchir (le linge) à neuf.

clear-starching ['kliəstɑ:tʃiŋ], *s. A:* blanchissage *m* de fin, à neuf.

clearstory ['kliəstɔ:ri], *s.* = CLERESTORY.

clear-toned ['kliə'tound], *a.* au timbre clair, pur.

clear-up ['kliərʌp], *s.* (*a*) remise *f* en ordre (d'une chambre); (*b*) solde *m* (d'un compte).

clearway ['kliəwei], *s. Adm:* grande route à stationnement interdit.

clearweed ['kliəwi:d], *s. Bot:* pilea *m* pumila.

clearwing ['kliəwiŋ], *s. Ent:* lépidoptère *m* aux ailes transparentes, (i) égérie *f*; (ii) sésie *f*; **hornet c. moth,** sésie apiforme.

cleat[1] [kli:t], *s.* **1.** (*a*) (*strip of wood*) tasseau *m*, agrafe *f*, languette *f* (de bois); **stop c.,** taquet *m* d'arrêt; *Nau:* cabrion *m* d'arrêt; (*b*) **girder c.,** attache *f* de poutre; **roof-purlin c.,** échantignole *f*. **2.** *Nau:* **(belaying-)c.,** taquet (de tournage); **shroud c.,** taquet de hauban; **comb c.,** pomme gougée. **3.** *El:* serre-câble(s) *m inv.*, serre-fils *m inv*, barrette *f* de connexion. **4.** *pl. Min:* **cleats,** plans *m* de clivage (de la houille).

cleat[2], *v.tr.* assujettir (un cordage à un taquet, etc.).

cleavability [kli:və'biliti], *s.* fissilité *f*.

cleavable ['kli:vəbl], *a.* **1.** qui peut se fendre; fissile. **2.** *Geol: Miner:* clivable.

cleavage ['kli:vidʒ], *s.* **1.** (*a*) fendage *m*; *Geol: Miner:* clivage *m*; (*in schists*) délit *m*; **fracture c., flux c.,** clivage de fracture, de flux; **c. plane,** plan *m* de clivage; (*b*) *Biol:* division *f* (d'une cellule); **bilateral c.,** segmentation bilatérale; **c. cavity,** cavité *f* de segmentation; **c. cell, c. globule,** blastomère *m*; (*c*) sillon *m* mammaire (qui se laisse voir par une échancrure provocante du corsage). **2.** fissure *f*, scission *f* (dans un parti).

cleave[1] [kli:v], *v.* (*p.t.* **cleaved, cleft** [kleft], *Lit:* **clove** [klouv], *B:* **clave** [kleiv]; *p.p.* **cleaved, cleft,** *Lit:* **cloven** [klouvn]) **1.** *v.tr.* (*a*) *Lit:* fendre (le bois, le fer); **to c. a tree in two, asunder,** fendre un arbre en deux; (*b*) *Geol: Miner:* cliver (un cristal); (*c*) (*of bird, ship*) fendre (l'air, les eaux); **to c. the waves,** tailler la lame; **to c. (one's way through) the crowd,** fendre la foule. **2.** *v.i.* (*a*) *Lit:* **to c. (asunder),** se fendre, se feuilleter; (*b*) (*of crystals*) se cliver; (*c*) **to c. through the water, the crowd,** fendre l'eau, la foule.

cleave[2], *v.i.* (*p.t.* **cleaved** [kli:vd], *Lit:* **clave** [kleiv]; *p.p.* **cleaved**) adhérer. **1.** *Lit:* **to c. to s.o., to a party, to a principle, to a practice,** s'attacher, être fidèle, à qn, à un parti; être fidèle à un principe; conserver, garder, un usage; **to c. to an opinion,** adhérer à une opinion. **2.** *A:* (*of thg*) **to c. to sth.,** s'attacher, (se) coller, adhérer, à qch.; **his tongue clave to his palate,** sa langue se colla à son palais; la langue lui colla au palais.

cleaver ['kli:vər], *s.* **1.** (*pers.*) fendeur *m*. **2.** *Tls:* fendoir *m*; (*for meat*) couperet *m*, osseret *m*; (*for wood*) merlin *m*.

cleavers ['kli:vəz], *s. Bot:* gaillet accrochant; grat(t)eron *m*.

cleaving ['kli:viŋ], *s.* fendage *m*; refente *f* (du bois); *Miner:* clivage *m*; **c. axe,** hache *f* de fendage; merlin *m*; **c. saw,** scie *f* à refendre; **c. knife,** fendoir *m*.

cleek [kli:k], *s. Golf:* cleek *m*.

clef [klef], *s. Mus:* clef *f*; **bass c.,** clef de fa; **treble c.,** clef de sol; **C c.,** clef d'ut.

cleft[1] [kleft], *a.* fendu; **c. stick,** piquet fourchu; *Fig:* **to be in a c. stick,** se trouver dans une impasse, dans une mauvaise passe; *Med:* **c. palate,** palais fendu.

cleft[2], *s.* fente *f*, fissure *f*, crevasse *f*; interstice *m*; *Anat:* scissure *f*; *Metall:* paille *f*.

cleft-graft ['kleftgrɑ:ft], *v.tr. Arb:* greffer en fente simple.

cleg [kleg], *s. Dial:* (*esp. Scot:*) taon *m*.

cleidorrhexis [klaidou'reksis], *s. Obst:* cléidorrhexie *f*.

cleidotomy [klai'dɔtəmi], *s. Obst:* cléidotomie *f*.

cleistocarp ['klaistoukɑ:p], *s. Fung:* cléistocarpe *f*.

cleistocarpous [klaistou'kɑ:pəs], *a. Bot:* cléistocarpe, cléistocarpique.

cleistogamic [klaistou'gæmik], **cleistogamous** [klai'stɔgəməs], *a. Bot:* cléistogame.

cleistogamy [klai'stɔgəmi], *s. Bot:* cléistogamie *f*.

clem [klem], *v.* **(clemmed)** *Dial:* **1.** *v.tr.* faire mourir (qn) de faim ou de soif. **2.** *v.i.* mourir, *P:* crever, de faim ou de soif; être transi de froid.

clematis ['klemətis, klə'meitis], *s. Bot:* clématite *f* (vigne-blanche); *F:* vigne *f* de Salomon; vigne blanche; viorne *f* des pauvres; herbe *f* aux gueux; berceau *m* de la Vierge.

clemency, *pl.* **-cies** ['klemənsi, -siz], *s.* **1.** clémence *f*, indulgence *f* (to, envers). **2.** douceur *f*, clémence (du temps).

clement[1] ['klemənt], *a.* **1.** (*of pers.*) clément, indulgent (to, envers, pour). **2.** (*of weather*) doux, *f.* douce; clément.

Clement[2], *Pr.n.m.* Clément.

Clementina [klemən'ti:nə], *Pr.n.f.* Clémentine.

Clementine ['klemənti:n, -ain]. **1.** *Pr.n.f.* Clémentine. **2.** *s. Hort:* **clementine,** clémentine *f*. **3.** *a.* **the C. Constitutions,** les Clémentines *f*.

clemently ['kleməntli], *adv.* avec clémence, avec indulgence.

clench[1] [klen(t)ʃ]. **1.** *v.tr.* = CLINCH[2] **1.** **2.** *v.tr.* serrer (les dents, le poing); **with clenched hands,** les mains crispées; **with teeth clenched in the effort to control himself,** les mâchoires contractées dans un effort de volonté; **to c. sth. in, with, one's hand,** serrer qch. dans la main. **3.** *v.i.* (*of teeth, the hands*) se serrer; (*of the hands*) se crisper.

clench[2], *s.* **1.** serrage *m*, étreinte *f* (de la main). **2.** pointe abattue (d'un clou rivé); **c. nail,** clou rivé, à river; rivet *m*.

clencher ['klen(t)ʃər], *s.* = CLINCHER.

cleome ['kli:oum], *s. Bot:* cléome *m*.

Cleopatra [kliə'pætrə], *Pr.n.f. A.Hist:* Cléopâtre; **Cleopatra's needle,** l'Obélisque *m* de Cléopâtre.

clepsydra ['klepsidrə], *s.* clepsydre *f*.

clerestory ['kliəstɔ:ri], *s.* **1.** *Ecc.Arch:* fenêtres hautes. **2.** *Const:* lanterneau *m* (de toit).

clergy ['klə:dʒi], *s.* (*no pl.*) **1.** *coll.* clergé *m*; **c. house,** presbytère *m*. **2.** (*with pl.const.*) membres *m* du clergé; **at least five hundred c. were present at the ceremony,** au moins cinq cents ecclésiastiques *m* ont assisté à la cérémonie. **3.** *A:* clergie *f*; *Hist:* **benefit of c.,** bénéfice *m* de clergie; *F:* **to live, take up, with s.o. without benefit of c.,** se marier avec qn de la main gauche.

clergyman, *pl.* **-men** ['klə:dʒimən], *s.m.* ecclésiastique; ministre (du culte); pasteur (protestant); prêtre (catholique ou anglican); clergyman, *pl.* -men (anglais ou américain); *F:* **clergyman's (sore) throat,** pharyngite *f* chronique.

cleric ['klerik]. **1.** *s.* = CLERGYMAN. **2.** *a. A:* = CLERICAL 1.

clerical ['klerik(ə)l]. **1.** *a.* clérical, -aux; (i) du parti du clergé; (ii) du clergé; **to wear c. dress,** *F:* **to wear clericals,** porter l'habit ecclésiastique; **c. outfitter,** chasublier *m*; **c. outfitters,** chasublerie *f*; **c. voice,** voix affectée, voix d'ainsi-soit-il. **2.** *a.* (*a*) **c. error,** faute *f* de copiste; erreur *f* de plume; *Book-k:* erreur d'écritures; (*b*) **c. work,** travail *m* d'écritures, de bureau; **c. staff,** personnel *m* de bureau; employés *mpl* de bureau; commis *mpl* aux écritures; (*in lawyer's office*) cléricature *f*. **3.** *s.pl. Pol:* **the clericals,** les cléricaux *m*.

clericalism ['klerikəlizm], *s. Pol: Pej:* cléricalisme *m*; *P:* la calotte.

clericalist ['klerikəlist], *s. Pol: Pej:* cléricaliste *m*; *P:* calotin *m*.

clericalize ['klerikəlaiz], *v.tr. Pol:* cléricaliser (les écoles, etc.).

clerically ['klerik(ə)li], *adv.* cléricalement.

clerico-political ['klerikoupə'litik(ə)l], *a.* politico-religieux, -euse, *pl.* politico-religieux, -euses.

clerid ['klerid], *s. Ent:* cléridé *m*.

clerihew ['klerihju:], *s.* poème amusant en deux couplets.

clerk[1] [klɑ:k, *NAm:* klə:k], *s.* **1.** (*a*) employé, -ée, de bureau; commis *m*; clerc *m* (d'avoué); **bank c.,** employé, -ée, de banque; **chief c., senior c., head c., managing c.,** chef *m* de bureau; commis principal; premier commis; (*in lawyer's office*) premier clerc, maître-clerc, *pl.* maîtres-clercs; **junior c.,** petit employé; *F:* saute-ruisseau *m inv*; **copying c.,** expéditionnaire *m*, *F:* gratte-papier *m inv*; **filing c.,** *U.S:* **file c.,** fichiste *m*, employé au classement; **records c.,** archiviste *m*; **shipping c.,** (commis) expéditionnaire, employé de l'expédition; *Rail:* **booking c.,** préposé à la distribution, délivrance, des billets; employé du guichet; *Post:* **telegraph c.,** employé(e) du télégraphe, buraliste *mf*; (*b*) *Jur:* **c. of the court,** greffier *m* (du tribunal); **c. of the court's office,** greffe *m*; **you should apply to the c. of the court,** il faut vous adresser au greffe. **2.** *Ecc:* (*a*) **c. (in holy orders),** clerc; ecclésiastique *m*; *R.C.Ch:* **c. regular,** clerc régulier; (*b*) (*of cathedral choir*) chantre *m*; (*c*) **parish c.,** clerc de paroisse. **3.** *A:* (*scholar*) savant *m*, clerc; **I'm no great c.,** je ne suis pas grand clerc. **4.** (*a*) **c. of (the) works,** (i) *Const:* conducteur *m* des travaux; (ii) *Civ.E:* conducteur des ponts et chaussées; (*b*) *F:* **the C. of the weather,** la providence qui régit la pluie et le beau temps; (*c*) *Rac:* **c. of the course,** commissaire *m* de la piste. **5.** *NAm:* (*a*) vendeur, -euse (de magasin), commis (de magasin); (*b*) préposé(e) à la réception (d'un hôtel).

clerk[2], *v.i.* **1.** travailler comme employé(e) de bureau. **2.** *NAm:* **to c. in a store,** travailler comme vendeur, euse, dans un magasin.

clerkess ['klɑ:kes], *s.f. A: & Dial:* employée.

clerkly ['klɑ:kli], *a. A:* **1.** de bureau; **c. hand,** (i) écriture moulée; (ii) écriture de bureau. **2.** docte, savant, lettré.

clerkship ['klɑ:kʃip], *s.* **1.** *Adm: Com:* emploi *m*, place *f*, de commis, d'employé. **2.** *Jur:* (*a*) emploi, place, de clerc (de *solicitor*, etc.); cléricature *f*; (*b*) **c. to the court,** fonctions *fpl*, place, de greffier.

clerodendron [klerə'dendrən], *s. Bot:* clerodendron *m*.

cleruch ['kleruk], *s. Gr.Hist:* clérouque *m*.

cleruchy ['kleruki], *s. Gr.Hist:* clérouquie *f*.

clethra ['kli:θrə, 'kleθ-], *s. Bot:* clèthre *m*.

cleveite ['kli:vait], *s. Miner:* clévéite *f*.

clever ['klevər], *a.* **1.** (*dexterous*) habile, adroit; **he is c. with his hands,** il est adroit, agile, de ses mains, des mains; il a la main adroite; *F:* il n'est pas manchot; **footballer c. at footwork,** joueur de football adroit des pieds; **c. at his trade,** habile dans son métier; **c. at doing sth.,** habile, adroit, ingénieux, à faire qch.; **to be c. with one's pencil,** savoir bien dessiner; *F:* **to play (it) c., to box c.,** jouer serré. **2.** (*a*) intelligent; qui a de l'esprit; (chien, etc.) savant; **to be c.,** être intelligent; **a c. child,** un enfant à l'intelligence éveillée; *Sch:* **c. at mathematics,** fort en mathématiques; **c. at making sauces,** savant à préparer les sauces; *F: Pej:* **that's clever!** ça c'est intelligent! (*b*) (*smart*) *Pej: F:* **a c. Dick, stick,** un je-sais-tout; **c.-c. style,** style ampoulé; **he was too c. for us,** il nous a roulés; il nous a mis dedans; (*c*) (*done with skill*) bien fait; **c. parody,** parodie pleine de finesse; (*d*) **c. device,** dispositif ingénieux **3.** *NAm:* obligeant; aimable. **4.** *Austr: F:* **not to be too c.,** se sentir peu valide; n'être pas dans son assiette.

cleverly ['klevəli], *adv.* habilement, adroitement; avec adresse; avec intelligence; bien.

cleverness ['klevənis], *s.* **1.** habileté *f*, adresse *f*, dextérité *f*; **c. at doing sth.,** habileté à faire qch. **2.** intelligence *f*; **at an early age he showed great c.,** dès sa jeunesse il se révéla très intelligent, il montra de grands moyens. **3.** ingéniosité *f* (d'une invention, d'un mécanisme).

clevis ['klevis], *s.* **1.** crochet *m* à ressort, crochet de sûreté. **2.** manille *f* d'assemblage; maillon *m* d'attache, de jonction, chape *f*; étrier *m*; **c.-pin,** axe *m* de chape; broche *f* d'étrier.

clew[1] [klu:], *s.* **1.** (*a*) pelote *f* (de fil); (*b*) *Myth:* fil conducteur (du Labyrinthe); **Ariadne's c.,** le fil d'Ariane. **2.** *Nau:* (*a*) araignée *f* (de hamac); (*b*) point *m* d'écoute (de voile); **weather c.,** point de vent; **lee c.,** point sous le vent; **c. garnet,** cargue-point *m* (de basse voile), *pl.* cargues-points; **c. line,** cargue-point (de haute voile); amure *f* (de voile); **c. rope,** faux point. **3.** (*in N. of Engl., Scot: & NAm:*) = CLUE[1] 2.

clew[2], *v.tr.* **1.** *Nau:* **to c. (up) the sails,** carguer les voiles. **2.** = CLUE[2].

cliché ['kli:ʃei], *s.* **1.** *Typ:* cliché *m*. **2.** (*stereotyped phrase*) cliché.

click[1] [klik], *s.* **1.** bruit sec, clic *m* (d'un pistolet qu'on arme, etc.); cliquetis *m* (d'épées); *Tg:* claquement *m* (du manipulateur); **c. clack,** tic-tac *m* (d'un moulin, d'un métier à tisser); *Ent:* **c. beetle,** élatère *m*; *F:* taupin *m*; scarabée *m* à ressort; tape-marteau *m*, *pl.* tape-marteaux. **2.** **c. (of the tongue),** coup *m* de langue; *Equit:* appel *m* de langue; *Ling:* clic. **3.** *Tchn:* cliquet *m*, chien *m*; doigt *m* d'encliquetage; déclic *m*; détente *f*;

c. and ratchet, encliquetage *m*; **c. wheel,** roue *f* à cliquet, à rochet, à chien; *Fish:* **c. reel,** moulinet *m* à cliquet.

click[2]. **1.** *v.i.* cliqueter, faire tic-tac; (*of horse*) forger; **cameras were clicking all round,** partout les déclics des appareils; **the two parts c. together,** les deux parties s'assemblent avec un bruit sec. **2.** *v.tr.* **to c. one's heels,** (faire) claquer les talons (en saluant); **to c. one's tongue,** claquer la langue, clapper de la langue; **to c. the shutter of a camera,** déclencher l'obturateur d'un appareil. **3.** *v.i. P:* (*a*) (*of two pers.*) se plaire du premier coup; s'entendre à merveille dès l'abord; **they've clicked,** ils se plaisent; ils sont inséparables; **he's clicked with her,** il a une touche avec elle; (*b*) (*of things*) aller ensemble; (*c*) **that clicks!** ça me rappelle quelque chose! (*d*) atteindre son but; (*of play, etc.*) réussir; (*in business*) décrocher la timbale; gagner le gros lot; (*e*) *O:* concevoir; **she told him she'd clicked and he must marry her,** elle lui a dit que ça y était et qu'il fallait qu'il l'épouse; (*f*) *Mil:* être tué; *P:* passer l'arme à gauche. **4.** *v.tr. P:* (*a*) *O:* **to c. it,** écoper; **to c. a bad attack of malaria,** attraper une crise de paludisme; (*b*) *v.ind.tr. Mil:* **to c. for a fatigue,** écoper d'une corvée.

click[3], *s. Wr:* croc-en-jambe *m*, *pl.* crocs-en-jambe.

clicker ['klikər], *s.* **1.** *Typ:* metteur *m* en pages. **2.** *Toys: F:* criquet *m*.

clickety-click ['klikəti'klik], (*a*) *s.* & *adv.* clic-clac (*m*), clic-clic (*m*); (*b*) *s. F:* soixante-six.

clicking ['klikiŋ], *s.* = CLICK[1] 1, 2.

client ['klaiənt], *s.* **1.** *Rom.Ant:* client *m* (d'un patricien). **2.** (*a*) client, -ente (dans les professions libérales); (*of stockbroker*) donneur *m* d'ordres; (*b*) *Com:* client, -ente (d'un magasin).

clientage ['klaiəntidʒ], **clientele, clientèle** [kliɑn'tel, kliɑ̃tel], *s.* clientèle *f* (i) *Rom.Ant:* d'un patricien, (ii) dans les professions libérales, (iii) d'un magasin, etc.

Clifden blue ['klifdən'blu:], *s. Ent:* (papillon) adonis *m*.

cliff [klif], *s.* **1.** à-pic *m*, *pl.* à-pics; falaise *f*; *Mount:* varappe *f*; **c. climber,** escaladeur *m* de falaises; varappeur *m*; **c.-climbing expedition,** varappée *f*; **c. dweller,** (i) *Prehist:* **c.-dwellers,** cliff dwellers *m*; (ii) troglodyte *m*; (iii) *NAm:* locataire *mf* d'un gratte-ciel. **2.** *Golf:* face *f* (d'une banquette).

cliff-chat ['kliftʃæt], *s. Orn:* traquet *m* de roche.

cliffed [klift], *a.* en falaise; escarpé; à pic.

cliffhang ['klifhæŋ], *v.i.* être au bord du précipice, du gouffre.

cliffhanger ['klifhæŋər], *s. Journ:* roman-feuilleton *m*, *pl.* romans-feuilletons (dont chaque épisode se termine par un suspense); film *m*, pièce *f* de théâtre, à gros effets, mélodramatique; **the election, race, was a c.,** le résultat de l'élection, de la course, a été douteux jusqu'au dernier moment.

cliffsman, *pl.* **-men** ['klifsmən], *s.m.* escaladeur de falaises; varappeur.

cliffy ['klifi], *a.* = CLIFFED.

Clifton blue ['kliftən'blu:], *s. Ent:* (papillon *m*) adonis.

climacteric [klai'mæktərik]. **1.** *a. A.Med:* climatérique; **the c. years,** les années climatériques (multiples de 7); **c. diseases,** maladies climatériques, dues à la sénilité. **2.** *s.* (*a*) **the (grand) c.,** la grande climatérique (63 ans); (*b*) ménopause *f*.

climactic [klai'mæktik], *a. Rh: etc:* **1.** (arrangement *m*) par gradation, en série ascendante. **2.** arrivé à son apogée.

climate ['klaimət], *s.* climat *m*; **I have lived in all climates,** j'ai vécu sous tous les climats; **she must avoid a hot c.,** il faut qu'elle évite les pays chauds; *Fig:* **I can't work in a hostile c.,** je ne peux pas travailler dans un climat, une ambiance, hostile; **the c. of public opinion,** l'état *m* de l'opinion (publique).

climatic [klai'mætik], *a.* (*a*) (zone *f*, etc.) climatique; **c. conditions,** conditions *f* climatiques; climature *f*; **c. diseases,** maladies spéciales à certains climats, maladies climatiques; **c. influence,** influence *f* climatique; (*b*) *Biol:* **c. variation,** variation *f* climatologique.

climatize ['klaimətaiz], *v.tr.* acclimater (une plante, etc.).

climatological [klaimətə'lɔdʒik(ə)l], *a.* climatologique; **c. conditions,** climature *f*.

climatologist [klaimə'tɔlədʒist], *s.* climatologue *mf*, climatologiste *mf*.

climatology [klaimə'tɔlədʒi], *s.* climatologie *f*.

climatotherapeutic ['klaimətouθerə'pju:tik], *a.* climatothérapeutique, climatothérapique.

climatotherapy ['klaimətou'θerəpi], *s.* climatothérapie *f*.

climature ['klaimətʃər, -tjər], *s.* climature *f*, climat *m*.

climax[1] ['klaimæks], *s.* **1.** *Rh:* gradation (ascendante). **2.** comble *m*, apogée *m*, faîte *m*, point culminant, plus haut point (de la renommée, etc.); **c. of an illness,** l'apogée d'une maladie; **the c. of a fine life,** le couronnement d'une belle vie; **this brought matters to a c.,** ce fut le comble; **to work up to a c.,** (i) procéder par gradation (ascendante); (ii) *Th: etc: F:* corser l'action; amener la grande scène; **at the c. of the epidemic,** au plus fort de l'épidémie; **to form a c.,** mettre le comble à l'étonnement, à la joie, à la terreur, etc.; **as a c. to the entertainment . . .,** comme bouquet de la fête . . .. **3.** *Bot:* climax *m*; **edaphic c.,** climax édaphique; **climatic c.,** formation climatique finale, formation climacique. **4.** *Physiol:* orgasme *m*.

climax[2]. **1.** *v.tr.* amener (qch.) au point culminant. **2.** *v.i.* atteindre le point culminant, le comble.

climaxing ['klaimæksiŋ], *a.* culminant; **that was the c. stroke,** ce fut le comble.

climb[1] [klaim], *s.* **1.** (*a*) ascension *f*, montée *f*; *Mount:* course *f* (dans les montagnes); escalade *f*, ascension (d'une paroi abrupte); *Aut:* **hill c.,** course de côte; (*b*) *Av:* **rate of c.,** vitesse ascensionnelle, de montée. **2.** côte *f*, montée, rampe *f*, remontée *f* (d'une route, etc.); **steep c.,** grimpette *f*.

climb[2]. **1.** *v.i.* & *tr.* monter, gravir (l'escalier); grimper à (un arbre); monter à (l'échelle); escalader (une falaise, une varappe); *Aut:* **to c. a hill in top (gear),** monter une côte en prise directe; **to c. (up) to the top of sth.,** monter au sommet de qch.; **to c. (up) a mountain,** gravir une montagne; faire l'ascension *f* d'une montagne; **to c. up a wall,** (*of pers.*) se hisser le long d'un mur; escalader un mur; (*of snail, creeper, etc.*) grimper sur un mur; *F:* **it was enough to make you c. up the wall,** il y avait de quoi devenir fou; **to c. over the wall,** escalader, franchir, le mur; **to c. on to the roof,** monter, grimper, sur le toit; **to c. down the cliff,** descendre la falaise; **to c. down the tree, the ladder,** descendre de l'arbre, de l'échelle; **to c. through an opening,** se hisser par une ouverture; **to c. out of a hole,** grimper, se hisser, en dehors d'un trou; se tirer d'un trou; **to c. into bed,** grimper dans son lit; **to c. into a pair of overalls,** enfiler des bleus; **if you knew how many stairs we climbed!** si vous saviez les escaliers qu'on a monté(s)! **to c. a rung of the social ladder,** gravir un échelon social. **2.** *v.i.* (*a*) **the road climbs,** la route monte, va en montant; **prices are climbing,** les prix montent, augmentent; (*b*) (*of mountaineer*) (i) faire des ascensions; (ii) faire de la varappe, varapper; (*c*) **to c. to power,** s'élever au pouvoir; **to c. (socially, in the world),** faire son chemin; parvenir; (*d*) *Av:* prendre de l'altitude, de la hauteur; monter. **3.** *v.i.* **to c. down,** (*a*) descendre (**from a tree,** d'un arbre); **it took us two hours to c. down,** il nous a fallu deux heures pour descendre; (*b*) *F:* en rabattre; reculer; baisser pavillon; changer de gamme, rétracter ses paroles; se rétracter; *P:* caner; se dégonfler.

climbable ['klaiməbl], *a.* qui peut être (i) gravi, (ii) escaladé; **c. tree,** arbre où il est facile de grimper.

climb-down ['klaim'daun], *s.* **1.** descente *f*. **2.** *F:* abandon *m* de ses prétentions; défaite *f*; reculade *f*; **a miserable c.-d.,** une honteuse reculade.

climber ['klaimər], *s.* **1.** (*a*) alpiniste *mf*; varappeur *m* (d'un à-pic); grimpeur *m* (à un arbre); (*b*) *P:* cambrioleur *m* acrobatique; monte-en-l'air *m inv*; (*c*) **(social) c.,** arriviste *mf*. **2.** *A:* **this car is a good c.,** cette voiture est bonne grimpeuse; **these planes are good climbers,** ces avions montent vite. **3.** *Bot:* plante grimpante. **4.** *Orn:* grimpeur. **5.** *pl.* **climbers,** crampons *m*, grappins *m*, grimpettes *f*. **6.** *Rail:* roue dentée (de wagon de chemin de fer à crémaillère).

climbing[1] ['klaimiŋ], *a.* **c. bird,** (oiseau) grimpeur; *A:* **c. boy,** petit ramoneur; petit savoyard; *Bot:* **c. plant,** plante grimpante; *Av:* **c. flight,** vol ascendant.

climbing[2], *s.* **1.** escalade *f*; montée *f*; ascension *f* (d'un arbre); *Av:* remontée *f* (après descente); **c. irons,** crampons *m*, grappins *m*, grimpettes *f*; griffes *f* de monteur; étriers *m* (pour l'ascension des arbres); **alpine c., mountain c.,** alpinisme *m*; *Mount:* **artificial c.,** escalade artificielle; **c. speed,** *Aut:* vitesse *f* en montée; *Av:* vitesse ascensionnelle; *Aut:* **c. ability,** tenue *f* en côte (d'une voiture); *Aut: Rail: etc:* **c. power,** pouvoir *m* de traction en rampe, en côte. **2. the art of c.,** l'art *m* de parvenir; l'arrivisme *m*.

clime [klaim], *s. Poet:* climat *m*; pays *m*, région *f*; **to live in foreign climes,** vivre sous un ciel étranger.

climograph ['klaiməgræf], *s. Meteor:* climatogramme *m*.

clinandrium, *pl.* **-ia** [kli'nændriəm, -iə], *s. Bot:* clinandre *m*.

clinch[1] [klin(t)ʃ], *s.* **1.** (*a*) (i) rivet *m*, crampon *m*; (ii) pointe abattue (d'un clou rivé); **c. bolt,** rivet; **c. nail,** clou rivé, à river; rivet; (*b*) *Nau:* étalingure *f*; **anchor c.,** étalingure sur l'ancre; **inner c.,** étalingure du puits; (*c*) = CLINCHER 3. **2.** (*a*) *Box:* corps-à-corps *m*; clinch *m*; accrochage *m*; **to break a c.,** briser un corps-à-corps; **to go into a c.,** se prendre corps à corps; s'accrocher; (*b*) *F:* étreinte *f* (d'amoureux); **to go into a c.,** s'étreindre. **3. c. button,** bouton *m* fermoir.

clinch[2]. **1.** *v.tr.* (*a*) river (un clou); abattre, aplatir (un rivet, la pointe du clou); (*b*) *Nau:* étalinguer (une chaîne); **to c. the cables to the anchor,** étalinguer la chaîne; (*c*) conclure, clore, *F:* accrocher, boucler (un marché); confirmer (un argument); **that clinches the argument, that clinches it,** *F:* voilà qui vous rive votre clou; **clinching argument,** argument décisif. **2.** *v.i.* (*a*) *Box:* en venir aux prises; se prendre corps à corps; s'accrocher; (*b*) *F:* (*of lovers*) s'étreindre.

clincher ['klin(t)ʃər], *s.* **1.** *F:* argument *m* irréfutable, sans réplique; argument-massue *m*; **that was a c. for him!** ça lui a rivé son clou! **2.** (*a*) crampon *m*; (*b*) *Nau:* étalingure *f*. **3.** *Cy:* (*of wheel-rim*) accrochage *m*, gouttière *f*; **c. rim, c. tyre,** jante *f*, pneu *m*, à talon.

clincher-built ['klin(t)ʃə'bilt], *a.* = CLINKER-BUILT.

cline [klain], *s. Nat.Hist:* cline *f*.

cling[1] [kliŋ], *v.i.* (**clung** [klʌŋ]; **clung**) (*a*) (*of pers.*) s'attacher, s'accrocher, s'agriffer, s'agripper, se cramponner (**to s.o., to sth.,** à qn, à qch.); (*of burr*) s'attraper (to, à); **she clung to me,** elle se prit à moi; **to c. close to s.o.,** se serrer, se coller, contre qn; **to c. together, to one another,** (i) rester attachés l'un à l'autre; rester étroitement unis; (ii) se tenir étroitement enlacés; **village clinging to the hillside,** village accroché au flanc de la colline; (*b*) **to c. to an opinion,** rester attaché à une opinion; s'opiniâtrer, s'obstiner, dans une opinion; ne pas abandonner une opinion; **he clings to his principles,** il reste à cheval sur ses principes; **to c. to a hope,** se raccrocher, se cramponner, à un espoir; (*c*) adhérer (to, à); (*of plants*) s'attacher, s'accrocher (aux murs); **ivy clings to the tree,** le lierre s'attache, se noue, à l'arbre; (*of garment*) **to c. to the figure,** coller au corps; mouler le corps; épouser la forme du corps.

cling[2], *s.* **c. (peach),** = CLINGSTONE 1.

cling-fish ['kliŋ'fiʃ], *s. Ich:* gobiesocidé *m*.

clinginess ['kliŋinis], *s.* **1.** adhésivité *f* (de l'argile, etc.). **2.** (*of garment*) tendance *f* à s'attacher au corps.

clinging[1] ['kliŋiŋ], *a.* qui s'attache; qui colle; qui s'accroche; **c. garment, material,** vêtement collant; tissu *m* qui moule le corps; vêtement, étoffe, qui tend à s'attacher au corps; **c. nature,** naturel affectueux; **c. perfume,** parfum *m* tenace; *Bot:* **c. root,** crampon *m*.

clinging[2], *s.* attachement *m* (à une opinion, etc.).

clingstone ['kliŋstoun], *s.* **1. c. (peach),** (pavie *f*) alberge (*f*); pêche *f* à noyau adhérent. **2. c. (tree),** albergier *m*.

clingy ['kliŋi], *a.* (*of mud, garment, etc.*) collant.

clinic ['klinik], *s.* **1.** (*bedside instruction, class*) clinique *f*. **2.** (*treatment centre*) dispensaire *m*; **V.D. c.,** dispensaire antivénérien. **3.** (*nursing home*) clinique.

clinical ['klinik(ə)l], *a.* **1.** clinique; **c. lecture,** (leçon) clinique *f*; **c. thermometer,** thermomètre médical, de clinique. **2.** froid; **to examine a social problem with c. detachment,** examiner un problème social avec un détachement dépourvu de toute émotion; **her kitchen, all in white, is positively c.,** la blancheur de sa cuisine rappelle une salle d'opérations.

clinically ['klinik(ə)li], *adv.* **1.** *Med:* d'après la méthode clinique. **2.** froidement; sans émotion.

clinician [kli'niʃ(ə)n], *s.* clinicien *m*.

clinique [kli'ni:k], *s.* = CLINIC.

clink[1] [kliŋk], *s.* **1.** tintement *m*, choc *m* (de verres); cliquetis *m* (d'épées). **2.** *pl. U.S: P:* **clinks,** (i) monnaie *f*, argent *m*; (ii) glaçons *mpl* (dans un cocktail). **3.** *Civ.E:* pointe en acier (enfoncée au gros marteau pour casser le béton, etc.). **4.** *Metall:* tapure *f* (dans l'acier, etc.).

clink[2]. **1.** *v.i.* (*of glasses, etc.*) tinter. **2.** *v.tr.* faire tinter, faire résonner; **to c. glasses,** choquer les verres; trinquer. **3.** *v.tr. Metall:* produire des tapures dans (l'acier, etc.).

clink[3], *s. P:* cellule *f* (de prison); *Mil:* salle *f* de police; *P:* bloc *m*, boîte *f*, taule *f*; **to go to c., to be put in c.,** être fourré au bloc, être fourré dedans; se faire boucler; **to be in c.,** être bouclé; faire de la taule; être au bloc.

clinker[1] ['kliŋkər], *s.* **1.** (*a*) brique hollandaise (pour carrelage); (*b*) brique vitrifiée; brique à four. **2.** mâchefer *m* (de forge, etc.); scories vitreuses; escarbilles *fpl*; (*iron slag*) crasse *f* de fonte; **c. bar,** ringard *m*; **c. pit,** dépôt *m* de scories du foyer. **3.** (*in cement making*) clinker *m*. **4.** *NAm: P:* (*a*) gaffe *f*, bévue *f*; (*b*) *Cin: Th:* four *m*, fiasco *m*; (*c*) *Mus:* fausse note; canard *m*, couac *m* (sur la clarinette, etc.).

clinker[2]. **1.** *v.i.* (*of furnace*) former des scories, du mâchefer; (*of coal*) laisser du mâchefer. **2.** *v.tr.* décrasser (un foyer, etc.).

clinker[3], *s.* **1.** (*a*) = CLINCHER 1; (*b*) *F: O:* personne, chose, épatante. **2.** (*a*) clou rivé, à river; rivet *m*; (*b*) *Bootm:* clou à ferrer (les souliers); gros clou.

clinker-built ['kliŋkəbilt], *a. N.Arch:* bordé à clin(s); encouturé.

clinkering ['kliŋkəriŋ], *s.* décrassement *m*, décrassage *m* (du foyer); **c. tool,** ringard *m*.

clinker work ['kliŋkəwə:k], *s. N.Arch:* bordage *m* à clin(s).

clinking[1] ['kliŋkiŋ], *a.* **1.** (*a*) (verres *m*, etc.) qui s'entrechoquent; cliquetant. **2.** *F: O:* épatant, bath.

clinking[2], *s.* tintement *m*, choc *m* (de verres); cliquetis *m* (d'épées).

clinkstone ['kliŋkstoun], *s. Miner: A:* phonolit(h)e *f*.

clinocephaly [klainou'sefəli], *s. Ter:* clinocéphalie *f*.

clinochlore ['klainouklo:r], *s. Miner:* clinochlore *m*.

clinoclase ['klainoukleis, -kleiz], **clinoclasite** ['klainou'kleisait], *s. Miner:* clinoclase *f*, clinoclasite *f*.

clino(h)edrite [klainou'(h)i:drait], *s. Miner:* clinoédrite *f*.

clinohumite [klainou'hju:mait], *s. Miner:* clinohumite *f*.

clinoid ['klainɔid], *a. Anat:* (apophyse *f*) clinoïde.

clinometer [klai'nɔmitər], *s.* (*a*) *Surv: Nau:* clinomètre *m*, clitographe *m*; éclimètre *m*; niveau *m*; **bead c.,** clinomètre à bulle; (*b*) *Anthr:* clinomètre.

clinopodium [klainou'poudiəm], *s. Bot:* clinopode *m*.

clinorhombic [klainou'rɔmbik], *a. Cryst:* clinorhombique.

clinorhomboidal ['klainourɔm'bɔid(ə)l], *a. Cryst:* (système *m*) asymétrique, triclinique.

clinostat ['klainoustæt], *s. Bot:* clinostat *m*.

clint [klint], *s. Dial: Geol:* lapié *m*, lapiaz *m*.

clintonite ['klintənait], *s. Miner:* clintonite *f*.

Clio [kli(:)ou], *Pr.n.f.* Clio.

cliona [kli'ounə], *s. Spong:* clione *f*.

clip[1] [klip], *s.* **1.** pince *f*, serre *f*, attache *f*; patte *f* d'attache; griffe *f*, collier *m*, étrier *m*, de serrage; brabant *m* à patte; *Jewel:* (*on ear, shoulder, etc.*) clip *m*; *Hairdr:* (i) pince (pour mise en plis); (ii) (*ornament*) barrette *f*; **hold-down c.,** attache de fixation; **spring c.,** pince à ressort; **rubber-tube c.,** pince d'arrêt; **paper c.,** (i) agrafe *f*, happeur *m* (pour papiers); attache-papiers *m inv.*; serre-papiers *m inv.*; pince-notes *m inv.*; pince-feuilles *m inv.*; pince à papiers; (ii) attache métallique, parisienne *f*, de bureau; **wire paper c., slide-on c.,** (attache) trombone *m*; **fountain pen c.,** bague-agrafe *f*, *pl.* bagues-agrafes; clip; *Cost: A:* **dress c.,** page *m* de robe, relève-jupe *m inv.*; **tie c.,** pince à cravate, fixe-cravate *m*, *pl.* fixe-cravates; *Cy:* **trouser c., bicycle c.,** pince à pantalon, pince-pantalon *m inv.*, crochet *m* de cycliste; **pump c.,** fixe-pompe *m*, *pl.* fixe-pompes; **toe c.,** (i) *Cy:* cale-pieds *m inv.*; arrêt *m* de pied; (ii) *Farr:* pinçon *m*; *Mec.E:* **Bowden c.,** attache Bowden; **c. of a lathe chuck,** mordache *f* de mandrin de tour; *Surg:* **artery c.,** pince hémostatique; **suture c.,** agrafe; **c. of a microscope stage,** valet *m* de la platine d'un microscope. **2.** *El:* cosse *f* (de fil, de câble); **bonding c.,** collier *m* de masse; **battery-charging c.,** pince terminale (pour chargement de batteries); *Sm.a:* **loading c.,** lame *f* chargeur; chargeur *m* (pour cartouches); **c.-loading rifle, c. loader,** fusil *m* à (alimentation par) chargeurs. **3.** *Rail:* serre-rail(s) *m inv.*; crapaud *m*.

clip[2], *v.tr.* (**clipped** [klipt]) pincer, serrer; **to c. papers together,** agrafer des papiers; **to c. an attachment on to sth.,** attacher une pièce mobile à qch. avec une agrafe, un étrier.

clip[3], *v.tr.* **1.** tondre (un mouton, un cheval, le gazon); faire le poil à (un cheval); couper, ébarber, tailler (une haie); rogner, cisailler (la monnaie); couper, trancher, cisailler (une tôle); **to c. an article out of a paper,** découper un article dans un journal; **to c. the wings of a bird,** rogner les ailes à une volaille; **to c. s.o.'s wings,** **claws,** rogner les ongles, les griffes, à qn; **to c. s.o.'s hair,** passer les cheveux de qn à la tondeuse; **to c. one's words,** manger, écourter, ses mots; **to c. expenses,** rogner les dépenses; **to c. ten seconds off a record,** réduire un record par dix secondes; *Ten:* **to c. the line,** mordre la ligne. **2.** poinçonner, contrôler (un billet de chemin de fer). **3.** (*a*) donner un coup sec à (qch.); *Cr:* **to c. the ball to the boundary,** envoyer la balle jusqu'aux limites du terrain d'un coup sec; (*b*) *P:* **to c. s.o.'s ear,** flanquer une taloche à qn. **4.** *NAm:* voler, filouter (qn); (*overcharge*) donner le coup de barre à (un client); **to c. s.o. for a thousand pounds,** filouter qn de mille livres.

clip[4], *s.* **1.** (*a*) tonte *f* (de moutons); (*b*) **the (wool) c.,** la tonte de la saison. **2.** *pl.* **clips** = CLIPPER[1] 2. **3.** (*a*) *NAm:* **at one c.,** d'un seul coup; (*b*) *P:* **taloche** *f*; beigne *f*; marron *m*; *Box:* **c. on the jaw,** coup sec à la mâchoire. **4.** *P: O:* (grande) vitesse; **at a rare, good, c.,** à toute vitesse; comme un bolide. **5.** *NAm: P:* escroquerie *f*, filouterie *f*; **c. artist,** carotteur *m*; **the c. game,** l'escroquerie; **c. joint,** boîte *f* de nuit, restaurant *m*, où l'on reçoit le coup de barre. **6.** (*a*) *Cin:* extrait *m* de film; (*b*) *U.S: Journ:* coupure *f* (de journal); **c. sheet,** feuille de journal imprimée d'un seul côté.

clipboard ['klipbɔ:d], *s.* plaque *f* porte-blois; tablette *f* à croquis; planchette *f* porte-papiers.

clip-on ['klipɔn], *a.* qui s'attache avec une agrafe, un étrier; **c.-o. tie,** cravate *f* à système.

clippable ['klipəbl], *a.* (gazon, etc.) que l'on peut tondre.

clipped [klipt], *a.* **c. speech,** manière de parler saccadée; **c. pronunciation,** prononciation écourtée.

clipper[1] ['klipər], *s.* **1.** (*pers.*) tondeur, -euse; rogneur, -euse. **2.** *Tls:* (*a*) **clipper(s),** (*for the hair, etc.*) tondeuse; **hedge clipper(s),** taille-buissons *m inv*, cisaille *f* à haies; **nail clippers,** coupe-ongles *m inv*, taille-ongles *m inv*; (*b*) **bolt c.,** cisaille à boulons. **3.** (*a*) *Nau: A:* clipper *m*, fin voilier; **c.-built,** (navire) à formes élancées et à mâts inclinés vers l'arrière; **c. bow,** avant *m* à guibre; (*b*) cheval *m* très vite, qui va comme le vent. **4.** *P: O:* type épatant; **she was a c.,** elle était épatante.

clipper[2], *s. Min:* accrocheur *m* (de cuffats).

clippety-clop ['klipəti'klɔp], *s. Onomat:* clic-clac *m*.

clippie ['klipi], *s.f. F: O:* receveuse, poinçonneuse (d'autobus).

clipping[1] ['klipiŋ], *s.* serrage *m*; **c. together,** agrafage *m* (de papiers).

clipping[2], *s.* **1.** (*a*) tondage *m* (de chevaux, etc.); tondaison *f*, tonte *f* (de moutons); (*b*) contrôle *m*, poinçonnage *m* (de billets). **2.** (*a*) coupure *f* (de journal); *U.S:* **c. bureau,** agence *f* de coupures de presse; (*b*) *pl.* rognures *f* (de papiers, d'ongles, de monnaie, etc.); **clippings of hides,** rognures de peaux (dans l'industrie de la colle forte). **3.** contrôle *m*, poinçonnage *m* (d'un billet de chemin de fer, etc.).

clipping[3], *a. P: A:* épatant, bath.

clique [kli:k], *s.* (*a*) coterie *f*, petite chapelle; *F:* clan *m*; **literary c., artistic c.,** cénacle *m*; (*b*) *Pej:* clique *f*.

cliquiness ['kli:kinis], *s.* = CLIQUISHNESS.

cliquish ['kli:kiʃ], *a. F:* (*a*) attaché aux intérêts de sa coterie; (*b*) (gens) qui s'en tiennent à leur coterie.

cliquishness ['kli:kiʃnis], *s. F:* camaraderie *f*; esprit *m* de coterie.

cliqu(e)y ['kli:ki], *a. F:* **1.** (endroit) plein de coteries. **2.** = CLIQUISH.

clitellum, *pl.* **-ella** [kli'teləm, -elə], *s. Ann:* clitellum *m*.

clitocybe [klai'tɔsibi], *s. Fung:* clitocybe *m*.

clitocybin(e) [klai'tɔsibin, -bi:n], *s. Med:* clitocybine *f*.

clitoridectomy [klitɔri'dektəmi, klai-], *s. Surg:* clitoridectomie *f*.

clitoris, *pl.* **-ides** ['klitəris, 'klai-, -'tɔridi:z], *s. Anat:* clitoris *m*.

clitorism ['klitərizm, 'klai-], *s. Med:* clitorisme *m*.

clivers ['klivəz], *s. Bot:* gaillet accrochant; grat(t)eron *m*.

clivia ['klaiviə], *s. Bot:* clivia *m*, clivie *f*.

cloaca, *pl.* **-ae** [klou'ɑ:kə, -'eikə, -i:], *s.* **1.** (*a*) cloaque *m*; *Lit:* **c. of infamy,** bourbier *m* de vice; (*b*) *Rom.Ant:* **the C. Maxima,** la Grande Cloaque. **2.** *Z:* cloaque *m* (des poissons, des oiseaux et des reptiles).

cloacal [klou'eik(ə)l], *a. Z:* **c. sac,** poche cloacale.

cloacitis [klouə'saitis], *s. Vet:* inflammation *f* du cloaque.

cloak[1] [klouk], *s.* **1.** (*a*) manteau *m*; **evening c.,** manteau de soir (pour dame); sortie *f* de bal, de théâtre; **c. of snow, of moss,** manteau de neige, de mousse; **under the c. of night,** sous le couvert, le voile, de la nuit; **under the c. of religion,** sous le manteau de la religion; sous les dehors *m*, le prétexte, l'apparence *f*, le voile, le masque, de la religion; sous couverture de religion; **c.-and-dagger story, c.-and-sword story,** roman *m* de cape et d'épée; *F:* **the c.-and-dagger boys,** les barbouzes *f*; (*b*) *Ecc. Cost:* camail *m*, *pl.* camails. **2.** *F:* **ladies' cloaks,** toilettes *f* des dames.

cloak[2], **1.** *v.tr.* (*a*) couvrir, revêtir, (qn) d'un manteau; (*b*) masquer, voiler (ses projets, ses pensées). **2.** *v.i.* mettre son manteau; se revêtir d'un manteau.

cloakroom ['kloukru:m], *s.* **1.** vestiaire *m*; (*b*) toilettes *fpl*; **ladies' c.,** dames; **c. attendant,** préposé(e) (i) au vestiaire, (ii) aux cabinets de toilette; *P:* dame *f* pipi. **2.** *Rail: etc:* consigne *f*; **to leave one's luggage in the c.,** déposer, mettre, ses bagages à la consigne; consigner ses bagages.

clobber[1] ['klɔbər], *s. F:* **1.** frusques *fpl*, hardes *fpl*. **2.** effets *mpl*; **bring all your c. with you,** apporte toutes tes affaires, tout ton bazar.

clobber[2], *v.i. P: O:* **to c. out, up,** s'attifer; se frusquer.

clobber[3], *v.tr. P:* **1.** (*a*) (*thrash*) rosser (qn); (*b*) (*reprimand*) tancer, étriller (qn); (*c*) battre (un adversaire) à plates coutures. **2.** *Mil:* (*a*) pilonner (une ville ennemie, etc.); (*b*) abattre (un avion).

clobbering ['klɔbəriŋ], *s. P:* **1. to get a c.,** être (i) rossé; (ii) tancé, étrillé; (iii) battu à plates coutures. **2.** *Mil:* (*a*) pilonnage *m*; (*b*) abattage *m* (d'un avion).

cloche[1] [klɔʃ, klouʃ], *s.* **1.** *Hort:* cloche *f* cloche continue, cloche tunnel; **tent c.,** cloche tente; **to put (melons, etc.) under a c.,** mettre sous cloche; clocher. **2. c. hat,** cloche.

cloche[2], *v.tr. Hort:* clocher; mettre (des melons, etc.) sous cloche.

clock[1] [klɔk], *s.* **1.** (*a*) (*large*) horloge *f*; (*smaller*) pendule *f*; *Aut: Nau:* montre *f*; **ship's c.,** horloge marine; montre de bord; *Aut:* **dashboard c.,** montre de bord; **town c.,** horloge de ville; **grandfather('s) c.,** horloge de parquet; horloge comtoise; horloge normande; pendule à gaine; **grandmother c.,** horloge de parquet de petit modèle; **carriage c., travelling c.,** pendulette *f*; **wall c., hanging c.,** pendule murale; cartel *m*; **mantelpiece c.,** pendule à poser, de cheminée; **bedside c.,** montre-chevalet *f*, *pl.* montres-chevalet; **Dutch c.,** (pendule à) coucou (*m*); **eight-day c.,** huitaine *f*; **weight-driven c.,** horloge à poids; **hand-wound c.,** horloge à remontage à la main; **spring c.,** horloge à ressort; **pendulum c.,** horloge à pendule, à balancier; **water c.,** clepsydre *f*; **electric c.,** horloge, pendule, électrique; **battery c.,** pendule à pile; **electronic c.,** horloge électronique; **quartz (crystal) c.,** horloge à quartz; **digital c.,** pendule digitale; *Tp:* **speaking c.,** horloge parlante; *Ind: etc:* **master c.,** horloge mère; *Clockm:* horloge fiducielle; **slave c.,** horloge réceptrice; **watchman's c.,** contrôleur *m* de ronde; mouchard *m*; **time c.,** enregistreur *m* de temps; horodateur *m*; *A:* **at six of the c.** (= O'CLOCK), à six heures; **it's two by the c.,** il est deux heures à l'horloge; **I waited for a full hour by the c.,** j'ai attendu une bonne heure d'horloge; **it took him ten minutes by the c.,** cela lui a pris dix minutes montre en main; **to sleep the c. round,** faire le tour du cadran; **to work round the c.,** travailler vingt-quatre heures sur vingt-quatre; *Ind:* faire les trois-huits *m*; **a race against the c.,** une course contre la montre; **to beat the c.,** arriver avant temps; **to set, put, the c. back,** (i) retarder la pendule; (ii) rétrogresser; (*b*) *P: O:* montre; *P:* toquante *f*; (*c*) (i) *Aut:* compteur *m* de vitesse; (ii) **c. of a taxi,** compteur *m* horokilométrique. **2.** *Cmptr:* (i) horloge; (ii) base *f* de temps; (iii) générateur *m* de rythme; **digital c.,** horloge à signaux numériques, horloge numérique; **master c.,** horloge pilote, mère; rythmeur *m*; **real-time c.,** horloge binaire; **c. number, c. frequency,** fréquence de base (de temps); **c. pulse,** impulsion *f* de synchronisation, d'horloge; **c. track,** piste *f* de référence, de base de temps, de synchronisation; piste horloge. **3.** *P:* (*a*) visage *m*; *P:* ciboulot *m*; (*b*) coup *m*, gnon *m*; beigne *f*.

clock[2], **1.** *v.tr. F:* (*a*) chronométrer (un coureur, etc.); **to be clocked at ten seconds, to c. ten seconds,** être crédité d'un temps de dix secondes; (*b*) *Aut:* **to c. ninety,** taper le 145; (*c*) *P:* donner, flanquer, un gnon, une beigne, à (qn). **2.** *v.i. Av:* (*of engine*) **to c. over,** tourner au (grand) ralenti. **3.** *v.i. Ind: Com:* **to c. in, on,** pointer à l'arrivée; **to c. out, off,** pointer à la sortie.

clock[3], *s.* (*Com: pl. often* **clox**) (*on sock, etc.*) baguette *f*, grisotte *f*, coin *m*; **openwork clocks,** baguettes à jour.

clock[4], *v.tr. & i. N.Dial:* (*of hen*) couver (des œufs).

clocked [klɔkt], *a.* (bas *m*) à baguettes, à grisottes, à coins.

clocker[1] ['klɔkər], *s.* chronométreur (sportif).

clocker[2], *s. N.Dial:* poule couveuse.

clock-golf ['klɔk'gɔlf], *s.* jeu *m* de clock-golf.

clocking ['klɔkiŋ], *s. Sp:* chronométrage *m*. **2.** *Ind: Com:* **c. in, on,** pointage *m* à l'arrivée; **c. off, out,** pointage à la sortie.

clocklike ['klɔklaik], *a.* (d'une régularité) d'horloge; (d'une régularité) monotone.

clockmaker ['klɔkmeikər], *s.* horloger *m*.

clock-watcher ['klɔkwɔtʃər], *s.* employé(e) qui ne pense qu'à l'heure de sortie, qui a l'œil rivé à l'horloge.

clockwise ['klɔkwaiz], *adv. & a.* dans le sens des aiguilles d'une montre; à droite.

clockwork ['klɔkwə:k], *s.* rouage *m* d'horloge; mouvement *m* d'horlogerie; mécanisme *m* à ressort; *Toys:* **c. train,** chemin *m* de fer mécanique; *Exp:* **c. delay mechanism,** mécanisme d'horlogerie à retardement; **c.-driven,** mû, entraîné, par un mouvement d'horlogerie; **everything is done with c. precision,** tout est réglé comme une montre; **everything's going like c.,** tout va, marche, comme sur des roulettes.

clod[1] [klɔd], *s.* **1.** (*a*) motte *f* (de terre); *Agr:* **to break (up) the clods,** émotter la terre; **breaking up of the clods,** émottage *m*; *Tls:* **c. beetle,** émottoir *m*; **c. breaker, c. crusher,** (i) (*pers.*) émotteur, -euse; (ii) (*machine*) (rouleau *m*) brise-mottes *m inv*; casse-mottes *m inv*; émotteuse *f*; (iii) *F:* **c. crushers,** gros souliers; godasses *f*; godillots *m*; (*b*) *F:* **the c.,** la terre (des champs); (*c*) *Lit:* **the c.,** le corps (opposé à l'âme); la matière. **2.** *F:* (*a*) rustre *m*, lourdaud *m*, manant *m*; (*b*) stupide *mf*; **what a c.!** quel abruti! **3.** *Cu:* talon *m* de collier (de bœuf).

clod[2], *v.* **(clodded) 1.** *v.i.* (*of earth*) s'agglomérer. **2.** *v.tr.* motter (un chien, etc.); lancer des mottes à (un chien, un mouton).

cloddish ['klɔdiʃ], *a.* **1.** (champ *m*) à mottes. **2.** lourdaud; à l'esprit balourd; campagnard.

cloddishness ['klɔdiʃnis], *s.* caractère grossier; mœurs *fpl* de campagnard; rustrerie *f*.

cloddy ['klɔdi], *a.* (sol) rempli de mottes, qui se casse en mottes.

clodhopper ['klɔdhɔpər], *s.* **1.** rustre *m*, lourdaud *m*, balourd *m*, manant *m*; *F:* cul-terreux *m*, *pl.* culs-terreux. **2.** *pl.* **clodhoppers,** gros souliers; *F:* godasses *f*; godillots *m*.

clodhopping ['klɔdhɔpiŋ], *a.* rustre; **c. boots,** sabots *m* de campagnard.

Cloelia ['kli:liə], *Pr.n.f.* Clélie.

clog[1] [klɔg], *s.* **1.** (*a*) entrave *f* (pour cheval); billot *m* (pour vache); (*b*) empêchement *m*, embarras *m*, entrave; **these restrictions are a c. upon industry,** ces restrictions *f* entravent l'industrie. **2.** (*a*) (*overshoe*) socque *f*; (*b*) gros brodequin à semelle de bois et à bout ferré; galoche *f*; **c. dance,** sabotière *f*; **c. dancer,** danseur, -euse, de sabotière.

clog[2], *v.* **(clogged) 1.** *v.tr.* (*a*) entraver (un animal); (*b*) entraver, embarrasser, empêcher, gêner (une entreprise, etc.); (*c*) boucher, obstruer (une artère, un tuyau, etc.); encrasser, cambouiser (une arme à feu, une machine); colmater (un filtre); empâter (une lime); embarrasser (l'estomac); **metal that clogs the file,** métal *m* qui graisse la lime; **our boots got clogged with mud,** nos souliers se crottaient dans la boue; **to c. one's memory with useless facts,** se charger la mémoire de faits inutiles; *Phot:* **clogged negative,** cliché empâté. **2.** *v.i.* se boucher, s'obstruer, s'encrasser; (*of filter*) se colmater; (*of file*) s'empâter; **streets clogged with cars,** rues bouchées, obstruées, encombrées, de voitures.

clogger ['klɔgər], **clogmaker** ['klɔgmeikər], *s.* fabricant *m* de galoches, de brodequins à semelle de bois; **clogmaker's knife, stock,** rogne *f*.

clogging ['klɔgiŋ], *s.* obstruction *f*, encrassement *m*; colmatage *m* (d'un filtre); empâtement *m* (d'une lime, d'un cliché).

cloisonné [klwɑ:'zɔnei, *NAm:* klɔizə'nei], *a. & s. Ind: Art:* **c. (enamel),** cloisonné (*m*).

cloister[1] ['klɔistər], *s.* **1.** monastère *m*. **2.** (*usu. pl.*) cloitre *m*.

cloister[2], *v.tr.* cloîtrer.

cloistered ['klɔistəd], *a.* **1. c. life,** vie *f* de cloître; **to lead a c. life,** mener une vie monacale. **2. c. quadrangle,** cour cloîtrée, entourée de cloîtres, bordée d'un cloître.

cloisterer ['klɔistərər], *s.* cloîtrier, -ière.

cloistral ['klɔistr(ə)l], *a.* claustral, -aux.

cloke [klouk], *s. & v.tr. A:* = CLOAK[1,2].

clone [kloun], *s. Bot: Biol:* clone *m*.

cloned [klound], *a. Biol:* en lignée; **c. colonies,** colonies *f* en lignée pure.

clonic ['klɔnik], *a. Med:* clonique; **c. spasms,** convulsions *f* cloniques.

clonism [['klounizm], *s. Med:* clonisme *m*.

clonk[1] [klɔŋk], *s.* coup sourd.

clonk[2], *v.i.* rendre un son sourd.

clonus ['klounəs], *s. Med:* clonus *m*.

Clootie ['klu:ti], *Pr.n.m. Scot:* **(old) C.,** le Diable (aux pieds fourchus).

close[1] [klous], *a. & adv.*

I. *a.* **1.** (*a*) bien fermé, clos; **c. harbour,** port fermé; *Metall:* **c. annealing,** recuit *m* en vase clos; *Ling:* **c. vowel,** voyelle fermée, entravée; (*b*) **c. air,** air renfermé; **c. smell,** odeur *f* de renfermé; **the room smells c.,** ça sent le renfermé ici; **c. weather,** temps lourd; (*c*) **c. secret, silence,** secret *m*, silence *m*, impénétrable; (*d*) (*limited*) **c. corporation,** société exclusive, fermée; **c. scholarship,** bourse *f* pour une catégorie restreinte de candidats; (*e*) (*closed*) *Ven:* **c. time, c. season,** période *f* d'interdiction; chasse fermée; temps prohibé; **fish for which there is no c. season,** poissons indifférents; **to shoot in c. time,** braconner. **2.** serré, dense; (*a*) **c. rain,** pluie serrée, drue; **c. thicket, c. wood,** fourré, bois, épaiss, touffu; (*b*) (*of metal, stone, wood, etc.*) **c. grain,** grain fin, dense; **c. texture,** (con)texture serrée, tissu serré; *Const:* **c. mortar,** mortier épais, compact; *Typ:* **c. matter,** composition compacte; (*c*) *Mil:* **c. formations,** formations serrées; **in c. order,** (i) en ordre serré, en rangs serrés; (ii) *Navy:* à distance serrée; **c.-order drill,** exercice *m* d'ordre serré, de rangs serrés; **in c. ranks,** en rangs serrés, au coude à coude et dos contre poitrine. **3.** (*near*) rapproché; (*a*) **c. intervals,** intervalles rapprochés, serrés; **c. proximity,** proximité immédiate; *F:* **that was a close thing,** nous l'avons échappé belle; il était moins cinq; **at c. quarters,** tout près l'un de l'autre; **when I saw him at c. quarters,** quand je l'ai vu de près; **to come to c. quarters,** en venir aux mains; **c. correspondence,** correspondance suivie; (*b*) *Mil:* **c. approach,** approche *f* à proximité de l'ennemi; **c. billets,** cantonnement(s) *m* d'alerte; **c. combat, c. quarters fighting,** (i) (combat *m*) corps à corps (*m*); (ii) *Navy:* combat bord à bord; **c. defence,** défense rapprochée; *Navy:* **c.(-range) action,** combat rapproché; **c. range,** courte portée, courte distance; **c.-range weapon,** arme *f* à courte portée; **to fire at c. range,** tirer à très courte distance, à bout portant; **c. support,** appui direct, tactique; **c.-support weapon,** engin *m* d'accompagnement. **4.** (*tight*) (*a*) ajusté, serré; **c. carpeting,** tapis ajusté; *Mec.E:* **c. fit,** montage, ajustage, serré; frottement dur; **c. joint,** joint *m* étanche; *El:* **c. coupling,** couplage serré; (*b*) étroit; **c. co-ordination,** coordination étroite; **c. connection between two facts,** rapport étroit entre deux faits; **Italian is c. to French,** l'italien est proche du français; **c. friend,** ami intime; **c. friendship,** amitié étroite, solide amitié. **5.** (*a*) minutieux, attentif; **c. attention,** attention soutenue, suivie; **c. observer,** observateur attentif, assidu; **c. study,** étude minutieuse, approfondie; **to put s.o. through a c. examination,** soumettre qn à un interrogatoire, examen, minutieux; soumettre qn à un interrogatoire serré; **on closer examination it was discovered that . . .,** en y regardant de plus près on s'aperçut que . . .; **after c. consideration,** après mûre considération; **c. reasoning,** raisonnement rigoureux, serré; **to keep c. watch on s.o., sth.,** surveiller qn, qch., de près, étroitement; **he keeps a c. watch on us,** il a toujours l'œil braqué sur nous; **to keep a c. control over expenditure,** contrôler de près, étroitement, les dépenses; (*b*) rigoureux, strict; **c. blockade,** blocus rigoureux; **c. imprisonment,** emprisonnement rigoureux; **c. prisoner,** prisonnier étroitement gardé, mis au secret; (*c*) exact, précis; **c. copy,** copie exacte; **c. resemblance,** ressemblance exacte; **c. translation,** traduction exacte, fidèle, serrée, qui serre le texte de près, très près de l'original. **6.** (*a*) serré; **to cut (hair, etc.) c.,** couper (les cheveux, etc.) ras; *Com:* **c. price,** prix calculé au plus juste, qui ne laisse pas de marge; (*b*) (*of contest*) à chances, à forces, égales; **c. election,** élection vivement contestée; **c. match,** match serré; **c. struggle,** lutte serrée; *Rac:* **c. finish,** arrivée serrée. **7.** (*confined*) **c. alley,** allée étroite; **I can put you up if you don't mind c. quarters,** je peux vous loger si cela ne vous fait rien d'être à l'étroit. **8.** (*secret*) (homme) peu communicatif, réservé, renfermé, concentré, très boutonné, *F:* cachottier; **to be c. about sth., to keep sth. c.,** ne rien dire de qch.; être réservé à l'égard de qch., sur qch.; **to play a c. game,** jouer serré, cacher ses cartes. **9.** (*stingy*) avare, ladre, regardant. **10.** *Vet:* (*of horses*) **c. tendon,** tendon failli.

II. *adv.* **1.** (*tightly*) **c. shut,** étroitement, bien, hermétiquement, fermé ou bouché. **2.** (*near*) près, de près, auprès; **to be, follow, c. behind s.o.,** suivre qn de près; être sur les talons de qn; **stay c. by me,** restez (tout) auprès de moi; **to keep c. to the door,** se tenir tout près de la porte; **to stand c. against a wall,** se coller contre un mur; **to set two planks closer,** rapprocher deux planches; (*of garment*) **to fit c.,** bien prendre la taille; *Prov:* **c. my shirt but closer my skin,** la chemise est plus proche que le pourpoint; **houses c. together,** maisons serrées; **houses very c. to one another,** maisons très rapprochées; **to sit, stand, c. together,** être, se tenir, serrés, coude à coude; **sit closer (together)!** serrez-vous! **to look closer,** regarder de plus près; **the closer we look into the question the more we are convinced that . . .,** plus nous examinons la question de près, plus nous sommes convaincus que . . .. **3. to keep, lie, c.,** se tenir caché, rester caché, se tenir retiré, se tenir tapi. **4.** (*a*) **c. at hand, c. by,** tout près, tout proche, tout attenant, tout contre; à peu de distance; à deux pas; (*b*) **c. in;** *Nau:* **to stand c. in (to the land),** serrer la terre; (*c*) **c. on nine (o'clock),** tout près de neuf heures; **to be c. on fifty,** friser la cinquantaine; toucher à la cinquantaine; **they are c. on us,** ils nous serrent de près; ils nous talonnent; (*d*) **c. to, c. by (s.o., sth.),** (tout) près de, à proximité de (qn, qch.); **here is the church, the house is c. to it, the house is c. to,** voici l'église, la maison est tout auprès, *F:* à deux pas (de là); **he lives c. to here,** il demeure tout près, à deux pas (d'ici); **to come, draw, c., closer, to s.o.,** s'approcher, se rapprocher, de qn; **to keep c. to s.o.,** s'attacher à qn; se tenir tout près de qn; **he kept c. to the coast,** il serrait la côte de près; **ship c. to the shore,** navire près de terre; **I saw someone pass c. by the wall,** j'ai vu quelqu'un qui rasait le mur; **c. to the door,** tout contre la porte; **c. to the ground,** à fleur de terre; à ras de terre; au ras du sol; **to keep c. to the text,** serrer le texte de près.

close[2] [klous], *s.* **1.** *A: & Jur:* clôture *f*; **breach of c.,** effraction *f*; bris *m*, violation *f*, de clôture. **2.** (*a*) clos *m*, enclos *m*; (*b*) enceinte *f* (de cathédrale). **3.** (*a*) *Scot:* passage *m*, allée *f* (donnant accès aux portes d'entrée ou aux escaliers); (*b*) *Town P:* impasse *f*; cul-de-sac *m*, *pl.* culs-de-sac; **number 10 Forest C.,** numéro *m* dix de l'impasse de la Forêt.

close[3] [klouz], *s.* **1.** fin *f*, conclusion *f*, terminaison *f* (d'une action, d'un discours, etc.); fin, bout *m* (de l'année); clôture *f*, levée *f* (d'une séance); fin (du jour); **at the c. of the meeting,** à l'issue *f* de la réunion; *Lit:* **at c. of day,** à la chute du jour; à la tombée de la nuit; au jour tombant; **the day, the year, draws to a c.,** le jour, l'année, tire à sa fin, s'achève; **the evening was drawing to a c.,** la soirée touchait à sa fin; **the evening drew to a c.,** la soirée prit fin; **to bring sth. to a c.,** mettre fin à qch.; terminer, achever, qch.; **before bringing my letter to a c. . . .,** avant d'achever ma lettre . . .; **at the c. of the financial period,** à l'achèvement *m* de la période budgétaire; *Fish: Ven:* **c. of the season,** fermeture *f*, clôture *f*, de la pêche, de la chasse. **2.** corps-à-corps *m inv*; (*of wrestlers, etc.*) **to come to a c.,** en venir au corps-à-corps. **3.** *Mus: A:* cadence *f*; **perfect c.,** cadence parfaite; **interrupted c.,** cadence (inter)rompue; **avoided c.,** cadence évitée; **trilled c.,** cadence brisée.

close[4] [klouz], *v.*

I. *v.tr. & i.* **1.** *v.tr.* (*a*) fermer (une porte, les yeux, un livre, un parc, un circuit électrique, etc.); fermer, replier (un parapluie); barrer (une rue); *Nau:* bâcler (un port); boucher (un trou); *I.C.E:* recouvrir (les orifices d'échappement); *Rail:* bloquer (une section); **closed to troops,** consigné aux militaires; **road closed to motor traffic,** route interdite à la circulation automobile; **this victory closed the Aegean to our fleet,** cette victoire ferma la mer Égée à notre flotte; **cold closes the pores,** le froid resserre les pores; *I.C.E:* **valve closed by a spring,** soupape rappelée sur son siège par un ressort; *Book-k:* **to c. the books,** régler les livres; boucler, balancer, les comptes; (*b*) conclure, terminer (une série, une affaire, etc.); clore (une serie); lever, clore (une séance); arrêter (un marché); fermer (un débat); fermer, clôturer, arrêter (un compte); *St.Exch:* liquider (une opération); *Jur:* clôturer (une faillite); **to c. one's days,** finir ses jours; **the fire brigade closed the procession,** les pompiers fermaient le cortège; **he closed his speech with a few witty allusions to his opponents,** il termina par quelques allusions spirituelles à ses adversaires; **to declare the discussion closed,** prononcer la clôture des débats; **let the subject be closed,** qu'il n'en soit plus question; *v.i.* **I will now c. with a story,** pour terminer je vais vous raconter une histoire; **I don't want to c. on a note of sadness,** je ne voudrais pas finir sur une note triste; (*c*) (i) **to c. the ranks,** serrer les rangs; *Navy:* **to c. the columns,** resserrer les colonnes; (ii) *Nau:* **to c. one headland with another,** fermer un promontoire par un autre; (*d*) *Metalw:* **to c. a rivet,** refouler un rivet. **2.** *v.i.* (*a*) (*of door, etc.*) (se) fermer; (*of wound*) **to c. (up),** se refermer; se rejoindre; se cicatriser; **to arrive as the gates are closing,** arriver à la fermeture des portes; **the waters closed over him,** les flots se refermèrent sur sa tête; il disparut sous les flots; **his fingers closed on his revolver,** ses doigts se fermèrent sur son revolver; **the theatre will c. for a month,** le théâtre fermera ses portes pendant un mois; **theatres c. on Good Friday,** les théâtres font relâche le vendredi saint; (*b*) finir, se terminer; **the day is closing,** le jour tire à sa fin, s'achève; *St.Exch:* **the shares closed at £1,** les actions ont terminé à £1; (*c*) **to c. about, round, s.o.,** cerner qn, se presser autour de qn; **to c. about an army,** envelopper, encercler, une armée; (*d*) **to c. with s.o.,** (i) conclure le marché avec qn; toper; (ii) se prendre corps à corps avec qn; en venir aux mains avec qn; **to c. with a bargain,** accepter une offre; *F:* toper.

II. (*compound verbs*) **1. close down;** (*a*) *v.tr.* fermer (une usine, etc.); *F:* **to c. down,** *U.S:* **c. down on, a revolutionary movement,** mettre fin à, étouffer, un mouvement de révolte; (*b*) *v.i.* (i) (*of factory, etc.*) fermer; cesser la production; chômer; (*of shop*) fermer boutique; **closing down,** cessation *f* de commerce; (ii) *W.Tel: T.V:* terminer l'émission.

2. close in; (*a*) *v.tr.* clôturer (un terrain, etc.); entourer (un édifice, etc.) d'une clôture; recouvrir (une rigole, etc.); **closed-in culvert,** canal *m* à ciel couvert; (*b*) *v.i.* (i) **the night is closing in,** la nuit tombe; le jour baisse; **when night closes in,** à la tombée de la nuit; **the days are closing in,** les jours (se) raccourcissent; (ii) **to c. in on s.o.,** cerner qn de près; **darkness closed in (up)on us,** la nuit nous enveloppa.

3. close out, *NAm:* (*a*) *v.tr.* (i) solder; écouler (des marchandises) à bas prix; se défaire de (ses marchandises, ses titres); (ii) fermer, arrêter, clôturer (un compte); (*b*) *v.i.* fermer boutique.

4. close up; (*a*) *v.tr.* (i) boucher, obturer (une ouverture); barrer (un chemin); (ii) *Typ:* **to c. up the type,** rapprocher les caractères; *Mil:* **to c. up the ranks,** serrer les rangs; (iii) **to c. up the rear,** venir en queue (d'un cortège); *Mil:* fermer la marche; (*b*) *v.i.* (i) (*of aperture*) s'obturer; (ii) (*of people*) se serrer, se tasser; *Mil: etc:* **c. up!** serrez (les rangs)! **to c. up to the right, left,** serrer à droite, gauche.

close-carpet ['klous'kɑːpit], *v.tr.* **to c.-c. a room,** recouvrir le plancher d'une pièce d'un tapis ajusté.

close-clipped ['klous'klipt], *a.* (mouton) tondu de près; (*of moustache*) très court.

close-cropped ['klous'krɔpt], **close-cut**[1] ['klous'kʌt], *a.* (*of hair*) coupé ras; (*of grass*) rasé, tondu, de près.

close-cut[2], *v.tr. Phot.Engr:* détourer (un profil, etc.).

closed [klouzd], *a.* **1.** (*a*) fermé; (*of pipe, etc.*) obturé, bouché; **c. conveyance,** voiture fermée; **with c. eyes,** les yeux clos; **road c.,** rue barrée; *Mus:* **c. note** (*on horn*), son bouché; (*b*) *P.N: Th:* **c.,** relâche; **c. for the season,** clôture; *Ven:* **c. season,** période *f* d'interdiction; chasse fermée. **2.** (*a*) **c. professions,** professions fermées; *Ind:* **c. shop,** atelier *m*, chantier *m*, etc., qui n'admet pas de travailleurs non syndiqués; **c.-shop policy,** exclusivité syndicale. **3.** *El:* **c. circuit,** circuit fermé; **c. circuit television,** télévision *f* à circuit fermé; **c. loop control,** fonctionnement *m* en boucle fermé; *Cmptr:* **c. routine,** programme fermé, en boucle. **4.** *For:* **c. wood,** bois mis en défends.

closedown ['klouzdaun], *s.* **1.** fermeture *f*, clôture *f* (d'ateliers). **2.** *W.Tel: T.V:* fin *f* d'émission.

close-fisted ['klous'fistid], *a.* ladre, serré, peu donnant; *F:* pingre, dur à la détente; **to be c.-f.,** avoir la main fermée; avoir les doigts crochus, les mains crochues; être dur à la desserre.

close-fistedness ['klous'fistidnis], *s.* ladrerie *f*, pingrerie *f*.

close-fitting ['klous'fitiŋ], *a. Dressm: etc:* (vêtement) qui prend (bien) la taille, ajusté, collant; **c.-f. over the hips,** bien ajusté aux hanches.

close-grained ['klous'greind], *a.* **1.** (*of wood*) serré, fin; à grain(s) fin(s), serré(s). **2.** *Metall:* à grains fins; à fine cristallisation.

close-haul ['klous'hɔːl], *v.tr. Nau:* choquer (les écoutes).

close-hauled ['klous'hɔːld], *a. Nau:* au plus près serré; **to sail c.-h.,** marcher à l'allure du plus près; courir au plus serré; cingler au plus près; naviguer, aller, à la bouline; **vessel running c.-h. on the port tack,** navire courant au plus près bâbord amures; **sailing c.-h.,** boulinage *m*.

close-in ['klouz'in], *s. Aut: Av:* pincement *m* (des roues).

close-knit ['klous'nit], *a.* (*of family*) lié, joint, étroitement.

close-lipped ['klous'lipt], *a.* taciturne; la bouche cousue; muet comme une carpe.

closely ['klousli], *adv.* **1.** = CLOSE[1] II. 1. **2.** (*a*) **to clasp sth., s.o., c. to one,** serrer qch., qn, contre soi; **c. guarded,** étroitement gardé; **c. connected,** lié étroitement, intimement; (*with sth.*) en rapport intime (avec qch.); **you are the most c. concerned,** c'est vous le premier intéressé; (*b*) **c. cut,** tondu ras; **c. contested,** vivement contesté; (*c*) (ressemblant) exactement; (examiné) de près, attentivement; (suivi, observé, traduit) de près; mûrement (considéré); strictement (obéi); **to watch s.o. c.,** surveiller qn de près; **you must watch them more c.,** il faut mieux les surveiller; **to go c. into a matter,** examiner une affaire de près; examiner minutieusement une affaire; **to follow an argument c.,** prêter, donner, une attention suivie à un raisonnement; **to listen c.,** écouter attentivement. **3.** serré, l'un près de l'autre; **c. packed in a box,** serrés dans une boîte; **two c. written pages,** deux pages d'une écriture serrée.

close-meshed ['klous'meʃt], *a.* à petites mailles.

close-mouthed [klous'mauðd], *a.* économe de paroles; peu communicatif.

closen ['klousn], *v.tr.* rapprocher; **to c. the contact,** rendre le contact plus intime.

closeness ['klousnis], *s.* **1.** (*a*) rapprochement *m*, proximité *f*; **c. of contact,** intimité *f* de contact; **the c. of their relationship, of their friendship,** leur proche parenté *f*, leur grande intimité; **the c. of their connection,** leurs rapports étroits; (*b*) contexture serrée (d'une étoffe, etc.); compacité *f* (du mortier, etc.); (*c*) **the c. of the pursuit,** la vigueur de la poursuite; **the c. of his questions,** ses questions pressantes; la rigueur de son interrogatoire. **2.** exactitude *f* (d'une description, etc.); **the c. of the resemblance,** la très grande ressemblance; la ressemblance frappante; **the c. of the translation,** la fidélité, l'exactitude, de la traduction. **3.** (*a*) manque *m* d'air (d'une salle); (*b*) lourdeur *f* (du temps, de l'atmosphère). **4.** réserve *f*, caractère réservé, peu communicatif (de qn). **5.** avarice *f*, ladrerie *f*.

closer ['klouzər], *s.* **1.** celui qui ferme ou qui a fermé (la porte, etc.). **2.** (*a*) appareil *m* de fermeture; (*b*) *Const:* clausoir *m*, closoir *m* (d'une assise).

close-ranked ['klous'ræŋkt], *a.* en rangs serrés.

close-reef ['klous'riːf], *s. Nau:* bas ris.

close-reefed ['klous'riːft], *a. Nau:* au bas ris.

close-set ['klous'set], *a.* **1.** (*of eyes, etc.*) rapprochés; **c.-s. teeth,** dents serrées, rapprochées. **2.** (*of onions, etc.*) (plantés) en rangs serrés; **c.-s. grass,** herbe drue; **c.-s. hedge,** haie épaisse.

close-shaven ['klous'ʃeivn], *a.* rasé de près.

close-shut ['klous'ʃʌt], *a.* bien fermé; hermétiquement fermé.

close-stool ['klousstuːl], *s. A:* chaise percée.

closet[1] ['klɔzit], *s.* **1.** (*a*) cabinet *m*; **storage c.,** (i) cabinet de débarras; (ii) *Ind:* petit magasin; (*b*) *A:* boudoir *m*; cabinet de travail; cabinet particulier; *F: O:* **c. strategists,** stratégistes *m* en chambre; **c. play,** pièce *f* de théâtre à lire, non destinée à la scène; (*c*) (*water closet*) les cabinets; **chemical c.,** w.c. *m* chimique. **2.** placard *m*; *U.S:* armoire *f*; (*under stairs*) soupente *f*.

closet[2], *v.tr.* (**closeted**) **1.** *A:* **to c. oneself,** se claquemurer, se cloîtrer. **2. to be closeted with s.o.,** être enfermé dans son cabinet, être en tête-à-tête, avec qn.

close-tongued ['klous'tʌŋd], *a.* taciturne.

close-up ['klousʌp], *s.* **1.** *Cin: T.V:* plan rapproché, gros plan; *T.V:* plan serré; **big c.-u.,** très gros plan; **c.-up detail,** détail vu de près. **2.** *Journ:* portrait-interview, *pl.* portraits-interview.

close-woven ['klous'wouvn], *a.* (toile *f*) d'un tissu serré; (tissu) à contexture serrée.

closing[1] ['klouziŋ], *a.* (*a*) qui (se) ferme; (*b*) dernier; final, -als; **the c. date for applications is . . .,** le registre d'inscriptions sera clos le . . .; **the c. days of March,** les derniers jours de mars; **the c. years of life,** les dernières années, l'arrière-saison *f*, de la vie; **the c. bid,** la dernière enchère; **the c. speech,** le discours de fin de séance; **c. session,** séance *f* de clôture; **c. prices,** derniers cours; prix *m* de clôture; **the c. quotations,** les cotes *f* en clôture.

closing[2], *s.* **1.** fermeture *f* (des magasins, etc.); clôture *f* (d'un théâtre, etc.); barrage *m* (d'une rue); bâclage *m* (d'un port); cicatrisation *f* (d'une blessure); **at the c. of the gates,** à la fermeture des portes; **c.(-down) of a factory,** fermeture, chômage *m*, d'une usine; *Com:* **Sunday c.,** chômage du dimanche; repos *m* hebdomadaire; **c. time,** heure *f* de la fermeture; **c. time!** on ferme! **early c. day,** jour *m* où les magasins sont fermés l'après-midi. **2.** clôture (d'un compte, d'une séance, etc.); levée *f* (d'une séance); arrêté *m*, règlement *m* (d'un compte).

closing out ['klouziŋ'aut], *s. NAm:* fermeture *f* (d'un magasin); **c.-o. sale,** solde *m* de fermeture.

closing up ['klouziŋ'ʌp], *s. Metalw:* refoulement *m*, rivetage *m* (du corps d'un rivet).

clostridial [klɔs'tridiəl], *a. Bac:* qui ressemble à un clostridion; **c. infection,** infection provoquée par les clostridions.

clostridium, *pl.* **-ia** [klɔs'tridiəm, -iə], *s. Bac:* clostridium *m inv*, clostridion *m*.

closure[1] ['klouʒər], *s.* **1.** (*a*) clôture *f*, fermeture *f* (d'une séance, etc.); (*b*) *Parl:* clôture; **to move the c.,** voter la clôture; **to apply the c. to a debate,** clôturer un débat. **2.** fermeture, occlusion *f*; **full c. of a valve,** fermeture, occlusion, complète d'une soupape; *El:* **c. of the current,** lancement *m* du courant; *Ling:* **c. of a vowel,** fermeture (d'une voyelle). **3.** *Med:* **epiphyseal c.,** soudure *f* des épiphyses.

closure[2], *v.tr.* clôturer (un débat); appliquer la clôture à (un débat).

clot[1] [klɔt], *s.* **1.** caillot *m* (de sang, de lait); bourbillon *m* (d'encre); **c. of blood,** caillot sanguin; *Med: F:* **c. on the brain,** embolie cérébrale. **2.** *Physiol:* **the c.,** le coagulum (du sang). **3.** *P:* idiot, -ote, imbécile *mf*, cruche *f*.

clot[2], *v.* (**clotted**) **1.** *v.i.* se grumeler; former des grumeaux; (*of milk*) se cailler, se caillebotter; (*of blood*) se figer, se coaguler; (*of soap, etc.*) s'engrumeler. **2.** *v.tr.* (*a*) caillebotter (le lait, la crème); cailler (le lait); figer (le sang); (*b*) (*of blood, etc.*) coller, faire attacher (les cheveux).

clotbur ['klɔtbər], *s. Bot:* xanthium *m*; bardane *f*.

cloth, *pl.* **cloths** [klɔθ, klɔθs], *s.* **1.** (*a*) étoffe *f* de laine; drap *m*; **c. trousers,** pantalon *m* de drap; **c.-covered buttons,** boutons drapés; *F:* **story made up out of whole c.,** histoire inventée de toutes pièces; **c. hall,** halle *f* aux draps; **c. maker, manufacturer,** fabricant *m* de draps; drapier *m*; **c. merchant,** négociant *m* en draps; **c. trade,** commerce *m* des draps; draperie *f*; **c. worker,** ouvrier drapier; (*b*) (*linen, cotton*) toile *f*; **map mounted on c.,** carte entoilée; **abrasive c.,** toile émeri; **glass c.,** toile verrée; **c. binding,** reliure *f* en toile, en percaline; **bound in c., c.-bound,** relié toile; **bound in c. boards,** cartonnage *m* pleine toile; (*c*) **American c.,** (i) toile cirée; (ii) molesquine *f*, moleskine *f*; **floor c.,** linoléum *m*; (*d*) **c. of gold,** drap d'or; (*e*) *P:* **c. head,** idiot *m*, imbécile *m*; **to have c. ears,** être dur d'oreille. **2.** (*a*) linge *m*; (*for cleaning*) (i) torchon *m*; (ii) serpillière *f*; **to wipe sth. with a dry c.,** essuyer qch. avec un linge sec; **to use a soft c.,** se servir d'un linge fin, d'un chiffon doux; (*b*) (= *tablecloth*) nappe *f*; **to lay the c.,** (i) mettre la nappe; (ii) dresser, mettre, le couvert; **to remove the c.,** (i) ôter la nappe; (ii) desservir; (*c*) tapis *m* (*de billard*); (*d*) *Th:* toile (de décor); (*e*) *Nau:* bande *f*, laize *f*, cueille *f*; **sail of so many cloths,** voile *f* de tant de laizes; (*f*) *Nau:* **ship that spreads much c.,** navire *m* qui porte une forte voilure. **3.** *F:* **the c.,** (i) l'habit *m* ecclésiastique, la soutane; (ii) le clergé; **the respect due to the c.,** le respect dû au clergé, à la soutane.

clothe [klouð], *v.tr.* (*p.t. & p.p.* **clad** [klad] *or* **clothed** [klouðd]) vêtir, revêtir, habiller (**in, with,** de); **to c. oneself in wool,** se vêtir de laine; **warmly clad, lightly clad,** chaudement vêtu, légèrement vêtu; **clad in armour,** revêtu d'une armure; **wall clad with ivy, ivy-clad wall,** mur revêtu, tapissé, de lierre; **vine-clad hills,** collines couvertes de vignes; *B:* **to be clothed with righteousness,** être tout revêtu de droiture; *Fig:* **to be clothed and in one's right mind,** avoir l'esprit bien équilibré.

clothes [klouðz], *s.pl.* **1.** vêtements *m*, habits *m*, effets *m*, *F:* frusques *f*; **c. make the man,** l'habit fait l'homme; **suit of c.,** complet *m*; **old c.,** vieux habits; **in one's best c.,** dans ses habits de cérémonie; *F:* sur son trente et un; endimanché; (*of woman*) dans ses plus beaux atours; (*of woman*) **to be fond of c.,** aimer la toilette; *F:* **he looks as if he'd gone to bed in his c., his c. look as if they'd been slept in,** son complet est (toujours) tout fripé; **to put on, take off, one's c.,** s'habiller, se vêtir; se déshabiller, se dévêtir; **to put on one's c. again,** se rhabiller; **pack up your c.,** ramassez vos effets; *F:* faites votre baluchon; **to go to bed, to sleep, with one's c. on, in one's c.,** se coucher tout habillé; **c. brush,** brosse *f* à habits; **c. hook,** patère *f* à habits; portemanteau *m*; **c. rack,** porte-habit(s) *m inv.*; **c. press,** armoire *f* à linge; armoire-étagère, *pl.* armoires-étagères; *NAm:* **c. tree,** porte-chapeaux *m inv.* **2.** linge *m*; **dirty c.,** linge sale; **(dirty) c. basket,** panier *m* à linge, au linge sale; **c. horse,** (i) chevalet *m* pour linge; séchoir *m*; (ii) *F: Pej:* élégant, -ante, gommeux, -euse; **c. line, rope,** corde *f* à (étendre le) linge; étendoir *m*; tendoir *m*; *Nau:* cartahu *m* (de linge); *F:* **I can sleep on a c. line,** moi, je peux dormir n'importe où, n'importe comment; **c. peg, pin,** (i) pince *f*; épingle *f* à linge; (ii) fichoir *m*; **c. prop,** *NAm:* **pole,** perche *f* d'étendoir, de corde à linge; fourche *f* de soutien. **3.** (= *bedclothes*) couvertures *fpl* et draps *mpl* de lit; couchage *m*.

clothier ['klouðiər], *s.* **1.** fabricant *m* de draps; drapier *m*. **2.** (*a*) marchand *m* de draps; drapier; (*b*) marchand de confections; confectionneur *m*.

clothing ['klouðiŋ], *s.* **1.** (*a*) action *f* de vêtir, de se vêtir; (*b*) *Ecc:* prise *f* d'habit. **2.** *coll.* habillement *m*, vêtements *mpl*; **soiled c.,** linge *m* sale; **articles of c.,** (i) vêtements; (ii) linge de corps; **the c. trade,** l'industrie *f* du vêtement, de l'habillement; **c. store,** (i) *Mil:* magasin *m* d'habillement; (ii) *NAm:* magasin de drapier, magasin de confections; *Hist:* **c. book** = carte *f* d'habillement. **3.** *Const:* revêtement *m* (d'une charpente de fer).

clothyard ['klɔθjɑːd], *s.* aune *f* de drapier; *Hist:* **c. shaft,** flèche d'archer longue d'un *yard*.

Clotilda [klə'tildə], *Pr.n.f.* Clotilde.

clotted ['klɔtid], *a.* **1. c. blood,** sang coagulé; *Cu:* **c. cream,** crème caillée, caillebottée (par l'échaudage); **c. oil,** huile grenue; *Lit: Art:* **c. style,** style pâteux; *F:* **c. nonsense,** un tas d'absurdités. **2. c. hair,** cheveux collés ensemble (par la boue, le sang, etc.).

clotting ['klɔtiŋ], *s.* caillement *m*, figement *m*.

cloud[1] [klaud], *s.* **1.** nuage *m*; *Poet:* nuée *f*, nue *f*; **masses of c.,** masses *f* de nuages; **c. bank,** banc *m*, panne *f*, de nuages; **c. drift,** nuages flottants; **c. banner, banner c.,** nuages en bannière; **rain c.,** nuage de pluie, pluvieux; nimbus *m*; **small black c.** (*announcing a storm*), point noir; *Nau:* **c. ring** (= *doldrums*), le pot au noir; *Fig:* **to be in the clouds,** (i) être distrait; être, se perdre, dans les nuages; (ii) être aux anges; **he is always in the clouds,** il est toujours entre (le) ciel et (la) terre; *U.S:* **to be on c. seven, on c. nine, on a c.,** être aux anges; (*of stranger*) **to drop from the clouds,** tomber des nues, de la lune, du ciel; *Prov:* **every c. has a silver lining,** après la pluie le beau temps; dans toute chose il y a un bon côté; **there was a c. on his face,** son visage était sombre, soucieux;

the c. on his brow, son front assombri; **to be under a c.,** (i) être en défaveur; (ii) être l'objet de soupçons; être mal vu; être regardé d'un mauvais œil; **he is under a c.,** sa réputation a subi une forte atteinte; *Phot:* **c. negative,** cliché *m*, négatif *m*, de nuages. **2.** (*a*) nuage, voile *m* (de fumée, de poussière); tourbillon *m* (de poussière); **the dust rises in clouds,** la poussière monte en tourbillons; *Fig:* **under the c. of night,** sous le voile de la nuit; *Mil: O:* **c. attack,** attaque *f* par vague, nuage, chimique, de gaz; **atomic c.,** nuage radioactif; *Artil:* **bursting c.,** fumée *f* d'éclatement; (*b*) *Atom.Ph:* **c. chamber,** chambre *f* de détente, d'ionisation; **Wilson's c. chamber,** chambre (à condensation) de Wilson. **3.** (*in liquid*) nuage, turbidité *f*; (*on glass*) buée *f*; (*on marble*) tache *f*; (*in precious stone*) nuée; (*on horse's head*) tache noire. **4.** nuée (de sauterelles, flèches); *Lit:* **c. of witnesses,** nuée de témoins.

cloud[2]. **1.** *v.tr.* (*a*) couvrir, voiler, obscurcir (le ciel); troubler, rendre trouble (un liquide); couvrir (une vitre) de buée; embuer (une vitre); ternir (un miroir); **eyes clouded with tears,** yeux voilés, embués, de larmes; **to c. s.o.'s happiness,** troubler le bonheur de qn; **cares have clouded his brow,** les chagrins ont assombri son front; **to c. s.o.'s mind,** troubler, obscurcir, la raison de qn; **to c. the issue,** embrouiller la question; **to c. s.o's reputation,** flétrir, ternir, la réputation de qn; (*b*) *Tex:* chiner (un tissu); (*c*) marbrer (le bois, le cuir). **2.** *v.i.* (*of sky*) **to c. (up, over),** se couvrir, se voiler, de nuages; se rembrunir, s'assombrir, s'embrumer, s'embrouiller, se brouiller, s'obscurcir; **his brow clouded (over),** son front s'assombrit, se rembrunit.

cloudberry ['klaudberi], *s. Bot:* ronce *f* faux mûrier.

cloudburst ['klaudbə:st], *s.* trombe *f*; rafale *f* de pluie.

cloud-cannon ['klaudkænən], *s.* canon *m* paragrêle.

cloud-capped ['klaudkæpt], *a.* couronné de nuages; perdu dans les nues.

cloud-cuckoo-land, -town ['klaud'kuku:lænd, -taun], *s.* **1.** *Gr.Lit:* néphélococcygie *f*. **2.** *Fig:* pays *m*, ville *f*, imaginaire; pays de cocagne.

clouded ['klaudid], *a.* **c. sky,** ciel couvert (de nuages); **c. glass,** (i) verre embué, couvert de buée; (ii) verre dépoli; **c. liquid,** liquide *m* trouble; **c. gem,** pierre nuageuse, tachetée; **c. coat of fur,** poil nuagé; *Z:* **c. leopard,** panthère *f* longibande; **to become c.,** (*of sky*), se couvrir; (*of mind*) s'obscurcir; **c. brow,** front assombri, rembruni, nébuleux; **c. mind,** esprit obnubilé.

cloudily ['klaudili], *adv.* nuageusement, obscurément.

cloudiness ['klaudinis], *s.* **1.** aspect nuageux (du ciel). **2.** turbidité *f* (d'un liquide); obscurité *f* (de style).

clouding ['klaudiŋ], *s.* **c. (over) of the sky, the mind,** obscurcissement *m* du ciel, de l'esprit.

cloudland ['klaudlænd], **cloud-world** ['klaudwə:ld], *s.* (le) pays des songes.

cloudless ['klaudlis], *a.* (ciel *m*) sans nuages; *Fig:* **c. days,** jours sereins; **c. days of happiness,** jours de bonheur sans nuages.

cloudlet ['klaudlit], *s.* petit nuage.

cloudscape ['klaudskeip], *s. Art:* étude *f* de nuages.

cloudy ['klaudi], *a.* **1. c. weather,** temps couvert; **c. sky,** ciel nuageux, assombri; **it's c.,** le temps est couvert; il fait un temps couvert. **2. c. liquid,** liquide *m* trouble; (*of liquid*) **to turn c.,** louchir; **c. wine,** vin *m* louche; *Med:* **c. urine,** urine chargée; *Paperm:* **c. paper,** papier nuageux, floconneux, moutonneux (par transparence); **c. gem,** pierre nuageuse, pâteuse, sourde; **c. style,** style obscur, nuageux; **c. ideas,** idées fumeuses, nébuleuses.

cloué ['klu:ei], *a. Her:* cloué.

clough [klʌf], *s. Geog:* ravin *m*, gorge *f*; couloir *m*.

clout[1] [klaut], *s.* **1.** *A: & Dial:* (*a*) morceau (de toile, cuir, tôle) destiné à remettre une pièce (à un vêtement, la carène d'un navire, etc.); (*b*) pièce (remise à un vêtement, etc.); (*c*) ferrure *f* (de sabot); (*d*) *Veh:* happe *f* (de l'essieu). **2.** *A:* (*a*) chiffon *m*, linge *m*, torchon *m*; **dish-c.,** torchon; (*b*) *P:* mouchoir *m*; (*c*) *P:* serviette *f* hygiénique; bande *f*, linge, périodique. **3.** *usu. pl. F: A:* frusques *f*, nippes *f*; (*of women*) jupons *m*, dessous *mpl*; *Prov:* **ne'er cast a c. till May be out** = en avril ne quitte pas un fil. **4.** (*a*) but *m* (de tir à l'arc); centre *m* de la cible; (*b*) flèche *f* qui a atteint le but. **5.** *F:* beigne *f*; claque *f*, taloche *f* (sur la tête). **6.** *Carp: Const:* **c. (nail),** clou *m* à tête plate; caboche *f*.

clout[2], *v.tr.* **1.** *A: & Dial:* (*a*) rapiécer, rapetasser (un vieil habit); (*b*) ferrer (un sabot); (*c*) *Nau:* mailleter (la carène). **2.** *F:* **to c. s.o. on, over, the head,** flanquer une taloche, une beigne, à qn; talocher qn.

clouting ['klautiŋ], *s.* (*a*) rapiéçage *m*, rapiècement *m*, rapetassage *m*; (*b*) *Nau:* mailletage *m* (de la carène).

clove[1] [klouv], *s. Bot:* caïeu *m*; **c. of garlic,** gousse *f* d'ail.

clove[2], *s.* **1.** (*a*) clou *m* de girofle; **mother c.,** mère *f* de girofle, clou-matrice *m*, *pl.* clous-matrices; **oil of cloves, c. oil,** essence *f* de girofle; (*b*) *Bot:* **c. tree,** giroflier *m*. **2.** *Bot:* **c. (gillyflower), c. pink,** œillet-giroflée *m*, *pl.* œillets-giroflées; œillet *m* des fleuristes, à bouquet.

clove hitch ['klouvhitʃ], *s. Nau:* demi-clefs *fpl* à capeler; **c.-h. inverted,** deux demi-clefs renversées.

clove hook ['klouvhuk], *s.* croc *m* à ciseaux.

cloven ['klouvn], *a.* **1. c. hoof,** pied fendu, fourchu; **to show, display, the c. hoof,** montrer le pied fourchu; laisser passer le bout de l'oreille; se trahir. **2.** *Com:* **c. timber,** bois *m* de fente.

cloven-footed, -hoofed ['klouvn'futid, '-huft], *a. Z:* fissipède; qui a le pied fourchu, fendu, bisulque.

clover ['klouvər], *s. Bot:* trèfle *m*; *F:* lupinelle *f*, mignonnet *m*; **crimson c., French c., flesh-coloured c.,** trèfle incarnat, anglais, du Roussillon; (trèfle) farouche *m*; **white c., Dutch c., New Zealand c.,** trèfle rampant; petit trèfle blanc; triolet *m*; traînelle *f*; **Japan(ese), bush, c.,** lespedeza *m*; **wild white c.,** trèfle blanc; **sweet c.,** mélilot *m*; **heart c.,** medicago maculé; **hop c.,** trèfle jaune, luzerne *f* houblon, trèfle minette, lupuline *f*; **hare's foot c.,** *U.S:* **rabbit-foot c.,** patte-de-lièvre *f*, *pl.* pattes-de-lièvre; **prairie c.,** petalostemon *m*; **c. field,** tréflière *f*; **c. leaf,** feuille *f* de trèfle; **four-leaved c.,** trèfle à quatre feuilles (qui porte bonheur); *F:* **to be, live, in c., to live like pigs in c.,** vivre comme un coq en pâte, comme un porc à l'auge; être logé dans un fromage; avoir les pieds au chaud; *P:* boire du lait.

cloverleaf, *pl.* **-leafs, -leaves** ['klouvəli:f, -li:fs, -li:vz], *s. Civ.E:* **c. (intersection),** croisement *m*, carrefour *m*, en (as de) trèfle.

Clovis ['klouvis], *Pr.n.m.* Clovis.

clown[1] [klaun], *s.* **1.** *A:* paysan *m*. **2.** *A:* rustre *m*, manant *m*, baptiste *m*, Baptiste *m*. **3.** *Th:* (*a*) bouffon *m*, paillasse *m*, gille *m*, pitre *m*; (*in old farce*) le Barbouillé; (*b*) clown *m* (de cirque); (*c*) *F:* **you c.!** espèce d'imbécile, d'idiot!

clown[2]. **1.** *v.i.* faire le clown, le bouffon, le pitre. **2.** *v.tr.* charger, travestir (un rôle).

clownery ['klaunəri], **clowning** ['klauniŋ], *s.* **1.** (i) bouffonnerie *f*, pitrerie *f*, paillasserie *f*; (ii) clownerie *f* (de cirque); **piece of c.,** (i) pitrerie, paillasserie; (ii) clownerie. **2.** *pl.* (i) tours *m* de paillasse; (ii) clowneries.

clownish ['klauniʃ], *a.* **1.** *A:* campagnard, agreste. **2.** (*a*) gauche, empoté; (*b*) grossier, mal élevé; **c. conduct,** conduite *f* digne d'un rustre. **3.** (tour *m*) de paillasse, de clown (de cirque); clownesque; **c. trick,** clownerie *f*.

clownishly ['klauniʃli], *adv.* **1.** gauchement, d'un air empoté. **2.** en rustre; grossièrement.

clownishness ['klauniʃnis], *s.* **1.** (*a*) gaucherie *f*, rusticité *f*; (*b*) grossièreté *f*. **2.** (*a*) paillasserie *f*; (*b*) **piece of c.,** clownerie *f*.

cloy [klɔi], *v.tr.* (*of food, etc.*) rassasier; écœurer; **cloyed with pleasure,** rassasié de plaisir; blasé sur les plaisirs; **to c. the palate,** blaser le palais; **to c. the appetite,** affadir le cœur; *Lit:* **delights that never c.,** plaisirs dont on ne se lasse pas.

cloying[1] ['klɔiiŋ], *a.* rassasiant, affadissant.

cloying[2], *s.* satiété *f*; affadissement *m*.

club[1] [klʌb], *s.* **1.** (*a*) massue *f*, gourdin *m*; **c. law,** la loi du plus fort, du bâton; *Mec.E:* **c. tooth,** dent *f* conique; *Gym:* **Indian c.,** mil *m*; bouteille *f* en bois; (*b*) *Golf:* club *m*, crosse *f*, canne *f*; (*c*) *Bot: Z:* massue; *Bot:* **c. fungus,** clavaire *f*; **c. rush,** scirpe *m*; (*d*) *A:* (*of hair*) catogan *m*. **2.** *Cards:* trèfle *m*; **to play clubs, a c.,** jouer (un) trèfle; **ace of clubs,** as *m* de trèfle. **3.** (*a*) club *m* (politique, littéraire, etc., offrant à ses membres tout le confort d'un hôtel); *F:* **the best c. in London,** le palais du Parlement; **c. chair,** (fauteuil *m*) club *m*; **c. sandwich,** sandwich *m* copieusement garni de viande, laitue, tomate, etc.; *F:* **c. story,** histoire égrillarde, à raconter entre hommes; **to tell c. stories,** en raconter de salées; dire des gaudrioles; (*b*) cercle *m*; **literary c.,** cercle, cénacle *m*, littéraire; **supper c.,** dancing *m*; **gambling c.,** cercle (de jeu); *Mil:* **officers' c.,** cercle militaire; cercle des officiers; (*c*) association *f*; société *f*; club; **benefit c.,** société de secours mutuels; **social c.,** société où l'on se distrait en famille; **c. for young people, youth c.,** foyer *m* des jeunes; (*associated with church*) patronage *m*; **tennis c.,** société, club, de tennis; **alpine c.,** club alpin; **yacht c.,** club de yachting; *F:* **the nuclear power c.,** les puissances *f* nucléaires; *P:* **to be in the (pudding) c.,** être enceinte; *P:* avoir un polichinelle dans le tiroir; **c. money,** (i) cotisation *f*; (ii) caisse *f* (d'une société de secours mutuels); **c. tie,** cravate *f* aux couleurs d'une association sportive; (*d*) **book c.,** club, guilde *f*, du livre.

club[2], *v.* (**clubbed**) **1.** *v.tr.* (*a*) frapper (qn) avec une massue, avec un gourdin; **to c. s.o. to death,** assommer qn à coups de gourdin; **to c. s.o. with a rifle,** frapper qn à coups de crosse; (*b*) *Mil:* **to c. one's rifle,** saisir son fusil par le canon; **with clubbed rifle,** la crosse en l'air. **2.** *v.tr.* (*a*) **to c. (persons) together,** joindre, réunir (des personnes); former un noyau (d'adhérents, etc.); (*b*) *Mil:* **to c. a battalion,** mettre un bataillon en cohue, en pagaïe; (*c*) (*of several pers.*) **to c. one's resources (together),** mettre ses ressources en commun; faire bourse commune; boursiller. **3.** *v.i.* (*a*) **to c. with others for sth., to do sth.,** se réunir, s'associer, avec d'autres pour qch., pour faire qch.; (*b*) **to c. together to purchase sth.,** se cotiser, mettre son argent en commun, pour acheter qch.; (*c*) *Mil:* (*of battalion, company, etc.*) se mettre en cohue, en pagaïe; (*d*) *Nau:* (*of ship*) **to c. (down),** déraper sur son ancre.

clubbable ['klʌbəbl], *a.* (homme) sociable.

clubbed [klʌbd], *a. Nat.Hist:* claviforme, clavé; en forme de massue.

clubbing ['klʌbiŋ], *s.* **1.** = CLUBROOT. **2.** (*a*) association *f*, réunion *f* (de personnes); (*b*) **c. of resources,** mise *f* en commun de fonds, de ressources.

clubfoot ['klʌbfut], *s.* pied bot, pied équin.

clubfooted ['klʌbfutid], *a.* (qui a le) pied bot; *Tchn:* **c. magnet,** électro-aimant boiteux.

clubhaul ['klʌbhɔ:l], *v.tr. & i. Nau: A:* **to c. (a ship),** virer vent devant en mouillant l'ancre sous le vent.

clubhouse ['klʌbhaus], *s.* (local *m* du) cercle; club *m*; *Golf: Ten: etc:* pavillon *m*.

Clubionidae [klʌbi'ɔnidi:], *s.pl. Arach:* clubionidés *m*.

clubland ['klʌblænd], *s.* quartier *m* des clubs à Londres (St James' et Piccadilly).

clubman, *pl.* **-men** ['klʌbmən], *s.m.* **1.** habitué d'un club ou des clubs; cercleux, clubiste, clubman, -men. **2.** *U.S:* homme du monde.

clubmoss ['klʌbmɔs], *s. Bot:* lycopode *m* en massue; *F:* herbe *f* aux massues; soufre végétal; pied-de-loup *m*, *pl.* pieds-de-loup.

clubroom ['klʌbru:m], *s.* local, -aux *m*, salle *f*, de réunion.

clubroot ['klʌbru:t], *s. Hort:* hernie *f* (des choux, des navets).

club-shaped ['klʌbʃeipt], *a. Nat.Hist:* claviforme, clavé; en forme de massue.

clubwoman, *pl.* **-women** ['klʌbwumən, -wimin], *s.f.* membre d'un club féminin.

cluck[1] [klʌk], *s.* **1.** (*of hens*) gloussement *m*; **the hen gave a c.,** la poule a gloussé. **2.** *P:* **dumb c.,** sot, sotte; niais, -aise; idiot, -ote.

cluck[2], *v.i.* (*a*) (*of hen*) glousser; (*b*) *F:* (*of pers.*) faire claquer sa langue.

clucker ['klʌkər], *s. F:* bavard, -arde.

clucking ['klʌkiŋ], *s.* gloussement *m*.

clucky ['klʌki], *a.* (poule) couveuse.

clue[1] [klu:], *s.* **1.** = CLEW[1] 1, 2. **2.** (*a*) fil *m*, indication *f*, indice *m*; **to have the c.,** tenir le bout du fil; *F:* avoir trouvé le joint; **to get, find, the c. to sth.,** trouver, découvrir, la clef de qch., le fin mot; **to give s.o. a c.,** mettre qn sur la voie, sur la piste; **the police have got a c.,** la police est sur la piste; **the revolver was the c. that led to his arrest,** le revolver fournit l'indice qui mena à son arrestation; (*b*) *F:* **I haven't a c.,** je n'en sais rien; je n'en ai pas la moindre idée; **he hasn't a c.,** il ne sait rien de rien, il ne sait jamais rien; (*c*) **the clues of a crossword puzzle,** les définitions *f* d'un problème de mots croisés.

clue[2], *v.tr.* **1. to c. a crossword puzzle,** donner les définitions d'un problème de mots croisés. **2.** *F:* **to c. s.o. (in, up),** renseigner qn, mettre qn à la page; **he's really clued up,** il sait de quoi il retourne.

clueless ['klu:lis], *a. F:* **he's quite c.,** il ne sait jamais rien; il ne sait, rien de rien, de quoi il retourne.

clumber ['klʌmbər], *s.* **c. (spaniel),** (épagneul) clumber *m*.

clump[1] [klʌmp], *s.* **1.** (*a*) bloc *m*, masse *f*, morceau *m* (de bois, d'argile, etc.); *Nau:* **mooring c.,** crapaud *m*; (*b*) groupe *m*, bouquet *m*, bosquet *m* (d'arbres); massif *m* (d'arbustes, de fleurs); touffe *f* (de fleurs); **c. of shoots,** cépée *f*; (*c*) *Med:* caillot *m* (de fibrine); *Bac:* agglutination *f* (de microbes). **2.** *Bootm:* **c.(-sole),** semelle *f* supplémentaire; patin *m* (de chaussure). **3.** *Nau:* **c.(-block),** moque *f* à rouet. **4.** pas lourd. **5.** *P:* taloche *f*, gnon *m*. **6.** *Typ:* lingot *m*.

clump[2]. **1.** (*a*) *v.i.* se grouper en masse compacte; (*of fibrine*) se cailler; (*of microbes*) s'agglutiner; (*b*) *v.tr.* grouper en masse compacte; semer (plusieurs graines) dans le même trou; planter (des arbustes, etc.) en massif. **2.** (*a*) *v.i.* **to c. (about),** marcher lourdement; **his heels went c., c., on the flagstones,** ses talons sonnaient lourdement sur les dalles; (*b*) *v.tr. P:* **to c. s.o.'s head,** flanquer une taloche à qn; (*c*) *v.tr.* **to c. a pair of shoes,** ajouter des patins *m*, une semelle supplémentaire, à des chaussures.

clumper ['klʌmpər], *s.* (i) gros soulier; (ii) botte *f* de marin.

clumsily ['klʌmzili], *adv.* **1.** maladroitement, gauchement, sans grâce. **2.** grossièrement; **c. built,** mal bâti. **3.** sans tact.

clumsiness ['klʌmzinis], *s.* **1.** maladresse *f,* gaucherie *f;* manque *m* de grâce. **2.** (*of shape*) grossièreté *f,* lourdeur *f.* **3.** manque *m* de tact.

clumsy ['klʌmzi], *a.* **1.** (*of pers., movement, etc.*) maladroit, malhabile, gauche, empoté, mal dégourdi. **2.** (*of shape*) lourd, disgracieux, informe; **c. boots,** godillots *mpl;* **she has a c. figure,** elle est mal bâtie. **3. c. verse,** vers lourds, mal faits; **c. forgery,** contre-façon grossière; **c. apology,** excuse maladroite, gauche; **c. praise,** éloges maladroits, qui manquent de tact.

clunch [klʌn(t)ʃ], *s.* **1.** *Geol:* barre *f* (dans une couche de houille). **2.** *Const:* argile schisteuse (employée comme pierre à bâtir à l'intérieur des édifices).

Cluniac ['klu:niæk], *a.* (ordre, édifice) clunisien; *a. & s.* (moine) cluniste (*m*).

Clunist ['klu:nist], *s. Ecc:* cluniste *m.*

clunk[1] [klʌŋk], *v.tr.* battre, cogner; **to c. s.o.'s ears, head,** flanquer une taloche à qn; *U.S:* **to c. down the money,** allonger l'argent; casquer.

clunk[2], *s.* **1.** bruit sourd; son mat. **2.** *U.S: F:* sot, sotte; niais, -aise.

clunker ['klʌnkər], *s. U.S: F:* auto délabrée; vieille bagnole.

clupea ['klu:piə], *s. Ich:* clupéa *f.*

clupeid ['klu:piid], *s. Ich:* clupe *f.*

Clupeidae [clu:'pi:idi:], *s.pl. Ich:* clupéidés *m.*

clupeine ['klu:piin], *s. Ch:* clupéine *f.*

cluricaune ['kluərikɔ:n], *s. Irish Myth:* farfadet *m,* lutin *m.*

cluse [klu:z], *s. Geol:* cluse *f.*

Clusiaceae [klu:zi'eisii:], *s.pl. Bot:* clusiacées *f.*

cluster[1] ['klʌstər], *s.* bouquet *m* (de fleurs, de cerises); bouquet, touffe *f,* massif *m,* groupe *m* (d'arbres); grappe *f* (de raisins, de cerises); glane *f* (de poires; régime *m* (de bananes); épi *m,* nœud *m* (de diamants); amas *m* (d'étoiles); essaim *m* (d'abeilles); peloton *m* (de chenilles); groupe, rassemblement *m* (de personnes); agglomération *f* (d'îles); pâté *m* (de maisons); faisceau *m* (d'ampoules électriques); *Bot:* trochet *m* (de fruits, de fleurs); **houses scattered in clusters,** maisons éparses en grappes; **hair in thick clusters,** cheveux *mpl* en grosses boucles; **c. candlestick,** candélabre *m;* **c. sampling,** sondage *m* en grappes; *Astr:* **galactic c.,** amas ouvert, galactique: **globular c.,** amas globulaire; *Mil:* **c. bomb,** (type *m* de) bombe *f* antipersonnel.

cluster[2]. **1.** *v.tr.* grouper (en grappes); rassembler (des objets) en groupes. **2.** *v.i.* (*a*) (*of fruit*) se former, croître, en grappes; (*b*) (*of bees*) se pelotonner; (*of pers.*) **to c. round s.o., sth.,** se grouper, se rassembler, s'attrouper, autour de qn, de qch.; **they clustered round the door,** ils se tenaient à la porte; **village clustering round its church,** village ramassé autour de son église; (*c*) (*of particles, etc.*) **to c. together,** se conglomérer, s'agglomérer.

clustered ['klʌstəd], *a.* **1. c. vine,** vigne chargée de grappes; **heavy-c. branch,** branche grappue, lourdement chargée. **2.** *Arch:* **c. columns,** colonnes *f* en faisceau; **c. pillar,** pilier *m* à colonnes engagées.

clustering[1] ['klʌstəriŋ], *a.* **c. grapes,** raisins *m* en grappes; **c. curls,** boucles épaisses.

clustering[2], *s.* **1.** croissance *f* en grappes. **2.** agglomération *f.* **3.** groupage *m* (en grappes).

clutch[1] [klʌtʃ], *s.* **1.** (*a*) griffe *f* (d'un animal); serre *f* (d'un oiseau de proie); **to fall into s.o.'s clutches,** tomber sous la patte de qn; **to be in the clutches of a blackmailer,** être la proie, être entre les griffes, d'un chanteur; **to escape from s.o.'s clutches,** se tirer des pattes de qn; (*b*) action *f* de saisir, d'agripper; geste *m* fait pour agripper; prise *f;* **to make a c. at sth.,** essayer de saisir qch.; **only a c. at his companion's arm saved him from falling,** s'il n'avait pas saisi le bras de son compagnon il serait tombé. **2.** (*a*) *Mec.E: Aut:* embrayage *m;* **automatic c.,** embrayage automatique; autodébrayage *m;* **hydraulic c.,** embrayage hydraulique; **(electro-) magnetic c.,** embrayage (électro-)magnétique; **centrifugal c.,** embrayage centrifugal; **cone c.,** embrayage à cône; **band c.,** embrayage à courroies, à ruban; **friction c.,** embrayage à friction; **(single-)disc c.,** embrayage à disque (unique); **multi(ple)-disc c.,** embrayage à disques multiples; **(single-)plate c.,** embrayage à plateau (unique); **multi(ple)-plate c.,** embrayage à plateaux multiples; **dog c., claw c., jaw c.,** embrayage à clabots, à griffe(s); clabot *m;* clabotage *m;* accouplement *m* à griffe(s); **direct-drive dog c.,** crabot *m;* **disconnecting c.,** manchon *m* de débrayage; **c. control,** commande *f* d'embrayage; **c. disc, plate,** disque *m,* plateau *m,* d'embrayage; **c. fork, lever,** fourche *f* d'embrayage; **c. facing, lining,** garniture *f* d'embrayage; **c. housing,** carter *m* d'embrayage; **c. arm,** levier *m* d'embrayage; **c. guide,** guide *m* d'embrayage; **c. pedal,** pédale *f* d'embrayage, de débrayage; **c. spring,** ressort *m* d'embrayage; **c. linkage,** timonerie *f* d'embrayage; **c. stop,** frein *m* d'embrayage, de débrayage; **to let in the c.,** embrayer; **to release, let out, the c.,** débrayer; (*b*) *Const: etc:* accouplement *m* à griffes.

clutch[2], *v.tr. & ind.tr.* saisir, empoigner, étreindre, agripper; agriffer; **to c. sth. with both hands,** saisir qch. à deux mains; **to c. at sth., to c. hold of sth.,** se retenir, se raccrocher, s'agripper, s'agriffer, se cramponner, à qch.; **to c. at any straw,** se raccrocher à n'importe quoi; **the pistol which he was still clutching,** le pistolet qu'il étreignait encore.

clutch[3], *s.* (*a*) couvée *f* (d'œufs, de poussins); (*b*) *F:* **a c. of journalists covering a story,** un groupe de journalistes qui faisaient un reportage.

clutch bag ['klʌtʃbæg], *s.* pochette *f.*

clutter[1] ['klʌtər], *s.* **1.** *A:* tapage *m,* remue-ménage *m.* **2.** encombrement *m,* méli-mélo *m,* confusion *f;* entassement *m* (de mobilier, etc.); **everything's in a c.,** tout est en désordre, en confusion, en pagaille. **3.** *Rad:* échos *m pl* parasites; **fixed, permanent, c.,** échos fixes; **ground c.,** échos de sol; **rain c.,** échos parasites dus à la pluie; **sea c.,** échos parasites en mer.

clutter[2]. **1.** *v.i. A:* = CLATTER[2]. **2.** *v.tr.* **to c. up a room,** encombrer une pièce (**with,** de); **desk cluttered with papers,** bureau encombré de papiers, où des papiers traînent partout; **to c. up one's mind with useless facts,** charger sa mémoire de faits inutiles.

cluttered ['klʌtəd], *a.* encombré (**with,** de).

Clydesdale ['klaidzdeil], *s.* **1.** (cheval *m* de trait) clydesdale *m.* **2.** (chien terrier) clydesdale.

Clymenia [klai'mi:niə], *s. Paleont:* clymenia *f,* clyménie *f.*

clymenid ['klaiminid], *s. Paleont:* clyménidé *m.*

Clymenidae [klai'menidi:], *s.pl. Paleont:* clyménidés *m.*

Clypeastridea [klipiæ'stridiə], **Clypeastrina** [klipiæ'strainə], **Clypeastroid(e)a** [klipiæ'strɔid(i)ə], *s.pl. Echin:* clypéastrides *m,* clypéastroïdes *m.*

clypeate ['klipieit], *a. Ent:* clypéacé.

clypeiform ['klipiifɔ:m], *a. Ent:* clypéiforme.

clypeus, *pl.* **-ei** ['klipiəs, -iai], *s. Ent:* clypeus *m,* chaperon *m,* épistome *m.*

clysmian ['klizmiən], *a. Geol:* clysmien.

clyster ['klistər], *s. Med: A:* clystère *m.*

Clytemnestra [kl(a)item'nestrə], *Pr.n.f. Gr.Lit:* Clytemnestre.

cneorum [ni:'ɔrəm], *s. Bot:* cneorum *m;* camélée *f.*

cnida, *pl.* **-ae** ['naidə, -i:], *s. Coel:* cnidoblaste *m,* nématocyste *m.*

Cnidaria [nai'dɛəriə], *s.pl. Coel:* cnidaires *m.*

Cnidian ['naidiən], *A.Geog:* (*a*) *a.* cnidien; (*b*) *s.* Cnidien, -ienne.

cnidoblast ['naidoublæst], *s. Biol:* cnidoblaste *m.*

cnidocil ['naidousil], *s. Biol:* cnidocil *m.*

cnidocyst ['naidousist], *s. Biol:* cnidocyste *f.*

cnidosis [nai'dousis], *s. Med:* cnidose *f.*

Cnidosporidia [naidouspɔ'ridiə], *s.pl. Prot:* cnidosporidies *m.*

Cnidus ['naidəs], *Pr.n. A.Geog:* Cnide.

Cnossos, Cnossus ['nɔsəs], *Pr.n. A.Geog:* Cnosse, Cnossos.

co- [kou], *pref.* co-.

coacervate [kou'æsəveit], *s. Ch:* coacervat *m.*

coacervation [kouæsə'veiʃ(ə)n], *s. Ch:* coacervation *f.*

coach[1] [koutʃ], *s.* **1.** (*a*) *A.Veh:* carrosse *m;* coche *m;* **stage c.,** diligence *m;* **c. and six,** carrosse, coche, à six chevaux; **to drive a c. and four through an Act of Parliament,** passer outre la loi; *F:* **his story has holes that you could drive a c. and four through,** son histoire ne tient pas debout; **c. horse,** (i) cheval *m* de carrosse, de diligence; carrossier *m;* (ii) *Ent:* **devil's c. horse,** staphylin *m;* **c. dog,** chien *m* de Dalmatie; **c. box,** siège *m* du cocher; (*b*) *Aut: A: & N Am:* conduite intérieure à deux portes, coach *m;* (*c*) autocar *m,* car *m;* **c. station,** gare routière. **2.** *Rail:* voiture *f,* wagon *m;* **the train has four coaches for Glasgow,** le train comporte une rame de quatre wagons sur Glasgow. **3.** *Navy: A:* chambre *f* du conseil; chambre de galerie. **4.** (*a*) *Sch:* professeur *m* qui donne des leçons particulières; répétiteur *m;* (*b*) *Sp:* entraîneur *m.*

coach[2]. **1.** *v.tr.* (*a*) *Sch:* donner des leçons particulières, **to be coached,** prendre des leçons particulières; **to c. s.o. to do sth.,** faire la leçon à qn; catéchiser qn; seriner son rôle à qn; *Th:* **to c. s.o. for a part,** faire répéter son rôle à qn; (*b*) *Sp:* entraîner (une équipe). **2.** *v.i.* (*a*) voyager (i) *A:* en carrosse, en diligence, (ii) en autocar; (*b*) *Sch:* donner des leçons particulières.

coachbuilder ['koutʃbildər], *s.* carrossier *m.*

coachbuilding ['koutʃbildiŋ], *s.* carrosserie *f.*

coachbuilt ['koutʃbilt], *a. Aut:* (voiture) carrossée.

coachhouse ['koutʃhaus], *s.* remise *f* (pour voitures à chevaux); **in the c.,** sous la remise.

coaching ['koutʃiŋ]. **1.** les voyages en carosse, en coche, en diligence; **in the old c. days,** au temps des diligences; **c. inn, c. house,** relais *m.* **2.** (*a*) *Sch:* leçons particulières; répétitions *fpl;* **to give private c.,** donner des leçons particulières; (*b*) *Sp:* entraînement *m* (d'une équipe).

coachman, *pl.* **-men** ['koutʃmən], *s.m.* cocher.

coachsmith ['koutʃsmiθ], *s.* serrurier *m* charron; **coachsmith's work,** serrurerie *f* en charronnage.

coachsmithing ['koutʃsmiθiŋ], *s.* serrurerie *f* en charronnage.

coachwheel ['koutʃ(h)wi:l], *s.* **1.** roue *f* de carrosse. **2.** *Num: A: F:* pièce *f* d'une couronne (cinq shillings).

coachwhip ['koutʃ(h)wip], *s.* **1.** fouet *m* de cocher. **2.** *Rept:* **c. (snake),** masticophis *m,* serpent-fouet *m, pl.* serpents-fouets. **3. c. bird,** psophode *m,* oiseau-cocher *m, pl.* oiseaux-cochers.

coachwork ['koutʃwə:k], *s.* carrosserie *f.*

coact [kou'ækt], *v.i.* agir ensemble.

coadjacent ['kouə'dʒeis(ə)nt], *a.* contigu, -uë (**with,** à).

coadjutor [kou'ædʒutər], *s.* aide *m,* collègue *m; Ecc:* coadjuteur *m.*

coadjutorship [kouæ'dʒu:təʃip], *s. Ecc:* coadjutorerie *f.*

coadjutrix [kou'ædʒutriks], *s.f. Ecc:* coadjutrice.

co-administration ['kouədmini'streiʃ(ə)n], *s.* cogérance *f.*

co-administrator, -trix ['kouəd'ministreitər, -triks], *s.* cogérant, -ante.

coadunate [kou'ædjuneit], *a. Physiol: Bot:* coadné.

coagulability [kouægjulə'biliti], *s.* coagulabilité *f.*

coagulable [kou'ægjuləbl], *a.* coagulable, concrescible.

coagulant [kou'ægjulənt], *s.* coagulant *m.*

coagulase [kou'ægjuleis], *s. Biol:* coagulase *f.*

coagulate [kou'ægjuleit]. **1.** *v.tr.* coaguler, figer; cailler, caillebotter (le lait). **2.** *v.i.* se coaguler, se figer, (se) prendre en masse; (*of milk*) se cailler.

coagulation [kouægju'leiʃ(ə)n], *s.* coagulation *f,* figement *m,* caillement *m;* concrétion *f; Med:* **c. time,** temps *m* de coagulation (du sang).

coagulative [kou'ægjulətiv], *a.* **1.** coagulateur, -trice. **2.** concrescible.

coagulator [kou'ægjuleitər], *s.* coagulant *m.*

coagulum [kou'ægjuləm], *s.* coagulum *m.*

coaita [kouai'tɑ:], *s. Z:* singe-araignée *m, pl.* singes-araignées; atèle *m.*

coak[1] [kouk], *s. Carp:* goujon *m.*

coak[2], *v.tr. Carp:* goujonner (des planches).

coal[1] [koul], *s.* (*a*) charbon *m* (de terre); houille *f;* **hard c.,** houille anthraciteuse; **soft, bituminous, caking, c.,** houille grasse, collante; **semi-bituminous c.,** houille demi-grasse; **lean, non-caking, c.,** houille maigre, sèche, non collante; **steam c.,** houille de chaudière; charbon à vapeur; **smokeless c.,** charbon sans fumée; **smokeless steam c.,** houille à vapeur sans fumée; **splint c.,** houille flambante; **boghead c.,** boghead *m;* **cannel c.,** cannel-coal *m;* **coking c.,** charbon à coke; **small c.,** menu charbon; charbon fin; houille menue; menus *mpl;* fines *fpl;* menuaille *f,* charbonnaille *f,* gailleterie *f,* gailletin *m,* gaillettes *fpl;* **slack c.,** (i) menus (de houille); (ii) poussier *m;* **c. dust,** poussier; charbon en poussière; **c.-dust explosion,** coup *m* de poussière; **house(hold) c.,** charbon (pour usage) domestique; (*b*) **the c.(-mining) industry,** l'industrie houillère, charbonnière; **c. mine,** mine *f* de charbon, de houille; houillère *f;* charbonnage *m;* **c. basin,** houillère; bassin houiller; **c. mining,** exploitation *f* de la houille; **c. miner,** (ouvrier) mineur *m,* houilleur *m;* **c. measure, bed, seam,** couche *f* de houille; gisement houiller; filon houiller; **c.-bearing strata,** couches carbonifères, houillères; **c. face, c. wall,** front *m* de taille; **c. strike,** (i) *Min:* rencontre *f* d'un (nouveau) filon de charbon; (ii) *Ind:* grève *f* des mineurs; **c. barge,** chaland *m* à charbon; **c. lighter,** charbonnière *f;* **c. ship,** (navire) charbonnier *m;* **c. wharf,** quai *m* à houille; **c. depot,** parc *m* à charbon; dépôt *m* de charbon; **c. owner,** propriétaire *m* de mines de charbon; **c. merchant,** (i) négociant *m* en charbon; (ii) marchand *m* de charbon; charbonnier *m;* **c. heaver,** porteur *m,* coltineur *m,* de charbon; déchargeur *m* de charbon; *A:* **c. whipper,** (i) (*pers.*) déchargeur de charbon; (ii) (*machine*) grue *f* à charbon; **c. cutter,** (i) (*pers.*) haveur *m;* soucheur *m;* (ii) (*machine*) haveuse *f;* **c. breaker, cracker,** concasseur *m* à charbon; **c. bag, sack,** sac *m* à charbon; *Ind:* **c. tip,** culbuteur *m,* basculeur *m* (de wagons à charbon); estacade *f;* **c. car,** enfourneuse *f,* chariot *m* à charbon; *Mch:* **c. firing,** chauffe *f* au charbon; **c.-fired, c.-fed,** alimenté au charbon; **c. bunker,** (i) *Nau:* soute *f* à charbon; (ii) *Dom.Ec:*

coffre *m* à charbon; **c. bin,** coffre à charbon; **c. box,** (i) boîte *f*, bac *m*, caisse *f*, à charbon; charbonnière *f*; (ii) garde-fraisil *m inv* (de forge); **c. cellar,** cave *f* au charbon; **c. hole,** (i) cave, réduit *m*, à carbon; (ii) soupirail *m*; **c. flap,** tampon *m* (donnant accès à la cave à charbon); **c. scuttle, hod, bucket,** seau *m* à charbon; charbonnière; **c. shovel, scoop,** pelle *f* à charbon; (*c*) **c. gas,** gaz *m* de houille; **c. naphtha,** benzine *f*, huile légère de houille; **c. tar,** goudron *m* de houille; co(a)ltar *m*; **c.-tar soap,** savon *m* coaltar; *U.S:* **c. oil,** huile lourde de houille; (*d*) *usu. pl.* monceau *m* de charbon; **live coals,** braise *f*; charbon ardent; **to put a few coals on the fire,** remettre du charbon au feu; **to carry coals to Newcastle,** porter de l'eau à la rivière, à la mer; **to heap coals of fire on s.o.'s head,** faire repentir qn de son ingratitude, etc.; *F:* **to haul s.o. over the coals,** réprimander, semoncer, qn; laver la tête, donner un savon, à qn; **to get hauled over the coals,** se faire attraper; prendre quelque chose pour son rhume.

coal[2], *v.tr.* **1.** charbonner (du bois). **2.** approvisionner (un navire) de charbon; **to c. ship,** *v.i.* **to coal,** s'approvisionner de charbon; faire le charbon; embarquer du charbon.

coal-black ['koul'blæk], *a.* noir comme du charbon.

coaler ['koulər], *s.* (navire) charbonnier *m.*

coalesce [kouə'les], *v.i.* **1.** (*a*) s'unir; se fondre (ensemble); (*of edges of a wound*) se souder; **the two vowels have coalesced,** les deux voyelles se sont assimilées; (*b*) *Ch:* se combiner. **2.** (*of parties, etc.*) fusionner.

coalescence [kouə'lesəns], *s.* (*a*) coalescence *f*, union *f*, fusion *f*; (*b*) *Ch:* combinaison *f*.

coalescent [kouə'lesnt], *a. Nat.Hist:* coalescent.

coalescing [kouə'lesiŋ], *s.* **1.** union *f*, coalescence *f*; *Psy:* **c. of ideas,** condensation *f* des idées. **2.** fusion *f*, fusionnement *m* (de partis).

coaley ['kouli], *s. F:* **1.** *O:* porteur *m*, coltineur *m*, de charbon. **2.** *Ich: F:* = COALFISH.

coalfield ['koulfi:ld], *s. Min:* bassin houiller; région *f* carbonifère; charbonnages *mpl*; centre charbonnier.

coalfish ['koulfiʃ], *s. Ich:* charbonnier *m*, colin *m*; merlan noir; morue noire; lieu noir.

coalie ['kouli], *s. Ich: F:* = COALFISH.

coaling ['kouliŋ], *s. Nau:* charbonnement *m*; **c. port, station,** port *m* à charbon.

Coalite ['koulait], *s. R.t.m:* semi-coke *m*; Coalite *f*.

coalition [kouə'liʃ(ə)n], *s.* coalition *f*; *Pol:* **the left wing c.,** le cartel, le bloc, des Gauches; **to form a c.,** se coaliser.

coalitionist [kouə'liʃənist], *s.* coalitionniste *m.*

coalman, *pl.* **-men** ['koulmæn, -men], *s.* (petit) marchand de charbon; charbonnier.

coal tit ['koultit], *s. Orn:* petite charbonnière; mésange noire; *F:* moinotin *m.*

coalshed ['koulʃed], *s.* hangar *m* à charbon.

coaly[1] ['kouli], *a.* **1.** houilleux; riche en charbon. **2.** couleur de charbon, noir comme le charbon.

coaly[2], *s.* = COALEY.

coaming ['koumiŋ], *s. Nau:* hiloire *f* (d'écoutille, de panneau); surbau *m.*

coaptation ['kouæp'teiʃ(ə)n], *s. Surg:* coaptation *f*; réduction *f* d'une fracture, d'une luxation.

coarctate [kou'ɑ:kteit], *a.* **1.** *Ent:* **c. chrysalis,** chrysalide coarctée. **2.** *Med:* (pouls) coarcté.

coarctation [kouɑ:k'teiʃ(ə)n], *s. Med:* constriction *f*, rétrécissement *m* (d'un conduit); coarctation *f* (du pouls).

coarse [kɔ:s], *a.* **1.** grossier, vulgaire; brutal, -aux; **c. laugh,** rire canaille, brutal; gros rire; **c. voice,** voix commune; **c. individual,** grossier personnage; **c. features,** traits grossiers; **c. words,** mots grossiers; grossièretés *f*; **c. language,** langage *m* de charretier; **to use c. language,** être mal embouché; **c. joke,** plaisanterie grossière, crue, de caserne, de corps de garde; **c. satire,** satire *f* au gros sel; **to have c. tastes,** avoir des goûts vulgaires. **2.** (*a*) (*of material*) gros, grossier, rude; **wrapped up in a c. cloth,** enveloppé de grosse toile; **c. needle,** grosse aiguille; **c. hair,** cheveux *m* rudes; **c. salt,** gros sel; **c. sugar,** sucre brut; **to have a c. skin,** avoir la peau rude; (*b*) (*of food*) grossier; **c. fish,** poissons (i) d'eau douce (sauf truites et saumons); (ii) communs; **c. fishing,** pêche *f* de poissons (i) d'eau douce, (ii) ordinaires; (*c*) *Mec.E:* **c. adjustment,** réglage approximatif.

coarse-cut ['kɔ:s'kʌt], *a.* haché gros; **c.-c. tobacco,** tabac *m* de grosse coupe.

coarse-featured ['kɔ:s'fi:tjəd], *a.* aux traits grossiers, épais.

coarse-fibred, -grained, -textured ['kɔ:s'faibəd, -'greind, -'tekstjəd], *a.* (*of metal, etc.*) à gros grain(s), à grain grossier; (*of wood*) à gros fil; **c.-grained leather,** cuir *m* gros grain.

coarsely ['kɔ:sli], *adv.* grossièrement; brutalement.

coarse-minded ['kɔ:s'maindid], *a.* peu raffiné; peu délicat; à l'esprit grossier.

coarsen ['kɔ:sn]. **1.** *v.tr.* (*a*) rendre plus grossier, plus rude; **life in the bush had coarsened him,** la vie de la brousse lui avait donné quelque chose de rude, de fruste, l'avait un peu décivilisé; **drink had coarsened his features,** il avait les traits épaissis par la boisson; (*b*) **sun coarsens the skin,** le soleil rend la peau plus rude. **2.** *v.i.* devenir plus grossier; (*of features*) s'épaissir.

coarseness ['kɔ:snis], *s.* **1.** grossièreté *f*, brutalité *f* (des manières, etc.); crudité *f* (d'une plaisanterie, etc.); **to avoid c. in one's writing,** éviter le grossier dans ses écrits. **2.** rudesse *f* (de la peau, des cheveux); grosseur *f* de fil (d'une étoffe); gros grain (de la pierre, du bois); *Phot:* granulosité *f* (d'un cliché).

coast[1] [koust], *s.* **1.** côte *f*, rivage *m*; (*extensive*) littoral *m*; **the c. of France,** les côtes, le littoral, de la France; **from c. to c.,** d'une mer à l'autre, d'un océan à l'autre; **by the c. road,** (i) par bord de mer; (ii) par la corniche; **c. defence,** défense côtière. **2.** (*a*) *U.S:* piste *f* (de toboggan); (*b*) descente *f* (en toboggan); *Cy: Aut:* descente en roue libre, au débrayé.

coast[2], *v.i. & tr.* **1.** *Nau:* (*a*) **to c. (along),** suivre la côte; côtoyer le rivage; **to c. a headland, to c. along a shore,** prolonger un promontoire, une côte; (*b*) *Com:* caboter. **2.** (*a*) **to c. (down a hill),** descendre (une côte) en toboggan; *Cy:* descendre en roue libre; *Aut:* (i) descendre (une côte) le moteur débrayé; marcher au débrayé; (ii) lâcher l'accélérateur; (iii) couper l'allumage; (*b*) (*of bird*) planer; (*c*) (*of spacecraft*) se déplacer, se mouvoir, par inertie, sur sa lancée; effectuer un vol inertiel.

coastal ['koust(ə)l], *a.* côtier; **c. zone,** zone côtière; **c. mountains,** montagnes littorales; **c. navigation,** navigation côtière; cabotage *m*; **limited c. navigation,** bornage *m*; **c. defence,** défense côtière; défense des côtes; **C. Command,** Commandement *m* de l'Aviation (de défense) côtière, (Aviation *f* de) Défense côtière; **c.-defence ship,** bâtiment *m* garde-côte, **c.-defence submarine,** sous-marin *m* côtier, de défense côtière.

coaster ['koustər], *s.* **1.** (*of pers., ship*) cabotier *m*, caboteur *m*. **2.** *O:* **c. brake** (*of bicycle*), frein *m* à contre-pédalage. **3.** (*for bottle, decanter*) dessous *m* de bouteille, de carafe; porte-bouteille *m*, *pl.* porte-bouteilles; porte-carafe *m*, *pl.* porte-carafes.

coastguard ['koustgɑ:d], *s.* **1.** *coll.* la garde des côtes; les gardes-côte *m*. **2.** (*also* **coastguard(s)man** [koust'gɑ:d(z)mən]) garde-côte *m*, *pl.* gardes-côte. **3.** *attrib.* **c. path,** sentier douanier; *Nau:* **c. cutter,** aviso *m* garde côte.

coasting ['koustiŋ], *s.* **1.** (*a*) navigation côtière; (*b*) cabotage *m*; **c. trade,** commerce caboteur; cabotage; **to be in the c. trade,** naviguer au cabotage; faire le cabotage; **c. vessel,** caboteur *m*; **master of a c. vessel,** capitaine *m* au cabotage; maître *m* au cabotage. **2.** (*a*) *Cy: Aut:* descente *f* (de côte) en roue libre; *Aut:* marche *f* au débrayé, avec l'allumage coupé; (*b*) (*of bird*) vol plané; (*c*) (*of spacecraft*) vol innertiel; **c. method,** méthode *f* d'inertie.

coastline ['koustlain], *s.* littoral *m.*

coastward(s) ['koustwəd(z)], *adv.* vers la côte.

coastwatcher ['koustwɔtʃər], *s.* garde-côte, *pl.* gardes-côte.

coastwatching ['koustwɔtʃiŋ], *s.* surveillance *f* des côtes.

coastwise ['koustwaiz]. **1.** *adv.* le long de la côte. **2.** *a.* **c. trade,** commerce caboteur, cabotage *m.*

coat[1] [kout], *s.* **1.** (*a*) *Cost:* (*short*) veste *f*, veston *m*; (*long*) manteau *m*, (*for men*) pardessus *m*; **dress c., tail c.,** habit *m* à queue, *F:* queue-de pie *f*, *pl.* queues-de-pie; **morning c.,** jaquette *f*, *F:* queue-de-morue *f*, *pl.* queues-de-morue; **frock c.,** redingote *f*; *O:* **c. dress, c. frock,** robe *f* manteau; *O:* **c. and skirt,** (costume *m*) tailleur *m*; **car c.,** autocoat *m*; **watch c.,** (i) *Mil:* capote *f* de guérite; (ii) *Nau:* capote; *Mil: A:* **buff c.,** pourpoint *m* de cuir épais; *Arm:* **c. of mail,** cotte *f* de mailles, cotte annelée; **c. hook, c. peg,** patère *f*; **to cut one's c. according to one's cloth,** tailler la robe selon le corps; subordonner ses dépenses à son revenu; régler ses dépenses sur son revenu; (*b*) *A:* casaque *f* (de livrée); **to turn one's c.,** tourner casaque; tourner sa veste; changer d'écharpe, de parti; **to wear the King's c.,** être soldat; (*c*) *Her:* **c. armour,** cotte d'armes, **c. of arms,** armes *fpl*, armoiries *fpl*, écusson *m*. **2.** (*a*) robe (d'un chien, d'un cheval, d'une vache); pelage *m* (d'un cheval, d'un cerf, d'un fauve); livrée *f* (d'un cheval, d'un cerf); (*b*) enveloppe *f*, tunique *f*, peau *f* (de bulbe, d'oignon); (*c*) manteau, couche *f* (de neige, etc.). **3.** (*a*) couche, application *f* (de peinture); pelure *f* (de vernis); enduit *m* (de goudron); **ground c., first c., priming c.,** première couche, couche d'impression; **final c., finishing c.,** couche de teinte, de finition; **rough c.** (**of plaster**), crépi *m*; (*b*) *Anat:* paroi *f* (de l'estomac, du crâne). **4.** *Nau:* braie *f* (d'un mât, de la pompe, etc.).

coat[2], *v.tr.* enduire (qch. de peinture, de goudron, etc.); enrober (qch. de chocolat, etc.); **to c. a pill,** dragéifier une pilule; **to c. a cable,** revêtir, couvrir, armer, un câble (**with,** de); **to c. with cadmium,** cadmier; **to c. paper,** coucher du papier; **to c. (sth.) with dust,** couvrir (qch.) de poussière; **drink that coats the palate,** boisson *f* qui empâte la bouche.

coated ['koutid], *a.* enduit, couvert, recouvert, enrobé (**with,** de); **c. electrode,** électrode enrobée; **c. tongue,** langue chargée, pâteuse; *Med:* langue saburrale; *Paperm:* **c. paper,** papier couché; *Phot:* **c. lens,** objectif bleuté, traité; *Pharm:* **c. tablet,** comprimé dragéifié, enrobé; **c. with dust,** couvert de poussière.

coatee [kou'ti:], *s.* (*a*) *A:* habit *m* à courtes basques; (*b*) *Mil: A:* tunique *f*; (*c*) jaquette courte (de dame); (*d*) petite veste (d'enfant).

coathanger ['kouthæŋər], *s.* cintre *m*; porte-vêtements *m inv.*

coati [kou'ɑ:ti], *s. Z:* coati *m.*

coating ['koutiŋ], *s.* **1.** enduisage *m*. **2.** enduit *m*, revêtement *m*, couche *f* (de peinture, etc.); pelure *f* (de vernis); enrobage *m*, enrobement *m* (de goudron, etc.); pellicule *f* (de gélatine); peau *f* (de lait bouilli, etc.); *El:* armature *f* (d'une bouteille de Leyde); *Artil: Sm.a:* enveloppe *f* (d'un projectile); *Anat:* paroi *m* (de l'estomac); *Tchn:* **c. (layer),** apport *m*; **protective c.,** couche protective, enduit protecteur; **transparent c.,** glacis *m*; **rough c.** (*of plaster*), crépi *m*; **c. machine,** enrobeuse *f*; **to give sth. a fresh c. of. . .,** renduire qch. de. . . . **3.** *Com:* tissu *m* pour manteaux; **winter coatings,** tissus d'hiver.

coatrack ['koutræk], *s.* portemanteau *m.*

co-author [kou'ɔ:θər], *s.* coauteur *m.*

coax [kouks], *v.tr.* cajoler, enjôler, câliner; **to c. s.o. to do sth.,** encourager qn à faire qch. (en le cajolant); **to c. s.o. into doing sth.,** faire faire qch. à qn à force de cajoleries; **he was coaxed into it,** on l'a enjôlé; **to c. s.o. out of doing sth.,** persuader qn de ne pas faire qch. (à force de cajoleries); **he was coaxed out of it,** on est parvenu à l'en dissuader; **to c. sth. out of s.o.,** obtenir qch. de qn, soutirer qch. à qn, en le cajolant; **to c. (up) the fire,** raviver, tisonner, doucement le feu.

coaxer ['kouksər], *s.* cajoleur, -euse; enjôleur, -euse, câlin, -e, amadoueur, -euse.

coaxial [kou'æksiəl], *a. Mth: Mec:* coaxial, -aux; ayant le même axe.

coaxing[1] ['kouksiŋ], *a.* (enfant, ton, etc.) câlin, cajoleur; **c. ways,** cajoleries *f*, câlineries *f*, chatteries *f*.

coaxing[2], *s.* cajolerie *f*, enjôlement *m*; **he took a lot of c. before he consented,** il s'est fait tirer l'oreille pour consentir.

coaxingly ['kouksiŋli], *adv.* d'un ton câlin, cajoleur.

cob[1] [kɔb], *s.* **1.** (*horse*) cob *m*, bidet, *m*; (cheval) goussant *m*, goussaut *m*. **2. c. (swan),** cygne *m* mâle. **3.** aveline *f*, grosse noisette. **4. (corn) c.,** (i) (*with grain*) épi *m* de maïs; (ii) (*without grain*) rafle *f*; **c. meal,** farine *f* de maïs (y compris l'épi et les grains); **c. pipe,** pipe *f* (à tabac) dont le fourneau est fait d'un épi de maïs; pipe de maïs; *Cu:* **corn on the c.,** maïs frais poché, maïs en épi(s). **5.** *Dial:* (*a*) boule *f* (de terre, de pâte, etc.); (*b*) miche *f* (de pain); (*c*) *Husb:* gob(b)e *f* (pour empâter la volaille). **6.** *Min:* **c. (coal), cobs,** gaillette *f*, gailleterie *f*, gailletin *m.*

cob[2], *v.tr. Min:* scheider (le minerai); **cobbed ore,** minerai de scheidage.

cob[3], *s. Const:* pisé *m*, torchis *m*; paillebart *m*; **c. wall,** mur *m* en torchis, en pisé, en bousillage; **c. mortar,** mortier *m* de terre; **c. work,** construction *f* en pisé; **to work in c.,** torcher; **worker in c.,** torcher *m.*

cobaea [kɔ'bi:ə], *s. Bot:* cobéa *m*, cobée *f*.

cobalt ['koubɔ:lt, kou'bɔ:lt], *s. Ch:* cobalt *m*; *Miner:* **earthy c.,** asbolite *f*, asbolane *f*, wad *m*; **red c.** cobalt arséniaté; érythrine *f*; **c. blue,** cobalt d'outremer; bleu *m* de cobalt; *Ind:* **c. plating,** (i) (*process*) cobaltage *m*; (ii) couche *f* de cobalt; *Med:* **c. 60,** cobalt radio-actif; **c. 60 therapy,** cobalthérapie *f*, cobaltothérapie *f*; **c. bomb,** bombe *f* au cobalt.

cobaltammine ['koubɔ:lt'æmain], *s. Ch:* cobalt(i)ammine *f*.

cobaltic [kou'bɔ:ltik], *a. Ch:* cobaltique.

cobaltiferous [koubɔ:l'tifərəs], *a.* cobaltifère.

cobaltine [kou'bɔ:ltain], *s. Miner:* cobaltine *f*; cobalt gris.

cobaltinitrite [koubɔ:lti'naitrait], *s. Ch:* cobaltinitrite *m.*

cobaltous [kou'bɔ:ltəs], *a. Ch:* cobalteux.

cobber ['kɔbər], *s. Austr: F:* camarade *m*, copain *m*.
cobbing ['kɔbiŋ], *s. Min:* scheidage *m*; **c. hammer,** marteau *m* de scheidage.
cobble[1] ['kɔbl], *s.* **1.** galet *m*, caillou *m* (de chaussée); **c. pavement,** pavé *m* en cailloutis; **to drive slowly over the cobbles,** avancer lentement sur le pavé. **2.** *pl. Com: Min:* charbon *m* en morceaux; gaillette(s) *f(pl)*; gailleterie *f*, gailletins *mpl*.
cobble[2], *v.tr.* paver (une cour, une route) de galets, en cailloutis.
cobble[3], *v.tr.* **1.** carreler (des chaussures). **2.** rapetasser (des vêtements).
cobbler ['kɔblər], *s.* **1.** *(a)* cordonnier *m* (qui fait les raccommodages); savetier *m*; **cobbler's wax,** poix *f* de cordonnier, cire grasse; *Prov:* **the cobbler's wife is always the worst shod,** les cordonniers sont toujours les plus mal chaussés; *(b)* rapetasseur *m*. **2.** *NAm:* boisson rafraîchissante (faite de rhum, de vin, de jus de fruits, etc.).
cobblestone ['kɔblstoun], *s.* caillou *m* (de chaussée); **we had to go slowly over the cobblestones,** nous avons dû avancer lentement sur le caillou.
cobbly ['kɔbli], *a.* (rue, route) mal empierrée, en mauvais cailloutis.
cobby ['kɔbi], *a.* *(of horse)* bouleux; ramassé (et un peu lourd); goussant, goussaut, ragot.
Cobdenism ['kɔbdənizm], *s. Pol.Ec:* Cobdenisme *m*; doctrine *f* du libre-échange et de la coopération internationale.
cobelligerent ['koubə'lidʒərənt], *a. & s.* cobelligérant, -ante.
Cobitidae [kɔ'bitidi:], *s.pl. Ich:* cobitidés *m*.
coble ['koubl], *s. Fish:* barque *f* de pêche à fond plat (à six rames et à une voile).
Coblen(t)z [kə'blen(t)s], *Pr.n. Geog:* Coblence *f*.
Coblenzian [kə'blen(t)siən], *a. & s. Geol:* coblencien (*m*), coblenzien (*m*).
cobloaf ['kɔblouf], *s.* pain rond.
cobnut ['kɔbnʌt], *s.* aveline *f*, grosse noisette.
cobra ['koubrə, 'kɔb-], *s. Rept:* cobra(-capello) *m*; serpent *m* à coiffe, à lunettes; **black-necked c., spitting c.,** cobra à cou noir, serpent cracheur; **king c.,** cobra royal.
Coburg ['koubə:g], *Pr.n. Geog:* Cobourg *m*.
cobweb ['kɔbweb], *s.* **1.** toile *f* d'araignée; **to brush, sweep, away the cobwebs from sth., to clear sth. of cobwebs,** ôter les toiles d'araignées de qch.; araigner (le plafond, etc.); **to go for a walk to blow away the cobwebs,** prendre l'air pour se rafraîchir les idées; *Lit:* **the cobwebs of the law, of diplomacy,** les arcanes *m* de la loi, de la diplomatie; *Pol.Ec:* **c. theorem,** théorème *m* de la toile d'araignée; *P: O:* **c. throat,** gueule *f* de bois. **2.** fil *m* d'araignée.
cobweb-like ['kɔbweblaik], *a.* aranéeux, arachnéen.
cobwebby ['kɔbwebi], *a.* **1.** (plafond) couvert de toiles d'araignées. **2.** *(of texture, etc.)* arachnéen.
cobwork ['kɔbwə:k], *s. Const:* construction *f* en pisé.
coca ['koukə], *s. Bot: Pharm:* coca *m or f*.
cocaine [kou'kein], *s. Pharm:* cocaïne *f*; **the c. habit,** la cocaïnomanie; **c. addict,** cocaïnomane *mf*.
cocainism [kou'keinizm], *s.* cocaïnisme *m*, cocaïsme *m*.
cocainist [kou'keinist], *s.* cocaïnomane *mf*.
cocainization [koukeinai'zeiʃ(ə)n], *s.* cocaïnisation *f*.
cocainize [kou'keinaiz], *v.tr.* **1.** *Pharm:* cocaïniser. **2.** *Med:* anesthésier (un organe, etc.) à la cocaïne.
cocarboxylase [koukɑ:'bɔksileiz], *s. Bio-Ch:* cocarboxylase *f*.
Coccaceae [kɔ'keisii:], *s.pl. Bac:* coccacées *f*.
Coccidae ['kɔksidi:], *s.pl. Ent:* coccidés *m*.
Coccidia [kɔk'sidiə], *s.pl. Prot:* coccidies *f*.
coccidian [kɔk'sidiən], *a.* coccidien.
Coccidiomorpha [kɔksidiou'mɔ:fə], *s.pl. Prot:* coccidiomorphes *m*.
coccidiosis [kɔksidi'ousis], *s. Vet:* coccidiose *f*.
coccidium [kɔk'sidiəm], *s. Prot:* coccidie *f*.
coccinella [kɔksi'nelə], *s. Ent:* coccinelle *f*.
Coccinellidae [kɔksi'nelidi:], *s.pl. Ent:* coccinellidés *m*.
coccobacillus [kɔkou'bæsiləs], *s. Bac:* coccobacille *m*.
coccoid ['kɔkɔid], *s. Bac:* coccoïde *m*.
coccolite ['kɔkəlait], *s. Miner:* coccolit(h)e *f*.
coccolith ['kɔkəliθ], *s. Geol:* coccolit(h)e *f*.
Coccolithophoridae [kɔkouliθou'fɔridi:], *s.pl. Paleont:* coccolithophoridés *m*.
coccus, *pl.* **cocci** ['kɔkəs, 'kɔksai], *s.* **1.** *Ent: Bac:* coccus *m*. **2.** *Bot:* coque *f* (d'un fruit schistocarpe).
coccygeal [kɔk'sidʒiəl], **coccygean** [kɔk'sidʒiən], *a. Anat:* coccygien.
coccyx [''kɔksiks], *s. Anat:* coccyx *m*.
Cochinchina ['kɔtʃin'tʃainə]. **1.** *Pr.n. Geog:* Cochinchine *f*. **2.** *s. Husb:* **C. (fowl),** cochinchinois, -oise.

cochineal ['kɔtʃini:l], *s.* **1.** *Dy:* cochenille *f*; **to dye a tissue with c.,** cocheniller un tissu. **2.** *Ent:* cochenille; *Bot:* **c. fig, cactus,** cochenillier *m*, nopal *m*.
cochlea ['kɔkliə], *s. Anat: Arch:* cochlée *f*; *Anat:* limaçon *m* (de l'oreille).
cochlear ['kɔkliər], *a. Bot:* cochléaire.
cochlearia [kɔkli'ɛəriə], *s. Bot:* cochléaria *m*.
cochleariform [kɔkli'ɛərifɔ:m], *a.* **1.** cochléaire; *Nat.Hist:* cochléiforme. **2.** cochléariforme.
cochleate(d) ['kɔklieit(id)], *a.* cochléaire.
Cochlidiidae [kɔkli'daiidi:], *s.pl. Ent:* cochlidiidés *m*.
cochylis ['kɔkilis], *s. Ent:* cochylis *f*.
cock[1] [kɔk], *s.* **1.** *(a)* coq *m*; **as bold as, like, a c. on its, his, own dunghill,** hardi comme un coq sur son fumier; **fighting c.,** coq de combat; **to live like a fighting c.,** être comme un coq en pâte; *A:* **that c. won't fight,** ça ne prend, ne prendra, pas; il faut chercher une meilleure excuse, une meilleure raison; *F:* **c. of the walk, of the roost,** coq du village, de la paroisse; *P:* **well, old c.!** eh bien, mon vieux! **wotcher, c.!** ça gaze, ma vieille branche? *(b)* *(male)* **c. bird,** oiseau *m* mâle; **c. pheasant,** coq faisan; **c. partridge,** coq de la perdrix; **c. canary,** serin *m*; **c. sparrow,** moineau *m* mâle; *F:* *(of pers.)* **he's just a little c. sparrow,** ce n'est qu'un petit suffisant; **c. lobster,** homard *m* mâle; *(c)* *Orn:* **c. of the wood,** coq de bruyère; grand tétras; **c. of the north,** pinson *m* des Ardennes; **c. of the rock,** coq de roche, rupicole *m*; **sage c.,** centrocerque *m* des montagnes Rocheuses; **snow c.,** tétraogalle *m*; *(d)* *Ich:* **sea c.,** coq de mer; *(e)* **c. loft,** grenier *m*; galetas *m*. **2.** *(a)* robinet *m*; **c. metal, c. brass,** bronze *m*, potin *m*, pour robinetterie; *Plumb: Hyd.E:* **straight-nose c.,** robinet à bec droit; **swan-neck c.,** robinet à col de cygne; **plug c.,** robinet à clef; **taper-plug c.,** robinet tournant; **two-way, three-way, c.,** robinet à deux, à trois, voies; **feed c.,** robinet d'alimentation, de remplissage; **overflow c.,** robinet de trop-plein; **scum c.,** robinet d'extraction à la surface, robinet de purge; **priming c.,** amorceur *m*; **self-closing c.,** robinet à repoussoir; **c. valve,** robinet à boisseau; *(b)* *Mec: Mec.E:* **feed c.,** robinet de refoulement; **test c.,** robinet de vérification; **blow-off, blow-through, c., waste c., bleeding c.** *(of air reservoir)*, robinet d'extraction, (robinet) purgeur *m*; **drain c., drip c.,** (robinet) purgeur *m*, robinet de purge, de vidange; *I.C.E:* robinet de décompression; **pet c.,** robinet de vidange, de décharge; **mud c.,** robinet d'ébouage; purgeur; **gauge c.,** robinet de jauge, de hauteur d'eau; **steam c.,** prise *f* de vapeur; robinet de, à, vapeur; **grease c.,** robinet graisseur; *(c)* *Nau:* **sea c.,** robinet de prise d'eau à la mer; **flooding c.,** robinet de noyage. **3.** *(a)* *Sm.a:* chien *m* (de fusil); **c. notch,** cran *m* de l'armé; **at full c.,** au cran d'armé; armé (à fond); au bandé; **pistol at full c.,** pistolet *m* avec le chien armé; **at half c.,** au repos, au cran de sûreté; *Fig:* **to go off at half c.,** mal démarrer; *(b)* *(of balance)* aiguille *f*; *(of sundial)* style *m*; *(of clock)* coq; *(of watch)* pont *m* de rouage. **4.** *(a)* *V:* pénis *m*, queue *f*; *(b)* *P:* bêtises *fpl*, sottises *fpl*; conneries *fpl*; **to talk c.,** déconner.
cock[2], *s.* **1.** (mouvement de côté) **c. of the eye,** coup *m* d'œil. **2.** *(a)* **the c. of his hat,** (i) le retroussis de son chapeau; (ii) son chapeau (qu'il portait) sur l'oreille; **the c. of his nose,** son nez retroussé; *(b)* *A:* corne *f* (de chapeau à cornes).
cock[3], *v.tr.* **1.** *(a)* **to c. one's eye at s.o., sth.,** donner un coup d'œil à qn, qch.; *(b)* *(of horse, F: of pers.)* **to c. (up) its ears, to c. one's ears,** dresser les oreilles; dresser l'oreille; **to c. one's nose,** relever le nez (d'un air de mépris); **to c. one's nose at sth.,** renifler sur qch.; **to c. one's nose at s.o.,** regarder qn de haut en bas; toiser qn (dédaigneusement). **2. to c. one's hat,** (i) mettre son chapeau de côté, de travers, sur l'oreille; (ii) relever, retrousser, son chapeau. **3. to c. a gun,** armer un fusil; armer, bander, le chien; **in the cocked position,** à l'armé.
cock[4], *s. Agr:* meulon *m*, meule *f* (de foin).
cock[5], *v.tr. Agr:* mettre (du foin) en meulons, en meules.
cockabondy [kɔkə'bɔndi], *s. Fish:* (variété *f* de) mouche artificielle.
cockade [kɔ'keid], *s.* cocarde *f*.
cockaded [kɔ'keidid], *a.* (chapeau *m*) à cocarde.
cock-a-doodle-doo ['kɔkədu:dl'du:], *F:* **1.** *s.* *(child's word)* coq *m*, poule *f*, cocotte *f*. **2.** *int.* cocorico!
cock-a-hoop ['kɔkə'hu:p], *a. & adv.* (en) jubilant; triomphant, exultant; **he was all c.-a-h.,** il était fier comme un coq; **you're looking very c.-a-h. this morning!** comme vous avez l'air jubilant ce matin!
Cockaigne, Cockayne [kɔ'kein], *Pr.n. Lit:* le pays de Cocagne *f*.
cock-a-leekie ['kɔkə'li:ki], *s. Cu: Scot:* potage *m* (de coq au pot avec poireaux).
cockalorum [kɔkə'lɔ:rəm], *s. O:* **1.** *F:* jeune prodige *m*; petit fat. **2.** *Games:* **hey-c., high-c.,** cheval-fondu *m*.
cock-and-bull ['kɔk(ə)nd'bul], *a. F:* **c.-a.-b. story,** histoire abracadabrante, de pure invention; conte *m* à dormir debout; conte bleu.
cock-and-hen ['kɔk(ə)nd'hen], *a. F:* **c.-a.-h. club,** club *m*, cercle *m*, mixte (auquel l'on admet les hommes et les femmes).
cockatiel [kɔkə'ti:l], *s. Orn:* perruche *f* calopsitte.
cockatoo [kɔkə'tu:], *s.* **1.** *Orn:* cacatoès *m*; **funereal c., yellow-tailed black c.,** cacatoès funèbre; **gang-gang c.,** cacatoès à tête rouge; **Leadbeater's c.,** cacatoès de Leadbeater; **palm c.,** microglosse *m*; **roseate c.,** cacatoès rosalbin; **salmon-crested c.,** cacatoès des Moluques; **slender-billed c.,** cacatoès nasique. **2.** *F: Austr:* petit agriculteur, paysan *m*.
cockatrice ['kɔkətrais], *s. Myth:* basilic *m*, cocatris *m*.
cock bead ['kɔkbi:d], *s. Join:* noix *F: Tls:* **c.-b. plane,** noix.
cock-bill ['kɔkbil], *v.tr. Nau:* apiquer (une vergue, etc.); *A:* **to c.-b. the anchor,** faire péneau; mettre l'ancre en veille.
cockboat ['kɔkbout], *s. Nau:* petit canot; coquet *m*.
cockchafer ['kɔktʃeifər], *s. Ent:* hanneton *m*; **c. grub,** ver blanc.
cockcrow ['kɔkkrou], *s.* chant *m* du coq; **to rise at c.,** se lever au (premier) chant du coq, à l'aube, avec les coqs.
cocked [kɔkt], *a.* **1. c. hat,** (i) chapeau *m* à cornes; *(two-pointed)* bicorne *m*; (chapeau à) claque *m*; *(three-pointed)* tricorne *m*; (ii) billet plié en triangle; (iii) *Surv:* chapeau d'erreur; *F:* **to knock s.o. into a c. hat,** (i) battre qn à plates coutures; démolir qn; démolir les arguments de qn; pulvériser qn; (ii) abasourdir qn; **when he told me I was absolutely knocked into a c. hat,** quand il m'a dit ça j'en ai été absolument renversé, sidéré. **2.** *Const:* **c. centre,** cintre retroussé.
cocker[1] ['kɔkər], *s.* **c. (spaniel),** (épagneul *m*) cocker *m*.
cocker[2], *v.tr.* **to c. s.o. (up),** choyer, gâter, câliner, dorloter, qn; *F:* mitonner qn.
Cocker[3], *Pr.n. F:* **according to C.,** conforme à la règle; réglementaire; (faire qch.) dans les formes.
cockerel ['kɔk(ə)r(ə)l], *s.* jeune coq *m*; cochet *m*, cochelet *m*.
cocket ['kɔkit], *s. Cust: A:* acquit-à-caution *m*, *pl.* acquits-à-caution.
cockeye[1] ['kɔkai], *s. Harn:* ganse *f* de trait.
cockeye[2], *s. F:* **1.** œil *m* qui louche. **2.** *attrib. Austr: F:* (orage) violent (et inattendu).
cockeyed ['kɔkaid], *a. F:* **1.** *(of pers.)* qui louche, qui a un œil qui dit zut à l'autre. **2.** *(a)* de travers, de guingois; *(b)* confus, brouillé; **c. story,** histoire *f* à dormir debout; **c. scheme,** projet biscornu; *(c)* ivre, rétamé à bloc.
cockfight ['kɔkfait], *s.* combat *m*, joute *f*, de coqs.
cockfighting ['kɔkfaitiŋ], *s.* combats *mpl*, concours *m* de coqs; *Furn:* **c. chair,** voyeuse *f*.
cockhorse [kɔk'hɔ:s], *s.* **1.** *(a)* *A:* cheval *m* de bois; dada *m*; *(b)* *(of child)* **to ride a c.,** faire dada (sur les genoux de qn). **2.** *A.Trans:* cheval *m* de renfort.
cockily ['kɔkili], *adv. F:* effrontément; avec suffisance.
cockiness ['kɔkinis], *s. F:* effronterie *f*, toupet *m*.
cocking ['kɔkiŋ], *s. Sm.a:* armement *m*, armé *m* (d'un fusil, d'un pistolet); **c. piece,** chien *m*; **c. handle,** levier *m* d'armement; **self-c.,** armé automatique.
cockle[1] ['kɔkl], *s.* **1.** *Bot:* *(a)* **(corn) c.,** nielle *f* des champs, des blés; githago *m*; agrostemme *f*; *F:* oreille *f* de lièvre; gerzeau *m*, lampette *f*; *(b)* ivraie *f*, vorge *f*. **2.** *Agr:* *(disease)* nielle.
cockle[2], *s.* **1.** *(a)* *Moll:* coque *f*, sourdon *m*, fausse praire, *Dial:* rigadeau *m*; **beaked c.,** anomie *f*; *(b)* *Hist:* coquille *f* de pèlerin; *(c)* *A:* **cockles of the heart,** le cœur; **that will warm the cockles of your heart,** voilà qui vous réchauffera. **2.** *Games: A:* **hot cockles,** main chaude; **to play at hot cockles,** jouer à la main chaude.
cockle[3]. **1.** *v.tr.* *(a)* (re)coquiller (une feuille de papier); faire goder (une étoffe); *(b)* froisser, chiffonner (une étoffe). **2.** *v.i.* **to c. (up),** *(a)* se recroqueviller; *(of paper)* (se) gondoler; se crisper; *(of tissue)* goder, coquiller; *(b)* se chiffonner, se froisser.
cocklebur(r) ['kɔklbə:r], *s. Bot:* xanthium *m*.
cockle-shell ['kɔklʃel], *s.* **1.** coquillage *m*. **2.** *F:* *(boat)* coquille *f* de noix; coque *f*; **it's a mere c.,** c'est une vraie coquille de noix.
cockle stove ['kɔklstouv], *s. O:* calorifère *m*, poêle *m* (d'appartement).
cockling[1] ['kɔkliŋ], *s.* *(a)* gondolement *m*, gondolage *m*; crispation *f*; *(b)* chiffonnement *m*.
cockling[2], *s.* la pêche aux coques, aux coquillages.
Cockney ['kɔkni]. **1.** *(a)* *a.* londonien; **c. accent,** accent londonien populaire; *(b)* *s.* Londonien, -ienne (des quartiers populaires de l'est de Londres). **2.** *s. U.S:* citadin, -ine.

cockneyism ['kɔkniizm], *s.* (*a*). locution londonienne (des quartiers populaires de l'est de Londres); (*b*) particularité *f* de prononciation propre aux Londoniens.

cockpit ['kɔkpit], *s.* **1.** arène *f*, parc *m*, de combats de coqs; *Hist:* **the c. of Europe,** le champ clos de l'Europe. **2.** *Navy: A:* poste *m* des blessés. **3.** (*a*) *Av:* habitacle *m* (du pilote); cockpit *m*; (*b*) *Aut:* (*in racing car*) siège *m* du conducteur.

cockroach ['kɔkroutʃ], *s. Ent:* blatte *f*, cancrelat *m*; cafard *m*, meunier *m*; **German c.,** papin *m*, phyllodromie *f*.

cockscomb ['kɔkskoum], *s.* **1.** crête *f* de coq. **2.** *Bot:* célosie *f* à crête(s); crête-de-coq *f*, *pl.* crêtes-de-coq; passe-velours *m inv*, amarante *f* crête-de-coq. **3.** = COXCOMB.

cocksfoot ['kɔksfut], *s. Bot:* **c. (grass),** dactyle pelotonné; chiendent *m* à brossettes.

cockshead ['kɔkshed], *s. Bot:* sainfoin *m* des prés; éparcet *m*, éparcette *f*.

cockshot ['kɔkʃɔt], *s.* **1.** but *m* à viser. **2.** coup visé; **to have a c. at s.o., at sth.,** lancer une pierre, etc., à, contre, qn, qch.

cockshy ['kɔkʃai], *s.* **1.** = COCKSHOT. **2.** jeu *m* de massacre.

cockspur ['kɔkspəːr], *s.* **1.** ergot *m* de coq. **2.** *A:* **c. (burner),** bec *m* (de gaz) à trois trous. **3.** *Bot:* (*a*) dactyle pelotonné; (*b*) pisonia *m*; (*c*) cenchrus *m*; (*d*) **c. flower,** plectanthrus *m*.

cocksure ['kɔk'ʃjuər], sûr de soi; suffisant, outrecuidant; **to be c. of, about, sth.,** n'avoir aucun doute sur qch.; être sûr et certain de qch.

cocksureness ['kɔk'ʃjuənis], *s.* assurance *f*, confiance *f*, en soi-même, outrecuidance *f*.

cocktail ['kɔkteil], *s.* **1.** (*a*) *A:* cheval anglaisé; (*b*) *Breed:* cheval demi-sang. **2.** *A:* parvenu *m*. **3.** *Ent:* staphylin *m*. **4.** (*a*) (*drink*) cocktail *m*; **c. cabinet,** bar *m* (à cocktails); **c. mixer, shaker,** frappe-cocktail *m*, *pl.* frappe-cocktails; **c. snack,** amuse-gueule *m*, *pl.* amuse-gueules; **c. party,** cocktail; **c. dress,** robe *f* cocktail; (*b*) *Exp:* **Molotov c.,** cocktail Molotov; (*c*) *Med:* **lytic c.,** cocktail lytique.

cocktailed ['kɔkteild], *a. A:* (cheval *m*) à queue anglaisée.

cock-throttled ['kɔkθrɔtld], *a.* (cheval *m*) à encolure de cygne.

cockup[1] ['kɔkʌp], *s. Ich:* latès *m*.

cockup[2], *s. Typ:* **1.** lettre supérieure. **2.** (lettre) initiale *f*.

cockup[3], *s. P:* gâchis *m*, couillonnade *f*.

cocky[1] ['kɔki], *a. F:* effronté, suffisant, outrecuidant; qui a du toupet; qui fait l'important.

cocky[2], *s. Austr: F:* petit agriculteur, éleveur, de la brousse; **cow c.,** éleveur de bovins; **fruit c.,** cultivateur *m* de fruits.

cockyolly [kɔki'ɔli], *s. F:* (*child's word*) **c. (bird),** petit oiseau.

cocoa ['koukou], *s.* **1.** (*a*) cacao *m*; **c. bean,** graine *f*, fève *f*, de cacao; **c. nib,** graine, fève, de cacao décortiquée; **c. butter,** beurre *m* de cacao; **c. pod,** cabosse *f*; (*b*) **c. tree,** cacaotier *m*, cacaoyer *m*. **2.** (*a*) **c. plum** (*also* **coco plum**), (i) (prune *f* d') icaque *f*; prune des anses, de coton, de coco; (ii) (*tree*) icaquier *m*; (*b*) *Bot: U.S:* **c. grass** (*also* **coco grass**), souchet rond.

coconut ['koukənʌt], *s.* (*a*) (noix *f* de) coco *m*; **c. palm, tree,** cocotier *m*; **c. plantation,** cocoteraie *f*; **c. milk,** eau *f*, lait *m*, de coco; **desiccated c.,** noix de coco déshydratée; **c. butter,** beurre *m* de coco; **c. oil,** huile *f* de coprah; **c. fibre,** fibre *f* de coco; coir *m*; **c. fibre mat,** tapis-brosse *m*, *pl.* tapis brosses; paillasson *m*; **c. matting,** natte *f*, tapis *m*, en fibres de coco; **c. shy,** jeu *m* de massacre (où on essaie d'abattre des noix de coco); (*b*) **double c., sea c.,** coco de mer, des Maldives, des Seychelles.

cocoon[1] [kə'kuːn], *s.* **1.** cocon *m* (de ver à soie, etc.); **the c. trade,** l'industrie coconnière. **2.** *Mil:* **equipment in c.,** matériel en cocon, encoconné.

cocoon[2]. **1.** *v.i.* (*of caterpillar*) coconner; filer son cocon. **2.** *v.tr. Metall: etc:* appliquer un produit plastique à (qch.).

cocoonery [kə'kuːnəri], *s.* magnanerie *f*; coconnière *f*.

co creditor [kou'kreditər], *s. Jur:* cocréancier, -ière.

coction ['kɔkʃ(ə)n], *s. A:* coction *f*.

cod[1] [kɔd], *s. Ich:* (*a*) morue *f*; **fresh c.,** morue fraîche, franche; cabillaud *m*; **salt c.,** morue salée, sèche; **dried c.,** morue sèche; merluche *f*; **c. roe,** œufs *mpl* de morue, (*salted*) rabes *fpl*; *Pharm:* **c.-liver oil,** huile *f* de foie de morue; *Fish:* **c. bank,** banc *m* de morues; **c. fisher,** morutier *m*, moruyer *m*; **c. smack,** défileur *m*; (*b*) **black c.,** charbonnier *m*; (*c*) **butterfly c.,** dragon *m* de mer.

cod[2], *s. P: O:* (*take-in*) attrape *f*; *attrib.* **c. auction,** enchères *fpl* pour rire.

cod[3], *v.tr. & i.* (**codded**) *P: O:* tromper (qn); mettre (qn) dedans; faire marcher (qn); se payer la tête de (qn); la faire à l'oseille à (qn).

cod[4], *s. Anat: A:* scrotum *m*; *Cost: A:* **c.(-)piece,** braguette, brayette *f*.

coda ['koudə], *s. Mus:* coda *f*.

codamine ['koudəmiːn, -in], *s. Ch:* codamine *f*.

coddle ['kɔdl], *v.tr.* **1.** *Cu:* faire cuire (des œufs) à l'eau frémissante. **2. to c. s.o.,** gâter, choyer, câliner, dorloter, mitonner, chouchouter, douilletter, qn; élever qn dans le coton, dans la ouate; **coddled by his mother,** gâté par sa mère; **the child has been too much coddled,** cet enfant a été élevé trop délicatement; **to c. oneself,** s'écouter; se dodiner; se dorloter; se mijoter.

code[1] [koud], *s.* **1.** code *m*; **c. of honour,** code, règles *fpl*, de l'honneur; **c. of good manners,** code de la politesse; **the duelling c., the c. of honour,** les règles du duel; **Highway C.** = Code de la route; **International Seamen's C.,** Statut international des marins; *Jur:* **c. of criminal procedure,** code d'instruction criminelle. **2.** (*a*) *Tg: etc:* **telegraphic c.,** code télégraphique; **signal(ling) c.,** code de signalisations, de transmissions; *Nau:* **International C. of Signals,** Code international des signaux; **c. letter, number,** indicatif littéral, numérique; *Tp:* **codes and numbers,** caractères *mpl*; **(dialling) c.,** indicatif (départemental); **c. word,** mot télégraphique, convenu; *Av:* **c. beacon,** balise *f* code, à occultations codées; **c. sign,** indicatif (d'une station); **c. signal,** signal conventionnel; **map-reference c., coordinate c.,** code de coordonnées cartographiques; (*b*) (*secret*) code, chiffre *m*; **c. letter,** lettre *f* code; **c. group,** groupe *m* (de lettres, de chiffres) code; **c. name,** nom conventionnel; **air-ground (liaison) c.,** code (de liaison) air-sol; **panel c.,** code de signalisation par panneaux; **identification panel c.,** code d'identification par panneaux; **to write a message, a dispatch, in c.,** chiffrer un message, une dépêche; **c. message,** message chiffré; **c. book,** code, carnet *m*, (i) de chiffrement; (ii) de déchiffrement; (*c*) *Cmptr:* code; **computer c.,** code machine; **c. character,** caractère *m* d'un code; **alphabetic(al), alphanumeric, c.,** code alphabétique, alphanumérique; **binary c.,** code binaire; **punch-tape c.,** code de bande perforée; **c. chart,** tableau *m* de code; **c. check,** contrôle *m* de programmation; **c. converter,** convertisseur *m* de code; **c. pattern,** combinaison *f* de perforations; **c. disc, wheel,** disque codeur; **c. translation,** transcodage *m*.

code[2], *v.tr.* (*a*) coder, chiffrer, mettre en code, en chiffre (un message, une dépêche, etc.); (*b*) *Cmptr:* coder, programmer, écrire (une séquence, etc.); **to c. check,** contrôler la programmation.

co-declination ['koudekli'neiʃ(ə)n], *s. Astr:* complément *m* de la déclinaison.

coded ['koudid], *a.* (*a*) (*of message, dispatch, etc.*) codé, chiffré; (*b*) *Cmptr:* codé, programmé; **c. character,** caractère codé; **c. stop,** arrêt programmé.

co-defendant ['koudi'fendənt], *s.* coaccusé, -ée; codéfendeur *m*.

codeine ['koudiːn], *s. Pharm:* codéine *f*.

coder ['koudər], *s.* (*a*) chiffreur *m*; (*b*) *Cmptr:* codeur *m*, codifieur *m*, programmeur, -euse.

codex, *pl.* **-ices** ['koudeks, -isiːz], *s.* **1.** manuscrit (ancien). **2.** *Pharm:* codex *m*.

codger ['kɔdʒər], *s. F: O:* type *m*; **an old c.,** un vieux bonhomme; **he's a comical, funny, old c.,** c'est un numéro, un drôle de type.

codhauler ['kɔdhɔːlər], *s. Can: P:* (*pers.*) Terre-neuvien, -ienne.

codicil ['kɔdisil], *s.* codicille *m* (d'un testament); avenant *m* (d'un traité).

codicillary [kɔdi'siləri], *a.* codicillaire.

codicology [kɔdi'kɔlədʒi], *s.* codicologie *f*.

codification [kɔdifi'keiʃ(ə)n], *s.* codification *f*.

codifier ['koudifaiər], *s.* codificateur *m*.

codify ['koudifai], *v.tr.* codifier (les lois, des signaux, etc.).

coding ['koudiŋ], *s.* (*a*) codification *f*; codage *m*; chiffrage *m*, mise *f* en chiffres; (*b*) *Cmptr:* codage, programmation *f*, écriture *f*; séquence *f* de programmation, d'instructions; **c. error,** erreur *f* de programmation; **c. form, line,** feuille *f*, ligne *f*, de programmation; **c. sequence,** séquence programmée; **c. clerk,** codeur *m*; **absolute c., specific c.,** codage en langage machine; **relative c.,** programmation relative.

co-director ['koud(a)i'rektər], *s.* codirecteur, -trice; coadministrateur *m*.

codling[1] ['kɔdliŋ], *s. Ich:* petite morue.

codlin(g)[2] ['kɔdlin, -iŋ], *s.* **1.** (*a*) *Hort:* pomme *f* à cuire; (*b*) *Ent:* **c. moth,** pyrale *f* des pommes, carpocapse *f*. **2.** *Bot:* **codlin(g)s and cream,** épilobe *m* à épi.

codman, *pl.* **-men** ['kɔdmæn, -men], *s. Nau:* défileur *m*.

codswallop ['kɔdzwɔləp], *s. P:* **1.** bêtises *fpl*, tissu *m* d'âneries; **it's a load of (old) c.,** c'est du bidon. **2.** bière *f* de mauvaise qualité, bibine *f*.

coecilian [siː'siliən], *s. Amph:* cécilie *f*.

co-ed ['kou'ed], *F:* **1.** *a. & s.* (école *f*) mixte. **2.** *s.* élève *f* d'une école mixte.

coeducate ['kou'edjukeit], *v.tr.* instruire ensemble (garçons et filles).

coeducation ['kouedju'keiʃ(ə)n], *s.* coéducation *f*; enseignement *m* mixte.

coeducational ['kouedju'keiʃənl], *a.* coéducationnel; **c. school,** école mixte.

coefficient [koui'fiʃənt], *s.* coefficient *m*; *Mth:* **literal, numerical, c.,** coefficient littéral, numérique; **differential c.,** coefficient différentiel; dérivée *f*; **correlation c., c. of correlation,** coefficient de corrélation; *Ph: etc:* **c. of absorption,** coefficient d'absorption; **c. of expansion,** coefficient de dilatation; **c. of elasticity,** coefficient d'élasticité; **scatter c.,** coefficient de dispersion; *El:* **beam coupling c.,** coefficient du couplage électronique; *Mec.E: etc:* **c. of safety,** facteur *m* de sûreté, de sécurité; **c. of efficiency,** coefficient d'effet utile, de rendement; *Av:* **lift c.,** coefficient de force ascensionnelle, de portance, de sustentation; **thrust c.,** coefficient de traction; **drag c.,** coefficient de traînage; *Pol.Ec: etc:* **c. of depreciation,** coefficient d'amortissement; **discount c.,** coefficient d'actualisation.

coelacanth ['siːləkænθ], *s. Ich:* coelacanthe *m*.

Coelacanthidae [siːlə'kænθidiː], *s.pl. Ich:* cœlacanthidés *m*.

Coelenterata [siːlentə'reitə], *s.pl. Z:* cœlentérés *m*.

cœlestine [siː'lestain], *s. Miner:* célestine *f*.

coeliac ['siːliæk], *a. Anat:* (artère *f*, etc.) cœliaque.

coelialgia [siːli'ældʒiə], *s. Med:* cœlialgie *f*.

coelioscopy [siːli'ɔskəpi], *s. Med:* cœlioscopie *f*.

coeliotomy [siːli'ɔtəmi], *s. Surg:* cœliotomie *f*.

coeloblastula [siːlou'blæstjulə], *s. Biol:* cœloblastula *m*.

coeloglossum [siːlou'glɔs(ə)m], *s. Bot:* cœloglossum *m*.

coelogyne ['siːloudʒain], *s. Bot:* cœlogyne *m*.

coelom(e) ['siːləm, oum], *s. Ann:* cœlome *m*.

Coelomata [siːlə'meitə], *s.pl. Z:* cœlomates *m*.

coelomic [siː'lɔmik], *a. Anat:* cœlomique.

coelostat ['siːloustæt], *s. Astr:* cœlostat *m*.

coemption [kou'em(p)ʃ(ə)n], *s.* **1.** *Rom.Jur:* (mariage *m* par) coemption *f*. **2.** *Jur:* accaparement *m*.

coenaesthesia [siːnes'θiːziə], **coenaesthesis** [siːnes'θiːsis], *s.* cénesthésie *f*.

coendou [kou'enduː], *s. Z:* coendou *m*.

coenenchyma [siː'neŋkimə], *s. Z:* cœnenchyme *m*.

coenobite ['siːnoubait], *s.* cénobite *m*.

coenobitic [siːnou'bitik], *a.* cénobitique.

coenobium [siː'noubiəm], *s. Biol:* cœnobe *m*.

coenocyte ['siːnousait], *s. Biol:* cœnocyte *m*.

cœnogamete [siːnougæ'miːt], *s. Bot:* cœnogamète *m*.

Coenolestidae [siːnou'lestidiː], *s.pl. Z:* cœnolestidés *m*.

cœnosarc ['siːnousɑːk], *s. Z:* cœnosarque *m*, cœnosarc *m*.

coenure ['siːnjuər], **coenurus** [siː'njuːrəs], *s. Ann: Vet:* cœnure *m*, cénure *m*.

co-enzyme ['kou'enzaim], *s. Biol:* coenzyme *f*.

coerce [kou'əːs], *v.tr.* **1.** forcer, contraindre (**s.o. into doing sth.,** qn à faire qch.); réprimer, réduire (un peuple). **2.** réprimer par la force.

coercibility [kouəːsi'biliti], *s. Ph:* coercibilité *f* (des gaz, etc.).

coercible [kou'əːsibl], *a.* **1.** (*of pers.*) contraignable. **2.** (*of gas, etc.*) coercible.

coercion [kou'əːʃ(ə)n], *s.* coercition *f*, contrainte *f*; *Jur:* coaction *f*; **to employ means of c.,** mettre en action des moyens de coercition; **to act under c.,** agir par contrainte; agir à son corps défendant; **he will pay under c.,** il payera s'il y est contraint; **C. Act,** loi *f* qui suspend les droits civils.

coercionist [kou'əːʃ(ə)nist], *s.* partisan *m* des mesures coercitives (*Hist:* dans l'administration de l'Irlande).

coercive [kou'əːsiv], *a.* **1.** coercitif; *Jur:* coactif; **c. weapon,** sanction (pénale); *Jur:* **c. measures,** procédure coercitive. **2.** *Magn:* **c. force,** force coercitive; coercitivité *f* (d'un aimant).

coercively [kou'əːsivli], *adv.* par la force, par contrainte; de force.

coerciveness [kou'əːsivnis], *s.* coactivité *f*.

coercivity [kouəː'siviti], *s. Magn:* coercitivité *f*.

Coerebidae [siː'rebidiː], *s.pl. Orn:* cœrébidés *m*.

coerulignone [siə'rulignoun], *s. Ch:* cérulignone *f*.

coessential ['koui'senʃ(ə)l], *a.* de même essence.

coeternal ['koui'təːnl], *a.* coéternel.

coeternity ['koui'təːniti], *s. Theol:* coéternité *f*.

coeval [kou'iːv(ə)l], *esp. Lit:* **1.** *a.* **c. with sth.,** contemporain de qch.; du même âge que qch.; de l'âge de qch.; **worlds c. with the sun,** des mondes *m* du même âge que le soleil. 2. s. contemporain, -aine.

co-executor, -trix [ˈkouigˈzekjutər, -triks], s. Jur: coexécuteur, -trice (testamentaire).

coexist [ˈkouigˈzist], v.i. coexister (with, avec).

coexistence [ˈkouigˈzistəns], s. coexistence f (with, avec); concomitance f; Pol: peaceful c., coexistence f pacifique.

coexistent [ˈkouigˈzistənt], a. coexistant (with, avec).

coextensive [ˈkouiksˈtensiv], a. de même étendue, de même durée (with, que); Log: coextensif.

coffee [ˈkɔfi], s. (a) café m; roasted c., café torréfié; unroasted c., café vert; c. burner, roaster, brûloir m, torréfacteur m; c. mill, moulin m à café; ground c., café moulu; c. grounds, grouts, marc m de café; instant c., café en poudre; black c., café noir, café nature; three black coffees, trois cafés (noirs); white c., café au lait; café crème; let's go and have a c. together, allons prendre un café (ensemble); (ordering breakfast) c. and rolls, café complet; c. pot, cafetière f; (with straight handle) verseuse f; c. percolator, percolateur m; cafetière automatique, russe; c. cup, tasse f à café; c. spoon, cuillère f (i) à café, (ii) (small) à moka; c. set, service, service m à café; c. table, table f de salon; c.-table book, livre de grand format profusément illustré; c. morning, réunion matinale de dames (qui prennent le café ensemble et vendent des objets en faveur d'une œuvre de bienfaisance); c. break, pause-café f, pl. pauses-café; A: c. house, café (où on ne sert que du café); c. bar, café (où on sert du café, des boissons non-alcooliques et des sandwichs); O: c. room, salle f des voyageurs, salle à manger (d'hôtel); c. stall, bar m, cantine f, de coin de rue (où on sert des boissons non-alcooliques et repas sur le pouce); (b) c. shrub, tree, caféier m, cafier m; (Kentucky) c. tree, Kentucky c. nut, gymnocladus m, chicot m de Canada; c.-leaf disease, rouillle f du caféier; c. bean, grain m de café; c. berry, fruit m, cerise f, de caféier; (c) Comest: c. cream, chocolat fourré au café; (d) a. c.(-coloured), (i) café inv; (ii) café au lait inv.

coffer[1] [ˈkɔfər], s. 1. coffre m; the coffers of State, les coffres de l'État; les fonds publics. 2. (a) Arch: caisson m (de plafond); Join: (sunk panel) arrière-corps m inv; (b) Const: caisson (pour pisé, etc.). 3. Hyd.E: (a) chambre f, bassin m, sas m (d'écluse); (b) = COFFERDAM. 4. Nau: bassin m à flot; chantier m à flot.

coffer[2], v.tr. 1. Min: Civ.E: coffrer, glaiser (un puits). 2. diviser (un plafond) en caissons.

cofferdam [ˈkɔfədæm], s. 1. Hyd.E: coffre m, bâtardeau m; caisson m hydraulique. 2. Nau: A: cofferdam m.

coffered [ˈkɔfəd], a. Arch: (plafond m) à caissons.

cofferfish [ˈkɔfəfiʃ], s. Ich: coffre m.

coffering [ˈkɔf(ə)riŋ], s. coffrage m, glaisage m.

cofferwork [ˈkɔfəwəːk], s. Const: pisé m.

coffin[1] [ˈkɔfin], s. 1. cercueil m; bière f; deal c., sapinière f; c. plate, plaque f de cercueil; P: c. nail, cigarette f, sèche f; F: that's another nail in his c., (i) c'est (pour lui) un pas de plus vers la tombe; (ii) avec ça il va se faire renvoyer. 2. cavité f du sabot (d'un cheval); c. bone, phalangette f; c. joint, articulation f de la phalangette.

coffin[2], v.tr. 1. mettre (qn) en bière. 2. A: mettre de côté, mettre au rancart; to live coffined in a dark basement, vivre enterré dans un sous-sol mal éclairé.

coffining [ˈkɔfiniŋ], s. mise f en bière.

coffle [ˈkɔfl], s. convoi m (d'esclaves ou de bêtes) à la chaîne; chaîne (d'esclaves).

cofounder [ˈkouˈfaundər], s. cofondateur, -trice.

cog[1] [kɔg], s. 1. Mec.E: (a) dent f (d'une roue dentée); esp. alluchon m (de roue dentée à mortaises); dent rapportée; the cogs, la denture; I am only a c. in the machinery, je ne suis qu'un rouage de la machine; to slip a c., (i) (of pawl) glisser sur une dent; (ii) F: (of the mind) avoir un moment d'absence; (b) levée f (de came, etc.); c.-shaft, arbre m de levée; (c) c. rail, crémaillère f; c. railway, U.S: railroad, chemin m de fer à crémaillère. 2. Farr: crampon m (d'un fer à cheval).

cog[2], v. (cogged; cogging) 1. v.tr. (a) denter, endenter (une roue); garnir (une roue) de dents; cogged wheel = COGWHEEL; (b) cramponner (un fer à cheval); (c) Metall: ébaucher (le fer). 2. v.i. (of wheels) s'engrener.

cog[3], v.tr. piper (des dés); cogged dice, dés pipés.

cog[4], s. Carp: adent m, tenon m; c. joint, joint m à adent, en adent.

cogency [ˈkoudʒənsi], s. 1. force f, puissance f (d'un argument); Jur: bien-fondé m (d'une cause, d'une réclamation). 2. urgence f (d'un cas).

cogent [ˈkoudʒənt], a. 1. (argument m) irrésistible; (motif) puissant; (raison) valable, incontestable, convaincante. 2. (cas) urgent.

cogently [ˈkoudʒəntli], adv. avec force, fortement, incontestablement; d'une façon convaincante.

cogging [ˈkɔgiŋ], s. Metall: ébauchage m.

cogitate [ˈkɔdʒiteit]. 1. v.i. méditer, réfléchir (on, over, sur). 2. v.tr. (a) projeter, imaginer (un plan, etc.); (b) Phil: concevoir.

cogitation [kɔdʒiˈteiʃ(ə)n], s. 1. réflexion f, cogitation f, méditation f, délibération f (on, over, sur); after much c., après avoir longuement réfléchi. 2. these cogitations lead to nothing, ces méditations, tous ces projets, ne mènent à rien, n'aboutissent à rien.

cogitative [ˈkɔdʒitətiv], a. qui réfléchit; méditatif.

cognac [ˈkɔnjæk], s. cognac m.

cognate [ˈkɔgneit]. 1. s. Jur: (a) cognat m; parent m; (b) Scot: etc: parent du côté maternel; cognat. 2. (a) a. c. (with sth.), qui a du rapport (avec qch.); qui est parent (de qch.); analogue (à qch.); de la même origine, du même genre (que qch.); de même nature (que qch.); c. words, mots de même origine, de même racine, de même famille; mots congénères, apparentés; (b) s. mot, locution f, etc., de même origine; deceptive cognates, faux-amis m, mots-pièges m.

cognateness [ˈkɔgneitnis], s. rapport m, analogie f, parenté f.

cognatic [ˈkɔgnætik], a. Jur: cognatique.

cognation [kɔgˈneiʃ(ə)n], s. 1. Jur: cognation f. 2. Ling: identité f de source, de racine; parenté f.

cognition [kɔgˈniʃ(ə)n], s. 1. Phil: Psy: connaissance f, cognition f. 2. Jur: Scot: = COGNIZANCE.

cognitive [ˈkɔgnitiv], a. Psy: c. faculty, faculté cognitive; c. of sth., ayant connaissance de qch.

cognizable [ˈkɔgnizəbl, Jur: ˈkɔnizəbl], a. 1. Phil: Psy: (a) connaissable, perceptible; (b) reconnaissable. 2. Jur: c. by a court, qui est du ressort, de la compétence, d'un tribunal; c. offence, (i) délit m qui tombe sous le coup de la loi; (ii) A: (in India) délit justifiant l'arrestation du coupable sans mandat d'arrêt.

cognizance [ˈkɔgnizəns, Jur: ˈkɔnizəns], s. 1. (a) Phil: connaissance f, perception f; (b) Jur: connaissance; to take c. of sth., prendre connaissance de qch.; (i) connaître de qch.; (ii) prendre acte de qch.; (c) Jur: the child acted without c., l'enfant a agi sans discernement. 2. Jur: compétence f; within, under, the c. of a court, du ressort, de la compétence, d'une cour; that falls within, goes beyond, my c., cela est, n'est pas, de ma compétence. 3. Her: insigne m, emblème m (d'une maison noble, porté par tous ses serviteurs et vassaux); armes fpl, armoiries fpl, marque distinctive.

cognizant [ˈkɔgnizənt, Jur: ˈkɔnizənt], a. 1. ayant connaissance (of, de); to be c. of a fact, être instruit d'un fait. 2. Jur: court c. of an offence, tribunal compétent pour juger un délit.

cognize [kɔgˈnaiz], v.tr. Phil: avoir conscience de (qch.).

cognomen [kɔgˈnoumen], s. 1. Rom.Hist: cognomen m. 2. (a) surnom m, sobriquet m; (b) nom m de famille.

cognosce [kɔgˈnɔs], v. Jur: (Scot.) 1. v.i. connaître de la cause; faire une enquête. 2. v.tr. to c. a case, connaître d'une cause; juger une cause.

cognoscibility [kɔgnɔsiˈbiliti], s. Phil: cognoscibilité f.

cognoscible [kɔgˈnɔsibl], a. Phil: cognoscible, connaissable.

cognovit [kɔgˈnouvit], s. Jur: aveu (signé par le défendeur et reconnaissant le bien-fondé de la requête du demandeur).

cogwheel [ˈkɔg(h)wiːl], s. Mec.E: roue à dents, dentée, encliquetée; roue d'engrenage; c. railway, chemin m de fer à crémaillère.

cohabit [ˈkouˈhæbit], v.i. (cohabited) cohabiter, vivre maritalement (with, avec).

cohabitant [ˈkouˈhæbitənt], s. cohabitant, -ante.

cohabitation [ˈkouhæbiˈteiʃ(ə)n], s. cohabitation f (with, avec).

coheir [ˈkouˈɛər], **coheiress** [ˈkouˈɛəris], s. cohéritier, -ière.

cohenite [ˈkouənait], s. Miner: cohénite f.

cohere [kouˈhiər]. 1. v.i. (a) (of whole, of parts) se tenir ensemble, rester uni(s); adhérer; rester aggloméré; (b) s'agglomérer; (c) (of argument, style) être conséquent; se suivre (logiquement); se tenir, tenir ensemble; to c. with sth., être d'accord avec, conforme à, qch. 2. v.tr. faire tenir ensemble, agglomérer (des matériaux, etc.).

coherence [kouˈhiər(ə)ns], **coherency** [kouˈhiər(ə)nsi], s. 1. cohésion f; adhérence f. 2. (of argument, style) suite f (logique); cohérence f.

coherent [kouˈhiər(ə)nt], a. 1. (a) (of whole, of parts) cohérent(s); lié(s) ensemble; Bot: c. stamens, étamines cohérentes; (b) Ph: cohérent. 2. (of plan, speech, etc.) conséquent, cohérent, (of thinker) qui a de la suite dans ses idées; c. argument, raisonnement bien suivi, bien développé.

coherently [kouˈhiərəntli], adv. (parler) d'une manière cohérente, avec cohérence.

coherer [kouˈhiərər], s. Ph: cohéreur m, radioconducteur m; A: Branly c., tube m de Branly; tube à limaille.

coheritor [ˈkouˈheritər], s. = COHEIR.

cohesion [kouˈhiːʒ(ə)n], s. (a) cohésion f; adhérence f; (b) attack that lacks c., attaque f qui manque d'ensemble; (c) Bot: cohérence f (des étamines, etc.).

cohesive [kouˈhiːsiv], a. 1. cohésif; Ph: c. force, force f de cohésion; attraction f moléculaire; c. metal, métal m tenace. 2. cohésif, susceptible de cohésion.

cohesively [kouˈhiːsivli], adv. cohésivement.

cohesiveness [kouˈhiːsivnis], s. cohésion f.

cohobate [ˈkouhoubeit], v.tr. Ch: Dist: cohober.

cohobation [kouhouˈbeiʃ(ə)n], s. Ch: Dist: cohobation f.

cohort [ˈkouhɔːt], s. 1. (a) Rom.Mil.Hist: cohorte f; (b) cohorte, bande f (de guerriers); armée f; (c) F: cohorte, troupe f (de gens quelconques); (d) N.Am: Pol.Ec: c. of women born in 1940, cohorte des femmes nées en 1940. 2. Nat.Hist: A: ordre m. 3. esp. N.Am: F: satellite m; complice mf.

coif [kɔif], s. 1. Cost: (a) A: coiffe f, béguin m; (b) cornette f (de nonne); (c) A: calotte blanche des avocats (serjeants at law); F: A: a Brother of the c., un serjeant at law. 2. Bot: calyptre f, coiffe (des mousses).

coiffure[1] [kwɑːˈfjuər], s. coiffure f.

coiffure[2], v.tr. hair beautifully coiffured, cheveux bien coiffés; coiffure magnifique.

coign [kɔin], s. 1. A: coin m (qui avance); Lit: c. of vantage, position avantageuse. 2. Typ: A: coin, cale f.

coil[1] [kɔil], s. 1. (a) rouleau m (de corde); Nau: glène f; cueille f (de filin, de câble); roue f (de câble); paquet m (de corde); rouleau, couronne f, botte f (de fil métallique); torque f (de fil métallique, de tabac à chiquer); (b) Hairdr: enroulement m, rouleau (de cheveux); chignon m; (c) (coiled tube) serpentin m; c. of metal piping, serpentin métallique; (d) (contraceptive device) stérilet m. 2. (a) pli m, repli m (d'un cordage); repli, nœud m, anneau m (d'un serpent); (b) coils of smoke, tourbillons m de fumée. 3. El: enroulement m, bobinage m; bobine f; primary, secondary, c., enroulement, bobine, primaire, secondaire; bucking c., bobine de compensation; search c., bobine exploratrice; slit c., bobine à prises; plug-in c., bobine à fiche; shunt c., bobine en dérivation; double-wound c., bobine à double enroulement; single-layer, multi-layer, c., bobine à couche unique, à couche multiple; c. tap, prise f de bobine; c.-loaded cable, câble pupinisé.

coil[2]. 1. v.tr. (en)rouler, gléner, rouer (un cordage, etc.); El: bobiner (des fils); (of snake) to c. (itself) up, s'enrouler, se lover, se replier; to c. (itself) round a tree, s'enrouler autour d'un arbre; the cat coiled itself up, le chat s'est pelotonné, s'est mis en rond; (of pers.) to c. (oneself) up in an armchair, se blottir, se pelotonner, dans un fauteuil; Nau: etc: to c. (down) a rope, lover, cueillir, un cordage. 2. v.i. avancer en ondulant; serpenter; the serpent was coiling through the grass, le serpent se glissait à travers l'herbe.

coiled [kɔild], a. (en)roulé, gléné, roué, lové; c. piping, tuyau enroulé en couronne; serpentin m; c. spring, ressort m en spirale; ressort à boudin; c. snake, couleuvre lovée.

coiler [ˈkɔilər], s. (a) Ind: bobineur, -euse; (b) Nau: loveur m.

coiling [ˈkɔiliŋ], s. enroulement m, enroulage m; bobinage m.

Coimbra [kouˈimbrə], Pr.n. Geog: Coïmbre f.

coin[1] [kɔin], s. 1. pièce f de monnaie; gold coins, pièces d'or; a false c., une fausse pièce, une pièce fausse; c. balance, trébuchet m. 2. coll. (no pl.) monnaie(s) f, pièces, numéraire m, espèces fpl; small c., subsidiary c., monnaie divisionnaire; on the table was a small heap of c., sur la table il y avait un petit tas de pièces de monnaie; c. and bullion, métal monnayé et métal en barres; false c., de la fausse monnaie; in coin, en espèces, en numéraire; to pay in c. of the realm, payer en espèces (sonnantes et trébuchantes); to pay s.o. back in his own c., rendre la pareille à qn; Prov: much c. much care, qui terre a guerre a. 3. attrib. c. machine, c.-operated machine, c.-in-the-slot machine, distributeur m automatique; Tp: c.-operated box = taxiphone m; U.S: c. purse, porte-monnaie m inv.

coin[2], v.tr. 1. to c. money, frapper de la monnaie, battre monnaie; F: he's simply coining money, coining it, il est en train de faire fortune; il fait des affaires d'or. 2. monnayer (des lingots). 3. inventer, forger, fabriquer, créer (un mot nouveau); to c. a phrase, (i) pour créer, inventer, un idiotisme; (ii) Iron: pour se servir du cliché habituel; si je puis m'exprimer ainsi.

coinage [ˈkɔinidʒ], s. 1. (a) monnayage m; frappe f (de la monnaie); right of c., droit m de frappe; droit de battre monnaie; c. offence, crime m de fausse monnaie, de faux monnayage; (*b*) invention *f*, fabrication *f*, création *f* (d'un mot); **words of modern c.**, mots *m* de création nouvelle. **2.** (*a*) système *m* monétaire (d'un pays); (*b*) monnaie(s) *f*; numéraire *m*; (*c*) mot inventé; **chortle is a c. of Lewis Carroll's,** Lewis Carroll a inventé le mot *chortle*.

coinbox ['kɔinbɔks], *s.* **1.** tirelire *f*. **2.** boîte *f* aux sous (d'un distributeur automatique, etc.); **c. (telephone)** = taxiphone *m*.

coincide [kouin'said], *v.i.* **1.** (*in space, time*) coïncider (**with,** avec); **events that c.,** événements *m* qui concourent; *Mth:* **the two lines c.,** les deux lignes coïncident. **2.** coïncider, s'accorder, être d'accord (**with,** avec); **his interests c. with his duty,** ses intérêts *m* s'accordent avec son devoir. **3.** (*of pers.*) **to c. in an opinion,** être d'accord sur un point.

coincidence [kou'insidəns], *s.* **1.** (*in space, time*) coïncidence *f*; *Ph: etc:* **delayed c.,** coïncidence retardée; **random c.,** coïncidence fortuite; **true c.,** coïncidence vraie; *El:* **phase c.,** coïncidence, concordance *f*, de phase; **c. circuit,** circuit *m* à coïncidence; **c. counter,** compteur *m* à coïncidence; **c. loss,** perte *f* par coïncidence; **c. selector,** sélecteur *m* à coïncidences; *Opt:* **c. telemeter,** télémètre *m* à coïncidence. **2.** coïncidence, rencontre *f*, concours *m* (d'événements); **what a c.!** quelle coïncidence! comme ça se rencontre! comme ça tombe!

coincident [kou'insidənt], *a.* coïncident; d'accord (**with,** avec).

coincidental [kouinsi'dentl], *a.* (effet *m*) de coïncidence; **entirely c. occurrences,** faits *m* de pure coïncidence.

coincidently [kou'insidəntli], *adv.* coïncidemment; d'accord (**with,** avec).

coined [kɔind], *a.* **1.** (argent) monnayé. **2.** (mot) inventé, forgé, pour l'occasion, pour les besoins de la cause.

coiner ['kɔinər], *s.* **1.** monnayeur *m*. **2.** faux monnayeur. **3.** fabricateur, -trice, inventeur, -trice, forgeur, -euse (d'un nouveau mot, d'un mensonge, etc.).

coining ['kɔiniŋ], *s.* = COINAGE 1.

coin shell ['kɔinʃel], *s. Moll:* lepton *m*.

coinstantaneity ['kouinstæntə'ni:iti], *s.* simultanéité *f*.

coinstantaneous ['kouinstən'teiniəs], *a.* simultané.

coinstantaneously ['kouinstən'teiniəsli], *adv.* simultanément.

co-insurance ['kouin'sju:rəns], *s.* coassurance *f*.

coir ['kɔiər], *s.* coir *m*; fibre *f* de coco, de cocotier; bastin *m*; **c. broom, matting, rope,** balai *m*, natte *f*, cordage *m*, en coco; **c. mat,** paillasson *m*; tapis brosse *m*, *pl.* tapis-brosses.

coition [kou'iʃ(ə)n], *s.* **coitus** ['kouitəs], *s.*, coït *m*; **coitus interruptus,** rapport interrompu.

coix [kouiks], *s. Bot:* coix *m*.

coke[1] [kouk], *s.* coke *m*; **foundry c.,** coke de fonderie; **gas c.,** coke de gaz, d'usine à gaz; **c. oven,** four *m* à coke; **c.-oven gas,** gaz *m* de coke; **c. iron,** fer *m*, fonte *f*, au coke; **c. breaker,** casse-coke *m inv*; concasseur *m* de coke; **c. car,** wagon *m* d'extinction, chariot *m* à coke; **c. maker, manufacturer,** coketier *m*, cokerier *m*; *P: A:* **go and eat c.!** va te faire voir!

coke[2], *v.tr.* (*a*) coké(i)fier; convertir (de la houille) en coke; (*b*) (*of coal, with passive force*) se coké(i)fier, se convertir en coke.

coke[3], *s. P:* (= cocaine) coco *f*, neige *f*.

coke[4], *v.tr. & i.* **to c. oneself, c. up, get coked (up),** se droguer (à la cocaïne), se bourrer (de cocaïne).

coke[5], *s. F:* Coca-Cola *m* (*R.t.m.*).

cokehead ['koukhed], *s. P:* camé, -ée.

cokeman, *pl.* **-men** ['koukmæn, -men], *s.m. Ind:* coketier, cokerier.

cokernut ['koukənʌt], *s. P:* = COCONUT.

cokey, cokie ['kouki], *s. P:* camé, -ée.

coking ['koukiŋ]. **1.** *a.* cokéfiable, cokéfiant; **c. coal,** charbon *m* cokéfiable; **2.** *s.* (*a*) cokéfaction *f*, coké(i)fication *f*; **c. plant,** cokerie *f*; (*b*) *Petr:* cokage *m*.

coky[1] ['kouki], *a.* semblable au coke.

coky[2], *s. P:* camé, -ée.

col [kɔl], *s.* **1.** *Geog:* (*a*) col *m*; (*b*) ensellement *m*. **2.** *Meteor:* col (séparant deux anticyclones).

cola ['koulə], *s. Bot:* cola *m*, kola *m*.

colander ['kʌləndər], *s.* **1.** *Dom.Ec:* passoire *f*. **2.** *Ind:* chantepleure *f*.

colarin ['kɔlərin], *s. Arch:* colarin *m*.

co-latitude ['kou'lætitju:d], *s. Astr:* colatitude *f*.

colchicine ['kɔltʃisi:n], *s. Pharm:* colchicine *f*.

colchicum ['kɔltʃikəm], *s.* **1.** *Bot:* colchique *m*; **autumn c.,** colchique d'automne. **2.** *Pharm:* colchique.

Colchis ['kɔlkis], *Pr.n. Geog:* Colchide *f*; *Myth:* **the dragon of C.,** le dragon colchique.

colcothar ['kɔlkouθɑ:r], *s. Ch:* colcot(h)ar *m*.

cold[1] [kould], *a. & adv.*

I. *a.* **1.** (*a*) (*of temperature*) froid; **it's c.,** il fait froid; **do you find it c. here?** est-ce que vous trouvez qu'il fait froid ici? **it's getting colder,** la température baisse; *Meteor:* **c. front,** front froid; **c. wave,** (i) *Meteor:* vague *f* de froid; (ii) *Hairdr:* indéfrisable *f* à froid; **to get, grow, c.,** se refroidir; **as c. as charity, as marble,** froid comme le marbre; **c. steel,** l'arme blanche; *Com:* **c. storage,** conservation *f* par le froid; **c. room, store,** chambre *f*, entrepôt *m*, frigorifique; **c. storage plant, industry,** installation *f*, industrie *f*, du froid; *F:* **to put sth. in c. storage,** mettre qch. aux oubliettes; *P: A:* **to be in c. storage,** faire de la prison, être à l'ombre; **c. bath,** bain froid; **c. engine,** moteur froid; **c. meal,** repas froid; **c. meat,** (i) viandes froides; (ii) *P: O:* cadavre *m*; *P: O:* **c. meat train,** train *m* mortuaire; *P: O:* **c. meat party,** enterrement *m*; *F:* **to make c. meat of s.o.,** tuer, refroidir, qn; *F:* **out c.,** sans connaissance, inanimé; **to knock s.o. (out) c.,** (i) étendre qn raide (d'un coup); (ii) stupéfier qn; *F:* **I've got him (stone) c.,** je l'ai à ma merci; *F:* **c. pig,** douche *f* d'eau froide (jetée sur qn qui dort, pour le réveiller); **to give s.o. the c. shoulder,** battre froid à qn; tourner le dos à qn; snober qn; *Th: etc: F:* **c. performance,** représentation *f* sans musique, sans orchestre; *Pol: F:* **c. war,** guerre froide; (*b*) (*of pers.*) **to be, feel, c.,** avoir froid; **my hands are c.,** j'ai les mains froides, j'ai froid aux mains; **my feet are as c. as ice,** j'ai les pieds glacés; *F:* **to have c. feet,** avoir la frousse; *Prov:* **c. hands, warm heart,** froides mains, chaudes amours; (*c*) *Ven:* **c. scent,** piste froide; (*d*) *Med:* **c. abscess,** abcès froid; (*e*) **c. tint,** ton froid, tirant sur le bleu; (*f*) *Atom.Ph: F:* non radioactif. **2.** (*a*) (*of pers., manner*) froid; **c. reception, welcome,** accueil froid; **to be c. with s.o.,** se montrer froid avec qn; **to have a c. heart,** avoir un cœur de marbre; **to be as c. as marble,** être en marbre; **c. eloquence,** éloquence *f* sans chaleur; *F:* **that leaves me c.,** cela me laisse froid; *F:* **he's a c. fish,** c'est un pisse-froid; (*b*) (*of woman*) (**sexually**) **c.,** froid. **3.** *Tchn:* (*in compounds*) à froid; **c.-pressed,** embouti à froid; **c. rivetting,** rivure *f* à froid; **c.-worked, c.-strained,** écroui; **c. working,** écrouissage *m*.

II. *adv.* (*a*) **the wind blows c.,** il fait un vent froid; (*b*) *U.S:* (tout) net; carrément; (*c*) *U.S:* **to know sth. c.,** connaître qch. à fond; (*d*) *Surg:* **to operate c.,** opérer à froid.

cold[2], *s.* **1.** (*in atmosphere*) froid *m*; **c. wave,** vague *f* de froid; coup *m* de froid; *Ph:* **unit of c.,** unité *f* de froid; **I feel the c.,** je suis très frileux; **to protect oneself against the c.,** se protéger contre le froid; **don't leave the plants in the c.,** ne laissez pas les plantes au froid; *F:* **to leave s.o. out in the c.,** laisser qn à l'écart; ne pas inviter qn; ne pas s'inquiéter de qn; **to be left out in the c.,** rester en carafe, sur le carreau; **to come in from the c.,** rentrer en faveur. **2.** *Med:* (**common**) **c.,** rhume *m*; **to have a c.,** être enrhumé; avoir un rhume; **bad, heavy, c.,** gros rhume; *F:* rhume carabiné; **c. in the head, head c.,** rhume de cerveau; **to have a c. in the head,** être enrhumé du cerveau; **c. on the chest, chest c.,** rhume de poitrine; **feverish c.,** rhume accompagné de fièvre; fièvre catarrhale; **to catch (a) c.,** attraper un rhume; s'enrhumer; prendre froid; **to catch c. again,** reprendre froid; **I can't get rid of my c.,** je n'arrive pas à me désenrhumer; **c. in the eye,** coup *m* d'air dans l'œil; **c. sore,** herpès *m*; *F:* **you'll catch your death of c.,** vous allez crever de froid.

cold-blooded ['kould'blʌdid], *a.* **1.** *Z:* (animal) à sang froid. **2.** (*of pers.*) froid, insensible; (*of action*) prémédité, délibéré; accompli de sang-froid; **in a c.-b. way,** sans pitié.

cold-bloodedly ['kould'blʌdidli], *adv.* de, avec, sang-froid; avec insensibilité.

cold-bloodedness ['kould'blʌdidnis], *s.* sang-froid *m*, insensibilité *f*.

cold cream ['kould'kri:m], *s. Toil:* cold-cream *m*.

cold-draw ['kould'drɔ:], *v.tr.* **1.** *Metalw:* étirer (le fil de fer) à froid; écrouir. **2.** *Pharm:* exprimer (l'huile de ricin) à froid.

cold-drawing ['kould'drɔ:iŋ], *s. Metalw:* étirage *m* à froid; écrouissage *m*.

cold-drawn ['kould'drɔ:n], *a.* **1.** *Metalw:* étiré à froid. **2.** *Pharm:* exprimé à froid.

cold-hammer ['kould'hæmər], *v.tr. Metalw:* écrouir (le fer); battre, marteler, (le fer) à froid.

cold-hammered ['kould'hæməd], *a. Metalw:* façonné à froid.

cold hammering ['kould'hæməriŋ], *s. Metalw:* battage *m* à froid; martelage *m* à froid; écrouissage *m*.

coldhearted ['kould'hɑ:tid], *a.* au cœur froid, sec; insensible; sans pitié.

coldheartedly ['kould'hɑ:tidli], *adv.* froidement, avec insensibilité; sans pitié.

coldheartedness ['kould'hɑ:tidnis], *s.* froideur *f*, sécheresse *f*, du cœur; insensibilité *f*.

coldish ['kouldiʃ], *a.* un peu froid; plutôt, assez, froid; (*of weather*) frais, frisquet.

coldly ['kouldli], *adv.* froidement; (regarder qch.) avec froideur, d'un œil indifférent.

coldness ['kouldnis], *s.* **1.** froideur *f*; froidure *f* (du climat, etc.). **2.** froideur (de caractère, de style, d'un accueil); **there is a c. between them,** il y a de la froideur, du froid, entre eux.

cold-press ['kould'pres], *v.tr. Tex: etc:* catir, satiner, (le drap) à froid; satiner (le papier) à froid; *Metalw:* emboutir (la tôle) à froid; *Petr:* filtrer (des huiles) à froid.

cold pressing ['kould'presiŋ], *s. Tex: etc:* catinage *m* à froid; *Metalw:* emboutissage *m* à froid; *Petr:* filtration *f* à froid.

coldproof ['kouldpru:f], *a.* à l'épreuve du froid.

cold-roll ['kould'roul], *v.tr. Metalw:* écrouir (le métal).

cold rolling ['kould'rouliŋ], *s. Metalw:* écrouissage *m*; cylindrage *m*, laminage *m*, à froid; **c.-r. mill,** laminoir *m* à froid.

cold-short ['kould'ʃɔ:t]. **1.** *a. Metall:* (fer) cassant à froid; tendre, aigre. **2.** *s. Metalw:* mauvaise soudure par forgeage.

cold-shortness ['kould'ʃɔ:tnis], *s. Metall:* fragilité *f* à froid.

cold-shoulder ['kould'ʃouldər], *v.tr.* battre froid à (qn); tourner le dos à (qn); snober (qn).

cold turkey ['kould'tə:ki], *s. U.S: F:* **1. to talk c. t.,** dire les faits sans ménagements. **2. to be a c. t.,** être froid, insensible. **3. c.-t. cure,** sevrage *m* de drogues (par privation radicale).

cole [koul], *s. Hort: A:* **1.** navette *f*. **2.** chou-marin *m*, *pl.* choux-marins.

colectomy [kə'lektəmi], *s. Surg:* colectomie *f*.

co-legatee ['koulegə'ti:], *s.* colégataire *mf*; légataire conjoint(e).

coleophorid [kɔli'ɔfərid], *s. Ent:* coléophoride *m*.

Coleophoridae [kɔliə'fɔridi:], *s.pl. Ent:* coléophorides *m*.

coleopter [kɔli'ɔptər], *s. Ent:* coléoptère *m*.

Coleoptera [kɔli'ɔptərə], *s.pl. Ent:* coléoptères *m*.

coleopterist [kɔli'ɔptərist], *s. Ent:* coléoptériste *mf*.

Coleopteroidea [kɔliɔptə'rɔidiə], *s.pl. Ent:* coléoptéroïdes *m*.

coleopterous [kɔli'ɔptərəs], *a. Ent:* coléoptère.

coleoptile [kɔli'ɔptail], *s. Bot:* coléoptile *m*.

coleorhiza, *pl.* **-ae** [kɔliou'raizə, -i:], *s. Bot:* coléorhize *f*.

Coleorhyncha [kɔliou'riŋkə], *s.pl. Ent:* coléorhynches *m*.

colerape ['koulreip], *s. Bot:* rave *f*.

coleseed ['koulsi:d], *s. Bot:* **1.** graine *f* de colza. **2.** colza *m*.

coleslaw ['koulslɔ:], *s. Cu:* salade *f* de chou cru.

colewort ['koulwə:t], *s. Bot:* (*a*) chou *m* fourrager; (*b*) chou non pommé; (*c*) chou vert.

coli- ['koul(a)i], *pref.* coli-.

colibacillosis ['koulibæsi'lousis], *s. Med:* colibacillose *f*.

colibri ['kɔlibri], *s. Orn:* colibri *m*.

colic ['kɔlik]. **1.** *a. Anat:* (artère *f*, etc.) colique. **2.** *s.* (*a*) *Med:* colique *f*, épreintes *fpl*; **lead c.,** colique de plomb, colique saturnine; **painter's c.,** colique saturnine; **wind c.,** colique flatulente; **to be suffering from c.,** (i) avoir mal au ventre; (ii) souffrir de coliques; *A:* **c. belt,** ceinture *f* de flanelle; (*b*) *Vet:* tranchées *fpl*; **violent c.** (*in horses*), tranchées rouges.

colicky ['kɔliki], *a.* coliqueux.

Coliidae [kə'liidi:], *s.pl. Orn:* coliidés *m*, les colious *m*.

Coliiformes [kɔlii'fɔ:mi:z], *s.pl. Orn:* coliiformes *m*.

co-liquidator ['kou'likwideitər], *s.* coliquidateur *m* (d'une faillite).

Coliseum (the) [ðəkɔli'siəm], *s. Rom.Ant:* le Colisée.

colitic [kə'litik], *a. Med:* colitique.

colitis [kə'laitis], *s. Med:* colite *f*.

collaborate [kə'læbəreit], *v.i.* (*a*) collaborer (**with,** avec; **on,** à); **a group of students collaborated on the project,** un groupe d'étudiants a collaboré au projet; (*b*) **to c. with the enemy,** collaborer avec l'ennemi.

collaboration [kəlæbə'reiʃ(ə)n], *s.* (*a*) collaboration *f*; (*b*) *Pol:* collaboration (avec l'ennemi).

collaborationism [kəlæbə'reiʃənizm], *s.* collaborationnisme *m*.

collaborationist [kəlæbə'reiʃənist], *s. Pol: etc: Pej:* collaborationniste *mf*.

collaborator [kə'læbəreitər], *s.* (*a*) collaborateur, -trice; coauteur *m*; **to secure the help of a c.,** s'associer, s'assurer, un auxiliaire, un collaborateur; (*b*) *Pol:* collaborateur, -trice (avec l'ennemi).

collage ['kɔlɑ:ʒ], *s. Art:* collage *m*.

collagen ['kɔlədʒen], *s. Biol:* collagène *m*.

collagenous [kə'lædʒinəs], *a.* collagène.

collapsable [kə'læpsəbl], *a.* = COLLAPSIBLE.

collapse[1] [kə'læps], *s.* **1.** (*a*) écroulement *m*, effondrement *m* (d'un édifice, d'un empire, d'espoirs); effondrement, éboulement *m* (de terre, de sable); dégonflement *m* (d'un ballon); affaissement *m* (d'un pneu); culbute *f* (d'un ministère); débâcle *f* (d'un établissement, d'un pays); (*b*) *Mec.E: etc:* déformation *f*, gauchissement *m*, flambage *m*, voilage *m*, flexion *f* (d'une plaque, etc.); (*c*) *Com:* chute subite (de prix); *Fin:* **the c. of the market,** l'effondrement du marché; **the c. of the franc,** la dégringolade du franc. **2.** (*a*) *Med:* affaissement subit (au cours d'une maladie, par choc traumatique, etc.); collapsus *m*, prostration *f*; **c. therapy,** collapsothérapie *f*; (*b*) effondrement moral.

collapse[2], *v.*

I. *v.i.* **1.** (*a*) (*of building, institution, etc.*) s'affaisser, s'écrouler, s'effondrer; (*of balloon, etc.*) se dégonfler, s'aplatir; (*of ministry*) faire la culbute; (*of pers.*) s'effondrer, tomber comme une masse; **to cause sth. to c.,** faire affaisser qch.; **she collapsed,** elle tomba accablée; **he collapsed into an armchair,** il s'effondra dans un fauteuil; (*b*) *Mec.E: etc:* (*of support, wheel, etc.*) gauchir, fléchir, se déformer; se voiler; flamber; (*c*) *O:* (*of car hood*) se rabattre; (*d*) (*of prices*) s'effondrer. **2.** *Med:* (*of pers.*) s'affaisser (subitement).

II. *v.tr.* **1.** effondrer, affaisser (un bâtiment, etc.); dégonfler (un ballon, etc.). **2.** *U.S:* fermer (une lunette d'approche). **3.** *Med:* **to c. a lung,** collaber un poumon.

collapsible [kə'læpsəbl], *a.* **1.** (*of chair, boat, etc.*) pliant, repliable, démontable; (*of handle, etc.*) rabattable; *Nau:* **c. Berthon boat,** berthon *m* repliable; *Aut:* **c. hood,** capote pliante, rabattable. **2.** *Mec.E:* **c. load,** effort *m* de compression axiale.

collapsing [kə'læpsiŋ], *s. Med:* collapsus *m* (du poumon).

collar[1] ['kɔlər], *s.* **1.** *Cost:* col *m* (de robe, de chemise, de pardessus); collet *m* (de manteau); tour *m* de cou (en fourrure, etc.); collier *m* (d'un ordre, etc.); **lace c.,** collerette *f* en dentelle; **sailor c.,** col marin; **shirt with c. attached,** chemise *f* à col tenant; **(detachable) c.,** faux col; **soft c.,** col souple; **stiff c.,** col raide, empesé; **butterfly, wing, c.,** col cassé; **Eton c.,** grand col rabattu (d'écolier); **Peter Pan c.,** col Claudine; **button-down c.,** col à pointes boutonnées; **clerical c.,** col romain; **size in collars,** encolure *f*; **white-c. worker,** employé *m* (de bureau), *Fr.C:* collet-blanc *m, pl.* collets-blancs; **blue-c. worker,** ouvrier manuel, *Fr.C:* col bleu; **to seize,** *F:* **grab, s.o. by the c.,** prendre, saisir, qn au collet; *F:* **to get hot under the c.,** se ficher en rogne. **2.** (*a*) collier (de chien, de cheval); bourrelet *m* (de cheval); **dog c.,** (i) collier de chien; (ii) *F:* col romain; (*b*) *A:* **to work against the c.,** travailler sans plaisir; rechigner au travail; **out of the c.,** sans travail, en chômage; inoccupé. **3.** (*a*) *Mec.E:* anneau *m*, collier *m*, collet *m*, frette *f*, bague *f*, virole *f*, bride *f*; (*of axle*) collet, champignon *m*, heurtequin *m*, talon *m*; (*of pipe*) collet; **shaft c.,** collet d'arbre; embase *f* d'arbre; **set c.,** bague d'arrêt, de butée, de sûreté; **sliding c.,** collier coulissant, bague coulissante; baladeur *m*; **stop c.,** collier, bague d'arrêt; bague de butée; **drive c.,** collier d'entraînement; **c. bearing,** palier *m* à cannelures; **c.-slip bearing,** crapaudine *f* annulaire; **screw c.,** collier-écrou *m, pl.* colliers-écrous; **thrust c.,** bague de butée; collet de butée; *Mch:* **c. nut,** écrou *m* à embase; *Veh:* **axle-tree c.,** couvre-essieu *m, pl.* couvre-essieux; *I.C.E:* (*on valve stem*) clavette *f* de soupape; (*b*) *Nau:* collier (d'étai); (*c*) *Const:* **c. beam, tie,** entrait retroussé; faux entrait; (*between rafters*) traversière *f*. **4.** (*a*) *Z:* collier (d'oiseau, de quadrupède); (*b*) *Bot:* collet (de racine). **5.** *Cu:* roulade *f* (de bœuf, de veau, de poisson). **6.** *Min:* (*of mine shaft*) cadre *m* de la surface. **7.** *Furn: Arch:* frette *f*.

collar[2], *v.tr.* **1.** (*a*) colleter (qn); saisir, prendre, (qn) au collet; (*b*) *Rugby: Fb:* arrêter (l'adversaire qui détient le ballon); **to c. s.o. low,** ceinturer qn; (*c*) *F: O:* saisir, empoigner, pincer, mettre la main sur (qn, qch.); chiper (qch.); cravater (qn); **the burglars collared all the silver,** les cambrioleurs ont raflé toute l'argenterie. **2.** *Cu:* rouler (de la viande) pour la ficeler; mettre (du bœuf, du poisson) en roulades. **3.** *Mec.E:* baguer, fretter.

collarbone ['kɔləboun], *s. Anat:* clavicule *f*; **to break one's c.,** se fracturer la clavicule.

collared ['kɔləd], *a.* **1.** *Mec.E:* **c. coupling,** manchon *m* à frettes. **2.** *Cu:* (viande *f*, poisson *m*) roulé(e), mis(e) en roulades; **c. head,** fromage *m* de tête.

collaret(te) [kɔlə'ret], *s. Cost:* collerette *f*.

collargol [kɔ'lɑːgɔl], *s. Ch:* collargol *m*.

collate [kɔ'leit], *v.tr.* **1.** (*a*) rassembler (des documents, des données); *Bookb:* assembler, collationner (les feuilles); (*b*) collationner, conférer (un texte) **(with,** avec); (*c*) *Cmptr:* interclasser (des cartes). **2.** *Ecc:* **to c. a cleric to a benefice,** *abs.* **to c.,** nommer un ecclésiastique à un bénéfice; conférer un bénéfice à un ecclésiastique.

collateral [kɔ'lætər(ə)l], *a.* **1.** (*of street, etc.*) collatéral, -aux; parallèle; *Anat:* **c. (artery),** (artère) collatérale *f*. **2.** *a. & s.* (*of branch of family*) collatéral, -ale. **3.** (*a*) (*of knowledge, fact*) concomitant, additionnel; (*b*) (*of phenomenon*) correspondant, parallèle. **4.** (*of cause, etc.*) accessoire, subsidiaire, indirect; *Com: Jur:* **c. security,** *s.* **c.,** garantie additionnelle, accessoire; nantissement *m* subsidiaire.

collaterally [kɔ'læt(ə)rəli], *adv.* **1.** parallèlement **(with,** à). **2.** (*a*) indirectement, subsidiairement; (*b*) *Jur:* collatéralement; **c. related (to s.o.),** parent (de qn) en ligne collatérale.

collating [kə'leitiŋ], *s.* **1.** collationnement *m*. **2.** *Bookb:* assemblage *m*. **3.** *Cmptr:* interclassement *m*.

collation [kə'leiʃ(ə)n], *s.* **1.** (*a*) rassemblement *m* (de documents, de données); *Bookb:* assemblage *m*, collationnement *m* (des feuilles); (*b*) collation *f*, conférence *f*, confrontation *f* (de textes); (*c*) *Cmptr:* interclassement *m* (des cartes); **c. file,** fichier *m* d'interclassement; **c. tape,** bande *f* d'interclassement. **2.** (*meal*) collation; **cold c.,** repas froid. **3.** *Ecc:* collation (d'un bénéfice).

collative [kə'leitiv], *a.* collatif.

collator [kə'leitər], *s.* **1.** (*a*) **the c. of the two texts,** celui qui a collationné les deux textes; (*b*) *Bookb:* collateur *m* (de feuillets). **2.** *Ecc:* collateur (d'un bénéfice). **3.** *Cmptr:* interclasseuse *f*.

colleague ['kɔliːg], *s.* collègue *mf*; confrère *m*; collaborateur, -trice.

collect[1] ['kɔlekt], *s. Ecc:* (*prayer*) collecte *f*.

collect[2] [kə'lekt]. **1.** *v.tr.* (*a*) rassembler (la foule, ses effets); assembler (des matériaux); réunir, assembler (des amis); amasser (une fortune); recueillir (des données, des nouvelles); récolter (des documents, des anecdotes, etc.); *Mil:* **to c. the wounded,** ramasser les blessés; **to c. the dead,** ramasser, enlever, les morts; *Post:* **to c. the letters,** lever les lettres; faire la levée des lettres; **to c. (the) eggs,** ramasser les œufs; **milk collected over a wide area,** lait *m* de grand ramassage; *Rail: etc: A:* **to c. the luggage (in advance),** prendre les bagages à domicile; **I'll c. you with the car at midday,** je passerai vous prendre à midi; *Hyd.E:* **to c. the water,** capter, réunir, les eaux; *El:* **to c. the current,** recueillir, capter, le courant; *Ost:* **to c. oysters** (*from the beds*), déparquer des huîtres; (*b*) collectionner (des timbres, des livres, etc.); **I c. paintings,** je fais collection de peintures; (*c*) percevoir, lever, recouvrer (les impôts); toucher (une traite); **to c. a debt,** recouvrer, récupérer, faire rentrer, une créance; faire un recouvrement; *Com: Fin:* **to c. moneys due,** faire la recette (des traites, etc.); (*of bank*) **to c. a cheque,** encaisser un chèque; *Sch:* **to c. the candidates' papers,** ramasser les copies; *v.i.* **to c. for charity,** quêter, faire la quête, pour une œuvre de bienfaisance; (*d*) aller chercher (sa valise, etc.); (*e*) recueillir, rassembler (ses idées); ramasser, recueillir (ses forces); **to c. oneself,** se reprendre, se reconnaître; reprendre son sang-froid; se calmer, se remettre; **to c. one's thoughts,** se recueillir; se reprendre; (*f*) *Equit:* (r)assembler (un cheval). **2.** *v.i.* (*of people*) s'assembler, se rassembler, se réunir; (*of thgs*) s'amasser.

collect[3], *a. & adv. Post: NAm:* en port dû; **to send a telegram c.,** envoyer un télégramme en port dû; *Tp:* **c. call,** communication *f* en, avec, P.C.V.; **to call (s.o.) c.,** appeler (qn) avec P.C.V.

collectable, -ible [kə'lektəbl], *a.* (*of money*) recouvrable, récupérable; (*of tax*) percevable, perceptible; (*of coupon*) encaissable; touchable.

collected [kə'lektid], *a.* (*a*) recueilli; (*b*) (plein) de sang-froid; maître de soi, *f.* maîtresse de soi.

collectedly [kə'lektidli], *adv.* (*a*) avec recueillement; (*b*) avec calme; avec sang-froid; de sens rassis.

collecting[1] [kə'lektiŋ], *a.* **1.** collecteur, -trice; **c. clerk,** garçon *m* de recettes. **2.** *Bot:* **c. hairs,** poils collecteurs.

collecting[2], *s.* **1.** = COLLECTION 1. **2.** *Mil:* **c. of the wounded,** ramassage *m* des blessés; **c. of the dead,** ramassage, enlèvement *m* des morts; **casualty c. post,** section *f* de ramassage (des blessés); **medical c. unit,** unité médicale de ramassage (des blessés); **c. station,** poste *m*, centre *m*, de triage et de premier traitement (des blessés, malades, etc.); **c. point,** point *m*, poste *m*, centre *m* de ramassage, de rassemblement (du personnel, du matériel, etc.).

collection [kə'lekʃ(ə)n], *s.* **1.** rassemblement *m*, réunion *f*, assemblage *m* (de personnes, de choses); ramassage *m* (des blessés); recouvrement *m*, récupération *f* (d'une somme); perception *f*, recouvrement, levée *f*, rentrée *f* (des impôts); encaissement *m* (d'un billet); levée (des lettres); enlèvement *m*, prise *f* à domicile (de colis); captation *f*, captage *m* (d'eau, de courant électrique, etc.); collectionnement *m* (de tableaux, de livres); recueil *m* (de renseignements, de données); **c. of eggs,** collecte *f*, ramassage *m*, des œufs; **c. round,** tournée *f* de collecte, de ramassage, collecte *f* (du lait dans les fermes, etc.). **2.** *Ecc: etc:* quête *f*, collecte; **to take up a c.,** faire la quête; faire une collecte; **c. box,** tronc *m* (d'église, de quêteur); **c. plate,** plat *m*, plateau *m*, de quête. **3.** amas *m*, assemblage, entassement *m*, réunion. **4.** collection *f* (de papillons, de timbres); recueil *m* (de proverbes, de bons mots, de chansons); **c. of plants,** collection de plantes; herbier *m*; **c. of medals,** collection de médailles; médaillier *m*; *Dressm: etc:* **spring c.,** collection de printemps. **5.** *pl. Sch:* **collections,** examen trimestriel (à Oxford, Durham, etc.).

collective [kə'lektiv], *a.* **1.** collectif; *Jur:* **c. ownership,** propriété collective; possession *f* en commun; **c. farm,** ferme collective; *Pol.Ec:* **c. bargaining,** (négociation *f* de) convention collective; *Pol:* **c. security,** sécurité collective; *Dipl:* **c. note,** note collective; *Gram:* **c. noun,** nom collectif. **2.** *Bot:* (fruit) multiple, agrégé.

collectively [kə'lektivli], *adv.* collectivement; (possédé, etc.) en commun.

collectivism [kə'lektivizm], *s. Pol.Ec:* collectivisme *m*.

collectivist [kə'lektivist], *Pol.Ec:* **1.** *s.* collectiviste *mf*. **2.** *a.* collectiviste; **c. economies,** économies *f* collectivistes.

collectivity [kɔlek'tiviti], *s.* **1.** collectivité *f*. **2.** propriété *f* en commun; possession *f* en commun.

collectivization [kəlektivai'zeiʃ(ə)n], *s.* collectivisation *f*.

collectivize [kə'lektivaiz], *v.tr.* collectiviser.

collector [kə'lektər], *s.* **1.** (*pers.*) (*a*) encaisseur *m* (d'un chèque, d'un billet); quêteur, -euse (d'aumônes); collecteur, -trice (de cotisations); ramasseur *m* (de lait, etc.); *Rail:* **ticket c.,** contrôleur *m* (de billets); (*b*) encaisseur (de la Compagnie du gaz, etc.); *Adm:* percepteur *m* (des contributions directes); receveur *m* (des contributions indirectes); (*c*) collectionneur, -euse; amateur *m* (de tableaux, de livres); amasseur, -euse (de curiosités, etc.); **stamp c.,** collectionneur, -euse, de timbres-poste; philatéliste *mf*; **collector's piece,** pièce *f* de collection. **2.** *Mec.E: etc:* collecteur (d'huile, de vapeur, etc.); récepteur *m* (de trop-plein, etc.); *Hyd.E: etc:* **c. of waters, steam,** réceptacle *m*; *El:* **current c.,** prise *f* de courant; **plough c.,** sabot *m*, charrue *f*, chariot *m*, de prise de courant; **c. (ring),** bague collectrice (de dynamo, etc.); anneau *m* (de prise de courant); commutateur(-collecteur) *m*; collecteur; **brush c.,** commutateur à balais.

collectorship [kə'lektəʃip], *s.* fonctions *fpl* de percepteur, de receveur; perception *f*, recette *f*.

colleen ['kɔliːn], *s. Dial:* (*in Ireland*) jeune fille *f*.

college ['kɔlidʒ], *s.* **1.** collège *m*; *Rom.Ant:* **the C. of Augurs,** le Collège des augures; *Ecc:* **the Sacred C., the C. of Cardinals,** le sacré Collège; le Collège des cardinaux; **the Heralds' C., the C. of Arms,** le Collège des hérauts; *Pol:* **electoral c.,** collège électoral. **2.** *Sch:* (*a*) collège (d'université britannique); (*b*) *F:* l'université; **when I was at c.,** quand j'étais à la faculté; (*c*) **military, naval, c.,** école *f* militaire, navale; *Av:* **R.F.C.** = école de l'air; (*d*) **c. of education,** *A:* **(teachers') training c.** = école normale; **agricultural c.** = institut *m* agronomique; (*e*) = lycée *m*; **technical c.** = lycée technique; (*as Pr.n.*) **Eton C.,** le collège d'Eton; (*f*) *Cu:* **c. pudding,** (variété de) pouding *m* aux raisins. **3.** *P: A:* prison *f*.

colleger ['kɔlidʒər], *s. Sch:* **1.** (*at Eton*) boursier *m*. **2.** *NAm:* = lycéen, -éenne.

collegial [kə'liːdʒiəl], *a.* collégial, -aux; de collège.

collegian [kə'liːdʒiən], *s.* **1.** membre *m* d'un collège (universitaire). **2.** *P: A:* (*a*) prisonnier *m*; (*b*) débiteur emprisonné.

collegiate [kə'liːdʒiət], *a.* collégial, -aux. **1. c. life,** la vie à l'université, dans les collèges *m* universitaires. **2. c. church,** collégiale *f*.

Collembola [kə'lembələ], *s.pl. Ent:* collemboles *m*.

collenchyma, *pl.* **-mata** [kə'leŋkima, kɔleŋ'kimətə], *s. Bot:* collenchyme *m*.

collenchymatous [kɔlen'kimətəs], *a. Bot:* collenchymateux.

collet[1] ['kɔlit], *s.* **1.** *Tchn:* douille *f* (de serrage), mandrin *m*, bague *f*; **die-holding c.,** lunette *f*, douille, de filière; manchon *m* porte-filière; **c. for drills,** mandrin porte-foret. **2.** *Lap:* chaton *m* (de bague); sertissure *f*. **3.** anneau *m* d'ivoire (isolant l'anse d'une cafetière, d'une théière, etc.).

collet[2], *v.tr.* sertir (un diamant, etc.).

collet[3], *s. Lap:* culasse *f* (de diamant taillé en brilliant).

colleter [kə'li:tər], *s. Bot:* collétère *m.*

Colletes [kɔ'li:ti:z], *s. Ent:* collète *m.*

colletia [kɔ'li:ʃiə], *s. Bot:* collétie *f.*

colletotrichum [kɔli'tɔtrikəm], *s. Fung:* colletotrichum *m.*

collide [kə'laid], **1.** *v.i.* (*of vehicles, etc.*) se rencontrer, se heurter, se tamponner, s'entrechoquer; entrer en collision; **the trains collided at the points,** les deux trains se sont pris en écharpe; **to c. with sth.,** rencontrer, heurter, tamponner, qch.; entrer en collision avec qch.; *Nau:* aborder (un navire); (*of pers.*) **to c. with s.o., sth.,** se heurter à, contre, qn, qch.; heurter qch. **2. to c. with s.o's ideas, with s.o.'s interests,** heurter, aller contre, les idées, les intérêts de qn.

collidin(e) ['kɔlidin, -ɑin], *s. Ch:* collidine *f.*

colliding [kə'laidiŋ], *s.* = COLLISION.

collie ['kɔli], *s.* **c. (dog),** chien de berger écossais; colley *m.*

collier ['kɔliər], *s.* **1.** (*pers.*) houilleur *m*; mineur *m* (de charbon). **2.** *Nau:* (navire *m*) charbonnier *m.*

colliery ['kɔljəri], *s.* houillère *f*; mine *f* de houille, de charbon.

colligate ['kɔligeit], *v.tr.* colliger; rapprocher, réunir (des idées, des faits).

colligation [kɔli'geiʃ(ə)n], *s.* colligation *f.*

colligative [kə'ligətiv], *a. Ch:* colligatif.

collimate ['kɔlimeit], *v.tr. Opt:* collimater (des lentilles, un faisceau lumineux); **collimating lens,** collimateur *m.*

collimation [kɔli'meiʃ(ə)n], *s. Opt:* collimation *f.*

collimator ['kɔlimeitər], *s. Opt:* collimateur *m.*

collinear [kɔ'liniər, kou-], *a. Mth:* (points) situés sur la même droite; **c. with the line A B,** dans le prolongement de la ligne A B.

Collins ['kɔlinz], *s. F: A:* lettre de remerciement écrite à un hôte (d'un personnage de Jane Austen).

colliquation [kɔli'kweiʃ(ə)n], *s. Med:* colliquation *f.*

collision [kə'liʒ(ə)n], *s.* **1.** (*a*). collision *f*, rencontre *f*; heurt *m*; tamponnement *m* (de trains); abordage *m*, collision (de navires); **head-on c.,** collision frontale; **there was a head-on c.,** les deux voitures se sont embouties; **to come into c. with. . .,** tamponner (un train, une auto), entrer en collision avec (un train, un navire, etc.), aborder (un navire), se heurter à, contre (qn, qch.); **ship that has been in c. with another,** navire qui a été abordé par un autre; **the two cars had a slight c.,** les deux voitures se sont accrochées légèrement; *Nau:* **c. door,** porte *f* étanche; cloison *f* d'abordage; **c. mat,** paillet lardé, Makarov *m*; **head on c.,** abordage droit debout; (*b*) choc *m* (de consonnes); (*c*) **c. course,** cap *m* de collision (d'un navire, d'un projectile anti-aérien, d'un engin anti-missile); (*d*) *Atom.Ph:* choc, collision (des particules); **c. of the first, of the second, kind,** choc de première, de deuxième, espèce; **elastic, inelastic, c.,** collision élastique, inélastique; **effective c. cross section,** section *f* efficace de choc; **total effective c. cross section,** section spécifique de choc; (*e*) *Ph:* **c. excitation,** excitation *f* (d'un gaz) par choc; **c. ionization,** ionisation *f* (d'un gaz) par choc. **2.** collision, choc, conflit *m* (d'intérêts).

colloblast ['kɔləblæst], *s. Biol:* colloblaste *m.*

collocate ['kɔloukeit], *v.tr. Lit:* colloquer, arranger, disposer (des troupes, des faits).

collocation [kɔlou'keiʃ(ə)n], *s. Lit:* collocation *f*, arrangement *m*; alliance *f* (de mots).

collocutor [kɔ'lɔkjutər], *s. Lit:* interlocuteur, -trice.

collodion [kə'loudiən], *s.* collodion *m*; *Phot:* **c.-coated,** celloïdin.

collodionize [kə'loudiənaiz], *v.tr.* collodionner.

collogue [kɔ'loug], *v.i. A:* **1.** comploter, manigancer, s'entendre (**with s.o. to do sth.,** avec qn pour faire qch.). **2.** s'entretenir (**with s.o.,** avec qn).

colloid ['kɔlɔid], *a. & s. Ch:* colloïde (*m*); *Med:* **c. degeneration,** dégénérescence colloïde; **c. cancer, carcinoma,** tumeur *f* colloïde.

colloidal [kə'lɔidl], *a. Ch:* colloïdal, -aux.

collop ['kɔləp], *s.* **1.** *Cu:* tranche *f* de viande; **minced collops,** hachis *m*; **Scotch collops,** bifteck *m* aux oignons. **2.** *B:* repli *m* (de graisse).

colloquial [kə'loukwiəl], *a.* familier; de (la) conversation; (langue) parlée; **c. English,** l'anglais parlé.

colloquialism [kə'loukwiəlizm], *s.* expression familière.

colloquially [kə'loukwi(ə)li], *adv.* familièrement; dans le langage de la conversation; en style familier.

colloquist ['kɔləkwist], *s. Lit:* interlocuteur, -trice.

colloquium [kə'loukwiəm], **colloquy** ['kɔləkwi], *s.* colloque *m.*

collotype ['kɔlətaip], *s.* **1. c. (plate),** phototype *m.* **2. c. (process),** phototypie *f*; *occ.* collotypie *f.*

colloxylin [kɔ'lɔksilin], *s. Ch:* colloxyline *f.*

collude [kə'l(j)u:d], *v.i. A:* être d'intelligence; s'entendre (**with,** avec).

collum ['kɔləm], *s. Anat:* col *m*; sillon *m.*

collusion [kə'l(j)u:ʒ(ə)n], *s.* collusion *f*; **to act in c. with s.o.,** agir de complicité, de connivence, avec qn: **they are acting in c.,** ils se sont donné le mot; **to be in c. with s.o.,** être d'intelligence, *F:* de mèche, avec qn.

collusive [kə'l(j)u:siv], *a.* collusoire.

collusively [kə'l(j)u:sivli], *adv.* collusoirement.

colluvial [kə'lu:viəl], *a. Geog:* **c. deposits,** colluvion *f.*

colluvium [kə'lu:viəm], *s. Geog:* colluvion *f.*

collybia [kə'libiə], *s. Fung:* collybie *f.*

collyrite ['kɔlirait], *s. Miner:* collyrite *m.*

collyrium [kə'liriəm], *s. Pharm:* collyre *m.*

collywobbles ['kɔliwɔblz], *s.pl. F:* **to have the c.,** avoir mal au ventre.

coloboma, *pl.* **-mata** [kɔlə'boumə, -mətə], *s. Med:* colobome *m.*

colobus ['kɔləbəs], *s. Z:* colobe *m*; **white-mantled c.,** colobe à manteau blanc, guéréza *m*; **black c.,** colobe noir.

colocynth ['kɔləsinθ], *s. Bot:* coloquinte *f.*

colog ['koulɔg], *s. Mth: F:* colog *m.*

cologarithm ['kou'lɔgəriθm], *s.* cologarithme *m.*

Cologne [kə'loun], *Pr.n. Geog:* Cologne; *Toil:* **eau de C.,** eau *f* de Cologne; *s.* **cologne,** eau de toilette.

Colombia [kə'lʌmbiə], *Pr.n. Geog:* Colombie *f.*

Colombian [kə'lʌmbiən], *Geog:* (*a*) *a.* colombien; (*b*) *s.* Colombien, -ienne.

colon[1] ['koulən], *s. Anat:* côlon *m*; *Med:* **c. bacillus,** colibacille *m.*

colon[2], *s.* deux-points *m*; *Typ:* comma *m.*

colonel ['kə:n(ə)l], *s. Mil:* colonel *m*; *Mil.Av: U.S:* colonel (de l'Armée de l'air); **c. commandant,** général *m* de brigade; **Queen Elizabeth, c.-in-chief of the London Scottish,** la reine Élisabeth, colonelle d'honneur des *London Scottish.*

colonelcy ['kə:nəlsi], **colonelship** ['kə:nəlʃip], *s.* grade *m* de colonel.

colonial [kə'louniəl], *a. & s.* (*a*) colonial, -aux; *Adm: A:* **the C. Office,** le ministère des Colonies; (*b*) *Arch: etc: U.S:* (style) du dix-huitième siècle.

colonialism [kə'louniəlizm], *s.* **1.** *O:* (la) vie coloniale. **2.** *O:* expression coloniale. **3.** colonialisme *m*; **economic c.,** colonialisme économique.

colonialist [kə'louniəlist], *a. & s.* colonialiste (*mf*).

colonic [kə'lɔnik], *a. Med:* **c. irrigation,** irrigation *f* du côlon.

colonist ['kɔlənist], *s.* colon *m.*

colonization [kɔlənai'zeiʃ(ə)n], *s.* colonisation *f.*

colonizationist [kɔlənai'zeiʃ(ə)nist], *s. Pol: U.S:* coloniste *mf.*

colonize ['kɔlənaiz]. **1.** *v.tr.* coloniser. **2.** *v.i.* former une colonie, des colonies; s'établir (dans un pays nouveau).

colonizer ['kɔlənaizər], *s.* colonisateur *m.*

colonnade [kɔlə'neid], *s.* colonnade *f.*

colonnette [kɔlə'net], *s. Arch:* colonnette *f.*

Colonus [kɔ'lounəs], *Pr.n. A.Geog:* Colone *f.*

colony ['kɔləni], *s.* **1.** colonie *f*; **to live in the colonies,** vivre aux colonies; **the English c. in Paris,** la colonie anglaise à Paris. **2.** (*a*) *Biol:* colonie; (*b*) **c. of crystals,** colonie, amas *m*, de cristaux.

colopexia [kɔlou'peksiə], **colopexy** [kɔlou'peksi], *s. Surg:* colopexie *f.*

colophanite [kɔ'lɔfənait], *s. Miner:* colophanite *f.*

colophene ['kɔloufi:n], *s. Ch:* colophène *m.*

Colophon[1] ['kɔləfən], *Pr. n. A Geog:* Colophon *m*; **the C. oracle,** l'oracle *m* de Claros.

colophon[2], *s. Typ:* **1.** *A:* colophon *m*; **from title page to c.,** de la première page à la dernière; du commencement jusqu'à la fin. **2.** chiffre *m* (de l'éditeur, de l'imprimeur); marque *f* typographique.

colophony [kɔ'lɔfəni], *s.* colophane *f.*

Colorado [kɔlə'rɑ:dou], *Pr.n.* **1.** *Geog:* Colorado *m.* **2.** *Ent:* **C. beetle,** doryphore *m.*

coloration [kʌlə'reiʃ(ə)n], **colorization** [kʌlərai'zeiʃ(ə)n], *s.* coloration *f*; coloris *m*; (*of textiles, etc.*) colorisation *f.*

coloratura [kɔlərə'tjuərə], *s. Mus:* (*a*) chant agrémenté de fioritures; vocalisation *f*, vocalise *f*; (*b*) **c. (soprano),** vocalisatrice *f*, coloratur *f.*

colorcast ['kʌləkɑ:st], *s. U.S: T.V:* émission-couleur *f*, *pl.* émissions-couleur.

colorectitis [kɔlərek'taitis], *s. Med:* colorectite *f.*

colorimeter [kʌlə'rimitər], *s.* colorimètre *m.*

colorimetric(al) [kʌləri'metrik(l)], *a.* colorimétrique.

colorimetrics [kʌləri'metriks], *s.pl.* (*usu. with sg. const.*), **colorimetry** [kʌlə'rimitri], *s.* colorimétrie *f.*

colorrhaphy [kə'lɔrəfi], *s. Surg:* colorraphie *f.*

Colossae [kə'lɔsi:], *Pr.n. A.Geog:* Colosses *f.*

colossal [kə'lɔsl], *a.* (*a*) colossal, -aux; démesuré; (*b*) (*intensive*) **c. success,** succès colossal; **c. liar,** menteur colossal, achevé, démesuré.

colossally [kə'lɔsəli], *adv.* colossalement, démesurément.

Colosseum [kɔlə'siəm], *s. Rom.Ant:* **the C.,** le Colisée.

Colossian [kə'lɔsiən], *A.Geog:* (*a*) *a.* colossien; (*b*) *s.* Colossien, -ienne.

colossus, *pl.* **-i, -uses** [kə'lɔsəs, -ai, -əsiz], *s.* colosse *m*; **the C. of Rhodes,** le Colosse de Rhodes.

colostomy [kə'lɔstəmi], *s. Surg:* colostomie *f*; **transverse c.,** transversostomie *f.*

colostrum [kə'lɔstrəm], *s. Physiol:* colostrum *m.*

colotomy [kə'lɔtəmi], *s. Surg:* côlotomie *f.*

colour[1] ['kʌlər], *s.* **1.** couleur *f*; (*a*) **primary colours,** couleurs primaires, génératrices; *Dy:* couleurs matrices; **secondary colours,** couleurs composites, binaires; **what c. is it?** de quelle couleur est-ce? **the water was the c. of blood,** l'eau était d'une couleur de sang; **to take the c. out of sth.,** décolorer qch.; *B:* **coat of many colours,** robe bigarrée; *Anat: etc:* **c. cell,** chrom(at)ocyte *m*, cellule *f* pigmentaire; **the c. problem,** le problème des races de couleur; **c. bar,** *U.S:* **c. line,** discrimination raciale; ségrégation raciale; **style full of c.,** style coloré; **to paint sth. in bright, dark, colours,** présenter une affaire sous un jour favorable, peu favorable; **local c.,** couleur locale; **to see sth. in its true colours,** voir qch. sous son vrai jour; **to see things in their true colours,** voir les choses comme elles sont; *F:* **I've still to see the c. of his money,** je n'ai pas encore vu la couleur de son argent; **c. photography, television,** photographie *f*, télévision *f*, en couleur(s); **c. print,** reproduction *f* en couleurs; (*b*) *Art: etc:* coloris *m*; **light colours,** coloris clairs; **c. value,** valeur *f* chromatique; **balance of colours,** harmonie *f* des couleurs; **c. scale, range,** échelle *f*, gamme *f*, des colorations; échelle des couleurs; *Com:* **wide range of colours,** grand choix de couleurs. **2.** (*material*) matière colorante; pigment *m*; **oil c.,** couleur à l'huile; **to paint in water c.,** peindre à l'aquarelle; **box of colours,** boîte *f* de couleurs. **3.** teint *m*, couleurs; **to lose c.,** perdre ses couleurs; devenir pâle; **his cheeks have lost their c.,** ses joues *f* ont pâli; **to get back one's c.,** retrouver ses couleurs; **to change c.,** rougir (ou pâlir); changer de visage; **her c. came and went,** elle pâlit et rougit tour à tour; **indignation brought the c. to his cheeks,** l'indignation *f* colorait ses joues; **to have a fresh c.,** avoir le teint frais, de fraîches couleurs; **high c.,** vivacité *f* de teint; **to have a high c.,** avoir de la coloration; *F:* **to be off c.,** être souffrant; ne pas être dans son assiette; *F:* **off-c. joke,** plaisanterie (très) osée. **4.** *usu. pl.* (*a*) couleurs (d'un parti); *Nau:* pavillon *m*, couleurs; **the national colours,** les couleurs nationales; le pavillon, le drapeau, national; **to show, display, one's colours,** montrer son pavillon; montrer les couleurs; *Mil:* **(regimental) colours,** le fanion, le drapeau particulier, du régiment; **c. party,** garde *f* du drapeau; **c. bearer,** porte-drapeau *m inv*; **c. sergeant,** sergent chef (de la garde du drapeau); **to serve with the colours,** servir sous les drapeaux; **to beat, sound, to the c.,** battre, sonner, au drapeau; **hoisting, lowering of, the colours,** lever *m*, salut *m*, du drapeau; *Navy: Mus:* **colours,** au drapeau; **with colours high,** pavillon haut; **with colours flying,** (à) enseignes déployées; **to pass (an examination) with flying colours,** passer haut la main; **to come off with flying colours,** s'en tirer à son honneur; s'acquitter brillamment; **to sail under British colours,** naviguer sous (le) pavillon britannique; **to sail under false colours,** (i) naviguer sous un faux pavillon; (ii) *F:* se faire passer pour quelqu'un d'autre; afficher un faux nom; *Nau:* **to fire a shot under one's true colours,** appuyer son pavillon; **to stick to one's (true) colours,** rester fidèle à ses principes; **to come out in, show oneself in, one's true colours,** se révéler tel qu'on est; se démasquer; jeter le masque; se montrer sous son vrai jour; **to nail one's colours to the mast,** clouer son pavillon; *Fig:* prendre un parti irrévocable; (*b*) *Turf: Sp:* couleurs (d'un jockey, d'une équipe); **to play in a club's colours,** jouer sous les couleurs d'une équipe; (*c*) *Sp: Sch:* (i) **to be awarded one's colours,** recevoir une haute distinction sportive; (ii) **there were two colours in the team,** il y avait deux membres couronnés dans l'équipe. **5.** (*a*) **the political c. of a journal,** la couleur d'un journal; **the Conservative majority gave its c. to the coalition,** le bloc était fortement coloré par la majorité conservatrice; **to take one's c. from one's companions,** prendre le ton ou les opinions de ses camarades; (*b*) **the story has some c. of truth,** l'histoire *f* est vraisemblable; **to give, lend, c. to a story,** rendre une histoire vraisemblable; colorer un récit; **these facts give c. to his statement,** ces faits donnent de la vraisemblance à son affirmation; **his testimony gave c. to the rumour,** son témoignage accrédita le bruit; **to put a false c. on things,** mal voir les choses; *Jur:* **claim under c. of title,** revendication immobilière appuyée sur un droit non vérifié; (*c*) prétexte *m*, couleur, fausse apparence; **under c. of law, of reason,** sous l'apparence de la légalité, du bon sens; **under c. of doing sth.,** sous prétexte, sous couleur, de faire qch.; **the spies worked under c. of an official mission,** les espions *m* agissaient sous le couvert d'une prétendue mission officielle.

colour[2]. **1.** *v.tr.* (*a*) colorer; colorier (une carte, un dessin); enluminer (une gravure); mettre (une surface) en couleur; culotter (une pipe); **to c. sth. blue,** colorer qch. en bleu; (*b*) donner de l'éclat à (une description); imager (son style, un discours); (*c*) présenter (un fait) sous un faux jour; dénaturer (les faits); **to c. a lie,** déguiser un mensonge; **resentment will c. one's opinions,** le ressentiment agit sur, fausse, les opinions. **2.** *v.i.* (*a*) (*of thg.*) se colorer; (*of pipe*) se culotter; (*of fruit, etc.*) tourner; (*b*) (*of pers.*) rougir.

colourable ['kʌlərəbl], *a.* **1.** plausible, vraisemblable; (argument) spécieux. **2.** trompeur; **c. imitation,** imitation à laquelle on pourrait se laisser prendre; *Jur:* imitation (d'un article de commerce, etc.) entachée de dol; contrefaçon *f.*

colourably ['kʌlərəbli], *adv.* **1.** plausiblement, vraisemblablement, spécieusement. **2.** trompeusement.

colouration [kʌlə'reiʃ(ə)n], *s.* = COLORATION.

colourblind ['kʌləblaind], *a.* **1.** (*a*) daltonien, atteint de daltonisme; (*b*) insensible aux couleurs. **2.** *U.S:* qui n'est pas raciste; qui est contre le racisme.

colourblindness ['kʌləblaindnis], *s.* (*a*) daltonisme *m*, achromatopsie *f*; (*b*) insensibilité *f* aux couleurs.

coloured ['kʌləd], *a.* **1.** coloré; (*of drawing*) colorié; **dark-c.,** sombre; **light-c.,** clair; **c. shirt,** chemise *f* de couleur; **c. person,** personne *f* de couleur; métis, -isse; **c. sketch,** croquis *m* en couleurs; **hand-c.,** colorié à la main; **gaily c. butterfly,** papillon *m* multicolore. **2.** **highly c. narrative,** récit coloré; **the evidence was c.,** les témoignages étaient tendancieux. **3.** *s. F:* (*a*) (*clothes*) **coloureds,** couleurs *fpl*; (*b*) **the coloureds,** les gens *m* de couleur.

colourer ['kʌlərər], *s.* coloriste *mf*; coloriste enlumineur (de cartes-postales, etc.); colorieur *m* (de faïence, de cartes).

colourful ['kʌləful], *a.* (ciel, etc.) coloré; **c. style,** style coloré, pittoresque; **c. portrait,** portrait vif, brillant; **c. landscape,** paysage éclatant; **a c. character,** un original.

colouring[1] ['kʌləriŋ], *a.* colorant; **c. matter,** colorant *m.*

colouring[2], *s.* **1.** (*a*) coloration *f*; *Ind:* mettage *m* en couleur; (*b*) **c. of maps, etc.,** coloriage *m* des cartes, etc.; (*c*) **the sudden c. of her face,** la rougeur qui lui monta aux joues. **2.** (*a*) coloris *m* (de la peinture, du style, des fruits); (*b*) teint *m* (d'une personne); **people with high c.,** gens hauts en couleur. **3.** apparence *f*; **to give a false c. to the facts,** dénaturer, travestir, les faits.

colourist ['kʌlərist], *s. Art: Lit:* coloriste *m.*

colourless ['kʌləlis], *a.* **1.** sans couleur; incolore; (*of living things*) dépigmenté; **c. glass,** verre blanc; *Ph:* **c. flame,** flamme *f* achrome; **water is c.,** l'eau *f* est incolore. **2.** (*a*) terne, incolore; (visage) décoloré; (teint) délavé; (lumière) pâle, falote; **c. cheeks,** joues pâles, décolorées; (*b*) **c. style,** style *m* incolore, insipide, fade; **c. voice,** voix *f* veule, terne; **c. individual,** individu *m* sans caractère, sans personnalité; **to lead a c. existence,** mener une existence terne, veule.

colourlessly ['kʌləlisli], *adv.* sans expression; insipidement; veulement.

colourlessness ['kʌləlisnis], *s.* **1.** absence *f* de couleur. **2.** décoloration *f* (du teint); *Lit:* fadeur *f*, insipidité *f* (du style); veulerie *f* (de l'existence).

colourman, *pl.* **-men** ['kʌləmæn, -men], *s.m.* marchand de couleurs; droguiste.

colour-producing ['kʌləprə'dju:siŋ], *a. Biol:* chromogène.

colour-sensitive ['kʌlə'sensitiv], *a. Phot:* orthochromatique, chromosensible.

colourwash[1] ['kʌləwɔʃ], *s.* badigeon *m.*

colourwash[2], *v.tr.* badigeonner (un mur, etc.).

colourwashing ['kʌləwɔʃiŋ], *s.* badigeonnage *m.*

coloury ['kʌləri], *a.* (café, houblon) d'une bonne couleur.

colpo- ['kɔlpou, kɔl'pɔ], *pref.* colpo-.

colpocele ['kɔlpousi:l], *s. Med:* colpocèle *f.*

colpohysterectomy ['kɔlpouhistə'rektəmi], *s. Surg:* colpo-hystérectomie *f.*

colpoperin(a)eoplasty ['kɔlpouperini:ou'plæsti], *s. Surg:* colpopérinéoplastie *f.*

colpoperin(a)eorrhaphy ['kɔlpouperini:'ɔrəfi], *s. Surg:* colpopérinéorraphie *f.*

colpoplasty ['kɔlpou'plæsti], *s. Surg:* colpoplastie *f.*

colporrhaphy [kɔl'pɔrəfi], *s. Surg:* colpor(r)aphie *f.*

colposcope ['kɔlpouskoup], *s. Med:* colposcope *m.*

colposcopy [kɔl'pɔskəpi], *s. Med:* colposcopie *f.*

colpostenosis ['kɔlpoustə'nousis], *s. Med:* colposténose *f.*

colpotomy [kɔl'pɔtəmi], *s. Surg:* colpotomie *f.*

colt[1] [koult], *s.* **1.** poulain *m*, pouliche *f*; (*as opposed to* **filly**) poulain; **baby c.,** poulichon *m.* **2.** personne inexercée; débutant, -ante; novice *mf*; poulain (d'un éditeur, etc.); *Cr:* professionnel *m* à ses débuts; *Box:* poulain; *Rugby: Fb:* poussin *m*; **he is only a c.,** il est encore jeune. **3.** *Nau: A:* corde *f* à nœud, garcette *f* (de châtiment).

Colt[2], *Pr.n. Sm.a:* **C. pistol,** pistolet *m* automatique; **C. automatic machine gun,** mitrailleuse *f* Colt.

colter ['koultər], *s. U.S:* coutre *m* (de charrue).

coltish ['koultiʃ], *a.* **1.** sans expérience; jeunet. **2.** folâtre.

coltsfoot ['koultsfut], *s. Bot:* tussilage *m*; *F:* pas-d'âne *m*; **sweet-scented c.,** pétasite commun.

colt's tail ['koultsteil], *s. Meteor:* cirrus *m*; *F:* queue-de-chat *f.*

Colubridae [kɔ'lju:bridi:], *s.pl. Rept:* colubridés *m.*

colubriform [kɔ'lju:brifɔ:m], *a. Rept:* colubriforme.

colubrine ['kɔljubrain], *a.* **1.** *Rept:* colubrin. **2.** *A:* rusé, fourbe.

Columba[1] [kə'lʌmbə], *Pr.n.m.* Colomba.

Columba[2], *Pr.n.m.* **St. C.,** saint Colomban.

columba[3], *s. Bot:* colombo *m*, columbo *m.*

columbarium [kɔləm'bɛəriəm], *s.* **1.** columbarium *m*, colombaire *m* (de crématorium). **2.** (*a*) colombier *m*, pigeonnier *m*; (*b*) boulin *m* (de pigeonnier).

columbella [kɔləm'belə], *s. Moll:* colombelle *f.*

Columbia [kə'lʌmbiə], *Pr.n. Geog:* **1.** *A: Poet:* l'Amérique *f.* **2.** **British C.,** Colombie britannique, *Fr.C:* canadienne. **3.** **(District of) C.,** (District fédéral de) Columbia.

Columbidae [kə'lʌmbidi:], *s.pl. Orn:* columbidés *m.*

Columbiformes [kəlʌmbi'fɔ:mi:z], *s.pl. Orn:* columbiformes *m.*

columbin [kə'lʌmbin], *s. Pharm:* colombine *f.*

columbine[1] ['kɔləmbain], *a.* colombin; (simplicité *f*, innocence *f*) de colombe.

columbine[2], *s. Bot:* colombine *f*, ancolie *f*; *F:* éperonnière *f*, aquilégie *f*; gant *m* de bergère; gant de Notre-Dame; manteau royal.

Columbine[3], *Pr.n.f. Th:* Colombine.

columbite ['kɔləmbait], *s. Miner:* colombite *f*, columbite *f.*

columbium [kə'lʌmbiəm], *s. Ch:* colombium *m*, niobium *m.*

Columbus [kə'lʌmbəs], *Pr.n.m.* **Christopher C.,** Christophe Colomb.

columella[1] [kɔlju'melə], *s. Nat.Hist:* columelle *f.*

Columella[2], *Pr.n.m. Lt.Lit:* Columelle.

columellar [kɔlju'melər], *a. Nat.Hist:* columellaire.

column ['kɔləm], *s.* **1.** colonne *f*; (*a*) *Arch:* **Doric, Corinthian, Ionic, c.,** colonne dorique, corinthienne, ionique; **fluted c.,** colonne cannelée; **banded c.,** colonne annelée, baguée; **grouped columns,** colonnes accouplées; (*b*) *Anat:* **spinal c.,** colonne vertébrale; (*c*) *Bot:* gynostème *m* (des orchidées); (*d*) **c. of mercury, of smoke,** colonne de mercure, de fumée; (*e*) *Mec.E:* colonne (d'une fraisure); montant *m* (d'une machine); *Aut:* **steering c.,** colonne de direction; *Av:* **control c.,** levier *m* de commande; (*f*) *Min:* **tube c.,** colonne de tubage; *Petr:* **baffle c.,** colonne à chicanes; **flash c.,** colonne de détente; **bulb fractioning c.,** colonne à cloche. **2.** (*a*) *Mil: Nau:* colonne; ligne *f* de file; *Mil:* **c. of files,** colonne par un; **c. of twos, threes, fours,** colonne par deux, par trois, par quatre; **to march in c., in two columns,** marcher en colonne, en deux colonnes; **in extended c.,** en colonne diluée; **c. on the march,** colonne en marche; **leading c., rear c.,** colonne de tête, de queue; **head, rear, of the c.,** tête *f*, queue *f*, de colonne; **to break into column(s),** (se) former en colonne(s); **to open out a c.,** déployer, faire éclater, une colonne; **assaulting, attacking, c.,** colonne d'assaut, d'attaque; **supply c.,** colonne de ravitaillement; convoi administratif; **relief c.,** colonne de secours; **flying c.,** colonne mobile, volante; **mechanized, motorized, c.,** colonne motorisée; *F:* **to dodge the c.,** tirer au flanc; (*b*) *Pol:* **fifth c.,** cinquième colonne. **3.** *Journ: Publ:* **page of two columns,** page de deux colonnes; **sports c.,** rubrique, chronique, sportive; **theatrical c.,** courrier *m*, rubrique, des théâtres; **this kind of article never appears in our columns,** ce genre d'article ne paraît jamais dans nos colonnes, dans notre journal.

columnar [kə'lʌmnər], *a.* colomnaire; en colonnes; en forme de colonne.

columned ['kɔləmd], *a. Arch:* à colonnes.

columniferous [kɔləm'nifərəs], *a. Bot:* colomnifère.

columniform [kə'lʌmnifɔ:m], *a.* en forme de colonnes.

columnism ['kɔləm(n)izm], *s. Pol:* **fifth c.,** action *f* de la cinquième colonne.

columnist ['kɔləm(n)ist], *s.* **1.** *Journ:* rubriqueur *m*, chroniqueur *m*, courriériste *m*; **sports c.,** rubriqueur aux sports. **2.** *Pol:* **fifth c.,** membre *m* de la cinquième colonne.

columnization [kɔləmnai'zeiʃ(ə)n], **columnizing** ['kɔləmnaiziŋ], *s. Med:* columnisation *f.*

colure [kə'ljuər, 'kouljuər], *s. Astr:* colure *f.*

coly ['kouli], *s. Orn:* coliou *m*, *F:* oiseau-souris *m*, *pl.* oiseaux-souris.

Colymbidae [kə'limbidi:], *s.pl. Orn:* colymbidés *m*, gaviidés *m.*

Colymbiformes [kəlimbi'fɔ:mi:z], *s.pl. Orn:* colymbiformes *m.*

colza ['kɔlzə], *s. Bot:* colza *m*; **c. oil,** huile *f* de colza.

coma[1] ['koumə], *s. Med:* coma *m*; **deep c.,** carus *m*; (*of disease*) **c.-inducing,** soporeux, comatogène.

coma[2], *pl.* **-ae** ['koumə, -i:], *s.* **1.** *Bot:* coma *m*, barbe *f*, chevelure *f* (d'une graine, d'un ananas). **2.** *Astr:* (*a*) chevelure (d'une comète); (*b*) **c. Berenices,** [berə'naisi:z], la Chevelure de Bérénice. **3.** *Opt:* aigrette *f*, coma *f.*

Comagenian [koumə'dʒi:niən], *A.Geog:* (*a*) *a.* comagénien; (*b*) *s.* Comagénien, -ienne.

comagmatic [koumæg'mætik], *a. Geol:* comagmatique.

Comanches [kə'mæntʃiz], *Pr.n. pl. Ethn:* (Indiens) comanches *m.*

comanic [kou'mænik], *a. Ch:* (acide) comanique.

comate ['koumeit], *a. Bot:* (*of seed*) chevelu.

comatic [kou'mætik], *a. Opt:* comatique.

comatose ['koumətous], *a. Med:* **1.** (état) comateux, carotique; (sommeil) soporeux. **2.** (*pers.*) dans le coma.

comatulid [kə'mætjulid], *s. Echin:* comatule *f.*

Comatulidae [kɔmæ'tju:lidi:], *s.pl. Echin:* comatulidés *m.*

comb[1] [koum], *s.* **1.** *Toil:* peigne *m*; **hair c.,** peigne de coiffure; **dressing c., rake c.,** démêloir *m*; peigne râteau; **to run a c. through one's hair,** se donner un coup de peigne; **c. maker, manufacturer,** peignier, -ière. **2.** (*a*) *Tex:* peigne, carde *f*; (*b*) *Paint: Tchn:* peigne (à décor, à fileter); (*c*) *El:* collecteur *m* (d'électricité statique); (*d*) peigne (de palier d'arrivée d'un escalier roulant); **c. escalator,** escalier roulant à tasseaux. **3.** (*a*) crête *f* (de coq); (*b*) *Lit:* crête (de colline, de vague). **4.** busc *m* (d'une crosse de fusil). **5.** *Ap:* rayon *m*; **c. foundation,** gaufre *f*, gâteau *m*, de cire; **honey in the c.,** miel *m* en rayon. **6.** (*a*) *Moll:* **c. (shell),** coquille *f* (Saint-Jacques); pèlerine *f*; (*b*) *Coel:* **c. jelly,** cténophore *m.*

comb[2], *s.* **to give one's hair a c.,** donner un coup de peigne à ses cheveux.

comb[3], *v.*

I. *v.tr. & i.* **1.** *v.tr.* (*a*) peigner (les cheveux de qn); **to c. one's hair,** se peigner; **to c. a child's hair,** peigner un enfant; *P: O:* **I'll c. his hair for him,** je vais lui laver la tête; **to c. down a horse,** étriller un cheval; (*b*) *Tex: etc:* peigner, carder, houpper (la laine, etc.); (*c*) (*of police, etc.*) ratisser, fouiller; passer au peigne fin. **2.** *v.i.* (*of wave*) (i) se briser en écumant; déferler; (ii) s'ourler; **the waves combed over the vessel,** les vagues *f* déferlaient sur le navire.

II. (*compound verb*) **comb out,** *v.tr.* **1.** (*a*) démêler (les cheveux); (*b*) carder (un matelas, etc.). **2.** *F:* (*a*) (*of police*) **to c. out a district, criminal haunts,** faire une rafle (de suspects); (*b*) **to c. out a department, a works,** éliminer les incapables, les non-valeurs, d'un service, d'une usine; (*c*) *Mil:* **to c. out a (captured) position,** nettoyer les tranchées *f* d'une position.

combassou [kɔm'bæsu:], *s. Orn:* combassou *m.*

combat[1] ['kɔmbæt], *s.* combat *m*; (*a*) **single c.,** combat singulier; **unequal c.,** combat inégal; *Hist:* **trial by c.,** combat judiciaire; **c. of wits,** joute *f*, assaut *m*, d'esprit; (*b*) *Mil: etc:* **close c.,** combat rapproché; **mock c.,** combat simulé; **air, aerial, c.,** combat aérien; **c. mission,** mission *f* tactique, de combat; **c. reconnaissance,** reconnaissance *f* tactique; **c. firing,** *U.S:* **c. practice,** (exercice de) tir(s) réel(s), tir(s) de combat; **c. zone,** zone *f* de combat; **c. dispositions,** dispositif *m* de combat; **c. effectiveness,** valeur combative; **c. ready,** (i) apte au combat; (tactiquement) instruit, entraîné; (ii) en état d'alerte; *U.S:* **c. fatigue,** psychose *f* traumatique; syndrome commotionnel; (*c*) *Mil: etc:* *U.S:* **c. command,** groupement blindé; **regimental c. team,** groupement tactique; **battalion c. team,** sous-groupement *m* (tactique); **(air) c. group,** escadre *f* (d'aviation); (*d*) **camouflaged c. clothing,** tenue *f* léopard.

combat[2], *v.* **(combated) 1.** *v.i.* combattre (**with, against,** contre). **2.** *v.tr.* lutter contre, combattre (une maladie, un préjugé).

combatable ['kɔmbətəbl], *a.* combattable.

combatant ['kɔmbətənt], *a. & s.* combattant (*m*); *Her:* **lions combat(t)ant,** lions affrontés.

combative ['kɔmbətiv], *a.* combatif; batailleur; agressif.

combatively ['kɔmbətivli], *adv.* d'un air, d'un ton, batailleur; agressivement.

combativeness ['kɔmbətivnis], **combativity** [kɔmbə'tiviti], *s.* combativité *f*; humeur guerroyante; caractère batailleur; agressivité *f.*

combe [ku:m], *s.* combe *f*, vallon *m.*

comber ['koumər], *s.* **1.** *Tex:* (*a*) (*pers.*) peigneur, -euse; cardeur, -euse (de laine); (*b*) (*machine*) peigneuse *f.* **2.** *Lit:* longue vague déferlante. **3.** *Ich:* serran *m.*

combinable [kəm'bainəbl], *a.* combinable.

combination [ˌkɔmbi'neiʃ(ə)n], *s.* **1.** combinaison *f*; (*a*) **the c. of two elements with one another,** la combinaison, l'alliage *m*, de deux corps simples; **c. of sounds, of atoms, of circumstances,** concours *m* de sons, d'atomes, de circonstances; **to enter into c. with . . .,** se combiner avec . . .; **nitrogen in c. with oxygen,** l'azote combiné avec l'oxygène; *Mth:* **combinations of *n* things taken *r* at a time (nCr),** combinaisons de *n* objets *r* à *r*; (*b*) *Ch:* combiné *m*, mélange *m*; (*c*) *Phot:* **c. print,** épreuve *f* avec fond rapporté; (*d*) **smokers' c.,** nettoie-pipes *m inv* (en métal). **2.** association *f* (de personnes, d'ouvriers, etc.); **to enter into a c. with . . .,** s'associer, se combiner, avec . . .; **right of c.,** droit *m* d'association; droit de se syndiquer; *Sch:* (*at Cambridge*) **c. room** = salle *f* des professeurs. **3.** *pl. Cost: O:* **(pair of) combinations,** combinaison-culotte *f*, *pl.* combinaisons-culottes. **4. c. lock,** serrure *f* à combinaisons; serrure secrète; **safe with c. lock,** coffre *m* à combinaisons. **5.** *Aut:* motocyclette *f* avec sidecar.

combinative ['kɔmbinətiv], **combinatory** [kɔmbi'neitəri], *a.* combinateur, -trice; cumulatif; combinatoire.

combinatorial [kɔmbinə'tɔ:riəl], *a.* combinatoire.

combine[1] ['kɔmbain], *s.* **1.** *Com: Fin:* combinaison financière; entente industrielle; cartel *m*; trust *m*; **horizontal c.,** cartel horizontal; consortium *m* **2.** *Agr:* **c. (harvester),** moissonneuse-batteuse *f*, *pl.* moissonneuses-batteuses.

combine[2] [kəm'bain]. **1.** *v.tr.* combiner; allier (des qualités, des mots, etc.) **(with,** à); (*of pers.*) (ré)unir, allier; **to c. forces, one's efforts,** joindre ses forces, ses efforts; **to c. strength of body with strength of mind,** allier la force du corps à celle de l'âme; **he combined the jobs of butcher and cook,** il cumulait les métiers de boucher et de cuisinier; **to c. business with pleasure,** joindre l'utile à l'agréable; unir les plaisirs aux affaires; **to c. two electoral lists,** fusionner deux listes électorales; *Artil:* **to c. sights,** conjuguer les hausses. **2.** *v.i.* (*a*) (*of pers.*) s'unir, se réunir, s'associer, s'allier; se liguer **(against,** contre); (*of workers*) se syndiquer; (*b*) *Pol:* (*of parties*) fusionner; (*of party*) **to c. with a majority,** s'intégrer dans une majorité; (*c*) **everything combined to give me this impression,** tout concourait à me donner cette impression; **everything is combining against me,** tout se ligue contre moi; **lighting effects that c. well,** effets *m* de lumière qui s'agencent bien; (*d*) *Ch:* (*of elements*) se combiner.

combined [kəm'baind], *a.* **c. fleets,** flottes combinées; **c. efforts,** efforts réunis, conjugués; **c. work,** travail fait en collaboration; **c. movement,** mouvement *m* d'ensemble; *Mec.E:* **c. strength,** résistance composée; *Artil:* **c. sights,** hausses combinées, conjuguées; *Rail:* **c. rail and road ticket,** billet *m* mixte; *Mch.Tls:* **c. machine,** machine *f* multiple; *El:* **c. coupling,** couplage *m* mixte; *Cmptr:* **c. head,** tête *f* simple de lecture-écriture; **c. read-write head,** tête double de lecture-écriture; *Mil: etc:* **c. staff operation,** opération *f* interarmes; **c. operation,** opération combinée, amphibie; opération interarmées; **c. force,** force *f* mixte.

combiner [kəm'bainər], *s.* combinateur, -trice.

combing[1] ['koumiŋ], *a.* **c. wave,** (i) vague déferlante; (ii) vague ourlée.

combing[2], *s.* **1.** (*a*) coup *m* de peigne; (*b*) *Tex:* peignage *m*, cardage *m*, **c. machine,** peigneuse *f*; **c. machine tenter,** peigneur, -euse; (*c*) ratissage *m* (par la police). **2.** *pl.* **combings,** (*a*) peignures *f*, démêlures *f*; (*b*) *Tex:* blousse *f.*

combing out ['koumiŋ'aut], *s.* **1.** démêlage *m* (des cheveux). **2.** *F:* (*a*) épluchage *m* (de services administratifs, etc.); (*b*) rafle *f*, ratissage *m* (par la police); (*c*) *Mil:* nettoyage *m* (des tranchées).

combining [kəm'bainiŋ], *s.* combinaison *f*; *Ling:* **c. form** (*of a word*), forme *f* en combinaison (*p. ex.* anglo-, franco-).

combo ['kɔmbou], *s. F:* combinaison *f.*

comb-out ['koumaut], *s.* (*a*) *Hairdr:* coup *m* de peigne; (*b*) *F:* rafle *f*, ratissage *m* (par la police, etc.).

Combretaceae [kɔmbri'teisii:], *s.pl. Bot:* combrétacées *f.*

combretum [kɔm'bri:təm], *s. Bot:* combretum *m.*

combs[1] [koumz], *s.pl. Brew:* **malt c.,** touraillon *m.*

combs[2] [kɔmz], *s.pl.* (*usu. with sg. const.*) *Cost: F: O:* combinaison-culotte *f.*

comb-shaped ['koumʃeipt], *a. Nat.Hist:* pectiné.

combust [kəm'bʌst], *v.i. Tchn:* entrer en combustion; brûler.

combustibility [kəmbʌsti'biliti], *s.* combustibilité *f.*

combustible [kəm'bʌstibl]. **1.** *a.* (*a*) combustible; (*b*) (*of a crowd, etc.*) inflammable; prompt à se soulever. **2.** *s.* (*a*) matière *f* inflammable; (*b*) (*fuel*) combustible *m.*

combustion [kəm'bʌstʃ(ə)n], *s.* combustion *f*; **detonating c.,** combustion détonante; **spontaneous c.,** inflammation spontanée; auto-allumage *m*; **internal c. engine,** moteur *m* à explosion, à combustion interne, à carburation; *I.C.E:* **c. chamber,** chambre *f* de combustion, d'explosion; espace mort; *Ch:* **c. furnace,** grille *f* à analyse; **slow-c. stove,** poêle *m* à combustion continue, à feu continu.

combustive [kəm'bʌstiv], *a. Ch: etc:* comburant.

come [kʌm], *v.* **(came** [keim]; **come).**

I. *v.i.* **1.** venir, arriver; (*a*) **to c. to a place,** venir, arriver, à un endroit; **he has just c. from Paris,** il arrive de Paris; **in the year after he came to Paris,** l'année qui suivit son arrivée à Paris; **he came up to me,** il est venu à moi, vers moi; il est venu me parler; **there came a soldier who . . .,** il arriva un soldat qui . . .; **I can see the children coming, here c. the children,** voici les enfants qui arrivent, qui viennent; *F:* **let 'em all c.!** (i) qu'ils viennent tous! ils seront tous les bienvenus; (ii) à tout venant beau jeu! **I'm coming with you,** je viens avec vous; je vous accompagne; **he came to the station with me,** il m'a accompagné jusqu'à la gare; **he comes this way every week,** il passe par ici tous les huit jours; **here he comes!** le voilà qui arrive! le voilà qui vient! **c. here!** venez ici! *F:* viens là! amène-toi! (*to dog*) (viens) ici! **coming!** voilà! on y va! j'y vais! je viens! **you go on, I'm just coming,** partez, je vous suis; **to c. to see s.o.,** venir trouver qn; **c. and see me tomorrow,** venez me voir, me trouver, demain; **I have c. to see you,** je viens vous voir; **to c. for s.o., for sth.,** venir chercher qn, qch.; *F:* **the dog came for, at, me,** le chien m'a attaqué; **to c. to s.o.,** venir à qn; venir trouver qn; **to c. to s.o. for advice, for an explanation,** venir demander conseil, une explication, à qn; **you have c. to the wrong person,** vous vous adressez mal; vous tombez mal; vous vous trompez d'adresse; **to c. to the throne,** monter sur le trône; **to c. to years of discretion,** arriver à l'âge de discrétion, de raison; **we c. now to the verb,** nous en venons maintenant au verbe; **a crisis is coming,** une crise se prépare; **what are things coming to?** où allons-nous? **dinner came at last,** enfin on a servi le dîner; **he came riding, running (up),** il est arrivé à cheval, en courant; **the mast came crashing down,** le mât s'abattit; **letters came pouring in,** ce fut une avalanche de lettres; **he has c. a long way,** (i) il arrive de loin; (ii) *Fig:* il a fait son chemin; **to c. and go,** aller et venir; **people were constantly coming and going,** c'étaient des allées et venues continuelles, un va-et-vient continuel; **I don't know whether I'm coming or going,** j'ai la tête à l'envers; **after many years had c. and gone,** quand bien des années se furent écoulées; **the idea came to me, came into my mind, that . . .,** il m'est venu à l'esprit que . . .; **suddenly it came to me,** tout d'un coup je m'en suis souvenu; **to c. to the surface again,** remonter sur l'eau; **a smile came to his lips,** un sourire parut sur ses lèvres; **his colour came and went,** il pâlit et rougit tour à tour; *int.* **c. now! c., c.!** allons! voyons! **c. on, cheer up!** allons, prenez courage! *Prov:* **easy c. easy go; light c. light go,** ce qui vient par la flûte s'en va par le tambour; l'argent ne lui coûte guère; (*b*) **to c. to oneself,** (i) reprendre connaissance; (ii) recouvrer sa raison; (iii) revenir de ses erreurs; se ressaisir; (*c*) *F:* **c. summer (and) we shall meet again,** vienne l'été, on se retrouvera tous; **I saw him a week c. Tuesday,** je l'ai vu il y aura mardi huit jours; **he will be ten c. January,** il aura dix ans en janvier, au mois de janvier; **it'll be a year c. Monday since he left,** il y aura lundi prochain un an qu'il est parti. **2.** (*occur, happen*) (*a*) **that comes on the next page,** cela se trouve, se rencontre, à la page suivante; **we must take things as they c.,** il faut prendre les choses comme elles viennent; **I've got £500 coming to me,** je vais (bientôt) toucher £500; *F:* **you've got it coming to you,** (i) ça vous pend au nez; (ii) vous ne perdez rien pour attendre; **c. what may,** advienne que pourra; quoi qu'il arrive; quoi qu'il advienne; vaille que vaille; **when his turn came, when it came to his turn,** quand ce fut son tour, quand ce fut à lui; (*b*) **how does the door c. to be open?** d'où vient que la porte est ouverte? *Lit:* **how comes it that . . .?** comment se fait-il que +*sub.*; **how do you c. to know that?** comment avez-vous pu savoir cela? *F:* **how c.?** pourquoi? **now that I c. to think of it,** maintenant que j'y songe; **this theory has c. to be accepted,** on en est venu à accepter cette théorie; **I have c. to believe that . . .,** j'en suis venu, j'en suis arrivé, à croire que . . .; **the church has c. to be used as a concert hall,** cette église en est venue à servir de salle de concert; **this plan came to be realized,** ce projet finit par se réaliser; **the (motor) car is coming to be realized as a menace,** on est en voie de se rendre compte que l'automobile est un fléau; **I came to like him,** il m'est devenu sympathique; **when I came to know her better,** lorsque j'ai appris à la mieux connaître. **3.** (*result, spring from*) (*a*) **what will c. of it?** qu'en adviendra-t-il? qu'en résultera-t-il? **what came of it?** que s'en est-il suivi? **what do you think will c. of it?** qu'en augurez-vous? **no good will c. of it,** cela tournera mal; **that's what comes of doing . . .,** voilà ce qu'il en est de faire . . .; **it comes from,** *F:* **of, his being so shy,** cela tient à ce qu'il est si timide; cela tient à sa timidité; (*b*) **word that comes from Latin,** mot *m* qui (pro)vient du latin; **I tried to explain but the words wouldn't c.,** j'ai essayé de l'expliquer mais les mots me manquaient; **to c. of a good family,** être, sortir, d'une bonne famille; **he comes of peasant stock,** il descend d'une famille de paysans; **horse that comes from a good stud,** cheval *m* qui sort d'un bon haras; **he comes from Paris,** il vient de Paris; **this is astounding coming from him,** cela étonne de sa part. **4.** (*a*) (*amount*) **the total comes to fifty francs,** la somme monte, s'élève, à cinquante francs; **how much does it c. to?** combien cela fait-il? **it comes to this, that . . .,** cela revient à ceci, que . . .; **this is what his argument comes to,** voici à quoi se ramène, se borne, se réduit, son raisonnement; **what he knows doesn't c. to much,** ce qu'il sait ce n'est pas grand-chose; *F:* il n'en sait pas lourd; *F:* **it won't c. to much,** ça ne va pas chercher loin; (*b*) **if it comes to that . . .,** à ce compte là . . .; **if it comes to that I would just as soon . . .,** pour tant faire, tant qu'à faire, j'aimerais autant . . .; **it must c. to that,** il faudra bien en arriver là, en venir là; **I hope it won't c. to that,** ce serait un pis-aller; **you haven't c. to that yet!** vous n'en êtes pas (encore) là! **how did you c. to this?** comment en êtes-vous (arrivé) là?; **c. to that, what are you doing here?** pendant que j'y suis, qu'est-ce que vous faites ici? **if it comes to buying a house, I may as well buy a nice one,** pour tant faire qu'acheter une maison, pour tant faire que d'acheter une maison, autant en acheter une belle; **he will never c. to much,** il ne sera, ne fera, jamais grand-chose; (*c*) **that doesn't c. within my duties,** cela ne rentre pas dans mes fonctions; **it doesn't c. into the same category,** cela ne rentre pas dans la même catégorie. **5.** (*a*) **that comes easy, natural, to him,** cela lui est facile, naturel; **to c. expensive, cheap,** coûter cher, revenir cher; coûter peu; (*b*) (*become*) **to c. apart,** se séparer; se décoller; (*of seam, etc.*) **to c. apart, unstitched, unsewn,** se découdre; (*of tie, knot, bootlaces, etc.*) **to c. undone, untied, loose, etc.,** se dénouer, se délacer, se défaire, se détacher, se desserrer; (*of beads, etc.*) se défiler; *F:* **she's coming fifteen,** elle va sur ses quinze ans; (*c*) **you c. first,** vous venez en premier; c'est vous le premier; **you c. third,** vous êtes le troisième. **6. in the days to c.,** dans les temps à venir; à l'avenir; **the life to c.,** la vie future; **orders to c.,** ordres ultérieurs; **for three months to c.,** pendant trois mois encore; **that will not be for several years to c., for some time to c.,** cela n'arrivera pas d'ici plusieurs années, avant de nombreuses années, d'ici à quelque temps. **7.** (*of butter*) prendre forme; (*of fruit, etc.*) venir; **when the teeth begin to c.,** lorsque les dents commencent à sortir. **8.** *F:* **to c. it strong,** exagérer; crâner; charrier; faire de l'épate; **that's coming it a bit strong,** ça, c'est un peu fort; **he tried to c. it over me,** il a essayé de m'en mettre plein les yeux; *P:* **don't you c. it with me!** charrie pas avec moi! **to c. the heavy husband,** prendre un ton de mari autoritaire. **9.** *P:* (*reach orgasm*) jouir.

II. (*compound verbs*) **1. come about,** *v.i.* (*a*) (*of event, occurrence, etc.*) arriver, se passer, se produire, avoir lieu; **it came about that,** il arriva, il advint, que . . .; **how does it c. about that . . .?** comment se fait-il que . . .? **how could such a misunderstanding c. about?** comment un pareil malentendu a-t-il pu se produire? (*b*) (i) *Nau:* virer de bord; (ii) (*of the wind*) tourner.

2. come across, *v.i.* (*a*) trouver, rencontrer, (qn, qch.) par hasard, sur son chemin; tomber sur (qn); **everything they c. across,** tout ce qui leur tombe sous la main; **it is a curio that I came across,** c'est un bibelot de

rencontre; (*b*) (*adverbial use*) *F:* (i) payer ce que l'on doit; (ii) = COME OVER (*b*); (iii) se décider à dire la vérité; *P:* accoucher.
3. come along, *v.i.* (*a*) arriver, venir; **c. along!** (i) amène-toi! arrive! (ii) allons-y! allons-nous-en! **do c. along!** mais venez donc! (*b*) arriver; se passer; **these things c. along when you least expect them,** ces choses-là arrivent quand on s'y attend le moins.
4. come around, *v.i.* = COME ROUND.
5. come at, *v.i.* (*a*) *O:* **to c. at the truth,** parvenir à la vérité; découvrir la vérité; (*b*) **it isn't easy to c. at,** il me serait difficile de mettre la main dessus; (*c*) *O:* arriver à voir (qn); (*d*) *Austr: N.Z: P:* **I won't c. at that again,** c'est la dernière fois que j'essaie ce coup-là.
6. come away, *v.i.* (*a*) (i) **to c. away (from a place),** partir, s'en aller (d'un lieu); quitter (un lieu); **c. away!** allons, partons! (ii) **c. away with it!** allons, racontez-nous la chose! (*b*) se détacher; se décoller; **the handle came away (in his hand),** l'anse s'est détachée, lui est restée dans la main.
7. come back, *v.i.* revenir; **to c. back (home),** rentrer; *F:* **c. back all I said,** mettons que je n'ai rien dit; (*a*) **he came back with me a little way,** il m'a fait un bout de reconduite; **we are coming back to rail travel,** on revient au chemin de fer; **the names are coming back to me,** les noms me reviennent à l'esprit; **it's all coming back to me,** cela me revient à la mémoire; **to c. back to what I was saying. . .,** pour en revenir à ce que je disais . . .; *Nau:* **to c. back on board,** rentrer à bord; (*b*) revenir à soi; reprendre connaissance; (*c*) (*of fashion, etc.*) revenir en vogue; (*d*) *U.S: F:* répliquer; riposter.
8. come by, *v.i.* (*a*) (i) **to c. by the house,** passer par la maison; (ii) **to c. by money,** obtenir de l'argent; **how did you c. by that money?** comment êtes-vous devenu possesseur de cet argent? *A:* **to c. by one's death,** trouver la mort; **(money) hard to c. by,** (argent) dur à gagner, à obtenir; **honestly c. by,** honnêtement acquis; (*b*) (i) **I heard him c. by,** je l'ai entendu passer; **to c. by again,** repasser; **we shoot them as they c. by,** nous les tirons à leur passage; (ii) *esp. U.S:* entrer en passant.
9. come down, *v.i.* (*a*) descendre (l'échelle, l'escalier); faire la descente de (la montagne, etc.); (*b*) (i) **to c. down to breakfast, to dinner,** descendre déjeuner, dîner; **to c. down from a tree,** descendre d'un arbre; **as he came down from the pulpit,** à sa descente de chaire; **to c. down (in the world),** déchoir; **to c. down to earth,** descendre des nues; **he had c. down to begging,** il en était venu à mendier; **prices are coming down,** les prix *m* baissent, sont en baisse; (ii) *F:* **to c. down on s.o.,** tomber sur le dos à qn; **to c. down on s.o. for ten pounds,** faire casquer qn de dix livres; (iii) *F:* **I had to c. down with a five-pound note,** il a fallu me fendre de cinq livres; (iv) (*of rain, etc.*) tomber; **her hair was coming down,** ses cheveux se dénouaient, se déroulaient; (v) (*reach*) **her hair came down to her waist,** ses cheveux lui descendaient jusqu'à la taille; **the snow comes down to the 1500 m level,** la neige descend jusqu'à la cote de 1500 m; (vi) (*of tale, tradition*) venir (de nos aïeux); **the tales that have c. down to us,** les contes qui nous sont parvenus; (vii) (*of pers., horse*) s'abattre; (*of structure*) s'écrouler; **these houses are coming down soon,** on démolira, abattra, bientôt ces maisons; (viii) (*amount to*) (*of problem, etc.*) se résumer, se ramener, revenir, se borner **(to,** à); **this is what his argument comes down to,** voici à quoi se ramène, se borne, se réduit, son raisonnement; **the whole difficulty comes down to the question whether . . .,** toute la difficulté se réduit à savoir si . . ..
10. come forward, *v.i.* se proposer (pour faire qch.); *Iron:* **he's not backward in coming forward,** il ne se gêne pas; **to c. forward as a candidate,** se présenter comme candidat, se porter candidat, poser sa candidature **(for,** à); se mettre sur les rangs **(for,** pour).
11. come in, *v.i.* (*a*) entrer; **to c. in again,** rentrer; **after my walk I came in,** après ma promenade je suis rentré; **at eight o'clock His Excellency came in,** à huit heures Son Excellence a fait son entrée; **c. in!** entrez! *F:* **Mrs B. comes in twice a week,** Madame B. vient faire le ménage deux fois par semaine; **the business was my father's; I came in when I was twenty-one,** la maison appartenait à mon père; j'y suis entré (comme associé) à vingt et un ans; **the water was coming in on all sides,** l'eau faisait irruption de toutes parts; *F:* **that's where I c. in,** voilà où je peux vous aider; ça c'est mon rayon; **this is where I came in,** j'ai déjà entendu, vu, tout ça; (*b*) (*of tide*) monter; (*of ship*) arriver; (*of year*) commencer; (*of custom, etc.*) s'introduire, devenir la mode; **this fashion is coming in again,** cette mode reprend; **this fashion came in last year,** cette mode est entrée en vogue l'année dernière; **as soon as oysters c. in,** dès que commence la saison des huîtres; dès que les huîtres sont de saison; **this produce is sold the day it comes in,** ces denrées sont vendues le jour même de leur arrivée; (*of funds*) rentrer; **money is coming in well,** la recette est bonne; (*c*) (i) *Pol:* (*of party*) arriver, parvenir, au pouvoir; (ii) *Cr:* (*of batsman*) venir prendre son tour au guichet; (*d*) *Pred:* (i) **to c. in useful to s.o., for sth., for doing sth.,** servir à qn, à qch., à, pour, faire qch.; (ii) *Sp:* **to c. in first, second,** arriver premier, second; (*e*) (i) **to c. in for a share of sth.,** avoir part à qch.; **to c. in for a fortune,** succéder à une fortune; *F:* **and where do I c. in?** et moi, qu'est-ce que j'y gagne? (ii) **to c. in for a scolding, for praise,** recevoir, s'attirer, une semonce, des éloges; (*f*) (i) être admis dans une affaire; **we don't want Thomas to c. in,** nous ne voulons pas que Thomas en soit; (ii) intervenir **(between,** entre).
12. come into, *v.i.* (*prepositional use*) (*a*) (i) entrer dans (une chambre); **to c. into the world,** venir au monde; **to c. into power,** arriver, parvenir, au pouvoir; (*of idea*) **to c. into s.o.'s mind,** se présenter à l'esprit de qn; **a look of perplexity came into his face,** son visage prit un air perplexe; **I came into the business when I was twenty-one,** je suis entré dans la maison (comme associé) à l'âge de vingt et un ans; (ii) **Cullen comes into Scottish history,** Cullen figure dans l'histoire d'Écosse; (*b*) **to c. into a property,** entrer en possession d'un domaine; hériter d'une terre; **to c. into an inheritance, an estate,** recueillir une succession; **the property he came into from his father,** la propriété qu'il a eue de son père.
13. come off, *v.i.* (*a*) (i) descendre de (la table, etc.); sortir de (la chaîne de fabrication); **to c. off a ship,** débarquer (d'un navire); **c. off it!** en voilà assez! la barbe! (ii) **to c. off one's horse,** tomber de (son) cheval; (iii) **to c. off the gold standard,** abandonner l'étalon or; (*b*) (i) (*of button, etc.*) se détacher, sauter; (*of smell, etc.*) se dégager; (*of paint, stain, etc.*) s'enlever, s'en aller, partir; (*of fabric, etc.*) se décoller; **the colour came off on my dress,** la couleur a déteint sur ma robe; **hydrogen comes off at the cathode,** l'hydrogène est mis en liberté, se dégage, à la cathode; (ii) (*of ship aground*) se déséchouer; partir; (iii) (*of event*) avoir lieu; (*of plan, attempt, etc.*) réussir, aboutir; **did it c. off all right?** ça s'est bien passé? **not to c. off,** ne pas avoir lieu; n'aboutir à rien; **my little trip abroad didn't c. off,** mon petit voyage à l'étranger ne s'est pas réalisé, *F:* est tombé à l'eau; **I don't know whether the marriage will c. off,** je ne sais pas si le mariage se fera; **the marriage didn't c. off,** le mariage ne s'est pas fait; **the trick, the experiment, came off,** le tour, l'expérience, a réussi; **sneezes that don't c. off,** éternûments qui ne viennent pas, qui n'aboutissent pas; (iv) (*of pers.*) **to c. off badly, with flying colours,** s'en mal tirer; s'acquitter brillamment; **he came off victorious,** il en sortit vainqueur; **to c. off with a few scratches,** s'en tirer avec quelques égratignures; en être quitte pour quelques égratignures; (v) *P:* (=*to have an orgasm*) jouir.
14. come on, *v.i.* (*a*) s'avancer; aller de l'avant; **you go first; I'll c. on,** partez en avant; je vous suis; **c. on, let's have a game!** allons! faisons une partie! **c. on!** (i) en avant! (ii) arrivez! (iii) *F:* (*as a challenge*) viens-y donc! (iv) *F:* (*incredulity*) allons donc! qu'est-ce que vous chantez là? (*b*) (*of plants, children, etc.*) (bien) venir; se développer; faire des progrès; **your picture is coming on,** votre tableau avance, vient bien; **the team is coming on,** l'équipe vient en forme; **the harvest is coming on,** la récolte s'annonce bien; **he has c. on surprisingly (well),** il a fait des progrès étonnants; (*c*) (*of rain, illness, etc.*) survenir; (*of winter, etc.*) venir, arriver; (*of night*) tomber; **I feel a cold coming on,** je m'enrhume; **autumn is coming on, the leaves are falling,** voici l'automne, les feuilles tombent; **when it comes on to blow,** quand le vent se met à souffler; **it came on to rain,** il a commencé à pleuvoir; **the rain came on worse than ever,** la pluie a repris de plus belle; (*d*) (*of question*) **to c. on (for discussion),** venir en discussion; venir sur le tapis; (*of lawsuit*) **to c. on for trial,** venir devant la cour; **the case comes on tomorrow,** la cause sera entendue demain, se plaidera demain; l'affaire passe demain; (*e*) *Th:* (*of actor*) entrer en scène; (*f*) **the play, the film, is coming on next week,** on va donner la pièce, le film va passer, la semaine prochaine; **I see** *Hamlet* **is coming on again,** je vois qu'on redonne *Hamlet*.
15. come out, *v.i.* (*a*) **to c. out of a place,** sortir d'un lieu; **on coming out of . . ., as I came out of . . .,** au sortir de . . .; (*b*) (i) sortir; **it's too cold for you to c. out,** il fait trop froid pour que vous sortiez; **my tooth is aching, the stopping has come out,** ma dent me fait mal, le plombage est parti; *Ind:* **to c. out (on strike),** se mettre en grève; (ii) **do c. out to India,** venez donc nous retrouver aux Indes! (iii) **to c. badly out of an affair,** se tirer mal d'une affaire; **to c. well out of an affair,** se bien tirer d'affaire; **he came safely out of it,** il s'en est tiré sain et sauf; *Sch:* **to c. out first, second,** sortir premier, second; être reçu premier, second; (iv) (*of sun, stars*) paraître; (*of buds*) éclore; *Phot:* (*of image*) se développer, venir, se révéler; (*of rash, pimples*) sortir, se montrer; (*of the truth*) se découvrir; **the trees are coming out again,** les arbres *m* bourgeonnent de nouveau; (*of pers.*) **to c. out in a rash,** avoir une éruption (de boutons, etc.); avoir une poussée d'urticaire; **everything comes out in time,** tout se sait avec le temps; **as soon as the news came out . . .,** dès qu'on sut la nouvelle. . .; **how did the news c. out?** comment cela s'est-il su? **at last the truth is coming out,** enfin la vérité se dégage, se fait jour; **it came out that . . .,** il ressortit, apparut, que . . .; le fait se révéla que . . .; (v) (α) *Art: etc:* (*of details*) ressortir; se détacher **(against the background,** sur le fond); (β) *Phot:* (*of detail in negative*) apparaître; venir; (γ) *Phot:* **you have come out well (in the group),** vous êtes très réussi; c'est bien vous; **he always comes out well,** il est photogénique; (vi) (*of stains*) s'enlever, s'effacer; **the colour soon comes out of this material,** c'est une étoffe qui se déteint vite; (vii) (*of book, journal*) paraître, sortir; (viii) (*of problem*) se résoudre; **her sums would never c. out right,** elle n'arrivait jamais à la solution juste; (*of average, total, etc.*) **to c. out at . . .,** être de . . ., se monter à . . .; *Com:* **this article comes out at 95p.,** cet article vous reviendra à 95p.; (ix) (*of pers.*) débuter (au théâtre); débuter, faire son entrée dans le monde; **my daughter comes out next spring,** ma fille débutera au printemps; (x) *F:* **to c. out with a remark,** lâcher, laisser échapper, une observation; **to c. out strongly,** se prononcer avec vigueur **(for,** pour; **against,** contre); **to c. out with a long story,** sortir une longue histoire.
16. come over, *v.i.* (*a*) (i) traverser (la mer, les champs); (ii) envahir, gagner, saisir (qn); **a change has come over him,** un changement s'est produit, s'est opéré, en lui; **what has come over you?** qu'est-ce qui vous est arrivé? qu'est-ce qui vous prend? **a fit of dizziness came over her,** un vertige la gagna; (*b*) (i) **to c. over from a place,** arriver, venir, d'un lieu (situé de l'autre côté de la mer, du pont, de la montagne, etc.); **family that came over with the Conqueror,** famille *f* qui traversa la Manche avec Guillaume le Conquérant; **he's coming over to London for the summer school,** il vient à Londres pour les cours de vacances; *F:* **do c. over and see us sometimes,** poussez donc une pointe jusque chez nous de temps en temps; (ii) **to c. over to s.o.'s side,** passer dans le parti de qn, du côté de qn; **to c. over to an opinion,** se convertir, se ranger, à une opinion; (iii) **how did he c. over?** quelle impression vous a-t-il faite? **he doesn't c. over well on television,** il manque de relief à la télévision; *Rec:* **her voice comes over well,** sa voix se reproduit bien; (iv) *F:* **to c. over funny, dizzy,** être pris d'un malaise, d'un vertige; *F:* se sentir tout chose.
17. come round, *v.i.* (*a*) faire le tour; **the road is blocked; I had to c. round by the village,** la route est bloquée; j'ai dû faire le tour, faire un détour, par le village; **conversation that comes round to the same subjects again,** conversation *f* qui retombe sur les mêmes sujets; (*b*) *F:* **c. round and see me one day,** venez me voir un de ces jours; (*c*) **the time has c. round,** les temps sont révolus; **Sunday will soon c. round,** dimanche viendra bientôt; **as soon as Christmas comes round . . .,** dès que revient Noël. . .; **when it came round to me to take duty . . .,** quand mon tour fut venu d'être de service . . .; quand ce fut de nouveau mon tour de service . . .; (*d*) reprendre connaissance; reprendre ses esprits, ses sens; revenir à soi; (*e*) **to c. round to s.o.'s way of thinking,** se convertir à l'opinion de qn; se rallier, se ranger, à l'avis de qn; **I have c. round to your way of thinking,** j'en suis venu à votre manière de penser; **he has c. round,** il a cédé; il a consenti; (*f*) *Nau:* (i) (*of ship*) venir dans le vent; (ii) (*of wind*) remonter; (*g*) *Av:* **to c. round again (to land),** faire une deuxième présentation.
18. come through, *v.i.* (*a*) (i) **to c. through the wood,** passer par, à travers, le bois; **the rain has c. through my coat,** la pluie a traversé, percé, mon pardessus; (ii) **to c. through trials, sufferings,** passer par des épreuves; éprouver des souffrances; **he had come through the Great War,** il était réchappé de la Grande Guerre; **to c. through an illness,** surmonter une maladie; (*b*) (i) **the water, the rain, is coming through,** l'eau *f,* la pluie, pénètre; (ii) **he came through without a scratch,** il s'en est tiré indemne; **he has c. through with clean hands,** il en est sorti les mains nettes.
19. come to, *v.i.* (*a*) = COME ROUND (*d*); (*b*) *Nau:* (*of ship*) loffer, venir dans le vent.

20. come together, *v.i.* (*a*) s'assembler, se réunir; (*of troops*) opérer une jonction; **the election has compelled the parties to c. together,** l'élection *f* a imposé l'union des partis; **we shall c. together again in Paris,** nous nous retrouverons à Paris; *B:* **before they came together,** avant qu'ils eussent mené vie commune; (*b*) se rencontrer.

21. come up, *v.i.* (*a*) monter (l'échelle, l'escalier, etc.); **I saw him coming up the hill,** je l'aperçus qui gravissait la colline, qui montait, grimpait, la côte; (*b*) (i) monter; **come up to my rooms,** montez chez moi; **come up and have a drink,** montez donc prendre un verre; **your coffee coming up, sir!** (voilà) votre café, monsieur! **it was worth (while) coming up for the view; the view was worth coming up for,** le panorama valait le déplacement; **to c. up out of the abyss,** surgir de l'abime; **to c. up after a dive,** revenir à la surface après un plongeon, (*of submarine*) après une plongée; **to c. up to the surface again,** remonter sur l'eau; *F:* **everything he eats comes up again,** il rejette tout ce qu'il mange; *Nau:* (*of land, etc.*) **to c. up on the horizon,** commencer à paraître à l'horizon; (ii) **to c. up to town,** venir en ville, venir à Londres; **to c. up (to the university),** commencer ses études *f* (à Oxford, Cambridge, etc.); **the students will be coming up on October 10,** la rentrée universitaire est le dix octobre; (iii) **to c. up to s.o.,** s'approcher de qn; venir à, s'avancer vers, qn; **up came a man,** voilà qu'un homme arriva; **the tide is coming up,** la marée monte; *Ten:* **to c. up to the net,** monter au filet; *Jur:* **to c. up before the Court,** comparaître (devant le tribunal); (iv) *Nau:* (*of ship*) **to c. up into the wind,** s'effacer dans le lit du vent; **don't let her c. up!** défiez l'aulof(f)ée! (v) (*of plants*) sortir de terre; pousser; (vi) **to c. up (for discussion),** venir en discussion; venir sur le tapis; **this question has never yet come up,** cette question n'a encore jamais été soulevée; *Sch:* cette question n'est jamais encore sortie (à l'examen); *F:* **we haven't c. up with an answer to this problem yet,** nous n'avons pas encore trouvé la solution de ce problème; **the case comes up for hearing tomorrow,** la cause sera entendue demain; l'affaire passera demain; (vii) (*reach*) **to c. up to sth.,** atteindre, s'élever, jusqu'à qch; **the water came up to my knees,** l'eau *f* me montait jusqu'aux genoux; **the water came up over the houses,** l'eau a submergé les maisons; **he does not c. up to my waist,** il ne me vient pas à la ceinture; (*to a horse*) **c. up!** allons, hop! (viii) égaler; **as a violinist he doesn't c. up to X,** comme violoniste il n'égale pas X, il ne vaut pas X; **his talents do not c. up to yours,** ses talents *m* n'égalent pas, ne valent pas, les vôtres; (ix) **the table comes up well when you polish it,** la table revient bien à l'astiquage.

22. come upon, *v.i.* (*a*) *esp. Lit:* tomber, fondre, s'abattre, sur (un adversaire, etc.); **fear came upon him,** la peur l'envahit, le saisit, s'empara de lui; **the calamity that has c. upon us,** le malheur qui nous frappe; (*b*) *A:* **to c. upon s.o. for a sum,** réclamer une somme à qn; s'adresser, s'en prendre, à qn pour une somme; (*c*) *A:* **to c. upon the parish,** tomber à la charge de la paroisse; (*d*) **to c. upon sth., s.o.,** trouver qch., rencontrer qn, par hasard; **to c. upon a secret,** surprendre un secret; (*e*) *O:* (*of idea*) **to c. upon s.o.,** venir à l'esprit, à la mémoire, de qn; **it came upon me that I had seen this man before,** j'eus le sentiment d'avoir déjà vu cet homme; **it came upon me that calamity lay ahead,** j'eus le pressentiment d'un malheur.

come-at-able [kʌm'ætəbl], *a. F:* (endroit *m*) accessible; (homme *m*) abordable, accessible.

comeback ['kʌmbæk], *s.* **1.** retour *m* (en vogue); retour au pouvoir (d'un homme politique, etc.); retour à la scène, à l'écran (d'un acteur). **2.** *esp. U.S:* revanche *f*. **3.** *F:* réplique *f*.

comedian [kə'mi:diən], *s.* **1.** *Th:* (*a*) comédien, -ienne; (*b*) comique *m* (de music-hall, etc.). **2.** auteur *m* de comédies; auteur comique; poète *m* comique.

comedienne [kɔmi:di'en], *s.f. Th:* (*a*) comédienne; (*b*) actrice comique (de music-hall, etc.).

comedo, *pl.* **comedones** ['kɔmi:dou, kɔmi:'douni:z], *s. Med:* **1.** comédon *m*; point noir. **2.** acné *f*.

comedown ['kʌmdaun], *s. F:* humiliation *f*; déchéance *f*; **what a c.!** quelle dégringolade! **to live in furnished apartments would have been a c. (in the world),** vivre en meublé l'aurait dégradé; vivre en meublé, ç'aurait été déchoir.

comedy ['kɔmedi], *s.* **1.** comédie *f*; le genre comique; **high, low, c.,** la haute comédie; le bas comique; **c. of manners, social c.,** comédie de mœurs; **domestic c.,** comédie bourgeoise; **musical c.,** opérette *f*; comédie musicale; **black c.,** comédie noire. **2.** (*play*) comédie; **the comedies of Shakespeare,** les comédies de Shakespeare; **the human c.,** la comédie humaine; **we weren't taken in by her little c.,** sa petite comédie n'a pas pris. **3.** *Ital.Lit:* **the Divine C.,** la Divine Comédie.

come-hither [kʌm'hiðər], *a. F:* (regard) aguichant.

comeliness ['kʌmlinis], *s.* **1.** *O:* mine avenante. **2.** *A:* bienséance *f*.

comely ['kʌmli], *a.* **1.** (*of pers.*) avenant. **2.** *A:* (*of behaviour, etc.*) convenable, digne, bienséant.

comenic [kə'mi:nik], *a. Ch:* coménique.

come-on ['kʌmɔn], *s.* **1.** *Av: etc: F:* signal *m* d'approche. **2.** *P:* **to give s.o. the c.-o.,** encourager les avances sexuelles de qn.

come-out ['kʌmaut], *s. F:* (*of girl*) début *m* (dans le monde).

Comephoridae [kɔmi'fɔridi:], *s.pl. Ich:* coméphoridés *m*.

comer ['kʌmər], *s.* **1.** arrivant, -ante; venant, -ante; **comers and goers,** allants *m* et venants *m*; entrants *m* et sortants *m*; **pleasant to all comers,** affable à tout le monde, à tout venant, à tous. **2. first c.,** premier venu, premier arrivant, premier arrivé; **latest c.,** dernier venu.

comestible [kə'mestibl]. **1.** *a. esp. NAm:* comestible. **2.** *s.* (*usu. pl.*) comestible *m*.

comet ['kɔmet], *s.* **1.** comète *f*; **the C. year,** l'année *f* de la comète (1811); **c. wine,** vin *m* de la comète. **2.** *Orn:* colibri *m* sapho.

cometary ['kɔmetəri], **cometic** [kɔ'metik], *a. Astr:* cométaire; qui ressemble à une comète.

comeuppance [kʌm'ʌpəns], *s. F:* **she got her c.,** (i) elle a ce qu'elle mérite; (ii) on lui a dit son fait.

comfit ['kʌmfit], *s.* bonbon *m*; fruit confit; dragée *f*; **c. box,** bonbonnière *f*.

comfort[1] ['kʌmfət], *s.* **1.** consolation *f*; motif *m* de consolation; soulagement *m*; **a grain of c.,** un brin de consolation; **a few words of c.,** quelques paroles de réconfort; **to take c.,** se consoler; **that's cold c.,** cela n'est guère consolant; c'est là une piètre consolation; **too close for c.,** plutôt dangereux; **to be a great c. to s.o.,** être un grand sujet de consolation à qn; **she is a great c. to me,** elle me rend la vie douce; **child who is a c. to his mother,** enfant qui donne de la satisfaction à sa mère; **it's a c. to know, think, that . . .,** c'est une satisfaction que . . .; **it is a c. to tell one's woes,** on soulage ses maux à les raconter; **no one knows, that's one c.,** personne ne le sait, c'est déjà une consolation; *F: A:* **a little drop of c.,** un petit verre. **2.** (*wellbeing*) bien-être *m*; **I like c.,** j'aime mes aises *f*. **3.** (*a*) confort *m*; confortable *m*; aisance *f*; (*at hotel, etc.*) **every modern c.,** tout le confort moderne; **to live in c.,** vivre dans l'aisance, à l'aise; (*b*) *U.S:* **c. station,** toilette *f*. **4.** *pl.* commodités *f*; **the comforts of life,** les commodités, les agréments *m*, les douceurs *f*, de la vie; **to like one's comforts,** aimer le confortable, ses aises. **5.** *A: & NAm:* couvre-pied *inv* piqué.

comfort[2], *v.tr.* **1.** consoler, soulager; **to c. s.o. for a loss,** consoler qn d'une perte; **to be comforted,** être consolé; se consoler. **2.** (*a*) (*of beverage, etc.*) réconforter; (*b*) redonner du courage à (qn); **we were comforted by the sight of land,** à la vue de la terre nous avons repris courage.

comfortable ['kʌmfətəbl], *a.* **1.** (*a*) (*of bed, armchair, etc.*) confortable; (*of dress*) commode, aisé; (*of warmth, sensation*) agréable, doux, *f.* douce; **these shoes are c.,** on est à l'aise dans ces chaussures; **to make s.o. c. in an armchair,** accommoder qn dans un fauteuil; **you will be more c. in this armchair,** vous serez mieux dans ce fauteuil; **to make oneself c.,** se mettre à son aise; **to be c.,** être à l'aise, à son aise; **to feel c.,** se trouver bien, à son aise; se sentir à l'aise; **it is so c. here,** on est si bien ici; il fait si bon ici; **we are quite c. here,** nous ne sommes pas mal ici; **we had a c. journey,** nous avons fait un bon voyage; **seated by a c. fire,** assis auprès d'un bon feu; (*b*) (*of patient*) **to be c.,** ne pas souffrir; **he had a c. night,** la nuit a été bonne; (*c*) **I never feel c. with him,** je ne me sens jamais à mon aise avec lui. **2. c. income,** revenu suffisant; ample revenu; **to make s.o. c. for the rest of his days,** assurer la vie de qn pour le restant de ses jours; **to be in c. circumstances,** être fort aisé, dans l'aisance. **3.** (*free from anxiety*) sans inquiétude; tranquille; rassuré; **make yourself c. about that,** tranquillisez-vous, rassurez-vous, là-dessus. **4.** *s. NAm:* = COMFORT[1] 5.

comfortably ['kʌmfətəbli], *adv.* confortablement, commodément, agréablement; **to be c. off,** avoir de quoi (vivre); être à l'aise; jouir d'une honnête aisance; **to live c.,** vivre à l'aise, à son aise; **to be c. housed, dressed,** être logé, vêtu, commodément; **c. heated room,** pièce bien chauffée; **this car holds six people c.,** cette voiture tient bien six personnes; on tient à l'aise à six dans cette voiture; **we can get there c. in an hour,** une heure suffira amplement pour y aller; on peut y aller en une heure sans se presser.

comforter ['kʌmfətər], *s.* **1.** consolateur, -trice; *Ecc:* **the C.,** le Consolateur; le Saint-Esprit. **2.** (*a*) cache-nez *m inv* (de laine); (*b*) *NAm:* = COMFORT[1] 5. **3.** (*baby's*) tétine *f* (sur anneau); sucette *f*.

comforting ['kʌmfətiŋ], *a.* réconfortant; **c. words,** paroles *f* de consolation, de réconfort.

comfortless ['kʌmfətlis], *a.* **1.** sans confort; peu confortable; **I had to spend an hour in a c. waiting room,** j'ai dû passer une heure dans une triste salle d'attente. **2.** abandonné; sans consolation; *B:* **I will not leave you c.,** je ne vous laisserai point orphelins.

comfrey ['kʌmfri], *s. Bot:* consoude *f*.

comfy ['kʌmfi], *a. F:* = COMFORTABLE 1 (*a*).

comic ['kɔmik]. **1.** *a.* comique; **c. song,** chansonnette *f* comique; **c. paper,** journal amusant, journal pour rire; **to see the c. side of a situation,** voir le comique, le côté ridicule, d'une situation; **c. opera,** opéra *m* bouffe; *Journ:* **c. strip,** bande dessinée. **2.** *s.* comédien, -ienne (de music-hall); comique *m*. **3.** *s. Journ:* (*a*) journal *m* de bandes dessinées; (*b*) *pl. NAm: F:* **comics,** (la page des) bandes dessinées.

comical ['kɔmikl], *a.* comique, risible; drôle; cocasse; **to have a c. face,** avoir du comique dans la figure; avoir une mine burlesque; **the c. thing about it is . . .,** le (plus) plaisant de l'affaire c'est que . . .; **it is most c.,** c'est du dernier comique; c'est tout à fait cocasse; **what a c. idea!** quelle drôle d'idée!

comicality [kɔmi'kæliti], *s.* **1.** caractère *m* comique; comique *m* (d'une situation). **2.** (*a*) **a speech full of comicalities,** un discours rempli de drôleries *f*; (*b*) *F: A:* **a queer little c.,** un drôle de petit bonhomme; une drôle de petite bonne femme.

comically ['kɔmik(ə)li], *adv.* comiquement, d'une manière comique; drôlement.

comicalness ['kɔmik(ə)lnis], *s.* = COMICALITY 1.

comice ['kɔmis], *s. Hort:* poire *f* comice.

Cominform (the) [ðə'kɔminfɔ:m], *s.* Kominform *m*.

coming[1] ['kʌmiŋ], *a.* **1.** qui vient, qui arrive, qui approche; futur; **the c. year,** l'année qui vient, l'année prochaine; **the c. storm,** l'orage *m* qui approche; **c. generations,** les générations futures; **c. fashions,** la mode de demain; **its the up-and-c. sport,** c'est le sport de l'avenir; **a c. man,** un homme d'avenir; l'homme de demain; *Sp:* **a c. player,** un joueur d'avenir. **2.** *A: & Lit:* accueillant.

coming[2], *s.* venue *f*, arrivée *f* (de qn); approche *f* (de la nuit); avènement *m* (du Messie); **the Second C.,** le second avènement, la seconde venue; **comings and goings,** allées *f* et venues.

coming out ['kʌmiŋ'aut], *s.* (*a*) sortie *f* (du public après une représentation, etc.); chute *f* (de cheveux); (*b*) apparition *f* (du soleil, etc.); éclosion *f* (des fleurs); (*c*) apparition, parution *f* (d'un livre); (*d*) début *m* (au théâtre, dans le monde); **c.-o. ball,** bal donné en l'honneur des débuts d'une jeune fille.

Comintern (the) [ðə'kɔmintə:n], *s.* (*in Russia*) le Komintern; le Parti communiste international.

comitia [kə'miʃiə], *s.pl. Rom.Ant:* comices *m*.

comitial [kə'miʃiəl], *a.* comitial, -aux.

comity ['kɔmiti], *s. Lit:* courtoisie *f*, politesse *f*; **the c. of nations,** (i) le bon accord entre les nations; la courtoisie internationale; (ii) (par erreur d'interprétation) l'ensemble *m* des nations unies par des liens de courtoisie.

comma ['kɔmə], *s.* **1.** (*a*) virgule *f*; (*b*) **inverted commas,** guillemets *m*; **to put a word in, between, inverted commas,** mettre un mot entre guillemets; guillemeter un mot; encadrer un mot de guillemets; **to begin, to close, the inverted commas,** ouvrir, fermer, les guillemets. **2.** *Mus:* comma *m*. **3.** (*a*) *Ent: F:* robert-le-diable *m*; (*b*) **c. bacillus,** bacille *m* virgule.

command[1] [kə'mɑ:nd], *s.* **1.** ordre *m*, commandement *m*; **to do sth. at, by, s.o.'s c.,** agir d'après les ordres, suivant l'ordre, de qn; **to be at s.o.'s c.,** être aux ordres de qn; **word of c.,** commandement; **at the word of c., on a gesture of c.,** au signal donné; **God's commands,** les commandements de Dieu; **to attend a ball at Court by royal c.,** assister à un bal à la Cour sur l'ordre, sur l'invitation, du souverain; *Th:* **c. performance,** représentation *f* de commande, commandée par le souverain. **2.** *Mil:* (*a*) commandement, ordre; **cautionary c.,** commandement préparatoire; **executive c., c. of execution,** commandement d'exécution; **to give the c. at drill,** commander l'exercice; *U.S:* **fire at c.,** tir *m* au commandement; (*b*) commandement (**of, de; over, sur**); gouvernement *m* (d'une place forte); **supreme c.,** commandement suprême; **the Higher C.,** (*of the British Army*) le Commandement Supérieur; **c. of an army, of an expedition,** commandement, conduite *f*, d'une armée, d'une expédition; **to be in c. of a battalion,** avoir le commandement d'un bataillon, commander un bataillon; **to be first, second, in c.,** commander en premier, en second; **to take over c. from . . .,** recevoir, prendre (i) le commandement, (ii) les consignes, de . . .; **to hand over c. to . . .,** remettre, passer, (i) le commandement, (ii) les consignes, à . . .; **under (the) c. of . . .,** sous le commandement, sous les ordres, de . . .; **c. channel, chain of c.,** voie *f* hiérarchique, hiérarchie *f* militaire; **c. structure,** articulation *f*, structure *f*, du commandement; **c. car,** voiture *f* de liaison; *U.S:* **c. post,** poste *m* de commandement; **c. post exercise,** exercice *m* de cadres, de postes de commandement; *Navy:* **sea-going c.,** commandement à la mer; **c. of shore establishment,** commandement à terre; (*c*) (*troops*) **to be responsible for one's c.,** être responsable de ses troupes, de ses hommes; *Av:* **bomber, fighter, c.,** aviation *f* de bombardement, de chasse; **transport c.,** aviation de transport; *U.S:* **base c.,** l'ensemble *m* des troupes affectées à la défense d'une base; (*d*) (*territory, etc., under command*) **Scottish c., Northern c.,** la région militaire d'Écosse, du Nord; **air c.,** région aérienne; **naval c.,** région maritime. **3.** (*a*) **to be in c. of a pass, etc.,** commander, dominer, un défilé, etc.; **fort with low c.,** fort *m* de faible commandement; (*b*) **c. of a language,** connaissance *f*, maîtrise *f*, d'une langue; **to have several languages at one's c.; to have a c. of several languages,** avoir l'intelligence *f* de plusieurs langues; posséder plusieurs langues; **c. of language,** facilité *f* d'expression; *Com:* **c. of world markets,** supériorité *f* sur les marchés mondiaux; (*c*) *Nau:* **ship not under c.,** navire *m* qui n'est pas maître de sa manœuvre; (*d*) **c. over oneself,** maîtrise de soi; **he has a wonderful c. over himself,** il se possède à merveille; **he has no c. over himself,** il ne sait pas se maîtriser; (*e*) **c. of the seas,** maîtrise des mers; (*f*) **the money at my c.,** les fonds *m* à ma disposition, dont je peux disposer.

command², *v.tr.* **1.** ordonner, commander (**sth.,** qch.; **s.o. to do sth.,** à qn de faire qch.); **he did what, as, I commanded him (to do),** il a fait ce que je lui ai commandé, ordonné (de faire); *v.i.* **it is I who c.,** c'est moi qui commande; c'est moi qui donne les ordres. **2.** (*a*) commander (un navire, un régiment); *v.i.* **to c. in chief,** commander en chef; (*b*) **to c. oneself,** rester maître de soi; **to c. one's passions,** commander à ses passions; être maître de ses passions; **to c. one's temper,** se contenir; (*c*) **with money one commands the world,** avec de l'argent on est maître du monde. **3.** avoir (qch.) à sa disposition; **all the skill he could c.,** toute l'habileté qu'il possédait; **in an emergency I can c. a thousand pounds,** au besoin je pourrais disposer de mille livres; **you may c. me,** vous pouvez disposer de moi; **yours to c.,** à vos ordres; votre obéissant serviteur. **4.** (*a*) **to c. respect, admiration,** commander, inspirer, le respect, l'admiration; **to c. attention,** forcer l'attention; **he always commands the attention of his audience,** il est toujours maître de son auditoire; **to c. the market,** être maître du marché; (*b*) **to c. a high price,** se vendre à un haut prix. **5.** (*a*) (*of fort, etc.*) commander, dominer (une ville, l'entrée d'un détroit, etc.); **battery that commands the gorge,** batterie *f* qui défend le défilé; **window that commands a view over the valley,** fenêtre *f* qui domine la vallée, qui a vue sur la vallée; (*b*) *Cards:* **to c. a suit,** avoir les cartes maîtresses d'une couleur; être maître dans une couleur.

commandant [kɔmən'dænt], *s.* **1.** commandant *m* (d'un arsenal, d'un camp, etc.); gouverneur *m* (d'une place forte). **2.** *Hist:* (*S. Africa*) chef *m* de commando.

commandeer [kɔmən'diər], *v.tr.* réquisitionner.

commandeering [kɔmən'diəriŋ], *s.* réquisitionnement *m*, réquisition *f*.

commander [kə'mɑːndər], *s.* **1.** (*a*) *Mil:* commandant *m*; **army, battalion, company, c.,** commandant d'armée, de bataillon, de compagnie; **platoon, squad, c.,** chef *m* de section, de groupe; **tank c.,** chef de char; **c.-in-chief,** commandant en chef; généralissime *m*; **to be c.-in-chief of an interallied force,** commander en chef une force interalliée; **garrison, station, c.,** *U.S:* **post c.,** commandant d'armes; (*b*) *Mil.Av:* chef de bord (d'un avion, etc.); **wing c.,** lieutenant-colonel *m* (d'aviation), *pl.* lieutenants-colonels; (*c*) *Navy:* capitaine *m* de frégate; **lieutenant c.,** capitaine de corvette. **2.** (*a*) (*of knights*) commandeur *m*; (*b*) (*of caliph*) **C. of the Faithful,** commandeur des croyants. **3.** *Tls:* dame *f*, demoiselle *f*; *Nau:* masse *f* (en bois); mailloche *f*.

command(e)ry [kə'mɑːndəri], *s. Hist:* commanderie *f*.

commanding [kə'mɑːndiŋ], *a.* **1.** *Mil:* **c. officer,** officier commandant; chef *m* de corps. **2. c. tone,** ton *m* d'autorité, de commandement. **3. c. presence,** air, port, imposant; **c. beauty,** beauté majestueuse. **4.** (lieu) éminent; **c. position,** position dominante, importante; **shop in a c. position,** magasin admirablement situé; **c. spot,** éminence *f* (de terrain).

commandment [kə'mɑːndmənt], *s.* commandement (divin); **the Ten Commandments,** les Dix Commandements; **to break a c.,** violer un commandement; **to keep the commandments,** observer les commandements.

commando [kə'mɑːndou], *s.* (*a*) *Hist:* (*in S. Africa*) commando *m*; (*b*) *Mil:* commando, corps franc, groupe franc; (*c*) soldat *m* membre d'un commando.

commelina [kɔmi'lainə], *s. Bot:* commélyne *f*.

Commelinaceae [kɔmili'neisiː], *s.pl. Bot:* commélynacées *f*.

commemorate [kə'meməreit], *v.tr.* commémorer (qn, le souvenir de qn); solenniser, célébrer, rappeler, le souvenir de (qn, qch.); **prize to c. s.o.,** prix destiné à honorer la mémoire de qn.

commemoration [kəmemə'reiʃ(ə)n], *s.* **1.** commémoration *f*; **in c. of s.o., of sth.,** en commémoration, en mémoire, de qn, de qch. **2.** *Ecc:* commémoraison *f*.

commemorative [kə'memərətiv], *a.* commémoratif (**of,** de); *Ecc:* **c. prayer,** commémoraison *f*.

commence [kə'mens], *v.tr. & i.* commencer (qch., à faire qch., par faire qch.); *Jur:* **to c. an action against s.o.,** intenter un procès contre qn; *Mil:* **to c. operations,** entamer les opérations.

commencement [kə'mensmənt], *s.* **1.** commencement *m*, début *m*; *Ins:* **c. of a policy,** effet *m* d'une police. **2.** *Sch: NAm:* (i) distribution *f* des prix; (ii) remise *f* des diplômes.

commencing [kə'mensiŋ], *a.* qui commence; **at a c. salary of . . .,** aux appointements *m* de début de . . ..

commend [kə'mend], *v.tr.* **1.** (*a*) *Lit:* **to c. sth. to s.o., to s.o.'s care,** recommander, confier, qch. à qn, aux soins de qn; remettre qch. entre les mains de qn; **to c. one's soul to God,** recommander son âme à Dieu; *Hist:* **to c. a vassal to an overlord,** mettre un vassal sous la protection d'un suzerain; (*b*) *Ecc:* commender (un bénéfice). **2.** (*a*) faire l'éloge de (qn); louer (qn, qch.); approuver (qch.); **to c. s.o. for bravery,** louer qn de sa bravoure; **to c. one's wares,** faire valoir ses marchandises; **to c. s.o. for doing sth.,** applaudir, approuver, qn d'avoir fait qch.; **she is to be commended for having persevered,** elle est louable d'avoir persévéré; (*b*) **if this view commends itself to the public,** si le public se range à cet avis; **a course of action that did not c. itself to me,** une ligne de conduite qui n'était pas à mon goût, à laquelle je ne pouvais pas donner mon approbation. **3.** *A:* **c. me to him,** saluez-le de ma part.

commendable [kə'mendəbl], *a.* louable; (action *f*) digne d'éloges; **he acted with c. promptness,** il a pris des mesures avec une louable promptitude.

commendably [kə'mendəbli], *adv.* louablement, d'une manière louable.

commendam [kə'mendæm], *s. Ecc: A:* commende *f*; **to give a benefice in c.,** commender un bénéfice.

commendation [kɔmen'deiʃ(ə)n], *s.* **1.** éloge *m*, louange *f*, approbation *f* (**of,** de). **2. letters of c.,** lettres *f* de recommandation.

commendatory [kə'mendət(ə)ri], *a.* **1.** élogieux. **2. c. prayer,** prière *f* pour un mourant, pour un agonisant. **3.** *Ecc:* (abbé *m*, abbaye *f*) commendataire.

commensal [kə'mens(ə)l], *s.* **1.** *s. esp. Biol:* commensal *m*, -aux. **2.** *a.* (*a*) *A:* qui mange à la même table; (*b*) *Biol:* commensal.

commensalism [kə'mensəlizm], *s. Biol:* commensalisme *m*.

commensurability [kəmens(j)ərə'biliti, -ʃər-], **commensurableness** [kə'mens(j)ərəblnis, -ʃər-], *s.* commensurabilité *f* (**with,** avec).

commensurable [kə'mens(j)ərəbl, -ʃər-], *a.* **1.** (*of number, etc.*) commensurable (**with, to,** avec); **mind and space are not c.,** l'esprit *m* et l'espace *m* n'ont pas de commune mesure. **2.** = COMMENSURATE 2.

commensurate [kə'mens(j)ərət, -ʃər-], *a.* **1.** coétendu (**with,** à). **2.** proportionné (**to, with,** à); **his success was not c. with his efforts,** son succès ne répondit pas à ses efforts; **the salary offered will be c. with experience,** les appointements offerts seront en fonction de l'expérience.

commensurately [kə'mens(j)ərətli, -ʃər-], *adv.* proportionnellement (**to, with,** à).

commensurateness [kə'mens(j)ərətnis, -ʃər-], *s.* commensurabilité *f*.

commensuration [kəmens(j)ə'reiʃ(ə)n, -ʃər-], *s. Mth:* commensuration *f*.

comment¹ ['kɔment], *s.* (*a*) *A:* (= COMMENTARY) commentaire *m*; (*b*) **comments on a text,** observations *f* critiques, gloses *f*, sur un texte; **c. is needless,** voilà qui se passe de commentaire; **to make a c. on sth.,** faire des observations sur qch.; **no c.,** je n'ai rien à dire (à ce sujet); sans commentaire, rien à dire là-dessus; **no comments, please!** point d'observations, de commentaires, s'il vous plaît! **to call for c.,** provoquer des critiques, des commentaires; *Com:* **for comments,** pour observations; *Jur:* **the judge's c.,** l'appréciation *f* du juge; (*c*) *Cmptr:* commentaire; **comments card,** carte *f* commentaires.

comment², *v.i.* **1. to c. on a text,** commenter un texte; faire le commentaire d'un texte. **2. to c. on s.o.'s behaviour,** commenter (sur), critiquer, la conduite de qn; **several people commented on his absence,** plusieurs personnes ont fait des observations sur son absence; **nobody commented on it,** cela n'a suscité aucun commentaire.

commentary ['kɔmənt(ə)ri], *s.* **1.** (*a*) commentaire *m*, glose *f*; (*b*) *Lt.Lit:* **Caesar's Commentaries, the Commentaries on the Gallic War,** les Commentaires de César, les Commentaires de la Guerre des Gaules. **2. running c.,** (i) commentaire point par point; radioreportage *m*, reportage *m* en direct (d'un match, etc.).

commentate ['kɔmənteit], *v.i. Journ:* faire le commentaire (d'un événement).

commentator ['kɔmənteitər], *s.* **1.** commentateur, -trice; annotateur, -trice; glossateur *m*. **2.** *W.Tel:* radioreporter *m*; *T.V:* commentateur.

commerce ['kɔməːs], *s.* **1.** commerce *m* (en gros); négoce *m*; les affaires *f*; **Chamber of C.,** Chambre *f* de commerce. **2.** *Jur:* commerce; rapports sexuels. **3.** *A:* **man of good c.,** homme *m* d'un commerce agréable.

commercial [kə'məːʃəl]. **1.** *a.* (*a*) commercial, -aux; **the c. world,** le commerce; **c. bank,** banque commerciale, de commerce; **c. port,** port *m* de commerce; **c. law,** droit commercial; le Code de commerce; **c. court,** tribunal *m* de commerce; **c. vehicle,** véhicule *m* utilitaire; **c. college,** école *f* de commerce; *O:* **c. traveller,** voyageur *m* de commerce; représentant *m*; **c. room,** salle réservée aux représentants (dans un hôtel); **c. artist,** artiste *mf* en publicité; **c. value,** valeur marchande, vénale; **c. efficiency (of a machine),** rendement *m* économique, effet *m* utile (d'une machine); *Dipl:* **c. attaché,** attaché commercial; (*b*) *usu. Pej:* (esprit) mercantile, commercial. **2.** *s.* (*a*) *F: A:* voyageur de commerce; (*b*) *W.Tel: T.V:* émission *f* publicitaire.

commercialese [kəməːʃə'liːz], *s. Pej:* (mauvais) style du commerce.

commercialism [kə'məːʃəlizm], *s.* esprit commercial; *Pej:* mercantilisme *m*.

commercialistic [kəməːʃə'listik], *s. Pej:* mercantile, commercial.

commercialization [kəməːʃəlai'zeiʃ(ə)n], *s.* commercialisation *f*.

commercialize [kə'məːʃəlaiz], *v.tr.* commercialiser.

commercially [kə'məːʃəli], *adv.* commercialement.

commie ['kɔmi], *s. F:* communiste *mf*.

commination [kɔmi'neiʃ(ə)n], *s.* **1.** *Ecc:* commination *f*. **2.** *Lit:* dénonciation *f*; menaces *fpl*.

comminatory ['kɔminət(ə)ri], *a.* comminatoire.

commingle [kɔ'miŋgl]. **1.** *v.tr.* (*a*) mêler ensemble; mélanger; (*b*) emmêler, entremêler. **2.** *v.i.* se mêler (**with,** avec); se mélanger.

comminute ['kɔminjuːt], *v.tr.* **1.** pulvériser, porphyriser, réduire en fragments (du marbre, etc.); grenailler (un métal); *Surg:* comminuer (un os); **comminuted fracture,** fracture esquilleuse, comminutive; comminution *f*. **2.** morceler (une propriété).

comminution [kɔmi'njuːʃ(ə)n], *s.* **1.** comminution *f* (d'un os); pulvérisation *f*, porphyrisation *f* (du marbre); *Metalw: etc:* grenaillement *m*. **2.** morcellement *m*.

Commiphora [kə'mifərə], *s. Bot:* commiphora *m*.

commiserate [kə'mizəreit], *v.tr. & i.* **to c. s.o., with s.o.,** s'apitoyer sur le sort de qn; compatir à la misère de qn; témoigner de la commisération à qn.

commiseration [kəmizə'reiʃ(ə)n], *s.* commisération *f*, compassion *f* (**with,** pour).

commiserative [kə'mizərətiv], *a.* compatissant.

commiseratively [kə'mizərətivli], *adv.* avec compassion.

commissar [kɔmi'sɑːr], *s.* commissaire *m* (du peuple).

commissariat [kɔmi'seəriət], *s.* **1.** *Mil:* (*a*) intendance *f* (militaire); **Navy c.,** commissariat *m* de la Marine; (*b*) les vivres *m*; **c. department,** (i) *Mil:* l'intendance vivres; (ii) *Navy:* le commissariat. **2.** *Hist:* (*U.S.S.R.*) service *m*, ministère *m*.

commissary ['kɔmisəri], *s.* **1.** commissaire *m*, délégué *m*; **High C.,** Haut-Commissaire *m*. **2.** *Mil:* (*a*) officier *m* d'intendance; intendant *m*; **c. general,** intendant général d'armée; (*b*) *U.S:* (i) dépôt *m* de vivres; (ii) *pl.* vivres *m*. **3.** *Ecc:* vicaire *m* général.

commission¹ [kə'miʃ(ə)n], *s.* **1.** commission *f*; délégation *f* (de devoirs, d'autorité). **2.** (*a*) brevet *m*, titre *m*; **c. of the peace,** charge *f* de juge de tribunal d'instance; *Jur:* **c. day,** jour *m* de l'ouverture des assises (où il était autrefois donné lecture du mandat du juge); **to have a roving c.,** (i) *Navy:* avoir liberté de manœuvre, de croisière; (ii) avoir carte blanche (pour chercher des débouchés, etc.); (*b*) *Mil:* = brevet (d'officier); **to resign, throw up, one's c.,** démissionner, donner sa démission; **to get a, one's, c.,** être nommé officier, passer officier, gagner l'épaulette. **3.** ordre *m*, mandat *m*, commande *f*, mission *f*; **work done on c.,** travail fait sur commande; **to carry out a c.,** s'acquitter d'une commission, d'un mandat, d'une mission. **4.** commission (parlementaire, etc.); **fact-finding c.,** commission d'enquête; *Pol:* **Royal C.,** commission d'enquête ordonnée par décret parlementaire; **the Ecclesiastical C.,** la commission d'administration des biens de l'Église anglicane. **5.** *Nau:* armement *m* (d'un navire); **to put a ship into c.,** armer un navire; **ship in c.,** navire en commission, en armement; **to put a factory into c.,** mettre une usine en service; **aircraft in c.,** avion *m* en service; (*of ship*) **out of c.,** désarmé, en réserve; **to put a ship out of c.,** désarmer un navire, mettre un navire en réserve; **my car is out of c.,** ma voiture est en réparation, en panne. **6.** *Com:* commission; pourcentage *m*; **sale on c.,** vente *f* à la commission; **three per cent c.,** trois pour cent de commission; **to charge 5% c.,** prendre une commission de 5%; **to appoint s.o. as buyer on c.,** commissionner qn; **illicit c.,** remise *f* illicite; *F:* pot *m* de vin; **c. agent,** (i) représentant *m* à la commission; commissionnaire *m* en marchandises; (ii) *Turf:* bookmaker *m*. **7.** perpétration *f* (d'un crime).

commission², **1.** *v.tr.* (*a*) commissionner (qn); **to c. s.o. to do sth.,** charger qn de faire qch.; **to c. s.o. to buy sth.,** donner à qn pleins pouvoirs pour acheter qch., la commission d'acheter qch.; **to c. an artist to paint a portrait,** faire à un artiste la commande d'un portrait; **to c. a painting,** commander une peinture; **to be commissioned to do sth.,** être chargé, avoir mission, avoir la commission, de faire qch.; (*b*) préposer, déléguer, (qn) à une fonction; investir (qn) d'un pouvoir; nommer (un officier) à un commandement; (*c*) commander (un livre, un tableau); **work commissioned by the publisher,** ouvrage écrit sur la commande de l'éditeur. **2.** (*a*) *v.tr.* armer (un navire); mettre (une usine) en service; (*b*) *v.i.* (*of ship*) armer; entrer en armement.

commissionaire [kəmiʃə'nɛər], *s.* **1.** commissionnaire *m*; chasseur *m* (d'hôtel). **2.** messager patenté (sociétaire du *Corps of Commissionaires*, association de vétérans d'une capacité et d'une probité éprouvées).

commissioned [kə'miʃənd], *a.* **1.** muni de pouvoirs; commissionné, délégué. **2.** (navire) en commission, en armement; (navire) armé. **3.** *Mil:* **c. officer,** officier *m*; **to be c.,** être nommé officier; obtenir, recevoir, son brevet d'officier.

commissioner [kə'miʃ(ə)nər], *s.* commissaire *m*; (*a*) membre *m* d'une commission; (*b*) délégué *m* d'une commission; **c. of police** = préfet *m* de police; **the Commissioners of Inland Revenue** = le fisc; *Adm:* **C. of audit,** auditeur *m* à la Cour des Comptes; **the Civil Service Commissioners,** le corps chargé du recrutement des fonctionnaires (par voie de concours); **c. for oaths,** officier ministériel (le plus souvent un *solicitor*) ayant qualité pour recevoir les déclarations sous serment; **Lord High C.,** délégué de la Couronne à l'Assemblée générale de l'Église d'Écosse; **Wreck C.,** commissaire des naufrages; **the Charity Commissioners,** la Commission de surveillance de bienfaisance; **the Ecclesiastical Commissioners,** la Commission d'administration des biens de l'Église anglicane.

commissioning [kə'miʃəniŋ], *s.* **1.** délégation *f*. **2.** nomination *f* (d'un officier) à un commandement. **3.** *Nau:* armement *m*.

commissoria lex [kɔmi'sɔːriə'leks], *s. Jur:* clause *f*, pacte *m*, commissoire.

commissural [kə'miʃərəl], *a. Anat: etc:* commissural, -aux.

commissure ['kɔmiʃuər], *s. Anat: Biol: Arch:* commissure *f*; *Anat:* **optic c.,** chiasma *m*; **the great c.,** la grande commissure cérébrale.

commit [kə'mit], *v.tr.* (**committed**) **1.** commettre, confier, livrer, remettre (**s.o., sth., to s.o.'s care,** qn, qch., aux soins, à la garde, de qn); **to c. a body to the earth,** livrer un corps à la terre; **to c. one's soul to God,** remettre, résigner, rendre, son âme à Dieu; **to c. oneself to Providence,** s'abandonner à la Providence; **to c. sth. to writing,** coucher qch. par écrit; **to c. sth. to memory,** apprendre qch. par cœur; se mettre, *F:* se loger, qch. dans la mémoire. **2.** *Jur:* **to c. s.o. to prison,** *abs.* **to c. s.o.,** (i) délivrer un mandat de dépôt contre qn; (ii) envoyer qn en prison; écrouer qn; **to c. s.o. for trial,** (i) mettre qn en accusation; (ii) renvoyer (un prévenu) aux assises; **committed for trial,** détenu préventivement; en état de prévention; renvoyé devant la cour d'assises. **3.** *Pol:* **to c. a bill,** renvoyer un projet de loi à une commission. **4.** (*a*) engager (sa parole d'honneur, etc.); **to be committed to sth., to do sth.,** être engagé à (faire) qch., être tenu de faire qch.; (*b*) **to c. troops,** engager des troupes à fond; **the troops were too deeply committed to be withdrawn,** les troupes étaient trop engagées pour qu'il fût possible de les rappeler; (*c*) **to c. oneself,** se compromettre; **to refuse to c. oneself,** se tenir sur la réserve; **without committing myself,** sans me compromettre; sous toutes réserves; sans m'engager. **5.** commettre, *Jur:* perpétrer (un crime); commettre (une erreur, une indiscrétion); **to c. an offence against the law,** commettre une infraction à la loi; commettre un délit, un crime, puni par la loi; **to c. suicide,** se suicider.

commitment [kə'mitmənt], *s.* **1.** (*a*) dépôt *m* (d'un document chez un notaire, etc.); (*b*) *Jur:* emprisonnement *m*, mise *f* en prison; (*c*) *esp. NAm:* internement *m* (d'un aliéné) dans un hôpital psychiatrique. **2.** engagement *m* (financier ou autre); **c. to withdraw troops,** engagement, promesse *f*, de retirer, faire replier, des troupes; **our commitments to developing countries,** nos engagements, nos obligations *f*, envers les pays en voie de développement; **I cannot do it because of other commitments,** d'autres obligations m'empêchent de le faire.

committable [kə'mitəbl], *a. Jur:* (prévenu *m*) qu'il y a lieu de renvoyer aux assises.

committal [kə'mitl], *s.* **1.** (*a*) mise *f* en terre (d'un cadavre); **c. to the deep,** immersion *f* (d'un cadavre); **c. service, prayers,** prières *f* au bord de la tombe; (*b*) *Jur:* emprisonnement *m*, mise en prison; incarcération *f*; **c. order,** mandat *m* de dépôt (d'un prévenu); **c. for trial,** détention préventive, mise en prévention, en accusation; **c. to a higher court,** renvoi *m* à un tribunal supérieur; (*c*) *esp. NAm:* internement *m* (d'un aliéné) dans un hôpital psychiatrique; (*d*) renvoi (d'un projet de loi) à une commission. **2.** perpétration *f* (d'un délit, etc.).

committed [kə'mitid], *a.* (*a*) engagé; **c. literature,** littérature engagée; (*b*) *Pej:* partial, -aux.

committee¹ [kə'miti], *s.* comité *m*; commission *f*; conseil *m*; **to be on, sit on, a c.,** être membre, faire partie, d'un comité, etc.; **c. meeting,** réunion *f* d'un comité, etc.; **executive c.,** (i) bureau *m* (d'une société); (ii) commission exécutive (d'un parti politique, d'un syndicat, etc.); **management c.,** conseil d'administration; **joint production c.,** comité d'entreprise; **advisory c.,** comité consultatif; **defence c.,** commission de défense; *Sp: etc:* **organizing c.,** comité d'organisation; *Th: etc:* **selection c., reading c.,** comité de lecture; *Art:* **hanging c.,** comité de réception, jury *m* d'admission, des tableaux (au Salon, à Paris, à la Royal Academy à Londres, etc.); **the Stock Exchange C.** = la Chambre syndicale des agents de change; *Jur:* **c. of inspection,** délégation *f* de créanciers chargés de la surveillance d'une faillite; *Parl:* **the House resolves itself, goes, into c.,** la Chambre se constitue en comité; **to send a bill to a c.,** renvoyer un projet de loi à, devant, une commission; **standing c.,** commission permanente; **select c.,** conseil, commission, d'enquête; **steering c.,** comité-directeur *m, pl.* comités-directeurs; **C. of ways and means, c. of supply** = Commission du budget; **interdepartmental c.,** comité interministériel; **c. rooms** (*of parliamentary candidate*), permanence électorale; **c. man, woman, member,** membre *m* d'un comité.

committee² [kɔmi'tiː], *s. Jur:* tuteur, -trice, curateur, -trice, d'un dément, d'un faible d'esprit (désigné(e) par le *Lord Chancellor*).

commix [kɔ'miks], *v.i.* mélanger.

commixture [kɔ'mikstjər], *s.* mélange *m*.

commodatary [kɔmə'deitəri], *s. Jur:* commodataire *m*.

commodate ['kɔmədeit], **commodatum,** *pl.* **-data** [kɔmə'deitəm, -'deitə], *s. Jur:* commodat *m*; prêt *m* à usage.

commode [kə'moud], *s.* **1.** *Furn:* commode *f*. **2.** (**night**) **c.,** chaise percée. **3.** *A.Cost:* (*woman's headdress*) commode.

commodious [kə'moudiəs], *a.* spacieux.

commodiously [kə'moudiəsli], *adv.* spacieusement.

commodiousness [kə'moudiəsnis], *s.* spaciosité *f*, amples dimensions *f* (d'une maison, d'une pièce, etc.).

commodity [kə'mɔditi], *s.* marchandise *f*, denrée *f*, produit *m*; **commodities such as meat, fats and sugar,** denrées telles que la viande, les matières grasses et le sucre; **primary c., basic c.,** produit de base; **standard c.,** bien *m* étalon; article *m* de référence; **coffee is the staple c. of Brazil,** le café est la ressource principale du Brésil; **c. market,** marché *m* de matières premières; **c. exchange,** bourse *f* (de marchandises); **c. credits,** crédits commerciaux; **c. money,** monnaie marchandise; **international c. agreements,** accords internationaux sur les produits de base.

commodore ['kɔmədɔːr], *s.* **1.** (*a*) *Navy:* chef *m* de division (par intérim); (*b*) *Navy: Nau:* (i) le commandant de bâtiment le plus ancien (d'un détachement); (ii) (*in wartime*) le chef de convoi (navires marchands escortés); (*c*) le capitaine le plus ancien d'une flotte marchande; (*d*) le capitaine (d'un corps de pilotes, d'un yacht-club). **2.** (*a*) *Mil.Av:* **air c.,** général *m* de brigade; (*b*) *U.S: Av:* commandant de bord. **3.** (*ship*) le navire (d'un convoi ou d'une flotte marchande) sur lequel se trouve le commodore.

Commodus ['kɔmədəs], *Pr.n.m. Rom.Hist:* Commode.

common¹ ['kɔmən], *a.* commun. **1.** (*a*) **staircase c. to two flats,** escalier commun à deux appartements; *Sch:* **c. room,** (i) salle commune; (ii) salle des professeurs; (iii) *F:* le personnel enseignant; **c. wall,** mur commun, mitoyen; **c. report,** rumeur publique; *Jur:* commune renommée; **c. property,** choses communes; propriété possédée en commun; **c. land,** champs communs; **we have c. interests,** nous avons des intérêts communs; **the c. opinion,** l'opinion courante; **it has been our c. experience,** cela nous est arrivé à tous; **it is to our c. credit,** c'est à notre honneur à tous; **to make c. cause with s.o.,** s'allier à qn; *Gram:* **c. noun,** nom commun; *Mth:* **c. divisor, factor,** commun diviseur; *Rail:* **c. user engine,** locomotive conduite en banalité; (*b*) public; **the c. gaol,** la maison d'arrêt (commune); **the c. hangman,** le bourreau (au service de l'État). **2.** (*a*) ordinaire; **c. occurrence,** chose fréquente, qui arrive souvent; **c. name (of a plant),** nom vulgaire (d'une plante); **c. honesty,** la probité la plus élémentaire; **in c. use,** d'usage courant; **in c. parlance,** en langage ordinaire; (*of news, etc.*) **to be c. talk,** courir les rues; **it is c. (practice) to dine in the evening,** il est d'usage de dîner le soir; *A:* **the c. soldiery,** les simples soldats *m*; **c. salt,** sel commun, sel de cuisine; **c. or garden cabbage,** chou commun; *F:* **it's just a c. or garden detective story,** ce n'est qu'un roman policier tout à fait ordinaire, banal; **they are as c. as blackberries, as dirt,** les rues en sont pavées; (*b*) **the c. people,** les gens du peuple; **he lacks the c. touch,** il manque de doigté, il ne sait pas parler aux gens; (*c*) de peu de valeur. **3.** vulgaire, trivial; **c. manners,** manières vulgaires, communes; **c. accent,** accent faubourien, plébéien; **the duchess was rather c.,** la duchesse manquait de distinction; **he's rather a c. little man,** il est assez vulgaire; **he's dead c., as c. as dirt,** c'est le dernier des derniers; **c. expression,** expression triviale, trivialité *f*.

common², *s.* **1.** (*a*) terrain, pré, communal; *Jur:* vaine pâture; **the village c.,** les communaux du village; (*b*) *Jur:* **c. (right), (right of) c.,** (droits *mpl* de) servitude *f*; usage *m*; *esp.* droit de pâturage, de (vaine) pâture; **c. of pasture, of pasturage,** droit(s) de pâture, de pacage. **2. to have sth. in c. with s.o.,** avoir qch. en commun avec qn; **to have interests in c.,** avoir des intérêts communs; **they have nothing in c.,** ils n'ont rien de commun; *F:* ils ne se chauffent pas du même bois; **out of the c.,** hors ligne; **it's out of the c.,** cela sort de l'ordinaire; **nothing out of the c.,** rien d'extraordinaire. **3.** *R.C.Ch:* **the c. of martyrs,** le commun des martyrs.

commonage ['kɔmənidʒ], *s.* **1.** (*a*) (i) droit *m* de vaine pâture; (ii) droit de parcours; (*b*) vaine pâture. **2.** communauté *f* (de jouissance, etc.). **3.** le tiers état; le peuple.

commonality [kɔmən'æliti], *s.* **1.** = COMMONALTY. **2.** *Mec.E:* normalisation *f* (des pièces); **greater c. of car wheels,** normalisation plus poussée des roues de voitures.

commonalty ['kɔmənəlti], *s.* **the c.,** (i) le commun des hommes; (ii) le tiers état; *A:* les roturiers, la roture; (iii) corporation *f*, corps *m*.

commoner ['kɔmənər], *s.* **1.** homme *m*, femme *f*, du peuple; bourgeois, -oise; *A:* roturier *m*. **2.** *Jur:* (*having right of common*) usager *m* d'une servitude, *p. ex.* du droit de vaine pâture. **3.** *occ.* membre *m* de la Chambre des Communes; *F:* **the First C.,** le président des Communes; *Hist:* **the Great C.,** Lord Chatham. **4.** *Sch:* (*at Oxford*) étudiant *m* ordinaire (qui n'est pas boursier).

commonly ['kɔmənli], *adv.* **1.** communément, ordinairement, généralement; d'habitude; pour la plupart; **that c. happens,** ça arrive souvent; **what is c. known as . . .,** ce qu'en langage courant on appelle . . .. **2.** vulgairement, de façon vulgaire.

commonness ['kɔmənnis], *s.* **1.** fréquence *f* (d'un événement). **2.** banalité *f* (de style); vulgarité *f* (d'une personne).

commonplace ['kɔmənpleis]. **1.** *s.* (*a*) vérité *f* d'ordre général; lieu commun; (*b*) banalité *f,* trivialité *f*; **conversational commonplaces,** phrases *f* d'usage; **to write nothing but commonplaces,** n'écrire que des platitudes, des pauvretés; (*c*) **c. book,** mémorandum *m*; recueil *m* de faits notables, de citations, de lieux communs. **2.** *a.* banal, -als; terre à terre; **c. person,** personne médiocre; **he is a very c. kind of man,** c'est un homme très quelconque; **it is becoming c.,** cela tombe dans le banal; **in a c. manner,** banalement.

commonplaceness ['kɔmənpleisnis], *s.* banalité *f.*

commons ['kɔmənz], *s.* **1.** (*a*) le peuple; le tiers état; (*b*) **the House of C.,** la Chambre des Communes; **he sits in the C.,** il siège aux Communes. **2.** *Sch:* (*a*) *A:* ordinaire *m* (de la table); *Fig:* **to be on short c.,** faire maigre chère; être réduit à une maigre pitance; **to keep s.o. on short c.,** compter les morceaux à qn; mesurer la nourriture à qn; **during the siege we were on short c.,** pendant le siège nous étions rationnés; (*b*) (*at Oxford and Cambridge*) portions à prix fixe délivrées aux étudiants par la dépense du collège. **3.** *A:* (*with sg. concord*) table *f* de l'ordinaire.

commonweal (the) [ðə'kɔmənwi:l], *s.* le bien de la patrie; le bien public.

commonwealth ['kɔmənwelθ], *s.* **1.** état *m*; **the C.,** la chose publique. **2.** (*a*) *Hist:* **the C. of England,** la République d'Angleterre (1649–60); **the C. of Australia,** le Commonwealth d'Australie; (*b*) **the British C. (of Nations),** le Commonwealth, la Communauté britannique. **3.** *A:* = COMMONWEAL.

commorientes ['kɔmmɔ:ri'enti:z], *s.pl. Jur:* comourants *m.*

commotion [kə'mouʃ(ə)n], *s.* **1.** agitation *f,* commotion *f,* ébranlement *m*; **in a state of c.,** en émoi; **the news made a great c.,** la nouvelle occasionna un grand branle-bas; **the c. in the streets,** le brouhaha de la rue; **to create a c.,** faire de l'éclat; **to make a c. (about sth.),** (i) faire des histoires, des embarras (à propos de qch.); (ii) faire de l'esclandre. **2.** troubles *mpl*; agitation (parmi le peuple).

commove [kə'mu:v], *v.tr.* (*a*) mettre en mouvement; (*b*) agiter.

communal ['kɔmjun(ə)l], *a.* **1.** (*a*) *A:* (moulin, four) banal; (*b*) communal, communautaire; **c. forest,** forêt communale; **c. life,** la vie commune, de communauté, communautaire; *Jur:* **c. estate,** communauté (conjugale); **to bring one's property into the c. estate,** ameublir ses immeubles; **inclusion of realty in the c. estate,** ameublissement *m* d'immeubles. **2.** *Fr.Hist:* (*1871*) de la Commune.

communalism ['kɔmjunəlizm], *s.* théorie *f* communaliste de l'État; théorie de la décentralisation des pouvoirs.

communalist ['kɔmjunəlist], *s. Fr.Pol:* communaliste *mf.*

communalistic [kɔmjunə'listik], *a.* communaliste.

communalization [kɔmjunəlai'zeiʃ(ə)n], communalisation *f.*

communalize ['kɔmjunəlaiːz], *v.tr.* communaliser.

communally ['kɔmjunəli], *adv.* communalement.

commune[1] ['kɔmju:n], *s.* commune *f*; communauté *f.*

commune[2] [kə'mju:n], *v.i.* **1.** *Lit:* converser, s'entretenir (**with s.o.,** avec qn); **to c. with oneself,** rentrer en soi-même; se recueillir (sur soi-même). **2.** *Ecc: U.S:* communier.

communicability [kəmju:nikə'biliti], **communicableness** [kə'mju:nikəblnis], *s.* communicabilité *f.*

communicable [kə'mju:nikəbl], *a.* communicable; *Med:* contagieux.

communicant [kə'mju:nikənt], *s.* **1.** informateur, -trice. **2.** *Ecc:* communiant, -ante; **to be a regular c.,** fréquenter les sacrements.

communicate [kə'mju:nikeit]. **1.** *v.tr.* **to s. (sth.) to sth., to s.o.,** communiquer (la chaleur, le mouvement, etc.) à qch.; communiquer, faire connaître, faire parvenir, (une nouvelle, etc.) à qn; donner (une maladie) à qn; **to c. a document to s.o.,** donner communication d'un document à qn. **2.** *v.i.* (*a*) **to c. with s.o.,** communiquer avec qn; entrer en communication, en relations, en rapport, avec qn; **to c. with the police,** se mettre en rapport avec la police; **to c. by letter,** communiquer par lettre; (*of two pers.*) s'écrire; correspondre; **he finds it difficult to c.,** il lui est difficile d'entrer en rapport avec les autres; (*b*) **rooms that c. with one another,** chambres qui communiquent entre elles, qui se commandent; **door that communicates with the garden,** porte *f* qui communique au, avec le, jardin, qui donne accès au jardin; **bell that communicates with the porter's lodge,** sonnette *f* qui sonne chez le concierge. **3.** *Ecc:* (*a*) *v.tr.* communier (qn); (*b*) *v.i.* communier; recevoir la communion.

communicating [kə'mju:nikeitiŋ], *a.* communicant; **c. rooms,** chambres *f* qui se commandent, qui communiquent entre elles; **c. doors,** portes *f* de communication; *Mil:* **c. trench,** boyau *m* de communication.

communication [kəmju:ni'keiʃ(ə)n], *s.* communication *f.* **1.** (*a*) **c. of a piece of news to s.o.,** communication d'une nouvelle à qn; (*b*) **to read a c.,** lire une communication; **please regard our c. as confidential,** veuillez bien considérer ces renseignements comme confidentiels; **you'll be getting another unpleasant c.,** *F:* vous allez encore recevoir du papier timbré. **2. to get into c. with s.o.,** communiquer avec qn; se mettre, entrer, en communication, en relations, avec qn; **to be in c. with . . .,** être en relation avec . . .; **to be in close c. with one another,** être en relations suivies; **to be in (secret) c. with the enemy,** avoir des intelligences avec l'ennemi; **to break off all c. with s.o.,** rompre tout commerce, toutes relations, avec qn. **3.** (*a*) voie *f* d'accès; **line of c.,** voie d'intercommunication, *Mil:* ligne *f* de communication; **means of c.,** moyens *m* (i) de communication, (ii) de transport; **rail communications,** liaisons ferroviaires; *Mil:* **communications zone,** zone *f* de communications; *Rail:* **c. cord,** corde *f* de signal d'alarme; corde de secours; sonnette *f* d'alarme; *Mil:* **c. lines,** lignes *f* de communication; (*b*) *Mil:* transmissions *f,* liaison(s) *f*; **c. facilities,** réseau *m* de transmissions; **signal communications,** *U.S:* **communications,** les transmissions; **wire c.,** liaison, transmission, par fil; **radio c.,** liaison, transmission, par radio; **air-ground communications,** liaisons, transmissions, aéro-terrestres; **point-to-point c.,** liaison, transmission, poste à poste; **main artery, line, axis, of (signal) communications,** axe *m* des transmissions; (*c*) *Med:* **(abnormal) interventricular, interauricular, c.,** communication inter-ventriculaire, inter-auriculaire.

communicative [kə'mju:nikətiv], *a.* **1.** communicatif; expansif. **2.** *A:* contagieux.

communicatively [kə'mju:nikətivli], *adv.* **to be c. disposed,** être disposé à l'expansion; être d'humeur bavarde, expansive.

communicativeness [kə'mju:nikətivnis], *s.* caractère communicatif, expansif; humeur bavarde.

communicator [kə'mju:nikeitər], *s.* **1.** (*pers.*) débiteur, -euse (de nouvelles). **2.** *Mec.E:* communicateur *m* (de mouvement, etc.); *Tg:* communicateur.

communion [kə'mju:njən], *s.* **1.** *usu. Lit:* communication *f,* commerce *m,* relations *fpl,* rapports *mpl* (**with s.o.,** avec qn); **to hold c. with s.o.,** être en communion d'esprit avec qn; **self c.,** recueillement *m.* **2.** union *f* dans une même foi; communion *f*; **to belong to the same c.,** appartenir à la même communion; **the c. of saints,** la communion des saints. **3.** *Ecc:* **the (Holy) C.,** la sainte communion, la (Sainte) Cène; **the c. service,** la célébration de la communion; **c. wine,** (i) (*in Protestant Ch.*) vin *m* de communion; (ii) *R.C.Ch:* vin de messe; **c. cloth,** nappe *f* de communion; **c. cup,** calice *m*; **the c. table,** la Sainte Table; **to administer Holy C. to s.o.,** administrer la sainte communion à qn; donner la communion à qn; communier qn; **to take (Holy) C.,** communier; recevoir la (sainte) communion; s'approcher de la Sainte Table; **to make one's Easter C.,** faire sa communion pascale; *F:* faire ses pâques.

communiqué [kə'mju:nikei], *s.* communiqué *m*; **joint c.,** communiqué publié conjointement.

communism ['kɔmjunizm], *s.* communisme *m.*

communist ['kɔmjunist]. **1.** *a.* & *s.* communiste (*mf*). **2.** *Fr.Hist:* *F:* (1871) communard *m.*

communistic [kɔmju'nistik], *a.* communiste; communisant; **a trade union with c. tendencies,** un syndicat ouvrier à tendances communisantes.

community [kə'mju:niti], *s.* **1.** communauté *f* (de biens, d'intérêts, etc.); communité *f* (de biens); solidarité *f* (d'intérêts). **2.** communauté, identité *f* (de goûts, etc.). **3.** *Ecc:* communauté (religieuse); ordre *m* (monastique). **4.** (*a*) **the c.,** l'État *m,* le public; **harmful to the c.,** nuisible au public, à la communauté; **all classes of the c.,** toutes les classes de la société; (*b*) société (de personnes); collectivité *f*; **the European c.,** la communauté européenne; **the Jewish c.,** la communauté juive; (*c*) **c. singing,** chansons populaires reprises en chœur par l'assistance; (*d*) **c. centre,** centre social; *U.S:* **c. chest,** fonds *m* de secours.

communization ['kɔmjunaizeiʃ(ə)n], *s.* communisation *f.*

communize ['kɔmjuna:iz], *v.tr.* **1.** répartir (les biens) en commun. **2.** *Pol:* communiser.

commutability [kəmju:tə'biliti], *s.* **1.** permutabilité *f.* **2.** *Jur:* commuabilité *f* (d'une peine).

commutable [kə'mju:təbl], *a.* **1.** permutable; interchangeable. **2.** *Jur:* (peine *f*) commuable; **offences not c. by fine,** délits *m* dont la peine ne peut être commuée en amende.

commutate ['kɔmjuteit], *v.tr. El:* commuter, permuter (le courant).

commutating ['kɔmjuteitiŋ], *s.* commutation *f*; **c.-machine,** commutatrice *f*; machine *f* à courant redressé.

commutation [kɔmju'teiʃ(ə)n], *s.* **1.** (*a*) commutation *f*; *Jur:* **c. of sentence,** commutation de peine; (*b*) *Jur:* **c. of an easement, of a right of user,** rachat *m* d'une servitude; *Hist:* **the C. Act** (1836), loi *f* autorisant la commutation en rente annuelle des dîmes payées en nature. **2.** *Rail: U.S:* **c. ticket,** carte *f* d'abonnement; **c. passenger,** abonné, -ée. **3.** *Mil:* indemnité (compensatrice); **c. of heat and light,** indemnité de chauffage et d'éclairage; **c. value,** équivalent *m* de la ration de vivres en deniers; indemnité (compensatrice) de repas.

commutative [kə'mjutətiv, 'kɔmjuteitiv], *a.* commutatif; *esp. Jur:* **c. contract,** contrat commutatif.

commutator ['kɔmjuteitər], *s. El:* commutateur *m*; collecteur *m*; **c. ring,** bague *f* de collecteur; **c. rectifier, rectifying c.,** permutatrice *f*; **c. bar,** lame *f,* touche *f,* segment *m,* de collecteur.

commute [kə'mju:t], *v.tr.* **1.** permuter, interchanger (des emplois). **2.** (*a*) échanger (**for, into,** pour, contre); racheter (une servitude); **to c. an annuity into, for, a lump sum,** racheter une rente par un versement global; (*b*) *Jur:* **to c. a penalty into, for, another,** commuer une peine en une autre; (*c*) *U.S: Rail:* (i) **to c. a fare,** prendre un abonnement; (ii) *v.i. U.S: Rail:* s'abonner; prendre un abonnement; (iii) *v.i.* faire un long trajet journalier entre sa résidence et son bureau; faire la navette. **3.** *El:* = COMMUTATE.

commuter [kə'mju:tər], *s. Rail:* abonné, -ée; personne *f* qui fait un long trajet journalier entre sa résidence et son lieu de travail; **c. belt,** zone *f* de villes dortoirs.

commuterdom [kə'mju:tədəm], *s.* **commuterland** [kə'mju:təlænd], *s.* grande banlieue.

commuting [kə'mju:tiŋ], *s.* (action *f* de faire un) long trajet journalier par le chemin de fer etc. entre la résidence et le lieu de travail; *Pol.Ec:* migrations alternantes; migration pendulaire.

commy ['kɔmi], *s. F:* communiste *mf.*

Como ['koumou], *Pr.n. Geog:* Côme; **Lake C.,** le lac de Côme.

Comoro ['kɔmərou], *Pr.n. Geog:* **the C. Islands,** les (îles) Comores *f.*

comose ['koumous], *a.* = COMATE.

compact[1] ['kɔmpækt], *s.* convention *f,* accord *m,* pacte *m,* contrat *m*; **the social c.,** le contrat social; **by general c.,** d'un commun accord; *Hist:* **the Family C.,** le Pacte de famille (entre les Bourbons).

compact[2] [kəm'pækt], *a.* **1.** compact; de faible encombrement; serré, resserré, tassé; (terrain) liant; (style) concis; **the machine is c. without being cramped,** bien que resserrés tous les organes (de la machine) sont accessibles; **his c. little figure,** sa petite personne trapue. **2.** *Lit:* formé, composé (**of,** de); **mind c. of formulas,** esprit bourré; pétri, de formules.

compact[3] ['kɔmpækt], *s.* **1.** *Toil:* (*a*) *A:* poudre compacte; fard compact; (*b*) poudrier *m* (de sac à main); boîte *f* à poudre. **2.** *Metall:* comprimé *m.* **3.** *Aut: U.S:* compacte *f.*

compact[4] [kəm'pækt], *v.tr.* **1.** (*a*) rendre (qch.) compact; unir (des éléments), tasser (de la neige); (*b*) *Civ.E:* compacter. **2. to be compacted of . . .,** être formé, composé, de . . .

compaction [kəm'pækʃ(ə)n], *s.* (*a*) *Geol:* tassement *m*; (*b*) *Civ.E:* compactage *m.*

compactly [kəm'pæktli], *adv.* d'une manière compacte.

compactness [kəm'pæktnəs], *s.* caractère compact, compacité *f* (d'une masse, etc.); concision *f* (de style).

compandor [kəm'pændər], *s. Cmptr:* compresseur-extenseur *m.*

companion[1] [kəm'pænjən], *s.* **1.** (*a*) compagnon *f*; compagne; **companions in distress,** compagnons d'infortune; **c. in arms,** compagnon d'armes; **his faithful c.,** son fidèle Achate; **he was my c. in all my travels,** il m'a accompagné dans tous mes voyages; **bad companions,** mauvaises fréquentations; (*b*) **(lady) c.,** dame *f,* demoiselle *f,* de compagnie; (*c*) compagnon (d'un ordre). **2.** (*a*) (*as title of book*) manuel *m,* vade-mecum *m;* (*b*) *A:* **lady's c.,** nécessaire *m* à ouvrage. **3.** pendant *m* (à un livre, un tableau, etc.); **this is a c. picture to the other,** ce tableau fait pendant à l'autre. **4.** *attrib.* **c. crops,** cultures associées.

companion[2], *A:* **1.** *v.tr.* tenir compagnie à (qn); accompagner (qn, qch.). **2.** *v.i.* **to c. with s.o.,** tenir compagnie à qn; fréquenter qn; **to c. with sth.,** aller de pair avec qch.

companion[3], *s. Nau:* **c. (hatch, head),** capot *m* (de descente, d'échelle); dôme *m.* **2. c. (ladder),** échelle *f* de commandement; (ii) échelle des cabines; **c. (way),** escalier *m* des cabines.

companionable [kəm'pænjənəbl], *a.* sociable; d'une société agréable.

companionableness [kəm'pænjənəblnis], *s.* sociabilité *f.*

companionably [kəm'pænjənəbli], *adv.* sociablement; amicalement.

companionate [kəm'pænjəneit], *a. U.S:* **c. marriage,** union *f* libre (et stérile).

companionship [kəm'pænjənʃip], *s.* **1.** *(a)* compagnie *f*; **I enjoyed his c. during the whole journey,** je l'ai eu comme compagnon pendant tout le voyage; **we lived in close c.,** nous vivions entre nous; **c. of one's fellows,** société *f* de ses semblables; *(b)* camaraderie *f.* **2.** *Typ:* commandite *f*; équipe *f* travaillant en commandite. **3.** dignité *f* de compagnon (d'un ordre).

company[1] ['kʌmpəni], *s.* **1.** *(a)* *(companionship)* compagnie *f*; **to be in s.o.'s c.,** être en compagnie de qn; **to keep s.o. c.,** tenir compagnie à qn; *P: O:* **to keep c. with s.o.,** courtiser une jeune fille; être courtisée par un jeune homme; sortir avec un jeune homme, une jeune fille; **to go with s.o. for (the sake of) c.,** accompagner qn pour avoir le plaisir de sa société, pour ne pas rester seul; **we enjoy each other's c.,** nous aimons être ensemble; **he's very good c.,** c'est un compagnon agréable; **he's poor c.,** il est plutôt ennuyeux; **I like my own c.,** j'aime à être seul; **if I'm wrong I'm in good c.,** si je me trompe je ne suis pas le seul; *Prov:* **two's c., three's a crowd, three's none,** deux s'amusent, trois s'embêtent; **to part c. with s.o.,** (i) se séparer de qn; (ii) ne plus être d'accord avec qn; **Mrs X requests the pleasure of your c. at dinner,** Mme X vous prie de lui faire le plaisir de venir dîner; *(b)* *(associates, associations)* compagnie, société *f*; **a man is known by the c. he keeps,** on connaît un homme par ses fréquentations; dis-moi qui tu hantes, je te dirai qui tu es; **we don't keep the same c.,** nous ne fréquentons pas le même milieu; **to avoid bad c.,** éviter les mauvaises fréquentations; **he is no fit c. for you,** ce n'est pas une fréquentation pour vous; sa société n'est pas ce qu'il vous faut. **2.** *(a)* *(group of people, etc.)* assemblée *f*, compagnie; bande *f* (de promeneurs, etc.); troupe *f* (de lions); **a large c.,** une compagnie, une société, nombreuse; **present c. excepted,** les présents exceptés; *(b)* *(guests)* monde *m*; invités *m pl*; **we have c. to dinner today,** nous avons du monde, des invités, à dîner aujourd'hui; **to put on one's c. manners,** soigner sa tenue, son langage; s'observer; **it isn't done in c.,** cela ne se fait pas en compagnie, devant le monde. **3.** *Com: Ind:* *(a)* compagnie; société; entreprise *f*; **joint stock c.,** société par actions; **limited c.,** société avec limitation de la responsabilité des associés au capital; **private c.** = société à responsabilité limitée; **public c.** = société anonyme; **affiliated c.,** filiale *f*; **assurance c.,** compagnie d'assurances; **real estate c.,** société immobilière; **shipping c.,** compagnie de navigation; **companies' act,** loi *f* sur les sociétés; **(the firm of) Thomas and Company** *(usu. & Co.),* (la maison) Thomas et Compagnie (et Cie.); **to form, incorporate, a c.,** constituer une société; **to liquidate, wind up, a c.,** liquider une société; **the senior staff have c. cars,** la maison fournit des voitures aux cadres; **a (good) c. man,** homme qui se dévoue aux intérêts de l'entreprise; *NAm:* **c. union,** syndicat *m* dont les membres appartiennent à une seule entreprise; *NAm:* **c. town,** agglomération construite pour les employés d'une entreprise; *(b)* corporation *f* de marchands; **the City Companies,** les corporations de la Cité de Londres. **4.** *(a)* *Th:* troupe *f*; **touring c.,** troupe ambulante, en tournée; *(b)* *Nau:* **the ship's c.,** l'équipage *m* (au complet, y compris les officiers); tous les hommes du bord; *(c)* *Scout:* compagnie (de guides). **5.** *Mil:* compagnie; **separate c.,** compagnie autonome; **skeleton c.,** compagnie cadre; **rifle c.,** compagnie de fusiliers, de voltigeurs; **support c.,** *U.S:* **heavy weapons c.,** compagnie d'accompagnement; **machine gun c.,** compagnie de mitrailleuses; **tank c.,** escadron *m* de chars; **field c.,** *U.S:* **combat engineer c.,** compagnie du génie divisionnaire, d'armée; compagnie du génie de combat; **headquarters c.,** compagnie de commandement et des services; **c. headquarters,** (i) section *f* de commandement (de la compagnie); (ii) poste *m* de commandement de compagnie; **c. officer,** officier *m* subalterne, officier de compagnie; **to get one's c.,** être promu commandant; recevoir le commandement d'une compagnie.

company[2], *v.i. A:* **to c. with s.o.,** (i) fréquenter qn; (ii) vivre, voyager, etc., en compagnie de qn.

comparability [kɔmpərə'biliti], *s.* comparabilité *f.*

comparable ['kɔmpərəbl], *a.* comparable **(with, to,** avec, à); assimilable **(to,** à).

comparably ['kɔmpərəbli], *adv.* comparablement.

comparatist [kəm'pærətist], *s.* comparatiste *mf.*

comparative [kəm'pærətiv], *a.* **1.** *(a)* comparatif; **c. method of investigation,** étude *f* par la méthode comparative; *Gram:* **c. adverb,** adverbe comparatif; **c. degree,** le comparatif; *s.* **adjective in the c.,** adjectif au comparatif; *(b)* **c. grammar, philology,** la grammaire, la philologie, comparée. **2.** relatif; **c. advantages,** avantages relatifs, comparatifs, comparés; **c. cost,** coût comparatif, relatif; **c. economics,** économie comparée; **c. statistics,** statistique comparative; **this would be c. wealth,** ce serait l'aisance relative; **he's a c. stranger to me,** je ne le connais guère.

comparatively [kəm'pærətivli], *adv.* **1.** comparativement, par comparaison **(to,** à). **2.** relativement; **the next examination is c. easy,** l'examen *m* qui suit est relativement facile.

comparativist [kəm'pærətivist], *s. Ling:* comparatiste *mf.*

comparator ['kɔmpəreitər], *s. Meas:* comparateur *m*; **dial c.,** comparateur à cadran; *Cmptr:* **digital c.,** comparateur numérique; **tape c.,** comparateur de bandes (perforées).

compare[1] [kəm'pɛər], *s. Lit:* **beyond, past, c.,** sans comparaison; hors de comparaison; hors de pair; incomparable; **beauty without c.,** beauté sans pareille.

compare[2]. **1.** *v.tr.* comparer, rapprocher (des faits, des idées); confronter (des résultats, etc.); **to c. sth. to, with, sth.,** comparer qch. à, avec, qch.; assimiler qch. à qch.; **to c. s.o. with s.o.,** mettre qn en parallèle avec qn; **c. the two things!** faites la comparaison! **not to be compared to . . .,** pas comparable à . . ., qui ne peut être comparé à . . .; **they are not to be compared,** on ne saurait les comparer; **magnificent work, nothing to be compared with it,** œuvre *f* magnifique, il n'y a rien à mettre auprès; **compared with, to . . .,** en comparaison de . . ., à côté de . . ., auprès de . . .; **he is short compared with his brother,** il est de petite taille si on le compare à son frère; **he is wealthy compared with the rest of the inhabitants,** il est riche par rapport au reste des habitants; **my troubles are small compared with yours,** mes maux sont petits à côté des vôtres; **it is little compared with what I had hoped for,** c'est peu de chose auprès de ce que j'espérais; **to c. a copy with the original,** comparer, confronter, une copie avec l'original; **to c. two documents,** collationner, conférer, deux documents; *Com:* **to c. the books,** collationner les livres, les écritures; **to c. notes,** échanger ses impressions; échanger des idées, des opinions, avec qn; *(b)* *Gram:* **to c. an adjective, an adverb,** former les degrés de comparaison d'un adjectif, d'un adverbe. **2.** *v.i.* être comparable **(with,** à); **he can't c. with you,** il ne vous est pas comparable; **he can c. with the best,** il peut rivaliser, s'aligner, avec les meilleurs; **to c. favourably with sth.,** ne le céder en rien à qch.; **his plays cannot c. with those of his father,** ses pièces ne supportent pas la comparaison avec celles de son père.

comparing [kəm'pɛəriŋ], *s.* comparaison *f* (de deux personnes, de deux choses); rapprochement *m* (de faits); confrontation *f* (de résultats, de documents); collationnement *m* (de documents); *Cmptr:* **c. control change,** rupture *f* de contrôle par comparaison (de zones).

comparison [kəm'pæris(ə)n], *s.* comparaison *f*; *(of documents, etc.)* collation *f*, conférence *f*, confrontation *f*; **to make, draw, a c. between sth. and sth.,** faire la comparaison de qch. avec qch.; **in, by, c.,** en comparaison; **in c. with . . .,** en comparaison de . . ., par rapport à . . ., à côté de . . ., auprès de . . .; **to bear, stand, c. with . . .,** soutenir, supporter, la comparaison avec . . .; **without c.; out of, beyond, all c.,** sans comparaison; **comparisons are odious,** comparaison n'est pas raison; *Gram:* **degrees of c.,** degrés *m* de comparaison.

compart [kəm'pɑ:t], *v.tr.* diviser (une surface, etc.) en compartiments; compartimenter.

compartment[1] [kəm'pɑ:tmənt], *s.* **1.** *(a)* compartiment *m*; **watertight c.,** compartiment étanche; **each department is kept in a watertight c.,** il y a des cloisons étanches entre les différents services; *N.Arch:* **cellular c.,** tranche *f* cellulaire; *Rail:* **smoking c.,** compartiment fumeurs; **sleeping c.,** compartiment couchette; *Av:* **crew c.,** habitacle *m*; **flight c.,** poste *m* de pilotage; *Aut:* **glove c.,** boîte *f* à gants, vide-poches *m inv*; *Trans:* **luggage c.,** soute *f* à bagages; *Arms:* **ammunition c.,** compartiment des munitions; **ten-round c.,** compartiment pour dix cartouches; *Mil:* *(of tank)* **fighting c.,** poste de tir; *(b)* *For:* parcelle *f* (de forêt); **sub c.,** sous-parcelle *f.* **2.** case *f* (d'un tiroir, etc.). **3.** *Parl:* section *f* (d'un projet de loi); **to closure a bill by compartments,** appliquer la clôture à un projet de loi par sections successives.

compartment[2], *v.tr.* compartimenter.

compartmental [kɔmpɑ:t'mentl], *a.* compartimenté.

compartmentalization [kɔmpɑ:t'mentəlai'zeiʃ(ə)n], *s.* compartimentage *m* rigide.

compartmentalize [kɔmpɑ:t'mentəlaiz], *v.tr.* compartimenter.

compartmentation [kɔmpɑ:tmen'teiʃ(ə)n], *s.* *(a)* *N.Arch:* compartimentage *m*; *Const:* cloisonnement *m*; *(b)* *Adm: etc:* compartimentage.

compass[1] ['kʌmpəs], *s.* **1. (a pair of) compasses,** un compas; **proportional compasses,** compas à, de, réduction; **elliptic compasses,** compas d'ellipse; compas elliptique; **c. point,** pointe *f* de compas; **compasses with pencil point,** compas porte-crayon; **beam c.,** compas à trusquin, à verge (de dessinateur); **bow c.,** compas à balustre; **draught c.,** compas à pointes échangeantes; **hair c.,** compas à cheveu, de précision; **pen c.,** compas à tire-ligne; **scribing c.,** rouanne *f.* **2.** *(a)* limite(s) *f(pl)*, borne(s) *f(pl)* (d'un endroit); *(b)* *A:* **c. of a building,** pourtour *m* d'un bâtiment; **to be twenty kilometres in c.,** avoir vingt kilomètres de tour; *(c)* *Const:* **c. brick,** brique *f* circulaire; **c. timber,** bois *m* courbe; bois courbant; **c. window,** fenêtre *f* en saillie ronde; *Carp:* **c. plane,** rabot cintré, à semelle cintrée; **c. saw,** scie *f* à guichet. **3.** *(a)* étendue *f* (d'un endroit, du savoir); espace *m* (de temps); portée *f* (de l'esprit); étendue, portée (de la voix); **within the c. of a day,** dans l'espace d'un jour; **knowledge within, beyond, my c.,** connaissances *f* à la portée de mon esprit, à ma portée, au-dessus de ma portée; **beyond the c. of the human mind,** que l'esprit humain ne saurait embrasser; **in small c.,** sous un volume restreint; sur une petite échelle; dans des limites étroites; *(b)* *Mus:* étendue, diapason *m*, registre *m* (de la voix); clavier *m* (de la clarinette, etc.). **4.** *Nau: Surv: etc:* *(with moving needle)* boussole *f*; *(with moving card)* compas; **pocket c., marching c.,** boussole de poche; *(in hunter case)* boussole savonnette; **mariner's c.,** compas (de mer); **steering c.,** compas de route; **standard c.,** compas étalon; **binnacle c.,** compas d'habitacle; **fluid c., liquid c.,** compas liquide; **azimuth c.,** compas de relèvement; **c. error,** erreur *f* du compas, déviation *f*; **the c. is disturbed,** le compas s'affole; **projector, reflector, c.,** compas à répétition optique; **c. repeater,** compas répétiteur; **the points of the c.,** les aires *f* de vent; quart *m* du vent, **c. card,** rose *f* des vents; *Surv:* **trough c., surveyor's c.,** déclinateur *m*; **transit c.,** théodolite *m* à boussole; **to set (the plane table) by the c.,** décliner la planchette; *Nau:* **to take a c. bearing,** prendre un relèvement au compas; **c. variation,** déclinaison magnétique locale.

compass[2], *v.tr.* **1.** *A:* faire le tour de (qch.). **2.** *Lit:* **to c. sth. (about, round) with sth.,** entourer, environner, qch. de qch.; **compassed about by, with, enemies,** entouré d'ennemis. **3.** embrasser (par l'esprit); comprendre; saisir. **4.** *Jur:* comploter (la mort, la ruine, de qn). **5.** *Lit:* atteindre (son but); en venir à (ses fins); accomplir (une tâche); **to resort to every stratagem in order to c. one's ends,** recourir à tous les stratagèmes pour arriver à ses fins, à son but. **6.** *Carp: N.Arch:* courber, cintrer (une membrure, etc.).

compassion [kəm'pæʃ(ə)n], *s.* compassion *f*; **to have c. on s.o.,** avoir compassion de qn; avoir pitié de qn; avoir de la compassion pour qn; s'apitoyer sur le sort de qn; **to arouse c.,** faire pitié; exciter la compassion; **to do sth. out of c. for s.o.,** faire qch. par compassion pour qn.

compassionate[1] [kəm'pæʃənət], *a.* compatissant **(to, towards,** à, pour); porté à l'apitoiement; (regard) attendri; **on c. grounds,** pour des raisons d'humanité; *Mil: Adm:* **c. leave,** permission exceptionnelle (pour raisons familiales).

compassionate[2], *v.tr. A:* compatir (aux malheurs de qn); témoigner de la commisération à (qn).

compassionately [kəm'pæʃənətli], *adv.* avec compassion.

compatibility [kəmpætə'biliti], *s.* compatibilité *f*; *Cmptr: etc:* **equipment c.,** compatibilité entre équipements.

compatible [kəm'pætəbl], *a.* compatible **(with,** avec); **pleasure c. with work,** plaisir *m* compatible avec le travail; **c. ideas,** idées compatibles; **heat is c. with moisture,** la chaleur peut aller avec l'humidité; *Cmptr:* **computer c.,** compatible avec plusieurs (types de) calculateurs.

compatibly [kəm'pætibli], *adv.* d'une manière compatible **(with,** avec).

compatriot [kəm'pætriət, -'pei-], *s.* compatriote *mf.*
compear [kəm'piər], *v.i. Jur: Scot:* comparaître.
compearance [kəm'piərəns], *s. Jur: Scot:* comparution *f.*
compeer ['kɔmpiər], *s. A: & Lit:* égal *m,* pair *m.*
compel [kəm'pel], *v.tr.* **(compelled)** contraindre, astreindre, forcer, obliger; **to c. s.o. to do sth.,** contraindre, forcer, obliger, qn à, *occ.* de, faire qch.; violenter qn pour lui faire faire qch.; mettre qn dans la nécessité de faire qch.; **to be compelled to do sth.,** être contraint, être astreint, se voir forcé, obligé, dans l'obligation, de faire qch.; **to c. admiration, respect, from s.o.,** forcer, commander, l'admiration, le respect, de qn; se faire admirer, respecter, de qn; **he compels respect,** il impose le respect; **he compels applause from his very opponents,** ses adversaires mêmes sont forcés d'applaudir; **the election has compelled the parties to come together,** les élections *f* ont imposé l'union des partis.
compellable [kəm'peləbl], *a.* contraignable **(to sth., to do sth.,** à qch., à faire qch.).
compelling [kəm'peliŋ], *a.* **c. force,** force compulsive; **c. curiosity,** curiosité *f* irrésistible; **c. orator, speaker,** orateur *m* qui attire, qui convainc, son auditoire.
compendious [kəm'pendiəs], *a. Lit:* abrégé, succinct, concis, sommaire; *A:* compendieux.
compendiousness [kəm'pendiəsnis], *s. Lit:* **1.** forme succincte; concision *f.* **2.** peu *m* d'encombrement (d'une substance).
compendium, *pl.* **-ums** [kəm'pendiəm(z)], *s.* **1.** abrégé *m,* précis *m,* compendium *m* (d'une science, etc.); **c. of laws,** recueil *m* des lois; **he wrote a c. of science,** il a écrit un abrégé de toutes les sciences. **2.** *Com:* (*a*) *O:* pochette *f* (de papeterie); (*b*) *A:* **c. of games,** malle *f* de jeux.
compensable [kəm'pensəbl], *a.* compensable; indemnisable; (*of loss*) payable à titre de dédommagement; **not c.,** incompensable.
compensate ['kɔmpenseit]. **1.** *v.tr.* (*a*) **to c. s.o. for sth.,** dédommager, indemniser, qn de qch.; **to c. a workman for injuries,** dédommager un ouvrier pour blessures; (*b*) rémunérer (qn); (*c*) *Mec:* compenser (un pendule, etc.); **to c. torque reaction,** neutraliser l'effort de torsion; **these errors c. one another,** ces erreurs *f* se compensent. **2.** *v.i.* **to c. for sth.,** (i) remplacer, racheter, qch.; (ii) compenser qch.; **skill may c. for lack of strength,** l'adresse *f* peut compenser, racheter, le manque de force; **to c. for errors of workmanship,** corriger, racheter, les erreurs d'exécution; *Mec.E:* **to c. for wear,** compenser, rattraper, rappeler, l'usure.
compensated ['kɔmpenseitid], *a.* compensé; *El: Elcs: etc:* **c. loop (of direction finder),** cadre compensé (de radiogoniomètre); **c. lead,** connexion compensée; **c.-winding motor,** moteur (électrique) compensé; *Av:* **c. propeller,** hélice compensée.
compensating ['kɔmpenseitiŋ], *a.* compensateur, -trice; (*a*) **c. payment,** règlement *m* en compensation; **c. errors,** erreurs *f* qui se compensent; **c. qualities,** qualités *f* qui rachètent les défauts; *Pol.Ec:* **c. variation in income,** variation compensatrice de revenu; (*b*) *Mec.E: etc:* **c. valve,** soupape *f* de compensation; **c. spring,** ressort compensateur; **c. coupling,** manchon *m* élastique; **c. arm,** bras *m* de rappel; **c. gear,** engrenage différentiel; *El: etc:* **c. magnet,** aimant correcteur, de correction; **c. winding,** enroulement compensateur, de compensation; **c. coil,** bobine compensatrice, de compensation; **c. network,** circuit compensateur.
compensation [kɔmpen'seiʃ(ə)n], *s.* **1.** (*a*) compensation *f*; (*for loss, injury*) dédommagement *m*; (*for damage*) indemnité *f,* indemnisation *f*; *Jur:* réparation civile; composition *f*; *Post:* **c. fee parcel** = paquet recommandé; **pecuniary c.,** réparation pécuniaire; rétribution *f*; **war damage c.,** dommages *m pl* de guerre; **to pay s.o. c. in cash,** indemniser qn en argent; **Workmen's C. Act,** loi *f* sur les accidents du travail; **c. for industrial diseases,** indemnité pour maladies industrielles; **by way of c., in c.,** en compensation, en dédommagement (**for,** de); **by way of c. I'll take you to the theatre,** pour compenser je vous emmènerai au théâtre; **in c.,** (i) à titre de compensation; (ii) en revanche; **if the flat is small, in c. we have a magnificent view,** si l'appartement est petit, en compensation nous avons une vue magnifique; (*b*) *Mec.E: etc:* **c. for wear,** compensation, rattrapage *m,* de l'usure; système *m* rattrape-jeu; **c. bar,** palonnier *m*; **c. pipe,** tube *m* de compensation; **temperature c.,** compensation des températures; *Ph:* **c. pendulum,** pendule compensé; balancier compensateur; *Opt:* **c. screen, filter,** écran, filtre, compensateur. **2.** *NAm:* rémunération *f* (des salariés).
compensative [kəm'pensətiv], *a.* compensateur, -trice; compensatif; compensant.
compensator ['kɔmpenseitər], *s. El: Ph:* compensateur *m*; *Aut:* palonnier *m* (du frein); *I.C.E:* **c. jet,** compensateur (du carburateur); *El:* **voltage c.,** compensateur de voltage; *Elcs:* **bass c.,** circuit correcteur de basses fréquences; compensateur des basses fréquences; *Cmptr:* **level c.,** compensateur des niveaux.
compensatory [kɔmpen'seit(ə)ri], *a.* compensatoire; compensateur, -trice; compensatif; compensant; **c. measures,** mesures *f* compensatoires; *Pol.Ec:* **c. official financing,** financement compensatoire officiel.
compère[1] ['kɔmpεər], *s. Th: T.V: etc:* animateur *m,* présentateur, -trice (d'un spectacle, d'un programme).
compère[2], *v.tr. Th: T.V: etc:* présenter, animer (un spectacle, un programme).
compete [kəm'pi:t], *v.i.* **1. to c. with s.o.,** faire concurrence à qn; concurrencer qn; aller, courir, sur les brisées de qn; *Com:* **we cannot c. successfully with . . .,** nous ne pouvons pas soutenir la concurrence de . . .; nous ne pouvons pas lutter contre . . .; **to c. with one another,** se faire concurrence. **2. to c. for a prize,** concourir pour un prix; **to c. with s.o. for a prize,** disputer un prix à qn; **I intend to c.,** j'ai l'intention de me mettre sur les rangs; **the cup will be competed for tomorrow,** la coupe se courra demain; **non competing,** hors concours. **3. to c. with s.o. in virtue, talent, grace,** le disputer en vertu, en talent, avec qn; rivaliser de grâce avec qn.
competence ['kɔmpitəns], *s.* **1.** suffisance *f* de moyens d'existence; **to have, enjoy, a c.,** avoir de quoi vivre; jouir d'une honnête aisance; avoir un revenu raisonnable; **he has a small c.,** c'est un petit rentier; **to have a bare c.,** avoir tout juste de quoi vivre. **2.** (*a*) **c. in a subject,** compétence *f* en un sujet; **c. for sth., to do sth.,** aptitude *f* à (faire) qch.; capacité *f* pour (faire) qch.; (*b*) *Geog:* **c. of a stream,** compétence (de prise en charge) d'un cours d'eau. **3.** attributions *fpl* (d'un fonctionnaire); *Jur:* compétence; **this lies within his c.,** cela rentre dans ses attributions; **to be within, beyond, the c. of a court,** être, ne pas être, de la compétence, du ressort, d'un tribunal; **to fall within the c. of. . .,** rentrer dans la compétence de . . .; **it lies beyond my c.,** cela dépasse ma compétence; c'est en dehors de mon pouvoir; **to disclaim c.,** se récuser.
competency ['kɔmpitənsi], *s.* = COMPETENCE.
competent ['kɔmpitənt], *a.* **1.** capable; **I am looking for a c. manager,** je cherche un gérant capable. **2.** (*a*) compétent **(in a matter,** en une matière); **c. to do sth.,** capable de faire qch.; compétent, qualifié, pour faire qch.; **I am not c. to speak on the matter,** je ne suis pas compétent dans la matière; (*b*) *Jur:* **c. to inherit,** habile à succéder. **3.** *Jur:* (tribunal) compétent. **4.** *A: & Lit:* **it is c. to him to accept or decline,** il lui est loisible d'accepter ou de refuser. **5. c. knowledge of English,** bonne connaissance de l'anglais.
competently ['kɔmpitəntli], *adv.* avec compétence; d'une manière capable.
competing [kəm'pi:tiŋ], *a.* concurrent; concurrentiel; **c. products,** produits concurrents; **c. firm,** entreprise concurrentielle.
competition [kɔmpi'tiʃ(ə)n], *s.* **1.** rivalité *f,* concurrence *f*; **to enter into c. with s.o.,** concurrencer, faire concurrence à, qn; **there was keen c. (for it),** il y avait un grand nombre de concurrents. **2.** concours *m*; épreuve *f*; meeting (sportif); compétition (sportive); **fishing c.,** concours de pêche; **chess c.,** tournoi *m* d'échecs; **c. for a prize,** concours pour un prix; **to win a prize in open c.,** remporter un prix au concours, de haute lutte; **the post will be filled by open c.,** l'emploi sera mis au concours; **not for c.,** hors concours; *Aut:* **endurance c.,** course *f* d'endurance; **open c.,** course ouverte. **3.** *Com: Pol.Ec:* concurrence; **free c.,** libre concurrence; **monopolistic c.,** concurrence monopolistique; **unfair c.,** concurrence déloyale; **price defying all c.,** prix défiant toute concurrence. **4.** *Biol:* concurrence.
competitive [kəm'petitiv], *a.* **1. c. spirit,** esprit *m* de concurrence, de rivalité; **c. power,** capacité *f* de concurrence. **2. c. examination,** concours *m*; **admitted by c. examination,** admis sur, par voie de, après, concours. **3.** *Com: Pol.Ec:* concurrentiel; concurrent; compétitif; **in c. conditions,** en conditions de concurrence; **c. price,** prix concurrentiel, compétitif; **c. products,** produits concurrents, compétitifs; **full c. costs,** coûts concurrentiels intégraux; **c. supply and demand,** l'offre et la demande concurrentielles; **c. bidding,** appel *m* d'offres; **c. bidding for new securities,** émission *f* d'actions nouvelles sur le marché.
competitively [kəm'petitivli], *adv.* **1.** en esprit de concurrence, de rivalité. **2. gained, obtained, c.,** obtenu au concours.
competitiveness [kəm'petitivnis], *s.* compétitivité *f*; concurrence *f* (d'un produit sur le marché).
competitor [kəm'petitər], *s.* (*a*) concurrent, -ente; rival, -ale, -aux, -ales; **my competitors in trade,** mes concurrents; **the competitors in the race,** les concurrents; (*b*) **the competitors for the prize,** les compétiteurs, -trices, pour le prix; **to be a c.,** être sur les rangs.
compilation [kɔmp(a)i'leiʃ(ə)n], *s.* **1.** rédaction *f* (d'un dictionnaire, etc.); confection *f* (d'un inventaire). **2.** compilation *f,* recueil *m.*
compile [kəm'pail], *v.tr.* rédiger, composer (un dictionnaire, un recueil); recueillir (des matériaux pour une œuvre); **to c. a catalogue,** dresser un catalogue; **compiled from . . .,** établi d'après . . ., extrait de . . ..
compiler [kəm'pailər], *s.* **1.** compilateur, -trice; rédacteur, -trice (d'un dictionnaire, etc.). **2.** *Cmptr:* compilateur; programme *m* de compilation.
compiling [kəm'pailiŋ], *s.* compilation *f*; *Cmptr:* **c. program(me), c. routine,** programme *m* de compilation; **c. computer,** calculateur *m* de compilation; **c. duration, phase,** durée *f,* phase *f,* de compilation.
complacence [kəm'pleis(ə)ns], **complacency** [kəm'pleisənsi], *s.* **1.** satisfaction *f,* contentement *m.* **2.** (*a*) **(self) c.,** contentement de soi-même; suffisance *f*; (*b*) **the elections have not given the government any grounds for complacency,** les élections n'ont pas permis au gouvernement de se reposer sur ses lauriers, de rester passif.
complacent [kəm'pleis(ə)nt], *a.* **1.** (*of pers.*) content de soi-même; suffisant; **c. air,** air suffisant, de suffisance; **c. optimism,** optimisme béat. **2.** = COMPLAISANT.
complacently [kəm'pleisəntli], *adv.* **1.** (*a*) avec contentement, avec satisfaction; (*b*) d'un air, d'un ton, suffisant; avec suffisance. **2.** = COMPLAISANTLY.
complain [kəm'plein], *v.i.* **1.** se plaindre **(of,** de); **to c. that. . .,** se plaindre que + *sub. or ind.*; **he complained that he was not paid punctually,** il se plaignait qu'on ne le payait pas exactement, qu'on ne le payât pas exactement; **he complains of the heat, of rheumatism,** il se plaint de la chaleur, de rhumatismes; **she complained of giddiness,** (i) elle se disait sujette à des étourdissements; (ii) elle se plaignit d'un étourdissement; **I have nothing to c. of,** je n'ai pas à me plaindre; je n'ai à me plaindre de rien; **what have you to c. of?** de quoi vous plaignez-vous? **that is what I am complaining about,** voilà ce dont je me plains, voilà de quoi je me plains. **2.** formuler une plainte; adresser une réclamation **(to,** à); porter plainte **(against s.o.,** contre qn); se plaindre **(to,** à); réclamer **(against sth.,** contre qch.); **what have you to c. of? what do you c. of?** sur quoi porte votre plainte? **3.** *Poet:* (*lament*) pousser des plaintes; se lamenter; geindre.
complainant [kəm'pleinənt], *s. Jur:* plaignant, -ante.
complainer [kəm'pleinər], *s.* **1.** (*a*) réclamant, -ante; réclameur, -euse; (*b*) *Jur:* = COMPLAINANT. **2.** mécontent, -ente; grondeur, -euse; *F:* ronchonneur, -euse.
complaint [kəm'pleint], *s.* **1.** *A: & Lit:* (*a*) plainte *f,* doléances *fpl*; **to make c.,** se plaindre, se lamenter; (*b*) *Lit.Hist:* complainte *f* (chanson populaire). **2.** (*a*) grief *m*; sujet *m* de plainte; **it is a general c.,** tout le monde s'en plaint; **the complaints by the employers of the scarcity of labour,** les plaintes formulées par les patrons sur la rareté de la main-d'œuvre; **I have no cause for c., no grounds for c.,** je n'ai aucun sujet de plainte, aucun motif de plainte; **he's full of complaints,** il est toujours à se plaindre; *F:* **any complaints?** tout va bien? **what's your c.?** de quoi vous plaignez-vous? (*b*) plainte, réclamation *f*; **to lodge, make, a c. against s.o.,** porter plainte, dresser une plainte, déposer, formuler, une plainte, contre qn; **to lodge a c. with s.o.,** réclamer auprès de qn; **to remove a cause of c.,** faire droit à une réclamation; *Adm: Com:* **complaints office,** service *m* des réclamations; (*c*) *Jur: U.S:* plainte en justice; instance *f* en justice. **3.** maladie *f*; mal *m,* affection *f*; **liver c.,** maladie de foie; affection du foie; **bowel c.,** affection intestinale; **childish complaints,** maladies de l'enfance.
complaisance [kəm'pleiz(ə)ns], *s.* complaisance *f,* obligeance *f*; *Pej:* facilité *f*; **to do sth. out of c.,** faire qch. par complaisance.
complaisant [kəm'pleiz(ə)nt], *a.* (*a*) complaisant, obligeant; (*b*) *Pej:* **c. husband,** mari complaisant.
complaisantly [kəm'pleizəntli], *adv.* complaisamment, avec complaisance.
complected [kəm'plektid], *a. Bot:* complectif.
complement[1] ['kɔmplimənt], *s.* **1.** (*a*) plein *m*; **ship that has taken in its c. of fuel.** navire *m* qui a fait son plein de combustibles; **when the bus had its full c. of passengers,** lorsque le car eut pris sa charge complète de voyageurs; (*b*) *Navy: etc:* effectif *m*; **full c.,** effectif complet; **to have its full c.,** être au grand complet; (*of ship*) avoir son effectif au complet; **ship with a full c. of officers and men,** navire au complet en officiers et en

hommes; (*c*) personnel *m*; **engine-room c.,** personnel des machines. **2.** (*a*) complément *m* (d'un verbe, d'un angle, d'un logarithme, etc.); *Gram:* attribut *m*; (*b*) *Bio-Ch:* complément; **c. deviation, deviation of the c.,** déviation *f* du complément (d'un sérum); (*c*) *Cmptr:* **nines c., c. on nine,** complément à neuf; **diminished radix c., radix-minus-one c.,** complément à base diminuée (de un).

complement[2] ['kɔmpliment], *v.tr.* compléter; être, faire, le complément de (qch.).

complementary [kɔmpli'ment(ə)ri], *a.* (angle *m*, etc.) complémentaire; **the two books are c. to one another,** les deux volumes se complètent (l'un l'autre); *Cmptr:* **c. operation, operator,** opération *f*, opérateur *m*, complémentaire.

complete[1] [kəm'pli:t], *a.* **1.** (*a*) complet, entier, total; **c. success,** succès complet, franc succès; **c. circuit,** circuit total; **to have c. charge of the business,** avoir l'entière direction de la maison; **two opinions at c. variance with one another,** deux opinions *f* en contradiction absolue; **c. rest,** repos complet; **c. surprise,** surprise complète, absolue; **c. knowledge,** connaissance intégrale; **is the pack c.?** le jeu est-il complet? **c. with,** avec, comprenant; *Com:* **c. with battery,** livré avec batterie; **he arrived, c. with all his family,** il est arrivé accompagné de toute sa famille; **my happiness is c.,** rien ne manque à mon bonheur; mon bonheur est au comble; **the staff is c.,** le personnel est au complet; **give the sentence c.,** donnez la phrase en entier; **to give a c. account,** donner tout le détail; *Cmptr:* **c. carry,** report total; **c. instruction,** instruction complète; **c. operation,** opération complète; (*b*) terminé; **my report is not yet c.,** mon rapport n'est pas encore achevé. **2.** parfait, achevé, accompli; **the c. angler,** le pêcheur accompli; le parfait pêcheur; **a c. civil servant,** un fonctionnaire parfait; un vrai fonctionnaire; **a c. scoundrel,** un coquin accompli, un vrai coquin; **c. (and utter) failure,** échec total; **the operation has been a c. success,** l'opération *f* a pleinement réussi.

complete[2], *v.tr.* **1.** compléter, parachever (qch.); parfaire, achever, terminer (un travail, etc.); accomplir, mener à bien (une tâche); accomplir (son apprentissage); **to c. the sense,** compléter le sens; **to c. payment,** parfaire le paiement; solder l'achat; **to c. s.o.'s sufferings,** mettre le comble aux maux de qn; **to c. the misfortune,** pour comble de malheur. **2.** compléter (une collection, un nombre); rapparier (une paire); rapparciller (un service à thé); **to c. a battalion, a crew,** compléter un bataillon, un équipage; *Com:* **to c. an order,** compléter une commande. **3. to c. a form, a questionnaire,** remplir une formule, un questionnaire.

completely [kəm'pli:tli], *adv.* complètement, totalement, absolument; **two c. opposite opinions,** deux opinions en contradiction totale.

completeness [kəm'pli:tnis], *s.* état complet; perfection *f*; plénitude *f* (d'une victoire, d'un succès).

completing [kəm'pli:tiŋ], *s.* achèvement *m*, parachèvement *m*.

completion [kəm'pli:ʃ(ə)n], *s.* **1.** achèvement *m*, parachèvement *m* (d'un ouvrage); complètement *m* (d'une collection); *Petr:* complétion *f*; *Mch:* **c. of the power stroke,** fin *f* de la course de détente; **in process of c.,** en (cours d')achèvement; **near c.,** près d'être achevé; **to reach c.,** s'achever; **date of c. of a mandate,** terme *m* d'un mandat; **occupation (of property) on c. (of contract),** prise *f* de possession dès la signature du contrat. **2.** *Lit:* accomplissement *m* (d'un vœu, d'une prophétie); pleine réalisation (d'un désir, etc.).

completive [kəm'pli:tiv], *a.* complétif.

complex ['kɔmpleks]. **1.** *a.* complexe; *Gram:* **c. sentence,** phrase *f* complexe; *Mth:* **c. number, quantity (involving an imaginary),** quantité *f* complexe. **2.** *s.* (*a*) tout (formé de parties); **industrial c.,** complexe industriel; (*b*) *Ch:* complexe; (*c*) *Psy:* complexe; **the Œdipus c.,** le complexe d'Œdipe; **inferiority c.,** complexe d'infériorité; (*d*) *F:* **to have a c. about sth.,** avoir des préjugés contre qch.

complexification [kəmpleksifi'keiʃ(ə)n], *s.* complexification *f*.

complexify [kəm'pleksifai], *v.tr.* & *i.* (se) complexifier.

complexion [kəm'plekʃ(ə)n], *s.* **1.** teint *m*; **to have a fine c.,** avoir un joli teint, de belles couleurs; *Com:* **c. cream,** crème *f* de beauté. **2.** nature *f*, caractère *m* (de qch.); **that puts a new, a different, c. on it,** voilà qui change la thèse, qui complique la situation; **the matter has taken on a serious c.,** l'affaire *f* a pris un caractère grave.

complexity [kəm'pleksiti], *s.* complexité *f*; **question of the greatest c.,** question très compliquée.

complexly ['kɔmpleksli], *adv.* d'une manière complexe, compliquée.

complexus [kəm'pleksəs], *s. Anat:* complexus *m*.

compliance [kəm'plaiəns], *s.* **1.** (*a*) action *f* de conformer (**with,** à); acquiescement *m* (**with,** à); **in c. with your wishes,** conformément à vos désirs; **to refuse c. with an order,** refuser d'obéir à un ordre; (*b*) *Pej:* soumission (abjecte). **2.** *Elcs: etc:* **(acoustic) c.,** élasticité *f* acoustique, compliance *f*.

compliant [kəm'plaiənt], *a.* (*a*) complaisant, obligeant, accommodant; (*b*) *Pej:* d'une complaisance servile; souple.

compliantly [kəm'plaiəntli], *adv.* (*a*) complaisamment; (*b*) *Pej:* servilement.

complicacy ['kɔmplikəsi], *s. Lit:* complexité *f*; nature *f*, caractère *m*, complexe, nature compliquée (de qch.).

complicate ['kɔmplikeit], *v.tr.* compliquer (**with,** de); **that complicates matters,** cela complique la situation; voilà qui embrouille tout.

complicated ['kɔmplikeitid], *a.* compliqué; (*of situation, etc.*) **to become c.,** se compliquer; **a c. business,** une affaire embrouillée, compliquée, difficile à démêler.

complication [kɔmpli'keiʃ(ə)n], *s.* complication *f*; **c. of circumstances,** engrenage *m* de circonstances; *Med:* **if no complications set in,** s'il ne survient pas de complications; **pneumonia is always a serious c.,** la pneumonie est toujours une complication grave; **you're always making complications!** tu compliques toujours les choses!

complicity [kəm'plisiti], *s.* complicité *f* (**in,** à); connivence *f*.

compliment[1] ['kɔmplimənt], *s.* **1.** (*a*) compliment *m*; **to pay a c. to s.o.,** faire, adresser, un compliment à qn; **I never pay compliments,** je ne fais jamais de compliments; **to exchange compliments,** faire échange de politesses; **to return s.o. the c.,** répondre à qn sur le même ton, du tac au tac; *Iron:* **then compliments began to fly,** il y eut alors un échange d'aménités *f*; **to pay one's compliments to s.o.,** faire une visite (de politesse) à qn; *Mil: Navy:* **to pay compliments,** rendre les honneurs *m*; (*b*) **do me the c. of listening,** faites-moi la politesse, le plaisir, l'honneur, d'écouter; **your presence is a great c. to us,** votre présence *f* est un grand honneur pour nous. **2.** (*at end of letter*) **to present, send, one's compliments to s.o.,** se rappeler au bon souvenir de qn; présenter ses hommages *m* à (une dame); **compliments of the season,** meilleurs souhaits de nouvel an; souhaits de bonne année; **with the author's, publisher's, compliments,** hommage, envoi *m*, de l'auteur, de l'éditeur; **by way of c.,** à titre gracieux.

compliment[2] ['kɔmpliment], *v.tr.* complimenter, féliciter (qn); faire des compliments à (qn) (**on, de, on doing sth.,** d'avoir fait qch.).

complimentary [kɔmpli'ment(ə)ri], *a.* (*a*) flatteur, -euse; de félicitation; **c. allusion,** allusion flatteuse; **c. remarks,** compliments *mpl*; félicitations *fpl*; (*b*) gratuit; gracieux; **c. ticket,** billet *m* de faveur; billet donné à titre gracieux; *Publ:* **c. copy,** exemplaire envoyé à titre gracieux.

complin(e) ['kɔmpl(a)in], *s. Ecc:* complies *fpl*.

comply [kəm'plai], *v.i.* **1. to c. with (sth.),** se conformer à, remplir, accomplir (une clause d'un traité, une formalité, etc.); se soumettre à (la loi); observer (une règle, les bienséances); satisfaire à (une règle); accéder, répondre, faire droit, à (une demande); déférer à (un désir); obéir à, obtempérer à (un ordre); **to c. with a clause in a contract,** respecter une clause d'un contrat; **to c. with the public taste,** se plier au goût du public; **he complied gracefully,** il s'exécuta avec grâce; **in order to c. with s.o.'s wishes,** par complaisance pour qn; **your wishes have been complied with,** vos désirs ont reçu satisfaction; **ready to c. with every wish of his employer,** souple, soumis, à toutes les volontés de son patron. **2.** *A:* (*of result, etc.*) **to c. with the formula,** répondre à la formule; **the Jewish year did not c. with the Solar year,** l'année juive ne répondait pas à l'année solaire.

compo[1] ['kɔmpou], *s. Const: F:* (*composition*) stuc *m*.

compo[2], *s. Austr: N.Z: F:* = COMPENSATION.

component [kəm'pounənt]. **1.** *a.* composant, constituant, constitutif; **c. parts,** parties constituantes, composantes; *Ind:* pièces détachées; *Mec:* **c. forces,** forces composantes. **2.** *s.* (*a*) composant *m*; partie composante; *Ind:* pièce détachée; *Mec:* composante *f* (d'une force, etc.); (*b*) organe *m* (d'une machine); (*c*) *Opt:* lentille *f* (d'objectif); **four-c. lens,** objectif *m* à quatre lentilles.

compony ['kɔmpəni], *a.* & *s. Her:* compon(n)é.

comport[1] [kəm'pɔ:t]. **1.** *v.i.* s'accorder, convenir (**with,** à); **this would not c. with his position,** cela n'irait pas avec sa position (sociale). **2.** *v.pr.* **to c. oneself,** se comporter, se conduire; **he comported himself well,** il s'est bien comporté.

comport[2] ['kɔmpɔ:t], *s. Cer: etc:* compotier *m*.

comportment [kəm'pɔ:tmənt], *s.* conduite *f*, maintien *m*, comportement *m*.

compos ['kɔmpɔs], *a.* (*a*) *Lt.phr. Jur:* **c. mentis,** sain d'esprit; **non c. (mentis),** aliéné; (*b*) *F:* **is he quite c.?** est-ce qu'il a (toute) sa tête? **he doesn't seem c. to me,** à mon avis il est cinglé.

compose [kəm'pouz], *v.tr.* **1.** (*a*) composer (un poème, une symphonie, etc.); (*b*) mettre (des paroles) en musique; (*c*) *Typ:* **to c. a line,** composer une ligne. **2.** constituer, composer; **the parts that c. the whole,** les parties *f* qui composent l'ensemble; **to be composed of sth.,** se composer, être composé, de qch.; **an engine is composed of many parts,** un moteur se compose, est composé, de nombreux organes; *Jur:* **estate composed of wood and meadow land,** propriété consistante en bois et prés, en consistance de bois et prés. **3.** *Art:* **to c. the figures in a picture,** arranger, agencer, les personnages d'un tableau. **4.** arranger, accommoder, ajuster, régler (un différend, etc.). **5.** (*a*) **to c. one's features,** se composer le visage; **to c. one's thoughts for action,** se recueillir avant d'agir; **to c. oneself to sleep,** se disposer au sommeil, à dormir; (*b*) calmer, tranquilliser, remettre, rasseoir (l'esprit); **c. yourself!** calmez-vous!

composed [kəm'pouzd], *a.* **1.** calme, tranquille. **2. c. manner, countenance,** manière composée, visage composé.

composedly [kəm'pouzidli], *adv.* tranquillement; avec calme.

composedness [kəm'pouzidnis], *s.* tranquillité *f*, calme *m*.

composer [kəm'pouzər], *s.* (*a*) *Mus:* compositeur, -trice; (*b*) *Lit: etc:* auteur *m* (de tragédies, etc.).

composing [kəm'pouziŋ], *s.* composition *f*; *Typ:* **c. frame,** rang *m*, casse *f* de compositeur; **c.-rule,** filet *m* de composition; **c.-machine,** composeuse *f*; **c.-stick,** composteur *m*.

Compositae [kəm'pɔziti:], *s.pl. Bot:* composacées *f*.

composite ['kɔmpəzit]. **1.** *a.* (*a*) *Bot:* (fleur) composée; *Arch.* (base *f*, chapiteau *m*) composite; **c. arch,** arc *m* en lancette; (*b*) *Rail:* (train *m*) mixte; **c. coach,** voiture *f* mixte; *Ind:* **c. materials,** matériaux *m* composites; *Tp: Tg:* **c. circuit,** circuit approprié; *Geol:* **c. cone,** cône *m* mixte; (*c*) *Cin:* **c. shot,** impression combinée. **2.** *s.* (*a*) composé *m*; corps composé; (*b*) *Bot:* composée *f*.

composition [kɔmpə'ziʃ(ə)n], *s.* **1.** (*a*) action *f* de composer; composition *f* (de qch.); **an ode, a sonata, of his own c.,** une ode, une sonate, de sa composition; *Mec:* **c. of forces,** la composition des forces; *Cryst:* **c. plane,** plan *m* d'accolement; *Mus:* **the rules of c.,** les règles *f* de la composition; *Typ:* **hand c.,** composition à la main; **machine c.,** composition mécanique; (*b*) composition, constitution *f* (de l'air, de l'eau, etc.); **ingredients that enter into the c. of sth.,** ingrédients *m* qui entrent dans la composition de qch., qui composent qch.; **there is a touch of madness in his c.,** il y a un brin de folie dans son caractère; (*c*) *Art:* (distribution des figures, arrangement des draperies, etc.) composition. **2.** (*a*) mélange *m*, composé *m*, composition; **c. of vinegar and molasses,** mélange de vinaigre et de mélasse; **c. of selfishness and generosity,** mélange, composé *m*, d'égoïsme et de générosité; **non-conducting c.,** enduit *m* calorifuge; *Typ:* **roller c.,** pâte *f* à rouleaux; (*b*) *Const:* stuc *m*; simili marbre *m*. **3.** (*a*) **a musical c.,** une composition musicale; (*b*) *Sch:* dissertation *f*, rédaction *f*, narration *f*; **he was first in English c.,** il a été premier en dissertation anglaise; (*c*) *Sch: O:* **prose c.,** thème *m*. **4.** (*a*) *Lit:* accommodement *m*, entente *f* (avec ses ennemis, etc.); **to enter into a c. with s.o. over sth.,** entrer en composition avec qn sur qch.; **to make a c. with one's conscience,** capituler avec sa conscience; **to come to a c.,** venir à composition; arriver à une entente; (*b*) transaction *f*; **c. for stamp duty,** (taxe *f* d')abonnement *m* au timbre; **c. tax,** impôt forfaitaire fixé par voie d'abonnement; (*c*) *Com:* atermoiement *m* (avec ses créanciers); (*d*) arrangement *m*, accommodement (avec des créanciers); concordat préventif (à la faillite); **to make a c.,** composer; **c. of fifty pence in the pound,** décharge *f* de cinquante pour cent.

compositive [kəm'pɔzitiv], *a.* synthétique.

compositor [kəm'pɔzitər], *s. Typ:* compositeur *m*, typographe *m*.

compost[1] ['kɔmpɔst], *s. Hort:* compost *m*; terreau *m* de feuilles.

compost[2], *v.tr.* composter, terreauter (un parterre, etc.).

composure [kəm'pouʒər], *s.* calme *m*, quiétude *f*; sang-froid *m*; recueillement *m* d'esprit; **to act with the utmost c.,** agir avec le plus grand calme; **to retain one's c.,** garder son sang froid; **to regain one's c.,** (re)trouver son sang-froid; se calmer.

compote ['kɔmpout, -pɔt], *s.* **1.** compote *f* (de fruits). **2. c. (dish),** compotier *m.*

compound[1] ['kɔmpaund]. **1.** *a.* (*a*) composé; combiné; **c. microscope,** microscope composé; *Arch:* **c. order,** ordre *m* composite; *Gram:* **c. word,** mot composé; *Mus:* **c. time,** mesure composée; *Book-k:* **c. entry,** article composé, collectif, récapitulatif; *Fin:* **c. interest,** intérêts composés; *Min:* **c. wedge,** coin *m* multiple; *Mec.E:* **c. motion,** mouvement composé; (*b*) complexe; *Mth:* **c. number,** nombre *m* complexe; **c. addition, subtraction,** addition *f,* soustraction *f,* des nombres complexes; *Gram:* **c. subject,** sujet *m* complexe; (*c*) compound *inv*; *Metall:* **c. steel,** acier *m* compound; *El:* **c. winding,** enroulement *m* compound; **c. wound,** à enroulement compoundé, à double enroulement. **2.** *s.* (*a*) (corps *m*) composé *m*; **chemical c.,** composé chimique; **binary c.,** composé binaire; (*b*) *Tchn:* composition *f,* mastic *m,* pâte *f,* compound *m*; (*c*) *Gram:* mot composé.

compound[2] [kəm'paund]. **1.** *v.tr.* (*a*) composer, mélanger (une boisson, etc.); combiner (des éléments); composer, préparer (une drogue); (*b*) accommoder, arranger (un différend); régler (un différend) à l'amiable; **to c. a debt,** passer, faire, une transaction pour le règlement d'une dette; (*c*) *Jur:* **to c. a felony,** fermer les yeux sur un crime; pactiser avec un crime; entrer en composition avec le coupable; (*d*) *El:* compounder (une dynamo, le courant). **2.** *v.i.* (*a*) s'arranger, composer (**with s.o.,** avec qn); entrer en arrangement, en composition (avec qn); venir à composition (avec qn); transiger (avec qn, avec sa conscience); **to c. for a tax,** (i) payer un impôt à forfait; (ii) se rédimer d'un impôt; (*b*) *Com:* composer, transiger, concorder, arriver à un concordat, faire un compromis, s'accommoder, s'arranger (avec ses créanciers); (*c*) *Rac:* (*of horse*) flancher.

compound[3] ['kɔmpaund], *s.* (*a*) *A:* (*in Far East*) enceinte européenne; (*b*) (*in S. Africa*) quartier *m* des noirs (dans une mine d'or, etc.); (*c*) (*in S. Africa*) parc *m* à bétail; (*d*) cour *f* (d'une prison); (*e*) *Av: etc:* **visitors' c.,** aire *f* de visite; *P.N:* réservé aux visiteurs.

compoundable [kəm'paundəbl], *a.* (différend *m,* dette *f*) qui peuvent s'arranger à l'amiable, sur lesquels on peut entrer en composition, venir à composition.

compounder [kəm'paundər], *s.* **1.** (*pers.*) *Jur:* compositeur *m* à l'amiable; *Gasm:* combinateur *m.*

compounding [kəm'paundiŋ], *s.* **1.** composition *f*; confection *f* (de drogues). **2.** capitulation *f* (de conscience). **3.** *El:* compoundage *m.*

comprehend [kɔmpri'hend], *v.tr.* comprendre.

comprehending [kɔmpri'hendiŋ], *a.* qui comprend; plein de compréhension; compréhensif.

comprehensibility ['kɔmprihensə'biliti], *s.* compréhensibilité *f,* intelligibilité *f.*

comprehensible [kɔmpri'hensəbl], *a.* **1.** compréhensible, intelligible. **2.** qui peut être contenu, renfermé, englobé (**in,** dans).

comprehensibly [kɔmpri'hensibli], *adv.* d'une manière compréhensible, intelligible.

comprehension [kɔmpri'henʃ(ə)n], *s.* compréhension *f.* **1.** (*a*) entendement *m*; *Phil:* intellection *f*; **it is above, beyond, my c., it passes my c.,** cela passe mon entendement; cela me dépasse; (*b*) **for the clearer c. of what follows,** pour bien comprendre ce qui va suivre. **2.** portée *f,* étendue *f*; **words of the widest c.,** mots *m* d'une portée très étendue; *Log:* **term of wide c.,** terme *m* d'une compréhension très étendue, très large. **3.** *Ecc.Hist:* politique *f* de tolérance et d'inclusion des sectes dissidentes dans l'Église établie.

comprehensive [kɔmpri'hensiv], *a.* compréhensif. **1.** *Phil:* **the c. faculty,** la faculté de comprendre, de concevoir; l'entendement *m.* **2. c. study,** étude *f* d'ensemble; étude complète; **c. knowledge,** vastes connaissances *fpl*; **c. school** = centre *m* d'études secondaires; **c. view,** vue *f* d'ensemble; **c. term,** terme au sens très large; terme compréhensif; **c. offer,** offre *f* qui embrasse toutes les matières en discussion; **c. programme,** programme détaillé et complet; **to take a more c. view of sth.,** envisager qch. de plus haut.

comprehensively [kɔmpri'hensivli], *adv.* dans un sens très étendu; largement.

comprehensiveness [kɔmpri'hensivnis], *s.* **1.** *Phil:* compréhensivité *f*; faculté *f* de compréhension. **2.** étendue *f,* portée *f* (d'un mot, d'une offre).

compress[1] ['kɔmpres], *s. Med:* compresse *f.*

compress[2] [kəm'pres], *v.tr.* **1.** (*a*) comprimer (un gaz, l'air, etc.); bander (un ressort); (*of compressor*) refouler (l'air, etc.); (*b*) (*with passive force*) (*of gas, etc.*) se comprimer; (*of spring*) fléchir. **2.** (*condense*) condenser (un discours, ses pensées, etc.); resserrer (un récit); concentrer (son style).

compressed [kəm'prest], *a.* comprimé; *Husb:* **c. fodder,** biscuit *m* de fourrage; *Geol:* **c. fold,** pli serré; **she stood with c. lips,** elle se tenait là les lèvres serrées, pincées.

compressibility [kəmpresi'biliti], *s.* compressibilité *f.*

compressible [kəm'presəbl], *a.* compressible, comprimable.

compressing [kəm'presiŋ], *a.* comprimant; *Mec.E:* **c. fan,** ventilateur soufflant, foulant.

compression [kəm'preʃ(ə)n], *s.* **1.** compression *f* (d'un gaz, d'un ressort, etc.); bande *f,* bandé *m* (d'un ressort); **gas under high c.,** gaz surpressé; **c. of bellows,** foulée *f* d'un soufflet; **force of c.,** effort *m* de compression; *I.C.E: etc:* **c. tap,** robinet *m* de décompression, robinet décompresseur; purgeur *m*; **c. stroke,** (temps *m* de) compression; **c. ratio,** compression volumétrique; **c. ignition engine,** moteur *m* à allumage par compression; **high c. engine,** moteur à haute compression; **c. pump,** pompe *f* à compression; *Mec.E:* **member in c.,** pièce comprimée; **c. test,** essai *m* à la compression. **2.** concentration *f* (de la pensée, du style, etc.).

compressive [kəm'presiv], *a.* compressif; *Mec.E:* **c. strain,** déformation due à la compression; **c. stress,** effort *m* de compression; **c. strength,** résistance *f* à l'écrasement.

compressometer [kɔmpre'sɔmitər], *s. Civ.E:* compressimètre *m.*

compressor [kəm'presər], *s.* **1.** compresseur *m* (de gaz, d'air, etc.); **air c.,** motocompresseur *m.* **2.** (*a*) *Nau:* étrangloir *m* (de câble); stoppeur *m*; (*b*) *Artil:* (*buffer*) frein *m*; **to set up the compressors,** régler les freins.

comprisable [kəm'praizəbl], *a.* qui peut être compris, renfermé, englobé (**in,** dans).

comprise [kəm'praiz], *v.tr.* comprendre, contenir, renfermer; comporter; **the house comprises three reception rooms and five bedrooms,** la maison comprend trois pièces au rez-de-chaussée et cinq chambres (à coucher).

compromise[1] ['kɔmprəmaiz], *s.* compromis *m,* transaction *f*; **c. with one's conscience,** transaction avec sa conscience; capitulation *f* de conscience; **to agree to a c.,** accepter une transaction; consentir à transiger; **to make, reach, a c., to arrive at a c.,** composer (**with s.o.,** avec qn); arriver à une solution transactionnelle; transiger; **policy of c.,** politique *f* de compromis, d'accommodements; **policy of no c.,** politique intransigeante; **a. c. between two widely different opinions,** moyen terme entre deux opinions très différentes; **c. agreement arrived at by the parties,** arrangement intervenu entre les parties.

compromise[2]. **1.** *v.tr.* (*a*) compromettre (qn, son honneur, etc.); **to c. oneself with s.o.,** se compromettre avec qn; *F:* (*of woman*) se laisser aller avec qn; (*b*) arranger (un différend); transiger sur (un différend). **2.** *v.i.* compromettre, transiger, composer; **to c. with s.o.,** s'accommoder avec qn; **to c. with one's conscience,** pactiser avec sa conscience; **if he agrees to c.,** s'il accepte un compromis.

compromising[1] ['kɔmprəmaiziŋ], *a.* compromettant.

compromising[2], *s.* **1.** compromission *f* (de son honneur). **2.** composition *f* (d'un différend).

compsognathus [kɔmp'sɔgnəθəs], *s. Paleont:* compsognathus *m.*

comptometer [kɔmp'tɔmitər], *s. R.t.m:* machine *f* à calculer.

comptroller [kən'troulər], *s. Adm:* **1.** administrateur *m* (d'une maison royale, etc.). **2.** contrôleur *m*; vérificateur *m* (de comptes).

compulsion [kəm'pʌlʃ(ə)n], *s.* **1.** contrainte *f*; compulsion *f*; **under c., on c.,** par contrainte; **to be under c. to do sth.,** être astreint à faire qch.; **to obey only under c.,** n'obéir qu'à son corps défendant; n'obéir que contraint et forcé, que si on y est contraint; céder à la contrainte; **to pay under c.,** payer à son corps défendant. **2.** *Psy:* compulsion; **c. neurosis,** névrose obsessionnelle.

compulsive [kəm'pʌlsiv], *a.* **1.** (voix, manière, etc.) qui commande l'obéissance. **2.** *Psy:* compulsif; **c. thinking,** pensée obsédante; **c. smoker, gambler,** fumeur, -euse, joueur, -euse, chronique; **to be a c. drinker,** être obsédé par la boisson.

compulsively [kəm'pʌlsivli], *adv.* **1.** par force, par contrainte. **2.** par besoin; **to drink c.,** être obsédé par la boisson.

compulsorily [kəm'pʌlsərili], *adv.* obligatoirement; *Adm: etc:* **to be retired c.,** être mis à la retraite d'office.

compulsory [kəm'pʌls(ə)ri], *a.* **1.** obligatoire, forcé, par contrainte; **c. loan, liquidation,** emprunt forcé, liquidation forcée; **c. school attendance,** scolarité *f* obligatoire; obligation *f* scolaire; *Sch:* **c. Latin,** latin obligatoire. **2.** coercitif; **magistrate invested with c. powers,** magistrat investi de pouvoirs coercitifs.

compunction [kəm'pʌŋ(k)ʃ(ə)n], *s.* componction *f*; remords *m*; **without c.,** sans (aucune) componction; sans scrupule; **to be seized with c.,** avoir un retour de conscience.

compunctious [kəm'pʌŋ(k)ʃəs], *a.* plein de componction.

compunctiously [kəm'pʌŋ(k)ʃəsli], *adv.* avec un air de componction.

compurgation [kɔmpəː'geiʃ(ə)n], *s. Jur: A:* témoignage justificateur (porté par les amis de l'accusé); justification *f* (de l'accusé).

compurgator ['kɔmpəːgeitər], *s. Jur: A:* témoin justificateur.

compurgatory [kəm'pəːgət(ə)ri], *a. Jur: A:* **c. oath,** serment prêté par témoin justificateur.

computable [kəm'pjuːtəbl], *a.* calculable.

computation [kɔmpju'teiʃ(ə)n], *s.* (*a*) compte *m,* calcul *m,* supputation *f,* estimation *f*; **to make a c. of sth.,** faire le calcul de qch.; calculer qch.; estimer (les dépenses, etc.); **at the lowest c., it will cost. . .,** en mettant les choses au plus bas, cela va coûter. . .; **beyond c.,** incalculable; (*b*) **electronic c.,** calcul électronique; *Cmptr:* **address c.,** calcul d'adresse; **scientific c.,** calcul scientifique; **c. centre,** centre *m* de calcul; (*c*) *Ecc:* comput *m* (du temps).

computational [kɔmpju'teiʃənl], *a.* de calcul; **c. error,** erreur *f* de calcul; *Cmptr:* **c. load,** volume *m* des calculs.

compute[1] [kəm'pjuːt], *v.tr.* computer, compter, calculer, évaluer, estimer, supputer; **computed distance,** distance estimée; **the population has been computed at 7000,** on a estimé la population à 7000.

compute[2]. **1.** *a. Cmptr:* **c. mode,** état *m* de fonctionnement; **c. bound, c. limited,** tributaire de la vitesse de calcul. **2.** *s.* **beyond c.,** incalculable.

computer [kəm'pjuːtər], *s.* **1.** (*pers.*) calculateur, -trice. **2.** (*machine*) calculateur *m*; ordinateur *m*; (*a*) **electronic c.,** calculateur électronique; ordinateur; **all-purpose c.,** calculateur universel; **analog(ue) c.,** calculateur analogique; **automatic c.,** calculateur automatique; **digital c.,** calculateur numérique; **sequential c.,** calculateur séquentiel; **the c. age,** l'ère *f* des ordinateurs; **c. control,** gestion *f* par ordinateur; **c. operation,** opération *f* machine; **c. program(me),** programme *m* machine; **c. instruction, language,** instruction *f,* langage *m,* machine; **c. department, service,** service *m* informatique; **c. population,** parc *m* d'ordinateurs; **c. room,** salle *f* des machines, de l'ordinateur; **c. file,** fichier *m* mécanographique; **c. accounting,** comptabilité *f* mécanographique (sur ordinateur); **c.-assisted instruction,** enseignement *m* à l'aide d'un ordinateur; (*pers.*) **c. expert,** informaticien, -ienne; **c. analyst,** analyste *mf* en informatique; **c. engineer,** ingénieur *m* informaticien; **c. programmer,** programmeur, -euse; (*b*) *Artil:* **fire data c.,** calculateur de tir; **wind and parallax c.,** calculateur de vent et de parallaxe; *Mil.Av:* **gun sight c.,** calculateur de tir; *Av:* **course-line c.,** calculateur de route.

computerese [kəmpjutə'riːz], *s.* jargon *m* de l'informatique.

computerizable [kəmpjutə'raizəbl], *a.* mécanisable, automatisable, informatisable.

computerization [kəmpjutərai'zeiʃ(ə)n], *s.* mécanisation *f,* automatisation *f,* informatisation *f.*

computerize [kəm'pjuːtəraiz], *v.tr.* mécaniser, automatiser, informatiser; équiper (une organisation) d'ordinateurs.

computerized [kəm'pjuːtəraizd], *a.* **c. data,** données *f* mécanographiques; **c. file,** fichier mécanisé; **c. solution,** solution *f* mécanographique, solution ordinateur; **c. type setting,** composition *f* automatique.

computing [kəm'pjuːtiŋ], *s.* évaluation *f,* estimation *f*; calcul *m*; **c. machine,** machine *f* à calcul; **c. equipment,** matériel *m* mécanographique; **c. speed, time,** vitesse *f,* durée *f,* de calcul.

comrade ['kɔmreid, -ræd, -rəd], *s.* (*a*) camarade *m,* compagnon *m*; **comrades in arms, in exile,** compagnons d'armes, d'exil; (*b*) (*as term of address*) camarade *mf.*

comradeship ['kɔmreidʃip, -ræd, -rəd-], *s.* camaraderie *f.*

comsat ['kɔmsæt], *s. F:* satellite *m* de télécommunications.

con[1] [kɔn], *v.tr.* (**conned**) étudier (une leçon, un rôle); **to c. over,** repasser, répéter (une leçon, etc.).

con[2], *v.tr.* (**conned**) *Nau:* gouverner (un navire); **to c. the ship,** diriger, commander, la manœuvre; **conning tower,** blockhaus *m*; kiosque *m,* baignoire *f* (d'un sous-marin).

con[3]. **1.** *s.* **to consider the pros and (the) cons,** considérer le pour et le contre. **2.** *prep.* **much was said pro and c. the proposal,** on a beaucoup parlé pour et contre le projet.

con[4], *a. F:* (=*confidence*) **c. man,** escroc *m,* chevalier *m* d'industrie, voleur *m* à l'américaine.

con[5], *s. F:* déception *f,* duperie *f,* supercherie *f,* escroquerie *f.*

con[6], *v.tr.* **(conned)** *F:* escroquer (surtout après avoir gagné la confiance de la victime); **I've been conned,** on m'a eu.

conation [kou'neiʃ(ə)n], *s. Phil:* conation *f*; volition *f*; mise *f* en action de la volonté.

conative ['kounətiv], *a.* (*a*) *Phil:* volitif; (*b*) *Ling:* conatif.

concameration [kɔnkæmə'reiʃ(ə)n], *s. Arch:* concamération *f.*

concatenate [kɔn'kætineit], *v.tr.* enchaîner, lier (des idées); concaténer; *Pros:* **concatenated stanzas,** strophes concaténées.

concatenation [kɔnkæti'neiʃ(ə)n], *s.* concaténation *f,* chaîne *f*; enchaînement *m* (d'idées, de causes et d'effets); concours *m* (de circonstances).

concave[1] ['kɔnkeiv]. **1.** *a.* concave, incurvé. **2.** *s. A: & Lit:* surface *f* concave.

concave[2]. **1.** *v.tr.* rendre concave. **2.** *v.i.* devenir concave.

concavely [kɔn'keivli], *adv.* en se creusant.

concavity [kɔn'kæviti], *s.* concavité *f.*

concavo-concave [kɔn'keivou'kɔnkeiv], *a.* biconcave; concavo-concave; double-concave.

concavo-convex [kɔn'keivou'kɔnveks], *a.* concavo-convexe; concave-convexe.

conceal [kən'si:l], *v.tr.* (*a*) cacher (qn, qch.); celer, dissimuler (la vérité, son chagrin, etc.); masquer (ses projets, une fenêtre); voiler (ses pensées, ses desseins); tenir secret (un projet, etc.); **I do not c. the fact (that it is so),** je ne dissimule pas qu'il en est ainsi, qu'il n'en soit ainsi; **to c. one's intentions,** cacher, déguiser, son jeu; masquer ses batteries; **to c. s.o.'s physical defects,** dissimuler les défauts de conformation; **to c. sth. from s.o.,** cacher qch. à qn; taire qch. à qn; **to c. one's movements from the enemy,** dérober sa marche à l'ennemi; (*b*) *Jur:* receler (un malfaiteur, un enfant, un objet volé).

concealable [kən'si:ləbl], *a.* que l'on peut cacher; *Ind: etc:* (pièce *f*) escamotable, éclipsable.

concealed [kən'si:ld], *a.* caché, dissimulé, invisible, masqué; **c. turning,** virage masqué; *Geol:* **c. outcrop,** affleurement masqué; **c. lighting,** éclairage indirect.

concealer [kən'si:lər], *s. Jur:* receleur, -euse.

concealment [kən'si:lmənt], *s.* **1.** dissimulation *f,* déguisement *m* (de ses sentiments, etc.). **2.** *Jur:* (*a*) recel *m,* cel *m,* recèlement *m* (de malfaiteurs, d'objets volés); (*b*) réticence *f*; dissimulation (de certains faits, *p. ex.* fait de cacher un défaut de la marchandise) (donnant lieu à rescission du contrat); **c. of birth,** recel d'enfant; suppression *f* d'enfant; non-présentation *f* d'enfant; *Fin:* **c. of assets,** dissimulation d'actif. **3.** action *f* de (se) cacher; **to keep s.o. in c.,** tenir qn caché; **to find a place of c.,** trouver une cachette, une retraite; *Mil:* **c. from the air,** dissimulation aux vues aériennes; **c. from enemy observation,** dissimulation aux vues de l'ennemi; **c. area,** zone *f* de défilement. **4.** retraite (cachée); **the hills offered safe c. to the fugitives,** les montagnes *f* offraient aux fugitifs des retraites sûres.

concede [kən'si:d], *v.tr.* **1.** concéder (un privilège, etc.); **I will c. nothing,** je ne ferai aucune concession; *Games:* **to c. points to one's opponent,** donner, rendre, des points à son adversaire; *v.tr. or i. Pol: etc:* **to c. (defeat),** s'avouer vaincu. **2. to c. that one is wrong,** concéder, admettre, qu'on a tort.

concededly [kən'si:didli], *adv. U.S:* à vrai dire; indisputablement.

conceit [kən'si:t], *s.* **1.** vanité *f,* suffisance *f*; affectation *f*; **I'll take the c. out of him,** je vais le remettre à sa place; je vais le dégonfler; **eaten up with c.,** pétri, pourri, d'amour-propre. **2.** *A:* opinion *f* favorable; jugement *m* favorable; **he is a very big man in his own c.,** il se croit un très grand homme; **he has a very good c. of himself,** il est très satisfait de sa petite personne; il se croit quelqu'un; il se gobe; **to be out of c. with sth., with oneself,** être dégoûté, mécontent, de qch., de soi; **to put s.o. out of c. with his own work,** dégoûter qn de son propre travail. **3.** *A: & Lit:* trait *m* d'esprit (ingénieux); *pl.* **conceits,** concetti *m.*

conceited [kən'si:tid], *a.* suffisant, vaniteux; infatué de soi-même; prétentieux; (air) suffisant, affecté, avantageux; **he looks very c.,** il a l'air bien suffisant; **he is unbearably c.,** il est d'une suffisance insupportable; **a c. puppy,** un jeune prétentieux.

conceitedly [kən'si:tidli], *adv.* avec suffisance, avec vanité; d'un air suffisant, avantageux.

conceitedness [kən'si:tidnis], *s.* suffisance *f,* vanité *f.*

conceivability [kənsi:və'biliti], **conceivableness** [kən'si:vəbəlnis], *s.* conceptibilité *f.*

conceivable [kən'si:vəbl], *a.* concevable, imaginable; **it is c. that . . .,** il est concevable que + *sub.* **every means c.,** tous les moyens imaginables; **it is the best c.,** c'est le mieux que l'on puisse imaginer.

conceivably [kən'si:vəbli], *adv.* d'une façon concevable; **he may c. have reached the summit,** il est concevable qu'il ait pu atteindre jusqu'au sommet.

conceive [kən'si:v], *v.tr.* **1.** (*a*) concevoir (un enfant); *v.i.* concevoir; devenir enceinte; (*b*) (*of child*) **to be conceived,** être conçu; *Ecc:* **conceived by the Holy Ghost,** conçu de l'Esprit Saint. **2.** (*a*) concevoir (un projet, de l'amour); **to c. a great friendship for s.o.,** concevoir une grande amitié pour qn; se prendre d'une vive amitié pour qn; **to c. a dislike for s.o.,** prendre qn en aversion; (*b*) **I cannot c. why you should allow it,** je n'imagine pas, ne conçois pas, pourquoi vous le permettriez; **I conceived that some difficulties might arise,** je concevais bien qu'il pourrait se présenter quelques difficultés; j'envisageais bien quelques difficultés. **3.** (*of document*) **conceived as follows,** ainsi conçu; rédigé dans les termes suivants, comme suit. **4.** *v.i.* (*a*) **things that have never been conceived of,** choses qu'on n'a jamais imaginées; (*b*) **that is not the case, as you may well c.,** vous pouvez bien vous imaginer qu'il n'en est pas ainsi.

concentrate[1] ['kɔnsəntreit], *s.* (*a*) minerai concentré; (*b*) concentré *m* (de tomates, etc.); *Husb:* **to feed the cows on concentrates,** donner du concentré aux vaches.

concentrate[2]. **1.** *v.tr.* concentrer (des troupes, son attention, un liquide, etc.); *Ch: Ind:* déflegmer (l'alcool); grouper (des efforts); *Mil:* **to c. the fire of a battery,** faire converger les feux d'une batterie; **concentrated fire,** tir convergent; **concentrated milk,** lait concentré; *Ind:* **concentrated sulphuric acid,** acide sulfurique concentré; **with concentrated fury,** avec une fureur concentrée; *Art:* **concentrated composition, painting,** composition, peinture, ramassée. **2.** *v.i.* (*a*) se concentrer; **population tends to c. in cities,** la population tend à se concentrer dans les villes; *Th:* **interest concentrates on the fourth act,** l'intérêt se concentre sur le quatrième acte, (*b*) **to c. on sth., on doing sth.,** concentrer son attention sur qch.; porter toute son attention sur qch.; s'appliquer à faire qch.; **you must learn to c.,** il faut apprendre à appliquer votre pensée, à vous concentrer.

concentration [kɔnsən'treiʃ(ə)n], *s.* **1.** (*a*) concentration *f* (d'une solution, des troupes, etc.); *Mil:* convergence *f* (des feux); *Ch: Ind:* déflegmation *f* (de l'alcool); **c. of effort,** convergence des efforts; **c. camp,** camp *m* de concentration; **prisoner in a c. camp,** concentrationnaire *mf*; *Aut: Sp:* **c. point,** parc *m* d'étape (de course sur routes); (*b*) *Ch:* **(degree of) c.,** titre *m* (d'un acide, etc.); **at high c.,** concentré. **2.** concentration, application *f* (de l'esprit); **power of c.,** faculté *f* de concentration, d'application; **to lose c.,** être déconcentré, perdre sa concentration. **3. enemy c.,** rassemblement ennemi; **the large urban concentrations,** les grandes agglomérations urbaines.

concentrative ['kɔnsəntreitiv], *a.* qui tend à la concentration; *Psy:* **c. act,** acte *m* de concentration, d'application (de l'esprit).

concentrator ['kɔnsəntreitər], *s. Ch: Min: etc:* (appareil *m*; dispositif *m*) concentrateur *m.*

concentric [kɔn'sentrik], *a.* (*of circles, cable, lens, etc.*) concentrique; (*of lens*) homocentrique.

concentrically [kɔn'sentrik(ə)li], *adv.* concentriquement.

concentricity [kɔnsen'trisiti], *s.* **1.** arrangement *m* concentrique. **2.** *Tchn:* centrage *m.*

concept ['kɔnsept], *s.* concept *m*; idée générale; (*in vocabulary, etc.*) **c. does not exist, no corresponding c.,** notion absente.

conceptacle [kən'septəkl], *s. Bot:* conceptacle *m.*

conception [kən'sepʃ(ə)n], *s.* **1.** conception *f* (d'un enfant, d'une idée, etc.); **c. control,** procédés anticonceptionnels. **2. conceptions of a writer,** conceptions, imaginations *f,* d'un auteur; **to have a high c. of one's duty,** avoir une haute idée de son devoir; **to have a clear c. of sth.,** se représenter clairement qch. par la pensée; *F:* **I haven't the remotest c.,** je n'en ai pas la moindre idée.

conceptional [kən'sepʃən(ə)l], *a.* conceptionnel.

conceptism ['kɔnseptizm], *s. Lit:* conceptisme *m.*

conceptive [kən'septiv], *a.* **conceptual** [kən'septjuəl], *a.* conceptuel.

conceptualism [kən'septjuəlizm], *s. Phil:* conceptualisme *m.*

conceptualist [kən'septjuəlist], *s. Phil:* conceptualiste *mf.*

conceptualist(ic) [kənseptjuə'list(ik)], *a. Phil:* conceptualiste.

conceptualization [kən'septjuəlai'zeiʃ(ə)n], *s.* conceptualisation *f.*

conceptualize [kən'septjuəlaiz], *Phil:* **1.** *v.tr.* conceptualiser (une théorie, etc.), concevoir; former un concept, une idée, de (qch.). **2.** *v.i.* conceptualiser.

conceptually [kən'septjuəli], *adv.* comme concept; essentiellement.

concern[1] [kən'sə:n], *s.* **1.** (*a*) *A:* rapport *m*; **to have no c. with sth.,** n'avoir pas de rapport avec qch.; (*b*) intérêt *m* **(in,** dans); **it's not my c.; it's no c. of mine,** cela ne me regarde pas; cela ne me concerne pas; ce n'est pas mon affaire; je ne me soucie pas de cela; **it's no c. of yours,** cela ne vous intéresse pas; vous n'avez rien à y voir; ne vous en mêlez pas. **2.** (*a*) souci *m*; **my c. for your welfare,** le souci que j'ai de votre bien-être; **my only c. has been to ensure . . .,** ma seule préoccupation a été d'assurer . . .; **a problem likely to be a major c. of the new administration,** problème *m* susceptible d'être parmi les préoccupations les plus importantes de la nouvelle administration; (*b*) souci, anxiété *f,* inquiétude *f*; **he showed great c. about you,** il s'est montré inquiet à votre égard; **he enquired with c. . . .,** il a demandé avec sollicitude *f*. . .; **he showed deep c. at the news,** il s'est montré très affecté de cette nouvelle. **3.** (*a*) *Com: Ind:* entreprise *f,* affaire *f,* exploitation *f*; maison *f* (de commerce, etc.); fonds *m* de commerce; **the whole c. is for sale,** toute l'entreprise est mise en vente, est à vendre; **running a large c. is a complicated business,** la gestion d'une grosse entreprise est bien compliquée; **going c.,** affaire qui marche; **the business is a going c.,** la maison marche bien, est en pleine activité; (*of shop, etc.*) **to be sold as a going c.,** à vendre avec fonds; (*b*) *F:* **I'm sick of, fed up with, the whole c.,** j'en ai marre de tout le bataclan; (*c*) *F:* appareil *m,* machin *m,* truc *m.*

concern[2], *v.tr.* **1.** (*a*) concerner, regarder, toucher, intéresser (qn, qch.); se rapporter à (qn, qch.); avoir rapport à (qch.); **this does not c. you,** (i) ceci ne vous concerne pas, ne vous touche pas; (ii) ceci n'est pas votre affaire; vous n'avez rien à y voir; **action that concerns me alone,** action *f* qui est mon affaire à moi seul; **that does not c. me,** cela ne me regarde pas, ne m'intéresse pas, ne me touche pas, ne touche pas à mes intérêts; **you are the most closely concerned,** c'est vous le premier intéressé; **it concerns him to know . . .,** il lui importe de savoir . . .; **law that concerns Alsace,** loi *f* qui affecte l'Alsace; **matters that c. the public,** choses *f* qui intéressent le public; **to whom it may c.,** pour qui de droit; à toutes fins utiles; (*b*) **to c. oneself with, about, in, sth.,** s'intéresser à, s'occuper de, qch. **2.** (*a*) **to be concerned in, with, sth.,** s'intéresser à, s'occuper de, qch.; être en cause; **question in which the whole world is concerned,** question *f* qui intéresse le monde entier; **to be concerned in a plot,** être impliqué dans un complot; **you are in no way concerned in the business,** vous n'entrez pour rien dans l'affaire; **the parties, persons, concerned,** les intéressés; **to notify the persons concerned,** aviser qui de droit; *Com: etc:* **to pass on to the department concerned,** transmettre au service compétent; **all the treaties concerned,** tous les traités envisagés; **as far as I am concerned,** en ce qui me concerne; en ce qui me regarde; quant à moi; pour mon compte; **well, that's all right as far as he is concerned,** enfin, passe pour lui; **as far as this question is concerned,** en ce qui touche à cette question; **we are not particularly concerned with tracing their history,** nous n'avons pas à tâche de retracer leur histoire; **optics is concerned with the laws of light,** l'optique *f* a pour objet les lois de la lumière; **art is not concerned with politics,** l'art n'a rien à voir avec la politique; **this book is concerned with politics,** ce livre traite de la politique; dans ce livre il s'agit de politique; (*b*) **to be concerned about s.o., sth.,** s'inquiéter, être inquiet, de qn, de qch.; **I am concerned to hear that . . .,** j'apprends avec regret, avec peine, que . . .; **I am concerned for his health,** l'état *m* de sa santé me donne des inquiétudes *f*; **he looked very much concerned,** il avait l'air très inquiet, très soucieux; **he didn't look in the least concerned,** (i) il n'avait l'air aucunement inquiet; (ii) cela a paru le laisser indifférent; **I feel concerned for his safety,** je crains qu'il ne lui arrive, ne lui soit arrivé, quelque chose; **I feel concerned about the matter,** cette affaire me cause de l'inquiétude, me donne du souci; **I feel concerned at his failure,** son échec me donne du souci; **I am not concerned about what they say,** je ne m'inquiète guère de ce qu'on dit.

concernedly [kən'sə:nidli], *adv.* avec inquiétude; d'un air soucieux.

concerning [kən'sə:niŋ], *prep.* (*usu. considered poor style;* **about** *is preferable*) concernant, touchant, en ce qui concerne, au sujet de, à l'égard de (qn, qch.); relatif à (qn, qch.); **I have heard much c. this,** j'ai appris beaucoup de choses à ce sujet.

concert[1] ['kɔnsət], *s.* **1.** concert *m*, accord *m*; (*a*) **to sing in c.,** chanter à l'unisson *m*; **to act in c. (with s.o.),** agir de concert, d'accord, de compagnie (avec qn); agir d'ensemble; se concerter (avec qn); (*b*) *Hist:* **the C. of Europe,** le concert européen. **2.** *Mus:* concert; séance musicale; **a Wagner c.,** un festival Wagner; **broadcast, televised, c.,** concert radiodiffusé, télévisé; **c. performer,** concertant, -ante; concertiste *mf*; **c. hall,** salle *f* de concert; **c. grand,** piano *m* de concert; **c. flute,** grande flûte; **c. pitch,** (i) diapason *m* de concert anglais (la = 440 vibrations); (ii) *Fig:* pleine forme; **to keep up to c. pitch,** se maintenir en pleine forme; **to work at c. pitch,** travailler au maximum.

concert[2] [kən'sə:t]. **1.** *v.tr.* concerter (des mesures, etc.); **we had concerted a code of signals,** nous avions arrangé d'avance un code de signaux. **2.** *v.i.* se concerter, tenir conseil (**with,** avec).

concertante [kɔntʃə(:)'tænti], *a. Mus:* **c. part,** partie concertante.

concerted [kən'sə:tid], *a.* concerté; **with no c. plan,** sans plan concerté; **c. action,** action *f* d'ensemble; **c. music, piece,** musique *f*, morceau *m*, d'ensemble; morceau concertant.

concertina[1] [kɔnsə'ti:nə], *s.* **1.** *Mus:* concertina *m*. **2.** *Rail:* **c. vestibule** (*joining coaches*), soufflet *m*.

concertina[2], *v.i.* (**concertinaed**) se fermer en accordéon; *F:* (*of cars, etc. in collision*) former un accordéon; **her stockings concertinaed round her ankles,** ses bas tombaient en accordéon autour de ses chevilles.

concertino [kɔntʃə'ti:nou], *s. Mus:* concertino *m*.

concerto [kən'tʃə:tou], *s. Mus:* concerto *m*; **piano, violin, c.,** concerto pour piano, pour violon.

concessible [kən'sesibl], *a.* concessible.

concession [kən'seʃ(ə)n], *s.* (*a*) concession *f* (de terrain, d'opinion, etc.); **mining c.,** concession minière; **to make concessions,** faire des concessions; **to make concessions to the prejudices of the time,** sacrifier aux préjugés de l'époque; **we must make some c. to the weakness of old age,** il faut savoir déférer quelque chose à la faiblesse des vieillards; (*b*) *Com:* réduction *f*.

concession(n)aire [kənseʃə'nɛər], *s.* concessionnaire *mf*.

concessionary [kən'seʃən(ə)ri]. **1.** *a.* (*a*) (compagnie *f*, etc.) concessionnaire; (*b*) (subside, etc.) concédé. **2.** *s.* = CONCESSION(N)AIRE.

concessive [kən'sesiv], *a.* concessif; *Gram:* **c. clause, conjunction,** proposition, conjonction, concessive.

concetti [kɔn'tʃeti], *s.pl. Lit.Hist:* concetti *m*.

concettism [kɔn'tʃetizm], *s. Lit.Hist:* abus *m* des concetti; préciosité *f*.

conch [kɔŋk, kɔn(t)ʃ], *s.* **1.** *Moll:* (*a*) conque *f* (de moullusque); **Triton's c.,** la conque de Triton; (*b*) conque; **king c.,** strombe géant; **queen c.,** casque *m*; **horse c.,** fasciolaria *f*. **2.** = CONCHA 1. **3.** *P: Pej:* **Conch,** habitant, -ante, des Bahamas.

concha, *pl.* **-ae** ['kɔŋkə, -i:], *s.* **1.** *Anat:* conque *f* (de l'oreille); oreille *f* externe. **2.** *Arch:* (*a*) voûte *f* d'abside; (*b*) abside *f*.

conchate ['kɔŋkeit], *a.* conchiforme.

conchie ['kɔn(t)ʃi], *s. F:* objecteur *m* de conscience; réfractaire *m*.

Conchifera [kɔŋ'kifərə], *s.pl. Moll:* conchifères *m*.

conchiferous [kɔŋ'kifərəs], *a.* conchifère.

conchiform ['kɔŋkifɔ:m], *a.* conchiforme.

conchoid ['kɔŋkɔid]. **1.** *a.* conchoïde. **2.** *s. Mth:* conchoïde *f*.

conchoidal [kɔŋ'kɔidl], *a.* (*a*) *Mth: etc:* conchoïdal, -aux; conchoïde; (*b*) **c. fracture,** cassure *f* conchoïdale.

conchological [kɔŋkou'lɔdʒikl], *a.* conchyliologique.

conchologist [kɔŋ'kɔlədʒist], *s.* conchyliologiste *mf*.

conchology [kɔŋ'kɔlədʒi], *s.* conchyliologie *f*.

Conchostraca [kɔŋ'kɔstrəkə], *s.pl. Crust:* conchostracés *m*.

conchy ['kɔn(t)ʃi], *s.* = CONCHIE.

conciliar [kən'siliər], *a.* conciliaire; *Ecc.Hist:* **c. records and decrees,** conciles *m*.

conciliate [kən'silieit], *v.tr.* (*a*) concilier, réconcilier (des théories contraires, des intérêts opposés); **it is difficult to c. the views of labour and management on this point,** il est difficile de concilier le point de vue des travailleurs et de la direction en cette matière; (*b*) **he conciliated her mother,** il a réussi à gagner la bonne volonté de sa mère.

conciliation [kənsili'eiʃ(ə)n], *s.* conciliation *f*; *Jur:* **court of c.,** bureau *m* de conciliation; (*in industrial dispute*) **c. board,** conseil *m* d'arbitrage, = conseil des prud'hommes.

conciliative [kən'siliətiv], *a.* conciliant.

conciliator [kən'silieitər], *s.* conciliateur, -trice.

conciliatory [kən'siliət(ə)ri], *a.* conciliatoire, conciliant; **c. spirit,** esprit *m* de conciliation.

concise [kən'sais], *a.* concis; (style) serré, ramassé.

concisely [kən'saisli], *adv.* brièvement, avec concision; **to put it c.,** en un mot (comme en cent).

conciseness [kən'saisnis], **concision** [kən'siʒ(ə)n], *s.* concision *f*; **to aim at c.,** serrer son style; essayer d'être concis.

conclave ['kɔŋkleiv], *s.* **1.** (*a*) *R.C.Ch:* conclave *m* (le lieu d'assemblée ou l'assemblée des cardinaux); (*b*) **the c.,** les cardinaux *m*. **2.** (*a*) assemblée *f*, réunion *f* (à huis clos); (*b*) conseil (tenu à huis clos); **to be in c. with s.o.,** tenir conseil avec qn; (*c*) **decisions arrived at in c.,** décisions prises en assemblée plénière.

conclavist ['kɔŋkleivist], *s. Ecc:* conclaviste *m*.

conclude [kən'klu:d]. **1.** *v.tr.* conclure (une affaire, la paix, un traité, etc.); arranger, régler (une affaire, un contrat). **2.** (*a*) terminer, conclure, finir, achever (un discours, un ouvrage); clôturer (une session); *v.i.* (*at end of speech, etc.*) **to c.,** en conclusion; en terminant; finalement; (*of serial story*) **to be concluded (in our next),** la fin au prochain numéro; **concluded,** suite et fin; (*b*) *v.i.* **the report concludes as follows,** le rapport aboutit à la conclusion suivante; le rapport se termine comme il suit. **3.** *v.tr.* (*infer*) **from this I c. that . . .,** de ceci je conclus, je juge, j'estime, que . . . . **4.** *v.tr. NAm:* **we concluded to wait for fine weather,** nous avons décidé d'attendre le beau temps.

concluding [kən'klu:diŋ], *a.* (mot, chapitre) final (*pl.* -als).

conclusion [kən'klu:ʒ(ə)n]. **1.** conclusion *f* (de la paix, d'un traité, etc.). **2.** fin *f*, conclusion (d'une lettre, d'un ouvrage, etc.); clôture *f* (d'une session, etc.); **in c.,** pour conclure; en conclusion; finalement; **to bring a matter to a successful c.,** mener une affaire à bonne fin, à bon terme; faire aboutir une affaire. **3.** (*a*) *Log:* conséquent *m*, conclusion (d'un syllogisme); (*b*) **without coming to a c., to conclusions,** sans rien conclure; **conclusions arrived at (at a meeting),** décisions prises (par une assemblée); **to draw a c. from sth.,** tirer une déduction, une conclusion, de qch.; **to come to a c. about sth.,** (i) arriver à une décision, (ii) se prononcer, sur une question; **to come to the c. that . . .,** conclure que . . .; **to come to the c. that the scheme is impossible,** conclure à l'impossibilité du projet; **it was a foregone c.,** l'issue n'était pas douteuse; c'était prévu; *F:* **to try conclusions with s.o.,** se mesurer, lutter, avec, contre, qn; **to jump to a c.,** arriver (i) immédiatement, (ii) prématurément, trop vite, à une conclusion; **it's up to you to draw your own conclusions,** à vous d'en juger.

conclusive [kən'klu:siv], *a.* (*of argument*) concluant, décisif; (*of test*) probant.

conclusively [kən'klu:sivli], *adv.* décisivement; d'une manière décisive, concluante.

conclusiveness [kən'klu:sivnis], *s.* évidence *f* (d'un argument, etc.); caractère probant (d'une épreuve).

concoct [kən'kɔkt], *v.tr.* **1.** mixtionner (une potion); composer (un cocktail, etc.); confectionner, mitonner (un plat). . . . **2.** imaginer, inventer, combiner (un plan); tramer, machiner (un complot); **to c. a lie, a charge against s.o.,** forger un mensonge, une accusation contre qn.

concoction [kən'kɔkʃ(ə)n], *s.* **1.** (*a*) confectionnement *m*, confection *f* (d'un plat, etc.); *F:* **it's just a c. of mine,** c'est un plat que j'ai inventé; (*b*) mixtion *f*; *esp.* boisson *f*, potion *f*. **2.** (*a*) conception *f*, élaboration *f* (d'un plan); machination *f* (d'un complot); (*b*) **I have never heard such a c. of lies,** jamais je n'ai entendu un pareil tissu de mensonges; **the whole story was a c.,** l'histoire était inventée à plaisir.

concoctor, -er [kən'kɔktər], *s.* **1.** confectionneur, -euse (d'un plat). **2.** auteur *m* (d'un projet, etc.); machinateur, -trice (d'une intrigue).

concolorate [kɔn'kʌləreit], **concolorous** [kɔn'kʌlərəs], *a. Nat.Hist:* de couleur uniforme; concolore.

concomitance [kən'kɔmitəns], **concomitancy** [kən'kɔmitənsi], *s.* (*a*) concomitance *f*; (*b*) *Theol:* **the Body is present in the wine by c.,** le Corps est sous le vin par concomitance.

concomitant [kən'kɔmit(ə)nt]. **1.** *a.* concomitant (**with,** de). **2.** *s.* accessoire *m*, accompagnement *m*; **these infirmities are the concomitants of old age,** ces infirmités *f* forment le cortège de la vieillesse.

concord[1] ['kɔŋkɔ:d], *s.* **1.** concorde *f*, bonne entente, harmonie *f* (entre personnes); **to live in c.,** vivre en bon accord, de bon accord (**with,** avec). **2.** *Gram:* concordance *f*; **the concords,** les règles *f* d'accord; **to be in c. with . . .,** s'accorder avec . . . . **3.** *Mus:* accord.

concord[2] [kən'kɔ:d], *v.i.* concorder, s'accorder, être d'accord.

concordance [kən'kɔ:d(ə)ns], *s.* **1.** concordance *f*, accord *m* (**with,** avec); harmonie *f*; **the c. of the evidence,** la concordance des témoignages. **2.** index *m*, concordance (de la Bible, des œuvres d'un auteur).

concordant [kən'kɔ:d(ə)nt], *a.* **1.** (*a*) qui s'accorde, concordant, en harmonie (**with,** avec); **c. depositions,** témoignages concordants; (*b*) *Geol:* concordant. **2.** *Mus:* consonant, harmonieux.

concordantly [kən'kɔ:dəntli], *adv.* d'une manière concordante, harmonieuse.

concordat [kɔn'kɔ:dæt], *s.* concordat *m* (entre l'État et le Saint-Siège).

concordatory [kɔn'kɔ:dət(ə)ri], *a.* concordataire.

concours [kɔ̃ku:r], *s.* **c. d'élégance,** concours *m* d'élégance; **hors c.,** hors concours.

concourse ['kɔŋkɔ:s], *s.* **1.** (*a*) foule, *f*, rassemblement *m*, affluence *f*, concours *m* (de personnes); (*b*) convergence *f* d'allées (dans une forêt, etc.); carrefour *m*; *NAm:* confluent *m* (de deux rivières); (*c*) (i) lieu *m* de rassemblement; (ii) *NAm:* hall *m* (de gare). **2.** **fortuitous c. of atoms,** concours fortuit d'atomes; *Lit:* **unforeseen c. of circumstances,** concours inattendu de circonstances. **3.** *Jur: Scot:* homologation *f* (d'un procès au criminel intenté par un particulier).

concrescence [kən'kres(ə)ns], *s. Bot:* concrescence *f*.

concrete[1] ['kɔŋkri:t]. **1.** (*a*) concret, -ète; *Gram: Log:* **c. term,** terme concret; *Jur:* **c. case,** cas *m* d'espèce; *Psy:* **c. operations,** opérations concrètes; **c. music,** musique concrète; **c. suggestion, proposal,** suggestion *f*, proposition *f*, pratique, concrète; **c. example,** exemple concret; **to take a c. case,** concréter, concrétiser, un cas; (*b*) *Bot:* concrescent. **2.** *s. A: & Lit:* agrégation *f* (de faits, d'éléments disparates). **3.** *s. Civ.E: Const:* (*a*) béton *m* (de ciment); **to face a wall with c.,** bétonner une paroi; **reinforced c., armoured c.,** béton armé; ciment armé; **vibrated c.,** béton désaéré; **hooped c.,** béton cerclé, fretté; **c. block,** bloc *m* de, en, béton; **c. masonry,** maçonnerie *f* de béton; **c. mixer,** malaxeur *m* de béton; bétonnière *f*; bétonneuse *f*; **c. work,** bétonnage *m*; (*of new town*) *F:* **c. jungle,** forêt *f* de béton; (*b*) **tar c.,** béton de goudron et cailloux.

concrete[2] [kən'kri:t]. **1.** *v.tr.* (*a*) concrétiser (une idée, un cas); (*b*) concréter, solidifier (une matière); (*c*) ['kɔŋkri:t] *Civ.E: Const:* bétonner (une paroi, etc.) **2.** *v.i.* se solidifier; se concréter; se prendre en masse.

concretely ['kɔŋkri:tli], *adv.* d'une manière concrète; sous forme concrète.

concreteness ['kɔŋkri:tnis], *s.* caractère concret (d'un exemple, etc.).

concreting ['kɔŋkri:tiŋ], *s. Civ.E: etc:* bétonnage *m*.

concretion [kən'kri:ʃ(ə)n], *s. Med: Geol: etc:* concrétion *f*; *Med:* **biliary concretions,** concrétions biliaires.

concretionary [kən'kri:ʃn(ə)ri], *a. Geol:* concrétionné.

concretism ['kɔŋkri:tizm], *s. Phil:* chosisme *m*.

concretization ['kɔŋkri:tai'zeiʃ(ə)n], *s.* concrétisation *f*.

concretize ['kɔŋkri:taiz]. **1.** *v.tr.* concrétiser (une idée, un avantage). **2.** *v.i.* se concrétiser.

concubinage [kɔn'kju:binidʒ], *s.* concubinage *m*, concubinat *m*.

concubinary [kɔn'kju:binəri]. **1.** *a.* concubin. **2.** *s.* concubinaire *m*.

concubine ['kɔŋkjubain], *s.f.* **1.** concubine. **2.** seconde femme (chez les polygames).

concupiscence [kən'kju:pis(ə)ns], *s.* concupiscence *f*.

concupiscent [kən'kju:pis(ə)nt], *a.* concupiscent, libidineux.

concur [kən'kə:r], *v.i.* (**concurred**) **1.** (*a*) (*of events*) concourir, se rencontrer, coïncider; (*b*) **to c. in a result,** concourir à un résultat; **to c. to produce a result,** contribuer à produire un résultat. **2.** (*of pers.*) être d'accord (**with s.o.,** avec qn); (*of two pers.*) s'accorder ensemble (**in doing sth.,** pour faire qch.); être du même avis (que qn). **3.** *Jur:* (*of rights*) se heurter, s'opposer.

concurrence [kən'kʌr(ə)ns], *s.* **1.** (*a*) concours *m* (de lignes, de circonstances); coopération *f* (de personnes); *Geom:* **point of c.,** point *m* de concours; (*b*) simultanéité *f*. **2.** (*of pers.*) (*a*) accord *m*, concours; (*b*) assentiment *m*, consentement *m* (**in,** à); approbation *f*. **3.** *Jur:* conflit *m*, concurrence *f* (de droits).

concurrent [kən'kʌr(ə)nt], *a.* **1.** (*a*) concourant; *Mth:* **c. lines,** lignes concourantes; *Mec:* **c. forces,** forces concourantes; *Jur:* **c. powers,** pouvoirs communs; **c. fire insurance,** Assurance-Incendie répartie à conditions identiques entre plusieurs assureurs; (*b*) (*in time*) simultané; coexistant; *Jur:* **c. lease,** bail sujet à la servitude d'une autre fin de bail à courir; **two c. sentences,** confusion *f* de deux peines; (*c*) **c. cause,** cause contribuante. **2.** (*in agreement*) unanime, concordant, d'accord; **the c. views of several experts,** les opinions concordantes de plusieurs experts. **3.** (*a*) *Jur:* (*of rights*) qui se heurtent; opposés.

concurrently [kən'kʌrəntli], *adv.* concurremment (**with,** avec); **strikes and economic crises often happen c.,** les grèves vont souvent de pair avec les crises économiques; *Jur:* **the two sentences to run c.,** avec confusion des deux peines.

concuss [kən'kʌs], *v.tr.* **1.** (*a*) ébranler, secouer (qch.); (*b*) *Med:* commotionner (le cerveau). **2.** *Jur:* intimider (qn); **to c. s.o. into doing sth.,** faire commettre une action à qn sous le coup de l'intimidation.

concussion [kən'kʌʃ(ə)n], *s.* secousse *f*, choc *m*, ébranlement *m*; *Med:* commotion (cérébrale); **suffering from c.,** commotionné; *Artil:* **c. fuse,** fusée percutante.

concussive [kən'kʌsiv], *a. Med:* qui cause une commotion cérébrale.

condemn [kən'dem], *v.tr.* condamner. **1.** (*a*) **to c. s.o. to death, to be beheaded,** condamner qn à (la)mort, à être décapité; **the condemned man (on the scaffold),** le patient; *Theol:* **condemned by God's decree,** réprouvé; (*b*) **he was condemned by the doctors,** il a été condamné par les médecins; **condemned to lead a hopeless existence,** condamné à vivre sans espoir. **2.** condamner (une fenêtre, une porte, etc.); **these slums have been condemned,** ces taudis ont été condamnés à être démolis, à la démolition; **the bridge has been condemned as unfit for traffic,** le pont a été fermé à la circulation à cause de son mauvais état. **3.** déclarer coupable; **he was condemned of high treason,** il fut convaincu de haute trahison; **his looks c. him,** sa mine, rien que son apparence *f*, le condamne, le trahit. **4.** censurer, blâmer; **many people condemned the government's policy in this matter,** beaucoup de gens ont censuré, ont condamné, la politique du gouvernement vis-à-vis cette affaire.

condemnable [kən'dem(n)əbl], *a.* condamnable, blâmable.

condemnation [kɔndem'neiʃ(ə)n], *s.* **1.** (*a*) condamnation *f* (d'un coupable); (*b*) **his silence was his c.,** son silence le condamnait; *B:* **this is the c.,** or c'est ici le sujet de la condamnation; (*c*) censure *f*, blâme *m*; **I did not deserve his c.,** je ne méritais pas sa condamnation. **2.** condamnation (d'une porte, etc.); *Mil:* réforme *f* (du matériel).

condemnatory [kən'demnət(ə)ri], *a.* (silence *m*, *Jur:* sentence *f*) condamnatoire.

condemned [kən'demd], *a.* **c. man,** condamné *m*; **c. cell,** cellule *f* des condamnés.

condensability [kəndensə'biliti], *s.* condensabilité *f*.

condensable [kən'densəbl], *a.* condensable.

condensate [kɔn'denseit, 'kɔndenseit], *s. Mch:* eau *f* de condensation; **condensate,** *v.tr. & i.* condenser.

condensation [kɔnden'seiʃ(ə)n], *s.* **1.** *Ph: Ch: Meteor: etc:* condensation *f* (de la vapeur, d'un gaz, d'un produit synthétique, d'un discours, d'idées, etc.); *Av:* **c. trail,** traînée *f* de condensation. **2.** liquide condensé; (*of water*) eau *f* de condensation; **a slight c. on the inside of the flask,** une rosée sur la paroi interne de l'ampoule. **3. c. code,** code *m* d'abréviations.

condense [kən'dens]. **1.** *v.tr.* (*a*) condenser (un gaz, un produit, une pensée, un discours, etc.); serrer (son style); concentrer (un produit); **to c. a chapter into a single paragraph,** condenser, resserrer, un chapitre en un seul paragraphe; (*b*) **to c. a beam of light,** concentrer un faisceau de rayons. **2.** *v.i.* se condenser.

condensed [kən'denst], *a.* condensé; **c. milk,** lait concentré, condensé; *Cmptr:* **c. keyboard,** clavier réduit.

condenser [kən'densər], *s.* **1.** (*a*) *Mch: Gasm: etc:* condenseur *m*; **surface c.,** condenseur par surface; **jet c.,** condenseur à injection, condenseur à, par, mélange; **c. of a still,** réfrigérant *m*; **syphon c.,** condenseur à siphon; **regenerative c.,** condenseur à récupération; **evaporative c., counter-current c.,** condenseur à ruissellement; **single action c.,** condenseur à simple effet; **c. by contact,** condenseur tubulaire; **c. gauge,** baromètre *m* de condenseur; (*b*) *Nau:* **freshwater c.,** distillateur *m*. **2.** *El:* condensateur *m*; **plate c.,** condensateur à plaques, à plateaux; **air-dielectric c.,** condensateur à air; **mica c.,** condensateur isolé au mica; **sliding c.,** condensateur à armatures *f* mobiles; **by-pass c.,** condensateur de fuite, shunté; *W.Tel:* **tuning c.,** condensateur d'accord, de syntonisation; **variable c., adjustable c.,** condensateur (à capacité *f*) réglable; condensateur variable; **ganged condensers,** condensateurs à blocs combinés; **two-gang c.,** condensateur à deux blocs; **grid c.,** condensateur de la grille. **3.** *Opt:* condensateur; lentille condensatrice (d'un projecteur); **Abbe** ['æbe] **c.,** condensateur d'Abbe, éclaireur *m* d'Abbe (d'un microscope); **prismatic c.,** condensateur prismatique, de Fresnel; **cardioid c.,** condensateur cardioïde.

condensing[1] [kən'densiŋ], *a.* condensant; condensateur, -trice; **c. engine,** machine *f* à vapeur à condensation; *Mch:* **non-c.,** (machine *f*) sans condensation, à échappement libre.

condensing[2], *s.* condensation *f*.

condescend [kɔndi'send], *v.i.* **1.** condescendre (**to sth., to do sth.,** à qch., à faire qch.); s'abaisser, descendre (à, jusqu'à, faire qch.). **2.** (*a*) se montrer condescendant (to s.o., envers qn); user de condescendance (envers qn); (*b*) **I won't be condescended to,** je n'aime pas qu'on me traite de haut en bas; (*c*) **to c. to one's public,** s'abaisser au niveau de son public; **he wouldn't c. to take a bribe,** il ne s'abaisserait pas jusqu'à se laisser corrompre. **3.** *Jur: Scot:* (*of pursuer*) **to c. upon particulars,** spécifier les détails de sa plainte.

condescendance [kɔndi'sendəns], *s.* **1.** = CONDESCENSION. **2.** *Jur: Scot:* spécification *f* (par le plaignant) des détails (d'une action au criminel).

condescending [kɔndi'sendiŋ], *a.* condescendant (to, envers); **ironic and c. smile,** sourire ironique et condescendant.

condescendingly [kɔndi'sendiŋli], *adv.* avec condescendance; du haut de sa grandeur; **to treat s.o. c.,** traiter qn de haut en bas; **he spoke to me very c.,** il m'a parlé d'une manière condescendante.

condescension [kɔndi'senʃ(ə)n], *s.* **1.** condescendance *f* (to, envers, pour); **his c. annoys me intensely,** son air de condescendance, de supériorité, me répugne. **2.** *O:* complaisance *f*.

condign [kən'dain], *a. Lit:* (châtiment) mérité, exemplaire; **c. punishment,** juste punition *f*; **this reverse of fortune was c. punishment for his crimes,** ce revers de fortune fut la juste récompense de ses crimes; **he was brought to c. punishment as a traitor,** il subit le châtiment mérité des traîtres.

condignly [kən'dainli], *adv. Lit:* (puni) justement, exemplairement.

condiment ['kɔndimənt], *s.* condiment *m*; assaisonnement *m*; **to add condiments to a sauce,** relever une sauce; **c. set,** ménagère *f*.

condisciple [kɔndi'saipl], *s.* condisciple *m*, compagnon *m* d'études.

condition[1] [kən'diʃ(ə)n], *s.* condition *f*. **1. to impose conditions on s.o.; to lay down conditions to s.o.,** poser des conditions à qn; **conditions of sale,** conditions de vente; **conditions laid down in an agreement,** stipulations *f* d'un contrat; **conditions of the contract,** cahier *m* des charges; *Fin:* **terms and conditions of an issue,** modalités *f* d'une émission; *Jur:* **express c.,** condition expresse; **implied c.,** condition tacite; *Log: Mth:* **necessary and sufficient c.,** condition nécessaire et suffisante; **on c. that . . .,** à (la) condition, avec condition, que . . .; **on that c. I accept,** à cette condition, à ces conditions, j'accepte; **I accept, but on c. that I may do as much for you some other time,** j'accepte, mais à charge de revanche; **on c. that you pay,** à charge pour vous de payer; **under these conditions,** dans ces conditions. **2.** (*a*) état *m*, situation *f*; état d'entretien (du matériel, etc.), **the c. of the workers,** la situation des travailleurs; **working conditions (in a factory),** conditions de travail (dans une usine); (*of machine*) **normal working conditions,** régime *m* de marche normal; **weather, atmospheric, conditions,** conditions atmosphériques; **road conditions,** l'état des routes; **it depends on the c. of the road,** cela dépend de l'état de viabilité de la route; **to travel under the most favourable conditions,** voyager dans les meilleures conditions; *Aut:* **town conditions,** régime de ville; **climatic conditions,** régime climatérique; **in (good) c.,** en (bonne) condition, en bon état; **in bad c., in a poor c.,** en mauvais état; (*of goods*) **in fair c.,** acceptable(s); (*of person*) **to keep oneself in c.,** se maintenir en forme; **I'm (in bad) out of c.,** je ne suis pas en forme; *O:* **she's in an interesting c.,** elle est enceinte; elle est dans une situation intéressante; **I'm not in a (fit) c. to do it,** je ne suis pas à même, en état, de le faire; **horse in c.,** cheval *m* en chair, en condition; *Pol.Ec:* **economic conditions,** conditions économiques; **the c. of the market,** l'état du marché; **competitive conditions,** conditions de concurrence; **minimum cost c.,** hypothèse *f* du coût minimum; **living conditions,** conditions de vie; **the human c.,** la condition humaine; (*b*) état (civil); **to change one's c.,** changer d'état; se marier; (*c*) *O:* **people of humble c.,** gens *m* de simple condition.

condition[2], *v.tr.* **1. to c. to do sth., that sth. be done,** stipuler de faire qch., qu'on fasse qch. **2.** soumettre (qch.) à une condition; conditionner (qch.); imposer des conditions à (qch.); **man's life is conditioned by natural laws,** la vie de l'homme dépend des lois naturelles; **everything that conditions laws,** tout ce qui conditionne les lois; **factors that c. each other,** considérations *f* solidaires. **3.** *Ind: Com:* (*a*) conditionner (la soie, la laine, etc.); (*b*) vérifier l'état (d'humidité, etc.) (d'une marchandise, particulièrement des soieries). **4.** *Psy:* établir une réaction conditionnelle (chez un sujet).

conditional [kən'diʃənl]. **1.** *a.* conditionnel; (*a*) **my promise was c.,** ma promesse était soumise à certaines réserves; *Ecc:* **c. absolution,** absolution *f* à cautèle; (*b*) **c. on sth.,** dépendant de qch.; **my promise is c. on his satisfactory answer, on his getting married,** ma promesse est valable dans le cas où il répondrait d'une manière satisfaisante, à (la) condition qu'il se mariera; **cheapness is c. upon abundance,** le bon marché est fonction de l'abondance; (*c*) *Gram:* **c. clause,** proposition conditionnelle; **c. mood,** mode conditionnel. **2.** *s. Gram:* **verb in the c.,** verbe *m* au conditionnel.

conditionalism [kən'diʃənəlizm], *s. Theol:* conditionnalisme *m*.

conditionality [kəndiʃə'næliti], *s.* état conditionnel; limitation *f* par certaines conditions.

conditionally [kən'diʃən(ə)li], *adv.* conditionnellement; sous condition; sous certaines conditions; sous bénéfice d'inventaire; **c. on,** à la condition que.

conditioned [kən'diʃənd], *a.* conditionné. **1. if I were so c.,** si j'étais (i) dans une position semblable, (ii) soumis à de telles conditions; *Psy: Med:* **c. reflex,** réflexe conditionné. **2.** (*of proposition, etc.*) conditionné.

conditioner [kən'diʃənər], *s. Ind:* appareil *m* à conditionner (la soie, etc.); régulateur *m* d'air (d'un cinéma, etc.); **air c.,** climatiseur *m*, conditionneur *m* d'air; *Toil:* **hair c.,** lotion *f* capillaire.

conditioning [kən'diʃəniŋ], *s.* **1.** conditionnement *m* (des textiles, etc.); **air c.,** conditionnement de l'air; climatisation *f*. **2.** *Psy:* conditionnement.

condolatory [kən'doulət(ə)ri], *a.* (lettre *f*, etc.) de condoléance.

condole [kən'doul], *v.i.* **to c. with s.o.,** partager la douleur de qn; (*formally*) faire, exprimer, ses condoléances à qn.

condolence [kən'douləns], *s.* condoléance *f*; **to offer s.o. one's condolences,** offrir, présenter, ses condoléances à qn; **letter of c.,** lettre *f* de condoléance.

condom ['kɔndəm], *s. Hyg:* condom *m*.

condominium [kɔndou'miniəm], *s.* condominium *m*.

condonable [kən'dounəbl], *a.* (faute *f*) excusable, rémissible.

condonation [kɔndou'neiʃ(ə)n], *s.* pardon *m* (**of an offence,** d'une faute); indulgence *f* (of, pour); *Jur:* **c. (of matrimonial infidelity),** (i) pardon d'une offense conjugale; (ii) réconciliation *f* (des époux).

condone [kən'doun], *v.tr.* **1.** trouver des excuses pour (qch.); pardonner (un adultère). **2.** (*of action*) racheter (une offense); **that fact alone would c. many shortcomings,** ce fait à lui seul rachète bien des défaillances.

condonement [kən'dounmənt], *s.* = CONDONATION.

condoning[1] [kən'douniŋ], *a.* indulgent.

condoning[2], *s.* = CONDONATION.

condor ['kɔndɔːr], *s. Orn:* condor *m*.

condottiere, *pl.* **-ri** [kɔndɔ'tjεərei, -ri], *s. Hist:* capitaine *m* (de bande, de mercenaires); condottiere *m*, *pl.* -ri.

conduce [kən'djuːs], *v.i.* (*of action or thg*) contribuer, tendre (to, à); **to c. to a result,** conduire à un résultat; **virtues that c. to success,** vertus *f* qui favorisent le succès, qui mènent au succès.

conducive [kən'djuːsiv], *a.* qui contribue (à qch.); favorable (à qch.); **this weather is not c. to work,** ce temps n'incite pas au travail.

conduct[1] ['kɔndʌkt], *s.* conduite *f*. **1.** (*a*) **c. of affairs,** conduite, gestion *f*, maniement *m*, des affaires; **safe c.,** sauf-conduit *m*, *pl.* sauf-conduits; (*b*) *Art:* conduite (d'un tableau). **2.** allure *f*, manière *f* de se conduire (d'une personne); **c. towards s.o.,** conduite à l'égard de, avec, envers, qn; **laxity of c.,** inconduite *f*; **insolent c.,** insolence *f*; **good c. certificate,** certificat *m* de moralité; *Sch:* **good c. prize,** prix *m* de sagesse; *Jur:* **c. money,** frais *mpl* de déplacement, indemnité *f* de voyage (d'un témoin); **to lay down a line of c. to s.o.,** tracer une ligne de conduite à qn; *Mil: Navy:* **c. book,** (i) registre *m* de punitions; (ii) (*private*) livret *m* matricule; **c. sheet,** feuille *f* de punitions.

conduct[2] [kən'dʌkt], *v.tr.* **1. to c. s.o.,** conduire, (a)mener, qn; **conducted tours,** voyages organisés. **2.** (*a*) mener, gérer (des affaires); diriger (des opérations); effectuer, mener (une expérience); **to c. the correspondence** (*of a firm*), rédiger la correspondance; **to c. a campaign against s.o.,** mener une campagne contre qn; **who will c. the negotiations?** qui va mener les negociations? *Ecc:* **to c. a service,** diriger un office; *Jur:* **to c. one's own case,** plaider soi-même sa cause; *Ind:* **to c. a test,** exécuter un essai; (*b*) *Mus:* **to c. an orchestra,** diriger un orchestre; *v.i.* **Mr X will c.,** l'orchestre sera sous la direction de M. X. **3. to c. onself,** se comporter, se conduire (bien, mal). **4.** *Ph:* être conducteur de . . .; **substance that conducts heat, electricity,** substance conductrice de la chaleur, de

l'électricité.
conduct[3] ['kɔndʌkt], *s. Sch: Ecc: (at Eton)* aumônier *m.*
conductance [kən'dʌktəns], *s. El:* conductivité *f* spécifique; conductance *f*; **forward c.,** conductance directe; **back c.,** conductance inverse; **leakage c.,** perditance *f*; **mutual c.,** conductance mutuelle; **thermal c.,** conductance thermique.
conductibility [kəndʌktə'biliti], *s. Ph:* conductibilité *f.*
conductible [kən'dʌktəbl], *a. Ph:* conductible.
conductimeter [kəndʌk'timitər], *s. Ph: El:* conductimètre *m.*
conductimetric [kəndʌkti'metrik], *a. Ph: El:* conductimétrique.
conductimetry [kəndʌk'timitri], *s. Ph: El:* conductimétrie *f.*
conducting[1] [kən'dʌktiŋ], *a.* conducteur, -trice; *El:* **the c. parts,** les organes conducteurs; **current-c. ring,** bague *f* d'amenée de courant.
conducting[2], *s.* **1.** conduite *f* (de touristes, etc.). **2.** exécution *f* (d'un essai, etc.); conduite (d'une entreprise, d'une expérience); art *m* de diriger (un orchestre).
conduction [kən'dʌkʃ(ə)n], *s.* **1.** *Ph:* (*a*) conduction *f,* transmission *f* (de la chaleur); (*b*) *El:* **c. current,** courant *m* de conduction, courant conduit. **2.** conduite *f* (d'un liquide par tubes, etc.). **3.** *Physiol:* conduction *f.*
conductive [kən'dʌktiv], *a.* conducteur, -trice; *El:* **highly c.,** de haute conductibilité; bon conducteur.
conductivity [kɔndʌk'tiviti], *s. Ph:* conductivité *f,* conductibilité *f,* conductance *f*; **thermal c.,** conductibilité calorique; **electric c.,** conductivité électrique; **c. of an electrolyte,** conductance d'un électrolyte.
conductometer [kəndʌk'tɔmitər], *s. Ph: El:* conductimètre *m.*
conductometric [kəndʌktə'metrik], *a. Ph: El:* conductimétrique.
conductometry [kəndʌk'tɔmitri], *s. Ph: El:* conductimétrie *f.*
conductor [kən'dʌktər], *s.* **1.** (*pers.*) (*a*) conducteur, -trice, guide *m* (de personnes); accompagnateur, -trice (de touristes); (*b*) receveur *m,* (receveur-)encaisseur *m* (d'un autobus); *Rail: U.S:* chef *m* de train; (*c*) *Mus:* chef d'orchestre; **deputy c.,** sous-chef *m.* **2.** conducteur (de la chaleur, de l'électricité, etc.); *El:* **earthed, grounded, c.,** conducteur de terre; **c. wire,** fil *m* conducteur; *El:* **bare c.,** conducteur nu; **live c.,** conducteur chargé, en charge; **screened c.,** conducteur blindé; **resistor c.,** conducteur résistant; **equalizing c.,** fil neutre, fil d'équilibre; **lightning c.,** conducteur de paratonnerre; paratonnerre *m*; **neutral c.,** conducteur neutre, conducteur d'équilibre; fil intermédiaire, médian; fil de compensation; *Ph:* **non c.,** non-conducteur *m,* mauvais conducteur; (*of heat*) calorifuge *m*; (*of electricity*) isolant *m,* inconducteur *m*; *Rail:* **c. rail,** rail *m* de contact; rail de, du, courant; rail conducteur, électrisé, sous tension.
conductorship [kən'dʌktəʃip], *s.* direction *f* (d'un orchestre).
conductress [kən'dʌktris], *s.f.* receveuse (d'un autobus).
conduit ['kɔnd(w)it], *s.* canalisation *f.* **1.** (*a*) *Hyd.E:* **c. (pipe),** conduit *m*; tuyau conducteur; (tuyau de) conduite *f*; **water c.,** aqueduc *m*; (*b*) *Mch: etc:* tuyau de communication; (*c*) *El:* **cable c.,** tube *m* guide-fils; gaine *f* ou carter *m* de câbles; manchon *m* pour câbles. **2.** (*of electric trains*) caniveau (souterrain). **3.** passage souterrain, secret. **4.** *A:* fontaine (jaillissante); jet *m* d'eau.
conduplicate [kɔn'dju:plikeit], *a. Bot:* condupliqué.
condurango [kɔndju'ræŋgou], *s. Bot:* condurango *m.*
condylar ['kɔndilər], *a. Anat:* condylien.
condyle ['kɔndail], *s. Anat:* condyle *m.*
condyloid ['kɔndilɔid], *a. Anat:* condyloïde.
condyloma, *pl.* **-ata** [kɔndi'loumə, -ətə], *s. Med:* condylome *m.*
cone[1] [koun], *s.* **1.** (*a*) *Mth:* cône *m*; **truncated c.,** cône tronqué; tronc *m* de cône; **c. of revolution,** cône de révolution; **right c.,** cône droit; **right circular c.,** cône droit (à base) circulaire; **curvilinear c.,** cône parabolique; **vertex of a c.,** sommet *m* d'un cône; (*b*) *Artil:* **c. of dispersion, of spread,** cône de dispersion; gerbe *f* de dispersion; *Ind:* **white c. (of oxidizing flame),** panache *m* (de chalumeau); **inner c. of a flame,** noyau *m* d'une flamme; (*c*) *Opt:* **c. of light, of rays,** cône de lumière; (*d*) *Nau: etc:* **signal c.,** cône de signalisation; **storm c.,** cône de tempête, de mauvais temps; (*e*) *Comest:* cornet *m* (de glace, de crème glacée). **2.** *Geol:* (*a*) cône (d'un volcan); **parasitic, lateral, c.,** cône adventif; **cinder c.,** cône de cendres, de scories; **lava c.,** cône de coulée, de lave; cône lavique; **tuff c., debris c.,** cône de débris; **nested, ringed, c.,** cône emboîté; (*b*) **alluvial c., c. delta,** cône de déjection. **3.** (*a*) *Mec.E:* **driving c.,** cône de commande; **driven c.,** cône conduit; **clutch c.,** cône d'embrayage; **c. clutch,** embrayage *m* à cônes; **exhaust c.,** cône d'échappement; **adjusting c.,** cône de réglage; **c. of gears,** cône d'engrenage; **gearing c.,** cône d'entraînement; **direct c.,** cône direct; **inverted c.,** cône inversé, renversé; **c. brake,** frein *m* à cônes; **c. wheel,** roue *f* conique (à friction); **male, female, c.,** cône mâle, femelle; **expanding c.,** cône extensible; **friction c.,** cône à, de, friction; **speed c., (stepped-)c. pulley,** cône de vitesse, de transmission; cône-poulie *m, pl.* cônes-poulies; poulie étagée, à gradins; poire *f*; **belt c.,** cône à courroies; *I.C.E:* **spray c.,** diffuseur *m*; **atomizer, atomizing, c.,** champignon (pulvérisateur); *Mch:* **steam c.,** ajutage *m* à vapeur; (*b*) *Metall:* cône de fermeture, cloche *f,* trémie *f* (d'un haut fourneau); (*c*) *Av:* **nose c., shock c.,** cône avant, souris *f* (d'un avion); **spinner c., propeller c., hub c.,** cône de pénétration de l'hélice; **propeller hub securing c.,** cône d'appui du moyeu de l'hélice; **entrance, exit, c.** (*of wind tunnel*), cône d'entrée, de sortie: *Aer:* **mooring c.,** cône d'ancrage; (*d*) *Mus:* **tuning c.,** accordoir *m* (d'accordeur d'orgues). **4.** *Bot:* pomme *f,* cône (de pin); strobile *m* (de houblon, de pin); **c.-bearing,** conifère, strobilifère. **5.** (*a*) *Anat:* cône (de la rétine); (*b*) *Moll:* cône. **6.** *El: Elcs:* cône (de tube cathodique); **c. of silence,** cône de silence; **fake c. of silence,** faux cône de silence; *Rad:* **blind c.,** cône mort. **7.** *Cer:* **Seger c.,** cône de Seger; **pyrometric c.,** cône pyrométrique. **8.** *Agr:* **c. wheat, cones,** blé poulard.
cone[2]. **1.** *v.tr.* (*a*) *Mec.E:* côner (une surface); (*b*) bobiner (la soie, etc.) sur un cône; (*c*) *Av:* attraper, prendre, (un avion) dans un cône de projecteurs. **2.** *v.i.* (*of conifer*) produire des cônes, des pommes.
coneflower ['kounflauər], *s. Bot:* rudbeckie *f.*
cone-in-cone ['kouninkoun], *a. Geol:* (structure) cône-en-cône *inv.*
conenose ['kounnouz], *s. Ent: U.S:* (*also* **cone-nose(d) bug**), conorhine *m,* triatome *m.*
conepate ['kounei'pɑ:tei], *s. Z:* conépate *m.*
cone-shaped ['kounʃeipt], *a.* en forme de cône, coniforme; côné, conique; *Bot:* strobiliforme.
conessine ['kounisain], *s. Ch:* conessine *f.*
coney ['kouni], *s.* (*a*) lapin *m*; *Com:* **c. (skin),** peau *f* de lapin; **c. seal,** fourrure *f* genre loutre; (*b*) **Salinas c.,** lièvre patagon, mara *m*; (*c*) daman *m*; (*d*) *Her:* connil *m.*
confab[1] ['kɔnfæb], *s. F:* (= CONFABULATION) causerie *f*; entretien *m*; **there's a family c. going on in the dining room,** toute la famille est en train de conférer, est assemblée en conseil, en conclave, dans la salle à manger.
confab[2], *v.i. F:* causer, s'entretenir.
confabulate [kən'fæbjuleit], *v.i.* **1.** tenir un colloque; s'entretenir, *F:* causer. **2.** *Med: Psy:* fabuler.
confabulation [kənfæbju'leiʃ(ə)n], *s.* **1.** conciliabule *m*; causerie *f* intime; entretien familier; colloque *m*; **to have a c. with an old friend,** bavarder avec une vieille connaissance. **2.** *Med: Psy:* (con)fabulation *f.*
confect [kən'fekt], *v.tr. A: & U.S:* (*a*) confectionner (un plat, un médicament, etc.); conserver (des fruits, des légumes, etc.); confire (des fruits); (*b*) composer, écrire (un poème, etc.); (*c*) confectionner (une robe).
confection[1] [kən'fekʃ(ə)n], *s.* **1.** confectionnement *m,* confection *f* (de qch.). **2.** (*a*) *Pharm:* confection; (*b*) *Cu: A: & NAm:* confit *m,* friandise *f,* bonbon *m,* sucrerie *f*; (= *preserve*) conserve *f.* **3.** *Dressm: A: & NAm:* confection.
confection[2], *v.tr. A:* **1.** confectionner (des vêtements). **2.** confire (des fruits); fabriquer (des bonbons).
confectionary [kən'fekʃn(ə)ri], *a. A:* de confection.
confectioner [kən'fekʃ(ə)nər], *s. Com:* (*a*) confiseur, -euse; (*b*) pâtissier, -ière; **baker and c.,** boulanger-pâtissier *m, pl.* boulangers-pâtissiers; (*c*) **I bought them at the confectioner's,** je les ai achetés (i) à la confiserie, (ii) à la pâtisserie.
confectionery [kən'fekʃən(ə)ri], *s.* confiserie *f,* bonbons *mpl.*
confederacy [kən'fed(ə)rəsi], *s.* **1.** confédération *f* (d'États); *U.S.Hist:* **the Southern C.,** les (États) confédérés (1860–65). **2.** (*a*) conspiration *f*; (*b*) *A:* **they are in c.,** il y a entente entre eux.
confederate[1] [kən'fed(ə)rət]. **1.** *a.* confédéré (**with,** avec); *U.S.Hist:* **the C. States,** les États confédérés (1860–65). **2.** *s.* (*a*) confédéré *m*; (*b*) *Jur:* complice *mf* (**with,** de); (*c*) compère *m,* acolyte *m*; **conjuror's c.,** comparse *m.*
confederate[2] [kən'fedəreit]. **1.** *v.tr.* confédérer (des États); **to c. oneself with . . .,** se liguer avec . . .. **2.** *v.i.* (*a*) se confédérer (**with,** avec); former une confédération; (*b*) conspirer, comploter (**with, against,** avec, contre).
confederating [kən'fedəreitiŋ], *a.* confédérateur, -trice.
confederation [kənfedə'reiʃ(ə)n], *s.* confédération *f.*
confer [kən'fə:r], *v.* (**conferred**) **1.** *v.tr.* conférer (**a title on s.o.,** un titre à qn); **to c. a favour on s.o.,** accorder une faveur à qn; **to c. a benefit on s.o.,** (i) faire du bien à qn; (ii) attribuer un avantage à qn; **to c. a reward on s.o.,** adjuger une récompense à qn. **2.** *v.i.* conférer, entrer en consultation (**with s.o. on sth., about sth.,** avec qn sur qch.); **counsel and solicitor conferred,** l'avocat et le *solicitor* ont conféré.
conference ['kɔnfərəns], *s.* **1.** (*a*) conférence *f,* entretien *m,* consultation *f*; **c. of doctors,** consultation entre médecins; **clinico-pathological c.,** confrontation *f* radio-anatomo-clinique; **press c., news c.,** conférence de presse; **to be in c. with one's colleagues,** être en conférence, en consultation, avec ses collègues; **Mr Martin is in c.,** M. Martin est occupé; **round-table c.,** table ronde; **around the c. table,** à la table des conférences; autour du tapis vert. **2.** (*a*) congrès *m*; conférence; colloque *m*; **publishers' c.,** congrès d'éditeurs; **international c.,** congrès international; **modern-language c.,** congrès des professeurs de langues vivantes; **he is going to Paris for a c.,** il va assister à un congrès, un colloque, à Paris; (*b*) *Pol:* **Conservative Party C.,** congrès annuel du parti conservateur; *Ecc:* **the (Methodist) C.,** la conférence annuelle (des méthodistes).
conferment [kən'fə:mənt], *s.* **1.** collation *f* (d'un titre, d'un grade); **c. of a title on s.o.,** anoblissement *m* de qn. **2.** octroi *m* (d'une faveur).
conferrable [kən'fə:rəbl], *a.* que l'on peut conférer; accordable.
conferring [kən'fə:riŋ], *s.* **1.** = CONFERMENT. **2.** consultation *f.*
conferva, *pl.* **-ae** [kən'fə:və, -i:], *s. Algae:* conferve *f.*
Confervaceae [kɔnfə:'veisii:], *s.pl. Algae:* confervacées *f.*
confess [kən'fes], *v.tr.* **1.** (*a*) confesser, avouer (une faute); **to c. oneself (to be) guilty,** s'avouer coupable; **he confessed that he was the man who had written the article,** il avoua être l'auteur de l'article; **I was wrong, I c.,** j'admets que j'ai eu tort; j'ai eu tort, je l'avoue, j'en conviens; *Prov:* **a fault confessed is half redressed,** péché avoué est à demi pardonné; une faute avouée est à demi pardonnée; (*b*) *v.i.* (*of criminal*) faire des aveux; (*c*) *v.ind.tr.* **to c. to a crime,** avouer un crime; **to c. to (having) a dread of . . .,** avouer avoir peur de . . .; **to c. to a liking for . . .,** avouer avoir un penchant, un faible, pour . . .; **to c. to having done sth.,** se confesser de qch. **2.** *Ecc:* (*a*) **to c. one's sins,** confesser ses péchés; se confesser de ses péchés; **to c. (oneself),** se confesser (**to s.o.,** à qn, auprès de qn); (*b*) (*of priest*) confesser (un pénitent). **3.** *A: & Poet:* attester; **to c. the faith,** confesser, attester, sa foi.
confessant [kən'fes(ə)nt], *s. Ecc:* confessant, -ante; pénitent, -ente (à confesse).
confessed [kən'fest], *a.* (crime) confessé, avoué; (pénitent) confessé; **a c. difficulty,** une difficulté reconnue; **the c. murderer of . . .,** le meurtrier avoué de . . .; **to stand c. as . . .,** se révéler, s'accuser, se faire reconnaître, comme . . ..
confessedly [kən'fesidli], *adv.* **1.** de l'aveu général; **c. difficult,** reconnu comme difficile. **2.** de son propre aveu; ouvertement; **to become c. an enemy of s.o.,** s'avouer franchement ennemi de qn.
confession [kən'feʃ(ə)n], *s.* **1.** confession *f,* aveu *m* (de qch.); **to make a full c.,** faire des aveux complets; **on their own c.,** de leur propre aveu; **by general c.,** de l'aveu de tout le monde. **2.** *Jur:* **c. of defence, of plea; c. and avoidance,** désistement *m.* **3.** *Ecc:* **(auricular) c.,** confession (auriculaire, privée); **the seal of c.,** le secret de la confession; le secret du confessionnal; **to go to c.,** aller à confesse; se confesser; **to hear s.o.'s c.,** confesser qn; entendre la confession de qn. **4.** (*a*) **c. of faith,** confession (de foi); **the C. of Augsburg,** la Confession d'Augsbourg; (*b*) **the various confessions of the European people,** les confessions diverses des peuples de l'Europe. **5.** (*also* **confessio**) confession, tombe *f* (d'un martyr, d'un confesseur).
confessional [kən'feʃənl]. **1.** *a.* confessionnel. **2.** *s. Ecc:* confessionnal *m*; **the secrets of the c.,** les secrets *m* du confessionnal.
confessionary [kən'feʃən(ə)ri]. **1.** *a.* confessionnaire. **2.** *s. A:* = CONFESSION 5.
confessionist [kən'feʃənist], *s. Rel.H:* confessionniste *m*; luthérien *m.*
confessor [kən'fesər], *s.* **1.** personne *f* qui avoue (un crime); *Ecc:* personne qui se confesse; pénitent, -ente. **2.** *Ecc:* (*priest*) confesseur *m.* **3.** confesseur (de sa foi); *Hist:* **Edward the C.,** Édouard le Confesseur.
confetti [kən'feti(:)], *s.pl.* confetti *m.*

confidant, *f.* **confidante** [kɔnfi'dænt], *s.* confident, -ente; affidé, -ée.

confide [kən'faid]. **1.** *v.tr.* confier; (*a*) **to c. a secret to s.o.,** confier un secret à qn; **he confided to me that . . .,** il m'a avoué en confidence que . . .; **he hadn't confided his plans to anyone,** il n'avait révélé ses projets à qui que ce soit; **to c. sth. to s.o.'s care,** confier qch. à la garde de qn. **2.** *v.i.* (*a*) **to c. in s.o.,** se fier à qn; se confier, se livrer, à qn; compter sur qn; mettre sa confiance en qn; (*b*) **to c. in s.o. about one's private affairs,** confier ses affaires personnelles à qn; parler de ses affaires personnelles à qn; **I have not one friend to c. in,** je n'ai pas un ami à qui je puisse confier un secret.

confidence ['kɔnfidəns], *s.* **1.** (*a*) confiance *f* **(in,** en); **to place, put, repose, one's c. in s.o.,** placer, mettre, sa confiance en qn; donner, accorder, sa confiance à qn; faire confiance à qn; **to have every c. in s.o.,** faire toute confiance à qn; **you can buy it with complete c.,** vous pouvez l'acheter en toute assurance; **to lose the c. of the public,** perdre toute créance; **well-placed c.,** confiance bien placée; **the c. placed in me,** la confiance qui m'a été témoignée; **to deserve s.o.'s c.,** répondre à la confiance de qn; **to restore (public) c.,** faire renaître la confiance; *Parl:* **vote of c.,** vote *m* de confiance; **to ask for a vote of c.,** poser la question de confiance; **to receive a vote of c.,** se voir accorder un vote de confiance; **motion of no c.,** motion *f* de défiance; (*b*) assurance *f*, confiance, hardiesse *f*; **to act with c.,** agir avec confiance, avec assurance; **to answer with c.,** répondre avec assurance, avec hardiesse; **to gather c.,** prendre confiance; **I have every c. that he will succeed,** j'ai l'assurance qu'il réussira; (*c*) *Cmptr:* **c. check,** test *m* de sécurité (des circuits). **2.** confidence *f*; **to be in s.o.'s c.,** (i) partager (tous) les secrets de qn; (ii) être dans le secret; **to take s.o. into one's c.,** se confier à qn; mettre qn dans le secret; **I was warned in c. that . . .,** on m'a prévenu confidentiellement que . . .; **to tell s.o. sth. in c.,** dire qch. à qn en confidence; **in strict c.,** à titre essentiellement confidentiel. **3. to make a c. to s.o.,** faire une confidence à qn; **guilty of repeating a c.,** coupable d'avoir répété une chose dite en confidence. **4. c. trick,** *NAm:* **c. game,** vol *m* à l'américaine, *P:* à la goure; *P:* charriage *m*; **to play the c. trick on s.o.,** voler qn à l'américaine; *P:* charrier qn; **c. trickster,** escroc *m*; chevalier *m* d'industrie, voleur *m* à l'américaine.

confident ['kɔnfidənt]. **1.** *a.* (*a*) assuré, sûr **(of,** de); confiant; **to be c. of the future,** avoir foi en l'avenir; **c. of success,** sûr de réussir; **feeling c. that . . .,** convaincu, assuré, que . . .; dans la conviction que . . .; **in a c. tone,** d'un ton assuré; d'un ton plein d'assurance; **c. hope,** ferme espoir *m*; **we are c. that . . .,** nous sommes persuadés que + *ind.*; nous ne doutons pas que . . . (ne) + *sub.* (*b*) *Pej:* plein de hardiesse; effronté. **2.** *s.* confident, -ente.

confidential [kɔnfi'denʃl], *a.* **1.** (avis, etc.) confidentiel. **2. to be c. (with s.o.),** faire des confidences (à qn); **he became quite c. with me,** il s'ouvrit tout entier à moi. **3. c. clerk, post,** homme *m*, poste *m*, de confiance; **c. secretary,** secrétaire particulier; **c. agent,** homme de confiance; *Pej:* affidé *m*.

confidentiality [kɔnfidenʃi'æliti], **confidentialness** [kɔnfi'denʃ(ə)lnis], *s.* caractère confidentiel (de qch.).

confidentially [kɔnfi'denʃəli], *adv.* confidentiellement; en confidence; à titre confidentiel.

confidently ['kɔnfidəntli], *adv.* (*a*) avec confiance; en toute confiance; **to rely c. on sth., on s.o.,** avoir pleine confiance en qch.; se reposer sur qn; (*b*) avec assurance; d'un ton assuré.

confiding [kən'faidiŋ], *a.* confiant; sans soupçons; **to be of a c. nature,** être peu soupçonneux, peu méfiant, de caractère.

confidingly [kən'faidiŋli], *adv.* avec confiance; d'un air, d'un ton, confiant.

configuration [kənfigju'reiʃ(ə)n], *s.* **1.** (*a*) configuration *f* (de la terre, etc.); profil *m* (d'une route, etc.); (*b*) **electronic c.,** configuration électronique; (*c*) *Cmptr:* configuration, composition *f* (d'un ordinateur); combinaison *f* (de perforations, de bits); **bit c.,** configuration binaire; **object c.,** configuration objet. **2.** *Astr:* configuration (des planètes).

configurator [kən'figjureitər], *s.* configurateur *m*.

configure [kən'figər], *v.tr.* configurer (qch.); *Cmptr:* composer (un ensemble), réaliser une configuration.

confine [kən'fain]. **1.** *v.tr.* (*a*) *A:* (*banish*) confiner **(s.o. to a place,** qn dans un lieu); (*b*) (r)enfermer (qn dans une prison, etc.); **confined within four walls,** renfermé entre quatre murs; (*c*) (re)tenir (un malade dans son lit), cantonner (des animaux malades); **to be confined to one's room, to the house,** (être obligé de) garder la chambre, la maison; être confiné au logis; **to be confined to bed,** être obligé de garder le lit; être alité; (*d*) **happiness is not confined to any particular class,** le bonheur ne se limite pas à une seule classe, n'est pas l'apanage d'une seule classe; **to c. oneself to sth., to doing sth.,** se borner, se limiter, s'en tenir, se restreindre, à qch., à faire qch.; **to c. oneself to a field of study,** se cantonner dans un champ d'études; **to c. oneself to one's instructions,** s'en tenir à ses instructions; **to c. oneself to facts,** s'en tenir aux faits; se retrancher derrière les faits; **all their knowledge is confined to this,** toute leur science se borne à cela; (*e*) resserrer (une rivière dans son lit, etc.); **to be confined (for space),** être à l'étroit; **confined air,** air confiné, renfermé; **confined space,** espace resserré, restreint; (*f*) (*of woman*) **to be confined,** faire ses couches; accoucher; **she has just been confined,** elle relève de (ses) couches. **2.** *v.i. occ.Lit:* **to c. with, on, to, a country,** confiner à un pays; être limitrophe d'un pays.

confinement [kən'fainmənt], *s.* **1.** emprisonnement *m*, encellulement *m*, réclusion *f*; **three months' c.,** trois mois *m* de prison *f*; **solitary c.,** prison cellulaire, emprisonnement cellulaire, encellulement; *Jur:* réclusion; **three months' solitary c.,** trois mois de cellule *f*; **to be in c.,** être renfermé, en prison, en cellule; être étroitement gardé; **in close c., in solitary c.,** au secret; dans une réclusion rigoureuse. **2.** couches *fpl*, accouchement *m*; **home c.,** accouchement à domicile; (*of doctor*) **to attend a c.,** faire un accouchement. **3.** limitation *f*, restriction *f* **(to,** à).

confines ['kɔnfainz], *s.pl.* (*a*) *Lit:* confins *m* (d'un lieu, etc.); **within the c. of Judea,** en deçà des confins de la Judée; **on the c. of the city and the Temple,** aux confins de la cité et du Temple; **at the extreme c. of the earth,** aux derniers confins de la terre; **the utmost c. of space,** les dernières limites de l'espace; (*b*) eaux *f* (d'un port).

confirm [kən'fə:m], *v.tr.* **1.** (*strengthen*) (r)affermir, assurer (son pouvoir); fortifier (une résolution, des soupçons); confirmer, affermir (qn dans une opinion); consolider (la paix, une alliance); **example that confirms the reading,** exemple *m* qui sanctionne la leçon; **to c. s.o.'s hopes,** répondre, correspondre, aux espérances de qn; réaliser, remplir, les espérances de qn. **2.** (*ratify*) confirmer (un traité, un privilège, etc.); approuver (une nomination); adhérer à, entériner (une décision); valider (une élection); *Jur:* homologuer (un arrêt); **to c. s.o. in a title,** assurer un titre à qn. **3.** (*a*) (*corroborate*) confirmer, corroborer (une nouvelle, des soupçons); **confirming my letter,** en confirmation de ma lettre; (*b*) *Av:* **flight confirmed,** vol confirmé. **4.** *Ecc:* confirmer; donner la confirmation à (qn); **to be confirmed,** recevoir la confirmation.

confirmand [kɔnfə:'mænd], *s. Ecc:* confirmand, -ande.

confirmation [kɔnfə'meiʃ(ə)n], *s.* **1.** (r)affermissement *m* (de l'autorité de qn); confirmation *f* (d'un traité, d'une nouvelle, etc.); corroboration *f* (d'un témoignage, etc.); *Jur:* homologation *f* (d'un concordat); **in c. of . . .,** à l'appui de . . .; pour confirmer . . . **2.** *Ecc:* confirmation.

confirmative [kən'fə:mətiv], *a.* confirmatif **(of,** de).

confirmatory [kən'fə:mət(ə)ri], *a.* confirmatoire **(of,** de).

confirmed [kən'fə:md], *a.* (habitude *f*) invétérée; (ivrogne) incorrigible, fieffé; **c. bachelor,** célibataire endurci; **c. invalid,** valétudinaire *mf* de longue date.

confirmee [kɔnfə:'mi:], *s. Ecc:* confirmé, -ée.

confirmer [kən'fə:mər], *s.* confirmateur, -trice.

confiscable [kən'fiskəbl], *a.* confiscable.

confiscate ['kɔnfiskeit], *v.tr.* confisquer **(from s.o.,** à qn).

confiscation [kɔnfis'keiʃ(ə)n], *s.* confiscation *f*.

confiscator ['kɔnfiskeitər], *s.* confiscateur, -trice.

confiscatory [kɔnfis'keitəri], *a.* (mesures *f*, etc.) de confiscation.

confiteor [kɔn'fitiɔ:r], *s. Ecc:* confiteor *m*.

conflagration [kɔnflə'greiʃ(ə)n], *s.* (*a*) conflagration *f*, embrasement *m*; (*b*) incendie *m*; sinistre *m* (par incendie).

conflict[1] ['kɔnflikt], *s.* **1.** conflit *m*, lutte *f* (de personnes); conflit, antagonisme *m*, contradiction *f* (de lois, de sentiments, d'intérêts); **to come into c. with s.o., with s.o.'s opinions,** entrer en conflit, en lutte, avec qn, avec les opinions de qn; froisser les opinions de qn; **to be in c. with s.o.,** être en conflit, en désaccord, avec qn; **to bring interests into c.,** mettre des intérêts aux prises. **2.** *A:* entrechoquement *m* (de deux masses).

conflict[2] [kən'flikt], *v.i.* **1.** *A:* lutter **(with,** contre); **he had to c. with great difficulties,** il eut à lutter contre de grandes difficultés. **2.** être en conflit, en contradiction, en désaccord **(with sth.,** avec qch.); **duties that c. with each other,** fonctions *f* incompatibles; **when interests c.,** lorsque les intérêts se heurtent; lorsqu'il y a un heurt d'intérêts.

conflicting [kən'fliktiŋ], *a.* opposé **(with,** à); incompatible **(with,** avec); **c. passions,** passions opposées, contradictoires; **c. evidence,** témoignages discordants, contradictoires.

confliction [kən'flikʃ(ə)n], *s. Lit:* incompatibilité *f*, antagonisme *m* (de deux textes, etc.).

conflictual [kən'fliktjuəl], *a.* conflictuel.

confluence ['kɔnfluəns], *s.* **1.** *Geog:* confluent *m*, confluence *f* (de deux cours d'eau, deux glaciers). **2.** *A:* & *Lit:* affluence *f*, concours *m* (de monde). **3.** *Med:* confluence *f* (de la petite vérole).

confluent ['kɔnfluənt]. **1.** *a.* (*a*) (*of streams*) qui confluent; (*of valleys*) qui se rejoignent, se réunissent; (*of marks, spots*) qui se confondent; *Med:* **c. smallpox,** petite vérole confluente; (*b*) *Bot:* (*of leaves, etc.*) confluent. **2.** *s.* affluent *m* (d'un fleuve).

conform [kən'fɔ:m]. **1.** *v.tr.* conformer **(sth. to sth.,** qch. à qch.). **2.** *v.i.* se conformer **(to, with, sth.,** à qch.); (*a*) **to c. to fashion,** suivre la mode; **to c. with an order,** se conformer, se soumettre, à un ordre; **to c. to a discipline, to the law,** se plier à une discipline; obéir aux lois; **to make a law c. to a principle,** mettre une loi d'accord avec un principe; **not to c. to a principle, to a clause,** déroger à un principe, à un article (du traité); **this does not c. with our arrangements,** cela ne va pas avec les dispositions que nous avons prises; (*b*) (*of a part*) **to c. (in shape) to another part,** épouser la forme d'une autre pièce; s'adapter à une autre pièce; (*c*) *Rel.H:* **to c.,** faire acte de soumission à la religion d'État; faire acte de conformité.

conformability [kənfɔ:mə'biliti], *s. Geol: etc:* conformité *f*.

conformable [kən'fɔ:məbl], *a.* **1.** (*a*) (*of thg*) conforme **(to,** à); **c. to reason,** compatible avec la raison; (*b*) auquel l'on peut se conformer, s'accommoder. **2.** (*of pers.*) (*a*) accommodant, complaisant; (*b*) docile, soumis **(to,** à); (*c*) *Rel.H:* soumis, rallié, à la religion d'État. **3.** *Geol:* **c. strata,** couches concordantes.

conformably [kən'fɔ:məbli], *adv.* conformément (à); en conformité (de).

conformance [kən'fɔ:məns], *s.* conformité *f*; soumission *f* **(to,** à).

conformation [kɔnfɔ:'meiʃ(ə)n], *s.* **1.** action *f* de rendre conforme **(to,** à); **the c. of our lives to the duties of morality,** le devoir qui nous incombe de vivre conformément à la morale. **2.** conformation *f*, structure *f* (d'un corps, etc.); configuration *f* (des montagnes, d'une route, etc.); profil *m*.

conformator ['kɔnfɔ:meitər], *s.* conformateur *m* (de chapelier).

conformism [kən'fɔ:mizm], *s.* (*a*) *Rel:* conformisme *m*; (*b*) conformisme; traditionalisme *m*.

conformist [kən'fɔ:mist], *s.* (*a*) *Rel:* conformiste *mf*; adhérent, -ente, de la religion d'État, de l'Église anglicane; (*b*) conformiste; traditionaliste *mf*.

conformity [kən'fɔ:miti], *s.* **1.** conformité *f* **(to, with,** à); **in c. with . . .,** en conformité de . . ., conformément à . . ., à l'avenant de . . .; **in c. with your instructions,** d'après vos instructions; conformément à vos ordres; **action in c. with the law,** action *f* conforme à la loi; **to bring a law into c. with a principle,** mettre une loi d'accord avec un principe. **2.** (*a*) *U.S:* conformisme *m*; (*b*) *Rel:* conformisme; conformité; orthodoxie *f*; soumission *f* à la religion d'État.

confound [kən'faund], *v.tr.* **1.** confondre, déconcerter, renverser (les plans de qn); **events often c. our hopes,** souvent les événements *m* réduisent à rien nos espérances. **2.** (*a*) bouleverser, troubler, confondre (qn); (*b*) *A:* rendre (qn) confus; couvrir (qn) de confusion; *B:* **to be confounded,** être confus. **3.** *Lit:* (*a*) mêler, brouiller; mettre la confusion, le désordre, dans (les choses); (*b*) **to c. sth. with sth.,** confondre qch. avec qch.; prendre qch. pour qch. d'autre. **4.** *F:* envoyer (qn) au diable; **c. him!** que le diable l'emporte! **c. it!** zut alors!

confounded [kən'faundid], *a. F:* maudit, sacré; **shut that c. window!** ferme cette sacrée fenêtre! **you c. idiot!** espèce d'idiot! **his c. dog,** son sacré chien.

confoundedly [kən'faundidli], *adv. F:* furieusement, diablement; **c. cold,** bigrement froid.

confraternity [kɔnfrə'tə:niti], *s.* **1.** confrérie *f*. **2. treaty of c.,** traité *m* de confraternité.

confrere, confrère ['kɔnfreər], *s.* confrère *m*.

confront [kən'frʌnt], *v.tr.* **1. to c. s.o., sth.,** être en face, se trouver en présence, de qn, de qch.; **many difficulties c. us,** nous avons bien des difficultés à envisager; **to be confronted by, with, a difficulty,** se trouver en face, en présence, d'une difficulté; se trouver devant une difficulté. **2. to c. the enemy, a danger,** affronter, faire face à, l'ennemi, un danger; tenir tête à l'ennemi. **3. to c. s.o. with witnesses,** confronter qn avec des témoins; **to c. s.o. with sth.,** mettre qn en présence, en face, de qch.; **to c. two witnesses,** mettre deux témoins face à face; confronter deux témoins. **4.** confronter, comparer (des documents, etc.).

confrontation [kɔnfrʌn'teiʃ(ə)n], *s.* **1.** confrontation *f* (de témoins, etc.). **2.** affrontement *m.*

confronting [kən'frʌntiŋ], *a.* **c. armies,** armées opposées, se faisant front.

Confucian [kən'fju:ʃiən], *a. & s.* confucien, -ienne; confucianiste *mf.*

Confucianism [kən'fju:ʃiənizm], *s.* confucianisme *m.*

Confucianist [kən'fju:ʃiənist], *a. & s.* confucianiste (*mf*).

confuse [kən'fju:z], *v.tr.* **1.** mêler, brouiller; mettre la confusion, le désordre, dans (les choses); **to c. accounts,** embrouiller des comptes. **2. to c. sth. with sth.,** confondre qch. avec qch.; **I confused you with your brother,** je vous ai confondu avec votre frère; **to c. dates,** confondre des dates. **3.** (*a*) embrouiller (qn); **to get confused,** s'embrouiller; *F:* perdre le nord; **to be utterly confused,** avoir la raison à l'envers; **my memory is getting confused,** ma mémoire se brouille; (*b*) confondre, bouleverser, ahurir, dérouter, troubler (qn); (*c*) rendre (qn) confus; **to get confused,** se troubler; devenir confus.

confused [kən'fju:zd], *a.* **1.** (*a*) embrouillé; **c. mind, conscience,** esprit *m* trouble; conscience *f* trouble; **I have only a c. memory of the facts,** je n'ai plus qu'un souvenir confus des faits, qu'un vague souvenir des faits; (*b*) bouleversé, ahuri; (*c*) confus, interdit, honteux. **2.** (*of thg*) confus, enchevêtré; **c. speech,** discours confus, embrouillé, entortillé; **c. voices,** voix confuses; **a c. mass of twisted girders,** un enchevêtrement de poutres tordues; *Nau:* **c. sea,** mer tourmentée.

confusedly [kən'fju:zidli], *adv.* **1.** confusément. **2.** (regarder qn) avec confusion, d'un air confus, interdit.

confusedness [kən'fju:zidnis], *s.* confusion *f.*

confusing [kən'fju:ziŋ], *a.* embrouillant; **it's very c.,** c'est à ne pas s'y reconnaître; on s'y perd.

confusion [kən'fju:ʒ(ə)n], *s.* **1.** *A:* déconfiture *f*, ruine *f*; **to drink to the c. of one's enemies,** boire à la déconfiture de ses ennemis. **2.** (*of pers.*) confusion *f*; (*a*) **his extravagant praise caused her a great deal of c.,** ses louanges exagérées l'ont couverte de confusion; **in his c. he forgot his appointment,** tout confus, il a oublié son rendez-vous; (*b*) **to put s.o. to c.,** couvrir qn de confusion, de honte; confondre qn. **3.** (*a*) action *f* de brouiller; **the c. of tongues,** la confusion des langues; (*b*) confusion, désordre *m*, désarroi *m*, remue-ménage *m*; **everything was in c.,** tout était en désordre; tout était sens dessus dessous; tout était pêle-mêle; **this event threw the household into utter c.,** cet événement a mis la maison aux cent coups; **to throw the army into c.,** mettre la confusion, le désarroi, dans l'armée; jeter le désordre dans l'armée; **to spread c. everywhere,** jeter partout le désordre; mettre tout en confusion; **to retire in c.,** se retirer en désordre, à la débandade; **to fall into c.,** se désorganiser, se désordonner; *Lit:* **c. worse confounded,** le comble de la confusion. **4. c. of sth. with sth.,** confusion de qch. avec qch.; **the c. of knowledge with wisdom,** la confusion du savoir avec la sagesse; **there has been a c. of names,** il y a eu confusion de noms. **5.** mélange *m*, fondu *m*; *Opt: Phot:* **circle of c.,** cercle *m* de diffusion *f.* **6.** *Med:* état confusionnel, confusion mentale.

confutable [kən'fju:təbl], *a.* réfutable.

confutation [kɔnfju:'teiʃ(ə)n], *s.* réfutation *f.*

confute [kən'fju:t], *v.tr.* **1.** convaincre (qn) d'erreur; démolir les arguments de (qn). **2.** réfuter (un argument).

confuter [kən'fju:tər], *s.* réfutateur, -trice.

conga ['kɔŋgə], *s. Danc:* conga *f.*

congé ['kɔnʒei], *s.* **1.** congé *m*; **to give s.o. his c.,** signifier son congé à qn. **2.** *Arch:* congé (d'une colonne); apophyge *f.*

congeal [kən'dʒi:l]. **1.** *v.tr.* (*a*) congeler, geler; (*b*) coaguler; cailler (le sang); figer (l'huile, le sang); concréter (l'huile, etc.). **2.** *v.i.* (*a*) se congeler; geler; (*b*) (*of oil, blood*) se figer; (*of blood*) se coaguler; (*of jelly, milk*) se prendre; (*of oil, etc.*) se concréter.

congealability [kəndʒi:lə'biliti], **congealableness** [kən'dʒi:ləblnis], *s.* congélabilité *f.*

congealable [kən'dʒi:ləbl], *a.* congelable; concrescible.

congealment [kən'dʒi:lmənt], **congelation** [kəndʒi'leiʃ(ə)n], *s.* congélation *f.*

congelifluction [kəndʒeli'flʌkʃ(ə)n], *s. Geol:* gélifluxion *f.*

congelifraction [kəndʒeli'frækʃ(ə)n], *s. Geol:* gélifraction *f*, gélivation *f.*

congeliturbation [kəndʒelitə:'beiʃ(ə)n], *s. Geol:* géliturbation *f.*

congener ['kɔndʒinər]. **1.** *s.* congénère *m* (**of,** de). **2.** *a.* congénère (**to,** de).

congeneric ['kɔndʒe'nerik], *a.* congénère.

congenerous [kən'dʒenərəs], *a. Anat:* (muscles *m*) congénères.

congenial [kən'dʒi:niəl], *a.* **1.** (*a*) **c. with sth.,** du même caractère, de la même nature, que qch.; **we have c. tastes,** nous avons des goûts en commun; **my tastes are c. with yours,** mes goûts s'accordent avec les vôtres; (*b*) **c. spirit,** esprit *m* sympathique, aimable; **c. surroundings,** entourage *m* sympathique; **c. employment,** travail *m* agréable. **2.** propre, convenable, qui convient (**to,** à); **if I could find some c. employment,** si je pouvais trouver un emploi qui me convienne; **work c. to an old soldier,** travail *m* qui convient, qui conviendrait, à un ancien soldat.

congeniality [kəndʒi:ni'æliti], *s.* **1.** accord *m* de sentiments, d'humeur; **c. of tastes,** communauté *f* de goûts. **2. the c. of my employment,** le caractère agréable de mon travail.

congenially [kən'dʒi:niəli], *adv.* agréablement; d'une manière aimable, sympathique.

congenital [kən'dʒenitl], *a.* congénital, -aux; **c. hernia,** hernie congénitale; **c. idiot,** (i) idiot de naissance; (ii) *F:* parfait idiot.

congenitally [kən'dʒenitəli], *adv.* congénitalement; de naissance.

conger ['kɔŋgər], *s. Ich:* **c. (eel),** congre *m*; anguille *f* de mer.

congeries [kən'dʒiəri:z], *s. A: & Lit:* entassement *m*, amas *m*, accumulation *f*, masse *f* (d'objets disparates, etc.).

congest [kən'dʒest]. **1.** *v.tr.* (*a*) *Med:* congestionner; engorger; (*b*) encombrer, embouteiller (la circulation, les rues, etc.). **2.** *v.i.* (*a*) *Med:* se congestionner; (*b*) (*of traffic, etc.*) s'accumuler, s'embouteiller.

congested [kən'dʒestid], *a.* **1.** *Med:* congestionné, hyperémié; injecté (de sang). **2.** (*of traffic, etc.*) encombré, embarrassé, embouteillé; **c. area,** région surpeuplée; **c. streets,** rues surchargées de circulation; rues encombrées; **the c. state of the roads,** l'encombrement *m* des routes.

congestion [kən'dʒestʃ(ə)n], *s.* **1.** *Med:* congestion *f*; engorgement *m*, injection *f* (des capillaires, etc.); **c. of the brain, of the lungs,** congestion cérébrale, pulmonaire; **to relieve the c. in the lungs, etc.,** décongestionner les poumons, etc. **2.** (*a*) encombrement *m* (de circulation, etc.); embouteillage *m*; **the new road will relieve the c. in the centre of the town,** la nouvelle route va décongestionner le centre de la ville; **the bus queues were causing c. on the pavement,** les queues de gens qui attendaient l'autobus bloquaient, encombraient, le trottoir; (*b*) (*overcrowding*) surpeuplement *m.*

congestive [kən'dʒestiv], *a. Med:* congestif.

congius ['kɔndʒiəs], *s. Meas:* **1.** *Rom.Ant:* conge *m.* **2.** *Pharm:* gallon *m.*

conglobate[1] ['kɔngloubeit], *a. Nat.Hist:* conglobé.

conglobate[2], **conglobe** [kən'gloub]. **1.** *v.tr.* conglober. **2.** *v.i.* se conglober.

conglomerate[1] [kən'glɔmərət]. **1.** *a.* congloméré; *Anat:* **c. glands,** glandes conglomérées, glandes en grappes. **2.** *s.* (*a*) *Geol:* conglomérat *m*, aggloméré *m*; (*b*) *Pol.Ec:* conglomérat.

conglomerate[2] [kən'glɔməreit]. **1.** *v.tr.* conglomérer. **2.** *v.i.* se conglomérer; *Geol:* s'agglomérer.

conglomeratic [kən'glɔmərətik], *a.* conglomératique.

conglomeration [kənglɔmə'reiʃ(ə)n], *s.* conglomération *f*; agrégation *f* (de roches, etc.).

conglutinant [kən'glu:tinənt], *a.* conglutinant.

conglutinate[1] [kən'glu:tineit], *a.* conglutiné.

conglutinate[2]. **1.** *v.tr.* conglutiner. **2.** *v.i.* se conglutiner; adhérer.

conglutination [kənglu:ti'neiʃ(ə)n], *s.* conglutination *f*; adhésion *f.*

conglutinative [kən'glu:tinətiv], *a.* conglutinant.

Congo ['kɔŋgou], *Pr.n.* **1.** *Geog:* **the (River) C.,** le Congo. **2.** *Geog: Hist:* **Republic of the C.,** République *f* du Congo; *Hist:* **the Belgian C.,** le Congo belge. **3.** *Amph:* **c. snake, c. eel,** amphiume *m*, amphiuma *m.* **4.** *Dy:* **C. red,** rouge Congo; **C. yellow,** jaune Congo.

Congolese [kɔŋgou'li:z], *Geog:* (*a*) *a.* congolais; **the C. Republic,** la République démocratique du Congo; (*b*) *s.* Congolais, -aise.

congou ['kɔŋgu; 'kɔŋgou], *s.* (thé) congou *m*; thé noir (de Chine).

congratulate [kən'grætjuleit], *v.tr.* **to c. s.o. on sth.,** féliciter qn de qch.; complimenter qn sur qch., de qch.; **I c. you,** je vous en félicite; (je vous en fais) mes compliments; **allow me to c. you,** permettez-moi de vous offrir mes félicitations; **to c. s.o. on having done sth.,** féliciter qn d'avoir fait qch., pour avoir fait qch., de ce qu'il a fait qch.; **to c. oneself on sth., on having done sth.,** se féliciter, s'applaudir, se louer, de qch., d'avoir fait qch.

congratulation [kəngrætju'leiʃ(ə)n], *s.* félicitation *f*; **congratulations!** je vous en félicite! félicitations! **to offer s.o. one's congratulations on sth.,** faire (son) compliment, adresser ses compliments, à qn de, sur, qch.

congratulator [kən'grætjuleitər], *s.* congratulateur, -trice.

congratulatory [kən'grætjuleitəri], *a.* de félicitation; **c. letter,** lettre *f* de félicitations.

congregate ['kɔŋgrigeit]. **1.** *v.tr.* rassembler, réunir. **2.** *v.i.* se rassembler, s'assembler.

congregation [kɔŋgri'geiʃ(ə)n], *s.* **1.** rassemblement *m.* **2.** (*body of people*) (*a*) *A: & Lit:* assemblée *f*; *R.C.Ch:* **Consistorial C.,** congrégation *f* consistoire; **the C. de propaganda fide,** la Congrégation de la propagande; *B:* **all the c. of Israel,** toute l'assemblée d'Israël; **the c. of saints,** l'assemblée des saints; (*b*) (*in church*) assemblée des fidèles; assistance *f*, paroissiens *m*; **to preach to a large c.,** prêcher devant une nombreuse assistance, devant un grand auditoire; (*c*) *Sch:* (*at Oxford, Cambridge*) assemblée générale (des professeurs, des membres de l'université).

congregational [kɔŋgri'geiʃənl], *a. Ecc:* **1.** en assemblée; **c. worship,** culte public. **2. the C. Church,** l'Église *f* congrégationaliste.

congregationalism [kɔŋgri'geiʃnəlizm], *s. Ecc:* congrégationalisme *m.*

congregationalist [kɔŋgri'geiʃnəlist], *s. Ecc:* congrégationaliste *mf.*

congress ['kɔŋgres], *s.* **1.** réunion *f* (d'atomes, de personnes, etc.); *Nat.Hist: A:* **birds of c.,** oiseaux *m* grégaires. **2.** (*a*) congrès *m* (de l'enseignement, d'une Église, d'hommes d'État, etc.); *Hist:* **the C. of Vienna,** le Congrès de Vienne; (*b*) *Parl:* (*in Fr. & U.S.*) Congrès (du Sénat et de la Chambre); (*c*) *U.S:* session *f* du Congrès; (*d*) *Pol:* **C. (Party),** Congrès (national indien).

congressional [kɔŋ'greʃən(ə)l], *a.* (réunion *f*, etc.) du congrès; congressionnel.

congressman, -woman; *pl.* **-men, -women** ['kɔŋgresmæn, -wumən; -men, -wimin], *s. Pol: esp. U.S:* membre *m* du Congrès; congressiste *mf*; parlementaire *mf.*

congruence ['kɔŋgruəns], **congruency** ['kɔŋgruənsi]. *s.* **1.** conformité *f*, convenance *f* (**with,** avec). **2.** *Mth:* congruence *f* (de nombres, de lignes).

congruent ['kɔŋgruənt], *a.* **1.** conforme (**with,** à). **2.** *Mth:* congruent (**with,** à); **c. figures,** figures *f* conformes; **c. triangles,** triangles congrus; **c. integers,** entiers congrus.

congruism ['kɔŋgruizm], *s. Theol:* congruisme *m.*

congruist ['kɔŋgruist], *s. Theol:* congruiste *mf.*

congruity [kɔŋ'gruiti], *s.* conformité *f* (**with,** à).

congruous ['kɔŋgruəs], *a.* conforme (**with,** à).

congruously ['kɔŋgruəsli], *adv.* congrûment, convenablement, conformément (**to, with,** à).

conic ['kɔnik], *a. Mth:* conique; **c. sections,** sections coniques.

conical ['kɔnikl], *a.* conique; *Mapm:* **c. projection,** projection *f* conique.

conicity [kɔ'nisiti], *s.* conicité *f.*

conico-cylindrical ['kɔnikousi'lindrikl], *a.* cylindro-conique.

conics ['kɔniks], *s.pl.* (*usu. with sg. const.*) *Mth:* sections *f* coniques.

Conidae ['kounidi:], *s.pl. Moll:* conidés *m.*

conidiospore [kə'nidiouspɔ:r], **conidium,** *pl.* **-ia** [kə'nidiəm, -iə], *s. Biol:* conidie *f.*

conifer ['kounifər], *s. Bot:* conifère *m.*

coniferous [kə'nifərəs], *a. Bot:* conifère; **c. forest,** forêt de conifères.

coniform ['kounifɔ:m], *a.* coniforme.

coni(i)ne ['koun(i)ain], *s. Ch:* conine *f*, conicine *f*, conéine *f*, cicutine *f.*

coniosis [kouni'ousis], *s. Med:* coniose *f.*

coniroster [kouni'rɔstər], *s. Orn:* conirostre *m.*

conirostral [kouni'rɔstrəl], *a. Orn:* conirostre.

conjecturable [kən'dʒektjərəbl], *a.* qui peut être conjecturé.

conjectural [kən'dʒektjərəl], *a.* conjectural, -aux; **these emendations are entirely c.,** ces variantes qui ont été proposées reposent entièrement sur des conjectures.

conjecturally [kən'dʒektjərəli], *adv.* conjecturalement; par conjecture.

conjecture[1] [kən'dʒektjər], *s.* conjecture *f*; **to hazard a c.,** risquer une hypothèse, une supposition; **to be reduced to c.,** être réduit à des conjectures; **to be right in a c.,** supposer juste.

conjecture[2], *v.tr.* conjecturer, supposer, soupçonner;

faire une hypothèse.

conjoin [kən'dʒɔin]. **1.** *v.tr.* conjoindre. **2.** *v.i.* s'unir; se joindre ensemble; s'associer.

conjoined [kən'dʒɔind], *a.* conjoint; *Her:* accolé; *Astr:* (planètes *f*) en conjonction.

conjoint ['kɔndʒɔint], *a.* conjoint, associé; **the c. labour of. . .**, le travail en commun de . . .; *Mus:* **c. degrees,** degrés conjoints.

conjointly [kɔn'dʒɔintli], *adv.* conjointement, ensemble; l'un avec l'autre; **to act c. with s.o.,** agir conjointement, de concert, avec qn; **to inherit c.,** cohériter.

conjugal ['kɔndʒugl], *a.* conjugal, -aux; **c. rights,** droits conjugaux.

conjugality [kɔndʒu'gæliti], *s.* état conjugal, mariage *m.*

conjugally [kɔn'dʒugəli], *adv.* conjugalement.

Conjugatae [kɔndʒu'geiti:], *s.pl. Algae:* conjuguées *f.*

conjugate[1] ['kɔndʒugeit], *a.* (*a*) *Mth: Opt:* conjugué; **c. diameters,** diamètres conjugués; **c. lines,** droites conjuguées; **c. foci,** foyers conjugués; **c. hyperbolae,** hyperboles conjuguées; **c. mirrors,** miroirs conjugués; **c. planes, points,** plans, points, conjugués; *El:* **c. impedances,** impédances conjuguées; *Bot:* **c. leaves,** feuilles conjuguées; (*b*) *Ch:* conjugué.

conjugate[2]. **1.** *v.tr.* (*a*) *Lit:* conjuguer, unir; (*b*) *Gram:* conjuguer (un verbe). **2.** *v.i.* (*a*) *Biol:* (*of cells*) se conjuguer; s'unir par conjugaison; (*b*) s'unir charnellement; s'accoupler.

conjugated ['kɔndʒugeitid], *a.* conjugué.

conjugation [kɔndʒu'geiʃ(ə)n], *s.* **1.** *Gram:* conjugaison *f.* **2.** *Biol:* conjugaison, zygose *f.* **3.** *Atom.Ph:* **charge c.,** conjugaison de charge.

conjugational [kɔndʒu'geiʃənl], *a.* conjugatif.

conjunct [kən'dʒʌŋ(k)t]. **1.** *a.* conjoint, associé; *Ling:* **c. letter, consonant,** lettre conjointe, consonne conjointe (en sanscrit); *Mus:* **c. degrees,** degrés conjoints. **2.** *s.* (*a*) associé, -ée; (*b*) chose liée (à une autre).

conjunction [kən'dʒʌŋ(k)ʃ(ə)n], *s.* **1.** (*a*) conjonction *f*; **in c. with s.o.,** conjointement, de concert, avec qn; **in c. with sth.,** concurremment avec qch.; **c. of circumstances,** concours *m* de circonstances; *Astr:* **planets in c.,** planètes *f* en conjonction; (*b*) *Cmptr:* opération *f* ET, intersection *f.* **2.** *Gram:* conjonction.

conjunctional [kən'dʒʌŋ(k)ʃənl], *a.* conjonctionnel.

conjunctiva [kɔndʒʌŋ(k)'taivə], *s. Anat:* conjonctive *f* (de l'œil).

conjunctive [kən'dʒʌŋ(k)tiv]. **1.** *a.* (tissu, etc.) conjonctif. **2.** *a.* & *s.* *Gram:* (mode) conjonctif (*m*); **c. particle,** particule conjonctive.

conjunctively [kən'dʒʌŋ(k)tivli], *adv.* **1.** conjointement. **2.** *Gram:* **words used c.,** locution conjonctive.

conjunctivitis [kəndʒʌŋ(k)ti'vaitis], *s. Med:* conjonctivite *f*; **granular c.,** conjonctivite granuleuse; trachome *m.*

conjunctly [kən'dʒʌŋ(k)tli], *adv.* conjointement.

conjuncture [kən'dʒʌŋ(k)tjər], *s.* conjoncture *f*, circonstance *f*, occasion *f*; **at this c.,** dans cette conjoncture.

conjuration [kɔndʒu(ə)'reiʃ(ə)n], *s.* conjuration *f.* **1.** *A:* prières *fpl.*; supplications *fpl.* **2.** (*a*) évocation *f* (des démons); (*b*) incantation *f.* **3.** complot *m.*

conjure, *v.* **1.** [kən'dʒuər], *v.tr.* conjurer (**s.o. to do sth.,** qn de faire qch.). **2.** ['kʌndʒər] (*a*) *v.tr.* conjurer (un démon); **to c. up,** évoquer (un esprit, un démon); **to c. up ideas, memories,** évoquer des idées, des souvenirs; **place that conjures up old memories,** lieu évocateur d'anciens souvenirs; **to c. s.o. away,** faire disparaître qn (comme par enchantement); **to c. sth. away from s.o.,** escamoter qch. à qn; **to c. a rabbit out of a top hat,** (faire) sortir un lapin d'un chapeau haut de forme; **a name to c. with,** un nom tout-puissant; un nom évocateur; (*b*) *v.i.* faire de tours de passe-passe.

conjurer, conjuror ['kʌndʒərər], *s.* **1.** *A:* & *Lit:* conjurateur *m* (d'esprits). **2.** prestidigitateur *m*, escamoteur *m*, illusionniste *mf*; **a man, without being a c., might guess that. . .,** point n'est besoin d'être sorcier pour deviner que . . .

conjuring ['kʌndʒəriŋ], *s.* **1.** conjuration *f* (des esprits); **c. up,** évocation *f.* **2.** prestidigitation *f*, escamotage *m*; tours *mpl* de passe-passe.

conk[1] [kɔŋk], *s. P:* **1.** nez *m*, blair *m*, pif *m.* **2.** tête *f*, caboche *f.* **3.** coup *m*, gnon *m.*

conk[2], *v.tr. P:* flanquer un gnon à (qn).

conk[3], *v.i. F:* **to c. (out),** (i) (*of machinery, etc.*) caler, tomber en panne; (ii) (*of pers.*) s'évanouir, tomber dans les pommes; (iii) (*of pers.*) mourir, casser sa pipe.

conk[4], *s. esp. U.S: Fung:* tramète *m.*

conker ['kɔŋkər], *s. F:* **1.** marron *m* d'Inde. **2. to play at conkers,** jouer à qui démolira le marron de son adversaire (chacun des joueurs tenant son marron suspendu au bout d'une ficelle).

conky ['kɔŋki], *a. P:* au nez fort; piffard.

connate ['kɔneit], *a.* **1.** (*a*) inné; **c. ideas,** idées innées; (*b*) **c. with . . .,** né en même temps, à la même date, que . . .; (*c*) *Med:* congénital. **2.** *Bot: Z:* conné, coadné. **3.** *Geol:* conné, fossile.

connatural [kɔ'nætjər(ə)l], *a.* **1.** inné (**to,** chez, à); inhérent (**to,** à). **2.** congénère.

connect[1] [kə'nekt]. **1.** *v.tr.* (*a*) (re)lier, (ré)unir; rattacher, joindre (**sth. with, to, sth.,** qch. à qch.); faire communiquer; mettre en communication (avec); **train that connects (up) fifteen small towns,** train *m* qui dessert quinze petites villes; **a system of railways connects Paris with all the large towns,** un réseau de voies ferrées relie Paris à toutes les grandes villes; **connected by telephone,** relié par téléphone; *Tp:* **to c. two subscribers,** mettre deux abonnés en communication; **to c. pipes,** joindre, raccorder, des tuyaux; *El:* **to c. to earth,** relier, connecter, à la terre; **to c. circuits,** interconnecter des circuits; **to c. a lamp to a plug,** brancher une lampe sur une prise de courant; **to c. (up) the cells,** (ac)coupler, assembler, monter, grouper, la batterie; (*of power stations*) **connected up,** interconnectés; *Mec.E:* **to c. (up) two parts (of a machine),** connecter, mettre en communication, deux pièces d'une machine; **to c. two shafts,** embrayer deux arbres; (*b*) associer (**s.o., sth., with s.o., sth.,** qn, qch., avec qn, à qch.); relier (des idées); **to be connected with . . .,** (*of pers.*) avoir des relations, des rapports, avec . . .; (*of thg*) se lier, se rattacher, se rapporter, à . . .; **the traditions that c. the present with the past,** les traditions *f* qui relient le présent au passé; **questions connected with a subject,** questions relatives à un sujet; (*c*) (*of pers.*) **to be connected with a family,** être allié à, avec, une famille; être parent de l'une famille; être apparenté à une famille; **to c. two families by marriage,** unir deux familles par le mariage; apparenter deux familles; (*d*) *v.tr.* & *i.* *esp. U.S: F:* **to c. (with) s.o.,** rencontrer, trouver, qn; se mettre en rapport avec qn (*esp.* pour acheter des stupéfiants). **2.** *v.i.* (*a*) se lier, se relier, se joindre, s'unir (**with,** à); se réunir, se raccorder; *Trans:* **to c. with a train, a boat,** faire correspondance, assurer la correspondance, avec un train, un bateau; **the two train services c. at Crewe,** les deux services *m* correspondent à Crewe; **side streets that c. with the main arteries,** rues latérales qui vont rejoindre les grandes voies; (*b*) *F:* (*of blow, punch*) atteindre son but; (*c*) *F:* **I tried to explain it to him but it didn't c.,** j'ai essayé de le lui expliquer mais il n'a pas compris.

connect[2], *s. Cmptr:* connexion *f*; **c. time,** durée *f* (d'établissement) de la connexion.

connected [kə'nektid], *a.* **1.** (*a*) **c. speech,** discours suivi, conséquent, cohérent; **arguments that are c.,** arguments *m* qui se suivent bien; (*b*) **two closely c. trades,** deux métiers connexes, proches voisins; (*c*) **c. graph,** graphe *m* connexe. **2.** (*of pers.*) **to be well c.,** être bien apparenté; être de bonne famille; appartenir à une bonne famille. **3.** *Bot: Jur: etc:* connexe.

connectedly [kə'nektidli], *adv.* d'une manière cohérente; **to think c.,** penser avec suite; avoir de la suite dans les idées.

connecter [kə'nektər], *s.* = CONNECTOR.

connectible [kə'nektəbl], *a.* qui peut se lier, se raccorder, se joindre (**with,** à).

connecting[1] [kə'nektiŋ], *a.* (*a*) qui sert à joindre, à unir; **c. link,** (i) trait *m* d'union (**between . . . and,** entre . . . et); (ii) fausse maille (de chaîne); *Harn:* **c. piece,** alliance *f*; **c. wire,** fil *m* de connexion; **c. pipe,** tuyau *m* de communication, de jonction; *El:* **c. box,** boîte *f* de raccordement (pour câbles); **c. gear,** embrayage *m*; **c. rod,** (i) *Mec.E:* bielle *f*, tiraille *f*, tige *f*, tringle *f*, barre *f*, de connexion; (ii) *Mch: I.C.E:* bielle motrice; (iii) *El:* tige conductrice; **articulated c. rod,** biellette articulée; **back-acting c. rod,** bielle renversée; **c. rod shank, body,** corps *m* de bielle; **c.-rod bearings,** embiellage *m*; (*b*) *Trans:* **c. flight, train,** correspondance *f* (d'un vol, d'un train, avec un autre).

connecting[2], *s.* **1.** association *f* (de piles, etc.). **2.** *El:* **c. up,** (i) montage *m*; (ii) mise *f* en circuit.

connection [kə'nekʃ(ə)n], *s.* **1.** rapport *m*, liaison *f* (des choses); connexité *f* (entre deux choses); connexion *f*, suite *f* (des idées); **close c. between two facts,** relation étroite entre deux faits; connexité de deux faits; **to have a c. with . . .,** avoir rapport à . . .; **this question has no c. with . . .,** cette question n'a rien à voir avec . . .; **in c. with . . .,** à propos de . . ., relativement à . . ., relatif à . . .; **in this c.,** à ce propos; à cet égard; dans cet ordre d'idées; **in another c.,** d'autre part; par ailleurs. **2.** (*a*) **c. of s.o. with s.o.,** relations *fpl*, rapports *mpl*, commerce *m*, liaison, de qn avec qn; **to form a c. with s.o.,** établir des rapports avec qn; **to break off a c.,** rompre des relations, rompre une attache; **I have broken off all c. with him,** j'ai cessé toutes relations avec lui; (*b*) **sexual c.,** coït *m.* **3.** (*a*) (*relationship*) parenté *f*; apparentage *m*; liens *mpl* de famille; **to form a c. by marriage with a good family,** s'allier à, avec, une bonne famille; (*b*) parent, -ente; (*by marriage*) allié, -ée; *Jur:* affin *m*; **he, she, is a c. of mine,** c'est un(e) de mes parent(e)s; (*c*) *coll.O:* **the whole c.,** toute la famille. **4.** *Ecc:* (= DENOMINATION) secte *f*; **the Methodist c.,** la secte méthodiste, l'Église *f* méthodiste. **5.** (*a*) *Com:* clientèle *f*; **wide c.,** belle clientèle; belles relations d'affaires; **representative with a wide c.,** représentant bien relationné; **to open up a business c.,** entrer en relations (d'affaires) avec une maison; (*b*) *esp. U.S: P:* contact *m*, inter *m* (qui fournit des narcotiques). **6.** *Trans:* correspondance *f*; train, avion, bateau, correspondant; (*of train, etc.*) **to have, make, a c. with . . .,** être en correspondance, assurer la correspondance, avec . . .; **I missed my c. at Crewe,** j'ai manqué, *F:* raté, ma correspondance à Crewe. **7.** (*a*) *Mec.E: etc:* connexion; assemblage *m*, raccordement *m*, réunion *f* (de deux éléments, tuyaux, fils, etc.); accouplement *m*, embrayage *m*, engrenage *m* (des organes d'une machine); **hinged c.,** assemblage à charnière; **ball c.,** assemblage à rotule; **conical c.,** accouplement, embrayage, à cônes; (*b*) *El:* raccordement, connexion; branchement *m*; montage *m*; **bridge c.,** montage en pont; **c. bridge,** pont *m* de raccordement; **shunt c.,** montage en dérivation; **series c.,** montage en série; **c. layout, diagram,** (schéma *m* de) câblage *m*; **wrong c.,** (i) *El:* fausse connexion; (ii) *Tp:* fausse communication; (*c*) *Cmptr:* connexion, branchement, liaison *f*; **c. box,** (i) boîtier *m* de connexion; (ii) symbole *m* de renvoi (dans un organigramme). **8.** (*a*) raccord *m*, liaison, connexion, attache *f* (entre deux tuyaux, fils, etc.); **pipe connections,** tuyauteries *f*; **flexible c.,** raccord souple; **rubber c.,** raccord en caoutchouc; **swivel c.,** raccord orientable; **sleeve c.,** raccord à manchon; **banjo c.,** raccord banjo; (*b*) *El:* contact *m*; prise *f* (de courant); **earth,** *U.S:* **ground, c.,** (i) prise de terre, contact à la terre; (ii) *Aut: etc:* mise *f* à la masse; (*c*) *Civ.E:* point *m* d'attache; **connections of a framework,** attaches, liaisons, d'une charpente, d'une structure.

connective [kə'nektiv]. **1.** *a.* connectif; *Anat:* **c. tissue,** tissu cellulaire, connectif, conjonctif. **2.** *s.* (*a*) *Bot:* connectif *m*; (*b*) *Cmptr:* **logical c.,** opérateur *m* logique; (*c*) *Gram:* conjonction *f*; particule ou locution conjonctive.

connector [kə'nektər], *s.* **1.** (*a*) *Ch:* ajutage *m*; (*b*) raccord *m* (de pompe à graisse, de gonfleur de pneus, etc.); (*c*) *Rail:* attelage *m*; (*d*) articulation *f*; (*e*) *Mec.E: etc:* **c. base,** embase *f* de raccordement. **2.** (*a*) connecteur *m*, raccord *m*; *El:* prise *f*; **(cable) c.,** pince *f* de raccordement, attache-fil(s) *m inv*; **forked c.,** chape *f*; **c. of a battery, cell-to-cell c.,** bande *f* de connexion des éléments; lame *f* de jonction; pont *m* polaire; étrier *m* de raccordement; (*b*) *Cmptr:* (i) connecteur (multibroche); (ii) symbole *m* de renvoi (dans un organigramme); **logical c.,** opérateur *m* logique.

connexion [kə'nekʃ(ə)n], *s.* = CONNECTION.

connexity [kə'neksiti], *s.* connexité *f* (de faits, de cas).

connivance [kə'naiv(ə)ns], *s.* connivence *f*, collusion *f*; **c. at, in, a crime,** complicité *f* dans un crime; participation *f* à un crime; **to be in c. with s.o.,** être de connivence, d'intelligence, avec qn; **this was done with his c.,** cela s'est fait de connivence, d'intelligence, avec lui.

connive [kə'naiv], *v.i.* **1. to c. at an abuse,** fermer les yeux sur un abus; tolérer un abus; *A:* conniver à un abus. **2.** *A:* **to c. at a crime,** être de connivence dans un crime; être complice d'un crime; être fauteur d'un crime.

connivent [kə'naiv(ə)nt], *a. Anat: Bot: Ent:* connivent; **c. valves,** valvules conniventes (de l'intestin); **c. wings,** ailes conniventes (d'un insecte).

connoisseur [kɔnə'səːr], *s.* (bon) connaisseur (**of, in,** en); **to be a c. of paintings,** se connaître en peinture, en tableaux.

connotation [kɔnou'teiʃ(ə)n], *s.* **1.** (*a*) connotation *f* (d'un terme); (*b*) signification *f* (d'un mot). **2.** *Phil:* totalité *f* des idées qu'enferme un nom générique; compréhension *f* (d'un nom générique).

connotative [kɔ'noutətiv], *a.* connotatif.

connote [kɔ'nout], *v.tr.* **1.** *Log:* connoter. **2.** comporter (des conséquences, une signification secondaire, etc.). **3.** signifier, vouloir dire; donner à entendre; impliquer.

connubial [kə'nju:biəl], *a.* conjugal, -aux; matrimonial, -aux; du mariage.

connubiality [kənju:bi'æliti], *s.* **1.** état conjugal. **2.** (*a*) pratique *f* du mariage; (*b*) droit *m* de se marier.

conocarpus [kounou'kɑ:pəs], *s. Bot:* conocarpe *m.*

conocephalum [kounou'sefələm], *s. Ent:* conocéphale *m.*

conoid ['kounɔid], *a.* & *s.* **1.** *Mth:* conoïde (*m*). **2.** *Anat:* **c. (gland),** glande pinéale.

conoidal [kou'nɔidl], *a.* conoïde, conoïdal, -aux.

conolophus [kə'nɔləfəs], *s. Rept:* conolophe *m.*
Conopidae [kə'nɔpidi:], *s.pl. Ent:* conopidés *m.*
conquer ['kɔŋkər], *v.tr.* **1.** conquérir (un pays, l'amour de qn). **2.** vaincre (un ennemi, une difficulté, sa timidité); surmonter (une difficulté, sa timidité); vaincre, dompter (ses passions); **Everest was conquered in 1953,** la première ascension du Mont Everest a eu lieu en 1953.
conquerable ['kɔŋk(ə)rəbl], *a.* qui peut être vaincu, conquis; (passion *f*) domptable.
conquering ['kɔŋk(ə)riŋ], *a.* **1.** conquérant. **2.** victorieux; **the c. hero,** le héros triomphant.
conqueror ['kɔŋk(ə)rər], *s.* **1.** conquérant *m* (d'un pays); *Hist:* **(William) the C.,** Guillaume le Conquérant. **2.** vainqueur *m.* **3.** *Cards:* **to play the c.,** jouer la belle.
conquest ['kɔŋkwest], *s.* **1.** conquête *f* (d'un pays, d'un cœur); *Hist:* **the (Norman) C.,** la conquête de l'Angleterre (1066). **2.** conquête, pays de conquête; **to make a c. (of s.o., of s.o.'s heart),** faire la conquête de qn, du cœur de qn.
consanguine [kɔn'sæŋgwin], **consanguineous** [kɔnsæŋ'gwiniəs], *a.* consanguin.
consanguinity [kɔnsæŋ'gwiniti], *s.* consanguinité *f.*
conscience ['kɔnʃ(ə)ns], *s.* **1.** conscience *f*; **to have an easy, a clean, clear, c.,** avoir la conscience nette, tranquille, pure; **with a clear c.,** en (toute) sûreté de conscience; **to have a guilty, bad, c.,** avoir une mauvaise conscience; avoir la conscience chargée; ne pas avoir la conscience tranquille; **to have sth. on one's c.,** avoir qch. (qui pèse) sur la conscience; (*in an act*) **c. clause,** article *m* sauvegardant la liberté de conscience (de ceux qui auraient des scrupules à se conformer à la loi); **c. money,** somme restituée par remords de conscience; restitution *f* (d'une somme due); **to have no c.,** n'avoir point de conscience; être sans conscience; **point of c.,** cas *m* de conscience; **a matter of c.,** une affaire de conscience; **for conscience(')sake,** par acquit de conscience; **I shall do it for conscience(') sake, I shall make it a matter of c. to do it,** je le ferai par acquit de conscience; *O:* **upon my c.,** sur ma conscience; par ma foi; sur ma parole; la main sur la conscience; **in all c.,** (i) en conscience, en vérité, assurément; en toute franchise; (ii) raisonnablement; **I can assure you in all c. that . . .,** je puis vous assurer, la main sur la conscience, en toute sincérité, que . . .; **one cannot in all c. believe that . . .,** on ne peut pas raisonnablement croire que . . .; **it would be, go, against my c. to do it,** cela irait contre ma conscience de le faire; **liberty of c.,** liberté *f* de conscience; *Lit:* **c. doth make cowards of us all,** à conscience troublée, jambes molles. **2.** *Tls:* plastron *m* conscience, estomac *m* (de vilebrequin).
conscienceless ['kɔnʃənslis], *a.* sans scrupule; sans conscience; incapable de remords.
consciencestricken ['kɔnʃənsstrik(ə)n], *a.* pris de remords; atteint, bourrelé, de remords.
conscientious [kɔnʃi'enʃəs], *a.* **1.** (travailleur, travail) consciencieux; (travail) fait en conscience; **to have a c. approach to one's work,** travailler avec une conscience professionnelle. **2. c. scruple,** scrupule *m* de conscience; **c. objector,** réfractaire *m*; objecteur *m* de conscience (en matière de service militaire, de vaccination); **c. objection,** objection *f* de conscience.
conscientiously [kɔnʃi'enʃəsli], *adv.* consciencieusement; **to carry out a piece of work c.,** s'acquitter en conscience, consciencieusement, d'une tâche.
conscientiousness [kɔnʃi'enʃəsnis], *s.* conscience *f*; délicatesse *f* de conscience; droiture *f*; **his c. about his work,** la conscience qu'il apporte à son travail.
conscious ['kɔnʃəs], *a.* **1.** (*a*) **to be c. of sth.,** avoir conscience de qch.; être conscient, avoir le sentiment, de qch.; savoir, sentir, qch.; **I was c. of faces watching me,** j'avais conscience de visages qui m'épiaient; **I was not c. of having moved,** je n'avais pas conscience d'avoir bougé; je ne me rendais pas compte que j'avais bougé; **to become c. of sth.,** s'apercevoir de qch.; **I was, became, c. of a smell of fish,** mon odorat était, fut, affecté par une odeur de poisson; **I was c. that he was looking at me,** je sentais qu'il me regardait; **c. of being capable of . . .,** se sachant capable de . . .; (*b*) **c. movement,** mouvement conscient; **his c. superiority,** le sentiment qu'il a de sa supériorité; **the dog wore an air of c. guilt,** on voyait bien à la mine du chien qu'il se savait coupable; (*c*) **fashion c.,** qui suit de près la mode; **food c.,** qui se préoccupe beaucoup de sa nourriture; **horse c.,** qui aime beaucoup les chevaux (et s'en occupe beaucoup); (*d*) *Phil:* conscient; **man as a c. being,** l'homme en tant qu'être conscient. **2. to be c.,** avoir sa connaissance; être en pleine connaissance; **to become c.,** reprendre connaissance; reprendre ses sens; revenir de son évanouissement.
consciously ['kɔnʃəsli], *adv.* consciemment, d'une façon consciente; sciemment.
consciousness ['kɔnʃəsnis], *s.* **1.** (*a*) conscience *f*, sentiment *m* (of, de); **to act in full c. of the consequences,** agir avec la pleine conscience des conséquences; **the c. of being watched,** le fait de savoir qu'on vous regarde; le sentiment qu'on vous regarde; **when I awoke to the c. of my misfortune,** lorsque j'ai pris conscience de mon malheur; (*b*) sentiment intime, persuasion *f* intime; **the c. that all was not well kept me awake,** un pressentiment de malheur m'empêchait de dormir. **2.** *Phil:* (*a*) conscience (de l'être conscient); (*b*) **moral c.,** conscience morale. **3.** connaissance *f*; **to lose c.,** perdre connaissance; s'évanouir; tomber en défaillance; **to regain c.,** reprendre connaissance; revenir à soi; reprendre ses esprits, ses sens.
conscribable [kən'skraibəbl], *a.* conscriptible.
conscribe [kən'skraib], *v.tr. A:* = CONSCRIPT².
conscript¹ ['kɔnskript]. **1.** *Mil: etc:* (*a*) *a.* conscrit, appelé sous les drapeaux; **c. army,** armée nationale, recrutée par conscription; (*b*) *s.* conscrit *m.* **2.** *a.* **the c. fathers,** (i) *Rom.Hist:* les pères conscrits; (ii) *esp.NAm:* les sénateurs *m*; les législateurs *m.*
conscript² [kən'skript], *v.tr.* enrôler, engager, (des troupes) par la conscription.
conscription [kən'skripʃ(ə)n], *s.* conscription *f*; *A:* **seaboard c. for the Navy,** inscription *f* maritime; **c. of wealth,** conscription des fortunes.
consecrate¹ ['kɔnsikreit], *a. A:* consacré (to, à).
consecrate², *v.tr.* **1.** (*a*) *Ecc:* consacrer (une église, l'hostie, le calice); bénir (le pain, un cimetière, un drapeau); sacrer (un roi, un évêque); **he was consecrated Bishop of London,** il fut sacré évêque de Londres; (*b*) **custom consecrated by time,** coutume consacrée par le temps. **2. to consecrate one's life to a work,** consacrer, vouer, sa vie à un travail; se vouer à un travail.
consecrated ['kɔnsikreitid], *a.* (*of church, phrase, etc.*) consacré; (*of bread*) bénit; **c. taper,** cierge bénit; **in c. ground,** en terre sainte, en terre bénite.
consecration [kɔnsi'kreiʃ(ə)n], *s.* **1.** consécration *f* (d'une église, de l'hostie, du vin, etc.); bénédiction *f* (d'une cloche, d'un drapeau); sacre *m* (d'un roi, d'un évêque). **2. the c. of a whole life to a single object,** le dévouement d'une vie entière à un seul but.
consecrator ['kɔnsikreitər], *s.* consacrant *m.*
consecution [kɔnsi'kju:ʃ(ə)n], *s.* **1.** consécution *f*; *Mus:* **c. of thirds,** suite *f* de tierces. **2.** *Gram:* concordance *f* (des temps).
consecutive [kən'sekjutiv], *a.* consécutif. **1.** *pl.* qui se suivent; **on three c. days,** trois jours consécutifs; trois jours de suite, d'affilée; *Mus:* **c. fifths,** quintes consécutives. **2.** *Gram:* **c. clause,** proposition consécutive.
consecutively [kən'sekjutivli], *adv.* consécutivement, de suite; par ordre de date.
consecutiveness [kən'sekjutivnis], *s.* succession *f*, suite *f*, enchaînement *m.*
consensual [kən'sensjuəl], *a.* **1.** *Jur:* **c. contract,** contrat consensuel; **c. obligation,** obligation consensuelle. **2.** *Physiol:* **c. reflexes,** réflexes consensuels.
consensus [kən'sensəs], *s.* **1.** consensus *m*, unanimité *f* (d'opinions, de témoignages, etc.); accord *m* pour ainsi dire unanime. **2.** *Physiol:* consensus, sympathie *f* (de plusieurs organes).
consent¹ [kən'sent], *s.* consentement *m*, assentiment *m*, approbation *f*, acquiescement *m*; **c. to a request,** agrément donné à une requête; **to give one's c. to sth.,** donner son consentement à qch.; **to obtain s.o.'s c. to do sth.,** obtenir le consentement, l'aveu *m*, la permission, de qn pour faire qch.; **by common c.,** d'une commune voix; de l'aveu, au dire, de tout le monde; **with one c.,** d'un commun accord; à l'unanimité; unanimement; **by mutual c.,** de gré à gré; (divorce *m*) par consentement mutuel; *Jur:* **age of c.,** âge *m* nubile.
consent², *v.i.* **to c. to sth., to do sth.,** consentir à qch., à faire qch.; **I c.,** j'y consens; je veux bien; **to c. to sth. being done,** consentir à ce que qch. se fasse; **he has consented to being president,** il a accepté la présidence; *Com:* **to c. to a reduction in price,** consentir une réduction de prix.
consentient [kən'senʃ(ə)nt], *a.* **1.** d'accord; d'un même sentiment; unanime (**in,** sur). **2. c. forces,** forces concourantes. **3.** consentant (**to,** à).
consenting [kən'sentiŋ], *a.* (*a*) **c. parties,** parties consentantes; (*b*) *F:* **c. adult,** homosexuel *m.*
consequence ['kɔnsikwəns], *s.* **1.** (*a*) conséquence *f*; suites *fpl*; **the c. is that . . .,** il en résulte, il s'ensuit, que . . .; **the c. of all that will be to annoy him,** tout cela aura pour effet de le fâcher; **in c.,** par conséquent; **in c. of . . .,** par suite de . . ., en conséquence de . . .; **to take the consequences, to put up with the consequences,** subir, accepter, les conséquences; *F:* **to hell with the consequences!** je me fiche pas mal des conséquences! **the thing is done and we must face the consequences,** le vin est tiré, il faut le boire; **(game of) consequences,** (jeu *m* des) petits papiers; (*b*) *Log:* conséquent *m* (d'un syllogisme). **2.** importance *f*; conséquence; **it is of no c.,** cela n'a pas d'importance; cela ne tire pas à conséquence; n'importe; cela ne signifie rien; cela ne fait rien; **he is of no c.,** il ne compte pas; **to set up as a man of c.,** faire l'homme d'importance; faire l'important; **all the people of c. in the town,** toutes les personnalités de la ville.
consequent¹ ['kɔnsikwənt], *s.* **1.** conséquence *f.* **2.** (*a*) *Mth:* conséquent *m*; (*b*) *Log:* conclusion *f.*
consequent², *a.* **1.** (*a*) résultant; qui suit; **c. upon sth.,** qui est la conséquence de qch.; qui résulte de, qui découle de, qui vient à la suite de, qch.; **infirmity c. on a wound,** infirmité consécutive à une blessure; (*b*) *Geog:* **c. stream,** cours d'eau conséquent, cataclinal. **2.** *Log:* conséquent (**from,** de). **3.** (*consistent*) conséquent; **to be c., he ought to have shown that . . .,** pour être logique il aurait dû démontrer que . . ..
consequential [kɔnsi'kwenʃ(ə)l], *a.* **1.** conséquent (**to,** à); dû (**to,** à); consécutif (**to,** à); *Jur:* **c. effects of an action,** répercussions *f* d'une action; **c. damages,** dommages indirects. **2.** (*of pers.*) suffisant, important, plein de soi; plein d'importance; **to have a c. manner,** faire l'important.
consequentiality [kɔnsikwenʃi'æliti], *s.* **1.** *Log:* conséquence *f*, suite *f* (dans les idées). **2.** (*of pers.*) importance *f*, suffisance *f.*
consequentially [kɔnsi'kwenʃəli], *adv.* **1.** indirectement, secondairement. **2.** avec importance; d'un air important; d'un air d'importance.
consequently ['kɔnsikwəntli]. **1.** *adv. & conj.* par conséquent, conséquemment; dès lors; il en résulte que . . .; donc. **2.** *adv.* logiquement; avec suite.
conservancy [kən'sə:v(ə)nsi], *s.* **1.** commission *f* de conservation (d'une forêt, d'un fleuve, etc.); **the Thames C.,** la Commission fluviale (de la Tamise). **2.** conservation *f*, protection *f*, préservation *f* (des forêts, etc.); gardiennage *m* (des ports); **fire c.,** protection contre le feu; **c. staff,** personnel préposé aux mesures de protection.
conservation [kɔnsə(:)'veiʃ(ə)n], *s.* conservation *f*; **measures of c.,** mesures *f* conservatoires; mesures de protection; **forest c.,** conservation forestière; *Ph:* **c. of energy,** conservation de l'énergie; *Astr:* **c. of areas,** conservation des aires.
conservationist [kɔnsə'veiʃənist], *s.* partisan, -ane, de la conservation (des sites pittoresques, etc.).
conservatism [kən'sə:vətizm], *s. Pol:* conservatisme *m.*
conservative [kən'sə:vətiv]. **1.** *a.* (*a*) préservatif; préservateur, -trice; conservateur, -trice; (*b*) **c. estimate,** évaluation prudente; **the distances quoted are c.,** les distances citées sont plutôt en deçà de la vérité; **at a c. estimate,** au minimum; au bas mot; **on c. lines,** selon la méthode consacrée par l'usage; (*c*) *Pol:* conservateur, -trice. **2.** *s. Pol:* conservateur, -trice.
conservatively [kən'sə:vətivli], *adv.* **it was c. estimated . . .,** selon des estimations modérées . . ..
conservatoire [kən'sə:vətwɑ:r], *s.* conservatoire *m* (de musique).
conservator ['kɔnsə(:)veitər, kən'sə:vətər], *s.* (*a*) conservateur, -trice; *Adm:* **c. of a forest, of a river,** conservateur d'une forêt, d'un cours d'eau; *For:* **deputy c.,** inspecteur *m*; **assistant c.,** inspecteur adjoint; **c. of a museum,** conservateur d'un musée; (*b*) *Jur:* **the Conservators of the Peace,** les Gardiens *m* de la paix (le Roi, le Chancelier, et les juges).
conservatory [kən'sə:vətri]. **1.** *a.* (*a*) (principe, etc.) conservateur, préservateur; (*b*) (fonctions *f*) de conservateur. **2.** *s.* (*a*) *Hort:* serre *f*; (*b*) *U.S:* = CONSERVATOIRE.
conserve¹ [kən'sə:v], *s.* **1.** *Pharm:* conserve *f*; préparation sucrée. **2.** *pl. Cu:* **conserves,** confiture(s) *f*, conserves (de fruits).
conserve², *v.tr.* conserver, préserver (un monument ancien, etc.).
conshie, conshy ['kɔnʃi], *s. P:* objecteur *m* de conscience.
consider [kən'sidər], *v.tr.* **1.** *A:* (*look at*) considérer, contempler. **2.** (*a*) (*reflect upon*) considérer (une question); songer à, réfléchir à (qch.); **to c. the facts,** interroger les faits; **to c. a possibility,** envisager une possibilité; **among the measures considered up to the present time,** parmi les mesures envisagées jusqu'ici; **I will c. it,** j'y réfléchirai; j'y songerai; **to c. one's actions,** composer ses actions; agir avec délibération; **considered opinion,** opinion motivée, réfléchie; **all things considered,** tout bien considéré; tout compte fait; (toute) réflexion faite; à tout prendre; eu égard aux circonstances; en fin de compte; en dernière analyse; **he paused to c.,** il s'est

arrêté pour réfléchir; (*b*) **to c. an offer,** prendre une offre en considération; **to c. a proposal,** étudier, examiner, une proposition; **the jury retired to c. its verdict,** le jury se retira pour délibérer. **3.** (*a*) **to c. s.o.'s feelings,** avoir égard à la sensibilité de qn; **to c. the expense,** regarder à la dépense; **we must c. him a little,** il faut lui montrer de la considération, le ménager; **he is a man to be considered,** c'est un homme dont il faut tenir compte; (*b*) **when one considers that he is only twenty . . .,** quand on pense qu'il n'a que vingt ans . . .. **4.** (*a*) **I c. him (to be) crazy,** je le considère, regarde, comme fou; je le tiens pour fou; **the doctor considers his case hopeless,** le médecin le juge perdu; **c. it as done,** tenez cela pour fait; **c. yourself dismissed,** tenez-vous pour congédié; considérez-vous comme congédié; **I c. the book bad,** je trouve le livre mauvais; **he is considered rich,** il passe pour riche; on le dit riche; **to c. oneself happy,** s'estimer heureux; **I c. it my duty to . . .,** j'estime qu'il est de mon devoir de . . .; **the measures considered necessary,** les mesures *f* dont on envisage la nécessité; (*b*) **we c. that he ought to do it,** à notre avis il doit le faire; (*c*) **he was considering whether to go out when the telephone rang,** il se demandait s'il sortirait quand le téléphone a sonné.

considerable [kən'sid(ə)rəbl], *a.* considérable. **1.** (*a*) digne d'attention; (*b*) (*of pers.*) notable, grand, important. **2.** grand, fort; **a c. section of the country,** une bonne partie du pays; **a c. number of . . .,** un nombre considérable de, un grand nombre de, pas mal de . . .; **to a c. extent,** dans une forte mesure; **c. difference,** différence *f* sensible; *adv. U.S: F:* **a c. long time ago,** il y a assez longtemps; il y a pas mal de temps.

considerably [kən'sid(ə)rəbli], *adv.* considérablement; bien, fort, beaucoup, dans des proportions considérables; **the patient has improved c.,** il y a un mieux sensible dans l'état du malade.

considerate [kən'sidərət], *a.* **1.** (*a*) **c. (towards, to, s.o.),** attentif (à qn), prévenant, plein d'égards, bon, attentionné (pour, envers, qn); **it's very c. of you,** c'est très aimable de votre part, très aimable à vous; (*b*) **if you had shown yourself more c.,** si vous aviez tenu compte des circonstances, de son état, etc.; si vous aviez montré plus de discrétion, plus de délicatesse. **2.** *A:* (*of conduct, etc.*) considéré, réfléchi; (*of pers.*) avisé, prudent.

considerately [kən'sidərətli], *adv.* **1.** avec considération, avec égards, avec prévenance, avec bonté; **he acted very c.,** il a agi avec beaucoup de considération, avec une grande délicatesse. **2.** *A:* d'une manière réfléchie; considérément, prudemment.

considerateness [kən'sidərətnis], *s.* **1.** attentions *fpl*, égards *mpl*, délicatesse *f* (**to, for,** envers, pour). **2.** *A:* caractère réfléchi; prudence *f*.

consideration [kənsidə'reiʃ(ə)n], *s.* **1.** considération *f*; (*a*) **to take sth. into c.,** prendre qch. en considération; tenir compte de qch.; faire entrer qch. en ligne de compte; **to take into c. that . . .,** tenir compte (de ce) que . . .; **taking all things into c.,** tout bien considéré, pesé; **to leave a point out of c.,** faire abstraction d'un point; **a fact that has been left out of c.,** un fait auquel on n'a pas pris garde; **leaving patriotism out of c., I should like to . . .,** patriotisme à part, je voudrais . . .; **in c. of . . .,** en considération de . . ., eu égard à . . ., attendu . . .; **he was let off in c. of his youth,** on lui fit grâce en faveur de sa jeunesse; **in c. of the payment of a sum of money,** moyennant paiement d'une somme; en retour d'une somme; **this requires c.,** ceci exige de la réflexion; **question under c.,** question envisagée, en délibération, à l'examen, à l'étude; **to give c. to a question,** mettre une question à l'étude; **to take a request into c.,** faire bon accueil à une demande; **after due c.,** à la réflexion; après mûre réflexion; tout bien considéré; toute réflexion faite, après délibération; **a list for your c.,** une liste que nous vous prions de bien vouloir examiner; **to act without due c.,** agir hâtivement, sans réfléchir, à la légère; (*b*) **these considerations made me pause,** ces considérations m'arrêtèrent; **there is another c.,** il y a autre chose dont il faut tenir compte; **money is always the first c.,** la question d'argent vient toujours en premier; **to rise above material considerations,** s'élever au-dessus des préoccupations matérielles; **on, under, no c.,** à aucun prix, pour rien au monde. **2.** (*reward*) compensation *f*, rémunération *f*, prix *m*; *Com: etc:* **for a c.,** moyennant paiement; moyennant contrepartie; **he will do it for a c.,** il le fera si vous le payez, si vous le remboursez; (*in contract*) **absence, lack, of c.,** absence *f* de contre partie; **agreed c.,** prix convenu; contre partie convenue; *Jur:* **property acquired for valuable c.,** propriété acquise à titre onéreux; **for good c.,** (i) à titre amical; (ii) à titre onéreux. **3.** *Jur: Fin: Com:* cause *f*, provision *f* (**for,** de); **to give c. for a bill,** provisionner une lettre de change; **c. given for a bill of exchange,** cause d'un billet. **4.** (= CONSIDERATENESS 1) **to have no c. for anyone,** n'avoir de considération pour personne; **out of c. for s.o.,** par égard, par considération, pour qn; **a little c. would have cost you nothing,** un peu d'égards *m* ne vous auraient rien coûté; **to treat s.o. with c.,** ménager qn; **he showed me no c.,** il n'a gardé aucun ménagement à mon égard. **5.** (*a*) *A:* (*importance*) **of much, of no, c.,** de grande importance; de nulle, d'aucune, importance; **a man of the first c.,** un homme de première importance; (*b*) **he is well off, and money is no c.,** il est à l'aise, et l'argent n'entre pas en ligne de compte, et la question d'argent n'a pas d'importance.

considering [kən'sid(ə)riŋ], *prep.* eu égard à (qch.); **c. his age,** étant donné son âge; **c. the circumstances,** vu les circonstances; *conj.phr.* **c. that . . .,** vu, attendu, que . . .; **c. (that) he is so young,** vu, attendu, étant donné, qu'il est si jeune; *F:* (*elliptically*) **it's not so bad c.,** ce n'est pas si mauvais après tout, malgré tout, vu les circonstances; somme toute, ce n'est pas si mal.

consign [kən'sain], *v.tr.* **1.** *Com:* consigner, envoyer, expédier (des marchandises) (**to s.o.,** à qn, à l'adresse de qn); envoyer (des marchandises) en consignation (à qn). **2.** confier, remettre, livrer (**sth. to s.o.'s care,** qch. à qn, entre les mains de qn); **to c. sth. to oblivion,** ensevelir qch. dans l'oubli; livrer qch. à l'oubli; **to c. a body to the grave,** livrer un corps à la tombe; **to c. a picture to the attic,** reléguer un tableau au grenier. **3.** déposer, consigner (de l'argent dans une banque).

consignation [kɔnsai'neiʃ(ə)n], *s.* consignation *f*. **1.** **to ship goods to the c. of s.o.,** consigner des marchandises à qn; envoyer des marchandises en consignation à qn. **2.** dépôt *m* en banque.

consignee [kɔnsai'niː], *s.* consignataire *mf*; destinataire *mf*; **bareboat c.,** consignataire de la coque.

consignment [kən'sainmənt], *s.* **1.** (*a*) envoi *m*, expédition *f* (de marchandises); **goods for c. to the provinces and abroad,** articles *m* à destination de la province et de l'étranger; **c. note,** (i) lettre *f* de voiture; note *f*, bordereau *m*, de consignation; (ii) *Rail:* récépissé *m*; (*b*) *Com:* **on c.,** en consignation, en dépôt (permanent); **to send s.o. goods on c.,** livrer à qn une marchandise en dépôt permanent. **2.** (*goods sent*) envoi, arrivage *m* (de marchandises); **your c. of books has duly come to hand,** votre envoi de livres nous est bien parvenu; **I am expecting a heavy c. of . . .,** j'attends un fort arrivage de . . ..

consignor [kən'sainər], *s. Com:* consignateur, -trice, expéditeur, -trice.

consist [kən'sist], *v.i.* **1.** (*a*) **to c. of sth.,** consister en, dans, se composer de, qch.; **his fortune consisted of consols,** sa fortune consistait en rentes sur l'État; **life consists of what we put into it,** la vie est faite de ce que nous y mettons; *Jur:* **inheritance consisting of a house,** héritage *m* en consistance d'une maison, consistant en une maison; (*b*) **true happiness consists in desiring little,** le vrai bonheur consiste à modérer ses désirs; **all the difficulty consists in this, that . . .,** toute la difficulté réside en ceci, que . . .. **2.** *A:* **to c. with sth.,** s'accorder, être compatible, avec qch. **3.** *B:* **by him all things c.,** toutes choses subsistent par lui.

consistence [kən'sist(ə)ns], *s.* = CONSISTENCY 1.

consistency [kən'sistənsi], *s.* **1.** consistance *f* (d'un liquide, d'un solide); compacité *f* (du sol, etc.). **2.** (*a*) uniformité *f* (de conduite, etc.); cohérence *f* (d'un raisonnement, etc.); suite *f*, logique *f* (dans les idées); *Phil:* conséquence *f*; (*b*) *Med:* **self, internal, c.,** structure mentale cohérente; (*c*) *Cmptr:* **c. check,** contrôle *m* de cohérence, d'uniformité, d'homogénéité.

consistent [kən'sist(ə)nt], *a.* **1.** (*a*) (*of pers.*) conséquent; (*of conduct, etc.*) uniforme, logique; (*of reasoning, etc.*) cohérent; **ideas that are not c.,** idées qui ne sont pas cohérentes, qui ne tiennent pas, qui manquent de suite; *F:* **he may be pigheaded, but at least he's c.,** il est entêté si vous voulez, mais il a quand même de la suite dans ses idées; (*b*) *Cmptr:* cohérent, homogène; **c. unit,** élément cohérent; (*c*) **c. advocate of free trade,** partisan constant du libre-échange; *Com:* **c. buying,** achats suivis. **2.** compatible, d'accord (**with,** avec); **action c. with the law,** action *f* conforme à la loi; **theory which is not c. with the facts,** théorie *f* qui ne s'accorde pas avec les faits; **this action is not c. with his character,** cette action n'est pas en harmonie avec son caractère; **speed is not always c. with safety,** la vitesse n'est pas toujours compatible, ne va pas toujours de pair, avec la sécurité; **the means of transport must be c. with the nature of the goods,** le moyen de transport doit être fonction de la nature des marchandises; *Pol.Ec:* **c. expectations,** prévisions concordantes.

consistently [kən'sistəntli], *adv.* **1.** uniformément, conséquemment; logiquement; **c. ironic tone,** ton *m* uniformément ironique; **one cannot c. defend such dishonesty,** on ne peut pas logiquement défendre une telle malhonnêteté. **2.** **c. with one's principles,** conformément à, en conformité avec, ses principes.

consistometer [kɔnsis'tɔmitər], *s. Tchn:* consistomètre *m*.

consistorial [kɔnsis'tɔːriəl], *a. Ecc:* consistorial, -aux.

consistory [kən'sistəri], *s. Ecc:* **1.** consistoire (pontifical). **2.** **C. Court,** tribunal *m* ecclésiastique (d'un diocèse).

consol ['kɔnsɔl], *s. Nav: Av:* consol *m*.

consolable [kən'souləbl], *a.* consolable.

consolation [kɔnsə'leiʃ(ə)n], *s.* consolation *f*; (*a*) **words of c.,** paroles consolatrices; (*b*) **that's one c.,** c'est déjà une consolation; (*c*) *Games: Sp:* **c. prize,** prix *m* des perdants; **c. match,** match *m*, course *f*, de consolation.

consolatory [kən'sɔlət(ə)ri], *a.* consolant; consolateur, -trice; consolatoire.

console[1] ['kɔnsoul], *s.* **1.** *Arch:* console *f*, arc-boutant *m* (d'un balcon, etc.); *pl.* arcs-boutants; aileron *m* (d'un portail, etc.). **2.** (*a*) console (d'orgue); (*b*) **c. (table),** (table *f*) console; (*c*) meuble *m* pour radio, pour télévision; (*d*) *Av:* tableau *m* de bord; (*d*) *Elcs:* console; *Cmptr:* **c. (desk), control c.,** pupitre *m* de commande; **c. printer,** imprimante *f* de pupitre; **c. operator,** pupitreur, -euse.

console[2] [kən'soul], *v.tr.* consoler (**s.o. for a loss,** qn d'une perte).

consoleer [kɔnsə'liər], *s. Cmptr:* pupitreur, -euse.

consoler [kən'soulər], *s.* **1.** consolateur, -trice. **2.** *A:* **baby's c.,** sucette *f*, tétine *f*.

consolidate [kən'sɔlideit]. **1.** *v.tr.* (*a*) consolider, (r)affermir (des fondements, un empire, etc.); cimenter (une alliance); **to c. the road surface,** tasser la chaussée; *Mil: etc:* **to c. a position,** consolider une position; (*b*) consolider, unir, réunir (deux propriétés, deux entreprises, etc.); regrouper, fusionner; *Jur:* joindre (des instances); (*c*) *Fin:* consolider, unifier (une dette). **2.** *v.i.* se consolider; (*of road, etc.*) se tasser.

consolidated [kən'sɔlideitid], *a.* consolidé, unifié; *Fin:* **c. accounts,** comptes consolidés; **c. annuities,** fonds consolidés; **c. cash transactions,** récapitulation *f*, regroupement *m*, des opérations de caisse.

consolidation [kənsɔli'deiʃ(ə)n], *s.* **1.** consolidation *f*, (r)affermissement *m* (de fondements, de sa position, de pouvoir, etc.); tassement *m* (de terres, de l'opinion publique); *Mil:* colmatage *m* (d'une position). **2.** consolidation, unification *f* (des lois, de la dette publique, etc.); *Pol.Ec: Agr:* (i) remembrement *m*, réorganisation foncière; (ii) remaniement *m*, regroupement *m* parcellaire; *Cmptr:* groupage *m*, regroupement *m*, fusion *f*; *Fin:* regroupement (d'actions); *Jur:* **c. of actions,** jonction *f* d'instances; *Pol.Ec:* **c. of the floating debt,** consolidation de la dette flottante.

consolidator [kən'sɔlideitər], *s.* auteur *m* d'une consolidation. **1.** (r)affermisseur *m*. **2.** unificateur *m*.

consolidatory [kənsɔli'deitəri], *a.* consolidant; consolidatif.

consoling [kən'souliŋ], *a.* consolant, consolateur, -trice.

consols ['kɔnsɔlz, kən'sɔlz], *s.pl. Fin:* (fonds) consolidés *m*; **c. certificate,** titre consolidé.

consommé [kən'sɔmei], *s. Cu:* consommé *m*.

consonance ['kɔnsənəns], *s.* **1.** *Mus: Ling:* consonance *f*; *Mus:* accord *m*. **2.** accord, conformité *f*, communion *f* (d'idées, de sentiments, etc.); *Lit:* **this action is not in c. with his character,** cette action ne s'accorde pas, n'est pas en harmonie, avec son caractère. **3.** *Ph:* résonance *f*.

consonant[1] ['kɔnsənənt], *a.* **1.** *Mus: Ling:* consonant; *Mus:* harmonieux. **2.** *A: & Lit:* **c. with one's duty,** conforme à, d'accord avec, qui s'accorde avec, son devoir; **part c. with your dignity,** rôle *m* en rapport avec votre dignité.

consonant[2], *s. Ling:* consonne *f*; **breath c.,** consonne soufflée; **back c.,** vélaire *f*.

consonantal [kɔnsə'næntl], *a. Ling:* consonantique.

consonantism ['kɔnsənəntizm], *s. Ling:* consonantisme *m*.

consort[1] ['kɔnsɔːt], *s.* **1.** (*a*) époux, -ouse; conjoint, -ointe; **prince c., queen c.,** prince consort, reine consort(e); (*b*) *Nau:* (*ship*) conserve *f*. **2.** (*a*) **to act in c. with s.o.,** agir d'accord, de concert, avec qn; (*b*) *Nau:* **to sail in c.,** naviguer de conserve.

consort[2] [kən'sɔːt], *v.i.* **1.** (*of pers.*) **to c. with s.o.,** s'associer avec qn; frayer avec qn; fréquenter qn. **2.** (*of thg*) *Lit:* **to c. with sth.,** s'accorder avec qch.

consortium [kən'sɔːtiəm], *s. Com: Fin:* consortium *m*.

conspectus [kən'spektəs], *s.* (*a*) aperçu général; vue *f* d'ensemble; étude *f* d'ensemble; (*b*) tableau *m* synoptique.

conspicuity [kɔnspi'kjuːiti], *s.* = CONSPICUOUSNESS.

conspicuous [kən'spikjuəs], *a.* **1.** (*a*) visible, apparent, manifeste; qui donne dans la vue; **in a c. position,** bien en évidence; dans une situation très en relief; (*in a crowd, etc.*) **to be c.,** être en évidence; attirer les regards, l'attention; *F:* **to be c. by one's absence,** briller par son absence; (*b*) (*of monument, landmark*) voyant; (*c*) *Pol.Ec:* **c. consumption, waste,** consommation *f* ostentatoire. **2.** remarquable, frappant, marquant; éminent, insigne; **to make oneself c.,** se faire remarquer; se singulariser; se signaler (**by, through,** par); **she flaunts these hats in order to make herself c.,** elle affiche ces chapeaux par désir de se singulariser; **to play a c. part,** jouer un rôle marquant; **mentioned in dispatches for c. gallantry,** cité à l'ordre du jour pour un acte de bravoure insigne; **c. personality,** personnalité *f* en vue; **to cut a c. figure,** (i) marquer; (ii) se faire remarquer; **c. violation of a rule,** manquement *m* manifeste, insigne, à une règle.

conspicuously [kən'spikjuəsli], *adv.* **1.** visiblement, manifestement; en évidence. **2.** remarquablement; éminemment.

conspicuousness [kən'spikjuəsnis], *s.* **1.** évidence *f*, visibilité *f* (de qch.); éclat *m*, voyant *m* (d'un uniforme, etc.). **2.** caractère *m* insigne (d'une action); éminence *f*.

conspiracy [kən'spirəsi], *s.* **1.** conspiration *f*, conjuration *f*, complot *m*, coalition *f*; **c. of silence,** conspiration du silence; **to be in the c.,** être dans le complot; **there is a c. between you to spoil my chances of success,** vous vous êtes entendus pour m'empêcher de réussir. **2.** *Jur:* entente délictueuse; coalition.

conspirator [kən'spirətər], *s.* conspirateur, -trice; conjuré, -ée.

conspiratorial [kənspirə'tɔ:riəl], *a.* (air *m*) de conspirateur.

conspiratorially [kənspirə'tɔ:riəli], *adv.* d'un air conspirateur.

conspire [kən'spaiər]. **1.** *v.i.* (*a*) conspirer (**against,** contre); **to c. together,** se conjurer; **to c. with s.o.,** agir de concert avec qn; **to c. to do sth.,** comploter de faire qch.; s'entendre pour faire qch.; conspirer (un acte); **his enemies c. to ruin him,** ses ennemis *m* concourent à le ruiner; (*b*) (*of events, etc.*) contribuer, concourir, conspirer (à produire un effet); **everything conspired to keep him late,** tout a contribué à le mettre en retard; **everything conspires to exaggerate the incident,** tout conspire à grossir l'incident. **2.** *v.tr. A:* méditer, conspirer, comploter (la ruine de qn).

conspiring [kən'spaiəriŋ], *s.* conspiration *f*; *Jur:* association *f*.

conspue [kən'spju:], *v.tr.* conspuer (qn, une politique).

constable ['kʌnstəbl], *s.* **1.** (*a*) *Hist:* connétable *m*; (*b*) **C. of the Tower of London, of Windsor Castle, etc.,** gouverneur *m* de la Tour de Londres, du château de Windsor, etc. **2.** **(police) c.** = (i) agent *m* de police; (ii) gendarme *m*; (iii) (*in rural areas*) garde *m* champêtre; **special c.** = supplétif *m*; **chief c.** = commissaire (central) de police.

constabulary [kən'stæbjuləri], *s. coll.* la police; **the mounted c.,** la police montée, à cheval; **the county c.** = la gendarmerie.

Constance ['kɔnstəns], *Pr.n.f.* Constance; **Lake C., the lake of C.,** le lac de Constance.

constancy ['kɔnst(ə)nsi], *s.* **1.** (*a*) constance *f*, fermeté *f* (de caractère, d'une personne); (*b*) fidélité *f* (d'un ami); (*c*) *Psy:* **perceptual c.,** constance perceptive. **2.** (*a*) constance (d'un élément de pile, de la température); (*b*) régularité *f* (du vent, etc.).

constant ['kɔnst(ə)nt]. **1.** *a.* (*a*) constant, qui ne varie pas; (équilibre *m*) stable; **c. pressure,** pression constante, invariable; *El:* **c. current,** courant continu, constant; *Hyd.E:* **to give a river a c. regime,** régler une rivière; **c.-level reservoir,** réservoir *m* à niveau constant; *Cmptr:* **c. data,** constantes *fpl*; **c. area,** zone de(s) constantes; **c. ratio code,** code *m* à rapport constant; (*b*) incessant, continuel; (soin, travail) assidu, soutenu; **through c. repetition,** à force de répéter; **c. rain,** pluie continuelle; (*c*) constant, ferme (dans le malheur, etc.); (*d*) (ami) constant, loyal, -aux; (au cœur) fidèle; **to remain c. to one's principles,** rester fidèle à ses principes. **2.** *s. Mth: Ph:* constante; **time c.,** constante de temps; *Cmptr:* **figurative c.,** constante figurative; **address c.,** adresse *f* de base, adresse origine.

constantan ['kɔnstəntæn], *s. Metall:* constantan *m*.

Constantia [kən'stænʃə]. **1.** *Pr.n.* Constance *f*. **2.** *s.* (*wine*) constance *m*.

Constantine ['kɔnst(ə)ntain], *Pr.n.* **1.** *Hist:* Constantin *m*. **2.** *Geog:* Constantine *f*.

Constantinopolitan ['kɔnstæntinou'pɔlit(ə)n], *Hist:* (*a*) *a.* Constantinopolitain; de Constantinople; (*b*) *s.* Constantinopolitain, -aine.

constantly ['kɔnstəntli], *adv.* constamment, continuellement; à tous coups, à tout coup.

constellate ['kɔnstəleit]. **1.** *v.tr.* consteller (**with,** de). **2.** *v.i.* (*a*) se former en constellations; (*b*) *Lit:* se grouper (**into,** en).

constellation [kɔnstə'leiʃ(ə)n], *s.* constellation *f*.

consternate ['kɔnstəneit], *v.tr.* consterner, atterrer, accabler.

consternated ['kɔnstəneitid], *a.* consterné (**by . . .,** de la mort de qn, etc., par une nouvelle, etc.); atterré.

consternation [kɔnstə'neiʃ(ə)n], *s.* consternation *f*; atterrement *m*; **look of c.,** air consterné; **they looked at each other in c.,** ils se regardaient atterrés; **to strike s.o. with c.; to cause great c. to s.o.,** jeter qn dans la consternation; consterner qn.

constipate ['kɔnstipeit], *v.tr. Med:* constiper.

constipated ['kɔnstipeitid], *a.* constipé.

constipating ['kɔnstipeitiŋ], *a.* constipant.

constipation [kɔnsti'peiʃ(ə)n], *s.* constipation *f*.

constituency [kən'stitjuənsi], *s.* **1.** collège (électoral); électeurs *mpl*; **the member and his c.,** le député et ses mandants; **my c.,** mes électeurs. **2.** circonscription électorale.

constituent [kən'stitjuənt]. **1.** *a.* (*a*) constituant, constitutif, composant; **the c. elements of air, of water,** les éléments constitutifs de l'air, de l'eau; **a c. part of our social life,** un des éléments de notre vie sociale; (*b*) *Fr.Hist:* **the C. Assembly,** l'Assemblée constituante; la Constituante. **2.** *s.* (*a*) élément constitutif; composant *m*; **the constituents of happiness,** les éléments du bonheur; (*b*) *Ling:* constituant *m*; **c. analysis,** analyse *f* en constituants. **3.** *s.* (*pers.*) (*a*) *Jur:* constituant *m* (d'un fondé de pouvoirs); commettant *m*; (*b*) *Pol:* **constituents of an M.P.,** les mandants, commettants, d'un député; **my constituents,** mes électeurs.

constitute ['kɔnstitjut], *v.tr.* constituer. **1.** (*a*) **to c. a tribunal,** constituer un tribunal; **to c. a threat to.,** constituer une menace pour . . .; **constituted authority,** les autorités constituées; (*b*) **to c. s.o. arbitrator,** constituer, nommer, qn arbitre; **he has constituted himself my mentor,** il s'est constitué mon conseiller. **2.** **to c. s.o.'s happiness,** constituer, faire, le bonheur de qn; **factors that c. an offence,** éléments constitutifs d'un délit. **3.** (*a*) **to be so constituted that . . .,** être ainsi fait que . . .; (*b*) **to be strongly constituted,** être fortement constitué; *F:* avoir une santé de fer.

constitution [kɔnsti'tju:ʃ(ə)n], *s.* **1.** constitution *f*, composition *f* (de qch.); **the c. of the air, of the solar spectrum,** la constitution de l'air, du spectre solaire. **2.** complexion *f*, constitution (du corps); **to have a good, strong, c.,** avoir une bonne constitution; être d'une complexion solide; **to have an iron c.,** avoir une santé, une constitution, de fer; **of (a) delicate c.,** de santé délicate; **mental c.,** idiosyncrasie *f*. **3.** *Pol:* constitution (d'un État); **monarchic c.,** constitution monarchique; **the economic c. of France,** le statut économique de la France; **the written c.,** la constitution écrite. **4.** *pl.* **constitutions,** arrêts *m*; **the Clementine Constitutions** (**of Pope Clement V**), les Clémentines *f*.

constitutional [kɔnsti'tju:ʃənl]. **1.** *a.* (*a*) (monarque, régime) constitutionnel; (*b*) *Med:* (affection) diathésique, constitutionnelle. **2.** *s.* promenade *f* (hygiénique); **to take one's daily c.,** faire sa promenade quotidienne.

constitutionalist [kɔnsti'tju:ʃənəlist], *s.* **1.** spécialiste *m*, historien *m*, des constitutions politiques. **2.** *Pol:* (*a*) constitutionnel *m*; (*b*) *Eng.Hist:* = Conservateur *m*.

constitutionality [kɔnstitju:ʃə'næliti], *s.* constitutionnalité *f*; légitimité *f* (d'un décret, etc.).

constitutionalize [kɔnsti'tju:ʃənəlaiz], *v.tr.* constitutionnaliser, rendre constitutionnel; légitimer (un décret, etc.).

constitutionally [kɔnsti'tju:ʃən(ə)li], *adv.* constitutionnellement. **1.** conformément à la constitution (de l'État). **2.** par tempérament; **he was c. inaccurate,** il était inexact par nature.

constitutive [kən'stitjutiv], *a.* constitutif; **the c. elements of the human body,** les éléments constitutifs du corps humain.

constrain [kən'strein], *v.tr.* **1.** **to c. s.o. to do sth.,** contraindre, forcer, qn à, de, faire qch.; faire faire qch. à qn; **to find oneself, to feel, constrained to do sth.,** se voir, être, dans la nécessité, dans l'obligation, de faire qch. **2.** (*a*) (*of clothing, etc.*) gêner (les mouvements); comprimer (le corps); (*b*) retenir (qn) de force; contenir (qn); tenir (qn) en contrainte; **planets constrained in their orbits,** planètes contenues, renfermées, dans leurs orbites; (*c*) *A:* enfermer, emprisonner (qn).

constrained [kən'streind], *a.* **1.** **c. manner,** air gêné; **c. voice,** voix forcée; **c. smile,** sourire forcé, embarrassé, bridé. **2.** *Mec:* **c. movement,** mouvement commandé.

constrainedly [kən'streinidli], *adv.* **1.** par contrainte. **2.** **to smile c.,** sourire d'un air gêné, d'un air contraint.

constraint [kən'streint], *s.* **1.** (*a*) contrainte *f*; (*b*) *Jur: etc:* contrainte par corps, coercition *f*; **to put s.o. under c.,** retenir qn de force; enfermer, interner (un aliéné, etc.). **2.** (*a*) (*of manner*) gêne *f*, contrainte; (*b*) **you should show some c.,** vous devriez observer une certaine retenue; **he writes to me without c.,** il m'écrit d'un ton entièrement dégagé, à cœur ouvert.

constrict [kən'strikt], *v.tr.* **1.** resserrer, étrangler, rétrécir (une ouverture). **2.** (*a*) brider, serrer, gêner (le corps, etc.); (*b*) *Physiol:* resserrer (les fibres, les tissus).

constriction [kən'strikʃ(ə)n], *s.* resserrement *m*, étranglement *m*, rétrécissement *m*; *Med:* constriction *f*, strangulation *f*; angustie *f* (du cœur, des artères); *Physiol:* constriction (des fibres, des pores).

constrictive [kən'striktiv], *a.* constrictif.

constrictor [kən'striktər], *s.* **1.** *Anat:* (muscle) constricteur (*m*). **2.** **boa c.,** boa constricteur. **3.** *Surg:* (*instrument*) compresseur *m*.

constringent [kən'strin(d)ʒ(ə)nt], *a.* constringent; *Med:* astringent.

construct[1] ['kɔnstrʌkt], *s.* construction *f* ((i) de l'esprit, (ii) géométrique).

construct[2] [kən'strʌkt], *v.tr.* construire (une machine, une phrase, un triangle, etc.); construire, bâtir (un édifice); confectionner, charpenter (un drame, un roman); *Cmptr:* constituer, créer (une table, etc.); **to c. a dam, a railway,** établir un barrage, un chemin de fer; **badly constructed sentences,** phrases mal agencées; **well constructed play,** pièce de théâtre bien charpentée.

constructible [kən'strʌktəbl], *a.* constructible.

construction [kən'strʌkʃ(ə)n], *s.* **1.** (*a*) construction *f* (d'un bâtiment, etc.); construction, réalisation *f* (d'une machine, etc.); **under c., in course of c.,** en (cours de) construction; **c. site,** chantier *m* de construction; *P.N: NAm:* **c. (works)!** travaux! (*b*) manière *f* dont une machine, etc. a été réalisée; **compact c.,** réalisation peu encombrante; (*c*) *Cmptr: etc:* constitution *f* (d'une table, etc.); **c. of index numbers,** établissement *m* d'indices; (*d*) (*thing constructed*) construction; édifice *m*; bâtiment *m*; immeuble *m*; **a huge c. of reinforced concrete,** un bâtiment énorme en béton armé; **all-metal c.,** construction entièrement métallique; **composite c.,** construction mixte. **2.** (*a*) *Gram:* construction (d'une phrase); **c. of a novel,** construction d'un roman; (*b*) interprétation *f*; **c. of a law,** interprétation d'une loi; **c. of a provision,** interprétation d'une disposition (d'un contrat); **to put a good, bad, c. on s.o.'s words,** interpréter en bien, en mal, les paroles de qn; **to put a wrong c. on an action,** tourner une action en mal; **this is a charitable c. of his action,** c'est interpréter son action avec beaucoup de charité; **to put another c. on sth.,** interpréter qch. autrement, d'une autre façon; **you're putting a wrong c. on it,** vous l'interprétez mal; vous ne le comprenez pas. **3.** *Art:* sculpture *f* constructiviste.

constructional [kən'strʌkʃənl], *a.* de construction; **c. defect,** défaut *m*, vice *m*, de construction; **c. engineering,** construction *f* mécanique; **c. toy,** jeu *m* de construction.

constructive [kən'strʌktiv], *a.* **1.** constructif; **c. criticism,** critique constructive; **c. mind,** esprit créateur. **2.** *Ind:* constructeur, -trice; de construction. **3.** *Jur:* par interprétation; par déduction; **c. treason,** trahison *f* implicite; *Ins:* **c. total loss,** perte censée totale. **4.** *Th: Art:* **c. movement,** constructivisme *m*.

constructively [kən'strʌktivli], *adv.* **1.** d'une manière constructive, pratique. **2.** *Jur:* par interprétation, par induction.

constructivism [kən'strʌktivizm], *s. Th: Art:* constructivisme *m*.

constructivist [kən'strʌktivist], *a. Art:* **the c. manifesto,** le manifeste constructiviste.

constructor [kən'strʌktər], *s.* constructeur *m*; **naval c.,** ingénieur *m* des constructions navales, du génie maritime.

construe[1] ['kɔnstru:], *s. O:* (*a*) *Gram:* décomposition *f*, mot à mot *m*, analyse *f* (d'une phrase); (*b*) **c. of a Greek author,** explication *f* d'un auteur grec.

construe[2] [kən'stru:], *v.tr.* **1.** *O:* (*a*) *Sch:* faire le mot à mot (d'un passage); analyser, décomposer (une phrase); **to c. Homer,** expliquer Homère; (*with passive force*) **sentence that does not c.,** phrase *f* qui manque de construction, qui pèche contre la grammaire; (*b*) *Gram:* **preposition that is construed with the dative,** préposition qui gouverne le datif, qui est suivie du datif. **2.** interpréter (les paroles de qn); expliquer (la conduite de qn); **to c. an unskilfully drawn will,** interpréter les volontés du testateur d'après un testament mal rédigé.

construing [kən'stru:iŋ], *s.* = CONSTRUE[1].

consubstantial [kɔnsəb'stænsjəl], *a. Theol:* consubstantiel; **the Son is c. with the Father,** le Fils est consubstantiel au Père, avec le Père.

consubstantiality [kɔnsəbstænsi'æliti], *s. Theol:* consubstantialité *f* **(with,** avec).

consubstantially [kɔnsəb'stænsjəli], *adv.* consubstantiellement.

consubstantiate [kɔnsəb'stænsieit], *Theol:* **1.** *v.tr.* unir (qch.) dans une seule et même substance **(with,** à). **2.** *v.i.* s'unir en une seule et même substance.

consuetude ['kɔnswitju:d], *s.* **1.** *Jur: Scot:* coutume *f*; usage local. **2.** *A: & Lit:* relations sociales.

consuetudinary [kɔnswi'tju:dinəri]. **1.** *a. Jur:* (droit) coutumier. **2.** *s. Ecc:* recueil *m* de la coutume (d'un couvent, d'une abbaye); coutumier *m.*

consul ['kɔns(ə)l], *s.* **1.** *Rom. & Fr.Hist:* consul *m*; **the C. Regulus,** le consul Régulus. **2.** *Dipl:* consul; **c. general,** consul général; **the French C. in London,** le consul de France à Londres.

consulage ['kɔnsjulidʒ], *s. Dipl:* droits *m* consulaires.

consular ['kɔnsjulər], *a.* consulaire.

consulate ['kɔnsjulət], *s.* **1.** *(a) Rom.Hist:* consulat *m*; *(b) Fr.Hist:* **the C.,** le Consulat (1799–1804). **2.** *Dipl:* consulat; **C. General,** Consulat Général; **the British C. in Paris,** le consulat de Grande-Bretagne, *F:* le consulat d'Angleterre, à Paris.

consulship ['kɔnsəlʃip], *s. Rom.Hist: etc:* consulat *m* ((i) fonctions de consul, (ii) durée du mandat d'un consul).

consult [kən'sʌlt]. **1.** *v.tr.* *(a)* consulter **(s.o. on, about, sth.,** qn sur qch.); **to c. a dictionary,** consulter un dictionnaire; *(b)* **to c. one's own interests, one's own safety,** consulter ses intérêts; pourvoir à son propre salut; **to c. s.o.'s feelings,** avoir égard à la sensibilité de qn; ménager qn. **2.** *v.i.* consulter (avec qn); **to c. together,** délibérer; se consulter; **we have consulted about the matter,** (i) nous nous sommes consultés, nous avons conféré, sur cette affaire; (ii) nous avons consulté un avocat sur cette affaire.

consultable [kən'sʌltəbl], *a.* consultable.

consultancy [kən'sʌltənsi], *s.* **1.** *Med:* **to be appointed to a c.,** être nommé médecin consultant, chirurgien consultant. **2.** *Ind: etc:* **c. firm,** cabinet *m* d'experts conseils.

consultant [kən'sʌltənt], *s.* **1.** consultant *m* (qui interroge un oracle, etc.). **2.** *(a)* médecin, chirurgien, consultant; *(b) Ind: etc:* expert-conseil *m, pl.* experts-conseils; **engineering c.,** ingénieur *m* conseil; **management c.,** conseiller *m,* ingénieur conseil, en organisation; **data-processing c.,** conseiller, ingénieur conseil, en informatique; **c. service,** assistance *f* technique.

consultation [kɔnsəl'teiʃ(ə)n], *s.* **1.** consultation *f* (d'un dictionnaire, etc.). **2.** *(a)* consultation, délibération *f* (entre médecins, etc.); **after c. with my colleagues,** après avoir consulté mes collègues; **to hold a c.,** consulter, délibérer, conférer; **the doctors held a c.,** les médecins se sont consultés; *(b) Jur:* consultation entre plusieurs avocats.

consultative [kən'sʌltətiv], *a.* consultatif.

consulter [kən'sʌltər], *s.* consultant *m* (d'un oracle, d'un médecin, etc.).

consulting[1] [kən'sʌltiŋ], *a.* **c. physician,** médecin consultant; **c. chemist, engineer,** chimiste *m* conseil, ingénieur *m* conseil.

consulting[2], *s.* consultation *f*; *Med: etc:* **c. hours,** heures *f* de consultation; **c. room,** cabinet *m* de consultation.

consultor [kən'sʌltər], *s.m. R.C.Ch:* consulteur *m* (du Saint-Office, etc.).

consumable [kən'sju:məbl], *a.* **1.** consumable (par le feu). **2.** *(a)* (aliment *m*) consommable; *Pol.Ec:* consomptible; **c. goods,** produits *m* de consommation courante; *(b) s.pl.* **consumables,** aliments *m,* comestibles *m,* denrées *f.*

consume [kən'sju:m]. **1.** *v.tr.* *(a) (of fire)* consumer, dévorer; **the town was consumed by fire,** la ville a été incendiée, a été la proie des flammes; *(b)* consommer (des vivres); **the English c. a great deal of meat,** les Anglais consomment beaucoup de viande; *(c)* **engine that consumes a ton of coal per hour,** machine *f* qui consomme, qui brûle, une tonne de charbon par heure; *(d)* **to c. one's life, one's time (in doing sth.),** (i) perdre, gaspiller; (ii) passer, dépenser, sa vie, son temps (à faire qch.); *(e)* **to be consumed with thirst,** être consumé par la soif; **to be consumed with desire, jealousy,** brûler de désir; être dévoré, rongé, de jalousie; être miné par l'envie; **to be consumed with impatience, with boredom,** sécher d'impatience, d'ennui; *(f)* épuiser (ses vivres, etc.); **gambling has consumed his fortune,** le jeu a absorbé sa fortune. **2.** *v.i.* se consumer.

consumedly [kən'sju:midli], *adv. A:* excessivement, énormément; **to laugh c.,** se pâmer de rire.

consumer [kən'sju:mər], *s.* consommateur, -trice (d'une denrée, etc.); **gas, electricity, consumers,** abonnés *m* au gaz, à l'électricité; *Pol.Ec:* **producers and consumers,** producteurs *m* et consommateurs; **c. council,** comité (consultatif) des consommateurs; **c. goods,** biens *m* de consommation; **c. durables,** biens de consommation durables; **c. credit,** crédit *m* à la consommation; **c. education,** éducation *f* des consommateurs.

consuming [kən'sju:miŋ], *a. (of fire, passion, etc.)* dévorant.

consummate[1] [kən'sʌmət, 'kɔnsəmət], *a.* *(a)* (art, artiste) consommé, achevé, parfait, complet; **to be a c. master, mistress, of one's craft,** connaître à fond son métier; être passé(e) maître(sse) dans son métier; *(b)* **c. liar, hypocrite,** menteur, hypocrite, achevé.

consummate[2] ['kɔnsʌmeit, -sju-], *v.tr.* consommer (un mariage, un sacrifice, un crime).

consummately ['kənsʌmətli], *adv.* parfaitement, complètement; avec une maîtrise achevée.

consummation [kɔnsʌ'meiʃ(ə)n], *s.* **1.** consommation *f* (d'un mariage, d'un crime, etc.). **2.** consommation, achèvement *m,* fin *f*; **the c. of the world, of all things, the final c.,** la consommation, la fin, des temps, des siècles, du monde. **3.** perfection *f* (d'un art, etc.). **4.** fin; but *m*; comble *m* (des désirs); **the c. of a splendid life,** le couronnement d'une belle vie; *Lit:* **this is a c. devoutly to be wished,** puisse cette fin se réaliser!

consumption [kən'sʌm(p)ʃ(ə)n], *s.* **1.** *(a)* consommation *f* (des denrées, etc.); **increased price causes a decreased c.,** la hausse des prix abaisse la consommation; *Pol.Ec:* **home c.,** consommation intérieure; **public, private, c.,** consommation publique, privée; **for current c.,** destiné à la consommation courante; **unfit for human c.,** non comestible; **we took some food for c. on the journey,** nous avons apporté de quoi manger en cours de route; *(b)* consommation, dépense *f* (de chaleur, de charbon, d'essence); *Mch: etc:* **cruising c.,** consommation à la vitesse, au régime, économique; **c. per hour,** consommation horaire; **car with a petrol c. of 25 miles per gallon** = voiture avec une consommation d'essence de 11 litres aux 100 kms, *F:* qui fait 11 litres aux 100 kms. **2.** *(a)* destruction *f*; *Lit:* **till the c. of the world,** jusqu'à la fin du monde; *(b) Med: O:* **(pulmonary) c.,** phtisie *f*; consomption *f* pulmonaire; *A:* **to go into c.,** devenir phtisique, poitrinaire.

consumptive [kən'sʌm(p)tiv], *a.* **1.** *(a)* (pouvoir *m,* etc.) de consommation; *(b)* **work too c. of time,** travail *m* qui prend, gaspille, trop de temps. **2.** destructeur, -trice **(of,** de); destructif. **3.** *a. & s. Med:* poitrinaire *(mf),* phtisique *(mf),* tuberculeux, -euse; **a c. cough,** une toux de poitrinaire.

contabescence [kɔntə'bes(ə)ns], *s. Bot: Med:* contabescence *f.*

contabescent [kɔntə'bes(ə)nt], *a.* contabescent.

contact[1] ['kɔntækt], *s.* **1.** *(a)* contact *m*; attouchement *m,* touche *f*; portée *f* (d'une dent de roue); **point of c.,** point *m* de contact, de tangence, d'attouchement (de deux courbes, etc.); *Opt:* **c. lens,** verre *m,* lentille *f,* de contact; *Phot:* **c. print,** épreuve *f,* copie *f,* par contact; *Geol:* **c. lode, vein,** filon *m,* veine *f,* de contact; **c. metamorphism,** métamorphisme *m* de contact; *(b)* rapport *m,* contact; **preliminary contacts,** prise *f* de contact; **to be in c., to come into c., with s.o.,** être, entrer, se mettre, en contact, en rapport, avec qn; **I'll put you in c. with him,** je vais vous mettre en contact, en rapport, avec lui; *Mil:* **to establish, lose, c. with the enemy,** prendre, perdre, contact avec l'ennemi; *Av: O:* **c. flying,** vol *m* en vue de la terre; navigation *f* par points de repère; *Com: etc:* **c. man,** agent *m* de liaison; *(c) Med:* personne *f* ayant approché un malade contagieux; *F:* **to have plenty of contacts,** avoir de nombreuses relations, connaître un tas de gens; **I have a c. who may be able to help you,** je connais quelqu'un, un type, qui pourrait vous aider. **2.** *El: etc:* *(a)* contact; **c. to earth,** contact avec la terre; mise *f* à terre; **frictional c.,** contact par frottement; **c. point,** point de contact; **c. fault,** défaut *m* de contact; **c. losses,** pertes dues au contact; **c. knife,** couteau *m* de contact; **c. plug,** fiche *f,* cheville *f,* de contact; **c. screw,** vis *f* de contact; **c. electrode,** électrode *f* de contact; **c. microphone,** microphone *f* de contact; **to make c.,** établir le contact; **c. maker,** contacteur *m*; **to break c.,** rompre le contact; interrompre le courant; couper le circuit; **c. breaker,** dispositif *m,* levier *m,* de rupture; (inter)rupteur *m*; trembleur *m*; *Cmptr:* **c. pin,** épingle *f* de contact (de tableau de connexion); *Av: O:* **to ask the pilot for c.,** demander le contact au pilote; *(b)* contact, touche; **fixed, mobile, c.,** contact fixe, mobile; **sliding c.,** contact glissant; **spring c.,** contact élastique; **plug c.,** contact à cheville, à fiche; **relay c.,** contact à relais; **c. rectifier,** contact redresseur; **c. point (of switchboard),** goutte-de-suif *f, pl.* gouttes-de-suif; **c. stud,** plot *m*; **single-c., double-c., base,** culot *m* à plot central, à deux plots (de lampe électrique); **single-c. bulb,** lampe *f* à un plot; *Tg:* **back, break, resting, c.,** contact de repos; **make c.,** contact de travail; **make-and-break c.,** contact repos-travail.

contact[2], *v.tr.* **to c. s.o.,** se mettre en contact, en rapport, en relation, avec qn; *F:* contacter qn.

contactor [kən'tæktər], *s. El:* contacteur *m*; interrupteur *m* automatique.

contagion [kən'teidʒ(ə)n], *s.* **1.** contagion *f.* **2.** maladie contagieus, contagion.

contagious [kən'teidʒəs], *a.* **1.** *(of disease, laughter, etc.)* contagieux; *(of laughter)* communicatif; **to communicate a c. disease to s.o.,** contagier qn. **2.** *Vet:* **c. disease,** épizootie *f*; **c. abortion,** brucellose *f,* avortement *m* épizootique.

contagiously [kən'teidʒəsli], *adv.* *(a)* par contagion; *(b)* (rire) d'une façon contagieuse.

contagiousness [kən'teidʒəsnis], *s.* contagiosité *f*; **the c. of laughter,** la contagion du rire.

contagium, *pl.* **-ia** [kən'teidʒiəm, -iə], *s. Med:* contage *m*; virus *m* de contagion.

contain [kən'tein], *v.tr.* **1.** *(a) (hold)* contenir; **all the land contained within the limits of the estate,** toute la terre contenue entre les bornes du domaine; **this jug will not c. a litre,** ce pot a une capacité de moins d'un litre; **a litre jug containing only a few drops of milk,** pot d'un litre qui ne contenait que quelques gouttes de lait; **what did the old trunk c.?** qu'est-ce qu'il y avait dans la vieille malle? *(b) (comprise, include)* contenir, renfermer, comprendre, comporter; **book that contains many errors,** livre qui contient, qui renferme, beaucoup d'erreurs; **his letter contained interesting news,** sa lettre nous apportait des nouvelles intéressantes; **medicine that contains arsenic,** médicament *m* qui renferme, où il entre, de l'arsenic; **ore containing a high percentage of iron,** minerai *m* à forte teneur en fer; **machine containing all the latest improvements,** machine *f* qui comporte tous les derniers perfectionnements. **2.** *(restrain)* contenir, maîtriser (son indignation); retenir, refouler (ses sentiments); contenir, enrayer, juguler (l'inflation, une attaque, la montée des eaux, etc.); **he was unable to c. his laughter,** il ne pouvait pas s'empêcher de rire; *F:* **there's no containing him!** impossible de freiner son exubérance, son enthousiasme! *Lit.* **to c. oneself,** se contenir, se maîtriser; *F:* **I hope I can c. myself until the end of the film,** espérons que je ne serai pas obligé d'aller à la toilette avant la fin du film. **3.** *Mil:* contenir, maintenir (l'ennemi); **containing force,** corps de troupes destiné à contenir, à arrêter, l'ennemi. **4.** *Mth: O: (of number)* être divisible par (un nombre).

containable [kən'teinəbl], *a.* qui peut être contenu, maintenu, maîtrisé.

contained [kən'teind], *a. (of passions, behaviour)* retenu.

container [kən'teinər], *s.* *(a)* récipient *m*; réservoir *m*; bac *m* (pour aliments); *El:* bac (d'accumulateur), vase *m*; ampoule *f* (d'une bouteille isolante); *(b) Com: etc:* boîte *f,* récipient, logement *m*; coffret *m,* boîte (pour bande magnétique, etc.); **slotted (cardboard) c.,** caisse *f* (en carton) à rabats; *(c) Trans:* conteneur *m, F:* container *m*; cadre *m* (de déménagement); *Av:* **(supply) c.,** récipient, conteneur, de parachutage; **c. plane, ship,** avion *m,* navire *m,* porte-conteneurs; **c. shipping,** transports *m* maritimes par conteneurs; **c. berth,** poste *m* à quai pour navires porte-conteneurs.

containerization [kənteinərai'zeiʃ(ə)n], *s. Trans:* transport *m* par conteneurs; **the dock strike was against c.,** la grève des dockers avait pour origine l'opposition à l'adoption des conteneurs.

containment [kən'teinmənt], *s.* *(a)* retenue *f* (dans la conduite); refoulement *m,* maîtrise *f* (de ses sentiments, etc.); *(b)* endiguement *m,* enrayement *m,* freinage *m* (de l'inflation, de l'inondation, d'une attaque, etc.); **policy of c.,** politique *f* d'endiguement.

contaminant [kən'tæminənt], *a. & s.* contaminant *(m).*

contaminate[1] [kən'tæmineit], *v.tr.* contaminer; corrompre; souiller; **to breathe contaminated air,** respirer un air vicié, contaminé.

contaminate[2] [kən'tæminət], *s. Ch: Petr:* *(a)* impuretés *fpl*; *(b)* contaminat *m.*

contaminating [kən'tæmineitiŋ], *a.* contaminant; viciateur, -trice.

contamination [kəntæmi'neiʃ(ə)n], *s.* contamination *f.*

contango[1], *pl.* **-oes** [kən'tæŋgou, -ouz], *s. St.Exch:* report *m*; taux *m* du report; **c. day,** jour *m* des reports; **money on c.,** capitaux *mpl* en report; **contangoes are heavy, low,** les reports sont chers, bon marché; **payer of c.,** reporté *m.*

contango[2], *v.tr. & i. St.Exch:* reporter (une position).

contangoable [kən'tæŋgouəbl], *a. St.Exch:* reportable.

contangoing [kən'tæŋgouiŋ], *s. St.Exch:* report *m.*
contemn [kən'tem], *v.tr. A: & Lit:* mépriser; traiter (qn, qch.) avec mépris; *B:* **they contemned the counsel of the Most High,** ils ont méprisé, rejeté par mépris, le conseil du Souverain.
contemner [kən'tem(n)ər], *s. (a) A: & Lit:* contempteur, -trice; *(b) Jur:* celui qui s'est rendu coupable d'une offense à la Cour.
contemplate ['kɔntempleit]. **1.** *(a) v.tr.* contempler, considérer (qn, qch.); *Lit:* **to c. bygone ages,** planer sur les siècles passés; *(b) v.i.* se recueillir; méditer. **2.** *v.tr. (a)* prévoir, envisager, s'attendre à (qch.), avoir (qch.) en vue; *(b)* **to c. (doing) sth.,** projeter, méditer, se proposer, qch.; projeter de, se proposer de, songer à, faire qch.; **to c. suicide,** songer au suicide; **to c. a journey,** projeter un voyage; **that was never contemplated,** il n'a jamais été question de cela; **I do not c. staying here,** je n'ai pas l'intention de rester ici.
contemplation [kɔntem'pleiʃ(ə)n], *s.* **1.** *(a)* contemplation *f* (d'un tableau, d'une vitrine, etc.); **I found him in c. before . . .,** je l'ai trouvé en contemplation devant . . .; *(b)* recueillement *m,* méditation *f,* contemplation. **2.** *(a)* **to have sth. in c.,** avoir qch. en vue; projeter qch.; **it is as yet only in c.,** ce n'est encore qu'à l'état de projet; ce n'est encore qu'un projet; *(b)* **they had taken precautions in c. of an attack,** ils avaient pris des mesures en prévision *f* d'une attaque, dans l'attente *f* d'une attaque.
contemplative [kən'templətiv], *a. (of character, religious life, etc.)* contemplatif, recueilli; **c. eyes,** regard songeur, pensif.
contemplatively [kən'templətivli], *adv.* contemplativement; **he looked at me c.,** il m'a regardé pensivement, d'un air songeur.
contemplator ['kɔntempleitər], *s.* contemplateur, -trice.
contemporaneous [kəntempə'reiniəs], *a.* contemporain (**with,** de).
contemporaneously [kəntempə'reiniəsli], *adv.* **c. with . . .,** au même temps que . . .; à la même époque que . . ..
contemporaneousness [kəntempə'reiniəsnis], **contemporaneity** [kəntempərə'ni:iti], *s.* contemporanéité *f.*
contemporary [kən'temp(ə)rəri], *a. & s. (a)* contemporain, -aine (**with,** de); **he was c. with Homer, he was a c. of Homer's, he and Homer were contemporaries,** il était contemporain d'Homère; *(b)* **c. literature,** littérature contemporaine, d'aujourd'hui; **c. furniture,** meubles contemporains, modernes; **c. events,** événements actuels; **our contemporaries,** nos contemporains.
contempt [kən'tem(p)t], *s.* **1.** mépris *m*; dédain *m*; **to show c. for s.o., sth., to hold s.o., sth., in c.,** mépriser qn, qch.; tenir qn, qch., en mépris; avoir du mépris, du dédain, pour qn, qch.; **to treat s.o., sth., with c.,** traiter qn avec dédain, avec mépris; montrer du mépris pour qn, qch.; **to incur s.o.'s c.,** subir le mépris de qn; **(absolutely) beneath c.,** tout ce qu'il y a de plus méprisable. **2.** *(a) Jur:* **c. of court,** (i) outrage *m* au tribunal, offense *f* à la cour, aux magistrats; désobéissance *f*; (ii) *(non appearance)* défaut *m*; refus *m* de comparaître; contumace *f*; *(b) (at meeting, etc.)* **c. of the chair,** manquement *m* à l'autorité du président.
contemptible [kən'tem(p)təbl], *a.* méprisable; **he made a c. apology,** il fit de plates excuses; **c. conduct,** conduite *f* indigne; *Hist: s.* **the Old Contemptibles,** les survivants *m* de "la misérable petite armée britannique" de 1914.
contemptibleness [kən'tem(p)təblnis], **contemptibility** [kəntem(p)tə'biliti], *s.* caractère *m* méprisable; platitude *f,* bassesse *f* (d'une action).
contemptibly [kən'tem(p)təbli], *adv.* d'une manière méprisable; platement; bassement; **to behave c.,** se conduire d'une façon indigne.
contemptuous [kən'tem(p)tjuəs], *a.* **1. c. of sth.,** dédaigneux de qch.; **he was c. of praise,** il faisait peu de cas des louanges. **2.** (air) méprisant, (geste *m,* parole *f*) de mépris; **with an air of c. indifference,** d'un air d'indifférence dédaigneuse.
contemptuously [kən'tem(p)tjuəsli], *adv.* avec mépris; avec dédain; d'un air, d'un ton, méprisant.
contemptuousness [kən'tem(p)tjuəsnis], *s.* mépris *m*; caractère méprisant.
contend [kən'tend]. **1.** *v.i.* combattre, lutter (**with, against,** contre); disputer, discuter (**with s.o. about sth.,** avec qn sur qch.); **to have a powerful enemy to c. with,** avoir affaire à forte partie; **to c. with s.o. for sth.,** disputer, contester, qch. à qn; **to c. with a difficulty, with one's passions,** combattre, lutter contre, une difficulté; combattre ses passions; **the difficulties with which I have to c.,** les difficultés avec lesquelles je suis aux prises. **2.** *v.tr.* **to c. that . . .,** prétendre, soutenir, affirmer, que + *ind.*; **I have always contended that . . .,** j'ai toujours soutenu que . . ..
contender [kən'tendər], *s. (a)* concurrent, -ente; compétiteur, -trice; **he was a c. in the municipal elections,** il était candidat aux élections municipales; *(b) Sp:* challenger *m.*
contending [kən'tendiŋ], *a.* **c. parties,** contestants *m,* partis *m* en lutte, partis en présence; **the c. armies,** les armées opposées; les combattants *m.*
content[1] ['kɔntent], *s.* **1.** *(a)* contenu *m,* volume *m* (d'un solide); contenance *f,* capacité *f* (d'un vase); contenance, superficie *f* (d'un champ); *(b) pl.* **contents,** contenu (d'une bouteille, d'un livre, d'une lettre, etc.); *(of book)* **(table of) contents,** table *f* des matières. **2.** *Ch: Miner: etc:* teneur *f,* titre *m*; **gold c.,** teneur en or; **heat c. of a mixture,** contenance *f* thermique d'un mélange; **moisture c. of a gas,** teneur en humidité d'un gaz; **bacterial c.,** teneur microbienne; **with low radioactive c.,** légèrement radioactif; **with a high protein c.,** riche en protéine.
content[2] [kən'tent], *s.* **1.** *(a)* contentement *m,* satisfaction *f*; *(b) A:* **to take sth. upon c.,** accepter (une affirmation, etc.) sans examen. **2.** *(in House of Lords) (a)* vote affirmatif; voix *f* pour; *(b)* membre *m* qui a voté pour la motion.
content[3] [kən'tent], *a.* **1.** satisfait (**with,** de); **I am perfectly c.,** je n'en demande pas davantage, mieux; **I'll be c. to spend a quiet holiday in the country,** il me suffit de passer des vacances paisibles à la campagne; **would you be c. to wait until tomorrow?** cela ne vous dérange pas d'attendre jusqu'à demain? **yes, I'm quite c.,** oui, je veux bien, je consens, cela m'est égal; **to be c. with sth.,** se contenter de qch.; **I am not c. with your explanation,** je ne trouve pas votre explication satisfaisante, suffisante; **I am not c. with guesses,** je ne me satisfais pas de conjectures; **not c. with robbing us, he is now bringing an action against us,** comme si ce n'était pas assez de nous voler, voilà qu'il nous cite en justice! *Cards:* **content!** je m'y tiens! ça va! **2.** *(in House of Lords)* **the House then divided; content 84, not content 23,** la Chambre procéda au vote: pour, 84, contre, 23.
content[4] [kən'tent], *v.tr.* **1.** contenter, satisfaire (qn). **2. to c. oneself with sth., with doing sth.,** se contenter de qch., de faire qch.; se borner à faire qch.
contented [kən'tentid], *a.* content; satisfait; **he's a very c. person,** c'est un heureux; **he's never c.,** il n'est jamais satisfait; **a c. smile,** un sourire de satisfaction, de contentement; **I try to keep the children c.,** j'essaie de rendre les enfants contents, heureux; **c. with life,** content de son sort.
contentedly [kən'tentidli], *adv.* avec contentement; sans se plaindre; **to live c.,** vivre content, heureux.
contentedness [kən'tentidnis], *s.* contentement *m* (de son sort).
contention [kən'tenʃ(ə)n], *s.* **1.** lutte *f,* dispute *f,* discussion *f,* démêlé *m,* débat *m*; **bone of c.,** pomme *f* de discorde; sujet *m* de dispute; l'objet *m* du litige. **2.** émulation *f,* rivalité *f.* **3.** affirmation *f,* prétention *f*; **my c. is that . . .,** je soutiens que + *ind.*; ce que j'affirme, c'est que . . ..
contentious [kən'tenʃəs], *a.* **1.** *(of pers., humour)* disputeur, -euse; querelleur, -euse; disputailleur, -euse; chicaneur, -euse; chicanier, -ière. **2.** *(of issue, etc.)* contentieux. **3. c. jurisdiction,** droit *m* d'intervention entre plaideurs.
contentiously [kən'tenʃəsli], *adv.* **1.** en chicanant. **2.** *Jur:* contentieusement.
contentiousness [kən'tenʃəsnis], *s.* humeur querelleuse, chicanière.
contentment [kən'tentmənt], *s.* contentement *m*; *Prov:* **c. is better than riches,** contentement passe richesse.
contest[1] ['kɔntest], *s. (a)* combat *m,* lutte *f* (**with,** avec, contre; **between,** entre); *(b) (competition)* concours *m,* épreuve *f,* match *m,* partie *f*; *Sp:* critérium *m*; **musical c.,** concours de musique; **speed c.,** course *f* de vitesse; **c. of eloquence,** joute *f* oratoire; **beauty c.,** concours de beauté; *W.Tel: etc:* **talent c.,** crochet *m,* jeu *m* (radiophonique); *(c) Lit:* controverse *f,* débat *m,* contestation *f*; **a noisy c. arose between the spectators,** il s'éleva entre les assistants une contestation bruyante; **beyond c.** [kən'test], sans contestation possible; sans conteste; *(d) U.S: Jur:* **no c.,** pas de témoins à charge.
contest[2] [kən'test]. **1.** *v.tr. (a)* contester, disputer, débattre (une question) (**with, against,** avec); *(b)* **to c. s.o.'s right to do sth.,** contester à qn le droit de faire qch.; **to c. the victory, the day, with s.o.,** disputer la victoire à qn; *Sp:* **to c. a race,** se mettre sur les rangs; *(c)* **to c. a seat in Parliament,** disputer un siège au Parlement; se poser candidat pour un siège au Parlement; *(d) Jur:* attaquer (un testament); contester (une succession, une dette). **2.** *v.i. (a)* se disputer, entrer en discussion (**with, against,** avec); *(b)* **to c. for a prize,** disputer un prix; se mettre sur les rangs (pour remporter un prix).
contestable [kən'testəbl], *a.* contestable; (question *f*) débattable; (testament *m*) attaquable.
contestant [kən'testənt], *s.* **1.** contestant, -ante; *Pol:* contestataire *mf.* **2.** compétiteur, -trice; concurrent *m* (d'un concours agricole, etc.).
contestation [kɔntes'teiʃ(ə)n], *s.* **1.** *(a)* contestation *f* (d'un droit, etc.); **matters in c.,** matières *f* en contestation, en litige *m*; *(b)* affirmation *f,* prétention *f*; **his c. was that . . .,** il soutenait que . . .. **2.** *A:* témoignage *m.* **3.** *Ecc: A:* contestation (de la messe).
contesting [kən'testiŋ], *a.* contestant.
context ['kɔntekst], *s.* contexte *m*; **in this c.,** à ce propos; *Sch:* **c. (question),** extrait *m* à commenter (d'un livre au programme).
contextual [kən'tekstjuəl], *a.* contextuel; d'après le contexte.
contexture [kən'tekstjər], *s.* **1.** (con)texture *f* (des os, etc.); texture (d'un tissu). **2.** *Lit:* contexture, facture *f* (d'un discours, d'un poème, etc.).
contiguity [kɔnti'gju:iti], *s.* contiguïté *f*; proximité immédiate; **in c.,** contigu, -uë (**with,** à); *Surg:* **amputation in c.,** amputation *f* dans la contiguïté.
contiguous [kən'tigjuəs], *a.* **1.** *(a)* contigu, -uë (à qch., avec qch.); attenant (à qch.); adjacent; (terres *f,* maisons *f*) d'un seul tenant, d'une seule tenue; *(of gardens, etc.)* **to be c.,** se toucher; *Mth:* **c. angles,** angles adjacents; *(b)* **c. moments of time,** moments *m* dans le temps qui se suivent immédiatement. **2.** tout proche, voisin (to, de).
contiguously [kən'tigjuəsli], *adv.* en contiguïté (**to,** avec).
continence ['kɔntinəns], *s.* continence *f*; chasteté *f.*
continent[1] ['kɔntinənt], *a. (a)* continent; chaste; *(b) Med:* continent.
continent[2], *s. Geog: (a)* continent *m*; **the five continents,** les cinq parties *f* du monde; *(b)* **the C.,** l'Europe continentale; **we went for a long trip to the C.,** nous avons fait une grande randonnée en Europe, outre-Manche.
continental [kɔnti'nentl]. **1.** *a. (a)* continental, -aux; *Hist:* **the C. System,** le Blocus continental; *Geog:* **c. climate,** climat continental; **c. shelf,** plate-forme continentale, plateau continental; *(b) (usu. cap.* C) de l'Europe continentale; **the C. attitude to this problem,** l'attitude européenne envers ce problème; *Dom.Ec:* **c. quilt,** duvet *m.* **2.** *s. (a)* continental, -ale; habitant de l'Europe (continentale); *(b) U.S.Hist:* billet, assignat, émis par le Congrès continental (1774–76); *NAm: F:* **it's not worth a c.,** ça ne vaut pas un sou.
continentalism [kɔnti'nentəlizm], *s.* continentalisme *m.*
continentalize [kɔnti'nentəlaiz], *v.tr.* continentaliser.
contingence [kən'tindʒəns], *s. Mth:* **angle of c.,** angle *m* de contingence *f.*
contingency [kən'tindʒənsi], *s.* **1.** contingence *f* (d'événements); éventualité *f* (d'un événement). **2.** *(a)* éventualité; (cas) imprévu *m*; événement incertain; **should a c. arise; in case of a c.,** en cas d'imprévu; en cas d'accident; **prepared for all contingencies,** préparé à tous les événements, à toutes les éventualités; **result depending on contingencies,** résultat *m* aléatoire; *(b) Ind: Com:* **contingencies,** faux frais divers; **to provide for, allow for, contingencies,** parer à l'imprévu; tenir compte de l'imprévu.
contingent [kən'tindʒənt]. **1.** *a. (a) Phil:* contingent; *Log:* **c. matter,** proposition contingente; *(b)* éventuel, fortuit, accidentel, aléatoire; **c. expenses,** dépenses imprévues; **c. profit,** profit *m* aléatoire; *(c)* conditionnel; **c. on sth.,** sous (la) réserve de qch.; *(of event)* **to be c. upon sth.,** dépendre de qch.; *Jur:* **c. condition,** condition casuelle. **2.** *s. (a) A:* événement fortuit; *(b)* contingent *m*; *Mil:* **the annual c. (of recruits),** le contingent annuel; *F:* la classe.
contingently [kən'tindʒəntli], *adv.* **1.** éventuellement, accidentellement, fortuitement, aléatoirement. **2. c. upon an event,** à condition qu'un cas survienne, se produise.
continuable [kən'tinjuəbl], *a. (a)* qui peut être continué; *(b) St.Exch: (of stock)* reportable.
continual [kən'tinjuəl], *a.* continuel; **c. complaints,** plaintes incessantes.
continually [kən'tinjuəli], *adv.* continuellement; sans cesse, sans arrêt.
continuance [kən'tinjuəns], *s.* **1.** *(a)* continuation *f* (d'une action); perpétuation *f* (de l'espèce); *(b) Jur:* ajournement *m* (d'un procès). **2.** *(a)* continuation, persistance *f,* durée *f*; **of short c.,** de courte durée; **of long c.,** continu, prolongé; de longue durée; *(b)* **c. in a place,** (continuation de) séjour *m* (dans un endroit).
continuant [kən'tinjuənt], *Ling:* **1.** *a.* continu. **2.** *s.* (consonne) continue *f.*

continuation [kəntinju'eiʃ(ə)n], *s.* **1.** continuation *f* (de l'espèce, d'une route, d'une histoire, etc.). **2.** (*a*) prolongement *m* (d'un mur, etc.); suite *f* (d'un roman); **this story is a c. of . . .**, cette histoire fait suite à . . .; *Min:* **c. of a vein,** sillage *m* (de charbon); *Cmptr:* **c. card, file,** carte *f*, fichier *m*, "suite"; (*b*) *pl. F: A:* **continuations,** (i) guêtres *f*; (ii) pantalon *m*, *P:* grimpant *m*. **3.** *St.Exch:* report *m*; **c. day,** jour *m* des reports ; **c. rate,** taux *m* du report.

continuator [kən'tinjueitər], *s.* continuateur, -trice (d'un roman, etc.).

continue [kən'tinju:]. **1.** *v.tr.* (*a*) continuer (un ouvrage, sa carrière, etc.); prolonger (une droite); poursuivre (un travail); continuer, reprendre (une conversation); **to c. one's studies,** (i) poursuivre, continuer, ses études; (ii) se remettre à, reprendre, ses études; *Journ:* **to be continued,** à suivre; **continued on page 30,** suite *f* à la page 30; (*b*) perpétuer (la race, une tradition); (*c*) **to c. one's way,** *v.i.* **to c. on one's way,** continuer son chemin; se remettre en marche; (*d*) **to c. to do sth., doing sth.,** continuer à, de, faire qch.; **they continued to be friends,** leur amitié a continué; **in spite of his misfortunes he continued cheerful,** en dépit de ses malheurs il gardait le sourire; **after lunch we continued working,** après le déjeuner nous avons repris notre travail; **he continued whistling,** il a continué à siffler; (*e*) *Jur:* ajourner (un procès); (*f*) *St.Exch:* reporter (des titres). **2.** *v.i.* (*a*) (se) continuer; se soutenir; (*of line*) se prolonger; **the road continues beyond the last houses of the village,** la route continue au delà des dernières maisons du village; (*b*) **"and then", he continued,** "et puis", continua-t-il; (*c*) **to c. impenitent,** rester, demeurer, impénitent; **to c. in office,** (i) garder sa charge; (ii) (*of political party*) rester au pouvoir; **kingdom which will not c.,** royaume *m* qui ne durera pas; **his bad luck continues,** ses malheurs *m* continuent, se poursuivent; la malchance ne le quitte pas; (*d*) *v.tr. & i.* **to c. (staying) in, at, a place,** continuer son séjour dans un endroit; *O:* **I shall c. in Paris for a time,** je vais rester à Paris pendant quelque temps.

continued [kən'tinju:d], *a.* **c. existence of a race,** permanence *f* d'une race; **c. interest,** intérêt soutenu; **c. effort,** effort soutenu, prolongé; *Med:* **c. fever,** fièvre continue, continente, continuelle; *Mth:* **c. fraction,** fraction continue; **c. proportion,** proportion continue.

continuing [kən'tinju:iŋ], *a.* continu; soutenu; permanent; **on a c. basis,** de manière permanente.

continuity [kɔnti'nju:iti], *s.* **1.** continuité *f*; **solution of c.,** solution *f* de continuité; **to break the c. of s.o.'s ideas,** rompre la chaîne, couper le fil, des idées de qn; *El:* **c. of the current,** uniformité *f* du courant; *Phil:* **the principle of c.,** la loi de continuité. **2.** *Cin:* (*a*) scénario *m*, découpage *m*; (*b*) **c. title,** titre *m* de liaison *f*; **c. man,** découpeur *m*; **c. girl,** script-girl *f*, *pl.* script-girls.

continuous [kən'tinjuəs], *a.* continu; **c. succession of visits,** suite continue, ininterrompue, de visites; **c. studies,** études suivies; *Mth:* **c. function,** fonction continue; *El:* **c. waves,** ondes entretenues, non amorties; *Cin:* **c. performance,** spectacle permanent; *Nau: Jur: Ins:* **c. voyage,** continuité *f* du voyage; *Rail:* **c. brake,** freins continus; *Cmptr:* **c. cards,** cartes *f* en continu; **c. form,** papier (imprimé) en continu; **c. forms burster,** rupteuse *f*.

continuously [kən'tinjuəsli], *adv.* continûment; sans interruption; **c. printed,** imprimé en continu.

continuousness [kən'tinjuəsnis], *s.* continuité *f*.

continuum, *pl.* **-ua** [kən'tinjuəm, -juə], *s. Ph: Phil:* continu *m*; *Mth:* **metrical c.,** continuum *m* métrique; **space-time c.,** continuum espace-temps.

contorniate(d) [kən'tɔ:nieit(id)], *a. Num:* (médaille *f*) contorniate.

contort [kən'tɔ:t], *v.tr.* tordre, contourner (les traits, etc.); dévier (un organe, etc.); **face contorted by anger, by pain,** visage contracté, crispé, par la colère, la douleur.

Contortae [kən'tɔ:ti:], *s.pl. Bot:* contortées *f*.

contorted [kən'tɔ:tid], *a.* **1.** contorsionné, contourné, déformé, tors, tourmenté; (visage, etc.) crispé. **2.** *Bot:* (*of petal*) contorté.

contortion [kən'tɔ:ʃ(ə)n], *s.* **1.** contorsion *f* (des traits, etc.). **2. these contortions can hardly be called dancing,** ces contorsions méritent à peine le nom de danse.

contortionist [kən'tɔ:ʃənist], *s.* contorsionniste *mf*; *F:* homme-caoutchouc *m*, *pl.* hommes caoutchouc; disloqué *m*; homme-serpent *m*, *pl.* hommes-serpents; femme-serpent *f*, *pl.* femmes-serpents.

contour[1] ['kɔntuər], *s.* (*a*) contour *m* (d'un objet, d'une colonne); profil *m* (du terrain, du visage); tracé *m* (d'un plan); **irregular c.,** profil irrégulier; *F:* **contours,** rondeurs *fpl*; (féminines); (*b*) *Surv: Mapm:* **c. (line),** courbe *f* de niveau, courbe hypsométrique; (*for sea bed, lake bed*) courbe bathymétrique; **c. interval,** équidistance *f* des courbes; **master c.,** courbe maîtresse; **intercalary c.,** courbe intercalaire; **c. map,** carte *f* en courbes de niveau; carte hypsométrique; (*c*) **c. farming,** culture *f* en courbes de niveau; **strip c. farming,** culture en bandes de niveau; (*d*) *Orn:* **c. feathers,** pennes *f*.

contour[2], *v.tr.* **1.** *Surv:* lever les courbes de niveau de (la région, etc.); **contoured survey,** lever *m* dénivelé. **2.** *Civ.E:* construire (une route) en corniche.

contra[1] ['kɔntrə]. **1.** *prep.* (*frequently abbreviated to* **con.**) contre. **2.** *s. Book-k:* **per c.,** par contre; **as per c.,** en contrepartie, porté ci-contre; **settlement per c.,** compensation *f*; **to settle a debt per c.,** compenser une dette avec une autre; **c. entry,** article *m* inverse, écriture *f* inverse; **c. account,** compte *m* d'autre part; compte contrepartie; jumelage *m*.

contra[2], *v.tr. Book-k:* contre-passer (des écritures, etc.).

contra- ['kɔntrə], *pref.* contre-; contra-.

contraband ['kɔntrəbænd], *s.* contrebande *f*; **c. of war,** contrebande de guerre; *attrib.* **c. goods,** marchandises *f* de contrebande; **c. vessel,** vaisseau contrebandier.

contrabandist ['kɔntrəbændist], *s.* contrebandier *m*.

contrabass ['kɔntrəbeis], *s. Mus:* (*a*) contrebasse *f* (à cordes); (*b*) **c. tuba,** bombardon *m*; contrebasse en si bémol.

contra-bassoon [kɔntrəbə'su:n], *s. Mus:* contrebasson *m*.

contraception [kɔntrə'sepʃ(ə)n], *s.* contraception *f*.

contraceptive [kɔntrə'septiv], *a. & s.* contraceptif (*m*).

contract[1] ['kɔntrækt], *s.* **1.** (*a*) pacte *m*, contrat *m*, convention *f*; **marriage c.,** contrat de mariage; *Jur:* **c. of benevolence,** contrat unilatéral; **to bind oneself by c.,** s'engager par contrat, contractuellement; (*b*) acte *m* de vente; contrat translatif de propriété; *Jur:* **c. of record,** contrat enregistré, ou résultant d'une décision judiciaire; **simple c.,** convention verbale, tacite; **law of c.,** droit *m* des obligations; **c. note,** note *f*, bordereau *m*, de contrat, d'achat ou de vente; *St.Exch:* avis *m* d'exécution; **by private c.,** à l'amiable; de gré à gré. **2.** *Ind: Com:* entreprise *f*; soumission *f*; adjudication *f*; convention forfaitaire; marché *m*; **to make a c. for a supply of coal,** passer marché pour une fourniture de charbon; **c. for a bridge, etc.,** entreprise d'un pont, etc.; **c. work, work on c.,** travail *m* à l'entreprise, à forfait; **c. price,** prix *m* à forfait; *Adm:* prix de série; **to enter into a c.,** (i) (*of pers.*) passer (un) contrat (**with,** avec); (ii) (*of thg*) faire partie d'un contrat; **worker on c.,** contractuel, -elle; **to put work up for c.,** mettre un travail en adjudication; **to put work out to c.,** mettre un travail à l'entreprise; **to place, give, award, a c.,** concéder, adjuger, l'exécution (d'un travail); passer un contrat (à qn) pour l'exécution (d'un travail); **to tender for a c.,** soumissionner à une adjudication; **to get, secure, a c. for sth.,** être déclaré adjudicataire de qch.; **conditions of c.,** cahier *m* des charges; **conditions as per c.,** conditions contractuelles; **c. date,** date contractuelle; **breach of c.,** rupture *f* de contrat; *Jur:* **action for breach of c.,** action *f* en rescision pour inexécution d'un contrat; action contractuelle; **action for specific performance of c.,** action en exécution de contrat; **penalty for non-fulfilment of c.,** peine contractuelle; **c. labour,** main-d'œuvre contractuelle; travailleurs engagés sur contrat. **3.** *Rail:* (carte *f* d')abonnement *m*. **4.** *Cards:* déclaration *f*; contrat; **to make one's c.,** réaliser son contrat; **game c.,** contrat de manche; **c. bridge,** bridge *m* contrat, (bridge) plafond.

contract[2] [kən'trækt], *v.* **1.** *v.tr.* (*a*) contracter (une obligation, un mariage, une maladie); prendre, contracter (une habitude); (*b*) *Com:* **to c. to do sth.,** entreprendre de faire qch.; s'engager par traité à faire qch. **2.** *v.i. Com:* **to c. for a supply of sth.,** entreprendre une fourniture de qch.; **to c. for work,** entreprendre des travaux à forfait; **to c. with s.o. for sth.,** traiter avec qn pour qch.; faire, passer, (un) marché avec qn pour qch.; *Ind: Adm:* **to c. out,** renoncer par contrat, par entente préalable (à certaines dispositions); **to c. in,** s'engager par contrat préalable.

contract[3] [kən'trækt], *v.* **1.** *v.tr.* (*a*) (*make smaller*) contracter (les métaux, les muscles, etc.); contracter, crisper (les traits); rétrécir (un tissu, une ouverture); resserrer (les tissus); froncer (les sourcils); **the rails had been contracted by the cold,** les rails s'étaient contractés, raccourcis, sous l'influence du froid; (*b*) *Ling:* **to c.** *shall not* **into** *shan't*, contracter *shall not* en *shan't*. **2.** *v.i.* (*a*) se contracter, se resserrer, se rétrécir; **the pupil contracts in the daylight,** la prunelle se contracte, s'étrécit, au grand jour; (*b*) *Ling:* ***cannot* contracts into *can't*,** *cannot* se contracte en *can't*.

contractable [kən'træktəbl], *a.* contractable.

contracted [kən'træktid], *a.* contracté; (*of outlook*) rétréci.

contractibility [kəntræktə'biliti], *s.* contractilité *f*.

contractible [kən'træktəbl], *a.* contractile; susceptible de contraction.

contractile [kən'træktail], *a.* **1.** contractile. **2. c. force,** force *f* de contraction.

contractility [kɔntræk'tiliti], *s.* contractilité *f*.

contracting[1] [kən'træktiŋ], *a.* (*a*) contractant; **high c. parties,** hautes parties contractantes; (*b*) *Com: Ind:* **c. party,** contractant *m*; *esp.* partie *f* adjudicataire.

contracting[2], *s.* (*a*) affermage *m* (pour annonces, etc.); (*b*) *Ind:* recours *m* à l'entreprise.

contraction [kən'trækʃ(ə)n], *s.* **1.** (*a*) contraction *f*; striction *f*, rétrécissement *m*; rétraction *f*, raccourcissement *m*, resserrement *m*; **c. of cooling metals,** retrait *m* des métaux lors du refroidissement; **c. of the pupil,** contraction, rétrécissement, de la pupille; **c. of a muscle,** contraction d'un muscle; *Mec.E:* (*of bar under tension test*) **c. of area,** striction; *Metalw:* **c. rule,** mètre *m* à retrait; (*b*) *Com:* **c. of credit,** amoindrissement *m* de crédit. **2.** *Ling:* (*a*) contraction (de deux mots en un seul, etc.); écrasement *m*; (*b*) mot contracté; contraction. **3. c. of debts,** endettement *m*.

contractive [kən'træktiv], *a.* (*of force, etc.*) contractif.

contractor [kən'træktər], *s.* **1.** entrepreneur *m*, pourvoyeur *m*; (*of public works*) adjudicataire *m*; **c. to the government,** fournisseur *m*, entrepreneur, du gouvernement; **army c.,** fournisseur de l'armée; **labour c.,** embaucheur *m*; **haulage c.,** entrepreneur de transports; *Ind:* **prime c.,** maître *m* d'œuvre. **2.** *Anat:* (i) (muscle) -échisseur *m*; (ii) constricteur *m*.

contractual [kən'træktjuəl], *a.* contractuel; **c. claims,** créances contractuelles.

contracture [kən'træktʃər], *s.* **1.** *Med:* contracture *f* (des muscles, des articulations). **2.** *Arch:* contracture (d'une colonne).

contradict [kɔntrə'dikt], *v.tr.* contredire (qn); démentir (qn, un bruit); **to c. oneself,** se contredire, se démentir; **to c. a statement,** opposer, donner, un démenti à une déclaration; **there's no contradicting it,** il n'y a pas de contradiction possible; **the statements of the witnesses c. each other,** les dépositions *f* des témoins se contredisent.

contradictable [kɔntrə'diktəbl], *a.* que l'on peut démentir.

contradiction [kɔntrə'dikʃ(ə)n], *s.* contradiction *f*. **1.** démenti *m* (d'une nouvelle, d'un mensonge); **to give a flat c. to a statement,** démentir formellement une assertion; donner un démenti formel à une assertion. **2.** *Phil:* antinomie *f*, contradiction, incompatibilité *f* (entre deux principes); **in c. with,** en contradiction, en désaccord, avec; incompatible avec; **c. in terms,** contradiction dans les termes; **to imply c.,** impliquer contradiction.

contradictious [kɔntrə'dikʃəs], *a. F:* contredisant; raisonneur, -euse; ergoteur, -euse.

contradictor [kɔntrə'diktər], *s.* contradicteur *m*.

contradictorily [kɔntrə'dikt(ə)rəli], *adv.* **1.** *Log:* contradictoirement. **2.** d'un ton de contradiction.

contradictoriness [kɔntrə'dikt(ə)rinis], *s.* **1.** nature *f* contradictoire; contradiction *f*. **2.** esprit *m* de contradiction.

contradictory [kɔntrə'dikt(ə)ri], *a.* **1.** (*a*) (*of statement, etc.*) contradictoire; opposé **(to,** à); (*b*) *Log:* **c. propositions, s. contradictories,** propositions *f* contradictoires; contradictoires *f*. **2.** (*of pers.*) raisonneur, -euse.

contradistinction ['kɔntrədis'tiŋ(k)ʃ(ə)n], *s.* opposition *f*, contraste *m*; **in c. to . . .,** par opposition à, par contraste avec, au contraire de . . ..

contradistinctive ['kɔntrədis'tiŋ(k)tiv], *a.* contrasté **(with,** avec); distingué **(from,** de); opposé **(to,** à).

contradistinguish ['kɔntrədis'tiŋgwiʃ], *v.tr. Lit:* distinguer **(from,** de); contraster **(from,** avec).

contragredience ['kɔntrə'gri:diəns], *s. Mth:* contragrédience *f* (de deux systèmes de variables).

contragredient ['kɔntrə'gri:diənt], *a. Mth:* contragrédient; **transformations c. to one another,** transformations contra-grédientes l'une de l'autre.

contrail ['kɔntreil], *s. Av:* traînée *f* (de condensation laissée par un avion).

contra-indicate ['kɔntrə'indikeit], *v.tr. Med:* contre-indiquer (un régime, etc.).

contra-indication ['kɔntrəindi'keiʃ(ə)n], *s. Med:* contre indication *f*, *pl.* contre-indications.

contralateral ['kɔntrə'læt(ə)rəl], *a. Med:* contra-latéral, -aux, contro-latéral, -aux.

contralto [kən'træltou, -'tru:l-], *a. & s. Mus:* contralto (*m*), contralte (*m*).

contraposition ['kɔntrəpə'ziʃ(ə)n], *s.* **1.** *Log:* contraposition *f*. **2.** antithèse *f*, opposition *f*.

contrapositive ['kɔntrə'pɔzitiv], *a.* contrapositif, inverse.
contraprop ['kɔntrəprɔp], *s. Av: Nau: etc: F:* hélice contrarotative.
contraption [kən'træpʃ(ə)n], *s. F:* dispositif *m*, machin *m*, truc *m*, engin *m*; invention *f* baroque.
contrapuntal ['kɔntrə'pʌntl], *a. Mus:* (morceau *m*, accompagnement *m*, etc.) en contrepoint.
contrapuntist ['kɔntrə'pʌntist], *s. Mus:* contrapontiste *m*, contrapuntiste *m*, contrepointiste *m*.
contrariety [kɔntrə'raiəti], *s.* contrariété *f* (d'intérêts, d'opinions).
contrarily, *adv.* **1.** ['kɔntrərili], contrairement (**to**, à). **2.** *F:* [kən'trɛərili], obstinément; avec obstination; par esprit de contradiction.
contrariness [kən'trɛərinis], *s.* disposition *f* à tout contrarier; esprit contrariant; esprit de contradiction, de contrariété.
contrarious [kən'trɛəriəs], *a. A: & Dial:* **1.** (*of event, etc.*) contrariant; (*of pers.*) indocile; revêche; qui prend plaisir à contrarier. **2.** (*of weather, wind*) contraire.
contrariwise ['kɔntrəriwaiz], *adv.* **1.** au contraire; d'autre part. **2.** en sens opposé; à contre-biais; **to do c.**, faire l'opposé, le contraire. **3.** *F:* [kən'trɛəriwaiz] par esprit de contradiction.
contrarotating ['kɔntrərou'teitiŋ], *a. Mec.E:* contrarotatif; *Av: Nau: etc:* **c. propeller**, hélice contrarotative.
contrary ['kɔntrəri]. **1.** *a.* (*a*) contraire (**to**, à); (*of interests, etc.*) opposé (à), en opposition (avec); **in a c. direction**, en sens opposé; à contre-sens; en sens inverse; **c. to nature**, contre (la) nature; **c. to reason**, qui répugne à la raison, qui choque la raison, contraire à la raison; *Log:* **c. propositions**, propositions *f* contraires; (*b*) (*unfavourable*) **c. winds**, vents *m* contraires; (*c*) *F:* [kən'trɛəri] (*of pers.*) opiniâtre; qui a l'esprit de contradiction. **2.** *s.* (*a*) contraire *m*; **quite the c.**, bien le contraire; tout au contraire; c'est tout l'opposé; **on the c.**, au contraire; **by rule of contraries**, par raison des contraires; **the direct c. of, to, sth.**, l'antithèse *f* de qch.; **notification to the c.**, contravis *m*; **unless you hear to the c.**, à moins d'avis contraire; sauf contravis; sauf contrordre; sauf avis contraire; **for anything I know to the c., he is still in London**, il est encore à Londres, autant que je sache; **I have nothing to say to the c.**, je n'ai rien à objecter; je n'ai rien à dire contre, à l'encontre; **I know nothing to the c.**, je ne sais rien qui contredise ces faits, cette nouvelle, etc.; **dreams go by contraries**, il faut interpréter les rêves à rebours; (*b*) *pl. Paperm:* **contraries**, impuretés *f*; corps étrangers. **3.** *adv.* contrairement (**to**, à); en opposition (**to**, à, avec); à contrepied (**to**, de); à, au, rebours (**to**, de); **to act c. to s.o.'s views, to one's principles**, agir en opposition avec la manière de voir de qn; faire violence à ses principes; **to act c. to instructions**, contrevenir aux ordres reçus; **c. to accepted opinions**, à l'encontre des idées reçues; contrairement aux idées reçues; **c. to my expectation**, contre mon attente; **c. to the statements in the papers**, quoi qu'en aient dit les journaux.
contrast[1] ['kɔntrɑ:st], *s.* contraste *m* (**between**, entre); **to give c. to one's style**, donner du relief à son style; **in c. with sth.**, par contraste avec qch.; **the c. between light and shade**, le contraste de la lumière et de l'ombre; **colours in c.**, couleurs *f* en contraste, en opposition; **to form a c. to . . .**, faire contraste avec . . .; **as a c. to . . .**, comme contraste à . . .; **to stand out in sharp c. to sth.**, se détacher nettement sur qch.; faire un contraste frappant avec qch.; *Phot:* **c. picture**, image contrastée; **c. range**, intervalle *m* de noircissement (de l'émulsion); **c. filter**, écran *m* pour contrastes.
contrast[2] [kən'trɑ:st]. **1.** *v.tr.* faire contraster, mettre en contraste (**with**, avec); *Art:* contraster (ses personnages, etc.); **to c. vice with virtue**, opposer le vice à la vertu. **2.** *v.i.* contraster, faire contraste (**with**, avec); **to c. strongly**, trancher (**with**, sur).
contrasting [kən'trɑ:stiŋ], *a.* qui fait contraste; **c. colours**, tons opposés.
contrate ['kɔntreit], *a. Clockm:* **c. wheel**, roue *f* de champ.
contra tempo ['kɔntrə'tempou], *adv.phr. Mus:* à contre-temps.
contravallation ['kɔntrəvə'leiʃ(ə)n], *s. Hist: Fort:* contrevallation *f*.
contravariant ['kɔntrə'vɛəriənt], *a. Mth:* contrevariant.
contravene [kɔntrə'vi:n], *v.tr.* **1.** transgresser, enfreindre (la loi, etc.); **to c. the regulations**, contrevenir aux règlements; être en contravention avec les règlements. **2.** aller à l'encontre de (qch.); **laws that c. the first principles of equity**, lois *f* qui violent, qui sont en opposition avec, les premiers principes de l'équité; **to c. s.o.'s plans**, aller à l'encontre de, contrarier, les projets de qn.
contravener [kɔntrə'vi:nər], *s.* transgresseur *m* (**of**, de); *Jur:* contrevenant, -ante (**of**, à).
contravention [kɔntrə'venʃ(ə)n], *s.* **c. of a law**, contravention *f*, infraction *f*, à la loi; **to act in c. of a rule, a right**, agir en violation d'une règle, en opposition avec un droit.
contretemps ['kɔntrətɑ̃], *s.* contretemps *m*.
contribute [kən'tribjut], *v.tr. & i.* **to c. one's share**, payer sa (quote-)part; **to c. a sum of money**, contribuer pour une somme; **to c. to a charity**, contribuer à, souscrire pour, une bonne œuvre; **to c. newspaper articles**, écrire des articles pour un journal; **to c. to a newspaper**, collaborer à un journal; **to c. to the success**, aider au succès; **everything contributed to make him happy**, tout contribuait, concourait, à le rendre heureux; *Ecc: etc:* **everybody is expected to c. according to his means**, l'offrande *f*, la contribution, est selon ses moyens.
contribution [kɔntri'bju:ʃ(ə)n], *s.* **1.** contribution *f*, apport *m*; cotisation *f*; **to pay one's c.**, payer sa cotisation; **they made a handsome c. to it**, ils y ont contribué pour une bonne part; **c.** *pro rata*, quote-part *f*, *pl.* quotes-parts; *Fin:* **c. of capital**, apport *m* de capitaux; **c. to the capital of a company**, contribution, versement *m*, au capital, à la masse sociale, d'une compagnie; *Jur:* **c. of each party in a marriage settlement**, apport des époux; (*b*) *Mil: etc:* contribution; réquisition *f*; **forced contributions (by inhabitants of occupied territory)**, impôts *m* de guerre. **2. c. to a newspaper**, article écrit pour un journal.
contributive [kən'tribjutiv], *a.* contributif; qui contribue (**to**, à).
contributor [kən'tribjutər], *s.* **1.** (*a*) *A:* contribuant *m*, contributaire *mf*; (*b*) *Fin:* **c. of capital**, apporteur *m* de capitaux. **2.** collaborateur, -trice (**to a paper**, d'un journal); **a regular c. to the** *Times*, un collaborateur régulier du *Times*.
contributory [kən'tribjut(ə)ri]. **1.** *a.* contribuant, contributif; **c. causes**, causes contribuantes; **his enthusiasm played a c. part in the success of the undertaking**, son enthousiasme a contribué au succès de l'entreprise; *Jur: Ins:* **c. negligence**, manque *m* de précautions, imprudence *f* (de la part de l'accidenté, du sinistré, de la victime). **2.** *s.* (*a*) contributaire *mf*; (*b*) actionnaire *mf* qui doit, en cas de liquidation de la société, contribuer au paiement des dettes.
contrite ['kɔntrait], *a.* contrit, pénitent, repentant.
contritely ['kɔntraitli], *adv.* d'un air contrit, pénitent; avec contrition.
contrition [kən'triʃ(ə)n], *s.* contrition *f*, pénitence *f*.
contrivable [kən'traivəbl], *a.* que l'on peut inventer, arranger, combiner; réalisable.
contrivance [kən'traiv(ə)ns], *s.* **1.** (*a*) invention *f* (d'un appareil, etc.); combinaison *f*, adaptation *f* (d'un moyen); **beyond human c.**, qui dépasse l'invention humaine; au-delà de l'invention humaine; (*b*) **to escape by the c. of one's friends**, s'échapper grâce à (l'ingéniosité de) ses amis. **2.** (*a*) invention, projet *m*; artifice *m*, combinaison *f*; (*b*) *Pej:* machination *f*; manigance *f*. **3.** appareil *m*, dispositif *m*, engin *m*; *F:* truc *m*; **mechanical c.**, dispositif *m* mécanique.
contrive [kən'traiv], *v.tr.* (*a*) (*devise*) inventer, concevoir, imaginer, combiner; (*b*) (*effect*) arranger, pratiquer, ménager; **to c. a means to do sth.**, trouver moyen de faire qch.; **to c. to do sth.**, trouver moyen de, s'ingénier à, s'arranger pour, parvenir à, réussir à, venir à bout de, faire qch.; **I contrived to warn him in time**, j'ai pu l'avertir à temps; **I shall c. to be there**, je m'arrangerai pour être là; je trouverai moyen d'être là; **at last he contrived to get rid of it**, il a trouvé enfin moyen de s'en débarrassr; (*c*) *Pej:* machiner, ourdir (un complot, etc.); (*d*) *v.i. O:* se débrouiller; se tirer d'affaire; s'arranger; **I don't know how she contrives**, je ne sais pas comment elle se débrouille.
contriver [kən'traivər], *s.* (*a*) inventeur, -trice (de qch.); auteur *m* (d'une combinaison, etc.); combinateur, -trice; agenceur, -euse; *O:* **he is a good c.**, c'est un débrouillard; il a de la res ource; (*b*) *Pej:* machinateur *m*, ourdisseur *m* (d'un complot, etc.).
control[1] [kən'troul], *s.* **1.** (*power, authority*) autorité *f*; **state c.**, étatisme *m*; **he has c. over a whole province**, *Adm:* **over several departments**, il administre toute une province, plusieurs services; **his c. extended to the Nile**, son autorité s'exerçait jusqu'au Nil; **to be given c. over s.o., over sth.**, être chargé du contrôle de qn, de qch.; **to have c. of a business**, être à la tête d'une entreprise. **2.** (*check, restraint*) contrôle *m*; maîtrise *f*; contrainte *f*; surveillance *f*; (*a*) **circumstances beyond our c.**, circonstances indépendantes de notre volonté, qui ne dépendent pas de nous; **these things are beyond our c.**, ces choses-là *f* ne se commandent pas; **to keep s.o. under (strict) c.**, tenir, surveiller, qn de près; exercer un contrôle sévère sur la conduite de qn; **to have s.o. under absolute c.**, **to have absolute c. over s.o.**, avoir un empire absolu, un énorme ascendant, sur qn; avoir la haute main sur qn; **she has no c. over the children**, elle n'a aucune autorité sur les enfants; *Sch:* elle ne sait pas tenir ses élèves; **to get out of c.**, échapper à, s'affranchir de, toute autorité; **to have one's horse under c.**, avoir son cheval bien en main; **to have a horse well under the c. of the hand and legs**, renfermer un cheval; **the fire brigade had the flames under c.**, les pompiers étaient maîtres du feu; **self c.**, contrôle de soi-même; **to lose c. of oneself**, ne plus être maître de soi; ne plus se maîtriser; perdre tout empire sur soi-même; **to regain c. of oneself**, se ressaisir; **to keep one's feelings under c.**, contenir ses sentiments; **everything is under c.**, tout est fin prêt; **to bring a disease under c.**, enrayer une maladie; **mosquito c.**, lutte préventive contre les moustiques; (*b*) *Pol.Ec: etc:* **budgetary c.**, contrôle budgétaire; (**foreign**) **exchange c.**, contrôle des changes; **price c.**, taxation *f* (des prix); **rent c.**, contrôle, réglementation *f*, des loyers; **birth c.**, contrôle, régulation *f*, limitation *f*, des naissances; (*c*) (*verification*) *Med:* **c. case**, cas *m* témoin; *Metall:* **c. assay**, essai *m* contradictoire; (*d*) *Tchn:* asservissement *m*, commande *f* (d'un mécanisme); gouverne *f*, manœuvre *f* (d'un train, d'un avion, d'un navire, etc.); **to bring a mechanism under c.**, asservir un mécanisme; **automatic c.**, réglage *m* automatique; **dual c.**, double commande; **c. gear**, (i) appareil *m* de commande; (ii) dispositif *m* de manœuvre; **c. lever**, levier *m* de commande, d'asservissement; **c. mechanism, wheel**, appareil *m*, roue *f*, de commande; *Av:* **c. column**, levier de commande; *I.C.E:* **c. of the mixture**, dosage *m* du mélange; **to be in c., lose c., of one's car**, être maître, ne plus être maître, de sa voiture; perdre contrôle de sa voiture; **ship out of c.**, navire qui n'est plus maître de sa manœuvre; *Rail:* **c. system**, régulation; **c. office**, poste *m* de régulation; **c. lock**, verrou *m* de blocage; *Sp: Aut:* **c. point**, contrôle (du passage de voitures, etc.); *Av:* **air c.**, (i) maîtrise *f* de l'air; (ii) contrôle aérien; (**tactical**) **air c. centre**, centre *m* de contrôle tactique aérien; **approach c.**, contrôle d'approche; **ground c. approach**, station *f* de contrôle d'approche; **c. tower**, tour *f* de contrôle; *Mil: etc:* **gunnery c., fire c.**, conduite *f*, direction *f*, du tir; **radar fire c.**, commande de tir par radar; **remote c.**, télécommande *f*, commande à distance; *Navy:* **fore c.**, contrôle de direction de tir; **aft c.**, poste de direction de tir arrière; (*of submarine*) **c. room**, poste central; **Naval c. service**, Direction *f* des routes; *El: Elcs: etc:* **frequency c.**, contrôle de fréquence; **amplitude c.**, contrôle d'amplitude; **volume c.**, contrôle de volume; réglage de puissance, d'intensité; **radar c.**, contrôle radar; **thermostat c.**, commande par thermostat; **temperature c.**, régulation thermique; **attitude c. (of satellite)**, contrôle d'attitude (d'un satellite); *Cmptr:* **data c.**, contrôle de données; **program(me) c.**, commande par calculateur; **feedback c.**, régulation par réaction; **c. desk, console**, pupitre *m* de commande. **3.** *Tchn:* (organe *m* de) commande; **the controls**, les commandes; *I.C.E:* **ignition c.**, commande d'allumage; **throttle c.**, (i) *I.C.E:* manette *f* de commande des gaz; (ii) *Mch:* levier de papillon; *Av:* **flying controls**, commandes de vol; **elevator c.**, vérin *m* de commande de la profondeur; **aileron c.**, vérin de l'aileron; **flap c.**, vérin de volet; **altitude c.**, commande altimétrique; *W.Tel: etc:* **volume c.**, bouton *m* de puissance. **4.** *Psychics:* contrôleur, -euse (d'un médium); esprit contrôleur.
control[2], *v.tr.* **1.** *A:* vérifier, contrôler (des comptes). **2.** (*be in authority over*) diriger, réglementer (des affaires, la production); régler (la dépense, le cours des événements); commander (aux éléments, le mouvement d'une machine); **to c. men's, one's fate**, commander aux hommes, au destin; **he cannot c. his pupils**, il ne sait pas tenir ses élèves; **to c. a business**, diriger une entreprise; être à la tête d'une entreprise; *Artil: etc:* **to c. the fire**, diriger le feu, le tir; *Adm:* **to c. the traffic**, réglementer la circulation; *Mil:* **to c. a strategic area**, contrôler une région stratégique. **3.** (*restrain*) (*a*) maîtriser, tenir, gouverner (un cheval); réprimer (un soulèvement); contenir (des hordes sauvages); gouverner, refréner, dompter, commander à (ses passions); contrôler (ses réactions, etc.); **to c. inflation**, contenir l'inflation; **to c. the rise in the cost of living**, enrayer la hausse du coût de la vie; **to c. one's tears**, retenir ses larmes; **to c. oneself**, se contrôler, se maîtriser, se surmonter, se retenir, se commander, se contraindre, se dominer; **c. yourself!** voyons! modérez-vous! retenez-vous! de la retenue! **to try to c. oneself**, faire un effort sur soi-même; (*b*) *Med:* **to c. diabetes**, équilibrer un diabète.
controllability [kən'trulə'biliti], *s.* maniabilité *f*,

manœuvrabilité *f*, (d'une voiture, d'une navire); docilité *f* (d'un cheval).

controllable [kən'trouləbl], *a.* **1.** *A:* (témoignage *m*, etc.) vérifiable, contrôlable. **2.** qui peut être gouverné; (machine *f*, navire *m*) maniable, manœuvrable. **3.** (passion *f*, cheval *m*) maîtrisable; (passion, foule) contenable; *Ch:* (réaction) qui peut être freinée.

controlled [kən'trould], *a.* (*a*) (*of pers.*) qui sait se contenir; (bien) équilibré; (*b*) *Pol.Ec:* **c. economy,** économie dirigée; **c. currency,** monnaie dirigée; **c. prices,** prix taxés; **to fix a c. price for a product,** taxer une denrée; **c. market,** marché réglementé; (*c*) *Adm:* (*in street*) **c. crossing,** passage réglementé (par un agent de police, etc.); (*d*) *Med:* **c. diabetes,** diabète équilibré.

controller [kən'troulər], *s.* **1.** (*pers.*) (*a*) contrôleur, -euse; **c. in bankruptcy,** contrôleur aux liquidations; *Av:* **air traffic c.,** contrôleur de la circulation aérienne, *F:* aiguilleur *m* du ciel; **air defence c.,** contrôleur de défense aérienne; (*b*) *A:* contrôleur, vérificateur *m* de comptes. **2.** (*apparatus*) contrôleur; commande *f*; *Rail:* régulateur *m*; *Av:* **flight c.,** contrôleur de vol.

controllership [kən'trouləʃip], *s.* office *m* de contrôleur.

controlling[1] [kən'trouliŋ], *a.* **1.** qui gouverne, dirige; **c. power,** puissance dirigeante; *Mec:* **c. force,** force *f* antagoniste; *Ind: etc:* **c. operation,** opération *f* d'enclenchement; **c. unit,** unité directrice; **c. interest,** participation *f* donnant le contrôle. **2.** répressif.

controlling[2], *s.* **1.** *A:* vérification *f* (de comptes). **2.** direction *f* (des affaires); réglementation *f* (de la circulation, etc.); commande *f* (de mécanisme). **3.** maîtrise *f* (des passions, etc.); domination *f* (de soi-même).

controversial [kɔntrə'vəːʃ(ə)l], *a.* **1.** (*of question, opinion, etc.*) controversable, controversé. **2.** (esprit *m*) de controverse. **3.** (*of pers.*) enclin à la controverse, à la polémique; disputailleur.

controversialist [kɔntrə'vəːʃəlist], *s.* controversiste *mf*, polémiste *mf*.

controversially [kɔntrə'vəːʃəli], *adv.* **c. inclined,** enclin à la polémique; chicaneur.

controversy ['kɔntrəvəːsi, kən'trɔvəsi], *s.* polémique *f*; (*religious, philosophical*) controverse *f*; **press c.,** polémique de presse; **to hold, carry on, a c. (with, against, s.o.) on sth.,** soutenir une polémique, une controverse, (contre qn) au sujet de qch.; **the fact is beyond c.,** le fait ne souffre pas de discussion, est hors de controverse; **question that has given rise to much c.,** question fort controversée.

controvert ['kɔntrəvəːt], *v.tr.* **1.** controverser (une question). **2.** disputer, mettre en doute (la vérité de qch.); disputer, discuter (un droit).

controvertible [kɔntrə'vəːtəbl], *a.* controversable.

controvertibly [kɔntrə'vəːtibli], *adv.* d'une façon controversable.

controvertist ['kɔntrəvəːtist, kən'trɔvəːtist], *s.* = CONTROVERSIALIST.

contumacious [kɔntju'meiʃəs], *a.* **1.** (*a*) entêté, rebelle, récalcitrant; **c. assembly,** assemblée *f* réfractaire; (*b*) *Jur:* contumace, contumax, rebelle. **2.** (ton *m*) rogue.

contumaciously [kɔntju'meiʃəsli], *adv.* avec entêtement; obstinément.

contumaciousness [kɔntju'meiʃəsnis], **contumacy** ['kɔntjuməsi, kən'tjuː-], *s.* (*a*) entêtement *m*, obstination *f*, opiniâtreté *f*; (*b*) *Jur:* contumace *f*; désobéissance *f*; rébellion *f*.

contumelious [kɔntju'miːliəs], *a. Lit:* **1.** (*of words, actions*) injurieux outrageant. **2.** (*of pers.*) dédaigneux, insolent.

contumely [kən'tjuːm(ə)li], *s.* **1.** insolence *f*, injure *f*, outrage *m*; **to treat s.o. with c.,** traiter qn avec (un souverain) mépris; ravaler qn. **2.** honte *f*; **to cover s.o. with c.,** couvrir qn de honte.

contuse [kən'tjuːz], *v.tr.* contusionner, meurtrir; **contused wound,** plaie contuse.

contusion [kən'tjuːʒ(ə)n], *s.* contusion *f*; meurtrissure *f*; *Surg:* coup *m* orbe.

contusive [kən'tjuːziv], *a.* (coup, instrument) contondant.

conundrum [kə'nʌndrəm], *s.* **1.** devinette *f*. **2.** énigme *f*; **to speak in conundrums,** parler par énigmes.

conurbation [kɔnəː'beiʃ(ə)n], *s.* conurbation *f*.

convalesce [kɔnvə'les], *v.i.* être en convalescence; relever de maladie; **he is convalescing at Brighton,** il est en convalescence à Brighton.

convalescence [kɔnvə'les(ə)ns], *s.* convalescence *f*.

convalescent [kɔnvə'les(ə)nt], *a. & s.* **1.** convalescent, -ente. **2. c. home,** maison *f* de convalescence.

convallaria [kɔnvə'lɛəriə], *s. Bot:* convallaire *f*.

convection [kən'vekʃ(ə)n], *s. Ph: El: etc:* convection *f* (de la chaleur, d'un courant électrique); **c. currents,** courants *m* de convection; *Dom.Ec:* **c. heater,** radiateur *m* à convection.

convectional [kən'vekʃənl], *a.* (courant, etc.) de convection; (chauffage) par convection.

convector [kən'vektər], *s.* appareil *m* de chauffage par convection, radiateur *m* à convection.

convenable [kən'viːnəbl], *a.* sujet à convocation; qui peut être assemblé; **committee not easily c. at short notice,** comité *m* qu'il serait difficile de réunir à bref délai.

convene [kən'viːn]. **1.** *v.tr.* (*a*) convoquer, réunir (une assemblée); réunir, assembler (une conférence, etc.); (*b*) *Jur:* **to c. s.o. before a court,** citer qn devant un tribunal. **2.** *v.i.* (*a*) s'assembler, se réunir, se rencontrer; (*b*) *A:* s'accorder, s'harmoniser.

convener [kən'viːnər], *s.* membre *m* (du bureau, de la commission) à qui il incombe de convoquer ses collègues.

convenience [kən'viːnjəns], *s.* **1.** commodité *f*, convenance *f*; **marriage of c.,** mariage *m* de convenance, de raison; **for (the sake of) c.,** pour la commodité, pour plus de commodité; **at your c.,** à votre convenance, à votre bon plaisir; **do it at your c.,** faites-le à loisir; **at your earliest c.,** à la première occasion; au premier moment favorable; le plus tôt possible; d'urgence; **this is a great c.,** cela est bien commode; **to make a c. of s.o.,** abuser de la bonté de qn; *Nau:* **flag of c.,** pavillon *m* de complaisance. **2. (public) c.,** w.c. (publics), toilettes *fpl*. **3.** *pl.* commodités *f*, facilités *f*, agréments *m*; **rooms fitted with all modern conveniences,** chambres installées avec tout le confort moderne.

convenient [kən'viːniənt], *a.* **1.** commode, pratique; *F:* **that's a c. little gadget!** voilà un petit truc bien pratique!; **to be c. to s.o. to do sth.,** convenir à qn de faire qch.; **if it is c. to you,** si cela vous convient; si cela ne vous dérange pas; si vous n'y voyez pas d'inconvénient; **if it is not c. for you to come,** s'il ne vous est pas commode de venir; **to make it c. to do sth.,** s'arranger de manière à faire qch.; **to find a c. opportunity to do sth.,** trouver l'occasion *f* de faire qch. **2. c. to the hand,** à portée de la main.

conveniently [kən'viːniəntli], *adv.* commodément; sans inconvénient; **if you can c. wait until tomorrow,** si cela ne vous dérange pas d'attendre jusqu'à demain; **have your tools c. to hand,** ayez vos outils à portée de la main, sous la main.

convent ['kɔnvənt], *s.* couvent *m*; *esp.* couvent de femmes; **to enter a c.,** entrer au couvent; **she goes to the c.,** elle fait ses études au couvent, *F:* chez les bonnes sœurs.

conventicle [kən'ventikl], *s.* **1.** conventicule *m*, conciliabule *m*; *esp. Ecc.Hist:* conventicule de dissidents (pendant les persécutions de Charles II et de Jacques II). **2.** *Pej:* lieu *m* de réunion; temple *m* (de dissidents).

convention [kən'venʃ(ə)n], *s.* **1.** (*a*) convention *f* (**on,** relative à); **the Hague Conventions,** les conventions, les actes *m*, de la Haye; **the Berne C.,** la Convention de Berne; *Cards:* **the conventions of bridge,** les conventions du bridge; (*b*) accord *m*, contrat *m*; *Jur:* **Leonine c.,** contrat *m* léonin. **2.** *often pl.* convenances *fpl*, bienséances *fpl*, décorum *m*; **social conventions,** les conventions sociales, la civilité, le protocole; **to defy conventions,** braver les convenances; **to be a slave to c.,** être l'esclave des conventions sociales. **3.** *Pol:* assemblée *f*, convention *f*; **medical c.,** congrès médical; *Fr.Hist:* **the C.,** la Convention (nationale) (1792).

conventional [kən'venʃən(ə)l], *a.* **1.** conventionnel; de convention; **c. propriety,** les convenances admises; *Art:* **c. design,** dessin stylisé; *Cards:* **c. play,** jeu *m* d'après les conventions. **2.** (*a*) courant, ordinaire, classique; **c. car,** voiture *f* ordinaire, classique; *Mil:* **c. warfare, c. weapon,** guerre *f*, arme *f*, classique; *Const:* **c. material,** matériau traditionnel; (*b*) *Pej:* sans originalité; *Art: Lit: etc: s.* **the c.,** le poncif, le conventionnel, le banal. **3.** *Hist: Pol:* **c. assembly,** assemblée conventionnelle; convention *f*.

conventionalism [kən'venʃənəlizm], *s.* **1.** conventionalisme *m*; les conventions (sociales); le respect des convenances; conformalisme *m*. **2.** *Art:* (culte *m* du) poncif *m*; formalisme *m*.

conventionalist [kən'venʃənəlist], *s.* **1.** conformiste *mf*; *Art:* formaliste *mf*. **2.** *Hist:* conventionnel *m*.

conventionality [kənvenʃə'næliti], *s.* **1.** (*a*) convention *f*; usage admis; (*b*) les conventions (sociales); les bienséances *f*. **2.** (*a*) caractère conventionnel, ordinaire (du dernier Salon, etc.); (*b*) *Art: Lit:* le poncif; le banal.

conventionalize [kən'venʃənəlaiz], *v.tr.* (*a*) rendre conventionnel; *Art:* styliser (un décor, etc.); **conventionalized flowers,** fleurs stylisées; (*b*) banaliser (son style, son coloris, etc.).

conventionally [kən'venʃənəli], *adv.* **1.** conventionnellement. **2.** banalement, d'une façon banale; sans originalité.

conventual [kən'ventjuəl]. **1.** *a.* conventuel. **2.** *s.* religieux, -euse; conventuel, -elle.

converge [kən'vəːdʒ]. **1.** *v.i.* converger (**on,** sur); **the main railway systems c. on London,** les grands réseaux de chemins de fer aboutissent à Londres; **three armies were converging on Paris,** trois armées convergeaient sur Paris. **2.** *v.tr.* faire converger (des rayons lumineux, etc.).

convergence [kən'vəːdʒ(ə)ns], *s.* convergence *f* (de lignes, d'opinions, *Nat.Hist:* d'espèces); *Mth:* focalisation *f*; *Geog:* **Antarctic, subtropical, c.,** convergence antarctique, subtropicale; **c. of the meridians,** convergence des méridiens.

convergency [kən'vəːdʒənsi], = CONVERGENCE.

convergent [kən'vəːdʒ(ə)nt], *a.* convergent; *Mth:* **c. series,** série convergente.

converging [kən'vəːdʒiŋ], *a.* **1.** convergent, concourant; **c. point,** point *m* de concours. **2.** *Opt:* **c. lens,** lentille convergente.

conversable [kən'vəːsəbl], *a. Lit:* de bonne conversation; sociable; de commerce agréable.

conversance [kən'vəːs(ə)ns], **conversancy** [kən'vəːsənsi], *s. A: & Lit:* familiarité *f* (**with,** avec); connaissance *f*, habitude *f* (**with,** de).

conversant [kən'vəːs(ə)nt], *a.* (*a*) *A: & Lit:* **c. with s.o.,** familier, intime, avec qn; (*b*) **c. with sth.,** versé dans, au courant de, qch.; **c. with finance,** compétent en matière de finance.

conversation [kɔnvə'seiʃ(ə)n], *s.* **1.** conversation *f*, entretien *m*; *Cmptr:* dialogue *m*; **preliminary c.,** prise *f* de contact; **to have a twenty minutes' c. with s.o.,** avoir une conversation, un entretien, de vingt minutes avec qn; **to hold a c. with s.o.,** s'entretenir avec qn; **to carry on the c.,** continuer la conversation; **to change the c.,** changer de conversation, de propos; détourner la conversation; **to take part, to join, in the c.,** être dans la conversation; prendre part à la conversation; **to enter, fall, into c., (with s.o.),** entrer en conversation (avec qn); lier, nouer, conversation, engager une conversation (avec qn); **to make c.,** alimenter la conversation; **to be the subject of c.,** défrayer la conversation; faire les frais *m* de la conversation; **he's only making c.,** il parle pour ne rien dire, pour dire quelque chose; *Art:* **c. piece,** scène *f* d'intérieur; tableau *m* de genre. **2.** *A:* commerce *m*; *Jur:* **criminal c.,** *F:* **crim. con.,** adultère *m*.

conversational [kɔnvə'seiʃən(ə)l], *a.* **1.** (*a*) de (la) conversation; **in a c. tone,** sur le ton de la conversation; (*b*) *Cmptr:* **c. mode,** mode *m* dialogue; **c. programming,** programmation *f* conversationnelle. **2.** (*of pers.*) qui aime à parler; loquace; **c. style,** style *m* de la conversation, style familier.

conversationalist [kɔnvə'seiʃənəlist], *s.* **to be a good c.,** (i) bien parler; (ii) aimer la conversation.

conversationally [kɔnvə'seiʃən(ə)li], *adv.* **to write c.,** écrire comme on parle.

conversazione, *pl.* **-es, -i** [kɔnvəsætsi'ouni, -iz, -iː], *s. A:* réunion *f* (littéraire, artistique).

converse[1] ['kɔnvəːs], *s. A:* **1.** = CONVERSATION 1. **2.** commerce *m*, relations *fpl*, rapports *mpl* (**with,** avec).

converse[2] [kən'vəːs], *v.i.* parler; **to c. with s.o. on, about, sth.,** converser avec qn sur qch.; parler, s'entretenir, avec qn de qch.

converse[3] ['kɔnvəːs], *a. & s.* **1.** *Log:* (proposition) converse (*f*). **2.** *Mth:* (proposition) réciproque (*f*).

conversely [kən'vəːsli], *adv.* réciproquement; vice versa; inversement.

conversion [kən'vəːʃ(ə)n], *s.* **1.** conversion *f* (de qn); **c. to Christianity,** conversion au christianisme. **2.** (*transformation*) conversion; (*a*) **c. of water into steam,** conversion de l'eau en vapeur; *Metall:* **c. of iron into steel,** conversion, transformation *f*, du fer en acier; affinage *m* au convertisseur; **c. pig,** fonte *f* d'affinage; *Fin:* **c. of 4% stock into $3\frac{1}{2}$ per cents,** conversion, convertissement *m*, de la rente 4% en $3\frac{1}{2}$%; *Jur:* **c. (of realty) into personalty,** ameublissement *m* (de biens immeubles); **c. of funds to one's own use; improper c. of funds,** détournement *m* de fonds; *Jur:* **fraudulent c.,** carambouillage *m*, *St. Exch:* **fraudulent c. of stocks,** lavage *m* des titres; *Cmptr: etc:* **multiway c.,** multiconversion *f*; *Log:* **c. of a proposition,** conversion, transformation, d'une proposition; (*b*) **c. of timber,** façonnage *m*, débit *m*, du bois en grume; (*c*) **c. of a room to office use,** aménagement *m*, transformation *f*, d'une pièce en bureau; (*d*) *Sp:* (*Rugby Fb:*) transformation. **3.** *Mil: A:* conversion; changement *m* de front.

convert[1] ['kɔnvəːt], *s.* converti, -ie; **to become a c. to sth.,** se convertir à qch.; **to make a c. of s.o.,** convertir qn; **the new converts,** les nouveaux convertis, les nouvelles converties.

convert[2] [kən'vəːt], *v.tr.* **1.** convertir (qn) (à une religion); **to be converted to Christianity,** se convertir au christianisme; **to c. s.o. to an opinion,** convertir, amener, qn à une opinion. **2.** transformer, changer, convertir (**sth. into sth.,** qch. en qch.); (*a*) **to c. a defeat into a rout,** changer une défaite en déroute; *Metall:* **to c. iron into steel,** convertir le fer en acier; effectuer l'affinage (au convertisseur); *Log:* **to c. a proposition,** convertir, transformer, une proposition; *Jur:* **to c. one's realty into personalty,** ameublir ses biens immeubles; *Rugby Fb:* **to c. a try,** transformer un essai; **converted goal,** transformation *f*; (*b*) **to c. timber,** débiter, façonner, le bois en grume; (*c*) **converted traffic,** circulation modifiée, changement *m* dans la circulation; **converted cowshed,** étable aménagée. **3. to c. funds to another purpose,** affecter des fonds à un autre usage, à d'autres fins; *Jur:* **to c. funds to one's own use,** détourner des fonds; **to c. (property) fraudulently,** carambouiller.

converter [kən'və:tər], *s.* **1.** (*pers.*) convertisseur, -euse (des infidèles, etc.). **2.** (appareil) convertisseur *m*; (*a*) *Metall:* **steel c., Bessemer c.,** convertisseir Bessemer; **c. pig,** fonte *f* d'affinage; (*b*) *El: W.Tel: etc:* adapteur *m*; **static c.,** convertisseur, transformateur *m*; **rotary c., c. unit,** commutatrice *f*; groupe convertisseur; **c. to direct current,** transformateur alternatif-continu; **c. to alternating current,** transformateur continu-alternatif; (*c*) machine *f* à chiffrer.

convertibility [kənvə:tə'biliti], *s.* convertibilité *f*.

convertible [kəf'və:təbl], *a.* **1.** (*of pers.*) convertissable (**to,** à). **2.** (*a*) (*of thg*) convertible, convertissable, transformable (**into,** en); *Phot:* (**objectif** *m*) dédoublable; *s.* voiture *f* décapotable, convertible *f*. **3.** (*a*) **c. terms,** termes *m* synonymes, interchangeables, réciproques; (*b*) *Fin:* **c. bond,** obligation *f* convertible; **c. currencies,** monnaies *f* convertibles.

convertibly [kən'və:tibli], *adv.* convertiblement, réciproquement.

converting [kən'və:tiŋ], *s.* = CONVERSION 1, 2.

convertiplane [kən'və:tiplein], *s. Av:* convertible *m*.

convex ['kɔnveks], *a.* **1.** convexe; **double c.,** biconvexe. **2. c. lid (of box, etc.),** couvercle *m* en bahut. **3.** *U.S:* **c. road,** route, chaussée, bombée.

convexity [kən'veksiti], *s.* convexité *f*.

convexo-concave [kən'veksou'kɔŋkeiv], *a. Opt:* convexo-concave; **converging c.-c. lens,** ménisque *m*.

convey [kən'vei], *v.tr.* **1.** transporter, porter, conduire (qch., qn); (a)mener (qn); voiturer (des marchandises); **they were conveyed to the station in a bus,** un car les a transportés à la gare; **to c. (passengers) across (the river, etc.),** passer (des voyageurs); **to c. crude oil to the refinery,** acheminer le pétrole brut sur la raffinerie. **2.** (*a*) (*of air, etc.*) transmettre (le son, une odeur); (*b*) **to c. a disease,** servir de véhicule à la contagion d'une maladie. **3.** transmettre (un ordre, des remerciements); donner (une idée); communiquer (une nouvelle) (**to,** à); **please c. my good wishes to the young couple,** veuillez transmettre, présenter, tous mes vœux aux jeunes époux; **to c. an author's meaning,** rendre, donner, le sens d'un auteur; **to c. one's meaning,** communiquer, rendre, sa pensée; **to c. the suggestion that . . .,** donner à penser que . . .; **to c. to s.o. that . . .,** faire comprendre à qn que . . .; **these words c. nothing to me,** ces paroles *f* n'ont pas de sens pour moi; **the name conveys nothing to me,** ce nom ne me dit rien; **superfluous words that c. nothing,** mots superflus qui ne disent rien, qui n'expriment rien. **4.** *Jur:* (*a*) faire cession (d'un bien); transmettre, transférer, céder (un bien) (**to,** à); (*b*) (*of solicitor*) dresser, rédiger, l'acte de cession (d'une terre, etc.), ou l'acte translatif de propriété.

conveyable [kən'veiəbl], *a.* **1.** transportable, portable. **2.** communicable. **3.** *Jur:* transférable, cessible.

conveyance [kən'veiəns], *s.* **1.** transport *m*; moyen *m* de transport; charriage *m*, transmission *f*, convoyage *m*; acheminement *m*; **public means of c.,** les transports en commun; **we have no means of c.,** nous ne disposons d'aucun moyen de transport. **2.** (*a*) transmission, communication *f* (de qch. à qn); (*b*) *Ph:* **c. of sound, of heat,** transmission du son, de la chaleur; (*c*) *Jur:* transmission, translation *f*, transfert *m*, cession *f*, disposition *f* (de biens); **c. of actual chattels,** apport effectif; **c. of real estate,** transport d'immeubles; **c. of a patent,** transmission de propriété d'un brevet. **3.** *Jur:* acte translatif de propriété; acte de transmission, de cession; contrat translatif de propriété. **4.** véhicule *m* (de transport); voiture *f*; *Jur:* **public c.,** véhicule de transport(s) en commun; voiture publique.

conveyancer [kən'veiənsər], *s. Jur: solicitor: m* qui se consacre spécialement à la rédaction des actes translatifs de propriété; = notaire *m*.

conveyancing [kən'veiənsiŋ], *s. Jur:* **1.** rédaction *f* des actes de cession, des actes translatifs de propriété; **c.** lawyer = CONVEYANCER. **2.** procédure translative de propriété, ((i) assignation *f*; (ii) cession *f* constitutive de biens).

conveying [kən'veiiŋ], *s.* **1.** transport *m*, charriage *m*, transmission *f*; *Ind:* **c. belt,** courroie *f* de transport; **c. screw,** transporteur *m* à vis. **2.** transmission, communication *f* (de qch. à qn); *Mec.E:* **c. of movement,** transmission du movement. **3.** *Jur:* = CONVEYANCE 2 (*c*).

conveyor, conveyer [kən'veiər], *s.* **1.** (*pers.*) (*a*) porteur, -euse (d'une lettre, d'un paquet); (*b*) voiturier *m*. **2.** *Ind:* (appareil) transporteur *m*; transporteuse *f*; convoyeur *m*; **coal c.,** transporteur à charbon; **portable c.,** transporteur à courroies mobile, sauterelle *f*; **roller c.,** transporteur à rouleaux; **c. belt, belt c.,** bande transporteuse; courroie *f* de transport; ruban roulant; transporteur à ruban, à courroie, à bande; **bucket c.,** transporteur à godets, à augets; **apron c., trough c.,** transporteur *m* à éléments articulés; **suction c.,** aspirateur *m*; **spiral c., screw c.,** hélice, vis, transporteuse; spirale transporteuse; transporteur à vis (sans fin); vis de transport, d'Archimède; **shaker c.,** couloir *m* à secousses; *Mec.E:* **assembly c.,** chaîne *f* de montage; tapis roulant; **work on the c. belt,** travail *m* à la chaîne; *Min:* **c. trough,** rigole *f* de chargement. **3.** conducteur *m* (d'électricité).

convict[1] ['kɔnvikt], *s.* **1.** *A:* condamné *m*. **2.** (*a*) détenu, -ue; (*b*) forçat *m*; bagnard *m*; **gang of convicts,** équipe *f* de forçats; **c. prison** = maison centrale; **former c.,** repris *m* de justice; (*c*) *A:* (i) déporté *m*; (ii) (*on the hulks*) bagnard, galérien *m*; **c. station,** pénitencier *m*; **c. colony,** colonie *f* pénitenciaire, de déportation; **gang of convicts,** chiourme *f*; **c. ship,** bagne flottant.

convict[2] [kən'vikt], *v.tr.* (*a*) **to c. s.o. of a crime,** convaincre qn d'un crime; déclarer qn coupable d'un crime; **he was convicted,** il fut déclaré, reconnu, coupable; il fut condamné; (*b*) **to c. s.o. of error,** convaincre qn d'erreur; **to be convicted of lying,** être convaincu de mensonge; (*c*) **you stand convicted by your own words,** vos propres paroles vous condamnent.

conviction [kən'vikʃ(ə)n], *s.* **1.** condamnation *f*; *Jur:* **previous convictions,** condamnations antérieures; dossier *m* du prévenu. **2.** persuasion *f*, conviction *f*; **to be open to c.,** être accessible à la persuasion, à la conviction; ne demander qu'à être convaincu. **3.** (*belief*) conviction; **to act according to one's convictions,** agir d'après ses convictions; **to act from c.,** agir par conviction; **to have the courage of one's convictions,** avoir le courage de ses convictions; (*of evidence, etc.*) **to carry c.,** emporter conviction; **it is my c. that he is innocent,** je suis persuadé qu'il est innocent; **that is his firm c.,** il ne sort pas de là; il n'en sort pas.

convictive [kən'viktiv], *a. Jur:* convictionnel.

convince [kən'vins], *v.tr.* convaincre, persuader (**s.o. of sth., that . . .,** qn de qch., que . . .); **I am convinced that he is still alive,** j'ai la conviction, je suis persuadé, qu'il est encore vivant; **to allow oneself to be convinced,** se laisser convaincre.

convinced [kən'vinst], *a.* convaincu; **c. communist,** communiste convaincu, de conviction.

convincedly [kən'vinsidli], *adv.* d'un air, d'un ton, convaincu.

convincible [kən'vinsəbl], *a.* disposé à se laisser convaincre.

convincing [kən'vinsiŋ], *a.* (*a*) (argument) convaincant; (langage) persuasif; (*b*) **his rendering of the part is quite c.,** son interprétation du rôle emporte conviction, est saisissant de vérité.

convincingly [kən'vinsiŋli], *adv.* d'une façon convaincante.

convincingness [kən'vinsiŋnis], *s.* force *f* (d'un argument, d'une preuve); vérité évidente (des paroles de qn); vérité (d'une interprétation).

convivial [kən'viviəl], *a.* qui a rapport aux plaisirs de la table. **1. c. evening,** dîner *m* entre camarades; soirée passée à table ou à boire; **man of c. habits,** amateur *m* des plaisirs de la table; bon vivant (entre convives); bon convive; *Lit:* **c. verse,** vers *m* anacréontiques. **2.** (*of pers.*) joyeux, jovial (à table), bon convive.

conviviality [kənvivi'æliti], *s.* **1.** franche gaieté (dans un repas); esprit *m* de société. **2.** *O:* **convivialities,** noces *f* et festins; soirées passées à table, à banqueter.

convivially [kən'viviəli], *adv.* joyeusement, jovialement; **the two teams spent the evening c.,** les deux équipes ont passé la soirée joyeusement.

convocation [kɔnvə'keiʃ(ə)n], *a.* **1.** convocation *f* (d'une assemblée, d'un comité); *Ecc:* indiction *f* (d'un concile). **2.** (*a*) *Ecc:* assemblée, synode *m* (du clergé d'un diocèse); **the C. of Canterbury, of York,** le synode de Cantorbéry, d'York; **C. house,** (i) lieu *m* d'assemblée du synode; (ii) le synode; (*b*) *Sch:* (*at Oxford*) assemblée délibérante des maîtres ès arts de l'Université.

convocator ['kɔnvəkeitər], **convoker** [kən'voukər], *s.* convocateur, -trice.

convoke [kən'vouk], *v.tr.* convoquer (une assemblée).

Convoluta [kɔnvə'lju:tə], *s. Ann:* convoluta *m*, convolute *m*, planaire *f*.

convolute ['kɔnvəljut]. **1.** *a.* (*a*) *Bot:* convoluté, contourné, contorté; (*b*) *Conch:* contourné. **2.** *s. Nat.Hist: etc:* enroulement *m*.

convoluted ['kɔnvəljutid], *a. Nat.Hist:* convoluté; *Anat:* circonvolutionnaire.

convolution [kɔnvə'lju:ʃ(ə)n], *s.* circonvolution *f*. **1.** repli *m*, sinuosité *f*; *Anat:* **cerebral convolutions,** circonvolutions cérébrales, du cerveau. **2.** enroulement *m*, spire *f*.

convolutionary [kɔnvə'lju:ʃən(ə)ri], *a. Anat:* circonvolutionnaire, circonvolutif.

convolvulaceous [kənvɔlvu'leiʃəs], *a. Bot:* convolvulacé, convolvulé.

convolvulus, *pl.* **-uses** [kən'vɔlvjuləs, -əsiz], *s. Bot:* volubilis *m*, convolvulus *m*, liseron *m*; belle-de-jour *f*, *pl.* belles-de-jour; **wild c.,** liseron des champs.

convoy[1] ['kɔnvɔi], *s. Mil: Nau:* (i) convoi *m*; (ii) (*now rare*) escorte *f* (d'un convoi); **c. ship,** (i) bâtiment convoyé; (ii) (*now rare*) bâtiment convoyeur; (bâtiment d')escorte; escorteur *m*; **ship under, in, c.,** bâtiment convoyé, en convoi; **to sail, to proceed, under, in, c.,** naviguer en convoi, de conserve; *Mil:* **c. guard,** escorte de convoi; *Nau: Navy:* **c. escort,** (i) escorte de convoi; (ii) escorteur.

convoy[2], *v.tr. Mil: Nau:* convoyer, escorter; **ship convoyed by . . .,** navire *m* sous l'escorte de . . ..

convulse [kən'vʌls], *v.tr.* **1.** convulsionner, bouleverser (un état); bouleverser (qn, la vie de qn); ébranler (la terre). **2.** *Med:* convulsionner; convulser (un muscle); donner des convulsions à (qn); **to be convulsed,** être convulsé. **3. to be convulsed with laughter, with pain,** se tordre de rire, de douleur; se pâmer de rire; **scene that convulses the audience,** scène *f* qui fait tordre de rire toute la salle; **face convulsed by, with, terror, with anger,** visage convulsé, décomposé, par la terreur, par la colère.

convulsion [kən'vʌlʃ(ə)n], *s.* **1.** *Med:* (*usu. pl.*) convulsion *f*; **to throw s.o. into convulsions,** donner des convulsions à qn; **infantile convulsions,** convulsions des enfants. **2. to be seized with convulsions of laughter,** se tordre de rire; rire à se tordre. **3. political convulsions,** convulsions, bouleversements *m*, politiques. **4.** agitation violente (de la mer); bouleversement, commotion *f* (de la terre).

convulsionary [kən'vʌlʃən(ə)ri]. **1.** *a.* convulsionnaire. **2.** *s. Fr.Hist:* convulsionnaire *mf* (de Saint-Médard).

convulsive [kən'vʌlsiv], *a.* (mouvement, etc.) convulsif; **c. movements (of the limbs),** soubresauts *m*.

convulsively [kən'vʌlsivli], *adv.* convulsivement.

cony ['kouni], *s.* = CONEY.

coo[1] [ku:]. **1.** *s.* roucoulement *m*. **2.** *int. P:* tiens! ça alors!

coo[2], *v.i.* (*of dove, F: of pers.*) roucouler; (*of baby*) gazouiller; *F:* (*of pers.*) **to bill and c.,** faire les tourtereaux; s'aimer comme deux tourtereaux.

co-obligant ['kou'ɔbligənt], **co-obligor** ['kou'ɔbligər], *s. Jur:* co-obligé, -ée.

co-occurrence ['kouə'kʌrəns], *s. Ling:* co-occurrence *f*.

co-occurrent ['kouə'kʌrənt], *a. & s. Ling:* co-occurrent (*m*).

co-occurring ['kouə'kə:riŋ], *a. Ling:* co-occurrent.

cooee, cooey ['ku:'i:], *F:* (*a*) *int.* ohé! (*b*) *s. Austr:* **to be within c. of a place,** être à deux pas d'un endroit.

cooing ['ku:iŋ], *s.* roucoulement *m*.

cook[1] [kuk], *s.* (*a*) cuisinier, -ère; **head c.,** chef *m*; **she's a first-rate c.,** c'est un cordon bleu; **plain c.,** cuisinière bourgeoise; **c. general,** cuisinière et bonne à tout faire; *F:* **head c. and bottle washer,** (i) factotum *m*; (ii) homme qui mène toute l'affaire; *Prov:* **too many cooks spoil the broth,** trop de cuisinières gâtent la sauce; (*b*) *Nau:* cuisinier; maître-coq *m*, *pl.* maîtres-coqs; (*c*) *Mil: Nau: F:* cuistot *m*.

cook[2], *v.*

I. *v.tr. & i.* **1.** *v.tr.* (*a*) (faire) cuire (de la viande, etc.); *v.i.* faire la cuisine; cuisiner; **she's (busy) cooking,** elle prépare le repas; **who's going to c. the dinner?** qui est-ce qui va faire le dîner? qui va s'occuper du dîner? **well cooked vegetables,** légumes bien accommodés, bien apprêtés; **half-cooked,** demi-cuit, à moitié cuit; **ready-cooked food,** aliments tout cuits; plats *mpl* cuisinés, à emporter; *F:* **to c. s.o.'s goose,** (i) renverser, bouleverser, les projets de qn; contrecarrer qn; (ii) faire son affaire à qn; tuer, ruiner, qn; **that's, I've, cooked my goose!** je suis fait! *P:* **he's cooked,** (i) *A:* (*drunk*) il a sa cuite; (ii) il est à bout de forces; il n'en peut plus; il est à plat; (*b*) *F:* **to c. the accounts, the books,** falsifier les comptes; truquer, tripatouiller, tripoter, les comptes; (*c*) *Phot: F:* trop développer (un film). **2.** *v.i.* (*a*) (*of food*) cuire; **I'll lay the table while the meat's cooking,** je vais mettre la table pendant que la viande est en train de cuire; (*b*) *F:* **what's cooking?** qu'est-ce qui se passe? **II.** (*compound verb*) **cook up,** *v.tr. F:* inventer, imaginer (une excuse, etc.); forger (un mensonge); mijoter (une revanche); **I wonder what (mischief) he's cooking up,** je me demande ce qu'il fricote.

cook[3], *s. Chess:* problème vicié par une solution alternative (et non prévue par l'auteur).

cookbook ['kukbuk], *s. esp. NAm:* livre *m* de cuisine.

cooker ['kukər], *s.* **1.** (*a*) (*kitchen stove*) cuisinière *f*; **electric c.,** cuisinière électrique; **gas c.,** cuisinière à gaz; réchaud *m* à gaz (à plusieurs feux); (*b*) **pressure c.,** auto-cuiseur *m*, cocotte-minute *f* (*R.t.m.*). **2.** fruit *m* à cuire, *esp.* pomme *f* à cuire; **these pears are good cookers,** ces poires se cuisent facilement.

cookery ['kukəri], *s.* (l'art de la) cuisine; **c. book,** livre *m* de cuisine.

cookhouse ['kukhaus], *s.* (*a*) *Mil: Nau:* cuisine *f*; (*b*) *Nau:* (*on wharf*) coquerie *f*.

cookie ['kuki], *s.* (*a*) *Scot:* petit pain au lait; (*b*) *esp. NAm:* (i) petit gâteau, (ii) biscuit *m*; (*c*) *NAm: F:* **that's the way the c. crumbles!** c'est la vie (que veux -tu)!

cooking ['kukiŋ], *s.* **1.** cuisson *f* (de la viande, etc.); (*of food*) **to take a lot of c.,** être dur à cuire; **c. apples,** pommes à cuire; **c. fat,** matière grasse (pour la cuisine). **2.** cuisine *f*; **plain c.,** cuisine bourgeoise; **to do the c.,** faire la cuisine; **c. utensils,** batterie *f* de cuisine; **c. oil,** huile *f* (de cuisine). **3.** *F:* **c. of accounts,** falsification *f*, trucage *m*, des comptes, irrégularités *fpl* d'écriture; tripotages *mpl* de caisse.

cookout ['kukaut], *s. NAm:* pique-nique où on fait cuire des plats (en plein air).

cookroom ['kukru:m], *s. U.S:* cuisine *f*.

cooks hop ['kukʃɔp], *s. NAm:* **1.** rôtisserie *f*. **2.** petit restaurant.

cookstove ['kukstouv], *s. NAm:* (*stove*) cuisinière *f*.

cooky ['kuki], *s.* **1.** *F: O:* (*pers.*) cuisinière *f*. **2.** *NAm:* = COOKIE.

cool[1] [ku:l]. **1.** *a.* (*a*) frais, *f* fraîche; **c. wind,** vent frais; **c. drink,** boisson rafraîchissante; **to get c.,** se refraîchir, se refroidir; **it's c.,** il fait frais; **it's getting c.,** le temps se rafraîchit; *Com: etc:* **to be kept in a c. place,** craint la chaleur; tenir au frais; mettre au frais; *Metalw:* **c. time,** temps mort; (*b*) tiède; (*c*) calme; de sang-froid; **to keep c. and collected, to keep one's c.,** garder son sang-froid; conserver sa tête; **as c. as a cucumber,** avec un sang froid imperturbable; **keep c.!** calmez-vous! du calme! *F:* ne vous emballez pas! (*d*) (*of pers., etc.*) froid, tiède; **c. reception,** accueil froid; (*e*) *F:* hardi; sans gêne; peu gêné; **I call that c.!** ça, c'est du toupet! quelle audace! **well, you're a c. customer!** eh bien, vous avez de l'aplomb, du culot, du toupet! **he answered as c. as you please,** il a répondu sans se laisser démonter; (*f*) *F:* **I lost a c. thousand,** j'ai perdu mille livres bien comptées, rien (de) moins que mille livres; **it cost me a c. hundred,** je l'ai payé cent livres, pas un sou de moins; (*g*) *Ven:* **c. scent,** voie légère. **2.** *s.* frais *m*, fraîcheur *f*; **in the c. of the evening,** dans la fraîcheur du soir; à la fraîche. **3.** *adv. F:* **to play it c.,** (i) jouer (en) décontracté; (ii) être décontracté.

cool[2], *v.*

I. *v.tr. & i.* **1.** *v.tr.* rafraîchir, refroidir, réfrigérer (l'eau, l'air); rafraîchir (le sang); refroidir, attiédir (qn, le zèle de qn); *F:* **c. it!** calme-toi! *Mec.E:* **to c. a bearing,** rafraîchir un portage; **to c. one's heels,** croquer le marmot; faire le pied de grue; poireauter. **2.** *v.i.* (*of liquid*) se rafraîchir, (se) refroidir; (*of anger, friendship, etc.*) se refroidir; tiédir, s'attiédir; **to put the wine to c. in the cellar,** mettre le vin à rafraîchir à la cave; **his anger soon cooled,** sa colère a vite passé.

II. (*compound verbs*) **1. cool down** (*a*) *v.i.* (i) (*after exertion*) se rafraîchir; (ii) (*after anger*) s'apaiser, se calmer, se modérer; **his anger is cooling down,** sa colère se détend; (*b*) *v.tr.* apaiser, calmer (qn).

2. cool off, (*a*) *v.i. F:* (*of affection, enthusiasm*) se refroidir, tiédir; (*b*) *v.tr. F:* **the government's mistakes have cooled off his enthusiasm for the party,** les fautes du gouvernement ont refroidi son enthousiasme pour le parti.

coolant ['ku:lənt], *s.* agent *m* de refroidissement; agent frigorigène.

cooler [ku:lər], *s.* **1.** (*a*) (appareil) rafraîchisseur *m*; rafraîchissoir *m*, **butter c.,** beurrier refroidisseur; **wine c.,** rafraîchissoir *m*, refroidisseur *m* (à vin); (*b*) *Ind:* réfrigérant *m*, réfrigérateur *m*, refroidisseur *m*; **surface c.,** réfrigérant à ruissellement; **forced-draught c.,** réfrigérant soufflé; *I.C.E:* **oil c.,** radiateur *m* d'huile; **air-intake oil c.,** radiateur *m* (d'huile) monté sur l'entrée d'air; **multi-element oil c.,** réservoir (d'huile) refroidisseur. **2.** *F:* (*drink*) boisson rafraîchissante. **3.** *P:* gnouf *m*, taule *f*, prison *f*.

cool-headed ['ku:l'hedid], *a.* (personne *f*) de sang-froid, calme, à l'esprit calme, que rien ne démonte; imperturbable.

coolie ['ku:li], *s. A:* homme *m* de peine; coolie *m*, couli *m*.

cooling[1] ['ku:liŋ], *a.* (*a*) rafraîchissant; **c. draught,** breuvage *m* apyrétique; (*b*) *Ind: etc:* réfrigérant, refroidissant; **c. agent,** agent *m* de refroidissement.

cooling[2], *s.* rafraîchissement *m*, refroidissement *m* (de la température, etc.), attiédissement *m* (d'un liquide); *Ind:* réfrigération *f*; **air c.,** refroidissement par air; **effusion c.,** refroidissement par diffusion; **evaporative, sweat, transpiration, c.,** refroidissement par sudation; **surface c.,** rafraîchissement superficiel; *Cin:* **c. tank,** cuvette *f* de refroidissement; cuve *f* à eau; *I.C.E: etc:* **c. flange,** ailette *f*, nervure *f*, de refroidissement; **c. jacket,** chemise *f* d'eau, de circulation, chambre *f* d'eau; *Ind:* **c. tower,** tour *f* de réfrigération; réfrigérant *m* à cheminée; refroidisseur *m*; **c. fan,** ventilateur *m* (de refroidissement); **c. system,** système *m* de refroidissement.

coolish ['ku:liʃ], *a.* un peu frais, *f* fraiche.

coolly ['ku:l(l)i], *adv.* **1.** fraîchement. **2.** (agir) avec calme, de sang-froid, de sens rassis, à tête reposée. **3.** (recevoir qn) avec froideur, froidement. **4.** *F:* hardiment, effrontément; sans gêne.

coolness ['ku:lnis], *s.* **1.** fraîcheur *f* (de l'air, du soir). **2.** (*a*) calme *m*, sang-froid *m*, flegme *m*; (*b*) *F:* aplomb *m*; culot *m*; toupet *m*. **3.** froideur *f* (de qn, d'un accueil).

coolwort ['ku:lwə:t], *s. Bot:* tiarella *m*.

coomb [ku:m], *s. Geog:* combe *f*, vallon *m*.

coon [ku:n], *s. U.S:* **1.** *Z:* raton laveur. **2.** *P:* (*a*) (*pers.*) type *m*; **he's a gone c.,** c'(en) est fait de lui; il est fichu; c'est un type fichu; (*b*) un malin. **3.** *F:* nègre *m* (des plantations); **c. songs,** chansons *f* nègres.

coop[1] [ku:p], *s.* (*a*) cage *f* à poules; mue *f*; **fattening c.,** cageot *m* d'engraissement; épinette *f*; séminaire *m*; (*b*) poussinière *f*; (*c*) *Fish:* casier *m*, (*d*) *F.* prison *f*, taule *f*; *U.S:* **to fly the c.,** s'évader.

coop[2], *v.tr.* enfermer (des poules) dans une mue; **to c. s.o. up,** tenir qn enfermé; claquemurer, parquer, cloîtrer, qn; **to feel cooped up,** se sentir à l'étroit.

co-op ['kou'ɔp], *s.* (*shop*) coop *f*

cooper[1] ['ku:pər], *s.* **1.** tonnelier *m*, cerclier *m*, barilleur *m*; **dry c.,** fabricant *m* de caques, de barils pour solides; boisselier *m*; **wet c.,** fabricant de tonneaux, de fûts pour liquides; tonnelier; **white c.,** boisselier; **cooper's wood,** bois *m* de tonnellerie; merrain *m*; **cooper's block,** charpi *m*. **2.** *F: A:* mélange *m* de porter et de stout.

cooper[2], *v.tr.* réparer, remettre à neuf (les tonneaux).

cooperage ['ku:pəridʒ], *s.* tonnellerie *f*, barillage *m*; **white c.,** boissellerie *f*.

co-operate [kou'ɔpəreit], *v.i.* **1.** coopérer (**with s.o. in sth.,** avec qn à qch.); **to c. in the success of sth.,** coopérer au succès de qch.; **to c. to achieve a result,** agir en commun pour atteindre un résultat. **2.** (*of thgs*) concourir, contribuer (**in,** à).

co-operation [kouɔpə'reiʃ(ə)n], *s.* **1.** (*a*) coopération *f*; (*b*) concours *m* (**in,** à). **2.** *Pol.Ec:* coopération, coopératisme *m*.

co-operative [kou'ɔp(ə)rətiv], *a.* **1.** (*a*) coopératif; **c. society,** société coopérative; **c. (supply) stores,** société coopérative de consommation; coopérative *f*; **c. dairy,** coopérative laitière; **farmer's c.,** coopérative agricole; (*b*) *s.* coopérative; **we sell our produce, our grapes, to the c.,** nous vendons notre récolte, nos raisins, à la coopérative (agricole, vinicole); (*c*) **to be c.,** prêter son aide; **do be a little more c.,** voyons, donnez-vous la peine de m'aider; **you're not a bit c.,** vous ne m'aidez guère; on ne peut pas travailler avec vous. **2. c. forces,** forces concurrentes.

co-operatively [kou'ɔpərətivili], *adv.* coopérativement.

co-operativeness [kou'ɔp(ə)rətivnis], *s.* coopération *f*; aide *f*.

co-operator [kou'ɔpəreitər], *s.* coopérateur, -trice.

cooperite ['ku:pərait], *s. Miner:* coopérite *f*.

coopery ['ku:pəri], *s.* tonnellerie *f*.

co-opt [kou'ɔpt], *v.tr.* coopter; **the co-opted members,** les membres cooptés (du conseil, etc.).

co-optation [kouɔp'teiʃ(ə)n], **co-opting** [kou'ɔptiŋ], **co-option** [kou'ɔpʃ(ə)n], *s.* cooptation *f*.

co-op(ta)tive [kou'ɔp(tə)tiv], *a.* **c. body,** corps *m* dont les membres sont choisis par cooptation.

co-ordinate[1] [kou'ɔ:dinət]. **1.** *a.* (*a*) égal, -aux (**with,** à); de même rang (**with,** que); (*b*) *Gram:* **c. clauses,** propositions coordonnées; (*c*) **c. geometry,** géométrie *f* analytique; **c. axes,** axes *m* de coordonnées; (*d*) *Ch:* coordiné. **2.** *s.* (*a*) *Hist:* égal *m* (par le rang ou l'importance); (*b*) *Mth: etc:* **co-ordinates,** coordonnées *f*; *Mth: Astr:* **astronomical co-ordinates,** coordonnées astronomiques; **Cartesian co-ordinates,** coordonnées cartésiennes; **celestial co-ordinates,** coordonnées célestes; **equatorial co-ordinates,** coordonnées équatoriales; **horizontal co-ordinates,** coordonnées horizontales; **polar, bipolar, co-ordinates,** coordonnées polaires, bipolaires; **rectangular co-ordinates,** coordonnées rectangulaires; **spherical co-ordinates,** coordonnées sphériques; **space-time co-ordinates,** coordonnées espace-temps; *Geog:* **geographic co-ordinates,** coordonnées géographiques; **map co-ordinates,** coordonnées topographiques, cartographiques; **grid, hectometric, co-ordinates,** coordonnées hectométriques; **lettered co-ordinates,** coordonnées littérales; (*c*) *Cost: Com:* **co(-)ordinates,** coordonnées.

co-ordinate[2] [kou'ɔ:dineit], *v.tr.* coordonner (**with,** à, avec); **co-ordinated movement,** mouvement *m* d'ensemble.

co-ordinating [kou'ɔ:dineitiŋ], *a.* **1.** coordonnateur, -trice. **2.** *Gram:* (*of conjunction, etc.*) coordonnant.

co-ordination [kouɔ:di'neiʃ(ə)n], *s.* coordination *f*; **efforts that lack c.,** efforts *m* qui manquent de coordination; *Ch:* **c. number,** indice *m* de coordination, coordinence *f*.

co-ordinative [kou'ɔ:dineitiv], *a.* coordonnateur, -trice.

co-ordinator [kou'ɔ:dineitər], *s.* coordonnateur, -trice.

coot [ku:t], *s.* **1.** *Orn:* **(common, bald) c.,** *NAm:* **European c.,** foulque *f* (macroule), *Fr.C:* foulque noire; **(American) c.,** foulque américaine; **crested c.,** foulque à crête; *F:* **as bald as a c.,** chauve comme un genou, comme un œuf, comme une bille. **2.** *F:* (*pers.*) idiot, -ote; gourde *f*.

cooter ['ku:tər], *s. U.S: F:* petite tortue.

cootie, cooty ['ku:ti], *s. Mil: P: O:* toto *m*, pou *m*, *pl.* poux.

co-owner ['kou'ounər], *s.* copropriétaire *mf*.

co-ownership ['kou'ounəʃip], *s.* copropriété *f*.

cop[1] [kɔp], *s. Tex:* cannette *f* de fil; **c. yarn,** fil *m* de coton sur cannettes; **c. winder,** cannetière *f*.

cop[2], *s. F:* agent *m* de police, flic *m*; **courtesy c., speed c.,** motard *m*; **to play cops and robbers,** jouer aux gendarmes et aux voleurs.

cop[3], *s. P:* **1. it's a fair c.!** je suis, vous êtes, pris sur le fait. **2. it's no c., not much c.,** ça ne vaut pas grand-chose; ça ne me tente pas; ce n'est pas le Pérou.

cop[4], *v.tr. P:* attraper, piger, pincer (qn); **to get copped,** se faire pincer (par la police, par le patron etc.); **to c. five years' hard labour,** écoper de cinq ans de travaux forcés; **to c. it,** (i) attiger; se faire attiger; écoper; recevoir une blessure, être touché; (ii) recevoir un savon.

copaiba [kə'paibə], **copaiva** [kə'paivə], *s. Pharm: etc:* copahu *m*; **c. balsam,** baume *m* de copahu.

copaifera [kɔpei'ifərə], *s. Bot:* copaïfera *m or f*, copayer *m*.

copal ['koupəl], *s.* **(gum) c.,** copal *m*; **courbaril c.,** animé *f*; **Congo c.,** copal Congo; **jackass c.,** copal cru de Zanzibar; **fossil c.,** copaline *f*, copal dur; **c. tree,** copalier *m*; **c. varnish,** vernis *m* au copal.

copaline ['kɔpəlain], **copalite** ['kɔpəlait], *s. Miner:* copaline *f*, copalite *f*.

copalm ['koupɑ:m], *s. Pharm:* **c. balsam,** (baume *m*) copalme *m*, *Bot:* **c. balsam tree,** copalme.

coparcenary ['kou'pɑ:sən(ə)ri], *s. Jur:* **1.** copartage *m* (d'une succession); indivision *f*. **2.** copropriété *f*.

coparcener ['kou'pɑ:sənər], *s. Jur:* copartageant, -ante; cohéritier, -ière; propriétaire indivis; indivisaire *m*.

copartner ['kou'pɑ:tnər], *s. Com:* coassocié, -ée; coparticipant, -ante.

copartnership ['kou'pɑ:tnəʃip], *s.* coassociation *f*; coparticipation *f*; société *f* en nom collectif; **industrial c.,** actionnariat ouvrier.

cope[1] [koup], *s.* **1.** *Ecc:* chape *f*; pluvial *m*, -aux; **c. chest,** chapier *m*. **2.** *Lit:* **the c. of heaven,** la voûte céleste, la calotte des cieux; **under the c. of night,** sous le voile, le manteau, de la nuit. **3.** *Const:* chaperon *m*, couronnement *m* (d'un mur, etc.); *Hort:* chaperon d'abri (d'un espalier); *Const:* **c. stone,** pierre *f* de couronnement. **4.** *Metall:* dessus *m*, chapeau *m* (de châssis, de moulage).

cope[2]. **1.** *v.tr.* (*a*) mettre la chape à (un évêque); **coped and mitred,** chapé et mitré; (*b*) *Const:* chaperonner (un mur); mettre un couronnement à (un mur); *Hort:* abriter (un espalier) d'un chaperon; (*c*) recouvrir d'une voûte; *Lit:* **the night which coped the earth,** la nuit qui couvrait la terre de son voile, de son manteau. **2.** *v.i.* (*of course of bricks, etc.*) **to c. over,** faire saillie; surplomber.

cope[3], *v.i.* (*a*) **to c. with s.o., with the enemy,** tenir tête à qn, à l'ennemi; **I'll c. with him,** je m'en occuperai; **people who don't have to c. with children don't know what life is,** les gens qui n'ont pas à faire à, à se débattre avec, des enfants ne savent pas ce que c'est que la vie; (*b*) **to c. with a situation, a danger,** faire face à une situation, un danger; **to c. with a difficulty,** venir à bout d'une difficulté; **to be able to c. with a job,** être à la hauteur d'une tâche; **I just can't c.,** c'est au-dessus de mes forces; **I'll c. with it,** je m'en chargerai, m'en occuperai; **I'll c.,** je me débrouillerai.

cope[4], *v.tr. Dial: O:* échanger, troquer.

copeck ['koupek], *s. Num:* copeck *m.*

Copenhagen [koupən'heig(ə)n], *Pr.n.* Copenhague *f.*

Copenhagener [koupən'heignər], *s.* habitant, -ante, de Copenhague.

copepod ['koupipɔd], *s. Crust:* copépode *m.*

Copepoda [kou'pepədə], *s.pl. Crust:* copépodes *m.*

coper ['koupər], *s.* **horse c.,** marchand *m* de chevaux; maquignon *m.*

Copernican [kə'pə:nikən], *a.* copernicien, -ienne; **the C. system, theory,** le système de Copernic.

Copernicus [kə'pə:nikəs], *Pr.n.m.* Copernic.

copier ['kɔpiər], *s.* **1.** copiste *mf.* **2.** copiste, imitateur, -trice. **3.** duplicateur *m,* copieur *m.*

co-pilot ['kou'pailət], *s. Av:* copilote *m.*

coping ['koupiŋ], *s. Const: etc:* chaperon *m,* crête *f,* couronnement *m* (d'un mur, d'une paroi en pierre); chaperon d'abri (d'un espalier); **c. stone,** pierre *f* de couronnement.

copious ['koupiəs], *a.* copieux, abondant, ample; **c. notes,** des notes abondantes; **c. amounts of beer,** de grandes quantités de bière.

copiously ['koupiəsli], *adv.* copieusement, abondamment, amplement.

copiousness ['koupiəsnis], *s.* abondance *f,* profusion *f;* ampleur *f* (de style).

co-plaintiff ['kou'pleintif], *s. Jur:* codemandeur, -eresse.

coplanar ['kou'pleinər], *a. Mth:* coplanaire.

copolymer ['kou'pɔlimiər], *s. Ch:* copolymère *m.*

copolymerization ['koupɔlimiərai'zeiʃ(ə)n], *s. Ch:* copolymérisation *f.*

copper[1] ['kɔpər], *s.* **1.** (*a*) cuivre *m* (rouge); *Miner:* **red c.,** cuivre vitreux rouge; cuprite *f;* **c. ore,** minerai *m* de cuivre; **blue c. ore,** azurite *f;* **grey c. ore,** cuivre gris, panabase *f;* **c. pyrites,** chalcopyrite *f;* **c. glance,** chalcocite *f,* chalcosine *f,* cuivre sulfuré; **c. blende,** kupferblende *f; Metall: etc:* **phosphor c.,** cuivre phosphoreux; **manganese c.,** cuivre manganésé, au manganèse; **soft c.,** cuivre doux; **c. sulphate,** sulfate *m* de cuivre; **c. foundry,** fonderie *f* de cuivre; **to turn the colour of c.,** se cuivrer; **the C. Age,** l'âge de cuivre; (*b*) *St.Exch:* **coppers,** valeurs *f* cuprifères; (*c*) *Ent:* lycène *f.* **2.** (*a*) *Dom.Ec:* cuve *f* à lessive, lessiveuse *f; Brew:* brassin *m,* chaudière *f;* **hop c.,** chaudière à houblon; (*b*) **coppers,** petite monnaie, sous *m;* **to give a beggar a few coppers,** donner des sous à un mendiant; (*c*) *P: A:* **to have hot coppers,** avoir la gueule de bois; **to cool one's coppers,** se rincer le gosier. **3.** *attrib.* (*a*) de cuivre; en cuivre; **c. wire,** fil *m* de cuivre; **c. fittings,** cuivreries *f;* **c. bath,** bain *m* de cuivrage; (*b*) **c.(-coloured),** cuivré, cuivreux; **c.-skinned,** au teint cuivré, bronzé; *Bot:* **c. beech,** hêtre *m* rouge.

copper[2], *v.tr.* **1.** *Metalw:* cuivrer (un métal). **2.** *N.Arch: etc:* doubler (un navire, etc.).

copper[3], *s. F:* (*policeman*) flic *m.*

copperas ['kɔpərəs], *s. Miner:* **1.** (**green**) **c.,** couperose verte, vitriol vert, sulfate ferreux. **2.** *A:* **white c.,** couperose blanche, vitriol blanc, sulfate de zinc; **blue c.,** vitriol bleu, sulfate de cuivre.

copper-asbestos ['kɔpəræs'bestɔs], *a. Tchn:* **c.-a. gasket,** joint *m* métalloplastique.

copper-bearing ['kɔpəbεəriŋ], *a.* cuprifère.

copper-bottomed ['kɔpə'bɔtəmd], *a.* (*a*) à fond de cuivre; *Nau: etc:* doublé en cuivre; (*b*) *Fin: etc:* sûr; (*c*) *F:* à outrance; **a c.-b. conservative,** un vieux de la vieille.

copperhead ['kɔpəhed], *s. Rept:* trigonocéphale *m; F:* mocassin *m.*

coppering ['kɔpəriŋ], *s.* **1.** cuivrage *m.* **2.** doublage *m.*

copperplate[1] ['kɔpəpleit], *s.* **1.** plaque *f* de cuivre; cuivre *m* en plaque(s); tôle *f* de cuivre. **2.** *Engr:* taille-douce *f;* **c. engraving,** (gravure *f* en) taille-douce, gravure sur cuivre; **c. printing,** impression *f* en creux, en taille-douce; **c. printer,** taille-doucier *m, pl.* taille-douciers; **c. (writing),** écriture moulée, calligraphiée.

copperplate[2], *v.tr.* cuivrer (un métal).

copperplating ['kɔpəpleitiŋ], *s. Metall:* **1.** (*action*) cuivrage *m.* **2.** (*material*) cuivrure *f.*

copperskin ['kɔpəskin], *s. U.S:* peau-rouge *m, pl.* peaux-rouges.

coppersmith ['kɔpəsmiθ], *s.* **1.** chaudronnier *m* en, de, cuivre. **2.** *Orn:* barbu *m* à front rouge.

copper-solder ['kɔpə'sɔ:ldər], *v.tr. Metalw:* braser au cuivre.

coppertop ['kɔpətɔp], *s. F:* **1.** cheveux roux. **2.** (*of pers.*) roux, *f* rousse; rouquin, -ine.

copperware ['kɔpəwεər], *s.* dinanderie *f.*

copper-wound ['kɔpəwaund], *a. El:* **c.-w. armature,** induit bobiné en, de, cuivre.

coppery ['kɔpəri], *a.* cuivreux; **to turn c.,** se cuivrer.

coppice ['kɔpis], *s.* taillis *m,* hallier *m,* gaulis *m; Ven:* breuil *m;* **c. clump,** cépée *f;* **c. wood,** bois *m* de taille; **c. with standards,** taillis sous futaie; **bark c.,** taillis à écorce.

copra(h) ['kɔprə], *s. Com:* copra(h) *m.*

coprinus ['kɔprinəs, kə'prainəs], *s. Fung:* coprin *m.*

coproduction ['kouprə'dʌkʃ(ə)n], *s.* coproduction *f.*

coprolalia [kɔprə'leiliə], *s. Med:* coprolalie *f.*

coprolite ['kɔprəlait], *s. Paleont:* coprolit(h)e *m.*

coprolith ['kɔprəliθ], *s. Med:* coprolit(h)e *m.*

coprology [kə'prɔlədʒi], *s.* coprologie *f,* scatologie *f.*

co-property ['kou'prɔpəti], *s. Jur:* copropriété *f.*

coprophagan [kə'prɔfəgən], *s. Ent:* coprophage *m.*

coprophagia [kɔprə'feidʒiə], **coprophagy** [kə'prɔfədʒi], *s. Ent:* coprophagie *f.*

coprophagous [kə'prɔfəgəs], *a. Ent:* coprophage, merdivore.

coprophilous [kə'prɔfiləs], *a. Ent:* coprophile.

co-proprietor ['kouprə'praiətər], *s. Jur:* copropriétaire *mf.*

cops(e) [kɔps], *s. Harn: etc:* fer *m* en U.

copse[1] [kɔps], *s.* taillis *m.*

copse[2], *v.tr.* planter (un terrain) en taillis.

copsewood ['kɔpswud], *s.* bois *m* de taille.

Copt [kɔpt], *s.* Copte *mf.*

Coptic ['kɔptik]. **1.** *a.* coptique, copte. **2.** *s. Ling:* copte *m.*

coptis ['kɔptis], *s. Bot:* coptis *m.*

copula ['kɔpjulə], *s.* **1.** *Gram: Log:* copule *f.* **2.** *Mus:* (*of organ*) pédale *f* d'accouplement.

copulate ['kɔpjuleit], *v.i.* s'accoupler.

copulation [kɔpju'leiʃ(ə)n], *s. Physiol:* copulation *f;* coït *m;* accouplement *m.*

copulative ['kɔpjulətiv, -leitiv]. **1.** *a.* (*a*) *Gram: Log:* copulatif; (*b*) *Physiol: Anat:* copulateur, -trice. **2.** *s. Gram:* copulative *f.*

copulatory ['kɔpjulət(ə)ri], *a. Physiol: Anat:* copulateur, -trice; (organe *m*) de copulation.

copy[1] ['kɔpi], *s.* copie *f.* **1.** (*imitation*) **this picture is only a c.,** ce tableau n'est qu'une copie, qu'une reproduction; (**traced**) **c.,** calque *m.* **2.** (*a*) (*transcription*) copie, transcription *f* (d'une lettre, d'un texte, d'un devoir); *Typ:* double *m;* **top c.,** original *m;* **rough c.,** brouillon *m; Jur: etc:* **fair c.,** copie (au net); **to make, write, a fair c. of a letter, of an exercise,** mettre une lettre, un devoir, au net; **to take a c. of a letter,** prendre copie d'une lettre; **each competitor should submit five copies of his work,** chaque concurrent doit présenter son ouvrage en cinq exemplaires *m;* (*b*) *Jur:* expédition *f* (d'un acte, d'un titre); **certified c.,** copie authentique; ampliation *f;* **certified true c.,** pour copie conforme; copie certifiée (conforme); copie authentique; **true c.,** copie conforme; **file c.,** exemplaire des archives; **to make a c. of a deed,** expédier un acte; **first authentic c.,** grosse *f* exécutoire, première expédition; (*c*) *Jur:* extrait *m* du livre censier, du rôle de la cour seigneuriale (tenant lieu de titre de propriété terrienne). **3.** modèle *m* (de dessin); exemple *m,* modèle (d'écriture). **4.** exemplaire *m* (d'un livre); numéro *m* (d'un journal); **only 500 copies of the book were printed,** le livre n'a été tiré qu'à 500 exemplaires; **review, press, c.,** exemplaire de publicité, exemplaire de service de presse. **5.** *Typ:* (*a*) manuscrit (destiné à l'impression); copie; **to wait c., to be out of c.,** manquer de copie; être à court de copie; (*b*) *Journ:* matière *f* à reportage; sujet *m* d'article; **this would make good c.,** voilà un bon sujet d'article, de reportage; **the supernatural is always good c.,** les articles sur le surnaturel plaisent toujours, se lisent toujours; **he would make c. out of his grandmother's funeral,** pour gagner cent sous il ferait du reportage sur l'enterrement de sa grand-mère; **c. writer,** articlier *m.* **6.** *Rec:* copie. **7.** *Cmptr:* **hard c.,** copie sur papier; copie en clair; **c. check,** contrôle *m* par duplication.

copy[2], *v.tr.* copier. **1.** (*a*) imiter, reproduire (une œuvre d'art, etc.); **to c. a plan,** suivre un dessin; (*b*) **to c. s.o.,** se modeler, se calquer, sur qn; **to c. s.o.'s walk, s.o.'s style,** imiter la démarche, le style, de qn; *Art: Lit: Mus:* **to c. s.o.'s style,** copier, pasticher, le style de qn; (*c*) *v.i. Sch:* **to c.,** copier (sur un autre élève); (*d*) *Journ:* (*of announcement*) **Australian papers please c.,** les journaux d'Australie sont priés de reproduire; "prière d'insérer dans les journaux australiens"; (*e*) calquer (qch.) (**from,** sur) **expression copied from the English,** expression calquée sur l'anglais. **2. to c.** (**out**) **a letter, etc.,** copier, transcrire, une lettre, etc.; **to c. out a passage from a book,** extraire un passage d'un livre; **to c. sth. from nature,** copier qch. d'après nature.

copybook ['kɔpibuk], *s.* (*a*) cahier *m* d'écriture; *O:* **c. maxims,** maximes banales; lieux communs; *F:* **to blot one's c.,** ternir sa réputation; (*b*) *attrib.* selon les règles.

copycat ['kɔpikæt], *s. F:* imitateur, -trice; singe *m.*

copyhold ['kɔpihould], *s. A.Jur:* **1.** tenure *f* en vertu d'une copie du rôle de la Cour seigneuriale; tenure censitaire. **2. c.** (**estate**), terre occupée en vertu d'une copie du rôle.

copyholder ['kɔpihouldər], *s.* **1.** *A.Jur:* censitaire *m;* **c. tenure,** tenure censuelle. **2.** (*a*) *Typ: Typew:* porte-copie *m;* (*b*) *Typ:* (*reader's assistant*) teneur *m* de copie.

copying[1] ['kɔpiiŋ], *a. Com: etc: A:* **c. clerk,** expéditionnaire *m.*

copying[2], *s.* transcription *f,* imitation *f; Sch:* copiage *m;* **c. machine,** duplicateur *m;* copieur *m;* **c. ink,** encre *f* à copier; encre communicative; **c. press,** presse *f* à copier.

copyist ['kɔpiist], *s.* copiste *mf;* scribe *m.*

copyright[1] ['kɔpirait], *s.* droit *m* d'auteur (sur son œuvre); propriété *f* littéraire; copyright *m;* **out of c.,** (tombé) dans le domaine public; *Jur:* **c. case; action for infringement of c.,** procès *m* en contrefaçon; **the International C. Union,** l'Union internationale de Berne; **c. reserved,** tous droits réservés; droit de publication réservé; **terms of c.,** délai *m* de protection (littéraire); **c. notice,** mention *f* de réserve; *Journ:* mention d'interdiction.

copyright[2], *v.tr. Publ:* déposer (un livre); copyrighter.

copyright[3], *a.* (livre) qui est protégé par des droits d'auteur; (article *m*) dont le droit de reproduction est réservé; (livre) qui n'est pas dans le domaine public; **c. (in all countries),** tous droits de reproduction et de traduction réservés (pour tous pays).

copyrighted ['kɔpiraitid], *a. Publ:* (*of book*) déposé.

copyrighting ['kɔpiraitiŋ], *s.* dépôt légal (d'une publication).

coquetry ['koukitri], *s.* coquetterie *f.*

coquette[1] [kə'ket], *s.* **1.** coquette *f.* **2.** *Orn:* coquet *m.*

coquet(te)[2], *v.i. O:* faire la coquette; flirter; *A:* coqueter; **to c. with s.o.,** faire des coquetteries, des avances, à qn; faire la coquette, flirter, avec qn; **to c. with an idea,** jouer avec une idée; caresser une idée.

coquettish [kə'ketiʃ], *a.* **1.** flirteuse. **2.** (*a*) (petit chapeau, etc.) coquet; (*b*) (sourire, etc.) provocant, *F:* aguichant.

coquettishly [kə'ketiʃli], *adv.* d'un air provocant.

coquilla nut [kə'kilənʌt], *s. Bot:* attalée *f* à cordes.

coquito [kə'ki:tou], *s. Bot:* jubéa *m.*

cor[1] [kɔ:r], *s. Mus:* **c. anglais,** cor anglais.

cor[2], *int. P:* ça alors! **c.! she's a smasher!** merde! ce qu'elle est belle!

Coraciidae [kɔræ'si:idi:], *s.pl. Orn:* coraciadidés *m,* les rolliers *m.*

Coraciiformes [kɔræsii'fɔ:mi:z], *s.pl. Orn:* coraciadiformes *m.*

coracite ['kɔrəsait], *s. Miner:* coracite *f.*

coracle ['kɔrəkl], *s.* coracle *m* (canot *m* de pêcheur à carcasse en osier).

coraco-clavicular ['kɔrəkoukla'vikjulər], *a. Anat:* coraco-claviculaire.

coracoid ['kɔrəkɔid], *a. & s.* coracoïde; *Anat:* **c. process,** apophyse *f* coracoïde.

coral ['kɔrəl], *a.* **1.** (*a*) corail *m, pl.* coraux; **organ-pipe c.,** orgue *m* de mer; tubipore *m;* **cup c.,** caryophyllie *f;* corail simple; **c. fisher,** corailleur *m;* **c. fishery,** la pêche du corail; **c.-fishing boat,** corallière *f,* corailleur *m;* **c. island,** île corallienne, de corail; **c. reef,** récif corallien, de corail; **c. shoal,** banc *m* de corail; **c. red,** corallin; *Geol:* **c. limestone,** calcaire *m* corallien; **c. rag,** coralrag *m;* (*b*) *a. & s.* (*colour*) (de) corail. **2.** œufs *mpl* de homard. **3.** *Bot:* **c. tree,** érythrine *f,* flamboyant *m;* **c. plant,** aveline purgative; **c. pea, creeper,** kennedya *m;* **c. fungus,** clavaire *f.* **4. c. snake,** serpent-corail *m, pl.* serpents-corail.

coralliferous [kɔrə'lifərəs], *a.* corallifère, coralligère.

coralliform [kə'rælifɔ:m], *a.* coralliforme.

coralligenous [kɔrə'lidʒinəs], *a.* coralligène.

coralligerous [kɔrə'lidʒərəs], *a.* coralligère.

Coralliida [kɔrə'li:idi:], *s.pl. Coel:* corallidés *m.*

coralline[1] ['kɔrəl(a)in], *s.* **1.** *Miner:* coralline *f.* **2.** *Biol:* bryozoaire *m; Oc:* **c. zone,** zone *f* des bryozoaires (30 à 100 m.).

coralline[2], *a.* (*a*) corallien; coralleux; **c. limestone,** calcaire *m* corallien; (*b*) (*pinkish-red*) corallin.

corallite ['kɔrəlait], *s.* **1.** *Paleont:* corallite *m.* **2.** *Geol:*

marbre corallin.

coralloid ['kɔrəlɔid], *a.* coralloïde, corallaire.

coralwort ['kɔrəlwə:t], *s. Bot:* dentaire *f.*

corbel[1] ['kɔ:bl], *s.* **1.** *Arch:* corbeau *m*, console *f*; **c. table,** encorbellement *m*; **arched c. table,** bandes lombardes. **2.** *Const:* **c. (block),** chapeau *m* (de montant), semelle *f* (d'encastrement de poutre).

corbel[2], *v.tr. Const:* encorbeller; *Arch: Civ.E:* **to be corbelled out,** *v.i.* **to c. out,** porter en saillie; former un encorbellement.

corbelled ['kɔ:bəld], *a. Arch:* en encorbellement.

corbelling ['kɔ:bəliŋ], *s.* encorbellement *m.*

corbicula, *pl.* **-ae** [kɔ:'bikjulə, -i:], *s.* corbeille *f* (d'abeille).

corbie ['kɔ:bi], *s. Scot: Orn:* corbeau *m*; *Arch:* **c. gable,** pignon *m* à redans; **c. steps,** redans *m* (d'un pignon crénelé).

Corcyra [kɔ:'saiərə], *Pr.n. A.Geog:* Corcyre *f.*

cord[1] [kɔ:d], *s.* **1.** (*a*) corde *f* (mince); cordon *m*; ficelle *f*; **stranded, twisted, c.,** cordon câblé; **laid c.,** ficelle tordue; *Miner: etc:* **c.-shaped,** funiforme; (*b*) *El:* conducteur *m* souple; cordon; **armoured c.,** cordon armé; **twine c.,** cordon double; (*c*) bandereau *m* (de trompette); *Dressm: Tail:* ganse *f* (de couture de vêtement); **silk c.,** rondelette *f*; *Bookb:* nerf *m* (de dos de livre); (*d*) *Anat:* **the vocal cords,** les cordes vocales; **the spinal c.,** le cordon médullaire; la moelle épinière; **the umbilical c.,** le cordon ombilical; (*e*) *Min:* cordeau *m*, mèche *f*; (*f*) *A: & Lit:* lien *m*; **cords of affection,** liens d'amitié. **2.** *A. Meas:* corde (de bois de chauffage); **c. wood,** bois *m* de stère; bois à brûler. **3.** (*a*) *Tex:* côte *f* (de velours côtelé, etc.); **Bedford c.,** bedford *m*; (*b*) *pl.* **cords,** pantalon *m* de velours côtelé.

cord[2], *v.tr.* **1.** corder; attacher, lier, avec une corde; ligoter (un fagot, etc.). **2.** *A.Meas:* corder, mesurer (du bois de chauffage). **3.** *Bookb:* Mettre (un livre) en presse (entre deux ais).

cordage ['kɔ:didʒ], *s.* (*a*) cordage *m*, filin *m*; (*b*) *coll.* cordages, filin; *Nau:* **the c. store,** la soute à filin.

cordate ['kɔ:deit], *a. Bot: etc:* cordé, cordiforme; en forme de cœur; **with c. leaves,** cordiforme.

corded ['kɔ:did], *a.* **1.** (*a*) *Tex:* côtelé, à côtes; vergé; **c. fabric,** étoffe croisée; (*b*) *Knit: etc:* **c. cotton,** coton perlé. **2.** *Aut: etc:* **c. tyre,** pneu *m* à cordes.

cordelier [kɔ:də'liər], *s. Ecc:* cordelier *m.*

cordelière [kɔ:də'ljɛər], *s. Her:* cordelière *f.*

cordial ['kɔ:diəl]. **1.** *a.* (accueil) cordial, chaleureux; **they were very c.,** ils ont été très cordiaux; ils m'ont fait un accueil chaleureux. **2.** *s.* cordial *m.*

cordiality [kɔ:di'æliti], *s.* cordialité *f*; **exchange of cordialities,** échange *m* de cordialités.

cordially ['kɔ:diəli], *adv.* cordialement, chaleureusement; de tout cœur; de grand cœur; de bon cœur; **to be received c. by s.o.,** trouver un chaleureux accueil chez qn; *U.S:* (*at end of letter*) **c. yours,** bien sincèrement.

cordierite ['kɔ:diərait], *s. Miner:* cordiérite *f.*

cordiform ['kɔ:difɔ:m], *a. Anat: etc:* cordiforme.

cordillera [kɔ:di'ljɛərə], *s. Geog:* cordillère *f*; **the Great C.,** la Cordillère des Andes.

cording ['kɔ:diŋ], *s.* **1.** encordage *m*, cordage *m* (d'un paquet, etc.). **2.** *coll. Tex:* **c. and healds of a loom,** encordage d'un métier.

cordite ['kɔ:dait], *s. Exp:* cordite *f.*

cordleaf ['kɔ:dli:f], *s. Bot:* restio *m.*

Cordoba ['kɔ:dəbə], *Pr.n. Geog:* **1.** Cordoue (Espagne). **2.** Cordoba (Argentine).

cordon[1] ['kɔ:d(ə)n], *s.* **1.** (*a*) *Dressm:* cordon *m*, tresse *f*; (*b*) [kɔr'dɔ̃] cordon (d'un ordre de chevalerie), **the Blue C.,** le Cordon bleu (de l'ordre du Saint-Esprit); (*c*) **c. bleu,** cordon(-)bleu. **2. c. of police, of troops,** cordon de police, de troupes; *Med:* **sanitary c.,** cordon sanitaire. **3.** *Arch:* cordon (de corniche). **4.** *Hort:* **c. (tree),** cordon. **5.** *Orn:* **red-cheeked c. bleu,** cordon-bleu *m.*

cordon[2], *v.tr.* **the street was cordoned off by the police,** on isola la rue par un cordon de police, on établit un cordon de police aux entrées de la rue.

cordoned ['kɔ:dənd], *a. Arch:* cordonné.

cordotomy [kɔ:'dɔtəmi], *s. Surg:* cordotomie *f.*

Cordova ['kɔ:dəvə], *Pr.n. Geog:* Cordoue *f.*

Cordovan ['kɔ:dəvən]. **1.** *Geog:* (*a*) *a.* cordouan, de Cordoue; (*b*) *s.* Cordouan, -ane. **2.** *s. Leath: A:* cuir de Cordoue, d'Espagne; cordouan *m.*

cordulia [kɔ:'dju:liə], *s. Ent:* cordulie *f.*

corduroy[1] ['kɔ:d(j)ərɔi], *s. & a.* (*a*) *Tex:* velours (de coton) côtelé; *Cost:* **c. trousers, breeches,** *s.* **corduroys,** pantalon *m*, culotte *f*, de velours côtelé; **c. velvet,** velours cannelé, coulissé, côtelé; velours de chasse; (*b*) **c. road,** chaussée formée de troncs d'arbres; chemin *m* de rondins; piste *f* en rondins; route fascinée; (*c*) *Min: etc:* corduroy *m.*

corduroy[2], *v.tr. U.S:* garnir (un chemin) de rondins; fasciner (un chemin).

cordwainer ['kɔ:dweinər], *s. A:* cordonnier *m*; **the Cordwainers' Company,** corporation *f* des cordonniers de la Cité de Londres.

Cordylidae [kɔ:'dilidi:], *s.pl. Rept:* cordylidés *m.*

cordyline ['kɔ:dilain], *s. Bot:* cordyline *m.*

core[1] [kɔ:r], *s.* centre *m*, partie centrale (d'une masse). **1.** cœur *m* (du bois, etc.); trognon *m* (d'une pomme, etc.); tripe *f* (de cigare); **hard c.,** noyau *m*; **to get to the c. of the matter,** approfondir une affaire; **selfish to the c.,** d'un égoïsme foncier; **French to the c.,** Français jusqu'au fond du cœur; **false to the c.,** faux comme un jeton; *F:* **he's rotten to the c.,** il est pourri de vices; il est corrompu jusqu'à la moelle des os; **to touch s.o. to the c.,** toucher qn profondément; *Lit:* **in my heart's c.,** au plus profond de mon cœur. **2.** (*a*) bourbillon *m* (d'un abcès); cornillon *m* (d'un cor, d'une corne); (*b*) *Vet:* (i) bouteille *f* (des moutons); (ii) cachexie aqueuse, pourriture *f* (des moutons). **3.** (*a*) *Geol: etc:* noyau; **c. (of the earth),** nifé *m*; *Min:* **c. sample,** carotte *f*, témoin *m*, échantillon carotté; **c. section,** section *f* de carotte; **c. drilling, sampling, boring,** carottage *m*; **c. bit, cutter,** (trépan *m*) carottier *m*; **c. drill,** perforateur creux, perforatrice creuse; (*b*) *Metall:* noyau; **false cores,** pièces *f* de rapport; **c. frame,** armature *f* de noyau; **c. box,** boîte *f* à noyau(x); (*c*) *El:* noyau (d'un aimant); **c. losses,** pertes *f* dans le noyau; (*d*) *Civ.E: etc:* **watertight c.,** noyau d'étanchéité; **c. wall,** âme *f* imperméable (d'un barrage); (*e*) mèche *f*, âme *f* (d'un câble); (*f*) *Atom.Ph:* cœur (d'une pile atomique); (*g*) *Cmptr:* noyau, tore *m* (magnétique); **c. memory, store, storage,** mémoire *f* à tores (magnétiques); **c. size,** capacité *f* de mémoire.

core[2], *v.tr.* **1. to c. an apple,** enlever le cœur d'une pomme; vider une pomme. **2. to c. out (a casting, etc.),** enlever le noyau (d'une pièce de fonte, etc.); **to c. out a mould,** noyauter, creuser, évider, un moule; **to c. up a mould,** rem(m)ouler un moule. **3.** *Min:* carotter.

corcboard ['kɔ:bɔ:d], *s.* latté *m.*

cored [kɔ:d], *a.* **1.** évidé. **2.** *Metall:* pourvu d'un noyau; *El:* **c. carbon,** charbon *m* à mèche.

co-regency ['kou'ri:dʒənsi], *s.* corégence *f.*

co-regent ['kou'ri:dʒənt], *s.* corégent *m*; corégnant *m.*

co-regnant ['kou'regnənt], *a.* corégnant.

coregonid [kɔri'gɔnid], *s. Ich:* corégone *m.*

Coregonidae [kɔri'gɔnidi:], *s. pl. Ich:* corégones *m.*

Coreidae [kɔ'ri:idi:], *s.pl. Ent:* coréidés *m.*

co-religionist ['kouri'lidʒənist], *s.* coreligionnaire *mf.*

corella [kə'relə], *s. Orn:* **little c.,** cacatoès *m* à œil nu; **long-billed c.,** cacatoès nasique.

coreopsis [kɔri'ɔpsis], *s. Bot:* coréopsis *m.*

corer ['kɔ:rər], *s.* (*a*) *Dom.Ec:* **apple c.,** vide-pomme *m*, *pl.* vide-pommes; (*b*) *Min: etc:* perforateur creux, perforatrice creuse.

co-respondent ['kouri'spɔndənt], *s.* (*a*) *Jur:* complice *m* de la femme (en adultère); codéfendeur *m* (en adultère); (*b*) **co-respondent('s) shoes,** chaussures *f* bicolores (de mauvais goût).

corf, *pl.* **corves** [kɔ:f, kɔ:vz], *s.* **1.** *Min:* berline *f*, banne *f*, benne *f*, manne *f*, wagonnet *m* (d'extraction). **2.** *Fish:* banneton *m.*

Corfiot ['kɔ:fiət]. *Geog:* (*a*) *a.* corfiote; (*b*) *s.* Corfiote *mf.*

Corfu [kɔ:'fu:], *Pr.n. Geog:* Corfou *m.*

corgi ['kɔ:gi], *s.* corgi *m.*

coriaceous [kɔri'eiʃəs], *a.* coriace; *Nat.Hist:* coriacé.

coriander [kɔri'ændər], *s. Bot:* coriandre *f*; **c. seed,** semences *fpl* de coriandre.

coring ['kɔ:riŋ], *s.* (*a*) *Metall:* noyautage *m* (d'un moule); (*b*) *Min:* carottage *m*; **side wall c.,** échantillonnage latéral des formations.

Corinna [kə'rinə], *Pr.n.f. Gr.Lit:* Corinne.

Corinth ['kɔrinθ], *Pr.n. Geog:* Corinthe *f.*

Corinthian [kə'rinθiən]. **1.** (*a*) *a. Geog:* corinthien; *Arch:* **C. order, capital,** ordre, chapiteau, corinthien; (*b*) *s. Geog:* Corinthien, -ienne. **2.** *s.* (*a*) *A:* viveur *m*; (*b*) *A: & U.S:* gentleman amateur d'un sport; sport(s)man *m*, *pl.* sport(s)men; yachtman *m*, *pl.* yachtmen.

Coriolanus [kɔriə'leinəs], *Pr.n.m. Rom.Hist:* Coriolan.

corium ['kɔ:riəm], *s.* **1.** *Anat:* c(h)orion *m.* **2.** *Ent:* corion.

corixid [kə'riksid], *a. Ent:* corixidé.

Corixidae [kə'riksidi:], **Corizidae** [kə'rizidi:], *s.pl. Ent:* corisidés *m*, corixidés *m.*

cork[1] [kɔ:k], *s.* **1.** (*a*) *Bot:* liège *m*; **male c.,** liège mâle, vierge; **female c.,** liège femelle; **c. elm,** orme-liège *m*, *pl.* ormes-lièges; **c. oak,** chêne-liège *m*, *pl.* chênes-lièges; **c. sole,** semelle *f* de, en, liège; **c. jacket,** corset *m* de liège; ceinture *f*, gilet *m*, de sauvetage; cuirasse marine, flottante; **c. tipped cigarettes,** cigarettes *f* à bouts de liège; *F:* **c. leg,** jambe artificielle; (*b*) *Miner: F:* **fossil c.,** liège de montagne; amiante *m.* **2.** (*for float, bottle stopper*) bouchon *m* (de liège); *Tls:* **c. drawer,** débouchoir *m*; **c. borer,** perce-bouchon *m*, *pl.* perce-bouchons; **c. cutter,** (i) (*pers.*) bouchonnier *m*; (ii) (*machine*) tubeuse *f*; **to draw the c. (of a bottle),** déboucher une bouteille; (*of champagne, etc.*) faire sauter le bouchon; **c. wire,** muselet *m*; **crown c.,** capsule *f* (métallique) de bouteille (tenant lieu de bouchon); *Box: P:* **to draw a c.,** faire saigner le nez de l'adversaire.

cork[2], *v.tr.* **1.** (*a*) **to c. (up) a bottle,** boucher une bouteille; *F:* **to c. up one's feelings,** étouffer ses sentiments; *P:* **to c. s.o. up,** clore le bec à qn; (*b*) garnir (un filet, etc.) de bouchons. **2. to c. one's face,** se grimer avec un bouchon brûlé; se noircir le visage au bouchon.

corkage ['kɔ:kidʒ], *s.* (*in restaurant, etc.*) droit *m* (de débouchage) sur un vin qui n'est pas de la maison, qui a été apporté par les consommateurs.

corkboard ['kɔ:kbɔ:d], *s.* liège aggloméré.

corked [kɔ:kt], *a.* (*of wine*) qui sent le bouchon; qui a un goût de bouchon.

corker ['kɔ:kər], *s. P: A:* **1.** (*a*) mensonge *m*, blague *f*; **that's a c.!** ça, c'est un peu fort (de café)! (*b*) réponse *f* qui vous en bouche un coin, qui vous clôt le bec; **that's a c.!** bien répondu! **2. he's a c.,** c'est un type épatant; **she's a c.,** ce qu'elle est belle! **it's a c.,** c'est le dernier cri.

corking[1] ['kɔ:kiŋ], *a. P: A:* épatant, fameux; bath.

corking[2], *s.* **1.** bouchage *m*; **bottle-c. machine,** bouche-bouteilles *m inv.* **2.** détérioration *f* du vin qui prend un goût de bouchon.

corkscrew[1] ['kɔ:kskru:], *s.* tire-bouchon *m*, *pl.* tire-bouchons; *Hairdr:* **c. curl,** tire-bouchon; boudin *m*; anglaise *f*; **hair in c. curls,** cheveux tire-bouchonnés; **c. staircase,** escalier tournant, hélicoïdal; escalier en vis, à vis; escalier en spirale, en escargot, en (co)limaçon; escalier à noyau plein; escargot *m*, colimaçon *m.*

corkscrew[2]. **1.** *v.tr.* **to c. a line,** tracer une ligne en spirale. **2.** *v.i.* (*a*) (*of wire, etc.*) vriller, vrillonner; (*b*) (*of stair, etc.*) tourner en vrille.

corkwood ['kɔ:kwud], *s. Bot:* (*a*) bois *m* de liège; (*b*) balsa *m.*

corky ['kɔ:ki], *a.* **1.** semblable au liège; *Bot:* **c. layer,** couche subéreus; **the c. character of the tissues,** la subérosité des tissus. **2.** (vin *m*) qui sent le bouchon. **3.** *F: A:* joyeux, enjoué; plein d'entrain.

Corliss ['kɔ:lis], *Pr.n. Mch:* **C. valve,** distributeur *m* Corliss; **C. engine,** machine *f* à vapeur Corliss.

corm [kɔ:m], *s. Bot:* bulbe *m* solide.

cormidium [kɔ:'midiəm], *s. Coel:* cormidie *f.*

Cormophyta [kɔ:'mɔfitə], *s.pl. Bot:* cormophytes *m.*

cormorant ['kɔ:mərənt], *s.* **1.** *Orn:* cormoran *m*; (*phalacrocorax carbo*) grand cormoran; **pygmy c.,** cormoran pygmée; **southern c.,** cormoran moyen, **green c.,** cormoran huppé; **flightless c.,** cormoran de Harris; **guanay c.,** cormoran de Bougainville; **Indian c.,** cormoran à cou brun; **reed c.,** cormoran africain; **Brandt's c.,** cormoran de Brandt; **double-crested c.,** cormoran à aigrettes, à double huppe; **pelagic, Baird's, c.,** cormoran pélagique; **red-faced c.,** cormoran à face rouge. **2.** *F:* (*a*) *O:* homme *m* d'une rapacité de cormoran; grippe-sou *m*, *pl.* grippe-sou(s); affameur *m*; **he's a regular c.,** il a les doigts crochus, les mains crochues; il n'en a jamais assez; (*b*) glouton, -onne.

corn[1] [kɔ:n], *s.* **1.** grain *m* (de blé, de poivre, de poudre à fusil, etc.). **2.** *coll.* (*a*) grains; blé(s) *m* (*pl*); céréales *fpl*; **winter c.,** semis *m* d'hiver; **C. Exchange,** bourse *f* des céréales; halle *f* aux blés; **c. chandler, dealer, merchant,** marchand *m* de blé, de grains; grainetier *m*; **c. trade,** commerce *m* des grains, des céréales; *Bot:* **c. cockle,** nielle *f* des blés; githago *m*; agrostemme *f*; oreille *f* de lièvre; gerzeau *m*; lampette *f*; *Ent:* **c. moth,** (fausse) teigne des blés, des grains; alucite *f*; *Husb.* (*for feeding*) **mixed c.,** farrago *m*; **dredge c.,** mélange *m* d'orge et d'avoine; *Hist:* **the c. laws,** les lois *f* (sur les céréales); (*b*) *esp. NAm:* **(Indian) c.,** maïs *m*; **c. picker,** ramasseuse *f* de maïs, corn-picker *m*, *pl.* corn-pickers; **c. sheller,** égreneuse *f* de maïs; **c. silk,** barbe *f* de maïs; **c. bread, c. pone,** pain *m* de maïs; **c. on the cob,** maïs en épi; **c. (whiskey),** whisky *m* de maïs; *Geog:* **c. belt,** région *f* du maïs; *U.S:* **the c. states,** les états producteurs de maïs; (*c*) *esp. Scot:* avoine *f*; **to give one's horse a feed of c.,** donner un picotin à son cheval. **3.** (*a*) *Bot:* **c. marigold,** marguerite dorée; **c. poppy,** coquelicot *m*, pavot *m* rouge, des moissons; **c. spurrey,** spergule *f* des champs, spargoule *f*; **c. rattle,** (rhinanthe *m*) crête de coq *f*; croquette *f*, rougette blanche; **c. salad,** mâche *f*; salade *f* de blé; bourcette *f*, boursette *f*, doucette *f*, clairette *f*, valérianelle *f*; miroir *m* de Vénus; (*b*) *Rept: US:* **c. snake,** serpent *m* des blés. **4.** *F:* banalité *f*; lieu commun; **that's just c.,** ça, c'est vieux jeu.

corn[2], *s.* **1.** cor *m* (à l'orteil, etc.); oignon *m* (au pied);

durillon *m* (sous le pied); **soft c.,** œil-de-perdrix *m, pl.* œils-de-perdrix; **c. cure, c. plaster,** coricide *m*; remède *m* contre les cors; **c. cutter, knife, razor,** coupe-cors *m inv*; *F:* **to tread on s.o.'s corns,** marcher sur les pieds de qn; froisser qn; toucher, blesser, qn à l'endroit sensible. **2.** *Vet:* bleime *f.*

corn[3], *v.tr.* (*a*) saler (du bœuf); **corned beef,** bœuf de conserve; *Mil: F:* singe *m*; (*b*) grainer, grener (le métal, etc.); granuler (la poudre).

Cornaceae [kɔ:'neisii:], *s.pl. Bot:* cornacées *f.*

cornbind ['kɔ:nbaind], *s. Bot:* (*also U.S:* **corn bindweed**) liseron *m.*

cornbottle ['kɔ:nbɔtl], *s. Bot:* bl(e)uet *m,* barbeau *m*; centaurée *f* bluet.

corncob ['kɔ:nkɔb], *s.* **1.** épi *m* de maïs. **2.** pipe *f* en épi de maïs.

corncrake ['kɔ:nkreik], *s. Orn:* râle *m* des genêts; *F:* **he's got a voice like a c.,** il a une voix de crécelle.

cornea ['kɔ:niə], *s. Anat:* cornée *f* (de l'œil).

corneal ['kɔ:niəl], *a. Anat:* cornéal, -aux; cornéen; *Ent:* (*of compound eye*) **c. surface,** cornéule *f*; *Med:* **c. grafting,** greffe *f* de la cornée.

corneitis [kɔ:ni'aitis], *s. Med:* cornéite *f,* kératite *f.*

cornel ['kɔ:nl], *s. Bot:* **c. berry, cherry,** corne *f,* cornouille *f*; **c. tree,** cornouiller *m*; *NAm:* cornouiller sanguin.

Cornelia [kɔ:'ni:liə], *Pr.n.f.* Cornélie.

cornelian[1] [kɔ'ni:liən], *s.* (*a*) *Lap:* cornaline *f*; (*b*) *Miner:* cornéliane *f.*

Cornelian[2], *a. Lit:* cornélien.

corneous ['kɔ:niəs], *a. Nat.Hist:* corné.

corner[1] ['kɔ:nər], *s.* **1.** coin *m,* angle *m*; carre *f* (d'un champ); carne *f* (d'une pierre); **to turn down the c. of a page,** faire une corne à une page; **rear c. (of a car),** coin arrière (d'une voiture); *Const:* **stone c.,** jambe *f* d'encoignure; **c. post,** poteau *m* d'angle; borne *f*; *For:* **c. tree,** pied cornier; *F:* **that will rub the corners off him,** cela va le décrasser, le dégourdir, le dégrossir. **2.** (*a*) coin; encoignure *f* (d'une pièce, etc.); *Const:* **c. plate,** équerre *f* en fer, en tôle; **c. iron,** harpe *f* de fer; **c. rafter,** arêtier *m*; **c. tile,** tuile cornière; *Tls:* **c. (bit) brace,** vilebrequin *m* d'angle; *Furn:* **c. cupboard,** armoire *f* d'angle, de coin; **c. chair,** coin de feu; **chimney c.,** coin de feu; (*in railway compartment*) **c. seat,** (place *f* de) coin; **to put a child in the c.,** mettre un enfant en pénitence, au coin; **to drive s.o. into a c.,** (i) acculer qn; (ii) mettre qn au pied du mur; enfermer qn dans un dilemme, dans une impasse; **driven into a c.,** (i) (*of animal*) à l'accul; (ii) (*of pers.*) au pied du mur; **we have him in a c.,** le voilà acculé; il n'en sortira pas; **in a tight c.,** en mauvaise passe; (*b*) **the four corners of the earth,** les quatre coins du monde; **quiet c. of Brittany,** coin retiré de la Bretagne; **nooks and corners,** coins et recoins; **to search every (nook and) c. of the house,** chercher dans tous les coins et recoins de la maison; (*c*) *Fb:* **c. (kick),** coup *m* de pied de coin; corner *m*; **c. flag,** piquet *m* de coin; (*d*) commissure *f* (des lèvres, de l'œil); **to look out of the c. of one's eye,** regarder du coin de l'œil; (*of horse*) **c. tooth,** (dent *f* de) coin. **3.** (*a*) coin, angle (de rue); **situated at the c.,** situé au coin; **c. house,** maison *f* du coin, qui fait le coin, l'angle, de la rue; **c. shop,** magasin *m* d'angle; *P:* **c. boy,** voyou *m*; batteur *m* de pavé; traîne-cul *m, pl.* traîne-culs; **he lives round the c.,** il habite (i) dans la rue qui fait le coin, (ii) tout près, à côté; **you'll find the grocer's round the c.,** vous trouverez l'épicerie en tournant le coin; **the grocer round the c.,** l'épicier du coin; **spring is just round the c.,** ce sera bientôt le printemps; **with the elections just round the c.,** avec les élections qui approchent; **to turn the c.,** (i) tourner le coin; (ii) franchir le passage difficile; surmonter des difficultés; passer le moment critique; (iii) (*of invalid*) surmonter la crise; être hors de danger; *Turf:* **the C.** = Tattersall's; (*b*) (*bend*) tournant; *Aut: etc:* virage *m*; **right-angled c.,** tournant à angle droit; **sharp c.,** tournant brusque; **dangerous c.,** virage dangereux; **blind c.,** virage masqué, sans visibilité; tournant encaissé; *Mount:* **open c.,** dièdre *m*; **he disappeared round the c.,** il a disparu au tournant; **to cut off a c.,** prendre le plus court; **that cuts off a c.,** cela évite un détour; *Aut: etc:* **to take a c.,** prendre un virage; virer; **to cut a c. (close),** (i) prendre un virage à la corde; (ii) virer court; **to cut corners,** (i) prendre le chemin le plus court; (ii) faire des économies (d'argent, de temps); *F:* **to stand one's c.,** payer sa tournée, son écot. **4.** *Com:* monopole *m*; trust *m* d'accapareurs; corner *m*; **to make a c. in wheat,** accaparer le blé.

corner[2], *v.tr.* **1.** (*a*) mettre (qch.) dans un coin; (*b*) acculer, coincer (qn); mettre (un animal) à l'accul; (*c*) mettre (qn) au pied du mur, dans une impasse; mettre (qn) à quia. **2. building cornered with pillars,** bâtiment *m* avec des piliers aux angles. **3. to c. timber,** biseauter le bois. **4.** *Com:* accaparer (une denrée, le marché). **5.** *v.i. Aut: etc:* prendre un virage; virer; **to c. sharply,** virer court; **this car corners well,** cette voiture prend bien les virages.

cornered ['kɔ:nəd], *a.* **1.** acculé; coincé; à l'accul. **2.** (*with a. or num. prefixed*) **sharp-c.,** à angles saillants; **three-c.,** à trois coins; triangulaire; (chapeau) tricorne.

cornering ['kɔ:n(ə)riŋ], *s.* **1.** (*a*) acculement *m* (d'un animal); (*b*) mise *f* à quia (de qn). **2.** accaparement *m* (d'une denrée). **3.** virage *m.*

cornerpiece ['kɔ:nəpi:s], *s.* coin *m*; *Const:* écoinçon *m.*

cornerstone ['kɔ:nəstoun], *s.* **1.** *Const:* pierre *f* angulaire; écoinçon *m*; pierre *f* de refend; **cornerstones (of brick-work, etc.),** chaîne *f* d'encoignure; **the c. of civilization,** la pierre angulaire de la civilisation. **2.** *Surv: etc:* borne *f.*

cornerways, -wise ['kɔ:nəweiz, -waiz], *adv.* diagonalement; en diagonale; en coin.

cornet[1] ['kɔ:nit], *s.* **1.** *Mus:* (*a*) cornet *m* à pistons; piston *m*; **soprano c. (in E flat),** petit bugle; (*b*) (*organ stop*) cornet; (*c*) (*pers.*) cornettiste *m,* piston. **2. (paper) c.,** cornet (en papier). **3.** *Bot:* cornet (de l'enveloppe florale). **4.** (*a*) *Comest:* oublie *f,* plaisir *m* (en cornet); (*b*) **ice-cream c.,** cornet *m* de crème glacée, de glace.

cornet[2], *s.* **1.** (*a*) *A.Cost:* cornette *f*; (*b*) *Ecc:* cornette (de religieuse) **2.** *Mil: A:* étendard *m* (de cavalerie). **3.** *Mil: A:* (*pers.*) cornette *m* (qui portait l'étendard).

cornetcy ['kɔ:nitsi], *s. Mil: A:* grade *m* de cornette.

cornetist ['kɔ:nitist], *s. Mus:* cornettiste *mf.*

cornfactor ['kɔ:nfæktər], *s.* négociant *m,* commissionnaire *m,* en blé, en grains.

corn-fed ['kɔ:n'fed], *a.* nourri de grain, *NAm:* de maïs; **c.-f. pullet,** poulet *m* de grain.

cornfield ['kɔ:nfi:ld], *s.* champ *m* de blé, *NAm:* de maïs.

cornflag ['kɔ:nflæg], *s. Bot:* glaïeul *m.*

cornflakes ['kɔ:nfleiks], *s.pl. Comest:* pétales *f,* paillettes *f,* flocons *m,* de maïs; cornflakes *m.*

cornflour ['kɔ:nflauər], *s.* farine *f* de maïs.

cornflower ['kɔ:nflauər], *s. Bot:* bleuet *m,* bluet *m,* barbeau *m*; centaurée *f* bluet; **c. blue,** bleu centaurée *inv*; bleu barbeau *inv.*

cornice ['kɔ:nis], *s.* **1.** *Arch:* corniche *f.* **2.** *Furn:* (*a*) galerie *f* (cachant la tête des rideaux); (*b*) chapiteau *m* (d'armoire). **3.** *Mount:* corniche (de neige).

corniced ['kɔ:nist], *a.* à corniche.

cornicle ['kɔ:nikl], *s. Ent:* cornicule *f.*

corniculate [kɔ:'nikjuleit], *a. Ent:* corniculé.

cornification [kɔ:nifi'keiʃ(ə)n], *s.* racornissement *m.*

corniform ['kɔ:nifɔ:m], *a.* corniforme.

cornigerous [kɔ:'nidʒərəs], *a.* cornigère.

Cornish ['kɔ:niʃ]. **1.** *a.* (*a*) *Geog:* cornouaillais (du sud-ouest de l'Angleterre); cornique; (*b*) *Cu:* **C. pasty,** chausson *m* de viande. **2.** *s. Ling:* cornique *m.*

Cornishman, -woman, *pl.* **-men, -women** ['kɔ:niʃmən, -wumən; -mən, -wimin], *s. Geog:* Cornouaillais, -aise (du sud-ouest de l'Angleterre).

cornland ['kɔ:nlænd], *s.* terre *f,* région *f,* à blé, *NAm:* à maïs.

cornmeal ['kɔ:nmi:l], *s. NAm:* farine *f* de maïs.

cornopean [kɔ:'noupiən], *s. Mus: A:* cornet *m* à pistons.

cornstalk ['kɔ:nstɔ:k], *s.* **1.** *NAm:* tige *f* de maïs. **2.** *F:* (*pers.*) (*a*) grand échalas, grande perche; (*b*) *Austr:* Néo-gallois, -oise.

cornstarch ['kɔ:nsta:tʃ], *s. NAm:* farine *f* de maïs.

cornucopia, *pl.* **-as** [kɔ:nju'koupjə, -əz], *s.* corne *f* d'abondance.

Cornwall ['kɔ:nw(ə)l], *Pr.n. Geog:* Cornouailles *f.*

Cornwallis ['kɔ:nwɔlis], *Pr.n. Geog:* **C. Island,** l'île *f* de Cornouaille.

cornwallite ['kɔ:nwəlait], *s. Miner:* cornwallite *f.*

corny ['kɔ:ni], *a. F:* usé; vieux, vieille; banal; rebattu; **c. joke,** plaisanterie usée.

corolla [kə'rɔlə], *s. Bot:* corolle *f.*

corollaceous [kɔrə'leiʃəs], *a. Bot:* corollacé.

corollary [kə'rɔləri]. **1.** *s.* (*a*) *Log: Mth:* corollaire *m*; **as a c. to . . .,** corollairement à . . .; (*b*) conséquence *f* (découlant d'un fait). **2.** *a.* corollaire.

corollate(d) ['kɔrəleit(id)], *a. Bot:* corollé.

corolliferous [kɔrə'lifərəs], *a. Bot:* corollifère.

corollifloral, corolliflorous [kərɔli'flɔ:rl, -'flɔ:rəs], *a. Bot:* corolliflore.

corolliform [kə'rɔlifɔ:m], *a.* corolliforme.

corolline [kə'rɔlain], *a. Bot:* corollaire, corollin.

Coromandel [kɔrou'mændl], *Pr.n. Geog:* **the C. coast,** la côte de Coromandel; **C. lacquer,** laque *f* de Coromandel.

corona, *pl.* **-ae** [kə'rounə, -i:], *s.* **1.** (*a*) *Astr: Bot: Mus: etc:* couronne *f*; *Ecc:* couronne de lumière (suspendue à la voûte); *Astr:* **solar c.,** couronne solaire; **c. of a tooth,** couronne d'une dent; *El:* **c. round the conductor,** couronne électrique; gaine lumineuse; **c. effect,** effet *m* corona, de couronne; (*b*) *Meteor:* halo *m* (du soleil, de la lune). **2.** *Arch:* larmier *m* (de corniche).

coronach ['kɔrənæχ], *s. Scot: Irish:* coronach *m*; chant *m* funèbre.

coronadite [kɔrə'neidait], *s. Miner:* coronadite *f.*

coronagraph [kə'rounəgræf], *s. Astr:* coronographe *m.*

coronal[1] ['kɔrənl], *s.* **1.** = CORONET 1. **2.** guirlande *f,* couronne *f* (de fleurs). **3.** *A.Arms:* frette *f* (de lance).

coronal[2] [kə'rounl], *a.* **1.** *Anat:* coronal, -aux; **the c. bone,** l'os coronal; le coronal. **2.** *Astr:* (*of light, atmosphere*) coronal.

coronaritis [kərounə'raitis], *s. Med:* coronarite *f.*

coronary ['kɔrən(ə)ri]. (*a*) *a.* & *s. Anat:* coronaire; **c. (artery),** artère *f* coronaire; *Med:* **c. (thrombosis),** infarctus *m* du myocarde; (*b*) *a. Med:* coronarien; **c. insufficiency, disease,** insuffisance, maladie, coronarienne; (*c*) *a.* **c. cushion, band, ring,** bourrelet *m* (de pied de cheval).

coronate(d) ['kɔrəneit(id)], *a. Bot:* couronné; à couronne.

coronation [kɔrə'neiʃ(ə)n], *s.* couronnement *m*; sacre *m*; **c. day,** jour *m* du couronnement; **c. mug,** tasse commémorative du couronnement (du roi, de la reine).

coronella [kɔrə'nelə], *s. Rept:* coronelle *f.*

coroner ['kɔrənər], *s. Jur:* coroner *m* (officier civil chargé d'instruire, assisté d'un jury, en cas d mort violente ou subite).

coronet ['kɔrənit], *s.* **1.** (*a*) (petite) couronne, cercle *m*; **Earl's c.,** couronne de comte; **Ducal c.,** couronne ducale; **Baron's c.,** tortil *m* de baron; (*b*) (*lady's*) diadème *m*; bandeau *m.* **2.** fraise *f* (de bois de cerf). **3.** (*of horse*) couronne (du pâturon); *Vet:* **swelling under the c.,** javart encorné.

coroneted ['kɔrənitid], *a.* couronné; portant une couronne (de pair d'Angleterre).

coroniform [kə'rounifɔ:m], *a.* coroniforme.

coronilla [kɔrə'nilə], *s. Bot:* coronille *f,* coronilla *f.*

coronograph [kə'rounəgræf], *s. Astr:* coronographe *m.*

coronoid ['kɔrənɔid], *a. Anat:* coronoïde; **c. process,** apophyse *f* coronoïde.

coronule ['kɔrənjul], *s. Crust:* coronule *f.*

corophium [kə'roufiəm], *s. Crust:* corophie *f.*

corozo [kə'rouzou], *s. Bot:* **c. (palm),** corozo *m*; ivoire végétal; arbre *m* à ivoire; **c. nut,** graine *f* d'arbre à ivoire.

corporal[1] ['kɔ:pər(ə)l], *a.* corporel; **c. punishment,** punition corporelle; **c. defect,** défectuosité *f* physique; *A:* **c. oath,** serment prêté en appuyant la main sur un objet sacré.

corporal[2], *s. Ecc:* (*also* **c. cloth**) corporal *m,* -aux.

corporal[3], *s.* (*a*) *Mil:* (*of infantry*) caporal *m,* -aux; (*of cavalry, artillery*) brigadier *m*; **senior c.,** caporal-chef *m, pl.* caporaux-chefs; **c. of the guard,** caporal de garde; **mess c.,** caporal d'ordinaire; (*b*) *Mil.Av:* caporal-chef *m*; (*c*) (*women's services*) sixième catégorie *f*; (*d*) *Nau:* **ship's c.,** caporal d'armes.

corporality [kɔ:pə'ræliti], *s.* **1.** corporéité *f.* **2.** *pl.* besoins matériels.

corporally ['kɔ:p(ə)rəli], *adv.* (punir qn) corporellement.

corporate ['kɔ:p(ə)rət], *a.* **1.** constitué (en corps); formant (un) corps; *Jur:* **body c., c. body,** corps constitué; corporation *f*; personne morale, civile, juridique; **status of body c.,** personnalité civile; **c. town,** municipalité *f.* **2.** (*a*) de corporation, de corps; **c. feeling,** esprit *m* de corps; (*b*) *Com:* corporatif, de société; **c. name,** raison sociale; **c. profit,** profit *m* des sociétés; **c. image,** image *f* de la firme.

corporation [kɔ:pə'reiʃ(ə)n], *s.* **1.** (*a*) corporation *f*; corps constitué; (*b*) *Hist:* corps de métier. **2.** *Com:* société enregistrée; compagnie *f*; **public c.,** entreprise publique. **3.** *Jur:* personne morale, civile; **c. aggregate,** personne morale formée par plusieurs individus; **c. sole,** personne morale constituée par un seul individu. **4. municipal c.,** conseil municipal; corps municipal; municipalité *f*; **the mayor and c.,** le maire et les conseillers *m*; *Fin:* **c. stocks,** emprunts *mpl* de ville; **c. tax,** impôt sur le revenu des personnes morales. **5.** *F:* bedaine *f,* bedon *m,* gros ventre, ventre rebondi; **he's beginning to get a c.,** il commence à prendre du ventre, à bedonner.

corporatism ['kɔ:pərətizm], *s. Pol.Ec: etc:* corporatisme *m.*

corporatist ['kɔ:pərətist], *a.* & *s.* corporatiste (*m*).

corporative ['kɔ:p(ə)rətiv], *a.* corporatif.

corporativism ['kɔ:p(ə)rətivizm], *s. Pol.Ec: etc:* corporatisme *m.*

corporator ['kɔ:pəreitər], *s.* membre *m* du corps municipal.

corporeal [kɔ:'pɔ:riəl], *a.* **1.** corporel, matériel. **2.** *Jur:* **c. hereditament,** biens matériels transmissibles par héritage; terres et immeubles. **3.** *Med:* corporéal, -aux.

corporeality [kɔ:pɔ:ri'æliti], *s. Phil: Theol:* matérialité *f.*

corporealize [kɔː'pɔːriəlaiz], *v.tr.* corporifier, matérialiser.
corporeally [kɔː'pɔːriəli], *adv.* corporellement.
corporeity [kɔːpə'riːiti], *s.* corporéité *f.*
corposant ['kɔːpəzænt], *s.* feu *m* de Saint-Elme.
corps [kɔːr, *pl.* kɔːz], *s.inv.* (*a*) corps *m*; **the diplomatic c.,** le corps diplomatique; (*b*) *Mil:* corps d'armée; **air c.,** corps d'armée aérienne; **cavalry c.,** corps de cavalerie; **tank c.,** formation *f* de chars; **c. troops, c. units,** éléments *m* organiques de corps d'armée; **c. area,** zone *f* (d'action) du corps d'armée; **c. d'élite,** corps d'élite; (*c*) **c. de ballet** [də'bælei], corps de ballet.
corpse [kɔːps], *s.* (*a*) cadavre *m*; corps (mort); (*at a burial*) dépouille mortelle; **c. candle,** feu follet (des cimetières, annonçant une mort); (*b*) **the c. of a city once so beautiful,** les ruines d'une ville autrefois si belle; (*c*) *F:* **c. reviver,** remontant *m*; (*d*) *Bot:* **c. plant, c. light,** monotrope *m.*
corpulence ['kɔːpjuləns], **corpulency** ['kɔːpjulənsi], *s.* corpulence *f*, obésité *f.*
corpulent ['kɔːpjulənt], *a.* corpulent, obèse.
corpus ['kɔːpəs], *s.* **1.** (*a*) corpus *m*, recueil *m* (d'inscriptions, etc.); **c. juris,** corpus juris; (*b*) *Jur:* **c. delicti** [di'liktai], le corps du délit. **2.** *Anat:* **c. striatum,** corps strié; **c. luteum,** corps progestatif, corps jaune; **corpora quadrigemina,** les tubercules quadrijumeaux (de la moelle allongée). **3.** *Ecc:* (*R.C.Ch.*) **Corpus Christi** ['kristi], la Fête-Dieu.
corpuscle ['kɔːpʌsl], **corpuscule** [kɔː'pʌskjul], *s.* **1.** corpuscule *m*; **blood corpuscules,** globules sanguins; **red blood corpuscles,** globules rouges; **white blood corpuscules,** globules blancs. **2.** *Ph:* *F:* = atome *m*, molécule *f*, etc.
corpuscular [kɔː'pʌskjulər], *a.* corpusculaire.
corrade [kɔ'reid], *v.tr.* *Geog:* (*of stream, etc.*) abrader (ses rives).
corral[1] [kɔ'rɑːl], *s.* corral *m*, *pl.* -als.
corral[2], *v.tr.* **1.** renfermer (des bestiaux, chevaux, etc.) dans un corral. **2.** parquer (les chariots) en rond (en guise de clôture). **3.** *NAm:* *F:* s'emparer de (qch.); mettre la main sur (qch.).
corrasion [kɔ'reiʒən], *s.* *Geog:* corrasion *f.*
correct[1] [kə'rekt], *v.tr.* **1.** relever les fautes (d'un thème, etc.); corriger (une épreuve d'imprimerie, un thème, etc.); **to c. a bad habit,** corriger une mauvaise habitude. **2.** rectifier (une erreur); modifier, redresser (le réglage d'un instrument); *Av:* **route corrected for drift,** route corrigée de la dérive; *Ph:* **volume corrected for temperature and pressure,** volume ramené aux conditions normales de température et de pression; *Book-k:* **correcting entry,** écriture *f* de redressement; *Com:* **corrected invoice,** facture rectificative. **3.** (*a*) reprendre, admonester (qn); faire la leçon à (un enfant, etc.); **to c. s.o.'s faults,** reprendre les fautes de qn; corriger qn de ses fautes; **to stand corrected,** reconnaître son erreur, ses torts; avouer qu'on a tort; **to c. oneself,** se reprendre; (*b*) punir, châtier, infliger une correction à (un coupable, etc.). **4.** neutraliser, contrebalancer, annuler (une influence, un goût).
correct[2], *a.* **1.** correct, exact; **c. style,** style correct, pur; **c. description,** description correcte, exacte, conforme à la vérité; **c. statement,** déclaration exacte; **c. answer,** réponse *f* juste; **c. working (of a machine),** marche régulière, normale (d'une machine); **c. weight,** poids exact, juste; **c. to a millimetre,** exact à un millimètre près; **his prediction proved c.,** sa prédiction s'est vérifiée; **events have proved our views c.,** les événements ont donné raison à nos prévisions, ont prouvé l'exactitude de nos prévisions; **if my memory is c.,** si j'ai bonne mémoire. **2.** bienséant, correct, conforme à l'usage; **(strictly) c. conduct,** conduite *f* d'une correction irréprochable; **it's the c. thing to . . .,** il est de rigueur de . . ., la politesse veut que . . .; **c. young man,** jeune homme bien élevé, comme il faut.
correction [kə'rekʃ(ə)n], *s.* **1.** correction *f* (d'une épreuve, d'un devoir d'école, etc.); redressement *m* (d'un compte); **under c.,** (i) sauf erreur, sauf correction; (ii) en train d'être corrigé; **subject to c.,** sous toutes réserves, sauf correction; **may I make the following c.,** permettez-moi la mise au point suivante. **2.** correction, châtiment *m*, punition *f.* **3.** (*a*) *Ph:* *Meteor:* *etc:* correction (d'une cote, d'un système optique, etc.); **barometer corrections,** corrections barométriques; *Ph:* **Bouguer c.,** correction Bouguer; (*b*) *Artil:* *etc:* **meteorological, metro, c.,** correction aérologique; **drift c.,** correction de dérive; **deflection c.,** correction de gisement; **range c.,** correction en portée; **wind c.,** correction du vent; **elevation c.,** correction en site; (*c*) *Mec.E:* *etc:* **c. for temperature,** correction de température; **index c. (of measuring instrument),** correction du zéro (d'un appareil de mesure); *Surv:* **c. for alignment,** correction d'alignement; *Elcs:* **tone c.,** correction de tonalité; **frequency c.,** correction de fréquence; (*d*) *Opt:* *etc:* **c. for astigmatism, for parallax, for refraction,** correction de l'astigmatisme, de la parallaxe, de la réfraction.
correctional [kə'rekʃənl], *a.* correctionnel.
correctitude [kə'rektitjud], *s.* correction *f* (diplomatique, etc.).
corrective [kə'rektiv]. **1.** *s.* *Med:* correctif *m.* **2.** *a.* (*a*) correctif, rectifiant; **c. exercises,** gymnastique médicale, corrective; *Opt:* **c. lens,** verre correcteur; (*b*) punitif; de correction.
correctively [kə'rektivli], *adv.* correctivement.
correctly [kə'rektli], *adv.* **1.** correctement, exactement, justement; **to speak c.,** parler correctement, avec correction; **or to put it more c.,** ou pour mieux dire. **2.** conformément à l'usage; suivant la bienséance.
correctness [kə'rektnis], *s.* correction *f*, convenance *f* (de tenue, etc.); exactitude *f*, justesse *f*, précision *f* (d'une description); pureté *f* (de style); justesse (d'une balance); rectitude *f* (de jugement).
corrector [kə'rektər], *s.* **1.** (*pers.*) (*a*) correcteur, -trice; (*b*) *Typ:* **press c.,** correcteur *m* (d'épreuves); corrigeur *m.* **2.** *Tchn:* (appareil, dispositif) correcteur; *Artil:* **c. gear (of fuse setting),** corrigeur.
Correggio [kɔ'redʒiou], *Pr.n.m.* *Hist. of Art:* le Corrège.
correlate[1] ['kɔrileit], *s.* corrélatif *m.*
correlate[2]. **1.** *v.i.* correspondre, être corrélatif, rapporter, **(with, to,** à); être en corrélation **(with,** avec) *Stat:* correler. **2.** *v.tr.* mettre (qch.) en corrélation **(with,** avec); mettre (deux choses) en corrélation.
correlation [kɔri'leiʃ(ə)n], *s.* corrélation *f*; *Mth:* **c. coefficient,** coefficient *m* de corrélation; **c. curve,** corrélogramme *m.*
correlational [kɔri'leiʃənl], *a.* corrélationnel.
correlative [kɔ'relətiv], *a.* & *s.* corrélatif (*m*); en corrélation **(with,** avec).
correlatively [kɔ'relətivli], *adv.* corrélativement.
correlogram [kɔ'relougræm], *s.* *Mth:* corrélogramme *m.*
correspond [kɔris'pɔnd], *v.i.* **1.** (*a*) (*be in harmony*) correspondre, être conforme **(with, to,** à); **his actions do not c. with his words,** ses actions *f* ne s'accordent pas avec ses paroles; *Com:* **to c. to sample,** être conforme à l'échantillon; (*b*) (*be similar*) correspondre **(to,** avec); **the two windows do not c.,** les deux fenêtres ne correspondent pas, ne se répondent pas, ne sont pas symétriques (l'une avec l'autre). **2.** (*communicate*) correspondre **(with s.o.,** avec qn); écrire (à qn); échanger des lettres (avec qn).
correspondence [kɔris'pɔndəns], *s.* **1.** correspondance *f* **(with, to,** avec); **the c. between cause and effect,** la correspondance, le rapport, entre la cause et l'effet. **2.** (*a*) correspondance, commerce *m* de lettres; **to be in c. with s.o.,** être en correspondance avec qn; **there has been some c. between us,** nous avons échangé quelques lettres; **to keep up a secret c. with s.o.,** entretenir des intelligences avec qn; (*b*) correspondance, courrier *m*; **to do, attend to, the c.,** faire la correspondance; *Com:* **c. clerk,** correspondancier *m*; *Mil:* *etc:* **c. section,** le courrier (d'un état-major); *Sch:* **c. course,** cours *m* par correspondance.
correspondent [kɔris'pɔndənt]. **1.** *s.* correspondant, -ante; **regular c.,** correspondant régulier, fidèle; **this bank has correspondents in many countries,** cette banque a des correspondants dans de nombreux pays; *Journ:* **parliamentary c.,** rédacteur *m* parlementaire; **war c.,** correspondant de guerre; **our Washington c.,** notre correspondant à Washington; **from our special c.,** de notre envoyé spécial. **2.** *a.* **to be c. to, with, sth.,** correspondre, s'accorder, avec qch.; être conforme à qch.
correspondently [kɔris'pɔndəntli], *adv.* d'une manière correspondante.
corresponding [kɔris'pɔndiŋ], *a.* **1.** (*a*) correspondant **(to,** à); **c. to the original,** conforme à l'original; *Book-k:* **c. entry,** écriture *f* conforme, de conformité; (*b*) *Mth:* **c. angles,** angles correspondants; **c. sides of two similar triangles,** côtés homologues de deux triangles semblables. **2. c. member of a society,** membre correspondant d'une société.
correspondingly [kɔris'pɔndiŋli], *adv.* également, à l'avenant.
corridor ['kɔridɔːr], *s.* couloir *m*, corridor *m*; **c. train,** train *m* à couloir; **air c.,** couloir, corridor, aérien; *Meteor:* **low pressure c.,** couloir de basse pression; *Hist:* *Geog:* **the Polish C.,** le corridor polonais, le corridor, le couloir, de Dantzig.
corrie ['kɔri], *s.* (*a*) *Geog:* cirque *m*; (*b*) *Ven:* entonnoir *m*, creux *m* (où gîte le cerf).
Corrigan ['kɔrigən], *Pr.n.* *Med:* **Corrigan's disease,** maladie *f* de Corrigan, insuffisance *f* aortique; **Corrigan's pulse,** pouls *m* de Corrigan.
corrigendum, *pl.* **-da** [kɔri'dʒendəm, -də], *s.* *Typ:* erratum *m*, *pl.* errata *m*; *Adm:* **c. to a circular,** rectificatif *m* d'un bulletin.
corrigible ['kɔridʒibl], *a.* corrigible.
corroborant [kə'rɔbər(ə)nt]. **1.** *a.* (*of proof, etc.*) corroborant, corroboratif. **2.** *a.* & *s.* *Med:* *A:* corroborant (*m*); confortant (*m*); fortifiant (*m*).
corroborate [kə'rɔbəreit], *v.tr.* corroborer, confirmer (une déclaration); **to c. s.o.'s statement,** confirmer le dire de qn; **the facts c. his statements,** les faits *m* témoignent en faveur de son dire, viennent à l'appui de ce qu'il dit.
corroboration [kərɔbə'reiʃ(ə)n], *s.* corroboration *f*, confirmation *f*; **in c. of . . .,** à l'appui de . . ..
corroborative [kə'rɔb(ə)rətiv], *a.* corroboratif, corroborant.
corroborator [kə'rɔbəreitər], *s.* témoin *m* à l'appui; personne *f*, chose *f*, qui corrobore.
corroboratory [kə'rɔbətɔri], *a.* corroboratif.
corroboree[1] [kə'rɔbəri], *s.* *Austr:* (*a*) (i) danse *f*, (ii) chant *m*, des aborigènes; (*b*) réunion *f*, festivité *f.*
corroboree[2], *v.i.* *Austr:* danser un *corroboree.*
corrode [kə'roud]. **1.** *v.tr.* corroder, attaquer (le métal); ronger (le métal, le cœur). **2.** *v.i.* se corroder.
corrodent [kə'roud(ə)nt], *s.* corrodant *m.*
corrodibility [kəroudi'biliti], **corrosibility** [kərouzi'biliti], *s.* corrodabilité *f.*
corrosion [kə'rouʒ(ə)n], *s.* corrosion *f*; **electrolytic c.,** corrosion électrolytique; **cracking c.,** corrosion fissurante; **c. on battery terminals,** sulfatage *m* des bornes; *Geol:* **karstic c.,** corrosion karstique.
corrosive [kə'rousiv], *a.* & *s.* corrosif (*m*), corrodant (*m*); **c. power,** pouvoir corrosif; **non-corrosive,** inoxydable.
corrosively [kə'rousivli], *adv.* corrosivement.
corrosiveness [kə'rousivnis], *s.* corrosiveté *f*; action corrosive; mordant *m*, mordacité *f* (d'un acide).
corrugate ['kɔrugeit]. **1.** *v.tr.* strier de nervures; rider, plisser (une surface); strier (le verre); onduler (la tôle); gaufrer (le papier). **2.** *v.i.* se plisser, se rider; onduler.
corrugated ['kɔrugeitid], *a.* ridé, plissé, rugueux; **c. glass,** verre strié, cannelé; **c. iron,** tôle ondulée, ridée; **c. iron roof,** toit en tôle ondulée; **c. paper,** papier ondulé, gaufré; **c. cardboard,** carton ondulé; **c. lens,** lentille *f* à gradins; lentille prismatique de Fresnel; **c. mirror,** miroir cannelé.
corrugating ['kɔrugeitiŋ], *s.* gaufrage *m* (du papier).
corrugation [kɔru'geiʃ(ə)n], *s.* plissement *m*, ondulation *f*, cannelure *f*, striure *f*, strie *f*, gaufrage *m*, rugosité *f*; **honeycomb c.,** gaufrage en nid d'abeilles.
corrugator ['kɔrugeitər], *s.* *Anat:* (muscle) corrugateur *m* (du front); (muscle) sourcilier *m.*
corrupt[1] [kə'rʌpt], *a.* corrompu; (*a*) **c. practices,** (i) tractations malhonnêtes; brigues *f*; abus *m*; (ii) trafic *m* d'influence; **c. press,** presse vénale; **c. administration (of funds, etc.),** déprédation *f*; (*b*) **c. text,** texte corrompu, altéré.
corrupt[2]. **1.** *v.tr.* corrompre, altérer (la viande, un texte, le caractère, etc.); démoraliser (qn); suborner (un témoin); **to c. youth,** dépraver, dévoyer, la jeunesse; **to c. the electorate,** corrompre, soudoyer, acheter, les électeurs; **to c. the world with unsound doctrines,** empoisonner le monde de mauvaises doctrines. **2.** *v.i.* se corrompre; (*a*) se putréfier; (*b*) se dépraver; (*c*) *O:* (*of language, etc.*) s'altérer.
corrupter [kə'rʌptər], *s.* corrupteur, -trice, démoralisateur, -trice.
corruptibility [kərʌptə'biliti], *s.* corruptibilité *f*; vénalité *f.*
corruptible [kə'rʌptəbl], *a.* corruptible; vénal, -aux.
corrupting [kə'rʌptiŋ], *a.* **1.** (*a*) corrompant; corruptif; corrupteur, -trice; (*b*) dépravant. **2.** en train de se putréfier; en putréfaction.
corruption [kə'rʌpʃ(ə)n], *s.* **1.** (*a*) corruption *f*, putréfaction *f*; (*b*) corruption, dépravation *f.* **2.** action *f* de corrompre; corruption; *Jur:* **c. of witnesses,** subornation *f* de témoins; **proof against c.,** incorruptible; **bribery and c.,** corruption, subornation; *Jur:* *A:* **c. of blood,** corruption du sang; mort civile.
corruptive [kə'rʌptiv], *a.* corruptif.
corruptly [kə'rʌptli], *adv.* d'une manière corrompue; par corruption; vénalement.
corruptness [kə'rʌptnis], *s.* corruption *f*; vénalité *f* (des juges, etc.).
corsage [kɔː'sɑːʒ], *s.* **1.** *Cost:* corsage *m.* **2.** boutonnière (portée au corsage).
corsair ['kɔːsɛər], *s.* **1.** corsaire *m* (navire ou marin). **2.** flibustier *m*, pirate *m.*

corsak ['kɔːsæk], *s. Z:* karagan *m*, corsac *m*.

corse [kɔːs], *s.* (*a*) *Lit: A:* cadavre *m*; (*b*) *Ecc: A:* **c. present,** droit *m* mortuaire.

corselet ['kɔːslet], *s.* **1.** *A.Arm: Ent:* corselet *m.* **2.** *Cost:* (*also* **corselette**) gaine-combinaison *f*, *pl.* gaines-combinaisons, combiné *m*.

corset[1] ['kɔːsit], *s. Cost:* **a c.,** *F: O:* **a pair of corsets,** un corset; **my corsets are hurting me,** mon corset me fait mal; **orthopaedic, surgical, c.,** corset orthopédique; **c. maker,** corsetier, -ière.

corset[2], *v.tr.* corseter (qn).

corsetry ['kɔːsitri], *s.* **1.** (i) fabrique *f*, (ii) vente *f*, de corsets. **2.** *coll.* corsets *mpl*.

Corsica ['kɔːsikə], *Pr.n. Geog:* la Corse.

Corsican ['kɔːsikən]. (*a*) *a. Geog:* corse; *Bot:* **C. pine, fir, larch,** pin *m* Laricio; (*b*) *s. Geog:* Corse *mf.*

corslet ['kɔːslet], *s.* = CORSELET.

cortège [kɔː'teʒ], *s.* **funeral c.,** convoi *m*, cortège *m*, funèbre.

Cortes (the) [ðə'kɔːtiːz], *s.pl.* les Cortès *f* (d'Espagne, du Portugal).

cortex, *pl.* **-ices** ['kɔːteks, -isiːz], *s.* (*a*) *Bot:* cortex *m*; écorce *f* (d'un arbre); (*b*) *Anat:* cortex (cérébral, surrénal).

cortical ['kɔːtikl], *a. Bot: Anat:* cortical, -aux.

corticate(d) ['kɔːtikeit(id)], *a. Bot:* cortiqué; couvert d'écorce.

cortication [kɔːti'keiʃ(ə)n], *s. Bot:* cortication *f.*

corticectomy [kɔːti'sektəmi], *s. Surg:* corticectomie *f.*

corticiferous [kɔːti'sifərəs], *a. Bot:* corticifère.

corticiform [kɔː'tisifɔːm], *a.* corticiforme.

corticin ['kɔːtisin], *s. Bot: Ch:* corticine *f.*

corticoid ['kɔːtikɔid], *s. Bio-Ch:* corticoïde *m*.

corticose ['kɔːtikous], **corticous** ['kɔːtikəs], *a. Bot:* cortiqueux.

corticosteroid ['kɔːtikou'sterɔid], *s. Bio-Ch:* corticostéroïde *m*.

corticosterone ['kɔːtikou'steroun], *s. Bio-Ch:* corticostérone *f.*

corticosurrenaloma ['kɔːtikousjuriːnə'loumə], *s. Med:* corticosurrénalome *m*.

corticotherapy [kɔːtikou'θerəpi], *s. Med:* corticothérapie *f.*

corticotrop(h)ic ['kɔːtikou'trɔpik, -'trɔfik], *a. Bio-Ch:* corticotrope.

corticotrop(h)in ['kɔːtikou'trɔpin, -'trɔfin], *s. Bio-Ch:* corticotrop(h)ine *f.*

cortin ['kɔːtin], *s. Bio-Ch:* cortine *f.*

cortina, *pl.* **-ae** ['kɔːtinə, -iː], *s. Fung:* cortine *f.*

cortisol ['kɔːtisɔl], *s. Bio-Ch:* cortisol *m*.

cortisone ['kɔːtizoun], *s. Bio-Ch: Med:* cortisone *f*; **c. derivatives,** dérivés *m* cortisoniques.

corundophilite [kɔrən'dɔfilait], *s. Miner:* corundophyllite *f.*

corundum [kə'rʌndəm], *s. Miner:* corindon *m*; spath adamantin; *Ind:* **c. wheel,** meule *f* en corindon.

Corunna [kə'rʌnə], *Pr.n. Geog:* la Corogne.

coruscant [kə'rʌskənt], *a.* = CORUSCATING.

coruscate ['kɔrəskeit], *v.i.* briller; scintiller.

coruscating ['kɔrəskeitiŋ], *a.* coruscant, scintillant.

coruscation [kɔrəs'keiʃ(ə)n], *s.* **1.** *Meteor: etc:* coruscation *f* (de l'aurore boréale, etc.). **2.** (*a*) vif éclat; (*b*) (*of metals*) éclair *m* d'argent; (*c*) *Lit:* **c. of wit,** paillettes *fpl* d'esprit.

corvette [kɔː'vet], *s. Nau:* corvette *f.*

Corvidae ['kɔːvidiː], *s.pl. Orn:* corvidés *m*, les corbeaux *m*.

corvine ['kɔːvain], *a. Orn:* corvin.

corvusite ['kɔːvəsait], *s. Miner:* corvusite *f.*

corybant, *pl.* **corybants, corybantes** ['kɔribænt(s), kɔri'bæntiːz], *s.* corybante *m*; prêtre *m* de Cybèle.

corybantiasm [kɔri'bæntiæzm], *s. Med:* corybantiasme *m*.

corybantic [kɔri'bæntik], *a.* corybantique; **c. frenzy,** corybantiasme *m*.

Corycia [kə'risiə], *A.Geog:* Coryce *f.*

Corycian [kə'risiən], *A.Geog:* (*a*) *a.* corycien; (*b*) *s.* Corycien, -ienne.

corycium [kə'risiəm], *s. Geol:* corycium *m*.

Corydalidae [kɔri'dælidiː], *s.pl. Ent:* corydalidés *m*.

corydalis [kɔ'ridəlis], *s.* **1.** *Bot:* corydale *m*, corydal(l)is *m.* **2.** *Ent:* = CORYDALUS.

corydalus [kə'ridələs], *s. Ent:* corydale *m*, corydal(l)is *m*.

Corydon ['kɔridən], *Pr.n.m. Lit:* Corydon; berger (de pastorale).

corylus ['kɔriləs], *s. Bot:* corylus *m*.

corymb ['kɔrimb], *s. Bot:* corymbe *m*.

corymbiferous [kɔrim'bifərəs], *a. Bot:* corymbifère, corymbiflore.

corymbiform [kɔ'rimbifɔːm], *a.* corymbiforme.

corymbose [kɔrim'bous], **corymbous** [kɔ'rimbəs], *a. Bot:* corymbé, corymbeux.

corynebacterium, *pl.* **-ia** ['kɔrinibæk'tiːriəm, -iə], *s.* corynébactérie *f*, corynébactérium *m*.

coryphaeus [kɔri'fiːəs], *s.* **1.** coryphée *m* (du théâtre antique). **2.** coryphée; chef *m* d'école, de secte, de parti.

coryphodon [kɔ'rifədən], *s. Paleont:* coryphodon *m*.

corystes [kɔ'ristiːz], *s. Crust:* coryste(s) *m*.

coryza [kə'raizə], *s. Med:* coryza *m*; rhume *m* de cerveau.

Cos[1] [kɔs]. (*a*) *Pr.n. Geog:* (l'île *f* de) Cos; (*b*) *s. Hort:* **c. (lettuce),** (laitue) romaine *f*, *F:* chicon *m*.

cos[2], *s. Mth: F:* (= **cosine**) cos *m*.

cosalite ['kouzəlait], *s. Miner:* cosalite *f.*

cose [kouz], *v.i. F:* se douilletter (au coin du feu, etc.); lézarder (au soleil).

cosecant ['kou'siːk(ə)nt], *s. Mth:* (*F:* **cosec** ['kousek]) cosécante *f*, *F:* cosec.

coseismal [kou'saizm(ə)l], *a. Geol:* cosismal, -aux; **c. line,** cosiste *f.*

cosh[1] [kɔʃ], *s. F:* matraque *f*, assommoir *m*; nerf *m* de bœuf; **c. boy, bandit,** matraqueur *m*; *A:* **c. carrier,** souteneur *m*, *P:* marlou *m*.

cosh[2] [kɔʃ], *v.tr. F:* assommer, matraquer (qn); frapper (qn) avec un assommoir; asséner un coup sur la tête de (qn).

cosh[3] [kɔs'eitʃ, kɔʃ], *s. Mth:* cosinus *m* hyperbolique, ch.

cosher ['kɔʃər, 'kou-], *a. Jew. Rel:* casher, cawcher.

co-signatory ['kou'signət(ə)ri], *a. & s.* cosignataire (*mf*).

cosily ['kouzili], *adv.* confortablement; bien au chaud; douillettement; **c. wrapped up,** enveloppé frileusement.

Cosimo ['kɔsimou], *Pr.n.m.* Cosme.

cosine ['kousain], *s. Mth:* cosinus *m*; **c. curve,** cosinusoïde *f.*

cosiness ['kouzinis], *s.* confortable *m* (d'un fauteuil, d'un petit coin intime); chaleur *f* agréable (du coin du feu, etc.).

Cosmas ['kɔsməs], *Pr.n.m. Ecc.Hist:* Cosme.

cosmetic [kɔz'metik], *a. & s.* cosmétique (*m*); *s.pl.* **cosmetics,** produits *m* de beauté; **c. surgery,** chirurgie *f* esthétique.

cosmetician [kɔzme'tiʃ(ə)n], *s.* esthéticien, -ienne.

cosmetologist [kɔzme'tɔlədʒist], *s.* cosmétologiste *mf.*

cosmetology [kɔzme'tɔlədʒi], *s.* cosmétologie *f.*

cosmia ['kɔzmiə], *s. Ent:* cosmie *f*, cosmia *f.*

cosmic ['kɔzmik], *a.* (*a*) cosmique; **c. rays,** rayons *m* cosmiques; **c. radiation,** rayonnement *m* cosmique; **c. dust,** poussières *f* cosmiques; (*b*) vaste, immense, infini; **this c. boredom,** cet ennui qui envahit tout.

cosmical ['kɔzmikl], *a. Astr:* **c. rising, setting, of a star,** lever *m*, coucher *m*, cosmique d'une étoile.

cosmo- ['kɔzmou, kɔz'mɔ], *pref.* cosmo-.

cosmobiology ['kɔzmoubai'ɔlədʒi], *s.* cosmobiologie *f.*

cosmodrome ['kɔzmoudroum], *s. Space:* cosmodrome *m*.

cosmogenic [kɔzmou'dʒenik], *a.* cosmogénique.

cosmogeny [kɔz'mɔdʒəni], *s.* cosmogénie *f.*

cosmogonic [kɔzmou'gɔnik], *a.* cosmogonique.

cosmogony [kɔz'mɔgəni], *s.* cosmogonie *f.*

cosmographer [kɔz'mɔgrəfər], *s.* cosmographe *m*.

cosmographic(al) [kɔzmou'græfik(l)], *a.* cosmographique.

cosmography [kɔz'mɔgrəfi], *s.* cosmographie *f.*

cosmological [kɔzmou'lɔdʒikl], *a.* cosmologique.

cosmologist [kɔz'mɔlədʒist], *s.* cosmologue *m*, cosmologiste *m*.

cosmology [kɔz'mɔlədʒi], *s.* cosmologie *f.*

cosmonaut ['kɔzmounɔːt], *s.* cosmonaute *mf.*

cosmonautics [kɔzmou'nɔːtiks], *s.pl.* (*usu. with sg. const.*) cosmonautique *f.*

cosmonette ['kɔzmounet], *s.* cosmonette *f.*

cosmopolis [kɔz'mɔpəlis], *s.* cité *f* cosmopolite.

cosmopolitan [kɔzmə'pɔlit(ə)n], *a. & s.* cosmopolite (*mf*).

cosmopolit(an)ism [kɔzmə'pɔlit(ən)izm], *s.* cosmopolitisme *m*.

cosmopolite [kɔz'mɔpəlait]. **1.** *s.* cosmopolite *mf.* **2.** *Occ.a.* = COSMOPOLITAN.

cosmorama [kɔzmə'rɑːmə], *s.* cosmorama *m*.

cosmos ['kɔzmɔs], *s.* **1.** cosmos *m*; **the c.,** l'univers *m.* **2.** *Bot:* cosmos.

cosmotron ['kɔzmoutrɔn], *s. Atom.Ph:* cosmotron *m*.

Cossack ['kɔsæk], *a. & s.* **1.** cosaque (*mf*); *Mil: A:* **C. post,** avant-poste *m* à la Cosaque. **2.** *pl. Com: A:* **cossacks,** pantalon (bouffant).

cosset[1] ['kɔsit], *s.* agneau élevé au biberon; agneau favori.

cosset[2], *v.tr.* dorloter, choyer, gâter, câliner, chouchouter (qn).

cossette [kɔ'set], *s. Sug.-R:* cossette *f* (de betterave).

Cossidae ['kɔsidiː], *s.pl. Ent:* cossidés *m*.

cossus ['kɔsəs], *s. Ent:* cossus *m*.

cost[1] [kɔst], *s.* **1.** coût *m*, frais *mpl*; **c. of living,** coût de la vie; **increased c. of living,** renchérissement *m* de la vie; **c.-of-living allowance, bonus,** indemnité *f* de cherté de vie, de vie chère; **the c. of an undertaking,** les frais d'une entreprise; **costs to be borne by . . .,** frais à la charge de . . .; **at the c. of one's life,** au prix de sa vie; **at a c. of much time, trouble,** au prix de beaucoup de temps, de peine; avec beaucoup de peine; **at little c.,** à peu de frais; **at great c.,** à grands frais; au prix de dépenses énormes; **at such great c.,** si coûteusement; **at any c., at all costs,** à tout prix; à toute force; coûte que coûte, vaille que vaille; **without c.,** sans frais, sans dépens; **I learnt it to my c.,** je l'ai appris à mes dépens, à mon détriment, pour mon malheur; j'ai payé, je suis payé, pour le savoir; **I tried to help him, to my c.,** j'ai voulu l'aider, mais il m'en a coûté; **they spare no c.,** ils ne regardent pas à la dépense; **to do sth. without counting the c.,** faire qch. sans considérer (i) la dépense, (ii) le danger, (iii) l'effort à fournir; *Ind: Com:* **first c., prime c.,** coût premier; prix initial; **actual c., net c., c. price,** prix de revient; prix d'achat; prix coûtant; **gross c.,** prix de revient brut; **to sell at c.,** vendre au prix coûtant; **to sell under c. price,** vendre à perte; **c. analysis,** analyse *f* des coûts; **c.-effectiveness analysis,** étude *f* de coût et d'efficacité; **c.-benefit analysis,** analyse des coûts et rendements; **operating costs,** frais d'exploitation; **c., insurance and freight,** coût, assurance, fret (CAF); **c. keeping,** comptabilité *f* de prix coûtants; **c. account,** compte *m* des charges; **c. book,** livre *m* de(s) charges; *St.Exch:* **c. of a share,** valeur *f* d'achat d'une action; **c. of acquisition and disposal (of securities),** frais d'acquisition et de cession (de titres). **2.** *pl. Jur:* frais d'instance; dépens *mpl*; **court costs,** frais de justice; **to carry costs,** entraîner les dépens; **to allow costs,** accorder les frais et dépens; **to pay costs,** payer, acquitter, les condamnations, les frais et dépens; **they were ordered to pay costs, costs were given against them,** ils furent condamnés aux frais; **order to pay costs,** exécutoire *m* de dépens; **untaxable costs,** faux frais.

cost[2]. **1.** *v.i. & tr.* **(cost; cost)** coûter; **how much does it c.?** combien cela coûte-t-il? **it costs five pounds,** cela coûte cinq livres; **his house has cost him £30,000,** sa maison lui revient à £30,000; **that will c. him a great deal of money, of trouble,** cela lui coûtera beaucoup d'argent, beaucoup de peine; *P:* **that'll c. you!** ça vous reviendra cher! **the ten pounds which the clock c. me,** les dix livres que la pendule m'a coûté; **to c. a fortune, a pretty penny, the earth,** coûter un argent fou, coûter les yeux de la tête; **those things c. money,** ces choses-là se paient; **the attempt c. him his life,** cette tentative lui coûta la vie; **the battle c. 2000 men their lives,** la bataille coûta la vie à 2000 hommes; **it c. him an arm,** il lui en a coûté un bras; **to c. s.o. dearly,** coûter cher à qn; **c. what it may,** coûte que coûte; **it must have c. him something to admit that,** il a dû lui en coûter de l'avouer; **it merely c. me a little politeness,** j'en ai été quitte pour une petite politesse. **2.** *v.tr.* **(costed; costed)** *Com: Ind:* **to c. an article,** établir le prix de revient d'un article; **to c. a job,** évaluer le coût d'une entreprise, d'un travail.

costal ['kɔstl], *a. Anat:* costal, -aux; **c. respiration,** respiration costale.

costar[1] ['koustɑːr], *s. Cin: etc:* acteur, actrice, qui partage la vedette avec un(e) autre.

costar[2], *v.i. Cin: etc:* partager la vedette.

costard ['kɔstəd], *s. Hort:* grosse pomme côtelée.

costate ['kɔsteit], *a. Nat.Hist:* à côtes.

costean [kɔs'tiːn], *v.i. Min:* (*in Cornwall*) opérer des trous de prospection, des sondages.

costectomy [kɔs'tektəmi], *s. Surg:* costectomie *f.*

coster(monger) ['kɔstər ('kɔstəmʌŋgər)], *s.* marchand ambulant (de fruits, de poisson, etc.); marchand des quatre saisons; **coster's cart,** baladeuse *f*; voiture *f* à bras.

costiasis [kɔs'taiəsis], *s. Ich:* costiase *f.*

costing ['kɔstiŋ], *s. Ind: Com:* établissement *m* du, des, prix de revient; évaluation *f* du coût; **c. department,** bureau *m* de prix.

costive ['kɔstiv], *a.* **1.** (*a*) constipé; (*b*) *A:* au travail laborieux. **2.** *A:* ladre, pingre; dur à la détente.

costiveness ['kɔstivnis], *s.* **1.** (*a*) constipation *f*; (*b*) *A:* manque *m* de facilité. **2.** *A:* pingrerie *f.*

costless ['kɔstlis], *a.* qui ne coûte rien; sans frais; gratis *inv.*

costliness ['kɔstlinis], *s.* **1.** richesse *f*, somptuosité *f* (de l'ameublement, etc.). **2.** haut prix, prix élevé, cherté *f.*

costly ['kɔstli], *a.* **1.** (*a*) précieux, de grand prix; (*b*) (ameublement, etc.) riche, somptueux; de luxe. **2.** coûteux, dispendieux, cher.
costmary ['kɔstmɛəri], *s. Bot:* balsamite *f*; baume *m* des jardins; herbe *f* au coq; menthe-coq *f*.
costo- ['kɔstou], *pref. Anat:* costo-.
costo-abdominal ['kɔstouæb'dɔminl], *a. & s.* costo-abdominal (*m*), *pl.* costo-abdominaux.
costotome ['kɔstətoum], *s. Surg:* costotome *m*.
cost-saver ['kɔstseivər], *s.* économiseur *m*; **to be a c.-s.,** être économique.
costula, *pl.* **-ae** ['kɔstjulə, -i:], *s. Moll: etc:* costule *f*.
costume[1] ['kɔstjum], *s.* costume *m*; (*a*) **national c.,** costume national; **c. jewellery,** bijoux *m* de fantaisie; *Th:* **c. play,** pièce historique; (*b*) **bathing c.,** costume, maillot *m*, de bain; *O:* **(lady's tailormade) c.,** (costume) tailleur *m*.
costume[2] ['kɔstjum, kɔs'tju:m], *v.tr.* costumer (qn, *Th:* une pièce).
costum(i)er [kɔs'tju:m(i)ər], *s.* costumier *m*; **theatrical c.,** costumier de théâtre.
cosurety ['kou'sjurəti], *s. Jur:* cofidéjusseur *m*.
cosy ['kouzi]. **1.** *a.* (*of place, thg*) chaud, confortable, commode; (*of pers.*) bien au chaud; installé douillettement; à l'aise; **c. room,** pièce confortable, douillette; **c. little house,** petite maison sympathique, confortable; **it's c., cosier, here,** il fait bon, meilleur, ici; *F:* **a c. little job,** un lit de plumes; une sinécure; un filon; un bon petit fromage. **2.** *s.* (*a*) **egg c.,** cosy *m* (pour œufs à la coque); **tea c.,** couvre-théière *m*, chauffe-théière *m*, *pl.* couvre-, chauffe-théières; (*b*) *Furn: A:* causeuse *f*.
cot[1] [kɔt], *s.* **1.** *esp. Poet:* (*a*) petite maison; (*thatched*) chaumière *f*; (*b*) cabane *f*. **2.** (*a*) abri *m*; **bell c.,** abri en porte-à-faux pour cloches; (*b*) *NAm: Med:* doigtier *m*.
cot[2], *s.* **1.** lit *m* d'enfant, lit à galerie; **basket c.,** moïse *m*; **basket c. on wheels,** berceau, chariot, alsacien; **c. death,** mort inattendue d'un enfant (dans son lit). **2.** (*a*) *esp. NAm:* petit lit (pliant); lit de camp; **c. bed,** lit (étroit) à une personne; *Med: F:* **c. case,** malade alité; (*b*) *Nau:* cadre *m*, couchette *f*; hamac *m* à cadre, à l'anglaise.
cot[3], *s. Mth: F:* (= **cotangent**) cot *f*.
cotangent ['kou'tæn(d)ʒ(ə)nt], *s. Mth:* cotangente *f*.
cote [kout], *s.* **1.** *Scot: A:* petite ferme. **2.** (*a*) colombier *m*, pigeonnier *m*; (*b*) abri *m*; **bell c.,** abri en porte-à-faux pour cloches.
cotehardie ['kout(h)ɑ:di], *s. A.Cost:* cotte-hardie *f*, *pl.* cottes-hardies.
cotenant ['kou'tenənt], *s.* colocataire *mf*.
coterie ['koutəri], *s.* coterie *f*; *Lit: Art:* petite église, petite chapelle (de disciples); cénacle *m* (littéraire, etc.).
cothurnus [kou'θə:nəs], *s. Ant:* cothurne *m*.
cotidal ['kou'taidl], *a.* cotidal, -aux; (ligne *f*) des marées simultanées.
cotill(i)on[1] [kə'tiljən], *s. Danc:* **1.** cotillon *m*. **2.** *U.S:* quadrille *m*.
cotill(i)on[2], *v.i.* **1.** cotillonner. **2.** *U.S:* danser le quadrille.
cotinga [kou'tiŋgə], *s. Orn:* cotinga *m*.
cotise ['kɔtis], *s. Her:* cotice *f*.
cotised ['kɔtist], *a. Her:* coticé.
cotoneaster [kətouni'æstər], *s. Bot:* cotonéaster *m*.
co-trustee ['koutrʌs'ti:], *s. Jur:* coadministrateur, -trice.
cottage ['kɔtidʒ], *s.* (*a*) petite maison (à la campagne); **thatched c.,** chaumière *f*; **country c.,** cottage *m*; **weekend c., c. in the country,** résidence *f* secondaire; **c. industry,** artisanat *m*; industrie artisanale; **c. loaf** = pain *m* de ménage; **c. cheese,** fromage blanc; **c. hospital,** hôpital *m* de médecine générale (où on ne traite pas les cas sérieux); (*b*) *Austr:* maison sans étage.
cottager ['kɔtidʒər], *s.* villageois, -oise (qui habite une petite maison de campagne).
cottar[1], **cotter**[1] ['kɔtər], *s. Scot:* **1.** = COTTAGER. **2.** valet *m* de ferme (locataire d'une des maisons de la propriété).
cottar[2], **cotter**[2], *s. Mec.E: etc:* **c. (pin),** clavette *f*, goupille *f*; **c(-shaped) c.,** goupille en C; **split c.,** goupille fendue; clavette à fourche; **to remove the c. from a nut,** dégoupiller un écrou; **c. bolt,** boulon *m* à clavette; **c. joint,** agrafe *f* à clavette; **c. plate,** bride *f*; **c. wire,** fil *m* pour goupilles; *Tls:* **c. driver,** chasse-clavette *m*, *pl.* chasse-clavettes; **c. puller,** arrache-clavettes *m inv*.
cotter[3], *v.tr. Mec.E:* claveter; goupiller; caler (une pièce); **to c. a pin into a slot,** claveter une goupille dans une mortaise; **cottered joint,** assemblage *m* par clavette en coin; **to c. a nut,** goupiller un écrou.
cottering ['kɔtəriŋ], *s.* clavet(t)age *m*; goupillage *m*; calage *m*.
cotterite ['kɔtərait], *s. Miner:* cottérite *f*.
cotterpin ['kɔtəpin], *v.tr. Mec.E:* claveter, goupiller.
Cottian ['kɔtiən], *a. Geog:* (Alpes) Cottiennes.
Cottidae ['kɔtidi:], *s.pl. Ich:* cottidés *m*.
cottise ['kɔtis], *s. Her:* cotice *f*.
cotton[1] ['kɔtn], *s.* **1.** (*a*) *Bot:* **c. (plant),** cotonnier *m*; **c. plantation,** cotonnerie *f*; (*b*) coton *m*; **black-seed c., long-staple c.,** coton (en) longue soie; **green-seed c., short-staple c.,** coton (en) courte soie; **raw c.,** coton brut; **c. growing,** culture *f* du coton; cotonnerie; **the c. regions,** les régions cotonnières; *U.S:* **c. belt,** région du coton; **c. industry,** industrie cotonnière; **c. mill,** filature *f* de coton; cotonnerie; **c. trade,** commerce *m* des cotons; **c. broker,** courtier *m* en coton; *Pharm:* **c. wool,** *U.S:* **absorbent c.,** ouate *f* (de coton), coton hydrophile; *F:* **he's been wrapped up in c. wool,** on l'a élevé dans du coton, dans une boîte; **my legs feel like c. wool,** j'ai, je me sens, les jambes en coton; **c. waste,** déchets *mpl*, bourre *f*, de coton; chiffons *mpl*; étoupe *f*, chiffons, de nettoyage; *Husb:* **c. cake,** tourteau *m* (de graines de coton); (*c*) *Bot:* **c. tree,** bombax *m*, fromager *m*; **silk c.,** bombycine *f*; **c. grass,** linaigrette *f*; lin *m* des marais; **c. thistle,** (i) chardonnette *f*; chardon *m* aux ânes; (ii) onoporde *f*, acanthe *f* sauvage; (*d*) *Ent:* **c. moth,** noctuelle *f* du coton; (*e*) *U.S: Comest:* **c. candy,** barbe *f* à papa. **2.** *Tex:* (*a*) **c. yarn,** coton filé; fil *m* de coton; (*b*) **c. goods, stuffs,** tissus *m* de coton; cotonnades *f*; **c. (cloth),** (toile *f* de) coton; cotonnade, percale *f*, percaline *f*; **coarse c.,** rouennerie *f*; **printed c., c. print,** coton imprimé; indienne *f*; **c. printer,** rouennier *m*; **c. spinner,** (i) (*owner*) filateur *m* de coton; (ii) (*worker*) fileur, -euse, de coton; cotonnier, -ière; (iii) *Echin:* holothurie *f*; **c. canvas,** cotonnerie. **3.** *Dom.Ec:* **sewing c.,** fil à coudre; fil d'Écosse; fil de coton; **sewing machine c.,** câblé *m*; **embroidery c.,** coton à broder.
cotton[2], *v.i.* **1.** *A:* (*of material, etc.*) (se) cotonner. **2.** *F: O:* **to c. (with s.o.),** s'accorder, faire bon ménage (avec qn). **3.** *A:* **to c. up to s.o.,** faire des avances à qn. **4.** (*a*) *F:* **to c. (on) to s.o.,** se sentir attiré par qn; prendre qn en amitié; (*b*) **to c. on to (s.o.),** s'attacher à (qn). **5.** *F:* (*a*) **to c. on to sth.,** piger qch.; **I don't c. on,** je n'y suis pas; **I don't c. on to what he's up to,** je ne pige pas ce qu'il veut faire; (*b*) **to c. on to s.o.,** pénétrer les intentions de qn.
cotton-covered ['kɔtnkʌvəd], *a. El:* (fil) à guipage en coton, guipé coton.
cottonmouth ['kɔtnmauθ], *s. Rept:* mocassin *m* d'eau.
cotton-picking ['kɔtnpikiŋ], *a. U.S: P:* sale, fichu.
cottonseed ['kɔtnsi:d], *s.* graine *f* de coton; **c. oil,** huile *f* de coton.
cottontail ['kɔtnteil], *s. U.S:* lapin *m* (de garenne).
cottonweed ['kɔtnwi:d], *s. Bot:* cotonnière *f*.
cottonwood ['kɔtnwud], *s.* **1.** *Bot:* (variété *f* de) peuplier *m*; **river c., swamp c.,** peuplier des marais; **black c.,** peuplier du Canada. **2.** bois *m* de peuplier.
cottony ['kɔtni], *a.* cotonneux.
cottus ['kɔtəs], *s. Ich:* cotte *m*.
cotula ['kɔtjulə], *s. Bot:* cotule *f*.
cotunnite [kə'tʌnait], *s. Miner:* cotunnite *f*.
cotyle ['kɔtili], *s. Gr.Ant: Anat:* cotyle *f*.
cotyledon [kɔti'li:d(ə)n], *s.* **1.** *Bot:* cotylédon *m*. **2.** *Anat: Z:* cotylédon.
cotyledonary [kɔti'li:dən(ə)ri], *a.* cotylédonaire.
cotyledonous [kɔti'li:dənəs], *a.* cotylédoné.
cotyligerous [kɔti'lidʒərəs], *a.* cotylifère.
cotyloid ['kɔtilɔid], *a. Anat: Ent:* cotyloïde; *Anat:* **the c. cavity,** la cavité cotyloïde (où s'emboîte l'os du fémur).
cotylosaur ['kɔtilousɔ:r], *s. Paleont:* cotylosaurien *m*.
Cotylosauria [kɔtilou'sɔ:riə], *s.pl. Paleont:* cotylosauriens *m*.
cotype ['koutaip], *s. Biol:* cotype *m*.
coua ['ku:ɔ], *s. Orn:* coua *m*.
coucal ['ku:kl], *s. Orn:* coucal *m*.
couch[1] [kautʃ], *s.* **1.** *Lit: Poet:* lit *m*, couche *f*. **2.** *Furn:* canapé *m*, divan *m*; lit de repos; **S-shaped c.,** vis-à-vis *m inv*; **studio c.,** banquette-lit *f*, *pl.* banquettes-lits. **3.** *Brew:* couche, lit (de grains). **4.** *esp. NAm:* couche (de peinture, etc.).
couch[2]. **1.** *v.tr.* (*a*) *Lit:* (*of pers., animal*) **to be couched on the ground,** être couché par terre; (*b*) *Brew:* coucher (le grain); mettre (le grain) en couche; *Paperm:* coucher (une feuille) sur les feutres; *Needlew:* **couched threads,** fils couchés; *A:* **garment couched with gold,** vêtement brodé d'or; (*c*) mettre (sa lance) en arrêt; (*d*) *Surg:* faire une kératotomie; *F:* enlever, extraire, une cataracte; (*e*) *A: & Adm:* **to c. a request in writing,** coucher une demande par écrit; **to c. a demand in certain terms,** rédiger une réclamation en certains termes; **the letter was couched in these terms,** la lettre était ainsi conçue, ainsi rédigée. **2.** *v.i. A: & Lit:* (*a*) (*of animal*) se coucher, être couché (dans sa tanière, etc.); se terrer; gîter; (*b*) (*of dog, pers.*) se tapir (devant qn); (*of pers.*) courber l'échine; s'aplatir; (*c*) (*of animal, pers.*) se tapir (pour se dérober à la vue); (*of pers.*) se tenir embusqué.
couch[3] **(grass)** ['ku:tʃ(grɑ:s), 'kautʃ-], *s. Bot:* chiendent *m* (officinal, des boutiques).
couchant ['kautʃənt], *a. Her:* couché; accroupi.
couché ['ku:ʃei], *a. Her:* (chevron) couché.
couched [kautʃt], *a.* **1.** *Her:* couché; **chevron c.,** chevron couché. **2.** *Needlew:* **c. threads,** fils couchés.
coucher ['kautʃər], *s. Paperm:* (*pers.*) coucheur *m*, couchart *m*.
couchette [ku'ʃet], *s. Trans:* couchette *f*.
couching ['kautʃiŋ], *s.* **1.** *Surg:* kératotomie *f*. **2.** *Needlew:* broderie *f* sur fils couchés. **3.** *Paperm:* **c. felt,** (feutre) coucheur *m*.
Couéism ['ku:eiizm], *s. Med:* couéisme *m*.
cougar ['ku:gər], *s. Z:* couguar *m*, puma *m*; lion *m* d'Amérique.
cough[1] [kɔf], *s.* toux *f*; **to have a c.,** tousser; **to have a bad c.,** avoir une mauvaise toux; **dry c.,** toux sèche; **loose c.,** toux grasse; **spasmodic c.,** toux férine; *F:* **churchyard c.,** toux qui sent le sapin; **whooping c.,** coqueluche *f*; **he gave a c. to warn me,** il toussa pour m'avertir; **c. mixture,** sirop *m* contre la toux; **c. drop, lozenge,** pastille pectorale, contre la toux; *P: A:* **he's a c. drop,** c'est un numéro, un drôle de type.
cough[2]. **1.** *v.i.* (*of pers., of animal, F: of engine*) tousser. **2.** *v.tr.* **to c. up, out, sth.,** cracher qch. (en toussant); **to c. up phlegm,** cracher des glaires; tousser gras; **to c. up blood,** cracher du, le, sang; *F:* **to c. up money,** *v.i.* **to c. up,** payer, *P:* cracher; **I had to c. up a hundred francs,** il m'a fallu cracher cent francs; **c. it up!** mais accouche donc!
coughing ['kɔfiŋ], *s.* toux *f*; **fit of c.,** accès *m*, quinte *f*, de toux.
couldn't-care-less ['kudntkɛə'les], *a.* **c.-c.-l. attitude,** je-m'en-fichisme *m*, je-m'en-foutisme *m*.
coulee, coulie ['ku:li:], **coulée** ['ku:lei], *s. Geol:* **1.** coulée *f* de lave. **2.** *U.S:* ravin *m*.
couloir ['ku:lwɑ:r], *s. Geog:* couloir *m*, ravin *m*.
coulomb ['ku:lɔm], *s. El.Meas:* coulomb *m*.
coulom(b)meter [ku'lɔmitər], *s.* coulombmètre *m*; voltamètre *m*.
coulter ['koultər], *s. Agr:* coutre *m* (de charrue); **skim c.,** rasette *f*.
coumalic [ku'mælik], *a. Ch:* coumalique.
coumalin(e) ['ku:məl(ə)in], *s. Ch:* coumaline *f*.
coumaran(e) ['ku:mərən], *s. Ch:* coumaranne *m*.
coumaric [ku'mærik], *a. Ch:* coumarique.
coumarin(e) ['ku:mər(a)in], *s. Ch:* coumarine *f*.
coumarinic [kumə'rinik], *a. Ch:* coumarinique.
coumarone ['ku:məroun], *s. Ch:* coumarone *f*; **c. resin,** résine *f* de coumarone.
coumarou ['ku:məru:], *s. Bot:* coumarou(na) *m*.
council ['kaunsəl], *s.* **1.** conseil *m*; *Adm:* **district c.** = conseil municipal; *Hist:* **rural district c.** = conseil municipal (d'un groupe de petites communes); **town, borough, city, urban district, municipal, c.,** conseil municipal; *A:* **c. school** = école communale; **c. house** = habitation *f* à loyer modéré, H.L.M.; **the Court of Common C.,** le conseil municipal de la Cité de Londres; **county c.,** conseil général, conseil départemental; **to hold c.; to be, meet, in c.,** tenir conseil; tenir chapitre; **c. chamber,** chambre *f*, salle *f*, du conseil; **C. of State,** Conseil d'État; **cabinet c.,** conseil de cabinet, des ministres; **order in C.** = décret présidentiel, arrêté ministériel; décret-loi *m*, *pl.* décrets-lois; **the King, Queen, Crown, in C.,** le Conseil privé; **the Privy C.,** le Conseil privé (du souverain); **the Army C.,** le Conseil supérieur de la Guerre; **C. of Europe,** Conseil de l'Europe; *Hist:* **the Supreme War C.,** le Conseil supérieur interallié; (*of higher command, etc.*) **to hold a c. of war,** se réunir en conseil; délibérer; *Pol.Ec:* **consumer c.,** comité (consultatif) des consommateurs. **2.** (*a*) *Ecc:* concile *m* (œcuménique, etc.); **the C. of Trent,** le concile de Trente; (*b*) *B:* (le) conseil.
councillor ['kaunsilər], *s.* conseiller *m*; membre *m* du conseil; **county c.** = conseiller général.
councillorship ['kaunsiləʃip], *s.* **1.** dignité *f* de conseiller. **2.** période *f* d'exercice des fonctions de conseiller.
counsel[1] ['kauns(ə)l], *s.* **1.** délibération *f*; consultation *f*; **to take c. with s.o.,** (i) prendre conseil de qn; (ii) délibérer, consulter, avec qn; se concerter avec qn **(about,** sur); **to take c. (together),** se consulter, se concerter. **2.** conseil *m*, avis *m*; *Theol:* **evangelical counsels, counsels of perfection,** les conseils évangéliques, les conseils de perfection; *Lit:* **c. of perfection,** idéal *m* difficile à atteindre. **3.** dessein *m*, in-

tention *f*; **to keep one's (own) c.,** garder ses projets pour soi; garder le secret; observer le silence; ne pas parler; ne pas bavarder; se taire; **keep your own c.,** (i) n'en parlez à personne; (ii) laissez dire. **4.** *Jur:* (*a*) avocat *m*; conseil *m*; avocat-conseil *m, pl.* avocats-conseils; **to hear c. on both sides,** entendre les avocats des deux parties; **to act as c. for s.o.,** plaider la cause de qn; **to be represented by c.,** comparaître par avoué; **c. in chambers, chamber c.,** avocat consultant; **c. for the defence,** défenseur *m*; (*in civil law*) avocat du défendeur, de la défense; **junior c.,** avocat en second; **counsel's opinion,** consultation écrite délivrée par un avocat; avis motivé; **to take counsel's opinion,** consulter un avocat, un conseiller juridique; (*b*) **King's, Queen's, c.,** conseiller du Roi, de la Reine; conseiller de la Couronne; (*c*) *coll.* (i) le barreau; les avocats; (ii) **the King's, Queen's, C.,** le Conseil de la Couronne.

counsel[2], *v.tr.* **(counselled)** *Lit:* **1.** recommander (une ligne de conduite); **he counselled patience,** il (me, nous) recommanda la patience. **2. to c. s.o. to do sth.,** conseiller, recommander, à qn de faire qch.

counsellor ['kauns(ə)lər], *s.* (*a*) *Dipl:* conseiller *m* d'ambassade; (*b*) conseiller *m* (qui offre des conseils); **he proved a wise c.,** ses conseils m'ont été précieux; je me suis trouvé bien d'avoir suivi ses conseils; les événements ont démontré la sagesse de ses conseils.

count[1] [kaunt], *s.* **1.** (*a*) compte *m*, calcul *m*; (*of votes*) dépouillement *m*; (*of people*) dénombrement *m*; **to keep c. of. . .,** compter, énumérer . . .; tenir le compte de. . .; **to lose c.,** perdre le compte; s'embrouiller; **to lose c. of time,** perdre la notion du temps; oublier les heures; **they lost all c. of time while chatting,** elles s'oublièrent à bavarder; **to ask for a c.,** demander le scrutin; *Med:* **blood c.,** dénombrement des hématies; numération *f* globulaire; **blood-count cell,** hématimètre *m*; (*b*) total *m*; **this is short of the c.,** cela ne fait pas le compte; le total n'y est pas; (*c*) *Cmptr:* comptage *m*; nombre *m*; **c. field,** zone *f* de comptage; **c.-controlled loop,** boucle d'itération commandée par compteur. **2.** *Jur:* **counts of an indictment,** chefs *m* d'accusation; **the most important c.,** le premier chef. **3.** (*House of Commons*) **c. out,** ajournement *m* (quand il y a moins de quarante membres présents). **4.** *Tex:* numéro *m* (du fil). **5.** *Box:* compte (de dix secondes); **to take the c. (out),** rester sur le plancher pour le compte; *F:* **to be out for the c.,** (i) avoir son compte; (ii) être profondément endormi.

count[2], *v.*

I. *v.tr. & i.* **1.** *v.tr.* (*a*) compter; **to c. the cost,** compter, calculer, la dépense; *v.i.* **to c. up to ten,** compter jusqu'à dix; **to c. up sth.,** compter, faire le compte de, qch.; **to c. one's flocks,** dénombrer, prendre le nombre de, ses troupeaux; (*at election*) **to c. the votes,** compter, recenser, les votes; dépouiller le scrutin; **without counting . . .,** sans compter . . .; **counting from tomorrow . . .,** à compter de demain . . .; (*b*) **to c. s.o. among one's friends,** compter qn parmi ses amis; **to c. s.o. among the greatest writers,** mettre qn au rang des plus grands écrivains; (*c*) **to c. s.o., sth., (to be) sth.,** tenir qn, qch., pour qch.; **to c. s.o. as dead,** compter qn pour mort; **to be counted as a member,** être compté au nombre des membres; **I c. it an honour to . . .,** je considère comme un honneur de . . .. **2.** *v.i.* (*a*) **to c. on doing sth.,** compter faire qch.; **to c. without one's host,** compter sans son hôte; (*b*) **to c. on, upon, s.o., sth.,** compter sur qn, qch.; faire son compte de qch.; faire fond sur qch.; **I am counting on you to help me,** je compte sur vous pour m'aider; **to c. on human foolishness,** compter, faire fond, sur la bêtise humaine; **I can c. on his protection,** sa protection m'est acquise; **don't c. on me,** ne comptez pas sur moi; (*c*) *v.tr.* **he counted me out twenty £1 notes,** il m'a compté un à un vingt billets d'une livre; *Box:* **to be counted out,** rester sur le plancher pour le compte; *F:* être compté dehors; *Pol:* **to c. out the House,** ajourner la Chambre faute d'un quorum; **(you can) c. me out,** ne comptez pas sur moi; je ne vous accompagnerai pas; je ne serai pas des vôtres; **c. me in,** vous pouvez compter sur moi; je serai des vôtres. **3.** *v.i.* (*a*) **he counts among my best friends,** il compte parmi, il est au nombre de, mes meilleurs amis; *Cards:* **card that counts,** (carte) marquante *f*; *Bill:* **a cannon counts two,** pour un carambolage on compte deux; **two children c. as one adult,** deux enfants comptent comme un adulte; **he doesn't c. for much,** il ne compte guère; **he doesn't c.,** il ne compte pas; (*b*) avoir de l'importance; **every vote counts,** chaque voix fait nombre, a son importance; **every minute counts,** il n'y a pas une minute à perdre; **every penny counts,** il faut regarder à chaque sou; **everything counts,** tout fait somme; **money counts with him more than anything,** l'argent *m* fait sur lui plus que tout.

II. (*compound verb*) **count down,** *v.i.* compter à rebours.

count[3], *s.m.* (*title*) comte; **the C. of Monte Cristo,** le comte de Monte Cristo; *Hist:* **the Counts Palatine,** les comtes palatins.

countable ['kauntəbl], *a.* dénombrable.

countdown ['kauntdaun], *s.* compte *m* à rebours; comptage régressif, décomptage *m*.

countenance[1] ['kauntinəns], *s. esp. Lit:* **1.** expression *f* du visage; visage, figure *f*, mine *f*, air *m*, maintien *m*, contenance *f*; **to change c.,** changer de visage, de contenance; **to keep one's c.,** (i) ne pas se laisser décontenancer; (ii) se donner, se faire, une contenance; garder son sérieux; **to keep myself in c.,** pour me donner une contenance, par contenance, pour me donner un maintien; **to put s.o. out of c.,** décontenancer qn; **to lose c.,** se décontenancer; perdre contenance; **to stare s.o. out of c.,** dévisager qn; faire baisser les yeux à qn; faire perdre contenance a qn; **to keep s.o. in c.,** soutenir qn; aider qn à faire bon visage (lors d'une entrevue, etc.); **his c. fell,** son visage, sa figure, s'allongea; *B:* **the light of His c.,** la clarté de son visage. **2.** faveur *f*, appui *m*, encouragement *m*; **to give, lend, c. to s.o., to sth.,** appuyer, favoriser, encourager, qn, qch.; accréditer (une nouvelle, etc.).

countenance[2], *v.tr.* **1.** autoriser, approuver, sanctionner (une action); **to c. a fraud,** se prêter à une fraude. **2.** encourager, appuyer, soutenir (qn) **(in,** dans).

counter[1] ['kauntər], *s.* **1.** (*pers.*) compteur, -euse. **2.** (*a*) *Mec.E:* compteur *m*; **speed c., revolution c.,** compteur de tours, compte-tours *m inv.* **set-back c.,** compteur avec remise à zéro; (*b*) *Cmptr:* compteur, registre *m*; **binary c.,** compteur binaire; **instruction c.,** registre d'adresses, d'instruction; **pulse c.,** compteur d'impulsions. **3.** *Games:* (i) (*square*) fiche *f* (en os, etc.); (ii) (*round*) jeton *m*; *Ind:* jeton. **4.** (*a*) (*in bank, etc.*) guichets *mpl*; caisse *f*; **payable over the c.,** payable au guichet; (*b*) (*in shop*) comptoir *m*; (*in supermarket*) rayon *m*; **sold over the c.,** vendu (au) comptant; **to sell under the c.,** vendre en cachette; **goods from under the c.,** des marchandises de l'arrière-boutique; **c. hand,** vendeur, -euse.

counter[2], *s.* **1.** poitrail *m* (d'un cheval). **2.** *N.Arch:* voûte *f* d'arcasse; voûte arrière. **3.** creux *m* (d'un poinçon, etc.). **4.** contre-poinçon *m*.

counter[3], *s. Bootm:* contrefort *m*.

counter[4]. **1.** *s.* (*a*) *Fenc:* contre *m*; (*b*) *Box:* parade *f* d'un bras et riposte simultanée de l'autre; coup *m* d'arrêt; contre; **cross c.,** cross *m*. **2.** *a.* (*a*) contraire, opposé **(to,** à); (*b*) contre-; **c. advice,** contravis *m*; *Fort:* **c. approaches,** contre-approches *f*; **c. attraction,** (i) attraction opposée; (ii) attraction destinée à faire concurrence au clou de la fête, etc.; **c. declaration,** contre-déclaration *f*; **c. effort,** contre-effort *m*; *Med:* **c. extension,** contre-extension *f*; **c. reaction,** contre-réaction *f*; **c. reformation,** contre-réformation *f*; **c. revolution,** contre-révolution *f*; **c. revolutionary,** contre-révolutionnaire *mf*; *Fenc:* **c. riposte,** contre-riposte *f*; *Com:* **c. sample,** contretype *m*; *Nau:* **c. sea,** mer à contre vent; **c. tide,** contre-marée *f*. **3.** *adv.* en sens inverse; à contre-sens; **to run, go, act, c. to one's orders,** agir contrairement à ses instructions; aller à l'encontre de ses instructions; **to run c. to a prejudice,** heurter de front un préjugé; **to run c. to the law,** aller à l'encontre de la loi; contrarier la loi; **to run c. to interests, all conventions,** heurter des intérêts, toutes les idées reçues; **tendency that runs c. to modern evolution,** tendance *f* qui va à l'encontre de l'évolution moderne; *Ven:* **to hunt, run, go, c.,** suivre, prendre, le contre-pied.

counter[5], *v.tr.* **1.** aller à l'encontre de, contrarier (qn, qch.); **to c. s.o.'s designs,** aller à l'encontre des desseins de qn; contrecarrer les desseins de qn; **to c. an opinion,** prendre le contre-pied d'une opinion; *Mec.E:* **to c. a motion,** arrêter, stopper, un mouvement; *Box:* **to c. (a blow),** parer, bloquer (un coup) et riposter en même temps; *Chess:* **to c. a move,** contrer un coup; riposter à un coup. **2.** *Mec.E:* renvoyer (le mouvement).

counter- ['kauntər], *pref.* contre-. NOTE: *to form the pl. of French words with the pref.* **contre-**, *the second part takes the pl. ending and* **contre-** is invariable.

counteract [kauntə'rækt], *v.tr.* **1.** contrarier, contrecarrer, déjouer (un projet); **to c. an influence,** contrecarrer une influence, riposter à une influence. **2.** neutraliser (une influence), parer à (un résultat), riposter à, contrecarrer, contrer (un effet).

counteraction [kauntə'rækʃ(ə)n], *s.* **1.** action *f* contraire; mouvement opposé; opposition *f*; antagonisme *m* réciproque (entre deux choses). **2.** neutralisation *f* (d'une influence, etc.).

counteractive [kauntə'ræktiv]. **1.** *a.* tendant à agir en opposition; contraire, opposé **(to,** à). **2.** *s.* tendance opposée; action *f* contraire.

counteragent ['kauntəreidʒ(ə)nt], *s.* = COUNTERACTIVE 2.

counterarch ['kauntərɑ:tʃ], *s. Arch:* voûtin *m*.

counterargument [kauntə'rɑ:gjumənt], *s.* argument *m* contraire.

counterattack[1] ['kauntərətæk], *s. Mil:* contre-attaque *f*; retour offensif.

counterattack[2], *v.tr. & i.* contre-attaquer.

counterbalance[1] ['kauntəbæləns], *s.* contrepoids *m*; *Tchn:* contrebalancier *m*, équilibrier *m*.

counterbalance[2] [kauntə'bæləns], *v.tr.* contrebalancer; faire contrepoids à (qch.); compenser (une force, etc.); faire équilibre à (une force); **forces that c. each other,** forces qui s'annulent; **counterbalanced lever,** levier équilibré par contrepoids.

counterbalancing [kauntə'bælənsiŋ], *s.* équilibrage *m*.

counterbattery ['kauntəbæt(ə)ri], *s. Mil:* contrebatterie *f*.

counterblast ['kauntəblɑ:st], *s.* réplique *f*, riposte *f* **(to,** à).

counterblow ['kauntəblou], *s.* contrecoup *m*.

counter-bond ['kauntəbɔnd], *s. Jur:* contre-promesse *f*.

counterbore[1] ['kauntəbɔər], *s. Tls:* **1.** = COUNTERSINK[1] 1. **2.** outil *m* à repercer; alésoir *m*; mèche *f* d'alésage; contre-alésage *m*.

counterbore[2], *v.tr. Mec.E:* = COUNTERSINK[2] 1. **2.** réaléser, contre-aléser; agrandir (un trou).

counterboring ['kauntəbɔ:riŋ], *s.* contre-alésage *m*.

counterbrace[1] ['kauntəbreis], *s. Civ.E:* contre-tirant *m*; entretoise *f*; raidisseur *m*.

counterbrace[2], *v.tr.* entretoiser, contre-brasser; raidir.

counterbracing ['kauntəbreisiŋ], *s.* entretoisement *m*, contre-appui *m*, raidissement *m*.

countercharge ['kauntətʃɑ:dʒ], *s. Jur:* contre-accusation *f*; contre-plainte *f*.

countercheck[1] ['kauntətʃek], *s.* **1.** *Mec:* force opposée; force antagoniste. **2.** recoupement *m*; recoupage *m*; vérification *f*.

countercheck[2], *v.tr.* recouper; vérifier.

counter-claim[1] ['kauntəkleim], *s. Jur:* demande reconventionnelle, compensatoire; reconvention *f*; contre-demande *f*; défense *f* au contraire.

counter-claim[2], *v.tr. Jur:* faire, opposer, une demande reconventionnelle (en dommages-intérêts, etc.).

counterclockwise [kauntə'klɔkwaiz], *adv.* dans le sens contraire des aiguilles d'une montre; en sens inverse des aiguilles d'une montre; à l'envers, à l'encontre, des aiguilles d'une montre; dans le sens négatif; à gauche; sinistrorsum.

countercriticism [kauntə'kritisizm], *s.* contre-critique *f*.

countercurrent ['kauntəkʌrənt], *s.* contre-courant *m*.

countercurve ['kauntəkə:v], *s. Arch:* contre-courbe *f*.

counter-deed ['kauntədi:d], *s. Jur:* contre-lettre *f*.

counterdemonstrate [kauntə'demənstreit], *v.i. Pol:* contre-manifester.

counterdemonstration [kauntədemən'streiʃ(ə)n], *s.* contre-manifestation *f*.

counterdemonstrator [kauntə'demənstreitər], *s.* contre-manifestant, -ante.

counterdisengage ['kauntədisin'geidʒ], *v.tr. & i. Fenc:* contre-dégager.

counterdisengagement ['kauntədisin'geidʒmənt], *s. Fenc:* contre-dégagement *m*.

counterdraw ['kauntədrɔ:], *v.tr. Engr:* contre-tirer (une gravure).

counter-enquiry ['kauntərin'kwaiəri], *s. Jur:* contre-enquête *f*.

counter-ermine ['kauntərə:min], *s. Her:* contre-hermine *f*.

counterespionage [kauntər'espiənɑ:ʒ], *s.* contre-espionnage *m*.

counteretching ['kauntər'etʃiŋ], *s. Engr:* décapage *m*; **c. solution,** solution *f* de décapage.

counterextension ['kauntərik'stenʃ(ə)n], *s. Surg:* contrextension *f*.

counter-faced ['kauntəfeist], *a. Her:* contre-barré.

counterfeit[1] ['kauntəfi(:)t]. **1.** *a.* contrefait; faux; **c. coin,** fausse monnaie; **c. emotions,** émotions simulées. **2.** *s.* contrefaçon *f*; (*of document*) faux *m*.

counterfeit[2], *v.tr.* **1.** contrefaire (la monnaie, etc.). **2.** simuler, feindre (une passion, etc.); **to c. poverty,** faire le pauvre.

counterfeiter ['kauntəfi(:)tər], *s.* **1.** contrefacteur *m*; faux monnayeur. **2.** simulateur, -trice.

counterfeiting ['kauntəfi(:)tiŋ], *s.* **1.** contrefaction *f*; contrefaçon *f*. **2.** simulation *f*.

counterfire ['kauntəfaiər], *s. For:* contre-feu *m*.

counterflow ['kauntəflou], *s. El:* contre-courant *m*.

counterfoil [ˈkauntəfɔil], *s.* souche *f*, talon *m* (de chèque, de quittance); **c. book,** cahier *m*, carnet *m*, registre *m*, livre *m* à souche.
counterforce [ˈkauntəfɔːs], *s. Mil: U.S:* attaque(s) *f* (à la bombe atomique) des bases aériennes, des bases de lancement d'engins ennemis.
counterfort [ˈkauntəfɔːt], *s.* **1.** *Arch:* éperon *m* (d'un mur, etc.). **2.** *Ph.Geog:* contrefort *m*.
counterfugue [ˈkauntəfjuːg], *s. Mus:* contre-fugue *f*.
countergear(ing) [ˈkauntəgiə(riŋ)], *s. Mec.E:* renvoi *m* de mouvement; mécanisme *m* de renvoi.
counterguard [ˈkauntəgɑːd], *s. Fort:* contre-garde *f*.
countering [ˈkaunt(ə)riŋ], *s.* **1.** parade *f* et riposte *f*. **2.** *Mec.E:* **c. of a motion,** stoppage *m* d'un mouvement.
counter-inquiry [ˈkauntərinˈkwaiəri], *s. Jur:* contre-enquête *f*.
counterintelligence [ˈkauntərinˈtelidʒəns], *s. Mil: etc:* contre-renseignement *m*, *pl.* contre-renseignements; contre-intelligence *f*, *pl.* contre-intelligences.
counter-irritant [ˈkauntərˈirit(ə)nt], *a. & s. Med:* (médicament) révulsif (*m*), dérivatif (*m*); contre-stimulant (*m*) *pl.* contre-stimulants; émollient (*m*).
counterirritate [ˈkauntərˈiriteit], *v.tr. Med:* révulser.
counter-irritation [ˈkauntəririˈteiʃ(ə)n], *s. Med:* révulsion *f*, dérivation *f*.
counterjumper [ˈkauntədʒʌmpər], *s. A: & U.S: Pej:* (*of pers.*) commis *m* (de magasin); vendeur, -euse.
counterlath[1] [ˈkauntəlæθ], *s. Const:* contre-latte *f*.
counterlath[2], *v.tr. Const:* contre-latter.
countermand[1] [ˈkauntəmɑːnd], *s.* contremandement *m*, contrordre *m*, contravis *m*.
countermand[2], *v.tr.* contremander; décommander (une grève, etc.); révoquer, rappeler, annuler (un ordre); *Com:* **to c. the order for sth.,** décommander qch.; **unless countermanded,** sauf contrordre, sauf contravis.
countermanding [ˈkauntəmɑːndiŋ], *s.* décommandement *m*; révocation *f*, rappel *m* (d'un ordre).
countermanœuvre [ˈkauntəməˈnuːvər], *s.* contre-manœuvre *f*, *pl.* contre-manœuvres.
countermarch[1] [ˈkauntəmɑːtʃ], *s.* contremarche *f*.
countermarch[2]. **1.** *v.i.* contremarcher. **2.** *v.tr.* faire contremarcher (des troupes).
countermark[1] [ˈkauntəmɑːk], *s. Com: Farr: etc:* contremarque *f*.
countermark[2], *v.tr.* contremarquer.
countermeasure [ˈkauntəmeʒər], *s.* contre-mesure *f*, *pl.* contre-mesures; disposition *f* (prise) contre . . .; **electronic c.,** mesure *f* contre-électronique; contre-mesure électronique.
countermelody [ˈkauntəˈmeləḍi], *s. Mus:* contre-chant *m*.
countermine[1] [ˈkauntəmain], *s.* contre(-)mine *f*.
countermine[2] [kauntəˈmain], *v.tr. & i.* contre(-)miner (une mine, *Navy:* une passe, etc.).
counterminer [ˈkauntəmainər], *s.* contre(-)mineur *m*.
countermotion [ˈkauntəmouʃ(ə)n], *s. Mec.E:* transmission secondaire, intermédiaire; renvoi *m* de mouvement.
countermove [ˈkauntəmuːv], *s.* contre-mesure *f*, *pl.* contre-mesures; contre-opération *f*, *pl.* contre-opérations; **move and c.,** avance *f* et recul *m* stratégiques.
countermovement [kauntəˈmuːvmənt], *s.* mouvement *m* contraire.
countermure[1] [ˈkauntəmjuər], *s. Mil:* contre-mur *m*.
countermure[2] [kauntəˈmjuər], *v.tr. Mil:* contre-murer.
counteroffensive [ˈkauntərəˈfensiv], *s. Mil:* contre-offensive *f*.
counteropening [ˈkauntərˈoup(ə)niŋ], *s. esp. Surg:* contre-ouverture *f*.
counterorder [ˈkauntərɔːdər], *s.* contrordre *m*.
counterpane [ˈkauntəpein], *s.* courtepointe *f*; couvre-lit *m*, *pl.* couvre-lits; couvre-pied(s) *m*.
counterpart [ˈkauntəpɑːt], *s.* **1.** (*a*) contre-partie *f*; analogue *m*; pendant *m* (d'un tableau, etc.); *Phot:* contre-type *m* (positif ou négatif); **to be the c. of . . .,** aller de pair avec . . .; (*b*) homologue *m*, équivalent *m*. **2.** duplicata *m*, double *m* (d'un document); contre-partie; **tally c.,** souche *f* (d'un reçu).
counterpetition[1] [ˈkauntəpiˈtiʃ(ə)n], *s.* contre-pétition *f*.
counterpetition[2], *v.i.* contre-pétitionner.
counterpetitioner [ˈkauntəpiˈtiʃənər], *s.* contre-pétitionnaire *mf*.
counterpierce [ˈkauntəpiəs], *v.tr.* contrepercer.
counterplan [ˈkauntəplæn], *s.* contre-projet *m*.
counter-plea [ˈkauntəpliː], *s. Jur:* réplique *f*.
counterplot[1] [ˈkauntəplɔt], *s.* contre-ruse *f*, contre-trame *f*.
counterplot[2]. **1.** *v.i.* inventer une contre-ruse (**against s.o.,** contre qn). **2.** *v.tr.* frustrer (qn); déjouer (un dessein) par une contre-ruse.

counterpoint [ˈkauntəpɔint], *s. Mus:* contrepoint *m*; **florid c.,** contrepoint fleuri, contrepoint figuré; figuré *m*.
counterpoise[1] [ˈkauntəpɔiz], *s.* **1.** contrepoids *m*; masse *f* d'équilibrage; **c. bridge,** pont *m* à bascule; **c. barrier,** tapecul *m*. **2.** équilibre; **in c.,** en équilibre.
counterpoise[2], *v.tr.* contrebalancer; faire contrepoids à (qch.).
counterpoison [ˈkauntəˈpɔiz(ə)n], *s.* contrepoison *m*.
counterpreparation [ˈkauntəprepəˈreiʃ(ə)n], *s. Mil:* contre-préparation *f*.
counterpressure [ˈkauntəpreʃər], *s.* contre-pression *f*.
counterproductive [ˈkauntəprəˈdʌktiv], *a.* contre-productif.
counterproof [ˈkauntəpruːf], *s. Engr:* contre-épreuve *f*; **to take a c. of an engraving,** contre-tirer une gravure.
counterproposal, counterproposition [ˈkauntəprəˈpouz(ə)l, -prɔpəˈziʃ(ə)n], *s.* contre-proposition *f*.
counterprove [ˈkauntəpruːv], *v.tr. Engr:* contre-épreuver.
counterpunch [ˈkauntəpʌntʃ], *s. Tls.* contre-poinçon *m*.
counter-quartered [ˈkauntəˈkwɔːtəd], *a. Her:* contre-écartelé.
counter-rotating [ˈkauntərouˈteitiŋ], *a. Mec.E:* contrarotatif.
counterscarp [ˈkauntəskɑːp], *s. Fort:* contrescarpe *f*.
counterseal[1] [ˈkauntəsiːl], *s.* contre-sceau *m*.
counterseal[2], *v.tr.* contre-sceller.
countersection [ˈkauntəsekʃ(ə)n], *s. Surv:* recoupement *m*.
counter-security [ˈkauntəsiˈkjuːriti], *s. Jur:* contre-sûreté *f*.
countershaft [ˈkauntəʃɑːft], *s. Mec.E:* arbre *m* intermédiaire, mécanisme *m* de renvoi; renvoi *m* de mouvement; *Aut:* contre-arbre *m*.
countersign[1] [ˈkauntəsain], *s.* **1.** contreseing *m*. **2.** *Mil: etc:* mot *m* d'ordre; mot de ralliement; **advance and give the c.,** avance à l'ordre.
countersign[2], *v.tr.* contresigner, signer en second, viser (un ordre, etc.); ratifier (un ordre).
countersignal [ˈkauntəsignl], *s. Mil: etc:* contre-signal *m*, *pl.* contre-signaux; *Tp:* contre-appel *m*.
countersignature [ˈkauntəˈsignətjər], *s.* **1.** contreseing *m*. **2.** approuvé *m*.
countersink[1] [ˈkauntəsiŋk], *s.* **1.** *Tls:* fraise *f*; foret *m* conique; **c. bit,** fraisoir *m*, louche *f*; **plain c.,** fraise simple; **snail c.,** fraise à couteau; **rose-bit c.,** fraise taillée, fraise à roder, fraise champignon. **2. c. (hole),** (i) avant trou *m* (de perçage); (ii) fraisure *f* (d'un trou); noyure *f* (pour tête de vis).
countersink[2], *v.tr.* (**countersunk; countersunk**) *Carp: Mec.E: etc:* **1.** fraiser, ébiseler, chanfreiner, *Nau:* gourbiller. **2.** encastrer (la tête d'un rivet); noyer (la tête d'une vis); **countersunk rivet,** rivet *m* à tête encastrée, fraisée; **flat countersunk rivet,** rivet à tête noyée; **countersunk screw,** vis à tête noyée, à tête perdue; **screw with countersunk head,** vis à tête plate.
counterslope [ˈkauntəsloup], *s.* contre-pente *f*.
countersloped [ˈkauntəsloupt], *a.* (mur) recoupé.
counterspring [ˈkauntəspriŋ], *s.* contre-ressort *m*.
counterspy [ˈkauntəspai], *s.* agent *m* de contre-espionnage.
counterstamp [ˈkauntəstæmp], *s.* contre-timbre *m*.
counter-statement [ˈkauntəˈsteitmənt], *s. Jur:* contre-mémoire *m*.
counterstratagem [ˈkauntəˈstrætədʒəm], *s.* contre-finesse *f*; contre-ruse *f*.
counterstroke [ˈkauntəstrouk], *s. Mil:* retour offensif.
countersubject [ˈkauntəsʌbdʒikt], *s. Mus:* partie conséquente (d'une fugue); conséquent *m*; contre-sujet *m*.
counter-surety [ˈkauntəˈsjuərəti], *s. Jur:* contre-sûreté *f*.
counter-tenor [ˈkauntətenər], *s. Mus:* haute-contre *f*, *pl.* hautes-contre; alto *m*.
counterterrorism [ˈkauntəˈterərizm], *s.* contre-terrorisme *m*.
counterterrorist [ˈkauntəˈterərist], *a. & s.* contre-terroriste (*mf*).
counterthreat [ˈkauntəθret], *s.* **threats and counter-threats,** menaces *f* de part et d'autre.
countertrade [ˈkauntətreid], *s. Meteor:* contre-alizé *m*.
countertransference [ˈkauntəˈtrænsfərəns], *s. Psy:* contre-transfert *m*.
countervail [ˈkauntəveil]. **1.** *v.tr. Lit:* contrebalancer, compenser. **2.** *v.i.* prévaloir (**against,** contre).
countervailing [ˈkauntəveiliŋ], *a. Fin: etc:* compensatoire, compensateur.
countervair [ˈkauntəveər], *s. Her:* contre-vair *m*.
countervaluation [ˈkauntəvæljuˈeiʃ(ə)n], *s.* contre-expertise *f*.

counterverification [ˈkauntəverifiˈkeiʃ(ə)n], *s. Adm:* contre-épreuve *f* des voix (à une élection).
counterweigh [ˈkauntəwei], *v.tr.* **1.** contrebalancer; avoir plus de poids (qu'un autre argument, etc.). **2.** comparer les poids de (deux objets); peser (deux arguments) l'un contre l'autre.
counterweight[1] [ˈkauntəweit], *s.* contrepoids *m*; **door c.,** valet *m*; **c. cable,** câble *m* de contrepoids.
counterweight[2], *v.tr.* contrebalancer; équilibrer; munir (un appareil) d'un contrepoids.
counterwork[1] [ˈkauntəwəːk], *s.* **1.** contre-ruse *f*. **2.** *pl. Fort:* contre-attaques *f*.
counterwork[2], *v.tr.* **1.** contrarier, frustrer, contrecarrer. **2.** *Fort:* contre-attaquer.
countess [ˈkauntis], *s.* comtesse *f* (femme d'un COUNT, *q.v.*, ou d'un EARL, *q.v.*).
counting [ˈkauntiŋ], *s.* compte *m*, calcul *m*; dépouillement *m* (du scrutin); dénombrement *m* (de personnes); **c. mechanism,** mécanisme *m* compteur (de tours, etc.); minuterie *f* (d'enregistrement) (d'un compteur à gaz, etc.); **c. frame,** boulier *m* compteur.
counting house [ˈkauntiŋhaus], *s. Com:* bureau *m*, service *m*, de la comptabilité; la comptabilité.
countless [ˈkauntlis], *a.* innombrable; **c. races inhabit India,** un nombre incalculable de races habite les Indes.
countrified, countryfied [ˈkʌntrifaid], *a.* aux allures campagnardes, provinciales, agrestes; *Pej:* **to become c.,** se provincialiser; **they are very c.,** ils sont très province.
country [ˈkʌntri], *s.* **1.** (*expanse of land*) pays *m*, région *f*; terrain *m*; **broken c.,** pays, terrain, accidenté, coupé, compartimenté; **rough c.,** pays, terrain, accidenté, raboteux; **close c.,** pays, terrain, couvert; **open c.,** pays, terrain, découvert; rase campagne; **undulating, rolling, c.,** pays, terrain, vallonné, onduleux; **flat c.,** pays de plaine(s); terrain plat; **rich, fertile, c.,** pays riche, fertile; **wheat-growing c.,** région à blé; **back c.,** arrière-pays *m inv*; région non développée; **to go up c.,** remonter vers l'intérieur (du pays); pénétrer dans le pays; *Geol:* **c. rock,** stampe *f* (entre les veines métallifères); roche encaissante. **2.** (*a*) (*political entity*) pays; **the countries of Europe,** les pays de l'Europe; **industrial, agricultural, countries,** pays industriels, agricoles; *Pol.* **to go to the c.,** aller devant le pays; **to go back to the c.,** retourner devant les électeurs; *Mil:* **to carry war into the enemy's c.,** porter la guerre chez l'ennemi; **God's own c.,** (i) un paradis terrestre; (ii) *U.S:* les États-Unis; (*b*) **one's native c.,** sa patrie; **to betray one's c.,** trahir sa patrie, son pays; **to love one's c.,** aimer son pays; **to die for one's c.,** mourir pour sa patrie. **3.** (*a*) (*opposed to the capital*) la province; **a quiet little c. town,** une petite ville tranquille de province; **c. bank,** banque provinciale; **c. cousin,** cousin de province; **young man fresh from the c.,** jeune homme nouvellement débarqué de province; (*b*) (*opposed to the town*) campagne *f*; **in the c.,** à la campagne; **c. life,** vie de, à la, campagne; vie champêtre, rurale; **she's a real c. girl,** elle n'aime que la vie de campagne; **c. gentleman,** gentilhomme propriétaire, campagnard; **c. seat,** manoir *m*, gentilhommière *f*; **c. house,** (i) maison *f* de campagne; (ii) manoir, gentilhommière; **c. houses open to the public,** châteaux ouverts au public; **c. club,** club (sportif, etc.) situé à la campagne; **c. dance,** danse *f* rustique, folklorique; **to spend a day in the c.,** passer une journée à la campagne.
countryfolk [ˈkʌntrifouk], *s.pl.* gens *m* de la campagne.
countryman, -woman, *pl.* **-men, -women** [ˈkʌntrimən, -wumən; -men, -wimin], *s.* (*a*) campagnard, -arde; personne *f* qui habite à la campagne; (*b*) **fellow c.,** compatriote *mf*.
countryside [ˈkʌntrisaid], *s.* (*a*) **beautiful c.,** beau paysage; (*b*) pays *m*; région *f*; **the whole c. was horrified by the news,** tout le pays a été bouleversé par la nouvelle.
countrystyle [ˈkʌntristail], *a.* **c. cooking,** cuisine campagnarde.
countship [ˈkauntʃip], *s.* dignité *f* de comte; comté *m*.
county [ˈkaunti], *s.* comté *m*. **1.** (*a*) *Hist:* territoire *m* sous la haute juridiction d'un comte; (*b*) *Hist:* **the counties palatine,** les comtés palatins (Cheshire, Lancashire, Durham). **2.** (*a*) division territoriale et administrative (i) de la Grande-Bretagne et de l'Irlande, (ii) *U.S:* d'un *State*; **the c. of Kent,** le comté de Kent; (*In Ireland no article*) **C. Mayo,** le comté de Mayo; *U.S:* **Chester C., New York C.,** le comté de Chester, de New York; (*b*) les habitants *m* du comté; **the whole c. wants it,** tout le comté le désire; **c. town,** chef-lieu *m* de comté, *pl.* chefs-lieux; *Fin:* **c. stocks,** emprunts *m*

des comtés; **a c. family,** une des familles terriennes du comté; **c. society,** l'aristocratie et la haute bourgeoisie du comté; *Cr:* **the c. team,** l'équipe *f* qui joue pour le comté; **c. cricket,** les grands matches entre les équipes de comté; **c. cricketer,** membre *m* de l'équipe du comté.

county-court ['kaunti'kɔ:t], *v.tr. A:* citer, assigner (un débiteur).

coup [ku:], *s.* **1.** (*a*) coup (audacieux); **to bring off a c.,** faire un coup, réussir un coup; (*b*) *l'anglais a emprunté du français* (*dans le même sens*); **c. d'état, c. de grâce, c. de main, c. d'œil, c. de théâtre. 2.** *Bill:* envoi *m* de la bille dans une des blouses, sans avoir touché une des deux autres billes.

coup-de-poing ['ku:də'pwɛ̃(ŋ)], *s. Prehist:* coup-de-poing *m, pl.* coups-de-poing.

coupe [ku:p], *s. For:* (= **felling**) coupe *f.*

coupé[1] ['ku:pei], *s. Veh:* coupé *m*; *Aut:* **sports c.,** coupé sport(s).

coupé[2], **couped** ['ku:pt], *a. Her:* coupé; **cross c.,** croix alésée.

couple[1] ['kʌpl], *s.* **1.** couple *f* (d'attache, pour chiens de chasse). **2.** (*a*) couple *f* (de pigeons, d'œufs, etc.); **a c. of seconds,** deux secondes; **to work in couples,** se mettre à deux pour travailler; *F:* **we'll stop (at the pub) for a c.,** on va s'arrêter boire un coup; **to have had a c.,** être gris; (*b*) *El:* **astatic c.,** couple *m,* paire *f,* d'aiguilles astatique. **3.** (*a*) couple *m* (de chiens de chasse); **thirty c. of dogs,** trente couples de chiens; (*of pers.*) **to go, hunt, run, in couples,** être toujours ensemble; (*b*) couple *m* (d'époux, de danseurs); **the married c.,** les (deux) époux *m*; **the newly married c.,** les nouveaux mariés; le nouveau ménage; **the young c.,** les deux jeunes époux; **an old c.,** un vieux ménage; *Journ:* **reliable c. wanted,** on demande un ménage recommandable; *Danc:* (*quadrille*) **top c.,** couple numéro un; **bottom c.,** couple numéro deux; **side top c.,** couple numéro trois; **side bottom c.,** couple numéro quatre. **4.** *Const:* paire *f* de chevrons; moise *f.* **5.** *Mec:* couple *m* (de torsion, de rotation); couple moteur. **6.** *El:* thermocouple *m*; **copper-constantan c.,** élément *m* cuivre-constantan.

couple[2]. **1.** *v.tr.* (*a*) coupler, accoupler (des bœufs, deux idées); accoupler, apparier (le mâle et la femelle); associer, accoler (des noms, etc.); relier (des personnes, des objets); **coupled with the fact that . . .,** ajouté au fait que . . .; **common sense coupled with intelligence,** le bon sens joint à l'intelligence; *Ven:* **to c. hounds (in fours or sixes),** harder des chiens courants (par quatre ou par six); *Mus:* (*organ*) **to c. two manuals,** accoupler deux claviers; *Arch:* **coupled columns,** colonnes accouplées; **coupled posts,** poteaux jumelés, accolés; (*b*) *Mec.E: etc:* engrener, embrayer (une machine); conjuguer (des mouvements); raccorder (des tuyaux); emmancher, assembler (des tiges de sonde); **coupled direct to the motor,** en prise directe avec le moteur; **coupled brakes,** freinage conjugué; (*c*) *El:* associer, grouper, accoupler (des piles); faire communiquer, assembler, brancher (des organes); **coupled direct to the condenser,** en communication directe avec le condenseur; (*d*) *Rail:* **to c. up, c. on, a carriage,** atteler, accrocher, un wagon; **the dining car is coupled up at Leeds,** le wagon-restaurant est accroché à Leeds. **2.** *v.i.* (*of male and female*) s'accoupler.

coupler ['kʌplər], *s.* **1.** *Mus:* (*organ*) (i) tirant *m* à accoupler; (ii) pédale *f* d'accouplement; **pedal c.,** tirasse *f*; **octave c.,** double-main *f, pl.* double-mains; **draw the c.,** tirant à accoupler. **2.** (*a*) *Rail:* attelage *m*; (*b*) *El: etc:* **wire c.,** attache-fils *m inv*; **longitudinal beam c.,** coupleur *m* de faisceau longitudinal.

couplet ['kʌplit], *s. Pros:* distique *m.*

coupling ['kʌpliŋ], *s.* **1.** accouplement *m* (de deux choses); appariement *m* (des animaux); association *f* (d'idées, etc.); accolement *m* (de deux noms). **2.** *Tchn:* (*a*) accouplement, raccordement *m,* assemblage *m,* couplage *m* (de deux roues, etc.); emmanchage *m,* emmanchement *m,* raccord *m* (de deux tuyaux); **pin c.,** accouplement par cheville, par goupille; **c. pin,** cheville *f,* boulon *m,* d'accouplement; **c. rod,** (i) allonge *f*; (ii) bielle *f* d'accouplement (de roues de locomotive); **axle-tree c. band,** sous(-)bande *f* d'essieu; **c. box, c. sleeve,** manchon *m* d'accouplement; (*b*) *Rail:* attelage *m,* accrochage *m* (des wagons); **c. chain,** chaîne *f* d'attelage; **c. hook,** crochet *m* d'attelage, de traction; **c. lever,** levier *m* de décrochage; **c. buffer,** tampon *m* d'attelage; (*c*) *El: etc:* couplage, association *f,* groupement *m* (d'éléments de pile, etc.); **c. in parallel,** couplage en parallèle; **c. in series,** couplage en série, en tension; **induction c.,** couplage par induction; **beam c.,** couplage électronique; **c. coefficient,** coefficient *m* de couplage; **close c., tight c.,** accouplement serré; **loose c.,** accouplement lâche; connexion inductive. **3.** (*coupling device*) (*a*) (*static*) accouplement, raccord, joint *m*; *Rail:* attelage; **universal c.,** raccord, joint, universel; **bayonet c.,** raccord, joint, à baïonnette; **pawl c.,** accouplement à cliquet; **jointed c.,** accouplement à articulation; **friction c.,** accouplement, manchon, à friction; **jump c.,** assemblage à manchon taraudé; **screw c.,** manchon, union *f,* à vis; **sleeve c.,** accouplement à douille, à manchon; (*b*) (*for transmitting motion*) accouplement, embrayage *m*; **flexible, compensating, c.,** (i) manchon élastique; (ii) entraîneur *m* flexible; **clutch c.,** accouplement à débrayage; **cone c.,** accouplement à cônes; **plate c.,** accouplement à plateaux, à disques; **shaft c.,** (i) accouplement d'arbres; (ii) manchon d'accouplement, d'assemblage (d'arbres).

coupon ['ku:pɔn], *s.* **1.** coupon *m*; *Post:* **international reply c.,** coupon-réponse international, *pl.* coupons-réponse; *Com:* **(free) gift c.,** bon-prime *m, pl.* bons-primes; **c. redeemable for cash,** timbre *m* ristourne; *Adm:* **petrol c.,** bon *m* d'essence; **bread c.,** ticket *m* de pain; **clothing coupons,** points *m* textiles; *Sp:* **football c., pools c.,** formulaire *m* de concours de pronostics de football; *Fin:* **interest c.,** coupon d'intérêts; **cum c., ex c.,** coupon attaché, détaché; **due date of c.,** échéance *f* de coupon; **outstanding coupons,** coupons en souffrance. **2.** *Pol:* recommandation officielle donnée à un candidat par le chef d'un parti; **c. candidate,** candidat recommandé.

courage ['kʌridʒ], *s.* courage *m*; **to have c.,** avoir du courage, du cœur; **to have the c. to do sth.,** avoir le courage de faire qch.; **to have the c. of one's convictions,** avoir le courage de ses opinions; **to take, pluck up, screw up, muster up, c.,** prendre son courage à deux mains; s'enhardir; s'armer de courage; faire appel à tout son courage; **that will put a little c. into him,** cela va lui donner du cœur; **to restore s.o.'s c.,** rencourager qn; **c.!** du courage! **my c. failed me,** le courage m'a manqué; **I tried to keep my c. up,** j'ai essayé de ne pas perdre courage.

courageous [kə'reidʒəs], *a.* courageux.

courageously [kə'reidʒəsli], *adv.* courageusement; avec courage.

couratari ['kurə'tɑ:ri], *s. Bot:* couratari *m.*

courbaril ['kuəbəril], *s. Bot:* courbaril *m*; **c. copal,** animé *f.*

courgette [kuə'ʒet], *s. Hort:* courgette *f.*

courier ['kuriər], *s.* **1.** (*a*) courrier *m,* messager *m*; (*b*) accompagnateur, -trice (de touristes). **2.** *A:* valet *m* de place; courrier (qui devançait son maître à l'étape). **3.** *Journ:* **the Northern C.,** le Courrier du Nord.

courlan ['kuələn], *s. Orn:* courlan *m.*

course[1] [kɔ:s], *s.* **1.** (*a*) cours *m* (d'un fleuve, du temps); courant *m* (des affaires, etc.); cours, ordre *m,* marche *f* (des événements); cours, trajet *m* (d'une balle, d'une artère, etc.); évolution *f* (d'une maladie); *Geol:* direction *f* (d'un filon); **upper, middle, lower, c. (of a river),** cours supérieur, moyen, inférieur (d'une rivière); **in the c. of the sitting,** au cours de la séance; **in the c. of conversation,** au cours de la conversation; **in the c. of the morning, of the week, of the year,** au cours de la matinée, de la semaine; dans la matinée, dans la semaine; dans le courant de l'année; **in the c. of centuries,** dans la suite des siècles; **this will probably happen in the c. of the next three or four months,** ceci se produira probablement d'ici trois ou quatre mois; **in (the) c. of time,** avec le temps; dans la suite, le cours, des temps; à la longue; **in the c. of nature, in the ordinary c. of things,** normalement; **in the c. of his inquiry he discovered that . . .,** il découvrit, au cours de son enquête, que . . .; **to do sth. in due c.,** faire qch. en temps voulu, en temps utile, en temps et lieu; **we shall write to you in due c.,** nous vous écrirons en temps utile; **it happened in due c. that. . .,** le moment arriva où . . .; **building in c. of construction,** bâtiment *m* en cours de construction; **the fever must run its c.,** il faut que la fièvre suive son cours; **the sun had run its c.,** le soleil avait terminé sa carrière; **to let nature take her c.,** donner libre cours à la nature; **justice will take its c.,** la justice suivra son cours; **let things take their c.,** laissez couler l'eau; laissez faire; *Jur:* **by c. of law,** d'après, suivant, la loi; **nothing could stop Napoleon in his c.,** rien n'arrêtait Napoléon dans sa course, dans sa carrière; (*b*) **of c.,** bien entendu, naturellement; bien sûr; **of c. not!** bien sûr que non! **have you seen it?—of c. (I have),** l'avez-vous vu?—bien sûr! naturellement! **may I come in?—(why,) of c.!** puis-je entrer?—mais oui, évidemment! je vous en prie! **of c. I shall pay you interest,** comme de juste je vous paierai des intérêts; (*c*) **that is a matter of c.,** cela va sans dire; cela va de soi; **as a matter of c.,** comme de juste, tout naturellement, comme de raison; **you will be my best man as a matter of c.,** tu es mon garçon d'honneur obligé; **it is a matter of c. that. . .,** il va de soi que. . . . **2.** (*a*) *Sch:* cours; **c. of public lectures,** cours public; série *f* de conférences; **general c. of education,** programme *m* d'instruction générale; **to give a c. of lectures,** professer un cours; **to take, follow, a c.,** (i) suivre un cours (de physique, etc.); (ii) (*of nurse, etc.*) faire son stage; **he has published a French c.,** il a publié une méthode de français; (*b*) *Med:* traitement *m,* régime *m*; **to take a c. of three treatments at the doctor's,** aller faire un traitement de trois séances chez le médecin; **a c. of injections,** une série de piqûres; (*c*) *Agr:* assolement *m*; **four-c. rotation, four-field c.,** assolement quadriennal. **3.** (*a*) route *f,* direction *f*; **to hold (on) one's c.,** suivre la voie que l'on s'est tracée; continuer sa route; suivre tout droit son chemin; *Nau:* se soutenir dans sa route; **to keep one's c.,** ne pas dévier de sa route; *Nau:* maintenir son cap; conserver le même cap; se soutenir dans sa route; **to change one's c.,** changer de direction; *Nau:* changer le cap, changer de route; *Nau:* **to shape, set, the c. (on the chart),** tracer la route (sur la carte); **to be on (the) c.,** suivre le cap fixé; **to veer off one's c.,** dévier du cap fixé; **to steer a c.,** suivre une route; **ships steering the same c.,** navires faisant la même route; **compass c.,** route au compas; **true c.,** route vraie, corrigée; **what c. are we steering?** quel est notre cap? **to alter c. to starboard,** venir sur tribord, venir cap à tribord; (*of ship*) **to be driven out of its c.,** être drossé, dépalé; *Av:* **track c.,** angle *m* de cap; (*b*) **to take a c. of action,** prendre un parti; adopter une ligne de conduite; **to take a drastic c.,** employer de grands moyens; **to follow one's own c.,** agir à sa guise; **there is only one c. open,** il n'y a qu'un parti à prendre; **it is the only c. open to me,** c'est la seule voie que je puisse suivre, c'est ma seule ressource; **there was no c. open to me but flight,** je n'avais d'autre ressource que la fuite; **to hesitate between two courses,** hésiter entre deux partis; **you are entering on a dangerous c.,** vous vous engagez dans une voie dangereuse; **the better c. to take,** ce qu'il y a de mieux à faire; **the c. to adopt,** la marche à suivre; **I always take, adopt, this c.,** c'est le parti que je prends toujours; **the best c., the right c.,** le parti le plus sûr; la bonne voie; **courses of action open to the enemy,** possibilités offertes à l'ennemi; *A:* **evil courses,** vie déréglée, désordonnée; (*c*) *Mch:* **upward c. of a piston,** course ascendante, ascensionnelle, d'un piston; **downward c.,** course descendante. **4.** (*of meal*) service *m,* plat *m*; **four-c. dinner,** dîner *m* à quatre services; **three courses and a sweet,** trois plats et un dessert; **main c.,** plat principal. **5.** *Sp: etc:* (*a*) champ *m,* terrain *m* (de courses); **golf c.,** terrain, parcours *m,* de golf, *F:* golf *m*; *F:* (*of horse, etc.*) **to be down the c.,** être dans les choux; (*b*) piste *f*; *Golf:* **the c.,** le parcours; (*c*) **closed c.,** circuit *m* (sur piste, sur route, dans l'air, etc.); (*d*) *Av:* **speed c.,** base *f* de vitesse; **straight c.,** trajectoire *m* rectiligne. **6.** (*a*) *Hyd.E:* canal *m*; bief *m*; **mill c.,** canal, courant *m,* bief, de moulin; (*b*) *Min:* galerie *f*; **ventilating c.,** galerie d'aérage. **7.** *Const:* assise *f*; **c. of bricks, of timber,** assise de briques, de charpente; **c. of large stones,** assise de grand appareil; **last c., levelling c.,** arasement *m* (des briques, des pierres); **base c.,** couche *f* de liaison; **brick-on-end c.,** assise de bout; assise debout; **damp c.,** couche isolante, hydrofuge, d'isolement. **8.** *Nau:* basse voile, voile basse; **main c.,** basse voile du grand mât; **force c.,** basse voile de misaine. **9.** *Physiol: A:* **courses,** menstrues *f.*

course[2]. **1.** *v.tr.* (*a*) *Ven:* courir (un lièvre); *v.i.* courir le lièvre; (*b*) faire courir (un chien, un cheval). **2.** *v.i.* (*of liquids*) courir, couler; **the blood courses through the veins,** le sang circule dans les veines; *Lit:* **the tears coursed down her cheeks,** les larmes couraient, coulaient, sur, le long de, ses joues, lui coulaient le long des joues.

coursed [kɔ:st], *a. Const:* **c. work,** maçonnerie *f* par assises; assises réglées.

courser ['kɔ:sər], *s.* **1.** *Lit:* coursier *m.* **2.** *Orn:* courvite *m*; **cream-coloured c.,** courvite isabelle, gaulois.

coursing ['kɔ:siŋ], *s.* **1.** *Ven:* chasse *f* à courre au lièvre; chasse au lévrier; **to go c.,** chasser au lièvre. **2.** *Sp:* concours *m* de vitesse entre lévriers lâchés sur un lièvre en champ clos; coursing *m.*

court[1] [kɔ:t], *s.* **1.** (*a*) (*courtyard*) cour *f*; *B:* **the C. of Solomon's temple,** le parvis du temple de Salomon; *Lit:* **the courts of heaven,** les célestes parvis; (*b*) (*in names of blocks of flats*) = résidence *f*; (*in names of palaces, etc., e.g.* **Hampton C.**) château *m*; palais *m*; manoir *m*; (*c*) *NAm:* **motor c., tourist c.,** motel *m*; (*d*) ruelle *f,* impasse *f,* cul-de-sac *m, pl.* culs-de-sac. **2.** (*a*) cour (royale); **the King, Queen, will hold a c.,** il y aura réception à la cour; **the c. has gone to Windsor,** la cour vient de se rendre à Windsor; **Ambassador to the C. of**

St James's, ambassadeur *m* auprès du roi, de la reine, d'Angleterre; **c. dress,** (i) habit *m*, (ii) robe *f*, de cour; *Cards:* **c. card,** figure *f*; carte peinte; *Lit:* **c. epic,** épopée courtoise; (*b*) **to pay c. to s.o.,** faire la cour à qn. **3.** *Jur:* (*a*) (i) cour, tribunal *m*; (ii) (*courtroom*) (salle *f* d')audience *f*; auditoire *m* de tribunal; **the c. was shocked by the revelations of the witness,** l'audience fut scandalisée par les révélations du témoin; **law c., c. of law, c. of justice,** tribunal; cour de justice; **the Law Courts,** le palais de justice; **civil c.,** tribunal civil; **Criminal C.,** tribunal criminel; **the Central Criminal C.,** le tribunal principal de Londres en matière criminelle; la cour d'assises de Londres; **commercial c.,** tribunal de commerce; **the High C. of Justice,** la Haute Cour de Justice (siégeant à Londres); **High C. of Parliament,** Haute Cour du Parlement; **magistrate's c.** = tribunal d'instance; **Crown c.,** *A:* **county c.,** = tribunal de grande instance, *A:* de première instance; **c. of appeal,** cour d'appel; **supreme c. (of judicature),** cour souveraine de justice; **to go to c.,** aller en justice; **we will have to go to c.,** il faudra plaider; **to misconduct oneself in c.,** se mal conduire devant le tribunal, en plein tribunal; **in open c.,** en plein tribunal, en pleine audience; à huis ouvert; **case before the c.,** affaire *f* en cause; **to come before the c.,** comparaître devant le tribunal; paraître à la barre; **to bring s.o. into c.,** amener qn devant la cour; **to arrange, settle, a case out of c.,** arranger une affaire à l'amiable; **the case was settled out of c.,** la plainte a été retirée; **to be ruled, put, out of c.,** être mis hors de cour; être débouté de sa demande; **to rule (a plaintiff, an argument) out of c.,** mettre (un demandeur, un argument) hors de cour; **sale by order of the c.,** vente *f* judiciaire; **barrister, expert, appointed by the c.,** avocat, expert, nommé d'office; (*b*) *Mil: Navy:* **c. of inquiry,** conseil *m* d'enquête, commission *f* d'enquête (sur une question de discipline). **4.** (*a*) *NAm:* **c. tennis,** jeu *m* de paume; (*b*) **tennis c.,** court *m* (de tennis), tennis *m*; **grass c.,** court sur gazon; **hard c.,** court dur; **service c.,** rectangle *m* de service.

court², *v.tr.* **1.** courtiser; faire la cour à (une femme). **2.** briguer, rechercher (une alliance, etc.); (re)chercher, solliciter (l'amitié de qn, les applaudissements, etc.); **to c. s.o.'s favour,** briguer la faveur de qn; **to c. popularity,** chercher à se faire bien voir; **to c. praise, applause,** rechercher les éloges; **to c. danger, defeat,** s'offrir au danger; aller au-devant du danger, d'une défaite; **to c. death,** braver la mort; **to c. disaster,** courir à un échec; aller au-devant d'un échec; **to c. disappointment,** se ménager une déception; aller au-devant d'une déception; **to c. one's own ruin,** chercher sa ruine. **3.** *A.* attirer, allécher (qn); **to c. s.o. into doing sth.,** amener qn à faire qch.

courteous ['kə:tiəs], *a.* courtois, poli, gracieux (**to, towards,** envers).

courteously ['kə:tiəsli], *adv.* courtoisement; poliment, avec politesse.

courteousness ['kə:tiəsnis], *s.* courtoisie *f*, politesse *f*.

courtesan [kɔ:ti'zæn], *s.* courtisane *f*.

courtesy ['kə:təsi], *s.* **1.** courtoisie *f*, politesse *f*; *Mil:* marques extérieures de respect; **common c.,** la politesse la plus élémentaire; **by c., as a matter of c.,** à titre gracieux; **by c. of. . .,** avec la gracieuse permission de . . .; avec l'aimable concours de . . .; **he did me the c. to ask my permission,** il a eu la courtoisie de me demander ma permission; *Journ:* **may I, through the c. of your columns, enquire. . .,** je me permets de solliciter l'hospitalité de vos colonnes pour demander . . .; **road c.,** courtoisie, politesse, entre automobilistes; **exchange of courtesies,** échange *m* de bons procédés; *F:* **c. cop,** motard *m* (de la route); *Aut:* **c. light,** éclairage intérieur automatique; **c. title,** titre *m* de courtoisie; *A:* **arms of c.,** armes courtoises. **2.** *A:* = CURTSY. **3.** *Jur: A:* **the C. of England,** droit *m* d'usufruit par le veuf de certains biens de l'épouse.

courthouse ['kɔ:thaus], *s.* palais *m* de justice; tribunal *m*.

courtier ['kɔ:tiər], *s.* courtisan *m*.

courting ['kɔ:tiŋ], *s.* cour (faite à une femme); **c. couple,** couple *m* d'amoureux; *Furn: O:* **c. chair,** causeuse *f*.

courtliness ['kɔ:tlinis], *s.* **1.** courtoisie *f*. **2.** élégance *f*; grand air.

courtly ['kɔ:tli], *a.* **1.** (*a*) courtois; d'une politesse raffinée; (*b*) élégant; à l'air digne et aristocratique. **2.** *A:* obséquieux, servile.

court-martial¹ ['kɔ:t'mɑ:ʃəl], *s.* (*pl.* **courts martial**) *Mil:* conseil *m* de guerre; **to be tried by c.-m.,** passer en conseil de guerre; **drumhead c.-m.,** conseil de guerre prévôtal (en campagne); **regulations for field courts-martial,** procédure *f* militaire en campagne.

court-martial², *v.tr.* (**court-martialled**) faire passer (qn) en conseil de guerre; **to be court-martialled,** être traduit, passer, en conseil de guerre.

courtroom ['kɔ:tru:m], *s.* *Jur:* salle *f* d'audience; auditoire *m* de tribunal.

courtship ['kɔ:tʃip], *s.* cour (faite à une femme); **after two years of c. . . .,** après lui avoir fait la cour pendant deux ans . . .; *Nat.Hist:* **c. display,** parade nuptiale.

courtyard ['kɔ:tjɑ:d], *s.* cour *f* (de maison, de château, de ferme).

couscous ['kuskus], *s.* *Cu:* couscous *m*.

cousin ['kʌzn], *s.* **1.** cousin, -ine; **first c., full c., c. german,** cousin(e) germain(e); **second c.,** cousin(e) issu(e) de germain; cousin(e) au second degré; petit(e)-cousin(e); **first c. once removed,** (i) oncle *m*, tante *f*, à la mode de Bretagne; (ii) neveu *m*, nièce *f*, à la mode de Bretagne; **distant c.,** arrière-cousin(e); *A:* **to call cousins with s.o.,** se dire, se prétendre, parent de qn. **2.** *Hist:* (*term of address used by sovereign, etc.*) cousin(e); **our c. the King of Scots,** notre cousin le roi d'Écosse.

coussinet ['kusinet], *s.* *Arch: Civ.E:* coussinet *m* (de colonne ionique, de pied-droit).

couture ['ku:'tjuər], *s.* *Dressm:* **haute c.,** haute couture.

couturier, *f.* **-ière** [ku:'tju(ə)riei, -iɛər], *s.* *Dressm:* (*a*) grand couturier, grande couturière; (*b*) directeur, -trice, d'une maison de haute couture.

couxia, couxio ['ku:ʃiə, -ioul, *s.* *Z:* saki *m*.

covalence, covalency ['kou'veiləns, -ənsi], *s.* *Ch:* covalence *f*.

covalent ['kou'veilənt], *a.* *Ch:* covalent.

covariance ['kou'vɛəriəns], *s.* *Mth: etc:* covariance *f*; **c. analysis,** analyse *f* de covariance.

covariant ['kou'vɛəriənt], *s.* *Mth:* covariant *m*; *a.* **c. functions,** fonctions covariantes.

co-variation ['kouvɛəri'eiʃ(ə)n], *s.* *Biol: Mth:* covariation *f* (de deux espèces, etc.).

cove¹ [kouv], *s.* **1.** *Geog:* (*a*) anse *f*; petite baie; havre *m*; (*b*) *U.S:* (i) dépression *f* de terrain; cuvette *f*; (ii) gorge *f*, passe *f*. **2.** *Arch:* (*a*) grande gorge; (*b*) voûte *f* (de plafond).

cove², *v.tr.* **1.** cintrer, voûter (un foyer de cheminée, etc.). **2.** raccorder (un plafond) avec une grande gorge; **coved ceiling,** (i) plafond voûté; (ii) plafond plan à grandes gorges.

cove³, *s.* *P:* type *m*, individu *m*, gonze *m*; **a queer c.,** un drôle de pistolet.

covelline, covellite ['kouvəlain, -ait], *s.* *Miner:* covelline *f*, covellite *f*.

coven ['kʌv(ə)n], *s.* (*a*) bande *f* de sorcières; (*b*) réunion *f* de sorcières.

covenant¹ ['kʌvənənt], *s.* **1.** *Jur:* convention *f*, contrat *m*. **2.** *Pol:* pacte *m*, traité *m*; *Hist:* **the C. of the League of Nations,** le Pacte de la Société des Nations. **3.** (*a*) *B:* alliance *f* (entre Dieu et les Israélites); (*b*) *Rel.H:* pacte, covenant *m*.

covenant². **1.** *v.tr.* (*a*) promettre, accorder, (qch.) par contrat; (*b*) stipuler (une somme); (*c*) **to c. to do sth., that sth. shall be done,** convenir de, s'engager à, faire qch.; convenir que qch. se fera. **2.** *v.i.* **to c. with s.o. for sth.,** convenir (par contrat) de qch. avec qn; *B:* **they covenanted with him for thirty pieces of silver,** ils lui comptèrent trente pièces d'argent.

covenanted ['kʌvənəntid], *a.* stipulé par contrat; contractuel.

covenantee [kʌvənən'ti:], *s.* *Jur:* créancier *m*.

covenanter ['kʌvənəntər], *s.* **1.** (*a*) partie contractante; (*b*) débiteur *m*. **2.** *Rel.H:* covenantaire *m*.

co-vendor ['kou'vendər], *s.* *Jur:* covendeur, -euse; colicitant *m*.

Coventry ['kʌvəntri, 'kɔv-], *Pr.n.* **1.** *Geog:* Coventry. **2.** *F:* **to send s.o. to C.,** mettre qn en quarantaine, au ban; frapper qn d'ostracisme.

cover¹ ['kʌvər], *s.* **1.** (*a*) couverture *f* (de lit, de cheval, etc.); dessus *m* (de buffet, etc.); fourreau *m* (de parapluie); *O:* bâche *f* (d'automobile); *Nau:* étui *m* (de canot, de voile); (*for chair*) **loose c.,** housse *f*; *Aut:* **car c.,** housse; **outer c. (of tyre),** enveloppe *f* (de pneu); **spare-wheel c.,** housse de la roue de secours; *Av:* **propeller c.,** housse d'hélice; (*b*) *Meteor:* **heavy cloud c.,** forte nébulosité. **2.** (*a*) couvercle *m* (de marmite, etc.); cloche *f* (pour plat); tampon *m*, plaque *f* (d'égout); capuchon *m* (de ventilateur); calotte *f* (d'une pompe); fond *m*, plateau *m* (de cylindre à vapeur); *Metall:* cône *m* (de haut fourneau); *Nau:* capot *m* (de cheminée, de panneau, de cabestan); **steel hatch c.,** opercule *m* d'acier; *Ind: Mec.E: etc:* **protection c.,** chape protectrice; **chain c.,** carter *m* de chaîne; *I.C.E:* **timing-case c.,** couvercle de distribution; **breech c.** (*of gun*), coiffe *f* de culasse; *Mec.E: etc:* **condenser c.,** coquille *f* de condenseur; **c. band,** bride *f* de fermeture; **c. plate,** plaque de couverture; tôle *f* de recouvrement; plaque-couvercle *f*, *pl.* plaques-couvercles; *Tchn:* **c. glass, slip,** (lamelle *f*) couvre-objet *m* (d'une préparation microscopique), *pl.* couvre-objets; *Mil:* **cap c.,** manchon *m* de képi; *Nau:* **white cap c.,** coiffe blanche; (*b*) *Bot:* involucre *m*. **3.** couverture (d'un livre); *Bookb:* les plats *m*; **to read a book from c. to c.,** lire un livre d'un bout à l'autre; **c. girl,** cover-girl *f*, *pl.* cover-girls. **4.** *Post:* enveloppe, pli *m*; **under separate c.,** sous pli séparé; (*for philatelists*) **first-day c.,** enveloppe (du) premier jour; **wreck c.,** accidenté *m*. **5.** (*a*) abri *m*; **to give s.o. c.,** abriter qn; **to seek, take, c.,** se mettre à l'abri; s'abriter; **to take c. from an explosion,** se garer d'une explosion; **take c.!** garez-vous! **to be under c.,** être à couvert, à l'abri; **under c. of a tree,** à l'abri d'un arbre; (*b*) *Ven:* (i) abri, couvert *m*, fourré *m*, hallier *m*; (ii) gîte *m*, retraite *f*, remise *f*; **to take c.,** se remiser; **to break c.,** (i) sortir de son terrier, d'un bois, d'un fourré; débucher; (ii) *F:* (*of pers.*) sortir de son terrier, de sa retraite; **to force (an animal) from c.,** faire débucher, faire bouquer (un animal); **breaking of c.,** débucher *m*; (*of stag*) **to turn back to c.,** s'embûcher, se rembucher; **to drive (stag, etc.) to c.,** embûcher, rembucher (un cerf); *For:* **trees that grow in thick c.,** arbres *m* qui croissent en massif; (*c*) *Mil: etc:* couvert, abri; défilement *m*; **under c.,** à couvert, à l'abri; dissimulé, abrité; dans une position défilée; **to take c.,** se mettre à couvert, se défiler, s'abriter; s'embusquer; **approach under c.,** cheminement défilé; **c. from fire,** couvert, abri, contre le(s) feu(x); **to take c. from enemy fire,** se mettre à couvert contre le, se défiler du, feu adverse; **without c.,** (à) découvert. **6.** (*a*) couvert, voile *m*, masque *m*; **under (the) c. of darkness, under c. of the night,** sous le couvert de la nuit; sous le manteau de la nuit; à la faveur de la nuit; **under (the) c. of friendship, of religion,** sous le masque de l'amitié, sous de faux semblants d'amitié; sous le voile, sous le couvert, de la religion; **under c. of his name,** à l'abri de son nom; (*b*) *Mil.Av:* **air c.,** couverture aérienne; **fighter c.,** couverture de chasse; **radar c.,** couverture radar; (*c*) organisation camouflée; **c. plan,** plan *m* de couverture; (*d*) *Com: Ins:* couverture, provision *f*, marge *f*, garantie *f*; **to operate with, without, c.,** opérer avec couverture, à découvert; *Fin:* **call for additional c.,** appel *m* de marge; *Ins:* **full c.,** garantie totale; *Jur: Com:* **to lodge stock as c.,** déposer des titres en nantissement. **7.** (*at table*) couvert; **covers were laid for four,** la table était de quatre couverts; on avait mis quatre couverts; (*in restaurant*) **c. charge,** couvert.

cover², *v.*

I. *v.tr.* **1.** (*a*) couvrir (qn, qch.) (**with,** de); **covered with snow,** couvert de neige, par la neige; *Cards:* **to c. a card,** couvrir une carte; **balcony covering the pavement,** balcon *m* en surplomb sur le trottoir; **to c. one's head,** se couvrir (la tête), se coiffer; *A:* **to stand covered,** se tenir la tête couverte; rester couvert; **to be well covered,** (i) être bien couvert, chaudement vêtu; (ii) *F:* être bien en chair; (*b*) **to c. s.o. with ridicule,** couvrir, larder, cribler, qn de ridicule; **covered with shame, with confusion,** couvert de honte, de confusion. **2.** (*a*) (*protect*) **the frontier is covered by a chain of forts,** la frontière est protégée, défendue, par une chaîne de forts; **the cavalry covered the retreat,** la cavalerie couvrait la retraite; *Navy:* **the flag covers the cargo,** le pavillon couvre la marchandise; *Mil:* **to c. a battery from fire,** dérober une batterie aux coups; *Ten:* (*of player*) **to c. as much of the court as possible,** couvrir autant de terrain qu'il est possible; (*b*) (*support*) *Cr:* **to c. a fielder,** se tenir en arrière, en soutien, d'un autre chasseur (pour attraper les balles qu'il n'aurait pu arrêter); (*c*) *v.i.* *Box: etc:* se couvrir. **3.** couvrir, recouvrir, gainer, envelopper, revêtir; **the walls are covered with yellow paper,** un papier jaune tapisse les murs; **wall covered with advertisements, with ivy,** mur tapissé d'affiches, de lierre; **to c. a book,** couvrir un livre; *v.i.* **paint that covers well,** peinture *f* qui s'étale bien, qui couvre bien; *El: etc:* **to c. a wire,** guiper, recouvrir, un fil conducteur; **to c. a cable,** chemiser un câble; *v.tr. & ind.tr.* **to c. (in) (a drainage system, etc.),** recouvrir (une canalisation sous terre, etc.); **to c. in a trench,** remplir une tranchée; **to c. over a well,** fermer un puits (à la surface). **4. to c. a distance,** couvrir, franchir, parcourir, une distance; **to c. ten kilometres on foot,** faire, abattre, dix kilomètres à pied; **to c. a great deal of ground,** (i) faire beaucoup de chemin; (ii) parcourir un champ très vaste. **5.** couvrir, dissimuler (son inquiétude, etc.); **he laughed to c. his confusion,** il riait pour dissimuler sa confusion. **6. to c. s.o. with a rifle, with a pistol,** mettre, tenir, qn en joue; braquer un pistolet sur qn; *F:* **I've got you covered,** je te tiens! tu ne peux pas m'échapper! **7.** comprendre, englober, embrasser; **this explanation does not c. all the facts,** cette explication n'embrasse pas tous les faits, ne tient pas compte de tous les faits; **in order to c. all eventualities,** pour parer à toute éventualité. **8.** (*a*) couvrir (un risque, son banquier); (*of creditor*) **to be covered,** être à couvert; **to c. a bill,** faire la provision d'une lettre de change; *St.Exch:* **to c. short sales, shorts,** se racheter; **to c. a short account,** couvrir un découvert; **to c. by buying back,** se couvrir en rachetant; **the application is covered,** la souscription est couverte; *Ins:* **the policy covers the risk of loss,** la police couvre le risque de perte; (*b*) **to c. (one's) expenses,** couvrir, faire, ses frais; couvrir ses dépenses; **to c. the requirements of. . .,** répondre aux besoins de . . .; **to c. a deficit,** combler un déficit; (*c*) *Journ:* couvrir (un événement sportif, etc.); **to c. a meeting,** assurer le compte rendu d'une réunion. **9.** *Breed:* couvrir, saillir, aligner (la femelle); sauter, monter (la jument).

II. (*compound verb*) **cover up.** (*a*) *v.tr.* couvrir entièrement, recouvrir; dissimuler (la vérité, des illégalités); **to c. up a picture,** cacher un tableau; **to c. up one's tracks,** dépister ses adversaires; (*b*) *v.i. Box:* se couvrir; **to c. up for s.o.,** servir de couverture à qn.

coverage ['kʌvəridʒ], *s.* couverture *f*; champ *m* d'application (d'une activité, etc.); champ d'action (d'un appareil, etc.); *Com: Ins:* couverture, provision *f*, marge *f*, garantie *f*; *Journ:* **news c.,** (ensemble *m* des) informations *fpl*; **complete world c.,** portée mondiale; *Mapm:* **map c.,** couverture cartographique; *Meteor:* **c. area,** zone *f*, champ, d'observation; *Phot:* **(lens) c.,** champ de couverture.

coverall(s) ['kʌvərɔ:l(z)], *s.(pl.) NAm:* bleu(s) *m(pl)* (de travail).

covered ['kʌvəd], *a.* (*a*) couvert; abrité; **c. market,** marché couvert; **c. terrace,** terrasse couverte; **c. way,** chemin couvert; *esp. U.S:* **c. wagon,** charrette *f* à bâche; (*b*) (risque) couvert (par les assurances); (*c*) *El:* **c. dynamo,** dynamo cuirassée.

coverer ['kʌvərər], *s.* couvreur, -euse; habilleur, -euse (de cartonnage de livre); couseur, -euse (de parapluies).

covering[1] ['kʌv(ə)riŋ], *a.* **1. c. letter,** lettre confirmative (d'une autre); lettre d'introduction, de couverture; lettre annexe; lettre d'envoi; *Com:* **c. note,** garantie *f*. **2.** *Mil:* **c. forces, troops,** forces *f*, troupes *f*, de couverture; **c. position,** position *f* de couverture; **c. fire,** tir *m* de soutien, de protection; **c.-fire unit,** base *f* de couverture, de feu; unité *f* d'appui de feu; *Artil:* **c. crest, ridge, mark,** masse couvrante. **3.** *St.Exch:* **c. purchases,** rachats *m*.

covering[2], *s.* **1.** (*a*) action *f* de couvrir; recouvrement *m* (de qch.); **c. plate,** plaque *f* de recouvrement; (*b*) *Breed:* action de couvrir (la femelle). **2.** (*a*) couverture *f*; enveloppe *f*, revêtement *m*, recouvrement *m*, gainage *m*; *El:* guipage *m* (d'un câble, etc.); **lead c.,** gaine *f* en plomb; *A:* **fabric c.,** entoilage *m* (d'un avion, etc.); (*b*) *Nau: etc:* bâche *f*; **iron c.,** bâche de fonte (d'une turbine, etc.); (*c*) *Furn:* housse *f*; (*d*) **don't go out in the rain without any c. on your head,** ne sortez pas sous la pluie sans vous couvrir la tête.

covering up ['kʌv(ə)riŋ'ʌp], *s.* (*a*) recouvrement *m* (de qch. à protéger); (*b*) dissimulation *f* (de la vérité); (*c*) **c. up (for s.o.),** couverture *f* (de qn).

coverlet ['kʌvəlit], *s.* couvre-lit *m*, *pl.* couvre-lits; dessus *m* de lit; couvre-pied(s) *m inv*.

coverpoint ['kʌvəpɔint], *s. Cr:* joueur qui double celui qui est posté à droite du guichet.

covert[1] ['kʌvət], *a.* **1.** (*of threat, etc.*) caché, voilé; clandestin; **c. action,** action clandestine; **c. attack,** attaque indirecte, préparée en secret, dans la clandestinité; **c. enemy,** ennemi secret, clandestin, opérant dans la clandestinité. **2.** *Jur:* **feme c.,** femme *f* en puissance de mari. **3.** *occ.* abrité; *Fort:* **c. way,** chemin couvert.

covert[2], *s.* **1.** *Ven:* = COVER[1] 5 (*b*). **2.** *Orn:* **tail coverts, wing coverts,** plumes tectrices de la queue, des ailes; **upper tail coverts,** plumes sus-caudales; **lower tail coverts,** plumes sous-caudales.

covert-coat ['kʌvətkout], *s. Tail:* paletot *m* en cover-coat (pour équitation).

covert-coating ['kʌvət'koutiŋ], *s. Tex:* cover-coat *m inv*.

covertly ['kʌvətli], *adv.* secrètement; en secret, en cachette; clandestinement.

coverture ['kʌvətjər], *s.* **1.** *A: & Lit:* refuge *m*, abri *m*. **2.** *Jur:* **under c.,** en puissance de mari.

cover-up ['kʌvərʌp], *s.* dissimulation *f* (d'une irrégularité, etc.); **to act as a c.-up,** se prêter à une dissimulation.

covet ['kʌvit], *v.tr.* **(coveted)** (*a*) convoiter; (*b*) ambitionner (qch.), aspirer à (qch.); **appointments that are becoming more and more coveted,** postes qui sont de plus en plus brigués, recherchés.

covetable ['kʌvitəbl], *a.* convoitable.

coveter ['kʌvitər], *s.* convoiteur, -euse.

covetous ['kʌvitəs], *a.* **1.** avide **(of gain,** de gain); **c. man,** homme *m* avare, cupide. **2. to be c. of s.o. else's property,** convoiter les biens d'autrui; **c. glance,** regard *m* de convoitise; **to cast c. eyes on sth.,** convoiter qch. des yeux; regarder qch. d'un œil de convoitise; **to arouse c. desires,** allumer des convoitises.

covetously ['kʌvitəsli], *adv.* avec convoitise; avidement; **to look c. at sth.,** regarder qch. d'un œil de convoitise.

covetousness ['kʌvitəsnis], *s.* **1.** cupidité *f*, avidité *f*. **2.** convoitise *f*.

covey ['kʌvi], *s.* **1.** compagnie *f*, vol *m* (de perdrix, de coqs de bruyère). **2.** *F:* troupe *f*, bande *f* (de personnes).

covin ['kʌvin], *s.* **1.** *A: & Jur:* collusion *f*. **2.** *A: & Scot:* bande *f* (de sorcières, etc.).

coving ['kouviŋ], *s. Arch:* voussure *f*.

cow[1] [kau], *s.* **1.** (*a*) vache *f*; **milch c., milking c.,** vache laitière; *F:* (*of pers.*) **milch c.,** vache à lait; **c. in, with, calf,** vache pleine; **c. pat(ch),** bouse *f* de vache; *Austr: N.Z: F:* **c. banger, c. cocky, c. spanker,** (i) éleveur *m* de vaches laitières; (ii) vacher *m*, cowboy *m*; *U.S:* **c. town,** ville *f* de marché (d'une région laitière); *P:* **c. juice,** lait *m*; *F:* **to wait until the cows come home,** attendre jusqu'à la semaine des quatre jeudis, jusqu'à la Saint-Glinglin; (*b*) **sacred c.,** (i) *Rel:* vache sacrée; (ii) *F:* institution *f* intouchable; (*c*) *P:* (*woman*) **old c.,** vache, vieille chipie, vieille bique; *Austr:* **silly c.,** idiot *m*, drôle *m* de type; **fair c.,** (i) (*esp. of man*) salaud *m*, sale type *m*; (ii) sale affaire *f*; **he's, it's, (a) fair c.,** ce qu'il est, que c'est, moche; (*d*) (*of horse, dog*) **c. hock,** jarret clos; **c.-hocked,** (cheval, chien) clos de derrière, serré du derrière; (jument *f*) panard; (*of horse*) **c. kick,** coup *m* de pied en vache; **to give a c. kick,** ruer en vache. **2.** (*of elephant, whale, seal, etc.*) femelle *f*; **c. rhinoceros,** rhinocéros *m* femelle; **c. buffalo,** bufflette *f*, bufflonne *f*. **3.** (*a*) *Bot:* **c. parsley, c. weed,** cerfeuil *m* sauvage; **c. parsnip,** berce *f*; acanthe *f* d'Allemagne; angélique *f* sauvage; **c. lily,** (i) renoncule *f* des marais; (ii) nuphar *m* des étangs, lis *m* jaune; **c. wheat,** mélampyre *m* des champs, *F:* blé *m* des vaches, rougeole *f*, rougeotte *f*, rouget *m*, queue-de-renard *f*, queue-de-loup *f*, cornette *f*; **c. tree,** galactodendron *m*, arbre *m* à la vache; (*b*) *Z:* **Steller's sea c.,** rhytine *f* de Steller, stellère *mf*; *Coel:* **c. paps,** alcyon *m*.

cow[2], *v.tr.* **1.** intimider, dompter (qn); **to be cowed in s.o.'s presence,** être, se sentir, intimidé en présence de qn; **to look cowed,** avoir l'air d'un chien battu. **2.** accouardir (un chien, etc.).

cowage ['kauidʒ], *s. Bot:* **1.** mucune *f*. **2. creeping c.,** tragie *f*. **3. c. cherry,** moureiller *m*; cerisier *m* des Antilles.

coward ['kauəd], *s. & a.* lâche (*mf*); *A:* couard, -e; *F:* capon, -onne; *Her:* **lion c.,** lion couard; **to turn a man, an animal, into a c.,** accouardir un homme, un animal; **to turn c.,** s'accouardir; **I'm a terrible c. in the dark,** je suis très poltron, j'ai bien peur, quand il fait nuit.

cowardice ['kauədis], **cowardliness** ['kauədlinəs], *s.* lâcheté *f*; poltronnerie *f*.

cowardly ['kauədli], *a.* lâche; poltron.

cowbane ['kaubein], *s. Bot:* cicutaire *f* aquatique; ciguë vireuse, ciguë aquatique.

cowbell ['kaubel], *s.* **1.** clochette *f*, sonnette *f*, clarine *f*, sonnaille *f* (pour bétail). **2.** *Bot: U.S:* silène enflé; béhen blanc.

cowberry ['kauberi], *s. Bot:* myrtille *f* rouge; airelle ponctuée.

cowbird ['kaubə:d], *s. Orn:* molothre *m*, carouge *m*, *Fr.C:* vacher *m*; **shiny c.,** carouge brillant; **bay-winged c.,** molothre à ailes baies; **screaming c.,** molothre bruyant; **North-American c.,** molothre des troupeaux.

cowboy ['kaubɔi], *s.* vacher *m*; cowboy *m*.

cowcatcher ['kaukætʃər], *s. U.S:* cow-catcher *m*, chasse-bestiaux *m inv*, fender *m* (de locomotive).

cower ['kauər], *v.i.* **1.** se blottir, se tapir (à terre); se faire tout petit. **2. to c. before s.o.,** trembler, se faire tout petit, devant qn.

cowfish ['kaufiʃ], *s.* **1.** *Z:* lamantin *m*; vache marine. **2.** *Ich:* coffre (cornu), vache *f* des mers.

cowgirl ['kaugə:l], *s.* vachère *f*.

cowgrass ['kaugrɑ:s], *s. Bot:* trèfle *m* des prés.

cowhage ['kauidʒ], *s.* = COWAGE.

cowhand ['kauhænd], *s.* vacher *m*; cowboy *m*.

cowheel ['kauhi:l], *s. Cu:* pied *m* de vache en gelée.

cowherd ['kauhə:d], *s.* vacher *m*; bouvier *m*.

cowhide[1] ['kauhaid], *s.* **1.** *Leath:* peau *f* de vache; cuir *m* de vache; vache *f*; **soft c.,** vache souple; **grained c.,** vache maroquinée. **2.** *esp. U.S:* gros fouet en cuir de vache.

cowhide[2], *v.tr. U.S:* administrer une volée de coups de fouet à (qn).

cowhouse ['kauhaus], *s.* vacherie *f*, étable *f*.

cowl[1] [kaul], *s.* **1.** *Ecc:* (*a*) capuchon *m*, capuce *m* (de moine); **penitent's c.,** cagoule *f*; *Prov:* **the c. does not make the monk,** l'habit ne fait pas le moine; **to take the c.,** prendre le capuchon; (*b*) têtière *f* (d'un capuchon de moine). **2.** (*a*) capuchon, capote *f*, chapeau *m*, champignon *m*, mitre *f*, abat-vent *m inv*, tabourin *m*, gueule-de-loup *f*, *pl.* gueules-de-loup (de cheminée, de ventilateur); **rotating, revolving, c.,** girouette *f* à fumée; (*b*) *Av: Nau:* capot *m* (de moteur, de cheminée).

cowl[2], *v.tr.* capuchonner (une cheminée, etc.).

cowled [kauld], *a.* (en)capuchonné.

cowlick ['kaulik], *s. F:* épi *m* (de cheveux).

cowling ['kauliŋ], *s.* **1.** capuchonnement *m* (d'une cheminée). **2.** capot *m*, capotage *m* (de moteur).

cowl-shaped ['kaulʃeipt], *a.* cuculliforme.

cowman, *pl.* **-men** ['kaumæn, -men], *s.m.* (*a*) vacher; cowboy; (*b*) *U.S:* propriétaire d'un ranch.

cowperitis [kaupə'raitis, ku:-], *s. Med:* cowpérite *f*.

cowpoke ['kaupouk], *s. NAm: F:* = COWBOY.

cowpox ['kaupɔks], *s.* (*a*) *Vet:* variole *f* des vaches, cowpox *m*; (*b*) *Med:* **inoculated c.,** vaccine *f*.

cowpuncher ['kaupʌntʃər], *s.m. U.S:* cowboy; conducteur de bestiaux.

cowrie ['kauəri], *s.* **1.** *Conch: Moll:* porcelaine *f*; *F:* pucelage *m*. **2.** (*money*) cauri(s) *m*.

cowry bird ['kauribə:d], *s. Orn:* damier *m*.

cowshed ['kauʃed], *s.* étable *f*.

cowskin ['kauskin], *s.* = COWHIDE[1].

cowslip ['kauslip], *s. Bot:* (fleur *f* de) coucou *m*; primevère commune; primevère des champs.

cowslipping ['kauslipiŋ], *s.* cueillette *f* des fleurs de coucou.

cowtail ['kauteil], *s. Tex:* écouailles *fpl*.

cox[1] [kɔks], *s. Row:* barreur *m*.

cox[2], *v.tr. & i. Row:* diriger, gouverner (un canot); barrer.

cox[3], *s. Hort:* (*from Pr.n.,* **Cox's orange pippins**) = reinette *f*.

coxa, *pl.* **-ae** ['kɔksə, -i:], *s.* **1.** *Anat:* (*a*) hanche *f*; (*b*) ischion *m*. **2.** *Ent:* hanche, coxa *f*, article *m* coxal.

coxal ['kɔksəl], *a. Anat: etc:* coxal, -aux.

coxalgia [kɔks'ældʒiə], *s. Med:* coxalgie *f*.

coxalgic [kɔks'ældʒik], *a. Med:* coxalgique.

coxcomb ['kɔkskoum], *s. O:* petit-maître *m*, *pl.* petits-maîtres; fat *m*, freluquet *m*, avantageux *m*, prétentieux *m*, vaniteux *m*.

coxed [kɔkst], *a. Row:* **a c. pair,** un deux barré; **a c. four,** un quatre barré.

coxitis [kɔks'aitis], *s. Med:* **senile c.,** coxarthrie *f*, coxarthrose *f*.

coxless ['kɔkslis], *a. Row:* **a c. four,** un quatre sans barreur.

coxodynia [kɔksou'diniə], *s. Med:* coxodynie *f*.

coxofemoral [kɔksou'femərl], *a. Anat:* coxo-fémoral, -aux.

coxopodite [kɔks'ɔpədait], *s. Crust:* coxopodite *m*.

coxwain[1] ['kɔksn], *s.* **1.** *Nau:* patron *m* (d'une chaloupe, d'un canot); **Admiral's c.,** patron de la vedette de l'amiral. **2.** *Row:* barreur *m*.

coxwain[2], *v.tr.* = COX[2].

coxwainless ['kɔks(ə)nlis], *a. Row:* sans barreur; **a c. pair, four,** un deux, quatre, sans barreur.

coy [kɔi], *a.* (*esp. of girl*) (*a*) timide, réservée, modeste, farouche, sauvage; **not over-coy,** peu farouche; (*b*) qui fait la sainte-nitouche.

coyly ['kɔili], *adv.* modestement, timidement; avec réserve.

coyness ['kɔinis], *s.* timidité *f*, modestie *f*, réserve *f*.

coyote [kɔi'jouti], *s.* **1.** *Z:* coyote *m*. **2.** *F: O:* fripouille *f*, vaurien *m*.

coyp(o)u ['kɔipu:], *s. Z:* coypou *m*, ragondin *m*.

coz [kʌz], *s. F: A:* cousin, -ine.

coze[1] [kouz], *s. F: A:* causerie *f* intime (entre amis); causette *f*.

coze[2], *v.i. F: A:* s'entretenir familièrement; faire la causette.

cozen ['kʌzn], *v.tr. A:* tromper, duper (qn); **to c. s.o. out of sth.,** dépouiller qn de qch.; filouter qch. à qn; **to c. s.o. into doing sth.,** user d'artifices pour amener qn à faire qch.

cozenage ['kʌzənidʒ], *s. A:* fourberie *f*, tromperie *f*.

conzener ['kʌzənər], *s. A:* fourbe *m*; trompeur *m*.

cozy ['kouzi], *a.* = COSY.

cozymase [kou'zaimeis], *s. Bio-Ch:* cozymase *f*.

crab[1] [kræb], *s.* **1.** (*a*) *Crust:* crabe *m*; cancre *m*; **angular c.,** gonoplax *m*; **box c.,** calappe *m*, coq *m* de mer; crabe honteux; **coconut c.,** crabe des cocotiers; **edible c.,** tourteau dormeur, poupart *m,* houvet *m;* **fiddler c.,** crabe appelant; **furrowed c.,** crabe sillonné; **green c.,** crabe enragé; carcin *m;* **hairy porcelain c.,** petit crabe velu; porcellane *f;* **hermit c.,** pagure *m,* bernard-l'ermite *m inv;* **king c.,** crabe des Moluques; limule *m;* **land c.,** crabe terrestre, de terre; tourlourou *m;* gécarcin *m;* **masked c.,** crabe masqué; **robber c., trees c.,** crabe des cocotiers; **shore c.,** crabe enragé, carcin; **soldier c.,** soldat marin, bernard-l'ermite; **spider c.,** araignée *f* de mer; maïa *m;* **swimming c.,** crabe laineux, anglais; étrille *f;* **c.-eating,** (phoque, raton, etc.) crabbier; *Fish:* **c. pot,** nasse *f,* casier *m* (à crabes); *Aer:* **c.-pot (valve),** clapet *m* (d'isolement), valve *f,* manchon *m* (de dirigeable); *Austr:* **c. hole,** trou creusé par un crabe terrestre; *Row: F:* **to catch a c.,** (i) engager un aviron; (ii) attaquer en sifflet; faire fausse rame; (*b*) *P:* **c. (louse),** pou *m* du pubis, *P:* morpion *m.* **2.** *Astr:* **the C.,** (i) (*constellation*) le Cancer; (ii) (*nebula*) le Crabe. **3.** *Av:* vol *m* en crabe. **4.** *Ind: etc:* treuil (roulant, portatif); chèvre *f;* singe *m;* **crane c.,** chariot *m* de pont roulant; **ceiling c.,** chariot (transporteur) à poutre de plafond; **bracket c.,** treuil d'applique; **c. winch, c. windlass,** treuil à manivelle; (*with vertical barrel*) vindas *m,* vindau *m.* **5.** *Gaming:* **to throw crabs,** amener deux as; *F:* (*of enterprise, etc.*) **to turn out crabs,** échouer. **6.** *pl. Publ:* **crabs,** rendus *m;* invendus (renvoyés aux éditeurs).

crab[2] **(crabbed) 1.** *v.i.* (*of pers.*) marcher, avancer, en crabe; *Nau:* (*of ship*) marcher en dépendant; dériver. **2.** *v.tr. Av:* faire avancer (l'appareil) diagonalement. **3.** *v.i.* prendre les crabes.

crab[3], *s.* **1.** *Bot:* **c. (apple),** pomme *f* sauvage; **c. (tree),** pommier *m* sauvage. **2. c. (stick),** (*a*) (i) bâton *m* de pommier sauvage; (ii) (*any sort of cudgel*) bâton épineux; (*b*) *F:* personne *f* revêche, maussade; bâton épineux; *P:* bâton merdeux.

crab[4], *v.tr.* **1.** (*of hawks*) **to c. each other,** se griffer, se battre. **2.** *F:* (*a*) critiquer, décrier, déprécier, dénigrer (qn, qch.); chiner, débiner, charrier (qn); (*b*) mettre des bâtons dans les roues à (qn); **to c. a scheme,** se mettre en travers d'un projet; faire échouer un projet.

crab[5], *s. F: O:* critique *f;* **my c. to them is . . .,** ce que je leur reproche, c'est . . .; **that's the c.!** voilà le chiendent!

crabbed ['kræb(i)d], *a.* **1.** (*of pers., character*) maussade, désagréable, grognon, grincheux, revêche, rêche, rechigné, aigre; *F:* grinchu; (*of woman*) acariâtre; **you're very c. today!** comme vous êtes désagréable aujourd'hui! **c. face,** visage renfrogné. **2. c. style,** style pénible, difficile, entortillé, rébarbatif; **c. writing,** écriture *f* illisible, en pattes de mouche.

crabbedly ['kræbidli], *adv.* **1.** d'un ton bourru, d'un air revêche, aigrement, maussadement. **2. to write c.,** (i) avoir une écriture difficile à lire; (ii) avoir le style pénible.

crabbedness ['kræbidnis], *s.* humeur *f* aigre, acariâtre; maussaderie *f,* âpreté *f,* aspérité *f.*

crabber[1] ['kræbər], *s.* bateau pêcheur de crabes.

crabber[2], *s.* ronchonneur, -euse.

crabby ['kræbi], *a.* = CRABBED 1; **you're very c. today,** comme vous êtes désagréable aujourd'hui!

crabeater ['kræbi:tər], *s. Orn: Z:* (*heron, racoon, etc.*) crabier *m.*

crabgrass ['kræbgrɑ:s], *s. Bot:* digitaria *m.*

crablike ['kræblaik], *a.* de crabe, comme un crabe.

crab plover ['kræbplʌvər], *s. Orn:* drome *m* (ardéole); dromas *m.*

crab's eyes ['kræbzaiz], **crabstones** ['kræbstounz], *s. pl.* **1.** *Crust: A.Med:* yeux *m* d'écrevisse, pierres *f* d'écrevisse. **2.** graines de l'abrus precatorius (utilisées dans la confection de chapelets).

crabwise ['kræbwaiz], *adv.* comme un crabe; **to walk c.,** marcher en crabe, de biais; *Nau:* **to edge away c.,** s'éloigner en dépendant.

Cracidae ['kræsidi:], *s.pl. Orn:* cracidés *m;* les hoccos *m.*

crack[1] [kræk], *s. & a.*

I. *s.* **1.** (*a*) craquement *m,* crac *m* (de branches, de glace, etc.); claquement *m,* clic-clac *m* (de fouet); détonation *f,* claquement sec (d'une arme à feu); crépitement *m* (d'une fusillade); *F:* **in a c.,** en un clin d'œil; (*b*) *F:* **c. on the head,** (i) coup sec sur la tête; (ii) taloche *f;* (*c*) *F:* **to have, take, a c. at sth.,** essayer de faire qch.; **have, take, a c. at it!** essayez le coup! essayez un peu! **to give s.o. a c. at sth.,** laisser qn tenter le coup; **you can have (the) first c.,** à vous le premier coup, le premier essai; **at one c.,** d'un seul coup, dès le premier essai. **2.** (*a*) fente *f,* fissure *f;* (*in skin, wood, metal*) gerçure *f,* crevasse *f;* (*in stone*) flache *f;* (*in wrought steel, etc.*) tapure *f,* criqûre *f,* crique *f* (de chauffage); (*in wall, ground*) crevasse, lézarde *f,* bâillement *m;* (*in cliff*) avalure *f;* (*in varnish, enamel*) craquelure *f,* trésaillure *f;* (*in glass, pottery, bell, cylinder head, etc.*) fêlure *f;* **radial c.** (*in glass, etc.*), étoile *f* (*wood, ground*) **heat c.,** fente de sécheresse; **frost c.,** gélivure *f* (du bois); **shrinkage c.,** (i) *Geol:* gerçure (due au soleil); fente, cassure *f,* de retrait; (ii) *Metall:* tapure *f* (dans le métal coulé); *Metall:* **fire c.,** crique, criqûre, de recuit; tapure de chauffage; **season c.,** crique saisonnière; **c. detection,** ressuage *m;* **magnetic c. detector,** métalloscope *m;* **ground showing numerous cracks,** terrain crevassé de nombreuses fissures; *Vet:* **toe c.,** soie *f* dans le sabot; **sand c.,** seime *f;* **the cracks in the social structure,** les fissures de l'édifice social; **to paper over the cracks in a scheme,** masquer les défauts d'un projet; *U.S: P:* **to walk the c.,** marcher le long d'une fente entre les ais du plancher (comme preuve qu'on n'est pas ivre); (*b*) entrebâillement *m* (d'une porte, etc.); *F:* **open the window a c.,** ouvrez la fenêtre un petit peu; (*c*) **the c. of dawn,** la pointe du jour; les premières lueurs de l'aube. **3.** *Scot:* causerie *f,* causette *f;* **to have a c. with s.o.,** tailler une bavette avec qn. **4.** *F:* cheval *m,* joueur *m,* etc., de premier ordre; *Sp:* crack *m.* **5.** *P:* (*a*) cambrioleur *m;* (*b*) cambriolage *m.* **6.** *F:* bon mot; saillie *f;* plaisanterie *f;* **nasty c.,** plaisanterie acérée; **that was a nasty, dirty, c.,** ça, c'est plutôt vache, rosse.

II. *a. F:* fameux; d'élite; de première force; de la première volée; **c. shot,** fin tireur; tireur de premier ordre; tireur d'élite; **c. regiment,** régiment *m* d'élite; *Sp:* **c. club,** club *m* vedette; **c. horse,** crack *m;* **c. player,** as *m,* crack; **he's a c. tennis player,** il est de première force au tennis; *Aut:* **c. racing driver,** as du volant; *Rail:* **c. train** = train *m* de luxe, train drapeau.

crack[2], *int.* clac! crac! pan!

crack[3], *v.*

I. *v.tr.* **1.** faire claquer (un fouet); faire craquer (ses doigts); *F:* **to c. s.o. over the head,** asséner un coup sur la tête à qn; assommer qn. **2.** (*a*) fêler (une cloche, un verre); gercer, crevasser (la peau); lézarder, crevasser (un mur, la terre); fendre, fendiller (une pierre, etc.); fracturer (un os); (*b*) (i) casser (une noisette); (ii) croquer (une noisette) sous la dent; **to c. one's skull,** se casser la tête; *F:* **to c. a bottle of wine (with s.o.),** déboucher une bouteille de vin; vider, boire, une bouteille (avec qn); *Sp:* **to c. a record,** battre un record; (*c*) *F:* **to c. a problem,** résoudre un problème; trouver la solution d'un problème; **to c. a code,** décrypter un chiffre; trouver la clef d'un chiffre; **to c. a safe,** percer un coffre-fort; *P:* **to c. a crib,** cambrioler une maison; (*d*) *Ind:* fractionner, craquer (une huile lourde). **3. to c. a joke,** faire, lâcher, lancer, une plaisanterie; **to c. jokes,** débiter des drôleries; dire des facéties, des joyeusetés; **to c. jokes at s.o.'s expense,** s'amuser aux dépens de qn; prendre qn comme tête de Turc. **4.** *U.S:* **to c. the door,** ouvrir la porte un petit peu; *Aut:* **to c. the throttle,** ouvrir, mettre, les gaz un tout petit peu.

II. *v.i.* **1.** craquer; (*of whip*) claquer; **a rifle cracked,** un coup de fusil partit; on entendit un coup de fusil. **2.** se fêler; se fissurer; se crevasser; (*of wall*) se lézarder, travailler; (*of skin*) se gercer; se fendre, se fendiller, se craqueter; (*of steel*) s'égrener; (*of steel under the smith's hammer*) criquer; *F:* **the social structure is cracking,** l'édifice social est en train de craquer. **3.** (*a*) (*of voice*) se casser, se fausser; (*at puberty*) muer; (*b*) **after five hours' questioning he cracked,** après cinq heures d'interrogatoire il s'effondra; (*c*) *Rac:* (*of horse*) s'effondrer. **4.** *Scot: F:* causer, faire la causette (avec qn). **5.** *Austr: N.Z:* **to c. hearty,** faire bonne mine, bon cœur (à mauvais jeu). **6.** *U.S:* (*of dawn*) poindre. **7.** *F:* **to get cracking,** s'y mettre; **get cracking!** grouille-toi! magne-toi!

III. (*compound verbs*) **1. crack along,** *v.i. F: Sp: Aut: etc:* faire de la vitesse.

2. crack back, *v.i. F:* **to c. back at s.o.,** répliquer vivement à qn.

3. crack down, *v.i. F:* **to c. down on s.o.,** (i) laver la tête à qn; *P:* engueuler qn; (ii) devenir plus strict avec qn; serrer les pouces à qn; **to c. down on smuggling,** prendre des mesures sévères contre la contrebande.

4. crack on. (*a*) *v.tr. Nau:* **to c. on sail,** faire force de voiles; **cracking on,** couvert de toile; à toc de toile; *U.S: F:* **to c. on another tax,** imposer une nouvelle taxe; (*b*) *v.i. F:* continuer à parler, à se plaindre.

5. crack up. (*a*) *v.tr.* (i) mettre (qch.) en morceaux; (ii) **to c. (s.o., sth.) up (to the nines),** vanter, prôner (qn, qch.); préconiser (un remède, etc.); faire mousser (qch.); **it's not all it's cracked up to be,** ce n'est pas tout ce qu'on en dit; (*b*) *v.i.* (*of empire, etc.*) se démembrer; *F:* craquer; (*of firm*) faire faillite; (*of bank*) faire un krach; *F:* (*of pers.*) défaillir; **he's cracking up,** il n'y a plus d'huile dans la lampe.

crackajack ['krækədʒæk], *s. & a.* = CRACKERJACK.

crackbrain ['krækbrein], *s. F:* cerveau fêlé.

crackbrained ['krækbreind], *a. F:* au cerveau timbré, fêlé, piqué; à l'esprit fêlé; **a c. creature,** un échappé de Charenton; **c. notion,** idée folle.

crack(-)down ['krækdaun], *s.* mesure *f* énergique; **public opinion demanded an immediate c. on the illicit drug trade,** l'opinion demandait qu'on prît immédiatement des mesures sévères contre le trafic illicite des stupéfiants.

cracked [krækt], *a.* **1.** fêlé, fendu; (*of wall*) lézardé; (*of tree, timber*) gerçuré; **tree, stone, c. by frost,** arbre gélif, pierre gélive; **c. voice,** voix cassée; **to sound c.,** sonner le fêlé; *Vet:* **c. heel,** crevasses *fpl* (au pied du cheval); mule traversière, mule traversine. **2.** *F:* timbré, toqué; loufoque, maboul, marteau, dingue; **to be c.,** avoir le cerveau, le timbre, le coco, fêlé; **to be slightly c.,** avoir un grain, une fêlure; être un peu toc-toc; **to be c. on, about, s.o.,** être entiché de qn. **3.** *Petr:* **c. petrol,** essence *f* de craquage.

cracker ['krækər], *s.* **1.** (*pers.*) (*a*) **c. of jokes,** faiseur, -euse, de plaisanteries; (*b*) *P:* **c. of cribs,** cambrioleur *m;* (*c*) *F:* **c.-up,** prôneur, -euse; (*d*) *U.S: P:* blanc, *f* blanche, sans fortune. **2.** *F:* mensonge *m,* craque *f;* fanfaronnade *f.* **3.** (*a*) pétard *m;* **jumping c.,** crapaud *m;* (*b*) **(Christmas) c.,** diablotin *m;* papillote *f* à pétard; **c. poetry,** vers *mpl* de mirliton; (*c*) mèche *f* (de fouet). **4. (nut) crackers,** casse-noisette(s) *m inv,* casse noix *m inv.* **5.** biscuit sec; craquelin *m,* croquet *m.* **6.** *Hairdr: F: A:* **crackers,** papillotes. **7.** *F: A:* **to go a c.,** (i) flancher; (ii) aller à un train d'enfer. **8.** *Petr:* appareil *m,* installation *f,* matériel *m,* de craquage.

cracker barrel, box ['krækəbærl, -bɔks]. *NAm:* **1.** *s.* baril *m* à biscuits. **2.** *a.* simple, rustique; **c.-b. philosopher,** philosophe *m* de chambre, du Café du Commerce.

crackerjack ['krækədʒæk], *NAm: F:* **1.** *s.* (*a*) gros bonnet, grosse légume; expert *m;* (*b*) *R.t.m:* **Cracker Jack,** maïs grillé, éclaté et enduit de caramel. **2.** *a.* rupin, chouette.

crackers ['krækəz], *a. F:* **he's c.,** il est cinglé, maboule, loufoque; **to go c.,** perdre la raison.

cracking[1] ['krækiŋ], *a. F:* excellent, épatant; **a c. good dinner,** un dîner à la hauteur, qui en vaut la peine; **to be in c. (good) form,** être en pleine forme, dans une forme à tout casser.

cracking[2], *s.* **1.** claquement *m,* craquement *m,* clic-clac *m.* **2.** fendillement *m;* craquelure *f,* craquelage *m* (de la peinture); décollements *mpl* (dans les papiers couchés); fissuration *f.* **3.** fractionnement *m,* craquage *m,* cracking *m* (d'une huile lourde); **catalytic c., thermal c.,** craquage catalytique, thermal; **c. plant, installation,** appareil *m,* installation *f,* matériel *m,* de craquage; cracking *m;* **c. unit,** unité *f* de cracking; **c. furnace, kiln,** four *m* de craquage. **4.** *Vet:* **c. off of a horse's hoof,** avalure *f* du sabot d'un cheval.

crackjaw ['krækdʒɔ:], *a. F:* (nom, etc.) impossible à prononcer, *F:* à vous décrocher la mâchoire.

crackle[1] ['krækl], *s.* **1.** craquement *m,* craquètement *m,* craquettement *m;* crépitement *m,* crépitation *f;* cri *m* (de l'étain); *W.Tel:* crachements *mpl;* friture *f;* crachotements *mpl.* **2.** fendillement *m;* trésaillure *f* (de peinture, de porcelaine); *Cer:* **c. finish,** craquelage *m;* **(black and) c. finish,** surface granitée; *Glassm:* **c. mark,** crachat *m.* **3.** *Cer:* **c. (ware, china, glass),** craquelé *m.*

crackle[2]. **1.** *v.i.* (*a*) craqueter; (*of dried leaves, etc.*) craquer; (*of shots, salt on fire, etc.*) crépiter; (*of snow, something frying*) grésiller; (*of fire*) pétiller; *W.Tel:* crachoter; (*b*) se fendiller; se craqueler. **2.** *v.tr.* fendiller; *Cer:* craqueler.

crackled ['krækld], *a.* **1.** (*of oil painting*) fendillé, faïencé; (*of painting, chinaware*) trésaillé; (*of chinaware*) truité. **2.** *Cer:* craquelé.

crackler ['kræklər], *s. Crust:* craquelot *m,* craquelin *m.*

crackling[1] ['krækliŋ], *a.* pétillant, crépitant, grésillant; *Tp: W.Tel:* **c. noise,** friture *f.*

crackling[2], *s.* **1.** (*a*) = CRACKLE[1] 1, 2; (*b*) *Cer:* (*process*) craquelage *m,* craquèlement *m,* craquellement *m.* **2.** *Cu:* (*a*) peau croquante (du porc rôti); couenne *f;* (*b*) *Dial:* **cracklings,** cretons *m,* fritons *m;* (*c*) *P:* **a nice bit of c.,** une croquignole, un prix de Diane.

cracknel ['krækn(ə)l], *s.* (*biscuit*) craquelin *m,* croquignole *f.*

crackpot ['krækpɔt]. *F:* **1.** *s.* cerveau fêlé; **he's a c.,** il est dingo, cinglé. **2.** *a.* **a c. idea,** une idée folle.

cracksman, *pl.* **-men** ['kræksmən], *s. F:* cambrioleur *m.*

crack-up ['krækʌp], *s.* **1.** débâcle *f* (d'un système, d'un gouvernement, de la santé); **mental c. up,** effondrement *m* de la raison. **2.** destruction complète (d'un avion, etc.).

crack-voiced ['krækvɔist], *a.* à la voix fêlée; (*of boy*) à la voix qui mue.

cracky ['kræki], *a. F:* **1.** fendillé. **2.** fragile, cassant. **3.** (*of pers.*) **to be a bit c.,** avoir le cerveau, le timbre, fêlé. **4.** *Scot:* causeur, -euse; bavard, -arde.

Cracovian [krə'kouviən]. *Geog:* (*a*) *a.* cracovien; (*b*) *s.* Cracovien, -ienne.

Cracow ['krækau], *s. Geog:* Cracovie *f.*

cracowe ['krækou], *s. A.Cost:* soulier *m* à la poulaine.

cradle[1] ['kreidl], *s.* **1.** (*a*) berceau *m* (d'un enfant, d'une science, d'un art, d'une civilisation); **wicker c.,** moïse *m*; **child in the c.,** enfant au berceau; **to have been changed in the c.,** avoir été changé en nourrice; **from the c.,** dès le berceau; **I have known this from my c.,** j'ai appris cela au berceau; **from the c. to the grave,** du berceau au tombeau; (*b*) *Nau:* cadre *m* (d'hôpital). **2.** *Ind:* berceau (d'une machine, etc.); cadre; *N.Arch:* ber *m* (de lancement); *Nau:* **boat c.,** chantier *m*; *Nau: Av:* **starting c.,** chariot *m* de lancement (d'un avion à bord); *Artil:* **c. mounting,** affût *m* à berceau. **3.** (*a*) *Const: Min:* échafaud(age) volant; pont volant; **c.-iron, c.-stirrup,** étrier *m* d'échafaudage; (*b*) sellette *f* (de peintre, de calfateur). **4.** (*a*) *Min:* (*for gold*) **c. (rocker),** berceau, cradle *m*; sas *m* mobile; (*b*) *Cin:* **c. head,** trépied *m* à bascule (pour prise de vues). **5.** *Agr:* râteau *m*, crochets *mpl* (d'une faux); **c. scythe,** faux *f* à râteau. **6.** *Engr:* berceau (pour donner du grain à la planche). **7.** *Med:* (*a*) (*splint*) gouttière *f* (de contention); (*b*) (*over bed*) cerceau *m*, arceau *m*, archet *m*. **8.** *Vet:* chapelet *m* (pour empêcher un cheval de se lécher). **9.** *Tp:* étrier *m*, fourche interruptrice (de récepteur); support *m* (de combiné).

cradle[2], *v.tr.* **1.** mettre, coucher, (qn) dans un berceau; **cradled in luxury,** bercé dans le luxe; **to be cradled in a doctrine,** sucer une doctrine avec le lait. **2.** mettre (un navire) dans un ber. **3.** *Tp:* remettre (le combiné) dans le support, (le récepteur) dans la fourche, dans l'étrier. **4.** *Agr:* faucher (le blé) avec la faux à râteau. **5.** *Min:* **to c. out gold,** extraire de l'or au berceau.

cradleboard ['kreidlbɔ:d], *s. NAm:* porte-bébé(s) (porté dans le dos par les Amérindiens).

cradle books ['kreidlbuks], *s.pl. Typ:* incunables *m.*

cradlesnatcher ['kreidlsnætʃər], *s. F:* **he's, she's, a c.,** il, elle, les prend au berceau, au biberon.

cradlesnatching ['kreidlsnætʃiŋ], *s. F:* **I don't go in for c.,** je ne les prends pas au berceau, au biberon.

cradlesong ['kreidlsɔŋ], *s.* berceuse *f.*

cradle vault ['kreidlvɔ:lt], *s. Arch:* (voûte *f* en) tonnelle *f*; (voûte en) berceau *m.*

cradling ['kreidliŋ], *s. Const:* cintre *m* (de voûte).

craft[1] [krɑ:ft], *s.* **1.** (*a*) habileté *f*, adresse *f*; (*b*) *Pej:* ruse *f*; artifice *m*; fourberie *f*. **2.** (*a*) (i) métier manuel; (ii) profession *f*; **questions relating to crafts,** questions artisanales; **arts and crafts,** (i) artisanat *m* d'expression; (ii) *Sch:* travaux manuels; *Prov:* **every man to his c.,** chacun son métier; **painter, sculptor, who is master of his c.,** peintre *m*, sculpteur *m*, qui a du métier; **c.-bowl,** bol ouvré; (*b*) *Sch: A:* **the seven crafts,** les sept arts (des universités du moyen âge). **3.** (*a*) corps *m* de métier; **c. union,** syndicat *m* dont les membres appartiennent au même corps de métier; (*b*) **the C.,** la franc-maçonnerie. **4.** (*pl.* **craft**) *Nau:* embarcation *f*, petit navire; **small c.,** canots *mpl*, petits bâtiments, petits bateaux; **hundreds of small c.,** des centaines d'embarcations; *Navy:* **harbour c.,** bâtiments de servitude. **5.** *Nau:* outillage *m* de pêche (à la baleine, etc.).

craft[2], *v.tr.* **fine crafted furniture,** de beaux meubles fabriqués, ouvrés, par des experts.

craftily ['krɑ:ftili], *adv.* artificieusement, astucieusement; cauteleusement, subtilement.

craftiness ['krɑ:ftinis], *s.* ruse *f*, astuce *f*, sournoiserie *f*; *F:* roublardise *f.*

craftsman, *pl.* **-men** ['krɑ:ftsmən], *s.m.* **1.** artisan, ouvrier qualifié. **2.** artiste dans son métier; **that great c. William Morris,** William Morris, ce grand artiste dans tous les métiers qu'il exerça.

craftsmanship ['krɑ:ftsmənʃip], *s.* **1.** dextérité manuelle; art consommé; **old furniture of marvellous c.,** vieux meubles d'une exécution merveilleuse; **bad c.,** travail *m* indigne d'un bon ouvrier; **a wonderful piece of c.,** un chef-d'œuvre merveilleux. **2.** (*in writer, etc.*) (connaissance *f* du) métier.

crafty ['krɑ:fti], *a.* artificieux, astucieux, sournois, rusé, cauteleux; *F:* roublard.

crag [kræg], *s.* **1.** (*a*) rocher, flanc, de montagne escarpé; rocher à pic; **overhanging c.,** rocher en surplomb; (*b*) *Mount:* varappe *f*. **2.** *Geol:* crag *m.*

cragged ['krægid], *a.* = CRAGGY.

craggedness ['krægidnis], **cragginess** ['kræginis], *s.* aspect anfractueux, rocailleux (d'une montagne); anfractuosité(s) *f*(*pl*).

craggy ['krægi], *a.* **1.** rocailleux, anfractueux; **mountains with c. sides,** montagnes aux flancs rocailleux, aux flancs escarpés. **2. c. face,** visage anguleux, taillé à coups de serpe.

cragsman, *pl.* **-men** ['krægzmən], *s.m.* ascensionniste de rochers, de varappes; varappeur.

crake[1] [kreik], *s.* **1.** *Orn:* râle *m*; **water c., spotted c.,** râle marouette, marouette ponctuée; **Carolina c.,** marouette de la Caroline; **little c.,** marouette poussin, râle poussin; **Baillon's c.,** râle, marouette, de Baillon. **2.** cri *m* du râle.

crake[2], *v.i.* (*of corncrake*) crier.

crakow ['krækou], *s. A.Cost:* soulier *m* à la poulaine.

cram[1] [kræm], *s.* **1.** (*a*) *Husb: Dial:* gavée *f*; (*b*) *Sch: F:* chauffage *m* (pour un examen); = bachotage *m*; **c. shop** = boîte *f* à bachot. **2.** *F:* presse *f* à étouffer; foule serrée. **3.** *F: A:* mensonge *m*, craque *f.*

cram[2], *v.* (**crammed**) **1.** *v.tr.* (*a*) fourrer (**sth. into sth.,** qch. dans qch.); **the 146 prisoners were crammed into a small guard-room,** les 146 prisonniers furent entassés dans un étroit corps de garde; **to c. sth. down one's throat,** se fourrer qch. dans le gosier; **to c. one's hat over one ear,** enfoncer son chapeau sur l'oreille; **book crammed with quotations,** livre *m* qui regorge de citations; *Th:* **the house was crammed,** la salle était bondée; **room crammed to suffocation,** pièce tellement bondée que l'on y suffoque; salle *f* où l'on s'étouffe; **cupboards crammed with linen,** armoires bourrées de linge; (*b*) **to c. s.o. with sth.,** bourrer qn de qch.; *F:* **to c. s.o. (up) with lies,** faire avaler des mensonges à qn; (*c*) *Husb:* empâter, appâter, gaver, engraisser, emboquer, gorger (de la volaille); (*d*) *F:* empiffrer (qn) de nourriture; **to c. oneself with food,** s'empiffrer, se bâfrer; **he crammed them with good things to eat,** il les creva de bonne chère; **to c. a child with sweets,** fourrer des bonbons à un enfant; (*e*) *Sch:* chauffer (un candidat pour un examen); **to c. a pupil with Greek,** bourrer, gaver, farcir, un élève de grec; **he crams me with Latin and Greek,** il me fourre du latin et du grec; (*of student*) **to c. maths,** potasser ferme, bûcher, les math; (*f*) *F:* **to c. a horse,** forcer un cheval. **2.** *v.i. F:* (*a*) s'entasser; **we all crammed into a luggage van,** nous nous sommes entassés dans un fourgon à bagages; (*b*) se gorger de nourriture; s'empiffrer, se gaver (**with,** de); (*c*) *Sch: F:* potasser; **to c. for an exam,** préparer un examen; *F:* se bourrer le crâne en vue d'un examen; = bachoter; (*d*) *F: A:* mentir, raconter des craques.

crambe ['kræmbi], *s. Bot:* crambe *m*, crambé *m.*

crambo ['kræmbou], *s.* bouts-rimés; corbillon *m*; **dumb c.,** charade mimée.

crambus ['kræmbəs], *s. Ent:* crambus *m.*

cramfull ['kræm'ful], *a.* tout plein, regorgeant (**of,** de); **to be c. of sth.,** regorger de qch.

cram-jam ['kræm'dʒæm], *adv. U.S: F:* **c.-j. full,** tout plein; plein à craquer.

crammer ['kræmər], *s.* **1.** *Husb:* (*a*) (*pers.*) gaveur, -euse; (*b*) (*appliance*) gaveuse. **2.** *Sch: F:* (*a*) chauffeur *m*; préparateur *m*; colleur *m*; = bachoteur *m*; (*b*) directeur *m*, *F:* patron *m*, de boîte à bachot; (*c*) boîte *f* à bachot. **3.** *F: A:* mensonge *m*, craque *f.*

cramming ['kræmiŋ], *s.* **1.** entassement *m* (des voyageurs dans un autobus, etc.). **2.** *Husb:* gavage *m*. **3.** *Sch: F:* chauffage *m* (pour un examen); **c. shop,** boîte *f* à bachot. **4.** *Plumb:* bouchage *m* temporaire (d'un tuyau).

cramp[1] [kræmp], *s. Med:* crampe *f*; **writer's c.,** crampe des écrivains; **to be seized with c.,** *F:* **with the c.,** être pris, saisi, d'une crampe; **to have c. in the stomach,** avoir des crampes d'estomac.

cramp[2], *s.* **1.** (*a*) *Const: etc:* **c. (iron),** crampon *m*, crampe *f*, happe *f*, agrafe *f*, ancre *f*, tirant *m*, ancrure *f*; *Carp:* clameau *m*, crochet *m* d'assemblage; **small c. (iron),** cramponnet *m*; (*b*) *Tls:* (*for tightening*) serre-joint(s) *m inv*; *F:* sergeant *m*; presse *f* à vis; bride *f* de serrage, à capote; **joiner's c.,** étau *m* d'ébéniste; **flooring c.,** étreignoir *m*; *Coop:* **hoop c.,** traitoir *m*; (*c*) *Typ:* cornière *f*. **2.** *F: O:* entrave *f*; contrainte *f.*

cramp[3], *v.tr.* **1.** donner des crampes à (qn); *usu. in the passive;* **limbs cramped by the cold,** membres engourdis par le froid. **2.** gêner (les mouvements, l'esprit, etc.); **to be cramped up in a small space,** être à l'étroit; *F:* **to c. s.o.'s style,** priver qn de ses moyens; enlever les moyens à qn. **3.** (*a*) *Const:* cramponner, agrafer (des pierres, etc.); **to c. down a beam,** retenir une poutre; (*b*) *Carp: etc:* presser, serrer (à l'étau, au serre-joint). **4.** *U.S:* virer (un bateau); *Cy:* tourner (la roue directrice à droite, à gauche); *v.i.* (*of boat*) **to c. to the left,** virer à gauche.

cramped [kræmpt], *a.* à l'étroit; gêné; **c. position,** fausse position; position étriquée; **to be, feel, c. for room,** être, se sentir, à l'étroit; n'avoir pas les, ses, coudées franches; **c. courtyard,** cour étriquée; **c. handwriting,** écriture gênée; pattes *fpl* de mouche; **c. style,** style contraint.

crampfish ['kræmpfiʃ], *s. Ich:* torpille *f*, crampe *f.*

crampon ['kræmpən], *s.* **1.** (*a*) crampon *m* à glace; (*b*) *Tchn:* grappin *m*. **2.** *Bot:* crampon.

cramponnee [kræm'pɔni], *a. Her:* **cross c.,** croix cramponnée.

cran [kræn], *s. Fish:* cran *m* (de harengs).

cranage ['kreinidʒ], *s.* droits *mpl* de grue; frais *mpl* de grue.

cranberry ['krænbəri], *s. Bot:* canneberge *f*; airelle *f* cousinette; *U.S: P:* **c. eye,** œil injecté (des ivrognes).

cranberrying ['krænbəriiŋ], *s.* cueillette *f* des airelles.

crane[1] [krein], *s.* **1.** *Orn:* (*a*) grue *f*; **young c.,** gruau *m*; **common c.,** grue cendrée; **Asiatic white c.,** grue sibérienne; **Balearic c., crowned c.,** grue couronnée; **demoiselle c.,** demoiselle *f* de Numidie; **Manchurian c.,** grue (blanche) de Mandchourie; **blue c., Stanley c., paradise c.,** grue de paradis; **sandhill c.,** grue du Canada, *Fr.C:* grue canadienne; **sarus c.,** grue antigone; **whooping c.,** grue blanche américaine; (*b*) *Dial:* (i) cigogne *f*; (ii) héron *m*. **2.** *Mec.E: etc:* grue; **balance c.,** grue à contrepoids; **bridge c., overhead travelling c.,** pont-grue *m*, *pl.* ponts-grues; pont roulant (à voie aérienne); (chariot *m*) transporteur *m*; grue à chariot, à pont roulant; **flying c.,** grue volante, du ciel; **gantry c.,** grue à portique; **giant c., Titan c.,** grue Titan; **Goliath c.,** grue chevalet; **grabbing c.,** grue à benne preneuse; **hammer-head c.,** grue marteau; **hand c.,** grue à bras; **hydraulic c.,** grue hydraulique; **jib c.,** grue à volée, à flèche, à bras; **loco(motive) c., travelling c.,** grue mobile, transportable, roulante; **mast c.,** mât-grue *m*, *pl.* mâts-grues; bigue *f*; **pillar c.,** grue à colonne, à fût; **portal jib c.,** grue à flèche horizontale; **semi-portal bridge c.,** semi-portique *m*, *pl.* semi-portiques; **steam c.,** grue à vapeur; **swing(ing) c., slewing c., revolving c.,** grue pivotante, à pivot; **tower c.,** grue à pylône; **wall c.,** grue murale, à potence, à console; grue d'applique; *Aut:* **breakdown c., salvage c.,** grue de dépannage; grue dépanneuse; *Nau:* **dock c.,** crône *m*; **floating c.,** grue flottante; ponton-grue *m*, *pl.* pontons-grues; *Metall:* **pouring c.,** pont *m* de coulée; *attrib.* **c.-driver,** conducteur *m* de grue; grutier *m*; **c. post,** arbre *m*, fût *m*, de grue; **c. way,** voie *f* pour grues; *Const:* **c. tower,** sapine *f*; *El:* **c. magnet,** électro-aimant *m*, *pl.* électro-aimants, porteur. **3.** *Cin:* (i) grue (de prise de vue); (ii) **light c.,** chariot porte-lampes (de studio). **4.** (*a*) siphon *m*; (*b*) *Rail:* **(water) c.,** grue d'alimentation; bouche *f* d'eau; colonne *f* (d'eau) alimentaire. **5.** console *f* en fer (de crémaillère de cheminée). **6.** *Veh:* **c.(-neck),** cou *m* de cygne.

crane[2]. **1.** *v.tr.* (*a*) lever, hisser, ou descendre, décharger, (des fardeaux) au moyen d'une grue; (*b*) tendre, allonger (le cou); **to c. one's neck to see sth.,** se hausser pour voir qch. **2.** *v.i.* (*a*) **to c. forward,** allonger le cou, la tête, en avant; **to c. out of the window,** se pencher à, par, la fenêtre; (*b*) *Equit:* (*of horse*) **to c. at a hedge,** refuser (devant une haie); *F: O:* **to c. at a difficulty,** hésiter, reculer, devant une difficulté; (*c*) *Cin:* (*of camera*) **to c. up, down,** être dirigé en haut, en bas.

cranefly ['kreinflai], *s. Ent:* tipule *f*; **winter c.,** trichocère *f.*

craneman, *pl.* **-men** ['kreinmən], *s.m.* conducteur de grue; grutier.

craner ['kreinər], *s. O:* **1.** = CRANEMAN. **2.** *Equit:* cheval enclin à refuser.

crane's-bill, cranesbill ['kreinzbil], *s. Bot:* bec-de-grue, *m*, *pl.* becs-de-grue; géranium *m*; **meadow c.-b.,** géranium des prés; **alpine c.-b.,** géranium à feuilles d'aconit.

crang [kræŋ], *s.* carcasse de baleine dépouillée de son lard.

crania ['kreiniə], *s. Moll:* crania *f.*

cranial ['kreiniəl], *a. Anat:* (nerf, etc.) crânien; *Anthr:* **c. index,** indice *m* céphalique.

Craniata [kreini'eitə], *s.pl. Z:* vertébrés *m.*

craniectomy [kreini'ektəmi], *s. Surg:* crâniectomie *f.*

crani(o)- [kreini('ɔ)-, 'kreini(ou)-], *comb.fm.* crani(o)-.

cranioclasis [kreiniou'kleisis], *s. Obst:* cranioclasie *f.*

cranioclast ['kreiniouklæst], *s. Obst:* cranioclaste *m.*

craniograph ['kreiniougræf], *s.* craniographe *m.*

craniological [kreiniou'lɔdʒikl], *a.* craniologique.

craniologist [kreini'ɔlədʒist], *s.* craniologiste *mf*, craniologue *mf.*

craniology [kreini'ɔlədʒi], *s.* craniologie *f.*

craniomalacia ['kreinioumə'leiʃə], *s. Med:* craniomalacie *f.*

craniometer [kreini'ɔmitər], *s. Anthr:* craniomètre *m.*

craniometric [kreiniou'metrik], *a.* craniométrique.

craniometry [kreini'ɔmitri], *s.* craniométrie *f*, céphalométrie *f*.

craniophore ['kreinioufɔ:r], *s. Anthr:* craniophore *m*, craniostat *m*.

cranioplasty ['kreiniouplæsti], *s. Surg:* cranioplastie *f*.

cranioscopy [kreini'ɔskəpi], *s.* cranioscopie *f*.

craniotabes ['kreiniou'teibi:z], *s. Med:* craniotabès *m*.

craniotome ['kreiniətoum], *s. Obst:* craniotome *m*.

craniotomy [kreini'ɔtəmi], *s. Surg:* craniotomie *f*.

cranium, *pl.* **-ia** ['kreiniəm, -iə], *s.* **1.** *Anat:* crâne *m*. **2.** *F:* tête *f*, crâne.

crank[1] [kræŋk], *s.* **1.** *Mec.E:* (*a*) manivelle *f*; cigogne *f* (de meule à aiguiser); **operating c.,** manivelle de manœuvre; *Artil:* **elevating c.,** manivelle de pointage en hauteur; *Mch:* **c. connecting-rod system,** système *m* bielle-manivelle; **disc c., wheel c.,** manivelle à plateau; plateau-manivelle *m*, *pl.* plateaux-manivelles; **throw c.,** arbre, vilebrequin, coudé, à manetons; **treadle c.,** manivelle à pédale; *attrib.* **c. arm,** bras *m*, corps *m*, flasque *m*, de manivelle; **c. axle,** (i) essieu coudé; (ii) *Cy:* axe pédalier; **c. boss,** moyeu *m* de manivelle; **c. brace,** vilebrequin (de menuisier); **c. chamber** = CRANKCASE; **c. cheek,** corps *m* de manivelle; **c. disk,** plateau-manivelle; **c. engine,** moteur *m* avec arbre manivelle, à vilebrequin; **c. head,** tête *f* de bielle; **c. lever,** cigogne; **c. pit,** cuvette *f* de l'arbre coudé; **c. web,** bras *m*, flasque, joue *f*, de manivelle; (*b*) coude *m*. **2.** bascule *f* (d'une cloche).

crank[2], *v.tr.* **1.** *Mec.E:* couder (un essieu). **2. to c. up a car,** lancer une voiture à la main; mettre en route une voiture à la manivelle; **to c. up the engine,** décoller le moteur à la main; lancer le moteur; **to c. away,** continuer à tourner la manivelle de mise en marche.

crank[3], *s. F:* **1.** (*a*) marotte *f*, manie *f*; (*b*) *O:* mot plaisant; paradoxe *m*; *pl.* extravagances *f*, originalités *f*; **quips and cranks,** pointes *f* et bons mots. **2.** (*pers.*) (*a*) maniaque *mf*, excentrique *mf*, original *m*; **he's a fresh air c.,** il a la manie d'ouvrir toutes les fenêtres; (*b*) rouspéteur, -euse; ronchonneur, -euse; geignard, arde.

crank[4], *a.* (*of machinery, apparatus*) qui fonctionne mal ou irrégulièrement; détraqué; délabré.

crank[5], *a.* **c.(-sided) ship,** navire instable, rouleux, chavirable, mal équilibré.

crank[6], *v.i.* (*of wheels, etc.*) grincer.

crankcase ['kræŋkkeis], *s. I.C.E:* carter *m* (du moteur); **dummy c.,** faux carter; **upper, lower, c.,** demi-carter supérieur, inférieur; **barrel-type c.,** carter tubulaire.

cranked [kræŋkt], *a.* coudé, bicoudé.

crankily ['kræŋkili], *adv.* **1.** (répondre, etc.) d'un ton maussade; avec humeur. **2.** (la machine fonctionne) par à-coups, en geignant, capricieusement.

crankiness ['kræŋkinis], *s.* **1.** (*a*) humeur *f* difficile; (*b*) excentricité *f*. **2.** (*a*) mauvais fonctionnement (d'une machine); état délabré; (*b*) *Nau:* chavirabilité *f*, instabilité *f* (d'un navire).

crankpin ['kræŋkpin], *s. Mch: etc:* (i) (*of engine crank*) maneton *m*, tourillon *m*; bouton *m* de manivelle, de vilebrequin; (ii) (*of hand crank*) soie *f*; *I.C.E:* **c. of the crankshaft,** maneton du vilebrequin; **c. sleeve,** douille *f* de maneton; *Sm.a:* **c. of a Maxim gun,** vilebrequin *m* d'une mitrailleuse Maxim.

crankshaft ['kræŋkʃɑ:ft], *s.* vilebrequin *m*; arbre-vilebrequin *m*, *pl.* arbres-vilebrequins; arbre coudé; **five-bearing c.,** vilebrequin à cinq paliers; **double-throw, multi-throw, c.,** vilebrequin à double coude, à coudes multiples; **c. housing,** carter *m* de vilebrequin; **c. throw,** coude *m* de vilebrequin.

cranky ['kræŋki], *a.* **1.** (*of pers.*) (*a*) d'humeur difficile; au caractère épineux; capricieux; (*b*) excentrique; maniaque; **c. ideas,** idées biscornues. **2.** (*a*) = CRANK[4]; (*b*) = CRANK[5].

crannied ['krænid], *a.* (*a*) lézardé, crevassé; (*b*) plein de coins et recoins; plein de niches.

crannog ['krænɔg], *s.* (*in Scot: & Ireland*) crannoge *m*; habitation *f* lacustre.

cranny[1] ['kræni], *s.* (*a*) fente *f*, lézarde *f*, crevasse *f*; (*b*) enfoncement *m*, niche *f*; **nooks and crannies,** coins *m* et recoins *m*.

cranny[2], *v.i.* (*of wood*) se gercer; (*of rock*) se fissurer.

crap[1] [kræp], *s. P:* (*not in decent use*) **1.** merde *f*. **2.** (*a*) (*foolish act*) couillonnade *f*, connerie *f*; (*b*) **to talk a lot of c.,** dire des couillonnades; (*c*) (*rubbishy goods*) fatras *m*, camelote *f*; (*d*) (*things of no importance*) foutaises *fpl*.

crap[2], *v.i.* (**crapped**) *P:* (*not in decent use*) **1.** chier. **2. to c. around, about,** (i) faire des bêtises; faire le con; (ii) dire des bêtises; déconner, dire des conneries; **3.** *v.tr.* **to c. s.o.,** dire des mensonges à qn.

crap[3], *s. U.S:* jeu *m* de dés; **c. house, c. table,** maison *f*, table *f*, de jeu (où l'on joue aux dés).

crapaudine [kræpə'di:n], *s.* **1.** crapaudine *f* (de porte, etc.). **2.** *Vet:* crapaudine.

crape[1] [kreip], *s. Tex:* **1.** crêpe noir (de soie, de rayonne); **black mourning c.,** crêpe anglais; **c. band** (*round the arm*), brassard *m* de crêpe. **2. Canton c., oriental c.,** crêpe de Chine. **3.** *Med:* **c. bandage,** bande *f* Velpeau; velpeau *m*. **4.** *Ferns:* **c. fern,** Todea superba. **5.** *Astr:* **the C. Ring,** l'anneau *m* de Crêpe (de Saturne).

crape[2], *v.tr.* draper, garnir, de crêpe (en signe de deuil).

crape[3], *v.tr.* crêper (les cheveux).

craped[1] [kreipt], *a.* portant le crêpe; (chapeau, etc.) garni de crêpe; **c. flag, flag furled and c.,** drapeau *m* en berne.

craped[2], *a.* (cheveux) crêpés, frisés.

crapehanger ['kreiphæŋər], *s. U.S: F:* rabat-joie *m inv*.

crapette [kræ'pet], *s. Cards:* crapette *f*.

crappie ['kræpi], *s. Ich: NAm:* crapet *m* (*Fr.C.*).

crappy ['kræpi], *a. P:* (*not in decent use*) misérable; sale *P:* débectant; dégueulasse.

craps [kræps], *s.pl.* (*often with sg. const.*) *NAm:* **to shoot c.,** jouer aux dés.

crapshooter ['kræpʃu:tər], *s.* joueur *m* de dés.

crapulence ['kræpjuləns], *s.* crapule *f*; crapulerie *f*; débauche *f*.

crapulent ['kræpjulənt], **crapulous** ['kræpjuləs], *a.* **1.** crapuleux, *P:* arsouille. **2.** adonné à la boisson; abruti par la boisson.

crapulosity [kræpju'lɔsiti], **crapulousness** ['kræpjuləsnis], *s.* **1.** crapulerie *f*. **2.** ivrognerie *f*.

craquelé ['krækleɪ], *a. Cer:* craquelé.

craquelure ['kræk(ə)ljuər], *s. Art:* craquelures *fpl*.

crash[1] [kræʃ], *s.* **1.** (*a*) fracas *m*; **to fall with a c.,** tomber et se briser avec fracas; **the c. of thunder,** le fracas du tonnerre; **a c. of thunder,** un coup de tonnerre; *W.Tel:* **crashes,** bruits (parasites) violents; (*b*) *Ven:* cri *m* de la meute au débucher. **2.** catastrophe *f*, débâcle *f*, chute *f*, effondrement *m*; **the final c.,** l'effondrement final, la catastrophe finale; **financial c., business c.,** débâcle financière; krach *m*; *P:* pouf *m*. **3.** écrasement *m* (à la suite d'un heurt brutal); chute (accidentelle); *Aut:* collision *f*, accident *m*; *Aut:Adm:* **c. barrier,** glissière *f*; *Rail: Av:* accident; catastrophe. **4.** *attrib.* (*a*) *Aut: Av: etc:* **c. ambulance,** *U.S:* **c. truck, c. wagon,** ambulance *f* (d'aérodrome en cas d'accident); **c. belt,** ceinture *f* de sécurité; **c. boat,** canot *m*, bateau *m*, de sauvetage; **c. crew,** équipe *f* de secours (en cas d'accident); **c. dive,** (i) *Navy:* plongée *f* raide (d'un sous-marin); (ii) *Av:* piqué *m* catastrophique; **c. helmet,** casque protecteur, de protection; **c.-helmeted,** coiffé d'un casque protecteur; **c. landing,** atterrissage brutal; crash; **c.-landing strip,** piste *f* pour atterrissage de détresse; **c. pad,** bourrelet *m*, tampon *m*, de protection, de sécurité; **c.-proof,** antichoc *inv.*; résistant aux chocs; (*b*) *F:* **c. course,** cours (d'instruction) accéléré; *Adm:* **c. programme,** programme choc, accéléré, d'urgence. **5.** *int:* patatras! **c. went the vase,** le vase tomba avec un grand fracas; **he went, drove, c. into the wall,** il est allé s'emboutir contre le mur.

crash[2]. **1.** *v.i.* (*a*) retenir; éclater avec fracas; **the thunder crashed,** (i) il y eut un violent coup de tonnerre; (ii) le tonnerre retentissait; (*b*) **to c. (down),** tomber avec fracas; s'abattre; **the vase crashed to the ground,** le vase tomba et se brisa avec fracas; **the mast came crashing down,** le mât s'abattit; **the roof crashed in,** le toit s'effondra; **to c. into a shop window,** enfoncer une vitrine; **the seats crashed over,** les bancs *m* se renversèrent; **to c. through sth.,** passer à travers qch. avec fracas; (*with cogn. acc.*) **the herd crashed its way through the jungle,** le troupeau avançait à travers la jungle, brisant tout sur son passage; *Aut:* **to c. into a tree,** s'emboutir sur un arbre; *F:* tamponner un arbre, entrer dans un arbre; **the two cars crashed head on,** les deux voitures se sont tamponnées de front, par l'avant, se sont heurtées de plein fouet; (*c*) *Av:* (i) (*of plane*) s'écraser sur le sol; (ii) (*of pilot*) atterrir brutalement; *F:* casser du bois, faire de la casse; bousiller son appareil; (*d*) (*of business, government, etc.*) sauter; (*of prices*) s'effondrer; (*e*) *P:* se coucher. **2.** *v.tr.* briser, fracasser; *Av:* écraser (son appareil) sur le sol; *Aut:* **to c. the lights,** brûler les signaux; **to c. the gears,** faire grincer la boîte de vitesses. **3.** *v.tr. & i. F:* **to c. (in, into) a party, to c. the gate,** resquiller, aller à une réunion sans être invité; **to c. (into) a closed profession,** s'introduire dans une profession fermée par fraude.

crash[3], *s. Tex:* toile *f* à serviettes (de toilette); toile de jute.

crash-dive ['kræʃdaiv], *v. Navy:* **1.** *v.tr.* faire plonger raide (un sous-marin). **2.** *v.i.* plonger raide.

crasher ['kræʃər], *s. F:* **1.** (*a*) coup retentissant; (*b*) coup accablant. **2.** resquilleur, -euse; invité(e) de contrebande; intrus(e); (*at theatre*) hirondelle *f*.

crashing ['kræʃiŋ], *a.* **1.** (bruit) fracassant. **2.** *F:* superbe; *F:* épatant, formidable; **a c. bore,** (i) une personne assommante; (ii) une soirée, besogne, etc., assommante.

crash-land ['kræʃ'lænd], *v.i. Av:* atterrir brutalement; *F:* casser du bois; faire un crash.

crashworthiness ['kræʃwə:θinəs], *s.* résistance *f* aux collisions.

crasis ['kreisis], *s. Gr.Gram:* crase *f*.

craspedote ['kræspidout], *a. Coel:* craspédote.

crass [kræs], *a.* épais, -aisse; grossier; *now only in a few phr., esp.* **c. minds,** esprits épais; **c. stupidity,** stupidité grossière; **c. ignorance,** ignorance *f* crasse.

crassilingual [kræsi'liŋgwəl], *a. Rept:* crassilingue.

crassitude ['kræsitju:d], **crassness** ['kræsnis], *s.* épaisseur *f* (d'esprit); profondeur *f* (de l'ignorance).

crassly ['kræsli], *adv.* grossièrement, stupidement; **c. ignorant,** d'une ignorance crasse.

crassula ['kræsjulə], *s. Bot:* crassule *f*.

Crassulaceae [kræsju'leisii:], *s.pl. Bot:* crassulacées *f*.

crataegin [krə'ti:dʒin], *s. Ch:* cratégine *f*.

crataegus [krə'ti:gəs], *s. Bot:* cratægus *m*.

crataeva [krə'ti:və], *s. Bot:* cratæva *m*.

cratch [krætʃ], *s. Agr:* râtelier *m*.

crate[1] [kreit], *s.* **1.** caisse *f* ou cadre *m* à claire-voie, en voliges; cageot *m*, cageotte *f*; (*for glass, bicycle, etc.*) harasse *f*; (*small, for fruit, etc.*) basquet *m*; **wicker c.,** mannequin *m*. **2.** *P:* (i) *Aut:* bagnole *f*, coucou *m*; (ii) *Av:* appareil *m*; *P:* zinc *m*, coucou.

crate[2], *v.tr.* emballer (des marchandises) dans une caisse à claire-voie.

crateful ['kreitful], *s.* (plein une) caisse, harasse (de marchandises).

crater[1] ['kreitər], *s.* **1.** *Gr.Ant:* cratère *m*. **2.** *Geol:* cratère; **explosion c.,** cratère d'explosion; **impact c.,** cratère météorique; **parasitic c., lateral c.,** cratère adventif; **ringed c., nested c.,** cônes emboîtés; **moon craters,** cratères lunaires; **c. lake,** lac *m* de cratère; **c.-like,** cratériforme. **3.** (*shell hole*) entonnoir *m*, cratère. **4.** *El:* cratère (de l'arc électrique).

crater[2], **1.** *v.i.* (*of carbon rod*) se creuser (en cratère). **2.** *v.tr. Mil:* défoncer (une route).

cratered ['kreitəd], *a.* couvert de cratères; *Mil:* (route) défoncée.

craterellus [kreitə'reləs], *s. Fung:* craterelle *f*.

crateriform ['kreitərifɔ:m], *a.* cratériforme.

crating ['kreitiŋ], *s.* emballage *m* (de bicyclettes, etc.).

Cratinian [kræ'tiniən], *a. Gr.Pros:* (vers) cratinien.

Cratippus [krə'tipəs], *Pr.n.m. Gr.Hist:* Cratippe.

craton ['kreitən], *s. Geol:* craton *m*, bouclier *m*.

cravat [krə'væt], *s.* **1.** *A:* (*neck-tie*) cravate *f*; *F: A:* **the hempen c.,** la corde de la potence; *F:* la cravate de chanvre. **2.** foulard *m*.

cravatted [krə'vætid], *a.* **1.** *A:* portant une cravate; cravaté. **2.** portant un foulard.

crave [kreiv], *v.tr. & i.* **1.** *Lit:* **to c. sth. from s.o., of s.o.,** demander avec instance qch. à qn; implorer qch. de qn; **to c. s.o.'s pardon,** demander pardon à qn; **to c. the attention of the audience,** solliciter l'attention du public; **to c. indulgence,** solliciter l'indulgence. **2. to c. for, after, sth.,** désirer ardemment, réclamer, qch.; être affamé de qch; **child that craves for affection,** enfant affamé d'affection; **the more you drink the more you c. (for drink),** plus on boit plus on a envie de boire.

craven ['kreivn], *a. & s. Lit: O:* poltron (*m*), lâche (*m*); **to cry c.,** se rendre; mettre les pouces.

cravenly ['kreivənli], *adv. A: & Lit:* lâchement, couardement.

cravenness ['kreivənnis], *s. A: & Lit:* lâcheté *f*, couardise *f*.

craving[1] ['kreiviŋ], *a.* **c. appetite,** appétit dévorant; boulimie *f*; **c. desire,** désir ardent.

craving[2], *s.* désir ardent, obsédant; besoin *m* irrésistible, appétit *m* insatiable (**for,** de); **to have a c. for praise,** être assoiffé de louanges; avoir soif de louanges; **c. for strong drink,** passion *f* de l'alcool; besoin d'alcool; **his sexual c.,** sa fringale érotique.

craw [krɔ:], *s.* **1.** jabot *m* (d'un oiseau). **2.** estomac *m* (d'un animal).

craw-craw ['krɔ:krɔ:], *s. Med: F:* onchocercose *f*.

crawfish[1] ['krɔ:fiʃ], *s. Crust:* = CRAYFISH.

crawfish[2], *v.i. NAm: F:* se dérober, *P:* caner.

crawl[1] [krɔ:l], *s.* (*a*) vivier *m*, bordigue *f*, serre *f*, bouchot *m*; (*b*) parc *m* (à tortues, à homards).

crawl[2], *s.* **1.** rampement *m* (d'un serpent). **2.** (*a*) **to go along at a c.,** traîner les pieds; se traîner; *F:* **taxi on the c.,** taxi *m* en maraude; (*b*) *F:* **pub c.,** tournée *f* des bars, des cafés. **3.** *Swim:* crawl *m*; **back c.,** crawl sur le dos; dos crawlé; **to do, swim, the c.,** crawler; **c. swimmer,** crawleur, -euse. **4.** *T.V:* **line c.,** défilement *m* (des lignes).

crawl[3], *v.i.* **1.** (*of reptile, etc.*) ramper; **to c. in, out,** entrer, sortir, en rampant; **to c. into a hole,** se glisser dans un trou; s'introduire dans un trou en rampant; **to c. to the door,** gagner la porte en rampant; *F:* **to c. to, before, s.o.,** ramper, s'aplatir, devant qn; faire le chien couchant auprès de qn; **I refuse to c.,** je refuse de m'aplatir. **2.** (*a*) (*of pers.*) **to c. (along),** se traîner; **he crawled to the ditch,** il se traîna jusqu'au fossé; **(he is so weak that) he can hardly c.,** il ne peut pas mettre un pied devant l'autre; **to c. on one's hands and knees,** aller à quatre pattes; (*b*) avancer lentement; (*of taxi*) marauder; *Aut: F:* faire du surplace. **3.** (*a*) **to c. with vermin, to be crawling with vermin,** grouiller de vermine; **the floor was crawling with insects,** le plancher fourmillait d'insectes; *F:* **the streets were crawling with troops,** les rues fourmillaient, grouillaient, de militaires; (*b*) **to c. all over,** se sentir des fourmillements par tout le corps. **4.** *U.S:* (*of plant*) grimper. **5.** *Swim:* crawler; faire du crawl.

crawler ['krɔːlər], *s.* **1.** (*a*) reptile *m*; animal *m*, bébé *m*, qui rampe; (*b*) *F:* lèche-bottes *m inv*; (*c*) traînard, -arde; *F:* **pub c.,** coureur *m* de cabarets, de bars; (*d*) taxi *m* en maraude; maraudeur *m*. **2.** *Swim:* crawleur, -euse. **3.** *pl.* **crawlers,** barboteuse *f* (pour enfants). **4.** (*a*) **c. tractor,** tracteur *m* à chenilles; (*b*) plateforme chenillée (pour le transport des fusées géantes).

crawling[1] ['krɔːliŋ], *a.* **1.** rampant. **2. c. cab,** taxi *m* en maraude. **3.** grouillant **(with,** de); **cheese c. with maggots,** fromage *m* qui grouille de vers.

crawling[2], *s.* **1.** (*a*) *Z:* reptation *f*; (*b*) = CRAWL[2]. **2.** *Cer:* retirement *m* (de la glaçure).

crawlway ['krɔːlwei], *s.* passage souterrain, galerie *f* d'accès (que l'on ne peut suivre qu'en rampant).

crawly ['krɔːli], *a.* **1.** (*of pers.*) qui se sent des fourmillements. **2. c. feeling,** (i) fourmillement *m*; (ii) chair *f* de poule.

cray [krei], *s. Austr. & N.Z:* langouste *f*, palinure *m*, homard épineux; **c. fishing,** (i) pêche *f* des langoustes; (ii) *Austr: F:* **the truth and no c. fishing,** la vérité sans faux-fuyants.

crayer [kreər], *s. Nau.Hist:* crayer *m*.

crayfish ['kreifiʃ], *s. Crust:* **1. (freshwater) c.,** écrevisse *f*; **c. breeding,** astaciculture *f*; **c. breeder,** astaciculteur *m*. **2.** *Com: F:* **(sea) c.,** langouste *f*, palinure *m*, homard épineux.

crayon[1] ['kreiɔn, -ən], *s.* **1.** craie *f* à dessiner; pastel *m*; crayon *m* pastel; **coloured c.,** crayon de couleur; **Conté c.,** crayon Conté; **drawn in c.,** dessiné au pastel, au crayon Conté; pastellé; **c. holder,** porte-fusain *m inv*; *Lith:* **litho c.,** *U.S:* **grease c.,** crayon litho. **2.** dessin *m* au pastel, au crayon Conté; pastel. **3.** *El:* crayon (d'une lampe à arc).

crayon[2], *v.tr.* **1.** dessiner (qch.) au pastel, au crayon Conté. **2.** crayonner (une esquisse); esquisser (un portrait, etc.).

craze[1] [kreiz], *s.* **1.** manie *f*, toquade *f* **(for sth.,** de qch.); **the telly c.,** l'engouement *m* pour la télé; **she has a c. for travelling,** elle a la fureur des voyages; **discotheques are all the c.,** les discothèques font fureur. **2.** *Cer: Paint:* fendilles *fpl*, craquelures *fpl*.

craze[2]. **1.** *v.tr.* (*a*) rendre (qn) fou; déranger (l'esprit); (*b*) *Cer:* fendiller, craqueler (la porcelaine). **2.** *v.i. Cer:* se fendiller, se craqueler.

crazed [kreizd], *a.* **1.** = CRAZY 1 (*a*). **2.** *Cer: Paint:* fendillé, craquelé.

crazily ['kreizili], *adv.* follement.

craziness ['kreizinis], *s.* **1.** (*of pers.*) folie *f*, démence *f*. **2.** (*of building, furniture, etc.*) décrépitude *f*.

crazing ['kreiziŋ], *s. Cer: Paint:* (*a*) fendillement *m*; (*b*) fendilles *fpl*, craquelures *fpl*.

crazy ['kreizi], *a.* **1.** (*a*) (*of pers.*) fou, *f* folle (à lier); toqué; (*of idea, etc.*) fou, saugrenu; **c. with grief,** fou de douleur; **c. with fear,** affolé (de terreur); *F:* **to go c.,** perdre la tête; devenir fou **(with anger,** de colère); **he was half c.,** il n'avait plus sa tête à lui; **to drive, send, s.o. c.,** rendre qn fou; affoler qn; *F:* faire tourner qn en bourrique; faire damner qn; **you're c.!** vous êtes fou! vous divaguez! vous extravaguez! **to be c. about, over, s.o., sth.,** être fou de qn, qch.; **to be c. about music, to be music c.,** ne rêver que musique; être fou de musique; **to be c. to do sth.,** brûler de faire qch.; *U.S: F:* **to rush around like c.,** courir çà et là comme un enragé; (*b*) *U.S:* **the c. bone,** le petit juif (à l'articulation du coude); (*c*) *F:* (*of dress, etc.*) bizarre; qui se fait remarquer; (*d*) *U.S: F:* merveilleux; épatant; **we had a c. time,** nous nous sommes rudement bien amusés. **2.** (*a*) (*of building, etc.*) délabré; qui menace ruine; **c. furniture,** meubles branlants, boiteux; **c. ship,** navire *m* hors d'état de tenir la mer; *F:* craquelin *m*; (*b*) (*of machinery, etc.*) qui fonctionne mal, irrégulièrement; détraqué; délabré. **3.** composé de morceaux rapportés; irrégulier; **c. path,** allée couverte de dalles rapportées (de formes irrégulières), pavée en opus incertum; **c. paving,** dallage irrégulier en pierres plates; **c. quilt,** courtepointe *f* en pièces rapportées de toutes couleurs. **4.** *s. F:* fou, *f* folle; détraqué, -ée.

creak[1] [kriːk], *s.* cri *m*, grincement *m* (de gonds, etc.); craquement *m* (du bois, de chaussures neuves, etc.).

creak[2], *v.i.* (*of hinge, etc.*) crier, grincer; (*of timber, shoes*) craquer; **the door creaks,** la porte grince, crie, chante, sur ses gonds; **the car creaked to a halt,** la voiture s'est arrêtée en grinçant.

creakily ['kriːkili], *adv.* en grinçant, en gémissant.

creaking[1] ['kriːkiŋ], *a.* qui crie, qui grince; *Prov:* **c. gates hang, last, longest,** tout ce qui branle ne tombe pas; pot fêlé dure longtemps.

creaking[2], *s.* **1.** = CREAK[1]. **2.** *Med:* **dry-leather c.,** bruits *mpl* de parchemin (du poumon).

creaky ['kriːki], *a.* = CREAKING[1].

cream[1] [kriːm], *s.* **1.** (*a*) crème *f* (du lait); **strawberries and c.,** fraises *f* à la crème; **clotted c., Devonshire c.,** crème caillée (par échaudage); **whipped c.,** crème fouettée; **whipping c.,** crème à fouetter; **c. bun, c. puff,** chou *m* à la crème; mirliton *m*; puits *m* d'amour; **c. horn,** cornet *m* de pâte feuilletée garni de confiture et de crème; **to take the c. off the milk,** écrémer le lait; **c. jug,** pot *m* à crème; crémière *f*; **c.-setting pan,** crémeuse *f*; (*b*) *F:* (le) meilleur; (le) dessus du panier; *F:* la fleur des pois; **the c. of society,** la crème de la société; **the c. of s.o.'s works,** la fleur des œuvres de qn; **the c. of the joke, business, is that . . .,** le plus drôle, le plus beau, le piquant, de l'histoire, l'affaire, c'est que . . .; **to take the c. off sth.,** écrémer qch. **2.** (*a*) **coffee c.,** crème au café; (*b*) **c. of tomato, asparagus, soup,** crème de tomate, d'asperges; (*c*) **c. of tartar,** *Com:* crème de tartre; *Ch:* bitartrate *m* de potasse; (*d*) **shoe c., boot c.,** crème pour chaussures; **furniture c.,** encaustique *f* en pâte; (*e*) crème (de toilette, de beauté); **night c.,** crème de nuit; (*f*) *Rubberm:* caillot *m*, coagulum *m* (de caoutchouc). **3.** *attrib.* **c.(-coloured),** (dentelles) crème *inv*; (cheval) soupe-de-lait *inv*, soupe-au-lait *inv*; (cheval) isabelle *inv*; *Paperm:* **c.(-)laid,** (papier) vergé blanc; **c.(-)wove,** (papier) vélin blanc.

cream[2]. **1.** *v.tr.* (*a*) **to c. (off),** écrémer (le lait; *F:* une bibliothèque, les œuvres d'un auteur, etc.); (*b*) ajouter de la crème à (son café, etc.); (*c*) battre (du beurre) en crème; *Rubberm:* coaguler (le latex); (*d*) *Toil:* étendre de la crème sur (la peau, etc.). **2.** *v.i.* (*of milk*) se couvrir de crème, crémer; (*of ale*) mousser; *Rubberm:* (*of latex*) se coaguler.

creambush ['kriːmbuʃ], *s. Bot:* holodiscus *m*.

creamcups ['kriːmkʌps], *s. Bot:* (*a*) platystémon *m*; (*b*) holodiscus *m*.

creamed [kriːmd], *a.* **1.** (lait) écrémé. **2.** *Cu:* (poulet, etc.) à la crème. **3.** (teint) velouté.

creamer ['kriːmər], *s.* **1.** (*pan*) crémeuse *f*. **2.** écrémeuse *f* centrifuge.

creamery ['kriːməri], *s.* **1.** crémerie *f*; **bought at the c.,** acheté chez le crémier, à la crémerie. **2.** coopérative laitière; **c. butter,** beurre laitier.

creaminess ['kriːminis], *s.* **1.** abondance *f* en crème. **2.** velouté *m* (de la peau, de la voix).

creaming[1] ['kriːmiŋ], *a.* (vin) crémant.

creaming[2], *s.* production *f* de la crème; *Rubberm:* coagulation *f* (du latex).

creamy ['kriːmi], *a.* **1.** crémeux. **2. rich c. voice,** voix veloutée; **c. complexion,** teint velouté.

creance ['kriːəns], *s. Ven:* créance *f*.

crease[1] [kriːs], *s.* **1.** (*a*) (faux) pli; (*in paper, etc.*) fronce *f*; *Tex:* ancrure *f*; **linen that shows creases,** linge qui plisse mal; **to remove the creases from material,** éclancher l'étoffe; **c.-resisting, c.-resistant,** infroissable; (*b*) pli (d'un pantalon, etc.); *Dressm: etc:* **c. edge,** cassure *f* (du col, du revers). **2.** *Sp:* ligne blanche; ligne de limite; *Cr:* **batting c.,** limite *f* du batteur; **bowling c.,** ligne du bôleur, de service.

crease[2]. **1.** *v.tr.* (*a*) plisser, faire des plis, des fronces, à (qch.); **well-creased trousers,** pantalon avec un pli impeccable, bien marqué d'un pli; (*b*) faire des faux plis à, friper, chiffonner, froisser (une robe, etc.); (*c*) *P:* **to c. s.o.,** (i) assommer, étourdir, qn; (ii) épuiser, éreinter, qn; (iii) assommer, tuer, qn; **to c. it,** mourir; *P:* casser sa pipe; (*d*) *Metalw:* suager (le fer blanc); tomber (un bord). **2.** *v.i.* (*a*) se plisser; prendre un (faux) pli; (*b*) se friper, se chiffonner, se froisser.

crease[3], *s.* criss (malais).

creaseable ['kriːsəbl], *a.* froissable.

creaseless ['kriːslis], *a.* **1.** sans faux plis. **2.** (cravate, etc.) infroissable.

creaser ['kriːsər], *s. Tls: Metalw:* suage *m*.

creasing ['kriːsiŋ], *s.* **1.** plissement *m*; froncement *m*. **2.** pli *m*. **3.** *P:* (i) abattage *m*; (ii) épuisement *m* (de qn). **4.** *Metalw:* **c. hammer, c. tool,** suage *m*.

creasy ['kriːsi], *a.* chiffonné, froissé.

create [kri'eit], *v.tr.* **1.** créer (le monde, un pair, *Th:* un rôle); *pred.* **to c. s.o. a knight, an earl,** créer qn chevalier, comte. **2.** (*a*) créer, faire naître, susciter (une difficulté); faire, produire (une impression); provoquer (un rire); faire, susciter (des ennemis); **to c. a vacuum,** faire, produire, le vide; **to c. a draught,** créer, provoquer, un courant d'air; **to c. sth. out of nothing,** créer qch. de toutes pièces; **to c. a mortgage,** constituer une hypothèque; **to c. a scandal,** (i) causer un scandale; (ii) faire de l'esclandre; **to c. a disturbance,** troubler l'ordre public; (*hence*) *v.i. P:* **to c.,** faire du tapage, de l'esclandre; faire une scène, rouspéter **(about,** à propos de); *P:* **he doesn't half c.,** qu'est-ce qu'il peut râler! **to c. at s.o.,** faire une scène à qn; s'en prendre à qn; (*b*) **to c. a fashion,** lancer, créer, une mode; **costume created by So-and-so,** création *f* de la maison une telle.

creatine ['kriːəti(ː)n], *s. Bio-Ch:* créatine *f*.

creatininaemia [kri'ætiniˈniːmiə], *s. Med:* créatininémie *f*.

creatinine [kri'ætiniːn], *s. Bio-Ch:* créatinine *f*.

creation [kri'eiʃ(ə)n], *s.* **1.** création *f* (du monde, d'un titre, d'un rôle, d'une maison de commerce); *Lit:* **phantasms of their own c.,** fantômes *m* qu'ils se créent, se forgent, eux-mêmes. **2.** (*created beings*) **the wonders of c.,** les merveilles de la création; **the brute c.,** l'espèce animale; les bêtes *fpl*; *F: A:* **that beats c.!** ça dépasse tout au monde! ça c'est fort! *A:* **when in all c. will you have finished?** quand diable aurez-vous fini? **3.** (*thing created*) création, produit *m*, œuvre *f*; **her dress was a c. by Venus & Co.,** sa robe était une création de chez Vénus et Cie; **the latest creations,** les dernières modes.

creationism [kri'eiʃ(ə)nizm], *s.* **1.** *Theol:* créationisme *m*. **2.** *Biol:* créationisme, fixisme *m*.

creationist [kri'eiʃ(ə)nist], *s.* **1.** *Theol:* créationiste *mf*. **2.** *Biol:* créationiste; fixiste *mf*.

creative [kri'eitiv], *a.* créateur, -trice; **c. drive,** impulsion créatrice; *Phil:* **c. evolution,** évolution créatrice; **circumstances c. of despondency,** circonstances *f* qui engendrent le découragement; **a c. job,** un métier stimulant.

creatively [kri'eitivli], *adv.* d'une façon créatrice.

creativeness [kri'eitivnis], **creativity** [kriə'tiviti], *s.* faculté *f* de créer; puissance créatrice; esprit *m* de création; créativité *f*.

creator [kri'eitər], *s.* (*f. occ.* **creatress, -trix** [kri'eitris, -triks]) créateur, -trice; **the C.,** le Créateur; *Th:* **c. of a rôle,** créateur, -trice, d'un rôle.

creature ['kriːtʃər], *s.* **1.** *A:* création *f*, produit *m*, œuvre *f*. **2.** créature *f*, être *m*; *esp.* être vivant. **3.** animal *m*, bête *f*; **dumb creatures,** les bêtes, les animaux. **4.** (*of pers.*) **vile, pretty, c.,** vile, jolie, créature; **poor c.!** le pauvre homme! la pauvre femme! le, la, pauvre enfant! **not a c. was to be seen,** il n'y avait personne en vue; on ne voyait âme qui vive. **5. to be the c. of some great man,** être la créature, l'âme damnée, d'un homme puissant; **c. of the Government,** homme vendu au gouvernement; instrument *m* du gouvernement. **6. man is the c. of circumstances,** l'homme dépend des circonstances; **we are creatures of habit,** nous sommes tels que nous fait l'habitude. **7.** *P:* **the c.,** l'eau-de-vie *f*; le whisky. **8.** *attrib.* **to make provision for s.o.'s c. comforts,** assurer l'aisance matérielle à qn.

crèche [kreiʃ, kreʃ], *s.* **1.** (*a*) crèche *f*; pouponnière *f*; (*b*) *U.S:* orphelinat *m*. **2.** *Ecc:* crèche.

Crécy ['kresi], *Pr.n. Geog: Hist:* Crécy.

credal ['kriːdl], *a.* (préjugé, etc.) provenant d'une croyance religieuse.

credence ['kriːd(ə)ns], *s.* **1.** créance *f*, croyance *f*, foi *f*; **to give, attach, c. to sth.,** ajouter foi à qch.; donner créance à qch.; **news that is gaining c.,** nouvelle en voie de trouver créance, *Lit:* qui prend crédit; **worthy of c.,** digne de foi; **letter of c.,** lettre *f* de créance. **2.** *Ecc:* **c. (table),** crédence *f*.

credentialled [kri'denʃ(ə)ld], *a.* pourvu de lettres de créance.

credentials [kri'denʃ(ə)lz], *s.pl.* **1.** (*a*) lettres *f* de créance; (*of delegate*) **to come without full c.,** se présenter sans pouvoirs réguliers; (*b*) certificat *m* (d'un domestique, etc.); **to show one's c.,** (i) montrer ses pouvoirs; (ii) faire preuve de ses titres; *A:* **a man without c.,** un homme sans distinction, de rien. **2.** papiers *m* d'identité; pièces justificatives d'identité; **car c.,** les papiers de la voiture.

credenza [kri'denzə], *s. Furn:* buffet *m*, crédence *f*.

credibility [kredi'biliti], *s.* crédibilité *f*; **c. gap,** (i) perte *f* de confiance (entre deux personnes, etc.); (ii) divergence *f*; (iii) refus *m* de croire (à qch.); **there is a c. gap between their claims and their achievements,** leurs affirmations et leurs œuvres ne cadrent pas; *Cmptr:* **c. check,** contrôle *m* de vraisemblance.

credible ['kredibl], *a.* croyable; digne de foi, de créance; **it is hardly c. that . . .,** il n'est pas vraisemblable que + *sub.*; **a nuclear deterrent is more c. than conventional weapons,** la dissuasion nucléaire est plus crédible que les armements classiques.

credibly ['kredibli], *adv.* d'une façon qui inspire confiance; **to be c. informed of sth.,** tenir qch. de bonne source.

credit[1] ['kredit], *s.* **1.** croyance *f*, créance *f*, foi *f*; **to give c. to a report,** ajouter foi à un bruit; (*of report*) **to gain c.,** s'accréditer; **rumour that is gaining c.,** bruit qui prend de la consistance; **facts that lend c. to a rumour,** faits *m* qui accréditent un bruit. **2.** crédit *m*, influence *f*, réputation *f* (**with,** auprès de); **to use one's c. in s.o.'s favour,** employer son crédit en faveur de qn; s'employer pour qn; **he has c. at court,** il est bien en cour; **he has lost c. with the public,** son crédit a décliné; il a perdu sa réputation; *F:* c'est un saint qu'on ne fête plus; **he is losing his c.,** *F:* ses actions sont en baisse; *Lit:* **John Gilpin was a citizen of c. and renown,** John Gilpin était un citoyen estimé, dont la renommée s'étendait au loin. **3.** (*a*) mérite *m*, honneur *m*; **to take c. for an action,** s'attribuer le mérite d'une action; **to take c. to oneself for generosity, for doing sth.,** se flatter de générosité, d'avoir fait qch.; **to get c. for another's work,** se voir attribuer le mérite du travail d'autrui; **to acquit oneself with c.,** s'acquitter honorablement; **he came out of it with c.,** il en est sorti à son honneur; *Sch:* **to pass an examination with c.,** être reçu à un examen avec mention assez bien; **to give s.o. c. for superior intelligence,** créditer qn d'une intelligence supérieure; **I gave him c. for more sense,** je lui croyais, lui supposais, plus de jugement; **I give him c. for his good intentions,** je lui tiens compte de ses bonnes intentions; **to give s.o. full c. for a discovery,** rendre à qn l'hommage d'une découverte; **to give s.o. c. for his zeal,** rendre justice au zèle de qn; **it must be said to his c. that . . .,** on doit dire à son honneur, il faut dire à son mérite, que . . .; **that is all to his c.,** c'est tout à son honneur; **it does him c., it reflects great c. on him,** cela lui fait (grand) honneur; **step that does you c.,** démarche *f* qui vous honore; **he is a c. to the school,** il fait honneur à l'école; (*b*) *Cln:* **c. titles, credits,** générique *m*; *Th:* crédits, remerciements, *m*. **4.** *Com: Fin:* (*a*) crédit; **to give s.o. c.,** faire crédit à qn; **to sell on c.,** vendre à crédit, à terme; **long c.,** crédit à long terme; **blank c., open c.,** crédit en blanc, à découvert; lettre *f* de crédit dont le montant n'est pas spécifié; **c. bank, c. establishment,** banque *f*, établissement *m*, de crédit; *NAm:* **c. union,** société *f* de crédit; *Bank:* **letter of c.,** lettre de créance, de crédit, accréditive; accréditif *m*; **documentary letter of c.,** crédit documentaire; **permanent c.,** accréditif permanent; **c. account,** compte créditeur; **to open a c. account with s.o.,** ouvrir un crédit chez qn; **to open a c. account in s.o.'s favour,** ouvrir un crédit à qn; **to open a c.,** loger un accréditif; **to give s.o. a bank c.,** ouvrir un crédit en banque à qn; **c. card,** carte *f* de crédit; **c. circulation,** circulation *f* fiduciaire; **c. insurance,** assurance *f* contre les mauvaises créances; **c. rating,** degré *m* de solvabilité; **c.(-)worthy,** qui a une réputation de solvabilité; digne de confiance; **c. worthiness,** degré, réputation, de solvabilité; **to live on c.,** vivre à crédit; *Com:* **no c.,** on ne fait pas (de) crédit; (*b*) *Book-k:* **debit and c.,** doit *m* et avoir *m*; **c. side,** avoir; **c. balance,** solde créditeur; **account showing a c. balance, account in c.,** compte bénéficiaire; **c. note,** note *f*, facture *f*, d'avoir, de crédit; bordereau *m* de crédit; **c. slip,** bulletin *m* de versement; **to enter, put, a sum to s.o.'s c.,** porter une somme au crédit, à l'actif, de qn; **to pay in a sum to s.o.'s c.,** payer une somme à la décharge de qn; **bank c.,** crédit bancaire; **tax credits,** déductions fiscales; **frozen credits,** créances gelées; **another good action to your c.,** encore une bonne action à votre actif. **5.** réputation de solvabilité; crédit; **his c. is good,** on lui fait toute confiance. **6.** *Parl:* = douzième *m* provisoire; **to pass a c. vote,** voter un douzième provisoire. **7.** *Pol:* **social c.,** crédit social.

credit[2], *v.tr.* **1.** ajouter foi à, attacher foi à, donner croyance à, donner, accorder, crédit, créance, à, croire (un bruit); croire (qn); **these stories are no longer credited,** ces récits ne trouvent plus créance; *F:* **I wouldn't have credited it,** je ne l'aurais pas cru possible; **you wouldn't c. it,** c'est à ne pas croire. **2.** (*attribute*) attribuer, prêter (**s.o. with a quality,** une qualité à qn); **to c. s.o. with superior intelligence,** créditer qn d'une intelligence supérieure; **I credited you with more sense,** je vous croyais, supposais, plus de jugement; **I didn't c. him with so much energy,** je ne pensais pas qu'il eût tant d'énergie; je ne lui croyais pas tant d'énergie; **to be credited with having done sth.,** passer pour avoir fait qch.; **I have been credited with this discovery,** on m'a fait l'honneur de cette découverte; **to c. s.o. with an intention,** prêter une intention à qn; **he has not the talents you c. him with,** il n'a pas les talents que vous lui prêtez; **I am credited with speeches of which I am guiltless,** on me prête des discours dont je suis innocent; **he hasn't as much money as people c. him with,** il n'a pas la grosse fortune qu'on lui prête; **people had credited him with being a miser,** on lui avait fait une réputation d'avare; (*b*) **to c. s.o. with a quality,** reconnaître une qualité à qn. **3.** *Com:* **to c. s.o., an account, with a sum, to c. a sum to s.o., to an account,** créditer qn, un compte, d'une somme; créditer une somme à qn, à un compte; porter une somme au crédit de qn, d'un compte; mettre une somme à l'actif de qn; bonifier une somme à qn.

creditable ['kreditəbl], *a.* (action) estimable, honorable, digne d'éloges.

creditably ['kreditəbli], *adv.* honorablement, avec honneur.

Creditiste [kredi'ti:st], *a.* & *s.* *Can:* (adhérent, -ente, député) du Crédit social.

creditor ['kreditər], *s.* **1.** créancier, -ière; **to be s.o.'s c. for 1000 francs,** être en avance avec qn de 1000 francs; **simple-contract c.,** créancier chirographaire; créancier en vertu d'un contrat sous seing privé; **joint c.,** cocréancier, -ière; **c. of a c.** (*in bankruptcy*), créancier en sous-ordre. **2.** *attrib.* créditeur, -trice; *Book-k:* **c. side** (*of balance*), compte créditeur; compte avoir; *Pol.Ec:* **c. nation,** nation créditrice.

crednerite ['krednərait], *s. Miner:* crednérite *f*.

credo, *pl.* **-os** ['kri:dou, 'krei-, -ouz], *s. Ecc: Mus:* credo *m inv.*

credulity [kri'dju:liti], *s.* crédulité *f*.

credulous ['kredjuləs], *a.* crédule.

credulously ['kredjuləsli], *adv.* crédulement; avec crédulité.

credulousness ['kredjuləsnis], *s.* crédulité *f*.

creed[1] [kri:d], *s.* **1.** *Theol:* credo *m inv*, symbole *m*; **the (Apostles') C.,** le symbole des Apôtres; le credo. **2.** croyance *f*, foi (confessionnelle); **school open to every c.,** école ouverte à toutes les confessions. **3.** profession *f* de foi; **political c.,** credo politique.

Creed[2], *Pr.n. Tg:* **C. printer,** appareil *m* téléimprimeur Creed.

creek[1] [kri:k], *s.* **1.** crique *f*, anse *f*; *Nau:* accul *m*, alise *f*. **2.** *NAm: Austr: N.Z:* (*a*) ruisseau *m*, petit cours d'eau; affluent *m*; (*b*) petite vallée. **3.** *P:* **to be up the c.,** (i) être dans l'embarras, *P:* dans la merde; (ii) (*of woman*) être enceinte; (iii) être maboul, loufoque.

Creek[2]. **1.** *Ethn:* (*a*) *a.* des Muskogees, des Creeks; (*b*) *s.* (*pl.* **Creek(s)**) Muskogee *m*, Creek *m*. **2.** *s. Ling:* la langue des Muskogees, des Creeks.

creel [kri:l], *s.* **1.** *Fish:* (*a*) panier *m* de pêche; glène *f*, gline *f*; (*b*) casier *m* à homards; (*c*) **fishwife's c.,** manne *f* à marée. **2.** *Tex:* râtelier *m* (à bobines); porte-bobines *m inv.*

creep[1] [kri:p], *s.* **1.** *F:* (*a*) *pl.* chair *f* de poule; **to give s.o. the creeps,** donner la chair de poule à qn; **it gives me the creeps,** ça me met les nerfs en pelote, en boule; (*b*) personnage répugnant; *P:* type *m* dégueulasse. **2.** (*a*) action *f* de ramper; **c. (hole),** (i) trou *m* de refuge; abri souterrain; (ii) passage étroit, trou (dans une haie, etc.); (*b*) cheminement *m* (des couches géologiques, des rails de chemin de fer); *Metall:* fluage *m*; *Mec.E:* glissement *m* (d'une courroie de transmission); *Aut: etc:* glissement, cheminement (d'un pneu sur la jante); *Geog:* creep(ing) *m*; ((i) reptation *f*, (ii) saltation *f* (des débris)); reptation (d'un toit en plomb, etc.); (*c*) *Ch:* grimpement *m* (des liquides, etc.). **3.** *Min:* gonflement *m*; boursouflement *m* (de la sole, du mur).

creep[2], *v.* (*p.t.* & *p.p.* **crept** [krept])

I. *v.i.* **1.** (*a*) (*of insect, animal, plant*) ramper; (*of roots*) tracer; (*of pers.*) se traîner, se glisser; *F:* ramper (devant les grands); **to c. into bed,** se glisser dans son lit; **to c. along a ditch on all fours,** ramper à quatre pattes dans un fossé; **to c. along the wall,** se faufiler le long du mur; **he crept into the room,** il entra tout doucement, furtivement, à pas de loup, dans la chambre; **to c. into a hole,** se couler dans un trou; **to c. into s.o.'s favour,** s'insinuer dans la faveur de qn; **abuse that has crept into the State,** abus qui s'est introduit furtivement dans l'État; **a feeling of uneasiness crept over me,** un sentiment de gêne commençait à me gagner, s'insinuait en moi; (*b*) **to make s.o.'s flesh c.,** donner la chair de poule à qn; horripiler qn. **2.** (*a*) *Min:* (*of floor*) gonfler, se boursoufler; (*b*) (*of rails, geological strata, etc.*) cheminer; (*of transmission belt*) glisser, ramper; (*of tyre*) glisser, cheminer, sur la jante. **3.** *Nau:* **to c. for (sth. under water),** draguer (qch.). **4.** (*a*) (*of plant*) grimper; (*b*) (*of liquid, esp. of acid*) grimper.

II. (*compound verbs*) **1. creep along,** *v.i.* s'avancer en rampant, furtivement; *F:* marcher à pas de loup.

2. creep away, *v.i.* (*a*) s'éloigner en rampant; (*b*) s'éloigner à pas de loup.

3. creep by, *v.i.* **time, the hours, crept slowly by,** les heures passaient, défilaient, lentement.

4. creep down, *v.i.* descendre en rampant, doucement.

5. creep on, *v.i.* avancer lentement; **old age is creeping on,** la vieillesse s'approche à pas lents; **time creeps on,** le temps passe insensiblement.

6. creep up, *v.i.* (*a*) se traîner jusqu'en haut; (*b*) s'approcher en rampant; avancer lentement; **the speedometer needle crept up to 120,** l'aiguille de l'indicateur de vitesse avança lentement, monta tout doucement, jusqu'à 120; (*c*) **to c. up on s.o.,** surprendre qn, prendre qn à l'improviste; **old age has crept up on me,** j'ai vieilli sans m'en rendre compte.

creepage ['kri:pidʒ], *s.* grimpement *m*, ascension *f* capillaire (de l'acide d'un accu, des sels d'une solution, etc.); *El:* décharge superficielle (sur un isolateur).

creeper ['kri:pər], *s.* **1.** *Bot:* plante (i) rampante, (ii) grimpante. **2.** *Orn:* grimpereau *m*; **common c., brown c., tree c.,** grimpereau familier, des bois; *Fr.C:* grimpereau brun; **short-toed tree c.,** grimpereau des jardins; **wall c.,** grimpereau, tichodrome *m*, des murailles; (tichodrome) échelette *f*. **3.** *Nau:* grappin *m* (à main); *F:* chatte *f*. **4.** *Ind:* vis *f* de transport. **5.** *pl.* *NAm:* **creepers:** (*a*) chaussons *m*, souliers *m*, à semelles de crêpe; (*b*) crampons *m* à verglas; (*c*) barboteuse *f* (d'enfant). **6.** *P: O:* flagorneur, -euse; lèche-bottes *m inv.* **7.** *O:* élève planteur dans les théeries de Ceylan.

creepie ['kri:pi], *s. Scot: F:* petit escabeau.

creeping[1] ['kri:piŋ], *a.* **1.** (*a*) (*of animal, plant, inflation, etc.*) rampant; (brouillard) qui s'avance au ras du sol; *Med:* **c. paralysis,** paralysie progressive; (*b*) (homme) servile, rampant; *P:* **c. Jesus,** (i) type servile, obséquieux; (ii) faux bigot. **2.** (*climbing*) (*a*) (*of plant*) grimpant; (*b*) *El:* **c. salts,** sels grimpants (d'un accu, etc.).

creeping[2], *s.* **1.** rampement *m*; *Z:* reptation *f*; *Mch: etc:* **c. speed,** grand ralenti. **2.** grimpement *m*, ascension *f* capillaire (de l'acide d'un accu, des sels d'une solution, etc.). **3.** (*of skin*) chair *f* de poule. **4.** = CREEP[1] 2, 3.

creepy ['kri:pi], *a.* *F:* **1.** rampant; **I could feel c. things on my leg,** je sentais sur ma jambe des choses qui rampaient. **2. to feel c.,** avoir la chair de poule; **c. story,** récit *m* qui donne la chair de poule. **3.** *U.S:* (homme) misérable, miteux, moche.

creepy-crawly ['kri:pi'krɔ:li], *F:* **1.** *a.* (*a*) **c.-c. feeling,** (i) fourmillement *m*; (ii) chair *f* de poule; (*b*) (*of pers.*) rampant, servile. **2.** *s.* bête rampante; vermine *f*.

creese [kri:s], *s.* criss (malais).

cremaster [krə'mæstə:r], *s. Anat: Ent:* crémaster *m*.

cremate [kri'meit], *v.tr.* incinérer, crémer (un mort).

cremation [kri'meiʃ(ə)n], *s.* incinération *f*; crémation *f*.

cremator [kri'meitər], *s.* **1.** personne *f* qui incinère (les cadavres). **2.** (four *m*) crématoire *m*.

crematorium, *pl.* **-ia** [kremə'tɔ:riəm, -iə], **crematory**[1] ['kremətəri], *s.* **1.** (*building*) crématoire *m*. **2.** (*furnace*) (four *m*) crématoire *m*; crématorium.

crematory[2], *a.* crématoire.

crème [kreim], *s.* crème *f*; **c. caramel** ['kærəmel], crème (renversée) au caramel; crème (au) caramel; **c. brûlée** ['bru:lei], crème brûlée; **c. de menthe** [də'mɑ:nt], crème de menthe; **c. pâtissière** [pæ'ti:sjɛər], crème pâtissière; *F:* **the c. de la c. of society,** la crème de la société.

Cremona[1] [kri'mounə]. **1.** *Pr.n. Geog:* Crémone *f*. **2.** *s. Mus:* violon *m* de Crémone; crémone *m*.

cremona[2], *s. Mus:* **1.** *A:* cromorne *m*, tournebout *m*. **2.** (*organ stop*) cromorne.

crenate ['kri:neit], **crenated** ['kri:neitid], *a. Bot: Z:* crénelé.

crenation [kri'neiʃ(ə)n], **crenature** ['kri:nətjər], *s. Bot: Z:* crénelure *f*.

crenel[1] ['kren(ə)l], **crenelle** [kri'nel], *s.* créneau *m*, meurtrière *f*.

crenel[2], **crenel(l)ate** ['krenəleit], *v.tr.* créneler (une muraille).

crenel(l)ation [krenə'leiʃ(ə)n], *s.* crénelure *f*, crénelage *m*; créneaux *mpl.*

crenelled ['krenld], *a. Bot:* (*of leaf*) crénelé.

crenelling ['krenəliŋ], *s. Bot:* crénelure *f* (d'une feuille).

crenotherapy ['krenou'θerəpi], *s. Med:* crénothérapie *f*.

crenulate ['krenjuleit], *a. Bot:* (*of leaf*) crénulé; *Geog:* (*of coastline*) échancré.

creodont ['kriədɔnt], *s. Paleont:* créodonte *m*.

Creole ['kri:oul]. **1.** *Ethn:* *a.* & *s.* (*a*) créole (*mf*); (*b*) *U.S:* (descendant, -ante) des colons français ou espagnols de la Louisiane. **2.** *s. Ling:* le créole. **3.** *a.* (*of animal,*

plant) acclimaté (aux Indes occidentales).
creolize ['kri:əlaiz], *v.tr. Ling:* créoliser (une langue).
Creon ['kri:ən], *Pr.n.m. Gr.Lit:* Créon.
creosol ['kri(:)əsɔl], *s. Ch:* créosol *m.*
creosote[1] ['kri(:)əsout], *s. Ch:* créosote *f*; **coal-tar c., c. oil,** créosote de houille, huile lourde de houille, huile de créosote; *Com:* acide *m* carbolique.
creosote[2], *v.tr.* créosoter, injecter (le bois) à la créosote.
creosoting ['kri(:)əsoutiŋ], *s.* créosotage *m.*
crepance ['krepəns], *s. Vet:* entretaillure *f.*
crêpe [kreip], *s.* **1.** *Tex:* (i) crêpe *m*; (ii) simili-crêpe *m*; **soft c.,** crêpe lisse, français; **crisped c., hard c.,** crêpe crêpé; **satin c.,** crêpe satin; **c. de Chine,** crêpe de Chine; **c. nylon socks,** chaussettes *f* crêpe mousse; *Med:* **c. bandage,** bande *f* Velpeau; velpeau *m.* **2. c.(-rubber) soles,** semelles *f* (de) crêpe. **3. c. paper,** papier *m* crêpé. **4.** *Cu:* **c. Suzette,** crêpe Suzette.
crêpehanger ['kreiphæŋər], *s. U.S: F:* rabat-joie *m inv.*
crépeline ['kreipəli:n], *s. Tex:* crépeline *f.*
crepidula [kre'pidjulə], *s. Moll:* crepidula *f.*
crepis ['kri:pis], *s. Bot:* crépide *m,* crépis *m.*
crepitant ['krepitənt], *a.* crépitant.
crepitate ['krepiteit], *v.i.* crépiter.
crepitation [krepi'teiʃ(ə)n], *s.* crépitation *f.*
crepitus ['krepitəs], *s. Med: Surg:* crépitation *f.*
crêpoline ['kreipəli:n], *s. Tex:* crêpeline *f.*
crépon ['kreipɔn], *s. Tex:* crépon *m.*
crepuscular [kre'pʌskjulər], *a.* (lumière, papillon, etc.) crépusculaire.
Crepuscularia [krepʌskju'lεəriə], *s.pl. Ent: A:* crépusculaires *m.*
crescendo[1] [kri'ʃendou]. **1.** *adv. Mus:* crescendo; en augmentant. **2.** *s.* crescendo *m inv.*
crescendo[2], *v.i.* aller en augmentant; aller crescendo.
crescent ['kres(ə)nt]. **1.** *s.* (*a*) premier quartier de la lune; (*b*) croissant *m* (de la lune qui croit ou décroît); (*c*) *Her: etc:* croissant; **the Red C.,** le Croissant Rouge; **the Turkish C.,** le croissant turc; *Hist:* **the C.,** l'Empire turc; le Croissant; *Mus:* **a Turkish c.,** un pavillon chinois; (*d*) rue *f* ou côté *m* de rue en arc de cercle; maisons *fpl* formant demi-lune (souvent nom de rue, *e.g. Mornington C.*); (*e*) *Bak:* **c. (roll),** croissant; (*f*) *Tls:* clé *f* à molette. **2.** *a.* (*a*) croissant; augmentant; **the c. moon,** la lune dans son croissant, le croissant de la lune; (*b*) **c.(-shaped),** en forme de croissant, de demi-lune; *U.S:* **the C. City,** la Nouvelle-Orléans.
cresol ['kresɔl, 'kri:-], *s. Ch:* crésol *m.*
cresorcin [kri'sɔ:sin], *s. Ch:* crésorcine *m.*
cress [kres], *s. Bot:* cresson *m*; **garden c., golden c.,** cresson alénois; passerage cultivée; **wall c.,** arabette *f*; **winter c.,** barbarée *f*; roquette *f* des jardins; **c. bed,** cressonnière *f.*
cresset ['kresit], *s. A:* torchère *f,* fanal *m,* -aux (d'une tour, des anciens phares, etc.).
crest[1] [krest], *s.* **1.** crête *f* (de coq, reptile); huppe *f* (d'alouette); aigrette *f* (de paon). **2.** cimier *m,* crête (de casque). **3.** (*a*) crête, sommet *m,* arête *f* (de colline); crête, sommet (d'une vague); houppe *f* (d'un arbre); *Geog:* **c. line,** ligne *f* de faîte; (*b*) *Ph:* crête, point haut (d'une onde); *El:* **c. value,** valeur maximale, de crête; *U.S:* **c. speed,** vitesse normale maximum sur parcours libre. **4.** *Arch:* crête, faîte *m,* faîtage *m*; *Fort:* crête (d'un parapet); *Civ.E:* crête, couronnement *m* (d'un barrage); *Const:* **c. tile,** (tuile *f*) faîtière *f*; *Artil:* **c. clearance,** évitement *m* du masque, de (la) crête. **5.** *Anat:* crête, arête (d'un os). **6.** (*a*) crête du cou (d'un animal); (*b*) crinière *f* (de cheval). **7.** (*a*) *Her:* (*on helmet*) cimier *m*; (*on escutcheon*) timbre *m*; (*b*) (*on seal, note-paper, etc.*) armoiries *fpl*; écusson *m*; emblème *m* héraldique; **car c.,** écusson de voiture; *Av:* **company c.,** cocarde *f*; *Sp: NAm:* **club c.,** insigne sportif.
crest[2]. **1.** *v.tr.* orner (qch.) d'un cimier, d'une crête; mettre une crête à (un mur); mettre un faîte à (un comble). **2.** *v.tr.* (*a*) gravir (une colline) jusqu'à la crête; surmonter (une colline); (*b*) franchir la crête d'(une vague). **3.** *v.i.* (*of wave*) monter en crête; moutonner.
crested ['krestid], *a.* **1.** *Orn:* à crête, à huppe; huppé, houppé; *Z:* à crête, crêté; *Bot:* cristé; **white-c. waves,** vagues *f* aux crêtes blanches. **2.** (*a*) (*of helmet*) orné d'un cimier; panaché; *Her:* (écusson) timbré; (coq) crêté; (*b*) *F:* armorié; orné d'un écusson.
crestfallen ['krestfɔ:ln], *a.* (*of pers.*) abattu, découragé; (*of look*) déconfit, penaud; **to look c.,** baisser l'oreille, la crête, le nez; *F:* faire un nez (long d'une aune).
cresting ['krestiŋ], *s. Furn:* galerie *f* (de dos de chaise).
crestmoreite ['krestmɔ:rait], *s. Miner:* crestmoréite *f.*
cresyl[1] ['kresil, 'kri:-], *s. Ch:* crésyle *m.*
Cresyl[2], *s. R.t.m:* Crésyl *m*; **to disinfect with C.,** crésyler; **disinfecting with C.,** crésylage *m.*
cresylate ['kresileit], *s. Ch:* crésylate *m.*
cresylene ['kresili:n], *s. Ch:* crésylène *m.*
cresylic [krə'silik], *a. Ch:* (acide *m*) crésylique.
cresylite ['kresilait], *s. Exp:* crésylite *m.*
cretaceous [kri'teiʃəs]. **1.** *a.* crétacé; crayeux. **2.** *a. & s. Geol:* crétacé (*m*); **middle c.,** mésocrétacé *m*; **upper, lower, c.,** crétacé supérieur, inférieur.
Cretan ['kri:t(ə)n], *Geog:* **1.** *a.* crétois. **2.** *s.* Crétois, -oise.
Crete [kri:t], *Pr.n. Geog:* la Crète; *A:* (l'île *f* de) Candie *f.*
cretic ['kri:tik]. **1.** *a. Geog:* **C.,** crétois. **2.** *Pros:* (*a*) *a.* crétique; (*b*) *s.* crétique *m,* amphimacre *m.*
cretification [kri:tifi'keiʃ(ə)n], *s. Med:* crétification *f*; dégénération *f* calcaire.
cretin ['kretin], *s. Med:* crétin *m.*
cretinism ['kretinizm], *s. Med:* crétinisme *m.*
cretinize ['kretinaiz], *v.tr.* crétiniser.
cretinoid ['kretinɔid], *a. Med:* crétinoïde.
cretinous ['kretinəs], *a. Med:* crétineux.
cretonne [kre'tɔn, 'kretɔn], *s. Tex:* cretonne *f*; **tapestry c.,** cretonne d'ameublement.
Creusa [kri'ju:zə], *Pr.n.f. Gr.Lit:* Créuse.
creutzer ['krɔitsər], *s. A.Num:* kreutzer *m.*
crevasse[1] [kri'væs], *s.* **1.** crevasse *f* (glaciaire). **2.** *U.S:* crevasse, fissure *f* (dans une levée de fleuve).
crevasse[2], *v.i.* (*of ice, embankment*) se crevasser, se fissurer.
crevassing [kri'væsiŋ], *s.* fissuration *f.*
crevice ['krevis], *s.* fente *f*; crevasse *f,* lézarde *f* (de mur); fissure *f* (de rocher); avalure *f* (dans une falaise).
creviced ['krevist], *a.* (mur) lézardé; (roc) fissuré.
crew[1] [kru:], *s.* **1.** *Nau:* équipage *m*; les hommes *m*; l'armement *m*; *Row: etc:* équipe *f*; les canotiers *m*; les équipiers *m*; **the c. space,** le poste d'équipage; les logements *m,* les aménagements *m*; *Cost:* **c. neck (of sweater),** col ras le cou. **2.** (*gang, team*) équipe; équipage; **c. of a lorry,** équipage d'un camion; *Av:* **air c., flight c.,** équipage (d'avion); **ground c.,** équipe au sol; *Ind:* **maintenance c.,** équipe d'entretien; *Petr:* **drilling rig c.,** équipe de forage; *Rail:* **engine c.,** équipe de conduite, de locomotive; *esp. NAm:* **train c.,** personnel *m* du train; **gun c.,** *Mil: etc:* équipe de pièce; *Navy:* les servants *m* (d'une pièce); **c.-served weapon,** arme collective; **tank c.,** équipage de char; **c. member,** membre *m* d'équipage, d'équipe (d'avion, de char, etc.); servant (d'une pièce d'artillerie, de mitrailleuse, etc.); *Cin:* groupiste *m.* **3.** *Pej:* bande *f,* troupe *f*; **sorry c.,** triste engeance *f.*
crew[2]. **1.** *v.tr.* (*a*) armer (un navire d'un équipage); fournir (un avion, etc.) d'un équipage; (*b*) désigner (qn) à un équipage, à une équipe; (*c*) **to c. a yacht,** faire partie de l'équipe d'un yacht; **yacht that can't be crewed by less than six,** yacht qui exige un équipage de six au moins. **2.** *v.i.* **to c. for s.o.,** servir d'équipier à qn.
crewel ['kru:əl], *s.* laine *f* (i) à broder, (ii) à tapisserie; **c. needle,** aiguille *f* à tapisserie.
crewelwork ['kru:əlwə:k], *s.* tapisserie *f* (sur canevas).
crewman, *pl.* **-men** ['kru:mən], *s.* équipier *m.*
crib[1] [krib], *s.* **1.** (*a*) *Husb:* mangeoire *f*; râtelier *m*; **c. biter,** (cheval) tiqueur; (jument) tiqueuse; **c. biting,** tic rongeur; (*b*) *NAm:* huche *f,* coffre *m* (pour le maïs, sel, etc.); armoire *f* (à outils). **2.** (*a*) cabane *f,* hutte *f*; bicoque *f*; (*b*) *P:* habitation *f*; maison *f*; **to crack a c.,** cambrioler une maison; **c. cracker,** cambrioleur *m.* **3.** (*a*) lit *m* d'enfant; couchette *f*; *Ecc:* crèche *f*; **c. death,** mort inattendue d'un enfant (dans son lit); (*b*) *occ.* berceau *m.* **4.** (*a*) *Hyd.E: Min:* cadre porteur; roue *f,* rouet *m,* de fondation (de revêtement de puits); (*b*) *Civ.E:* encoffrement *m* en charpente; boisage *m.* **5.** *Fish:* sac *m* (d'un verveux). **6.** *F:* (*a*) plagiat *m*; (*b*) *Sch:* traduction *f* (d'auteur), corrigé *m* (de thèmes, etc.) (employés subrepticement). **7.** *F: O:* emploi *m,* place *f*; **he's got a good c. with a City firm,** il a une bonne situation dans une maison de la Cité. **8.** *P:* café *m,* cabaret *m,* borgne; *F:* trou *m* borgne.
crib[2], *v.tr.* (**cribbed**) **1.** *A:* claquemurer, enfermer; *Lit:* **to be cabined, cribbed, and confined,** (i) être à l'étroit; (ii) être enfermé (dans les limites d'un sujet, etc.). **2.** *Min:* boiser, bâcher (un puits). **3.** *F:* (*a*) voler, chiper (**sth. from s.o.,** qch. à qn); (*b*) **to c. a passage from an author,** reproduire, copier, un passage d'un auteur; *v.i.* **to c. from an author,** plagier un auteur; faire un plagiat à un auteur; **to c. from the works of others,** fourrager dans les œuvres d'autrui; (*c*) *Sch:* (i) **to c. an exercise from another boy,** copier un devoir sur un camarade; (ii) *v.i.* se servir de traductions, de corrigés. **4.** *v.i.* (*a*) (*of horse*) tiquer; (*b*) *F:* (*of pers.*) se plaindre; **to c. about sth.,** ronchonner, maugréer, contre qch.
cribbage ['kribidʒ], *s. Cards:* cribbage *m.*
cribbing ['kribiŋ], *s.* **1.** boisage *m* (d'un puits). **2.** *Sch:* (*a*) emploi déloyal de traductions, de corrigés; tuyautage *m*; (*b*) copiage *m.* **3.** *Vet:* tic rongeur.
cribellated ['kribəleitid], *a. Arach:* cribellate, cribellaté.
cribellum, *pl.* **-a** [kri'beləm, -ə], *s. Arach:* cribellum *m.*
criblé ['kri:blei], *a. A.Engr:* **c. process,** crible *m.*
cribriform ['kribrifɔ:m], *a. Nat.Hist:* cribriforme.
cribrose ['kribrous], *a. Nat.Hist:* cribreux, cribleux.
cribwork ['kribwə:k], *s. Civ.E:* boisage *m* (d'un puits, etc.); cribwork *m.*
Cricetidae [kri'setidi:], *s.pl. Z:* cricétidés *m.*
crick[1] [krik], *s.* **1.** crampe *f*; **c. in the neck,** torticolis *m.* **2.** effort *m,* foulure *f*; **c. in the back,** tour *m* de reins.
crick[2], *v.tr.* **to c. one's neck,** se donner le torticolis; **to c. one's back,** se donner un tour de reins.
cricket[1] ['krikit], *s. Ent:* grillon *m*; **domestic c., house c.,** grillon domestique, de boulangerie; *F:* cricri *m,* cri-cri *m, pl.* cri-cris; **field c.,** grillon des champs; **tree c.,** œcanthe *m*; **the c. on the hearth,** le grillon du foyer; *F:* **as merry as a c.,** gai comme un pinson.
cricket[2], *s. Sp:* cricket *m*; **to play c.,** (i) jouer au cricket; (ii) *Fig:* agir loyalement; *Fig:* **that's not c.,** cela n'est pas de jeu, passe le jeu, n'est pas loyal, n'est pas juste, ne se fait pas; **c. field, c. ground,** terrain *m* de cricket; terrain de jeu; **c. shirt,** chemise blanche à col ouvert.
cricket[3], *v.i.* jouer au cricket.
cricket[4], *s. Dial: NAm:* escabeau *m.*
cricketer ['krikitər], *s.* cricketeur *m*; joueur *m* de cricket.
cricoarytenoid ['kraikouæri'ti:nɔid], *a. Anat:* crico-aryténoïdien.
cricoid ['kraikɔid], *a. & s. Anat:* (cartilage *m*) cricoïde *m.*
cricothyroid [kraikou'θairɔid], *a. Anat:* crico-thyroïdien, -ienne.
cri de, du, cœur [kridə, dju, kɔ:r], *s.* cri *m* du cœur.
crier ['kraiər], *s.* (*a*) crieur *m* (à une vente, etc.); (*b*) **public c., town c.,** crieur public, municipal; tambourineur *m*; (*c*) **court c.,** audiencier *m* (du tribunal); huissier audiencier.
crikey ['kraiki], *int. P:* mazette! mince alors! sapristi!
crime[1] [kraim], *s.* (*a*) crime *m*; **capital c.,** crime capital; **victim of a c.,** victime *f* d'un attentat; **the blackest of crimes,** le plus grand, noir, des crimes; **they are linked by c.,** il y a un cadavre entre eux; *Fig:* **it's a c. to touch up these pictures,** c'est un meurtre, un crime, de retoucher ces tableaux; **it's not (really) a c.,** ce n'est pas un grand crime; (*b*) délit *m*; **punishment out of all proportion to the c.,** châtiment *m* hors de proportion avec la faute, l'offense *f*; (*c*) **to make a study of c.,** étudier le crime, la criminalité; **c. fiction,** romans (i) noirs, (ii) policiers; **c. writer,** auteur *m* de romans (i) noirs, (ii) policiers; **c. reporter,** journaliste *mf* qui fait la chronique des tribunaux; (*d*) *Mil:* manquement *m* à la discipline; infraction *f,* faute *f*; **c. sheet,** feuille *f* de punitions.
crime[2], *v.tr. Mil:* **1.** accuser (qn) d'un délit. **2.** condamner (un accusé).
Crimea (the) [ðəkrai'miə], *Pr.n. Geog:* la Crimée.
Crimean [krai'miən], *Geog:* **1.** *a.* criméen; *Hist:* **the C. War,** la guerre de Crimée; **C. veteran,** ancien combattant de la guerre de Crimée. **2.** *s.* Criméen, -éenne.
criminal ['krimin(ə)l]. **1.** *a.* criminel; (*a*) **c. act, behaviour,** action, conduite, criminelle; (*b*) (*concerning crime*) **c. action, c. case,** action *f,* cas *m,* au criminel; **to take c. proceedings against s.o.,** poursuivre qn criminellement, au criminel; **c. law,** droit criminel, pénal; **c. jurist,** criminaliste *m*; **c. lawyer,** avocat *m* au criminel, d'assises; **the C. Investigation Department,** *F:* **the C.I.D.** ['si:'ai:'di:] = la Police judiciaire; *F:* la P.J.; **c. record,** casier *m* judiciaire; **the C. Records Office** = l'Identité *f* judiciaire; le Bureau d'identité; (*c*) **it would be c. to cut down these trees,** ce serait un crime, criminel, d'abattre ces arbres. **2.** *s.* (*a*) criminel, -elle; **habitual c.,** repris *m* de justice; récidiviste *mf*; (*b*) (le) coupable.
criminalism ['kriminəlizm], *s.* criminalisme *m.*
criminalist ['kriminəlist], *s.* criminaliste *m.*
criminalistic [kriminə'listik], *a.* criminalistique.
criminalistics [kriminə'listiks], *s.pl.* (*usu. with sg. const.*) criminalistique *f.*
criminality [krimi'næliti], *s.* criminalité *f.*
criminally ['kriminəli], *adv.* criminellement.
criminate ['krimineit], *v.tr.* **1.** incriminer, accuser (qn). **2.** convaincre (qn) d'un crime; **to c. oneself,** fournir des preuves contre soi-même. **3.** blâmer, incriminer (qch.).
crimination [krimi'neiʃ(ə)n], *s.* incrimination *f.*
criminative ['kriminətiv], **criminatory** ['kriminətəri], *a.* criminatoire.
crimine ['krimini], *int. A:* = CRIKEY.
criminogenic [kriminou'dʒenik], *a.* criminogène.
criminological [kriminə'lɔdʒikl], *a.* criminologique.
criminologist [krimi'nɔlədʒist], *s.* criminologiste *mf,* criminologue *mf.*
criminology [krimi'nɔlədʒi], *s.* criminologie *f.*
criminous ['kriminəs], *a. Jur:* **c. clerk,** prêtre *m* coupable.

criminy ['krimini], *int. P: A:* = CRIKEY.
crimp[1] [krimp], *s. A:* racoleur *m*, embaucheur *m* (de marins, etc.).
crimp[2], *v.tr. A:* racoler, embaucher (des marins, etc.).
crimp[3], *s.* **1.** gaufrage *m*; pli *m* (d'un drap); frisure *f* (des cheveux, de la laine, etc.); gaufrage, sertissage *m* (d'une cartouche, etc.); *NAm: P:* **to put a c. in a scheme,** mettre des bâtons dans les roues. **2.** sertissure *f* (d'une cartouche, boîte de conserve, etc.).
crimp[4], *v.tr.* **1.** (*a*) gaufrer (à la paille), plisser, crêper, friser (de l'étoffe, etc.); (*b*) friser, frisotter, onduler, crêper (les cheveux); **crimped hair,** cheveux crêpelés à gaufrures; (*c*) onduler (la tôle); (*d*) *NAm: P:* **business was crimped by high taxation,** les affaires étaient gênées, restreintes, par la fiscalité excessive. **2.** (*a*) sertir (une cartouche, une boîte de conserve, etc.); (*b*) *Bootm:* emboutir (les empeignes de chaussures). **3.** taillader (le poisson fraîchement pêché).
crimping[1] ['krimpiŋ], *s. A:* racolage *m*, embauchage *m*.
crimping[2], *s.* **1.** (*a*) plissement *m*, gaufrage *m*, crêpage *m*; (*b*) frisage *m*, crêpage (des cheveux). **2.** (*a*) sertissage *m* (de cartouches); **c. tool,** sertisseur *m*; (*b*) emboutissage *m* (du cuir).
crimpy ['krimpi], *a.* frisé, crêpé.
crimson[1] ['krimz(ə)n], *a. & s.* cramoisi (*m*); pourpre (*m*); **c. with rage,** rouge de colère; **he turned c.,** il est devenu pourpre; le pourpre lui est monté au visage; **the sky was turning c.,** le ciel s'empourprait.
crimson[2]. **1.** *v.tr.* teindre (qch.) en cramoisi. **2.** *v.i.* devenir cramoisi, pourpre; (*of cheeks, sky, etc.*) s'empourprer.
cringe[1] [krindʒ], *s.* **1.** mouvement craintif (pour se dérober). **2.** courbette servile, obséquieuse.
cringe[2], *v.i.* **1.** se faire tout petit; se tapir, se blottir (de peur); se dérober (par crainte d'un coup); **he did not c.,** il n'a pas bronché, n'a pas sourcillé. **2.** s'humilier, ramper, s'aplatir, se mettre à plat ventre, faire des courbettes, courber l'échine, courber les épaules (**to c. before, s.o.,** devant qn); *F:* faire le chien couchant (auprès de qn).
cringer ['krindʒər], *s.* personne obséquieuse, servile; *F:* chien couchant.
cringing ['krindʒiŋ], *a.* **1.** (geste) craintif. **2.** servile, obséquieux.
cringingly ['krindʒiŋli], *adv.* **1.** craintivement. **2.** servilement, obséquieusement; en courbant l'échine.
cringle ['kriŋgl], *s. Nau:* patte *f* de bouline; andaillot *m*; **iron c.,** anneau *m* en fer; **reef c.,** patte de ris.
crinite[1] ['krainait], *a. Nat.Hist:* velu, chevelu.
crinite[2], *s. Paleont:* encrine *f*.
crinkle[1] ['kriŋkl], *s.* pli *m*, ride *f*; *Tchn:* froncé *f* (dans le papier); *Hort:* crinkle *m* (des pommes, des pommes de terre); frisolée *f*, fris(el)ée *f* (des pommes de terre).
crinkle[2]. **1.** *v.tr.* froisser, chiffonner (du papier); **crinkled paper,** papier plissé, ondulé, bourdonné, gaufré; papier crêpe, crêpé. **2.** *v.i.* (*a*) se froisser; (*of felt*) **to c. (up),** grigner; (*b*) rendre un son de papier froissé; (*c*) (*of apples, potatoes*) se rider.
crinkling ['kriŋkliŋ], *s.* plissage *m*, froissement *m*, gaufrage *m*.
crinkly ['kriŋkli], *a.* **1.** plein de rides. **2. c. sound,** froufrou *m*, *pl.* frous-frous; son *m* de papier froissé.
crinoid ['krinɔid]. **1.** *a.* crinoïde; en forme de lis. **2.** *s. Echin: Paleont:* crinoïde *m*; lis *m* à bras; lis de mer; encrine *f*.
crinoidal [kri'nɔid(ə)l], *a. Echin: Paleont:* crinoïde.
Crinoidea [kri'nɔidiə], *s.pl. Echin: Paleont:* crinoïdes *m*.
crinoline ['krinəli(:)n], *s. A.Tex: Cost:* crinoline *f*.
crinum ['krainəm], *s. Bot:* crinum *m*.
crioceras [kri'ɔsərəs], *s. Paleont:* criocéras *m*.
Crioceratites [kriou'serətaits], *s.pl. Paleont:* criocératidés *m*.
crioceris [kri'ɔsəris], *s. Ent:* criocère *m*.
criollo ['kriɔlou], *s.* **1.** Hispano-américain, -aine (surtout de sang espagnol pur). **2.** *Bot:* criollo *m*.
cripes [kraips], *int. P: O:* mazette! sapristi!
cripple[1] ['kripl], *s.* **1.** estropié, -ée; boiteux, -euse; impotent, -ente; infirme *mf*; *F:* (*on crutches*) béquillard, -arde. **2.** échafaud volant (de peintre en bâtiment, etc.). **3.** *Carp:* **c. timber,** empannon *m*, chevron *m* en croupe.
cripple[2], *v.tr.* **1.** estropier (qn); **the men who were crippled in the war,** les mutilés de guerre. **2.** disloquer (une machine, un système); mettre (une machine) hors service, hors de fonctionnement; désemparer (un navire); condamner (une industrie) à dépérir, paralyser (l'industrie, la volonté).
crippled ['kripld], *a.* **1.** estropié; **c. with rheumatism,** perclus de rhumatismes; **to have a c. foot,** être estropié du pied; **he's c. in his left arm,** il est infirme du bras gauche. **2.** (*a*) **c. ship,** vaisseau désemparé; **a c. ship makes little headway,** avec des avaries un vaisseau avance lentement; (*b*) (machine) hors service, hors de fonctionnement; (*c*) *Cmptr:* **c. leapfrog test,** test saute-mouton restreint.
crippling ['kripliŋ], *a.* (*a*) (*of disease, etc.*) estropiant; (*b*) (*of taxation, etc.*) paralysant.
crisis, *pl.* **-es** ['kraisis, -i:z], *s.* crise *f* (d'une maladie, dans les affaires, etc.); **the present acute c.,** la crise qui sévit actuellement; **things are coming to a c.,** le moment décisif approche; **to go, pass, through a c.,** passer par une crise; **to end a c.,** mettre fin à, dénouer, résoudre, une crise.
crisp[1] [krisp]. **1.** *a.* (*a*) (cheveux) crêpés, crépus, frisés; (*b*) (biscuit, etc.) croquant, croustillant, cassant; **c. almond,** praline *f*; **c. lettuce,** laitue croquante; **the snow was c. under foot,** la neige craquait sous nos pas; (*c*) (style) nerveux; (ton) tranchant; **c. touch (on the piano),** doigté nerveux et perlé; (*d*) **the c. air of an autumn morning,** l'air vif d'une matinée d'automne. **2.** *s.* (*a*) *F: A:* **crisps,** billets *m* de banque; (*b*) **cooked to a c.,** rôti à point pour croustiller, croquer, sous la dent; (*c*) *Cu:* **(potato) crisps,** croustilles *f*; (pommes *f*) chips (*m*).
crisp[2]. **1.** *v.tr.* (*a*) crêper (les cheveux); froncer (du crêpe); (*b*) donner du croustillant, du croquant, à (des biscuits, etc.); praliner (des amandes, etc.). **2.** *v.i.* (*a*) (*of hair, cloth, etc.*) se crêper; (*b*) (*of leaves, etc.*) se dessécher, se parcheminer.
crispate ['krispeit], *a. Nat.Hist:* crépu; aux bords crépus.
crispation [kris'peiʃ(ə)n], *s.* **1.** frisure *f* (des cheveux); crispation *f* (du cuir par la chaleur, etc.). **2.** crispation (des nerfs); chair *f* de poule. **3.** *Ph:* ondulation *f*.
crispbread ['krispbred], *s.* biscuit fait de grains (de blé, de seigle, etc.) égrugés.
crisped [krispt], *a. Bot:* crépu; aux bords crépus.
crisper ['krispər], *s.* bac *m* à légumes (d'un réfrigérateur); *Fr.C:* hydrateur *m*.
crispifloral [krispi'flɔ:r(ə)l], *a. Bot:* crispiflore.
crispifolious [krispi'fouliəs], *a. Bot:* crispifolié.
Crispin ['krispin], *Pr.n.m.* Crépin.
crisply ['krispli], *adv.* (parler) d'un ton tranchant; (écrire) d'un style nerveux, net; nettement.
crispness ['krispnis], *s.* **1.** crêpure *f* (des cheveux). **2.** qualité croustillante (d'un gâteau, etc.); dureté *f* (de la neige); état parcheminé (du papier, etc.); (*of fabric, etc.*) **to lose its c.,** se défraîchir. **3.** netteté *f* (de style, d'articulation, *Mus:* d'exécution). **4.** froid vif (de l'air).
crispy ['krispi], *a.* **1.** (*of hair*) crépu. **2.** (biscuit) croquant; **c. noodles,** nouilles frites. **3.** (air) frisquet, (matinée) frisquette.
criss [kri:s], *s.* criss (malais).
criss-cross[1], **crisscross**[1] ['kriskrɔs]. **1.** *a.* entrecroisé, intriqué, treillissé; *Rad:* **c.-c. jamming,** brouillage *m* en treillis. **2.** *adv.* **everything went c.-c. from the start,** dès le commencement tout a marché de travers. **3.** *s.* entrecroisement *m*; **c.-c. of wires,** enchevêtrement *m* de fils de fer; **riddled with a c.-c. of footpaths,** couvert d'un réseau de sentiers; *F:* **there is a certain amount of c.-c. between the ministries,** il y a un certain nombre de malentendus *m* entre les ministères.
criss-cross[2], **crisscross**[2]. **1.** *v.tr.* entrecroiser (des fils, etc.); **brow criss-crossed with wrinkles,** front craquelé de rides. **2.** *v.i.* s'entrecroiser.
criss-cross-row ['kriskrɔs'rou], *s. A:* croix *f* de par Dieu; alphabet *m*.
crista, *pl.* **-ae** ['kristə, -i:], *s. Nat.Hist:* crête *f*.
cristate ['kristeit], *a. Nat.Hist:* crêté, cristé.
cristatella [kristə'telə], *s. Z:* cristatelle *f*.
cristobalite [kris'toubəlait], *s. Miner:* cristobalite *f*.
crit [krit], *s. F:* critique *f* (d'une pièce de théâtre, etc.).
criteriology [kraitiəri'ɔlədʒi], *s.* critériologie *f*.
criterion, *pl.* **-ia** [krai'tiəriən, -iə], *s.* critère *m*; *O:* critérium *m*; *F:* pierre *f* de touche; **the criteria of truth,** les critériums de la vérité; *Cmptr:* **cycle c.,** (i) nombre *m*, (ii) compteur *m*, d'itérations.
crith [kriθ], *s. Ph:* poids d'un litre d'hydrogène ramené aux conditions normales de température et pression.
critic ['kritik], *s.* (*a*) critique *m*; **music, drama(tic), literary, c.,** critique musical, dramatique, littéraire; **severe c.,** critique acerbe; **ill-natured c.,** criticailleur *m*; **armchair c.,** critique en chambre; *Lit:* **psychological c.,** psychocritique *m*; (*b*) censeur *m* (de la conduite d'autrui); critiqueur *m*.
critical ['kritik(ə)l]. **1.** *a.* critique; (*a*) qui aime à censurer, à blâmer; exigeant; **to play before a c. audience,** jouer devant des auditeurs critiques, exigeants; **c. mind,** esprit *m* critique; **to look on sth. with a c. eye,** regarder qch. d'un œil (de) connaisseur, d'un œil scrutateur, sévère; (*b*) **c. treatise,** dissertation *f* critique; **c. study of Homer,** étude *f* critique d'Homère; **textual and c. notes,** remarques littérales et critiques; **c. philosophy,** criticisme *m*; **c. philosopher,** criticiste *m*; (*c*) **c. situation,** situation critique, dangereuse, pleine de risque; *Med:* **in a c. state,** dans un état critique; **at a c. moment,** à un moment critique, décisif; **the c. age,** l'âge *m* critique; **c. year,** année *f* climatérique; **she is going through a c. time,** elle subit, traverse, une crise en ce moment; (*d*) *Mth: Ph: etc:* (point) de transition; *Ph:* **c. temperature,** température critique, de transformation; **c. density,** densité *f* limite; *El:* **c. voltage,** tension *f* critique; *Mch:* **c. speed,** vitesse *f* limite, optima; *Hyd.E:* **c. level,** cote *f* d'alerte; *Opt:* **c. angle,** angle *m* limite, critique; (*e*) *Opt:* **c. definition,** netteté *f*. **2.** *s. Atom.Ph:* **delayed c.,** critique différé, retardé; **prompt c.,** critique instantané.
criticality [kriti'kæliti], *s. Atom.Ph:* criticalité *f*.
critically ['kritik(ə)li], *adv.* **1. to look at sth. c.,** considérer qch. en critique; regarder qch. d'un œil (de) connaisseur, d'un œil scrutateur, sévère. **2. c. ill,** dangereusement malade; **c. situated,** dans une situation critique.
criticaster ['kritikæstər], *s.* un Zoïle, criticailleur *m*.
criticism ['kritisizm], *s.* **1.** (*action, act, of criticizing*) critique *f*; **to lay oneself open to c.,** s'exposer à la critique; **it passed without c.,** on n'en a fait aucune critique. **2.** *Lit: Art: etc:* (*a*) critique; **c. should be impersonal,** la critique devrait être divorcée de tout élément personnel; **bible c.,** critique biblique, exégèse *f* biblique; **historical c., higher c.,** critique des sources; **textual c., verbal c.,** critique des textes; critique verbale; *Lit:* **psychological c.,** psychocritique *f*; (*b*) **to write a c. of a book, etc.,** faire la critique d'un livre, etc. **3.** *Phil:* criticisme *m*.
criticizable ['kritisaizəbl], *a.* critiquable.
criticize ['kritisaiz], *v.tr.* **1.** critiquer, faire la critique de (qch.). **2.** censurer, blâmer, commenter (sur); faire le procès de (qn); **to c. sth. severely,** se répandre en critiques sur qch.; **to c. the defects of a work,** relever les fautes d'un ouvrage.
criticizer ['kritisaizər], *s.* critiqueur, -euse; censeur *m*.
critique [kri'ti:k], *s.* **1.** critique *f*; article *m* critique (sur une œuvre littéraire, etc.); (*Kant's*) **C. of Pure Reason,** Critique de la raison pure. **2.** l'art *m* de la critique.
Crito ['kraitou], *Pr.n.m. Gr.Lit:* Criton.
croak[1] [krouk], *s.* coassement *m* (de grenouille); croassement *m* (de corbeau).
croak[2], *v.i.* **1.** (*of frog*) coasser; (*of raven*) croasser. **2.** *F:* (*of pers.*) (*a*) grogner, ronchonner; croasser; (*b*) voir l'avenir en noir; **croaking pessimist,** sombre pessimiste *m*. **3.** *P:* (*a*) mourir, claquer; (*b*) *v.tr.* assassiner, descendre (qn).
croaker ['kroukər], *s.* **1.** ronchonneur, -euse; grogneur, -euse; grognon *mf*; pessimiste *mf*. **2.** prophète *m* de malheur; prêche-malheur *mf inv*; (*in war*) défaitiste *mf*. **3.** *P:* docteur *m*, toubib *m*.
croakily ['kroukili], *adv.* d'une voix enrouée, rauque.
croaking ['kroukiŋ], *s.* coassement *m* (de grenouille); croassement *m* (de corbeau).
croaky ['krouki], *a.* (voix) enrouée, rauque.
Croat ['krouæt], *s.* (*a*) *Geog:* Croate *mf*; (*b*) *Ling:* croate *m*.
Croatia [krou'eiʃə], *Pr.n. Geog:* Croatie *f*.
Croatian [krou'eiʃən]. **1.** *Geog:* (*a*) *a.* croate; (*b*) *s.* Croate *mf*. **2.** *s. Ling:* croate *m*.
croc [krɔk], *s. F:* crocodile *m*.
croceate ['krousieit], *a.* safrané; jaune safran *inv*.
crocein(e) ['krousiin, -ain], *s. Ch:* crocéine *f*.
crochet[1] ['krouʃei, -ʃi], *s.* **1.** (travail *m* au) crochet *m*; **single c.,** maille coulée; **double c.,** maille serrée; **art c.,** crochet d'art; **c. wool,** laine perlée; **c. hook,** crochet. **2.** **c. (work),** ouvrage *m*, travail *m*, dentelle *f*, au crochet.
crochet[2] **(crocheted)** ['krouʃeid, -ʃid], (*a*) *v.tr.* faire (qch.) au crochet; (*b*) *v.i.* faire du crochet.
crocheting ['krouʃeiiŋ, -ʃiin], *s.* (travail *m* au) crochet *m*.
crocidolite [krou'sidəlait], *s. Miner:* crocidolite *f*.
crocidura, *pl.* **-ae** [krɔsi'dju:rə, -i:], *s. Z:* crocidure *f*.
crocin ['krousin], *s. Ch:* crocine *f*.
crock[1] [krɔk], *s.* **1.** (*a*) cruche *f*; (*b*) pot *m* de terre. **2.** *Hort:* tesson *m* (pour couvrir le trou d'un pot de fleurs).
crock[2], *s. F:* (*a*) cheval claqué; vieille rosse; cagne *f*; (*b*) *Scot:* vieille brebis finie; (*c*) (*of pers.*) **to be a bit of a c.,** être mal portant; **old c.,** (i) (*pers.*) vieux bonhomme fini, croulant *m*; **old c. of 90,** vieux type de 90 ans; **I'm too much of an old c. to play football,** le football n'est plus de mon âge; (ii) (*car*) vieux clou, tacot *m*, vieille guimbarde, vieille bagnole.
crock[3], *F:* **1.** *v.i.* **to c. (up),** tomber malade. **2.** *v.tr.* mettre (un athlète) hors de combat; claquer, abîmer (un cheval); **I crocked my leg on Saturday,** je me suis abîmé la jambe samedi; **to get badly crocked (up),** se faire abîmer.
crocked [krɔkt], *a. F:* abîmé; (cheval) claqué; hors de combat.
crockery ['krɔkəri], *s.* (*a*) faïence *f*, poterie *f*; (*b*) *coll.*

vaisselle *f* de table, de cuisine.

crocket ['krɔkit], *s. Arch:* crochet *m* (de pignon gothique, etc.).

crocky ['krɔki], *a. F:* mal en point; mal fichu; **his illness left him with a c. heart,** il est resté avec un cœur affaibli depuis sa maladie.

crocodile ['krɔkədail], *s.* **1.** (*a*) crocodile *m*; **c. tears,** larmes *f* de crocodile, de commande; pleurs *m* de commande; (*b*) **c. (skin),** peau *f* de crocodile. *F:* croco *m*; **c. handbag,** sac *m* à main en crocodile; (*c*) (i) élèves d'un pensionnat marchant deux à deux, en rang(s) d'oignons; (ii) *O:* procession *f*, défilé *m* (d'automobiles). **2.** *attrib.* **c. spanner,** clef *f* à mâchoires dentées; clef crocodile; *Metalw:* **c. shears,** cisailleuse *f* à guillotine. **3.** *Orn:* **c. bird,** pluvian *m*.

crocodilian [krɔkə'diliən], *a. & s.* crocodilien (*m*).

Crocodilidae [krɔkə'dilidi:], *s.pl. Rept:* crocodilidés *m*.

crocodiling ['krɔkədailiŋ], *s. Const:* crocodilage *m*, formation *f* de frisures, fendillement *m* (du vernis, etc.).

crocoisite ['krɔkɔizait], **crocoite** ['krɔkouait], *s. Miner:* crocoïse *f*, crocoïte *f*.

croconic [krə'kɔnik], *a. Ch:* (acide) croconique.

crocus, *pl.* **-uses** ['kroukəs, -əsiz], *s.* **1.** *Bot:* crocus *m*; **c. sativus,** safran *m*; **autumn c.,** safran cultivé, safran officinal; **prairie c.,** (espèce d')anémone *f*. **2.** *Ch:* rouge *m* à polir.

Croesus ['kri:səs], *Pr.n.m.* Crésus; **as rich as C.,** riche comme Crésus.

croft[1] [krɔft], *s.* **1.** petit clos, closerie *f*. **2.** petite frme.

croft[2], *v.tr. Tex:* herber (des toiles).

crofter ['krɔftər], *s.* (*a*) petit fermier; (*b*) (*N. Scot.*) fermier d'une terre divisée entre affermataires.

croissant ['krwæsɑ̃], *s. Cu:* croissant *m*.

croissanté [krwæ'sɑ̃tei], *a. Her:* croissanté.

Cro-Magnon ['krou'mæɲɔn], *Pr.n. Prehist:* **C.-M. man,** homme *m* de Cro-Magnon.

cromaltite ['kroumɔltait], *s. Miner:* cromaltite *f*.

crombec ['krɔmbek], *s. Orn:* sylviette *f*.

cromlech ['krɔmlek, -leχ], *s. Prehist:* cromlech *m*.

cromorne [krou'mɔ:n], *s. Mus:* **1.** *A:* cromorne *m*, tournebout *m*. **2.** (*organ stop*) cromorne.

crone [kroun], *s.* **1.** vieille (femme); commère *f*. **2.** vieille brebis.

cronk [krɔŋk], *a. Austr: P:* **1.** *Turf:* (cheval *m*) hors de forme. **2.** (*of business, financier, transaction*) véreux; **c. fortune,** fortune mal acquise; *Turf:* **c. race,** course déloyale.

cronstedtite ['krɔnstetait], *s. Miner:* cronstedtite *f*.

crony ['krouni], *s.* (old) **c.,** ami(e) intime; vieil(le) ami(e); vieux copain, vieille copine.

crook[1] [kruk], *s.* **1.** (*a*) croc *m*, crochet *m*; (*b*) houlette *f* (de berger); crosse *f* (d'évêque); (*c*) *Mus:* ton *m* de rechange, corps *m* de rechange (d'un cor d'harmonie). **2.** (*a*) angle *m*, courbure *f*; (*of river, path, etc.*) détour *m*, coude *m*; (*b*) *F: O:* **to get sth. on the c.,** obtenir qch. par fraude, malhonnêtement. **3.** *A:* action *f* de courber, de plier; **c. of the knee,** flexion *f* du genou; génuflexion *f*. **4.** *F:* (*pers.*) escroc *m*; chevalier *m* d'industrie.

crook[2]. **1.** *v.tr.* courber, recourber; *F:* **to c. the little finger, the elbow,** lever le coude. **2.** *v.i.* se courber, se recourber.

crook[3], *a. Austr: F:* **1.** (*of pers.*) (*a*) malade, mal fichu, patraque; (*b*) en colère, furieux; **to go c. at s.o.,** se mettre en colère, fulminer, contre qn. **2.** (*a*) (*of machinery, etc.*) en panne; **there's something c. with the car,** la voiture (i) ne marche pas comme il faut, (ii) est en panne; (*b*) mal choisi; moche; **what a c. place for a dance!** quel drôle d'endroit pour un bal!

crookback ['krukbæk], *s. F:* bossu, -ue.

crookbacked ['krukbækt], *a. F:* bossu; qui a le dos voûté.

crooked ['krukid], *a.* **1.** (*a*) courbé (en crosse); crochu; tordu, recourbé; (*of wood*) courbant, tors; (*of path*) tortueux; (*of limb, tree*) contourné, déjeté; **c. nose,** nez crochu, de travers; **c. legs,** jambes torses; **a c. little man,** un petit homme difforme; **to wear one's hat c.,** porter son chapeau de travers; (*b*) tortueux; malhonnête, déshonnête; **c. reasoning,** raisonnement tortu; **c. advice,** conseils pervers; **c. means,** moyens *m* obliques; **to resort to c. means in order to attain an end,** prendre des détours *m* pour arriver à un but; *B:* **a perverse and c. generation,** une génération perverse et revêche; (*c*) *Can:* **c. knife,** couteau croché. **2.** [krukt] (canne *f*, etc.) à béquille.

crookedly ['krukidli], *adv.* **1.** tortueusement; d'une façon tortueuse. **2.** de travers.

crookedness ['krukidnis], *s.* **1.** irrégularité *f* (des contours, etc.). **2.** (*a*) perversité *f*; (*b*) manque *m* de franchise, de droiture, de loyauté; malhonnêteté *f*. **3.** difformité *f* (de stature); déjettement *m* (de la colonne vertébrale).

Crookes [kruks], *Pr.n. Ph:* **C. tube,** tube *m* de Crookes.

crookesite ['kruksait], *s. Miner:* crookésite *f*.

croon[1] [kru:n], *s.* (*a*) chanson *f* à demi-voix; fredonnement *m*; (*b*) plainte *f*, gémissement plaintif.

croon[2], *v.tr.* chantonner; fredonner (une chanson); chanter à demi-voix.

crooner ['kru:nər], *s.* **1.** (*a*) fredonneur, -euse; (*b*) chanteur, -euse, de charme. **2.** *Ich: Scot:* grondin gris.

crop[1] [krɔp], *s.* **1.** jabot *m*; *F:* gave *f* (d'un oiseau). **2.** manche *m* (d'un fouet); **hunting c.,** stick *m* de chasse. **3.** (*a*) récolte *f*, moisson *f*; (*of fruit, etc.*) cueillette *f*; **under c., in c.,** (terres *fpl*) en culture; **out of c.,** en friche, en jachère; **second c.,** regain *m*; **catch c., snatch c.,** culture dérobée; **cash c.,** culture de rapport, culture commerciale; **cover c.,** (i) plante de couverture, plante améliorante; (ii) (*machine*) cultivateur à disques lourds; **standing, growing, crops,** récoltes sur pied; **break c.,** culture de rechange; **food crops,** récoltes alimentaires; **bread crops,** céréales *f* panifiables; **fruit crops,** cultures fruitières; **companion crops,** cultures associées; **to harvest the crops,** faire la récolte, la moisson; **if there is a good c. of wheat this year,** si les blés donnent cette année; **a c. of lies,** un tas de mensonges; **a fine c. of hair,** une belle chevelure; (*b*) *For:* peuplement *m*; **c. density,** consistance *f* du peuplement. **4.** coupe *f* (des cheveux); **to give s.o. a close c.,** tondre les cheveux de qn; *O:* **Eton c.,** cheveux *mpl* à la garçonne; 'cheveux garçon. **5.** bout coupé; morceau coupé; **c. end,** bout affranchi, chute *f* au bout (d'une barre de fer, etc.). **6.** *Cu:* paleron *m*. **7.** *Tan:* **c. (hide),** (i) peau entière; (ii) cuir fort, gros cuir.

crop[2], *v.* **(cropped)**

I. *v.tr. & i.* **1.** *v.tr.* (*a*) tondre, tailler, couper (une haie, les cheveux, etc.); émarger (un livre); affranchir (une barre de fer); écourter, couper (les oreilles, la queue); essoriller (un chien); *Tex:* tondre, raser (une étoffe); *Leath:* crouponner; **hair cropped close,** cheveux coupés ras; (*b*) (*of cattle*) brouter, paître (l'herbe); **the sheep were cropping the grass,** les brebis *f* tondaient l'herbe. **2.** (*a*) *v.i.* (*of land*) donner une récolte; (*b*) *v.tr.* cultiver (les pommes de terre, etc.); **to c. land with corn,** mettre une terre en blé; emblaver une terre.

II. (*compound verbs*) **1. crop out,** *v.i. Geol:* affleurer.

2. crop up, *v.i.* (*a*) **once the hay is in, these plants c. up full of life,** la fenaison faite, ces plantes surgissent pleines de vie; (*b*) se produire, se présenter, survenir, surgir; **a question has cropped up,** une question a surgi; **these questions c. up,** ces questions se posent (d'elles-mêmes); **the question has cropped up again,** la question est revenue en discussion.

crop-eared ['krɔpi:əd], *a.* **1.** courtaud, essorillé. **2.** *Hist:* (têtes-rondes) aux cheveux coupés ras, aux oreilles apparentes.

cropper[1] ['krɔpər], *s.* **1.** (*a*) (*pers.*) tondeur *m* (de drap); *Leath:* crouponneur *m*; (*b*) *Metalw:* cisailleuse *f*. **2.** (pigeon *m*) boulant *m*. **3.** *Agr:* (*a*) (*pers.*) cultivateur *m*; (*b*) **good, bad, c.,** plante *f*, qui donne de bonnes, de mauvaises, récoltes, qui donne bien, mal. **4.** *F:* **to come a c.,** (i) faire une chute; ramasser une pelle, une gamelle, un gadin, une bûche; s'aplatir, se flanquer par terre; prendre un billet de parterre; (ii) *Com: etc:* faire faillite, faire la culbute, boire un bouillon; (iii) se heurter à un obstacle imprévu; (iv) *Gaming:* prendre une culotte; **to come a c. over sth.,** se casser les dents sur qch.; **he'd come a c. at the least obstacle,** il se noierait dans une goutte d'eau; **he came a nasty c. over some gambling debts,** il s'est attiré des histoires à propos de dettes de jeu; *Sch:* **I came a c. in history,** j'ai été collé en histoire.

cropper[2], *s. Typ:* (*jobbing machine*) minerve (imaginée par H. S. Cropper, 1866).

cropping ['krɔpiŋ], *s.* **1.** tondage *m*; affranchissement *m* (d'une barre de fer); *Tex:* affinage *m* (des draps); *Leath:* crouponnage *m*; **c. flock,** (bourre *f*) tontisse *f*. **2.** mise *f* en culture, (*with cereals*) emblavage *m* (d'une terre).

croquet[1] ['kroukei, -ki], *s.* **1.** (jeu *m* de) croquet *m*. **2.** coup roqué; **tight c.,** coup croqué.

croquet[2], *v.tr.* **(croqueted** ['kroukeid, -kid]) **to (tight-)c.,** croquer (la boule); **to (loose-)c.,** roquer (la boule).

croquette [krɔ'ket], *s. Cu:* croquette *f*.

crosier ['krouziər], *s. Ecc:* **1.** *A:* (*a*) porte-croix *m inv*; (*b*) porte-crosse *m inv.* **2.** crosse *f* (d'évêque, d'abbé).

cross[1] [krɔs], *s.* **1.** croix *f*; (*a*) **the stations of the C.,** le chemin de la Croix; **the descent from the C.,** la descente de Croix; **to bear one's c.,** porter sa croix; **everyone must bear his own c.,** à chacun sa croix; **no c. no crown,** nul bien sans peine; **the sign of the c.,** le signe de la croix; **to make the sign of the c.,** tracer, faire, le signe de la croix, un signe de croix; se signer; (*b*) **processional c.,** croix processionnelle; **c. bearer,** porte-croix *m inv*; **fiery c.,** croix de feu, croix sanglante; (*of crusader*) **to take the c.,** prendre la croix; se croiser; **market c.,** croix de la place du marché; (*to child*) **ride a cock horse to Banbury C.,** joue à dada sur mon bidet; (*c*) **St Andrew's c.,** croix de Saint-André; **St Anthony's c.,** croix de Saint-Antoine; croix en tau; **Maltese c.,** croix de Malte; **Greek c.,** croix grecque; **the Red C.,** la Croix rouge (de Genève); **Victoria C.,** croix de Victoria (croix de bronze décernée pour acte d'héroïsme sur le champ de bataille); **C. of the Legion of Honour,** croix de la Légion d'honneur; **Military C.,** Croix de Guerre; **C. of Lorraine,** Croix de Lorraine; *Astr:* **Southern C.,** Croix du Sud; (*d*) **to sign with a c.,** signer d'une croix; (*e*) **c.(-)shaped,** cruciforme, en forme de croix; **c. headed screw, screwdriver,** vis *f*, tournevis *m*, cruciforme. **2.** contrariété *f*, ennui *m*; **he had known crosses and disappointments,** il avait connu les revers *m* et les déceptions *f*; **the slightest c. puts him in bad humour,** la moindre contrariété le met de mauvaise humeur. **3.** *Husb:* (*a*) croisement *m* (de races) **(between . . . and . . .,** entre . . . et . . .); (*b*) métis, -isse; produit *m* de croisement; **to be a c. between sth. and sth.,** être un mélange de qch. et de qch. **4.** *Nau:* **c. in the hawse,** tour *m* de chaîne. **5.** (*a*) (*of material*) biais *m*; **on the c.,** en biais; (*b*) *F: A:* **to be on the c.,** vivre d'escroquerie. **6.** *Box:* (*a*) cross *m*, coup croisé; (*b*) arrangement *m* illicite, combine *f* (entre adversaires); **the fight was a c.,** le match était du chiqué.

cross[2], *v.*

I. *v.tr. & i.* **1.** *v.tr.* (*a*) croiser (deux bâtons, etc.); **to c. one's legs,** croiser les jambes; (*b*) *Ecc:* **to c. oneself,** faire le signe de la croix; se signer; *F:* **c. my heart,** croix de bois croix de fer; boule de feu boule de fer; Normand, cochon, qui s'en dédit; **to c. a fortune teller's palm with silver,** donner une pièce d'argent à une diseuse de bonne aventure; (*c*) barrer (un chèque); mettre les barres à (ses t); **crossed cheque,** chèque barré; *A:* **to c. one's correspondence,** écrire ses lettres en travers (des lignes déjà écrites); (*d*) passer (la mer, un fleuve); traverser (la rue, la mer, une salle); franchir (le seuil, la frontière, une salle); **he crossed the street again,** il repassa de l'autre côté de la rue; **the bridge that crosses the river,** le pont qui traverse la rivière; **to c. a bridge,** passer (sur) un pont, traverser un pont; **the river is easy to c.,** la rivière est de passage facile; **he had not crossed the threshold for two years,** il y avait deux ans qu'il n'avait passé la porte, qu'il n'avait franchi le pas de la porte; *Pol:* **to c. the floor (of the House),** changer de parti (politique); **wood crossed by numerous paths,** bois sillonné de nombreux sentiers; *Nau:* **to c. the line,** passer l'équateur; *Nau:* couper la ligne; (*of thought*) **to c. s.o.'s mind,** se présenter à l'esprit de qn; passer par, traverser, l'esprit de qn; (*e*) *O:* **to c. a horse, a saddle,** enfourcher un cheval; monter à cheval; monter en selle; **he'll never c. a saddle again,** on ne le reverra jamais en selle; (*f*) croiser (qn dans la rue); **to c. s.o.'s path,** (i) se trouver sur le chemin de qn; (ii) se mettre en travers de la volonté, des visées, de qn; (*g*) contrarier, contrecarrer (qn, les desseins de qn); susciter des difficultés à (qn); **to be crossed in love,** avoir une déception amoureuse; être contrarié dans ses amours; **he's very unpleasant when crossed,** il est très désagréable quand on va à l'encontre de ses projets; *Sp:* (*polo, etc.*) **to c. an opponent,** couper un adversaire; (*h*) *F:* tromper (qn); trahir (qn); **he crossed his accomplices and got away with the whole of the loot,** il a trompé ses complices et a saisi tout le butin; (*i*) *Breed:* **to c. breeds,** croiser, métisser, des races; faire des croisements (de races); (*j*) *Mec.E:* **to c. a screw,** fausser une vis. **2.** *v.i.* (*a*) (*of roads, letters, breeds, etc.*) se croiser; (*of lines*) se croiser, s'entrecroiser; (*of wires*) chevaucher; **ships crossing,** navires *m* se coupant la route; (*b*) passer (d'un lieu à un autre); **to c. from Dover to Calais,** faire la traversée de Douvres à Calais.

II. (*compound verbs*) **1. cross off,** *v.tr.* rayer (un nom sur une liste, etc.).

2. cross out, *v.tr.* biffer, barrer, rayer, raturer (un mot, une phrase, etc.).

3. cross over, *v.i.* **he crossed over to speak to me,** il a traversé la rue, etc., pour me parler; **they crossed over to Cherbourg in their yacht,** ils ont fait la traversée jusqu'à Cherbourg dans leur yacht.

cross[3]. **1.** *a. & comb.fm.* (*a*) transversal, -aux; oblique; mis en travers; **c. girder,** poutre transversale; *Civ.E: Aut: etc:* **c. member,** traverse *f*, entretoise *f* (de châssis, etc.); *Metall:* **c. cracks,** travers *m*; *Geol:* **c. fault,** faille *f* oblique; faille de plongement; *Hyd.E:* **c. dyke,** duit *m* (dans un cours d'eau); *Cmptr: etc:* **c. total,** total horizontal; (*b*) (*intersecting*) (entre) croisé; **c. lines,** lignes *f* qui se croisent; *Tex:* **c. fabric,** tissu *m* droit fil; *Nau:* **c. bearings,** relèvements croisés, simultanés; **to**

take c. bearings, faire le point par relèvements; *Geol:* c. bedding, stratification entrecroisée, oblique; *Opt:* c. hairs, c. threads, c. wires, fils *m* en croix, fils d'araignée; réticule *m*; *Pol.Ec: etc:* c. elasticity of demand, élasticité croisée de la demande; c. effects, effets *m* réciproques; *Cmptr:* c. modulation, intermodulation *f*, transmodulation *f*; (*c*) (*opposed*) contraire, opposé (to, à); *Nau:* c. sea, mer du travers; mer, houle, battue; *Jur:* c. action, action contraire, reconventionnelle; reconvention *f*, opposition *f*. 2. *a.* (*of pers.*) maussade, de mauvaise humeur, fâché; to be as c. as two sticks, as a bear with a sore head, être d'une humeur massacrante, de méchante humeur, d'une humeur de chien; être inabordable; he looks c., il a l'air fâché; don't be c. with me, il ne faut pas m'en vouloir; he is c. with me for being late, il est de mauvaise humeur parce que je suis en retard; you never hear a c. word, jamais on n'entend un mot vif.

crossarm ['krɔsɑːm], *s.* traverse *f* (d'un poteau télégraphique, etc.); verge *f* (d'une presse à balancier); croisillon *m*.

crossbar ['krɔsbɑːr], *s.* (*a*) (barre *f* de) traverse *f*, entretoise *f*; (*of window*) croisillon *m*; (*of door*) épar(t) *m*; (*of sword*) quillon *m*; lower c., sommier *m* (d'une grille); (*b*) *Aut:* barre d'accouplement, de connexion (des roues avant); *Artil:* traverse (de la hausse); (*c*) *Fb: etc:* barre transversale; (*d*) *attrib. Comptr:* c. switch, commutateur *m* crossbar, à barres croisées; c. system, système *m* crossbar.

crossbeam ['krɔsbiːm], *s.* 1. *Const:* sommier *m*, traverse *f*; hip crossbeams (of roof), herses *f* de (la) croupe. 2. (*a*) *N.Arch:* barrotin *m*; (*b*) *Civ.E:* chapeau *m* (de pilotis, etc.). 3. *Gym:* portique *m*.

crossbelt ['krɔsbelt], *s. Mil: etc:* bandoulière *f*.

crossbench ['krɔsbentʃ], *s.* banquette transversale; *Parl:* to sit on the c. = être (un député) indépendant.

crossbencher ['krɔsbentʃər], *s. Parl:* = député indépendant.

crossbill ['krɔsbil], *s. Orn:* bec-croisé *m*, *pl.* becs-croisés; (*NAm:* red) c., bec-croisé *m* des sapins, *Fr.C:* bec-croisé rouge; two-barred, *NAm:* white-winged, c., bec-croisé bifascié, *Fr.C:* à ailes blanches; parrot c., bec-croisé perroquet.

crossbones ['krɔsbounz], *s.pl.* os *m* en croix; os de mort; skull and c., tête *f* de mort et tibias (du pavillon des pirates).

crossbow ['krɔsbou], *s.* arbalète *f*.

crossbowman, *pl.* -men ['krɔsboumən], *s.* arbalétrier *m*.

cross brace ['krɔsbreis], *s. Const: etc:* entretoise *f*; croisillon *m*.

cross-brace ['krɔsbreis], *v.tr. Const: etc:* entretoiser; croisillonner.

crossbred ['krɔsbred], *a.* métis, -isse; c. horse, échappé *m*.

crossbreed[1] ['krɔsbriːd], *s.* 1. *Breed:* race croisée; produit *m* d'un croisement. 2. *F:* métis, -isse.

crossbreed[2], *v.tr.* (*p.t. & p.p.* crossbred) croiser, métisser (des races, etc.).

crossbreeding ['krɔs'briːdiŋ], *s.* croisement *m* de races; hybridation *f*; métissage *m*.

cross-buttock[1] ['krɔs'bʌtək], *s. Wr:* = tour *m* de hanche.

cross-buttock[2], *v.tr. Wr:* tomber (son adversaire) par un tour de hanche.

cross-check[1] ['krɔs'tʃek], *s.* contre-vérification *f*, moyen *m* de recoupement; double contrôle *m*; *Surv: etc:* recoupement *m*.

cross-check[2], *v.tr.* contre-vérifier.

cross-checking ['krɔs'tʃekiŋ], *s.* contrôle *m* par balance carrée, contre-vérification *f*.

cross-connect ['krɔskə'nekt], *v.tr. El: etc:* raccorder transversalement.

cross connection ['krɔskə'nekʃ(ə)n], *s.* raccordement transversal.

cross correspondence ['krɔskɔris'pɔnd(ə)ns], *s. Psychics:* correspondances croisées.

cross counter ['krɔs'kauntər], *s. Box:* cross *m*.

cross-country ['krɔs'kʌntri], *a.* (chemin *m*, promenade *f*, etc.) à travers champs; (vol *m*, etc.) à travers la campagne; (véhicule) tout-terrain; *Sp:* c.-c. running, le cross; c.-c. runner, crossman *m*, *pl.* crossmen.

crosscurrent ['krɔskʌrənt], *s.* renvoi *m* de courant.

crosscut[1] ['krɔskʌt], *s.* 1. (*a*) coupe *f* en travers; c. saw, scie *f* passe-partout; (*b*) contre-taille *f*; c. file, lime *f* à taille croisée. 2. raccourci *m*; traverse *f*; chemin *m* de traverse. 3. *Min:* travers-banc *m inv*, bouvette *f*.

crosscut[2], *v.* (crosscut) 1. *v.tr.* (*a*) couper, scier, (le bois) en travers, de travers; traverser; (*b*) couper (un tissu) de biais, en biais; (*c*) contre-tailler (une lime, etc.). 2. *v.i. Min:* percer en travers-banc.

crosse [krɔs], *s. Sp:* crosse *f* (du jeu de la crosse).

crossette [krɔ'set], *s. Arch:* crossette *f*.

cross-examination ['krɔsigzæmi'neiʃ(ə)n], *s.* contre-interrogatoire *m*, *pl.* contre-interrogatoires; interrogatoire *m* contradictoire.

cross-examine ['krɔsig'zæmin], *v.tr. Jur:* procéder à l'interrogatoire de (qn); interroger (qn) contradictoirement.

cross-examiner ['krɔsig'zæminər], *s.* interrogateur, -trice.

cross-eye ['krɔsai], *s. Med:* strabisme *m*.

cross-eyed ['krɔsaid], *a.* louche, qui louche; strabique; to be c.-e., loucher.

crossfall ['krɔsfɔːl], *s. U.S:* bombement *m* (d'une chaussée).

cross-feed ['krɔsfiːd], *s. Mec.E:* avance transversale; (*of lathe*) c.-f. screw, vis *f* d'avance transversale.

cross-fertilization ['krɔsfəːtilai'zeiʃ(ə)n], *s. Bot:* (*a*) fécondation croisée; pollinisation croisée; allogamie *f*; (*b*) hybridation *f*.

cross-fertilize ['krɔs'fəːtilaiz], *v.tr. Bot:* hybrider (deux espèces).

cross-file ['krɔsfail], *s. Tls:* lime double demi-ronde; feuille-de-sauge *f*, *pl.* feuilles-de-sauge.

cross-fingering ['krɔs'fiŋg(ə)riŋ], *s. Mus:* fourchu *m*, doigté fourchu (sur instruments à vent).

crossfire[1] ['krɔsfaiər], *s.* (*a*) *Mil: etc:* feu croisé; exposed to c., pris entre deux feux; (*b*) *Cmptr:* courant perturbateur; receiving-end c., courant perturbateur côté réception.

crossfire[2], *v.i. Mil: etc:* croiser les feux.

crossfoot[1] ['krɔsfut], *s. Cmptr:* (*also* crossfooting) opération horizontale; c. total, total horizontal.

crossfoot[2], *v.i. Cmptr:* faire une opération horizontale.

crossfooter ['krɔsfutər], *s. Cmptr:* compteur *m* à opération horizontale.

crossgrain ['krɔsgrein], *s. Carp: etc:* 1. fibre torse. 2. coupe transversale.

crossgrained ['krɔsgreind], *a.* 1. (*of wood*) aux fibres irrégulières; à fibres torses; tortillard, tortillart. 2. *F:* (*of pers.*) (*a*) revêche, rêche, grincheux; qui a l'esprit mal tourné, à rebours; (*of woman*) acariâtre; he's c., c'est un fagot d'épines; (*b*) bourru, ronchonneur.

crosshatch[1] ['krɔshætʃ], *s. Engr:* contre-taille *f*, *pl.* contre-tailles.

crosshatch[2], *v.tr. Engr:* contre-hacher, contre-tailler.

crosshatching ['krɔs'hætʃiŋ], *s.* 1. contre-hachure *f*, *pl.* contre-hachures; système *m* de hachures croisées. 2. *Typ:* (*as a defect in half-tone work*) moirage *m*.

crosshead ['krɔshed], *s.* 1. *Mch:* pied *m* de bielle; crosse *f*, crossette *f*, tête *f* (de piston); c. guide, guide *m* de la tête du piston. 2. (barre *f* de) traverse *f*; *Mch:* joug *m*. 3. *Journ:* (*of article*) sous-titre *m*, *pl.* sous-titres.

crossheading ['krɔs'hediŋ], *s.* 1. *Min:* recoupe *f* d'aérage; galerie transversale. 2. *Journ:* sous-titre *m*, *pl.* sous-titres.

crossing ['krɔsiŋ], *s.* 1. barrement *m*, barrage *m* (d'un chèque). 2. *Ecc:* signe *m* de croix. 3. (*a*) traversée *f* (de la mer); passage *m* (d'un fleuve, des Alpes); *Mil: etc:* franchissement *m* (d'un fleuve, etc.); *Mil:* c. capacity, capacité *f* de franchissement; *Nau:* we had a fine, good, c., nous avons eu, fait, une belle traversée; to make an east-west c., faire une traversée dans le sens est-ouest; this is my first Channel c., c'est la première fois que je traverse la Manche; c'est ma première traversée de la Manche; (*b*) street c., passage (d'un trottoir à l'autre); pedestrian c., passage pour piétons, passage clouté; underground c., passage souterrain; overhead c., passage supérieur; *O:* c. sweeper, balayeur *m* des rues. 4. (*a*) croisement *m*, entrecroisement *m* (de lignes, de fils, etc.); (*b*) *Ecc.Arch:* croisée *f* du transept. 5. (*a*) (*of roads, railway lines, etc.*) croisement, intersection *f*, de voies; point *m* d'intersection; jonction *f*; (*of two railway lines*) traversée *f*; (*b*) *Rail:* level, *NAm:* grade, c., passage à niveau. 6. *Breed:* croisement, mélange *m* (de deux espèces).

crossing-over ['krɔsiŋ'ouvər], *s. Biol:* crossing-over *m inv*, enjambement *m*.

crossite ['krɔsait], *s. Miner:* crossite *f*.

cross-jetted ['krɔs'dʒetid], *a. Tail:* (poche *f*) sans patte.

cross keys ['krɔs'kiːz], *s.pl. Her: etc:* clefs *f* en sautoir.

cross-legged ['krɔs'leg(i)d], *a.* les jambes croisées; to sit c.-l., être assis en tailleur, à la Turque.

crosslet ['krɔslet]. *Her:* (*a*) *s.* croisette *f*; (*b*) *a.* cross c., croix recroisetée.

crossleted ['krɔsletid], *a. Her:* croiset(t)é; (*of cross*) recroisetée.

crosslight ['krɔslait], *s. Art:* faux jour (par rapport à l'éclairage principal du tableau); rayon *m* oblique, de côté.

crosslighting ['krɔs'laitiŋ], *s. Th: etc:* éclairage *m* à feux croisés.

crossline ['krɔslain], *s.* 1. ligne transversale. 2. *Engr:* contre-taille *f*. 3. *pl. Opt:* cross-lines, fils croisés (de viseur, etc.).

cross link ['krɔsliŋk], *s. Ch:* liaison croisée, transversale.

crossly ['krɔsli], *adv.* avec mauvaise humeur; d'un air, d'un ton, maussade, fâché.

crossness ['krɔsnis], *s.* mauvaise humeur; maussaderie *f*.

Crossopterygia, Crossopterygii [krɔsɔptə'ridʒiə, -iai], *s.pl. Ich: Paleont:* crossoptérygiens *m*.

crossopterygian [krɔsɔptə'ridʒiən], *s.* crossoptérygien *m*.

crossout ['krɔsaut], *attrib.* c. key, touche *f* x (de machine à écrire).

crossover ['krɔsouvər], *s.* 1. croisement *m*; c. of the current, renvoi *m* du courant vers l'autre rive (d'un cours d'eau); *Mec.E: etc:* c. bend, coude *m* de croisement (d'un tube, d'une canalisation); *Rail:* c. (road), voie *f* de croisement, de passage; voie diagonale; diagonal *m*; (voie de) jonction *f*; traversée *f*, bretelle *f*. 2. *Cost:* croisure *f* (d'un habit).

crosspatch ['krɔspætʃ], *s. F: O:* (*usu. f.*) grincheux, -euse; grognon *mf*; pelote *f* d'épingles; bâton épineux; a little c., une petite fille grognon, *occ.* grognonne.

cross-perforate ['krɔs'pəːfəreit], *v.tr. Cmptr:* faire un moletage transversal (d'une liasse en continu).

cross perforation ['krɔspəːfə'reiʃ(ə)n], *s. Cmptr:* moletage transversal.

crosspiece ['krɔspiːs], *s.* (barre *f* de) traverse *f*; entretoise *f*; moise *f*; potence *f*; *W.Tel:* gabie *f* (d'antenne).

cross question[1] ['krɔs'kwestjən], *s.* 1. *Jur:* question (faite au témoin) par la partie adverse. 2. *Games: A:* c. questions and crooked answers, propos interrompus.

cross-question[2], *v.tr.* = CROSS-EXAMINE.

cross reference[1] ['krɔs'ref(ə)rəns], *s.* renvoi *m*; correspondance *f*; c.-r. listing, table, liste *f*, table *f*, des correspondances.

cross-reference[2], (*a*) *v.tr.* numéroter (des lettres); to c.-r. a book, établir les renvois d'un livre; to c.-r. all allusions to subjects treated elsewhere, mettre des renvois à toutes les allusions aux sujets traités ailleurs; (*b*) *v.i. Cmptr: etc:* établir des correspondances, des renvois croisés.

crossroad ['krɔsroud], *s.* 1. chemin *m* de traverse. 2. crossroads, (i) carrefour *m*, croisement *m* de routes, croisée *f* de chemins; (ii) *U.S:* amorce *f* de bourg (à un carrefour); at the crossroads, à la croisée des chemins; (*occ. with sg. const.*) when you come to a crossroad, quand vous arriverez à un croisement de routes; we are now at the crossroads, c'est l'heure des décisions irrévocables; democracy is at the crossroads, la démocratie va décider de son sort.

cross-rule ['krɔsruːl], *v.tr.* quadriller (du papier, une carte).

cross-ruling ['krɔs'ruːliŋ], *s.* quadrillage *m*.

cross-section[1] ['krɔs'sekʃ(ə)n], *s.* coupe *f* en travers; coupe, section, transversale; coupe droite; profil transversal; profil en travers, vue *f* en coupe; carre *f* (d'une planche); *Draw:* section droite; rod of uniform c.-s., tige *f* à section constante; a c.-s. of life, une tranche de vie; a c.-s. of the population, un groupe représentant les différents étages de la société.

cross-section[2], *v.tr.* 1. couper (qch.) en travers. 2. établir le profil en travers de (qch.).

cross-sectional ['krɔs'sekʃən(ə)l], *a.* en coupe; c.-s. drawing, vue *f* en coupe.

cross-staff ['krɔsstɑːf], *s. Surv:* équerre *f* d'arpenteur.

cross-stitch ['krɔsstitʃ], *s. Needlew:* point croisé.

crosstalk ['krɔstɔːk], *s.* 1. répliques *fpl.* 2. *Tp: Elcs: etc:* diaphonie *f*; interférence *f*; far-end c., télédiaphonie *f*; near-end c., paradiaphonie *f*; c. attenuation, affaiblissement *m* diaphonique.

cross-thread ['krɔs'θred], *v.tr.* to c.-t. (a bolt), fausser le filetage (d'un boulon).

cross(-)tie ['krɔstai], *s.* 1. *Const: etc:* ventrière *f*; tirant *m*. 2. *Rail: U.S:* traverse *f*.

crosstown ['krɔstaun], *a. U.S:* c. artery, voie *f*, artère *f*, de dégagement, de grande circulation; voie transurbaine; c. highway, boulevard *m* à grande circulation; route transurbaine.

crosstrees ['krɔstriːz], *s.pl. Nau:* barres (de hune) traversières; barres de travers.

crosswalk ['krɔswɔːk], *s. NAm:* passage *m* pour piétons, passage clouté.

crossway ['krɔswei], *s. NAm:* carrefour *m*.

crossways ['krɔsweiz], *adv.* (*a*) en (forme de) croix; en sautoir; (*b*) en travers; diagonalement, en diagonale.

crosswind ['krɔswind], *s.* vent *m* de travers.

cross-wind ['krɔs'waind], *v.tr.* bobiner (la laine, etc.) à fils croisés.
crosswise ['krɔswaiz], *adv.* = CROSSWAYS.
crossword ['krɔswə:d], *s.* **c. (puzzle),** mots croisés, en croix, en damier.
crosswort ['krɔswə:t], *s. Bot:* croisette *f*, crucianelle *f*, rubéole *f*.
Crotalidae [krou'tælidi:], *s.pl. Rept:* crotalidés *m*.
crotalum ['krɔtələm], *s. Gr.Ant:* crotale *m*.
crotalus ['krɔtələs], *s. Rept:* crotale *m*; serpent *m* à sonnettes.
crotch [krɔtʃ], *s.* **1.** fourche *f*, enfourchure *f* (d'un arbre). **2.** (*a*) entrecuisse *m*; (*b*) *Tail: etc:* fourche, entre(-)jambe *m inv* (d'un pantalon, d'un slip).
crotched [krɔtʃt], *a.* fourchu.
crotchet ['krɔtʃit], *s.* **1.** crochet *m*. **2.** *Mus:* noire *f*. **3.** *F:* (*a*) lubie *f*, caprice *m*, toquade *f*; **to be full of crotchets,** avoir des lubies; (*b*) idée *f* fixe; manie *f*; (*c*) *pl.* préjugés *m*.
crotchetiness ['krɔtʃətinis], *s.* caractère capricieux; inégalité *f* d'humeur.
crotchety ['krɔtʃəti], *a.* sujet à des lubies; capricieux, fantasque, maniaque; (esprit) biscornu; (humeur *f*) difficile.
croton ['krout(ə)n], *s.* (*a*) *Bot:* croton *m*; *Pharm:* **c. oil,** huile *f* de croton; **c. seed,** pignon *m* d'Inde; (*b*) *Ent:* **c. bug,** papin *m*, phyllodromie *f*.
Crotona [krə'tounə], *Pr.n. Geog:* Crotone *f*.
crotonaldehyde [kroutə'nældihaid], *s. Ch:* aldéhyde *m* crotonique.
crotonic [krou'tɔnik], *a. Ch:* (acide) crotonique.
crotylic [krou'tilik], *a. Ch:* crotylique.
crouch[1] [krautʃ], *s.* accroupissement *m*.
crouch[2], *v.i.* se blottir, se tapir, s'accroupir; **tiger crouching for a spring,** tigre accroupi avant de sauter; **to c. before springing,** se raccourcir, se ramasser, ramasser son corps, avant de sauter.
croup[1] [kru:p], *s.* croupe *f* (de cheval, etc.); croupion *m* (d'un oiseau); **drooping c.,** croupe avalée.
croup[2], *s. Med:* croup *m*; laryngite *f* diphtérique; **false c.,** faux croup, laryngite striduleuse.
croupade [kru:'pɑ:d], *s. Equit:* croupade *f*.
croupier ['kru:piər], *s.* croupier *m*.
croupière ['kru:piɛər], *s. A.Arm:* croupière *f*.
croupous ['kru:pəs], **croupy** ['kru:pi], *a.* (*a*) (enfant) croupeux; (*b*) (toux) croupale.
croustade [kru:'stɑ:d], *s. Cu:* croustade *f*.
crouton ['kru:tɔn], *s. Cu:* croûton *m*.
crow[1] [krou], *s.* **1.** (*a*) *Orn:* corneille *f*; **the crows (as a class),** les corbeaux *m*; **common, American, c.,** corneille américaine; *NAm:* **Northwestern c.,** corneille du nord-ouest; **carrion c.,** corneille noire, corbeau-corneille *m*, *pl.* corbeaux-corneilles; **bald c.,** picatharte *m*; **wattled c.,** corneille caronculée, kokako *m*; **fruit c.,** coracine *f*, piauhau *m*; **paradise c.,** lycocorax *m*; **piping c.,** gymnorhine *m*, *F:* (corbeau) flûteur *m*; **hooded, Royston, saddleback, grey(-back), c.,** corneille mantelée, *F:* religieuse *f*; **red-legged c.,** crave *m*; **crow's nest,** (i) nid *m* de corneille; (ii) *Nau:* nid *m* de corbeau, de pie; hune *f* de vigie; *A:* **c. quill,** (i) plume *f* de corbeau (pour écrire); (ii) plume tubulaire de dessinateur; **as the c. flies,** à vol d'oiseau; en ligne droite; *esp. NAm: F:* **to have a c. to pick, pluck, with s.o.,** avoir maille à partir avec qn; *U.S: F:* **to eat c.,** avaler des couleuvres; (*b*) *Orn: Dial: esp. Scot:* freux *m*: (*c*) **white c.,** (i) *Orn:* néophron *m*; (ii) merle blanc; (*d*) *Orn:* **c. pheasant,** coucal *m*, *F:* coq *m* des pagodes; (*e*) *P:* (i) prêtre *m*, corbeau; (ii) (*woman*) **old c.,** vieille bique; (*f*) *esp. U.S: Pej:* **Jim C.,** un noir. **2.** = CROWBAR.
crow[2], *s. Cu:* fraise *f*, toilette *f* (de porc).
crow[3], *s.* **1.** chant *m* du coq; *F:* coquerico *m*, cocorico *m*. **2.** gazouillement *m* (de bébé).
crow[4], *v.i.* **1.** (*of cock*) chanter; *F:* faire cocorico; coqueriquer; (*of pheasant*) rappeler; *F:* **to c. over s.o.,** chanter victoire sur qn; narguer qn; traiter qn avec jactance. **2.** (*of infant*) gazouiller; pousser de petits cris de joie.
crowbar ['kroubɑ:r], *s. Tls:* pince *f* (à levier); levier *m*, anspect *m*, pied-de-biche *m*, *pl.* pieds-de-biche, bec-de-corbin *m*, *pl.* becs-de-corbin; loup *m*.
crowberry ['kroubəri], *s. Bot:* camarine noire; empêtre *m* à fruits noirs, myrtille *f*.
crowbill, crow's bill ['krou(z)bil], *s.* **1.** *Surg:* (*instrument*) bec-de-corbin *m*, *pl.* becs-de-corbin; bec-de-corbeau *m*, *pl.* becs-de-corbeau. **2.** *Anat: F:* apophyse *f* coracoïde.
crowd[1] [kraud], *s.* **1.** (*a*) foule *f*; affluence *f*; rassemblement *m*; cohue *f*; **to come in a c., in crowds,** venir en foule; **a great c. had gathered,** une vaste foule s'était réunie; **to force one's way through the c.,** fendre la foule, se frayer un chemin à travers la foule; **to draw crowds,** faire foule, attirer la foule; (*b*) **to rise above the c.,** s'élever au-dessus de la foule, du vulgaire; **to stand out from, above, the c.,** se distinguer. **2.** *F:* grande quantité, tas *m* (de choses); **a whole c. of cousins,** toute une foule de cousins. **3.** (*a*) *F:* bande *f*, troupe *f*, groupe *m* (de personnes); **they're a good c.,** ce sont de bons types; **we often go out with their c.,** nous sortons souvent avec leur (petite) bande; **they stick to their own c.,** ils font bande à part; ils s'en tiennent à leur clique; (*b*) *Th: Cin:* **the c.,** les figurants *m*, les cachets *m*; **c. artist,** figurant, cachet; **c. scene,** scène *f* de masses. **4.** *Nau:* **the c. of sail made her heel over dangerously,** la voilure trop chargée lui donnait une bande dangereuse; **under a c. of sail,** toutes voiles dehors.
crowd[2], *v.*
I. *v.tr. & i.* **1.** *v.tr.* (*a*) serrer, (en)tasser (des personnes, des choses); **crowded together,** pressés, serrés, l'un contre l'autre; **we are too crowded here,** on est gêné ici; **three families crowded into one small room,** trois familles entassées dans une seule petite pièce; **the boats are crowded together in a corner of the harbour,** les bateaux se tassent dans un coin du port; **to c. a great many facts into a few lines,** faire tenir beaucoup de faits en peu de lignes; (*b*) remplir, bourrer, encombrer (**with,** de); **room crowded with furniture,** pièce encombrée de meubles; **the hall was crowded with people,** la salle regorgeait de monde, était bondée; **the streets were crowded,** il y avait foule dans les rues; les rues étaient encombrées; **everywhere was crowded,** la foule se pressait partout; partout il y avait un monde fou; **streets crowded with traffic,** rues *f* à circulation intense; **memory crowded with facts,** mémoire bourrée de faits; (*c*) *Sp:* **to c. a competitor,** tasser un concurrent; **to c. another car,** serrer une autre voiture; *U.S:* **his horse crowded him against the wall,** son cheval l'a froissé contre le mur; (*d*) *U.S:* **to c. matters,** presser les affaires; **to c. a debtor,** importuner, relancer, un débiteur; **to c. s.o. into doing sth.,** amener, forcer, qn à faire qch.; (*e*) forcer; **to be crowded off the pavement,** être forcé de quitter le trottoir; (*f*) *Cmptr:* tasser (l'information, les données); (*g*) *Nau:* **to c. (on) sail,** forcer les voiles, faire force de voiles, de toile; augmenter de toile; se couvrir de toile. **2.** *v.i.* (*a*) **to c. (together),** se presser en foule; s'attrouper; se serrer, s'entasser, se tasser, se pelotonner; *F:* s'empiler (dans un compartiment, etc.); **to c. round s.o.,** se presser, faire foule, autour de qn; entourer qn en foule; assiéger qn; **they crowded into the square,** ils arrivèrent en foule sur la place; **people were crowding in through the gates,** on passait les barrières en foule; **they were crowding to board the bus,** ils se pressaient pour monter dans l'autobus; **to c. to a place,** affluer à, dans, un endroit; **here memories c. in on me, upon my mind,** ici des souvenirs *m* se pressent dans ma mémoire, des souvenirs m'assaillent en foule, une foule de souvenirs se présente(nt) à mon esprit; (*b*) *Nau:* se hâter, se presser; (*of sailing ship*) courir à toutes voiles.
II. (*compound verb*) **crowd out,** *v.tr.* (*a*) ne pas laisser de place à (qn qch.); **there was an overflow meeting for those who were crowded out,** il y a eu une réunion supplémentaire pour ceux qui n'avaient pu entrer; **your article was crowded out,** la publication de votre article a été retardée par suite de l'abondance de matières; *Journ:* **matter crowded out,** matière restée sur le marbre; (*b*) *U.S:* évincer (qn).
crowded ['kraudid], *a.* **c. streets,** rues encombrées; **c. cities,** villes surpeuplées; **c. room,** pièce (i) bondée (de gens), (ii) encombrée (de meubles); **c. train,** train bondé, très chargé; **c. profession,** profession encombrée; **the c. events of that day,** les nombreux événements de cette journée.
crowding ['kraudiŋ], *s.* encombrement *m*; entassement *m*; *Sp:* tassage *m* (d'un concurrent); *Cmptr:* tassement *m* (de données); *Dent:* **tooth c.,** encombrement dentaire.
crowfoot[1] ['kroufut], *s.* (*pl. usu.* **crowfoots**) *Bot:* renoncule *f* (âcre), *F:* pied-de-corbeau *m*, *pl.* pieds-de-corbeau; **water c.,** renoncule flottante; grenouillette *f*; **creeping c.,** renoncule rampante; **glacier c.,** renoncule glaciaire; **celery-leaved c.,** scélérate *f*; mort *f* aux vaches.
crowfoot[2], *s.* (*pl.* **crowfeet**) = CROW'S FOOT.
crowing ['krouiŋ], *s.* **1.** (*a*) chant *m* (du coq); (*b*) *Med:* faux croup, laryngite striduleuse. **2.** gazouillement *m* (de bébé).
crown[1] [kraun], *s.* **1.** (*a*) couronne *f* (de fleurs, d'or); **the martyr's c.,** la couronne du martyre; (*b*) **royal c.,** couronne royale; **to assume the c.,** prendre la couronne; (*c*) la Couronne (symbole de l'État monarchique); **C. lands, estates,** terres domaniales, relevantes de la Couronne, appartenantes à la Couronne; **C. timber,** bois *mpl* de la Couronne, de l'État; bois domaniaux; **C. prince,** prince héritier; prince royal, impérial; (*in modern Greece*) diadoque *m*; **C. princess,** princesse royale, impériale; **the c. jewels,** les joyaux *m* de la Couronne; **C. Colony,** colonie *f* de la Couronne; *Jur:* **C. law,** droit criminel; **C. lawyer,** avocat *m* du gouvernement; **C. witness,** témoin *m* à charge; **C. court** = tribunal *m* de grande instance; **the C. office,** les services administratifs de la Cour suprême; (*d*) couronnement *m* (de la vie, d'une carrière); comble *m* (des bonheurs, des malheurs); (*e*) *Bot:* **c. imperial,** couronne impériale; (*f*) couronnure *f* (des bois d'un cerf). **2.** *Num:* (*a*) couronne (de cinq shillings); *A:* **half a c.,** une demi-couronne; (*b*) écu *m*. **3.** (*a*) sommet *m*, haut *m* (de la tête); (*b*) **c. of a hat,** (i) (*outside*) calotte *f*, forme *f*, carre *f*; (ii) (*inside*) fond *m* (d'un chapeau). **4.** couronne *f* (de dent); sommet, clef *f* (d'une voûte); bombement *m*, heurt *m* (d'un pont, d'une chaussée); griffe *f* (d'asperge); cîme *f* (d'un arbre); *For:* houppier *m* (d'un arbre ébranché); crête *f* (de colline); faîte *m* (de toit); croisée *f*, diamant *m*, collet *m*, encolure *f* (d'ancre); table *f*, aire *f* (d'enclume); couronne, arche *f*, voûte *f* (de fourneau); *N.Arch:* **c. of the deck,** tonture *f* du pont; *Aut: etc:* **to drive on the c. of the road,** conduire sur l'axe de la chaussée; *Sp:* (*bowls*) **c. green,** terrain bombé; *Mch:* **fire box c.,** plafond *m*, ciel *m*, de la boîte à feu; **c. bar of the fire box,** ferme *f* de ciel du foyer; *Mec.E:* **c. wheel, c. gear,** roue dentée sur une surface latérale; roue de champ; couronne; hérisson *m* de côté; *Aut:* **c. wheel and pinion,** pignon *m* et couronne d'entraînement, engrenage *m* hypoïde; *Tls:* **c. saw,** trépan *m* (à couronne); *Min:* **c. borer,** perforatrice *f* à rotation; *Const:* **c. post,** poinçon *m* (de faîte); *Hyd.E:* **c. gate,** porte *f* d'amont (d'une écluse de canal); *Ind:* **c. glass,** crown-glass *m*, crown *m*, verre *m* à boudine; *Opt:* **c. lens,** lentille *f* en crown-glass (d'une lentille achromatique); *Com:* **c. cork,** *U.S:* **c. cap,** capsule *f* (métallique) de bouteille; **c. cork opener,** décapsulateur *m*; **to take off a c. cork,** décapsuler (une bouteille). **5.** *Paperm:* **c. paper,** papier *m* couronne.
crown[2], *v.tr.* **1.** couronner (qn, la tête de qn) (**with,** de); **to c. s.o. king,** couronner, sacrer, qn roi; **crowned with roses,** couronné de roses; **building crowned with statues,** édifice couronné de statues; **column crowned by a cross,** colonne surmontée d'une croix; *P:* **I'll c. you (for that)!** je vais te flanquer un de ces coups sur la tête! **2.** (*a*) couronner, récompenser (les efforts de qn); combler, couronner (les désirs, le bonheur, de qn); *F:* mettre le sceau à (la réputation de qn); (*b*) *F:* **to c. all,** pour comble de malheur, de bonheur; pour y mettre le comble; **that crowns all!** il ne manquait plus que cela! **3.** (*at draughts*) damer (un pion). **4.** couronner (une dent, etc.). **5.** (*a*) bomber (une route); (*b*) *v.i.* (*of road, etc.*) avoir de la cambrure; bomber.
crowning[1] ['krauniŋ], *a.* final, -als; suprême; qui met le comble; **that would be the c. mistake, offence, etc.,** il ne manquerait plus que cela! cela serait le comble! **as a c. folly,** pour comble de folie; *F:* pour renfort de potage; **as a c. happiness,** pour surcroît de bonheur.
crowning[2], *s.* **1.** couronnement *m* (d'un prince, etc.). **2.** bombement *m* (d'une poulie, d'une route, etc.); **c. tool,** outil *m* à bomber.
crownwork ['kraunwə:k], *s.* **1.** *Fort:* couronnement *m*, couronne *f*. **2.** *Dent:* (*a*) travail *m* des couronnes; (*b*) les couronnes *f*.
crow-pick ['kroupik], *v.tr. Min:* ramasser les pierres dans (la houille).
crow-picker ['kroupikər], *s. Min:* ramasseur *m* de pierres (dans la houille).
crow's bill ['krouzbil], *s.* = CROW BILL.
crow's(-)foot, *pl.* **-feet** ['krouzfut, -fi:t], *s.* **1.** patte *f* d'oie (au coin de l'œil). **2.** *Mil: A:* chausse-trape *f*, *pl.* chausse-trapes. **3.** *Tls: Min:* caracole *f* (pour extraire les tiges de sonde). **4.** araignée *f* (d'une tente, d'un hamac).
crow's(-)footed ['krouzfutid], *a.* (yeux) éperonnés.
crow silk ['krousilk], *s. Algae:* conferve *f*.
crowstep ['kroustep], *s. Arch:* redent *m*, redan *m* (d'un pignon).
crowstepped ['kroustept], *a.* à redents, à redans.
croze[1] [krouz], *s.* **1.** *Coop:* jable *m*, peigne *m* (du fût). **2.** *Tls:* jabloir *m*; **c. iron,** peigne *m* à jabler.
croze[2], *v.tr. Coop:* jabler (une douve).
crozier ['krouziər], *s.* = CROSIER.
crucial ['kru:siəl, -ʃ(ə)l], *a.* **1.** (point, etc.) décisif, critique, crucial, -aux; **the c. test,** l'épreuve décisive; *Phil:* **c. experiment,** expérience cruciale. **2.** (*a*) *Anat:* (ligaments *m*) cruciformes; (*b*) *Surg:* (incision) cruciale, en croix; (*c*) (*of bandage*) croisé.
crucian ['kru:ʃ(ə)n], *s. Ich:* **c. (carp),** carrassin *m*.

crucianella [kru:ʃə'nelə], *s. Bot:* crucianella *f.*

cruciate ['kru:ʃieit], *a. Bot: Z:* en forme de croix; croisé, cruciforme.

crucible ['kru:sibl], *s.* **1.** *Ch: Ind:* creuset *m*; pot *m*; *Metall:* **case-hardening c.,** creuset de cémentation; *Lit:* **to be tested in the c. of adversity,** passer par le creuset de l'adversité. **2.** *Metall:* ouvrage *m*, creuset (de haut fourneau); cassetin *m* (de four catalan, etc.); **c. steel,** acier (fondu) au creuset.

crucifer ['kru:sifər], *s.* **1.** *Ecc:* porte-croix *m inv.* **2.** *Bot:* crucifère *f.*

Cruciferae [kru:'sifəri:], *s.pl. Bot:* cruciféracées *f*, crucifères *f.*

cruciferous [kru:'sifərəs], *a.* **1.** portant une croix; orné d'une croix; (colonne *f*, etc.) crucifère. **2.** *Bot:* crucifère.

crucifix ['kru:sifiks], *s.* crucifix *m*, christ *m*; **roadside c.,** calvaire *m.*

crucifixion [kru:si'fikʃ(ə)n], *s.* crucifixion *f*, crucifiement *m*; mise *f* en croix; *Art:* **the C.,** le Crucifiement.

cruciform ['kru:sifɔ:m], *a.* cruciforme; **c. iron, girder,** fer *m*, poutre *f*, en croix.

crucify ['kru:sifai], *v.tr.* crucifier (qn, la chair, etc.); mettre (qn) en croix; mortifier (la chair); **Christ Crucified,** le Crucifié.

crude [kru:d], *a.* **1.** (*a*) (*of metal, material, etc.*) (à l'état) brut; **c. iron,** fer brut; **c. oil, petroleum,** pétrole brut; (*b*) (*of fruit*) vert, aigre; (*of colour*) cru, aigre; **c. colouring, c. lights, of a picture,** tons crus d'un tableau; **c. expression,** expression crue, malsonnante; (*c*) (*of method, idea, style, etc.*) informe, grossier; **c. manners,** manières *f* frustes, rudes; **c. statement of the facts,** exposition brutale des faits; **to make a c. attempt at sth.,** essayer de faire qch. sans beaucoup de succès; (*d*) (*of literary work*) indigeste; qui manque de fini; **c. opinions,** opinions sommaires, à peine ébauchées. **2.** (*a*) *Physiol:* (aliment) non assimilé, non digéré; (suc, etc.) non élaboré; (*b*) *Med:* (*of disease*) non encore développé. **3.** *Gram:* **c. form (of a word),** forme sans désinence, sans inflexions.

crudely ['kru:dli], *adv.* **1.** crûment, grossièrement; **to speak c.,** parler avec crudité. **2.** d'une manière fruste.

crudeness ['kru:dnis], *s.* **1.** crudité *f* (de l'eau, d'expression, *Art:* de tons). **2.** nature grossière, informe, fruste (de la pensée, du style).

crudity ['kru:diti], *s.* **1.** = CRUDENESS. **2.** *Med. A:* crudité *f* (d'estomac).

cruel ['kruəl], *a.* cruel; (*a*) **a c. and ambitious policy,** une politique cruelle et ambitieuse; **c. disposition,** naturel brutal; (*b*) **a c. death, fate,** une mort cruelle, un destin cruel.

cruelly ['kruəli], *adv.* cruellement.

cruelty ['kruəlti], *s.* (*a*) cruauté *f* (**to, towards,** envers); **society for the prevention of c. to animals, to children,** société protectrice des animaux, de l'enfance; **a piece, an act, of c.,** une cruauté; (*b*) *Jur:* sévices *mpl* (**to one's wife,** envers sa femme); **extreme c.,** sévices graves.

cruet ['kruit], *s.* (*a*) *Ecc:* **altar c.,** burette *f*; (*b*) *Dom.Ec:* **c. (stand),** ménagère *f*, huilier *m.*

cruise[1] [kru:z], *s.* (*a*) *Nau:* croisière *f*; **to go for a c.,** faire une croisière; faire un voyage (en mer); **pleasure c.,** excursion *f*, voyage d'agrément (en mer); **on a c., on the c.,** en croisière; *Navy:* **long c.,** campagne *f*; **distant c.,** campagne lointaine; (*b*) *Mil:* **c.(-type) missile,** engin *m* atmosphérique.

cruise[2], *v.i.* **1.** *Nau:* croiser; être en croisière; **to c. about,** battre la mer, faire des croisières; (*of yachts*) faire des promenades en mer; *Navy:* **to be cruising (in . . .),** tenir croisière (dans . . .). **2.** (*of taxi*) marauder; faire la maraude. **3. to c. at (a speed of . . .),** avoir une vitesse de croisière, une vitesse économique (de tant de km par heure). **4.** *For:* **to c. a forest,** parcourir une forêt pour estimer le rendement de bois.

cruiser ['kru:zər], *s. Nau:* **1.** croiseur *m*; **armoured c.,** croiseur cuirassé; **battle c.,** croiseur de combat, de bataille; **armed merchant c.,** croiseur auxiliaire; **light c.,** croiseur léger; **missile-launching c.,** croiseur lance-engins. **2.** yacht *m* de plaisance, de croisière. **3.** *a. & s. Box:* **c. weight,** poids mi-lourd.

cruising[1] ['kru:ziŋ], *a.* **1.** en croisière; **c. fleet,** (flotte *f* en) croisière *f.* **2.** (*of taxi*) en maraude.

cruising[2], *s.* **1.** croisière(s) *f*(*pl*); **c. holiday,** croisière; **c. speed,** vitesse économique, de croisière. **2.** (*of taxi*) maraude *f.*

crulve [kru:v], *s. Fish: Scot:* nasse *f* à saumon.

cruller ['krʌlər], *s. Cu: U.S:* roussette *f.*

crumb[1] [krʌm], *s.* **1.** miette *f* (de pain); **he didn't leave a c.,** il n'en a pas laissé une miette; **c. scoop,** ramasse-miettes *m inv*; *Lit:* **c. of comfort,** brin *m* de consolation. **2.** (*opposed to crust*) mie *f* (de pain). **3.** *P:* (*a*) *esp. U.S:* pou *m* (du corps); (*b*) pauvre mec *m*; (*c*) *a. U.S:* moche. **4.** *int. F:* **crumbs!** ça alors!

crumb[2], *v.tr.* **1.** *A:* émietter. **3.** *Cu:* paner (des côtelettes, etc.); couvrir de chapelure.

crumble[1] ['krʌmbl]. **1.** *v.tr.* émietter (du pain); désagréger, effriter (les pierres); **to c. glass,** gruger le verre; **to c. sth. up,** réduire qch. en miettes; **to c. up an estate,** morceler un domaine. **2.** *v.i.* (*of bread*) s'émietter; (*of stone, etc.*) se déliter, se désagréger, s'épaufrer, s'effriter, brésiller; (*of masonry*) s'écrouler; (*of earth*) s'ébouler; (*of empire*) s'effondrer, crouler; *St.Exch:* (*of prices*) s'effriter; **wood that crumbles into dust,** bois *m* qui s'effrite en poudre; **everything is crumbling to dust,** tout tombe, s'en va, en poussière; **the empire crumbled into a number of small kingdoms,** l'empire *m* se morcela, s'émietta, en une multitude de petits royaumes.

crumble[2] **1.** *s. Cu:* **apple c.,** genreole charlotte aux pommes. **2.** *s.pl. Husb:* miettes *fpl.*

crumbling[1] ['krʌmbliŋ], *a.* qui s'écroule, qui s'éboule, qui s'effrite; **c. walls,** murs croulants, qui tombent en ruine; **c. empire,** empire *m* qui croule.

crumbling[2], *s.* **1.** émiettement *m*, effritement *m*, désagrégation *f*; *St.Exch:* effritement (des cours). **2.** éboulement *m*; écroulement *m.*

crumbly ['krʌmbli], *a.* friable, ébouleux.

crumby ['krʌmi], *a.* **1.** (pain *m*) qui s'émiette trop, qui a beaucoup de mie. **2.** = CRUMMY 3.

crummy ['krʌmi], *a.* **1.** = CRUMBY. **2.** *F: A:* (*a*) (femme) bien en chair, *P:* gironde; (*b*) (femme) avenante. **3.** *F: A:* riche, galetteux. **4.** *P:* dégoûtant; pouilleux; miteux; moche; **what a c. joint!** quelle sale boîte!

crump[1] [krʌmp], *s. F:* **1.** coup violent. **2.** chute *f*, pelle *f.* **3.** *O:* obus *m* qui éclate; **c. hole,** entonnoir *m.*

crump[2], *v.tr. F:* (*a*) frapper violemment, cogner dur; (*b*) *Mil: O:* bombarder, marmiter (une position).

crumpet ['krʌmpit], *s.* **1.** (*a*) *Cu:* (sorte de) crêpe (servie rôtie et beurrée); (*b*) *F: O:* **you stupid little c.!** petite sotte! **2.** *F: O:* tête *f*, caboche *f*; **off one's c.,** maboul, loufoque. **3. a nice bit of c.,** (i) *F:* une jolie fille; (ii) *P:* une belle pépée.

crumple ['krʌmpl]. **1.** *v.tr.* friper, froisser (du drap, etc.); **to c. (up) paper,** (i) chiffonner, froisser, du papier; (ii) faire une boule avec du papier. **2.** *v.i.* **to c. (up):** (*a*) se friper, se froisser, se chiffonner, se bouchonner, s'écraser; (*of leaves, parchment*) se recroqueviller, se ratatiner; (*b*) (*of opposition, etc.*) s'effondrer; *Sp:* (*of pers., horse*) s'effondrer, lâcher; (*c*) (*of mudguard, car*) se mettre en accordéon; (*of railway coaches*) se télescoper.

crumpled ['krʌmpld], *a.* fripé, froissé, chiffonné, recroquevillé; **cow with c. horns,** vache *f* à cornes recourbées.

crumpling ['krʌmpliŋ], *s.* **1.** froissement *m*, chiffonnage *m*; ratatinement *m*; *Ph:* **crumplings in the Einsteinian space,** rides *f* de l'espace einsteinien. **2.** écrasement *m.*

crunch[1] [krʌn(t)ʃ], *s.* **1.** coup *m* de dents; **he disposed of each sweet at one c.,** il broyait chaque bonbon d'un seul coup de dents. **2.** bruit *m* de broiement; craquement *m*, grincement *m*; **the c. of the gravel under the wheels,** le crissement du sable sous les roues. **3.** moment *m* difficile, critique; **when it comes to the c.,** au moment critique.

crunch[2]. **1.** (*a*) *v.tr.* croquer, broyer (qch. avec les dents); broyer (des pierres, etc.); écraser (la neige durcie); (*b*) *v.i., or with cogn. acc.* **we crunched (our way) through the snow to the station,** nous avons gagné la gare à travers la neige qui s'écrasait sous nos pas. **2.** *v.i.* crier, craquer, grincer, crisser; **hard snow crunches under foot,** la neige durcie craque, s'écrase, crisse, sous les pieds.

crunching ['krʌn(t)ʃiŋ], *s.* = CRUNCH[1] 2.

crunchy ['krʌn(t)ʃi], *a.* **1.** croquant. **2.** qui craque (sous les pas).

cruor ['kru:ɔ:r], *s. Physiol:* cruor *m*, sang figé.

crupper ['krʌpər], *s.* **1.** *Harn:* croupière *f*, culière *f.* **2.** (*a*) croupe *f* (de cheval); **to take s.o. up on the c.,** prendre qn en croupe; **c. loop,** culeron *m*; (*b*) *F: O:* fesses *fpl*, derrière *m*, cul *m.*

crural ['kruərəl], *a. Anat:* crural, -aux.

crusade[1] [kru:'seid], *s.* **1.** croisade *f*; **to go on a c.,** partir en croisade. **2.** campagne *f* (contre le vice, etc.); **to start a c. against ignorance,** lancer une croisade, partir en campagne, contre l'ignorance.

crusade[2], *v.i.* **1.** aller ou être en croisade. **2.** mener une campagne, une croisade (**against,** contre).

crusader [kru:'seidər], *s.* croisé *m.*

cruse [kru:z], *s. A: & B:* pot *m*, cruche *f*, jarre *f*; *B:* **neither did the c. of oil fail,** l'huile *f* de la fiole ne tarit point; **it's like the widow's c.,** c'est une source intarissable.

crush[1] [krʌʃ], *s.* **1.** (*a*) écrasement *m*; **c. syndrome,** syndrome *m* de broiement; (*b*) *Min:* écrasée *f*; (*c*) *Cmptr:* bourrage *m* (de cartes); (*d*) **c. hat,** (i) (chapeau) claque *m*; gibus *m*; (ii) *U.S:* chapeau mou, souple; (*e*) *Comest:* **orange, lemon, c.,** orangeade *f*, citronnade *f.* **2.** (*a*) presse *f*, foule *f*, cohue *f*; bousculade *f*; **there was a terrible c.,** il y avait un monde fou; **c. barrier,** barrière *f* pour contenir la foule; (*b*) *F: A:* réunion mondaine (où l'on s'étouffe, s'écrase). **3.** *F:* **to have a c. on s.o.,** avoir un béguin pour qn; être entiché de qn; en pincer pour qn.

crush[2]. **1.** *v.tr.* (*a*) écraser (qn, qch.); aplatir (un chapeau, etc.); pressurer (des fruits); exprimer le jus (des raisins, etc.); détriter (des olives, etc.); étouffer, réprimer, écraser (une révolte); (*of boa constrictor*) enserrer (sa victime); (*of people*) **crushed together,** tassés, serrés; **to c. sth. into a box,** enfoncer, fourrer, qch. dans une boîte; **we were nearly crushed to death,** la presse était à mourir; *A:* **to c. a cup of wine,** vider, avaler, une coupe de vin; (*b*) **to c. the enemy,** écraser, anéantir, l'ennemi; **to be crushed by the news,** être atterré par la nouvelle; **crushed with grief,** accablé de douleur; (*c*) froisser (une robe); (*on velvet*) **crushed spot,** écrasure *f*; (*d*) *Min: etc:* broyer, concasser, bocarder, briser, désintégrer (du minerai, des pierres). **2.** *v.i.* se presser en foule, se bousculer (pour entrer dans un endroit); s'entasser (dans un endroit); **people crushed in,** on se bousculait, s'étouffait, pour entrer; *with cogn. acc.* **to c. one's way through the crowd,** fendre la foule; se frayer un chemin à travers la foule.

crusher ['krʌʃər], *s.* **1.** *Min: etc:* broyeur *m*, écraseur *m*; bocardeur *m*, concasseur *m*; **gypsum c.,** concasseur à plâtre; **ore c.,** pileur *m* de minerai, moulin *m* à minerai; désintégrateur *m*; **jaw c.,** broyeur à mâchoires; **fine, medium, coarse, c.,** broyeur des fins, des mixtes, des gros; **oil c.,** moulin à huile; *Mec:* **c. gauge,** dynamomètre *m* à écrasement; *F:* **beetle crushers,** grosses chaussures, godillots *m*, godasses *f.* **2.** malheur accablant, coup *m* de massue, d'assommoir.

crushing[1] ['krʌʃiŋ], *a.* **1.** *Tchn:* (*of roller, etc.*) concasseur. **2.** (*of news, defeat, etc.*) écrasant; atterrant; **c. reply,** réponse cinglante, humiliante; **to treat s.o. with c. contempt,** écraser qn de son mépris.

crushing[2], *s.* forte pression; aplatissage *m*, écrasement *m*; détritage *m* (des olives); broyage *m* (du minerai, de la pierre); bocardage *m*, concassage *m* (du minerai); écrasage *m* (du minerai, des graines oléagineuses); **wet c.,** broyage à l'eau, par voie humide; **dry c.,** broyage à sec, par voie sèche; **fine, medium, coarse, c.,** broyage fin, moyen, grossier; **c. mill,** (i) détritoir *m* (d'olives); (ii) aplatisseur *m* (de graines); bocard *m*; broyeur *m* (de minerai).

crushingly ['krʌʃiŋli], *adv.* (répondre, parler) d'un ton écrasant.

Crusoe ['kru:sou], *Pr.n.m. Lit:* **Robinson C.,** Robinson Crusoé.

crust[1] [krʌst], *s.* **1.** (*a*) croûte *f* (de pain, de pâté); **not a c. to eat,** pas une croûte à manger; **to beg for crusts,** mendier son pain; (*b*) **piece of c.,** croûton *m.* **2.** écorce *f*, croûte (terrestre); carapace *f* (de homard, etc.); paroi *f* (de sabot de cheval); croûte, couche *f* (de rouille); *Meteor:* **ice c.,** verglas *m*; **a c. of indifference,** une couche, une croûte, d'indifférence; *F: O:* **the upper c.,** la fine fleur de la société; *P:* la haute, le gratin. **3.** dépôt *m* (de vin en bouteille). **4.** croûte (d'une plaie); escarre *f*; **do not touch the burn till the c. comes off,** ne touchez pas à la brûlure avant que la croûte tombe. **5.** *P:* **he's got a c.!** il en a une couche! il a du toupet!

crust[2]. **1.** *v.tr.* encroûter; couvrir d'une croûte (de rouille, de sel, etc.). **2.** *v.i.* se couvrir d'une croûte; (*a*) s'incruster (de rouille, etc.); (*b*) (*of wound, etc.*) faire croûte.

crusta ['krʌstə], *s.* **1.** *Med:* croûte *f*; escarre *f.* **2.** *Crust:* carapace *f.*

Crustacea [krʌs'teisiə, -ʃə], *s.pl.* crustacés *m.*

crustacean [krʌs'teiʃən]. **1.** *a.* crustacéen. **2.** *s.* crustacé *m.*

crustaceologist [krʌsteisi'ɔlədʒist], *s.* crustacéologue *mf.*

crustaceology [krʌsteisi'ɔlədʒi], *s.* crustacéologie *f.*

crustaceous [krʌs'teiʃəs], *a.* **1.** *Bot: Z:* crustacé; à carapace. **2.** crustacéen.

crustation [krʌs'teiʃ(ə)n], *s.* incrustation *f.*

crusted ['krʌstid], *a.* **1. c. over,** couvert d'une croûte; **c. snow,** (neige) tôlée *f*; **c. prejudices,** préjugés invétérés; **c. Tories,** conservateurs encroûtés, de la vieille roche, aux opinions surannées. **2.** (vin *m*) qui a du dépôt; **old c. port,** vieux porto de derrière les fagots, qui a des années de bouteille; **fine old c. joke,** plaisanterie *f* qui a de la bouteille.

crustily ['krʌstili], *adv.* d'un ton (i) bourru, (ii) hargneux, irritable.

crustiness ['krʌstinis], *s.* **1.** texture croustillante, appétissante (d'un pain, etc.). **2.** humeur bourrue.

crusty ['krʌsti], *a.* **1.** *Cu:* (*a*) (pain *m*) qui a une forte croûte; (*b*) (biscuit, etc.) croustillant, qui croque sous la dent; (*c*) = CRUSTED 2. **2.** (*of pers.*) (*a*) bourru; **a c. old man,** un vieux bourru; (*b*) hargneux, irritable; **he's a c. fellow,** c'est un ours, un fagot d'épines.

crutch[1] [krʌtʃ], *s.* **1.** béquille *f*; **a c. to lean on,** un soutien; **to go about, walk, on crutches,** marcher avec des béquilles; **elbow crutches,** cannes anglaises; (*of shovel, etc.*) **c. handle,** manche *m* à poignée en croisillon; **c. handled umbrella,** parapluie *m* à béquille; **c.-handled walking stick,** béquillon *m*; **c. key,** béquille (d'un robinet). **2.** (*a*) *Ind: Const: etc:* support *m*, soutien; béquille; étançon *m*; **c. bridge,** pont *m* à béquilles; (*b*) *Equit:* corne *f* d'arçon, fourche *f* (d'une selle de femme); (*c*) *Nau:* support, chandelier *m* (à fourche); chantier *m* (d'une embarcation à bord); toletière *f*; (*d*) *Row:* tolet *m* à fourche; (*e*) *Cy:* support arrière (de motocyclette). **3.** (*a*) entrecuisse *m*; (*b*) *Tail:* fourche, entre(-)jambe *m inv* (d'un pantalon, d'un slip).

crutch[2], *v.tr.* étayer, soutenir, étançonner.

crutched [krʌtʃt], *a.* **1. with a c. handle,** (canne *f*) à bec de corbin, à béquille; (bêche *f*) à poignée à croisillon. **2.** *Ecc:* **c. friar,** frère *m* de la Sainte-Croix.

crux, *pl.* **cruxes,** *also* **cruces** [krʌks, 'krʌksiz, 'kru:siz], *s.* nœud *m* (d'une difficulté, *Lit:* d'une pièce de théâtre, etc.); point capital, crucial (d'une discussion, etc.); **the c. of the matter,** le nœud de la question.

cruzeiro [kru:'zeirou], *s. Num:* cruzeiro *m*.

crwth [kru:θ], *s. A.Mus:* crouth *m*.

cry[1] [krai], *s.* **1.** cri *m* (d'une personne, d'un animal); **within c.,** à portée de voix; **to give, set up, raise, utter, a c.,** pousser un cri; **it is a long, a far, c. from here to . . .,** il y a loin d'ici à . . .; **hunting cries,** cris de chasse; **the (street) cries of London,** les cris de Londres; **battle c.,** (i) cri de bataille; (ii) cri de ralliement; **war c.,** cri de guerre; (*of hounds*) **to be in full c.,** donner de la voix; **the pack is in full c.,** toute la meute aboie; **the thief fled with the street in full c. after him,** le voleur détala avec toute la rue à ses trousses; **to follow the c.,** suivre la meute, le mouvement; *Prov:* **much c. and little wool,** beaucoup de façons pour rien; la montagne qui accouche; grand bruit et petite besogne; il fait, vous faites, plus de remous que de sillage; **there was a c. for peace,** l'opinion *f* réclamait la paix. **2.** cri (de douleur); plainte *f*. **3.** action *f* de pleurer; pleurs *mpl*; **to have a good c.,** donner libre cours à ses larmes; **to have one's c. out,** pleurer tout son content; **when she had had her c. out,** quand elle eut bien pleuré.

cry[2], *v.* **(cried** [kraid]; **cried)**

I. *v.tr. & i.* **1.** *v.tr. & i.* (*a*) crier; pousser un cri, des cris; **to c. aloud,** pousser de grands cris; **to c. (un)to God,** crier vers Dieu; implorer Dieu; invoquer Dieu; **to c. for help,** crier au secours; **to c. for mercy,** demander grâce, crier grâce; **he cries before he's hurt,** il crie avant qu'on l'écorche; *F:* **for crying out loud!** nom de nom! (*b*) **to c. fish, etc. (for sale),** crier son poisson, etc. (dans la rue); *F: O:* **to c. stinking fish,** dénigrer, déprécier, décrier, sa propre marchandise; dire du mal de ses propres affaires ou de ses parents; décrier les siens; (*c*) *O:* **to have sth. cried,** faire crier un objet perdu; publier qch. à son de caisse; **to c. a lost ring,** tambouriner une bague perdue; (*d*) *Ven:* (*of hounds*) donner de la voix; aboyer. **2.** *v.i.* s'écrier; **"that is false!" he cried,** "c'est faux!" s'écria-t-il. **3.** (*a*) *v.i.* pleurer; verser des larmes; **to c. over sth.,** pleurer, verser des pleurs, sur qch.; **to c. for joy,** pleurer de joie; **to c. for sth.,** demander qch. en pleurant; (*b*) *v.tr.* **to c. one's eyes out,** pleurer toutes les larmes de ses yeux; se perdre les yeux, se brûler les yeux, à force de pleurer; pleurer à chaudes larmes; pleurer comme une Madeleine; **she cried herself to sleep,** à force de pleurer elle s'est endormie.

II. (*compound verbs*) **1. cry down,** *v.tr.* décrier, déprécier (qn, qch.).

2. cry off. (*a*) *v.i.* se dédire, se récuser; se faire excuser; retirer son enjeu, quitter la partie; renoncer à un projet; (*b*) *v.tr.* **to c. off a deal, a bargain,** annuler une affaire.

3. cry out, *v.i.* (*a*) pousser des cris; s'écrier; (*b*) **abuse that cries out for a remedy,** abus *m* qui réclame un remède.

4. cry up, *v.tr.* prôner (qch.).

cryanaesthesia [kraiænis'θi:ziə], *s.* cryanesthésie *f*.

crybaby ['kraibeibi], *s. F:* pleurard, -arde; pleurnicheur, -euse; pleurnichard, -arde; *m*; enfant douillet; chialeur, -euse.

crying[1] ['kraiiŋ], *a.* **1.** criant; **c. injustice,** injustice criante; **c. evil,** abus scandaleux, qui réclame l'attention; **to supply the c. needs of the people,** subvenir aux besoins les plus urgents du peuple; **it is a c. shame that . . .,** il est scandaleux que + *sub.* **2.** pleurant, qui pleure. **3.** *Ich:* **(Chinese) c. fish,** poisson criard.

crying[2], *s.* **1.** *O:* **public c. of an event, etc.,** annonce publique d'un événement; ban *m* d'un événement; tambourinage *m* (d'un objet perdu). **2.** cri(s) *m(pl)*; clameur *f*. **3.** pleurs *mpl*, larmes *fpl*; **fit of c.,** crise *f* de larmes.

crymotherapy [kraimou'θerəpi], *s. Med:* crymothérapie *f*.

cryobiology ['kraioubai'ɔlədʒi], *s.* cryobiologie *f*.

cryoconite [krai'ɔkənait], *s. Geol:* cryoconite *f*.

cryogen ['kraioudʒen], *s. Ph:* cryogène *m*; réfrigérant *m*.

cryogenic [kraiou'dʒenik], *a. Ph:* cryogénique; *Cmptr:* **c. computer,** ordinateur *m* cryogénique; **c. store, storage,** mémoire *f* cryogénique.

cryogenics [kraiou'dʒeniks], *s.pl. Ph:* (*usu. with sg. const.*) cryogénie *f*.

cryogeny [krai'ɔdʒəni], *s.* cryogénie *f*.

cryohydrate [kraiou'haidreit], *s. Ch:* cryohydrate *m*.

cryolite ['kraioulait], *s. Miner:* cryolit(h)e *f*.

cryomagnetism [kraiou'mægnətizm], *s.* cryomagnétisme *m*.

cryometer [krai'ɔmitər], *s. Ph:* cryomètre *m*.

cryometry [krai'ɔmətri], *s. Ph:* cryométrie *f*.

cryophorous [krai'ɔfərəs], *a. Ph:* cryophore.

cryoplanation [kraiouplæ'neiʃ(ə)n], *s. Geog:* cryoplanation *f*.

cryosar ['kraiousa:r], *s. Cmptr:* cryosar *m*.

cryoscope ['kraiouskoup], *s. Ph:* cryoscope *m*.

cryoscopic [kraiou'skɔpik], *a. Ph:* cryoscopique.

cryoscopy [krai'ɔskəpi], *s. Ph:* cryoscopie *f*.

cryostat ['kraioustæt], *s. Ph:* cryostat *m*.

cryotherapy [kraiou'θerəpi], *s. Med:* cryothérapie *f*.

cryotron ['kraioutrɔn], *s. Elcs:* cryotron *m*.

cryoturbation [kraiouta'beiʃ(ə)n], *s. Geol:* cryoturbation *f*.

crypt [kript], *s.* **1.** *Ecc.Arch: etc:* crypte *f*. **2.** *Anat:* crypte, follicule *m*.

cryptaesthesia [kriptis'θi:ziə], *s. Psy:* cryptesthésie *f*.

cryptal ['kriptl], *a. Anat:* cryptique; en forme de crypte.

cryptanalysis [kriptə'nælisis], *s.* lecture *f* des messages dont on ne connaît pas le chiffre; décryptement *m*.

cryptic ['kriptik], *a.* cryptique; secret, caché, occulte; sibyllin; **author who makes a point of remaining c.,** auteur *m* qui s'attache à être cryptique, hermétique; **to maintain a c. silence,** se renfermer dans un silence énigmatique.

cryptically ['kriptik(ə)li], *adv.* (parler) à mots couverts.

crypto ['kriptou], *a. Mil: etc:* **c. system,** procédé *m* de chiffrement; **c. security violation,** infraction *f* à la sécurité du chiffre.

crypto- ['kriptou, krip'tɔ], *pref.* crypto-.

cryptobranchiate [kriptou'bræŋkieit], *s. Amph:* cryptobranche *m*.

Cryptobranchidae [kriptou'bræŋkidi:], *s.pl. Amph:* cryptobranchidés *m*, les salamandres géantes.

crypto-Calvinism ['kriptou'kælvinizm], *s.* cryptocalvinisme *m*.

crypto-Calvinist ['kriptou'kælvinist], *s.* cryptocalviniste *mf*.

crypto-Calvinistic ['kriptoukælvi'nistik], *a.* cryptocalviniste.

Cryptocephala [kriptou'sefələ], *s.pl. Ent:* cryptocéphales *m*.

Cryptocerata ['kriptousə'reitə], *s.pl. Ent:* cryptocérates *m*.

crypto-communism ['kriptou'kɔmjunizm], *s.* cryptocommunisme *m*.

crypto-communist ['kriptou'kɔmjunist], *a. & s.* cryptocommuniste *mf*, *pl.* crypto-communistes.

Cryptodira [kriptou'dairə], *s.pl. Rept:* cryptodères *m*.

cryptogam ['kriptougæm], *s. Bot:* cryptogame *f*.

cryptogamic [kriptou'gæmik], **cryptogamous** [krip'tɔgəməs], *a. Bot:* cryptogamique.

cryptogamist [krip'tɔgəmist], *s.* cryptogamiste *mf*.

cryptogamy [krip'tɔgəmi], *s. Bot:* cryptogamie *f*.

cryptogenetic, cryptogenic ['kriptoudʒə'netik, -'dʒenik], *a. Med:* cryptogénique, cryptogénétique.

cryptogram ['kriptougræm], *s.* cryptogramme *m*.

cryptograph ['kriptougræf], *s.* cryptographe *m*, machine *f* à chiffrer.

cryptographer [krip'tɔgrəfər], *s.* chiffreur, -euse, cryptographe *mf*.

cryptographic [kriptou'græfik], *a.* cryptographique.

cryptographist [krip'tɔgrəfist], *s.* cryptographe *mf*.

cryptography [krip'tɔgrəfi], *s.* cryptographie *f*.

cryptolite ['kriptoulait], *s. Miner:* cryptolite *f*.

cryptologist [krip'tɔlədʒist], *s.* cryptologue *mf*.

cryptology [krip'tɔlədʒi], *s.* cryptologie *f*.

cryptomeria [kriptou'miəriə], *s. Bot:* cryptomeria *m*.

cryptomnesia [kriptɔm'ni:ziə], *s.* cryptomnésie *f*.

Cryptomonadales ['kriptoumɔnə'deili:z], *s.pl. Algae:* cryptomonadales *m*.

crypton ['kriptɔn], *s. Ch:* crypton *m*.

Cryptonemiales ['kriptounemi'eili:z], *s.pl. Algae:* cryptonémiales *f*.

cryptonym ['kriptounim], *s.* cryptonyme *m*.

cryptonymous [krip'tɔniməs], *a.* cryptonyme.

Cryptophagidae ['kriptou'fædʒidi:], *s.pl. Ent:* cryptophagidés *m*.

cryptophthalmos [kriptɔf'θælmɔs], *s. Med:* cryptophtalmie *f*.

cryptophyte ['kriptoufait], *s. Bot:* cryptophyte *f*.

cryptopine ['kriptoupain], *s. Ch:* cryptopine *f*.

cryptoporticus ['kriptou'pɔ:tikəs], *s. Arch:* cryptoportique *m*.

cryptorchid [kript'ɔ:kid], *a. & s. Med: Vet:* cryptorchide (*m*).

cryptorchidism [kript'ɔ:kidizm], *s. Med: Vet:* cryptorchidie *f*.

cryptorhynchus ['kriptou'riŋkəs], *s. Ent:* cryptorhynque *m*, cryptorhynchus *m*.

cryptostegia [kriptou'sti:dʒiə], *s. Bot:* cryptostegia *m*.

cryptozygosity ['kriptouzi'gɔsiti], *s. Anthr:* cryptozygie *f*.

cryptozygous [krip'tɔzigəs], *a. Anthr:* cryptozyge.

crystal ['kristl], *s.* **1.** *Ch: Miner:* cristal *m*, -aux; **right-, left-handed c.,** cristal droit, gauche; **(optically) positive c.,** cristal attractif; **(optically) negative c.,** cristal répulsif; **twin(ned) c.,** macle *f*; **rock c.,** cristal de roche. **2.** (*a*) *a. & s.* **c. (glass),** cristal; **c. factory,** cristallerie *f*; (*b*) *a.* **c.(-clear),** clair, limpide, cristallin; *Fig:* **c.-clear,** clair comme le jour, comme de l'eau de roche; *Lit:* **the c. waters of the fountain,** les eaux cristallines, limpides, de la source. **3.** (*a*) *U.S:* verre *m* de montre; (*b*) *pl.* pendeloques *f* (d'un lustre). **4.** *Psychics:* **c. (ball),** boule *f* de cristal; **c. gazer,** cristallomancien, -ienne, voyant, -ante (qui pratique la divination par le cristal); **c. gazing,** cristallomancie *f*, divination *f* par la boule de cristal. **5.** *Elcs: etc:* quartz *m*, cristal; **c. control, drive,** pilotage *m* piézo-électrique, par quartz; **c.-controlled,** piloté par quartz; **c. oscillator,** oscillateur à quartz, piloté par quartz; **c. microphone, loudspeaker, pickup,** microphone *m*, haut-parleur *m*, pick-up *m*, piézo-électrique; *W.Tel: A:* **c. set,** poste *m* à galène.

crystalliferous [kristə'lifərəs], *a.* cristallifère.

crystalline ['kristəlain], *a.* cristallin; *Anat:* **c. lens (of the eye),** cristallin *m*; **c. humour (of the eye),** humeur cristalline; *A.Astr:* **the c. circles, spheres,** les cristallins *m*.

crystallinity [kristə'liniti], *s.* cristallinité *f*.

crystallite ['kristəlait], *s. Miner:* cristallite *f*.

crystallitic [kristə'litik], *a.* cristallitique.

crystallizable ['kristəlaizəbl], *a.* cristallisable.

crystallization [kristəlai'zeiʃ(ə)n], *s.* cristallisation *f*.

crystallize ['kristəlaiz]. **1.** *v.tr.* (*a*) cristalliser; (*b*) **to c. sugar,** faire candir du sucre; **crystallized fruits,** fruits confits. **2.** *v.i.* (*a*) (se) cristalliser; **to c. (out),** se dissocier en cristaux; (*of salt*) se séparer à l'état cristallin; **his opinions were beginning to c.,** ses opinions commençaient à se cristalliser, se fixer; (*b*) (*of sugar*) se candir.

crystallizer ['kristəlaizər], *s. Ch:* cristallisoir *m*.

crystalloblastic [kristəlou'blæstik], *a.* cristalloblastique.

crystallogenesis [kristəlou'dʒenəsis], *s.* cristallogénèse *f*.

crystallogenic [kristəlou'dʒenik], *a.* cristallogénique.

crystallogeny [kristə'lɔdʒəni], *s.* cristallogénie *f*.

crystallographer [kristə'lɔgrəfər], *s.* cristallographe *mf*.

crystallographic(al) [kristəlou'græfik(l)], *a.* cristallographique.

crystallography [kristə'lɔgrəfi], *s.* cristallographie *f*.

crystalloid ['kristəlɔid], *a. & s.* cristalloïde (*m*).

crystalloidal [kristə'lɔidl], *a.* cristalloïdal.

crystalloluminescence ['kristəloulu:mi'nes(ə)ns], *s.* cristalloluminescence *f*.

crystallomancy ['kristəlou'mænsi], *s.* cristallomancie *f*.

crystallometric ['kristəlou'metrik], *a.* cristallométrique.

crystallometry [kristə'lɔmitri], *s.* cristallométrie *f*.

csardas ['tʃa:da:ʃ, 'tʃa:dæʃ], *s. Danc:* csardas *f*; czardas *f*.

ctenidium [tə'nidiəm], *s. Moll: Ent:* cténidie *f*.

ctenocephalus [tenou'sefələs], *s. Ent:* cténocéphale *m*.

Ctenodactylidae [tenoudæk'tilidi:], *s.pl. Z:* cténodactylidés *m*.

ctenoid ['tenɔid, 'ti:-], *a. Ich:* cténoïde, pectiné.

Ctenomyidae [tenou'maiidi:], *s.pl. Z:* cténomyidés *m*.

Ctenophora [te'nɔfərə], *s.pl. Coel:* cténophores *m*.

cub[1] [kʌb], *s.* **1.** petit *m* (d'un animal); (*of fox*) renardeau *m*; (*of bear*) ourson *m*; (*of lion*) lionceau *m*; (*of wolf*)

louveteau *m*; *Ven:* **c. hunting,** chasse *f* au renardeau. **2.** *F:* (*a*) apprenti *m*; blanc-bec *m, pl.* blancs-becs; (*b*) jeune homme mal appris; **unlicked c.,** ours mal léché. **3.** *Scout:* louveteau.
cub², *v.i.* (**cubbed**) **1.** (*of fox, bear, etc.*) mettre bas (des petits); (*of wolf*) louveter. **2.** *Ven:* faire la chasse au renardeau.
Cuba ['kju:bə], *Pr.n. Geog:* (l'île de) Cuba *m*; **in C.,** à Cuba.
cubage ['kju:bidʒ], **cubature** ['kju:bətjər], *s.* cubage *m.*
Cuban ['kju:bən], *Geog:* (*a*) *a.* cubain; (*b*) *s.* Cubain, -aine.
cubanite ['kju:bənait], *s. Miner:* cubanite *f.*
cubbing ['kʌbiŋ], *s.* **1.** *Z:* mise bas *f* (des fauves, etc.). **2.** chasse *f* au renardeau.
cubbish ['kʌbiʃ], *a. F: O:* mal léché; gauche.
cubbyhole ['kʌbihoul], *s.* **1.** (*a*) retraite *f*, cachette *f*, abri *m*; (*b*) (toute) petite pièce, chambre. **2.** (*a*) placard *m*; (*b*) *Aut:* vide-poche(s) *m inv.*
cube¹ [kju:b], *s.* **1.** *Mth:* cube *m*; **c. root,** racine *f* cubique; **expressed by the c. root,** sous-triplé. **2.** morceau *m* cubique (de sucre); tablette *f* (de potage); dé *m* (de pain, etc.).
cube², *v.tr.* **1.** *Mth:* cuber; élever (un nombre) au cube. **2.** (*measure*) cuber (du bois, etc.).
cubeb ['kju:beb], *s. Bot:* cubèbe *m*; *F:* poivre *m* à queue; *Pharm:* cubèbe.
cubebin ['kju:bibin], *s. Ch:* cubébin *m*, cubébine *f.*
cubic ['kju:bik], *a.* **1.** (*cube-shaped*) cubique. **2.** *Meas:* **c. metre,** mètre *m* cube; **c. measurement,** cubage *m*; **c. contents,** cubage; contenance *f* cubique; volume *m*; **c. capacity,** volume; *Mch:* cylindrée *f*; **c. measures,** mesures *f* de volume. **3.** *Mth:* **c. equation,** équation *f* du troisième degré; **c. curve,** *s.* **cubic,** courbe *f* cubique; cubique *f.*
cubical ['kju:bikl], *a.* cubique, en (forme de) cube.
cubicle ['kju:bikl], *s.* **1.** (*a*) compartiment cloisonné, alcôve *f*, (d'un dortoir); **cubicles,** alcôves de dortoir; (*b*) *Cmptr:* caisson *m*, armoire *f*, baie *f.* **2.** cabine *f* (d'une piscine, etc.); (**tailor's**) **trying-on c.,** cabine d'essayage; *El:* **switch-gear c.,** guérite *f* de la distribution.
cubiform ['kju:bifɔ:m], *a.* cubique; en (forme de) cube.
cubism ['kju:bizm], *s. Art:* cubisme *m.*
cubist ['kju:bist], *a. & s. Art:* cubiste (*mf*).
cubit ['kju:bit], *s. A.Meas:* coudée *f.*
cubital ['kju:bitl], *a.* cubital, -aux. **1.** *Anat:* de l'avant-bras. **2.** *A:* long d'une coudée.
cubitière [kju:'bitiɛər], *s. A.Arm:* cubitière *f.*
cubito-palmar ['kju:bitou'pælmər], *a. Anat:* cubito palmaire.
cubitoradial ['kju:bitou'reidiəl], *a. & s. Anat:* radio-cubital, -aux (*m*); cubito-radial, -aux (*m*).
cubitus ['kju:bitəs], *s. Anat:* cubitus *m.*
cubmaster ['kʌbma:stər], *s.m. or f. Scout:* (*always a woman in Fr.*) chef(e)taine *f* (de louveteaux).
cubo-cubo-cube ['kju:bou'kju:bou'kju:b], *s. A.Mth:* neuvième puissance *f*; *A:* cubocube *m.*
cubo-dodecahedron ['kjuboudoudekə'hi:drən], *s. Cryst:* cubo-dodécaèdre *m*, cubo-dodécaèdres.
cuboid ['kju:bɔid], *a. & s.* **1.** *Mth:* cuboïde (*m*). **2.** *Anat:* **c.** (**bone**), (os *m*) cuboïde (du pied).
cub(o)-octahedron ['kju:b(ou)ɔktə'hi:drən], *s. Cryst:* cubo-octaèdre *m*, cubo-octaèdres.
cuchia ['ku:tʃiə], *s. Ich:* cuchia *f.*
cucking-stool ['kʌkiŋstu:l], *s. A:* sellette *f* de correction, chaise percée (pour la punition des mégères et des marchands malhonnêtes).
cuckold¹ ['kʌkɔld], *s.* cocu *m.*
cuckold², *v.tr.* coucfier; tromper (un mari).
cuckoldom ['kʌkəldəm], *s.* cocuage *m.*
cuckoldry ['kʌkəldri], *s.* adultère *m* (d'une femme).
cuckoo¹ ['kuku:], *s.* **1.** (*a*) *Orn:* coucou *m*; (*b*) *Orn:* coulicou *m*; **black-billed c.,** coulicou à bec noir; **yellow-billed c.,** coulicou à bec jaune; **great spotted c.,** coucougeai *m*, oxylophe *m* geai; **channel-billed c.,** scythrops *m*; (*Austr.*) **swamp c.,** coucal *m*; **ground c.,** coucou terrestre; **hawk c.,** coucou-épervier *m*; **emerald c.,** foliotocol *m*; **long-tailed c.** (**of Tahiti**), coucou à longue queue (de Tahiti); (*c*) *Orn:* **c. roller,** courol *m*; **c. shrike,** échenilleur *m*, choucari *m*; (*d*) **c. clock,** (pendule *f* à) coucou; (*e*) *int.* coucou! **2.** (*a*) *Ent:* **c. bee,** psithyre *m*; **c. spit,** crachat *m* de coucou, de grenouille; écume printanière; (*b*) *Bot:* **c. bread,** pain-coucou *m*, pain *m* de coucou, oseille *f* des bois; **c. pint,** (i) arum maculé; pied-de-veau *m*; gouet *m*; (ii) lychnide *f* des prés, fleur *f* de coucou. **3.** *F:* niais *m*, benêt *m*; **to go c.,** devenir loufoque, maboul; perdre la boule.
cuckoo², *v.i.* coucouer, coucouler.
cuckooflower ['kuku:flauər], *s. Bot:* cardamine *f* des prés; cresson élégant, cresson des prés.

cucujid [kə'ku:dʒid], *s. Ent:* cucuje *m*, cucujus *m.*
Cucujidae [kə'ku:djidi:], *s.pl. Ent:* cucujidés *m.*
Cuculidae [kə'k(j)u:lidi:], *s.pl. Orn:* cuculidés *m*, les coucous *m.*
Cuculiformes [kək(j)u:li'fɔ:mi:z], *s.pl.* cuculiformes *m.*
cucullate(d) ['kju:kəleit(id)], *a. Nat.Hist:* cucullifère, capuchonné, encapuchonné; cuculé.
cuculliform [kju(:)'kʌlifɔ:m], *a.* cuculliforme.
Cucumariidae [kju:k(j)u:mə'raiidi:], *s.pl. Echin:* cucumaridés *m.*
cucumber ['kju:kʌmbər], *s.* **1.** (*a*) *Hort:* concombre *m*; (*b*) *Bot:* **squirting c.,** giclet *m*, ecballium *m*; **bitter c.,** coloquinte *f*; **c. tree,** carambolier *m* cylindrique. **2.** *Echin:* **sea c.,** (i) holothurie *f*, concombre de mer; (ii) tripang *m*, trépang *m*, *F:* bêche-de-mer *f*, *pl.* bêches-de-mer.
cucurbit [kju'kə:bit], *s.* **1.** *A:* cucurbite *f* (d'un alambic). **2.** *Bot:* courge *f.*
Cucurbitaceae [kjukə:bi'teisii:], *s.pl. Bot:* cucurbitacées *f.*
cucurbitaceous [kjukə:bi'teiʃəs], *a. Bot:* cucurbitacé.
cud [kʌd], *s.* bol *m* alimentaire (d'un ruminant); **to chew the c.,** (i) ruminer; (ii) *F:* (*of pers.*) ruminer une idée; méditer.
cudbear ['kʌdbɛər], *s. Bot: Dy:* orseille *f* de terre.
cuddle¹ ['kʌdl], *s.* étreinte *f*, embrassade *f*; pelotage *m.*
cuddle². **1.** *v.tr.* serrer (qn) doucement dans ses bras; s'appuyer amoureusement contre (qn); *F:* peloter (qn). **2.** *v.i.* (*a*) se peloter (l'un l'autre); (*b*) **to c. up to s.o.,** se blottir, se pelotonner, contre qn; (*c*) se mettre en chien de fusil (dans son lit); (*to child*) **c. down and go to sleep,** enfonce-toi bien sous la couverture et fais dodo.
cuddlesome ['kʌdlsəm], **cuddly** ['kʌdli], *a. F:* (enfant, etc.) qui invite aux caresses; (femme) gironde; (poupée *f*, etc.) qu'on peut serrer dans ses bras.
cuddling ['kʌdliŋ], *s.* étreintes *fpl*; embrassades *fpl*; pelotage *m.*
cuddy¹ ['kʌdi], *s.* **1.** *Nau:* tille *f*; cabine *f*, chambre *f*, arrière; (*of barge*) rouf *m.* **2.** (*a*) armoire *f*, placard *m*; (*b*) cabinet *m*, buffet *m.*
cuddy², *s. Scot: F:* **1.** bourricot *m.* **2.** sot *m*, bêta *m*, nigaud *m.*
cudgel¹ ['kʌdʒəl], *s.* bâton *m*, gourdin *m*, trique *f*; **to take up the cudgels for s.o., on s.o.'s behalf,** prendre fait et cause pour qn; prendre querelle pour qn; prendre la défense de qn; prendre, épouser, le parti de qn; livrer bataille pour qn; se mettre en campagne pour qn.
cudgel², *v.tr.* (**cudgelled**) bâtonner; donner des coups de bâton à (qn); **to c. s.o. to death,** assommer qn à coups de gourdin, de trique, faire périr qn sous le bâton; **to c. one's brains,** se creuser le cerveau, l'esprit.
cudgelling ['kʌdʒ(ə)liŋ], *s.* (volée *f* de) coups *mpl* de bâton.
cudweed ['kʌdwi:d], *s. Bot: F:* (i) filage *m*, cotonnière *f*; (ii) gnaphale *m.*
cue¹ [kju:], *s.* **1.** (*a*) *Th:* fin *f* de tirade; réplique *f*; **to take** (**up**) **one's c.,** donner la réplique; **to give s.o. his c.,** donner la réplique à qn; (*b*) *Cmptr:* caractère indicateur; **c. symbol,** caractère spécial; (*c*) avis *m*, mot *m*, indication *f*; **to give s.o. a c.,** mettre qn sur la voie; **to give s.o. the c.,** donner le mot à qn; **to take one's c. from s.o.,** prendre exemple sur qn; régler sa conduite sur qn; s'ajuster sur qn; **Hungary takes her c. from Russia,** la Hongrie s'aligne sur la Russie; **on c.,** au bon moment; (*d*) *Mus:* indication de rentrée (d'un instrument). **2.** *A:* rôle *m*; interprétation *f* de rôle. **3.** *A:* humeur *f*, veine *f*; **I am not in the c. for reading,** je n'ai aucune envie de lire.
cue², *v.tr. Cmptr:* intercaler, insérer.
cue³, *s.* **1.** *A:* queue *f* (de cheveux, de perruque). **2.** queue (de billard); **c. rack,** porte-queues *m inv*; **c. tip,** procédé *m.*
cueist ['kju:ist], *s. O:* joueur *m* de billard.
cuesta ['kwestə], *s. Geol:* cuesta *f.*
cuff¹ [kʌf], *s.* **1.** (*a*) poignet *m* (de chemise); (*starched*) manchette *f*; *Dressm:* mancheron *m*, manchette, poignet; **double c., turnback c., gauntlet c.,** manchette mousquetaire, à revers; **c. protector,** poignet de manche; garde-manche *m*, *pl.* garde-manches; **c. links,** boutons (de manchette) jumelés; (*b*) (*of coat sleeve*) parement *m*; **double c.,** parement mousquetaire; (*c*) *F:* (**speech, etc.**) **off the c.,** (discours, etc.) impromptu; **to do sth. off the c.,** faire qch. impromptu; *NAm:* **on the c.,** à crédit. **2.** *NAm:* (**trouser**) **cuffs,** revers *mpl* de pantalon.
cuff², *s.* taloche *f*, calotte *f.*
cuff³, *v.tr.* talocher, calotter (qn); flanquer une taloche, une calotte, des taloches, à (qn).
cuffing ['kʌfiŋ], *s.* volée *f* de taloches, de calottes; échange *m* de taloches; **he gave him such a c. that . . .,** il lui a frotté si bien les oreilles que . . .

Cufic ['kju:fik], *a. & s. Pal:* (alphabet *m*) koufique.
cui bono ['kwi:'bounou], *interr. Lt.phr:* **1.** *Jur:* qui en a profité? à qui cela profitera-t-il? **2.** à quoi bon? dans quel but?
cuirass¹ [kwi'ræs], *s.* **1.** cuirasse *f* (de cuir, d'acier). **2.** *Ich: N.Arch: etc:* cuirasse.
cuirass², *v.tr. N.Arch: A.Mil:* cuirasser (qch., qn).
cuirassier [kwirə'siər], *s. A.Mil:* cuirassier *m.*
cuir-bouilli ['kwiəbu:'ji:], *s.* cuir *m* bouilli.
cuisse [kwis], **cuish** [kwiʃ], *s. A.Arm:* cuissard *m.*
cuisse-madame ['kwi:smæ'dæm], *s. Hort:* cuisse-madame *f*, *pl.* cuisses-madame.
culch [kʌltʃ], *s. Ost:* collecteur *m* pour huîtres; ruche *f.*
cul-de-lampe ['kʌldə'læmp], *s.* (*pl.* **culs-de-lampe**) *Arch: Typ:* cul-de-lampe *m*, *pl.* culs-de-lampe.
cul-de-sac ['kʌldəsæk], *s.* (*pl.* **culs-de-sac, cul-de-sacs**) cul-de-sac *m*, *pl.* culs de sac; impasse *f.*
culet ['kju:lit], *s. Lap:* culasse *f* (de diamant taillé en brillant).
culicicide [kju(:)'lisisaid], *s.* insecticide *m* (contre les culicidés).
Culicidae [kju(:)'lisidi:], *s.pl. Ent:* culicidés *m.*
culiciform [kju(:)'lisifɔ:m], *a. Ent:* culiciforme.
culicifuge [kju(:)'lisifju:dʒ], *a. Pharm:* préparation *f* anti-moustiques.
culinary ['kʌlinəri], *a.* de cuisine; culinaire.
cull¹ [kʌl], *s.* **1.** *Husb:* bête *f* à éliminer du troupeau. **2.** *pl. U.S:* **culls,** déchet *m*, rebut *m* (de bois en grume, etc.).
cull², *v.tr.* **1.** *Lit:* (*a*) cueillir (des fleurs, des fruits); (*b*) choisir, recueillir (**from,** dans). **2.** *Husb:* (*a*) débarrasser (un troupeau) des sujets malsains; (*b*) éliminer (les sujets malsains) d'un troupeau.
cull³, *s. F: A:* = CULLY.
cullender ['kʌlindər], *s. Dom.Ec:* passoire *f.*
cullet ['kʌlit], *s. Glassm:* **1.** calcin *m*, grésil *m*, groisil *m*, graisin *m*; rognures *fpl* de verre. **2.** tessons *mpl* de bouteille.
cully ['kʌli], *s. P:* (*a*) *A:* nigaud *m*, benêt *m*, jobard *m*; (*b*) copain *m.*
culm¹ [kʌlm], *s.* **1.** (*a*) poussier *m* d'anthracite; (*b*) *Dial:* anthracite *m.* **2.** *Geol:* culm *m.*
culm², *s. Bot:* chaume *m*, stipe *m*, tige *f* (des graminées).
culmiferous [kʌl'mifərəs], *a. Bot:* culmifère.
culminant ['kʌlminənt], *a.* **1.** *Astr:* (astre) culminant, au méridien. **2.** (point) culminant, (point) le plus haut.
culminate ['kʌlmineit], *v.i.* **1.** *Astr:* (*of star, etc.*) culminer; passer au méridien. **2.** atteindre son plus haut point, son apogée; **to c. in sth.,** se terminer en qch.; finir par qch.; aboutir à, dans, en qch.
culminating ['kʌlmineitiŋ], *a.* culminant; **c. point,** (i) point culminant, sommet *m*; (ii) *Med:* (*of illness or fit*) paroxysme *m*; **the c. point of the drama,** le moment culminant du drame.
culmination [kʌlmi'neiʃ(ə)n], *s.* **1.** *Astr:* culmination *f*; passage *m* au méridien. **2.** point culminant; sommet *m*; aboutissement *m*; apogée *m* (de la gloire, etc.).
culotte [kju(:)'lɔt], *s. Cost:* jupe-culotte *f*, *pl.* jupes-culottes.
culpability [kʌlpə'biliti], **culpableness** ['kʌlpəb(ə)lnis], *s.* culpabilité *f.*
culpable ['kʌlpəbl], *a.* **1.** (faiblesse *f*, négligence *f*, etc.) coupable. **2.** *A:* (personne *f*) coupable; (*still so used in*) **to hold s.o. c.,** tenir qn pour coupable. **3.** *Jur:* **c. of punishment, of death,** digne de punition, de mort.
culpably ['kʌlpəbli], *adv.* coupablement; d'une manière coupable.
culprit ['kʌlprit], *s.* **1.** *Jur:* accusé, -ée; prévenu, -ue. **2.** coupable *mf.*
cult [kʌlt], *s.* (*a*) *Ecc:* culte *m* (**of,** de); (*b*) **the Wordsworth c.,** le culte de Wordsworth; **to make a c. of sth.,** avoir un culte pour qch.; **c. figure,** idole *f.*
cultch¹ [kʌltʃ], *s. Ost:* collecteur *m* pour huîtres; ruche *f.*
cultch², *s. P:* **we did a few museums for a bit of c.,** on a visité des musées pour se stimuler les méninges.
cultellation [kʌlte'leiʃ(ə)n], *s. Surv:* cultellation *f.*
cultism ['kʌltizm], *s.* gongorisme *m*, cultisme *m.*
cultist ['kʌltist], *s.* gongoriste *mf*, cultiste *mf.*
cultivable ['kʌltivəbl], *a.* cultivable.
cultivar ['kʌltivɑ:r], *s. Bot:* cultivar *m.*
cultivate ['kʌltiveit], *v.tr.* **1.** (*a*) cultiver, exploiter (la terre, un champ); mettre (des terres) en valeur; **badly cultivated fields,** champs mal exploités; (*b*) cultiver (des légumes, etc.); (*c*) *Agr:* travailler (le sol) avec un cultivateur, un extirpateur, ou autre engin. **2. to c. a bacillus,** faire une culture (sur bouillon) d'un bacille. **3.** (*a*) **to c. one's friends, s.o.'s friendship, s.o.'s acquaintance,** cultiver ses amis, l'amitié de qn, la connaissance de qn; **this is a connection that should be cultivated,** c'est une relation à cultiver; **to c. the Muses,** se vouer au culte des Muses; cultiver les Muses; (*b*) **to c. an art,** cultiver un art; **to c. an easy manner,** arrondir ses

manières; to **c. bluntness,** afficher une franchise bourrue.

cultivated ['kʌltiveitid], *a.* (*a*) (voix *f*, etc.) qui dénote, accuse, une bonne éducation; (esprit) cultivé; **his c. mind,** la culture de son esprit; (*b*) **c. land,** terre cultivée.

cultivation [kʌlti'veiʃ(ə)n], *s.* culture *f*; **field in, under, c.,** champ cultivé, en culture; **fields under c.,** cultures *fpl*; **to bring land into c.,** défricher du terrain; mettre des terres en valeur; **extensive, intensive, c.,** culture extensive, intensive.

cultivator ['kʌltiveitər], *s. Agr:* **1.** (*pers.*) cultivateur, -trice; exploitant, -ante. **2.** (*machine*) cultivateur *m*; motoculteur *m*; **rotary c.,** rotavator *m*.

cultrate ['kʌltreit], *a. Nat.Hist:* cultellaire, cultriforme.

cultriform ['kʌltrifɔːm], *a. Nat.Hist:* cultriforme.

cultrirostral [kʌltri'rɔstr(ə)l], *a. Orn:* cultrirostre.

cultual ['kʌltjuəl], *a.* cultuel.

cultural ['kʌltjər(ə)l], *a.* **1.** (*pertaining to agriculture*) cultural, -aux. **2.** (*pertaining to intellectual culture*) culturel; (organisation) pour la culture.

culture[1] ['kʌltjər], *s.* **1.** culture *f* (des champs, des abeilles, d'un bacille, de l'esprit). **2.** *Bac:* culture; **c. tube,** tube *m* à culture. **3. the c. of his mind,** la culture de son esprit; son esprit cultivé; **he lacks c.,** il n'a aucune culture.

culture[2], *v.tr. Bac:* faire une culture (d'un bacille).

cultured ['kʌltjəd], *a.* (*a*) cultivé, lettré; **his c. mind,** son esprit cultivé; la culture de son esprit; **highly c. man,** homme *m* de forte culture; **c. people,** gens cultivés; (*b*) **c. pearl,** perle *f* de culture.

culturist ['kʌltjərist], *s.* **1.** (*a*) cultivateur, -trice; (*b*) éleveur *m*; pisciculteur *m*; **oyster c.,** ostréiculteur *m*. **2.** partisan *m* de l'instruction générale.

culver ['kʌlvər], *s. Orn:* (pigeon *m*) ramier *m*.

culverin ['kʌlvərin], *s. A.Artil:* couleuvrine *f*.

culvert ['kʌlvət], *s.* **1.** *Civ.E:* (*a*) ponceau *m*; pont dormant, aqueduc *m*; (*b*) canal *m*, -aux; **open c.,** canal (à ciel) ouvert; rigole *f*, cassis *m*; **closed c.,** canal (à ciel) couvert. **2.** *El:* conduit souterrain.

cum [kʌm], *Lt. prep.* avec; *St.Exch:* **c. dividend,** coupon attaché.

Cumacea [kju'meisiə], *s.pl. Crust:* cumacés *m*.

Cumae ['kjuːmiː], *Pr.n. A.Geog:* Cumes *f*.

Cumaean [kju'miːən], *a. A.Geog:* cuméen, éenne.

cumaldehyde [kju'mældihaid], *s. Ch:* aldéhyde *m* cuminique.

cumara ['kuːmərə], **cumaru** ['kuːməruː], *s. Bot:* coumarou(na) *m*.

cumarin ['kuːmərin], *s. Ch:* coumarine *f*.

cumber[1] ['kʌmbər], *s. A:* embarras *m*, encombrement *m*, obstacle *m*.

cumber[2], *v.tr.* embarrasser, encombrer, gêner (**with,** de); **to c. s.o. with parcels,** charger qn de paquets; *B:* **why cumbereth it the ground?** pourquoi occupe-t-il inutilement la terre?

cumberlandite ['kʌmbəlændait], *s. Miner:* cumberlandite *f*.

cumbersome ['kʌmbəsəm], *a.* embarrassant, encombrant, gênant, incommode; peu facile à remuer; lourd.

cumbersomeness ['kʌmbəsəmnis], *s.* incommodité *f* (d'un objet lourd ou encombrant); lourdeur *f* (d'un carrosse, etc.).

cumbraite ['kʌmbreiait], *s. Miner:* cumbraïte *f*.

Cumbrian ['kʌmbriən], *Geog:* (*a*) *a.* **the C. mountains,** les monts *m* Cumbrian; (*b*) *a. & s.* (habitant, -ante) (i) *Hist:* du Cumberland; (ii) du comté de Cumbria.

cumbrous ['kʌmbrəs], *a.* = CUMBERSOME.

cumbrously ['kʌmbrəsli], *s. adv.* d'une manière encombrante; lourdement.

cumbrousness ['kʌmbrəsnis], *s.* = CUMBERSOMENESS.

cumene ['kjuːmiːn], *s. Ch:* cumène *m*.

cumeng(e)ite [kju'mendʒait], *s. Miner:* cumengéite *f*.

cumidine ['kjuːmidain], *s. Ch:* cumidine *f*.

cumin ['kʌmin, 'kjuː-], *s. Bot:* cumin *m*; **wild c.,** cumin bâtard.

cuminic [kjuː'minik], *a. Ch:* (acide *m*, etc.) cuminique.

cuminoin [kjuː'minɔin], *s. Ch:* cuminoïne *f*.

cummer ['kʌmər], *s.f. A: & Dial: Scot:* **1.** commère (marraine ou vieille bavarde). **2.** la mère (une telle); sage-femme; vieille sorcière. **3.** femme, jeune fille (en général).

cummerbund ['kʌməbʌnd], *s.* large ceinture *f* (de mousseline, etc.); ceinture turban; **c. vest,** ceinture giletière.

cummin ['kʌmin], *s. Bot:* = CUMIN.

cummings ['kʌmiŋz], *s.pl. Brew:* touraillon *m*.

cummingtonite ['kʌmiŋtənait], *s. Miner:* cummingtonite *f*.

cumquat ['kʌmkwɔt], *s. Bot:* koumquat *m*, kumquat *m*.

cumulate[1] ['kjuːmjuleit], *a.* (ac)cumulé.

cumulate[2], *v.tr. & i.* (ac)cumuler; *Jur:* **to c. proofs,** cumuler les preuves.

cumulated ['kjuːmjuleitid], *a.* (ac)cumulé; **c. percentages,** pourcentages cumulés; **cumulated clouds,** cumulus *mpl*; nuages amoncelés.

cumulative ['kjuːmjulətiv], *a.* cumulatif; *Jur:* **c. evidence,** accumulation *f* de témoignages; **c. voting,** faculté *f* de réunir sur un seul candidat toutes les voix dont on dispose; *Cmptr: etc:* **c. costs,** cumul *m* des frais; **c. error,** erreur cumulée; **c. index,** index cumulatif; **c. total,** cumul; *Fin:* **c. interest,** intérêts cumulatifs; **c. preference shares,** actions de priorité cumulatives.

cumulatively ['kjuːmjulətivli], *adv.* cumulativement; en cumulé.

cumulo-nimbus ['kjuːmjulou'nimbəs], *s. Meteor:* cumulo-nimbus *m inv*.

cumulo-stratus ['kjuːmjulou'streitəs, -'strɑː-], *s. Meteor:* cumulo-stratus *m inv*.

cumulous ['kjuːmjuləs], *a. Meteor:* (nuage) amoncelé en cumulus.

cumulovolcano ['kjuːmjulouvɔl'keinou], *s. Geog:* cumulo-volcan *m*, *pl.* cumulo-volcans.

cumulus, *pl.* **-li** ['kjuːmjuləs, -lai], *s. Meteor:* cumulus *m*.

cumyl ['kjuːmil], *s. Ch:* cumyle *m*.

Cunarder [kjuː'nɑːdər], *s.* paquebot *m* de la Compagnie Cunard.

cuneate ['kjuːnieit], *a. Bot: etc:* cunéaire; (feuille) cunéiforme; **c.-leaved,** cunéifolié.

Cunegonde ['kjuːnigɔnd], *Pr.n.f.* Cunégonde.

cuneiform [kju'neiifɔːm], *a. & s.* (os *m*, écriture *f*) cunéiforme (*m*).

cunette [kjuː'net], *s. Fort:* cunette *f*.

cunning[1] ['kʌniŋ], *s.* **1.** (*guile*) (*a*) ruse *f*, finesse *f*, art *m*; astuce *f*; (*b*) *Pej:* (**low**) **c.,** fourberie *f*, sournoiserie *f*; astuce; **piece of c.,** (i) finasserie *f*; (ii) *Pej:* fourberie; **to play c.,** finasser. **2.** (*skill*) adresse *f*, habileté *f*; **his hand has not lost its c.,** il n'a rien perdu de son adresse.

cunning[2], *a.* **1.** rusé; malin, *f*; maligne; fin, madré, artificieux; *F:* roublard; (*of child*) futé; (*of look*) sournois. **2.** (*a*) *A:* adroit, habile, expérimenté; (*b*) **c. device,** dispositif ingénieux. **3.** *esp: NAm: F:* (*of child, small animal, etc.*) mignon, -onne; gentillet, -ette; intéressant.

cunningly ['kʌniŋli], *adv.* **1.** avec ruse, avec finesse; astucieusement, sournoisement. **2.** *A:* adroitement, habilement.

cunt [kʌnt], *s. V:* (*not in decent use*) (*a*) vulve *f*, con *m*; (*b*) (*pers.*) con *m*, connasse *f*.

cuon ['kjuːən], *s. Z:* cyon *m*, chien *m* sauvage d'Asie.

cup[1] [kʌp], *s.* **1.** (*a*) tasse *f*; **coffee c.,** tasse à café; **c. of coffee, of tea,** tasse de café, de thé; *F:* **that's my c. of tea,** c'est tout à fait dans mes cordes; **that's, it's, not my c. of tea,** je ne mange pas de ce pain-là, ce ne sont pas mes oignons; **that's another c. of tea,** ça, c'est autre chose, une autre affaire, une autre paire de manches; **that's not everyone's c. of tea,** ce n'est pas au goût de tout le monde; *Cu:* **take a c. of flour,** prenez une tasse (= *approx.* 200 grammes) de farine; (*b*) (**metal**) **c.,** gobelet *m*, timbale *f*; *Mil:* **tin c., canteen c.,** quart *m*. **2.** (*a*) *Lit:* coupe *f*; *Ecc:* calice *m* (du saint Sacrement); **c. bearer,** échanson *m*; **the stirrup c., parting c.,** le coup de l'étrier; **to drink, drain, the c. of pleasure to the dregs,** vider la coupe des plaisirs jusqu'à la lie; **to drink a bitter c.,** vider un calice amer; **to drain the c.** (**of sorrow**) **to the dregs,** boire le calice jusqu'à la lie; épuiser tous les chagrins; *B:* **my c. is full, runneth over,** ma coupe est comble, est remplie, déborde; *Prov:* **there's many a slip 'twixt the c. and the lip,** il y a loin de la coupe aux lèvres; il arrive beaucoup de choses entre la bouche et le verre; vin versé n'est pas avalé; *F:* **to be in one's cups,** être pris de boisson, de vin; être dans les vignes du Seigneur; être gris; **over one's cups,** en buvant; (*b*) *Sp:* coupe; **to win a c.,** emporter une coupe; *Ten:* **the Davis C.,** la coupe Davis; *Fb:* **c. tie,** match *m* éliminatoire, de coupe; **c. final,** finale *f* du championnat, de coupe. **3. champagne c., wine c.,** marquise *f*; **cider c.,** boisson glacée au cidre (avec des fruits). **4.** (*cup-shaped object*) (*a*) *Bot:* (i) calice (d'une fleur); (ii) cupule *f*; *W.Tel: A:* **c. of the crystal,** cupule, capsule *f*, de la galène; (*b*) *Anat:* emboîture *f* (d'un os); (*c*) **c. and ball,** (jeu *m* de) bilboquet *m*; *Mec.E:* **c.-and-ball joint,** joint *m* à rotule; (*d*) *Artil:* **gas-check c.,** coupelle *f* (de douille d'obus); **fuse c.,** porte-amorce *m inv*; (*e*) *Tchn: Paint:* godet *m*; *Mec.E:* godet, cuvette *f*; **oil-retainer c.,** cuvette d'étanchéité; **lubricating c.,** godet graisseur; **c. valve,** soupape *f* à cloche; **cups of a wind gauge,** coquilles *f* d'un anémomètre; (*f*) *A.Med:* (i) **dry c.,** ventouse sèche; **wet c.,** ventouse scarifiée; sangsue artificielle; (ii) (*for blistering*) cloche *f*; (*g*) *Cost:* (*of brassière*) bonnet *m*. **5.** creux *m* de terrain; cuvette. **6.** (*a*) *Arb:* **c. shake,** roulure *f*; (*b*) *Bot:* **c. moss,** cladonie *f*; (*c*) *Coel:* **c. coral,** corail simple; **Devonshire c. coral,** carophyllie *f*.

cup[2], *v.tr.* (**cupped**) **1.** *A: Med:* ventouser (qn); appliquer, faire, des ventouses à (qn). **2. with her chin cupped in her hand,** le menton dans le creux de la main; **to c. one's hand behind one's ear,** mettre sa main en cornet; **to c. one's hand round one's mouth,** mettre la main en porte-voix. **3.** *Ind:* rendre convexe, bomber (une tôle, etc.).

cup-and-saucer ['kʌpnd'sɔːsər], *a. & s. Moll: F:* **c.-and-s.** (**limpet**), calyptrée *f*.

cupboard ['kʌbəd], *s.* armoire *f*; (*in wall*) placard *m*; **corner c.,** armoire de coin; **store c.,** armoire à provisions; **staircase c.,** caveau *m*, soupente *f* d'escalier; **airing c.,** chauffe-linge *m inv*; *F:* **c. love,** amour intéressé.

cupel[1] ['kjuːpəl], *s. Metall:* coupelle *f* (d'essai); têt *m* de coupellation.

cupel[2], *v.tr.* (*p.t. & p.p.* **cupelled** ['kjuːpəld]) *Metall:* coupeller (l'or, l'argent).

cupellation [kjuːpə'leiʃ(ə)n], *s. Metall:* coupellation *f* (de l'argent, etc.).

cupful ['kʌpful], *s.* pleine tasse, pleine coupe (**of,** de); **add two cupfuls of milk,** ajouter deux tasses de lait.

cuphea [kjuː'fiə], *s. Bot:* cuphæa *m*.

Cupid ['kjuːpid]. **1.** *Pr.n.m.* Cupidon; *Miner:* **Cupid's darts,** flèches *f* d'amour. **2.** *s.* **to paint little Cupids,** peindre des petits Amours; **chubby little Cupids,** Amours joufflus.

cupidity [kjuː'piditi], *s.* cupidité *f*; convoitise *f*; **to arouse c.,** faire naître, allumer, des convoitises.

cupola ['kjuːpələ], *s. Arch:* coupole *f*, dôme *m*; *Navy:* **c. of a gun turret,** coupole de tourelle cuirassée; *Metall:* **c.** (**furnace**), cubilot *m*.

cuppa ['kʌpə], *s. P:* tasse *f* de thé.

cupped [kʌpt], *a.* en forme de tasse, de cuvette; évasé.

cupper ['kʌpər], *s. A.Med:* ventouseur, -euse.

cupping ['kʌpiŋ], *s.* **1.** *A.Med:* application *f* de ventouses; **c. glass,** ventouse *f*. **2.** (*a*) taillage *m* en forme de cuvette; évasement *m*; (*b*) bombement *m* (d'une tôle, etc.); (*c*) **c.** (**of tape**), courbure transversale (de la bande).

cuprammonium [kjuːprə'mouniəm], *s. Ch: Paperm: etc:* cuprammonium *m*; cuproammoniaque *f*; liqueur ammoniacale de cuivre; liqueur cuproammoniacale; réactif *m* de Schweitzer; *Ind: A:* **c. silk,** rayonne *f* à la liqueur ammoniacale de cuivre.

cuprate ['kjuːpreit], *s. Ch:* cuprate *m*.

cuprea [kjuː'priə], *s. Pharm:* **c. bark,** écorce *f* de rémijia.

cuprene ['kjuːpriːn], *s. Ch:* cuprène *m*.

cupreous ['kjuːpriəs], *a.* cuivreux.

Cupressaceae [kjuːpre'seisiːː], *s.pl. Bot:* cupressacées *f*.

cupric ['kjuːprik], *a. Ch:* cuivrique; (acide *m*) cuprique.

cupride ['kjuːpraid], *s. Ch:* cupride *m*.

cupriferous [kjuː'prifərəs], *a.* cuprifère.

cuprite ['kjuːprait], *s. Miner:* cuprite *f*.

cupro-ammonia ['kjuːprouə'mouniə], *s. Ch:* = CUPRAMMONIUM.

cupro-ammoniacal ['kjuːprouæmə'naiəkl], *a. Ch:* cupro-ammoniacal, -aux.

cuprodescloizite ['kjuːproudez'klɔizait], *s. Miner:* cuprodescloizite *f*.

cupromanganese ['kjuːpro'mæŋgəniːz], *s.* cupromanganèse *m*.

cupronickel ['kjuːprou'nikl], *s. Metall:* cupronickel *m*.

cuproscheelite ['kjuːprou'ʃiːlait], *s. Miner:* cuproscheelite *f*.

cuprosilicon ['kjuːprou'silikən], *s. Metall:* cuprosilicium *m*.

cuprotungstite ['kjuːprou'tʌŋstait], *s. Miner:* cupritungstite *f*.

cuprous ['kjuːprəs], *a. Ch:* cuivreux.

cuproxide [kjuː'prɔksaid], *s. Ch:* cuproxyde *m*; *El:* **c. valve,** valve redresseuse au cuproxyde; valve cuproxyde.

cup-shaped ['kʌpʃeipt], *a. Bot:* cupulaire, cupuliforme.

cupular ['kjuːpjulər], *a. Bot:* cupulaire.

cupulate ['kjuːpjuleit], *a. Bot:* cupulé.

cupule ['kjuːpjuːl], *s. Bot: Z:* cupule *f*.

Cupuliferae [kjuːpju'lifəriː], *s.pl. Bot:* cupuliféracées *f*, *A:* cupulifères *f*.

cupuliferous [kjuːpju'lifərəs], *a. Bot:* cupulifère.

cupuliform [kjuː'pjulifɔːm], *a.* cupuliforme.

cur [kəːr], *s.* **1.** cabot *m*, roquet *m*; chien *m* sans race. **2.** *F:* (*of pers.*) homme *m* méprisable; malotru *m*, sale type *m*.

curability [kjuərə'biliti], *s.* curabilité *f*.

curable ['kjuərəbl], *a.* guérissable; (mal) curable.

curaçao, curaçoa ['kjuərəsou], *s.* curaçao *m*.

curacy ['kjuərəsi], *s. Ecc:* vicariat *m*, vicairie *f*.

curare [kjuə'rɑːri], *s.* curare *m*.

curariform [kju'rɑ:rifɔ:m], *a.* curarisant.

curarine [kju'rɑ:r(a)in], *s. Ch:* curarine *f.*

curarization [kju'rɑ:ri'zeiʃ(ə)n], *s. Med:* curarisation *f.*

curarize [kju'rɑ:raiz], *v.tr.* curariser (un animal, etc.).

curassow ['kjuərəsou], *s. Orn:* hocco *m*; **crested c.,** hocco à crête; **galeated c.,** hocco à casque; **globose c.,** hocco globigère; **razor-billed c.,** hocco à bec-en-rasoir, mitu *m.*

curate ['kjuərət], *s.* **1.** vicaire *m*; **c. in charge,** desservant *m*; **perpetual c.,** vicaire titulaire d'une église succursale. **2.** *F: A:* petit tisonnier (plus maniable que celui de la garniture de foyer).

curative ['kjuərətiv]. **1.** *a.* curatif; médicateur, -trice; (onguent *m*) sanatoire. **2.** *s.* remède *m.*

curator [kjuə'reitər], *s.* **1.** conservateur *m* (de musée); curateur *m* (d'université). **2.** *Jur: Scot:* tuteur, -trice, curateur (d'un dément).

curatorship [kjuə'reitəʃip], *s.* fonction *f* de conservateur, de curateur.

curb[1] [kə:b], *s.* **1.** *Harn:* gourmette *f*; **c. bit,** mors *m* de bride, à gourmette; **c. reins,** rênes *f* de mors; **c. chain,** (i) *Harn:* tranchefil *m*; (ii) *Jewel:* gourmette; **to put a c. on one's passions,** refréner, mettre un frein à, ses passions. **2.** (*a*) bord *m*, bordure *f* garde-pavé *m* (de trottoir); rebord *m* de trottoir; margelle *f*, murette *f* (de fontaine, de puits); *Aut:* **to hit the c.,** heurter le trottoir; (*b*) *Arch:* **c. roof,** comble brisé; toit *m*, comble, en mansarde. **3.** *Hyd.E: Min:* cadre porteur; roue *f*, rouet *m*, de fondation (de revêtement de puits); *Min:* roulisse *f.* **4.** *Vet:* tumeur osseuse (à la jambe d'un cheval); courbe *f.*

curb[2], *v.tr.* **1.** gourmer, mettre la gourmette à (un cheval). **2.** réprimer, refréner, contenir, retenir (sa colère); assujettir, maîtriser, brider, refréner, restreindre (ses passions); commander à, modérer (son impatience); freiner (une inflation, etc.). **3.** (*more usu.* KERB) border (un puits, un trottoir); mettre la bordure à (un trottoir).

curbing ['kə:biŋ], *s.* **1.** mise *f* de la gourmette à (un cheval). **2.** refrènement *m* (des instincts).

curbstone ['kə:bstoun], *s.* **1.** pierre *f* (de rebord de trottoir). **2.** *attrib. St.Exch: F: U.S:* **c. market,** marché *m* hors cote, coulisse *f*; **c. broker** (*also* **curbstoner**), coulissier *m.*

Curculionidae [kə:kjuli'ɔnidi:], *s.pl. Ent:* curculionidés *m.*

curcuma ['kə:kjumə], *s.* **1.** *Bot:* curcuma *m.* **2.** *Ch:* **c. paper,** papier *m* curcuma.

curcumin(e) ['kə:kjum(a)in], *s. Ch:* curcumine *f.*

curd [kə:d], *s.* **1.** (lait) caillé *m*; caillebotte *f*; **curds and whey,** lait caillé sucré; **lemon c.,** pâte composée d'œufs, de beurre et de jus de citron. **2. soap curds,** grumeaux *m* de savon.

curdle ['kə:dl]. **1.** *v.tr.* (*a*) cailler (le lait); figer, coaguler (un liquide); glacer, figer (le sang); (*b*) engrumeler (le savon, etc.). **2.** *v.i.* (*of milk*) se cailler, se caillebotter, prendre; (*of blood*) se figer; **my blood curdled,** mon sang s'est figé, s'est glacé; (*b*) (*of soap*) se grumeler, s'engrumeler; se mettre en grumeaux; former des grumeaux.

curdled ['kə:dld], *a.* **1.** coagulé; figé. **2.** grumeleux.

curdy ['kə:di], *a.* caillebotté; ressemblant à du lait caillé.

cure[1] [kjuər], *s.* **1.** guérison *f*; **to achieve, bring about, a c. you must . . .,** pour réaliser, assurer, la guérison il faudra . . .. **2.** (*a*) cure *f*; **milk c.,** cure de lait; **grape c.,** cure de raisins; **rest c.,** cure de repos; **to take a c.,** faire une cure, suivre un traitement; **a three weeks' c. at Vichy,** une saison, une cure, de trois semaines à Vichy; (*b*) remède *m*; **past c.,** (*of pers.*) incurable; (*of thg*) irrémédiable, irréparable; **the c. is worse than the disease,** le remède est pire que le mal; **there is a c. for everything but death,** il y a remède à tout fors la mort. **3.** vulcanisation *f* (du caoutchouc); **hot c., cold c.,** vulcanisation à chaud, à froid. **4.** *Ecc:* **c. of souls,** cure, charge *f*, d'âmes; **benefice with c. of souls,** bénéfice *m* avec cure.

cure[2], *v.tr.* **1. to c. s.o. of an illness, of bad habits,** guérir qn d'une maladie; corriger qn de ses mauvaises habitudes; **to c. an evil,** remédier à un mal; porter remède à un mal; **it has cured my headache,** cela a fait passer mon mal de tête; **he is too far gone to be cured,** sa maladie est trop avancée pour qu'il puisse en guérir; *Prov:* **what can't be cured must be endured,** il faut souffrir ce qu'on ne peut empêcher; où il n'y a pas de remède il faut se résigner. **2.** (*a*) saler, fumer, boucaner (la viande, etc.); sécher (la viande); confire (des sardines); saurer (des harengs); **well cured ham,** jambon *m* d'un bon sel; (*b*) *Leath:* saler (les peaux); (*c*) vulcaniser, cuire (le caoutchouc); *v.i.* (*of rubber*) se vulcaniser; (*d*) conserver (le béton).

cure[3], *s. F: A:* drôle de garçon, drôle de fille; original *m*, -aux; **he's a c.!** c'est un numéro!

cure-all ['kjuərɔ:l], *s.* panacée *f.*

cureless ['kjuəlis], *a.* sans remède; impossible à guérir.

curer ['kjuərər], *s.* **1.** guérisseur, -euse. **2.** saleur *m* (de viande, etc.); confiseur, -euse (de sardines); **herring c.,** caqueur, -euse.

curettage [kjuə'retidʒ], *s. Med:* curettage *m.*

curette[1] [kjuə'ret], *s. Med:* (*instrument*) curette *f.*

curette[2], *v.tr.* **to c. the ear, the womb,** cureter, opérer le curettage de, l'oreille, de l'utérus.

curfew ['kə:fju:], *s.* couvre-feu *m*; **to ring the c. (bell),** sonner le couvre-feu.

curia ['kjuəriə], *s.* (*a*) *Rom.Hist: Ecc:* curie *f*; (*b*) *Hist:* cour *f* de justice.

curial ['kjuəriəl], *a. Rom.Hist: Ecc:* curial, -aux.

Curiatii [kjuəri'eiʃiai], *Pr.n.m.pl. Rom.Hist:* les Curiaces.

curie ['kjuəri], *s. Rad.-A: Meas:* curie *m*; **C. point,** point *m* de Curie.

curietherapy [kjuəri'θerəpi], *s. Med:* curiethérapie *f.*

curing ['kjuəriŋ], *s.* **1.** guérison *f.* **2.** (*a*) salaison *f*, boucanage *m*; confiserie *f* (à l'huile); (*b*) vulcanisation *f*, cuisson *f* (du caoutchouc); (*c*) conservation *f* (du béton); (*d*) *Sug.-R:* **c. house,** purgerie *f.*

curio ['kjuəriou], *s.* curiosité *f*; bibelot *m*; petit objet d'art; **Chinese c.,** chinoiserie *f*; **Japanese curios,** japonaiseries *f*; **c. hunter,** bibeloteur *m*; dénicheur *m* de curiosités; **c.-hunting,** bibelotage *m*; **to go c.-hunting,** aller bibeloter; **c. dealer,** antiquaire *m*; brocanteur, -euse; marchand *m* de curiosités; **c. shop,** magasin *m* d'antiquités, de curiosités; brocante *f.*

curiologic(al) [kjuəriou'lɔdʒik(l)], *a.* curiologique, kyriologique.

curiosity [kjuəri'ɔsiti], *s.* **1.** curiosité *f*; **out of c., from c.,** par curiosité; **I was dying of c., burning with c.,** je mourais de curiosité; je brûlais d'en savoir plus long; **as a matter of c. tell me whether . . .,** je suis curieux de savoir si . . .. **2.** (*curiousness*) **I mentioned it as a matter of c.,** j'en ai fait mention pour la curiosité, la singularité, la rareté, du fait. **3.** (*a*) (*curious object*) curiosité, rareté; **we were taken to see all the curiosities of the town,** on nous a fait voir toutes les curiosités de la ville; **old curiosities,** antiquités *f*, curiosités; bibelots *m* antiques; bric-à-brac *m*; (*b*) (*of pers.*) original *m*, -aux; excentrique *m.*

curious ['kjuəriəs], *a.* **1.** (*a*) (*desirous of knowing*) curieux; **to be c. to see sth.,** avoir la curiosité, être curieux, de voir qch.; **I felt c. to know whether . . .,** j'étais curieux de savoir si . . .; **were you never c. enough to find out who lived in this house?** n'avez-vous jamais eu la curiosité de savoir qui vivait dans cette maison? (*b*) *Pej:* curieux; indiscret, -ète. **2.** (*a*) (*strange*) curieux, singulier; **the c. part about it,** le curieux de l'affaire; **c. sight,** chose curieuse à voir; **a c.-looking object,** un objet d'un aspect bizarre, singulier; (*b*) (*in booksellers' catalogues*) **c. books,** livres curieux (c.-à-d. occultes, érotiques, etc.). **3. c. inquiry,** examen exact, fait avec soin minutieux.

curiously ['kjuəriəsli], *adv.* **1.** curieusement, singulièrement, bizarrement; **c. enough . . .,** chose assez curieuse, assez singulière . . .. **2. c. made,** curieusement ouvré; d'une facture minutieuse. **3.** avec curiosité; indiscrètement.

curiousness ['kjuəriəsnis], *s.* (*a*) curiosité *f*; *Pej:* indiscrétion *f*; (*b*) curieux *m*, étrangeté *f*, singularité *f*, curiosité *f* (d'un lieu, d'un fait).

curium ['kjuəriəm], *s. Ph:* curium *m.*

curl[1] [kə:l], *s.* **1.** (*a*) boucle *f* (de cheveux); frisure *f*, frison *m*; anneau *m* (de cheveux); **large, loose curls,** boucles éparses; **side curls,** *F:* guiches *f*; **to wear one's hair in curls,** porter les cheveux en frisons, en boucles; (*of hair*) **to fall in curls,** tomber en boucles; **false curls,** *F:* chichis *m*; *O:* **c. papers,** papillotes *f*; (*b*) spirale *f* (de fumée); crête recourbée, volute *f* (d'une vague); ondulation *f*, ronce *f* (dans le grain du bois); *Navy:* boucle (du galon porté sur la manche); (*c*) *Metalw:* bordure *f*, bordage *m* (d'une tôle, etc.); **half c.,** bordure rabattue à moitié; **full c.,** bordure terminée. **2.** (*a*) action *f* de se recourber; **c. of the lips,** moue *f* de dédain; **with a c. of the lips,** avec une moue dédaigneuse; (*b*) état bouclé; (*of hair*) **in c.,** bouclé, frisé; **to go out of c.,** (i) (*of hair*) se défriser; (ii) *P: A:* (*of pers.*) perdre son énergie; se sentir (mou) comme une chiffe; **my hair is out of c.,** je suis toute défrisée. **3.** (*a*) *Agr:* early blight *m* (des pommes de terre); enroulement *m* (des feuilles); (*b*) cloque *f* (du pêcher).

curl[2], *v.*

I. *v.tr. & i.* **1.** *v.tr.* (*a*) boucler, friser (les cheveux); **to c. the moustache,** donner un coup de fer à la moustache; **why don't you get your hair curled?** pourquoi ne vous faites-vous pas friser? (*b*) rider, faire onduler (les vagues); **to c. one's lip,** faire la moue, la lippe; abaisser ou retrousser les coins des lèvres (avec dédain); (*c*) *Metalw:* border (une tôle, etc.); (*d*) **to c. sth. round sth.,** enrouler qch. autour de qch. **2.** *v.i.* (*a*) (*of hair*) boucler, friser; (*of paper*) se recroqueviller, se crisper; *F:* **stories that make your hair c.,** histoires *f* qui vous donnent le frisson, qui font dresser les cheveux; *P:* **you drink that, it'll make your hair c.,** buvez-moi ça, ça vous ressuscitera, ça vous fouettera le sang; (*b*) (*of smoke*) s'élever en spirales; tire-bouchonner, tourbillonner; (*of waves*) onduler ou déferler; (*of lip*) se relever, ou s'abaisser, avec dédain; **the smoke is curling up(wards),** la fumée monte en spirales; (*c*) (*of serpent, plant, etc.*) **to c. round sth.,** s'enrouler autour de qch.; (*d*) *Agr:* (*of potatoes*) être atteint de l'early blight. **3.** *v.i. Games: Scot:* jouer au *curling.*

II. (*compound verb*) **curl up. 1.** *v.tr.* (*a*) **to c. up one's lip,** retrousser la lèvre; **to c. up one's moustache,** porter la moustache en croc; (*b*) **to c. (oneself) up,** se rouler en boule; (*of cat, etc.*) se mettre en rond; **to c. (oneself) up in an armchair,** se pelotonner, se blottir, dans un fauteuil; **curled up in bed,** couché en chien de fusil; **cat curled up on a sofa,** chat couché en rond sur un canapé. **2.** *v.i.* (*a*) (*of leaves, paper, etc.*) s'enrouler; (*of nail, point*) se rebrousser; (*of thread, rope*) vriller; (*b*) (*of hedgehog*) se mettre en boule; *F:* (*of pers.*) se renfermer dans le silence; **when we mention it he curls up (like a hedgehog),** quand on lui en parle il se hérisse, se met en boule; (*c*) **he has a bitter tongue, and I have seen him make his opponent absolutely c. up,** il a une langue acérée, et je l'ai vu faire tortiller ses adversaires; (*d*) *Sp: etc: F:* (*of pers.*) s'effondrer; être obligé de renoncer.

curled ['kə:ld], *a.* **1.** (*a*) (*of hair*) frisé; (*of leaf*) crépu; vrillé; **c. moustache,** moustache *f* en croc; (*b*) (tôle) bordée. **2.** *Com:* **c. maple,** (bois d')érable madré. **3.** *Agr:* (pomme de terre) atteinte de l'early blight; *Hort:* (pêcher) cloqué.

curler ['kə:lər], *s.* **1. (hair) c.,** bigoudi *m.* **2.** (*wave*) lame déferlante. **3.** *Scot:* joueur *m* de *curling*;

curlew ['kə:lju:], *s. Orn:* courlis *m*; (*numenius arquata*) courlis cendré, grand courlis; **eskimo c.,** courlis esquimau; **slender-billed c.,** courlis à bec grêle; **long-billed c.,** courlis à long bec; **stone c.,** œdicnème *m* (criard), courlis de terre; **c. jack,** turlu(i) *m*; **c. sandpiper,** (bécasseau *m*) cocorli *m.*

curlicue ['kə:likju:], *s.* **1.** (*with the pen*) trait *m* de plume en parafe; enjolivure *f.* **2.** (*in skating*) figure compliquée.

curling ['kə:liŋ], *s.* **1.** (*a*) frisure *f* (des cheveux); ondulation *f* (des cheveux, des vagues); **c. irons, c. tongs,** fer *m* à friser, frisoir *m*; (*b*) *Metalw:* bordage *m* (des tôles, etc.); **c. tool,** outil *m* de bordage. **2.** *Games:* curling *m* (jeu écossais semblable au jeu de boules; se joue sur la glace en y lançant de grosses pierres plates (*curling stones*) munies d'une poignée).

curliness ['kə:linis], *s.* **1.** frisure *f.* **2.** ondulations *fpl*; sinuosité *f.*

curly ['kə:li], *a.* **1.** (*a*) bouclé, frisé; en spirale; (laitue) frisée; **she had short c. hair,** elle était court bouclée; (*b*) *Typ: F:* **c. bracket,** accolade *f.* **2.** (bois *m*) à grain ondulé; (chemin) sinueux. **3.** *Agr:* (pomme de terre) atteinte de l'early blight; *Hort:* (pêcher) cloqué.

curly-headed, -haired ['kə:lihedid, -hɛəd], *a.* à la tête bouclée, aux cheveux frisés; (*of negro*) crépu.

curly-pate ['kə:lipeit] *s. O:* personne *f* dont les cheveux frisent naturellement; frisé, -ée.

curly-tailed ['kə:li'teild], *a.* **1.** à queue en tire-bouchon. **2.** à queue recourbée.

curmudgeon [kə:'mʌdʒ(ə)n], *s.* **1.** bourru *m.* **2.** grippe-sou *m. pl.* grippe-sou(s); pingre *m.*

currach, curragh[1] ['kʌrəχ, -ək], *s.* coracle *m.*

curragh[2], *s. Dial:* (*Irish*) fondrière *f*; plaine marécageuse; **the C.,** grande plaine du comté de Kildare (centre *m* de camps militaires, champ *m* de courses).

currant ['kʌrənt], *s.* **1.** *Hort:* groseille *f* (à grappes); **red c.,** groseille rouge; **white c.,** groseille blanche; **black c.,** cassis *m*; **c. bush,** groseillier *m*; **red-flowering c., bloody c.,** groseillier sanguin; **red c. jelly,** gelée *f* de groseilles. **2.** *Com:* raisin *m* de Corinthe. **3.** *Ent:* **c. moth,** zérène *f* du groseiller, phalène mouchetée.

currawong ['kʌrəwɔŋ], *s. Orn:* réveilleur *m*, strépère *m.*

currency ['kʌrənsi], *s.* **1.** circulation *f*, cours *m* (de l'argent, des idées); vogue *f*, crédit *m* (des idées); **to give c. to a rumour,** mettre un bruit en circulation; répandre un bruit; (*of news, etc.*) **to gain c.,** s'accréditer. **2.** terme *m* d'échéance, échéance *f* (d'une lettre de change). **3.** unité *f* monétaire (d'un pays); numéraire *m*; monnaie *f*; **payable in c.,** payable en espèces de cours; **foreign c.,** (i) monnaie étrangère; (ii) devise étrangère; **bill in foreign c.,** effet *m* en devise; **foreign c. allowance,** allocation *f* en devises; **c. area,** zone *f* monétaire; **hard,**

soft, c., devise forte, faible; **countries with hard currencies,** pays *m* à change élevé, à devises fortes; **legal (tender) c.,** monnaie légale, courante, libératoire; **paper c.,** papier-monnaie *m*; papiers-valeur *mpl*; numéraire fictif; circulation fiduciaire; **silver c.,** monnaie, numéraire, d'argent; **c. note,** coupure *f* (d'une livre); currency-note *f*; **questions of c.,** questions *f* monétaires.

current[1] [ˈkʌrənt], *a.* (*a*) courant, en cours; *Cmptr:* (carte) en cours de (i) perforation, (ii) lecture; (programme) en cours d'exécution; **c. work,** travail *m* en cours; **c. file,** dossier *m* en train; **to keep a file c.,** tenir un dossier à jour; **c. month,** mois *m* en cours; **c. events,** actualités *f*; **c. number (of a periodical),** dernier numéro (d'une revue); numéro du jour; **the c. treasurer of the association,** l'actuel trésorier de l'association; *Fin: etc:* **c. account,** compte courant; *St.Exch:* liquidation courante; **money on c. account,** dépôt *m* à vue; **c. liabilities,** passif *m* exigible; exigibilités *fpl*; **c. assets,** actif *m* réalisable et disponible, actifs de roulement; **c. price,** prix courant; prix de marché; **the rate of exchange c. in Paris,** le taux de change en cours à Paris; **c. quotations,** cours actuels; **c. income,** revenu courant, présent; **money that is no longer c.,** monnaie qui n'est plus courante, en cours, de mise; **c. loan,** prêt en cours, non remboursé, consenti; (*b*) courant, admis, reçu; **a c. opinion,** une opinion courante; **to be c.,** être accepté, de mise, en vogue; avoir cours; **in c. use,** d'usage courant; très usité; **the word is in c. use,** le mot s'emploie couramment, est d'usage courant; **c. rumours,** bruits *m* qui circulent, qui courent.

current[2], *s.* **1.** courant *m* (d'un cours d'eau, de la marée, etc.); fil *m* de l'eau; **drift c.,** courant de dérive; **flood, ebb, c.,** courant de flot, de jusant; *Nau:* **back c., reverse c.,** revolin *m*; *Hyd.E:* **rip c.,** courant d'attachement; **c. meter,** (i) *Hyd.E:* moulinet *m*; (ii) *Oc:* courantographe *m*; *Meteor:* **air c.,** courant d'air; **to drift with the c.,** se laisser aller au fil de l'eau; *Fig:* suivre le courant; aller à vau-l'eau; **he goes whichever way the c. takes him,** il va comme on le pousse; **to go against the c.,** remonter le courant; *Fig:* aller à contre-courant. **2.** *El: etc:* **electric c.,** courant électrique; **constant c., closed-circuit c.,** courant permanent; **break c., c. at breaking,** courant de rupture; **c. at making,** courant de fermeture; **direct c.,** courant continu; **alternating c.,** courant alternatif; **quiescent c.,** courant de repos; **no-load c.,** courant à vide; **back c.,** courant de retour; **forward c.,** courant direct; **dark c.,** courant d'obscurité; **inverse, reverse, echo, c.,** courant inverse; **interference c.,** courant perturbateur; **eddy, Foucault, currents,** courants de Foucault; **balanced c.,** courant équilibré; **c. balance, c. weigher,** balance *f* de courant; **peak c.,** courant de crête, de pointe; **effective c.,** intensité *f* efficace; **electronic c.,** courant électronique; **space c.,** courant spatial; (*of cathode ray tube*) **beam c.,** courant de faisceau; *Cmptr:* **erasure c.,** courant d'effacement.

currently [ˈkʌrəntli], *adv.* (*a*) actuellement; **it is c. reported that . . .,** le bruit court que . . .; (*b*) couramment, ordinairement, généralement, communément.

curricle [ˈkʌrikl], *s. A.Veh:* voiture *f*, cabriolet *m*, à deux roues et à deux chevaux.

curriculum, *pl.* **-a** [kəˈrikjuləm, -ə], *s.* (*a*) *Sch:* programme *m* d'études; plan *m* d'études; **the c. is too extensive,** le programme est trop chargé; (*b*) **c. vitae,** curriculum vitae *m*.

currier [ˈkʌriər], *s.* corroyeur *m*.

currish [ˈkəːriʃ], *a. O:* **1.** qui ne vaut pas mieux qu'un roquet, qu'un cabot. **2.** hargneux.

currishly [ˈkəːriʃli], *adv. O:* **1.** bassement. **2.** hargneusement.

currishness [ˈkəːriʃnis], *s. O:* **1.** bassesse *f* (d'esprit). **2.** nature hargneuse, querelleuse.

curry[1] [ˈkʌri], *s. Cu:* (*powder or dish*) cari *m*, carry *m*, curry *m*.

curry[2], *v.tr. Cu:* **to c. eggs, etc.,** apprêter des œufs, etc., au cari, au curry; **curried eggs,** œufs *m* à l'indienne.

curry[3], *v.tr.* **1.** (*a*) étriller (un cheval); (*b*) *F: A:* étriller, rosser (qn). **2.** corroyer (le cuir). **3. to c. favour with s.o.,** s'insinuer dans les bonnes grâces de qn; chercher à plaire à qn; s'efforcer de gagner les bonnes grâces de qn; faire sa cour à qn.

currycomb [ˈkʌrikoum], *s.* étrille *f*.

curse[1] [kəːs], *s.* **1.** malédiction *f*, anathème *m*; **a c. on the day when . . .!** maudit soit le jour où . . .! **to lie under a c.,** être sous le coup d'une malédiction; **to call down curses from heaven upon s.o.,** appeler les malédictions du ciel sur qn; lancer des imprécations *f* contre qn; **(chickens and) curses come home to roost,** les malédictions se retournent contre leur auteur; quand on crache en l'air cela vous retombe sur le nez; (*b*) chose maudite, abomination *f*; *B:* **I will make this city a c. to all nations,** je livrerai cette ville en malédiction à toutes les nations de la terre; (*c*) imprécation; juron *m*; gros mot; **to let fly a c.,** lâcher un juron. **2.** (*a*) fléau *m*, calamité *f*; **gambling was his c.,** il avait un penchant invétéré pour le jeu; **here the rabbits are a c.,** ici les lapins sont un fléau; *F:* **the c. of Scotland,** le neuf de carreau; *F:* **it's a perfect c.,** quelle barbe! (*b*) *F:* (*of woman*) **to have the c.,** avoir ses règles.

curse[2]. **1.** *v.tr.* (*a*) maudire, anathématiser (qn, qch.); *Lit:* **cursed** [ˈkəːrsid], **be this people!** anathème sur ce peuple! **cursed be he who moves my bones!** maudit soit celui qui dérangera mes os! **to be cursed** [kəːrst] **by one's subjects,** encourir les malédictions de ses sujets; **to c. s.o. with bell, book, and candle,** invoquer les malédictions de Dieu et de tous les saints sur qn; fulminer une excommunication contre qn; **he is cursed with a violent temper,** il est affligé d'un mauvais caractère; il a pour son malheur un tempérament très violent; **c. (it)!** malédiction! le diable l'emporte! (*b*) **to c. God,** blasphémer le saint nom de Dieu; blasphémer contre Dieu. **2.** *v.i.* blasphémer; sacrer, jurer; **to c. and swear,** jurer et sacrer.

cursed [ˈkəːsid, kəːst], *a.* **1.** maudit; **the spot is c.,** ce lieu est maudit. **2.** *F:* **it's a c. nuisance,** c'est bigrement embêtant, c'est une sale histoire; **what c. weather!** quel fichu, sale, sacré, temps! quel temps abominable! **3.** *A:* (*of pers.*) acariâtre, méchant.

cursedly [ˈkəːsidli], *adv. F:* (*intensive*) diablement, bigrement; salement, rudement (embêtant).

cursedness [ˈkəːsidnis, ˈkʌs-], *s. F:* **the c. of things,** la contrariété des choses.

cursing [ˈkəːsiŋ], *s.* **1.** malédiction(s) *f*. **2.** blasphèmes *mpl*. **3.** jurons *mpl*; gros mots *pl*.

cursitor [ˈkəːsitər], *s. Jur.Hist:* greffier *m* de la Cour de Chancellerie.

cursive [ˈkəːsiv], *a.* cursif; **c. handwriting,** *s.* **cursive,** écriture courante, cursive; cursive *f*.

cursor [ˈkəːsər], *s.* curseur *m* (de règle à calcul).

cursorial [kəːˈsɔːriəl], *a. Z:* **c. birds,** (oiseaux) coureurs *m*.

cursorily [ˈkəːsərili], *adv.* rapidement, à la hâte, en courant; superficiellement.

cursoriness [ˈkəːsərinis], *s.* rapidité *f*, caractère superficiel (d'un examen, d'un coup d'œil).

cursory [ˈkəːsəri], *a.* (coup d'œil) rapide, superficiel; (examen) rapide, hâtif, fait à la hâte; **at a c. glance,** à première vue.

curst [kəːst], *a. A:* = CURSED.

curt [kəːt], *a.* (*of manner, answer, etc.*) brusque; sec, *f* sèche; cassant; bref; **c. answer,** réponse sèche, brève; **he might have been a little less c.,** il aurait pu le prendre sur un ton un peu moins cassant; il aurait pu montrer moins de brusquerie.

curtail [kəːˈteil], *v.tr.* **1.** raccourcir, abréger; écourter (**of,** de); accourcir (une dissertation); tronquer (un ouvrage); *F:* amputer (un article, etc.). **2.** diminuer, restreindre, amoindrir (l'autorité de qn); réduire, rogner, restreindre (ses dépenses); **to c. the output,** restreindre, contingenter, la production. **3. to c. s.o. of his privileges,** enlever ses privilèges à qn; priver qn de ses privilèges.

curtailment [kəːˈteilmənt], *s.* raccourcissement *m*; restriction *f*, diminution *f* (d'autorité, etc.); réduction *f* (de dépenses); *F:* amputation *f* (d'un livre, etc.).

curtail step [ˈkəːtlstep], *s. Const:* marche *f* de départ (d'un escalier).

curtain[1] [ˈkəːtn], *s.* **1.** (*a*) rideau *m*; **to draw the c.,** (i) tirer, ouvrir, (ii) tirer, fermer, le rideau; *F:* **it will be best to draw a c. over what followed,** mieux vaut tirer le rideau, jeter un voile, sur ce qui s'ensuivit; **hung with curtains,** garni de rideaux; **door c.,** portière *f*; *Nau:* **awning curtains,** rideaux de tentes; *Pol:* **the Iron C.,** le rideau de fer; *Arch:* **c. wall,** mur-rideau *m*, *pl.* murs-rideaux; *Mil: etc:* **fire c.,** rideau de feu; *Artil:* **c. fire,** (tir *m* de) barrage *m*; *attrib.* **c. ring, loop, rod,** anneau *m*, embrasse *f*, tringle *f*, de rideau; **c. holder, hook,** patère *f* à embrasse; rinceau *m*; *F:* **c. lecture,** semonce conjugale; sermon *m* d'alcôve; (*b*) *O:* **blind c.,** store *m*; *Aut: etc:* **spring c.,** store, rideau, à enroulement automatique. **2.** *Th:* rideau, toile *f*; **to raise, drop, the c.,** lever, baisser, le rideau; **to ring down the c.,** sonner pour le baisser du rideau; *Fig:* **let us ring down the c. on this scene,** baissons le rideau sur cette scène; **the c. rises at eight sharp,** rideau à huit heures précises; **the c. falls, drops,** le rideau tombe, se baisse; **fireproof c., safety c.,** rideau métallique; rideau de fer; **advertisement c.,** rideau-réclame *m*, *pl.* rideaux-réclame; *F: O:* (*in narrative*) **c.!** tableau! *P:* **it'll be curtains for you if . . .,** vous y laisserez votre peau si . . .; *attrib.* **c. speech,** allocution *f* au baisser du rideau; **c. call,** rappel *m* (d'un acteur) devant le rideau; **to take three c. calls,** être rappelé trois fois; (*short play*) **c. raiser,** lever *m* de rideau; piécette *f*. **3.** (*a*) *Fort:* courtine *f*; (*b*) **c. of troops,** rideau de troupes. **4.** *Locksm:* cache-entrée *m inv* (de clef).

curtain[2], *v.tr.* **1.** garnir (une alcôve, etc.) de rideaux. **2. to c. off a part of a room,** masquer une partie d'une pièce par un rideau.

curtained [ˈkəːtənd], *a.* garni, entouré, de rideaux; (porte) garnie d'une portière; **red.-c. bed,** lit *m* à rideaux rouges.

curtana [kəːˈtɑːnə, -ˈteinə], *s.* épée *f* d'armes à pointe émoussée, portée devant le roi à la cérémonie du sacre (comme symbole de clémence).

curtate[1] [ˈkəːteit], *a. Mth:* **c. cycloid,** cycloïde raccourcie.

curtate[2], *s. Cmptr:* portion horizontale (d'une carte); **lower c., upper c.,** partie basse, haute; portion des rangées inférieures, supérieures.

Curthose [ˈkəːthouz], *Pr.n. Hist:* **Robert C.,** Robert Courte-heuse.

curtilage [ˈkəːtilidʒ], *s. Jur:* pièce *f* de terre attenant à une maison d'habitation; enclos *m* avec habitation.

curtly [ˈkəːtli], *adv.* brusquement, sèchement; d'un ton cassant; d'un ton péremptoire.

curtness [ˈkəːtnis], *s.* brusquerie *f* (de paroles); ton cassant.

curts(e)y[1] [ˈkəːtsi], *s.* révérence *f* (que fait une femme en pliant le genou); **to make, drop, a c. to s.o.,** faire une révérence à qn.

curts(e)y[2]. (*of woman*) **1.** *v.i.* (*a*) faire une révérence (**to s.o.,** à qn); faire la, sa, révérence (à qn); (*b*) *O:* (*with cogn. acc.*) **to c. one's acquiescence,** signifier son consentement par une révérence. **2.** *v.tr.* **she curtsied herself out,** elle fit une révérence et sortit; elle sortit en faisant ses révérences.

curule [ˈkjuərjul], *a. Rom.Ant:* **c. chair, magistracy,** chaise *f* curule, magistrature *f* curule.

curvaceous [kəːˈveiʃəs], *a. F:* (*of woman*) bien roulée, bien carrossée.

curvature [ˈkəːvətjər], *s.* courbure *f*; inflexion *f*; sphéricité *f* (de la terre, etc.); *Mth:* **radius of c.,** rayon *m* de courbure; cintre *m*; *Med:* **c. of the spine,** déviation *f*, déjettement *m*, de la colonne vertébrale; **accident that gave him c. of the spine,** accident *m* qui lui a dévié la colonne vertébrale; *Ph:* **c. of space,** courbure de l'espace; *Opt:* **c. of field,** courbure de champ.

curve[1] [kəːv], *s.* **1.** (*a*) courbe *f*; (*in road*) tournant *m*, virage *m*; **radius of a c.,** rayon *m* de courbure; *Civ.E:* rayon d'une courbe; **c. of small radius,** courbe de faible rayon; **long-radius c., sweeping c.,** courbe à grand rayon; **to take a c.,** (i) (*of train, etc.*) inscrire une courbe; (ii) *Aut: etc:* prendre un virage; *Arch: Const:* **c. of a beam,** cambrure *f* d'une poutre; **c. of an arch,** voussure *f* d'une voûte; **to reverse the c. of a moulding,** contre-profiler une moulure; (*b*) (*of pers.*) *pl.* **curves,** rondeurs *f*, formes *f*; (*c*) *Mth: etc:* **c. of the first, second, degree,** courbe du premier, du second, degré; **to plot a c.,** tracer une courbe; **plane c.,** courbe plane; **polar c.,** courbe polaire; **asymptotic c.,** courbe asymptote; **anallagmatic c.,** anallagmatique *f*; **cosine c.,** cosinusoïde *f*; **harmonic c.,** sinusoïde *f*; **hyperbolic c.,** hyperbole *f*; **probability c.,** courbe en cloche, de probabilité; **loci c.,** courbe de lieux géométriques; **c. fitting,** ajustement *m* de courbe; ajustement statistique; **fitting of an exponential c.,** ajustement par une exponentielle; *Cmptr:* **c. follower,** lecteur *m* de courbe; **c. plotter,** traceur *m* de courbe; *Mec:* **potential energy c.,** courbe d'énergie potentielle; *Ph:* **characteristic c.,** courbe caractéristique; *Opt:* **visibility c.,** courbe de visibilité; *Atom.Ph:* **decay c.,** courbe de décroissance; **dose-effect c.,** courbe d'effet de dose; *El: Elcs:* **load c.,** courbe de charge, de débit; **resonance c.,** courbe de résonance; **magnetization c., B-H c.,** courbe de magnétisation, d'aimantation. **2.** *Draw:* **French c.,** pistolet *m* (de dessinateur).

curve[2]. **1.** *v.tr.* courber, recourber, cintrer, arquer; replier; **to c. the back,** courber le dos; *Const:* **to c. a plate,** cintrer une plaque; *Carp:* **to c. a timber,** dévirer une pièce de bois. **2.** *v.i.* se courber; décrire une courbe; **the road curves round the castle,** la route décrit une (ligne) courbe autour du château; **to c. inwards,** s'infléchir.

curved [ˈkəːvd], *a.* courbé, courbe, cintré, arqué; *Com:* **c. timber,** bois courbe, courbant; **c. nose,** nez busqué; **sharply c.,** à courbure accentuée; **bird with a c. beak,** oiseau *m* au bec retors.

curvet[1] [kəːˈvet], *s. Equit:* courbette *f*.

curvet[2], *v.i.* (**curvet(t)ed**) *Equit:* faire des courbettes, des sauts.

curvi- [ˈkəːvi], *comb.fm.* curvi-.

curvicaudate [ˈkəːviˈkɔːdeit], *a. Z:* curvicaude.

curvidentate ['kə:vi'denteit], *a. Z:* curvidenté.
curvifoliate ['kə:vi'foulieit], *a. Bot:* curvifolié.
curviform ['kə:vifɔ:m], *a.* curviforme.
curvilineal ['kə:vi'liniəl], *a.* curviligne.
curvilinear ['kə:vi'liniər], *a.* curviligne; *Mth: etc:* **c. relationship,** corrélation *f* curvilinéaire; *Mec.E:* **c. motion,** mouvement *m* curviligne.
curvinervate ['kə:vi'nə:veit], *a. Bot:* curvinervé.
curvirostral ['kə:vi'rɔstr(ə)l], *a. Orn:* curvirostre.
curvograph ['kə:vougræf], *s. Mth:* curvigraphe *m.*
curvometer [kə:'vɔmitər], *s. Surv:* curvimètre *m.*
cuscus[1] ['kʌskəs], *s. Bot:* vétiver *m.*
cuscus[2], *s. Z:* couscou *m.*
cuscuta [kə'sk(j)u:tə], *s. Bot:* cuscute *f.*
cusec ['kju:sek], *s. Hyd.E.Meas:* pied *m* cubique par seconde.
cushat ['kʌʃət], *s. Orn: Scot:* (pigeon *m*) ramier *m.*
cush-cush ['kʌʃkʌʃ], *s. Bot:* colocase *f.*
cushion[1] ['kuʃ(ə)n], *s.* **1.** (*a*) coussin *m*; **leather c.,** coussin de cuir; **plain c.,** coussin tendu; **scatter c.,** petit coussin décoratif; **upholstered c.,** coussin capitonné; **c. of fat,** bourrelet *m* de graisse, de chair; (*b*) **(lace) c.,** métier *m*, carreau *m*, coussin, oreiller *m* (pour dentelle aux fuseaux); (*c*) (*hair pad*) crépon *m.* **2.** *Bill:* bande *f*; **the short cushions,** les petites bandes; **square c.,** bande à arête vive; **bevelled c.,** bande à arête abattue; **off the c.,** par la bande; **stroke off the c.,** doublé *m*; **to play off the c.,** bricoler; jouer au doublé; jouer par la bande; faire des effets de bande. **3.** *Mch:* **steam c.,** matelas *m* de vapeur (dans le cylindre); contre-vapeur *f.* **4.** (i) bourrelet, (ii) fourchette *f* (de sabot de cheval). **5.** *Cu:* culotte *f* (de porc, etc.); noix *f* (de veau). **6.** *Arch: Civ.E:* coussinet *m* (de colonne ionique, de pied-droit). **7.** *Bot:* (*a*) **leaf c.,** coussinet foliaire; (*b*) **c. aloe,** haworthia *m.*
cushion[2], *v.tr.* **1.** (*a*) garnir (un siège, etc.) de coussins; (*b*) rembourrer (un siège, etc.). **2.** (*a*) faire asseoir (qn) sur un coussin, des coussins; **to c. s.o. up,** soutenir qn par des coussins; (*b*) dorloter (qn). **3.** amortir (un coup); *Mch:* matelasser (le piston). **4.** *Bill:* acculer (une bille) à la bande.
cushioncraft ['kuʃənkrɑ:ft], *s.* véhicule *m* à coussin d'air.
cushioned ['kuʃənd], *a.* **1.** (*a*) garni de coussins; (siège *m*) à coussins; (*b*) *Rail: etc:* **c. seat,** banquette rembourrée; **leather-c.,** (i) à coussins de cuir; (ii) garni en cuir. **2.** installé sur des coussins. **3.** (coup) amorti; *Tls:* **c. hammer,** marteau amorti. **4.** (voix) ouatée.
cushioning[1] ['kuʃəniŋ], *a.* (effet) amortisseur.
cushioning[2], *s.* **1.** (*a*) garnissage *m* avec des coussins; (*b*) garniture *f* de coussins. **2.** amortissement *m* (des chocs, des cahots, etc.); matelassure *f*, rembourrage *m* antichoc; **air c.,** amortissement pneumatique, par air.
cushion star ['kuʃənstɑ:r], *s. Echin:* poranie *f.*
cushy ['kuʃi], *a. F:* (vie, etc.) facile, pépère; **c. job,** prébende *f*, fromage *m*, filon *m*, (bonne) planque; **to have a c. time of it,** l'avoir pépère.
cusk [kʌsk], *s. Ich:* torsk *m*, brosme *m.*
cusp [kʌsp], *s.* **1.** pointe *f*; *Astr:* **c. of the moon,** corne *f* de la lune. **2.** *Mth:* point *m* de rebroussement, sommet *m* (d'une courbe). **3.** *Arch:* redent *m.* **4.** *Anat: Bot:* cuspide *f*; *Dent:* **supplemental c.,** cuspide secondaire.
cuspal ['kʌsp(ə)l], *a. Dent:* **c. wear,** abrasion *f* des cuspides.
cuspate ['kʌspeit], *a. Arch:* redenté.
cusped [kʌspt], *a.* (*of moon*) à cornes; (*of arch*) redenté.
cuspid ['kʌspid], *s.* (dent) canine (*f*).
cuspidal ['kʌspid(ə)l], *a.* **1.** *Mth:* **c. edge (of developable curve),** arête *f* de rebroussement. **2.** (dent) canine.
cuspidate(d) ['kʌspideit(id)], *a.* **1.** *Bot:* (*of leaf, etc.*) cuspidé; **cuspidate-leaved,** cuspidifolié. **2. cuspidate tooth,** dent canine.
cuspidine ['kʌspidain], *s. Miner:* cuspidine *f.*
cuspidor ['kʌspidɔ:r], *s.* crachoir *m.*
cuss [kʌs], *s. F:* **1.** malédiction *f*; juron *m*; **it isn't worth a (tinker's) c.,** ça ne vaut pas un pet de lapin, le pet d'un âne mort; ça ne vaut pas un clou; *O:* **c.-word,** juron; gros mot. **2.** (*of pers.*) individu *m*, type *m*, client *m*; **an awkward c.,** un mauvais coucheur.
cussed ['kʌsid], *a. F:* (*a*) damné, sacré; **it's a c. nuisance,** c'est bigrement embêtant, c'est une sale histoire; (*b*) (*of pers.*) entêté.
cussedly ['kʌsidli], *adv. F:* bigrement.
cussedness ['kʌsidnis], *s. F:* (= *cursedness*) perversité *f*, entêtement *m*; **out of pure, sheer, c.,** par esprit de contradiction; rien que pour embêter le monde; de parti pris; **the c. of things,** l'ironie *f* des choses.
custard ['kʌstəd], *s.* **1.** **(egg) c.,** crème anglaise; **baked c.,** crème cuite au four; flan *m*; **caramel c.,** crème brûlée, renversée, au caramel; **c. powder,** (poudre pour faire la) crème anglaise; crème express. **2.** *Cin: etc:* **c. pie,** tarte à la crème (utilisée comme projectile). **3.** *Bot:* **c. apple,** anone réticulée, muriquée; *F:* cachiment *m*, corossol *m*, cœur-de-bœuf *m*; **c.-apple (tree),** corossolier *m*, asiminier *m.*
custerite ['kʌstərait], *s. Miner:* cuspidine *f.*
custodial [kʌs'toudiəl]. **1.** *a.* (fonctions *fpl*, responsabilité *f*) de gardien, de surveillance. **2.** *s. Ecc:* custode *f* (recouvrant le saint ciboire, pour reliques, etc.).
custodian [kʌs'toudiən], *s.* gardien, -ienne; (*of museum, etc.*) conservateur *m.*
custody ['kʌstədi], *s.* **1.** garde *f* (d'enfants, etc.); **to have c. of s.o., of sth.,** avoir la garde de qn, de qch.; **the children remain in the c. of their father,** les enfants demeurent à la garde du père; **to be in the c. of s.o.,** être confié à la garde de qn; être sous la garde de qn; **to leave a sum of money in s.o.'s c.,** laisser une somme d'argent à la garde de qn; **in safe c.,** sous bonne garde, en lieu sûr; *F:* sous les verrous; **to place securities in safe c.,** déposer des titres en garde; mettre des titres en dépôt; **safe-c. receipt,** récépissé *m* de dépôt. **2.** emprisonnement *m*; détention *f*; **to take s.o. into c.,** arrêter qn; mettre qn en état d'arrestation; constituer qn prisonnier; **to give s.o. into c.,** faire arrêter qn; remettre qn aux mains de la police; **to be in c.,** être en détention préventive; être détenu préventivement; être en état de prévention; **he was taken away in c.,** il fut emmené prisonnier.
custom ['kʌstəm], *s.* **1.** coutume *f*, usage *m*, habitude *f*; **according to c.,** selon l'usage; **it is the c. of the country,** c'est la pratique, l'habitude, la coutume, du pays; **it is becoming quite the c. to. . .,** cela devient l'habitude, la coutume, de . . .; **it was a c. with him to. . .,** il avait l'habitude, coutume, de . . .; **the manners and customs (of a country),** les us *m* et coutumes (d'un pays). **2.** *Jur:* droit coutumier, coutume (d'un pays). **3.** *pl. Adm:* **customs,** douane *f*; **custom(s) officer,** douanier *m*; **customs broker,** agent *m* en douanes; **customs station, post, house,** (poste *m*, bureau *m*, de) douane; **custom(s) duties,** droits *m* de douane; **customs declaration,** déclaration *f* de, en, douane; **customs regime, tariff,** régime, tarif, douanier; **customs union,** union douanière; **to pass, get through, the customs,** passer la douane, en douane, par la douane; **to clear one's luggage through the customs,** dédouaner ses bagages; **customs examination, formalities,** visite douanière; visite de la douane; la visite en douane; vérification *f* en douane; **customs clearance,** expédition douanière; expédition en douane; **to effect customs clearance,** procéder aux formalités de la douane; *Aut: O:* **International Customs Pass,** carnet *m* de passage en douane, de passages en douanes; **customs permit,** acquit-à-caution *m*, *pl.* acquits-à-caution. **4.** *Com:* (*a*) (*of business*) clientèle *f*; **we should lose all our c.,** nous perdrions toute notre clientèle; *F:* ça nous coulerait; (*b*) patronage *m*, pratique *f* (du client); **to lose s.o.'s c.,** perdre un client; (*c*) *attrib.* **c. built, c. designed, c. made,** fait, fabriqué, sur commande, sur demande; hors série, personnalisé; adapté aux besoins particuliers de l'utilisateur; *Aut:* **c. built body,** carrosserie spéciale; *Tail:* **c.(-made) clothes,** vêtements (faits) sur mesure.
customable ['kʌstəməbl], *a.* soumis aux droits de douane.
customarily ['kʌstəmərili], *adv.* ordinairement, habituellement, d'habitude.
customariness ['kʌstəmərinis], *s.* habitude *f*, fréquence *f.*
customary ['kʌstəm(ə)ri]. **1.** *a.* (*a*) accoutumé, habituel, ordinaire, d'usage; **a. c. evil,** un mal habituel, coutumier; **the c. toasts were drunk,** on a porté les toasts rituels, les toasts d'usage; **at the c. hour,** à l'heure accoutumée; **it is c. to. . .,** il est de coutume, d'usage, de . . .; **it is c. to pay him a visit,** il est de règle de lui rendre visite, qu'on lui rende visite; **as is c.,** comme il est d'usage, comme à l'accoutumée; (*b*) *Jur:* **c. law,** droit coutumier; coutume *f* (d'une province, etc.); **c. right,** droit *m* d'usage; **c. clause,** clause *f* d'usage. **2.** *s. Jur:* (*collection of customs*) coutumier *m*; coutume *f* (d'un lieu).
customer ['kʌstəmər], *s.* **1.** (*a*) (*of shop, etc.*) client, -ente; (*of bank, etc.*) déposant, -ante; (*of public house, etc.*) consommateur *m*; (*of restaurant, etc.*) **regular c.,** habitué, -ée; **he's a c. of ours,** c'est un de nos clients; il se fournit chez nous; (*b*) *Cmptr:* **c. file,** fichier *m* (des) clients; **c. engineer,** inspecteur *m* (en clientèle); technicien *m* d'entretien; **c.-developed program(me),** programme écrit par l'utilisateur, par le client. **2.** *F:* individu *m*, type *m*; **an odd, queer, c.,** un drôle de type, de numéro; **a rough, ugly, c.,** un sale type, un mauvais coucheur; un brutal; **an awkward c.,** un type pas commode.
customizable [kʌstə'maizəbl], *a.* personnalisable.
customization [kʌstəmai'zeiʃ(ə)n], *s.* adaptation *f* aux besoins du client; personnalisation *f.*
customize ['kʌstəmaiz], *v.tr.* faire sur commande; personnaliser, adapter (un appareil, etc.) en vue d'une utilisation particulière.
custos, *pl.* **-odes** ['kʌstɔs, kʌs'toudi:z], *s.* gardien *m*; *Hist:* **c. rotulorum,** garde *m* des archives (fonction exercée par le doyen des juges de paix du comté).
cut[1] [kʌt], *s.* **1.** (*a*) coupe *f*; **to make a clean c.,** trancher net; **the first c.,** l'entame *f*; **crew c.,** cheveux (taillés) en brosse; **(power, electricity) c.,** coupure *f* de courant; (*b*) coupure (dans une pièce de théâtre, etc.); **the censor made some cuts in the film,** le censeur a fait des coupures dans le film; *Journ: etc:* **to make cuts in an article,** faire des coupes dans un article; (*c*) *Cin:* **c. from one shot to another,** raccord *m* de deux plans; **jump c.,** ellipse *f*; (*d*) *Com: etc:* réduction *f* (de prix, de dépenses); **wage cuts, cuts in wages,** réductions de salaires, sur le traitement; **to restore the cuts,** supprimer les réductions; (*e*) *Cards:* coupe; **c. for partners,** tirage *m* pour les places; (*f*) *Cr: Ten:* coup tranchant; (*g*) *F: O:* **to give s.o. the c. direct,** passer près de qn sans le saluer; faire à qn l'insulte de ne pas le reconnaître. **2.** (*a*) coup *m* (de couteau, d'épée); taillade *f*; **sabre c.,** coup de sabre; **to go for s.o. c. and thrust,** attaquer qn d'estoc et de taille; **c.-and-thrust blade,** lame faite pour frapper d'estoc et de taille; **it was c. and thrust,** c'était une lutte acharnée; **the c. and thrust of parliamentary debate,** le jeu d'attaques et de ripostes des débats parlementaires; **c.-and-thrust character,** caractère batailleur; (*b*) **c. with a whip,** coup de fouet; sanglade *f*, cinglon *m*; **to give s.o. a c. with one's whip,** sangler un coup de fouet à qn; **c. with a cane,** coup de canne, de badine; (*c*) coup, revers *m* (de fortune); trait acéré; sarcasme blessant; **the unkindest c. of all,** le coup de pied de l'âne. **3.** *Metalw: etc:* (*a*) taille *f*, entaille *f* (d'une lime); **rough c.,** grosse taille; **single c.,** taille simple; **second c.,** taille seconde, taille demi-douce; **smooth c.,** taille douce; **cross c.,** taille croisée; (*b*) passe *f* (de machine-outil); **heavy c.,** passe profonde; forte passe; **finishing c.,** passe de finition, de finissage; dernière passe; **to make, take, a c.,** exécuter une passe; prendre une passe; **depth of c.,** profondeur *f* de passe; (*c*) **milling c.,** dressage *m* à la fraise; (*d*) **saw c.,** trait *m* de scie; (*e*) *Min:* havée *f*; coupe. **4.** (*a*) (*wound, gash*) coupure, estafilade *f*; balafre *f*, entaille; **c. in the arm,** coupure, entaille, au bras; (*in sword fight*) **c. in the forearm,** estafilade à l'avant-bras; **c. across the cheek,** balafre à la joue; **the surgeon made a small c. in the finger,** le chirurgien fit une légère incision au doigt; (*b*) *Hort:* enture *f*; (*c*) *Civ.E: Rail:* fouille *f*, saignée *f*, tranchée *f*, déblai *m*; *Mec.E:* saignée (pour graissage); (*d*) *U.S: Rail:* (voie *f* en) déblai; (*e*) *For:* **allowable c.,** possibilité *f* de coupe. **5.** (*a*) illustration *f*, gravure *f*, vignette *f*; planche *f*; *Typ:* **letterpress and cuts,** texte *m* et illustrations; (*b*) diagramme *m*, schéma *m.* **6.** *Th:* trappillon *m* (pour les fermes). **7.** coupe (d'un vêtement, d'une voile); taille (d'une pierre précieuse). **8.** (*a*) *F:* **to be a c. above s.o., sth.,** être supérieur à qn, de meilleure qualité que qch.; **she was a c. above the other girls,** elle appartenait à un niveau social au-dessus des autres; (*b*) **to draw cuts,** tirer à la courte paille. **9.** (*a*) *Cu:* **c. off the joint,** tranche *f*, morceau *m*, de rôti; **prime c.,** morceau de (premier) choix; **cheap cuts,** bas morceaux; *U.S:* **cold cuts,** assiette anglaise; (*b*) *F:* commission *f*; gratte *f*; **he gets his c.,** il a part au gâteau. **10. short c.,** raccourci *m*, chemin *m* de traverse; **to take a short c.,** couper au plus court; prendre (par) un raccourci; **I took the short c.,** j'ai pris par le plus court, j'ai pris la traverse; **this is a short c. to the town,** ce chemin est plus court pour la ville. **11.** *Danc:* entrechat *m.* **12.** *F:* absence *f* (d'une classe, etc.) sans permission.
cut[2], *v.*
I. *v.tr. & i.* **(cut; cut; pr.p. cutting) 1.** couper, tailler; (*in slices*) trancher; hacher (le tabac, etc.); **to c. one's finger,** s'entailler, se couper, le doigt; se couper, se faire une entaille, au doigt; **he was badly c. (about),** il a reçu de nombreuses blessures; **my article has been all c. about,** mon article a été mutilé; **to c. one's nails,** se couper les ongles; **to have one's hair c.,** se faire couper les cheveux; se faire tailler les cheveux; **the wind c. his face,** le vent lui coupait, lui cinglait, le visage; **this remark c. him to the quick,** cette parole l'a piqué au vif; **to c. the hay,** couper, faucher, les foins; **once the hay is cut,** une fois la fenaison faite; **tool that cuts well,** outil *m* qui coupe, tranche, bien; **knife that cuts like a razor,** couteau *m* qui tranche comme un rasoir; (*with passive force*) **cloth that cuts easily,** tissu *m* qui se coupe facilement; **fog you could c. with a knife,** brouillard *m* à couper au couteau; **to c. and thrust,** frapper d'estoc et de taille; **that cuts both ways,** c'est une épée, un argument, à deux tranchants, une arme à double tranchant;

to c. and come again, revenir au plat; y revenir; *F:* y repiquer; **to have enough to c. and come again,** en avoir à bouche que veux-tu; **to c. at s.o.,** décocher un coup d'épée, de fouet, etc., à qn; **to c. (away) at sth.,** (i) couper assidûment, (ii) coupailler, qch.; **to c. into a loaf,** entamer un pain; **to c. into a pie,** faire une brèche dans un pâté; **to c. the wedding cake,** entamer le gâteau de noces; **to c. into the bark,** inciser l'écorce; **the work cuts into my free time,** ce travail empiète sur mes heures de liberté; **the string is cutting (into) me,** le cordon me coupe la chair; **this cuts across all my principles,** ceci va à l'encontre de tous mes principes; *Bill:* **to c. the cloth,** faire un accroc au tapis; *Bookb:* **to c. the edges,** rogner les tranches; **to c. the boards,** rabaisser les cartons; *Com:* **to c. prices,** baisser les prix; *Aut: etc:* **to c. a corner (close),** prendre un virage à la corde; *usu. Pej:* **to c. a corner, corners,** (i) faire des économies, lésiner, (ii) y aller trop vite, couper court, contourner les règlements, (iii) contourner la loi (pour atteindre son but); **to c. a piece to length,** couper une pièce à la longueur; **to c. wood to measure,** débiter du bois; *Metalw:* **to c. a piece to pattern,** profiler une pièce sur modèle; *Nau:* **to c. one's moorings,** couper, filer, ses amarres; **to c. and run,** (i) *Nau:* filer le câble; (ii) *F:* filer (en vitesse); prendre ses jambes à son cou; montrer les talons, jouer des talons; décamper, se sauver; *F: A:* **to c. (it),** se trotter; se la casser; *F:* **c. along (now)!** sauve-toi! file! *U.S:* **to c. loose,** (i) s'émanciper; (ii) s'évader, **to c. loose with an axe,** frapper comme un fou avec une hache; **to c. a connection with s.o.,** rompre les relations avec qn. **2.** (*a*) **to c. sth. in two, in(to) pieces,** couper qch. en deux; couper qch. en, par, morceaux; dépecer (un poulet, etc.); **to c. an army to pieces,** tailler une armée en pièces; écharper une armée; **to c. sth. to ribbons, to bits,** déchiqueter qch.; *F:* **to c. a play to pieces,** soumettre une pièce à une critique sanglante; éreinter une pièce; **to c. an animal loose,** délier, détacher, une bête; **to c. oneself loose from sth.,** se séparer, se libérer, de qch.; (*b*) **to c. an actor's part, lines,** faire des coupures dans le rôle d'un acteur; **the film had to be c. to satisfy the censor,** on a dû faire des coupures dans le film pour satisfaire le censeur; **to c. sth. short,** couper court à qch.; **to c. a speech, a visit, short,** abréger un discours, une visite; raccourcir un discours; écourter une visite; **to c. s.o. short,** couper la parole à qn; **to c. a long story short,** pour abréger; pour dire la chose en deux mots; pour le trancher net; en un mot comme en cent; pour en finir; en fin de compte; à la fin du compte; *F:* **c. it short!** soyez bref! *P:* **c. the cackle!** assez jacassé! la ferme! **to c. the engine,** couper les gaz; *Cin: Rec: etc:* **c.!** coupez! (*c*) *Cin:* (*edit*) procéder au montage (d'un film). **3.** (*a*) couper, tailler, entailler (une pierre, du verre, etc.); percer, creuser (un canal); pratiquer (une ouverture); graver, ciseler, sculpter (des caractères sur le métal ou la pierre); couper, tailler (un habit); **to c. an opening, a staircase, in a wall,** pratiquer une ouverture, un escalier, dans un mur; **there was a new name c. on his tombstone,** il y avait sur sa pierre un nouveau nom de gravé; *Mount:* **to c. steps,** tailler; *Rec:* **to c. a disc,** faire un disque; (*b*) **to c. velvet,** ciseler le velours; (*c*) **to c. a screw,** fileter, décolleter, une vis; **to c. a screw-hole,** tarauder un trou; **to c. a new thread inside a nut,** retaper un écrou; (*d*) *Min:* haver. **4.** (*a*) **to c. one's way through the wood,** se frayer, s'ouvrir, un chemin à travers le bois; **to c. across the fields, across country,** couper à travers champs; **to c. through sth.,** passer à travers qch.; transpercer qch.; **to c. through the waves, the air,** fendre les eaux, l'air; **the place where the lines, the roads, c. one another,** l'endroit où les lignes, les routes, se croisent, se coupent; (*b*) **to c. into the conversation,** intervenir dans, interrompre brusquement, la conversation; (*c*) *F: A:* **c. down, along, the street and see if he's there,** cours jusqu'au bout de la rue voir s'il est là; **c. out and get some sausages,** cours acheter des saucisses. **5.** (*general meaning*) **to c. capers, a dash, a tooth, etc.,** faire des cabrioles, de l'effet, une dent, etc. **6.** *Cards:* **(cut; cut;** *pr.p.* **cutting)** (*for deal*) tirer pour les places, pour la donne. **7.** *Cr: Ten:* trancher, couper (la balle). **8. to c. s.o. (dead),** faire semblant de ne pas voir qn; passer près de qn sans le saluer; tourner le dos à qn; **he c. me dead,** il m'a passé raide (sans me saluer). **9.** *F:* (*a*) manquer exprès à (un rendez-vous); *Sch:* sécher (un cours, une classe); **to c. school,** faire l'école buissonnière; (*b*) **to c. the whole concern,** abandonner l'affaire; renoncer à l'affaire. **10.** *Vet:* châtrer (un cheval). **11.** *v.i.* (*of horse*) s'entretailler. **12.** *Danc:* battre des entrechats.

II. (*compound verbs*) **1. cut away,** *v.tr.* (*a*) couper, ôter, retrancher, élaguer; (*b*) évider, entailler; *Wood-Engr:* échopper; (*c*) donner du dégagement à (une pièce).

2. cut back, (*a*) *v.tr.* (i) élaguer, recéper, rabattre (un arbre, une vigne, etc.); (ii) baisser (les prix); diminuer (la production, etc.); (*b*) *v.i.* (i) s'en retourner; rebrousser chemin; (ii) *Cin:* (*of action*) revenir en arrière.

3. cut down, *v.tr.* (*a*) (i) couper, abattre (un arbre); couper (le blé); **I want that tree c. down,** je voudrais faire abattre cet arbre-là; (ii) sabrer, abattre (un adversaire); faucher (les troupes ennemies); (*b*) recéper (des arbustes); menuiser (le bois); abréger, élaguer, émonder (un discours, etc.); tronquer (un ouvrage); couper, réduire, restreindre, rogner (des dépenses); *Ind:* restreindre (la production); **to c. down s.o.'s allowance or profits,** *F:* rogner les morceaux à qn; **to c. down expenses,** restreindre les dépenses; réduire les frais; *F:* mettre de l'eau dans son vin; (*c*) **to c. down a man who is hanging,** couper la corde d'un pendu; (*d*) **to c. down trousers (to make shorts),** raccourcir un pantalon; **she cuts down her dresses for the child,** elle taille dans ses robes pour habiller la petite; (*e*) *Sp: Turf:* **to c. down (the field),** démarrer (et passer ses concurrents); (*f*) *v.i.* **to c. down on cigarettes,** fumer moins.

4. cut in, *v.i.* (*a*) *Cards:* (r)entrer dans le jeu (à la place du joueur écarté au sort); (*b*) (i) se mêler à la conversation; placer son mot; intervenir; (ii) *Tp:* faire intrusion (dans une conversation); (*c*) *Danc:* enlever la danseuse de qn; (*d*) *Rac:* couper la ligne; couper un concurrent; *Aut:* couper la route à qn (après avoir doublé), faire une queue de poisson; croiser une voiture; **he cut in (on my car),** sa voiture croisa, coupa, la mienne; (*e*) (i) *El:* (*of cutout*) se fermer; coller; **the cutout cuts in too late,** le conjoncteur se ferme trop tard; (ii) *v.tr. El:* **to c. in a resistance,** intercaler une résistance; (iii) *v.tr. F:* **to c. s.o. in,** donner à qn sa part du gâteau.

5. cut off, *v.tr.* (*a*) couper, découper, trancher (un morceau); détacher (un coupon de rente); **to c. off a piece of sth. (from sth.),** détacher, retrancher, un morceau de qch. (de qch.); lever un morceau (sur qch.); **to c. off a sample,** prélever un échantillon; **to c. off s.o.'s head,** couper, trancher, la tête à qn; **to c. off a limb, s.o.'s limb,** amputer un membre; amputer qn; **to c. off one's finger,** se couper le doigt; (i) perdre un doigt; (ii) se mutiler d'un doigt; **to c. off the head of a pile,** couper, araser, la tête d'un pieu; **to c. off a rivet,** cisailler un rivet; *Lit:* **to be c. off in the prime of life, in one's prime,** être emporté, fauché, à la fleur de l'âge; (*b*) **to c. off s.o.'s retreat,** couper la retraite à qn; **to c. off the enemy,** couper la ligne de retraite, la route, de l'ennemi; **army c. off from the sea,** armée coupée de ses communications avec la mer; **to be c. off from the main body,** être coupé du gros de l'armée; se trouver isolé; **c. off from all the enjoyments of life,** privé de toutes les jouissances de la vie; **to c. oneself off from the world,** se retirer du monde, dans la solitude; **paper c. off from news,** journal sevré d'informations; (*c*) *Tp:* couper (qn); **don't c. me off,** ne coupez pas; (*d*) couper, supprimer, détendre, intercepter (la vapeur, etc.); *El:* **to c. off the current,** couper, interrompre, le courant; *I.C.E:* **to c. off the ignition,** couper l'allumage; *Av:* **to land with the engine c. off,** atterrir hélice calée; **to c. off s.o.'s water, gas,** couper, supprimer, l'eau, le gaz, à qn; *Aut:* **to c. off the petrol,** couper l'arrivée de l'essence; **to c. off s.o.'s supplies,** couper, supprimer, les vivres à qn; priver qn d'approvisionnements; **to c. s.o. off with a shilling,** déshériter qn; (*e*) **to c. off the negotiations,** couper court aux négociations ((i) les interrompre, (ii) y mettre fin).

6. cut out, *v.tr.* (*a*) (i) couper, enlever (qch.); retrancher (un passage d'un livre); **to c. out details,** élaguer des détails; *Surg:* exciser (une tumeur, etc.); (ii) *F:* **to c. s.o. out,** couper l'herbe sous le pied de qn; supplanter qn; souffler la place à qn; éclipser qn; **he's trying to c. me out with my girlfriend,** il voudrait m'évincer auprès de mon amie; **big traders c. out the small,** les gros poissons mangent les petits; (iii) **to c. out cattle from a herd,** détacher des bêtes d'un troupeau; (*b*) (i) **to c. out pictures from a book,** découper des images dans un livre; **to c. out a garment,** couper, tailler, découper, un vêtement; **to c. out a pattern, etc. (with stamping press),** frapper un patron; **to be c. out for sth.,** être fait, taillé, pour qch.; être né pour qch.; avoir des dispositions pour qch.; **he's c. out for teaching,** il a la vocation du professorat; **he's not c. out to be, for, a leader,** il n'est pas de taille à être chef; il n'est pas taillé, fait, pour commander; il n'a pas l'étoffe d'un grand capitaine; (ii) échancrer (une robe, etc.); (iii) **to c. a statue out of wood,** tailler une statue dans le bois; (*c*) (i) *Mec.E: etc:* **to c. out a part,** supprimer, retrancher, un organe; *El:* mettre un organe hors (de) circuit; *Ind: Nau:* **to c. out a boiler,** isoler une chaudière; **on Sundays we c. out tea,** le dimanche nous supprimons le goûter; **to c. out everything that is not necessary,** s'en tenir au principal; **to c. out luxuries,** se retrancher tout luxe; **to c. out smoking,** renoncer à fumer; *F:* **c. out the threats!** pas de menaces! **c. it out!** ça suffit maintenant! ça va comme ça! (ii) *v.i. El:* (*of cutout*) s'ouvrir; décoller; **to c. out too soon,** s'ouvrir trop tôt; (*d*) *v.i. Cards:* couper à qui se retirera du jeu (pour admettre un joueur qui attend son tour).

7. cut up, *v.tr.* (*a*) couper, débiter (le bois, la viande); détailler (une pièce, etc.); découper, dépecer, démembrer (une volaille, etc.); équarrir (un cheval, etc.); hacher (des légumes, etc.); défoncer, effondrer (un chemin, le terrain); tailler en pièces, défoncer (une armée); *F:* critiquer sévèrement, éreinter (un livre); *F:* (*of pers., with passive force*) **to c. up well,** *A:* **to c. up fat,** laisser une fortune considérable; **to c. up the bread,** tailler le pain par morceaux; (*for soup*) tailler la soupe; **crops c. up by the hail,** récoltes hachées par la grêle; **the army was badly c. up in the fight,** l'armée a souffert de fortes pertes, a été fort maltraitée, dans le combat; **coast c. up into deep bays,** côte découpée en golfes profonds, échancrée, dentelée, de golfes profonds; (*b*) *F:* (i) **to be very c. up by a piece of news,** être démonté, profondément affecté, affligé, par une nouvelle; **don't be so c. up about it,** ne vous affligez pas ainsi; (ii) *v.i.* **to c. up rough,** se fâcher; se mettre en colère; grincher; **he c. up very rough (about it),** il a très mal pris la chose.

cut[3], *a.* **1. c. glass,** cristal taillé; **c. diamond,** diamant taillé; **c. velvet,** velours ciselé; **c. nail,** clou découpé, étampé; **well-c. suit,** complet *m* de bonne coupe; **low-c. dress,** robe décolletée; **c. and dried,** *occ.* **c. and dry, opinions, programme,** opinions toutes faites; programme arrangé, préparé, d'avance; **the work is c. and dried,** la besogne est toute taillée. **2. c. prices,** prix réduits; **c.-price goods,** marchandises vendues au rabais. **3.** *P: A:* (*a*) ivre, pompette; (*b*) stupide, bête.

cutaneous [kju'teiniəs], *a.* cutané.

cutaway ['kʌtəwei]. **1.** *a.* entaillé; évidé; **c. illustration,** vue *f* en coupe. **2.** *a. & s.* **c. (coat),** jaquette *f.* **3.** *s.* **c.,** dégagement *m* d'une charnière, etc.). **4.** *a. & s. Cin:* **c. (shot),** parenthèse *f.*

cutback ['kʌtbæk], *s.* **1.** *Cin: A:* retour *m* en arrière. **2.** réduction *f* (de la production, d'un budget). **3.** *Arb:* plant ravalé. **4.** *Civ.E:* cut-back *m*; **c. asphalt,** brai fluxé, asphalte *m* de pétrole fluxé.

cutch [kʌtʃ], *s. Com:* = CATECHU.

cute [kju:t], *a. F:* **1.** (*a*) (*of pers.*) malin, -igne; rusé, dégourdi, déluré; (*b*) **c. idea,** idée originale. **2.** *esp. U.S:* (*of pers., thg*) gentil, mignon; *Pej:* mièvre.

cutely ['kju:tli], *adv. F:* **1.** avec ruse, habilement; ingénieusement. **2.** joliment, d'une manière charmante.

cuteness ['kju:tnis], *s. F:* **1.** intelligence *f,* finesse *f.* **2.** charme *m*; *usu. Pej:* mièvrerie *f.*

cutey ['kju:ti], *s.f. esp. U.S: F:* **1.** petite rusée; petite délurée. **2.** mignonne, poupée.

cuticle ['kju:tikl], *s.* **1.** *Anat:* épiderme *m,* cuticule *f*; *Toil:* **c. pen,** repousse-peaux *minv,* repoussoir *m.* **2.** *Bot: Biol:* cuticule; pellicule *f* (du riz, etc.).

cuticular [kju'tikjulər], *a.* cuticulaire, cuticuleux.

cutie ['kju:ti], *s.f.* = CUTEY.

cut-in ['kʌtin], *s.* **1.** *Cin:* plan *m* raccord. **2.** *El:* conjoncteur *m.*

cutin ['kju:tin], *s. Bot:* cutine *f.*

cutinization [kjutini'zeiʃ(ə)n], *s. Bot:* cutinisation *f.*

cutinized ['kjutinaizd], *a. Bot:* **c. membrane,** membrane cutinisée; **to become c.,** se cutiniser.

cutis ['kju:tis], *s. Anat:* derme *m.*

cutlass ['kʌtləs], *s.* **1.** *Nau:* sabre *m* d'abordage. **2.** *U.S:* couteau *m* de chasse. **3.** *Ich:* **c. fish,** ceinture *f* d'argent.

cutler ['kʌtlər], *s.* coutelier *m.*

cutlery ['kʌtləri], *s.* **1.** coutellerie *f.* **2.** *Com:* coutellerie et argenterie *f* de table; **canteen of c., c. cabinet,** coffre *m* de coutellerie et orfèvrerie de table; ménagère *f*; **c. basket,** ramasse-couverts *m inv*; **c. works,** (fabrique *f* de) coutellerie *f.*

cutlet ['kʌtlit], *s. Cu:* **1.** côtelette *f* (de mouton, de veau). **2.** croquette *f* (de volaille, etc.) en forme de côtelette.

cutoff ['kʌtɔf], *s.* **1.** (*a*) *Geog:* nouveau lit (coupé par une rivière en évitant un bras mort, etc.); **c. meander,** méandre recoupé; (*b*) *U.S:* chemin *m* de traverse; raccourci *m.* **2.** *Mch:* (*a*) obturateur *m* (du cylindre); (*b*) fermeture *f* de l'admission; occlusion *f,* exclusion *f* (de la vapeur); **c. valve,** dispositif *m* de détente; **c. at 10% of stroke,** détente *f* au dixième; *I.C.E:* **late c.,** retard *m* à la fermeture de l'admission. **3.** *Cin:* (*a*) écran *m* de sûreté (d'un projecteur); (*b*) **c. period,** intervalle *m* d'obscuration; phase *f* d'escamotage. **4.** *Civ.E:* parafouille *f*; rideau *m,* masque *m,* d'étanchéité.

cutout ['kʌtaut], *s.* **1.** (*a*) coupure *f* (d'une pièce de théâtre); (*b*) *Cin:* déchet *m* de film. **2.** *Bookb:* carton (détaché d'une feuille entière). **3.** *El:* coupe-circuit *m inv*, brise-circuit *m inv*; (*a*) conjoncteur-disjoncteur *m*, *pl.* conjoncteurs-disjoncteurs; interrupteur *m*; **double c.,** interrupteur double; **overload c.,** interrupteur à maximum, de surcharge; disjoncteur *m* à maximum; **zero c.,** commutateur *m* à zéro; (*b*) fusible *m* (de sûreté); plomb *m* (fusible, de sûreté). **4.** *I.C.E: Aut:* (soupape *f* d')échappement *m* libre (du silencieux); échappement libre. **5.** (*a*) *Th: Cin:* décor découpé; (*b*) *Photo-Engr: etc:* portrait détouré; (*c*) (*child's game*) **to do cutouts,** faire des découpures *f*, des découpages *m*. **6.** *Rail:* (voie *f* en) déblai *m*.

cutpurse ['kʌtpə:s], *s. A:* coupeur *m* de bourses; malandrin *m*.

cutter ['kʌtər], *s.* **1.** (*pers.*) (*a*) coupeur *m*; tailleur *m* (de pierre, etc.); **coal c.,** (i) haveur *m*; (ii) soucheveur *m*; **gem c.,** tailleur, polisseur *m*, de pierres précieuses; (*b*) *Tail:* coupeur; (*c*) *Husb:* châtreur *m*; (*d*) *Cin:* monteur, -euse. **2.** *Tls:* coupoir *m*, lame *f*, couteau *m*; **anvil c.,** tranchet *m* (d'enclume); **rotary c.,** roue *f* à couteaux; **milling c., milled c.,** fraise *f*; **c. spindle, arbor,** mandrin *m* de fraisage; **coal c.,** haveuse *f*; *Typ:* **rule c.,** coupoir pour filets; **angle c.,** fraise *f* d'angle, biconique; **circle c.,** mèche *f* circulaire; **face c.,** fraise de face; **c. with a lead,** fraise hélicoïdale; **milled tooth c.,** fraise à dents fraisées; **inserted-tooth c.,** fraise à lames rapportées; **shank-type c.,** fraise à queue; **profile c.,** fraise à profiler, fraise commune; **thread-milling c.,** fraise à fileter, fraise-mère *f*, *pl.* fraises-mères; **gear c.,** fraise à tailler les engrenages; **roughing, finishing, gear c.,** fraise à dégrossir, à finir, les engrenages; **rack-tooth c.,** fraise à tailler les crémaillères; **stocking c.,** fraise éboucheuse; **bar c.,** cisailles *fpl.* à barres; *Cu:* **pastry c.,** emporte-pièce *m inv.* **3.** *Const:* brique *f* tendre. **4.** *Nau:* (*a*) canot *m* (d'un bâtiment de guerre); *Navy:* **cruising c.,** aviso *m* de croisière; (*b*) **revenue c.,** vedette *f* de la douane; (*c*) cotre *m*, cutter *m*. **5.** *U.S:* traineau *m*. **6.** *Cards:* **c. in,** rentrant, -ante.

cutthroat ['kʌtθrout], *s.* **1.** (*a*) coupe-jarret *m*, *pl.* coupe-jarrets; escarpe *m*; **c. den,** coupe-gorge *m inv*; égorgeoir *m*; (*b*) **c. (razor),** rasoir *m* à manche, *F:* coupe-choux *m inv.* **2.** *Orn:* **c. (bird),** cou coupé *m*. **3.** (*a*) **c. competition,** concurrence acharnée; (*b*) *Cards:* **c. (bridge),** bridge *m* à trois.

cutting[1] ['kʌtiŋ], *a.* **1. c. edge,** arête tranchante; coupant *m*, tranchant *m*; fil *m* (d'un outil). **2. c. wind, rain,** vent cinglant, glacial; pluie cinglante; vent à vous couper la figure en quatre. **3. c. remark,** réponse mordante, blessante, piquante, caustique, cinglon *m*, coup *m* de langue; **c. criticism,** critique incisive; **c. way of saying things, c. tongue,** langue acérée; **c. words,** mots *m* à l'emporte-pièce; **he is very c.,** c'est un emporte-pièce.

cutting[2], *s.* **1.** (*a*) coupe *f*, coupage *m* (d'une branche, des foins, etc.); *Metalw:* cisaillage *m*, cisaillement *m* (d'une barre de fer, etc.); *Bookb:* rognage *m* (des bords); *Surg:* **c. out,** excision *f*; **c. off,** découpage *m*, tranchage *m*; suppression *f* (des vivres, etc.); **c. press,** balancier *m* découpoir, cisaille *f*; **cable c.,** coupe des câbles sous-marins; **c. of velvet,** ciselage *m* du velours; *Typewr:* **c. of wax stencils,** préparation *f* de clichés au stencil; *Mec.E:* **c. action,** cisaillement; **c. angle,** angle *m* de coupe; **c. bench,** banc *m* à couper; **c. back,** ravalement *m* (d'un arbre); *Mount:* **step c.,** taille *f*; **c. away,** enlèvement *m*, élagage *m*, retranchement *m*; évidement *m*; *Engr:* échoppage *m*; (*b*) **c. (down),** coupe, coupage, abattage *m* (des arbres); *For:* **c. area,** parterre *m* de la coupe; **to make periodical cuttings in a wood,** mettre un bois en coupe réglée; (*c*) entaillage *m* (d'une coche, etc.); percement *m* (d'un canal); (*d*) taille *f* (d'un diamant, d'une haie, d'un rosier, etc.); **file c.,** taillage *m* de limes; **c. of screw threads,** filetage *m*; (*e*) découpage *m* (de la tôle, de la viande, etc.); *Cin:* montage *m*; *Leath:* **c. board,** écoffret *m*; *Tail:* **c. out,** découpage *m*; **c. out table,** table *f* de coupe; **c. up,** découpage *m*, dépècement *m*, démembrement *m*; équarrissage *m*; (*of cloth, meat, etc.*) détail *m*; **c. (up) of timber,** débit *m* du bois; **c. (of timber) on the quarter,** débit sur maille, sur quartier; **c. (down) to size (of timber),** menuisage *m*; *Metalw:* **blow-torch c.,** découpage au chalumeau; **arc c.,** (dé)coupage à l'arc; (*f*) *Min:* havage *m* (du charbon); (*g*) **c. of wages, c. (down) of prices,** réduction *f* des salaires, des prix; rabais *m* des prix. **2.** (*piece cut off*) (*a*) coupon *m*, bout *m* (d'étoffe, etc.); **c. from a newspaper,** coupure prise dans un journal; *Metalw:* **c. from the plate,** cisaille *f*; (*b*) *pl.* **cuttings,** copeaux *m*, rognures *f*, recoupe *f* (de bois, de métal, etc.); (*c*) *pl. Civ.E:* déblais *m*, débris *m* (de forage); havrits *m* (de havage); (*d*) *Hort:* bouture *f*; (*of vine*) sarment *m*. **3.** (*a*) *Civ.E: etc:* coupure *f*, tranchée *f*, excavation *f*, déblai *m*; voie *f* en tranchée; **road running through a c.,** route encaissée; **railway c.,** (voie *f* en) déblai; (*b*) (*in forest*) percée *f*, tranchée, laie *f*, layon *m*.

cutting in ['kʌtiŋ'in], *s.* intervention *f*; *Aut:* croisement *m* d'une autre voiture après l'avoir doublée, queue *f* de poisson.

cuttingly ['kʌtiŋli], *adv.* caustiquement, d'un ton piquant.

cuttle(fish) ['kʌtl(fiʃ)], *s.* seiche *f*, sèche *f*, sépia *f*.

cuttlebone ['kʌtlboun], *s.* os *m* de seiche, biscuit *m* de mer, sépion *m*.

cutty ['kʌti], *Scot:* **1.** *a.* petit, court; **c. sark,** chemise (de femme) écourtée. **2.** *s. F:* (*a*) brûle-gueule *m inv*; (*b*) coquine *f*.

cutty-stool ['kʌtistu:l], *s. Scot:* **1.** petit escabeau. **2.** *Ecc: A:* sellette *f*.

cutwater ['kʌtwo:tər], *s.* **1.** *N.Arch:* tailler-mer *m inv*; éperon *m*; guibre *f*; **c. stem,** étrave *f* à guibre. **2.** *Civ.E:* bec *m* (d'une pile de pont); **downstream c.,** arrière-bec *m*, *pl.* arrière-becs; **upstream c.,** avant-bec *m*, *pl.* avant-becs.

cutwork ['kʌtwə:k], *s. Needlew:* broderie ajourée; broderie de Madère.

cutworm ['kʌtwə:m], *s. Ent:* agrotis *f* des moissons, ver gris, ver des moissons.

cuvette [kju'vet], *s.* **1.** *Fort:* cunette *f*. **2.** *Geol:* cuvette *f*.

Cuzco ['kʌzkou], *Pr.n.* **1.** *Geog:* Cuzco. **2.** *Pharm: etc:* **c. bark,** quinquina *m*, cinchona *m*.

cwm [ku(:)m], *s. Geog:* (*in Wales*) vallon *m*; **C. Rhondda,** la vallée du Rhondda; (*b*) cirque *m*.

cyamelid(e) [sai'æməl(a)id], *s. Ch:* cyamélide *f*.

cyamus [sai'eiməs], *s. Crust:* cyame *m*, cyamus *m*.

cyan ['saiæn], *s. Phot:* cyan *m*.

cyanacetic [saiənæ'si:tik], *a. Ch:* cyanacétique.

cyanamide [sai'ænəmaid], *s. Ch:* cyanamide *f*; **calcium c.,** cyanamide calcique.

cyanate ['saiəneit], *s. Ch:* cyanate *m*.

cyanea [sai'æniə, -'einiə], *s. Coel:* cyanée *f*, cyanéa *f*.

cyanhydric [saiən'haidrik], *a. Ch:* cyanhydrique.

cyanhydrin [saiən'haidrin], *s. Ch:* cyanhydrine *f*.

cyanic [sai'ænik], *a. Ch:* cyanique.

cyanidation [saiənai'deiʃ(ə)n], *s. Min:* cyanuration *f*.

cyanide[1] ['saiənaid], *s. Ch:* cyanure *m*; **potassium c.,** cyanure de potassium; prussiate *m* de potasse ; **c. solution,** dissolution cyanurée; **c. process,** procédé *m* de cyanuration; extraction *f* de l'or par cyanuration; *Metall:* **c. hardening,** cyanuration *f* (de l'acier).

cyanide[2]. **1.** *v.tr.* cyanurer (l'or, l'acier; *Hort:* une serre, etc.). **2.** *v.i.* se cyanurer.

cyaniding ['saiənaidiŋ], *s. Ch: Min:* cyanuration *f*; cyanurage *m* (pour la destruction de certains parasites).

cyanidrosis [saiəni'drousis], *s. Med:* cyanidrose *f*, cyanéphidrose *f*.

cyanin ['saiənin], *s. Bot: Ch:* cyanine *f*.

cyanine ['saiənain], *s. Ch: Dy:* cyanine *f*.

cyanite ['saiənait], *s. Miner:* cyanite *m*.

cyanize ['saiənaiz], *v.tr. Ch:* cyaniser; cyanurer (des matières organiques).

cyano- ['saiənou, saiə'nɔ], *comb.fm.* cyano-.

cyano-acetic ['saiənouə'si:tik], *a.* cyanacétique.

cyanocobalamin ['saiənoukou'bæləmin], *s. Bio-Ch:* cyanocobalamine *f*.

cyanogen [sai'ænədʒin], *s. Ch:* cyanogène *m*.

cyanogenesis ['saiənou'dʒenisis], *s.* cyanogénèse *f*.

cyanogenetic ['saiənoudʒə'netik], **cyanogenic** ['saiənou'dʒi:nik], *a.* cyanogénétique.

cyanohydrin ['saiənou'haidrin], *s. Ch:* cyanhydrine *f*.

cyanometer [saiə'nɔmitər], *s. Meteor:* cyanomètre *m*.

Cyanophyceae ['saiənou'faisii:], *s.pl. Algae:* cyanophycées *f*.

Cyanophyta [saiə'nɔfitə], *s.pl. Algae:* cyanophytes *f*.

cyanose ['saiənous], **cyanosite** [sai'ænousait], *s. Miner:* cyanose *f*; couperose bleue.

cyanosed ['saiənouzd, -noust], *a. Med:* cyanosé.

cyanosis [saiə'nousis], *s. Med:* cyanose *f*; maladie bleue; couperose bleue; ictère bleu.

cyanotic [saiə'noutik], *a. Med:* cyanotique.

cyanotrichite [saiə'nɔtrikait], *s. Miner:* cyanotrichite *f*.

cyanuric [saiə'nju:rik], *a. Ch:* cyanurique.

Cyatheaceae [saiəθ'eisii:], *s.pl. Bot:* cyathacées *f*, cyathéacées *f*.

cyathium [sai'æθiəm], *s. Bot:* cyathium *m*.

Cyathophyllidae ['saiəθou'filidi:], *s.pl. Paleont:* cyathophyllidés *m*.

cyathus, *pl.* **-i** ['saiəθəs, -ai, -i:], *s.* **1.** *Gr.Ant:* cyathe *m*. **2.** *Fung:* cyathe, cyathus *m*.

Cybele ['sibili], *Pr.n.f. Myth:* Cybèle.

cybernetic [saibə'netik], *a.* cybernétique.

cyberneticist [saibə'netisist], **cybernetician** [saibəne'tiʃ(ə)n], *s.* cybernéticien, -ienne.

cybernetics [saibə'netiks], *s.* cybernétique *f*.

cybernocratic [saibənou'krætik], *a.* cybernocratique.

cybister [si'bistər, 'sib-], *s. Ent:* cybister *m*.

cybotactic [sibou'tæktik], *a. Ph:* cybotactique.

cycad ['saikæd], *s. Bot:* cycas *m*.

Cycadaceae [saikə'deisii:], *s.pl. Bot:* cycadacées *f*, cycadées *f*.

Cycadales [saikə'deili:z], *s.pl. Bot:* cycadales *f*.

Cycadophyta [saikə'dɔfitə], *s.pl. Bot: Paleont:* cycadophytes *f*.

Cyclades (the) [ðə'sikləd i:z], *Pr.n.pl. Geog:* les Cyclades *f*.

Cycladic [si'klædik], *a. Geog:* des Cyclades.

cyclamen ['sikləmən]. **1.** *s. Bot:* cyclamen *m*. **2.** *a.* (rose) cyclamen *inv*.

cyclamin ['sikləmin], *s. Ch:* cyclamine *f*.

cyclane ['siklein], *s. Ch:* cyclane *m*.

Cyclanthaceae [siklæn'θeisii:], *s.pl. Bot:* cyclanthacées *f*.

cyclas ['sikləs], *s.* **1.** *Gr.Ant:* cyclas *f*, tunique *f*. **2.** *A.Cost:* cotte *f* d'armes. **3.** *Moll:* cyclade *f*.

cycle[1] ['saikl], *s.* **1.** cycle *m* (de mouvements, etc.); **trade c.,** cycle économique; **geological c.,** cycle géologique; *Geog:* **c. of erosion,** cycle d'érosion; *Astr:* **lunar, metonic, c.,** cycle lunaire; *Ph:* **Carnot's c.,** le cycle de Carnot; **reversible c.,** cycle réversible; *Ch:* **nitrogen, carbon, c.,** cycle de l'azote, du carbone; *Atom.Ph:* **reaction c.,** cycle de réaction; **breeding c.,** cycle de régénération, de surgénération; **fuel c.,** cycle du combustible; **Bethe c., carbon-nitrogen c.,** cycle de Bethe, de carbone-azote; *Magn:* **hysteresis c.,** cycle d'aimantation; *Elcs: etc:* **c.(-rate) counter,** compteur *m* de cycles; *Cmptr:* **memory c., store, storage, c.,** cycle (de) mémoire; **control c.,** cycle (i) de commande, (ii) opératoire; **dot c.,** fréquence *f* de points; **reset c.,** cycle de remise à l'état initial; **c. reset,** retour *m* du compteur (de cycles) à la valeur initiale; *I.C.E:* **four-stroke c.,** cycle à quatre temps; **bacterial life c.,** cycle de l'évolution des bactéries; *Physiol:* **menstrual c.,** cycle menstruel; **cardiac c.,** cycle cardiaque. **2. (pedal) c.,** bicyclette *f*, vélo *m*; **c. track,** piste *f* cyclable; **c. racing,** courses *fpl* de bicyclettes; épreuves *f* cyclistes; **c.-racing track,** vélodrome *m*.

cycle[2]. **1.** *v.tr. Cmptr:* (i) itérer, répéter; (ii) boucler (un cycle); **to c. down,** mettre (la machine) progressivement hors tension; **to c. through,** tourner sur une boucle. **2.** *v.i.* faire de la bicyclette, du vélo; aller à bicyclette.

cyclecar ['saiklkɑ:r], *s.* cyclecar *m*, tri-car *m*, tri-voiturette *f*.

cyclene ['saikli:n], *s. Ch.* cyclène *m*.

cycler ['saiklər], *s. U.S:* cycliste *mf*.

cyclic ['s(a)iklik], *a.* (*of movement, chemical compound, poem, etc.*) cyclique; **c. novel,** roman-fleuve *m*, *pl.* romans-fleuves, roman-cycle *m*, *pl.* romans-cycles; *Mth:* **c. permutations,** permutations *f* circulaires; *Cmptr:* **c. store, storage,** mémoire circulante, cyclique; **c. code,** code *m* cyclique; **c. binary code,** code Gray, code binaire réfléchi; **c. shift,** décalage *m* circulaire.

cyclical ['siklikl], *a.* **1.** = CYCLIC. **2.** *Pol.Ec:* conjoncturel; **c. component,** composante cyclique, conjoncturelle.

cyclide ['siklaid], *s. Mth:* cyclide *f*.

cycling ['saikliŋ], *s.* **1.** *Tchn:* cyclage *m*; *Cmptr:* itération *f*. **2.** cyclisme *m*; **c. paper,** journal *m* cycliste, de cyclisme; **c. track,** vélodrome *m*.

cyclist ['saiklist], *s.* cycliste *mf*.

cyclitis [si'klaitis], *s. Med:* cyclite *f*.

cyclization [siklai'zeiʃ(ə)n], *s. Ch:* cyclisation *f*.

cyclize ['saiklaiz], *v.tr. Ch:* cycliser.

cyclo- ['saiklou, sai'klɔ], *comb.fm.* cyclo-.

cyclobranchiate ['saiklou'bræŋkieit], *a.* cyclobranche.

cyclobutane ['saiklou'bju:tein], *s. Ch:* cyclobutane *m*.

cyclocephalian ['saiklousə'feiliən], *a. & s. Ter:* cyclocéphale (*mf*).

cyclo-cross ['saikloukrɔs], *s. Sp:* cyclo-cross *m*.

cyclogenesis ['saiklou'dʒenisis], *s. Meteor:* cyclogénèse *f*.

cyclograph ['saiklougræf], *s. Draw:* cyclographe *m*.

cycloheptane ['saiklou'heptein], *s. Ch:* cycloheptane *m*.

cyclohexane ['saiklou'heksein], *s. Ch:* cyclohexane *m*.

cyclohexanol ['saiklou'heksənɔl], *s. Ch:* cyclohexanol *m*.

cyclohexanone ['saiklou'heksənoun], *s. Ch:* cyclohexanone *f*.

cyclohexene ['saiklou'heksi:n], *s. Ch:* cyclohexène *m*.

cyclohexyl ['saiklou'heksil], *s. Ch:* cyclohexyle *m*.

cycloid ['saiklɔid], **1.** *s. Mth:* cycloïde *f*; **curtate c.,** cycloïde raccourcie; **prolate c.,** cycloïde allongée. **2.** *a. Ich:* **c. scales,** écailles *f* cycloïdes. **3.** *Med:* (*a*) *a.* cycloïdique; (*b*) *s.* cycloïde *mf*.

cycloidal [sai'klɔidl], *a. Mth: etc:* cycloïdal, -aux; **c. pen-**

dulum, pendule cycloïdal; **clock with a c. pendulum,** horloge *f* à cycloïde; **c. curve,** anse *f*, cycloïde *f*.

cyclometer [sai'klɔmitər], *s.* **1.** cyclomètre *m*; curvimètre *m*. **2.** compteur *m* kilométrique (pour bicyclettes).

cyclometry [sai'klɔmitri], *s.* cyclométrie *f*.

cyclonal [sai'klounl], *a. Meteor:* cyclonal, -aux.

cyclone ['saikloun], *s.* **1.** *Meteor:* cyclone *m*; **centre of c.,** œil *m* de cyclone; *U.S:* **c. cellar,** abri *m* anticyclone. **2.** *Tchn:* **c. separator,** (séparateur *m* à) cyclone.

cyclonic [sai'klɔnik], *a.* cyclonique; cyclonal, -aux.

cyclonite ['saiklənait], *s. Ch:* cyclonite *f*.

cyclopaedia [saiklə'pi:diə], *s.* encyclopédie *f*.

Cyclopean, Cyclopian [sai'kloupiən], *a.* (*a*) cyclopéen, gigantesque; (*b*) *Arch:* **c. wall, etc.,** mur, etc., cyclopéen; *Civ.E:* **c. concrete,** béton cyclopéen; (*c*) *Ter:* cyclopien.

cyclopentadiene ['saikloupentə'daii:n], *s. Ch:* cyclopentadiène *m*.

cyclopentane ['saiklou'pentein], *s. Ch:* cyclopentane *m*.

cyclopentanone ['saiklou'pentənoun], *s. Ch:* cyclopentanone *f*.

cyclopentene ['saiklou'penti:n], *s. Ch:* cyclopentène *m*.

cyclopes [sai'kloupi:z], *s. Z:* cyclope *m*.

cyclophrenia ['saiklou'fri:niə], *s. Med:* cyclophrénie *f*.

Cyclophyllidea ['saikloufi'lidiə], *s.pl. Ann:* cyclophyllidiens *m*.

cyclopia [sai'kloupiə], *s. Ter:* cyclopie *f*.

cycloplegia ['saiklou'pli:dʒiə], *s. Med:* cycloplégie *f*.

cyclopropane ['saiklou'proupein], *s. Med:* cyclopropane *m*.

Cyclops ['saiklɔps], *s.* **1.** *Myth:* cyclope *m*. **2.** *Crust:* cyclops *m*, cyclope.

Cyclopteridae ['saiklɔp'teridi:], *s.pl. Ich:* cycloptéridés *m*.

cyclopteroid [sai'klɔptərɔid], *s. Ich:* cycloptère *m*; cycloptéridé *m*.

cyclorama [saiklə'rɑ:mə], *s. Th: etc:* cyclorama *m*, cyclo *m*.

Cyclorrhapha [sai'klɔrəfə], *s.pl. Ent:* cyclorraphes *m*.

cycloserine ['saiklou'seri:n], *s. Med:* cyclosérine *f*.

cyclosis [sai'klousis], *s. Biol:* cyclose *f*.

Cyclostomata ['saiklou'stɔmətə], *s.pl. Ich:* cyclostomes *m*, agnathes *m*.

cyclostome ['saikloustoum], *s. Ich:* cyclostome *m*.

cyclostrophic [saiklou'strɔfik], *a. Meteor:* cyclostrophique.

cyclostyle[1] ['saikloustail], *s. O:* autocopiste *m* (à stencils).

cyclostyle[2], *v.tr. O:* autocopier, polycopier (au moyen d'un stencil).

cyclostyling ['saikloustailiŋ], *s. O:* autocopie *f*.

cyclothyme ['saiklouθaim], *s. Med:* cyclothyme *mf*, cyclothymique *mf*.

cyclothymia ['saiklou'θaimiə], *s. Med:* cyclothymie *f*.

cyclothymic ['saiklou'θaimik], *a. Med:* cyclothymique.

Cyclotornidae ['saiklou'tɔ:nidi:], *s.pl. Ent:* cyclotornidés *m*.

cyclotron ['saikloutrɔn], *a. Atom.Ph:* cyclotron *m*.

cycnoches ['siknəki:z], *s. Bot:* cycnoche *m*, cycnoque *m*.

cygnet ['signit], *s. Orn:* jeune cygne *m*.

cylinder ['silindər], *s.* **1.** *Mth:* cylindre *m*; **right c.,** cylindre droit; **oblique c.,** cylindre oblique. **2.** *Tchn:* cylindre; corps *m*, barillet *m* (de pompe); barillet (de revolver); *El:* tambour *m* (de bobine électrique); *Typewr:* rouleau *m* porte-papier; *Tex:* cochonnet *m* (pour impressions d'indiennes, etc.); *Mch: I.C.E:* **piston c.,** cylindre de piston; **c. bore,** alésage *m* du cylindre; **c. block,** bloc *m* cylindres; **c. sleeve,** chemise *f* de cylindre; **c. jacket,** chemise, enveloppe *f*, soufflage *m*, du cylindre; **c. barrel,** (corps *m* du) cylindre; **c. cover,** plateau *m* de cylindre; **c. head,** culasse *f*, calotte *f*; **detachable c. head,** culasse rapportée, amovible; **four-c. engine,** moteur *m* à quatre cylindres; **a four-c. car,** une quatre cylindres; *Min: etc:* **sorting c.,** tambour à assortir; *Metall:* **roughing c.,** cylindre dégrossisseur, ébaucheur; *Typ:* **c. press,** presse *f* à cylindre(s); **printing c.,** cylindre imprimeur, d'impression; **blanket c.,** cylindre de blanchet; **plate c.,** cylindre de plaque; **packed c.,** cylindre habillé; **c. packing,** habillement *m* de cylindre; *Mus:* **cylinders (of a brass instrument),** cylindres (d'un instrument à cuivre); *Paperm:* **c.-dried,** séché à la machine; **(compressed) gas c.,** bouteille *f* à gaz (comprimé); tube *m* de gaz comprimé; *Ch:* **measuring c.,** (tube) mesureur *m*; *Archeol:* **c. seal,** cylindre-sceau *m*, *pl.* cylindres-sceaux. **3.** *Bot:* **vascular c.,** stèle *f*, cylindre central.

cylinderful ['silindəful], *s.* cylindrée *f*.

cylindraceous [silin'dreiʃəs], *a. Nat.Hist:* cylindracé.

cylindrical [si'lindrikl], *a.* cylindrique.

cylindricity [silin'drisiti], *s.* cylindricité *f*.

cylindriform [si'lindrifɔ:m], *a.* cylindriforme.

cylindrite ['silindrait], *s. Miner:* cylindrite *f*.

cylindro-conical ['silindrou'kɔnikl], *a.* cylindro-conique, *pl.* cylindro-coniques.

cylindroid [si'lindrɔid], *a. & s. Mth:* cylindroïde (*m*); *s.* cylindre *m* elliptique.

cylinduria [silin'dru:riə], *s. Med:* cylindrurie *f*.

cyma, *pl.* **-mas** ['saimə(z)], *s.* **1.** *Arch:* cimaise *f*, cymaise *f* (de corniche); **c. recta,** cimaise droite; **c. reversa, inversa,** cimaise renversée. **2.** *Bot:* cyme *f*.

cymbal ['simb(ə)l], *s.* cymbale *f*; **c. player,** cymbalier *m*.

cymbalist ['simbəlist], *s.* cymbalier *m*.

cymbalo(m) ['simbəlou, -ləm], *s. Mus:* cymbalum *m*, tympanon *m*.

cymbiform ['simbifɔ:m], *a. Bot:* cymbiforme.

cyme [saim], *s. Bot:* cyme *f*.

cymene ['saimi:n], *s. Ch:* cymène *m*.

cymograph ['saimougræf], *s. Med:* kymographe *m*.

cymometer [sai'mɔmitər], *s. W.Tel: A:* cymomètre *m*, ondemètre *m*.

cymophane ['saiməfein], *s. Miner:* cymophane *f*, chrysobéryl *m*.

cymophanous [sai'mɔfənəs], *a.* chatoyant.

cymoscope ['saiməskoup], *s. El: etc:* cymoscope *m*.

cymose [sai'mous], *a. Bot:* en cyme, cymeux.

Cymric ['kimrik], *a.* kymrique, cymrique; gallois.

cynanchum [si'næŋkəm], *s. Bot:* cynanque *m*, cynanchum *m*.

cynegetic [saini'dʒetik], *a.* cynégétique.

cynegetics [saini'dʒetiks], *s.pl.* (*usu. with sg. const.*) cynégétique *f*.

cynic ['sinik], *a. & s.* **1.** (*a*) *Hist. of Phil:* cynique (*m*); (*b*) *Med:* **c. spasm,** spasme *m* cynique. **2.** (*a*) *a.* = CYNICAL; (*b*) *s.* cynique *m*, censeur *m* caustique, sarcastique; railleur *m*; sceptique *m*, incrédule *m*.

cynical ['sinikl], *a.* **1.** *Hist. of Phil:* cynique. **2.** cynique; (*a*) sarcastique, railleur; sceptique, incrédule; désabusé; (*b*) (sourire *m*, comédie *f*) rosse.

cynically ['sinikəli], *adv.* cyniquement; (*a*) d'un ton sceptique; railleusement, caustiquement; (*b*) d'un ton rosse.

cynicism ['sinisizm], *s.* **1.** *Hist. of Phil:* cynisme *m*. **2.** cynisme; désillusionnement *m*; scepticisme railleur; esprit *m* de blague. **3.** (*a*) mot *m* caustique; (*b*) **cynicisms,** rosseries *f*.

Cynipidae [si'nipidi:], *s.pl. Ent:* cynipidés *m*.

cynips ['sinips], *s. Ent:* cynips *m*.

cynocephalous [sainou'sefələs], *a. Z:* cynocéphale.

cynocephalus [sainou'sefələs], *s.* cynocéphale *m*.

cynodon ['sainoudɔn], *s. Bot:* cynodon *m*.

Cynodontia [sainou'dɔntiə], *s.pl. Paleont:* cynodontes *m*.

cynoglossum [sainou'glɔsəm], *s. Bot:* cynoglosse *f*.

cynomys ['sainoumis], *s. Z:* cynomys *m*, chien *m* des prairies.

cynopithecus [sainoupi'θi:kəs], *s. Z:* cynopithèque *m*.

Cynoscephalae [sainou'sefəli:], *Pr.n. A.Geog:* (les) Cyno(s)céphales *f*.

cynosure ['sainousjuər], *s. Astr:* cynosure *f*; la Petite Ourse; *Lit:* **the c. of every eye,** le point de mire de tous les yeux.

cynosurus [sainou'sju:rəs], *s. Bot:* cynosure *f*.

Cyperaceae [saipə'reisii:], *s.pl. Bot:* cypéracées *f*.

cyperus ['saipərəs], *s. Bot:* souchet *m*; (*genus*) cyperus *m*; **sweet c.,** souchet long.

cypher ['saifər], *s.* = CIPHER.

cyphomandra [saifou'mændrə], *s. Bot:* cyphomandra *m*, tomate *f* en arbre.

cyphoscoliosis ['saifouskouli'ousis], *s. Med:* cyphoscoliose *f*.

cyphosis [sai'fousis], *s. Med:* cyphose *f*.

Cypraeidae [sai'pri:ədi:], *s.pl. Moll:* cypréidés *m*.

cypres ['si:'prei], *Fr. adv. phr. Jur:* aussi exactement que faire se pourra; (autorisation donnée par la Cour de suivre d'aussi près que possible les intentions du testateur, en matière de fondations charitables).

cypress ['saiprəs], *s. Bot:* cyprès *m*; **black, bald, deciduous, c.,** taxaudier *m*, taxodier *m*, taxodium *m*; cyprès chauve; arbre *m* de Chypre; **c. grove, plantation,** cyprière *f*.

Cyprian[1] ['sipriən], *Pr.n.m.* Cyprien.

Cyprian[2]. **1.** *Geog:* (*a*) *a.* cypriote, chypriote; *Lit:* **C. Venus,** Cypris *f*; (*b*) *s.* Cypriote *mf*; Chypriote *mf*. **2.** *A: & Lit:* (*a*) *a.* débauché, dévergondé; (*b*) *s.f.* courtisane; prostituée.

Cypridinidae [sipri'dainidi:], *s.pl. Crust:* cypridin(id)és *m*.

cyprina [si'prainə], *s. Moll:* cyprine *f*.

cyprinid ['siprinid], *a. & s. Ich:* cyprinide (*m*), cyprinidé (*m*).

Cyprinidae [si'prinidi:], *s.pl. Ich:* cyprinidés *m*.

Cyprinodontidae [siprinou'dɔntidi], *s.pl. Ich:* cyprinodontes *m*, cyprinodontidés *m*.

Cypriot(e) ['sipriət], *Geog:* (*a*) *a.* chypriote, cypriote; (*b*) *s.* Chypriote *mf*, Cypriote *mf*.

cypripedium [sipri'pi:diəm], *s. Bot:* cypripède *m*, *F:* sabot *m* de Vénus.

Cypris ['saipris]. **1.** *Pr.n.f. A.Lit:* Cypris. **2.** *s. Crust:* cypris *f*.

Cyprus ['saiprəs], *Pr.n. Geog:* l'île de Chypre, Chypre *f*.

Cyrenaic [sai(ə)ri'neiik], *a. & s. Phil:* cyrénaïque (*m*).

Cyrenaica [sai(ə)ri'neiikə], *Pr.n. Geog:* Cyrénaïque *f*.

Cyrene [sai(ə)'ri:ni], *Pr.n. A.Geog:* Cyrène *f*.

Cyrenian [sai(ə)'ri:niən], *A.Geog:* (*a*) *a.* cyrénéen; (*b*) *s.* Cyrénéen, -enne.

Cyril ['sir(ə)l], *Pr.n.m.* Cyrille.

Cyrillian [si'riliən], **Cyrillic** [si'rilik], *a.* cyrillien; (alphabet) cyrillique.

Cyropaedia (the) [ðəsaiərə'pi:diə], *s. Gr.Lit:* la Cyropédie.

cyrtometer [sə:'tɔmitər], *s.* cyrtomètre *m*.

cyst [sist], *s.* **1.** (*a*) *Biol: Anat:* sac *m*; vésicule *f*; **bile c.,** vésicule du fiel; (*b*) *Bot:* kyste *m*, cyste *m*. **2.** *Med:* kyste; **branchial, dermoid, epithelial, c.,** kyste branchial, dermoïde, épithélial; **mucous c.,** kyste mucoïde, muqueux; **bone c.,** kyste intra-osseux; **dental, odontogenic, c.,** kyste (d'origine) dentaire.

cyst-, cysti-, cysto- [sist(i, -ou, -ə)], *comb.fm.* cyst-, cysti-, cysto-.

cystalgia [sis'tældʒiə], *s. Med:* cystalgie *f*.

cystectomy [sis'tektəmi], *s. Surg:* cystectomie *f*.

cystein ['sist(i)i:n], *s. Ch:* cystéine *f*.

cysthepatic [sisti'pætik], *a. Med:* cysthépatique.

cystic ['sistik], *a. Anat: Med:* kystique, cystique.

cysticercosis [sistisə:'kousis], *s. Med:* cysticercose *f*.

cysticercus [sisti'sə:kəs], *s. Ann:* cysticerque *m*.

cystidium [sis'tidiəm], *s. Fung:* cystide *f*.

cystiform ['sistifɔ:m], *a.* en forme de kyste.

cystin(e) ['sistain, 'sisti:n], *s. Ch:* cystine *f*.

cystinuria [sisti'nju:riə], *s. Med:* cystinurie *f*.

cystirrh(o)ea [sisti'ri:ə], *s. Med:* cistirrhée *f*.

cystitis [sis'taitis], *s. Med: Vet:* cystite *f*.

cystocarp ['sistoukɑ:p], *s. Bot:* cystocarpe *m*.

cystocele ['sistousi:l], *s. Med:* cystocèle *f*.

cystodynia [sistou'dainiə], *s. Med:* cystodynie *f*.

cystography [sis'tɔgrəfi], *s. Med:* cystographie *f*.

cystoid ['sistɔid], *a.* cystoïde.

Cystoidea [sis'tɔidiə], *s.pl. Paleont:* cystidés *m*, cystoïdes *m*.

cystolith ['sistouliθ], *s. Bot: Med:* cystolithe *m*.

cystometry [sis'tɔmitri], *s. Med:* cystométrie *f*.

cystophora [sis'tɔfərə], *s. Z:* cystophore *m*, phoque *m* à capuchon.

cystoplasty ['sistouplæsti], *s. Surg:* cystoplastie *f*.

cystorrhea [sistou'ri:ə], *s. Med:* cystirrhée *f*.

cystoscope ['sistəskoup], *s. Med:* cystoscope *m*.

cystoscopy [sis'tɔskəpi], *s. Med:* cystoscopie *f*.

cystostomy [sis'tɔstəmi], *s. Med:* cystostomie *f*.

cystotome ['sistətoum], *s. Surg:* cystotome *m*.

cystotomy [sis'tɔtəmi], *s. Surg:* cystotomie *f*.

cytase ['saiteis], *s. Bio-Ch:* cytase *f*, cellulase *f*.

cytaster [sai'tæstər], *s. Biol:* cytaster *m*.

cyte [sait], *s. Biol:* cyte *mf*.

Cythera [si'θiərə, 'siθərə], *Pr.n. A.Geog:* Cythère *f*.

cytinus ['saitinəs], *s. Bot:* cytinet *m*, cytinus *m*.

cytisine ['saitisi:n], *s. Bio-Ch:* cytisine *f*.

cytisus ['saitisəs], *s. Bot:* cytisus *m*; genêt *m* d'Espagne.

cyto- ['saitou], *comb.fm.* cyto-.

cytoblast ['saitoublæst], *s. Biol:* cytoblaste *m*.

cytochemistry ['saitou'kemistri], *s.* cytochimie *f*.

cytochrome ['saitoukroum], *s. Biol:* cytochrome *m*.

cytode ['saitoud], *s. Biol:* cytode *m*.

cytodiaeresis ['saitoudai'iərəsis, -'er-], *s. Biol:* cytodiérèse *f*.

cytodiagnosis ['saitoudaiəg'nousis], *s. Med:* cytodiagnostic *m*.

cytogamy [sai'tɔgəmi], *s. Biol:* cytogamie *f*.

cytogenesis ['saitou'dʒenisis], *s. Biol:* cytogénie *f*.

cytogenetic ['saitoudʒə'netik], *a.* cytogénétique.

cytogenous [sai'tɔdʒənəs], *a. Biol:* cytogène.

cytoid ['saitɔid], *a. Bot: Med:* cytoïde.

cytokinesis [saitouk(a)i'ni:sis], *s. Biol:* cytodiérèse *f*.

cytologist [sai'tɔlədʒist], *s.* cytologiste *mf*.

cytology [sai'tɔlədʒi], *s. Biol:* cytologie *f*.

cytolysis [sai'tɔlisis], *s. Biol:* cytolyse *f*.

cytopathology ['saitoupæ'θɔlədʒi], *s.* cytopathologie *f*.

cytophaga [sai'tɔfəgə], *s. Bac:* cytophaga *f*.

cytopharynx [saitou'færiŋks], *s. Prot:* cytopharynx *m*.

cytoplasm ['saitouplæzm], *s. Biol:* cytoplasme *m*.

cytoplasmic [saitou'plæzmik], *a. Biol:* cytoplasmique; **c. heredity, c. inheritance,** hérédité *f* cytoplasmique.
cytoproct ['saitouprɔkt], *s. Prot:* cytoprocte *m.*
cytosine ['saitousi:n], *s. Bio-Ch:* cytosine *f.*
cytostome ['saitoustoum], *s. Prot:* cytostome *m.*
cytotheca [saitou'θi:kə], *s. Ent:* cytothèque *f.*
cytotoxic [saitou'tɔksik], *a.* cytotoxique.
cytotoxin(e) [saitou'tɔksin], *s. Bio-Ch:* cytotoxine *f.*
cytotropism [sai'tɔtrəpizm], *s. Biol:* cytotropisme *m.*
cytozoon, *pl.* **-zoa** [saitou'zouən, -'zouə], *s. Prot:* cytozoaire *m.*
Cyzicene ['sizisi:n], *A.Geog:* (*a*) *a.* cyzicénien; (*b*) *s.* Cyzicénien, -ienne.
Cyzicus ['sizikəs], *Pr.n. A.Geog:* Cyzique.
czar [zɑ:r], *s.* czar *m,* tsar *m.*
czarevitch ['zɑ:rəvitʃ], *s.* czarévitch *m,* tsarévitch *m.*
czarina [zɑ:'ri:nə], *s.* czarine *f,* tsarine *f.*
Czech [tʃek], *Geog:* **1.** (*a*) *a.* tchèque; (*b*) *s.* Tchèque *mf.* tchèque (*mf*). **2.** *s. Ling:* tchèque *m.*
Czechoslovakia [tʃekousləˈvækiə], *Pr.n. Geog:* Tchécoslovaquie *f.*

D

D, d [di:], *s.* **1.** (la lettre) D, d *m*; *Tp:* **D for David,** D comme Désiré; *Mch:* **D valve,** tiroir *m* en D; *Mil: etc:* **D day,** le jour J. **2.** *Mus:* ré *m*. **3.** *A.Num:* (*abbr. for Lt.* **denarius**) penny *m*, pence *mpl*; **6d.,** six pence.

dab[1] [dæb], *s.* **1.** coup léger, tape *f*; (*of bird*) coup de bec; **to give s.o. a d. in the eye,** donner à qn une tape dans l'œil. **2.** (*a*) tache *f* (d'encre, de peinture); éclaboussure *f* (de boue); **a d. of butter,** un petit morceau de beurre; **a little d. of rouge on her cheek,** un rien, une touche, de rouge sur sa joue; (*b*) *F:* **dabs,** empreintes digitales.

dab[2], *v.tr.* (**dabbed**) **1.** donner un petit coup, une tape, à (qn); (*of bird*) lancer un coup de bec à (qch., qn). **2.** tapoter, frapper légèrement; (*with pad*) tamponner; **to d. one's cheeks with powder,** se tamponner les joues avec de la poudre; *F:* **to d. it on thick,** (i) se poudrer à l'excès, s'en mettre jusqu'aux yeux; (ii) exagérer; **to d. one's eyes with a handkerchief,** se tamponner, s'éponger, les yeux; **to d. paint on sth., to d. on paint,** donner un coup de peinture à qch. **3.** *F:* prendre les empreintes digitales (de qn).

dab[3], *s. Ich:* limande *f*, calimande *f*; **lemon d.,** plie *f* sole; limande sole.

dab[4], *a. & s. F:* **to be a d. (hand) at sth., at doing sth.,** s'entendre à qch., à faire qch.; être passé maître en qch., en l'art de faire qch., s'y connaître en qch.; être calé en qch.

dabber ['dæbər], *s.* tampon *m*; *Typ:* balle *f*; *Engr:* poupée *f*.

dabble ['dæbl]. **1.** *v.tr.* (*a*) humecter, mouiller; (*b*) **to d. one's hands in the water,** tremper ses mains dans l'eau; faire éclabousser l'eau. **2.** *v.i.* (*a*) barboter, tripoter (dans l'eau); (*b*) *F:* **to d. in, at, law, medicine, etc.,** se mêler, s'occuper, un peu de droit; faire un peu de droit, etc.; étudier la médecine en amateur; **to d. on the Stock Exchange,** boursicoter; **to d. in politics,** se mêler de politique, *F: Pej:* politicailler.

dabbler ['dæblər], *s.* **to be a d. in sth.,** se mêler, s'occuper, un peu de qch.; faire qch. en amateur; **d. on the Stock Exchange,** boursicoteur *m*, boursicotier *m*.

dabbling ['dæbliŋ], *s.* amateurisme *m*; *St.Exch:* boursicotage *m*.

dabchick ['dæbtʃik], *s.* **1.** *Orn:* grèbe castagneux; petit grèbe. **2.** *Y:* yacht qui jauge cinq tonneaux ou au-dessous.

daboia, daboya [dæ'bɔiə], *s. Rept:* daboia *m*.

dabster ['dæbstər], *s. F:* **1.** expert *m*. **2.** amateur *m*; *Art:* barbouilleur, -euse.

dace [deis], *s. Ich:* vandoise *f*; dard *m*.

dachshund ['dækshund], *s.* (*F:* **dachs** [dæks]) dachshund *m*, teckel *m*, basset allemand.

Dacia ['deisiə], *Pr.n. A.Geog:* Dacie *f*.

Dacian ['deisiən], *A.Geog:* (*a*) *a.* dace, dacique; (*b*) *s.* Dace *mf*.

dacite ['deisait], *s. Miner:* dacite *f*.

dacitic [dei'sitik], *a. Geol:* dacitique.

dacnis ['dæknis], *s. Orn:* dacnis *m*.

dacoit [də'kɔit], *s. Hist:* dacoït *m*.

dacoity [də'kɔiti], *s. Hist:* **1.** (*armed-gang robbery in India*) dacoïtisme *m*. **2.** (*act of such robbery*) dacoït *m*.

dacrydium [dæ'kridiəm], *s. Bot:* dacryde *f*, dacrydion *m*, dacrydium *m*.

dacry(o)adenitis ['dækri(ou)ædə'naitis], *s. Med:* dacry(o)adénite *f*.

dacryocyst ['dækriousist], *s. Anat:* dacryocyste *m*.

dacryocystitis ['dækriousis'taitis], *s. Med:* dacryocystite *f*.

dacryolith ['dækriouliθ], *s. Med:* dacryolithe *m*.

dacryon ['dækriɔn], *s. Anat:* dacryon *m*.

dacryops ['dækriɔps], *s. Med:* dacryops *m*.

dactyl ['dæktil], *s. Pros:* dactyle *m*.

dactylate ['dæktileit], *a. Nat.Hist:* dactylé.

dactylic [dæk'tilik], *a.* (hexamètre *m*, etc.) dactylique; *s.* **written in dactylics,** composé en vers dactyliques.

dactyliography [dæktili'ɔgrəfi], *s. Archeol:* dactyliographie *f*.

dactyliology [dæktili'ɔlədʒi], *s. Archeol:* dactyliologie *f*.

dactyliomancy [dæktiliou'mænsi], *s.* dactyliomancie *f*.

dactylion [dæk'tiliən], *s.* **1.** *Mus:* dactylion *m*. **2.** *Nat.Hist: Anat:* dactylion; syndactylie *f*.

dactyliotheca [dæktiliou'θi:kə], *s.* dactyliothèque *f*.

dactylis ['dæktilis], *s. Bot:* dactyle *m*, *F:* patte-de-lièvre *f*, herbe *f* des vergers.

dactylitis [dækti'laitis], *s. Med:* dactylite *f*.

dactylogram [dæk'tilougræm], *s.* dactylogramme *m*; empreinte digitale.

dactylography [dækti'lɔgrəfi], *s.* **1.** dactylographie *f*, dactylologie *f*. **2.** dactyloscopie *f*.

dactyloid ['dæktilɔid], *a.* dactyloïde.

dactylology [dækti'lɔlədʒi], *s.* dactylologie *f*.

dactylomegaly ['dæktilou'megəli], *s. Med:* dactylomégalie *f*.

dactylonomy [dækti'lɔnəmi], *s.* dactylonomie *f*.

dactylopius [dækti'loupiəs], *s. Ent:* dactylopius *m*.

dactylopodite [dækti'lɔpədait], *s. Crust:* dactylopodite *m*.

Dactylopteridae [dæktilɔp'teridi:], *s.pl. Ich:* dactyloptères *m*.

dactylopterous [dækti'lɔptərəs], *a. Ich:* dactyloptère.

dactylopterus [dækti'lɔptərəs], *s. Ich:* dactyloptère *m*.

dactyloscopy [dækti'lɔskəpi], *s.* dactyloscopie *f*, étude *f* des empreintes digitales.

dactylozooid [dæktilou'zouɔid], *s. Z:* dactylozoïde *m*.

dacus ['deikəs], *s. Ent:* dacus *m*.

dad [dæd], *s. F:* papa *m*.

Dada ['dɑ:dɑ:], *a. & s. Art: Lit:* dada *m*, dadaïsme *m*; **the D. movement,** le mouvement dada.

Dadaism ['dɑ:dɑ:izm], *s. Art: Lit:* dadaïsme *m*.

Dadaist ['dɑ:dɑ:ist], *s. Art: Lit:* dadaïste *m*.

Dadaistic [dɑ:dɑ:'istik], *a. Art: Lit:* dadaïste.

daddy ['dædi], *s. F:* **1.** papa *m*; **sugar d.,** protecteur âgé, papa gâteau. **2.** *Th:* le régisseur.

daddy longlegs ['dædi'lɔŋlegz], *s. F:* **1.** *Ent:* tipule *f*, cousin *m*. **2.** *Arach: U.S:* faucheux *m*.

daddynut ['dædinʌt], *s. Bot:* tilleul *m* d'Amérique.

dado ['deidou], *s.* **1.** *Arch:* (*a*) dé *m* (de piédestal); (*b*) cimaise *f*. **2.** lambris *m* (d'appui) (d'une salle).

dadoed ['deidoud], *a.* (*of room*) lambrissé.

dadoxylon [dæ'dɔksilɔn], *s. Paleont:* dadoxylon *m*.

Daedalian [di'deiliən], *a.* de Dédale, dédalien, dédaléen, dédalique, compliqué, inextricable.

Daedalus ['di:dələs], *Pr.n.m. Gr.Myth:* Dédale.

daemon ['di:mɔn], **daemonic** [di:'mɔnik], *etc.* = DEMON, DEMONIC, *etc.*

daff [dæf], *s. F:* = DAFFODIL; **a bunch of daffs,** un bouquet de jonquilles.

daffodil ['dæfədil]. **1.** *s. Bot:* (narcisse *m*) jonquille *f*; **a bunch of daffodils,** un bouquet de jonquilles. **2.** *a.* **d. (yellow),** jonquille *inv*.

daffy ['dæfi], *a. F:* = DAFT.

daft [dɑ:ft], *a. F:* écervelé, évaporé; timbré, toqué, cinglé, maboul(e); **to go d. over sth., over s.o.,** s'enticher de qch., de qn; **he's gone completely d.,** il a perdu l'esprit, la boule; **as d. as they come, as they make 'em,** bête comme ses pieds; *adv.* **don't talk d.!** ne dis pas de bêtises!

daftie, dafty ['dɑ:fti], *s. F:* cruche *f*, crétin *m*, loufoque *m*.

daftness ['dɑ:ftnis], *s. F:* stupidité *f*, bêtise *f*, loufoquerie *f*.

dag[1] [dæg], *s.* (*of sheep*) couaille *f*.

dag[2], *s.* (*of deer*) dague *f*.

dagger ['dægər], *s.* **1.** poignard *m*, dague *f*; *F:* **to be at daggers drawn,** être à couteaux tirés (**with,** avec); **to look daggers at s.o.,** lancer un regard furibond, fulgurant, foudroyant, à qn; foudroyer qn du regard. **2.** *Typ:* croix *f*, obèle *m*; **double d.,** diésis *m*. **3.** *Bot:* **d. plant, Spanish d.,** yucca *m*.

dago ['deigou], *s. P: Pej:* = métèque *m*.

daguerreotype[1] [də'geroutaip], *s.* daguerréotype *m*.

daguerreotype[2], *v.tr.* daguerréotyper.

daguerreotypy [də'gerətaipi], *s.* daguerréotypie *f*.

dahlia ['deiliə], *s. Bot:* dahlia *m*; **cactus d.,** dahlia cactus.

dahllite ['dɑ:lait], *s. Miner:* dahllite *f*.

Dahoman [də'houmən], *Geog:* (*a*) *a.* dahoméen; (*b*) *s.* Dahoméen, -enne.

Dahomey [də'houmi], *Pr.n. Geog:* Dahomey *m*.

daikon ['daikən], *s. Bot:* daikon *m*.

Dail Eireann ['dɔil'ɛərən], *s.* chambre *f* des Députés de la République d'Irlande.

daily ['deili]. **1.** *a.* journalier, quotidien, de tous les jours; **d. paper,** (journal) quotidien *m*; **d. experience,** expérience *f* de tous les jours; **d. task,** tâche quotidienne; *Com:* **d. returns,** recettes journalières, relevés journaliers; *Fin:* **d. loans,** prêts *m* au jour je jour; *St.Exch:* **d. closing prices,** cours de clôture quotidiens; *Dom.Ec:* **d. woman, help,** femme *f* de ménage; *Ecc:* **give us this day our d. bread,** donne-nous aujourd'hui notre pain de ce jour. **2.** *adv.* (*a*) journellement, quotidiennement, tous les jours; (*b*) **to expect sth. d.,** attendre qch. d'un jour à l'autre. **3.** *s.* (*a*) *Journ:* quotidien *m*; **our leading dailies,** nos grands quotidiens; (*b*) *F:* femme de ménage.

daimio ['daimiou], *s. Hist:* daïmio *m* (seigneur féodal du Japon).

daincha ['deintʃə], *s. Bot:* sesbania *f*, sesbanie *f*.

daintily ['deintili], *adv.* (*a*) délicatement, coquettement; d'une manière raffinée; (*b*) avec friandise; (*c*) **to eat d.,** manger d'une manière délicate.

daintiness ['deintinis], *s.* délicatesse *f*, raffinement *m* (de goût, de manières); recherche *f*, coquetterie *f* (de toilette).

dainty[1] ['deinti], *s.* friandise *f*; mets délicat; gourmandise *f*; petit morceau de choix.

dainty[2], *a.* **1.** (*of dish, food*) friand, délicat. **2.** (*of pers., thg*) délicat; gentil; coquet; mignon; **she's a d. little thing,** elle est mignonne. **3.** délicat, friand, difficile; **to**

be d., faire le délicat, le difficile; faire la petite bouche; **these animals are d. feeders,** ces animaux (i) mangent très proprement, (ii) sont délicats sur la nourriture; **she was born with a d. tooth,** elle a toujours été (i) friande de bonnes choses, (ii) difficile sur la nourriture.

dairy ['dεəri], *s.* **1.** laiterie *f*; **co-operative d.,** coopérative laitière; **d. farm,** ferme laitière; **d. farming,** laiterie *f*, industrie laitière; **d. herd, d. cattle,** (troupeau *m* de) vaches laitières; **d. butter,** beurre laitier; **d. produce,** produits laitiers. **2.** (*shop*) laiterie; crémerie *f*.

dairying ['dεəriiŋ], *s.* l'industrie laitière.

dairymaid ['dεərimeid], *s.f.* fille de laiterie.

dairyman, *pl.* **-men** ['dεərimən], *s.m.* **1.** *Husb:* nourrisseur. **2.** *Com:* laitier; crémier.

dais ['deiis], *s.* (*a*) estrade *f* (d'honneur); dais *m*; (*b*) dais (recouvrant l'estrade); (*c*) (*freemasonry*) **the d.,** les chefs *m* de l'atelier (qui occupent l'estrade).

daisied ['deizid], *a. Lit:* couvert de pâquerettes; parsemé, émaillé, de pâquerettes.

daisy ['deizi], *s.* **1.** *Bot:* marguerite *f*; **common d.,** pâquerette *f*; **Michaelmas d.,** aster *m* œil-du-Christ, marguerite de la Saint-Michel, d'automne; **oxeye d.,** grande marguerite, marguerite des champs, œil-de-bœuf *m*, chrysanthème *m* des prés; **Paris d.,** chrysanthème frutescent; **globe d.,** globulaire *f*; **red d.,** épervière *f*; **d. chain,** guirlande *f* de pâquerettes, de marguerites; **as fresh as a d.,** frais, fraîche, comme une rose; *P:* **he's pushing up the daisies,** il est mort et enterré, il mange les pissenlits par les racines, les choux par les trognons; *F:* **d. cutter,** (i) *Equit: O:* cheval *m* qui rase le turf; (ii) *Cr: Ten: etc:* balle *f* qui rase le sol; (iii) *esp. U.S:* bombe *f* à fragmentation, bombe antipersonnel; (iv) *Av:* atterrissage parfait. **2.** *a. & s. F:* (personne, chose) épatante; **she's a d.,** c'est une perle. **3.** *U.S: Cu:* jambon d'épaule fumé et désossé.

Dalai Lama ['dælai'lɑ:mə], *s.* Dalaï-lama *m*.

dalbergia [dæl'bə:dʒiə], *s. Bot:* dalbergie *f*, dalbergia *m*.

dale[1] [deil], *s.* vallée *f*, vallon *m*; **d. land,** basses terres (d'une région).

dale[2], *s. Nau:* dalot *m* de pompe.

dalesman, *pl.* **-men** ['deilzmən], *s.m.* habitant des vallées (du nord de l'Angleterre).

dalliance ['dæliəns], *s. Lit:* **1.** échange *m* de tendresses; badinage *m*. **2.** *A:* lanternerie *f*, baguenauderie *f*.

dally ['dæli], *v.i. esp. Lit:* **1.** (*a*) folâtrer, folichonner (**with s.o.,** avec qn); **to d. with an idea,** caresser une idée; **people still dallying with bygone ideas,** gens attardés à des conceptions d'hier; **he dallied with several professions,** il essaya (sans ardeur) de plusieurs professions; (*b*) badiner, flirter (**with,** avec); (*c*) se jouer, se moquer (**with s.o.,** de qn). **2.** tarder, lambiner, baguenauder, traînasser; **to d. over sth.,** s'attarder à qch.; *v.tr.* **to d. the time away,** gaspiller son temps (en s'amusant, etc.).

Dalmanites [dælmə'naiti:z], *s. Paleont:* dalmanites *f*.

Dalmatia [dæl'meiʃə], *Pr.n. Geog:* Dalmatie *f*.

Dalmatian [dæl'meiʃən]. **1.** *Geog:* (*a*) *a.* dalmate; (*b*) *s.* Dalmate *mf*. **2.** *a. & s.* **D. (dog),** braque *m* de Bengale, chien *m* de Dalmatie.

dalmatic [dæl'mætik], *s. Ecc.Cost:* dalmatique *f*.

Daltonian [dɔ:l'tounjən], *a. & s. Med:* daltonien, -ienne.

daltonism ['dɔ:ltənizm], *s. Med:* daltonisme *m*.

dam[1] [dæm], *s.* **1.** *Hyd.E:* (*a*) barrage *m* (de retenue); digue *f* (de canal); bâtardeau *m*, décharge *f* (de rivière); dame *f* (dans un canal en construction); **storage d.,** barrage-réservoir *m*; **filter d.,** barrage criblant; **needle d.,** barrage à fermettes; **earth d.,** barrage en terre; **gravity d.,** barrage poids; **arch d.,** barrage voûte; **arch gravity d.,** barrage voûte-poids; **rock fill d.,** barrage en enrochements; **river d., low head d.,** barrage au fil de l'eau; (*b*) eau retenue (par un barrage); retenue *f*; **he was drowned in a d.,** il s'est noyé dans un réservoir; (*c*) **floating d.,** bâtardeau mobile (de cale sèche). **2.** *Min:* serrement *m*, serrage *m* (pour retenir l'eau); estouffée *f* (contre l'incendie).

dam[2], *v.tr.* **(dammed) to d. (up),** contenir, endiguer (un cours d'eau, un lac); construire un barrage en aval (d'une vallée); obstruer (un caniveau, etc.); **to d. the torrent of s.o.'s eloquence,** opposer une digue aux flots d'éloquence de qn.

dam[3], *s.* **1.** mère *f* (en parlant des animaux); **the cubs with their sires and their dams,** les petits *m* avec leurs pères et leurs mères. **2.** *Pej:* **that devil's d.,** cette femme (sortie de l'enfer); **the Devil and his d.,** le diable et sa mère; l'enfer déchaîné.

dam[4], *s. Metall:* **d. (stone),** dame *f* (de haut fourneau); **d. plate,** plaque *f* de dame.

damage[1] ['dæmidʒ], *s.* **1.** dommage(s) *m(pl)*, dégâts *mpl*; (*to engine, ship, etc.*) avarie(s) *f(pl)*; **war d.,** dommages de guerre; **storm d.,** méfaits *mpl* d'un orage; dégâts causés par un orage; **d. in transit,** avaries de route; **sea d.,** avaries de mer; **serious d.,** dégâts importants; avaries sérieuses, majeures; *Ins:* **d. survey,** expertise *f* des dégâts, des avaries; **to estimate the d.,** évaluer les dégâts; **to pay for the d.,** payer les dégâts, les détériorations; *Jur:* **cattle d. feasant,** bétail trouvé en dommage; **there's no great d. done,** il n'y a pas grand mal. **2.** préjudice *m*, tort *m*; **to cause s.o. d.,** porter préjudice, faire du tort, à qn; **this press campaign has done our cause irreparable d.,** cette campagne de presse a fait à notre cause un tort irréparable. **3.** *pl. Jur:* dommages-intérêts *m*, indemnité *f*; **to sue s.o. for damages, to bring an action for damages against s.o.,** poursuivre qn en dommages-intérêts; (*in criminal case*) **plaintiff claiming damages,** partie civile; **to be liable for damages,** être tenu des dommages-intérêts; (*in respect of act committed by third party*) être civilement responsable; **to pay the damages,** payer, acquitter, les condamnations. **4.** *F:* prix *m*, frais *mpl*; **what's the d.?** c'est combien?

damage[2], *v.tr.* **1.** endommager; avarier (une marchandise, une machine); abîmer, détériorer (qch.); faire subir des dégâts, des avaries, à (qch.); accidenter (une voiture); **the damp has damaged the fruit,** l'humidité *f* a taré les fruits; **the hail has damaged the wheat,** la grêle a gâté le blé; **the vines have been damaged by the frost,** les vignes *f* ont souffert de la gelée. **2.** faire tort, nuire, à (qn); léser, heurter (des intérêts); porter atteinte à, tarer (la réputation de qn, etc.).

damageable ['dæmidʒəbl], *a.* susceptible de s'avarier; avariable.

damaged ['dæmidʒd], *a.* avarié, endommagé, abîmé, taré; (*of fruits*) gâcheux; **d. goods,** marchandises avariées; **d. car,** voiture accidentée.

damaging ['dæmədʒiŋ], *a.* préjudiciable, nuisible; **d. admission,** aveu *m* préjudiciable; **this was a most d. admission,** cet aveu était de nature à lui faire beaucoup de tort.

daman ['dæmən], *s. Z:* daman *m* (de Syrie).

Damascene[1] [dæmə'si:n], *Geog:* (*a*) *a.* de Damas; damascène; **D. work,** damasquinage *m*, damasquinure *f*; *A:* **D. plum,** prune *f* de Damas; (*b*) *s.* Damascène *mf*.

damascene[2], *v.tr. Metalw:* damasquiner.

damascener [dæmə'si:nər], *s.Metalw:* damasquineur *m*.

damascening [dæmə'si:niŋ], *s.* damasquinage *m*, damasquinerie *f*, damasquinure *f*.

Damascus [də'mæskəs, -'mɑ:-], *Pr.n. Geog:* Damas *m*.

damask[1] ['dæməsk], *a. & s.* **1.** *Tex:* **d. (silk, linen),** damas *m*; soie damassée, linge damassé; soierie *f*, linge, de Damas; **d. linen manufacture, trade,** damasserie *f*; **d. weaver,** damasseur, -euse. **2.** *Metall:* **d. steel,** acier damassé; **d. (blade),** (lame *f* de) damas *m*; lame damasquinée; **d. work,** damasquinage *m*. **3. d. rose,** (i) *Bot:* rose *f* de Provins; (ii) *Hort:* rose de Damas, rose incarnate. **4. d. (colour),** rose foncé *m inv*; incarnat *m*; *Lit:* **her d. cheeks,** l'incarnat de ses joues; ses joues vermeilles.

damask[2], *v.tr.* **1.** *Tex:* damasser (une étoffe). **2.** = DAMASCENE[2].

damaskeen [dæmə'ski:n], *v.tr.* = DAMASCENE[2].

damassé [dæ'mæsei], *a. & Tex:* damassé *m*.

damassin ['dæməsin], *s. A.Tex:* damasquette *f*.

dambonite ['dæmbənait], **dambonitol** [dæm'bɔnitɔl], *s. Ch:* dambonite *f*.

dambose ['dæmbous], *s. Ch:* dambose *m*.

dame [deim], *s.* **1.** (*a*) *A:* dame *f*; maîtresse *f* de maison; (*b*) **an old d.,** une vieille femme; (*c*) *P:* femme *f*, gonzesse *f*; (*d*) *Th:* (*in pantomime*) vieille femme comique (rôle joué généralement par un homme). **2.** (*title*) (*a*) *Jur: A:* (*title of wife of knight or baronet*) dame; (*b*) seigneur *m* (de Sercq); (*c*) dame (titre accordé aux femmes titulaires de certaines décorations); (*d*) *Ecc:* sœur professe; dame; (*e*) *Lit:* **D. Nature,** dame Nature; *A:* **D. Alice,** dame Alice; la mère Alice. **3.** *Sch:* (*a*) *A:* maîtresse *f* (d'école enfantine); **d. school,** école enfantine (tenue par une femme); (*b*) = intendante *f* (au collège d'Eton). **4.** *Bot:* **dame's violet,** julienne *f* des dames; cassolette *f*, damas *m*.

damfool ['dæm'fu:l], *s. P:* (= *damned fool*) sacré idiot; imbécile *mf*; crétin *m*; *a.* **that's a d. reason!** en voilà une raison!

damfoolery ['dæm'fu:ləri], **damfoolishness** ['dæm'fu:liʃnis], *s. P:* ineptie *f*, sacrée imbécillité.

Damietta [dæmi'etə], *Pr.n. Geog:* Damiette *f*.

dammar ['dæmər], *s.* **1.** *Com:* **d. (resin),** (résine *f*) dammar *m*. **2.** *Bot:* **d. (pine, tree),** dammara *m*.

dammara ['dæmərə], *s. Bot:* dammara *m*.

damme ['dæmi], *int. A:* Dieu me damne!

dammer ['dæmər], *s. Hyd.E:* constructeur *m* de barrages.

damming ['dæmiŋ], *s. Hyd.E:* barrage *m*, endiguement *m*.

dammit ['dæmit]. *F:* (*a*) *int.* sacristi! sacrebleu! nom d'un chien! (*b*) *s.* **it was as near as d.,** il était moins une.

damn[1] [dæm], *s. F:* juron *m*, gros mot; **it's not worth a (tuppenny) d.,** ça ne vaut pas un pet de lapin; ça vaut deux fois rien; **I don't give, care, a d. (for it, him),** je m'en moque, m'en soucie, m'en fiche, comme de ma première culotte.

damn[2], *v.tr.* **1.** (*a*) condamner, critiquer défavorablement (un livre, etc.); éreinter (une pièce de théâtre); **to d. a work with faint praise,** assommer une œuvre avec des fleurs; éreinter une œuvre sous couleur d'éloge; (*b*) perdre, ruiner (qn, un projet); tomber (une pièce). **2.** (*a*) *Theol:* damner; (*of God*) réprouver; (*b*) *F:* **well I'm damned!** ça c'est trop fort! **I'm, I'll be, damned if I'll do it,** si tu crois que je vais le faire . . .! **I'll see him damned first!** qu'il aille au diable! **be damned to you!** va te faire fiche! **good cook be damned! she can't even boil an egg!** bonne cuisinière, tu parles! elle n'est pas fichue de faire cuire un œuf! **3.** *F:* (*a*) jurer après (qn); envoyer (qn) au diable; **d. you, your eyes, your impudence!** que le diable vous emporte! va te faire fiche! (*b*) **d. (it)!** zut! **d. and blast (it)!** sacré nom d'un chien! sacré nom de Dieu!

damn[3], *a. F:* **1.** = DAMNED 2 (*a*), (*b*). **2.** *adv.* **he's doing d. all,** il ne fiche rien; **he knows d. all about it,** il en sait moins que rien, deux fois rien; il n'y connaît (absolument) rien; il n'y pige rien.

damnable ['dæmnəbl], *a.* **1.** damnable. **2.** *F:* maudit, odieux, exécrable, détestable.

damnably ['dæmnəbli], *adv.* **1.** damnablement. **2.** odieusement, détestablement; diablement, bigrement, vachement (difficile, etc.).

damnation [dæm'neiʃ(ə)n]. **1.** *s.* damnation *f*; *Theol:* **eternal d.,** la peine du dam. **2.** *int. F:* zut!

damnatory ['dæmnət(ə)ri], *a.* **1.** = DAMNING[1]. **2.** *Theol:* qui a rapport à la damnation.

damned ['dæmd]. **1.** *a.* damné, réprouvé; **the d.,** les damnés; **to suffer the tortures of the d.,** souffrir comme un damné. **2.** *F:* (*a*) *a.* sacré, satané; **you d. fool!** sacré imbécile! espèce d'idiot! **one d. thing after another,** tout le diable et son train, tuile sur tuile; **what a d. nuisance!** quel empoisonnement! **he's a d. nuisance!** ce qu'il est embêtant, casse-pieds! (*b*) *adv.* (*intensive*) diablement, vachement, bigrement, rudement, joliment; **it's d. hot,** il fait bigrement, rudement, chaud; **it's d. hard,** c'est vachement difficile; **it serves you d. well right!** tu l'as bien mérité! **you can do what you d. well like!** fais ce que tu veux, je m'en fiche! (*c*) *s.* **to do one's damn(e)dest** ['dæmdist], faire tout son possible; faire un effort de tous les diables; **you can do your damn(e)dest!** je me moque bien de vos menaces!

damnification [dæmnifi'keiʃ(ə)n], *s. Jur: A:* lésion *f*.

damnify ['dæmnifai], *v.tr. Jur: A:* léser, faire du tort à (qn); nuire à (qn).

damning[1] ['dæmiŋ], *a.* portant condamnation; qui condamne, qui perd; **these are d. facts,** ce sont là des faits accablants; **d. evidence,** preuves écrasantes, accablantes, confondantes; *F:* **d. praise,** éreintement *m* avec des fleurs.

damning[2], *s.* **1.** condamnation *f*. **2.** damnation *f*. **3.** *Th: etc:* éreintement *m*.

Damocles ['dæməkli:z], *Pr.n.m. A.Hist:* Damoclès; **the sword of D.,** l'épée *f* de Damoclès.

damourite [dæ'mu:rait], *s. Miner:* damourite *f*.

damp[1] [dæmp], *s.* **1.** (*a*) humidité *f* (de l'air, d'un logement, etc.); moiteur *f* (de la peau); **the morning mist and the evening d.,** les brumes *f* du matin et l'humidité du soir, et le serein; **to catch a chill in the evening d.,** prendre froid au serein; prendre le serein; **don't sit in the d.,** ne vous asseyez pas sur le sol humide, ne restez pas à l'humidité; **d. mark, stain,** mouillure *f*; tache *f* d'humidité; *Const:* **d. course, coursing,** couche *f* d'isolement; couche isolante, hydrofuge; plaques isolatrices; (*b*) refroidissement *m* d'ardeur; nuage *m* de tristesse, d'abattement; *O:* **to strike a d. over the company,** jeter un froid sur la compagnie. **2.** *Min:* **(choke) d.,** mofette *f*; touffe *f*; gaz étouffant, méphitique; **fire d.,** grisou *m*; méthane *m*; mofette inflammable.

damp[2], *v.*

I. *v.tr.* **1.** mouiller; humecter (le linge, etc.); amoitir (la peau); madéfier (un emplâtre, etc.). **2.** étouffer (le feu); étouffer, assourdir (un son); **to d. down a furnace,** boucher un haut fourneau; *Pol.Ec:* **to d. down the market,** freiner le marché; **to d. down consumption,** réduire la consommation. **3.** *Ph: Mec: etc:* (*a*) **to d. (out) an oscillation,** amortir, éteindre, une oscillation; **damped waves,** ondes amorties; **to d. the spring reaction,** freiner l'action des ressorts; *El:* **to d. a magnetic needle,** modérer une aiguille aimantée; **damped oscillation,** oscillation forcée, amortie; **to d. the strings of a piano, one's footsteps,** étouffer les cordes d'un piano;

étouffer, feutrer, ses pas; (*b*) *v.i.* **the oscillations d. down,** les vibrations *f* s'amortissent. **4.** (*a*) (*of dish, unpleasant sight, etc.*) **to d. the appetite,** couper l'appétit (à qn); (*b*) abattre, affaiblir (le zèle, le courage, de qn); rabattre, troubler (la joie de qn); refroidir (la sympathie de qn); **to d. s.o.'s spirits,** décourager qn; abattre le courage de qn; déprimer qn; **to d. initiative,** étouffer l'initiative.

II. (*compound verb*) **damp off,** *v.i. Hort:* (*of seedlings, etc.*) périr de moisissure, d'excès d'humidité.

damp[3], *a.* humide; (*of skin*) moite; **to sleep in a d. bed,** coucher dans un lit humide; **his hands are always d.,** il a toujours les mains moites; **she had been washing up, and her hands were still d.,** elle venait de laver la vaisselle, et ses mains étaient encore humides; **d. heat,** chaleur *f* humide, moite; **this house is d.,** cette maison est humide; **the powder was d. and the gun missed fire,** la poudre était humide, mouillée, et le fusil rata; *F:* **d. squib,** affaire ratée; coup raté.

dampen ['dæmp(ə)n]. **1.** *v.tr.* = DAMP[2] I 1, 4 (*b*). **2.** *v.i.* (*a*) devenir humide, moite; (*b*) (*of ardour, etc.*) se refroidir.

dampener ['dæmp(ə)nər], *s.* **1.** mouilleur *m* (pour linge, etc.). **2.** *F:* douche froide (sur l'enthousiasme, etc.).

damper ['dæmpər], *s.* **1.** *F:* (*a*) (*pers.*) rabat-joie *m inv*; (*b*) événement déprimant, décourageant; douche froide (sur l'enthousiasme, etc.); **to put a d. on the company,** jeter un froid sur la compagnie; (*c*) *P: A:* quelque chose à boire; une consommation; **let's have a d.,** si on se mouillait le gosier? **2.** *Austr:* pain *m* en galette, sans levain, et cuit sous la cendre. **3.** *Mus:* (*of piano, sound*) étouffoir *m*; **d. pedal,** grande pédale (du piano). **4.** (*a*) registre *m* (de foyer, de cheminée); soupape *f* de réglage, à papillon (d'un tuyau de poêle); **sliding d.,** registre à guillotine; (*b*) *Ind:* registre, barrette *f,* tirette *f* (de fourneau); clapet *m* (de cendrier); *Mch:* **expansion d.,** papillon *m* de la détente. **5.** (*a*) *Mec.E: El:* amortisseur *m*; étouffoir *m*; frein *m*; modérateur *m* (d'une aiguille aimantée); *W.Tel:* sourdine *f*; **vibration d.,** étouffeur *m* de vibration (pour les tuyauteries rigides); *Aut:* **inertia d.,** batteur *m* à inertie; *Ind:* **flame d.,** anti-retour *m inv* de flammes; *Aut:* **steering d.,** frein de direction; (*b*) *F: A:* plat bourrant; abat-faim *m inv*; plat bourratif. **6.** mouilleur *m* (pour timbres, enveloppes); mouille-étiquettes *m inv.*

damping ['dæmpiŋ], *s.* **1.** (*a*) humectation *f*; mouillage *m* (du linge à repasser, etc.); madéfaction *f* (d'un emplâtre); *Dom.Ec:* **d. cloth,** pattemouille *f*; (*b*) **a general d. of spirits,** un froid général jeté sur la compagnie. **2.** (*a*) *Mec.E: etc:* amortissement *m*; effet *m* de freinage; **aerodynamic d.,** résistance *f* aux forces aérodynamiques; **d. device,** amortisseur *m*; (*b*) *El:* **spark d.,** amortissement des étincelles; **d. grid,** amortisseur; **d. winding,** enroulement *m* d'amortisseur; *Cin: etc:* **sound d.,** amortissement acoustique; insonorisation *f.* **3.** *Hort:* **d. off,** fonte *f* des semis.

dampish ['dæmpiʃ], *a.* un peu humide; (chaleur *f,* peau *f*) moite.

damply ['dæmpli], *adv.* humidement.

dampness ['dæmpnis], *s.* humidité *f*; moiteur *f* (de la peau).

damp-proof ['dæmppru:f], *a.* hydrofuge; imperméable; étanche à l'eau.

damp-proofing ['dæmppru:fiŋ], *s.* isolation *f* contre l'humidité; imperméabilisation *f*; **d.-p. compound,** isolant *m.*

damsel ['dæmz(ə)l], *s.* **1.** *A: & Lit:* demoiselle *f,* jeune fille *f.* **2.** (*a*) *Ich:* **d. fish,** poisson *m* ange, demoiselle; (*b*) *Ent:* **d. fly,** demoiselle.

damson ['dæmz(ə)n]. **1.** *s.* (*a*) prune *f* de Damas; (*b*) **d. (tree),** prunier *m* de Damas. **2.** *a.* (*colour*) prune *inv.*

Dan[1] [dæn], *Pr.n. B.Geog:* Dan *m*; **from D. to Beersheba,** d'un bout à l'autre du pays.

Dan[2], *Pr.n.m.* (*dim. of Daniel*) Daniel.

dan[3], *s. Sp:* (*judo*) dan *m.*

Danaë ['dæneii:]. **1.** *Pr.n.f. Gr.Myth:* Danaé. **2.** *s. Bot:* danaé *f,* laurier *m* d'Alexandrie.

Danaid ['dæneiid]. **1.** *s.f. Gr.Myth:* Danaïde; **the Danaides** [dæ'neiidi:z], les Danaïdes. **2.** *s. Ent:* danaïde *f.*

danaite ['deinəait], *s. Miner:* danaïte *f.*

danalite ['deinəlait], *s. Miner:* danalite *f.*

danburite ['dænbjurait], *s. Miner:* danburite *f.*

dance[1] [dɑ:ns], *s.* **1.** (*a*) danse *f*; **d. music,** musique *f* de danse; **to join the d.,** entrer en danse; **to lead, begin, the d.,** mener la danse; **solo d.,** pas seul; *F:* **to lead s.o. a d.,** (i) en faire voir de grises, de bleues, de toutes les couleurs, à qn; donner du fil à retordre à qn; faire valser qn; (ii) faire voir bien du chemin à qn; **country d.,** danse rustique; **folk d.,** danse villageoise, rustique; **figure d.,** danse figurée; **toe d.,** danse sur la pointe des pieds; **d. hostess,** entraîneuse *f*; **d. band,** orchestre *m* de musique de danse; **d. dress,** robe *f* de bal; **d. hall,** salle *f* de danse; dancing *m*; (*b*) (air *m* de) danse. **2.** bal *m, pl.* bals; soirée dansante; **informal d.,** sauterie *f*; **to go to a d.,** aller au bal; aller danser. **3.** *Ent:* **d. fly,** empididé *m.*

dance[2]. **1.** *v.i.* (*a*) danser; **to d. with s.o.,** danser avec qn; faire danser qn; **to d. to s.o.'s piping,** (i) se laisser mener par qn; (ii) s'accommoder aux désirs de qn; **I'll make him d. to a different tune!** je vais le faire chanter sur un autre ton; (*b*) **to d. for joy,** danser de joie; **to d. with rage,** piétiner, trépigner, de colère; *P: A:* **to d. on nothing,** être pendu; danser en l'air; **to d. along, in, out,** avancer, entrer, sortir, en dansant; **to d. about,** sauter, gambader; **they danced away,** (i) ils continuaient à danser; (ii) ils sont sortis en dansant; **to d. away the time,** passer le temps à danser. **2.** *v.tr.* (*a*) danser (une valse, etc.); **the polka is no longer danced,** la polka ne se danse plus; (*b*) faire danser (un ours, un pantin); **to d. a baby on one's knee,** faire sauter un bébé sur son genou; (*c*) **to d. attendance on s.o.,** (i) faire antichambre, faire le pied de grue, chez qn; (ii) être toujours aux côtés de qn; faire l'empressé auprès de qn; faire les trente-six volontés de qn; faire le cavalier servant auprès d'une dame; (*d*) *Const:* **to d. a step,** (faire) balancer une marche; faire le balancement d'une marche.

danceable ['dɑ:nsəbl], *a.* dansable.

dancer ['dɑ:nsər], *s.* danseur, -euse; **ballet d.,** danseur, -euse, de ballet; *f,* ballerine *f*; **rope d.,** danseur, -euse, de corde; *Lit: Scot:* **the merry dancers,** l'aurore boréale.

dancetté [dɑ:n'setei], **dancetty** [dɑ:n'seti], *a. Her:* (*of fess, etc.*) vivré.

dancing[1] ['dɑ:nsiŋ], *a.* **1.** dansant; **d. dervish,** derviche tourneur. **2.** *Tchn:* (*a*) **d. seat of a valve,** siège branlant d'une soupape; (*b*) *Const:* **d. step,** marche balançante, marche balancée.

dancing[2], *s.* danse *f*; **toe d.,** pointes *fpl*; **d. school,** école *f* de danse; **d. master, mistress,** maître, maîtresse, de danse; **d. partner,** (i) cavalier *m,* dame *f*; partenaire *mf*; (ii) partenaire rétribué(e); danseur mondain, *Pej:* gigolo *m*; **Indian d. girl,** bayadère *f.*

dandelion ['dændilaiən], *s. Bot:* pissenlit *m*; *NAm:* **fall d.,** léontodon *m*; **d. clock,** boule *f,* aigrette *f,* de pissenlit; *F:* chandelle *f,* voyageur *m.*

dander[1] ['dændər], *s. F:* **to get s.o.'s d. up, to raise s.o.'s d.,** mettre qn en colère; faire sortir qn de ses gonds; **to get one's d. up,** prendre la mouche; **he got his d. up,** la moutarde lui a monté au nez.

dander[2], *s. Scot:* petite promenade.

dander[3], *s.* = DANDRUFF.

dandified ['dændifaid], *a. O:* (*a*) (*of pers.*) vêtu en dandy; adonisé; **d. young man,** (i) jeune gommeux; (ii) jeune fat; jeune homme qui fait des manières; (*b*) (*of style*) affecté, recherché, maniéré.

dandle ['dændl], *v.tr.* **1.** (*a*) faire sauter (un enfant, sur ses genoux); (*b*) dodeliner, dandiner (un enfant). **2.** *Dial:* câliner, choyer, dorloter (qn).

dandruff ['dændrəf], *s.* pellicules *fpl* (du cuir chevelu).

dandy[1] ['dændi]. **1.** *s.* (*a*) (*pers.*) dandy *m,* gommeux *m,* élégant *m*; (*b*) (*for horse*) **d. brush,** brosse *f* de pansage. **2.** *s.* (*a*) *Nau: A:* dindet *m,* dandy *m*; (*b*) *Ind:* brouette *f* (de fonderie, etc.); (*c*) *Paperm:* **d. roll(er),** rouleau égoutteur; (rouleau) vergeur (*m*). **3.** *a. NAm: F:* épatant, chic, chouette; **everything's just d.,** tout marche à merveille.

dandy[2], *s. Med: F:* **d. (fever),** dengue *f.*

dandyish ['dændiiʃ], *a.* élégant, gommeux, fashionable.

dandyism ['dændiizm], *s.* dandysme *m*; recherche *f* d'élégance.

Dane [dein], *s.* **1.** *Ethn: Geog:* danois, -oise. **2.** (*dog*) **(Great) D.,** (grand) danois; **lesser D.,** (petit) danois; **Harlequin D.,** arlequin *m.* **3.** *Bot:* **d. flower,** coquelourde *f*; **Dane's blood,** (i) coquelourde; (ii) sureau *m* hièble; petit sureau.

Danegeld ['deingeld], *s. Hist:* l'impôt danois; le Danegeld.

daneweed ['deinwi:d], **danewort** ['deinwə:t], *s. Bot:* sureau *m* hièble; petit sureau.

dang [dæŋ], **danged** [dæŋd], *P:* = DAMN[2] 3, DAMNED 2.

danger ['dein(d)ʒər], *s.* danger *m*; péril *m*; **d. zone,** zone dangereuse; **d. point,** point *m* d'alerte; **to be in d.,** courir un danger; **out of d.,** hors de danger; hors d'affaire; **to keep out of d.,** rester à l'abri du danger; **to run into d.,** s'exposer au danger; **to be in d. of falling,** courir le risque, être en danger, de tomber; **in d. of (losing) his life,** en danger de mort; **building in d. of falling down,** bâtiment *m* qui menace ruine; **territory in d. of invasion,** territoire menacé d'invasion; **he is in d. of becoming ridiculous,** il s'expose à devenir ridicule; **to avert, ward off, a d.,** écarter un danger; **a d. to national security,** un danger pour la sécurité nationale; **rock that is a d. to navigation,** écueil dangereux pour la navigation; **he realized his d.,** il se rendait compte du danger qu'il courait; **there is some d. that . . .,** il y a quelque danger que . . . (ne) + *sub.*; **there was no d. of Clara getting stout,** il n'y avait pas de danger que Clara engraissât; *P.N:* **d., road up,** attention aux travaux; *Rail: etc:* **signal at d., d. signal,** signal *m* à l'arrêt.

dangerous ['dein(d)ʒ(ə)rəs], *a.* (*a*) dangereux, périlleux; **a d. opponent,** un dangereux adversaire; **d. illness,** maladie *f* grave; **it's not so d. as all that,** ce n'est pas dangereux à ce point-là; est bien malade qui en meurt; **to go to d. lengths,** passer la mesure; **you are on d. ground,** vous êtes sur un terrain brûlant; **d. situation,** mauvais pas; **the river is d. to bathe in,** c'est une rivière qui est dangereuse pour les baigneurs; **a d. river to cross,** une rivière dangereuse à traverser; (*b*) **d. example, maxim,** exemple pernicieux, maxime pernicieuse.

dangerously ['dein(d)ʒərəsli], *adv.* dangereusement; **d. ill,** gravement malade.

dangle ['dæŋgl]. **1.** *v.i.* pendiller, pendre, (se) balancer, brimbaler; **with one's legs dangling,** les jambes ballantes; *F:* **to d. after, round, a woman,** être pendu aux trousses, aux jupes, d'une femme; tournailler autour d'une femme; **he's been dangling round her, about her, after her, for a week,** voilà huit jours qu'il tourne autour d'elle. **2.** *v.tr.* balancer (qch. au bout d'un cordon, etc.); faire pendiller; **to d. one's arms,** laisser baller ses bras; *O:* **to d. a prospect before s.o.'s eyes,** faire miroiter une perspective aux yeux de qn.

dangling ['dæŋgliŋ], *a.* pendillant, pendu; (*of arms, legs*) ballant.

Danian ['deiniən], *a. & s. Geol:* danien (*m*).

Daniel ['dæniəl], *Pr.n.m.* Daniel; *B:* **D. in the lion's den,** Daniel dans la fosse aux lions; *Lit:* **a D. come to judgement,** un juge intègre, un homme au jugement infaillible.

Daniell ['dæniəl], *Pr.n. Ph:* **D. hygrometer,** hygromètre *m* de Daniell; *El:* **D. cell,** pile *f* de Daniell.

Danish ['deiniʃ]. **1.** *a.* danois. **2.** *s. Ling:* danois *m.*

dank [dæŋk], *a.* (temps, cachot) humide (et froid); (humidité *f*) désagréable.

dannemorite [dæni'mɔ:rait], *s. Miner:* dannemorite *f.*

danseur [dɔn'sə:r], *s.* (*in ballet*) danseur *m*; **d. noble,** premier danseur.

danseuse [dɔn'sə:z], *s.* ballerine *f.*

Dantesque [dæn'tesk], *a.* dantesque.

Danube (the) [ðə'dænju:b], *Pr.n. Geog:* le Danube.

Danubian [dæ'nju:biən], *a. Geog:* danubien; du Danube.

Danzig ['dæntzig], *Pr.n.f. Geog:* Dantzig.

Danziger ['dæntzigər], *s. Geog:* Dantzikois, -oise.

dap[1] [dæp], *s. Fish:* dandinette *f.*

dap[2]. **1.** *v.i.* (*a*) *Fish:* faire trembloter l'appât à la surface de l'eau; pêcher à la trembleuse, à la dandinette; (*b*) (*of ball*) rebondir. **2.** *v.tr.* (*a*) *Fish:* **to d. the bait,** faire sauter l'appât; (*b*) **to d. a ball,** faire rebondir une balle (du sol à la main).

Daphne ['dæfni]. **1.** *Pr.n.f. Myth:* Daphné. **2.** *s. Bot:* daphné *m*; (*a*) (*mezereon*) bois gentil; malherbe *f*; (*b*) (*spurge laurel*) lauréole *f.*

daphnetin ['dæfnitin], *s. Ch:* daphnétine *f.*

daphnia ['dæfniə], **daphnid** ['dæfnid], *s. Crust:* daphnie *f.*

daphnin ['dæfnin], *s. Ch:* daphnine *f.*

daphnite ['dæfnait], *s. Miner:* daphnite *f.*

dapper ['dæpər], *a.* **1.** pimpant, coquet, correct; **a d. little man,** un petit homme tiré à quatre épingles, bien troussé. **2.** vif, éveillé.

dapping ['dæpiŋ], *s.* pêche *f* à la trembleuse, à la dandinette.

dapple[1] ['dæpl], *s.* **1.** (*a*) tache *f* de couleur (sur la robe d'un cheval, etc.); (*b*) tacheture *f.* **2.** cheval pommelé, cheval (bai) miroité, à miroir; **d. grey,** (cheval) gris pommelé.

dapple[2]. **1.** *v.tr.* tacheter. **2.** *v.i.* se tacheter; (*of sky*) se pommeler.

darbies ['dɑ:biz], *s.pl. P: O:* menottes *f.*

Darby ['dɑ:bi], *Pr.n.* **D. and Joan** = Philémon et Baucis; Monsieur et Madame Denis; Robin et Marion; **D. and Joan club,** club *m* des vieux, du troisième âge.

Darbyism ['dɑ:biizm], *s. Rel:* darbysme *m.*

darcy ['dɑ:si], *s. Ph.Meas:* darcy *m.*

dare[1] [dɛər], *v.* **1.** *modal aux.* (*3rd. sg.pr.* **dare;** *p.t.* **dared, dare,** *A: & Lit:* **durst** [də:st]; *no p.p.*; **d. not** *often contracted to* **daren't**) oser; **I d. not, daren't speak to him,** je n'ose pas lui parler; **he knew it was true but he dare(d) not say so,** il savait que c'était vrai mais il n'osait pas le dire; **he dared not contradict me,** il n'a pas osé me contredire; **he didn't d. turn his head,** il n'a pas osé tourner la tête; **don't you d. touch him!** ne touchez pas un cheveu de sa tête! **I d. say that. . .,** (i) j'ose affirmer que . . .; (ii) je suppose que . . .; **I d. say,** sans doute; peut-être bien; je (le) crois bien; c'est fort probable; **I d. say he'll come,** sans doute, il est probable, qu'il viendra. **2.** *v.tr.* (*3rd sg.pr.* **dares;** *p.t.* **dared;** *p.p.* **dared**) (*a*) oser; **to d. to do sth.,** oser faire qch.; **he did not d. to contradict me,** il n'a pas osé me contredire; il n'a pas eu la hardiesse de me contredire; **no one dared to propose it,** personne n'osait le proposer; **if he dares to go alone,** s'il ose y aller seul; **how d. you!** vous avez cette audace! **let him do it if he dare(s)!** qu'il le fasse s'il l'ose! **to d. all things,** tout oser; (*b*) braver, affronter (le danger, la mort, etc.); **to d. the perils of a journey,** affronter, risquer, les périls d'un voyage; (*c*) **to d. s.o. to do sth.,** défier qn de faire qch.; **if he dares me to contradict him,** s'il me met au défi de le contredire.

dare[2], *s.* (*a*) coup *m* d'audace; (*b*) défi *m.*

daredevil ['dɛədevl]. **1.** *s.* casse-cou *m inv*; cervelle brûlée; téméraire *m*; risque-tout *m inv.* **2.** *a.* qui ne craint ni Dieu ni diable.

daring[1] ['dɛəriŋ], *a.* (i) audacieux, hardi; (ii) téméraire; **d. dress,** robe provocante; **greatly d.,** bien osé, fort osé.

daring[2], *s.* (i) audace *f*, hardiesse *f*; (ii) témérité *f*; **to lose one's d.,** perdre de son audace; s'accouardir.

daringly ['dɛəriŋli], *adv.* audacieusement, témérairement, hardiment.

dariole ['dæriəl], *s. Cu:* dariole *f.*

dark[1] [dɑ:k], *a.* **1.** sombre, obscur; noir; **d. glasses,** lunettes noires, de soleil; *A:* **d. lantern,** lanterne sourde; **it's d.,** il fait nuit, il fait noir; **it is getting, growing, d.,** il commence à faire sombre, à faire nuit; **the sky grew d.,** le ciel se rembrunit; **it was very d. in the room,** il faisait très sombre dans la pièce; **to make sth. dark(er),** rembrunir qch.; **everything became d.,** tout s'assombrit; **d. dungeon, d. forests,** cachot ténébreux, forêts ténébreuses. **2.** (*of colour*) foncé, sombre; **d. blue (dresses),** (robes *f*) bleu foncé; **to draw a picture of the situation in the darkest colours,** peindre la situation sous les couleurs les plus sombres. **3.** (*of pers.*) brun; (*of complexion*) basané, brun; (*of hair*) **to become d.,** brunir; **she has d. hair,** elle est brune; **a d. beauty,** une belle brune. **4.** (*a*) sombre, triste; **d. future,** sombre avenir *m*; noire destinée; **to look on, to see, the d. side of things,** envisager, voir, les choses par leur mauvais côté; voir tout en noir; **d. thoughts,** pensées tristes; (*b*) ténébreux, mauvais, sinistre; **d. thoughts,** pensées ténébreuses, sinistres; **to harbour d. designs,** nourrir de noirs desseins. **5.** mystérieux; secret, -ète; **d. saying,** mot mystérieux; énigme *f*; **Heraclitus was called the Dark Philosopher,** on appelait Héraclite le philosophe ténébreux; **d. words,** paroles obscures; **to keep sth. d.,** tenir qch. secret; cacher son jeu; **keep it d.!** gardez le secret! motus! **a d. horse,** (*Turf: or pers.*) un outsider; (*pers.*) un concurrent inconnu, une quantité inconnue. **6.** *Hist:* **the D. Ages,** le haut moyen âge; les premiers siècles du moyen âge; **the D. Continent,** le Continent noir, l'Afrique *f*; **to live in darkest ignorance,** croupir dans l'ignorance. **7.** *Ph:* **d. heat,** chaleur obscure.

dark[2], *s.* **1.** (*a*) ténèbres *fpl*, obscurité *f*; noir *m*; **in the d.,** dans l'obscurité, dans le noir; **to look for sth. in the d.,** chercher qch. à l'aveuglette, à tâtons; **the child is afraid of the d.,** l'enfant a peur du noir, dans le noir; **after d.,** à, après, la tombée de la nuit; la nuit tombée, venue; **until d.,** jusqu'à la tombée de la nuit; **the d. of the moon,** la nouvelle lune; *P: O:* **to be in the d.,** être en prison, à l'ombre; (*b*) **darks of a picture,** ombres *f* d'un tableau; noirs d'une gravure. **2. to be (kept) in the d.,** être (laissé) dans l'ignorance; **they like to keep people in the d. about what they are doing,** ils aiment faire un mystère de ce qu'ils font; ils n'aiment pas trop qu'on sache ce qu'ils font; **he is entirely in the d.,** il ne sait rien de rien (de l'affaire); **with this new technique we find ourselves working in the d.,** avec ces nouvelles techniques nous avons l'impression de marcher à l'aveuglette, d'avancer comme dans un tunnel.

darken ['dɑ:k(ə)n]. **1.** *v.tr.* obscurcir (une chambre, etc.); assombrir, rembrunir (le ciel, l'avenir, le front de qn); brunir (le teint); foncer (une couleur); ternir (l'éclat de qch.); attrister (la vie de qn); troubler (la raison); **fears that d. the future,** craintes *f* qui embrument l'avenir; **a cloud darkened the sun,** un nuage a voilé la face du soleil; **never d. my doors again!** ne remettez plus les pieds chez moi! **we were shown into a darkened room,** on nous a fait entrer dans une pièce (i) à volets clos, (ii) à rideaux tirés. **2.** *v.i.* s'obscurcir; (*of sky, brow*) s'assombrir, se rembrunir; (*of colour*) se foncer; **these pictures have darkened,** ces tableaux ont tiré au noir, ont poussé au noir (avec le temps).

darkening ['dɑ:kniŋ], *s.* (*a*) assombrissement *m*; noircissement *m* (d'un tableau, d'un cliché, etc.); (*b*) *Lit:* **at the d.,** à la tombée de la nuit.

dark(e)y, darkie ['dɑ:ki], *s. P: Pej:* nègre, *f.* négresse; moricaud, -aude.

dark-eyed ['dɑ:k'aid], *a.* aux yeux noirs.

darkish ['dɑ:kiʃ], *a.* un peu sombre; (*of hair*) **d. brown,** châtain.

darkle ['dɑ:kl], *v.i. Lit:* **1.** s'assombrir. **2.** se dissimuler à l'ombre.

darkling ['dɑ:kliŋ], *a. Lit:* **1.** sombre, obscur. **2.** dans l'obscurité.

darkly ['dɑ:kli], *adv.* (*a*) obscurément; (*b*) **to look d. at s.o.,** regarder qn (i) d'un air sombre, (ii) d'un air menaçant.

darkness ['dɑ:knis], *s.* **1.** obscurité *f*, ténèbres *fpl*; **the room was in complete d.,** il faisait tout à fait noir dans la pièce; **the Prince of D.,** le prince des ténèbres; **the d. of death,** les affres *f* de la mort. **2.** (*of colour*) teinte foncée; **d. of complexion,** teint bronzé, basané. **3.** ignorance *f*; **I am in complete d. about his plans,** j'ignore entièrement ses projets; je ne sais rien de ses projets.

darkroom ['dɑ:kru:m], *s. Phot:* chambre noire (pour manipulations); cabinet noir; laboratoire obscur.

dark-skinned ['dɑ:k'skind], *a.* à peau brune; qui a la peau brune; brun.

darksome ['dɑ:ksəm], *a. A: & Lit:* sombre.

darling[1] ['dɑ:liŋ], *s. & a.* favori, -ite; chéri(e); bien-aimé(e); **(my) d.!** mon cheri! ma chérie! mon chou! mon petit chat! ma petite chatte! **she's a little d.,** c'est un petit amour; **she was a perfect d. about it,** elle s'est montrée très compréhensive; **a mother's d.,** un enfant gâté, *F:* le chouchou de sa maman; **fortune's d.,** l'enfant gâté de la fortune; **the d. of the people,** l'idole *f* du peuple; **a d. little place,** un petit endroit charmant, délicieux.

Darling[2], *Pr.n. Geog:* (le fleuve) Darling *m*; *Austr:* **D. shower,** tourbillon *m* de poussière.

darn[1] [dɑ:n], *s.* reprise *f*, passefilure *f*; *Nau:* (*in sail*) videlle *f.*

darn[2], *v.tr.* raccommoder, ravauder, repriser; passefiler (des bas); remplir (un trou).

darn[3], *a. F:* sacré; **it's a d. nuisance,** c'est vachement embêtant.

darn[4], *v.tr. & i. F:* **d. (it)!** zut!

darned ['dɑ:nd], *a. F:* = DARN[3].

darnel ['dɑ:nl], *s. Bot:* **(bearded) d.,** ivraie (enivrante), *F:* vorge *f.*

darner ['dɑ:nər], *s.* **1.** (*pers.*) repriseur, -euse, ravaudeur, -euse; **fine d.,** stoppeur, -euse. **2.** (*a*) aiguille *f* à repriser; (*b*) boule *f*, œuf *m*, à repriser.

darning ['dɑ:niŋ], *s.* reprise *f*, reprisage *m*, ravaudage *m*, passefilage *m*; **fine d.,** stoppage *m*; **invisible d.,** reprise perdue; **d. ball, egg, mushroom,** boule *f*, œuf *m*, à repriser; **d. cotton, wool,** coton *m*, laine *f*, à repriser; **d. needle,** aiguille *f* à repriser; *Ent:* **devil's d. needle,** demoiselle *f*, libellule *f.*

dart[1] [dɑ:t], *s.* **1.** (*a*) dard *m*, trait *m*, javelot *m*; *Mil:* **aerial d.,** fléchette *f* d'avion; **(paper) d.,** avion *m* (de, en, papier); *Lit:* **the lightning's vivid darts,** les traits aveuglants de la foudre; (*b*) *Games:* fléchette; **game of darts,** jeu *m* de fléchettes; (*c*) dard (de serpent, d'abeille, de sarcasme); (*d*) *Dressm:* pince *f.* **2.** mouvement soudain en avant; élan *m*; **to make a sudden d. on sth.,** foncer, se précipiter, sur qch.; **the child made a d. after the ball,** l'enfant s'est élancé pour rattraper la balle. **3.** *Ent:* **d. moth,** agrotide *f*, agrotis *f*, des moissons.

dart[2]. **1.** *v.tr.* (*a*) darder (des rayons, un aiguillon); lancer, darder (un harpon, un regard); lancer, décocher (un sarcasme); **his eyes darted triumph,** un regard de triomphe jaillissait de ses yeux; (*b*) *A:* **to d. a whale,** darder une baleine. **2.** *v.i.* se précipiter, s'élancer, foncer (**at, upon, s.o., sth.,** sur qn, qch.); **he darted down, across, the road,** il descendit, traversa, la rue comme une flèche, comme un bolide; **to d. in, out, away, off,** entrer, sortir, partir, vivement, comme une flèche, comme un trait; **to d. up,** (i) se lever d'un bond; (ii) accourir à toute vitesse; **a deer darted out of the copse,** un cerf s'élança du taillis. **3.** *v.tr. Dressm:* faire des pinces à (une robe, etc.).

dartboard ['dɑ:tbɔ:d], *s.* cible *f* (de jeu de fléchettes).

darter ['dɑ:tər], *s.* **1.** *Ich:* toxote *m*, archer *m*. **2.** *Orn:* anhinga *m*, *F:* oiseau-serpent *m.*

dartre ['dɑ:tər], *s. Med:* (*a*) dartre *f*; (*b*) affection *f* herpétique.

dartrous ['dɑ:trəs], *a. Med:* dartreux; herpétique.

Darwinian [dɑ:winiən], *a.* darwinien, darwiniste.

Darwinism ['dɑ:winizm], *s.* darwinisme *m.*

Darwinist ['dɑ:winist], *s.* darwiniste *mf.*

dash[1] [dæʃ], *s.* **1.** coup *m*, heurt *m*, choc *m*; choc, floc *m* (sur l'eau); **I could hear the d. of oars,** j'entendais le choc des avirons sur l'eau; **a d. of cold water will revive her,** quelques gouttes d'eau froide au visage la ranimera. **2.** soupçon *m*, goutte *f*, larme *f* (de cognac, etc.); pointe *f* (de vanille, etc.); filet *m* (de vinaigre); **coffee with a d. of spirits,** café additionné d'un doigt d'eau-de-vie, d'une goutte d'eau-de-vie; **add a d. of lemon,** ajoutez-y un filet de citron. **3. d. of colour,** tache *f* de couleur (dans le paysage, etc.); touche *f* de couleur (dans un tableau). **4.** trait *m* (de plume, de l'alphabet Morse); *Typ:* (i) tiret *m*; (ii) moins *m*; *Mth:* **A dash (A′),** a prime; **A double d. (A″),** a seconde. **5.** (*a*) (i) attaque soudaine; (ii) course *f* à toute vitesse; élan *m*; ruée *f*; **to make a d. forward,** s'élancer en avant; **to make a d. at sth.,** se précipiter, se ruer, sur qch.; foncer (sur l'ennemi); **d. for liberty,** évasion *f*; **to make a d. for liberty,** saisir l'occasion de s'enfuir; *Hist:* **the d. for the Channel ports,** la ruée sur les ports de la Manche; *Fb:* **a d. by the forwards,** une descente des avants; (*b*) *F: O:* **to have a d. at sth.,** tenter, essayer (un examen, etc.); **to have a d. at it,** essayer (le coup); (*c*) *Sp: U.S:* course sans épreuves éliminatoires. **6.** élan, impétuosité *f*, fougue *f*, entrain *m*, allant *m*; **troops full of d.,** troupes pleines d'allant, qui ont du cran; **artist full of d.,** artiste plein(e) de brio *m*; *Mus:* **to play with d.,** jouer avec brio. **7. to cut a d.,** faire (brillante) figure; faire de l'effet; faire de l'épate. **8.** *Aut: F:* = DASHBOARD 2.

dash[2], *v.*

I. *v.tr. & i.* **1.** *v.tr.* (*a*) heurter, choquer, lancer, violemment (qch. contre qch.); jeter, *F:* flanquer (qch. par terre); **the ship was dashed against a rock,** le navire fut jeté sur un écueil, contre un rocher; **to d. sth. to pieces,** fracasser qch.; briser qch. en morceaux; **to d. one's head against sth.,** se casser la tête contre qch.; (*b*) déconcerter, confondre (qn); anéantir, détruire, renverser (les espérances); refroidir (l'enthousiasme); **to d. s.o.'s spirits,** abattre le courage, l'entrain, de qn; abattre qn; **he saw his hopes dashed (to the ground),** il a vu sombrer, fondre, tomber à l'eau, ses espérances; **he was somewhat dashed by the news,** il a été un peu déconcerté par la nouvelle; (*c*) *F:* **d. (it)!** zut! **2.** *v.i.* (*a*) **to d. against sth.,** se heurter, se jeter, se cogner, donner, contre qch.; (*of car*) **to d. into a wall, etc.,** s'emboutir contre un mur, etc.; (*b*) (*meaning little more than 'move precipitately'*) **I must d.,** il faut que je file; **to come dashing up, in,** arriver, entrer, comme un éclair, comme un bolide; arriver, entrer, en trombe; **they went dashing away, off, out,** ils partaient, s'éloignaient, en coup de vent; **cars dashing along (the road),** voitures qui filent, foncent, à toute vitesse; **to d. at s.o., at sth.,** se précipiter, s'élancer, sur qn, qch.; **to d. into the sea,** se jeter, se précipiter, dans la mer; **to d. down the street,** descendre la rue à toute vitesse, comme un bolide; **to d. down the hill,** dévaler la pente à toute vitesse; **to d. up, down, the stairs,** monter, descendre, l'escalier quatre à quatre; **to d. into the room,** entrer précipitamment, en trombe, en coup de vent, dans la salle; **to d. out of the room,** s'élancer hors de la pièce; **to d. through France,** traverser la France au galop, à la galopade, à la galope.

II. (*compound verbs*) **1. dash aside,** *v.tr.* écarter (qn, un coup) brusquement, violemment.

2. dash away, *v.tr.* **to d. away a tear,** essuyer furtivement une larme.

3. dash off, *v.tr.* faire (qch.) en vitesse, à la six-quatre-deux; dessiner, faire (un croquis) rapidement, en un tour de main; écrire (une lettre) en vitesse.

4. dash out, *v.tr.* **to d. out one's brains,** se fracasser la cervelle.

dashboard ['dæʃbɔ:d], *s.* **1.** *A: Veh:* garde-crotte *m inv*, garde-boue *m inv*, pare-boue *m inv.* **2.** *Aut: etc:* tableau *m* de bord; **d. light, lamp,** voyant (lumineux), lampe *f* de tableau de bord.

dashed [dæʃt], *a.* = DAMNED 2.

dasher ['dæʃər], *s.* **1.** *F:* (*a*) *A:* élégant *m*, gommeux *m*; (*b*) *Pej:* épateur *m*. **2.** *Husb:* batte *f* à beurre; babeurre *m*; palette *f* (de baratte); barat(t)on *m.*

dashing ['dæʃiŋ], *a.* (*of pers.*) impétueux; plein d'élan; qui a de l'allant; (*of horse*) fougueux, fringant; **d. young man,** beau cavalier; **he's a d. fellow,** il a du panache; *Sp:* **d. player,** joueur brillant, plein d'allant, mais peu prudent.

dashingly ['dæʃiŋli], *adv.* (se conduire) avec fougue, avec brio; *O:* (s'habiller) avec une élégance tapageuse.

dashpot ['dæʃpɔt], *s. Mec.E: Aut:* dash-pot *m*; amortisseur *m*; **oil d.,** amortisseur à huile.

dassie, dassy ['dæsi], *s. Z:* daman *m*; **d. rat,** pétromys *m.*

dastard [ˈdæstəd], *s. Lit:* **1.** lâche *m.* **2.** personnage *m* ignoble.

dastardliness [ˈdæstədlinis], *s. Lit:* **1.** lâcheté *f.* **2.** caractère *m* infâme, ignoble (d'une action).

dastardly [ˈdæstədli], *a. Lit:* **1.** lâche. **2.** (crime *m*, etc.) infâme, ignoble.

Dasyatidae [dæsiˈætidi], *s.pl. Ich:* dasyatidés *m.*

dasyphyllous [dæsiˈfiləs], *a. Bot:* dasyphylle.

Dasypodidae [dæsiˈpɔdidi:], *s.pl. Z:* dasypodidés *m*, les tatous *m.*

Dasyproctidae [dæsiˈprɔktidi:], *s.pl. Z:* dasyproctidés *m.*

dasyure [ˈdæsijuər], *s. Z:* dasyure *m.*

Dasyuridae [dæsiˈju:ridi:], *s.pl. Z:* dasyuridés *m.*

data [ˈdeitə], *s.pl.* (*occ. with sg. const.*) données *f*; renseignements *m*; *Cmptr: etc:* **d. processing,** (i) l'informatique *f*; (ii) traitement *m* de l'information, des données; **d. gathering,** collecte *f*, rassemblement *m*, de données; **d. handling,** exploitation *f*, interprétation *f*, manipulation *f*, traitement, de données, de l'information, des informations; **raw d.,** données brutes, non traitées, à traiter; **control d.,** données de contrôle; **master d.,** données de base; **d. bank,** banque *f* de données; fichier central; **d.-processing card,** carte perforée, mécanographique; **d.-processing department,** service *m* informatique, mécanographique; **d. convertor,** convertisseur *m* de données, d'éléments; **d. recorder,** enregistreur *m* de données, d'éléments; mémoire *f*; *Meteor:* **weather d.,** données, renseignements, météorologiques; **upper air d.,** observations *f* en altitude; **sea, swell and surf d.,** données, renseignements, sur l'état de la mer, de la houle, du ressac; *Surv: Mapm:* **survey d.,** (i) indications *f* topographiques; (ii) éléments topographiques de base; **grid d.,** éléments numériques du quadrillage; **marginal d.,** renseignements en marge (de la carte); *Artil:* **firing, fire, d.,** éléments de, du, tir; **prediction d.,** éléments extrapolés.

datable [ˈdeitəbl], *a.* datable, qu'on peut dater (**from,** à partir de).

dataller [ˈdeitələr], *s. Ind: A:* ouvrier *m* à la journée; journalier *m.*

datary [ˈdeitəri], *s. Ecc:* (*a*) dataire *m*; (*b*) daterie *f.*

date[1] [deit], *s.* **1.** *Bot:* datte *f*; **d. palm,** dattier *m.* **2.** *Bot:* **d. plum,** plaqueminier *m.* **3.** *Bot: U.S:* palmier-éventail *m, pl.* palmiers-éventails. **4.** *Moll:* **d. mussel, shell,** datte de mer.

date[2], *s.* (*a*) date *f*; (*on coins, books, etc.*) millésime *m*; (*of month*) quantième *m*; **d. of birth,** date de naissance; **what's the d. (today)?** quelle est la date (aujourd'hui)? quel jour (du mois) sommes-nous? **what is the d. of this paper?** de quand est ce journal? **to fix a d. for sth.,** prendre date pour qch.; **we'll fix the d. later,** nous conviendrons d'un jour plus tard, par la suite; **d. stamp, d. marker,** dateur *m*, timbre *m* à date; *Geog:* **d. line,** ligne *f* de changement de date (le méridien 180°); (*b*) **up to d.,** à jour; **to be up to d. with one's work,** être à jour pour, dans, son travail; **I'm not up to d. with the latest developments,** je ne suis pas au courant des derniers développements; **to bring, keep, a diary, the accounts, a catalogue, etc., up to d.,** mettre, tenir, à jour son journal, les écritures, un catalogue, etc.; **he's not, his ideas aren't, exactly up to d.,** il n'est pas de son temps, *F:* dans le mouvement, dans le vent, à la page; il ne suit pas les derniers progrès; il n'est pas au courant des méthodes modernes; **to d.,** à ce jour; **interest to d.,** intérêts *mpl* à ce jour; **to d. we have received fifty orders,** à ce jour nous avons reçu cinquante commandes; (*c*) **out of d.,** périmé; démodé; **this style is out of d.,** ce style date, est démodé; **theory that is out of d.,** théorie qui a eu son temps; **your father's quite out of d.** votre père est de la vieille école, *F:* n'est pas à la page, dans le vent; (*d*) *Com: Fin:* **d. of a bill,** terme *m*, échéance *f*, d'un billet; **three months after d., at three months' d.,** à trois mois de date, d'échéance; **d. of maturity, due d.,** (date d')échéance; **final, latest, d.,** terme de rigueur; **to buy at long d.,** acheter à long terme; **to pay at fixed dates,** payer à échéances fixes; *A: & Lit:* **all has its d. below,** tout ici-bas a son terme; (*e*) *F:* (i) rendez-vous *m inv*; **double d.,** partie carrée, rendez-vous à quatre; **blind d.,** rendez-vous avec quelqu'un qu'on ne connaît pas; **to make a d.,** fixer un rendez-vous; (ii) ami(e) (avec qui on a fixé un rendez-vous); **my d. didn't turn up,** mon ami(e) n'est pas venu(e).

date[3]. **1.** *v.tr.* (*a*) dater (une lettre, etc.); millésimer (une bouteille de vin, etc.); composter (un billet); **dating and numbering machine,** composteur *m*; **coin dated . . .,** pièce *f* au millésime de . . .; **to d. back,** antidater; **to d. forward,** postdater; (*b*) **work of art, (etc.), that is difficult to d.,** œuvre d'art (etc.) à laquelle il est difficile d'assigner une date; (*c*) **his clothes d. him,** ses vêtements démodés montrent qu'il n'est jeune; (*d*) *F:* **to d. s.o.,** fixer un rendez-vous avec qn. **2.** *v.i.* (*a*) dater (**from,** de); **church dating from, dating back to, the XIIIth century,** église *f* qui remonte au XIIIe siècle, qui date du XIIIe siècle; **the house dates back to the reign of Elizabeth,** la maison remonte au règne d'Élisabeth; **this debt dates back several years,** cette dette remonte à plusieurs années; **the improvements d. from this period,** c'est à partir de cette époque qu'on constate des améliorations; **friendship dating back to the days of their youth,** amitié *f* qui remonte à leur jeunesse; *U.S: F:* **I can d. back to . . .,** mes souvenirs remontent jusqu'à . . .; (*b*) **his style has dated, his car is beginning to d.,** son style, sa voiture, commence à dater.

date-cancel [ˈdeitkænsl], *v.tr.* (**-cancelled**) oblitérer (un timbre).

dated [ˈdeitid], *a.* (*a*) démodé; **his style is rather d.,** son style commence à dater; (*b*) (*in compounds*) *Fin:* **long-d., short-d.,** à longue, à courte, échéance.

dateless [ˈdeitlis], *a.* (*of letter, etc.*) sans date, non daté.

dater [ˈdeitər], *s.* dateur *m*; timbre-dateur *m, pl.* timbres-dateurs; composteur *m.*

dating [ˈdeitiŋ], *s.* (*a*) datage *m* (d'un document, etc.); (*b*) compostage *m* (de billets de chemin de fer, etc.); (*c*) *Archeol: etc:* datation *f*; **d. by radiocarbon, carbon 14,** datation par radio-carbone, par (le) carbone 14.

dation [ˈdeiʃ(ə)n], *s. Jur:* dation *f* (d'une tutelle, etc.).

datisca [dæˈtiskə], *s. Bot:* datisque *m*, datisca *f.*

Datiscaceae [dætisˈkeisii:], *s.pl. Bot:* datiscacées *f.*

datiscin [ˈdætisin], *s. Ch:* datiscine *f.*

dative [ˈdeitiv], *a. & s.* **1.** *Gram:* **d. (case),** (cas) datif *m*; **in the d.,** au datif. **2.** *Jur:* **tutory d.,** tutelle dative.

datolite [ˈdætəlait], *s. Miner:* datolite *f.*

datum [ˈdeitəm], *s.* (*pl. usu.* **data,** *q.v.*) donnée *f*, élément *m* (d'information); renseignement *m*; indication *f*; (*a*) *Surv: etc:* **d. point,** (i) élément de base; (ii) point *m* de référence; (iii) (point de) repère *m*; **d. line,** (i) ligne *f* de base, de référence, d'opérations; base *f* (d'opérations); (ii) *Av:* axe *m* de référence; **d. plane, level,** plan *m* de référence; **ordnance d.,** système de références établi par le service géographique de l'armée; (*b*) *Mec.E: etc:* (point de) repère.

datura [dəˈtju:rə], *s. Bot:* datura *m*; **d. stramonium,** stramoine *f*; pomme épineuse.

daturic [dəˈtju:rik], *a. Ch:* daturique.

daturine [ˈdætjurin], *s. Bio-Ch:* daturine *f.*

daub[1] [dɔ:b], *s.* **1.** (*a*) enduit *m*, barbouillage *m*; (*b*) *Const:* torchis *m*, gobetage *m*, enduit. **2.** (*of picture*) croûte *f*, barbouillage.

daub[2], *v.tr.* **1.** (*a*) barbouiller, enduire (**with,** de); **the tables were daubed with green paint,** les tables étaient grossièrement enduites de vert, étaient barbouillées de vert; **she daubs her face with rouge,** elle se plâtre le visage de rouge; (*b*) **wherever there is a flaw, they d. on the paint,** partout où se montre une fêlure, on plâtre de la couleur; (*c*) **to daub a wall (with clay, etc.),** gobeter, torcher, un mur; **wall daubed with clay,** mur enduit de torchis. **2.** *Art: F:* peintur(lur)er, barbouiller (une toile).

Daubentoniidae [doubentoˈnaiidi:], *s.pl. Z:* daubentoniidés *m*, les ayes-ayes *m.*

dauber [ˈdɔ:bər], **daubster** [ˈdɔ:bstər], *s. Art: F:* barbouilleur, -euse; peintur(lur)eur, -euse; peintraillon *m.*

daubre(e)ite [ˈdɔ:bri:ait, douˈbreiait], *s. Miner:* daubréite *f.*

daubreelite [ˈdɔ:bri:lait, douˈbreilait], *s. Miner:* daubréelite *f.*

daughter [ˈdɔ:tər], *s.f.* (*a*) fille; **three sons and one d.,** trois fils et une fille; (*b*) *Ecc:* **d. house,** filiale *f.*

daughter-in-law [ˈdɔ:tərinlɔ:], *s.f.* (*a*) belle-fille, *pl.* belles-filles; bru; (*b*) *A:* (= *stepdaughter*) belle-fille.

daughterly [ˈdɔ:təli], *a.* filial, -aux.

daunt [dɔ:nt], *v.tr.* intimider, décourager, abattre (qn); démonter (qn); **he is never daunted,** il ne se décourage jamais; rien ne le démonte; **nothing daunted,** intrépide(ment); nullement, aucunement, intimidé; sans se laisser intimider; **daunting,** intimidant.

dauntless [ˈdɔ:ntlis], *a.* intrépide; sans peur.

dauntlessly [ˈdɔ:ntlisli], *adv.* intrépidement; sans peur.

dauntlessness [ˈdɔ:ntlisnis], *s.* intrépidité *f.*

Dauphin, Dauphine [ˈdɔ:fin, -i:n], *s.* **1.** *Fr.Hist:* Dauphin, -ine. **2.** *Cu:* **dauphine potatoes,** pommes dauphine.

Davallia [dəˈvæliə], *s. Bot:* davallie *f*, davallia *f.*

davenport [ˈdævnpɔ:t], *s.* **1.** petit bureau-pupitre, *pl.* bureaux-pupitres; secrétaire *m* (de salon). **2.** *NAm:* canapé *m*, divan *m.*

David [ˈdeivid]. **1.** *Pr.n.m.* David. **2.** *Bot:* **David's harp,** sceau *m* de Salomon.

davidsonite [ˈdeividsənait], *s. Miner:* davidsonite *f.*

daviesite [ˈdeivisait], *s. Miner:* daviésite *f.*

davit [ˈdævit], *s.* (*a*) *Nau:* bossoir *m*, davier *m* (d'embarcation); portemanteau *m*; potence *f*; **d. guys,** bras *m* de bossoir; **d. span,** entremise *f* de bossoir; (*b*) *Artil:* **loading d.,** potence, grue *f* (de chargement).

davy[1] [ˈdeivi], *s. F: A:* (*affidavit*) **to take one's d. that . . .,** donner sa parole que . . .; **I'll take my d. on it,** je vous en donne mon billet.

Davy[2], *Pr.n.m.* (*dim. of David*) David; *Nau: F:* **D. Jones's locker,** le port des navires perdus, le fond de la mer; **to go to D. Jones's locker,** boire à la grande tasse.

Davy[3], *Pr.n. Min:* **D. lamp,** lampe *f* de Davy.

daw [dɔ:], *s. Orn:* choucas *m* des tours.

dawdle[1] [ˈdɔ:dl]. **1.** *v.i.* flâner, musarder, muser, traîner, traînasser, lambiner; **to d. on the way,** s'amuser en chemin; **to d. along, d. away one's time, one's life,** passer son temps, sa vie, à flâner; gaspiller le temps.

dawdle[2], *s.* flânerie *f*, musardise *f.*

dawdler [ˈdɔ:dlər], *s.* flâneur, -euse; musard, -arde; lambin, -ine; traînard, -arde.

dawdling[1] [ˈdɔ:dliŋ], *a.* flâneur, musard, lambin; **d. step,** pas traînard, qui traîne.

dawdling[2], *s.* flânerie *f*, musardise *f*, musarderie *f*, traînerie *f.*

dawn[1] [dɔ:n], *s.* **1.** aube *f*, aurore *f*; *Lit:* **rosy-fingered d.,** l'aurore aux doigts de rose; **at d.,** au point du jour; aux premières lueurs du jour; **at early d., at the first streak of d., at the break of d., at crack of d.,** à la pointe du jour; dès le patron-jaquet, dès le patron-minet; **it is almost d.,** le jour va paraître; **the d. chorus,** le chant des oiseaux à l'aube. **2.** aurore, aube (de la vie, de l'histoire); commencement *m* (de la civilisation); naissance *f* (d'une idée); **since the d. of the motoring age,** depuis l'avènement de l'automobile; *attrib. Bot:* **d. redwood,** métaséquoia *m.*

dawn[2], *v.i.* (*of day, morning*) poindre; (commencer à) paraître; naître; **day is dawning,** le jour se lève; **finally the truth dawned on him,** enfin la vérité s'est fait jour dans son esprit; enfin il a compris la vérité; **it dawned on me that . . .,** il m'est venu à l'esprit que . . .; j'ai commencé à avoir conscience que . . ., à me rendre compte que . . .; **I saw a smile dawning on her lips,** j'ai vu poindre un sourire sur ses lèvres.

dawning[1] [ˈdɔ:niŋ], *a.* (jour, espoir) naissant.

dawning[2], *s.* **1.** = DAWN[1]; **the first dawnings,** les premières lueurs (de l'aube, de la civilisation, etc.). **2.** *Poet:* l'orient *m*, l'est *m.*

dawsonite [ˈdɔ:sənait], *s. Miner:* dawsonite *f.*

day [dei], *s.* **1.** (*a*) jour *m*; (*considered as a day's work, earnings, etc.*) journée *f*; **it's a fine d.,** il fait beau aujourd'hui; **it has been a sunny d.,** il a fait une journée de soleil; **it has been a wet d.,** il a plu toute la journée; **to work d. and night,** travailler nuit et jour; **to work all d. (long),** travailler toute la journée, tout le long du jour; **he does nothing all d.,** il ne fait rien de toute la journée; **to work by the day,** travailler à la journée; **it's all in a day's work,** ça fait partie de ma routine; j'en vois bien d'autres! **eight hour d.,** journée de huit heures; **it's a day's journey (from here),** c'est à un jour de voyage; **in the course of the d.,** dans la journée; **twice a d.,** deux fois par jour; **this d. of all days,** ce jour entre tous; **this d. of all days the telephone was out of order,** ce jour-là, comme un fait exprès, le téléphone ne marchait pas; **I remember it to this (very) d.,** je m'en souviens encore aujourd'hui; **this d. week,** (d')aujourd'hui en huit; **this d. next year,** dans un an jour pour jour; l'an prochain à pareil jour, à pareille date; **this d. last week,** il y a aujourd'hui huit jours; **this d. last year,** l'an dernier à pareille date, à pareil jour; il y a aujourd'hui un an; **it was ten years ago to this very d.,** il y a de cela dix ans jour pour jour; **the d. before (he came),** la veille (de son arrivée); **two days before (his wedding),** l'avant-veille *f* (de son mariage); **the d. after (his arrival),** le lendemain (de son arrivée); **two days after, later,** deux jours après, plus tard; le surlendemain; **the case was adjourned for two days,** la cause fut renvoyée au surlendemain; **every other d.,** *O:* **d. about,** tous les deux jours; un jour sur deux; **d. after d., d. in d. out,** jour après jour; un jour après l'autre; tous les jours; de jour en jour; à la longueur de la journée; sans trêve; **d. after d., year after year,** au fil des jours et des ans; **d. after d. passed,** les jours se succédaient; **d. by d.,** jour par jour; de jour en jour; **from d. to d.,** de jour en jour, d'un jour à l'autre, du jour au lendemain; **to live from d. to d.,** vivre au jour le jour; **from that d. to this,** à partir de ce jour; **he's sixty if he's a d.,** il a soixante ans bien sonnés; *Mil: etc:* **one day's, two days', rations,** un jour, deux jours, de vivres; **officer, sergeant, of the d.,** officier *m*, sergent *m*, de jour; **pay d.,** jour de paie, de paiement; *Mil:* jour de solde; *St.Exch:* jour de liquidation, de règlement; *F:*

let's call it a d., we'd better call it a d., ça suffit pour aujourd'hui; assez travaillé pour aujourd'hui; **they decided to call it a d.,** ils ont décidé de s'en tenir là; (*b*) **d. of battle,** journée de bataille; **to carry, win, the d.,** gagner la journée, la bataille; remporter la victoire; être victorieux; (*in lawsuit*) avoir gain de cause; **to lose the d.,** perdre la bataille; **the d. is ours,** la victoire est à nous; **it was a great d.,** ce fut un beau jour, une grande journée; *F:* **that'll be the d.!** il fera chaud! demain on rase gratis! (*c*) *attrib.* **d. labour,** travail *m* à la journée; **d. labourer,** journalier *m,* ouvrier *m* à la journée; *Ind:* **d. shift,** équipe *f* du jour; (*of workman*) **to be on d. shift,** être de jour; **d. duty,** service *m* de jour; *Med:* **d. nurse,** infirmier, -ière, qui est de service de jour; *Sch:* **d. school,** externat *m*; **d. pupil, d. student, d. boy, girl,** externe *mf*; **d. boarder,** demi-pensionnaire *mf, pl.* demi-pensionnaires; **d. nursery,** (i) pouponnière *f,* crèche *f*; garderie *f* d'enfants; (ii) (*in house*) salle *f* des enfants; *Meteor:* **d. temperature,** température *f* diurne; *Rail: etc:* **d. ticket, d. return,** (billet *m* d')aller et retour *m* valable pour un jour; *Med:* **d.(-)blind,** nyctalope, nyctalopique; **d. blindness,** nyctalopie *f*; *Fin:* **d. bill,** effet *m* à date fixe; **d.-to-d. loan,** prêt *m* au jour le jour; **one-d. option,** prime *f* au lendemain; **last-d. money,** emprunt *m* remboursable fin courant; *Min:* **d. drift,** fendue *f*; *Bot:* **d. lily,** hémérocalle *f*; *Orn:* **d. owl,** chouette épervière. **2.** (*a*) (*dawn*) **before d.,** avant le jour; **at break of d.,** au point du jour; (*b*) (*daylight*) **full d., broad d.,** grand jour; **in the full light of d.,** en plein midi; **to travel, etc., by d.,** voyager, etc., le jour, de jour, pendant le jour. **3.** (*24 hours*) **solar, astronomical, d.,** jour solaire, astronomique; **mean solar d.,** jour solaire moyen; **sidereal d.,** jour sidéral; **apparent d.,** jour apparent; **civil d.,** jour civil; *Jur: etc:* **clear d.,** jour franc. plein; **ten clear days' notice,** préavis *m* de dix jours francs. **4.** (*point in time*) (*a*) **d. of the month,** quantième *m* du mois; **what d. (of the week) is it (today)?** quel jour de la semaine sommes-nous? **to pass the time of d. with s.o.,** échanger quelques paroles de politesse avec qn; **one fine summer d.,** par un beau jour d'été; **one d., some d., one of these (fine) days,** un jour ou l'autre; un de ces (beaux) jours; un de ces quatre matins; **I shall write to you in a d. or so,** je vous écrirai bientôt, dans un ou deux jours; **I saw him the other d.,** je l'ai vu l'autre jour; **come any d. (you like),** venez n'importe quel jour; **he may arrive any d.,** il peut arriver d'un jour à l'autre, du jour au lendemain; **it will be many a long d. before I go there again,** il fera beau quand j'y retournerai; **it will be many a long d. before anything is done,** on a le temps d'attendre avant que quelque chose se fasse; **it's many a long d. since you went there,** il y a bien longtemps que vous n'y avez pas mis les pieds; *O:* **to have a d., an at-home d.,** avoir un jour (de réception); *Sch:* **parents' d., open d.,** jour où les parents d'élèves sont invités à visiter le lycée, l'école, etc.; **the maid's d. out,** le jour de congé de la bonne; **to take, get, a d. off,** prendre, obtenir, un jour de congé; **wedding d.,** jour de mariage; *F:* **to name the d.,** fixer le jour du mariage; *Prov:* **(the) better the d. (the) better the deed,** bon jour bonne œuvre; *Ecc:* **the last d., the d. of judgement,** le jour du jugement; (*b*) fête *f*; **All Saints' D.,** (la fête de) la Toussaint; **All Souls' D.,** le Jour des Morts; **Easter D.,** le jour de Pâques; **Lady D.,** la fête de l'Annonciation (le 25 mars); *F:* **let's make it a d., let's make a d. of it!** allons faire fête, faire la noce! **5.** (*period of time*) **the good old days,** le bon vieux temps; **in the days of . . .,** au, du, temps de . . .; au vivant de . . .; **in my young days,** au, du, temps de ma jeunesse; **in those days,** en ce temps-là; alors; **(in) these days, in our days,** de notre temps; *Lit:* **in the days of old,** autrefois; au temps jadis; du temps que Berthe filait; **I was a student in those days,** j'étais étudiant à ce moment-là, à cette époque-là; **those were the days, those were happy days,** c'était la bonne, la belle, vie (alors); c'était le bon temps; **in his d.,** de, en, son vivant; **he ended his days in poverty,** il a fini ses jours, il est mort, pauvre; **he was a great man in his d.,** ce fut un grand homme dans son temps; **she was a great beauty in her d.,** elle a été d'une beauté ravissante; **in days to come,** à l'avenir; **novels of the d.,** romans contemporains, du jour; **the man of the d.,** l'homme du jour; (*of theory, fashion, etc.*) **to have had its d.,** avoir fait son temps; être passé de vogue, de mode; être démodé; **I've had my d.,** je suis vieux, vieille; **the d. of individualism is gone,** les jours de l'individualisme sont révolus; *Prov:* **everything has its d.,** chaque chose a son temps.

dayal [dɑː'jɑːl], *s. Orn:* **d. (bird),** dyal *m.*

daybed ['deibed], *s. Furn:* lit *m* de repos.

daybook ['deibuk], *s. Com:* (livre) journal *m,* -aux; sommier *m,* mémorial, -aux; main courante, brouillard *m.*

daybreak ['deibreik], *s.* point *m* du jour; lever *m* du jour; aube *f* (du jour); **at d.,** au jour levant.

daydream[1] ['deidriːm], *s.* rêverie *f,* songerie *f,* rêvasserie *f*; **to lose oneself in daydreams,** se perdre dans le bleu, dans les nues.

daydream[2], *v.i.* rêver tout éveillé; rêver creux; rêvasser, songer.

daydreamer ['deidriːmər], *s.* rêveur, -euse; songe-creux *m inv*; songeur, -euse; visionnaire *mf.*

daydreaming ['deidriːmiŋ], *s.* rêverie *f,* songerie *f*; **given to d.,** porté au rêve et à la paresse.

dayflower ['deiflauər], *s. Bot:* (i) commélyne *f*; (ii) ciste *m* de Crète.

daylight ['deilait], *s.* **1.** (*a*) jour *m*; lumière *f* du jour; *attrib.* de jour; **d. bombing,** bombardement *m* de jour; **by d.,** de jour, le jour; **to work by d.,** travailler à la lumière du jour; *F:* **to burn d.,** gâcher son temps; **in broad d.,** en plein jour; au grand jour; en plein midi; au su et vu de tous; **it is broad d.,** il fait grand jour; **bring it into the d.,** mettez cela au grand jour; *Adm: O:* **d. saving,** économie *f* de lumière par l'adoption de l'heure d'été; **d.-saving time,** l'heure *f* d'été; *Phot:* **d. loading,** chargement *m* (de l'appareil) en plein jour, en pleine lumière; (*b*) l'aube *f*; le point du jour; **before d.,** avant le jour. **2.** (*open space, opening*) espace *m* libre; ouverture *f* (d'une machine-outil, etc.); jour, intervalle *m*; *Equit:* **to show d. when trotting,** faire du trot enlevé; trotter à l'anglaise; *Fig:* **to (begin to) see d.,** (i) apercevoir la fin (du travail); approcher du but; (ii) (commencer à) voir clair (dans une affaire). **3.** *pl. P: A:* **the daylights,** les yeux *m,* les mirettes *f.* **4.** *F:* **to knock, beat, the living daylights out of s.o.,** battre qn comme plâtre, jusqu'à ce qu'il ne voie plus que du noir; **to scare the (living) daylights out of s.o.,** causer une peur bleue à qn; *P:* **to let d. into s.o.,** donner à qn un coup de fusil, un coup d'épée.

daylong ['deilɔŋ], *O: & Lit:* **1.** *a.* qui dure toute la journée; **during his d. work,** pendant ses longues heures de travail. **2.** *adv.* toute la journée, tout le long du jour.

daymark ['deimɑːk], *s. Nau:* amer *m.*

dayspring ['deispriŋ], *s. Poet:* jour naissant, aurore *f,* aube *f.*

daystar ['deistɑːr], *s. Poet:* **1.** l'étoile *f* du matin. **2.** l'astre du jour, le soleil.

daytime ['deitaim], *s.* le jour, la journée; **in the d.,** pendant la journée; de jour.

daze[1] [deiz], *s.* **1.** étourdissement *m,* stupéfaction *f,* ahurissement *m*; **to be in a d.,** être hébété, stupéfait, ahuri; **he acts as if he were in a d.,** il agit comme un hébété. **2.** *Miner: F:* mica *m.*

daze[2], *v.tr.* **1.** (*a*) (*of drug, etc.*) stupéfier, hébéter; (*b*) (*of blow*) étourdir; (*c*) abasourdir, ahurir, méduser (qn). **2.** = DAZZLE[2].

dazed [deizd], *a.* **1.** (*a*) stupéfié (par un narcotique); hébété; (*b*) tout étourdi (par un coup); (*c*) abasourdi, ahuri, sidéré; **I am absolutely d. by what has happened,** je suis abasourdi, tout abruti, de ce qui vient de se passer; **d. expression,** expression ahurie; **in a d. condition,** ahuri; commotionné. **2.** = DAZZLED.

dazedly ['deizidli], *adv.* d'un air, d'un ton, hébété, ahuri.

dazzle[1] ['dæzl], *s.* **1.** éblouissement *m*; aveuglement *m.* **2.** *Navy:* camouflage *m.*

dazzle[2], *v.tr.* **1.** éblouir, aveugler; **dazzled with, by, the light,** ébloui, aveuglé, par la lumière; **dazzled by such a brilliant prospect,** ébloui par une si brillante perspective. **2.** *Navy:* **to d.-paint a ship,** camoufler un navire; **d.-painted,** camouflé.

dazzled ['dæzld], *a.* ébloui.

dazzlement ['dæzlmənt], *s.* éblouissement *m.*

dazzling ['dæzliŋ], *a.* éblouissant, aveuglant; **d. sky,** ciel radieux; **d. success,** succès éclatant.

dazzlingly ['dæzliŋli], *adv.* d'une manière éblouissante; **d. beautiful,** d'une beauté éblouissante.

de- [diː], *pref.* dé-.

deacidification ['diːæsidifi'keiʃ(ə)n], *s. Ch:* déacidification *f.*

deacidize [diː'æsidaiz], *v.tr. Ch:* déacidifier.

deacidizing [diː'æsidaiziŋ], *s. Ch:* déacidification *f.*

deacon[1] ['diːkən], *s. Ecc:* **1.** diacre *m.* **2.** (*a*) (*Non-Conformist Ch.*) membre *m* du Conseil de fabrique; (*b*) (*Congregational Ch.*) ancien *m.* **3.** *Leath: U.S:* **d. (hide),** veau mort-né.

deacon[2], *v.tr. U.S:* **1.** *F:* **to d. a basket of apples,** mettre les plus belles pommes en dessus; **to d. wine,** frelater le vin. **2.** tuer (un veau nouveau-né).

deaconess ['diːkənis], *s.f.* diaconesse.

deaconry ['diːkənri], *s. Ecc:* **1.** diaconat *m.* **2.** la maison du diacre. **3.** *coll.* les diacres.

deaconship ['diːkənʃip], *s. Ecc:* diaconat *m*; office *m* de diacre.

de-activate [diː'æktiveit], *v.tr. El: Cmptr:* mettre (un appareil, etc.) hors tension.

dead [ded], *a., s. & adv.*

I. *a.* **1.** mort; (*a*) **he is d.,** il est mort, décédé; **the d. man, woman,** le mort, la morte; **if you move you are a d. man,** si vous bougez vous êtes un homme mort; **he is practically a d. man,** il est condamné; *Prov:* **d. men tell no tales, d. dogs do not bite,** les morts ne parlent pas; morte la bête mort le venin; chien mort ne mord pas; **to strike, kill, s.o. (stone) d.,** tuer qn raide; **to drop (down) d., to fall (stone) d.,** tomber (raide) mort; **to shoot s.o. d.,** tuer qn raide, net (d'un coup de fusil, de revolver); *F:* **d. as a doornail, d. as mutton,** mort et bien mort; tombé dans un oubli complet; **d. and gone, d. and buried,** mort et enterré, *F:* parti pour le royaume des taupes; **half d. with fright,** plus mort que vif; *F:* **he's d. and done for,** il est flambé, fichu, fini; c'en est fait de lui; son compte est réglé, son affaire est faite; *P:* **drop d.!** ta gueule! **d. to the world,** (i) mort pour le monde; (ii) profondément endormi, dans les bras de Morphée; (iii) *F:* ivre mort, bourré à bloc; *F:* **d. from the neck up,** bête, idiot, bouché à l'émeri; **d. water,** eau stagnante, morte; *Nau:* remous *m* de sillage; *Geog:* **the D. Sea,** la Mer Morte; (*of regulation*) **to become a d. letter,** tomber en désuétude; rester lettre morte; *Post:* **d. letters,** lettres tombées au rebut; lettres de rebut; **d.-letter office,** bureau *m* des rebuts; **d. language,** langue morte; (*b*) **d. tree, hedge,** arbre mort, haie morte; **d. wood,** (i) bois mort, bois chablis; (ii) *N.Arch:* bois de remplissage, contre-étrave *f,* étambot *m*; (iii) personnel *m* incapable; matériel démodé, inutile; **we shall have to cut out some of the d. wood (from the staff),** il va falloir élaguer, déblayer, le personnel; (*c*) (doigt) mort, engourdi par le froid; (*of limb*) **to go d.,** s'engourdir; (*d*) *F:* **d. man,** bouteille vidée, cadavre *m.* **2.** (*hardened against*) **d. to all sense of honour,** insensible à tout sentiment d'honneur; **d. to reason,** sourd à la raison. **3.** (*extinct*) **d. fire,** feu mort; **d. coal,** charbon éteint; **d. colour,** (i) couleur *f* terne; (ii) première couche de couleur; **d. white,** blanc mat; **d. gold,** or mat; **d. sound,** son mat; **d. well,** puits perdu; *El:* **d. wire,** fil *m* (i) hors courant, (ii) sans tension, sans courant; *Mch:* **d. steam,** vapeur *f* d'échappement; *Metall:* **d. sand,** sable brûlé; *El:* **d. cell,** pile épuisée; *Min:* **d. lode,** filon épuisé; **d. ground,** mort-terrain *m, pl.* morts-terrains; *Typ:* **d. matter,** composition devenue inutile; matière *f* à distribuer. **4.** (*inactive*) **d. season,** morte-saison, *pl.* mortes-saisons; **the d. hours,** (i) la nuit; (ii) *Ind: etc:* les heures creuses; **d. period,** période *f* d'inactivité; **d. city,** ville morte; **d. centre,** (i) *Mch:* point mort (du piston); (ii) (*of lathe*) pointe *f* de la poupée mobile; contre pointe *f*; centre *m* fixe; **top, bottom, d. centre,** haut *m,* fond *m,* de course, point mort haut, bas; *Mch:* **d. plate,** table *f* de foyer; *Rail:* **d. block,** tampon sec (de wagon de marchandises); *Av:* **d. propeller,** hélice calée; *Mec.E:* **d. spring,** ressort *m* qui a perdu son élasticité; ressort détendu; **d. axle,** essieu *m* fixe; **d. bolt,** pêne dormant; **d. window,** fausse fenêtre; fenêtre feinte, aveugle; **d. hole,** trou aveugle, borgne; *Civ.E:* **d. load,** poids mort; charge constante; *Fb:* **d. ball,** ballon mort; (*bowls*) **d. bowl,** boule noyée; *Mil:* **d. angle, ground,** angle, terrain, privé de feu, mort; *Fin:* **d. money,** argent mort, qui dort; **d. loan,** emprunt *m* irrécouvrable; *Com:* **d. market,** marché mort; **d. freight,** faux fret; dédit *m* pour défaut de chargement; *Metalw: etc:* **d. acid,** acide décomposé; *Ph:* **d. beat,** oscillation amortie. **5.** (*abrupt, complete, exact*) **d. stop, halt,** arrêt *m* brusque, halte *f* subie; **to come to a d. stop,** s'arrêter net; **to bring the enemy, etc., to a d. stop,** arrêter net l'ennemi, etc.; *Nau:* **d. calm,** calme plat; **d. silence,** silence *m* de mort; **d. secret,** profond secret; **d. level,** niveau parfait; *Med:* (*of disease*) plateau *m,* point mort; **on a d. level,** absolument de niveau; à franc niveau; **d. wall,** mur orbe; mur blanc; **d. loss,** (i) perte sèche; (ii) *F:* (*pers.*) propre *m* à rien, crétin *m*; **to be in d. earnest,** être tout à fait sérieux; **he's a d. shot,** il ne manque, ne rate, jamais son coup; c'est un tireur sûr de son coup; *Golf:* (*of ball*) **to lie d.,** être au bord du trou; *El:* **d. earth,** contact parfait avec le sol.

II. *s.* **1.** *pl.* **the d.,** les morts *m*; *Lit:* les trépassés; *Ecc:* **the Office for the d.,** l'office *m* des morts; **to rise from the d.,** ressusciter des morts; **bring out your d.!** sortez vos morts! *attrib. Mus:* **d. march,** marche *f* funèbre. **2.** **at d. of night,** au plus profond, dans le silence, au milieu, de la nuit; **in the d. of winter,** au cœur, au (plus) fort, de l'hiver. **3.** *pl. Min:* **deads,** stériles *m* de mine; déchets *m,* déblais *m,* de mine; *Metall:* gangue *f.*

III. *adv.* (*a*) absolument; **d. drunk,** ivre mort; **d. asleep,** profondément endormi; **d. tired,** mort de fatigue; éreinté; fourbu; **d. sure,** absolument certain; **d. on time, on the hour,** à l'heure tapante, pile; **he was d.**

right, il avait absolument raison; *F:* **d. broke,** fauché; complètement ruiné; absolument décavé; *Nau:* **to sail d. south,** faire route droit vers le sud; **wind d. ahead,** vent droit debout; **to go d. slow,** marcher aussi lentement que possible; *Aut:* **to take a corner d. slow,** prendre un virage au grand ralenti; *P.N:* **d. slow,** au pas; (*b*) **to stop d.,** s'arrêter net; (*c*) **with the tide running d. against us,** avec le courant en plein contre nous; (*of pers.*) **to be d. against sth.,** être absolument opposé à qch.; (*d*) **piece that fits d. true, d. square,** pièce *f* à ajustage parfait; **d. smooth surface,** surface parfaitement plane; **d. smooth file cut,** taille *f* de lime très douce; *Cr:* **d. on the middle stump,** en plein sur le piquet du milieu.

dead-and-alive ['dednda'laiv], *a.* mort, triste, sans animation; **a d.-and-a. hole,** un petit trou à moitié mort, un bled.

deadbeat ['dedbi:t], *a. El:* (instrument *m*) apériodique; (galvanomètre *m*) à oscillations amorties; *Clockm:* **d. escapement,** échappement *m* à repos.

dead(-)beat ['ded'bi:t]. **1.** *a. F:* rendu, épuisé, éreinté, exténué, fourbu, vanné, moulu; recru de fatigue; brisé de fatigue; (cheval) tordu; **I'm d.(-)b.,** je n'en puis plus; je suis anéanti; je tombe de faiblesse. **2.** *s. P:* (*a*) *esp. Austr:* chemineau *m*; (*b*) *esp. U.S:* tapeur *m*, quémandeur *m*, filou *m*.

deaden ['dedn]. **1.** *v.tr.* amortir (un coup, un choc, les vibrations, les passions); assourdir, étouffer, amortir (un son); hourder (un plancher, une cloison); émousser, assoupir, aveulir, abrutir (les sens); (a)matir (l'or, etc.); **to d. one's footsteps,** ouater, feutrer, ses pas; *Nau:* **to d. a ship's way,** amortir l'erre d'un bâtiment. **2.** *v.i.* s'amortir; (*of sound*) s'assourdir; (*of senses*) s'émousser.

dead end ['ded'end], *s.* **1.** cul-de-sac *m*, *pl.* culs-de-sac; impasse *f*; (*of pipe*) bout aveugle, fermé, *Min:* accul *m*; *attrib.* **d.-e. job,** emploi *m* sans avenir; *F:* **d.-e. kids,** enfants sans avenir (élevés dans des taudis). **2.** *El: W.Tel:* bout mort.

deadening ['ded(ə)niŋ], *s.* amortissement *m*; assourdissement *m* (du bruit, d'un son).

deader ['dedər], *s. P:* cadavre *m*, macchabée *m*, refroidi *m*.

deadeye ['dedai], *s. Nau:* cap *m* de mouton; moque *f*.

deadfall ['dedfɔ:l], *s.* **1.** *Ven:* (piège *m*) assommoir *m*; traquenard *m*. **2.** enchevêtrement *m* d'arbres morts (dans une forêt). **3.** *U.S:* (*gambling den*) assommoir.

deadhead ['dedhed], *s.* **1.** (*a*) *Metall:* masselotte *f*; (*b*) (*of lathe*) contre-pointe *f*, contre-poupée *f*. **2.** *F:* (*a*) *esp. U.S: Th: Rail: etc:* personne *f* en possession d'un billet de faveur; spectateur *m* qui entre gratuitement *F:* qui entre à l'œil; (*b*) individu *m* (i) bête, (ii) qui ne contribue rien au travail, à l'entreprise.

dead-head, *v.tr. Hort:* **to d.-h. the roses,** ôter les fleurs mortes des rosiers.

deading ['dediŋ], *s. Tchn:* enveloppe *f*, garniture *f*.

dead-leaf ['dedli:f], *a.* **1.** *Ent:* **d.-l. butterfly,** feuille-morte *f*, *pl.* feuilles-mortes. **2.** *Av: A:* **d.-l. descent,** descente *f* en feuille morte.

deadlight ['dedlait], *s.* **1.** *Nau: F:* (*a*) contre-sabord *m*, mantelet *m* de sabord; tape *f*, opercule *m* de hublot; (*b*) couvercle *m* de panneau, panneau *m* de claire-voie; (*c*) faux hublot. **2.** *Const:* fausse fenêtre. **3.** *Dial: Scot:* feu follet (de cimetière).

deadline ['dedlain], *s.* **1.** (*a*) ligne *f* de délimitation; limites *fpl* (d'une prison pour forçats, d'un camp de prisonniers de guerre); (*b*) bornes *fpl* que l'on ne saurait franchir; (*c*) date *f* limite. **2.** *Typ:* ligne de repère (du marbre d'une presse à cylindre).

deadliness ['dedlinis], *s.* nature mortelle (d'un poison, etc.); *F:* ennui mortel (d'un endroit).

deadlock ['dedlɔk], *s.* **1.** serrure *f* à pêne dormant. **2.** impasse *f*; point mort; situation *f* inextricable, insoluble; **to come to a d.,** aboutir à une impasse (au cours de négociations, etc.).

deadly ['dedli]. **1.** *a.* (*a*) (*of poison, blow, etc.*) mortel; **d. weapon,** arme meurtrière; **d. hatred,** haine mortelle, implacable; **d. combat,** combat meurtrier, à mort; **d. insult,** insulte mortelle, sanglante; **d. evidence,** témoignage accablant; **d. scourge,** fléau redoutable, meurtrier; **d. sin,** péché mortel; **the seven d. sins,** les sept péchés capitaux; (*b*) = DEATHLIKE; (*c*) **to be in d. earnest,** être tout à fait sérieux; (*d*) **the men had a good time, but the women's lives were d.,** les hommes s'amusaient, mais les femmes s'ennuyaient mortellement. **2.** *adv.* mortellement, comme la mort; **d. pale,** d'une pâleur mortelle; **it was d. cold,** il faisait un froid mortel, un froid de loup.

deadman, *pl.* **-men** ['dedmæn, men], *s.* **1.** (*a*) (*in place names*) mort *m*; **Deadman's Bay,** Baie *f* des Morts; (*b*) *Rail: etc:* **deadman's handle, control, brake,** l'homme mort. **2.** *Bot:* **deadmen's bones,** linaire *f*; **deadman's hand,** (i) *Algae:* laminaire *f*; (ii) fougère *f* mâle.

deadness ['dednis], *s.* **1.** torpeur *f*; engourdissement *m* (des membres); stagnation *f* (des affaires); matité *f* (des couleurs). **2.** indifférence *f*, insensibilité *f* (**to,** envers).

deadpan[1] ['dedpæn]. **1.** *a.* (visage) impassible, figé, sans expression; **d. humour,** humour *m* à froid, de pince-sans-rire. **2.** *s.* pince-sans-rire *m inv.*; **master of d.,** roi *m* du pince-sans-rire.

deadpan[2], *v.i.* être, faire le, pince-sans-rire.

deadweight ['dedweit], *s.* **1.** poids mort, poids inerte; poids accablant (de dettes, etc.); **he's a d.,** c'est un poids mort. **2.** *Nau:* portée *f* en poids, chargement *m*, port *m*, en lourd; **d. cargo,** marchandises lourdes; **d. cargo capacity,** port en marchandises; **ton d.,** tonneau *m* de portée en lourd, d'affrètement.

dead work ['dedwə:k], *s.* **1.** *Min:* travaux *mpl* de premier établissement, travaux préparatoires. **2.** *pl. N.Arch:* œuvres mortes.

deaerate [di:'ɛəreit], *v.tr.* désaérer.

deaf [def], *a.* **1.** (*a*) sourd; **d. in one ear,** sourd d'une oreille; **he's d. in that ear, on that side,** il n'entend pas de cette oreille-là; **d. and dumb,** sourd-muet, *f.* sourde-muette; **d. and dumbness,** surdi-mutité *f*; **d. as a (door)post, as an adder,** sourd comme un pot, comme une bécasse; **d. to entreaties,** sourd aux supplications; *Prov:* **there are none so d. as those that will not hear,** il n'y a pire sourd que celui qui ne veut (pas) entendre; **to turn a d. ear to s.o., to entreaties,** faire la sourde oreille à ce que dit qn, refuser d'écouter qn; rester sourd aux prières; **I have not turned a d. ear to your words,** je ne suis pas resté sourd à vos paroles; **to preach to d. ears,** prêcher dans le désert; parler aux murs; (*b*) *Rept:* **d. adder,** orvet *m*; serpent *m* de verre. **2.** (noisette *f*) vide, sans amande.

deafen ['defn], *v.tr.* **1.** assourdir (qn); rendre (qn) sourd; **you're deafening me,** vous me percez les oreilles; vous me cassez la tête. **2.** *A:* étouffer (la voix, un son). **3.** *Const:* hourder (un plancher, une cloison).

deafening ['def(ə)niŋ], *a.* assourdissant; **the din was d.,** le bruit était assourdissant; ce fut à ne plus s'entendre; on n'aurait pas entendu Dieu tonner; **the waves broke with a d. roar,** les vagues déferlaient avec fracas.

deafly ['defli], *adv.* comme un sourd.

deaf-mute ['def'mju:t], *s.* sourd-muet, *f*; sourde-muette, *pl.* sourds-muets, sourdes-muettes.

deaf-muteness, -mutism ['def'mju:tnis, -'mju:tizm], *s.* surdi-mutité *f*.

deafness ['defnis], *s.* surdité *f*; **temporary d.,** assourdissement *m*; **tone d.,** surdité musicale; **word d.,** surdité tonale.

deal[1] [di:l], *s.* (*usu.* **a great d., a good d.**) (grande) quantité, beaucoup; **I have a good d.,** *F:* **a d., to do,** j'ai beaucoup à faire, j'ai bien des choses, à faire; **a great d. of the paper is damaged,** une bonne partie du papier est avariée; **there's a great d. of truth in that,** il y a beaucoup de vrai là-dedans; **that's saying a good d.,** ce n'est pas peu dire; **I felt it a good d.,** cela m'a beaucoup affecté; **I think a great d. of you,** (i) je pense beaucoup à vous; (ii) je vous estime beaucoup; *adv.* **he is a good d. better,** il va beaucoup mieux; **he is a great d. wiser than you,** il est de beaucoup plus sage que vous; **you are a good d. too zealous,** vous êtes par trop zélé.

deal[2], *s.* **1.** *Cards:* donne *f*; main *f*; **whose d. is it?** à qui de donner, de faire? à qui main? **your d.!** à vous la donne! à vous de faire! (*at baccarat, etc.*) **to pass the d.,** passer la main. **2.** *Com: etc:* affaire *f*; marché *m*; **firm d.,** marché ferme; **cash d.,** transaction *f* au comptant; **d. on joint account,** opération *f* en participation; **option d.,** opération à prime; **package d.,** contrat global; **even deal,** opération blanche; **swap credit d.,** facilités *fpl* de crédit réciproques; **big d.,** (i) grosse affaire; (ii) *F: Iron:* la belle affaire! **oh, big d.!** merci de rien! **d. on the Stock Exchange,** coup *m* de Bourse; **it's a d.!** d'accord! entendu! *F:* tope là! *Pol:* **d. between parties,** tractation *f* entre partis; **ministerial deals,** tractations ministérielles; **to give s.o. a fair, a square, d.,** agir loyalement envers qn; **to give s.o. a raw d.,** en faire voir de dures à qn; **it's a raw, a poor, d.!** c'est dur à avaler!

deal[3], *v.* (**dealt** [delt]; **dealt**).

I. *v.tr.* **1. to d. out provisions, gifts,** distribuer, répartir, partager, des vivres, des dons (**to, among,** entre); **to d. out justice,** rendre la justice. **2. to d. a blow,** donner, porter, allonger, asséner, un coup; **to d. a blow at s.o., to d. s.o. a blow,** porter, lancer, un coup à qn. **3.** donner, distribuer (les cartes); **I was dealt eight trumps,** j'ai reçu huit atouts.

II. *v.i.* **1.** (*a*) **to (have to) d. with s.o.,** avoir affaire à, avec, qn; **man easy to d. with,** homme commode, accommodant, de bonne composition; **difficult to d. with,** peu accommodant, pas commode; **I refuse to d. with him,** je refuse d'avoir aucun rapport avec lui, de traiter avec lui; (*b*) **to d. with a subject,** traiter, s'occuper, d'un sujet; **the matter dealt with in your letter,** la question dont vous parlez dans votre lettre; **letter dealing with . . .,** lettre *f* qui traite de . . ., lettre concernant . . .; **before dealing with this problem . . .,** avant d'aborder ce problème . . .; **resolution dealing with a matter,** résolution *f* portant sur une question; **article in the treaty under which a case is dealt with,** article *m* du traité qui prévoit un cas. **2.** (*a*) **to d. with a piece of business,** conclure, terminer, une affaire; **to d. with a difficulty,** venir à bout d'une difficulté; **the difficulties I have to d. with,** les difficultés avec lesquelles je suis aux prises; **to (take steps to) d. with a situation,** aviser à une situation; **all right, I'll d. with it,** bon, j'en fais mon affaire; *Jur:* **to d. with a grievance,** connaître d'un grief; **to d. with a case,** statuer sur un cas; *Com:* **to d. with an order,** donner suite à une commande; (*b*) **to d. with s.o.,** prendre des mesures à l'égard de qn; **to d. with a culprit,** disposer d'un coupable, faire justice à un coupable; **let me d. with him,** laissez-moi en user à ma guise avec lui; **I know how to d. with him,** je sais comment m'y prendre avec lui; je sais comment il faut le traiter; **to d. leniently with s.o.,** traiter qn avec indulgence; **to d. roughly with s.o.,** agir rudement envers qn; **to d. well, badly, by s.o.,** bien, mal, traiter qn; en user bien, mal, avec qn; **I have been hardly dealt with, dealt by,** on m'a traité avec dureté, avec rigueur, avec peu de générosité. **3.** *Com:* **to d. with s.o.,** traiter, négocier, commercer, avec qn; **to d. with such and such a grocer,** se fournir, se servir, faire ses achats, chez tel ou tel épicier; **to d. in leather, in wool, etc.,** faire le commerce des cuirs, des laines, etc., faire les cuirs, les laines, etc.; **he deals in toilet requisites in a small way,** il fait un petit commerce d'objets de toilette; **I don't d. in that line,** je ne fais pas cet article; *Fin:* **to d. in options,** faire le commerce des primes; **to d. in politics,** se mêler, s'occuper, de politique; *Lit:* **to d. in lies,** faire métier et marchandise de mensonges. **4.** *Cards:* faire la donne; donner; *F:* faire.

deal[4], *s.* **1.** (*a*) madrier *m*; (*b*) planche *f* (à planchéier); sapine *f*. **2.** (bois *m* de) pin *m*, de sapin *m*; **white d.,** sapin blanc, bois blanc; **red d.,** sapin rouge; **d. furniture,** meubles *mpl* en bois blanc.

dealbation [di:æl'beiʃ(ə)n], *s.* déalbation *f*.

dealer ['di:lər], *s.* **1.** *Cards:* donneur *m*; serveur, -euse. **2.** *Com:* (*a*) négociant *m* (**in,** en); distributeur *m* (**in,** de); *Aut: etc:* stockiste *m*; (*b*) marchand, -ande, fournisseur *m* (**in,** de); **retail d.,** détaillant, -ante; **wholesale d.,** grossiste *mf*; **secondhand d.,** revendeur, -euse; brocanteur, -euse; **exchange d.,** courtier *m* de change, cambiste *m*; **authorized d.,** cambiste agréé; **licensed d.,** commerçant patenté; **picture d.,** marchand, -ande, de tableaux; **record d.,** disquaire *m*; **you can obtain this article from your usual d.,** vous trouverez cet article chez votre fournisseur habituel; (*c*) *St.Exch:* marchand de titres; (*d*) **double d.,** homme *m* à deux visages; trompeur, -euse.

dealfish ['di:lfiʃ], *s. Ich:* trachyptère *m*, gros-argentin *m*, *pl.* gros-argentins.

dealing ['di:liŋ], *s.* **1. d. (out),** distribution *f* (de dons, etc.); distribution, donne *f* (de cartes). **2.** *Com:* **d. in wool, in wines,** commerce *m* des laines, des vins; *St.Exch:* **dealings for the account, for the settlement,** négociations *f* à terme; **forward dealings,** négociations, opérations *f*, de change à terme; **option dealing(s),** opérations, négociations, à prime, à option. **3.** *pl.* (*a*) relations *f*, rapports *m*; **to have dealings with s.o.,** avoir des relations, des rapports, entretenir des relations, avec qn: être en relations d'affaires, faire des affaires, traiter d'affaires, avec qn; **I am glad to have no further dealings with them,** je suis heureux de n'avoir plus rien à faire avec eux, de n'avoir plus affaire à eux; (*b*) *Pej:* accointances *f*, tractations *f* (**with,** avec); tripotage *m*; **underhand dealings,** menées sourdes, sournoises; **to have dealings with the enemy,** avoir, pratiquer, des intelligences avec l'ennemi. **4.** (*a*) conduite *f*, procédé *m*, manière *f* d'agir; **fair, square, d.,** loyauté *f*, honnêteté *f* (en affaires), procédés honnêtes; probité *f*; bonne foi; (*b*) **d. with s.o.,** traitement *m* de qn, conduite *f* envers qn; **one's dealings with the world,** le commerce de la vie.

dealkylate [di:'ælkileit], *v.tr. Ch:* désalkyler.

dealkylation [di:ælki'leiʃ(ə)n], *s. Ch:* désalkylation *f*.

deallocation [di:ælou'keiʃ(ə)n], *s. Cmptr: etc:* désaffectation *f*, libération *f*, (d'un appareil).

deambulation [diæmbju'leiʃ(ə)n], *s. Lit:* déambulation *f*, promenade *f*.

deambulatory [di'æmbjulətəri], *a. Lit:* déambulatoire.

dean [diːn], *s.* **1.** *Ecc:* doyen *m* d'une cathédrale, du chapitre, *R.C.Ch:* du Sacré collège); **rural d.,** doyen rural. **2.** *Sch:* doyen (de faculté, de collège universitaire).

deanery [ˈdiːnəri], *s. Ecc:* **1.** doyenné *m.* **2.** résidence *f* du doyen.

deanship [ˈdiːnʃip], *s.* **1.** *Ecc:* doyenné *m*, décanat *m.* **2.** *Sch:* doyennat *m.*

dear [diər], *a., s., adv. & int.*

I. *a.* **1.** (*a*) cher, chère (**to,** à); **he is d. to me,** il m'est cher; **all that I hold d.,** tout ce qui m'est cher; **what a d. little child!** quel amour d'enfant! **a d. little house,** une petite maison coquette; **d. old Mr. Martin,** ce bon M. Martin; **my d. chap!** mon cher! cher ami! **my d. girl!** (i) chère amie! (ii) ma pauvre petite! **my d. child!** mon cher enfant! ma chère enfant! **to run, work, for d. life,** courir, travailler, de toutes ses forces, aussi vite, aussi fort, que possible; (*b*) *Corr:* **D. Sir,** Monsieur; **D. Madam,** Madame, Mademoiselle; **D. Mr Thomas,** Cher Monsieur; **D. Daniel,** Cher Daniel; **My d. Alice,** Ma chère Alice. **2.** cher, coûteux; **these cigars are too d.,** ces cigares sont trop chers; (*of food, etc.*) **to get d., dearer,** enchérir, renchérir; **fruit is much dearer this year,** le prix des fruits a beaucoup augmenté cette année; **the dearer petrol has scarcely reduced the traffic at all,** l'augmentation *f* du prix de l'essence n'a guère diminué la circulation.

II. *s.* cher, *f.* chère; chéri, chérie; **my d.,** cher ami, chère amie, mon ami(e), mon petit chou; **(my) dearest,** (mon) chéri, (ma) chérie; **you're a d.!** t'es un amour! **be a d.!** sois un amour! **be a d. and . . .,** sois gentil(le) et . . .; **come with me, there's a d.,** viens avec moi, ça sera gentil de ta part, tu seras bien gentil(le); sois bien gentil(le) et viens avec moi; **your doctor's an old d.,** j'adore votre vieux bonhomme de médecin; **your aunt's a d.,** votre tante *f* est un ange.

III. *adv.* **1.** (vendre, acheter, coûter, payer) cher. **2. he sold his life d.,** il vendit chèrement sa vie.

IV. *int.* **d. d.! d. me!** mon Dieu, mon Dieu! vraiment? pas possible! **oh d.!** (i) oh là là! diable! (ii) hélas! **oh d. no!** (oh) que non! certainement pas!

dearie [ˈdiəri], *s.* (*a*) *F: O:* mon (petit) chéri, ma (petite) chérie; (*b*) *P:* (*said by shopkeeper, etc.*) ma petite dame.

dearly [ˈdiəli], *adv.* **1.** cher, chèrement; **they sold their lives d.,** ils vendirent chèrement leur vie; **you shall pay d. for this,** cela vous coûtera cher. **2. d. loved,** tendrement aimé(e), bien aimé(e); **I love him d.,** je l'aime tendrement; **you know how d. I love you,** vous savez l'amour que je vous porte; **he d. loves his house,** il est fort attaché à sa maison; **he d. loves to play jokes on people,** il trouve tout son plaisir à jouer des tours aux gens; *Ecc:* **d. beloved brethren,** mes bien chers frères.

dearness [ˈdiənis], *s.* **1.** cherté *f* (des vivres, etc.). **2.** tendresse *f.*

dearomatization [diːərouməta iˈzeiʃ(ə)n], **dearomatizing** [diːəˈroumətaiziŋ], *s.* désaromatisation *f.*

dearomatize [diːəˈroumətaiz], *v.tr.* désaromatiser.

dearth [dəːθ], *s.* disette *f*, pénurie *f* (de vivres, d'idées, de livres, etc.); dénuement *m*, stérilité *f*, pauvreté *f* (d'idées); **in times of d. and famine,** par les temps de disette et de famine; **there is a d. of young women,** les jeunes filles manquent, il y a un manque de jeunes filles; **there was no great d. of young men,** les jeunes gens *m* ne manquaient pas; *St.Exch:* **d. of stock,** pénurie de titres.

deary [ˈdiəri]. **1.** *s.* = DEARIE. **2.** *int. F: O:* **d. me!** mon Dieu! diable!

de-asphalt [diːˈæsfælt], *v.tr. Petr:* désasphalter.

de-asphalting [diːˈæsfæltiŋ], *s. Petr:* désasphaltage *m.*

death [deθ], *s.* (*a*) mort *f*; *Lit:* trépas *m*; **lingering d.,** lente agonie; *Hist:* **the Black D.,** la peste noire; **in the hour of d.,** au moment de mourir, *Lit:* à l'heure suprême; **to be at death's door, at the point of d., on the verge of d.,** être sur le point de mourir, à l'article de la mort, à deux doigts de la mort; agoniser, être à l'agonie; **he has been at death's door,** il revient de loin; **to look d. in the face,** voir la mort de près; **to meet d. calmly,** affronter la mort avec calme; bien mourir; **to die a natural d.,** mourir de sa belle mort; **to die a violent d.,** mourir de mort violente; **we do not know how he met his d.,** nous ne savons pas comment il est mort; **on his father's d. he returned to France,** à la mort de son père il est rentré en France; **at (the time of) his d. he was the owner of the estate,** à sa mort la propriété lui appartenait; **until d.,** pour la vie; **faithful unto d.,** fidèle jusqu'au tombeau; *Lit:* **to be sick (un)to d.,** être malade à mourir; *F:* **to be sick to d. of sth.,** en avoir marre de qch.; *Psy:* **d. wish, instinct,** pulsion *f* de mort; **d. wound,** blessure *f* mortelle; **d. rattle,** râle *m*, râlement *m* (de la mort); **d. mask,** masque *m* mortuaire; **death's head,** tête *f* de mort; *Ent:* **death's head moth,** (sphinx *m*) atropos *m*, *F:* tête-de-mort; **d. roll,** liste *f* des morts; **the earthquake caused a d. toll of 500,** 500 personnes sont mortes dans le tremblement de terre; **d. chamber,** chambre *f* mortuaire; **d. house,** (i) *U.S: Jur:* salle *f* d'exécution (dans une prison); (ii) *Journ:* maison *f* du mort, de la morte; *esp.* maison où le meurtre a été commis; **d. knell,** glas *m*; **this speech appeared to sound the d. knell of their plans,** ce discours semblait mettre fin à leurs projets; **you are running to certain d.,** vous courez à la mort; **he fell 100 metres to his d.,** il a fait une chute mortelle de 100 mètres; **it was d. to enter the temple,** quiconque entrait dans le temple mourait sur-le-champ; **you'll catch your d. of cold if you go out in this weather,** vous allez attraper la mort si vous sortez par ce temps; *F:* **he'll be the d. of me,** (i) il me fera mourir; (ii) il me fait mourir de rire; **it would be the d. of him,** ce serait sa mort; **it is the d. of all my hopes,** cela met fin à tous mes espoirs; **to be d. on game,** faire mouche à tout coup; **to be d. on sth.,** faire la guerre à qch.; ne pas souffrir qch.; **she was d. on dust,** elle pourchassait, faisait la guerre à, la poussière; **to put s.o. to d.,** mettre qn à mort; exécuter qn; faire périr qn; **condemned to d., under sentence of d.,** condamné à mort; *F:* **to do s.o. to d.,** tuer qn; assassiner qn; **this meat has been done to d.,** cette viande est archicuite, carbonisée; **fashion that has been done to d.,** mode qui a été copiée jusqu'à la nausée; **to torture s.o. to d.,** torturer qn à mort; **war to the d.,** guerre *f* à mort, à outrance; **to drink oneself to d.,** se tuer à force de boire; **he died the d.,** (i) il fut exécuté; (ii) (*of actor*) il est tombé à vide; **d. to traitors!** à mort les traîtres! **to be in at the d.,** (i) *Ven:* être à la curée, à l'hallali; (ii) *F:* être présent au bon moment, pour le bouquet; être là pour voir aboutir l'affaire; *F:* **to look like d. (warmed up),** avoir une figure de cadavre, un air de cadavre ambulant; (*b*) *Lit:* **D. (the Reaper),** la Mort; **no one can cheat D.,** nul ne peut tromper la Mort; (*c*) *Jur: Adm:* décès *m*, **to notify a d.,** notifier un décès; **proof of d.,** constatation *f* de décès; **d. certificate,** extrait *m* d'acte de décès; **register of births, marriages and deaths,** registre *m* de l'état civil; **there were three deaths on board,** il y a eu trois cas de mort, trois décès, à bord; *Journ:* **deaths, d. notices,** nécrologie *f*; avis *m* mortuaires; **d. rate,** (taux *m* de la) mortalité *f*; **crude d. rates,** taux bruts de mortalité; **d. duties,** *U.S:* **d. taxes,** droits *m* de succession; droits de mutation par décès; *Jur:* **d. warrant,** ordre *m* d'exécution; arrêt *m* de mort; **to sign s.o.'s d. warrant,** signer l'ordre d'exécution de qn; **to sign one's own d. warrant,** se condamner par ses propres actes, ses propres paroles; **to sign the d. warrant of an enterprise,** condamner une entreprise, prononcer l'arrêt de mort d'une entreprise; (*d*) *Jur:* **civil d.,** mort civile; (*e*) *Rept:* **d. adder,** acanthopis *m*; *F:* vipère *f* de la mort; (*f*) *Fung:* **d. cap, d. cup,** amanite *f* phalloïde; (*g*) **d. sand,** poussière radioactive.

deathbed [ˈdeθbed], *s.* lit *m* de mort; **long-protracted d.,** lente agonie; **d. confession,** aveu fait au lit de mort.

deathblow [ˈdeθblou], *s.* coup mortel, fatal; **to give the d. to one's opponent,** porter le coup mortel à son adversaire; **to strike a d. to s.o.'s hopes,** porter un coup mortel aux espérances de qn.

death-come-quickly [ˈdeθˈkʌmˈkwikli], *s. Bot: F:* géranium *m* robertin.

death-dealing [ˈdeθdiːliŋ], *a.* (engin *m*, etc.) meurtrier.

deathless [ˈdeθlis], *a.* impérissable, immortel.

deathlessly [ˈdeθlisli], *adv.* immortellement, impérissablement.

deathlessness [ˈdeθlisnis], *s.* immortalité *f.*

deathlike [ˈdeθlaik], *a.* de mort; semblable à la mort; **d. pallor,** pâleur *f* de mort; pâleur sépulcrale; teint çadavéreux; **d. stillness, sleep,** silence *m*, sommeil *m*, de mort.

deathly [ˈdeθli]. **1.** *a.* (*a*) = DEADLY 1 (*a*); (*b*) = DEATHLIKE. **2.** *adv.* comme la mort; **d. pale,** d'une pâleur de mort; d'une pâleur mortelle.

deathtrap [ˈdeθtræp], *s.* endroit dangereux pour la vie; coupe-gorge *m inv*, casse-cou *m inv*; souricière *f*; *Aut: etc:* croisement *m* de routes dangereux.

deathwatch [ˈdeθwɔːtʃ], *s.* **1.** veillée *f* d'un mourant, d'un mort; veillée de corps. **2.** *Ent:* **d. (beetle),** psoque *m*, atropos *m*, anobion *m*, anobie *m*, *F:* horloge *f* de la mort, vrillette *f.*

de-atomize [diːˈætəmaiz], *v.tr.* désatomiser.

deb [deb], *s.f. F:* débutante.

débâcle, debacle [deiˈbɑːkl], *s.* débâcle *f.*

debag [diːˈbæg], *v.tr.* **(debagged)** *F:* déculotter.

debar [diˈbɑːr], *v.tr.* **(debarred) 1. to d. s.o. from sth.,** exclure, priver, qn de qch., interdire qch. à qn; **countries debarred from commerce,** pays fermés au commerce; **to d. s.o. from doing sth.,** défendre, interdire, à qn de faire qch.; **his age debars him from competing,** son âge l'empêche de concourir; *Jur:* **debarred from succeeding, from inheriting,** indigne de succéder; exclu d'une succession pour cause d'indignité. **2. to d. s.o. a right,** refuser un droit à qn; priver qn d'un droit. **3.** *A:* empêcher, interdire (qch.).

debark[1] [diːˈbɑːk], *v.tr. & i.* désembarquer; débarquer.

debark[2], *v.tr.* écorcer (un arbre).

debarkation [diːbɑːˈkeiʃ(ə)n], *s.* débarquement *m*; désembarquement *m.*

debase [diˈbeis], *v.tr.* **1.** avilir, ravaler, dégrader (qn); rabaisser, trivialiser (son style, la langue); altérer (la langue); **I would not d. myself as far as to . . .,** je ne m'abaisserais pas jusqu'à . . .; **the candidature of X debases the political image even further,** la candidature de X ramène à un niveau encore plus bas l'image de la vie politique. **2.** (*a*) **to d. the coinage,** adultérer, écharser, les monnaies; (*b*) **to d. the currency,** déprécier, avilir, la monnaie.

debasement [diˈbeismənt], *s.* **1.** avilissement *m*, dégradation *f*, abrutissement *m* (de qn). **2.** altération *f*, adultération *f* (des monnaies).

debaser [diˈbeisər], *s.* **1. journalists who are great debasers of the English language,** journalistes qui respectent peu la pureté de la langue anglaise. **2.** altérateur *m*, adultérateur *m* (de la monnaie).

debasing[1] [diˈbeisiŋ], *a.* avilissant.

debasing[2], *s.* = DEBASEMENT.

debatable [diˈbeitəbl], *a.* contestable, discutable, débattable; (frontière *f*, etc.) en litige; *Cmptr:* **d. time,** temps *m* non imputable; **it's d., a d. point,** cela est contestable.

debate[1] [diˈbeit], *s.* débat *m*, discussion *f*, délibération *f*; conférence *f* contradictoire; **the question in d., under d.,** la question en discussion; **after much d. . . .,** après de longues discussions . . .; **full-dress d.,** grand débat (à la Chambre, etc.).

debate[2]. **1.** *v.tr.* (*a*) débattre contradictoirement, discuter, agiter (une question, etc.); **to d. a subject,** mettre un sujet en discussion; **the question is being, has been, debated again,** la question est revenue en discussion; **a much debated question,** une question fort controversée, **I was debating with myself, in my mind, whether I would go or not,** je délibérais si j'irais ou non; (*b*) *Lit: A:* disputer (la victoire, etc.). **2.** *v.i.* discuter, disputer **(with s.o. on sth.,** avec qn sur qch.).

debater [diˈbeitər], *s.* orateur *m* (qui brille dans les débats); débatteur *m.*

debating [diˈbeitiŋ], *s.* **d. society,** association *f* ayant pour but l'organisation de débats, des conférences contradictoires, où les gens peuvent s'exercer à la parole; **d. point,** sujet *m* qui prête à discussion.

debauch[1] [diˈbɔːtʃ], *s.* **1.** la débauche. **2.** débauche, orgie *f.*

debauch[2], *v.tr.* débaucher, corrompre (qn); séduire, débaucher (une femme); corrompre, vicier (le goût).

debauched [diˈbɔːtʃt], *a.* débauché, corrompu.

debauchee [diebɔːˈtʃiː], *s.* débauché, -ée.

debaucher [diˈbɔːtʃər], *s.* corrupteur, -trice (des gens ou mœurs); séducteur *m* (de femmes).

debauchery [diˈbɔːtʃəri], *s.* **1.** débauche *f*; dérèglement *m* de mœurs; **to turn to d.,** se débaucher; *Jur:* **d. of youth,** corruption *f* de mineurs. **2.** *A:* débauchement *m*, débauchage *m* (des troupes, etc.).

debeaking [diːˈbiːkiŋ], *s.* débecquage *m* (des poules).

debenture [diˈbentjər], *s.* **1.** *Cust:* certificat *m* de drawback. **2.** *Fin:* obligation *f*; **first, second, third, d.,** obligation de premier, de deuxième, de troisième, rang; **bearer d.,** obligation au porteur; **mortgage d.,** obligation hypothécaire; **unissued debentures,** obligations à la souche; **d. bond,** titre *m*, certificat *m*, d'obligation; **d. loan,** emprunt *m* obligataire; **d. capital,** capital-obligations *m*; **d. stock,** obligations sans garantie, non remboursables; **d. holder,** porteur, -euse, d'obligations; obligataire *mf.*

debenzolize [diːˈbenzəlaiz], *v.tr. Ch:* débenzoler.

debilitant [diˈbilitənt], *a. & s. Med:* débilitant (*m*).

debilitate [diˈbiliteit], *v.tr.* débiliter.

debilitating [diˈbiliteitiŋ], *a.* débilitant.

debilitation [dibiliˈteiʃ(ə)n], *s. Med:* débilitation *f.*

debility [diˈbiliti], *s.* **1.** *Med:* débilité *f*, asthénie *f.* **2.** *Lit:* **d. of purpose,** faiblesse *f* de caractère; irrésolution *f.*

debit[1] [ˈdebit], *s. Book-k:* débit *m*, doit *m*; (*a*) **d. and credit,** doit et avoir *m*; **d. (entry),** article *m* au débit; **every d. has a corresponding credit,** chaque débit a un crédit correspondant; (*b*) **to enter sth. on the d. (side) of an account,** porter qch. au débit, au doit, d'un compte; **d. note,** note *f*, bordereau *m*, de débit; **d. account,** compte débiteur; **d. balance,** solde débiteur; **account**

showing a d. balance, compte *m* déficitaire; **account that shows a d. balance of so much,** compte qui se balance de tant au passif; **d. column,** colonne débitrice; (*c*) *Bank:* **direct d.,** prélèvement *m* bancaire.

debit[2], *v.tr. Book-k:* **1.** débiter (un article, un compte); **to whom shall I d. the amount?** au débit de qui dois-je porter le montant? **2. to d. s.o. with a sum,** inscrire, porter, une somme au débit de qn; débiter (le compte de) qn d'une somme.

debitable ['debitəbl], *a.* **charge d. to the profit and loss account,** charge *f* à porter au débit du compte profits et pertes.

debituminization [di:bitjuminai'zeiʃ(ə)n], *s.* débituminisation *f.*

debituminize [di:bi'tju:minaiz], *v.tr.* débituminiser.

deblock [di:'blɔk], *v.tr.* **1.** libérer (le transfert des monnaies, etc.). **2.** *Cmptr:* dégrouper (des articles groupés par blocs).

debonair [debə'nɛər], *a. Lit:* **1.** jovial, -aux. **2.** *A:* débonnaire.

debouch [di'bautʃ], *v.i.* déboucher; **the army debouched into the plain,** l'armée déboucha dans la plaine; **roads debouching into the market place,** rues *f* qui débouchent sur la place du marché.

debouchment [di'bautʃmənt], *s.* **1.** débouchement *m* (de troupes, d'un fleuve). **2.** débouché *m*, sortie *f* (d'un défilé, etc.).

debride [dei'bri:d, də-], *v.tr. Surg:* débrider.

debridement [dei'bri:dmɑ̃(ŋ), -mənt], *s. Surg:* débridement *m.*

debrief [di:'bri:f], *v.tr. Pol: Av: etc:* interroger (un réfugié, un pilote, etc.).

debriefing [di:'bri:fiŋ], *s. Pol: Av: etc:* interrogation *f* (d'un réfugié, d'un pilote, etc.).

debris ['debri:], *s.* débris *mpl*; détritus *m* (géologiques).

debt [det], *s.* dette *f*; créance *f*; **bad d.,** mauvaise créance, créance douteuse, irrécouvrable; **good d.,** bonne créance, dette; **d. due,** créance exigible; **secured d.,** créance garantie; **privileged d.,** dette privilégiée; **d. owed by us, by the firm,** dette passive; **d. owed to us,** dette active; créance *f*; **d. of honour,** dette d'honneur; **to be in d.,** être endetté; avoir des dettes; **he is in d. to everybody,** il doit à tout le monde; *F:* **to be head over ears, up to the ears, eyes, in d.,** devoir à Dieu et au diable; être criblé, accablé, cousu, de dettes; avoir des dettes par-dessus la tête; être dans les dettes jusqu'au cou; être perdu de dettes; **how much am I in your d.?** combien vous dois-je? **I shall always be in your d.,** je vous serai toujours redevable; **I am no longer in your d.,** je suis quitte envers vous; **to be x francs in d.,** avoir x francs de dette; être endetté de x francs; **to be out of d.,** être quitte de dettes; n'avoir plus de dettes; avoir ses dettes réglées; **to get out of d.,** se désendetter; s'acquitter de ses dettes; payer ses dettes; **to be out of s.o.'s d.,** être quitte envers qn; **the Public D., the National D.,** la Dette publique, nationale; **the National D. Register,** le Grand-Livre de la Dette publique; **funded d., consolidated d.,** fonds consolidés; dette consolidée; dette publique en rentes sur l'État; **floating d.,** dette publique flottante, non consolidée; dette courante; **war d.,** dette de guerre; **d. collector,** agent *m* de recouvrements; **to pay the d. of nature, to pay one's last d.,** mourir; payer le tribut, sa dette, à la nature.

debtor ['detər], *s.* **1.** débiteur, -trice; **joint d.,** codébiteur, -trice; *A:* **debtors' prison,** prison *f* pour dettes; **I am your d. for £100,** je vous dois £100, je vous suis redevable de £100. **2.** *Book-k:* **d. side,** débit *m*, doit *m*; **d. account,** compte débiteur; **d. and creditor account,** compte par doit et avoir.

debug [di:'bʌg], *v.tr. F:* **1.** éliminer les insectes d'(une plante). **2.** (*a*) éliminer les erreurs et les imperfections d'(un prototype, etc.); *Cmptr:* mettre (un programme) au point; dépanner (une machine); (*b*) éliminer les microphones clandestins, cachés, dans (une pièce, etc.).

debugger [di:'bʌgər], *s. Cmptr:* sous-programme *m* de mise au point.

debugging [di:'bʌgiŋ], *s. F:* **1.** élimination *f* des insectes. **2.** (*a*) élimination des imperfections (d'un prototype, etc.); *Cmptr:* mise *f* au point (d'un programme); dépannage *m* (d'une machine); **d. run,** passage *m* de mise au point; (*b*) élimination des microphones cachés.

debunk [di:'bʌŋk], *v.tr. F:* **1.** faire descendre (un grand homme) de son piédestal; déboulonner (un grand homme). **2.** démystifier, pénétrer le mystère (d'un sujet d'effroi); ramener (une nouvelle alarmiste, etc.) à ses justes proportions.

debunking [di:'bʌŋkiŋ], *s. F:* **1.** dégonflement *m* (d'une réputation, etc.); déboulonnage *m*. **2.** démystification *f* (d'un sujet, etc.).

debus [di:'bʌs], *v.tr. & i.* (**debussed** [di:'bʌst]) (faire) débarquer (des troupes, etc.) des autobus, etc.

debussing [di:'bʌsiŋ], *s.* débarquement *m* (des troupes, etc.) des autobus, etc.; **d. point,** chantier *m*, point *m*, de débarquement; **d. area,** zone *f* de débarquement.

début ['deibju:], *s.* début *m*; (*in society*) entrée *f* dans le monde; **to make one's d.,** faire son début, ses débuts; débuter.

debutanization [di:bju:tənai'zeiʃ(ə)n], *s. Petr:* débutanisation *f.*

debutanize [di:'bju:tənaiz], *v.tr. Petr:* débutaniser.

debutanizer [di:'bju:tənaizər], *s. Petr:* débutaniseur *m.*

débutante ['debjutɑ̃t, -tænt], *s.f.* débutante.

dec(a)- ['dek(ə)], *comb.fm.* déc(a)-.

decacanthous [dekə'kænθəs], *a. Bot: Z:* décacanthe.

decachord ['dekəkɔ:d], *s. Mus:* décac(h)orde *m.*

decadactylous [dekə'dæktiləs], *a. Nat.Hist:* décadactyle.

decadal ['dekədl], *a. Fr.Hist:* décadaire.

decade ['dekəd, -keid, di'keid], *s.* **1.** (*a*) décennie *f*, décade *f*, période *f* de dix ans; (*b*) *Fr.Hist:* (*period of ten days*) décade (du calendrier républicain). **2.** *Lt.Lit:* (*set of ten*) **the Decades of Livy,** les Décades de Tite-Live. **3.** *Ecc:* dizaine *f* (d'un chapelet).

decadence ['dekəd(ə)ns], *s.* **1.** décadence *f*. **2.** *Lit: Art:* décadentisme *m.*

decadent ['dekəd(ə)nt]. **1.** *a.* en décadence; décadent. **2.** *s. Lit: Art:* décadent *m.*

decadentism ['dekədəntizm], *s. Lit: Art:* décadentisme *m.*

decaffeinate [di:'kæfi:ineit], *v.tr.* décaféiner.

decaffeinization [di:kæfi:inai'zeiʃ(ə)n], *s.* décaféinisation *f.*

decaffeinize [di:'kæfi:inaiz], *v.tr.* décaféiner.

decagon ['dekəgən], *s. Mth:* décagone *m.*

decagonal [di'kægən(ə)l], *a. Mth:* décagonal, -aux; décagone.

decagram(me) ['dekəgræm], *s. Meas:* décagramme *m.*

decagynian [dekə'dʒiniən], **decagynous** [de'kædʒinəs], *a. Bot:* décagyne.

decahedral [dekə'hedr(ə)l, -'hi:-], *a. Mth:* décaèdre.

decahedron [dekə'hedr(ə)n, -'hi:-], *s. Mth:* décaèdre *m.*

decalage [dekə'lɑ:ʒ, dei-], *s.* décalage *m* (des ailes d'un avion).

decalcification ['di:kælsifi'keiʃ(ə)n], *s.* décalcification *f.*

decalcify [di:'kælsifai], *v.tr.* décalcifier (les os, une roche).

decalcomania [di:kælkou'meiniə], *s. Cer: etc:* décalcomanie *f.*

decalitre ['dekəli:tər], *s. Meas:* décalitre *m.*

decalobate [dekə'loubeit], *a. Bot:* décalobé.

decalogue ['dekəlɔg], *s.* décalogue *m.*

Decameron (the) [ðədi'kæmər(ə)n], *s. Lit:* le Décaméron *m.*

decametre ['dekəmi:tər], *s. Meas:* décamètre *m.*

decametric [dekə'metrik], *a.* décamétrique; *W.Tel: etc:* **d. wave,** onde *f* décamétrique.

decamp [di'kæmp], *v.i.* **1.** *Mil:* lever le camp. **2.** *F:* détaler, décamper, filer; prendre la poudre d'escampette; prendre, fiche(r), le camp; prendre la clef des champs; prendre le large; ne pas demander son reste.

decampment [di'kæmpmənt], *s. Mil:* levée *f* du camp.

decan ['dekən], *s. Astrol:* décan *m.*

decanal [di'kein(ə)l], *a. Ecc:* (*a*) décanal, -aux; (*b*) **the d. side of the choir,** le côté sud du chœur (où se trouve la stalle du doyen).

decandrian [de'kændriən], **decandrous** [de'kændrəs], *a. Bot:* décandre.

decane [de'kein], *s. Ch:* décane *m.*

decani [di'keinai], *adj. Ecc.Mus:* (partie de l'antienne à chanter) du côté du doyen.

decanol ['dekənɔl], *s. Ch:* décanol *m.*

decant [di'kænt], *v.tr.* (*a*) décanter, transvaser (un liquide); tirer (un liquide) au clair; **to d. a bottle of wine,** décanter une bouteille de vin dans une carafe; (*b*) *F:* **the tourists were decanted from the coach in front of the hotel,** le car a déversé les touristes devant l'hôtel.

decantation [di:kæn'teiʃ(ə)n], *s.* décantation *f*, décantage *m*; transvasement *m.*

decanter [di'kæntər], *s.* **1.** carafe *f* (à liqueur, à vin); **small d.,** carafon *m*; **d. stand,** porte-carafe *m*, *pl.* porte-carafes. **2.** *Tchn:* décanteur *m.*

decanting [di'kæntiŋ], *s.* = DECANTATION.

decapetalous [dekə'petələs], *a. Bot:* décapétale.

decapitate [di'kæpiteit], *v.tr.* décapiter (qn, *F:* une fleur, etc.); couper la tête à (qn).

decapitation [dikæpi'teiʃ(ə)n], *s.* **1.** décapitation *f*; *B:* décollation *f* (de saint Jean-Baptiste). **2.** *Obst:* décollation (du fœtus).

decapod ['dekəpɔd], *s.* **1.** *Crust:* décapode *m*. **2.** *Rail:* décapod *m.*

Decapoda [di'kæpədə], *s.pl. Crust:* décapodes *m.*

decapodal [di'kæpədl], **decapodous** [di'kæpədəs], *a. Crust:* décapode.

Decapolis [di'kæpəlis], *Pr.n. A.Geog:* la Décapole.

decapsulate [di:'kæpsjuleit], *v.tr. Surg:* décapsuler.

decapsulation ['di:kæpsju'leiʃ(ə)n], *s. Surg:* décapsulation *f* (d'un rein).

decarbonate [di:'kɑ:bəneit], *v.tr. Ch:* décarbonater.

decarbonated [di:'kɑ:bəneitid], *a.* décarbonaté.

decarbonation [di:kɑ:bə'neiʃ(ə)n], *s. Ch:* décarbonatation *f.*

decarbonization [di:kɑ:bənai'zeiʃ(ə)n], *s.* **1.** *Metall: Ind:* décarburation *f* (de l'acier, etc.). **2.** *I.C.E:* décalaminage *m*, détartrage *m*, décrassage *m* (du moteur).

decarbonize [di:'kɑ:bənaiz], *v.tr.* **1.** *Metall: Ind:* décarburer, décarboniser (la fonte, l'acier, etc.). **2.** *I.C.E:* **to d. a cylinder head,** décalaminer, désencrasser, une culasse.

decarbonizer [di:'kɑ:bənaizər], *s.* **1.** *Ch: Ind:* décarburant *m*. **2.** *I.C.E:* décalaminant *m.*

decarbonizing [di:'kɑ:bənaiziŋ], *a. Metall: Ind:* décarburant.

decarboxylase [di:kɑ:'bɔksileis], *s. Ch:* décarboxylase *f.*

decarboxylation [di:kɑ:bɔksi'leiʃ(ə)n], *s. Ch:* décarboxylation *f.*

decarburization [di:kɑ:bju(ə)rai'zeiʃ(ə)n], *s. Ind:* décarburation *f.*

decarburize [di:'kɑ:bju(ə)raiz], *v.tr. Ind:* décarburer, décarboniser.

decarburizer [di:'kɑ:bju(ə)raizər], *s. Ind:* décarburant *m.*

decartelization [di:kɑ:təlai'zeiʃ(ə)n], *s. Pol.Ec:* décartellisation *f.*

decartelize [di:'kɑ:təlaiz], *v.tr. Pol.Ec:* décartelliser.

decastere ['dekəstiər], *s. Meas:* décastère *m.*

decastyle ['dekəstail], *s. Arch:* décastyle *m.*

decasualization ['di:kæʒjuəlai'zeiʃ(ə)n], *s.* régularisation *f* du travail (des dockers, etc.).

decasualize [di:'kæʒju(ə)laiz], *v.tr. Ind:* régulariser le travail des (dockers, etc.); supprimer la main-d'œuvre d'emploi intermittent dans (une industrie).

decasyllabic ['dekəsi'læbik], *a.* décasyllabe, décasyllabique.

decasyllable ['dekə'siləbl], *a. & s. Pros:* décasyllabe (*m*).

decathlon [de'kæθlɔn], *s. Sp:* décathlon *m.*

decatholicize [di:kə'θɔlisaiz], *v.tr.* décatholiciser (un pays, etc.).

decatize ['dekətaiz], *v.tr. Tex:* décatir (des étoffes).

decay[1] [di'kei], *s.* **1.** décadence *f*, déchéance *f* (d'une famille, d'un pays, d'un art, du commerce); décrépitude *f* (d'une nation); déclin *m* (de la beauté, d'une fortune); caducité *f*, ruine *f*, délabrement *m* (d'un bâtiment, d'un état); délabrement (de la santé, d'un vêtement); dépérissement *m* (d'une plante, de la morale); affaiblissement (du corps, de la vue, du pouvoir); **d. of intellectual power,** affaiblissement, avachissement *m*, de l'esprit; **senile d.,** affaiblissement sénile; gâtisme *m*; **suffering from senile d.,** gâteux, -euse; **to fall into d.,** (*of house*) tomber en ruine, se délabrer; (*of state*) tomber en décadence; (*of custom*) tomber en désuétude; **houses falling into d. for lack of upkeep,** maisons *f* qui dépérissent faute d'entretien; **to be in a state of d.,** être en ruine, en décadence; **the Empire was already in d.,** l'Empire déclinait déjà; **seeds of d.,** germes *mpl* de déchéance, de mort; **idleness leads to moral d.,** l'oisiveté amène la déchéance individuelle; *Ling:* **phonetic d.,** usure *f* phonique; *Pol.Ec:* **use, d. and obsolescence,** l'usure *f*, le dépérissement et la désuétude. **2.** (*a*) pourriture *f*, corruption *f*, décomposition *f*, putréfaction *f* (du bois, etc.); altération *f* (du caoutchouc, etc.); **prevention of d.,** imputrescibilisation *f*; (*b*) pourriture; carie *f* (des os, des dents); (*c*) *Atom.Ph:* désintégration *f*; **alpha, beta, d.,** désintégration alpha, bêta; (*d*) *Cmptr:* **d. time,** période *f* d'extinction.

decay[2]. **1.** *v.i.* (*a*) (*of nation, family, commerce, art*) tomber en décadence; (*of building*) tomber en ruine; se délabrer; (*of race, tree, plant*) dépérir; (*of empire*) décliner; (*of beauty, flowers*), (se) passer, se flétrir; (*of health*) décliner, se délabrer; (*of eyesight*) s'affaiblir; (*of custom*) se perdre; (*of hope*) s'évanouir; (*of friendships*) s'en aller une à une; (*b*) (*of meat, fruit*) se gâter, s'altérer, s'avarier, pourrir; (*of timber*) pourrir; (*of teeth*) se carier; (*of rubber*) s'altérer; (*c*) *Atom.Ph:* désintégrer. **2.** *v.tr.* (*a*) pourrir (le bois, etc.); (*b*) carier (les dents).

decayed [di'keid], *a.* **1.** (famille) déchue, ruinée; (fleur, beauté) passée, flétrie; (maison, fortune) délabrée; **d. gentlewoman,** dame (bien née) tombée dans la gêne. **2.** (bois) pourri; (fruit) gâté; **d. tooth,** dent gâtée, cariée, malade.

decaying [di'keiiŋ], *a.* **1.** (nation) en décadence; (arbre) dépérissant; (maison) caduque. **2.** en pourriture; en train de s'avarier, de se carier.

Deccan ['dekæn], *Pr.n. Geog:* Deccan *m*, Dekkan *m*.

decease[1] [di'si:s], *s. Jur: Adm:* décès *m*.

decease[2], *v.i. Jur: Adm:* décéder; **he deceased without heirs,** il est décédé sans laisser d'héritiers.

deceased [di'si:st], *esp. Jur:* **1.** *a.* (*a*) décédé; **son of parents d.,** fils de père et mère décédés, défunts; **son of Robert Martin, d.,** fils de feu M. Robert Martin; **Anne Gilbert, d.,** feue Mme. Anne Gilbert; (*b*) d'un décédé; **d. estate,** succession *f*. **2.** *s.* **the d.,** le défunt, la défunte; **the house of the d.,** la maison mortuaire.

decedent [di'si:dnt], *a. & s. Jur: NAm:* = DECEASED; **decedent's estate,** succession *f*.

deceit [di'si:t], *s.* **1.** tromperie *f*, duperie *f*, fourberie *f*; *Jur:* fraude *f*, dol *m*; **a piece of d.,** une supercherie. **2.** = DECEITFULNESS.

deceitful [di'si:tf(u)l], *a.* trompeur, -euse; fourbe; faux, *f.* fausse; (regard) mensonger.

deceitfully [di'si:tfuli], *adv.* **1.** frauduleusement; par supercherie. **2.** faussement; avec duplicité.

deceitfulness [di'si:tf(u)lnis], *s.* nature trompeuse; fausseté *f*.

deceivable [di'si:vəbl], *a.* décevable; facile à tromper.

deceive [di'si:v], *v.tr.* (*a*) tromper, abuser (qn); induire (qn) en erreur; en imposer à (qn); *F:* en conter à (qn); faire marcher (qn); **to d. oneself,** se tromper, s'abuser; se faire illusion à soi-même; **to d. oneself with a fond hope,** se leurrer d'un espoir; **I have been deceived in you,** je me suis abusé sur votre compte; **to d. s.o.'s hopes,** tromper, décevoir, les espérances de qn; **I thought my eyes were deceiving me,** je ne pouvais pas en croire mes yeux; j'ai cru avoir la berlue; *v.i.* **I did not mean to d.,** je n'ai voulu tromper personne; (*b*) tromper (son mari, sa femme); **deceived husband,** mari trompé; *F:* cocu *m*.

deceiver [di'si:vər], *s.* trompeur, -euse; attrapeur, -euse; fourbe *m*.

deceiving [di'si:viŋ], *a.* trompeur, -euse; décevant.

deceivingly [di'si:viŋli], *adv.* trompeusement.

decelerate [di:'seləreit], *v.i. & tr.* décélérer; ralentir; freiner.

deceleration [di:selə'reiʃ(ə)n], *s.* décélération *f*; accélération négative, contre-accélération *f*; ralentissement *m*; freinage *m*; *Av:* **landing d.,** freinage à l'atterrissage; *Space:* **re-entry d.,** freinage lors de la rentrée dans l'atmosphère; **d. device,** décélérateur *m*, ralentisseur *m*, dispositif *m* de freinage; *Av:* **d. parachute,** parachute *m* de freinage (à l'atterrissage); *Aut: U.S:* **d. lane,** voie *f*, bande *f*, de ralentissement; *Cmptr: etc:* **d. time,** temps *m* de décélération, d'arrêt.

decelerator [di:'seləreitər], *s.* décélérateur *m*; ralentisseur *m*; frein *m* (de ralentissement).

decelerometer [di:selə'rəmitər], *s.* décéléromètre *m*.

December [di'sembər], *s.* décembre *m*; **in D.,** au mois de décembre, en décembre; **(on) the first, the seventh, of D.,** le premier, le sept, décembre.

Decembrist [di'sembrist], *s. Russ: Hist:* décembriste *m*, décabriste *m*.

decemvir [di'semvər], *s. Rom.Hist:* décemvir *m*; **the decemvirs, decemviri** [di'semvirai], les décemvirs.

decemvirate [di'semvireit], *s.* décemvirat *m*.

decency ['di:sənsi], *s.* **1.** décence *f*, bienséance *f* (de costume, etc.). **2.** bienséance, convenance(s) *f(pl)*, décence, honnêteté *f*; **the decencies, common d.,** les convenances (sociales); le respect humain; **for decency's sake,** par convenance; pour garder les convenances; **ordinary d. demands that . . .,** la simple honnêteté exige que + *sub;* **in common d., he ought to have written to her,** la simple politesse, le simple savoir-vivre, exigeait qu'il lui écrivît; **I can't with d. refuse,** je ne peux pas décemment refuser.

decennary [di'senəri]. **1.** *a.* = DECENNIAL. **2.** *s.* = DECENNIUM.

decennial [di'seniəl]. **1.** *a.* décennal, -aux. **2.** *s. esp. NAm:* dixième anniversaire *m*.

decennially [di'seniəli], *adv.* tous les dix ans.

decennium [di'seniəm], *s.* décennie *f*, (période *f* de) dix ans.

decent ['di:snt], *a.* **1.** (*a*) bienséant, convenable; *F:* **are you d.?** es-tu habillé (convenablement)? (*b*) décent, honnête, modeste. **2.** passable; assez bon; **to have a d. income,** avoir une honnête aisance; **this wine is quite d.,** ce vin est très buvable, très acceptable; **the food is d. enough,** la nourriture n'est pas mauvaise. **3.** *F:* **a d. sort of man,** un très bon garçon; un brave garçon; **it's very d. of you,** c'est trop aimable à vous; c'est très gentil de votre part; **to do the d. thing by s.o.,** redresser ses torts envers qn. **4.** *adv.* (*in compound adjs*) **d.-sized house,** maison *f* d'une grandeur raisonnable.

decently ['di:səntli], *adv.* **1.** décemment, convenablement, honnêtement; avec bienséance, avec décence. **2.** passablement; **he is doing quite d.,** (i) il travaille assez bien; (ii) il fait pas mal de progrès; (iii) ses affaires ne marchent pas mal; il gagne de quoi vivre convenablement.

decentralism [di:'sentrəlizm], *s. Pol:* décentralisme *m*.

decentralist [di:'sentrəlist], *s. Pol:* décentraliste *mf*, décentralisateur, -trice.

decentralization [di:sentrəlai'zeiʃ(ə)n], *s.* décentralisation (administrative, etc.).

decentralize [di:'sentrəlaiz], *v.tr.* décentraliser (l'administration, etc.).

decentralizing [di:'sentrəlaiziŋ], *a.* décentralisateur, -trice.

decentration [di:sen'treiʃ(ə)n], *s. Opt:* décentration *f*.

decentre [di:'sentər], *v.tr. Opt: etc:* décentrer.

decentring [di:'sentriŋ], *s.* décentrage *m*, décentration *f*, décentrement *m*.

deception [di'sepʃ(ə)n], *s.* **1.** tromperie *f*, duperie *f*; fraude *f*; **he is incapable of d.,** il est incapable de tromper; *Mil: etc:* **d. plan,** plan *m* de déception; **visual d.,** trompe-l'œil *m inv.* **2.** erreur *f*, duperie. **3. (piece of) d.,** supercherie *f*.

deceptive [di'septiv], *a.* (*a*) (*of thg, appearance*) trompeur, -euse; décevant, mensonger; menteur, -euse; **d. advertising,** publicité déloyale; *Prov:* **appearances are d.,** les apparences sont trompeuses; (*b*) *Mus:* **d. cadence,** cadence (inter)rompue; (*c*) **he, his manner, is very d.,** on ne peut jamais deviner ce qu'il va faire, dire.

deceptively [di'septivli], *adv.* trompeusement; **he has a d. quiet manner,** il a un air tranquille (bien) trompeur; il n'est pas toujours si tranquille qu'il en a l'air.

deceptiveness [di'septivnis], *s.* caractère mensonger, trompeur (de qch.).

decerebrate[1] [di:'seribreit], *a.* **d. rigidity,** rigidité décérébrée.

decerebrate[2], *v.tr.* décérébrer (un animal).

decerebration [di:seri'breiʃ(ə)n], *s.* décérébration *f* (d'un animal).

dechenite ['dekənait], *s. Miner:* déchénite *f*.

dechloridation [di:klɔri'deiʃ(ə)n], *s. Med:* déchloruration *f*.

dechloridize [di:'klɔridaiz], *v.tr. Med:* déchlorurer.

dechristianization [di:kristjənai'zeiʃ(ə)n], *s.* déchristianisation *f*.

dechristianize [di:'kristjənaiz], *v.tr.* déchristianiser.

deci- ['desi], *comb.fm.* déci-.

Decian ['di:siən], *a. Hist:* **the D. persecution,** la persécution de Decius.

deciare ['desieər], *s. Meas:* déciare *m*.

decibel ['desibel], *s. Ph:* décibel *m*.

decibelmeter ['desibelmi:tər], *s. Ph:* décibelmètre *m*.

decidable [di'saidəbl], *a.* que l'on peut décider.

decide [di'said]. **1.** *v.tr.* (*a*) (*to settle, judge*) décider (une question, une querelle); trancher (une question); juger (un différend); statuer sur (une affaire); **the matter is decided,** c'est une affaire jugée, délibérée; **only a long trial will d. which of the two processes is the better,** seule une longue pratique pourra dire lequel des deux procédés vaut le mieux; *Jur:* **to d. a case,** rendre un jugement; (*b*) (*to settle, fix*) décider de (qch.); **to d. s.o.'s fate,** décider du sort de qn; **event that decided his career,** événement *m* qui décida de sa carrière; **his fate is now being decided,** son sort se décide maintenant; **the artillery decided the battle,** l'artillerie *f* décida du sort de la bataille; **nothing has been, is, decided yet,** il n'y a rien de décidé pour le moment; il n'y a encore rien de décidé; (*c*) **to d. s.o. to do sth.,** décider qn à faire qch.; **that decided me (to depart),** cela me décida (à partir); (*d*) (*to make up one's mind*) **to d. to do sth.,** se décider, se résoudre, à faire qch.; décider, résoudre, de faire qch.; prendre le parti de faire qch.; *Impers:* **it was decided to await his reply,** on a décidé d'attendre sa réponse; **I have not yet decided what I shall do, what answer I shall give, whether I shall go,** je n'ai pas encore décidé ce que je ferai, quelle réponse je ferai, si j'irai; **I have decided what I shall do, which course I shall adopt,** mon parti est pris. **2.** *v.i.* **to d. on sth.,** se décider à qch.; conclure à qch.; **have you decided?** avez-vous pris un parti? êtes-vous décidé? **to d. on doing sth.,** se décider à, décider de, faire qch.; **to d. on sth. being done,** opiner pour que, à ce que, qch. se fasse; **to d. on a line of action,** arrêter un plan de conduite; **to d. on a method of work,** déterminer une méthode de travail; **to d. on a day,** fixer un jour; **the Assembly decided upon war,** l'Assemblée décida, résolut, la guerre, vota pour la guerre; **to d. for, in favour of, s.o.,** se décider pour, en faveur de, qn; donner raison à qn; **to d. against sth., s.o.,** se prononcer contre qch.; donner tort à qn; **to d. between opinions,** départager des opinions.

decided [di'saidid], *a.* **1.** (*a*) (*of pers.*) décidé; **they are quite d. about it,** ils sont tout à fait décidés (à agir, etc.); (*b*) **d. opinion,** opinion (bien) arrêtée; **d. manner,** allure décidée; **in a d. tone,** d'un ton net, résolu, tranchant; **a d. refusal, a d. 'no,'** un refus, un 'non,' catégorique. **2.** incontestable, indéniable, prononcé, décidé, très marqué; **to have a d. superiority over s.o.,** avoir une supériorité marquée sur qn; **a d. difference,** une différence marquée; **d. alteration for the better,** amélioration marquée, sensible, positive; **a d. success,** un succès indéniable, incontestable; **this is a d. step forward,** c'est un progrès très marqué.

decidedly [di'saididli], *adv.* **1.** (agir, répondre) résolument, avec décision. **2.** incontestablement, décidément; d'une façon marquée; **he is d. the best,** c'est lui le meilleur, sans contredit; **he is d. better,** il va décidément mieux; il y a un mieux très marqué.

decidedness [di'saididnis], *s.* résolution *f*, fermeté *f*; décision *f* (de caractère).

decider [di'saidər], *s.* **1.** (*pers.*) arbitre *m*, juge *m* **(of,** de). **2.** (*a*) *Games:* la belle; (*b*) *Sp:* (*after dead heat*) course *f* de décision.

deciding [di'saidiŋ], *a.* décisif; **d. factor,** facteur décisif; **the d. game, set, rubber,** la belle.

decidua [di'sidjuə], *s. Obst:* membrane caduque; caduque *f*.

deciduoma [disidju'oumə], *s. Med:* déciduome *m*.

deciduous [di'sidjuəs], *a.* **1.** (*a*) *Bot:* décidu; caduc, *f.* caduque; **d. leaf,** feuille décidue; **d. tree,** arbre *m* à feuillage caduc, à feuilles caduques; (*b*) **d. forest,** forêt feuillue. **2.** *Z:* (*of antlers, etc.*) caduc; *Obst:* **d. membrane,** membrane caduque; caduque *f*; *Ent:* **d. insects,** insectes *m* à ailes caduques. **3.** *A: & Lit:* éphémère.

deciduousness [di'sidjuəsnis], *s.* caducité *f*.

decigram(me) ['desigræm], *s. Meas:* décigramme *m*.

decile ['desail, -il], *s.* décile *m*.

decilitre ['desili:tər], *s. Meas:* décilitre *m*.

decillion [di'siliən], *s.* (*a*) un billion d'octillions (10^{60}); (*b*) *NAm:* mille quintillions (10^{33}).

decimal ['desiml]. **1.** *a.* (*of numeration, fraction, system, coinage, etc.*) décimal, -aux; *Mth:* **d. logarithm,** logarithme *m* ordinaire, à base 10; **terminate d. fraction,** fraction décimale exacte; **d. point,** virgule (décimale), *Fr.C:* point (décimal); **d. place,** (i) décimale *f*; (ii) *Cmptr:* position décimale; *Cmptr:* **coded d. number,** nombre décimal codé; **binary to d. conversion,** conversion *f* binaire (à) décimal, de binaire en décimal. **2.** *s.* (*a*) décimale; **recurring d.,** fraction *f* périodique; **correct to five places of decimals,** exact jusqu'à la cinquième décimale; **to give one's answer to two places of decimals,** donner le résultat à deux décimales près; (*b*) *pl.* **decimals,** calcul décimal; **I'm bad at, can't do, decimals,** je ne suis pas bon en calcul décimal.

decimalization [desiməlai'zeiʃ(ə)n], *s.* décimalisation *f*.

decimalize ['desiməlaiz], *v.tr.* décimaliser.

decimate ['desimeit], *v.tr.* décimer (des mutinés, etc.); **the plague decimated the population,** la peste décima le peuple.

decimation [desi'meiʃ(ə)n], *s.* décimation *f*.

decimetre ['desimi:tər], *s.* **1.** *Meas:* décimètre *m*; **square d.,** décimètre carré; **cubic d.,** décimètre cube. **2.** *Ph:* **d. waves,** ondes *f* décimétriques.

decimo-octavo ['desimouɔk'teivou], *s. Typ:* in-dix-huit *m*.

decineper [desi'ni:pər], *s. Ph.Meas:* décineper *m*.

decinormal [desi'nɔ:m(ə)l], *a. Ch:* (*of solution*) décinormal, -aux.

decipher[1] [di'saifər], *s.* déchiffrement *m*; transcription *f* en clair.

decipher[2], *v.tr.* **1.** déchiffrer (des hiéroglyphes); déchiffrer, décoder, transcrire en clair (une dépêche chiffrée); décrypter (un cryptogramme). **2. handwriting difficult to d.,** écriture *f* difficile à déchiffrer, à débrouiller.

decipherable [di'saif(ə)rəbl], *a.* déchiffrable.

deciphering [di'saif(ə)riŋ], *s.* déchiffrement *m*; transcription *f* en clair; décryptement *m*.

decipherment [di'saifəmənt], *s.* déchiffrement *m* (des hiéroglyphes, des inscriptions).

decision [di'siʒ(ə)n], *s.* **1.** (*a*) décision *f* (d'une question, d'une affaire, de faire qch.); vote *m* (sur une question); délibération *f* (d'une assemblée); **to bring a question to a d.,** décider, dénouer, une question; **to make known a d.,** faire connaître une décision; (*b*) décision, jugement *m*, arrêt *m*, arrêté *m*; **to give a d. on a case,** décider, statuer sur, un cas; **the d. of the Commission of Arbitration,** la sentence de la Commission arbitrale. **2.** (*a*) décision, résolution *f*; **to come to, make, arrive at, reach, a d. (about sth.),** arriver à une décision, prendre une décision, un parti (quant à, touchant, qch.); se décider, se prononcer; **not to know what d. to make,** ne savoir quel parti prendre; **to abide by one's d.,** s'en tenir à sa décision; **to reverse one's d.,** revenir sur sa décision; se déjuger; *Jur:* **judicial decisions,** réponses *f* de droit; (*b*) *attrib. Cmptr: etc:* **d. instruction,** instruction *f* de branchement; **d. box,** symbole *m* de décision (dans un organigramme); aiguillage *m*; **d. criterion,** critère *m* de choix, de décision; **d. element,** élément *m* de seuil; **d. maker,** décideur *m*, technicien *m* qui prend des décisions; **d. making,** prise *f* de décision. **3.** résolution (de caractère); fermeté *f*; **d. of character,** fermeté, décision, de caractère; **look of d.,** air décidé, résolu; **to act with d.,** agir avec décision.

decisive [di'saisiv], *a.* **1.** (*of question, battle, etc.*) décisif; (*of experiment, etc.*) concluant; **d. proof,** preuve victorieuse; *Lit:* **this incident was d. of his fate,** cet incident décida de son sort; *Jur:* **d. oath,** serment *m* décisoire. **2. d. manner, tone,** allure décidée; ton tranchant, net.

decisively [di'saisivli], *adv.* décisivement; d'une façon décisive; affirmativement; d'un ton décidé.

decisiveness [di'saisivnis], *s.* **1.** caractère décisif, concluant (d'une expérience, etc.). **2.** = DECISION 3.

decistere ['desistiər], *s. Meas:* décistère *m.*

decivilization [di:sivilai'zeiʃ(ə)n], *s.* décivilisation *f.*

decivilize [di:'sivilaiz], *v.tr.* déciviliser.

deck[1] [dek], *s.* **1.** (*a*) *Nau:* pont *m*; tillac *m*; **flush d.,** pont entier, ras; **flush-d. ship,** navire *m* à pont ras; **fore d., forecastle d.,** gaillard *m* d'avant; plage *f*, pont, avant; **aft(er) d., quarter d., poop d.,** pont, plage, arrière; gaillard d'arrière; dunette *f*; **lower d.,** pont inférieur; **middle d.,** pont intermédiaire; entrepont *m*; **upper d., weather d.,** premier pont; pont supérieur; **shelter d.,** pont-abri *m*, *pl.* ponts-abris; **promenade d., sun d.,** pont(-)promenade, *pl.* ponts(-)promenades; **bridge d.,** pont de passerelle; **boat d.,** pont des embarcations; **main d.,** pont principal; franc tillac; **spar d.,** pont volant, spardeck *m*; **well d.,** (pont à) coffre *m*; **orlop d.,** faux pont; **armoured d.,** pont cuirassé; pont blindé; **battery d., gun d.,** (pont de) batterie *f*; *Av:* **angled d.,** pont oblique; **flight d.,** pont d'envol; pont d'atterrissage; **d. officer, passenger,** officier *m*, passager *m*, de pont; **d. boy,** mousse *m* de pont; **d. cargo, load,** pontée *f*; *Navy:* **the lower d. (ratings),** le personnel non officier; **mess d.,** poste *m* de l'équipage, des hommes; **to come, go, on d.,** monter sur le pont; **clear lower d.!** en haut tout le monde! **to clear the decks for action,** (i) faire le branle-bas de combat; (ii) *Fig:* se préparer à agir; *N.Arch:* **d. plank,** bordé *m* de pont; **d. bolt,** boulon *m* de pont; cervelle *f*; **d. nail,** (clou *m* de) cervelle; (*b*) *Veh:* plate-forme *f*, *pl.* plates-formes; (*of bus*) **top d.,** impériale *f*; **single-d. bus,** autobus *m* sans impériale. **2.** *Av:* plan *m* (d'avion). **3.** *Civ.E:* tablier *m*; plancher *m* (d'un pont). **4.** *Const:* faux comble (de comble en mansarde). **5.** *Min:* plancher (d'une cage d'extraction). **6.** (*a*) *NAm:* **d. of cards,** jeu *m* de cartes; *F:* **to play with a stacked d.,** (i) jouer avec des cartes biseautées, maquillées; (ii) avoir l'avantage sur qn; (*b*) *Cmptr:* paquet *m* (de cartes); **source d.,** paquet de cartes en langage source; **assembled card d.,** paquet de cartes-programme en langage machine; **d. arrangement, set-up,** composition *f* du paquet de cartes; (*c*) *Rec:* tourne-disques *m inv*; platine *f*; **cassette d.,** lecteur *m* de cassettes, platine à cassette; **tape d.,** platine, dérouleur *m*, unité *f*, de bande magnétique. **7.** *U.S: Aut:* (*a*) coffre *m*; malle *f*; (*b*) couvercle *m* du coffre. **8.** *F:* sol *m*; **to hit the d.,** tomber à plat ventre. **9.** *P:* petite quantité de drogues, prise *f*, boulette *f*.

deck[2], *v.tr.* **1.** parer, orner, agrémenter (**sth. with sth.,** qch. de qch.); **balcony decked with flowers,** balcon fleuri; **to d. a house with flags,** pavoiser une maison; **to d. oneself out,** s'endimancher; se mettre sur son trente et un, dans ses plus beaux atours. **2.** (*a*) *N.Arch:* **to d. (over, in) a ship,** ponter un navire; (*b*) *Civ.E:* poser le tablier, le plancher (d'un pont). **3.** *Min:* encager (les wagons).

decker ['dekər], *s.* **1.** *U.S:* appartement *m*. **2.** (*with number, etc., prefixed, e.g.*) *Nau:* **a three-d.,** un navire à trois ponts; un trois-ponts; *Trans:* **single-d. (bus),** autobus *m* sans impériale; **double-d. (bus),** autobus à impériale; *Comest:* **double-d. sandwich,** sandwich *m* double.

deckhand ['dekhænd], *s.* homme *m*, matelot *m*, de pont.

deckhouse ['dekhaus], *s. Nau:* rouf *m*, teugue *f*.

decking ['dekiŋ], *s.* **1. decking (out),** décoration *f*; pavoisement *m* (des rues); endimanchement *m* (de qn). **2.** (*a*) pontage *m* (d'un navire); (*b*) *Civ.E:* pose *f* du tablier, du plancher (d'un pont). **3.** *coll.* (*a*) (les) ponts *m* (d'un navire); (*b*) *Civ.E:* = DECK[1] 3.

deckle ['dekl], *s. Paperm:* cadre volant, rebord *m* (de la forme); **d. edge,** barbes *fpl* (du papier); bords baveux; témoins *mpl.*

deckled ['dekld], *a. Paperm:* **1.** (bord) non ébarbé, déchiqueté. **2.** = DECKLE-EDGED.

deckle-edged ['dekl'edʒd], *a.* (papier *m* à (la) forme) à bords non ébarbés; (papier) à bords déchiquetés, à bords moyen âge.

declaim [di'kleim]. **1.** *v.i.* déclamer (**against,** contre). **2.** *v.tr.* déclamer (des vers, etc.).

declaimer [di'kleimər], *s.* déclamateur, -trice.

declamation [deklə'meiʃ(ə)n], *s.* déclamation *f.*

declamatory [di'klæmət(ə)ri], *a.* (style) déclamatoire.

declarant [di'kleərənt], *s. Jur:* déclarant, -ante.

declaration [deklə'reiʃ(ə)n], *s.* (*a*) déclaration *f*; **d. of war,** déclaration de guerre; **d. of the poll,** proclamation *f* du résultat du scrutin; *Hist:* **the D. of Rights,** la Déclaration des droits; **d. of intent,** déclaration d'intention; (*b*) **statutory d.,** attestation *f*; **d. of income,** déclaration de revenu; **customs d.,** déclaration de, en, douane; (*c*) *Cards:* annonce *f*; déclaration; (*d*) *St.Exch:* **d. of options,** réponse *f* des primes; (*e*) *A:* offre *f* de mariage.

declarative [di'klærətiv], *a.* (*a*) qui déclare; **d. statement,** phrase déclarative; (*b*) *Jur:* déclaratif; déclaratoire.

declaratory [di'klærət(ə)ri], *a. Jur:* déclaratif; déclaratoire; **d. act,** acte déclaratif; **d. judgement,** jugement déclaratoire.

declare [di'kleər]. **1.** *v.tr.* (*a*) déclarer (**sth. to s.o.,** qch. à qn); assurer (**sth. to s.o.,** qch. à qn, qn de qch.); **he declared he had seen nothing,** il déclara, affirma, n'avoir rien vu; *B:* **the heavens d. the glory of God,** les cieux *m* proclament la gloire de Dieu; **to d. war,** déclarer la guerre (**on, against,** à); **the text of the treaty declares that . . .,** le texte du traité porte que . . .; *Cust:* **have you anything to d.?** avez-vous quelque chose à déclarer? **to d. a strike,** proclamer la grève; *Bill:* **to d. a shot,** annoncer le coup qu'on va jouer; *St.Exch:* **to d. an option,** répondre, donner la réponse, à une prime; *Fin:* **to d. a dividend of ten per cent,** déclarer un dividende de dix pour cent; *O:F:* **well, I d.!** par exemple! (*b*) **to d. s.o., oneself (to be) guilty,** déclarer qn, se déclarer, coupable; **he was declared to have done the best,** il fut proclamé vainqueur; **to d. s.o. a deserter,** porter qn déserteur; *Jur:* **to d. s.o. a lunatic,** interdire qn en démence; **to d. the bargain off,** rompre le marché; **the whole thing has been declared off,** on ne donnera pas suite au projet; *F:* l'affaire est tombée dans l'eau; *Cr:* **to d. an innings closed,** *v.i.* **to d.,** fermer son jeu (avant la chute des dix guichets); s'annoncer satisfait du nombre des points marqués; *v.i. Turf:* **to d.,** déclarer forfait; (*c*) *Cards:* **to d. trumps, a suit,** appeler l'atout, une couleur; *v.i.* **to d.,** annoncer son jeu; *Fig:* **to d. one's hand,** avouer ses intentions; (*d*) **to d. oneself,** (i) prendre parti; (ii) (*of lover*) faire sa déclaration; **he declared himself for war,** il se déclara pour la guerre, en faveur de la guerre; (*of disease*) **to d. itself,** se déclarer, éclater. **2.** *v.i.* (*a*) **to d. for, against, sth.,** se déclarer, se prononcer, pour, contre, qch.; **to d. in favour of sth.,** conclure à qch.; (*b*) **to d. off,** se retirer, y renoncer; retirer son enjeu.

declared [di'kleəd], *a.* ouvert, avoué, déclaré; **d. enemy,** ennemi juré, déclaré; **he is a d. Socialist,** il est socialiste de son plein aveu; **d. value,** valeur déclarée.

declaredly [di'kleəridli], *adv.* ouvertement; (i) formellement, (ii) franchement, de son propre aveu.

declarer [di'kleərər], *s.* **1.** déclarateur, -trice. **2.** *Cards:* déclarant, -ante; demandeur, -euse.

declassification [di:klæsifi'keiʃ(ə)n], *s.* déclassement *m* (d'un document secret, etc.).

declassify [di:'klæsifai], *v.tr.* déclasser (un document secret, etc.).

declension [di'klenʃ(ə)n], *s.* **1.** *Lit:* décadence *f*, déclin *m*, dépérissement *m* (d'un empire); altération *f* (du caractère, etc.). **2.** *Gram:* déclinaison *f*; **first d. noun,** nom *m* de la première déclinaison.

declinable [di'klainəbl], *a. Gram:* déclinable.

declinate ['deklineit], *a. Bot:* décliné.

declination [dekli'neiʃ(ə)n], *s.* **1.** (*a*) *A:* déclin *m*, pente *f*; (*b*) *Astr:* déclinaison *f*; **d. circle,** cercle *m* de déclinaison; *Magn:* **magnetic d.,** déclinaison magnétique; **d. compass,** déclinomètre *m*; *Mapm:* **grid d.,** déclinaison de quadrillage. **2.** *NAm:* refus courtois, formel.

declinatory [di'klainətəri], *a. Jur: A:* **d. plea,** déclinatoire *m.*

decline[1] [di'klain], *s.* **1.** déclin *m* (du jour, de la vie, d'un empire); **d. in prices,** baisse *f* de prix; **d. of business,** ralentissement *m* des affaires; **to be on the d.,** être sur le déclin; décliner; (*of pers.*) être sur le retour (d'âge); (*of fame*) être à son couchant; (*of prices*) être en baisse, baisser; **these shares have experienced a d.,** ces actions *f* ont éprouvé une baisse; **the D. and Fall of the Roman Empire,** la Décadence et la chute de l'Empire romain. **2.** *Med: A:* maladie *f* de langueur; marasme *m*; consomption *f*, étisie *f*; **to be in a d.,** être atteint d'une maladie de langueur; *esp.* être atteint, attaqué, de la poitrine; **to go into a d.,** entrer en consomption.

decline[2], *v.tr. & i.*

I. *v.tr.* **1.** *A:* pencher (la tête, etc.). **2.** (*a*) refuser courtoisement (une invitation, une offre); décliner (un honneur); *v.i.* s'excuser; se faire excuser; **I declined with thanks,** j'ai refusé en le remerciant; (*b*) refuser; repousser (l'intervention de qn); *Mil:* **to d. battle,** refuser le combat; *Chess:* **to d. a gambit,** refuser un gambit; **to d. to do sth., to d. doing sth.,** (i) s'excuser; (ii) refuser de faire qch.; **I d. to be intimidated,** on ne m'intimide pas. **3.** *Gram:* décliner (un nom, etc.).

II. *v.i.* **1.** (*a*) (*of ground, etc.*) s'incliner, pencher; être en pente; (*b*) *A:* s'écarter (**from,** de); dévier (**from,** de); *Lit:* **to d. from virtue,** se détourner de la vertu. **2.** (*a*) (*of day, sun, etc.*) décliner; (*of day*) tirer à sa fin; baisser, tomber; (*b*) (*of health, influence, etc.*) décliner, baisser; (*of empire*) tomber en décadence; (*of tree, plant*) dépérir; *Com:* (*of prices*) fléchir, baisser; être en baisse; **business is declining,** les affaires *f* sont en baisse.

declining[1] [di'klainiŋ], *a.* (*a*) sur son déclin; **d. sun,** soleil couchant, baissant; *Lit:* **the d. day,** le jour à son déclin; **in one's d. years,** au déclin de la vie; (*b*) *Pol.Ec:* **d. industries,** industries déclinantes; **d. market,** marché *m* en baisse; **d. marginal value,** valeur marginale décroissante.

declining[2], *s.* **1.** refus *m* (d'une invitation, etc.). **2.** dépérissement *m*. **3.** *Gram:* déclinaison *f*.

declinometer [dekli'nɔmitər], *s. Magn:* déclinomètre *m.*

declivitous [di'klivitəs], *a. Lit:* déclive; en pente abrupte; escarpé.

declivity [di'kliviti], *s.* déclivité *f*, pente *f*; **a steep d.,** une descente rapide.

decloche [di:'klɔʃ], *v.tr. Hort:* déclocher (des melons, etc.).

declutch [di:'klʌtʃ], *v.i. Aut:* débrayer.

declutching [di:'klʌtʃiŋ], *s. Aut:* débrayage *m.*

decoct [di'kɔkt], *v.tr.* (faire) bouillir (des herbes, etc., pour en extraire les parties solubles).

decoction [di'kɔkʃ(ə)n], *s.* **1.** (*process*) décoction *f*. **2.** (*resultant liquid*) décoction; *Pharm:* décocté *m*.

decode [di:'koud], *v.tr.* déchiffrer, décoder, traduire, transcrire en clair (une dépêche).

decoded [di:'koudid], *a.* en clair.

decoder [di:'koudər], *s.* décodeur *m*; déchiffreur *m*; décrypteur *m.*

decoding [di:'koudiŋ], *s.* déchiffrement *m*; décodage *m*; transcription *f* en clair; *Cmptr:* **d. circuit,** circuit décodeur, de décodage.

decohere [di:kou'hiər], *v.tr. W.Tel: A:* décohérer.

decoherence [di:kou'hiərəns], *s. A:* décohésion *f* (magnétique).

decoherer [di:kou'hiərər], *s. W.Tel: A:* décohéreur *m.*

decoke[1] [di:'kouk], *v.tr. Aut: F:* décalaminer (le moteur).

decoke[2], **decoking** [di:'koukiŋ], *s. Aut: F:* décalaminage *m.*

decollate [di'kɔleit], *v.tr.* **1.** décoller, décapiter (qn). **2.** *Cmptr:* déliasser; **decollating machine,** déliasseuse *f*.

decollation [di:kɔ'leiʃ(ə)n], *s.* (*a*) décollation *f* (de saint Jean-Baptiste); (*b*) *Obst:* décollation (du fœtus); (*c*) *Cmptr:* déliassage *m.*

decollator [di:kɔ'leitər], *s. Cmptr:* déliasseuse *f*.

décollement [dei'kɔlmənt], *s. Surg: Geol:* décollement *m.*

décolletage [dei'kɔltɑ:ʒ], *s.* décolleté *m*; **square d.,** décolleté carré; **V d.,** décolleté en pointe.

décolleté [dei'kɔltei]. **1.** *a.* (vêtement) décolleté; (personne) décolletée. **2.** *s.* décolletage *m.*

decolonization [di:kɔlənai'zeiʃ(ə)n], *s.* décolonisation *f*.

decolonize [di:'kɔlənaiz], *v.tr.* décoloniser.

decolorant [di:'kʌlər(ə)nt], **1.** *a. & s.* décolorant (*m*).

decolorization [di:kʌlərai'zeiʃ(ə)n], *s.* décoloration *f*.

decolorize [di:'kʌləraiz], *v.tr.* décolorer.

decolorizer [di:'kʌləraizər], *s.* décolorant *m.*

decommission [di:kə'miʃ(ə)n], *v.tr.* désarmer (un navire).

decompensated [di:'kɔmpenseitid], *a. Med:* décompensé.

decompensation [di:kɔmpen'seiʃ(ə)n], *s.* décompensation *f*; *Med:* **cardiac d.,** décompensation cardiaque.

decomposable [di:kəm'pouzəbl], *a.* (*a*) décomposable (**into,** en); (*b*) *Ch:* (*of double salts*) dédoublable.

decompose [di:kəm'pouz]. **1.** *v.tr.* (*a*) décomposer, analyser (un composé, une force, la lumière, une pensée, etc.); *Ch:* dédoubler (un sel double); (*b*) décomposer, corrompre (la matière). **2.** *v.i.* (*a*) se décomposer; (*b*) entrer en décomposition; pourrir.

decomposing [di:kəm'pouziŋ], *a.* **1.** (*of force, agent*) décomposant. **2.** (matières *fpl*) en décomposition, en putréfaction.

decomposite [di:'kɔmpəzit]. **1.** *a.* (*a*) surcomposé; (*b*) *Bot:* décomposé. **2.** *s. Ling:* mot surcomposé, doublement composé.

decomposition ['di:kɔmpə'ziʃ(ə)n], *s.* décomposition *f.* **1.** résolution *f* en parties simples; *Ch:* **double d.,** dédoublement *m.* **2.** altération *f,* désintégration *f;* putréfaction *f;* **the d. of society,** la désintégration de la société.

decompound [di:'kɔmpaund], *a.* = DECOMPOSITE 1.

decompress [di:kəm'pres], *v.tr.* (*a*) décomprimer (un gaz, etc.); *Civ.E:* **to d. a workman,** faire séjourner un ouvrier dans le sas de décompression; (*b*) *Surg:* décompresser (le cerveau, etc.).

decompression [di:kəm'preʃ(ə)n], *s.* (*a*) *Mch: etc:* décompression *f*; *Civ.E:* séjournement *m* (d'un ouvrier) dans le sas de décompression; **d. chamber,** chambre *f* de décompression; *Med:* **d. sickness,** mal, maladie, des caissons; (*b*) *Surg:* soulagement *m* de l'hypertension cérébrale.

decompressor [di:kəm'presər], *s. I.C.E:* décompresseur *m.*

decondition [di:kən'diʃ(ə)n], *v.tr.* déconditionner.

decongest [di:kən'dʒest], *v.tr.* décongestionner.

decongestant [di:kən'dʒest(ə)nt], *a.* & *s. Med:* décongestionnant (*m*).

decongestion [di:kən'dʒestjən], *s. Med:* décongestion *f.*

decongestive [di:kən'dʒestiv], *a. Med:* décongestionnant.

deconsecrate [di:'kɔnsikreit], *v.tr.* prononcer l'exécration (d'une église); séculariser, désaffecter (une église).

deconsecration [di:kɔnsi'kreiʃ(ə)n], *s.* exécration *f* (d'une église, etc.); sécularisation *f,* désaffectation *f.*

decontaminate [di:kən'tæmineit], *v.tr.* **1.** désinfecter. **2.** décontaminer.

decontamination [di:kəntæmi'neiʃ(ə)n], *s.* **1.** désinfection *f.* **2.** décontamination *f.*

decontrol [di:kən'troul], *v.tr.* (*a*) libérer (le commerce, etc.) des contraintes du gouvernement; **to d. the price of meat,** détaxer la viande; (*b*) *Adm:* **decontrolled road,** route sur laquelle on a supprimé la limite de vitesse.

décor ['deikɔ:r], *s. Th:* décor *m.*

decorate ['dekəreit], *v.tr.* **1.** (*a*) décorer, orner, agrémenter (**sth. with sth.,** qch. de qch.); pavoiser (une rue, un édifice); (*b*) peindre et tapisser, décorer (un appartement). **2.** médailler, décorer (un soldat, etc.); remettre une décoration à (qn).

decorated ['dekəreitid], *a.* (*a*) décoré; (*b*) *Arch:* **d. period,** époque *f* du gothique rayonnant.

decoration [dekə'reiʃ(ə)n], *s.* **1.** (*a*) décoration *f*; parement *m* (d'une façade, etc.), pavoisement *m* (des rues, etc.); peinture *f* et collage *m* de la tapisserie, décoration (d'une pièce); **interior d.,** décoration intérieure, d'intérieur; *U.S:* **D. day,** le 30 mai (jour où l'on fleurit les tombes de ceux qui tombèrent sur les champs de bataille de la Guerre civile); (*b*) remise *f* d'une décoration (à qn). **2.** (*a*) *usu. pl.* (les) décorations (d'une ville en fête, etc.); décor *m* (d'un appartement, etc.); (*b*) décoration, médaille *f*; **holders of war decorations,** décorés de guerre; (*c*) *Pyr:* garniture *f* (de fusée volante).

decorative ['dek(ə)rətiv], *a.* décoratif; **d. arts,** arts décoratifs; **d. drawing,** dessin *m* d'ornement; **d. artist,** artiste décorateur; ensemblier *m.*

decoratively ['dek(ə)rətivli], *adv.* décorativement.

decorator ['dekəreitər], *s.* décorateur *m*; (**painter and**) **d.,** peintre décorateur (d'appartements); tapissier *m*; **interior d.,** décorateur-ensemblier *m, pl.* décorateurs-ensembliers.

decorous ['dekərəs], *a.* bienséant, convenable; comme il faut; approprié aux circonstances; **d. behaviour,** conduite *f* modeste, convenable.

decorously ['dekərəsli], *adv.* avec bienséance; convenablement; comme il faut; avec dignité; **to do sth. d.,** faire qch. dans les formes.

decorticate [di:'kɔ:tikeit], *v.tr.* décortiquer (le riz, etc.).

decortication [dikɔ:ti'keiʃ(ə)n], *s.* **1.** *Surg:* décortication *f* (d'un poumon, etc.). **2.** décortication, décortiquage *m* (du riz, etc.).

decorticator [di:'kɔ:tikeitər], *s.* (*pers. or machine*) décortiqueur *m,* décortiqueuse *f.*

decorum [di'kɔ:rəm], *s.* décorum *m,* bienséance *f,* retenue *f* honnête; **a breach of d.,** une inconvenance; **to have a sense of d.,** avoir de la tenue, de la dignité dans le maintien; **with d.,** avec dignité; **with due d.,** dans les formes.

decouple [di:'kʌpl], *v.tr. El: etc:* découpler.

decoupling [di:'kʌpliŋ], *s. El: etc:* découplage *m*; **d. condenser,** condensateur *m* de découplage.

decoy[1] [di'kɔi], *s.* **1.** (*a*) appât *m,* piège *m,* leurre *m,* amorce *f*; **d.** (**bird**), (oiseau *m* de) leurre; appeau *m,* moquette *f*; (oiseau) appelant *m*; *F:* chanterelle *f*; *Ap:* **d. comb,** amorce; *Navy:* **d. ship,** bateau-piège *m, pl.* bateaux-pièges; (*b*) **d.** (**pond**), canardière *f.* **2.** (*a*) compère *m* (d'un escroc); (*b*) amorceur, -euse (d'une maison de débauche, etc.).

decoy[2], *v.tr.* **1.** piper, leurrer (des oiseaux). **2.** leurrer, amorcer (qn); **to d. s.o. into a trap,** entraîner, attirer, qn dans un piège; **he had been decoyed across the frontier,** on lui avait fait passer la frontière à son insu; on l'avait attiré de l'autre côté de la frontière; *Jur:* **to d. a girl under age,** attirer, dévoyer, séduire, une mineure.

decrease[1] ['di:kri:s], *s.* diminution *f,* décroissement *m,* décroissance *f,* amoindrissement *m*; **d. in price,** baisse *f* de prix; **d. in value,** diminution de valeur; moins-value *f*; **d. in speed,** ralentissement *m*; **the d. in wheat,** la raréfaction du blé; *El:* **d. in current,** baisse de courant; **d. of load,** diminution de charge; **our imports are on the d.,** nos importations *f* sont en décroissance, en baisse; **proportionate d.,** diminution proportionnelle.

decrease[2] [di'kri:s]. **1.** *v.tr.* (*a*) diminuer, faire décroître; (*b*) *Knit:* **d. three stitches,** diminuer de trois mailles. **2.** *v.i.* (*a*) diminuer; décroître; s'amoindrir; aller en diminuant, en décroissant; **our imports are decreasing,** nos importations *f* sont en décroissance; (*b*) *Knit:* diminuer, faire des diminutions.

decreasing [di'kri:siŋ], *a.* décroissant, diminuant; **d. order,** ordre décroissant; *Pol.Ec:* **d. marginal cost,** coût marginal décroissant; *Mth:* **d. series,** progression descendante.

decreasingly [di'kri:siŋli], *adv.* de moins en moins.

decree[1] [di'kri:], *s.* **1.** *Adm:* decret *m,* édit *m,* arrêté *m*; ordonnance (royale); **to pass a d.,** prendre un arrêté; **to issue a d.,** promulguer un décret, un édit. **2.** *Theol: Ecc:* décret; **the decrees of God, of Providence,** les décrets de Dieu, de la Providence; **the Decrees of the Popes, of the Councils,** les décrets des Papes, des Conciles; les décrétales *f* des Papes. **3.** *Jur:* décision *f,* arrêté, arrêt *m,* jugement *m*; ordonnance (de divorce, etc.); **d. nisi** ['naisai], jugement provisoire (en matière de divorce); **d. in bankruptcy,** jugement déclaratif de faillite.

decree[2], *v.tr.* **1.** décréter, ordonner; *Jur:* arrêter; **it had been decreed that . . .,** il avait été décrété que . . .. **2.** décerner, accorder par décret (des honneurs, un prix) (**to,** à).

decrement[1] ['dekrimənt], *s.* **1.** décroissement *m,* décroissance *f*; *Her:* **moon in d.,** croissant contourné. **2.** (*a*) perte *f,* diminution *f*; **sound d.,** atténuation *f* des sons; amortissement *m* acoustique; (*b*) *Mth: etc:* décrément *m*; **logarithmic d.,** décrément logarithmique; *Cmptr:* **d. field,** zone *f* de modification d'adresse.

decrement[2], *v.i.* & *tr. Cmptr:* décrémenter, diminuer, faire régresser; **to d. by one,** diminuer d'une unité; **to d. to,** ramener à.

decrementation [dekrimen'teiʃ(ə)n], *s. Cmptr:* diminution *f,* régression *f.*

decremeter [di'krimitər], *s. Elcs:* décremètre *m.*

decrepit [di'krepit], *a.* **1.** (*of pers.*) décrépit; caduc, -uque; **d. old age,** la vieillesse décrépite. **2.** (*of thg*) vermoulu; qui tombe en ruine; délabré.

decrepitate [di'krepiteit]. **1.** *v.tr.* calciner (un sel, etc.). **2.** *v.i.* (*of salt, etc.*) décrépiter; pétiller (au feu).

decrepitation [dikrepi'teiʃ(ə)n], *s.* **1.** calcination *f* (d'un sel, etc.). **2.** décrépitation *f.*

decrepitude [di'krepitjud], *s.* **1.** décrépitude *f*; caducité *f* (d'une personne). **2.** vermoulure *f*; état délabré (d'un mobilier, etc.).

decrescendo [di:kri'ʃendou], *adv.* & *s. Mus:* decrescendo (*m*).

decrescent [di'kres(ə)nt], *a.* décroissant; en décroissance; décrescent; *Her:* **d. moon,** croissant contourné.

decretal [di'kri:tl], *s. R.C.Ch:* décrétale *f*; **the Gregorian Decretals,** les Décrétales de Grégoire.

decret(al)ist [di'kri:t(əl)ist], *s.* décrétaliste *m,* canoniste *m.*

decry [di'krai], *v.tr.* (*a*) décrier, déprécier, dénigrer (qn, qch.); (*b*) conspuer (qn).

decrying [di'kraiiŋ], *s.* dénigrement *m,* dépréciation *f.*

decrypt(ograph) [di:'kript(ougræf)], *v.tr.* déchiffrer (un cryptogramme); décrypter (un message).

decubitus [di:'kju:bitəs], *s.* **1.** décubitus (ventral, latéral, etc.); **dorsal d.,** décubitus dorsal. **2.** (*bedsore*) **d.** (**ulcer**), escarre *f,* eschare *f,* décubitus.

decumbent [di'kʌmbənt], *a. Bot:* décombant; **d. stem,** tige décombante.

decumulation [dikjumju'leiʃ(ə)n], *s. Pol.Ec:* décumulation *f*; **capital d.,** diminution *f* du capital.

decuple[1] ['dekjupl], *a.* & *s.* décuple (*m*).

decuple[2]. **1.** *v.tr.* décupler. **2.** *v.i.* se décupler.

decurion [di'kjuəriən], *s. Rom.Ant:* décurion *m.*

decurrence, decurrency [di:'kʌrəns, -si], *s. Bot:* décurrence *f.*

decurrent [di'kʌrənt], *a. Bot:* décurrent.

decursive [di:'kə:siv], *a. Bot:* décursif; décurrent.

decury ['dekjuri], *s. Rom.Ant:* décurie *f.*

decussate[1] [di'kʌseit], *a.* croisé en X; *Bot:* décussé.

decussate[2]. **1.** *v.tr.* disposer en croix de Saint-André, en X, en sautoir. **2.** *v.i.* (*of nerves, etc.*) se croiser (en forme d'X).

decussation [di:kʌ'seiʃ(ə)n], *s.* décussation *f.*

decyl ['desil], *s. Ch:* décyle *m*; **d. alcohol,** alcool *m* décylique.

decylene ['desili:n], *s. Ch:* décylène *m.*

dedendum, *pl.* **-da** [di'dendəm, -də], *s. Mec.E:* creux *m* de l'engrenage au-dessous de la circonférence primitive; **d. line, circle,** ligne *f* de racine; cercle intérieur, cercle de pied, cercle de racine (d'une roue dentée).

dedicate ['dedikeit], *v.tr.* **1.** (*a*) dédier, consacrer (une église); **to d. a temple to a god,** vouer un temple à un dieu; **church dedicated to Saint Peter,** église sous le vocable de saint Pierre; **to d. oneself, one's life, to s.o., to sth.,** se vouer à qn, à qch.; se consacrer à qch.; **we are dedicated to the revision of the Standard Dictionary,** nous nous consacrons à la révision du *Standard Dictionary*; **to d. a day to pleasure,** dédier un jour au plaisir; (*b*) *esp. N.Am:* inaugurer (un édifice, etc.). **2.** dédicacer, dédier (un livre, etc.) (**to,** à). **3.** *Jur:* **to d. a highway,** rendre publique une voie privée (par des actes dont il ressort une intention manifeste).

dedicated ['dedikeitid], *a.* **1.** (*of pers.*) dédié à sa profession, etc.; **d. doctor,** médecin *m* par vocation; **d. dancer,** danseur passionné par son métier; **d. life,** vie *f* de dédication. **2.** *Cmptr:* spécialisé; **d.** (**application**) **computer,** ordinateur spécialisé; **d. core locations,** positions réservées en mémoire; **d. uses,** applications spéciales.

dedicatee [dedikə'ti:], *s.* dédicataire *mf.*

dedication [dedi'keiʃ(ə)n], *s.* **1.** dédicace *f,* consécration *f* (d'une église). **2.** dédicace (d'un livre); **to write a d. in a book,** dédicacer un livre. **3.** attachement *m* (à un maître, à un idéal). **4.** *Cmptr:* (*a*) inauguration *f*; (*b*) spécialisation *f.*

dedicative ['dedikeitiv], *a.* dédicatoire.

dedicator ['dedikeitər], *a.* dédicateur, -trice.

dedicatory [dedi'keitəri], *a.* (épître *f,* etc.) dédicatoire.

dedifferentiation ['di:difərensi'eiʃ(ə)n], *s. Biol:* dédifférenciation *f.*

deduce [di'dju:s], *v.tr.* **1.** *Lit:* retracer, suivre (l'histoire d'un peuple, etc.) en partant des origines; **to d. one's descent, one's family, from the Conquest to the present day,** établir sa descendance à partir de la Conquête jusqu'à nos jours; **to d. one's descent from Norman stock,** faire remonter sa descendance à une souche normande. **2.** déduire, inférer, conclure (**from,** de); **the knowledge of causes is deduced from their effects,** la connaissance des causes se déduit de leurs effets; **to d. sth. from a fact,** arguer qch. d'un fait; **other evidence may be deduced from his work,** de son travail on peut tirer encore d'autres preuves.

deducible [di'dju:səbl], *a.* que l'on peut déduire, conclure, inférer (**from,** de).

deduct [di'dʌkt], *v.tr.* déduire, défalquer, retrancher (**from,** de); **to d. sth. from the price,** déduire qch. du prix; rabattre qch. sur le prix; **to d. a sum** (**of money**), compter une somme en moins; **you may d. that,** vous compterez cela en moins; **to d. the discount** (**before payment**), retenir l'escompte; **to d. 5% from the wages,** faire une retenue de 5% sur les salaires; **after deducting . . .,** après déduction de . . .; déduction faite de . . .; **to be deducted,** à déduire; **brokerage is deducted from sales,** le courtage vient en déduction des ventes; **this number must be deducted from the total,** il faut déduire ce nombre du total.

deductible [di'dʌktəbl], *a.* déductible.

deduction [di'dʌkʃ(ə)n], *s.* **1.** déduction *f,* défalcation *f,* imputation *f* (**from a quantity,** sur une quantité); (*of pay*) retenue *f*; **after d. of taxes,** après déduction des impôts; **d. from wages,** prélèvement *m* sur le salaire; **d. at source,** stoppage *m* à la source; *Cmptr:* **d. card,**

carte *f* (de) retenue. **2.** (*a*) raisonnement déductif; déduction; (*b*) déduction, conclusion *f* (**from,** tirée de); **fallacious d.,** déduction erronée.

deductive [di'dʌktiv], *a.* (raisonnement) déductif, par déduction; (mécanisme) déductif; (méthode) déductive; **d. economics,** économie déductive.

deductively [di'dʌktivli], *adv.* déductivement, par déduction.

dee [di:], *s.* (*a*) la lettre d; (*b*) **d. (ring),** dé *m,* enchapure *f* (d'une courroie, d'un ceinturon).

deed[1] [di:d], *s.* **1.** (*a*) action *f,* acte *m*; **good d.,** bonne action; *Scout:* **to do one's good d. for the day,** faire sa bonne action, sa B.A., quotidienne; **man of deeds,** homme *m* d'action, d'exécution; **bold in word and d.,** audacieux en paroles et en actions; **this requires deeds, not words,** il faut des actes, non (pas) des paroles, de vaines promesses; (*b*) *Lit:* **d. of valour,** haut fait; exploit *m*; **deeds of daring,** bravoures *fpl*; (*c*) **foul d.,** forfait *m*; **it is he who has done this d.,** c'est lui qui a commis cette action, ce forfait; c'est lui qui a fait le coup; (*d*) fait; *Lit:* **in very d. . . .,** dans le fait . . ., par le fait . . ., de fait . . ., en réalité . . ., en vérité . . .; **he was ruler in d., though not in name,** c'était lui, dans le fait, qui était le chef, bien qu'il n'en portât pas le titre. **2.** *Jur:* acte notarié, sur papier timbré, et signé par les parties; **d. privately executed by the parties, private d.,** acte sous seing privé; **d. executed by a solicitor, etc.,** acte authentique; **d. of arrangement,** contrat *m* d'arrangement; **d. of transfer,** feuille *f* de transfert; **d. of assignment,** acte attributif; acte de transfert; **mortgage d.,** acte hypothécaire; **d. poll,** acte unilatéral; contrat *m* à titre gratuit; **to change one's name by d. poll,** changer légalement son nom; **to draw up a d.,** rédiger un acte; **d. box,** coffre *m* à documents.

deed[2], *v.tr. NAm:* transférer (qch.) par un acte.

deejay ['di:'dʒei], *s. W.Tel: T.V: F:* présentateur *m* de disques.

deem [di:m], *v.tr. A: & Lit:* juger, estimer, croire; **I do not d. it necessary to . . .,** je ne juge pas, ne crois pas, nécessaire de . . .; **I deemed it proper to depart,** je jugeai convenable , à propos, de partir; **I deemed that he was an American,** je jugeai qu'il était Américain; **I d. it an honour to serve you,** je regarde comme un honneur de vous servir; **he was deemed (to be) unfortunate,** (i) il fut considéré, regardé, comme malheureux; (ii) il passait pour (être) malheureux; il était censé être malheureux; il était réputé malheureux; **to d. highly of s.o.,** avoir une haute opinion de qn; **to d. s.o. clever,** tenir qn pour habile; **answer deemed final,** réponse considérée comme définitive.

de-emphasis [di:'emfəsis], *s. esp. U.S:* **1.** abaissement *m,* atténuation *f,* de l'importance (de qch.). **2.** *W.Tel: etc:* suppression *f* (des tons aigres, discordants).

de-emphasize [di:'emfəsaiz], *v.tr. esp. U.S:* **1.** abaisser, atténuer, l'importance de (qch.). **2.** *W.Tel: etc:* supprimer (des tons aigres, discordants).

deemster ['di:mstər], *s.* juge *m* (dans l'île de Man).

deemstership ['di:mstəʃip], *s.* office *m* de deemster.

de-energization [di:enədʒai'zeiʃ(ə)n], *s. Cmptr:* désexcitation *f* (d'un relais).

de-energize [di'enədʒaiz], *v.tr. Cmptr:* désexciter (un relais).

deep [di:p], *a., adv. & s.*

I. *a.* **1.** (*a*) profond; **d. well,** puits profond; **to be ten metres d.,** avoir dix mètres de profondeur, avoir une profondeur de dix mètres; être profond de dix mètres; **in water 3 metres d.,** par trois mètres de fond; **the road was one metre d. in snow,** la route était enfouie sous un mètre de neige; **d. end,** bout le plus profond (de la piscine); *F:* **to go off the d. end,** (i) se mettre en colère, prendre la mouche; monter, s'emporter, comme une soupe au lait; (ii) prendre les choses au tragique; s'affoler; **d. valley,** vallée profonde, encaissée, enfoncée; **a shady valley lies d. between the hills,** un vallon ombrageux se creuse entre les collines; *Min:* **d. boring,** sondage *m* à grande profondeur; **d. in debt, in study, in meditation, in thought,** criblé de dettes; absorbé, plongé, enfoncé, dans l'étude; plongé dans la méditation; abîmé dans ses pensées; **he was d. in his book, in his paper,** il était absorbé dans la lecture de son livre; il était plongé dans son journal; (*b*) **d. cave,** caverne profonde; **d. wound,** blessure profonde; (*of weapon*) **to inflict a d. wound,** pénétrer très avant; **d. wrinkles,** rides très accusées; **his eyes are very d. in his head,** ses yeux sont très enfoncés; **d. insight into human nature,** connaissance profonde de la nature humaine; (*c*) **d. shelves,** rayons *m* larges; *Mil:* **two, four, d.,** sur deux, quatre, rangs; **form two d.!** par deux, marche! **the crowd on the pavement was twelve d.,** sur le trottoir la foule formait une haie d'une douzaine de rangs; (*d*) **d. sigh,** profond soupir, long soupir; **d. bow,** profonde révérence; **d thinker,** penseur profond; **his d. learning,** ses connaissances profondes. **2.** (*a*) (*of colour*) foncé, sombre; **d. blue,** bleu foncé, bleu intense; (*b*) (*of sound*) profond, grave; **the d. notes of the bassoon,** les notes *f* graves du basson; **in a d. voice,** d'une voix profonde; d'une voix de basse-taille. **3.** (*a*) **the d. veins of the body,** les veines profondes du corps; (*b*) (*of emotion, etc.*) **d. sorrow, despair,** chagrin profond, profond désespoir; **d. concern,** vive préoccupation; **to listen with d. interest,** écouter avec un intérêt profond, avec un vif intérêt; **the deeper causes of the social unrest,** les causes profondes du malaise social; (*c*) (*of conduct*) difficile à pénétrer; (*of pers.*) rusé, malin, ténébreux, astucieux, sournois; **he's a d. one,** c'est un malin!

II. *adv.* **1.** profondément; **secret hidden d. in his heart,** secret caché au plus profond de son cœur; **hands stuck d. in one's pockets,** les mains enfoncées dans les poches; **the difference goes d.,** il y a une profonde différence; **d.-lying causes,** causes profondes; *Prov:* **still waters run d.,** il n'y a pire eau que l'eau qui dort. **2. the harpoon sank d. into the flesh,** le harpon pénétra très avant dans les chairs; **to work d. into the night,** travailler très avant dans la nuit. **3.** *A:* **to play d.,** jouer gros jeu; *O:* **to drink d.,** boire copieusement, largement, à longs traits, à plein verre, à tire-larigot; *Lit:* **he had drunk d. of the pleasures of life,** il s'était abreuvé des plaisirs de cette vie.

III. *s.* **1. the d.,** (*a*) les profondeurs *f,* l'abîme *m,* le gouffre; *Oc:* **ocean d.,** fosse *f*; **the ocean deeps,** les grands fonds; *Oc:* la région abyssale; **the unfathomed d.,** les abîmes insondables de l'océan; *B:* **d. calleth to d.,** un abîme appelle un autre abîme; (*b*) l'océan *m*; **to commit a body to the d.,** immerger un mort; **committal to the d.,** immersion *f.* **2. in the d. of winter,** au plus profond, au plus fort, de l'hiver; **in the d. of night,** au milieu de la nuit; en pleine nuit. **3.** *Nau:* brassiage *m* intermédiaire entre deux marques de la ligne de sonde.

deep-chested ['di:p'tʃestid], *a.* (homme) à forte poitrine.

deep-drawn ['di:p'drɔ:n], *a.* (soupir) profond.

deepen ['di:p(ə)n]. **1.** *v.tr.* (*a*) approfondir, creuser (un chenal, un puits, etc.); (*b*) augmenter (les sentiments); rendre (un sentiment) plus intense; **this only deepened his love, his resentment,** cela n'a fait qu'augmenter son amour, son ressentiment; (*c*) foncer (une couleur); rendre (un son) plus grave, plus sonore; (*d*) rendre (les ténèbres) plus épaisses. **2.** *v.i.* (*a*) devenir plus profond, s'approfondir; **the river deepens below London,** le fleuve prend de la profondeur en aval de Londres; (*b*) (*of colour*) devenir plus foncé; (*of sound*) devenir plus grave; (*c*) **the shadows deepen,** les ombres *f* s'épaississent; la nuit devient plus profonde; **the silence deepened,** le silence est devenu plus profond; **the evening had deepened into starlight,** la nuit s'était faite, et les étoiles brillaient.

deepening[1] ['di:p(ə)niŋ], *a.* **1.** qui s'approfondit. **2.** (couleur) qui se fonce; (son) qui devient plus grave; (ténèbres) qui s'épaississent; (nuit) qui se fait.

deepening[2], *s.* **1.** approfondissement *m.* **2.** augmentation *f* de profondeur, d'intensité. **3. d. of a depression,** creusement *m* d'une dépression.

deep-freeze ['di:p'fri:z], *v.tr.* surgeler, congeler.

deep freeze(r) ['di:p'fri:z(ər)], *s.* congélateur *m.*

deep freezing ['di:p'fri:ziŋ], *s.* congélation *f.*

deep-fry ['di:p'frai], *v.tr. & i.* (faire) cuire (du poisson, etc.) dans la friture.

deep-laid ['di:p'leid], *a.* (complot) ténébreux, habilement ourdi, *F:* habilement combiné.

deep-level ['di:p'levl], *a.* (mine *f*) à grande profondeur.

deeply ['di:pli], *adv.* profondément; **to go d. into sth.,** pénétrer, entrer, creuser, fort avant dans qch.; approfondir qch.; **to be d. indebted to s.o.,** être extrêmement redevable à qn; **to fall d. in love with s.o.,** tomber profondément amoureux de qn; **d. interesting,** profondément, fort, intéressant; **d. offended,** grièvement, vivement, offensé; **to be d. read in a subject,** avoir une profonde connaissance d'un sujet.

deep-mouthed ['di:p'mauðd], *a. Ven:* (*of hound*) à l'aboi profond.

deepness ['di:pnis], *s.* **1.** profondeur *f* (de la voix, etc.); *Mus:* gravité *f* (d'un son). **2.** astuce *f* (d'une personne).

deep-rooted ['di:p'ru:tid], *a.* profondément enraciné; (arbre) à enracinement profond; (affection) aux racines profondes; (préjugé) vivace; **idea d.-r. in the mind,** idée ancrée dans la tête; **the change is even deeper-rooted than that,** le changement tient à des causes encore plus profondes.

deep-sea ['di:p'si:], *attrib:* **d.-s. fishery, fishing,** (i) pêche hauturière; (ii) grande pêche (de Terre-Neuve, etc.); **d.-s. animal, plant,** animal *m,* plante *f,* pélagique; **d.-s. current,** courant sous-marin; **d.-s. lead,** grande sonde.

deep-seated ['di:p'si:tid], *a.* profond, enraciné, fermement établi; **d.-s. conviction,** conviction *f* intime; *Geol:* **d.-s. rocks,** roches *f* d'intrusion; roches sous-jacentes; *Med:* **d.-s. abscess,** abcès profond; **d.-s. cough,** toux bronchiale; **d.-s. cold,** rhume *m* de poitrine.

deep-set ['di:p'set], *a.* (yeux) enfoncés, creux, caves; (fenêtre) profonde.

deep-toned ['di:p'tound], *a.* sonore; au ton grave.

deepwater ['di:pwɔ:tər], *a.* (*a*) (navire) hauturier; (*b*) (port *m*) en eau profonde, de toute marée.

deer ['diər], *s. inv.* **(red) d.,** cerf commun; **fallow d.,** daim *m*; **roe d.,** chevreuil *m*; **axis d.,** (cerf) axis (*m*); **barking d.,** muntjac *m,* muntjak *m*; **hog d.,** cerf-cochon *m, pl.* cerfs-cochons; **jackass d.,** (i) sing-sing *m, pl.* sing-sings; (ii) (*also* **mule d., burro d., blacktailed d.**) cerf à queue noire; **musk d.,** (i) (chevrotain *m*) porte-musc (*m inv*), musc *m*; (ii) (*also* **mouse d.**) chevrotain; **Père David's d.,** cerf du Père David; **Szechwan d.,** cerf du Kashmir; **Chinese water d.,** hydropote *m,* cerf d'eau; **Andean d.,** cerf andin, huemal *m*; **Virginia d., (Virginian) whitetailed d.,** cerf de Virginie, chevreuil à queue blanche; cariacou *m*; **d. park, forest,** chasse gardée pour le cerf; **he runs like a d.,** c'est un cerf à la course; il court comme un cerf.

deerhound ['diəhaund], *s. Z:* limier *m*; lévrier *m* d'Écosse.

deerskin ['diəskin], *s.* peau *f* de daim; *Com:* daim *m*; **d. gloves,** gants *m* de daim.

deerstalker ['diəstɔ:kər], *s.* **1.** chasseur *m* (de cerf) à l'approche; affûteur *m* (de cerfs). **2.** *Cost:* chapeau *m* de chasse (en drap et à petits bords); tapabor(d) *m.*

deerstalking ['diəstɔ:kiŋ], *s.* chasse *f* (au cerf) à l'approche.

de-escalation [di:eskə'leiʃ(ə)n], *s.* désescalade *f.*

de-ethanization [di:eθənai'zeiʃ(ə)n], *s. Petr:* déséthanisation *f.*

de-ethanize [di:'eθənaiz], *v.tr. Petr:* déséthaniser.

de-ethanizer [di:'eθənaizər], *s. Petr:* déséthaniseur *m.*

deface [di'feis], *v.tr.* **1.** défigurer (qch.); mutiler (une statue); dégrader (une porte, un mur); lacérer (une affiche); **to d. the coinage,** défigurer la monnaie. **2.** effacer, oblitérer; **to d. a stamp,** oblitérer un timbre.

defacement [di'feismənt], *s.* **1.** défiguration *f,* mutilation *f* (d'une statue, etc.); dégradation *f*; lacération *f* (d'une affiche). **2.** effacement *m,* oblitération *f.*

defacer [di'feisər], *s.* mutilateur, -trice.

defacing [di'feisiŋ], *s.* = DEFACEMENT.

de facto ['di:'fæktou], *Lt. phr: Jur:* de facto; *Jur:* **de f. and de jure,** de droit et de fait.

defalcate [di(:)'fælkeit], *v.i.* détourner des fonds; commettre des détournements (de fonds).

defalcation [di:fæl'keiʃ(ə)n], *s.* **1.** détournement *m* de fonds. **2.** fonds manquants; déficit *m* (de caisse); **to make up defalcations to the extent of £1000,** combler un déficit de caisse de £1000.

defalcator ['di:fælkeitər], *s.* détourneur *m* de fonds; (*of public money*) concussionnaire *m.*

defamation [defə'meiʃ(ə)n], *s.* diffamation *f*; injures *fpl.*

defamatory [di'fæmət(ə)ri], *a.* diffamatoire, diffamant, infamant.

defame [di'feim], *v.tr.* diffamer (qn); salir le nom de (qn).

defamed [di'feimd], *a. Her:* (lion, etc.) diffamé.

defamer [di'feimər], *s.* diffamateur, -trice; avilisseur, -euse.

default[1] [di'fɔ:lt], *s.* **1.** (*a*) *A:* manquement *m* (à un engagement); (*b*) *St.Exch:* déconfiture *f.* **2.** *Jur:* défaut *m*; non comparution *f*; (*criminal law*) contumace *f*; **to make d.,** faire défaut; être en état de contumace; **judgment by d.,** jugement *m,* arrêt *m,* par défaut, par contumace; défaut contre partie; **to deliver judgment by d.,** juger par défaut; *Sp:* **match won by d.,** match gagné par forfait. **3.** carence *f*; (*a*) *Com:* **d. in paying,** défaut de paiement; **d. interest,** intérêts *mpl* pour défaut de paiement, intérêts compensatoires; **d. risk,** risque *m* de défaillance; (*b*) *Jur:* **d. of heirs,** déshérence *f*; (*c*) *prep.phr.* **in d. of. . .,** à, au, défaut de . . .; faute de . . ..

default[2]. **1.** *v.i.* (*a*) *Jur:* faire défaut, être en état de contumace; ne pas comparaître; (*b*) *St.Exch:* ne pas faire face à ses engagements; manquer, faillir, à ses engagements; tomber en déconfiture. **2.** *v.tr. Jur:* condamner (qn) par défaut, par contumace.

defaulter [di'fɔ:ltər], *s.* **1.** (*a*) délinquant, -ante; (*b*) *Jur:* défaillant, -ante; non-comparant, -ante; contumace *mf.* **2.** *Mil: Navy:* (*a*) retardataire *m,* réfractaire *m*; (*b*) (*undergoing punishment*) consigné *m*; homme puni; **defaulters' book,** cahier *m* des punitions. **3.** auteur *m* de détournements de fonds; (*of public money*) concussionnaire *m*; **tax d.,** fraudeur *m* du fisc. **4.** *St.Exch:* défaillant *m,* failli *m,* retardataire *m*; agent *m* en défaut; **purchasing, selling, against a d.,** rachat *m,* revente *f*, d'un défaillant.

defaulting[1] [di'fɔ:ltiŋ], *a.* **1.** *St.Exch: etc:* défaillant; en défaut. **2.** *Jur:* (témoin, etc.) défaillant, qui n'a pas comparu.

defaulting[2], *s.* **1.** (*of debtor, etc.*) manquement *m* à ses engagements. **2.** *Jur:* non comparution *f*.

defaunation [di:fɔ:'neiʃ(ə)n], *s.* défaunation *f*.

defeasance [di'fi:z(ə)ns], *s. Jur:* **1.** (*a*) annulation *f*, abrogation *f*; (*b*) contre-lettre *f*. **2. d. clause,** clause *f* résolutoire (de contrat).

defeasibility [difi:zə'biliti], *s. Jur:* annulabilité *f*.

defeasible [di'fi:zəbl], *a. Jur:* annulable.

defeat[1] [di'fi:t], *s.* **1.** (*a*) défaite *f*, écrasement *m* (d'une armée); (*b*) **to suffer, sustain, a d.,** essuyer une défaite. **2.** (*a*) renversement *m* (d'un projet, d'une espérance); insuccès *m* (d'une entreprise); (*b*) échec *m* (d'une mesure); défaite (du gouvernement). **3.** *Jur:* annulation *f*.

defeat[2], *v.tr.* **1.** (*a*) battre, vaincre, mettre en déroute (une armée); (*b*) *A:* **to d. s.o. of his hopes, of his plans,** frustrer les espérances de qn; faire échouer les projets de qn; (*c*) **this defeats me,** cela me dépasse; cela dépasse ma compétence, mes forces, mes moyens, mon entendement. **2.** (*a*) renverser, détruire, déjouer, faire échouer (un projet); frustrer, renverser, ruiner (une espérance); **to be defeated in one's plans,** voir échouer, voir avorter, ses projets; **such a development would d. the purpose of the scheme,** si les choses tournaient ainsi, cela irait contre les intentions de l'entreprise; **to d. the ends of justice,** contrarier la justice; **to d. one's own object,** aller contre, à l'encontre de, ses propres intentions; (*b*) mettre en minorité *f*; **the government was defeated in Parliament,** le Gouvernement a été mis en minorité au Parlement. **3.** *Jur:* annuler.

defeatism [di'fi:tizm], *s.* défaitisme *m*.

defeatist [di'fi:tist], *s.* défaitiste *mf*.

defecate ['defəkeit, 'di:-], *v.tr.* **1.** déféquer, purifier, clarifier (un liquide). **2.** (*a*) extraire, expulser, ôter (des impuretés); (*b*) *v.i. Physiol:* décharger son ventre.

defecation [defi'keiʃ(ə)n, di:-], *s. Ind: Physiol:* défécation *f*.

defecator ['defikeitər, 'di:-], *s. Sug.-R:* **1.** (*operative*) défécateur *m*. **2.** défécateur; chaudière *f* à défécation.

defect[1] [di'fekt], *s.* **1.** défaut *m*, insuffisance *f*, manque *m* (of, de); **to supply a d.,** suppléer, remédier, à un défaut, à une insuffisance. **2.** défaut, imperfection *f*, défectuosité *f*, vice *m* (de construction), tare *f*; **to have the defects of one's qualities,** avoir les défauts de ses qualités; **d. of eyesight,** trouble visuel; **d. in pronunciation,** défaut, vice, de prononciation; **physical d.,** défaut, vice, de conformation; **d. in wood,** malandre *f*; **d. due to warping,** défaut de déformation; *El:* **d. in insulation,** défaut d'isolement; *Metall:* **d. in a casting,** loup *m* d'une pièce coulée; chambre *f* de fonderie. **3.** *A:* manquant *m*, déficit *m*.

defect[2], *v.i. Mil: etc:* déserter, passer à l'ennemi; **the spy defected to the enemy,** l'espion est passé au service de l'ennemi.

defection [di'fekʃ(ə)n], *s.* **1.** défection *f*; (*from religion*) apostasie *f*. **2.** *A:* **d. of memory, of courage,** défaillance *f* de mémoire, de courage.

defective [di'fektiv]. **1.** *a.* (*a*) défectueux, imparfait; (*of formation, development*) vicieux; **d. child,** enfant anormal; **to be d. in sth.,** manquer de qch.; fauter par un endroit; **d. memory,** mémoire *f* infidèle; **d. brakes,** freins en mauvais état; freins mauvais; *Ind:* **d. piece,** pièce défectueuse; *Cmptr:* **d. modulation,** modulation incorrecte; (*b*) *Gram:* (verbe, etc.) défectif. **2.** *s.* **mental d.,** arriéré, -ée; imbécile *mf*; faible *mf* d'esprit.

defectively [di'fektivli], *adv.* défectueusement.

defectiveness [di'fektivnis], *s.* **1.** état défectueux; défectuosité *f*, imperfection *f*. **2.** *Gram:* défectivité *f*.

defector [di'fektər], *s. Mil: etc:* transfuge *mf*; déserteur *m*.

defectoscope [di'fektəskoup], *s.* défectoscope *m*.

defence [di'fens], *s.* **1.** (*a*) défense *f*, protection *f*; **the best form of d. is attack,** la meilleure défense c'est l'attaque; **to fight in d. of one's country,** combattre, lutter, pour la défense de son pays; **to put up a stubborn d.,** opposer une défense acharnée, obstinée; se défendre avec acharnement, obstinément; **self d.,** autodéfense *f*; *Hist:* **the D. of the Realm Act,** l'Ordonnance *f* du mois d'août 1914 pour l'extension des pouvoirs du gouvernement (en vue de la défense du royaume); *Mil: etc:* **distance, close(-in), local d.,** défense éloignée, rapprochée, immédiate; **all-round d.,** défense circulaire, en point d'appui fermé, tous azimuts; **hedgehog d.,** défense en hérisson; **active, passive, d.,** défense active, passive; **civil d.** = défense passive, protection civile; **zone d., d. in depth,** défense en profondeur; **hasty d.,** défense hâtive, sommaire; **deliberate d.,** défense méthodique, mûrement préparée; **mobile, static, d.,** défense mobile, statique; **air d.,** défense aérienne; **air d. operations centre,** centre *m* d'opérations de défense aérienne; *Navy:* **air d. ship,** bâtiment directeur de défense aérienne; **harbour d. craft,** bâtiment de défense des ports, du port; **seaward d. craft,** bâtiment de défense des ports, du port, de défense vers le large; **d. expenditure,** dépenses *fpl* de défense nationale. **2.** (*a*) ouvrage *m*, barrière *f*, de défense (**against,** contre); dispositif défensif; *pl.* défenses; (*of port*) **seaward, landward, defences,** ouvrages de défense face à la mer, à la terre, côté mer, côté terre; **d. boom,** estacade *f*; (*b*) *Mil: etc:* **the d.,** les défenseurs *m*. **3.** (*a*) défense, justification *f*, apologie *f*; **to speak in d. of s.o.,** défendre qn; faire l'apologie de qn; (*b*) *Jur:* défense; **counsel for the d.,** défenseur *m*; (*in civil law*) avocat *m* du défendeur, de la défense; **witness for the d.,** témoin *m* à décharge; **to set up a d.,** établir, présenter, une défense; **to reserve one's d.,** réserver ses moyens *m* de défense; **to conduct one's own d.,** défendre soi-même sa cause; **in his d. it may be said that . . .,** l'on pourrait dire, à sa décharge, que . . ..

defenceless [di'fenslis], *a.* sans défense. **1.** (*a*) sans protection; (*b*) trop faible pour se défendre; incapable de se défendre. **2.** désarmé; sans moyen de défense; **to strike a d. opponent,** frapper un adversaire désarmé.

defencelessness [di'fenslisnis], *s.* incapacité *f* de se défendre; faiblesse *f*.

defend [di'fend], *v.tr.* **1.** défendre, protéger (**from, against,** contre). **2.** (*a*) faire l'apologie de (qn); (*b*) défendre, justifier (une opinion). **3.** *Jur:* défendre (un accusé); assumer, soutenir, la défense de (qn). **4.** *A:* (i) écarter (un danger); (ii) défendre, interdire; **God d.!** que Dieu nous en préserve! à Dieu ne plaise!

defendant [di'fendənt], *a.* & *s. Jur:* (*a*) défendeur, -eresse; **defendant denied the words,** le défendeur nia avoir prononcé ces paroles; (*b*) (*on appeal*) intimé, -ée; (*c*) (*in criminal case*) accusé, -ée.

defender [di'fendər], *s.* **1.** (*a*) défenseur *m*; **D. of the Faith,** défenseur de la foi; (*b*) *Sp:* détenteur, -trice (d'une coupe). **2.** *Jur: Scot:* = DEFENDANT.

defenestration ['di:fenis'treiʃ(ə)n], *s. Hist:* défenestration *f*.

defensibility [difensi'biliti], *s.* **1.** (*of frontier, etc.*) susceptibilité *f* d'être défendu, d'être mis en état de défense; possibilités *fpl* de défense. **2.** caractère *m* justifiable (d'une opinion); bien-fondé *m* (d'une action).

defensible [di'fensəbl], *a.* **1.** (frontière *f*, cause *f*) défendable; (position *f*) tenable. **2.** (opinion *f*) justifiable, soutenable.

defensibly [di'fensibli], *adv.* d'une manière justifiable.

defensive [di'fensiv]. **1.** *a.* défensif, de défense; *Mil: etc:* **d. action, operation, war,** action, opération, guerre, défensive; **d. system,** dispositif défensif, de défense; **d. position,** position défensive, de défense; **d. alliance,** alliance défensive; *Psy:* **d. neurosis,** névrose *f* de défense. **2.** *s.* défensive *f*; **to be on the d.,** se tenir sur la défensive; **to take up, assume, the d.,** se mettre sur la défensive; *Fenc:* **to remain (entirely) on the d.,** parer au mur.

defensively [di'fensivli], *adv.* défensivement.

defensiveness [di'fensivnis], *s.* attitude *f* de défense.

defer[1] [di'fə:r], *v.* (**deferred**) **1.** *v.tr.* (*a*) différer, ajourner, remettre, renvoyer, retarder (une affaire); remettre, arriérer, reculer (un paiement); suspendre (un jugement); **to d. doing sth.,** différer de faire qch.; **to d. sth. to a later date,** remettre, reporter, qch. à plus tard; **it's only a pleasure deferred,** c'est partie remise; **to d. a payment,** différer le paiement; **to d. a project,** ajourner un projet; (*b*) *Mil: etc:* mettre (qn) en sursis (d'appel); **to d. s.o. on medical grounds,** ajourner qn; réformer qn (temporairement). **2.** *v.i.* différer; **without deferring any longer,** sans plus tarder, sans plus attendre.

defer[2], *v.i.* déférer (**to custom,** à l'usage); **to d. to s.o.'s wishes, decision,** se soumettre à la volonté, à la décision, de qn; s'incliner devant la volonté, etc., de qn; **to d. to s.o.'s opinion,** déférer, se rendre, à l'avis, à l'opinion, de qn.

deference ['defər(ə)ns], *s.* déférence *f*; **to pay, show, d. to s.o., to an opinion,** témoigner de la déférence à, envers, qn, pour une opinion; traiter qn avec respect; **to be wanting in d. to s.o.,** manquer de respect à qn; **in, out of, d. to . . .,** par déférence pour . . .; **in d. to your request . . .,** comme suite à votre demande. . .; **with all due d. to you,** avec tout le respect que je vous dois; sauf le respect que je vous dois; **with all due d. to your father,** n'en déplaise à monsieur votre père; **with all due d. I think that . . .,** sauf meilleur avis je crois que . . ..

deferent ['defərənt]. **1.** *a. Anat:* **d. duct,** canal déférent; **d. artery,** artère déférentielle. **2.** *s. A.Astr:* (cercle) déférent *m*.

deferential [defə'renʃl], *a.* (*a*) (air *m*, ton *m*) de déférence; respectueux; plein de déférence; **to be d. to s.o.,** se montrer plein de déférence pour, envers, qn; avoir de la déférence pour qn; (*b*) *Anat:* **d. artery,** artère déférentielle.

deferentially [defə'renʃəli], *adv.* avec déférence.

deferentitis [deferen'taitis], *s. Med:* déférentite *f*.

deferment [di'fə:mənt], *s.* (*a*) ajournement *m*, remise *f* (d'une affaire); (*b*) *Mil: etc:* ajournement *m* (pour raison de santé); **to be on d.,** être en sursis; **to apply for d. (of call up),** faire une demande de sursis (d'appel).

deferred [di'fə:d], *a.* (*of share, etc.*) différé; **deferred stock,** actions différées; **d. calls on shares,** appels différés sur actions; **d. results,** résultats *m* à longue échéance; **d. payment,** paiement (i) différé, (ii) par versements échelonnés; **our goods can be supplied on d. payments,** nous livrons nos marchandises avec facilités *fpl* de paiement; **d. annuity,** rente *f* à paiement différé; *Post:* **d. telegram,** télégramme différé; **d. rate,** tarif *m* des télégrammes différés; **d. pay,** *Mil: Navy:* arriéré *m* de solde (payable lors de la libération); *Adm: etc:* rappel *m* de traitement; *Cmptr:* **d. entry, exit,** entrée, sortie, différée; **d. printing,** impression *f* en différé; **d. addressing,** adressage différé; adressage indirect à plusieurs niveaux.

deferrization [di:ferai'zeiʃ(ə)n], *s.* déferrisation *f*.

deferrize [di:'feraiz], *v.tr.* déferriser.

defervescence [di:fə'vesns], *s.* défervescence *f*.

defiance [di'faiəns], *s.* défi *m*; **to bid d. to s.o., to hurl d. at s.o.,** lancer, porter, jeter, un défi à qn; lancer des provocations *f* à qn; **to set s.o. at d.,** défier, braver, narguer, qn; aller à l'encontre des ordres de qn; **to set the law at d.,** aller à l'encontre de la loi; passer outre, faire échec, à la loi; **in d. of the law, of an order,** au mépris de la loi, d'un ordre; **in d. of s.o.,** en dépit de qn; **to act in d. of the law, of common sense,** agir au mépris de la loi, du bon sens.

defiant [di'faiənt], *a.* **1.** (*a*) provocant; (regard *m*, parole *f*) de défi; **to be insolently d. to s.o.,** braver qn avec insolence; (*b*) qui repousse les avances; intraitable; réfractaire. **2.** *occ.* méfiant, défiant.

defiantly [di'faiəntli], *adv.* d'un air, d'un ton, provocant; d'un air de défi; **to look d. at s.o.,** regarder qn avec insolence, défiance, *F:* sous le nez.

defibrillation [di:faibri'leiʃ(ə)n], *s. Med:* défibrillation *f* (du cœur).

defibrillator [di:'faibrileitər], *s.* défibrillateur *m*.

defibrinate [di:'faibrineit], *v.tr.* défibriner.

defibrination [di:faibri'neiʃ(ə)n], *s.* défibrination *f*.

deficiency [di'fiʃənsi], *s.* **1.** manque *m*, insuffisance *f*, défaut *m* (of, de). **2.** défaut *m*, faiblesse *f*, imperfection *f*; **art has supplied the deficiencies of nature,** l'art *m* a remédié aux imperfections, aux insuffisances, de la nature. **3.** (*a*) manquant *m*, déficit *m*; *Com:* découvert *m*; **to make up a d.,** combler un déficit; (*b*) déficit budgétaire; découvert; **d. bills,** avances *f* provisoires; crédits *m* budgétaires intérimaires; collectifs *m* budgétaires; (*c*) **d. payment,** subvention compensatrice (aux agriculteurs, etc.). **4.** *Med:* carence *f* (**in, of,** de); déficience *f*; **d. disease,** maladie carentielle; maladie de, par, carence; **physical d.,** déficience physique.

deficient [di'fiʃənt], *a.* (*a*) défectueux, insuffisant, incomplet; *Mth:* **d. hyperbola,** hyperbole défective; **to be d. in sth.,** manquer de qch., être dépourvu de qch.; **he is d. in courage,** le courage lui manque; (*b*) (personne *f*) à petite mentalité; *s.* **a mental d.,** un(e) déficient(e), un(e) débile mental(e); (*c*) *Mth:* **d. number,** nombre déficient; (*d*) *A.Chr:* **d. month, year,** mois *m* cave, année *f* cave.

deficiently [di'fiʃəntli], *adv.* défectueusement, insuffisamment, incomplètement.

deficit ['defisit], *s. Fin: Com:* excédent *m* de dépenses; déficit *m*; découvert *m*; **budget that shows a d.,** budget *m* en déficit, budget déficitaire; **to make good, make up, the d.,** combler le déficit.

defilade[1] [defi'leid], *s. Fort:* défilement *m*.

defilade[2], *v.tr. Fort:* défiler (un ouvrage).

defile[1] ['di:fail], *s. Geog:* défilé *m*; gorge *f* (entre montagnes).

defile[2] [di'fail], *v.i. Mil: etc:* (*of troops, procession*) défiler.

defile[3] [di'fail], *v.tr.* **1.** souiller, salir, tacher; **hands defiled with the blood of martyrs,** mains souillées du sang des martyrs; **to d. a sacred place,** polluer, profaner, un lieu saint; **to d. the marriage bed,** souiller, déshonorer, la couche nuptiale. **2.** *A:* & *B:* débaucher, déflorer, violer.

defilement [di'failmənt], *s.* **1.** souillure *f*; profanation *f*, pollution *f* (d'un lieu saint). **2.** souillure, salissure *f*, tache *f*; **free from d.,** sans tache, sans souillure.

defiler [di'failər], *s.* celui qui salit, qui souille; profanateur, -trice (d'un lieu saint).

definable [di'fainəbl], *a.* définissable; déterminable.

define [di'fain], *v.tr.* **1.** définir (un mot, un objet); *Gram:* **defining clause,** incidente déterminative. **2. to d. one's position,** préciser son attitude (politique, etc.); formuler sa position. **3.** déterminer (l'étendue, les limites, de qch.); délimiter (un territoire, des pouvoirs); **well-defined limits,** limites bien déterminées. **4.** *(a)* dessiner, dégager (les formes de qn, de qch.); *esp. in passive:* **well-defined outlines,** contours nettement dessinés, nettement dégagés; *(b)* **the properties which d. this species,** les propriétés qui distinguent cette espèce.

definer [di'fainər], *s.* définisseur *m*; **the lexicographer is a d.,** le lexicographe est un définisseur.

definite ['definit], *a.* **1.** défini; bien déterminé; **at a d. time,** à une heure déterminée; **there is no d. frontier,** il n'y a pas de frontière bien déterminée; **d. answer,** réponse précise, catégorique; **d. situation,** situation *f* de fait; **d. intentions,** intentions bien arrêtées; **to come to a d. understanding,** s'entendre clairement; arriver à une entente qui ne laisse aucune imprécision; **to answer d. needs,** répondre à des besoins précis; **to give s.o. d. information about one's intentions,** fixer qn sur ses intentions; **you are not d. enough,** vous ne précisez pas assez; *Com:* **d. order, sale,** commande *f*, vente *f*, ferme. **2.** *Gram:* **d. article,** article défini; **past d.,** passé défini. **3.** *Bot:* *(a)* (étamines *fpl*, etc.) en nombre défini; *(b)* (inflorescence) définie. **4.** *Mth:* **d. integral,** intégrale définie.

definitely ['definitli], *adv.* d'une manière précise, bien déterminée; précisément, exactement, nettement, catégoriquement; **he has been d. forbidden to . . .,** il lui est formellement interdit de . . .; **he is d. coming,** nous avons l'assurance formelle qu'il viendra; **he is d. going,** il est décidé qu'il ira; **he is d. better,** il va décidément mieux; **he is d. mad,** il est fou à n'en pas douter; sa folie est bien établie; **quite d. things are improving,** il n'y a pas de doute qu'il y a une amélioration; **this book is d. pacifist,** ce livre est nettement pacifiste; **d. superior,** nettement supérieur.

definiteness ['definitnis], *s.* nature définie, déterminée (**of,** de); précision *f*, exactitude *f*, netteté *f*.

definition [defi'niʃ(ə)n], *s.* **1.** définition *f*; **standard definitions,** définitions normalisées; **to give the d. of sth.,** donner la définition de qch.; **homicide that falls under the d. of murder,** homicide *m* qualifiable de meurtre. **2.** *Ecc: etc:* décision *f*, définition; **the definitions of the councils,** les définitions des conciles. **3.** *Opt:* netteté *f* (de l'image); *Phot:* **negative with fine d.,** cliché très fouillé; **bad d.,** manque *m* de netteté; flou *m*; *T.V:* **French television has a d. of 819 lines,** la télévision française a une définition de 819 lignes. **4.** *A:* délimitation *f*.

definitional [defi'niʃənl], *a.* définitionnel.

definitive [di'finitiv], *a.* (jugement, résultat) définitif; (réponse) définitive; **d. edition,** édition définitive, ne varietur.

definitively [di'finitivli], *adv.* définitivement; en définitive.

definitor [di'finitɔ:r], *s. Ecc:* définiteur *m*.

deflagrate ['defləgreit], *Ch:* **1.** *v.tr.* faire déflagrer (du salpêtre, etc.). **2.** *v.i.* déflagrer, fuser.

deflagration [deflə'greiʃ(ə)n], *s. Ch:* déflagration *f*.

deflagrator ['defləgreitər], *s.* (appareil) déflagrateur *m*, inflammateur *m*.

deflate [di:'fleit]. **1.** *v.tr.* *(a)* dégonfler (un ballon, un pneu); *Cy: Aut:* **deflated tyre,** pneu aplati, à plat; **to become deflated,** s'aplatir; *(b)* *Pol.Ec:* **to d. (the currency),** amener la déflation de la monnaie; diminuer la circulation du papier-monnaie; faire (de) la déflation; *(c)* *F:* **to d. s.o.,** remettre qn à sa place. **2.** *v.i.* (*of tyre, etc.*) se dégonfler.

deflation [di:'fleiʃ(ə)n], *s.* **1.** dégonflement *m* (d'un ballon, d'un pneu); aplatissage *m*, crevaison *f* (d'un pneu). **2.** *Fin:* déflation *f*. **3.** *Geol:* *esp. U.S:* érosion éolienne.

deflationary [di:'fleiʃən(ə)ri], *a. Pol.Ec:* (politique, etc.) de déflation; (mesures *f*) déflationnistes.

deflationist [di'fleiʃənist], *a. & s. Pol.Ec:* déflationniste (*mf*).

deflator [di:'fleitər], *s.* dégonfleur *m* (de pneus, etc.).

deflect [di'flekt]. **1.** *v.tr.* *(a)* (faire) dévier; détourner, défléchir; **to d. a needle (on a dial),** faire dévier, défléchir, une aiguille; *Aut:* **to d. the front wheels,** braquer les roues avant; **to d. a stream,** détourner un cours d'eau; *Artil:* (*of projectile*) **to be deflected,** dériver; *Min:* **to d. a well,** dévier un puits; *(b)* incurver, cintrer. **2.** *v.i.* *(a)* (se) dévier, se détourner, défléchir; *(b)* s'incurver, se cintrer; faire flèche.

deflecting [di'flektiŋ], *a.* **d. force,** (i) force *f* de déviation; force déviatrice; (ii) force fléchissante (d'une poutre); *El:* **d. action of a current,** action déviatrice d'un courant; **d. field,** champ *m* de déviation; **d. coil, yoke,** bobine *f* de déviation; *Elcs: etc:* **d. plate,** plaque déflectrice, de déviation.

deflection, deflexion [di'flekʃ(ə)n], *s.* **1.** déflection *f*, déflexion *f* (de la lumière, d'un rayon); déviation *f* (de l'aiguille sur le cadran, de l'aiguille du compas); *Mch:* **angle of d. of the arms of the governor,** écart *m*, angle *m* d'écartement, des boules du régulateur. **2.** déjettement *m*, déformation *f*; (*sag*) flèche *f*, flexion *f*; fléchissement *m* (d'un ressort); **elastic d.,** déformation élastique; **d. under load,** flexion, affaissement *m*, sous charge; *Mec.E:* **d. for a given load,** flèche, affaissement, correspondant à la charge. **3.** *Nav.Artil:* **d. in knots,** (i) dérive *f* (du projectile); (ii) correction *f* de dérive. **4.** *Aut:* braquage *m* (des roues avant). **5.** *El:* *Elcs:* (*of voltmeter, etc.*) déviation, déflexion, valeur *f* d'élongation; **d. coefficient, factor,** coefficient *m*, facteur *m*, de déviation; **d. defocusing,** défocalisation *f* de déflexion; **d. plate,** plaque *f* de déflexion, plaque *f* de déviation; **d. tube,** tube *m* à parcours électronique dirigé; **d. sensitivity,** sensibilité *f* de déviation.

deflector [di'flektər], *s.* (dispositif) déflecteur *m*; *I.C.E: etc:* chicane *f*; *Rail:* aiguillage *m* de caténaire; *Mec.E:* **oil d.,** renvoi *m* d'huile; **sound d.,** abat-son(s) *m inv*; *El:* **d. coil,** bobine déflectrice, de déviation.

deflocculant [di'flɔkjulənt], *s. Ch:* défloculant *m*.

deflocculate [di'flɔkjuleit], *v.tr. Ch:* défloculer.

deflocculation [diflɔkju'leiʃ(ə)n], *s. Ch:* défloculation *f*.

defloration [di:flɔ:'reiʃ(ə)n], *s.* défloration *f*, séduction *f*, *F:* dépucelage *m* (d'une vierge).

deflower [di:'flauər], *v.tr.* **1.** déflorer, *F:* dépuceler (une vierge). **2.** déflorer, défleurir, gâter (un sujet, le paysage, etc.). **3.** défleurir, déflorer (une plante, etc.).

defluent ['defluənt]. **1.** *a.* découlant. **2.** *s.* partie découlante (d'un glacier).

defoliant [di:'fouliənt], *s. Agr:* défoliant *m*.

defoliate [di:'foulieit], *v.tr.* défeuiller (un arbuste, etc.).

defoliation [di:fouli'eiʃ(ə)n], *s.* défoliation *f*, défeuillaison *f*.

deforce [di'fɔ:s], *v.tr. Jur:* **1.** *(a)* **to d. sth. from its owner,** usurper qch. sur son propriétaire; *(b)* **to d. s.o. of a right,** usurper un droit sur qn. **2.** *Scot:* **to d. an officer of the law,** entraver un huissier, etc., dans l'exercice de ses fonctions.

deforcement [di'fɔ:smənt], *s. Jur:* usurpation *f*; détention illégale.

deforest [di:'fɔrist], *v.tr.* **1.** déboiser. **2.** défricher.

deforestation [di:fɔris'teiʃ(ə)n], *s.* **1.** déboisement *m*. **2.** défrichement *m*.

deform [di'fɔ:m], *v.tr.* **1.** défigurer, enlaidir (qn, qch.). **2.** déformer, contourner; *Mec.E:* fausser (une poutre, etc.); déformer (un ressort); **body deformed by illness,** corps contrefait par la maladie.

deformation [di:fɔ:'meiʃ(ə)n], *s.* **1.** défiguration *f*. **2.** déformation *f* (d'un os, d'une surface, etc.); **lateral d.,** déviation latérale; *El:* **field d.,** torsion *f* de champ. **3.** changement *m* en mal, altération *f*. **4.** *Ling:* déformation, altération.

deformed [di'fɔ:md], *a.* **1.** (*of pers.*) contrefait, difforme. **2.** *W.Tel:* **d. wave,** onde faussée, déformée.

deformity [di'fɔ:miti], *s.* *(a)* difformité *f*; *(b)* *A:* laideur *f* (de caractère).

defraud [di'frɔ:d], *v.tr.* **1.** frauder (le fisc, etc.). **2.** *(a)* *Jur:* léser (qn); frustrer (ses créanciers); *(b)* **to d. s.o. of sth.,** frustrer qn de qch.; escroquer qch. à qn; faire tort à qn de qch.

defrauder [di'frɔ:dər], *s.* **1.** fraudeur *m* (du fisc). **2.** escroc *m*.

defrauding [di'frɔ:diŋ], *s.* **1.** fraude *f*. **2.** frustration *f* (de ses créanciers, etc.).

defray [di'frei], *v.tr.* **to d. s.o.'s expenses,** défrayer qn; fournir aux dépenses de qn; rembourser les frais de qn; **to d. the cost of sth.,** couvrir les frais de qch.; subvenir, pourvoir, aux frais de qch.; prendre à sa charge toutes les dépenses.

defrayable [di'freiəbl], *a.* à la charge (**by,** de); **the upkeep of the roads is d. by the town,** l'entretien *m* des routes est à la charge de la ville; **expenses d. out of local contributions,** frias *m* imputables à la localité.

defrayal [di'freiəl], **defrayment** [di'freimənt], *s.* paiement *m*, remboursement *m* (des frais).

defreeze [di:'fri:z], *v.tr.* décongeler.

defreezing [di:'fri:ziŋ], *s.* décongélation *f*.

defrock [di:'frɔk], *v.tr.* défroquer (un prêtre).

defrost [di:'frɔst], *v.tr.* **1.** dégivrer (un réfrigérateur, un pare-brise, etc.). **2.** décongeler (la viande frigorifiée, etc.).

defroster [di:'frɔstər], *s.* dégivreur *m*, dispositif *m* antigel; **electric, hot-air, d.,** dégivreur électrique, à air chaud.

deft [deft], *a.* adroit, habile; **with a d. hand,** d'une main exercée; d'une main preste.

deftly ['deftli], *adv.* adroitement, prestement; d'une main exercée, d'une main preste.

deftness ['deftnis], *s.* adresse *f*, habileté *f*, dextérité *f*, prestesse *f*; *Art:* **d. of touch,** prestesse dans le maniement du pinceau.

defunct [di'fʌŋkt], *a.* défunt, -e; décédé, -ée; *s.* **the d.,** le défunt, la défunte.

defuse [di:'fju:z], *v.tr.* *(a)* désamorcer; *(b)* **to d. a crisis,** alléger une crise.

defy [di'fai], *v.tr.* défier (qn); mettre (qn) au défi; braver (qn, un ordre, la loi); **I d. you to do it,** je vous mets au défi, je vous défie, de le faire; **to d. description,** échapper à toute description; **the fortress defied every attack,** la forteresse résista à toutes les attaques; **constitution that defies every climate,** tempérament *m* qui résiste à tous les climats; tempérament à l'épreuve de tous les climats; **goods that defy competition,** marchandises *f* qui ne craignent pas la concurrence.

dégagé[1] [dei'gæʒei], *s. Danc:* dégagé *m*.

dégagé[2], *v.i. Danc:* dégager.

degallicize [di:'gælisaiz], *v.tr.* défranciser.

degas [di:'gæs], *v.tr.* dégazer.

degasification [di:gæsifi'keiʃ(ə)n], *s.* dégazage *m*.

degasify [di:'gæsifai], *v.tr.* dégazer.

de Gaullism [də'goulizm], *s. Pol:* gaullisme *m*.

de Gaullist [də'goulist], *s. Pol:* gaulliste *mf*.

degauss [di'gaus], *v.tr.* dégausser, démagnétiser.

degaussing[1] [di'gausiŋ], *a.* dégaussant, de démagnétisation, de dégaussage, de dégaussement; **d. equipment,** matériel *m* de démagnétisation; **d. lane, girdle,** parcours *m*, ceinture *f*, de démagnétisation.

degaussing[2], *s.* démagnétisation *f*, dégaussage *m*, dégaussement *m*.

degeneracy [di'dʒen(ə)rəsi], *s.* dégénération *f*, abâtardissement *m*.

degenerate[1] [di'dʒen(ə)rət], *a. & s.* *(a)* dégénéré, -ée; abâtardi, -ie; **to make d.,** abâtardir; *(b)* *Ph:* **d. matter,** matière dégénérée.

degenerate[2] [di'dʒenəreit]. **1.** *v.i.* dégénérer (**from,** de; **into,** en); s'abâtardir; **to cause to d.,** abâtardir; **thrift that degenerates into avarice,** économie *f* qui tourne à l'avarice. **2.** *v.tr.* *A:* occasionner la dégénérescence de (qn).

degeneration [didʒenə'reiʃ(ə)n], *s.* dégénérescence *f*, dégénération *f*; appauvrissement *m* (d'une race); abâtardissement *m*; **diseases consequent on d.,** maladies *f* de dégénérescence; *Med:* **black d.,** mélanose *f*; **waxy d.,** amylose *f* (du foie, etc.); **fatty d.,** dégénérescence graisseuse; stéatose *f*.

degerm(inate) [di:'dʒə:m(ineit)], *v.tr. Brew:* égermer, dégermer (l'orge).

degerming [di:'dʒə:miŋ], *s. Brew:* égermage *m* (de l'orge).

deglaciation [di:gleisi'eiʃ(ə)n], *s. Geol:* déglaciation *f*.

deglutition [di:glu:'tiʃ(ə)n], *s. Physiol:* déglutition *f*; action *f* d'avaler.

degradation [degrə'deiʃ(ə)n], *s.* **1.** dégradation *f*; cassation *f* (d'un officier, etc.). **2.** avilissement *m*, dégradation, abrutissement *m*; **to live a life of d.,** vivre dans la dégradation. **3.** *(a)* *Ph:* dégradation (de l'énergie); *(b)* *Geol:* dégradation, effritement *m*, désagrégation *f* (des roches). **4.** *Art:* dégradation (des teintes). **5.** *Cmptr:* fonctionnement *m* en mode dégradé.

degrade [di'greid]. **1.** *v.tr.* *(a)* dégrader, casser (un officier, etc.); dépouiller (qn) de ses dignités, de ses titres, de son rang; *(b)* avilir, dégrader (qn); profaner (ses talents); **to d. man to the level of the beasts,** réduire, ravaler, les hommes à l'état des animaux; **to d. thought,** encanailler la pensée; *(c)* *Ph:* dégrader (l'énergie); *(d)* *Geol:* désagréger, effriter, dégrader (des roches); *(e)* *Art: Paint:* dégrader (les teintes). **2.** *v.i.* *(a)* (*of race, etc.*) dégénérer; *(b)* *Geol:* (*of rock*) se dégrader, s'effriter. **3.** *v.i. Sch:* *A:* (*at Cambridge*) remettre d'un an son examen du *Tripos*.

degrading [di'greidiŋ], *a.* avilissant, dégradant; **d. affair,** affaire infamante, honteuse.

degras [dei'grɑ:], *s. Leath:* dégras *m*.

degrease [di:'gri:s], *v.tr.* dégraisser.

degree [di'gri:], *s.* **1.** *A:* degré *m*, marche *f* (d'autel, etc.); *Ecc:* **song of degrees,** psaume graduel. **2.** *(a)* **to some, to a certain d.,** à un certain degré; (jusqu')à un certain point; to, in, a high d., éminemment; **in the highest d.,** au plus haut degré, au suprême degré, au dernier degré; par excellence; au plus haut point; **beautiful in**

the highest d., d'une suprême beauté; **in some d.,** jusqu'à un certain point; dans une certaine mesure; **in a lesser d.,** dans une plus faible mesure; **not in the slightest d.,** pas le moins du monde; **by imperceptible degrees,** imperceptiblement; **it's a question of d.,** cela dépend de ce qu'on veut, de ce qu'on pense; **scrupulous to a d.,** scrupuleux au superlatif, au possible, au plus haut degré; scrupuleux à l'excès; éminemment scrupuleux; **to such a d. that . . .,** à tel point que . . .; **to the last d.,** au dernier degré, au dernier point; **by degrees,** par degrés; peu à peu; petit à petit; insensiblement; **the fire was spreading by degrees,** le feu s'étendait petit à petit; (*of pers.*) **to rise by degrees,** monter par échelons; **by slow degrees,** graduellement, lentement; **d. of wear,** degré d'usure; *Tchn:* **d. of inherent distortion,** degré de distorsion propre; *Gram:* **d. of comparison,** degré de comparaison; **adverb of d.,** adverbe quantitatif; *Mec.E: Metall:* **d. of hardness,** degré de dureté; *Ph:* **d. of humidity,** titre *m* d'eau, d'humidité; teneur *f* en eau; *Jur:* **d. of relationship,** degré de parenté; **d. of consanguinity, of affinity,** degré de parenté, d'alliance; **marriage within the prohibited, forbidden, degrees,** mariage *m* entre parents ou alliés au degré prohibé; (*b*) **third d.,** (i) (*freemasonry*) troisième degré; (ii) passage *m* à tabac; cuisinage *m*; **to put a prisoner through the third d.,** passer un accusé à tabac; cuisiner un prisonnier; (*c*) *Ph: Geog: etc:* degré (d'un cercle, de latitude, de température); **angle of 30 degrees,** angle *m* de 30 degrés; **ten degrees of frost,** dix degrés au-dessous de zéro; **there were eight degrees of frost,** il a gelé à moins huit; **the thermometer registers 15 degrees (centigrade),** le thermomètre marque 15 degrés (centigrades); **we were 30° North,** nous étions par 30 degrés de latitude nord; **twenty degrees west of Greenwich,** sous le méridien de vingt degrés à l'ouest de Greenwich; (*d*) *Mth:* **equation of the second, of the third, d.,** équation *f* du second, du troisième, degré. **3.** *Mus:* échelon *m* (de la gamme); degré (de la portée). **4.** *A: & Lit:* rang *m*, condition *f*; **of high d.,** de haut rang, de haut lignage; **of low d.,** de bas étage. **5.** *Sch:* grade *m* (universitaire); **bachelor's d.** = licence *f* (ès lettres, ès sciences, en droit); **to take, sit for, one's d.** = passer son examen de licence; **he has his d.** = il a sa licence, est licencié; il a ses diplômes.

degression [di'greʃ(ə)n], *s.* dégression *f*, diminution progressive; dégressivité *f* (de l'impôt).

degressive [di'gresiv], *a.* **d. taxation,** impôt dégressif.

degum [di:'gʌm], *v.tr. Tex:* décreuser, cuire (la soie grège); **degummed silk,** soie cuite.

degumming [di:'gʌmiŋ], *s. Tex:* décreusage *m*, décruage *m*, décrûment *m*, décrusage *m*, décrusement *m*.

dehair [di:'hɛər], *v.tr. Leath:* dépiler, peler, débourrer, ébourrer.

dehisce [di'his], *v.i. Bot:* (*of seed vessel, etc.*) s'ouvrir (le long d'une suture préexistante); s'entr'ouvrir.

dehiscence [di'his(ə)ns], *s. Bot:* déhiscence *f*.

dehiscent [di'his(ə)nt], *a. Bot:* déhiscent.

dehorn [di:'hɔ:n], *v.tr.* décorner (un bœuf, etc.).

dehumanization [di:hjumənai'zeiʃ(ə)n], *s.* déshumanisation *f*.

dehumanize [di:'hju:mənaiz], *v.tr.* déshumaniser.

dehumidification [di:hjumidifi'keiʃ(ə)n], *s.* déshumidification *f*.

dehumidifier [di:hju'midifaiər], *s.* déshumidificateur *m*; déshydratant *m*.

dehumidify [di:hju'midifai], *v.tr.* déshumidifier; déshydrater (l'air, etc.).

dehydracetic [di:haidrə'si:tik], *a. Ch:* déhydracétique.

dehydrase [di:'haidreis], *s. Bio-Ch:* déshydrase *f*.

dehydrate [di:'haidreit], *v.tr.* déshydrater; **to become dehydrated,** se déshydrater; **dehydrated eggs,** œufs *m* en poudre; **dehydrated vegetables,** (i) légumes déshydratés; (ii) légumes secs.

dehydration [di:hai'dreiʃ(ə)n], *s.* anhydrisation *f*; déshydratation *f*; dessiccation *f*.

dehydrator [di:'haidreitər], *s.* déshydrateur *m*.

dehydrogenase [di:'haidroudʒəneis], *s. Bio-Ch:* déshydrogénase *m*.

dehydrogenate [di:'haidrədʒəneit, -haid'rɔdʒ-], *v.tr. Ch:* déshydrogéner.

dehydrogenated [di:hai'drɔdʒəneitid], *a. Ch:* déshydrogéné.

dehydrogenation [di:haidrədʒə'neiʃ(ə)n], *s. Ch:* déshydrogénation *f*.

dehypnotize [di:'hipnətaiz], *v.tr.* réveiller (un hypnotisé).

Deianira [diə'nairə], *Pr.n.f. Gr.Myth:* Déjanire.

de-ice [di:'ais], *v.tr.* dégivrer.

de-icer [di:'aisər], *s.* dégivreur *m*.

deicide[1] ['di:isaid], *s.* (*pers.*) déicide *mf*.

deicide[2], *s.* (crime *m* de) déicide *m*.

de-icing [di:'aisiŋ], *s.* dégivrage *m*.

deictic ['daiktik], *a.* **1.** *Log:* qui prouve directement. **2.** *Ling:* déictique.

deification [di:ifi'keiʃ(ə)n], *s.* déification *f*; apothéose *f*.

deiform ['di:ifɔ:m], *a.* déiforme.

deify ['di:ifai], *v.tr.* déifier (qn); apothéoser.

deign [dein], *v.tr.* **1. to d. to do sth.,** daigner faire qch.; condescendre à faire qch.; **without deigning to look at me,** sans daigner me regarder. **2.** *A: & Lit: usu. neg.* **he did not d. me an answer, a reply,** il ne daigna pas me répondre; il ne m'accorda pas de réponse.

deionization [di:aiənai'zeiʃ(ə)n], *s. Ph: etc:* dé(s)ionisation *f*.

deism ['di:izm], *s.* déisme *m*.

deist ['di:ist], *s.* déiste *mf*.

deistic [di:'istik], *a.* déiste.

Deiters ['di:tə:z], *Pr.n. Anat:* **nucleus of D.,** noyau *m* de Deiters.

deity ['di:iti], *s.* **1.** divinité *f* (de Jésus-Christ, etc.). **2.** (*a*) dieu *m*, déesse *f*; déité *f*, divinité; **the pagan deities,** les divinités païennes; (*b*) *Theol:* **the D.,** la Divinité; Dieu *m*; l'Être *m* suprême.

deject [di'dʒekt], *v.tr.* abattre, décourager, déprimer (qn).

dejecta [di'dʒektə], *s.pl.* (*a*) *Med:* déjections *f*, excréments *m*; (*b*) *Geol:* déjections (d'un volcan).

dejected [di'dʒektid], *a.* triste, abattu, déprimé, affaissé, découragé, morne; **to become d.,** se décourager; perdre sa gaieté; se laisser abattre.

dejectedly [di'dʒektidli], *adv.* d'un air abattu, découragé; tristement.

dejection [di'dʒekʃ(ə)n], *s.* **1.** découragement *m*, accablement *m*; tristesse *f*, abattement *m*; affaissement *m*; mélancolie *f*; **deep d.,** profond abattement; **he went away in d.,** il s'en est allé d'un air abattu. **2.** (*a*) *Med:* déjection *f*; évacuation *f* (du ventre); (*b*) *pl.* = DEJECTA.

de jure [dei'dʒuəri], *Lt. adv. phr.* de jure.

Dekatron ['dekətrɔn], *s. Elcs: R.t.m:* Décatron *m*.

dekko ['dekou], *s. P: O:* regard *m*, coup *m* d'œil; **let's have a d.,** fais, faites, voir; **dekko!** pige-moi ça!

del [del], *s. Mth:* (opérateur *m*) nabla *m*.

delabialization [di:leibiəlai'zeiʃ(ə)n], *s. Ling:* délabialisation *f*.

delabialize [di:'leibiəlaiz], *v.tr. Ling:* délabialiser.

delafossite [delə'fɔsait], *s. Miner:* delafossite *f*.

delaine [di'lein], *s. Tex:* mousseline *f* de laine.

delasting [di:'la:stiŋ], *s. Boom:* déformage *m*.

delate [di'leit], *v.tr. A:* dénoncer (qn, un méfait, etc.).

delation [di'leiʃ(ə)n], *s. A:* délation *f*; dénonciation *f*.

delator [di'leitər], *s. A:* délateur *m*.

delay[1] [di'lei], *s.* **1.** sursis *m*, remise *f*; délai *m*, retard *m*; **we shall have to start without d.,** il nous faut partir sans délai, sans nous attarder, tout de suite; **without (any) further d.,** sans plus tarder; **an hour's d.,** une heure de retard; **to make no d.,** ne pas traîner, ne pas tarder (à faire qch.); *Jur:* **to obtain a d. of payment,** obtenir un atermoiement, un délai. **2.** retardement *m*, arrêt *m*, entrave *f* (du progrès); **excusable d.,** retard justifié; **the road works caused traffic delays,** les travaux *m* (sur la route) ont retardé, bloqué, la circulation; **operating delays,** retards d'exploitation, retards dus aux opérateurs; *Com:* **claim for d. in transit,** réclamation *f* pour retard; *Cmptr:* **d. equalizer,** compensateur *m* de phase; **d. line store, storage,** mémoire *f* à propagation, à ligne à retard.

delay[2]. **1.** *v.tr.* (*a*) différer, retarder, remettre, ajourner (une affaire); différer, arriérer (un paiement); **to d. one's departure,** différer, remettre, son départ; **the King's return is still being delayed,** le retour du roi est toujours reculé; **these payments have long been delayed,** ces paiements *m* ont subi un long retard; **delayed-action fuse,** fusée *f* à retardement; (*b*) retenir, arrêter, retarder (qn); entraver, retarder (le progrès); **ship delayed by bad weather,** navire retardé par le mauvais temps; **to d. the traffic,** gêner, entraver, la circulation. **2.** *v.i.* (*a*) tarder, différer (**in doing sth.,** à faire qch.); *Mil:* **delaying action,** action retardatrice, combat retardateur; (*b*) s'attarder.

del credere [del'kredəri], *a. & s. Com:* **d. c. (commission),** (commission *f*) ducroire *m*.

dele[1] ['di:li(:)], *Lt. imp. & s. Typ:* deleatur (*m*).

dele[2], *v.tr. Typ: F:* marquer (une lettre, etc.) d'un deleatur; supprimer (une lettre); indiquer la suppression (d'une lettre).

deleave [di:'li:v], *v.tr. Cmptr:* déliasser.

deleaver [di:'li:vər], *s. Cmptr:* déliasseuse *f*.

deleaving [di:'li:viŋ], *s. Cmptr:* déliassage *m*; **d. machine,** déliasseuse *f*.

delectable [di'lektəbl], *a.* délectable, délicieux; **d. reading,** une savoureuse lecture.

delectableness [di'lektəblnis], *s. Lit:* nature délicieuse (de qch.); délices *fpl* (d'un endroit, etc.).

delectably [di'lektəbli], *adv.* délectablement.

delectation [di:lek'teiʃ(ə)n], *s.* délectation *f*.

delegacy ['deligəsi], *s.* délégation *f* ((i) action de déléguer; (ii) pouvoirs de délégué; (iii) corps des délégués).

delegant ['deligənt], *s. Jur:* délégateur, -trice.

delegate[1] ['deligət], *s.* délégué, -ée.

delegate[2] ['deligeit], *v.tr.* **1.** déléguer (qn); **to d. s.o. to do sth.,** députer, déléguer, qn pour faire qch. **2. to d. powers,** déléguer des pouvoirs.

delegation [deli'geiʃ(ə)n], *s.* **1.** (*a*) délégation *f*, subrogation *f* (de droits, etc.); (*b*) délégation (de qn); nomination *f*, désignation *f* (de qn comme délégué). **2.** *Hist:* **the German Peace D.,** la Délégation allemande de la Paix; **the Delegations,** les Délégations austro-hongroises.

delegator ['deligeitər], *s. Jur:* délégateur, -trice.

delete[1] [di'li:t], *v.tr.* effacer, raturer, rayer (un mot, etc.); *F:* biffer (un mot); *Typ:* à supprimer; (*on form*) **d. where inapplicable,** rayer les mentions inutiles; *Cmptr:* **deleted representation,** oblitération *f*.

delete[2], *s. Cmptr:* (i) effacement *m*; (ii) élimination *f*, suppression *f*; **d. character,** caractère *m* d'effacement, d'annulation.

deleter [di'li:tər], *s. Cmptr:* **blank d.,** suppresseur *m* d'espaces.

deleterious [deli'tiəriəs], *a.* **1.** nuisible à la santé; *A:* nuisible aux mœurs. **2.** *A:* (gaz *m*, etc.) délétère.

deleteriously [deli'tiəriəsli], *adv.* nuisiblement, d'une manière nuisible.

deletion [di'li:ʃ(ə)n], *s.* **1.** rature *f*, annulation *f*; suppression *f* (d'un passage). **2.** passage effacé, raturé, supprimé, *F:* biffé. **3.** *Biol:* délétion *f*. **4.** *Cmptr:* élimination *f*, effacement *m*; **d. record,** article éliminé; enregistrement *m* d'annulation.

delft [delf(t)], *s. Cer:* faïence *f* de Delft; hollande *f*; **d. blue,** bleu *m* de faïence.

Delian ['di:liən]. **1.** *a. Geog: etc:* délien, déliaque; *Ant:* **D. Apollo,** Apollon délien; *Hist:* **D. League,** confédération *f* de Délos; *Mth:* **D. problem,** problème *m* déliaque. **2.** *s. Geog:* Délien, -ienne.

deliberate[1] [di'lib(ə)rət], *a.* **1.** délibéré, prémédité, réfléchi, intentionnel, voulu; **d. trap,** piège tendu à dessein; **d. insolence,** insolence calculée; **d. insult,** insulte préméditée; **d. attack, defence,** attaque, défense, préparée. **2.** (*of pers.*) (*a*) réfléchi, circonspect, avisé; **d. action,** action réfléchie; (*b*) lent, sans hâte, mesuré; **d. tread,** pas mesuré.

deliberate[2] [di'libəreit], *v.tr. & i.* délibérer (**on,** de, sur); réfléchir (**on,** sur); **to d. over, on, a question,** délibérer une question, d'une question; **I was deliberating whether I should go or not,** je délibérais si j'irais ou non.

deliberately [di'libərətli], *adv.* **1.** de propos délibéré; de parti pris; de sang-froid; à dessein; par calcul; avec intention; exprès; à bon escient. **2.** (agir) posément, sans hâte, sans précipitation, délibérément; **to answer d.,** répondre sans se presser.

deliberateness [di'lib(ə)rətnis], *s.* **1.** intention marquée (d'une insulte, etc.). **2.** sage lenteur *f*, mesure *f* (dans les actions).

deliberation [dilibə'reiʃ(ə)n], *s.* **1.** (*a*) délibération *f*; **after due d.,** après mûre délibération; après mûre réflexion; **after two hours' d.,** après avoir délibéré pendant deux heures; **the time for d. is past,** le temps de délibérer est passé; (*b*) **the deliberations of an assembly,** les débats *m* d'une assemblée. **2.** (*a*) **to act with d.,** agir avec circonspection, après réflexion; (*b*) sage lenteur *f*; mesure *f*; **with d.,** posément, avec lenteur, sans se hâter, sans hâte; **he always speaks with d.,** il prend toujours le temps de mesurer, de peser, ses paroles; **d. in answering,** lenteur réfléchie à répondre.

deliberative [di'libərətiv], *a.* **1.** (*of function*) délibératif; (*a*) *A:* **d. voice,** voix délibérative; droit *m* de vote; (*b*) **d. assembly,** assemblée délibérante. **2. in a d. moment,** dans un temps de délibération, de réflexion.

delicacy ['delikəsi], *s.* **1.** (*a*) délicatesse *f*; **d. of a design,** délicatesse, finesse *f*, d'un dessin; **d. of hearing, of the ear,** finesse *f* de l'ouïe; délicatesse, sensibilité *f*, de l'oreille; **d. of a precision instrument,** sensibilité d'un instrument de précision; (*b*) délicatesse, faiblesse *f* (de santé); mièvrerie *f* (d'un enfant); *Art:* morbidesse *f* (de teintes carnées); (*c*) légèreté *f* (de touche, de pinceau, de doigté); (*d*) **to have no sense of d.,** manquer de délicatesse, de tact *m*; **to shock s.o.'s d.,** faire outrage à la délicatesse, à la pudeur, à la modestie, de qn; **to feel a d. about doing sth.,** se faire scrupule de faire qch.; (*e*) **negotiations of the utmost d.,** négociations très délicates. **2.** (**table**) **delicacies,** délicatesses, friandises *f*, de table; petits plats soignés; mets délicats.

delicate [ˈdelikət], *a.* **1.** délicat; (*a*) **d. pink,** rose délicat, doux, tendre; **d. features,** traits fins, délicats; **to have a d. touch,** avoir de la légèreté de touche, de doigté; (*of painter*) avoir un pinceau léger, délicat; (*of sculptor*) avoir un ciseau délicat; **to have a d. wit,** avoir l'esprit fin; **d. ear,** oreille délicate, fine, sensible; **d. piece of machinery,** mécanisme délicat; (*b*) **d. feelings,** sentiments délicats, raffinés; sentiments de délicatesse; (*c*) *A:* efféminé. **2.** difficile, délicat; **to handle a d. situation,** manier une situation délicate, difficile; **d. question,** question épineuse; **to tread on d. ground,** toucher à des questions délicates; *F:* marcher sur des œufs; **you are on d. ground,** vous risquez d'être indiscret; n'insistez pas. **3. d. health,** santé délicate, faible; **d. child,** enfant mièvre, chétif; **d. from childhood,** délicat dès son enfance; **to be d.,** être délicat; ne pas avoir de santé; *F: O:* **to be in a d. condition, in a d. state of health,** être enceinte, être dans un état intéressant; *Art:* **d. flesh tints,** chairs *f* morbides.

delicately [ˈdelikətli], *adv.* délicatement; avec délicatesse; *B:* **Agag came d. to him,** Agag vint à lui faisant le gracieux.

delicateness [ˈdelikətnis], *s.* = DELICACY 1.

delicatessen [delikəˈtes(ə)n], *s.* charcuterie *f*.

delicious [diˈliʃəs], *a.* exquis; (mets) délicieux.

deliciously [diˈliʃəsli], *adv.* délicieusement.

deliciousness [diˈliʃəsnis], *s.* goût délicieux (d'un mets); délices *fpl* (de l'oisiveté).

delict [ˈdi:likt], *s. Jur:* délit *m*; *used only in phr.*; **in flagrant d.,** en flagrant délit.

delight[1] [diˈlait], *s.* **1.** délices *fpl*, délice *m*, délectation *f*, bonheur *m*, plaisir *m*; **the fragrance of the flowers was a sheer d.,** le parfum des fleurs caressait délicieusement l'odorat; **it is a d. to hear him talk,** c'est un délice de l'entendre parler; **it is such a d. to . . .,** c'est si bon de . . .; **to be s.o.'s d.,** faire les délices, le bonheur, de qn. **2.** joie *f*; **much to the d. of . . ., to the great d. of . . .,** au grand plaisir de . . ., à la grande joie de . . .; **to my great d. I was allowed to . . .,** à ma grande joie on me permit de . . .. **3. to take d. in (doing) sth.,** aimer beaucoup (faire) qch.; trouver son bonheur dans, à faire, qch.; prendre grand plaisir à faire qch.

delight[2]. **1.** *v.tr.* enchanter, ravir, réjouir (qn); faire les délices de (qn); **music that delights the ears,** musique *f* qui charme les oreilles; **to d. the eye,** réjouir, charmer, flatter, le regard; **I shall be delighted to come,** je serai enchanté, ravi, de venir; ça me donnera grand plaisir de venir; je ne demande pas mieux que de venir; **I'm delighted with it,** j'en suis ravi, enchanté. **2.** *v.i.* **to d. in sth., in doing sth.,** se délecter à, de (qch.); aimer beaucoup (faire) qch.; se faire un plaisir, une joie, de faire qch.; trouver son bonheur dans, à faire, qch.; **she delights in her garden,** elle aime passionnément son jardin.

delighted [diˈlaitid], *a.* (air) ravi, rayonnant; (sourire) radieux.

delightedly [diˈlaitidli], *adv.* avec enchantement; avec délices; avec joie; **he looked at us d.,** il nous a regardés d'un œil ravi.

delightful [diˈlaitful], *a.* délicieux, ravissant; enchanteur, -eresse; charmant; **d. voice,** voix enchanteresse; **d. smile,** sourire ravissant; **d. sight,** spectacle *m* à ravir; **it is d. to live like this,** c'est un délice de vivre ainsi.

delightfully [diˈlaitfəli], *adv.* délicieusement; **she sings d.,** elle chante à ravir.

delignification [di:lignifiˈkeiʃ(ə)n], *s. Tchn:* délignification *f*.

delignify [di:ˈlignifai], *v.tr. Tchn:* délignifier.

Delilah [diˈlailə], *Pr.n.f.* Dalila.

delime [di:ˈlaim], *v.tr. Tan:* déchauler.

deliming [di:ˈlaimiŋ], *s. Tan:* déchaulage *m*.

delimit [di:ˈlimit], *v.tr.* délimiter, borner (un terrain, des pouvoirs, etc.); aborner (une frontière).

delimitation [dilimiˈteiʃ(ə)n], *s.* délimitation *f*; abornement *m* (d'une frontière).

delimiter [di:ˈlimitər], *s. Cmptr:* séparateur *m*, borne *f*, délimiteur *m*.

delimiting [di:ˈlimitiŋ], *s. Cmptr:* séparation *f*; **d. comma,** virgule *f* de séparation.

delineate [diˈlinieit], *v.tr.* **1.** tracer, décrire, dessiner au trait (un triangle, etc.). **2.** esquisser (un projet); donner un exposé sommaire (d'un procédé, etc.). **3.** dessiner, peindre (un paysage, les traits de qn); délinéer (un profil); **mountains clearly delineated on the horizon,** montagnes *f* qui se détachent clairement à l'horizon. **4.** tracer, décrire, peindre (verbalement) (le portrait de qn, etc.).

delineation [diliniˈeiʃ(ə)n], *s.* **1.** délinéation *f*; **d. of a character,** description *f*, peinture *f*, d'un caractère. **2.** tracé *m*, dessin *m*.

delineator [diˈlinieitər], *s.* **1.** (*pers.*) dessinateur *m*, délinéateur *m*. **2.** instrument traceur.

delink [di:ˈliŋk], *v.tr. Cmptr:* détacher.

delinquency [diˈliŋkwənsi], *s.* **1.** culpabilité *f*. **2.** (*a*) délit *m*, faute *f*; écart *m* de conduite; (*b*) *NAm:* défaut *m* de paiement. **3.** délinquance *f*; **juvenile d.,** criminalité *f*, délinquance, juvénile.

delinquent [diˈliŋkwənt], *a.* & *s.* **1.** délinquant, -ante; coupable (*mf*), contrevenant, -ante; **juvenile d.,** délinquant juvénile, enfant délinquant. **2.** *NAm:* **d. taxes,** impôts non payés.

deliquesce [deliˈkwes], *v.i.* **1.** *Ch:* tomber en déliquescence. **2.** fondre; s'en aller en eau.

deliquescence [deliˈkwesəns], *s.* déliquescence *f*; *F:* **the room was so hot that we were all in a state of d.,** la pièce était tellement surchauffée qu'on fondait à vue d'œil.

deliquescent [deliˈkwesənt], *a.* déliquescent.

deliquium [diˈlikwiəm], *s. Ph: A:* déliquium *m*.

delirious [diˈliriəs], *a.* (malade) en délire, dans le délire; délirant; (divagations) du délire; **to be d.,** avoir, être dans, le délire; délirer; **to become d.,** être pris de délire; tomber en délire; **d. with joy,** ivre, fou, délirant, de joie.

deliriously [diˈliriəsli], *adv.* frénétiquement; **d. happy,** fou de joie, délirant de joie.

delirium [diˈliriəm], *s.* délire *m*; **fit of d.,** accès *m* de délire; transport *m* au cerveau; **fever accompanied by d.,** fièvre délirante; **d. tremens,** delirium *m* tremens.

delitescence [deliˈtes(ə)ns], *s. Med:* délitescence *f* (d'une tumeur, etc.).

delitescent [deliˈtes(ə)nt], *a. Med:* caché, latent.

deliver [diˈlivər], *v.tr.* **1.** délivrer (**s.o. from sth.,** qn de qch.); **to d. s.o. from death,** sauver qn de la mort; arracher qn à la mort; *Ecc:* **d. us from evil,** délivre-nous du mal; **to d. s.o. from, out of, captivity,** (re)tirer qn de (la) captivité; mettre qn en liberté; **to d. s.o. from his enemies,** délivrer qn de ses ennemis. **2.** (*a*) *Obst:* **to d. a woman (of a child),** (faire) accoucher une femme; (*of a child or the after-birth*), délivrer une femme; (*b*) **to be delivered of a child,** accoucher d'un enfant; *A:* & *Lit:* **to be delivered of a sonnet, of an epigram,** accoucher d'un sonnet, d'une épigramme; (*c*) *Lit:* **to d. oneself of an opinion,** émettre, lancer, exprimer, une opinion; **when he had delivered himself thus . . .,** après s'être exprimé en ces termes . . .; **I have already delivered myself against the bill,** j'ai déjà dit tout ce que j'avais à dire contre ce projet. **3.** (*a*) **to d. s.o., sth., (up, over) to s.o.,** livrer, délivrer, qn, qch., à qn; **to d. s.o. into the hands of the enemy,** livrer qn aux mains de l'ennemi; **they were delivered over to execution,** ils furent livrés au bourreau, au supplice; **hunger compelled them to d. the fortress,** la faim les contraignit à rendre la place; (*b*) **to d. up,** restituer, rendre (**to,** à); **the fox delivered up its prey,** le renard a rendu, a abandonné, sa proie; **the thief delivered up the stolen rings,** le voleur a restitué les bagues volées; (*c*) **to d. over,** céder, transférer, transmettre (un bien, etc.) (**to,** à); **to d. over an estate to one's son,** se défaire d'un bien en faveur de son fils; transmettre un bien à son fils. **4.** remettre, rendre, délivrer (un paquet, un télégramme, etc.); distribuer (des lettres); livrer (des marchandises); rendre (des marchandises) à destination; *Jur:* signifier (un acte); **to d. sth. into s.o.'s charge,** confier qch. à qn, à la garde de qn, aux mains de qn; **to d. a message,** faire une commission; s'acquitter d'une commission; délivrer un message; **to d. sth. at s.o.'s house,** livrer qch. à domicile; **to d. milk (at the door),** porter le lait à domicile; *Com:* **delivered free,** rendu à domicile; livraison franco; **delivered on board,** rendu à bord; **goods delivered at any address,** livraison *f* à domicile; **to d. the goods,** (i) livrer les marchandises; (ii) *F:* remplir ses engagements; tenir parole; *Rail:* **to d. luggage,** remettre les bagages à domicile. **5.** porter, donner (un coup); lancer (un projectile, etc.); effectuer, lancer (une attaque, etc.); livrer (bataille); *Mil:* **to d. fire,** ouvrir le feu; *Navy:* **to d. a broadside,** envoyer, lâcher, une bordée; *Games:* **to d. the ball,** lancer la balle, le ballon. **6.** faire, prononcer (un discours); faire (une conférence); *Jur:* prononcer, rendre (un jugement). **7.** (*a*) *Mec.E: etc:* (*of engine*) **to d. normal power,** développer sa puissance normale; (*of pump, injector, etc.*) refouler (l'eau, etc.); (*of machine, dynamo, etc.*) débiter, fournir (du courant); **to d. current to a machine,** alimenter une machine en courant; (*b*) *Cer: Metall:* **to d. a pattern from the mould,** sortir un modèle du moule; (*with passive force*) (*of mould*) **to d. easily,** offrir de la dépouille.

deliverance [diˈliv(ə)rəns], *s.* **1.** délivrance *f*, libération *f* (**from,** de). **2.** déclaration *f*, expression *f* (d'opinion). **3.** *Jur: Scot:* (*a*) prononcé *m*, jugement *m*; (*b*) verdict *m* (du jury).

deliverer [diˈliv(ə)rər], *s.* **1.** libérateur, -trice; sauveur *m*. **2.** distributeur, -trice (de prospectus, etc.); livreur, -euse (de marchandises).

delivery [diˈliv(ə)ri], *s.* **1.** *Obst:* accouchement *m*, délivrance *f* (d'une femme). **2.** *A:* = DELIVERANCE 1. **3.** *Mil:* **d. of a town, of a prisoner,** reddition *f* d'une ville, d'un prisonnier. **4.** (*a*) **d. of a message,** exécution *f* d'une commission; (*b*) livraison *f*, délivrance, remise *f* (d'un paquet, etc.); remise (d'une lettre); distribution *f* (des lettres); *Jur:* **d. of a writ,** signification *f* d'un acte; **charge for d.,** (frais *m* de) port *m* (d'un télégramme, etc.); *Post:* **times of d.,** heures *f* d'arrivée; *U.S:* **general d.,** poste restante; **d. of goods,** livraison, (*from railway*) factage *m*, de marchandises; **parcels awaiting d.,** colis *m* en souffrance; **d. note,** bulletin *m* de livraison; **certificate of d.,** vu-arriver *m inv*; **d. of luggage,** remise de bagages à domicile; **for immediate d.,** à livrer de suite; **free d.,** livraison franco; **d. within a month,** délai *m* de livraison, un mois; **d. man, boy, girl,** livreur, -euse; **to pay on d.,** payer à, sur, livraison; payer au reçu; **d. date,** date *f* de livraison; **d. schedule,** calendrier *m* de livraison; **purchase for future d.,** achat *m* à terme; **notice of d.,** accusé *m* de réception; **d. price,** prix rendu; **to accept d. of sth.,** prendre qch. en recette; (*c*) *Fin:* **d. of stocks,** cession *f*, remise, de titres; **to take d. of stocks,** prendre livraison des titres; (*of stocks*) **for d.,** au comptant; **to sell for d.,** vendre à couvert; **sale for d.,** vente *f* à livrer; (*d*) *Jur:* tradition *f* (d'un bien, d'une marchandise); délivrance (d'un legs, etc.) (**to,** à). **5.** (*a*) *Games:* **d. of the ball,** (i) lancement *m*, envoi *m* (de la balle); (ii) manière *f* de lancer la balle; (*b*) *Mil:* lancement (d'un missile, d'une fusée, etc.); **d. unit,** (i) unité *f* de lancement (de missiles, de fusées, etc.); (ii) unité de livraison (des armes atomiques). **6.** (*a*) **d. of a speech,** prononciation *f* d'un discours; (*b*) débit *m*, diction *f* (d'un orateur); **to have a good d.,** avoir un bon débit; **his d. is calm,** il a la parole calme; **he had a very rapid d.,** il parlait toujours très vite. **7.** (*a*) distribution (de courant électrique, etc.); (*b*) débit (d'eau, de courant, etc.); refoulement *m* (d'une pompe); **d. valve,** soupape *f* de refoulement, de décharge; **d. pipe,** tuyau *m*, conduite *f*, d'amenée, d'arrivée, de refoulement; **d. hopper,** magasin *m* d'alimentation; *Mch: I.C.E: etc:* **d. tube,** ajutage *m*, ajutoir *m*; *I.C.E:* **d. space,** conque *f*; *Tex:* **d. roll,** cylindre délivreur; cylindre de décharge; *Cin: Cmptr:* **d. spool,** bobine débitrice, dérouleuse; *Typ:* **d. of the sheets (from the press),** sortie *f* des feuilles; *Metall:* **d. of the pattern (from the mould),** sortie du modèle.

dell [del], *s.* vallon *m*, combe *f*.

delocalization [di:loukəlaiˈzeiʃ(ə)n], *s.* délocalisation *f*.

delocalize [di:ˈloukəlaiz], *v.tr.* **1.** délocaliser (des intérêts, etc.). **2.** déplacer, envoyer au loin (des archives, etc.).

delorenzite [di:ləˈrenzait], *s. Miner:* delorenzite *f*.

Delos [ˈdi:lɔs], *Pr.n. Geog:* Délos *f*.

delouse [di:ˈlaus], *v.tr.* (*a*) ôter les poux de (qch., qn); épouiller (qn); (*b*) *Mil: F:* déminer (un terrain).

delousing [di:ˈlausiŋ], *s.* (*a*) épouillage *m*; *Adm: Mil:* **d. station,** poste *m* d'épouillage; (*b*) *Mil: F:* déminage *m*.

Delphi [ˈdelf(a)i], *Pr.n. Geog:* Delphes *f*.

Delphian [ˈdelfiən], **Delphic** [ˈdelfik], *a.* **1.** delphien; delphique; de Delphes; **the Delphic Oracle,** l'Oracle *m* de Delphes. **2.** *Lit:* obscur, sibyllin.

Delphin [ˈdelfin], *a.* **the D. classics,** les dauphins *m*; **D. edition,** édition dauphine, édition des dauphins; édition *ad usum Delphini.*

delphinapterus [delfinˈæptərəs], *s. Z:* bélouga *m*.

Delphinidae [delˈfinidi:], *s.pl. Z:* delphinidés *m*.

delphinin [ˈdelfinin], *s. Bio-Ch:* (*glycoside derived from larkspur*) *Ch:* delphinine *f*.

delphinine [ˈdelfini:n], *s. Bio-Ch:* (*alkaloid derived from stavesacre*) delphinine *f*.

delphinium [delˈfiniəm], *s. Bot:* delphinium *m*, *F:* pied-d'alouette *m*, *pl.* pieds-d'alouette; dauphinelle *f*.

delta [ˈdeltə], *s.* **1.** *Gr.Alph:* delta *m inv.* **2.** *Geog:* delta *m*, *pl.* deltas; **cone d.,** cône *m* de déjection; **fan d.,** cône d'éboulis. **3.** *El:* triangle *m*, delta; **d. connection,** montage *m* en triangle, en delta; **star d. connection,** montage en étoile-triangle; groupement *m* en étoile-triangle. **4.** *Ph:* **d. rays,** rayons *m* delta. **5.** *Metall:* **d. metal,** métal *m* delta (cuivre, zinc, et fer). **6.** *Av:* **d. wing,** aile *f* (en) delta.

deltaic [delˈteiik], *a.* deltaïque.

delthyrium [delˈθairiəm], *s. Moll:* delthyridium *m*.

deltidial [delˈtidiəl], *a. Moll:* deltidial.

deltidium [delˈtidiəm], *s. Moll:* deltidium *m*.

deltoid [ˈdeltɔid]. **1.** *a. Geog:* deltaïque; (feuille *f*)

deltoïde, en delta. **2.** *a. & s. Anat:* (muscle *m*) deltoïde *m.*
deltoidal [del'tɔidl], *a. Anat: Bot:* deltoïdien.
delude [di'l(j)u:d], *v.tr.* **1.** abuser, tromper (qn); induire (qn) en erreur; **to d. s.o. with vain promises,** abuser, bercer, qn de vaines promesses, par de fausses promesses; **his promises deluded us,** ses promesses nous ont fait illusion; **to d. oneself,** s'abuser, se faire illusion, s'illusionner; se leurrer d'illusions; **to d. oneself with false hopes,** se bercer, s'illusionner, se leurrer, de vaines espérances; **to d. oneself into the belief that . . .,** s'abuser au point de croire que . . .. **2.** duper (qn); en faire accroire à (qn); **to d. s.o. into a belief that . . .,** faire (ac)croire à qn que . . .; **to d. the public,** tromper le public.
deluge[1] ['delju:dʒ], *s.* déluge *m*; (*a*) **a d. of rain,** une pluie diluvienne; *B:* **the D.,** le Déluge; (*b*) **a d. of words, of tears,** un déluge de paroles, de larmes; **a d. of letters, of bills,** une avalanche de lettres, de notes.
deluge[2], *v.tr.* (*a*) inonder (**with,** de); (*b*) **to be deluged with letters, with bills, with requests,** être accablé de lettres, de notes; être assailli de demandes.
delusion [di'lu:ʒ(ə)n], *s.* **1.** illusion *f,* hallucination *f,* erreur *f*; **to be under a d.,** se faire illusion; s'abuser; être dans l'erreur; s'illusionner; **to suffer from delusions,** être sujet à des hallucinations; **delusions of grandeur,** folie *f* des grandeurs; **a fond d.,** une douce illusion. **2.** action *f* de tromper, de duper.
delusive [di'lu:siv], *a.* illusoire, illusionnant; trompeur, -euse.
delusively [di'lu:sivli], *adv.* illusoirement; trompeusement.
delusiveness [di'lu:sivnis], *s.* caractère illusoire, trompeur (d'une apparence, d'une promesse).
delusory [di'lu:səri], *a. Lit:* = DELUSIVE.
delustre [di'lʌstər], *v.tr. Tex:* délustrer.
de luxe [di'lʌks], *a.* **de l. hotel,** palace *m*; *Aut: etc:* **de l. model,** modèle *m* de luxe.
delvauxine [del'vɔksi:n], *s. Miner:* delvauxine *f.*
delve [delv]. **1.** *v.tr. A: & Lit:* (*a*) fouiller, creuser (le sol); (*b*) **to d. up, out,** déterrer, exhumer (un trésor, des faits). **2.** *v.i.* (*a*) *A: & Lit:* fouiller le sol; (*b*) (*of path, etc.*) s'abaisser; (*c*) **to d. into one's pocket for one's handkerchief,** fouiller dans sa poche pour y prendre son mouchoir; **to d. into the past,** fouiller, remonter, dans le passé.
demagnetization [di:mægnitai'zeiʃ(ə)n], *s.* démagnétisation *f*; désaimantation *f.*
demagnetize [di:'mægnitaiz]. **1.** *v.tr.* démagnétiser; désaimanter. **2.** *v.i.* se démagnétiser; se désaimanter.
demagnetizing [di:'mægnitaiziŋ], *s.* = DEMAGNETIZATION.
demagogic [demə'gɔgic], *a.* démagogique.
demagogism ['deməgɔgizm], *s.* démagogisme *m.*
demagogue ['deməgɔg], *s.* démagogue *m.*
demagogy ['deməgɔgi], démagogie *f.*
demand[1] [di'mɑ:nd], *s.* **1.** demande *f,* réclamation *f,* revendication *f,* requête *f*; *Jur:* sommation *f*; **to put down one's demands in writing,** coucher par écrit ses réclamations; **the demands of labour,** les revendications ouvrières; **payable on d.,** payable sur demande, à vue, à bureau ouvert, à présentation; **promissory note payable on d.,** billet *m* payable à volonté; **d. note** (*for rates, taxes*), feuille *f* de contributions; avertissement *m*; *Com:* **d. bill,** traite *f* à vue; *Fin:* **d. deposit,** dépôt *m* à vue; *Cmptr:* **d. processing,** traitement immédiat, à la demande. **2.** *Pol.E:* demande; **supply and d.,** l'offre *f* et la demande; **to be in (great, little) d.,** être (très, peu) demandé, recherché; **there is little d. for these goods,** ces marchandises *f* ont peu de vente, peu de débit; **there is a great d. for this line,** cet article a un écoulement considérable. **3.** *pl.* **demands,** nécessités *f*; exigences *f*; **moderate in one's demands on s.o.,** modéré envers qn; **to make great demands on s.o.'s energy, on s.o.'s good nature,** exiger de qn beaucoup d'énergie, de bonhomie; **you make too many demands on my patience,** vous abusez de ma patience; **I have many demands on my time,** je suis très pris; **his excessive demands,** ses prétentions excessives; **my just demands,** ce qui m'est dû.
demand[2], *v.tr.* **1. to d. sth. of, from, s.o.,** demander (formellement), réclamer, qch. à qn; exiger qch. de qn; **to d. to do sth.,** demander absolument à faire qch.; **to d. to know whether . . .,** insister pour savoir si . . .; **to d. that . . .,** demander, exiger, que + *sub*; **I demanded that the money be returned to me,** j'ai réclamé mon argent; **I d. it,** je le veux absolument; **to d. assistance,** requérir aide et assistance. **2.** (*of thg*) demander, exiger; **the matter demands great care,** l'affaire *f* demande, exige, réclame, beaucoup de soin; **the care which the situation demands,** les soins *m* que comporte la situation; **elementary prudence demands that . . .,** la simple prudence veut que + *sub.* **3.** *A:* demander; s'enquérir de (qch.); *Ecc:* **then the priest shall d. the name of the child,** puis le prêtre demandera le nom de l'enfant.
demandant [di'mɑ:ndənt], *s. Jur:* demandeur, -eresse; plaignant, -ante; réclamant, -ante.
demander [di'mɑ:ndər], *s.* **1.** *Pol.Ec:* acheteur, -euse; demandeur, -euse, preneur, -euse. **2.** *Jur:* = DEMANDANT.
demanding [di'mɑ:ndiŋ], *a.* (*a*) exigeant, accaparant, assujettissant; (*b*) revendicatif.
demantoid [di'mæntɔid], *s. Miner:* démantoïde *f.*
demarcate ['di:mɑ:keit], *v.tr.* **1.** délimiter (un terrain); aborner (une frontière). **2. to d. one subject from another,** tracer une ligne de démarcation entre un sujet et un autre.
demarcating ['di:mɑ:keitiŋ], *a.* démarcatif.
demarcation [di:mɑ:'keiʃ(ə)n], *s.* démarcation *f*; délimitation *f*; abornement *m* (d'une frontière); **line of d.,** ligne de démarcation, ligne démarcative; *Ind:* **d. dispute,** conflit industriel (au sujet du domaine d'activité de chaque corps de métier); *Cmptr:* **d. character,** caractère *m* de délimitation.
demarcator ['di:mɑ:keitər], *s.* délimitateur, -trice.
démarche [dei'mɑ:ʃ], *s.* démarche *f* (politique, diplomatique).
dematerialization [di:mətiəriəlai'zeiʃ(ə)n], *s.* dématérialisation *f*; *Atom.Ph:* annihilation *f.*
dematerialize [di:mə'tiəriəlaiz], *v.tr. & i.* (se) dématérialiser.
Dematiaceae [demæti'eisii:], *s.pl. Fung:* dématiacées *f.*
deme [di:m], *s. Biol:* dème *m.*
demean[1] [di'mi:n], *v.pr. A: & Lit:* **to d. oneself honourably, like a man of honour, etc.,** se conduire, se comporter, en homme d'honneur, etc.
demean[2], *v.tr.* (*usu. v.pr., and usu. with an affectation of grandiloquence*) **to d. oneself,** s'abaisser, se dégrader, s'avilir, se ravaler; **to d. oneself so far as to do sth.,** s'abaisser (jusqu'à) faire qch.
demeanour [di'mi:nər], *s.* façon *f* de se comporter; air *m,* tenue *f,* maintien *m*; **to have a fine d.,** avoir bon air, belle allure; **his supercilious d.,** son attitude hautaine.
dement[1] [di'ment], *v.tr. A:* rendre fou (qn); faire perdre la raison à (qn).
dement[2] ['di:ment, di'ment], *s. U.S:* dément, -ente; fou *m,* folle *f.*
demented [di'mentid], *a.* fou, *f.* folle; dément; en démence; **to become d.,** tomber en démence; **he was running like one d.,** il courait comme un fou; **a poor d. creature,** un pauvre dément, une pauvre démente.
dementedly [di'mentidli], *adv.* comme un fou; comme un affolé.
dementia [di'menʃiə], *s. Med:* démence *f*; **d. praecox,** démence précoce; **senile d.,** démence sénile.
Demerara [demə'rεərə], *Pr.n. Geog:* Demerara; **D. sugar** = cassonade *f*; *Bot:* **D. greenheart,** nectandra *m,* nectandre *m,* laurier marbré.
demerit [di:'merit], *s.* démérite *m*; **the merits and demerits of the case,** le pour et le contre de l'affaire.
demersal [di:'mə:s(ə)l], *a. Ich:* démersal, -aux.
demesh [di:'meʃ]. **1.** *v.tr.* désengrener. **2.** *v.i.* se désengrener (**from,** d'avec).
demesmerization [di:mezmərai'zeiʃ(ə)n], *s.* démagnétisation *f* (d'un hypnotisé).
demesmerize [di:'mezməraiz], *v.tr.* démagnétiser (un hypnotisé).
demesne [də'mein], *s.* **1.** *Jur:* possession *f*; **to hold sth. in d.,** posséder qch. (en toute propriété). **2.** domaine *m*; **d. of the Crown, Royal d.,** domaine de la Couronne; **State d.,** domaine de l'État; **d. lands,** terres domaniales. **3.** *Lit:* = DOMAIN.
Demeter [di'mi:tər], *Pr.n.f. Myth:* Déméter.
demethylate ['di:'meθileit], *v.tr. Ch:* déméthyliser.
Demetrius [di'mi:triəs], *Pr.n.m.* Démétrius.
demi- ['demi], *pref.* demi-.
demicannon ['demikæn(ə)n], *s. A.Artil:* demi-canon *m, pl.* demi-canons.
demicircle ['demisə:kl], *s. Surv:* demi-cercle *m, pl.* demi-cercles.
demigod ['demigɔd], *s.* demi-dieu *m, pl.* demi-dieux.
demijohn ['demidʒɔn], *s. Ind: etc:* dame-jeanne *f, pl.* dames-jeannes; bonbonne *f*; bouteille clissée (d'une contenance de 15 à 25 litres); tourie *f*; jacqueline *f*; bac *m* à acide.
demilitarization [di:milit(ə)rai'zeiʃ(ə)n], *s.* démilitarisation *f.*
demilitarize [di:'militəraiz], *v.tr.* démilitariser.
demilune ['demilu:n], *s. Fort:* demi-lune *f, pl.* demi-lunes.
demi-mondaine ['demi'mɔndein], *s.* demi-mondaine *f, pl.* demi-mondaines.
demi-monde ['demi'mɔ̃:(n)d], *s.* demi-monde *m.*
demineralization [di:minərəlai'zeiʃ(ə)n], *s.* déminéralisation *f.*
demineralize [di:'minərəlaiz], *v.tr.* déminéraliser *f.*
demi pension ['demi'penʃən], *s.* demi-pension *f, pl.* demi-pensions.
demisable [di'maizəbl], *a. Jur:* **1.** (*of land*) affermable. **2.** cessible; transmissible.
demi sang ['demi'sɑ̃:(g)], *s.* (*horse*) demi-sang *m inv.*
demise[1] [di'maiz], *s.* **1.** *Jur:* affermage *m* (d'un terrain); cession *f* à bail. **2.** *Jur:* cession, transmission *f* (par testament, etc.); transfert *m* (d'un titre, etc.); **d. of the crown,** transmission de la couronne. **3.** *Adm:* décès *m,* mort *f* (de qn).
demise[2], *v.tr. Jur:* **1.** céder à bail, affermer (une terre, etc.). **2.** (*a*) céder, transmettre (un bien, un titre, la couronne); (*b*) léguer (un bien).
demisemiquaver ['demisemikweivər], *s. Mus:* triple croche *f*; **d. rest,** demi-quart *m* de soupir.
demission [di'miʃ(ə)n], *s.* **1.** abdication *f* (**of,** de). **2.** démission *f.*
demist [di:'mist], *v.tr.* désembuer.
demister [di:'mistər], *s. Aut:* (dispositif) antibuée *m.*
demisting [di:'mistiŋ], *s.* désembuage *m.*
demit [di'mit] (**demitted**) (*a*) *v.tr.* **to d. office,** se démettre de ses fonctions; résigner sa charge, ses fonctions; remettre sa charge; (*b*) *v.i.* se démettre (de sa charge); démissionner; **they must either submit or d.,** il leur faudra se soumettre ou se démettre.
demitasse ['demitæs], *s. NAm:* (*a*) (petite) tasse à café; (*b*) tasse de café (noir).
demiurge ['demiə:dʒ], *s. A.Phil:* démiurge *m.*
demiurgic [demi'ə:dʒik], *a. A.Phil:* démiurgique.
demivolte ['demivɔlt], *s. Equit:* demi-volte *f, pl.* demi-voltes.
demo ['demo], *s. F:* manif *f.*
demob [di:'mɔb], *v.tr.* (**demobbed**) *F:* démobiliser.
demobilization [di:moubilai'zeiʃ(ə)n], *s.* (*F:* **demob**) démobilisation *f.*
demobilize [di:'moubilaiz], *v.tr. & i.* démobiliser.
democracy [di'mɔkrəsi], *s.* démocratie *f*; **people's d.,** démocratie populaire; **social d.,** social-démocratie *f.*
democrat ['deməkræt], *s.* **1.** démocrate *mf*; **social d.,** social-démocrate *mf, m.pl.* sociaux-démocrates; **Christian D.,** démocrate chrétien, -ienne; *coll.* **the Christian Democrats,** la démocratie chrétienne; *U.S:* **the Democrats,** le parti démocrate. **2.** *A.Veh: U.S:* **d. (waggon),** charrette anglaise à deux chevaux.
democratic [demə'krætik], *a.* démocratique; *U.S:* **D. Party,** parti *m* démocrate.
democratically [demə'krætik(ə)li], *adv.* démocratiquement.
democratism [di'mɔkrətizm], *s.* démocratisme *m.*
democratization [dimɔkrətai'zeiʃ(ə)n], *s.* démocratisation *f.*
democratize [di'mɔkrətaiz]. **1.** *v.tr.* démocratiser. **2.** *v.i.* se démocratiser.
Democritus [di'mɔkritəs], *Pr.n.m. Gr.Phil:* Démocrite.
démodé [dei'mɔdei], *a.* démodé.
demodectic [di:mə'dektik], *a. Vet:* démodécique; **d. mange,** démodécie *f.*
demodex ['di:mədeks], *s. Arach:* démodex *m.*
demodicosis [di:moudi'kousis], *s. Vet:* démodécie *f.*
demodulate [di:'mɔdjuleit], *v.tr. Elcs:* démoduler.
demodulation [di:mɔdju'leiʃ(ə)n], *s. Elcs:* démodulation *f.*
demodulator [di:'mɔdjuleitər], *s. Elcs:* démodulateur *m.*
Demogorgon [di:mou'gɔ:gən], *Pr.n.m. Myth:* Démogorgon.
demographer [di'mɔgrəfər], *s.* démographe *mf.*
demographic [demɔ'græfik], *a.* démographique; **d. survey,** enquête *f* démographique.
demography [di'mɔgrəfi], *s.* démographie *f.*
demoiselle [demwæ'zel], *s.* **1.** *Orn:* demoiselle *f* de Numidie. **2.** *Ent:* libellule *f,* demoiselle, agrion *m.*
demolish [di'mɔliʃ], *v.tr.* démolir; démanteler (des fortifications, etc.); **to d. s.o.'s arguments,** démolir les arguments de qn; démonter les batteries de qn; *F:* **he had soon demolished most of the tart,** il eut bientôt avalé, dévoré, les trois quarts de la tarte.
demolisher [di'mɔliʃər], *s.* démolisseur, -euse (**of,** dc).
demolition [demə'liʃ(ə)n, di:-], *s.* démolition *f*; **d. materials,** matériaux *m* de démolition; **d. contractor,** démolisseur *m*; *Mil:* **d. party, squad,** équipe chargée, détachement chargé, (d'effectuer) des destructions; **atomic d. munition, mine,** charge *f* nucléaire de démolition, de destruction; **d. fire,** tir *m* de destruction, à démolir; **d. bomb,** bombe de destruction, bombe explosive à effet de souffle.

demon [ˈdiːmən], *s.* **1.** (*a*) *Gr.Myth:* démon *m*, esprit *m*; (*b*) *Myth:* démon, génie *m*. **2.** (*a*) démon, diable *m*; **the D.,** le Démon, l'Esprit malin; **the d. of jealousy,** le démon de la jalousie; *F:* **that child's a little d.,** cet enfant est un petit démon; (*b*) (*intensive*) *F:* **he's a d. for work,** c'est un travailleur acharné; c'est un cheval à l'ouvrage, un bœuf pour le travail; **he's a d. at tennis,** c'est un as du tennis.
demonetization [diːmʌnitaiˈzeiʃ(ə)n], *s.* démonétisation *f*.
demonetize [diːˈmʌnitaiz], *v.tr.* démonétiser (une monnaie).
demoniac [diˈmouniæk], *a.* & *s.* démoniaque (*mf*); **d. frenzy,** frénésie *f* démoniaque, diabolique.
demoniacal [diːməˈnaiəkl], *a.* démoniaque; **d. possession,** possession *f* diabolique; **d. fury,** fureur *f* diabolique.
demonic [diːˈmɔnik], *a.* **1.** démoniaque, diabolique; du démon, de l'esprit malin. **2.** génial, -aux.
demonism [ˈdiːmənizm], *s. Rel.H:* démonisme *m*.
demonist [ˈdiːmənist], *s.* démoniste *m*.
demonolatry [diːməˈnɔlətri], *s.* démonolâtrie *f*.
demonologic(al) [diːmənəˈlɔdʒik(l)], *a.* démonologique.
demonologist [diːməˈnɔlədʒist], *s.* démonologue *mf*.
demonology [diːməˈnɔlədʒi], *s.* démonologie *f*.
demonomania [diːmənouˈmeiniə], *s. Psy:* démonomanie *f*.
demonry [ˈdiːmənri], *s. Rel.H:* pratique *f* du Démon; sorcellerie *f*.
demonstrability [dimɔnstrəˈbiliti], *s.* démontrabilité *f*.
demonstrable [diˈmɔnstrəbl, ˈdemən-], *a.* démontrable; susceptible de démonstration; *Phil:* **clearly d. proposition,** proposition *f* apodictique.
demonstrably [diˈmɔnstrəbli, ˈdemən-], *adv.* **statement d. true, false,** affirmation *f* dont la vérité, la fausseté, est susceptible de démonstration, peut être prouvée; affirmation dont la vérité s'impose.
demonstrate [ˈdemənstreit]. **1.** *v.tr.* (*a*) démontrer (une vérité); (*b*) décrire, expliquer (un système); **to d. an apparatus,** donner une démonstration pratique du fonctionnement d'un appareil; *Com:* **to d. a car,** montrer une voiture à un client; (*c*) *A:* manifester, témoigner (son émotion, etc.). **2.** *v.i.* (*a*) *Pol: etc:* manifester; faire une manifestation; prendre part à une manifestation; (*b*) *Mil:* faire une démonstration (pour dérouter l'ennemi).
demonstration [demənˈstreiʃ(ə)n], *s.* **1.** (*a*) démonstration *f* (d'une vérité); **proved to d.,** prouvé sans contredit, indiscutablement; (*b*) **practical d. (of an apparatus),** démonstration pratique (d'un appareil); **d. car, flight,** voiture *f*, vol *m*, de démonstration; *Cmptr:* **d. deck,** jeu *m* de démonstration; (*c*) *Sch:* **d. (class, lecture),** (séance *f* de) démonstration; **d. farm, forest,** ferme *f*, forêt *f*, d'étude. **2. demonstrations of love,** témoignages *m*, démonstrations, effusions *f*, de tendresse. **3.** (*a*) manifestation *f* (politique); **to make a d.,** manifester; (*b*) *Mil:* **to make a d. (in order to mislead the enemy),** faire une démonstration (pour dérouter l'ennemi).
demonstrative [diˈmɔnstrətiv], *a.* **1.** (argument, etc.) démonstratif; **action d. of a generous character,** action *f* qui démontre un caractère généreux. **2.** (*of pers.*) démonstratif, expansif. **3.** *Gram:* (adjectif, etc.) démonstratif. **4.** (vérité *f*, etc.) démontrable.
demonstratively [diˈmɔnstrətivli], *adv.* **1.** (prouver, etc.) démonstrativement. **2.** (accueillir qn) avec de grandes démonstrations d'amitié, avec effusion.
demonstrativeness [diˈmɔnstrətivnis], *s.* **1.** caractère démonstratif, expansif (de qn); expansivité *f*. **2.** démonstrations *f* de joie, d'amitié (de qn); sauts *m* de joie (d'un chien, etc.).
demonstrator [ˈdemənstreitər], *s.* **1.** démonstrateur, -trice; *Sch:* préparateur, -trice (d'un professeur de sciences, etc.); chargé, -ée, de travaux; **d. in, of, anatomy,** démonstrateur en anatomie; prosecteur *m*. **2.** manifestant, -ante (politique).
demoralization [dimɔrəlaiˈzeiʃ(ə)n], *s.* démoralisation *f*; **the army was in a state of utter d.,** l'armée était complètement démoralisée.
demoralize [diˈmɔrəlaiz], *v.tr.* **1.** dépraver, corrompre. **2.** démoraliser (les troupes, etc.); *Pol.Ec:* **the market has become demoralized,** le marché a perdu toute confiance, est démoralisé.
Demospongia, -giae [diːmouˈspɔndʒiə, -dʒiiː], *s.pl. Spong:* démosponges *m*.
Demosthenes [diˈmɔsθəniːz], *Pr.n.m. Gr.Hist:* Démosthène.
demote [diˈmout], *v.tr. Mil: Adm: Sch:* réduire à un grade inférieur, à une classe inférieure; faire descendre d'une classe.
demotic [diˈmɔtik], *a.* **1.** du peuple. **2.** *Pal:* (écriture *f*) démotique (des Égyptiens); *s.* **written in d.,** écrit en cursive *f* populaire. **3.** *a.* & *s. Ling:* démotique (*m*).
demotion [diˈmouʃ(ə)n], *s. Mil: Adm:* réduction *f* à un grade inférieur, à une classe inférieure, rétrogradation *f*.
demulcent [diˈmʌlsənt], *a.* & *s. Med:* adoucissant (*m*), émollient (*m*).
demulsification [diːmʌlsifiˈkeiʃ(ə)n], *s. Ch:* désémulsification *f*.
demulsify [diːˈmʌlsifai], *v.tr. Ch:* désémulsionner.
demulsifying [diːˈmʌlsifaiiŋ], *s. Ch:* désémulsification *f*.
demultiplexing [diːˈmʌltipleksiŋ], *s. Cmptr:* démultiplexage *m*.
demultiplying [diːˈmʌltiplaiiŋ], *a. Mec.E:* (*of gearing*) démultiplicateur, -trice.
demur[1] [diˈməːr], *s.* hésitation *f*; **to make no d.,** ne faire aucune difficulté, aucune objection; ne pas hésiter; **without d.,** sans faire d'objection; sans hésitation; **he made no further d.,** il n'opposa plus d'objection.
demur[2], *v.* (**demurred**) **1.** (*a*) *v.i.* faire des difficultés; manifester des scrupules; soulever des objections (**at, to,** contre); hésiter (devant); s'opposer (à); se refuser (à); **without demurring,** sans y regarder à deux fois; (*b*) *v.tr. A:* **I d. the inference,** je n'accepte pas cette conclusion. **2.** *v.i. Jur:* opposer, produire, une exception..
demure [diˈmjuər], *a.* (*used chiefly of young women*) **1.** posé(e), grave, sérieux, -euse; modeste, réservé(e). **2.** d'une modestie affectée; **d. manner, countenance,** manière composée, visage composé; **d. look,** petit air de sainte nitouche.
demurely [diˈmjuəli], *adv.* **1.** d'un air posé, modeste; gravement; avec réserve. **2.** avec une modestie affectée; sans vouloir avoir l'air; d'un air de sainte nitouche.
demureness [diˈmjuənis], *s.* **1.** gravité *f* de maintien (d'une jeune fille). **2.** modestie affectée; air *m* de sainte nitouche.
demurrable [diˈmʌrəbl], *a. Jur:* opposable.
demurrage [diˈmʌridʒ], *s.* **1.** *Nau:* (*a*) surestarie(s) *f*(*pl*); (*b*) indemnité *f* de, pour, surestaries. **2.** *Rail:* (*a*) magasinage *m*; (*b*) droits *mpl* de magasinage. **3.** *Fin:* retenue pour frais de fabrication (perçue sur l'or en barres versé à la Banque d'Angleterre).
demurrer [diˈmʌrər], *s. Jur:* exception *f* péremptoire; fin *f* de non-recevoir.
demy [diˈmai], *s.* **1.** *Paperm:* coquille *f*; (format) carré *m*. **2.** *Sch:* boursier *m* (de Magdalen College, Oxford) (qui autrefois avait droit à des demi-portions).
demystify [diːˈmistifai], *v.tr.* démystifier.
den [den], *s.* **1.** tanière *f*, antre *m*, repaire *m* (de bêtes féroces); repaire, caverne *f*; *F:* nid *m* (de brigands); *B:* **d. of lions,** fosse *f* aux lions; **d. of thieves,** retraite *f* de voleurs; coupe-gorge *m inv.* **2.** petite chambre privée; cabinet *m* de travail; fumoir *m*. **3.** bouge *m*, bauge *f*, taudis *m*; **gambling d.,** maison *f* de jeu, tripot *m*; **opium d.,** fumerie *f* d'opium.
denarius [diˈnɛəriəs], *s.* **1.** *Rom.Ant:* denier *m*. **2.** *A:* (*abbreviated* **d.**) = PENNY.
denary [ˈdiːnəri], *a. Mth:* (système *m*) dénaire; décimal, -aux.
denasalization [diːneizəlaiˈzeiʃ(ə)n], *s. Ling:* dénasalisation *f*.
denasalize [diːˈneizəlaiz], *v.tr. Ling:* dénasaliser; (*of vowel*) **to be denasalized,** se dénasaliser.
denatant [diːˈneitənt], *a. Ich:* qui suit le courant.
denationalization [diːnæʃnəlaiˈzeiʃ(ə)n], *s.* dénationalisation *f*.
denationalize [diːˈnæʃnəlaiz], *v.tr.* **1.** dénationaliser (qn). **2.** aliéner (une propriété) du domaine public; dénationaliser (une industrie).
denaturalization [diːnætjərəlaiˈzeiʃ(ə)n], *s.* dénaturalisation *f*.
denaturalize [diːˈnætjərəlaiz], *v.tr.* **1.** dénaturer (qch.). **2. to d. oneself,** se dénaturaliser, se dénationaliser.
denaturant [diːˈneitjərənt], *s.* dénaturant *m* (de l'alcool, etc.); **nuclear d.,** dénaturant nucléaire.
denaturation [diːneitjəˈreiʃ(ə)n], *s.* dénaturation *f* (de l'alcool, etc.).
denature [diːˈneitjər], **denaturize** [diːˈneitjəraiz], *v.tr.* dénaturer (un produit); **denatured alcohol,** alcool dénaturé.
denaturing[1] [diːˈneitjəriŋ], *a.* dénaturant.
denaturing[2], *s.* dénaturation *f*.
denazification [diːnɑːtsifiˈkeiʃ(ə)n], *s.* dénazification *f*.
denazify [diːˈnɑːtsifai], *v.tr.* dénazifier.
dendraspis [denˈdræspis], *s. Rept:* dendraspis *m*.
dendriform [ˈdendrifɔːm], *a.* dendriforme.
dendrite [ˈdendrait], *s. Miner: Cryst:* arborisation *f*, dendrite *f*.
dendritic [denˈdritik], *a. Miner:* dendritique; arborisé, herborisé; **d. markings,** arborisations *f* (de cristaux, etc.); **d. agate,** agate arborisée.
dendro- [ˈdendrou, denˈdrɔ], *pref.* dendro-.
Dendrobates [denˈdrɔbətiːz], *s. Amph:* dendrobate *m*, dendrobates *m*.
Dendrochirota [dendroukaiˈroutə], *s.pl. Echin:* dendrochirotes *m*.
dendrochronology [dendroukrəˈnɔlədʒi], *s. Archeol:* dendrochronologie *f*.
dendroctonus [denˈdrɔktənəs], *s. Ent:* dendroctone *m*.
dendrocygna [dendrouˈsignə], *s. Orn:* dendrocygne *m*, canard *m* d'arbre.
dendroeca [denˈdriːkə], *s. Orn:* dendroïque *m*.
dendrograph [ˈdendrougræf], *s.* dendromètre *m*.
dendrographic [dendrouˈgræfik], *a.* dendrographique.
dendrography [denˈdrɔgrəfi], *s.* (*a*) dendrographie *f*; (*b*) dendrométrie *f*.
dendroid [ˈdendrɔid], *a.* dendroïde.
dendrolagus [denˈdrɔləgəs], *s. Z:* dendrolague *m*, kangourou *m* arboricole.
dendrologist [denˈdrɔlədʒist], *s.* dendrographe *m*.
dendrology [denˈdrɔlədʒi], *s.* dendrologie *f*.
dendrometer [denˈdrɔmitər], *s.* dendromètre *m*.
dene[1] [diːn], *s. A:* dune(s) *f*(*pl*).
dene[2], *s.* vallon *m*.
denegation [diːniˈgeiʃ(ə)n], *s. A:* dénégation *f*.
denehole [ˈdiːnhoul], *s. Archeol:* puits artificiel qui débouche dans une caverne souterraine dans le calcaire.
denervate [diːˈnəːveit], *v.tr. Surg:* énerver.
denervation [diːnəːˈveiʃ(ə)n], *s. Surg:* énervation *f*.
dengue [ˈdeŋgi], *s. Med:* **d. (fever),** dengue *f*.
deniable [diˈnaiəbl], *a.* niable.
denial [diˈnaiəl], *s.* **1.** (*refusal*) déni *m*, refus *m*; **d. of justice,** déni de justice; **the d. of a hearing to Mr X was a serious blunder,** le refus d'entendre M. X a été une grosse faute; **I will take no d.,** il faut absolument que vous veniez, que vous le fassiez, etc. **2.** dénégation *f*, démenti *m* (de la vérité de qch.); **d. of responsibility,** dénégation de responsabilité; **absolute d.,** dénégation absolue; **to give a formal d. to a statement,** opposer un démenti formel à une affirmation. **3.** *B:* **Peter's d.,** le reniement de saint Pierre. **4.** *Mil:* interdiction *f*; **the d. of vital areas to the enemy,** l'interdiction à l'ennemi des zones essentielles; **d. of penetration,** interdiction de survol.
denicotine, dinicotinize [diːˈnikətiːn, -tiːnaiz], *v.tr.* dénicotiniser.
denicotinizing [diːnikətiːˈnaiziŋ], *s.* dénicotinisation *f*.
denier[1] [diˈnaiər], *s.* dénégateur, -trice.
denier[2] [ˈdeniər], *s. Tex:* (*hosiery*) denier *m*; **a 30 denier stocking,** un bas 30 deniers.
denigrate [ˈdenigreit], *v.tr. Lit:* (*a*) noircir (la réputation de qn); diffamer (qn); (*b*) dénigrer (qn, un projet).
denigration [deniˈgreiʃ(ə)n], *s. Lit:* (*a*) diffamation *f*; (*b*) dénigrement *m*.
denigrator [ˈdenigreitər], *s. Lit:* (*a*) diffamateur, -trice; (*b*) dénigreur, -euse.
denim [ˈdenim], *s.* **1.** *Tex:* croisé *m* de coton; tissu (grossier) de coton sergé. **2.** *pl. Cost:* **denims,** bleus *m* (de travail), *Mil:* treillis *m*.
denitrate [diːˈnaitreit], *v.tr. Ch: Ind: Agr:* dénitrifier, désazoter (la terre, etc.).
denitration [diːnaiˈtreiʃ(ə)n], **denitrification** [diːnaitrifiˈkeiʃ(ə)n], *s. Ch: Ind: Agr:* dénitrification *f*, désazotation *f*.
denitrator [diːˈnaitreitər], *s. Ind:* dénitreur *m*; **d. tower,** tour, colonne, dénitrante.
denitrify [diːˈnaitrifai], *v.tr. Ch: Ind: Agr:* dénitrifier, désazoter.
denization [deniˈzeiʃ(ə)n], *s. A:* octroi *m* (à un étranger) de petites lettres de naturalisation.
denizen[1] [ˈdeniz(ə)n], *s.* **1.** *Poet:* citoyen, -enne; habitant, -ante; **denizens of the forest,** hôtes *m*, habitants, des bois. **2.** *A:* étranger admis à la *denization*; titulaire *m* de petites lettres de naturalisation. **3.** (*a*) animal acclimaté, plante acclimatée; (*b*) mot (étranger) naturalisé, adopté dans la langue.
denizen[2], *v.tr. A:* accorder à (qn) les droits de *denization*; donner le droit de cité à (un étranger).
denizenship [ˈdenizənʃip], *s. A:* état *m* de demi-naturalisé; bénéfice *m* de la "denization."
Denmark [ˈdenmɑːk], *Pr.n. Geog:* Danemark *m*; **in D.,** au Danemark.
denominate [diˈnɔmineit], *v.tr.* dénommer.
denominating [diˈnɔmineitiŋ], *s.* dénommement *m*.
denomination [dinɔmiˈneiʃ(ə)n], *s.* **1.** dénomination *f*, dénommement *m*; **they were known under all these denominations,** on leur attribuait tous ces noms, toutes ces dénominations. **2.** (*sect*) culte *m*, communion *f*, secte *f*, confession *f*; **meeting attended by all**

sects and denominations, réunion à laquelle ont assisté des membres de toutes les sectes et de toutes les confessions. **3.** (*a*) (*class, category*) *Mth:* **to reduce fractions to the same d.,** réduire des fractions au même dénominateur; *Fin:* **fractional shares in denominations of multiples of ten pounds,** coupures *f* de diix livres et multiples; **money of small denominations,** (i) petite monnaie, (ii) coupures; **coins of all denominations,** pièces *f* de toutes valeurs; **(notes of) small, large, denominations,** petites, grosses, coupures; (*b*) unité *f* (de poids, de mesure, etc.); **in measures of length the smallest d. is the millimetre,** dans les mesures de longueur la plus petite unité est le millimètre.

denominative [di'nɔminətiv], *a.* dénominatif.

denominator [di'nɔmineitər], *s. Mth:* dénominateur *m*; **common d.,** dénominateur commun.

denotation [diːnou'teiʃ(ə)n], *s.* **1.** indication *f*; désignation *f* **(of sth. by sth.,** de qch. par qch.). **2.** *Lit:* **denotations of an uneasy conscience,** signes *m*, indices *m*, d'une conscience troublée. **3.** (*a*) signification *f* (d'un mot); (*b*) *Log:* dénotation *f*; extension *f* (d'un terme).

denotative [di'noutətiv], *a.* **1.** (signe, etc.) indicatif **(of,** de). **2.** *Log:* (*of meaning, etc.*) extensif.

denote [di'nout], *v.tr.* **1.** dénoter, marquer, montrer; **face that denotes energy,** visage *m* qui dénote l'énergie; **signs that d. that a crisis is approaching,** signes qui annoncent une crise, qui indiquent, dénotent, qu'une crise se prépare; signes avant-coureurs d'une crise; **here everything denotes peace,** ici tout respire la paix. **2.** (*a*) signifier; (*b*) *Log:* (*of term*) s'étendre à (plusieurs objets, etc.).

dénouement [dei'nuːmɑ̃ː(ŋ)], *s.* dénouement *m*.

denounce [di'nauns], *v.tr.* **1.** (*a*) dénoncer (un criminel, un crime); **to d. one's accomplices,** dénoncer, informer contre, ses complices; **to d. s.o. to the authorities,** déférer qn à la justice, en justice; signaler qn à la justice; (*b*) démasquer (un imposteur, etc.); dévoiler (une fourberie); (*c*) **to d. s.o. as an impostor,** taxer qn d'imposture; **this doctrine is denounced as erroneous,** on taxe d'erreur cette doctrine. **2.** invectiver contre, tonner contre (une hérésie, etc.); s'élever contre (un abus); faire le procès (d'un ministre, etc.); condamner (l'art moderne, etc.); exposer (qn) à la vindicte publique. **3.** *A:* annoncer, prédire (un malheur); prononcer (une peine, un jugement); crier (vengeance). **4. to d. a treaty, a truce,** dénoncer un traité, une trêve.

denouncer [di'naunsər], *s.* dénonciateur, -trice.

de novo [diː'nouvou], *Lt.adv.phr.* à nouveau.

dense [dens], *a.* **1.** (*a*) *Ph:* (*of body, metal, etc.*) dense, *Mth:* **d. set,** ensemble *m* dense; (*b*) *Cmptr:* condensé, dense; **d. binary code,** code binaire saturé. **2.** (*of smoke, etc.*) épais, aisse; **d. darkness,** obscurité profonde; **d. fog,** brouillard épais; *F:* brouillard à couper au couteau; **d. crowd,** foule compacte; **d. population,** population nombreuse, dense; **cloth of d. texture,** étoffe *f* à trame serrée; *For:* **d. crop,** peuplement serré. **3.** stupide, bête; **d. ignorance,** ignorance crasse; **d. mind,** esprit lourd, obtus, bouché; **I am not any denser than anyone else,** je ne suis pas plus bouché qu'un autre. **4.** *Phot:* **d. negative,** cliché *m* opaque, dense, intense.

densely ['densli], *adv.* **1. d. wooded country,** pays couvert de forêts épaisses; **d. crowded streets,** rues *f* où se presse une foule compacte; **d. populated region,** région très peuplée. **2. d. ignorant,** d'une ignorance crasse. **3.** *F:* (agir, etc.) stupidement.

denseness ['densnis], *s.* **1.** épaisseur *f* (du brouillard); encombrement *m* (de la circulation). **2.** stupidité *f*.

densher, denshire ['denʃər], *v.tr. Agr: A:* brûler, écobuer (le sol) (pratique originaire du Devonshire); **patch of denshered land,** brûlis *m*.

denshering ['denʃəriŋ], *s. Agr: A:* brûlage *m*, écobuage *m*.

densify ['densifai], *v.tr.* densifier; **densified wood,** bois densifié.

densimeter [den'simitər], *s.* densimètre *m* (à gaz, etc.).

densimetric [densi'metrik], *a.* densimétrique.

densimetry [den'simitri], *s.* densimétrie *f*.

densitometer [densi'tɔmitər], *s.* **1.** densimètre *m*. **2.** *Phot:* densitomètre *m*.

density ['densiti], *s.* **1.** densité *f*; (*a*) *Ph:* **average, mean, d.,** densité moyenne; **gravimetric d.,** densité gravimétrique; *Ch:* **deposition d.,** densité de précipitation; (*b*) *El: Elcs:* **pulse d.,** densité d'impulsion; *Rec: etc:* **tape d., recording d.,** densité d'enregistrement; *Cmptr:* **bit d.,** densité en (nombre de) bits; (*c*) *Atom.Ph::* **collision d.,** densité de chocs; **slowing-down d.,** densité de ralentissement; **radiant-flux d.,** densité du flux de radiation(s); **ion, neutron, d.,** densité ionique, neutronique. **2.** (*a*) épaisseur *f* (du brouillard, de la fumée, etc.); compacité *f* (du sol, etc.); densité (de la population); densité (de la circulation routière); (*b*) *Mil:* densité (du feu, du tir, des coups, des points d'impact); **d. of target,** densité de l'objectif. **3.** (*of pers.*) stupidité *f*. **4.** *Phot:* densité, opacité *f* (d'un cliché); intensité *f* de noircissement.

dent[1] [dent], *s.* (*a*) marque *f* de coup; bossellement *m*, bosselure *f* (d'une théière, etc.); creux *m*, renfoncement *m*; fistule *f* (dans la boiserie); **to remove the dents from an object,** débosseler un objet; (*b*) brèche *f*, hoche *f* (dans une lame); *F:* **to make a d. in one's fortune,** faire une brèche à sa fortune.

dent[2], *v.tr.* (*a*) bosseler, bossuer, cabosser; (*b*) ébrécher, hocher (une lame).

dental ['dentl], *a.* **1.** (pulpe *f*, etc.) dentaire; **d. formula,** formule *f* dentaire; **d. plate,** prothèse *f* dentaire; **d. surgery,** chirurgie *f* dentaire; **d. surgeon,** chirurgien *m* dentiste; **d. student,** étudiant, -ante, en dentisterie; **d. practice, surgery,** *NAm:* **office,** cabinet *m* de dentiste; **d. hospital** = institut *m* dentaire; **d. school,** école *f* dentaire; **d. mechanic, technician,** mécanicien-dentiste *m*, *pl.* mécaniciens-dentistes. **2.** *Ling:* dental, -aux; **d. consonant,** (consonne) dentale *f*; **d. r,** r cacuminale.

dentalium [den'teiliəm], *s. Moll:* dentale *m*.

dentaria [den'tɛəriə], *s. Bot:* dentaire *f*.

dentary ['dentəri], *a. Anat:* (arcade *f*, etc.) dentaire.

dentate ['denteit], *a.* **1.** *Z:* denté. **2.** *Bot:* dentelé, denté.

dentation [den'teiʃ(ə)n], *s.* dentelure *f*.

dented ['dentid], *a.* **1.** bosselé, cabossé; *Aut:* **d. wing,** aile bossuée, bosselée, faussée. **2.** (*a*) ébréché; (*b*) dentelé.

dentex ['denteks], *s. Ich:* denté *m*.

denticle ['dentikl], *s.* **1.** (*small tooth*) denticule *m*. **2.** *Arch:* denticule *m*.

denticular [den'tikjulər], **denticulate(d)** [den'tikjuleit(id)], *a.* denticulé, découpé; garni de denticules.

denticulation [dentikju'leiʃ(ə)n], *s.* dentelure *f*.

dentiform ['dentifɔːm], *a.* dentiforme.

dentifrice ['dentifris], *s.* dentifrice *m*.

dentil ['dentil], *s. Arch:* denticule *m*; **d. moulding, band, cornice,** denticules.

dentine ['dentiːn], *s. Anat:* dentine *f*; substance éburnée.

dentist ['dentist], *s.* dentiste *mf*; **dentist's chair,** fauteuil *m* de dentiste; **to go to the dentist's,** aller chez le dentiste.

dentistry ['dentistri], *s.* dentisterie *f*; art *m* du dentiste, art dentaire.

dentition [den'tiʃ(ə)n], *s.* **1.** (*teething*) dentition *f*; poussée *f* dentaire. **2.** *Anat:* dentition; arrangement *m* des dents.

denture ['dentjər], *s.* **1.** *Z:* denture *f*. **2.** (*of artificial teeth*) dentier *m*; prothèse *f* dentaire; pièce *f* dentaire; denture artificielle; *F:* râtelier *m*.

denunclearization [diːnjuːkliərai'zeiʃ(ə)n], *s.* dénucléarisation *f*.

denuclearize [diː'njuːkliəraiz], *v.tr.* dénucléariser.

denudation [diːnjuː'deiʃ(ə)n], *s.* dénudation *f*; mise *f* à nu; *Geol:* érosion *f*, ablation *f*; *For: etc:* enlèvement *m* de la couverture; dénudation du terrain.

denudative [di'njuːdətiv], *a.* dénudant, de dénudation.

denude [di'njuːd], *v.tr.* dénuder (qch.); mettre (qch.) à nu; **tree denuded of leaves,** arbre dénudé; **denuded mountains,** montagnes mises à nu, dénudées, pelées.

denunciation [dinʌnsi'eiʃ(ə)n], *s.* **1.** dénonciation *f*, délation *f* (d'un complice, etc.), dévoilement *m* (d'une fourberie). **2.** (*a*) condamnation *f* (d'un abus, de l'art moderne, etc.); (*b*) accusation publique (de qn). **3.** *A:* prédication *f*, annonce *f* (du malheur, etc.). **4.** dénonciation (d'un traité, d'une trêve).

denunciative [di'nʌnsiətiv], **denunciatory** [dinʌnsi'eitəri, di'nʌnsiətri], *a.* **1.** (écrit *m*, etc.) dénonciateur, -trice. **2.** (discours *m*, etc.) condamnatoire; *Ecc: Jur:* (décret *m*, etc.) comminatoire.

denunciator [di'nʌnsieitər], *s.* **1.** dénonciateur, -trice (d'un coupable, etc.). **2.** condamnateur *m* (des abus).

denutrition [diːnjuː'triʃ(ə)n], *s. Med:* dénutrition *f*.

deny [di'nai], *v.tr.* **1.** nier (un fait, une vérité); démentir (une nouvelle); *Jur:* dénier (un crime); repousser (une accusation); **to d. a statement,** opposer un démenti à une déclaration; **I don't, cannot, d. it,** je n'en disconviens pas; je n'en déconviens pas; je ne m'en défends pas; **the accused denies the charge,** l'accusé nie; **defendant denied the words,** le défendeur nia avoir prononcé ces paroles; **to d. having done sth.,** nier avoir fait qch.; se défendre d'avoir fait qch.; **to d. that this is so, to d. this to be so,** nier qu'il en soit ainsi; disconvenir que cela (ne) soit; **to d. that s.o. has any talent,** refuser tout talent à qn; **I don't d. that he is clever,** je ne disconviens pas qu'il est intelligent, qu'il ne soit intelligent; **I do not d. that we have common interests,** je ne nie pas que nous ayons, que nous ayons, des intérêts communs; **I cannot d. (but) that you are right,** je ne saurais nier que vous n'ayez raison; **there is no denying the fact,** c'est un fait indéniable; **I do not d. the fact that. . .,** j'apprécie le fait que . . .; **there's no denying it,** il n'y a pas à le nier; il n'y a pas de contradiction possible; **there's no denying that. . .,** pas moyen de nier, on ne saurait nier, que . . .; **one can hardly d. that these concessions are dangerous,** on ne saurait nier que ces concessions soient dangereuses. **2.** (*a*) renier (qn, sa foi); **to d. God,** nier Dieu; nier l'existence de Dieu; **those who d. Providence,** les négateurs *m* de la Providence; (*b*) **to d. one's signature,** démentir, désavouer, sa signature; **to d. an agreement,** renier un contrat. **3. to d. s.o. sth., sth. to s.o.,** refuser qch. à qn; **to d. the door to s.o.,** fermer sa porte à qn; **to d. a request,** refuser une prière; **if I am denied . . .,** si l'on m'oppose un refus . . .; **to be denied one's request,** se voir refuser sa demande; **to be denied a right,** se voir frustré d'un droit; **this was denied (to) me, I was denied this,** on me l'a refusé; **he was denied access to the Queen,** on ne le laissa pas approcher de la Reine; **he is not to be denied,** il le veut à tout prix; il n'acceptera pas de refus; **to d. access, admission, to . . .,** interdire l'accès à . . .; *Mil:* **to d. the Baltic to the enemy,** interdire à l'ennemi l'accès de la Baltique. **4.** (*a*) **to d. oneself sth.,** se refuser qch.; se priver de qch.; **to d. oneself nothing,** ne se faire faute de rien; (*b*) **to d. oneself,** faire abnégation de soi-même; **to d. oneself for one's children,** se priver pour ses enfants.

deobstruant [diːɔb'struənt], *a. & s. Med:* désobstruant (*m*), désobstructif, -ive.

deodar ['diːoudɑːr], *s. Bot:* **d. (cedar),** déodar *m*, déodore *m*, cèdre *m* de l'Himalaya.

deodara [diːou'dɑːrə], *s. Bot:* = DEODAR.

deodorant [diː'oudərənt], *s.* désodorisant *m*; **d. stick,** bâtonnet désodorisant.

deodorization [diːoudərai'zeiʃ(ə)n], *s.* désodorisation *f*; enlèvement des odeurs malsaines.

deodorize [diː'oudəraiz], *v.tr.* désodoriser.

deodorizer [diː'oudəraizər], *s.* désodorisateur *m*, désodorisant *m*.

deodorizing [diː'oudəraiziŋ], *s.* = DEODORIZATION.

de-oil [diː'ɔil], *v.tr.* déshuiler.

de-oiling [diː'ɔiliŋ], *s.* deshuilage *m*.

deontological [diːɔntou'lɔdʒikl], *a. Phil:* déontologique.

deontology [diːɔn'tɔlədʒi], *s. Phil:* déontologie *f*.

deoxid(iz)ation [diːɔksi'deiʃ(ə)n, diːɔksidai'zeiʃ(ə)n], *s. Ch:* désoxydation *f*.

deoxidize [diː'ɔksidaiz], *v.tr. Ch: Ind:* désoxyder; **deoxidizing agent,** désoxydant *m*.

deoxidizer [diː'ɔksidaizər], *s.* désoxydant *m*.

deoxy- [di(ː)'ɔksi], *pref.* désoxy-.

deoxycorticosterone [diɔksi'kɔːtikou'steroun], **deoxycortone** [diɔksi'kɔːtoun], *s. Bio-Ch:* désoxycorticostérone *f*.

deoxygenate [diː'ɔksidʒəneit], *v.tr. Ch: Ind:* désoxyder.

deoxygenating [diː'ɔksidʒəneitiŋ], **deoxygenation** [diɔksidʒə'neiʃ(ə)n], *s.* désoxygénation *f*.

deoxygenize [diː'ɔksidʒənaiz], *v.tr.* désoxygéner.

deoxyribonuclease [diɔksiribou'njuːklieis], *s. Bio-Ch:* désoxyribonucléase *f*.

deoxyribonucleic [diɔksiribou'njuːkliik], *a. Bio-Ch:* désoxyribonucléique.

deoxyribose [diɔksi'ribous], *s. Bio-Ch:* désoxyribose *m*.

depart [di'pɑːt], *v.i.* **1.** (*a*) s'en aller, partir; (*of train*) partir; **to d. from a place,** quitter un lieu; s'éloigner d'un lieu; **to be on the point of departing,** être sur son départ; (*b*) mourir; **to d. (from) this life,** quitter cette vie; quitter ce monde; sortir de la vie; partir de ce monde. **2.** (*diverge*) **to d. from one's duty,** se départir, s'écarter, de son devoir; **to d. from a rule,** sortir d'une règle; se départir d'une règle; **to d. from a custom,** déroger à un usage; **to d. from one's subject,** sortir de son sujet; **without ever departing from one of his principles,** sans jamais démordre d'un de ses principes.

departed [di'pɑːtid], *a.* **1.** (*of glory, etc.*) passé, évanoui. **2.** mort, défunt, décédé, disparu; *s.* **the d.,** le mort, la morte, etc.; **to pray for the souls of the d.,** prier pour les âmes des trépassés.

department [di'pɑːtmənt], *s.* **1.** (*a*) *Adm: etc:* département *m*, service *m*; branche *f* (d'une compagnie d'assurances, etc.); **(capital-)issue d.,** service des émissions; **personnel d.,** service du personnel; *Ind: etc:* **accounts d.,** service de la comptabilité; **purchasing d.,** service des achats; **dispatch d.,** service des expéditions; **supply, equipment, d.,** service du matériel; **design d.,** bloc *m* technique; *Trans:* **traffic d.,** service de l'exploitation; *Rail:* **permanent way d.,** service de la voie; **locomotive d.,** service de la traction; *Med: (in hospital)* **surgical d.,** service de chirurgie; **out-patients' d.,** service des consultations externes; **head of d.,** chef *m* de service; **to solve a problem between the departments concerned,** résoudre un problème interdépartementalement; (*b*) *Mil:* **A, I, G, Q, Department,** Premier, Deuxième, Troisième, Quatrième, Bureau; *Navy:* **Naval Personnel D.,** Premier Bureau; **Administrative Planning D.,** Quatrième Bureau; (*c*) *Com: (in shop)* rayon *m*; comptoir *m*; **glove d.,** rayon des gants; **d. store,** grand magasin, magasin à rayons multiples; (*d*) **that's not (really) my d.,** ce n'est pas mon rayon. **2.** ministère *m*; **D. of Education and Science** = Ministère de l'Éducation; *U.S:* **War D.,** Ministère de la Guerre. **3.** *Geog: (in Fr.)* département.

departmental [di:pɑ:t'mentl], *a.* (*a*) départemental, -aux; qui se rapporte à un service; **d. committee,** commission ministérielle; **d. manager,** chef *m* de service; (*b*) **d. store,** grand magasin, magasin à rayons multiples.

departmentalization [di:pɑ:tmentəlai'zeiʃ(ə)n], *s.* division *f* en services (d'une administration, d'une entreprise); division en rayons (d'un magasin); compartimentage *m* (de la connaissance).

departmentalize [di:pɑ:t'mentəlaiz], *v.tr.* diviser (une administration, une entreprise) en services, (un magasin) en rayons.

departmentally [di:pɑ:t'mentəli], *adv.* départementalement.

departure [di'pɑ:tjər], *s.* **1.** départ *m* (de qn, d'un train, d'un autobus, etc.); *Trans:* **departures,** départs; *Av:* **d. lounge,** départs: salle *f* d'attente; **to take one's d.,** s'en aller, partir; prendre congé. **2.** déviation *f* (d'un principe); dérogation *f* (à une loi); **departures from the general rule,** exceptions *f* à la règle générale; **d. from the truth,** manquement *m* à la vérité; **that is an obvious d. from the truth,** c'est s'écarter manifestement de la vérité; **a d. from his usual habits,** action *f,* procédé *m,* contraire à ses habitudes. **3. a new d.,** une nouvelle tendance, direction, orientation; une nouveauté; **computerization will be a new d. for the firm,** l'emploi *m* des ordinateurs ouvrira des horizons nouveaux, donnera une nouvelle orientation, à l'entreprise. **4.** *Nau:* (*a*) chemin *m* est et ouest; (*b*) point *m* de départ; **to take (a bearing of) the d.,** prendre le point de départ.

depauperize [di:'pɔ:pəraiz], *v.tr.* (*a*) (re)tirer (qn) de l'indigence; (*b*) abolir l'indigence, le paupérisme, dans (une région).

depend [di'pend], *v.i.* **1.** *A: & Poet:* pendre (**from,** à); être suspendu (à). **2.** dépendre (**on,** de); **it depends on you whether you succeed,** il dépend de vous de réussir, que vous réussissiez; **that depends entirely on you,** cela ne tient qu'à vous; **that depends, it all depends,** cela dépend, *F:* c'est selon; **the service depends on the number of travellers,** le service est subordonné au nombre des voyageurs; **the whole of human life depends on chance,** toute la vie humaine roule sur des probabilités; **it depends on whether you are in a hurry or not,** cela dépend si vous êtes pressé ou non; **it depends on whether he's married (or not),** ça dépend s'il est marié; **depending on whether . . .,** suivant que . . .. **3.** (*a*) **to d. on s.o.,** (i) *A:* vivre sous la protection de qn; (ii) être à la charge de qn; (iii) recevoir une pension de qn; (*b*) **to d. on imports from abroad,** être tributaire de l'étranger; **she depends on her piano for her livelihood,** elle n'a que son piano pour vivre; **to d. on oneself,** voler de ses propres ailes. **4.** (*rely*) **to d. on s.o., sth.,** compter sur, se reposer sur, s'appuyer sur, se fier à, avoir confiance en, qn, qch.; **you can d. on him,** vous pouvez avoir confiance en lui, compter sur lui; **you can never d. on his being on time,** on ne peut jamais se fier à sa ponctualité; **you can never d. on what he says,** on ne peut pas se fier à ce qu'il dit; **you can d. on him to help you,** vous pouvez compter sur lui pour vous aider; **you can d. on it that what I say is true,** soyez certain que je dis la vérité; **d. (up)on it,** comptez là-dessus, soyez-en sûr, croyez-le bien; vous pouvez m'en croire. **5.** *Jur: (of suit, bill)* être pendant.

dependability [dipendə'biliti], *s.* (*a*) confiance *f* que l'on inspire; **his great quality is his d.,** sa grande qualité, c'est qu'on peut compter sur lui; (*b*) sécurité *f* (de fonctionnement), fiabilité *f* (d'une machine).

dependable [di'pendəbl], *a.* (*of pers.*) digne de confiance; sûr; (*of information*) sûr, bien fondé; **d. machine,** machine *f* d'un fonctionnement sûr, d'une sécurité absolue; **he is not d.,** on ne peut pas se fier à lui, compter sur lui.

dependably [di'pendəbli], *adv.* d'une manière (i) digne de confiance, (ii) digne de foi.

dependant [di'pendənt], *s.* (*a*) *O:* protégé, -ée; (*b*) pensionnaire *mf* (de qn); (*c*) personne *f* à charge; **dependants,** (i) *O:* domesticité *f*; (ii) charges *f* de famille.

dependence [di'pendəns], *s.* **1.** (*a*) **d. on s.o., on sth.,** dépendance *f* de qn, de qch.; sujétion *f* à qn, à qch.; **d. of an effect upon a cause,** subordination *f* d'un effet à une cause; **he aimed at freeing the Crown from its d. on Parliament,** il visait à affranchir la Couronne de toute dépendance du Parlement; (*b*) **d. on s.o.,** le fait d'être à la charge de qn. **2.** confiance *f* (**on,** en); **to place d. on s.o., on s.o.'s word,** se fier à qn, aux paroles de qn. **3.** *Med:* assuétude *f.*

dependency [di'pendənsi], *s.* **1.** *A:* dépendance *f* (de qn, de qch.). **2.** dépendance, annexe *f* (d'une ville, d'un État); **the parish and its dependencies,** la commune et ses écarts; **dependencies of a (manor) house, of an estate,** dépendances d'une demeure, d'une terre.

dependent [di'pendənt], *a.* (*a*) dépendant (**on,** de); sujet (**on,** à); *Jur:* relevant (**on,** de); **to be d. on s.o., on sth.,** dépendre, relever, de qn, de qch.; **he is entirely d. on himself,** il ne peut compter que sur lui-même; **institution d. on voluntary contributions,** institution soutenue par des contributions bénévoles; **to be d. on imports from abroad,** être tributaire de l'étranger; *Ind:* **d. process,** opération enclenchée; *Mth:* **d. variable,** variable dépendante; (*b*) *Gram:* **d. clause,** proposition dépendante, subordonnée; (*c*) **to be d. on s.o.,** (i) être à la charge de qn, à charge à qn; (ii) recevoir une pension de qn; **two d. children,** deux enfants à charge; (*d*) *Med:* **d. drainage,** drainage *m* au point déclive; (*e*) **the value of the electromotive force is d. on the rate of change of current,** la valeur de la force électromotrice est fonction du taux de variation du courant.

depentanize [di:'pentənaiz], *v.tr. Petr:* dépentaniser.

depersonalization [di:pə:sənəlai'zeiʃ(ə)n], *s.* dépersonnalisation *f.*

depersonalize [di:'pə:sənəlaiz], *v.tr.* dépersonnaliser.

dephase [di:'feiz], *v.tr. El:* déphaser (le courant).

dephasing [di:'feiziŋ], *s. El:* déphasage *m.*

dephosphorization ['di:fɔsfərai'zeiʃ(ə)n], *s. Metall:* déphosphoration *f.*

dephosphorize [di:'fɔsfəraiz], *v.tr. Metall:* déphosphorer (le fer).

depict [di'pikt], *v.tr.* peindre, dépeindre, décrire, représenter; **the terror depicted in his face,** la terreur peinte sur son visage; **bible scenes depicted in tapestry,** scènes de l'histoire sainte représentées en tapisserie.

depicter, depictor [di'piktər], *s.* peintre *m,* descripteur *m.*

depiction [di'pikʃ(ə)n], *s.* peinture *f,* description *f.*

depigment [di'pigmənt], *v.tr.* dépigmenter.

dipigmentation [di:pigmen'teiʃ(ə)n], *s.* dépigmentation *f.*

depilate ['depileit], *v.tr. Leath:* dépiler, peler; *Toil:* épiler.

depilation [depi'leiʃ(ə)n], *s. Leath:* dépilage *m,* épilage *m*; *Toil:* épilation *f.*

depilator [di'pilətər], *s.* épileur, -euse.

depilatory [di'pilətəri]. *Toil:* **1.** *a.* dépilatoire; (pommade *f,* pâte *f*) épilatoire; (onguent) dépilatif. **2.** *s.* dépilatoire *m.*

deplane [di:'plein], *v.i.* descendre d'avion.

deplasmolysis [di:plæz'mɔlisis], *s. Biol:* déplasmolyse *f.*

deplete [di'pli:t], *v.tr.* (*a*) épuiser (des provisions, des munitions, etc.); (*b*) **to d. a garrison of troops,** démunir une garnison de ses troupes.

depletion [di'pli:ʃ(ə)n], *s.* **1.** (*a*) épuisement *m* (des ressources, etc.); (*b*) dégarnissement *m* (d'une place forte, etc.); (*c*) *For:* prélèvement global, dépeuplement *m.* **2.** *Med:* (*a*) déplétion *f*; (*b*) épuisement.

deplorable [di'plɔ:rəbl], *a.* déplorable, lamentable.

deplorably [di'plɔ:rəbli], *adv.* déplorablement, lamentablement; d'une façon lamentable.

deplore [di'plɔ:r], *v.tr.* déplorer; regretter vivement (une méprise, etc.); **his behaviour is to be deplored,** sa conduite est lamentable.

deploy [di'plɔi]. *Mil: etc:* **1.** *v.tr.* déployer (une colonne, une unité, des navires); articuler (des troupes, des dépôts, etc., sur le terrain); faire prendre (aux navires) leur poste de combat; déployer (un parachute). **2.** *v.i.* se déployer; (*of troops*) s'articuler (sur le terrain); **to d. in extended order, as skirmishers,** se déployer en tirailleurs; **to d. from route formation to battle formation,** passer de la formation de marche à la formation de combat; se déployer en formation de combat à partir de la formation de route; **to d. in width, in depth,** s'articuler en largeur, en profondeur.

deployment [di'plɔimənt], *s. Mil: etc:* répartition *f* (de troupes); déploiement *m* (d'une colonne, d'une unité, des navires); articulation *f* (de troupes, de dépôts, etc., sur le terrain); mise *f* en place (des navires) à leur poste de combat; déploiement (d'un parachute); **d. area,** zone *f* de déploiement.

deplumation [di:plu(:)'meiʃ(ə)n], *s.* perte *f* du plumage; mue *f.*

deplume [di'plu:m], *v.tr.* déplumer.

depolarization [di:poulərai'zeiʃ(ə)n], *s. Opt: El:* dépolarisation *f.*

depolarize [di:'pouləraiz], *v.tr. Opt: El:* dépolariser.

depolarizer [di:'pouləraizər], *s. El:* dépolarisant *m.*

depoliticization [di:pɔlitisai'zeiʃ(ə)n], *s.* dépolitisation *f.*

depoliticize [di:pɔ'litisaiz], *v.tr.* dépolitiser.

depolymerization [di:pɔlimərai'zeiʃ(ə)n], *s. Ch:* dépolymérisation *f.*

depolymerize [di:'pɔliməraiz], *v.tr. Ch:* dépolymériser.

depone [di'poun], *v.tr. & i. Jur:* = DEPOSE 2.

deponent [di'pounənt], *a. & s.* **1.** *Gram:* (verbe) déponent *m.* **2.** *Jur:* (témoin) déposant *m.*

depopulate [di:'pɔpjuleit], *v.tr. & i.* (se) dépeupler.

depopulation [di:pɔpju'leiʃ(ə)n], *s.* dépopulation *f* (d'un pays); dépeuplement *m* (d'un pays, d'une forêt); **rural d.,** exode rural, désertion *f* des campagnes.

deport [di'pɔ:t]. **1.** *v.tr.* (*a*) expulser (un étranger); (*b*) *Hist: (in India)* mettre (qn) en détention préventive; (*c*) déporter (un condamné politique, etc.). **2.** *v.pr. Lit:* **to d. oneself,** se comporter, se conduire (bien, mal).

deportation [di:pɔ:'teiʃ(ə)n], *s.* **1.** expulsion *f* (d'un étranger); **d. order,** arrêté *m* d'expulsion. **2.** *Hist: (in India)* détention préventive. **3.** déportation *f* (d'un condamné politique, etc.); **d. camp,** camp *m* de déportation.

deportee [di:pɔ:'ti:], *s.* déporté, -ée.

deportment [di'pɔ:tmənt], *s.* **1.** (*a*) tenue *f,* maintien *m*; **lessons in d.,** leçons *f* de maintien; (*b*) conduite *f*; manière *f* d'agir. **2.** *Ch:* action *f* (d'un métal).

depose [di'pouz], *v.tr.* **1.** (*a*) *A:* poser, déposer (qch.); (*b*) déposer (un roi, etc.). **2.** *Jur:* (*a*) affirmer, déposer, témoigner, attester (**that,** que + *ind.*); (*b*) *v.i.* faire une déposition; déposer; **to d. to a fact,** témoigner d'un fait.

deposit[1] di'pɔzit], *s.* **1.** *Bank:* dépôt *m*; **bank d.,** dépôt bancaire, en banque; **d. money,** monnaie scripturale; **minimum d.,** acompte *m* minimum; **on d.,** en dépôt; **d. account,** compte *m* à terme; **fixed d., d. for a fixed period,** dépôt à échéance fixe; argent *m* en dépôt à terme; **d. at seven days' notice,** dépôt à sept jours de préavis; **d. slip,** bulletin *m* de versement; **safe d.,** dépôt en coffre-fort; *Jur:* **D. and Consignment Office,** Caisse *f* de dépôts et consignations. **2.** (*pledge*) consignation *f* (d'une somme); cautionnement *m*; arrhes *fpl*; (*on renting*) denier *m* à Dieu; **to leave a d. on sth.,** verser une somme, un acompte, en garantie de qch.; laisser une somme en gage pour qch.; **to leave £10 as (a) d.,** laisser £10 comme arrhes; **to pay a d.,** verser une provision, des provisions, une caution, des arrhes; verser une somme à titre de provision; *Pol:* **one of the candidates lost his d.** = un des candidats a perdu sa caution. **3.** (*a*) (*sediment*) dépôt(s); précipité *m,* sédiment *m*; **alluvial deposits,** alluvions *f*; **there are deposits of sand at the mouth of the river,** il y a des alluvions sablonneuses à l'embouchure du fleuve; **salty d.,** grumeaux *mpl* de sel; *Med:* **chalky d.,** encroûtement *m,* dépôt, calcique; *I.C.E:* **carbon d.,** calamine *f*; (*b*) *Geol:* gisement *m*; gîte *m*; couche *f*; **coal d.,** gisement houiller; (*c*) *Techn:* (*coating layer*) apport *m*; **electrolytic metal d.,** précipité, dépôt, de métal électrolytique, **d. of silver,** précipité d'argent.

deposit[2], *v.tr.* **1.** déposer, poser (**sth. on sth.,** qch. sur qch.); **these insects d. their eggs in the ground,** ces insectes déposent leurs œufs dans la terre. **2.** (*a*) déposer (de l'argent à la banque); **to d. documents with a bank,** mettre des documents en dépôt dans une banque; *Publ:* **to d. duty copies of a book (for copyright),** déposer des exemplaires d'un livre; (*b*) **to d. £100,** verser £100 comme arrhes, à titre de provision; *Cust:* **to d. the duty (repayable),** cautionner les droits. **3.** *v.tr. & i.* (*of liquid*) déposer (un sédiment); **the flood waters deposited a layer of mud in the street,** les inondations ont laissé un dépôt de boue dans la rue.

depositary [di'pɔzit(ə)ri], *s.* dépositaire *mf,* consignataire *mf*; *Jur:* séquestre *m* (de biens séquestrés); **she was the d. of all his troubles,** c'est à elle qu'il confiait tous ses ennuis.

depositing [di'pɔzitiŋ], *s.* dépôt *m*; *Jur:* **d. of documents (in a suit),** apport *m* de pièces.

deposition [di:pə'ziʃ(ə)n], *s.* **1.** déposition *f* (d'un roi, etc.). **2.** *Jur:* déposition, témoignage *m.* **3.** dépôt *m* (d'un sédiment). **4.** *Art:* **the D. from the Cross,** la Déposition, la Descente, de Croix.

depositor [di'pɔzitər], *s. Bank:* déposant, -ante; **depositor's book,** livret nominatif.

depository [di'pɔzit(ə)ri], *s.* **1.** dépôt *m,* magasin *m,* entrepôt *m*; **furniture d.,** garde-meubles *m inv.* **2.** = DEPOSITARY.

depot, *s.* **1.** ['depou] dépôt *m*; (*a*) *Mil: etc:* **regimental d.,** dépôt de régiment, de corps de troupe; **advanced d.,** dépôt d'armée; **general d.,** dépôt central; **branch d.,** dépôt particulier; **intermediate d.,** dépôt intermédiaire, dépôt de la zone des communications; **base d.,** (i) = dépôt ministériel, dépôt de (la zone de) l'intérieur; (ii) *U.S:* dépôt de base (arrière); **supply d.,** dépôt de ravitaillement; **ammunition d.,** dépôt de munitions; **engineer d.,** dépôt de matériel du génie; **salvage d.,** dépôt de récupération (du matériel); **air force d.,** dépôt de l'aéronautique, de matériel d'aviation; *Navy:* **d. ship,** bâtiment-base *m,* bâtiment-caserne *m,* ravitailleur *m*; (*b*) *Com: etc:* dépôt, entrepôt *m*; **goods d.,** dépôt des marchandises, hangar *m* à marchandises; **coal d.,** dépôt de charbon; **petrol storage d.,** dépôt d'essence; *Rail:* **locomotive d.,** garage *m,* dépôt, de(s) locomotives. **2.** ['di:pou] *U.S:* (*a*) (**railroad**) **d.,** gare *f* (de chemin de fer); **freight d.,** gare des marchandises; **shunting d.,** gare de triage; (*b*) (**bus**) **d.,** gare routière; (*c*) aérogare *f.*

depravation [deprə'veiʃ(ə)n], *s.* dépravation *f* (de l'âme, du bon goût, etc.).

deprave [di'preiv], *v.tr.* dépraver.

depraved [di'preivd], *a.* (homme, goût) dépravé.

depravity [di'præviti], *s.* **1.** (état *m* de) dépravation *f*; perversité *f.* **2.** *Theol:* **total d.,** état de corruption entière et originelle (de l'homme).

deprecate ['deprikeit], *v.tr.* **1.** *A:* chercher à écarter (la colère divine, etc.) par des prières. **2.** désapprouver, désavouer, déconseiller (une action).

deprecating [depri'keitiŋ], *a.* désapprobateur, -trice; (sourire *m,* etc.) de désapprobation.

deprecatingly [depri'keitiŋli], *adv.* d'un air, d'un ton, de désapprobation.

deprecation [depri'keiʃ(ə)n], *s.* **1.** *Theol: A:* déprécation *f.* **2.** désapprobation *f,* désaveu *m* (**of,** de).

deprecative ['deprəkətiv], *a.* = DEPRECATORY 1.

deprecatory ['deprəkeitəri], *a.* **1.** *Theol: A:* déprécatoire, déprécatif. **2.** (rire *m,* etc.) qui va audevant des reproches, de la critique.

depreciate [di'pri:ʃieit]. **1.** *v.tr.* (*a*) déprécier, rabaisser (la valeur de qch.); avilir (les marchandises); **to d. the franc,** déprécier, dévaloriser, le franc; (*b*) déprécier, dénigrer, rabaisser, ravaler (qn); parler avec mépris de (qn, qch.); (*c*) *Com: Ind:* amortir (le mobilier, l'outillage, etc.). **2.** *v.i.* se déprécier; diminuer de valeur; (*of prices, shares, etc.*) baisser.

depreciatingly [di'pri:ʃicitiŋli], *adv.* d'un air de dépréciation, de mépris, de dénigrement.

depreciation [dipri:ʃi'eiʃ(ə)n], *s.* **1.** (*a*) dépréciation *f* (de l'argent, *Ind:* du matériel, etc.); moins-value *f*; avilissement *m* (des marchandises); dévalorisation *f* (de la monnaie); **shares that show a d.,** actions *f* qui ont enregistré une moins-value, une baisse (de prix); (*b*) *Ind: Book-k:* **annual d.,** dépréciation annuelle, amortissement *m* annuel. **2.** dépréciation, dénigrement *m* (d'une bonne action, de qn).

depreciative [di'pri:ʃiətiv], **depreciatory** [di'pri:ʃiətəri], *a.* dépréciateur, -trice; péjoratif; *Ling:* **depreciatory suffix,** suffixe dépréciatif.

depreciator [di'pri:ʃieitər], *s.* dépréciateur, -trice; dénigreur, -euse (du mérite de qn).

depredation [depri'deiʃ(ə)n], *s.* (*a*) déprédation *f,* pillage *m*; (*b*) *A.Jur:* **d. of decedent's estate,** expilation *f* d'hérédité.

depredator ['deprideitər], *s.* déprédateur, -trice; pillard, -arde; pilleur, -euse.

depredatory [di'predət(ə)ri], *a.* (habitudes *fpl,* etc.) de déprédation.

depress [di'pres], *v.tr.* **1.** (*a*) abaisser; diminuer la hauteur de (qch.); baisser (qch.); *Artil:* abaisser (un canon); *Aut: etc:* **to d. the pedal,** appuyer sur la pédale; enfoncer la pédale; (*b*) *Mth:* abaisser (une équation). **2.** (*a*) abattre (les forces); faire languir, faire végéter (le commerce); faire baisser (le prix de qch.); (*b*) attrister, décourager, accabler, oppresser, affaisser (qn); *F:* donner le cafard à (qn).

depressant [di'pres(ə)nt]. **1.** *Med:* (*a*) *a.* déprimant; sédatif; (*b*) *s.* sédatif *m*; **appetite d.,** anorexigène *m*; dépresseur *m* de l'appétit. **2.** *s. Tchn:* dépresseur, déprimant *m* (pour le traitement des minerais). **3.** *s.* (*also* **depressent**) quelque chose de décourageant, de déprimant.

depressed [di'prest], *a.* **1.** (*a*) *Arch:* (arc) surbaissé, déprimé; (*b*) *Orn:* (bec) aplati. **2.** *Com:* (marché) languissant, déprimé, dans le marasme; **d. area,** région touchée par la crise. **3.** triste, abattu, déprimé; (malade) affaissé, en proie à la dépression; **he looks d.,** il a l'air découragé, déprimé; **to become d.,** se laisser abattre, décourager; **to be easily d.,** se laisser décourager facilement; **to feel d.,** être découragé, déprimé, *F:* avoir le cafard.

depressing [di'presiŋ], *a.* attristant, contristant; déprimant, décourageant; **d. landscape,** paysage *m* triste, maussade; **d. book,** livre décourageant.

depression [di'preʃ(ə)n], *s.* **1.** (*a*) abaissement *m* (de qch.); *Aut:* **full d. of the pedal,** enfoncement total de la pédale; (*b*) *Artil:* pointage négatif; **angle of d.,** angle *m* de dépression, angle de site négatif; (*c*) *Astr:* dépression *f* (d'un astre, de l'horizon). **2.** abaissement (d'un son, du mercure); *Meteor:* dépression; zone *f* dépressionnaire; (*in isobar*) **squall d.,** crochet *m* de grain. **3.** (*a*) dépression, dénivellement *m,* enfoncement *m,* creux *m* (de terrain); cuvette *f*; *Agr:* baissière *f*; (*b*) affaissement *m,* consentement *m* (d'un rail, etc.); (*c*) trou *m,* godet *m,* poche *f* (dans une plaque, etc.). **4.** *Com:* crise *f,* affaissement, marasme *m,* stagnation *f* (des affaires); **economic d.,** dépression économique. **5.** découragement *m,* affaissement, abattement *m*; *F:* le cafard; **he found her in a state of deep d.,** il l'a trouvée dans un état de profond découragement, de profond abattement.

depressive [di'presiv], *a.* dépressif.

depressor [di'presər], *s.* **1.** *Anat:* (muscle) abaisseur *m.* **2.** *Med:* dépressoir *m,* dépressoire *f.* **3.** *Ch:* dépresseur *m.*

depressurize [di:'preʃəraiz], *v.tr. & i. Av:* dépressuriser.

deprival [di'praiv(ə)l], *s.* privation *f* (**of,** de).

deprivation [depri'veiʃ(ə)n], *s.* **1.** privation *f,* perte *f* (de droits, etc.); **d. of civil rights,** (i) (*temporary*) interdiction légale, civile, judiciaire; (ii) (*permanent*) dégradation *f* civique. **2.** dépossession *f* (d'un office); destitution *f,* révocation *f* (d'un ecclésiastique, etc.); *Adm: etc:* **d. of office,** retrait *m* d'emploi.

deprive [di'praiv], *v.tr.* **1. to d. s.o. of sth.,** priver qn de qch., enlever qch. à qn, supprimer qch. à qn; dénantir (un créancier de ses nantissements); **to d. a man of a week's pay,** suspendre la solde d'un homme pour huit jours; **to d. s.o. of food,** priver qn de nourriture; affamer qn; **to d. oneself,** s'infliger des privations, des jeûnes. **2.** déposséder (qn) d'une charge; destituer (un prêtre).

deprived [di'praivd], *a.* (enfant) déshérité.

depropanization [di:prɔpənaizeiʃ(ə)n], *s. Petr:* dépropanisation *f.*

depropanize [di:'prɔpənaiz], *v.tr. Petr:* dépropaniser.

depropanizer [di:'prɔpənaizər], *s. Petr:* dépropanis(at)eur *m.*

depth [depθ], *s.* **1.** profondeur *f* (d'une rivière, de la pensée, des sentiments, etc.); **perpendicular d.,** profondeur perpendiculaire; *Mth:* abattement *m*; **in d.,** en profondeur, dans le sens de la profondeur; **the pond is three metres in d.,** l'étang *m* a trois mètres de profondeur; **at a d. of 50 fathoms,** par 50 brasses de fond; *attrib. Oc:* **d. finder, d. sounder,** sondeur *m*; *Navy:* **d. charge, d. bomb,** grenade sous-marine; **d. charging,** grenadage *m.* **2.** fond *m,* hauteur *f* (de l'eau); **to go, get, beyond, out of, one's d.,** (i) perdre pied; ne pas avoir pied; (ii) *Fig:* sortir de sa sphère, de sa compétence; parler de ce qu'on ignore; **to be out of one's d.,** (i) avoir perdu pied; (ii) *Fig:* ne pas être à la hauteur du sujet traité (par le conférencier, etc.); ne plus être sur son terrain; **to get back into one's d.,** reprendre pied; **to be within one's d.,** avoir pied; *Nau:* **to try the depth(s),** (essayer de) prendre le fond; trouver le fond. **3.** hauteur (d'un piston, d'un faux col, d'une frange, etc.); épaisseur *f* (d'une couche); **d. of a bridge arch,** hauteur d'une arche de pont; *Mec.E:* **d. of tooth,** hauteur de dent (d'une roue); **d. of thread of a screw,** hauteur, profondeur, du filet d'une vis; *Mil:* **d. (of formation) of a battalion,** profondeur d'un bataillon. **4.** (*a*) gravité *f* (d'un son); (*b*) portée *f* (de l'intelligence); (*c*) vigueur *f,* intensité *f* (de coloris). **5.** fond (d'une forêt, d'une caverne, etc.); milieu *m* (de la nuit); **in the d. of winter,** au cœur, au milieu, de l'hiver; au gros de l'hiver; en plein hiver; au plus fort de l'hiver. **6.** *Tchn:* (*a*) *Mec.E:* **d. of cut,** (i) avancement *m*; (ii) profondeur de passe, de coupe (d'une machine-outil); (*b*) *Opt:* **d. of focus,** profondeur de foyer; (*c*) *N.Arch:* creux *m* (d'un navire); **moulded d.,** creux sur quille. **7.** *pl.* **the depths:** (*a*) *Lit:* l'abîme *m,* le gouffre; **the depths of unrecorded time,** l'abîme des temps qui n'ont pas laissé d'histoire; *B:* **out of the depths have I cried unto thee, O Lord,** O Éternel, je t'invoque des lieux profonds; (*b*) profondeurs (de l'océan, etc.); ténèbres *f* (de l'ignorance, etc.); abîme (de l'affliction); **in the depths of despair,** dans le plus profond désespoir; **the lowest depths,** le dernier degré, le plus profond, le fin fond, le comble (de la honte, etc.).

depurant [di'pjuərənt, 'depjurənt], *a. & s. Med:* dépuratif (*m*).

depurate ['depjureit], *v.tr. Med:* dépurer, purifier (le sang).

depuration [depju'reiʃ(ə)n], *s. Med:* dépuration *f.*

depurative [di'pju:rətiv, 'depjureitiv], *a. & s. Med:* dépuratif (*m*); *a.* dépuratoire.

deputation [depju'teiʃ(ə)n], *s.* **1.** députation *f,* délégation *f* (de qn). **2.** *coll.* députation (composée de délégués); **to send a d. to confer with s.o.,** envoyer une députation pour conférer avec qn.

depute[1] [di'pju:t], *v.tr.* **1.** déléguer (**powers to s.o.,** des pouvoirs à qn). **2. to d. s.o. to do sth.,** députer, déléguer, qn pour faire qch.

depute[2] ['depjut], *a. & (s.)* adjoint (*m*).

deputize ['depjutaiz], *v.i.* **to d. for s.o.,** faire l'intérim de qn, remplacer qn; remplir une suppléance; *Th:* doubler (un acteur absent); **the Home Secretary, deputizing for the Premier, replied . . .,** le Ministre de l'Intérieur, qui remplaçait le Premier Ministre, a répondu . . . .

deputy ['depjuti], *s.* **1.** fondé *m* de pouvoir; représentant *m* (de qn); substitut *m,* suppléant *m* (d'un juge etc.); délégué *m* (d'un fonctionnaire); **to act as d. for s.o.,** suppléer qn; **to find a d.,** se faire suppléer; **d. chairman,** vice-président *m*; **d. governor,** sous-gouverneur *m*; **d. judge,** juge *m* suppléant; **d. manager, manageress;** sous-directeur, -trice; vice-gérant, -ante; **d. chief clerk,** sous-chef *m*; **d. director,** directeur adjoint. **2.** délégué, ambassadeur *m,* représentant (d'une association, etc.).

deracinate [di:'ræsineit], *v.tr.* déraciner, extirper (une plante, un préjugé).

deracination [di:ræsi'neiʃ(ə)n], *s.* déracinement *m,* extirpation *f.*

derail [di(:)'reil]. *Rail:* **1.** *v.tr.* faire dérailler (un train); **to be derailed,** sortir des rails; dérailler. **2.** *v.i.* dérailler; quitter la voie.

derailleur [dera'jœ:r, di'reilər], *s. Cy:* **d. gear,** dérailleur *m.*

derailment [di(:)'reilmənt], *s.* déraillement *m.*

derange [di'rein(d)ʒ], *v.tr.* **1.** déranger, dérégler, détraquer, fausser (une machine). **2.** (*a*) déranger (qn, la santé); **to d. s.o.'s plans,** déranger, désorganiser, bouleverser, les projets de qn; (*b*) aliéner (l'esprit); déranger le cerveau de (qn); jeter le trouble dans l'esprit de (qn); **he, his mind, is deranged,** il a le cerveau détraqué, il n'a plus sa raison, il a perdu l'esprit; c'est un détraqué.

derangement [di'rein(d)ʒmənt], *s.* **1.** déréglage *m* (d'un appareil); **apparatus liable to d., subject to d.,** appareil susceptible de se détraquer. **2.** (*a*) **d. of mind,** dérangement *m* d'esprit; aliénation mentale, confusion mentale; dérèglement *m* d'esprit; (*b*) **d. of digestion,** troubles *mpl* de digestion.

derate [di:'reit], *v.tr.* dégrever (une industrie, etc.).

derating [di:'reitiŋ], *s.* dégrèvement *m.*

deration [di:'ræʃ(ə)n], *v.tr.* dérationner, mettre en vente libre.

derationing [di:'ræʃəniŋ], *s.* mise *f* en vente libre.

deratization [di:rætai'zeiʃ(ə)n], *s.* dératisation *f* (d'une ferme, etc.); extermination *f* des rats.

Derby ['da:bi]. **1.** *Pr.n. Geog:* Derby; **D. (porcelain, china),** porcelaine fabriquée à Derby. **2.** *s. Sp:* (*a*) *Turf:* **the D.,** le derby d'Epsom; *F: A:* **D. dog,** (i) chien fatal qui traverse la piste au moment psychologique; (ii) incident fâcheux et imprévu (qui survient à la dernière minute); (*b*) **donkey D.,** course *f* d'ânes; (*c*) *Fb:* **local d.,** derby. **3.** *s. Cost:* (*a*) *U.S:* ['də:bi] chapeau *m* melon; (*b*) (*shoe*) derby.

Derbyshire ['da:biʃ(i)ər], *Pr.n. Geog:* le comté de Derby; *Med: F:* **D. neck,** goitre *m*; *Miner:* **D. spar,** spath *m* fluor.

deregister [di:'redʒistər], *v.tr.* radier (qn, une société, etc.); rayer (qn, etc.) du registre.

deregistration [di:redʒis'treiʃ(ə)n], *s.* radiation *f* (de qn, d'une association, etc.).

derelict ['derəlikt]. **1.** *a.* abandonné, délaissé, à l'abandon; **d. land,** relais *m.* **2.** *s.* (*a*) objet abandonné; bien *m* sans maître; *Jur:* épave *f*; *esp. Nau:* navire abandonné (en mer); épave; (*b*) délaissé, -ée; épave humaine. **3.** *a. U.S:* (*of pers.*) **to be d. (in one's duty),** être, se montrer, négligent de son devoir.

dereliction [deri'likʃ(ə)n], *s.* **1.** abandon *m,* délaissement *m,* déréliction *f.* **2.** retrait *m,* recul *m* (de la mer). **3.** négligence *f,* oubli *m* (de son devoir); **d. of duty,** négligence dans le service; manquement *m* au devoir.

derequisition[1] [di:rekwi'ziʃ(ə)n], *s.* déréquisition *f.*

derequisition[2], *v.tr.* déréquisitionner.

derestrict [di:ri'strikt], *v.tr. Adm: Aut:* **to d. a road,** libérer une route de toute restriction de vitesse.

deride [di'raid], *v.tr.* tourner (qn, qch.) en dérision; bafouer, railler, ridiculiser (qn); se moquer, se rire, se gausser (de qn, de qch.).

derider [di'raidər], *s.* moqueur, -euse, railleur, -euse.

derision [di'riʒ(ə)n], *s.* **1.** dérision *f*; **object of d.,** objet *m* de risée; **to hold s.o. in d.,** se moquer de qn; **to be held in d. by all,** être l'objet de la risée universelle; **to bring s.o. into d.,** tourner qn en dérision, en ridicule; **to say, do, sth. in d.,** dire, faire, qch. par dérision. **2.** objet *m* de dérision.

derisive [di'raisiv], **derisory** [di'raisəri], *a.* **1.** moqueur, ironique; **d. laughter,** rires moqueurs; **d. cheers,** acclamations *f* ironiques. **2. d. offer,** offre *f* dérisoire, à faire rire, à se moquer du monde.

derisively [di'raisivli], *adv.* **1.** d'un air moqueur; ironiquement. **2.** dérisoirement; **d. small (offer, etc.),** (offre *f*, etc.) dérisoire.

derivable [di'raivəbl], *a.* **1.** dérivable; (mot *m*, etc.) que l'on peut tirer, que l'on peut dériver (**from,** de). **2. income d. from an investment,** revenu *m* que l'on peut tirer d'un placement.

derivation [deri'veiʃ(ə)n], *s.* dérivation *f*. **1.** (*a*) **d. of a doctrine from a source,** emprunt *m* d'une doctrine à une source; **d. of a word from Latin,** dérivation d'un mot du latin; **to find the d. of a word,** trouver la dérivation, l'origine *f*, d'un mot; (*b*) (*thing derived*) **doctrine that is but a d. of an old heresy,** doctrine *f* qui n'est qu'un rejeton d'une ancienne hérésie. **2.** *Mth:* **d. of a function,** dérivation d'une fonction. **3.** *Med: A:* **d. of the blood from an organ,** dérivation du sang d'un organe.

derivative [di'rivətiv]. **1.** (*a*) *a.* & *s.* *Gram:* (mot) dérivé (*m*); (*b*) *a.* *Geol:* **d. rocks,** roches dérivées; (*c*) influencé par (qch.); **d. writer,** auteur *m* sans originalité. **2.** *s.* (*a*) *Ch: Ind:* dérivé *m*; **petroleum d.,** dérivé du pétrole; (*b*) *Mth:* dérivée *f*; *pl.* **derivatives,** dérivées continues; (*c*) *Mus:* accord dérivé; (*d*) *Med:* dérivatif *m*.

derivatively [di'rivətivli], *adv.* (*a*) par dérivation; (*b*) dans un style d'emprunt.

derive [di'raiv], *v.tr.* & *i.* **1.** (*a*) **to d. sth. from sth.,** tirer (son origine, etc.) de qch.; devoir (son bonheur, etc.) à qch.; tirer, retirer (des revenus, des renseignements, etc.) de qch.; tenir (des nouvelles) de qch.; trouver, prendre (du plaisir) à qch.; **income derived from an investment,** revenu *m* provenant d'un placement; **the moon derives its light from the sun,** la lune reçoit, emprunte, sa lumière du soleil; **to d. consolation from religion,** puiser des consolations dans la religion; **doctrine from which one derives great satisfaction,** doctrine *f* où l'on goûte de vives satisfactions; (*b*) *Ch:* **to d. one compound from another,** dériver un composé d'un autre; (*c*) *Ling:* **to d. a word from Latin,** dériver, faire dériver, tirer, un mot du latin; **word derived from Latin,** mot qui vient du latin. **2. to be derived,** *v.i.* **to derive,** dériver, tirer son origine, (pro)venir, émaner (**from,** de); **obligations that d. from a clause,** obligations *f* qui émanent d'une clause; **consequences that d. from a principle,** conséquences *f* qui découlent d'un principe. **3.** *Med: A:* dériver (le sang).

derm(a) ['dəːm(ə)], *s.* *Anat:* derme *m*.

dermabrasion [dəːmə'breiʒ(ə)n], *s.* *Surg:* abrasion *f* (pour détruire une cicatrice, etc.).

dermal ['dəːm(ə)l], *a.* *Anat:* **1.** cutané. **2.** dermique.

Dermaptera [dəː'mæptərə], *s.pl.* *Ent:* dermaptères *m*.

Dermapteroidea [dəːmæptə'rɔidiə], *s.pl.* *Ent:* dermaptéroïdes *m*.

dermatitis [dəːmə'taitis], *s.* *Med:* dermite *f*, dermatite *f*.

dermatobia [dəːmə'toubiə], *s.* *Ent:* dermatobie *f*.

dermatological [dəːmətə'lɔdʒikl], *a.* dermatologique.

dermatologist [dəːmə'tɔlədʒist], *s.* dermatologue *mf*, dermatologiste *mf*.

dermatology [dəːmə'tɔlədʒi], *s.* dermatologie *f*.

dermatome ['dəːmətoum], *s.* dermatome *m*.

dermatomycosis ['dəːmətoumai'kousis], *s.* *Med:* dermatomycose *f*.

dermatomyositis ['dəːmətoumaiou'saitis], *s.* *Med:* dermatomyosite *f*.

dermatophyte [dəː'mætoufait], *s.* *Fung:* dermatophyte *m*.

dermatosis [dəːmə'tousis], *s.* dermatose *f*.

dermestes [dəː'mestiːz], *s.* *Ent:* dermeste *m*.

dermic ['dəːmik], *a.* dermique.

dermographia [dəːmou'græfiə], *s.* *Med:* dermographie *f*.

dermographism [dəː'mɔgrəfizm], *s.* *Med:* dermographisme *m*.

dermoid ['dəːmɔid], *a.* & *s.* *Med:* dermoïde; **d. (cyst),** kyste *m* dermoïde.

Dermoptera [dəː'mɔptərə], *s.pl.* *Z:* dermoptères *m*.

dermopteran [dəː'mɔptərən], *a.* & *s.* *Z:* dermoptère (*m*).

dermopterous [dəː'mɔptərəs], *a.* *Z:* dermoptère.

dermovaccine [dəːmou'væksin], *s.* *Med:* dermovaccin *m*.

derogate ['derəgeit], *v.i.* **1.** *A:* **to d. from a right, from a liberty, etc.,** porter atteinte à un droit, à une liberté, etc.; **to d. from s.o.'s authority,** diminuer l'autorité de qn; déprécier la compétence de qn. **2. to d.** (**from one's dignity, position, etc.**), déroger (à sa dignité, à son rang, etc.).

derogation [derə'geiʃ(ə)n], *s.* **1. d. of a law,** dérogation *f* à une loi. **2.** (*a*) **d. from a right, from a privilege,** atteinte portée à un droit, à un privilège; (*b*) **papal usurpations to the d. of the Crown,** usurpations *f* de la papauté au détriment de la Couronne. **3.** abaissement *m*, ravalement *m* (de qn); **without d.,** sans déroger (**from dignity, etc.,** à la dignité, etc.).

derogatory [di'rɔgət(ə)ri], *a.* **1.** (*a*) dérogatoire (**from,** à); (*b*) **d. to, from, a right,** attentatoire, qui porte atteinte, à un droit. **2.** dérogeant, qui déroge (**to,** à); **conduct d. to his rank,** conduite *f* indigne de son rang; **to do sth. d. to one's position,** se manquer à soi-même. **3.** dépréciateur, -trice; qui abaisse, déprécie (**to s.o.,** qn); **this word has acquired a d. meaning,** ce mot a acquis un sens péjoratif.

derotation [diːrou'teiʃ(ə)n], *s.* *Surg:* dérotation *f*.

derrick ['derik], *s.* **1.** *A:* (*a*) (*pers.*) bourreau *m*; (*b*) potence *f*. **2.** (*a*) derrick *m*; tour *f* de forage; (grue *f* de) chevalement *m*; chèvre *f*; **floating d.,** grue flottante, ponton-grue *m*, *pl.* pontons-grues; (*b*) *Nau:* mât *m* de charge; grue mâtée; **d. span,** martinet *m* du mât de charge.

derring-do ['deriŋ'duː], *s.* *A:* bravoure *f*; **deeds of d.-do,** hauts faits; bravoures.

derringer ['derin(d)ʒər], *s.* *Sm.a:* derringer *m*; pistolet *m* de gros calibre.

derris ['deris], *s.* *Bot:* derris *m*.

derv [dəːv], *s.* (*initials of Diesel-engined road vehicles*) gas-oil *m*, gaz-oil *m*.

dervish ['dəːviʃ], *s.* derviche *m*; **whirling, dancing, d.,** derviche tourneur.

desalination [diːsæli'neiʃ(ə)n], **desalinization** [diːsælinai'zeiʃ(ə)n], *s.* *Ind:* dessalaison *f*; dessalement *m* (de l'eau de mer).

desalt [diː'sɔlt], *v.tr.* dessaler (l'eau de mer).

desalter [diː'sɔltər], *s.* dessaleur *m*.

desand [diː'sænd], *v.tr.* dessabler.

desanding [diː'sændiŋ], *s.* dessablage *m*, dessablement *m*.

descale [diː'skeil], *v.tr.* (*a*) *Dent:* détartrer; (*b*) *Aut: etc:* décalaminer.

descaling [diː'skeiliŋ], *s.* (*a*) *Dent:* détartrage *m*; (*b*) *Aut: etc:* décalaminage *m*.

descant[1] ['deskænt], *s.* **1.** *Mus:* (*a*) déchant *m*; (*b*) dessus *m*. **2.** mélodie *f*, harmonie *f*; prélude *m*.

descant[2] [dis'kænt], *v.i.* **1.** *Mus:* accompagner (les notes du plain-chant) en déchant. **2.** *A:* & *Lit:* discourir, faire des discours, disserter, s'étendre (**on,** sur).

descend [di'send]. **1.** *v.i.* (*a*) descendre; (*of rain*) tomber; **the angel descended from heaven,** l'ange est descendu du ciel; **the Spirit of God has descended upon him,** l'Esprit de Dieu a descendu sur lui; **a feeling of sadness descended upon him,** un sentiment de tristesse s'empara de lui; une tristesse s'abattit sur lui; (*b*) **to d. on s.o.,** s'abattre, tomber, sur qn; **the Goths descended (up)on Rome,** les Goths descendirent sur Rome; *F:* **they descended on us without warning,** ils ont fait irruption chez nous sans nous prévenir; (*c*) **to d. to s.o.'s level, to doing sth.,** s'abaisser au niveau de qn, (jusqu')à faire qch.; **to d. to lying,** descendre jusqu'au mensonge; (*d*) **to d., be descended, from s.o.,** descendre de qn; être le descendant de qn; tirer son origine (d'une maison royale, etc.); être issu (de sang royal); sortir, venir (d'une bonne famille); (*e*) (*of property, privilege*) **to d. from s.o. to s.o.,** passer de qn à qn. **2.** *v.tr.* descendre, dévaler (une colline, un escalier).

descendant, -ent [di'sendənt], *s.* descendant, -ante; *pl.* **descendants,** descendance *f*, postérité *f*; **to leave no descendants,** ne point laisser de race, de descendants.

descendance, -ence [di'sendəns], *s.* **1.** (*lineage*) descendance *f*. **2.** descendance *f*, postérité *f*, descendants *mpl*.

descending [di'sendiŋ], *a.* **1.** descendant; *Mus:* **d. scale,** gamme descendante; *Mth:* **d. series,** progression décroissante; **in d. order,** en ordre décroissant. **2. d. motion,** mouvement *m* de descente; *Min:* **d. shaft,** descente *f* de mine; descenderie *f*. **3.** *Typ:* (lettre) à queue inférieure.

descensional [di'senʃən(ə)l], *a.* descensionnel.

descent [di'sent], *s.* **1.** descente *f* (d'un alpiniste, d'un aéronaute, etc.); *Theol:* **the D.,** la descente de Jésus-Christ aux enfers; *Art:* **the D. from the Cross,** la Descente de Croix. **2.** descente, pente *f*; **sharp d.,** descente rapide, brusque. **3.** (*attack*) descente, irruption *f* (**on,** dans, à, sur); **the police made a d. on the night club,** la police fit une descente, a descendu, dans la boîte de nuit. **4.** (*a*) (*lineage*) descendance *f*; **to trace one's d. back to William the Conqueror,** faire remonter sa famille à Guillaume le Conquérant; **to boast a long d.,** se vanter d'une longue généalogie; (*b*) *A:* génération *f*; **this land was theirs during four descents,** cette terre leur appartint pendant quatre générations. **5.** *Jur:* transmission *f* (d'un bien) par droit de succession, par héritage.

descloizite [dei'klɔizait], *s.* *Miner:* descloizite *f*.

describable [dis'kraibəbl], *a.* descriptible.

describe [dis'kraib], *v.tr.* **1.** (*a*) décrire, dépeindre (qn, qch.); **words cannot d. the scene,** la parole est impuissante à dépeindre la scène; (*b*) **to d. s.o., sth., as . . .,** qualifier qn, qch., de . . ., représenter qn comme . . .; **to d. oneself as an actor,** se représenter comme acteur; se prétendre acteur; **my decision has been described as arbitrary,** on a qualifié ma décision d'arbitraire; (*c*) *Jur:* désigner (des titres de propriété, des marchandises, etc.); (*d*) donner le signalement (d'un déserteur, d'un homme recherché par la police); (*e*) **to d. an escutcheon heraldically,** blasonner un écu. **2.** décrire (une courbe, un cercle); **to d. a circle about a polygon,** circonscrire un cercle à un polygone; **to d. a triangle,** tracer un triangle.

description [dis'kripʃ(ə)n], *s.* **1.** (*a*) description *f* (de qn, de qch.); **to give a true d. of s.o.,** dépeindre qn tel qu'il est; **beyond d.,** indescriptible; **d. of the morals of the period,** peinture *f* des mœurs de l'époque; **the sittings have been stormy beyond d.,** les séances ont été orageuses, c'était quelque chose d'indescriptible; (*b*) (*formally*) (i) (*for police purposes*) signalement *m*; (*in a card index*) fiche *f* signalétique; (ii) (*on passports, etc.*) profession *f*, qualité *f*; **to answer to the d.,** répondre au signalement; (iii) *Com:* désignation *f* (de marchandises). **2.** sorte *f*, espèce *f*, genre *m*; **people of this d.,** les gens *m* de cette espèce, de cette sorte; **a scoundrel of the worst d.,** le pire des coquins.

descriptive [dis'kriptiv], *a.* **1.** (*a*) descriptif; **d. geometry,** géométrie descriptive; **d. catalogue,** catalogue raisonné; (*b*) *Adm:* signalétique; *esp. Mil:* **d. return,** état *m* signalétique. **2. d. talent,** talent *m* de description.

descriptively [dis'kriptivli], *adv.* d'une manière descriptive.

descry [dis'krai], *v.tr.* *Lit:* apercevoir, aviser, découvrir, distinguer; **we descried a house in the distance,** on discernait une maison dans le lointain.

Desdemona [dezdi'mounə], *Pr.n.f.* Desdémone.

desecrate ['desikreit], *v.tr.* **1.** profaner (un lieu saint); outrager (l'hospitalité); violer (une sépulture). **2.** profaner; rendre à un usage profane; **sacred vessels must be desecrated before they are repaired,** pour réparer les vases sacrés il faut d'abord les profaner.

desecration [desi'kreiʃ(ə)n], *s.* profanation *f*; **d. of a grave,** violation *f* de sépulture.

desecrator ['desikreitər], *s.* profanateur, -trice.

desegregate [diː'segrigeit], *v.tr.* & *i.* mettre fin à la ségrégation.

desegregation [diːsegri'geiʃ(ə)n], *s.* déségrégation *f*.

densensitization [diːsensitai'zeiʃ(ə)n], *s.* désensibilisation *f*.

desensitize [diː'sensitaiz], *v.tr.* *Phot: Med:* désensibiliser.

desensitizer [diː'sensitaizər], *s.* *Phot:* désensibilisateur *m*; réducteur *m* de sensibilité.

desensitizing[1] [diː'sensitaiziŋ], *a.* désensibilisateur, -trice.

desensitizing[2], *s.* désensibilisation *f*.

desert[1] [di'zəːt], *s.* **1.** mérite *m*; **each shall be given a place according to his d.,** chacun sera placé en son rang selon son mérite. **2.** *usu. pl.* mérites; ce qu'on mérite; dû *m*; **according to one's deserts,** selon ses mérites; **to each according to his deserts,** à chacun son dû; **to deal with s.o. according to his deserts,** faire justice à qn; **to get, meet with, come by, one's deserts,** avoir ce que l'on mérite; être récompensé selon ses mérites; **he has only got his deserts,** il n'a que ce qu'il mérite.

desert[2] ['dezət]. **1.** *a.* (région *f*, flore *f*) désertique; (région) déserte; (sujet *m*, etc.) aride, stérile; *A:* **the d. air,** le vide de l'air. **2.** *s.* désert *m*; **the Sahara D.,** le désert du Sahara; **the deserts of Africa,** l'Afrique *f* désertique. **3.** *attrib.* **d. rat,** (i) *Z:* rat sauteur; (ii) *Mil: F:* (*World War II*) militaire *m* qui a fait la campagne de l'Afrique du Nord.

desert[3] [di'zəːt], *v.tr.* (*a*) déserter, quitter (un lieu); déserter, abandonner (son poste); *v.i.* *Mil:* déserter; **to d. from the army,** déserter l'armée; (*b*) abandonner, délaisser (qn); **his friends are deserting him,** ses amis l'abandonnent; **his courage deserted him,** son courage l'a abandonné; *Pol:* **to d. one's party,** faire défection; tourner casaque.

deserted [di'zə:tid], *a.* (*of pers.*) abandonné; (*of place*) désert.

deserter [di'zə:tər], *s.* déserteur *m.*

desertic [di'zə:tik], *a. Geog:* désertique.

desertion [di'zə:ʃ(ə)n], *s.* **1.** abandon *m*, délaissement (de qn); *Jur:* **wife d.,** abandon criminel de l'épouse et des enfants. **2.** *Mil:* désertion *f*; abandon *m* de poste; *Pol:* **d. of one's party,** défection *f.*

deserve [di'zə:v]n *v.tr.* mériter (qch.); **he deserves to be punished,** il mérite d'être puni, qu'on le punisse; **to d. hanging,** être digne, mériter, d'être pendu; **to d. praise,** être digne d'éloges; **to d. one's victory, to win a deserved victory,** remporter une victoire bien méritée; **the penalties which these crimes d.,** la peine due à ces forfaits; **he richly, thoroughly, deserves it!** il ne l'a pas volé! *v.i.* **to d. well of s.o., of one's country,** bien mériter de qn, de sa patrie; **as you d.,** selon vos mérites.

deservedly [di'zə:vidli], *adv.* justement, dignement; à juste titre, à bon droit.

deservedness [di'zə:vidnis], *s.* justice *f* (d'une punition).

deserving [di'zə:viŋ], *a.* (*of pers.*) méritant, de mérite; (*of action*) méritoire; **the least d. candidate,** le candidat le moins méritant; **however d. he may be,** quel que soit son mérite; **d. case,** cas *m* digne d'intérêt.

desex(ualize) [di:'seks(uəlaiz)], *v.tr.* **1.** désexualiser. **2.** châtrer.

déshabille [dezæ'bi:(j)], **déshabillé** [dezæ'bi:jei], *s.* **1.** déshabillé *m*; **in d.,** en déshabillé, en négligé. **2.** *Cost:* négligé *m*, peignoir *m.*

desiccant ['desikənt], *a.* & *s.* desséchant (*m*); déshydratant (*m*).

desiccate ['desikeit], *v.tr.* dessécher, sécher; déshydrater; charquer (la viande à conserver); **to become dessicated,** se déshydrater; **dessicated coconut,** noix de coco déshydratée.

desiccation [desi'keiʃ(ə)n], *s.* dessiccation *f*; dessèchement *m.*

desiccative [de'sikətiv], *a.* & *s.* siccatif (*m*); dessiccatif (*m*).

desiccator ['desikeitər], *s.* dessiccateur *m*, exsiccateur *m*, séchoir *m.*

desiderate [di'zidəreit], *v.tr. Lit:* soupirer après (qch.); sentir le besoin de (qch.); **the reforms desiderated by the public,** les réformes *f* que réclame le public.

desiderative [di'zidəreitiv], *a.* & *s. Gram:* (verbe) désidératif (*m*), méditatif.

desideratum, *pl.* **-a** [dizidə'rɑ:təm, 'reitəm; -ə], *s.* desideratum *m*, *pl.* desiderata.

design[1] [di'zain], *s.* **1.** (*a*) dessein *m*, intention *f*, projet *m*, conception *f*; **by d.,** à dessein; **to have designs on s.o.,** avoir des desseins, des projets, sur qn; *esp.* avoir des vues matrimoniales sur qn; **to have designs on sth.,** avoir des desseins sur qch.; *F:* jeter son dévolu sur qch.; *Phil:* **argument from d.,** preuve *f* par les causes finales; (*b*) (*end*) but *m*; **what is your d.?** quel est votre but? **with this design . . .,** dans ce but . . .; **the designs of France,** les visées *f* de la France. **2.** (*a*) **(decorative) design,** dessin *m* d'ornement; (*in embroidery*) modèle *m*; (*b*) *Tex:* armure *f.* **3.** (*a*) plan *m* (d'un roman, etc.); grandes lignes, ébauche *f* (d'un tableau, etc.); (*b*) *Ind: etc:* étude *f*, avant-projet *m* (d'une machine, etc.); calcul *m* (d'un organe); **industrial d.,** esthétique industrielle; **d. office,** service *m*, bureau *m*, d'études. **4.** (*a*) dessin, représentation *f*, forme *f* (d'une machine, etc.); **machine of faulty d.,** machine mal étudiée, de construction fautive; **in marketing an article d. is as important as construction,** pour le lancement d'un article sur le marché la présentation a autant d'importance que la fabrication; (*b*) type *m*; **houses of different designs,** maisons *f* de types différents; *Com:* **our latest d.,** notre dernier modèle; **car of the latest d.,** voiture *f* dernier modèle; **d. centre,** centre *m* d'exposition (de modèles).

design[2], *v.tr.* **1.** destiner (**for,** à); (*a*) **I had designed this bedroom for you,** c'est à votre intention que j'avais aménagé cette chambre; je vous réservais cette chambre; (*b*) *O:* **to d. s.o. for the church, for the bar,** destiner qn à la prêtrise, au barreau; (*c*) **to d. sth. for a purpose,** destiner qch. à un usage; **boats designed for river traffic, for a speed of 20 knots,** bateaux destinés à la navigation fluviale, établis en vue d'une vitesse de 20 nœuds; **designed speed (of a ship),** vitesse prévue, vitesse contractuelle (d'un navire); **machine designed for a special purpose,** machine construite, étudiée, dans un but spécial; **vessel designed to launch torpedoes,** bâtiment conçu pour lancer des torpilles. **2.** *Jur: Scot:* = DESIGNATE[2] 1 (*a*). **3.** *A:* projeter, se proposer (qch.); **to d. to do, doing, sth.,** projeter, se proposer, avoir le dessein, de faire qch. **4.** (*a*) préparer (un projet); (*b*) étudier, calculer, projeter, concevoir; dessiner d'original (un bâtiment, une robe, une œuvre d'art, des ornements); établir le plan (d'un bâtiment, d'un avion, etc.); créer, inventer (une robe, un chapeau); établir, dimensionner (un mécanisme, un avion, etc.); *Tex:* **to d. a cloth,** mettre un tissu en carte; **binding designed by . . .,** reliure établie par . . .; **well designed premises,** local bien agencé; **the new model is much better designed,** le nouveau modèle est bien mieux compris; **well designed furniture,** meubles *m* aux lignes étudiées.

designate[1] ['dezigneit], *a.* (évêque, etc.) désigné.

designate, *v.tr.* **1.** (*a*) désigner, nommer (**s.o. to an office,** qn à une fonction); (*b*) **to d. s.o. as, for, one's successor,** désigner qn pour, comme, son successeur. **2.** désigner, nommer, appeler; **designated by the name of . . .,** désigné sous le nom de . . .; **he has been designated (as) the most generous man of his age,** il a été représenté comme, il a été appelé, l'homme le plus généreux de son époque; **rulings designated as arbitrary,** décisions qualifiées d'arbitraires. **3.** *O:* (*of things*) indiquer (qch.); **his dress designated (that he was) a person of importance,** son costume indiquait (qu'il était) un homme d'importance.

designation [dezig'neiʃ(ə)n], *s.* **1.** *Adm:* désignation *f* (d'une personne, d'une marchandise); **the d. shall include a statement of profession and residence,** la désignation devra mentionner la profession et le domicile. **2.** désignation, nomination *f* (d'un successeur); **d. to a post,** nomination à un emploi. **3.** désignation, nom *m*, dénomination *f*; **known under several designations,** connu sous plusieurs noms.

designative ['dezigneitiv], *a.* désignatif.

designedly [di'zainidli], *adv.* à dessein, avec dessein; de dessein prémédité; avec préméditation, avec intention; de propos délibéré; intentionnellement.

designer [di'zainər], *s.* **1.** (*a*) *Art: Ind:* dessinateur, -trice, projeteur *m* (qui établit les types d'une invention, d'un article de commerce, etc.); *Th:* **stage d.,** décorateur *m* de théâtre; (*b*) auteur *m*, inventeur, -trice (d'un projet). **2.** intrigant, -ante. **3.** *Tex:* metteur, -euse, en carte.

designing[1] [di'zainiŋ], *a.* artificieux, intrigant.

designing[2], *s.* dessin *m*, création *f*, étude *f* (d'une machine, d'un navire, etc.); dessin, création (d'une robe, d'un chapeau); *Tex:* mise *f* en carte (d'un tissu).

designingly [di'zainiŋli], *adv.* artificieusement; avec ruse.

desilver [di:'silvər], **desilverize** [di:'silvəraiz], *v.tr.* désargenter.

desilverization [di:silvərai'zeiʃ(ə)n], *s.* désargentage *m*; désargentation *f.*

desinence ['desinəns], *s. Ling:* désinence *f.*

desinential [desi'nenʃəl], *a. Ling:* désinentiel.

desirability [dizaiərə'biliti], **desirableness** [di'zaiərəblnis], *s.* caractère *m* désirable; avantage *m* (d'une ligne de conduite, etc.); attrait *m* (d'une femme).

desirable [di'zaiərəbl]. **1.** *a.* (*a*) désirable; à désirer; souhaitable, à souhaiter; opportun; avantageux; **it is most d. to know . . .,** il serait opportun de savoir . . ., il importe de savoir . . .; **it is most d. that he should do it,** il y a le plus haut intérêt à ce qu'il le fasse; il est grandement à désirer qu'il le fasse; *Com:* **this d. property to be sold or let,** belle maison de maître à vendre ou à louer; (*b*) (*of pers., esp. of woman*) attrayant. **2.** *s. usu. pl.* (*a*) *Adm:* **the desirables and the undesirables,** les désirables et les indésirables; (*b*) *F: O:* **young Martin was one of the desirables,** le jeune Martin était parmi les bon partis.

desirably [di'zaiərəbli], *adv.* d'une manière désirable; avantageusement.

desire[1] [di'zaiər], *s.* **1.** (*a*) désir *m*, souhait *m*; **to have a d. to do sth.,** désirer faire qch., avoir le désir, avoir envie, de faire qch.; **I feel no d. to . . .,** je n'éprouve aucune envie de . . .; **all my desires have been met,** on a déféré à tous mes désirs; tous mes désirs ont été comblés; (*b*) appétit (charnel); désir; **consumed with d.,** consumé par le désir. **2.** demande *f*, prière *f*; **at, by, s.o.'s d.,** à, sur, la demande de qn; sur, selon, le désir de qn.

desire[2], *v.tr.* **1.** désirer (qch.); avoir envie de (qch.); vouloir (qch.); **to d. to do sth.,** désirer faire qch.; avoir envie de faire qch.; **to d. that . . .,** désirer que + *sub.*; **it is to be desired that . . .,** il est souhaitable que + *sub.*; **if you d. your child to live . . .,** si vous désirez que votre enfant vive . . .; **I d. to know whether . . .,** je tiens à savoir si . . ., je suis désireux de savoir si . . .; **since you d. it,** puisque vous y tenez; **it leaves much to be desired,** cela laisse beaucoup à désirer. **2.** (*a*) **to d. sth. of s.o.,** demander qch. à qn; désirer qch. de qn; (*b*) **to d. s.o. to do sth.,** prier qn de faire qch.

desirous [di'zaiərəs], *a.* désireux (**of,** de).

desist [di'zist], *v.i. Lit:* **1.** cesser (**from doing sth.,** de faire qch.). **2. to d. from sth.,** renoncer à qch.; se désister de qch.; **to d. from a candidature,** se désister d'une candidature; se désister.

desistance [di'zistəns], *s. Lit:* désistement *m* (**from,** de).

desk [desk], *s.* **1.** (*a*) (**office**) **d.,** bureau *m*; (**writing**) **d.,** secrétaire *m*; (**school**) **d.,** pupitre *m* (d'écolier); **roll-top d.,** bureau à cylindre, à rideau; bureau américain; **d. pad,** sous-main *m inv*; bloc-notes *m*, *pl.* blocs-notes; **reading d.,** pupitre; *Ecc:* lutrin *m*; *Sch:* **master's d.,** chaire *f*; *Publ:* **d. copy,** livre *m* du professeur (fourni à titre gratuit); (*b*) *journ: esp. NAm:* **the d.,** le secrétariat de la rédaction. **2.** *Com:* caisse *f*; **pay at the d.,** payez à la caisse. **3.** (*a*) *El:* **switch d.,** pupitre de distribution; (*b*) *Cmptr:* **control d.,** pupitre de commande.

desman ['desmən], *s. Z:* desman *m.*

Desmidiales [dezmidi'eili:z], *s.pl. Algae:* desmidiales *f.*

desmine ['desmin, -i:n], *s. Miner:* desmine *f*, stilbite *f.*

Desmodium [dez'moudiəm], *s. Bot:* desmodium *m.*

Desmodonta [dezmə'dɔntə], *s.pl. Moll:* desmodontes *m.*

Desmodontidae [dezmə'dɔntidi:], *s.pl. Z:* desmodontidés *m.*

desmognathus [dezmɔg'neiθəs], *s. Z:* desmognathe *m.*

desmography [dez'mɔgrəfi], *s. Anat:* desmographie *f.*

desmolase ['dezməleis], *s. Biol:* desmolase *f.*

desmology [dez'mɔlədʒi], *s. Anat:* desmologie *f.*

desmolysis [dez'mɔlisis], *s. Ch:* desmolyse *f.*

desmoncus [dez'mɔŋkəs], *s. Bot:* desmoncus *m.*

desmotomy [dez'mɔtəmi], *s. Surg:* desmotomie *f.*

desmotropism [dez'mɔtrəpizm], **desmotropy** [dez'mɔtrəpi], *s. Ch:* desmotropie *f.*

desolate[1] ['desələt], *a.* désolé. **1.** solitaire, abandonné; laissé seul. **2.** (lieu) désert, vide, ravagé; **d. region,** pays déshérité. **3.** (*a*) affligé plongé dans l'affliction; (*b*) **d. cry,** cri *m* de désolation.

desolate[2] ['desəleit], *v.tr.* désoler. **1.** (*a*) ravager (un pays, etc.); **the civil wars that desolated Germany,** les guerres *f* civiles qui désolèrent l'Allemagne; (*b*) (*of epidemic, etc.*) dépeupler (une ville). **2.** affliger (qn); mettre (qn) dans la désolation.

desolately ['desələtli], *adv.* **1.** seul, dans la solitude. **2.** d'un air désolé; avec désolation.

desolateness ['desələtnis], *s.* désolation *f*, aspect vide, déshérité (d'un pays, etc.).

desolating ['desəleitiŋ], *a.* (*of news, etc.*) affligeant, désolant.

desolation [desə'leiʃ(ə)n], *s.* **1.** désolation *f*, dévastation *f* (d'un pays vaincu, etc.). **2.** (*a*) désolation, état désolé (d'un paysage, etc.); **the d. of the times,** la misère des temps; (*b*) désolation, chagrin *m*, affliction *f.*

desorb [di'sɔ:b], *v.tr.* désorber.

desorption [di'sɔ:pʃ(ə)n], *s.* désorption *f.*

desoxy- [di'zɔksi], *pref.* = DEOXY.

despair[1] [dis'pɛər], *s.* **1.** désespoir *m*; **to be in d.,** être au désespoir; se désespérer; **a dumb d.,** un accablement muet; **to give up (the attempt) in d.,** y renoncer en désespoir de cause; **to drive s.o. to d.,** désespérer qn; réduire qn au désespoir; **these forms to be filled up drive me to d.,** ces formules *f* à remplir font mon désespoir; **to give way to d.,** s'abandonner au désespoir; **to sink into d.,** tomber dans le désespoir; **act of d.,** coup *m* de désespoir. **2.** *F:* **child who is the d. of his parents,** enfant qui fait le désespoir des siens.

despair[2], *v.i.* (*a*) désespérer (**of,** de); **to d. of doing sth.,** désespérer de faire qch.; **I d. of his succeeding,** je désespère de le voir réussir; **his life is despaired of,** on désespère de sa vie; on n'a plus d'espoir; **to d. of the future,** envisager l'avenir sans espoir; (*b*) perdre espoir; (se) désespérer.

despairing [dis'pɛəriŋ], *a.* désespéré; **in a d. tone,** d'un ton de désespoir.

despairingly [dis'pɛəriŋli], *adv.* désespérément; avec désespoir; **he clung on d.,** il s'accrochait en désespéré.

despatch [dis'pætʃ], *s.* & *v.* = DISPATCH[1,2].

despecialization [di:speʃəlai'zeiʃ(ə)n], *s.* déspécialisation *f.*

despecialize [di:'speʃəlaiz], *v.tr.* déspécialiser.

desperado [despə'rɑ:dou], *s.m.* homme capable de tout; cerveau brûlé; risque-tout *inv.*

desperate ['desp(ə)rət], *a.* **1.** (*a*) (*of condition, illness, etc.*) désespéré; sans espoir; (*b*) **d. remedy,** remède héroïque, désespéré; **d. cases require d. remedies,** aux grands maux les grands remèdes; (*c*) (homme) capable de tout. **2.** (*a*) **a d. man,** un désespéré; un homme aux abois, poussé à bout; (*b*) **d. energy,** l'énergie *f* du désespoir; **d. conflict,** combat acharné; lutte désespérée; **d. resistance,** résistance acharnée, éperdue; **to do something d.,** faire un malheur. **3.** (*intensive*) terrible, affreux, épouvantable; **to have a d. thirst,** avoir une soif affreuse.

desperately ['desp(ə)rətli], *adv.* **1.** (lutter, etc.)

désespérément, en desespéré, avec acharnement, avec fureur, à outrance; **to rush d. into the fight,** se jeter à corps perdu dans la mêlée; **men fighting d. against each other,** hommes acharnés les uns contre les autres. **2. d. ill,** gravement malade; près de la mort. **3.** (*intensive*) éperdument; **to be d. in love with s.o.,** aimer qn à la folie, à en mourir.

desperateness ['desp(ə)rətnis], *s.* état désespéré.

desperation [despə'reiʃ(ə)n], *s.* (outrance *f* du) désespoir *m*; **to drive s.o. to d.,** pousser qn à bout, réduire qn au désespoir; **in d. I wrote to my uncle,** en désespoir de cause, j'ai écrit à mon oncle; **I was in d.,** j'étais aux cent coups; **the people rose in d.,** poussé à bout, le peuple se souleva.

despicable [des'pikəbl, 'despikəbl], *a.* (conduite *f*, action *f*) méprisable, mesquine, digne de mépris.

despicably [des'pikəbli], *adv.* bassement, abjectement; **to behave d.,** se conduire en pleutre, en goujat; (*of woman*) se conduire comme la dernière des dernières.

despise [di'spaiz], *v.tr.* (*a*) mépriser (qn, qch.); faire mépris de (qch.); faire fi (d'une menace); *B:* **he is despised and rejected of men,** il est le méprisé et le rejeté des hommes; (*b*) dédaigner (qch.); **these things are not to be despised,** cela n'est pas à dédaigner.

despiser [dis'paizər], *s.* contempteur, -trice; dénigreur, -euse.

despite [dis'pait]. **1.** *s.* (*a*) *A:* outrage *m*; (*b*) *A:* aversion *f*, rancune *f*; (*c*) *Lit:* sentiment *m* de colère; dépit *m*. **2.** *prep & prep.phr.* **d., in d. of (sth.),** en dépit de, malgré (qch.); **d. what she says,** en dépit de ce qu'elle dit, quoi qu'elle en dise.

despoil [dis'pɔil], *v.tr.* dépouiller, piller, spolier (qn, qch.); **to d. s.o. of sth.,** dépouiller, spolier, qn de qch.; **to d. a tomb,** violer, spolier, un tombeau.

despoiler [dis'pɔilər], *s.* spoliateur, -trice.

despoilment [dis'pɔilmənt], **despoliation** [dispouli'eiʃ(ə)n], *s.* spoliation *f*.

despond[1] [dis'pɔnd], *s. Lit: A:* désespérance *f*, découragement *m*; **the slough of d.,** le bourbier du découragement; l'abîme *m* du désespoir.

despond[2], *v.i.* perdre courage; se décourager, se laisser abattre; voir tout en noir.

despondency [dis'pɔndənsi], *s.* découragement *m*, abattement *m*, accablement *m*, affaissement *m*, mélancolie *f*; **to fall into d.,** tomber dans l'accablement.

despondent [dis'pɔndənt], *a.* découragé, abattu; **he does not allow himself to become d. on account of failure,** il ne se laisse pas abattre par l'insuccès; **to feel d.,** se sentir déprimé; voir tout en noir; **d. gesture,** geste *m* de découragement.

despondently [dis'pɔndəntli], *adv.* d'un air découragé, abattu; avec découragement.

despot ['despɔt], *s.* despote *m*; tyran *m*.

despotic [dis'pɔtik], *a.* **1.** (gouvernement *m*, pouvoir *m*) despotique. **2.** (*of pers.*) arbitraire, despote.

despotically [dis'pɔtik(ə)li], *adv.* despotiquement; arbitrairement.

despotism ['despətizm], *s.* despotisme *m*; **under iron d.,** sous un sceptre de fer.

despun ['di:spʌn], *a. Elcs: Space:* **d. antenna,** antenne antirotative.

desquamate ['deskwəmeit]. **1.** *v.tr. A:* desquamer. **2.** *v.i.* se desquamer, s'exfolier.

desquamation [deskwə'meiʃ(ə)n], *s.* desquamation *f*, exfoliation *f*.

desquamative [des'kwæmətiv], *a.* desquamatif.

dessert [di'zə:t], *s.* dessert *m*; entremets sucré; **d. knife, fork, spoon, plate,** couteau *m*, fourchette *f*, cuillère *f*, assiette *f*, à dessert; **d. service,** service *m* à dessert; **d. wine,** vin *m* de liqueur.

destalinization [di:sta:linai'zeiʃ(ə)n], *s. Pol:* déstalinisation *f*.

destalinize [di:'sta:linaiz], *v.tr. Pol:* déstaliniser.

destearinate [di:'stiərineit], *v.tr.* démargariner (les huiles).

destination [desti'neiʃ(ə)n], *s.* destination *f*; **to forward a letter to its d.,** faire suivre une lettre à son adresse; **to reach one's d.,** arriver à sa destination.

destine ['destin], *v.tr.* **1.** destiner (**s.o. to a calling,** qn à une carrière); **he was destined for the church,** il fut destiné à l'église. **2.** (*usu. in pass.*) **I was destined to be unhappy,** j'étais destiné à être malheureux; **he was destined to succeed,** il lui était réservé de réussir; **he was destined never to see her again,** il ne devait plus la revoir; **it was destined that . . .,** il était écrit que . . .; **the destined hour,** l'heure fatale; l'heure marquée par le destin. **3.** *Lit:* **to be destined for a place,** être en route pour un endroit; être sur le point de partir pour un endroit.

destiny ['destini], *s.* **1.** destin *m*, destinée *f*; le sort; **such was his d.,** telle fut sa destinée; **carried along by ruthless d.,** emporté par un sort impitoyable. **2.** *Myth:* (*a*) le Destin; (*b*) **the Destinies,** les Parques *f*.

destitute ['destitju:t], *a.* **1.** dépourvu, dénué (**of,** de); **a barren waste d. of trees,** un désert aride et dénué d'arbres; **d. of common sense,** dénué de bon sens. **2.** indigent; sans ressources; *F:* sans le sou, sans un sou vaillant; *s.* **the destitute,** les pauvres, les indigents, les miséreux; **to be utterly d.,** manquer de tout; être dans un dénuement complet; **these losses have left him absolutely d.,** ces pertes *f* l'ont laissé sans le sou; **in my d. condition,** dans le dénuement où je me trouvais, me trouve.

destitution [desti'tju:ʃ(ə)n], *s.* **1.** dénûment *m*, dénuement *m*, indigence *f*; misère *f*. **2.** *A:* (*deprivation of office*) destitution *f*.

destrier ['destriər], *s. A: & Lit:* destrier *m*; cheval *m* de bataille.

destroy [dis'trɔi], *v.tr.* **1.** détruire, annihiler (qch.); anéantir (des espérances, etc.); *Artil:* **to d. an obstacle,** disperser un obstacle; **the house was destroyed by the flames,** la maison a été la proie des flammes; **the bad weather had destroyed everything,** le mauvais temps avait tout détruit; **excesses that d. our powers of resistance to disease,** excès *m* qui mettent à bas la résistance vitale; **to d. the discipline of troops,** démoraliser des troupes; saper la discipline. **2.** tuer, abattre (un animal); **to d. an injured horse,** abattre un cheval blessé; **to d. oneself,** se suicider; se détruire.

destroyer [dis'trɔiər], *s.* **1.** destructeur, -trice; démolisseur, -euse. **2.** (*a*) *Navy:* contre-torpilleur *m*; *F:* destroyer *m*; **d. escort,** escorteur *m* rapide; **fleet d.,** escorteur d'escadre; **radar-picket d.,** destroyer picket radar; **d. flotilla, division, squadron,** escadrille *f*, division *f*, escadre *m*, de contre-torpilleurs; **d. leader,** *U.S:* **d. frigate,** destroyer chef de flottille, chef *m* d'escadrille; (*b*) *Mil:* **tank d.,** chasseur *m* de chars.

destroying [dis'trɔiiŋ], *a.* destructeur, -trice.

destruct [dis'trʌkt], *v.tr. Mil: esp. U.S:* détruire (un engin balistique, etc.).

destructible [dis'trʌktibl], *a.* destructible.

destruction [dis'trʌkʃ(ə)n], *s.* **1.** (*a*) destruction *f*, anéantissement *m* (de qch.); consomption *f* (de qch. par le feu); déperdition *f* (de tissu); **d. of a road by a torrent,** rupture *f* d'une route par un torrent; **malicious d. (of property),** sabotage *m*; (*b*) **he is rushing to his own d.,** il court à sa perte; **for the soul to avoid utter d. . . .,** pour échapper à la perdition . . .. **2. the d. caused by the fire, by the storm,** les ravages *m* du feu, de la tempête. **3.** (*cause of destruction*) **gambling was his d.,** le jeu fut sa ruine, causa sa perte; **drink was his d.,** c'est la boisson qui l'a perdu.

destructional [dis'trʌkʃən(ə)l], *a. Geol:* (agent *m*) de dénudation.

destructive [dis'trʌktiv], *a.* destructeur, -trice; destructif; **d. effect of . . .,** effet destructeur de . . .; **d. criticism,** critique destructive; **d. of, to, health,** qui ruine la santé; fatal à la santé; **d. child,** enfant qui détruit tout; brise-tout *m inv*.

destructively [dis'trʌktivli], *adv.* d'une façon funeste.

destructiveness [dis'trʌktivnis], *s.* **1.** effet destructeur, pouvoir destructeur (d'un explosif, etc.). **2.** (*of child, etc.*) penchant *m* à détruire, à tout briser; (*in phrenology*) destructivité *f*.

destructor [dis'trʌktər], *s.* **1.** destructeur, -trice. **2.** *Tchn:* **refuse d.,** destructeur *m* de déchets; incinérateur *m* (d'ordures).

desuetude [di'sju:itju:d], *s.* désuétude *f*; **to fall into d.,** tomber en désuétude; *Jur:* **law fallen into d.,** loi caduque, tombée en désuétude, désuète.

desugar(ize) [di:'ʃugə(raiz)], *v.tr.* désucrer.

(*d*)**desulphurate** [di:'sʌlfəreit, -'sʌlfju-], *v.tr.* = DESULPHURIZE.

desulphurization [di:sʌlfərai'zeiʃ(ə)n, -sʌlfju-], *s. Ch: Ind:* désulfuration *f*, désoufrage *m*.

desulphurize [di:'sʌlfəraiz, -'sʌlfju-], *v.tr. Ch: Ind:* désulfurer, désoufrer, dessoufrer.

desultorily ['desəlt(ə)rili], *adv.* d'une manière décousue; sans suite, sans méthode, à bâtons rompus.

desultoriness ['desəlt(ə)rinis], *s.* manque *m* de suite, de méthode; **the d. of my reading,** le décousu de mes lectures.

desultory ['desəlt(ə)ri], *a.* qui saute d'un sujet à un autre; décousu, sans suite; **d. conversation,** propos interrompus; conversation *f* à bâtons rompus; **d. reading,** lectures décousues; lecture sans méthode.

desurger [di:'sə:dʒər], *s. Hyd.E:* antibélier *m*.

desynchronize [di:'siŋkrənaiz], *v.tr.* désynchroniser.

detach [di'tætʃ], *v.tr.* **1.** détacher, séparer (**from,** de); dételer, désatteler (des wagons); décoller (un timbre, etc.); **to d. s.o. from his party,** détacher qn de son parti; **to d. oneself from the world,** se détacher du monde. **2.** *Mil: Navy:* détacher (des troupes, un navire, etc.); envoyer (des troupes) en détachement. **3.** *Mus:* **to d. the notes,** détacher les notes.

detachability [ditæ:tʃə'biliti], *s.* amovibilité *f* (d'une pièce).

detachable [di'tætʃəbl], *a.* détachable; démontable; (*of parts of machine*) amovible, mobile; **d. cover,** couvercle *m* amovible, enlevable; **d. lens,** objectif *m* mobile; **vice with d. jaws,** étau *m* à mâchoires rapportées; *I.C.E:* **engine with d. head,** moteur *m* à culasse rapportée; *Aut:* **d. rim,** jante *f* amovible.

detached [di'tætʃt], *a.* **1.** détaché, séparé (**from,** de); **one cannot judge the work from d. extracts,** on ne saurait juger de l'œuvre d'après des extraits détachés; **d. house,** maison séparée; *Fort:* **d. works,** ouvrages détachés; *Mil:* **d. post,** poste isolé; **d. battalion,** bataillon détaché, isolé; **d. officer,** officier détaché, en affectation spéciale. **2.** (*a*) (*of pers.*) désintéressé; sans préjugés; (*b*) **d. manner,** manière *f* désinvolte; air détaché, indifférent, nonchalant; **in a d. tone,** d'un ton insouciant, détaché. **3. to live d. from the world,** vivre loin du monde.

detachedly [di'tætʃidli], *adv.* **1.** séparément; à part. **2.** d'un air insouciant, détaché.

detachedness [di'tætʃtnis], *s.* **1.** séparation *f*, isolement *m*, éloignement *m* (**from,** de). **2.** insouciance *f*, détachement *m*.

detachment [di'tætʃmənt], *s.* **1.** (*a*) action *f* de détacher; séparation *f* (**from,** de); dételage *m*, désattelage *m* (de wagons); (*b*) action de se détacher; décollement *m* (d'un timbre, etc.); *Med:* **d. of the retina,** décollement de la rétine. **2.** (*a*) détachement *m* (de l'esprit) (**from,** de); liberté *f* d'esprit; désintéressement *m*; (*b*) indifférence *f* (**from,** envers); incuriosité *f*; insouciance *f*; (*c*) **d. from the world,** détachement du monde. **3.** *Mil:* détachement; **gun d.,** peloton *m* (des servants); **on d.,** détaché.

detail[1] ['di:teil], *s.* **1.** détail *m*; particularité *f*; **to go, enter, into all the details,** donner, entrer dans, s'étendre sur, tous les détails; raconter les choses par le menu; **to go into the smallest details,** descendre jusqu'aux plus petits détails; **in d.,** en détail; **in every d.,** de point en point; **in the fullest d.,** dans le plus grand détail; **to do sth. with minute d.,** faire qch. avec minutie; **to do the d. work,** exécuter les détails; **to go through a movement in details,** exécuter un mouvement en décomposant; **minor details,** (i) menus détails; (ii) l'accessoire *m*, les accessoires; **I cannot give you any details,** je ne peux vous donner aucune précision; **let us have the exact details,** précisons; **but that's a d.,** mais c'est là un détail; **there are points of d. to be settled,** il y a des questions de détail à régler; *Mil:* **war of d.,** guerre *f* de détail; *Art:* **to paint with care for d.,** soigner les détails; *Surv:* **plotting d. (of road, etc.),** détail de tracé (de route, etc.). **2.** organe *m*, pièce composante (d'une machine). **3.** *Mil:* extrait *m* de l'ordre du jour; **details,** l'ordre *m* du jour. **4.** détachement *m* (*Mil:* de corvée, etc., *esp. U.S:* de policiers). **5.** *U.S:* **d. man,** représentant *m* en pharmacie.

detail[2], *tr.* **1.** détailler; raconter en détail; **to d. the facts,** énumérer les faits. **2.** *Mil: etc:* **to d. s.o. for a duty,** désigner, détacher, qn pour un service; affecter qn à un service.

detailed ['di:teild], *a.* détaillé; (récit) circonstancié, détaillé; **to give a d. account of sth.,** raconter qch. en détail; *Surv:* **d. survey,** levé *m* de détail; **d. plotting (of road, etc.),** tracé détaillé (de route, etc.); **d. work,** travail minutieux; travail très fouillé; **to do the d. work,** exécuter les détails.

detain [di'tein], *v.tr.* **1.** détenir (qn en prison); garder (qn à l'hôpital). **2.** (*a*) retenir, retarder, arrêter (qn); empêcher (qn) de partir; **ship detained by ice,** navire retenu par les glaces; **this question need not d. us,** cette question ne nous retiendra pas; (*b*) consigner (un élève). **3.** retenir, détenir (l'argent de qn, etc.).

detainee [ditei'ni:], *s.* détenu, -ue; prisonnier, -ière.

detainer [di'teinər], *s. Jur:* **1.** détention (d'un objet); **forcible d.,** prise *f* de possession d'un immeuble sans autorisation légale. **2. (writ of) d.,** ordre *m* d'incarcération; mandat *m* de dépôt.

detainment [di'teinmənt], *s.* détention *f* (de qn, d'une somme).

detect [di'tekt], *v.tr.* **1.** (*a*) découvrir (le coupable, etc.); déceler (un crime, etc.); dépister (une maladie); **to d. s.o. in the act,** surprendre qn sur le fait; prendre qn en flagrant délit; **I have detected several mistakes,** j'ai découvert plusieurs erreurs; (*b*) **to d. a noise,** percevoir un bruit; **speech in which jealousy could be detected,** discours *m* où perçait la jalousie. **2.** trouver; localiser; détecter; **to d. a leakage of gas,** (i) localiser, (ii) chercher, une fuite de gaz. **3.** *W.Tel: A:* démoduler. **4.**

v.i. faire le métier de détective.
detectable, -ible [di'tektəbl], *a.* discernable; détectable.
detectaphone [di'tektəfoun], *s.* espion *m.*
detecting [di'tektiŋ], *a.* détecteur, -trice.
detection [di'tekʃ(ə)n], *s.* **1.** découverte *f*; **to escape d.,** (i) se dérober aux recherches; (ii) (*of mistake, etc.*) passer inaperçu; **to avoid d.,** éviter de se faire prendre, d'être découvert. **2.** détection *f*; (*a*) *Elcs: etc:* **d. device,** appareil *m* de détection; **d. head,** tête *f* de détection; **d. range,** portée *f* de détection; **radar d.,** détection radar; **sound d.,** détection par le son; **parabolic, square-law, d.,** détection quadratique; **submarine, underwater, d.,** détection sous-marine; *W.Tel:* **grid, bias, d.,** détection grille; **anode d.,** détection plaque; (*b*) *Mil: etc:* **mine d.,** détection des mines; **d. of low-flying aircraft,** détection des avions volant bas; (*c*) *Atom.Ph:* détection. **3.** *W.Tel: A:* démodulation *f.*
detective [di'tektiv]. **1.** *a.* révélateur, -trice; (appareil) révélateur (de fuites, etc.). **2.** *s.* agent *m* de la police judiciaire, de la sûreté; détective *m*; **private d.,** détective (privé); **d. story,** roman policier.
detector [di'tektər], *s.* **1.** (*pers.*) découvreur, -euse (d'erreurs, etc.). **2.** *Tchn:* détecteur *m*; (*a*) **smoke d.,** détecteur de fumée; **metal d.,** détecteur d'objets, de corps, métalliques; *Mil:* **mine d.,** détecteur de mines; **sound d.,** détecteur (d'armes, d'engins) par le son; appareil *m* de repérage par le son; *Min:* **gas d.,** détecteur de grisou; indicateur *m* de gaz; *Jur:* **lie d.,** détecteur de mensonges; (*b*) *Mec.E: etc:* **deviation d.,** détecteur d'écarts; **fault d., leak d.,** détecteur, déceleur *m*, de fuites; indique-fuites *m inv*; **thermal d.,** détecteur thermique, de température; *Metall:* **crack d.,** détecteur de fissures; (*c*) *El: Elcs: etc:* **contact d.,** détecteur à contact; **crystal d.,** détecteur à cristal, à quartz; **valve d.,** détecteur à lampe; **vacuum tube d.,** détecteur à tube à vide; **wave d.,** détecteur d'ondes; **quadratic, square-law, d.,** détecteur quadratique; **pole d.,** chercheur *m* de pôles; **regenerative d.,** détectrice *f* à régénération, à réaction; (*d*) *Atom.Ph:* **radiation d.,** détecteur de rayonnement, de radiations; **gas-flow d.,** détecteur à balayage, à courant, gazeux; **scintillation d.,** détecteur à scintillation(s); **high-resolution, high-resolving power, d.,** détecteur à séparation élevée; **nuclear test d.,** détecteur d'expériences nucléaires.
detent [di'tent], *s. Mec.E:* détente *f*; (dispositif *m* d')arrêt *m*; ergot *m*; linguet *m*; cliquet *m*; chien *m* (d'arrêt); **d. pin,** pivot *m*, goupille *f*, d'arrêt.
détente [del'tɑ̃:nt], *s.* detente *f* (dans les relations politiques, etc.).
detention [di'tenʃ(ə)n], *s.* **1.** (*a*) détention *f* (en prison); **d. on suspicion, d. awaiting trial,** détention préventive; **d. barracks,** prison *f* militaire, locaux *m* disciplinaires; *Mil:* **six weeks' d.,** six semaines de prison, *F:* de taule; *O:* **d. camp,** camp *m* d'internement; (*b*) *Sch:* consigne *f*, retenue *f*; **to give a boy d.,** mettre un élève en retenue; consigner un élève. **2.** (*a*) retard *m* (inévitable); arrêt *m*; *Mil:* **d. allowance,** indemnité journalière; (*b*) *Nau:* arrêt (d'un navire); **to order the d. of a ship,** mettre arrêt sur un navire. **3.** *Jur:* détention (d'une somme due, etc.).
deter [di'tər], *v.tr.* **(deterred)** détourner, décourager, empêcher (**s.o. from doing sth.,** qn de faire qch.) (à cause du danger); **nothing will d. him,** rien ne le fera hésiter.
deterge [di'tə:dʒ], *v.tr. Med:* déterger (une plaie, etc.).
detergency [di'tə:dʒənsi], *s. Ch:* détergence *f.*
detergent [di'tə:dʒənt]. (*a*) *a. & s.* détergent (*m*), détersif (*m*); (*b*) *s.* lessive *f.*
deteriorate [di'tiərəreit]. **1.** *v.tr.* (*a*) détériorer, altérer, avarier; (*b*) déprécier, avilir; enlever de la valeur à (une terre, etc.). **2.** *v.i.* (*a*) (se) détériorer, s'altérer, s'avarier, se tarer; **grain deteriorates with age,** le grain perd en vieillissant; (*b*) diminuer de valeur; perdre de sa valeur; (*c*) (*of race, etc.*) dégénérer; **art is deteriorating,** les arts *m* dégénèrent.
deterioration [ditiərə'reiʃ(ə)n], *s.* (*a*) détérioration *f*, altération *f*; dépérissement *m* (de l'outillage); **d. in quality, in morals,** baisse *f* de qualité, de la moralité; (*b*) diminution *f* de valeur; (*c*) dégénération *f* (d'une race); déchéance *f* (des arts).
deteriorative [di'tiərərəitiv], *a.* nuisible (**to,** à).
determent [di'tə:mənt], *s.* action *f* de détourner (qn) (**from an action,** d'une action); **they had set mantraps for the d. of poachers,** ils avaient tendu des pièges à loups pour arrêter, effrayer, tenir à distance, les braconniers.
determinability [ditə:minə'biliti], *s.* déterminabilité *f.*
determinable [di'tə:minəbl], *a.* **1.** (*a*) (quantité *f*) déterminable; *Ch: etc:* (constituant *m*) dosable; (*b*) (conditions, etc.) que l'on peut préciser, que l'on peut fixer. **2.** *Jur:* (contrat *m*) résoluble.
determinant [di'tə:minənt]. **1.** *a.* déterminant; **d. of sth.,** qui détermine qch. **2.** *s.* (*a*) cause déterminante (**of,** de); (*b*) *Mth:* déterminant *m*; (*c*) *Biol:* déterminant.
determinate [di'tə:minət], *a.* (*a*) déterminé; précis; bien défini; **in a d. sense,** dans un sens déterminé; (*b*) définitif; (*c*) *Bot:* **d. inflorescence,** inflorescence définie.
determination [ditə:mi'neiʃ(ə)n], *s.* **1.** (*a*) détermination *f* (d'une date, de la position d'un astre); **d. of compensation,** fixation *f* des indemnités; **d. of penalty,** application *f* de peine; (*b*) délimitation *f* (d'une frontière); (*c*) *Ch:* **quantity d. (of ingredients),** dosage *m*; **blank d.,** dosage témoin, expérience *f* à blanc. **2.** (*of pers.*) (*a*) détermination, résolution *f*; **his d. to build,** son intention arrêtée de bâtir; **to come to a d.,** se décider; arriver à une décision; prendre une détermination; **air of d.,** air résolu, décidé, déterminé; (*b*) *Phil:* détermination. **3.** *Jur:* (*a*) décision *f* (d'une affaire); (*b*) arrêt *m*, décision, sentence *f*. **4.** (*a*) *Jur:* résolution, résiliation *f*, résiliment *m* (d'un contrat, etc.); (*b*) expiration *f* (d'un contrat, etc.). **5.** (*a*) *Ph: etc:* détermination, tendance *f* **(towards,** vers); (*b*) *Physiol:* **d. of blood to the head,** détermination, afflux *m*, du sang à la tête.
determinative [di'tə:minətiv]. **1.** *a.* déterminant; **an incident d. of his career,** incident *m* qui décida de sa carrière. **2.** *a. & s. Gram:* déterminatif (*m*); (pronom, etc.) démonstratif.
determine [di'tə:min], *v.tr. & i.* **1.** (*a*) déterminer, fixer (une date, des règles, etc.); **conditions to be determined,** conditions *f* à définir; **the price is determined by the amount on the market,** le prix est réglé, fixé, par l'offre; (*b*) déterminer, délimiter (une frontière); (*c*) déterminer, constater (la nature, les dimensions, de qch.); déterminer (une famille de plantes); apprécier (une distance, etc.). **2.** décider, résoudre (une question, etc.); régler (un point en litige); **to d. s.o.'s fate,** décider du sort de qn. **3.** (*a*) **to d. to do sth., to d. on doing sth.,** décider, résoudre, de faire qch.; se décider, se déterminer, se résoudre, à faire qch.; **to d. that. . .,** décider, résoudre, que . . .; (*b*) **to be determined to do sth.,** être résolu à, vouloir absolument, faire qch.; **we were determined to buy a dishwasher,** nous voulions à tout prix acheter un lave-vaisselle. **4. to d. s.o. to do sth.,** décider, déterminer, qn à faire qch.; **these reflections determined me to do something,** ces réflexions *f* me décidèrent à agir. **5.** *Jur:* (*a*) *v.tr.* résoudre, résilier (un contrat, un bail); (*b*) *v.i.* (*of lease, agreement, etc.*) prendre fin; expirer (à telle ou telle date).
determined [di'tə:mind], *a.* **1.** (prix) déterminé; (limite) déterminée. **2.** (*of pers.*) déterminé, résolu, volontaire; **d. character,** caractère décidé; **d. chin,** menton *m* volontaire, **he is more d. than ever,** il est plus décidé que jamais.
determinedly [di'tə:mindli], *adv.* résolument; d'un air décidé; avec détermination.
determining [di'tə:miniŋ], *a.* déterminant.
determinism [di'tə:minizm], *s. Phil:* déterminisme *m.*
determinist [di'tə:minist], *a. & s. Phil:* déterministe (*mf*).
deterrence [di'terəns], *s. Mil: Pol:* emploi *m* des armes de dissuasion.
deterrent [di'terənt]. **1.** *a.* (*a*) (effet) préventif (d'une peine); (*b*) **we were kept in port by d. weather,** nous étions retenus au port sous la menace de gros temps. **2.** *s.* (*of penalty, etc.*) **to act as a d. of crime,** servir de préventif *m*, exercer un effet préventif, contre le crime. **3.** *s. Mil: Pol:* arme *f* de dissuasion.
detersion [di'tə:ʃ(ə)n], *s. Med:* détersion *f.*
detersive [di'tə:siv], *a. & s. Med:* détersif (*m*).
detest [di'test], *v.tr.* détester; abhorrer; **detested by all,** détesté de tous; **I d. being interrupted,** je déteste être dérangé; je déteste qu'on vienne me déranger.
detestable [di'testəbl], *a.* détestable.
detestableness [di'testəb(ə)lnis], **detestability** [ditestə'biliti], *s.* caractère *m* détestable (de qch.).
destestably [di'testəbli], *adv.* détestablement.
detestation [di:tes'teiʃ(ə)n], *s.* **1.** détestation *f* (**of,** de); **to have, hold, sth. in d.,** avoir qch. en horreur; détester qch. **2.** chose *f* détestable; (objet *m* d')horreur *f*; abomination *f.*
detester [di'testər], *s.* ennemi, -ie (**of,** de).
dethrone [di'θroun], *v.tr.* détrôner.
dethronement [di'θrounmənt], *s.* détrônement *m*, déposition *f.*
detin [di:'tin], *v.tr. Metalw:* désétamer.
detinning [di:'tiniŋ], *s. Metalw:* désétamage *m.*
detinue ['detinju:], *s. Jur:* détention (illégale); *used only in* **action of d.,** action *f* en revendication, en restitution.
detonate ['detəneit]. **1.** *v.tr.* faire détoner (un explosif); faire sauter (une mine); **to d. a fog signal,** faire éclater un détonateur, un pétard. **2.** *v.i.* (*a*) détoner; (*b*) *I.C.E:* (*of engine*) cogner.
detonating ['detəneitiŋ], *a. & s.* détonant, explosif; **d. mixture,** mélange détonant; *I.C.E: etc:* **non-detonating mixture,** mélange anti-détonant; **d. gas,** gaz tonnant; **d. temperature,** température *f* de détonation; **d. wave,** onde explosive; *Ph:* **d. bulb,** larme *f* batavique; bombe-chandelle *f*, *pl.* bombes-chandelles; *Exp:* **d. fuse,** cordeau détonant; **d. set,** appareil *m*, engin *m*, à détonateur.
detonation [detə'neiʃ(ə)n], *s.* **1.** détonation *f*, explosion *f*. **2.** *I.C.E:* cognement *m*, cliquetis *m* (du moteur).
detonative ['detəneitiv], *a.* détonant, explosif; **d. power,** force explosive.
detonator ['detəneitər], *s.* (*a*) *Exp:* détonateur *m*; amorce *f*; **primer d.,** détonateur primaire; amorce détonateur; **burster d.,** détonateur de la charge d'éclatement; **percussion d.,** détonateur à éclatement; **percussion d.,** détonateur à percussion; **contact mine d.,** détonateur de mine à percussion; **chemical, electrical, d.,** détonateur chimique, électrique; (*b*) *Rail:* (*fog signal*) détonateur.
detour[1], **détour** ['deituər, 'di:-], *s.* (*a*) détour *m*; (*b*) *U.S:* déviation *f* (d'itinéraire, etc.); *Rail:* **d. ticket,** billet *m* de changement d'itinéraire.
detour[2], *v.* **1.** *v.tr. U.S:* dévier (la circulation). **2.** *v.i.* **to d. to the right round an obstacle,** contourner à droite un obstacle.
detoxicate [di:'tɔksikeit], *v.tr. Med:* (*a*) désintoxiquer; (*b*) détoxiquer.
detoxication [di:tɔksi'keiʃ(ə)n], *s. Med:* (*a*) désintoxication *f*; (*b*) détoxication *f.*
detoxification [di:tɔksifi'keiʃ(ə)n], *s.* détoxification *f.*
detoxifier [di:'tɔksifaiər], *s.* détoxifiant *m.*
detract [di'trækt]. **1.** *v.i.* **to d. from s.o.'s merit, reputation, etc.,** rabaisser, amoindrir, le mérite de qn; nuire, porter atteinte, à la réputation de qn. **2.** *v.tr.* (*a*) **to d. something, a great deal, from s.o.'s pleasure,** diminuer un peu, de beaucoup, le plaisir de qn; (*b*) *A:* déprécier, dénigrer (qn); *A:* détracter (qn).
detraction [di'trækʃ(ə)n], *s.* (*a*) dénigrement *m*; (*b*) **this is no d. from his merits,** ceci n'enlève rien à son mérite.
detractive [di'træktiv], *a.* (esprit) détracteur.
detractor [di'træktər], *s.* détracteur, -trice; avilisseur, -euse; dénigreur, -euse.
detrain [di:'trein]. **1.** *v.tr.* débarquer (des troupes) d'un train. **2.** *v.i.* (*of troops*) débarquer (du train).
detraining, *s.* [di:'treiniŋ], **detrainment** [di:'treinmənt], *s.* débarquement *m* (d'un train); **d. point,** chantier *m*, point *m*, de débarquement.
detriment ['detrimənt], *s.* détriment *m*, dommage *m*, préjudice *m*; **to the d. of . . .,** au détriment, au préjudice, de . . .; **without d. to . . .,** sans préjudice de (mes droits, etc.); sans nuire à . . ..
detrimental [detri'mentl], *a.* nuisible, préjudiciable (**to,** à); **it would be d. to my interests,** cela desservirait mes intérêts.
detrimentally [detri'mentəli], *adv.* nuisiblement; d'une manière préjudiciable, nuisible (**to,** à).
detrital [di'trait(ə)l], *a. Geol:* (dépôt *m*, etc.) détritique.
detrition [di'triʃ(ə)n], *s. Geol:* détrition *f*; usure *f*; frottement *m.*
detritivorous [detri'tivə:rəs], *a. Ent:* détritophage.
detritus [di'traitəs], *s. Geol:* détritus *m(pl)*; **drift d.,** détritus charriés.
detruck [di:'trʌk], *U.S: Mil:* **1.** *v.tr.* (faire) débarquer (des troupes, etc., de véhicules automobiles). **2.** *v.i.* (*of troops, etc.*) débarquer.
detrucking [di:'trʌkiŋ], *s. U.S: Mil:* débarquement *m* (de véhicules automobiles); **d. point,** chantier *m*, point *m*, de débarquement; **d. area,** zone *f* de débarquement.
detumescence [di:tju'mesəns], *s. Med:* détumescence *f.*
detune [di:'tju:n], *v.tr. Elcs: etc:* désaccorder.
deuce[1] [dju:s], *s.* **1.** (*of dice, dominoes, cards*) deux *m*; **d. ace,** (coup *m* de dés de) deux et un. **2.** *Ten:* à deux; égalité *f* (à quarante); quarante à, quarante partout; (*after one player has had advantage*) avantage détruit; **d. set,** partie *f* où il y a (eu) cinq partout.
deuce[2], *s. F: O:* diantre *m*, diable *m*; **what the d. does he mean?** que diable veut-il dire? **he's the d. of a liar,** c'est un satané menteur; **a d. of a mess,** un joli gâchis; **that was a d. of a time ago,** il y a diantrement, diablement, longtemps de cela.
deuced ['dju:sid]. *F: O:* **1.** *a.* **a d. lot of trouble,** une peine du diable; **I was in a d. mess!** j'étais dans de beaux draps! **2.** *adv.* **what d. bad weather!** quel diable de temps!
deucedly ['dju:sidli], *adv. F: O:* diablement, diantrement.
deuteragonist [dju:tər'ægənist], *s. Gr.Th:* deutéragoniste *m.*
deuteranomaly [dju:tərə'nɔməli], *s. Opt:*

deutéranomalie *f.*
deuteranope ['dju:tərənoup], *s. Opt:* deutéranope *mf.*
deuteranopia [dju:tərə'noupiə], *s. Opt:* deutéranopie *f.*
deuteranopic [dju:tərə'noupik], *a. Opt:* deutéranope.
deuteride ['dju:təraid], *s. Ch:* hydrure lourd.
deuterium [dju:'tiəriəm], *s. Ch:* deutérium *m.*
deuterocanonical ['dju:təroukə'nɔnikl], *a. B.Hist:* deutérocanonique.
deuterograph ['dju:tərəgræf], *s.* passage *m* double (de l'Ancien Testament).
Deuteromycetes ['dju:təroumai'si:ti:z], *s.pl. Fung:* deutéromycètes *m.*
deuteron ['dju:tərɔn], *s. Ch:* deutéron *m*, deuton *m.*
Deuteronomy [dju(:)tə'ɔnəmi], *s. B:* Deutéronome *m.*
deuteropathy [djutə'rɔpəθi], *s. Med:* deutéropathie *f.*
deuteroscopy [djutə'rɔskəpi], *s.* deutéroscopie *f.*
deuton ['dju:tɔn], *s. Ch:* deuton *m*, deutéron *m.*
deutoplasm ['dju:touplæzm], *s.* deutoplasma *m.*
deutzia ['dju:tsiə, 'dɔitsiə], *s. Bot:* deutzie *f.*
devalorization [di:vælərai'zeiʃ(ə)n], *s. Pol.Ec:* dévalorisation *f.*
devalorize [di:'væləraiz], *v.tr.* dévaloriser (la monnaie).
devaluate [di:'væljueit], *v.tr. Pol.Ec:* dévaluer.
devaluation [di:vælju'eiʃ(ə)n], *s. Pol.Ec:* dévaluation *f.*
devalue [di:'vælju], *v.tr. Pol.Ec:* dévaluer.
devastate ['devəsteit], *v.tr.* dévaster, ravager; **the war had devastated the whole country,** la guerre avait dévasté, ravagé, tout le pays; **the storm devastated everything,** la tempête a tout moissonné.
devastating ['devəsteitiŋ], *a.* **1.** (*of storm, etc.*) dévastateur, -trice; ravageur, -euse; destructeur, -trice. **2.** (argument) accablant; (charme) fatal; **d. shyness,** timidité excessive, embarrassante; *F:* **a d. bore,** un casse-pieds sans égal; *Iron:* **how d.!** quel malheur!
devastatingly ['devəsteitiŋli], *adv.* d'une manière désastreuse, désespérante; **d. beautiful,** d'une beauté incomparable; **d. funny,** d'un comique à se tordre.
devastation [devəs'teiʃ(ə)n], *s.* **1.** dévastation *f.* **2.** *Jur:* dilapidation *f* (d'une succession par le curateur).
devastator ['devəsteitər], *s.* dévastateur, -trice.
devastavit [di:væs'teivit], *s. Jur:* action *f* en dilapidation (contre un curateur); action en maladministration (des biens d'un mineur).
develop [di'veləp], *v.* **(developed** [di'veləpt]**)**
I. *v.tr.* **1.** *Mth:* développer (une surface, une fonction). **2.** (*a*) développer (les facultés, etc.); **gymnastics d. the body,** la gymnastique développe le corps; (*b*) développer, exposer graduellement, amplifier, élargir (une pensée, etc.); (*c*) *Mil:* **to d. an attack,** développer une attaque; (*d*) *Chess:* **to d. one's pieces, one's game,** déployer son jeu. **3.** (*a*) **to d. a district, a coal basin,** exploiter, mettre en valeur, faire valoir, une région, un bassin houiller; développer les ressources d'une région; **to d. a building site,** lotir, faire des lotissements; *Min:* **to d. a new level,** tracer une nouvelle galerie; (*b*) *Tchn:* réaliser, mettre au point (un nouveau dessin, etc.). **4.** **to d. heat,** engendrer de la chaleur; **heat developed,** chaleur développée, engendrée. **5.** (*a*) contracter (une maladie); **to d. fever, whooping cough,** faire de la fièvre, de la coqueluche; **he developed a tumour,** il lui est venu une tumeur; (*b*) contracter (une mauvaise habitude); manifester (une tendance à . . .); **at school he developed a great gift for mathematics,** à l'école il s'est révélé très doué pour les mathématiques. **6.** (*a*) *Phot:* révéler, développer (une plaque, une épreuve); (*b*) *NAm:* **the inquiry has developed some new facts,** l'enquête *f* a mis à jour, a révélé, a fait connaître, des faits nouveaux.
II. *v.i.* **1.** (*a*) (*of the body, the faculties, etc.*) se développer; **young man whose character is developing,** jeune homme qui se fait; **fully developed horse,** cheval fait; **we must let the scheme d., let things d.,** il faut laisser couver le projet, laisser dérouler les choses; **they had met but the acquaintance had not developed,** ils s'étaient rencontrés mais sans entrer en relations suivies; *Bot:* (*of plant*) **to d. imperfectly,** avorter; (*b*) **London developed into the general mart of Europe,** Londres devint peu à peu le grand marché de l'Europe. **2.** se manifester, se révéler; (*of crisis*) se produire; (*a*) **fever developed,** la fièvre s'est déclarée; **an abscess had developed,** il s'était formé un abcès; (*b*) *NAm:* **a new feature of the case developed today,** l'affaire a pris aujourd'hui une nouvelle tournure; **it developed today that . . .,** nous apprenons aujourd'hui que . . ..
developable [di'veləpəbl], *a.* **1.** *Mth:* (surface *f*) développable. **2.** *Town P:* **d. site,** terrain *m* exploitable, à lotir.
developer [di'veləpər], *s.* **1.** (*a*) personne *f* qui développe, qui met en valeur (une région, etc.); promoteur *m*; *Town P:* lotisseur *m*; (*b*) *Phot:* (*pers.*) développeur *m*; (*c*) **late d.,** enfant *m* qui se développe sur le tard. **2.** *Phot:* (agent) révélateur *m.* **3.** *Gym:* sandow *m*, exerciseur *m.*
developing[1] [di'veləpiŋ], *a.* **1.** développant. **2.** qui se développe, qui fait des progrès, qui se fait; **d. countries,** pays *m* en voie de développement.
developing[2], *s.* **1.** développement *m*, exploitation *f*, mise *f* en valeur (d'une région, etc.); *Chess:* déploiement *m* (des pièces). **2.** *Phot:* développement; **d. of prints,** tirage *m* par développement; **d. bath,** (bain) révélateur *m*; bain de développement; **d. dish, d. tray,** cuvette *f*; **d. tank,** cuve *f* à développement; *Cin:* **d. rack,** châssis *m*, cadre *m*, de développement; *O:* **d. (out) paper,** papier *m* à image latente.
development [di'veləpmənt], *s.* **1.** *Mth:* (*a*) développement *m* (d'une surface, d'une fonction); (*b*) développée *f* (d'une spirale). **2.** (*a*) développement (du corps, des facultés); (*b*) développement, amplification *f* (d'un sujet); élargissement *m* (d'une idée); (*c*) *Chess:* **d. of one's game, of one's pieces,** déploiement *m* de ses pièces. **3.** (*a*) exploitation *f*, mise *f* en valeur (d'une région, etc.); *Town P:* aménagement *m*; lotissement *m* (d'un terrain à bâtir); *Min:* traçage *m* (d'une nouvelle galerie); **d. companies,** sociétés *f* d'exploitation; *Pol.Ec:* **national d.,** aménagement du territoire; (*b*) *Tchn:* réalisation *f*, mise au point (d'un nouveau dessin, etc.). **4.** *Phot:* développement. **5.** (*a*) développement *m*, progrès *m*; déroulement *m* (des événements, etc.); (*b*) évolution *f* (des événements, de la pensée, des animaux). **6.** fait nouveau; **a new d. occurred,** un nouveau fait se produisit; **to await further developments,** attendre pour voir quelle tournure prendront les choses; attendre les événements.
developmental [diveləp'mentl], *a.* développemental, -aux; qui appartient à l'évolution; **d. ailments,** troubles *m* de croissance.
développé [deivə'lɔpei], *s. Danc:* développé *m.*
deverbal [di:'və:bəl], **deverbative** [di:'və:bətiv], *a. & s. Gram:* déverbal, -aux (*m*); déverbatif (*m*).
deviance ['di:viəns], **deviancy** ['di:viənsi], *s. Psy:* déviance *f.*
deviant ['di:viənt], *a. & s. Psy:* aberrant, -ante.
deviate ['di:vieit], *v.i.* dévier, s'écarter (**from,** de); *Ph:* (*of beam*) s'infléchir; *Ball:* (*of projectile*) dériver; **to d. from one's duty,** se départir, s'éloigner, sortir, de son devoir; s'écarter du devoir; *El: etc:* **deviating power,** force *f* de déviation.
deviation [di:vi'eiʃ(ə)n], *s.* **1.** déviation *f* (d'une aiguille aimantée, d'un rayon lumineux, etc.); écart *m* (de la norme, etc.); **absolute d.,** écart absolu; **mean d.,** écart moyen; **d. from one's instructions,** dérogation *f* à ses instructions; *Med:* **conjugate d. of the eyes,** déviation conjuguée des yeux; *Ball:* **lateral d.,** dérivation *f*; **vertical d.,** écart en hauteur. **2.** *Com: Ins:* déroutement *m* (d'un navire, entraînant l'annulation des polices d'assurance et de la charte-partie).
deviationism [di:vi'eiʃənizm], *s.* déviationnisme *m.*
deviationist [di:vi'eiʃənist], *a. & s.* déviationniste (*mf*).
deviatory ['di:viətəri], *a.* déviateur, -trice.
device [di'vais], *s.* **1.** (*a*) expédient *m*, moyen *m*; **temporary devices,** moyens temporaires; (*b*) *esp. pl.* inclination *f*, caprices *mpl*; **to leave s.o. to his own devices,** abandonner qn à ses propres moyens; laisser qn s'occuper comme bon lui semble; livrer qn à lui-même; (*c*) stratagème *m*, ruse *f*; **through this d. he put the police off the scent,** grâce à cette ruse il a pu dépister la police. **2.** dispositif *m*, appareil *m*, mécanisme *m*, invention *f*, arrangement *m*; **ignition d.,** dispositif d'allumage; **lubricating devices,** appareils de graissage; *Mil:* **light and smoke devices,** artifices *mpl*; **adjusting d.,** dispositif, système *m*, de réglage; **locking d.,** dispositif, système, de verrouillage, de fermeture; **safety d.,** dispositif, système, de sécurité; *Artil:* **aiming d.,** instrument *m* de pointage. **3.** (*a*) *A:* forme *f*, figure *f*, image *f*, dessin *m*; (*b*) emblème *m*, devise *f*; **a banner with a strange d.,** une bannière portant une devise étrange; (*c*) *Her:* devise, meuble *m* (de l'écu).
devil[1] ['devl], *s.* **1.** (*a*) diable *m*; **Jesus was tempted by the d.,** Jésus fut tenté par le diable; **devil's advocate,** avocat *m* du diable; **to be between the d. and the deep (blue) sea,** être pris entre deux feux; se trouver entre l'arbre et l'écorce; être entre l'enclume et le marteau, entre Charybde et Scylla; **talk of the d. (and his horns will appear, and he's sure to appear),** quand on parle du loup, on en voit la queue; **needs must when the d. drives,** il faut marcher quand le diable est à vos trousses; **to paint the d. blacker than he is,** faire le diable plus noir qu'il n'est; **the d. rebuking sin,** le diable qui s'est fait ermite; *O:* **d. take it!** que le diable l'emporte! **to send s.o. to the d.,** envoyer qn au diable, à tous les diables; *P:* envoyer dinguer qn; **to go to the d.,** se ruiner, se perdre, se couler; *F:* **go to the d.!** allez vous promener! *P:* va te faire fiche! **to play the d.,** faire le diable à quatre; **to play the (very) d. with s.o., sth.,** faire un mal du diable à qn; mettre la confusion dans qch.; ruiner qch.; **drinking has played the d. with his health,** la boisson a ruiné sa santé; **to raise the d. about sth.,** faire un boucan de tous les diables au sujet de qch.; faire un bruit infernal; **he's the d. incarnate,** c'est un vrai démon; c'est un diable incarné, un diable à quatre; **that child's a little d.,** cet enfant est un petit monstre; **the devil's in it!** le diable s'en mêle! *A:* **the devil's bones,** les dés *m*; *A:* **the devil's picture book,** les cartes *f*; *Cards:* **the devil's bedpost,** le quatre de trèfle; (*b*) *F:* **what the d. are you doing?** que diable faites-vous là? **how the d. . . .?** comment diable . . .? **to work like the d.,** travailler avec acharnement; **to run like the d.,** courir comme un dératé; **there'll be the d. to pay,** ça nous, vous, coûtera cher; (*of a task, etc.*) **it's the d.,** c'est le diable (à confesser); **it's the d. and all to get him to consent,** c'est la croix et la bannière pour le faire consentir; **it's the d. of a way,** c'est au diable vauvert; **a d. of a wind,** un vent du diable; **a d. of a business,** une diable d'affaire; **a d. of a row, of a job,** un vacarme, un bruit, un travail, de tous les diables; **to have the d. of a job (to do sth.),** avoir un mal de chien, un mal de tous les diables (à faire qch.); **he's a d. of a fellow,** c'est un garçon terrible; **he's got the d. of a temper,** il a un fichu caractère; il est mauvais coucheur; **to be in the, a, d. of a funk,** avoir une frousse, un trac, de tous les diables; *O:* **d. a one!** pas un! personne! **d. a bit!** pas du tout! pas le moins du monde! **2.** démon *m*; **she-d.,** (i) diablesse *f*; (ii) *F:* mégère *f*; **prince of devils,** prince *m* des démons; **to raise a d.,** évoquer un démon; *F:* **to raise the d. in s.o.,** mettre qn dans une colère folle; **to cast out a d.,** chasser un démon; **d. worship,** démonolâtrie *f*; *F:* **blue devils,** diables bleus; humeur noire; le cafard; *F:* **poor d.!** pauvre diable! **he's a bit of a d.,** (i) c'est une tête brûlée; (ii) il est quelque peu rageur; **the silly d.!** quel espèce d'idiot! **3.** *F:* (*a*) nègre *m* (d'un écrivain, d'un avocat); (*b*) *Typ:* **printer's d.,** apprenti imprimeur. **4.** (*a*) pot *m* à feu; brasero *m*; (*b*) lampe *f* (de peintre en bâtiments). **5.** *Ind:* nom de dispositifs divers à dents ou à pointes; *Tex: Paperm:* dérompoir *m*, effilocheuse *f*; *Mec.E:* **devil's claw,** tendeur *m* à pouce articulé; chien *m.* **6.** (*a*) *Meteor:* **dust d.,** tourbillon *m* de poussière; (*b*) *NAm: Ent: F:* **devil's horse,** mante religieuse; **devil's darning needle,** (i) libellule *f*; (ii) *Bot:* sparte *m*, alfa *m*; (*c*) *Bot: F:* **d. in the bush,** nigelle *f*; **devil's bit,** scabieuse tronquée, mors *m* du diable, herbe *f* de Saint-Joseph; **devil's guts,** *Austr:* **devil's twine,** cuscute *f*; **devil's milk,** (i) euphorbe *f* réveille-matin; (ii) grande chélidoine; (*d*) *Rept: F:* **thorny d.,** moloch épineux; (*e*) *Cu:* **devils on horseback,** huîtres frites enveloppées de bacon; **devil's food cake,** gâteau *m* au chocolat.
devil[2], *v.* **(devilled) 1.** *v.i. F:* **to d. for s.o.,** servir de nègre à (un avocat, etc.). **2.** *v.tr.* (*a*) *Cu:* faire griller et poivrer fortement (de la viande); **devilled grill,** grillade *f* au feu d'enfer; (*b*) *Paperm: etc:* effilocher (des chiffons, etc.); (*c*) *NAm: F:* **to d. s.o. with questions,** harceler qn de questions.
devil-dodger ['devldɔdʒər], *s. P:* curé *m*, corbeau *m*, ratichon *m.*
devilfish ['devlfiʃ], *s.* **1.** *Ich:* mante *f*, raie *f* manta, diable *m* de mer. **2.** *Moll:* pieuvre *f*; poulpe *m.*
devilish ['devliʃ]. **1.** *a.* (*a*) diabolique; **a d. plot to ruin you,** un complot diabolique pour vous perdre; (*b*) *F:* de diable, du diable, maudit, satané. **2.** *adv. F: O:* **it's d. hot!** il fait rudement chaud! il fait une chaleur du diable.
devilishly ['devliʃli], *adv.* **1.** diaboliquement. **2.** *F:* diablement, rudement, bigrement; **d. pretty,** diablement joli(e); **d. hot,** rudement chaud.
devilishness ['devliʃnis], *s.* **1.** nature *f* diabolique (d'une invention, etc.). **2.** *F:* diablerie *f* (d'un enfant, etc.).
devilism ['devlizm], *s.* satanisme *m.*
devil-like ['devllaik], *a.* (cruauté *f*, etc.) diabolique.
devil-may-care ['devlmei'kɛər], *a. & s.* **d.-m.-c. (person),** cerveau brûlé; tête brûlée; casse-cou *m inv*; un j'm'en-fichiste; **d.-m.-c. spirit,** esprit (i) téméraire, (ii) insouciant.
devilment ['devlmənt], **devilry** ['devlri], *s.* **1.** (*a*) action *f* diabolique; (*b*) magie (noire); (*c*) méchanceté *f*; **there's some d. afoot,** il se trame quelque chose. **2.** diablerie *f*; **to be full of d.,** (i) avoir le diable au corps; (ii) avoir le cerveau brûlé.
deviltry ['devltri], *s. Scot. & NAm:* = DEVILRY.
devious ['di:viəs], *a.* **1.** (*of course, way*) détourné, tortueux, oblique; **to achieve one's ends by d. ways,** prendre des voies détournées pour arriver à son but. **2.** (*of pers.*) retors. **3.** *A:* (*of place*) écarté, détourné.
deviously ['di:viəsli], *adv.* d'une façon détournée; par

des détours.
deviousness ['di:viəsnis], *s.* détours *mpl*, tortuosité *f* (d'un sentier, de la pensée); caractère retors (de qn).
devirilization [di:virilai'zeiʃ(ə)n], *s.* dévirilisation *f.*
devirilize [di:'virilaiz], *v.tr.* efféminer.
devisable [di'vaizəbl], *a.* **1.** imaginable. **2.** *Jur:* (bien immobilier) disponible (par testament).
devise[1] [di'vaiz], *s. Jur:* **1.** dispositions *f* testamentaires de biens immobiliers. **2.** legs (immobilier).
devise[2], *v.tr.* **1.** combiner (un projet); inventer, imaginer, trouver (un appareil, un expédient); tramer (un complot); **to d. a good plan,** s'aviser d'un bon expédient; **if you can d. a way of doing it,** si vous pouvez trouver le moyen de le faire; **speech devised to impress,** discours destiné à frapper les esprits. **2.** *Jur:* disposer par testament de (biens immobiliers); léguer (des biens immobiliers).
devisee [divai'zi:], *s. Jur:* institué, -ée; légataire *mf* (de biens immobiliers); héritier, -ière, testamentaire.
deviser [di'vaizər], *s.* inventeur *m* (de qch.).
devising [di'vaiziŋ], *s.* **1.** invention *f* (d'un appareil, etc.); **the plot of the play is of his own d.,** il a inventé, imaginé, lui-même l'intrigue de la pièce. **2.** *Jur:* disposition *f* par testament.
devisor [di'vaizɔ:r], *s. Jur:* testateur, -trice.
devitalize [di:'vaitəlaiz], *v.tr.* dévitaliser (une dent, etc.).
devitaminized [di:'vitəminaizd], *a.* dévitaminé.
devitrification [di:vitrifi'keiʃ(ə)n], *s.* dévitrification *f* (du verre).
devitrify [di:'vitrifai], *v.tr.* dévitrifier (le verre).
devocalization [di:voukəlai'zeiʃ(ə)n], *s.* dévocalisation *f.*
devoid [di'vɔid], *a.* **1.** dénué, dépourvu (**of,** de); **d. of sense,** dépourvu de sens, vide de sens. **2. d. of cares,** exempt de soucis.
devoir ['devwɑ:r], *s. A:* devoir *m*; *esp. in the phr.* **to pay one's devoirs to s.o.,** rendre ses devoirs à qn.
devolution [di:və'l(j)u:ʃ(ə)n], *s.* **1.** *Biol:* dégénération *f* (d'une espèce); dégénérescence *f.* **2.** *Jur:* (*a*) dévolution *f*; transmission *f* par succession; *Hist:* **the War of D.,** la Guerre de Dévolution; (*b*) déchéance *f* (d'un droit) (en faveur de l'ultime propriétaire); *Ecc:* dévolution, dévolu *m* (d'un bénéfice). **3.** *Pol:* (*a*) délégation *f* (de pouvoir); (*b*) décentralisation administrative.
devolutionary [di:və'l(j)u:ʃən(ə)ri], *a. Jur:* dévolutif.
devolve [di'vɔlv]. **1.** *v.tr.* (*a*) **to d. a duty, a responsibility, to, (up)on, s.o.,** se décharger sur qn d'un devoir, d'une responsabilité; (*b*) **to d. duties, powers, to s.o.,** déléguer, transmettre, des fonctions, des pouvoirs, à qn. **2.** *v.i.* (*a*) revenir, incomber, échoir (**on, upon,** à); **the responsibility that devolves on the tenant,** la responsabilité qui incombe au locataire; **the duty devolved on me to . . .,** le devoir m'échut de . . .; **upon him would d. the chief labour,** c'est à lui que reviendrait la partie la plus importance du travail; **it devolves upon me to . . .,** c'est à moi (qu'il incombe) de . . .; **all the responsibility devolves on me,** toute la responsabilité retombe sur moi; (*b*) *Jur:* (*of property*) **to d. to, upon, s.o.,** être dévolu à qn; **the estate devolved upon him,** c'est lui qui a hérité.
Devonian [de'vouniən], *a. & s.* **1.** (habitant, -ante, natif, -ive) du Devon. **2.** *Geol:* dévonien (*m*); **middle D.,** mésodévonien (*m*).
devonite ['devənait], *s. Miner:* dévonite *f.*
Devonshire ['devənʃ(i)ər], *attrib.* du comté de Devon; **D. cream,** crème caillée.
devote [di'vout], *v.tr.* vouer, consacrer (**s.o., sth., to sth.,** qn, qch., à qch.); consacrer, dévouer (son temps, son argent, etc., à qn, à qch.); affecter, appliquer (une somme à qch.); accorder (du temps à qch.); vouer, condamner (qch. à la destruction); **to d. all one's energies to doing sth.,** employer toute son énergie à faire qch.; **review specially devoted to history and geography,** revue spéciale à l'histoire et à la géographie; **two columns are devoted to book reviews,** deux colonnes sont affectées aux revues littéraires; **to d. oneself to sth.,** se vouer, se consacrer (à Dieu, à une occupation); se dévouer (à sa patrie); se livrer (au plaisir); s'adonner, se livrer (à l'étude, etc.); **to d. oneself to the Muses,** se vouer au culte des Muses.
devoted [di'voutid], *a.* **1.** dévoué, attaché (**to,** à); **a few d. friends,** quelques amis dévoués; **to be wholly d. to s.o., to s.o.'s cause,** être tout acquis, entièrement acquis, à qn; **a tribute from a few d. admirers,** un hommage de quelques fervents admirateurs; **they are d. to each other,** ils sont dévoués l'un à l'autre; **d. to work,** assidu au travail. **2.** *A: & Lit:* voué au malheur; condamné à la ruine; **blows fell thick and fast upon his d. head,** il courbait la tête sous les coups du malheur.
devotedly [di'voutidli], *adv.* avec dévouement; **d. attached to s.o.,** dévoué à qn; profondément attaché à qn; **to be d. attached to tradition,** avoir le culte de la tradition; **to serve one's master d.,** servir son maître avec (un sincère) dévouement.
devotedness [di'voutidnis], *s.* dévouement *m.*
devotee [devou'ti:], *s.* **1.** *A: & Lit:* (*a*) dévot, -ote; **from a profligate he became a d.,** il passa du libertinage à la dévotion; (*b*) **d. of a faith,** adepte *m* d'un culte. **2.** fervent, -ente, fanatique *m* (**of sport, etc.,** du sport, etc.); **he is a d. of music,** c'est un fervent, un passionné, de la musique; **surrounded by his devotees,** entouré d'admirateurs.
devoting [di'voutiŋ], *s.* consécration *f* (de sa vie à qch., etc.); affectation *f* (d'une somme à qch.).
devotion [di'vouʃ(ə)n], *s.* **1.** dévotion *f* (à Dieu); **to show special d. to a saint,** avoir dévotion à un saint; **feast of d.,** fête *f* de dévotion. **2.** prière *f*; **morning, evening, d.,** prière du matin, du soir; *used esp. in the pl.* **to be at one's devotions,** faire ses dévotions, ses prières. **3.** dévouement *m* (**to s.o.,** à, pour, qn); **d. to science,** dévouement à la science; **d. to duty,** dévouement; **d. to work,** assiduité *f* au travail; **d. to pleasure,** amour *m* du plaisir. **4.** consécration *f* (de sa vie à qch., etc.).
devotional [di'vouʃən(ə)l], *a.* (livre, etc.) de dévotion; (livre) dévot, de piété; (esprit) religieux, pieux; **d. attitude,** attitude *f* de prière; attitude dévote; **d. helps,** aides *f* à la dévotion, à la prière; **d. articles,** articles *m* de piété; *F: Pej:* bondieuseries *f.*
devotionalist [di'vouʃənəlist], *s.* personne confite en dévotion; *Pej:* bigot, -ote.
devotionally [di'vouʃən(ə)li], *adv.* **1.** avec dévotion. **2. d. inclined,** porté à la dévotion.
devour [di'vauər], *v.tr.* (*of beast, pers.; of fire*) dévorer; **his body was devoured by vultures,** son corps servit de pâture aux vautours; *F:* **to d. s.o. with one's eyes,** dévorer, avaler, qn des yeux; **to d. a fortune,** manger une fortune; **to d. a book,** dévorer un livre; **machine that devours fuel,** machine *f* qui mange le combustible; **devoured by anxiety,** dévoré d'inquiétude; en proie aux plus vives inquiétudes; *v.i.* **they sat and devoured,** ils mangeaient avec voracité; ils dévoraient.
devourer [di'vauərər], *s.* dévorateur, -trice (**of,** de).
devouring [di'vauəriŋ], *a.* dévorant; dévorateur, -trice.
devout [di'vaut], *a.* **1.** dévot, pieux. **2.** (*of wish, etc.*) fervent, sincère.
devoutly [di'vautli], *adv.* **1.** dévotement, pieusement, avec dévotion. **2.** sincèrement; **it is d. to be hoped that . . .,** on ne saurait trop espérer que . . ..
devoutness [di'vautnis], *s.* dévotion *f*, piété *f.*
devulgarize [di:'vʌlgəraiz], *v.tr.* dévulgariser.
dew[1] [dju:], *s.* **1.** rosée *f*; *Ven:* aiguail *m*; **evening d.,** serein *m*; rosée du soir; **the morning d.,** la rosée du matin; **d. is falling,** il tombe de la rosée; **d. point,** point *m* de rosée, de condensation; **d.-point hygrometer,** hygromètre *m* à condensation; **d. bow,** arc-en-terre *m*, *pl.* arcs-en-terre. **2.** *F: A:* **mountain d.,** whisky *m* d'Écosse.
dew[2], *v.tr.* **1.** humecter (l'herbe, etc.) de rosée. **2.** (*esp. in passive*) arroser, mouiller (**with,** de); **brow dewed with sweat,** front perlé de sueur; **eyes dewed with tears,** yeux mouillés de larmes; yeux où perlent des larmes.
Dewar ['dju:ər], *Pr.n. Ch:* **D. flask,** vase *m* de Dewar.
de-water [di:'wɔ:tər], *v.tr.* assécher (un bassin de radoub); dénoyer (une mine).
dewax [di:'wæks], *v.tr. Petr:* déparaffiner.
dewaxing [di:'wæksiŋ], *s. Petr:* déparaffinage *m.*
dewberry ['dju:beri], *s. Bot:* (*a*) (*fruit*) mûre *f* des haies; (*b*) (*shrub*) ronce bleue.
dewclaw ['dju:klɔ:], *s. Z:* ergot *m* (des chiens, etc.).
dewclawed ['dju:klɔ:d], *a.* (chien, etc.) bien ergoté.
dewdrop ['dju:drɔp], *s.* **1.** (*a*) goutte *f* de rosée; (*on leaves*) aiguail *m*; (*b*) *F:* goutte au bout du nez; roupie *f.* **2.** petite perle de verre.
deweylite ['dju:ilait], *s. Miner:* deweylite *f.*
dewfall ['dju:fɔ:l], *s.* serein *m.*
dewlap ['dju:læp], *s.* **1.** fanon *m* (de la vache). **2.** *F:* peau flasque et pendante (sous le menton de qn); double menton; **he had dewlaps,** il avait des peaux sous le menton.
dewlapped ['dju:læpt], *a.* **1.** (bœuf *m*, vache *f*) à fanon. **2.** *F:* (*of pers.*) qui a des peaux sous le menton; qui a un double menton.
dewpond ['dju:pɔnd], *s.* mare artificielle (au sommet d'une colline) qui s'alimente de rosée.
dew-ret ['dju:ret], *v.tr.* (**-retted**) *Tex:* rouir (le lin) sur pré.
dew-worm ['dju:wə:m], *s. Ann:* ver *m* de terre (qui sort au moment de la rosée).
dewy ['dju:i], *a.* couvert de rosée, humide de rosée, humecté de rosée.
dexter ['dekstər], *a.* **1.** droit. **2.** *Her:* dextre; *adv.* **a sun, dexter a star,** à un soleil adextré d'une étoile.
dexterity [deks'teriti], *s.* dextérité *f*, doigté *m*; habileté *f*, adresse *f*, art *m*; **d. in doing sth.,** adresse, dextérité, à faire qch.; **manual d.,** habileté manuelle.
dext(e)rous ['dekst(ə)rəs], *a.* **1.** adroit, habile (**in doing sth.,** à faire qch.). **2.** droitier, -ière.
dext(e)rously ['dekstrəsli], *adv.* avec dextérité; adroitement, habilement.
dextral ['dekstrəl], *a.* **1.** (*of pers.*) droitier, -ière. **2.** situé à droite; *Her:* dextre. **3.** *Conch:* dextrorsum *inv.*
dextran ['dekstrən], *s. Ch: Med:* dextran *m.*
dextrin(e) ['dekstrin, -i:n], *s. Ch: Ind:* dextrine *f.*
dextro(-) ['dekstrou], *comb.fm.* dextro-; *Ch:* **d. compound,** composé *m* dextrogyre.
dextrocardia ['dekstrou'kɑ:diə], *s. Med:* dextrocardie *f.*
dextroglucose ['dekstrou'glu:kouz], *s. Ch:* dextrose *m.*
dextrogyre ['dekstroudʒaiər], **dextrogyrous** ['dekstrou'dʒaiərəs], *a.* dextrogyre.
dextrorotation ['dekstrourou'teiʃ(ə)n], *s.* rotation *f* dextrorsum.
dextrorotatory ['dekstrourou'teitəri], *a.* dextrogyre.
dextrorse [deks'trɔ:s], *a. & adv.* dextrorsum *inv.*
destrose ['dekstrous], *s. Ch:* dextrose *m.*
Dey [dei], *s. Hist:* dey *m.*
dezinc [di:'ziŋk], *v.tr.* dézinguer.
dezin(cifi)cation ['di:ziŋ(kifi)'keiʃ(ə)n], *s.* dézincage *m*, dézingage *m.*
dhobi ['doubi], *s.* **1.** (*in India*) blanchisseur *m.* **2.** *Navy: F:* lessive *f.*
dhoti ['douti], *s.* (*in India*) pagne *m.*
dhow [dau], *s. Nau:* dhaw *m.*
dhurra ['dʌrə], *s. Agr:* doura *m.*
di- [dai], *pref.* di-; bi-.
dia- ['daiə, dai'æ], *pref.* dia-.
diabase ['daiəbeis], *s. Miner:* diabase *f.*
diabetes [daiə'bi:ti:z], *s. Med:* diabète *m*; (*a*) **d. mellitus,** diabète sucré; glucosurie *f*, méliturie *f*; (*b*) **d. insipidus,** diabète insipide.
diabetic [daiə'betik], *a. & s. Med:* diabétique (*mf*).
diabetogenic [daiəbe'tɔdʒənik], *a.* diabétogène.
diabetometer [daiəbe'tɔmitər], *s.* diabétomètre.
diablerie [di'ɑ:bləri], *s.* diablerie *f.*
diabolic [daiə'bɔlik], *a.* (rire *m*, grimace *f*, etc.) diabolique.
diabolical [daiə'bɔlikl], *a.* (cruauté *f*) diabolique, atroce; (complot) infernal, -aux; **d. grin,** ricanement *m* satanique.
diabolically [daiə'bɔlik(ə)li], *adv.* diaboliquement.
diabolism [dai'æbəlizm], *s.* **1.** diablerie *f*, magie noire; sorcellerie *f.* **2.** satanisme *m*, diabolisme *m.*
diabolist[1] [dai'æbəlist], *s.* (*a*) démoniste *m*; (*b*) démonolâtre *mf.*
diabolist[2] [di'æbəlist], *s.* joueur, -euse, de diabolo.
diabolize [dai'æbəlaiz], *v.tr.* rendre démoniaque; soumettre (qn) à une influence démoniaque.
diabolo [di'æbəlou], *s. Games:* diabolo *m.*
diacaustic [daiə'kɔ:stik], *a. & s. Opt:* (courbe) diacaustique *f.*
diacetic [daiə'si:tik], *a. Ch:* (acide *m*) diacétique.
diacetonuria [daiəsi:tou'nju:riə], **diaceturia** [daiæsi'tju:riə], *s. Med:* diacéturie *f.*
diacetyl [dai'æsitil], *s. Ch:* diacétyle *m.*
diachronic [daiə'krɔnik], **diachronistic** [daiəkrə'nistik], **diachronous** [dai'ækrənəs], *a. Ling:* diachronique.
diachronically [daiə'krɔnik(ə)li], **diachronistically** [daiəkrə'nistik(ə)li], *adv. Ling:* diachroniquement.
diachronism [dai'ækrənizm], **diachrony** [dai'ækrəni], *s. Ling:* diachronie *f.*
diachylon, -lum [dai'ækilən, -ləm], *s. Pharm:* diachylon *m*, diachylum *m*; **d. plaster,** emplâtre *m* diachylum.
diacid [dai'æsid], *a. Ch:* diacide, biacide.
diaclase ['daiəkleiz], *s. Geol:* diaclase *f.*
diaclastic [daiə'klæstik], *a. Geol:* diaclasé.
diacodion, -ium [daiə'koudiən, -iəm], *s. Pharm:* (sirop) diacode *m.*
diaconal [dai'ækənl], *a. Ecc:* diaconal, -aux.
diaconate [dai'ækəneit], *s. Ecc:* **1.** diaconat *m.* **2.** le corps des diacres.
diacritic [daiə'kritik], *a. & s. Gram:* (signe) diacritique *m*; accent grammatical.
diacritical [daiə'kritikl], *a.* **1.** *Gram:* (signe *m*) diacritique. **2. d. mind,** esprit *m* capable d'apprécier les distinctions; esprit qui juge avec discernement; esprit fin.
diactinic [daiæk'tinik], *a. Opt:* perméable aux rayons actiniques.
diad ['daiæd], *s.* **1.** *Phil: Poet:* dyade *f.* **2.** *Ch:* radical divalent.
diadelphian [daiə'delfiən], **diadelphous** [daiə'delfəs], *a. Bot:* diadelphe.
diadem ['daiədem], *s.* diadème *m*, bandeau royal; *Lit:* **to**

assume the d., ceindre le diadème.
diadochite [dai'ædəkait], *s. Miner:* diadochite *f.*
diaeresis, *pl.* **-eses** [dai'erəsis, -əsi:z], *s.* **1.** *Ling:* diérèse *f.* **2.** *Gram:* tréma *m.* **3.** *Surg:* diérèse.
diagenesis [daiə'dʒenəsis], *s. Geol:* diagénèse *f.*
diagnosable [daiəg'nouzəbl], *a. Med:* susceptible d'un diagnostic.
diagnose ['daiəgnouz], *v.tr.* diagnostiquer (une maladie, une panne du moteur, etc.); faire le diagnostic (d'une maladie).
diagnosis, *pl.* **-ses** [daiəg'nousis, -si:z], *s.* **1.** *Bot:* diagnose *f* (d'une plante). **2.** *Med:* (*a*) diagnostic *m* (d'une maladie); (*b*) (*the art*) diagnose.
diagnostic [daiəg'nɔstik]. **1.** *a.* diagnostique. **2.** *s. Med:* (*a*) signe *m* diagnostique; symptôme *m*; (*b*) *pl.* **diagnostics,** la diagnose.
diagnostician [daiəgnɔs'tiʃ(ə)n], *s.* diagnostiqueur *m*; bon diagnosticien.
diagometer [daiə'gɔmitər], *s. El:* diagomètre *m.*
diagonal [dai'ægənl]. **1.** *a. Mth:* diagonal, -aux; *Const:* (*of beam, etc.*) en écharpe; **d. stay,** étai *m* en sautoir; *Tex:* **d. cloth,** *s.* **diagonal,** diagonale *f.* **2.** *s. Mth:* diagonale *f.*
diagonally [dai'ægən(ə)li], *adv.* diagonalement, en diagonale; en écharpe; obliquement.
diagram[1] ['daiəgræm], *s.* **1.** diagramme *m*, tracé *m*, schéma *m*; figure *f*, dessin *m* schématique; plan *m*, dessin, graphique; épure *f*; **geometrical d.,** figure géométrique; **block d.,** bloc-diagramme *m*, *pl.* blocs-diagrammes; *El: etc:* **connection d., wiring d.,** schéma des connexions; schéma de montage; plan de pose; *Bot:* **floral d.,** diagramme d'une fleur. **2.** (*a*) *Ph: etc:* graphique *m*, courbe *f* (de température, de pression, etc.); (*b*) *Mec.E: Mch:* **indicator d.,** diagramme d'indicateur; **engine d.,** diagramme, caractéristique *f*, de la machine, du moteur; **flow d.,** (i) *Ind:* diagramme des opérations successives; (ii) *Cmptr:* organigramme *m*; graphique *m* d'écoulement, de débit; *Cmptr:* **working, running, d.,** graphique de marche.
diagram[2], *v.tr.* représenter schématiquement (un appareil, etc.).
diagrammatic [daiəgrə'mætik], *a.* schématique; **d. representation,** représentation *f* graphique.
diagrammatically [daiəgrə'mætik(ə)li], *adv.* schématiquement.
diagrammatize [daiə'græmətaiz], *v.tr.* représenter (qch.) par un diagramme; schématiser; représenter schématiquement (un appareil, etc.); **this arrangement, which is diagrammatized by arrows in the figure,** cette disposition, schématisée par des flèches sur la figure.
diagraph ['daiəgræf], *s. Draw:* diagraphe *m.*
diagraphics [daiə'græfiks], *s.* (*usu. with sg. const.*) diagraphie *f.*
diakinesis [daiək(a)i'ni:sis], *s. Biol:* diacinèse *f.*
dial[1] ['daiəl], *s.* **1.** (*a*) **d. (plate),** cadran *m* (d'horloge, de baromètre, etc.); **d. case,** cartel *m*; **d. work,** cadrature *f*; (*b*) *Nau:* **compass d.,** rose *f* des vents; **floating d.,** rose mobile; (*c*) *Tp:* cadran (d'appel, d'abonné); (*d*) cadran (d'un instrument scientifique, etc.); **graduated, calibrated, d.,** cadran gradué; **vernier d.,** cadran démultiplicateur; **slow-motion d.,** cadran démultiplié; **rotary d.,** cadran rotatif; (*e*) *Artil:* **d. sight,** hausse *f* à cadran; hausse circulaire; goniomètre *m*; **range d.,** cadran de pointage. **2.** *P:* visage *m*, museau *m*, gueule *f.*
dial[2], *v.tr.* **(dialled** (*a*) *Tp:* **to d. (a number),** composer, faire, un numéro; **to d. 999** = appeler Police Secours; (*b*) *Cmptr:* composer (un cadran); sélectionner.
dial bird ['daiəlbə:d], *s. Orn:* dyal *m.*
dialcohol [dai'ælkəhɔl], *s. Ch:* dialcool *m.*
dialdehyde [dai'ældihaid], *s. Ch:* dialdéhyde *m.*
dialect ['daiəlekt], *s.* dialecte *m*, parler *m*, idiome *m*; **provincial d.,** patois *m.*
dialectal [daiə'lektl], *a. Ling:* dialectal, -aux; dialectique; **d. differences between the counties,** différences *f* de dialectes entre les comtés.
dialectic(s) [daiə'lektik(s)], *s. Phil:* dialectique *f.*
dialectic(al) [daiə'lektik(l)], *a.* **1.** *Phil:* dialectique; **d. materialism,** matérialisme *m* dialectique; **d. materialist,** matérialiste dialecticien. **2.** *Ling:* = DIALECTAL.
dialectically [daiə'lektik(ə)li], *adv.* dialectiquement.
dialectician [daiəlek'tiʃ(ə)n], *s.* dialecticien, -ienne.
dialectologist [daiəlek'tɔlədʒist], *s. Ling:* dialectologue *mf.*
dialectology [daiəlek'tɔlədʒi], *s. Ling:* dialectologie *f*; étude *f* des dialectes.
diallage ['daiəlidʒ], *s. Miner:* diallage *f.*
diallagic [daiə'lædʒik], *a. Miner:* diallagique.
diallelon [daiə'li:lɔn], *s. Log:* diallèle *m.*
dialling ['daiəliŋ], *s. Tp:* composition *f* du numéro; **d. tone,** signal *m* de ligne, de manœuvre; tonalité (continue); **d. code,** indicatif (départemental); *Cmptr:* signal de sélection; *Cmptr:* **automatic d. unit,** dispositif *m* automatique de sélection.
dial(l)ogite [dai'ælədʒait], *s. Miner:* dial(l)ogite *f.*
dialogic(al) [daiə'lɔdʒik(l)], *a.* (traité *m*, etc.) dialogique, en forme de dialogue.
dialogist [dai'ælədʒist], *s. Cin: etc:* dialoguiste *mf.*
dialogize [dai'ælədʒaiz], *v.tr. Cin: etc:* dialoguer (une scène, etc.).
dialogue ['daiəlɔg], *s.* dialogue *m.*
dialuric [daiə'lju:rik], *a. Ch:* **d. acid,** acide *m* dialurique, tartronylurée *f.*
Dialypetalae [daiəli'petəli:], *s.pl. Bot:* dialypétales *f.*
dialypetalous [daiəli'petələs], *a. Bot:* (corolle *f*) dialypétale.
dialysable [daiə'laizəbl], *a. Ch:* dialysable.
dialysate [daiə'laiseit], *s. Ch:* dialysat *m.*
dialyse ['daiəlaiz], *v.tr. Ch:* dialyser.
dialysepalous [daiəli'sepələs], *a. Bot:* (calice *m*) dialysépale.
dialyser ['daiəlaizər], *s. Ch:* dialyseur *m.*
dialysis, *pl.* **-es** [dai'ælisis, -i:z], *s. Ch: Surg: Rh:* dialyse *f.*
dialytic [daiə'litik], *a. Ch:* dialytique.
diamagnetic [daiəmæg'netik], *a.* diamagnétique.
diamagnetism [daiə'mægnətizm], *s.* diamagnétisme *m.*
diamanté [daiə'mæntei], *s.* broderie diamantée; **d. buttons,** boutons diamantés.
diamantiferous [daiəmæn'tifərəs], *a.* (sable *m*) diamantifère.
diamantine [daiə'mæntain], *s.* diamantine *f.*
diamantoid [daiə'mæntɔid], *a.* diamantin.
diameter [dai'æmitər], *s.* (*a*) diamètre *m*; **the wheel is 60 cm in d.,** la roue a 60 cm de diamètre; **external d.,** diamètre extérieur; **internal d.,** diamètre intérieur; calibre *m* (d'un tube); *I.C.E: etc:* alésage *m* (d'un cylindre, etc.); **double-d. cylinder,** cylindre à deux alésages; **throat d. (of a screw),** diamètre intérieur, à fond de gorge (d'une vis); *Mec.E:* **pitch, effective, d.,** diamètre primitif (d'une roue dentée); *Tls:* **d. gauge** (*for standing timber*), compas forestier; *Nau:* **final, tactical, d.,** diamètre de giration, d'évolution; (*b*) *Opt:* unité *f* de grossissement (d'une lentille, d'un télescope); **glass with a magnification of eight diameters,** lunette *f* avec un grossissement de huit fois.
diametral [dai'æmitrl], *a. Mth: Cryst:* diamétral, -aux; **d. plane,** plan diamétral (d'un solide).
diametric(al) [daiə'metrik(l)], *a.* **1.** *Mth: etc:* = DIAMETRAL. **2. I hold opinions in d. opposition to his,** j'ai des opinions diamétralement opposées aux siennes.
diametrically [daiə'metrik(ə)li], *adv.* diamétralement; **pieces of evidence d. opposed to one another,** témoignages diamétralement opposés, directement contradictoires; **opinions d. opposed to ours,** des opinions à rebours des nôtres; **that is d. opposed to the truth,** c'est le rebours de la vérité; cela est en contradiction absolue avec la vérité.
diamide ['daiəmaid], *s. Ch:* diamide *m.*
diamidophenol [dai'æmidou'fi:nɔl], *s. Ch:* diamidophénol.
diamido- [dai'æmidou], *pref. Ch:* diamido-.
diamine ['daiəmain], *s. Ch:* diamine *f.*
diamino- [dai'æminou], *pref. Ch: etc:* diamino-.
diammonium [daiə'mouniəm], *a. Ch:* diammonique.
diamond ['daiəmənd], *s.* **1.** (*a*) diamant *m*; **d. of the first water,** diamant de première eau; **rough d., uncut d.,** diamant brut, qui n'est pas taillé; **he's a rough d.,** c'est un diamant dans sa gangue; **cut d.,** diamant taillé; **point d.,** diamant à pointes naïves; **rose(-cut) d.,** diamant (taillé) en rose; **table(-cut) d.,** diamant en table; **brown d.,** diamant savoyard; **black d.,** diamant noir; carbonado *m*; *O:* **black diamonds,** la houille; *Prov:* **d. cut d.,** fin contre fin; à fourbe fourbe et demi; à malin malin et demi; à bon chat, bon rat; **hands loaded with diamonds,** mains endiamantées; **d. necklace, d. ring,** collier *m*, bague *f*, de diamants; **d. merchant,** diamantaire *m*, négociant *m* en diamants; **d. cutting,** taille *f* du diamant; (*pers.*) **d. cutter,** tailleur *m* de diamants; diamantaire *m*; **d. dust,** poussière *f* de diamant; *Ind:* égrisée *f*; *Mec.E:* **d. grinding tool** outil *m* diamant (pour rectification); *Tls:* **(cutting) d.,** diamant de vitrier; **d. point,** outil *m* en pointe de diamant; *Min:* **d. drill,** perforatrice diamantée, à diamants; **d. mine,** mine *f* de diamants; **d. field,** champ *m* diamantifère; *Geol:* **d. pipe,** cheminée *f*, puits *f*, *m*, diamantifère; **d. mining,** exploitation *f* de mines de diamants; l'industrie minière diamantifère; **d. fragments,** boort *m*; *St.Exch:* **d. shares, diamonds,** valeurs *f* diamantifères; **d. wedding,** noces *fpl* de diamant; (*b*) *Rec:* **biradial, elliptical, d.,** diamant elliptique. **2.** *Miner:* **d. spar,** corindon *m*; **Bristol d., Cornish d.,** cristal *m* de quartz. **3.** (*a*) losange *m*, rhombe *m*; **d. pattern,** dessin *m* en losanges; **d. panes,** vitres *f* en forme de losange; **d. nail,** clou *m* à tête de diamant; *Cy: A:* **d. frame,** cadre *m* (de bicyclette); *Rail:* **d. crossing,** traversée *f*, croisement *m*, oblique; coupement *m* de voie; **d. switch,** traversée-bretelle *f*, *pl.* traversées-bretelles; *Vet:* **d. skin disease,** rouget *m*; (*b*) *Cards:* carreau *m*; **to play a d., diamonds,** jouer du carreau; *Aut:* **d. interchange,** jonction *f* en as de carreau; (*c*) *Sp:* terrain *m* de baseball. **4.** *Typ:* corps *m* quatre; perle *f*; **d. edition,** édition imprimée en corps quatre. **5.** (*a*) *Orn:* **d. bird, d. sparrow,** pardalote *m*; (*b*) *Ent:* **d. beetle,** entime *m*; (*c*) *Rept:* **d. snake,** morélie *f.*
diamondback ['daiəməndbæk], *a. & s.* **1.** *Rept:* (*a*) terrapin *m*; (*b*) **d.-b. (rattlesnake),** diamantin *m.* **2.** *Ent:* **d.-b. (moth),** plutelle *f.*
diamond-bearing ['daiəməndbɛəriŋ], *a.* diamantifère, gemmifère.
diamondiferous [daiəmən'difərəs], *a.* diamantifère.
diamond-shaped ['daiəməndʃeipt], *a.* en losange.
diamond-yielding ['daiəməndji:ldiŋ], *a.* diamantifère.
Diana [dai'ænə]. **1.** *Pr.n.f. Myth: etc:* Diane. **2.** *s.f.* (*a*) *Lit:* amazone; chasseresse; (*b*) *Poet:* Diane; la lune; (*c*) *Ent:* **D. butterfly,** diane *f.*
diandrous [dai'ændrəs], *a. Bot:* diandrique, diandre.
dianite ['daiənait], *s. Miner:* dianite *f.*
dianthera [dai'ænθərə], *s. Bot:* dianthera *m.*
diapason [daiə'peisən], *s. Mus:* **1.** (*a*) *A: & Lit:* accord *m*, harmonie *f*; *esp.* crescendo harmonieux; (*b*) diapason *m*, étendue *f* (de la voix, d'un instrument). **2.** (*pitch*) diapason, (hauteur *f* du) ton *m* (d'un instrument). **3.** principaux jeux de fond (d'un orgue) (prestant *m*, diapason, montre *f*, etc.).
diapause ['daiəpɔ:z], *s. Ent: etc:* diapause *f.*
diapedesis [daiəpe'di:sis], *s. Physiol:* diapédèse *f.*
diaper[1] ['daiəpər], *s.* **1.** *Tex:* linge ouvré; damassé *m*; toile diaprée, gaufrée. **2.** *NAm:* couche *f*, lange *m* (de bébé). **3.** motif *m* (d'ornementation) en simples formes géométriques.
diaper[2], *v.tr.* **1.** *Needlew:* ouvrer (le linge); *Tex:* gaufrer (la toile). **2.** losanger (une surface). **3.** *NAm:* changer (un bébé).
diapered ['daiəpəd], *a.* **1.** (*of linen*) ouvré; gaufré. **2.** (*of pattern, wall*) découpé en simples formes géométriques. **3.** *Her:* (champ) diapré.
diaphaneity [daiəfə'ni:iti], *s.* diaphanéité *f.*
diaphanoscope [daiə'fænəskoup], *s. Med:* diaphanoscope *m.*
diaphanoscopy [daiəfə'nɔskəpi], *s. Med:* diaphanoscopie *f.*
diaphanous [dai'æfənəs], *a.* diaphane.
diaphony [dai'æfəni], *s. Mus:* diaphonie *f.*
diaphoresis [daiəfə'ri:sis], *s. Med:* diaphorèse *f.*
diaphoretic [daiəfə'retik], *a. & s. Med:* diaphorétique (*m*).
diaphorite [dai'æfərait], *s. Miner:* diaphorite *f.*
diaphragm[1] ['daiəfræm], *s.* **1.** *Anat:* diaphragme *m.* **2.** (*a*) diaphragme, membrane *f*; cloison *f*; **porous d.,** membrane poreuse; *Tp:* **d. of a telephone,** membrane (vibrante), plaque vibrante, d'un téléphone; **carbon d.,** membrane de charbon; *Rec: etc: A:* **d. of the sound box,** membrane du diaphragme; (*c*) *Phot:* **iris d.,** diaphragme iris; **d. aperture,** ouverture *f* du diaphragme; (*c*) *Med:* diaphragme (contraceptif).
diaphragm[2], *v.tr. Opt: Phot:* **to d. (down) a lens,** diaphragmer une lentille, un objectif.
diaphragmatic [daiəfræg'mætik], *a. Anat: Med:* diaphragmatique.
diaphysis [dai'æfisis], *s. Anat: Bot:* diaphyse *f.*
diapir ['daiəpiər], *s. Geol:* diapir *m.*
diapiric [daiə'piərik], *a. Geol:* diapirique.
diapirism [dai'æpiərizm], *s. Geol:* diapirisme *m.*
diaplegia [daiə'pli:dʒiə], *s. Med:* diaplégie *f.*
diapositive [daiə'pɔzitiv], *s. Phot:* diapositive *f.*
diarch ['daiɑ:k], *a. Bot:* diarche.
diarchal [dai'ɑ:kl], **diarchic** [dai'ɑ:kik], *a. Pol:* dyarchique.
diarchy ['daiɑ:ki], *s.* **1.** *Pol:* dyarchie *f.* **2.** *Bot:* structure *f* diarche.
diarist ['daiərist], *s.* auteur *m* d'un journal (intime); diariste *m.*
diarrhoea [daiə'riə], *s. Med:* diarrhée *f*; *Vet:* (*bacillary*) **white d.,** diarrhée blanche, crayeuse (des poussins).
diarrhoeal, diarrhoeic [daiə'riəl, -'ri:ik], *a.* diarrhéique.
diarthrodial [daiɑ:'θroudiəl], *a. Anat:* diarthrodial, -aux.
diarthrosis [daiɑ:'θrousis], *s. Anat:* diarthrose *f.*

diary ['daiəri], *s.* **1.** journal *m* (intime); *Mil: etc:* **war, field, d.,** journal de marche; *Journ:* **d. of social events,** carnet mondain. **2.** agenda *m*; calendrier *m*; **desk d.,** bloc *m* calendrier; *Com:* **bill d.,** carnet *m* d'échéances; échéancier *m*.
diaschisis [dai'æskisis], *s. Med:* diaschisis *m*.
diascope ['daiəskoup], *s. Med:* diascope *m*.
diascopy [dai'æskəpi], *s. Opt:* diascopie *f*.
diascordium [daiəs'kɔ:diəm], *s. Pharm:* diascordium *m*.
diaspis [dai'æspis], *s. Ent:* diaspis *m*.
Diaspora (the) [ðədai'æspərə], *s. Jew.Rel:* la Diaspora.
diaspore ['daiəspɔ:r], *s.* **1.** *Miner:* diaspore *m*. **2.** *Bot:* diaspore *f*.
diastaltic [daiə'stæltik], *a. Physiol:* (réflexe *m*) diastaltique.
diastase ['daiəsteis], *s. Bio-Ch:* diastase *f*.
diastasis [dai'æstəsis], *s. Med:* diastasis *m*, diastase *f*.
diastatic [daiə'stætik], *a. Bio-Ch:* diastatique.
diastem ['daiəstem], *s. Anat: Biol:* diastème *f*.
diastema [dai'æstəmə], *s. Z:* diastème *f*.
diastole [dai'æstəli], *s. Physiol:* diastole *f*.
diastolic [daiə'stɔlik], *a. Physiol:* diastolique.
diathermance, -mancy [daiə'θə:məns, -mənsi], **diathermaneity** [daiəθəmə'ni:iti], diathermansie *f*, diathermanéité *f*.
diathermanous [daiə'θə:mənəs], **diathermic** [daiə'θə:mik], *a. Ph:* diathermique, diathermane.
diathermy ['daiəθə:mi], *s. Med:* diathermie *f*; **treatment by d.,** (d')arsonvalisation *f*.
diathesis, *pl.* **-ses** [dai'æθisis, -si:z], *s. Med:* diathèse *f*; **sanguine d.,** diathèse sanguine; **arthritic d.,** prédisposition *f* à l'arthrite; tempérament *m* arthritique.
diathetic [daiə'θetik], *a. Med:* diathésique.
diatom ['daiətəm], *s. Algae:* diatomée *f*; *Geol:* **d. earth,** diatomite *f*; **d. ooze,** boue *f* à diatomées.
Diatoma [daiə'toumə], *s.pl. Algae:* diatomées *f*.
diatomaceous [daiətə'meiʃəs], *a. Geol:* **d. earth,** diatomite *f*, terre *f* d'infusoires, kieselguhr *m*.
diatomic [daiə'tɔmik], *a. Ch:* **1.** diatomique, biatomique. **2.** *occ.* = DIVALENT.
diatomite [dai'ætəmait], *s. Geol:* diatomite *f*.
diatonic [daiə'tɔnik], *a. Mus:* (gamme *f*, chant *m*) diatonique.
diatribe ['daiətraib], *s.* diatribe *f*; catilinaire *f* (**against,** contre).
diaulos [dai'auləs], *s. Gr.Ant:* **1.** *Mus:* diaule *f*. **2.** *Sp:* diaule.
diazo [dai'eizou, 'daiəzou], *a. & s. Ch:* **d. (compound),** diazoïque *m*, *F:* diazo *m*; **d. reaction,** diazo-réaction *f*.
diazoaminobenzene [dai'eizouæ'mainouben'zi:n], *s. Ch:* diazoaminobenzène *m*.
diazoanhydride [dai'eizouæn'haidraid], *s. Ch:* diazoanhydride *m*.
diazobenzene [dai'eizouben'zi:n], *s. Ch:* diazobenzène *m*.
diazole ['daiəzoul], *s. Ch:* diazole *m*.
diazoma [dai'æzəmə], *s. A.Gr.Arch:* diazoma *m*.
diazomethane [dai'eizou'meθein, -'mi:-], *s. Ch:* diazométhane *m*.
diazoimide [daiə'zoimaid], *s. Ch:* diazoïmide *m*.
diazomine [dai'æzoumain], *s. Ch:* diazominé *m*.
diazotize [dai'æzoutaiz], *v.tr. Ch:* diazoter.
dib [dib], *v.i.* **(dibbed)** *Fish:* faire trembler l'appât à la surface de l'eau; pêcher à la trembleuse, à la dandinette.
dibasic [dai'beisik], *a. Ch:* bibasique, dibasique.
dibber ['dibər], **dibble**[1] ['dibl], *s. Tls:* plantoir *m*.
dibble[2]. **1.** *v.tr.* (*a*) faire des trous dans (la terre) avec le plantoir; (*b*) semer (des graines), repiquer (des plantes), au plantoir; (*c*) *Fish:* faire sauter (l'appât). **2.** *v.i.* se servir du plantoir; semer, repiquer, au plantoir.
dibbling ['dibliŋ], *s.* semis *m* en poquets.
dibenzopyrrole [daibenzou'pirɔl], *s. Ch:* dibenzopyrrole *m*.
dibenzoyl [dai'benzoil], *a. Ch:* dibenzoyle.
dibenzyl [dai'benzil], *s. Ch:* dibenzyle *m*.
dibenzylamine [daibenzil'æmi:n], *s.* dibenzylamine *f*.
Dibranchia(ta) [dai'bræŋkiə, -bræŋki'u:tə], *s.pl. Moll:* dibranches *m*.
dibromobenzene [daibroumouben'zi:n], *s. Ch:* dibromobenzène *m*.
dibromohydrin [daibroumou'haidrin], *s. Ch:* dibromohydrine *f*.
dibromosuccinic [daibroumousʌk'sinik], *a. Ch:* dibromosuccinique.
dibs [dibz], *s.pl.* **1.** (*game*) osselets *mpl*; **to play at d.,** jouer aux osselets. **2.** *Games:* jetons *mpl*. **3.** *F:* argent *m*, fric *m*; **he's got the d.,** (i) il a de l'argent, du fric; (ii) c'est un richard.
dibutyrin [dai'bju:tirin], *s. Ch:* dibutyrine *f*.
Dicaeidae [dai'si:idi:], *s.pl. Orn:* dicaéidés *m*.
dicaryon [dai'kæriən], *s. Bot:* dicaryon *m*.
dicaryotic [daikæri'ɔtik], *a. Bot:* dicaryotique.
dicast ['dikæst], *s. Gr.Hist:* dicaste *m*.
dicastery [di'kæstəri], *s. Gr.Hist:* dicastère *m*.
dice[1] [dais], *s.pl. Games:* dés *m*; **d. box,** cornet *m* à dés.
dice[2]. **1.** *v.i.* (*a*) jouer aux dés; (*b*) **to d. with death,** risquer sa vie. **2.** *v.tr.* (*a*) **to d. away a fortune,** perdre une fortune au jeu; (*b*) *Cu:* couper (des légumes) en cubes; (*c*) quadriller (l'étoffe). **3.** *v.i. Av: F:* attaquer en rase-mottes.
dicentra [dai'sentrə], *s. Bot:* dicentre *m*.
dicephalism [dai'sefəlizm], *s. Ter:* dicéphalie *f*.
dicer ['daisər], *s.* joueur, -euse, de dés.
dicerion [dai'siəriən], *s. Ecc:* dicérion *m*.
dicey ['daisi], *a. F:* hasardeux; risqué.
dichapetalum [daikə'petələm], *s. Bot:* dichapétale *m*.
dichlamydeous [daiklə'midiəs], *a. Bot:* dichlamydé, à double périanthe.
dichloracetic [daiklɔræ'si:tik], *a. Ch:* dichloracétique.
dichloride [dai'klɔ:raid], *s. Ch:* bichlorure *m*.
dichloroacetone [daiklɔ:rou'æsitoun], *s. Ch:* dichloracétone *f*.
dichlorobenzene [daiklɔ:rouben'zi:n], *s. Ch:* dichlorobenzène *m*.
dichloroethane [daiklɔ:rou'eθein], *s. Ch:* dichloréthane *f*.
dichlorohydrin [daiklɔ:rou'haidrin], *s. Ch:* dichlorohydrine *f*.
dichogamous [dai'kɔgəməs], *a. Bot:* dichogame.
dichogamy [dai'kɔgəmi], *s. Bot:* dichogamie *f*.
dichotomic [daikɔ'tɔmik], *a.* dichotomique.
dichotomically [daikɔ'tɔmik(ə)li], *adv.* dichotomiquement.
dichotomize [dai'kɔtəmaiz], *v.tr. & i.* (se) dichotomiser.
dichotomous [dai'kɔtəməs], *a.* **1.** *Nat.Hist:* dichotome; bifurqué. **2.** *Log: etc:* dichotomique.
dichotomy [dai'kɔtəmi], *s. Astr: Bot: Log: etc:* dichotomie *f*.
dichroic [dai'krouik], *a.* **1.** (cristal *m*) dichroïque. **2.** *Phot:* **d. fog,** voile *m* dichroïque; voile jaune; **d. filter,** filtre *m* dichroïque.
dichroism ['daikrouizm], *s. Cryst:* dichroïsme *m*.
dichroite ['daikrouait], *s. Miner:* dichroïte *f*.
dichromate [dai'kroumeit], *s. Ch:* bichromate *m*.
dichromatic [daikrou'mætik], *a.* **1.** dichromatique. **2.** *Cryst:* dichroïque. **3.** *Bot:* dicroanthe.
dichromic [dai'kroumik], *a. Med:* **d. vision,** vision affectée de daltonisme dichromatique.
dichroscopic [daikrou'skɔpik], *a.* dichroscopique.
dicing ['daisiŋ], *s.* (*a*) le jeu de dés; (*b*) les dés *m*, le jeu.
Dick[1] [dik], *Pr.n.m. F:* Richard; **any Tom, D. or Harry,** tout le monde; le premier venu.
dick[2], *s. F: A:* **1. to take one's d. that. . .,** jurer, affirmer, que. . . . **2. up to d.,** (i) malin, rusé; (ii) très bien, à la hauteur.
dick[3], *s. F:* policier *m*, flic *m*; détective *m*.
dick[4], *s. V:* pénis *m*.
dickcissel [dik'sis(ə)l], *s. Orn: Fr.C:* dickcissel *m*.
dickens ['dikinz], *s. F:* **what the d. are you doing?** que diable fais-tu? **the d. of a row,** (i) un bruit de tous les diables; (ii) une dispute à tout casser.
Dickensian [di'kensiən]. **1.** *a.* (caractère, etc.) qu'on dirait tiré d'un roman de Dickens. **2.** *s.* admirateur, -trice, de Dickens.
dicker[1] ['dikər], *s. Com:* dizaine *f* (de peaux, de cuirs).
dicker[2], *v.tr. & i. U.S: F:* marchander.
dickey ['diki], *s. F:* = DICKY[1].
dickinsonite ['dikinsənait], *s. Miner:* dickinsonite *f*.
dicksonia [dik'souniə], *s. Bot:* dicksonia *m*.
Dicksoniaceae [diksouni'eisii:], *s.pl. Bot:* dicksoniacées *f*.
dicky[1] ['diki], *s. F:* **1.** *Dial:* bourricot *m*, âne *m*. **2.** (*child's language*) **d. (bird),** (petit) oiseau. **3.** (*shirt-front*) plastron *m* mobile, faux plastron (de chemise). **4.** (*a*) *A.Veh:* **d.(seat),** (i) siège *m* du cocher; (ii) siège de derrière (pour les valets); (*b*) *A.Aut:* spider *m*; **two-seater with a d.,** spider.
dicky[2], *a. F:* (*a*) défectueux, peu solide, peu sûr; **furniture in a d. condition,** meubles délabrés, boiteux, peu solides; (*b*) malade, indisposé; **to feel d.,** se sentir tout chose; ne pas être dans son assiette; se sentir peu solide.
diclinous [di'klainəs], *a. Bot:* dicline.
dicotyledon [daikɔti'li:d(ə)n], *s. Bot:* dicotylédone *f*, dicotylédonée *f*.
dicotyledonous [daikɔti'li:dənəs], *a. Bot:* dicotylédone, dicotylédoné.
dicoumarin [dai'koumərin], **dicoumarol** [dai'koumərɔl], *s. Med:* dicoumarine *f*, dicoumarol *m*.
dicrotic [dai'krɔtik], *a. Med:* (pouls *m*) dicrotique.
dicrotism ['daikroutizm], *s. Med:* dicrotisme *m* (du pouls).
Dicruridae [dai'kru:ridi:], *s.pl. Orn:* dicruridés *m*, les drongos *m*.
dictagraph ['diktəgræf], *s.* dictagraphe *m*.
dictamnus [dik'tæmnəs], *s. Bot:* dictame *m*, fraxinelle *f*.
Dictaphone ['diktəfoun], *s. R.t.m:* Dictaphone *m*, machine *f* à dicter.
dictate[1] ['dikteit], *s.* ordre *m*, commandement *m*, précepte *m*; **the dictates of conscience,** la voix de la conscience; **to follow the dictates of one's conscience,** écouter sa conscience; **the dictates of fashion,** les exigences (*f*) de la mode.
dictate[2] [dik'teit]. **1.** *v.tr.* (*a*) dicter (une lettre, un passage); (*b*) dicter (des conditions de paix, etc.); *v.i.* faire la loi; (*c*) **his words are dictated by wisdom,** c'est la sagesse qui dicte, qui inspire, ses paroles; **to d. a line of action,** prescrire, indiquer, une ligne de conduite. **2.** *v.i.* **to d. to s.o.,** régenter qn; faire la loi, la leçon, à qn; **I won't be dictated to,** je n'ai pas d'ordres à recevoir; on ne me donne pas d'ordres.
dictating [dik'teitiŋ], *s.* dictée *f* (d'une lettre); **d. machine,** machine *f* à dicter.
dictation [dik'teiʃ(ə)n], *s.* **1.** dictée *f*; (*a*) **to write at, from, to, s.o.'s d.,** écrire sous la dictée de qn; **passage taken down from d.,** passage dicté; (*b*) *Sch:* **to do d.,** faire la dictée. **2.** étalage *m* d'autorité; ordres *mpl*; **it would be unsafe to attempt d. or repression,** il serait dangereux de faire acte d'autorité ou de répression; **these people won't submit to d.,** on ne fait pas la loi à ces gens-là.
dictator [dik'teitər], *s.* **1.** personne *f* qui dicte (une lettre, etc.). **2.** (*a*) *Pol:* dictateur *m*; (*b*) dictateur, prescripteur *m* (d'une mode, etc.).
dictatorial [diktə'tɔ:riəl], *a.* **1.** (pouvoir) dictatorial, -aux. **2.** (ton) impérieux, autoritaire, de dictateur; **he's very d.,** il est très autoritaire; c'est un vrai dictateur.
dictatorially [diktə'tɔ:riəli], *adv.* dictatorialement, impérieusement; autoritairement.
dictatorship [dik'teitəʃip], *s.* dictature *f*.
diction ['dikʃ(ə)n], *s.* **1.** style *m* (d'un orateur). **2.** diction *f*.
dictionary ['dikʃən(ə)ri], *s.* dictionnaire *m*; **English-French d.,** dictionnaire anglais-français; **d. making,** lexicographie *f*; *F:* **he's a walking, living, d., he's swallowed the d.,** c'est un dictionnaire ambulant, vivant; **it's just a d. word, nobody ever uses it,** c'est un mot qui se trouve dans les dictionnaires mais dont personne ne se sert.
dictograph ['diktəgræf], *s.* dictagraphe *m*.
dictum, *pl.* **-ums, -a** ['diktəm, -əmz, -ə], *s.* **1.** affirmation *f*, dire *m*. **2.** maxime *f*, sentence *f*, dicton *m*, mot *m*. **3.** *Jur:* (*a*) opinion prononcée par un juge; (*b*) *Hist:* dictum *m*, *pl.* dictums; jugement *m*, arrêt *m*.
Dictynidae [dik'tinidi:], *s.pl. Arach:* dictynidés *m*.
Dictyoptera [dikti'ɔptərə], *s.pl. Ent:* dictyoptères *m*.
dictyosome ['diktiəsoum], *s. Biol:* dictyosome *m*.
dictyospore ['diktiouspɔ:r], *s. Fung:* dictyospore *f*, spore *f* mûriforme.
dictyota [dikti'outə], *s. Algae:* dictyota *f*.
Dictyotales [diktiou'teiliz], *s.pl. Algae:* dictyotales *f*.
dicyanodiamide [daisaiənou'daiəmaid], *s. Ch:* dicyanodiamide *m*.
Dicynodontidae [daisainou'dɔntidi:], *s.pl. Paleont:* dicynodontidés *m*.
didactic [d(a)i'dæktik], *a.* didactique.
didactically [d(a)i'dæktik(ə)li], *adv.* didactiquement.
didacticism [d(a)i'dæktisizm], *s.* le didactique.
didactics [d(a)i'dæktiks], *s.pl.* (*usu. with sg. const.*) la didactique.
didactyl(e) [dai'dæktil, -tail], *a.* didactyle.
Didactyla [dai'dæktilə], *s.pl. Z:* didactyles *m*.
didactylous [dai'dæktiləs], *a.* didactyle.
didapper ['daidæpər], *s. Orn:* castagneux *m*; petit grèbe.
diddies ['didiz], *s.pl. P:* seins *m*, nénés *m*.
diddle ['didl], *v.tr. F:* duper, refaire, rouler, carotter (qn); **to d. s.o. out of his money,** soutirer son argent à qn; tirer une carotte à qn; **he diddled me out of £1000,** il m'a refait, roulé, de £1000; il m'a soufflé £1000.
diddler ['didlər], *s. F:* voleur *m*, -euse, carotteur, -euse.
diddums ['didəmz], *int. F:* (*to child*) pauvre petit! tu t'es fait mal? ça t'a fait bobo?
Didelphia [dai'delfiə], *s.pl. Z:* didelphes *m*, didelphiens *m*.
didelphic [dai'delfik], *a. Anat:* didelphe.
Didelphidae [dai'delfidi:], *s.pl. Z:* didelphidés *m*, les opossums *m*.
Dido[1] ['daidou], *Pr.n.f. Lt.Lit:* Didon.
dido[2], *s. F: A:* frasque *f*.
didodecahedral [daidoudekə'hi:drəl], *a. Cryst:* didodécaèdre.

diduncculus [dai'dʌŋkjuləs], *s. Orn:* diduncule *m*, diduncculus *m*.
Didyma ['didimə], *Pr.n. A.Geog:* Didyme *f*.
didymium [di'dimiəm], *s. Ch:* didyme *m*, didymium *m*.
didymous ['didiməs], *a. Bot:* didyme.
Didymus ['didiməs], *Pr.n.m. B.Hist:* Didyme.
didynamian [didi'neimiən], **didynamous** [di'dinəməs], *a. Bot:* didyname, didynamique.
die[1] [dai], *s.*
I. (*pl.* **dice,** *q.v.*) dé *m* (à jouer); (*with twelve faces*) cochonnet *m*; **the cast of the d.,** le coup de dés; **the d. is cast,** le sort en est jeté, les dés sont jetés; **to play dice,** jouer aux dés.
II. (*pl.* **dies** [daiz]) **1.** *Arch:* dé, tympan *m*. **2.** *Num:* (*in minting*) coin *m*; **ring d.,** virole *f*. **3.** (*a*) *Metalw:* (*for stamping and moulding*) matrice *f*; coquille *f* (de moulage); dé; **master d.,** matrice type; **stamping, embossing, d.,** matrice, machine *f* à estamper; étampe *f*; **cutting d., cut-off d., blanking d.,** matrice à, pour, découper; **form d.,** matrice à façonner, à mettre en forme; **pressing d.,** matrice d'emboutissage; **hydro-press d.,** matrice de presse hydraulique; **(wire-)drawing d., threading d.,** filière *f* (à étirer), matrice d'étirage; **riveting d.,** bouterolle *f*; **screw-cutting d.,** mère *f* (de filet de vis); filière, coussinet *m*, lunette *f* (à fileter, à tarauder); **to run a d. over a bolt,** fileter un boulon; **d. forging,** (i) forgeage *m* par matriçage; (ii) pièce forgée à dé; **d. casting,** moulage *m* en coquille; **pressure d. casting,** moulage sous pression; **d. stamping,** matriçage *m*; **d. nut,** écrou taraudeur; **d. plate,** filière simple, à truelle, à cage; **d. head,** porte-coussinet *m*, *pl.* porte-coussinets; porte-lunette *m*, *pl.* porte-lunettes; **d. stock,** porte-filière *m*, *pl.* porte-filières; **d. holder,** (i) (semelle *f*) porte-matrice *m*, *pl.* porte-matrices; (ii) porte-filière; (*pers.*) **d. sinker,** graveur *m* d'étampes, de matrices; médailleur *m*; (*b*) (*for hand punching*) poinçonneuse *f* (à main); (*c*) *Bookb:* **d. stamp,** balancier *m*. **4.** *Min:* dé (de bocard).
die[2], *v.* (**died** [daid]; **died; dying** ['daiiŋ])
I. *v.i.* **1.** mourir; (*of plant, animal, P: of pers.*) crever; **to be dying,** se mourir; être à l'agonie; **when did he d.?** quand est-il mort? **he died yesterday,** il est mort hier; **it is five years since he died,** il y a cinq ans qu'il est mort; **when about to d.,** au moment de mourir; **I feel that I am dying,** je sens que je (me) meurs; **he'll d. there,** il y laissera ses os; **to d. in one's bed, to d. a natural death,** mourir dans son lit; mourir de mort naturelle, de sa belle mort; **this fashion has died a natural death,** cette mode a passé comme on pouvait s'y attendre; **to d. before one's time,** mourir avant l'âge, prématurément; **to d. in harness,** mourir à la peine, à la tâche, en pleine activité; *F:* **to d. in one's boots, one's shoes, to d. with one's boots on,** (i) mourir d'un accident, de mort violente; (ii) combattre jusqu'à la mort; *U.S:* **the plan died on the vine,** le projet n'a abouti à rien; *Aut: F:* **the engine died on me,** le moteur a calé; *F:* **he died on me,** il m'a fait le coup de mourir; *Ecc:* **to d. well,** faire une bonne mort, une bonne fin; **to d. a martyr to the cause,** mourir martyr pour une cause; **to d. rich, a millionaire,** mourir riche, millionnaire; **they died like heroes,** ils sont morts en héros; **to d. a glorious death,** périr d'une mort glorieuse; **to d. of grief,** mourir de chagrin; **to d. from, of, a wound,** mourir des suites d'une blessure; **to d. through neglect,** mourir faute de soins; **to d. of starvation,** mourir de faim, d'inanition; **to d. poisoned,** mourir empoisonné; *Lit:* **to d. by the sword,** périr par le fer; **to d. by one's own hand,** se suicider, périr de sa propre main; **to d. by inches,** mourir à petit feu; **to d. hard,** (i) vendre chèrement sa vie; vendre cher sa peau; se défendre jusqu'à la dernière minute; (ii) se montrer irréductible; **these old superstitions d. hard,** ces vieilles superstitions ont la vie dure; **to d. in the last ditch,** combattre jusqu'à la mort; **never say d.!** (i) il ne faut jamais désespérer; (ii) courage! tenez bon! **I shall carry on to the end, live or d.,** j'irai jusqu'au bout, quitte à en mourir; **many animals died because of the drought,** beaucoup d'animaux sont morts, ont crevé, à cause de la sécheresse; **if you don't water those flowers they'll d.,** arrosez ces fleurs ou elles crèveront. **2. I nearly died laughing, with laughter,** je mourais de rire; **I'm dying with sleep,** je tombe de sommeil; **we were dying of cold,** nous mourions, *F:* crevions, de froid; **to be dying to do sth.,** brûler, mourir, d'envie de faire qch.; **I was dying to tell him,** je mourais d'envie de le lui dire; **I'm dying for you to tell me,** vous me faites mourir d'impatience; **she's dying to go on the stage,** elle veut à tout prix être actrice. **3. day is dying,** le jour s'en va; **his fortune dies with him,** sa fortune s'éteindra avec lui; **his secret died with him,** il a emporté son secret dans le tombeau; *Lit:* **my heart died within me,** mon cœur se serra, défaillit; mon courage s'évanouit; *Theol:* **to d. to sin, to the world,** mourir au péché, au monde.
II. (*compound verbs*). **1. die away,** *v.i.* se mourir; (*of sound*) s'affaiblir, s'assourdir, s'assoupir; s'en aller en mourant; s'évanouir; (*of voice*) s'éteindre, expirer (peu à peu); (*of wind*) s'apaiser, tomber; (*of jealousy, etc.*) s'éteindre peu à peu; disparaître; **the sound was dying away in the distance,** le son se perdait au lointain; *Mus:* **to let the sound d. away,** éteindre le son.
2. die back, *v.i. Hort:* dépérir; mourir de froid.f **3. die down,** *v.i.* (*of fire, etc.*) baisser; s'éteindre peu à peu; (*of wind*) s'apaiser, tomber; (*of sound*) s'éteindre; (*of plant*) perdre ses feuilles; (*of excitement*) se calmer; **the storm has died down,** la tempête s'est calmée.
4. die off, *v.i.* (*a*) (*of leaves*) se faner; (*c*) *F:* **they're dying off like flies,** ils meurent les uns après les autres, comme des mouches.
5. die out, *v.i.* se mourir; (*of fire, etc.*) s'éteindre; (*of family, etc.*) s'éteindre, disparaître; *Nat.Hist:* (*of species*) se faire rare; disparaître.
dieback ['daibæk], *s. Hort:* dépérissement *m*.
die-cast ['daikɑ:st], *v.tr. Metalw:* couler sous pression.
diecast ['daikɑ:st], *a. Metalw:* coulé sous pression, en matrice; matricé; **d. moulding,** moulage matricé.
diehard ['daihɑ:d], *s. Pol:* conservateur *m* à outrance; immobiliste *m*; intransigeant *m*; réactionnaire *m* à fond, à tous crins; jusqu'auboutiste *m*; **the diehards,** les irréductibles *m*; les enragés; le parti immobiliste; les ultras *m*; **d. policy,** (politique *f* d')immobilisme *m*; politique outrancière.
dieing ['daiiŋ], *s. Metalw:* matriçage *m*.
dielectric [daii'lektrik]. **1.** *a.* diélectrique; **d. constant,** constante *f* diélectrique. **2.** *s.* diélectrique *m*.
diencephalic [daiense'fælik], *a. Anat:* diencéphalique.
diencephalon [daien'sefələn], *s. Anat:* diencéphale *m*.
diene ['daien], *s. Ch:* diène *m*.
diesel ['di:z(ə)l]. **1.** *a.* **d. engine, locomotive,** moteur *m*, locomotive *f*, diesel; **semi-d. engine,** moteur semi-diesel; **multiple-unit d. train,** train automoteur; **d. oil, fuel,** gas-oil *m*, gaz-oil *m*, diesel-oil *m*. **2.** *s.* diesel *m*.
diesel-electric [di:zəli'lektrik], *a.* diesel-électrique, *pl.* diesel-électriques.
diesel-hydraulic [di:zəlhai'drɔ:lik], *a.* diesel-hydraulique, *pl.* diesel-hydrauliques.
dieselization [di:zəlai'zeiʃ(ə)n], *s.* diésélisation *f*.
dieselize ['di:ʒəlaiz], *v.tr.* diéséliser.
diesis, *pl.* **-eses** [dai'i:sis, -'i:si:z], *s.* **1.** *Mus:* **enharmonic d.,** dièse *m* enharmonique. **2.** *Typ:* diésis *m*.
dies non ['daii:z'nɔn], *s. Jur:* **1.** jour férié. **2.** jour dont il n'est pas tenu compte.
diet[1] ['daiət], *s.* **1.** alimentation *f*, nourriture *f*; **the d. of this tribe consists mainly of fish,** la nourriture de cette tribu se compose essentiellement de poisson. **2.** *Med:* (*way of feeding*) (*a*) régime *m* (alimentaire); **to be on a d.,** être au régime; **to go on a milk d.,** se mettre au lait; **milk d.,** régime lacté, diète lactée; **milk and vegetable d.,** régime lacto-végétarien; **d. bread,** pain *m* de régime; (*b*) **short, low, d.,** diète; **starvation d.,** diète absolue; régime affamant.
diet[2], *v.i.* se mettre, être, au régime.
diet[3], *s. Pol:* diète *f*; *Hist:* **the D. of Worms,** la Diète de Worms.
dietary ['daiət(ə)ri]. **1.** *s.* régime *m* (alimentaire) (d'un malade, d'une prison, etc.). **2.** *a.* diététique; **d. survey,** enquête *f* alimentaire.
dietetic [daiə'tetik], *a.* diététique.
dietetician [daiəte'tiʃ(ə)n], *s.* diététicien, -ienne; expert *m* en matière d'alimentation.
dietetics [daiə'tetiks], *s.pl.* (*usu. with sg. const.*) diététique *f*.
diethanolamine [daieθənɔl'æmain], *s.* diéthanolamine *f*.
diethylenic [daieθi'li:nik], *a. Ch:* diéthylénique.
dietist ['daiətist], *s.* expert *m* en diététique.
dietitian [daiə'tiʃ(ə)n], *s.* diététicien, -ienne.
dietrichite ['di:trikait], *s. Miner:* diétrichite *f*.
dietzeite ['di:tziait], *s. Miner:* dietzéite *f*.
differ ['difər], *v.i.* **1.** différer (**from,** de); être différent (de); **to d. from s.o. in age,** différer de qn par l'âge; **your opinion does not d. much from mine,** votre opinion *f* ne s'éloigne pas beaucoup de la mienne. **2.** (*disagree*) **to d. in opinion,** différer d'opinion, d'avis; **to d. (in opinion) from, with, s.o.,** n'être pas de l'avis de qn; être en désaccord avec qn; **to d. about sth.,** ne pas s'accorder sur qch.; **they d. on this point,** ils diffèrent (entre eux) sur ce point; **I beg to d.,** permettez-moi d'être d'un autre avis; **to agree to d.,** garder chacun son opinion; **the witnesses d.,** les témoins *m* ne sont pas d'accord; les témoins sont en désaccord.
difference[1] ['dif(ə)rəns], *s.* **1.** (*a*) différence *f*, écart *m* (**between,** entre); **the d. between A and B,** la différence de A et B, entre A et B, de A et de B; **d. between two versions of a text,** différence entre deux versions d'un texte; **d. in age,** différence d'âge; **d. in altitude,** différence d'altitude; **d. in temperature,** écart de température; **d. in expansion,** inégalité *f* de dilatation; **differences of taste,** différence de goûts; **I don't quite see the d.,** je ne saisis pas la nuance; **to tell the d.,** faire la différence; **I can't tell the d., make any d., between these two wines,** je ne peux pas faire de différence entre ces deux vins; (*of schoolmistress, etc.*) **she doesn't make any d. between the children,** elle traite tous les enfants de la même manière; elle ne fait pas de distinction entre les enfants; **it doesn't make any d., a shred of d.,** *F:* **a ha'p'orth of d.,** cela ne fait aucune différence; cela revient absolument au même; **it makes no d. (to me),** cela ne (me) fait rien, m'est parfaitement égal; c'est tout un; **it makes a great (deal of) d.,** cela fait une grande différence; **it doesn't make much d.,** cela ne fait pas grande différence; **that makes all the d.,** voilà qui change complètement les choses, qui change les choses du tout au tout; **that's making a distinction without a d.,** ça c'est couper les cheveux en quatre; *F:* **he doesn't know the d. between chalk and cheese,** il ne sait rien de rien; **what a d. between him and his brother!** quelle différence entre lui et son frère! **what a d. with last week's weather!** quel changement de temps depuis la semaine dernière! **they are alike, with the d. that . . .,** ils se ressemblent, à la différence, avec cette différence, que . . .; *F:* **he's a businessman, but with a d.,** c'est bien un homme d'affaires, mais pas comme le reste, les autres; (*b*) différence (entre deux nombres, etc.); *Mth:* **common d. of an arithmetical progression,** raison *f* d'une progression arithmétique; **differences in price,** écarts de prix; **the d. between the wholesale and retail price,** l'écart entre le prix de gros et le prix de détail; **give me £10 and I'll pay the d.,** donnez-moi £10 et je paierai le reste; **to split the d.,** (i) *Com:* partager le différend; *F:* couper la fève, la poire, la paille, en deux; (ii) faire un compromis; *St.Exch:* **d. between cash and settlement prices,** report *m*; **speculation in differences and contangoes,** spéculation *f* sur les différences et les reports. **2.** dispute *f*, désaccord *m*, différend *m*, querelle *f*; **to have a d. with s.o. about sth.,** avoir un différend avec qn au sujet de qch.; **to settle a d.,** régler un différend; se mettre d'accord; **we sometimes have our differences,** nous ne sommes pas toujours d'accord. **3.** *Her:* brisure *f*.
difference[2], *v.tr.* **1.** *esp. U.S:* différencier (**from,** de). **2.** *Her:* briser (des armoiries).
different ['dif(ə)rənt], *a.* différent (**from,** de); (*a*) (*unlike, dissimilar*) **they have d. customs from ours,** leurs mœurs sont différentes des nôtres; **d. styles of architecture,** différents styles d'architecture; **d. ideas,** des idées tout à fait différentes; **the d. nature of two things,** la différence de nature de deux choses; (*b*) (*changed*) **I feel a d. man,** je me sens tout autre; je ne me sens plus le même; **quite a d. woman,** une tout autre femme; **when I saw him again I found him completely d.,** quand je l'ai revu je l'ai trouvé tout autre, complètement changé; **that dress makes you look d.,** cette robe vous change; (*c*) (*not the same*) **they live in d. houses,** ils habitent des maisons différentes; **she wears a d. dress every day,** elle porte une robe différente, une nouvelle robe, tous les jours; **I do it in a d. way,** je le fais d'une façon différente: je m'y prends tout autrement; **I saw it in a d. way, light, from before,** je l'ai vu sous un tout autre jour qu'auparavant; **to do sth. quite d.,** faire tout autre chose; **that's quite a d. matter,** ça c'est une autre affaire; (*d*) (*various*) **d. colours,** couleurs diverses, variées; **d. kinds of . . .,** diverses, différentes, espèces de . . .; **d. people saw him,** différentes personnes l'ont vu; **at d. times,** à différentes, diverses, reprises; (*e*) (*superior; striking*) au-dessus de l'ordinaire; *Com:* **if you are looking for an article that is d.,** si vous cherchez un article supérieur, qui sort de l'ordinaire; *F:* **he just wants to be d.,** il cherche à se singulariser, à se faire remarquer; il ne peut rien faire comme tout le monde.
differentia, *pl.* **-iae** [difə'renʃiə, -ii:], *s. Log:* différence *f* spécifique; attribut distinctif.
differentiable [difə'renʃiəbl], *a.* différentiable.
differential [difə'renʃ(ə)l]. **1.** *a.* (*a*) (*of tariff charges, diagnosis, etc.*) différentiel; *Psy:* **d. threshold,** seuil différentiel; *Mth:* **d. calculus,** calcul différentiel; *Mec.E:* **d. action,** action différentielle; **d. gear,** (i) train *m* d'engrenages épicycloïdal sphérique; (ii) *Aut:* engrenage différentiel; (iii) *Turb:* compensateur différentiel; **d. screw,** vis *f* à filets différentiels; **d. axle,** arbre différentiel; *Nau: etc:* **d. purchase, tackle,** palan différentiel; *Cmptr:* **d. analyser,** analyseur différentiel; (*b*) distinctif. **2.** *s.* (*a*) *Mth:* différentielle *f*; **to obtain the**

d. of an equation, différentier une équation; (*b*) *Aut:* différentiel *m*; **bevel-gear d.,** différentiel à couple conique, à pignons d'angle; **helical-gear d.,** différentiel à pignons hélicoïdaux; **worm-gear d.,** différentiel à, par, vis sans fin; *attrib.* **d. case, housing,** carter *m* de différentiel; **d. carrier,** porte-pignons *m inv*, porte-satellites *m inv* (de différentiel); **d. drive pinion,** pignon *m* du différentiel; **d. pinion gear,** satellite *m* de différentiel; **d. ring gear,** couronne *f* de différentiel; **d. side gear,** planétaire *m* de différentiel; (*c*) **weight d.,** différence *f* de poids.

differentially [difə'renʃəli], *adv.* **1.** *Mec.E: etc:* par action différentielle. **2.** distinctivement.

differentiate [difə'renʃieit]. **1.** *v.tr.* (*a*) différencier (**sth. from sth.,** qch. de qch.); **reason differentiates man from other animals,** la raison distingue l'homme des autres animaux; *v.i.* **to d. between two things,** faire la différence, différencier, établir les distinctions, entre deux choses; (*b*) *Mth:* différentier (une fonction). **2.** *v.i. Biol: etc:* se différencier.

differentiating [difə'renʃieitiŋ], *a.* (*a*) qui différencie, fait une distinction (entre deux choses); (*b*) *Cmptr:* **d. amplifier,** amplificateur *m* différentiateur; **d. circuit,** *US:* **network,** montage *m* différentiateur.

differentiation [difərenʃi'eiʃ(ə)n], *s.* **1.** différenciation *f* (d'espèces, etc.). **2.** *Mth:* différentiation *f* (d'une équation).

differentiator [difə'renʃieitər], *s. Cmptr:* (*a*) différentiateur *m*; (*b*) circuit *m* différentiateur.

differently ['dif(ə)rəntli], *adv.* (*a*) différemment; d'une façon différente; **he speaks d. from you,** il ne parle pas de la même manière que vous; (*b*) diversement, différemment; **a group of girls d. dressed,** un groupe de jeunes filles différemment, diversement, habillées.

difficult ['difikəlt], *a.* (*a*) difficile; ardu; penible; **a d. job, problem,** une tâche, un problème, difficile; **the most d. part is done,** le plus fort, le plus difficile, est fait; **there's nothing very d. about that, that's not so very d.,** cela ne présente aucune difficulté; **only the beginning is d.,** il n'y a que le premier pas qui coûte; **onions are d. to digest,** les oignons sont difficiles à digérer, se digèrent difficilement; **this question is d. to answer,** il est difficile de répondre à cette question; **he is d. to approach,** il est difficile d'accès, **it is d. to deny that . . .,** on ne saurait nier que . . .; **I find it d., it is d. for me, to . . .,** j'ai (de la) peine à . . ., j'ai du mal à . . .; **it is d. to believe that . . .,** on a peine à croire que . . . + *sub.*; **it is d. for pupils to express their ideas,** il est difficile pour les, aux, élèves d'exprimer leurs idées; **this loss has made things d. for us,** cette perte nous a rendu la vie difficile; (*b*) (*of pers.*) difficile, peu comode; **he's d. to get on with,** il est peu commode, difficile à vivre, d'un caractère difficile; **don't be so d.!** ne fais pas le, la, difficile!

difficultly ['difikəltli], *adv.* **we are d. situated,** nous sommes dans une situation difficile.

difficultness ['difikətnis], *s.* caractère *m* difficile (de qn).

difficulty ['difikəlti], *s.* **1.** difficulté *f*; **to have d. in doing sth.,** éprouver de la difficulté à faire qch.; avoir du mal, de la peine, à faire qch.; **to have d. in breathing,** avoir de la gêne dans la respiration; **I had the utmost d. in finding it,** j'ai eu toutes les peines du monde à le trouver; **there will be no d. in getting you a copy,** il n'y aura aucune difficulté à vous en procurer un exemplaire; **there will be no d. about that,** cela ne fera pas de difficultés; **the d. is to . . .,** le difficile, c'est de . . .; **I realize the d. of answering this question,** je me rends compte combien il est difficile de répondre à cette question; **the d. of choice,** l'embarras *m* du choix; **with d.,** avec difficulté, avec peine, difficilement; **to act under circumstances of the greatest d.,** agir dans les circonstances *f* les plus difficiles. **2.** obstacle *m*, difficulté, anicroche *f*, accroc *m*; **I see no d. about it,** je n'y vois pas d'obstacle, d'inconvénient; **to raise, make, difficulties,** soulever des objections *f*; faire, élever, susciter, des difficultés; **to make no d., difficulties, about doing sth.,** ne faire aucune difficulté pour exécuter qch.; **there's the d.!** voilà la difficulté! **to surmount, to get over, to overcome, a d.,** surmonter une difficulté; triompher d'un obstacle; supprimer un inconvénient; **to remove a d.,** lever, aplanir, une difficulté; **to get round, evade, a d.,** tourner une difficulté; **to look for difficulties where there are none,** chercher midi à quatorze heures. **3.** embarras *m*, ennui *m*; **to be in a d.,** être dans l'embarras, dans une situation difficile; **ship in difficulties,** navire *m* en détresse; **to add to s.o.'s difficulties,** ajouter aux embarras de qn; **financial difficulties,** embarras pécuniaire, financier; pénurie *f* d'argent; soucis *mpl* d'argent; la gêne; **to lead s.o. into difficulties,** attirer des désagréments *m* à qn; **to involve oneself in difficulties, to get into difficulties,** (i) se créer des ennuis; s'attirer des ennuis; (ii) se mettre dans un mauvais pas; **to do sth., under difficulties,** accomplir qch. dans des circonstances difficiles, au milieu de toutes sortes de difficultés; **if you knew the difficulties I was in!** si vous saviez les difficultés que j'ai eues à surmonter! **to get out of one's difficulties,** se tirer d'affaire; **he knows how to get out of a d.,** il sait se retourner; il sait se débrouiller.

diffidence ['difidəns], *s.* manque *m* de confiance en soi-même; manque d'assurance; défiance *f* de soi-même; modestie excessive; **speaking with d., I imagine that . . .,** si j'ose hasarder une conjecture, je croirais volontiers que . . ..

diffident ['difidənt], *a.* qui manque d'assurance, de confiance en soi-même; **to be d.,** se défier de soi-même; **I was d. about speaking to him,** j'hésitais à lui parler; **d. smile,** sourire embarrassé, timide; **d. tone,** ton hésitant.

diffidently ['difidəntli], *adv.* timidement; en hésitant; avec quelque hésitation.

diffluence ['difluəns], *s.* diffluence *f*.

diffluent ['difluənt], *a.* diffluent.

difformed [di'fɔːmd], *a. Bot:* de forme anormale.

diffract [di'frækt], *v.tr. Opt:* diffracter.

diffracting [di'fræktiŋ], *a. Opt:* diffractif, diffringent.

diffraction [di'frækʃ(ə)n], *s. Opt:* diffraction *f*; **d. fringes,** franges *f* de Fresnel.

diffractive [di'fræktiv], *a. Opt:* diffractif, diffringent.

diffractometer [difræk'təmitər], *s. Cryst:* diffractomètre *m*.

diffuse[1] [di'fjuːs], *a.* (*of light*) diffus; (*of style*) diffus, prolixe; *Med:* (*of aneurism, etc.*) diffus.

diffuse[2] (*a*) [di'fjuːz]. **1.** *v.tr.* répandre (la lumière, une nouvelle, la gaieté, etc.); diffuser (la lumière); *W.Tel:* **to d. news,** diffuser des nouvelles. **2.** *v.i.* se répandre; rayonner; (*of light*) se diffuser; *Ch:* **to d. in water,** se diffuser dans l'eau.

diffused [di'fjuːzd], *a.* diffus, diffusé; *Phot:* **d.-focus lens,** objectif *m* anachromatique; **d. lighting,** éclairage diffusé.

diffusedly [di'fjuːzidli], *adv.* en tout lieu, de tous côtés.

diffusely [di'fjuːsli], *adv.* **1.** de tous les côtés; partout. **2.** (parler, écrire) d'une manière diffuse; diffusément; avec prolixité.

diffuseness [di'fjuːsnis], *s.* prolixité *f*, caractère diffus (du style).

diffuser [di'fjuːzər], *s. El: I.C.E: etc:* diffuseur *m*; *Ill:* paralume *m*.

diffusibility [difjuːzi'biliti], *s.* diffusibilité *f*.

diffusible [di'fjuːzibl], *a.* diffusible.

diffusiometer [difjuzi'ɔmitər], *s.* diffusiomètre *m*.

diffusion [di'fjuːʒ(ə)n], *s.* diffusion *f* (d'un fluide, du style, etc.); rayonnement *m* (des idées, d'un art); *Ph:* dispersion *f* (des rayons); *W.Tel: etc:* diffusion (de nouvelles); **the d. of French culture,** le rayonnement français; *Phot:* **d. screen,** écran diffuseur; *Sug.-R:* **d. battery,** diffuseur *m*.

diffusive [di'fjuːsiv], *a.* **1.** diffusif. **2.** (style) diffus, prolixe; **he is less d. than usual,** il est moins prolixe que d'habitude.

dig[1] [dig], *s.* **1.** (*a*) **I've been having a d. in the garden,** je viens de donner un coup de bêche au jardin; (*b*) *Archeol: F:* **they were working on a d. in Egypt,** ils faisaient des fouilles en Égypte. **2.** *F:* (*a*) **he gave me a d. in the ribs,** il m'a donné un coup de coude dans les côtes; **you'll have to give him a d. in the ribs to get him started,** il faut le secouer un peu pour le faire agir; (*b*) **to have, make, a d. at s.o., to get in a d. at s.o.,** faire une allusion (critique) à qn; lancer un coup de patte à qn; **that's a d. at you,** cette remarque est à votre intention; c'est une pierre dans votre jardin. **3.** *Sch: U.S: F:* piocheur, -euse. **4.** *P:* piqûre *f*, piquouse *f*.

dig[2], *v.* (**dug** [dʌg]; **dug; digging** ['digiŋ])

I. *v.tr. & i.* **1.** (*a*) *v.tr.* bêcher, retourner (la terre); labourer (la terre) à la bêche; (*with a pick*) piocher (la terre); (*b*) *v.tr.* **to d. potatoes,** arracher des pommes de terre; **to d. peat,** creuser la tourbe; (*c*) *v.tr.* creuser (un trou, un puits, etc.); **to d. a grave,** creuser une fosse; (*d*) *v.i.* travailler la terre; fouir; *Archeol:* faire des fouilles; **to d. for gold, for information,** faire des fouilles pour trouver de l'or, des renseignements; **to d. into, through, sth.,** creuser, percer, qch.; (*of wheels, etc.*) **to d. into the snow,** mordre dans la neige. **2.** *v.tr.* enfoncer (**sth. into sth.,** qch. dans qch.); *F:* **to d. a spoon into the dish,** pêcher au plat; *F:* **to d. s.o. in the ribs,** (i) donner un coup de coude à qn; (ii) secouer qn (pour le faire agir). **3.** *v.i. F:* loger en garni; **where do you d.?** où est-ce que vous habitez? **4.** *v.tr. P:* (*a*) comprendre, piger (qch.); (*b*) aimer (qn, qch.); **I d. that,** ça me plaît, me botte.

II. (*compound verbs*) **1. dig in.** (*a*) *v.tr.* enterrer (le fumier, etc.); **to d. one's toes in,** (i) s'assurer; se tenir de pied ferme; (ii) s'enfermer dans son opiniâtreté; s'entêter; *F:* **to d. oneself in,** s'incruster, s'ancrer, s'accrocher (chez qn, etc.); (*b*) *v.i.* (i) *Mil:* s'établir (en creusant des tranchées); (ii) *F:* manger, bouffer; piocher (dans le plat).

2. dig out, *v.tr.* (*a*) extraire, déterrer (qch.); **we had to d. the car out of the snow,** il a fallu des bêches pour tirer la voiture de la neige; (*b*) déterrer (qn de sa solitude, un secret, de vieux manuscrits, etc.); **documents dug out of the archives,** documents exhumés des archives.

3. dig round, *v.tr. For:* cerner (un arbre).

4. dig up, *v.tr.* déraciner (une plante, etc.); mettre à jour (un trésor); retourner (la terre); piocher (la rue, etc.); désenterrer (de vieux griefs); déterrer, exhumer (un corps); *F:* **where did you d. that up?** où as-tu déniché ça?

digamma [dai'gæmə], *s. Gr.Alph:* digamma *m*.

digamous ['digəməs], *a. Jur:* remarié(e).

digamy[1] ['digəmi], *s. Jur:* remariage *m*.

digamy[2], *s. Bot:* digamie *f*.

digastric [dai'gæstrik], *a. & s. Anat:* (muscle) digastrique (*m*).

digenesis [dai'dʒenisis], *s. Biol:* digénèse *f*.

digest[1] ['daidʒest], *s.* **1.** sommaire *m*, abrégé *m*, aperçu *m*, résumé *m* (d'une science). **2.** digeste *m*; codification *f* (des lois); recueil *m* de lois; **the Digest,** le Digeste (de Justinien). **3.** *Journ:* condensé *m*, *F:* digest(e) *m*.

digest[2] [d(a)i'dʒest], *v.tr.* **1.** (*a*) mettre en ordre (des faits); faire un digeste de (la législation); (*b*) résumer (un compte rendu), faire un résumé de (qch.). **2.** digérer, élaborer (un projet); **ill-digested schemes,** plans mal digérés. **3.** (*a*) *Physiol:* digérer (les aliments); **food difficult to d., that does not d. (easily),** nourriture *f* qui se digère mal, d'une digestion laborieuse; (*b*) *F:* **to d. an insult,** digérer, avaler, une insulte, un affront; (*c*) **to d. what one reads,** digérer, s'assimiler, ce qu'on lit. **4.** *Ch: Pharm:* (faire) digérer (une substance dans l'alcool, etc.).

digester ['daidʒestər], *s.* **1.** rédacteur *m* d'un digeste, d'un résumé. **2.** *Ch: Pharm: etc:* digesteur *m*; marmite *f* autoclave; autoclave *m*; **Papin's d.,** marmite de Papin. **3.** *Med: etc:* aide *f* à la digestion; digestif *m*.

digestibility [didʒestə'biliti], *s.* digestibilité *f*.

digestible [di'dʒestəbl], *a.* digestible.

digestion [d(a)i'dʒestʃ(ə)n], *s.* **1.** (*a*) digestion *f*; *Physiol:* coction *f* (des aliments); (*of food*) **to be easy, hard, of d.,** être facile, difficile, à digérer; être d'une digestion facile, difficile; **the d. of a philosophical treatise,** la digestion, l'assimilation *f*, d'un traité de philosophie; (*b*) (*of pers.*) **sluggish d.,** digestion laborieuse; **exercise that is good for the d.,** exercice *m* qui aide à digérer; **to spoil one's d.,** s'abîmer l'estomac; *F:* **to have the d. of an ostrich,** avoir un estomac d'autruche. **2.** *Ch: etc:* digestion (d'une substance); *Phot:* **d. of the emulsion,** maturation *f* de l'émulsion.

digestive [dai'dʒestiv]. **1.** *a.* digestif; **d. system,** appareil digestif; **d. troubles,** troubles digestifs, de digestion. **2.** *s. Pharm:* (*a*) digestif *m*; (*b*) suppuratif *m*. **3.** *s.* digestif *m*.

digger ['digər], *s.* **1.** (*a*) (*with spade*) bêcheur *m*; piqueur *m* (de la houille, de la tourbe); terrassier *m* (de fossés); fouilleur *m* (de monuments); (*b*) *U.S: F:* **D. (Indian),** Indien Shoshone de l'Utah (qui se nourrit de racines); (*c*) *F:* (i) *Austr: F: O:* chercheur *m* d'or; (ii) soldat australien ou néo-zélandais (1914–18); (iii) Australien *m*; Néo-zélandais *m*. **2.** (*a*) *Tls:* truelle *f*, plantoir *m*; (*b*) *Agr:* défonceuse *f*, arrachoir *m*. **3.** *Ent:* **d. (wasp, bee),** fouisseur *m*; guêpe, abeille, fouisseuse, ammophile, terrassière.

digging ['digiŋ], *s.* **1.** (*a*) bêchage *m* (de la terre), labour *m* à la bêche; creusement *m*, terrassement *m* (des fossés, etc.); excavation *f* (d'un puits); (*b*) fouilles *fpl*; mise *f* à découvert (des monuments antiques); (*c*) piquage *m* (de la tourbe, etc.). **2.** *pl. Min:* placer *m*; gisements *m* alluvionnaires; minière *f*.

diggings ['digiŋz], *s.pl. F: O:* = DIGS.

dight [dait], *a. A: & Poet:* paré, orné (**with, in,** de).

digit ['didʒit], *s.* **1.** (*a*) doigt *m*; (*b*) doigt de pied; orteil *m*. **2.** *Meas: A:* (grandeur *f* d'un travers de) doigt; trois quarts de pouce. **3.** (*a*) *Mth:* chiffre *m* (arabe); **the ten digits,** les neuf chiffres et le zéro; (*b*) *Cmptr:* **binary d.,** chiffre binaire, bit *m*; **sign d.,** caractère *m* de signe; **check d.,** clef *f*, chiffre, de contrôle; **d. key,** touche *f* de chiffre; **d. punch, row,** perforation *f*, ligne *f*, numérique; **d. selector,** sélecteur *m* d'indice; **d. time,** temps *m* élémentaire. **4.** *Astr:* doigt, douzième partie *f* (du diamètre du soleil ou de la lune).

digital ['didʒitl]. **1.** *a.* (*a*) *Anat: etc:* digital, -aux; (*b*) *Cmptr:* numérique; **d. computer,** calculateur *m* numérique; **d. multiplicator, divider,** multiplicateur *m*, diviseur *m*, numérique; **d. keyboard,** clavier *m*

numérique; **d. clock,** pendule *f* à lecture directe, digitale; **d. tape transport,** dérouleur *m* de bande magnétique. **2.** *s. Mus:* touche *f* (du piano, de l'orgue).
digitalein [didʒi'teiliin], *s. Ch:* digitaléine *f.*
digitalin [didʒi'teilin], *s. Ch: Pharm:* digitaline *f.*
digitalis [didʒi'teilis], *s.* **1.** *Bot:* digitale *f*; **purple d.,** digitale pourprée; *F:* claquet *m.* **2.** *Pharm:* digitaline *f.*
digitalization [didʒitəlai'zeiʃ(ə)n], *s. Med: Mth: etc:* digitalisation *f.*
digitalize[1] ['didʒitəlaiz], *v.tr. Med:* digitaliser.
digitalize[2], *v.tr. Cmptr: etc:* convertir en numérique.
digitally ['didʒitəli], *adv.* numériquement, sous forme digitale; **d. controlled,** à commande numérique; **d. programmed machine tool,** machine-outil *m* à commande numérique.
digitate(d) ['didʒiteit(id)], *a. Nat.Hist:* digité; **digitate-leaved,** digitifolié.
digitation [didʒi'teiʃ(ə)n], *s. Nat.Hist:* digitation *f.*
digitiform ['didʒitifɔ:m], *a.* digitiforme.
digitigrade ['didʒitigreid], *a. & s. Z:* digitigrade (*m*).
digitinervate, -nerved ['didʒiti'nə:veit, -'nə:vd], *a. Bot:* digitinervé, digitinerve.
digitipinnate ['didʒiti'pineit], *a. Bot:* digitipenné.
digitize ['didʒitaiz], *v.tr. Cmptr: etc:* convertir en numérique.
digitizer ['didʒitaizər], *s. Cmptr:* convertisseur *m* analogique-numérique.
digitoxin [didʒi'tɔksin], *s. Pharm:* digitoxine *f.*
digitoxose [didʒi'tɔksouz], *s. Pharm:* digitoxose *f.*
diglossia [dai'glɔsiə], *s. Ling:* diglossie *f.*
diglyph ['daiglif], *s. Arch:* diglyphe *m.*
dignified ['dignifaid], *a.* plein de dignité; (air *m*) digne; **to have d. manners,** avoir de la dignité, de la tenue.
dignify ['dignifai], *v.tr.* (*a*) donner de la dignité à (qch.); revêtir (qch.) d'un air de majesté; (*b*) appeler (qch.) par un nom plus prétentieux, moins banal; **to try to d. a little dissertation by calling it a thesis,** essayer de hausser la valeur d'une petite dissertation en l'appelant thèse.
dignitary ['dignit(ə)ri], *s.* dignitaire *m.*
dignity ['digniti], *s.* **1.** dignité *f*; (*a*) **to preserve one's d.,** soutenir sa dignité; **to be, stand, on one's d. (with s.o.),** se tenir sur son quant-à-soi; se retrancher derrière sa dignité; le prendre de haut (avec qn); **it is beneath your d. to accept,** vous ne pouvez pas vous abaisser (jusqu')à accepter; ce serait indigne de vous d'accepter; (*b*) **the d. of labour,** la dignité du travail. **2.** dignité, haut rang; **d. of chancellor,** dignité de chancelier; **to maintain the d. of one's position,** représenter dignement son rang, sa position. **3.** *A:* dignitaire *m.*
digraph ['daigræf], *s. Gram: Typ:* digramme *m.*
digraphic [dai'græfik], *a. Typ:* digraphe.
digress [dai'gres], *v.i.* **1.** faire une digression, des digressions (**from,** de); s'écarter (du sujet); digresser; se lancer dans une digression. **2.** *O:* s'écarter de son chemin.
digression [dai'greʃ(ə)n], *s.* **1.** digression *f,* écart *m*; **this by way of d.,** ceci soit dit en passant; **to engage in a d.,** se lancer dans une digression; **to ramble off into, to lose oneself in, a d.,** se lancer, se perdre, dans une digression. **2.** *Astr: Ph:* digression, élongation *f.*
digressive [dai'gresiv], *a.* digressif; (*of pers.*) enclin aux digressions.
digressively [dai'gresivli], *adv.* digressivement.
digs [digz], *s.pl. F:* logement *m*; **to live in d.,** loger en garni, en meublé; **I called at his d.,** je suis passé chez lui.
diguanide ['daigwænaid], *s. Ch:* diguanide *f,* biguanide *f.*
digynous ['daidʒinəs], *a. Bot:* digyne.
dihedral [dai'hi:drəl]. **1.** *a.* (angle *m*) dièdre. **2.** *s.* (*a*) angle *m* dièdre; (*b*) *Av:* dièdre *m.*
dihedron [dai'hi:drən], *s. Mth:* dièdre *m.*
dihybrid [dai'haibrid], *s. Biol:* dihybride *m.*
dihybridism [dai'haibridizm], *s. Biol:* dihybridisme *m.*
dihydrate [dai'haidreit], *s. Ch:* dihydrate *m.*
dihydrite [dai'haidrait], *s. Miner:* dihydrite *f.*
dihydroacridine ['daihaidrou'ækridain], *s.* dihydracridine *f.*
dihydroanthracene [daihaidrou'ænθrəsi:n], *s. Ch:* dihydroanthracène *m.*
dihydrobenzene [daihaidrouben'zi:n], *s. Ch:* dihydrobenzène *m.*
dihydrocarveol [daihaidrou'kɑ:viəl], *s. Ch:* dihydrocarvéol *m.*
dihydrocarvone [daihaidrou'kɑ:voun], *s. Ch:* dihydrocarvone *f.*
dyhydroergotamine [daihaidrouə:'gɔtəmain], *s. Ch:* dihydroergotamine *f.*
dihydronaphthalene [daihaidrou'næfθəli:n], *s. Ch:* dihydronaphtalène *m.*
dihydrostreptomycin [daihaidroustreptou'maisin], *s. Ch:* dihydrostreptomycine *f.*
dihydroxyacetone [daihaidrɔksi'æsitoun], *s. Ch:* dihydroxyacétone *m.*
dihydroxyanthracene [daihaidrɔksi'ænθrəsi:n], *s. Ch:* dihydroxyanthracène *m.*
dihydroxybenzoic [daihaidrɔksiben'zouik], *a. Ch:* dihydroxybenzoïque.
diiamb(us) [daii'æmb(əs)], *s. Pros:* diiambe *m.*
diiodobenzene [daiaioudouben'zi:n], *s. Ch:* diiodobenzène *m.*
diiodoform [daiai'oudoufɔ:m], *s.* diiodoforme *m.*
dikaryon [dai'kεəriən], *s. Bot:* dic(h)aryon *m.*
dikaryotic [daikεəri'ɔtik], *a. Bot:* dicaryotique.
dik-dik ['dikdik], *s. Z:* dik-dik *m.*
dike[1,2] [daik], *s. & v.tr.* = DYKE[1,2].
dike[3], *v.i. U.S: F:* **to d. out, up,** s'attifer; se mettre sur son trente et un; **diked out,** endimanché.
dikerion [dai'kiəriən], *s. Ecc:* dicérion *m.*
diketone [dai'ki:toun], *s. Ch:* dicétone *f.*
diktat ['diktæt], *s. Pej:* diktat *m.*
dilacerate [di'læsəreit], *v.tr.* dilacérer, déchirer (une victime, etc.).
dilaceration [dilæsə'reiʃ(ə)n], *s.* dilacération *f,* déchirement *m.*
dilapidate [di'læpideit]. **1.** *v.tr.* (*a*) délabrer, dégrader (un édifice, etc.); (*b*) dilapider (une fortune). **2.** *v.i.* se délabrer, se dégrader; tomber en ruines.
dilapidated [di'læpideitid], *a.* (*of building, etc.*) délabré, décrépit; dans un état de délabrement; **d. hat,** chapeau dépenaillé; **d. fortune,** fortune dilapidée.
dilapidation [dilæpi'deiʃ(ə)n], *s.* **1.** (*a*) délabrement *m,* dépérissement *m,* dégradation *f* (d'un mur, etc.); (*b*) *pl. Jur:* **dilapidations,** détériorations *f,* dégradations; **the outgoing tenant is liable for all dilapidations,** les dégradations sont à la charge du locataire sortant. **2.** dilapidation *f* (d'une fortune, etc.). **3.** *Geol:* éboulement *m*; désagrégation *f.*
dilatability [daileitə'biliti], *s.* dilatabilité *f,* expansibilité *f.*
dilatable [dai'leitəbl], *a.* dilatable, expansible.
dilatant [dai'leitənt], *a.* dilatant.
dilatation [dailei'teiʃ(ə)n], *s.* dilatation *f*; *Med:* élargissement *m* (du cœur, etc.).
dilatator [dailei'teitər], *s.* = DILATOR.
dilate [dai'leit]. **1.** *v.tr.* dilater. **2.** *v.i.* (*a*) (*of eyes, etc.*) se dilater; (*b*) **to d. on a topic,** s'étendre sur un sujet.
dilating [dai'leitiŋ], *a.* dilatateur, -trice.
dilation [dai'leiʃ(ə)n], *s.* = DILATATION.
dilatometer [dailə'tɔmitər], *s. Ph:* dilatomètre *m.*
dilatometry [dailə'tɔmitri], *s. Ph:* dilatométrie *f.*
dilator [dai'leitər], *s.* **1.** *Anat:* dilatateur *m.* **2.** *Med:* (*instrument*) dilatateur.
dilatorily ['dilətərili], *adv.* dilatoirement, d'une façon lente, dilatoire.
dilatoriness ['dilət(ə)rinis], *s.* lenteur *f* (à agir, etc.); **d. in answering,** lenteur à répondre.
dilatory ['dilət(ə)ri], *a.* **1.** (*of pers.*) lent (à agir); (*of action*) tardif. **2. d. methods,** moyens *m* dilatoires; *Jur:* **d. exception,** exception *f* dilatoire.
dilection [di'lekʃ(ə)n], *s.* dilection *f.*
dilemma [dai'lemə], *s.* **1.** *Log:* dilemme *m*; **to be on the horns of a d., reduced to a d.,** être enfermé dans un dilemme. **2.** embarras *m*; **to be in a d.,** être fort embarrassé; être entre l'enclume *f* et le marteau.
dilemmatic [daili'mætik, dili-], *a. Log:* dilemmatique.
dilettante, *pl.* **-ti** [dili'tænti, -ti]. **1.** *s.* dilettante *m*; amateur *m.* **2.** *a.* en dilettante, en amateur; **to work in a d. manner,** travailler en dilettante, en amateur.
dilettantish [dili'tæntiʃ], **dilettantist** [dili'tæntist], *a.* de dilettante.
dilettantism [dili'tæntizm], *s.* dilettantisme *m.*
diligence ['dilidʒ(ə)ns], *s.* **1.** assiduité *f,* application *f,* diligence *f,* soin *m*; **to d. of the bee,** l'industrie *f* de l'abeille. **2.** *Jur: Scot:* (*a*) saisie-arrêt *f, pl.* saisies-arrêts; (*b*) assignation, citation (signifiée à un témoin).
diligent ['dilidʒ(ə)nt], *a.* (*of pers., work*) assidu, appliqué, diligent.
diligently ['dilidʒəntli], *adv.* avec assiduité, avec application; diligemment, assidûment.
dill[1] [dil], *s. Bot:* aneth odorant; fenouil bâtard; *Pharm:* **d. water,** eau *f* d'aneth.
dill[2], *s. Austr: F:* idiot, -ote; andouille *f.*
dillybag ['dilibæg], *s. Austr: F:* petit sac (à provisions, etc.).
dillydaller ['dili'dæliər], *s. F:* traînard, -arde.
dillydally ['dili'dæli], *v.i.* (**dillydallied**) traîner, traînasser.
dilogy ['dilədʒi], *s. Rh:* dilogie *f.*
diluent ['diljuənt], *a. & s.* délayant (*m*), diluant (*m*).
dilute[1] [dai'lju:t, di-], *a.* **1.** (*of acid, etc.*) dilué, étendu. **2.** (*of colour*) délayé, adouci. **3.** atténué; (socialisme *m,* etc.) à l'eau de rose.
dilute[2], *v.tr.* **1.** diluer, étendre (un acide); mouiller, arroser (le vin, le lait); allonger (une sauce) (**with,** de); **to d. wine with water,** étendre, couper, du vin avec de l'eau; **wine diluted with water,** vin trempé; eau rougie; **to become diluted,** se diluer; **alcohol diluted with water,** alcool additionné d'eau; *Ind: O:* **to d. (skilled) labour,** adjoindre de la main-d'œuvre non professionnelle au travail spécialisé. **2.** délayer, adoucir, délaver (une couleur). **3.** atténuer, édulcorer (une doctrine, etc.); **diluted radicalism,** radicalisme *m* à l'eau de rose.
dilutee [dail(j)u:'ti:], *s. Ind: O:* manœuvre *m* adjoint à un ouvrier specialisé.
diluter [dai'l(j)u:tər], *s.* diluant *m.*
dilution [dai'l(j)u:ʃ(ə)n, di-], *s.* **1.** dilution *f*; réduction *f* (d'un acide); délayage *m,* délayement *m* (d'une couleur); mouillage *m* (du vin); *I.C.E: etc:* **oil d.,** dilution d'huile. **2.** *O:* **d. of labour,** adjonction *f* de main-d'œuvre non professionnelle.
diluvial [di'l(j)u:viəl], **diluvian** [di'lju:viən], *a. Geol:* diluvien; diluvial, -aux; **diluvial deposits, formations,** dépôts, terrains, diluviens; sédiments diluviaux; **diluvian epoch,** première époque du champlainien.
diluvium [di'l(j)u:viəm], *s. Geol:* diluvium *m.*
dim[1] [dim], *a.* (**dimmer, dimmest**) (*of light*) faible, pâle, indistinct, obscur; (*of colour*) effacé, terne, mat; (*of sight*) faible, trouble; (*of forest, room, lighting*) sombre; (*of sound*) sourd, mat; (*of outline, memory*) incertain, indécis, imprécis, vague, faible, indistinct, estompé; (*of intelligence*) vague, obtus, confus; **the d. light of dawn,** le jour douteux de l'aube; **eyes d. with tears,** yeux obscurcis par les larmes; yeux voilés, brouillés, de larmes; **d. forebodings,** d'obscurs pressentiments; **the fire was d.,** le feu brûlait faiblement; **to grow d.,** (*of light, faculties*) baisser, s'éteindre; (*of recollection*) s'effacer; (*of understanding*) s'affaiblir; (*of sight*) se troubler, s'obscurcir; (*of colour*) s'effacer, pâlir, se ternir; (*of outline*) s'effacer, s'estomper; **light that is getting dimmer,** lumière *f* qui décroît, qui s'atténue; *F:* **to take a d. view of sth.,** avoir une piètre opinion de qch.; **the outlook is pretty d.,** il n'y a guère d'espoir; **he's a d. type,** (i) c'est un idiot, une andouille (ii) c'est une nullité, une perte sèche; **don't be so d.!** sois pas si bête, si obtus!
dim[2], *v.* (**dimmed**)
I. *v.tr. & i.* **1.** *v.tr.* (*a*) obscurcir (la vue); troubler, affaiblir (la mémoire, l'intelligence); ternir (la beauté de qn, la surface d'un miroir); **eyes dimmed with weeping, with tears,** yeux ternis de pleurs, troublés de larmes, obscurcis par les larmes; (*b*) atténuer, réduire (la lumière); **to d. the lights,** baisser les lumières; (*c*) rejeter dans l'ombre (la gloire de qn); **his great deeds were dimmed by those of his son,** ses hauts faits ont été éclipsés, obscurcis, par ceux de son fils. **2.** *v.i.* (*of light*) baisser; s'éteindre; (*of eyes*) s'obscurcir; (*of polished surface, of beauty*) se ternir; (*of outlines*) s'effacer, s'estomper.
II. (*compound verb*) **dim out,** *v.tr. U.S:* faire un blackout partiel à (une ville).
dime [daim], *s. U.S:* dime *f* (= un dixième de dollar); *F:* **d. novels,** romans *m* à quatre sous; **they're a d. a dozen,** ça ne vaut pas cher.
dimension[1] [dai'menʃ(ə)n, di-], *s.* **1.** dimension *f*; étendue *f*; *Ind:* cote *f*; **linear d.,** dimension linéaire; **overall dimensions,** encombrement *m* hors tout; cotes d'encombrement; **of large dimensions,** de grandes dimensions; **to reduce sth. to the required dimensions,** (i) (*on plan*) réduire qch. au tracé nécessaire; (ii) (*on lathe, etc.*) réduire une pièce aux cotes requises; mettre une pièce à dimension; **d. figures of a machine,** cotes d'une machine; **specified d.,** cote de dessin; **d. line,** ligne *f* de cote; trait *m* de cote. **2.** *Ind: Const: etc:* échantillon *m*; *Com:* **d.-timber, -stone,** bois *m* d'échantillon, pierre *f* d'échantillon. **3.** *Mth:* dimension; **the fourth d.,** la quatrième dimension.
dimension[2], *v.tr. Ind:* **1.** déterminer, calculer, les dimensions (d'une machine, etc.). **2.** coter (un dessin, etc.).
dimensional [dai'menʃənəl, di-], *a.* dimensionnel; **two-, three-d. space,** espace *m* à deux, à trois, dimensions *f*; **fourth-d.,** de la quatrième dimension; surnaturel; **three-d. model,** modèle *m* à trois dimensions; *Cin:* **three-d., 3 D., film,** film *m* à réfraction, en relief.
dimensioned [dai'menʃənd, di-], *a.* **1.** dimensionné; **two-, three-d.,** à deux, à trois, dimensions *f.* **2.** *Ind:* (dessin, etc.) coté.
dimensionless [dai'menʃənlis, di-], *a.* **1.** sans dimensions. **2.** illimité.
dimer ['daimər], *s. Ch:* dimère *m.*
dimeric [dai'merik], *a. Ch:* dimère.
dimerous ['dimərəs], *a. Bot: Ent:* (feuille *f,* tarse *m*)

dimère.
dimeter ['dimitər], *s. Pros:* dimètre *m.*
dimethyl [dai'meθil], *s. Ch:* diméthyle *m.*
dimethylacetic [daimeθilə'si:tik], *a. Ch:* diméthylacétique.
dimethylamine [daimeθil'æmain], *s. Ch:* diméthylamine *f.*
dimethylaniline [daimeθil'ænilain], *s. Ch:* diméthylaniline *f.*
dimethylarsine [daimeθil'ɑ:sain], *s. Ch:* diméthylarsine *f.*
dimethylbenzene [daimeθilben'zi:n], *s. Ch:* diméthylbenzène *m.*
dimidiate [di'midieit, dai-], *a. Nat.Hist:* dimidié.
diminish [di'miniʃ]. **1.** *v.tr.* (*a*) diminuer, réduire, amoindrir, atténuer; **country diminished in power,** pays amoindri dans sa puissance; (*b*) *Carp: Metalw:* amincir (une tige, etc.). **2.** *v.i.* diminuer, s'amoindrir, s'atténuer, décroître; aller en diminuant; subir une diminution; **his business has diminished,** ses affaires *f* ont reculé, ont baissé.
diminishable [di'miniʃəbl], *a.* que l'on peut diminuer.
diminished [di'miniʃt], *a.* diminué, amoindri; *Arch:* **d. column,** colonne diminuée; *Mus:* **d. interval,** intervalle diminué; **d. fifth,** quinte diminuée; fausse quinte; *Jur:* **d. responsibility,** responsabilité atténuée.
diminishing[1] [di'miniʃiŋ], *a.* **1.** décroissant; qui diminue, qui va en diminuant; (*of value, etc.*) baissant; **d. scale,** échelle fuyante; *N.Arch:* **d. planks,** bordages *m* de diminution; *Pol.Ec:* **law of d. returns,** loi *f* des rendements non-proportionnels, décroissants. **2. d. glass,** lunette *f* qui rapetisse les objets; lentille concave, divergente.
diminishing[2], *s.* diminution *f*; atténuation *f.*
diminuendo [diminju'endou], *adv. & s. Mus:* diminuendo (*m*).
diminution [dimi'nju:ʃ(ə)n], *s.* diminution *f*; réduction *f*; amoindrissement *m*; abaissement *m*; **request for d. of taxes,** demande *f* en dégrèvement d'impôt; **our takings show a considerable d.,** nos recettes accusent une baisse sensible.
diminutive [di'minjutiv]. **1.** *a. & s. Gram:* diminutif (*m*). **2.** *a.* tout petit; minuscule; mince; exigu, -uë; **he was small, almost d., in stature,** il était de taille médiocre, presque exiguë.
diminutively [di'minjutivli], *adv.* **ending used d.,** terminaison employée comme diminutif.
diminutiveness [di'minjutivnis], *s.* petitesse *f*, exiguïté *f.*
dimissory [di'misəri], *a. Ecc:* **d. letter, letters d.,** lettres dimissoriales; dimissoire *m* (octroyé par l'évêque).
dimity ['dimiti], *s. Tex:* basin *m*, brillanté *m.*
dimly ['dimli], *adv.* (brûler) faiblement, sans éclat; (voir) imparfaitement, indistinctement, à peine; (sentir, se souvenir) vaguement, indistinctement; **d. lit room,** pièce mal, faiblement, éclairée.
dimmer ['dimər], *s. El:* résistance *f*; interrupteur *m* à gradation de lumière; régulateur *m* de tension; réducteur *m* d'éclairage; *Aut: A:* dispositif anti-éblouissant; *Cin:* obscurateur *m* de salle; **d. bulb,** lampe *f* satellite; ampoule *f* veilleuse; *Th:* **stage d.,** régulateur d'éclairage de scène.
dimming ['dimiŋ], *s.* **1.** (*a*) obscurcissement *m*; atténuation *f* (de la lumière); ternissement *m* (d'un miroir); affaiblissement *m* (de la mémoire, de la vue, etc.); (*b*) mise *f* en veilleuse (d'une lampe, etc.); (*c*) *Aut: A:* mise en code (des phares). **2.** baisse *f* (de la lumière, p. ex. par insuffisance du courant).
dimness ['dimnis], *s.* **1.** faiblesse *f* (d'éclairage, de la vue); obscurité *f* (d'une pièce); aspect *m* terne (d'une couleur, d'une surface polie). **2.** imprécision *f*, vague *m* (d'un contour, d'un souvenir). **3.** *F:* stupidité *f*, bêtise *f.*
dimorphic [dai'mɔ:fik], **dimorphous** [dai'mɔ:fəs], *a. Cryst: Biol: etc:* dimorphe.
dimorphism [dai'mɔ:fizm], *s. Cryst: Biol: etc:* dimorphisme *m*, dimorphie *f.*
dimout ['dimaut], *s. U.S:* blackout partiel.
dimple[1] ['dimpl], *s.* **1.** (*on cheek, chin*) fossette *f.* **2.** (*on water, ground*) ride *f*, ondulation *f.*
dimple[2]. **1.** *v.tr.* (*a*) (*of smile*) former, creuser, des fossettes *f* dans (les joues de qn); (*b*) (*of wind*) rider (la surface de l'eau). **2.** *v.i.* (*of cheeks*) se former en fossettes; (*of water*) onduler; **she dimpled with laughter,** son rire lui mettait des fossettes aux joues.
dimpled ['dimpld], *a.* (joue *f*) à fossette.
dim-sighted [dim'saitid], *a.* qui a la vue trouble, faible; **to be d.-s.,** voir mal.
dimwit ['dimwit], *s. F:* idiot, -ote, andouille *f*; **you d.!** espèce d'idiot!
dimwitted [dim'witid], *a. F:* obtus, stupide, bête.
din[1] [din], *s.* tapage *m*, tumulte *m*, fracas *m*, vacarme *m*; *F:* boucan *m*, tintamarre *m*; **the d. of battle,** le bruit, le fracas, de la bataille; *F:* **to kick up a d., no end of a d.,** faire un charivari, un tapage, de tous les diables; **what a din!** quel vacarme!
din[2], *v.* (**dinned**) **1.** *v.tr.* (*a*) assourdir, étourdir (les oreilles de qn); **I had my ears dinned by hooters,** j'étais assourdi par les sirènes; (*b*) **to d. sth. into s.o.'s ears,** corner qch. aux oreilles de qn; rebattre les oreilles à qn de qch.; **you have to d. it into him,** il faut le lui crier dans les oreilles, le lui enfoncer à coups répétés dans la tête; **to d. a part into s.o.,** seriner un rôle à qn. **2.** *v.i.* (*of voice, etc.*) **to d. in s.o.'s ears,** résonner à l'oreille, retentir dans l'oreille, de qn.
Dinantian [dai'nænʃ(ə)n], *a. & s. Geol:* dinantien (*m*).
dinaphthyl [dai'næfθil], *s. Ch:* dinaphtyle *m.*
dinar ['di:nɑ:r], *s. Num:* dinar *m.*
Dinaric [dai'nærik], *a. Geog:* **the D. Alps,** les Alpes *f* Dinariques.
dine [dain]. **1.** *v.i.* dîner; **we dined off the remains of the roast lamb,** nous avons dîné des restes du gigot; **to d. at a restaurant, at s.o.'s house,** dîner à un restaurant, chez qn; **to d. out,** dîner (i) en ville, à un restaurant, (ii) chez des amis; **to d. in, at home,** dîner à la maison; *A:* **to d. with Duke Humphrey,** dîner avec les chevaux de bois. **2.** *v.tr.* (*a*) offrir un dîner à (qn); **to wine and d. s.o.,** fêter qn; (*b*) **the table dines twenty,** on peut dîner à vingt autour de la table.
diner ['dainər], *s.* **1.** (*pers.*) dîneur, -euse; **he's a great d. out,** (i) il dîne souvent au restaurant, chez des amis; (ii) *Pej:* c'est un coureur de dîners. **2.** (*a*) *Rail:* wagon-restaurant *m*, *pl.* wagons-restaurants; (*b*) *NAm:* petit restaurant (au bord d'une route).
dinette [dai'net], *s.* coin *m* (des) repas.
dineutron [dai'nju:trɔn], *s. Ph:* dineutron *m.*
ding [diŋ], *v.i.* résonner, retentir.
ding-dong ['diŋ'dɔŋ]. **1.** *adv.* digue-din-don. **2.** *s.* tintement *m* (des cloches); digue-din-don *m inv.* **3.** (*a*) *s.* **the d.-d. of public argument,** l'échange *m* de ripostes des discussions en public; (*b*) **a d.-d. match,** partie où l'avantage passe constamment d'un côté à l'autre; partie durement disputée.
dinghy ['diŋ(g)i], *s. Nau:* canot *m*, youyou *m*; **collapsible d.,** berthon *m*; **sailing d.,** dinghy *m*, *pl.* dinghies.
dinginess ['dindʒinis], *s.* aspect sombre, enfumé (d'une ville, d'une maison); couleur *f* terne; manque *m* de fraîcheur (du mobilier, des rideaux); propreté douteuse (d'une maison, du mobilier, des vêtements).
dingle ['diŋgl], *s.* vallon (boisé).
dingo[1] ['diŋgou], *s. Z:* dingo *m*, chien *m* sauvage (de l'Australie).
dingo[2], *a. P: O:* un peu toqué; dingo, *f.* dingote; dingue.
dingy ['dindʒi], *a.* qui manque d'éclat, de fraîcheur; (*of room, furniture, etc.*) défraîchi, enfumé; (*of colour*) terne, sale; (*of sky*) fuligineux; **d. hotel, linen,** hôtel *m*, linge *m*, d'une propreté douteuse; **d. white,** d'un blanc sale; **the d. towns of the Midlands,** les villes enfumées des comtés du centre; **his clothes were getting dingier and dingier,** ses vêtements se défraîchissaient de plus en plus; **all these d. acquaintances sponged on him,** tous ces déchards, ces décheux, le tapaient tant et plus.
dining ['dainiŋ], *attrib.* **d. room,** salle *f* à manger; **d. alcove,** coin *m* (des) repas; **d. hall,** réfectoire *m*; *Rail:* **d. car,** wagon-restaurant *m*, *pl.* wagons-restaurants.
dinitrobenzene [dainaitrouben'zi:n], *s. Ch:* dinitrobenzène *m.*
dinitrocresol [dainaitrou'kresɔl], *s. Ch:* dinitrocrésol *m.*
dinitromethane [dainaitrou'meθein, -'mi:-], *s. Ch:* dinitrométhane *m.*
dinitronaphthalene [dainaitrou'næfθəli:n], dinitronaphtalène *m.*
dinitrophenol ['dainaitrou'finɔl], *s. Ch:* dinitrophénol *m.*
dinitrotoluene [dainaitrou'tɔljui:n], *s. Ch:* dinitrotoluène *m.*
dinkum ['diŋkəm]. *Austr: F:* **1.** *a.* (*of pers.*) franc, *f*; franche; sincère; (*of thg*) authentique; **faire d.,** régulier, vrai de vrai; **a d. Aussie,** un vrai Australien, une vraie Australienne; **d. oil,** la vérité; un bon tuyau. **2.** *s.* Australien, -ienne, de naissance; Kangourou *m.* **3.** *adv.* franchement; vraiment.
dinky ['diŋki], *a. F:* coquet, mignon, gentil; **a d. little hat,** un petit chapeau coquet.
dinkydie [diŋki'dai], *a. Austr: F:* sincère; authentique.
dinner ['dinər], *s.* (*a*) dîner *m*, *Fr.C:* souper *m*; **to be at d.,** être à table; **we were having d.,** nous étions en train de dîner; **to finish d.,** sortir de table; **to have a good d.,** faire un bon dîner; **after a good d.,** après avoir bien mangé; **to go out to d.,** dîner (i) en ville, dans un restaurant, (ii) chez des amis; **public d.,** banquet *m*; *Mil:* **regimental d.,** repas *m* de corps; *Rail: etc:* **first, second, d.,** premier, deuxième, service; **d. party,** (i) dîner sur invitation; (ii) les convives; **to give a d. party,** avoir du monde à dîner; **we are going to a big d. party this evening,** nous allons à un grand dîner ce soir; **dolls' d. party,** dînette *f* (de poupées); **d. dance,** dîner-dansant *m*, *pl.* dîners-dansant; **d. dress,** (i) (*for women*) robe *f* de soirée; (ii) (*for men*) tenue *f* de soirée; **d. jacket,** smoking *m*; **d. service,** service *m* de table; **d. knife, fork,** couteau *m*, fourchette *f*, de table; **d. mat,** dessous *m* de plat, d'assiette; **d. table,** table *f* de salle à manger; **d. trolley, wagon,** table (desserte) roulante, à roulettes; **d. wine,** vin *m* de table; **d. time,** l'heure *f* du dîner; **after-d. speech,** discours *m* d'après-dîner; (*b*) (*mid-day*) **d.,** déjeuner *m*; **d. can, pail,** gamelle *f*, porte-manger *m inv* (d'ouvrier, etc.); *Sch:* **d. hour,** l'heure du déjeuner; **to do d. duty,** surveiller, faire le service de, la cantine; surveiller au réfectoire; **to give the dog his d.,** donner à manger au chien; *F:* **it looks like the dog's d.,** (i) c'est un beau gâchis; (ii) quel plat! *P:* **to be got up like a dog's d.,** être endimanché.
dinnerware ['dinəweər], *s. NAm:* vaisselle *f* et verrerie *f* de table.
dinoceras [dai'nɔsərəs], *s. Paleont:* dinocéras *m.*
Dinoflagellata [dainouflædʒə'leitə], *s.pl. Nat.Hist:* dinoflagellés *m.*
Dinomyidae [dainou'maiidi:], *s.pl. Z:* dinomyidés *m.*
dinornis [dai'nɔ:nis], *s. Paleont:* dinornis *m.*
dinosaur ['dainousɔ:r]n **dinosaurian** [dainou'sɔ:riən], *s. Paleont:* dinosaure *m*, dinosaurien *m.*
Dinosauria [dainə'sɔ:riə], *s.pl. Paleont:* dinosauriens *m.*
dinotherium [dainə'θiəriəm], *s. Paleont:* dinotherium *m.*
dint[1] [dint], *s.* **1.** = DENT[1]. **2.** *A:* violence *f*, force *f*; *still so used in the prep. phr.;* **by d. of,** à force de; **by d. of hard work we achieved success,** à force de travailler dur nous avons réussi.
dint[2], *v.tr.* = DENT[2].
diocesan [dai'ɔsisən]. *Ecc:* **1.** *a.* diocésain. **2.** *s.* diocésain *m*, évêque *m.*
diocese ['daiəsis], *s. Ecc:* diocèse *m.*
dioch ['daiɔk], *s. Orn:* dioch *m*, quelea *m*, *F:* travailleur *m.*
Diocletian [daiə'kli:ʃ(ə)n], *Pr.n.m.* Dioclétien.
diode ['daioud], *s. Elcs:* (lampe *f*) diode *f*, **double d.,** diode bianodique; **double-base d.,** diode à double base; **cross-connected d.,** diode en montage croisé; **detector d.,** diode détectrice; **cat whisker d.,** diode à pointe; **d. detection,** détection *f* par diode.
diodon ['daiədɔn], *s. Ich:* diodon *m.*
dioecious [dai'i:ʃəs], *a. Bot: Z:* dioïque.
Diogenes [dai'ɔdʒəni:z], *Pr.n.m.* Diogène; **Diogenes' tub,** le tonneau de Diogène; **the lantern of D.,** la lanterne de Diogène.
Diomede(s) ['daiəmi:d, daiə'mi:di:z], *Pr.n.m. Gr.Lit:* Diomède.
Diomedeidae [daiəmi'di:idi:], *s.pl. Orn:* diomédéidés *m.*
dionaea [daiə'ni:ə], *s. Bot:* dionée *f*; *F:* attrape-mouche(s) *m inv.*
Dionysia [daiə'niziə], *s.pl. Gr.Ant:* dionysies *f.*
Dionysiac [daiə'niziæk], *a. Gr.Ant:* dionysiaque.
Dionysius [daiə'naisiəs, -niʃiəs], *Pr.n.m. Gr.Ant:* Denys (le Tyran).
Dionysus [daiə'naisəs], *Pr.n.m. Gr.Myth:* Dionysos.
Diophantine [daiə'fænti:n, -tain], *a. Mth:* **D. analysis,** analyse *f* diophantine.
Diophantos [daiə'fæntɔs], *Pr.n.m. Hist. of Mth:* Diophante.
diopside [dai'ɔpsaid], *s. Miner:* diopside *m.*
dioptase [dai'ɔpteis], *s. Miner:* dioptase *f.*
diopter [dai'ɔptər], *s. Opt.Meas:* dioptrie *f.*
Dioptidae [dai'ɔptidi:], *s.pl. Ent:* dioptides *m.*
dioptric [dai'ɔptrik]. **1.** *a.* dioptrique. **2.** *s. Opt.Meas:* dioptrie *f.*
dioptrics [dai'ɔptriks], *s.pl.* (*usu. with sg. const.*) dioptrique *f.*
diorama [daiə'rɑ:mə], *s.* diorama *m.*
dioramic [daiə'ræmik], *a.* dioramique.
diorite ['daiərait], *s. Geol:* diorite *f.*
Dioscoreaceae [daiɔskɔri'eisii:], *s.pl. Bot:* dioscoréacées *f.*
Dioscuri (the) [ðədaiɔs'kju:rai], *Pr.n.pl. Gr.Myth:* les Dioscures *m.*
diosphenol [daiɔs'fenɔl, -'fi:-], *s. Ch:* diosphénol *m.*
dioxane [dai'ɔksein], *s. Ch:* dioxane *m.*
dioxide [dai'ɔksaid], *s. Ch:* dioxyde *m*, bioxyde *m*; **carbon d.,** dioxyde de carbone.
dioxime [dai'ɔksaim], *s. Ch:* dioxime *m.*
dioxytartaric [daiɔksita:'tærik], *a. Ch:* dioxytartrique.
dip[1] [dip], *s.* **1.** (*a*) plongement *m*, immersion *f*, plongée *f*, plongeon *m* (de qch. dans un liquide, etc.); *Metalw:*

hot d., immersion à chaud; **I'll have a d. into this book,** je vais jeter un coup d'œil dans ce livre; (*b*) tirant *m* d'eau (d'un navire); hauteur *f* d'immersion (d'une roue à aubes). **2.** (*a*) inclinaison *f* (d'une aiguille aimantée); (*b*) inclinaison, abaissement *m*, dépression *f*, creux *m*, pente *f*, dénivellement *m*, dénivellation *f*, plongée *f* (du terrain); déclivité *f* (de terrain); *Geol:* pendage *m* (d'une couche); *Min:* vallée *f*; *Agr: etc:* baissière *f*; (*in road*) caniveau *m*; *Geol:* **d. slope,** pente douce; **d. fault,** faille *f* de plongement; **d. meter,** pendagemètre *m*; (*c*) *Mth:* **d. in a curve,** inflexion *f* d'une courbe; flèche *f*; (*d*) dépression (de l'horizon); (*e*) *esp. NAm:* baisse *f*, repli *m* (dans les prix, etc.). **3.** *Nau:* salut *m* (avec le pavillon); **flag at the d.,** pavillon à mi-drisse. **4.** baignade *f*; **I'm going for a d.,** je vais me baigner. **5.** (*a*) *Ind:* solution *f*, bain *m* (de décapage, de dorure, etc.); (*b*) (**sheep**) **d.,** bain parasiticide (pour moutons, etc.). **6.** chandelle plongée à la baguette. **7.** *P:* voleur *m* à la tire.

dip[2], *v.* (**dipped**)

I. *v.tr.* **1.** plonger, tremper (les mains, etc., dans l'eau); tremper (une plume dans l'encre, etc.); **to d. one's feet in a stream,** baigner ses pieds dans un ruisseau; **I'm always dipping my hand into my pocket,** je suis toujours à débourser. **2.** (*a*) *Ind:* traiter par immersion; immerger, décaper, dérocher (un métal); teindre (la laine, un tissu); *Metalw:* **to d. a wire,** étamer un fil métallique; *Tan:* **to d. skins,** confire les peaux; (*b*) **to d. sheep,** baigner, laver, les moutons (dans un bain parasiticide); (*c*) **to d. candles,** plonger des chandelles. **3.** baisser (qch.) subitement; **to d. the scale pan,** faire pencher la balance; *Aut:* **to d. (one's headlights),** se mettre en code; *Nau:* **to d. a flag, a signal,** (faire) marquer un pavillon, un signal; **to d. one's flag,** *v.i.* **to d. (to a ship),** saluer (un navire avec son pavillon).

II. *v.i.* **1.** plonger (dans l'eau, etc.); *Mec.E:* (*of gear, etc.*) **to d. in oil,** barboter dans l'huile; **to d. into a book,** feuilleter un livre; **to d. into a subject,** effleurer un sujet; **to d. into one's capital,** prendre dans son capital; **I'm always dipping into my pocket,** je suis toujours à débourser; **to d. into the past,** sonder le passé. **2.** (*a*) (*of compass needle*) incliner; (*of scale*) pencher; (*of suspended wire, etc.*) faire flèche; (*of ground*) s'abaisser, descendre; (*of strata*) s'incliner; **the road dips sharply,** la route plonge, descend, brusquement; (*b*) **the sun dipped below the horizon,** le soleil est descendu derrière l'horizon; (*c*) *esp. NAm:* (*of prices, etc.*) baisser; (*d*) (*of bird in flight, of aircraft*) piquer.

dipalmitin [di'pælmitin], *s. Ch:* dipalmitine *f*.

diparachlorobenzyl [daipærəklɔ:rou'benzil], *s. Ch:* diparachlorobenzyle *m*.

diphase ['daifeiz], **diphasic** [dai'feizik], *a. El:* (circuit, etc.) diphasé.

diphead ['diphed], *s. Min:* vallée *f*.

diphenic [dai'fi:nik], *a. Ch:* diphénique.

diphenyl [dai'fenil], *s. Ch:* diphényle *m*.

diphenylacetylene [daifenilæ'setili:n], *s. Ch:* diphénylacétylène *f*.

diphenylamine [daifenil'æmain], *s. Ch:* diphénylamine *f*.

diphenyline [dai'fenilain], *s. Ch:* diphényline *f*.

diphenylmethane [daifenil'meθein, -'mi:-], *s. Ch:* diphénylméthane *m*.

diphtheria [dif'θiəriə], *s. Med:* diphtérie *f*; **d. vaccine,** vaccin *m* antidiphtérique.

diphtherial [dif'θiəriəl], **diphtheric** [dif'θerik], *a. Med:* diphtérique.

diphtheritic [difθə'ritik], *a. Med:* atteint de diphtérie; **d. membrane,** membrane couenneuse.

diphtheroid ['difθərɔid], *a. Med:* diphtéroïde.

diphthong[1] ['difθɔŋ], *s. Ling:* diphtongue *f*.

diphthong[2], *v.tr. Ling:* diphtonguer.

diphthongal [dif'θɔŋ(ə)l], *a. Ling:* diphtongal, -aux.

diphthongization [difθɔŋai'zeiʃ(ə)n], **dipthongism** ['difθɔŋizm], *s. Ling:* diphtongaison *f*.

diphthongize ['difθɔŋaiz]. **1.** *v.tr.* diphtonguer, diphtonguifier. **2.** *v.i.* (*of vowel*) se diphtonguer.

diphyletic [daifi'letik], *a. Nat.Hist:* diphylétique.

diphyodont [dai'faioudɔnt], *a. & s. Z:* diphyodonte (*m*).

dipicrylamine [dai'pikrilәmi:n], *s. Exp:* hexyl *m*.

diplacusis [diplə'kju:sis], *s. Med:* diplacousie *f*.

diplegia [dai'pli:dʒiə], *s. Med:* diplégie *f*; paralysie bilatérale.

diplex[1] ['daipleks], *a. & s. W.Tel: etc:* duplex (*m inv*), diplex (*m inv*).

diplex[2], *v.tr. W.Tel: etc:* duplexer, dupliquer.

diplexer [dai'pleksər], *s. Elcs:* diplexeur *m*.

diplexing [dai'pleksiŋ], *s. W.Tel: etc:* duplication *f*; duplexage *m*.

diplo- ['diplou], *comb.fm.* diplo-.

diplocephalous [diplouselfələs], *a. Ter:* diplocéphale.

diplocephalus [diplou'sefələs], *s. Ter:* diplocéphale *m*.

diplocephaly [diplou'sefəli], *s. Ter:* diplocéphalie *f*.

diplococcus, *pl.* **-cocci** [diplou'kɔkəs, -'kɔksai], *s. Bac:* diplocoque *m*.

diplodocus [di'plɔdəkəs], *s. Paleont:* diplodocus *m*.

diplogenesis [diplou'dʒenəsis], *s. Biol:* diplogénèse *f*.

diploglossus [diplou'glɔsəs], *s. Rept:* diploglosse *m*.

diplohedral [diplou'hi:dr(ə)l], *a.* diploédrique.

diplohedron [diplou'hi:dr(ə)n], *s. Cryst:* diploèdre *m*.

diploid ['diplɔid], *a. Biol:* diploïde.

diploidy ['diplɔidi], *s. Biol:* diploïdie *f*.

diploma [di'ploumə], *s.* **1.** diplôme *m*; *Sch:* **teacher's d.** = C.A.P. (Certificat d'aptitude pédagogique); **D. of Education** = C.A.P.E.S. (Certificat d'aptitude au professorat de l'enseignement secondaire). **2.** *Hist: Pal:* diplôme, charte *f*.

diplomacy [di'plouməsi], *s.* (*a*) diplomatie *f*; (*b*) diplomatie, adresse *f*, tact *m*; **to attain one's ends by d.,** faire de la diplomatie, user d'adresse, pour atteindre son but.

diplomat ['dipləmæt], *s.* diplomate *m*.

diplomatic[1] [diplə'mætik], *a.* **1.** diplomatique; **the d. corps,** le corps diplomatique; **to enter the d. service,** entrer dans la diplomatie, *F:* dans la Carrière. **2.** politique, adroit, prudent, diplomatique; **d. answer,** réponse *f* politique; **he knows how to be d.,** il a beaucoup de souplesse.

diplomatic[2], *a. Pal:* diplomatique; **d. copy,** copie exacte de l'original.

diplomatically [diplə'mætik(ə)li], *adv.* **1.** diplomatiqement. **2.** avec adresse; avec tact; en usant de subterfuges.

diplomatics [diplə'mætiks], *s.pl.* (*usu. with sg. const.*) diplomatique *f*.

diplomatist [di'ploumətist], *s.* diplomate *m*.

diplomatize [di'plomətaiz], *v.i.* agir en diplomate; faire de la diplomatie.

diplophase ['diploufeiz], *s. Biol:* diplophase *f*.

diplopia [di'ploupiə], *s. Med:* diplopie *f*.

diplopod ['diploupɔd], *s. Ent:* diplopode *m*.

Diplopoda [di'plɔpədə], *s.pl. Ent:* diplopodes *m*.

Diploptera [di'plɔptərə], *s.pl. Ent:* diploptères *m*.

diplopterous [di'plɔptərəs], *a. Ent:* diploptère.

diplosome ['diplousoum], *s.* diplosome *m*.

diplozoon [diplou'zouən], *s. Prot:* diplozoon *m*.

Diplura [di'plju:rə], *s.pl. Ent:* diploures *m*.

dip net ['dipnet], *s. Fish:* épuisette *f*.

dipneumonous [dai'nju:mənəs], *a. Z:* dipneumone.

Dipneusti [dip'nju:stai], *s.pl. Ich:* dipneustes *m*.

Dipnoi [dip'nouai], *s.pl. Ich:* dipnoïques *m*, dipneustes *m*.

Dipodidae [dai'pɔdidi:], *s.pl. Z:* dipodidés *m*.

dipodous ['dipədəs], *a. Biol:* dipode.

dipolar [dai'poulər], *a.* **1.** (aimant) bipolaire. **2.** *El:* dipolaire.

dipole ['daipoul], *s. El:* dipôle *m*; **d. moment,** moment *m* dipolaire, d'un dipôle; *W.Tel: etc:* **d. aerial,** antenne *f* dipôle.

dipped [dipt], *a.* (*a*) incliné; (*b*) (*of chair seat, etc.*) surbaissé; (*c*) *Aut:* (*of headlights*) en code.

dipper ['dipər], *s.* **1** (*pers.*) plongeur, -euse; (*in pottery, glazing, etc.*) trempeur *m*; *Paperm:* puiseur *m*, plongeur; ouvrier *m* de cuve. **2.** *Rel: F:* baptiste *mf*; anabaptiste *mf*. **3.** *Orn: F:* (*a*) cincle plongeur, cincle américain; merle *m* d'eau; (*b*) *esp. NAm:* martin-pêcheur *m*, *pl.* martins-pêcheurs. **4.** (*a*) cuillère *f* à pot; louche *f*; (*b*) *Astr: NAm:* **the Great, Big, D.,** la Grande Ourse; **the Little D.,** la Petite Ourse; (*c*) (*on fair ground*) **big d.,** le grand huit. **5.** (*a*) *I.C.E:* **oil d.,** plongeur *m*, cuiller *f* d'huile (de tête de bielle); (*b*) *Aut: F:* jauge *f* à tige, d'huile; (*c*) *Paint:* pincelier *m*. **6.** *Aut:* basculeur *m* (de phares).

dipping[1] ['dipiŋ], *a.* incliné; plongeant; *Min:* **steeply d. seam, lode,** dressant *m*.

dipping[2], *s.* (*a*) plongée *f*, immersion *f*; *Metalw:* dérochage *m*, décapage *m*; **d. liquid,** bain *m* de dérochage; *Paperm:* **d. rolls,** rouleaux *m* d'immersion; (*b*) **sheep d.,** baignage *m* des moutons; (*c*) *Fish:* **d. net,** pêchette *f*; épuisette *f*; (*square*) carrelet *m*.

dippy ['dipi], *a. P: O:* maboul, loufoque, timbré.

diprotodon [dai'proutədɔn], *s. Paleont:* diprotodon *m*.

Diprotodontia [daiproutou'dɔntiə], *s.pl. Z:* diprotodontes *m*.

diproton [dai'proutɔn], *s. Atom.Ph:* diproton *m*.

Dipsacaceae [dipsə'keisii:], *s.pl. Bot:* dipsacacées *f*.

Dipsaceae [dip'seisii:], *s.pl. Bot:* dipsacées *f*.

Dipsadinae [dip'sædini:], *s.pl. Rept:* dipsadinés *m*.

dipsomania [dipsə'meiniə], *s.* dipsomanie *f*.

dipsomaniac [dipsə'meiniæk], *a. & s.* dipsomane (*mf*).

dipstick ['dipstik], *s. Aut:* jauge *f* à tige, jauge de carter.

dipter ['diptər], *s. Ent:* diptère *m*.

Diptera ['diptərə], *s.pl. Ent:* diptères *m*.

dipteral ['diptər(ə)l], *a. Arch:* (temple *m*) diptère.

dipteran ['diptərən], *s. Ent:* diptère *m*.

Dipterocarpaceae [diptəroukɑ:'peisii:], *s.pl. Bot:* diptérocarpacées *f*.

dipterous ['diltərəs], *a. Ent:* diptère.

diptych ['diptik], *s.* **1.** *Ant:* diptyque *m*, diptyques *mpl*. **2.** *Art:* diptyque.

dipyre ['daipaiər], *s. Miner:* dipyre *m*.

dipyrenous [dai'pirənəs], *a. Bot:* dipyréné.

dire ['daiər], *a.* désastreux, néfaste, terrible, affreux; **d. necessity,** dure nécessité, nécessité implacable; **d. forebodings,** pressentiments *m* lugubres; **to be in d. poverty, distress, straits,** se trouver dans la dernière misère, dans la plus grande détresse; **exposed to the direst dangers,** exposé aux pires dangers; **this decision will have d. consequences,** cette décision aura des conséquences néfastes; **I'm in d. need of sleep,** il me faut absolument dormir.

direct[1] [dai'rekt, di-], *v.tr.* **1.** adresser (une lettre, des observations, etc.) (**to s.o.,** à qn); **letter directed to s.o.,** lettre à l'adresse de qn; **please d. it to me care of my father,** je vous prie de me l'adresser aux bons soins de mon père. **2.** gouverner (sa conduite); conduire (une armée, ses affaires, un orchestre); diriger, mener, gérer, régir, administrer (une entreprise); *NAm: Th:* **to d. a play,** mettre une pièce en scène. **3.** (*a*) **to d. s.o.'s attention to sth.,** appeler, attirer, l'attention de qn sur qch.; **to d. one's attention to sth.,** diriger son attention sur qch.; **to d. a telescope towards sth.,** orienter, braquer, une lunette sur qch.; (*b*) **accusation directed against s.o.,** accusation *f* visant, qui vise, qn; **measures were directed against this abuse,** on a pris des mesures contre cet abus; (*c*) **to d. one's steps towards . . .,** diriger ses pas, se diriger, vers . . .; (*d*) *Mil:* **to d. the fire on a target,** appliquer, diriger, le feu sur un objectif; battre un objectif. **4. can you d. me to the station?** pouvez-vous m'indiquer le chemin de la gare? **5.** (*a*) **to d. s.o. to do sth.,** ordonner, dire, à qn de faire qch.; **as directed,** (i) conformément aux ordres; (ii) selon les instructions, les indications données; **they were directed to work in a munitions factory** = ils étaient mobilisés dans une usine de munitions; **the officer directed the troops to advance,** l'officier a donné aux troupes l'ordre d'avancer; **he is directed by his conscience,** sa conscience lui dicte son devoir; (*b*) *Jur:* (*of judge*) **to d. the jury,** instruire le jury (sur un point de droit).

direct[2]. **1.** *a.* (*a*) direct; **the d. way, road,** le chemin direct, le plus court; **d. cause,** cause immédiate; **he had d. charge of the library,** la bibliothèque était directement sous ses ordres; **to be a d. descendant of s.o.,** descendre de qn en ligne directe; **to have a d. interest in sth.,** avoir un intérêt personnel dans qch.; **in d. contradiction,** en contradiction directe; **the d. opposite of sth.,** juste l'opposé *m* de qch.; *Gram:* **d. object,** complément direct; **d. speech,** discours direct; **d. action, control,** action, commande, directe; *Ind:* **to take d. action,** se mettre en grève; *Jur:* **d. evidence,** preuve directe; *Mec.E:* **d. drive,** commande, prise, directe; **d. drive engine,** moteur direct, sans démultiplicateur; **d.-coupled,** en prise directe; *Artil: etc:* **d. fire,** tir (i) direct, (ii) de plein fouet; **d. laying, aiming,** pointage direct; **d. hit,** coup *m* (i) au but, (ii) de plein fouet; *Pol.Ec:* **d. tax,** impôt direct; **d. taxation,** contributions directes; *Mth:* **in d. ratio to distance,** en raison directe de la distance; proportionnellement à la distance; *Tchn:* **d.-reading instrument,** instrument *m* à lecture directe; *Cmptr:* **d. access,** accès direct, sélectif; **d. address,** adresse absolue; **d. instruction,** instruction *f* à opérande directe; (*b*) (*of pers.*) franc, *f.* franche; ouvert; (*c*) absolu, formel, exprès; catégorique; **I want a d. answer,** il me faut une réponse catégorique, sans détours; (*d*) *El:* **d. current,** courant continu; **d. voltage,** tension continue; **fed with d. current,** alimenté en continu; **d.-current dynamo,** dynamo *m* à courant continu; *Metalw:* **d. casting,** coulée *f* en première fusion; *Dy:* **d. dyeing,** teinture *f* sans mordant; *Phot:* **d. (vision) finder,** viseur direct, clair, iconométrique; viseur à cadre (sans lentille). **2.** *adv.* (aller) directement, tout droit; **to dispatch goods d. to s.o.,** expédier des marchandises directement à qn; **I shall communicate with you d.,** je vous écrirai directement; *W.Tel: T.V:* **the concert will be transmitted d. from Paris,** ce concert sera transmis en direct de Paris.

directing [dai'rektiŋ, di-], *a.* (*a*) directeur, -trice; dirigeant; directif; (*b*) *Artil:* **d. gun,** pièce directrice; **d. mark,** jalon *m*.

direction [dai'rekʃ(ə)n, di-], *s.* **1.** (*a*) direction *f*, administration *f* (d'une société, etc.); conduite *f* (des affaires); **under the d. of . . .,** sous la direction, la conduite, de . . .; (*b*) **d. of the traffic,** réglementation *f* de la circulation. **2.** *A:* adresse *f* (d'une lettre). **3.** (*a*) direction, sens *m*; *Aut:* **d. sign,** panneau *m* de signalisation; **in the d. of . . .,** dans la direction de . . .; **we were going in the d. of Paris,** nous nous dirigions vers Paris; **in every d.,** en tous sens; dans tous les sens; de-ci, de-là; **to run about in all directions,** courir de côté et d'autre; **in the opposite d.,** en sens inverse; **in which d.?** de quel côté? **d. of the traffic,** sens de la circulation (*see also* 1 (*b*)); **to put s.o. in the right d., mettre qn dans la bonne voie; you are not looking in the right d.,** vous ne regardez pas du bon côté; **to lose one's sense of d.,** perdre le sens de l'orientation; **change of d.,** changement *m* de direction; *Aer: Nau:* changement de cap *m*; *Mth:* **positive d.,** sens direct; **negative d.,** sens rétrograde; *Elcs:* **d. finding,** (radio)goniométrie *f*; **d.-finding apparatus, station,** appareil *m*, station *f*, radiogoniométrique; **position by d. findings,** position donnée par gonio, par relèvements radiogoniométriques; **d. finder,** (radio)goniomètre *m*; indicateur *m* de gisement; **cathode-ray d. finder,** (radio)goniomètre à oscilloscope; **compensated-loop d. finder,** (radio)goniomètre à cadre compensé; (*b*) **improvements in many directions,** améliorations *f* sous bien des rapports. **4.** (*a*) *pl.* **directions,** instructions *f*; directives *f*; **you have been given the wrong directions,** on vous a mal renseigné; **stage directions,** indications *f* scéniques; **directions for carrying out an experiment,** mode *m* opératoire; **directions (for use),** notice (explicative); (*b*) *Jur:* **d. to the jury,** exposé de la loi fait par le juge au jury.

directional [dai'rekʃənl, di-], *a.* **1.** *Elcs: etc:* directionnel, dirigé; **d. aerial, antenna,** antenne directionnelle, dirigée; **d. coupler,** dispositif *m* de couplage directionnel; détecteur directionnel de mesures; **d. radio, d. transmission,** liaison(s) radio, liaison(s) hertzienne(s), dirigée(s); **d. relay,** relais directionnel. **2.** *Av:* **d. gyro,** conservateur *m* de cap (gyroscopique); **d.-gyro card,** rose *f* des vents du conservateur de cap; **d. stability,** stabilité de direction, de route. **3.** (*of committee, authority, etc.*) dirigeant, de direction.

directive[1] [dai'rektiv, di-], *a.* directif; **d. function,** fonction directrice.

directive[2], *s. Mil: etc:* directive *f*.

directivity [dairek'tiviti], *s. El: etc:* directivité *f*.

directly [d(a)i'rektli]. **1.** *adv.* (*a*) (aller, conduire) directement, tout droit, sans détours; **to go d. to the point,** aller droit au fait; **to be d. descended from . . .,** descendre en droite ligne de . . .; **to be d. under s.o.'s influence,** être soumis immédiatement à l'influence de qn; **I am not d. concerned,** cela ne m'intéresse pas personnellement; (*b*) absolument, complètement, nettement; **d. contrary,** diamétralement opposé, nettement opposé (**to,** à); **a. d. opposite effect,** un effet exactement contraire; **the land lies d. to the north,** le terrain se trouve juste au nord; **he lives d. opposite the church,** il demeure juste en face de l'église, directement en face de l'église; (*c*) tout de suite, tout à l'heure, immédiatement; **I'm coming d.,** je viens tout de suite; **the doctor came d.,** le médecin est venu aussitôt. **2.** *conj. F:* aussitôt que, dès que; **I'll come d. I've finished,** je viendrai dès que j'aurai fini.

directness [d(a)i'rektnis], *s.* **1.** (*a*) franchise *f* (d'une réponse, etc.); (*b*) franchise bourrue; **his d. of speech,** son parler carré. **2. the d. of my information,** la source directe à laquelle je dois ce renseignement.

director [d(a)i'rektər], *s.* **1.** (*pers.*) (*a*) administrateur *m*, directeur *m* (d'une société, etc.); chef *m*, gérant *m* (d'une entreprise); **managing d.,** administrateur délégué, gérant; **board of directors,** conseil *m* d'administration; **d. of music,** (i) *Ecc:* maître *m* de chapelle, (ii) *Mil: etc:* chef de musique; *Adm:* **d. of studies,** *approx.* = inspecteur d'Académie; *Th:* **d. of (operatic) chorus,** répétiteur *m*; (*b*) *Fr.Hist:* directeur; membre *m* du Directoire; (*c*) *R.C.Ch:* directeur de conscience; (*d*) *Jur:* **d. of public prosecutions,** *approx.* = chef de parquet; (*e*) *Th: Cin: Mth:* metteur *m* en scène; *Cin:* directeur écraniste; réalisateur *m*; **assistant d.,** régisseur *m*. **2.** (*a*) directrice *f*; (*of ellipse, hyperbola*) **d. circle,** cercle directeur; (*b*) *Navy:* **d. top,** hune *f* de télépointage; le télépointage; (*c*) appareil *m* de visée (de torpille); (*d*) *Mec.E: etc:* guide *m* (d'un mouvement).

directorate [d(a)i'rektər(e)it], *s.* **1.** fonctions *fpl* d'administrateur, directorat *m*. **2.** (conseil *m* d')administration *f*; direction *f* (des chemins de fer, etc.).

directorial [dairek'tɔ:riəl], *a.* directorial, -aux.

directorship [d(a)i'rektəʃip], *s.* **1.** directorat *m*; poste *m*, fonctions *fpl*, de directeur, d'administrateur. **2. during my d.,** au cours de mon administration.

directory[1] [d(a)i'rektəri], *a.* directeur, -trice.

directory[2], *s.* **1.** répertoire *m* d'adresses; (*in France*) = le Bottin; annuaire *m* (des téléphones, etc.); **commercial d.,** annuaire du commerce. **2.** (*a*) *Fr.Hist:* **the D.,** le Directoire; (*b*) *U.S:* conseil *m* d'administration (d'une compagnie, etc.). **3.** *Ecc:* (*book*) directoire (des offices).

directress [d(a)i'rektris], *s. NAm:* (*pers.*) directrice *f*.

directrix, *pl.* **-ices** [d(a)i'rektriks, -isi:z], *s. Mth:* directrice *f* (d'une conique).

direful ['daiəful], *a. Lit:* = DIRE.

direfully ['daiəfuli], **direly** ['daiəli], *adv. Lit:* désastreusement, affreusement; lugubrement.

direness ['daiənis], *s. Lit:* horreur *f*; caractère désastreux, funeste, lugubre (**of,** de).

dirge [də:dʒ], *s.* hymne *m*, chant *m*, funèbre.

dirigibility [diridʒi'biliti], *s.* dirigeabilité *f*.

dirigible ['diridʒibl], *a. & s.* **d. (balloon),** (ballon *m*) dirigeable (*m*).

dirigism(e) ['diridʒizm], *s. Pol.Ec:* dirigisme *m*.

dirigist(ic) [diri'dʒist(ik)], *a. Pol.Ec:* dirigiste.

diriment ['dirimənt], *a. Jur:* **d. impediment (to marriage),** empêchement dirimant de mariage; cause dirimante de mariage.

dirk[1] [də:k], *s.* poignard *m* (des Écossais, des aspirants de marine).

dirk[2], *v.tr.* poignarder.

dirt[1] [də:t], *s.* **1.** saleté *f*; boue *f*, crotte *f*, fange *f*; (*unwashed*) crasse *f*; (*from drains*) curure *f*; (*excrement*) ordure *f*; **hands ingrained with d.,** mains encrassées; (*of material*) **to show the d.,** être salissant; *F:* **to throw d. at s.o.,** calomnier qn, couvrir qn de boue, traîner qn dans la boue; *F:* **to eat d.,** avaler son amour-propre, avaler des couleuvres; *F:* **to treat s.o. like (so much) d.,** traiter qn comme le dernier des derniers; *Ind: etc:* **d. money,** indemnité *f* de travail salissant; *F:* **to be d. poor,** être extrêmement pauvre, ne pas avoir un sou; *F:* **d. cheap,** à vil prix, pour rien; **I bought it d. cheap,** je l'ai eu pour (deux fois) rien; *P:* **(yellow) d.,** de l'argent *m*, du pognon, de la braise; (*b*) corps étranger(s), saletés (dans une machine, une solution, etc.); **d. in the carburettor,** des saletés dans le carburateur; (*c*) *Min:* terre *f*, alluvion *f*, aurifère; (*d*) *attrib.* **d. road,** chemin *m* en terre, de terre battue; chemin non macadamisé; **d. floor,** plancher *m* en terre battue; *U.S:* **d. roof,** toiture *f* en tourbe; *NAm:* **d. farmer,** exploitant *m* agricole; **d. farming,** exploitation *f* agricole; *Sp:* **d. track,** piste *f* en cendrée; **d.-track racing,** courses *f* (motocyclistes) sur cendrée; *Geol:* **d. band,** bande *f* de moraine intraglaciaire. **2.** (*a*) saleté, malpropreté; **to live in a state of d.,** vivre dans la saleté; (*b*) *F:* obscénités *fpl*, cochonneries *fpl*; pornographie *f*; **to talk d.,** dire des saletés, raconter des cochonneries; *P:* **to have the d. on s.o.,** savoir des choses peu relevées sur qn; *P:* **to spill, dish out, the d.,** raconter des scandales, ragoter, cancaner, potiner; *P:* **to do d. on s.o., to do s.o. dirt,** faire un sale coup à qn.

dirt[2], *v.tr.* **1.** *A: & P:* salir. **2.** *Hort: etc:* rechausser (un arbre, etc.).

dirtily ['də:tili], *adv.* **1.** salement, malpropremet, d'une façon malpropre; **these animals eat d.,** ces animaux mangent salement. **2.** bassement; grossièrement, d'une façon grossière.

dirtiness ['də:tinis], *s.* **1.** saleté *f*, malpropreté *f*. **2.** (*of atom bomb, etc.*) capacité *f* de contamination radioactive; importance *f* des retombées radioactives. **3.** *F:* (*of speech*) saleté; (*of action*) bassesse *f*.

dirt-proof ['də:tpru:f], *a.* **1.** insalissable. **2.** à l'abri de la saleté, de l'encrassement.

dirty[1] ['də:ti], *a.* **1.** (*a*) sale, malpropre, souillé, crasseux; (*with mud*) fangeux, crotté; (*of valves, pistons, etc.*) encrassé; **d. hands,** mains *f* sales; **d. face,** visage barbouillé; **d. old coat,** vieux manteau crasseux; **d. shoes,** chaussures sales, crottées; **d. clothes, linen,** linge *m* sale; **d. streets,** rues sales, malpropres, fangeuses; *Med:* **d. wound,** plaie *f* septique; *El:* **d. contact,** contact encrassé; *I.C.E: etc:* **d. oil,** huile usée; (*to child*) **try not to get (your clothes) d.,** essaie de ne pas te salir; (*b*) **d. weather,** mauvais, sale, temps; *Nau:* gros temps, temps de bran; **we're going to have d. weather,** le temps se barbouille; (*c*) *Typ:* **d. copy,** manuscrit brouillé, peu clair; (*d*) **d. money,** (i) *Ind: etc:* indemnité *f*, prime *f*, de travail salissant; (ii) argent mal acquis; gratte *f*; (*e*) (*of atom bomb, etc.*) sale, aux retombées importantes; (*f*) *Orn: F:* **d. Allan,** stercoraire *m* parasite. **2.** (*a*) **d. mind,** esprit mal tourné, *F:* esprit cochon; **d. word,** (i) mot grossier; (ii) *F:* mot qui a acquis un sens péjoratif; **he's a d. old man,** (i) c'est un vieillard malpropre, un vieux crasseux; (ii) *F:* il a l'esprit mal tourné; (iii) *F:* c'est un vieux coureur de jupons; **d. story,** histoire sale, graveleuse; **to tell d. stories,** raconter des saletés; **d. book,** livre pornographique; (*b*) *F:* **d. trick,** saleté, sale tour *m*; **to play s.o. a d. trick,** *s.* **to do the d. on s.o.,** jouer un sale tour, un sale coup, un tour de cochon, à qn; **it's a d. business,** c'est une sale affaire, une affaire louche; **there's been d. work at the crossroads,** c'était un sale coup; **I always get the d. work, the d. end of the stick,** c'est toujours à moi de faire la grosse, la sale, besogne; **d. look,** sale coup *m* d'œil; (*pers.*) **d. sort, type, rat,** *O:* **dog,** sale type *m*. **3.** *adv. F:* (*intensive*) **a d. great lorry,** un camion maous(se); **a d. big suitcase,** une valise qui se pose là.

dirty[2]. **1.** *v.tr.* (*a*) salir, crotter, encrasser; (ses habits, etc.); **to d. one's hands,** se salir les mains; (*b*) (*of atom bomb, etc.*) contaminer par voie de retombées radioactives. **2.** *v.i.* se souiller, se salir; (*of material*) **to d. easily,** se salir facilement.

dis [dis], *v.tr. Typ: F:* (= *distribute*) distribuer (la composition).

dis- [dis], *pref.* dis-, dés-, dé-, des-.

disa ['daisə], *s. Bot:* disa *f*.

disability [disə'biliti], *s.* **1.** (*a*) incapacité *f*, impuissance *f* (**to do, for doing, sth.,** de faire qch.); **under a d.,** incapable; (*b*) **(physical) d.,** infirmité *f*; (*c*) *Adm:* invalidité *f*; **d. pension,** pension *f* d'invalidité; **temporary, partial, total, d.,** invalidité temporaire, partielle, totale. **2.** *Jur:* (*a*) incapacité légale; inhabilité *f* (à faire qch.); (*b*) (*imposed on property*) servitude *f*.

disable [dis'eibl], *v.tr.* **1.** mettre (qn) hors de combat; estropier (qn); désemparer (un navire, un canon); mettre (une machine) hors de service; **he was disabled by rheumatism,** les rhumatismes *m* l'avaient rendu impotent, il était perclus de rhumatismes; **to d. s.o. from doing sth.,** mettre qn dans l'impuissance, mettre qn hors d'état, de faire qch.; (*of machine, ship*) **to be disabled,** avoir des avaries, être avarié; être en panne; être désemparé; être hors de service. **2.** *Jur:* **to d. s.o. from doing sth.,** prononcer qn incapable de, inhabile à (tester, etc.).

disabled [dis'eibld], *a.* infirme; (*as result of accident, etc.*) estropié; mutilé; **d. ex-serviceman,** mutilé *m*, invalide *m* de guerre; réformé *m* de guerre avec pension d'invalidité; *s.* **the badly d.,** les grands infirmes; les grands mutilés.

disablement [dis'eiblmənt], *s.* **1.** mise *f* hors de combat. **2.** invalidité *f*, incapacité *f* de travail; *Adm:* **degree of d.,** coefficient *m* d'invalidité; **permanent d.,** incapacité, infirmité, permanente.

disabuse [disə'bju:z], *v.tr.* désabuser (**of,** de); désaveugler (qn).

disaccharide, disaccharose [dai'sækəraid, -ous], *s. Ch:* disaccharide *f*.

disaccord[1] [disə'kɔ:d], *s.* désaccord *m* (**with,** avec).

disaccord[2], *v.i.* être en désaccord (**with,** avec).

disaccustom [disə'kʌstəm], *v.tr.* désaccoutumer, déshabituer (**s.o. to sth., to doing sth.,** qn de qch., de faire qch.).

disadvantage[1] [disəd'vɑ:ntidʒ], *s.* désavantage *m*, inconvénient *m*; **it is no d. to be young,** ce n'est pas un désavantage d'être jeune; **to take s.o. at a d.,** prendre qn dans de mauvaises conditions, au dépourvu; surprendre qn dans un moment embarrassant; **to be at a d. owing to sth.,** être désavantagé par qch.; **to be seen, to show oneself, at a d., to d.,** être vu, se montrer, à son désavantage, sous un jour désavantageux; **to sell at a d.,** vendre à perte; **to labour, lie, under a d., under the d. of . . .,** avoir le désavantage (de) . . .; **the machine has two main disadvantages,** cette machine a deux principaux inconvénients; **this book has the d. of being written in a tedious style,** le style plat nuit à la valeur de ce livre.

disadvantage[2], *v.tr.* désavantager (qn); handicaper (qn).

disadvantaged [disəd'vɑ:ntidʒd], *a.* désavantagé, déshérité.

disadvantageous [disædvæn'teidʒəs], *a.* désavantageux, défavorable (**to,** à).

disaffect [disə'fekt], *v.tr. A:* désaffectionner (qn); aliéner (une tribu).

disaffected [disə'fektid], *a.* mal disposé (**to, towards,** à l'égard de, envers); mécontent; dissident; désaffectionné; en dissidence.

disaffectedness, disaffection [disə'fektidnis, -'fekʃ(ə)n], *s.* désaffection *f* (**to, towards,** à l'égard de, envers); mécontentement *m*.

disaffiliate [disə'filieit], *v.tr.* désaffilier.

disaffiliation [disəfili'eiʃ(ə)n], *s.* désaffiliation *f*.

disaffirm [disə'fə:m], *v.tr. Jur:* annuler, rapporter, casser (un jugement); défaire (une convention); dénoncer (un contrat).

disaffirmation [disæfə'meiʃ(ə)n], *s. Jur:* annulation *f*, cassation *f*.

disafforest [disə'fɔrist], *v.tr.* **1.** déboiser (une terre). **2.** *Jur.* déclarer (un terrain, un bois) hors du régime forestier.

disafforestation [disæfɔris'teiʃ(ə)n], *s.* déboisement *m* (d'une terre).

disagree [disə'gri:], *v.i.* **1.** (*a*) être en désaccord, ne pas être d'accord (**with,** avec); **the accounts d.,** les récits *m* diffèrent, sont en désaccord, ne concordent pas; **the witnesses d.,** les témoins *m* ne sont pas d'accord; (*b*) **to d. with s.o.,** ne pas être du même avis que qn; donner tort à qn; **those who d. with the author,** ceux qui se trouvent en désaccord avec l'auteur; **I d.,** je ne suis pas de cet avis. **2.** (*a*) (*quarrel*) se brouiller (**with,** avec); (*b*) **they had always disagreed,** ils avaient toujours vécu en mésintelligence. **3.** ne pas convenir (**with,** à); **the climate disagrees with him,** le climat ne lui convient pas, ne lui va pas; **wine disagrees with him,** le vin lui est contraire; **the salmon disagreed with me,** je n'ai pas digéré le saumon.

disagreeable [disə'gri:əbl]. **1.** *a.* (*a*) désagréable (**to,** à); déplaisant (**to,** à); **d. smell,** odeur *f* désagréable, qui déplaît; (*b*) fâcheux, incommode; **a d. incident,** un incident fâcheux; (*c*) désagréable, maussade; **how d. you are today!** comme vous êtes désagréable aujourd'hui! **d. person,** personne désobligeante. **2.** *s.pl. A: & Lit:* désagréments *m.*

disagreeableness [disə'gri:əblnis], *s.* **1.** désagrément *m*; ce que qch. a de désagréable, de fâcheux. **2.** (*a*) mauvaise humeur; maussaderie *f*; (*b*) désobligeance *f* (**to,** envers).

disagreeably [disə'gri:əbli], *adv.* désagréablement; fâcheusement; d'un ton désobligeant.

disagreement [disə'gri:mənt], *s.* **1.** différence *f* (**between,** entre); discordance *f.* **2.** désaccord *m* (**with s.o. on, about, sth.,** avec qn sur qch.); conflit *m* d'opinions; **to be in d. with s.o.,** ne pas partager l'avis de qn. **3.** (*a*) brouille *f,* différend *m,* querelle *f*; (*b*) mésintelligence *f,* mésentente *f* (**between,** entre).

disalign [disə'lain], *v.tr.* désaligner.

disalignment [disə'lainm(ə)nt], *s.* défaut *m* d'alignement; désalignement *m*; (*vertically*) dénivellation *f*; *Veh: etc:* non-parallélisme *m* (des roues).

disallow [disə'lau], *v.tr.* **1.** ne pas admettre, ne pas reconnaître (une réclamation, un article d'un compte, une hypothèse, etc.); rejeter (un article d'un compte); refuser (un privilège); *Jur:* rejeter (un témoignage) **2.** ne pas permettre; interdire. **3.** *Fb: etc:* annuler (un but).

disallowance [disə'lauəns], *s.* refus *m* de reconnaître la validité (d'une réclamation, etc.); rejet *m*; *Jur:* **d. of a plea, of costs,** rejet d'une défense, de frais.

disappear [disə'piər]. **1.** *v.i.* disparaître (**from a place,** d'un endroit); (*of difficulties*) s'aplanir; *Ling:* (*of sound*) s'amuir; **he disappeared from our sight,** il a disparu à nos yeux; **to d. in the darkness,** s'enfoncer dans l'ombre; **to d. in, into, the crowd,** se couler, se perdre, dans la foule; **to d. to America,** filer sur l'Amérique; **since he disappeared,** depuis sa disparition; **all this money has disappeared into thin air,** tout cet argent a passé au bleu; **may I d. for a moment?** excusez-moi un instant. **2.** *v.tr.* (*of conjuror*) faire disparaître (un lapin, etc.).

disappearance [disə'piərəns], *s.* disparition *f*; *Ling:* amuissement *m* (d'un son); **to return after a year's d.,** revenir après une éclipse d'un an.

disappearing[1] [disə'piəriŋ], *a.* (cible *f,* etc.) à éclipse; escamotable; *U.S:* **d. bed,** lit *m* escamotable.

disappearing[2], *s.* disparition *f*; *F:* **to do a d. trick, act,** (i) partir, s'esquiver; (ii) déménager à la cloche de bois.

disappoint [disə'pɔint], *v.tr.* (*a*) désappointer (qn); (*after promising*) manquer de parole à (qn); **don't d. me,** ne manquez pas à votre parole, à votre promesse; je compte sur vous; ne me faites pas faux bond; (*b*) décevoir, chagriner (qn); **he was rather disappointed at not being invited,** il fut un peu déçu de ce qu'on ne l'invitait pas; **are you disappointed?** c'est une déception? **he was greatly disappointed,** il a eu une grave déception; **to be disappointed in love,** avoir des chagrins d'amour; **disappointed ambition,** ambition déçue; (*c*) tromper, décevoir (les espérances de qn); tromper (l'attente de qn); **I am disappointed in, with, you,** vous avez trompé, démenti, mon espoir, mes espérances; **to be disappointed in sth.,** trouver du décompte à qch.; **I was very much disappointed in it, with it,** cela m'a beaucoup déçu; cela ne répondait aucunement à mon attente.

disappointed [disə'pɔintid], *a.* désappointé; déçu; **d. hopes,** espoirs déçus; **d. customers,** clients déçus, mal satisfaits; **d. candidate,** candidat refusé.

disappointedly [disə'pɔintidli], *adv.* d'un ton, d'un air, désappointé, déçu.

disappointing [disə'pɔintiŋ], *a.* **1.** décevant; qui ne répond pas, qui n'a pas répondu, à l'attente. **2. how d.!** quel contretemps!

disappointingly [disə'pɔintiŋli], *adv.* **d. slow,** d'une lenteur décourageante; *Sch:* **d. weak paper,** composition *f* d'une faiblesse décourageante.

disappointment [disə'pɔintmənt], *s.* déception *f,* désappointement *m*; déboire *m*; contretemps *m,* mécompte *m*; **bitter d.,** vive contrariété; crève-cœur *m inv*; **this is a d. to my expectations,** c'est un démenti à mes espérances; **this year's Salon leaves a feeling of d.,** le Salon de cette année nous laisse un sentiment de découragement; **d. in love,** chagrin *m* d'amour; **to suffer many disappointments,** essuyer bien des déboires.

disapprobation [disæprou'beiʃ(ə)n], *s.* désapprobation *f* (**of,** de); improbation *f.*

disapprobative [disæprə'beitiv], **disapprobatory** [disæprə'beitəri], *a.* désapprobateur, -trice; improbateur, -trice.

disappropriate [disə'prouprieit], *v.tr. Jur:* désapproprier.

disapproval [disə'pru:v(ə)l], *s.* désapprobation *f* (**of,** de); improbation *f*; **look of d.,** regard désapprobateur, improbateur.

disapprove [disə'pru:v]. **1.** *v.tr.* désapprouver (qn); réprouver, blâmer (qn, un usage); trouver mauvais (un usage, etc.). **2.** *v.i.* (*a*) **to d. of sth.,** désapprouver qch.; trouver à redire à qch.; **to d. of sth. being done,** désapprouver, trouver mauvais, que l'on fasse qch.; **I have heard of her engagement, and entirely d.,** j'ai appris ses fiançailles et je suis absolument contre; (*c*) **she disapproves of her son-in-law,** son gendre n'est pas à son goût.

disapproving [disə'pru:viŋ], *a.* désapprobateur, -trice.

disapprovingly [disə'pru:viŋli], *adv.* avec désapprobation; d'un air, d'un ton, désapprobateur.

disarm [dis'ɑ:m]. **1.** *v.tr.* désarmer (un prisonnier, une nation, la critique, etc.); désamorcer (une bombe); **to d. s.o. of his rifle,** désarmer qn de son fusil. **2.** *v.i.* désarmer.

disarmament [dis'ɑ:məmənt], *s.* désarmement *m*; **D. Conference,** Conférence *f* du désarmement.

disarmed [dis'ɑ:md], *a.* désarmé; *Her:* **lion d.,** lion morné.

disarmer [dis'ɑ:mər], *s.* partisan, -ane, avocat, -ate, du désarmement (nucléaire).

disarming[1] [dis'ɑ:miŋ], *a.* (sourire, idéalisme, etc) désarmant.

disarming[2], *s.* désarmement *m.*

disarmingly [dis'ɑ:miŋli], *adv.* **he was d. frank,** il montrait une franchise désarmante; **she smiled d. at me,** elle m'a fait un sourire désarmant.

disarrange [disə'reindʒ], *v.tr.* déranger, désajuster; mettre (qch.) en désordre; dérégler (des habitudes, etc.); désagencer (une machine, etc.); **disarranged hair,** cheveux défaits; **to d. s.o.'s plans,** déranger, bouleverser, les projets de qn.

disarrangement [disə'reindʒmənt], *s.* dérangement *m,* désajustement *m,* désordre *m,* désagencement *m.*

disarray[1] [disə'rei], *s.* (*a*) désarroi *m*; désordre *m*; (*b*) *A:* (*of pers.*) **in d.,** à demi vêtu, à demi habillé.

disarray[2], *v.tr.* **1.** *Lit:* (*a*) mettre (des troupes) en désarroi, en déroute; (*b*) mettre en désordre. **2.** *A: & Poet:* mettre le désordre dans le vêtements de (qn); dévêtir (qn).

disarticulate [disɑ:'tikjuleit], *v.tr.* **1.** désarticuler; démembrer (un poulet, etc.). **2.** disjoindre, démonter (un mécanisme, etc.).

disarticulation [disɑ:tikju'leiʃ(ə)n], *s.* **1.** désarticulation *f*; démembrement *m.* **2.** démontage *m.*

disassemble [disə'sembl], *v.tr.* démonter, désassembler, démembrer (une machine, etc.).

disassembler [disə'semblər], *s. Ind:* démonteur, -euse.

disassembly [disə'sembli], *s.* démontage *m,* désassemblement *m.*

disassimilate [disə'simileit], *v.tr. Biol:* désassimiler.

disassimilation [disəsimi'leiʃ(ə)n], *s. Biol:* désassimilation *f.*

disassociate [disə'sousieit], *v.tr.* dissocier.

disassociation [disəsousi'eiʃ(ə)n], *s.* dissociation *f.*

disaster [di'zɑ:stər], *s.* désastre *m*; (*by shipwreck, fire, flood*) sinistre *m*; **the d. area,** la scène du désastre, du sinistre; **public d.,** calamité publique; **railway d.,** accident *m,* catastrophe *f,* de chemin de fer; **villages that have suffered d.,** villages sinistrés; **our journey was a series of disasters,** notre voyage n'a été qu'une suite de malheurs; **to scent d.,** sentir le cadavre; **he is heading for, courting, d.,** il court à sa perte; **it would be a d.!** ce serait le désastre!

disastrous [di'zɑ:strəs], *a.* désastreux; néfaste, funeste; **we had a d. trip,** notre voyage n'a été qu'une suite de malheurs.

disastrously [di'zɑ:strəsli], *adv.* désastreusement.

disavow [disə'vau], *v.tr.* désavouer, répudier (une doctrine, un enfant, etc.); renier (sa foi, une action).

disavowal [disə'vauəl], *s.* désaveu *m,* répudiation *f* (d'une obligation, etc.); reniement *m* (de sa foi, etc.).

disazo [dis'æzou], *a.* **d. dyes,** colorants *m* disazoïques.

disband [dis'bænd]. **1.** *v.tr.* licencier (des troupes, etc.); dissoudre (un comité, une unité, etc.); **the commission was disbanded,** la commission a été dissoute, a cessé ses travaux. **2.** *v.i.* (*of troops*) (i) se débander, fuir à la débandade; (ii) être licencié; (*of committee, unit*) être dissout.

disbanding [dis'bændiŋ], *s.* (*a*) (fuite *f* en) débandade *f*; (*b*) licenciement *m* (des troupes, etc.); dissolution *f* (d'une commission, etc.).

disbandment [dis'bændmənt], *s.* licenciement *m.*

disbar [dis'bɑ:r], *v.tr.* (**disbarred**) rayer (un avocat) du barreau, du tableau de l'ordre.

disbarment [dis'bɑ:mənt], *s.* radiation *f* (d'un avocat) du tableau de l'ordre, de la liste du barreau.

disbelief [disbi'li:f], *s.* **1. d. in sth.,** incrédulité *f* à l'égard de qch.; refus *m* de croire à qch. **2.** *Theol:* incrédulité, mécréance *f.*

disbelieve [disbi'li:v]. **1.** *v.tr.* ne pas croire, refuser de croire (qn, qch.); refuser créance à (qn); **to d. every word,** ne pas en croire un seul mot. **2.** *v.i.* **to d. in s.o., in sth.,** ne pas croire à qn, à qch.

disbeliever [disbi'li:vər], *s.* incrédule *mf.*

disbranch [dis'brɑ:n(t)ʃ], *v.tr.* ébrancher (un arbre).

disbud [dis'bʌd], *v.tr.* (**disbudded**) *Arb:* ébourgeonner, escionner, épincer, éborgner (un arbre fruitier).

disbudding [dis'bʌdiŋ], *s.* ébourgeonnement *m,* escionnement *m,* épinçage *m,* ébourgeonnage *m,* éborgnage *m.*

disburden [dis'bə:dn], *v.tr. Lit:* **1.** décharger, soulager (**s.o. of sth.,** qn de qch.); **to d. one's mind of a secret,** décharger sa conscience d'un secret; se décharger la conscience. **2.** déposer, mettre bas (un fardeau).

disbursal [dis'bə:s(ə)l], *s.* déboursement *m.*

disburse [dis'bə:s], *v.tr.* débourser (de l'argent).

disbursement [dis'bə:smənt], *s.* **1.** déboursement *m*; **heavy d.,** gros paiement. **2.** *pl.* **disbursements,** déboursés *m,* frais *mpl*; *Com:* débours *mpl.*

disc [disk], *s.* **1.** (*a*) disque *m* (de la lune, etc.); *Archeol:* **winged d., sun d.,** disque ailé; (*b*) *Mil: etc:* **identity d., identification d.,** plaque *f* d'identité; *Aut:* **parking d.,** disque de stationnement; (*c*) *Tchn:* disque, plateau *m*; rondelle *f* (en carton, etc.); *Mec.E:* manchon *m* (d'excentrique); *Mec.E:* **d. crank,** manivelle *f* à plateau; plateau-manivelle *m, pl.* plateaux-manivelles; *Aut:* **d. brakes,** freins *m* à disque; **wheel d.,** enjoliveur *m*; **d. wheel,** roue pleine, disque, à voile plein; *Rail:* **d. signal, target d.,** disque; (*d*) *Agr:* **d. harrow,** pulvériseur *m*; **d. plough,** charrue *f* à disques; **one-way d.,** déchaumeuse *f* à disques; (*e*) *El:* **d. winding,** enroulement *m,* bobinage *m,* en disque; (*f*) *Tp:* **call indicator d.,** volet *m* d'appel; (*in automatic system*) **calling d.,** disque d'appel; (*g*) *Rec:* (= *record*) disque; **recording d.,** disque d'enregistrement; *W.Tel:* **d. jockey,** présentateur *m* de disques; (*h*) *Cmptr:* **d.-oriented computer,** ordinateur *m* à disques; **d. storage,** mémoire *f* à disques; **magnetic d.,** disque magnétique; (*i*) *Anat:* **red blood d.,** plaque sanguine; (**intervertebral**) **d.,** disque intervertébral; *Med:* **slipped d.,** hernie discale; **to slip a d.,** se faire une hernie discale. **2.** gâteau *m* (de coton-poudre, etc.).

discalceate(d) [dis'kælsieit(id)], **discalced** [dis'kælst], *a. Ecc:* (moine, etc.) déchaussé, *A:* déchaux.

discant[1,2] ['diskænt, dis'kænt], *s. & v.i. A.Mus:* = DESCANT[1,2].

discard[1] ['diskɑ:d], *s.* **1.** *Cards:* (*a*) (*at cribbage, etc.*) écart *m* (action ou carte); (*b*) (*at bridge, etc.*) défausse *f.* **2.** *Ind: etc:* pièce *f* de rebut; déchet *m.*

discard[2] [dis'kɑ:d], *v.tr.* **1.** *Cards:* (*a*) (*at cribbage, etc.*) écarter (une carte); (*b*) (*at bridge, etc.*) **to d. a suit,** se défausser d'une couleur; se faire une renonce à une couleur; **to d. a sequence,** filer les cartes; *v.i.* **to d.,** se défausser. **2.** mettre, laisser, (qch.) de côté; se défaire de (qch.); mettre (une pièce) au rebut; abandonner (un projet); quitter (une habitude); renoncer à (une croyance); mettre (une théorie) au rancart; **to d. one's winter clothing,** laisser de côté ses vêtements d'hiver; **to d. the unessential,** laisser tomber ce qui n'est pas essentiel; **to d. an old hat,** mettre au rebut un vieux chapeau; *Av: etc:* **to d. sth. in flight,** larguer, lâcher, qch. en plein vol. **3.** *A:* renvoyer, congédier, supprimer (une partie de ses domestiques, etc.).

discarding [dis'kɑ:diŋ], *s.* **1.** *Cards:* (*a*) écart *m*; (*b*) (*at bridge*) défausse *f.* **2.** mise *f* de côté (de qch.); abandon *m* (d'un projet); mise au rancart (d'une théorie). **3.** *A:* renvoi *m,* congédiement *m* (d'un domestique, etc.).

discarnate [dis'kɑ:neit], *a. A: & Lit:* **d. bones,** os

décharnés; **d. soul,** âme libérée du corps.
discarnation [diskɑː'neiʃ(ə)n], *s.* séparation *f* de l'âme de sa dépouille mortelle.
discentre [dis'sentər], *v.tr. Arch:* décintrer.
discern [di'səːn, -'zəːn], *v.tr.* (*a*) distinguer, discerner, reconnaître, apercevoir, percevoir; **to d. a distant object,** discerner, reconnaître, un objet dans le lointain; **to d. no difference,** ne percevoir aucune différence; (*b*) **to d. good and bad, good from bad, between good and bad,** discerner le bien du mal, d'avec le mal; faire la distinction, le départ, entre le bien et le mal.
discernible [di'səːnibl, -'zəː-], *a.* perceptible.
discernibly [di'səːnibli, -'zəː-], *adv.* perceptiblement.
discerning[1] [di'səːniŋ, -'zəː-], *a.* (*of pers.*) éclairé, judicieux; plein de discernement; (*of intelligence*) pénétrant, subtil; (*of taste*) sûr, délicat.
discerning[2], *s.* = DISCERNMENT 1.
discernment [di'səːnmənt, -'zəː-], *s.* **1.** discernement *m* (**between . . . and . . .,** de . . . et de . . .). **2.** discernement; intelligence pénétrante; clairvoyance *f*; jugement *m*; **d. of character,** pénétration *f* des caractères.
discharge[1] ['distʃɑːdʒ], *s.* **1.** déchargement *m* (d'un navire); déchargement, débarquement *m*, débardage *m* (d'une cargaison); défournage *m* (du coke). **2.** décharge *f* (d'artillerie); départ *m* (d'une arme à feu); décochement *m* (d'une flèche); volée *f* (de flèches). **3.** (*a*) décharge, déversement *m*, vidange *f*, vidage *m*, évacuation *f*, dépense *f*, épanchement *m* (d'eau, etc.); décharge, dégagement *m* (de gaz); échappement *m* (de vapeur); débit *m*, refoulement *m* (d'une pompe); débit, portée *f*, écoulement *m* (d'un cours d'eau, d'un déversoir); **convective d.,** décharge convective; *Hyd.E:* **d. head,** hauteur *f* de refoulement; **d. header,** collecteur *m* de refoulement; **d. pipe,** tuyau *m* de décharge, de débit, d'évacuation, de vidange; **d. pump,** pompe *f* d'extraction, d'épuisement; (*b*) *El:* décharge (d'électricité); **brush d., silent d.,** décharge en brosse, en aigrette; décharge rayonnante; aigrette *f*, effluve *m*; **dark d.,** décharge obscure; *Cin:* **d. lamp,** lampe *f* à luminescence, à lueur (pour enregistrement sonore); (*c*) *El:* décharge (d'une pile, d'un accumulateur); (*d*) *Med:* (i) écoulement, perte *f*; (ii) suppuration *f*; (*e*) (*from factory, etc.*) eaux usées. **4.** (*a*) renvoi *m*, congé *m* (d'un employé); (*b*) libération (temporaire ou définitive); congé; (*after active service*) démobilisation *f*; *Navy:* débarquement *m*; *Mil: Navy:* **to take one's d.,** prendre son congé; *Navy:* **d. note,** ordre *m* de débarquement; (*c*) *Mil: Navy:* (*for unfitness*) réforme *f*; **d. with allowance,** réforme No 1; **d. without allowance,** réforme No 2; (*d*) (*from hospital*) exéat *m*; **order of d.,** billet *m*, autorisation *f*, de sortie. **5.** *Jur:* (*a*) mise *f* en liberté, libération, élargissement *m*, relaxation *f*, relaxe *f* (d'un prisonnier); **d. from prison,** levée *f* d'écrou; (*b*) acquittement *m* (d'un accusé); (*c*) **d. in bankruptcy, order of d.,** réhabilitation *f* (d'un failli); **to apply for, to get, one's d.,** demander, obtenir, sa réhabilitation. **6.** accomplissement *m* (d'un devoir, d'un vœu); *Jur:* solution *f* (d'une obligation); **d. of, from, an engagement,** acquit *m* d'un engagement; **in the d. of his duty,** en faisant son devoir; **in the d. of his duties,** dans l'exercice *m* de ses fonctions. **7.** (*a*) paiement *m* (d'une dette); (*b*) quittance *f*, décharge, libération, acquit; **in full d.,** pour acquit; **final d.,** quitus *m*. **8.** *Arch:* décharge. **9.** *Dy:* (*a*) décoloration *f* (d'un tissu); (*b*) décolorant *m*.
discharge[2] [dis'tʃɑːdʒ], *v.*
I. *v.tr.* **1.** (*a*) décharger (un navire, un réservoir, etc.); (*b*) *Arch:* **to d. a beam,** décharger une poutre; **discharging arch,** arc *m* en décharge. **2.** (*a*) décharger, tirer, faire partir (une arme à feu); (*b*) *El:* décharger (une pile, etc.); **discharged battery,** accu *m* à vide, *F:* à plat. **3.** (*a*) décharger, débarquer, débarder (une cargaison); (*b*) (*of vehicle*) **to d. passengers,** déposer des voyageurs. **4.** (*a*) congédier, renvoyer, remercier (un employé); débaucher (un ouvrier); destituer (un fonctionnaire); (*b*) licencier (des troupes); congédier, mettre en congé (un militaire, etc.); donner son congé à, désenrôler (un militaire); libérer (un homme) du service militaire; renvoyer (un homme) dans ses foyers; *Navy:* débarquer (un homme, un équipage); **to be discharged from the force,** être congédié; (*c*) *Mil: Navy:* (*for unfitness*) réformer (un homme); (*d*) **to d. a patient (from hospital),** renvoyer un malade guéri; **he was discharged from hospital yesterday,** il est sorti de l'hôpital hier; (*e*) *Jur:* **to d. the jury,** congédier les jurés. **5.** *Jur:* (*a*) libérer, élargir, mettre en liberté (un prisonnier); (*b*) acquitter, renvoyer (un accusé); **he was discharged,** il a bénéficié d'une ordonnance de non-lieu; **to d. the accused on every count,** relaxer l'accusé des fins de toute poursuite. **6.** (*a*) **to d. s.o. of an obligation,** décharger, libérer, acquitter, qn d'une obligation; *Jur:* **to d. a surety,** libérer un garant; (*b*) *Jur:* réhabiliter, décharger (un failli); **discharged bankrupt,** failli réhabilité. **7.** (*a*) lancer (un projectile, une torpille); décocher (une flèche, un trait); (*b*) (*of abscess*) **to d. pus,** jeter du pus; *v.i.* (*of abscess*) **to d.,** se dégorger, jeter du pus; (*of wound*) suppurer; (*c*) (*of chemical reaction, etc.*) dégager, émettre (un gaz); dégager (de la vapeur); (*of gland*) **to d. hormones,** sécréter des hormones; (*d*) (*of reservoir, etc.*) déverser (de l'eau); (*of pump*) débiter, refouler (de l'eau); **river that discharges its water into a lake,** rivière qui se jette, s'évacue, se déverse, se décharge, débouche, déverse ses eaux, dans un lac; (*e*) *Dy:* (*of material*) **to d. (its colour),** décharger (sa couleur); se décolorer. **8.** (*a*) accomplir (un devoir); s'acquitter de (son devoir); remplir, s'acquitter de (ses fonctions); (*b*) acquitter, liquider, solder (une dette); payer (une dette, une amende, un compte); apurer (un compte, une obligation); faire l'apurement (d'un compte); **to d. one's liabilities in full,** acquitter intégralement le montant de son passif; *Jur:* **until discharged in full,** jusqu'à parfaite solution; jusqu'à libération complète. **9.** *Jur:* **to d. an order of the court,** réformer, annuler, un arrêt.
II. *v.i.* **1.** (*a*) (*of ship, etc.*) se décharger; être en déchargement; (*b*) *El:* **discharging accumulator,** accu *m* en décharge. **2.** (*of gun*) partir, se décharger.
dischargeable [dis'tʃɑːdʒəbl], *a.* **1.** (*a*) (soldat *m*) congédiable; (*b*) (*for unfitness*) réformable. **2.** (failli *m*) réhabilitable. **3.** (dette *f*) acquittable, payable.
dischargee [distʃɑː'dʒiː], *s.* soldat (i) congédié, (ii) réformé.
discharger [dis'tʃɑːdʒər], *s. El:* excitateur *m*; **static d.,** déperditeur *m* (de potentiel).
discharging [dis'tʃɑːdʒiŋ], *s.* (*a*) décharge *f*, déchargement *m*; (*b*) *Tex:* décr(c)usage *m* (de soie grège, etc.).
disciflorál, disciflorous [diski'flɔːrəl, -'flɔːrəs], *a. Bot:* disciflore.
disciple [di'saipl], *s.* disciple *m*.
discipleship [di'saiplʃip], *s.* état *m*, qualité *f*, de disciple.
disciplinable ['disiplinəbl], *a.* **1.** disciplinable. **2.** soumis à la discipline; docile. **3. d. offence,** infraction *f* à la discipline; délit *m*.
disciplinarian [disipli'nɛəriən], *s.* **1.** disciplinaire *m*; **he is a good d.,** il a une bonne discipline; il a de la discipline; **he is a strict d.,** il est strict en matière de discipline; **he's no d.,** il n'a pas de discipline. **2.** partisan, -ane, d'une forte discipline.
disciplinary ['disiplinəri], *a.* **1.** (punition *f*, etc.) disciplinaire; (établissement, etc.) de discipline; *Mil:* **d. companies,** sections spéciales. **2. an excellent d. instrument for the formation of character,** un excellent instrument de discipline pour former le caractère.
discipline[1] ['disiplin], *s.* discipline *f*; (*a*) **iron d.,** discipline de fer, à la prussienne; **to put, keep, children under d.,** soumettre les enfants à la discipline; **to keep (strict) d., to enforce d.,** maintenir la discipline, une discipline rigoureuse; **he cannot keep d.,** il ne sait pas maintenir la discipline; **to undermine, destroy, the d. of the troops,** démoraliser les troupes; (*b*) (*branch of learning*) discipline; (*c*) *A:* châtiment *m*; (*d*) *Ecc:* (*penitential scourge*) discipline.
discipline[2], *v.tr.* **1.** (*a*) discipliner (des élèves, des troupes); (*b*) former (le caractère); **disciplined in the school of adversity,** formé, élevé, à l'école de l'adversité; (*c*) punir. **2.** (*a*) *A:* discipliner, châtier (un religieux); (*b*) *R.C.Ch:* **to d.** (= *scourge*) **oneself,** se donner la discipline.
disciplining ['disipliniŋ], *s.* disciplinement *m*.
discipular [di'sipjulər], *a.* de disciple.
discission [di'siʃən], *s. Surg:* discission *f*.
discitis [dis'kaitis], *s. Med:* discite *f*.
disclaim [dis'kleim], *v.tr.* **1.** *Jur:* se désister de, renoncer à (un droit, etc.). **2.** refuser d'admettre, désavouer (qch.); **to d. all intention of doing sth.,** se défendre d'avoir l'intention de faire qch.; se défendre de la moindre intention de faire qch.; **to d. all responsibility,** dénier toute responsabilité. **3.** rejeter, renier (l'autorité de qn).
disclaimer [dis'kleimər], *s.* **1.** (*a*) *Jur:* désistement *m*; **d. of a right,** renonciation *f* à un droit; (*b*) **d. of authorship (of a work),** désaveu *m* (d'une œuvre); **d. of responsibility,** déni *m*, dénégation *f*, de responsabilité; **to send a d. to the press,** envoyer un démenti à la presse. **2.** personne *f* qui désavoue, qui renie.
disclimax [dis'klaimæks], *s. Geog:* disclimax *m*.
disclose [dis'klouz], *v.tr.* **1.** découvrir, laisser voir, mettre à découvert, révéler (qch.); **to d. one's point of view,** se découvrir; déclarer, laisser voir, sa pensée. **2.** divulguer, déceler, dévoiler (un secret, etc.).
disclosure [dis'klouʒər], *s.* **1.** mise *f* à découvert (d'un trésor, etc.); révélation *f* (de sa pensée, de son amour, etc.). **2.** divulgation *f* (d'un secret).
disco ['diskou], *s. F:* discothèque *f*.
discoblastula [diskou'blæstjulə], *s. Biol:* discoblastula *f*.
discobolus [dis'kɔbələs], *s. Gr.Ant: Ich:* discobole *m*.
discodactyl(ous) [diskou'dæktil(əs)], *a. Z:* discodactyle.
discogastrula [diskou'gæstrjulə], *s. Biol:* discogastrula *f*.
discoglossid [diskou'glɔsid], *a. & s. Amph:* discoglosse (*m*).
Discoglossidae [diskou'glɔsidiː], *s.pl. Amph:* discoglossidés *m*.
discography [dis'kɔgrəfi], *s.* discographie *f*.
discoid(al) ['diskɔid, dis'kɔid(ə)l], *a.* discoïde.
discolichen [diskou'laikən], *s. Moss:* discolichen *m*.
discolour [dis'kʌlər]. **1.** *v.tr.* (*a*) décolorer; **discoloured teeth,** dents jaunies; (*b*) ternir, délaver (un tissu, etc.); **to become discoloured,** (i) se décolorer; changer de teinte; (ii) se ternir. **2.** *v.i.* (*a*) se décolorer; (*b*) se ternir.
discolo(u)ration [diskʌlə'reiʃ(ə)n], *s.* **1.** décoloration *f*. **2.** (*a*) ternissement *m*; (*b*) ternissure *f*.
discomfit [dis'kʌmfit], *v.tr.* **1.** *Lit:* déconfire, défaire (une armée). **2.** décontenancer, contrarier, déconcerter (qn); *O:* **discomfited lover,** amoureux bafoué.
discomfiture [dis'kʌmfitjər], *s.* **1.** *Lit:* déconfiture *f*, déroute *f* (d'une armée). **2.** (*a*) mise *f* à quia (de qn); (*b*) déconvenue *f* (de qn).
discomfort[1] [dis'kʌmfət], *s.* **1.** *A:* chagrin *m*, inquiétude *f*. **2.** (*a*) manque *m* de confort, inconfort *m*; (*b*) malaise *m*, gêne *f*, incommodité *f*.
discomfort[2], *v.tr.* **1.** *A:* chagriner, affliger, attrister. **2.** incommoder, gêner.
discommode [diskə'moud], *v.tr.* **1.** incommoder, gêner (qn). **2.** importuner (qn).
discommon [dis'kɔmən], *v.tr.* **1.** *Sch: A:* **to d. a tradesman,** retirer la permission donnée à un marchand de fournir les étudiants. **2.** *Jur:* enclore (des terrains communaux).
discompose [diskəm'pouz], *v.tr. Lit:* déranger, troubler, agiter (qn).
discomposure [diskəm'pouʒər], *s.* trouble *m*, agitation *f*; perturbation *f* (d'esprit), altération *f* (des traits).
Discomycetes [diskoumai'siːtiːz], *s.pl. Fung:* discomycètes *m*.
disconcert [diskən'səːt], *v.tr.* **1.** déconcerter; déranger (un projet, etc.). **2.** déconcerter, troubler, interloquer (qn); **it completely disconcerted him,** cela lui a fait perdre contenance; **he is not so easily disconcerted,** il ne se démonte pas pour si peu; *v.i.* **attitude that surprises and disconcerts,** attitude surprenante et déconcertante.
disconcerted [diskən'səːtid], *a.* (air) déconcerté.
disconcertedly [diskən'səːtidli], *adv.* d'un air déconcerté.
disconcerting [diskən'səːtiŋ], *a.* déconcertant, troublant.
disconcertingly [diskən'səːtiŋli], *adv.* d'une manière déconcertante.
disconcertment [diskən'səːtmənt], *s.* **1.** action *f* de déconcerter; mise *f* à quia (de qn). **2.** embarras *m*, trouble *m*, confusion *f*.
disconformable [diskən'fɔːməbl], *a. Geol:* discordant.
disconformity [diskən'fɔːmiti], *s. Geol:* discordance *f*.
disconnect [diskə'nekt], *v.tr.* **1.** désunir, disjoindre, séparer, détacher (**sth. with, from, sth.,** qch. de qch.); désaccoupler, désassembler (des raccords, etc.); décrocher (des wagons); débrayer, désembrayer, affoler (une machine); *Aut:* **to d. the engine,** supprimer l'action du moteur; supprimer l'accouplement; **to d. the dynamo,** débrayer la dynamo. **2.** *El:* mettre (un accumulateur, etc.) hors circuit; débrancher (un accu, etc.); ouvrir, rompre (un circuit); *Tp:* débrancher, couper (la ligne); **I've been disconnected,** on a coupé la communication.
disconnected [diskə'nektid], *a.* **1.** (*a*) détaché, isolé; (*b*) *Mec.E:* débrayé; *El:* débranché, hors circuit. **2.** (*of speech, style, etc.*) décousu, sans suite, sans cohésion; (histoire *f*) sans queue ni tête; (conversation *f*) à bâtons rompus.
disconnectedly [diskə'nektidli], *adv.* (parler, penser) confusément, sans suite, d'une façon décousue; à bâtons rompus.
disconnectedness [diskə'nektidnis], *s.* incohérence *f*, nature décousue, manque *m* de suite (des idées); **the d. of his conversation,** les sauts et ressauts de sa conversation; sa conversation à bâtons rompus.
disconnecting [diskə'nektiŋ], *s.* **1.** désunion *f* (des parties d'une machine); désassemblage *m* (des raccords,

etc.); décrochage *m* (d'un wagon, etc.); débrayage *m*, désembrayage *m* (d'une machine); *Aut: etc:* **d. clutch,** manchon *m* de débrayage. **2.** *El:* mise *f* (d'un accu, etc.) hors circuit, coupe *f* du circuit; **d. plug,** bouton disjoncteur; **d. switch,** sectionneur *m*.

disconnection, disconnexion [diskə'nekʃ(ə)n], *s.* **1.** = DISCONNECTING. **2.** séparation *f* **(between,** entre). **3.** = DISCONNECTEDNESS.

disconsolate [dis'kɔnsələt], *a.* **1.** tout triste; inconsolable; désolé; **d. cry,** cri *m* de désolation. **2.** (*of landscape, light, etc.*) triste, maussade, morne.

disconsolately [dis'kɔnsələtli], *adv.* tristement; d'un air, d'un ton, désolé.

discontent[1] [diskən'tent]. **1.** *s.* (*a*) mécontentement *m*; **general d.,** mécontentement général; fermentation *f* des esprits; (*b*) sujet *m* de mécontentement; grief *m*. **2.** *a. O:* mécontent **(with,** de); peu satisfait (de).

discontent[2], *v.tr.* mécontenter.

discontented [diskən'tentid], *a.* (*a*) mécontent **(with,** de); peu satisfait (de son sort, etc.); aigri; (*b*) **d. spirits,** esprits factieux.

discontentedly [diskən'tentidli], *adv.* avec mécontentement; sans satisfaction, sans joie; **to work d.,** travailler en rechignant; rechigner au travail.

discontentedness [diskən'tentidnis], *s.* mécontentement *m* (de son sort, etc.).

discontiguous [diskən'tigjuəs], *a. Jur: Scot:* (bien) morcelé.

discontinuance [diskən'tinju(:)əns], *s.* **1.** discontinuation *f*, cessation *f*, renoncement *m* **(of sth.,** à qch.). **2.** *Jur:* abandon *m* (d'un procès).

discontinue [diskən'tinju:], *v.tr.* (*a*) **to d. sth., doing sth.,** discontinuer qch., de faire qch.; cesser de faire qch.; (*b*) *Jur:* abandonner (un procès).

discontinuity ['diskɔnti'nju:iti], *s.* **1.** discontinuité *f*; *Phil:* **the concepts of continuity and d.,** les concepts *m* du continu et du discontinu; **d. of ideas,** manque *m* de suite dans les idées. **2.** solution *f* de continuité; intervalle *m*.

discontinuous [diskən'tinjuəs], *a.* (i) discontinu; (ii) intermittent; *Mth:* **d. quantity,** quantité discrète; **d. function,** fonction discontinue.

discontinuously [diskən'tinjuəsli], *adv.* sans continuité; de façon intermittente.

discophile ['diskoufail], *s.* discophile *mf*.

discord[1] ['diskɔ:d], *s.* **1.** discorde *f*, désunion *f*, désaccord *m*; **to bring d. into a family,** mettre la division, semer la discorde, apporter la dissension, la désunion, du trouble, dans une famille; **civil d.,** dissensions civiles. **2.** bruit discordant; discordance *f*, désaccord *m* (des voix, etc.). **3.** *Mus:* (i) dissonance *f* (de deux notes); (ii) dissonance, accord dissonant, faux accord; (iii) intervalle dissonant; (iv) note dissonante; **to resolve a d.,** résoudre une dissonance.

discord[2] [dis'kɔ:d], *v.i.* **1.** (*a*) (*of pers.*) être en désaccord **(with, from,** avec); (*b*) (*of actions, etc.*) être en désaccord, discorder. **2.** (*of sounds*) dissoner, discorder; *Mus:* former une dissonance.

discordance [dis'kɔ:d(ə)ns], *s.* **1.** (*a*) discordance *f* (des sons); (*b*) *Geol:* discordance (de stratification). **2. d. of opinions,** désaccord *m* d'opinions; **the d. between custom and law,** le désaccord entre l'usage et la loi.

discordant [dis'kɔ:d(ə)nt], *a.* **1.** (*a*) (*of sound*) discordant; peu harmonieux; **d. voice,** voix criarde; (*b*) *Mus:* dissonant. **2.** (faction, etc.) en désaccord; **d. opinions,** opinions opposées. **3.** *Geol:* **d. stratification,** stratification discordante.

discordantly [dis'kɔ:dəntli], *adv.* **1.** (sonner, etc.) d'une manière discordante. **2.** (vivre, etc.) en désaccord.

discotheque ['diskoutek], *s.* discothèque *f*.

discount[1] ['diskaunt], *s.* **1.** *Com:* remise *f*, rabais *m*, ristourne *f*; **to sell sth. at a d.,** vendre qch. au rabais; **d. for quantities,** réductions *fpl* sur la quantité; **d. for cash, cash d.,** escompte *m* au comptant; escompte de caisse; rabais en cas de paiement comptant; **trade d.,** remise sur les marchandises; **additional d.,** surremise *f*; **to allow a d. of 10%,** consentir un rabais de 10%; **d. price,** prix *m* faible. **2.** (*a*) *Fin:* escompte; **bank d.,** escompte en dehors; **true d.,** escompte en dedans; **d. bank,** banque *f* d'escompte; (*of shares*) **to be, stand, at a d.,** être en perte; accuser une perte; se trouver en moins-value; (*b*) **sentiment is at a d.,** la sensiblerie est en défaveur, est peu estimée; **politeness is at a d.,** on fait peu de cas de la politesse.

discount[2] [dis'kaunt, 'diskaunt], *v.tr.* **1.** *Fin:* escompter; prendre (un effet) à l'escompte; faire l'escompte (d'un effet); **to d. a rise in shares,** escompter sur une hausse des valeurs; **discounted value,** valeur escomptée. **2.** (*a*) ne pas tenir compte de (qn, qch.); (*b*) faire peu de cas de (l'avis de qn, un avertissement); **to d. news,** faire la part de l'exagération dans une nouvelle; **you must d. half of what he says,** il faut rabattre la moitié de ce qu'il dit; **my gains ae largely discounted by my previous losses,** en calculant mes profits il faut tenir largement compte de mes pertes antérieures.

discountable [dis'kauntəbl], *a.* **1.** escomptable. **2.** (nouvelle *f*, etc.) dont il faut rabattre la moitié.

discountenance [dis'kauntinəns], *v.tr.* **1.** décontenancer, déconcerter (qn); faire rougir (qn). **2.** décourager (un projet); désapprouver, s'opposer à (qch.); être contre (qch.); se montrer défavorable à (un projet).

discounter ['diskauntər], *s* **1.** (*pers.*) escompteur *m*. **2.** *U.S:* magasin *m* de vente à marges réduites.

discounting ['diskauntiŋ], *s.* escompte *m*; actualisation *f*; **d. banker,** banquier *m* escompteur.

discourage [dis'kʌridʒ], *v.tr.* **1.** décourager, abattre (qn); **to become discouraged,** se décourager, s'abattre, se rebuter; **don't be discouraged by one or two failures,** ne vous laissez pas rebuter par un ou deux échecs; ne vous découragez pas pour un ou deux échecs. **2.** (*a*) décourager (un projet, etc.); rebuter (un soupirant, la critique, etc.); (*b*) **to d. s.o. from sth., from doing sth.,** décourager, détourner, qn de qch.; décourager qn de faire qch.

discouragement [dis'kʌridʒmənt], *s.* **1.** découragement *m*, écœurement *m*; *F:* affalement *m*; **he has never known d.,** il n'a jamais connu le découragement; **to meet with d.,** essuyer des déboires *m*. **2.** désapprobation *f* (d'un projet, etc.).

discouraging [dis'kʌridʒiŋ], *a.* décourageant.

discouragingly [dis'kʌridʒiŋli], *adv.* d'une manière décourageante; d'un ton décourageant.

discourse[1] ['diskɔ:s], *s.* **1.** *Lit:* (*a*) discours *m*; (*b*) discours, dissertation *f* **(on,** sur). **2.** *A:* entretien *m*, conversation *f*; **to hold d. wih s.o.,** s'entretenir avec qn **(on,** de).

discourse[2] [dis'kɔ:s]. *Lit:* **1.** *v.i.* (*a*) discourir, disserter **(on, of,** sur); **he discoursed on Eastern affairs,** il a parlé des affaires de l'Orient; (*b*) parler, s'entretenir (de). **2.** *v.tr. A:* faire entendre (de la musique).

discourser [dis'kɔ:sər], *s. A:* discoureur, -euse.

discourteous [dis'kə:tiəs], *a.* discourtois, impoli.

discourteously [dis'kə:tiəsli], *adv.* impoliment; d'une façon impolie, discourtoise; (parler) brusquement; **to behave d. to s.o.,** faire une impolitesse à qn; traiter qn d'une façon impolie.

discourtesy [dis'kə:təsi], *s.* discourtoisie *f*, impolitesse *f*.

discover [dis'kʌvər], *v.tr.* **1.** découvrir, trouver; (*a*) **to d. a new gas, the cause of an illness, an island,** découvrir un gaz nouveau, la cause d'une maladie, une île; **he set out to d. the North-West passage,** il se lança à la découverte du passage nord-ouest; **to d. a secret,** découvrir, surprendre, un secret; **we have discovered a good chauffeur,** nous avons déniché un bon chauffeur; (*b*) **I discovered too late that . . .,** je me suis rendu compte trop tard que . . .; **when she came in from the garden she discovered that she was cold,** en rentrant du jardin elle s'est aperçu, s'est rendu compte, qu'elle avait froid; **she discovered that her aunt was a little better,** elle a trouvé que sa tante allait un peu mieux. **2.** (*a*) *A: & Lit:* révéler, laisser voir (qch.); divulguer (un secret); **to d. oneself,** se révéler, se faire connaître; **to d. a secret to one's friends,** dévoiler un secret à ses amis; (*b*) *Th:* **to be discovered at the rise of the curtain,** être en scène au lever du rideau; (*c*) *Chess:* **discovered check,** échec *m* à la découverte.

discoverable [dis'kʌvərəbl], *a.* que l'on peut découvrir; décelable; **its effects are d. everywhere,** on en découvre partout les effets; les effets *m* en sont partout visibles.

discoverer [dis'kʌvərər], *s.* **1.** découvreur, -euse (de l'Amérique, etc.). **2.** *A:* révélateur *m* (d'un complot, etc.).

discovert [dis'kʌvət], *a. Jur:* qui n'est pas en puissance de mari; (femme) (i) non mariée, (ii) veuve.

discovery [dis'kʌvəri], *s.* **1.** découverte *f*; (*a*) **the d. of Australia,** la découverte de l'Australie; **voyage of d.,** voyage *m* d'exploration *f*; (*b*) **to make a d.,** faire une découverte; **the d. of argon,** la découverte de l'argon; **a great d.,** (i) une grande découverte; (ii) (*of a find*) une trouvaille. **2.** (*a*) *Jur:* **to give d. of documents,** donner communication, donner connaissance, de pièces, de documents; (*b*) *A: & Lit:* révélation *f* (d'un secret); divulgation *f*; **he made a d. of the whole plot,** il divulgua tout le complot.

discredit[1] [dis'kredit], *s.* **1.** doute *m*; **to throw d. on a statement,** mettre en doute une affirmation. **2.** (*a*) discrédit *m* (de qn, de qch.); déconsidération *f* (de qn); **to bring d. on s.o.'s authority,** discréditer l'autorité de qn; décréditer qn; **to bring d. on oneself,** se discréditer, se décréditer; **to throw d. on s.o.,** jeter le discrédit sur qn; décréditer, discréditer, qn; **to reflect d. on . . .,** jeter du discrédit sur . . .; **to fall into d.,** se décréditer, se discréditer; se perdre de réputation; tomber dans un discrédit absolu; **this brand has fallen into d.,** cette marque a perdu sa réputation; (*b*) *Com:* discrédit (d'un billet, d'un commerçant).

discredit[2], *v.tr.* **1.** ne pas croire (un bruit); ne pas ajouter foi à (un bruit); mettre en doute (un bruit); **to d. s.o.'s evidence,** nier, contester, la véracité du témoignage de qn. **2.** discréditer (qn, une opinion); déconsidérer (qn); décréditer (l'honneur de qn); dévaloriser (qn, un projet); **his conduct has discredited him with the public,** sa conduite lui a fait perdre la considération du public; **discredited science,** science déconsidérée, tombée en déconsidération.

discreditable [dis'kreditəbl], *a.* **1.** peu digne, peu honorable; **conduct d. to a barrister,** conduite *f* indigne d'un avocat; **d. acquaintances, profession,** connaissances *f* interlopes, profession *f* interlope. **2. d. examination paper,** composition *f* qui ne fait pas honneur au candidat; **her performance was far from d.,** elle ne s'est pas mal acquittée; elle ne s'en est pas mal tirée.

discreditably [dis'kreditəbli], *adv.* de façon indigne, déshonorante.

discreet [dis'kri:t], *a.* **1.** avisé, prudent, judicieux, sage; **d. young man,** jeune homme sage; **a d. smile,** un petit sourire contenu. **2.** discret, -ète; **to maintain a d. silence,** observer un silence discret, plein de réserve; **he is an absolutely d. person,** il est la discrétion même, *F:* c'est le tombeau des secrets.

discreetly [dis'kri:tli], *adv.* **1.** avec réserve, avec retenue, prudemment. **2.** discrètement; avec discrétion.

discrepancy [dis'krepənsi], *s.* désaccord *m*, opposition *f*, écart *m*, antinomie *f*; **there is a d. between the two stories,** les deux récits *m* ne cadrent pas; **statistical d.,** écart statistique; **there is a d. in the accounts,** les comptes *m* ne sont pas justes, *F:* ne collent pas.

discrepant [dis'krepənt], *a.* différent **(from,** de); **d. accounts,** récits contradictoires, opposés, qui ne cadrent pas.

discrete [dis'kri:t], *a.* **1.** (*a*) *Mth:* discret, -ète; discontinu; **d. quantity,** quantité discrète; *Cmptr:* **d. representation,** représentation discrète; (*b*) *Med:* **d. smallpox,** variole discrète. **2.** *Phil:* abstrait.

discretion [dis'kreʃ(ə)n], *s.* **1.** (*liberty of action*) discrétion *f*; **I shall use my own d.,** je ferai comme bon me semblera, comme je jugerai à propos; **to have full d. to act,** avoir toute liberté, latitude, pour agir; **it is within my d. to go or not,** je suis libre d'y aller ou non; **to leave sth. to s.o.'s d.,** laisser qch. à la discrétion, à l'arbitraire, de qn; **the method of recording accidents might be left to the d. of each country,** il vaudrait mieux laisser chaque pays libre de déterminer comme il l'entend le mode de recensement des accidents; **at your d.,** comme vous voudrez; *Jur:* **fine at, left to, the d. of the judge,** amende *f* arbitraire; *Mil:* **to surrender at d.,** se rendre à discrétion. **2.** (*judgment*) sagesse *f*, jugement *m*, prudence *f*; **he is the soul of d.,** il est la discrétion même; **to use d.,** agir avec discrétion; **at the age, at years, of d.,** en âge de connaissance; à l'âge de discrétion, de discernement, de raison; **to come to years of d.,** atteindre l'âge de raison; **the better part of valour is d.,** l'essentiel du courage c'est la prudence; **he thought d. the better part of valour,** (i) il abandonna le champ à de plus dignes; (ii) il resta coi; **to have an air of d.,** avoir un air diplomatique. **3.** discrétion, réserve *f*; silence judicieux.

discretionary [dis'kreʃən(ə)ri], *a. Jur:* (pouvoir *m*) discrétionnaire; (peine *f*) arbitraire; **to give s.o. d. powers to act,** faire confiance à qn pour toute action à poursuivre; *St.Exch:* **d. order,** ordre *m* à appréciation; **d. number,** nombre choisi à priori; **d. value,** valeur librement choisie.

discriminant [dis'kriminənt], *a. & s. Mth:* discriminant (*m*); **d. analysis,** analyse discriminante.

discriminate[1] [dis'krimineit]. **1.** *v.tr.* distinguer **(from,** de, d'avec); **his great stature discriminated him from his companions,** sa haute taille le distinguait, le faisait distinguer, de ses compagnons. **2.** *v.i.* (*a*) distinguer, établir une distinction, faire le départ **(between,** entre); faire la différence (entre deux choses, d'une chose avec une autre); discerner (qch. de qch.); **to d. between A and B,** distinguer, faire la distinction, entre A et B; (*b*) **to d. in favour of s.o., against s.o.,** faire des distinctions en faveur de qn, contre qn; **to d. against other candidates,** évincer d'autres concurrents.

discriminate[2], *a.* (*of action, conduct*) judicieux.

discriminating [dis'krimineitiŋ], *a.* **1.** (signe, etc.) distinctif. **2.** (*of pers.*) plein de discernement; capable de juger; judicieux; **d. purchaser,** acheteur avisé, averti; **d. ear,** oreille fine, délicate. **3.** (loi) qui fait la distinction des personnes; *Adm:* **d. duty, tariff,** droit, tarif, différentiel.

discriminatingly [dis'krimineitiŋli], *adv.* avec discernement; judicieusement.

discrimination [diskrimi'neiʃ(ə)n], *s.* **1.** discrimination *f*, discernement *m* (**between . . . and,** entre . . . et); **d. between error and truth,** séparation *f* de l'erreur et de la vérité. **2.** jugement *m*, discernement; **man of d.,** homme judicieux, plein de discernement. **3.** discrimination, distinction *f*; mesures *f* discriminatoires; **law that applies to everyone without d.,** loi *f* qui s'applique à tous, sans discrimination; **race, racial, d.,** discrimination raciale; **d. in favour of non-union men,** préférence donnée aux ouvriers non-syndiqués. **4.** *Cmptr:* **frequency d.,** sélection *f* d'une fréquence; **d. instruction,** instruction *f* de décision.

discriminative [dis'krimineitiv], *a.* = DISCRIMINATING.

discriminator [dis'krimineitər], *s.* *El: etc:* discriminateur *m*; **pulse amplitude d.,** discriminateur d'amplitude; **d. curve,** courbe *f* de discrimination; **d. threshold value,** seuil *m* de discrimination.

discriminatory [dis'kriinət(ə)ri], *a.* discriminatoire.

disc-shaped ['diskʃeipt], *a.* en forme de disque; discoïde.

disculpate [dis'kʌlpeit], *v.tr.* disculper.

discursive [dis'kə:siv], *a.* **1.** (*a*) qui passe agréablement d'un sujet à un autre; (*b*) (style, etc.) décousu, sans suite; **he is too d.,** il ne s'attache pas assez à son sujet. **2.** *Log:* discursif, déductif.

discursively [dis'kə:sivli], *adv.* **1.** (*a*) en passant d'un sujet à un autre; (*b*) d'une manière décousue; sans suite. **2.** *Log:* par déduction.

discursiveness [dis'kə:sivnis], *s.* tendance *f* à s'écarter du sujet.

discus ['diskəs], *s.* *Sp:* disque *m*; **d. thrower,** lanceur, -euse, de disque.

discuss [dis'kʌs], *v.tr.* **1.** discuter, débattre (un problème, etc.); délibérer, s'entretenir (d'une question); agiter (une question); **much discussed question,** question très débattue; **I know they were discussing me,** je sais qu'on parlait de moi; **we are discussing who should be invited,** nous sommes en train de débattre la liste des invités; **we were discussing where to go and what to do,** nous discutions de notre destination et de ce que nous allions faire; **d. the matter with him,** concertez-vous avec lui là-dessus. **2.** *F: O:* **to d. a bottle,** déguster, vider, une bouteille; **to d. a pâté,** tâter d'un pâté, expédier un pâté. **3.** *Jur:* discuter (le débiteur principal). **4.** *Med: A:* résoudre, dissoudre (une tumeur).

discussible [dis'kʌsibl], *a.* discutable.

discussion [dis'kʌʃ(ə)n], *s.* **1.** discussion *f*; étude *f*, examen *m* (d'une question); **a subject for d.,** un sujet de discussion; **d. on a question,** délibération *f* touchant une affaire; **question under d.,** question *f* en discussion, en dispute; question qu'on discute; **to start a d.,** entamer une discussion; **after much d. of sth.,** après avoir longtemps discuté, débattu, qch.; **the question will come up for d. tomorrow,** la question sera discutée, débattue, demain; on abordera cette question demain; **this question needs d.,** cette question demande à être débattue. **2.** *F: O:* **an hour was spent over the d. of a bottle of port,** on passait une heure à boire, à déguster, une bouteille de porto. **3.** *Jur:* **benefit of d.,** bénéfice *m* de discussion.

disdain[1] [dis'dein], *s.* dédain *m* (**of,** de); mépris (altier).

disdain[2], *v.tr.* dédaigner (qn, qch.); **to d. to do, doing, sth.,** dédaigner de faire qch.

disdainful [dis'deinful], *a.* dédaigneux (**of,** de).

disdainfully [dis'deinfuli], *adv.* dédaigneusement.

disease [di'zi:z], *s.* **1.** maladie *f*; **to die of d.,** mourir de maladie. **2.** (*a*) maladie, mal *m*, affection *f*; **d. process,** processus *m* morbide; **diseases of the mind,** maladies mentales; **skin d.,** maladie de la peau; dermatose *f*; **Bright's d.,** maladie de Bright, brightisme *m*; **Graves' d.,** maladie de Graves, goître *m* exophtalmique; **Parkinson's d.,** maladie de Parkinson, paralysie agitante; **Pott's d.,** mal de Pott; **foot and mouth d.,** fièvre aphteuse; (*b*) **potato d.,** maladie des pommes de terre; **Dutch elm d.,** thyllose *f* parasitaire de l'orme, maladie des ormes; **diseases of wines,** maladies des vins. **3.** [dis'i:z], *A:* malaise *m*; sentiment *m* de gêne.

diseased [di'zi:zd], *a.* **1.** malade; **d. in body and mind,** malade d'esprit et de corps; **d. liver,** foie atteint, malade. **2. d. wine,** vin *m* malade. **3.** morbide.

disembark [disem'bɑ:k], *v.tr. & i.* débarquer (**from,** de).

disembarkation [disembɑ:'keiʃ(ə)n], **disembarkment** [disem'bɑ:kmənt], *s.* débarquement *m*.

disembarrass [disim'bærəs], *v.tr.* **1.** débarrasser (**s.o., sth., of sth.,** qn, qch., de qch.). **2.** (*disentangle*) dégager, démêler (**sth. from sth.,** qch. de qch.).

disembodiment [disim'bɔdimənt], *s.* **1. d. of the soul,** affranchissement *m* de l'âme de sa dépouille mortelle. **2.** *Mil: A:* désincorporation *f*, licenciement *m* (de troupes).

disembody [disim'bɔdi], *v.tr.* **1. to d. the soul,** dépouiller, affranchir, l'âme du corps; **disembodied spirit,** esprit désincarné. **2.** *Mil: A:* désincorporer, licencier (des troupes).

disembogue [disim'boug]. **1.** *v.i.* (*a*) (*of river*) déboucher; (*b*) (*of ship*) débouquer. **2.** *v.tr.* **the river disembogues its waters, itself, into the lake,** la rivière verse ses eaux, débouche, dans le lac.

disembowel [disim'bauəl], *v.tr.* éventrer; éviscérer.

disemplane [disem'plein], *v.i.* descendre d'avion.

disenchant [disin'tʃɑ:nt], *v.tr.* (*a*) désenchanter, désensorceler (qn); (*b*) désillusionner (qn).

disenchanted [disin'tʃɑ:ntid], *a.* (*a*) désenchanté, désensorcelé; (*b*) désillusionné.

disenchantment [disin'tʃɑ:ntmənt], *s.* (*a*) désenchantement *m*, désensorcellement *m*; (*b*) désillusion *f*.

disencumber [disin'kʌmbər], *v.tr.* (*a*) débarrasser (**sth. of, from, sth.,** qch. de qch.); désencombrer (qn, qch.); **disencumbered of his armour,** débarrassé de son armure; (*b*) *Jur:* dégrever, déshypothéquer (une propriété); purger l'hypothèque sur (une terre).

disendow [disin'dau], *v.tr.* priver (une église, etc.) de ses dotations, de ses biens.

disendowment [disin'daumənt], *s.* sécularisation *f* des biens et dotations (d'une église, etc.).

disengage[1] [disin'geidʒ], *s.* *Fenc:* dégagement *m*.

disengage[2]. **1.** *v.tr.* (*a*) dégager, débarrasser, dépêtrer (**s.o., sth., from sth.,** qn, qch., de qch.); (*b*) *A:* dégager, libérer, délier (**s.o. from a pledge,** qn d'une promesse); (*c*) *Mec.E:* **to d. a catch,** déclencher un déclic; **to d. a toothed wheel,** désengrener une roue dentée; **to d. a part,** débrayer, désembrayer, un organe; (*d*) *Ch:* **to d. oxygen, hydrogen, etc.,** dégager de l'oxygène, de l'hydrogène, etc.; (*e*) *v.i.* *Fenc:* dégager (le fer). **2.** *v.i.* (*a*) se dégager; (*b*) se déclencher, se défaire.

disengaged [disin'geidʒd], *a.* **1.** (*of pers.*) (*a*) libre, inoccupé, visible; (*b*) sans engagement. **2.** (*of seat, room, etc.*) libre, pas occupé. **3.** *Mec.E: etc:* (*of part*) hors fonction.

disengagement [disin'geidʒmənt], *s.* **1.** détachement *m*, dégagement *m* (**from,** de). **2.** = DISENGAGING[2] 1, 2. **3.** dégagement, détachement (de l'esprit); air dégagé. **4.** rupture *f* de fiançailles. **5.** (*a*) *Fenc:* dégagement; (*b*) *Pol. Mil.* dégagement, *F:* désengagement *m*.

disengaging[1] [disin'geidʒiŋ], *a.* *Mec.E:* **d. coupling,** accouplement *m* débrayable, amovible.

disengaging[2], *s.* **1.** dégagement *m* (de gaz). **2.** débrayage *m* (d'un organe); désengrenage *m* (de roues dentées); **d. gear,** (i) *Mec.E:* appareil *m*, dispositif *m*, de débrayage; (appareil) déclencheur *m*; (ii) *Mch:* modificateur *m*; (iii) accouplement *m* à débrayage; **d. lever,** (i) *Mec.E:* levier *m* de débrayage; (ii) *Rail:* désengageur *m*.

disentail [disin'teil], *v.tr.* *Jur:* libérer (une propriété substituée).

disentangle [disin'tæŋgl]. **1.** *v.tr.* démêler; (*a*) débarrasser, *F:* dépêtrer (**s.o., sth., from sth.,** qn, qch., de qch.); (*b*) débrouiller, désenchevêtrer, désentortiller (une ficelle); dénouer (un différend, une intrigue, une situation). **2.** *v.i.* se démêler, se débrouiller, se désenchevêtrer; **this skein won't d.,** cet écheveau ne veut pas se démêler.

disentanglement [disin'tæŋglmənt], *s.* débrouillement *m*, dégagement *m*; dénouement *m*, démêlement *m* (d'une intrigue); démêlage *m* (d'un écheveau).

disentomb [disin'tu:m], *v.tr.* désensevelir, exhumer; tirer (un cadavre, une momie) de sa tombe.

disentombment [disin'tu:mmənt], *s.* exhumation *f*.

disequilibrium [disi:kwi'libriəm], *s.* déséquilibre *m*.

disestablish [disis'tæbliʃ], *v.tr.* séparer (l'Église) de l'État.

disestablishment [disis'tæbliʃmənt], *s.* **d. of the Church,** séparation *f* de l'Eglise et de l'Etat.

diseur, *f.* **diseuse** [di:'zə:r, di:'zə:z], *s.* *Th:* diseur, *f.* diseuse.

disfavour[1] [dis'feivər], *s.* **1.** défaveur *f*; **to fall into d.,** tomber en disgrâce, en défaveur; **to be in d. with s.o.,** être mal vu de qn; **in s.o.'s disfavour,** au désavantage de qn; **at the risk of incurring s.o.'s d.,** au risque de déplaire à qn. **2.** désapprobation *f* (**of,** de).

disfavour[2], *v.tr.* désapprouver (qch.); voir (qch.) avec défaveur; se montrer défavorable à (un projet).

disfigure [dis'figər], *v.tr.* défigurer (qn, une statue, etc.); désembellir (une jeune fille, etc.); déparer, enlaidir (le visage); **factory chimneys that d. the landscape,** cheminées *f* d'usine qui gâtent, abîment, le paysage.

disfigured [dis'figəd], *a.* défiguré; (visage) ravagé (par une blessure, etc.).

disfigurement [dis'figəmənt], *s.* défiguration *f* (de qn, d'une statue); enlaidissement *m*; **to be a d. to sth.,** défigurer qch.; **these factories are a d. to our countryside,** ces usines *f* déparent nos campagnes; **she goes out very little since her d.,** depuis cet accident qui l'a enlaidie, elle sort très peu.

disfranchise [dis'fræn(t)ʃaiz], *v.tr.* priver (qn) du droit électoral, de ses droits civiques; priver (un bourg pourri, etc.) de ses droits de représentation.

disfranchisement [dis'fræn(t)ʃizmənt], *s.* privation *f* du droit de vote, des droits civiques; *Hist:* **the d. of the rotten boroughs,** l'abolition *f* des bourgs pourris.

disfunction [dis'fʌŋkʃən], *s.* *Med:* dysfonctionnement *m*.

disgorge [dis'gɔ:dʒ], *v.tr.* **1.** (*a*) dégorger, rendre, vomir (la nourriture); **to make a bird d. its prey,** faire dégorger un oiseau; (*b*) **river that disgorges itself, its waters, into . . .,** *abs.* **river that disgorges into . . .,** rivière *f* qui décharge ses eaux, qui se décharge, dans . . .; (*c*) *F:* dégorger, regorger (ce qu'on a volé, etc.); *v.i.* **to make s.o. d.,** faire rendre gorge à qn; faire dégorger qn. **2.** dégorger, faire dégorger (des sangsues).

disgorger [dis'gɔ:dʒər], *s.* **1.** *Wine-m:* (*pers.*) dégorgeur *m* (de vins mousseux). **2.** *Fish:* dégorgeoir *m*.

disgrace[1] [dis'greis], *s.* **1.** disgrâce *f*, défaveur *f*; **to fall into d. (with s.o.),** tomber en disgrâce, en défaveur (auprès de qn); **to be in d.,** être en disgrâce; (*of child*) être en pénitence *f*; **to be in deep d.,** être couvert d'opprobre *m*; **he was sent away in d.,** (i) il fut renvoyé en disgrâce; (ii) l'enfant fut envoyé en pénitence; **to bring s.o. into d.,** faire tomber qn en disgrâce, faire disgracier (un courtisan); attirer une disgrâce à qn; faire punir (un enfant). **2.** (*a*) honte *f*, déshonneur *m*, infamie *f*; **there is no d. in doing that,** il n'y a pas de honte à faire cela; il n'est pas infamant de faire cela; **to bring d. on one's family,** déshonorer sa famille; (*b*) honte; **to be a d. to, the d. of, one's family,** être la honte de sa famille; faire honte à sa famille; **these slums are a d. to the town,** ces taudis *m* sont la honte de la ville; **to be a d. to mankind,** être l'opprobre du genre humain.

disgrace[2], *v.tr.* **1.** disgracier (un courtisan, etc.); (*esp. in passive*) **he was disgraced for refusing to betray his friends,** il fut disgracié pour avoir refusé de trahir ses amis. **2.** déshonorer; faire déshonneur à (qn); **to d. oneself,** (i) se conduire indignement; (ii) se couvrir de honte; (iii) *F:* (*of dog, etc.*) s'oublier.

disgraceful [dis'greisful], *a.* honteux, déshonorant, infâme, ignoble; **it is d. that he has not yet settled his debts,** il est scandaleux qu'il n'ait pas encore payé ses dettes; **an action d. to all concerned,** action *f* qui déshonore tous ceux qui y ont participé.

disgracefully [dis'greisfuli], *adv.* honteusement; d'une manière scandaleuse; **he acted d.,** sa conduite a été indigne.

disgracefulness [dis'greisfulnis], *s.* honte *f*, ignominie *f*, infamie *f*; **the d. of the whole proceedings,** la façon indigne dont a été menée toute l'affaire.

disgruntle [dis'grʌntl], *v.tr.* agacer, contrarier (qn); mettre (qn) de mauvaise humeur.

disgruntled [dis'grʌntld], *a.* contrarié, mécontent (**at,** de); maussade; de mauvaise humeur.

disguise[1] [dis'gaiz], *s.* **1.** déguisement *m*; travestissement *m*; **in d.,** déguisé; **he came in the d. of a clown,** il est venu déguisé, travesti, en clown; **to strip, relieve, s.o. of his d.,** désaffubler qn de son déguisement. **2.** feinte *f*; fausse apparence; **under the d. of charity,** sous le masque de la charité; **to throw off all d.,** laisser tomber le masque, lever le masque.

disguise[2], *v.tr.* **1.** déguiser, travestir (qn); **to d. oneself as a clown, with a false beard,** se travestir en clown; se déguiser à l'aide d'une fausse barbe. **2.** (*a*) déguiser (sa pensée, ses sentiments); **to d. one's voice, one's handwriting,** déguiser, contrefaire, sa voix, son écriture; **to d. a smell,** masquer une odeur; (*b*) **to d. the truth, the facts,** déguiser, *F:* farder, la vérité, les faits; **there is no disguising the fact that . . .,** il faut avouer que . . .; (*c*) **to d. one's sorrow, one's feelings,** dissimuler son chagrin, ses sentiments. **3.** *A:* **disguised (in liquor),** pris de boisson; gris.

disgust[1] [dis'gʌst], *s.* **1.** dégoût profond; aversion *f*, répugnance *f* (**at, for, towards,** pour); **to hold sth. in d.,** avoir un profond dégoût pour qch., de qch. **2.** profond mécontentement; **he resigned in d.,** dégoûté, écœuré, il donna sa démission; **to the d. of all decent people,** au grand scandale des gens de bien; **to her great d., she was given a walking-on part,** à son grand dépit, on lui attribua un rôle de figurante.

disgust[2], *v.tr.* dégoûter; inspirer du dégoût à (qn). **1.** donner la nausée à (qn); **remedies that d. the palate,**

remèdes *m* qui répugnent au goût, qui donnent la nausée; remèdes dégoûtants. **2.** indigner, écœurer; **his business methods d. me,** ses procédés en affaires me dégoûtent, me révoltent; **such language disgusts me,** un pareil langage m'écœure; **to be disgusted at, with, by, sth.,** être profondément mécontent de qch.; être écœuré de qch.; **I am disgusted with you,** vous me faites mal au cœur; **he is disgusted that . . .,** il est indigné, révolté, scandalisé, que + *sub.*, de ce que + *ind.*

disgusted [dis'gʌstid], *a.* dégoûté; écœuré; **d. expression,** expression *f* de dégoût.

disgustedly [dis'gʌstidli], *adv.* avec dégoût.

disgusting [dis'gʌstiŋ], *a.* dégoûtant. **1.** qui répugne au goût, à l'odorat, à la vue; répugnant. **2.** révoltant, écœurant; **all that's d.,** tout ça c'est dégoûtant! **it's d.!** c'est du propre! *F:* c'est à faire vomir!

disgustingly [dis'gʌstiŋli], *adv.* dégoûtamment; d'une manière dégoûtante; **he is d. mean,** il est d'une avarice dégoûtante; **he was d. drunk,** il était dans un état d'ivresse dégoûtant.

dish[1] [diʃ], *s.* **1.** (*a*) plat *m*; (*deep earthenware*) terrine *f*; **vegetable d.,** légumier *m*; **butter d.,** beurrier *m*; **jam d.,** confiturier *m*, pot *m* à confitures; **d. cover,** (i) couvercle *m* (de plat); dessus-de-plat *m inv*; (ii) cloche *f* (garde-manger); chape *f*; **d. rack, d. drainer,** égouttoir *m*; **d. warmer,** chauffe-plats *m inv*; (*b*) *coll.* **the dishes,** la vaisselle; **to wash the dishes,** faire la vaisselle; (*c*) (*contents*) **a d. of strawberries,** un plat de fraises; *A: & Dial:* **a d. of tea,** une tasse de thé. **2.** *Cu:* plat (de viande, de légumes, etc.); mets *m*; *A:* **side d.,** (i) entremets *m*; (ii) hors-d'œuvre *m inv*; **it's not a d. I often make,** ce n'est pas une recette que je prépare souvent. **3.** (*a*) récipient *m*; *A:* écuelle *f* (de mendiant); *Min:* écuelle; bat(t)ée *f*: *Phot:* cuvette *f*; *Ch:* capsule *f*; **evaporating d.,** capsule d'évaporation; (*b*) creux *m*, dénivellement *m* (de terrain, etc.); (*c*) *Veh:* écuanteur *f* (d'une roue); (*d*) *Rad: etc:* **d. antenna,** antenne *f* paraboloïde. **4.** *P:* belle fille, jolie pépée.

dish[2], *v.*

I. *v.tr.* **1.** apprêter, servir, dresser (la viande, etc.). **2.** *F:* achever, désarçonner, enfoncer (qn); **to d. one's opponents,** rouler, enfoncer, ses adversaires; **the publication of the letter dished all his chances,** la publication de cette lettre a mis fin à toutes ses chances de succès; **to d. oneself,** s'enferrer. **3.** donner une forme concave ou convexe à (une surface); bomber (une plaque de métal, etc.); *Metalw:* tomber le bord (d'une tôle); *Veh:* **to d. a wheel,** désaxer une roue; donner de l'écuanteur *f* à une roue. **4.** *v.i.* (*of horse*) faucher.

II. (*compound verbs*) **1. dish out,** *v.tr.* (*a*) servir (la viande, etc.); (*b*) *F:* **to d. out money,** payer, casquer, de l'argent; (*c*) *F:* **to d. out punishment,** (i) (*of boxer*) assener des coups (à son adversaire); (ii) (*of schoolmaster, etc.*) punir (ses élèves).

2. dish up, *v.tr.* (*a*) apprêter, servir, dresser (la viande, etc.); (*b*) *F:* **to d. up some excuse or other,** donner une excuse quelconque; **to d. up well-known facts in a new form,** faire un réchauffé de faits bien connus.

disharmonious [dishɑː'mouniəs], *a.* **1.** (opinions, etc.) en désaccord. **2.** (son) discordant.

disharmony [dis'hɑːməni], *s.* **1.** désaccord *m*; manque *m* d'harmonie; zizanie *f.* **2.** (*of sound*) dissonance *f.*

dishcloth ['diʃklɔθ], *O:* **dishclout** ['diʃklaut], *s.* torchon *m* (i) à laver, (ii) à essuyer, la vaisselle.

dishearten [dis'hɑːtn], *v.tr.* décourager, abattre, démoraliser, rebuter; **to become disheartened,** s'abattre, se rebuter; **don't get disheartened,** ne vous laissez pas abattre; ne perdez pas courage.

disheartening [dis'hɑːtniŋ], *a.* décourageant, désespérant; **d. work,** travail rebutant, ingrat.

disheartenment [dis'hɑːtənm(ə)nt], *s.* découragement *m*, abattement *m.*

dished [diʃt], *a.* **1.** en forme d'assiette ((i) (*inwards*) en cuvette; (ii) (*outwards*) ventru, en bahut); **d. end (of boiler, etc.),** fond convexe, bombé; *Veh:* **d. wheel,** roue désaxée; **d. hub,** moyeu déporté; *Metalw:* **d. plate,** tôle emboutie; tôle à bord tombé; tôle bombée; *El:* **d. electrode,** électrode capsulée, à capsule. **2.** *F:* flambé, fini, fichu.

disherison [dis'herizən], *s. Jur:* exhérédation *f.*

dishevel [di'ʃev(ə)l], *v.tr.* ébouriffer; mettre (les cheveux) en désordre.

dishevelled [di'ʃevəld], *a.* **1.** (*a*) (*of pers.*) échevelé, dépeigné; les cheveux en désordre, ébouriffés; (*b*) (*of hair*) en désordre; (cheveux) ébouriffés. **2.** (*of pers.*) aux vêtements chiffonnés, en désordre.

dischevelment [di'ʃevəlmənt], *s.* désordre *m* (des cheveux ou des vêtements).

dishful ['diʃful], *s.* platée *f*; plein un plat (**of,** de).

dishing ['diʃiŋ], *s.* concavité *f*; *Metalw:* bombage *m* (d'une tôle); emboutissage *m* (d'un fond); *Veh:* écuanteur *f* (d'une roue).

dishmop ['diʃmɔp], *s.* lavette *f* (à vaisselle).

dishonest [dis'ɔnist], *a.* malhonnête, peu honnête; déloyal, -aux; (caissier) indélicat, peu délicat; **d. business,** commerce *m* interlope; **to engage in a d. lawsuit,** engager un procès malhonnête.

dishonestly [dis'ɔnistli], *adv.* malhonnêtement.

dishonesty [dis'ɔnisti], *s.* improbité *f*, déloyauté *f*, malhonnêteté *f*, mauvaise foi; **she was dismissed for d.,** nous l'avons renvoyée parce qu'elle nous volait; **piece, act, of d.,** malhonnêteté.

dishonour[1] [dis'ɔnər], *s.* **1.** (*a*) déshonneur *m*; **to bring d. on one's family,** déshonorer sa famille; **to reap everlasting d.,** se tarer à jamais, pour toujours; (*b*) *A:* insulte *f*, affront *m*; **offer him no d.,** ne lui faites pas d'affront. **2.** chose déshonorante. **3.** non-paiement *m* (d'un chèque); non-acceptation *f* (d'un effet de commerce).

dishonour[2], *v.tr.* **1.** (*a*) déshonorer; **he stands dishonoured,** il a fait banqueroute à l'honneur; (*b*) *O:* **to d. a woman,** déshonorer, séduire, une femme. **2.** (*a*) **to d. one's word, one's promise,** manquer à sa parole; (*b*) *Com:* **to d. a bill,** ne pas honorer, ne pas accepter, un effet; laisser protester un effet; refuser de payer un effet; **dishonoured cheque,** chèque impayé.

dishonourable [dis'ɔnərəbl], *a.* **1.** (*of pers.*) sans honneur; infâme; dépourvu d'honneur. **2.** (*of action*) déshonorant, honteux, indigne; **to think it d. to . . .,** considérer comme déshonorant de . . .; *Lit:* tenir à déshonneur de . . ..

dishonourableness [dis'ɔnərəblnis], *s.* caractère déshonorant (d'une action).

dishonourably [dis'ɔnərəbli], *adv.* déshonorablement, d'une façon peu honorable.

dishorn [dis'hɔːn], *v.tr.* décorner, écorner (un taureau, etc.).

dishpan ['diʃpæn], *s. U.S:* bassine *f* (à vaisselle).

dishrag ['diʃræg], *s.* torchon *m* (à laver la vaisselle); *F:* **to feel like a (wet) d.,** être éreinté, à plat.

dishwash[1] ['diʃwɔʃ], *s. U.S: F:* des absurdités *f*, des bêtises *f.*

dishwash[2], *v.i. U.S:* faire la vaisselle.

dishwasher ['diʃwɔʃər], *s.* **1.** (*pers.*) laveur, -euse, de vaisselle; (*in restaurant*) plongeur, -euse. **2.** lave-vaisselle *m inv*; machine *f* à laver la vaisselle; *Fr.C:* laveuse *f* à vaisselle.

dishwater ['diʃwɔːtər], *s.* **1.** eau *f* de vaisselle, eau grasse. **2.** *F:* (*tasteless soup, coffee, etc.*) lavasse *f.*

dishy ['diʃi], *a. F:* chic, élégant; **he's, she's, d.,** ce qu'il, qu'elle, est beau, belle.

disilane [dai'silein], *s. Ch:* disilane *m.*

disillusion[1] [disi'ljuʒ(ə)n], *s.* désillusion *f*, désabusement *m*, désenchantement *m.*

disillusion[2], **disillusionize** [disi'ljuːʒənaiz], *v.tr.* désillusionner, désabuser, désenchanter.

disillusioned [disi'ljuːʒənd], *a.* désillusionné, désenchanté; désabusé (du monde).

disillusionment [disi'ljuːʒənmənt], *s.* désillusionnement *m*, désenchantement *m.*

disincarnate [disin'kɑːneit], *a.* désincarné.

disincarnation [disinkɑː'neiʃ(ə)n], *s.* désincarnation *f.*

disincentive [disin'sentiv], *s. Pol.Ec: etc:* facteur décourageant; frein *m*; **heavy taxation is a d. to expansion,** les taxes élevées freinent, découragent, toute expansion.

disinclination [disiŋkli'neiʃ(ə)n], *s.* répugnance *f*, aversion *f* (**for, to,** pour); **to have, show, a d. to do sth.,** n'être pas disposé, ne pas tenir, à faire qch.; montrer peu d'empressement à faire qch.; **he has a d. for work,** il a le travail en aversion; **his d. to meet people,** sa répugnance à frayer avec le monde.

disincline [disin'klain], *v.tr.* **to d. s.o. to, for, sth., to do sth.,** rendre qn peu disposé à qch., à faire qch.; éloigner, détourner, qn de qch.; **this hot weather disinclines you for meat, for work,** par cette chaleur on a le dégoût de la viande, on se sent peu disposé au travail, à travailler; **I am disinclined to do that,** je me sens peu disposé à faire ça.

disincorporate [disin'kɔːpəreit], *v.tr.* dissoudre (une société, etc.).

disinfect [disin'fekt], *v.tr.* désinfecter; assainir; étuver (des vêtements, la correspondance d'un hôpital, etc.).

disinfectant [disin'fektənt], *a. & s.* désinfectant (*m*).

disinfecting [disin'fektiŋ], *s.* = DISINFECTION.

disinfection [disin'fekʃ(ə)n], *s.* désinfection *f*; assainissement *m*; purge *f* (de marchandises); étuvage *m* (des vêtements, etc.).

disinfector [disin'fektər], *s.* désinfecteur *m.*

disinfest [disin'fest], *v.tr.* détruire la vermine dans (une maison, etc.); **to d. a cellar of rats,** dératiser une cave.

disinfestation [disinfes'teiʃ(ə)n], *s.* destruction *f* de la vermine; (*from rats*) dératisation *f*; (*from bugs*) épouillage *m.*

disingenuous [disin'dʒenjuəs], *a.* **1.** (*of pers.*) sans franchise, insincère, finaud, dissimulé, faux, *f.* fausse; **d. excuses,** mauvaises excuses; *F:* excuses à la noix (de coco). **2.** (*of scheme, etc.*) secret, sournois; **d. tricks,** finauderies *f.*

disingenuously [disin'dʒenjuəsli], *adv.* sans franchise.

disingenuousness [disin'dʒenjuəsnis], *s.* manque *m* de franchise; dissimulation *f*, sournoiserie *f*; mauvaise foi.

disinherit [disin'herit], *v.tr.* déshériter; *Jur:* exhéréder.

disinheritance [disin'herit(ə)ns], *s.* déshéritement *m*; *Jur:* exhérédation *f.*

disinheriting [disin'heritiŋ], *s.* = DISINHERITANCE.

disinsectization [disinsekti'zeiʃ(ə)n], *s.* désinsectisation *f.*

disintegrate [dis'intigreit]. **1.** *v.tr.* (*a*) désagréger; désintégrer (le minerai); effriter (la pierre); (*b*) *Sug.-R:* défibrer (les cannes). **2.** *v.i.* (*a*) (*of stone*) se désagréger, se désintégrer, s'effriter, se déliter; (*b*) (*of political party, etc.*) se désagréger.

disintegration [disinti'greiʃ(ə)n], *s.* (*a*) désagrégation *f*, désintégration *f*; effritement *m*, délitation *f*, détrition *f* (de la pierre); (*b*) *Sug.-R:* défibrage *m* (des cannes); (*c*) *Atom.Ph:* **(nuclear) d.,** désintégration *f*; **beta d.,** désintégration bêta; (*d*) désagrégation (de la société, etc.).

disintegrator [dis'intigreitər], *s.* **1.** (*a*) *Civ.E:* (appareil) désintégrateur *m*, broyeur *m*; casse-pierres *m inv*; (*b*) *Tex:* défibreur *m*; *Paperm:* concasseur *m.* **2. modern industry has been a great d. of family life,** l'industrie *f* moderne a contribué fortement à rompre les liens de la vie de famille.

disinter [disin'təːr], *v.tr.* **(disinterred),** déterrer, exhumer, désensevelir (un mort, des antiquités).

disinterest [dis'int(ə)rəst], *v.tr.* désintéresser; **to d. oneself in a question,** se désintéresser d'une question.

disinterested [dis'intərestid], *a.* **1.** désintéressé; **his action is not entirely d.,** ce qu'il en fait ce n'est pas entièrement désintéressé, n'est pas pour vos beaux yeux. **2.** non intéressé (**in,** dans); indifférent (**in,** à).

disinterestedly [dis'intərestidli], *adv.* avec désintéressement.

disinterestedness [dis'int(ə)restidnis], *s.* **1.** désintéressement *m*; **to establish one's d.,** faire preuve de désintéressement. **2.** détachement *m*, indifférence *f.*

disinterment [disin'təːmənt], *s.* déterrement *m*; exhumation *f.*

disinvagination [disinvædʒi'neiʃ(ə)n], *s. Surg:* désinvagination *f.*

disjoin [dis'dʒɔin]. **1.** *v.tr.* disjoindre, déjoindre, désunir, séparer, détacher. **2.** *v.i.* se disjoindre, se déjoindre, se séparer, se détacher, se désunir.

disjoint [dis'dʒɔint], *v.tr.* disjoindre, désassembler; démembrer (une volaille); *Med:* désarticuler (l'épaule, etc.).

disjointed [dis'dʒɔintid], *a.* disjoint, disloqué; (discours) sans suite, incohérent; (style) haché, décousu.

disjointedly [dis'dʒɔintidli], *adv.* **to speak, think, d.,** parler, penser, de façon décousue, à bâtons rompus; (*of author*) **he writes d.,** il a un style décousu, il va par sauts et par bonds.

disjointedness [dis'dʒɔintidnis], *s.* incohérence *f* (d'un discours); manque *m* de suite.

disjunct [dis'dʒʌŋkt], *a. Mus:* (mouvement) disjoint; **d. interval,** degré disjoint; saut *m.*

disjunction [dis'dʒʌŋ(k)ʃ(ə)n], *s.* disjonction *f*, séparation *f* (**from,** de).

disjunctive [dis'dʒʌŋ(k)tiv]. **1.** *a. Gram: Log: etc:* disjonctif; **d. proposition,** proposition disjonctive; **d. conjunction,** conjonction, particule, disjonctive. **2.** *s. Gram: Log:* disjonctive *f.*

disk [disk], *s.* = DISC.

dislike[1] [dis'laik], *s.* aversion *f*, dégoût *m*, répugnance *f* (**to, of, for,** pour); **to take, conceive, a d. to s.o.,** prendre qn en grippe, en aversion; **to conceive a d. for sth.,** prendre qch. en dégoût; **to have a strong d. for, of, sth.,** détester qch., ne pas pouvoir sentir qch.; **I have a particular d. for him,** il me déplaît beaucoup; **I have a d. for waste,** je n'aime rien gâcher, je n'aime pas le gaspillage.

dislike[2], *v.tr.* ne pas aimer; détester; **he dislikes you,** vous lui déplaisez; vous lui êtes antipathique; **I don't d. him,** il ne me déplaît pas; **to d. doing sth.,** détester, ne pas aimer, faire qch.; **to d. living in Paris,** se déplaire à Paris; **I d. his coming so often,** je n'aime pas, je trouve mauvais, qu'il vienne si souvent; **to be disliked by all,** être mal vu de tous; **you'll get yourself disliked!** vous allez vous mettre tout le monde à dos!

dislocate ['disləkeit], *v.tr.* (*a*) disloquer (une machine, l'écorce terrestre, un projet, etc.); désorganiser (la circulation, les affaires); bouleverser, dérouter (les projets de qn); démembrer (un empire); (*b*) luxer, déboîter, démancher, démettre, disloquer (un membre); **to d. one's jaw,** se décrocher la mâchoire; (*of horse*) **to d. its hip,** se déhancher.

dislocation [dislə'keiʃ(ə)n], *s.* (*a*) dislocation *f* (d'une machine, de l'écorce terrestre); bouleversement *m* (d'un projet, etc.); désorganisation *f* (de la circulation, des affaires); (*b*) luxation *f*, déboîtement *m*, dislocation, désarticulation *f* (d'un membre); *Med: Vet:* **d. of the hip,** déhanchement *m*.

dislodge [dis'lɔdʒ], *v.tr.* **1.** déloger, débusquer, chasser (**from,** de); *Ven:* débucher, faire débucher (un cerf); **to d. a fox,** faire sortir un renard de son terrier; dégiter un renard; **the enemy was easily dislodged from the hill,** on parvint sans peine à déloger, à débusquer, l'ennemi de la colline. **2.** détacher; **in climbing the cliff he dislodged a stone,** en escaladant la falaise il a fait dégringoler une pierre; **several bricks had become dislodged,** plusieurs briques s'étaient détachées.

dislodg(e)ment [dis'lɔdʒmənt], *s.* délogement *m*, débusquement *m* (de l'ennemi, etc.); *Ven:* débucher *m*.

disloyal [dis'lɔiəl], *a.* infidèle (à son roi, à l'amitié); perfide, déloyal, -aux; **a d. act,** une déloyauté.

disloyally [dis'lɔiəli], *adv.* infidèlement, perfidement, déloyalement.

disloyalty [dis'lɔiəlti], *s.* infidélité *f*, perfidie *f*, déloyauté *f*.

disluite ['disljuait], *s. Miner:* disluite *f*, dislyite *f*.

dismal ['dizməl], *a.* lugubre, sombre, triste; (paysage *m*, avenir *m*) morne; **d. face,** figure *f* de carême; visage *m* de croquemort; **a d. Jemmy,** un geignard, un broyeur de noir, un cafardeux.

dismally ['dizməli], *adv.* lugubrement, tristement.

dismalness ['dizməlnis], *s.* tristesse *f*; air *m* lugubre, morne.

dismantle [dis'mæntl], *v.tr.* **1.** (*a*) dégarnir, dépouiller (**of,** de); (*b*) raser, démolir (des murs). **2.** (*a*) démanteler (une forteresse, un vaisseau de guerre); désarmer, dégréer (un navire); (*b*) démonter, déséquiper, dégréer (une grue, etc.); démonter (une machine, un fusil, un lit, etc.).

dismantlement [dis'mæntlmənt], **dismantling** [dis'mæntliŋ], *s.* dégarnissement *m* (d'une chambre, etc.); démantèlement *m* (d'une forteresse); désarmement *m*, dégréement *m* (d'un navire); démontage *m* (d'une machine, etc.).

dismast [dis'mɑːst], *v.tr. Nau:* démâter.

dismasting [dis'mɑːstiŋ], *s.* démâtage *m*, démâtement *m*.

dismay[1] [dis'mei], *s.* consternation *f*, atterrement *m*; épouvante *f*, effroi *m*; effarement *m*, trouble *m*; **to strike s.o. with d.,** consterner qn; **to be seized with d.,** demeurer consterné; **in (blank) d.,** consterné, atterré; **exclamation of d.,** exclamation effarée.

dismay[2], *v.tr.* consterner, effarer, épouvanter; **we were dismayed at the news,** cette nouvelle nous jeta dans la consternation; **courage that nothing can d.,** courage *m* que rien ne peut ébranler, que rien ne peut démonter; *B:* **be not dismayed,** n'ayez point de crainte.

dismember [dis'membər], *v.tr.* **1.** démembrer (un poulet, un royaume, etc.); **his body was dismembered,** son corps fut écartelé. **2.** *A:* rayer (qn) des rôles (d'une société, etc.).

dismembering [dis'memb(ə)riŋ], **dismemberment** [dis'membəmənt], *s.* **1.** démembrement *m* (d'une volaille, d'un royaume). **2.** *A:* radiation *f* des rôles (d'une société, etc.).

dismiss[1] [dis'mis], *s. Mil:* **to sound the d.,** sonner la breloque.

dismiss[2], *v.tr.* **1.** congédier, remercier (qn); donner congé, signifier son congé, à (qn); mettre à pied (un employé); chasser (un domestique); révoquer, destituer (un fonctionnaire); relever (un fonctionnaire) de ses fonctions; démettre (un ministre) de ses fonctions; **to be, get, dismissed,** recevoir son congé; *Mil:* **to d. s.o. from the service,** (i) rayer qn des cadres *m* de l'armée; (ii) réformer qn; *Mil: Navy:* **to be dismissed the service,** être renvoyé du service; *Navy:* **dismissed his ship,** cassé de son grade. **2.** (*a*) congédier (aimablement) (qn); donner à (qn) la permission de se retirer; **the prince dismissed us with a few gracious words,** le prince nous congédia avec quelques paroles aimables; (*b*) congédier, éconduire (un importun, etc.); (*c*) dissoudre (une assemblée); (*d*) **to d. troops, reservists,** renvoyer des troupes, des réservistes, dans leurs foyers. **3. to d. sth. from one's thoughts, mind,** bannir, chasser, éloigner, qch. de ses pensées; **to d. any personal feeling,** écarter tout sentiment personnel; **to d. all thoughts of revenge,** écarter de son esprit toute pensée de vengeance; **to d. a threat,** ne tenir aucun compte d'une menace. **4.** quitter, abandonner (un sujet de conversation, etc.); **let us d. the subject,** n'en parlons plus; brisons là; **to d. a subject in a few words,** toucher quelques mots d'un sujet avant de passer outre; **the subject is not lightly to be dismissed,** l'on ne saurait écarter cette question aussi légèrement. **5.** (*a*) écarter (une proposition); *Jur:* rejeter (une demande, un appel); **to d. a case,** (i) classer une affaire; (ii) rendre une fin de non-recevoir; **to d. a charge,** rendre une ordonnance de non-lieu; **to d. s.o.'s appeal,** débouter qn de son appel; (*b*) **to d. the accused,** acquitter l'inculpé. **6.** *Mil:* **to d. a parade,** faire rompre les rangs *m* (aux troupes); **dismiss!** rompez (les rangs)! *Navy:* **to d. a boat's crew,** désarmer un canot. **7.** *Cr:* (*of batsman*) **dismissed for ten,** mis hors jeu quand il n'a marqué que dix points.

dismissal [dis'misəl], *s.* **1.** congédiement *m*, renvoi *m* (d'un employé); révocation *f*, destitution *f* (d'un fonctionnaire); renvoi (d'un ministre); **d. from the army,** (i) réforme *f* (d'un officier) par mesure de discipline; (ii) dégradation *f* militaire; **subject to d.,** (fonctionnaire) destituable, révocable; **he threatened him with d.,** il menaça de le renvoyer. **2.** *Jur:* (*a*) fin *f* de non-recevoir; rejet *m* (d'une demande, d'un appel); (*b*) acquittement *m* (de l'inculpé); ordonnance *f* d'acquit.

dismissible [dis'misibl], *a.* renvoyable; (fonctionnaire *m*) destituable, révocable, amovible.

dismount [dis'maunt]. **1.** *v.i.* **to d. (from a horse,** *A:* **from a carriage),** descendre (de cheval, de voiture); mettre pied à terre; sauter à terre; *v.tr.* **to d. one's horse,** descendre de cheval. **2.** *v.tr.* (*a*) démonter, désarçonner (un cavalier); faire descendre (qn) (de cheval); (*b*) *Mil:* mettre à pied (des troupes montées). **3.** *v.tr.* démonter (un canon, une machine).

dismounted [dis'mauntid], *a.* **1.** (*of pers.*) démonté; à pied; *Mil: A:* **d. action,** combat *m* à pied. **2.** (*of gun, machine*) démonté.

dismounting [dis'mauntiŋ], *s.* **1.** (*a*) descente *f* (de cheval, *A:* de voiture); (*b*) mise *f* à pied (d'une troupe montée). **2.** démontage *m* (d'une machine, etc.).

dismutation [dismju'teiʃ(ə)n], *s. Ch:* dismutation *f*.

disobedience [disə'biːdiəns], *s.* désobéissance *f* (**to s.o.,** à qn; **of a rule,** à une règle); **an act of d.,** une désobéissance; **civil d.,** résistance passive.

disobedient [disə'biːdiənt], *a.* désobéissant, (enfant) mutin; **to be d. to s.o.,** désobéir à qn; **stubbornly d. horse,** cheval rétif.

disobediently [disə'biːdiəntli], *adv.* en désobéissant; malgré les ordres donnés.

disobey [disə'bei], *v.tr.* désobéir (à qn, à un ordre); enfreindre (un ordre); violer, enfreindre (la loi); **my orders were disobeyed,** mes ordres ont été désobéis; **he refuses to be disobeyed,** il ne veut pas être désobéi; il ne veut pas qu'on lui désobéisse.

disoblige [disə'blaidʒ], *v.tr.* désobliger (qn).

disobliging [disə'blaidʒiŋ], *a.* désobligeant, peu complaisant (**to,** envers).

disobligingly [disə'blaidʒiŋli], *adv.* désobligeamment.

disobligingness [disə'blaidʒiŋnis], *s.* désobligeance *f*; manque *m* de complaisance (**to,** envers).

disodic, disodium [dai'soudik, -'soudiəm], *a. Ch:* disodique; **disodium phosphate,** phosphate *m* disodique.

disomic [dai'soumik], *a. Biol:* disomique.

disorder[1] [dis'ɔːdər], *s.* **1.** désordre *m*, confusion *f*, dérangement *m*; **in d.,** en désordre; **to throw the ranks into d.,** mettre le désordre, la confusion, dans les rangs; **to fall into d.,** se désordonner; **they fled in d.,** ils s'enfuirent à la débandade; *Nau:* **the convoy was falling into d.,** le convoi se mettait en pagaille, en pantenne. **2.** (*tumult*) désordre, trouble *m*, tumulte *m*; *F:* anarchie *f*; **serious d. has broken out,** de graves désordres ont éclaté. **3.** *Med:* désordre (dans les fonctions du corps); affection *f*; perturbation *f*; troubles (de digestion, etc.); **nervous d.,** troubles nerveux, affection nerveuse; **disorders of the mind,** dérangement d'esprit; **personality d., character d.,** trouble caractériel; **psychopatic d.,** trouble caractériel.

disorder[2], *v.tr.* **1.** déranger; mettre (qch.) en désordre; mettre le désordre, la confusion, dans (les rangs, etc.); jeter le trouble dans (le commerce, les esprits, etc.). **2.** déranger (l'estomac); affecter, *F:* détraquer (la santé, le foie, etc.).

disordered [dis'ɔːdəd], *a.* **1.** (*a*) (*of plans, ambition, etc.*) désordonné; (*b*) **d. hair,** cheveux *mpl*, coiffure *f*, en désordre. **2.** (estomac) dérangé; (foie, esprit) malade, *F:* détraqué; **d. imagination,** imagination désordonnée, troublée, délirante.

disorderliness [dis'ɔːdəlinis], *s.* **1.** désordre *m*; manque *m* d'ordre (dans un ménage, etc.). **2.** conduite *f* contraire aux bonnes mœurs; dérèglement *m*; **d. in a public place,** délit *m* contre l'ordre public. **3.** turbulence *f*; esprit *m* de trouble (parmi le peuple, etc.).

disorderly [dis'ɔːdəli], *a.* **1.** qui manque d'ordre; désordonné; en désordre, en confusion; **this d. rabble was all that remained of a crack battalion,** cette cohue était tout ce qui restait d'un de nos meilleurs bataillons. **2.** (*of mob, etc.*) turbulent, tumultueux; **the d. spirit now prevailing,** l'esprit *m* d'émeute qui règne actuellement. **3.** (*of pers., behaviour*) désordonné, déréglé; **to lead a d. life,** vivre dans le dérèglement, dans l'inconduite; *F:* mener une vie de bâton de chaise. **4.** *Jur:* **d. house,** (i) maison *f* de débauche; (ii) maison de jeu.

disorganization [disɔːgənai'zeiʃ(ə)n], *s.* désorganisation *f*, désagencement *m*.

disorganize [dis'ɔːgənaiz], *v.tr.* désorganiser; **to become disorganized,** se désorganiser.

disorient(ate) [dis'ɔːriənt(eit)], *v.tr.* désorienter.

disown [dis'oun], *v.tr.* **1.** désavouer (une œuvre); renier (l'autorité de qn); **to d. one's signature,** renier sa signature; **to d. a child,** refuser de reconnaître la paternité. **2.** *A:* refuser d'admettre, nier (un fait).

disparage [dis'pæridʒ], *v.tr.* **1.** déprécier, décrier, dénigrer, ravaler (qn, qch.); battre (qn) en brèche; **to d. everything,** peindre tout en laid. **2.** déshonorer, discréditer (qn, qch.).

disparagement [dis'pæridʒmənt], *s.* **1.** dénigrement *m*, dépréciation *f*, ravalement *m*; **to refer to s.o. in terms of d.,** faire une allusion méprisante à qn; **this is not written in d. of his work,** ceci n'est pas pour déprécier son œuvre. **2.** *A:* (*a*) mésalliance *f*; (*b*) déshonneur *m*.

disparager [dis'pæridʒər], *s.* dénigreur, -euse; détracteur, -trice.

disparaging [dis'pæridʒiŋ], *a.* **1.** (terme *m*) de dénigrement; dépréciateur, -trice. **2.** désavantageux; peu flatteur, -euse; déshonorant; **a comparison d. to . . .,** une comparaison qui rabaisse . . ., qui n'est pas à l'avantage de . . ..

disparagingly [dis'pæridʒiŋli], *adv.* d'un ton, d'un air, dépréciateur; **to speak d. of s.o.,** tenir des propos désobligeants pour qn; parler de qn en termes de mépris.

disparate ['dispəreit]. **1.** *a.* disparate. **2.** *s.pl.* **disparates,** disparates *f*.

disparation [dispæ'reiʃən], *s. Opt:* disparation rétinienne.

disparity [dis'pæriti], *s.* **1.** inégalité *f*, disconvenance *f* (**of,** de); **d. of age, in age,** inégalité, différence *f*, d'âge; **in spite of their d. in position,** malgré la différence de leurs positions (sociales). **2.** disparité *f*, disparate *f*, écart *m* (**between,** entre).

dispassionate [dis'pæʃənət], *a.* **1.** exempt de passion, sans passion; calme. **2.** impartial, -aux; **to take a d. view of things,** juger impartialement les choses.

dispassionately [dis'pæʃənətli], *adv.* **1.** sans passion; calmement, avec calme. **2.** sans parti pris; impartialement.

dispatch[1] [dis'pætʃ], *s.* **1.** expédition *f*; envoi *m* (de qn, de qch.); *Com:* **d. service,** service *m* des expéditions (d'une maison de commerce); **d. note,** bulletin *m*, bordereau *m*, d'expédition; *Post:* **office of d.,** bureau *m* d'origine. **2.** mise *f* à mort; exécution *f* (d'un condamné). **3.** (*a*) expédition (d'une affaire); **there is always somebody at the office for the d. of current business,** il y a une permanence pour l'expédition des affaires courantes; (*b*) promptitude *f*, célérité *f*, diligence *f*, rapidité *f*; **with d.,** promptement; **with all possible d., with the utmost d.,** en toute diligence; en toute hâte; au plus vite; avec la plus grande célérité; avec toute la promptitude possible; **to work with the greatest possible d.,** travailler avec la plus grande activité; **d. money,** prime *f* de rapidité. **4.** dépêche *f* (diplomatique, etc.); *Dipl: Adm: etc:* **d. box,** boîte *f* à documents; **d. case,** serviette *f* (en cuir); *Mil:* **d. rider,** estafette *f*; *Mil: etc:* **to be mentioned in dispatches,** être cité à l'ordre (du jour); **mention in dispatches,** citation *f* à l'ordre du jour. **5.** *Nau:* **d. boat,** mouche *f*.

dispatch[2], *v.tr.* **1.** dépêcher (un courrier); expédier (une lettre, des marchandises); envoyer (qn, une dépêche); faire partir (des troupes, etc.); mettre en route (un convoi, etc.); **to d. goods to a place,** acheminer des marchandises sur, vers, un endroit; **goods dispatched to Nantes,** marchandises acheminées sur Nantes. **2.** (*a*) achever (qn, un animal); donner le coup de grâce à (un animal); *Ven:* servir (un animal) au couteau; **he was knocked senseless and dispatched with a revolver,** il fut assommé puis achevé à coups de revolver; (*b*) expédier (qn) dans l'autre monde; tuer, égorger (qn); **the executioner soon dispatched the prisoners,** le bourreau eut vite fait d'expédier les prisonniers. **3.** expédier, *F:* trousser (une affaire); **to d. current business,** expédier les affaires courantes. **4.** *F:* expédier (un repas); **we soon dispatched our dinner,** nous avons vite expédié, avalé, notre dîner.

dispatcher [dis'pætʃər], *s.* (*a*) *Com: etc:* expéditeur, -trice; (*b*) *Trans: El: etc:* régulateur *m,* contrôleur *m* (du mouvement des trains, des avions, etc., de la répartition de l'énergie); *F:* dispatcher *m.*

dispatching [dis'pætʃiŋ], *s.* (*a*) *Com: etc:* expédition *f,* envoi *m,* acheminement *m* (des marchandises, etc.); (*b*) *Trans: El: etc:* régulation *f,* contrôle *m,* du mouvement, de l'utilisation (des véhicules, etc.), de la répartition (de l'énergie, etc.); *F:* dispatching *m*; (*c*) mise *f* en route (d'un convoi, etc.).

dispel [dis'pel], *v.tr.* **(dispelled)** chasser, dissiper (les nuages, les illusions, les craintes); **work dispels boredom,** le travail chasse l'ennui.

dispensable [dis'pensəbl], *a.* **1.** dont on peut se passer. **2.** *Ecc:* (vœu *m,* etc.) dispensable.

dispensary [dis'pensəri], *s.* **1.** *A:* **(charitable, public) d.,** dispensaire *m,* policlinique *f.* **2.** (*a*) officine *f* (d'une pharmacie); (*b*) pharmacie *f.*

dispensation [dispen'seiʃ(ə)n], *s.* **1.** dispensation *f,* distribution *f* (des récompenses, des aumônes). **2.** dispensation, administration *f* (des choses humaines). **3.** décret *m,* arrêt *m,* coup *m* (de la Providence). **4.** *Rel.H:* lois *fpl* (de Moïse, de l'Évangile); **the Mosaic d.,** la loi mosaïque. **5.** *Jur: Ecc:* **d. from sth., from doing sth.,** dispense *f* de qch., de faire qch.; **d. from fasting,** dispense du jeûne. **6. d. from sth., with sth.,** fait *m* d'être dispensé, de se dispenser, de qch.; **he asked for d. from the usual ceremonial visits,** il demanda à être dispensé des visites de cérémonie habituelles.

dispense [dis'pens]. **1.** *v.tr.* (*a*) dispenser, distribuer (des aumônes); départir (des bienfaits, des faveurs); (*b*) administrer, rendre (la justice); administrer (les derniers sacrements); (*c*) *Pharm:* préparer (des médicaments); **to d. a prescription,** exécuter une ordonnance; **dispensing chemist,** pharmacien diplômé (autorisé à exécuter les ordonnances). **2.** (*a*) *v.tr.* **to d. s.o. from sth., from doing sth.,** dispenser, exempter, qn de qch., de faire qch.; *Ecc:* **to d. s.o. from fasting,** dispenser qn du jeûne; *Mil:* **dispensed from all fatigues,** dispensé, exempté, de toutes corvées; (*b*) *v.i.* **the bishop may d.,** l'évêque peut accorder une dispense. **3.** *v.i.* (*a*) **to d. with s.o., with sth.,** se passer de qn, de qch.; **to d. with hand-labour,** supprimer la main-d'œuvre; (*b*) *Jur:* **to d. with an oath, with the signature of a witness,** ne pas exiger un serment, l'attestation d'un témoin.

dispenser [dis'pensər], *s.* **1.** (*a*) dispensateur, -trice, distributeur, -trice (d'aumônes, etc.); (*b*) *A:* (*in institution*) économe *mf*; (*c*) pharmacien, -ienne. **2.** administrateur *m* (de lois, etc.). **3.** distributeur *m* automatique (de cigarettes, de bonbons, etc.); **razor-blade d.,** distributeur de lames de rasoir.

dispensing [dis'pensiŋ], *s.* **1.** dispensation *f,* distribution *f* (des aumônes, etc.). **2.** *Pharm:* (*a*) préparation *f,* composition *f* (des ordonnances); (*b*) **d. department, counter,** rayon *m* d'ordonnances médicales.

dispermic [dai'spə:mik], *a. Biol:* dispermique.

dispersal [dis'pə:s(ə)l], *s.* dispersion *f*; *Mil: etc:* **d. area,** zone *f* de dispersion, *Av:* aire *f* de dispersion, *F:* dispersal *m*; *Mil:* **d. point (of a column),** point *m* de dispersion, de dislocation, d'éclatement (d'une colonne).

dispersant [dis'pə:sənt], *s. Ind:* dispersant *m.*

disperse[1] [dis'pə:s]. **1.** *v.tr.* (*a*) disperser, éparpiller, faire fuir (l'ennemi, une foule); dissiper, chasser (les nuages, l'obscurité); égailler (des oiseaux, des navires, etc.); (*b*) disperser (ses troupes, une belle collection, etc.); *Artil:* **to d. the fire,** disperser le tir; **our troops were too much dispersed,** nos troupes étaient trop éparpillées; (*c*) répandre, disséminer (des nouvelles, des plaintes); (*d*) *Med:* résoudre, dissoudre (une tumeur); (*e*) *Opt:* (*of prism,etc.*) disperser (la lumière). **2.** *v.i.* (*a*) (*of crowd*) se disperser, s'éparpiller, s'écouler; (*of light*) se disperser; (*of darkness*) se dissiper; **the rebels dispersed to their homes,** les insurgés se débandèrent et rentrèrent dans leurs familles; (*b*) *Mil:* rompre les postes de combat.

disperse[2], **dispersed** [dis'pəst], *a.* dispersé; éparpillé.

dispersibility [dispə:si'biliti], *s.* dispersibilité *f.*

dispersion [dis'pə:ʃ(ə)n], *s.* (*a*) dispersion *f*; *Rel.H:* **the D.,** la dispersion des Juifs; (*b*) dispersion, diffusion *f* (de la chaleur, etc.); (*c*) *Opt:* dispersion (d'un rayon lumineux); feux *mpl* (d'un diamant).

dispersive [dis'pə:siv], *a. Opt: etc:* (prisme, etc.) dispersif.

dispersiveness [dis'pə:sivnis], *s.* dispersivité *f.*

dispersoid [dis'pə:sɔid], *s. Ch:* dispersoïde *m.*

dispirit [dis'pirit], *v.tr.* décourager, abattre, rebuter (qn).

dispirited [dis'piritid], *a.* découragé, abattu.

dispiritedly [dis'piritidli], *adv.* d'un air, d'un ton, découragé; d'un air abattu.

dispiritedness [dis'piritidnis], *s.* découragement *m,* abattement *m.*

dispiriting [dis'piritiŋ], *a.* décourageant.

displace [dis'pleis], *v.tr.* **1.** déplacer (qch.); **someone had displaced the chair,** on avait déplacé la chaise; on avait changé la chaise de place; **weight of water displaced by a body,** poids *m* de l'eau déplacée par un corps; *El:* **to d. the brushes,** décaler les balais. **2.** (*a*) déplacer, destituer (un fonctionnaire, etc.); (*b*) remplacer **(by,** par); **the territorials were displaced by regulars,** les territoriaux furent remplacés par des troupes régulières; (*c*) évincer (qn); **to d. s.o. (in s.o.'s affections),** supplanter qn; (*d*) *St.Exch:* **displaced shares,** actions déclassées; (*e*) *Pol:* **displaced persons,** personnes déplacées.

displaceable [dis'pleisəbl], *a.* **1.** qui peut être déplacé; mobile. **2.** (fonctionnaire *m,* etc.) amovible.

displacement [dis'pleismənt], *s.* **1.** (*a*) déplacement *m* (de qch.); changement *m* de place; *El:* décalage *m* (des balais); *Med:* ectopie *f* (d'un organe); *Geol:* décrochement *m,* dislocation *f*; *Psy:* **affective d.,** déplacement affectif; (*b*) *St.Exch:* éclassement *m* (d'actions); (*c*) **volumetric d.,** déplacement volumétrique; *N.Arch:* déplacement, poids *m* (d'un navire); tonnage *m* (d'un navire de guerre); **d. light, light d.,** déplacement à vide; déplacement lège; **load d., d. loaded,** déplacement en charge; **ship of five thousand tons d.,** navire *m* d'un déplacement de 5000 tonnes, qui déplace 5000 tonnes. **2. d. of A by B,** remplacement *m* de A par B; substitution *f* de B à A.

display[1] [dis'plei], *s.* (*a*) étalage *m,* exposition *f* (d'objets, de marchandises); **d. window, cabinet, case,** vitrine *f* d'exposition; *Com:* **d. unit,** présentoir *m*; (*b*) affichage *m,* étalage, manifestation *f* (de sentiments, d'opinions, d'érudition, etc.); **d. of courage, of force,** déploiement *m* de courage, de force; démonstration *f* de force; **to make a great d. of sorrow,** se livrer à de grandes démonstrations de douleur; afficher, étaler, sa douleur; (*c*) étalage (de luxe); **to be fond of d.,** aimer l'ostentation; **to have a horror of d.,** avoir l'ostentation en horreur; (*d*) manifestation (artistique, sportive, etc.); **air d.,** fête *f* aéronautique; (*e*) *Typ:* lignes *fpl,* matières *fpl,* en vedette; **d. work,** composition *f* des titres, etc.; mise *f* en vedette; (*f*) *Rad:* (i) video *f,* représentation visuelle; (ii) indicateur *m*; **d. screen,** écran *m* (i) de visualisation, (ii) de veille; (*g*) *Elcs: etc:* affichage *m*; **data d. equipment,** appareillage *m* de présentation, de représentation visuelle, des données; (*h*) *Orn:* parade *m.*

display[2]. **1.** *v.tr.* (*a*) étaler, exposer (des objets, des marchandises); **to d. a notice,** afficher un avis; **to d. a flag,** déployer un drapeau; **she pulled up her sleeve to d. a scratch,** elle remonta sa manche pour montrer une égratignure; (*b*) afficher, déployer, étaler, manifester (un sentiment, une opinion, de l'érudition, etc.); **to d. courage,** faire preuve de courage, manifester du courage; **he displayed no sign of the emotion he was feeling,** il n'a rien laissé voir de l'émotion qu'il éprouvait; **to d. one's ignorance,** laisser paraître, révéler, son ignorance; (*c*) *Typ:* mettre (une ligne, etc.) en vedette; (*c*) *Elcs: etc:* afficher; visualiser. **2.** *v.i. Orn:* parader.

displayed [dis'pleid], *a. Her:* (aigle, etc.) éployé.

displease [dis'pli:z], (*a*) *v.tr.* déplaire à (qn); fâcher, contrarier, mécontenter, offenser (qn); (*b*) *v.i.* **to be displeased at, with, s.o., sth.,** être mécontent de qn, de qch.; être fâché contre qn, de qch.

displeasing [dis'pli:ziŋ], *a.* déplaisant, désagréable (to, à).

displeasingly [dis'pli:ziŋli], *adv.* désagréablement.

displeasure [dis'pleʒər], *s.* déplaisir *m,* mécontentement *m*; **to incur s.o.'s d.,** s'attirer le courroux de qn.

disport [dis'pɔ:t], *v.pr. & i.* **to d. (oneself),** (i) se divertir, s'amuser; (ii) s'ébattre, prendre ses ébats; folâtrer.

disporum [dis'pɔ:rəm], *s. Bot:* dispore *m.*

disposability [dispouzə'biliti], *s.* disponibilité *f.*

disposable [dis'pouzəbl], *a.* (*a*) disponible; **d. income, surplus,** revenu *m,* surplus *m,* disponible; **d. funds,** disponibilités *m*; fonds *m* disponible; *Jur:* **d. portion of property,** biens *m* disponibles par testament; (*b*) ne servant qu'une fois; (couche, etc.) jetable, à jeter (après usage).

disposal [dis'pouzl], *s.* **1.** (*a*) mise *f* au rebut; destruction *f,* enlèvement *m,* évacuation *f,* décharge *f* (des déchets, ordures, etc.); **d. area, ground, site,** terrain *m* de décharge; **(refuse) d. plant,** dépotoir *m*; **bomb d.,** désamorçage *m* et enlèvement des bombes non éclatées; désobusage *m*; déminage *m*; **bomb d. expert,** démineur *m*; **the d. of the corpse presented some difficulty,** il a été assez difficile de se débarrasser du cadavre; (*b*) **as far as the d. of the prisoner and his money was concerned,** quant à ce qu'il fallait faire du prisonnier et de son argent; (*c*) **to be at s.o.'s d.,** être à la disposition de qn; **I am entirely at your d.,** vous pouvez disposer de moi; je suis entièrement à votre service; **to put sth. at s.o.'s d.,** mettre qch. à la disposition de qn; **he has a large capital at his d.,** il dispose de gros capitaux; **to have a boat at one's d.,** disposer d'un bateau, avoir un bateau à sa disposition, avoir la jouissance d'un bateau; **the means at my d.,** les moyens *m* dont je dispose. **2.** (*a*) disposition, cession (onéreuse), vente *f* (de biens); **for d.,** à vendre; à céder; **d. of securities,** cession de titres; **we shall have to face the d. of these goods at a loss,** nous serons obligés de vendre ces marchandises à perte; (*b*) *Jur:* **d. of property,** dispositions testamentaires. **3.** arrangement *m* (des objets).

dispose [dis'pouz], *v.tr. & i.* **1.** (*a*) disposer, arranger, distribuer (des objets); aménager, ordonner (une maison, etc.); **God disposes all things according to His will,** Dieu ordonne toutes choses selon sa volonté; *Prov:* **man proposes, God disposes,** l'homme propose et Dieu dispose; (*b*) **to d. of one's time,** disposer de, employer, son temps. **2. to d. of sth., of s.o.,** se défaire, se débarrasser, de qch., de qn; mettre qch. au rebut; *F:* tuer, expédier, qn; **a squad arrived to d. of the bombs in the field,** une équipe est venue pour déminer le champ; **to d. of an opponent,** vaincre un adversaire; **to d. of an interrupter,** réduire un interrupteur au silence; river, clouer, le bec à un interrupteur; **to d. of a question,** résoudre, trancher, une question; **to d. of a matter,** régler une affaire; **to d. of an amendment,** statuer sur un amendement; **that disposes of any objections,** voilà qui supprime toutes les objections; **a young critic disposed of him in a couple of articles,** un jeune critique l'exécuta en deux articles; *F:* **to d. of a meal,** expédier un repas; **dinner was soon disposed of,** le dîner a été vite expédié; *Adm:* **permission to d. of a body,** permis *m* d'inhumer. **3.** *Com:* (*sell*) **to d. of goods, of an article,** écouler des marchandises; vendre, placer, un article; **to d. of one's business, of a lease,** céder son fonds, un bail; **to be disposed of,** à vendre, à céder; **goods easily disposed of,** marchandises *f* d'un écoulement facile, de vente facile; **article difficult to d. of,** article *m* difficile à écouler, à placer. **4.** disposer, incliner, porter **(s.o. to sth., to do sth.,** qn à qch., à faire qch.); **I am not (really) disposed to help him,** je ne suis pas disposé, prêt, à l'aider; **I am disposed to believe that . . .,** j'incline à croire que . . .. **5.** *Lit:* **to d. oneself to sleep, to meditation,** se disposer à dormir, à la méditation.

disposed [dis'pouzd], *a.* **1.** intentionné, disposé; **well, ill, d. to s.o., towards s.o.,** bien, mal, intentionné envers, pour, qn, à l'égard de qn; **so long as the army is well d.,** tant que l'armée a un bon esprit; **to be friendly d.,** être d'humeur affable; **if you feel so d.,** si le cœur vous en dit. **2. d. to sth.,** enclin, porté, à qch.; **to be d. to pity,** incliner à la pitié.

disposer [dis'pouzər], *s.* **1.** dispensateur, -trice, ordonnateur, -trice, arbitre *m* (des choses humaines, etc.). **2.** dispensateur, -trice (de bienfaits, etc.); **this minister, sovereign d. of royal favours,** ce ministre, souverain dispensateur des faveurs royales. **3.** *Jur:* vendeur, -euse.

disposition [dispə'ziʃ(ə)n], *s.* **1.** (*a*) disposition *f,* groupement *m,* arrangement *m*; agencement *m* (d'une maison, des mots dans une phrase, etc.); *Mil:* assiette *f* (d'un cantonnement, d'un camp); dispositif *m* (des troupes); **disposition(s) for battle,** dispositif de combat; (*b*) *Lit:* (*usu. pl.*) **to take one's dispositions to withstand an attack,** prendre des dispositions pour résister à une attaque; **God has the supreme d. of all things,** Dieu dispose de tout en dernier arbitre; (*c*) *Jur:* disposition (testamentaire). **2.** = DISPOSAL 1(*c*). **3.** caractère *m,* naturel *m,* nature *f,* complexion *f,* humeur *f,* aptitude *f*; **child of a pleasant d.,** enfant *mf* d'un bon naturel; **he is of a kindly d.,** c'est une bonne nature. **4.** (*a*) **d. to do sth.,** désir *m,* intention *f,* de faire qch.; inclination *f* à faire qch.; (*b*) penchant *m,* tendance *f* **(to sth., to do sth.,** à qch., à faire qch.); **to have a natural d. to catch cold,** avoir une prédisposition à s'enrhumer.

dispossess [dispə'zes], *v.tr.* **1.** (*a*) déposséder (qn); (*b*) exproprier (qn); **to d. s.o. of sth.,** déposséder, *Jur:* dessaisir, qn de qch. **2.** *A:* **to d. s.o., (of an evil spirit),** délivrer qn d'un démon.

dispossession [dispə'zeʃ(ə)n], *s.* (*a*) dépossession *f*; *Jur:* dessaisissement *m*; (*b*) expropriation *f.*

dispossessor [dispə'zesər], *s.* expropriateur, -trice.

disproportion [disprə'pɔ:ʃ(ə)n], *s.* disproportion *f,* défaut *m* de proportion **(between,** entre); **d. in age,** disconvenance *f* d'âge **(between . . . and . . .,** entre . . . et . . .).

disproportionally [disprə'pɔːʃən(ə)li], *adv.* disproportionnellement.
disproportionate [disprə'pɔːʃənət], *a.* disproportionné (**to,** à), hors de proportion (**to,** avec).
disproportionately [disprə'pɔːʃənətli], *adv.* d'une façon disproportionnée; hors de toute proportion (**to,** avec).
disproportioned [disprə'pɔːʃ(ə)nd], *a.* disproportionné, mal proportionné (**to,** à); hors de toute proportion (**to,** avec).
disprove [dis'pruːv], *v.tr.* (*p.p.* **disproved,** *Jur:* **disproven** [dis'prouvn]) réfuter (un dire); démontrer la fausseté (d'un dire).
disputable [dis'pjuːtəbl], *a.* contestable, controversable, disputable, douteux.
disputably [dis'pjuːtəbli], *adv.* contestablement; douteusement.
disputant [dis'pjuːtənt], *s.* discuteur, -euse; controversiste *mf.*
disputation [dispju'teiʃ(ə)n], *s.* (*a*) discussion *f* (d'un sujet, etc.); (*b*) discussion, controverse *f*, débat *m*; *Sch: A:* disputation *f.*
disputatious [dispju'teiʃəs], *a.* disputeur, -euse; chicanier, -ière; *F:* disputailleur, -euse.
dispute[1] ['dispjut, dis'pjuːt], *s.* **1.** contestation *f*, discussion *f*, controverse *f*, débat *m*; **the matter in d.,** (i) l'affaire contestée, en contestation; (ii) l'affaire dont il s'agit; **beyond, past, d.,** incontestable, indiscutable; hors de dispute, hors de contestation, hors de controverse; **the fact is beyond d.,** le fait ne souffre pas de discussion; **without d.,** sans contredit; *Jur:* **d. at law,** litige *m*; **case under d.,** cas *m* en litige; **to settle a d.,** trancher, vider, un débat ou un litige. **2.** querelle *f*, dispute *f*, altercation *f*, différend *m*, conflit *m* (**as to,** relatif, -ive, à); **to settle a d.,** régler une querelle; **industrial d.,** conflit *m* du travail.
dispute[2] [dis'pjuːt]. **1.** *v.i.* (*a*) *A:* **to d. with, against, s.o. about, on, sth.,** (i) débattre qch. avec qn; (ii) se disputer avec qn sur, au sujet de, qch.; (*b*) se disputer, se quereller. **2.** *v.tr.* (*a*) débattre, discuter (une question); controverser (un point de doctrine, etc.); contester (une affirmation, etc.); (*b*) **to d. (the possession of) sth. with s.o.,** disputer qch. à qn; **to d. every inch of the ground,** disputer le terrain; **I don't d. that he did it,** je ne conteste pas qu'il l'ait fait.
disputer [dis'pjuːtər], *s.* **1.** disputeur, -euse; discuteur, -euse; controversiste *mf.* **2.** contestant, -ante (**of,** pour).
disqualification [diskwɔlifi'keiʃ(ə)n], *s.* **1.** (*a*) incapacité *f*; *Jur:* inhabilité *f* (**to act,** à agir); (*b*) **d. of a director,** déchéance *f* d'un administrateur. **2.** cause *f* d'incapacité (**for,** à). **3.** (*a*) mise *f* en état d'incapacité; **why should a degree be a d. for business?** pourquoi un diplôme vous rendrait il inapte aux affaires? (*b*) *Sp:* diqualification *f*; exclusion *f* (d'un concours); *Rac:* distancement *m* (du gagnant).
disqualify [dis'kwɔlifai], *v.tr.* **1.** rendre incapable (**for sth.,** de faire qch.); **his timidity disqualified him for a profession,** sa timidité le rendait incapable d'exercer une profession, le mettait dans l'incapacité d'exercer une profession. **2.** (*a*) *Jur:* frapper (qn) d'incapacité; **disqualified from making a will,** incapable de tester, inhabile à tester; (*b*) **to be disqualified from a competition,** être exclus d'un concours; (*c*) **to d. s.o. from driving,** retirer le permis de conduire à qn. **3.** *Sp:* disqualifier (un joueur); *Rac:* distancer (le gagnant).
disqualifying[1] [dis'kwɔlifaiiŋ], *a.* **1.** (*a*) qui rend incapable, inhabile (à tester, etc.); (*b*) qui entraîne l'exclusion. **2.** *Box:* (coup) disqualificatif.
disqualifying[2], *s.* = DISQUALIFICATION 1 (*b*), 3 (*b*).
disquiet[1] [dis'kwaiət]. **1.** *a. A:* inquiet; agité. **2.** *s. Lit:* inquiétude *f.*
disquiet[2], **disquieten** [dis'kwaiət(ə)n], *v.tr.* inquiéter; troubler; **disquietened, disquieted, by apprehensions,** tourmenté, agité, par des appréhensions.
disquieting [dis'kwaiətiŋ], *a.* inquiétant, peu rassurant; troublant.
disquietingly [dis'kwaiətiŋli], *adv.* **d. high percentage of errors,** pourcentage de fautes inquiétant.
disquietude [dis'kwaiətjud], *s.* **1.** inquiétude *f*, anxiété *f.* **2.** *A:* manque *m* de calme; agitation *f*, malaise *m* (parmi le peuple, etc.).
disquisition [diskwi'ziʃ(ə)n], *s.* **1.** *A:* recherches *fpl*, étude *f*, examen *m*, enquête *f.* **2.** dissertation *f* (**on,** sur); **he made a long d. about it,** il a fait un long discours là-dessus.
disrate [dis'reit], *v.tr. Navy:* déclasser (un homme); réduire (un gradé) à un grade inférieur; rétrograder (un gradé).
disrating [dis'reitiŋ], *s. Navy:* déclassement *m*; réduction *f* (à un grade inférieur); rétrogradation *f.*
disregard[1] [disri'gɑːd], *s.* indifférence *f*, insouciance *f*, négligence *f* (**of, for,** à l'égard de); irrespect *m*; dédain *m* (pour); **d. of a rule,** désobéissance *f* à une règle; **d. of the law,** inobservation *f* de la loi; **d. for one's parents,** manque *m* d'égards envers ses parents.
disregard[2], *v.tr.* faire peu de cas de, ne tenir aucun compte de, ne pas faire attention à (qn, qch.); négliger (qn, qch.); méconnaitre (un devoir); ne pas s'inquiéter de, faire abstraction de (qch.); **to d. an objection,** passer outre à une objection; **to d. an order,** enfreindre un ordre; *Mil:* manquer à la consigne; forcer la consigne; **disregarding details,** abstraction faite des détails.
disremember [disri'membər], *v.tr. U.S: F:* oublier.
disrepair [disri'pɛər], *s.* (*no pl.*) délabrement *m* (d'une maison, etc.); **to fall into d.,** tomber en mauvais état; se délabrer, se dégrader; **walls in d.,** murs dégradés, croulants.
disreputable [dis'repjutəbl], *a.* **1.** (*of action*) déshonorant; peu honorable; honteux. **2.** (*a*) (*of pers.*) de mauvaise réputation; taré, perdu d'honneur; (*b*) **d. neighbourhood,** quartier (i) sordide, d'aspect minable, (ii) mal famé, louche, borgne. **3.** (*of garments, etc.*) minable, lamentable; **he was wearing a d. old hat,** il portait un vieux chapeau digne d'un chiffonnier.
disreputableness [dis'repjutəblnis], *s.* **1.** mauvaise réputation (de qn, d'un lieu). **2.** aspect *m* sordide.
disreputably [dis'repjutəbli], *adv.* **1.** honteusement; d'une façon peu honorable. **2. d. dressed,** habillé d'une façon lamentable.
disrepute [disri'pjuːt], *s.* discrédit *m*, déshonneur *m*, déconsidération *f*; mauvaise réputation; **to bring s.o., sth., into d.,** perdre qn de réputation; ruiner la réputation de qn; discréditer qch.; faire tomber qn dans le discrédit; **to fall into d.,** tomber dans le mépris, dans l'inconsidération, dans le décri; **to bring the law into d.,** discréditer la loi.
disrespect [disri'spekt], *s.* irrévérence *f*, irrespect *m*; manque *m* d'égards, de respect (**for,** envers); **to treat s.o., sth., with d.,** manquer de respect à qn, pour qch.; **d. to the flag,** insulte *f* au drapeau.
disrespectful [disri'spektful], *a.* irrespectueux, irrévérencieux, **to be d. to s.o.,** manquer de respect à qn.
disrespectfully [disri'spektfuli], *adv.* irrespectueusement, irrévérencieusement; **to speak d. of s.o.,** parler de qn sans respect.
disrobe [dis'roub]. **1.** *v.tr.* dévêtir, déshabiller (qn); dépouiller (qn) de ses vêtements; *esp.* aider (un magistrat, un prêtre) à se dévêtir de sa robe. **2.** *v.i.* se dévêtir, se déshabiller; *esp.* (*of judge, clergyman, etc.*) se dévêtir de sa robe.
disrupt [dis'rʌpt], *v.tr.* **1.** faire éclater (la pierre, etc.); rompre, briser; **ground disrupted by an earthquake,** terrain disloqué par un tremblement de terre. **2.** démembrer (un empire); faire crouler (un édifice), désorganiser (une administration, etc.); rompre (une coalition, l'unité nationale); **train services are often disrupted,** les relations ferroviaires sont souvent interrompues; **to d. our plans,** ruiner nos plans, nos projets; **to d. a public meeting,** interrompre avec fracas une séance publique.
disrupter [dis'rʌptər], *s.* = DISRUPTOR.
disruption [dis'rʌpʃ(ə)n], *s.* **1.** rupture *f*, éclatement *m*; dislocation (violente); **the accident caused a d. of the train service between London and Edinburgh,** l'accident a causé une interruption des relations ferroviaires entre Londres et Édimbourg. **2.** démembrement *m* (d'un empire). **3.** *Hist:* **the D.,** la scission qui eut lieu dans l'Église d'Écosse en 1843 (et qui eut pour résultat la création de l'Église libre).
disruptive [dis'rʌptiv], *a.* (*a*) disruptif; **d. explosives, s. disruptives,** explosifs brisants; *Mec:* **d. strength,** résistance disruptive; résistance à la perforation; (*b*) (argument, etc.) fallacieux; **he is a d. influence in the class,** il a une influence néfaste dans la classe.
disruptor [dis'rʌptər], *s. El: I.C.E:* disrupteur *m* (d'allumage); amplificateur *m* d'étincelles.
dissatisfaction [disætis'fækʃ(ə)n], *s.* dissatisfaction *f*, insatisfaction *f*, mécontentement *m* (**with,** de).
dissatisfactory [disætis'fækt(ə)ri], *a.* peu satisfaisant; qui laisse à désirer.
dissatisfied [di'sætisfaid], *a.* mécontent, insatisfait, mal satisfait (**with, at,** de).
dissatisfy [di'sætisfai], *v.tr.* dissatisfaire; mécontenter; ne pas satisfaire.
dissect [di'sekt], *v.tr.* **1.** disséquer (une plante, un cadavre; un compte, un ouvrage littéraire, etc.). **2.** découper. **3.** *Surg:* **to d. out,** exciser (une tumeur, etc.).
dissecting [di'sektiŋ], *s.* **1.** dissection *f.* **2.** (*a*) *Surg:* **d. out,** excision *f*; (*b*) *a. Med:* **d. aneurism,** anévrisme disséquant.
dissection [di'sekʃ(ə)n], *s.* **1.** dissection *f.* **2.** (*a*) découpage *m*; *Geol:* articulation *f*; (*b*) découpures *fpl.* **3.** *T.V:* **vertical d.,** exploration *f* par lignes verticales.
dissector [di'sektər], *s.* **1.** (*pers.*) dissecteur *m*, disséqueur *m.* **2.** *Tls:* scalpel *m.*
disseise, disseize [dis'siːz], *v.tr. Jur:* déposséder; **to d. s.o. of an estate,** déposséder, dessaisir, qn d'une terre; évincer qn.
disseisee, disseizee [dissiː'ziː], *s. Jur:* personne évincée, dépossédée.
disseisin, disseizin [dis'siːzin], *s. Jur:* dépossession (illégale); dessaisissement *m*; éviction *f.*
dissemble [di'sembl], *v.tr.* dissimuler, cacher, déguiser (ses sentiments, etc.); passer (un fait) sous silence; *v.i.* user de dissimulation; déguiser sa pensée; **dissembled thought,** arrière-pensée *f*, *pl.* arrière-pensées; **it is useless to attempt to d. the fact that . . .,** il serait vain de vouloir se dissimuler que . . . .
dissembler [di'semblər], *s.* dissimulateur, -trice; hypocrite *mf.*
dissembling [di'sembliŋ], *s.* dissimulation *f.*
disseminate [di'semineit], *v.tr.* disséminer, semer (le grain); propager, répandre, disséminer (des opinions, etc.).
dissemination [disemi'neiʃ(ə)n], *s.* dissémination *f*; propagation *f* (de la vérité, de l'Évangile, etc.); diffusion *f* (des connaissances techniques).
disseminator [di'semineitər], *s.* disséminateur, -trice, propagateur, -trice (d'idées nouvelles, etc.); semeur, -euse (de faux bruits).
dissension [di'senʃ(ə)n], *s.* dissension *f*; **to sow d.,** semer la dissension, le désaccord; **dissensions within the Church,** dissensions dans le sein de l'Église.
dissent[1] [di'sent], *s.* **1.** dissentiment *m*; avis *m* contraire. **2.** *Ecc:* (*a*) dissidence *f*; (*b*) *coll.* les dissidents *m.*
dissent[2], *v.i.* **1.** différer (**from s.o. about sth.,** de qn sur qch.); **to d. from s.o.'s opinion,** différer d'opinion avec qn; ne pas être du même avis que qn. **2.** *Ecc:* être dissident.
dissenter [di'sentər], *s.* dissident, -ente; *esp. Ecc:* personne qui n'appartient pas à l'Église anglicane; personne opposée en principe à une Église d'État.
dissentient [di'senʃjənt]. **1.** *a.* dissident; opposé (**from,** à); **there was not one d. voice,** pas une voix ne s'éleva contre; **passed without a d. voice,** voté à l'unanimité des voix, sans soulever la moindre objection; **with one d. vote,** à l'unanimité moins une voix. **2.** *s.* dissident, -ente; opposant, -ante (**from,** de).
dissenting [di'sentiŋ], *a.* dissident.
dissepiment [di'sepimənt], *s. Anat: Bot:* cloison *f*, septum *m*; dissépiment *m* (d'un polypier).
dissert [di'səːt], **dissertate** ['disəteit], *v.i. Lit:* disserter (**on,** sur).
dissertation [disə'teiʃ(ə)n], *s.* dissertation *f*; discours *m*, mémoire *m.*
disservice [di'səːvis], *s.* mauvais service rendu; **to do s.o. a d.,** desservir, messervir, qn; mal servir les intérêts de qn; rendre un mauvais service à qn.
dissidence ['disid(ə)ns], *s.* dissidence *f*; divergence *f* d'opinions; désaccord *m.*
dissident ['disid(ə)nt], *a. & s.* (*a*) dissident, -ente; (*b*) membre dissident (d'un parti); *Hist:* **the Polish Dissidents,** les dissidents de Pologne.
dissimilar [di'similər], *a.* dissemblable (**to,** à, de); différent (**to,** de).
dissimilarity [disimi'læriti], *s.* dissemblance *f*, dissimilarité *f*, dissimilitude *f* (**to,** de; **between,** entre).
dissimilate [di'simileit], *v.tr. Ling:* dissimiler (deux sons identiques).
dissimilation [disimi'leiʃ(ə)n], *s.* **1.** *Ling:* dissimilation *f.* **2.** *Biol:* catabolisme *m.*
dissimile [di'simili], *s. Rh:* dissimilitude *f.*
dissimilitude [disi'militjuːd]. *s.* dissimilitude *f*, diversité *f*, dissemblance *f.*
dissimulate [di'simjuleit], (*a*) *v.tr.* dissimuler; cacher (un fait); (*b*) *v.i.* dissimuler, feindre, cacher ses pensées.
dissimulation [disimju'leiʃ(ə)n], *s.* dissimulation *f.*
dissimulator [di'simjuleitər], *s.* dissimulateur, -trice.
dissipate ['disipeit]. **1.** *v.tr.* dissiper (les nuages, une fortune, etc.); gaspiller (une fortune); **to d. one's efforts,** disperser ses efforts. **2.** *v.i.* (*of cloud, heat, etc.*) se dissiper; *Ph:* (*of energy*) se dégrader; *Geog:* (*of drainage*) **dissipating area,** champ *m*, zone *f*, d'épandage.
dissipated ['disipeitid], *a.* dissipé; **to live a d. life,** mener une vie dissipée; vivre dans la dissipation; **to be d.,** se dissiper; s'adonner au plaisir.
dissipation [disi'peiʃ(ə)n], *s.* **1.** (*a*) dissipation *f* (du brouillard, de la chaleur, de ses biens); gaspillage *m* (d'une fortune); (*b*) dispersion *f* (de la chaleur, de l'électricité); *Ph:* dégradation *f* (de l'énergie); (*c*) **d. of**

mind, distraction *f.* 2. (*a*) divertissement *m*; **to allow oneself a little d.,** se permettre un peu de distraction; (*b*) dissipation, vie désordonnée.
dissipative ['disipeitiv], *a.* dispersif.
dissipator ['disipeitər], *s.* dissipateur, -trice (de son bien); *Ind: etc:* **heat d.,** évacuateur *m* de chaleur.
dissociability [disouʃə'biliti], *s.* dissociabilité *f.*
dissociable [di'souʃiəbl], *a. Ch: etc:* dissociable, séparable (**from,** de).
dissociate [di'sousieit]. 1. *v.tr.* (*a*) désassocier, dissocier (des personnes) (**from,** de); **to d. oneself from a question,** se désintéresser d'une affaire; (*b*) *Ch:* dissocier (un composé, etc.). 2. *v.i. Ch:* se dissocier.
dissociated [di'sousieitid], *a. Psy:* **d. personality,** personnalité simultanée; dédoublement *m* de personnalité.
dissociation [disousi'eiʃ(ə)n], *s.* 1. désassociation *f*, dissociation *f.* 2. *Ch:* dissociation; **coefficient of d.,** constante *f* de dissociation, d'affinité. 3. *Psy:* dédoublement *m* de la personnalité.
dissociative [di'sousieitiv], *a. Psy:* dissociatif.
dissolubility [disɔlju'biliti], *s. Ph: etc:* dissolubilité *f.*
dissoluble [di'sɔljubl], *a.* 1. *Ph: etc:* dissoluble (**in,** dans). 2. (mariage *m*, etc.) dissoluble.
dissolute ['disəljut], *a.* dissolu, débauché; **d. conduct,** conduite licencieuse; déportements *mpl*; **d. life,** vie désordonnée, déréglée; **to lead a d. life,** vivre dans la dissolution, dans la débauche, dans le dérèglement.
dissolutely ['disəljutli], *adv.* dissolument, licencieusement; (vivre) dans la débauche.
dissoluteness ['disəljutnis], *s.* dérèglement *m*, débauche *f.*
dissolution [disə'lju:ʃ(ə)n], *s.* 1. dissolution *f*, fonte *f*, liquéfaction *f.* 2. dissolution (d'une société, d'une assemblée, d'un mariage); **the signs of his approaching d.,** les signes *m* de sa dissolution prochaine, de sa mort prochaine; *Hist:* **the d. of the monasteries,** la suppression des monastères.
dissolvable [di'zɔlvəbl], *a.* 1. (assemblée *f*, etc.) dissoluble, dont on peut prononcer la dissolution; (association commerciale) terminable. 2. *A:* (substance *f*) dissoluble, liquéfiable.
dissolve[1] [di'zɔlv], *s. Cin:* fondu *m*; **d. in, out,** ouverture *f*, fermeture *f*, en fondu.
dissolve[2]. 1. *v.tr.* (*a*) dissoudre, faire dissoudre, faire fondre (qch.); déprendre (une substance coagulée); **dissolved in tears,** tout en larmes; (*b*) dissiper (un nuage); dissoudre, dissiper (une illusion); (*c*) dissoudre, disperser (une société, le parlement); dissoudre (un mariage); (*d*) *Cin:* **to d. a scene into the succeeding one,** fondre une scène dans la suivante. 2. *v.i.* (*a*) se dissoudre; fondre; **to d. into tears,** fondre en larmes; (*b*) se dissiper; (*of crowd*) se disperser, se séparer; **to d. into thin air,** partir, s'en aller, en fumée; (*c*) (*of Parliament*) se dissoudre.
dissolvent [di'zɔlvənt]. 1. *a. A:* dissolvant. 2. *s. Ph: etc:* dissolvant *m.*
dissolver [di'zɔlvər], *s.* 1. *Cin:* écran *m*, obturateur *m*, à bords dentelés (pour vues fondantes). 2. = DISSOLVENT 2.
dissolving [di'zɔlviŋ], *a.* 1. **d. views,** (i) *A:* tableaux fondants, (ii) *Cin:* vues fondantes; fondus *m.* 2. *Ch:* **d. agents,** solvants *m.*
dissonance ['disənəns], *s.* 1. *Mus:* dissonance *f.* 2. désaccord *m* (**between,** entre).
dissonant ['disənənt], *a.* 1. *Mus:* dissonant. 2. en désaccord (**from, to,** avec).
dissuade [di'sweid], *v.tr.* **to d. s.o. from sth., from doing sth.,** dissuader qn de qch., de faire qch.; déconseiller qch. à qn.
dissuasion [di'sweiʒ(ə)n], *s.* dissuasion *f* (**from,** de); **no d. could keep him from attempting the journey,** c'est en vain que l'on a essayé de le dissuader d'entreprendre ce voyage.
dissuasive [di'sweisiv], *a.* dissuasif; (air, ton) peu encourageant.
dissyllabic [disi'læbik], *a.* dissyllabique.
dissyllable [di'siləbl], *s.* dissyllabe *m.*
dissymmetrical [disi'metrikl], *a.* dissymétrique, asymétrique.
dissymmetry [di'simitri], *s.* dissymétrie *f*, asymétrie *f.*
distaff ['distɑ:f], *s.* quenouille *f*; **the d. side (of a family),** le côté maternel (d'une famille); **kingdom that falls to the d. side,** royaume *m* qui tombe en quenouille.
distal ['distəl], *a. Anat:* distal, -aux.
distance[1] ['distəns], *s.* 1. (*a*) distance *f*; éloignement *m*; **at a d. of 10 kilometres,** à une distance de 10 kilomètres; **it is within walking d.,** on peut s'y rendre, y aller, à pied; **within five minutes walking d.,** à cinq minutes de marche; **within speaking d.,** à portée de voix; **a short d., no d., away,** tout près; à deux pas; **to see sth. from a d.,** voir qch. de loin; **you can see nothing at that d.,** on ne peut rien voir à cette distance; **d. lends enchantment to the view,** (vu) de loin tout paraît beau; **to come from a d.,** venir de loin; **d. judging,** appréciation *f* des distances; *Mil:* **assaulting d.,** distance d'assaut; **within striking d.,** à portée des coups de fusil, de canon, etc.; à portée de l'ennemi; tout près de qch.; *Av:* **take-off d.,** parcours *m* de, au, décollage; **d. measuring equipment,** appareillage *m* de mesure de la distance; *Elcs: etc:* **d. control,** commande *f* à distance; (*b*) lointain *m*; *Art:* **the distances,** les lointains; **to see sth. in the d.,** voir qch. au loin, de loin, dans le lointain; **in the middle d.,** au second plan; à mi-distance; (*c*) **at this d. of time,** à cet intervalle de temps; après si longtemps. 2. (*a*) distance (entre deux endroits, *Mth:* deux points); **to go part of the d. on foot,** faire une partie du trajet à pied; (*b*) distance, intervalle (qui sépare deux personnes, deux choses); **to keep at a safe d. from s.o., from sth.,** se tenir à une distance respectueuse de qn, de qch.; **to keep s.o. at a d.,** tenir qn à distance; **I prefer him at a d.,** j'aime mieux qu'il soit loin; *Const: etc:* **d. block, piece,** entretoise *f*, entretoisement *m*; pièce *f* d'écartement; (*c*) *Sp:* (i) parcours; **to run the d. in record time,** établir un record pour le parcours; **long-d., medium-d., race,** course *f* de (grand) fond, de demi-fond; (ii) *Turf: U.S:* **the d.,** distance éliminatoire (dans une course d'élimination); *Fig:* **to go, last, stay, the d.,** tenir jusqu'au bout. 3. réserve *f*; air distant; **to keep one's d., to keep at a d.,** avoir un air distant; se tenir sur la réserve, sur son quant-à-soi.
distance[2], *v.tr.* 1. *A: & Lit:* (*a*) éloigner (**from,** de); (*b*) reculer, faire paraître éloigné. 2. distancer, dépasser (un concurrent, etc.).
distanced [distənst], *a. Turf: U.S:* (cheval) éliminé (dans une course d'élimination).
distant ['distənt], *a.* 1. *O:* **three miles d.,** distant de trois milles; à trois milles de distance; **not far d. from . . .,** à peu de distance de . . .. 2. (*a*) (endroit, objet, parent) éloigné; (pays) lointain; **to have a d. view of sth.,** voir qch. de loin; *Rail:* **d. signal,** signal à distance; signal avancé; *Elcs: etc:* **d. control,** commande *f* à distance; télécommande *f*; **d. allusion,** allusion indirecte; **d. look,** regard perdu dans le vague; **d. likeness,** faible, vague, ressemblance *f*; (*b*) (*in time*) éloigné, reculé; **d. age,** époque éloignée, reculée; **d. recollection,** souvenir lointain; **that day is still far d.,** ce jour est encore loin; **in the d. future,** dans un avenir lointain, reculé. 3. (*of pers., manner*) réservé, froid, hautain, distant; **to be d. with s.o.,** tenir qn à distance; se montrer réservé avec qn; **to treat s.o. in a markedly d. manner,** traiter qn avec un éloignement marqué.
distantly ['distəntli], *adv.* 1. de loin; **d. related,** d'une parenté éloignée. 2. avec hauteur, avec réserve, avec froideur; froidement; **d. polite,** d'une politesse hautaine.
distaste [dis'teist], *s.* dégoût *m* (**for,** de); aversion *f*, répugnance *f* (**for,** pour); **to conceive a d. for sth.,** prendre qch. en dégoût, en aversion; **he felt a d. for life,** il ressentait un dégoût de la vie.
distasteful [dis'teistful], *a.* 1. (*of food, etc.*) désagréable au goût. 2. désagréable, déplaisant, antipathique (**to,** à); **to be d. to s.o.,** répugner à qn; **it is d. to me to . . .,** cela me déplaît de . . .; **however d. it may be (to me),** quel que soit le dégoût que j'éprouve, malgré ma répugnance.
distastefulness [dis'teistfulnis], *s.* caractère désagréable, répugnant (d'une tâche, etc.).
distemper[1] [dis'tempər], *s.* 1. (*a*) *A:* maladie *f* (du corps ou de l'esprit); (*b*) *Vet:* maladie des chiens, maladie du jeune âge. 2. *A:* désordre *m* (dans l'État).
distemper[2], *v.tr. A:* rendre (qn) malade; déranger, troubler (l'esprit); **distempered mind,** esprit dérangé, troublé.
distemper[3], *s.* 1. *Art:* détrempe *f*; peinture *f* à la colle; **to paint in d.,** peindre en détrempe. 2. (*for house decoration*) détrempe, badigeon *m.*
distemper[4], *v.tr.* 1. *Art:* peindre (un tableau) en détrempe. 2. peindre (un mur) en détrempe; badigeonner (un mur) en couleur.
distempering [dis'temp(ə)riŋ], *s.* 1. peinture *f* en détrempe. 2. badigeonnage *m* en couleur.
distend [dis'tend]. 1. *v.tr.* (*a*) dilater, gonfler (un ballon); enfler, gonfler (les joues); dilater (les narines); (*b*) distendre, dilater, ballonner (l'estomac); *Vet:* météoriser (l'estomac). 2. *v.i.* (*a*) se dilater, enfler, se gonfler; (*b*) (*of stomach*) se ballonner, se distendre.
distended [dis'tendid], *a.* (*a*) dilaté, gonflé; (*b*) (estomac) ballonnant, ballonné, tendu.
distensible [dis'tensibl], *a.* dilatable.
distension [dis'tenʃ(ə)n], *s.* (*a*) dilatation *f*, distension *f*, gonflement *m*; (*b*) *Med:* ballonnement *m*, distension, dilatation, météorisation *f* (de l'estomac).
disthene ['disθi:n], *s. Miner:* disthène *m.*
distich ['distik], *s. Pros:* distique *m.*
distichous ['distikəs], *a. Bot:* distique.
distil [dis'til], *v.* (**distilled**) 1. *v.tr.* (*a*) *Ch: Ind:* distiller (de l'eau, du vin, des grains); brûler (le vin); raffiner (le pétrole); **to d. sth. from sth.,** extraire qch. de qch. par distillation; **to d. sth. into sth.,** changer qch. en qch. par la distillation; **to d. sth. off, out,** chasser qch. par la distillation; **they d. their own brandy,** ils brûlent leur vin; (*b*) laisser tomber goutte à goutte; (*of tree, etc.*) distiller (du suc); **to d. poison into s.o.'s mind,** faire couler du poison dans l'âme de qn. 2. *v.i.* (*a*) *Ch: Ind:* **to d. (over),** se distiller, passer; (*b*) (*of liquid, secretion, etc.*) distiller, tomber goutte à goutte, couler doucement (**from,** de).
distillable [dis'tiləbl], *a.* distillable.
distillage [dis'tilidʒ], *s. Ch: Ind:* distillat *m.*
distillate ['distileit], *s. Ch: Ind:* (produit *m* de) distillation *f*; distillat *m.*
distillation [disti'leiʃ(ə)n], *s.* 1. distillation *f*; **fractional d.,** distillation fractionnée; **dry d.,** distillation sèche; **batch d.,** distillation discontinue; **coal d.,** gazéification *f* du charbon. 2. (produit *m* de) distillation.
distillatory [dis'tilətəri], *a.* distillatoire.
distiller [dis'tilər], *s.* 1. (*pers.*) *Ind:* distillateur *m.* 2. *Nau:* appareil *m* distillatoire; distillateur; bouilleur *m.*
distillery [dis'tiləri], *s. Ind:* distillerie *f*; **oil d.,** raffinerie *f* de pétrole.
distilling [dis'tiliŋ], *s.* distillation *f*; **d. of oil,** raffinage *m* du pétrole; **d. apparatus,** appareil *m* de distillation; *Nau:* **d. condenser** = DISTILLER 2.
distinct [dis'tiŋ(k)t], *a.* 1. (*different*) distinct, différent (**from,** de); **to keep two things d.,** distinguer entre deux choses; **town life as d. from country life,** la vie des grandes villes, à la différence de celle de la campagne; **man as d. from animals,** l'homme en tant qu'il diffère des animaux. 2. (*clear*) distinct, net, *f.* nette, clair; (dessin, etc.) tranché; **d. refusal,** refu net; **d. recollection,** souvenir clair, net, précis; **d. utterance,** débit clair, bien articulé; **d. idea,** idée nette, distincte, précise; **d. orders,** ordres formels, précis; **d. promise,** promesse formelle; **in d. terms,** en termes précis; **the coast becomes more and more d.,** la côte se précise. 3. caractérisé, marqué; **d. preference, inclination,** préférence, inclination, marquée.
distinction [dis'tiŋ(k)ʃ(ə)n], *s.* 1. (*difference*) distinction *f* (**between,** entre); **to make a d. between two things,** faire une distinction entre deux choses; **that is making a d. without a difference,** c'est couper un cheveu en quatre; **without d. (of persons),** sans distinction de personnes; **without d. of rank, of age,** sans distinction de rang, d'âge; **class d.,** distinction des classes. 2. (*honour conferred*) **academic distinctions,** distinctions académiques. 3. (*a*) (*excellence*) distinction; **to gain d.,** se distinguer; **man of d.,** homme distingué, de marque, de distinction; *Sch:* **with d.,** avec mention; (*b*) **the book has d.,** ce livre a de la personnalité; **the lack of any d. in his dress,** le manque de distinction de sa toilette.
distinctive [dis'tiŋ(k)tiv], *a.* distinctif.
distinctively [dis'tiŋ(k)tivli], *adv.* distinctivement.
distinctiveness [dis'tiŋ(k)tivnis], *s.* caractère particulier, distinctif (**of,** de).
distinctly [dis'tiŋ(k)tli], *adv.* 1. (*a*) (parler, entendre, voir) distinctement, clairement; (*b*) **I told him d.,** je le lui ai dit expressément; **to promise d.,** promettre formellement. 2. (*unmistakably*) indéniablement, décidément, incontestablement; **a d. revolutionary paper,** un journal nettement révolutionnaire; **he is d. better,** il y a un mieux indéniable, sensible; **let it be d. understood that . . .,** il est bien entendu que . . ..
distinctness [dis'tiŋ(k)tnis], *s.* clarté *f*, netteté *f.*
distinguish [dis'tiŋgwiʃ]. 1. *v.tr.* (*a*) distinguer, discerner, démêler (un objet, un son); **I could not d. him among the crowd,** je n'ai pu le distinguer, le reconnaître, l'apercevoir, parmi la foule; (*b*) distinguer, différencier (**from,** de); **reason distinguishes man from the other animals,** la raison distingue, sépare, l'homme des autres animaux; **man is distinguished from the other animals by the gift of speech,** l'homme se distingue des autres animaux par le don de la parole; **distinguishing mark,** signe distinctif; **flowers may be distinguished by their scent,** on peut distinguer les fleurs à leur parfum; (*c*) **to d. oneself by . . .,** se distinguer, se signaler, se faire remarquer, par . . .; **he will d. himself,** il ira loin; *Iron:* **you** *have* **distinguished yourself!** ça c'est bien beau! 2. *v.i.* **to d. between two things,** distinguer entre, faire une distinction entre, deux choses; **to d. between people,** faire la distinction des personnes.

distinguishable [dis'tiŋgwiʃəbl], *a.* **1.** que l'on peut distinguer (**from,** de); **he is d. from his twin brother by the colour of his eyes,** il se distingue de son jumeau par la couleur de ses yeux. **2.** distinguable; reconnaissable; **hardly d. sound,** son *m* à peine saisissable, à peine perceptible; **the coast was hardly d. through the haze,** c'est à peine si l'on distinguait la côte à travers la brume.

distinguished [dis'tiŋgwiʃt], *a.* **1.** distingué; qui s'est distingué; **d. writer,** écrivain *m* de distinction; **d. people,** (i) personnages *mpl* de marque; (ii) gens distingués; **he is d. for his strength,** il est remarquable par sa force. **2. to look d.,** avoir l'air distingué; avoir bon air.

distinguo [dis'tiŋgwou], *s.* distinguo *m,* distinction *f.*

distome ['distoum], *s. Z: Vet:* distome *m.*

distomian [dis'toumiən], *s. Z:* (*a*) distome *m;* (*b*) (*order*) **Distomians,** distomiens *m.*

distort [dis'tɔ:t]. **1.** *v.tr.* (*a*) tordre, contourner (qch.); décomposer, déformer, défigurer (les traits, le visage); distordre (les membres); *Tchn:* déformer (le champ électrique, le champ visuel, la réception radiophonique, etc.); dévier la direction (du champ magnétique); fausser, déjeter (une tige, une surface); (*b*) altérer, fausser, déformer, défigurer (la vérité); fausser, dénaturer (les faits, des paroles); altérer (un texte); **to d. the meaning of a text,** dénaturer un texte; faire une entorse au sens d'un texte. **2.** *v.i.* se déformer, se fausser, se déjeter; gauchir.

distorted [dis'tɔ:tid], *a.* tordu, contourné, tourmenté; **face d. by rage,** visage convulsé par la fureur; **d. limbs,** membres tors, distors, tordus; **d. ideas,** idées biscornues; *Geol:* **d. seam,** couche tourmentée; *Phot:* **d. image,** image déformée; *Ac:* **d. sound,** son déformé; *El:* **d. field,** champ tors, tordu, déformé, décalé; *Mec.E:* **d. design,** type (de moteur) anormal.

distorting [dis'tɔ:tiŋ], *a.* déformant.

distortion [dis'tɔ:ʃ(ə)n], *s.* **1.** (*a*) distorsion *f;* décomposition *f,* altération *f* (des traits); (*b*) contorsion *f* (du corps); (*c*) altération (d'un texte); déformation *f* (des faits, de la vérité). **2.** (*a*) *Opt:* déformation, distorsion; **barrel (-shaped) d.,** distorsion en barillet; **pincushion d., pillow d.,** distorsion en coussinet, en croissant; (*b*) *Mec.E:* (i) distorsion (d'un organe); torsion *f,* déformation *f;* fléchissement *m;* voile *m;* **permanent d.,** déformation permanente; (ii) **d. of the design,** déformation anormale, exagération *f,* du modèle; (*c*) *Elcs: W.Tel: etc:* distorsion, déformation (de la transmission); (*of sound*) distorsion sonore; **d. factor,** taux *m* de distorsion; **d. meter,** distorsiomètre *m;* (*d*) déviation *f,* décalage *m* (du champ magnétique).

distract [dis'trækt], *v.tr.* **1.** (*a*) distraire, détourner, éloigner (**the mind, the attention, from,** l'esprit, l'attention, de); (*b*) brouiller, distraire (l'esprit); diviser (l'attention); **the radio distracts my attention when I'm working,** la radio me distrait quand je travaille; **go away! you're distracting me!** va-t'en! tu me déranges! **2.** troubler, tourmenter, affoler (qn); **distracted between hope and fear,** déchiré entre l'espoir et la crainte.

distracted [dis'træktid], *a.* affolé, bouleversé; hors de soi; fou, *f;* folle; éperdu; **I was almost d.,** j'en perdais presque la tête; **I shall go d.,** je deviendrai fou.

distractedly [dis'træktidli], *adv.* **1.** comme un affolé; comme un fou. **2.** (aimer qn) follement, éperdument, à la folie.

distracting [dis'træktiŋ], *a.* **1.** qui distrait l'attention; **I find noise d. when I'm working,** le bruit me dérange quand je travaille. **2.** affolant, tourmentant.

distractingly [dis'træktiŋli], *adv.* à rendre fou.

distraction [dis'trækʃ(ə)n], *s.* **1.** distraction *f;* (*a*) divertissement *m;* **he is seeking d.,** il cherche à se distraire; **he finds a healthy d. in golf,** il trouve dans le golf un salutaire dérivatif, une saine distraction; (*b*) interruption *f* (au milieu du travail, etc.). **2.** confusion *f,* trouble *m,* désordre *m.* **3.** folie *f,* démence *f,* affolement *m;* **to drive s.o. to d.,** rendre qn fou; mettre qn hors de soi, aux cent coups; faire perdre la tête à qn; **to love s.o. to d.,** aimer qn éperdument, à la folie.

distrain [dis'trein], *v.i. Jur:* **to d. upon s.o.'s belongings,** saisir les meubles de qn; opérer la saisie des meubles de qn; **to d. upon s.o.,** contraindre qn par saisie de biens; exercer la contrainte par saisie de biens; **to d. upon a debtor,** exécuter un débiteur.

distrainable [dis'treinəbl], *a. Jur:* saisissable; (biens *m*) exploitables.

distrainee [distrei'ni:], *s. Jur:* (débiteur) saisi *m.*

distrainer, distrainor [dis'treinər], *s. Jur:* saisissant *m.*

distraint [dis'treint], *s. Jur:* saisie *f,* (saisie-)exécution *f, pl.* (saisies-)exécutions; **d. of property** (*of debtor*), discussion *f* de biens; mainmise *f* sur les biens; **to levy a d.,** opérer une saisie; **furniture under d.,** meubles gagés, saisis.

distrait [dis'trei], *a.* distrait.

distraught [dis'trɔ:t], *a.* (*a*) angoissé, affolé; **to look d.,** avoir l'air affolé; (*b*) fou, folle (de douleur, etc.).

distress[1] [dis'tres], *s.* **1.** (*a*) (*anguish*) détresse *f,* angoisse *f,* affliction *f,* désolation *f;* (*b*) (*want*) misère (profonde); gêne *f.* **2.** (*misfortune*) détresse, embarras *m;* **companions in d.,** compagnons *m* d'infortune; *Nau:* **ship in d.,** navire *m* en détresse; **flag of d.,** pavillon *m* de détresse; **d. signal, gun,** signal *m,* canon *m,* de détresse. **3.** *Jur:* (*a*) saisie *f;* **d. warrant,** mandat *m,* ordre *m,* de saisie; (*b*) biens saisis; **d. sale,** vente publique de biens saisis. **4.** (*exhaustion*) épuisement *m;* **to show signs of d.,** commencer à donner des signes d'épuisement.

distress[2], *v.tr.* **1.** affliger, angoisser, désoler, chagriner, peiner; faire de la peine à (qn); **your letter has deeply distressed me,** votre lettre *f* m'a pénétré de douleur; votre lettre m'a désolé. **2.** *Com:* vieillir (un meuble).

distressed [dis'trest], *a.* **1.** affligé, désolé; **I am d. to hear . . .,** je suis désolé d'apprendre . . .; **to be d. about sth.,** s'affliger de qch.; être désolé d'apprendre qch. **2.** dans la détresse, dans la misère; **d. area,** (i) région frappée par le chômage, par une crise économique; (ii) zone sinistrée; *O:* **d. gentlewoman,** dame réduite à la misère. **3.** *Med:* **d. breathing,** respiration douloureuse. **4.** *Jur:* saisi.

distressing [dis'tresiŋ], *a.* affligeant, fâcheux, angoissant, désolant, pénible; douloureux à entendre ou à voir; **what is there so d. about that?** qu'y a-t-il d'affligeant à cela?

distressingly [dis'tresiŋli], *adv.* péniblement, douloureusement.

distributable [dis'tribjutəbl], *a.* distribuable, répartissable, partageable.

distributary [dis'tribjutəri]. **1.** *a.* (canal *m,* etc.) de distribution; distributeur, -trice. **2.** *s.* (*a*) défluent *m,* bras *m* (d'un delta, d'un cours d'eau anastomosé); (*b*) canal de distribution.

distribute [dis'tribju(:)t], *v.tr.* **1.** distribuer, répartir, partager; faire la distribution de (qch.); aménager (des provisions, etc.); répandre (de l'argent, l'aumône, etc.); départir (des faveurs); *Com:* être concessionnaire de, vendre (un produit); **to d. a dividend,** répartir un dividende. **2.** disperser, répartir (sur une surface, etc.); **to d. water evenly over a surface,** épandre de l'eau uniformément sur une surface; **load evenly distributed,** charge uniformément répartie; *El:* **distributed inductance,** inductance répartie. **3.** *Typ:* **to d. the type,** mettre la composition en casse; distribuer la composition. **4.** *Log:* employer (un terme) dans le sens distributif.

distributer [dis'tribjutər], *s.* = DISTRIBUTOR.

distributing [distri'bjutiŋ], *a.* & *s. El:* **d. board,** tableau *m* de distribution; **d. box,** boîte *f* de branchement, de dérivation; *Hyd. E:* **d. canal,** canal distributeur; *Typ:* **d. table,** encrier *m* (d'une machine à imprimer).

distribution [distri'bju:ʃ(ə)n], *s.* **1.** (*a*) (mise *f* en) distribution *f;* répartition *f;* partage *m;* diffusion *f* (d'un document officiel, etc.); **prize d.,** distribution des prix; **d. of tasks, duties,** répartition des tâches, des fonctions; *Mil:* **d. of troops,** répartition, implantation *f,* des troupes; *Fin:* (*in bankruptcy*) **d. of debts,** répartition des dettes; **final d.,** dernière répartition; **first and final d.,** première et unique répartition; *Com:* **d. channel,** circuit *m* de distribution; (*of automatic vending machine*) **d. slot,** sébile *f;* (*b*) *I.C.E:* **d. gear,** pignon *m* de commande de la distribution; *El: etc:* **d. cable, main,** câble *m,* artère *f,* de distribution; **d. (switch)board,** tableau *m,* panneau *m,* de distribution; **d. box,** boîte *f* de dérivation, de jonction; **d. network,** réseau *m* de distribution. **2.** (*a*) **population d.,** répartition de la population; **age d.,** distribution par âge; **d. of labour,** répartition de la main-d'œuvre; **d. of wealth,** distribution, répartition, des richesses; **d. of the flora (of a region),** répartition de la flore (d'une région); *Cards:* **d. of trumps,** répartition, partage, des atouts; *Mec:* **stress d.,** répartition des forces; *El:* **load d.,** répartition de charge; (*b*) *Mth:* **logarithmic d.,** distribution logarithmique; **binomial d.,** distribution binomiale; **multivariate d.,** distribution à plusieurs variables. **3.** *Typ:* mise en casse. **4.** *Log:* emploi *m* (d'un terme) dans le sens distributif.

distributional [distri'bju:ʃən(ə)l], *a.* distributionnel; **d. effect,** effet *m* sur la répartition.

distributive [dis'tribjutiv]. **1.** *a.* & *s. Log: Gram:* (terme, pronom) distributif (*m*). **2.** *a.* **d. justice,** justice distributive.

distributively [dis'tribjutivli], *adv.* distributivement.

distributor [dis'tribjutər], *s.* **1.** (*a*) distributeur, -trice; délivreur, -euse; (*b*) concessionnaire *m* (d'une marque d'automobiles, etc.). **2.** *Tchn:* (appareil, dispositif) distributeur *m;* *El: I.C.E:* distributeur (de courant); *I.C.E:* allumeur *m;* **d. gear,** pignon *m* de commande de la distribution; **d. timing mechanism,** mécanisme distributeur d'allumage; **d. arm,** rotor *m* du Delco; *Mch:* **steam d.,** distributeur de vapeur; **oil d.,** distributeur d'huile; rampe *f* de distribution d'huile, de graissage; *Mec.E:* **d. weight,** masselotte *f* de distributeur; *El: etc:* **d. cable,** câble *m* de distribution; **d. duct,** canalisation *f* (de réseau); **d. box,** boîte *f* de dérivation, de jonction.

district[1] ['distrikt], *s.* (*a*) région *f,* territoire *m,* district *m;* **mountainous d.,** région de montagnes; **frontier d.,** région frontalière; **mining d.,** région minière, district minier; **d. bank,** banque régionale; **d. manager,** directeur régional; *W.Tel: T.V:* **d. transmitter,** émetteur régional; (*b*) *Mil: etc:* région (militaire, aérienne, maritime); territoire (militaire); *Navy:* préfecture *f* maritime; (*c*) *Adm:* district, secteur *m;* **urban d.,** district urbain; **d. council** = conseil municipal; **postal d.,** circonscription *f* du bureau de poste; secteur postal; **electoral d.,** *U.S:* **congressional d.,** circonscription électorale; **federal d.,** district fédéral; *U.S: Jur:* **d. court** = tribunal *m* d'instance; *U.S:* **d. attorney** = procureur *m* (de la République); *A: & F:* **d. nurse,** infirmière visiteuse; (*d*) quartier *m* (d'une ville); *Adm:* = arrondissement *m* (d'une grande ville); **residential d.,** quartier résidentiel; **d. heating,** chauffage urbain; *A:* **d. visitor,** dame *f* de charité; visiteuse *f* des pauvres; (*e*) *Min:* quartier (d'une mine).

district[2], *v.tr. U.S:* diviser en districts; diviser (une région) en circonscriptions.

distringas [dis'triŋgæs], *s. Jur:* ordre *m* de saisie.

distrust[1] [dis'trʌst], *s.* méfiance *f,* défiance *f* (**of,** de); soupçons *mpl.*

distrust[2], *v.tr.* se méfier, se défier, de (qn, qch.); avoir de la méfiance envers, à l'égard de (qn); **to d. one's own eyes,** n'en pas croire ses propres yeux.

distrustful [dis'trʌstful], *a.* **1.** défiant, méfiant (**of,** de); soupçonneux; **a d. person,** un soupçonneur, une soupçonneuse. **2.** qui manque de confiance en soi; timide; **he was d. of his own capabilities,** il manquait de foi en ses propres capacités.

distrustfully [dis'trʌstfuli], *adv.* avec méfiance, avec défiance, d'un air défiant; soupçonneusement; **to look at s.o. d.,** regarder qn avec méfiance.

disturb [dis'tə:b], *v.tr.* **1.** déranger (qn); troubler (le repos, l'ordre public, etc.); agiter, remuer (une surface, la terre); déranger (des papiers, des projets); **don't d. him,** ne le dérangez pas; **I'm afraid of disturbing you,** je crains de vous être importun; **please don't d. yourself,** ne vous dérangez pas; **to d. a ceremony,** porter le trouble dans une cérémonie; *St.Exch:* **disturbed market,** marché agité. **2.** *Ph:* ébranler (l'éther); perturber, amener de la perturbation dans (le champ magnétique); affoler (l'aiguille aimantée). **3.** (*a*) inquiéter, troubler (qn); **to d. s.o.'s mind,** jeter le trouble dans l'esprit de qn; **he was much disturbed by what he heard,** il était fort ébranlé par ce qu'il apprenait; (*b*) *Jur:* inquiéter, troubler, (qn) dans la jouissance d'un droit, d'un bien.

disturbance [dis'tə:bəns], *s.* **1.** trouble *m;* dérangement *m,* perturbation *f;* **atmospheric d.,** perturbation atmosphérique; **magnetic d.,** perturbation magnétique. **2.** (*a*) bruit *m,* vacarme *m,* tumulte *m,* tapage *m,* remuement *m;* (*b*) bagarre *f,* soulèvement *m;* émeute *f;* **political disturbances,** troubles politiques; **to make, create, a d.,** troubler l'ordre public; soulever des troubles, le désordre. **3.** agitation *f,* trouble (d'esprit), inquiétude *f;* **emotional disturbances,** troubles émotifs. **4.** *Jur:* trouble de jouissance.

disturber [dis'tə:bər], *s.* **1.** dérangeur, -euse. **2.** perturbateur, -trice (de l'ordre, etc.).

disturbing [dis'tə:biŋ], *a.* perturbateur, -trice; (*a*) **d. factors,** éléments *m* d'instabilité; éléments perturbateurs; causes *f* de trouble; (*b*) **d. news,** nouvelle fâcheuse.

distyle ['d(a)istail], *a.* & *s. Arch:* distyle (*m*).

distylous [d(a)i'stailəs], *a. Bot:* distyle.

disubstituted [dai'sʌbstitjutid], *a: Ch:* disubstitué.

disulphide [dai'sʌlfaid], *s. Ch:* bisulfure *m,* disulfure *m;* **carbon d.,** carbosulfure *m;* sulfure *m* de carbone; **d. of tin,** or mussif.

disulphonic [daisʌl'fɔnik], *a. Ch:* disulfonique.

disunion [dis'ju:njən], *s.* **1.** désunion *f,* séparation *f.* **2.** désunion, brouille *f.*

disunite [disju'nait]. **1.** *v.tr.* (*a*) désunir, séparer; (*b*) **to d. a family,** jeter la désunion, la zizanie, dans une famille. **2.** *v.i.* se désunir.

disunity [dis'ju:niti], *s.* discordance *f;* désunion *f.*

disuse [dis'ju:s], *s.* **1.** désuétude *f* (d'un terme, etc.). **2.** abandon *m,* désemploi *m,* mise *f* au rancart (d'une machine, etc.); **to fall into d.,** (i) (*of word, custom*) tomber en désuétude; (*of law*) s'abroger; (ii) (*of object*) être abandonné, être mis au rancart; **institutions, customs, that are falling into d.,** institutions *f* qui s'oblitèrent; usages *m* qui se perdent.

disused [dis'ju:zd], *a.* hors d'usage; abandonné; mis au rancart; (*of public building*) désaffecté; (*of door, window*) condamné; (*of word*) désuet, vieilli; **d. mine,** mine abandonnée.

disyllabic [daisi'læbik, di-], *a.* (mot *m*) dissyllabe; (vers *m*) dissyllabique.

disyllable [dai'siləbl, di-], *s.* dissyllabe *m.*

ditch[1] [ditʃ], *s.* **1.** fossé *m*; (*along the roadside also*) rigole latérale; caniveau *m*; (*between fields*) douve *f*; **drainage d.,** saignée *f*; rigole d'écoulement, d'assèchement; *Rac:* **open d.,** douve; *El: Tp:* **cable d.,** caniveau *m* de câble; *Mil:* **anti-tank d.,** fossé antichars; **to die in a d.,** mourir sur le bord de la route, sur un fumier; **to die in the last d.,** résister jusqu'à la dernière extrémité; **2.** *Sp:* (*bowls*) rigole qui délimite le terrain.

ditch[2]. **1.** *v.tr.* (*a*) entourer (un champ) de fossés; creuser des fossés, faire des saignées, dans (un champ); (*b*) *F: Aut:* faire tomber (sa voiture) dans un fossé; *Rail: U.S:* faire dérailler (un train); (*c*) *F:* jeter (qch.); mettre (qch.) au rancart; se débarrasser de (qch.); abandonner (un projet, etc.); plaquer (qn); **to be ditched,** (i) échouer; (ii) être dans le pétrin; (*d*) *P:* **to d. stolen goods,** cacher des objets volés (avec l'intention de les récupérer plus tard). **2.** *v.i.* (*a*) curer les fossés; veiller à l'entretien des fossés; (*b*) *Av:* faire un amerrissage forcé.

ditcher ['ditʃər], *s.* **1.** (*pers.*) cureur *m* de fossés. **2.** *Civ.E:* (*machine*) excavatrice *f* pour fossés.

ditching ['ditʃiŋ], *s.* **1.** curage *m* de fossés; **hedging and d.,** entretien *m* des haies et fossés. **2.** *Av:* amérissage, amerrissage, forcé.

ditchwater ['ditʃwɔ:tər], *s.* eaux stagnantes (d'un fossé); *F:* **it's as clear as d.,** c'est la bouteille à l'encre, c'est clair comme du jus de chique; **as dull as d.,** ennuyeux comme la pluie, comme un jour de pluie.

ditheism ['daiθi:izm], *s. Rel:* dithéisme *m.*

ditheist ['daiθi:ist], *s. Rel:* dithéiste *mf.*

ditheistic [daiθi:'istik], *a. Rel:* dithéiste.

dither[1] ['diðər], *s. F:* **to be all of a d.,** (i) être tout agité, tout bouleversé; ne plus savoir où donner de la tête; (ii) (*also* **to have the dithers**) être tout tremblant.

dither[2], *v.i. F:* (*a*) branler, trembloter; trembler; (*b*) s'agiter sans but; (*c*) **don't d.!** décide-toi!

dithering grass ['diðəriŋgrɑ:s], *s. Bot:* brize moyenne; *F:* amourette *f*; pain *m* d'oiseau.

dithery ['diðəri], *a. F:* **to feel d.,** se sentir agité, nerveux; être tout tremblant; se sentir tout chose.

dithiobenzoic [daiθaiouben'zouik], *a. Ch:* dithiobenzoïque.

dithionate [dai'θaiəneit], *s. Ch:* dithionate *m.*

dithionic [daiθai'ɔnik], *a. Ch:* dithionique.

dithyramb ['diθiræm], *s. Lit:* dithyrambe *m.*

dithyrambic [diθi'ræmbik], *a. Lit:* dithyrambique.

ditolyl ['daitəlil], *s. Ch:* ditolyle *m.*

ditone ['daitoun], *s. Mus:* diton *m.*

dittany ['ditəni], *s. Bot:* **1. Cretan d.,** dictame *m* de Crète. **2.** dictame, fraxinelle *f.*

ditto ['ditou], *F:* **1.** *a. & s.* idem; de même; *Com:* dito *m inv*; **three white ties and six black d.,** trois cravates blanches et six dito noires; **he's been very foolish, and you d.,** il a agi très sottement, et vous de même, pareillement; **to say d.,** être du même avis. **2.** *adv.* **I'll act d.,** je ferai la même chose. **3.** *int.* d'accord!

dittography [di'tɔgrəfi], *s.* dittographie *f.*

dittology [di'tɔlədʒi], *s.* dittologie *f.*

ditty ['diti], *s.* chanson *f*, chansonnette *f*; **old ditties,** vieux refrains, vieilles chansons.

ditty bag, box ['ditibæg, -bɔks], *s. Nau:* nécessaire *m* de marin.

diuresis [daiju'ri:sis], *s. Med:* diurèse *f.*

diuretic [daiju'retik], *a. & s. Med:* diurétique (*m*).

diurnal [dai'ə:n(ə)l]. **1.** *a.* (*a*) *Astr:* **d. motion,** mouvement *m* diurne; (*b*) *Nat.Hist:* (oiseau *m*, papillon *m*, etc.) diurne; (*c*) *A:* journalier. **2.** *s.* (*a*) *Ecc:* diurnal *m*, -aux; (*b*) *A:* journal *m*, -aux.

diurnally [dai'ə:nəli], *adv.* **1.** de jour. **2.** *A:* journellement; tous les jours.

diva ['di:və], *s.f. Th: O:* diva, cantatrice.

divagate ['daivəgeit], *v.i.* divaguer. **1.** errer çà et là. **2.** s'écarter de son sujet.

divagation [daivə'geiʃ(ə)n], *s.* divagation *f.*

divalent [dai'veilənt], *a. & s. Ch:* divalent, bivalent.

divan [di'væn], *s.* **1.** *Hist:* (*a*) divan *m*, conseil *m* (d'un sultan); (*b*) divan, salle *f* du conseil. **2.** *Furn:* divan, ottomane *f*; **d. bed,** lit-divan *m*, *pl.* lits-divans. **3.** *A:* (*a*) fumoir *m*; (*b*) débit *m* de tabac.

divaricate[1] [dai'værikeit], *a. Nat.Hist:* divariqué.

divaricate[2], *v.i.* diverger, divariquer; (se) bifurquer.

divarication [daiværi'keiʃ(ə)n], *s.* divergence *f*, divarication *f*, bifurcation *f.*

divaricator [dai'værikeitər], *s. Nat.Hist:* (muscle) diducteur *m* (des brachiopodes, etc.).

dive[1] [daiv], *s.* **1.** (*a*) *Swim:* plongeon *m*; **high d.,** plongeon de haut vol; **pike d.,** plongeon à la hussarde; **surface d.,** *F:* **duck d.,** plongeon en canard; (*b*) *Nau:* plongée *f* (d'un sous-marin, d'un scaphandrier); (*c*) *Av:* **vertical d., nose d.,** descente piquée, piqué *m*; **to pull out of a d.,** effectuer une ressource, un rétablissement; **d. angle,** angle *m* de piqué; **d. brake,** frein *m* de piqué; **d. bombing,** bombardement *m*, attaque *f*, en piqué; **d. bomber,** bombardier *m* en piqué; (*d*) **he made a d. into his pocket,** il a plongé la main dans sa poche; **he made a d. for the shelter,** il s'est précipité vers l'abri. **2.** *F:* (**low**) **d.,** café *m*, bar *m*, borgne; bouge *m*; gargote *f.*

dive[2], *v.i.* (*p.t.* **dived,** *U.S: F:* **dove** [douv]; *p.p.* **dived**) (*a*) plonger (**into,** dans); (*headfirst*) piquer une tête; **to d. in again,** replonger; **to d. for sth.,** plonger à la recherche de qch.; **to d. for pearls, for coral,** pêcher des perles, du corail; *Nau: F:* (*of ship*) **to d. into it,** piquer du nez; mettre le nez dans la lame, dans la plume; (*b*) *Av:* **to d. down on an enemy,** piquer de haut sur un ennemi; (*c*) (*of submarine*) plonger, effectuer une plongée; s'immerger; (*d*) **to d. into a mystery,** chercher à pénétrer, à approfondir, un mystère; **to d. into one's pocket,** plonger (la main) dans sa poche; enfoncer la main dans sa poche; fouiller dans sa poche; **to d. into a doorway for shelter,** se précipiter, s'engouffrer, dans une entrée pour s'abriter.

dive-bomb ['daivbɔm], *v.tr. Av:* bombarder, attaquer en piqué.

diver ['daivər], *s.* **1.** (*a*) plongeur, -euse; **high d.,** plongeur de haut vol; **pearl d., sponge d.,** pêcheur *m* de perles, d'éponges; (*b*) scaphandrier *m*; **skin d.,** plongeur sous-marin autonome; **diver's paralysis,** mal *m* des caissons. **2.** *Orn:* plongeon *m*; **black-throated d.,** plongeon arctique, lumme *m*, plongeon à gorge noire; **great northern d.,** plongeon imbrin; imber *m*; **red-throated d.,** plongeon catmarin, plongeon à gorge rousse; **white-billed d.,** plongeon à bec blanc.

diverge [dai'və:dʒ]. **1.** *v.i.* (*of roads, lines, etc.*) diverger, s'écarter; **to d. from the beaten track,** s'écarter, dévier, du chemin battu; quitter le chemin battu. **2.** *v.tr.* faire diverger (des rayons, etc.).

divergence, divergency [dai'və:dʒəns, -'və:dʒənsi], *s.* divergence *f*; **d. between two results,** écart *m* entre deux résultats; *Biol:* **d. from type,** variation *f* des espèces.

divergent [dai'və:dʒənt], *a.* divergent; **we take d. views on certain points,** nos opinions *f* divergent, diffèrent, sur certains points; *Med:* **d. squint,** strabisme divergent.

diverging [dai'və:dʒiŋ], *a.* divergent.

divers ['daivəz]. *A:* **1.** *a. pl.* divers, plusieurs, quelques; **on d. occasions,** en diverses occasions; à diverses reprises. **2.** *s.pl.* **d. of them,** quelques-uns d'entre eux.

diverse [d(a)i'və:s], *a.* **1.** divers, différent. **2.** divers, varié, changeant.

diversely [d(a)i'və:sli], *adv.* diversement.

diverseness [d(a)i'və:snis], *s.* diversité *f.*

diversicoloured [d(a)i'və:sikʌləd], *a. Bot:* diversicolore.

diversification [d(a)ivə:sifi'keiʃ(ə)n], *s.* **1.** diversité *f* (de goûts, etc.); variété *f*; variation *f.* **2.** *Com: Fin: etc:* diversification *f.*

diversiflorous [d(a)ivə:si'flɔ:rəs], *a. Bot:* diversiflore.

diversiform [d(a)i'və:sifɔ:m], *a.* diversiforme.

diversify [d(a)i'və:sifai], *v.tr.* diversifier, varier.

diversion [d(a)i'və:ʃ(ə)n], *s.* **1.** (*a*) déviation *f*, détournement *m* (de la circulation, etc.); *Mil.Trans:* variantement *m* (d'un itinéraire); *Av:* **d. in flight,** déroutement *m* en vol; (*b*) *Hyd.E:* dérivation *f* (d'un cours d'eau); **d. canal,** canal *m* de dérivation; (*c*) *El:* dérivation. **2.** *Mil:* diversion *f.* **3.** (*a*) diversion (de l'esprit); **to create, make, a d.,** faire diversion; **to seek d. from sth.,** chercher à se distraire de qch.; (*b*) amusement *m*, divertissement *m*, délassement *m*, distraction *f*; **indoor diversions,** amusements de salon; **outdoor diversions,** jeux *m* de plein air.

diversionary [d(a)i'və:ʃən(ə)ri], *a.* **d.** (**demonstrations**), (des démonstrations) destinées à faire diversion; *Mil:* **d. landing,** débarquement *m* de diversion.

diversionist [d(a)i'və:ʃənist], *s. Pol:* saboteur, -euse.

diversity [d(a)i'və:siti], *s.* diversité *f*; *El: W.Tel: etc:* **d. system,** diversité en fréquence; **d.-coupled,** monté en diversité; **d. reception,** réception *f* en diversité; **d. receiver,** récepteur *m* en diversité; **d. radar,** radar *m* diversité.

divert [dai'və:t, di-], *v.tr.* **1.** détourner, dériver (un cours d'eau); parer, écarter (un coup); détourner, dévier (la circulation); *Nau:* dérouter; *Mil.Trans:* varianter (un itinéraire); détourner (l'attention, de l'argent) (**from,** de); dévoyer (un tuyau, etc.); **bus routes are diverted via . . .,** les itinéraires d'autobus sont détournés par . . .; *El:* **to d. the current,** dévier le courant; **to d. the conversation,** détourner la conversation; orienter la conversation sur d'autres sujets; **to d. s.o.'s attention, s.o.'s thoughts,** distraire l'attention, la pensée, de qn. **2.** (*a*) divertir, amuser, réjouir (qn); (*b*) divertir, distraire (qn); **to d. oneself by doing sth.,** faire qch. pour se distraire.

diverticulitis [daivə:tikju'laitis], *s. Med:* diverticulite *f.*

diverticulosis [daivə:tikju'lousis], *s. Med:* diverticulose *f.*

diverticulum [daivə:'tikjuləm], *s. Anat:* diverticule *m.*

divertimento [divə:ti'mentou], *s. Mus:* divertissement *m.*

diverting[1] [dai'və:tiŋ, di-], *a.* divertissant, amusant.

diverting[2], *s.* **1.** détournement *m*, déviation *f* (d'un cours d'eau, de la circulation, etc.). **2.** amusement *m* (de qn).

divertingly [dai'və:tiŋli, di-], *adv.* d'une façon amusante.

divertor [dai'və:tər], *s. Atom.Ph:* déflecteur *m.*

Dives ['daivi:z], *s.* **1.** *B:* le mauvais riche. **2.** *Jur:* **D. costs,** frais taxés au taux supérieur.

divest [dai'vest, di-], *v.tr.* **1.** *A:* **to d. s.o. of his clothes,** ôter, retirer, les habits à qn; dévêtir qn; débarrasser qn de ses vêtements. **2.** (*a*) dépouiller, priver, dénuer (qn de qch.); **to d. oneself of one's authority, of an office, of a right,** se dépouiller, se dévêtir, de son autorité; se désinvestir d'une fonction; renoncer à un droit; (*b*) *Jur:* déposséder (qn) (**of,** de).

divestiture [dai'vestitʃər, di-], *s. Jur:* dessaisissement *m*, dépossession *f.*

divi ['divi], *s. & v.tr. P:* = DIVVY[1,2].

dividable [di'vaidəbl], *a.* = DIVISIBLE.

divide[1] [di'vaid], *s. Geog:* ligne *f* de partage des eaux; **the Great D.,** la ligne de partage des eaux des Andes.

divide[2]. **1.** *v.tr.* (*a*) (*split into parts*) diviser (un héritage, etc.); scinder (une proposition, une question); **to d.** (**sth.**) (**up**), démembrer (un royaume); détailler (de la viande, etc.); morceler (un terrain); **to d. in two,** couper, diviser, en deux; **to d. into parts,** diviser en parties; sectionner, fractionner; **to d. a town into wards,** diviser une ville en, par, arrondissements; **tourists divided into five parties,** touristes répartis en cinq groupes; **divided between hatred and pity,** partagé entre la haine et la pitié; *Pol:* **to d. the House,** faire voter la Chambre; aller aux voix; voter; *Hort:* **to d. the roots,** sectionner, éclater, les racines; (*b*) (*share out*) partager, répartir, diviser (**among,** entre); **to d. the profits,** répartir les bénéfices; **to d. one's property among one's heirs,** départir ses biens entre ses héritiers; **we d. the work among us,** nous nous partageons le travail; (*c*) *Mth:* diviser; **to d. one number by another,** diviser un nombre par un autre; **two divides into all even numbers,** deux divise exactement tous les nombres pairs; (*with passive force*) **twelve divides by three,** douze est divisible par trois; (*d*) séparer (**from,** de); **the mountains that d. France from Spain,** les montagnes *f* qui divisent, séparent, la France d'avec l'Espagne; (*e*) diviser (une famille); mettre le désaccord dans (une famille); désunir (une famille); **a policy of d. and rule,** une politique de diviser pour régner; **house, army, divided against itself,** maison, armée, désunie; (*f*) **opinions are divided,** les avis sont partagés; **provinces divided in feelings and in interests,** provinces divisées de sentiments et d'intérêts. **2.** *v.i.* (*a*) se diviser, se partager (**into,** en); se séparer; se ramifier; (*of political party*) se scinder; (*of road*) faire fourche, fourcher; (*b*) *Pol:* aller aux voix; procéder au scrutin.

divided [di'vaidid], *a.* (*a*) divisé; partagé; **d. attention,** attention distraite; *Z:* **d. hoof,** ongle divisé; *Cost:* **d. skirt,** jupe-culotte *f*, *pl.* jupes-culottes; *I.C.E:* **d. exhaust,** échappement bifurqué; (*b*) *El:* **d. circuit,** circuit partagé; réseau *m* multiple; (*c*) (*of scale, thermometer, etc.*) gradué; **d. circle, dial,** cercle, cadran, gradué.

dividend ['dividend], *s.* **1.** *Mth:* dividende *m.* **2.** *Fin:* dividende; (*a*) **d. on shares,** dividende d'actions; **interim d.,** dividende par intérim; dividende provisoire; acompte *m* de, sur, dividende; **final d.,** solde *m* de dividende; **cum d.,** *U.S:* **d. on,** avec le dividende; coupon attaché; **ex d.,** *U.S:* **d. off,** ex-dividende; sans intérêt; **d. warrant,** chèque-dividende *m*, *pl.* chèques-dividendes; coupon *m* d'arrérages; **to draw one's dividends,** toucher ses arrérages; (*b*) (*to creditors of in-*

solvent estate) somme *f* à répartir; répartition *f*; **d. paid to each creditor,** dividende payé à chaque créancier.

divider [di'vaidər], *s.* **1.** personne (i) qui divise, partage, (ii) qui désunit. **2.** *Tls: Coop:* départoir *m* (pour fendre le merrain). **3.** *pl.* **dividers,** compas *m* à pointes sèches; compas droit (à pointes); compas de mesure; **dividers with arc, wing dividers,** quart *m* de cercle; **proportional dividers,** compas de proportion, de réduction.

dividing[1] [di'vaidiŋ], *a.* (ligne *f*) de démarcation; (machine *f*) à diviser; **d. wall,** mur mitoyen; mur de séparation, de cloison; *El:* **d. box,** boîte *f* de dérivation.

dividing[2], *s.* division *f*, partage *m*, répartition *f*; **d. (up) of work,** répartition du travail; *Rail:* **d. of load,** rupture *f* de charge.

divination [divi'neiʃ(ə)n], *s.* divination *f*.

divine[1] [di'vain]. **1.** *a.* (*a*) divin; (*b*) *F: O:* divin, admirable, parfait; **you look d. in that dress,** vous êtes divine, adorable, dans cette robe. **2.** *s.* (*a*) théologien *m*; (*b*) *A:* ecclésiastique *m*.

divine[2]. **1.** *v.tr.* deviner (l'avenir, l'intention de qn); pressentir (un malheur); **to d. what will be the future of . . .,** prédire quel sera l'avenir de . . .. **2.** *v.i.* prédire; faire de la divination.

divinely [di'vainli], *adv.* divinement; *F:* adorablement.

diviner [di'vainər], *s.* (*a*) devin *m*, devineresse *f*; divinateur, -trice; (*b*) **water d.,** radiesthésiste *m*; sourcier *m*.

diving ['daiviŋ], *s.* (*a*) *Swim:* plongeon *m*; **high d. event,** épreuve *f* de plongeon de haut vol; **d. board, stage, tower,** plongeoir *m*; **high d. board,** plongeoir de haut vol; **I'm no good at d.,** je plonge mal; je ne sais pas plonger; (*b*) plongée *f* (en scaphandre, d'un pêcheur d'éponges, etc.); **skin d., free d., scuba d.,** plongée sous-marine autonome; **d. suit,** (i) scaphandre *m*; (ii) vêtement *m* de plongée; **d. gear,** appareils *mpl*, matériel *m*, de plongée; **d. bell,** cloche *f* à plongeurs; **d. pump,** pompe *f* de scaphandre; **d. tender,** bâtiment *m* base pour plongeurs et scaphandriers; (*c*) *Nau:* **d. plane, d. rudder,** barre *f* d'immersion, gouvernail *m* de profondeur; (*d*) *Ent:* **d. beetle,** dytique *m*.

divining[1] [di'vainiŋ], *a.* divinateur, -trice.

divining[2], *s.* (*a*) divination *f*; (*b*) **water d.,** radiesthésie *f*; **d. rod,** baguette *f* de sourcier.

divinity [di'viniti], *s.* **1.** (*a*) (*divine nature*) divinité *f* (**of,** de); (*b*) **the D.,** la Divinité, Dieu. **2.** (*a*) théologie *f*; **Doctor of D.,** docteur *m* en théologie; **d. course,** cours *m* de théologie; (*b*) *Sch:* enseignement religieux; histoire sainte. **3.** *Bookb:* **d. calf,** reliure en veau dorée à froid.

divinization [divinai'zeiʃ(ə)n], *s.* divinisation *f*.

divinize ['divinaiz], *v.tr.* diviniser.

divinyl [dai'vainil], *s.* *Ch:* divinyle *m*.

divisi [di'vi:zi:], *adv. Mus:* à deux.

divisibility [divizi'biliti], *s.* divisibilité *f*.

divisible [di'vizibl], *a.* divisible (**by,** par); partageable; *Fin:* **d. profits,** profits *m* répartissables.

division [di'viʒ(ə)n], *s.* **1.** (*dividing*) (*a*) division *f*, partage *m* (**into,** en); scission *f* (d'un parti); morcellement *m* (des terres); sectionnement *m*; *Hort:* éclatage *m* (des racines); (*b*) graduation *f* (d'une échelle, d'un thermomètre, etc.). **2.** (*distribution*) répartition *f*, partage (des bénéfices, etc.); *Pol.Ec:* **d. of labour,** division du travail. **3.** (*discord*) division, désunion *f*, discorde *f*; **to bring d. into a family,** mettre la division, amener la désunion, dans une famille. **4.** *Log: Mth:* division; *Mth:* **short d.,** division par un diviseur inférieur à treize; **long d.,** division par un diviseur supérieur à douze; **simple d.** = division à un chiffre. **5.** *Parl:* vote *m*; **there will be a d.,** on ira aux voix; **to challenge a d.,** provoquer un vote; **to come to a d.,** voter; aller aux voix; **on a d.,** en allant aux voix; **without a d.,** sans aller aux voix; sans scrutin. **6.** (*section*) (*a*) division (d'un livre, d'un pays); subdivision *f* (d'un casier, etc.); *Jur: A:* **the first, second, third, d.,** les trois degrés de sévérité de l'incarcération; (*b*) *Biol:* groupe *m*, classe *f*; (*c*) *Geol:* étage *m*; **the Argovian d.,** l'étage argovien; (*d*) *Jur:* section *f*, chambre *f* (de la cour); (*e*) *Mil: etc:* division; **air d.,** division aérienne; **airborne d.,** division aéroportée; **armoured d.,** division blindée; **pentomic d.,** division pentomique; **square d.,** division quaternaire, carrée; **triangular d.,** division ternaire, triangulaire; **logistic d.,** division logistique; **Naval Intelligence D.,** Deuxième Bureau *m*; **Operations Divisions,** Troisième Bureau; *U.S:* **G1, G2, G3, G4, Division,** Premier, Deuxième, Troisième, Quatrième, Bureau; (*f*) *Pol:* **parliamentary d.,** circonscription électorale; (*g*) *esp. U.S: Rail:* section de ligne; (*h*) (*of scale*) degré *m* (d'une échelle, d'un thermomètre, etc.). **7.** *Const: etc:* cloison *f*, séparation *f*.

divisional [di'viʒən(ə)l], *a.* (*a*) *Mil:* divisionnaire; **d. staff,** état-major *m* divisionnaire; **d. headquarters,** poste *m* de commandement, quartier général divisionnaire; **d. troops,** éléments endivisionnés; **non-d. troops,** éléments non endivisionnés; (*b*) *Jur:* **d. court,** tribunal composé de deux ou plus de deux juges, prononçant sur les appels et en révision des décisions judiciaires antérieures.

divisionism [di'viʒənizm], *s. Art:* divisionnisme *m*.

divisionist [di'viʒənist], *a. & s. Art:* divisionniste (*mf*).

divisionistic [diviʒə'nistik], *a. Art:* divisionniste.

divisive [di'vaisiv], *a.* qui sème la discorde.

divisor [di'vaizər], *s. Mth:* diviseur *m*.

divisory [di'vaizəri], *a. Jur:* (action *f*) divisoire.

divorce[1] [di'vɔ:s], *s.* **1.** *Jur:* divorce *m*; **to sue for a d., to file a petition for d.,** demander le divorce; **he wishes to obtain a d.,** il veut divorcer; **to take, start, d. proceedings,** intenter une action en divorce; introduire une instance en divorce; **their d. proceedings are taking place,** ils sont en instance de divorce. **2.** divorce, séparation *f* (**between sth. and sth.,** de qch. et de qch.).

divorce[2], *v.tr.* (*a*) *Jur:* (*of judge*) prononcer le divorce (des époux); (*b*) (*of husband or wife*) **to be divorced from s.o., to d. s.o.,** divorcer d'avec qn; **they have been divorced,** ils sont divorcés; ils ont divorcé; (*c*) séparer (**from,** de); **to d. Church from State,** séparer l'Église et l'État; **passage divorced from the context,** passage détaché, isolé, du contexte.

divorcee; divorcé, *f.* **divorcée** [divɔ:'si:, -'sei], *s.* divorcé, -ée.

divorcement [di'vɔ:smənt], *s. A:* divorce *m*; *B:* **bill of d.,** lettre *f* de divorce; (*b*) **the d. of the written from the spoken language,** le divorce de la langue écrite et de la langue parlée.

divorcer [di'vɔ:sər], *s.* l'époux, l'épouse, en instance de divorce.

divot ['divət], *s.* motte *f* (de terre); *Golf:* escalope *f*; **to take a d.,** faire sauter une escalope.

divulgation [d(a)ivʌl'geiʃ(ə)n], **divulgement** [d(a)i'vʌldʒmənt], **divulgence** [d(a)i'vʌldʒəns], *s.* divulgation *f*.

divulge [di'vʌldʒ, dai-], *v.tr.* divulguer.

divulsion [dai'vʌlʃ(ə)n, di-], *s. Surg:* divulsion *f*.

divulsor [dai'vʌlsər, di-], *s. Surg:* divulseur *m*.

divvy[1] ['divi], *s. P:* (*a*) division *f*, partage *m*; (*b*) dividende *m*.

divvy[2], *v.tr. P:* (= *divide*) **to d. (up),** diviser, partager.

dixenite ['diksənait], *s. Miner:* dixénite *f*.

Dixie[1] ['diksi], *Pr.n. U.S: F:* **D. (land),** les États *m* du Sud.

dixie[2], **dixy**, *s. esp. Mil: F:* gamelle *f*; marmite *f* (de campement); bouteillon *m*.

dizygotic [daizai'gɔtik], *a. Biol:* dizygote, dizygotique.

dizzily ['dizili], *adv.* **1.** avec une sensation de vertige, d'étourdissement; **he walked d. across the room,** pris de vertige, il a traversé la pièce d'un pas incertain. **2.** vertigineusment; d'une manière vertigineuse; **they looked down at the river from a d. high bridge,** ils contemplaient la rivière de la hauteur vertigineuse du pont.

dizziness ['dizinis], *s.* étourdissement *m*, vertige(s) *m(pl)*; **fit of d.,** éblouissement *m*.

dizzy ['dizi], *a.* **1.** pris d'étourdissement; pris de vertige, de vertiges; **to feel d.,** avoir le vertige, des vertiges; **to make s.o. d.,** étourdir qn; donner le vertige à qn; **my head is d.,** la tête me tourne. **2.** (*of height, speed, etc.*) vertigineux. **3.** (*of wheel, stream, etc.*) tournoyant, tourbillonnant. **4.** *F:* **a d. blonde,** une blonde (i) tape-à-l'œil, (ii) évaporée.

do[1] [du:], *v.*

I. *v.tr.* (**do; doest** ['duest], *as aux.* **dost** [dʌst]; **does** [dʌz], *A:* **doth** [dʌθ], **doeth** ['dueθ]; *pl.* **do; did, didst, did,** *pl.* **did;** *pr.sub.sg. & pl.* **do;** *p.p.* **done** [dʌn]; *in the aux. use* **don't** [dount], **didn't** [didnt] *are common for* **do not, did not, doesn't,** *P:* **don't,** *for* **does not; d'you** *for* **do you.**) **1.** (*a*) (*perform*) faire (un travail, une bonne action, son devoir, des affaires); **what do you do (for a living)?** qu'est-ce que vous faites dans la vie? quel est votre métier? quelle est votre profession? **he has never needed to do anything,** il n'a jamais eu besoin de travailler; **what are you doing?** (i) qu'est-ce que vous faites? qu'est-ce que vous êtes en train de faire? (ii) mais qu'est-ce que tu es en train de faire? où as-tu la tête? (iii) que devenez-vous (ces temps-ci)? *F:* **what's the weather doing?** quel temps fait-il? **to do good, evil,** faire le bien, le mal; **to do right,** bien faire; bien agir; **to do wrong,** mal faire; mal agir; **he did brilliantly (in his examination),** il a réussi brillamment (son examen); **you would do well to . . .,** vous feriez bien de . . .; **do as you're told,** faites comme on vous dit; **to do one's duty, a task,** s'acquitter de son devoir, d'une tâche; **the amount of work he has done,** le travail qu'il a fourni; **I did the trip in ten hours,** j'ai fait le voyage en dix heures; **to do one's military service,** faire son service militaire; **I haven't done my homework,** (i) je n'ai pas fait mes devoirs; (ii) *F:* je n'ai pas suffisamment étudié la question; **this must be done again,** c'est à refaire; *F:* **it's been done to death,** on en a eu assez; **he is doing medicine,** il fait sa médecine; **are you doing German at school?** faites-vous de l'allemand à l'école? *F:* **we're doing Hamlet this term,** on étudie *Hamlet* ce trimestre-ci; *s. a.* I 2(*e*); **I can't do Latin,** je ne mords pas au latin; *P: A:* **I could do a beer,** je boirais bien un verre de bière; **to d. 10 kilometres on foot,** faire, abattre, 10 kilomètres à pied; **the car was doing sixty,** la voiture faisait du soixante; **this model can do 150 kilometres an hour,** ce modèle peut atteindre 150 kilomètres à l'heure; **to do ten years (in prison),** faire dix ans de prison; **what do you do when it's wet?** (i) comment vous arrangez-vous, (ii) à quoi vous occupez-vous, quand il pleut? **are you doing anything tomorrow?** avez-vous quelque chose en vue pour demain? **those things aren't done, it isn't done,** cela ne se fait pas; **it is quite commonly done,** c'est de pratique courante; **that's how it's usually done here,** voilà comment cela se fait ici; **it's as good as done,** c'est une affaire faite ou autant vaut; **that's so much done,** c'est autant de fait; *F:* **that's done it!** ça y est! ça c'est le bouquet! **I am building a summerhouse for something to do,** je bâtis un petit pavillon pour m'occuper; **it gives me something to do,** cela me donne de l'occupation ; **he makes her do anything he wants,** il la fait marcher au doigt et à l'œil; il la mène par le bout du nez; **I can't do it just now,** je ne peux pas m'y mettre à présent; *Prov:* **what's done is done, cannot be undone,** ce qui est fait est fait, à chose faite point de remède; **I shall do nothing of the sort, I shall do no such thing,** je n'en ferai rien; **don't do it again!** ne recommencez pas! **I'll never do it again,** cela ne m'arrivera plus; **what is there to do?** qu'est-ce qu'il y a à faire? **there's nothing to do here,** il n'y a rien à faire ici; **what is, was, to be done? what can, could, I, he, we, do?** que faire? **how is it to be done?** comment faire? le moyen? **it cannot, can't, be done,** cela n'est pas possible; c'est (chose) impossible; *F:* pas moyen! **there's nothing to be done,** il n'y a rien à faire, il n'y a pas de remède; on n'y peut rien; **don't just stand there,** *do* **something!** ne reste pas planté là, fais quelque chose! **she did nothing but cry,** elle ne faisait que pleurer; **I don't know what to do,** je ne sais que faire; **let's see what a bit of flattery will do,** essayons un peu de flatterie; **he has done a great deal for me,** il m'a été d'un grand secours; il m'a rendu de grands services; *F:* **this music doesn't do anything for me,** cette musique ne me dit rien; **by so doing, by doing so, you will save a good deal of money,** vous économiserez de la sorte pas mal d'argent; **we must do it (however reluctantly),** il faut nous y résoudre; **what can I do for you? can I do anything for you?** en quoi puis-je vous être utile, vous servir, vous aider? que puis-je faire pour vous, pour toi? **will you do sth. for me?** voulez-vous me rendre un petit service? *F:* tu veux être gentil(le)? *F:* **I must go and do sth. no one else can do for me,** je dois aller où on ne peut pas aller pour moi, où (même) le roi va seul; **what,** *O:* **how, do you do for, about, water?** comment faites-vous pour vous procurer de l'eau? **what are you going to do about it?** que vous proposez-vous de faire? quelles mesures allez-vous prendre? **what would he do without you?** que deviendrait-il sans vous? **you shouldn't do so much,** vous vous dépensez trop; **it was all I could do to lift it,** c'est à peine si j'ai pu le soulever; *A:* **I had much to do in getting him to come,** j'ai eu bien de la peine à le faire venir; **you must do as others do,** il faut faire comme les autres; **do what we would,** malgré tous nos efforts, en dépit de tous nos efforts; **we must do or die,** il faut vaincre ou mourir; **do-or-die attitude,** attitude *f* de détermination inébranlable; **when in Rome do as Rome does, as the Romans do,** il faut hurler avec les loups; **well done!** très bien! bravo! à la bonne heure! (*b*) (*with passive force*) **he came to see what was doing,** il est venu voir ce qui se faisait; *Com: etc:* **there's nothing doing,** les affaires *f* ne vont pas; le marché est mort, est nul; c'est le marasme; c'est la morte-saison; *F:* **nothing doing!** rien à faire! ça ne prend pas! *P:* tu peux te gratter, te taper! on ne me la fait pas! macache! des nèfles! **there was nothing doing,** il n'a rien voulu savoir; **nothing doing under 20%,** je ne marche pas à moins de 20%. **2.** (*a*) (*deal with*) faire (la correspondance, une chambre, le ménage); **to do s.o.'s hair,** (i) coiffer qn; (ii) faire une mise en plis à qn; **to do one's nails,** se faire les ongles; **to do out a room,** nettoyer, faire, une chambre; **he does repairs,** il fait des réparations; (*at barber's, etc.*) **I'll do you next, sir,** à votre tour, monsieur; (*b*) cuire, faire cuire (de la viande); **meat well done,** viande bien cuite; **done to a turn,** cuit à point; **is it done yet?** est-ce que c'est cuit? **they are best done with . . .,** ils s'accommodent mieux à, avec . . .; (*c*) **to do a sum, a problem,** faire un calcul; résoudre un problème; (*d*) faire (une traduction); (*e*) *F: (perform a play, act a part)* faire (Hamlet, etc.); *F: O:* **to do the polite, the agreeable,** faire l'aimable; **to do the interpreter,** faire l'interprète; (*f*) *F:* **to do a town, the Continent, a museum,** visiter, faire, une ville, le Continent, un musée; (*g*) *F: (cheat)* **to do s.o. (down),** refaire, faire, attraper, qn; mettre qn dedans; **I've been done** (*O:* **in the eye)!** j'ai été roulé! on m'a eu! **to do s.o. out of sth.,** soutirer, carotter, qch. à qn; frustrer, refaire, qn de qch.; **I've been done out of my money,** on m'a refait mon argent; **he's done me out of two thousand pounds,** il m'a mis dedans pour deux mille livres; **to do s.o. out of a job,** supplanter qn; (*h*) *F:* **they do you very well at this hotel,** on est très bien servi à cet hôtel; **how much do they do you for here?** la pension est de combien ici? **to do oneself well,** faire bonne chère; **cigars! your friend does himself well,** des cigares! il ne se refuse rien, votre ami! **you *have* done us well!** vous nous avez traités en prince! nous avons dîné somptueusement; (*i*) *Com: F:* **we can do you this article at . . .,** nous pouvons vous faire cet article à . . .. **3.** (*in perfect tenses and past participle*) (*make an end of*) (*a*) **to have done,** avoir fini; **one more question and I've, I'm, done,** encore une question et j'ai fini; **hurry up, or we shall never have done,** dépêchez-vous ou nous n'en sortirons pas; **it's done,** c'est fini, c'est fait; *F:* ça y est; **the day is done,** le jour est à son déclin; la journée tire à sa fin; **when you have, are, done, we'll go out,** quand vous aurez fini nous sortirons; *F:* **haven't you done eating yet?** est-ce que vous n'avez pas encore fini de manger? *A:* **have done (with) crying!** finissez de pleurer! assez de larmes! *F:* **have you done?** quand vous aurez fini! **will he never have done?** il n'en finira donc pas! *A:* **be done! have done!** finissez donc! en voilà assez! *U.S: P:* **have you done supper?** avez-vous soupé? avez-vous fini votre souper? (*b*) *P:* (*of pers.*) **to be done (to the world, to the wide),** être éreinté, exténué; n'en pouvoir plus; (*c*) (*after a bargain made*) **done!** entendu! d'accord! c'est marché fait! ça y est! tenu! **4. how do you do?** (i) comment allez-vous? (ii) (*on first introduction to s.o.*) enchanté (de faire votre connaissance); **to be doing well,** (*of pers.*) être en bonne voie, faire de bonnes affaires; faire son chemin; prospérer; (*of invalid*) être en voie de guérison; (*of business*) bien aller, réussir; (*of plant*) bien pousser, réussir, venir; **vines do well on hillsides,** la vigne se plait sur les coteaux; **how is he likely to do?** comment pense-t-on qu'il s'en tirera, qu'il s'en acquittera? **we're doing pretty well,** ça ne marche pas si mal; **that young man will do well,** c'est un garçon qui réussira; c'est un garçon d'avenir. **5.** (*to serve, suffice*) **that will do,** (i) c'est bien (comme cela); c'est bon; cela va; cela ira; cela fera l'affaire; (ii) cela suffira; ça suffit; c'est assez; assez comme ça; en voilà assez! **this room will do for the office,** cette pièce ira bien pour le bureau; **that will not do,** cela ne va pas; cela n'ira pas; cela ne fera pas l'affaire; cela ne peut pas aller, marcher, comme ça; **that won't do for me,** (i) cela ne me va pas, ne me convient pas; cela ne fera pas mon affaire; (ii) cela ne prend pas avec moi; **that won't do here,** cela ne passe pas ici; **that will never do,** cela n'ira jamais, ça n'ira pas du tout; ce n'est pas permis, tolérable; **will that do?** (i) cela va-t-il? cela fera-t-il l'affaire? est-ce bien comme cela? (ii) cela suffit-il? (*to child*) **that will do!** tais-toi! *F:* **will I do?** (i) est-ce que je fais l'affaire? (ii) suis-je bien comme ça? ça va-t-il comme ça? **it would hardly have done to . . .,** il n'aurait pas été convenable de . . .; **I will make it do,** je m'en arrangerai; **you *must* make do with what you have,** il faut vous arranger de, avec, ce que vous avez; **to be just able to make do,** vivre bien juste; **something one can make do with,** des moyens de fortune; *F:* **I have just enough to do me till the end of the year,** j'ai juste assez pour suffire à mes besoins jusqu'à la fin de l'année; **that will do me,** cela fera mon affaire; **a flat in town would do me,** un appartement en ville m'irait, m'accommoderait; **nothing would do,** rien n'y fit; **nothing would do but for me to go home with him,** il a fallu absolument que je rentre avec lui; **it would never do for them to see me,** il ne faudrait pas que je les rencontre.

II. *verb substitute.* **1.** (*replacing v.tr. or i.*) **I replied as the others had done,** j'ai répondu comme avaient fait les autres; **they work in the fields as their fathers did, as did their fathers,** ils travaillent aux champs comme le faisaient leurs pères; **why act as you do?** pourquoi agir comme vous le faites? **he writes better than he did,** il écrit mieux qu'autrefois; **he writes better than I do,** il écrit mieux que moi; **he acquitted himself much better than I could have done,** il s'en est acquitté beaucoup mieux que je n'aurais pu le faire. **2.** (*replacing v.tr. and taking its construction*) **he envies me as much as I do him,** il me porte autant d'envie que je lui en porte. **3.** (*replacing v.tr. and obj.*) **if you understood the question as well as I do,** si vous compreniez la question aussi bien que moi, aussi bien que je la comprends. **4.** (*elliptical auxiliary*) **may I open these letters?—(please) do,** puis-je ouvrir ces lettres?—faites donc! je vous en prie! **did you see him?—I did,** l'avez-vous vu?—oui (, je l'ai vu); **do you think of him?—yes, I do,** pensez-vous à lui?—oui, bien sûr; **do you like her?—I do not, no I don't,** l'aimez-vous?—non (, je ne l'aime pas); **don't you like it?—yes, I do,** vous ne l'aimez pas?—mais si; **he said he would sell the house, and he did,** il avait dit qu'il vendrait la maison, et il l'a vendue en effet, et il l'a fait; **I like coffee; do *you*?** j'aime le café; et vous? **I don't like tea; do *you*?** je n'aime pas le thé; et vous? **they travel a good deal.—do they? they do?** ils voyagent beaucoup.—c'est vrai? **you like him, don't you?** vous l'aimez, n'est-ce pas? **you had a disturbed night, didn't you?** vous avez eu une nuit troublée, n'est-ce pas? **you like him, do you?** vous l'aimez, alors? **he said so, did he?** il a dit cela, vraiment? **he lives here, doesn't he?** il demeure ici, n'est-ce pas? **that does you good, doesn't it?** ça fait du bien, hein? **don't!** ne faites pas ça! finissez! *F:* **he likes a wee drop, does the doctor,** il aime bien un petit verre, le docteur; **he needs to be taught manners, *he* does** ['hi: dʌz], il a besoin d'apprendre à vivre, cet homme-là. **5.** (*often with 'so', 'it', 'which'*) **I wanted to see him and I did so,** j'ai voulu le voir, et je l'ai vu; **you like Paris? so do I,** vous aimez Paris? moi aussi; **they have always existed, and do so still, and still do,** ils ont toujours existé, et existent encore; **passing through the square, which he seldom did,** en traversant la place, ce qu'il faisait rarement; **if you want to speak to him, do it now,** si vous désirez lui parler, faites-le maintenant.

III. *v.aux.* (*used with inf. for simple pr. and past*) **1.** (*a*) (*for emphasis*) **he *did* go,** il y est bien allé; **that's just what people *did* say,** c'est bien là en effet ce que disait le monde; **I *do* believe he is a thief,** je crois vraiment que c'est un voleur; **he threatened to go, and he *did* go, and go he *did,*** il menaçait de partir, et il est parti en effet; **the wisest men do say foolish things at times,** les plus sages, en effet, disent quelquefois des sottises; **he was determined not to fail, but fail he did,** il était résolu à ne pas échouer; il a échoué cependant; **it doesn't matter.—it *does* (matter)!** ça ne fait rien.—si, ça fait quelque chose! **why don't you work?—I *do* (work)!** pourquoi ne travaillez-vous pas?—mais si, je travaille! **you saved me; oh yes, you *did*!** vous m'avez sauvé; si, si, vous m'avez sauvé; **he couldn't have said that.—but he *did*,** il n'a pas pu dire cela.—mais si, il l'a dit; je vous dis que si; **he said so.—*did* he?** il a dit cela.—vraiment? **he never did (do that)!** cela, il ne l'a jamais fait! ***did* he indeed?** non vraiment? **do you remember him?—do I *remember* him!** vous souvenez-vous de lui?—si je m'en souviens! ***do* sit down,** asseyez-vous donc! ***do* tell me!** dites-le-moi donc! ***do* repeat it!** allons, répétez-le! ***do* give it me!** donnez-le-moi, je vous en prie! ***do* finish!** finissez donc! finissez, je vous en prie! ***do* shut up!** veux-tu bien te taire! mais tais-toi, donc! *A:* **do *you* go rather!** allez-y plutôt, vous! **that hairstyle *does* alter you!** ce que ça vous change, cette coiffure! **I *do* go to his house, but only on business,** je vais chez lui en effet, mais seulement pour affaires; **I *did* live in Paris, but I have moved,** je demeurais à Paris, en effet, mais j'ai déménagé; **yes, people *did* live there,** oui, des gens ont vécu là; **I do not say that . . ., but I *do* say that . . .,** je ne dis pas que . . ., mais j'affirme que . . .; **I don't like coffee, but I *do* like tea,** je n'aime pas le café, mais j'aime bien le thé; **I *do* like tea!** je raffole du thé; (*b*) *A: & Lit:* (*in sentences restricted by 'but'*) **the newcomers do but poorly replace those that have gone,** les nouveaux venus remplacent mal ceux qui sont partis; **he did but follow his inclination,** il n'a fait que suivre le penchant de son esprit. **2.** (*invention*) **never did I spend such a night,** jamais je n'ai passé une nuit pareille; **rarely does it happen that . . .,** il arrive rarement que . . .. **3.** *Ecc: & Jur:* **all the earth doth worship Thee, the Father everlasting,** toute la terre t'adore, ô Père d'éternité; **charged that he did on the 15th of August utter threats,** accusé d'avoir, le 15 août, proféré des menaces. **4.** (*usual form in questions and negative statements except with 'have', but cf.* HAVE, BE, *and modal verbs; also in negative commands*) **do you, did you, see him?** le voyez-vous? l'avez-vous vu? **do you dare ask him for it?** osez-vous le lui demander? **we do not know,** nous ne le savons pas; **do not speak!** ne parlez pas! **don't do it!** n'en faites rien! **don't be afraid,** n'ayez pas peur; **do you, d'you, mind?** ça ne vous fait rien? *F:* (*in frustrated irritation*) *do* **you mind!** (i) je vous en prie! *F:* fiche-moi la paix! (ii)je puis passer? *F:* bouge-toi!

IV. (*compound verbs*) **1. do away,** *v.i.* **to do away with,** abolir, proscrire, abandonner (un usage); supprimer, éliminer (des frais, etc.); détruire, faire disparaître (un édifice); tuer, *F:* supprimer (qn); se défaire de (qn); **the museum has been done away with,** on a fait disparaître le musée; **practice that has since been done away with,** usage qu'on a aboli depuis; **they had to do away with their old dog,** ils ont dû se défaire de leur vieux chien.

2. do by, *v.tr.* **to do well, badly, by s.o.,** bien, mal, agir, se bien, mal, conduire, envers qn; **he has been hard done by,** il a été traité durement, avec une sévérité excessive; **do as you would be done by,** agissez envers les autres comme vous voudriez qu'on agisse envers vous, comme vous voudriez qu'ils fissent envers vous; ne faites pas à autrui ce que vous ne voudriez pas qu'on vous fît.

3. *F:* **do for,** *v.tr.* (*a*) **to do for s.o.,** faire, tenir, le ménage de qn; (*b*) (*kill*) tuer (qn); faire son affaire à (qn); régler son compte à (qn); **he's done for,** c'est un homme mort; **another stroke would do for him,** une nouvelle congestion lui réglerait son compte; (*c*) (*ruin*) détruire, ruiner, couler (qn); mettre (qn) à bas; **this scandal has done for him,** ce scandale l'a coulé; **he's done for,** c'est un homme brûlé, coulé; *F:* il est flambé, frit, fichu; **but for you, I'd have been done for,** sans vous j'étais perdu, j'étais fichu.

4. do in, *v.tr. P:* (*a*) tuer, assassiner (qn); *F:* faire son affaire à (qn); faire un sort à (qn); *P:* estourbir, zigouiller (qn); (*b*) éreinter (qn); **I'm feeling absolutely done in,** je me sens absolument fourbu, vanné.

5. do up, *v.tr.* (*a*) (i) réparer (qch.); remettre (qch.) à neuf; retaper (un chapeau); décorer (une maison, etc.); *F:* **to do up one's face,** se farder; se maquiller; **to do oneself up,** faire toilette; (ii) apprêter (le linge); (*b*) *Cu: F:* accommoder (un plat, des restes); (*c*) faire, envelopper, ficeler (un paquet); emballer, empaqueter (des marchandises); mettre (un journal) sous bande; fermer, boutonner, agrafer (un vêtement); **dress that does up at the back,** robe *f* qui s'agrafe par derrière; **do me up, please,** veux-tu m'agrafer ma robe, s'il te plaît? (*d*) *F:* (*of pers., horse*) **to be done up,** être éreinté, fourbu, vanné, rompu, rendu; être sur le flanc; **I'm done up,** je n'en peux plus; j'ai les jambes rompues.

6. do with, *v.tr.* (*a*) **what is to be done with him?** que faire de lui? **what did you do with my umbrella?** qu'avez-vous fait de mon parapluie? **she didn't know what to do with herself,** elle ne savait que faire, à quoi s'occuper; (*for joy*) elle ne se tenait pas de joie; (*for awkwardness*) elle était fort embarrassée de sa personne; *F:* **he doesn't know what to do with his hands and feet,** il ne sait pas que faire de ses dix doigts; il est terriblement gauche; **tell me what you did with yourself yesterday,** dites-moi à quoi vous avez passé le temps hier; (*b*) **to have to do with s.o.,** avoir affaire à qn; **I want, I will have, nothing to do with him,** je ne veux pas avoir affaire à lui; *F:* **I just can't do with him,** je ne peux pas le sentir; **to have to do with sth.,** (*of pers.*) être mêlé à qch.; avoir à voir dans, à, qch.; (*of thg*) avoir rapport à, avec, qch.; avoir du rapport avec qch.; concerner qch.; **this has little to do with lexicography,** cela a peu de chose à voir avec la lexicographie; **to have something to do with a business,** (*of pers.*) être pour quelque chose dans une affaire; n'être pas étranger à une affaire; (*of thg*) avoir rapport à, avoir quelque rapport avec, une affaire; **philosophy has to do with all aspects of life,** la philosophie porte sur tous les aspects de la vie; **what's his work?—(it's) something to do with dictionaries, he's something to do with insurance,** qu'est-ce qu'il fait?—il s'occupe de dictionnaires, d'assurances; il est dans les assurances; **his description of everything to do with the engine,** sa description de tout ce qui regarde le fonctionnement du moteur; **to have nothing to do with a matter,** (i) (*of pers.*) n'être pour rien dans, être étranger à, n'avoir rien à voir avec, une affaire; (ii) (*of thg*) n'avoir rien à faire avec, n'avoir pas de rapport à, avec, une affaire; **you have nothing to do with it; it's nothing to do with you,** vous n'avez rien à voir là-dedans; vous n'avez rien à y voir; **it is nothing to do with drink,** la boisson n'a rien à y voir; la boisson n'y est pour rien, n'en est pas cause; **I had nothing to do with it,** je n'y suis pour rien; j'ai les mains nettes; **I'm sure she has something to do with it,** je suis sûr qu'elle y est pour quelque chose; elle y est sûrement pour quelque chose; **I'm sure she has nothing to do with it,** je suis sûr qu'elle n'y est pour rien; **jealousy has a lot to do with it,** la jalousie y est pour beaucoup; **favouritism has a great deal to do with promotion,** la faveur joue un très grand rôle dans l'avancement; (*c*) **to have done with sth.,** en avoir fini avec qch.; **let's have done with it!** finissons-en! **hurry up or we'll never have done with it,** dépêchez-vous ou nous n'en sortirons pas; *O:* **have done with compliments!** trêve de compliments! *O:* **have done with teasing him!** cessez de le taquiner! **I have done with politics,** je ne me mêle plus de politique; **I have done with teaching,** j'ai lâché l'enseignement; **if you have an old house you have never done with repairs,** à une vieille maison il y a toujours à refaire; **we've done with laughter,** c'est fini de rire; **I've done with love,** j'ai renoncé à l'amour; j'en ai assez de l'amour; **to have done with s.o.,** (i) n'avoir plus besoin de qn; (ii) avoir rompu avec qn; en avoir fini avec qn; ne plus s'occuper de qn; **he has done with her,** il ne veut plus entendre parler d'elle; **I haven't done with him yet!** je n'en ai pas encore fini avec lui! **that's all over and done with!** c'est fini, tout ça! (*d*) **I cannot do with any noise,** je ne peux pas supporter le bruit; **he does with very little food,** il s'accommode de très peu de nourriture; **I can do with little,** je sais me contenter de peu; (*e*) **how many can you do with?** combien en désirez-vous? combien vous en faut-il? **I think I can do with six,** je pense qu'il m'en faut six; **I could do with more sleep,** je dormirais volontiers davantage; **I could do with a cup of tea,** je prendrais bien une tasse de thé; **I could do with a drink,** je boirais bien quelque chose; **we can do with your help,** vous n'êtes pas de trop.

7. do without, *v.tr.* se passer de (qn, qch.); **I must do without,** il faut que je m'en passe; **I can do without it,** je peux m'en passer; **to do without food,** se passer de nourriture; *F:* **I could do without him,** je me passerais bien de lui; je ne peux pas le sentir.

do² [du:], *s.* **1.** (*a*) **the do's and don'ts of society,** les obligations *f* et les défenses *f* du monde; ce qui se fait et ce qui ne se fait pas dans le monde; **a diet with numerous do's and don'ts,** un régime comportant de nombreuses prescriptions et proscriptions; (*b*) *F:* manière *f* de traiter qn; **hotel where you get a poor do,** hôtel *m* où l'on est mal servi; **it's a poor do!** c'est plutôt minable! **come on, fair do's!** dis donc, (i) donne-moi ma part! (ii) sois juste! **that's not fair do's,** c'est pas juste! **2.** *F: O:* attrape *f*, escroquerie *f*; **it's a do,** c'est une attrape; on nous a mis dedans. **3.** *F:* (*a*) affaire *f*; *Mil:* **to take part in a big do,** prendre part à une grosse affaire; (*b*) réception *f*; réunion *f*; (*c*) exposition *f*; (*d*) *Mil: etc:* défilé *m*.

do³ [dou], *s. Mus:* **1.** (*fixed do*) do *m*, ut *m*. **2.** (*movable do, in tonic solfa* **doh**) la tonique.

do⁴ ['ditou] = DITTO.

doable ['du:əbl], *a.* faisable.

do-all ['du:ɔ:l], *s. A: & F:* factotum *m*.

doat [dout], *v.i. A:* = DOTE¹.

dobbie ['dɔbi], *s. Tex:* ratière *f*.

dobbin ['dɔbin], *s. F:* cheval *m* de trait, de labour.

dobby ['dɔbi], *s. Tex:* ratière *f*.

doberman(n) (pinscher) ['doubəmən('pinʃər)], *s.* (*dog*) doberman *m*, pinscher *m*.

Dobrudja (the) [ðədou'bru:dʒə], *Pr.n. Geog:* la Dobroudja; la Dobroutcha.

doc [dɔk], *s. F:* (= DOCTOR) toubib *m*.

doch-an-dorrach ['dɔχən'dɔrəχ], **doch-an-dorris** ['dɔχən'dɔris], *s. Scot:* coup *m* de l'étrier.

dochmiac ['dɔkmiak], *a. & s. Pros:* dochmiaque (*m*).

docile ['dousail], *a.* **1.** docile; (animal *m*) sage. **2.** (*of matter*) facile à travailler; souple; pliant; **d. ore,** minerai *m* docile.

docilely ['dousailli], *adv.* docilement.

docility [dou'siliti], *s.* docilité *f*.

docimasy ['dɔsiməsi], *s. Gr.Ant: Ch: Med:* docimasie *f*.

docimology [dɔsi'mɔlədʒi], *s.* docimologie *f*.

dock¹ [dɔk], *s. Bot:* patience *f*; **bloody d.,** patience rouge; **yellow d.,** parelle *f*; **sour d.,** oseille *f*; **water d.,** oseille aquatique.

dock², *s.* **1.** tronçon *m*, partie charnue (de la queue d'un cheval ou d'un chien). **2.** *Harn:* **d. (piece),** culeron *m*, trousse-queue *m inv*.

dock³, *v.tr.* **1.** (*a*) **to d. a horse('s tail), a dog('s tail),** couper la queue à, écourter, un cheval, un chien; (*b*) *A:* couper les cheveux à (qn). **2.** (*a*) diminuer, rogner, supprimer (le traitement de qn); **to d. sth. off a sum,** retrancher qch. sur une somme; (*b*) **to d. s.o. of his rations,** retrancher sa ration à qn; (*c*) *Jur:* **to d. an entail,** annuler une substitution.

dock⁴, *s.* **1.** *Nau:* (*a*) bassin *m* (d'un port); **outer d.,** avant-bassin *m*, *pl.* avant-bassins; **inner d.,** arrière-bassin *m*, *pl.* arrière-bassins; **flooding d., wet d.,** bassin à flot; (*in S. of Fr.*) darse *f*; **tidal d.,** bassin d'échouage; **to go into d.,** entrer au bassin; **to leave d.,** sortir du bassin; **the docks,** les docks *m*; **d. dues,** droits *m* de bassin; de port; **d. master,** officier *m* de port; directeur *m* des docks (et entrepôts); *F:* (*of car, plane*) **in d.,** en réparation; *Nau: Mil: P: A:* **in d.,** hospitalisé, à l'hôpital (surtout pour traitement d'une maladie vénérienne); (*b*) **dry d., graving d.,** cale sèche; bassin de radoub; forme *f* de radoub; dock de carénage; **ship in dry d.,** navire *m* en radoub; **to go into dry d.,** entrer en cale sèche; *P:* (*of pers.*) **to be in dry d.,** être sans emploi; (*c*) **floating d.,** dock flottant; chantier *m* à flot; **floating (dry) d.,** cale sèche flottante; (*d*) *pl.* **naval docks** = DOCKYARD; (*e*) *F:* (*wharf*) **loading d.,** embarcadère *m*; **unloading d.,** débarcadère *m*. **2.** (*a*) (*on river or canal*) gare *f* (d'eau); (*b*) *Rail:* quai *m* en cul-de-sac. **3.** *Th:* **scene d.,** remise *f* à décors. **4.** *Aer:* hangar *m*.

dock⁵. **1.** *v.tr.* (*a*) *Nau:* faire entrer (un navire) au bassin, au dock; faire passer (un navire) au(x) dock(s); (*b*) faire entrer (un navire) en cale sèche; (*c*) (*on canal, river*) garer (une péniche, etc.); (*d*) *Rail:* garer (un train); (*e*) arrimer (deux engins spatiaux). **2.** *v.tr.* fournir (un port) de docks. **3.** *v.i.* (*of ship*) entrer, passer, (i) au bassin, aux docks, (ii) en cale sèche.

dock⁶, *s. Jur:* banc *m*, box *m*, des accusés, des prévenus; **to be in the d.,** être au banc des prévenus; **d. brief,** entreprise *f* de la défense d'un prévenu indigent par un membre du barreau présent à l'audience.

dockage ['dɔkidʒ], *s.* **1.** *Adm:* droits *mpl* de quai, de bassin. **2.** outillage *m*, équipement *m*, de quai, de bassin. **3.** (*cereal trade*) déduction *f*, défalcation *f* (pour cause de perte de poids ou de diminution de qualité).

docker ['dɔkər], *s.* **1.** travailleur *m* aux docks; déchargeur *m*, docker *m*, débardeur *m*. **2.** marin *m* du port.

docket¹ ['dɔkit], *s.* **1.** *Jur:* (*a*) registre *m* des jugements rendus; (*b*) *U.S:* rôle *m* des causes; (*c*) bordereau *m* (des pièces d'un dossier). **2.** étiquette *f*, extrait *m*, fiche *f* (d'un document, d'une lettre); *Ind: etc:* **wages d.,** bordereau de paye. **3.** *Adm:* récépissé *m* de douane.

docket², *v.tr.* **1.** *Jur:* (*a*) enregistrer (un jugement rendu); (*b*) *U.S:* porter (une cause) sur le rôle des causes. **2.** étiqueter, classer (des papiers).

docketing ['dɔkitiŋ], *s.* classement *m*.

docking ['dɔkiŋ], *s.* (*a*) mise *f*, entrée *f*, au bassin; (*for repairs*) radoubage *m*, carénage *m*; **d. basin,** bassin *m* de desserte; (*b*) arrimage *m*, amarrage *m*, jonction *f* (de deux engins spatiaux); **d. manœuvre,** manœuvre *f* d'abordage.

dockland ['dɔklænd], *s.* les quartiers *m* des docks.

docksman, *pl.* **-men** ['dɔksmən, -men], *s.m.* ouvrier aux docks.

dock-tailed ['dɔkteild], *a.* **d.-t. horse,** courte-queue *m*, *pl.* courtes-queues.

dockyard ['dɔkjɑ:d], *s.* chantier *m* de construction de navires; *esp.* **naval d.,** arsenal *m* maritime, port *m* militaire; *Navy:* **d. staff,** maistrance *f*.

dockyardman, *pl.* **-men** ['dɔkjɑ:dmæn, -men], *s.m.* ouvrier d'un arsenal maritime.

doctor¹ ['dɔktər]. *s.* **1.** *A:* (*learned man*) docteur *m*; **the doctors of the Church,** les docteurs de l'Église. **2.** *Sch:* **D. of Divinity,** docteur en théologie; **D. of Laws,** docteur en droit; *A.Jur:* **Doctors' Commons,** collège *m* des docteurs en droit civil; **D. of Medicine,** docteur en médecine; **D. of Literature,** docteur ès lettres; **Miss X is a D. of Science,** Mlle X est docteur ès sciences; **he has taken his doctor's degree,** il a passé son doctorat. **3.** médecin *m*, docteur; **woman d.,** femme médecin; **Doctor** (*abbr.* **Dr**) **Martin,** (Monsieur) le docteur Martin; **to call in a d.,** appeler un médecin; **come in, D.,** entrez, docteur; **who is your d.?** quel est votre médecin (traitant)? **family d.,** médecin de famille; **factory, works, d.,** médecin du travail; **ship's d.,** médecin du bord; **army d.,** médecin militaire; **National Health (Service) d., N.H.S. d.,** médecin conventionné; *F:* **just what the d. ordered,** la bonne formule. **4.** *F: O:* raccommodeur, -euse (de parapluies, de stylos, etc.). **5.** (*a*) *Tchn: Typ:* raclette *f* (d'une presse rotative); *Tex: etc:* racle *f*, racloir *m*, essuyeur (d'une machine à rouleau); (*b*) *Petr:* **d. solution,** solution *f* au plombite. **6.** *Fish:* (variété *f* de) mouche artificielle.

doctor², *v.tr.* **1.** *F: A:* conférer le grade de docteur à (qn); recevoir (qn) docteur. **2.** (*a*) soigner, *F:* droguer, *Pej:* médicamenter (un malade); (*b*) *Turf: Pej:* droguer, doper (un cheval); (*c*) châtrer (un chat, etc.). **3.** *F: O:* réparer, raccommoder, retaper, rafistoler (un objet). **4.** *F:* falsifier, fausser, truquer, tripatouiller (des comptes, un texte); piper (un dé, des cartes); frelater, droguer (du vin, etc.); frelater (un aliment).

doctoral ['dɔktər(ə)l], *a.* doctoral, -aux; de docteur.

doctorand ['dɔktərænd], *s.* candidat *m* au doctorat.

doctorate ['dɔkt(ə)rət], *s. Sch:* doctorat *m*.

doct(o)ress ['dɔkt(ə)res], *s.f. F: O:* femme médecin, doctoresse.

doctorial [dɔk'tɔ:riəl], *a.* doctoral, -aux; de docteur.

doctoring ['dɔktəriŋ], *s.* **1.** (*a*) soins (**of s.o.,** donnés à qn); (*b*) *F:* doping *m* (d'un cheval); (*c*) castration *f* (d'un chat, etc.). **2.** *F:* profession *f* de médecin. **3.** *F:* falsification *f*.

doctrinaire [dɔktri'nɛər], **doctrinarian** [dɔktri'nɛəriən], *a. & s.* doctrinaire (*mf*).

doctrinairism [dɔktri'nɛərizm], **doctrinarianism** [dɔktri'nɛəriənizm], *s.* doctrinarisme *m*.

doctrinal [dɔk'train(ə)l], *a.* doctrinal, -aux.

doctrinally [dɔk'trainəli], *adv.* doctrinalement.

doctrine ['dɔktrin], *s.* doctrine *f*.

document¹ ['dɔkjumənt], *s.* document *m*, pièce *f*, titre *m*; papier *m*; *pl.* écritures *f*; **legal d.,** acte *m* authentique; **commercial documents,** papiers d'affaires; **working d.,** document de travail; *Cmptr:* **source d.,** document de base; *Jur:* **documents relating to a case,** dossier *m* d'une affaire; pièces en instance; **documents of title,** titres de propriété; **to draw up a d.,** dresser, rédiger, un acte; **d. case,** porte documents *m inv*.

document² ['dɔkjument], *v.tr.* **1.** documenter (une opinion); appuyer (une opinion) sur des documents; **well documented novel,** roman bien documenté. **2.** munir (qn) de documents; fournir des documents à (qn).

documental [dɔkju'ment(ə)l], *a.* = DOCUMENTARY 1.

documentarist [dɔkju'ment(ə)rist], *s. Cin: etc:* documentariste *mf*.

documentary [dɔkju'ment(ə)ri]. **1.** *a.* documentaire; *Com:* **d. bill,** traite documentaire; traite accompagnée de documents; **these maps have no d. authority,** ces cartes *f* ne font pas loi, ne font pas autorité. **2.** *s. Cin:* documentaire *m*.

documentation [dɔkjumen'teiʃ(ə)n], *s.* documentation *f*.

doda ['doudə], *s. Z:* tétracère *m*.

dodad ['du:dæd], *s. U.S: F:* truc *m*, machin *m*.

dodder¹ ['dɔdər], *s. Bot:* cuscute *f*; *F:* cheveux *mpl* du diable, barbe-de-moine *f*, *pl.* barbes-de-moine; teigne *f*.

dodder², *v.i.* (*of aged pers.*) trembloter; marcher d'un pas branlant; **to d. along,** (i) marcher en branlant bras et jambes; (ii) *Aut: etc: F:* aller, rouler, à la papa.

dodderer ['dɔdərər], *s. F:* **an old d.,** un vieux gâteux, une vieille gâteuse; un vieux gaga.

doddering ['dɔdəriŋ], *a.* **1. d. walk, head,** démarche, tête, branlante. **2.** (*of pers.*) gaga *inv*, gâteux.

doddery ['dɔdəri], *a. F:* tremblant, branlant, tremblotant.

dodec(a)- ['doudek(ə)], *comb.fm.* dodéc(a)-.

dodecagon [dou'dekəgən], *s. Geom:* dodécagone *m*.

dodecagonal [doude'kægən(ə)l], *a.* dodécagonal, -aux.

dodecahedral [doudekə'hi:drəl, -'hedrəl], *a.* dodécaèdre, dodécaédrique.

dodecahedron [doudekə'hi:drən, -'hedrən], *s.* dodécaèdre *m*.

dodecane ['doudəkein], *s. Ch:* dodécane *m*.

Dodecanese (the) [ðə'doudekə'ni:z]. *Pr.n. Geog:* le Dodécanèse.

dodecapartite [doudekə'pɑ:tait], *a.* dodécaparti, -ite.

dodecaphonic [doudekə'fɔnik], *a. Mus:* dodécaphonique.

dodecaphonist [doude'kæfənist], *s. Mus:* dodécaphoniste *mf*.

dodecaphony [doude'kæfəni], *s. Mus:* dodécaphonie *f*.

dodecastyle ['doudekəstail], *a. Arch:* dodécastyle.

dodecasyllable [doudekə'siləbl], *s. Pros:* dodécasyllabe *m*.

Dodecatheon [doude'kæθiən], *s. Bot:* dodécathéon *m*.

dodecuple [dou'dekjupl], *a.* dodécuple.

dodge¹ [dɔdʒ], *s.* **1.** mouvement *m* de côté; saut *m* de côté; *Box: Fb:* esquive *f*, évite *f*. **2.** (*a*) ruse *f*, artifice *m*; *F:* manigance *f*; **it was a d. to catch him out,** c'était une feinte pour le surprendre; **an old d.,** un coup classique; (*b*) truc *m*, ficelle *f*, tour *m* de main; **trade dodges,** recettes *f* de métier; **to be up to all the dodges,** connaître tous les trucs; la connaître dans les coins; **to discover the d. for doing sth.,** trouver le joint pour faire qch; (*c*) *P:* **to be on the d.,** (i) fricoter; trafiquer; (ii) se tenir coi (pour se dérober aux recherches de la police, etc.).

dodge². **1.** *v.i.* (*a*) se jeter de côté, s'esquiver; **to d. behind a tree,** se jeter derrière un arbre; **to d. about, in and out,** faire des tours et des détours; (*to child*) **don't d. about!** reste tranquille! (*b*) *Box: Fb:* esquiver, éviter; (*c*) biaiser, ruser, user d'artifices. **2.** *v.tr.* (*a*) se jeter de côté pour éviter (un coup); esquiver (un coup); éviter (qn);

esquiver, tourner, éluder (une difficulté); *F:* couper à (une punition); **to d. a question,** éluder, escamoter, une question; s'échapper par la tangente; *F:* **to d. the column,** tirer au flanc; **to d. military service,** se soustraire, *F:* couper, au service militaire; **to d. the law,** se dérober à l'atteinte de la loi; éluder la loi; *Nau:* **to d. a sea,** défier de la lame; (*b*) *A:* lanterner (qn.); se jouer de (qn).

dodgem ['dɔdʒəm], *a. & s.* **d. cars, dodgems,** autos tamponneuses.

dodger ['dɔdʒər], *s.* **1.** *F:* (*a*) *O:* **an artful d.,** un malin, un fin matois, un fin roublard; **an old d.,** un vieux malin; un vieux renard; (*b*) *Mil:* embusqué *m*; **column d.,** tire-au-flanc *m inv*; *U.S:* **draft d.,** homme qui essaie d'éviter le service militaire. **2.** *Nau:* toile *f* (de passerelle de commandement). **3.** *U.S:* *F:* prospectus *m*.

dodgy ['dɔdʒi], *a.* *F:* **1.** roublard. **2. d. situation,** situation délicate.

dodo, *pl.* **-oes, -os** ['doudou, -z], *s.* **1.** *Orn:* dronte *m*; dodo *m*. **2.** *F:* personne *f* vieux jeu; vieux fossile; **(as) dead as a d.,** (*a*) mort et enterré; (*b*) tombé dans un oubli complet.

Dodona [dou'dounə]. *Pr.n.* *A.Geog:* Dodone *f*.

Dodonaean [doudə'ni:ən], *a. & s.* *A.Geog:* Dodonéen, -enne.

doe [dou], *s.* *Z:* **1.** daine *f*; biche *f*; **d.-eyed,** aux yeux de biche. **2.** (*of rabbit*) lapine *f*; (*of wild rabbit and hare*) hase *f*.

doeglic ['dɔ:glik], *a.* *Ch:* (acide *m*) doéglique.

doegling ['dɔ:gliŋ], *s.* *Z:* rorqual *m*, -als, à bec; **d. oil,** huile *f* du rorqual à bec.

doer ['du(:)ər], *s.* **1.** (*a*) faiseur, -euse; *P:* **she's no end of a d.,** c'est une femme très agissante; (*b*) auteur *m* (d'une action). **2.** (*a*) (*of domestic animal*) **he's a good d.,** il profite bien (de sa nourriture); (*b*) *a.* (*of plant*) robuste, qui vient bien.

doeskin ['douskin]. **1.** *s.* (*a*) peau *f* de daim; (*b*) *Tex:* drap *m* imitant la peau de daim; simili-daim *m*. **2.** *attrib.* en peau de daim.

doff [dɔf], *v.tr.* **1.** *Lit:* enlever, ôter (un vêtement, son chapeau). **2.** *Tex:* (i) enlever (le ruban de la cardeuse); (ii) faire la levée (d'une bobine); **doffing cylinder,** peigneuse enleveuse; (cylindre) délivreur *m*; **doffing knife** = DOFFER.

doffer ['dɔfər], *s.* *Tex:* (*of carding machine*) peigne *m* d'abattage.

dog[1] [dɔg], *s.* **1.** (*a*) chien *m*; (*often also*) chienne *f*; **sporting, non-sporting, d.,** chien de chasse, de compagnie; **gun d., bird d.,** chien d'arrêt; **working d.,** chien de travail; **sheep d.,** chien de berger; **Shetland sheep d.,** berger *m* shetland; **Belgian, Groenendael, sheep d.,** groenendael *m*, chien de troupeaux belge; **Dutch shepherd d.,** chien de berger hollandais; **Australian cattle d.,** chien de troupeaux australien; **Bernese mountain d.,** berger de Berne; **Pyrenean mountain d.,** chien de montagne des Pyrénées; **tracker d., police d.,** chien policier; **guide d.,** chien d'aveugle; *Mil:* **ambulance d.,** chien sanitaire; *A:* **coach d., carriage d.,** braque *m* de Bengale; *F:* **spotted d.,** (i) braque de Bengale; chien de Dalmatie; (ii) pudding *m* aux raisins de Corinthe; *P.N:* **beware of the d.,** chien méchant; **d. racing,** *F:* **the dogs,** courses *fpl* de lévriers; *F:* **to go to the dogs,** (i) aller aux courses de lévriers; (ii) gâcher sa vie; se dégrader, se débaucher, mal tourner; (*of business*) aller à la ruine; **d. lover,** amateur, -trice, de chiens; **d.-loving,** qui aime les chiens; **d. show,** exposition canine; **d. biscuit,** biscuit *m*, gâteau *m*, de chien; **dog('s) meat,** pâtée *f* (pour chiens); **d. collar,** (i) collier *m* de chien; (ii) *F:* faux col d'ecclésiastique; *U.S:* **d. tag,** plaque *f* d'identité (de chien, *F:* de militaire); *Comest:* **hot d.,** (petit pain fourré d'une) saucisse de Francfort chaude; *F:* **dog's nose,** mélange *m* de bière et de gin; *F:* **d. Latin,** latin *m* de cuisine; *P:* **d. end,** mégot *m*; **to lead a dog's life,** mener une vie de chien; **to die like a d.,** mourir comme un chien; **to follow s.o. like a d.,** faire le chien après qn; **to help a lame d. over a stile,** aider qn dans l'embarras; tirer qn d'un mauvais pas; **you can't teach an old d. new tricks,** on ne peut pas apprendre aux vieux singes à faire des grimaces; *F:* **he doesn't stand a dog's chance,** il n'a pas l'ombre d'une chance; *F:* **to see a man about a d.,** aller faire un petit tour, *esp.* aller faire pipi; *F:* **to take a hair of the d. that bit you,** reprendre du poil de la bête; *F:* (*of new recipe*) **I'm trying it (out) on the d.,** j'en fais l'essai avec la famille, mon mari; *F:* **to put on d.,** poser, plastronner; faire de l'épate; *Provs:* **every d. has his day,** à chacun son heure de gloire; **give a d. a bad name (and hang him),** qui veut noyer son chien l'accuse de la rage; **let sleeping dogs lie,** ne réveillez pas le chat qui dort; **d. doesn't eat d.,** les loups ne se mangent pas entre eux; **a live d. is better than a dead lion,** mieux vaut un chien vivant qu'un lion mort; *F:* **to be a dead d.,** être inutile; (*b*) *Z:* **(African, Cape) hunting d.,** lycaon *m*; **forest wild d., bush d.,** chien forestier sud-américain; **prairie d.,** cynomys *m*; **d. town,** terrier (commun) de cynomys; (*c*) *Bot:* **d.-town grass,** aristide *f*; **d. cabbage,** cynocrambe *m*; **d. daisy,** grande marguerite; **dog's bane,** (i) apocyn *m*; (ii) aconit *m* tue-chien; **dog's tail (grass),** cynosure *f*, crételle *f*; **crested dog's tail,** crételle des prés; **d. fennel,** maroute *f*, camomille puante; **d. violet,** violette *f* des chiens; **dog's tooth (violet),** érythrone *m*, dent-de-chien *f*; **dog('s) tooth grass, d. grass,** chiendent *m*, pied-de-poule *m*. **2.** mâle *m* (de certains animaux); **d. fox,** renard *m* mâle; **d. hyena,** hyène *f* mâle. **3.** *F:* *O:* **sly d.,** rusé coquin, fin renard; **gay d.,** (i) coureur *m* (de femmes); viveur *m*, noceur *m*, fêtard *m*; (ii) joyeux gaillard; (iii) bon vivant, bon compagnon; **dirty d.,** salaud *m*, sale type *m*; *A:* **you d.!** coquin! **4.** *Astr:* **the Greater D., the D. Star,** Sirius *m*, le Grand Chien; **the Lesser D.,** le Petit Chien. **5.** *Tchn:* (*a*) (*pawl*) cliquet *m*; **holding d.,** cliquet d'arrêt; **d. wheel,** roue *f* à cliquet; **d. movement,** entraînement *m* à batteur; *Aut:* **(starting handle) dogs,** encliquetage *m* (de la manivelle); (*b*) (*of lathe*) toc *m* (d'entraînement); doguin *m*; (*of lathe-plate face*) mordache *f*; (*c*) *Mec.E:* crabot *m*; dent *f*; (*d*) *Metall:* agrafe *f*, serre *f* (de châssis de moulage); (*e*) valet *m*, sergent *m* (d'établi); sergent (de tonnelier); (*f*) bride *f* de couvercle (d'un trou d'homme); (*g*) *Min:* (*of cage or shaft*) **landing dogs,** taquets *m*, clichage *m*; (*of wagon*) **safety d.,** chambrière *f*; (*h*) *Tls:* **d. (hook),** griffe *f* de serrage, *Nau: etc:* renard *m*; (*i*) *Coop:* davis *m*. **6. (fire) d.,** chenet *m*. **7.** *P:* **dogs,** pieds *m*, panards *m*, nougats *m*; **to have dogs that bite, barking dogs,** avoir mal aux pattes. **8.** *U.S:* *P:* **what a d.!** que c'est moche! qu'elle est moche!

dog[2], *v.tr.* (**dogged** [dɔgd]) **1.** suivre (qn) à la piste; traquer, filer (qn); **to d. s.o.'s footsteps,** suivre qn pas à pas; s'attacher aux pas de qn; marcher sur les pas, sur les talons, de qn; talonner qn; **he's always dogging my footsteps,** il est attaché à mes pas; **he is dogged by misfortune,** il est poursuivi par la guigne; le malheur le poursuit; le malheur s'acharne après lui. **2.** (i) serrer, assujettir, (ii) saisir, (qch.) avec un clameau.

dogate ['dougeit], *s.* *Hist:* dogat *m* (dignité *f* de doge ou durée *f* de cette magistrature).

dogbane ['dɔgbein], *s.* *Bot:* **1.** apocyn *m*. **2.** aconit *m* tue-chien.

dogberry ['dɔgbəri], *s.* *Bot:* **1.** cornouille *f*. **2. d. (tree),** cornouiller *m*.

dog(-)cart ['dɔgkɑ:t], *s.* *Veh:* dog-cart *m*, *pl.* dog-carts; charrette anglaise.

dogcatcher ['dɔgkætʃər], *s.* preneur *m* de chiens.

doge [doudʒ], *s.* *Hist:* doge *m*; **doge's wife,** dogaresse *f*.

dog(-)ear ['dɔgiər], *s.* corne *f* (d'une page).

dogeate ['doudʒeit], **dogeship** ['doudʒʃip], *s.* = DOGATE.

dogey ['dougi], *s.* *U.S:* = DOGIE.

dogface ['dɔgfeis], *s.* *U.S:* *F:* soldat *m*.

dog-faced ['dɔgfeist], *a.* *Z:* cynocéphale.

dogfight ['dɔgfait], *s.* **1.** combat *m* de chiens. **2.** *F:* (*a*) *Mil: etc:* mêlée générale, affrontement général; (*b*) *Mil.Av:* engagement, duel, aérien; mêlée aérienne; *F:* carrousel *m*.

dogfish ['dɔgfiʃ], *s.* *Ich:* chien *m* de mer, cagnot *m*, roussette *f*, milandre *m*, squale *m*; **large spotted d.,** roussette à grandes taches, roussette rochier; **small spotted d.,** roussette à petites taches, gatangier *m*; **picked, spiny, d.,** aiguillat *m*.

dogfood ['dɔgfu:d], *s.* pâtée *f* (pour chiens).

dogged ['dɔgid], *a.* **1.** obstiné, résolu, persévérant, tenace, opiniâtre; **d. adherence to sth.,** attachement *m* inébranlable à qch.; **to meet with a d. resistance,** rencontrer une résistance obstinée; *F:* **it's d. (as) does it,** il faut persister, persévérer; il ne faut pas lâcher (le morceau). **2.** *A:* maussade.

doggedly ['dɔgidli], *adv.* obstinément; avec ténacité; opiniâtrement; **to work d.,** travailler sans relâche.

doggedness ['dɔgidnis], *s.* obstination *f*, entêtement *m*, résolution *f*; courage *m* tenace; persévérance *f*, persistance *f*.

dogger[1] ['dɔgər], *s.* *Nau:* **d. (boat),** dogre *m*.

dogger[2], *s.* *Geol:* dogger *m*.

Dogger[3], *Pr.n.* *Geog:* **the D. Bank,** le Dogger-bank.

doggerel ['dɔgərəl], *a. & s.* (i) (poésie *f*) burlesque, (ii) (vers *mpl*) de mirliton.

doggie ['dɔgi], *s.* *F:* **1.** toutou *m*, chienchien *m*. **2.** *Navy:* aspirant *m*, midship *m*, aide *m* au commandant.

doggish ['dɔgiʃ], *a.* **1.** *F:* qui ressemble à un chien; qui a un air de chien. **2.** *esp.* *U.S:* *F:* faraud; crâneur, -euse; plastronneur, -euse.

doggo ['dɔgou], *adv.* *F:* **to lie d.,** (i) rester coi; se tenir coi; faire le mort; se tenir peinard; (ii) ne pas montrer son jeu; (iii) faire l'ignorant.

doggone ['dɔ'gɔn], *a.* *U.S:* *F:* sacré; **d. it!** sacré nom de nom!

doggy ['dɔgi]. **1.** *a.* (*a*) canin, de chien; (*b*) *F:* qui se connaît en chiens; **a very d. family,** une famille qui adore les chiens; (*c*) *F:* *O:* chic. **2.** *s.* *F:* = DOGGIE.

dog-headed [dɔg'hedid], *a.* cynocéphale.

doghouse ['dɔghaus], *s.* (*a*) *esp.* *U.S:* chenil *m*; (*b*) *F:* **to be in the d.,** être en défaveur, en disgrâce (auprès de qn).

dogie ['dougi], *s.* *U.S:* veau *m*, génisse *f* (dont la mère est morte).

dogleg ['dɔgleg], *s.* (*a*) double courbure *f* (dans un tuyau, etc.); (*b*) *Space:* dog-leg *m*, coude *m* (de la trajectoire).

doglegged ['dɔglegd], *a.* **1.** *Tls:* **d. chisel,** butte-avant *m inv*, pousse-avant *m inv* (de graveur sur bois). **2. d. stair,** escalier *m* à limons superposés, en zigzag, sans jour médian.

doglike ['dɔglaik]. **1.** *a.* **d. devotion,** fidélité *f* de chien, de caniche. **2.** *adv.* comme un chien.

dogma, *pl.* **-as** ['dɔgmə, -əz], *s.* dogme *m*.

dogmatic [dɔg'mætik], *a.* **1.** dogmatique; **d. theology,** la dogmatique. **2.** autoritaire, tranchant, positif; **to be very d.,** trancher sur tout.

dogmatically [dɔg'mætik(ə)li], *adv.* d'un ton autoritaire, tranchant, décisif, positif.

dogmatics [dɔg'mætiks], *s.pl.* (*usu. with sg. const.*) théologie *f* dogmatique; la dogmatique.

dogmatism ['dɔgmətizm], *s.* **1.** dogmatisme *m*. **2.** tour d'esprit autoritaire, positif.

dogmatist ['dɔgmətist], *s.* **1.** dogmatiste *m*. **2.** individu positif, qui tranche sur tout.

dogmatization [dɔgmətai'zeiʃ(ə)n], *s.* dogmatisation *f*.

dogmatize ['dɔgmətaiz], *v.i.* dogmatiser; **I am not prepared to d. on the subject,** je ne voudrais pas dogmatiser, trancher, sur ce sujet.

dogmatizer ['dɔgmətaizər], *s.* dogmatiseur, -euse.

dogmeat ['dɔgmi:t], *s.* viande *f* pour chiens.

do-good ['du:'gud], *a.* *F:* *Pej:* charitable.

do-gooder ['du:'gudər], *s.* *F:* *Pej:* âme *f* charitable; philanthrope *mf*.

dogpaddle[1] ['dɔgpædl], *s.* *Swim:* nage *f* à la chien.

dogpaddle[2], *v.i.* nager à la chien.

dogrose ['dɔgrouz], *s.* *Bot:* **1.** églantine *f*; rose *f* de chien. **2.** (*bush*) rosier *m* sauvage, rosier de chien; églantier commun.

dogsbody[1] ['dɔgzbɔdi], *s.* *F:* subalterne *m*, nègre *m*; sous-fifre *m*; *Nau:* officier *m* subalterne.

dogsbody[2], *v.i.* faire le nègre (pour qn).

dogshore ['dɔgʃɔər], *s.* *N.Arch:* colombier *m*, poulain *m* (du ber).

dogskin ['dɔgskin]. **1.** *s.* peau *f* de chien. **2.** *attrib.* en peau de chien.

dog-tired ['dɔg'taiəd], *a.* *F:* éreinté, vanné, esquinté, claqué, rendu, fourbu; exténué, mort, brisé, de fatigue; n'en pouvant plus; las comme un chien; **I'm d.-t.,** les jambes me rentrent dans le corps.

dogtooth ['dɔgtu:θ]. (*a*) *a. & s.* *Arch:* dent-de-chien *f*, *pl.* dents-de-chien; (*b*) *a.* *Tex:* **d. check,** pied-de-poule *m*; (*c*) *a.* *Miner:* **d. spar,** calcite *f*; (*d*) *a. & s.* *Bot:* **d. (violet),** érythrone *m*; dent-de-chien, *F:* vioulte *f*; (*d*) *s.* *Tls:* dent-de-chien.

dogwood ['dɔgwud], *s.* **1.** *Bot:* cornouiller *m*; **red d.,** cornouiller sanguin; sanguin *m*; sanguinelle *f*; bois punais. **2.** *Com:* cornouiller.

dogy ['dougi], *s.* *U.S:* = DOGIE.

doh [dou], *s.* = DO[2] 2.

doily ['dɔili], *s.* **1.** petit napperon; garde-nappe(s) *m*; serviette *f* de dessert. **2.** dessus *m* d'assiette.

doing[1] ['du:iŋ], *s.* **1.** (*a*) **d. of sth.,** action *f* de faire qch.; **there is a great difference between d. and saying,** il y a loin du faire au dire; **talking is one thing, d. is another,** autre chose est de parler, autre chose d'agir; **that takes some d.,** ça ne se fait pas en un tour de main; ce n'est pas facile; (*b*) **this is so-and-so's d.,** c'est l'ouvrage d'un tel; **all this is your d.,** c'est vous qui êtes la cause de tout cela; tout cela c'est votre ouvrage; **it was none of my d.,** ce n'est pas à moi qu'il faut s'en prendre. **2.** (*usu. in pl.*) ce qu'on fait; (*a*) *Pej:* agissements *mpl* (de qn); **to be informed of s.o.'s doings,** être au courant des faits et gestes de qn; *O:* **fine doings these!** une jolie conduite! en voilà du joli! **that's some of Tom's doings!** c'est encore Tom qui a fait des siennes! **underhand doings,** menées secrètes; (*b*) *pl.* événements *m*, faits *m*; *F:* **there have been great doings at their house,** il y a eu bien du mouvement, de grandes fêtes, des réjouissances *f*, chez eux. **3.** *P:* *A:* **to give s.o. a d.,** faire une semonce à qn. **4.** *F:* **the doings,** le machin, le truc; les machins, les trucs; **have you brought the doings?** as-tu apporté les outils, etc.? **5.** (*a*) **d. away with sth.,**

suppression *f,* abandon *m,* proscription *f,* de qch.; (*b*) **d. out,** nettoyage *m* (d'une chambre); (*c*)**d. up,** remise *f* à neuf; réparations *fpl.*

doing[2] [dɔiŋ], *int. onomat:* dong!

doit [dɔit], *s.* **1.** *A:* pièce *f* de monnaie hollandaise d'une valeur infime. **2.** *F: A:* bagatelle *f,* rien *m;* **not to care a d. for sth.,** se moquer bien de qch.

do-it-yourself [duitjə'self], *s.* bricolage *m;* **a do-it-y. enthusiast,** un bricoleur passionné *F:* un mordu du bricolage; **do-it-y. kit,** panoplie *f* de construction (d'une table, d'un canot, etc.).

do-it-yourselfer [duitjə'selfər], *s. F:* bricoleur *m.*

dojo ['dou(d)ʒou], *s. Sp:* dojo *m;* salle *f* d'entraînement de judo.

dol [dɔl], *s. Med:* dol *m.*

dolabriform [də'læbrifɔːm], *a. Bot:* (feuille) en forme de doloire.

dolce ['dɔltʃei], *adv. Mus:* dolce.

dolcissimo [dɔl'tʃisimou], *adv. Mus:* dolcissimo.

doldrums (the) [ðə'dɔldrəmz], *s. pl.* (i) le cafard; idées noires; (ii) *Nau:* la Zone des calmes; le pot au noir; **to be in the d.,** (i) (*of pers.*) broyer du noir; avoir le cafard; (ii) *Nau:* être encalminé; être dans les calmes équatoriaux, dans le pot au noir; **business is in the d.,** les affaires sont dans le marasme.

dole[1] [doul], *s.* **1.** *A:* (*a*) portion échue en partage; (*b*) sort *m,* destinée *f.* **2.** (*a*) aumône *f;* don *m* charitable; charité *f;* **to live on doles,** vivre de charités, être à la charité; (*b*) *Adm: A:* allocation (faite par l'assistance publique); **unemployment d.,** secours *m,* allocation, ou indemnité *f* de chômage; **to be on the d.,** être à la charge de l'assistance publique; **to go on the d.,** s'inscrire au chômage; recevoir, toucher, une indemnité de chômage.

dole[2], *v.tr.* **to d. out sth.,** distribuer parcimonieusement qch.

dole[3], *s. Poet: A:* **1.** douleur *f,* chagrin *m.* **2. to make d.,** se lamenter.

doleful ['doulful], *a.* (mine *f*) lugubre; (cri) dolent, douloureux, plaintif; (*of pers.*) triste, larmoyant, affligé, dolent; **d. news,** nouvelles contristantes.

dolefully ['doulfuli], *adv.* tristement, douloureusement, plaintivement, lugubrement.

dolefulness ['doulfulnis], *s.* **1.** tristesse *f,* chagrin *m.* **2.** caractère contristant (d'une nouvelle, etc.).

dolerophanite [dolə'rɔfənait], *s. Miner:* dolérophane *f.*

doler-out ['doulərautl, *s.* distributeur, -trice, parcimonieux, -ieuse.

dolichocephal [dɔlikou'sefl], *s. Anthr:* dolichocéphale *mf.*

dolichocephalic ['dɔlikouse'fælik], **dolichocephalous** ['dɔlikou'sefələs], *a. Anthr:* dolichocéphale.

dolichocephalism ['dɔlikou'sefəlizm], **dolichocephaly** ['dɔlikou'sefəli], *s. Anthr:* dolichocéphalie *f.*

dolichocolon ['dɔlikou'koulən], *s. Med:* dolichocôlon *m.*

dolichocranial ['dɔlikou'kreiniəl], *a. Anthr:* dolichocrâne.

dolichocrany ['dɔlikou'kreini], *s. Anthr:* dolichocrânie *f.*

dolichos ['dɔlikɔs], *s. Bot:* dolic *m,* dolique *m.*

dolichosaurus ['dɔlikou'sɔːrəs], *s. Paleont:* dolichosaure *m.*

dolichotis [dɔli'koutis], *s. Z:* dolichotis *m;* mara *m,* lièvre *m* des Pampas.

Doliidae [də'liːidiː], *s. pl. Moll:* doliidés *m.*

doliiform [dou'liːifɔːm], **doliform** ['douliouf ɔːm], *a. Nat.Hist:* doliforme.

dolina, doline [dɔ'liːnə, '-liːn], *s. Geol:* doline *f.*

Doliolidae [douli'ɔlidiː], *s. pl. Z:* doliolidés *m.*

do-little ['duːlitl], *a.* & *s.* fainéant, -ante.

doll[1] [dɔl], *s.* **1.** (*a*) poupée *f;* **stuffed d., rag d.,** poupée en étoffe, en chiffons; **wax d.,** poupée (i) de cire, (ii) à tête de cire; **Dutch d., wooden d.,** poupée de bois; **baby d.,** *U.S:* **d. baby,** (poupée) bébé *m;* **to play with a d.,** jouer à la poupée; **too old to play with dolls,** trop âgée pour jouer à la poupée; **doll's house,** (i) maison *f* de poupée; (ii) jolie petite maisonnette; **she has a doll's face,** elle a un visage de poupée; (*b*) marionnette *f* (de ventriloque). **2.** *F:* (*a*) jolie femme (sans beaucoup d'intelligence); **she's a pretty little d.,** c'est une jolie poupée; (*b*) femme, jeune fille; (*c*) *U.S:* amoureuse *f,* bien-aimée *f.* **3.** *Rail: etc:* petit poteau de signal.

doll[2], *v.tr.* **to d. up a child, a woman,** pouponner un enfant, une femme; **to d. oneself up,** (*of woman*) se bichonner, se pomponner; (*of man*) se mignarder; **to be all dolled up,** être sur son tralala, en grand tralala.

dollar ['dɔlər], *s. Num:* **1.** *A:* thaler *m* (autrichien, etc.). **2.** (*a*) dollar (canadien, australien, malais, etc.); (*b*) dollar (des États-Unis); **the almighty d.,** le dollar qui ouvre toutes les portes; *F:* **I bet my bottom d. that . . .,** je parie jusqu'à mon dernier sou que . . .; *A:* **d. store,** magasin *m* à prix unique d'un dollar; *Pol.Ec:* **d. area,** zone *f* dollar; **d. diplomacy,** diplomatie *f* par allocation de crédits; diplomatie du dollar. **3.** *F: A:* (pièce *f* de) cinq shillings; **half a d.,** deux shillings et six pence.

dollar bird ['dɔləbəːd], *s. Orn:* eurystome *m,* rolle *m,* rollier *m* à large bec.

dollish ['dɔliʃ], *a.* poupin; (visage, etc.) de poupée.

dollop ['dɔləp], *s. F:* morceau *m* (informe); motte *f* (de qch. de mou); **she put a d. of butter on my bread,** elle a mis un gros morceau de beurre sur mon pain; **a good d. of jam,** une bonne cuillerée de confiture.

dolly[1] ['dɔli], *s.* **1.** *F:* (*a*) poupée *f;* *attrib.* **d. mixture,** petits bonbons assortis; *Sp: etc: F:* **d. shot,** coup *m* facile; (*b*) (*bandaged finger*) poupée. **2.** *Laund: Min:* agitateur *m* (pour le linge, le minerai); **d. tub,** (i) baquet *m* à lessive; (ii) *Min:* cuve *f* à rincer (l'or). **3.** *Metalw:* (*a*) tas *m* à river (de riveur); mandrin *m* d'abattage; (*b*) bouterolle *f* (de riveur); (*c*) tête bouterollée (de rivet); (*d*) étampe *f* (de forgeron). **4.** *Civ.E:* avant-pieu *m, pl.* avant-pieux. **5.** *Metalw:* brosse *f,* tampon *m,* de brunissage. **6.** *Rail:* (*a*) (*shunting engine*) chameau *m;* (*b*) berceau *m* de roulement. **7.** *Cin:* travelling *m;* chariot *m;* **d. shot,** travelling en poursuite.

dolly[2], *v.tr.* **1.** *Laund: Min:* agiter (le linge) dans le baquet, (le minerai) dans la cuve. **2.** *Metalw:* maintenir (un rivet) appuyé; *abs.* tenir coup aux chocs. **3.** *F: O:* **to d. up an old car, a tumbledown house,** enjoliver un vieux tacot, une maison délabrée. **4.** *v.i. Cin:* **to d. in, up,** avancer sur le travelling; **to d. out,** reculer sur le travelling.

Dolly[3], *Pr.n.f.* (*dim. of Dorothy*) Dorothée; *A. Cost:* **D. Varden hat,** chapeau de paille garni de fleurs; *s. Ich:* *NAm:* **D. Varden,** omble *m* du nord-ouest de l'Amérique.

dolly-shop ['dɔliʃɔp], *s. P: A:* **1.** petite boutique de fournitures pour la marine. **2.** (*a*) boutique de fripier; magasin *m* de chiffons; (*b*) boutique interlope de prêt sur gages.

dolman ['dɔlmən], *s. Cost:* **1.** (*Turkish*) doliman *m.* **2.** (*of hussar, etc.*) (*a*) dolman *m;* (*b*) pelisse portée à la fourragère. **3.** *A:* (i) dolman, (ii) pelisse (de femme).

dolmen ['dɔlmen], *s. Prehist:* dolmen *m.*

dolmenic [dɔl'menik], *a. Prehist:* dolménique.

dolomite ['dɔləmait]. **1.** *s.* (*a*) *Miner:* dolomite *f;* spath perlé; (*b*) *Geol:* (*rock*) dolomie *f;* calcaire magnésien. **2.** *Pr.n.pl. Geog:* **the Dolomites,** les Dolomites; les Alpes *f* Dolomitiques.

dolomitic [dɔlə'mitik], *a. Miner:* dolomitique.

dolomitization [dɔləmaiti'zeiʃ(ə)n], *s. Geol:* dolomitisation *f.*

dolomitize [dɔləmi'taiz], *v.tr. Geol:* changer (un calcaire) en dolomie.

dolorous ['dɔlərəs], *s. a.* & *Poet:* **1.** douloureux. **2.** triste, plaintif.

dolorously ['dɔlərəsli], *adv.* **1.** douloureusement. **2.** tristement, plaintivement.

dolose [də'lous], **dolous** ['douləs], *a. Jur:* dolosif.

dolostone ['dələstoun], *s. Geol:* dolomie *f.*

dolour ['dɔlər], *s. Poet:* douleur *f,* chagrin *m;* *Ecc:* **the Feast of the Seven Dolours of the B.V.M.,** la fête de Notre-Dame des Sept Douleurs.

dolphin ['dɔlfin], *s.* **1.** (*a*) *Z: Her:* dauphin *m;* *Z:* oie-de-mer *f, pl.* oies-de-mer; **bottlenose(d) d.,** tursiops *m;* souffleur *m;* **river d.,** plataniste *m;* **the d. genus,** les denticètes *m,* les denticétidés *m;* (*b*) *Ich:* coryphène *m.* **2.** *Hyd.E:* patte *f* d'oie (d'un pilier de pont). **3.** *Nau:* (*a*) baderne *f;* bourrelet *m* de défense (de mât); (*b*) bouée *f* de corps-mort; **to moor to a d.,** s'amarrer sur un corps-mort; (*c*) poteau *m* d'amarrage; duc-d'albe *m, pl.* ducs-d'albe; (*d*) *A:* anse *f* (de canon); (*e*) **d. striker,** arc-boutant *m, pl.* arcs-boutants, de martingale.

dolphinarium [dɔlfi'nɛəriəm], *s.* aquarium *m* pour dauphins.

dolt [doult], *s.* sot *m,* benêt *m;* lourdaud *m,* nigaud *m,* butor *m;* *P:* buse *f,* bûche *f,* cruche *f,* souche *f,* gourde *f.*

doltish ['doultiʃ], *a.* sot, lourdaud, bête, stupide.

doltishness ['doultiʃnis], *s.* sottise *f,* stupidité *f.*

dom [dɔm], *s. Ecc: etc:* (*title*) dom *m.*

domain [də'mein], *s.* domaine *m.* **1.** (*a*) terres *fpl,* propriété *f;* (*b*) **question within the d. of astronomy,** question qui est du domaine, rentre dans le domaine, de l'astronomie; **it doesn't come within my d.,** cela n'est pas de mon domaine; (*c*) *Mth:* **d. of a function,** domaine d'une fonction; (*d*) *Ph:* domaine (d'un corps ferromagnétique). **2.** possession *f* en toute propriété; *Jur:* **eminent d.,** (droit *m* de) domaine éminent.

domanial [də'meiniəl], *a. Jur:* domanial, -aux.

domatium, *pl.* **-ia** [də'meiʃəm, -iə], *s. Bot:* domatie *f.*

dombeya [dɔm'beiə], *s. Bot:* dombéya *m.*

dome[1] [doum], *s.* **1.** *Poet:* édifice *m.* **2.** *Arch:* dôme *m;* **d. roof,** comble *m* en dôme; **semi-d.,** cul-de-four *m* (d'abside), *pl.* culs-de-four; **d. lamp, d. light,** lampe *f* de plafonnier; plafonnier *m* (électrique). **3.** (*a*) *Metall:* dôme, voûte *f,* couronne *f* (de fourneau); (*b*) *Aut:* **d. (of saloon body, etc.),** pavillon *m;* *Rail:* **(vista) d., d. car,** vistadôme *m;* (*c*) *I.C.E:* **carburettor d. cap,** coiffe *f* à capuchon du carburateur; (*d*) *Mch:* **(steam) d.,** dôme de prise de vapeur; réceptacle *m* de la vapeur. **4.** (*a*) *Fig:* dôme, calotte *f* (des cieux); dôme (de verdure); sommet arrondi (d'une colline); calotte (du crâne); (*b*) *NAm: P:* tête *f,* *F:* crâne *m.* **5.** *Geog:* dôme; **salt d.,** dôme de sel; *Cryst:* prisme *m* rhombique. **6.** calotte (d'un bouton); **d. fastener,** bouton *m* à pression; bouton-pression *m, pl.* boutons-pression; fermeture *f* à pression; *Furn: R.t.m:* **domes of silence,** dômes du silence; patins *m* de chaise.

dome[2], *v.tr.* **1.** (*a*) couvrir (un espace) d'un dôme; (*b*) construire (un comble) en dôme. **2.** arrondir.

domed [doumd], *a.* (*a*) (édifice) à dôme; (*b*) en forme de dôme.

domelike ['doumlaik], *a.* en dôme.

Domesday ['duːmzdei], *attrib. Hist:* **D. Book,** (livre *m* du) cadastre de l'Angleterre (établi en 1086 sur l'ordre de Guillaume le Conquérant); le Grand Livre cadastral.

dome-shaped ['doumʃeipt], *a.* hémisphérique, bombé; en forme de dôme.

domestic [də'mestik], *a.* & *s.*

I. *a.* **1.** (vertu *f,* malheur *m*) domestique; (drame *m,* charbon *m*) de ménage; **d. duties, arrangements,** les affaires *f* du ménage; le ménage; **d. cares,** les soins *m,* les soucis *m,* du ménage; **d. quarrels,** scènes *f* de ménage; **d. life,** la vie de famille, la vie d'intérieur; **a model father in d. life,** un père modèle au sein de sa famille; **d. servant,** domestique *mf;* bonne *f;* servante *f;* **d. science,** (i) les arts ménagers; (ii) *Sch:* enseignement ménager; **d. economy,** économie *f* domestique; **d. workshop,** atelier *m* à domicile; **water for d. use,** eau ménagère; **non-d. water,** eau impropre à la consommation. **2.** (*a*) (commerce, etc.) intérieur; **d. production,** production nationale; **d. products,** denrées *f* du pays; *U.S:* **d. woolens,** laines *f* du pays; *Post: U.S:* **d. mail,** correspondance *f* à destination de l'intérieur; **d. postal rates,** tarif *m* d'affranchissement en régime intérieur; (*b*) (plante, etc.) indigène; (*c*) *Pol:* **d. quarrels,** dissensions intérieures; querelles intestines; **d. warfare,** guerres intestines, civiles, domestiques; (*d*) **d. animal,** animal *m* domestique. **3.** (*of pers.*) casanier; (femme) d'intérieur.

II. *s.* **1.** (*in formal speech*) domestique *mf,* bonne *f;* servante *f;* **d. agency,** bureau *m* de placement. **2.** (*a*) *Tex:* toile *f* de coton (i) uni, (ii) à carreaux; (*b*) *pl.* **domestics,** (i) articles *m* du pays; (ii) *U.S:* gros linge de maison.

domestically [də'mestik(ə)li], *adv.* dans le domestique; *A:* domestiquement.

domesticate [də'mestikeit], *v.tr.* **1.** domestiquer, apprivoiser (un animal); apprivoiser, civiliser (un sauvage); **animal that can be domesticated,** animal apprivoisable. **2.** (*a*) naturaliser (un étranger, *F:* un mot); (*b*) acclimater (un animal, une plante). **3.** rendre (qn) casanier; accoutumer (qn) à la vie d'intérieur; **domesticated woman,** femme *f* d'intérieur; **her husband isn't domesticated,** son mari (i) ne sait, (ii) ne veut, rien faire pour l'aider dans la maison; **to become domesticated,** se domestiquer.

domestication [dəmesti'keiʃ(ə)n], *s.* **1.** domestication *f,* apprivoisement *m* (d'un animal); civilisation *f* (d'une race sauvage, etc.). **2.** acclimatation *f* (d'un animal, d'une plante). **3.** attachement *m* à la vie d'intérieur, au foyer domestique.

domesticity [doumes'tisiti], *s.* **1.** domesticité *f* (d'un animal). **2.** (*a*) attachement *m* au foyer; goûts *m* domestiques; (*b*) vie casanière; vie de famille; (*c*) simplicité *f* (d'un intérieur). **3.** *pl.* **domesticities,** choses *f* domestiques, du ménage; affaires *f* domestiques; affaires de ménage.

domett [dou'met, 'dɔmit], *s. Tex:* domet *m.*

domeykite [dou'meikait], *s. Miner:* domeykite *f.*

domical ['dɔmikl], *a. Arch:* **d. vault,** voûte *f* en arc-de-cloître.

domicile[1] ['dɔmisail], *s. Com: Jur:* domicile *m;* **to elect d. at a place,** élire domicile dans un endroit.

domicile[2]. **1.** *v.tr.* (*a*) *Com:* domicilier (un effet); **bills domiciled in France,** traites *f* payables en France; (*b*) établir (qn) (dans un pays, dans un endroit). **2.** *v.i.* (*a*) se domicilier, s'établir (dans un endroit); (*b*) résider; **domiciled at Leeds,** domicilié, demeurant, à Leeds.

domiciliary [dɔmiˈsiljəri], *a.* (visite, etc.) domiciliaire; (assistance) à domicile; **d. nurse,** infirmière visiteuse.
domiciliate [dɔmiˈsilieit], *v.tr. & i.* = DOMICILE².
domiciliation [dɔmisiliˈeiʃ(ə)n], *s. Com:* domiciliation *f* (d'un effet).
dominance [ˈdɔminəns], *s.* **1.** dominance *f* (d'une maladie, espèce botanique, etc.); prédominance *f* (d'une race, passion). **2.** *Biol:* caractère dominant.
dominant [ˈdɔminənt]. **1.** *a.* dominant; dominateur, -trice; **d. height,** hauteur *f* qui domine le paysage; **d. passion,** passion maîtresse; *Biol:* **d. (character),** caractère dominant; *Jur:* **d. land, d. tenement,** fonds dominant. **2.** *s. Mus:* dominante *f*; *a.* **d. chord,** accord *m* de dominante; **d. seventh,** septième *f* de dominante; **chord of the d. seventh,** accord de sensible.
dominantly [ˈdɔminəntli], *adv.* d'une manière dominante; principalement.
dominate [ˈdɔmineit], *v.tr. & i.* **1. to d. (over) s.o., a people,** dominer (sur) qn, un peuple; **to be dominated by s.o.,** subir la loi de qn; **man dominated by ambition,** homme sous l'empire de, en proie à, l'ambition; homme que l'ambition domine; **to d. one's passions,** se dominer. **2.** (*of mountain, etc.*) **to d. (over) the landscape,** dominer le paysage; **the fortress dominates the town,** la forteresse commande la ville.
dominating [ˈdɔmineitiŋ], *a.* (*of feature, colour, etc.*) dominant; (*of personality, influence*) dominateur, -trice.
domination [dɔmiˈneiʃ(ə)n], *s.* **1.** domination *f* (over, sur); **to be under s.o.'s d.,** être sous la domination de, dominé par, qn. **2.** *pl. Theol:* **dominations,** dominations (d'anges).
dominative [ˈdɔmineitiv], *a.* dominatif; dominateur, -trice.
dominator [ˈdɔmineitər], *s.* dominateur, -trice.
domineer [dɔmiˈniər], *v.i.* se montrer autoritaire, tyrannique; **to d. over s.o.,** tyranniser, régenter, qn.
domineering [dɔminˈiəriŋ], *a.* (*of pers., character, etc.*) dominateur, -trice, impérieux, autoritaire, tyrannique.
domineeringly [dɔmiˈniəriŋli], *adv.* autoritairement, impérieusement.
Dominic [ˈdɔminik], *Pr.n.m.* Dominique.
Dominica [dəˈminikə], *Pr.n. Geog:* la Dominique.
dominical [dəˈminik(ə)l], *a. Ecc:* dominical, -aux; **d. letter,** lettre dominicale; **the d. year,** le premier an de Notre-Seigneur.
Dominican [dəˈminikən]. **1.** *a. & s. Ecc:* dominicain, -aine; (religieux, -euse) de l'ordre de Saint-Dominique. **2.** *Geog:* (*a*) *a.* dominicain; **the D. Republic,** la République Dominicaine; (*b*) *s.* Dominicain, -aine.
dominie [ˈdɔmini], *s.m. Scot:* maître d'école, magister.
dominigene [ˈdɔminidʒiːn], *s. Biol:* gène dominant.
dominion [dəˈminjən], *s.* **1.** domination *f*, maîtrise *f*, autorité *f*, empire *m*, ascendant *m*; **to have, hold, d. over . . .,** exercer son empire, dominer, sur . . .; **to be under s.o.'s d.,** être soumis à l'empire, au pouvoir, de qn; être sous l'autorité de qn. **2.** *Theol:* **dominions of angels,** dominations d'anges. **3.** dominion *m*; **the D. of Canada,** *F:* **the D.,** le Dominion (du Canada); *U.S:* **the Old D.,** la Virginie; *Can:* **D. Day,** fête nationale du Canada (le premier juillet); *attrib.* **to obtain d. status,** gagner le statut d'un dominion. **4.** *Jur:* possession *f* (en toute propriété).
domino, *pl.* **-oes** [ˈdɔminou, -ouz], *s.* **1.** (*a*) *Cost:* domino *m* (de bal masqué); **in a d.,** en domino; (*b*) (*pers.*) domino. **2.** (*a*) *Games:* domino; (i) *pl.* (*usu. with sg. const.*) **to play (at) dominoes,** jouer aux dominos; **game of dominoes,** partie *f* de dominos; **draw game of dominoes,** domino à la pioche, en pêchant, à la pêche; **passing game of dominoes,** domino en boudant; (ii) **to call 'd.', to make (the) d.,** faire domino; *P:* **it's d. with him,** il est fichu; (*b*) *P: O:* **box of dominoes,** piano *m*; **to rattle, punch, the dominoes,** taquiner l'ivoire; (*c*) *P:* **the dominoes,** les dents *f*, les dominos; **the d. box,** la bouche. **3. the d. theory,** la théorie des dominos (l'hypothèse qu'un événement sera suivi immédiatement par d'autres du même genre). **4. d. (paper),** domino.
dominoed [ˈdɔminoud], *a.* en domino (de bal).
domite [ˈdoumait], *s. Geol:* dômite *f*.
Domitian [dəˈmiʃ(ə)n], *Pr.n.m. Hist:* Domitien.
don¹ [dɔn], *s.m.* **1.** (*a*) (*Spanish title*) Don; **D. Quixote,** Don Quichotte; (*b*) *A:* gentilhomme espagnol. **2.** (*a*) *Sch: F:* professeur (d'université); (*b*) *F: O:* **he was a great d. at philology,** il était grand docteur en philologie.
don², *v.tr.* **(donned)** revêtir, endosser (un uniforme); mettre, coiffer (un chapeau); **to d. one's uniform again,** rendosser l'uniforme.
Donacidae [douˈnæsidiː], *s.pl. Moll:* donacidés *m*.
donat [ˈdounæt], **donate¹** [ˈdouneit], *s.m. Ecc:* donat.
donatary [ˈdounətəri], *s. Jur:* donataire *mf*.
donate² [dəˈneit], *v.tr.* **1.** faire un don de (qch.); **the floral decorations were donated by the growers,** les décorations florales ont été fournies gratuitement par les horticulteurs; *Med:* **to d. blood,** donner du sang, son sang; faire le don du sang. **2.** *NAm:* donner **(sth. to s.o.,** qch. à qn).
donation [dəˈneiʃ(ə)n], *s.* donation *f*, don *m*; *Jur:* don; **to make a d. of sth. to s.o.,** faire don de qch. à qn.
Donatism [ˈdounətizm], *s. Ecc.Hist:* donatisme *m*.
Donatist [ˈdounətist], *s. Ecc.Hist:* donatiste *m*.
donative [ˈdounətiv]. **1.** *s.* don *m*, donation *f*, présent *m*, largesse *f*. **2.** *a. & s. Ecc:* (bénéfice) qui peut être conféré par celui qui en dispose sans présentation du bénéficiaire à l'évêque.
donator [dəˈneitər], *s.* donateur, -trice.
donatory [ˈdounətəri], *s.* donataire *mf*.
donatrix [dəˈneitriks], *s.f. Jur:* donatrice.
Donatus [dəˈneitəs], *Pr.n.m. Ecc.Hist:* Donat.
donax [ˈdounæks], *s. Moll:* donace *f*; donax *m*.
donee [douˈniː], *s. Jur:* donataire *mf*.
Donegal [ˈdɔnigɔːl], *Pr.n. Geog:* Donegal; *Tex:* **D. (tweed),** tweed fabriqué en Donegal.
dong¹ [dɔŋ], *s. Austr: N.Z: P:* coup *m*, gnon *m*.
dong², *v.tr. Austr: N.Z: P:* donner, flanquer, un coup à (qn); cogner sur (qn).
donga [ˈdɔŋgə], *s.* (*S. Africa*) ravin *m*.
donjon [ˈdɔndʒən], *s.* donjon *m*.
Don Juan [dɔnˈdʒuən], *Pr.n.m.* Don Juan; *s.* **a D. J.,** un don Juan; **to act the D. J. with a woman,** libertiner avec une femme.
donjuanesque [dɔndʒuəˈnesk], *a.* donjuanesque.
donjuanism [dɔnˈdʒuənizm], *s.* donjuanisme *m*.
donkey [ˈdɔŋki], *s.* **1.** âne, *f*; ânesse; baudet *m*; bourricot *m*; bourrique *f*; **to ride a d.,** aller à âne; **d. ride,** promenade *f* à âne; **d. boy, d. driver,** ânier *m*; **d. load,** ânée *f*; **d. race,** course *f* d'ânes; *F:* **to win the d. race,** arriver dernier; *F:* faire lanterne rouge; **d. work,** le gros travail; **I want someone to do the d. work,** il me faut un nègre; *F:* **he, she, would talk the hind leg off a d.,** il a un bagout de commis voyageur; elle est bavarde, elle jase, comme une pie borgne; **I haven't seen him for donkey's years,** je ne l'ai pas vu depuis une éternité; il y a des éternités que je ne l'ai vu. **2.** *F:* imbécile *mf*; âne. **3. d. (engine),** (i) petit-cheval, *pl.* petits-chevaux; machine *f* auxiliaire, de renfort; (ii) treuil *m* à vapeur; guindeau *m* à vapeur; *Nau:* **d. boiler,** chaudière *f* auxiliaire; *Mch:* **d. pump,** pompe *f* alimentaire, d'alimentation; petit-cheval alimentaire; **d. winch,** treuil *m* à vapeur.
donkeyman, *pl.* **-men** [ˈdɔŋkimən], *s.m.* **1.** ânier *m*. **2.** *Nau: etc:* (i) homme du petit-cheval, de la machine auxiliaire; (ii) homme du treuil, du guindeau, à vapeur.
donnish [ˈdɔniʃ], *a.* pédant; **he's a bit d.,** il a un petit air professoral.
donor [ˈdounər], *s.* **1.** *Jur:* donateur, -trice. **2.** *Med:* donneur, -euse (de sang, d'un greffon rénal, etc.); **universal (blood) d.,** donneur, -euse, universel(le). **3.** *Elcs:* donneur.
do-nothing [ˈduːnʌθiŋ], *a. & s.* **1.** fainéant, -ante. **2.** (*a*) *a.* (politique, etc.) de laisser-faire; (*b*) *s.* personne *f* qui préconise, adopte, une politique de laisser-faire.
don't know [ˈdountˈnou], *s. F:* votant indécis.
donut [ˈdounʌt], *s.* **1.** *Cu: NAm:* sorte *f* de beignet fait avec de la pâte; *Fr.C:* beigne *f*. **2.** *Mth:* tore *m*; **d.-shaped,** torique.
doodad [ˈduːdæd], *s. NAm: P:* truc *m*, machine *m*.
doodah [ˈduːdɑː], *s. P:* **1.** truc *m*, machin *m*. **2. to be all of a d.,** avoir le trac.
doodle¹ [ˈduːdl], *v.tr. F:* griffonner, gribouiller, crayonner, faire des petits dessins, en pensant à autre chose.
doodle², *s. F:* griffonnage *m*, crayonnage *m*, gribouillage *m*.
doodle³, *s. P:* pénis *m*, verge *f*.
doodlebug [ˈduːdlbʌg], *s.* **1.** *Ent: NAm:* (i) larve *f* de cicindèle; (ii) cicindèle *f*. **2.** *Mil: F:* bombe volante.
doodle-doo [ˈduːdlˈduː], *int.* cocorico!
doohickey [ˈduːhiki], *s. NAm: P:* truc *m*, machin *m*.
doolan [ˈduːlən], *s. N.Z: P:* catholique irlandais.
doom¹ [duːm], *s.* **1.** destin *m* (funeste); sort (malheureux); **he met his d.,** (i) il trouva la mort; (ii) *P: Hum:* il s'est marié. **2.** perte *f*, ruine *f*; **his d. is sealed,** sa perte est arrêtée, assurée; c'en est fait de lui. **3. the Day of d.,** le jugement dernier; **until the crack of d.,** jusqu'au jugement dernier; jusqu'à la fin des temps. **4.** *Hist:* statut *m*, loi *f*, décret *m*. **5.** *A:* jugement, sentence *f*, condamnation *f*.
doom², *v.tr.* **1.** condamner **(to,** à); *esp. in p.p.* **doomed town,** ville condamnée; **doomed man,** homme perdu; **attempt doomed to failure,** tentative condamnée à l'insuccès, vouée à l'échec; **hopes doomed to disappointment,** espoirs destinés à être déçus; **poem doomed to oblivion,** poème voué à l'oubli. **2.** *A:* arrêter, décréter, décider (la mort de qn, etc.).
doom³, *s. Bot:* **d. (palm),** doum *m*.
doomsday [ˈduːmzdei], *s.* le (jour du) jugement dernier; **till d.,** (i) jusqu'à la fin du monde; (ii) *F:* indéfiniment; *F:* **to put off sth. till d.,** renvoyer qch. aux calendes grecques; **you may wait for me till d.,** attendez-moi sous l'orme; *Hist:* **D. Book** = DOMESDAY BOOK.
door [dɔːr], *s.* **1.** (*a*) porte *f* (de maison, etc.); **doors of a wardrobe,** portes, battants *m*, d'une armoire; **entrance d.,** *usu.* **front d., street d.,** porte de devant, d'entrée, de (la) rue; **back d.,** porte de derrière, de dégagement, de service; **to get into a profession through, by, the back d.,** entrer dans une profession par la petite porte, par la porte basse; **outer d.,** avant-porte *f*, *pl.* avant-portes; **inner d., screen d.,** contre-porte *f*, *pl.* contre-portes; **side d.,** porte latérale; **folding d.,** porte brisée, à brisures; **double d.,** porte à deux battants, à deux vantaux; **sliding d.,** porte coulissante; **revolving d.,** porte tournante, tambour *m*; **swing d., hanging d.,** porte battante, à bascule, porte va-et-vient; *Nau:* **cargo d.,** sabord *m* de charge; **watertight d.,** porte étanche; **behind, with(in), closed doors,** (à) portes closes; *Jur:* à huis clos; **two doors away, off,** deux portes plus loin; **to show s.o. the d.,** éconduire qn; montrer la porte à qn; **to show s.o. to the d.,** conduire qn à la porte; reconduire qn; *O:* **to keep within doors,** se tenir chez soi; rester à la maison; **it happened within doors,** cela eut lieu dans la maison; **to turn s.o. out of doors,** mettre qn à la porte; **to play, take one's meals, out of doors,** jouer, manger, dehors, en plein air; **to turn s.o. from the d.,** fermer la, sa, porte à qn; *O:* **to be denied the d.,** trouver porte close; **to open a d. to abuses,** prêter aux abus; **to open the d. to a settlement,** rendre possible un arrangement; **to close the d. behind, (up)on, s.o.,** fermer la porte derrière qn; **to close, shut, the d. to, against, s.o.,** fermer sa porte à, refuser de recevoir, qn; empêcher qn d'entrer; **to shut the d. in s.o.'s face,** fermer la porte au nez de qn; **to close the d. upon any discussion, to a settlement,** empêcher, rendre impossible, aucune discussion; rendre impossible tout arrangement; **I shall pay for these articles at the d.,** je vous réglerai cet envoi à domicile; **to pay at the d. (of an exhibition),** payer à l'entrée (d'une exposition); **to lay a charge at s.o.'s d.,** imputer qch. à qn; faire retomber une accusation sur qn; mettre qch. sur le compte de qn; s'en prendre à qn; **do not lay the blood of these men at our d.,** ne faites pas retomber sur nous le sang de ces hommes; **the fault lies at my d.,** la faute en est à moi, la faute retombe sur moi, la faute m'est imputable; **to lay a crime at s.o. else's d.,** rejeter un crime sur quelqu'un d'autre; **from d. to d.,** de domicile à domicile; **d.-to-d. transport, canvassing, selling,** porte-à-porte *m*; **to be a d.-to-d. salesman,** être placier *m*; faire du porte-à-porte; (*b*) *attrib.* **d. case, casing, frame,** dormant *m* (de porte); bâti (dormant); chambranle *m*, châssis *m*, de porte; huisserie *f*; **d. chain,** chaîne *f* de porte, de sûreté; **d. check, closer,** ferme-porte *m inv*; **d. curtain,** portière *f*; **d. handle,** poignée *f*, bouton *m*, de porte, de portière; *Aut:* **d. handle with locking device,** poignée à condamnation; **d. knocker,** marteau *m* de porte, heurtoir *m*; **d. money,** entrées *fpl*; *Furn:* **d. porter,** entrebâilleur *m*; **d. scraper,** décrottoir *m*; gratte-pieds *m inv*; **d. sill,** seuil *m*, traverse *f* (de la porte); **d. spring,** ferme-porte *m inv*. **2.** (*a*) portière *f* (de wagon, de voiture, etc.), porte (de voiture); (*b*) porte (de four, etc.); **soot d.,** registre *m* de ramonage. **3.** *Fish:* panneau *m* (de chalut).
doorbell [ˈdɔːbel], *s.* sonnette *f*; timbre *m*; *U.S: F:* **d. pusher,** démarcheur, -euse; placier *m*.
doorkeeper [ˈdɔːkiːpər], *s.* portier *m*, concierge *mf*.
doorknob [ˈdɔːnɔb], *s.* poignée (ronde) de porte; bouton *m*.
doorless [ˈdɔːlis], *a.* sans porte(s).
doorman, *pl.* **-men** [ˈdɔːmən], *s.m.* portier.
doormat [ˈdɔːmæt], *s.* **1.** paillasson *m* (d'entrée); essuie-pieds *m inv*. **2.** *Bot: Can:* renouée *f* des oiseaux; traînasse *f*; herbe *f* à cochon. **3.** *F:* (*pers.*) lavette *f*; **she lets her children make a d. of her,** elle se laisse mener par le nez par ses enfants.
doornail [ˈdɔːneil], *s.* clou *m* de porte; *F:* **(as) dead as a d.,** mort et bien mort.
doorplate [ˈdɔːpleit], *s.* plaque *f* de porte.
doorpost [ˈdɔːpoust], *s.* montant *m* de porte, poteau *m* d'huisserie.
doorstep [ˈdɔːstep], *s.* **1.** seuil *m*, pas *m* (de la porte); **sitting on the d.,** assis sur le pas de la porte; **he's never off our d.,** il est toujours fourré chez nous; **it happened right on my d.,** cela s'est passé à ma porte; **d.**

salesman, démarcheur *m,* placier *m.* **2.** *F:* grosse tranche de pain.
doorstop ['dɔːstɔp], *s.* **1.** butoir *m.* **2.** cale-porte *m, pl.* cale-portes.
doorstrip ['dɔːstrip], *s.* bourrelet *m* de porte.
doorway ['dɔːwei], *s.* (baie *f* de) porte, encadrement *m* de la porte; portail *m*; **in the d.,** sous la porte; dans l'encadrement de la porte.
dooryard ['dɔːjɑːd], *s. NAm:* (i) avant-cour *f, pl.* avant-cours; (ii) arrière-cour *f, pl.* arrière-cours.
dop [dɔp], *s.* **1.** *Diamond Ind:* dop *m.* **2.** eau *f* de vie de marc d'Afrique du Sud.
dopa reaction ['doupəri'ækʃ(ə)n], *s. Med:* dopa-réaction *f.*
dope[1] [doup], *s.* **1.** (liquide visqueux) *Av:* enduit *m*; *Aut:* enduit, laque *f* (de carrosserie). **2.** *Exp:* absorbant *m.* **3.** (*a*) stupéfiant *m,* narcotique *m,* drogue *f*; **d. fiend, d. addict,** morphinomane *mf,* toxicomane *mf*; **d. habit, d. addiction,** toxicomanie *f*; **d. peddler,** trafiquant, -ante, de, en, stupéfiants; (*b*) *Med: F:* anesthésique *m*; (*c*) *Rac:* doping *m,* stimulant *m.* **4.** *Petr:* additif *m,* adjuvant *m,* dope *m,* doping; **anti-detonating dopes,** produits anti-détonants. **5.** *P:* (*a*) *Rac: etc:* renseignement *m*; *P:* rencard *m,* tuyau *m*; **give us the d.,** dites-nous ce qui en est; mettez-nous au courant; **to get the d.,** se mettre au courant; se tuyauter; (*b*) faux renseignements; bourrage *m* de crâne; **to hand out the d.,** faire circuler des renseignements. **6.** *P:* (*a*) *NAm:* toxicomane; (*b*) **what a d.!** quelle nouille! quel crétin!
dope[2], *v.tr.* **1.** *Av:* enduire (les ailes); *Aut:* laquer (la carrosserie). **2.** (*a*) faire prendre, administrer, un narcotique à (qn); *Rac:* doper (un cheval); **to d. oneself,** *v.i.* **to d.,** prendre des stupéfiants, se doper; **he dopes,** il est toxicomane; (*b*) *Med: F:* anesthésier (qn). **3.** (*a*) *Aut: Av: A:* **to d. the engine,** introduire de l'essence dans les cylindres; (*b*) *Petr:* doper (l'essence); **doped fuel,** carburant dopé, additionné d'anti-détonant; (*c*) *El:* doper (un semi-conducteur). **4.** (*a*) mêler un narcotique à (un verre de vin); narcotiser (le vin de qn, une cigarette, etc.); (*b*) falsifier, sophistiquer, (une boisson, etc.). **5.** *U.S: Rac: etc: P:* (se procurer des tuyaux); **he knows how to d. out the winners,** il a le flair pour désigner les gagnants; **how did you d. it out?** comment avez-vous deviné ça? comment as-tu pigé cette combine-là?
doper ['doupər], *s.* **1.** toxicomane *mf.* **2.** personne qui dope un cheval.
dopester ['doupstər], *s.* pronostiqueur, -euse; *Rac:* tuyauteur, -cuse.
dopey ['doupi], *a. F:* **1.** (*a*) stupéfié, hébété (par un narcotique); (*b*) abruti (par la fatigue). **2.** engourdi, stupide.
dopiness ['doupinis], *s. F:* engourdissement *m,* stupidité *f.*
doping ['doupiŋ], *s.* **1.** enduisage *m* (des ailes d'un avion, etc.). **2.** *El: Petr:* dopage *m* (d'un semi-conducteur, d'un combustible). **3.** (*a*) administration *f* d'un narcotique (**of s.o.,** à qn); (*b*) dopage, doping *m* (d'un cheval, etc.). **4.** emploi *m* de stupéfiants; toxicomanie *f.*
doppelgänger ['dɔp(ə)lgæŋər], *s. Psychics:* double *m* (d'un vivant).
Doppler ['dɔplər], *Pr.n.m. Ph:* **D. effect,** effet *m* Doppler; **D. radar,** radar *m* Doppler.
dopy ['doupi], *a.* = DOPEY.
dor [dɔːr], *s. Ent:* = DOR-BEE, DOR-BEETLE.
Dora ['dɔːrə], *Pr.n.f.* **1.** (*dim. of Dorothy*) Dorothée. **2.** *Hist: F:* (*Defence of the Realm Act*) l'ordonnance *f* du mois d'août 1914 pour l'extension des pouvoirs du Gouvernement.
doradilla ['dɔrədilə], *s. Bot:* doradille *f.*
dorado [dɔ'rɑːdou]. **1.** *s. Ich:* coryphène *m.* **2.** *Pr.n. Astr:* **Dorado,** la Dorade.
dor-bee ['dɔːbiː], *s. Ent:* (i) bourdon *m*; (ii) frelon *m.*
dor-beetle ['dɔːbiːtl], *s. Ent:* **1.** géotrupe *m,* stercoraire *m,* bousier *m.* **2.** hanneton *m.*
Dorcas[1] ['dɔːkəs], *Pr.n.f.* Dorcas; **D. society,** œuvre *f* charitable, ouvroir *m* de dames, pour la confection de vêtements destinés aux pauvres de la paroisse.
dorcas[2], *s. Z:* dorcas *m,* gazelle africaine.
Dordonian [dɔː'douniən], *s. Geol:* dordonien *m,* maestrichtien *m.*
dorhawk ['dɔːhɔːk], *s. Orn:* engoulevent *m*; tette-chèvre *m, pl.* tette-chèvres.
Dorian ['dɔːriən], *Gr.Hist:* (*a*) *a.* dorien; *Mus:* **D. mode,** mode dorien; (*b*) *s.* Dorien, -ienne.
Doric ['dɔrik]. **1.** *Gr.Hist:* (*a*) *a.* dorien; (*b*) *s.* Dorien, -ienne. **2.** *a. & s. Arch:* dorique; **the D. (order),** l'ordre *m* dorique, le dorique. **3.** *s. Ling:* dorien *m.*
Dorididae [dɔ'rididiː], *s.pl. Moll:* doridiés *m.*
Doris ['dɔris]. **1.** *Pr.n.f. Gr.Myth:* Doris. **2.** ['dɔːris], *Pr.n. A.Geog:* la Doride. **3.** *s. Moll:* doris *f.*

dorm [dɔːm], *s. Sch: F:* dortoir *m.*
dormancy ['dɔːmənsi], *s. Nat.Hist:* dormance *f*; (**period of**) **d.,** (période *f* de) dormance; **summer d.,** estivation *f* (des serpents, etc.).
dormant ['dɔːmənt], *a.* **1.** (*a*) (*of passion, etc.*) assoupi, endormi; **to lie d.,** sommeiller, dormir, être en sommeil; **the passions d. in his heart,** les passions endormies, qui dorment, dans son cœur; (*b*) (*of plant, bud*) dormant; **to lift plants when d.,** arracher des plantes quand elles dorment; *Hort:* **d. grafting,** greffe *f* à l'œil dormant; (*c*) (volcan) assoupi, en repos. **2.** (titre) tombé en désuétude; **d. law,** loi inappliquée; *Jur:* **d. warrant,** mandat *m* en blanc; *Com:* **d. balance,** solde inactif; **d. accounts,** comptes dormants; **d. partner,** (associé) commanditaire (*m*); *Locksm:* **d. bolt,** pêne dormant; *Const:* **d. tree,** imposte *f.* **3.** *Her:* dormant.
dormer (window) ['dɔːmə('windou)], lucarne *f*; (fenêtre *f* en) mansarde *f.*
dormie ['dɔːmi], *a.* = DORMY.
dormition [dɔː'miʃ(ə)n], *s. Ecc:* dormition *f* (de la Sainte Vierge).
dormitive ['dɔːmitiv], *a. & s. Med:* dormitif (*m*).
dormitory ['dɔːmit(ə)ri], *s.* **1.** dortoir *m*; **the d. suburbs,** la grande banlieue; **d. town,** ville *f* dortoir; cité-dortoir *f, pl.* cités-dortoirs. **2.** *NAm:* maison *f* où logent les étudiants; maison, foyer *m,* d'étudiants.
dormouse, *pl.* **-mice** ['dɔːmaus, -mais], *s. Z:* (**fat**) **d.,** loir *m,* muscardin *m*; *F:* croque-noix *m inv*; croque-noisette *m, pl.* croque-noisettes; **garden d.,** lérot *m*; **edible d.,** loir gris.
dormy ['dɔːmi], *a. Golf:* **to be d. (one, three, four, etc.),** être sur le velours; être certain de ne pas perdre la partie.
doronicum [də'rɔnikəm], *s. Bot:* doronic *m,* doronicum *m.*
Dorothea [dɔrə'θiə], **Dorothy** ['dɔrəθi], *Pr.n.f.* **1.** Dorothée. **2.** *Hort:* **Dorothy Perkins,** variété *f* de rosier sarmenteux. **3. Dorothy bag,** sac (de dame) fermé par un cordon; aumônière *f.*
dorp [dɔːp], *s.* (*in S. Africa*) petite ville; village *m.*
dorsal ['dɔːs(ə)l]. **1.** *a. Nat.Hist:* dorsal, -aux; **d. fin,** nageoire dorsale (d'un poisson). **2.** *a. & s. Ling:* **d. (consonant),** consonne dorsale.
dorsalgia [dɔː'sældʒiə], *s. Med:* dorsalgie *f.*
dorsally ['dɔːsəli], *adv.* sur, vers, par, le dos.
dorsibranchiate ['dɔːsi'bræŋkiеit], *a. & s. Ann:* dorsibranche (*m*).
dorsiferous [dɔː'sifərəs], *a.* **1.** *Bot:* dorsifère, dorsigère. **2.** *Z:* qui porte ses petits sur le dos.
dorsifixed ['dɔːsifikst], *a. Bot:* dorsifixe.
dorsiventral ['dɔːsi'ventrəl], *a.* **1.** *Biol:* dorsiventral, -aux. **2.** *Bot:* dorso-ventral, -aux.
dorsiventrality ['dɔːsiven'træliti], *s. Biol:* dorsiventralité *f.*
dorsiventrally ['dɔːsi'ventrəli], *adv. Bot:* **d. symmetrical flower,** fleur *f* à symétrie dorso-ventrale.
dorsocostal ['dɔːsou'kɔst(ə)l], *a. Anat:* dorso-costal, -aux.
dorsodynia [dɔːsou'diniə], *s. Med:* douleurs aiguës dans les muscles dorsaux.
dorso-lateral ['dɔːsou'læt(ə)rəl], *a.* dorso-latéral, -aux.
dorso-lumbar ['dɔːsou'lʌmbər], *a. Anat:* dorso-lombaire, *pl.* dorso-lombaires.
dorsum, *pl.* **-a** ['dɔːsəm, -ə], *s. Anat: Z:* dos *m.*
dorter ['dɔːtər], *s.* dortoir *m* (d'un monastère).
dory[1] ['dɔːri], *s. Ich:* (**John**) **D.,** zée *m* forgeron; dorée *f,* dorade *f*; *F:* (Jean-)doré *m*; (poisson *m*) Saint-Pierre.
dory[2], *s. Nau:* doris *m.*
Doryanthes [dɔːri'ænθiːz], *s. Bot:* doryanthe *f.*
dorylaner [dɔːri'leinər], *s. Ent:* doryline *f*; fourmi chasseresse.
Dorylinae [dɔri'lainiː], *s.pl. Ent:* dorylinés *m.*
dosage ['dousidʒ], *s.* **1.** administration *f* d'un médicament (**of s.o.,** à qn). **2.** dosage *m,* posologie *f* (d'un médicament). **3.** *Atom.Ph:* dose *f*; **d. meter,** dosimètre *m.*
dose[1] [dous], *s.* **1.** (*a*) *Med:* dose *f* (d'un médicament); **d. of aspirin,** cachet *m,* prise *f,* d'aspirine; (*b*) *Atom.Ph:* dose. **2.** *P:* **to give s.o. a d. (of venereal infection),** plomber qn; **to get, cop, a d.,** (i) attraper quelque chose; se faire plomber; (ii) écoper de la prison.
dose[2], *v.tr.* **1.** doser (un médicament); **to d. out a drug to s.o.,** administrer une drogue à qn par petites doses. **2.** médicamenter, droguer (**s.o. with sth.,** qn de qch.); **she was heavily dosed with sedatives,** on lui administrait de fortes doses de sédatifs; **to d. oneself with quinine,** se soigner à la quinine. **3.** *Winem:* doser, alcooliser (le champagne).
dosimeter [dou'simitər], *s.* **1.** *Ch: etc:* dispositif *m* de dosage; doseur *m.* **2.** *Atom.Ph:* dosimètre *m.*
dosimetric [dousi'metrik], *a.* dosimétrique.

dosimetry [dous'imitri], *s.* dosimétrie *f.*
dosing ['dousiŋ], *s.* **1.** administration *f* d'un médicament (**of s.o.,** à qn). **2.** *Winem:* dosage *m* (du champagne).
dos(i)ology [dous(i)'ɔlədʒi], *s. Med:* posologie *f.*
doss[1] [dɔs], *s. P:* **1.** lit *m* (dans un asile de nuit); **d. house,** (i) asile de nuit; (ii) *U.S:* bordel *m*; **to sleep in a d. house,** (i) coucher à l'asile de nuit; (ii) dormir à la corde. **2. d. (down),** (i) lit de fortune, lit par terre; *P:* pieu *m*; (ii) sommeil *m,* assoupissement *m*; (*short*) somme *m*; **to have an hour's d. (down),** se coucher pendant une heure.
doss[2], *v.i. P:* **1.** (*a*) coucher à l'asile de nuit; (*b*) dormir à la corde. **2. to d. out,** coucher à la belle étoile; **to d. down,** se coucher; *P:* se pieuter; **where are you going to d. down tonight?** où allez-vous coucher ce soir?
dossal ['dɔsəl], *s. Ecc:* tenture *f* de fond de chœur.
dosser[1] ['dɔsər], *s.* hotte *f.*
dosser[2], *s.m. P:* clochard.
dosserful ['dɔsəful], *s.* hottée *f.*
dossier ['dɔsiei, -iər], *s.* (i) dossier *m,* documents *mpl* (d'une affaire); (ii) dossier (d'un fonctionnaire).
dossil ['dɔsil], *s.* **1.** *Surg:* bourdonnet *m.* **2.** *Typ:* tampon *m* (pour essuyer la plaque dans la gravure en taille douce).
dot[1] [dɔt], *s.* **1.** (*a*) point *m* (d'un trait pointillé); *Tg:* **dots and dashes,** points et traits *m*; **d. and dash line,** (ligne *f* en) trait mixte; *Cmptr:* **d. printer,** imprimante *f* par points; **d. printing,** impression *f* par points; **d. cycle,** fréquence *f* de points; *F:* **three o'clock on the d.,** trois heures pile; **he arrived on the d.,** il est arrivé recta, à l'heure tapante; **to pay on the d.,** payer argent comptant, recta; **since the year d.,** de temps immémorial; (*b*) point (d'un i, d'un j); (*c*) point (de ponctuation, etc.); **three dots,** trois points; plusieurs points; points de suspension; *Mth:* **d. product,** produit *m* scalaire. **2.** *Mus:* (*a*) point d'augmentation; (*b*) **staccato dots,** points détachés: (*c*) *P:* **the dots,** la musique. **3.** *F:* tout petit enfant; mioche *mf.* **4.** *P:* **to be off one's d.,** être toqué, piqué, maboul, timbré, loufoque.
dot[2], *v.tr.* (**dotted**) **1.** mettre un point sur (un i); *F:* **to d. one's i's (and cross one's t's),** mettre les points sur les i; observer les longues et les brèves. **2.** marquer (une surface) avec des points; pointiller (une ligne, un dessin); **feathers dotted with black (spots),** plumage parsemé de taches noires, piqueté de noir; **the meadow is dotted with flowers, flowers are dotted about, over, the meadow,** la prairie est semée de fleurs; les fleurs émaillent la prairie; **hillside dotted with chalets,** coteau parsemé de chalets; **the islands are dotted all round the coast,** les îles sont éparpillées, s'éparpillent, tout autour de la côte. **3.** *Mus:* pointer (une note). **4. to d. and carry one,** (i) *Mth: A:* poser et retenir; reporter un chiffre; (ii) *F:* boiter (en marchant); clopiner. **5.** *P:* **to d. s.o. one,** flanquer une beigne, un pain, à qn.
dotage ['doutidʒ], *s.* radotage *m*; seconde enfance; gâtisme *m*; **to fall into one's d.,** tomber dans le gâtisme.
dotal ['dout(ə)l], *a.* dotal, -aux.
dotard ['doutəd], *s.* (vieillard) radoteur; *F:* gâteux *m,* gaga *m*; vieux birbe.
dotation [dou'teiʃ(ə)n], *s.* dotation *f* (de sa fille, d'un hôpital, etc.).
dote[1] [dout], *v.i.* **1.** radoter; tomber dans la sénilité; retomber en enfance. **2. to d. on s.o.,** aimer qn à la folie; se passionner pour qn; raffoler, être fou, folle, de qn; adorer qn.
dote[2], *s.* pourriture *f* du bois.
doting[1] ['doutiŋ], *a.* **1.** qui radote; radoteur, sénile. **2.** qui montre une tendresse ou une indulgence ridicule; **d. mother,** mère *f* qui aime follement ses enfants, qui gâte ses enfants.
doting[2], *s.* raffolement *m* (**on,** de); engouement *m* (pour).
dotingly ['doutiŋli], *adv.* **1.** en radoteur. **2.** avec une tendresse, une indulgence, ridicule.
dotted ['dɔtid], *a.* **1.** (contour) pointillé; **d. line,** (ligne *f* en) pointillé *m*; ligne pointillée; trait pointillé; **d. line of lights,** égrènement *m* de lumières; **to sign on the d. line,** (i) signer à la place indiquée (sur une formule); (ii) *F:* se soumettre sans récriminer; capituler; **he'll sign on the d. line,** il marchera; *Engr:* **d. manner,** manière pointillée. **2.** *Mus:* **d. note,** note pointée, suivie d'un point.
dott(e)rel ['dɔt(ə)rəl], *s. Orn:* pluvier *m* guignard.
dottiness ['dɔtinis], *s. F:* stupidité *f*; loufoquerie *f.*
dotting ['dɔtiŋ], *s.* pointillage *m*; **d. pen,** (i) traulet *m*; (ii) tire-ligne *m* à pointiller, *pl.* tire-lignes; **d. wheel,** roue *f* à pointiller.
dottle ['dɔtl], *s. F:* culot *m* (de pipe).
dotty ['dɔti], *a.* **1.** marqué de points; moucheté; (dessin) pointillé. **2.** *F:* (*a*) toqué, piqué, maboul, timbré, loufoque; **to be d.,** avoir un coup de marteau; **to go d.,** déménager; perdre la boule; (*b*) **to be d. on one's legs,** être peu solide sur ses jambes.

doty ['douti], *a.* (bois) qui commence à pourrir.

double[1] ['dʌbl], *a., adv. & s.*

I. *a.* 1. (*a*) double; **d. chin,** double menton *m*; *F:* menton à double étage; **d. daffodil,** narcisse *m* double; *N.Arch:* **d. bottom,** double-fond *m, pl.* doubles-fonds (d'un navire); **d. boiler, d. saucepan,** bain-marie *m, pl.* bains-marie; **with a d. meaning,** (i) à deux, double, sens; (ii) ambigu, -uë; à double entente; **to give a d. knock,** frapper (à la porte) d'un coup redoublé; frapper deux coups à la porte; **d. bed,** lit *m* à deux places, grand lit; lit pour deux personnes; **d. bedroom,** chambre *f* pour deux personnes; **"all" is spelt "a, d. l",** "all" s'écrit "a, deux l"; **to reach d. figures,** atteindre les deux chiffres; *Av:* **d. bang,** double-bang *m, pl.* doubles-bangs; *Ch:* **d. salt,** sel *m* double; (*dicing; dominoes*) **d. ace,** double-as *m, pl.* doubles-as; **d. five, etc.,** double-cinq *m, pl.* doubles-cinq, etc.; (*dominoes*) **d. blank,** double-blanc *m, pl.* doubles-blancs; *Rail:* **d. track,** double voie *f*; ligne *f* à deux voies; *Tg:* **d. pole,** poteaux jumelés; *Turf: etc:* **to bet on the d. event,** jouer les deux courses; *F:* **a d. event,** (i) un double mariage; (ii) la naissance de jumeaux; **to play a d. game,** jouer double jeu; jouer deux rôles à la fois; ménager la chèvre et le chou; **d. agent,** agent *m* double; **to lead a d. life,** (*of criminal, etc.*) mener une vie double; (*of husband*) avoir deux ménages; **to run in d. harness,** (i) (*of horse*) être dressé à l'attelage en couple; être attelé en couple; (ii) *F: O:* être marié; *Mch:* **d. flow,** flux alternatif; (*b*) de grandeur double; de force double; **d. whisky, d. Scotch,** double (consommation *f* de) whisky *m*; **to be a d. traitor,** être doublement traître; *Mus:* **d. bassoon,** contrebasson *m*. 2. (*of material, etc.*) (plié) en deux; **to fold a sheet (of paper) d.,** plier une feuille en deux; (*of pers.*) **bent d.,** courbé en deux. 3. (*a*) **d. the number,** le double, deux fois autant; **to pay d. the value,** payer le double de la valeur; **to be d., the length of sth.,** avoir une longueur double de qch.; **I am d. your age,** je suis deux fois plus âgé que vous; (*b*) *Cmptr:* **d. length number,** nombre *m* en longueur double. 4. **d. time,** pas redoublé; **in d. time,** au pas redoublé, au pas gymnastique; *Mil:* **d. time,** (*as command*) **d. march!** pas de course (!).

II. *adv.* 1. **to see d.,** voir double. 2. **to sleep d.,** coucher à deux.

III. *s.* 1. double *m*, deux fois *f* autant; **I sold it for d. what it cost,** je l'ai vendu le double de ce qu'il m'a coûté; **to toss d. or quits,** jouer (à) quitte ou double. 2. (*a*) (*of spirit*) double *m* (d'un vivant); (*b*) (*of pers.*) double; *F:* sosie *m*, ménechme *m* (de qn); (*c*) *Th: Cin:* doublure *f*; doublant, -ante. 3. *F:* chambre *f* à deux personnes. 4. (*a*) détour *m* (d'un animal poursuivi, d'un fleuve); crochet *m* (d'un animal poursuivi); (*b*) *Bill:* doublé *m*. 5. *Mil:* **to break into the d.,** prendre le pas de course; **at the d.,** au pas de course, de charge; au pas gymnastique; **to come up at the d.,** arriver au pas de course. 6. *Ten:* (*a*) **men's, women's, mixed, doubles,** double messieurs, dames, mixte; (*b*) **d. (fault),** seconde faute, double faute. 7. *Turf:* (i) coup *m* de deux; (ii) pari couplé; **to bring off a d.,** réussir un double. 8. *Cards:* (*at bridge*) contre *m*; **informative d., penalty d.,** contre d'appel, de pénalité. 9. *Typ:* (*doubled letter, passage*) doublon *m*. 10. (*dominoes*) double.

double[2], *v.*

I. *v.tr.* 1. (*a*) doubler (un nombre, etc.); porter (un chiffre) au double; **even if it were doubled the salary would not be generous,** même porté au double le traitement ne serait pas généreux; *Nau:* **to d. a rope,** mettre une manœuvre en double; *Mil:* **to d. the files,** doubler les files; *Mus:* **to d. a note,** (re)doubler une note (à l'octave); **to d. the parts,** doubler les parties; *Th:* **to d. parts,** jouer deux rôles; **to d. a part,** doubler un rôle; *Gaming:* **to d. the stakes,** doubler la mise; **to d. one's stake (after a loss),** martingaler; **he doubled his stakes and lost,** il fit faux paroli; (*b*) *Tex:* doubler (le fil). 2. *Nau:* **to d. a cape,** doubler un cap. 3. **to d. (up) paper, material, etc.,** plier en deux, replier, doubler, du papier, de l'étoffe, etc.; **to d. (up) one's fist,** serrer le poing. 4. *Cards:* (*at bridge*) contrer; dire contre. 5. *Bill:* **to d. the red,** mettre la bille rouge dans la blouse en la faisant rebondir contre la bande; faire la rouge au doublé; doubler la rouge. 6. *F:* **to d. s.o. (up) with s.o. (in bedroom, cabin),** faire partager une chambre, une cabine, à qn avec qn; **to d. (up) two passengers,** mettre des passagers à deux.

II. *v.i.* 1. (*of population, etc.*) doubler, se doubler. 2. *Mil: etc:* prendre le pas gymnastique, le pas de course; courir au pas gymnastique. 3. (*a*) (*of pers., hunted animal, etc.*) **to d. (back),** faire un brusque crochet; doubler ses voies; **to d. on one's tracks,** revenir sur ses pas; (*b*) (*of road, etc.*) faire un détour, un crochet. 4. **to d. for s.o.,** remplacer qn; *Th:* doubler qn.

III. (*compound verbs*) 1. **double back,** (*a*) *v.tr.* replier, rabattre (une couverture, etc.); (*b*) *v.i. see* DOUBLE[2] II.3.

2. **double over,** (*a*) *v.i.* se plier; (*b*) *v.tr.* replier, rabattre.

3. **double up,** (*a*) *v.i.* (i) se plier (en deux); se courber (en deux); se replier; **to d. up with laughter,** se tordre de rire; *F:* se gondoler; **doubled up with his knees to his chin,** ployé les genoux au menton; (ii) accourir au pas gymnastique; *F:* **d. up!** dépêchez-vous! (*b*) *v.tr.* (i) replier (qch.); *s.a.* DOUBLE[2] I.3; (ii) (*of blow, etc.*) faire plier (qn) en deux; asseoir (qn) par terre; (iii) *see* DOUBLE[2] I.6; (*c*) *v.i.* **to d. up with s.o.,** partager une cabine, une chambre, avec qn.

double-acting ['dʌbl'æktiŋ], **double-action** ['dʌbl'ækʃ(ə)n], *a. Mec.E:* (cylindre, machine à vapeur) à double effet.

double-bank ['dʌbl'bæŋk]. 1. *v.tr.* (*a*) *Nau:* doubler (les avirons); (*b*) **to d.-b. the books on the shelves,** mettre les livres en deux rangs sur les rayons. 2. *v.i. Aut:* (i) aller, (ii) stationner, en file double.

double-banked ['dʌbl'bæŋkt], *a.* 1. *Nau:* (canot) armé à couple; **d.-b. oars,** avirons doublés. 2. (livres, etc.) en deux rangs; (automobiles) en file double.

double-barrelled ['dʌbl'bærəld], *a.* (fusil) à deux coups; **d.-b. telescope,** téléscope *m* binoculaire; **d.-b. air pump,** machine *f* pneumatique à deux corps; **d.-b. name,** patronymique *m* double (*p.ex.* Mr J. Wynn-Jones); nom *m* double; nom à rallonge, à tirette, à charnière; **d.-b. question,** question *f* équivoque.

double-bass ['dʌbl'beis], *s. Mus:* contrebasse *f* à cordes.

double-bedded ['dʌbl'bedid], *a.* (chambre) (i) à deux lits, (ii) *occ.* à grand lit.

double-bottomed ['dʌbl'bɔtəmd], *a.* (casserole, etc.) à double fond; *Nau:* (canot, etc.) à double coque.

double-breasted ['dʌbl'brestid], *a.* (gilet, pardessus) croisé.

double-buffered ['dʌbl'bʌfəd], *a. Cmptr:* (*of word channel*) à deux tampons.

double-check ['dʌbl'tʃek], *v.tr.* revérifier.

double-chinned ['dʌbl'tʃind], *a.* à double menton.

double-coated ['dʌbl'koutid], *a. Phot:* (film, etc.) à couche double.

double-concave ['dʌbl'kɔnkeiv], *a.* biconcave.

double-convex ['dʌbl'kɔnveks], *a.* biconvexe.

double-cross[1] ['dʌbl'krɔs], *v.tr. F:* duper, tromper, *F:* doubler (un associé).

double-cross[2], **double-crossing** ['dʌbl'krɔsiŋ], *s. F:* trahison *f*, duperie *f* (d'un associé).

double-crosser ['dʌbl'krɔsər], *s. F:* faux frère, faux jeton.

double-cuffed ['dʌbl'kʌft], *a.* (chemise) à manchettes doubles.

double-deal ['dʌbl'di:l], *v.i.* pratiquer la tromperie.

double dealer ['dʌbl'di:lər], *s.* homme à deux visages; fourbe *m*, trompeur *m*.

double-dealing[1] ['dʌbl'di:liŋ], *a.* fourbe, trompeur, -euse; faux, *f.* fausse.

double dealing[2], *s.* duplicité *f*, fourberie *f*, fausseté *f* de conduite; dissimulation *f*.

double-deck(ed) ['dʌbl'dek(t)], *a.* (autobus) à impériale.

double-decker ['dʌbl'dekər], *s.* 1. *Nau: Av:* deux-ponts *m*. 2. autobus *m* à impériale. 3. *F:* sandwich *m* double.

double-declutch ['dʌbl di'klʌtʃ], *v.i. Aut:* débrayer deux fois (pour changer de vitesse); exécuter un double débrayage.

double dome ['dʌbl'doum], *s. U.S: P:* intellectuel *m*; *F:* grosse tête, mandarin *m*.

double Dutch ['dʌbl'dʌtʃ], *s. F:* **to talk d. D.,** baragouiner, parler un langage inintelligible; **that's all d. D. to me,** (i) je ne puis rien comprendre à ce baragouin; (ii) c'est de l'hébreu pour moi.

double-dye ['dʌbl'dai], *v.tr.* teindre deux fois.

double-dyed ['dʌbl'daid], *a.* 1. *Tex:* (étoffe) bon teint *inv.* 2. *F:* **d.-d. scroundrel,** gredin fieffé.

double-edged ['dʌbl'edʒd], *a.* (épée, compliment, argument) à deux tranchants.

double-ended ['dʌbl'endid], *a.* à deux bouts; *Elcs:* **d.-e. amplifier,** amplificateur *m* push-pull.

double entendre ['du:blɑ̃n'tɑ̃ndr], *s. usu. Pej:* mot *m*, expression *f*, à double entente, à double sens.

double-faced ['dʌbl'feist], *a.* 1. *Tex:* **d.-f. cloth,** étoffe *f* sans envers, à double envers; double-face *f, pl.* doubles-faces. 2. (*of pers.*) à double face, à deux visages, fourbe, faux, *f.* fausse hypocrite.

double-fault ['dʌbl'fɔ(:)lt], *v.i. Ten:* faire une double faute.

double-feature ['dʌbl'fi:tjər], *a. Cin:* **d.-f. programme,** programme *m* double.

double-flanged ['dʌbl'flændʒd], *a.* à deux rebords; (roue) à gorge.

double-fronted ['dʌbl'frʌntid], *a.* **d.-f. house,** maison *f* à deux pignons en façade.

double-ganger ['dʌblgæŋər], *s.* (*spirit*) double *m* (d'un vivant).

double-geared ['dʌbl'giəd], *a. Mec.E:* 1. à double démultiplication. 2. à deux vitesses.

double-gild ['dʌbl'gild], *v.tr.* surdorer.

double-gilding ['dʌbl'gildiŋ], *s.* surdorure *f*.

double-gilt ['dʌbl'gilt], *a.* surdoré.

double-glazed ['dʌbl'gleizd], *a.* à double vitrage.

double-graft ['dʌbl'grɑ:ft], *v.tr. Hort:* contre-greffer, surgreffer.

double grafting ['dʌbl'grɑ:ftiŋ], *s. Hort:* surgreffage *m*.

double-handed ['dʌbl'hændid], *a.* 1. (canne à pêche, etc.) à deux mains. 2. à deux usages.

double-headed ['dʌbl'hedid], *a.* 1. à deux têtes; bicéphale; *Rail:* **d.-h. rail,** rail *m* à double champignon; **d.-h. train,** train *m* à deux locomotives, avec deux locomotives en tête. 2. *Her:* **d.-h. eagle,** aigle *f* à deux têtes; double aigle. 3. **d.-h. coin,** pièce *f* de monnaie à deux faces (pour tromper son adversaire au jeu de pile ou face).

double-header ['dʌbl'hedər], *s.* train *m* à deux locomotives, avec deux locomotives en tête.

double-iron ['dʌblaiən], *v.tr. Hist:* mettre des fers aux deux jambes de (qn).

double-jointed ['dʌbl'dʒɔintid], *a.* (*of pers., limb*) désarticulé.

double-leaded ['dʌbl'ledid], *a. Journ:* **d.-l. article,** article *m* à forts interlignes (pour attirer l'attention).

double-lock ['dʌbl'lɔk], *v.tr.* fermer (une porte, etc.) à double tour.

double-mesh ['dʌbl'meʃ], *v.tr. Fish:* contre-mailler (un filet).

double-opposed ['dʌblə'pouzd], *a. I.C.E:* (moteur) à deux cylindres opposés.

double-park ['dʌbl'pɑ:k], *v.tr. & i. Aut:* stationner en double file.

double parking ['dʌbl'pɑ:kiŋ], *s. Aut:* stationnement *m* en double file.

double-pole ['dʌbl'poul], *a. El:* **d.-p. switch,** interrupteur *m* bipolaire; inverseur *m* bipolaire.

double-quick ['dʌbl'kwik]. 1. *s.* pas *m* gymnastique. 2. *a. & adv.* **in d.-q. time, d.-q.,** (i) au pas gymnastique; (ii) *F:* en moins de rien, en vitesse; **to do sth. in d.-q. time,** *F:* mettre les bouchées doubles.

doubler ['dʌblər], *s.* 1. *Tex:* (*pers.*) doubleur, -euse (de laine, etc.). 2. *El:* duplicateur *m* électrique; **revolving d.,** duplicateur rotatif.

double-reading, double-scale ['dʌbl'ri:diŋ, -'skeil], *a.* (ampèremètre *m*) à deux échelles, à deux graduations.

double-reef ['dʌbl'ri:f], *v.tr. Nau:* prendre deux ris à, dans (une voile).

double-roping ['dʌbl'roupiŋ], *a. Mount:* **d.-r. technique,** escalade *f* à la double corde.

double-scull[1] ['dʌbl'skʌl], *s. Nau:* aviron *m* à couple.

double-scull[2], *v.i. Nau:* nager à, en, couple.

double-sculler ['dʌbl'skʌlər], *s. Row:* double-scull *m, pl.* doubles-sculls.

double sculling ['dʌbl'skʌliŋ], *s. Nau:* nage *f* à, en, couple.

double-seated ['dʌbl'si:tid], *a.* (pantalon) à double fond.

double-speak ['dʌblspi:k], *s. U.S:* 1. propos *mpl* nègre-blanc. 2. propos ambigus, insincères.

double-stitched ['dʌbl'stitʃt], *a.* (bords) à double couture.

double-stop ['dʌbl'stɔp], *v.i.* (**-stopped**) *Mus:* (*violin*) faire des doubles-cordes.

double stopping ['dʌbl'stɔpiŋ], *s. Mus:* double-corde *f*.

doublet ['dʌblit], *s.* 1. *A.Cost:* pourpoint *m*, doublet *m*. 2. *Ling:* doublet. 3. *B.Criticism:* passage *m* de la Bible qui en double un autre. 4. *Opt: Phot:* **d. (lens),** (i) objectif *m* double; (ii) objectif dédoublable. 5. *usu. pl.* **doublet(s),** (*at dice*) doublet. 6. *Shooting:* coup *m* double; doublé *m*. 7. *Lap:* doublet. 8. *El: W.Tel:* doublet.

double-talk ['dʌbltɔ:k], *s.* propos *mpl* nègre-blanc.

doubleton ['dʌbltən], *s. Cards:* bigleton *m*.

double-tongue ['dʌbl'tʌŋ], *v.i. Mus:* faire des doubles coups de langue (sur la flûte, etc.).

double-tongued ['dʌbl'tʌŋd], *a.* (*of pers.*) faux, *f.* fausse; peu sincère; fourbe; menteur, -euse.

double tonguing ['dʌbl'tʌŋiŋ], *s. Mus:* double coup *m* de langue.

double-width ['dʌbl'widθ], *a.* **d.-w. cloth,** tissu *m* grande largeur.

double-wound ['dʌbl'waund], *a.* (électro-aimant, etc.) à deux enroulements.

doubling [ˈdʌbliŋ], *s.* **1.** (*a*) doublement *m* (d'un nombre, etc.); (*b*) *Mus:* redoublement *m* (d'une note dans un accord). **2.** (*a*) *Tex:* doublage *m* (du fil, d'une étoffe); **d. frame,** doubleuse *f*; (*b*) *esp. Her:* doublure *f* (de l'étoffe). **3.** détour *m*, crochet *m*.

doubloon [dʌbˈluːn], *s. A.Num:* doublon *m*.

doubly [ˈdʌbli], *adv.* doublement; **d. bent,** bicoudé.

doubt[1] [daut], *s.* doute *m*; **to be in d.,** être en doute, dans le doute, dans l'incertitude *f*; **when in d.,** dans le doute; **the matter hangs in d.,** l'affaire reste douteuse, en suspens; **to cast doubts on sth.,** mettre qch. en doute; **to have one's doubts, to entertain doubts, about sth.,** avoir des doutes sur, au sujet de, à l'endroit de, qch.; **to raise doubts,** soulever des doutes; **in order that there may be no d. about . . .,** pour qu'il n'y ait pas d'équivoque sur . . .; **I have my doubts whether he will come,** je ne suis pas sûr qu'il viendra; je doute qu'il vienne; **I have my doubts whether this is true,** je doute que cela soit vrai; **it became a matter of d. whether . . .,** on commença à ne pas trop savoir si . . .; **there is no room for d.,** le doute n'est pas permis; **it is a matter of some d. with me whether I could . . .,** je doute de pouvoir . . .; **there is no d. of his adherence,** son adhésion ne fait pas question, ne fait pas de doute; **the result ceased to be a matter of d.,** le résultat cessa d'être douteux; **beyond d.,** hors de doute; sans le moindre doute; à n'en pas douter; indiscutablement; incontestablement; à coup sûr; **facts beyond d.,** faits avérés; **reputation beyond d.,** réputation indiscutée, indiscutable, au-dessus de toute discussion; **no d. he will come,** il viendra sans doute; sans doute qu'il viendra; **I have no d., little d., I shall see him before long,** je ne doute pas, guère, de le voir bientôt ; **there is, seems to be, no d. that . . .,** il n'est pas douteux, il n'est pas à douter, il ne semble faire aucun doute, que (ne) + *sub., more usu.* que + *ind.*; **without (a, any) d.,** sans aucun doute; **there is no d. about it,** il n'y a pas à dire; cela ne fait point de doute; **make no d. about it,** soyez-en certain.

doubt[2]. **1.** *v.tr.* douter; (*a*) **to d. s.o., s.o.'s word,** douter de qn, de la parole de qn; mettre en doute la parole de qn; **I d. it,** j'en doute; **there was no doubting the sincerity of their welcome,** on ne pouvait mettre en doute la sincérité de leur accueil; **to d. one's own eyes,** ne pas en croire ses yeux; **I d. whether, if, he will come,** je doute qu'il vienne, s'il viendra; je me demande s'il viendra; **I d. if I can come,** je doute de pouvoir venir; **I do not d. that he will come,** je ne doute pas qu'il ne vienne; **do you d. that I can do it?** doutez-vous que je puisse le faire? **I d. having said . . .,** je doute avoir dit . . .; (*b*) *Dial:* **I d. we are too late,** je crains (bien) que nous (ne) venions trop tard, que l'heure (ne) soit passée. **2.** *v.i.* (*a*) **he doubted no longer,** il n'hésita plus; (*b*) **we never doubted of your success,** nous n'avons jamais douté de votre succès.

doubter [ˈdautər], *s.* douteur, -euse, incrédule *mf*, sceptique *mf*.

doubtful [ˈdautful], *a.* **1.** (*of thg*) (*a*) douteux; **the result remains d.,** le résultat reste douteux, indécis, incertain; **it is d. whether . . .,** il est douteux, à douter, si . . .; *Pros:* **d. syllable, vowel,** syllabe, voyelle, douteuse; (*b*) *Com:* **d. debt,** créance douteuse; dette véreuse. **2.** (*of pers.*) (*a*) indécis, incertain; **I was still d. about speaking to him,** j'hésitais encore à lui parler; (*b*) **to be d. of, about, sth.,** douter de qch.; avoir des doutes sur qch.; **I am d. about his succeeding,** je doute qu'il réussisse, s'il réussira. **3.** (*questionable*) (caractère) équivoque, suspect; (question *f*) discutable; **in d. taste,** d'un goût douteux; **d. society,** compagnie *f* louche, équivoque; **story of d. authenticity,** histoire *f* apocryphe.

doubtfully [ˈdautfəli], *adv.* **1.** douteusement, d'une manière douteuse; d'un air de doute. **2.** en hésitant; d'une façon indécise; d'un ton indécis. **3.** vaguement.

doubtfulness [ˈdautfulnis], *s.* **1.** ambiguïté *f*; caractère incertain (d'un texte, etc.). **2.** incertitude *f* (du temps, de l'avenir). **3.** irrésolution *f*, indécision *f*.

doubting [ˈdautiŋ], *a.* incrédule, sceptique; **a d. Thomas,** un incrédule.

doubtless [ˈdautlis], *adv.* **1.** sans aucun doute. **2.** sans doute; très probablement.

douc [duːk], *s. Z:* douc *m*.

douceur [duːˈsəːr], *s.* **1.** gratification *f*, pourboire *m*, cadeau *m*. **2.** *Pej:* pot-de-vin *m*, *pl.* pots-de-vin.

douche[1] [duːʃ], *s.* **1.** *Toil:* douche *f*; *Fig:* **their enthusiasm got a cold d. from the minister,** le ministre a jeté une douche froide sur leur enthousiasme, a douché leur enthousiasme. **2.** *Med:* **d. (can),** bock *m*, irrigateur *m*.

douche[2]. **1.** *v.tr.* doucher; **douching stream,** jet *m* d'eau. **2.** *v.i.* se doucher.

doucin [ˈduːsin], *s. Hort:* **d. stock,** porte-greffes *m inv* doucin.

doucine [duːˈsiːn], *s. Arch:* doucine *f*.

dough [dou], *s.* **1.** pâte *f* (à pain); **heavy d.,** pâte mate; **d. knife,** coupe-pâte *m inv.* **2.** *P:* argent *m*; *P:* galette *f*, pognon *m*.

doughbird [ˈdoubəːd], *s. Orn: U.S:* courlis *m* du nord.

doughboy [ˈdoubɔi], *s. U.S:* **1.** *Cu: A:* boulette (de pâte) bouillie. **2.** *F:* simple soldat *m* = poilu *m*; *Hist:* (*World War I*) **the Doughboys,** les Américains.

doughface [ˈdoufeis], *s. U.S: F:* homme mou, sans caractère; lâche *m*.

doughiness [ˈdouinis], *s.* **1.** *Cu:* manque *m* de cuisson, mauvaise cuisson (du pain); lourdeur *f* (d'un gâteau, etc.). **2.** *F:* teint terreux (du visage).

doughnut [ˈdounʌt], *s.* **1.** *Cu:* sorte *f* de beignet fait avec de la pâte; *Fr.C:* beigne *f*. **2.** *Mth:* tore *m*; **d.-shaped,** en forme d'anneau; torique.

doughtily [ˈdautili], *adv. A: & Hum:* vaillamment: (s'acquitter) en preux chevalier.

doughtiness [ˈdautinis], *s. A: & Hum:* vaillance *f*.

doughty [ˈdauti], *a. A: & Hum:* vaillant, preux; **d. deeds,** haut faits.

doughy [ˈdoui], *a.* **1.** (pain) pâteux, mat. **2.** *F:* **d. face,** visage terreux.

Douglas [ˈdʌgləs], *Pr.n.* **1.** *Bot:* **D. fir,** douglas *m*. **2.** *Anat:* **Douglas's pouch,** cul-de-sac, *pl.* culs-de-sac, vagino rectal, -aux; cul-de-sac de Douglas.

douglasite [ˈdʌgləsait], *s. Miner:* douglasite *f*.

Doukhobors [ˈduːkoubɔːz], *s.pl. Rel.H:* Doukhobors *m*.

doum [duːm], *s. Bot:* **d. (palm),** doum *m*, doumier *m*, hyphaene *m*, hyphène *m*.

dour [duər], *a. Scot:* **1.** austère, froid, sévère; peu démonstratif. **2.** obstiné; (caractère *m*) qui se bute; buté.

dourine [ˈduəriːn], *s. Vet:* dourine *f*, mal *m* de coït.

dourly [ˈduəli], *adv. Scot:* **1.** avec une austérité froide. **2.** avec obstination.

dourness [ˈduənis], *s. Scot:* **1.** sévérité *f*, austérité *f* (de visage, de paroles). **2.** obstination *f*.

douro [ˈduərou], *s. Num:* douro *m*.

douroucouli [duːruːˈkuːli], *s. Z:* nyctipithèque *m*, singe *m* nocturne.

douse[1] [daus], *v.tr.* **1.** plonger, tremper, (qch.) dans l'eau. **2.** arroser, asperger, (qn) d'eau; doucher (qn); administrer une douche à (qn).

douse[2], *v.tr.* **1.** *Nau:* (*a*) amener rondement, ramasser (une voile); (*b*) fermer (un sabord). **2.** *F:* éteindre; **d. the light!** éteignez!

douser [ˈdausər], *s. Cin:* écran *m* de sûreté (du projecteur); écran pare-feu *inv*.

dousing [ˈdausiŋ], *s.* (*a*) plongeon *m*; (*b*) douche *f*; **he got a d.,** il a été trempé.

dove [dʌv]. **1.** *s.* (*a*) *Orn:* colombe *f*; *F:* pigeon *m*; **Barbary d.,** tourterelle rieuse; **collared d.,** tourterelle turque; **diamond d.,** colombe diamant; **emerald d.,** colombe turvert; **mourning d.,** *Fr.C:* tourterelle triste; **namaqua d.,** tourterelle à masque de fer; **pink-necked fruit d.,** colombe porphyre; **ring d., wood d.,** (pigeon) ramier (*m*); palombe *f*; **rock d.,** colombe, pigeon, de rocher; biset *m*; **stock d.,** petit ramier; colombin *m*; pigeon bleu; **tambourine d.,** colombe tambourette; **white-winged d.,** *Fr.C:* tourterelle à ailes blanches; **zenaida d.,** tourterelle zénaïde; **d. hawk,** busard bleu; oiseau *m* de Saint-Martin; soubuse *f*; (*b*) *F:* **my d.!** ma colombe! ma chérie! ma mie! (*c*) *N.Am:* femme douce, affectueuse, pleine de bonté; (*d*) *Pol:* *F:* **the doves and the hawks,** les colombes et les faucons. **2.** *a.* **d.(-coloured, -grey),** colombin; gorge-de-pigeon *inv*.

dovecot [ˈdʌvkɔt], **dovecote** [ˈdʌvkout, -kɔt], *s.* colombier *m*, pigeonnier *m*.

dovekie, dovekey [ˈdʌvkiː], *s. Orn: N.Am:* mergule nain.

dovelike [ˈdʌvlaik]. **1.** *a.* (douceur *f*, etc.) de colombe. **2.** *adv.* comme une colombe.

Dover[1] [ˈdouvər], *Pr.n. Geog:* Douvres; **the Straits of D.,** le Pas de Calais.

Dover[2], *Pr.n. Pharm:* **Dover's powder,** poudre anodine et diaphorétique qui contient de l'opium et de l'ipécacuana.

dove's foot [ˈdʌvzfut], *s. Bot:* bec-de-grue *m*, *pl.* becs-de-grue.

dovetail[1] [ˈdʌvteil], *s.* **1.** *Carp:* queue-d'aronde *f*, *pl.* queues d'aronde; adent *m*; **lapped, blind, concealed, secret, d.,** queue-d'aronde recouverte, à recouvrement; **countersunk d.,** embrèvement *m* à queue-d'aronde; **d. joint,** assemblage *m* à queue-d'aronde. **2.** *Sm.a:* grain-d'orge *m*, *pl.* grains-d'orge (de guidon)

dovetail[2]. **1.** *v.tr.* assembler à queue-d'aronde; adenter; **dovetailed joint,** assemblage *m* à queue-d'aronde. **2.** (*a*) *v.tr.* **to d. two schemes (together, into each other),** opérer le raccord entre deux entreprises; (*b*) *v.i.* (*of schemes, etc.*) se rejoindre, se raccorder.

dovetailing [ˈdʌvteiliŋ], *s.* **1.** *Carp:* assemblage *m* à queue-d'aronde. **2.** *Fig:* raccordement *m* (de deux projets, etc.).

dove tree [ˈdʌvtriː], *s. Bot:* davidia *m*.

dowager [ˈdauədʒər], *s.f.* **1.** douairière; **princess d., queen d.,** princesse douairière, reine douairière; **d.-duchess,** duchesse douairière. **2.** *F:* dame âgée (et d'aspect digne); douairière.

dowd [daud], *s.f.* femme peu élégante; caricature *f*.

dowdily [ˈdaudili], *adv.* (vêtue) sans élégance, sans goût.

dowdiness [ˈdaudinis], *s.* manque *m* d'élégance, de chic (dans la toilette d'une femme).

dowdy [ˈdaudi]. **1.** *a.* (femme, toilette) peu élégante, sans élégance, qui manque de chic; **her dress makes her look d.,** sa toilette la dépare; **a shy, d. young woman,** une jeune femme timide et mal habillée; **they were a d. lot,** elles étaient toutes habillées, *F:* fichues, comme quatre sous. **2.** *s.f.* **an old d.,** une vieille femme mal fagotée; une vieille caricature.

dowel[1] [ˈdauəl], *s.* *Carp:* **1. d. (pin),** goujon *m* (d'assemblage); goujon perdu; agrafe *f*; cheville *f* (en bois); goupille *f*; **d. bit,** foret *m*, mèche *f*, à cuiller; **d. hole,** enlaçure *f*; *Nau: etc:* **d. wedge,** épite *f*. **2. d. (wood),** fenton *m*. **3.** scellement *m*, tampon *m* (dans un mur pour recevoir un clou).

dowel[2], *v.tr.* **(dowelled)** *Carp:* goujonner, agrafer (des planches); enlacer (un joint à mortaise); **dowelled joint,** enlaçure *f*.

dowelling [ˈdauəliŋ], *s. Carp:* **1.** agrafage *m*. **2.** (*wood*) fenton *m*.

dowel-pin [ˈdauəlpin], *v.tr. Carp:* goupiller; goujonner; assembler (des pièces) au moyen de goujons.

dower[1] [ˈdauər], *s.* **1.** douaire *m* (de veuve); **d. house,** maison assignée en douaire. **2.** *A: & Lit:* dot *f*; *Jur:* apport dotal. **3.** *Lit:* don *m*, apanage *m*.

dower[2], *v.tr.* **1.** assigner un douaire à (une veuve). **2.** *A: & Lit:* doter (une jeune fille). **3.** *Lit:* **dowered with the most brilliant talents,** doué des plus brillantes qualités.

dowerless [ˈdauəlis], *a.* **1.** (veuve *f*) sans douaire. **2.** *A: & Lit:* (jeune fille) sans dot.

dowitcher [ˈdauitʃər], *s. Orn: N.Am:* limnodrome gris, *Fr.C:* bécasseau *m* à long bec.

dowlas [ˈdauləs], *s. Tex:* toile commune, toile grossière ((i) *A:* de lin, (ii) de coton).

down[1] [daun], *s. Geog:* **1.** dune *f*. **2.** *pl.* chaîne *f* de collines crétacées; **the (North, South) Downs,** les Downs *m*. **3. the Downs,** la rade au large de Deal.

down[2], *s.* **1.** duvet *m*; **d. feather,** plumule *f*; **d. mattress,** duvet; **d. pillow,** oreiller *m* de plumes. **2.** (*on pers.*) duvet, poil follet; cheveux follets. **3.** (*on plants*) poil, coton *m*, duvet; (*on buds*) bourre *f*; (*on fruit*) duvet, velouté *m*, fleur *f*.

down[3], *adv., prep., a. & s.*

I. *adv.* **1.** (*motion*) vers le bas; (de haut) en bas; à terre; par terre; (*a*) **to go d.,** aller en bas; descendre; **to lay d. one's arms,** mettre bas les armes; rendre les armes; **to shoot d., bring d., an aircraft,** abattre, *F:* descendre, un avion; **to fall d.,** tomber (i) à terre, (ii) par terre; *for* **come d., get d., let d., lie d., take d., etc.,** *see the verbs*; **music transposed one tone d.,** musique transposée d'un ton au-dessous; **money d., cash d.,** argent *m* (au) comptant, sur table, *F:* donnant donnant; **d. from the tree,** du haut de l'arbre; **d. to ground level, d. to the ground,** jusqu'au niveau de la terre, jusqu'à terre; (*b*) (*elliptical = imperative*) **d. with the traitors!** à bas les traîtres! les traîtres au poteau! conspuez les traîtres; (*of medicine, etc.*) **d. with it!** avalez! (*to child on a wall, etc.*) **d. with you!** descendez! (*to dog*) **d!** à bas! couché! **d. sir!** à bas les pattes! *Nau:* **d. (with the) helm!** la barre dessous! **hard d.!** amenez! **d. masts!** dématez! (*c*) (*crosswords*) verticalement. **2.** (*position*) **d. below,** (i) en bas, en contre-bas: (ii) *F:* en enfer; **d. there,** là-bas (en contre-bas); là en bas; **d. in the valley,** là-bas dans la vallée; **further d.,** plus bas; **ten lines (further) d.,** dix lignes plus bas; **d. in the country,** (au loin) à la campagne, en province; **he's d. at Folkestone,** il est parti à Folkestone; **d. here,** ici, dans ces parages; **d. under,** aux antipodes; **a man from d. under,** un voyageur des antipodes; *U.S:* **d. South,** aux États du sud; **d. East,** (i) *U.S:* en Nouvelle-Angleterre; au Maine; (ii) *Can:* aux provinces maritimes; **the blinds were d.,** les stores étaient baissés, tirés; **the curtains are d.,** on a enlevé les rideaux; **to lay sth. face d.,** placer qch. face en dessous, à l'envers; **head d.,** la tête en bas; **to be d.,** (i) être tombé (par terre), être à terre; (ii) (*of university student*) être rentré chez soi (à la fin du trimestre); (iii) (*of student*) n'être plus à l'université; **he is not d. (from his bedroom) yet,** il n'est pas encore descendu; **to hit a**

man when he's d., frapper un homme à terre; **that's hitting a man when he's d.,** c'est le coup de pied de l'âne; **to put, set, sth. d. (in black and white),** coucher qch. par écrit; **motion d. for today,** motion portée à l'ordre du jour; **he's d. for £20,** il est inscrit pour (une cotisation de) £20; **he's £20 d.,** il a un déficit de £20; **visitors were 20% d. on last year,** il y a eu 20% de visiteurs en moins, de moins, que l'année dernière; *F:* **the chips are d.,** c'est sérieux; **he is d. with influenza,** il est grippé; il est victime de la grippe; *F:* **that gets me d.,** je ne peux pas supporter cela; **he gets me d.,** je ne peux pas le sentir; **the sun is d.,** le soleil est couché; **the wind is d.,** le vent est tombé, s'est apaisé; **the tide is d.,** la mer est basse; **the sea is d.,** la mer s'est calmée; **the river is d.,** la rivière est basse, est rentrée dans son lit; **bread is d.,** le pain a baissé; **the clock has run d.,** on n'a pas remonté l'horloge; l'horloge est à bout (de remonte); **her hair is d.,** ses cheveux sont dénoués, défaits; *Aut: etc:* **your tyres are d.,** vos pneus sont dégonflés; **your tyres are d. flat,** vous pneus sont, *F:* vous êtes, à plat; *Cr:* **the wicket is d.,** le guichet est renversé; *Games:* **to be ten points d.,** avoir dix points de moins; être en perte de dix points; *Golf:* **two d. and three to play,** deux de moins et trois à jouer; *Cards:* **to be two d.,** avoir deux de chute; avoir chuté de deux levées; *Nau:* **hull d.,** coque noyée (sous l'horizon); **ship d. by the head, by the bows,** navire sur le nez, qui pique du nez; navire enfoncé par l'avant; (*of ship*) **to go d. by the bows,** piquer de l'avant; **d. by the stern,** enfoncé par, de, l'arrière; sur cul; **a funnel was d.,** une cheminée était dématée; **one of our masts is d.,** nous avons un mât par terre; *Artil:* (*in range finding*) **d. 300!** plus près 300! **3.** (*order, time*) **from prince d. to pedlar,** du prince jusqu'au colporteur; **he had eaten everything d. to his boots,** il avait mangé jusqu'à ses souliers; **d. to recent times,** jusqu'au temps présent; jusqu'à présent; **d. to date, d. to here, we have heard nothing,** jusqu'ici nous n'avons rien appris; **d. to here,** (en descendant) jusqu'ici. **4.** *miscellaneous phrases:* **to be d. on s.o.,** en vouloir à qn; tomber sur le dos de qn; *F:* **to come d. on s.o. like a ton of bricks,** rembarrer vertement qn; **everyone is d. on him,** tout le monde lui tombe dessus, est contre lui; **to be d. in the mouth,** être découragé, abattu, déprimé, tout triste; **he soon gets d. in the mouth,** il se déprime facilement; **he looks d. in the mouth,** il a l'air abattu, découragé; *F:* **to be d. and out,** être ruiné, vidé, décavé; être au bout de son rouleau, à bout de ressources, sur la paille, à fond de cale.

II. *prep.* **to lower s.o. d. a precipice,** descendre qn le long d'un précipice; **to slide d. the wall,** se laisser couler le long du mur; **the tears ran d. his face,** les larmes lui coulaient le long des joues; **her hair is hanging d. her back,** les cheveux lui pendent dans le dos; **to go d. the street, d. a hill,** descendre la rue, une colline; **to go d. the river,** descendre le fleuve; aller en aval; **he lives d. the river (from us),** il demeure en aval (de chez nous); **to fall d. the stairs,** tomber en bas de l'escalier; *Ven:* (*of game, etc.*) **to fly d. the wind,** aller à vau-vent; *Rail:* **d. the line,** en aval.

III. *a.* **1. d. leap,** saut *m* en bas, à terre. **2.** *Rail:* **d. train, d. platform,** train descendant, d'aller; quai descendant; **d. road, d. line,** voie impaire. **3.** *W.Tel:* **d. lead** [li:d], descente *f* d'antenne; *Telecom:* **d. link,** liaison descendante; *Tg:* **d. side,** aval *m*. **4.** *Mus:* (*violin*) **d. bow!** tirez! **with the d. bow,** en tirant. **5. d. payment,** acompte *m*; versement *m* à la commande. **6.** = DOWNHEARTED.

IV. *s.* **1. ups and downs,** ondulations *f* (du terrain); **the ups and downs of life,** les vicissitudes *f*, les péripéties *f*, les succès *m* et les revers *m*, les hauts et les bas, de la vie; **life is full of ups and downs,** la vie est remplie de succès et d'échecs; **a life of ups and downs,** une vie cahotée, mouvementée; **the ups and downs of politics, of the market,** les avatars *m* de la politique; les oscillations *f* du marché. **2.** *F:* **to have a d. on s.o.,** en vouloir à qn; nourrir de la rancune, *F:* avoir une dent, contre qn.

down[4], *v.tr.* **1.** (*a*) **to d. s.o.,** terrasser, abattre, qn; **to d. an aircraft,** descendre un avion; *Box: etc:* **to d. an opponent,** abattre un adversaire; **his horse had downed him three times,** son cheval l'avait désarçonné trois fois; (*b*) *P:* battre, vaincre (qn). **2.** *Ind:* **to d. tools,** débrayer; cesser le travail; mettre bas les outils; se mettre en grève; *P:* poser ses clous; **a d.-tools policy,** politique *f* d'action directe. **3.** *F:* **to d. a drink,** s'enfoncer une consommation, un verre.

Down[5], *Pr.n. Med:* **Down's syndrome,** maladie *f* de Down.

down-and-out ['daunən(d)'aut]. **1.** *a.* (*preceding the noun*) **a d.-a.-o. immigrant,** un immigré sans le sou, ruiné, décavé. **2.** *s.* (*also* **down-and-outer**) clochard *m*; épave *f*; crève-la-faim *m inv.*; sans-le-sou *m inv.*

down-at-heel ['daunət'hi:l], *a.* (*a*) (*of shoe*) éculé; (*b*) (*of pers.*) râpé; *F:* décheux.

downbeat[1] ['daunbi:t], *s. Mus:* temps fort; frappé *m*.

downbeat[2], *a. F:* triste, déprimé, abattu.

downcast[1] ['daunkɑ:st], *a.* **1.** (*of pers.*) abattu, déprimé; **to look d.,** avoir l'air découragé. **2.** (*of look, etc.*) baissé (vers la terre).

downcast[2], *s.* **1.** *Geol: Min:* rejet *m* en bas; **d. fault,** renfoncement *m*. **2.** *Min:* (*a*) courant d'air descendant; (*b*) **d. (shaft),** puits *m* d'appel (d'air); puits d'entrée (d'air).

downcome ['daunkʌm], *s.* **1.** déchéance *f*; débâcle *f*. **2.** *Metall:* prise de gaz latérale.

downcomer ['daunkʌmər], *s.* **1.** tuyau *m* de descente; descente *f* d'eau; gouttière *f*. **2.** *Metall:* prise de gaz latérale.

down-coming ['daunkʌmiŋ], *a.* descendant.

down country ['daunkʌntri], *s. U.S: N.Z:* (la) plaine; **d.-c. sheep farming,** l'élevage *m* des moutons dans les plaines.

down-draught ['daundrɑ:ft], *s.* (*a*) courant d'air descendant; *Ind:* tirage inférieur; *I.C.E:* **d.-d. carburettor,** carburateur à tirage descendant, à tirage en bas; carburateur inversé; (*b*) succion *f* (d'un navire qui coule, etc.).

down-easter [daun'i:stər], *s. NAm:* habitant, -ante, (i) de la Nouvelle-Angleterre, (ii) du Maine, (iii) des Provinces Maritimes du Canada.

downer ['daunər], *s.* **1.** *P: O:* **to have a d. on s.o.,** en vouloir à qn. **2.** *F:* tranquillisant *m*, sédatif *m*.

downfall ['daunfɔ:l], *s.* **1.** chute *f* (de neige, etc.). **2.** chute, ruine *f* (d'une personne); écroulement *m*, effondrement *m* (d'un empire, etc.); **d. of all my hopes,** écroulement de toutes mes espérances; **the d. of the ministry,** l'effondrement du ministère; **d. of a financier,** *F:* dégringolade *f* d'un financier; **drink was his d.,** la boisson l'a perdu. **3.** *Ven:* (*trap*) assommoir *m*.

downfold ['daunfould], *s. Geol:* pli synclinal, -aux.

downgrade[1]. **1.** *s.* ['daungreid], (*a*) *Rail: etc:* pente descendante; descente *f*, déclivité *f*; (*b*) décadence *f*; **to be on the d.,** baisser, être sur le déclin, *F:* sur le retour; **nation on the d.,** nation *f* en déchéance, en décrépitude; **at fifty a man is on the d.,** à cinquante ans on est sur l'autre versant; **his business, civilization, is on the d.,** ses affaires *f* périclitent; la civilisation recule. **2.** *adv.* ['daun'greid], sur une pente descendante.

downgrade[2] ['daungreid], *v.tr.* **1.** minimiser l'importance de (qch.). **2.** (*a*) classer (des marchandises) dans une catégorie inférieure; (*b*) déclasser (un employé) à une échelle de salaire inférieure. **3.** déclasser (un document classifié).

downgrading ['daungreidiŋ], *s.* **1.** baisse *f* de l'importance (de qch.). **2.** (*a*) classement *m* (des marchandises) dans une catégorie inférieure; (*b*) déclassement *m* (d'un employé) à une échelle de salaire inférieure. **3.** déclassement (d'un document secret).

down-haul ['daunhɔ:l], *s. Nau:* hale-bas *m inv*, calebas *m*.

downhearted [daun'hɑ:tid], *a.* découragé; déprimé, abattu; **don't be d.,** ne perdez pas courage; **to become d.,** se décourager; perdre courage.

downheartedly [daun'hɑ:tidli], *adv.* avec découragement.

downheartedness [daun'hɑ:tidnis], *s.* abattement moral; découragement *m*.

downhill ['daunhil]. **1.** *s.* descente *f*, déclivité *f*, pente *f*; *O:* **the d. of life,** le déclin de la vie. **2.** *a.* en pente, incliné; *O:* **the d. side of life,** le déclin de la vie. **3.** [daun'hil], *adv.* **to go d.,** (*of road*) aller en descendant; (*of cart, etc.*) descendre (la côte); *F:* (*of pers.*) être sur le déclin.

down-home ['daun'houm], *a. U.S:* (accent, etc.) des États du Sud.

downily ['daunili], *adv. F: O:* avec ruse; d'un ton, air, malin.

downiness ['dauninis], *s.* duveté *m*, velouté *m*; *Bot:* pubescence *f*.

downing ['dauniŋ], *s.* **1.** descente *f* (d'un avion) (par l'ennemi). **2. d. of tools,** cessation *f* du travail; *F:* débrayage *m*.

downingia [dau'niŋ(g)iə], *s. Bot:* downingie *f*.

Downing Street ['dauniŋ'stri:t], *Pr.n.* **1.** rue *f* où se trouve la résidence du premier ministre britannique. **2.** *Fig:* (i) le gouvernement; (ii) les Affaires étrangères.

downmost ['daunmoust]. **1.** *a.* le plus bas, la plus basse. **2.** *adv.* **to dive head d.,** plonger la tête en bas.

downpipe ['daunpaip], *s.* tuyau *m* de descente; descente *f* d'eau; gouttière *f*.

downpour ['daunpɔ:r], *s.* forte pluie; pluie battante, torrentielle, diluvienne; **sudden d.,** grosse averse; **what a d.!** quelle tombée! *F:* quelle rincée!

downright ['daunrait]. **1.** *adv.* (*a*) tout à fait, complètement, foncièrement; *F:* **this is d. good of you!** c'est vraiment trop de bonté de votre part! (*b*) nettement, catégoriquement, carrément; **he refused d.,** il a refusé catégoriquement. **2.** *a.* (*a*) (*of pers., language*) direct; franc, *f.* franche; carré; **he's a plain, d. fellow,** c'est un homme qui n'a ni si ni mais; (*b*) complet, absolu, véritable, vrai; **d. lie,** mensonge éclatant; **d. swindle,** véritable escroquerie *f*; **d. fool,** sot fieffé, sot achevé, sot en trois lettres, franc imbécile; **d. scoundrel,** franche canaille; **a d. no,** un non catégorique; **the d. truth,** la pure vérité.

downrightness ['daunraitnis], *s.* franchise *f*, droiture *f*; **d. of speech,** parler franc.

down-runner ['daunrʌnər], *s. Metall:* (trou *m*, jet *m* de) coulée *f*.

downslope. **1.** *s.* ['daunsloup] pente descendante. **2.** *adv.* ['daun'sloup] (aller, etc.) en descendant.

Downsman, *pl.* **-men** ['daunzmən], *s.m.* habitant des Downs.

downspout ['daunspaut], *s. NAm:* tuyau *m* de descente; descente *f* d'eau.

downstage ['daunsteidʒ], *Th:* **1.** *adv.* & *a.* sur le devant (de la scène); à l'avant-scène. **2.** *s.* avant-scène *f*.

downstairs. **1.** *adv.* [daun'stɛəz] (*a*) en bas (de l'escalier); **to come, go, d.,** descendre (l'escalier); **to fall, tumble, d.,** rouler en bas de l'escalier; tomber du haut de l'escalier; débouler du haut en bas de l'escalier; dégringoler, l'escalier; **to kick s.o. d.,** faire dégringoler l'escalier à qn; (*b*) en bas, au rez-de-chaussée; **our neighbours d.,** nos voisins (i) de l'étage au-dessous, (ii) du rez-de-chaussée; nos voisins d'en bas. **2.** *a.* ['daunstɛəz] **the d. rooms,** les pièces *f* d'en bas, du bas, du rez-de-chaussée. **3.** *s.pl. usu. with sg. const.* ['daunstɛəz] rez-de-chaussée *m inv*.

downstream. **1.** *adv.* ['daun'stri:m] en aval, à l'aval; **to go, drop, drift, d.,** aller en aval; suivre le courant; **going d.,** avalage *m*; **velocity d.,** vitesse *f* à l'aval; **he's going d.,** il est sur le déclin. **2.** *a.* ['daunstri:m] d'aval.

downstreet ['daun'stri:t], *adv. U.S:* **to go d.,** aller en ville.

down-striking ['daunstraikiŋ], *a. Civ.E: Const:* **d.-s. apparatus,** appareil *m* de décintrement.

downstroke ['daunstrouk], *s.* **1.** (*in writing*) jambage *m*, plein *m*. **2.** *Mch:* course descendante; mouvement *m* de descente (du piston). **3.** *Orn:* abaissée *f* (d'ailes).

downswept ['daunswept], *a. Aut:* (châssis) surbaissé.

downtake ['daunteik], *s.* **1.** *Metall:* prise de gaz latérale. **2.** *Mch:* **d. flue,** carneau *m* de descente.

down-the-line ['daunðəlain], *a.* (ballerine *f*) qui n'occupe qu'une place secondaire dans le corps de ballet.

downthrow ['daunθrou], *s. Geol: Min:* rejet *m* en bas; *Geol:* **d. side (of a fault),** lèvre affaissée (d'une faille).

downtime ['dauntaim], *s. Ind:* temps *m* de panne.

downtown [daun'taun], *NAm:* **1.** *adv.* vers (le centre de) la ville; **he gave me a lift d.,** il m'a descendu en ville. **2.** *a.* **d. New York,** le centre de New York. **3.** *s.* centre (d'une ville); quartier *m* des affaires.

downtowner [daun'taunər], *s. NAm:* habitant, -ante, du centre commercial (d'une ville).

downtrend ['dauntrend], *s. U.S:* tendance *f* à la baisse (des prix); ralentissement *m* (des affaires).

downtrodden ['dauntrɔdn], *a.* **1.** (*of grass, etc.*) foulé aux pieds; piétiné. **2.** (*of people*) opprimé, tyrannisé.

downturn ['dauntə:n], *s. Pol.Ec: etc:* diminution *f*, baisse *f*; régression *f*.

downward ['daunwəd]. **1.** *a.* (mouvement, sentier) descendant; (regard) dirigé en bas; **d. curve,** courbe descendante; **d. tendency (of prices),** tendance *f* à la baisse; *Fig:* **the d. path,** la pente fatale, la pente du mal; **to be on the d. path,** être (i) sur le penchant de sa ruine, (ii) sur le déclin; **heavenly body on its d. course,** astre penchant; *Artil:* **d. fire,** tir fichant, surbaissé. **2.** *adv.* = DOWNWARDS.

downwards ['daunwədz], *adv.* (*a*) de haut en bas; vers le bas, en descendant; (*on river*) en aval; **to look d.,** regarder en bas; **hanging head d.,** pendu la tête en bas; **to lay sth. face d.,** placer qch. face en dessous; **the road runs d.,** la route va en descendant; **measurement taken d.,** mesure prise en contrebas; (*b*) **from the twelfth century d.,** à partir du douzième siècle; depuis le douzième siècle; (*c*) **children of five and d.,** enfants *m* de cinq ans et au-dessous.

downwarp ['daunwɔ:p], *s. Geol:* fond *m* de bateau.

downwash ['daunwɔʃ], *s. Aer:* déplacement *m* d'air vers le bas; déflexion *f*, écoulement *m*, vers le bas des filets d'air; **d. angle,** angle *m* de déflexion des filets d'air.

downwind. **1.** *adv.* ['daun'wind], *Av:* (atterrir, etc.) vent arrière; *Ven:* (chasser) à vau-vent. **2.** *a.* ['daunwind], (atterrissage) vent arrière; *Ven:* à vau-vent.

downy ['dauni], *a.* **1.** (*a*) de duvet, duveteux, duveté; couvert de duvet; *Bot: etc:* lanugineux, pubescent; tomenteux; (*b*) (*of fruit*) velouté, pelucheux; (*of chin*) cotonné; **chin that is getting d.,** *F:* menton *m* qui commence à fleurir; (*c*) mou, molle; (lit) douillet, moelleux; *s. F: O:* **to seek the d.,** aller au plumard; (*d*) *F: O:* **a d. little bit,** un gentil brin de fille. **2.** *F: O:* **he's a d. bird,** c'est un malin, un rusé.

dowry ['dauri], *s.* **1.** dot *f*; *Jur:* apport dotal, -aux. **2.** *Lit:* don *m*; apanage *m*.

dowse[1] [dauz], *v.i.* employer la baguette de sourcier (pour reconnaître la présence de l'eau souterraine, etc.); faire de l'hydroscopie, de la radiesthésie.

dowse[2] [daus], *v.tr.* = DOUSE[1,2].

dowser[1] ['dauzər], *s.* sourcier *m*; hydroscope *m*; radiesthésiste *mf*; homme à baguette; tourneur *m* de baguette.

dowser[2] ['dausər, 'dauz-], *s. Cin:* écran *m* de sûreté (du projecteur); écran pare-feu *inv.*

dowsing[1] ['dauziŋ], *a.* radiesthésique; baguettisant.

dowsing[2], *s.* hydroscopie *f*; radiesthésie *f*; art *m* du sourcier; **d. rod,** baguette *f* divinatoire, de sourcier.

doxographer [dɔk'sɔgrəfər], *s. Gr.Lit:* doxographe *m.*

doxographic(al) [dɔksə'græfik(l)], *a. Gr.Lit:* doxographique.

doxography [dɔk'sɔgrəfi], *s.* doxographie *f.*

doxological [dɔksə'lɔdʒikl], *a.* doxologique.

doxology [dɔk'sɔlədʒi], *s. Ecc:* doxologie *f.*

doxy ['dɔksi], *s.f. P:* **1.** *A:* catin; maîtresse. **2.** *Dial:* bonne amie.

doyen ['dɔijən], *s.m.* doyen (du corps diplomatique).

doyenne[1] [dwai'jen, dɔi-], *s.f.* doyenne.

doyenne[2] [dwai'jen], **doyenné** [dwai'jenei], *s. Hort:* **d. (pear),** (poire *f* de) doyenné *m.*

doyley ['dɔili], *s.* = DOILY.

doze[1] [douz], *s.* petit somme; **to have a d.,** faire un petit somme; **to fall into a d.,** s'assoupir; **I found him in a d.,** je l'ai trouvé en train de faire un petit somme; je l'ai trouvé assoupi.

doze[2]. **1.** *v.i.* sommeiller, somnoler; *F:* dormailler; être assoupi; **to d. off,** s'assoupir; **to d. over one's work,** s'endormir sur son ouvrage. **2.** *v.tr.* **to d. away the time,** passer le temps à sommeiller.

doze[3], *v.tr.* déblayer, dégager, (un terrain) avec un bulldozer.

dozen ['dʌzn], *s.* douzaine *f.* **1.** (*inv. in pl.*) **a d. eggs,** une douzaine d'œufs; **half a d.,** une demi-douzaine; **six d. bottles of wine,** six douzaines de bouteilles de vin; **how many d. do you require?** combien de douzaines en voulez-vous? **I'll give you a d. reasons,** je vous donnerai vingt raisons; **about a d. people were there,** il y avait environ douze personnes; **in about ten years he produced a couple of d. comedies,** en une dizaine d'années il écrivit deux douzaines de comédies; **a couple of d. of his plays have never been staged,** deux douzaines de ses pièces n'ont jamais été jouées; *F:* **the daily d.,** la gymnastique matinale, quotidienne; **2.** (*pl.* **dozens) to sell articles in (sets of) dozens, by the d.,** vendre des articles à la douzaine; **they are to be had by the d.,** on les a par douzaines; **they arrived in their dozens,** ils arrivèrent par douzaines; **some dozens of their regular customers were unable to obtain admission,** quelques douzaines d'habitués n'ont pu se faire admettre; **dozens of people think as I do,** des douzaines de gens pensent comme moi; **dozens and dozens of times,** maintes et maintes fois; **a long d., a round d., a baker's, printer's, d., thirteen to the d.,** une bonne douzaine; treize douze; treize à la douzaine; **to sell eggs in bakers' dozens,** vendre des œufs à la treizaine, par treizaines, par demi-quarterons; *F:* **to talk thirteen, fifteen, nineteen, to the d.,** parler avec volubilité; bavarder, jaser, comme une pie borgne; avoir la langue bien pendue.

dozenth ['dʌznθ], *a. F:* **let me tell you for the d. time,** laissez-moi vous dire pour la douzième fois.

dozer ['douzər], *s.* bulldozer *m.*

dozily ['douzili], *adv.* d'un air somnolent.

doziness ['douzinis], *s.* somnolence *f,* assoupissement *m.*

dozing ['douziŋ], *s.* assoupissement *m.*

dozy ['douzi], *a.* somnolent; *F:* avachi.

drab[1] [dræb]. **1.** *a. & s.* (i) gris (*m*); (ii) brun (*m*); (iii) beige (*m*). **2.** *a.* (*a*) **she always wears d. clothes,** elle porte toujours des vêtements de couleurs ternes; (*b*) morne, monotone; **to lead a d. existence,** mener une existence terne, décolorée, veule. **3.** *s.* (*a*) *Tex:* drap *m* beige; toile bise; (*b*) *NAm: Mil:* tenue *f* d'un gris olivâtre.

drab[2], *s.f.* **1.** souillon. **2.** (*prostitute*) traînée, guenipe.

drab[3], *v.i.* **(drabbed)** *F:* courir la gueuse; *P:* putasser.

drab[4], *s.* **in dribs and drabs,** petit à petit; peu à peu; (mesurer qch.) au compte-gouttes.

draba ['dreibə], *s. Bot:* drave *f.*

drabbet ['dræbit], *s. Tex:* grosse toile bise croisée.

drabble ['dræbl]. **1.** *v.i.* (*a*) patauger, patouiller **(through the mud,** dans la boue); se crotter; (*b*) *Fish:* pêcher (le goujon, etc.) en traînant la ligne au fond. **2.** *v.tr.* traîner (qch.) dans la boue; crotter (qch.).

drabble-tail ['dræblteil], *s. F:* femme sans soin dans sa mise, toujours crottée; souillon *f*; traînée *f.*

drabbling ['dræbliŋ], *s.* **1.** pataugeage *m.* **2.** *Fish:* pêche *f* (au goujon, etc.) en traînant la ligne au fond.

drably ['dræbli], *adv.* mornement; monotonement; **to dress d.,** porter des vêtements de couleurs ternes.

dracaena [drə'si:nə], *s. Bot:* **1.** dracéna *m.* **2. d. palm,** dragonnier *m.*

dracena [drə'si:nə], *s. Bot:* dragonnier *m.*

drachm [dræm], *s.* **1.** *A.Num:* drachme *f.* **2.** *Meas:* drachme.

drachma, *pl.* **-mas, -mae** ['drækmə, -məz, -mi:], *s. Num:* drachme *f.*

Draco[1] ['dreikou], **Dracon** ['drækən], *Pr.n.m. Gr.Hist:* Dracon.

Draco[2], *Pr.n. Astr:* le Dragon.

dracocephalum [dreikou'sefələm], *s. Bot:* dracocephalum *m,* dracocéphale *m.*

Draconian [drə'kouniən], **Draconic**[1] [drə'kɔnik], *a.* (*a*) draconien; (*b*) (*of law, rule, etc.*) draconien, sévère, rigoureux.

draconic[2], *a.* draconien; qui ressemble à un dragon.

draconitic [drækə'nitik], *a. Astr:* draconitique, dracontique.

dracontiasis [drækən'taiəsis], *s. Med:* dracunculose *f*; dracontiase *m.*

dracontic [drə'kɔntik], *a. Astr:* dracontique, draconitique.

dracunculosis [drəkʌŋkju'lousis], *s. Med:* dracunculose *f,* draconculose *f.*

dracunculus [drə'kʌŋkjuləs], *s. Ann:* dracuncule *m,* draconcule *m.*

draff [dræf], *s.* **1.** *A:* (*a*) lie *f* (de vin); (*b*) lavure *f,* rinçure *f.* **2.** *Brew: Dist:* drêche *f*; drêche *f.*

draft[1] [drɑ:ft], *s.* **1.** *Mil:* (*a*) détachement *m* (de troupes); contingent *m* (de recrues); (*b*) membre *m* d'un détachement, d'un contingent; (*c*) *U.S:* conscription *f*; *F:* **d. dodger,** réfractaire *m.* **2.** troupeau *m* (de bétail, de moutons). **3.** *Com:* (*a*) tirage *m* (d'un effet); (*b*) traite *f*; lettre *f* de change; mandat *m,* disposition *f,* effet *m*; bon *m* (sur une banque); **banker's d.,** chèque *m* bancaire, de banque; **d. at sight, sight d.,** traite, effet, à vue; **time d.,** traite, effet, à terme; **to make a d. on s.o.,** faire traite, disposer, tirer, sur qn. **4.** *Arch: Mec.E: etc:* dessin *m* schématique; plan *m,* tracé *m*; ébauche *f*; esquisse *f*; (*of map, etc.*), **rough d.** canevas *m*; **eye d.,** dessin, esquisse, à vue; **drafts and estimates,** plans et devis *m.* **5.** (*a*) projet *m* (de loi); avant-projet *m, pl.* avant-projets (de traité); minute *f* (d'un acte); brouillon *m* (de lettre); **d. (of an) agreement,** projet de contrat, de convention; **first d. of a novel,** premier jet d'un roman; (*b*) *attrib.* provisoire; **d. scheme for a railway,** projet de chemin de fer. **6.** *Stonew:* plumée *f* (d'une pierre de taille).

draft[2], *v.tr.* **1.** *Mil:* (*a*) détacher, envoyer en détachement (des troupes); affecter (un militaire à un service); **to d. troops into . . .,** incorporer, faire passer, des troupes dans . . .; (*b*) *U.S:* appeler (des soldats) sous les drapeaux. **2. to d. s.o. to a post,** désigner qn pour, à, un poste. **3.** *Husb:* **to d. cattle, sheep,** trier du bétail, des moutons. **4.** rédiger (un acte, un procès-verbal, un projet); minuter, faire la minute ((d')un contrat, (d')une lettre); faire le brouillon (d'une lettre); **to d. a bill,** établir un projet de loi; **to d. a contract,** préparer, faire, le projet d'un contrat. **5.** *Stonew:* appareiller (des pierres de taille). **6.** *Tex:* **to d. the warp,** armer la lisse.

draft[3], *s.* = DRAUGHT[1].

draftee [drɑ:f'ti:], *s. U.S: Mil:* appelé *m,* conscrit *m,* recrue *f.*

drafter ['drɑ:ftər], *s.* rédacteur, -trice (d'un acte).

drafting ['drɑ:ftiŋ], *s.* **1.** rédaction *f* (d'un acte, etc.); **d. committee,** comité *m* de rédaction. **2.** *Husb:* triage *m* du bétail, des moutons. **3.** *Stonew:* appareillage *m.* **4.** *Tex:* armure *f* (de la lisse).

draftsman, *pl.* **-men** ['drɑ:ftsmən], *s.m.* **1.** = DRAUGHTSMAN 1. **2.** rédacteur (d'un acte).

draft tube ['drɑ:ft'tju:b], *s. Hyd:* tuyau *m* d'aspiration (de turbine).

drag[1] [dræg], *s.* **1.** (*a*) *Agr:* herse *f*; (*b*) traîneau (grossier); (*c*) *Ropem:* traîne *f*; (*d*) *Stonew:* rabotin *m.* **2.** *Veh:* drag *m,* mail-coach *m* (à quatre chevaux). **3.** (*a*) (*for dredging*) drague *f*; **peat d.,** puchette *f*; (*b*) (*for retrieving lost object*) araignée *f*; *Nau:* chatte *f,* grappin *m* à main; (*for drowning persons*) gaffe *f* de sauvetage; (*c*) *Fish:* = DRAGNET. **4.** (*a*) enrayure *f*; **d. (shoe),** sabot *m*; lugeon *m*; patin *m*; **to put a d. on a wheel,** enrayer une roue; *F:* (*of pers.*) **to put on the d.,** enrayer; (*b*) entrave *f*; **to be a d. on s.o.,** entraver qn; être un boulet au pied de qn; **he's a d. on me,** je le traîne comme un boulet; **his wife has been a d. on him all his life,** toute sa vie sa femme a été un obstacle à son avancement; **boy who is a d. on the class,** élève *m* qui ralentit le travail de la classe; (*c*) *F:* ennui *m*; scie *f*; **it was a frightful d.,** c'était la barbe et les cheveux; (*d*) *F:* (*pers.*) raseur, -euse; casse-pieds *m inv*; (*e*) *U.S: P:* bonne amie; *F:* gosse *f.* **5.** *Fish:* (*a*) frein *m* (de moulinet); (*b*) sillage *m* (de la ligne). **6.** *Aer:* guide-rope *m, pl.* guide-ropes. **7.** (*a*) tirage *m,* résistance *f* (à l'avancement); frottement excessif; **there is a slight d.,** il y a une légère résistance; (*b*) **an uphill d.,** une montée fatigante; **there is still a long d. ahead,** il y a encore toute une tirée; (*c*) *Av:* traînée *f*; résistance à l'avancement; **d. axis,** axe *m* de traînée; **skin-friction d.,** résistance aérodynamique; **profile d., wing d., tail d.,** traînée de profil, d'aile, de queue; **interference d.,** résistance de deux plans adjacents; **parasitic d.,** traînée parasite; (*d*) *Bill:* effet *m* rétrograde; *F:* rétro *m*; (*e*) ralentissement *m* (d'un moteur à ressort, etc.); (*f*) **to walk with a d.,** marcher en traînant la jambe. **8.** *P:* (*a*) **to have a d. (on a cigarette),** tirer une bouffée (d'une cigarette); (*b*) gorgée *f* (de boisson). **9.** *Ven:* (i) voie artificielle (hareng saur, etc.); (ii) **d. (hunt),** chasse *f* à courre où la meute suit une voie artificielle; drag *m.* **10.** (*a*) *P:* vêtements de femme portés par un homme; **he was in d.,** il portait des vêtements de femme; *Th:* il était en travesti; **d. show,** spectacle de travestis; (*b*) réunion *f* d'homosexuels. **11.** *NAm F:* **to have d.,** avoir du piston. **12.** *NAm: F:* rue *f*; **the main d.,** la grande rue. **13.** *NAm: Aut:* **d. (race),** concours *m* d'accélération.

drag[2], *v.* **(dragged** [drægd])

I. *v.tr. & i.* **1.** *v.tr.* (*a*) traîner, tirer (qn, qch.); entraîner (qn) (contre sa volonté); **to d. one's feet,** (i) traîner les pieds; (ii) *F:* (*also* **to d. one's heels**) montrer peu d'empressement (à faire qch.); **I could scarcely d. one foot after the other,** je pouvais à peine mettre un pied devant l'autre; **I cannot d. my feet another step,** je ne peux pas me traîner plus loin; je ne peux pas faire un pas de plus; **to d. s.o. from his home,** arracher qn de, à, son foyer; *F:* **we had to d. him here,** il a fallu le traîner ici; il n'est venu qu'à son corps défendant, **the partridge was dragging a wing,** la perdrix traînait (de) l'aile; (*b*) draguer (un étang, un fleuve); **to d. a pond** (for fish), pêcher un étang; (*c*) *Agr:* herser (le terrain); (*d*) enrayer (une roue, une charrette); (*e*) *Stonew:* dresser (une pierre) avec un rabotin; raboter (une pierre). **2.** *v.i.* (*a*) (*of pers.*) traîner, rester en arrière; (*of thg*) traîner (à terre); (*of lawsuit, etc.*) traîner en longueur; (*of conversation, action*) traîner, languir, s'éterniser; (*of garment*) gêner; **to have sth. dragging behind one,** avoir qch. à la traîne; **the conversation drags,** la conversation traîne, manque d'entrain; *Th:* **scene that drags,** scène *f* qui traîne en longueur; *St.Exch:* **rubber dragged,** les caoutchoucs *m* ont langui; *Med:* **dragging pain,** douleur gravative; (*b*) offrir de la résistance; (*of brakes*) frotter (sur les roues); (*c*) (i) draguer **(for sth.,** à la recherche de qch.); *Nau:* **to d. for (a cable, a wreck),** draguer (un câble, une épave); (ii) *Fish:* pêcher à la drague; **to d. for oysters,** pêcher les huîtres à la drague; (*e*) *F:* **to d. on, at, a cigarette,** tirer des bouffées d'une cigarette; (*f*) *Aut: NAm: F:* concourir dans une course d'accélération.

II. (*compound verbs*) **1. drag about,** (*a*) *v.tr.* traîner, *F:* trimbaler (qn, qch.); (*b*) *v.i.* **to d. about the streets,** traîner ses talons par les rues.

2. drag along, *v.tr.* traîner, entraîner (qn, qch.).

3. drag away, *v.tr.* (*a*) (i) entraîner, emmener, (qn) de force; (ii) arracher (qn) **(from,** à, de); (*b*) (i) traîner (qch.) dehors, hors de la salle, etc.; (ii) arracher (qch.) **(from,** de).

4. drag down, *v.tr.* tirer, entraîner, (qn, qch.) en bas; faire descendre (qn) de force; **he has dragged me down with him,** il m'a entraîné dans sa chute, dans sa perte; **she helped to d. him down,** elle a contribué à sa déchéance.

5. drag in, *v.tr.* (*a*) faire entrer de force (qn, qch.); *F:* **to d. a subject in (to a conversation, etc.),** amener un sujet à toute force; (*b*) traîner (un colis, etc.) jusque dans la salle, etc.

6. drag off, *v.tr.* = DRAG AWAY.

7. drag on, (*a*) *v.tr.* (i) entraîner (qn, qch.); (ii) **to d. on a miserable existence,** traîner une existence misérable, une vie de misère; (iii) prolonger, *F:* éterniser (une discussion, etc.); (*b*) *v.i.* (*of affair, etc.*) traîner en longueur; s'éterniser; **to let a matter d. on,** laisser traîner une affaire; *F:* s'endormir sur une affaire; **time**

drags on, les heures *f* se traînent.
8. drag out, *v.tr.* (*a*) faire sortir (qn, qch.) de force; arracher (qch.); **to d. s.o. out of bed,** tirer qn de son lit; **to d. the truth out of s.o.,** arracher la vérité à qn; (*b*) **to d. out an affair,** faire traîner une affaire; (*c*) **to d. out a wretched existence,** poursuivre, traîner, jusqu'à sa fin une existence misérable; **he dragged out his life for another ten years,** pendant dix ans encore il traîna une vie pénible; **another hour to d. out before lunch,** encore une heure à tirer d'ici le déjeuner.
9. drag up, *v.tr.* (*a*) entraîner, tirer, (qn, qch.) jusqu'en haut; (*b*) repêcher (un cadavre, etc.) à la drague; *F:* **why do you d. up that old story?** pourquoi ressortir cette vieille histoire? (*c*) *F:* (*of child*) **dragged up,** élevé à la diable, à la va-comme-je-te-pousse, tant bien que mal.

drag antenna ['dræg'æntenə], *s. W.Tel:* antenne traînante.

drag-bar ['drægbɑːr], *s.* barre *f* d'attelage, d'accouplement (de wagons, etc.).

drag-bench ['drægben(t)ʃ], *s. Metalw:* banc *m* à étirer, à tréfiler; machine *f* à étirer; étireur *m*; étireuse *f.*

drag-chain ['drægtʃein], *s.* **1.** chaîne *f* d'attelage (de wagons). **2.** chaîne d'enrayage (d'une charrette, etc.).

dragee ['drɑːʒei], *s. Pharm: etc:* dragée *f.*

dragger ['drægər], *s.* **1.** (*pers.*) tireur, -euse. **2.** *Fish:* (*boat*) chalutier *m.*

dragging ['drægiŋ], *s.* **1.** traînage *m*, traînement *m* (d'un fardeau derrière soi, etc.); *Nau:* **d. of the anchor,** dérapage *m*. **2.** (*a*) dragage *m* (d'un étang, etc.) (**for a dead body,** à la recherche d'un cadavre); (*b*) *Fish:* (pêche *f* à la) trôle.

draggle ['drægl]. **1.** *v.tr.* traîner (sa jupe, etc.) dans la boue; crotter (ses vêtements). **2.** *v.i.* (*a*) (*of skirt, etc.*) traîner (par terre); (*b*) (*of pers.*) traîner, rester en arrière; **to d. at the heels of the army,** traîner à la suite de l'armée.

draggle-tail ['drægl̩teil], *s.f. F:* femme qui laisse traîner le bas de sa jupe; femme sans soin dans sa mise, toujours crottée; souillon; traînée.

draggle-tailed ['drægl̩teild], *a.* (femme *f*) malpropre (dans sa mise), aux jupes qui traînent.

draggy ['drægi], *a. NAm: F:* peu intéressant; ennuyeux; *F:* assommant.

drag-hook ['drægshuk], *s.* **1.** crochet *m* de traction. **2.** crochet de chaîne d'enrayage. **3.** gaffe *f.*

drag lift ['dræglift], *s.* téléski *m.*

dragline ['dræglain], *s. Civ.E:* **d. (excavator),** dragline *m.*

drag-link ['dræglіŋk], *s.* **1.** (*a*) = DRAG-BAR; (*b*) *Aut:* bielle *f* de commande de direction; barre *f* (de connexion) de direction; **d.-l. connector,** boîte *f* à rotule de la barre de direction. **2.** *Mch:* (*a*) tringle *f* de relevage, d'entraînement; barre de rappel; (*b*) (barre d')accouplement *m.*

dragnet ['drægnet], *s.* **1.** *Fish:* drague *f*, chalon *m*, chalut *m*, seine *f*, gabare *f*, traîne *f*, traîneau *m*, bâche volante, bâche traînante; salabre *m*; filet *m* à la trôle; (*large*) hallope *m*. **2.** *Ven:* traîneau, traînasse *f*, tirasse *f*, tramail *m*, pantène *f*, pantière *f*. **3. to throw a d. round a district,** établir un cordon de police autour d'un quartier; **twenty suspects were picked up in the d.,** vingt personnes suspectes furent arrêtées dans la rafle, dans le coup de filet.

dragoman, *pl.* **-mans** ['drægoumən, -mənz], *s.* drogman *m*, dragoman *m*, truchement *m.*

dragon ['drægən], *s.* **1.** (*a*) *Myth:* dragon *m*; *F:* **d. of virtue,** dragon de vertu; femme d'une vertu farouche; (*b*) *F: A:* duègne *f*, dragon; (*c*) *Astr:* **the D.,** le Dragon; (*d*) *Rept:* **d. (lizard),** (i) dragon; draco *m*; (ii) dragon, varan *m*, de Komodo. **2.** *Mil:* (*a*) tracteur *m*; (*b*) **dragon's teeth,** rangées *fpl* de tétraèdres de béton, de cornières d'acier (comme défense antichar). **3.** *Bot:* **d. tree,** dragonnier *m*; dracéna *m*. **4.** *Com:* **dragon's blood,** sang-(de-)dragon *m*. **5.** *Const:* **d. tie,** aisselier *m*; contre-fiche *f*, *pl.* contre-fiches.

dragonet ['drægənet], *s.* **1.** *Myth:* petit dragon. **2.** *Ich:* dragonnet *m.*

dragonfish ['drægənfiʃ], *s. Ich:* (*a*) dragon *m* des mers; (*b*) dragonnet *m.*

dragonfly ['drægənflai], *s. Ent:* libellule *f*, odonate *m*, anisoptère *m*; *F:* demoiselle *f.*

dragonhead ['drægənhed], **dragon's head** ['drægənzhed], *s. Bot:* (*a*) dracocephalum *m*, dracocéphale *m*; (*b*) **false d.,** physostegia *m*, dracocéphale de Virginie.

dragon(n)ade [drægə'neid], *s. Fr.Hist:* dragonnade *f.*

dragonné, dragony ['drægəni], *a. Her:* dragonné.

dragonroot ['drægənruːt], *s. Bot:* arisaema *m.*

dragoon[1] [drə'guːn]. **1.** *Mil:* dragon *m*. **2.** *Orn:* (pigeon *m*) dragon.

dragoon[2], *v.tr.* **1.** *Hist:* dragonner (le peuple); persécuter (le peuple) par des dragonnades. **2.** *F:* tyranniser (qn); **to d. s.o. into doing sth.,** contraindre, forcer, qn à faire qch.

dragrope ['drægroup], *s.* **1.** *Artil:* (*for field gun*) bricole *f*, combleau *m*. **2.** *Fish:* fune *f* (d'une seine).

dragsaw ['drægsɔː], *s.* scie alternative à tronçonner.

drag screw ['drægskruː], *s.* vis *f* de rappel.

drag seine ['drægsein], *s. Fish:* seine *f.*

drag wire ['drægwaiər], *s. Av. A:* câble *m* de recul, de traînée.

drail[1] [dreil], *s. Fish:* traînée *f*, ligne *f* de fond.

drail[2], *v.tr. Fish:* pêcher à la traînée.

drain[1] [drein], *s.* **1.** (*a*) canal *m*, -aux (de décharge); tranchée *f*, caniveau *m*, rigole *f*, fossé *m*, d'écoulement; (*leading from source of water*) fossé de dérivation; *Agr:* fossé d'assainissement; échau *m*; **open d., surface d.,** (i) tranchée à ciel ouvert; *Agr:* saignée *f* d'irrigation; (ii) (*across road*) cassis *m*; **covered d.,** conduit souterrain; aqueduc *m*; **outlet d.,** colateur *m*; **French d.,** puits absorbant; **well d.,** puits d'écoulement; (*b*) *Civ.E:* cunette *f* (d'égout). **2.** (*a*) égout *m*; **smell of drains,** odeur *f* d'égout; *F:* **to go down the d.,** prendre le métro; **to throw money down the d.,** jeter son argent par la fenêtre; gâcher son argent; **that's five years' work down the d.,** voilà cinq années de travail perdues; **to laugh like a d.,** rire à gorge déployée; (*b*) **the drains of a house,** la canalisation sanitaire d'une maison. **3.** (*a*) *Mec.E: etc:* tuyau *m* d'écoulement, de vidange; *Mch:* tuyau de purge; **overflow d.,** (tube *m* de) trop-plein *m*, *pl.* trop-pleins; évacuation *f* du trop-plein; **box d.,** tuyau d'écoulement à section rectangulaire; (*b*) orifice *m* de trop-plein; (*c*) *Med:* drain *m*. **4.** *attrib.* **d. canal,** canal d'évacuation; **d. cock,** robinet *m* purgeur; purgeur *m*; robinet de purge, de vidange; **d. cup,** cuvette *f* d'égouttage; poche *f* de vidange; *Arch:* **d. hole,** chantepleure *f*, barbacane *f*, canonnière *f*; **d. manifold,** collecteur *m* d'évacuation, de purge; **d. plug,** bouchon *m* de vidange; **d. shaft,** puits *m* de drainage; **d. tank,** puisard *m*; **d. tap,** robinet de vidange, de soutirage; **d. tile,** tuile *f* de drainage; boisseau *m*; **d. trap,** siphon *m* (d'égout); **d. well,** puits absorbant; puits perdu; puisard *m*. **5.** perte *f*, fuite *f* (d'énergie, etc.); **d. of money, of bullion,** drainage *m* de capitaux; drainage, retrait *m*, d'or en lingots; **d. on the resources,** cause *f* d'épuisement des ressources; **constant d. on the resources,** saignée, hémorragie *f*, continuelle; *F:* ver rongeur; **the upkeep of two houses was too great a d. on my purse,** l'entretien de deux maisons était trop fort pour ma bourse; **the brain d.,** la fuite, l'exode *m*, le drainage, des cerveaux. **6.** *P:* **to have a d.,** pisser; se soulager.

drain[2]. **1.** *v.tr.* (*a*) **to d. water (away, off),** (i) évacuer, faire écouler, des eaux; (ii) faire égoutter l'eau; **to d. the wealth of a country,** drainer, épuiser, les richesses d'un pays; *Fin:* **to d. off excess liquidity,** éponger les liquidités en excédent; (*b*) boire (un liquide) jusqu'à la dernière goutte, *Lit:* jusqu'à la lie; vider (un fût, une coupe); (*c*) assécher (un terrain); dessécher, mettre à sec, vider (un étang); drainer, essorer, (faire) égoutter (un terrain); assainir (un champ, un terrain boisé); saigner (un fossé); assécher, drainer, épuiser (une mine); désamorcer (une pompe); purger (un cylindre); (faire) égoutter (des bouteilles, des légumes); essorer (le linge, etc.); *Leath:* écouler (des peaux); *I.C.E:* **to d. the sump,** vidanger le carter; *Med:* **to d. an abscess,** vider, drainer, un abcès; (*d*) épuiser, *F:* saigner (qn, la bourse); mettre (qn, etc.) à sec; **to d. a country of money,** épuiser l'argent d'un pays; **to d. one's purse,** mettre sa bourse à sec; **to d. s.o. of his strength,** épuiser les forces de qn; *F:* **to d. s.o. dry,** saigner qn à blanc; sucer qn jusqu'au dernier sou; **to d. s.o. body and soul,** vider qn. **2.** *v.i.* (*a*) (*of water, etc.*) **to d. away,** s'écouler; (*b*) (*of sponge, etc.*) (s')égoutter. **3.** *v.tr.* creuser des rigoles d'assèchement dans (une prairie, etc.).

drainable ['dreinəbl], *a.* drainable.

drainage ['dreinidʒ], *s.* **1.** = DRAINING 1; (*a*) **d. ditch,** saignée *f*; rigole *f* d'écoulement, d'assèchement; **d. hole, d. opening,** bonde *f* (de lac artificiel); *Min:* **d. level, d. gallery,** galerie *f* d'assèchement, d'exhaure; (*b*) *Geog:* **d. area, d. basin,** bassin *m* hydrographique; surface *f* de captation des eaux; bassin-versant *m*, *pl.* bassins-versants; bassin d'alimentation; **d. pattern,** réseau *m* hydrographique; (*c*) *Med:* **suction d.,** drainage *m* à vide; **dependent d.,** drainage au point déclive; **d. tube,** drain *m*. **2.** *Civ.E:* (i) système *m* d'écoulement des eaux; (ii) système d'égouts; **direct-to-sewer d., main d.,** tout-à-l'égout *m inv*. **3.** (i) eaux *f* de surface; *Min: etc:* eaux d'assèchement; (ii) eaux d'égout.

drainboard ['dreinbɔːd], *s. NAm:* égouttoir *m.*

drainer ['dreinər], *s.* **1.** (*a*) égouttoir *m*; **bottle d.,** égouttoir à bouteilles, hérisson *m*, if *m*; (*b*) vide-fûts *m inv*; **air-pressure d.,** vide-fûts à air comprimé. **2.** *Agr: etc:* (*pers.*) draineur *m.*

draining ['dreiniŋ], *s.* **1.** (*a*) écoulement *m*, épuisement *m* (des eaux); assèchement *m*, dessèchement *m* (d'un marais); drainage *m*, égouttement *m*, assainissement *m* (d'un terrain); purge *f* (d'un cylindre); égouttage *m*, égouttement (des bouteilles, etc.); vidange *f* (d'un tonneau, d'un carter, etc.); *Med:* drainage (d'une plaie); *Leath:* écoulage *m* (des peaux); *attrib.* **d. arch,** arche *f* de décharge (d'un pont); **d. board,** égouttoir *m*; **d. channel,** barbacane *f* (d'un pont); **d. engine,** machine *f* d'épuisement; épuise *f*; **d. rack,** égouttoir; (*for bottles*) égouttoir à bouteilles; if *m*; hérisson *m*; *Paperm: etc:* **d. tank,** caisse *f* d'égouttage; (**sunk**) **d. trap,** puisard *m*; (*b*) creusage *m* des rigoles d'assèchement (dans une prairie, etc.); **d. spade,** louchet *m*. **2.** *pl.* **drainings,** égoutture *f* (d'un verre, etc.).

drainpipe ['dreinpaip], *s.* tuyau *m* d'écoulement, d'échappement, de drainage; drain *m*; gouttière *f*; *F:* **d. trousers,** pantalon étroit; *F:* tuyaux *mpl* de poêle.

drake[1] [dreik], *s. Ent: Fish:* éphémère *m* vulgaire; manne *f* des poissons.

drake[2], *s. Orn:* canard *m* mâle; **wild d.,** malard *m*, malart *m.*

dram [dræm], *s.* **1.** *Pharm.Meas:* drachme *f*, gros *m* (= un seizième d'once = 1.77 gramme). **2.** *F:* (*O: & Scot:*) goutte *f* (à boire); petit verre; **to take a d.,** prendre un petit verre; **he likes a d.,** il aime la goutte; *NAm:* **d. shop,** débit *m* d'alcool, bistrot *m.*

drama ['drɑːmə], *s. Th:* **1. a d.,** un drame; **d. of ideas,** pièce *f* à thèse; **to make a d. out of a trivial incident,** faire un drame d'un incident sans importance; *F:* **no d.,** tout s'est bien passé. **2. (the) d.,** l'art *m* dramatique, la dramaturgie, le théâtre; **the masterpieces of French d.,** les chefs-d'œuvre de la scène française; **to succeed in d.,** réussir dans le dramatique.

dramatic [drə'mætik], *a.* (*a*) (ouvrage, style, situation, critique) dramatique; **the d. works of Corneille,** le théâtre de Corneille; **d. effect(s),** dramaturgie *f*; (*b*) effet théâtral; **story told with a view to d. effect,** récit poussé à l'effet théâtral; **to give a d. turn to an incident,** dramatiser un incident.

dramatically [drə'mætik(ə)li], *adv.* dramatiquement.

dramatics [drə'mætiks], *s.pl.* (*usu. with sg. const.*) le théâtre; **this is no time for d.,** ce n'est pas le moment de faire un drame, de dramatiser.

dramatis personæ ['dræmətispə:'souniː, -'sounai], *s. Th:* personnages *mpl.*

dramatist ['dræmətist], *s.* auteur *m* dramatique; dramaturge *m.*

dramatization [dræmətai'zeiʃ(ə)n], *s.* **1.** dramatisation *f*; adaptation *f* (d'un roman, etc.) à la scène. **2.** *Psy:* dramatisation.

dramatize ['dræmətaiz]. **1.** *v.tr.* (*a*) dramatiser; produire (un ouvrage) sur la scène; adapter (un roman) à la scène; tirer une pièce (d'un roman); (*b*) (*with passive force*) **novel that would d. well,** roman qui s'adapterait bien à la scène. **2.** *v.tr. & i.* **there's no need to d. (it),** il ne faut pas en faire un drame, (le) dramatiser.

dramatizer ['dræmətaizər], *s.* dramatiseur, -euse.

dramatizing[1] ['dræmətaiziŋ], *s.* **1.** dramatisation *f* (d'un roman, etc.). **2. no more d.!** plus de drame!

dramatizing[2], *a.* qui aime à faire un drame (de tout), à dramatiser.

dramaturge ['dræmətəːdʒ], *s.* dramaturge *m.*

dramaturgic [dræmə'təːdʒik], *a.* dramaturgique.

dramaturgy ['dræmətəːdʒi], *s.* dramaturgie *f.*

drape[1] [dreip]. **1.** *v.tr.* (*a*) draper, tendre (**with, in,** de); **gown draped with lace,** robe drapée de dentelle, ornée de dentelles; (*of church door, etc.*) **draped in black, in mourning,** drapé (de noir); **the church was draped in black,** l'église était tendue de noir, de voiles noirs; *A:* **black-draped horses,** chevaux caparaçonnés de noir; (*b*) *Art:* draper (une étoffe); (*c*) *F:* **she draped herself against the doorpost,** elle s'adossa élégamment contre le montant de la porte; **his legs draped over the arm of a chair,** ses jambes pendantes du bras d'un fauteuil; **the corpse was draped over the back of an armchair,** le cadavre était étendu par-dessus le dossier d'un fauteuil; (*of drunkard, etc.*) **to d. oneself round a lamp-post,** se coller contre un bec de gaz. **2.** *v.i.* (*a*) (*of hangings, etc.*) se draper; (*b*) *Cost:* (*of garment*) **to d. (loosely),** blouser.

drape[2], *s.* **1.** *Cost:* drapé *m* (d'une robe, etc.). **2.** (*a*) *pl.* tentures *f*; vêtements drapés; atours *m*; (*b*) *pl. NAm:* rideaux *m*. **3.** *NAm:* **d. (suit),** complet (affiné à la ligne allongeante).

draper ['dreipər], *s.* marchand, -ande, de tissus, de nouveautés; **linen d.,** marchand, -ande, de blanc, de toiles, de nouveautés; linger, -ère; **draper's shop,** magasin *m* de tissus, de nouveautés; mercerie *f*; **you will find it at a draper's,** vous trouverez cela dans un magasin de nouveautés.

draperied ['dreipərid], *a.* couvert de draperies.

drapery ['dreipəri], *s.* **1.** (*a*) **d. (trade),** draperie *f*; commerce *m* des tissus; (*b*) **d. (shop),** magasin *m* de tissus; mercerie *f*; **d. and fancy goods store,** magasin de nouveautés; (*c*) (articles *mpl* de) mercerie; **linen d.,** (articles *mpl* de) blanc *m*; toilerie *f*; lingerie *f*; nouveautés *fpl*. **2.** (*a*) tentures *fpl*; vêtements drapés; atours *mpl*; (*b*) *pl. NAm:* **draperies,** rideaux *mpl*; (*c*) *Furn: etc:* **d. panel,** panneau *m* à étoffe(s) pliée(s).

draping ['dreipiŋ], *s.* (*a*) (*action*) drapement *m*; drapage *m*; (*b*) (*result*) drapé *m*.

drappie ['dræpi], *s. Scot: F:* **wee d.,** petit verre, goutte *f* (de whisky).

drastic ['dræstik], *a.* **1.** violent; énergique; **to take d. measures,** prendre des mesures énergiques, rigoureuses, draconiennes; trancher dans le vif; **to make d. cuts in expenses, personnel,** faire des coupes sombres dans les dépenses, le personnel; *Com:* **d. reductions,** réductions colossales, incroyables, formidables. **2.** *Med:* (*a*) *a.* & *s.* drastique (*m*); (*b*) (remède *m*) énergique, de cheval.

drastically ['dræstik(ə)li], *adv.* énergiquement, rigoureusement.

drat [dræt], *v.tr. F:* (*used only in third pers. sing. sub.*) **d. (it)!** sacristi! nom de nom! bon sang! **d. the child!** au diable cet enfant! quel sacré mioche!

dratted ['drætid], *a. F:* maudit, sacré (mioche, etc.).

draught[1] [drɑːft], *s.* **1.** (*a*) traction *f*, tirage *m*; **oxen pull with a steadier d. than horses,** les bœufs donnent une traction moins saccadée que les chevaux; **d. animal,** animal *m*, -aux, bête *f*, de trait, d'attelage; **d. harness,** harnais *m* d'attelage; *Min:* **d. engine,** machine *f* d'extraction; *Rail:* **d. spring,** ressort *m* de traction; (*b*) (*way of harnessing*) attelage *m*; **pole d.,** attelage à l'allemande, à timon. **2.** *Fish:* coup *m* de filet; pêche (contenue dans le coup de filet); **d. net,** drague *f*; *B:* **the miraculous d. of fishes,** la pêche miraculeuse. **3.** (*drinking*) trait *m*, gorgée *f*; **at a d.,** d'un seul trait, d'un seul coup; d'une gorgée; *P:* d'une lampée; **you must drink it in one d., in three draughts,** il faut le boire en une fois, en trois fois; **in long draughts,** à longs traits; à grands traits. **4.** *Med:* potion *f*, breuvage *m*; **poisoned d.,** potion empoisonnée; *F:* bouillon *m* d'onze heures; *A:* **black d.,** purgatif *m*, médecine noire. **5.** (*a*) *Nau:* tirant *m* d'eau (d'un navire); **load d.,** tirant d'eau en charge; calaison *f*; **light d.,** tirant d'eau en lège; **shallow-d. ship,** navire à faible tirant d'eau; **deep-d. ship,** navire à, de, grand tirant d'eau; **d. mark(s),** marques *f* de tirant d'eau; (*b*) *Hyd.E:* (i) aire *f* (d'une vanne); (ii) aire des orifices d'entrée (d'une turbine); **d. tube,** tuyau *m* d'aspiration. **6.** *Tex:* (*a*) étirage *m* (d'un banc d'étirage); (*b*) armure *f* (de la lisse). **7.** *Metall:* dépouille *f* (d'un modèle). **8.** *pl.* **draughts,** (jeu *m* de) dames *fpl*; **to play a game of draughts,** faire une partie de dames; **d. board,** damier *m*. **9.** (*a*) (*in room*) courant *m* d'air; **I'm sitting in a d., I feel a d.,** je suis dans un courant d'air; **slight d.,** vent *m* coulis; **d. excluder, d. preventer, d. tube,** bourrelet *m* de porte; brise-bise *m inv*; **d. screen,** paravent *m*; **d.-proof,** à l'épreuve des courants d'air; calfeutré; **to make a d. with a fan,** faire du vent avec un éventail; *F:* **to feel a d.,** se sentir mal à l'aise; **a firm that reduces its advertising will soon feel a, the, d.,** une maison qui diminue sa publicité ne tarde pas à s'en ressentir; (*b*) tirage (d'une cheminée); appel *m* d'air; *Ind: etc:* entrée *f* d'air; venue *f* du vent; **natural d.,** tirage libre, naturel; **induced d.,** tirage induit, négatif; **forced-d. furnace,** four *m* à air forcé, soufflé; **back d.,** tirage inverti, renversé; contre-appel *m*, *pl.* contre-appels, contre-courant *m*, *pl.* contre-courants, d'air; contre-tirage *m*, *pl.* contre-tirages, contrevent *m*; (*in furnace*) **back d. of flames,** contre-feu *m*, *pl.* contre-feux; **d. gauge,** indicateur *m* du tirage; **d. hole,** aspirail *m*, -aux; (*of furnace*) ventouse *f*, regard *m*; **d. regulator,** registre (régulateur) de tirage. **10. beer on d.,** bière *f* à la pression; **d. beer,** bière au tonneau, détaillée du fût.

draught[2], *s.* = DRAFT[1].

draught[3], *v.tr.* = DRAFT[2].

draughtiness ['drɑːftinis], *s.* courants *mpl* d'air (d'une pièce, d'un coin de rue).

draughtsman, *pl.* **-men** ['drɑːftsmən], *s.* **1.** (*a*) *Ind:* dessinateur *m*, traceur *m* (de plans, d'épures, etc.); **architectural d.,** dessinateur en architecture; **engineering d., mechanical d.,** dessinateur industriel; *N.Arch:* **ship's d.,** gabarieur *m*; (*b*) *Art:* **he is a good d.,** il est bon dessinateur; il dessine bien. **2.** rédacteur *m* (d'un acte). **3.** *Games:* pion *m* (du jeu de dames).

draughtsmanship ['drɑːftsmənʃip], *s.* **1.** l'art *m* du dessin industriel; *Ind:* le dessin. **2.** talent *m* de dessinateur.

draughtswoman, *pl.* **-women** ['drɑːftswumən, -wimin], *s.f. Ind:* dessinatrice.

draughty ['drɑːfti], *a.* **1.** plein de courants d'air, de vents coulis. **2.** (coin de rue, etc.) exposé à tous les vents.

Dravidian [drə'vidiən], *a.* & *s. Ethn: Ling:* dravidien (*m*).

dravite ['drævait], *s. Miner:* dravite *f*.

draw[1] [drɔː], *s.* **1.** (*act of drawing*) tirage *m*; **it's your d.,** (*cards*) c'est à vous de tirer; (*dominoes*) c'est à vous de pêcher; **to take a d. at one's pipe, at a cigarette,** tirer une bouffée de sa pipe, d'une cigarette; *NAm:* **to have a d.,** fumer; *F:* griller une cigarette, en griller une; *F:* **to be quick on the d.,** (i) avoir la gâchette facile; (ii) avoir la répartie facile. **2.** (*thg. drawn*) (*a*) pont *m* (d'un pont-levis); (*b*) *Games:* carte tirée; (*dominoes*) pièce pêchée; (*c*) *U.S:* (= DRAWER) tiroir *m*; **two-d. desk,** bureau *m* à deux tiroirs. **3.** (*a*) tirage au sort; *F:* **that's just the luck of the d.,** ça c'est la vie! (*b*) loterie *f*; tombola *f*; (*c*) *Sp:* tableau *m* des concurrents à chaque tour d'une série d'épreuves de championnat, etc. **4.** (*thg. that draws*) (*a*) mots prononcés pour inviter qn à parler, à enfourcher son dada; **this was meant as a d. but he did not rise to it,** ceci était dit pour l'attirer sur ce sujet, mais il a laissé passer l'occasion, mais il n'a pas mordu; (*b*) attraction *f*; clou *m* (de la fête, etc.); *Th:* pièce *f* qui fait recette; pièce à succès; *Com: O:* marchandise *f* en réclame; (*of play, etc.*) **to be a d.,** faire recette; attirer un grand public. **5.** *Sp:* partie nulle; résultat nul; match *m* sans résultat; **the game ended in a d.,** la partie resta indécise; **to call a match a d.,** prononcer match nul. **6.** *Bill:* effet *m* rétrograde, de recul; **d. shot,** *F:* rétro *m*. **7.** *Metall:* **d. (taper),** dépouille *f*. **8.** *Metalw:* étirage *m*; **first d.,** premier étirage. **9.** *Geog: U.S:* ravin *m*; couloir *m*.

draw[2], *v.tr.* & *i.* (**drew** [druː], **drawn** [drɔːn])

I. *v.tr.* **1.** (*pull*) (*a*) tirer (un verrou); hâler (un filet) à bord; lever (un pont-levis); **to d. the curtains,** tirer les rideaux; (i) fermer, (ii) ouvrir, les rideaux; **to d. the blinds,** baisser les stores; **to d. one's hat over one's eyes,** ramener son chapeau sur ses yeux; **to d. one's hand across one's forehead,** passer la main sur son front; *Mus:* (*organ*) **draw . . .,** mettez . . .; **to d. a bow,** bander, tendre, un arc; *A:* **to d. the long bow,** exagérer; *Golf: etc:* **to d. the ball,** tirer la balle, le coup, à gauche; **astringents d. the mouth,** les astringents crispent la bouche; (*b*) tirer, traîner (une voiture, une remorque, etc.); **coach drawn by four horses,** carrosse attelé de quatre chevaux; **drawn by a locomotive,** remorqué par une locomotive; *A:* **to d. a criminal,** traîner un criminel (à l'échafaud) sur une claie. **2.** (*a*) (*take in*) tirer, aspirer (l'air dans ses poumons); **to d. acid up into a pipette,** aspirer de l'acide dans une pipette; (*b*) (*attract*) attirer; **a pretty girl drew his eye,** une jolie fille attira ses regards; **to d. a crowd, crowds,** attirer une foule; provoquer un rassemblement; **actor who draws the whole of Paris,** acteur qui fait courir tout Paris; *v.i.* **to d.,** attirer la foule, le public; **the play draws well,** la pièce fait de grosses recettes; **the play did not d.,** la pièce n'a pas pris; **in order to d. customers,** pour attirer, amadouer, les clients; **to d. s.o. into conversation,** entamer une conversation avec qn; **to d. s.o. into the conversation,** mêler qn à la conversation; faire entrer qn dans la conversation; **to d. s.o. into a conspiracy,** engager, entraîner, qn dans une conspiration; **to d. s.o. from a course,** détourner qn d'un projet; **to d. s.o. into doing sth.,** amener qn à faire qch.; **to d. vengeance upon oneself,** attirer la vengeance sur soi; **to feel drawn to s.o.,** se sentir attiré vers qn; se sentir de l'attrait pour qn; avoir de la sympathie, du sentiment, pour qn; se sentir quelque chose pour qn; **I feel drawn to him,** il m'est sympathique. **3.** (*a*) tirer, retirer, ôter (**sth. from, out of, sth.,** qch. de qch.); ôter (une vis); retirer, tirer, faire sauter (un bouchon); **to d. (one's sword),** tirer l'épée; dégainer; **to d. one's revolver,** sortir son revolver de l'étui, de sa poche; dégainer; **to d. on s.o.,** menacer qn de son épée, de son revolver; **to d. a card (from the pack),** tirer une carte; **to d. cards from the stock, stack, pile,** aller aux cartes; **to d. (cards) for partners,** tirer pour établir les partenaires; (*dominoes*) **to d. (from the pool),** pêcher, piocher; **to d. (lots) for sth., to d. sth. by lot,** tirer qch. au sort; tirer au sort pour qch.; **drawn by lot from amongst . . .,** tiré au sort parmi . . .; **the number that is, was, drawn,** le numéro sortant; **number five was drawn,** le numéro cinq sortit au tirage; **to d. a prize at a lottery,** gagner un lot à une loterie; *Fin:* (*of bonds*) **to be drawn,** sortir au tirage; **these bonds have not been drawn yet,** ces bons ne sont encore sortis à aucun tirage; **to d. a blank,** (i) tirer un mauvais numéro; (ii) éprouver une déception; ne pas avoir de chance, de veine; faire chou blanc; échouer; (iii) *Ven:* faire buisson creux; revenir bredouille; **to d. straws,** tirer à la courte paille; (*b*) arracher (un clou, une dent, etc.); **to d. a confession from s.o.,** arracher un aveu à qn; **to d. tears from s.o.,** tirer, arracher, des larmes à qn; *F:* **to d. s.o.'s teeth,** mettre qn hors d'état de nuire; (*c*) **to d. coal from a mine,** tirer, extraire, du charbon d'une mine; **to d. water from the river,** puiser, tirer, de l'eau à la rivière; **to have a bath drawn,** se faire préparer un bain; **to d. wine (from a barrel),** tirer du vin (d'un tonneau); *F: O:* **d. it mild!** n'exagérez pas! ne vous emballez pas! tout doux! **to d. consolation from sth.,** tirer consolation de qch.; puiser des consolations dans (la religion, etc.); **to d. strength from within oneself,** puiser des forces en soi-même; **to d. profit from sth.,** (re)tirer (du) profit de qch.; **to d. a conclusion from sth.,** tirer, déduire, une conclusion de qch.; (*d*) toucher (de l'argent, un salaire); *Mil:* **to d. rations,** toucher des rations; **to d. a commission on a transaction,** prélever une commission sur une opération; **to d. (one's) supplies from s.o.,** tirer des approvisionnements de qn; **to d. one's supplies from abroad,** être tributaire de l'étranger; *v.i.* **to d. on one's savings, the reserves,** prendre sur ses économies; mettre à contribution, prélever sur, les réserves; *F:* taper dans les réserves; **to d. on one's memory, one's imagination,** faire appel à sa mémoire; faire jouer son imagination; **to d. (up)on s.o.'s experiences for a novel,** s'inspirer, se servir, des expériences d'autrui pour un roman; (*e*) *Tchn:* **to d. the fire(s),** mettre bas les feux; décharger, sortir, éteindre, les feux; **to d. the furnace,** décharger les feux du fourneau; *Cer:* **to d. a batch of pottery,** défourner une fournée de poterie; *Metall:* **to d. a casting,** démouler un modèle; (*f*) *Ven:* **to d. a fox, a badger,** lancer, mettre debout, mettre sur pied, un renard, un blaireau; *Cards:* **to d. a card, trumps,** faire tomber une carte, les atouts; *Mil:* **to d. the enemy's fire,** attirer sur soi le feu de l'ennemi; se désigner au feu de l'ennemi; *Fig.* provoquer une attaque sur soi-même; **to try to d. the enemy,** tâter l'ennemi; *Fig:* **to try to d. s.o.,** essayer de faire parler qn; plaider le faux pour savoir le vrai; **that drew him,** cela l'a fait sortir de son silence; là-dessus il s'emballa; **his accusation drew an instant denial,** son accusation provoqua un démenti immédiat; **the government refused to be drawn,** le gouvernement refusa de se commettre. **4.** (*a*) vider (une volaille, etc.); *A:* **to be hanged, drawn and quartered,** être pendu, éviscéré et écartelé (tiré à quatre chevaux); (*b*) pêcher (un étang) au filet; *Ven:* **to d. a covert,** battre un bois, un taillis; *v.i.* **to d.,** faire le bois. **5.** *Med:* **to d. an abscess,** faire mûrir, faire aboutir, un abcès. **6.** *Metall:* (*a*) étirer, tirer (du fil, des tubes, etc.); tréfiler, fileter (un métal); (*b*) **to d. steel to the temper,** recuire l'acier après trempe; faire revenir l'acier. **7.** (*a*) (*trace*) tracer (un cercle, un plan); tirer, mener (une ligne); construire (des figures géométriques); **to d. a line between two points,** mener une ligne entre deux points; *F:* **I d. the line at that,** je n'accepte pas ça; (*b*) **to d. a map,** (i) (*of surveyor*) dresser une carte; (ii) (*of schoolboy*) faire, dessiner, une carte; (*c*) dessiner (un paysage, une figure); **to d. sth. in ink, in pencil,** dessiner qch. à l'encre, au crayon; **to d. a picture of s.o.,** faire le portrait de qn; **to d. s.o. as a Roman emperor,** représenter qn en empereur romain; **the author has drawn the characters skilfully,** l'auteur a tracé les personnages avec adresse; (*d*) **to d. a distinction between two things,** faire, établir, une distinction entre deux choses; **to d. comparisons,** faire, établir, des comparaisons. **8. to d. a cheque,** libeller, rédiger, formuler, un chèque; **to d. a cheque on a bank,** tirer, souscrire, un chèque sur une banque; **to d. a bill,** *v.i.* **to d., on s.o. for £ . . .,** tirer sur qn pour £ . . .; émettre, fournir, sur qn une traite de £ . . .; faire traite sur qn pour £ . . .; **to d. three months' bills on London,** fournir à trois mois sur Londres; **to d. on s.o. at sight,** tirer à vue sur qn. **9.** *Nau:* (*of ship*) **to d. twenty feet of water,** tirer, jauger, caler, vingt pieds d'eau; avoir vingt pieds de tirant d'eau. **10. to d. (a game) with s.o.,** faire partie nulle, match nul, avec qn; **the battle was drawn,** la bataille resta indécise. **11.** *Tex:* **to d. the warp,** armer la lisse.

II. *v.i.* **1.** (*move*) (*a*) **to d. near to s.o., close to s.o.,** se rapprocher de qn; s'approcher de qn; **when they drew near . . .,** à leur approche . . .; **he drew towards the door,** il se rapprocha de la porte; il se dirigea furtivement vers la porte; **on drawing near the mountains,** à leur approche des montagnes; **the crowd drew to one side,** la foule se rangea (de côté); **the train drew into the station,** le train entra en gare; **to d. ahead of s.o., a ship,** dépasser qn, un navire; gagner l'avant d'un navire, to

d. level with a competitor, arriver à (la) hauteur d'un concurrent; **to d. round the table,** s'assembler autour de la table; (*b*) (*of the day, of a play, etc.*) **to d. to an end,** tirer, toucher, à sa fin. **2.** (*a*) (*of chimney, pipe, etc.*) tirer; (*of pump*) aspirer; **the pump is drawing,** la pompe est prise, est chargée; la pompe marche; (*b*) *Med:* (*of plaster*) tirer. **3.** *Nau:* (*of sail*) porter; **the sails were drawing well,** les voiles *f* portaient plein. **4.** (*of tea*) infuser; **to let the tea d.,** laisser infuser le thé. **5.** faire du dessin; **he draws extremely well,** c'est un dessinateur de premier ordre.

III. (*compound verbs*) **1. draw along,** *v.tr.* traîner, entraîner (qn, qch.).

2. draw apart. (*a*) *v.tr.* séparer, écarter; (*b*) *v.i.* se séparer, s'écarter.

3. draw aside. (*a*) *v.tr.* (i) détourner, écarter (qch.); tirer, écarter (les rideaux); **to d. the curtains slightly aside,** entr'ouvrir les rideaux; (ii) tirer, prendre, (qn) à l'écart; (*b*) *v.i.* s'écarter; se ranger.

4. draw away. (*a*) *v.tr.* (i) entraîner (qn); (ii) détourner (**s.o. from sth.,** qn de qch.); (*b*) *v.i.* s'éloigner; *Sp:* **to d. away from a competitor,** prendre de l'avance sur un concurrent; **to d. away from the start,** prendre le départ.

5. draw back. (*a*) *v.tr.* (i) tirer (qch., qn) en arrière; retirer (sa main); **to d. back one's fist,** ramener le poing (en arrière); (ii) tirer, ouvrir (les rideaux); (*b*) *v.i.* (i) (se) reculer; se retirer en arrière; *Box: Fenc:* rompre; **to d. back against the wall,** se ranger contre le mur; (ii) se dédire; reprendre sa parole; **it is too late to d. back now,** *F:* le vin est tiré, il faut le boire.

6. draw down, *v.tr.* (*a*) tirer (qn, qch.) en bas; faire descendre (qn, qch); baisser (les stores); **to d. down wrath from heaven,** s'attirer la colère divine; **to d. one's hat down over one's eyes,** renfoncer son chapeau sur ses yeux; (*b*) *Metall:* dégrossir, étirer (un lingot, etc.).

7. draw forth, *v.tr. Lit:* (*a*) tirer (qn, qch.) en avant; faire sortir (qn); sortir (qch.); (*b*) soulever, exciter (les rires, les éloges); provoquer (les protestations); tirer (des larmes); arracher (des aveux).

8. draw forward, *v.i.* (*a*) (*of pers.*) s'avancer, s'approcher; (*b*) *Nau:* (*of wind*) refuser.

9. draw in. (*a*) *v.tr.* (i) (*of cat, etc.*) rentrer, rétracter (ses griffes); (*of horseman*) serrer (la bride); (ii) aspirer (l'air) (à pleins poumons); (iii) *Mil:* replier (un poste avancé); (iv) **to d. one's car in to the kerb,** ranger sa voiture le long du trottoir; (v) **to d. in one's horns,** réduire sa dépense; faire des économies; (*b*) *v.i.* (i) **the days are drawing in,** les jours décroissent, diminuent, (se) raccourcissent; (ii) **a car drew in to the kerb,** une voiture s'est rangée le long du trottoir.

10. draw off. (*a*) *v.tr.* (i) retirer, ôter (ses gants); (ii) retirer (des troupes); ramener (des troupes) en arrière; (iii) détourner (l'attention); (iv) soutirer (un liquide); *Med:* **to d. off blood,** prendre du sang, faire une prise de sang; *Mch:* **to d. off the sludge from a boiler,** décharger la boue d'une chaudière; (*b*) *v.i.* se retirer.

11. draw on. (*a*) *v.tr.* (i) mettre, enfiler (ses gants); passer, enfiler (un vêtement); **she drew on her gloves,** elle s'est gantée; (ii) **to d. s.o. on to do sth.,** entraîner, amener, qn à faire qch.; (*b*) *v.i.* (i) s'avancer; **the ship drew on,** le bâtiment s'avançait; (ii) **evening was drawing on,** la nuit approchait; **as time drew on his health improved,** avec le temps, dans le cours du temps, sa santé s'améliora.

12. draw out. (*a*) *v.tr.* (i) sortir, retirer (qch. de qch.); arracher (un clou, une dent); tirer, ouvrir (un tiroir); **to d. out money from the bank,** retirer de l'argent de la banque; (ii) encourager (qn) à sortir de sa réserve; provoquer l'expansion de (qn); faire parler (qn); faire briller (qn); **though he was shy I managed to d. him out,** malgré sa timidité je suis arrivé à le faire parler; (iii) allonger (un cordage); étirer (le fer); étendre (l'or); (iv) prolonger (un repas, un discours); tirer (une affaire) en longueur; (faire) traîner (une affaire); délayer (un discours); **long drawn out tale,** récit prolongé; conte *m* à n'en plus finir; **the third act is terribly drawn out,** le troisième acte est interminable; (v) tracer (un plan); (*b*) *v.i.* **the days are drawing out,** les journées se prolongent.

13. draw to, *v.tr.* **to d. the curtains to,** tirer, fermer, les rideaux.

14. draw together. (*a*) *v.tr.* (i) rassembler, réunir, rapprocher (des personnes, des choses); **the child's illness had drawn them together,** la maladie de l'enfant les avait rapprochés; (ii) tirer, fermer (les rideaux); (*b*) *v.i.* se rassembler; se rapprocher; se mettre en groupe.

15. draw up. (*a*) *v.tr.* (i) tirer (qn, qch.) en haut; faire (re)monter (qn, qch.); lever (un store); relever (ses manches); tirer, aspirer (de l'eau); **he drew the blankets up to his chin,** il ramena les couvertures jusqu'à son menton; **to d. oneself up (to one's full height),** se (re)dresser (de toute sa hauteur); **cat that draws itself up to spring,** chat qui se raccourcit pour bondir; *Nau:* **to d. up a boat (on the beach),** tirer un bateau à sec; **to d. up the nuts,** serrer les écrous; **nuts drawn up tight,** écrous serrés à refus; (ii) **to d. up a chair (to the table),** approcher une chaise (de la table); (iii) arrêter (une voiture); (iv) ranger, aligner (des troupes); **chairs drawn up along the pavement,** chaises en bordure du trottoir; (v) dresser, rédiger, minuter, libeller, instrumenter (un document); établir (un compte, un budget); **document drawn up before a lawyer,** acte passé devant (un) notaire; (vi) dresser, rédiger, arrêter (un programme); indiquer (une procédure); former, établir, élaborer (un projet); **to d. up an itinerary,** établir un itinéraire; (*b*) *v.i.* (i) **to d. up to the table,** s'approcher de la table; **to d. up with s.o.,** arriver à la hauteur de qn; *Nau:* **to d. up with a ship,** venir bord à bord avec un bâtiment; (ii) (*of car, etc.*) s'arrêter, stopper; **to d. up at the kerb,** se ranger, ranger la voiture, le long du trottoir; (iii) (*of troops*) se ranger, s'aligner; **to d. up in line,** se mettre en ligne, s'aligner.

drawback ['drɔːbæk], *s.* **1.** inconvénient *m*, désavantage *m*; **a d. to sth.,** un obstacle, un empêchement, à qch.; **there are drawbacks to her coming,** il y a des inconvénients à ce qu'elle vienne. **2.** (*a*) *Cust:* remboursement (à la sortie) des droits d'importation; prime *f* d'exportation, de réexportation; drawback *m*; (*b*) *A:* déduction *f* (**from,** de); remise *f*. **3.** *Metall:* tiroir *m*, pièce de rapport, pièce rapportée (de moule). **4.** *Mch: Mec.E:* **d. piston, d. spring,** piston *m*, ressort *m*, de rappel.

drawbar ['drɔːbɑːr], *s.* **1.** barre *f* extensible. **2.** *Rail: Aut: etc:* barre d'attelage, de tirage; crochet *m* de traction; *Rail:* tendeur *m*. **3.** *Glassm:* barre d'étirage (du procédé Pittsburgh).

drawbench ['drɔːben(t)ʃ], *s. Metalw:* banc *m* à étirer, à tréfiler; machine *f* à étirer; banc d'étirage; étireur *m*, étireuse *f*; argue *f*; **d. worker,** étireur *m*.

drawbox ['drɔːbɔks], *s. Tex:* banc *m* d'étirage (des rubans cardés).

drawbridge ['drɔːbridʒ], *s.* **1.** pont-levis *m*, *pl.* ponts-levis. **2.** *Civ.E:* pont basculant, pont à bascule, pont-levis, pont levant; **lever d.,** pont-levis à flèau, à balancier.

drawcard ['drɔːkɑːd], *s. U.S:* attraction *f*, *F:* clou *m* (d'une fête, etc.).

draw-chain ['drɔːtʃein], *s. Rail:* chaîne *f* d'attelage.

drawcord ['drɔːkɔːd], *s.* cordon *m* (de rideaux, etc.); lacet *m* (de capuchon, etc.).

draw curtains ['drɔːkəːtnz], *s.pl.* doubles rideaux *m*.

drawdown ['drɔːdaun], *s. Hyd.E:* abaissement *m* du niveau (d'un réservoir).

drawee [drɔː'iː], *s. Com:* tiré *m*, accepteur *m*, payeur *m* (d'une lettre de change).

drawer ['drɔːər], *s.* **1.** (*pers.*) (*a*) tireur, -euse; (*of water*) puiseur, -euse; (*of teeth, nails*) arracheur, -euse; (*b*) (i) tireur de vin, de bière; (ii) *A:* garçon *m* de cabaret; (*c*) *Min:* rouleur *m*, traîneur *m*, her(s)cheur *m*, meneur *m*; (*d*) *Com:* tireur, souscripteur *m* (d'une lettre de change); (*e*) dessinateur *m*, traceur *m*; (*f*) **d. (up) of a document,** rédacteur *m* d'un document; (*g*) *Tex:* **d. in,** passeur, -euse, de chaînes; (*h*) *Gasm:* **oven d.,** défourneur *m*. **2.** (*instrument*) extracteur *m*. **3.** [drɔːr], (*a*) tiroir *m*; **chest of drawers,** commode *f*; **nest of drawers,** (i) (*in home*) chiffonnier *m*; (ii) (*in office*) classeur *m* à tiroirs; **bottom d.,** trousseau *m* (de mariage); *F:* **they're not really (out of the) top d.,** ils n'appartiennent pas vraiment à l'élite; (*b*) *Com:* **cash d.,** tiroir-caisse *m*, *pl.* tiroirs-caisses. **4.** *pl. Cost: A:* **drawers** [drɔːz], (*underwear*) **(pair of) drawers,** (*for men*) caleçon *m*; (*for women*) culotte *f*.

drawerful ['drɔːful], *s.* plein tiroir (de papiers, etc.).

drawfile ['drɔːfail], *v.tr. Metalw:* donner un coup de lime longitudinal à (qch.); limer (une pièce) en long.

drawfiling ['drɔːfailiŋ], *s. Metalw:* limage *m* en long.

drawgate ['drɔːgeit], *s. Hyd.E:* vanne *f* (de barrage).

draw gear ['drɔːgiər], *s.* attelage *m*; appareil *m* de traction.

drawhole ['drɔːhoul], *s. Metalw:* trou *m* de coulée; trou de gueuse; œil *m* (de haut-fourneau).

drawhook ['drɔːhuk], *s.* crochet *m* (d'attelage).

draw-in ['drɔːin], *s.* (place *f* de) stationnement *m* (sur une route).

drawing ['drɔːiŋ], *s.* **1.** (*a*) tirage *m*; (*of water*) puisage *m*, puisement *m*; (*of teeth, nails, etc.*) arrachage *m*, extraction *f*; (*of lots*) tirage; **d. knife,** plane *f* (de charron); **straight d. knife,** plane droite; **d. of a fowl,** vidage *m* d'une volaille; *Ven:* **badger d.,** déterrage *m* du blaireau; chasse *f* au blaireau; (*b*) attraction *f* (**towards,** vers); **d. power,** pouvoir attractif, attirant; *U.S:* **d. card,** attraction, clou *m* (d'une fête, etc.); (*c*) *Metall:* démoulage *m* (des modèles); (*d*) *Metalw:* (i) étirage *m*, filetage *m* (des métaux); (*ii*) **d. bench, d. frame** = DRAWBENCH; **d. block** bobine *f* de tirerie; **d. mill,** tréfilerie *f*; **d. press,** presse *f* à tréfiler; (ii) **deep d.,** emboutissage profond; (*e*) *Tex:* étirage (des rubans cardés); **d. frame,** banc *m* d'étirage (des rubans cardés); machine *f* à étirer (les fils); (*f*) *Metall:* **d. temper,** recuit *m* (de l'acier après trempe); (*g*) *Min:* (i) roulage *m*, her(s)chage *m*; (ii) extraction, remontée *f* (du charbon, etc.); **d. engine,** machine d'extraction; **d. road,** galerie *f* de traînage; allée *f* de roulage; (*h*) *Fin:* traite *f* (de chèques, d'effets); **d. on s.o.,** disposition *f* sur qn; **d. account,** (i) compte courant; (ii) compte courant pour frais de représentation. **2.** *pl. Com: Fin:* **drawings,** prélèvements *m*, levées *f*, prises *f*. **3.** dessin *m*; (*a*) **to learn d.,** apprendre le dessin; **freehand d.,** dessin à main levée; **line d.,** dessin au trait; **rough d.,** ébauche *f*, croquis *m*; **scale d.,** dessin à l'échelle; **pen d., pencil d.,** dessin à la plume, au crayon; **out of d.,** mal dessiné; **in d.,** bien dessiné; **d. block,** bloc *m* à dessin; **d. board,** planche *f* à dessin; **plane, scheme, still on the d. board,** avion *m*, projet *m*, encore à l'étude; **d. book,** cahier *m* de dessin, album *m* à dessin; **d. ink,** encre *f* de dessin, de Chine; **d. master, d. teacher,** professeur *m* de dessin; **d. paper,** papier *m* à dessin; **d. pen,** tire-ligne *m*, *pl.* tire-lignes; **d. pin,** punaise *f* (pour papier à dessin); (*b*) *Ind: Mec.E:* dessin, épure *f*; **engineering d., mechanical d.,** dessin industriel, mécanique; **geometrical d.,** dessin géométrique, industriel; **assembly d.,** dessin de montage; **sectional d.,** (vue *f* en) coupe *f*; (vue en) section *f*; **to make a d. of sth.,** tracer qch.; **d. loft,** salle *f* des gabarits; **d. office,** salle de dessin; atelier *m*, bureau *m*, d'études.

drawing apart ['drɔːiŋə'pɑːt], *s.* séparation *f*, éloignement *m*.

drawing back ['drɔːiŋ'bæk], *s.* (*a*) (mouvement *m* de) recul *m*; (*b*) retraite *f*; défaite *f*.

drawing down ['drɔːiŋ'daun], *s. Metall:* dégrossage *m*.

drawing off ['drɔːiŋ'ɔf], *s.* soutirage *m* (du vin).

drawing out ['drɔːiŋ'aut], *s.* étirage *m*, étirement *m*, dégrossage *m* (du fer, etc.).

drawing room ['drɔːiŋruːm], *s.* **1.** (*a*) salon *m*; salle *f* de réception; *Mus:* **d.-r. piece,** morceau élégant; **it's not a d.-r. story,** ce n'est pas une histoire pour les jeunes filles; (*b*) *Rail: NAm:* voiture *f* salon, compartiment *m* salon. **2.** (*at Court*) réception *f*.

drawing together ['drɔːiŋtə'geðər], *s.* réunion *f*, rapprochement *m*.

drawing up ['drɔːiŋ'ʌp], *s.* **1.** rédaction *f*, dressement *m*, confection *f*, passation *f* (d'un acte); relèvement *m* (d'un compte). **2.** élaboration *f* (d'une constitution); indication *f* (d'une procédure). **3.** (*a*) arrêt *m* (d'une voiture, etc.); (*b*) alignement *m* (de troupes, etc.).

drawknife ['drɔːnaif], *s. Tls:* plane *f* (de charron); **straight d.,** plane droite.

drawl[1] [drɔːl], *s.* voix traînante; ton traînant; débit traînant; **to speak with an affected d.,** traîner la voix avec affectation.

drawl[2]. **1.** *v.i.* traîner la voix en parlant; parler d'une voix traînante, languissante; traîner ses paroles; **the speaker drawled on, drawled away,** l'orateur *m* continuait à traîner son discours. **2.** *v.tr.* **to d. out sth.,** (i) dire, prononcer, qch. avec une voix traînante, avec une nonchalance affectée; (ii) traîner (un discours).

drawleaf ['drɔːliːf], *attrib.* **d. table,** table *f* à rallonge(s) à l'italienne.

drawling[1] ['drɔːliŋ], *a.* (*of voice, etc.*) traînant.

drawling[2], *s.* affectation *f* de langueur dans le débit.

drawloom ['drɔːluːm], *s. Tex:* (métier *m* à la) tire.

drawn [drɔːn], *a.* **1. with d. sword(s),** sabre *m* au clair. **2.** (*a*) *Metalw:* **d. tube,** tube étiré; (*b*) *Hort:* (*of seedling*) étoilé; (*c*) (visage) hagard, abattu, altéré; **d. features,** traits tirés, contractés; (*d*) *Needlew:* **d.(-thread) work,** ouvrage *m*, travail *m*, à jour(s); **to do drawn(-thread) work,** faire des jours. **3. d. battle,** bataille indécise; **d. match,** partie égale, nulle, remise. **4. well-d., ill-d., picture,** tableau bien, mal, dessiné. **5.** *NAm: Cu:* **d. butter,** beurre fondu.

drawnet ['drɔːnet], *s.* = DRAGNET.

draw-off ['drɔːɔf], *s.* soutirage *m* (d'un liquide); *Mch:* décharge *f* (de la boue d'une chaudière); **d.-o. plug,** bouchon *m* de vidange; **d.-o. cock,** robinet *m* de purge.

draw pin ['drɔːpin], *s.* clavette *f*, cheville *f*, d'attelage.

drawplate ['drɔːpleit], *s. Metalw:* filière *f* (à étirer); plaque *f* filière.

draw screw ['drɔːskruː], *s. Mec.E:* vis *f* de rappel.

drawshave ['drɔːʃeiv], *s.* = DRAWKNIFE.

drawsheet ['drɔːʃiːt], *s. Med:* alèse *f*, alèze *f*.

draw slide ['drɔːslaid], *s. Opt:* tube *m* à tirage, tube de réglage, coulant *m* (d'un télescope, d'un microscope, etc.).

draw spring ['drɔːspriŋ], *s.* ressort *m* de traction.
draw step ['drɔːstep], *s. Danc:* pas *m* en arrière.
draw stop ['drɔːstɔp], *s. Mus:* bouton *m* d'appel, registre *m* (d'un jeu d'orgue).
drawstring ['drɔːstriŋ], *s.* lacet *m* (d'un capuchon, etc.).
draw table ['drɔteibl], *s.* table *f* (avec rallonge(s)) à l'italienne.
drawtongs ['drɔːtɔŋz], *s.pl. Metalw:* pinces *f* à tirer; baguettes *f*.
draw top ['drɔːtɔp], *s. Furn:* dessus *m* de table à l'italienne; **d.(-)t. table,** table *f* (avec rallonge(s)) à l'italienne.
drawtube ['drɔːtjuːb], *s. Opt:* = DRAW SLIDE.
draw vice ['drɔːvais], *s.* étau tendeur, étau tenseur (de fils téléphoniques, etc.); mâchoire *f* à tendre.
dray[1] [drei], *s. Veh:* **1.** (i) camion *m*, haquet *m* (de brasseur); (ii) fardier *m*; (iii) *Austr: N.Z:* charrette *f* à deux roues; **d. horse,** cheval *m* de camion, de charrette, de roulage. **2.** *NAm: Austr: N.Z:* traîneau allemand, schlitte *f* (pour le transport du bois abattu); **d. road,** chemin *m* de schlitte.
dray[2], *v.tr.* **1.** transporter sur (i) un camion, (ii) un fardier, (iii) une charrette. **2.** *NAm: Austr: N.Z:* schlitter (du bois).
dray[3], *s.* nid *m* d'écureuil.
drayage ['dreiidʒ], *s.* (*a*) camionnage *m*; (*b*) frais *mpl* de camionnage, de transport.
drayman, *pl.* **-men** ['dreimən], *s.m.* livreur de brasserie; camionneur; haquetier.
dread[1] [dred], *s.* crainte *f*, terreur *f*, épouvante *f*, appréhension *f*; effroi *m*; phobie *f*; **he was an object of d. to his enemies,** il était la terreur de ses ennemis; **in d. of doing sth.,** dans la crainte, de crainte, de faire qch.; **to be, stand, in d. of s.o., of sth.,** craindre, redouter, qn, qch. (comme le feu); **she has a positive d. of the telephone,** elle a une phobie du téléphone.
dread[2], *v.tr.* redouter, appréhender, craindre (qn, qch.); avoir la terreur de (qch.); **to d. that . . .,** redouter que (ne) + *sub.*; **to d. falling ill, to d. to fall ill,** redouter de tomber malade; **I d. nothing more than to . . .,** je redoute surtout de . . .; **I d. to think of it,** j'ai horreur d'y penser; *F:* **I d. telephoning,** j'ai le téléphone en horreur.
dread[3], *a. Lit: Poet:* **1.** = DREADFUL. **2.** vénérable, auguste.
dreadful ['dredful], **1.** *a.* terrible, redoutable. **2.** *a.* (*a*) (douleur *f*, bruit *m*, etc.) atroce, épouvantable; **it is something d.,** c'est quelque chose d'affreux; **it is d. that nothing can be done,** c'est affreux qu'on ne puisse rien faire; (*b*) *F:* (*intensive*) **what a d. time you've been!** vous y avez mis le temps! **it's a d. bore!** c'est assommant! c'est une scie! **I've been hearing d. things about you,** on m'a raconté des atrocités, des horreurs, sur votre compte. **3.** *s. A:* **penny d.,** feuilleton *m* à grands effets; roman *m* pour concierges, à deux sous, à sensation.
dreadfully ['dredf(u)li], *adv.* **1.** terriblement, affreusement, horriblement, atrocement; **I was d. frightened,** j'avais horriblement peur; j'avais une peur atroce. **2.** *F:* (*intensive*) **d. ugly,** affreusement laid; **I am d. sorry,** je regrette énormément, infiniment; **he was d. clumsy!** il était d'une maladresse!
dreadfulness ['dredf(ul)nis], *s.* nature *f* terrible (d'une action); caractère *m* redoutable (d'une éventualité); *F:* affreuseté *f*.
dreadnought ['drednɔːt], *s. A:* **1.** (*a*) *Cost:* paletot-pilote *m*, *pl.* paletots pilote; (*b*) *Tex:* frise *f*. **2.** *Navy:* (cuirassé *m* du type) dreadnought *m*; **super-d.,** super-dreadnought *m*.
dream[1] [driːm], *s.* rêve *m*; (*a*) songe *m*; **to have a d.,** *Lit:* **to dream a d.,** faire un rêve, un songe; **to have beautiful dreams,** faire de beaux rêves; *F:* rêver beau; **to have bad dreams,** avoir de mauvais rêves; **sweet dreams!** faites de beaux rêves! **to see sth. in a d.,** voir qch. en songe; **d. book,** clef *f* des songes; **d. reader,** interprète *mf* des rêves; *Psy:* **d. work,** travail *m* de rêve; **d. fantasies,** fantaisies *f* oniriques; **d. symbol,** symbole *m* onirique; (*b*) **waking d., day-d.,** rêve éveillé; **to cherish a d.,** caresser un rêve; **d. child,** l'enfant de nos rêveries, qui aurait pu être; **to be in a d.,** être dans un rêve; **all things of this world are but idle dreams,** toutes les choses de ce monde ne sont que fumée; **he was the husband of her dreams,** c'était pour elle le mari rêvé; **my d. house,** la maison de mes rêves; **the American d.,** les aspirations *f*, le rêve, des Américains; *F:* **a d. of a car,** la voiture rêvée, idéale; **it's a d.,** c'est le rêve; **it worked like a d.,** cela a réussi à merveille.
dream[2], *v.* (*p.t. & p.p.* **dreamt** [dremt], **dreamed** [dremt], *occ.* [driːmd])
I. *v.tr. & i.* **1.** (*during sleep*) **to d. of, about, s.o., sth.,** rêver de qn, de qch., **what did you d. about last night?** qu'avez-vous rêvé cette nuit? **you must have been dreaming! you must have dreamt it!** vous l'avez rêvé! **I dreamt (that) you were home,** j'ai rêvé que vous étiez de retour. **2.** laisser vaguer ses pensées; rêver creux; rêvasser; **to d. of one's youth,** rêver à sa jeunesse; **to d. of marriage,** rêver mariage; **to d. empty dreams,** se nourrir d'illusions; rêver creux. **3. I shouldn't d. of doing it,** jamais je ne m'aviserais de faire cela; je n'ai aucune intention de faire cela; **no one dreamt, would have dreamt, of suspecting him,** personne ne songeait, n'aurait songé, à le soupçonner; **I shouldn't have dreamt that . . .,** j'étais à mille lieues de supposer que . . .; **little did I d. that . . .,** je ne me doutais guère que . . .; je ne songeais guère que . . .; **I should never have dreamt of meeting you here!** c'est un rêve que de vous voir ici!
II. (*compound verbs*) **1. dream away,** *v.tr.* passer (son temps) à rêver.
2. dream up, *v.tr. F:* inventer, imaginer (une idée, etc.); **what have you dreamed up now?** qu'est-ce que tu as combiné?
dreamboat ['driːmbout], *s. NAm:* (i) chose rêvée; (ii) garçon, jeune fille, de nos rêves.
dreamer ['driːmər], *s.* **1.** rêveur, -euse. **2.** rêveur; (esprit) songeur *m*. **3.** *Pej:* cerveau creux; visionnaire *mf*; songe creux *m inv*; idéologue *m*.
dream-hole ['driːmhoul], *s. Arch: A:* rayère *f*.
dreamily ['driːmili], *adv.* **1.** d'un air, d'un ton, rêveur; rêveusement; **to think d. of the future,** rêvasser à l'avenir. **2.** (vaguer) comme dans un rêve.
dreaminess ['driːminis], *s.* (état *m* de) rêverie *f*; état d'esprit songeur; **the d. of her eyes,** ses yeux rêveurs.
dreaming ['driːmiŋ], *s.* rêves *mpl*, songes *mpl*.
dreamland ['driːmlænd], *s.* le pays, le monde, des rêves; le pays des songes, du bleu.
dreamless ['driːmlis], *a.* (sommeil) sans rêves.
dreamworld ['driːmwɔːld], *s.* = DREAMLAND.
dreamy ['driːmi], *a.* **1.** *Lit:* (*of sleep*) plein de rêves. **2.** (*of pers., mood, look*) rêveur, -euse; songeur, -euse; langoureux, -euse; **soft and d. eyes,** yeux *m* d'une douceur rêveuse; **d. look,** (i) air rêveur; (ii) *Pej:* air de songe-creux. **3.** (*of idea, memory, etc.*) vague, indistinct. **4.** *P:* magnifique, superbe.
drear [driər], *a.* (*a*) *Lit: Poet:* = DREARY; (*b*) *F:* **the meals are a bit d.,** les repas sont tant soit peu monotones.
drearily ['driərili], *adv.* tristement; d'un air, d'un ton, morne; lugubrement.
dreariness ['driərinis], *s.* tristesse *f* (de l'existence, etc.); aspect *m* morne (d'un paysage, etc.); manque *m* d'éclat, platitude *f* (d'un livre, d'un discours, etc.).
dreary ['driəri], *a.* (temps, paysage) triste, morne, lugubre; **d. outlook,** triste perspective; **d. speech,** discours morne, ennuyeux; **d. diet,** régime dépourvu de variété; monotone; **d. moor,** lande désolée.
dredge[1] [dredʒ], *s.* **1.** *Fish: Nau:* **d. (net),** (filet *m* de) drague *f*; **d. chain,** chaîne dragueuse. **2.** (*a*) **d. (boat),** (bateau *m*) dragueur *m*; bateau vasier; (*on canal*) revoyeur *m*; **d. master,** chef de drague; chef dragueur; capitaine (de bateau dragueur); (*b*) = DREDGER[1] 2(*b*); **d. bucket,** godet *m*, hotte *f*, de drague.
dredge[2], *v.tr. & i.* **1. to d. (out) a canal,** draguer, curer, dévaser (un canal); **to d. away mud,** enlever la vase avec une drague. **2. to d. for sth.,** draguer à la recherche de qch.; ramasser (des huîtres) à la drague. **3. to d. (up) mud,** enlever la vase avec une drague; **to d. up a sunken object,** pêcher, recueillir, un objet submergé avec une drague; *Fig:* **to d. up all the facts one can about sth.,** ramasser, déterrer, tous les faits qu'on peut trouver sur qch.
dredge[3], *v.tr. Cu:* saupoudrer; **to d. flour over meat,** saupoudrer la viande de farine; fariner la viande.
dredger[1] ['dredʒər], *s.* **1.** (*pers.*) (ouvrier) dragueur *m*; pêcheur *m* à la drague; **oyster d.,** dragueur d'huîtres. **2.** (*a*) (bateau *m*) dragueur; bateau vasier; (*on canal*) revoyeur *m*; (*b*) (*machine*) drague *f*; cure-môle *m*, *pl.* cure-môles; **bucket d.,** drague à godets; **grab d.,** drague à benne piocheuse; grappin *m*; **ladder d.,** drague à élinde, à échelle; **pump d., suction d.,** (drague) suceuse *f*; drague à suction; drague aspirante; extracteur *m* de dévasement; **shovel d.,** pelle *f* automatique.
dredger[2], *s. Cu:* boîte *f* à saupoudrer; saupoudroir *m* (à sucre, etc.).
dredging[1] ['dredʒiŋ], *s.* dragage *m*; **maintenance d.,** dragage d'entretien; **d. machine** = DREDGER[1] 2(*b*).
dredging[2], *s. Cu:* saupoudrage *m*.
dree [driː], *v.tr. A: & Scot:* (*only in*) **to d. one's weird,** se résigner à son sort; subir sa destinée.
dreg [dreg], *s.* (*usu. pl.*) **1. the dregs of the cup,** la lie, le fond, de la coupe; **to drink the cup to the dregs,** boire la coupe jusqu'à la lie; *F:* **the very dregs of the population,** la lie du peuple; **the dregs of society,** les bas-fonds *m*, le rebut, de la société; **he has only the dregs of his fortune,** il n'a que les restes *m* de sa fortune; *F:* **there is not a d. of truth in it,** il n'y a pas la moindre vérité là-dedans. **2. dregs of tar,** rache *f* (de goudron).
dreikanter ['draikæntər], *s. Geol:* dreikanter *m*.
drench[1] [dren(t)ʃ], *s.* **1.** *Vet:* breuvage *m*, purge *f*. **2.** *Med: A:* potion *f*, breuvage. **3. d. of rain,** grosse averse; *F:* saucée *f*. **4.** *Tan:* jusée *f*. **5.** *Agr:* aspersion *f*.
drench[2], *v.tr.* **1.** tremper, mouiller (**with,** de); **to get drenched (with rain),** *F:* se faire saucer; **drenched to the skin,** trempé jusqu'aux os; trempé comme une soupe; **drenched in blood,** noyé dans le sang; **flowers drenched with dew,** fleurs lavées de rosée. **2.** (*a*) arroser abondamment, abreuver (le sol); (*b*) *Tan:* tremper (les peaux); (*c*) *Fig:* **to d. oneself in the classics,** s'imprégner des classiques. **3.** *Vet:* donner, administrer, faire avaler, un breuvage à (une bête).
drencher ['dren(t)ʃər], *s.* **1.** grosse averse; *F:* saucée *f*. **2.** *Vet:* bidon *m* à breuvage.
drenching[1] ['dren(t)ʃiŋ], *a.* **d. rain,** pluie battante, diluvienne.
drenching[2], *s.* **1.** trempage *m* (des peaux, etc.). **2.** *F:* saucée *f*; **we got a d.,** nous avons été saucés. **3.** *Vet:* administration *f* d'un breuvage (à une bête); **d. gun,** bidon *m* à breuvage.
drepanaspis [drepə'næspis], *s. Paleont:* drepanaspis *m*.
Drepanididae [drepæ'nididiː], *s.pl. Orn:* drépanididés *m*.
drepanocytosis [drepənousai'tousis], *s. Med:* drépanocytose *f*.
Dresden ['drezdən], *Pr.n. Geog:* Dresde *f*; **D. china,** porcelaine *f* de Saxe.
dress[1] [dres], *s.* **1.** (*a*) (*attire*) habillement *m*; habits *mpl*; vêtements *mpl*; costume *m*; toilette *f*, mise *f*; tenue *f*; **articles of d.,** effets *m* d'habillement; **in full d.,** en grand costume; en tenue de cérémonie; en grande tenue; (*of women*) en grande toilette; **in morning d.,** (i) (*of women*) en négligé (*m*); (ii) (*of men*) en tenue de ville; (iii) (*of men*) en jaquette; **evening d.,** tenue de soirée; **it's a d. affair,** il faudra se mettre en tenue de soirée; **d. coat,** habit (de soirée); habit à queue, *F:* en queue-de-morue; **d. shirt,** chemise *f* de soirée; **d. suit,** habit; complet *m* de soirée; **d. sword,** épée *f* de parade; **faultless d.,** mise irréprochable; **she's very fond of d., very d. conscious,** elle aime beaucoup la toilette, la parure; elle fait beaucoup de toilette; **to talk d.,** causer chiffons; **he was wearing Turkish d.,** il était habillé en Turc; *Mil:* **service d.,** (i) tenue, uniforme *m*, réglementaire; (ii) tenue de service; (iii) tenue de campagne; (iv) *U.S:* tenue de ville, de sortie; **fatigue d.,** tenue de corvée; (jeu *m* de) treillis *m*; **mess d., formal d.,** tenue, uniforme, de cérémonie, de soirée; **full d.,** grande tenue; tenue, uniforme, de gala, de parade; **(full) d. parade,** parade *f* en grande tenue; **walking-out d.,** tenue de ville, de sortie; (*b*) **bird in its winter d.,** oiseau *m* dans son plumage d'hiver. **2.** (*single garment*) robe *f*, costume, toilette *f*; **walking d.,** robe de ville; **afternoon d.,** robe d'après-midi; **travelling d.,** costume de voyage; **ball d.,** robe de bal; **bathing d.,** costume, maillot *m*, de bain; *Com:* **ladies' dresses,** modes *f*; *A:* **d. basket,** panier *m* de voyage pour dames; **d. designer,** dessinateur, -trice, de robes; modéliste, modelliste *mf*; **d. hanger,** porte-robe *m*, *pl.* porte-robes; cintre *m*; *Cy:* **d. guard,** garde-jupe *m inv.*; *Cost: A:* **d. improver,** tournure *f*; *A:* **d. holder,** relève-jupe *m inv.*; **d. materials,** tissus *m* pour robes; **d. trunk,** malle bombée; chapelière *f*; **d. parade,** défilé *m* de modes; **d. preserver, d. shield,** dessous-de-bras *m inv.*; *Com:* **d. stand,** mannequin *m* (de vitrine, etc.). **3.** *Tex:* apprêt *m*.
dress[2], *v.* (**dressed** [drest])
I. 1. (*a*) *v.tr.* habiller, vêtir (qn); **to be dressed in black, in silk,** être vêtu de noir, de soie; **to be dressed in furs,** porter des fourrures; **well dressed,** bien habillé, bien mis; élégant; **meticulously well dressed,** d'une correction de toilette méticuleuse; **she was faultlessly but simply dressed,** elle était élégante sans recherche; **to be plainly dressed,** avoir une mise simple; **badly dressed,** mal habillé; mal mis; *Th:* **to d. a play,** costumer une pièce; (*b*) *v.pr. & i.* **to d. (oneself),** s'habiller, faire sa toilette; **she is dressing,** elle est à sa toilette; **to d. in black,** s'habiller de noir; **to d. with taste,** s'habiller avec goût; **to d. with care,** soigner sa toilette, sa mise; **to d. (for dinner),** (i) (*of man*) se mettre en habit, (ii) se mettre en toilette du soir (pour dîner). **2.** *v.tr.* orner, parer (**sth. with sth.,** qch. de qch.); *Com:* **to d. the window,** faire la vitrine; faire l'étalage; *Th:* **to d. the house,** remplir la salle de billets de faveur; *Nau:* **to d. (a) ship,** pavoiser un navire; **to d. (a ship) over all,** hisser le grand pavois; **to d. with masthead flags,** hisser le petit

pavois. **3.** *v.tr. Mil:* aligner (des troupes, des tentes, etc.); **to d. the ranks,** rectifier l'alignement, les rangs; *v.i.* (*of troops*) **to d. on the right, left, centre,** s'aligner sur la droite, la gauche, le centre; **right d.!** à droite, alignement! **on the centre, d.!** sur le centre, alignement! **4.** *v.tr. Med:* panser (une blessure, un blessé); faire un pansement à (un blessé). **5.** *v.tr.* (*a*) *Tchn:* apprêter (une surface); corroyer (le cuir); apprêter, habiller, chamoiser (les peaux); mégir (des peaux délicates); dresser, tailler, parer, piquer (des pierres); (r)habiller, repiquer, ribler (une meule); dresser, corroyer (le bois); habiller, sérancer (le lin); appareiller (des bas); préparer mécaniquement, trier (le minerai); préparer (une matière première, le coton, la laine, etc.); *Metall:* nettoyer, dessabler (une pièce coulée); **to d. timber roughly,** dégrossir le bois; **to d. cloth,** (i) apprêter, (ii) lainer, garnir, l'étoffe; *Typ:* **to d. a form,** garnir une forme; *Tex:* **to dress** (= *size*) **the warp,** basser la chaine; (*b*) **to d. s.o.'s hair,** accommoder, arranger, une coiffure; coiffer qn; **to d. one's hair,** se coiffer; (*c*) *Cu:* (i) habiller (une volaille, la viande); (ii) apprêter, accommoder, arranger (des mets); assaisonner, garnir (une salade); **dish that can be dressed with . . .,** mets accommodable à . . .; **dressed poultry,** volaille prête à cuire, parée; (*d*) *Fish:* **to d. a fly,** monter une mouche; (*e*) *Agr: Hort:* donner une façon à (un champ); **well dressed soil,** terre amoureuse; **to d. a tree with limewash,** traiter un arbre avec du lait de chaux; (*f*) *Hort:* tailler (un arbre fruitier, une vigne).

II. (*compound verbs*) **1. dress back,** *v.i. Mil:* se reculer pour se mettre à l'alignement; rentrer (le corps); **d. back!** rentrez!

2. dress down, *v.tr.* (*a*) panser (un cheval); (*b*) *F:* (i) flanquer une raclée, une volée, une peignée, à (qn); (ii) chapitrer (qn); donner un savon, un suif, à (qn); laver la tête à (qn); (*c*) *Metalw: etc:* dégrossir, dresser, roder (une pièce).

3. dress out, *v.tr.* parer, orner (qn); *F:* attifer, harnacher (qn); **dressed out in all her finery,** parée de tous ses atours.

4. dress up. (*a*) *v.tr.* habiller, parer, *F:* attifer (qn); poupiner (un enfant); **to d. oneself up,** *v.i.* **to d. up, as a soldier,** s'habiller, se costumer, en soldat; **to d. up for a part,** se costumer pour un rôle; **to d. (oneself) up,** (i) se mettre en travesti; (ii) se faire beau, belle; s'attifer; **children love to d. up,** les enfants aiment se costumer; *F:* **to be dressed up fit to kill,** *O:* **to the nines,** *O:* **to the knocker,** être sur son trente et un; **all dressed up,** tout attifé, tout endimanché; (*b*) *v.i. Mil:* avancer pour se mettre à l'alignement; sortir (le corps); **d. up!** sortez!

dressage ['dresɑːʒ], *s. Equit:* dressage (supérieur).

dresser[1] ['dresər], *s.* **1.** buffet *m* de cuisine; dressoir *m*; panetière *f*; vaisselier *m.* **2.** *NAm:* (table *f* de) toilette *f*; coiffeuse *f*; **d. set,** garniture *f* de toilette.

dresser[2], *s.* **1.** *Ind:* apprêteur, -euse; broyeur *m* (de cuirs, d'étoffes); dresseur, -euse (de gants); appareilleur *m* (de bas); équarrisseur *m* (de pierres); piqueur *m* (de granit); préparateur *m* (de pierres lithographiques); *Metall:* dessableur *m* (de pièces coulées); **flax d.,** filassier, -ière; racleur, -euse, de lin; **flax dresser's knife,** racloir *m* à lin; **floor d.,** aplanisseur *m* de parquets; **leather d.,** mégissier *m,* peaussier *m*; **vine d.,** vigneron, -onne. **2.** *Th:* habilleur, -euse. **3.** *Med: Surg:* externe *m* (des hôpitaux); panseur, -euse; assistant, -ante. **4. a good d.,** personne *f* qui s'habille bien. **5.** (*instrument*) (*a*) batte *f,* batte-plate *f* (de plombier), *pl.* battes-plates; rabattoir *m,* bourseau *m*; (*b*) *Min:* pointerolle *f*; (*c*) décrasse-meule *m, pl.* décrasse-meules.

dressiness ['dresinis], *s.* recherche *f* dans sa mise, sa toilette.

dressing ['dresiŋ], *s.* **1.** (*a*) habillement *m,* toilette *f*; **to take a long time over one's d.,** être long à sa toilette; **d. bell,** coup *m* de cloche d'avertissement qu'il est l'heure de s'habiller avant le dîner; **d. case,** nécessaire *m,* coffret *m,* trousse *f,* de toilette; (*fitted*) mallette garnie; **d. gown,** robe *f* de chambre; (*for women*) peignoir *m*; saut-de-lit *m, pl.* sauts-de-lit; *A:* **d. jacket,** liseuse *f*; **d. room,** (i) cabinet *m* de toilette; (ii) *Th: Cin:* loge *f* (d'acteur, d'actrice); **d. rooms,** loges des artistes; (iii) *Sp:* vestiaire *m*; **d. table,** (table *f* de) toilette; coiffeuse *f*; **d.-table set,** garniture *f* de toilette; (*b*) accommodage *m,* arrangement *m* (des cheveux); (*c*) *Agr: Hort:* façon *f*; **to give the soil a d.,** donner une façon à la terre; *Vit:* **first d.,** sombrage *m*; **to give the first d. to the vineyard,** sombrer la terre du vignoble; *Hort:* **d. of a fruit-tree with lime,** traitement *m* à la chaux d'un arbre fruitier; (*d*) *Cu:* habillage *m* (d'une volaille); accommodage, apprêt *m,* assaisonnement *m* (des mets); (*e*) *Med:* pansement *m* (d'une blessure); (*f*) *Mil:* alignement *m* (des troupes); **to get out of d.,** perdre l'alignement; (*g*) *Nau:* pavoisement *m* (d'un navire); (*h*) *Fish:* montage *m* (d'une mouche); (*i*) *Tchn:* apprêt *m,* habillage *m,* corroyage *m,* chamoisage *m,* mégisserie *f,* mégie *f,* peausserie *f* (des peaux); apprêtage *m,* apprêt (des étoffes); dressage *m,* taille *f* (des pierres); piquage *m* (du granit); dressage, corroyage, aplanissage *m,* aplanissement *m* (du bois); préparation *f* mécanique (du minerai); rhabillage *m* (d'une meule); *Metall:* nettoyage *m,* dessablage *m* (d'une pièce coulée); *Tex:* préparation, peignage *m,* drégeage *m* (du lin); **cotton d. machine,** machine *f* à préparer le coton; *Civ.E:* **surface d.,** enduisage *m* de surface; *Typ:* **d. stick,** composteur *m* d'apprêt. **2.** (*a*) *Cu:* (**salad**) **d.,** assaisonnement *m* (pour la salade) genre sauce mayonnaise; **French d.,** vinaigrette *f*; (*b*) produit *m* d'entretien; enduit *m* (pour cuirs, etc.); graisse *f* (pour courroies); *Toil:* fixateur *m* (pour les cheveux), lotion *f* capillaire; *Agr: Hort:* fumages *mpl,* fumades *fpl,* fumures *fpl,* fumaisons *fpl*; **a heavy d. of manure,** un gros apport de fumier; **light d.,** engrais légers; **surface d., top d.,** engrais en couverture, couche *f* d'engrais; **to give the ground a second d.,** biner la terre; *Civ.E:* **surface d.,** enduit *m* d'usure; (*c*) *Med:* pansement *m*; **dry, wet, d.,** pansement sec, humide; **fixed d.,** pansement à demeure; **improvised d.,** pansement de fortune; **occlusive d.,** pansement occlusif; **post-operative d.,** pansement post-opératoire; **to apply a d.,** appliquer, mettre, faire, un pansement; **after the first d., has been applied,** après l'application d'un premier pansement; **surgical d. case,** trousse de pansement; *Mil:* (**first**) **field d., first-aid d.,** pansement individuel, paquet individuel de pansement; **d. station,** poste *m* de secours; **field d. station,** antenne chirurgicale; **main d. station,** ambulance *f*; (*d*) *Tex:* apprêt, empois *m,* chas *m,* cati *m*; (*e*) *pl. Arch:* **dressings,** moulures *f,* saillies *f.*

dressing down ['dresiŋ'daun], *s.* **1.** *F:* (i) raclée *f,* volée *f,* tannée *f,* rincée *f*; (ii) verte semonce; savon *m*; **to give s.o. a d. d.,** (i) flanquer une raclée à qn; (ii) semoncer qn, *P:* suiffer qn; laver la tête à qn; donner un savon, *P:* un suif, à qn; **I gave him a good d. d.,** je l'ai arrangé, tancé, de la belle manière; *P:* je lui en ai donné d'une. **2.** dégrossissage *m,* dressage *m,* rodage *m.*

dressing up ['dresiŋ'ʌp], *s.* (*a*) **d. up does not appeal to most men,** la plupart des hommes n'aiment pas se mettre en tenue (de soirée); (*b*) déguisement *m*; **d.-up clothes,** vêtements *mpl* de travesti, de mascarade.

dressmaker ['dresmeikər], *s.* (i) couturière *f*; **dressmaker's hand, apprentice,** petite main, cousette *f,* arpette *f*; **visiting d.,** ouvrière *f* maison; couturière à la journée; (ii) couturier *m.*

dressmaking ['dresmeikiŋ], *s.* couture *f*; **to know d. and tailoring,** savoir faire le flou et le tailleur; **to be in the d. trade,** (i) être dans la (haute) couture; (ii) être dans la confection.

dress-up ['dresʌp], *attrib.* **d.-up party,** réunion pour laquelle il faut se mettre en tenue de soirée.

dressy ['dresi], *a.* **1.** (*of pers.*) mis avec recherche, luxueux dans sa mise; (*of woman*) qui aime la toilette, portée à la toilette; coquette; *P:* (*of man*) gommeux. **2.** (*of clothes, etc.*) chic, élégant; **a d. frock,** une robe habillée.

drey [drei], *s.* nid *m* d'écureuil.

drib [drib], *s.* (*short for* DRIBLET) *only used in* **in dribs and drabs,** petit à petit, peu à peu; (mesurer qch.) au compte-gouttes.

dribble[1] ['dribl], *s.* **1.** (*a*) (*of water, etc.*) dégouttement *m,* égouttage *m*; **a d. of rain,** quelques gouttes *f* de pluie; **d. glass,** verre baveur; (*b*) (*of pers.*) bave *f.* **2.** *Fb: etc:* dribble *m.*

dribble[2]. **1.** *v.i.* (*a*) (*of water, etc.*) dégoutter, tomber goutte à goutte; *F:* **the men came dribbling back,** les ouvriers revenaient par deux ou trois, par petits groupes; (*b*) (*of pers.*) baver; (*c*) *F:* pissoter; (*d*) *Bill:* (*of ball*) **to d. into the pocket,** rouler doucement dans la blouse. **2.** *v.tr.* (*a*) **to d. (out) a liquid,** laisser dégoutter un liquide; laisser couler un liquide goutte à goutte; (*b*) *Fb: etc:* dribbler (le ballon); (*c*) *Bill:* **to d. the ball into the pocket,** faire rouler tout doucement la bille dans la blouse.

dribbler ['driblər], *s.* **1.** baveur, -euse. **2.** *Fb: etc:* dribbleur *m.*

drib(b)let ['driblit], *s.* **1.** petite somme d'argent; **to pay in driblets,** payer sou par sou, petit à petit, par petits paquets; **payment in driblets,** paiement fractionné. **2.** petite quantité; **to dole out provisions in driblets,** mesurer les provisions au compte-gouttes. **3.** goutte *f* (d'eau, etc.).

dribbling ['dribliŋ], *s.* **1.** dégouttement *m,* égouttage *m* (d'un liquide). **2.** *Fb: etc:* dribbling *m.*

dried [draid], *a.* séché, desséché; **d. fruits,** fruits secs; **d. apples, d. pears,** pommes, poires, tapées; **d. eggs, milk,** œufs *m,* lait *m,* en poudre.

drier ['draiər], *s.* **1.** (*pers.*) dessécheur, -euse; *Dom.Ec:* **d.(-up),** essuyeur, -euse (de vaisselle). **2.** (*thg*) *Ind:* sécheur *m,* séchoir *m,* dessécheur *m,* dessiccateur *m*; (*place*) sécherie *f*; **centrifugal d.,** essoreuse *f* centrifuge; extracteur *m* centrifuge; **vacuum d.,** étuve *f* à vide; **steam d.,** (i) sécheuse *f,* séchoir, à vapeur; (ii) *Mch:* sécheur de vapeur; *Hairdr:* **hair d.,** (i) (*held in hand*) séchoir (à cheveux), sèche-cheveux *m inv*; (ii) casque *m* sèche-cheveux; *Laund:* **clothes d.,** séchoir (de plafond, pliant, etc.); **spin d.,** essoreuse (centrifuge); **tumbler d.,** essoreuse à tambour horizontal (à mouvement alterné); *Phot:* **plate d.,** sèche-cliché *m, pl.* sèche-clichés. **3.** *Paint: etc:* siccatif *m.*

drift[1] [drift], *s.* **1.** (*a*) *A:* impulsion *f*; (*b*) *Jur:* rassemblement *m* (à date fixe) du bétail (pour un recensement, etc.); (*c*) *Dial:* chemin *m* pour la conduite du bétail. **2.** (*a*) mouvement *m*; *Ph:* **ether d.,** mouvement (supposé) relatif de la terre et de l'éther; **continental d.,** dérive *f* des continents; **the d. of labour into the towns,** le mouvement progressif, la migration progressive, de la main-d'œuvre vers les villes; **the d. from the land,** la lente désertion des campagnes; (*b*) (i) direction *f,* sens *m* (d'un courant); (ii) vitesse *f* (d'un courant); *esp.* **d. of the tide,** vitesse de la marée; (*c*) cours *m,* marche *f* (des affaires, des événements). **3.** (*a*) dérive *f* (d'un avion, d'un navire); **d. meter, d. recorder,** dérivomètre *m,* indicateur *m* de dérive; **d. scale,** cadran *m* de dérive, échelle *f* des dérives; *Oc:* **longshore d., littoral d.,** dérive littorale; **d. current,** courant *m* de surface; **d. ice,** glaces flottantes; glaçons *mpl* en dérive; **d. sand, sand d.,** sable mouvant; **policy of d.,** politique *f* de laisser-faire; (*b*) dérivation *f* (d'un projectile, etc.); *Artil:* **wind d.,** dérivation due au vent; **d. slide,** (i) *Artil:* correcteur *m* de dérivation; (ii) *Sm.a:* curseur *m* de correction; *Civ.E:* **d. of a borehole,** déviation *f,* dérive, d'un trou de sonde; (*c*) *Elcs:* glissement *m*; **d. tube, d. tunnel,** tube *m,* tunnel *m,* de glissement; **d. transistor,** drift *m*; **d. corrected amplifier,** amplificateur *m* à compensation de dérive; **d. error,** erreur *f* de dérive. **4.** but *m,* tendance *f,* sens général, portée *f* (des paroles, des écrits, de qn); **I see his d.,** je vois où il veut en venir; *F:* **I get your d.,** je pige; **what is the d. of these questions?** où tendent ces questions? **what is the d. of all this?** où aboutira tout cela? **5.** (*a*) objet flottant (à la dérive); (*b*) **a d. of rain, of falling snow,** une rafale de pluie, de neige; **d. of clouds,** traînée *f* de nuages; *Hort:* **to plant snowdrops in drifts,** planter des perce-neige en bancs. **6.** amoncellement *m* (de sable, etc.); *Geog:* apport(s) *m(pl)* (de sable, de cailloux); congère *f* (de neige); **glacial d.,** moraine *f* de fond, argile *f* à blocaux. **7.** *Fish:* **d. (net),** filet traînant, dérivant, flottant; manet *m*; traîne *f.* **8.** *Min:* (i) direction (d'une galerie); (ii) (galerie de) chassage *m*; galerie chassante; (iii) galerie d'exploration, de recherche; **d. stope,** taille chassante; **d. stoping,** abattage *m* en taille chassante; **(cross-) d., cross d.,** recoupe *f*; (*gold mining*) **d. mining,** exploitation *f* par galeries. **9.** (*in S. Africa*) gué *m.* **10.** *Tls:* (*a*) **d. punch,** chasse-clef *m, pl.* chasse-clefs; chasse-clavette *m, pl.* chasse-clavettes; chasse-rivet(s) *m, pl.* chasse-rivets; chassoir *m,* poinçon *m,* repoussoir *m*; refouloir *m*; **d. bolt,** chasse-boulon *m, pl.* chasse-boulons, repoussoir *m*; **d. slot,** rainure *f* pour chasse-clavette; (*b*) (*for rivet holes*) **d. (pin),** broche *f* (d'assemblage); mandrin *m*; (*c*) (*broach*) alésoir *m.*

drift[2]. **1.** *v.i.* (*a*) flotter; être charrié, entraîné; *Nau:* dériver, aller en dérive; *Av:* déporter, marcher en crabe; *Ball:* (*of projectile*) dériver; *Nau:* **to d. to leeward,** être dépalé, drossé; **to d. on shore,** abattre à la côte; se laisser dépaler; **to d. downstream,** dériver à vau-l'eau; **to d. with the current,** se laisser aller au fil de l'eau; **much broken ice was drifting down the river,** le fleuve charriait de nombreux glaçons; **boats drifting on the waves,** barques *f* errant sur les flots; **wisps of smoke are drifting across the sky,** des fumées se traînent dans le ciel; **conversation drifted from one subject to another,** la conversation passait d'un sujet à un autre; **to d. apart,** (*of friends*) se perdre de vue; (*of married couple*) se séparer peu à peu; (*b*) **to d. into vice,** se laisser aller au vice; être entraîné vers le vice; **to d. into pessimism,** se laisser aller au pessimisme; **to let oneself d., to let things d.,** se laisser aller; laisser aller les choses; **he's just drifting,** il ne sait plus de quel bois faire flèche; **things are allowed to d.,** cela va comme il plaît à Dieu; (*c*) *F:* (*of pers.*) **to d. along,** flâner; marcher nonchalamment; **to d. around,** flâner, se balader; **to d. round to the library,** pousser (une pointe) jusqu'à la bibliothèque; **to d. in,** entrer en passant; s'amener (chez qn); **the audience started to d.**

out, l'assistance commençait à sortir silencieusement; (*d*) (*of sand, gravel, pebbles, etc.*) s'amonceler, s'amasser; (*of snow*) se former en congères, s'amasser; (*e*) *Min:* chasser; percer en direction; (*f*) (*of questions, events*) tendre (vers un but). **2.** *v.tr.* (*a*) flotter (du bois); (*of current*) charrier, entraîner (qch.); *Nau:* (*of wind, current*) drosser (le navire); *Fish:* laisser aller (la mouche) au fil de l'eau; (*b*) (*of wind*) amonceler, entasser (la neige, le sable); (*c*) (*of wind, etc.*) **to d. the fields with snow,** recouvrir les champs de neige, de congères; (*d*) *Mec.E:* brocher, mandriner (un trou de rivet); (*e*) *Dial: NAm:* conduire (du bétail) lentement (en laissant pâturer).

driftage ['driftidʒ], *s.* **1.** *Nau:* dérive *f.* **2.** laisses *fpl* (sur un rivage).

drifter ['driftər], *s.* **1.** *Min:* (*gold*) mineur *m* au rocher. **2.** *Fish:* (*a*) pêcheur *m* à filets traînants, dérivants; (*b*) bateau *m* de pêche à filets traînants, dérivants; chalutier *m*, cordier *m*, drifter *m*. **3.** vent *m* qui amoncelle la neige. **4. he was developing into a d.,** il commençait à se laisser aller à vau-l'eau. **5.** *Min:* perforatrice *f* à percussion (pour la taille chassante).

drifting[1] ['driftiŋ], *a.* en dérive; dérivant; **d. clouds,** nuages traînants, voguant dans le ciel; *Navy:* **d. mine,** mine dérivante.

drifting[2], *s.* **1.** entraînement *m* par le courant, par le vent. **2.** amoncellement *m* (des neiges). **3.** *Mec.E:* brochage *m*, mandrinage *m*. **4.** *Min:* chassage *m*; percement *m* (des galeries) dans la direction du filon.

driftway ['driftwei], *s.* **1.** *Min:* galerie *f* (en direction). **2.** (*a*) accotement *m* (d'une route); (*b*) chemin *m* pour la conduite du bétail.

driftweed ['driftwi:d], *s. Bot:* laminaires *fpl.*

driftwood ['driftwud], *s.* bois flottant, flotté; **d. from wrecked vessels,** débris *mpl* de navires naufragés; *Fig:* **human d.,** épaves humaines.

drill[1] [dril], *s.* **1.** *Metalw: Carp:* (*a*) foret *m*, mèche *f*, pointe *f* à forer; **twist d.,** *Carp:* mèche hélicoïdale; *Metalw:* foret hélicoïdal, à hélice, américain; **flat d., arrow-headed d., spearhead d.,** mèche à langue d'aspic, (en) fer de lance; **spoon d.,** cuiller *f*, cuillère *f*; **double-cutting d.,** mèche à deux tranches; **milling d.,** foret fraisé; **straight shank d.,** foret à queue cylindrique; **taper shank d.,** foret à queue conique; **right-hand d., left-hand d.,** foret à droite, à gauche; **d. grinder, d. sharpener,** machine *f* à affûter les mèches, les forets; **d. holder,** porte-foret *m*, *pl.* porte-forets; *Locksm:* **d. pin,** broche *f* (de serrure); (*b*) foreuse *f*, foret, drille *f*; (*power-driven*) perceuse *f*; **hand d.,** drille (à main); porte-foret à main, à engrenage; **electric (hand) d.,** perceuse à main; **foot d.,** machine à percer à (commande par) pédale; **breast d.,** drille à conscience; vilebrequin *m*, perceuse, à engrenages; chignolle *f*; **percussion d.,** perceuse percuteuse; **angle d., corner d.,** foret à angle; **snake d.,** foret flexible; **fiddle d., cord d., bow d.,** foret, drille, à arçon, à archet; touret *m*; **d. bow,** archet *m* de foret; **d. brace,** vilebrequin pour forerie; cliquet *m*, drille; **d. chuck,** mandrin *m* (de tour) porte-mèche; mandrin porte-foret; **d. plate,** disque *m* de perceuse; plastron *m*; **d. press,** machine à percer montée sur colonne; forerie *f* sur colonne; (*c*) (*broach, punch*) perce *f*, perceur *m*, perçoir *m*; **wall d. (for plug),** tamponnoir *m*. **2.** *Dent:* fraise *f*; *F:* roulette *f*. **3.** *Min: Civ.E:* (*a*) (i) perforateur *m*, perforatrice *f*; foreuse; (ii) (*taking borings*) sondeuse *f*, sonde *f*; **hand d.,** (i) perforatrice à main; (ii) sondeuse à bras; **air d., pneumatic d.,** perforatrice à air comprimé; marteau *m* pneumatique; **hammer d., percussion d.,** marteau perforateur; perforatrice à percussion; **cable d., churn d.,** foreuse à câble; **d. chain,** chaîne *f* d'allongement; **d. core,** témoin *m*, carotte *f*; **d. hole,** trou *m* de mine, de sonde; forage; sondage *m*; **d. pipe, d. rod,** tige *f* de forage, de sonde; **(rotary) d. string,** train *m* (des tiges) de sonde; (*b*) **d. (bit),** burin *m*, fleuret *m*, pistolet *m*. **4.** (*a*) *Gym: Mil: etc:* exercice(s) *m(pl)*; **physical d.,** exercice(s) physique(s), d'assouplissement; **fire d.,** exercices de sauvetage; *Mil:* **company d., battalion d.,** école *f* de compagnie, de bataillon; **recruit d.,** école du soldat; **firing d.,** exercice de tir; instruction *f* du tir; **bayonet d.,** escrime *f* à la baïonnette; **rifle d.,** maniement *m* du fusil; **gun (detachment) d.,** école de (la) pièce; **bridge d., pontoon d.,** exercice pratique, manœuvre *f* de pontage; **to do punishment d.,** faire la pelote; *F:* **to know the d.,** savoir ce qu'il faut faire, comment s'y prendre; **d. book,** (i) livret *m* d'exercices; (ii) *Mil:* théorie *f* (du soldat); **d. ground,** terrain *m* d'exercice, de manœuvres; **d. hall,** salle *f* d'exercice; **d. sergeant,** sergent instructeur; (*b*) *Sch:* **verb d.,** exercices oraux sur le(s) verbe(s).

drill[2]. **1.** *v.tr.* (*a*) (i) forer (un puits, etc.); perforer (une plaque); percer (un trou); *Min:* (per)forer, bosseyer (la roche, etc.); **to d. (metal) through a template,** contrepercer; **to d. (a hole) through sth.,** percer, perforer, qch.; *P:* **to d. (a hole in) s.o.,** (trans)percer qn d'un coup de revolver; fusiller qn; (ii) *Dent:* buriner, fraiser, *F:* passer la roulette sur (une dent); (iii) *v.ind. tr.* **to d. for oil, water,** forer pour rechercher du pétrole, de l'eau; (*b*) *Gym: etc:* faire faire l'exercice à (des hommes); *Mil:* instruire, exercer, faire manœuvrer (des soldats, matelots); *Nau:* **well-drilled crew,** équipage bien exercé; *F:* **to d. s.o. (in what he has to do, say),** faire la leçon à qn (sur ce qu'il doit faire, dire); **I can't d. (it) into him that . . .,** je ne peux pas lui enfoncer dans la tête, le faire comprendre, que . . .; *Sch:* **to d. the boys in French verbs,** faire faire aux élèves des exercices oraux sur les verbes français; (*c*) *Rail: NAm:* trier, classer (des wagons). **2.** *v.i.* (*of troops, etc.*) faire l'exercice; manœuvrer.

drill[3], *s. Agr: Hort:* **1.** ligne *f*, rayon *m*, sillon *m*; **to sow the grain in drills,** semer la graine en lignes, par sillons. **2.** semeuse *f* (à cuillers); semoir *m* en lignes; rayonneur *m*; drill *m*; **drop d.,** semoir en poquets; **d. harrow,** herse *f* à semer; **d. hoe,** rigoleur *m*; **d. planting,** plantation *f* en lignes; **d. plough,** sillonneur *m*.

drill[4], *v.tr. Agr:* semer (des navets, un champ) en lignes, en rayons; rayonner (un champ).

drill[5], *s. Z:* (singe *m*) drill (*m*).

drill[6], *s. Tex:* coutil *m*; (*for denims, etc.*) treillis *m*.

drillable ['driləbl], *a. Min:* forable.

driller ['drilər], *s.* **1.** (*pers.*) (*a*) perceur *m*; (*b*) foreur *m*, sondeur *m*. **2.** = DRILLING MACHINE; **gang d.,** perceuse *f* à forets multiples.

drillette [dri'let], *s.* croisé *m* coton fin.

drilling[1] ['driliŋ], *s.* **1.** (*a*) *Metalw:* forage *m*, perçage *m*, percement *m* (d'un trou); (*through template*) contreperçage *m*; *Min:* perforation *f* (des roches, etc.); **machine d.,** perforation mécanique; **d. gauge,** gabarit *m* de forage, de perçage; **d. guide,** canon *m* de forage, de perçage; **d. jig, d. template,** calibre *m* de forage, de perçage; **d. machine,** (i) *Mec.E:* (*also* **d. mill**) machine *f* à percer; perceuse *f*, foreuse *f*, aleseuse *f*, alésoir *m*; **single spindle d. machine,** perceuse monobroche; **multiple spindle d. machine,** perceuse à plusieurs broches; **radial d. machine,** perceuse radiale; **impact d. machine,** perceuse à percussion; **turret d. machine,** aléseuse à revolver; (ii) *Min:* **rock-d. machine,** perforatrice *f* mécanique; perforateur *m*; **d. pillar,** forerie *f* à colonne; **d. spindle,** arbre *m* porte-foret; broche *f* porte-mèche; (*b*) *Min:* forage, sondage *m* (d'un puits); **d. by percussion,** forage, sondage, par battage; **d. by rotation,** forage, sondage, par rodage; **d. bit,** trépan *m*; **d. machine,** sondeuse *f*, sonde *f*; **d. rope,** câble *m* de sondage; **rope d.,** sondage à la corde; sondage chinois; **(rotary) d. string,** train *m* (des tiges) de sonde; *Petr:* **oil d.,** forage pétrolier; **d. rig,** appareil *m* de sondage; installation *f* de forage; **offshore d. rig,** île *f* de forage; (*c*) *Dent:* alésage *m*; fraisage *m*. **2.** *Mil:* exercices *mpl*, manœuvres *fpl*. **3.** *NAm: Rail:* triage *m*, classement *m* (des wagons).

drilling[2], *s. Agr: Hort:* semis *m* par lignes, par rayons; rayonnage *m*.

drillmaster ['drilma:stər], *s. NAm:* (*a*) *Mil:* sergent instructeur; (*b*) *F:* chef *m* qui maintient une discipline rigoureuse; *F:* vrai garde-chiourme, *pl.* gardes-chiourmes.

drill track ['driltræk], *s. U.S: Rail:* voie *f* de classement, de triage.

drillyard ['drilja:d], *s. U.S: Rail:* gare *f* de triage.

drily ['draili], *adv.* = DRYLY.

drimys ['draimis], *s. Bot:* drimys *m*.

drink[1] [driŋk], *s.* **1.** (*liquid drunk*) (*a*) boire *m*; **food and d.,** le boire et le manger; **to give s.o. food and d.,** donner à boire et à manger à qn; *F:* **tobacco is meat and d. to me,** le tabac me tient lieu de tout; (*b*) **to give s.o., an animal, a d.,** donner à boire à qn, à un animal; faire boire qn; **to have a d.,** se désaltérer; boire quelque chose; **to have a long d.,** boire un bon coup; **give me a d. of water,** donnez-moi un peu d'eau à boire; (*c*) consommation *f*; **to have a d.,** prendre quelque chose; *F:* boire un coup; **he had been seen having a d. at a bar,** on l'avait vu consommer dans un bar; **to pay for the drinks,** payer les consommations; *F:* **long d.,** (grand) verre de bière, de cidre, etc.; gin *m*, whisky *m*, à l'eau; **short d.,** apéritif *m*; verre de vin, d'alcool, etc.; **(will you) have a d.?** voulez-vous boire quelque chose? prenez-vous un verre? **to stand s.o. a d.,** payer à boire à qn; **to finish one's d.,** vider son verre; (*d*) *Med: F:* potion *f*; (*e*) *F:* **the d.,** (i) *Nau:* la mer, la grande tasse; (ii) l'eau (d'un lac, d'une rivière); **to fall into the d.,** tomber (i) à la mer, (ii) dans l'eau. **2.** (*beverage*) boisson *f*, breuvage *m*; **strong d.,** liqueurs fortes; spiritueux *mpl*; **soft drinks,** boissons sans alcool; sirops *m*, limonades *f*, etc.; **I'll see to the drinks,** je vais m'occuper (i) de l'apéritif, (ii) des boissons; **come round for a d.,** venez prendre l'apéritif. **3.** boisson, ivrognerie *f*; **to take to d.,** s'adonner à la boisson, se mettre à boire; **to be addicted to d.,** être adonné à la boisson; **the poverty due to d.,** la misère imputable à l'alcoolisme *m*; **the d. question,** la question de l'alcoolisme; **to be in d., the worse for d., under the influence of d.,** avoir trop bu; être ivre, soûl, pris de vin, dans l'ivresse, sous l'empire de la boisson; *Jur:* être en état d'ébriété; **to drive a car while under the influence of d.,** conduire en état d'ébriété; **he died of d.,** il s'est tué à force de boire; **to drive s.o. to d.,** pousser qn à l'ivrognerie; **he, it, nearly drove me to d.,** il s'en est fallu de peu que je me mette à boire; **to smell of d.,** puer l'alcool; **d.-sodden,** abruti par la boisson.

drink[2], *v.* (*p.t.* **drank** [dræŋk]; *p.p.* **drunk** [drʌŋk], *Poet:* **drunken** ['drʌŋkən])

I. *v.tr. & i.* boire. **1.** (*a*) **to d. water, wine,** boire de l'eau, du vin; **d. your soup!** mange ta soupe! **he never drinks tea,** il ne prend jamais de thé; **will you have something to d.?** voulez-vous boire, prendre, quelque chose? **what will you have to d.?** qu'est-ce que vous allez prendre? **fit to d.,** bon à boire; buvable, potable; *Lit:* **to d. (of) the cup of joy, of sorrow,** boire, s'abreuver, à la coupe des plaisirs, des tristesses; **to d. (a toast) to s.o.,** boire, porter un toast, à qn; **to d. (to) s.o.'s health,** boire à la santé de qn; porter la santé de qn; **we d. the King,** nous buvons à la santé du Roi; **to d. success to s.o., to d. to s.o.'s success,** boire au succès de qn; (*b*) **to d. one's wages,** boire ses gages; **to d. oneself into debt, out of a job,** s'endetter à force de boire; se faire renvoyer pour ivrognerie; **to d. oneself drunk,** se soûler; **to d. s.o. under the table,** mettre qn sous la table. **2.** *v.i.* être adonné à la boisson; **he has taken to drinking,** il s'est mis à boire; **to d. hard, heavily,** (i) boire sec, raide; (ii) s'alcooliser; **to d. like a fish,** boire comme un trou, comme une éponge; **he drinks like a fish,** il boirait la mer et ses poissons; **he drinks (too much),** il boit (trop); c'est un buveur. **3.** *v.i.* **wine that drinks well after a year,** vin qui est bon à boire après un an.

II. (*compound verbs*) **1. drink away.** (*a*) *v.tr.* boire (sa fortune); noyer (ses soucis); (*b*) *v.i.* boire coup sur coup; continuer de boire.

2. drink down, *v.tr.* (*a*) boire, avaler (un breuvage); (*b*) *A:* mettre (qn) sous la table (à consommations égales).

3. drink in, *v.tr.* (*a*) absorber, boire (l'eau); s'imbiber (d'eau); *F:* **the earth drinks in the heat of the sun,** la terre se pénètre de la chaleur du soleil; (*b*) boire (les paroles de qn); **to d. in the beauties of the countryside,** boire des yeux les beautés du paysage; (*c*) **he drank it all in,** (i) pas un détail ne lui en a échappé; (ii) il a avalé ça doux comme lait.

4. drink off, *v.tr.* boire (un verre) d'un coup, d'un trait; avaler (une coupe de champagne).

5. drink up, *v.tr.* (*a*) achever de boire; avaler; boire (qch.) jusqu'à la dernière goutte; vider (un verre); *v.i.* **d. up!** videz vos verres! (*b*) (*of plants, etc.*) = DRINK IN (*a*).

drinkable ['driŋkəbl]. **1.** *a.* (*a*) (vin, etc.) buvable; **the wine's very d.,** ce vin se laisse boire; (*b*) (eau) potable. **2.** *s.pl. F: O:* **we've forgotten the drinkables,** nous avons oublié la boisson.

drinker ['driŋkər], *s.* **1.** buveur, -euse; (*a*) **water drinkers,** buveurs d'eau; (*b*) **heavy d., hard d.,** grand buveur, franc buveur, buveur intrépide; **hardened d.,** buveur impénitent. **2.** *Husb:* abreuvoir *m* (de poulailler, etc.).

drinking[1] ['driŋkiŋ], *a.* **he's a d. man,** c'est un (grand) buveur; il aime à boire; **I'm not a d. man,** je n'ai pas l'habitude de boire; **hard-d.,** adonné à la boisson.

drinking[2], *s.* **1.** boire *m*; **after d.,** après boire; **try eating without d.,** essayez donc des repas sans boisson; **d. fountain,** (i) borne-fontaine *f*, *pl.* bornes-fontaines; fontaine publique; (ii) *Ind: etc:* poste *m* d'eau potable; **d. glass,** verre *m* à boire; *Nau:* **d. tank,** charnier *m*; **d. trough,** abreuvoir *m*; **d. water,** eau *f* potable; eau de boisson. **2.** (*of alcoholic drinks*) (*a*) **d. saloon,** débit *m* de boissons; **d. song,** chanson *f* à boire; chanson bachique; (*b*) (*to excess*) ivrognerie *f*; alcoolisme *m*; la boisson; **his d. habits,** ses habitudes *f* de buveur, d'ivrognerie; **d. bout,** beuverie *f*, *P:* soûlerie *f*, soûlographie *f*; *F:* ribote *f*, **to have a d. bout,** faire ribote; tirer une bordée.

drinking up ['driŋkiŋ'ʌp], *s.* **d.-u. time,** les dix minutes pour vider les verres (avant la clôture des débits de boissons).

drip[1] [drip], *s.* **1.** dégouttement *m*; égout *m* (des eaux des toits, etc.); **the d. d., d. drop, from a tap,** le bruit que fait l'eau qui tombe goutte à goutte d'un robinet; l'égouttement *m* d'un robinet; *Jur:* **right of d.,** droit *m* de laisser s'écouler les eaux pluviales sur le fonds du voisin. 2. goutte *f*; *pl.* égoutture *f*, dégoutture *f*; **a d. fell on my nose,** une goutte me tomba sur le nez; **the drips from the trees,** les dégouttures, l'égoutture, des arbres. 3. *attrib. Mch:* **d. cock,** (robinet) purgeur; **d. coffee,** (café) filtre *m*; *Mch: etc:* **d. cup,** cuvette *f* d'égouttage; poche *f* de vidange; *Mch:* **d. feed,** distributeur *m* compte-gouttes (d'huile); **d.-feed lubricator,** (graisseur *m*) compte-gouttes *m inv*; *Med:* **d. feeding,** drip-feeding *m*; *Av:* **d. flap,** bande-gouttière *f*, *pl.* bandes-gouttières; rejéteau *m*, bavette *f*; **d. glass, ring,** bobèche *f* (de bougeoir); **d. mat,** dessous *m* de bouteille, de verre; **d. mould(ing),** rejéteau, jet *m* d'eau (de fenêtre, de porte); siccité *f* (d'une fenêtre); larmier *m*; *Aut:* chéneau *m* d'écoulement de pluie; *Mec.E:* **d. pan, d. tray,** attrape-gouttes *m inv*; cuvette *f* à huile; gatte *f*; *Mch:* **d. pump,** pompe *f* de purge; *Bot:* **d. tip,** alêne *f* (d'une feuille). 4. *Med:* goutte-à-goutte *m inv*; **intravenous d.,** goutte-à-goutte intraveineux; **Murphy d.,** goutte-à-goutte rectal. 5. *Arch:* larmier (de corniche); jet d'eau. 6. *P:* **he's, she's, a d.,** c'est une nouille.

drip[2], *v.* (**dripped**) 1. *v.i.* (d)égoutter, s'égoutter; tomber goutte à goutte; goutter; **your umbrella is dripping,** l'eau *f* dégoutte de votre parapluie; **wall that drips,** mur *m* qui suinte; **the water was dripping down the stairs,** *F:* l'eau dégoulinait le long de l'escalier; **the perspiration was dripping from his forehead,** la sueur lui dégouttait du front; son front ruisselait de sueur; *F:* **to be dripping with money,** être cousu d'or. 2. *v.tr.* faire dégoutter (du liquide); laisser tomber (du liquide) goutte à goutte.

drip-dry ['dripdrai], *a.* ne nécessitant aucun repassage; lavé-repassé *inv*.

drip-feed ['dripfi:d], *v.tr.* (**drip-fed**) *Med:* nourrir (un malade) par le drip-feeding.

dripping[1] ['dripiŋ], *a.* ruisselant, stillant; (roche *f*, robinet *m*) qui pleure; **to be d. wet,** être trempé (comme une soupe); être tout ruisselant; **d. joint,** rôti *m* qui jute; **d. with perspiration, with blood,** ruisselant de sueur, de sang.

dripping[2], *s.* 1. dégouttement *m*, égouttement *m*; stillation *f*; **constant d. wears away a stone,** l'eau *f* qui tombe goutte à goutte use, creuse, la pierre; **d. tube,** (pipette *f*) compte-gouttes *m inv*. 2. **the drippings from the trees, from the roof,** l'égoutture *f* des arbres; les dégouttures *f* du toit; les gouttes *f* qui tombent des arbres, du toit. 3. *Cu:* graisse *f* de rôti; **bread and d.,** tartine *f* à la graisse; **d. pan,** lèchefrite *f*.

dripstone ['dripstoun], *s.* 1. *Arch:* capucine *f*; larmier *m*. 2. *esp. U.S: Geog:* (i) stalagmite *f*; (ii) stalactite *f*.

drivage ['draividʒ], *s. Min:* (i) chassage *m*, percement *m*; (ii) galerie *f*.

drive[1] [draiv], *s.* 1. promenade *f* en voiture; course *f*; **a d. of 50 km,** un parcours, un trajet, de 50 km; **it's an hour's d. away,** c'est à une heure en voiture; **to go for a d.,** aller faire une promenade, *F:* un (petit) tour, en voiture; *Aut:* **trial d.,** conduite *f* d'essai. 2. (*a*) conduite (du bétail); **long drives have been replaced by trucking,** les longues marches ont été remplacées par le transport en camion; (*b*) *Ven:* battue *f* (du gibier); (*c*) *NAm:* (i) (transport *m* du bois par le) flottage; *Fr.C:* drave *f*; (ii) train *m* (de bois flotté). 3. (*a*) *Mec.E:* (mouvement *m* de) propulsion *f*; (i) attaque *f* (d'un organe); (ii) commande *f* (par un organe); transmission *f*, entraînement *m*, actionnement *m*; **mechanical d., power d.,** entraînement mécanique; **belt d.,** entraînement, transmission, par courroie; **chain d.,** entraînement, transmission, par chaîne; **gear d.,** commande par engrenages; **bevel d.,** transmission par pignons; **cardan d.,** transmission à cardan; **slow-motion d.,** commande à mouvement lent; **smooth d.,** entraînement régulier; *Av:* **supercharger d. ratio,** rapport *m* d'entraînement du compresseur centrifuge; **final d.,** commande finale; **d. wheel** = DRIVING WHEEL; *W.Tel:* **d. pin,** tige *f* (de haut-parleur); *Hyd.E:* **d. pipe,** conduite d'eau motrice; (*b*) *Aut:* **direct d.,** prise, attaque, directe; **speed on direct d.,** vitesse *f* en prise (directe); **car with front wheel d.,** voiture *f* à traction avant, à roues avant motrices; voiture tout-à-l'avant *inv*; **vehicle with four wheel d.,** véhicule *m* à quatre roues motrices; **differential d.,** (i) attaque du différentiel (par la transmission); (ii) commande (des roues arrière) par le différentiel; **fuel pump d.,** commande de la pompe à essence; (*c*) *Aut:* **rear d.,** pont *m* arrière. 4. *Aut:* conduite; **left-hand d.,** conduite à gauche. 5. *Sp:* (*a*) *Golf:* drive *m*, crossée *f* de départ; (*b*) *Ten:* drive; (**forearm**) **d.,** (drive de) coup droit; (*c*) *Cr:* coup droit long et appuyé. 6. (*a*) **the d. of business,** l'urgence *f* des affaires; (*b*) dynamisme *m*; **to have plenty of d.,** avoir de l'énergie; être énergique, dynamique, très entreprenant; aller toujours de l'avant; **to lack d.,** manquer de force, d'énergie. 7. (*a*) offensive *f*; **to launch a d. against a stronghold, an abuse,** déclencher une offensive contre une place forte, un abus; (*b*) campagne *f*; **sales d.,** campagne de vente; **higher output d.,** campagne en faveur de, pour, une production augmentée. 8. *Psy:* pulsion (sexuelle, etc.). 9. *U.S: P:* moment *m* d'exaltation, coup de fouet (dû à un stupéfiant). 10. (*a*) allée *f*, chemin *m* (dans un parc, etc.) pour les voitures; **scenic d.,** promenade *f* d'agrément; (*b*) avenue *f* (d'un château, etc.); route *f* de plaisance; entrée *f*; (*c*) *Ven:* routin *m* (dans une forêt). 11. *Min:* (*a*) galerie *f* en direction; **cross d.,** recoupe *f*; (*b*) **d. pipe, d. tube,** tube perforateur (de sondage); *Hyd: E:* **d. well,** puits abyssinien; abyssinienne *f*; puits instantané. 12. *Cards:* **bridge d., whist d.,** tournoi *m* de bridge, de whist. 13. *Equit:* chasse *f* (du bipède postérieur).

drive[2], *v.* (*p.t.* **drove** [drouv]; *p.p.* **driven** ['drivn])

I. *v.tr.* 1. (*a*) chasser, pousser, faire aller (devant soi); **to d. cattle to the fields,** conduire, mener, le bétail aux champs; **to d. the enemy down the hill,** (re)pousser l'ennemi jusqu'au bas de la colline; **to d. s.o. from, out of, the house,** chasser qn de la maison; **to d. the enemy from his positions,** déloger l'ennemi; *F:* **to d. sth. out of s.o.'s head,** faire oublier qch. à qn; **the wind is driving the rain against the window panes,** le vent chasse la pluie contre les vitres; **the wind is driving the tide,** la brise chasse la marée, *Nau:* vente la marée; **the waves drove the ship upon the rocks,** les vagues ont poussé, jeté, le navire contre les rochers; **to be driven off one's course,** être entraîné hors de sa route; **to be driven ashore,** être chassé, drossé, poussé, à la côte; (*of ship*) **tempest-driven,** battu par les tempêtes; **to d. water into a boiler,** refouler de l'eau dans une chaudière; (*b*) *Ven:* **to d. the game,** rabattre le gibier; **shooting of driven birds,** tir *m* du gibier rabattu sur les chasseurs; **to d. the country (for game),** battre la campagne; (*c*) **to d. a hoop,** faire courir, faire aller, un cerceau; jouer au cerceau. 2. (*a*) faire marcher (une machine); conduire (un cheval, une auto, une locomotive); *Rac:* driver (un trotteur); piloter (une voiture de course); **to d. three horses abreast,** mener trois chevaux de front; *v.i. & tr.* **can you d. (a car)?** savez-vous conduire? **are you going to d.?** vous allez conduire? vous allez prendre le volant? **to d. recklessly,** conduire avec imprudence, *F:* comme un fou; *F:* **to d. like mad,** filer à fond de train, à tombeau ouvert; **he was driving to the public danger,** il conduisait au mépris de la sécurité publique; *Aut:* **d. yourself service,** service de location sans chauffeur; (*b*) **to d. s.o. to a place,** conduire qn en voiture, en auto, quelque part; **to d. s.o. home,** reconduire qn chez lui (en voiture); (*c*) **to d. a timber raft,** diriger un flottage de bois; *Fr.C:* faire la drave. 3. (*a*) pousser (qn à une action); contraindre (qn à faire qch.); **to d. s.o. into doing sth., to do sth.,** pousser, contraindre, qn à faire qch.; **I was driven to resign,** force me fut, j'ai été forcé, de démissionner; **he was driven to it,** on lui a forcé la main; **he won't be driven,** on ne le mène pas comme on veut; (*b*) réduire (qn au désespoir, etc.); **to d. s.o. out of his mind, senses,** *F:* **round the bend,** rendre qn fou, affoler qn; **to d. s.o. wild,** mettre, pousser, qn à bout; faire sortir qn de ses gonds. 4. surcharger (qn) de travail; exploiter, excéder (qn); surmener (ses employés); **to d. oneself (too) hard,** se surmener. 5. enfoncer, chasser, refouler, ficher (un clou); foncer, enfoncer, battre, ficher (un pieu); serrer (une vis); **to d. a pipe into an opening,** engager un tube dans une ouverture; **to d. a knife into s.o.'s back,** enfoncer un couteau dans le dos à qn; **to d. a peg home,** enfoncer une cheville à fond, encocher une cheville; battre, enfoncer, une cheville (jusqu')à refus; **to d. the matter home,** faire aboutir l'affaire; *Mil:* **to d. a charge home,** faire une charge à fond; **I can't d. it home to him, d. it into his head, that . . .,** je ne peux pas lui enfoncer dans la tête que . . .. 6. (*a*) percer, forer, pousser, avancer (un tunnel, une galerie); pratiquer (une galerie); (*b*) **to d. a railway through the desert,** tracer, construire, une ligne de chemin de fer à travers le désert. 7. (*a*) **to d. a trade,** exercer un métier; faire un métier; (*b*) **to d. a bargain,** faire, conclure, passer, un marché; **to d. a hard bargain,** chercher à gagner le dernier centime; **to d. a hard bargain with s.o.,** imposer, faire, à qn des conditions très dures. 8. *Sp:* **to d. the ball,** *abs.* **to d.,** *Cr:* chasser la balle; *Ten:* jouer un drive; driver; *Golf:* jouer une crossée; driver. 9. (*a*) *Mec.E: Mch:* actionner, faire fonctionner, faire marcher, commander, animer, mouvoir (une machine); **to d. machines by steam,** actionner des machines par la vapeur; **driven by compressed air,** commandé par l'air comprimé; **this stream drives the mill,** ce cours d'eau sert le moulin; (*of part*) **to d. another part,** actionner, entraîner, attaquer, un organe; (*b*) *A:* (*of pers.*) **to d. a pen, a quill,** écrire; manier la plume; faire le métier de gratte-papier; gratter le papier.

II. *v.i.* 1. (*a*) (*of clouds, etc.*) **to d. before the wind,** chasser, être charrié, devant le vent; **the rain driving against the window panes,** la pluie qui fouette les vitres; **to let d. at s.o.,** (i) décocher un coup à qn; (ii) dire ses quatre vérités à qn; (*b*) (*of snow*) s'amonceler; (*c*) *Nau:* (*of ship*) dériver; **driving ashore,** dérivant à la côte; **to d. on to another ship,** tomber sur un autre navire; **to d. before the storm,** fuir devant la tempête. 2. **to d. along the road,** rouler sur la route; **to d. to a place,** se rendre en voiture à un endroit; **we were driving,** nous étions en voiture; **you will have some miles to d. from the station,** de la gare vous aurez quelques milles à faire en voiture; **will you walk or d.?** voulez-vous faire le trajet à pied ou en voiture? *Aut:* **we were driving by the map,** nous nous dirigions avec la carte; nous roulions suivant les indications de la carte; **I don't like to d. at night,** je n'aime pas conduire, voyager, la nuit; **to d. slowly,** marcher, rouler, à petite allure; **to d. on the right (of the road),** circuler à droite; tenir la droite. 3. (*with passive force*) (*a*) **nail that won't d.,** clou *f* qui ne se laisse pas enfoncer; **pile that won't d.,** pieu *m* qui refuse le mouton; (*b*) **car that drives well,** voiture *f* facile à conduire.

III. (*compound verbs*) 1. **drive along.** (*a*) *v.tr.* chasser, pousser (qn, qch.); (*b*) *v.i.* cheminer (en voiture); rouler; **I was driving along at 50 miles an hour,** je filais à 80 à l'heure; je roulais à 80.

2. **drive at,** *v.i.* (*a*) travailler à (qch.) sans relâche; *F:* bûcher (qch.); (*b*) **what are you driving at?** quel but poursuivez-vous? à quoi voulez-vous en venir? où tendent ces questions? **I see what you are driving at,** je comprends où vous voulez en venir; *F:* je vous vois venir.

3. **drive away.** (*a*) (i) *v.tr.* chasser, éloigner, écarter, repousser (qn, qch.); (ii) *v.i.* partir en voiture; s'en aller en voiture; *Aut:* démarrer; (*b*) *v.i.* **to d. away at one's work,** travailler d'arrache-pied; travailler comme un nègre, comme un cheval.

4. **drive back.** (*a*) *v.tr.* (i) repousser, refouler, faire reculer (qn, qch.); (ii) reconduire, ramener, (qn) en voiture; (*b*) *v.i.* rentrer, revenir, retourner, en voiture.

5. **drive down.** (*a*) *v.tr.* **to d. s.o. down to, into, the country,** conduire qn (en voiture) à la campagne; (*b*) *v.i.* se rendre en voiture (de la ville à la campagne, de Londres en province); **we shall d. down for the Sunday,** nous viendrons (en voiture) passer la journée du dimanche.

6. **drive in.** (*a*) *v.tr.* (i) enfoncer, renfoncer, brocher (un clou); visser (une vis); caler, chasser (une clavette); (ii) (*of chauffeur, etc.*) faire entrer (qn); (*b*) *v.i.* entrer (en voiture).

7. **drive off.** (*a*) *v.tr.* chasser, éloigner, écarter, repousser (qn, qch.); (*b*) *v.i.* partir, s'en aller, en voiture; démarrer.

8. **drive on.** (*a*) *v.tr.* (i) pousser, entraîner (qn); (ii) serrer (les cercles d'un tonneau); (*b*) *v.i.* continuer sa route; s'avancer; **d. on!** vous pouvez continuer!

9. **drive out.** (*a*) *v.tr.* chasser (qn, qch.); faire sortir (qn); (dé)chasser, refouler (un clou); *F:* **I've been driven out by the decorators,** les peintres m'ont chassé de chez moi; (*b*) *v.i.* (i) sortir (en voiture); (ii) *Typ:* (*of matter*) chasser.

10. **drive over.** (*a*) *v.tr. Typ:* faire sauter, chasser (un mot); (*b*) *v.i.* venir, se rendre (à un endroit) en voiture.

11. **drive through.** (*a*) *v.tr.* **to d. one's sword through s.o.'s body,** passer son sabre à travers le corps à qn; **to d. one's fist through the window pane,** enfoncer la vitre d'un coup de poing; (*b*) *v.i.* passer (par une ville) en voiture; **we are merely driving through,** nous ne faisons que passer.

12. **drive up.** (*a*) *v.i.* s'approcher; **a car drove up to the door,** une voiture vint s'arrêter devant la porte; (*b*) *v.tr.* faire monter (un piston, etc.).

drive-in ['draivin], *s. NAm:* **d.-in (cinema),** cinéma en plein air auquel on assiste en voiture; drive-in *m inv*; *Fr.C:* ciné-parc *m*, *pl.* ciné-parcs; **d.-in (restaurant),** restaurant *m* où les clients sont servis dans leurs voitures; **d.-in bank,** banque *f* dont les guichets sont accessibles aux clients dans leurs voitures.

drivel[1] ['drivl], *s.* 1. bave *f*. 2. *F:* radotage *m*; rabâchage *m*, bêtises *fpl*, balivernes *fpl*; **to talk d.,** radoter.

drivel[2], *v.i.* (**drivelled**) 1. baver. 2. *F:* radoter; **what is he drivelling about?** qu'est-ce qu'il bave? **he drivelled on, away,** il continuait de radoter.

driveller ['drivlər], *s.* 1. baveur, -euse. 2. *F:* radoteur, -euse.

drivelling ['drivliŋ], *a. F:* radoteur, -euse; imbécile; **you**

d. idiot! espèce d'imbécile!

driven ['drivn], *a.* **1. d. snow,** neige *f* vierge. **2.** *Mch: Mec.E:* **d. shaft,** arbre commandé, mené, récepteur, secondaire; **d. wheel,** roue menée; **d. gear,** engrenage mené; **d. side (of belt),** brin conduit, mené, mou; **d. end (of shaft),** bout *m* d'entraînement; **electrically d.,** actionné par l'électricité; à commande électrique; (voiture *f*) électromobile. **3.** *Hyd.E:* **d. well,** puits abyssinien, instantané; abyssinienne *f.*

driver ['draivər], *s.* **1.** *(a)* mécanicien *m,* mécanicien-conducteur, *pl.* mécaniciens-conducteurs (de locomotive); mécanicien, wattman *m* (de tramway); conducteur *m* (d'autobus); chauffeur, -euse (de taxi); conducteur, -trice (d'automobile); **he's a good d.,** il conduit bien; *Aut:* il tient bien le volant; *Aut:* **weekend d.,** conducteur du dimanche; **racing (car) d.,** coureur *m* (automobile); pilote *m*; *(b)* (*of horse-drawn vehicle*) conducteur, -trice; cocher *m* (de fiacre, etc.); voiturier *m* (de charrette); *Artil:* conducteur; *Rac:* driver *m* (de sulky); **to be a good d.,** conduire bien; tenir bien les guides; *F:* **to be in the driver's seat,** tenir les rênes; avoir la haute main (dans la maison); *(c)* conducteur (de bestiaux); *(d)* **(log) d.,** flotteur *m,* driver; *Fr.C:* draveur *m*; *(e)* surveillant *m* (d'esclaves); *(f)* homme, femme, qui fait marcher, trimer, son personnel, qui surmène ses employés; *F:* vrai garde-chiourme, *pl.* garde(s)-chiourme(s). **2.** *NAm:* cheval *m* d'attelage. **3.** *Tls:* *(a)* (*punch*) poinçon *m*; poussoir *m*; *(b)* (*key-drift*) chasse-clavette *m, pl.* chasse-clavettes; chasse-clef *m, pl.* chasse-clefs; *(c)* (*drift pin*) broche *f,* mandrin *m*; *(d)* (*Cooper's driver*) chassoir *m.* **4.** *Mec.E:* *(a)* = DRIVING WHEEL; *(b)* = DRIVING PULLEY; *(c)* tige *f,* doigt *m,* d'entraînement; (tige) pousse-toc *m, pl.* pousse-tocs; doguin *m* (de tour); *(d)* *I.C.E:* heurtoir *m* (d'une soupape); *(e)* *Tex:* tacot *m,* taquet *m* (du battant). **5.** *Golf:* driver *m.* **6.** *Elcs:* driver. **7.** *Ent:* **d. ant,** doryline *f.*

driveway ['draivwei], *s.* (i) allée *f,* chemin *m,* pour les voitures; (ii) entrée *f* (d'une demeure, etc.).

driving[1] ['draiviŋ], *a.* **1.** *Mec.E:* (*of wheel, etc.*) moteur, -trice; menant; **d. portion (of a pulley belt),** brin menant, tendu; brin conducteur; **d. force,** force motrice; *Fig:* **the d. force behind the scheme,** le moteur d'un projet; **d. band,** (i) *Artil:* ceinture *f* de, à, forcement (d'un obus); (ii) *Mec.E:* (*also* **d. belt**) courroie *f* de commande, d'entraînement, menante; **d. box,** boîte *f* d'essieu moteur (d'une locomotive); **d. chain,** chaîne *f* de transmission; **d. gear,** (i) (engrenage *m* de) transmission *f*; (organe(s) *m(pl)* de) commande *f*; (ii) engrenage menant; **d. pinion,** pignon *m* d'attaque; **d. power,** mobile *m*; **d. pulley,** poulie conductrice, menante, de commande, d'attaque; **d. rod,** bielle directrice (de machine à vapeur); **d. shaft,** arbre *m* de transmission, de commande, d'attaque, de couche, arbre moteur; **d. spring,** maître-ressort *m, pl.* maîtres-ressorts; **d. wheel,** (i) roue motrice (de locomotive, etc.); (ii) roue de transmission. **2. d. rain,** pluie battante.

driving[2], *s.* **1.** conduite *f* (d'une voiture, etc.); **the efficient d. of a car,** l'art *m* de bien conduire une automobile; **cross-country d.,** conduite à travers champs, conduite tous terrains; **d. box,** siège *m* (du cocher); **charged with d. to the public danger,** inculpé d'avoir conduit au mépris de la sécurité publique; *Aut:* **d. lessons,** leçons *f* de conduite; **d. school,** auto-école *f, pl.* auto-écoles; **d. test,** examen *m* pour permis de conduire; **to pass one's d. test,** passer son permis de conduire; **d. seat,** siège du chauffeur, du conducteur; *F:* **he's in the d. seat,** c'est lui qui mène l'affaire. **2. (log) d.,** flottage *m* du bois; *Fr.C:* drave *f.* **3.** *Mch: Mec.E:* commande *f,* transmission *f,* attaque *f.* **4.** *(a)* enfoncement *m* (d'un clou); enfoncement, battage *m* (d'un pieu); serrage *m* (d'une vis); *(b)* **d. (out),** chassage *m,* refoulement *m* (d'une goupille); **d. bolt,** repoussoir *m*; *(c)* *Min:* percement *m,* chassage (d'une galerie); **d. block,** bloc *m* de battage. **5.** *Golf:* **d. iron,** grand fer, driver *m.*

drizzle[1] ['drizl], *s.* **1.** bruine *f,* brouillasse *f,* crachin *m*; pluie fine et pénétrante; **the rain came down in a steady d.,** il pleuvait dru et menu. **2.** *U.S:* *P:* **he's, she's, a d. puss,** (i) c'est une nouille; (ii) c'est un chameau.

drizzle[2], *v.i.* **1.** bruiner, brouillasser, crachiner; pleuvoir à petites gouttes; *F:* pleuvoter, pluviner; **it was drizzling,** il bruinait; il faisait de la bruine. **2.** *A:* parfiler des galons d'or.

drizzly ['drizli], *a.* (jour) bruineux, de bruine.

drogue [droug], *s.* **1.** *Nau:* cône-ancre *m, pl.* cônes-ancres; ancre flottante, ancre de cape. **2.** *Av:* *(a)* parachute *m* de queue (pour freinage rapide); *(b)* sac *m* à vent (d'aérodrome); *(c)* cible remorquée; **A/A target d.,** marche *f*; *(d)* entonnoir *m* de ravitaillement en vol.

droit [drɔit], *s. Jur:* droit *m*; *A:* **droits of Admiralty,** droits provenant de la vente des prises ennemies.

droll [droul]. **1.** *s. A:* & *Lit:* bouffon *m,* triboulet *m.* **2.** *a.* drôle, drolatique, bouffon, plaisant; *F:* cocasse; *A:* **a d. fellow,** (i) un drôle de corps; (ii) un farceur.

drollery ['drouləri], *s.* **1.** drôlerie *f,* plaisanterie *f,* bouffonnerie *f.* **2.** = DROLLNESS.

drollness ['droulnis], *s.* caractère *m* drôle (de qch.).

drolly ['drouli], *adv.* drôlement, drolatiquement; d'une manière drôle, cocasse.

dromas ['drouməs], *s. Orn:* drome *m,* dromas *m.*

drome [droum], *s. F:* aérodrome *m.*

dromedarist ['drʌmədərist, 'drɔm-], *s.m.* méhariste.

dromedary ['drʌməd(ə)ri, 'drɔm-], *s.* dromadaire *m*; **fast, racing, d.,** méhari *m*; dromadaire coureur.

dromia ['droumiə], *s. Crust:* dromia *m,* dromie *f.*

dromomania [drɔmə'meiniə], *s. Med:* dromomanie *f.*

dromond ['drɔmənd], *s. A.Nau:* dromon(d) *m.*

dromotropic [drɔmə'trɔpik], *a. Physiol:* dromotrope.

drone[1] [droun], *s.* **1.** *(a)* *Ent:* abeille *f* mâle; faux-bourdon *m, pl.* faux-bourdons; *(b)* fainéant *m,* parasite *m*; **the drones,** les inutiles *m.* **2.** *(a)* bourdonnement *m* (des abeilles); rumeur *f*; **the parson's endless d.,** le débit monotone, la psalmodie intarissable, du pasteur; **the d. of an aircraft,** le ronronnement, le vrombissement, d'un avion; *(b)* *Mus:* (i) bourdon *m* (de cornemuse); (ii) **d. bass,** bourdon. **3.** *(a)* *Mil.Av:* (i) avion télécommandé, téléguidé; drone *m*; (ii) avion-cible *m, pl.* avions-cibles; *(b)* *Navy:* cible aérienne; bateau-cible télécommandé, téléguidé.

drone[2]. **1.** *v.i.* *(a)* (*of bee, etc.*) bourdonner; *(b)* (*of pers.*) parler d'un ton monotone; **to d. on and on, away,** ânonner; *(c)* (*of pers.*) fainéanter. **2.** *v.tr.* **to d. (out) sth.,** débiter (une prière, etc.) d'un ton monotone.

drongo ['drɔŋgou], *s.* **1.** *Orn:* drongo *m.* **2.** *Austr:* *F:* sot *m,* niais *m.*

droning[1] ['drouniŋ], *a.* (*of sound*) bourdonnant; (*of voice*) traînant.

droning[2], *s.* **1.** *(a)* bourdonnement *m*; *(b)* psalmodie *f,* récit *m* monotone (de qn); *(c)* ronronnement *m* (d'un moteur, etc.); vrombissement *m* (d'un avion). **2.** fainéantise *f.*

drool[1] [dru:l], *s.* **1.** bave *f.* **2.** radotage *m*; bêtises *fpl.*

drool[2], *v.i.* **1.** baver. **2.** radoter; dire des bêtises; **to d. over sth.,** s'extasier, se pâmer d'admiration, sur qch.

droop[1] [dru:p], *s.* **1.** *(a)* attitude penchée (de la tête); *(b)* abaissement *m* (des paupières). **2.** langueur *f,* abattement *m,* affaissement *m.*

droop[2]. **1.** *v.i.* *(a)* (*of head, etc.*) (se) pencher; (*of eyelids*) s'abaisser; (*of feathers*) pendre, retomber; (*of curve*) décroître; *(b)* (*of flower*) pencher, languir; *(c)* (*of pers.*) languir, s'alanguir; décliner, s'affaiblir, s'affaisser. **2.** *v.tr.* baisser, pencher, laisser tomber (la tête); baisser (les yeux); abaisser (les paupières); (*of bird*) laisser pendre (les ailes); *Mil:* *U.S:* **to d. the colour,** saluer du drapeau.

drooping[1] ['dru:piŋ], *a.* *(a)* (*of feather*) retombant, pendant; (*of shoulders*) tombant; (*of moustache*) tombant, pendant; (*of head*) baissé, penché; (*of eyelids*) abaissé; *Farr:* **d. croup (of horse),** croupe avalée; *(b)* (*of flower, pers.*) languissant; **to be like a d. lily,** prendre des airs penchés; **to revive the d. spirits (of a party),** remonter les esprits abattus; **to revive s.o.'s d. spirits,** remonter le courage à qn.

drooping[2], *s.* = DROOP[1].

droopingly ['dru:piŋli], *adv.* languissamment; d'un air languissant, abattu.

droopy ['dru:pi], *a.* *F:* (air) languissant, abattu, *F:* vaseux.

drop[1] [drɔp], *s.* **1.** *(a)* goutte *f* (d'eau, de pluie, de sang, de sueur); **water falling d. by d.,** eau qui tombe goutte à goutte; eau stillante; **the last d., which overflowed the cup,** la goutte qui fit déborder le vase; **cold drops of sweat,** sueur froide; *F:* **it's only a d. in the bucket, in the ocean,** ce n'est qu'une goutte d'eau dans la mer; **to drink the few drops remaining,** boire les égouttures *f* (d'une bouteille); **to drink to the last d.,** *F:* faire rubis sur l'ongle; *Metall:* **d. tin,** étain *m* en larmes, en grains; *(b)* *Pharm:* **drops,** gouttes; **nasal drops,** gouttes pour le nez; **I am having drops in my eyes,** on me met des gouttes dans les yeux; **d. bottle,** flacon *m* compte-gouttes; *(c)* **a d. of wine,** un coup, un doigt, une larme, de vin; **to take just a d. of rum in one's coffee,** prendre une larme de rhum dans son café; **I could do with a d. of something hot,** je prendrais bien une goutte de quelque chose de chaud; *Cu:* **a d., a few drops, of vinegar,** un filet de vinaigre; *(d)* *F:* **to take a d.,** boire la goutte; **he has had a d. too much,** il a bu un coup de trop; il a trop bu; il a sa pointe; **he's had a little d.,** il a sa pointe; il est un peu en train, un peu gris; **he likes a wee d.,** il aime bien prendre la goutte; *A:* **he has a d. in his eye,** il a un verre de trop dans le nez; *(e)* (*of necklace, chandelier, etc.*) pendant *m,* pendeloque *f*; *Arch:* goutte; *(f)* **peppermint, chocolate, d.,** pastille *f* de menthe, de chocolat. **2.** *(a)* chute *f* ((i) mouvement *m* de chute; (ii) dénivellation *f*); **path bordered by a d. of a hundred feet,** chemin qui contourne un à-pic de cent pieds; **the hangman gave him a six-foot d.,** le bourreau lui a ménagé une chute de six pieds; *F:* **to do sth. at the d. of a hat,** faire qch. sans hésiter, tout de suite, tout de go; **d. of a steam hammer,** (i) hauteur *f* de chute, (ii) chute, d'un pilon; *Hyd.E:* **d. of a lock,** chute d'un bief; *Surv:* **d. in the ground,** dénivellation du terrain; *NAm:* **to get the d. on s.o.,** prendre qn sans défense, au dépourvu; *(b)* *Av:* parachutage, *m,* droppage *m,* largage *m*; **delayed d.,** ouverture retardée (d'un parachute); **d. site, d. zone,** zone *f* de largage, de droppage; *Mil:* **d. angle,** angle *m* de bombardement, de largage de bombes, de visée; *(c)* chute, baisse *f,* abaissement *m*; **d. in prices,** chute, baisse, de prix; **considerable d. in prices,** baisse sensible de prix; **heavy d. in cottons,** débâcle *f* des cotons; **sales show a d. of 10%,** les ventes accusent une régression de 10%, sont en régression de 10%; *Fin:* **d. in value, in takings,** moins-value *f*; *El:* **d. in voltage,** perte *f* de charge; **inductive armature d.,** chute inductive de tension dans l'induit; **potential d.,** variation *f* brusque, chute, de potentiel, de tension; *Mec.E:* **pressure d.,** perte *f* de charge, de pression; *Ph:* **adiabatic d.,** chaleur *f* de la détente adiabatique. **3.** *(a)* (*of lock*) cache-entrée *m inv.*; *Tp:* *etc:* volet *m* (d'un tableau commutateur); **d. indicator, d. annunciator,** (i) annonciateur *m* (d'appel), indicateur *m,* à volets; (ii) *Rail:* (appareil *m* de) correspondance *f* à guichets; *(b)* *Th:* **d. (curtain),** rideau *m* d'entr'acte; *(c)* (*of gallows*) bascule *f,* trappe *f*; *F:* **the d.,** la potence, le gibet. **4.** *(a)* *Fb:* **d. (kick),** coup tombé; coup de pied à ras de terre; **d. goal,** drop-goal *m, pl.* drop-goals; drop *m*; *(b)* *Ten:* **d. shot, d. stroke,** volée amortie; *F:* carotte *f.* **5.** *Nau:* (*crane*) drop. **6.** *attrib.* *Arch:* **d. arch,** arc-ogive surbaissé, *pl.* arcs-ogives; *Surv:* **d. arrow,** fiche plombée; *N.Arch:* **d. bolt,** prisonnier *m,* cervelle *f*; **d. bottom,** fond *m* mobile; *Med:* **d. foot,** pied effondré; *Furn:* **d. front,** abattant *m* (de bureau); *Hyd.E:* **d. gate,** porte *f* à trappe; *Mch:* **d. grate,** jette-feu *m inv*; *Metall:* **d. hammer, d. press,** marteau-pilon *m* à friction, *pl.* marteaux-pilons; mouton *m*; **d. stamp,** martinet *m*; *Aut:* **d. head,** capote *f* rabattable; **d.-head coupé,** coupé *m* à capote rabattable, avec capote pliante, coupé décapotable; *Nau:* **d. keel,** dériveur *m*; aile *f* de dérive; *El:* **d. light,** suspension *f* électrique, suspension réglable; *Furn:* **d. leaf,** battant *m*; **d. leaf table,** table *f* à battants; **d. side,** paroi *f* à rabattement; **settee with d. sides,** divan *m* avec accotoirs *m* réversibles; **d. table,** abattant *m*; **d. letter,** (i) *Typ:* lettre *f* de deux-points; (ii) *NAm:* lettre envoyée par porteur; *Th:* **d. scene,** (i) toile *f* de fond; (ii) rideau *m* d'entr'acte; (iii) *F:* dernier acte (d'un drame de la vie réelle, etc.); *Phot:* **d. shutter,** obturateur *m* à guillotine; *Tex:* **d. stitch,** maille sautée; *Av:* **d. tank,** réservoir *m* largable; *Mec.E:* **d. test,** essai *m* au choc; épreuve *f* par choc; *Typ:* **d. title,** titre *m* de départ abaissé; *I.C.E:* **d. valve,** soupape renversée.

drop[2]. **(dropped** [drɔpt])

I. *v.i.* **1.** *(a)* (*fall in drops*) tomber goutte à goutte, dégoutter **(from,** de); s'égoutter; *(b)* *F:* (*of pers.*) **to d. at the nose,** avoir la roupie au nez. **2.** *(a)* tomber; (*of pers.*) se laisser tomber; (*of ground*) s'abaisser; *Med:* (*of womb, etc.*) descendre; (*of door*) **to d. (on its hinges),** s'affaisser; **a bomb dropped among the crowd,** une bombe est tombée, s'est abattue, au milieu de la foule; **the book dropped from, out of, his hands,** le livre lui tomba des mains; **the grapes are dropping from the vine,** les raisins s'égrènent; **a remark dropped from him,** il laissa échapper une remarque; **his jaw dropped,** son visage s'allongea; **to d. into a chair,** s'écrouler sur une chaise; s'affaler dans un fauteuil; *F:* **he almost dropped (with surprise),** il pensa tomber de son haut; **to work till one drops,** continuer de travailler jusqu'à ce qu'on meure, jusqu'à son dernier souffle; mourir à la tâche; **I am ready to d.,** (i) (*with fatigue*) je tombe de fatigue; je n'en puis plus; je ne me soutiens plus; je ne tiens plus sur mes jambes; (ii) (*with sleep*) je tombe de sommeil; **to d. (down) dead,** tomber mort; *P:* **d. dead!** allez au diable! *(b)* *Typ:* (*of letters*) **to d. out of place,** chevaucher; *(c)* *Ven:* (*of setter*) tomber en arrêt. **3.** (*of prices, temperature, etc.*) baisser; (*of wind*) tomber, s'apaiser, se calmer, faiblir; *Fin:* **receipts have dropped,** les recettes ont baissé, ont accusé une moins-value. **4. there the matter dropped,** l'affaire en resta là; **Mary came in, and the conversation dropped,** à l'entrée de Mary la conversation prit fin, en resta là; *F:* **d. it! let it d.!** n'en parlons plus! **5.** *(a)* **to d. to the rear,** rester en arrière; se laisser dépasser; *(b)* (*of boat*) **to d. downstream,** naviguer en aval; avaler; (*of pers., car,* *etc.*) **to d. into place,** prendre sa place (dans la file); prendre la file; (*b*) **to d. into the habit, the way, of. . .,** prendre l'habitude de . . .; **you will soon d. into our ways,** vous vous ferez bientôt à nos habitudes; **to d. into the local dialect,** retomber dans le dialecte. **6.** (*a*) **to d. into one's club, etc.,** entrer en passant à son cercle, etc.; **to d. in to see s.o.,** (i) aller, (ii) venir, faire une petite visite chez qn; (*b*) **to d. across, upon, s.o.,** rencontrer qn par hasard; **to d. (up)on sth.,** trouver, découvrir, qch. par hasard; **to d. on to a secret,** surprendre un secret; *U.S: F:* **to d. (down) to a fact,** se rendre compte d'un fait. **7.** *F:* **to d. on s.o. (like a ton of bricks),** (i) (*scold*) attraper qn; laver la tête à qn; (ii) (*snub*) rembarrer qn.

II. *v.tr.* **1.** verser (une larme); **to d. oil into sth.,** verser de l'huile goutte à goutte dans qch. **2.** (*a*) laisser tomber; lâcher (qch.); baisser (un voile, un rideau); lancer, larguer (une bombe); lâcher (un parachutiste); (*in knitting*) sauter (une maille), laisser échapper (une maille); (*to dog*) **d. it!** lâche ça! *Rugby:* **to d. a goal,** marquer un but sur coup tombé; *Cards:* **to d. the king,** (i) (*of holder of king*) se trouver forcé de jouer le roi sur l'as; (ii) (*of his opponent*) faire tomber le roi; *Nau:* **to d. the pilot,** débarquer le pilote; **to d. one's coil,** filer sa glène; *Mth:* **to d. a perpendicular to, on, a line,** abaisser une perpendiculaire à une ligne; (*b*) (*of sheep, etc.*) mettre bas (des petits); (*c*) laisser échapper (une observation); **to d. a word in s.o.'s ear, to d. s.o. a hint,** couler, glisser, un mot à l'oreille de qn; (*d*) **to d. a letter into the pillar box,** jeter une lettre à la poste; **to d. s.o. a line, a card,** envoyer, écrire, un mot, une carte, à qn. **3.** perdre (de l'argent) **(over sth.,** sur qch.); **it cost me a lot, but I wouldn't mind dropping a bit on it,** je l'ai payé cher, mais je consentirais à perdre quelque chose dessus. **4.** (*a*) (*lower*) **to d. the frame of a car,** surbaisser le châssis; **to d. the folding seat (of a taxi),** rabattre le strapontin; **to d. the hem of a dress,** allonger une robe; *Av:* **to d. a wing,** piquer de l'aile; (*b*) (*cause to drop*) abattre (qn, une pièce de gibier) (d'un coup de feu). **5.** (*set down*) déposer, descendre, (qn) (de voiture); **I shall d. you at your door,** je vous déposerai chez vous en passant; **will you d. this parcel at Mrs Smith's,** voulez-vous avoir l'obligeance de remettre ce paquet chez madame Smith. **6.** (*a*) omettre, supprimer (une lettre, une syllabe); **cases in which the article is dropped,** cas où l'on supprime l'article; (*b*) ne pas prononcer (les r, etc.); **to d. one's aitches,** ne pas aspirer les h. **7.** baisser, laisser tomber (les yeux, le bras, la voix, etc.). **8.** (*of woman*) **to d. a curtsey,** faire, tirer, une révérence. **9.** (*a*) abandonner, délaisser (un travail); cesser, lâcher (une poursuite); quitter (une habitude), se départir (d'une habitude); **to d. Latin,** *F:* lâcher le latin; **to d. the idea of doing sth.,** renoncer à (l'idée de) faire qch.; **I have dropped politics,** j'ai lâché la politique; **let us d. the subject,** laissons ce sujet! ne parlons plus de cela! brisons là! qu'il n'en soit plus question; *F:* **d. it!** finissez! cessez donc! en voilà assez! **to d. a newspaper,** se désabonner à un journal; (*b*) **to d. s.o.,** cesser de voir qn; cesser ses relations avec qn; laisser tomber qn; **we have dropped them,** nous ne les voyons plus; *F:* **to d. s.o. like a hot brick, a hot potato, a hot chestnut,** cesser du jour au lendemain toutes relations avec qn; *Sp:* **to d. a player,** laisser tomber, lâcher, un équipier.

III. (*compound verbs*) **1. drop back,** *v.i.* (*a*) retomber; (*b*) retourner en arrière; **to d. back towards the base,** se rabattre vers la base; (*c*) = DROP BEHIND.

2. drop behind, *v.i.* rester en arrière; se laisser distancer, dépasser, devancer.

3. drop down, *v.i.* (*a*) tomber par terre; **to d. down dead,** tomber mort; (*b*) *F:* **to d. down on s.o.,** flanquer un savon à qn; (*c*) (*of flap, etc.*) s'abaisser; basculer.

4. drop in. (*a*) *v.tr.* ajouter (qch.) goutte à goutte; glisser, laisser tomber, (qch.) dedans; (*b*) *v.i.* entrer en passant; **to d. in on s.o.,** (i) faire une petite visite, un bout de visite, à qn; (ii) venir en visite chez qn (sans être attendu); **I've just dropped in for a moment,** je ne fais qu'entrer et sortir; **do d. in some day,** passez donc nous voir un de ces jours.

5. drop off. (*a*) *v.i.* (i) (*of leaves, etc.*) tomber, se détacher; (ii) *F:* **to d. off (to sleep),** s'assoupir, s'endormir; **as soon as he was in bed he dropped right off,** aussitôt couché il s'endormit profondément; (iii) *P: A:* **to d. off (the hooks),** mourir; (iv) (*of membership, attendance, etc.*) diminuer; (*b*) *v.tr.* **d. me off at the corner,** déposez-moi au coin de la rue.

6. drop out. (*a*) *v.tr.* (i) laisser tomber (qch.) dehors; (ii) omettre, supprimer (une syllabe); omettre (un nom dans une liste, etc.); (*b*) *v.i.* (i) tomber dehors; (ii) **to d. out (of a contest),** se retirer; **two of the runners dropped out,** deux des coureurs ont renoncé; **to d. out (of a course of study, a class),** lâcher, abandonner, un cours; (iii) *Mil:* sortir des rangs; rester en arrière; (iv) *Typ: etc:* **the letter s has dropped out,** la lettre s a disparu, est tombée; **it dropped out of my mind,** cela m'est sorti de l'esprit.

drop-down ['drɔpdaun], *a. Sm.a:* (fusil) *m* à bascule.

drop-forge ['drɔpfɔ:dʒ], *v.tr. Metalw:* étamper, estamper; emboutir; forger à la presse; forger en matrices.

drop forging ['drɔpfɔ:dʒiŋ], *s. Metalw:* **1.** estampage *m*; matriçage *m*; **d.-f. press,** presse *f* hydraulique à estamper. **2.** pièce emboutie, étampée, matricée.

drophead ['drɔphed], *s. Aut:* capote *f* rabattable; **d. coupé,** coupé *m* à capote rabattable, avec capote pliante, coupé décapotable; *Dom.Ec:* **d. sewing machine,** machine *f* à coudre escamotable.

drop-in ['drɔpin], *s.* **1.** visiteur, -euse, inattendu(e). **2.** soirée, réunion, informelle. **3.** *Elcs:* information *f* parasite, signal *m*, -aux, parasite. **2.** *attrib.* **d.-in seat,** siège *m* amovible (d'une chaise).

droplet ['drɔplit], *s.* gouttelette *f*; *Med:* **d. infection,** transmission *f* des maladies infectieuses par projections salivaires en parlant; contagion *f*, contamination *f*, par projections salivaires en parlant.

drop-off ['drɔpɔf], *s.* **1.** pente descendante, acclivité *f* (d'un terrain) **2. d.-o. in attendance,** diminution *f* du nombre des assistants.

dropout ['drɔpaut], *s.* **1.** *El:* (courant *m*, tension *f*, puissance *f*, de) désexcitation *f*. **2.** *Fb:* (*Rugby*) coup *m* de renvoi; coup de vingt-deux mètres. **3.** *F:* (*a*) recalé, -ée, déchet *m* (d'une école, d'un collège); (*b*) (i) personne qui refuse la société, qui vit en marge de la société; (ii) vaurien, -ienne, mauvais garnement; *Psy:* déviant, -ante. **4.** *Elcs:* défaut *m* d'enregistrement.

droppable ['drɔpəbl], *a. Av:* (réservoir, canot de sauvetage, etc.) largable.

dropped [drɔpt], *a.* **1.** *Med:* **d. eyelid,** chute *f* de la paupière; ptosis *f*; **d. arches,** affaissement *m* de la surface plantaire; pied plat; **d. wrist,** paralysie *f* des extenseurs de la main; fléchissement *m* du poignet. **2.** *Aut: etc:* **d. axle, etc.,** essieu, etc., surbaissé; *Cy:* **d. handlebar,** guidon renversé. **3.** *Fb:* (*Rugby*) **d. goal,** drop-goal *m*, *pl.* drop-goals. **4.** *Cu: U.S:* **d. egg,** œuf poché.

dropper ['drɔpər], *s.* **1.** *Ch: Med: etc:* compte-gouttes *m inv*; *Cu:* stilligoutte *m*; **eye d.,** compte-gouttes pour les yeux. **2.** *Fish:* bout *m* de ligne. **3.** *NAm:* voleur armé; bandit *m*.

dropper-in ['drɔpə'rin], *s.* visiteur, -euse, inattendu(e).

dropping ['drɔpiŋ], *s.* **1.** (*a*) dégouttement *m* (d'un liquide); **d. bottle,** flacon *m* compte-gouttes; **d. tube,** pipette *f*, compte-gouttes *m inv*; *Cu:* stilligoutte *m*; (*b*) descente *f*, chute *f* (d'un objet); abaissement *m*, baisse *f*, chute (des prix); suppression *f* (d'un mot); abandon *m* (d'un projet); *Med:* descente, abaissement (de la matrice); *Typ:* chevauchage *m* (des caractères); (*c*) *Husb:* **d. (of young),** part *m*, mise *f* bas; agnelage *m*, vêlage *m*, etc.; (*d*) *Aut: etc:* **d. of the body, of the frame,** surbaissement *m* du châssis; (*e*) *Av:* lâchage *m*, largage *m* (d'un parachutiste, de colis); **d. site, d. zone,** zone *f* de largage, de droppage; *Mil:* **d. angle,** angle *m* de largage des bombes, de bombardement, de visée. **2.** *pl.* **droppings** (*a*) gouttes *fpl*; égoutture *f*; (*b*) (*of animals*) fiente *f*; (*of boars, wolves*) laissées *fpl*; (*of stags*) fumées *fpl*; (*of deer*) moquette *f*; (*of sheep*) crottes *fpl*.

dropping in ['drɔpiŋ'in], *s.* (*of visitors*) arrivée inattendue.

dropping off ['drɔpiŋ'ɔf], *s.* **1.** chute *f* (des feuilles). **2.** diminution *f* (de l'assistance). **3.** assoupissement *m*.

dropping out ['drɔpiŋ'aut], *s.* (*a*) abandon *m* (d'un cours, etc.); (*b*) désinsertion sociale.

dropseed ['drɔpsi:d], *s. Bot:* sporobolus *m*.

dropsical ['drɔpsik(ə)l], *a. Med:* hydropique.

dropsied ['drɔpsid], *a. F:* hydropique.

dropsy ['drɔpsi], *s. Med:* hydropisie *f*; **abdominal d.,** hydropisie abdominale; ascite *f*.

dropwort ['drɔpwə:t], *s. Bot:* filipendule *f*; **water d.,** ciguë aquatique, ciguë vireuse; œnanthe *m*.

drosera ['drɔsərə], *s. Bot:* droserè *f*, drosera *m*, rossolis *m*, rossolie *f*.

Droseraceae [drɔsə'reisii:], *s.pl. Bot:* droséracées *f*.

droshki ['drɔʃki], **droski** ['drɔski], *s. Veh:* droschki *m*.

drosometer [drɔ'sɔmitər], *s. Meteor:* drosomètre *m*.

drosophila [drɔ'sɔfilə], *s. Ent:* drosophile *f*, mouche *f* du vinaigre.

Drosophilidae [drɔsɔ'filidi:], *s.pl. Ent:* drosophilidés *m*.

drosophyllum [drɔsə'filəm], *s. Bot:* drosophyllum *m*.

dross[1] [drɔs], *s.* **1.** (*a*) *Metall:* scories *fpl*, crasse *f*, écume *f*, laitier *m*, *P:* chiasse *f* (du métal en fusion); (*at bottom of furnace*) cochon *m*, mâchefer *m*, crasses; (*b*) **anvil d.,** battitures *fpl*; (*c*) *Coal Min:* schlamm *m*. **2.** (*a*) impuretés *fpl* (de toutes sortes); déchet *m*; (*b*) *F:* rebut *m* (de la production littéraire, etc.).

dross[2], *v.tr. Metall:* écrémer, écumer (le métal en fusion).

drossing ['drɔsiŋ], *s. Metall:* écumage *m* (du métal en fusion).

drossy ['drɔsi], *a.* **1.** *Metall:* plein de scories; écumeux. **2.** (*a*) impur; (*b*) sans valeur; de rebut.

drought [draut], *s.* **1.** sécheresse *f*; disette *f* d'eau; rareté *f* des pluies; *Meteor:* (*in U.K.*) **absolute d.,** quinze jours avec moins de 0,2 mm de pluie par jour; **partial d.,** vingt-neuf jours dont aucun n'a eu 0,2 mm de pluie. **2.** *Dial:* soif *f*. **3.** *NAm:* manque *m*, disette *f* (de talent, etc.).

droughty ['drauti], *a.* **1.** sec, *f.* sèche; aride. **2.** *Dial:* qui a soif; altéré.

drouth [drauθ, *Scot:* druθ], *s.* **1.** *A: & NAm:* = DROUGHT 1. **2.** *Scot:* (*a*) soif *f*; (*b*) soif d'ivrogne.

drouthy ['drauθi, *Scot:* 'druθi], *a.* **1.** *A: & NAm:* = DROUGHTY 1. **2.** *Scot:* (*a*) qui a soif; altéré; (*b*) *F:* ivrogne.

drove [drouv], *s.* **1.** (*a*) troupeau *m* (de bœufs, etc.) en marche; (*b*) flots *mpl*, multitude *f*, foule *f* (de personnes en marche); **they walk about in droves,** ils se promènent en, par, grandes bandes. **2.** *Tls:* ciseau *m* large (de tailleur de pierres).

drover ['drouvər], *s.* conducteur *m* de bestiaux, de moutons; **(cattle) d.,** toucheur *m* de bestiaux, de bœufs; bouvier *m*.

drown [draun], *v.tr. & i.* **1.** noyer; **to d. oneself,** se noyer; **to be drowned (by accident),** se noyer, être noyé; **to stand idly by while somebody drowns,** rester à ne rien faire pendant que quelqu'un se noie; **he (was) nearly drowned,** il a failli se noyer; **drowned at sea,** noyé en mer; **to d. one's sorrow (in drink),** noyer son chagrin dans la boisson, dans son verre; s'étourdir dans la boisson; **they soon drowned their quarrel,** leurs libations leur firent bientôt oublier leur querelle; *F: A:* **to d. the miller,** mettre trop d'eau dans son vin; noyer son vin, son whisky. **2.** (*a*) inonder, submerger (une prairie); *F:* **eyes drowned in tears,** yeux noyés de larmes; (*b*) **to be drowned out,** être chassé (de sa demeure, etc.) par l'inondation. **3.** étouffer, couvrir (un son); **the noise of the waterfall drowns the voice,** le bruit de la cascade couvre la voix.

drowned [draund], *a.* **1.** noyé; **a d. man, woman,** un noyé, une noyée; *F:* **he came home like a d. rat,** il est rentré trempé comme une soupe. **2. d. lands,** terrains noyés, inondés; *Geog:* **d. valley,** vallée ennoyée.

drowning[1] ['drauniŋ], *a.* **a d. man,** un homme qui se noie; *Prov:* **a d. man will catch, clutch, at a straw,** un homme qui se noie s'attache à un brin de paille, se retient à tout.

drowning[2], *s.* **1. (case of) d.,** noyade *f*; **death by d.,** asphyxie *f* par submersion; **to save s.o. from d.,** sauver qn qui se noyait. **2.** inondation *f* (des champs).

drowse [drauz]. **1.** *v.i.* somnoler, s'assoupir; **to d. away, off,** s'assoupir. **2.** *v.tr.* (*a*) assoupir (qn); (*b*) **to d. the time away,** passer le temps à dormir, à somnoler.

drowsily ['drauzili], *adv.* d'un air, d'un ton, somnolent; à demi endormi.

drowsiness ['drauzinis], *s.* somnolence *f*, assoupissement *m*.

drowsy ['drauzi], *a.* assoupi, somnolent; **to grow d.,** s'assoupir; **to be, feel, d.,** avoir envie de dormir; avoir sommeil; *P:* taper de l'œil; **to make s.o. d.,** assoupir qn; **d. afternoon,** après-midi lourd.

drub [drʌb], *v.tr.* **(drubbed)** (*a*) battre, rosser (qn, l'ennemi); moudre (qn de coups); *F:* flanquer une raclée, une tripotée, à (qn); *A:* frotter l'échine à (qn); (*b*) **to d. sth. into s.o., out of s.o.,** faire entrer qch. de force dans la tête de qn; tirer qch. de qn à coups de bâton.

drubbing ['drʌbiŋ], *s.* (*a*) volée *f* de coups (de bâton, de poing); *F:* tripotée *f*; *P:* peignée *f*, trempée *f*; **to give s.o. a d.,** flanquer, administrer, une raclée à qn; bourrer qn de coups; *P:* secouer les puces à qn; (*b*) défaite *f*; **to give an opponent, the enemy, a d.,** battre un adversaire, l'ennemi, à plates coutures; infliger à l'ennemi une défaite écrasante.

drudge[1] [drʌdʒ], *s.* femme *f*, homme *m*, de peine; *F:* cheval *m* de bât; **to lead the life of a d.,** mener une vie d'esclave; **the d. of the household,** le chien, le souffre-douleur *inv*, de la maison; la cendrillon.

drudge[2], *v.i.* trimer, peiner; **to d. and slave,** mener une vie de forçat, de galérien; *v.tr.* **to d. away the best years of one's life,** sacrifier les meilleures années de sa vie à un travail ingrat.

drudgery ['drʌdʒəri], *s.* travail pénible, ingrat; besognes fastidieuses; corvée(s) *f*(*pl*); métier *m* d'esclave; **to go**

back to d., reprendre le collier de misère; **the d. of the office,** l'esclavage *m* du bureau.

drug[1] [drʌg], *s.* **1.** produit *m* pharmaceutique; drogue *f*; *Med: F:* **to be doing drugs,** faire ses études de pharmacologie; *F:* faire sa pharmacie. **2.** *(a)* **(narcotic) d.,** narcotique *m*, stupéfiant *m*; **to take drugs,** faire usage de stupéfiants, s'adonner aux stupéfiants; se droguer; **d. addict,** *F:* **d. fiend,** toxicomane *mf*; narcomane *mf*; cocaïnomane *mf*, héroïnomane *mf*, morphinomane *mf*, opiomane *mf*, etc.; **d. addiction, d. habit,** toxicomanie *f*, narcomanie *f*; cocaïnomanie *f*, héroïnomanie *f*, etc.; **d. traffic,** *F:* **d. pushing, d. peddling,** trafic *m* des stupéfiants; *(b) F:* **the truth d.,** le sérum de vérité. **3.** *(of goods)* **to be a d. on the market,** être invendable.

drug[2], *v.tr.* **(drugged) 1.** *(a)* donner, administrer, faire prendre, un narcotique, des stupéfiants, à (qn); *F:* endormir (qn); doper (un cheval); **to d. oneself,** (i) prendre un narcotique; (ii) *(habitually)* faire usage de stupéfiants; s'adonner aux stupéfiants; *(b) v.i.* **to d.,** faire usage de stupéfiants, s'adonner aux stupéfiants. **2. they had drugged his wine,** on avait mis, mêlé, un narcotique à son vin; *F:* on avait mis quelque chose dans son vin; **drugged cigarette,** cigarette narcotisée. **3.** *Lit:* rassasier; **drugged with pleasure,** rassasié de plaisirs.

drugger [drʌgər], *s.* toxicomane *mf*, narcomane *mf*.

drugget ['drʌgit], *s.* **1.** *Tex:* *(a)* droguet *m*; *(b) A:* bure *f*. **2.** carpette *f*, saut-de-lit *m* *(pl.* sauts-de-lit) de droguet.

druggist ['drʌgist], *s.* pharmacien *m*; **wholesale d.,** pharmacien en gros; droguiste *m*.

drugstore ['drʌgstɔːr], *s.* **1.** *NAm:* magasin *m* où l'on vend des produits pharmaceutiques, des articles de toilette, de la confiserie, de la papeterie, des journaux, et où l'on sert des repas rapides, *F:* drugstore *m*. **2.** *occ.* pharmacie *f*.

druid ['dru(ː)id], *s.m.* druide.

druidical [dru'idik(ə)l], *a.* druidique.

druidism ['dru(ː)idizm], *s.* druidisme *m*.

drum[1] [drʌm], *s.* **1.** *(a) Mus:* tambour *m*, caisse *f*; **big d., bass d.,** grosse caisse; **long d., tenor d.,** caisse roulante; **muffled d.,** tambour voilé; **d. parchment,** peau *f* de tambour; *Mil:* **the drums,** la batterie; *A:* **to follow the d.,** être soldat; **d. beat,** coup *m*, roulement *m*, batterie, de tambour; **to play, beat, the d.,** battre du tambour; *F:* **to bang, beat, the (big) d.,** faire du battage, battre la (grosse) caisse; faire de la réclame; faire de la publicité **(for s.o., sth.,** pour qn, qch.); *(in front of travelling booth)* battre la chamade; **with drums beating,** tambour(s) battant(s); **to announce sth. by beat of d.,** annoncer qch. au son du tambour; *NAm: F:* **d. beater,** agent *m* de publicité; *(b) Z:* caisse sonore (du singe hurleur). **2.** *(a)* tambourinage *m* (de la pluie contre les vitres, etc.); *(b)* **the d. of the woodpecker,** le tambourinage du pic-vert. **3.** *Anat:* (caisse, membrane *f* du) tympan. **4.** *(a)* tonneau *m* en fer, fût *m*, tonnelet *m*, récipient *m* cylindrique (pour fruits, etc.); gonne *f* (à goudron); bidon *m*, tambour, estagnon *m* (à huile); **air d.,** réservoir *m* d'air comprimé; *(b) Meteor: Nau:* **(storm) d.,** cylindre *m* de tempête. **5.** *Arch:* tambour (d'une colonne); vase *m* (d'un chapiteau). **6.** *(a) Mec.E: etc:* tambour, barillet *m*; **spring d.,** barillet de ressort, de mouvement d'horlogerie; *Mch:* **d. of a pressure gauge,** barillet d'un indicateur de pression; **d. cam,** came *f* à cylindre, à tambour; **d. drive,** commande *f*, entraînement *m*, transmission *f*, par tambour; *El:* **d. switch,** interrupteur *m* à tambour; *Tex:* **warp-folding d.,** tambourin *m*; *Sm.a:* **ammunition d.,** barillet; **d. magazine,** chargeur-tambour *m*, *pl.* chargeurs-tambours; **d. backsight,** hausse *f* à tambour; *(b) Civ.E: etc:* tambour, cylindre (pour lavage, malaxage, mélange, etc.); *Tan:* turbulent *m*; **concrete mixing d.,** (tambour, cylindre) mélangeur *m* à béton; bétonnière *f*; *Min: etc:* **sizing d., sorting d.,** tambour à assortir; trommel *m* classeur; *Mch:* **d. of a steam turbine,** tambour d'une turbine à vapeur; **steam d.** *(of tubular boiler)*, collecteur supérieur; **water d.** *(of tubular boiler)*, collecteur inférieur; *Dy:* **steaming d.,** tonneau *m* de vaporisage; *(c)* tambour, cylindre, touret *m* (de treuil); tambour (de moulinet); **capstan d.,** tambour, cloche *f*, de cabestan; **cable d.,** tambour, bobine *f*, dévidoir *m*, touret (pour câble électrique); **wire d.,** bobine à, de, fil; **d. barrow,** dévidoir; **d. shaft,** arbre *m* de, du, tambour; *El:* **d. armature,** induit *m* à tambour; **d. winding,** enroulement *m* en tambour; **d.-wound,** enroulé en tambour; *(d)* **d. (recorder),** enregistreur *m* à tambour; *Elcs:* **magnetic d.,** tambour magnétique; **programme d.,** tambour (de) programme; **d. memory,** mémoire *f* à tambour (magnétique); **d. speed,** (i) vitesse *f* de rotation du tambour; (ii) vitesse de balayage, d'exploration; *(e) Artil:* **deflection d.,** tambour des dérives; **elevation d., sight d.,** tambour des hausses; **site(-angle) d.,** tambour de site; **range d.,** tambour de portée. **7.** *A:* assemblée *f*; raout *m*. **8.** *Austr:* baluchon *m*, paquet *m* (de chemineau). **9.** *Austr: P:* tuyau *m*; **to give s.o. the d.,** tuyauter qn. **10.** *P:* logement *m*.

drum[2], *v.* **(drummed)**

I. *v.i.* *(a)* tambouriner; battre du tambour; *F:* *(of pers., rain)* **to d. on the window panes,** tambouriner sur les vitres; **her fingers were drumming on the tablecloth,** ses doigts pianotaient, tapotaient, sur la nappe; elle battait le rappel sur la nappe; *(b) (of insects)* bourdonner; *(of snipe)* crier; *(c) (of car, etc.)* ferrailler, tambouriner; *(d) NAm:* **to d. (for custom(ers)),** (i) voyager pour le commerce; (ii) faire de la réclame.

II. *v.tr.* **1. to d. a tune on sth.,** tambouriner un air sur qch.; **to d. one's feet on the floor,** tambouriner sur le plancher avec les pieds; **to d. sth. into s.o.'s head,** enfoncer, fourrer, qch. dans la tête de qn; **to d. sth. into s.o.'s ears,** corner qch. aux oreilles de qn; seriner qch. à qn. **2.** enfutailler, enfûter, embariller, entonner; *Leath:* agiter (des peaux) dans un turbulent. **3.** *Austr: P:* **to d. s.o. (up),** tuyauter qn.

III. *(compound verbs)* **1. drum out,** *v.tr.* *(a) Mil:* expulser (un militaire) au son du tambour; dégrader (un militaire); *(b) F:* expulser (qn d'un club, etc.) avec ignominie.

2. drum up. *(a) v.tr.* (i) racoler (des partisans); *F:* faire le rappel de (ses amis); **to d. up recruits,** faire du recrutement; **to d. up customers,** rechercher de la clientèle; racoler des clients; (ii) *Austr: P:* tuyauter (qn); *(b) v.i. P:* (i) faire le thé (en plein air); = faire le jus; (ii) (faire) réchauffer la marmite (en plein air).

drum-corporal ['drʌm'kɔːp(ə)rəl], *s.* *Mil:* caporal-tambour *m*, *pl.* caporaux-tambours.

drumfire ['drʌmfaiər], *s.* *Artil:* tir *m* de barrage; feu roulant.

drumfish ['drʌmfiʃ], *s.* *Ich:* tambour *m*.

drumhead ['drʌmhed], *s.* **1.** *(a)* peau *f* de tambour; *(b)* dessus *m* de tambour; *Mil:* **d. service,** office divin en plein air. **2.** *Nau:* tête *f*, chapeau *m* (de cabestan).

drumlin ['drʌmlin], *s.* *Geog:* drumlin *m*.

drum-major [drʌm'meidʒər], *s.* *Mil:* tambour-major *m*, *pl.* tambours-majors.

drum-majorette ['drʌmmeidʒə'ret], *s.f.* *U.S:* majorette.

drummer ['drʌmər], *s.* **1.** *(a)* tambour *m* (qui joue du tambour), *Mus:* qui fait la partie de tambour); *(player of kettle-drum)* timbalier *m*; *Mil: P:* tapin *m*; *(jazz)* batteur *m*; **big d.,** joueur *m* de la grosse caisse; *F:* la grosse caisse; **d. boy,** petit tambour; *(b) A:* tambourineur *m* (de nouvelles, etc.). **2.** *Com: esp. U.S:* commis voyageur; *(in town)* placier *m*.

drumming ['drʌmiŋ], *s.* **1.** *(a)* tambourinage *m*, bruit *m* de tambour; *(b)* bourdonnement *m* (d'un insecte, des oreilles); *(c) Orn:* tambourinage *m* (du pic épeiche); *(d) F:* ferraillement *m*, tambourinement *m*, bruit de ferraille (d'une vieille auto, etc.). **2.** *(a)* métier *m* de commis voyageur; *(b)* recherche *f* de la clientèle; racolage *m* des clients.

drumming out ['drʌmiŋ'aut], *s.* *(a) Mil:* expulsion *f* (d'un militaire) au son du tambour; *(b)* expulsion (de qn d'un club, etc.) avec ignominie.

drumming up ['drʌmiŋ'ʌp], *s.* racolage *m*, recrutement *m*.

Drummond ['drʌmənd], *Pr.n.* **D. light,** lumière *f* Drummond; lumière oxhydrique.

drumstick ['drʌmstik], *s.* **1.** *Mus:* baguette *f* de tambour, de timbale; **bass-d.,** tampon *m*, mailloche *f*; **d. holder** *(on drum)*, porte-baguette(s) *m*. **2.** *Cu:* pilon *m*, (bas *m* de la) cuisse (d'une volaille); **baby d.,** mini-pilon *m* de l'aile. **3.** *pl. F:* **drumsticks,** jambes fluettes; *F:* allumettes *f*.

drunk [drʌŋk]. **1.** *a.* *(a)* ivre, gris; soûl **(with,** de); **to be d.,** être pris de boisson; *P:* être schlass, bourré; avoir, tenir, une cuite; **to get, drink oneself, d.,** s'enivrer, se soûler; *P:* prendre une cuite, se cuiter; **to make s.o. d.,** griser, *F:* soûler, qn; **dead d.,** ivre mort; **blind d.,** soûl perdu; **d. as a fiddler, as a lord,** soûl comme un Polonais; plein comme une huître; *Jur:* **d. and disorderly, d. and incapable** = en état d'ivresse manifeste dans un lieu public; *(b)* enivré, grisé **(with opium, success,** par l'opium, le succès); **d. with blood, joy, tiredness,** ivre de sang, de joie, de fatigue. **2.** *s.* *(police-court term & F:)* homme pris de boisson; **the Saturday night drunks,** les ivrognes *m* du samedi soir. **3.** *s. F:* *(drunken bout)* soûlographie *f*; ribote *f*.

drunkard ['drʌŋkəd], *s.* alcoolique *mf*; ivrogne *m*, ivrognesse *f*; *F:* pochard *m*, poivrot *m*.

drunken ['drʌŋk(ə)n], *a.* **1. d. man,** (i) homme ivre; (ii) ivrogne *m*, soûlard *m*; **d. brawl,** querelle *f* d'ivrognes. **2. d. state,** état *m* d'ivresse, d'ébriété; *Jur:* **d. driving,** conduite *f* en état d'ivresse. **3.** *(a)* **d. chimney pot,** pot *m* de cheminée hors d'aplomb; *(b) Mec.E:* **d. screw,** excentrique *m* à gorge hélicoïdale; **d. cutter,** porte-lames *m inv* elliptique.

drunkenly ['drʌŋkənli], *adv.* **1.** en ivrogne; comme un ivrogne. **2. chimney leaning d. over the street,** cheminée penchée hors d'aplomb au-dessus de la rue.

drunkenness ['drʌŋk(ə)nnis], *s.* **1.** ivresse *f*. **2.** *(habitual)* intempérance *f*, ivrognerie *f*.

drunkometer [drʌŋ'kɔmitər], *s.* *NAm:* (appareil *m* de l')alcotest *m*.

drupaceous [dru'peiʃəs], *a.* *Bot:* drupacé.

drupe [druːp], *s.* *Bot:* drupe *m*.

drupel ['druːpl], **drupelet** ['druːplit], *s.* *Bot:* drupéole *m*, fructule *m*.

druse[1] [druːz], *s.* *Geol:* druse *f*, craque *f*, géode *f*; poche *f* à cristaux.

Druse[2], *s.* *Ethn: Geog:* Druse *m*, Druze *m*.

drusy ['druːzi], *a.* *Geol:* drusillaire.

dry[1] [drai], *a.* **(drier, driest)** sec, *f.* sèche. **1.** *(a) (of well, etc.)* tari, à sec; *(of pump)* désamorcé; *(of country)* aride; **d. land,** terre *f* ferme; **d. hole,** puits *m* stérile; **d. harbour,** port asséchant à basse mer; **d. nurse,** nourrice sèche; sevreuse; bonne *f* d'enfant, nurse *f*; **d. cow,** vache sèche; **to pump a well, d.,** épuiser l'eau d'un puits; assécher un puits; **the pump is d.,** la pompe est franche; **to make a valve quite d.,** rendre une soupape étanche; **to boil a liquid d.,** (faire) bouillir un liquide jusqu'à évaporation complète; **to wring linen d.,** essorer le linge; **to run d., go d.,** *(of channel)* se dessécher, (s')assécher; *(of spring, well)* s'épuiser, (se) tarir; *(of pump)* se désamorcer; *(of machinery)* manquer d'huile; manquer de graissage; **well run d.,** puits à sec; *(of speaker, writer)* **he soon runs d.,** il a l'haleine courte; **at the end of five minutes he had run d.,** au bout de cinq minutes il était à sec, au bout de son rouleau; **d. weather,** temps sec; **it has been d. (weather) for a week,** il fait sec depuis huit jours; **d. cold,** froid sec; **d. spell,** (i) période *f* de sécheresse; (ii) *Meteor:* *(in U.K.)* suite de quinze jours dont aucun n'a eu plus d'un millimètre de pluie; **d. farming,** dry farming *m*; *s.* *Austr:* **the d.,** (i) la saison sèche; (ii) le désert; *s.* **to stay in the d.,** rester au sec, à couvert; *Com:* **d. wine,** vin sec; **medium d. wine,** vin demi-sec, *pl* demi-secs; **extra d. champagne,** champagne brut; **d. juice,** suc concret; **d. toast,** rôtie *f* sans beurre; *(b) Ind: etc:* **d. process,** procédé *m* par voie sèche; **d. crushing,** broyage *m* à sec; *Metall:* **d. casting, d. moulding,** moulage *m* à sec, par voie sèche; *Const:* **d. masonry,** maçonnerie *f* à sec; **d. walling,** (i) murs *mpl* en pierres sèches; (ii) construction *f* en pierres sèches; *Ch:* **d. assay(ing),** essai *m*, analyse *f*, par voie sèche; *Mch:* **d. steam,** vapeur sèche; *Phot: A:* **d. plate,** plaque sèche; *El:* **d. joint,** mauvais contact à cause d'une faute de soudure; *(c)* **to put on d. clothing,** mettre des vêtements secs; **my child was d. at two years,** mon enfant était propre à deux ans; **d. wash,** blanchissage non calandré; **d. bread,** pain sec; **to be kept d.,** craint l'humidité; craint la pluie; à préserver de l'humidité; *F:* **as d. as a chip, as a bone, as tinder,** sec comme une allumette; *Fish:* **d. fly,** mouche sèche, flottante; *(d) F:* *(of pers.)* **to be, feel, d.,** avoir le gosier sec, la gorge sèche; avoir soif; *F:* avoir la pépie; **d. work,** travail qui donne soif, *F:* la pépie; *(e) Geol:* **d. valley,** vallée morte. **2.** *F:* **d. country,** pays sec (où les boissons alcooliques sont prohibées); **these States were d.,** ces États avaient le régime sec; **to go d.,** prohiber la consommation des boissons alcooliques; **to vote d.,** voter pour la prohibition; *s. F:* **a d.,** un prohibitionniste. **3.** *(a)* aride, fade, sans intérêt; **a d. subject,** un sujet aride; *(b)* **the d. facts,** les faits purs et simples; les simples faits. **4.** *(a)* **he has a d. manner,** il est d'une approche froide; *(b)* **d. smile,** sourire teinté d'ironie; **he gave a d. laugh,** il eut un petit rire ironique; **to answer with d. sarcasm,** répondre d'un air de pince-sans-rire; **d. humour,** esprit caustique, mordant; **a man of d. humour,** un pince-sans-rire; *(c)* **d. reception,** accueil peu cordial; **he was very d. with us,** il a été plutôt distant; il a manqué de cordialité. **5. d. run,** (i) *Mil:* exercices *mpl* d'entraînement avec munitions à blanc; (ii) coup *m* d'essai; *Elcs:* **d. running,** contrôle *m* de programmation; *W.Tel: Can:* **d. rehearsal,** répétition *f* sans technique, sans les décors. **6.** *Com:* *(a)* **d. money,** argent sec, liquide; *(b)* **d. goods,** (i) marchandises sèches; (ii) *NAm:* articles *mpl* de nouveauté; étoffes *fpl*, tissus *mpl*; mercerie *f*; **d. goods store,** magasin *m* de nouveautés; *Nau:* **d. cargo,** cargaison sèche.

dry[2], *v.* **(dried** [draid])

I. *v.tr.* sécher (qch.); faire sécher (le linge); *(with spin-drier)* essorer (le linge); ressuyer (la chaux, etc.); charquer (la viande à conserver); délaiter (le beurre); *Ind:* **to d. by heat, electricity,** sécher par le chauffage, électriquement; **to d. sth. with a cloth,** essuyer qch. avec un torchon; **to d. (up) the dishes,** essuyer la vaisselle, les plats; **it's my turn to d. (up),** c'est à moi d'essuyer le vaisselle; **to d. one's eyes,** s'essuyer les yeux; **to d. (away) one's tears,** sécher ses larmes; **the wind has dried (up) the roads,** le vent a séché, essuyé, ressuyé, les chemins; **wind that dries (up) the skin,** vent qui dessèche, ratatine, la peau; **to d. (up) secretions,** épuiser, supprimer, des sécrétions; **to d. (up) land,** étancher le terrain; **to d. (up) a pump, a spring,** (i) tarir une pompe, une source; (ii) désamorcer une pompe; *Husb:* **to d. (off) a cow,** faire tarir, faire sécher, une vache.

II. *v.i.* **1.** se sécher, se dessécher; (*of road, etc.*) se ressuyer; **to put sth. out to d.,** mettre qch. à sécher dehors; **ink that dries black,** encre qui vire au noir en séchant; **the streets have dried (up),** les rues sont sèches. **2.** *Husb:* (*of cow*) tarir, se sécher.

III. (*compound verbs*) **1. dry off, out,** (*a*) *v.tr.* faire évaporer (l'eau, etc.); (*b*) *v.i.* (*of moisture*) s'évaporer, sécher; (*c*) (i) *v.i.* (*of alcoholic, drug addict*) **to d. out,** subir un cours de désintoxication; (ii) *v.tr.* **to d. out an alcoholic,** faire subir un cours de désintoxication à un alcoolique.

2. dry up. (*a*) *v.i.* (i) (*of well, pool, etc.*) se dessécher, (s')assécher, tarir; **the well has dried up,** le puits est à sec; **little dried-up man,** petit homme sec; (ii) (*of author, etc.*) épuiser son inspiration; (iii) *F:* (*of speaker, etc.*) cesser de parler, se taire; rester court; rester en carafe; **he never dries up on this subject,** il est intarissable sur ce sujet; *P:* **d. up!** la ferme! ta bouche! (*b*) *v.tr. see* DRY[2] **I.**

dryad ['draiæd, -əd], *s.f. Myth:* dryade.

dryas ['draiəs], *s. Bot:* dryade *f.*

dryasdust ['draiəz'dʌst]. **1.** *s.* auteur prolixe et ennuyeux; pédant *m.* **2.** *a.* sec, aride, dépourvu d'intérêt.

dry-bulb ['draibʌlb], *a.* **d.-b. thermometer,** thermomètre à boule sèche; thermomètre sec.

dry-clean ['drai'kli:n], *v.tr.* nettoyer à sec; dégraisser (des vêtements).

dry-cleaner ['drai'kli:nər], *s.* nettoyeur *m* à sec; **the dry-cleaner's,** *F:* le pressing.

dry cleaning ['drai'kli:niŋ], *s.* nettoyage *m* à sec; dégraissage *m.*

dry-cure ['drai'kjuər], *v.tr.* saler et fumer (la viande).

dry-dock ['drai'dɔk]. **1.** *v.tr.* mettre (un navire) en cale sèche. **2.** *v.i.* (*of ship*) entrer, passer, en cale sèche.

dryer ['draiər], *s.* = DRIER.

dry-eyed ['drai'aid], *a.* **to look on d.-e.,** regarder d'un œil sec.

dry-fallen ['drai'fɔ:lən], *a. For:* (bois) mort.

dry-foot(ed) ['draifut(id)], *a. & adv.* à pied sec.

dry-grind ['drai'graind], *v.tr.* (*p.p. & p.t.* **dry-ground** ['drai'graund]) broyer à sec.

drying[1] ['draiiŋ], *a.* **1.** (vent, etc.) desséchant. **2.** **(quick-)d. oil, varnish,** huile siccative, vernis siccatif.

drying[2], *s.* **1.** séchage *m*; assèchement *m*, dessèchement *m*; (*with a cloth*) essuyage *m*; *Ind:* dessiccation *f* (du bois, de la viande, etc.); *Husb:* délaitement *m* (du beurre); **d. in the open air,** séchage à l'air; **vacuum d.,** séchage par le vide; **preliminary d.,** préséchage *m*; **d. apparatus,** séchoir *m*, sécherie *f*, sécheuse *f*; *Husb:* délaiteuse *f*; **d. room,** (i) *Laund:* séchoir *m* à linge; étendoir *m* à linge; (ii) *Ind:* chambre chaude; étuve *f* (à sécher); (iii) *Husb:* (*for cheese*) haloir *m*; *Tan:* **d. house,** penderie *f* (des peaux); **d. floor,** aire *f* de séchage; **d. ground, d. yard,** sécherie *f*, étendage *m*, étendoir *m*; *Dy:* **d. pole,** tendoir *m*; *Laund:* **d. cabinet,** armoire *f* sèche-linge; *Ind:* **d. cupboard, d. closet,** étuve, chambre chaude; **d. rack, d. drum,** châssis *m*, tambour *m*, de séchage; (*for fruit, etc.*) **d. factory,** séchage; (*for tobacco*) **d. barn,** suerie *f*; *Paperm:* **hot d. cylinders,** cylindres sécheurs. **2.** (*of varnish, etc.*) **d. quality,** siccativité *f.*

drying out ['draiiŋ'aut], *s.* **1.** assèchement *m*, dessèchement *m.* **2.** désintoxication *f* (d'un alcoolique).

drying up ['draiiŋ'ʌp], *s.* **1.** tarissement *m* (d'un cours d'eau, etc.). **2.** essuyage *m* (de la vaisselle).

dryly ['draili], *adv.* **1.** d'un ton sec; sèchement. **2.** avec une pointe d'ironie contenue; **to answer d.,** répondre d'un air de pince-sans-rire.

dryness ['drainəs, -nis], *s.* **1.** sécheresse *f* (d'une région); aridité *f* (du sol); sécheresse (du temps). **2.** sécheresse, sévérité *f* (de ton); aridité (d'un discours); causticité *f* (de l'esprit). **3. to evaporate a solution to d.,** évaporer une solution jusqu'à siccité *f.*

dry-nurse ['drai'nə:s], *v.tr.* **1.** élever (un enfant) au biberon. **2.** *F:* servir de mentor à (qn).

dryobalanops [draiou'bælənɔps], *s. Bot:* dryobalanops *m.*

dryopithecus [draioupi'θi:kəs], *s. Paleont:* dryopithèque *m*, dryopithecus *m.*

dryopteris [drai'ɔptəris], *s. Bot:* dryopteris *m.*

dry point ['draipɔint], *s. Engr:* **1.** *Tls:* pointe sèche. **2.** (*process or etched engraving*) gravure *f* à la pointe sèche; pointe-sèche *f*, *pl.* pointes-sèches.

dry-point, *v.tr.* exécuter (une gravure) à la pointe sèche.

dry rot ['drai'rɔt], *s.* carie sèche, pourriture sèche (du bois); *F:* (le) champignon.

dry-salt ['drai'sɔ:lt], *v.tr.* saler (de la viande) à sec.

drysalter [drai'sɔ:ltər], *s. O:* (*a*) marchand *m* de salaisons, de conserves au vinaigre, etc.; (*b*) marchand de produits chimiques, de couleurs; droguiste *m.*

drysaltery [drai'sɔ:ltəri], *s. O:* (*a*) produits *mpl* chimiques; (*b*) droguerie *f.*

dryshod ['draiʃɔd], *a. & adv.* à pied sec.

dry-topped ['draitɔpt], *a.* (arbre) mort en cime, couronné.

dual[1] ['dju(:)əl]. **1.** *a.* double; **d.-purpose,** (voiture, etc.) mixte, à deux fins; *I.C.E:* **d. ignition,** double allumage *m*; *Aut:* **d. wheels,** roues jumelées; *Av:* **d. wheel (assembly),** diabolo *m*; *Aut: Av: etc:* **d. control (system),** double-commande *f*, *pl.* doubles-commandes; **d.-control car, plane,** voiture *f*, avion *m*, à double commande; *Cin:* **d. programme,** programme *m* double, à deux longs métrages; *Psy:* **d. personality,** dédoublement *m* de la personnalité; personnalité simultanée; *Elcs:* **d. loudspeakers,** haut-parleurs accouplés; **d.-track tape,** bande *f* à deux pistes; *Cmptr:* **d. processor computer,** ordinateur *m* biprocesseur; **d. operation,** opération inverse (booléenne). **2.** *a. & s. Gram:* **d. (number),** duel (*m*). **3.** *a. Mth:* (nombre) dual.

dual[2], *v.tr.* **(dualled)** (re)construire (une route) en route à double piste.

dualin ['dju(:)əlin], *s. Exp:* dualine *f.*

dualism ['dju(:)əlizm], *s.* **1.** dualité *f.* **2.** *Phil:* dualisme *m.*

dualist ['dju(:)əlist], *s. Phil:* dualiste *m.*

dualistic [dju(:)ə'listik], *a.* **1.** *Phil:* dualiste. **2.** *Ch: A:* (notation, etc.) dualistique.

duality [dju(:)'æliti], *s.* dualité *f*; dédoublement *m* (de la personnalité, etc.).

dub[1] [dʌb], *v.tr.* **(dubbed) 1. to d. s.o. (a) knight,** armer, adouber, qn chevalier; donner l'accolade à qn. **2.** *Leath:* préparer (le cuir) avec le dégras. **3.** *Fish:* **to d. a fly,** monter une mouche (artificielle).

dub[2], *v.tr. Cin:* doubler (un film); postsynchroniser (un film en langue étrangère).

dub[3], *s. Elcs:* copie *f* (d'un enregistrement).

dub[4], *v.tr. & i. P:* **to d. up (a sum of money),** payer, *P:* cracher (une somme d'argent); **to d. in,** payer son écot, *P:* cracher.

dubbin[1] ['dʌbin], *s. Leath:* dégras *m.*

dubbin[2], *v.tr.* enduire (des chaussures) de dégras.

dubbing[1] ['dʌbiŋ], *s.* **1.** *Leath:* dégras *m.* **2.** *Fish:* matériel *m* de montage (de mouches artificielles).

dubbing[2], *s. Cin:* doublage *m*; postsynchronisation *f* (en langue étrangère).

dubiety [dju(:)'baiəti], *s. Lit:* (sentiment *m* de) doute *m*; incertitude *f* **(regarding,** à l'égard de).

dubious ['dju:biəs], *a.* **1.** douteux; (*a*) incertain, vague; **d. result,** résultat incertain; **d. light,** lumière douteuse, vague; **d. advantage,** avantage *m* contestable; (*b*) équivoque, louche; **d. honour,** honneur *m* équivoque; **d. company,** compagnie douteuse, louche; **financiers of d. character,** financiers véreux; *Fin:* **d. paper,** papier *m* de valeur douteuse; **shabby clothes and d. linen,** habits râpés et linge douteux. **2.** hésitant; qui doute; **d. expression,** air de doute; **d. as to what he should do,** incertain de, ne sachant trop, ce qu'il devait faire; **to be d. of s.o.'s honesty,** douter de la probité de qn; **I was d. (as to) whether I should interfere,** je me demandais si je devais intervenir; **I am d. about the weather,** je suis incertain du temps qu'il va faire; **we were d. about the scheme,** nous avions des doutes sur le projet.

dubiously ['dju:biəsli], *adv.* d'un air, d'un ton, de doute.

dubiousness ['dju:biəsnis], *s.* **1.** incertitude *f* (du résultat, etc.). **2.** caractère douteux, équivoque *f* (d'un compliment, etc.); *Fin: etc:* valeur douteuse (d'un billet, etc.).

dubitable ['dju:bitəbl], *a. Lit:* douteux.

dubitate ['dju:biteit], *v.i. Lit:* hésiter; rester incertain, indécis.

dubitation [dju:bi'teiʃ(ə)n], *s. Lit:* doute *m*, indécision *f*; *Rh:* dubitation *f.*

dubitative ['dju:bitətiv], *a.* **1.** dubitatif, plein de doute, hésitant. **2.** qui exprime le doute; *Gram:* dubitatif.

dubitatively ['dju:bitətivli], *adv.* dubitativement.

Dubliner ['dʌblinər], *s.* natif, -ive, habitant, -ante, de Dublin.

ducal ['dju:k(ə)l], *a.* ducal, -aux; **d. coronet,** couronne ducale, de duc.

ducally ['dju:kəli], *adv.* (se conduire) à la manière d'un duc; (vêtu) en duc.

ducat ['dʌkət], *s.* **1.** *A.Num:* ducat *m.* **2.** *P: A: & NAm:* billet *m* (d'entrée).

ducatoon [dʌkə'tu:n], *s. A.Num:* ducaton *m*; ducat *m* d'argent.

Duce (the) [ðə'du:tʃi], *s.m. Hist:* le duce.

duchess ['dʌtʃis], *s.* **1.** duchesse. **2.** *P:* (*a*) grande dame; (*b*) **the old d.,** ma femme, *P:* ma moitié, ma vieille, la bourgeoise; (*c*) *O:* **the d.,** maman. **3.** *Hort:* **d. pear,** poire *f* duchesse. **4.** *Paperm:* papier *m* à lettres de format 146 mm × 222 mm.

duchess(e) [dʌ'tʃes], *s.* **d. lace,** (guipure *f*) duchesse *f*; **d. satin,** (satin *m*) duchesse; **d. set,** garniture *f* de coiffeuse (en dentelles, etc.); *Cu:* **d. potatoes,** pommes *f* (de terre) duchesse.

duchy ['dʌtʃi], *s.* **1.** duché *m.* **2. the (Royal) Duchies,** les duchés de Cornouailles et de Lancastre.

duck[1] [dʌk], *s.* **1.** (*a*) (*female of drake*) cane *f*; (*b*) (*generic*) canard *m*; **domestic d.,** canard domestique; **wild d.,** canard sauvage; *Cu:* **d. and green peas,** canard aux petits pois; **Bombay d.,** poisson sec assaisonné de cari; **d. farm,** canarderie *f*; *Sm.a:* **d. gun,** canardière *f*; **d. shot,** plomb *m* à canard; **d. shooting,** chasse *f* aux canards (sauvages); **d. pond,** canardière; barbotière *f*, mare *f* aux canards; *F:* **to look like a dying d. (in a thunderstorm),** faire la carpe pâmée; faire des yeux de merlan frit; **he took to his new life like a d. to water,** il s'adonna à sa vie nouvelle comme s'il était né pour cela; **to take to Latin like a d. to water,** mordre au latin; **criticism runs off him like water off a duck's back,** il est impénétrable à la critique; **fine weather for (the) ducks,** temps *m* de pluie; beau temps pour les grenouilles; **to play at ducks and drakes,** faire des ricochets (sur l'eau); **to play (at) ducks and drakes with one's money, one's life,** gaspiller son argent, jeter son argent par les fenêtres; gâcher sa vie; *F:* **does, can, will, would, a d. swim?** tu parles! *P:* **to have duck's disease,** être courtaud; *NAm: P:* **it was d. soup for him,** pour lui, c'était simple comme bonjour; **he was d. soup for the crooks,** il était un jobard, une poire, pour les escrocs; (*c*) *Orn:* **black d.,** *Fr.C:* canard noir; **black-headed d.,** canard à tête noire; **buffle-headed d.,** garrot *m* albéole; *Fr.C:* petit garrot; **Carolina d.,** carolin *m*; **comb d., nutka d.,** oie *f* à crête, oie caronculée; **ferruginous d.,** fuligule *f* nyroca, canard nyroca; **harlequin d.,** garrot arlequin; *Fr.C:* canard arlequin; **Labrador d.,** *Fr.C:* canard du Labrador; **long-tailed d.,** harelde *f* de Miquelon, canard de Miquelon; *Fr.C:* canard kakawi; **marbled d.,** sarcelle marbrée; **Muscovy d., musk d.,** canard musqué, canard de Barbarie, canard turc; cane du Caire, de Guinée; **mussel d.,** morillon *m*; **Pekin(g) d.,** canard Pékin; **ring-necked d.,** *Fr.C:* morillon à collier; **ruddy d.,** *U.S:* **fool d.,** érismature roux; *Fr.C:* canard roux; **spoonbill d.,** souchet *m*; **steamer d.,** canard vapeur; **surf d.,** macreuse *f* à lunettes; **torrent d.,** merganette *f*; **tree d.,** dendrocygne *m*, canard d'arbre; **fulvous tree d.,** dendrocygne fauve; **white-faced tree d.,** dendrocygne veuf; **tufted d.,** fuligule morillon, canard morillon; **white-headed d.,** canard, érismature *m*, à tête blanche; **wood d.,** (i) (canard) carolin; *Fr.Can:* canard huppé; (ii) *Austr:* oie à crinière. **2.** *F:* (*a*) **a sitting d.,** une cible facile; **dead d.,** (i) pauvre type *m*; (ii) (*pers.*) raté, -ée; (*thg*) fiasco *m*; **lame d.,** (i) malheureux, -euse; (ii) pauvre type; (iii) *St. Exch:* spéculateur insolvable; failli *m*, décavé *m*; (iv) *U.S:* fonctionnaire mis à pied (après une élection); *Can:* **lame d. industry,** industrie qui marche mal, qui risque de faire faillite; (*b*) *F:* **a d. of a child,** un enfant joli à croquer; *O:* **a d. of a hat,** un amour de petit chapeau; **you're a d.!** tu es bien gentille! (*c*) *Com: P:* **what do you want, ducks?** et pour vous, ma petite dame? (*d*) *Cr:* **duck's egg, d. (egg),** zéro *m*; **to make a d.,** faire chou blanc; **to break one's d.,** marquer son premier point.

duck[2], *s. Tex:* coutil *m*; toile fine (pour voiles); toile légère; **cotton d.,** toile à voile coton; *Cost:* **ducks,** (i) pantalon *m*, (ii) complet, blanc, de coutil, de toile; **the crew were in ducks,** l'équipage *m* était en blanc.

duck[3], *s.* **1.** plongeon *m*, bain (inattendu, involontaire). **2.** mouvement instinctif de la tête (pour se dérober à un coup, etc.); *Box:* esquive *f.*

duck[4]. **1.** *v.i.* (*a*) plonger dans l'eau; faire le plongeon; (*of water fowl*) replonger; (*b*) baisser la tête, se baisser (subitement, instinctivement), faire une courbette (pour se dérober à un coup, etc.); *Mil: F:* saluer (les balles, les obus); *Box:* esquiver, éviter, de la tête; (*c*) *Cards:* (*at bridge, etc.*) esquicher. **2.** *v.tr.* (*a*) plonger (qn) dans l'eau, faire faire le plongeon à (qn); *Nau: A:* donner la cale à (un matelot); (*b*) baisser subitement (la tête); (*c*) *F:* se dérober à, esquiver (ses obligations, etc.); **to d. the issue,** s'esquiver, user de faux-fuyants, de fuites.

duck[5], *s. Mil:* voiture amphibie (chiffrée D.U.K.W. par le fabricant).

duckbill[1] ['dʌkbil], *s.* **1.** *Agr:* blé poulard. **2.** *Ich:* spatule *f.* **3.** *Z:* ornithor(h)ynque *m.*

duckbill[2], **duck-billed** ['dʌkbild], *a.* **1.** *Z:* **d. platypus,** platypus *m* à bec de canard; ornithor(h)ynque *m.* **2.** *Metalw:* **d. tongs,** tenaille *f* à bec recourbé, à cornières.

duckboard ['dʌkbɔːd], *s.usu. in pl.* **duckboards,** caillebotis *m*; plancher non glissant.

duckboarded ['dʌkbɔːdid], *a.* (*of walk*) couvert de caillebotis.

ducker ['dʌkər], *s. Orn:* (*a*) cincle plongeur; (*b*) petit grèbe.

duckfooted ['dʌkfutid], *a.* (*of pers.*) aux pieds plats tournés en dehors.

duckhawk ['dʌkhɔːk], *s. Orn:* **1.** busard *m* des marais. **2.** *U.S:* faucon commun; (faucon) pèlerin *m.*

ducking ['dʌkiŋ], *s.* (*a*) plongeon *m* (involontaire); bain forcé; **to give s.o. a d.,** faire boire une tasse à qn; *Hist:* **d. stool,** sellette à plongeon (destinée aux mégères); (*b*) *Hist: Nau:* (*punishment*) supplice *m,* peine *f,* de la cale.

duckling ['dʌkliŋ], *s. Orn:* canardeau *m*; (*drake*) caneton *m*; (*duck*) canette *f*; **the Ugly D.,** le vilain petit Canard.

duckmole ['dʌkmoul], *s. Z: F:* ornithor(h)ynque *m.*

duckwalk ['dʌkwɔːk], *s.* caillebotis *m.*

duckweed ['dʌkwiːd], *s. Bot:* lentille *f* d'eau; lenticule *f,* lemna *f,* lemne *f.*

ducky ['dʌki]. **1.** *s. F:* **(my) d.,** mon petit chat, ma petite chatte, mon petit chou, mon petit mimi, ma poupoule, ma cocotte. **2.** *a. F:* mignon, -onne; coquet, -ette; chic.

ducol ['djukɔl], *s. Cmptr:* **d. punched card system,** système *m* de perforation double par colonne.

duct[1] [dʌkt], *s.* **1.** conduit *m,* conduite *f*; *Civ.E: etc:* caniveau *m,* -aux, canalisation *f* (pour câbles, etc.); **air d.,** conduit, manche *f,* à air; gaine *f* (d'installation de ventilation); porte-vent *m inv*; *Av:* **slotted entry d.,** bec *m* d'attaque; *Mec.E:* **oil d.,** tube *m* de graissage; **elbow d.,** conduite d'angle. **2.** *Anat:* canal *m,* -aux, vaisseau *m,* -aux, voie *f*; **bile d.,** canal, voie, biliaire; **auditory d.,** conduit auditif; **Bellini's ducts,** tubes de Bellini; **choledoch d.,** canal cholédoque; **sweat d.,** canal excréteur (d'une glande sudoripare), conduit sudorifère; *Ich:* **air d.,** canal aérien (d'un poisson). **3.** *Bot:* trachée *f,* canal; **resin d.,** canal résinifère. **4.** *Typ:* encrier *m* (d'une presse à imprimer).

duct[2], *v.tr.* **to d. air,** transporter de l'air dans une gaine, un réseau de gaines, une conduite.

ductile ['dʌktail], *a.* **1.** ductile, malléable; (i) **d. metals,** métaux *m* ductiles; (ii) **d. character,** caractère *m* docile, malléable, souple. **2. d. clay,** argile *f* plastique.

ductility [dʌk'tiliti], *s.* **1.** (*a*) ductilité *f* (d'un métal); malléabilité *f*; (*b*) docilité *f,* souplesse *f* (de caractère). **2.** plasticité *f* (de l'argile).

ducting ['dʌktiŋ], *s. Tchn:* canalisation *f*; (réseau *m* de) gaines *fpl* (d'installation de ventilation).

ductless ['dʌktlis], *a. Anat:* **d. gland,** (glande *f*) endocrine *f*; glande à sécrétion interne, sans canal excrétoire.

ductor ['dʌktər], *s.* **1.** *Typ:* encrier *m* (d'une presse à imprimer). **2.** *Tex: Printing:* (rouleau) essuyeur *m.*

ductule ['dʌktjul], *s. Anat:* **efferent ductules,** vaisseaux efférents (de l'épididyme).

ductwork ['dʌktwəːk], *s.* = DUCTING.

dud [dʌd]. *F:* **1.** *s.pl. O:* **duds,** frusques *fpl,* nippes *fpl.* **2.** *s. & a.* (*a*) incapable; **he's a d.,** (i) c'est un type nul; (ii) c'est un raté; **I'm a d. at history,** je suis nul en histoire; **as a doctor he's a d.,** il ne vaut rien comme médecin; **d. artist,** artiste *mf* à la manque; **the duds,** (i) les élèves peu intéressants; *F:* les crétins *m*; (ii) les fruits secs (de la vie); (*b*) mauvais; *P:* moche; *Artil:* **d. (shell),** obus non éclaté, qui a raté, *F:* qui foire, a foiré; *Com:* **d. stock,** marchandises *fpl* hors de vente; rossignols *mpl*; **d. cheque,** chèque *m* sans provision; **d. note,** faux billet de banque; **the note was a d.,** le billet était faux; **it's a d. show,** c'est nul, moche, comme spectacle.

duddle arc ['dʌdl'ɑːk], *s. Elcs:* arc chantant.

dude[1] [djuːd], *s. U.S: F:* **1.** gommeux *m,* miché *m*; poseur *m.* **2.** (*a*) citadin *m*; (*b*) (*in the West*) touriste venu de l'est; *esp.* hôte *m* d'un ranch-hôtel; **d. ranch,** ranch-hôtel.

dude[2], *v.i. F:* **to d. up,** se mettre sur son trente et un.

dudgeon ['dʌdʒən], *s.* colère *f*; ressentiment *m*; **in (high) d.,** fort en colère; exaspéré, indigné.

due [djuː], *a., adv. & s.*

I. *a.* **1.** (*owing*) *Com: Fin:* (*of debt*) exigible; (*of bill*) échéant, échéable, échu; **bill d. on 1st May,** effet *m* payable le premier mai; **contributions still d.,** cotisations *f* à percevoir; **balance d.,** solde dû; **the balance d. to us,** le solde qui nous revient; **balance d. to us from Mr Martin,** redoit M. Martin; **the person from whom it is d.,** la personne qui en est débitrice; **debts d. to us, to the firm,** dettes actives; créances *f*; **debts d. by us, by the firm,** dettes passives; **sums d. from banks, d. to banks,** créances sur les banques, sommes dues aux banques; **bond d. for repayment,** obligation amortie; *U.S:* **d. bill,** reconnaissance *f* de dette; (*of bill, etc.*) **to fall, become, d.,** échoir, devenir payable, venir à (l')échéance; **falling d.,** échéance *f*; **when d.,** à l'échéance; **d. date,** échéance; **redemption before d. date,** remboursement anticipé. **2.** (*merited, proper*) dû, juste, mérité; **the first place is d. to Milton,** la première place revient à Milton; **it is d. to him to say . . .,** il n'est que juste envers lui de dire . . .; **the reward d. to his services, the d. reward of his services,** la récompense que méritent ses services; **to give s.o. d. warning,** avertir qn dans les formes; **to take all d. measures,** prendre toutes les mesures requises; **with d. care,** avec tout le soin requis; **he was received with d. ceremony,** il fut reçu avec tout le cérémonial qui lui était dû; **in d. form,** dans les formes voulues; en bonne forme: en règle; dans les règles; **contract drawn up in d. form,** contrat rédigé en bonne et due forme; **receipt in d. form,** quittance régulière; **within d. limits,** dans les limites prescrites, raisonnables; **after d. consideration,** après mûre réflexion; tout bien considéré. **3.** (*in consequence of*) **d. to . . .,** dû à . . ., occasionné, causé, par . . ., attribuable à . . .; **it is d. to him, to his negligence,** c'est lui, c'est sa négligence, qui en est (la) cause; **these advantages are d. to . . .,** ces avantages découlent de . . .; **his authority is d. to your support,** son autorité tient à votre appui; **what is it d. to?** à quoi cela tient-il? **lack of compression d. to a bent valve,** manque *m* de compression imputable à une soupape faussée; **this situation is d. to the fact that . . .,** cette situation s'explique par le fait que . . ., trouve son explication dans ce fait que . . .; **this chapter of accidents is d. to you,** ce chapitre de malheurs est votre ouvrage; *prep.phr. Journ:* **d. to . . .,** par suite de . . .; **d. to fog the boat arrived late,** par suite du brouillard, le bateau est arrivé en retard; **d. to unfounded rumours these shares crashed,** sous le coup de faux bruits ces actions ont subi une forte baisse. **4.** (*expected*) **the train is d. (to arrive), is d. in, at two o'clock,** le train arrive à deux heures; **the train was d. to start at ten,** le train partait à dix heures; **he is d. to arrive this evening,** il doit arriver ce soir; on l'attend ce soir; **I was d. to start early,** je devais me mettre en route de bonne heure; *F:* **I'm d. for a perm,** j'ai bien, grand, besoin d'une permanente; il serait temps que j'aie une permanente; **I'm d. for a rise,** j'attends une augmentation de salaire.

II. *adv.* **d. north,** droit vers le nord, plein nord.

III. *s.* **1.** dû *m*; **to give s.o. his d.,** donner à qn ce qui lui est dû, ce qui lui revient; rendre justice à qn; être juste à, envers, pour, qn; **one must give the devil his d.,** il faut faire la part du diable; à chacun son dû; à tout seigneur tout honneur; **to pay one's dues,** payer ce qu'on doit; payer ses redevances *f*; **to claim one's dues,** réclamer son dû. **2.** *pl.* **dues;** (*a*) droits *mpl,* frais *mpl*; **taxes and dues,** impôts *m* et taxes *f*; **market dues,** hallage *m*; **town dues,** (droits d')octroi *m*; *Nau:* **port dues,** droits de port; *Ecc:* **Easter dues,** offrande de Pâques (faite au prêtre de la paroisse); (*b*) (*club subscription*) cotisation annuelle. **3.** *adv.phr. Nau:* **for full d.,** (arrimé, etc.) définitivement.

due-date ['djuːdeit], *v.tr.* coter (un effet).

duel[1] ['dju(ː)əl], *s.* **1.** duel *m*; affaire *f* d'honneur; rencontre *f*; réparation *f* par les armes; **to fight a d.,** se battre en duel; aller sur le terrain; *F:* s'aligner sur le terrain; **d. to the death,** duel à mort; **pistol d.,** duel au pistolet; **d. with swords,** duel à l'épée. **2.** lutte *f,* contestation *f.*

duel[2], *v.i.* **(duelled)** se battre en duel.

dueller ['dju(ː)ələr], **duellist** ['dju(ː)əlist], *s.* duelliste *m.*

duelling ['dju(ː)əliŋ], *s.* le duel; **d. pistols, d. sword,** pistolets *m,* épée *f,* de combat.

duenna [dju(ː)'enə], *s.f.* duègne.

duet [dju(ː)'et], *s.* duo *m*; (*for piano*) morceau *m* à quatre mains; **d. stool,** banquette *f* de piano.

duettist [dju(ː)'etist], *s. Mus:* duettiste *mf.*

duff[1] [dʌf], *s.* **1.** *Dial:* pâte *f* à pain. **2. (plum) d.,** pudding *m* aux raisins. **3.** sol *m* sous une forêt. **4.** *Min:* (*coal*) fines *fpl.*

duff[2], *v.tr. F:* **1.** retaper (les vieux vêtements); dissimuler les défauts de (qch.). **2.** *Austr: O:* **to d. cattle,** changer les marques du bétail volé.

duff[3], *v.tr. F:* rater, *P:* bousiller (son coup, une affaire).

duff[4], *a. F:* de mauvaise qualité, moche; (*of work of art, banknote, etc.*) faux, *f.* fausse.

duffel ['dʌfl], *s.* **1.** *Tex:* drap molletonné; molleton *m*; **d. coat,** duffle-coat *m, pl.* duffle-coats; *NAm:* **d. sock,** (i) bande molletière de molleton; (ii) chausson *m* de molleton. **2.** (*a*) *NAm:* effets *mpl* (de voyageur, campeur, etc.); (*b*) **d. bag,** sac marin, de campeur.

duffer ['dʌfər], *s.* **1.** *P:* (*a*) *A:* colporteur *m* qui fait passer sa camelote pour des objets de valeur volés ou importés en contrebande; (*b*) *A:* colporteur; (*c*) *Austr:* voleur *m* de bétail (qui en change les marques). **2.** *F:* (*a*) bousilleur, -euse; *F:* savetier *m*; *Sch:* cancre *m,* croûte *f,* cruche *f*; *Sp:* maladroit, -oite; **well, you are a d.!** ce que tu es noix! **to be a d. at sth.,** n'entendre rien à qch.; **to be a d. at dancing,** danser comme une savate; **a perfect d. at history,** un élève nul en histoire; (*b*) godiche *mf,* gourde *f,* lourdaud *m,* ballot *m,* empoté *m.* **3.** *A:* (*a*) article mauvais, retapé, moche; œuvre d'art fausse; fausse pièce (de monnaie); (*b*) *Min: Austr:* placer improductif, sans valeur.

duffle ['dʌfl], *s.* = DUFFEL.

dufrenite [dju'freinait], *s. Miner:* dufrénite *f.*

dufrenoysite [djufrə'nɔizait], *s. Miner:* dufrénoysite *f.*

dug [dʌg], *s.* (*a*) mamelle *f* (d'un animal); pis *m* (de vache); (*b*) trayon *m,* tétin *m*; (*c*) *pl. P: O:* (*of woman*) **dugs,** seins *m*; nénés *m.*

dugong ['duːgɔŋ], *s. Z:* dugong *m*; vache marine.

dugout ['dʌgaut], *s.* **1.** canot creusé dans un tronc d'arbre; pirogue *f.* **2.** *Mil: etc:* (i) abri souterrain, enterré, blindé; *P:* cagna *f*; (ii) niche-abri *f, pl.* niches-abris; **deep d.,** abri-caverne *m, pl.* abris-cavernes. **3.** *Can:* bassin, réservoir d'eau (aménagé dans les Prairies). **4.** *P:* (i) *Mil:* officier en retraite rappelé en activité; vieille baderne; vieille culotte de peau; (ii) *A:* **school with a lot of old dugouts on the staff,** école *f* avec un grand nombre de professeurs en retraite parmi le personnel.

Duguet ['djugei], *Pr.n. Med:* **Duguet's ulcerations,** angine érythémateuse, de Duguet.

Duhring ['djuəriŋ], *Pr.n. Med:* **Duhring's disease,** dermatite *f* herpétiforme.

duiker ['daikər], *s.* **1.** *also* **duikerbok** ['daikəbɔk], *Z:* céphalophe *m*; *F:* biche-cochon *f, pl.* biches-cochons; **yellow-backed d.,** céphalophe à dos jaune; **black-fronted d.,** céphalophe à front noir; **blue d.,** céphalophe bleu. **2.** *Orn:* (*in S. Africa*) cormoran noir.

duke [djuːk], *s.* **1.** duc *m*; **my Lord D.,** monsieur le duc. **2.** *pl. P:* **dukes,** poings *m.*

dukedom ['djuːkdəm], *s.* **1.** duché *m.* **2.** (i) titre *m,* (ii) dignité *f,* de duc.

Dukeries ['djuːkəriz], *s.pl.* la région de Sherwood Forest, dans le comté de Nottingham, où se trouvent plusieurs domaines ducaux.

Dukhobors ['duːkoubɔːz], *s.pl. Rel.H:* Doukhobors *m.*

dulcet ['dʌlsit], *a. Lit:* (son) doux, suave, agréable.

dulcification [dʌlsifi'keiʃ(ə)n], *s.* dulcification *f.*

dulcify ['dʌlsifai], *v.tr.* dulcifier; adoucir.

dulcifying ['dʌlsifaiiŋ], *a.* dulcifiant.

dulcimer ['dʌlsimər], *s. A:Mus:* tympanon *m*; doulcemer *m.*

dulcin ['dʌlsin], **dulcine** ['dʌlsiːn], *s. Ch:* **1.** dulcine *f.* **2.** dulcite *f,* dulcitol *m.*

Dulcinea [dʌlsi'niə], *Pr.n.f. Span.Lit:* Dulcinée.

dulcite ['dʌlsait], **dulcitol** ['dʌlsitɔl], *s. Ch:* dulcite *f,* dulcitol *m.*

dulia [d(j)uː'laiə], *s. R.C.Ch:* dulie *f.*

dull[1] [dʌl], *a.* **1.** (*of pers.*) lent, lourd; **d. sense of touch, d. hearing,** toucher *m,* ouïe *f,* peu sensible; **d. look, eye,** regard *m* atone; **d.-eyed,** au regard terne; **to be d. of sight, d.-sighted,** avoir la vue faible; **to be d. of hearing,** avoir l'oreille dure, être dur d'oreille; **to be d.(-witted, -brained),** avoir l'esprit lourd, engourdi, obtus, lent, épais; avoir la tête dure, être pauvre d'esprit; *Sch:* **the d. boys,** les élèves peu brillants; *F:* les cancres *m*; *Prov:* **all work and no play makes Jack a d. boy,** à toujours travailler les enfants s'abrutissent. **2.** (*a*) (*of pain*) sourd; **a d. ache,** une douleur sourde; (*b*) (bruit) sourd, étouffé, mat; **I heard a d. blow,** j'entendis un coup sourd; **his heel gave a d. sound,** son talon sonna mat *inv.* **3.** *Com: Fin:* (marché) calme, inactif, lourd, plat, inanimé, languissant; **the d. season,** la morte-saison; **business, the market, is d.,** les affaires languissent; le marché est alourdi, sans activité; les affaires sont dans le marasme. **4.** (*depressed*) triste, morne, déprimé; **I feel d.,** je m'ennuie; j'ai le cafard; **in a d. mood,** maussade. **5.** (*tedious*) triste, ennuyeux, peu intéressant; **d. occupation,** occupation assoupissante; **d. life,** vie *f* monotone, atone; **as d. as ditchwater,** triste comme un bonnet de nuit, comme un enterrement; ennuyeux comme la pluie, comme un jour de pluie; **a deadly d. task,** une besogne abrutissante, assommante; **they find the work deadly d.,** ce travail les rebute; **it is deadly d. here, this is a deadly d. hole,** on s'ennuie à mourir ici; c'est mortellement ennuyeux ici; **I find it rather d. living here by myself,** je m'ennuie un peu à vivre ici tout seul; **a d. little town,** une petite ville sans mouvement; **a thoroughly d. evening,** une soirée tout à fait assommante. **6.** (*blunt*) émoussé; (*of tool, etc.*) **to become d.,** s'émousser. **7.** (*of colour*) terne, mat; (*of wine*) plat, mou, pâteux; **d. surface,** surface *f* terne, mate; **paper with a d. finish, d.-finish paper,** papier mat, non satiné; **d. style,** style *m* terne; **d. jewels,** bijoux sans éclat; **d. eyes,** yeux morts, sans regard, sans éclat; **a d. fire,** un feu triste; un pauvre feu; **the d. glow of the fire,** la rougeur sombre du feu; **the fire is getting d.,** le feu baisse; (*of paint*) **to become d.,** s'emboire. **8.** (*of weather*) lourd, triste, sombre, couvert.

dull[2], *v.tr. & i.*

I. *v.tr.* **1.** (*a*) hébéter (qn); (*b*) engourdir, alourdir, appesantir (l'esprit); émousser (les sens). **2.** émousser (un outil). **3.** (*a*) amortir, assourdir (le son); ternir, amatir (les couleurs, un miroir); dépolir (une surface); mater (un métal); (*b*) amortir (une douleur); rendre moins vif (le plaisir); **to d. pain by narcotics,** endormir la douleur au moyen de narcotiques; **sorrow is dulled by the passage of time,** le temps émousse la douleur; **enjoyment is dulled by anxiety,** l'anxiété émousse le plaisir.

II. *v.i.* **1.** (*of senses, etc.*) s'hébéter, s'engourdir, s'alourdir. **2.** (*of colour*) se ternir; (*of metal, etc.*) se dépolir; **the varnish dulls,** le vernis devient mat, perd son lustre.

dullard ['dʌləd], *s.* lourdaud *m*; *Sch:* cancre *m*, crétin *m*.

dulling ['dʌliŋ], *s.* **1.** alourdissement *m* (de l'esprit). **2.** émoussage *m* (d'un tranchant). **3.** (*a*) ternissage *m* (d'une couleur, etc.); dépolissement *m* (d'une surface); assourdissement *m* (du son); (*b*) apaisement *m* (de la douleur).

dullish ['dʌliʃ], *a.* **1.** un peu lourd (d'esprit). **2.** un peu triste. **3.** un peu terne, un peu sombre. **4.** quelque peu monotone; qui manque d'entrain.

dul(l)ness ['dʌlnis], *s.* **1.** lenteur *f*, pesanteur *f*, de l'esprit; épaisseur *f* de l'intelligence; émoussement *m* (des sens); **d. of hearing,** dureté *f* d'oreille; **increasing d. of the mind,** appesantissement *m* de l'esprit. **2.** matité *f* (d'un son); *Med:* **d. at the base of the lung,** matité à la base du poumon. **3.** ennui *m*, tristesse *f*; monotonie *f*, prosaïsme *m* (de la vie, d'un discours). **4.** *Com: Fin:* stagnation *f*, langueur *f*, marasme *m* (des affaires); inactivité *f*, inaction *f*, peu *m* d'activité (du marché). **5.** manque *m* de tranchant, de fil (d'une lame, d'un outil); émoussement (d'une pointe, d'un tranchant). **6.** manque d'éclat (d'une couleur); ternissure *f*; faiblesse *f* (d'un son, d'une lumière); bruit sourd (d'un coup).

dully ['dʌl(l)i], *adv.* **1.** lourdement, lentement. **2.** ennuyeusement; (vivre) dans l'ennui; tristement. **3.** sourdement, faiblement; sans éclat; **to burn d.,** donner peu de flamme.

dulosis [dju'lousis], *s. Ent:* esclavagisme *m* (des fourmis).

dulotic [dju'lɔtik], *a. Ent:* (fourmi *f*) esclavagiste.

dulse [dʌls], *s.* algue *f* comestible.

duly ['dju:li], *adv.* **1.** dûment, justement; comme de juste; convenablement; **members d. appointed,** membres régulièrement désignés; *Com:* **I d. received your letter of . . .,** j'ai bien reçu votre lettre du . . .. **2.** en temps voulu; en temps utile; **rent d. paid,** loyer payé exactement.

duma ['du:mə], *s. Russian Hist:* douma *f*.

dumb[1] [dʌm], *a.* **1.** muet, *f.* muette; **deaf and d.,** sourd-muet, *f.* sourde-muette; *F:* **d. as a fish, as an oyster,** muet comme un poisson, comme une carpe; *Pol: F:* **the d. millions,** les millions qui n'ont pas de voix; **d. animals,** les bêtes *f*, les animaux *m*; **our d. friends,** nos frères inférieurs; **question on which history is d.,** question sur laquelle l'histoire se tait; **to strike s.o. d.,** (i) frapper qn de mutisme; (ii) *F:* rendre qn muet; réduire qn au silence; abasourdir, *F:* sidérer, qn; **I was struck d. with astonishment,** la stupeur me rendit muet; **we are struck d. by the news,** nous restâmes abasourdis, interdits, de la nouvelle; **d. with fear,** muet de terreur; rendu muet par la peur; **d. show,** pantomime *f*; jeu muet; langage *m* mimique; *Th:* **d.-show performance,** pantomime, mimodrame *m*; **in d. show,** en pantomime; par (des) signes; **to act a scene in d. show,** mimer une scène; **to express one's sorrow, joy, in d. show,** mimer sa douleur, sa joie; **invitation conveyed in d. show,** invitation gesticulée. **2.** (*lacking some essential detail*) **d. piano,** piano *m* sans cordes; clavier *m* (pour l'étude du doigté, etc.); **d. peal (of bells),** volée de cloches assourdie; *Equit:* **d. jockey,** cavalier *m*, homme *m*, de bois; jockey *m*; *Min:* **d. drift,** galerie *f* en cul-de-sac; **d. furnace,** foyer *m* d'aérage; *Mch:* **d. plate,** plaque *f* d'avant-foyer; *Nau:* **d. craft,** bateaux *mpl* sans voiles; chalands *mpl*; **d. barge,** chaland (sans mât ni voiles). **3.** *Med: U.S:* **d. fever, d. ague,** fièvre intermittente. **4.** *F:* bête, sot, *f.* sotte; (garçon, esprit) bouché; **d. blonde,** blonde évaporée; **to play, act, d.,** faire le niais.

dumb[2], *v.tr.* amortir, assourdir (un son).

dumb-bell ['dʌmbel], *s.* **1.** haltère *m*. **2.** *P:* sot *m*, imbécile *m*.

dumbfound [dʌm'faund], *v.tr.* interdire, abasourdir, stupéfier, ahurir, confondre, ébahir, *F:* anéantir (qn); jeter (qn) dans l'étonnement; *P:* visser, asseoir (qn); **this news dumbfounded me,** la nouvelle m'a cassé les bras.

dumbfounded [dʌm'faundid], *a.* abasourdi, ahuri, stupéfié, ébahi, confondu, **(at, de); to be d.,** (penser) tomber de son haut; tomber de sa hauteur; être muet de stupeur; **I am d.,** je n'en reviens pas; les bras m'en tombent; **we were d. at the news,** nous restâmes abasourdis de la nouvelle; la nouvelle nous frappa de stupeur.

dumbfounding [dʌm'faundiŋ], *a.* abasourdissant; ahurissant; *F:* désarçonnant.

dumbhead ['dʌmhed], *s. NAm: P:* (*a*) lourdaud, -aude; malavisé, -ée; (*b*) imbécile; **you d.!** espèce d'idiot!

dumb iron ['dʌmaiən], *s. Aut:* main *f* (de ressort); **front, back, dumb irons,** main(s) avant, arrière.

dumbly ['dʌmli], *adv.* sans rien dire, sans mot dire; en silence.

dumbness ['dʌmnis], *s.* **1.** mutisme *m*; **deaf and d.,** surdi-mutité *f*. **2.** *F:* silence *m*. **3.** sottise *f*; bêtise *f*; niaiserie *f*.

dumbwaiter ['dʌmweitər], *s.* **1.** *Furn:* servante *f*; desserte *f*. **2.** *NAm:* monte-plats *m inv*.

dumdum ['dʌmdʌm], *s. Mil:* **d. bullet,** (balle) dum-dum *f*, *pl.* dum-dums.

dummy[1] ['dʌmi], *s.* **1.** *F:* muet, -ette. **2.** (*a*) homme *m* de paille; prête-nom *m inv*; (*b*) sot *m*, lourdaud *m*, niais *m*. **3.** (*a*) *Dressm: Tail:* mannequin *m*, poupée *f*; (*in shop window*) figure *f* de cire; **ventriloquist's d.,** poupée de ventriloque; *F:* **he's nothing but a tailor's d.,** il n'est qu'un dandy sans intelligence: **standing there like a stuffed d.,** planté comme un piquet; **couldn't you help me instead of sitting there like a stuffed d.?** tu ne pourrais pas m'aider au lieu de rester assis comme un empoté? (*b*) chose *f* factice, faux paquet; *Mil:* simulacre *m* (de grenade, etc.); *Publ:* maquette *f* (d'un livre); **these doors are dummies,** ces portes sont fausses; **shop window dressed with dummies,** devanture toute en fausses boîtes, en factices; *Fb:* **to sell the d.,** réussir une feinte de passe; *Mil:* **static d.,** simulacre fixe; **vertical screen d.,** simulacre-écran *m*, *pl.* simulacres-écrans; simulacre-panneau *m*, *pl.* simulacres-panneaux; (*c*) **(baby's) d.,** sucette *f*; tétine *f* sur anneau. **4.** *Cards:* (*player or hand at bridge, whist*) mort *m*; **to be, play, d.,** faire le mort; **d. bridge,** bridge *m* à trois personnes; **d. whist,** whist *m* avec un mort. **5.** *attrib.* (*a*) postiche; faux, *f* fausse; **d. work,** trucage *m*; **d. box (of chocolates, etc.)** boîte *f* factice; *Aut:* **d. hub,** faux moyeu; *Cmptr:* **d. instruction,** instruction fictive; *El:* **d. load,** charge factice; **d. plug,** fiche isolante; *Tp:* **d. ticket,** fiche témoin (de communication téléphonique); *Mil:* **d. tank,** char *m* factice, simulacre de char; **d. trench,** fausse tranchée; **d. headquarters,** faux quartier général; **d. cartridge,** (i) fausse cartouche; (ii) *Artil:* gargousse *f* sans poudre; *Artil:* **d. charge** *f* sans poudre; *Navy:* **d. head,** cône *m* d'exercice (de torpille); **d. run,** (i) *Navy:* évolution *f* d'entraînement; (ii) *MilAv:* incursion aérienne sans bombardement; (iii) *F:* coup *m* d'essai; *W.Tel:* **d. antenna,** antenna fictive; (*b*) (*in ciphers*) **d. letter,** nulle *f*.

dummy[2]. **1.** *v.i. NAm:* **to d. up,** demeurer bouche close. **2.** *v.tr. & i. Fb:* duper, tromper (un adversaire) avec une feinte de passe.

dumontite ['dju:mɔntait], *s. Miner:* dumontite *f*.

dumortierite [dju'mɔ:tiərait], *s. Miner:* dumortiérite *f*.

dump[1] [dʌmp], *s.* **1.** personne boulotte. **2.** *Games:* (*a*) jeton *m* (en plomb); (*b*) palet *m* (en plomb). **3.** gros bonbon en boule. **4.** *P: O:* (*a*) liard *m*; **it's not worth a d.,** cela ne vaut pas un patard, un rond, deux sous; (*b*) *pl.* **dumps,** argent *m*, galette *f*. **5.** *N.Arch:* clou *m*, boulon *m*, à bordage; gros clou de pont.

dump[2], *s.* **1.** coup sourd (d'une masse qui tombe). **2.** tas *m*, amas *m* (de déchets, de déblais, de minerai, etc.); *Min:* halde *f*, terris *m*, terril *m*; **ore on the d.,** minerai *m* sur la halde; *Ind:* **slag d.,** remblai *m*, halde, de scories. **3.** (*a*) chantier *m* de dépôt; dépôt *m* des déblais; (lieu *m* de) décharge *f*; déversement *m*; **refuse d.,** terrain *m* de décharge; **(council) refuse d., rubbish d.,** décharge publique; voirie *f*; **town (nightsoil) d.,** dépotoir *m*; (*b*) *F:* taudis *m*; **what a d.!** (i) (*of place*) quel trou! quel bled! (ii) (*of office, etc.*) quelle boîte! **4.** dépôt (de vivres, etc.); *Mil:* **ammunition d.,** dépôt, stockage *m*, de munitions; parc *m* à munitions. **5.** *Cmptr:* (*a*) coupure *f* (d'un courant électrique); (*b*) vidage *m*; mise *f* en réserve; **memory d., storage d., store d.,** vidage (de) mémoire. **6.** (*a*) *Civ.E: etc:* basculeur *m*, culbuteur *m*; **end d.,** basculeur en bout; (*b*) **d. cart,** tombereau *m*; **d. truck,** camion *m* à benne basculante; camion-benne *m*, *pl.* camions-bennes; **d. (car), d. (wagon),** wagon *m* à bascule; *Mch:* **d. grate,** jette-feu *m inv*; *Av:* **fuel d. valve,** vide-vite *m inv*. **7.** *Sp:* grosse vague (qui culbute un aquaplaniste).

dump[3], *v.tr. & i.*

I. *v.tr.* **1.** (*a*) décharger, déverser (une charretée de sable, de matériau, etc.); **to d. the contents of a lorry,** vider un camion (basculant); **to d. the refuse,** jeter les ordures à la voirie; (*b*) **to d. (down),** déposer, jeter, culbuter, (qch.) (avec un bruit sourd); laisser tomber lourdement (un ballot, etc.); **to d. a child in(to) its pushchair,** déposer un enfant rudement, flanquer un enfant, dans sa poussette; (*c*) *Av:* **to d. the cargo,** se délester de la cargaison; (*d*) *F:* **to d. s.o.,** (i) se débarrasser de qn; (ii) abandonner qn, laisser qn en plan, *F:* planquer qn. **2.** faire un dépôt de (vivres, etc.). **3.** *Com:* **to d. goods on a foreign market,** écouler à perte des marchandises à l'étranger; se débarrasser à l'étranger d'articles en surproduction; faire du dumping. **4.** *Cmptr:* (i) vider, (ii) mettre en réserve (un stockage); (*b*) couper (un courant électrique). **5.** *Austr:* mettre (la laine) en balles à la presse hydraulique. **6.** *Sp:* (*of wave*) culbuter (un aquaplaniste).

II. *v.i.* **1.** basculer, culbuter, se décharger. **2. to d. (down),** (i) (*of thg*) tomber lourdement; (ii) (*of pers.*) se laisser tomber (dans un fauteuil, etc.).

dumper ['dʌmpər], *s.* **1.** (*pers.*) (*a*) déchargeur *m* (de minerai, d'ordures, etc.); (*b*) *Com:* commerçant *m*, *esp.* exportateur *m*, qui surcharge le marché à vil prix du trop-plein de la production. **2.** *Civ.E: etc:* (i) wagon *m*, camion *m*, à bascule; (ii) motobrouette *f*, dumper *m*. **3.** *Sp:* grosse vague (qui culbute un aquaplaniste).

dumpiness ['dʌmpinis], *s.* taille trapue, apparence boulotte (de qn).

dumping ['dʌmpiŋ], *s.* **1.** (*a*) basculage *m*, basculement *m* (d'un camion, etc.); **lorry in a d. position,** camion en position de vidange; **d. bucket,** *U.S:* **d. body,** benne basculante; **d. cart,** tombereau *m*; **d. truck, d. wagon,** wagon *m* à bascule; camion-benne *m*, *pl.* camions-bennes; *Mch:* **d. grate,** jette-feu *m inv*; (*b*) dépôt *m*, versage *m*, déversement *m*; *Min:* mise *f* à terril, à terris; **d. ground,** (lieu *m* de) décharge *f*; déversement *m*; (*for rubbish*) dépotoir *m*; *F:* **my class is the d. ground for the whole school,** ma classe est le dépotoir de toute l'école. **2.** *Com:* dumping *m* (du trop-plein de la production). **3.** *Cmptr:* vidage *m* (d'une mémoire). **4.** *Med:* **d. syndrome,** dumping-syndrome *m*.

dumpling ['dʌmpliŋ], *s.* **1.** *Cu:* (*a*) boulette (de pâte) bouillie (servie avec le bœuf bouilli, etc.); (*b*) **apple d.,** pomme enrobée (dans de la pâte, et cuite au four); *Dial:* rabote *f*; petit bourdelot; *F: O:* **little d.,** petit boulot (d'enfant); **she's a regular little d.,** c'est une petite boule de suif; (*c*) *F:* **Norfolk d.,** habitant *m* du Norfolk. **2.** *Civ.E:* dame *f*, témoin *m*.

dumps [dʌmps], *s.pl. F:* cafard *m*; idées noires; **to be (down) in the d., to have the d.,** broyer du noir, avoir le spleen; se sentir déprimé; avoir le cafard; avoir le moral à zéro.

dumpty ['dʌm(p)ti], *s. Furn: F:* pouf *m*.

dumpy ['dʌmpi]. **1.** *a.* (*a*) trapu, boulot, ragot, replet, -ète; **a d. little man,** un petit homme replet; un courtaud; **d. horse,** ragot *m*; (*b*) *Surv:* **d. (level),** niveau *m* à lunette (fixe). **2.** *s.* (*a*) (*umbrella*) tom-pouce *m*, *pl.* tom-pouces; (*b*) *Furn:* pouf *m*.

dun[1] [dʌn]. **1.** *a.* (*a*) brun grisâtre; (*b*) *Poet:* sombre, obscur. **2.** *a. & s.* (cheval) gris louvet; **yellow d.,** bai doré, louvet. **3.** *s. Fish:* (*a*) subimago *m* (d'insecte); (*b*) **(artificial) d. (fly),** dun *f*; **blue d.,** subimago grisâtre; blue dun.

dun[2], *s.* **1.** (*a*) créancier importun; (*b*) agent *m* de recouvrement (de dettes). **2.** demande pressante (de paiement).

dun[3], *v.tr.* **(dunned)** importuner, harceler, pourchasser, relancer, assiéger, talonner (un débiteur); réclamer de l'argent à (un débiteur); **to be dunned on all sides,** être accablé de dettes criardes; **dunned by his creditors,** pressé par ses créanciers; **his creditors are dunning him,** ses créanciers le tourmentent.

dunbird ['dʌnbɔ:d], *s. Orn:* milouin *m*.

dunce [dʌns], *s.* ignorant, -ante; *F:* crétin, -ine; âne *m*, ânon *m*; *Sch: F:* cancre *m*, crétin; **dunce's cap,** bonnet *m* d'âne.

dundasite ['dʌndəsait], *s. Miner:* dundasite *f*.

Dundee [dʌn'di:], *Pr.n. Geog:* Dundee; *Cu:* **D. cake,** gâteau aux fruits couvert d'amandes grillées.

dunderhead ['dʌndəhed], *s. F:* (*a*) lourdaud, -aude; malavisé, -ée; (*b*) imbécile *mf*; **you d.!** espèce d'idiot!
dunderheaded ['dʌndəhedid], *a. F:* stupide.
dun diver ['dʌn'daivər], *s. Orn:* harle *m* bièvre.
Dundonian [dʌn'dounian], *s.* habitant, -ante, de Dundee.
Dundreary [dʌn'driəri], *Pr.n. F: A:* **D. whiskers,** *s.* **dundrearies,** longs favoris.
dune [dju:n], *s.* **(sand) d.,** dune *f*; **static d., fixed d.,** dune fixe; **active d.,** dune vive.
Dunedin [dʌ'ni:din], *Pr.n.* **1.** *Lit: Poet:* Édimbourg. **2.** *Geog:* [dʌ'ni:d(i)n], Dunedin (en Nouvelle-Zélande).
dung[1] [dʌŋ], *s.* **1.** (*a*) fiente *f*, crotte *f*; fumée *f* (de daim); bouse *f* (de vache), crottin *m* (de cheval); *Dy:* bouse; *Dy:* **d. bath,** bain *m* de bouse; *Ent:* **d. beetle,** bousier *m*, stercoraire *m*, escarbot *m*, ateuchus *m*, *F:* fouille-merde *m inv*; **d. fly,** scatophage *m*; *Nat.Hist:* **d. eating,** merdivore, scatophage; **d. loving,** scatophile; (*b*) *A:* excrément (humain). **2.** *Agr:* fumier *m*, engrais *m*; **d. fork,** fourche *f* à fumier.
dung[2]. **1.** *v.tr.* (*a*) *Agr:* fumer (un champ); (*b*) *Dy:* bouser (une étoffe). **2.** *v.i.* (*a*) (*of animal*) bouser; (*b*) *P:* (*not in decent use*) chier.
dungaree [dʌŋgə'ri:], *s.* **1.** *Tex:* étoffe de coton grossière (de l'Inde); cotonnade *f*, treillis *m*. **2.** *pl. Ind:* **dungarees,** combinaison *f*; *F:* salopette *f*; bleus *mpl* (de mécanicien); *Mil:* (jeu *m* de) treillis.
dungeon ['dʌn(d)ʒ(ə)n], *s.* **1.** cachot *m* (d'un château du moyen âge); **the deepest d.,** le cul de basse-fosse; **bottle d.,** cachot en cul de basse-fosse. **2.** (*tower*) donjon *m*.
dunghill ['dʌŋhil], *s.* tas *m* de fumier; pailler *m*, fumier *m*; **d. cock, d. hen,** coq *m*, poule *f*, de basse-cour; *F:* **to raise s.o. from the d.,** tirer qn de la poussière; **to be cock on one's own d.,** être sur son pailler.
dunging ['dʌŋiŋ], *s.* **1.** *Agr:* fumure *f*. **2.** *Dy:* bousage *m*.
dunite ['du:nait], *s. Geol:* dunite *f*.
dunk [dʌŋk], *v.tr.* **to d. one's croissant in one's coffee,** tremper son croissant dans son café; *F:* faire la trempette; *F:* **to d. s.o. (in a swimming pool),** plonger qn (dans une piscine); *F:* faire boire une tasse à qn.
dunking ['dʌŋkiŋ], *s.* trempage *m*.
Dunkirk ['dʌn'kə:k], *Pr.n. Geog:* Dunkerque *f*; *F:* **to do a D.,** réussir une retraite avec honneur; **to show the D. spirit,** montrer un courage inébranlable (en passant par de rudes épreuves).
dunlin ['dʌnlin], *s. Orn:* bécasseau *m* variable.
dunnage[1] ['dʌnidʒ], *s. Nau:* (*a*) fardage *m*, grenier *m*; bois *m* d'arrimage; parquet *m* de chargement; **to lay the d.,** faire son grenier; (*b*) *F:* effets personnels; sac *m* (de marin); **d. bag,** sac *m* (de) marin.
dunnage[2], *v.tr. & i. Nau:* faire un grenier; **to d. the floors well,** faire un bon grenier dans les cales.
dunning ['dʌniŋ], *a.* (créancier) criard.
dunno [dʌ'nou], *P:* (*corruption de* **(I) don't know**), sais pas!
dunnock ['dʌnək], *s. Orn:* accenteur *m* mouchet; fauvette *f* d'hiver; traîne-buisson *m inv*.
dunny ['dʌni], *s. P:* garde-robe *f*, *pl.* garde-robes; cabinets *mpl* sans eau courante.
duo ['dju(:)ou], *s. Mus:* duo *m*.
duodecennial [dju(:)oudi'senjəl], *a.* duodécennal, -aux.
duodecimal [dju(:)ou'desim(ə)l]. **1.** *a.* duodécimal, -aux. **2.** *s.pl. Mth:* **duodecimals,** multiplication duodécimale; calcul *m* par le système duodécimal.
duodecimo [dju(:)ou'desimou], *s. Typ:* in-douze *m inv*.
duodenal [dju(:)ə'di:n(ə)l], *a. Anat:* duodénal, -aux; *Med:* **d. ulcer,** ulcère duodénal.
duodenary [dju(:)ə'di:nəri], *a. Mth:* duodécimal, -aux.
duodenectomy [dju(:)oudi'nektəmi], *s. Surg:* duodénectomie *f*.
duodenitis [dju(:)ədi'naitis], *s. Med:* duodénite *f*.
duodeno-jejunostomy [dju(:)ou'di:noudʒidʒu'nɔstəmi], *s. Surg:* duodéno-jéjunostomie *f*.
duodeno-pancreatectomy [dju(:)ou'di:noupæŋkriə'tektəmi], *s. Surg:* duodéno-pancréatectomie *f*.
duodenostomy [dju(:)oudi'nɔstəmi], *s. Surg:* duodénostomie *f*.
duodenotomy [dju(:)oudi'nɔtəmi], *s. Surg:* duodénotomie *f*.
duodenum, *pl.* **-na, -nums** [dju(:)ə'di:nəm, -nə, -nəmz], *s. Anat:* duodénum *m*.
duodiode [dju(:)ou'daioud], *s. Elcs:* duodiode *f*.
duolateral [dju(:)ou'læt(ə)rəl], *a. El:* **d. coil,** bobine *f* en nid d'abeille.
duologue ['dju:əlɔg], *s.* **1.** dialogue *m*. **2.** *Th:* duodrame *m*.
Duomycin [djuou'maisin], *s. R.t.m:* = auréomycine *f*.
duopoly [dju'ɔpəli], *s.* duopole *m*.
duotone ['dju:ətoun], *a.* (automobile, etc.) de deux couleurs, de deux tons.
dupable ['dju:pəbl], *a.* facile à duper, à tromper; mystifiable.
dupe[1] [dju:p], *s.* dupe *f*; **to be the ready d. of s.o.,** se laisser facilement duper par qn.
dupe[2], *v.tr.* duper, tromper; *F:* dindonner, piper (qn); **to be duped,** se laisser duper; *F:* être le dindon de la farce.
dupe[3], *s. Cin: F:* contre-type *m*, *pl.* contre-types.
dupe[4], *v.tr. F:* = DUPLICATE[1] 2.
dupery ['dju:pəri], *s.* duperie *f*.
duple ['dju:pl], *a. Mus:* **d. time,** mesure *f* à deux temps, binaire.
duplet ['dju:plit], *s.* **1.** *Dice: Atom.Ph:* doublet *m*. **2.** *Mus:* duolet *m*.
duplex[1] ['dju:pleks], *a.* **1.** double; duplex *inv*; (*a*) *Mec.E: etc:* **d. boring machine,** aléseuse *f* à deux broches opposées; **d. lathe,** tour *m* à double outil; **d. compressor,** compresseur *m* double; **d. crank,** manivelle *f* double; **d. lever punch,** poinçonneuse *f* duplex; **d. pump,** pompe *f* double, duplex; **d. engine,** moteur *m*, machine *f*, bicylindrique; **d. steam engine,** machine à vapeur jumelle; (*b*) *El: Tp: Elcs:* duplex; **d. circuit,** ligne duplex, duplexée, bidirectionnelle; **d. channel,** voie duplex, duplexée; **d. communication,** liaison *f* (en) duplex; **d. telegraph, d. telegraphy,** télégraphe *m*, télégraphie *f* (en) duplex; **d. tube,** tube duplexeur; *Telecom:* **d. balance,** réseau équivalent, réseau d'équilibrage; **d. cable,** câble *m* à deux conducteurs torsadés; **d. operation,** exploitation *f*, fonctionnement *m*, en duplex; (*c*) *Paperm:* **d. paper, d. card,** papier *m*, carton *m*, duplex, bicolore. **2.** *NAm:* **d. (house),** pavillon *m*, maison *f*, pour deux familles; **d. (apartment),** appartement *m* à deux étages, en duplex; duplex *m*.
duplex[2], *v.tr.* **1.** doubler. **2.** *Telecom: etc:* duplexer, dupliquer.
duplexer ['dju:pleksər], *s. Telecom: etc:* duplexeur *m*.
duplexing ['dju:pleksiŋ], *s. Telecom: etc:* duplexage *m*, duplication *f*.
duplicate[1] ['dju:plikət]. **1.** *a.* double, en double; **d. set of tools,** outils *m* de rechange, en double; **d. parts,** pièces *f* de rechange; **d. receipt,** duplicata *m* de reçu; reçu *m* en duplicata; *Jur:* **d. document,** document ampliatif; *Cards:* **d. (bridge),** (bridge *m*) duplicate (*m*). **2.** *s.* (*a*) double *m*, répétition *f* (d'une œuvre d'art, etc.); *Phot: Cin:* contre(-)type *m* (*pl.* contre(-)types) (positif, négatif) (d'un film, etc.); (*b*) duplicata (d'un chèque egaré, etc.); double, contrepartie *f* (d'un écrit); ampliation *f* (d'un acte); **duplicates (of machine parts),** pièces *f* de rechange, en double; **in d.,** (en) double; en, par, duplicata; en double exemplaire, en double expédition; **to draw a bill of exchange in d.,** tirer une lettre de change par duplicata; (ii) reconnaissance *f* (de prêteur sur gages); (iii) *Com:* seconde *f* de change; (*c*) synonyme *m*.
duplicate[2] ['dju:plikeit], *v.tr. & i.* **1.** (*a*) faire le double de (qch.); copier (un document); reproduire (un document) en double exemplaire; répéter, reproduire (une pièce); *Typ:* surmouler (un cliché); *Cin:* contretyper; *Trans:* doubler (une ligne d'avions, etc.); dédoubler (un train); *Book-k:* (*of entry*) **to d. with another,** faire double emploi avec un autre; (*b*) **to d. a circular letter,** tirer plusieurs exemplaires d'une lettre circulaire au duplicateur; polycopier une lettre circulaire. **2.** *Ecc:* **to d. (masses),** biner.
duplicating ['dju:plikeitiŋ], *s.* **1.** duplication *f*, répétition *f*; *Typ:* surmoulage *m* (de clichés); **d. book,** carnet *m* multicopiste; manifold *m*. **2.** tirage *m* de plusieurs exemplaires (d'une lettre, etc.) au duplicateur; **d. machine,** duplicateur *m*; machine *f* à polycopier; **d. paper,** papier *m* pour duplicateurs.
duplication [dju:pli'keiʃ(ə)n], *s.* **1.** duplication *f*, répétition *f*, reproduction *f*; *Trans:* doublement *m* (d'une ligne d'avions, etc.), dédoublement *m* (d'un train); *Book-k:* double emploi *m* (d'une écriture); *Biol:* **d. of chromosomes,** duplication chromosomique; *Cmptr:* **d. check,** contrôle *m* par duplication. **2.** *Opt:* doublement (de l'image); dédoublement. **3.** *Ecc:* binage *m*.
duplicative ['dju:plikeitiv], *a.* duplicatif.
duplicator ['dju:plikeitər], *s.* duplicateur *m*, machine *f* à polycopier.
duplicature ['dju:plikeitʃər], *s. Anat:* duplicature *f*.
duplicident [dju'plisidənt], *a. Z:* duplicidenté.
Duplicidentata [djuplisiden'teitə], *s.pl. Z:* duplicidentés *m*.
duplicity [dju'plisiti], *s.* duplicité *f*; mauvaise foi.
Dupuytren [dju'pwitrən], *Pr.n. Med:* **Dupuytren's contraction, contracture,** maladie *f* de Dupuytren; **Dupuytren's fracture,** fracture *f* de Dupuytren.
durability [dju:rə'biliti], **durableness** ['dju:rəblnis], *s.* durabilité *f*; durée *f* (d'une étoffe, etc.); stabilité *f* (d'une administration); *Ind:* résistance *f* (des matériaux, etc.); longévité *f* (de l'équipement).
durable ['dju:rəbl], *a.* (*a*) durable; résistant; inusable; d'un bon user; **d. cloth,** étoffe résistante, de durée, qui fait de l'usage; **d. shoes,** chaussures *f* inusables; (*b*) *Com:* **d. goods,** *s.pl.* **(consumer) durables,** biens permanents, d'équipement; biens, produits *m*, d'usage.
durably ['dju:rəbli], *adv.* durablement, d'une façon durable.
durain ['djuərein], *s. Miner:* durain *m*.
Duralumin [dju(ə)'ræljumin], **Duraluminium** [dju(ə)rælju'miniəm], *s. R.t.m: Metall:* Duralumin *m*, Duraluminium *m*.
dura mater ['dju:rə'meitər], *s. Anat:* dure-mère *f*.
duramen [dju'reimen], *s.* duramen *m*; cœur *m* du bois, bois *m* de cœur; bois parfait.
durance ['dju:rəns], *s. Lit:* captivité *f*; *esp. in the phr.* **in d. vile,** dans un vil cachot; *Lit:* sur la paille humide des cachots.
duration [dju'reiʃ(ə)n], *s.* **1.** durée *f*; étendue *f* (de la vie); **d. of copyright,** délai *m*, durée, du droit d'auteur; **d. of a patent,** durée d'un brevet; **the peace was of short d.,** la paix fut de courte durée; *Mil:* **to enlist for the d. (of the war),** s'engager pour la durée de la guerre; *F:* **I thought that I was there for the d.,** je croyais que je serais là jusqu'à la Saint-Glinglin; *Tp:* **d. of call (in minutes),** durée de conversation; *Cmptr:* **response d.,** temps *m* de réponse. **2.** *Ind: Com:* **d. of the plant,** longévité *f* des machines.
durative ['djurətiv], *a. Gram:* duratif, -ive.
durbar ['də:ba:r], *s.* (*in India*) durbar *m* (la réception ou le local de la réception).
durdenite ['də:dənait], *s. Miner:* durdénite *f*.
durene ['dju:ri:n], *s. Ch:* durène *m*.
duress [dju'res], *s.* **1.** emprisonnement *m*. **2.** *Jur:* contrainte *f*, coercition *f*, violence *f*; **to act under d.,** agir à son corps défendant; céder à la force.
Durham ['dʌrəm], *Pr.n. Geog:* Durham; *Breed:* **D. cattle, Durhams,** durhams *m*.
durian, durion ['dju:riən], *s. Bot:* **1.** (*fruit*) durione *f*, durio *m*. **2.** (*tree*) durio(n) *m*.
duricrust ['dju:rikrʌst], *s. Geol:* croûte (calcaire, ferrugineuse, etc.).
during ['dju:riŋ], *prep.* pendant, durant; **d. his life,** pendant (toute) sa vie; sa vie durant; **d. the whole week,** tout le long de la semaine, d'un bout à l'autre de la semaine; **d. the winter,** au cours de l'hiver; **d. the march,** en cours de route; **d. the last year,** dans le courant de l'année dernière; **killed d. a brawl,** tué au cours d'une rixe; **d. that time,** (i) pendant ce temps; *Lit:* cependant; (ii) sur ces entrefaites.
durmast ['də:ma:st], *s. Bot:* **d. (oak),** (i) chêne pubescent, blanc; (ii) chêne à fleurs sessiles, à glands sessiles.
durn[1] [də:n], *v.tr. & i. F:* **d. (it),** zut!
durn[2], **durned** [də:nd], *a. F:* sacré; **it's a d. nuisance,** c'est vachement embêtant.
duro ['du:rou], *s. Num:* peso *m*.
Duroc ['d(j)u:rɔk], *s. NAm:* race *f* de porcs roux aux oreilles pendantes.
durometer [dju'rɔmitər], *s. Tchn:* duromètre *m*.
duroquinone ['dju:roukwi'noun], *s. Ch:* duroquinone *f*.
durra ['dʌrə], *s. Agr:* doura *m*.
durukuli [duru'ku:li], *s. Z:* douroucouli *m*, singe *m* de nuit.
durum ['dju:rəm], *s. Agr:* **d. (wheat),** blé dur.
dusk[1] [dʌsk]. **1.** *a.* (*a*) *A: & Poet:* = DUSKY; (*b*) **it is growing d.,** la nuit tombe. **2.** *s.* (*a*) obscurité *f*, ténèbres *fpl*; (*b*) crépuscule *m*; **at d.,** à la brune, à la nuit tombante; entre chien et loup; **in the d.,** dans la demi-obscurité.
dusk[2], *v. Lit:* **1.** *v.tr.* assombrir, obscurcir. **2.** *v.i.* s'assombrir, s'obscurcir.
duskiness ['dʌskinis], *s.* **1.** (*a*) obscurité *f*; (*b*) demi-jour *m*. **2.** (*of complexion*) (*a*) teint brun, bistré; (*b*) teint noiraud.
dusky ['dʌski], *a.* **1.** sombre, obscur. **2.** (*a*) (*of complexion*) brun foncé *inv*; (*b*) noirâtre; (*of pers.*) noiraud, moricaud.
dust[1] [dʌst], *s.* **1.** poussière *f*; *Poet:* poudre *f*; (*a*) **to lay the d.,** abattre la poussière; **to cover sth. with d.,** couvrir qch. de poussière; empoussiérer qch.; **to remove the d. from sth.,** dépoussiérer qch.; **removal of the d.,** dépoussiérage *m* **(from,** de); **to raise a cloud of d.,** soulever un nuage de poussière; **to raise the d.,** (i) faire de la poussière; (ii) *Ven:* (*of hunted hare*) poudrer; **to reduce sth. to d.,** réduire, mettre, qch. en poussière; **to humble onself in the d.,** s'humilier dans la poussière; **to trample s.o. in the d.,** fouler qn aux pieds; *Lit:* **to bite, lick, the d.,** mordre la poussière; **to shake the d. off one's feet,** secouer la poussière de ses pieds, ses souliers (en quittant un endroit dont on n'a pas eu lieu de se louer); *F:* **to throw d. in s.o.'s eyes,** jeter de la

poudre aux yeux de qn; **to kick up, raise, a d.,** faire une scène; *P:* faire du barouf, du raffut, du train; faire un train de tous les diables; faire de l'esclandre; rouspéter; (*b*) **brick d.,** poussière de brique; **marble d.,** sciure *f* de marbre; **stone d.,** poussier *m*; *Ph:* **cosmic d.,** poussière cosmique; (*c*) *attrib.* **d. bag,** (i) sac *m* à poussière; (ii) *Metall:* poncis *m* (de moule); **d. bath,** bain *m* de poussière, (*of bird*) **to take a d. bath,** s'ébrouer dans la poussière; faire la poudrette; *Mec.E:* **d. casing,** blindage *m* cache-poussière *inv*; **d. catcher, d. collector,** (appareil *m*) capteur *m*, collecteur *m*, de poussières; attrape-poussières *m inv*; *El:* **d. core,** noyau *m* à poudre de fer; **d. exhauster,** aspirateur *m* de poussière; **d.-exhausting plant,** installation *f* d'aspiration des poussières; **d. guard,** (i) pare-poussière *m inv*; garde-poussière *m inv*; écran *m* contre la poussière; (ii) *I.C.E:* cache-soupape(s) *m inv* (de soupape); **d. jacket, d. wrapper,** = DUSTCOVER 1; **d. laden,** (air) chargé de poussière; **d. prevention,** mesures préventives contre la poussière; défense *f* contre la poussière; **d. screen,** pare-poussière *m inv*; **d. sheet,** toile *f* de protection contre la poussière (pendant le nettoyage, etc.); housse *f*; **d. shield,** (i) plaque *f*, (ii) grille *f*, anti-poussière *inv*; *Mec.E: etc:* **d. sleeve,** (manchon *m*, manche *f*) cache-poussière *m inv*; **d. tight,** étanche, imperméable, à la poussière; **d. trap,** (i) attrape-poussières *m inv*; (ii) nid *m* à poussière; *A:* **d. veil,** pare-poussière. **2.** ordures ménagères; **d. destructor,** incinérateur *m* d'ordures; destructeur *m* de déchets; **d. hole,** trou *m* aux ordures; **d. shoot,** lieu *m* de décharge; dépotoir *m*. **3.** poussière fécondante, pollen *m* (des fleurs). **4.** cendres *fpl* (d'un mort); **ashes to ashes, d. to d.,** cendres aux cendres, poudre à la poudre; **to rake over the d. and ashes of the past,** tisonner les cendres du passé; **all their hopes had turned to d. and ashes,** tous leurs espoirs s'étaient anéantis. **5.** *NAm: P:* (*gold dust*) argent *m*; *P:* pognon *m*; **down with the d.!** payez! casquez! *P:* aboule la galette, le pèze!

dust², *v.tr.* **1.** (*a*) saupoudrer (un gâteau, etc.) (**with,** de); (*b*) *Metall:* tamponner (un moule, etc.). **2.** couvrir (qch.) de poussière; empoussiérer (qch.); *Hort:* poudrer. **3.** épousseter (une pièce, un meuble); **to be for ever dusting,** pourchasser la poussière; *F:* **to d. s.o.'s jacket, s.o.'s coat,** flanquer une raclée, une frottée, à qn; secouer les puces à qn; *A:* frotter l'échine à qn. **4.** *v.i.* (*of bird*) s'ébrouer dans la poussière; prendre un bain de poussière.

dustbin ['dʌs(t)bin], *s.* **1.** poubelle *f*; boîte *f*, bac *m*, à, aux, ordures ménagères; **d. raker,** chiffonnier, -ière. **2.** *Av: F:* tourelle de mitrailleuse inférieure; *F:* baignoire *f*.

dust bowl ['dʌs(t)boul], *s. Geog:* région dénudée; zone *f* semi-aride, semi-désertique (produite par l'érosion éolienne).

dust brand ['dʌstbrænd], *s. Agr:* charbon *m* du blé; rouille *f*.

dust cap ['dʌs(t)kæp], *s.* **1.** *Cost:* bonnet *m* anti-poussière; chapeau *m* à poussière; toquet *m*. **2.** *Mec.E: etc:* cache-poussière *m inv*; pare-poussière *m inv*; tamis *m* anti-poussière *inv* (de carburateur, etc.); **roller d. c.,** contre-galets *m inv*.

dustcart ['dʌs(t)kɑːt], *s.* camion *m* d'enlèvement des ordures ménagères; *F:* voiture *f* des boueurs.

dustcoat ['dʌs(t)kout], *s. Cost:* (*a*) *O:* peignoir *m*; (*b*) *O:* cache-poussière *m inv*, pare-poussière *m inv*; (*c*) manteau léger.

dust-colour(ed) ['dʌstkʌlə(d)], *a.* cendré.

dustcover ['dʌs(t)kʌvər], *s.* **1.** housse *f* (pour fauteuil, etc.). **2.** (*a*) *Bookb:* chemise *f*, jaquette *f* (d'un livre); couvre-livre *m*, *pl.* couvre-livres; protège-livre *m*, *pl.* protège-livres; couverture *f* (en papier); **to put a d. on a book,** enchemiser un livre; **putting on a d.,** enchemisage *m*; (*b*) liseuse *f*. **3.** *Mec.E: etc:* (*a*) = DUST CAP 2; (*b*) blindage *m* cache-poussière *inv*; *Aut:* blindage de roue.

dust devil ['dʌst'devl], *s. Meteor:* tourbillon *m* de poussière.

duster ['dʌstər], *s.* **1.** épousseteur, -euse. **2.** chiffon *m* (à épousseter); torchon *m*; essuie-meubles *m inv*; **feather d.,** plumeau *m*, époussette *f*; *Phot:* **plate d.,** blaireau *m*; *Sch:* **blackboard d.,** torchon. **3.** *Nau: P:* pavillon *m*; **red d.** = pavillon marchand. **4.** *NAm:* **d. (coat)** = DUSTCOAT. **5.** saupoudroir *m*; *Hort:* poudreuse *f*. **6.** *Min:* puits sec, improductif.

dustiness ['dʌstinis], *s.* état poudreux, poussiéreux; poudroiement *m* (de la route, etc.).

dusting ['dʌstiŋ], *s.* **1.** (*a*) saupoudrage *m* (d'un gâteau, etc.); *Phot:* poudrage *m*; **d. powder,** (i) *Toil:* (poudre *f* de) talc *m*; (ii) *Med:* poudre antiseptique; (*b*) *Metall:* tamponnement *m* (d'un moule). **2.** (*a*) époussetage *m* (d'une pièce, d'un meuble, etc.); (*b*) *F:* frottée *f*, raclée *f*, tripotée *f*. **3.** *Nau: F:* gros temps; *F:* tour *m* de danse; coup *m* de tabac.

dustman, *pl.* **-men** ['dʌs(t)mən], *s.m.* **1.** boueur, boueux. **2.** *F:* (*of sleepy child*) **the d. is coming,** le marchand de sable a passé.

dustpan ['dʌs(t)pæn], *s.* **1.** pelle *f* à main, à poussière, à ordures; ramasse-poussière *m inv*. **2.** tôle *f* de protection.

dustproof ['dʌs(t)pruːf], *a.* étanche, imperméable (à la poussière); à l'abri de la poussière.

dust shot ['dʌstʃɔt], *s. Sm.a:* cendrée *f*, menuisaille *f*; petit plomb.

duststorm ['dʌst(st)ɔːm], *s. Meteor:* tempête *f* de poussière.

dustup ['dʌstʌp], *s. F:* **1.** querelle *f*; *F:* coup *m* de torchon; prise *f* de bec; **to have a d. with s.o.,** se chamailler, se quereller, avec qn; **they had a d.,** il y a eu une scène. **2.** *Sp: A:* pointe *f* de vitesse; *Row:* enlevage *m*.

dusty ['dʌsti], *a.* **1.** (*a*) poussiéreux, poudreux; recouvert de poussière; **it is very d.,** il fait beaucoup de poussière; **to get d.,** se couvrir de poussière; (*b*) *Ch: etc:* pulvérulent. **2.** maride, dépourvu d'intérêt. **3.** *P: O:* **it's not so d.,** ce n'est pas si mauvais; c'est très passable; *F:* c'est pas mal du tout; *P:* c'est pas piqué des vers. **4.** *F:* **d. answer,** réponse décevante; **to get a d. answer,** éprouver une désillusion.

dusty miller ['dʌsti'milər], *s.* **1.** *Bot:* auricule *f*. **2.** (*a*) *Ent:* teigne *f*; (*b*) *Fish:* variété *f* de mouche artificielle.

Dutch¹ [dʌtʃ]. **1.** *a.* (*a*) hollandais; de Hollande; **the D. Government,** le Gouvernement néerlandais; **D. barn,** hangar *m* à récoltes; **D. cheese,** fromage *m* de Hollande; **D. clock,** (pendule *f* à) coucou *m*; **D. doll,** poupée *f* de bois; **D. elm disease,** maladie *f* des ormes; **D. garden,** jardin régulier à bordures de buis taillé; **D. gold,** oripeau *m*; **D. metal,** tombac *m*; **D. oven,** cuisinière *f*, rôtissoire *f*; **D. tile,** carreau *m* de céramique vernissée, carreau glacé; (*b*) *F:* **to do the D. act,** (i) s'enfuir; *F:* escamper; (ii) se suicider; **D. comfort,** piètre consolation *f*; **D. concert,** charivari *m*; **D. courage,** bravoure *f* après boire; courage arrosé, puisé dans la bouteille; **D. treat,** régal *m* où chacun paie son écot; *adv.* **to go D.,** payer son écot; **to talk to s.o. like a D. uncle,** faire la morale à qn; sermonner qn; faire à qn une semonce paternelle; (*c*) *A:* **High D., Low D.,** haut, bas, allemand, *f.* haut, bas, allemande; (*d*) *U.S:* allemand, de souche allemande. **2.** *s.* (*a*) **the D. (people),** les Hollandais *m*; *P:* **that beats the D.!** c'est le bouquet! il ne manquait plus que ça! (*b*) *Ling:* (i) le hollandais; (ii) *Hist:* **High D., Low D.,** haut, bas, allemand; (iii) *S. Africa:* **Cape D., South African D.,** afrikaans *m*; **High D.,** le hollandais; (*c*) *P:* **to be in D. with s.o.,** être mal vu de qn.

dutch², *s. P:* **my old d.,** ma femme; *F:* ma moitié, ma vieille, la bourgeoise.

Dutchie ['dʌtʃi], *s. P:* **1.** Hollandais, -aise. **2.** *occ.* Allemand, -ande.

Dutchman, *pl.* **-men** ['dʌtʃmən], *s.m.* **1.** Hollandais; *F:* **well, I'm a D.!** pas possible! **I'm a D. if. . .,** traite-moi de tous les noms si . . .; **you'll pay for it or I'm a D.,** vous me le payerez, je vous en donne ma parole; *Bot: NAm:* **Dutchman's breeches,** dicentra *m* cucullaria; **Dutchman's pipe,** aristoloche *f* siphon; *F:* pipe *f* de tabac. **2.** (*a*) *U.S:* Allemand; Américain de souche allemande; (*b*) *Nau:* matelot étranger; (*c*) *A:* vaisseau hollandais. **3.** *Carp: etc:* (*a*) morceau rapporté; flipot *m*; (*b*) cale *f* d'ajustage; garniture *f* d'ajustage.

Dutchy ['dʌtʃi], *s. P:* = DUTCHIE.

duteous ['djuːtiəs], *a. Lit:* soumis, respectueux.

duteously ['djuːtiəsli], *adv. Lit:* avec soumission; suivant son devoir.

dutiable ['djuːtiəbl], *a.* soumis à des droits; passible de droits; imposable, taxable; *Cust:* soumis aux droits de douane; *F:* déclarable.

dutiful ['djuːtif(u)l], *a.* (*of child, etc.*) respectueux, déférent, rangé, soumis; **d. and loyal subjects of the King,** sujets dévoués et fidèles du roi; **a d. husband,** un mari plein d'égards pour sa femme; **with all d. respect . . .,** sauf le respect que je vous dois . . ..

dutifully ['djuːtifuli], *adv.* avec soumission; suivant son devoir.

dutifulness ['djuːtif(u)lnis], *s.* obéissance *f*, soumission *f*.

duty ['djuːti], *s.* **1.** obéissance *f*, respect *m*; **to pay one's d. to s.o.,** présenter ses respects, ses hommages, à qn; **in d. to your wishes. . .,** par déférence pour vos désirs . . ., conformément à vos désirs . . .. **2.** devoir *m* (**to,** envers); **one's d. as a citizen,** nos devoirs de citoyen; **to do one's d.,** s'acquitter de son devoir; faire son devoir; **I know where my d. lies,** je sais ce qui est de mon devoir; **to do one's d. by, to, s.o.,** remplir son devoir, ses obligations, envers qn; **do your d. come what may,** fais ce que dois, advienne que pourra; **I shall make it my d. to . . ., I shall make it a point of d. to . . .,** je considérerai de mon devoir, je prendrai à tâche, de . . .; **he thought it his d. to retire,** il crut devoir se retirer; *Ecc:* **to go to, perform, one's duties,** accomplir ses devoirs religieux, faire ses dévotions; **to fail in one's d.,** manquer à son devoir; **it is my d. to make sure that . . ., to me falls the d. of making sure that . . .,** il m'appartient, c'est mon devoir, il m'incombe, de m'assurer que . . .; **you are in d. bound, are d. bound, to do it,** votre devoir vous y oblige; **as in duty b.,** comme il est de mon devoir; comme de juste; **from a sense of d.,** par devoir; **to pay a d. call,** faire une visite obligée, une visite de politesse; (*of mutineer, etc.*) **to return to d.,** rentrer dans le devoir; **that does not relieve you of the d. of keeping clear of another ship,** cela ne vous affranchit pas de l'obligation de vous écarter de la route d'un autre navire; *F:* **have you done your d.?** as-tu fait caca? **3.** (*a*) *usu.pl.* fonction(s) *f*(*pl*); attributions *fpl*; **public duties,** fonctions publiques; **the duties of various officials,** les attributions de divers fonctionnaires; **to enter upon, take up, one's duties,** entrer en fonctions, en charge; **to hand over one's duties,** (i) résigner ses fonctions; (ii) remettre, transmettre, ses fonctions (**to,** à); **in the course of my duties I was able to . . .,** au cours de ma carrière, à l'occasion de mon service, j'ai pu . . .; (*b*) *Mil:* mission *f*; tâche *f*; **the duties of infantry, artillery,** les missions, les tâches, de l'infanterie, de l'artillerie; **the chief duties of reconnaissance aircraft,** les principales missions des avions de reconnaissance; **rearguard d.,** mission d'arrière-garde; **on protective d.,** en mission d'éclairage, de couverture; en éclaireur(s); **to be on detached d.,** *U.S:* **on temporary d.,** être en mission, être détaché; être en position d'absence temporaire. **4.** service *m*; (*a*) **to be on d.,** être de service; (*in factory, playground, etc.*) être de surveillance; exercer la surveillance; *Navy:* être de service, de corvée; **to be on d. for the day, for the week,** être (de service) de jour, de semaine; **to be off d.,** ne pas être de service; être libre; *Mil:* avoir quartier libre; **what time do you go on, come off, d.?** à quelle heure prenez-vous, quittez-vous, votre service? *F:* **I'm never off d.,** mon travail n'en finit pas, ne finit jamais; **to hand over d. to s.o.,** remettre, passer, le service à qn; **to do d. for s.o.,** remplacer qn (dans son service); *F:* **settee that does d. for a bed,** canapé qui sert, fait office, tient lieu, de lit; *Ecc:* **to take s.o.'s d.,** officier pour qn; **d. chart, d. roster,** tableau *m* de service; (*b*) *Mil: Navy: etc:* **duties in barracks,** service intérieur; **d. covered by orders,** service commandé; **while on d.,** en service commandé; dans l'exécution du service; **active d.,** (i) service actif; (ii) activité *f* de service; **d. with troop,** service avec, dans, la troupe; **orderly d.,** service de planton; **on guard d.,** de service de garde; **to come off guard d.,** descendre de garde; **on sentry d.,** de, en, faction; **fatigue d.,** corvée *f*; **on fatigue d.,** de corvée; **extra d.,** (i) service supplémentaire; (ii) corvée supplémentaire; *Av:* **flying d.,** service en vol; heures *fpl* de vol; **d. men,** hommes de corvée; **d. officer, d. N.C.O.,** officier *m*, sous-officier *m*, de service; permanencier *m*; **d. tour, tour of d.,** tour *m* de service. **5.** droit *m*; (*a*) **customs d.,** droit(s) de douane, droits d'entrée; **liable to d.,** passible de droits; soumis aux droits; **d. on silk,** droits d'entrée sur les soieries; **d. paid,** franc de douane; douané; **to take the d. o goods,** exonérer une marchandise; (*b*) **stamp d.,** droit de timbre. **6.** *Mec.E: etc:* rendement *m*, débit *m* (d'une machine); **heavy-d. engine,** moteur de fatigue; **heavy-d. gear,** appareil soumis à un travail très dur; **heavy-d. jack,** cric *m* de force; (*of propeller, etc.*) **d. under service conditions,** rendement d'appropriation; **d. factor,** coefficient *m* d'utilisation; *El:* **d. cycle,** temps *m* de mise sous tension; **intermittent d., permanent d.,** service intermittent, permanent.

duty-free ['djuːti'friː], *a.* exempt de droit; franc de tout droit; (importé) en franchise; *Cust:* **d.-f. articles** (*of personal apparel, etc.*), effets usagers; **d.-f. shop,** boutique *f* hors taxe.

duumvir, *pl.* **-s, -viri** [dju(ː)'ʌmvər, -vəz, -vir(a)i], *s.m. Rom.Hist:* duumvir.

duumviral [dju(ː)'ʌmvirəl], *a. Rom.Hist:* duumviral -aux.

duumvirate [dju(ː)'ʌmvirət], *s. Rom.Hist:* duumvirat *m*.

duvet ['djuːvei], *s.* ((i) édredon *m*, (ii) sac *m* de couchage, de) duvet *m*.

dux [dʌks], *s. Sch: A:* premier, -ière (de la classe); élève *mf* qui a remporté le prix d'excellence; *F:* prix d'excellence.

dwale [dweil], *s. Bot: Poet:* belladone *f*; *F:* belle-dame *f*, *pl.* belles-dames.

dwang [dwæŋ], *s. Carp:* moise *f.*
dwarf[1] [dwɔ:f], *s. & a.* (*of pers.*) nain, *f.* naine; nabot, -ote; (*of plant*) (i) nain; (ii) rabougri; **d. tree,** arbre nain; *Astr:* **d. (star),** (étoile) naine; **white d.,** naine blanche; *Const:* **d. wall,** muret *m.*
dwarf[2], *v.tr.* **1.** empêcher (qn, qch.) de croître; rabougrir ou naniser (une plante). **2.** rapetisser (par contraste); **tower that dwarfs the main building,** tour *f* dont la hauteur écrase le corps de bâtiment.
dwarfed [dwɔ:ft], *a.* (arbre, arbuste) rabougri.
dwarfish ['dwɔ:fiʃ], *a.* (de) nain; chétif; (*of pers.*) nabot, -ote.
dwarfishness ['dwɔ:fiʃnis], **dwarfism** ['dwɔ:fizm], *s.* petite taille; nanisme *m.*
dwell[1] [dwel], *s. Mec.E:* arrêt momentané (du mouvement).
dwell[2], *v.i.* (*p.t. & p.p.* **dwelt**) **1.** *Lit:* **to d. in a place,** habiter (dans) un lieu; demeurer, résider, dans un lieu; être domicilié dans un lieu; **to d. in the country,** habiter (à) la campagne. **2.** rester; se fixer; être fixé; **her memory dwells with me,** son souvenir reste présent à ma mémoire; **this hope dwells within our hearts,** cet espoir repose dans notre cœur; **to let one's glance, one's eye, d. on s.o.,** appuyer son regard, arrêter son regard, sur qn. **3. to d. on (sth.),** insister sur, s'étendre sur, s'appesantir sur (un sujet); appuyer sur (une syllabe, etc.); faire ressortir (les difficultés); **to d. on a fact,** arrêter sa pensée, s'arrêter, sur un fait; **we will not d. on that,** glissons là-dessus; *Mus:* **to d. on a note,** appuyer (sur) une note; *F:* pauser sur une note. **4.** *Equit:* (*of horse*) s'arrêter, hésiter (avant de sauter ou après le saut).
dweller ['dwelər], *s.* **1.** habitant, -ante (**in, on,** de); *Prehist: etc:* **cave d.,** troglodyte *mf.* **2.** *Equit:* cheval *m* qui s'arrête, hésite, avant de sauter.
dwelling ['dweliŋ], *s.* **1.** (*a*) *Lit:* séjour *m,* habitation *f,* résidence *f* (dans un endroit); (*b*) insistance *f* (sur un fait, une note). **2. d. (place),** (i) *Lit:* lieu *m* de séjour; (ii) domicile *m,* habitation, logis *m,* demeure *f,* logement *m;* **d. house,** maison *f* d'habitation.
dwindle ['dwindl], *v.i.* **to d. (away),** diminuer, dépérir, s'affaiblir; (*of political party*) s'amenuiser; **to d. to nothing,** venir à rien; se réduire à rien.
dwindling[1] ['dwindliŋ], *a.* diminuant, faiblissant; **the d. production of wheat,** la raréfaction du blé.
dwindling[2], *s.* diminution *f,* dépérissement *m,* affaiblissement *m;* amenuisement *m* (d'un parti politique); *Fin:* déperdition *f,* dépérissement *m* (de capital).
dyad ['daiæd], *s. Phil: Poet: Biol:* dyade *f; Ch:* radical divalent.
dyadic [dai'ædik], *a.* dyadique; *Cmptr:* **d. operation,** opération *f* binaire à deux opérandes.
Dyak ['daiæk], *s. Ethn:* D(a)yak *m.*
dyarch ['daiɑ:k], *s.* dyarque *m.*
dyarchic [dai'ɑ:kik], *a.* dyarchique.
dyarchy ['daiɑ:ki], *s.* dyarchie *f.*
dye[1] [dai], *s.* **1.** (*a*) *Dy:* teinture *f,* teint *m;* **fast d.,** bon teint, grand teint; **fading d.,** petit teint; *Ind:* **to give the last d.,** parachever la teinture; (*b*) teinte *f; esp. F:* **villain of the deepest d.,** coquin fieffé; triple coquin; coquin de la plus belle eau, de la pire espèce. **2.** matière colorante; teinture, colorant *m;* **basic dyes,** colorants basiques; **synthetic dyes,** matières colorantes de synthèse; *Phot:* **d. solution,** bain colorant.
dye[2], *v.* (*pr.p.* **dyeing**) **1.** *v.tr.* (*a*) teindre; **to d. sth. black,** teindre qch. en noir; **to have a dress dyed,** faire teindre une robe; (*b*) teinter (un film, etc.). **2.** *v.i.* (se) teindre; **material that dyes well,** tissu qui prend bien la teinture.
dyeable ['daiəbl], *a.* qui prend bien la teinture.
dyed-in-the-wool ['daidinðə'wul], *a.* (drap) teint en laine; *F:* **a d.-in-t.-w. free-trader,** un libre-échangiste convaincu, bon teint, inébranlable; **a d.-in-t.-w. Englishman,** un Anglais pur sang, de bon aloi.
dyehouse ['daihaus], *s.* teinturerie *f.*
dyeing ['daiiŋ], *s.* **1.** (*a*) teinture *f* (d'étoffes, des cheveux); (*b*) teintage *m.* **2. d. (trade),** teinturerie *f.*
dyeline ['dailain], *a. Phot:* **d. process,** diazotypie *f.*
dyer ['daiər], *s.* **1.** teinturier *m;* **d. and cleaner,** teinturier dégraisseur. **2.** *Bot:* **dyer's greenweed,** (i) (*also* **dyer's weed, dyer's rocket**) réséda *m* des teinturiers; gaude *f;* (ii) genêt *m* des teinturiers; genestrol(l)e *f;* herbe *f* à jaunir; **dyer's moss,** orseille *f.*
dyestuff ['daistʌf], *s.* matière colorante; matière tinctoriale.
dyewood ['daiwud], *s.* bois *m* de teinture; bois tinctorial; **red d.,** bois de Brésil.
dyeworks ['daiwɔ:ks], *s.pl.* (*usu. with sg. const.*) teinturerie *f.*
dying[1] ['daiiŋ]. **1.** *a.* mourant, moribond, agonisant; **in a d. voice,** d'une voix éteinte; **the d. day,** le jour expirant. **2.** *s.pl.* **the dead and the d.,** les morts *m* et les moribonds *m;* **prayers for the d.,** prières *f* des agonisants.
dying[2], *s.* agonie *f,* mort *f;* **d. bed,** lit *m* de mort; **to one's d. day,** jusqu'au jour de la mort; jusqu'à la dernière heure; jusqu'à son dernier jour; jusqu'au dernier soupir; **I shall remember it to my d. day,** je m'en souviendrai jusqu'à la mort; **d. words,** dernières paroles; **with his d. breath,** de sa voix agonisante; **d. declaration,** déclaration faite (par un meurtrier) sur son lit de mort.
dying away ['daiiŋə'wei], *s.* affaiblissement *m,* assourdissement *m* (d'un son).
dying back ['daiiŋ'bæk], *s. Hort:* dépérissement *m* (d'une plante).
dying down ['daiiŋ'daun], *s.* **1.** effeuillaison *f* (d'une plante). **2.** extinction graduelle (du feu).
dying out ['daiiŋ'aut], *s.* extinction graduelle (d'une race); raréfaction *f* (d'un animal).
dyke[1] [daik], *s.* **1.** (*a*) *Hyd.E:* digue *f,* levée *f;* **strengthening d.,** contre-digue *f, pl.* contre-digues; **cross d.,** duit *m* (dans un cours d'eau); **d. reeve,** garde *m,* inspecteur *m,* des digues et écluses (des marécages de l'Est-Anglie); **to raise a d. against the barbarian hordes,** opposer une digue aux hordes des barbares; (*b*) chaussée surélevée, en remblai, en talus. **2.** fossé *m,* chenal *m,* -aux. **3.** *Geol: Min:* filon *m* d'injection; veine *f* de substance pierreuse; dyke *m;* **phonolitic d.,** dyke de phonolite. **4.** *esp. Scot:* **dry (stone) d.,** muraillon *m.*
dyke[2], *v.tr.* **1.** (*a*) endiguer (un cours d'eau); protéger (un terrain) par des digues; (*b*) drainer (un terrain) en faisant des fossés; creuser des fossés dans (un terrain). **2.** rouir (le lin, le chanvre).
dynameter [dai'næmitər], *s. Opt:* dynamètre *m.*
dynamic [dai'næmik]. **1.** *a.* (*a*) *Ph: etc:* (pouvoir, équilibre, unité, etc.) dynamique; **d. energy,** énergie actuelle; (*of force, etc.*) **to become d.,** se dynamiser; *Elcs:* **d. microphone,** micro(phone) *m* électrodynamique; **d. pick-up,** pick-up *m* électrodynamique; *Cmptr:* **d. storage,** mémoire *f* dynamique, cyclique; (*b*) *Fig:* **d. personality, d. character,** caractère *m* dynamique, énergique; dynamisme *m;* (*c*) *Med:* (trouble) fonctionnel; (*d*) *Mus:* **d. range,** dynamique *f* (d'un instrument). **2.** *s.* (*a*) *Ph:* force motrice; (*b*) *Phil:* dynamique; (*c*) *Mus:* dynamique.
dynamical [dai'næmik(ə)l], *a.* = DYNAMIC 1. (*a*).
dynamically [dai'næmik(ə)li], *adv.* dynamiquement.
dynamicizer [dai'næmisaizər], *s. Elcs:* convertisseur *m* parallèle-série.
dynamicism [dai'næmisizm], **dynamism** ['dainəmizm], *s.* dynamisme *m;* **group dynamism,** la dynamique des groupes.
dynamicist [dai'næmisist], **dynamist** ['dainəmist], *s.* dynamiste *m.*
dynamics [dai'næmiks], *s.pl.* (*usu. with sg.const.*) dynamique *f.*
dynamitard ['dainəmaitɑ:d], *s.* dynamiteur *m.*
dynamite[1] ['dainəmait], *s.* **1.** dynamite *f,* nobélite *f;* **gum d.,** dynamite gomme; gélatine explosive, détonante; **gelatine d.,** nitrogélatine *f;* dynamite-gélatine *f, pl.* dynamites-gélatines; **d. store, d. magazine,** dépôt *m* de dynamite; dynamitière *f;* **d. factory,** dynamiterie *f; F:* **subject that is political d.,** sujet explosif; *P:* **it's d.!** c'est du tonnerre! c'est sensas! **2.** *P:* stupéfiant *m; esp.* (i) héroïne *f;* (ii) marihuana *f.*
dynamite[2], *v.tr.* faire sauter (des roches, etc.) à la dynamite; dynamiter (un édifice, etc.).
dynamiter ['dainəmaitər], *s.* dynamiteur *m.*
dynamiting ['dainəmaitiŋ], *s.* dynamitage *m.*
dynamization ['dainəmai'zeiʃ(ə)n], *s.* dynamisation *f.*
dynamo, *pl.* **-os** ['dainəmou, -ouz], *s.* dynamo *f;* génératrice *f,* générateur *m* (de courant); **low-tension d.,** dynamo-quantité *f, pl.* dynamos-quantité; **high-tension d.,** dynamo-tension *f, pl.* dynamos-tension; **d. lighting,** éclairage *m* par dynamo; *Nau:* **d. room,** compartiment *m* des dynamos.
dynamoelectric(al) ['dainəmoui'lektrik(l)], *a. El:* dynamo-électrique, *pl.* dynamo-électriques.
dynamogenesis ['dainəmou'dʒenisis], *s. Physiol:* dynamogénie *f.*
dynamogenic ['dainəmou'dʒenik], **dynamogenous** [dainə'mɔdʒinəs], *a.* dynamogène, dynamogénique.
dynamograph ['dainəmougræf], *s.* dynamographe *m.*
dynamometamorphism ['dainəmoumetə'mɔ:fizm], *s. Geol:* dynamométamorphisme *m.*
dynamometer [dainə'mɔmitər], *s.* **1.** *Mec:* dynamomètre *m.* **2.** *Opt:* dynamomètre, dynamètre *m.*
dynamometric(al) ['dainəmo'metrik(l)], *a. El:* dynamométrique.
dynamometry [dainə'mɔmitri], *s. Mec:* dynamométrie *f.*
dynamotor ['dainəmoutər], *s. Aut:* dynamo démarreur *f, pl.* dynamos-démarreurs; dynastart *f;* dynamoteur *m;* convertisseur *m.*
dynast ['dinəst, 'dainæst], *s.* dynaste *m.*
dynastes [di'næsti:z], *s. Ent:* dynaste *m.*
dynastic [di'næstik, dai-], *a.* dynastique.
dynasty ['dinəsti], *s.* dynastie *f.*
dynatron ['dainətrɔn], *s. Elcs:* dynatron *m;* **d. effect,** effet *m* dynatron.
dyne [dain], *s. Ph.Meas:* dyne *f.*
dynode ['dainoud], *s. Elcs:* dynode *f.*
dypnone ['dipnoun], *s. Ch:* dypnone *f.*
dys- [dis], *pref.* dys-.
dysadaptation [disædæp'teiʃ(ə)n], *s. Med:* mauvaise adaptation (de l'œil).
dysaesthesia [disəs'θi:ziə], *s. Med:* dysesthésie *f.*
dysanalyte [dis'ænəlait], *s. Miner:* dysanalyte *f.*
dysarthria [dis'ɑ:θriə], *s. Med:* dysarthrie *f.*
dysbasia [dis'beisiə], *s. Med:* dysbasie *f.*
dyschromatopsia [diskroumə'tɔpsiə], *s. Med:* dyschromatopsie *f.*
dyschromia [dis'kroumiə], *s. Med:* dyschromie *f.*
dyscrasia [dis'kreiziə], *s. Med:* dyscrasie *f.*
dyscrasic [dis'kreizik], **dyscratic** [dis'krætik], *a. Med:* dyscrasique.
dyscrasite ['diskrəsait], *s. Miner:* dyscrase *f,* dyscrasite *f.*
dysenteric [disen'terik], *a. Med:* dysentérique.
dysenteriform ['disəntrifɔ:m], *a. Med:* dysentériforme.
dysentery ['disəntri], *s. Med:* dysenterie *f;* **amoebic d.,** dysenterie amibienne.
dysesthesia [disəs'θi:ziə], *s. Med:* dysesthésie *f.*
dysfunction [dis'fʌŋkʃ(ə)n], *s. Med:* dysfonctionnement *m.*
dysgenesis [dis'dʒenisis], *s. Biol:* dysgénésie *f.*
dysgenic [dis'dʒenik], *a. Biol:* contraire à l'eugénisme.
dysgraphia [dis'græfiə], *s. Med:* dysgraphie *f.*
dys(h)idrosis [dis(h)ai'drousis], *s. Med:* dys(h)idrose *f.*
dyskeratosis [diskerə'tousis], *s. Med:* dyskératose *f.*
dyskinesia [disk(a)i'ni:ziə], *s. Med:* dyscinésie *f,* dyskinésie *f.*
dyslalia [dis'leiliə], *s. Med:* dyslalie *f.*
dyslectic [dis'lektik], **dyslexic** [dis'leksik], *a. & s. Med:* dyslexique (*mf*).
dyslexia [dis'leksiə], *s. Med:* dyslexie *f.*
dyslogia [dis'loudʒiə], *s. Med:* dyslogie *f.*
dyslogistic [dislə'dʒistik], *a. Lit:* de désapprobation; péjoratif.
dysluite ['disluait], *s. Miner:* dysluite *f,* dyslyite *f.*
dysmenorrhoea [dismenə'riə], *s. Med:* dysménorrhée *f.*
dysmenorrhoeal [dismenə'riəl], *a. Med:* dysménorrhéique.
dysmetria [dis'metriə], *s. Med:* dysmétrie *f.*
dysmnesia [dis'ni:ziə], *s. Med:* dysmnésie *f.*
dysmorphophobia [dismɔ:sə'foubiə], *s. Med:* dysmorphophobie *f.*
dysorexia [disə'reksiə], *s. Med:* dysorexie *f.*
dyspepsia [dis'pepsiə], *s. Med:* dyspepsie *f;* **acid d.,** aigreurs *fpl* d'estomac; acidisme *m; F:* brûlures *fpl* d'estomac.
dyspeptic [dis'peptik]. **1.** *a. & s. Med:* dyspepsique (*mf*), dyspeptique (*mf*). **2.** *a. F:* mélancolique, morne; **to take a d. view of things,** broyer du noir.
dysphagia [dis'feidʒiə], *s. Med:* dysphagie *f.*
dysphagic [dis'fædʒik], *a. Med:* dysphagique.
dysphasia [dis'feiziə], *s. Med:* dysphasie *f.*
dysphonia [dis'founiə], *s. Med:* dysphonie *f.*
dysphoria [disfɔ:riə], *s.* dysphorie *f.*
disphrenia [dis'fri:niə], *s. Med:* dysphrénie *f.*
dysplasia [dis'pleiziə], *s. Med:* dysplasie *f.*
dysplastic [dis'plæstik], *a. Med:* caractérisé par la dysplasie.
dyspnoea [dis'(p)ni:ə], *s. Med:* dyspnée *f.*
dyspnoeal [dis'(p)ni:əl], **dyspnoeic** [dis'(p)ni:ik], *a. Med:* dyspnéique.
dysprosium [dis'prouziəm], *s. Ch:* dysprosium *m.*
dystetic [dis'tetik], *a. Ph:* **d. mixture,** mélange *m* dont la température de fusion reste constante.
dysthymia [dis'θaimiə], *s. Psy:* dysthymie *f.*
dysthyroidism [dis'θairɔidizm], *s. Med:* dysthyroïdie *f.*
dystocia [dis'touʃiə], **dystokia** [dis'toukiə], *s. Med:* dystocie *f.*
dystrophic [dis'trɔfik], *a. Med:* dystrophique.
dystrophy ['distrəfi], *s. Med:* dystrophie *f;* **muscular d.,** dystrophie musculaire progressive.
dysuria [dis'ju:riə], **dysury** ['disjuri], *s. Med:* dysurie *f.*
dysuric [dis'ju:rik], *a. Med:* dysurique.
dytiscid [di'tisid], *a. Ent:* dytique.
Dytiscidae [di'tisidi:], *s.pl. Ent:* dytiscidés *m.*
dytiscus [di'tiskəs], *s. Ent:* dyti(s)que *m.*
dziggetai ['(d)zigitai], *s. Z:* hémione *m.*
Dzungaria [(d)zuŋ'gɛəriə], *Pr.n. Geog:* Dzoungarie *f.*

E

E, e [i:], *s.* **1.** (la lettre) E, e *m*; *Tp:* **E for Edward,** E comme Eugène. **2.** *Mus:* mi *m*; **key of E flat,** clef *f* de mi bémol.

each [i:tʃ]. **1.** *a.* chaque; **e. man, e. woman,** chaque homme, chaque femme; **e. day,** chaque jour; tous les jours; **between e. course we dance,** entre chaque plat on danse; **e. elector has two votes,** chaque électeur, tout électeur, a deux voix; **e. one of us,** chacun, chacune, de nous, d'entre nous; (*emphatic*) **he gives figures to prove e. statement,** il cite des chiffres à l'appui de chacune de ses affirmations. **2.** *pron.* (*a*) chacun, -une; **e. of us,** (*emphatic*) **e. and all of us,** chacun de nous; chacun d'entre nous; **e. brought his offering,** chacun a apporté son offrande; ils ont apporté chacun leur offrande; **to e. according to his deserts,** à chacun selon ses mérites; **e. of them went on his way,** ils s'en allèrent chacun de leur côté; chacun s'en alla de son côté; **e. of them was handed a bouquet,** on leur remit à chacun un bouquet; **after e. of us had swallowed a cup of coffee we set out,** après avoir avalé chacun une tasse de café, nous sommes partis; **they stood still e. staring at the other,** ils restaient immobiles à se regarder; (*b*) **we e. earn £10, we earn £10 e.,** nous gagnons £10 chacun; **peaches at 5p e.,** pêches à 5p chacune, 5p pièce; **a little of e.,** un peu de chaque; (*c*) **e. other,** l'un l'autre, l'une l'autre; les uns les autres, les unes les autres; **for e. other,** l'un pour l'autre; **we call on e. other,** on va les uns chez les autres; **they are afraid of e. other,** ils ont peur l'un de l'autre; **separated from e. other,** séparés l'un de l'autre; **to fight e. other,** se battre; **to strike against e. other,** s'entrechoquer; **they flatter e. other,** ils se flattent réciproquement.

eager ['i:gər], *a.* (*a*) ardent, passionné; **e. student of . . .,** (étudiant) passionné de . . .; **the public was e. and receptive,** le public se montra vibrant et réceptif; **he was e. for praise,** il avait soif d'éloges; **e. for knowledge,** avide de tout savoir; **e. in pursuit of the enemy,** ardent à poursuivre l'ennemi; **to be e. to do sth.,** être impatient de faire qch., avoir une grande impatience de faire qch., désirer ardemment faire qch.; **e. to start,** impatient de partir; **to be e. to please,** être désireux, avoir un vif désir, de plaire; désirer vivement plaire; **to be too e. to accept,** montrer trop d'empressement à accepter; **passionately e. to undertake this journey,** passionné d'entreprendre ce voyage; *F:* **e. beaver,** fayot *m*; (*b*) **e. pursuit,** âpre poursuite *f*; *Ven:* **pack in e. pursuit,** meute acharnée à la poursuite; **e. desire,** vif désir; **e. hopes,** (i) espérances *f* avides; (ii) ardent espoir; vif espoir, vives espérances; **e. look,** regard *m* avide; (*c*) *A:* **e. air,** air *m* (d'un froid) piquant; **the e. morning air,** l'air âpre du matin.

eagerly ['i:gəli], *adv.* ardemment, passionnément, avidement; **to read sth. e.,** lire qch. avidement; **to desire sth. e.,** désirer qch. passionnément; **to listen e.,** écouter avidement, avec avidité, avec empressement; **to look at sth. e.,** regarder qch. d'un œil avide; *Ven:* **e. pursuing the game,** poursuivant âprement le gibier; poursuivant le gibier avec acharnement.

eagerness ['i:gənis], *s.* ardeur *f* (au travail, etc.); impatience *f* (de voir qn); empressement *m* (à se rendre utile, etc.); vif désir (d'apprendre qch. etc.); **e. in the pursuit of the enemy,** ardeur à poursuivre l'ennemi; **to show e. in doing sth.,** montrer un intérêt très vif à faire qch.; **e. to succeed,** ardent désir de réussir.

eagle ['i:gl], *s.* **1.** *Orn:* (*a*) aigle *m*; **mother e. and her young,** aigle *f* et ses aiglons; **golden e.,** aigle royal, fauve, doré; **crowned e.,** aigle couronné; **spotted e.,** aigle criard; **lesser spotted e.,** aigle pomarin; **tawny e.,** aigle ravisseur; **steppe e.,** aiole des steppes; **Bonelli's e.,** aigle de Bonelli, aigle à queue barrée; **imperial e., king e.,** aigle impérial; **booted e.,** aigle botté; **bateleur e.,** aigle bateleur; **monkey-eating e.,** aigle des singes; **crested serpent e.,** aigle serpentaire; (*b*) **sea e.,** pygargue *m*; **bald e.,** pygargue à tête blanche, *Fr.C:* aigle à tête blanche; **white-tailed e.,** *NAm:* **gray sea e.,** pygargue à queue blanche, *Fr.C:* aigle gris; **(African) fish e.,** pygargue vocifère; (*c*) **vulturine fish e.,** vautour *m* pêcheur, vautour des palmes; **harpy e.,** harpie *f*; **Chilean sea e.,** buse *f* aguia; **short-toed e.,** circaète *m* Jean-le-blanc; **wedge-tailed e.,** uraëte *m*, aigle audacieux. **2.** *Bot:* **e. fern,** fougère arborescente; fougère impériale, fougère à l'aigle. **3.** *Ich:* **e. ray,** aigle *m* de mer; tère *f*. **4.** (*a*) *Her:* aigle *f*; **double-headed e.,** double aigle; aigle à deux têtes; **e. displayed sable,** aigle de sable éployée; (*b*) **the Roman eagles,** les aigles romaines; **the Imperial Eagles,** les aigles impériales (des armées napoléoniennes); (*c*) **the Black E. of Prussia,** l'Aigle noir de Prusse; **the White E. of Poland,** l'Aigle blanc de Pologne; (*d*) *Mil: U.S:* aigle *m* (insigne de grade de colonel); (*e*) *A.Num: U.S:* (= *10 dollars*) aigle *m*; **double e.,** pièce *f* de vingt dollars; (*f*) *Ecc:* **e. lectern,** aigle *m*. **5.** *Golf:* deux coups *m* au-dessous de la normale du trou.

eagle-coloured ['i:glkʌləd], *a.* (cheval) aquilain, aquilant.

eagle-eyed ['i:gl'aid], *a.* aux yeux d'aigle; au regard d'aigle; **to be e.-e.,** avoir des yeux d'aigle.

eaglet ['i:glit], *s.* **1.** *Orn:* aiglon *m*. **2.** *Her:* aiglette *f*.

eaglewood ['i:glwud], *s.* bois *m* d'aigle, d'aloès, calambac *m*, calambour *m*, calambouc *m*.

eagre ['eigər, 'i:gər], *s. Oc:* mascaret *m*; raz *m* de marée; barre *f* d'eau.

ear[1] ['iər], *s.* **1.** oreille *f*; (*a*) *Anat:* **the external e.,** (i) (*also* **the outer e.**) l'oreille externe; (ii) le pavillon de l'oreille; la conque; **the middle e.,** l'oreille moyenne; le barillet; caisse *f* du tympan; **the internal e.,** l'oreille interne; le labyrinthe; *Med:* **e. specialist,** auriculiste *mf*, auriste *mf*; **e., nose and throat specialist,** oto-rhino-laryngologiste *mf*; (*b*) **e. trumpet,** cornet *m* acoustique; **e. muffs,** drapeaux *m* protège-oreilles; **e. protector,** (i) protège-tympan *m inv*; *Artil:* bonnet *m*, béguin *m*, protecteur *m* auriculaire (de canonnier); (ii) *Rugby Fb:* protège-oreilles *m inv*; **e. pendant,** pendant *m* d'oreille; **to wear rings in one's ears,** porter des anneaux aux oreilles; **a smile from e. to e.,** un sourire épanoui jusqu'aux deux oreilles; **to clip the ears of a dog,** écourter (les oreilles d' un chien; **to speak in(to) s.o.'s e.,** parler à l'oreille de qn; (*of words*) **to go in at one e. and out at the other,** entrer par une oreille et sortir par l'autre; **your ears must have burned, must have been tingling,** les oreilles ont dû vous corner, vous tinter; **to cock one's ears,** dresser, tendre, l'oreille; ouvrir grand les oreilles; **with his ear(s) cocked,** l'oreille tendue; **to prick (up) one's ears,** (i) (*of animal*) dresser les oreilles; (ii) (*of pers.*) tendre l'oreille, dresser l'oreille, ouvrir de grandes oreilles; *F:* **to be up to the ears, over head and ears, in work,** être accablé, surchargé, débordé, de travail; avoir du travail par-dessus la tête; **the ceiling fell about our ears,** le plafond nous tomba sur la tête, s'écroula sur nous; **to bring a storm about one's ears,** s'attirer une tempête de reproches, de protestations; **he's got nothing between his ears,** il est bête comme ses pieds; **I would give my ears for it, to have it,** je me ferais couper les oreilles pour l'avoir; **to set people by the ears,** brouiller les gens; mettre la discorde, semer la dissension, entre les gens, dans un groupe; *F:* **to be (thrown, pitched) out on one's e.,** être sorti, se faire sortir; **to send s.o. away with a flea in his e.,** (i) renvoyer qn avec un refus net et catégorique; (ii) éconduire qn avec une verte semonce; lui dire ses quatre vérités; **he went off with a flea in his e.,** il est parti l'oreille basse, tout penaud; **to box s.o.'s ears,** gifler, *F:* talocher, qn; flanquer une claque, une taloche, à qn; *P:* **to give s.o. a thick e.,** flanquer une gifle, une taloche, à qn; **to get a thick e.,** recevoir une gifle, une taloche; *Prov:* **walls have ears,** les murs ont des oreilles; *U.S: F:* **to get s.o. up on his ears,** fâcher qn; **dog's e.,** (i) corne faite à la page d'un livre; (ii) *Bookb:* larron *m*; témoin *m*; (*c*) **to have sharp ears,** avoir l'oreille, l'ouïe, fine; **to have a keen, sensitive, e.,** avoir l'oreille sensible, l'ouïe fine; **deaf in one e.,** sourd(e) d'une oreille; *Prov:* **little pitchers have long ears,** les petits enfants ont l'oreille fine; **to have an e., a fine e., for music; to have a good e.,** avoir l'oreille musicienne, musicale, juste; avoir de l'oreille; **to have a poor e., no e., (for music),** ne pas avoir d'oreille; **to play by e.,** jouer d'oreille; **to play it by e.,** aller au pifomètre; **to listen with one e. only, with only half an e.,** n'écouter que d'une oreille; **to listen with all one's ears, with both ears,** écouter de toutes ses oreilles; **to keep one's ears open, one's e. to the ground,** être, se tenir, aux écoutes; **she keeps her ears open for scandal,** *F:* **she has itching ears,** elle est toujours à l'affût du scandale; **to strain one's ears,** tendre l'oreille; **to have s.o.'s e.,** avoir, posséder, l'oreille de qn; **to gain s.o.'s e.,** (i) s'assurer l'attention bienveillante de qn; (ii) obtenir une audience avec qn; **to give e., lend an e., lend one's e., to s.o.,** prêter l'oreille à qn; **to give e. to s.o.'s petition,** écouter la requête de qn; **to give a cold e. to a request,** refuser d'entendre une requête; **to turn a sympathetic e., a ready e., to s.o.'s request,** prêter une oreille complaisante aux prières de qn; **to close one's ears to the truth,** fermer l'oreille à la vérité; **it has come to my e. that . . .,** il m'est venu à l'oreille, aux oreilles, que . . .; **if it should come to the ears of . . .,** si cela parvient aux oreilles de . . .; **you might drop this hint into his e.,** glissez-lui cet avis à l'oreille; dites-lui-en un mot dans le creux de l'oreille; *Lit:* (*of sound*) **to greet the e.,** frapper l'oreille; (*d*) *Bot:* **bear's e.,** oreille d'ours; auricule *f*; **elephant's e.,** bégonia *m*. **2.** *Tchn:* (*a*) anse *f*, oreille (de vase); anse, mentonnet *m* (d'une bombe); anse (de cloche); orillon *m* (d'une écuelle, etc.); happe *f* (d'une chaudière); languette *f* (d'une pièce de verrouillage, etc.); (*b*) *Conch:* oreillette *f* (d'un coquillage); (*c*) *Mec.E:* ouïe *f*, œillard *m* (de ventilateur, pompe, etc.); (*d*) *Cin:* pare-soleil *m inv*.

ear[2], *s.* épi *m* (de blé, de maïs); **wheat in the e.,** blé en épi; **e. cockle(s),** nielle *f* (des blés).

ear[3], *v.i.* monter en épi; épier.

earache ['i:əreik], *s.* mal *m*, maux *mpl*, d'oreille(s); douleur *f* d'oreille; *Med:* otalgie *f*; **to have e.,** avoir mal à l'oreille, aux oreilles; avoir des douleurs d'oreille.
eardrop ['i:ədrɔp], *s.* pendant *m* d'oreille; pendeloque *f*.
eardrum ['i:ədrʌm], *s.* tympan *m*.
eared[1] ['i:əd], *a.* **1.** *Bot:* auriculé. **2.** (*in compounds*) **long-e., short-e.,** aux oreilles longues, courtes; **long-e. bat,** oreillard *m*; **long-e. owl,** moyen duc; **pricked-e.,** (chien *m*) aux oreilles droites, pointues; **lop-e.,** (lapin *m*, etc.) aux oreilles pendantes, à oreilles avalées; (cheval) oreillard; **one-e.,** (lapin, etc.) monaut; **quick-e.,** à l'oreille fine; **to listen open-e.,** écouter de toutes ses oreilles.
eared[2], *a.* à épis; **e. wheat,** blé garni d'épis; blé en épi; blé épié; **full-e.,** à épis pleins.
earflap ['i:əflæp], *s.* **1.** lobe *m* de l'oreille. **2.** oreillette *f* (de casquette).
earful ['i:əful], *s.* (*a*) **I got an e. of water,** j'ai eu l'oreille pleine d'eau; (*b*) *F:* **to give s.o. an e.,** (i) donner une verte semonce à qn; (ii) dire son fait à qn; **I certainly got an e. in reply!** si vous aviez entendu ce qu'il m'a répondu!
earhole ['i:əhoul], *s.* trou *m* de l'oreille; *P: O:* **plug him one in the e.,** flanque-lui un pain sur l'oreille.
earing ['i:əriŋ], *s. Nau:* raban *m*, cosse *f*, d'empointure.
earl [ə:l], *s.m.* (*f.* **countess,** *q.v.*) comte; *Her:* **E. Marshal,** comte-maréchal *m*, *pl.* comtes-maréchaux; grand maréchal; président *m* du Collège des hérauts.
earldom ['ə:ldəm], *s.* comté *m*; titre *m* de comte.
earless[1] ['i:əlis], *a.* sans oreilles.
earless[2], *a. Bot:* sans épis.
earlet ['i:əlit], *s. Z:* oreillon *m* (de chauve-souris).
earliness ['ə:linis], *s.* **1.** (*a*) heure peu avancée (du jour); (*b*) heure prématurée (de la mort de qn). **2.** précocité *f* (d'un fruit, de l'hiver).
early ['ə:li], *a.* & *adv.*
I. *a.* **(earlier, earliest) 1.** qui appartient au commencement (du jour, de l'année, de la vie, etc.); (*a*) **the e. cock,** le coq matinal; **at this e. hour,** à cette heure matinale; **in the e. morning,** de bon matin; de grand matin; **e. morning tea,** tasse de thé prise au réveil; **e. morning walk,** promenade matinale; **in the e. quiet one could hear . . .,** dans le silence matinal on entendait . . .; **in the e. afternoon,** au commencement de l'après-midi; **to have an e. dinner,** dîner de bonne heure; **Tuesday is my e. evening,** le mardi je rentre de bonne heure; **e. rising,** l'habitude *f* de se lever de bonne heure, **to be an e. riser,** être (un) matineux; être toujours matinal; se lever (de bon) matin, de grand matin; **to be an e. bird,** (i) être toujours matinal; (ii) se coucher tôt; **I'm going to have an e. night (tonight),** je vais me coucher de bonne heure ce soir; *Prov:* **the e. bird catches the worm,** à qui se lève le matin Dieu aide et prête la main; heure du matin, heure du gain; *Med:* **e. case,** malade encore légèrement atteint; **an e. train,** un des premiers trains; **to keep e. hours,** se coucher tôt, de bonne heure; **in (the) e. summer, in the e. part of summer,** dans les premiers jours de l'été; aux premiers jours de l'été; au commencement de l'été; **a cold morning in e. spring,** une froide matinée du début du printemps; **during the earlier months of the year,** pendant les premiers mois de l'année; *Th:* **e. door,** admission *f* une demi-heure avant l'heure officielle (contre payement supplémentaire); *Com: etc:* **e. closing day,** jour où l'on ferme, où les magasins sont fermés, l'après-midi; **it's e. days yet,** il est encore trop tôt, bien tôt (**to,** pour); *I.C.E:* **e. admission,** admission anticipée; avance *f* à l'admission; **e. release,** échappement anticipé; avance à l'émission; (*b*) **e. ages,** premiers âges; **the earliest times,** les temps les plus reculés; **the e. Church,** l'Église primitive; **e. Christians,** les premiers chrétiens; **e. writers,** les anciens écrivains; **our e. poets,** nos vieux poètes; **an e. Victorian,** un Victorien de la première époque; un des premiers Victoriens; **in the e. nineteenth century,** au début du XIXe siècle; **in the early sixties,** un peu après 1960; dans les années qui suivirent 1960, au début des années soixante; **in the e. history of the Church,** dans l'histoire des premiers temps de l'Église; **in e. days,** (i) dans l'ancien temps; (ii) dans le temps passé; **at an e. date,** à une date reculée; **from the earliest times,** de toute ancienneté; **the earliest legends,** les premières légendes; *Art:* **the e. masters,** les primitifs; (*c*) **e. youth,** première jeunesse; **in his earliest youth,** dans sa toute jeunesse; dans sa prime jeunesse; **e. age,** âge tendre, bas âge, jeune âge, premier âge; **at an e. age,** tout jeune; dès l'enfance; **from the earliest age,** dès l'âge le plus tendre; dès la plus tendre enfance; **his genius manifested itself at an e. age,** son génie se manifesta de bonne heure; **e. remembrances,** souvenirs d'enfance; **my earliest recollections,** mes souvenirs les plus lointains; **e. errors,** erreurs *f* de jeunesse; **to retain one's e. freshness and youth,** conserver sa fraîcheur et sa jeunesse premières; **the poverty of his e. days,** sa pauvreté première; **he received his e. education at . . .,** il reçut sa première éducation à . . .. **2.** précoce, hâtif, *Mil:* anticipé; **e. marriage,** mariage *m* précoce; **e. death,** mort prématurée; **to be brought to an e. grave,** avoir une fin prématurée; **e. beans,** (i) haricots précoces, hâtifs; (ii) haricots de primeur; **e. flowers,** fleurs hâtives; **e. vegetables, e. fruit, e. produce,** primeurs *fpl*; **an e. spring,** un printemps précoce; **we're having an e. winter,** l'hiver *m* est précoce, commence de bonne heure. **3.** prochain, rapproché; **at an e. date,** prochainement; à une date rapprochée, prochaine; sous peu; bientôt; **at an earlier date,** (i) à une date antérieure; (ii) à une date plus rapprochée; **to take an e. opportunity to do sth.,** ne pas tarder à saisir l'occasion de faire qch.; faire qch. à la première occasion, aussitôt que possible; **I was warned of the e. arrival of the police,** on me prévint de l'arrivée prochaine de la police; **at the earliest possible moment,** dans le plus bref délai possible; au plus tôt; **it will be next week at the earliest,** ce sera la semaine prochaine au plus tôt; **what's the earliest you can come?** à quel moment pouvez-vous venir au plus tôt? **the earliest I can come,** le plus tôt que je puisse venir; **at your earliest convenience,** à la première occasion; au premier moment favorable; le plus tôt (qu'il vous sera) possible; d'urgence.
II. *adv.* **1.** (*a*) de bonne heure; tôt; **earlier,** plus tôt; **as I mentioned earlier,** comme j'ai mentionné (i) précédemment, plus tôt; (ii) ci-dessus, plus haut; **to make a meal earlier,** avancer l'heure d'un repas; **too e.,** trop tôt; de trop bonne heure; **to arrive five minutes too e.,** arriver avec cinq minutes d'avance; **too e. in the morning,** trop matin; **it is too e. to go to bed,** il est de trop bonne heure pour aller se coucher; **I am half an hour e.,** je suis en avance d'une demi-heure; **it was very e. (in the day),** il était grand matin; **e. in the morning,** le matin de bonne heure; de grand matin; **it was e. in the afternoon,** c'était au commencement de l'après-midi; **e. in the evening,** très tôt dans la soirée; à une heure peu avancée de la soirée; **to rise e.,** se lever de bonne heure; se lever (de bon) matin; être matineux, toujours matinal; **bright and e.,** de bon matin, de bonne heure; **e. enough,** à temps; **e. in the winter,** dans, des, les premiers jours de l'hiver; à l'entrée de l'hiver; **e. in the year,** au commencement, au début, de l'année; **he was ill e. on in the year,** il a été malade dans les commencements de l'année; **e. on it was apparent that . . .,** dès l'abord il a apparu que . . .; **e. in (his) life,** dans ses jeunes années; dans sa jeunesse; **e. in his career,** au début, dans le début, de sa carrière; **as e. as the tenth century,** dès le dixième siècle; **as e. as possible,** le plus tôt possible; **as e. as five o'clock,** dès (les) cinq heures; pas plus tard que cinq heures; **e. and late,** à toute heure du jour; du matin au soir; **e. or late,** tôt ou tard; (*b*) **to die e.,** (i) mourir jeune; (ii) mourir prématurément; **this species of flower blooms very e.,** cette espèce de fleur s'épanouit très précocement. **2. e. in the list,** tout au commencement de la liste.
early-warning ['ə:li'wɔ:niŋ], *a. Mil: etc:* **e.-w. system,** réseau *m* de radars de guet, de pré-alerte.
earlywood ['ə:liwud], *s. Arb:* bois *m* de printemps.
earmark[1] ['i:əma:k], *s.* **1.** *Husb:* marque à l'oreille (à laquelle on reconnaît les moutons, etc.). **2.** *Adm: etc:* marque particulière, distinctive.
earmark[2], *v.tr.* **1.** *Husb:* marquer (les moutons, etc.) en leur coupant ou en leur fendant l'oreille. **2.** (*a*) **to e. a document, a cheque,** faire une marque au coin d'un document, d'un chèque; (*b*) **to e. funds,** spécialiser des fonds; donner à des fonds une affectation spéciale, déterminée; **to e. funds for a purpose,** assigner, affecter, des fonds à un projet, à une entreprise; **funds earmarked for sth.,** fonds *m* applicables à qch.; *Fin:* **to e. securities,** mettre sous dossier des titres pour le compte d'une autre banque, sans déplacement effectif; *F:* **to e. sth. for oneself,** s'approprier qch.; se réserver qch.
earmarking ['i:əma:kiŋ], *s.* affectation *f*, assignation *f* (de fonds); *Fin:* **e. transaction,** transfert *m*, dépôt *m*; mise *f* sous dossier.
earn [ə:n], *v.tr.* **1.** gagner (de l'argent); **to e. one's living by writing,** gagner sa vie à écrire, en écrivant; **she earned a little by knitting,** elle se faisait un peu d'argent en tricotant; *Ind:* **earning capacity,** rapport *m* (d'une entreprise). **2.** mériter, gagner (des éloges, l'affection de qn); **to e. fame,** acquérir la renommée; **his conduct earned him universal praise,** sa conduite lui valut les éloges de tous; **this is what earned him this favour,** voilà ce qui lui a mérité cette faveur.
earnest[1] ['ə:nist]. **1.** *a.* (*a*) (*of pers.*) sérieux; **with an e. air,** d'un air pénétré, délibéré, grave; (*b*) **e. request,** demande pressante; **e. prayer,** prière fervente; **e. effort,** sérieux effort; effort soutenu; **e. desire,** profond désir. **2.** *s.* **in e.** sérieusement; pour de bon; tout de bon; *F:* pour tout de bon; **this reproach was not meant in e.,** ce reproche n'était pas fait sérieusement; **to be in e.,** être sérieux; ne pas plaisanter; **I'm in e.,** c'est sérieux; *F:* c'est (pour) de vrai; c'est pour de bon; **are you in e.?** parlez-vous sérieusement? c'est sérieux? *F:* vous dites cela pour de vrai? **you are not in e.,** vous n'êtes pas sérieux; **to speak in e.,** parler sérieusement; **I thought you were in e.,** je vous ai pris au sérieux; **he was only half in e.,** il ne l'a dit qu'à moitié sérieusement; **to work in real e.,** travailler sérieusement; **to set to work in e.,** se mettre sérieusement à l'ouvrage; **it's raining in real e.,** il pleut pour (tout) de bon; **he is in real e.,** il est de bonne foi; **he is very much in e.,** (i) il est terriblement convaincu; (ii) il prend son rôle à cœur; **to be in dead, deadly, e.,** être tout à fait sérieux; **half in jest, half in e.,** moitié plaisantant, moitié sérieux.
earnest[2], *s.* **1.** *Com: etc: O:* arrhes *fpl*; **to give an e. to s.o. (for goods, etc.),** arrher qn; donner des arrhes à qn; **e. money,** dépôt *m* de garantie; arrhes. **2.** *Lit:* gage *m*, garantie *f*; **to give an e. of one's talent,** laisser entrevoir son talent; **an e. of one's good intentions,** une preuve, un gage, de ses bonnes intentions; **an e. of more to come,** (i) un gage pour l'avenir; (ii) un avant-goût de ce que l'avenir nous réserve.
earnestly ['ə:nistli], *adv.* (parler) sérieusement, d'un ton convaincu, d'un ton sérieux; (travailler) de bon cœur, avec ardeur, avec zèle; **we e. hope that . . .,** nous espérons bien sincèrement que . . ..
earnestness ['ə:nistnis], *s.* caractère sérieux (d'une discussion, etc.); gravité *f*, sérieux *m* (de ton); ardeur *f*, ferveur *f* (d'une prière).
earning ['ə:niŋ], *a.* profitable, qui rapporte, lucratif; **e. capacity,** productivité, financière, rapport *m* (d'une entreprise).
earnings ['ə:niŋz], *s.pl.* **1.** salaire *m*, gages *mpl*; appointements *mpl*; **my e. are sufficient for our needs,** ce que je gagne suffit à nos besoins; *Adm:* **living on immoral e.,** vagabondage spécial. **2.** profits *mpl*, bénéfices *mpl* (d'une entreprise); **gross e. of a railway,** bénéfices bruts, recettes brutes, d'une ligne de chemin de fer; **net(t) e.,** bénéfices nets.
earphone ['i:əfoun], *s.* écouteur *m*; *pl.* casque *m*.
earpick ['i:əpik], *s.* cure-oreilles *m inv.*
earpiece ['i:əpi:s], *s. Tp:* écouteur *m*, pavillon *m* (de récepteur).
earpiercing ['iəpiəsiŋ], *a.* (cri) qui vous perce les oreilles, déchirant.
earplug ['i:əplʌg], *s.* protège-tympan *m inv*, antiphone *m*.
earring ['i:əriŋ], *s.* boucle *f* d'oreille; **stud e.,** dormeuse *f*; **drop e.,** pendant *m* d'oreille, pendeloque *f*.
ear-shaped ['i:əʃeipt], *a.* auriforme.
ear shell ['i:əʃel], *s. Conch:* oreille *f* de mer; ormeau *m*.
earshot ['i:əʃɔt], *s.* **within e.,** à portée de voix, de l'ouïe, de l'oreille; **out of e.,** hors de portée de la voix.
earsplitting ['i:əspliting], *a.* (cri) qui vous fend les oreilles; **e. noise,** bruit à briser, crever, le tympan; casse-tête *m inv*; **e. chatter,** caquetage *m* à vous fendre les oreilles.
earth[1] [ə:θ], *s.* **1.** terre *f*; (*a*) le monde; le globe terrestre; **the earth's crust,** l'écorce *f* terrestre; **the face of the e.,** la face du globe; **the earth's axis,** l'axe *m* (de rotation) de la terre; **the earth's atmosphere,** l'atmosphère *f* terrestre; **the bowels of the e.,** les entrailles, le sein, de la terre; **he's just back from the ends of the e.,** il revient du bout du monde; **on e.,** sur terre; **it's heaven on e.,** c'est le paradis sur terre; *B:* **in e. as it is in heaven,** sur la terre comme dans le ciel; *B:* **ye are the salt of the e.,** vous êtes le sel de la terre; **he's the salt of the e.,** c'est un homme comme il y en a peu; *F:* **where on e. have you been?** où diable êtes-vous allé? **why on e. . . .?** pourquoi diable . . .? **there's no reason on e.,** il n'y a absolument aucune raison; **nowhere on (God's) e.,** nulle part sur terre; *F:* **I feel like nothing on e.,** je ne sais pas ce que je ressens; je suis en proie à un fort malaise; je ne suis pas dans mon assiette; *F:* **it wouldn't cost the e.,** ça ne coûterait pas les yeux de la tête; *F:* **to promise s.o. the e.,** promettre monts et merveilles à qn; (*b*) le sol; *F:* **to come back to e.,** retomber sur terre; sortir de sa rêverie; **down to e.,** (i) réaliste, qui a les pieds sur terre; (ii) terre à terre, prosaïque. **2.** (*a*) *Agr: etc:* terre; **fat, heavy, e.,** terre(s) grasse(s), lourde(s); terrain gras; terroir gras; **light e.,** terre(s) légère(s); **loose e.,** terre(s) meuble(s); **meat e.,** terre végétale; **rammed, tamped, e.,** terre damée, pilonnée, battue; **green e.,** glauconie *f*; **heavy e.,** terre pesante; baryte *f*; **to till the e.,** cultiver la terre; **full of the fragrance of the e.,** fleurant bon la terre, le terroir; **to fill a pit with e.,** combler, remplir,

une fosse avec de la terre; **e. board,** versoir *m,* oreille *f,* de charrue; *Min:* **e. auger, borer,** cuiller *f,* cuillère *f,* tarière *f;* (*b*) *Ch:* **aluminous e.,** terre d'alumine; **alkaline e.,** terre alcaline; **rare earths,** terres rares; **fuller's e.,** terre savonneuse; terre à détacher; terre à foulon; marne *f* à foulon; glaise *f* à dégraisser; argile *f* smectique; smectite *f;* **e. oil,** huile *f* de roche; naphte minéral; (*c*) *Hyg:* **e. closet,** cabinets *mpl* sans eau courante; (*d*) *Geol:* **e. pillar,** nonne *f,* demoiselle *f;* colonne coiffée. **3.** *El:* (*a*) terre, masse *f;* perd-fluide *m inv;* **e. cable, wire, lead,** câble *m,* fil *m,* de terre; prise *f* de terre; **e. line,** ligne *f* de terre; **main e. lead,** collecteur *m* de terre; **e. connection,** conducteur *m,* contact *m,* à la terre; prise de terre; **e. plate,** prise *f,* fiche *f,* de terre; plaque *f* de masse; **e. leak(age),** fuite *f,* perte *f,* à la terre; **e. current,** (i) courant tellurique; (ii) courant de retour par la terre; **e. return,** retour par la terre; **e. conductivity,** conductivité *f* du sol; **e. telegraphy,** télégraphie par le sol; *W.Tel:* **e. antenna,** antenne *f* enterrée; (*b*) mise *f* à la terre; **e. fault,** mise à la terre accidentelle; contact *m* (accidentel) à la terre; **dead e.,** mise à la terre franche; contact parfait avec le sol; (*of car, etc.*) **e. to frame,** contact à la masse, mise à la masse; **e. electrode,** câble de mise à la terre; *W.Tel:* **e. plate,** plaque *f* de mise à la terre. **4.** terrier *m,* tanière *f* (de renard); renardière *f;* *Ven:* (*of fox*) **to go to e.,** se terrer; **to run to e.,** (i) chasser (un renard) jusqu'à son terrier; dépister (le gibier); (ii) *F:* découvrir la source, l'origine (d'une citation, d'une erreur de calcul, etc.); dépister, dénicher (qn); découvrir la retraite de (qn); **to drive the fox to e.,** mettre le renard à l'accul; **to stop an e.,** boucher un terrier.

earth[2]. **1.** *v.tr.* (*a*) *Hort:* **to e. (up),** butter, terrer, chausser (une plante); (*b*) *El:* mettre (le courant) à la terre, à la masse; (*c*) *Ven:* poursuivre, chasser, (un renard) jusqu'à son terrier. **2.** *v.i.* (*of fox*) se terrer.

earthborn ['ə:θbɔ:n], *a.* (*of pers.*) de naissance terrestre; (*of thoughts, etc.*) terrestre, terre à terre *inv.*

earthbound ['ə:θbaund], *a.* (*a*) terre à terre *inv;* (*b*) **e. spirit,** fantôme *m* (qui ne peut pas quitter le monde des vivants); (*c*) qui se dirige vers la terre.

earthed [ə:θt], *a. El:* mis à la terre, au sol; (*in engine, etc.*) relié à la masse; **e. conductor,** conducteur *m* au sol.

earthen ['ə:θ(ə)n], *a.* de terre; **e. jug,** cruche *f* en, de, terre (cuite).

earthenware ['ə:θ(ə)nwɛər], *s.* poterie *f* (de terre); argile cuite; **glazed e.,** (i) faïence *f;* (ii) grès flambé; **e. jug,** cruche *f* en, de, terre (cuite).

earthfall ['ə:θfɔ:l], *s.* éboulement *m* de terres.

earthiness ['ə:θinis], *s.* goût *m* de terre, du terroir.

earthing ['ə:θiŋ], *s.* **1.** buttage *m* (d'une plante). **2.** *El:* mise *f* à la terre, à la masse; **e. resistance,** résistance *f* de mise à la terre; **e. switch,** commutateur *m* de mise à la terre.

earthlight ['ə:θlait], *s. Astr:* lumière cendrée (de la lune).

earthliness ['ə:θlinis], *s.* **1.** caractère *m* terrestre. **2.** mondanité *f;* attachement *m* aux choses de ce monde.

earthling ['ə:θliŋ], *s.* habitant, -ante, de la terre.

earthly ['ə:θli], *a.* **1.** terrestre; **the E. Paradise,** le Paradis terrestre. **2.** *F:* **there's no e. reason for . . .,** il n'y a pas la moindre raison du monde pour . . .; **for no e. reason,** à propos de rien; à propos de bottes; comme à plaisir; **it's of no e. use to me,** ça n'a pour moi aucune utilité; ça ne me sert, ne me servirait, à rien; (*of remedy*) **it's no e. use,** c'est mettre un emplâtre sur une jambe de bois; **he hasn't an e. chance,** *F:* **he hasn't an e.,** il n'a pas la moindre chance; il n'a pas l'ombre d'une chance (de réussir). **3. e.-minded,** attaché aux choses d'ici-bas, aux choses de ce monde; terre à terre *inv.*

earthman, -woman, *pl.* **-men, -women** ['ə:θmæn, -wumən; -men, -wimin], *s.* terrien, -ienne.

earthmover ['ə:θmu:vər], *s. U.S:* (*a*) bulldozer *m;* (*b*) pelle *f* mécanique.

earthnut ['ə:θnʌt], *s. Bot:* **1.** gland *m* de terre; noix *f* de terre; terre-noix *f inv;* châtaigne *f* de terre; bunion bulbeux. **2.** arachide *f;* **e. oil,** huile *f* d'arachide.

earth pig ['ə:θpig], *s. Z:* oryctérope *m* (du Cap).

earthquake ['ə:θkweik], *s.* **1.** tremblement *m* de terre; *Tchn:* séisme *m;* **e. due to underground subsidence,** séisme par effondrement; **e. shock,** secousse *f* de tremblement de terre; secousse sismique. **2.** *F:* convulsion *f,* bouleversement *m* (politique, etc.); chambardement *m* (social, etc.).

earthshine ['ə:θʃain], *s.* = EARTHLIGHT.

earthwork ['ə:θwə:k], *s.* **1.** (travaux *mpl* de) terrassement *m;* **e. embankment,** terrassement en remblai; **e. contractor,** terrassier *m;* entrepreneur *m* de terrassements; **e. labourer,** terrassier. **2.** *pl.* **earthworks,** (i) *Prehist:* fortifications *f* en terre; (ii) *Civ.E: etc:* travaux en terre, de terrassement; terres *f* d'apport; **to execute earthworks,** effectuer des travaux de terrassement; **management of earthworks,** conduite *f* des travaux de terrassement.

earthworm ['ə:θwə:m], *s. Ann:* lombric *m;* *F:* ver *m* de terre.

earthy ['ə:θi], *a.* **1.** terreux; **e. taste,** goût *m* de terre; **to have an e. smell,** sentir la terre; *Miner:* **e. material, e. ore,** matières terreuses, minerai terreux; **e. cobalt,** cobalt oxydé noir. **2.** (*of pers.*) (i) *B:* tiré de la terre, terrestre; (ii) matériel, grossier; terre à terre *inv.*

earwig[1] ['i:əwig], *s. Ent:* **1.** forficule *f,* perce-oreille *m, pl.* perce-oreilles. **2.** *U.S:* mille-pattes *m inv.*

earwig[2], *v.tr. F: A:* **1.** harceler (qn) de requêtes. **2.** s'insinuer auprès de (qn).

ease[1] [i:z], *s.* **1.** (*a*) tranquillité *f* (d'esprit); repos *m,* bien-être *m,* aise *f* (du corps); **a moment's e.,** un moment de calme; **to be at e.,** avoir l'esprit tranquille; **ill at e.,** mal à l'aise; **to be ill at e.,** (i) être mal à l'aise; (ii) être inquiet; **to feel ill at e. about sth.,** se sentir inquiet au sujet de qch.; **to be at one's e.,** (i) être à son aise; (ii) être tranquille; **to set s.o. at e.,** (i) mettre qn à son aise; faire prendre ses aises à qn; (ii) tranquilliser qn; **to set s.o.'s mind at e.,** tirer qn de son inquiétude; dissiper les inquiétudes de qn; **set your mind at e.,** rassurez-vous; soyez tranquille; **to take one's e.,** prendre ses aises; se mettre à l'aise; paresser; *Mil: etc:* **to stand at e.,** se mettre, se tenir, au repos; se tenir dans la position hanchée; se hancher; **to be standing at e.,** être au repos; **stand at e.!** repos! (*b*) **e. from pain,** adoucissement *m* de la douleur; soulagement *m;* **chapel of e.,** (chapelle *f* de) secours *m,* (église) succursale *f;* annexe *f.* **2.** (*a*) loisir *m;* (*b*) oisiveté *f;* **to live a life of e.,** vivre dans l'oisiveté, vivre une vie de loisirs; **to live a life of e. and luxury,** vivre dans la mollesse. **3.** (*a*) aisance (de manières, etc.); moelleux *m* (des mouvements); (*b*) facilité *f* (d'élocution, etc.); simplicité *f* (de réglage); douceur *f,* facilité (de manœuvre); **e. of transport,** facilités de transport; **with e.,** facilement; aisément; avec aisance; **with the utmost e.,** avec la plus grande facilité; **to do sth. with great e.,** faire qch. en se jouant; **with the greatest of e.,** avec la plus grande aisance du monde.

ease[2], *v.*

I. *v.tr.* **1.** (*a*) adoucir, calmer, alléger, atténuer (la souffrance); soulager, apporter du soulagement à (un malade); *v.i.* **the pain has eased,** la douleur s'est atténuée; (*b*) calmer, tranquilliser (l'esprit); **to e. s.o.'s anxiety,** calmer les inquiétudes de qn; tranquilliser qn. **2.** débarrasser, délivrer **(s.o. of, from, sth.,** qn de qch.); **to e. oneself of a burden,** se soulager d'un fardeau; *F: A:* **to e. s.o. of his purse,** soulager qn de son porte-monnaie; subtiliser son porte-monnaie à qn. **3.** (*a*) détendre, relâcher, soulager (un cordage, un ressort); desserrer (une vis); *Nau:* larguer (une amarre); mollir (une manœuvre); *Mch: etc:* modérer, soulager (la pression); ralentir (la vitesse); **to e. (the strain on) a girder,** alléger, soulager, une poutre; **to e. the congestion in a street,** décongestionner la circulation d'une rue; **this has eased the situation,** *v.i.* **the situation has eased,** une détente s'est produite; la situation s'est détendue; *Nau:* **e. the engines!** lentement la machine! **e. her!** doucement! **to e. the helm (down),** mettre moins de barre; mettre la barre dessous, en douceur; mollir la barre; *Equit:* **to e. both reins,** rendre la bride, la main (au cheval); (*b*) *Dressm:* donner plus d'ampleur à (une robe); **to e. the elbows,** donner de l'aisance aux coudes; **to e. the collar on to the neck,** répartir le surplus du col; *Mec.E:* **to e. a part,** faciliter le jeu d'un organe; donner du jeu à un organe; *Civ.E:* **to e. a curve,** adoucir une courbe; *Const:* **to e. a door,** ajuster une porte. **4.** (*a*) déplacer doucement; **to e. a load off a cart,** faire glisser à terre la charge d'une charrette; (*b*) **to e. one's way through a crowd,** se faufiler à travers la foule.

II. (*compound verbs*) **1. ease down.** (*a*) *v.tr.* relâcher, diminuer (la vitesse, l'effort); (*b*) *v.i.* diminuer de vitesse; (*of effort*) se relâcher.

2. ease off. (*a*) *v.tr.* (i) *Nau:* filer, choquer (un cordage); **e. off the cable!** filez de la chaîne! **e. off the jib-sheet,** filez le foc; (ii) dégager (une surface d'appui, etc.); (*b*) *v.i.* (i) = EASE UP (*b*) (i); (ii) *St.Exch:* (*of rates*) se détendre; (iii) *Nau:* s'éloigner un peu du rivage.

3. ease up. (*a*) *v.tr. Nau:* soulager (le gui, un palan); (*b*) *v.i.* (i) se relâcher; moins travailler; (ii) diminuer la vitesse, l'allure; ralentir.

easeful ['i:zful], *a. Lit:* (*a*) (repos *m*) tranquille, paisible; (*b*) calmant.

easel ['i:zl], *s.* chevalet *m* (de peintre, etc.); *Art:* **e.-picture, piece,** tableau *m* de chevalet; *Phot:* **enlarging e.,** (panneau *m*) porte-papier *m inv;* chevalet d'agrandissement.

easeless ['i:zlis], *a. Lit:* **1.** qui manque d'aise, de confortable. **2.** que l'on ne saurait soulager.

easement ['i:zmənt], *s.* **1.** *Jur:* servitude *f;* service foncier; droit *m* d'usage; aisance *f* de voirie; **affirmative e.,** servitude active; **negative e.,** servitude passive; **easements are extinguished by non-user during thirty years,** les servitudes s'éteignent par le non-usage pendant trente ans; il y a prescription pour les servitudes après trente ans de non-usage. **2.** *Rail:* (i) raccordement *m* (entre deux voies); (ii) adoucissement *m* (d'une courbe). **3.** *Lit:* soulagement *m* (de la douleur).

easily ['i:zili], *adv.* **1.** tranquillement, à son aise, paisiblement; **the patient rests e.,** le malade repose paisiblement; **to live e.,** vivre dans l'aisance; **to take things, life, e.,** prendre le temps comme il vient; se laisser vivre; *F:* se la couler douce, bonne. **2.** (*a*) doucement, sans secousse, sans effort; **the door shuts e.,** la porte se ferme sans effort; (*b*) avec confort; **these shoes fit me e.,** je suis à l'aise dans ces souliers; **the car holds six people e.,** on tient à l'aise six dans cette voiture. **3.** facilement, sans difficulté, avec aisance; **to speak e.,** parler avec facilité; **the remedy is very e. used,** ce remède est d'un emploi des plus faciles; **you can e. imagine my disappointment,** vous concevez sans peine ma déception; **he is not e. satisfied,** il n'est pas facile, aisé, à satisfaire; **e. moved,** facile à émouvoir; **he came in e. first, last,** il est arrivé bon premier, bon dernier; **he is e. forty,** il a bien quarante ans; il a une bonne quarantaine.

easiness ['i:zinis], *s.* **1.** bien-être *m,* commodité *f.* **2.** aisance *f,* grâce *f* (des manières, du style, etc.). **3.** indifférence *f,* insouciance *f.* **4.** (*a*) facilité *f* (d'un travail); (*b*) **e. of belief,** facilité à croire. **5.** (*a*) complaisance *f,* humeur *f* facile, souplesse *f* de caractère (de qn); (*b*) jeu *m* facile (d'une machine); douceur *f* (de roulement). **6.** *Pol.Ec:* aisance, facilité, aise *f;* **e. of money,** facilité de l'argent; **monetary e. of the market,** aisance monétaire du marché.

easing ['i:ziŋ], *s.* **1.** (*a*) soulagement *m,* adoucissement *m* (de la souffrance); (*b*) allègement *m,* déchargement *m* (d'une poutre, etc.). **2.** *Civ.E:* adoucissement (d'une courbe). **3. e. of the tension in diplomatic circles,** détente *f* dans les milieux diplomatiques; **e. of the capital market,** détente, amélioration *f,* du marché des capitaux.

easing off ['i:ziŋ'ɔf], *s.* relâchement *m* **(from work,** du travail); *St.Exch:* détente *f* (des reports).

east [i:st]. **1.** *s.* (*a*) est *m,* orient *m,* levant *m;* **house facing (the) e.,** maison exposée à l'est; **on the e., to the e.,** à l'est (of, de); **look to the e.,** regardez vers l'est; (*b*) **the E.,** l'Orient, le Levant; **the Near E.,** le Proche-Orient; **the Middle E.,** le Moyen-Orient; **the Far E.,** l'Extrême-Orient; (*c*) **to live in the e. of England,** demeurer dans l'est de l'Angleterre; *U.S:* **the E.,** les États *m* de l'Est. **2.** *adv.* (*a*) à l'est, à l'orient; **to travel e.,** voyager vers l'est; **the town lies e. of the Rhine,** la ville est située à l'est du Rhin; **the wind blows e.,** le vent vient, souffle, de l'est; le vent est (d')est; *Nau:* **to sail due e.,** aller droit vers l'est; avoir le cap à l'est; faire de l'est; **e. by north,** est-quart-nord-est; **e. by south,** est-quart-sud-est; *Prov:* **too far e. is west,** les extrêmes se touchent; (*b*) **to go e.,** aller (i) dans l'Est, (ii) dans le Levant, en Orient. **3.** *a.* est; (vent *m*) d'est; (pays) de l'est, oriental; (mur, fenêtre) qui fait face à l'est; **e. aspect,** exposition à l'est; **e. coast,** côte *f* est; *Vet:* **e. coast fever,** theilériose *f;* **e. end,** chevet *m* (d'une église); **the E. End (of London),** les quartiers pauvres et populeux de la partie est de Londres; **E. Ender,** habitant, -ante, de *l'East End;* *Hist:* **the E. Indies,** les Indes orientales, les grandes Indes; *A:* **E. Indiaman,** navire *m* qui faisait le service des Indes orientales.

East Anglia [i:st'æŋgliə], *Pr.n. Geog:* l'Est-Anglie *f.*

East Anglian [i:st'æŋgliən], *a. & s. Geog:* (originaire, natif) de l'Est-Anglie.

eastbound ['i:stbaund], *a.* (*of train, etc.*) allant vers l'est; (*on underground*) en direction de la banlieue est.

Easter ['i:stər], *s.* **1.** Pâques *m;* **E. day, E. Sunday,** le jour, le dimanche, de Pâques; **E. Monday,** le lundi de Pâques; **E. week,** (i) la semaine de Pâques; (ii) la semaine sainte; **E. egg,** œuf de Pâques; œuf rouge; **to do one's E. duty,** faire ses Pâques; **E. dues, E. offering,** offrande de Pâques (faite au prêtre de la paroisse). **2.** *Geog:* **E. Island,** l'île *f* de Pâques.

easterly ['i:stəli]. **1.** *a.* **e. wind,** vent *m* (d')est; vent d'amont, qui vient de l'est; **e. current,** courant *m* qui se dirige vers l'est; **e. point,** point situé à, vers, l'est; **the e. region of a country,** la région est d'un pays. **2.** *adv.* vers l'est. **3.** *s.* vent *m* d'est.

eastern ['i:stən]. **1.** *a.* (*a*) est, de l'est; oriental, -aux; *Hist:* **the Near-E. question,** la question du Proche-Orient; **the E. question,** la question d'Orient; **the E. Church,** l'Église d'Orient; l'Église grecque (orthodoxe); **e. style,** style oriental; **e. trade,** commerce avec l'Orient; **e. voyages,** voyages en Orient; *U.S:* **the E. Shore,** les côtes de l'Est (du Maryland). **2.** *s.* (*a*) *U.S:* oriental, -ale; (*b*) membre *m* de l'Église grecque orthodoxe.

Easterner ['i:stənər], *s.* (*a*) oriental, -ale; (*b*) *U.S:* habitant, -ante, des États de l'est.

Eastertide ['i:stətaid], *s.* Pâques *m.*

easting ['i:stiŋ], *s.* **1.** *Nau:* marche *f*, route *f*, vers l'est; chemin *m* est. **2.** *Mapm:* longitude *f* est, abscisse *f.*

eastward ['i:stwəd]. **1.** *s.* est *m*; **to the e.,** vers l'est. **2.** *a.* (*a*) à l'est; dans l'est; (*b*) du côté de l'est; *Ecc:* **e. position,** position du célébrant quand il se tourne vers l'est. **3.** *adv.* = EASTWARDS.

eastwards ['i:stwədz], *adv.* à l'est; vers l'est; vers l'orient.

easy[1] ['i:zi], *a., adv., & s.*

I. *a.* **(easier, easiest) 1.** (*a*) à l'aise; **to feel easier,** se sentir plus à son aise, se sentir mieux; **my cough is getting easier,** ma toux est moins sèche; ma toux se dégage; *F:* **she's e. on the eye,** elle n'est pas désagréable, déplaisante, à regarder; (*b*) tranquille, sans inquiétude; **to make oneself, one's mind, e. about sth.,** se tranquilliser, se rassurer, sur qch.; **to be e. in one's mind,** avoir l'esprit tranquille; **with an e. conscience,** en toute tranquillité de conscience; la conscience tranquille; **e. life,** vie *f* sans souci, sans tracas; *F:* vie de chanoine; *F:* **to be in e. street,** être dans l'aisance *f*; **in e. circumstances,** dans l'aisance, à l'aise. **2.** (*a*) (*of manners, etc.*) aisé, libre, dégagé; **in an e. manner,** d'un air dégagé; **e. style,** style facile, naturel, coulant, aisé, inapprêté; (*b*) **my coat is an e. fit,** mon veston est ample, je suis à l'aise dans mon veston; (*c*) **e. movement,** mouvement moelleux; **e. stream,** cours *m* d'eau tranquille; *Nau:* **e. rolling,** roulis doux; **tenon that is too e. in its mortise,** tenon trop lâche, trop gai, dans sa mortaise; *Mec.E:* **e. fit,** ajustage *m* lâche, à jeu. **3.** (*a*) **e. task,** travail facile, aisé; **that is e. to see,** cela se voit; il y paraît; **it is e. for him to . . .,** il lui est facile de . . .; **it's e. to say . . .,** on a vite fait de dire . . ., il est aisé de dire . . .; **it's e. for you to say so,** vous en parlez bien à votre aise; **from which it is e. to deduce that . . .,** d'où l'on déduit facilement que . . .; **e. method,** méthode *f* simple; **this way will make your task easier,** ce procédé facilitera votre tâche; **it's only too e. to yield to temptation,** on a bientôt fait de céder à la tentation; **e. starting (of an engine),** facilité *f* de lancement, de mise en train; **e. to fix,** d'une mise en place facile; **the harbour is e. to enter,** le port est d'un accès facile; **within e. distance, within e. reach, of . . .,** à distance commode de . . .; *F:* **as e. as A B C, as e. as shelling peas, as e. as falling off a log, as e. as winking, as e. as e.,** simple comme bonjour; **it isn't e.,** ce n'est pas facile; *F:* ça ne va pas tout seul; **it's an e. matter,** c'est facile; *F:* ce n'est pas une affaire; *F:* **e. money,** argent gagné sans peine; *Fb:* **to miss an e. goal,** rater un but tout fait; *esp. U.S: F:* (*of pers.*) **e. mark,** jobard *m*; (*b*) (*of pers.*) facile, accommodant, coulant, complaisant; de bonne composition; débonnaire; **he's not e. to deal with,** il n'est pas accommodant; **e. to get on with,** d'un commerce facile; **e. to live with,** commode à vivre; facile à vivre; *F:* **I'm e.!** ça m'est égal! c'est comme tu veux! **woman of e. virtue,** femme de petite vertu, de mœurs faciles; (*c*) **to travel by e. stages,** voyager à petites étapes; **at an e. pace,** à petite vitesse, à une allure raisonnable; **at an e. trot,** au petit trot; (*of pers.*) **e. gait,** pas *m*, allure *f*, désinvolte; **horse of e. gait,** cheval coulant, d'allure coulante; **the road grows easier,** la route s'aplanit; *Com:* **by e. payments, on e. terms,** avec facilités *f* de paiement; *Nau:* **to keep under e. sail,** faire peu de toile; *Sp: etc:* **to come in an e. first,** arriver bon premier; *F:* **to have an e. time,** se la couler douce; *F:* **now we can take it e.,** maintenant on peut se la couler douce. **4.** *Com:* **e. market,** marché tranquille, calme; **easier market,** marché moins soutenu: **prices are (getting) easier,** les prix fléchissent; on accuse une détente dans les prix; **(the price of) corn is getting easier,** le blé mollit; **cotton was easier,** le coton a accusé une détente. **5.** *Cards: F:* **honours e.,** honneurs partagés.

II. *adv.* **1.** (*a*) **to take things e.,** prendre les choses en douceur; **to take it e.,** en prendre tout à son aise; se donner du bon temps; prendre les choses en douceur; ne pas se fouler la rate; *P:* faire qch. en peinard, en pénard; ne pas se la fouler; se la couler douce; **take it e.!** ne vous faites pas de bile! ne vous en faites pas! **I'll take it e.,** je ne me fatiguerai pas; **you'll have to go e. for a bit,** il va falloir freiner un peu; **to take life e.,** se laisser vivre; **to go e. with sth., s.o.,** ménager qch., qn; **e. does it!** (allez-y) doucement! allez-y en douceur! **go e. on the electricity,** allez-y doucement pour, sur, avec, l'électricité; **e.-riding car,** voiture bien suspendue; (*b*) *Nau: Row:* **e. (ahead)!** (en avant) doucement! **e. all!** stop(pe)! **to pull e.,** endurer; **he rides e.,** il ne fatigue pas à cheval; (*c*) *Mil:* **stand e.!** repos! **2.** *F:* **I can do it e.,** cela me sera facile; **I can do it easier than you,** cela m'est plus facile qu'à vous; **easier said than done,** c'est plus facile, plus aisé, à dire qu'à faire; c'est bientôt dit (mais pas sitôt fait); c'est bon à dire; *Prov:* **e. come e. go,** ce qui vient par la flûte s'en va par le tambour; l'argent ne lui coûte guère.

III. *s.* (*a*) *Row:* halte *f*; (*b*) *F:* **to have, take, an e.,** se reposer un peu.

easy[2], *v.i. Row:* cesser de nager.

easy-going ['i:zi'gouiŋ], *a.* **1.** (*of horse*) à l'allure douce; coulant; d'allure coulante. **2.** (*of pers.*) (*a*) qui prend les choses tranquillement, comme elles viennent; insouciant; qui ne se fait pas de bile; *F:* qui se la coule douce; **he is inconceivably e.-g.,** il est d'un sans-souci inconcevable; **he's a plain, e.-g. chap,** *P:* c'est un type tout à la flan; (*b*) (*not fussy*) accommodant, coulant; peu exigeant; peu tracassier; (*c*) (*good-tempered*) d'humeur facile; **an e.-g. man,** un homme facile à vivre; un bon garçon; (*d*) (*in matters of conscience*) qui a la conscience élastique.

eat [i:t], *v.* (**ate** [et, *esp. NAm:* eit]; **eaten** ['i:tn])

I. *v.tr.* **1.** (*a*) manger (du pain, de la soupe, etc.); **to e. again,** remanger; **to e. one's breakfast, dinner, supper,** déjeuner, dîner, souper; **to e. a good dinner,** faire un bon dîner; *Prov:* **you can't have your cake and e. it,** on ne peut pas avoir le drap et l'argent; *Ecc:* **to e. flesh,** faire gras; **to have nothing to e.,** n'avoir rien à manger, rien à se mettre sous la dent; **to ask for something to e.,** demander à manger; **fit to e.,** bon à manger; mangeable; **to e. next to nothing,** se nourrir de rien, avec rien; **to e. quickly,** mettre les bouchées doubles; **to e. like a wolf, like a horse,** manger comme un ogre; dévorer; **to e. oneself sick,** manger à se rendre malade; **to e. one's fill,** manger à sa faim, à son appétit, à sa suffisance; manger jusqu'à satiété; manger tout son content; se repaître; *F:* manger tout son soûl; **to e. one's heart out,** se ronger le cœur; se ronger dans l'inactivité; *v.i. A:* **to e. of a dish,** manger d'un plat; **the birds come and e. out of his hand,** les oiseaux viennent lui manger dans la main; *F:* **he eats out of my hand,** il fait tout ce que je veux; il m'obéit comme un chien; **to e. off plate,** manger dans de l'argenterie; *F:* **well, don't e. me!** vous n'allez pas me manger? **I thought he was going to e. me,** j'ai cru qu'il allait m'avaler; **to e. one's words,** (i) se rétracter; ravaler, rétracter, ses paroles; (ii) bafouiller, manger ses mots; **I shall make him e. his words,** je lui ferai rentrer les paroles dans la gorge, dans le ventre; *F:* **to e. dirt,** être forcé de faire des excuses, de se rétracter; *F:* avaler des couleuvres; *F:* **to e. humble pie,** s'humilier (devant qn); présenter d'humbles excuses; se rétracter, faire amende honorable; avouer être dans son tort; *F:* s'aplatir; filer doux; en rabattre; mettre les pouces; **if it comes off, I'll e. my hat,** si ça réussit, je mange mon chapeau!; **to e. s.o. out of hearth and home, out of house and home,** ruiner qn en nourriture; manger jusqu'au dernier sou à qn; manger la laine sur le dos de qn, à qn; gruger qn sans merci; (*with passive force*) **cheese eats well with apples,** le fromage se mange bien, va bien, avec les pommes; (*of insect, worm*) **to e. into wood,** ronger, mouliner, le bois; *Jur: F:* **to e. one's dinners, one's terms,** faire ses études d'avocat; (*b*) prendre ses repas; dîner; **we e. at seven,** nous dînons à sept heures; *F:* **let's e.!** à table! **2.** *F:* **what's eating you?** quelle mouche vous pique? qu'est-ce qui vous prend?

II. (*compound verbs*) **1. eat away.** (*a*) *v.i.* **to e. away steadily,** manger à belles dents; dévorer; (*b*) *v.tr.* (i) ronger, éroder, miner (des roches, une falaise); saper (des fondations); **the sea eats away the coastline, the cliffs,** la mer échancre le littoral, mine les falaises; (ii) (*of acid*) mordre, dissoudre, attaquer (un métal); *Phot:* **fixing bath that eats away the details,** fixateur qui ronge les détails.

2. eat off, *v.tr.* (*a*) (*of horse, etc.*) **to e. its head off,** s'engraisser à ne rien faire; coûter plus à nourrir qu'il ne vaut; *F:* (*of pers.*) **to e. one's head off,** s'empiffrer; (*b*) **to e. off a field,** (i) (*of flock*) manger toute l'herbe dans un champ; (ii) (*of farmer*) paître des troupeaux dans un champ.

3. eat up, *v.tr.* (*a*) manger jusqu'à la dernière miette (un gâteau, etc.); achever de manger (qch.); **e. up your bread!** finis ton pain! **he ate it all up (i.e. the chicken, etc.),** il le mangea en entier; il n'en a fait qu'une bouchée; *F:* **his opponent simply ate him up,** son adversaire n'en a fait qu'une bouchée; **to e. up the miles,** dévorer la route, manger le chemin, avaler les kilomètres; (*b*) réduire à néant les provisions de bouche (d'un pays); épuiser les provisions de (qn); (*c*) consumer (qch.) sans profit; **stove that eats up the coal,** poêle qui mange beaucoup de charbon; **to e. up all s.o.'s time,** faire perdre inutilement tout son temps à qn; (*d*) *F:* **to be eaten up (with sth.),** être dévoré (d'orgueil); être confit (de vanité), miné (par l'envie), consumé (par l'ambition), accablé, criblé (de dettes), perclus (de rhumatismes).

eatable ['i:təbl]. **1.** *a.* mangeable, bon à manger; **fruit that is quite e.,** fruit qui se laisse manger. **2.** *s.pl.* **eatables,** provisions *f* de bouche; comestibles *m.*

eater ['i:tər], *s.* **1.** mangeur, -euse; dîneur, -euse; **small e., great e.,** petit mangeur, gros mangeur; **he is not a big e.,** il ne mange pas beaucoup; **great e. of meat,** grand mangeur de viande. **2.** fruit *m* à couteau, de dessert; **these apples are good eaters,** ces pommes se laissent manger.

eating ['i:tiŋ], *s.* manger *m*; **pheasants are good e., excellent e.,** les faisans sont bons à manger, sont un mets excellent; **e. chocolate,** chocolat *m* à croquer; **e. apple,** pomme *f* à couteau, de dessert; **e. cherries,** cerises *f* de table.

eating away ['i:tiŋə'wei], *s.* corrosion *f* (du métal); érosion *f* (du littoral).

eating-house ['i:tiŋhaus], *s.* restaurant *m*; **cheap e.-h.,** gargote *f*; **e.-h. keeper,** (i) restaurateur *m*; (ii) *Pej:* gargotier *m*; **to keep an e.-h.,** donner à manger; tenir un restaurant ou une gargote.

eats [i:ts], *s.pl. F:* le manger; *P:* la boustifaille; **plenty of e. but nothing to drink,** amplement de quoi manger mais rien à boire.

eau-de-Cologne ['oudəkə'loun], *s. Toil:* eau *f* de Cologne.

eau-de-Nil ['oudə'ni:l]. **1.** *a.* (vert de) Nil. **2.** *s.* vert *m* (de) Nil.

eaves [i:vz], *s.pl. Const:* égout *m* (du toit); avance *f* (du toit); avant-toit *m*; gouttières *fpl*; *Tchn:* subgronde *f*; **e.-slate,** ardoise *f* de chéneau; **e.-board,** chanlat(t)e *f.*

eavesdrop ['i:vzdrɔp], *v.i.* **(eavesdropped)** écouter aux portes, à la porte; être aux écoutes.

eavesdropper ['i:vzdrɔpər], *s.* écouteur, -euse, aux portes; indiscret, -ète.

eavesdropping ['i:vzdrɔpiŋ], *s.* fait *m* d'écouter aux portes.

ebb[1] [eb], *s.* **1.** reflux *m*, jusant *m*; baisse *f*, déchalement *m* (de la marée); **the e. and flow,** le flux et le reflux; **e. tide,** marée descendante; marée de jusant; reflux *m*; **set of the e. (tide),** direction *f* du jusant; **slack of the e. (tide),** étale *m* du jusant; **the tide is on the e.,** la marée baisse; la mer, la marée, refoule; **when is the tide at its lowest e.?** quelle est l'heure de la marée basse? *Nau:* **e. anchor,** ancre *f* de jusant. **2.** déclin *m* (de la fortune, de la vie); **the patient is at a low e.,** le malade est très bas, est aussi mal que possible; *Lit:* **at the lowest e. of fortune,** au plus bas degré de la fortune; **to be at one's lowest e.,** être à bout de ressources; **his business is at a low e.,** ses affaires périclitent; *F:* les eaux sont basses chez lui.

ebb[2], *v.i.* **1.** (*of tide*) baisser, descendre; refluer, refouler; **to e. and flow,** monter et baisser; fluer et refluer; **the tide is ebbing,** la marée baisse; *F:* la marée perd. **2.** (*of life, etc.*) décliner; être sur le déclin; décroître, baisser; **to e. away,** s'écouler; **his life was rapidly ebbing away,** il baissait de jour en jour, d'heure en heure.

ebbing[1] ['ebiŋ], *a.* (*a*) (eaux) qui refluent; (*b*) (vie) sur le déclin; **e. strength,** forces diminuantes, qui s'en vont.

ebbing[2], *s.* **1.** reflux *m*, jusant *m*; baissant *m* (de l'eau). **2.** déclin *m.*

Ebenaceae [ebə'neisii:], *s.pl. Bot:* ébénacées *f.*

Ebenales [ebə'neili:z], *s.pl. Bot:* ébénales *f.*

Ebenezer [ebə'ni:zər]. **1.** *Pr.n.m.* (*a*) *B:* Eben-hézer; (*b*) (*baptismal name*) Ebenezer. **2.** *s. Rel:* (*a*) pierre commémorative; (*b*) petit temple (de secte dissidente).

Eberth ['i:bə:θ], *Pr.n. Med:* **Eberth's bacillus,** bacille *m* d'Eberth.

Ebionite ['ebiənait], *s. Rel.H:* ébionite *m.*

ebon ['ebən]. **1.** *a. Poet:* d'ébène. **2.** *s. U.S:* nègre, négresse.

ebonite ['ebənait], *s.* ébonite *f*; caoutchouc durci; vulcanite *f.*

ebonize ['ebənaiz], *v.tr.* ébéner (le bois); **ebonized wood,** bois noirci.

ebony ['ebəni], *s.* (*a*) ébène *f*; bois *m* d'ébène; *Com:* **red e.,** bois d'ébène rouge; grenadille *f*; **e. box,** boîte en bois d'ébène; *F:* **e. complexion,** teint (d'un noir) d'ébène; **as black as e.,** noir comme une taupe, comme un corbeau; d'un noir d'ébène; (*b*) **e. (tree),** ébénier *m*; plaqueminier ébénier.

ebracteate [i'bræktiət], *a. Bot:* ébracté.

ebriety [i:'braiəti], *s.* ébriété *f*, ivresse *f.*

ebrious ['i:briəs], *a.* en état d'ébriété; ivre; *occ.* ébrieux.

Ebro ['i:brou], *Pr.n. Geog:* l'Èbre *m.*

ebullience [i'bʌliəns], **ebulliency** [i'bʌliənsi], *s.* bouillonnement *m*, effervescence *f* (de la colère, de la jeunesse, etc.).

ebullient [i'bʌliənt], *a.* **1.** qui bout; bouillonnant, en ébullition. **2.** (sentiment) débordant, enthousiaste, exubérant; (homme) plein de vie.

ebulliometer [ibuli'ɔmitə(r)], *s. Ph:* ébulliomètre *m*, ébullioscope *m.*

ebulliometric [ibuliou'metrik], *a. Ph:* ébulliométrique.
ebulliometry [ibuli'ɔmitri], *s. Ph:* ébulliométrie *f*, ébullioscopie *f*.
ebullioscope [i'buliouskoup], *s. Ph:* ébullioscope *m*.
ebullioscopic [ibuliou'skɔpik], *a. Ph:* ébullioscopique.
ebullioscopy [ibuli'ɔskəpi], *s. Ph:* ébullioscopie *f*.
ebullition [i:bə'liʃ(ə)n], *s.* **1.** ébullition *f*, bouillonnement *m* (d'un liquide). **2.** *O:* (*a*) **e. of feeling,** transport *m*; **e. of wrath,** débordement *m* de colère; (*b*) insurrection *f*.
eburnation [i:bə:'neiʃ(ə)n], *s. Med:* éburnation *f*.
eburnean [i'bə:niən], *a.* éburnéen; éburné.
Eburones [ebju'rouni:z], *s.pl. Hist:* Éburons *m*.
ecad ['ekæd], *s. Biol:* écade *f*.
Ecardines [i:'kɑ:dini:z], *s.pl. Biol:* écardides *m*, écardines *m*, inarticulés *m*.
écarté [ei'kɑ:tei], *s. Cards:* écarté *m*.
écartelé [ei'kɑ:təlei], *a. Her:* écartelé.
ecbolic [ek'bɔlik], *a. & s. Obst:* abortif.
ecce homo ['eksi'houmou], *s. Art:* ecce homo *m*.
eccentric [ek'sentrik]. **1.** *a.* (*a*) *Mth: Astr:* (cercle *m*, etc.) excentrique; (*b*) *Mec.E:* **e. cam,** came désaxée; **e. catch,** demi-lune *f*; **e. load,** charge décentrée, excentrique; **e. shaft,** arbre *m* à excentrique(s); arbre excentré; **e. bushing,** douille excentrique, excentrée; **e. clamp,** levier *m* de coincement; **e. ring,** anneau *m* excentré; **e. sleeve,** manchon *m* excentré; **e. sliding-vane,** palette coulissante excentrée; *Min:* **e. bit,** trépan *m* excentrique; (*c*) (*of pers.*) excentrique; original, -aux. **2.** *s.* (*a*) *Mec.E:* excentrique *m*; **e. and collar, e. and strap,** excentrique à collier; **e. collar, e. hoop, e. strap,** collier *m* d'excentrique; **e. rod,** barre *f*, tige *f*, d'excentrique; **e. shaft,** arbre *m* à excentrique; **e. hook,** bec-de-cane *m*; pied-de-biche *m*; *Mch:* **fore e.,** excentrique *m* pour la marche avant; **forward e.,** excentrique de marche avant; (*b*) (*of pers.*) excentrique *mf*; original, -ale.
eccentrically [ek'sentrik(ə)li], *adv.* **1.** *Mec.E:* **e. bored spindle,** broche excentrée. **2.** (*of pers.*) excentriquement, originalement.
eccentricity [eksen'trisiti], *s.* **1.** (*a*) excentricité *f* (d'une ellipse); (*b*) *Mec.E:* excentricité, désaxage *m*, décentrement *m*. **2.** (*a*) excentricité (de caractère); bizarrerie *f*, originalité *f* (**in,** de); (*b*) **to bear with s.o.'s eccentricities,** supporter les excentricités de qn.
ecchondroma [ekɔn'droumə], **ecchondrosis** [ekɔn'drousis], *s. Med:* ecchondrome *m*, ecchondrose *f*.
ecchymosed ['ekimouzd], *a. Med:* ecchymosé.
ecchymosis [eki'mousis], *s. Med:* ecchymose *f*.
ecchymotic [eki'mɔtik], *a. Med:* ecchymotique.
Eccles ['eklz], *Pr.n. Geog:* Eccles; *Cu:* **E. cake,** (genre *m* de) pâtisserie *f* aux raisins secs.
ecclesia [i'kli:ziə], *s. Gr.Ant: Ecc:* ecclésie *f*, ecclésia *f*.
ecclesiarch [i'kli:siɑ:k], *s.* chef *m* (de l'Église).
Ecclesiast (the) [ðii'kli:ziæst], *Pr.n.m. B:* l'Ecclésiaste (auteur du Livre).
Ecclesiastes [ikli:zi'æsti:z], *Pr.n. B:* l'Ecclésiaste *m* (le Livre saint).
ecclesiastic [ikli:zi'æstik], *a. & s.* ecclésiastique (*m*).
ecclesiastical [ikli:zi'æstikl], *a.* ecclésiastique; **e. warehouse,** maison d'articles religieux; **the e. body,** le sacerdoce; *Adm:* **e. matters,** les cultes *m*; **the E. Commission,** la Commission d'administration des biens de l'Église anglicane.
ecclesiastically [ikli:zi'æstik(ə)li], *adv.* ecclésiastiquement.
ecclesiasticism [ikli:zi'æstisizm], *s.* esprit clérical; cléricalisme *m*.
Ecclesiasticus [ikli:zi'æstikəs], *Pr.n. B.Lit:* l'Ecclésiastique *m*.
ecclesiologist [ikli:zi'ɔlədʒist], *s.* ecclésiologue *m*.
ecclesiology [ikli:zi'ɔlədʒi], *s.* ecclésiologie *f*.
eccyclema [eksi'kli:mə], *s. A.Gr.Th:* eccyclème *m*.
ecdemic [ek'demik], *a.* ecdémique, non endémique.
ecdemite [ek'di:mait], *s. Miner:* ecdémite *f*.
ecdysiast [ek'diziæst], *s. NAm:* strippeuse *f*.
ecdysis ['ekdisis], *s. Ent: etc:* ecdysis *f*.
ecdyson(e) ['ekdisoun], *s. Physiol:* ecdysone *f*.
ecgonine ['ekgəni:n], *s. Ch:* ecgonine *f*.
echelon[1] ['eʃəlɔn], *s.* **1.** *Mil:* échelon *m*; **in e.,** en échelon; **movement in e.,** mouvement *m* en tiroir, par échelon(s) successif(s); **first, forward, e.,** premier échelon; **support e.,** deuxième échelon, échelon de soutien; **rear e.,** échelon arrière; **attack e.,** échelon d'attaque. **2.** *Ind: Com:* **the higher echelons of industry,** les niveaux supérieurs de l'industrie. **3.** *Opt:* **e. lens,** lentille *f* à échelons.
echelon[2], *v.tr. Mil:* échelonner (des troupes).
echeloned ['eʃəlɔnd], *a. Mil:* en échelon.
echelonment [eʃə'lɔnmənt], *s. Mil: etc:* échelonnement *m*.
echeveria [etʃivə'ri:ə], *s. Bot:* écheveria *m*.
echidna [e'kidnə], *s. Z:* échidné *m*.
Echimyidae [eki'maiədi], *s.pl. Z:* échimyidés *m*.
echinid [e'kainid], *s.* échinide *m*.
Echinidae [e'kainidi:], *s.pl.* échinides *m*.
Echinidea [eki'nidiə], *s.pl.* = ECHINOIDEA.
echinite ['ekinait], *s. Paleont:* échinide *m*, oursin *m*, fossile.
echinocactus [e'kainou'kæktəs], *s. Bot:* échinocactus *m*.
echinocaris [e'kainou'kɑ:ris], *s. Paleont:* échinocaris *m*.
echinocarpous [e'kainou'kɑ:pəs], *a. Bot:* échinocarpe.
echinocereus [e'kainou'si:riəs], *s. Bot:* échinocéreus *m*.
echinococcosis [e'kainoukɔ'kousis], *s. Med: Vet:* échinococcose *f*.
Echinococcus [e'kainou'kɔkəs], *s. Ann:* échinocoque *m*.
echinocystis [e'kainou'sistis], *s. Bot:* échinocystis *m*.
echinoderm [e'kainoudə:m], *s. Z:* échinoderme *m*.
Echinodermata [e'kainou'də:mətə], *s.pl.* échinodermes *m*.
echinodermatous [e'kainou'də:mətəs], *a.* échinoderme.
echinoid [e'kainɔid], *a. & s.* échinoïde (*m*).
Echinoidea [eki'nɔidiə], *s.pl.* échinidés *m*.
echinops ['ekinɔps], *s. Bot:* échinops *m*, échinope *m*.
echinorhynchus [e'kainou'riŋkəs], *s. Ann:* échinorynque *m*, échinorhynchus *m*.
echinulate [e'k(ə)injuleit], *a. Nat.Hist:* échinulé.
echinus [e'kainəs], *s.* **1.** échinus *m*; oursin *m*. **2.** *Arch:* échine *f* (de chapiteau).
Echis ['ekis], *s. Rept:* échis *m*.
Echites [e'kaiti:z], *s. Bot:* échitès *m*.
Echiurida [eki'ju:ridə], **Echiuroidea** [ekiju'rɔidiə], *s.pl. Ann:* échiures *m*, échiuriens *m*.
echo[1] ['ekou], *s.* **1.** (*pl.* **echoes**) (*a*) *Ac:* écho *m*, écho simple; **flutter e.,** écho multiple; **to applaud to the e.,** applaudir à tout rompre, frénétiquement; **e. sounding,** sondage *m* par le son, par ultra-sons; **e. sounder,** sondeur *m* par le son; (*b*) *Elcs: Ph:* écho; **fixed, permanent, e.,** écho fixe; **e. box,** cavité résonnante; **e. chamber,** chambre *f* à échos; **e. wave,** onde *f* d'écho; **e. image,** image *f* fantôme; **e. current,** courant *m* d'écho, courant réfléchi; **e. path,** itinéraire du, des courant(s) d'écho; **e. attenuation,** affaiblissement *m* des courants d'écho; **e. suppressor,** (dispositif) suppresseur *m* d'écho(s); (*c*) *Pros:* **e. verse,** rime *f* en écho, échoïque. **2.** *Pr.n.f. Gr.Myth:* Écho.
echo[2]. **1.** *v.tr.* répéter (en écho); **to e. s.o.'s opinions, s.o.'s words,** se faire l'écho des opinions de qn; faire écho aux paroles de qn; **to e. back a shout,** faire écho à un cri. **2.** *v.i.* (*a*) faire écho; **the woods echoed with the songs of birds,** les bois retentissaient des chants des oiseaux; **room that does not e.,** pièce sourde; **he made the valleys e. as he sang,** il réveillait de ses chants les échos des vallons; (*b*) retentir; **his voice echoes through the room,** sa voix retentit, résonne, dans la salle.
echogram ['ekougræm], *s.* échogramme *m*.
echograph ['ekougræf], *s.* échographe *m*.
echoic [e'kouik], *a.* échoïque.
echolalia [ekou'leiliə], *s. Med:* écholalie *f*.
echoless ['ekoulis], *a.* sans écho; *Cin:* **e. studio,** studio complètement sourd.
echolocation [ekoulou'keiʃ(ə)n], *s.* **1.** *Z:* audiodétection *f*, écholocation *f*. **2.** *Tch:* écholocalisation *f*.
echometer ['ekoumitər], *s. Elcs:* échomètre *m*.
echopraxia [ekou'præksiə], **echopraxis** [ekou'præksis], *s. Med:* échopraxie *f*.
eciton ['esitɔn], *s. Ent:* éciton *m*.
éclair [ei'klɛər, 'eiklɛər], *s. Cu:* éclair *m* (à la crème, etc.); **chocolate e.,** éclair au chocolat.
eclampsia [i'klæmpsiə], *s. Med:* éclampsie *f*.
eclamptic [i'klæmptik], *a. & s. Obst:* éclamptique (*f*).
éclat [ei'klɑ:, 'eiklɑ:], *s.* éclat *m*, gloire *f*.
eclectic [e'klektik], *a. & s.* éclectique (*m*).
eclectically [e'klektik(ə)li], *adv.* éclectiquement.
eclecticism [e'klektisizm], *s.* éclectisme *m*.
eclimeter [i'klimitər], *s. Surv:* éclimètre *m*.
eclipse[1] [i'klips], *s.* **1.** (*a*) *Astr:* éclipse *f*; **solar e., lunar e.,** éclipse de soleil, de lune; **total, partial, e.,** éclipse totale, partielle; (*b*) *Nau:* **the flash and the e. of a light,** l'éclat *m* et l'éclipse d'un phare; (*c*) **to suffer an e.,** être éclipsé; se trouver relégué à l'arrière-plan, dans l'ombre. **2.** *Orn:* **bird in e.,** oiseau qui a mué sa robe de noces; oiseau dans son plumage d'hiver.
eclipse[2], *v.tr.* éclipser (la lune, la lumière d'un phare, etc.); éclipser, surpasser, faire pâlir (la gloire de qn); faire ombre à (qn).
ecliptic [i'kliptik], *a. & s. Astr:* écliptique (*f*).
eclogite ['eklədʒait], *s. Miner:* éclogite *f*.
eclogue ['eklɔg], *s. Lit:* églogue *f*.
eclosion [i'klouʒən], *s. Ent:* éclosion *f*.
ecmnesia [ek'ni:ziə], *s. Med:* ecmnésie *f*.
ecological [i:kə'lɔdʒikl], *a.* écologique.
ecologist [i:'kɔlədʒist], *s.* écologiste *mf*.
ecology [i:'kɔlədʒi], *s.* écologie *f*.
econometrician [i:kɔnəme'triʃ(ə)n], *s.* économétricien, -ienne.
econometrics [i:kɔnə'metriks], *s.pl.* (*usu. with sg. const.*) économétrie *f*.
economic [i:kə'nɔmik], *a.* **1.** qui se rapporte à l'économie politique; (problème *m*) économique; **e. crisis,** crise *f* économique; **e. growth,** croissance *f* économique; **e. policy,** politique *f* économique; **European E. Community,** communauté économique européenne. **2. e. rent,** loyer *m* rentable.
economical [i:kə'nɔmikl], *a.* **1.** *A:* = ECONOMIC. **2.** (*a*) (*of pers.*) économe, ménager; **to be e. with sth.,** ménager, épargner, économiser, qch.; (*b*) (*of method, apparatus, etc.*) économique; **e. speed (of a ship, etc.),** vitesse *f* économique (d'un navire, etc.).
economically [i:kə'nɔmikli], *adv.* économiquement; **to use sth. e.,** ménager qch.
economics [i:kə'nɔmiks], *s.pl.* (*usu. with sg. const.*) **1.** les sciences *f* économiques; l'économie *f* politique; **welfare e.,** l'économie de bien-être. **2.** rentabilité *f* (d'un projet); **the e. of town planning,** les aspects financiers de l'urbanisme.
economism [i:'kɔnəmizm], *s.* économisme *m*.
economist [i(:)'kɔnəmist], *s.* **1.** *A:* (*a*) économe *m*, administrateur *m*; (*b*) ménagère *f*. **2.** personne *f* économe (**of,** de). **3.** (**political**) **e.,** économiste *m*; **agricultural e.,** agronome *m*.
economize [i(:)'kɔnəmaiz], *v.tr.* économiser, épargner, ménager (le temps, l'argent, etc.); *v.i.* économiser, faire des économies; **to e. on sth.,** économiser sur qch.
economizer [i(:)'kɔnəmaizər], *s.* **1.** personne *f* économe; économiseur, -euse. **2.** *Ind:* (*device*) économiseur *m*; **fuel e.,** économiseur de combustible.
economy [i(:)'kɔnəmi], *s.* **1.** économie *f* (d'argent, de temps, etc.); **e. in fuel consumption,** économie de, en, combustible; **to practise e.,** économiser; **to practise strict e.,** observer une stricte économie; se montrer extrêmement économe; vivre à l'étroit; **drawing showing great e. of line,** dessin *m* très sobre; **a good article is an e. in the long run,** on regagne le prix d'un article de bonne qualité; *Aut:* **e. run,** concours *m* de consommation; *Nau: Av:* **e. class,** classe *f* économique. **2.** (*a*) **political e.,** économie politique; **planned e.,** économie planifiée; **controlled e.,** économie dirigée; **open e.,** économie ouverte; (*b*) **to disturb the e. of the country,** déranger l'économie, le régime économique, du pays. **3. domestic e.,** économie domestique.
ecosystem ['ekousistəm], *s. Biol:* écosystème *m*.
écraseur [eikræ'zə:r], *s. Surg:* écraseur *m* (pour polypes, etc.).
ecrasite ['i:krəsait], *s. Exp: A:* écrasite *f*.
ecru ['eikru:], *a. & s. Tex:* écru (*m*).
ecstasied ['ekstəsid], *a.* extasié, en extase.
ecstasize ['ekstəsaiz]. **1.** *v.tr.* ravir (qn). **2.** *v.i.* s'extasier (**over sth.,** devant qch.).
ecstasy ['ekstəsi], *s.* **1.** transport *m* (de joie), joie délirante; ravissement *m*; **to be in an e. of joy,** se pâmer de joie; **to go into ecstasies over sth.,** s'extasier devant qch. **2.** (*a*) *Med:* extase *f*; (*b*) extase (religieuse, prophétique, poétique, etc.).
ecstatic [ek'stætik], *a.* extatique.
ecstatically [ek'stætik(ə)li], *adv.* avec extase, d'une manière extatique; **e. happy,** heureux jusqu'au ravissement; **to gaze e. at s.o.,** tomber en extase devant qn; contempler qn d'un air extasié.
ectasis ['ektəsis], *s.* **1.** *Gram:* ectase *f*. **2.** *Med:* ectasie *f*.
ecthyma [ek'θaimə], *s. Med: Vet:* ecthyma *m*.
ecto- ['ektou], *pref.* ecto-.
ectoblast ['ektoublæst], *s. Biol:* ectoblaste *m*.
ectocardia [ektou'kɑ:diə], *s. Med:* ectocardie *f*.
Ectocarpales [ektoukɑ:'peili:z], *s.pl. Algae:* ectocarpales *f*.
ectoderm ['ektoudə:m], *s. Biol:* ectoderme *m*.
ectodermal [ektou'də:m(ə)l], **ectodermic** [ektou'də:mik], *a.* ectodermique.
ectogenesis [ektou'dʒenəsis], *s. Biol:* ectogénèse *f*.
ectogenic [ektou'dʒenik], *a.* **1.** *Med:* exogène. **2.** = ECTOGENOUS.
ectogenous [ek'tɔdʒənəs], *a. Biol:* ectogène.
Ectognatha [ek'tɔgnəθə], *s.pl. Ent:* ectotrophes *m*.
ectolecithal [ektou'lesiθ(ə)l], *a. Biol:* ectolécithe.
ectomorph ['ektoumɔ:f], *s.* ectomorphe *mf*.
ectomorphic [ektou'mɔ:fik], *a.* ectomorphe.
ectomorphy ['ektoumɔ:fi], *s. Anthr:* ectomorphisme *m*, leptosomie *f*.
ectoparasite [ektou'pærəsait], *s. Ent:* ectoparasite *m*.
ectoparasitic [ektoupærə'sitik], *a. Ent:* ectoparasite.
ectopia [ek'toupiə], *s. Med:* ectopie *f*.
ectoplasm ['ektouplæzm], *s. Biol: Psychics:* ectoplasme *m*.
ectoplasmatic [ektouplæz'mætik], **ectoplasmic**

[ektou'plæzmik], *a.* ectoplasmique.

Ectoprocta [ektou'prɔktə], *s.pl. Nat.Hist:* ectoproctes *m.*

ectosome ['ektousoum], *s. Biol:* ectosome *m.*

Ectotrophi [ek'tɔtrəfai], *s.pl. Ent:* ectotrophes *m.*

ectotrophic [ektou'trɔfik], *a. Biol:* ectotrophe.

ectozoan [ektou'zouən], *a.* & *s. Nat.Hist:* ectozoaire (*m*).

ectozoon, *pl.* **-zoa** [ektou'zouɔn, -zouə], *s. Nat.Hist:* ectozoaire *m.*

ectrodactylia [ektroudæk'tiliə], **ectrodactylism** [ektrou'dæktilizm], **ectrodactyly** [ektrou'dæktili], *s.* ectrodactylie *f.*

ectrodactylous [ektrou'dæktiləs], *a.* ectrodactyle.

ectromelia [ektrou'mi:liə], *s. Ter:* ectromélie *f.*

ectromelian [ektrou'mi:liən], *a.* & *s. Ter:* ectromèle (*mf*).

ectropion [ek'troupiən], *s. Med:* ectropion *m*; éversion *f* (de la paupière).

ectypal ['ektipl, ek'taipl], *a. Phil:* ectypal.

ectype ['ektaip], *s.* ectype *f.*

Ecuador ['ekwədɔ:r], *Pr.n. Geog:* (la République de) l'Équateur *m.*

Ecuadorian [ekwə'dɔ:riən]. *Geog:* (*a*) *a.* écuadorien, équatorien; (*b*) *s.* Écuadorien, -ienne; Équatorien, -ienne.

ecumene ['ekjumi:n], *s. Geog:* écoumène *m,* œkoumène *m.*

ecumenical [i:kju'menikl], *a.* **1.** *Ecc:* (conseil *m*) œcuménique. **2.** universel.

ecumenicalism [i:kju'menik(ə)lizm], *s.* œcuménisme *m.*

ecumenically [i:kju'menik(ə)li], *adv.* œcuméniquement.

ecumenicity [i:kjumi'nisiti], *s.* œcuménicité *f.*

ecumenism [i:'kju:minizm], *s.* œcuménisme *m.*

eczema ['eksimə], *s. Med:* eczéma *m*; **moist e., weeping e.,** eczéma humide, suintant.

eczematization [eksimətai'zeiʃ(ə)n], *s.* eczématisation *f.*

eczematoid [ek'semətɔid], *a.* eczématiforme.

eczematous [ek'semətəs], *a.* eczémateux.

edacious [i'deiʃəs], *a.* vorace; glouton, -onne.

edacity [i'dæsiti], *s.* voracité *f,* gloutonnerie *f.*

edaphic [e'dæfik], *a. Biol:* édaphique.

edaphology [edə'fɔlədʒi], *s. Biol:* édaphologie *f.*

edaphon ['edəfɔn], *s. Biol:* édaphon *m.*

Edda ['edə], *s. Norse Lit:* Edda *f*; **the Older, Poetic, E.,** l'Edda poétique; **the Younger, Prose, E.,** l'Edda en prose.

Eddaic [e'deiik], **Eddic** ['edik], *a. Lit:* eddique.

eddy[1] [edi], *s.* **1.** (*of water, wind*) remous *m*; tourbillon *m*; tournoiement *m*; *Nau:* retour *m* de courant, revolin *m*; **e. chamber,** chambre *f* aérodynamique pour l'étude des remous; *Nau:* **e. wind,** revolin *m*; renvoi *m* de vent; *Aut: Av:* **e. current,** remous de courant. **2.** *El:* **e. currents,** courants *m* de Foucault; courants parasites; **e.-current circuit,** circuit *m* des courants parasites; **e.-current brake,** frein *m* magnétique.

eddy[2]. **1.** *v.i.* (*of water*) faire des remous; (*of wind*) tourbillonner, tournoyer. **2.** *v.tr.* faire tourbillonner.

eddying[1] ['ediiŋ], *a.* (*of water*) qui fait des remous, tournoyant; (*of wind*) tourbillonnant; **e. flow,** remous *m*; *Av:* **e. motion,** turbulence(s) *f*; courant(s) *m* tourbillonnaire(s).

eddying[2], *s.* tourbillonnement *m* (du vent); tournoiement *m,* remous *mpl* (de l'eau).

edelweiss ['eidlvais], *s. Bot:* édelweiss *m*; immortelle *f* des neiges.

edema [i:'di:mə], *s.* œdème *m.*

Eden ['i:dn]. *Pr.n. B:* (**the Garden of**) **E.,** l'Éden *m*; le Paradis terrestre.

edenite ['i:dənait], *s. Miner:* édénite *f.*

Edentata [i:den'teitə], *s.pl. Z:* édentés *m.*

edentate [i'denteit], *a.* & *s. Z:* édenté (*m*).

edentulous [i'dentjuləs], *a.* sans dents; édenté.

Edessa [i'desə], *Pr.n.* **1.** *A.Geog:* Édesse *f.* **2.** *Geog:* Ed(h)essa.

edestin [i'destin], *s. Bio-Ch:* édestine *f.*

edge[1] [edʒ], *s.* **1.** (*a*) fil *m,* tranchant *m,* taillant *m,* coupant *m,* arête tranchante, coupante (d'une lame); angle *m* (d'un outil); *Tls:* **wire e., feather e.,** morfil *m,* bavure *f*; **thin e. (of wedge),** tranchant (de coin); *F:* **it's the thin e. of the wedge,** c'est le premier pas (qui mène à une mauvaise habitude, etc.); **to give s.o. the rough e. of one's tongue,** dire son fait à qn; laver la tête à qn; *Sp:* (*karate*) **e. of the hand blow,** coup porté avec le tranchant de la main, coup du tranchant de la main; (*b*) **knife with an e., a keen e., on it,** couteau à tranchant aigu, acéré; **to put an e., a new e., a fine e., on, to, a tool, on a blade,** (re)donner du fil à un outil; aiguiser, affiler, acérer, aviver, un outil; (re)mettre la tranchant à une lame; **this knife has no e.,** ce couteau est émoussé, ne coupe plus; **to take the e. off a knife,** émousser un couteau; **e. tool,** outil tranchant, coupant; **e. tools,** taillanderie *f*; **e.-tool maker,** taillandier *m*; **e.-tool making,** taillanderie; *Min:* **e. mill,** broyeur *m* à meules verticales; **e. runner,** meule verticale; **to take the e. off, to dull the e. of, one's appetite,** (i) émousser l'appétit; (ii) étourdir la grosse faim; casser une croûte (pour attendre le repas); **to take the e. off pleasure,** gâter, gâcher, émousser, le plaisir; **to take the e. off an argument,** couper tout l'effet d'un argument; **style with an e. to it,** style acéré; **words with an e.,** paroles mordantes, caustiques; **not to put too fine an e. on it,** pour dire les choses carrément; pour ne pas mâcher les mots. **2.** (*a*) arête, angle (d'un cristal, d'une pierre, etc.); carne *f* (d'une pierre); accore *f* (d'un banc de sable, d'un écueil); **square e.,** bord *m* rectangulaire; **sharp e.,** arête vive; **rounded e., blunted e.,** arête mousse; *Carp: etc:* **feather e.,** biseau *m,* chanfrein *m*; bord *m* en biseau; **e. saw,** scie *f* à écorner; *Metalw:* **e. finishing,** ébarbage *m,* ébarbement *m*; **e.-finishing press,** presse à ébarber; **the e. of the kerb,** l'arête vive du trottoir; (*b*) (*of skating*) carre *f* (de patin); **inside e.,** dedans *m*; **outside e.,** dehors *m*; **to cut, do, the inside e.,** glisser sur les carres intérieures; faire des dedans; (*c*) *Mil:* **outside e. of a trench,** revers *m* d'une tranchée; (*d*) lèvre *f* (d'une plaie, d'une coupure); (*e*) *Tls: Carp:* **straight e.,** limande *f.* **3.** bord *m,* rebord *m* (de table, de vase); tranche *f,* can *m,* carne, rive *f,* chant *m* (d'une planche); ourlet *m* (d'un cratère); tranche (d'une médaille, d'une pièce de monnaie); tranchant (d'une raquette); rive (d'une feuille de papier); *Aut:* accrochage *m* (de la jante d'une roue); *Astr:* limbe *m* (du soleil, de la lune); *Bookb:* tranche (de livre); **gilt edges,** tranches dorées; **with gilt edges,** doré sur tranches; **gilt top e.,** tête dorée; (*of page*) **back e.,** petit fond; **fore e.,** gouttière *f*; **to set two boards e. to e.,** affronter deux planches; mettre deux planches bord à bord; *Num:* **milled e.,** crénelage *m,* grènetis *m,* cordon *m*; *Rail:* **e. rail,** (i) rail posé de chant; (ii) (*guard rail*) contre-rail *m, pl.* contre-rails; *N.Arch: Av:* **leading e.,** arêtier *m,* bord d'entrée, d'attaque; **trailing e.,** bord de fuite, de sortie, de chute; **on e.,** (i) (*of brick*) de chant, de can, sur can; (ii) (*of pers.*) énervé, nerveux; **to set on e.,** (i) mettre de chant, de can, sur can; canter (des briques); (ii) faire grincer (les dents à qn); agacer, crisper (les nerfs); crisper, énerver, horripiler (qn); **stones set on e.,** pierres posées de, sur, chant; **it sets my teeth on e.,** cela me fait mal aux dents; cela me crispe; **my nerves are all on e.,** j'ai les nerfs à fleur de peau; j'ai les nerfs à cran, à vif, en pelote; **the least worry puts him all on e.,** le moindre tracas lui donne sur les nerfs; **she is on e. today,** elle est nerveuse, elle a ses nerfs, aujourd'hui; *F:* **to have an, the, e. on s.o.,** (i) avoir barre sur qn; (ii) être avantagé par rapport à qn. **4.** lisière *f,* bordure *f,* orée *f* (d'un bois); bord, rive (d'une rivière); marge *f* (d'un chemin, d'un fossé); limite *f* (d'une plaine); pourtour *m* (d'une came, etc.); liséré *m,* bord (d'une étoffe, etc.); *Phot: etc:* (*of print*) **white e.,** liséré blanc; **safe e.,** cache *m*; *Min:* **e. seam, e. coal,** dressant *m*; *For:* **e. tree,** pied cornier; *Tls: Hort:* **e. trimmer, e. cutter,** coupe-bordure *m, pl.* coupe-bordure(s); **the e. of the road,** la bordure de la route; **houses built along, by, the e. of the road,** maisons bâties en bordure du chemin; **at the water's e.,** au bord de l'eau; **at the e. of a precipice,** au bord d'un précipice.

edge[2], *v.*

I. *v.tr.* & *i.* **1.** (*a*) affiler, aiguiser, donner un tranchant à (un couteau); affûter (un outil); (*b*) **to e. a grinding wheel,** repiquer une meule; (*c*) *Metalw:* tomber (un bord de tôle). **2.** (*a*) border (une étoffe, la route) (**with,** de); lisérer (une jupe); **road edged with poplars,** route bordée de peupliers; *Engr:* **to e. the plate with chalk,** marger la planche avec du blanc d'Espagne; (*b*) (*clip*) déborder (une tôle, un verre de lunette, etc.). **3.** **to e. (one's way) into, out of, a room; to e. in, out,** se faufiler, se glisser, dans une pièce; s'introduire doucement, de guingois, dans une pièce; sortir tout doucement d'une pièce; se dérober; *F:* se défiler; **to e. one's way into a job,** s'ingérer dans un emploi; **to e. in a word,** placer son mot; glisser un mot; **to e. a product out of the market,** faire disparaître insensiblement un produit du marché; **to e. s.o. out of a job,** évincer qn; **to e. one's chair nearer,** rapprocher, avancer, sa chaise peu à peu, tout doucement; *Nau:* **to e. to the north,** incliner la route vers le nord; **to e. to starboard,** obliquer sur tribord; **to e. to(wards) the right,** obliquer vers la droite. **4.** *A:* **to e. s.o. on,** pousser, inciter, qn (à faire qch.). **5.** *Cr:* **to e. a ball,** frapper la balle du bord de la batte.

II. (*compound verbs*) **1. edge away,** *v.i.* s'éloigner, se reculer, s'écarter, tout doucement (**from s.o.,** de qn); *Nau:* s'éloigner, laisser porter, en dépendant.

2. edge down, *v.i. Nau:* **to e. down upon a boat,** gouverner, arriver (sur un bateau) en dépendant; **to clear a point edging down,** doubler une pointe en dépendant.

3. edge off. (*a*) *v.tr.* (i) amincir (une lame, etc.); (ii) *Engr:* ébarber (une planche); (*b*) *v.i.* = EDGE AWAY.

edged [edʒd], *a.* **1.** (*of tool, etc.*) tranchant, acéré; *Fig:* **to play with e. tools,** jouer avec le feu; jouer un jeu dangereux. **2.** (*in compound adjs.*) (*a*) à tranchant; **chisel-e.,** taillé en lame; (*b*) **gilt-e.,** doré sur tranche; **deckle-e.,** (papier *m*) à bords non ébarbés, déchiquetés; (*c*) **double-e.,** (épée *f,* compliment *m*) à deux tranchants.

edgeless ['edʒlis], *a.* **1.** (*of sword, etc.*) émoussé. **2.** dépourvu de bords.

edger ['edʒər], *s. Tls: Hort:* coupe-bordure *m, pl.* coupe-bordure(s).

edgeways ['edʒweiz], **edgewise** ['edʒwaiz], *adv.* **1.** (vu) latéralement, de côté. **2.** de chant, sur chant, de côté; **to lay, set, a plank e.,** placer une planche de chant, de can, sur can; canter une planche; *F:* **I can't get a word in e.,** impossible de placer, de glisser, un mot (dans la conversation). **3.** (*of two things*) côte à côte; (*of two boards*) affronté.

edgily ['edʒili], *adv.* d'un air agacé.

edginess ['edʒinis], *s. F:* nervosité *f.*

edging ['edʒiŋ], *s.* **1.** (*a*) pose *f* d'un liséré, d'un cordonnet, d'une ganse (à une robe, etc.); entretien *m,* taillage *m,* de la bordure (d'une pelouse, etc.); **e. iron, e. tool,** coupe-gazon *m inv,* tranche-gazon *m inv,* molette *f*; **e. shears,** cisaille *f* à bordures; (*b*) (*clipping*) débordage *m* (d'une tôle, d'un verre de lunette). **2.** *Dressm: Furn: etc:* liséré *m,* cordonnet *m,* passement *m,* ganse *f*; garniture *f*; *Mil:* contour *m* (d'épaulette); *Nau:* gaine *f* (d'une voile); *Hort:* bordure *f* (de parterre, etc.); **box e.,** bordure *f* de buis; **e. strip,** bordure *f* (métallique, etc.).

edgy ['edʒi], *a.* **1.** (*of rock, etc.*) aux arêtes vives; (*of picture*) aux contours tranchés; aux lignes dures. **2.** *F:* (*of pers.*) (*a*) au caractère anguleux; (*b*) énervé, nerveux.

edibility [edi'biliti], *s.* comestibilité *f.*

edible ['edibl]. **1.** *a.* comestible; bon à manger; mangeable; **e. oil,** huile *f* comestible. **2.** *s.pl.* **edibles,** comestibles *m.*

edict ['i:dikt], *s. Hist:* édit *m*; *Hist:* **the E. of Nantes,** l'Édit de Nantes.

edictal [i'dikt(ə)l], *a.* édictal, -aux.

edification [edifi'keiʃ(ə)n], *s.* édification *f* (de la jeunesse, etc.); instruction *f*; **for your e.,** pour votre gouverne.

edifice ['edifis], *s.* édifice *m.*

edifier ['edifaiər], *s. usu. Iron:* **the edifiers of modern youth,** ceux qui se chargent de l'édification de la jeunesse moderne; les mentors *m* de la jeunesse moderne.

edify ['edifai], *v.tr.* **1.** *A:* édifier, bâtir, construire. **2.** édifier (qn).

edifying ['edifaiiŋ], *a.* édifiant.

Edinburgh ['edinbrə], *Pr.n. Geog:* Édimbourg, (**native, inhabitant) of E.,** édimbourgeois, -oise.

edingtonite ['ediŋtənait], *s. Miner:* édingtonite *f.*

Edison ['edisən], *Pr.n.m. El:* **E. accumulator,** accumulateur *m* fer-nickel; **E. screw cap,** culot *m* Edison, culot à vis; *Elcs:* **E. effect,** effet *m* Edison, effet redresseur.

edit ['edit], *v.tr.* (*a*) préparer (un texte) pour la publication; annoter, éditer (le texte d'un auteur); accompagner (un texte) de remarques; donner un texte critique, une édition annotée (d'une œuvre); diriger (une série de textes, etc.); (*b*) rédiger, diriger (un journal, une revue); **edited by . . .,** (série, journal, etc.) sous la direction de . . .; (*c*) *Cin:* monter (un film).

Edith ['i:diθ]. *Pr.n.f.* Édith(e).

editing ['editiŋ], *s.* (*a*) préparation *f,* annotation *f* (d'un texte); **book that would have been improved by careful e.,** livre qui aurait gagné à être revu soigneusement; (*b*) rédaction *f,* direction *f* (d'un journal); (*c*) *Cin:* montage *m* (d'un film).

edition [i'diʃ(ə)n], *s. Publ:* édition *f* (d'un ouvrage); **limited e.,** édition à tirage limité; **definitive e.,** édition ne varietur; **school e.,** édition scolaire; **popular e., cheap e.,** édition populaire, à bon marché; **book in its fourth e.,** livre à sa quatrième édition; **first e.,** édition princeps, édition originale.

editor ['editər], *s.* (*f. occ.* **editress** ['editris]) **1.** annotateur *m,* éditeur *m* (d'un texte); auteur *m* (d'une édition critique). **2.** (*a*) surveillant *m* de la publication; **e. of a series, of a dictionary,** directeur *m* d'une série, d'un dictionnaire; (*b*) rédacteur *m* en chef, directeur (d'une revue, d'un journal); **managing e.,** rédacteur gérant; **news e.,** rédacteur aux actualités, rédacteur de la chronique du jour, rédacteur au service des informations; (*c*) *Journ:* titulaire *m* d'une rubrique, chroniqueur *m*; **dramatic e.,** critique *m* dramatique; **sports e.,** rédacteur sportif; **city e.,** (i) rédacteur de la rubrique financière; (ii) *U.S:* rédacteur de la chronique du jour; *Fr.C:* chef *m* des nouvelles; (*d*) *W.Tel:* **programme e.,** éditorialiste *mf*; (*e*) *Cin:* monteur *m* (d'un film).

editorial [edi'tɔ:riəl]. **1.** *a.* éditorial, -aux; **e. office,** (salle *f* de) rédaction *f*; **the e. staff,** la rédaction. **2.** *s. Journ:* article *m* de fond, de tête; éditorial *m*.

editorially [edi'tɔ:riəli], *adv.* en qualité de rédacteur, de directeur.

editorship ['editəʃip], *s.* **1.** rôle *m* d'annotateur (d'un texte). **2.** direction *f* de publication; **series published under the e. of . . .,** série publiée sous la direction de . . .. **3.** fonctions *fpl* de rédacteur en chef; direction (d'un journal); rédaction *f*.

Edmund ['edmənd]. *Pr.n.m.* Edmond.

Edomite ['i:dəmait], *s. B.Hist:* Édomite *mf*.

Edones [i'douni:z], **Edoni** [i'douni:], *s.pl. Hist:* Édoniens *m*.

Edrioasteroidea [edriouæstə'rɔidiə], *s.pl. Paleont:* édrioastérides *m*.

Edriophthalma(ta) [edriɔf'θælmə, -ma:tə], *s.pl. Crust:* édriophtalmes *m*.

edriophthalmian [edriɔf'θælmiən], *s. Crust:* édriophtalme *m*.

edriophthalmic [edriɔf'θælmik], **edriophthalmatous** [edriɔf'θælmətəs], **edriophthalmous** [edriɔf'θælməs], *a. Crust:* édriophtalme.

educability [edjukə'biliti], *s.* éducabilité *f*.

educable ['edjukəbl], *a.* éducable.

educatability [edjukeitə'biliti], *s.* éducabilité *f*.

educatable ['edjukeitəbl], *a.* éducable.

educate ['edjukeit], *v.tr.* **1.** *A:* élever; *F:* éduquer. **2.** (*a*) donner de l'instruction à, instruire (qn); **he was educated in France,** il a fait ses études en France; **he is entirely self-educated,** il s'est instruit entièrement par lui-même; c'est un autodidacte; (*b*) faire faire ses études à (son enfant); **to e. one's son for the bar,** diriger son fils vers le barreau. **3.** former (qn, le goût de qn); **to e. s.o., oneself, to like sth.,** former le goût à qn, se former le goût, pour qch. **4.** dresser, éduquer (les animaux).

educated ['edjukeitid], *a.* **1. e. man,** homme instruit, lettré; esprit cultivé; **he is well e.,** il a reçu une forte éducation, une bonne instruction; **he is only half e.,** il a reçu une éducation rudimentaire; il n'a pas beaucoup d'instruction; il n'est que peu instruit; **where was he educated?** où a-t-il fait ses études?; **self e.,** autodidacte. **2.** (*of dog, etc.*) savant.

education [edju'keiʃ(ə)n], *s.* **1.** éducation *f*; **a man without e.,** un homme sans éducation; **a liberal e.,** une éducation libérale. **2.** enseignement *m*, instruction *f*, études *fpl*; **compulsory e.,** enseignement obligatoire; l'obligation *f* scolaire; **primary,** *A:* **elementary, e.,** enseignement primaire; **secondary e.,** enseignement secondaire; **higher, university, e.,** enseignement supérieur; études supérieures; **tertiary e.,** enseignement technologique; **further e.,** enseignement post-scolaire; **adult e.,** enseignement des adultes; formation continue; **technical e.,** enseignement technique; **commercial e.,** études commerciales; **general e.,** éducation de base, culture générale; **state e.,** enseignement public; **non-state, private e.,** enseignement libre; **Department of E. and Science,** *A:* **Board of E.** = Ministère *m* de l'Éducation nationale; **E. Act,** loi *f* sur l'enseignement; **he has had a classical e.,** il a fait des études classiques; **he has had a good e.,** il a reçu une bonne instruction; il a fait de fortes études. **3.** dressage *m* (des animaux).

educational [edju'keiʃən(ə)l], *a.* (maison, ouvrage) d'éducation, d'enseignement; (ouvrage) éducateur; (programme *m*) scolaire, des études; (procédé) éducatif, pédagogique; **e. film,** film éducatif; film d'enseignement; **the e. side of the cinema,** le côté culturel du cinéma; **for e. purposes,** pour l'enseignement; *U.S:* **E. Act,** loi *f* sur l'enseignement.

education(al)ist [edju'keiʃən(əl)ist], *s.* éducateur, -trice; pédagogue *mf*; spécialiste *mf* en matière d'enseignement.

educative ['edjukətiv], *a.* éducateur, -trice, éducatif.

educator ['edjukeitər], *s.* éducateur, -trice.

educe [i'dju:s, i:-], *v.tr.* **1.** (*a*) dégager, faire sortir, extraire (**out of,** de); (*b*) *Ch:* dégager (un gaz, etc.) (**from,** de). **2.** induire, inférer, déduire. **3.** évoquer (des actions, etc.).

educt ['i:dʌkt], *s.* **1.** *Ch:* produit *m* de décomposition. **2.** *Phil:* déduction *f*.

eduction [i'dʌkʃ(ə)n, i:-], *s.* **1.** (*a*) extraction *f*; (*b*) *Phil:* déduction *f*. **2.** *Mch: A:* échappement *m* (de vapeur, etc.); **e. pipe,** (i) *I.C.E:* tuyau *m*, conduite *f*, d'échappement; échappement *m*; (ii) *Mch:* tuyau d'évacuation, de refoulement, de décharge; déchargeoir *m*; *I.C.E: etc:* **e. port,** lumière *f*, fenêtre *f*, orifice *m*, d'échappement, d'évacuation; **e. valve,** soupape *f* d'échappement.

edulcorate [i'dʌlkəreit, i:-], *v.tr.* édulcorer.

edulcoration [idʌlkə'reiʃ(ə)n, i:-], *s.* édulcoration *f*.

Edward ['edwəd], *Pr.n.m.* Édouard.

Edwardian [ed'wɔ:diən], *a.* qui a rapport à l'époque (i) des rois Édouard I, II, III, (ii) du roi Édouard VI, (iii) du roi Édouard VII; **the E. Prayer Book,** le Livre de prières (anglican) autorisé par Édouard VI; **the E. era,** la belle époque.

eel [i:l], *s. Ich:* **1.** (*a*) anguille *f*; **small e.,** anguillette *f*; **silver e.,** (i) anguille argentée, anguille d'avalaison; (ii) *U.S:* trichiure *m*, ceinture *f* d'argent; **e. skin,** peau *f* d'anguille; **e. bed, e. pond, e. preserve,** anguillère *f*; **e. prong, e. spear,** foène *f*, fouëne *f*, fouine *f*; **e. basket, e. buck, e. pot, e. trap,** nasse *f* à anguilles; bosselle *f*; *Cu:* **jellied eels,** anguilles en gelée; **stewed eels,** matelote *f* d'anguille; **e. pie,** anguille(s) en pâte; *F:* **to be as slippery as an e.,** être souple, glissant, comme une anguille; **he's as slippery as an e.,** il vous glisse entre les doigts; (*b*) **conger e.,** congre *m*; anguille de mer; **e. pout,** lotte (commune); barbot *m*. **2. electric e.,** gymnote *m*; anguille électrique; **sand e.,** équille *f*, lançon *m*; anguille de sable; ammodyte *m*. **3.** *Amph:* **congo, blind, e.,** amphiuma *m*, amphiume *m*; *Ann:* **e. worm,** anguillule *f*; **hair e.,** gordius *m*; *F:* fil d'eau; crin *m* de fontaine, de mer; **vinegar e.,** anguille, anguillule, du vinaigre.

eelgrass ['i:lgra:s], *s. Bot:* **1.** vallisnérie spirale. **2.** *Algae:* zostère *f*.

eel-shaped ['i:lʃeipt], *a.* anguilliforme.

e'en[1] [i:n], *adv. Poet:* (= **even**) même; encore.

e'en[2], *s. Poet:* (= **evening**) soir *m*; soirée *f*.

e'er ['ɛər], *adv. Poet:* (= **ever**) (*a*) jamais; (*b*) toujours.

eerie, eery ['iəri], *a.* étrange, fantastique, mystérieux, surnaturel; qui inspire la peur; qui donne le frisson.

eerily ['iərili], *adv.* étrangement; d'une façon fantastique, mystérieuse, à donner le frisson.

eeriness ['iərinis], *s.* étrangeté mystérieuse, surnaturelle (d'un lieu, d'un son, etc.).

efface [i'feis], *v.tr.* (*a*) effacer; faire disparaître; oblitérer (une inscription, la mémoire de qch., etc.); **inscriptions that are becoming effaced,** inscriptions qui s'effacent; (*b*) effacer, éclipser (qn); faire ombre à (qn); (*c*) **to e. oneself,** s'effacer; se tenir à l'écart.

effaceable [i'feisəbl], *a.* effaçable.

effacement [i'feismənt], *s.* effacement *m*; **self-e.,** effacement (de soi-même).

effect[1] [i'fekt], *s.* **1.** (*a*) effet *m*, action *f*, influence *f*; résultat *m*, conséquence *f* (d'un fait); **the e. of heat on metals,** l'action de la chaleur sur les métaux; **the e. of a lever,** l'action d'un levier; **cause and e.,** la cause et l'effet; **no e. without a cause,** point d'effet sans cause; **the effects of the economic crisis,** les effets de la crise économique; **distributional effects,** effets sur la répartition; **indirect effects,** conséquences indirectes; **to feel the effects of an illness,** ressentir les effets d'une maladie; **after effects,** suites *fpl*, contre-coup *m*, répercussions *fpl* (d'un événement); séquelles *fpl*, reliquat *m* (d'une maladie); **side effects,** réactions secondaires; *Ch: etc:* réactions latérales; **to have an e. on s.o., sth.,** faire, produire, de l'effet sur qn, sur qch.; affecter qn, qch.; **to have no e.,** ne faire, ne produire, aucun effet; **it had little e.,** cela n'a pas fait grand-chose; **what e. will it have?** qu'en résultera-t-il? **I wonder what the effects will be,** je me demande quelles en seront les conséquences; **nothing has any e. on it,** rien n'y fait; (*b*) réalisation *f*; **to take e.,** (i) faire (son) effet; (ii) (*of regulation, etc.*) entrer en vigueur; (iii) (*of drugs*) agir, opérer; (*of vaccination*) prendre; (iv) (*of shot*) porter; *Adm: etc:* **to take e. on, with e. from, January 1st,** à compter du, applicable à partir du, qui entre en vigueur à partir du, premier janvier; **law that takes e., comes into e., today,** loi qui entre en vigueur à partir d'aujourd'hui; **of no e.,** (i) sans effet, inutile, inefficace; (ii) *Jur:* non avenu; **to no e.,** en vain, sans résultat; **to give e. to (sth.), to bring, carry (sth.) into e.,** mettre (qch.) à exécution; exécuter, effectuer, accomplir, réaliser (qch.); rendre (qch.) efficace; donner suite à (une décision, etc.); mettre (une loi) en vigueur; (*c*) sens *m*, teneur *f* (d'un document); **with a proviso to the e. that . . .,** avec une clause conditionnelle portant que . . ., dont la teneur est que . . .; **we have made provisions to this e.,** nous avons pris des dispositions dans ce sens; **that is what he said, or words to that e.,** voilà ce qu'il a dit, ou quelque chose d'approchant; (*d*) *Elcs: etc:* **Edison e.,** effet Edison; **Doppler-Fizeau e.,** effet Doppler-Fizeau; **Watson e.** = brouillage *m* par parasites; **photo-emissive e.,** effet photo-émissif; *El:* **electrophonic e.,** effet électrophonique; **flicker e.,** effet de scintillation; *Av:* **ram e.,** effet dynamique; *Ph:* **Kelvin e., skin e.,** effet pelliculaire, de peau; **Joule e.,** effet Joule; (*thermodynamics*) **Joule-Thomson e.,** détente *f* de Joule-Thomson; *Exp:* **blast e.,** effet de souffle. **2.** (*a*) **moonlight e.,** effet de lune; *Th: etc:* **stage effects,** effets, jeux *m*, scéniques; **sound effects,** bruitage *m*; *Cin: T.V: etc:* **special effects,** trucage *m*; (*b*) **words meant for e.,** phrases à effet; **to do sth. for e.,** faire qch. pour se faire remarquer, pour se donner un genre, pour se distinguer; **to wear a monocle for e.,** porter un monocle par genre, par chic; **it has a good e.,** cela fait bon effet. **3. in e.,** en fait, en réalité; **that is in e. a refusal,** c'est de fait un refus; de fait cela est un refus; cela équivaut à un refus; **Sparta was in e. a camp,** Sparte était proprement un camp. **4.** *pl.* **personal effects,** effets, biens, personnels; **household effects,** *Jur:* **movable effects,** biens, effets, mobiliers; **the dead man's effects were returned to his widow,** les effets du mort ont été rendus à sa veuve; *Bank:* **no effects,** pas de provision; défaut *m* de provision.

effect[2], *v.tr.* effectuer, accomplir, faire, opérer, réaliser, exécuter (qch.); **to e. one's purpose,** atteindre son but, accomplir son dessein; **to e. an entrance,** forcer la porte; entrer de force; **to e. a payment,** effectuer un paiement; **to e. customs clearance,** procéder aux formalités douanières; *Mil:* **to e. a retreat,** opérer une retraite; **to e. a settlement between two parties,** arriver à un accord entre deux parties; réussir à mettre les deux parties d'accord; **to e. an insurance, a policy of insurance,** prendre, souscrire, une police d'assurances; **to e. improvements in sth.,** apporter des améliorations à qch.; **meanwhile a great change has been effected,** un grand changement est intervenu; **to e. a cure, you will have to . . .,** pour réaliser la guérison, il vous faudra . . .; *Book-k:* **to e. a corresponding entry,** passer une écriture conforme.

effective [i'fektiv]. **1.** *a.* (*a*) efficace; qui fait, produit, de l'effet; **e. protection,** protection efficace; **the most e. method of doing sth.,** le meilleur moyen, le moyen le plus efficace, de faire qch.; **the medicine was e.,** le médicament était efficace, a produit son effet; **to make a machine more e.,** augmenter le rendement d'une machine; **e. shot,** coup *m* qui porte; *Artil:* **e. fire,** tir *m* d'efficacité; (*b*) effectif; *Pol.Ec:* **e. demand,** demande effective; **e. yield,** rendement effectif; **e. blockade,** blocus effectif; *Fin:* **e. money,** monnaie effective, réelle; *Mec.E:* **e. power,** rendement; effet *m* utile; puissance effective; puissance au frein; **e. horse power,** puissance (effective) en chevaux; puissance au frein en chevaux; cheval vapeur utile; *El:* **e. charge,** charge effective, efficace; **e. frequency,** fréquence *f* utile; **e. voltage,** tension *f* efficace; **e. reactance, resistance,** réactance, résistance, effective; **e. parallel resistance,** résistance parallèle équivalente; *Elcs;* **e. input, output, admittance,** admittance effective d'entrée, de sortie; *W.Tel: etc:* **e. height (of aerial),** hauteur effective, de rayonnement (d'une antenne); *Hyd.E:* **e. head,** chute effective, disponible, réelle; **e. range,** (i) *Elcs:* étendue *f* de mesure; (ii) portée *f* utile (d'une arme à feu); (iii) *Rad:* portée (efficace); (iv) *Av:* rayon *m* d'action; *Aer:* **e. angle of attack,** angle *m* d'incidence réel; *Opt:* **e. aperture,** ouverture *f* utile (d'un objectif); (*c*) frappant; **e. phrase,** expression heureuse, qui fait image; **e. contrast,** contraste frappant, saisissant; **e. reply,** réponse pleine d'à-propos; **e. picture, speech,** tableau *m*, discours *m*, qui fait, qui produit, de l'effet; **e. speaker,** orateur *m* dont les paroles portent; **e. style,** style vigoureux, à effets; **the trumpet part is very e.,** la partie de trompette fait beaucoup d'effet; (*d*) *Mil:* **e. troops,** troupes *f* valides; (*e*) *Adm:* **e. date,** date *f* d'application, d'entrée en vigueur; (*of decree, etc.*) **to become e.,** entrer en vigueur; **e. on, as from, October 10,** applicable à partir du 10 octobre. **2.** *s.pl. Mil:* **effectives,** effectifs *m*.

effectively [i'fektivli], *adv.* **1.** avec effet, efficacement, utilement. **2.** effectivement, en réalité. **3.** d'une façon frappante; avec beaucoup d'effet.

effectiveness [i'fektivnis], *s.* **1.** efficacité *f*; **the e. of the remedy,** les bons effets du remède. **2.** l'effet heureux (produit par un tableau, etc.).

effector [i'fektər], *a. Med:* effecteur, -trice.

effectual [i'fektjuəl], *a.* **1.** efficace. **2.** (contrat *m*) valide; (règlement) en vigueur.

effectually [i'fektjuəli], *adv.* efficacement.

effectuate [i'fektjueit], *v.tr. Lit:* effectuer (une guérison, etc.); réaliser, accomplir, opérer.

effectuation [ifektju'eiʃ(ə)n], *s. Lit:* accomplissement *m*, réalisation *f*.

effeminacy [i'feminəsi], *s.* **1.** caractère efféminé, mœurs efféminées; effémination, féminité *f*, mollesse *f*. **2.** *O:* homosexualité *f*.

effeminate[1] [i'feminət], *a.* & *s.* efféminé (*m*); **to grow e.,** s'amollir.

effeminate[2] [i'femineit], *v.tr.* efféminer, amollir; rendre (qn) efféminé.

effeminately [i'feminətli], *adv.* d'une manière efféminée; avec mollesse.

effeminateness [i'feminətnis], *s.* = EFFEMINACY.

effeminating[1] [i'femineitiŋ], *a.* (luxe) amollissant, énervant.

effeminating[2], **effemination** [ifemi'neiʃ(ə)n], *s.* effémination *f.*

efferent ['efərənt], *a. Physiol:* efférent.

effervesce [efə'ves], *v.i.* (*a*) être, entrer, en effervescence; faire effervescence; (*of drinks*) mousser; (*of gas*) se dégager (avec effervescence); (*b*) (*of pers.*) pétiller de joie, d'animation; bouillonner de colère.

effervescence [efə'ves(ə)ns], *s.* (*a*) effervescence *f* (d'un liquide); dégagement *m* (d'un gaz); (*b*) pétillement *m* (de la jeunesse, etc.); bouillonnement *m*, fermentation *f* (des esprits); effervescence.

effervescent [efə'ves(ə)nt], *a.* **1.** effervescent; **e. drinks,** boissons gazeuses. **2.** (*of pers.*) effervescent, bouillonnant.

effete [i'fi:t], *a.* (*a*) (*of material things*) épuisé, usé; (*b*) (*of civilization, method, etc.*) caduc, -uque; **an e. aristocracy,** une aristocratie qui a fait son temps.

effeteness [i'fi:tnis], *s.* (*a*) épuisement *m*; état *m* d'une chose usée; (*b*) caducité *f* (d'une civilisation, d'une méthode, etc.).

efficacious [efi'keiʃəs], *a.* efficace.

efficaciously [efi'keiʃəsli], *adv.* efficacement.

efficaciousness [efi'keiʃəsnis], **efficacity** [efi'kæsiti], **efficacy** ['efikəsi], *s.* efficacité *f*; énergie *f* (d'un remède); rendement *m* (d'une machine, etc.); *Theol:* efficace *f* (de la grâce).

efficiency [i'fiʃənsi], *s.* **1.** (*a*) efficacité *f* (du travail, d'un remède, etc.); **economic e.,** efficacité économique; **technical e.,** efficacité technique; **marginal e.,** efficacité marginale; **the work was carried out with increasing e.,** le travail a été accompli avec une efficacité, une compétence, toujours croissante; (*b*) rendement (d'une machine, etc.); *Mec.E:* effet *m* utile; **mean e.,** rendement moyen; **apparent e.,** rendement apparent; **overall e.,** rendement global; **propulsive e.,** rendement propulsif; **mechanical e.,** rendement mécanique; **heat, thermal, e.,** rendement calorifique, thermique; **e. of a joint,** résistance relative d'un assemblage; *I.C.E:* **volume, volumetric, e.,** rendement volumétrique; *Aut:* **actual e.,** rendement à la jante; **hill-climbing e.,** rendement en côte; **high-e. engine, machine,** moteur, machine, à grand, bon, rendement; moteur poussé; *Ind:* (*in chain production*) **motion e.,** rendement du geste; **e. expert,** expert *m* en organisation, en rendement; *Opt:* **luminous e.,** efficacité lumineuse; *Elcs:* **quantum e.,** rendement quantique; (*c*) bon fonctionnement (d'une administration, etc.). **2.** (*of pers.*) capacité *f*, valeur *f*, *F:* efficience *f*; valeur professionnelle (de la main-d'œuvre); *Mil: etc:* valeur opérationnelle (des troupes); **fighting e.,** aptitude *f* au combat, valeur opérationnelle (d'une troupe, d'une flotte, etc.); **e. rating,** *U.S:* **e. report,** notes *f* périodiques (d'un officier, etc.); *Ind:* **e. wages,** salaire proportionné à la production, basé sur le rendement.

efficient [i'fiʃ(ə)nt], *a.* (*a*) *A:* & *Phil:* efficient; *esp.* **e. cause,** cause efficiente; (*b*) (*of method, work*) effectif, efficace; **e. working (of apparatus),** bon fonctionnement (d'un appareil); (*c*) *Mec.E:* **e. machine,** (i) machine à bon rendement; (ii) machine d'un fonctionnement sûr; (*d*) (*of pers.*) capable, compétent, habile; *F:* efficient; **to be e. at doing sth.,** s'entendre à faire qch.; **to be e. in one's work,** être à la hauteur de sa tâche; se montrer capable dans son travail.

efficiently [i'fiʃəntli], *adv.* **1.** efficacement. **2.** avec compétence.

effigy ['efidʒi], *s.* effigie *f*; **coin bearing the e. of. . .,** monnaie frappée à l'effigie de . . .; **to burn, hang, s.o. in e.,** brûler, pendre, qn en effigie.

effleurage [e'flə:ridʒ], *s. Med:* effleurage *m.*

effloresce [eflə'res], *v.i.* **1.** *Lit:* fleurir. **2.** *Ch:* (s')effleurir; tomber en efflorescence; former une efflorescence.

efflorescence [eflə'res(ə)ns], *s.* **1.** *Bot:* effloraison *f*, floraison *f*. **2.** *Ch: etc:* efflorescence *f*, effleurissement *m*, délitescence *f*. **3.** *Med:* efflorescence.

efflorescent [eflə'res(ə)nt], *a.* **1.** *Bot:* efflorescent; en voie de fleurir; en floraison. **2.** *Ch:* efflorescent, délitescent.

effluence ['efluəns], *s.* émanation *f*, effluence *f*; écoulement *m.*

effluent ['efluənt]. **1.** *a.* effluent; **e. drain,** canalisation *f* de sortie (d'un collecteur d'eaux d'égout, etc.). **2.** *s.* (*a*) cours d'eau dérivé (d'un lac, d'une rivière, etc.); (*b*) effluent *m* (de collecteur d'eaux d'égout).

effluve [e'flu:v], *s. El:* effluve *m.*

effluvium, *pl.* **-ia** [i'flu:viəm, -iə], *s.* (*a*) effluve *m*, émanation *f*; (*b*) *Pej:* émanation désagréable, fétide; exhalaison *f.*

efflux ['eflʌks], *s.* flux *m*, écoulement *m* (de liquide); dégagement *m*, émanation *f* (de gaz); *Hyd.E:* **e. of water (in a given time),** dépense *f* d'eau; *Pol.Ec:* **e. of capital,** exode *m* des capitaux.

effluxion [i'flʌkʃ(ə)n], *s.* **1.** *A:* & *Lit:* = EFFLUX. **2.** *Jur:* **e.** of time, expiration *f* du terme.

effort ['efət], *s.* **1.** (*a*) effort *m*; **physical e.,** effort physique; **sustained e.,** effort soutenu; **without e.,** sans effort; **to make an e. to do sth.,** faire (un) effort pour faire qch.; s'efforcer de faire qch.; **make an e.!** (i) essayez toujours! (ii) secouez-vous! **to use every e. to do sth.,** faire tous ses efforts pour faire qch.; s'évertuer à faire qch.; **wasted e.,** peine perdue; **to make a great, a special, e.,** faire un grand effort, un effort spécial; **he spares no e.,** il ne s'épargne pas; rien ne lui coûte; **it required considerable e.,** cela a demandé un effort considérable; **it was an e. to let him go,** il nous en a coûté beaucoup de le laisser partir; **he does everything as if it were an e.,** tout est une corvée pour lui; tout lui coûte; (*b*) essai *m*; tentative *f*; **that's not a bad e.,** ce n'est pas mal réussi; **as a speech it was a pretty poor e.,** comme discours c'était plutôt pénible; (*c*) **literary, artistic, e.,** œuvre *f* littéraire, artistique; *F:* **what do you think of his latest e.?** qu'est-ce que vous pensez de ce qu'il vient de faire? **2.** *Mec:* effort (de traction, etc.); poussée *f*, travail *m.*

effortless ['efətlis], *a.* **1.** qui ne fait aucun effort. **2.** (*a*) sans effort; (*b*) facile.

effortlessly ['efətlisli], *adv.* sans effort.

effrontery [i'frʌntəri], *s.* effronterie *f*, cynisme *m.*

effulgence [i'fʌldʒəns], *s. Lit:* éclat *m*, splendeur *f*, rayonnement *m*; *Lit:* effulguration *f*; **e. of youth,** pétillement *m* de la jeunesse.

effulgent [i'fʌldʒənt], *a. Lit:* resplendissant, éclatant; **to be e. with light,** resplendir; **to be e. with joy,** rayonner de joie.

effuse[1] [i'fju:s], *a. Bot:* diffus.

effuse[2] [i'fju:z]. *Lit:* **1.** *v.tr.* verser (un liquide); déverser, répandre (la lumière). **2.** *v.i.* se répandre, se déverser; (*of blood, etc.*) s'extravaser, s'épancher.

effusion [i'fju:ʒ(ə)n], *s.* **1.** effusion *f*, épanchement *m* (du sang, etc.). **2.** (*a*) effusion (de tendresse, etc.); épanchement de cœur; (*b*) **poetical effusions,** effusions poétiques; **have you ever read such an e.?** avez-vous jamais lu une tartine pareille?

effusive [i'fju:siv], *a.* **1.** démonstratif, expansif; **e. style,** style exubérant; **e. compliments,** compliments sans fin; **to be e. in one's compliments,** se répandre en compliments; **to make an e. speech,** parler avec effusion; **to be e. in one's thanks,** se confondre en remerciements. **2.** *Geol:* effusif; **e. rock,** roche effusive, d'épanchement.

effusively [i'fju:sivli], *adv.* avec effusion; d'une manière (trop) démonstrative; **to thank s.o. e.,** se confondre en remerciements; **to welcome s.o. e.,** faire à qn un accueil empressé, exubérant.

effusiveness [i'fju:sivnis], *s.* effusion *f*; volubilité *f.*

eft [eft], *s. Amph: A: Dial:* triton *m.*

eftsoon(s) [eft'su:n(z)], *adv. Poet: A:* tout de suite (après); sur l'heure.

egad [i'gæd], *int. A:* parbleu! morbleu!

egalitarian [igæli'teəriən], *a.* & *s.* égalitaire *mf.*

egalitarianism [igæli'teəriənizm], *s.* égalitarisme *m.*

egeran ['eigərən], *s. Miner:* égérane *f.*

Egeria [i(:)'dʒiəriə], *Pr.n.f. Rom.Myth:* Égérie.

egest [i'dʒest], *v.tr. Physiol:* évacuer.

egestion [i'dʒestʃən], *s. Physiol:* évacuation *f*, éjection *f*, expulsion *f.*

egg[1] [eg], *s.* **1.** (*a*) *Biol:* œuf *m*; **e. tooth,** dent *f* d'éclosion; (*b*) œuf (d'oiseau); **wind e.,** (i) œuf non fécondé; œuf clair; (ii) œuf imparfait, blanc; œuf de couleuvre; *Comest:* **(farm) fresh e.,** œuf du jour; **newlaid e.,** œuf frais (pondu); **free-range eggs,** œufs de la ferme; *Cu:* **boiled e.,** œuf à la coque; **hard-boiled e.,** œuf dur; **soft-bolled e.,** œuf mollet, à la mouillette; **to boil an e.,** faire cuire un œuf à la coque; **fried e.,** œuf sur le plat; **poached e.,** œuf poché; **scrambled eggs,** œufs brouillés; **Scotch e.,** œuf dur entouré de chair de saucisse; **Russian eggs,** œufs à la russe; **eggs and bacon,** (i) des œufs au jambon; (ii) *Bot: F:* linaire *f*; **dried, dehydrated, eggs, e. powder,** œufs en poudre; **e. flip, e. nog** = lait *m* de poule; **e. beater, e. whisk,** batteur *m*, fouet *m* à œufs; *Av: F:* **e. beater,** hélicoptère *m*, hélico *m*, ventilateur *m*; **e. boiler,** coquetière *f*; **e. poacher,** pocheuse *f* à œufs, poche-œufs *m inv*; **e. slice,** pelle *f* à trous (pour retirer les œufs de la poêle); **e. holder,** œufrier *m* (en fil de fer); panier *m* à œufs; **e. timer,** sablier *m*; **e. stand,** œufrier (pour la table); **e. cutter, slicer, scissors,** coupe-œufs *m inv*; **e. spoon,** cuillère *f* à œufs; **e. dealer, merchant, e. man, woman,** coquetier, -ière; marchand, -ande, d'œufs; *F: A:* **at an e. trot,** au petit trot; **e. and spoon race,** course dans laquelle les coureurs doivent porter un œuf dans une cuillère; **the goose with the golden eggs,** la poule aux œufs d'or; *F:* **as sure as eggs is eggs,** aussi sûr que deux et deux font quatre; couru d'avance; aussi vrai qu'il fait jour; *F:* **go and teach your grandmother to suck eggs,** ce n'est pas aux vieux singes qu'on apprend à faire des grimaces; on n'apprend pas aux poissons à nager; **a bad e.,** (i) un œuf pourri; (ii) *F:* un propre à rien, un vaurien; *F: O:* **a good e.,** un type épatant; *F: O:* **good e.!** à la bonne heure! chouette! *F: A:* **I say, old e.!** dis donc, mon vieux! *F:* **it's like the curate's e.,** il y a à prendre et à laisser, à boire et à manger; c'est mi-figue, mi-raisin; *Prov:* **don't put all your eggs into one basket,** il ne faut pas mettre tous ses œufs dans le même panier; (*c*) œuf (d'insecte); lente *f* (de pou); **silkworms' eggs,** graines *f* de vers à soie; *Ent: Moll:* **e. capsule, e. sac,** oothèque *f*. **2.** *Arch:* ove *m* (de chapiteau dorique, etc.); **e.-and-anchor moulding,** godron *m* à oves. **3.** (*a*) **darning e.,** œuf à repriser; (*b*) **tea e.,** boule *f* à thé; (*c*) *Av: F:* bombe *f.*

egg[2], *v.tr.* **1.** *Cu:* **to e. (and breadcrumb),** passer à l'œuf; dorer. **2.** *U.S:* bombarder (qn) avec des œufs pourris.

egg[3], *v.tr.* **to e. s.o. on (to do sth.),** pousser, inciter, qn (à faire qch.).

egg-bound ['egbaund], *a.* (*of hen, etc.*) (poule, etc.) qui ne peut pas pondre, qui a l'œuf bloqué dans l'oviducte.

eggcup ['egkʌp], *s.* coquetier *m.*

egger (*occ.* **eggar**) ['egər], *s. Ent:* **(oak) e. (moth),** bombyx *m* du chêne; lasiocampe *m* (du chêne).

egghead ['eghed], *s. F:* intellectuel, -elle, cerveau *m*, grosse tête.

egg-laying ['egleiiŋ], (*a*) *a.* ovipare; (*b*) *s.* ponte *f.*

eggplant, *occ.* **eggfruit** ['egplɑ:nt, -fru:t], *s. Bot:* aubergine *f.*

egg-shaped ['egʃeipt], *a.* ovoïde; ovoïdal, -aux.

eggshell ['egʃel], *s.* coquille *f*, coque *f* (d'œuf); *Cer:* **e. china, ware,** coquille d'œuf; *Paint:* **e. finish,** fini *m* coquille d'œuf.

eggy ['egi], *a. F:* taché, souillé, de jaune d'œuf.

eglantine ['egləntain], *s. Bot:* **1.** églantine *f*. **2. e. (bush),** églantier *m.*

eglestonite ['egəlstounait], *s. Miner:* églestonite *f.*

ego ['egou, 'i:gou], *s.* **the e.,** le moi.

egocentric [egou'sentrik], *a. Psy:* égocentrique.

egocentricity [egousen'trisiti], **egocentrism** [egou'sentrizm], *s.* égocentrisme *m.*

egocerus [i'gɔsərəs], *s. Z:* égocère *m.*

egoism ['egouizm], *s.* égoïsme *m.*

egoist ['egouist], *s.* égoïste *mf.*

egoistic(al) [egou'istik(l)], *a.* égoïste.

egoistically [egou'istik(ə)li], *adv.* égoïstement.

egomania [egou'meiniə], *s.* manie *f* égocentrique.

egophonic [i'gɔfənik], *a. Med:* égophonique.

egophony [i'gɔfəni], *s. Med:* égophonie *f.*

egotism ['egətizm], *s.* égotisme *m.*

egotist ['egətist], *s.* égotiste *mf.*

egotistic(al) [egə'tistik(l)], *a.* égotiste, égotique.

egotize ['egoutaiz], *v.i.* rapporter tout à soi; **mettre en avant son moi.**

egregious [i'gri:dʒiəs], *a. Pej: O:* (sot, etc.) insigne, fieffé; fameux (sot); **e. blunder,** maladresse achevée, insigne, énorme.

egregiousness [i'gri:dʒiəsnis], *s. O:* énormité *f* (d'une maladresse).

egress ['i:gres], *s.* **1.** (*a*) sortie *f*, issue *f*; **right of free e.,** droit *m* de libre sortie; (*b*) *Mch: etc:* échappement *m*. **2.** *Astr:* émersion *f* (après une éclipse).

egression [i'greʃ(ə)n], *s.* **1.** *A:* & *Lit:* sortie *f*. **2.** *Mch: etc:* échappement *m.*

egret ['i:gret], *s.* **1.** *Orn:* aigrette *f*; **large e.,** *N.Am:* **common, American, e.,** aigrette blanche, grande aigrette; **little e., snowy e.,** aigrette garzette, petite aigrette; **cattle e.,** héron *m* garde-bœufs. **2.** *Bot:* aigrette (de chardon, etc.).

Egypt ['i:dʒipt], *Pr.n.* Égypte *f.*

Egyptian [i'dʒipʃ(ə)n]. **1.** *a.* (*a*) *Geog:* égyptien, d'Égypte; (*b*) *Bot:* **E. privet,** henné *m*; *Orn:* **E. goose,** oie *f* d'Égypte; **E. vulture,** percnoptère *m* d'Égypte. **2.** *s. Geog:* Égyptien, -ienne.

Egyptological [i:dʒiptə'lɔdʒikl], *a.* égyptologique.

Egyptologist [i:dʒip'tɔlədʒist], *s.* égyptologue *mf.*

Egyptology [i:dʒip'tɔlədʒi], *s.* égyptologie *f.*

eh [ei], *int.* eh! hé! hein?

ehlite ['eilait], *s. Miner:* ehlite *f.*

ehretia [i:'ri:ʃiə], *s. Bot:* éhrétie *f*, ehretia *f.*

Eichhornia [aik'(h)ɔ:niə], *s. Bot:* eichornia *m.*

eicosane ['aikousein], *s. Ch:* eicosane *m.*

eider ['aidər], *s. Orn:* eider *m* à duvet, *Fr.C:* eider commun; **king e.,** eider à tête grise, *Fr.C:* eider remarquable; **spectacled e.,** eider de Fischer, *Fr.C:* eider à lunettes; **Steller's e.,** eider de Steller.

eiderdown ['aidədaun], *s.* **1.** duvet *m* d'eider. **2. e. (quilt),** édredon (piqué, américain).

eidetic [ai'detik], *a.* eidétique.

Eidophor ['aidoufɔ:r], *s. T.V: R.t.m:* **E. system,** Éidophore *m.*

eifelian [ai'fi:liən], *s. Geol:* eifélien *m.*

eight [eit]. **1.** *num.a.* & *s.* huit (*m*); **twenty e.,** vingt-huit; **e. fives, five eights, are forty, eight times five is forty,** huit fois cinq, cinq fois huit, font quarante; *A:* **e. and six**

(pence), huit shillings six pence; **we have breakfast, dinner, at e.,** nous déjeunons, dînons, à huit heures; **the e.-thirty train,** le train de huit heures et demie; **to be e. (years old),** avoir huit ans; **a boy of e.,** un garçon de huit ans; **a mother of e.,** la mère de huit enfants; **e. of my pupils,** huit d'entre mes élèves; **there were e. of us,** nous étions huit; *Cards:* **the e. of spades,** le huit de pique; **to take eights in gloves,** avoir huit de pointure (pour les gants); **to take eights in shoes** = chausser du quarante-et-un; **e.-day clock,** huitaine *f*; *F:* **to have had one over the e.,** avoir bu un coup de trop; *Sp:* (*skating*) **to cut eights, figures of e.,** faire des huit; *U.S:* **e. ball,** (i) *Bill:* bille marquée d'un huit; (ii) (sorte de) jeu *m* de billard; (iii) *F:* microphone rond omnidirectionnel; (iv) *P:* bougnole *m*; *F:* **to be behind the e. ball,** être dans le pétrin. **2.** *s. Sp: Row:* (i) équipe *f* de huit rameurs; (ii) canot *m* à huit rameurs; huit de pointe; **the eights,** les régates *f* entre équipes de huit (à Oxford et Cambridge); **to be in the last e.,** être en huitième de finale.

eighteen [ei'ti:n], *num.a. & s.* dix-huit (*m*); **she is e. (years old),** elle a dix-huit ans; **e. houses,** dix-huit maisons; **the aircraft will land at e. (hundred) hours,** l'avion va atterrir à dix-huit heures; **the e.-thirty train,** le train de dix-huit heures trente.

eighteenmo [ei'ti:nmou], *a. & s. Typ:* (format, volume) in-dix-huit *m inv*, in-18 *m*.

eighteenth [ei'ti:nθ]. **1.** *num. a. & s.* (*a*) dix-huitième; **the e. house,** la dix-huitième maison; (*b*) **(on) the e. (of May),** le dix-huit (mai); **Louis the Eighteenth,** Louis Dix-huit. **2.** *s.* (*fractional*) dix-huitième *m*.

eighteenthly [ei'ti:θli], *adv.* dix-huitièmement.

eightfold ['eitfould]. **1.** *a.* octuple. **2.** *adv.* huit fois autant; **to increase e.,** octupler.

eighth [eitθ]. **1.** *num. a. & s.* (*a*) huitième; **he is e. in his class,** il est le huitième de sa classe; **in the e. place,** huitièmement; **you are the seventh or e. who has asked me that,** vous êtes le sept ou huitième qui me demandez cela; (*b*) **(on) the e. (of April),** le huit (avril); **Henry the E.,** Henri Huit. **2.** *s.* (*fractional*) huitième *m*; **three eighths,** trois huitièmes.

eighthly ['eitθli], *adv.* huitièmement; en huitième lieu.

eightieth ['eitiəθ], *num. a. & s.* quatre-vingtième (*m*); *Sw.Fr: Belg:* huitantième (*m*); *Sw.Fr: Fr.C:* octantième (*m*).

eightsome ['eitsəm], *a. & s. Danc:* **e. (reel),** danse écossaise pour huit personnes.

eighty ['eiti], *num. a. & s.* quatre-vingts (*m*); *Sw.Fr: Belg:* huitante (*m*); *Sw.Fr:* octante (*m*); **e. men,** quatre-vingts hommes; **e.-one,** quatre-vingt-un; **e.-first,** quatre-vingt-unième; **page e.,** page quatre-vingt; **in the eighties of last century,** entre 1880 et 1890; **the French novel of the eighties,** le roman français vers les années quatre-vingt (du dix-neuvième siècle); **in the eighties,** dans les années quatre-vingt; **she is in the eighties,** elle a quatre-vingts ans passés; *Pol: A:* **the E. Club,** club de Libéraux fondé en 1880.

eikon ['aikɔn], *s.* icône *f*.

Einhorn ['ainhɔ:n], *Pr.n. Med:* **Einhorn's tube,** sonde *f* d'Einhorn.

einkorn ['ainkɔ:n], *s. Agr:* engrain *m*; petit épeautre.

Einsteinian [ain'stainiən], *a.* einsténien, einsteinien.

einsteinium [ain'stainiəm], *s. Ch:* einsteinium *m*.

Eire ['ɛərə], *Pr.n. Geog:* Eire *f*.

eirenicon [ai'ri:nikɔn], *s. Rel:* proposition *f* irénique.

eisenkiesel ['aizənki:zl], *s. Miner:* eisenkiesel *m*, quartz *m* hématoïde.

eisteddfod, *pl.* **-fodau** [eis'teðvɔd, -'vɔdai], *s.* (*in Wales*) Eisteddfod *m* (concours de poésie et de chant; = jeux floraux).

either ['aiðər, *occ.* 'i:-]. **1.** *a. & pron.* (*a*) (*each of the two*) l'un(e) et l'autre, chaque, chacun(e); **on e. side, on e. of the sides,** de chaque côté; de chacun des deux côtés; des deux côtés; **they were sitting on e. side of the fire,** ils étaient assis au coin du feu, chacun de leur côté; ils étaient assis de chaque côté du feu; **the enemy overlooked us on e. flank,** nous étions dominés par l'ennemi sur l'un et l'autre flanc, de part et d'autre; (*b*) (*one or other of the two*) l'un(e) ou l'autre; **e. of them,** soit l'un(e), soit l'autre; **I don't believe e. of you,** je ne vous crois ni l'un ni l'autre; **e. of them will do it,** l'un ou l'autre le fera; ils le feront l'un ou l'autre; **e. candidate may win,** l'un ou l'autre candidat pourra l'emporter; **you can do it e. way,** vous pouvez le faire soit d'une manière, soit de l'autre, d'une manière ou de l'autre, des deux façons également; **there is no evidence e. way,** les preuves manquent de part et d'autre; **take e. cake, e. of the cakes,** prenez celui des gâteaux que vous voudrez; **without taking e. side,** sans prendre parti pour les uns ni pour les autres; **do you want this one or that one?—e.,** voulez-vous celui-ci ou celui-là?—l'un ou l'autre; n'importe lequel; **I do not want e. of them,** je ne veux ni l'un(e) ni l'autre; je n'en veux aucun(e); **if e. borrowed from the other, the borrower was probably Martin,** si l'un des deux a emprunté à l'autre, il est probable que l'emprunteur fut Martin. **2.** *conj. & adv.* (*a*) **e. . . ., or . . .,** ou . . ., ou . . .; soit . . ., soit . . .; **e. you or your brother,** (ou) vous ou votre frère; soit vous, soit votre frère; soit vous ou votre frère; **e. come in or go out,** entrez ou sortez; **I don't believe he is e. drunk or mad,** je ne crois pas qu'il soit ni soûl ni fou; (*b*) **not . . . e.,** ne . . . non plus; **if you don't go, I won't go e.,** si vous n'y allez pas je n'irai pas non plus; **nor I e.!** ni moi non plus; **if John had told me so, or William e., I could have believed it,** si Jean me l'avait dit ou même, ou encore, Guillaume, j'aurais pu le croire; (*c*) **in a gruff tone—not so very gruff e.—he told me to come in,** d'un ton bourru—et pas si bourru que ça, vraiment—il me dit d'entrer; **she's caught cold, and she isn't very strong e.,** elle s'est enrhumée, elle qui n'est déjà pas si forte.

ejaculate [i'dʒækjuleit], *v.tr. & i.* **1.** *Physiol:* éjaculer (une fluide, le sperme). **2.** prononcer, proférer (une parole, etc.); pousser (un cri); lancer (un juron, etc.).

ejaculation [idʒækju'leiʃ(ə)n], *s.* **1.** *Physiol:* éjaculation *f*. **2.** *Ecc:* éjaculation, courte prière. **3.** cri *m*, exclamation *f* (de joie, d'étonnement, etc.).

ejaculatory [i'dʒækjulət(ə)ri], *a.* **1.** *Physiol:* éjaculateur, -trice. **2.** (prière *f*) éjaculatoire.

eject[1] [i'dʒekt]. **1.** *v.tr.* jeter, émettre (des flammes, etc.); expulser, évacuer (de la bile); *Tchn:* éjecter (de la vapeur, une cartouche); **the volcano was ejecting ash,** le volcan projetait des cendres. **2.** *v.tr.* (*a*) **to e. an agitator from a meeting,** expulser un agitateur d'une réunion; (*b*) *Jur:* évincer, expulser (un locataire); (*c*) destituer (un fonctionnaire). **3.** *v.i. Av:* (*of pilot*) s'éjecter.

eject[2] ['i:dʒekt], *s.* **1.** *Phil:* éje(c)t *m*. **2.** article *m* de rebut, à rejeter.

ejecta [i'dʒektə], **ejectamenta** [idʒektə'mentə], *s.pl.* **1.** *Geol:* éjections *f* volcaniques, éjecta *m* (d'un volcan); rejets *m*, déjections *f*. **2.** *Med:* matières vomies.

ejection [i'dʒekʃ(ə)n], *s.* **1.** (*a*) jet *m* (de flammes); éjection *f* (de la vapeur, d'une cartouche); rejet *m* (de lave); expulsion *f* (de qn, de la bile); évacuation *f* (de la bile); *Sm.a:* **e. opening, slot,** fenêtre *f* d'éjection; *Av:* **e. seat,** siège *m* éjectable, éjecteur; (*b*) évincement *m*, éviction *f*, expulsion (d'un locataire); (*c*) destitution *f* (de qn de son emploi). **2.** *usu. pl.* éjections, matières éjectées.

ejective [i'dʒektiv], *a.* expulsif, évacuant, évacuatif.

ejectment [i'dʒektmənt], *s. Jur:* **1.** = EJECTION 1 (*b*). **2. action of e.,** action *f* en revendication de son bien; réintégrande *f*; **writ of e.,** réintégrande.

ejector [i'dʒektər], *s.* **1.** personne *f* qui expulse (qn), *Jur:* qui évince (un locataire, etc.). **2.** *Tchn:* (*a*) *Sm.a:* éjecteur *m* (d'étuis vides); (*b*) *Mch:* **steam-engine e.,** éjecteur; exhausteur *m* à jet. **3.** *Av:* **e. seat,** siège *m* éjectable, éjecteur.

eke[1] [i:k], *v.tr.* **to e. out,** suppléer à l'insuffisance de, augmenter (ses revenus, etc.); ménager, économiser, faire durer (les vivres); **to e. out the wine with cider,** suppléer à l'insuffisance de vin en buvant du cidre; **to e. out the soup, the sauce (with water),** allonger la soupe, la sauce; **to e. out a living,** subsister pauvrement; gagner une maigre pitance.

eke[2], *adv. A:* aussi; de même; également.

ekebergite ['i:kbəgait], *s. Miner:* ékebergite *f*.

ektoparasitic [ektoupærə'sitik], *a. Z:* ectoparasite.

elaborate[1] [i'læb(ə)rət], *a.* (*of tool, etc.*) compliqué; (*of work*) soigné, fini; (*of style*) travaillé; (*of work of art*) fouillé, poussé; raffiné; (*of inspection, research, etc.*) minutieux; (*of dress, etc.*) recherché; (*of hairstyle*) compliqué.

elaborate[2] [i'læbəreit]. **1.** *v.tr.* (*a*) élaborer (une théorie, un projet de loi, etc.); travailler, fouiller (son style); fouiller, pousser (une œuvre d'art); étudier (un projet) dans tous ses détails; **just e. your proposals a little,** si vous vouliez bien entrer dans plus de détails; (*b*) *Physiol:* élaborer (un suc, etc.) **(into, en). 2.** *v.i.* se compliquer.

elaborately [i'læbərətli], *adv.* minutieusement; d'une façon compliquée; d'une manière fouillée, approfondie; laborieusement.

elaborateness [i'læb(ə)rətnis], *s.* (*a*) fini *m* (d'un travail); soin *m*, minutie *f* (de recherches); (*b*) complication *f* (d'un mécanisme).

elaboration [ilæbə'reiʃ(ə)n], *s. Physiol: etc:* élaboration *f*; **the e. of this plan took three months,** la préparation de ce projet, l'étude détaillée de ce projet, a pris trois mois.

elaborative [i'læbərətiv], *a.* élaborateur, -trice; élaborant.

Elæagnaceae [eliæg'neisii:], *s.pl. Bot:* éléagnacées *f*.

elaeagnus [eli'ægnəs], *s. Bot:* élaeagnus *m*, olivier *m* de Bohême.

elaeis [e'li:əs], *s. Bot:* élæis *m*, éléis *m*.

Elaeocarpaceae [eliouka:'pei:sii:], *s.pl. Bot:* éléocarpacées *f*.

elaeodendron [eliou'dendrən], *s. Bot:* élaeodendron *m*.

elaeolite [e'li:oulait], *s. Miner:* éléolite *f*.

elaeometer [eli'ɔmitər], *s.* oléomètre *m*, éléomètre *m*.

Elagabalus [i:lə'gæbələs], *Pr.n.m. Rom.Hist:* Héliogabale, Élagabale.

elaidic [elə'idik], *a. Ch:* élaïdique.

elaidin [e'leiədin], *s. Ch:* élaïdine *f*.

Elamite ['i:ləmait]. *A.Geog:* (*a*) *a.* élamite; (*b*) *s.* Élamite *mf*.

Elamitic [i:lə'mitik], *s. Ling:* élamite *m*.

élan [e'lɑ̃], *s.* élan *m*, impétuosité *f*.

eland ['i:lənd], *s. Z:* **common e.,** éland *m* du Cap; **giant e., Lord Derby's e.,** éland de Derby.

elanus ['elənəs], *s. Orn:* élane *m*, élanion *m*, elanus *m*.

Elaphe ['eləfi], *s. Rept:* élaphé *f*.

elaphodus [e'læfədəs], *s. Z:* élaphode *m*, élaphodus *m*.

Elaphomyces [elæfou'maisi:z], *s. Fung:* élaphomycès *m*.

Elapidae [e'læpidi:], *s.pl. Rept:* élapidés *m*, les couleuvres venimeuses.

elaps ['i:læps], *s. Rept:* élaps *m*.

elapse [i'læps], *v.i.* (*of time*) s'écouler; (se) passer; **years have elapsed since then,** des années ont passé depuis.

Elasmobranchii [elæzmou'bræŋkiai], *s.pl. Ich:* élasmobranches *m*.

elasmosine [e'læsməsi:n], *s. Miner:* élasmose *f*.

elasmotherium [elæzmou'θiəriəm], *s. Paleont:* elasmotherium *m*.

elastase [e'læsteis], *s. Bio-Ch:* élastase *f*.

elastic [i'læstik]. **1.** *a.* (*a*) élastique; (bois, métal, etc.) flexible, obéissant; **to be e.,** faire ressort; *Ph: Mec:* **e. deformation,** déformation *f* élastique; **e. limit, strength,** limite *f* élastique, d'élasticité; **e. resilience,** résistance vive élastique; *Atom.Ph:* **e. collision, impact,** choc *m* élastique; **e. scattering,** diffusion *f* élastique; (*b*) élastique; résilient; **e. step,** pas élastique; *Mth:* **e. curve,** courbe *f* élastique; *Pol.Ec:* **e. supply, demand,** offre *f*, demande *f*, élastique; (*c*) *Anat:* **e. tissue,** tissu *m* élastique; (*d*) *Pej:* **e. conscience,** conscience *f* élastique. **2.** *s.* (*a*) élastique *m*; **e. braces,** bretelles *f* en élastique; **e.-sided boots,** bottines *f* à élastiques; *O:* **elastics,** jarretières *f* en élastique; (*b*) élastique, (bande *f* en) caoutchouc *m*.

elastically [i'læstik(ə)li], *adv.* d'une manière élastique; avec élasticité; **e. supple,** d'une souplesse élastique.

elasticity [i:læs'tisiti], *s.* **1.** élasticité *f* (des gaz, des membres, des règlements, de l'esprit); flexibilité *f*, obéissance *f* (du bois, d'un métal); ressort *m* (de caractère); souplesse *f* (de corps); *Med:* tonicité *f* (des muscles); *Mec:* **modulus, coefficient, of e.,** module *m*, coefficient *m*, d'élasticité; **tensile e.,** élasticité de traction; **metal with the greatest coefficient of e.,** le plus élastique des métaux. **2.** (*a*) élasticité; résilience *f*; **she struggled against her misfortunes with surprising e.,** elle luttait contre ses malheurs avec une élasticité surprenante; (*b*) **e. of interpretation of a law,** élasticité d'une loi; (*c*) *Pol.Ec:* **the e. of supply and demand,** l'élasticité de l'offre et de la demande.

elastin [e'læstin], *s. Bio-Ch:* élastine *f*.

elastomer [i'læstoumər], *s. Ch: etc:* élastomère *m*.

elastomeric [ilæstou'merik], *a. Ch: etc:* élastomère.

elastometry [i:læs'tɔmitri], *s.* élasticimétrie *f*.

elate[1] [i'leit], *v.tr.* exalter, transporter; **to be elated with success,** être transporté enivré de succès.

elate[2], *a. Lit:* **1.** *A:* haut, élevé. **2.** exalté, transporté.

elated [i'leitid], *a.* transporté, exultant; exalté; **to feel e.,** se sentir plein de joie; **to be e.,** (i) exulter; (ii) *F: O:* avoir bu un coup de trop; avoir son plumet; être parti pour la gloire.

elater ['elətər], *s.* **1.** *Ent:* élater *m*, élatère *m*; *F:* taupin *m*; scarabée *m* à ressort. **2.** *Bot:* élatère *f*.

elaterid [i'lætərid], *a. & s. Ent:* élatéridé *m*.

Elateridae [elə'teridi:], *s.pl. Ent:* élatéridés *m*.

elaterite [i'lætərait], *s. Miner:* élatérite *f*; caoutchouc minéral, fossile.

elaterium [elə'tiəriəm], *s.* **1.** *Bot:* élatérion *m*; concombre *m* sauvage. **2.** *Pharm:* élatérion.

Elatinaceae [elæti'neisii:], *s.pl. Bot:* élatinacées *f*.

elatine [i'lætini:], *s. Bot:* élatine *f*.

elation [i'leiʃ(ə)n], *s.* **1.** exaltation *f*; ivresse *f* (du succès). **2.** joie *f*, gaieté *f*.

elatrometer [elə'trɔmitər], *s. Tchn:* élatéromètre *m*.

Elba ['elbə], *Pr.n. Geog:* **the island of E.,** l'île *f* d'Elbe.

Elbe (the) [ði:'elb], *Pr.n. Geog:* l'Elbe *m*.

elbow ['elbou], *s.* **1.** (*a*) coude *m* (du bras); **e. joint,** articulation *f* du coude; **e. height,** hauteur *f* d'appui; **e.-high,** jusqu'au coude; à hauteur d'appui; **to lean, rest, one's e. on sth.,** s'accouder sur qch.; **to lean on one's elbow(s),** être accoudé; s'accouder; s'appuyer sur les coudes; **to touch elbows,** s'accouder; **they were standing e. to e.,** ils se tenaient coude à coude; **to be at s.o.'s**

e., être, se tenir, aux côtés de qn, tout à côté de qn; **to have a book at one's e.,** garder un livre à portée de sa main; **to rub elbows with all sorts of people,** coudoyer, fréquenter, toutes sortes de gens; **to have (enough) e. room,** avoir de la place pour se retourner; avoir ses coudées franches; avoir du large, du champ; *F:* **e. grease,** huile *f* de coude, de bras; **put a bit of e. grease into it!** mettez-y un peu de nerf! *F:* **to lift the e.,** lever le coude, être adonné à la boisson; *F:* **more power to your e.!** vas-y! bonne chance! *P:* **he doesn't know his arse from his e.,** il ne sait pas où il en est; *Furn:* **e. chair,** fauteuil *m*; **e. rest,** accoudoir *m,* accotoir *m*; *A.Arm:* **e. guard,** cubitière *f*; *Cost:* **e.-length sleeves,** manches *f* aux coudes, demi-manches *f*; **e.-length gloves,** gants longs (montant jusqu'au coude); (*b*) *Dressm: etc:* coude (d'une manche); (*of coat*) **out at elbows,** troué, percé, aux coudes; (*of pers.*) **to look out at elbows,** avoir l'air miteux, déguenillé; (*c*) *Z:* coude (de cheval). **2.** (*a*) coude, tournant *m* (d'une route, etc.); *Geog:* **e. of capture,** coude de capture (d'un cours d'eau); (*b*) coude, genou *m,* jarret *m* (d'un conduit, d'un tuyau); conduit coudé; **square e.,** genou vif; **e. duct,** conduite *f* d'angle; *Mec.E: etc:* **e. joint,** joint articulé, à genou; raccord coudé; **e. union,** raccord coudé, en équerre; *I.C.E:* **exhaust e. connexion,** pipe *f* de refoulement; *Tls:* **e. tongs,** tenaille(s) *f* (*pl*) à bec recourbé, à cornières; badine(s) *f*(*pl*); (*c*) (*corner piece*) coude; pièce *f* d'angle; (*d*) *Nau:* **e. in the hawse,** tour *m* dans les chaînes.

elbow[2], **1.** *v.tr.* (*a*) coudoyer (qn); pousser (qn) du coude ou des coudes; **to e. s.o. aside,** écarter qn d'un coup de coude; **to e. s.o. off, out of, sth.,** écarter, évincer, qn de qch.; **to be elbowed out,** être délogé, mis de côté; (*b*) **to e. one's way through the crowd,** s'ouvrir un passage, se frayer un passage, se frayer chemin, se faire jour, à travers la foule en jouant des coudes; jouer des coudes à travers la foule. **2.** *v.i.* (*of road, river, etc.*) faire coude.

elbowed ['elboud], *a. Nat.Hist:* géniculé.

elbowing ['elbouiŋ], *s.* **1.** (*a*) coudoiement *m*; (*b*) bousculade *f.* **2.** coup *m* de coude.

Elburz ['elbɔːz], *Pr.n. Geog:* **the E. Mountains,** l'Elbourz *m.*

elder[1] ['eldər]. **1.** *a.* (*a*) aîné, plus âgé (de deux personnes); **I was not an e. son,** je n'étais pas un fils aîné; **my e. brother,** mon frère aîné; **Pliny the E.,** Pline l'Ancien; *Pol:* **E. Statesmen,** les doyens des hommes politiques, les vétérans (de la politique), les hommes d'État chevronnés; (*b*) *Cards:* **e. hand,** premier *m* en main. **2.** *s.* (*a*) aîné, -ée; plus âgé, -ée (de deux personnes); **he is my e. by two years,** il est de deux ans mon aîné; **which is the e.?** quel est le plus vieux des deux? **children should obey their elders,** les enfants devraient obéir à leurs aînés; (*b*) *Hist: Ecc:* ancien *m.*

elder[2], *s. Bot:* **1. e. (tree),** sureau *m*; **common, black-berried, e.,** sureau noir, sureau proprement dit; **scarlet e.,** sureau rouge; **dwarf e.,** sureau hièble; hièble *f*; petit sureau; *U.S:* **red-berried e.,** sureau à grappes; **box e.,** négundo *m* (à feuilles de frêne), érable *m* négundo; **ground e.,** égopode *m,* herbe *f* aux goutteux. **2. marsh e., water e.,** sureau aquatique.

elderberry ['eldəberi], *s. Bot:* baie *f* de sureau; **e. wine,** vin *m* de sureau.

elderflower ['eldəflauər], *s.* fleur *f* de sureau.

elderly ['eldəli], *a.* d'un certain âge; d'un âge respectable; d'un âge mûr; un peu âgé; assez âgé; *Th:* **e. part,** rôle marqué.

eldership ['eldəʃip], *s. Ecc:* dignité *f* d'ancien.

eldest ['eldist], *a.* aîné; **my e. (son, daughter),** mon (fils) aîné, ma fille aînée, mon aînée.

El Dorado, Eldorado [eldə'rɑːdou], *Pr.n.* Eldorado *m.*

eldritch ['eldritʃ], *a.* surnaturel; mystérieux.

Elea ['iːliə], *Pr.n. A.Geog:* Élée *f.*

Elean ['iːliən], *A.Geog:* (*a*) *a.* éléen; (*b*) *s.* Éléen, -enne.

Eleanor ['elinər], *Pr.n.f.* Éléonore; *Hist:* **E. of Aquitaine,** Aliénor, Éléonore, de Guyenne, d'Aquitaine.

eleatic [eli'ætik]. *Hist. of Phil:* **1.** *a.* éléatique. **2.** *s.* Éléate *m,* éléatique *m.*

elecampane [elikæm'pein], *s. Bot:* au(l)née *f* hélène; inule *f*; *A.Pharm:* **e. root,** racine *f* d'aunée.

elect[1] [i'lekt], *a.* élu; **the president e.,** le président élu; **the mayor e.,** le futur maire; *s. Ecc:* **the e.,** les élus.

elect[2], *v.tr.* **1. to e. to do sth.,** choisir de faire qch.; se décider à, être d'avis de, faire qch.; **he had elected to become a priest,** il avait choisi de se faire prêtre. **2.** (*a*) élire (qn); *Pol:* **to e. s.o. (a) member, s.o. to be a member,** élire qn député; **to e. s.o. to the presidency,** élire qn à la présidence; nommer qn président; **he was elected to the Academy,** il fut élu à l'Académie; **the council elects the president from among its members,** le conseil élit le président dans son sein; **he was elected to serve on the committee,** il a été élu membre du comité; (*b*) *Jur:* **to e. domicile,** élire domicile; (*c*) *Theol:* **those whom God elects,** ceux que Dieu met parmi les élus.

election [i'lekʃ(ə)n], *s.* **1.** (*a*) élection *f* (d'un candidat, etc.); **to stand for e.,** poser sa candidature, se porter candidat; (*b*) *Pol:* **parliamentary, general, e.,** élections législatives; **by-e.,** *U.S:* **special e.,** élection partielle; **municipal elections,** élections municipales; **e. poster,** affiche électorale; **e. committee,** comité électoral, **e. agent,** agent électoral. **2.** *Jur:* (*choice between rights*) choix *m,* élection, option *f.* **3.** *Theol:* élection.

electioneer [ilekʃə'niər], *v.i.* faire une campagne électorale; faire de la propagande électorale; solliciter des voix.

electioneering [ilekʃə'niəriŋ], *s.* propagande électorale; manœuvres électorales.

elective [i'lektiv], *a.* **1.** (*a*) électif; *Hist:* **e. kings,** rois électifs; (*b*) (*of body, franchise, etc.*) électoral, -aux. **2.** *Ch:* **e. affinity,** affinité élective. **3.** *U.S:* (*of course of study, etc.*) facultatif.

electively [i'lektivli], *adv.* **1.** par (le) choix, par élection. **2.** électivement.

electiveness [i'lektivnis], **electivity** [ilek'tiviti], *s.* électivité *f.*

elector [i'lektər], *s.* **1.** électeur, -trice, votant, -ante; **the body of electors,** le Collège électoral. **2.** *Hist:* **the E. of Brandenburg, of Hanover, etc.,** l'Électeur de Brandebourg, de Hanovre, etc.

electoral [i'lektərəl], *a.* électoral, -aux; **e. body,** corps électoral; *U.S:* **the E. College,** le Collège électoral (qui élit le Président).

electorate [i'lektərət], *s.* **1.** *Hist:* électorat *m* ((i) dignité *f* de prince électeur; (ii) territoires soumis à un électeur). **2.** *Pol:* le corps électoral; les électeurs *m*; les votants *m.*

Electra [i'lektrə], *Pr.n.f. Gr.Lit:* Électre; *Psy:* **E. complex,** complexe *m* d'Électre.

electress [i'lektris], *s.f. Hist:* électrice; **the Electress Sophia,** Sophie, Électrice de Hanovre.

electric [i'lektrik]. **1.** *a.* électrique; (*a*) **e. current,** courant *m* électrique; **e. charge, discharge,** charge *f,* décharge *f,* électrique; **e. field,** champ *m* électrique; **e. spark,** étincelle *f* électrique; **e. induction,** induction *f* électrique, électrostatique; **e. wave,** onde *f* électrique, électromagnétique; onde hertzienne; **e. residuum,** électricité résiduelle; **e. power, energy,** énergie *f* électrique; **e. power station,** centrale *f* électrique; **e. generator,** générateur *m,* génératrice *f,* d'électricité; (*b*) **e. light,** lumière *f* électrique; **e. light bulb, e. lamp,** ampoule *f* électrique; **e. motor,** moteur *m* électrique, électromagnétique; électromoteur *m*; **e. fire,** radiateur *m* électrique; **e. cooker,** cuisinière *f* électrique; **e. iron,** fer *m* (à repasser) électrique; **e. typewriter,** machine *f* à écrire électrique; *U.S: Jur:* **e. chair,** chaise *f* électrique; (*c*) **e. blue,** bleu *m* électrique; (*d*) *Fig:* **the atmosphere of the meeting was e.,** l'atmosphère de la réunion était électrique, orageuse. **2.** *s.* (*a*) *A:* matériau, corps, etc. non conducteur de l'électricité; (*b*) *NAm: F:* (i) lampe *f* électrique; (ii) voiture *f,* locomotive *f,* train *m,* électrique; trolleybus *m.*

electrical [i'lektrikl], *a.* électrique; *used mainly in:* **e. engineering,** (i) électromécanique *f*; (ii) industrie *f* de l'équipement électrique; **e. engineer,** (i) ingénieur électricien; (ii) électromécanicien *m*; (monteur-)électricien.

electrically [i'lektrik(ə)li], *adv.* électriquement, par l'électricité; **e. driven,** actionné par électromoteur; **e. controlled,** à commande électrique.

electrician [ilek'triʃ(ə)n], *s.* (*a*) électrotechnicien, -ienne; (*b*) électromécanicien *m*; (monteur-)électricien; réparateur, -trice d'appareils électriques.

electricity [ilek'trisiti], *s.* électricité *f*; énergie *f* électrique; **positive, vitreous, e.,** électricité positive, vitrée; **negative, resinous, e.,** électricité négative, résineuse; **atmospheric, dynamic, static, e.,** électricité atmosphérique, dynamique, statique; **frictional e.,** électricité de friction; **lit by e.,** éclairé à l'électricité.

electrifiable [i'lektrifaiəbl], *a.* (*of substance, audience*) électrisable.

electrification [ilektrifi'keiʃ(ə)n], *s.* **1.** électrisation *f* (d'un corps, etc.). **2.** électrification *f* (d'une voie de chemin de fer, etc.).

electrified [i'lektrifaid], *a.* **1.** (*of substance, of audience*) électrisé. **2.** (*of railway line*) électrifié.

electrify [i'lektrifai], *v.tr.* **1.** électriser (un corps, un auditoire). **2.** électrifier (une ligne de chemin de fer, etc.).

electrifying[1] [i'lektrifaiiŋ], *a.* électrisant.

electrifying[2], *s.* **1.** électrisation *f.* **2.** électrification *f* (d'une ligne de chemin de fer, etc.).

electro [i'lektrou], *s. F:* électrotype *m, F:* galvano *m.*

electro- [i'lektrou], *pref.* électro-.

electroacoustic(al) [i'lektrouə'kuːstik(l)], *a.* électro(-)acoustique.

electroacoustics [i'lektrouə'kuːstiks], *s.pl.* (*usu. with sg. const.*) électro(-)acoustique *f.*

electro-affinity [i'lektrouə'finiti], *s.* électro-affinité *f.*

electroanalysis [i'lektrouə'næləsis], *s.* électro-analyse *f,* analyse *f* électrolytique.

electrobiological [i'lektroubaiə'lɔdʒikl], *a.* électrobiologique.

electrobiologist [i'lektroubai'ɔlədʒist], *s.* électrobiologiste *mf.*

electrobiology [i'lektroubai'ɔlədʒi], *s.* électrobiologie *f.*

electrocapillarity [i'lektroukæpi'læriti], *s.* électrocapillarité *f.*

electrocapillary [i'lektroukə'piləri], *a.* électrocapillaire.

electrocardiogram [i'lektrou'kɑːdiougræm], *s. Med:* électrocardiogramme *m.*

electrocardiograph [i'lektrou'kɑːdiougræf], *s. Med:* électrocardiographe *m.*

electrocardiography [i'lektroukɑːdi'ɔgrəfi], *s. Med:* électrocardiographie *f.*

electrocardioscope [i'lektrou'kɑːdiouskoup], *s. Med:* électrocardioscope *m.*

electrocauterization [i'lektroukɔːtərai'zeiʃ(ə)n], *s.* électrocaustique *f.*

electrocautery [i'lektrou'kɔːtəri], *s.* (*a*) électrocautère *m*; (*b*) électrocaustique *f.*

electro-cement [i'lektrousi'ment], *s.* électrobéton *m.*

electrochemical [i'lektrou'kemikl], *a.* électrochimique.

electrochemistry [i'lektrou'kemistri], *s.* électrochimie *f.*

electrocoagulation [i'lektroukouægju'leiʃ(ə)n], *s. Med:* électrocoagulation *f.*

electrocoating [i'lektrou'koutiŋ], *s.* peinture *f* par électrophorèse.

electrocoma [i'lektrou'koumə], *s. Med:* électrocoma *m.*

electroconvulsive [i'lektroukən'vʌlsiv], *a. Med:* **e. therapy, e. shock,** électrochoc *m.*

electrocorticogram [i'lektrou'kɔːtikougræm], *s* électrocorticogramme *m.*

electrocortin [i'lektru'kɔːtin], *s. Physiol:* électrocortine *f,* aldostérone *f.*

electroculture [i'lektro'kʌltjər], *s.* électroculture *f.*

electrocute [i'lektrəkjuːt], *v.tr.* électrocuter.

electrocuting [i'lektrəkjutiŋ], *a.* (courant) électrocuteur.

electrocution [ilektrə'kjuːʃ(ə)n], *s.* électrocution *f.*

electrocutor [i'lektrəkjuːtər], *s.* électrocuteur *m.*

electrode [i'lektroud], *s.* électrode *f*; **bare e.,** électrode nue; **coated e.,** électrode enrobée; **thin-coated e.,** électrode enduite; **easy-flowing e.,** électrode douce; **hard-metal e.,** électrode dure; **extruded e.,** électrode boudinée; **loop e.,** électrode en anse; **collector e.,** électrode collectrice; **input, output, e.,** électrode d'entrée, de sortie; **base e.,** électrode de base; **three-e. lamp, tube,** lampe *f* triode; **e. holder,** porte-électrodes *m inv*; **e. tip,** tête *f* d'électrode.

electrodeposit[1] [i'lektroudi'pɔzit], *s.* dépôt *m* électrolytique, galvanoplastique; précipité *m* galvanique.

electrodeposit[2], *v.tr.* déposer par électrolyse, par galvanoplastie, par voie galvanique, électrolytiquement.

electrodeposition [i'lektroudiːpou'ziʃ(ə)n], *s.* électrodéposition *f*; galvanoplastie *f.*

electrodiagnosis [i'lektroudaiəg'nousis], *s. Med:* électrodiagnostic *m.*

electrodialysis [i'lektroudai'ælisis], *s.* électrodialyse *f.*

electrodissolution [i'lektroudisə'luːʃ(ə)n], *s.* électrodissolution *f.*

electrodynamic [i'lektroudai'næmik], *a.* électrodynamique.

electrodynamics [i'lektroudai'næmiks], *s.* (*usu. with sg. const.*) électrodynamique *f.*

electrodynamometer [i'lektroudainə'mɔmitər], *s.* électrodynamomètre *m.*

electroencephalogram [i'lektrouen'sefəlougræm], *s. Med:* électroencéphalogramme *m.*

electroencephalograph [i'lektrouen'sefəlougræf], *s. Med:* électroencéphalographe *m.*

electroencephalography [i'lektrouensefə'lɔgrəfi], *s. Med:* électroencéphalographie *f.*

electroendosmosis [i'lektrouendɔz'mousis], *s.* électroendosmose *f.*

electroextraction [i'lektrouik'strækʃ(ə)n], *s. Min: etc:* électro-extraction *f*; extraction *f* électrolytique, électrochimique.

electroforming [ilektrou'fɔːmiŋ], *s. Tchn:* électroformage *m.*

electrogalvanize [i'lektrou'gælvənaiz], *v.tr.* électrogalvaniser.

electrogenesis [ilektrou'dʒenisis], *s.* électrogénèse *f,* électrogénie *f.*

electrograph [i'lektrougræf], *s. Tg:* électrographe *m.*

electrography [ilek'trɔgrəfi], *s. Tg:* électrographie *f.*
electrokinetic [i'lektrouk(a)i'netik], *a.* électrocinétique.
electroller [ilektrə'llər], *s.* lustre *m*, chandelier *m*, électrique.
electrology [ilek'trɔlədʒi], *s.* électrologie *f.*
electroluminescence [i'lektroulu:mi'nesəns], *s.* électroluminescence *f.*
electroluminescent [i'lektroulu:mi'nesənt], *a.* électroluminescent.
electrolysable [i'lektrou'laizəbl], *a.* électrolysable.
electrolyse [i'lektrəlaiz], *v.tr.* électrolyser.
electrolyser [i'lektrəlaizər], *s.* électrolyseur *m.*
electrolysis [ilek'trɔlisis], *s.* électrolyse *f.*
electrolyte [i'lektrəlait], *s. El:* électrolyte *m*; **foul e.,** électrolyte impropre.
electrolytic [i'lektrou'litik], *a.* électrolytique; **e. dissociation,** désintégration *f* électrolytique; **e. copper,** cuivre *m* électrolytique; **e. cell, vat,** cuve *f* électrolytique; **e. pickling,** décapage *m* électrolytique; **e. rectifier,** redresseur *m* électrolytique; **e. zinc process,** électrolyse *f* du zinc; **e. refining,** électroraffinage *m.*
electrolytically [i'lektrou'litik(ə)li], *adv.* électrolytiquement.
electromagnet [i'lektrou'mægnit], *s.* électro-aimant *m*, *pl.* électro-aimants.
electromagnetic [i'lektroumæg'netik], *a.* électromagnétique; **e. field,** champ *m* électromagnétique; **e. induction,** induction *f* électromagnétique; **e. leakage,** dispersion *f* électromagnétique; **e. wave,** onde *f* électromagnétique.
electromagnetism [i'lektrou'mægnitizm], *s.* électromagnétisme *m.*
electromechanic(al) [i'lektroumi'kænik(l)], *a.* électromécanique.
electromechanics [i'lektroumi'kæniks], *s.* (*usu. with sg. const.*) électromécanique *f.*
electromer [i'lektroumər], *s. Ch:* électromère *m.*
electromerism [ilektrou'merizm], *s. Ch:* électromérie *f.*
electrometallurgic [i'lektroumetə'lə:dʒik], *a.* électrométallurgique.
electrometallurgist [i'lektroume'tælədʒist], *s.* électrométallurgiste *m.*
electrometallurgy [i'lektroume'tælədʒi], *s.* électrométallurgie *f.*
electrometer [ilek'trɔmitər], *s.* électromètre *m*; **vibrating-reed e.,** électromètre à lame vibrante.
electrometric [ilektrou'metrik], *a.* électrométrique.
electrometry [ilek'trɔmitri], *s.* électrométrie *f.*
electromotive [i'lektrou'moutiv], *a.* électromoteur, -trice; **e. force,** force électromotrice; **e. (force) series,** tableau *m* des potentiels des réactions électrochimiques.
electromotor [i'lektrou'moutər], *s.* électromoteur *m*; machine électromotrice.
electromuscular [i'lektrou'mʌskjulər], *a.* électromusculaire.
electromyogram [i'lektrou'maiougræm], *s. Med:* électromyogramme *m.*
electromyograph [i'lektrou'maiougræf], *s. Med:* électromyographe *m.*
electromyography [i'lektroumai'ɔgrəfi], *s. Med:* électromyographie *f.*
electron [i'lektrɔn], *s. Ph:* électron *m*; **positive e.,** électron positif, posit(r)on *m*; **negative e.,** électron négatif, négat(r)on *m*; **primary, secondary, e.,** électron primaire, secondaire; **e. pair,** paire *f* d'électrons; **atomic, atom-bound, e.,** électron atomique; **nuclear, extranuclear, e.,** électron nucléaire, extra-nucléaire; **lone e.,** électron célibataire; **free e.,** électron libre; **trapped e.,** électron captif; **orbital, bound, e.,** électron lié; **planetary, orbital, e.,** électron planétaire, satellite; **inner(-shell), outer(-shell), e.,** électron interne, périphérique; **spinning e.,** électron tournant; **thermo e.,** électron thermique; **heavy e.,** électron lourd; **e. emission,** émission *f* électronique, d'électrons; **e. emitter,** émetteur *m* d'électrons; **e. multiplier,** multiplicateur *m* d'électrons; **e. accelerator,** accélérateur *m* d'électrons; **e. paths,** trajectoire *f* électronique; **e. shell,** couche *f* électronique; *T.V:* **e. gun,** canon *m* à électrons; **e. camera,** camera *f* électronique; **e. lens,** lentille *f* électronique; **e.-ray tube,** trèfle *m* cathodique; **e. captive, attachment,** électronation *f.*
electronarcosis [i'lektrouna:'kousis], *s. Med:* électronarcose *f.*
electronegative [ile'ktrou'negətiv], *a.* électronégatif.
electronegativity [i'lektrounegə'tiviti], *s.* électronégativité *f.*
electroneutrality [i'lektrounju':træliti], *s.* électroneutralité *f.*
electronic [ilek'trɔnik], *a.* électronique; **e. control,** commande *f* électronique; **e. recorder,** enregistreur *m* électronique; **e. computer,** calculateur *m* électronique; **e. brain,** cerveau *m* électronique; **e. storage,** mémoire *f* électronique; **e. engineer, e. specialist,** électronicien, -ienne; ingénieur électronicien.
electronically [ilek'trɔnik(ə)li], *adv.* électroniquement.
electronics [ilek'trɔniks], *s.pl.* (*usu. with sg. const.*) électronique *f*; **quantum physics of e.,** électronique quantique; **e. specialist, engineer, technician,** ingénieur électronicien; électronicien, -ienne; **e. industry,** industrie *f* électronique.
electron volt [i'lektrɔn'vɔlt], *s.* électron-volt *m*, *pl.* électrons-volts.
electro-optic(al) [i'lektrou'ɔptik, -l], *a.* électro-optique, *pl.* électro-optiques.
electro-optics [i'lektrou'ɔptiks], *s.* (*usu. with sg. const.*) électro-optique *f.*
electro-osmosis [i'lektrouɔz'mousis], *s. Ph:* électro-osmose *f.*
electro-osmotic [i'lektrouɔz'mɔtik], *a. Ph:* électro-osmotique.
electropathology [i'lektroupæ'θɔlədʒi], *s. Med:* électropathologie *f.*
electrophilic [i'lektrou'filik], *a. Ch:* électrophile.
electrophone [i'lektrəfoun], *s.* électrophone *m.*
electrophonic [i'lektrə'fɔnik], *a.* (effet) électrophonique.
electrophoresis [i'lektroufɔ'ri:sis], *s.* électrophorèse *f.*
electrophoretic [i'lektroufɔ'ri:tik], *a.* électrophorétique.
electrophorus, *pl.* **-i** [ilek'trɔfərəs, -ai], *s.* **1.** *Ph:* électrophore *m.* **2.** *Ich:* électrophore.
electrophotography [i'lektroufə'tɔgrəfi], *s.* électrophotographie *f.*
electrophotometer [i'lektroufɔ'tɔmitər], *s.* électrophotomètre *m.*
electrophysics [i'lektrou'fiziks], *s.* (*usu. with sg. const.*) électrophysique *f.*
electrophysiological [i'lektroufiziou'lɔdʒikl], *a.* électrophysiologique.
electrophysiologist [i'lektroufizi'ɔlədʒist], *s.* électrophysiologiste *mf.*
electrophysiology [i'lektroufizi'ɔlədʒi], *s.* électrophysiologie *f.*
electroplate[1] [i'lektroupleit], *s.* (métal) plaqué *m*; articles (i) plaqués, (ii) argentés.
electroplate[2], *v.tr.* (i) plaquer, (ii) argenter (un métal).
electroplax [i'lektrouplæks], *s. Ich:* électroplaxe *f.*
electropneumatic [i'lektrounju'mætik], *a.* électropneumatique.
electropositive [i'lektrou'pɔzitiv], *a.* électropositif.
electropositivity [i'lektroupɔzi'tiviti], *s.* électropositivité *f.*
electropuncture [i'lektrou'pʌŋktjər], *s. Med:* électropuncture *f*, électroponcture *f.*
electropyrexia [i'lektroupai'reksiə], *s. Med:* électropyrexie *f.*
electroradiologist [i'lektroureidi'ɔlədʒist], *s.* électroradiologiste *mf.*
electroradiology [i'lektroureidi'ɔlədʒi], *s.* électroradiologie *f.*
electrorefining [i'lektrouri'fainiŋ], *s. Ind:* électro-affinage *m*, électroraffinage *m.*
electroretinogram [i'lektroure'ti:nougræm], *s.* électrorétinogramme *m.*
electroscope [i'lektrəskoup], *s.* électroscope *m.*
electroshock [i'lektrou'ʃɔk], *a.* & *s.* **e. (therapy),** électrochoc *m.*
electrosiderurgy [i'lektrou'sidərə:dʒi], *s.* électrosidérurgie *f.*
electrosmosis [i'lektrɔz'mousis], *s.* électrosmose *f.*
electrostatic [i'lektrou'stætik], *a.* électrostatique; **e. generator,** générateur *m* électrostatique; **e. shield, screen,** blindage *m*, écran *m*, électrostatique; **e. transfer,** propagation *f* électrostatique; **e. voltmeter,** voltmètre *m* électrostatique.
electrostatics [i'lektrou'stætiks], *s.pl.* (*usu. with sg. const.*) électrostatique *f.*
electrostenolysis [i'lektrouste'nɔlisis], *s.* électrosténolyse *f.*
electrostriction [i'lektrou'strikʃ(ə)n], *s.* électrostriction *f.*
electrostrictive [i'lektrou'striktiv], *a.* **e. effect,** effet *m* d'électrostriction.
electrosurgery [i'lektrou'sə:dʒəri], *s.* électrochirurgie *f.*
electrosynthesis [i'lektrou'sinθəsis], *s. Ch:* électrosynthèse *f.*
electrotaxis [i'lektrou'tæksis], *s. Biol:* électrotaxis *f.*
electrotechnic(al) [i'lektrou'teknik(l)], *a.* électrotechnique.
electrotechnics [i'lektrou'tekniks], *s. pl.* (*usu. with sg. const.*) électrotechnique *f.*
electrotechnology [i'lektroutek'nɔlədʒi], *s.* électrotechnique *f.*
electrotherapeutic(al) [i'lektrouθerə'pju:tik(l)], *a. Med:* électrothérapeutique, électrothérapique.
electrotherapeutics [i'lektrouθerə'pju:tiks], *s. pl.* (*usu. with sg. const.*) *Med:* électrothérapie *f.*
electrotherapeutist [i'lektrouθerə'pju:tist], **electrotherapist** [i'lektrou'θerəpist], *s. Med:* électrothérapeute *mf.*
electrotherapy [i'lektrou'θerəpi], *s. Med:* électrothérapie *f.*
electrothermal, electrothermic [i'lektrou'θə:ml, -mik], *a.* électrothermique.
electrothermics [i'lektrou'θə:miks], *s.pl.* (*usu with sg. const.*) *Med:* électrothermie *f.*
electrotonic [i'lektrou'tɔnik], *a.* électrotonique.
electrotonus [ilek'trɔtənəs], *s. Physiol:* électrotonus *m.*
electrotropism [i'lektrou'trɔpizm], *s.* électrotropisme *m.*
electrotype[1] [i'lektroutaip], *s. Typ:* électrotype *m*; galvanotype *m.*
electrotype[2], *v.tr. Typ:* électrotyper; galvanotyper.
electrotyper [i'lektroutaipər], *s. Typ:* électrotypeur *m.*
electrotyping [i'lektroutaipiŋ], *s. Typ:* électrotypie *f*, galvanotypie *f.*
electrovalence, electrovalency [i'lektrou'veiləns, -'veilənsi], *s.* électrovalence *f.*
electro-valve [i'lektrouvælv], *s.* électro(-)valve *f.*
electrum [i'lektrəm], *s. Miner:* électrum *m.*
electuary [i'lektjuəri], *s. A.Pharm:* électuaire *m.*
eleemosynary [eli'mɔzinəri], *a. Lit:* & *U.S:* (*a*) charitable, de charité; **e. corporation,** société de bienfaisance; (*b*) qui vit de charités.
elegance ['eligəns], *Lit:* **elegancy** ['eligənsi], *s.* élégance *f.*
elegant ['eligənt], *a.* **1.** élégant; **e. figure,** taille élégante; **e. furniture,** meubles délicats, d'un goût raffiné; **life of e. ease,** vie luxueuse et raffinée. **2.** *NAm: F:* excellent; chic; de premier ordre.
elegantly ['eligəntli], *adv.* élégamment; avec élégance; **e. dressed,** habillé(e) avec élégance, avec recherche.
elegiac [eli'dʒaiək]. **1.** *a.* élégiaque. **2.** *s.pl.* **elegiacs,** vers *m* élégiaques.
elegiast [eli'dʒaiəst], **elegist** ['elidʒist], *s.* (poète *m*) élégiaque (*m*).
elegize ['elədʒaiz]. **1.** *v.i.* (*a*) écrire des élégies; (*b*) écrire d'une façon élégiaque. **2.** *v.tr.* écrire une élégie, des élégies, sur (qn, qch.).
elegy ['elidʒi], *s.* élégie *f.*
element ['elimənt], *s.* élément *m.* **1. the four elements,** les quatre éléments; *Alch:* la tétrasomie; **to brave the elements,** braver les éléments; **exposed to the elements,** exposé aux intempéries *fpl*; **water is the e. of the fish,** l'eau est l'élément du poisson; **to be in one's e.,** être dans son élément, dans son milieu, sur son terrain, à son affaire, *F:* comme un poisson dans l'eau; **to be out of one's e.,** être hors de son élément; être désorienté, dépaysé, hors de sa sphère, *F:* comme un poisson sur la paille. **2.** (*a*) **to reduce sth. to its elements,** réduire qch. à ses éléments; **e. of uncertainty,** élément d'incertitude; **character in which there is an e. of avarice,** caractère où il entre de l'avarice; **disturbing e.,** élément d'instabilité; **the personal e.,** le facteur humain; (*b*) élément, partie *f* (d'un tout); *El:* **battery of fifty elements,** batterie de cinquante éléments; **elements of a three-electrode valve,** électrodes *f* d'une lampe triode; *Cmptr:* **data e.,** élément d'information; *Const:* **the elements of a framework,** les membrières d'un cadre; *Atom.Ph:* (*for changing reactor*) **fuel e.,** charge *f*; (*c*) *Theol:* **the eucharistic elements,** les éléments de l'eucharistie; (*d*) *Mil:* **leading elements,** éléments de tête, de première ligne; **non-divisional elements,** éléments non endivisionnés; éléments de reconnaissance. **3.** *Ch:* corps *m* simple. **4.** *pl.* **elements,** rudiments *m* (d'une science); **Euclid's Elements,** les Éléments de Géométrie (d'Euclide).
elemental[1] [eli'ment(ə)l], *a.* **1.** qui appartient aux éléments, aux forces de la nature; qui est causé par les éléments, les forces de la nature; **e. force,** force *f* qui appartient à un élément de la nature; **e. spirit,** esprit élémental; **e. war,** guerre *f* des éléments; **e. grandeur,** grandeur transcendante, surnaturelle. **2.** élémentaire, à l'état brut, fruste, primitif, rudimentaire, sommaire. **3.** (*of substance*) élémentaire. **4.** fondamental, élémentaire, essentiel; **e. truths,** vérités premières.
elemental[2], *s.* **1.** esprit *m*, spectre *m*; **the elementals,** les esprits élémentaux. **2.** *pl.* **elementals,** (i) rudiments; (ii) éléments fondamentaux.
elementary [eli'ment(ə)ri], *a.* élémentaire; *Ch:* **e. analysis,** analyse *f* élémentaire; **e. body,** (i) *Ch:* corps *m* simple; (ii) *Med:* corps élémentaire; *Atom.Ph:* **e. particles,** particules *f* élémentaires; *A:* **e. school,** école *f* primaire; *Sch:* **e. algebra,** rudiments *mpl* d'algèbre; **e. prudence,** la prudence la plus élémentaire, simple prudence.
elemi ['eləmi], *s.* **(gum) e.,** élémi *m*; résine *f* d'amyris.

elemicin [ə'leməsin], *s. Ch:* élémicine *f.*

elench [i'leŋk], *s. Log:* réfutation *f*; élenchos *m*, élenchus *m.*

elenchus, *pl.* **-i** [i'leŋkəs, -ai], *s.* **1.** *Log:* = ELENCH. **2.** *Phil:* **Socratic e.,** méthode *f* socratique du dialogue.

elephant ['elifənt], *s.* **1.** (*a*) *Z:* éléphant *m*; **bull e.,** éléphant mâle; **cow e.,** éléphante *f*, éléphant femelle; **calf e., e. calf,** *F:* **baby e.,** éléphanteau *m*; **e. driver,** cornac *m*; **white e.,** (i) *Z:* éléphant blanc; (ii) *F:* objet *m*, cadeau *m*, d'une certaine valeur mais inutile et encombrant; attrape-poussières *m inv*; rossignol *m*; (iii) *Ind.Com: F:* loup *m*; *F:* **to see pink elephants,** voir double; *F:* **it's no more than a peanut to an e.,** c'est un grain de millet dans la bouche d'un âne; (*b*) **sea e., e. seal,** macrorhine *m*, *F:* éléphant de mer, phoque *m* à trompe; (*c*) *Ent:* **e. beetle,** mégasome *m*; (*d*) *Orn:* **e. bird,** pyornis *m*; (*e*) *Bot:* **elephant's, foot,** testudinaire *f*, pied d'éléphant; **elephant's ear,** bégonia *m.* **2.** *Paperm:* **e. (paper)** = papier *m* grand jésus; aigle *m*; **double e.,** grand aigle.

elephantiasic [elifən'taiəsik], *a. Med:* éléphantiasique.

elephantiasis [elifən'taiəsis], *s. Med:* éléphantiasis *f*, pachydermie *f.*

Elephantidae [eli'fæntidi:], *s.pl. Z:* éléphantidés *m.*

elephantine [eli'fæntain], *a.* **1.** éléphantin; **e. gambols,** gambades *f* gauches; **e. wit,** esprit lourd; **to display an e. wit,** être fin comme une dague de plomb. **2.** (*of proportions, etc.*) éléphantesque.

elephantopus [eli'fæntəpəs], *s. Bot:* éléphantopus *m.*

elettaria [elə'tɑ:riə], *s. Bot:* élettaria *m.*

eleusine [elju'saini], *s. Bot:* éleusine *f.*

Eleusinia [elju'siniə], *s.pl. Gr.Ant:* Éleusinies *f.*

Eleusinian [elju'siniən], *a.* d'Éleusis; **E. mysteries,** éleusinies *f.*

Eleutheria [elju'θiəriə], *s.pl. Gr.Ant:* Éleuthéries *f.*

eleutherodactylus [i'lju:θərou'dæktiləs], *s. Amph:* éleuthérodactyle *m.*

eleutheropetalous [i'lju:θərou'pet(ə)ləs], *a. Bot:* éleuthéropétale.

eleutherophyllous [i'lju:θərou'filəs], *a. Bot:* éleuthérophylle.

Eleutherozoa [i'lju:θərou'zouə], *s.pl. Echin:* éleuthérozoaires *m.*

elevate ['eliveit], *v.tr.* **1.** élever (l'hostie, etc.); élever, agrandir (qch., l'esprit); relever (une pensée, son style); hausser, élever (la voix); lever (les yeux); *Artil:* pointer (un canon) en hauteur; *Av:* cabrer (l'avion); *Ph:* (*capillarity*) **the liquid is elevated,** le liquide s'élève, mouille; **to e. s.o. to a high rank,** élever qn à un haut rang. **2.** exalter (qn); **the kind of sorrow that elevates,** la sorte de chagrin qui élève l'âme.

elevated ['eliveitid], *a.* **1.** élevé; **e. position,** position élevée; **e. thoughts,** hautes pensées; *F: A:* **to be slightly e.,** être un peu gris, un peu parti (pour la gloire). **2.** (*overhead*) surélevé; **e. railway,** *U.S:* **e. railroad,** (i) chemin de fer aérien; voie ferrée aérienne; (ii) (*also s. F:* **the e.**) métro aérien; **e. highway,** route surélevée.

elevating[1] ['eliveitiŋ], *a.* **1.** (*of discourse, etc.*) qui élève l'esprit; **e. principles,** principes moralisateurs. **2.** *Tchn:* élévatoire; élévateur; *Aer:* **e. power,** force ascensionnelle; *Mec: etc:* **e. machinery,** machines *fpl* élévatoires; *Artil:* **e. arc, e. rack,** secteur *m* denté; crémaillère *f* de pointage en hauteur; **e. crank, e. handle,** manivelle *f* de pointage en hauteur; **e. gear,** appareil *m* de pointage en hauteur; **e. screw,** (i) *Artil:* vis *f* de pointage en hauteur; vis télescopique; (ii) *Mec:* vis *f* monte-et-baisse; **e. wheel,** (i) *Artil:* volant *m* de pointage en hauteur, volant de hausse; (ii) *Mec:* roue *f* élévatoire; **e. plane,** gouvernail *m* d'altitude, de profondeur.

elevating[2], *s.* élévation *f*; levage *m*; relevage *m*; *Av:* cabrage *m* (de l'avion).

elevation [eli'veiʃ(ə)n], *s.* **1.** (*a*) élévation *f* (de qch. à une certaine hauteur, de qn à un rang supérieur); (*b*) *Ecc:* **the E. (of the Host),** l'Élévation. **2.** *Geog: Surv:* altitude *f*, hauteur *f*, cote *f*; **e. above sea level,** altitude, hauteur, au-dessus du niveau de la mer; **e. of 100 metres above sea level,** cote 100 (mètres); altitude de 100 mètres au-dessus du niveau de la mer; **the range rises to its highest e. at . . .,** la chaîne (de montagnes) atteint son point culminant à . . ., culmine à . . .. **3.** (*a*) (*hill*) élévation, éminence *f*; (*b*) *Geol:* exhaussement *m*, soulèvement *m*; **e. crater,** cratère *m* de soulèvement. **4.** hauteur angulaire; (*a*) *Astr:* élévation (d'un astre, etc.); (*b*) *Artil:* hausse *f*; pointage *m* en hauteur, pointage positif; **angle of e.,** angle *m* de hausse, de site positif; **e. index,** repère *m* de pointage en hauteur; **e. mechanism,** dispositif *m* de pointage en hauteur; **e. quadrant,** niveau de hausse; **quadrant e.,** angle au niveau; **e. scale,** échelle *f* de hausse; **to fire at extreme, maximum, e.,** tirer à portée extrême, à toute volée; **e.-tracking telescope,** lunette *f* de pointage en hauteur; *Ball:* (*missiles*) **quadrantal e.,** angle de tir. **5.** *Draw: Arch: etc:* élévation (d'un édifice, etc.); **sectional e.,** coupe verticale; élévation-coupe *f*; **front e.,** façade *f* (d'un édifice); élévation antérieure. **6.** élévation, dignité *f*, sublimité *f* (du style); élévation, noblesse *f*, grandeur *f* (du caractère); **the lack of any e. in his thought,** le terre à terre de sa pensée. **7.** *Rad:* **e. display,** indicateur *m* de site; **e.-position indicator,** radar *m* de position; indicateur de site et de distance; **e. position,** position site.

elevator ['eliveitər], *s.* **1.** (*a*) élévateur *m*, convoyeur *m*; *U.S:* (*for goods*) monte-charge(s) *m*; treuil *m* de chargement; (*for water, etc.*) pompe *f*; **bucket e.,** élévateur à godets, à augets; patenôtre *f*; **e. dredge,** drague *f* à (chaîne à) godets; **barrel e.,** élévateur à tonneaux; **pneumatic e., sucking e.,** élévateur, transporteur *m*, pneumatique; aspirateur *m*; (*b*) *N.Am:* ascenseur *m*; (*c*) **grain e.,** aspirateur à céréales, silo *m*, élévateur à grains, élévator *m.* **2.** *Av:* gouvernail *m* de profondeur, d'altitude; **e. lever,** guignol *m* de gouverne de profondeur; plan de profondeur (articulé); **e. angle,** angle *m* de braquage; **e. control,** commande *f* de profondeur; **e. aileron,** élevon *m.* **3.** *Bootm:* talonnette *f.* **4.** (*a*) *Surg:* élévatoire *m*; (*b*) *Dent:* élévateur *m*, langue-de-carpe *f*, *pl.* langues-de-carpe; trivelin *m.* **5.** *Anat:* (muscle) élévateur (de la paupière).

elevatory [eli'veitəri], *a.* (force *f*, etc.) élévatoire.

eleven [i'lev(ə)n]. **1.** *num.a. & s.* onze (*m*); **they are only e.,** ils ne sont que onze, *F:* qu'onze; **the e. o'clock train,** le train d'onze heures; *Sch:* **e. plus (examination)** = examen *m* d'entrée en 6ème. **2.** *s. Sp: Cr: Fb: etc:* équipe *f* de onze joueurs; le onze.

elevenses [i'levənziz], *s.pl. F:* collation *f*, casse-croûte *m inv*, café *m*, de onze heures (du matin).

eleventh [i'levənθ]. **1.** *num.a. & s.* onzième (*m*); **at the e. hour,** (i) *B:* à la onzième heure; (ii) au dernier moment; à la dernière heure; **an e.-hour change in the programme,** un changement de programme au dernier moment. **2.** *s.* (*fractional*) onzième.

eleventhly [i'levənθli], *adv.* onzièmement.

elevon ['elivɔn], *s. Av:* élevon *m.*

elf, *pl.* **elves** [elf, elvz], *s.* (*a*) *Myth:* elfe *m*, lutin *m*, lutine *f*; **e. child,** enfant changé en nourrice par les fées; (*b*) **e. arrow, e. bolt, e. dart, e. shot,** (i) tête *f* de flèche en silex; (ii) bélemnite *f*; (*c*) *F: O:* enfant *mf* espiègle; petit lutin, petite lutine.

elfin ['elfin]. **1.** *a.* (*a*) d'elfe, de lutin, de fée; **e. laugh,** rire *m* de lutin; rire espiègle; **e. landscape,** paysage *m* féerique; (*b*) **e. tree,** arbre rabougri (des Alpes). **2.** *s.* = ELF.

elfish ['elfiʃ], *a.* (*a*) des elfes, de lutin; (*b*) (*of child*) espiègle.

elfland ['elflænd], *s.* le royaume des elfes.

elflock ['elflɔk], *s.* (mèche *f* de) cheveux emmêlés.

Eli ['i:lai], *Pr.n.m. B.Hist:* Héli.

Eliakim [i'laiəkim], *Pr.n.m.* Éliacim, Éliakim.

Elian ['i:liən]. **1.** *a.* qui appartient à Charles Lamb; (caractère) tiré des *Essays of Elia.* **2.** *s.* admirateur, -trice, de Charles Lamb.

Elias [i'laiəs], *Pr.n.m.* Élie.

eliasite [i'laiəsait], *s. Miner:* éliasite *f.*

elicit[1] [e'lisit], *a. Phil:* **e. act,** acte *m* élicite.

elicit[2], *v.tr.* tirer, faire jaillir (qch. de caché); découvrir (la vérité); déduire, mettre au jour, mettre en lumière (des vérités d'après des données); **to e. the facts,** tirer les faits au clair; **to e. a reply from s.o.,** tirer, obtenir, une réponse de qn; **to e. an admission from s.o.,** arracher un aveu à qn; **to e. universal admiration,** être l'objet de l'admiration universelle; s'attirer, provoquer, l'admiration universelle.

elide [i'laid], *v.tr.* élider (une voyelle, etc.); (*at end of word*) **elided letter,** lettre apocopée; **e mute is elided before a vowel,** l'e muet s'élide devant une voyelle.

Eliezer [eli'i:zər], *Pr.n.m.* Éliézer.

eligibility [elidʒi'biliti], *s.* **1.** éligibilité *f* (en droit). **2.** acceptabilité *f* (d'un prétendant, etc.).

eligible ['elidʒibl], *a.* **1.** éligible (en droit) (**to,** à); **to be e.,** avoir droit (**for,** à). **2.** digne d'être élu, choisi; désirable; acceptable; **e. for an occupation,** admissible à un emploi; **e. young man,** jeune homme *m* acceptable; bon parti; parti sortable; **small town with no e. men,** petite ville où il n'y a pas de partis, pas d'épouseurs; **e. investment,** placement avantageux.

eligibleness ['elidʒiblnis], *s.* = ELIGIBILITY.

Eligius [i'lidʒiəs], *Pr.n.m. Rel.Hist:* Éloi.

Elihu [i'laihju:], *Pr.n.m. B:* Élihu.

Elijah [i'laidʒə], *Pr.n.m. B.Hist:* Élie.

eliminable [i'liminəbl], *a.* éliminable.

eliminate [i'limineit], *v.tr.* **1.** éliminer (des matières toxiques, des noms d'une liste, etc.); supprimer, écarter (des possibilités d'erreur, etc.); *Med:* **to e. a spasm,** lever un spasme; *Mth:* **to e. x, y,** éliminer x, y; faire évanouir x, y. **2.** tirer, extraire (de la nourriture du sol, etc.).

eliminating [i'limineitiŋ], *a.* éliminateur, -trice; *Sp:* **e. heats,** épreuves *f* éliminatoires.

elimination [ilimi'neiʃ(ə)n], *s.* élimination *f*; *Sp:* **e. trial,** épreuve *f* éliminatoire; *F:* éliminatoire *f*; **by process of e.,** en procédant par élimination.

eliminative [i'liminətiv], *a.* éliminateur, -trice.

eliminator [i'limineitər], *s.* éliminateur *m*; *Phot:* **hypo-e.,** éliminateur d'hypo; *Aut:* **shock e.,** amortisseur *m* (de chocs); *W.Tel:* **high-tension e.,** dispositif *m* de filtrage du courant du secteur (pour la haute tension); *W.Tel:* **battery e.,** éliminateur de batterie, appareil *m* remplaçant une batterie.

eliminatory [i'liminət(ə)ri], *a.* éliminatoire.

elinvar ['elinvɑ:r], *s. Metall:* élinvar *m.*

Elis ['i:lis], *Pr.n. Geog:* Élide *f.*

Eliseus [e'laisiəs], *Pr.n. B:* Élisée *m.*

Elisha [i'laiʃə], *Pr.n.m. B.Hist:* Élisée.

elision [i'liʒ(ə)n], *s.* élision *f* (d'une voyelle, etc.).

élite [ei'li:t], *s.* élite *f*; *Typewr:* **é. type,** caractères *m pl* élite.

elitism [ei'li:tizm], *s.* élitisme *m.*

elitist [ei'li:tist], *a. & s.* élitiste (*mf*).

elixir [i'liksər], *s.* élixir *m*; **the e. of life,** l'élixir de longue vie.

Eliza [i'laizə], *Pr.n.f.* Élise, Élisa.

Elizabeth [i'lizəbəθ], *Pr.n.f.* Élisabeth.

Elizabethan [ilizə'bi:θ(ə)n]. **1.** *a.* élisabéthain; qui appartient au règne de la reine Élisabeth. **2.** *s.* Élisabéthain, -aine.

elk [elk], *s. Z:* (*a*) **Scandinavian e.,** élan *m*; (*b*) **American e.,** wapiti *m.*

elkhound ['elkhaund], *s.* chien *m* pour la chasse à l'élan.

ell[1] [el], *s. A.Meas:* (*a*) aune *f*; **give him an inch and he'll take an e.,** donnez-lui-en grand comme le doigt et il en prendra long comme le bras; (*b*) aunée *f* (de drap, etc.).

ell[2], *s.* **1.** la lettre l. **2.** *Ind:* **e. (union),** raccord coudé en L. **3.** *N.Am:* aile *f* (d'un bâtiment) à angle droit avec le corps principal.

ellagic [e'lɑ:dʒik], *a. Ch:* ellagique.

ellagitannic [elɑ:dʒi'tænik], *a. Ch:* ellagotannique.

ellagitannin [elɑ:dʒi'tænin], *s. Ch:* acide *m* ellagotannique.

Ellen ['elən], *Pr.n.f.* Hélène.

ellipse [i'lips], *s. Mth:* ellipse *f*; **Cassinian e.,** cassionoïde *f*, ellipse de Cassini.

ellipsis, *pl.* **-ipses** [i'lipsis, -si:z], *s. Gram:* ellipse *f.*

ellipsograph [i'lipsəgræf], *s. Mth:* ellipsographe *m*; compas *m* à ellipse, à ovale.

ellipsoid [i'lipsɔid], *s. Mth:* ellipsoïde *m*; **e. of revolution,** ellipsoïde de rotation, de révolution.

ellipsoidal [ilip'sɔid(ə)l], *a.* ellipsoïdal, -aux; ellipsoïde.

elliptic(al) [i'liptik(ə)l], *a. Gram: Mth:* elliptique, **e. compass,** compas *m*; d'ellipse, compas elliptique; *Civ.E: etc:* **e. arch,** voûte elliptique; *Astr:* **e. galaxy,** galaxic elliptique.

elliptically [i'liptik(ə)li], *adv.* elliptiquement.

ellipticity [ilip'tisiti], *s.* ellipticité *f.*

elm [elm], *s. Bot:* orme *m*; ulmeau *m*, -eaux; **young elm,** ormeau *m*; **common e., English e.,** orme champêtre, à petites feuilles; **cork e., Dutch e.,** orme subéreux, orme liège; **red. slippery e.,** orme rouge orme de cèdre; **dwarf e.,** orme tortillard; **wych e., witch e., Scotch e.,** orme blanc, de(s) montagne(s); **broad-leaved e.,** orme à larges feuilles; ypréau *m*; **yoke e.,** charme *m*; **e. sapling,** ormille *f*; **e. grove,** ormaie *f*; **e. wood,** (bois *m* d')orme; **Dutch e. disease,** thyllose *f* parasitaire de l'orme, maladie *f* des ormes.

Elmo ['elmou], *Pr.n.m.* Elme; *Meteor:* **Saint Elmo's fire,** feu *m* Saint Elme.

elocute ['eləkju:t], *v.i. F:* (*a*) *U.S:* déclamer; réciter (en public); (*b*) parler avec une élégance voulue.

elocution [elə'kju:ʃ(ə)n], *s.* élocution *f*, diction *f.*

elocutionary [elə'kju:ʃənəri], *a.* d'élocution; **e. gifts,** dons *m* de déclamateur, dons de diction; **e. effects,** effets *m* oratoires.

elocutionist [elə'kju:ʃənist], *s.* (*a*) déclamateur, -trice; récitateur, -trice; (*b*) professeur *m* d'élocution, de diction.

elodea [e'loudiə], *s. Bot:* (h)élodée *f.*

Elohim [i'louhim], *Pr.n.m. B:* Élohim.

Elohist [i'louhist], *s.* (*Biblical criticism*) Élohiste *m.*

eloi(g)n [i'lɔin], *v.tr. A: & U.S: Jur:* éloigner.

elongate[1] ['i:lɔŋgeit]. **1.** *v.tr.* allonger, étendre. **2.** *v.i.* (*a*) *Bot: etc:* s'allonger, s'étendre; (*b*) *Astr:* se trouver en digression.

elongate[2], *a. Nat.Hist:* allongé.

elongated ['i:lɔŋgeitid], *a.* prolongé, allongé.

elongation [i:lɔŋ'geiʃ(ə)n], *s.* **1.** *Astr:* élongation *f*, digression *f.* **2.** (*a*) allongement *m*; *Mec.E:* **e. at rupture,** élongation, allongement, de rupture; ovalisation *f*; *Surg:* élongation; (*b*) allonge *f*; prolongement *m* (d'une ligne).

elope [i'loup], *v.i.* (*of daughter, wife*) s'enfuir de la maison paternelle, du domicile conjugal, avec un amant; se laisser enlever, se faire enlever (**with s.o.,** par qn); **they eloped,** ils ont pris la fuite.

elopement [i'loupmənt], *s.* fuite *f* de la maison paternelle, du domicile conjugal; enlèvement (consenti).

eloper [i'loupər], *s.* jeune fille *f* qui s'est fait enlever de chez ses parents; femme *f* qui a quitté le domicile conjugal; **the elopers,** les amoureux en fuite.

Elopidae [i'lɔpidi:], *s.pl. Ich:* élopidés *m*.

elops ['elɔps], *s. Ich:* élops *m*.

eloquence ['eləkwəns], *s.* **1.** éloquence *f*; **contest of e.,** joute *f* oratoire. **2.** *A:* rhétorique *f*; **professor of e.,** professeur *m* de rhétorique.

eloquent ['eləkwənt], *a.* éloquent; **to be an e. speaker,** être éloquent, disert; avoir de l'éloquence; **e. gesture,** geste éloquent, parlant; **to have an e. tongue,** être grand, beau, parleur; **to be naturally e.,** être né orateur; **e. look,** regard *m* qui en dit long; **to wax e. in support of. . .,** déployer toute son éloquence en faveur de. . .; *Lit:* **his whole attitude is e. of a generous nature,** toute son attitude annonce une nature généreuse.

eloquently ['eləkwəntli], *adv.* éloquemment.

elpasolite [el'pæsoulait], *s. Miner:* elpasolite *f*.

elpidite ['elpidait], *s. Miner:* elpidite *f*.

else [els]. **1.** *adv.* autrement; ou bien; **get up, or e. you'll be late,** lève-toi ou tu vas être en retard; **come tomorrow or e. it will be too late,** venez demain, autrement il sera trop tard; **he must be joking or e. he is mad,** il plaisante, ou bien alors il est fou; **do what I tell you or e. . . .!** fais ce que je te dis, sinon . . .! **I could not do anything e. but accept,** il m'a bien fallu accepter, je n'ai pu faire autrement que d'accepter. **2.** *(a) a. or adv. (with indef. or interr. pron. or adv.)* **anyone e., anybody e.,** (i) toute autre personne; tout autre, n'importe qui d'autre; un autre; **anyone e. would have missed that shot,** un autre aurait manqué le but; **he is no more stupid than anyone e.,** il n'est pas plus bête qu'un autre; (ii) *(Interrog.)* **can I speak to anyone e.?** y a-t-il quelqu'un d'autre à qui je puisse parler? **did you see anybody e.?** avez-vous vu encore quelqu'un? **anything e.,** (i) n'importe quoi d'autre; **anything e. will do,** n'importe quoi d'autre fera l'affaire; **say anything e., but not that,** dites tout ce que vous voudrez, mais pas cela; (ii) *(Interrog.)* **have you anything e. to do?** avez-vous autre chose à faire? *Com:* **anything e., madam?** encore quelque chose, madame? et avec cela, madame? **someone e., somebody e.,** quelqu'un d'autre, un autre; **you are taking me for someone e.,** vous me prenez pour quelqu'un d'autre, pour un autre; **he is engaged to someone e.,** il est fiancé par ailleurs, il est fiancé à une autre; **something e.,** quelque chose *m* d'autre; autre chose *m*; **I was thinking of something e.,** je pensais à autre chose; j'avais l'esprit ailleurs; **let's talk of something e.,** parlons d'autre chose; changeons de conversation; **he has something e. to think about,** il a bien autre chose à quoi penser; **no one e., nobody e.,** personne *m* d'autre, aucun autre, nul autre; **if it is not my business it is nobody else's,** si ce n'est pas mon affaire ce n'est celle de personne d'autre; **no one e. could do it but he,** il n'y avait que lui qui pût le faire; il était le seul à pouvoir le faire; **nothing e.,** rien *m* d'autre; **nothing e. will do,** rien d'autre ne fera l'affaire; **nothing e., thank you,** plus rien, merci; **who e.?** qui d'autre? qui encore? **who e. could have done it?** qui d'autre aurait pu l'accomplir? **whose e. can it be?** à qui d'autre, à quel autre, cela peut-il appartenir? **what e.?** quoi encore? quoi de plus? **what e. can I say?** qu'est-ce que je puis dire de plus? **what e. can I do?** que puis-je faire d'autre, de mieux? **are you a Londoner?—what e. should I be?** êtes-vous Londonien?—qu'est-ce que vous voulez que je sois? **everything e.,** tout le reste; **have a chop, sir? everything e. is off,** monsieur prendrait-il une côtelette? tous les autres plats sont épuisés; **everyone e. knows it,** tous les autres le savent; **in a small town everyone knows everyone e.,** dans une petite ville chacun se connaît; **everybody e.,** tous les autres; **little e.,** pas grand-chose *m* d'autre; **little e. remains to be done,** à part cela, il ne reste plus grand-chose à faire; **he is fit for little e.,** il n'est guère propre à autre chose; **he eats bread but little e.,** il ne mange guère que du pain; **much e.,** encore beaucoup; **there isn't much e. to be done,** il ne reste pas beaucoup à faire; *(b) adv.* **where e.?** (i) où encore? (ii) en quel autre lieu? **everywhere e.,** partout ailleurs; **somewhere e.,** autre part; ailleurs; **nowhere e.,** nulle autre part; nulle part ailleurs; en aucun autre lieu; **anywhere e.,** (i) n'importe où (ailleurs); partout ailleurs; (ii) *(Interrog.)* **can I find some anywhere e.?** puis-je en trouver ailleurs? **how e. would you set about it?** de quelle autre manière vous y prendriez-vous?

elsewhere ['els(h)wɛər], *adv.* ailleurs, autre part; **my thoughts were e.,** j'avais l'esprit ailleurs; **we shall refer to this again e.,** nous reviendrons là-dessus plus loin, d'autre part.

elsewhither ['els(h)wiðər], *adv. Lit:* (aller, s'en aller) ailleurs, autre part.

elsholtzia [el'ʃoultsiə], *s. Bot:* elsholtzia *m*.

Elsie ['elsi], *Pr.n.f.* Élise, Élisa.

Elsinore ['elsinɔ:r], *Pr.n. Geog:* Elseneur.

eluant ['eljuənt], *s. Ch:* éluant *m*.

eluate ['eljueit], *s. Ch:* éluat *m*.

elucidate [i'lju:sideit], *v.tr.* élucider, éclaircir, tirer au clair, mettre en lumière (un fait, une question); porter la lumière dans (une question); **to e. a passage,** dégager le sens d'un passage.

elucidation [ilju:si'deiʃ(ə)n], *s.* élucidation *f*, éclaircissement *m* (**of,** de).

elucidative [i'lju:sidətiv], *a.* éclaircissant.

elucidatory [iljusi'deitəri], *a.* éclaircissant.

elude [i'lju:d], *v.tr.* éluder (une question, une promesse); tromper (la loi); esquiver, éviter (un coup, une difficulté); échapper à (la poursuite, la mort); se soustraire à (la justice, ses obligations); **to e. s.o.'s grasp,** échapper aux mains de qn; **to e. the vigilance of one's guardians,** tromper la vigilance de ses gardes.

eluent ['eljuənt], *s. Ch:* éluant *m*.

elusion [i'lju:ʒ(ə)n], *s.* esquivement *m* (d'une question, de la loi); dérobade *f*; **his e. of danger,** sa manière d'échapper au danger.

elusive [i'lju:siv], *a.* insaisissable, intangible; **e. personality,** personnalité fuyante, flottante, qui se dérobe; **e. of sth.,** adroit à échapper à qch.; **e. reply,** réponse évasive, artificieuse.

elusively [i'lju:sivli], *adv.* évasivement.

elusiveness [i'lju:sivnis], *s.* nature *f* insaisissable; caractère évasif.

elusory [i'lju:səri], *a.* **1.** évasif. **2. an e. problem,** un problème qui vous échappe.

elute [i'lju:t], *v.tr. Ch:* éluer.

elution [i'lju:ʃən], *s. Ch:* élution *f*.

elutriate [i'lju:trieit], *v.tr.* séparer (un dépôt, etc.) par la décantation; décanter; *Ch: Metall:* départir (l'or, etc.).

elutriation [ilju:tri'eiʃ(ə)n], *s.* séparation *f* (d'un dépôt, etc.) par la décantation; *Ch: Metall:* départ *m*.

eluvial [i'lu:viəl], *a. Geol:* éluvial.

eluviation [ilu:vi'eiʃ(ə)n], *s. Geol:* éluviation *f*.

eluvium [i'lu:viəm], *s. Geol:* éluvion *f*, éluvium *m*.

elvan ['elvən], *s. Geol:* *(a)* *(also* **elvanite***)* elvan *m*; roches ignées d'intrusion; *(b)* filon *m* d'elvan.

elver ['elvər], *s. Ich:* civelle *f*; piballe *f*.

Elvira [el'vaiərə], *Pr.n.f.* Elvire.

elvish ['elviʃ], *a.* = ELFISH.

elymus ['eliməs], *s. Bot:* élyme *m*.

Elysia [i'liziə], *s. Moll:* élysie *f*, elysia *f*.

Elysian [i'liziən], *a. Myth:* élyséen; **the E. fields,** les Champs *m* Élysées.

Elysiidae [eli'saiidi:], *s.pl. Moll:* élysiidés *m*.

Elysium [i'liziəm], *Pr.n. Myth:* l'Élysée *m*.

elytral ['elitrəl], *a. Ent:* élytral.

elytrocele ['elitrəsi:l], *s. Med:* élytrocèle *f*.

elytron, *pl.* **-tra** ['elitrɔn, -trə], *s.* **1.** *Ent:* élytre *m*. **2.** *Anat:* vagin *m*.

Elzevir ['elziviər], *Pr.n.* Elzévir *m*; *attrib.* **E. edition,** édition elzévirienne; **E. type,** caractères elzéviriens; **the E. family,** les Elzévirs.

Elzevirian [elzi'viəriən], *a.* elzévirien, des Elzévirs.

em [em], *s.* (la lettre) m *m*; *Typ:* **em quadrat,** cadratin *m*.

em- [im], *pref.* em-, en-.

emaciate [i'meiʃieit, -'meisieit], *v.tr.* amaigrir; faire maigrir; émacier, dessécher (le corps); appauvrir (le sol); **body emaciated by illness,** corps desséché par la maladie, que la maladie a rendu squelettique.

emaciated [i'meiʃieitid, -'meis-], *a.* émacié, amaigri, décharné, hâve, étique; **to become e.,** s'atténuer, s'atrophier.

emaciation [imeisi'eiʃ(ə)n, -meiʃ-], *s.* amaigrissement *m*, émaciation *f*, dessèchement *m* (du corps); atrophie *f*; *Med:* tabescence *f*.

emanate ['eməneit], *v.i.* émaner, découler, tirer sa source, partir (**from,** de); **letters emanating from the Holy See,** lettres émanant, émanées, du Saint-Siège.

emanation [emə'neiʃ(ə)n], *s.* émanation (lumineuse, divine, du radium, etc.); effluve *m*.

emanationist [emə'neiʃənist], **emanatist** [emə'neitist], *s. Phil:* émaniste *mf*.

emancipate [i'mænsipeit], *v.tr.* émanciper (un mineur, une épouse, les femmes, etc.); affranchir (un esclave); *Eng.Hist:* réhabiliter (les catholiques).

emancipated [i'mænsipeitid], *a.* (mineur, etc.) émancipé; (esclave) affranchi.

emancipation [imænsi'peiʃ(ə)n], *s.* émancipation *f* (d'un mineur); affranchissement *m*, émancipation (d'un esclave, etc.); *Eng.Hist:* **the Catholic E.,** la réhabilitation des catholiques; *U.S:* **E. day,** le premier janvier 1863 (date de la loi qui affranchit les noirs des États du Sud).

emancipationist [imænsi'peiʃənist], *s.* *(a)* partisan *m* de l'affranchissement des esclaves; antiesclavagiste *mf*; *U.S.Hist:* abolitionniste *mf*; *(b) Eng.Hist:* partisan *m* de la réhabilitation des catholiques.

emancipator [i'mænsipeitər], *s.* émancipateur, -trice; affranchisseur *m*.

emancipatory [i'mænsipət(ə)ri], *a.* émancipateur, -trice; affranchissant.

emancipist [i'mænsipist], *s. A: Austr:* déporté(e) libéré(e); forçat libéré.

emanometer [emə'nɔmitər], *s.* émanomètre *m*.

emanometry [emə'nɔmitri], *s.* émanométrie *f*.

emanon ['emənɔn], *s. Ch:* émanon *m*.

emarginate [i'mɑ:dʒinit], **emarginated** [i'mɑ:dʒineitid], *a. Bot:* émarginé.

emargination [imɑ:dʒi'neiʃ(ə)n], *s. Nat.Hist:* émargination *f*.

emarginula [i:mɑ:'dʒinjulə], *s. Moll:* émarginule *f*.

emasculate[1] [i'mæskjuleit], *a.* = EMASCULATED.

emasculate[2], *v.tr.* émasculer; (i) châtrer (un animal); (ii) efféminer, énerver (son style, etc.); **to e. a literary work,** émasculer, châtrer, expurger, une œuvre littéraire.

emasculated [i'mæskjuleitid], *a.* émasculé, châtré; (style) énervé.

emasculating [i'mæskjuleitiŋ], *a.* efféminant, abâtardissant.

emasculation [imæskju'leiʃ(ə)n], *s.* émasculation *f* (d'un mâle, d'une œuvre littéraire, etc.); castration *f* (d'un animal).

emasculator [i'mæskjuleitər], *s. Vet:* émasculateur *m*.

Emballonuridae [embælə'nju:ridi:], *s.pl. Z:* emballonuridés *m*.

embalm [im'bɑ:m], *v.tr.* **1.** embaumer (un cadavre); *Lit:* conserver (la mémoire de qn, etc.). **2.** embaumer, parfumer (l'air, etc.).

embalmer [im'bɑ:mər], *s.* embaumeur *m*.

embalming [im'bɑ:miŋ], **embalmment** [im'bɑ:mmənt], *s.* embaumement *m*.

embank [im'bæŋk], *v.tr.* encaisser, endiguer (un fleuve); remblayer, taluter (une route); terrasser (un jardin).

embanked [im'bæŋkt], *a. (of road, etc.)* encaissé en remblai; *(of river)* endigué; **e. garden,** jardin *m* en terrasse.

embanking [im'bæŋkiŋ], *s.* endiguement *m* (d'un fleuve); remblayage *m*, remblai *m* (d'une route, etc.); terrassement *m*.

embankment [im'bæŋkmənt], *s.* **1.** = EMBANKING. **2.** *(a)* digue *f*; levée *f* de terre; *(b)* (terrassement *m* en) remblai *m*; talus *m*; remblai, banquette *f* (d'une route); **base of e.,** pied *m* du talus; **top of e.,** crête *f*, sommet *m*, du remblai, du talus; **road in e.,** route *f* en remblai; **river e.,** berge *f*, quai *m*, d'un fleuve.

embargo[1], *pl.* **-oes** [im'bɑ:gou, -ouz], *s.* embargo *m*, séquestre *m*; *Nau:* saisie *f*; **to lay an e. on a ship,** mettre l'embargo, l'arrêt, sur un navire; saisir un navire; **to take off an e. on a ship,** lever l'embargo, l'arrêt, sur un navire; *(of ship, goods)* **to be under an e.,** être séquestré; **to put an e. on the import of horses,** mettre un embargo sur, défendre, l'importation des chevaux.

embargo[2], *v.tr.* **1.** mettre l'embargo sur, séquestrer (un navire, des marchandises). **2.** réquisitionner (un navire, etc.).

embark [im'bɑ:k]. **1.** *v.tr.* *(a)* embarquer (des troupes, etc.); *(b) (of ship)* prendre à bord (des troupes, des marchandises, etc.). **2.** *v.i.* s'embarquer (à bord d'un navire, *Fig:* dans une mauvaise affaire); **to e. (up)on a dissertation about sth.,** s'embarquer dans, commencer, une dissertation sur qch.; **to e. on a course of action,** entreprendre une action.

embarkation [embɑ:'keiʃ(ə)n], *s. Nau:* embarquement *m*; **e. officer,** officier chargé de l'embarquement; **e. card,** carte d'accès à bord.

embarrass [im'bærəs], *v.tr.* embarrasser, gêner (qn, les mouvements de qn); déconcerter (qn); **to e. s.o. with indiscreet questions,** gêner qn par des questions indiscrètes; **embarrassed by his clothes, he was swimming with difficulty,** empêtré dans ses vêtements il avait grande peine à nager.

embarrassed [im'bærəst], *a.* embarrassé; dans l'embarras; gêné; **to feel (greatly) e.,** se sentir (extrêmement) gêné; éprouver une grande confusion; *Jur:* **e. estate,** propriété grevée d'hypothèques; *O:* **to be in e. circumstances,** avoir des embarras d'argent; être gêné.

embarrassing [im'bærəsiŋ], *a.* embarrassant; **to be in an e. situation,** se trouver dans une situation embarrassante.

embarrassingly [im'bærəsiŋli], *adv.* d'une manière embarrassante.

embarrassment [im'bærəsmənt], *s.* embarras *m*; gêne *f*; **blushing with e.,** rouge de confusion; **there was some e.**

on her side, elle se sentait gênée; **to be in a state of financial e.,** avoir des embarras d'argent.

embassy ['embəsi], *s.* **1.** ambassade *f* ((i) la fonction, (ii) l'hôtel de l'ambassadeur, (iii) l'ambassadeur et sa suite, et son personnel); **a ball at the French E.,** un bal à l'ambassade de France. **2. special e.,** mission spéciale.

embattle [im'bætl], *v.tr.* **1.** *Lit:* ranger (une armée) en bataille. **2.** *A:* fortifier (un château). **3.** garnir (des murailles) de remparts et de créneaux.

embattled [im'bætld], *a. Arch: Her:* crénelé; *Her:* bastillé.

embay [im'bei], *v.tr. Nau:* encaper; **to be embayed,** être encapé; être affalé sur la côte; **to get embayed on a leeshore,** s'affaler à la côte.

embayment [im'beimənt], *s.* **1.** baie *f.* **2.** enfoncement *m*; partie *f* en retrait (d'une côte).

embed [im'bed], *v.tr.* **(embedded)** enfoncer, noyer, enfouir (un clou dans un mur); poser (un câble dans le sable); encastrer, enchâsser, sceller (un châssis dans un mur); *Arch:* **embedded column,** colonne adossée, engagée; **embedded in concrete,** noyé dans le béton; enrobé de béton; **stone embedded in mortar, cement,** pierre perdue; *Cmptr:* **embedded blank,** espace *m* intercalaire.

embedding [im'bediŋ], *s.* enfoncement *m,* encastrement *m,* noyage *m.*

embedment [im'bedmənt], *s.* **1.** = EMBEDDING. **2.** (*the material*) encastrement *m* (mortier, terre, etc.); lit *m* (de matériau).

embellish [im'beliʃ], *v.tr.* embellir, orner, agrémenter (qch.); enjoliver (une robe, un récit); **to e. one's style,** orner, enjoliver, colorier, son style; **to e. the story,** enjoliver l'histoire, *F:* aider à la lettre.

embellisher [im'beliʃər], *s.* embellisseur, -euse; enjoliveur, -euse.

embellishment [im'beliʃmənt], *s.* embellissement *m,* ornement *m,* agrément *m*; enjolivure *f* (de robe, etc.); fioritures *fpl* (de style); *Jur:* **embellishments,** améliorations voluptuaires (apportées à un immeuble); **expenses for e.,** dépenses *f* voluptuaires.

ember[1] ['embər], *s.* (*usu. pl.*) braise *f*; charbons (ardents); cendres ardentes; **flying embers,** braisille *f*; *Lit:* **the embers of a dying passion,** les cendres d'une passion mourante.

Ember[2], *attrib. Ecc:* **E. days,** les Quatre-Temps *m*; **E. week,** semaine *f* des Quatre-Temps; **E. eve,** vigile *f* des Quatre-Temps; **to observe the E. fast,** jeûner les Quatre-Temps.

ember[3], *attrib. Orn:* **e. goose,** plongeon glacial, imbrim *m.*

embezzle [im'bezl]. (*a*) *v.tr.* détourner, distraire, s'approprier (des fonds); **to e. a large sum,** commettre un important détournement; (*b*) *v.i.* commettre des détournements.

embezzlement [im'bezəlm(ə)nt], *s.* détournement *m* (de fonds); appropriation *f* de fonds (par un salarié).

embezzler [im'bezlər], *s.* détourneur *m* de fonds; auteur *m* d'un détournement; déprédateur, -trice.

embia ['embiə], *s. Ent:* embie *m.*

Embiidae [em'baiidi:], *s.pl. Ent:* embiidés *m.*

Embioptera [embi'ɔptərə], *s.pl. Ent:* embioptères *m.*

embitter [im'bitər], *v.tr.* **1.** rendre (un liquide) amer. **2.** remplir d'amertume, enfieller (qn, le cœur); aigrir (le caractère); empoisonner (les plaisirs); envenimer, aggraver (une querelle, etc.); **to e. s.o. against s.o.,** exacerber, irriter, qn contre qn; **to e. s.o.'s life,** rendre la vie amère à qn; empoisonner la vie de qn; **he is getting more embittered every day,** il s'aigrit de jour en jour.

embittered [im'bitəd], *a.* aigri (**by,** par); (cœur) ulcéré.

embittering[1] [im'bit(ə)riŋ], *a.* qui vous remplit d'amertume, de rancune.

embittering[2], *s.* aigrissement *m* (de qn); envenimement *m,* aggravation *f* (d'une querelle).

embitterment [im'bitəmənt], *s.* **1.** = EMBITTERING[2]. **2.** amertume *f.*

emblazon [im'bleiz(ə)n], *v.tr.* **1.** blasonner; décorer d'armoiries; **emblazoned with the arms of the town,** peint aux armes de la ville. **2.** *Lit:* exalter, porter aux nues, célébrer (la gloire, etc., de qn).

emblazoned [im'bleizənd], *a.* blasonné.

emblazoner [im'bleizənər], *s.* armoriste *m*; peintre *m* d'armoiries.

emblazonry [im'bleizənri], *s.* **1.** blason *m*; science *f* héraldique. **2.** blason, armoiries *fpl.*

emblem[1] ['embləm], *s.* **1.** emblème *m,* symbole *m*; **the crown and sceptre are emblems of royalty,** la couronne et le sceptre sont des emblèmes, des attributs, de la royauté. **2.** (*a*) *Her:* emblème, devise *f*; (*b*) **sporting e.,** insigne sportif; *Aut:* **radiator e.,** écusson *m* de radiateur.

emblem[2], *v.tr. A: & Lit:* **to e. (forth),** symboliser; représenter d'une manière emblématique; être l'emblème de (une vertu, etc.).

emblematic(al) [emblə'mætik(l)], *a.* emblématique, figuratif; **the lion is e. of strength,** le lion est l'emblème de la force, symbolise la force.

emblematically [emblə'mætik(ə)li], *adv.* d'une manière emblématique, symboliquement.

emblements ['emblimənts], *s.pl. Jur:* fruits *m* de la terre; fruits civils, naturels; récoltes *f* sur pied.

embodied [im'bɔdid], *a.* **1.** incarné; **e. spirit,** esprit incarné. **2.** concrétisé; **e. art,** l'art mis en pratique. **3. e. troops,** troupes organisées; **e. army,** armée appelée en service.

embodiment [im'bɔdimənt], *s.* incorporation *f*; incarnation *f*; personnification *f*; **he is the e. of wisdom and kindness,** il est la sagesse et la bonté mêmes, la sagesse et la bonté incarnées; **the very e. of irresponsible gaiety,** l'incarnation même de l'insoucieuse gaieté.

embody [im'bɔdi], *v.tr.* **(embodied; embodying) 1.** incarner; revêtir (un esprit) d'un corps; unir (l'âme) au corps. **2.** réaliser (une conception); mettre en application (un principe); personnifier (une qualité). **3.** incorporer (un article dans une loi); renfermer, rédiger (ses principes dans un traité); **article that embodies the following regulations,** article *m* qui contient, renferme, les dispositions suivantes. **4.** réunir, rassembler, organiser (des troupes). **5.** donner du corps à (une couleur).

embog [im'bɔg], *v.tr.* **(embogged)** embourber (dans un marais); **embogged in a mass of calculations,** embourbé, empêtré, dans un tas de calculs.

embolden [im'bouldən], *v.tr.* enhardir (**s.o. to do sth.,** qn à faire qch.).

embolectomy [embə'lektəmi], *s. Surg:* embolectomie *f.*

embolic [em'bɔlik], *a. Med:* embolique.

embolism ['embəlizm], *s.* **1.** *Chr:* embolisme *m*; intercalation *f.* **2.** *Med:* embolie *f*; embolisation *f*; obstruction *f* (d'un vaisseau sanguin); **air e.,** embolie gazeuse.

embolismic [embə'lizmik], *a. Chr:* (mois *m,* etc.) embolismique, intercalaire.

embolite ['embəlait], *s. Miner:* embolite *f.*

embolus ['embələs], *s. Med:* embole *m,* embolus *m.*

embonpoint [ɑ̃bɔ̃'pwɛ̃], *s.* embonpoint *m,* rondeurs *fpl.*

emboss [im'bɔs], *v.tr.* graver en relief; relever en bosse; travailler en relief, en bosse; bosseler (le métal); repousser, estamper (le métal, le cuir); ciseler, frapper, gaufrer (le cuir); filigraner (le papier); gaufrer, brocher (un tissu); frapper (le velours, un papier tenture).

embossed [im'bɔst], *a.* (métal) gravé en relief, travaillé en bosse; bosselé; (métal, cuir) estampé, repoussé; (cuir, papier) gaufré; tissu, gaufré, broché; (velours) frappé; **e. ornament,** bosselure *f,* bosse *f*; **e. work,** travail *m* en relief, en repoussé, en bosse; gaufrage *m*; (*on document*) **e. stamp,** timbre fixe, timbre sec, à empreinte.

embosser [im'bɔsər], *s.* **1.** graveur *m* en relief. **2.** (*a*) repousseur *m* (de métaux, de cuir, etc.); (*b*) (*stamp-press operator*) estampeur *m,* gaufreur *m* (de métaux, de cuir, etc.).

embossing [im'bɔsiŋ], *s.* **1.** bosselage *m* (du métal); estampage *m,* repoussage *m* (du métal, du cuir); gaufrage *m,* frappage *m* (du cuir); frappage (du velours); brochage *m* (des étoffes); *Phot:* gaufrage (d'un film en couleurs); **e. iron,** ébauchoir *m,* talon *m* en fer; **e. punch,** repoussoir *m*; **e. loom,** brocheuse *f*; *Paperm:* **e. calender,** calandre gaufreuse, graineuse; laminoir *m* pour faux filigranage; **e. press,** (i) presse *f* à gaufrer, à imprimer en relief; (ii) (*handpress*) timbre sec. **2.** relief *m,* repoussé *m,* bosselure *f.*

embossment [im'bɔsmənt], *s.* relief *m*; *Paperm:* filigrane ombré.

embouchure [ɑ̃bu'ʃy:r], *s.* embouchure *f* ((i) d'un fleuve; (ii) d'un instrument à vent).

embowel [im'bauəl], *v.tr. A:* éventrer; éviscérer.

embower [im'bauər], *v.tr. Lit:* abriter (dans un berceau de verdure, etc.).

embrace[1] [im'breis], *s.* (*a*) étreinte *f,* embrassement *m*; **iron e.,** étreinte de fer; (*b*) étreinte amoureuse.

embrace[2], *v.tr.* **1.** embrasser, étreindre; accoler (qn); donner une accolade à (qn); *v.i.* **they embraced,** ils s'embrassèrent; **to e. the cross,** embrasser la croix. **2.** embrasser (une carrière, la foi, une religion, une occasion); adopter (une cause, une doctrine); **to e. s.o.'s cause,** se ranger sous les drapeaux de qn. **3.** (*include*) embrasser (**in,** dans); contenir, renfermer (**in,** dans); comporter, comprendre, englober (des sujets); **estate that embraces several villages,** domaine *m* qui englobe plusieurs villages. **4. to e. a situation,** envisager une situation sous tous ses aspects; **the view from the terrace embraces the whole valley,** de la terrasse, la vue s'étend sur toute la vallée, embrasse toute la vallée.

embrace[3], *v.tr. Jur:* suborner (un juré).

embracement [im'breismənt], *s.* **1.** embrassement *m,* embrassade *f,* étreinte *f.* **2.** adoption *f,* acceptation *f* (d'une opinion, etc.).

embracer [im'breisər], *s. Jur:* suborneur, -euse.

embracery [im'breisəri], *s. Jur:* subornation *f* (d'un juré).

embracing [im'breisiŋ], *a.* qui embrasse, qui renferme; **e. gesture,** geste ample, compréhensif; **all-e.,** qui embrasse tout; **all-e. knowledge,** vaste érudition *f.*

embranchment [im'brɑ:n(t)ʃmənt], *s.* embranchement *m*; bifurcation *f.*

embrangle [im'bræŋgl], *v.tr.* embrouiller, empêtrer (**in,** dans).

embranglement [im'bræŋglmənt], *s.* embrouillement *m,* confusion *f.*

embrasure [im'breiʒər], *s.* **1.** *Arch:* embrasure *f,* ébrasement *m.* **2.** *Artil:* embrasure, sabord *m.*

embrasured [im'breiʒəd], *a.* **1.** *Arch:* ébrasé, à embrasure. **2.** muni d'embrasures.

embrittlement [em'britlmənt], *s. Metalw:* fragilité *f*; fragilisation *f.*

embrocate ['embroukeit], *v.tr. Med:* appliquer une embrocation sur (un membre).

embrocation [embrə'keiʃ(ə)n], *s. Med:* embrocation *f.*

embroider [im'brɔidər], *v.tr.* **1.** *Needlew:* (*a*) broder; (*b*) *v.i.* faire de la broderie. **2.** broder, amplifier, enjoliver (un récit); **to e. the story,** broder l'histoire; broder sur le canevas.

embroiderer [im'brɔidərər], *s.* brodeur, -euse.

embroideress [im'brɔidəres], *s.f.* brodeuse.

embroidering [im'brɔid(ə)riŋ], *s.* **1.** (*a*) = EMBROIDERY; (*b*) **e. machine,** machine *f* à broder; métier *m* à broder; brodeuse *f.* **2.** enjolivement *m* (d'un récit).

embroidery [im'brɔidəri], *s.* **1.** *Needlew:* broderie *f*; **tulle e.,** broderie sur tulle; **raised e.,** broderie à plumetis; **e. scissors,** ciseaux *m* à broder; **e. frame,** métier *m* à broder; tambour *m* à broder. **2.** broderie, enjolivure *f* (d'un récit).

embroil [im'brɔil], *v.tr.* **1.** (*a*) brouiller, embrouiller (une affaire); **to e. matters,** brouiller les cartes; (*b*) brouiller (qn avec qn); **embroiled in a quarrel,** entraîné dans une querelle; **motorist embroiled with the law,** automobiliste aux prises avec la loi.

embroilment [im'brɔilmənt], *s.* **1.** brouillement *m,* embrouillement *m* (d'une affaire); **fearing new embroilments,** dans la crainte de nouvelles complications. **2.** brouille (entre deux personnes).

embryo, *pl.* **-os** ['embriou, -ouz], *s. Biol:* embryon *m*; **e. sac,** sac *m* embryonnaire; **in e.,** à l'état embryonnaire; **artist in e.,** artiste en puissance, en herbe; **plans still in e.,** projets *m* embryonnaires, encore en germe, en gestation.

embryocardia ['embriou'kɑ:diə], *s. Med:* embryocardie *f*; rythme fœtal.

embryogenesis ['embriou'dʒenisis], *s. Biol:* embryogénie *f,* embryogénèse *f.*

embryogenetic ['embrioudʒə'netik], **embryogenic** ['embriou'dʒenik], embryogénique.

embryogeny [embri'ɔdʒəni], *s.* = EMBRYOGENESIS.

embryography [embri'ɔgrəfi], *s.* embryographie *f.*

embryoid ['embriɔid], *a.* embryoïde.

embryologic(al) [embriə'lɔdʒik(əl)], *a.* embryologique.

embryologist [embri'ɔlədʒist], *s.* embryologiste *mf,* embryologue *mf.*

embryology [embri'ɔlədʒi], *s.* embryologie *f.*

embryoma [embri'oumə], *s. Med:* embryome *m.*

embryonary ['embriənəri], *a. Biol:* embryonnaire.

embryonic [embri'ɔnik], *a.* **1.** *Biol:* embryonnaire. **2.** en germe.

embryopathy [embri'ɔpəθi], *s. Med:* embryopathie *f.*

embryotega [embriou'ti:gə], *s. Bot:* embryotège *m.*

embryotome ['embrioutoum], *s. Obst:* (*instrument*) embryotome *m.*

embryotomy [embri'ɔtəmi], *s. Obst:* embryotomie *f.*

embryotrophic ['embriou'trɔfik], *a.* embryotrophique.

embryotrophy [embri'ɔtrəfi], *s.* embryotrophe *m.*

embus [im'bʌs], *O: & U.S:* **1.** *v.tr.* embarquer (des troupes) en autobus. **2.** *v.i.* s'embarquer dans un autobus.

emcee[1] ['em'si:], *s. NAm: F:* **1.** maître *m* de cérémonies. **2.** *W.Tel:* animateur, -trice.

emcee[2]. *NAm: F:* **1.** *v.i.* (*a*) être maître de cérémonies; (*b*) *W.Tel:* être animateur, -trice (d'un programme). **2.** *v.tr.* *W.Tel:* animer (un programme, etc.).

emend [i'mend], **emendate** ['i:mendeit], *v.tr.* corriger (un texte); apporter des émendations à (un texte).

emendation [i:men'deiʃ(ə)n], *s.* **1.** émendation *f,* correction *f* (d'un texte). **2.** variante proposée.

emendator ['i:mendeitər], *s.* correcteur, -trice.

emerald ['em(ə)rəld], *s.* **1.** émeraude *f*; **Brazilian e.,** émeraude du Brésil; **e. mine,** mine *f* d'émeraudes. **2.** *Typ:* caractère *m* de corps 6½ (entre la nonpareille et la mignonne). **3.** *a. & s.* **e. (green),** vert *m* d'émeraude; *a.* (*of stone*) smaragdin; **e. copper,** dioptase *f*; **the E. Isle,** l'île *f* d'Émeraude; la verte Erin, la verte Irlande.

emerge [i'mə:dʒ], *v.i.* **1.** émerger (**from,** de); surgir, s'élever (de l'eau, etc.); **to e. again,** revenir sur l'eau. **2.** déboucher (**from,** de); apparaître à l'orée (d'un bois); sortir (d'un trou, de la foule, de l'enfance, de l'obscurité); **the troops emerged from the pass,** les troupes *f* débouchèrent du défilé; **the moon is emerging from behind the clouds,** la lune se dégage des nuages. **3.** (*a*) (*of difficulty, etc.*) se dresser; surgir; (*b*) **from these facts it emerges that. . .,** de ces faits il apparaît, il ressort, que . . .; **two essential points emerged from, at, the discussion,** la discussion a permis de dégager deux points essentiels.

emergence [i'mə:dʒəns], *s.* émergence *f* (d'un rayon lumineux, d'une théorie, etc.); émersion *f*, exondation *f* (d'un rocher, etc.); apparition *f* (d'un nouvel état, d'un nouveau leader); *Tg:* **point of e. (of sea cable),** atterrissage *m* (d'un câble sous-marin).

emergency [i'mə:dʒənsi], *s.* circonstance *f* critique; nécessité urgente, pressante; cas urgent, cas pressant, cas imprévu, cas de nécessité; **to be ready for every e.,** être prêt à toute éventualité; **to provide for emergencies,** parer aux éventualités, à l'imprévu; **to deal with an e.,** (i) s'occuper d'urgence d'une question; (ii) parer à un cas urgent; **to meet an e.,** faire face à une situation critique; **to meet the e.,** tenir le coup; **to rise to the e.,** être, se montrer, à la hauteur de la situation, des circonstances; **in this e.,** dans ces circonstances; en cette conjoncture; en cette occurrence; dans ce cas imprévu; dans cette situation critique; **in case of e.,** au besoin; en cas d'imprévu; en cas de nécessité; en cas d'urgence; en cas d'événement; **e. repairs,** réparations *f* d'urgence, de fortune; **e. brake,** frein *m* de secours; **e. tank,** réservoir *m* auxiliaire, de secours; **e. exit,** issue *f*, sortie *f*, de secours; *Cin: etc:* **e. light, lighting,** éclairage *m* de sécurité; *El:* **e. switch,** interrupteur *m* d'urgence, de secours; **e. stock, snack, supply, etc.,** en-cas *m inv*; **e. vehicle,** voiture *f* de secours; **e. fund,** masse *f* de secours; **e. tax,** impôt *m* de crise; impôt extraordinaire; **e. department,** service *m* de secours, *A:* **e. man,** (i) *Sp:* remplaçant; (ii) (*in Ireland*) huissier *m*; agent *m* de poursuites; *Ind:* **e. hands,** ouvriers *m* supplémentaires (en cas d'urgence); extras *m*; **e. ration,** vivres *m* de réserve; **e. seat,** strapontin *m*; *Mil: etc:* **e. bridge,** (i) pont *m* de circonstance, de fortune; (ii) pont de secours; **e. leave, e. furlough, e. pass,** permission exceptionnelle; **state of e.,** état *m* d'urgence; **e. regulations,** mesures *f* d'exception; **e. government,** gouvernement *m* d'exception (après un coup d'état); **national e.,** catastrophe, calamité, nationale, péril national; *Med:* **an e.,** une urgence; **e. ward,** salle d'urgence; **e. operation (for appendicitis, etc.),** opération *f* à chaud (pour l'appendicite, etc.).

emergent [i'mə:dʒənt], *a. Geol: Opt: etc:* émergent; *Pol:* **e. nations,** nations émergentes.

emeritus [i'meritəs], *a.* (professeur *m*) honoraire, émérite.

emersion [i'mə:ʃ(ə)n], *s.* **1.** émersion *f*. **2.** *Astr:* émersion (après éclipse).

Emersonian [emə'souniən]. **1.** *a.* à la manière d'Emerson. **2.** *s.* admirateur, -trice, d'Emerson.

emery ['eməri], *s.* émeri *m*; **e. paper,** papier émerisé; papier d'émeri; *Toil:* **e. board,** lime *f* émeri, papier émerisé (pour manucure); lime de carton; *Ind:* **e. cloth,** toile *f* (d')émeri; **e. dust, powder, flour e.,** potée *f* d'émeri; poudre *f*, fleur *f* d'émeri; **e. grinder,** tour *m* à meuler; **e. machine,** polisseuse *f*; **e. stick,** rodoir *m* à l'émeri; **e. stopper,** bouchon *m* à l'émeri; **e. wheel,** meule *f* (en) émeri.

emesa [i'mi:sə], *s. Ent:* émèse *f*.

emetic [i'metik], *a. & s. Med:* émétique (*m*); *Pharm:* **tartar e.,** tartre stibié; tartrate *m* de potasse et d'antimoine; émétique *m* tartrique; **e. bowl,** haricot *m*.

emetin(e) ['emitin, -tain], *s. Ch:* émétine *f*.

emeto-cathartic ['emitoukə'θɑ:tik], *a. & s.* vomi-purgatif (*m*), *pl.* vomi-purgatifs.

emeu ['i:mju:], *s.* = EMU.

emiction [i'mikʃ(ə)n], *s. Med:* miction *f*.

emictory [i'miktəri], *a. Med:* diurétique.

emigrant ['emigrənt], *a. & s.* (*a*) émigrant, -ante; **e. ship,** navire *m* d'émigrants; (*b*) *Fr.Hist:* émigré, -ée.

emigrate ['emigreit]. **1.** *v.i.* (*a*) émigrer; (*b*) *U.S:* aller s'établir dans un autre État de l'Union. **2.** *v.tr.* faire émigrer (une population, etc.); assister l'émigration (d'une population).

emigrating ['emigreitiŋ], *a.* émigrant.

emigration [emi'greiʃ(ə)n], *s.* émigration *f*.

émigré ['emigrei], *s.* émigré, -ée.

Emilia. 1. [i'miliə] *Pr.n.f.* Émilie. **2.** [e'mi:liə, i'miliə], *Pr.n. Geog:* Émilie *f*.

Emilian [i'mi:liən], *Geog:* (*a*) *a.* émilien; (*b*) *s.* Émilien, -ienne.

Emily ['emili], *Pr.n.f.* Émilie.

eminence ['eminəns], *s.* **1.** (*a*) éminence *f*, élévation *f* (de terrain); monticule *m*; hauteur *f*; (*b*) *Anat:* éminence, saillie *f*. **2.** éminence, élévation (de caractère, etc.); grandeur *f*, distinction *f* (d'une charge); position éminente; **to rise to e.,** parvenir à une haute position, à un haut rang, à la célébrité; *F:* devenir un personnage; **the next Pope, the only Englishman to attain that e., was . . .,** le pape suivant, le seul Anglais à parvenir à cette haute dignité, fut . . .. **3.** *Ecc:* (*as title of cardinal*) Éminence; **your E. will kindly allow me to . . .,** votre Éminence voudra bien me permettre de . . ..

eminent ['eminənt], *a.* éminent; **e. doctor,** docteur célèbre, éminent; (*as title*) **Most E.,** (cardinal *m*) éminentissime; *Jur:* (*International law and U.S:*) **(right of) e. domain,** domaine éminent.

eminently ['eminəntli], *adv.* éminemment; par excellence; au suprême degré; **an e. respectable family,** une famille des plus honorables; **e. worthy of. . .,** digne au premier chef de . . ..

emir [e'miər], *s.* émir *m*.

emirate ['emireit], *s.* émirat *m*.

emissary ['emisəri]. **1.** *s.* émissaire *m*; messager, -ère. **2.** *a. Anat:* **e. vein,** émissaire. **3.** *s. Rom.Ant:* canal *m* de vidange; émissaire.

emission [i'miʃ(ə)n], *s.* **1.** émission *f*, dégagement *m* (de gaz, de chaleur, etc.); lancement *m* (de la vapeur); débordement *m* (d'étincelles); *Physiol:* éjaculation *f*; *Ph:* **the E. theory,** la théorie de l'émission; *Rad:* **e. spectrum,** spectre *m* d'émission; **e. current,** courant d'émission; **e. efficiency,** efficacité *f* (d'une cathode thermo-électronique). **2.** *Bank: etc:* **e. of bank notes, etc.,** émission de billets de banque, etc.

emissivity [imi'siviti], *s. Ph:* (*a*) pouvoir émissif, rayonnant (d'une source de lumière, etc.); (*b*) coefficient *m* d'émission.

emit [i'mit], *v.tr.* **1.** dégager (de la chaleur, de la fumée, etc.); exhaler, dégager, répandre (une odeur); lancer (de la vapeur); lancer, jeter (des étincelles); laisser échapper (un cri); rendre (un son). **2.** (*a*) émettre (du papier-monnaie); (*b*) émettre (une opinion); rendre (un avis).

emitter [i'mitər], *s.* **1.** (*pers.*) émetteur *m* (de papier-monnaie, etc.). **2.** *W.Tel:* **dull e. valve,** lampe *f* micro, de faible consommation, à filament obscur. **3.** *Atom.Ph:* émetteur; **alpha e.,** émetteur alpha.

emma[1] ['emə], *s. A: Tg:* la lettre e; *F:* **ack e.,** (i) *Mil: Tp:* (= **a.m.**) du matin; (ii) (= **air mechanic**) mécanicien *m* d'avion; *F:* **pip e.,** (= **p.m.**), (six heures, etc.) du soir.

Emma[2], *Pr.n.f.* Emma, Émilie.

Emmanuel [i'mænjuəl], *Pr.n.m.* Emmanuel.

Emmaus [i'meiəs], *Pr.n. A.Geog:* Emmaüs *m*.

emmenagogue [i'mi:nəgɔg], *s. Med:* emménagogue *m*.

emmensite ['emənsait], *s. Exp:* emmensite *f*.

emmet ['emit], *s. A: & Dial:* fourmi *f*.

emmetrope ['emitroup], *s.* emmétrope *mf*.

emmetropia [emi'troupiə], *s. Opt:* emmétropie *f*.

emmetropic [emi'trɔpik], *a.* emmétrope.

emodin ['emədin], *s. Ch:* émodine *f*.

emollient [i'mɔliənt], *a. & s. Med:* émollient (*m*), adoucissant (*m*).

emolument [i'mɔljumənt], *s.* (*usu. pl.*) émoluments *mpl*, appointements *mpl*, traitement *m*; **emoluments of a Member of Parliament,** indemnité *f* parlementaire.

emotion [i'mouʃ(ə)n], *s.* émotion *f*; émoi *m*; trouble *m*, attendrissement *m*; **to appeal to the emotions,** faire appel aux sentiments; **without showing the least e.,** sans montrer le moindre signe d'émotion; *F:* sans sourciller, sans broncher; **eyes brimming with e.,** yeux attendris; **voice touched with e.,** voix émue; **sudden e.,** soubresaut *m*; **to recall sth. with e.,** se souvenir de qch. avec attendrissement; **to look at s.o. with e.,** contempler qn d'un air ému; **to make a cheap display of e.,** faire de la sensiblerie.

emotional [i'mouʃən(ə)l], *a.* **1.** émotif; *Med:* **e. disturbances,** troubles émotifs; **for e. reasons,** pour des raisons émotives. **2.** (*liable to emotion*) émotif, émotionnable; **to be e.,** s'attendrir facilement; être facile à émouvoir; être émotionnel.

emotionalism [i'mouʃənəlizm], *s.* **1.** sensiblerie *f*; émotivité *f*. **2.** appel *m* aux émotions.

emotionalist [i'mouʃənəlist], *s.* **1.** personne *f* émotionnable. **2.** personne qui agit sur les émotions, sur la sensibilité (de la foule, etc.).

emotionality [imouʃə'næliti], *s.* émotivité *f*.

emotionally [i'mouʃən(ə)li], *adv.* **1.** avec beaucoup d'émotion; avec exaltation. **2. they are e. involved,** ils sont unis par des liens affectifs; **I cannot remain impartial because I am e. involved,** je ne peux rester impartial parce que cela me concerne de trop près, me touche trop.

emotionless [i'mouʃənlis], *a.* qui n'est pas susceptible d'émotion; indifférent; impassible.

emotionlessness [i'mouʃənlisnis], *s.* caractère *m* peu émotionnable; impassibilité *f*.

emotive [i'moutiv], *a.* émotif.

emotiveness [i'moutivnis], **emotivity** [imou'tiviti], *s.* émotivité *f*.

empale [im'peil], *v.tr.* empaler.

empanel [im'pæn(ə)l], *v.tr.* **(empanelled)** *Jur:* **to e. a jury,** former, dresser, la liste du jury; constituer le jury; former un tableau; **to e. a juror,** inscrire un juré sur la liste du jury.

empathy ['empəθi], *s. Psy:* empathie *f*.

Empedocles [im'pedəkli:z], *Pr.n.m. Gr.Ant:* Empédocle.

empennage [im'penidʒ], *s. Av:* empennage *m*.

emperor ['empərər], *s.* **1.** empereur *m*; **the E. Charles,** l'empereur Charles. **2.** (*a*) *Ent:* **purple e.,** grand mars; **e. moth,** saturnie *f*; *F:* paon *m* de nuit; (*b*) *Ich:* **e. (fish),** holacanthe *m* empereur; (*c*) *Orn:* **e. (penguin),** pingouin impérial; (*d*) *Rept:* **e. boa,** empereur.

Empetraceae [impe'treisii:], *s.pl. Bot:* empétracées *f*.

empetrum ['empitrəm], *s. Bot:* empêtre *m*.

emphasis ['emfəsis], *s.* **1.** force *f*; (énergie *f* d')accentuation *f*; **oratorical e.,** accent *m* oratoire. **2. to ask with e.,** demander avec insistance; **to lay e. on a fact, on a word,** appuyer, insister, sur un fait; souligner, faire ressortir, un fait, un mot. **3.** (*a*) *Gram:* mise *f* en relief; (*b*) *Ling:* accent *m* d'insistance (sur un mot ou une syllabe).

emphasize ['emfəsaiz], *v.tr.* accentuer, appuyer sur, souligner, mettre en valeur, faire valoir (un mot, un fait); attirer l'attention sur (un fait); faire ressortir, mettre en relief (une qualité, une situation, etc.); faire sortir (un trait de caractère, un rôle); *Mus:* marquer (la mélodie); *Mus:* **each entry well emphasized,** chaque attaque assez en dehors.

emphatic [im'fætik], *a.* **1.** (*a*) (manière *f*) énergique (de s'exprimer); (dénégation) absolue, énergique; (ton *m*) autoritaire; (orateur) vigoureux; (refus) positif, net, absolu; **e. gesture,** geste *m* énergique; **e. action,** acte significatif; (*b*) **e. syllable,** syllabe accentuée. **2.** (style *m*, mot *m*, etc.) emphatique.

emphatically [im'fætik(ə)li], *adv.* **1.** énergiquement, positivement; **to refuse e.,** refuser carrément, catégoriquement; refuser net. **2.** en termes pressants. **3.** (*intensive*) **he is most e. a leader,** c'est un chef s'il en fut jamais.

emphysema [emfi'si:mə], *s. Med:* emphysème *m*.

emphysematous [emfi'si:mətəs], *a.* emphysémateux.

Empididae [em'paididi:], *s.pl. Ent:* empididés *m*.

empire ['empaiər], *s.* empire *m*; (*a*) *A:* **to establish one's e. over sth.,** établir son empire sur qch.; (*b*) *Hist:* **the Roman E.,** l'Empire romain; **the Lower, the Later, E.,** le Bas Empire; **the (Holy Roman) E.,** le Saint Empire Romain Germanique; **the E.,** (i) l'Empire britannique; (ii) *Fr.Hist:* le Premier Empire; **the Second E.,** le second Empire (1852–70); **the Indian E.,** l'Empire des Indes; **the Middle E.,** l'Empire du milieu, l'Empire de la Chine; **e. builder,** constructeur *m* d'empires; **the paper is part of the Martin empire,** ce journal fait partie de l'Empire Martin; *attrib. A:* **E. day,** fête nationale de l'Empire britannique (célébrée le 24 mai); **E. furniture,** meubles *m* Empire; *U.S:* **the E. City, the E. State,** la ville, l'État, de New York.

empiric [em'pirik]. **1.** *a.* empirique. **2.** *s.* (*a*) empirique *m*, empiriste *m*; (*b*) *Pej:* charlatan *m*.

empirical [em'pirikl], *a.* empirique; **e. formula,** formule *f* empirique.

empirically [em'pirik(ə)li], *adv.* empiriquement.

empiricism [em'pirisizm], *s.* empirisme *m*.

empiricist [em'pirisist], *s.* empiriste *m*.

empiriocriticism [empiriou'kritisizm], *s. Phil:* empiriocriticisme *m*.

emplace [im'pleis], *v.tr. Artil:* mettre (un canon) en place.

emplacement [im'pleismənt], *s. Mil:* emplacement *m* (d'un canon).

emplane [im'plein]. **1.** *v.i.* monter en avion. **2.** *v.tr.* faire monter (qn, des troupes) en avion.

emplastic [im'plæstik], *a.* emplastique.

emplectite [im'plektait], *s. Miner:* emplectite *f*.

employ[1] [im'plɔi], *s. A:* emploi *m*; **out of e.,** sans emploi; **to be in s.o.'s e.,** être au service de qn; être employé par qn.

employ[2], *v.tr.* **1.** employer (des moyens, son temps, etc.); se servir de, faire usage de (la force, etc.); **to e. a method again,** reprendre un procédé; **to e. one's time in sth., in doing sth.,** employer son temps à qch., à faire qch. **2.** employer (qn) à son service; **to e. twenty workmen,** employer, occuper, vingt ouvriers; **to e. a man to look after the garden,** employer un homme pour entretenir le jardin; **to e. s.o. as secretary,** employer qn comme secrétaire. **3. to e. oneself (in doing sth.),** s'occuper (à faire qch.); **to be employed in doing sth.,** être occupé à faire qch.; **to keep s.o. well employed,** donner de quoi faire à qn.

employability [implɔiə'biliti], *s. Pol.Ec:* qualification *f* pour un emploi.

employable [im'plɔiəbl], *a.* employable.

employed [im'plɔid], (*a*) *a.* employé; **gainfully e.,** rémunéré; **the gainfully e. population,** la population active; (*b*) **employers and e.,** le patronat et le salariat.

employee [im'plɔii:, -plɔi'i:], *occ.* **employé, -ée** [ɑ̃'plwaje], *s.* employé, -ée; **the employees of Messrs Martin & Co.,** le personnel de la maison Martin; **relations between management and employees,** relations *f* entre la direction et le personnel.

employer [im'plɔiər], *s.* **1.** *Ind:* patron, patronne; maître, maîtresse; **the big employers of labour,** les grands employeurs de main-d'œuvre; **body of employers,** patronat *m*; **organization of employers, employers' association,** organisation patronale, syndicat patronal; **chamber of employers,** chambre patronale; **employers' liability insurance,** assurance *f* des patrons contre les accidents du travail; assurance réparation *f*. **2.** *Jur:* (*a*) employeur; (*b*) **e. and his agent,** commettant *m* et son représentant.

employment [im'plɔimənt], *s.* **1.** (*use*) emploi *m* (de l'argent, etc.); *Ind:* **e. of children,** admission *f* des enfants au travail. **2.** (*occupation*) emploi, travail *m*; place *f*, situation *f*; occupation *f*; **to be without e.,** être sans emploi, sans travail; chômer; **to find e. for s.o.,** placer, caser, qn; **to find alternative e. for an employee,** récupérer un employé; **to give s.o. e.,** donner un emploi à qn; **e. agency,** bureau *m*, agence *f*, office *m*, de placement; (*for workmen*) service *m* d'embauche; **security of e., guaranteed e.,** sécurité *f* de l'emploi.

empodium [im'poudiəm], *s. Ent:* empodium *m*.

empoison [im'pɔiz(ə)n], *v.tr. Lit:* empoisonner (les sentiments, *A:* la viande, etc.); **to e. s.o., s.o.'s mind, against s.o.,** enfieller qn, le cœur de qn, contre qn; monter la tête à qn contre qn.

emporium [im'pɔ:riəm], *s.* **1.** entrepôt *m*; centre *m* de commerce; marché *m*. **2.** grand magasin.

empower [im'pauər], *v.tr.* **1.** *Jur:* donner pouvoir, donner procuration, à (qn). **2. to e. s.o. to do sth.,** autoriser qn à faire qch.; permettre à qn de faire qch.; donner, conférer, plein(s) pouvoir(s) à qn pour faire qch.; **to be empowered to . . .,** recevoir, avoir, pleins pouvoirs pour . . ..

empress ['empres], *s.f.* impératrice.

emprise [em'praiz], *s. A:* & *Poet:* entreprise (courageuse); prouesse *f*; **knights of bold e.,** preux chevaliers.

emprosthotonos [emprɔs'θɔtənəs], *s. Med:* emprosthotonos *m*, emprosthotonie *f*.

emptiness ['em(p)tinis], *s.* **1.** vide *m* (d'une chambre, etc.); *F:* **to feel an e.,** se sentir l'estomac creux; **e. of mind,** nullité *f* d'esprit. **2.** néant *m*, vanité *f* (des plaisirs, etc.).

emption ['empʃ(ə)n], *s. Jur:* achat *m*; **right of e.,** droit *m* d'emption, droit d'achat.

empty[1] ['em(p)ti]. **1.** *a.* vide (**of,** de); (*a*) **e. street,** rue déserte; **e. purse,** bourse vide; *F:* bourse plate; **e. bottle,** bouteille *f* vide; **bottle partly e.,** bouteille en vidange; **e. waggon,** wagon *m* vide, sans chargement; **weight when e.,** poids *m* à vide; **to come back e.,** (*of lorry, etc.*) revenir à vide; (*of ship*) revenir sur lest; **building standing e.,** immeuble inoccupé; **e. stomach,** estomac creux; **to be taken on an e. stomach,** à prendre à jeun; **to feel e.,** se sentir l'estomac creux; avoir l'estomac dans les talons; *P:* n'avoir rien au fond de la caisse; *Cmptr:* **e. medium,** support vide; (*b*) *B:* **the rich he hath sent e. away,** il a renvoyé les riches les mains vides; (*c*) **e. head, mind,** tête *f* vide; esprit creux, nul; (*d*) **e. words,** vaines paroles; **e. threats,** menaces en l'air, vaines menaces; **an e. shadow,** une ombre vaine; **to pay s.o. in e. words,** payer qn de mots; *F:* payer qn en monnaie de singe; donner à qn de l'eau bénite de cour; (*e*) **word e. of meaning,** mot vide de sens; mot privé, dépouillé, dénué, de sens. **2.** *s.pl. Com:* **empties,** caisses *f* vides; bouteilles *f* vides; **returned empties,** emballages retournés vides; retournés *m* vides; **empties are not taken back,** on ne reprend pas les bouteilles, les caisses.

empty[2]. **1.** *v.tr.* vider (un verre, un tiroir, etc.) (**into,** dans); décharger, *Min:* verser (un wagon); dépeupler (les rues); débourrer (une pipe); assécher (un étang); épuiser (un puits); évacuer l'eau (d'une chaudière); vidanger (une fosse d'aisance, un carter); décombler (un fossé); **to e. a building,** faire écouler la foule; **they have emptied my shop,** ils ont dévalisé mon magasin. **2.** *v.i.* (*a*) (*of river, etc.*) se décharger, se déverser, se jeter, se vider, déboucher, tomber (**into,** dans); (*b*) (*of theatre*) se dégarnir, se vider.

empty handed ['em(p)ti'hændid], *a.* les mains vides; **to return e.-h.,** *F:* revenir bredouille.

empty-headed ['em(p)ti'hedid], *a.* sans cervelle; **to be e.-h.,** avoir la tête vide, avoir une tête de linotte.

emptying ['em(p)tiiŋ], *s.* **1.** vidage *m* (d'un verre, d'un tiroir, etc.); vidange *f* (d'un tonneau, etc.); déchargement *m*, *Min:* versage *m* (d'un wagon); asséchement *m* (d'un étang); épuisement *m* (d'un puits); décomblement *m* (d'un fossé); dépeuplement *m* (des rues); *Ind:* **gravity e. device,** dispositif *m* de vidange par gravité. **2.** *pl.* **emptyings,** fonds *m* (de verres, etc.).

empurple [im'pə:pl], *v.tr.* empourprer.

empusa [em'pju:zə], *s. Ent:* empuse *f*, empusa *f*.

empyema [empi'i:mə], *s. Med:* empyème *m*, pyothorax *m*.

empyreal [empai'riəl], *a.* empyrée; empyréal, -aux.

empyrean [empai'riən], *a.* & *s.* empyrée (*m*).

empyreuma [empi'ru:mə], *s.* empyreume *m*.

empyreumatic(al) [empiru:'mætik(l)], *a.* empyreumatique; **e. oil,** huile pyrogénée.

emu ['i:mju:], *s. Orn:* émeu *m*.

emulant ['emjulənt], *s.* = EMULATOR.

emulate ['emjuleit], *v.tr.* être l'émule de, marcher après (qn); marcher de pair avec (qn); rivaliser avec, imiter (qn, qch.); **he has emulated your courage,** il a été votre émule en courage.

emulation [emju'leiʃ(ə)n], *s.* émulation *f*; **in e. of each other,** à l'envi l'un de l'autre; à qui mieux mieux.

emulative ['emjulətiv], *a.* **1.** plein d'émulation. **2. e. of s.o., of sth.,** qui imite qn, qch.; qui rivalise avec qn.

emulator ['emjuleitər], *s.* **1.** émule *mf* (**of,** de). **2.** *Cmptr:* émulateur *m*.

emulgent [i'mʌldʒənt], *a. Physiol:* (vaisseau, etc.) émulgent.

emulous ['emjuləs], *a.* émulateur, -trice (**of,** de); **e. of honours,** ambitieux d'honneurs; **e. admirers,** émules *m*; **they worked with e. zeal,** ils travaillaient à qui mieux mieux.

emulously ['emjuləsli], *adv.* avec émulation; à l'envi; à qui mieux mieux.

emulsi(fia)bility [imʌlsi(faiə)'biliti], *s.* émulsibilité *f*.

emulsification [imʌlsifi'keiʃ(ə)n], *s. Med:* émulsionnement *m*.

emulsifier [i'mʌlsifaiər], *s.* émulsificateur *m*. **1.** (*substance*) émulsifiant *m*. **2.** (*device*) émulseur *m*, émulsionneur *m*.

emulsify [i'mʌlsifai], *v.tr.* emulsionner.

emulsifying [i'mʌlsifaiiŋ], *a.* émulsifiant.

emulsin [i'mʌlsin], *s. Ch:* émulsine *f*.

emulsion [i'mʌlʃ(ə)n], *s.* émulsion *f*; *Pharm:* looch *m*; *Phot:* **plate e.,** émulsion pour plaques.

emulsionize [i'mʌlʃənaiz], *v.tr.* émulsionner.

emulsive [i'mʌlsiv], *a.* émulsif.

emulsoid [i'mʌlsɔid], *s. Ch:* émulsoïde *m*.

emunctory [i'mʌŋktəri], *a.* & *s. Physiol:* émonctoire (*m*).

emyd ['emid], **emys** ['emis], *pl.* **emydes** ['emidi:z], *s. Rept:* émyde *f*; tortue *f* palustre.

Emydidae [e'midídi:], *s.pl. Rept:* émydidés *mpl*.

en [en], *s.* la lettre *n*; *Typ:* **en quadrat,** demi-cadrat *m*, demi-cadratin *m*.

en- [in], (*before b, m, p*) **em-** [im], *v.pref.* en-, em-.

enable [in'eibl], *v.tr.* **to e. s.o. to do sth.,** (i) rendre qn capable, mettre qn à même, mettre qn en état, permettre à qn, de faire qch.; (ii) *Jur:* habiliter qn à faire qch.; donner pouvoir à qn de faire qch.; **to be enabled to do sth.,** être, se trouver, à même de faire qch.; **this legacy enabled him to retire,** cet héritage lui permit, le mit à même, de prendre sa retraite; **this settlement enabled the work to be resumed,** cet arrangement permit de reprendre les travaux, rendit possible la reprise des travaux.

enabling [in'eibliŋ], *a. Jur:* habilitant; **e. act,** loi *f* qui habilite une personne juridique; *Cmptr:* **e. signal,** signal *m* de validation.

enact [in'ækt], *v.tr.* **1.** *Jur:* rendre, décréter (une loi); ordonner, arrêter, décréter (une mesure); **as by law enacted,** aux termes de la loi; **be it further enacted that . . .,** il est en outre ordonné, décrété, que. . . . **2.** *Lit:* jouer, représenter (une tragédie); remplir (un rôle); procéder à, accomplir (une cérémonie).

enacting [in'æktiŋ], *a. Jur:* **e. clauses of an act,** dispositif *m*, dispositions *fpl*, d'une loi.

enaction [in'ækʃ(ə)n], *s.* **1.** établissement *m*, promulgation *f* (d'une loi). **2.** loi, ordonnance *f*; décret (général, réglementaire); acte législatif; **by legislative e.,** par un texte législatif.

enactive [in'æktiv], *a.* = ENACTING.

enactment [in'æktmənt], *s.* = ENACTION.

enactor [in'æktər], *s.* **1.** auteur *m*, promoteur *m* (d'une loi). **2.** *A:* acteur *m* (d'une tragédie, etc.); interprète *mf* (d'un rôle).

enallage [i'næləd͡ʒi], *s. Gram:* énallage *f*.

enamel [i'næm(ə)l], *s.* **1.** émail *m*, *pl.* émaux; (*a*) *Art:* **champlevé e.,** émail champlevé; **niello enamels,** émaux de niellure; **cloisonné e.,** émail cloisonné; **e. work,** (i) émaillure *f*, émaillerie *f*; (ii) peinture *f* sur émail; **e. ware,** ustensiles *mpl* en fer émaillé; (*b*) *Anat:* **the e. of the teeth,** l'émail des dents; *Dent:* **e. prism, e. rod,** prisme *m* (de l'émail). **2.** (*a*) vernis *m*, émail, *pl.* émails; laque *f*; **enamels for leather,** vernis pour cuir; **black e. for iron,** vernis pour fer; **e. paint,** peinture *f* au vernis; **e. painting,** peinture en émail; **e. painter,** peintre en émail; *U.S:* **nail e.,** vernis *m* à ongles; (*b*) **baked (on) e.,** émail au four; **to finish a bicycle in baked e.,** émailler une bicyclette à chaud, au four; **cellulose e.,** émail cellulosique, à la cellulose; *Ind:* **glazed e.,** émail vitrifié. **3.** *Paperm: Com:* **bright enamels,** papiers glacés, brossés, émaillés.

enamel[2], *v.tr.* (**enamelled**). **1.** émailler (la porcelaine, etc.). **2.** ripoliner (une porte, etc.); vernir, vernisser (le fer, le cuir); glacer (le papier); *Phot:* émailler, satiner (une épreuve); *Cer:* vernisser (des briques, etc.).

enamelist [i'næməlist], *s.* émailleur, -euse.

enamelled [i'næməld], *a.* **1.** émaillé, d'émail, en émail; **e. saucepan,** casserole *f* en fer émaillé; **e. tile,** carreau verníssé; **e. brick,** brique émaillée; **stove e.,** émaillé au four. **2.** peint en émail; (cuir) verni, glacé; **white-e. furniture,** meubles laqués (de) blanc; **e. paper,** papier glacé; **e. iron,** tôle émaillée.

enameller [i'næmələr], *s.* **1.** (*pers.*) émailleur, -euse. **2.** *Phot:* presse *f* à satiner.

enamelling [i'næməliŋ], *s.* **1.** (*a*) émaillage *m*; (*b*) (*art of enamelling*) émaillure *f*, émaillerie *f*; (*c*) peinture *f* en émail; vernissage *m* (du fer, du cuir, etc.); glaçage *m* (du papier, etc.); **lacquer e.,** émaillage-vernissage *m*. **2.** = ENAMEL[1].

enamour [i'næmər], *v.tr. Lit:* enamourer (qn); rendre (qn) amoureux.

enamoured [i'næməd], *a. Lit:* amoureux (**of,** de); **to be e. of, with, s.o.,** être amoureux, épris, de qn; **to be e. of, with, sth.,** être passionné pour qch., être féru de qch.; avoir la passion de qch.; **to become e. of s.o.,** s'éprendre de qn.

enanthem [e'nænθəm], **enanthema,** *pl.* **-mata** [e'nænθəmə, -'mɑ:tə], *s. Med:* énanthème *m*.

enanthic [e'nænθik], *a. Bio Ch:* œnanthique.

enantiomorph [e'næntioumɔ:f], *s. Ch:* énantiomorphe *m*.

enantiomorphic [enæntiou'mɔ:fik], *a. Ch:* énantiomorphe.

enantiomorphism [enæntiou'mɔ:fizm], *s. Ch:* énantiomorphisme *m*, énantiomorphie *f*.

enantiomorphous [enæntiou'mɔ:fəs], *a. Min: Ch:* énantiomorphe.

enantiosis [enænti'ousis], *s. Phil:* énantiose *f*.

enantiotropic [enæntiou'trɔpik], *a. Ch:* énantiotrope.

enarch, enarchist ['enɑ:k, e'nɑ:kist], *s.* énarque *m*.

enargite ['enɑ:dʒait], *s. Miner:* énargite *f*.

enarme [en'ɑ:m], *s. A.Arm:* énarme *f*.

enarthrodial [enɑ:'θroudiəl], *a. Anat:* énarthrodial.

enarthrosis [enɑ:'θrousis], *s. Anat:* énarthrose *f*.

en bloc ['ɑ̃(n)'blɔk], *adv.* en bloc; *Com:* **to make one's orders en b.,** bloquer une commande.

encaenia [en'si:niə], *s.* **1.** *Ecc.Hist:* encénie *f*. **2.** *Sch:* (*at Oxford*) commémoration *f* des fondateurs.

encage [in'keidʒ], *v.tr.* encager; mettre (un animal) en cage.

encamp [in'kæmp]. **1.** *v.tr.* (faire) camper (une armée). **2.** *v.i.* camper.

encampment [in'kæmpmənt], *s.* campement *m*; camp *m*.

encapsulate [in'kæpsjuleit], *v.tr.* capsuler.

encapsulation [inkæpsju'leiʃ(ə)n], *s.* capsulage *m*.

encarpus [en'kɑ:pəs], *s. Arch:* encarpe *m*.

encase [in'keis], *v.tr.* **1.** encaisser, enfermer (**in,** dans); mettre (un objet) dans un étui. **2.** (*a*) munir (qch.) d'une enveloppe; blinder (une partie de machine, etc.); (*b*) revêtir, recouvrir (**s.o. in sth.,** qn de qch.).

encased [in'keist], *a. Mec.E:* habillé.

encasement [in'keismənt], *s.* **1.** revêtement *m*; enveloppe *f*. **2.** *Anat:* emboîtement *m* (de deux os).

encash [in'kæʃ], *v.tr.* **1.** encaisser (un chèque, de la monnaie); **when encashed,** après encaissement. **2.** toucher (un chèque, une somme).

encashable [in'kæʃəbl], *a.* encaissable.

encashment [in'kæʃmənt], *s.* **1.** encaissement *m*. **2.** recette *f*, rentrée *f*.

encasing [in'keisiŋ], *s.* **1.** mise *f* en caisse, en boîte, en étui. **2.** recouvrement *m*; blindage *m*.

encastage [in'kæstidʒ], *s. Cer:* encastage *m*.

encaustic [en'kɔ:stik]. **1.** *a.* (*a*) *Art:* (tableau *m*, etc.) à l'encaustique; (peinture *f*) encaustique; (*b*) *Cer:* **e. tile,** carreau *m* céramique. **2.** *s. Art:* encaustique *f*.

enceinte[1] [ɑ̃'sɛ̃:t], *a.f. Obst:* enceinte.

enceinte[2], *s. Fort:* enceinte *f*.

Enceladus [en'selədəs], *Pr.n.m. Gr.Myth:* Encelade.

encephalalgia [ensefæ'lældʒiə], *s. Med:* encéphalalgie *f*.

encephalic [ense'fælik], *a. Anat:* encéphalique.

encephalitic [ensefə'litik], *a.* encéphalitique.

encephalitis [ensefə'laitis], *s. Med:* encéphalite *f*, cérébrite *f*; **e. lethargica,** encéphalite épidémique, léthargique.

encephaloc(o)ele [en'sefəlousi:l], *s. Med:* encéphalocèle *f.*

encephalogram [en'sefələgræm], *s. Med:* (électro)encéphalogramme *m.*

encephalography [ensefə'lɔgrəfi], *s. Med:* (électro)encéphalographie *f.*

encephaloid [en'sefəlɔid], *a. Med:* encéphaloïde.

encephalolith [ense'fælouliθ], *s. Med:* encéphalolithe *m.*

encephalomalacia [en'sefəloumə'leisiə], *s. Med:* encéphalomalacie *f*; ramollissement cérébral, du cerveau.

encephalomyelitis [en'sefəloumaiə'laitis], *s. Med:* encéphalomyélite *f.*

encephalon, *pl.* **-a** [en'sefəlɔn, -ə], *s. Anat:* encéphale *m.*

encephalopathic [en'sefəlou'pæθik], *a. Med:* encéphalopathique.

encephalopathy [ensefə'lɔpəθi], *s.* encéphalopathie *f.*

encephalospinal [en'sefəlou'spainl], *a. Med:* cérébro-spinal, -aux.

enchain [in'tʃein], *v.tr. Lit:* enchaîner (une bête, les passions).

enchainment [in'tʃeinmənt], *s. Lit:* enchaînement *m* (d'une bête, des passions).

enchant [in'tʃɑ:nt], *v.tr.* **1.** enchanter, ensorceler. **2.** enchanter, charmer, ravir.

enchanted [in'tʃɑ:ntid], *a.* **1.** enchanté, ensorcelé. **2.** enchanté, charmé **(with,** de).

enchanter [in'tʃɑ:ntər], *s.* **1.** enchanteur *m.* **2.** *Bot:* **enchanter's nightshade,** circée *f*; sorcier *m*; herbe *f* à la magicienne.

enchanting [in'tʃɑ:ntiŋ], *a.* enchanteur, -eresse; ravissant, charmant.

enchantingly [in'tʃɑ:ntiŋli], *adv.* à ravir; d'une manière ravissante.

enchantment [in'tʃɑ:ntmənt], *s.* enchantement *m.* **1.** ensorcellement *m.* **2.** ravissement *m*; *Lit:* **distance lends e. to the view,** tout paraît beau (vu) de loin.

enchantress [in'tʃɑ:ntris], *s.f.* enchanteresse.

encharm [in'tʃɑ:m], *v.tr. A: & Lit:* mettre (qn) sous un charme; ensorceler.

enchase [in'tʃeis], *v.tr.* **1.** *(a)* enchâsser, sertir (une pierre) **(in,** dans); *(b)* **ring enchased with diamonds,** bague sertie de diamants. **2.** *(a)* ciseler, graver (une bague, etc.); *(b)* incruster (une bague, etc.) **(with,** de).

enchondroma, *pl.* **-mata** [enkɔn'droumə, -mətə], *s. Med:* enchondrome *m.*

enchylema [eŋki'li:mə], *s. Biol:* enchyléma *m*; suc *m* nucléaire.

Enchytraeidae [eŋki'tri:idi:], *s.pl. Ann:* enchytréidés *m.*

Enchytraeus [eŋki'tri:əs], *s. Ann:* enchytrée *m*, enchytraeus *m.*

encipher [in'saifər], *v.tr. Lit:* **1.** chiffrer (une dépêche). **2. to e. a letter with another,** combiner une lettre avec une autre (pour former un monogramme).

encircle [in'sə:kl], *v.tr.* ceindre, encercler; envelopper, cerner (une armée); entourer (une armée, la taille); *Art:* **to e. the faces (in a picture),** bordoyer les figures; *Lit:* **to e. one's head with . . .,** se ceindre la tête de . . .; **the equator encircles the earth,** l'équateur embrasse la terre; **a reputation which encircles the world,** une réputation qui a fait le tour du monde.

encirclement [in'sə:kəlmənt], *s.* encerclement *m.*

encircling [in'sə:kliŋ], *s.* encerclement *m*; *Mil: Navy:* **e. movement,** manœuvre *f* de débordement, d'enveloppement.

enclasp [in'klɑ:sp], *v.tr. Lit:* embrasser, étreindre.

enclave[1] ['enkleiv], *s.* **1.** enclave *f.* **2.** pièce *f* de terre en hache. **3.** *Biol: Bot: etc:* enclave.

enclave[2], *v.tr.* enclaver.

enclavement [en'kleivmənt], *s.* enclavement *m*, enclavure *f.*

enclisis, *pl.* **-es** ['eŋklisis, -i:z], *s. Ling:* enclise *f.*

enclitic [en'klitik], *(a) a. & s. Gram:* enclitique *(f)*; *(b) a. Obst:* se présentant obliquement.

enclose [in'klouz], *v.tr.* **1.** *(a)* enclore, clôturer, clore, enceindre (un champ) **(with,** de); entourer, enserrer, investir (l'ennemi, une ville); **the skull encloses the brain,** le crâne renferme le cerveau; **garden enclosed with, in, by, high walls,** jardin entouré de hauts murs; *(b)* blinder (un moteur électrique, etc.); enfermer (un mécanisme) dans un carter. **2.** *Ecc:* cloîtrer (une femme). **3.** inclure, renfermer, enfermer **(in,** dans); **to e. sth. in a letter,** joindre qch. à une lettre; **letter enclosing a cheque,** lettre contenant un chèque; **enclosed herewith,** sous ce pli; **enclosed please find . . .,** veuillez trouver ci-inclus, ci-joint, sous ce pli . . .

enclosed [in'klouzd], *a.* **1.** *(a) (of field, etc.)* clos, enclos, clôturé, enceint; *(of army)* entouré, cerné, enserré; *(of city)* investi; **e. space,** (i) espace clos; (ii) enceinte *f*; **e. ground (under cultivation),** clos *m*; *Geog:* **e. meander,** méandre encaissé; *(b) Ecc:* **e. monk,** moine cloîtré; cloîtrier *m*; **e. nun,** nonne cloîtrée; moniale *f.* **2.** recouvert, enfermé; en boîtier; en carter; *El:* **e. arc,** arc enfermé; **e. fuse,** fusible emboîté, renfermé; fusible sous couvercle; *Mec.E:* **e. gear,** engrenage blindé, recouvert d'une gaine protectrice; engrenage enfermé dans un carter; **e. dynamo,** dynamo blindée, cuirassée; *I.C.E: etc:* **e. condenser,** condensateur *m* à enveloppe étanche.

enclosing[1] [in'klouziŋ], *a.* *(a)* (mur *m*, etc.) de clôture; *(b)* qui renferme, qui recouvre; *Geol:* **e. matrix,** gangue enrobante, encaissante; *(c) Pros:* **e. rhymes,** rimes embrassées.

enclosing[2], *s.* *(a)* renfermement *m*; clôture *f* (d'un champ); entourage *m*, enserrage *m*, investissement *m* (de l'ennemi, d'une ville); *(b)* inclusion *f* (de qch. dans une lettre).

enclosure [in'klouʒər], *s.* **1.** *(a)* clôture *f*; *Ecc:* clôture, claustration *f* (de religieuses); **e. wall,** mur *m* de pourtour (d'une propriété, etc.); *Hist: Agr: Adm:* **e. system,** enclôture *f*; *(b)* enceinte *f*, clôture; **green enclosures,** haies vives. **2.** *(a)* enclos *m*, clos *m*, enceinte; *(b) Turf:* le pesage; **the public enclosures,** la pelouse; **the royal e.,** l'enceinte réservée pour la famille royale. **3.** *(a) Com:* pièce annexée, incluse; annexe *f*; le document ci-joint; **enclosures,** pièces jointes; *(b) Miner:* inclusion *f.*

enclothe [in'klouð], *v.tr. Lit:* revêtir **(with,** de).

encloud [in'klaud], *v.tr. Lit:* voiler, assombrir (l'horizon, le ciel, etc.); envelopper de nuages; **town enclouded in smoke,** ville voilée d'un nuage de fumée.

encode [en'koud], *v.tr.* chiffrer (un texte, une dépêche, etc.); *Cmptr:* coder.

encoder [en'koudər], *s. Cmptr:* **1.** codeur *m.* **2.** enregistreur *m*, encodeur *m*; **shaft position e.,** codeur *m* de position angulaire.

encoffin [in'kɔfin], *v.tr. Lit: A:* mettre (qn) en bière.

encolpion [en'kɔlpiən], **encolpium** [en'kɔlpiəm], *s. Ecc: A:* encolpion *m*, encolpium *m.*

encomiast [en'koumiæst], *s. A: & Lit:* panégyriste *m*, louangeur *m.*

encomium, *pl.* **-ums** [en'koumiəm(z)], *s. Lit:* panégyrique *m*, éloge *m*, louange *f.*

encompass [in'kʌmpəs], *v.tr.* **1.** entourer, environner, ceindre **(with,** de). **2.** envelopper, renfermer **(with, within,** dans). **3.** *A:* méditer, comploter, consommer (la mort, la ruine, de qn).

encore[1] [ɔŋ'kɔ:r], *s. & int.* *(a)* bis *m*; **e. (e.)!** bis! **he had two encores,** on l'a redemandé, bissé, deux fois; *(b)* chanson *f*, morceau, etc., exécuté à la fin d'un spectacle, d'un concert, etc., par un artiste que l'on a bissé; **to call for an e.,** bisser; **to call for a second e.,** trisser.

encore[2], *v.tr.* bisser (un passage, un acteur); *v.i.* crier bis, bisser; **to e. a second time,** trisser.

encounter[1] [in'kauntər], *s.* **1.** rencontre *f* (d'amis, etc.). **2.** *(a)* rencontre (hostile); combat *m*; **e. battle,** bataille *f* de rencontre; *(b)* duel *m*; *(c)* lutte *f*, assaut *m*; **e. of wits,** assaut d'esprit; *(d) Sp: Journ:* confrontation *f.*

encounter[2], *v.tr.* rencontrer (qn, un obstacle); éprouver, essuyer (des difficultés); affronter (l'ennemi); trouver (de la résistance); essuyer (une tempête); **the greatest danger that remains to be encountered,** le plus grand danger auquel il reste à parer.

encourage [in'kʌridʒ], *v.tr.* **1.** encourager, enhardir (qn). **2.** encourager, inciter, animer **(s.o. to do sth.,** qn à faire qch.); **to e. s.o. in well-doing,** encourager qn au bien. **3.** appuyer (une bonne œuvre, *Ven:* les chiens); favoriser (les arts); encourager (une croyance); **to e. production,** favoriser l'essor de la production.

encouragement [in'kʌridʒmənt], *s.* encouragement *m*; **to receive little e. to do sth.,** recevoir peu d'encouragement à faire qch.

encouraging [in'kʌridʒiŋ], *a.* encourageant.

encouragingly [in'kʌridʒiŋli], *adv.* d'une manière encourageante.

encrimson [in'krimzən], *v.tr. Lit:* empourprer (le ciel, etc.).

encrinite ['enkrinait], *s. Geol:* encrinite *f.*

encrinus [en'krainəs], *s. Echin:* encrine *f.*

encroach [in'kroutʃ], *v.i.* **to e. (up)on (sth.),** empiéter sur (une terre, etc.); entamer (son capital); usurper, *Jur:* léser (les droits de qn); anticiper sur (ses revenus, les droits de qn); abuser de (la bonté de qn); **the sea is encroaching on the land,** la mer gagne du terrain; **to e. on s.o.'s time,** abuser du temps de qn.

encroacher [in'kroutʃər], *s.* **every e. on my property,** tous ceux qui empiètent sur ma propriété; **e. on s.o.'s rights,** usurpateur *m* des droits de qn; **an e. on s.o.'s time,** un importun, un intrus.

encroaching [in'kroutʃiŋ], *a.* qui empiète; usurpateur, -trice; **e. sea,** mer *f* qui gagne sur la côte; **e. cattle,** bétail *m* paissant sur les terres d'autrui.

encroachment [in'kroutʃmənt], *s.* **1.** *Jur:* *(a)* **e. upon s.o.'s rights,** usurpation *f* des droits de qn, empiètement *m* sur les droits de qn; *(b)* empiètement (sur la voie publique). **2.** *(a)* **e. of a forest,** accrue *f* d'une forêt; *(b)* ingression *f* (de la mer).

encrust [in'krʌst]. **1.** *v.tr.* *(a)* incruster; **to e. ebony with mother of pearl,** incruster de la nacre dans l'ébène; *(b)* couvrir d'une croûte, encroûter, incruster **(with,** de). **2.** *v.i.* se couvrir d'une croûte; s'encroûter; s'incruster **(with,** de); s'entartrer.

encrusted [in'krʌstid], *a.* encroûté; revêtu d'incrustations; *(of boiler)* incrusté de tartre; entartré.

encrustment [in'krʌstmənt], *s.* croûte *f*, incrustation *f* (de tartre); entartrage *m.*

encumber [in'kʌmbər], *v.tr.* **1.** encombrer **(with,** de); embarrasser, gêner (qn, le mouvement); entraver (le commerce); *Fin:* surcharger (le marché); **to e. s.o. with parcels,** *F:* empêtrer qn de paquets; **to be encumbered with a family,** être chargé, surchargé, de famille. **2. encumbered estate,** propriété (i) grevée de dettes, obérée, (ii) grevée d'hypothèques.

encumbrance [in'kʌmbrəns], *s.* **1.** embarras *m*, charge *f*; **to be an e. to s.o.,** occasionner, causer, de l'embarras à qn; être à charge à qn; **man without (family) encumbrances,** homme *m* sans charges de famille; **free from all encumbrances,** libre de toute charge. **2.** *Jur:* *(a)* charges (d'une succession); **to free an estate from encumbrances,** dégrever une propriété; *(b)* servitude *f.*

encumbrancer [in'kʌmbrənsər], *s. Jur:* (créancier) hypothécaire *m.*

encyclic(al) [in'siklik(l)], *a. & s. R.C.Ch:* encyclique *(f).*

encyclopaedia [insaiklə'pi:diə], *s.* encyclopédie *f*; *F:* **walking e.,** bibliothèque, encyclopédie, ambulante; encyclopédie vivante; vrai bureau de renseignements.

encyclopaedic [insaiklə'pi:dik], *a.* encyclopédique.

encyclopaedism [insaiklə'pi:dizm], *s.* encyclopédisme *m.*

encyclopaedist [insaiklə'pi:dist], *s.* encyclopédiste *mf.*

Encyrtidae [en'sə:tidi:], *s.pl. Ent:* encyrtidés *m.*

encyst [en'sist], *v.tr. & i.* s'enkyster.

encystation [ensis'teiʃ(ə)n], **encystment** [en'sistmənt], *s. Biol:* enkystement *m.*

encysted [en'sistid], *a.* enkysté.

end[1] [end], *s.* **1.** *(a)* bout *m*, extrémité *f* (d'un bâton, d'une rue, etc.); fin *f* (d'un livre); queue *f* (d'une procession, etc.); chef *m* (d'une bande chirurgicale); about *m* (d'une poutre); **the e. of the table,** le bout de la table; *Rail:* **e. of line,** *Can:* **e. of steel,** tête *f* de ligne; **to come to the e. of the road,** (i) arriver au bout de la route; (ii) arriver au bout de sa carrière, de sa vie; (iii) être dans une impasse; *Ecc.Arch:* **east e.,** chevet *m* (d'une église); **west e.,** façade *f* ouest; *Geog:* **the East E. (of London),** les quartiers pauvres et populeux de la partie est de Londres; **the West E.,** les quartiers élégants de la partie ouest de Londres; **suit made by a West-E. tailor,** complet fait par un tailleur londonien renommé; **the office is at the Marble Arch e. of Oxford Street,** le bureau se trouve au bout d'Oxford Street près de Marble Arch; **the e. house of the street,** la dernière maison de la rue; **the e. arch of a bridge,** l'arche *f* de rive d'un pont; *Rail:* **the e. carriage,** le wagon de queue; *Tchn:* **e. piece,** embout *m*; **e. seal, protecting e., sealing e.,** embout obturateur, protecteur; *Carp:* **e. post,** montant *m* extrême; *Mec.E:* **e. thrust,** poussée axiale, longitudinale; **e. play,** jeu longitudinal, axial; jeu de bout, en bout; chasse axiale; **blind, blank, dead, e.,** joint plein; *El:* **e. ring,** anneau *m* de pointe; **the hauling e. of a rope,** le bon bout d'un câble; *F:* **to have the right e. of the stick,** tenir le bon bout; être dans la bonne voie; *F:* **to get hold of the wrong e. of the stick,** prendre quelque chose à contre-sens, saisir le mauvais bout, comprendre de travers; *F:* **to be at the receiving e. (of the stick),** recevoir les coups; *(of rope)* **loose e.,** bout pendant; *F:* **to be at a loose e.,** être désœuvré, se tourner les pouces, avoir du temps à perdre; **to begin, start, at the wrong e.,** écorcher l'anguille par la queue; brider son cheval, l'âne, par la queue; prendre une affaire à contre-poil; *Fb: etc:* **to change ends,** changer de camp; *(of swimming pool)* **the deep, the shallow, e.,** le grand, le petit, fond; *F:* **to be thrown in at the deep e.,** être mis en pleine eau, être tout de suite dans le bain; *F:* **to go off the deep e.,** s'énerver, se mettre en colère, sortir de ses gonds; **to keep one's e. up,** (i) *Cr:* maintenir son guichet intact; (ii) résister (à toutes les attaques); ne pas se laisser démonter; se défendre, tenir bon; (iii) faire sa part, y mettre du sien; **e. to e.,** bout à bout; **to join (two things) e. to e.,** joindre (deux choses) bout à bout; ajoindre, rabouter, raboutir (des planches); raccorder (des tuyaux); **to make both ends meet,** joindre les deux bouts; arriver à boucler son budget; s'en tirer; **from e. to e.,** d'un bout à l'autre; de bout en bout; *(of barrel, etc.)* **on e.,** debout, sur bout; **to stand a box (up) on e.,** dresser une boîte debout; **his hair was standing on e.,** ses cheveux se dressaient sur sa tête, se hérissaient; **five hours on e.,**

(pendant) cinq heures consécutives; cinq heures de suite, à la file, d'affilée; **e. on,** bout à bout; (*of ships*) **to meet e. on,** se rencontrer nez à nez; **two ships e. on to one another,** deux navires à l'encontre l'un de l'autre; **e.-on blow,** coup *m* sur le bout; *Aut: etc:* **e.-on collision,** collision *f* par l'arrière; *F:* **to beat s.o. all ends up,** battre qn à plate(s) couture(s); (*b*) *I.C.E:* **big e., small e.,** tête *f*, pied *m*, de bielle; **rod e.,** embout de bielle; (*c*) *Bootm:* **shoemaker's e.,** ligneul *m*, chégros *m*; fil poissé; (*d*) tronçon *m* (de mât, de lance, etc.); tronche *f* (de câble); bout (de chandelle); bout, *F:* mégot *m* (de cigare, de cigarette); *Carp:* **waste e. (cut off board),** tronçon de rebut, mouchure *f*. **2.** limite *f*, borne *f*; **to the ends of the earth,** jusqu'aux confins *m* de la terre; jusqu'au bout du monde; **to go to the ends of the earth to do sth.,** se mettre en quatre, se donner un mal fou, de faire qch.; *Med:* **e. point of effectiveness (of a vaccine, etc.),** limite d'efficacité (d'un vaccin, etc.). **3.** (*a*) bout, fin (du mois); fin (de travail); issue *f* (d'une réunion); terme *m* (d'un procès, etc.); **the third from the e.,** le troisième avant la fin; **the e. of the adventure,** le dénouement de l'aventure; **we shall never hear the e. of it,** on n'entendra jamais la fin; **I'll pay for it, and that will be the e. of the matter,** je payerai et tout sera dit; **and that's the e. of it!** et voilà tout! tout est dit! **he won't accept, and that's the e. of it!** il n'accepte pas, voilà tout! il n'y a plus rien à dire! **there's an e. to everything,** tout n'a qu'un temps; il y a terme à tout; **be more precise, or we shall never get to the e. of it,** soyez plus précis ou nous n'en sortirons jamais; **there's no e. to it,** c'est toujours à recommencer; cela n'en finit pas; *P:* **no e. of . . .,** infiniment de . . .; infinité de . . .; **it'll do you no e. of good,** ça te fera un bien énorme, énormément de bien; **no e. of money,** un argent fou; **it's no e. of a job,** c'est toute une histoire; **he thinks no e. of himself,** il se gobe, se croit; *F:* **that's (just about) the e.!** ça, c'est le comble! *F:* **he's the e.!** il est au-dessous de tout! **to make an e. of, put an e. to, (sth.),** en finir avec (qch.); achever (qch.); mettre fin à (un abus, etc.); abolir, dissiper (la haine, etc.); éteindre (les dissensions); supprimer (la concurrence); **death put an e. to the conquests of Alexander,** la mort mit un terme aux conquêtes d'Alexandre; **we must put an e. to this!** il faut en finir, en terminer! **to draw to an e.,** tirer, toucher, à sa fin; **to come to an e.,** prendre fin; arriver à son terme; (*of meeting, etc.*) se clore; **the meeting came to an abrupt e.,** la séance a pris fin, s'est terminée, abruptement; **with this speech the meeting came to an e.,** ce discours clôtura la séance; **our sugar is coming to an e.,** on n'a presque plus de sucre; **to be at an e.,** (i) (*of resources*) être épuisé; (ii) (*of time*) être accompli; (iii) (*of action, state*) être terminé, fini, achevé; **the war was at an e.,** la guerre était terminée; **to be at the e. of one's resources,** être au bout de ses ressources; **at the e. of the month, of the year, of (the) winter,** à la fin du mois, de l'année, de l'hiver; **at the e. of this period, of the six months allowed,** à l'expiration de cette période; au bout des six mois; **in the e.,** (i) à la longue, avec le temps; (ii) à la fin; enfin; en fin de compte; **in the e. he became a professor,** il finit par devenir professeur; **e. product,** (i) produit manufacturé, fabriqué; article fini; (ii) suite *f*, résultat *m*; (*b*) **e. of the world,** fin, consommation *f*, du monde; **until the e. of time,** jusqu'à la consommation des temps, des siècles; *Ecc:* **world without e.,** pour les siècles des siècles; **I felt that this was the e. of everything,** je me sentais sombrer; **it's not the e. of the world,** ce n'est pas la fin du monde; (*c*) fin, terme (de la vie); **to make a good e.,** avoir une belle mort; **to come to a bad e.,** mal finir; **to come to an untimely e.,** mourir avant l'âge; **to meet one's e.,** trouver la mort; rencontrer son destin; *F:* **he'll be the e. of me,** il me fera mourir. **4.** (*aim, purpose*) fin, but *m*, dessein *m*; **private ends,** intérêt(s) personnel(s); **to gain, attain, achieve, one's e.,** en arriver, en venir, parvenir, à ses fins; remplir son objet; atteindre son but; **to serve an e.,** répondre à des visées, à des vues; **what is the e. in view?** à quoi vise tout cela? **for, to, this e., with this e. in view,** dans ce dessein, cette intention, ce but; à cette fin, à cet effet; avec cet objectif en vue; *Prov:* **the e. justifies the means,** la fin justifie les moyens.

end². **1.** (*a*) *v.tr.* finir, terminer, achever (un ouvrage, sa vie, etc.); conclure (un discours); clore (une séance); **to e. one's days in peace,** terminer ses jours en paix; **to e. war,** mettre un terme aux guerres; **to e. a crisis,** mettre fin à, résoudre, une crise; **to e. a speech with a quotation,** conclure, terminer, un discours avec une citation; **it's all ended (and done with),** (i) c'est fini et bien fini; (ii) il n'y a plus à revenir là-dessus; (*b*) *v.i.* **I must e. by thanking Mr X,** pour conclure je dois remercier M. X; **let us e. with a song,** finissons par une chanson. **2.** *v.i.* finir, se terminer; aboutir (**at, in, dans, en**); **the first chapter ends with a murder,** le premier chapitre se termine par un meurtre; **the path ends at the lakeside,** le chemin aboutit, mène, au bord du lac; **term ending at Christmas,** trimestre *m* qui finit, qui se termine, à Noël; **your subscription ends on May 31,** votre abonnement expire le 31 mai; **this state of things must e.,** il faut mettre fin à cet état de choses; il faut que cela change; **I don't know how things will e.,** je ne sais pas comment cela finira, quelle en sera l'issue, à quoi cela aboutira; **to e. happily,** avoir une issue heureuse; **all stories e. like that,** toutes les histoires finissent de cette manière, comme ça; **he ended by insulting me,** il a fini par m'injurier; **his extravagance will e. by ruining him,** son extravagance aboutira à sa ruine; **to e. in a point,** aboutir, se terminer, en pointe; **to e. at a point,** aboutir, se terminer, à un point; **to e. (up) in smoke,** n'aboutir à rien; s'en aller en fumée; (*of plan*) avorter; **all's well that ends well,** tout est bien qui finit bien. **3.** *v.tr.* embouter (une canne, etc.).

end(-)all ['endɔ:l], *s.* fin *f*; *used in the phr.* **the be-all and e.-a.,** le but suprême, la fin des fins.

endamage [in'dæmidʒ], *v.tr. A: & Lit:* **1.** endommager. **2.** porter préjudice à (qn, des intérêts).

Endamoebidae [endə'mi:bidi:], *s.pl. Nat.Hist:* endamœbidés *m*.

endanger [in'deindʒər], *v.tr.* mettre (qn, qch.) en danger; exposer, hasarder, risquer (sa vie, etc.); léser, compromettre (des intérêts); **to e. a country,** porter atteinte à la sécurité d'un pays; **to e. an undertaking,** faire péricliter une entreprise.

endarteritis [enda:tə'raitis], *s. Med:* endartérite *f*.

endarterium [enda:'tiriəm], *s. Anat:* endartère *f*.

endear [in'diər], *v.tr.* rendre (qn, qch.) cher (**to,** à); **he has endeared himself to all,** il s'est fait universellement aimer.

endearing [in'diəriŋ], *a.* **1.** qui rend cher, qui inspire l'affection; **he has e. qualities,** il a des qualités qui le rendent sympathique. **2.** tendre, affectueux; **e. names,** termes d'amitié; mots doux.

endearingly [in'diəriŋli], *adv.* tendrement, affectueusement.

endearment [in'diəmənt], *s.* **1.** charme *m*, attrait *m*. **2.** *pl.* **endearments,** caresses *f*; mots *m* tendres.

endeavour¹ [in'devər], *s.* effort *m*, tentative *f*; **constant e.,** préoccupation constante, effort constant; **it will be my e. to satisfy you,** je m'efforcerai de vous contenter; **to use, make, every e. to . . .,** faire tous ses efforts, tout son possible, tous les efforts possibles, faire l'impossible, pour . . .; prendre à tâche de . . ..

endeavour², *v.i.* **to e. to do sth.,** s'efforcer, tenter, essayer, tâcher, de faire qch.; chercher à faire qch., travailler à faire qch.; **to e. to please s.o.,** s'étudier à faire plaisir à qn.

endecagon [en'dekəgən], *s.* hendécagone *m*.

ended ['endid], *a.* **1.** fini, terminé. **2.** (*with adj. or num. prefixed*) **round-e.,** à bout rond; **double-e.,** à deux bouts.

endemic [en'demik]. **1.** *a. Bot: Med:* endémique; **e. ulcer,** ulcère *f* d'Orient, bouton *m* d'Alep. **2.** *s. Med:* endémie *f*; maladie *f* endémique.

endemically [en'demik(ə)li], *adv.* endémiquement, d'une manière endémique.

endemicity [ende'misiti], *s.* endémicité *f*.

endemism ['endəmizm], *s.* endémisme *m*.

endermic [en'də:mik], *a.* endermique.

ending ['endiŋ], *s.* **1.** terminaison *f*, achèvement *m*. **2.** fin *f*, conclusion *f* (d'un ouvrage, d'un livre); terminaison; **happy e.,** dénouement heureux; **to come to an abrupt e.,** terminer court. **3.** *Gram:* désinence *f*, terminaison (d'un mot); **case e.,** flexion casuelle.

endive ['endiv], *s. Bot: Hort:* **1.** chicorée *f* endive; (**curled**) **e.,** chicorée frisée; **broad-leaved e., Batavian e.,** endive *f*, chicorée de Bruxelles, (e)scarole *f*. **2.** *U.S:* endive.

endless ['endlis], *a.* **1.** (*in space*) (*a*) sans fin; **e. journey,** voyage *m* sans fin, interminable; **e. cable, e. screw,** câble *m*, vis *f*, sans fin; *Cmptr:* **e. form,** imprimé *m* en continu; **e. tape,** bande *f* sans fin; (*b*) sans bornes, infini; **e. space,** l'infini *m*; **to take e. pains to do, over, sth.,** se donner une peine infinie à faire qch.; **man of e. resource,** homme inépuisable en ressources; **e. speculation,** raisonnements à perte de vue. **2.** (*in time*) (*a*) sans fin, éternel; **the conversation seemed e.,** l'entretien semblait s'éterniser; **e. discussions,** discussions à n'en plus finir, sans fin, interminables; **it's an e. task, it's e.,** cela n'en finit pas; c'est à n'en plus finir; (*b*) (*of pain, etc.*) continuel, incessant; (*of chatter, etc.*) intarissable.

endlessly ['endlisli], *adv.* sans fin, sans cesse, éternellement; perpétuellement, intarissablement.

endlessness ['endlisnis], *s.* **1.** perpétuité *f*; durée infinie. **2.** **the e. of her complaints,** ses plaintes *f* sans fin.

endlichite ['endlikait], *s. Miner:* endlichite *f*.

endo- ['endou], *comb.fm.* endo-.

endobiotic [endoubai'ɔtik], *a.* endobiotique.

endoblast ['endoublæst], *s. Biol:* endoblaste *m*.

endocardiac [endou'ka:diæk], **endocardial** [endou'ka:diəl], *a. Med:* (murmure *m*, etc.) endocardiaque.

endocarditic [endouka:'ditik], *a. Med:* endocarditique.

endocarditis [endouka:'daitis], *s. Med:* endocardite *f*.

endocardium [endou'ka:diəm], *s. Anat:* endocarde *m*.

endocarp ['endouka:p], *s. Bot:* endocarpe *m*.

endoceras [en'dɔsərəs], *s. Paleont:* endoceras *m*.

endocervicitis [endousəvi'saitis], *s.* endocervicite *f*.

endochondral [endou'kɔndrəl], *a.* endochondral.

endochrome ['endoukroum], *s. Biol:* endochrome *m*.

endocrane ['endoukrein], **endocranium** [endou'kreiniəm], *s. Anat:* endocrâne *m*.

endocranial [endou'kreiniəl], *a. Ant:* endocrânien.

endocrinal [endou'krainəl], *a. Physiol:* endocrinien.

endocrine ['endoukrain], *a. & s. Physiol:* **1.** (glande *f*) endocrine *f*, à sécrétion interne, sans canal excrétoire. **2.** (traitement, etc.) endocrinien.

endocrinology [endoukri'nɔlədʒi], *s. Physiol:* endocrinologie *f*.

endocrinopathic ['endoukrainou'pæθik], *a. Med:* dysendrocrinien.

endocrinopathy [endoukri'nɔpəθi], *s. Med:* dysendocrinie *f*.

endocyst ['endousist], *s. Z:* endocyste *m*.

endoderm ['endoudə:m], *s. Biol: Bot:* endoderme *m*.

endoergic [endou'ə:dʒik], *a.* endoénergétique.

endogamous [en'dɔgəməs], *a. Anthr:* (mariage *m*, tribu *f*) endogame.

endogamy [en'dɔgəmi], *s. Anthr:* endogamie *f*.

endogen ['endoudʒən], *s. Bot:* plante *f* endogène.

endogenetic [endoudʒə'netik], *a. Biol:* endogène; *Geol:* **e. rock,** roche *f* endogène.

endogenous [en'dɔdʒənəs], *a. Bot: Med:* (plante *f*, contagion *f*) endogène.

endogeny [en'dɔdʒəni], *s. Biol:* endogénèse *f*.

endolymph ['endoulimf], *s. Anat:* endolymphe *f*.

endolymphatic [endoulim'fætik], *a. Anat:* endolymphatique.

endometrioma, *pl.* **-mas, -mata** ['endoumi:tri'oumə, -məz, -mətə], *s. Med:* endométriome *m*.

endometriosis [endoumi:tri'ousis], *s. Med:* endométriose *f*.

endometritis [endoumi'traitis], *s. Med:* endométrite *f*.

endometrium [endou'metriəm], *s. Anat:* endomètre *m*.

endomitosis [endoumi'tousis], *s. Biol:* endomitose *f*.

endomixis [endou'miksis], *s. Biol:* endomixie *f*.

endomorph ['endoumɔ:f], *s. Miner:* endomorphe *m*.

endomorphic [endou'mɔ:fik], **endomorphous** [endou'mɔ:fəs], *a. Geol:* endomorphe.

endomorphism [endou'mɔ:fizm], *s. Geol:* endomorphisme *m*.

Endomycetaceae ['endoumaisi'teisii:], **Endomycetales** ['endoumaisi'teili:z], *s.pl. Fung:* endomycétacées *f*, endomycétales *f*.

endonephritis [endoune'fraitis], *s. Med:* endonéphrite *f*.

endoparasite [endou'pærəsait], *s. Z:* endoparasite *m*.

endophasia [endou'feiziə], *s.* endophasie *f*.

endophragm ['endoufræm], *s. Crust: etc:* endophragme *m*.

endophyte ['endoufait], *a. & s. Bot:* endophyte (*m*).

endoplasm ['endouplæzm], *s. Biol:* endoplasme *m*.

endopleura [endou'pluərə], *s. Bot:* endoplèvre *f*.

endopodite [endou'pɔdait], *s. Crust:* endopodite *m*.

endor(h)eic [endə'reiik], *a. Geol:* endoréique.

endor(h)eism [endə'reiizm], *s. Geol:* endoréisme *m*.

endorse [in'dɔ:s], *v.tr.* **1.** endosser (un document, un chèque, etc.); viser (un passeport); **to e. sth. on a document, to e. a document with sth.,** mentionner qch. au verso d'un document; *Post:* **endorsed not known,** mention *inconnu*; *Adm:* **to e. a motorist's licence,** inscrire les détails d'un délit sur le permis de conduire; *Com: Fin:* **to e. a bill,** avaliser, avaler, donner son aval à, un effet; **to honour an order endorsed by s.o.,** payer sur le visa approbatif de qn; **to e. a bill of exchange,** endosser une lettre de change; **to e. over a bill to s.o.,** transmettre par voie d'endossement une lettre de change à qn; **to e. back a bill to drawer,** contre-passer un effet au tireur. **2.** appuyer, sanctionner, venir à l'appui de, donner son adhésion à, s'associer à (une opinion, une action); souscrire à (une décision, une opinion); *Jur:* approuver (un appel); **I e. all you have done,** j'approuve tout ce que vous avez fait.

endorsee [indɔ:'si:], *s. Fin:* endossataire *mf*; bénéficiaire *mf* (d'un billet par endos); tiers porteur *m*; **e. of a cheque,** porteur d'un chèque.

endorsement [in'dɔ:smənt], *s.* **1.** (*a*) *Fin: etc:* endossement *m*, endos *m* (d'un chèque, d'une lettre de change); aval *m* (d'un effet); (*on envelope*) mention *f*; (*on passport, etc.*) mention spéciale; **blank e.,** endos en blanc; (*b*) *Ins:* avenant *m*. **2.** **e. of an action,** approbation *f* d'une action; **e. of an opinion,** adhésion *f* à une opinion.

endorser [in'dɔ:sər], *s. Fin:* endosseur *m*, cessionnaire *m* (d'un chèque, etc.); avaliste *m* (d'un effet); **second e. (of bill),** tiers porteur.

endoscope ['endəskoup], *s. Med:* endoscope *m*; photophore *m*.
endoscopic [endou'skɔpik], *a. Med:* endoscopique.
endoscopy [en'dɔskəpi], *s. Med:* endoscopie *f*.
endoskeleton [endou'skelitn], *s. Z:* squelette intérieur (des vertébrés).
endosmometer [endɔz'mɔmitər], *s. Ph:* endosmomètre *m*.
endosmosis [endɔz'mousis], *s. Med: Ph:* endosmose *f*.
endosmotic [endɔz'mɔtik], *a. Ph:* endosmotique.
endosome ['endousoum], *s. Biol:* endosome *m*.
endosperm ['endouspə:m], *s. Bot:* endosperme *m*.
endospermic [endou'spə:mik], *a. Bot:* endospermé.
endospore ['endouspɔ:r], *s. Bot:* endospore *m*.
endosporium [endou'spɔ:riəm], *s. Bot:* endhyménine *f*.
endostome ['endoustoum], *s. Bot:* endostome *m*.
endostyle ['endoustail], *s. Z:* endostyle *m*.
endotheca, *pl.* **-ae** [endou'θi:kə, -i:], *s. Nat.Hist:* endothèque *f*.
endothecium [endou'θi:siəm], *s. Bot:* endothecium *m*.
endothelial [endou'θi:liəl], *a. Physiol:* endothélial, -aux.
endothelioma [endouθi:li'oumə], *s. Med:* endothéliome *m*.
endothelium [endou'θi:liəm], *s. Physiol:* endothélium *m*.
endothermic [endou'θə:mik], *a. Ch:* (réaction *f*) endothermique.
endotoxin [endou'tɔksin], *s. Bac:* endotoxine *f*.
endow [in'dau], *v.tr.* **1.** doter (qn, une église, une société) **(with,** de); assurer un revenu à (sa fille, sa femme, une religieuse, etc.); **to e. a bed in a hospital,** fonder un lit dans un hôpital. **2. nature had endowed him with great talents,** la nature l'avait doué de grands talents; **woman endowed with great beauty,** femme dotée d'une grande beauté.
endowed [in'daud], *a.* (hôpital, etc.) doté, renté.
endowment [in'daumənt], *s.* **1.** *(a)* dotation *f* (l'action ou le fonds); *(b)* fondation (léguée à un hospice, etc.); *(c) Ins:* **(pure) e. assurance,** assurance *f* en cas de vie; assurance à capital différé, à terme fixe, à dotation; **(ordinary) e. assurance,** assurance mixte. **2.** don (naturel); talent *m*.
endpaper ['endpeipər], *s. Bookb:* (page *f* de) garde *f*; **front e.,** garde de tête, de front; **off e.,** garde de queue.
end-to-end ['endtuwend], *a. Surg:* termino-terminal, -aux.
endue [in'dju:], *v.tr. Lit:* **1.** *(a)* revêtir (un vêtement); *(b)* revêtir (qn) **(with,** de); **to e. s.o. with an office,** investir qn d'une fonction; *(in the Anglican Liturgy)* **e. Thy ministers with righteousness,** revêts de justice tes ministres. **2.** douer **(s.o. with sth.,** qn de qch.).
endurable [in'dju:rəbl], *a.* **1.** supportable, endurable. **2.** *Lit: (lasting)* durable.
endurance [in'dju:rəns], *s.* **1.** *(a)* résistance *f* (d'une personne, d'un animal); **physical e.,** endurance *f* (physique); **to have great powers of e.,** être dur à la fatigue, au mal, etc.; **beyond e.,** insupportable, intolérable; au-delà de ce qu'on peut supporter; *(b) Ind: etc: (resistance to fatigue)* endurance *f*; **e. test,** (i) *Mec.E:* essai *m* de durée; (ii) *Sp:* épreuve *f* d'endurance; *(c) Av:* autonomie *f*. **2.** patience *f*, longanimité *f*. **3.** *Lit:* durée *f*.
endure [in'dju:ər]. **1.** *v.tr.* supporter, endurer, souffrir avec patience (le mal, des insultes, etc.); soutenir (des reproches, etc.); **I can't e. being disturbed, to be disturbed,** je ne peux pas souffrir qu'on vienne me déranger; **he can't e. the brat,** il ne peut pas tolérer ce mioche; *Prov:* **what can't be cured must be endured,** il faut souffrir ce que l'on ne peut empêcher; où il n'y a pas de remède il faut se résigner. **2.** *v.i.* durer, rester; **work that will e.,** ouvrage *m* qui vivra, qui restera.
enduring [in'dju:riŋ], *a.* **1.** durable, qui dure, permanent; (paix *f*) stable; **e. evil,** mal persistant, qui persiste; **e. remorse,** remords *m* vivace; **the e. quality of these virtues,** la persistance de ces vertus. **2.** patient, longanime, endurant.
enduringly [in'dju:riŋli], *adv.* d'une manière durable, permanente.
enduringness [in'dju:riŋnis], *s.* durabilité *f*, permanence *f*.
endways, endwise ['endweiz, -waiz], *adv.* **1.** *(a)* de chant, sur chant, debout; *(b)* **e. on,** avec le bout en avant. **2.** *(end to end)* bout à bout. **3.** longitudinalement.
enema ['enəmə], *s. Med:* **1.** lavement *m*. **2.** appareil *m* à lavements; irrigateur *m*, énéma *m*; clyso-injecteur *m*, *pl.* clyso-injecteurs; clysoir *m*.
enemy ['enəmi]. **1.** *s. (a)* ennemi, -e; **e. No. 1,** ennemi n° 1; **man without an e.,** homme sans ennemis; **to be one's own (worst) e.,** se desservir soi-même; être le bourreau de soi-même; **he is no one's e. but his own,** il ne fait de tort qu'à lui-même; **they are deadly enemies,** ils sont à couteaux tirés; *U.S:* **public e.,** ennemi public; bandit *m*; *F: O:* **how goes the e.?** quelle heure est-il? *(b) coll:* **the e.,** l'ennemi, l'adversaire *m*; *Mil:* **potential e.,** l'ennemi virtuel, l'ennemi en puissance; **skeleton e.,** l'ennemi figuré, le plastron; **e.-occupied territories,** territoires occupés par l'ennemi. **2.** *a.* ennemi; **the e. fleet,** la flotte ennemie; **e. alien,** ressortissant, -ante, d'un pays ennemi; **e. dispositions,** dispositif ennemi.
energetic [enə'dʒetik]. **1.** *a.* (homme, nature, remède, mesure) énergique; **he is an e. man,** c'est un homme énergique, actif; *F:* c'est un homme à poigne, de poigne. **2.** *s.pl. (usu. with sg. const.)* **energetics,** l'énergétique *f*, l'énergétisme *m*.
energetically [enə'dʒetik(ə)li], *adv.* énergiquement; avec énergie; activement.
energize ['enədʒaiz]. **1.** *v.tr. (a)* donner de l'énergie à (qn); stimuler (qn); *(b) El:* (i) exciter, rendre actif, alimenter; (ii) amorcer (une dynamo); (iii) aimanter (l'âme d'une bobine, etc.). **2.** *v.i. (a) El:* (i) s'exciter, s'alimenter; (ii) *(of dynamo)* s'amorcer; (iii) *(of core of coil, etc.)* s'aimanter; *(b) Lit: (of pers.)* faire preuve d'énergie, agir avec vigueur.
energizer ['enədʒaizər], *s. (a)* excitateur *m*, agent *m* énergifiant; *(b)* amorceur *m*; *Av:* **external e.,** moteur de démarrage supplémentaire; moteur auxiliaire portatif de démarrage.
energizing[1] ['enədʒaiziŋ], *a.* **1.** qui donne de l'énergie; stimulant, activant; (médicament *m*, nourriture *f*) énergétique. **2.** *El:* **e. circuit,** (i) circuit d'excitation; (ii) circuit d'amorçage (d'une dynamo); (iii) circuit d'aimantation (d'une bobine).
energizing[2], *s. El:* amorçage *m* (d'un relais).
energumen [enə'gju:mən], *s.* énergumène *m*. **1.** démoniaque *m*. **2.** fanatique *m*.
energy ['enədʒi], *s.* **1.** énergie *f*, force *f*, vigueur *f*; **to have no e.,** ne pas avoir d'énergie; *F:* ne pas avoir de sang dans les veines; manquer d'allant, de nerf; **man of e.,** homme *m* énergique; **he even lacked the e. to go upstairs to bed,** il n'avait pas même l'énergie de monter se coucher; **e. in doing sth.,** énergie à faire qch.; **to devote, direct, apply, (all) one's energies to a task, to doing sth., to throw all one's e. into a task,** consacrer, apporter, appliquer, ses efforts, toutes ses facultés, toute son énergie, à une tâche, à faire qch.; mettre en œuvre toute son industrie à faire qch.; **you must put some e. into it,** il faut y mettre du vôtre; **e.-producing foods,** aliments *m* énergétiques. **2.** *(a) Mec:* énergie, puissance *f*, travail *m*; travail mécanique, travail moteur; **conservation of e.,** conservation *f* de l'énergie; **e. consumed,** puissance absorbée; **expenditure of e.,** dépense *f* énergétique; **indicated e.,** travail indiqué; **kinetic e.,** énergie cinétique, force vive; **potential e.,** énergie potentielle; **e. shift,** déplacement d'énergie; **sound e.,** énergie acoustique; **zero (point) e.,** énergie nulle; **radiant e.,** énergie radiante, rayonnante, de rayonnement; *Ind: Mec: Physiol:* **e. efficiency,** rendement énergétique; **to store up e.,** emmagasiner du travail; **stored e.,** énergie emmagasinée; *Ball:* **muzzle e.,** énergie à la bouche; **striking e.,** énergie au choc; *Elcs:* **e. band,** bande *f* d'énergie; **e. gap (between two bands),** écart *m* énergétique (entre deux bandes); **band edge e.,** énergie de la limite de bande; *(b)* **atomic e.,** énergie *f* atomique; **binding e.,** énergie de liaison; **repulsive e.,** énergie de répulsion; **disintegration e.,** énergie de désintégration; **e. barrier,** barrière *f* d'énergie; **e. equivalent,** équivalent *m* énergétique; **e. range,** gamme *f* d'énergie; **e. release,** dégagement *m* d'énergie, libération *f* d'énergie; **e. spectrum,** spectre *m* énergétique; **e. balance,** bilan *m* énergétique.
enervate[1] [i'nə:veit], *a.* **1.** *Lit: (of pers., character, style, etc.)* sans force; sans vigueur; (style) énervé. **2.** *Bot: (of leaf)* énerve, énervé.
enervate[2] ['enəveit], *v.tr.* affaiblir, amollir, énerver, aveulir (le corps, la volonté).
enervating[1] ['enəveitiŋ], *a.* (climat, etc.) amollissant, anémiant, débilitant, énervant, aveulissant.
enervating[2], *s.* = ENERVATION 1.
enervation [enə'veiʃ(ə)n], *s.* **1.** affaiblissement *m*, aveulissement *m*. **2.** mollesse *f*.
enface [in'feis], *v.tr. Fin:* **to e. the words . . . on a draft, to e. a draft with the words . . .,** inscrire les mots . . . au recto d'une traite; *St.Exch: A:* **enfaced paper,** rentes indiennes (payables à Londres).
enfacement [in'feismənt], *s. Fin:* formule inscrite, mots inscrits, au recto d'un effet de commerce.
enfant terrible [ɑ̃fɑ̃te'ri:blə], *s. (a)* enfant *mf* impossible; *(b)* **the e. t. of the Romantic movement,** l'enfant terrible du Romantisme.
enfeeble [in'fibl], *v.tr. (of pain, age)* affaiblir (qn, les facultés).
enfeeblement [in'fi:bəlm(ə)nt], *s.* affaiblissement *m*.
enfeoff [en'fi:f], *v.tr. A:* **1.** investir, ensaisiner, (qn) d'un fief. **2.** inféoder (une terre).
enfeoffment [en'fi:fmənt], *s. A:* inféodation *f*; acte *m* d'inféodation; ensaisinement *m*.
engetter [in'fetər], *v.tr. A:* enchaîner (qn, les passions, etc.).
enfilade[1] ['enfileid], *s. Mil:* enfilade *f*.
enfilade[2], *v.tr. Mil:* enfiler, battre de flanc, battre d'enfilade (une tranchée, etc.); prendre en enfilade.
enfilading [enfi'leidiŋ], *a.* d'enfilade; **e. battery, e. fire, e. shot,** batterie *f*, tir *m*, coup *m*, d'enfilade.
enfold [in'fould], *v.tr.* envelopper **(sth. in, with, sth.,** qch. dans qch.); **to e. s.o. in one's arms,** étreindre, embrasser, qn; *Surg:* **to e. a gastric ulcer,** envelopper un ulcère gastrique dans un pli de l'estomac.
enfolded [in'fouldid], *a.* **1.** enveloppé **(in, with,** dans). **2.** *Nat.Hist:* plissé.
enfolding[1] [in'fouldiŋ], *a.* (mouvement) enveloppant.
enfolding[2], *s.* enveloppement *m*; embrassement *m*.
enforce [in'fɔ:s], *v.tr.* **1.** donner de la force à, faire valoir (un argument); appuyer (une demande, *Nau:* un signal). **2.** mettre en vigueur, exécuter (une loi, etc.); **to e. one's rights,** faire valoir ses droits; **to e. the law,** faire respecter, faire obéir, la loi; appliquer la loi; **to e. the blockade,** rendre le blocus effectif. **3. to e. (respect for) a rule,** imposer, faire observer, un règlement; tenir la main à l'observation d'une règle; **to e. obedience,** se faire obéir; **to e. one's will on s.o.,** imposer sa volonté à qn; **to e. a certain line of conduct on s.o.,** obliger, contraindre, qn à une certaine conduite.
enforceability [infɔ:sə'biliti], *s.* **e. of a law,** possibilité *f* d'appliquer une loi.
enforceable [in'fɔ:səbl], *a. Jur:* (contrat *m*, jugement *m*) exécutoire.
enforced [in'fɔ:st], *a.* (silence, travail) forcé; **e. residence,** résidence forcée.
enforcement [in'fɔ:smənt], *s. Jur:* **1.** exécution *f*, mise *f* en vigueur, application *f* (d'une loi); **recognizances admit of direct e.,** les obligations sont directement exécutoires; **law e. officers,** fonctionnaires chargés de l'application de la loi. **2.** *A:* sanction (pénale). **3. e. action,** action coercitive.
enfranchise [in'fræn(t)ʃaiz], *v.tr.* **1.** affranchir (un esclave, une tenure). **2.** *Pol: (a)* admettre au suffrage (un citoyen); accorder le droit de vote à (qn); *(b)* conférer la franchise, des droits municipaux, à (une ville).
enfranchisement [in'fræn(t)ʃizmənt], *s.* **1.** affranchissement *m* (d'un esclave, d'une tenure). **2.** *Pol:* admission *f* (d'un citoyen) au suffrage; concession *f* de droits municipaux (à une ville).
engage [in'geidʒ], *v.tr. & i.* **1.** *(a)* engager (sa parole, son honneur); **to e. (oneself) to do sth.,** s'engager, s'obliger, à faire qch.; promettre formellement de faire qch.; *(b)* **to be engaged (to be married),** être fiancé(e); **to become engaged,** se fiancer. **2.** *(a)* engager, prendre (un domestique, etc.); embaucher (des ouvriers); *Navy:* recruter (des hommes); **I'll e. you,** je vous prends; *(b)* louer (un taxi); *O:* retenir, réserver (une chambre, etc.); **this seat is engaged,** cette place est retenue, réservée, occupée, prise; *(b) Tp:* **to e. the line for ten minutes,** occuper la ligne pendant dix minutes; **the number is engaged,** la ligne est occupée. **3.** occuper (qn); fixer (l'attention); attirer, gagner (l'affection, l'intérêt, de qn); **to e. in discussion, in conversation, with s.o., to e. s.o. in discussion, in conversation,** entrer en discussion, en conversation, avec qn; engager la conversation, lier conversation, avec qn; **are you engaged?** êtes-vous occupé? **I shall be engaged until three o'clock,** je serai occupé jusqu'à trois heures; je ne pourrai voir personne avant trois heures; **I can't come tonight as I am (otherwise) engaged,** je ne puis pas venir ce soir parce que je suis pris, puisque je suis déjà invité (ailleurs); **to be engaged in writing a novel,** être occupé à écrire un roman; **he's become very much engaged in politics,** il s'est livré à la politique. **4.** *Mil:* **to e. (in) combat, to e. the fight, to e. in action, to e. (with) the enemy,** engager le combat; intervenir dans la bataille; livrer bataille; **when two hostile forces are engaged,** quand deux forces adversaires sont aux prises; **to e. the fifth division,** engager, faire intervenir, la cinquième division; **to e. a target,** battre, ouvrir le feu sur, un objectif; prendre un objectif sous son feu; **to e. an enemy aircraft,** ouvrir le feu sur un appareil ennemi. **5.** *Mec.E: etc: (a)* mettre en prise (un engrenage, *Aut:* une vitesse); **to e. in first (gear),** mettre en première (vitesse); *(b) v.i. (of cog wheel)* (s')engrener, s'enclencher, (s')engager, se mettre en prise **(with,** avec); quotter; s'embrayer. **6.** *Fenc:* **to e. (the foil),** engager le fer.
engaged [in'geidʒd], *a.* **1.** fiancé; **the e. couple,** les fiancés. **2.** *(a)* **heavily e.,** très occupé; *(b) Tp:* **to get the e. signal,** entendre le signal de ligne occupée. **3.** *Mec.E: (of gear wheels, etc.)* en prise.
engagement [in'geidʒmənt], *s.* **1.** engagement *m*; *(a)*

promesse *f*, obligation *f*; **to enter into an e.,** prendre, contracter, un engagement; **to keep one's engagements,** être fidèle à, remplir, ses engagements; *Com:* **to carry out, meet, one's engagements,** faire face, faire honneur, à ses engagements; remplir ses engagements; (*b*) rendez-vous *m*; **owing to a previous e.,** à cause d'une promesse antérieure; **public e.,** engagement à paraître en public; **social engagements,** invitations *fpl* dans le monde; **to have an e.,** être pris, être occupé; ne pas être libre; **e. book,** agenda *m*. **2.** engagement (d'hommes, de domestiques); recrutement *m*. **3.** fiançailles; *fpl.* **e. ring,** anneau *m*, bague *f*, de fiançailles. **4.** *Mil: Navy:* (*a*) combat, *m*, engagement *m*; action *f*, rencontre *f*; **major e.,** combat, engagement, important; grande bataille; **minor e.,** combat, engagement, mineur; **meeting e.,** combat de rencontre; **only patrol engagements were reported,** on ne signale que des engagements de patrouille; (*b*) intervention, engagement (d'une unité dans la bataille); **the e. of the 5th division,** l'engagement, l'intervention, de la 5ème division; (*c*) **e. of a target,** prise *f* à partie d'un objectif; ouverture *f* du feu sur un objectif; **rules of e.** (**of targets**), dispositions *f* réglementant l'ouverture du feu, prescriptions *f* concernant l'ouverture du feu (sur les objectifs). **5.** *Mec.E:* (*a*) mise *f* en prise; emprise *f*; engrènement *m*; entraînement *m*; embrayage *m*; (*of dog clutch*) crabotage *m*; **gradual e.,** entraînement progressif; **side e.,** emprise latérale; (*b*) prise *f*, quottement *m* (d'un pignon avec une roue, etc.).

engaging [in'geidʒiŋ], *a.* (sourire, ton) engageant, attrayant, séduisant, attachant, attirant, qui attire; (ton) liant; (regard) sémillant; **to have an e. manner,** avoir du liant; **e. child,** enfant gentillet.

engagingly [in'geidʒiŋli], *adv.* d'une manière engageante, attrayante; **to smile e.,** (i) sourire gentiment; (ii) adresser un sourire provocant (**at s.o.,** à qn).

engarland [in'gɑ:lənd], *v.tr. Lit:* enguirlander.

engender [in'dʒendər], *v.tr.* **1.** *A:* engendrer (un enfant). **2.** faire naître, produire, causer (un effet); engendrer (une maladie, un sentiment).

engine[1] ['endʒin], *s.* **1.** (*a*) machine *f*, appareil *m*; **lifting e.,** engin *m* de levage; **fire e.,** pompe *f* à incendie; *Min:* **winding e.,** machine d'extraction, de hissage; **pumping e.,** pompe d'épuisement; *Paperm:* **beating e.,** pile défileuse; *Mil: A:* **engines of war,** engins, machines, de guerre; (*b*) *A:* instrument *m*, moyen *m*, agent *m*; **every e. at one's disposal,** tous les moyens dont on dispose. **2.** *Mec.E:* etc: (*a*) moteur *m*, machine; **compressed-air e.,** moteur, machine, à air comprimé; **hot-air e.,** moteur, machine, à air chaud; **heat, thermal, e.,** moteur, machine, thermique; **oil e.,** moteur, machine, à pétrole; **heavy-oil e.,** moteur à huile lourde; **Diesel e.,** moteur Diesel; **petrol e.,** *NAm:* **gas e.,** moteur, machine, à essence; **gas e.,** moteur, machine, à gaz; **producer-gas e.,** moteur, machine, à gaz pauvre; **waste-gas e.,** moteur, machine, à gaz perdu, brûlé; **wind e.,** moteur à vent; **hydraulic e.,** moteur hydraulique; **binary vapour e.,** machine à vapeurs combinées; **high-speed, low-speed, e.,** moteur, machine, à grande, à faible, vitesse; **upright, vertical, e.,** machine verticale, moteur vertical; **auxiliary e.,** moteur auxiliaire; **starting e.,** moteur de lancement; **rotary e.,** moteur rotatif; **stationary e.,** moteur, machine, fixe; **semi-portable e.,** moteur, machine, mi-fixe; **transportable e.,** locomobile *f*; (*of thresher*) agromotive *f*; **steam e.,** machine, moteur, à vapeur; **condensing, non-condensing, e.,** machine à condensation, sans condensation; **expansion, non-expansion, e.,** machine à détente, à expansion; machine sans expansion; **multiple expansion e.,** machine à multiple détente, à multiple expansion; **double-expansion e.,** machine à double expansion; **double-action e.,** machine à double effet; **high-pressure, low-pressure, e.,** machine à haute, à basse, pression; **condensing e.,** machine à condensation; *Aut:* **car, automobile, e.,** moteur de voiture, d'automobile; **internal combustion e.,** moteur à combustion interne, à explosion; **piston e.,** moteur à pistons; **two-stroke, four-stroke, e.,** moteur à deux, à quatre, temps; **injection e.,** moteur à injection; **direct-drive e.,** moteur en prise directe, sans démultiplicateur; **front-wheel drive e.,** moteur à traction avant; moteur attaquant directement l'essieu, les roues, avant; **left-handed, right-handed, e.,** moteur à rotation (à) gauche, (à) droite; **in-line e.,** moteur (à cylindres) en ligne; **radial e.,** moteur (à cylindres) en étoile; **V-type e.,** moteur (à cylindres) en V; **square e.,** moteur carré; **upright e.,** moteur droit; **inverted e.,** moteur inversé; **valve e.,** moteur à soupapes; **valve-in-head e.,** moteur à soupapes en tête; **side-valve e.,** moteur à soupapes latérales; **overhead-valve e.,** moteur à arbre à cames en tête; **valveless, sleeve-valve, e.,** moteur sans soupapes; **fluid-cooled, air-cooled, e.,** moteur à refroidissement par liquide, par air; *Av:* **aircraft e., aero(-)e.,** moteur d'avion, d'aviation; **jet e.,** moteur à réaction; **inboard, outboard, e.,** moteur intérieur, extérieur; **traction e.,** machine, locomotive, routière; tracteur *m*; remorqueur *m*, remorqueuse *f*; (**railway**) **e.,** locomotive *f*; **passenger, goods, e.,** locomotive à voyageurs, à marchandises; **emergency e.,** locomotive de réserve; **single-drive e.,** machine à roues libres, machine Crampton; **four(-wheel) coupled e.,** machine à deux essieux couplés, à quatre roues couplées; **to couple, uncouple, the e.,** accrocher, décrocher, la locomotive; **marine e.,** moteur marin; **nuclear e., atomic e.,** moteur nucléaire, atomique; **space(craft) e.,** moteur (de véhicule) spatial; **arc-jet e.,** moteur à arc; **photon e.,** moteur à photons; **plasma e.,** moteur à plasma; **ion e.,** moteur ionique; (*b*) *attrib.* **e. frame,** (i) bâti *m* de machine, de moteur; (ii) châssis *m* (de locomotive); **e. bed.,** bâti *m* (du) moteur; **e. compartment,** compartiment *m* des machines, du, des, moteur(s); *Mec.E:* **e. lathe,** tour *m* (marchant au moteur); *Mch:* **e. set,** groupe moto-propulseur; **e. oil,** huile *f* (i) de graissage, (ii) pour moteurs; **e. house,** bâtiment *m* des machines, des moteurs; dépôt *m* (de pompes à incendie, etc.); **e. room,** salle *f* des machines; *Nau:* chambre *f* des machines; **e.-room telegraph,** télégraphe *m* de la machine, chadburn *m*; *Rail:* **e. shed, shop,** garage *m*, dépôt *m*, remise *f*, atelier *m*, des locomotives; **circular e. shed,** rotonde *f*; *Rail:* **e. driver,** conducteur *m*, mécanicien *m*, machiniste *m* (de locomotive).

engine[2], *v.tr.* **1.** pourvoir (un navire) de machines; monter les machines (d'un navire). **2.** pourvoir, munir, d'un moteur.

engineer[1] [endʒi'niər], *s.* **1.** ingénieur *m*; (*a*) **civil e.,** (i) ingénieur des travaux publics; ingénieur constructeur; (ii) = ingénieur des ponts et chaussées; **metallurgical e.,** ingénieur métallurgiste; **marine e.,** ingénieur du génie maritime, des constructions mécaniques de la marine; **naval e.,** ingénieur de génie maritime militaire; **mechanical e.,** ingénieur mécanicien; **electrical e.,** ingénieur électricien; **electronics e.,** ingénieur électronicien; **hydraulic e.,** ingénieur hydraulicien; **mining e.,** ingénieur des mines; (*b*) **consulting e.,** ingénieur conseil; **patent e.** = ingénieur conseil; **management, industrial, e.,** ingénieur en organisation, d'exploitation, des méthodes; **project, design, e.,** ingénieur projecteur, d'études; **development e.,** ingénieur des mises au point; **planning, work-study, e.,** ingénieur de planification, en organisation; **programming e.,** ingénieur programmeur, de programmation; **production e.,** ingénieur (chargé) de la production; **sales e.,** ingénieur, chef *m* du service, des ventes; **technical sales e.,** ingénieur technico-commercial. **2.** (*a*) *Nau:* ingénieur, mécanicien *m*; **chief e.,** chef mécanicien; **watch e.,** *U.S:* **assistant e.,** mécanicien (chef) de quart; *Navy:* **e. officer,** ingénieur mécanicien; **second e.,** officier mécanicien en second; (*b*) *Av:* **flight e., operational e.,** (i) *Mil:* mécanicien navigant; (ii) (*civil*) mécanicien de bord; **aircraft e.,** mécanicien de piste; (*c*) *Mil:* soldat *m* du génie, sapeur *m*; **the engineers,** le génie, l'arme *f* du génie; **the Royal Engineers,** *U.S:* **the Corps of Engineers** = le Génie; **e. officer,** officier du génie; **chief e.,** (i) commandant *m* du génie (d'une grande unité); (ii) (général) directeur du génie; **electrical, mechanical, e.,** sapeur électricien, mécanicien; **armoured, airborne, engineers,** génie aéroporté, blindé; **divisional engineers,** génie divisionnaire; **e. intelligence,** service *m* de renseignement du génie; (*d*) *Rail: NAm:* conducteur *m*, mécanicien, machiniste *m* (de locomotive); (*e*) *Fig: O:* **the (chief) e. of the scheme, plot,** l'âme *f*, l'instigateur *m*, du projet, du complot.

engineer[2], *v.tr.* **1.** construire (en qualité d'ingénieur) (des ponts, des routes). **2.** arranger (un spectacle); *usu. Pej:* machiner (un coup); manigancer (une affaire).

engineering [endʒi'niəriŋ], *s.* (*a*) technogénie *f*, technique *f*, science *f*, de l'ingénieur; ingénierie *f*; **e. data,** données *f* technogéniques; **civil e.,** génie civil; les travaux publics; **marine e., naval e.,** génie maritime (militaire); **military e.,** génie militaire; **electrical e.,** électrotechnique *f*; **chemical e.,** génie chimique; chimie industrielle; **atomic, nuclear, e.,** génie atomique; **agricultural e.,** génie agricole, rural; **aeronautical e.,** génie aéronautique; construction *f* aéronautique; *Atom.Ph:* **e. reactor,** pile industrielle, réacteur industriel; (*b*) (**mechanical**) **e.,** mécanique *f*; constructions *f* mécaniques; **general e.,** mécanique générale; **precision e.,** mécanique de précision; **light e.,** petite mécanique; **e. works, factory,** atelier *m* de constructions mécaniques; **electrical e. industry,** industrie *f* de l'équipement électrique; (*c*) **industrial e.,** organisation industrielle; **management e.,** organisation de la gestion des entreprises; **production e.,** technique de la production; **methods e., process e.,** méthode industrielle; **e. department,** service *m* technique; **e. and design department,** bureau *m* d'études; **e. consultant,** ingénieur *m* conseil; **human e.,** psychanalyse (industrielle); (*d*) *Fig: usu. Pej:* machinations *fpl*, manœuvres *fpl*.

engineman, *pl.* **men** ['endʒinmæn, -men], *s.m. Rail: NAm:* mécanicien.

engine-sized ['endʒinsaizd], *a. Paperm:* (papier) encollé à la machine.

engine-turn ['endʒintə:n], *v.tr. Metalw:* guillocher; **engine-turned watch case,** boîtier de montre guilloché, vermiculé.

engine turner ['endʒintə:nər], *s. Metalw:* guillocheur *m*.

engine turning ['endʒintə:niŋ], *s. Metalw:* guillochage *m*.

engird [in'gə:d] (*p.p.* **engirt, engirdle** [in'gə:dl], *v.tr. Lit:* ceindre (**with,** de); entourer (de).

England ['iŋglənd], *Pr.n. Geog:* l'Angleterre *f*; **in E.,** en Angleterre; **to go to E.,** aller en Angleterre.

Englander ['iŋgləndər], *s. Hist:* **little E.,** partisan, -e, d'une "petite Angleterre"; opposant, -ante, de l'impérialisme britannique.

English[1] ['iŋgliʃ]. (*a*) *a.* anglais; **E. born, by birth,** de naissance anglaise; **E. boy, girl,** jeune Anglais, -aise; **E. products,** produits anglais; **E. history,** histoire *f* d'Angleterre; **the E. Channel,** la Manche; *Arch:* **early E. (style),** premier style gothique; *Typ:* **E. (type),** Saint-Augustin *m*; corps 13; **old E.,** gothique *f*; (*b*) *s.* **the E.,** les Anglais *m*; (*c*) *S. Ling:* anglais *m*, la langue anglaise; **E. E., British E.,** l'anglais d'Angleterre; **American, Australian, E.,** l'anglais américain, australien; **Canadian E.,** l'anglais canadien, du Canada; **the King's, Queen's, E.,** l'anglais correct; **E. speaking,** anglophone, de langue anglaise; **to study E.,** étudier l'anglais; **to speak E.,** parler anglais; **in E.,** en anglais; **what is the E. for . . .?** comment dit-on, traduit-on, en anglais . . .? **old E.,** l'ancien anglais (antérieur au XIIe siècle); l'anglo-saxon *m*; **middle E.,** le moyen anglais (1150–1500); **student, specialist, of E.,** angliste *mf*, angliciste *mf*, anglicisant, -ante; **professor, teacher, of E., E. master, mistress,** professeur *m* d'anglais; **in plain E.,** en bon anglais; **he can't understand plain E.,** il ne peut pas comprendre l'anglais quand on le lui parle; **let me tell you in plain E. that . . .,** je vais vous dire en mots de deux syllabes que . . .; **pidgin E.** = petit nègre.

English[2], *v.tr. A: & Lit:* **1.** traduire, rendre, (un livre) en anglais. **2.** angliciser (un mot, une nation).

Englishman, *pl.* **-men** ['iŋgliʃmən], *s.* **1.** Anglais *m*. **2.** *Nau: A:* vaisseau anglais.

Englishwoman, *pl.* **women** ['iŋgliʃwumən, -wimin], *s.f.* Anglaise.

engorge [in'gɔ:dʒ], *v.tr.* **1.** *Lit:* dévorer, engloutir (des aliments). **2.** (*a*) **to be engorged,** être engorgé, rempli outre mesure; (*of blast furnace, etc.*) **to become e.,** s'engorger; (*b*) **engorged (with blood),** gonflé de sang; congestionné; (*of blood vessel*) **to become engorged,** se congestionner.

engorgement [in'gɔ:dʒmənt], *s.* **1.** *Lit:* engloutissement *m*. **2.** (*a*) engorgement *m* (d'un haut fourneau, etc.); (*b*) *Med:* congestion *f* (d'un organe, etc.).

engouled [in'gu:ld], **engoulée** [ɔŋ'gu:lei], *a. Her:* engoulé.

engrailed [in'greild], *a. Her:* engrêlé.

engrain [in'grein], *v.tr. A.Tex:* teindre (une étoffe, etc.) grand teint.

engram ['engræm], *s. Psy:* engramme *m*.

engrave [in'greiv], *v.tr.* graver (des caractères, des formes); **to e. on wood,** graver sur bois; **to e. on metal,** graver au burin; **to e. on copper,** chalcographier; **plate engraved with an inscription,** plaque *f* portant gravée une inscription; **engraved on the memory,** gravé dans la mémoire.

engraver [in'greivər], *s.* **1.** (*pers.*) graveur *m*; **artist e., painter e.,** peintre-graveur *m*; **plate e.,** graveur à l'outil, au burin; **wood e.,** graveur sur bois; **e. on copper,** chalcographe *m*. **2.** *Tls:* (*a*) machine *f*, tour *m*, à graver; (*b*) burin *m* (de graveur).

engraving [in'greiviŋ], *s.* (*process or print*) gravure *f*; (*print*) estampe *f*; **e. needle,** pointe *f* pour taille-douce; **e. pen, e. tool,** poinçon *m* de graveur, crayon *m* vibreur; **copper-plate e., e. on copper,** taille-douce *f*; chalcographie *f*; **line e.,** gravure au trait, au burin, en taille-douce; **glass e.,** gravure sur verre, hyalographie *f*; **half-tone e.,** simili gravure; **process e.,** typogravure *f*; simili gravure *f*; **steel(-plate) e.,** gravure sur acier, en taille dure; sidérographie *f*; **stippled e.,** pointillé *m*; **stone e.,** gravure sur pierre, lithographie *f*; **wood e.,** gravure sur bois; xylographie *f*.

engross [in'grous], *v.tr.* **1.** *Jur:* (*a*) grossoyer, copier (un document); écrire (un document) en grosse; (*b*) rédiger (un document). **2.** (*a*) *Com: A:* accaparer (une denrée); (*b*) *A:* **to e. the conversation,** s'emparer de la conversation; accaparer la conversation. **3. to e. s.o., s.o.'s attention, s.o.'s time,** absorber, occuper, qn, l'attention, le temps, de qn; **his work engrosses him completely,** son travail l'absorbe entièrement; **engrossed in her reading,** toute à sa lecture; **to become engrossed in sth.,** s'abstraire, s'absorber, dans qch.

engrosser [in'grousər], *s. Jur:* rédacteur *m* d'une grosse.

engrossing[1] *a.* [in'grousiŋ], (*of work, study, etc.*) absorbant.

engrossing[2], *s.* = ENGROSSMENT.

engrossment [in'grousmənt], *s.* **1.** *Jur:* (*a*) rédaction *f* de la grosse; (*b*) grosse *f.* **2.** absorption *f* (de l'esprit, de l'attention) **(in,** dans). **3.** *A:* accaparement *m.*

engulf [in'gʌlf], *v.tr.* engloutir, engouffrer; **to be engulfed in the sea,** être englouti par les flots; s'engouffrer, sombrer, s'abîmer, dans les flots.

engulfment [in'gʌlfmənt], *s.* engouffrement *m,* engloutissement *m.*

enhance [in'hɑ:ns, -'hæns], *v.tr.* rehausser (le mérite, le prix, de qch.); augmenter, accroître (le plaisir); mettre en valeur, relever (la beauté de qn); agrandir (la réputation); **to e. the price of goods,** enchérir, renchérir, des marchandises; **to e. the value of land,** mettre une terre en valeur.

enhancement [in'hɑ:nsmənt, -'hæns-], *s.* renchérissement *m,* rehaussement *m,* hausse *f* (de prix); embellissement *m* (de charmes); augmentation *f* (de plaisir, etc.).

enharmonic [enhɑ:'mɔnik], *a. Mus:* (note *f,* gamme *f*) enharmonique; **e. change,** enharmonie *f.*

enhydra [en'haidrə], *s. Z:* enhydre *m.*

enhydros [en'haidrəs], *s. Miner:* enhydre *m.*

enhydrous [en'haidrəs], *a. Geol:* enhydre.

Enid ['i:nid], *Pr.n.f.* Énide.

enigma [i'nigmə], *s.* (*a*) énigme *f;* **to solve the e.,** trouver le mot de l'énigme; (*b*) personne énigmatique, mystérieuse.

enigmatic(al) [enig'mætik(l)], *a.* énigmatique; mystérieux.

enigmatically [enig'mætik(ə)li], *adv.* énigmatiquement, mystérieusement.

enjambment [in'dʒæm(b)mənt], *s. Pros:* enjambement *m.*

enjoin [in'dʒɔin], *v.tr.* **1.** enjoindre, ordonner, prescrire, imposer **(sth. on s.o.,** qch. à qn); **to e. s.o. to do sth.,** enjoindre, ordonner, à qn de faire qch.; **to e. s.o. not to do sth.,** défendre à qn de faire qch. **2.** *Jur:* interdire, prohiber.

enjoinment [in'dʒɔinmənt], *s.* **1.** injonction *f.* **2.** *Jur:* prohibition *f,* interdiction *f.*

enjoy [in'dʒɔi], *v.tr.* **1.** aimer, trouver bon, goûter; prendre plaisir à (qch.); **to e. one's dinner,** trouver le dîner bon; **to e. a meal at leisure,** savourer à loisir son repas; **to e. a pipe,** savourer une pipe; **to e. the fine weather,** jouir du beau temps; **he enjoyed his trips abroad,** il goûtait fort ses voyages à l'étranger; **how did you e. your holiday?** avez-vous passé de bonnes vacances? **to e. music, s.o.'s conversation,** goûter, prendre plaisir à, aimer, la musique, la conversation de qn; **to e. the humour of the situation,** savourer le comique de la situation; **he enjoyed music and the theatre,** il était amateur de musique et de théâtre; **to e. oneself,** s'amuser, se divertir; **he enjoys life,** il sait jouir de la vie; **e. yourself!** amusez-vous bien! **to e. a good laugh,** rire de bon cœur, tout son saoul; **to e. doing sth.,** aimer, prendre plaisir, trouver (du) plaisir, à faire qch.; **he did not e. writing his books,** il écrivait ses livres sans plaisir; **I e. a break from work for half an hour,** j'aime bien interrompre mon travail pendant une demi-heure; **I see you e. it,** je vois que cela vous fait plaisir, que cela vous plaît. **2.** (*a*) jouir de, posséder (une fortune, un droit, la confiance de qn); disposer (d'une fortune); (*b*) **to e. good, radiant, health,** jouir d'une bonne santé; avoir une santé florissante; *F:* **to e. bad, wretched, health,** avoir peu de santé; avoir la santé faible, une santé pitoyable; ne pas avoir de santé. **3.** *A:* posséder (une femme).

enjoyable [in'dʒɔiəbl], *a.* (chose) dont on peut jouir; (séjour *m,* excursion *f*) agréable; **we had a most e. evening,** nous avons passé une excellente soirée; **e. sensation,** sensation *f* agréable; **e. food,** mets *mpl* savoureux.

enjoyably [in'dʒɔiəbli], *adv.* agréablement; avec plaisir.

enjoyment [in'dʒɔimənt], *s.* **1.** jouissance *f* (d'un droit, etc.); *Jur:* **prevention of e.,** trouble de jouissance. **2.** plaisir *m.*

enkindle [en'kindl], *v.tr. Lit:* allumer (une flamme); enflammer, exciter (une passion, etc.).

enlace [in'leis], *v.tr.* enlacer; **tree enlaced with ivy,** arbre enlacé de lierre.

enlacement [in'leismənt], *s.* enlacement *m.*

enlarge [in'lɑ:dʒ]. **1.** *v.tr.* (*a*) agrandir; étendre (une propriété); accroître, augmenter (un nombre, sa fortune); dilater (un corps); élargir (un trou); (*ream out*) aléser (un trou); *Med:* hypertrophier (le cœur, le foie); *Phot:* agrandir (un cliché, etc.); **we are going to e. our premises,** nous allons nous agrandir; **enlarged edition,** édition augmentée; **enlarged copy,** reproduction *f* en grand; **enlarged pores,** pores dilatés; *Med:* **enlarged heart,** dilatation *f,* hypertrophie *f,* du cœur; cardiectasie *f;* **he has an enlarged heart,** il souffre d'une dilatation du cœur; **enlarged tonsils,** amygdales hypertrophiées; hypertrophie *f,* tuméfaction *f,* des amygdales; (*b*) développer, élargir (l'intelligence, une idée); (*c*) *A:* & *U.S:* élargir, relaxer (un prisonnier); (*d*) *Jur:* **to e. bail, a recognizance,** proroger une caution, un engagement. **2.** *v.i.* (*a*) s'agrandir, s'étendre, s'élargir; (*of bore of gun*) s'évaser; (*b*) **to e. on . . .,** s'étendre sur, discourir longuement sur (un sujet, les avantages, l'importance, de qch.).

enlargement [in'lɑ:dʒmənt], *s.* **1.** agrandissement *m;* extension *f* (d'une propriété); accroissement *m* (d'une fortune); élargissement *m,* alésage *m* (d'un trou); augmentation *f.* **2.** *Phot:* agrandissement; **carbon e.,** agrandissement en charbon, au charbon. **3.** *Med:* hypertrophie *f* (du cœur, de la rate). **4.** *A:* **e. upon a subject,** développement *m,* amplification *f,* d'un sujet. **5.** *A:* & *U.S:* élargissement, relaxation *f* (d'un prisonnier); mise *f* en liberté (d'un prisonnier, d'un animal).

enlarger [in'lɑ:dʒər], *s. Phot:* agrandisseur *m.*

enlighten [in'lait(ə)n], *v.tr.* **1.** *Poet:* illuminer. **2. to e. s.o. on a subject, as to sth.,** éclairer qn sur un sujet; ouvrir les yeux de qn, à qn, au sujet de qch.

enlightened [in'laitənd], *a.* (*of pers., mind*) éclairé; **e. criticism,** critique éclairée.

enlightenment [in'laitənm(ə)nt], *s.* **1.** (*a*) éclaircissement *mpl* **(on,** sur); (*b*) **for your e.,** pour votre édification. **2. the age of E.,** le siècle des lumières.

enlink [in'liŋk], *v.tr.* enchaîner, lier **(to, with,** à).

enlist [in'list]. **1.** *v.tr.* (*a*) *Mil:* enrôler, engager (un soldat); (*b*) **to e. supporters,** enrôler, recruter, des partisans; **to e. the services of s.o.,** s'assurer le concours de qn; s'adjoindre qn; **to e. s.o.'s support for a cause, etc., to e. s.o. in support of a cause, etc.,** rallier qn à une cause, etc.; **to e. public interest in a matter,** intéresser le public à une affaire. **2.** *v.i. Mil:* (*of soldier*) s'engager, s'enrôler.

enlisted [in'listid], *a.* enrôlé, engagé, appelé (sous les drapeaux); *Mil: U.S:* **e. man,** (i) homme de troupe; (ii) gradé *m;* **e. men, e. personnel,** les hommes de troupe et les gradés; *F:* la troupe (et les gradés).

enlistment [in'listmənt], *s. Mil:* engagement *m,* enrôlement *m;* **the Foreign E. Act,** la loi sur les engagements à l'étranger.

enliven [in'laiv(ə)n], *v.tr.* (*a*) animer, vivifier (qn, qch.); **to e. a discussion,** animer une discussion; **to e. business,** stimuler les affaires; (*b*) égayer (un tableau, une fête).

enlivening[1] [in'laivniŋ], *a.* **1.** (musique) animante; (air, climat) vivifiant. **2.** (récit) égayant.

enlivening[2], *s.* **1.** vivification *f;* animation *f* (de la conversation, etc.). **2.** égaiement *m.*

en masse ['ɑ̃ 'mæs], *adv.phr.* en masse, tous ensemble.

enmesh [in'meʃ], *v.tr.* **1.** (*a*) prendre (des poissons, etc.) au filet; (*b*) embarrasser, empêtrer (qn); prendre (qn) dans un piège. **2.** *Mec.E:* engrener.

enmeshing [in'meʃiŋ], *s. Mec.E:* engrènement *m.*

enmity ['enmiti], *s.* inimitié *f,* haine *f,* hostilité *f;* **to be at e. with s.o.,** être en inimitié déclarée, en guerre ouverte, avec qn.

ennead ['eniæd], *s.* ennéade *f.*

enneagon ['eniəgən], *s. Mth:* ennéagone *m.*

enneagonal [eni'ægən(ə)l], *a.* ennéagonal, -aux.

enneagynous [eni'ædʒinəs], *a. Bot:* ennéagyne.

enneandrous [eni'ændrəs], *a. Bot:* ennéandre.

enneapetalous [eniə'petələs], *a. Bot:* ennéapétale.

enneasyllabic [eniəsi'læbik], *a. Pros:* ennéasyllabe.

ennoble [i'noubl], *v.tr.* **1.** anoblir, faire noble (un roturier); **family recently ennobled,** famille de noblesse récente. **2.** ennoblir, rendre noble, grandir (qn, le caractère).

ennoblement [i'noublmənt], *s.* **1.** anoblissement *m* (d'un roturier). **2.** ennoblissement *m* (du caractère, etc.).

ennobling[1] [i'noubliŋ], *a.* (principe, influence) qui ennoblit.

ennobling[2], *s.* = ENNOBLEMENT.

ennui [ɑ̃nwi:], *s.* ennui *m;* lassitude morale.

Enoch ['i:nɔk], *Pr.n.m.* Énoch.

enol ['i:nɔl], *s. Ch:* énol *m.*

enolase ['i:nouleis], *s. Ch:* énolase *f.*

enolic [i:'nɔlik], *a. Ch:* énolique.

enolization [i:noulai'zeiʃ(ə)n], *s. Ch:* énolisation *f.*

enophthalmus [enɔf'θælməs], *s. Med:* énophtalmie *f.*

enormity [i'nɔ:miti], *s.* (*a*) énormité *f* (d'un crime, etc.); (*b*) **the enormities committed in the name of liberty,** les énormités, les atrocités, commises au nom de la liberté.

enormous [i'nɔ:məs], *a.* énorme; colossal, -aux; monumental, -aux; **an e. success,** un succès fou.

enormously [i'nɔ:məsli], *adv.* énormément, colossalement.

enormousness [i'nɔ:məsnis], *s.* énormité *f;* grandeur démesurée.

enosis [e'nousis], *s. Pol:* énosis *f.*

enostosis [enɔ'stousis], *s. Med:* énostose *f.*

enough [i'nʌf]. **1.** *a.* & *s.* assez; **e. potatoes, potatoes e., e. money, money e.,** assez de pommes de terre, assez d'argent; **e. food, e. wine, and e. of everything else,** assez de nourriture, assez de vin, et assez de toute autre chose; *A:* **take e. of it to cover a sixpence,** prenez-en de quoi couvrir une pièce de six pence; *F:* **I've had e. of it, of them,** j'en ai assez; **I've had e. of him,** je le porte sur mon dos; il me scie le dos; **I've had e. of your insults,** en voilà assez de vos injures; **I've had e. to drink, to eat,** j'ai assez bu, mangé; je n'ai plus soif, faim; **that's e. for me,** cela me suffit; **that's e.,** (i) c'est assez, c'est suffisant, cela suffit; (ii) en voilà assez! **more than e.,** plus qu'il n'en faut; plus que suffisant; assez et au delà; **there was more than e., e. and to spare,** il y en avait de reste; **quite e.,** bien suffisant; **talking is not e.,** c'est peu (que) de parler; **he cannot say e. about you,** il n'en finit pas de faire votre éloge; **to have not half e. money,** ne pas avoir à moitié près assez d'argent; **have you e. to pay the bill?** avez-vous de quoi payer? **a hundred francs will be e., I shall have e. with a hundred francs,** j'aurai assez de cent francs; **wages that are not e. to live on,** salaire *m* qui ne suffit pas pour vivre; **he has e. to live on,** il a de quoi vivre; **e. said!** assez parlé! brisons là! **you've drunk e.!** allons, assez bu! **e. of this nonsense!** assez de ces bêtises! **e.!** (i) il suffit! (ii) assez parlé! **one word was e. to prove that . . .,** il a suffi d'un mot pour prouver que . . .; **it was e. to drive one crazy, mad,** c'était à vous rendre fou; **this is e. to prevent the possibility of mistaking . . .,** cela suffit pour qu'on ne puisse se méprendre . . .; *Prov:* **e. is as good as a feast,** assez vaut (un) festin; trop et trop peu n'est pas mesure; le trop ne vaut rien. **2.** *adv.* (*a*) **good e., stupid e.,** assez bon, assez sot; **it's good e.,** c'est bien bon, ça fera bien; **good e.! fair e.!** ça va! d'accord! **it's a good e. reason,** c'est une raison comme une autre; **it is hardly cooked e.,** ce n'est pas tout à fait assez cuit; **she is not strong e. to go to school,** elle n'est pas assez forte pour aller à l'école; **he is wise e. to know what is expected of him,** il est assez sage pour savoir ce qu'on attend de lui; **to be near e. to see,** être assez près pour voir; (*b*) (*intensive*) **you know well e. what I mean,** vous savez très bien ce que je veux dire; **curiously, oddly, e., nobody knew anything about it,** chose curieuse, personne n'en savait rien; **I came across him in London, oddly e.,** par un hasard singulier je l'ai rencontré à Londres; (*c*) (*disparaging*) **she sings well e.,** elle chante passablement; **the house is comfortable e.,** la maison est assez confortable; **it is well e. in its way, but . . .,** ce n'est pas si mal en son genre, mais . . ..

enounce [i'nauns], *v.tr.* **1.** énoncer (un axiome). **2.** annoncer, déclarer (son opinion, etc.). **3.** prononcer (un mot, une syllabe).

enouncement [i'naunsmənt], *s.* **1.** énonciation *f.* **2.** déclaration *f.*

enow [i'nau], *a., s.,* & *adv. A:* & *Poet:* = ENOUGH.

en passant [ɑ̃:'pɑsɑ̃], *adv.* **1.** en passant, incidemment. **2.** *Chess:* **to take a pawn e. p.,** prendre un pion en passant.

enphytotic [enfi'tɔtik], *a.* & *s. Bot:* **e. (disease),** emphytie *f.*

enplane [in'plein], *v.i.* & *tr.* = EMPLANE.

enquire [iŋ'kwaiər], *v.tr.* & *i.* demander (qch.); s'informer (de qch.); se renseigner (sur qch.); faire des recherches des investigations (sur qch.).

enquiry [in'kwai(ə)ri], *s.* **1.** enquête *f,* recherche *f,* investigation *f.* **2.** demande *f* de renseignements.

enrage [in'reidʒ], *v.tr.* rendre (qn) furieux; faire enrager (qn); exaspérer (qn); **I'm enraged even to think of it,** même d'y penser m'enrage; **enraged beast,** bête furieuse.

enrapture [in'ræptjər], *v.tr.* ravir, enchanter, transporter (un auditoire, etc.); **to be enraptured with sth.,** s'extasier de, sur, devant, qch.; être en extase devant qch.

enraptured [in'ræptjəd], *a.* **1.** ravi, enchanté, transporté (d'admiration). **2.** extasié, extatique.

enregister [in'redʒistər], *v.tr.* enregistrer.

enrich [in'ritʃ], *v.tr.* enrichir (qn, une collection, une langue, un livre, etc.); meubler (l'esprit); fertiliser, amender (la terre); *Ch: etc:* enrichir; *I.C.E:* **to e. the mixture,** enrichir le mélange.

enriched [in'ritʃt], *a.* **e. with gold,** rehaussé d'or; **biography e. with new facts,** biographie accrue de faits nouveaux; *Atom.Ph:* **e. particle,** particule enrichie; **e. uranium,** uranium enrichi; **isotope-e.,** enrichi à l'isotope.

enriching [in'ritʃiŋ], *s.* enrichissement *m*; *Agr:* fertilisation *f,* amendement *m* (de la terre).

enrichment [in'ritʃmənt], *s.* enrichissement *m.*

enring [in'riŋ], *v.tr. Poet:* entourer, encercler (**with,** de).

enrobe [in'roub], *v.tr.* **1.** *Lit:* (*a*) vêtir, revêtir (qn) (**with, in,** de); (*b*) **to e. s.o.,** revêtir qn de sa robe, de sa toge (pour une cérémonie). **2.** *Ind:* enrober (des chocolats, etc.).

enrober [in'roubər], *s. Ind:* enrobeuse *f.*

enrockment [in'rɔkm(ə)nt], *s. Civ E: Hyd E:* enrochement *m.*

enrol, *occ.* **enroll** [in'roul], *v.tr.* (**enrolled**) **1.** *Mil: Nau: etc:* enrôler, encadrer (des recrues); engager (des ouvriers); embrigader, embaucher (des balayeurs, etc.); immatriculer (des étudiants); **to e. (oneself) in the army, in a society,** s'enrôler, s'engager, dans l'armée; s'inscrire à une société; **to e. for a course of lectures,** se faire inscrire pour un cours; **enrolled members,** membres inscrits; **to e. brains and talent,** s'adjoindre des capacités. **2.** *Jur:* enregistrer (un acte juridique, un jugement).

enrolment [in'roulmənt], *s.* **1.** enrôlement *m* (de soldats, etc.); engagement *m,* embauche *f* (d'ouvriers, etc.); embrigadement *m* (de balayeurs, etc.). **2.** *Jur:* enregistrement *m,* inscription *f* sur registre officiel (d'un acte juridique, d'un jugement, etc.).

en route [ɑ̃'ru:t], *Fr.phr.* en route.

ens [enz], *s. Phil:* ens *m.*

ensample [en'sɑ:mpl], *s. A:* = EXAMPLE.

ensanguine [in'sæŋgwin], *v.tr. Lit:* tacher de sang; ensanglanter.

ensconce [in'skɔns], *v.tr.* **to e. oneself in a corner,** se blottir, se nicher, dans un coin; se rencogner dans un angle; **to e. oneself in an armchair,** se camper dans un fauteuil; **statue ensconced in a recess,** statue nichée dans un enfoncement, abritée dans une niche.

ensellure [in'seljuər], *s. Anthr:* ensellure *f.*

ensemble [ɑ̃:'sɑ̃:bl], *s. Cost: Mus: etc:* ensemble *m.*

ensepulchre [en'seplkər], *v.tr. Lit:* mettre au tombeau.

ensete [en'si:ti], *s.* banane *f* d'Abyssinie.

enshrine [in'ʃrain], *v.tr.* enchâsser (une sainte relique, une image) (**in,** dans); **the casket that enshrined his bones,** la cassette qui enchâssait ses os.

enshrinement [in'ʃrainmənt], *s.* enchâssement *m.*

enshroud [in'ʃraud], *v.tr. Lit:* ensevelir (comme dans un linceul); cacher (**in,** sous); recouvrir (**in,** de); **the countryside was enshrouded in fog,** la campagne disparaissait, avait disparu, sous le brouillard.

ensiform ['ensifɔ:m], *a. Nat.Hist:* ensiforme; *Bot:* **e.-leaved,** ensifolié; *Anat:* **the e. cartilage,** le cartilage ensiforme, xiphoïde.

ensign ['ensain, 'ens(ə)n], *s.* **1.** enseigne *f;* (*a*) insigne *m,* symbole *m* (d'office, d'emploi); **those ensigns of authority, the keys,** les clefs, ces symboles de l'autorité; (*b*) drapeau *m; Nau:* pavillon national, de poupe; **white e.,** pavillon de la Marine anglaise et du Royal Yacht Squadron; **red e.** = pavillon marchand; **blue e.,** pavillon de la Marine de réserve. **2.** (*a*) *Mil: A:* porte-drapeau *m inv,* enseigne *m;* (*b*) *U.S. Navy:* enseigne *m* (de vaisseau de deuxième classe). **3.** *Ent:* **e. fly, wasp,** évanie *f.*

ensilage[1] ['ens(a)ilidʒ], **ensilation** [ensi'leiʃ(ə)n], *s. Agr:* **1.** ensilage *m,* (en)silotage *m;* **e. blower,** ensileuse *f.* **2. ensilage,** fourrage ensilé.

ensilage[2], **ensile** [en'sail], *v.tr.* ensiler (le fourrage, des grains, des racines, etc.).

enslave [in'sleiv], *v.tr.* réduire à l'esclavage; asservir; rendre (qn) esclave; **to e. hearts, the senses,** captiver, enjôler, les cœurs, les sens; **to be enslaved to habit, to superstition,** être l'esclave d'une habitude, de la superstition; **her beauty kept him enslaved,** il restait captif de sa beauté; sa beauté l'avait captivé, envoûté.

enslavement [in'sleivmənt], *s.* réduction *f* (d'une nation, etc.) à l'esclavage; asservissement *m;* assujettissement *m* (de qn à son devoir, etc.).

ensnare [in'snɛər], *v.tr.* prendre (qn) au piège; (*of woman*) attraper, séduire, enjôler (un homme).

ensnarl [in'snɑ:l], *v.tr.* enchevêtrer.

en-soi [ɑ̃'swa], *s. Phil:* en-soi *m inv.*

ensphere [in'sfiər], *v.tr. Poet:* envelopper, entourer (**with,** de).

enstatite ['enstətait], *s. Miner:* enstatite *f.*

ensuant [in'sju(:)ənt], *a.* **e. on . . .,** à la suite de . . .; **conditions e. on the war,** conditions qui découlent de la guerre.

ensue [in'sju:]. **1.** *v.i.* s'ensuivre; **the evils that ensued from this misunderstanding,** les maux qui se sont ensuivis, qui ont résulté, de ce malentendu; **a long silence ensued,** il se fit, il y eut, un long silence. **2.** *v.tr. B:* **let him seek peace and e. it,** qu'il recherche la paix et qu'il tâche de se la procurer.

ensuing [in'sju:iŋ], *a.* (an, jour) suivant; (événement) subséquent; **in the e. years,** au cours des années qui suivirent, qui suivront.

ensure [in'ʃuər], *v.tr.* **1.** assurer, rendre sûr (qn, qch.) (**against, from,** contre); garantir (qn) (**against, from,** de). **2.** (*a*) **if success is to be ensured . . .,** pour assurer le succès . . .; **to e. a cure, you must . . .,** pour réaliser la guérison, il vous faudra . . .; **I have taken steps to e. that everything shall be done in an orderly fashion,** j'ai pris des mesures pour que tout se fasse en ordre; **to e. good service,** assurer le service; (*b*) **to e. s.o. enough to live on,** assurer à qn de quoi vivre. **3.** *A:* = INSURE.

enswathe [in'sweið], *v.tr.* emmailloter, envelopper (**in,** dans).

entablature [in'tæblətjər], *s. Arch: Mec.E:* entablement *m* (d'un édifice, d'un marteau-pilon, etc.).

entablement [in'teiblmənt], *s. Arch:* table supérieure (d'un piédestal).

entail[1] ['enteil], *s.* **1.** *Jur:* substitution *f* (d'héritiers). **2.** (*a*) *Jur:* bien substitué; majorat *m;* (*b*) héritage *m* inéluctable.

entail[2] [en'teil], *v.tr.* **1.** *Jur:* **to e. an estate (on s.o.),** substituer un bien (au profit de qn); **entailed estate,** majorat *m;* bien substitué; bien indisponible, grevé, majoraté. **2.** (*of actions*) amener, entraîner (des dépenses, des conséquences); occasionner (des dépenses); imposer (beaucoup de travail) (**on,** à); comporter (des difficultés); **it entails trouble,** cela ne va pas sans peine; **your ruin will e. mine,** votre ruine entraînera la mienne.

entailment [en'teilmənt], *s. Jur:* substitution *f* (d'une propriété).

ental ['ent(ə)l], *a. Nat.Hist:* (*of surface, etc.*) intérieur.

entangle [in'tæŋgl], *v.tr.* **1.** (*a*) empêtrer; **to e. one's feet in a rope,** s'empêtrer les pieds dans un cordage; **to get, become, entangled in the seaweed,** s'empêtrer, dans les algues; (*b*) embarrasser, empêtrer (qn); **to get entangled in a shady business,** se trouver entraîné dans une affaire louche; **to get entangled with a woman,** avoir une affaire avec une femme; **he had got entangled,** il s'était fourré dans le pétrin. **2.** emmêler (les cheveux, du fil); enchevêtrer (du fil de fer); embrouiller (les idées); (*of thread, etc.*) **to get entangled,** s'emmêler, s'enchevêtrer, s'embrouiller; **hopelessly entangled style,** style *m* inextricable.

entanglement [in'tæŋglmənt], *s.* **1.** embrouillement *m,* enchevêtrement *m; Tp: etc:* **e. of the wires,** mélange *m* des fils; **wire e.,** réseau(x) *m(pl)* de fil de fer barbelé. **2.** embarras *m* (de voitures, etc.). **3. emotional entanglements,** complications sentimentales; **he had had an e. with a woman,** il avait eu une affaire avec une femme, une affaire de femme.

entangling [in'tæŋgliŋ], *a.* empêtrant, enchevêtrant.

entasis ['entəsis], *s. Arch:* renflement *m* imperceptible (d'une colonne); **pillar with e.,** colonne renflée.

enté ['entei], *a. Her:* **e. en point(e),** enté en pointe.

entelechy [en'teliki], *s. Phil:* entéléchie *f.*

entellus [en'teləs], *s. Z:* entelle *m.*

entente [ɑ̃:'tɑ̃:t], *s.* entente *f; esp. Dipl:* **e. cordiale,** entente cordiale; **the Little E.,** la petite Entente.

enter ['entər], *v.* (**entered**)

I. *v.i.* entrer (**into, through, etc.,** dans, par, etc.); *Th:* (*stage direction*) **e. Hamlet,** entre Hamlet; Hamlet entre.

II. *v.tr.* **1.** (*a*) entrer, pénétrer, dans (une maison, un pays); **the army entered the pass,** l'armée s'engagea dans le défilé; **to e. a highway,** (i) (*of road*) déboucher, (ii) (*of driver, of car*) s'engager, sur une route; **the bullet had entered his heart,** la balle lui était entrée, lui avait pénétré, dans le cœur; **the harbour is easy to e.,** le port est d'un accès facile; **it never entered my head, mind, that . . .,** il ne m'est pas venu à l'esprit que . . .; (*b*) faire entrer; *Artil: A:* **to e. the charge,** enfoncer la gargousse. **2.** (*a*) **to e. the Army, the Navy,** entrer au service; se faire soldat, se faire marin; **to e. the Church,** entrer dans les ordres; **to e. a university, a convent,** entrer à une université, dans un couvent; **to e. the fray,** descendre dans l'arène; **to e. the lists against s.o.,** entrer en lice contre qn; se mettre sur les rangs; descendre dans l'arène; **to e. s.o.'s service,** devenir le, la, domestique de qn, entrer au service de qn; (*b*) **to e. one's sixtieth year,** entrer dans sa soixantième année. **3.** (*a*) **to e. a name on a list,** inscrire, porter, un nom sur une liste; **to e. a seaman on the ship's books,** porter un homme au rôle de l'équipage; *Nau:* embarquer un homme; **to e. a student at a university,** admettre un étudiant à une université; **to e. a horse for a race,** engager un cheval dans une course; *v.i.* **to e. for a race,** se faire inscrire, s'engager, pour une course; **to e. for an examination,** se présenter à un examen; passer, subir, un examen; *Jur:* **to e. a deposition on the record,** consigner un témoignage sur le procès-verbal; **to e. a deed, a judgment,** enregistrer, minuter, un acte, un jugement; *U.S:* **to e. land,** se faire inscrire comme acquéreur d'une terre; *Cust:* **to e. goods,** déclarer des marchandises en douane; **to e. a ship inwards, outwards,** faire la déclaration d'entrée, de sortie; (*b*) *Com:* **to e. (up) an item in the ledger,** inscrire, porter, un article au grand livre; faire écriture d'un article au grand livre; **to e. (up) an amount in the expenditure, in the receipts,** employer une somme en dépense, en recette; **to e. (sth.) to, against, s.o.,** porter, inscrire, (qch.) au compte de qn; **e. that to me,** mettez cela à mon compte; (*c*) *Jur: etc:* **to e. an action against s.o.,** intenter un procès à qn; **to e. a protest,** faire une protestation par écrit, protester formellement; **to e. a mild protest,** protester mollement. **4.** commencer le dressage (d'un chien, d'un cheval).

III. (*compound verbs*) **1. enter into,** *v.i.* (*a*) **to e. into relations with s.o.,** entrer en relations avec qn; entamer des relations avec qn; **to e. into business,** entrer dans les affaires; **to e. into negotiations with s.o.,** engager des négociations avec qn; **to e. into partnership with s.o.,** entrer en association avec qn, s'associer avec qn; **to e. into a bargain, an agreement, a contract,** conclure un marché, un engagement, passer un contrat (**with,** avec); **to e. into service,** entrer en service; **the pecuniary obligations into which he has entered,** les engagements pécuniaires par lui contractés; **to e. into explanations,** fournir des explications; s'expliquer; **to e. into a conversation (with s.o.),** entrer en, lier, nouer, conversation (avec qn); engager une conversation, entrer en propos (avec qn); **to e. into the smallest details,** descendre jusqu'aux plus petits détails; (*b*) prendre part à (un complot, etc.); **when chance enters into it,** quand le hasard s'en mêle; **subjects that do not e. into the question,** sujets *m* qui n'entrent pas en ligne de compte, qui sont en dehors de l'affaire; **to e. into things,** être sociable, prendre part à la conversation, etc.; **to e. into the spirit of the game,** entrer dans le jeu, (*c*) *Jur:* **to e. into the rights of a creditor,** demeurer subrogé aux droits d'un créancier.

2. enter upon, *v.i. Jur:* **to e. upon a property,** entrer en possession, prendre possession, d'un bien.

enteric [en'terik], *a. Med:* entérique; **e. fever,** *s.* **e.,** fièvre intestinale; fièvre typhoïde.

entering[1] ['ent(ə)riŋ], *a.* **1.** (foule *f*) qui entre. **2.** (*a*) **e. stream (of fluid),** courant *m* d'entrée; (*b*) *Av:* **e. edge (of wing),** bord *m* d'attaque.

entering[2], *s.* **1.** entrée *f* (dans un endroit). **2.** (*a*) admission *f* (d'un étudiant); inscription *f* (de son nom); *Rac:* souscription *f* (d'un cheval engagé); (*b*) *Com:* **e. (up),** inscription, enregistrement *m,* comptabilisation *f;* **e. clerk,** commis *m* aux écritures. **3. e. tool,** outil *m* de pénétration.

enteritis [entə'raitis], *s. Med:* entérite *f.*

entero- ['entərou], *comb.fm. Med:* entéro-.

enteroc(o)ele ['entərousi:l], *s.* entérocèle *m.*

enterococcus, *pl.* **-cocci** ['entərou'kɔkəs, -'kɔksai], *s. Med:* entérocoque *m.*

enterocolitis ['entərouka'laitis], *s. Med:* entérocolite *f.*

enterokinase ['entərouki'neis], *s. Biol:* entérokinase *f.*

enterolith ['entərouliθ], *s. Med:* entérolithe *m.*

enteromorpha ['entərou'mɔ:fə], *s. Algae:* entéromorphe *f.*

enteron, *pl.* **-a** ['entərən, -ə], *s. Anat:* canal *m* alimentaire; intestin *m.*

Enteropneusta ['entərou'nju:stə], *s.pl. Ann:* entéropneustes *m.*

enteroptosis ['entərɔp'tousis], *s. Med:* entéroptose *f.*

enterorenal ['entərou'ri:nl], *a. Med:* entérorénal, -aux.

enterorrhagia ['entərou'reidʒiə], *s. Med:* entérorragie *f.*

enterotomy [entə'rɔtəmi], *s. Surg:* entérotomie *f.*

enterovaccine ['entərou'væksin], *s.* entérovaccin *m.*

enterprise[1] ['entəpraiz], *s.* **1.** (*a*) entreprise difficile, hardie; (*b*) *Pol.Ec:* **free e.,** la libre entreprise; **private e.,** l'entreprise privée; le secteur privé; **state e.,** secteur public; **small-scale e.,** entreprise artisanale. **2.** esprit; hardiesse *f;* **to show e.,** faire preuve d'un esprit entreprenant; **man of great e.,** homme entreprenant.

enterprise[2], *v.tr. A:* entreprendre.

enterprising ['entəpraiziŋ], *a.* (marchand, esprit) entreprenant.

enterprisingly ['entəpraiziŋli], *adv.* hardiment, résolument.

entertain [entə'tein], *v.tr.* **1.** (*a*) amuser, divertir (qn); I was greatly entertained by it, cela m'a beaucoup amusé, diverti; to e. s.o. with a story, raconter une histoire à qn pour le distraire; to e. the company, réjouir la compagnie; (b) faire la conversation à (qn). 2. (a) régaler, fêter (qn); faire fête à (un convive); v.i. offrir une réception; to e. s.o. to dinner, donner à dîner, offrir un dîner, à qn; v.i. they e. a great deal, ils reçoivent beaucoup (de monde) (chez eux); (b) loger; B: for thereby some have entertained angels unawares, car, par elle, quelques-uns ont logé des anges, n'en sachant rien. 3. admettre, accueillir (une proposition, une opinion); faire bon accueil, faire un accueil favorable, à (une demande). 4. avoir (une opinion); concevoir (une idée, des doutes); éprouver (des craintes, des soupçons); nourrir (un espoir, une idée, une passion, un doute); chérir (une illusion); caresser (des espérances); choyer (un espoir); être animé (d'un sentiment); to e. a kindly feeling for s.o., être animé d'un sentiment bienveillant pour qn; to e. hostile intentions towards s.o., nourrir des intentions hostiles contre qn. 5. A: & Lit: entretenir (une correspondance); to e. a discourse upon sth., disserter sur qch.

entertainer [entə'teinər], s. 1. hôte m, hôtesse f. 2. diseur, -euse (de monologues, de chansonnettes, etc.); comique m; fantaisiste mf.

entertaining[1] [entə'teiniŋ], a. amusant, divertissant.

entertaining[2], s. 1. divertissement m. 2. régal m, réception f (de convives). 3. admission f (d'une proposition, d'une idée).

entertainingly [entə'teiniŋli], adv. (a) (parler) d'une manière amusante, divertissante; (b) agréablement; d'une manière intéressante.

entertainment [entə'teinmənt], s. 1. (a) divertissement m, amusement m; much to the e. of the crowd, au grand amusement de la foule; (b) Th: spectacle m, divertissement; e. tax, taxe f sur les spectacles; (c) to give an e., donner un spectacle varié. 2. (a) hospitalité f; hébergement m; Adm: Com: e. expenses, frais mpl de représentation f; indemnité f de fonctions fpl; (b) réception f, fête f; (c) A: repas m, régal m, banquet m. 3. admission f, acceptation f (d'une idée, d'une proposition).

enthalpy ['enθælpi], s. Ph: enthalpie f.

enthetic [en'θetik], a. Med: exogène.

enthral(l) [in'θrɔ:l], v.tr. (enthralled) 1. captiver, charmer, ensorceler. 2. A: & Lit: asservir; rendre esclave; assujettir.

enthralling [in'θrɔ:liŋ], a. (spectacle, etc.) captivant.

enthralment [in'θrɔ:lmənt], s. 1. charme m, ensorcellement m. 2. A: & Lit: assujettissement m, asservissement m.

enthrone [in'θroun], v.tr. (a) introniser (un évêque); (b) mettre (un roi) sur le trône; to sit enthroned, trôner.

enthronement [in'θrounmənt], **enthronization** [inθrounai'zeiʃ(ə)n], s. intronisation f.

enthuse [in'θju:z], v.i. montrer de l'enthousiasme; s'enthousiasmer, s'exalter; to e. over, about, sth., s'enthousiasmer pour, se passionner de, pour, qch.; he didn't e. over our proposal, il a fait la moue à notre proposition.

enthusiasm [in'θju:ziæzm], s. enthousiasme m (for, about, pour); transports mpl; exaltation f; this life had killed all his enthusiasms, cette vie avait tué en lui tous les élans; he is easily moved to e., il s'enthousiasme facilement; book that arouses e., livre qui passionne; to receive s.o. without e., faire froide mine à qn.

enthusiast [in'θju:ziæst], s. enthousiaste mf (for, de); Wagner e., enthousiaste de Wagner; golf e., fervent(e) du golf; F: enragé(e) de golf; music e., passionné(e) de musique.

enthusiastic [inθjuzi'æstik], a. enthousiaste; e. fisherman, pêcheur passionné, enragé, fanatique; e. worker for a cause, zélateur m d'une cause; to become e. about sth., s'enthousiasmer sur qch.

enthusiastically [inθjuzi'æstik(ə)li], adv. avec enthousiasme; to accept e., accepter d'enthousiasme; they were e. in favour of the new king, ils se ralliaient d'enthousiasme au nouveau roi.

enthymeme ['enθimi:m], s. Log: enthymème m.

entice [in'tais], v.tr. attirer, séduire, allécher, affriander (qn); amorcer (un animal, une personne); to e. s.o. to do sth., entraîner qn à faire qch.; to e. s.o. away, entraîner qn à sa suite; to e. s.o. from his duty, détourner qn de son devoir; to e. s.o. into a place, attirer qn dans un endroit; to e. a bird into a trap, attirer un oiseau dans un piège; Jur: to e. women and girls, embaucher des femmes et des filles.

enticement [in'taismənt], s. 1. séduction f, entraînement m, allèchement m. 2. attrait m, charme m; novelist indifferent to the enticements of the screen, romancier indifférent aux invites f de l'écran. 3. appât m.

enticer [in'taisər], s. séducteur, -trice; tentateur, -trice.

enticing[1] [in'taisiŋ], a. (of offer, prospects) séduisant, tentant, attrayant, alléchant; (of dish) affriolant, affriandant, alléchant.

enticing[2], s. Jur: séduction f, embauchage m.

enticingly [in'taisiŋli], adv. d'une manière attrayante, séduisante.

entire [in'taiər]. 1. a. (a) entier, tout; the e. population, la population (tout) entière; the e. day, toute la journée; (b) entier, complet; an e. delusion, une illusion complète; A: not a window was left e., pas une vitre ne restait entière, intacte; to enjoy s.o.'s e. confidence, jouir de l'entière confiance de qn; the evening was voted an e. success, on déclara à l'unanimité que la soirée avait été une réussite complète; to be e. master of one's property, être maître absolu de ses biens; to reproduce an article e., reproduire un article en entier; Her: cross e., croix qui touche aux bords de l'écu; (c) Bot: e. leaves, feuilles entières; (d) e. horse, cheval entier. 2. s. cheval entier.

entirely [in'taiəli], adv. entièrement, tout à fait, complètement; to agree e. with s.o., être entièrement d'accord avec qn; être tout à fait du même avis que qn; it is e. unnecessary, c'est absolument inutile; to be e. different, différer du tout au tout; that e. alters the case, cela change les choses du tout au tout; you are e. mistaken, vous vous trompez du tout au tout; life e. given up to work, existence toute de travail; the invitation is e. formal, l'invitation est de pure forme.

entireness [in'taiənis], s. intégralité f.

entirety [in'taiərəti], s. 1. (a) intégralité f, intégrité f; in its e., en entier; totalement; to tell a story in its e., raconter une histoire d'un bout à l'autre; to fulfil an order in its e., exécuter intégralement une commande; (b) totalité f; the e. of the estate amounts to . . ., la totalité du domaine se monte à . . .. 2. Jur: by entireties, par indivis.

entitle [in'taitl], v.tr. 1. intituler (un livre, un chapitre). 2. donner à (qn) le titre de (duc, prince, etc.); the association shall be entitled . . ., la société prendra le titre de . . .. 3. donner à (qn) le droit (to, à); to e. s.o. to do sth., donner (le) droit à qn de faire qch.; these discoveries e. us to believe that . . ., ces découvertes autorisent à penser que . . .; to be entitled to sth., avoir droit à qch.; to be entitled to do sth., avoir le droit, être en droit, de faire qch.; Jur: être recevable à faire qch.; (of ambassador) avoir caractère pour faire qch.; to be entitled to say that . . ., pouvoir dire à juste titre que . . .; Jur: to be entitled to inherit, être apte, avoir habilité, à hériter.

entity ['entiti], s. 1. Phil: entité f. 2. legal e., personne morale, civile, juridique.

ento- ['entou], pref. Biol: Bot: ento-.

entobranchiate [entou'bræŋkieit], a. Ich: entobranche.

entoderm ['entoudə:m], s. Anat: entoderme m.

entoloma [entou'loumə], s. Fung: entolome m.

entomb [in'tu:m], v.tr. 1. mettre dans la tombe; mettre au tombeau; enterrer, ensevelir (un mort). 2. servir de tombeau à (un mort); the cave that entombed him, la caverne dans laquelle il était enseveli.

entombment [in'tu:mmənt], s. ensevelissement m, sépulture f; mise f au tombeau.

entomic [en'tɔmik], a. entomique.

entomolin [en'tɔməlin], s. Ch: Z: chitine f.

entomological [entəmə'lɔdʒikl], a. entomologique.

entomologist [entə'mɔlədʒist], s. entomologiste mf.

entomology [entə'mɔlədʒi], s. entomologie f.

entomophagous [entou'mɔfəgəs], a. Nat.Hist: entomophage, insectivore.

entomophilous [entou'mɔfiləs], a. Bot: entomophile; entomogame.

entomophily [entou'mɔfili], s. Bot: entomophilie f, entomogamie f.

Entomostraca [entoumɔs'treikə], s.pl. A: Moll: entomostracés.

entoparasite [entou'pærəsait], s. entoparasite m, endoparasite m.

entophyte ['entoufait], s. Bot: entophyte m.

Entoprocta [entou'prɔktə], s.pl. Nat.Hist: entoproctes m.

entoptic [en'tɔptik], a. Med: (of visual sensation, etc.) entoptique.

Entotrophi [entou'troufai], s.pl. Ent: entotrophes m.

entotrophic [entou'trɔfik], a. Ent: entotrophe.

entourage [ɔntu:'rɑ:ʒ], s. entourage m.

entozoon, pl. -oa [entou'zouən, -ouə], s. entozoaire m.

entracte ['ɑ̃(n)trækt], s. Th: entracte m.

entrails ['entreilz], s.pl. entrailles f (d'un animal, A: & Lit: de la terre, etc.).

entrain[1] [in'trein]. 1. v.tr. embarquer, faire embarquer (des troupes, etc.) en chemin de fer. 2. v.i. s'embarquer (en chemin de fer).

entrain[2], v.tr. (of fluid) entraîner (qch.).

entraining [in'treiniŋ], **entrainment** [in'treinmənt], s. embarquement m (en chemin de fer).

entrammel [in'træm(ə)l], v.tr. entraver, embarrasser, empêtrer.

entrance[1] ['entrəns], s. 1. entrée f; (a) to make one's e. into a room, etc., faire son entrée dans une salle, etc.; actor's e. on the stage, entrée en scène d'un acteur; to force an e. into a house, forcer l'entrée d'une maison; e. into office, upon one's duties, entrée en fonctions; initiation f; e. gate, barrière f; grille f d'entrée; e. hall, vestibule m (d'une maison); hall m (d'un grand hôtel); (b) pénétration f (de la poussière, etc.); (c) admission f, accès m; to give e. to s.o., to sth., livrer passage à, donner accès à, laisser entrer, admettre, qn, qch.; to pay one's e. (fee), payer son entrée; (to club, etc.) e. fee, droit m d'inscription; cotisation f (d'admission); e. examination, examen m d'entrée; (d) Opt: e. pupil, pupille f d'entrée. 2. (way in) wide, narrow, e., entrée large, étroite; main e., entrée principale; side e., entrée latérale; porte f de service; secret e., back-stair e., porte dérobée; (of bus, etc.) the e. is at the rear, l'entrée s'effectue par l'arrière; the e. to the harbour is blocked, l'entrée du port est bloquée. 3. Nau: formes fpl, façons fpl, d'avant.

entrance[2] [in'trɑ:ns], v.tr. 1. (a) plonger (qn) dans l'hypnose, dans un sommeil léthargique; (b) plonger (un mystique, etc.) dans l'extase. 2. extasier, ravir, transporter (qn); griser (with, de); to be, stand, entranced, être dans le ravissement; to be entranced by . . ., s'extasier sur, être en extase devant . . .; I was entranced with the music, j'étais enchanté par la musique.

entrancement [in'trɑ:nsmənt], s. extase f, ravissement m.

entrancing [in'trɑ:nsiŋ], a. (rêve) enchanteur; (conte) passionnant; e. melody, mélodie ravissante; e. beauty, beauté enchanteresse; e. landscape, paysage d'une beauté féerique.

entrancingly [in'trɑ:nsiŋli], adv. à ravir.

entrant ['entrənt], s. (a) débutant, -ante (dans une profession, etc.); (b) inscrit, -ite (pour une course).

entrap [in'træp], v.tr. (entrapped) prendre (qn) au piège; attraper (par des artifices).

entreat [in'tri:t], v.tr. to e. s.o. to do sth., prier, implorer, supplier, qn de faire qch.; demander en grâce à qn de faire qch.; demander instamment à qn de faire qch.; they entreated him to stay, ils le prièrent, ils lui demandèrent avec instance, de rester; leave me alone, I e. you, laissez-moi tranquille, je vous en prie; I e. your indulgence, je réclame votre indulgence; Lit: to e. sth. of s.o., demander (en grâce) qch. à qn.

entreating [in'tri:tiŋ], a. (ton, regard) suppliant.

entreatingly [in'tri:tiŋli], adv. d'une voix suppliante; d'un air, d'un ton suppliant; avec instance; instamment.

entreaty [in'tri:ti], s. prière f, supplication f; at s.o.'s urgent e., sur les vives instances, à la sollicitation pressante, de qn; to be open to e., être accessible aux prières; look of e., regard suppliant.

entrechat ['ɑ̃(n)trəʃa:], s. Danc: entrechat m.

entrée ['ɑ̃(n)trei], s. 1. entrée f (to, into, dans); to have the e. of a house, avoir ses entrées dans une maison; avoir ses entrées libres chez qn. 2. Cu: (a) entrée; (b) NAm: plat m de résistance.

entrench [in'tren(t)ʃ]. 1. v.tr. Mil: retrancher (un camp, une ville); v.i. faire des retranchements; to e. oneself behind, in (sth.), se retrancher, se terrer, derrière (des remparts, Fig: un prétexte); se cantonner dans (un travail, etc.); Geog: entrenched meander, méandre encaissé. 2. v.i. to e. (up)on, empiéter sur, enfreindre (un privilège, etc.).

entrenching [in'tren(t)ʃiŋ], s. retranchement m; e. spade, pelle-bêche f, pl. pelles-bêches; bêche portative; e. tool, outil m de terrassement, de tranchée.

entrenchment [in'tren(t)ʃmənt], s. 1. Mil: retranchement m. 2. défense f, garantie f.

entrepôt [ɑ̃(n)trəpou], s. entrepôt m; e. port, port franc.

entrepreneur [ɑ̃(n)trəprə'nə:r], s. 1. Mus: Th: O: impresario m. 2. Pol.Ec: entrepreneur m.

entresol ['ɑ̃(n)trəsɔl], s. Arch: entresol m.

entrochal ['entrəkl], a. Geol: Paleont: à entroques.

entrochite ['entrəkait], s. Paleont: entroque m.

entropion [en'troupiən], s. Med: entropion m.

entropy ['entrəpi], s. Ph: entropie f.

entruck [en'trʌk], v. U.S: 1. v.i. (of pers.) embarquer en camion. 2. v.tr. embarquer (des troupes, etc.) en camion.

entrust [in'trʌst], v.tr. to e. s.o. with sth., charger qn (d'une tâche, etc.), investir qn (d'une mission); to e.

(sth.) to s.o., confier (un secret, une direction, un enfant) à qn; **to e. s.o. with the care of sth., to e. the care of sth. to s.o.,** commettre qch. à la garde de qn; s'en remettre à qn du soin de qch.; laisser qch. aux soins de qn; **to e. s.o. with a sum of money, to e. a sum to s.o.,** remettre (en confiance) une somme (d'argent) à qn; **the position entrusted to him,** le poste à lui confié; **to be entrusted with the selling, with the sale, of sth.,** avoir charge de vendre qch.; être chargé de la vente de qch.; **to e. a question to a tribunal,** renvoyer une question devant, à, une juridiction; **we have entrusted this matter to our correspondent,** nous avons chargé notre correspondant de s'occuper de cette affaire.

entry ['entri], *s.* **1.** (*a*) entrée *f*; **lines of e. into France,** voies *f* donnant accès en France; **right of free e.,** droit *m* de passer librement les frontières; *P.N:* **no e.,** (i) (= *one way street*), sens interdit; (ii) passage interdit (au public); (*b*) **to make one's e.,** faire son entrée; entrer; (*of actor*) entrer en scène; **the e. of England on the scene,** l'entrée en scène de l'Angleterre; **the e. of the United States into world politics,** l'entrée des États-Unis dans la politique mondiale; (*c*) *Mus:* (i) entrée (d'un instrument); (ii) prise *f* (d'un sujet dans une fugue); (*d*) début *m* (dans la politique, etc.); (*e*) *Ven:* **the young e.,** les jeunes chiens qui vont, qui viennent de, joindre la meute. **2.** *Jur:* (*a*) prise de possession; entrée en jouissance; (*b*) **illegal e. (of a dwelling),** violation *f* de domicile. **3.** (*way in*) (*a*) **entrée (to a cave, to a mine,** d'une caverne, d'une mine); embouquement *m* (d'une passe); (*b*) *Min:* galerie principale; **single e.,** galerie simple; (*c*) *U.S:* = ENTRANCE[1] 2. **4.** (*a*) enregistrement *m* (d'un acte, etc.); inscription *f* (d'un nom sur une liste); (*b*) *Book-k:* (i) passation *f* d'écriture; inscription (dans un livre de commerce); **single, double, e.,** comptabilité *f* en partie simple, en partie double; (ii) (*item*) article *m*, poste *m*, écriture *f*; **to make an e.,** insérer un article; porter un article à compte; **to make an e. of a transaction,** passer une transaction en écriture; **to make an e. against s.o.,** débiter qn; **wrong e.,** faux emploi; **compound e.,** article composé, collectif, récapitulatif; **transfer e.,** article de contre-passement; **cross e.,** contre-passation *f*; **post e.,** écriture postérieure, subséquente; (*c*) (*in cataloguing*) **author entries,** fiches *f* auteur; **subject entries,** fiches sujet; (*d*) *Nau:* **e. in the log,** élément *m* du journal de bord; *Navy:* **e. book,** casernet *m*; (*e*) *Cust:* **custom-house e.,** passage *m* en douanes; **to make an e. of goods,** déclarer des marchandises à la douane; **(bill of) e., e. inwards,** déclaration *f* d'entrée (en douane); **e. under bond,** acquit-à-caution *m*; **post e.,** déclaration additionnelle. **5.** *Sp:* (*a*) liste *f* des inscrits, des engagés; (*b*) engagement *m*, inscription (d'un concurrent); **e. form,** feuille *f* d'inscription; **there are twenty entries,** il y a vingt engagés.

entwine [in'twain]. **1.** *v.tr.* (*a*) entrelacer (des rameaux, les doigts, etc.); **with arms entwined,** les bras entrelacés; (*b*) enlacer **(with,** de); embrasser; **the ivy entwines the elms,** le lierre enlace, embrasse, les ormes; **a creeper entwined the pillar,** une vigne vierge entourait, enlaçait, la colonne. **2.** *v.i.* (*a*) s'entrelacer; (*b*) s'enlacer **(round,** autour de).

enucleate[1] [i'nju:klieit], *v.tr.* **1.** *Surg: etc:* énucléer (un œil, une tumeur). **2.** *Lit:* **to e. a problem,** extraire le fond, faire ressortir l'essentiel, d'un problème; élucider un problème.

enucleate[2], *a.* énucléé.

enucleation [inju:kli'eiʃ(ə)n], *s.* **1.** énucléation *f.* **2.** élucidation *f.*

enumerate [i'nju:məreit], *v.tr.* (*a*) énumérer, détailler, dénombrer (les raisons, ses services); (*b*) *Jur:* articuler (les faits).

enumeration [inju:mə'reiʃ(ə)n], *s.* (*a*) enumération *f*, dénombrement *m*, recensement *m*; *For:* **e. survey,** dénombrement (des arbres); (*b*) *Jur:* articulation *f* (des faits).

enumerative [i'nju:mərətiv], *a.* énumératif.

enumerator [i'nju:məreitər], *s.* *Adm:* (*pers.*) énumérateur *m*, recenseur *m*.

enunciate [i'nʌnsieit]. **1.** *v.tr.* énoncer, exprimer, déclarer (une opinion, etc.). **2.** (*a*) *v.tr.* prononcer, articuler (des sons); **syllables easily enunciated,** syllabes qui s'énoncent, s'articulent, facilement; (*b*) *v.i.* **to e. clearly,** articuler distinctement.

enunciation [inʌnsi'eiʃ(ə)n], *s.* **1.** énonciation *f* (d'une opinion, etc.); *Mth:* énoncé *m* (d'un problème). **2.** prononciation *f* (d'un mot); articulation *f*, énonciation.

enunciative [i'nʌnsiətiv], *a.* énonciatif.

enunciator [i'nʌnsieitər], *s.* énonciateur, -trice.

enure [i'njuər]. **1.** *v.tr.* = INURE. **2.** *v.i. Jur:* (*of act, etc.*) entrer en vigueur; prendre effet; s'appliquer **(to,** à).

enuresis [enjuə'ri:sis], *s.* *Med:* énurèse *f*, énurésie *f*, énurésis *f*; incontinence *f* nocturne.

envelop [in'veləp], *v.tr.* **(enveloped)** envelopper **(in,** dans, de); **landscape enveloped in mist,** paysage enveloppé, voilé, de brume.

envelope ['envəloup, *occ.* 'ɔnvəloup], *s.* **1.** (*a*) (*covering*) enveloppe *f*; *Nat.Hist:* enveloppe, tunique *f* (d'un organe); *Sm.a:* chemise *f*, enveloppe (d'une balle); (*b*) enveloppe (d'une lettre); **window e., panel e.,** enveloppe à fenêtre (cristal rapportée), enveloppe vitrifié, à panneau transparent; **aperture e.,** enveloppe à panneau découpé, à fenêtre découpée; **adhesive e.,** enveloppe gommée; **e. with metal fastener,** pochette *f*; **to put a letter in an e.,** mettre une lettre sous enveloppe; **in a sealed e.,** sous pli cacheté; **e. file,** chemise *f* (de carton).

enveloping[1] [in'veləpiŋ], *a.* enveloppant; *Mil:* **e. movement,** manœuvre *f* d'enveloppement, mouvement enveloppant.

enveloping[2], *s.* enveloppement *m*.

envelopment [in'veləpmənt], *s.* enveloppement *m*.

envenom [in'venəm], *v.tr.* **1.** empoisonner (une arme, l'air, l'esprit). **2.** envenimer, aigrir (une discussion, une querelle).

envenoming [in'venəmiŋ], *s.* envenimement *m* (d'une discussion, etc.).

enviable ['enviəbl], *a.* enviable, digne d'envie.

enviably ['enviəbli], *adv.* d'une manière enviable.

envious ['enviəs], *a.* envieux; **e. looks,** regards d'envie; **to be e. of s.o.,** être envieux de qn; porter envie à qn; être jaloux de qn; **to look at s.o. with e. eyes,** regarder qn d'un œil d'envie, d'un œil jaloux; **to make s.o. e. of sth.,** faire envier qch. à qn; (*of things*) **to make s.o. e.,** faire envie à qn.

enviously ['enviəsli], *adv.* (parler, penser) avec envie; **to look e. at sth.,** regarder qch. d'un œil d'envie.

environ [in'vaiərən], *v.tr.* environner, entourer (qn, qch.) **(with,** de).

environment [in'vaiərənmənt], *s.* milieu *m*, entourage *m*; milieu ambiant; influences ambiantes; ambiance *f*, environnement *m*; *Av: Mil:* **ground e. (of radar system, air defence, etc.),** infrastructure *f* (radar, de défense aérienne, etc.); **Department of the E.** = ministère *m* de (la Protection de la Nature et de) l'Environnement.

environmental [invaiərən'mentl], *a.* (conditions, etc.) du milieu, qui ont rapport à l'environnement; **e. science,** science de l'environnement; **e. changes,** modifications (i) de l'environnement, (ii) produites par l'environnement.

environs [in'vaiərənz], *s.pl.* environs *m*, alentours *m* (d'une ville); abords *m*; voisinage *m*.

envisage [in'vizidʒ], *v.tr.* **1.** envisager (une difficulté, un danger); **I had not envisaged the matter in that light,** je n'avais pas regardé l'affaire sous cet aspect. **2.** regarder (un danger, etc.) en face; faire face à (un danger, etc.).

envisagement [in'vizidʒmənt], *s.* envisagement *m*.

envoy[1] ['envɔi], *s.* *Lit:* envoi *m* (à la suite des stances d'une ballade).

envoy[2], *s.* (*pers.*) envoyé, -ée (diplomatique); ambassadeur, -drice; **E. Extraordinary and Minister Plenipotentiary,** Envoyé extraordinaire et Ministre plénipotentiaire.

envy[1] ['envi], *s.* **1.** envie *f*, jalousie *f*; **to excite, raise, e.,** exciter l'envie; **to feel e. at sth., of sth.,** éprouver de l'envie au sujet de qch.; être envieux de qch.; **to be green with e.,** être dévoré d'envie; **to turn s.o. green with e.,** faire loucher qn d'envie, de jalousie; **he would be green with e.,** il en ferait une jaunisse; **she turned green with e.,** elle devint verte d'envie. **2.** objet *m* d'envie; **to be the e. of s.o.,** être l'objet d'envie de qn; être un objet d'envie pour qn; faire envie à qn; être envié par qn.

envy[2], *v.tr.* envier, porter envie à (qn); **to e. s.o. sth.,** envier qch. à qn; **to be envied by s.o.,** faire envie à qn, s'attirer l'envie de qn; **thing not to be envied,** chose qui n'est pas à envier, peu enviable; **it is better to be envied than pitied,** mieux vaut faire envie que pitié.

enwrap [in'ræp], *v.tr.* **(enwrapped) 1.** envelopper, enrouler **(in,** dans). **2.** *Lit:* **enwrapped in slumber, in thought,** plongé dans le sommeil, dans ses pensées.

enzootic [enzou'ɔtik]. *Vet:* **1.** *a.* (maladie *f*) enzootique. **2.** *s.* enzootie *f.*

enzymatic [enzi'mætik], *a.* *Bio-Ch:* enzymatique.

enzyme ['enzaim], **enzym** ['enzim], *s.* *Bio-Ch:* enzyme *f*, diastase *f*, zymase *f.*

enzymology [enzi'mɔlədʒi], *s.* *Bio-Ch:* enzymologie *f.*

eoanthropus [i(:)ou'ænθrəpəs], *s.* *Paleont:* eoanthropus *m*.

eocene ['i(:)əsi:n], *a.* & *s.* *Geol:* éocène (*m*); **lower e.,** paléocène *m*, éocène inférieur.

eohippus [i(:)ou'hipəs], *s.* *Paleont:* eohippus *m*.

Eolian [i(:)'ouliən], **Eolic** [i(:)'ɔlik], *a.* éolien.

eolith ['i(:)əliθ], *s.* *Prehist:* éolithe *m*.

eolithic [i(:)ə'liθik], *a.* éolithique.

eon ['i:ən], *s.* éon *m*.

eonism ['i(:)ənizm], *s.* *Psy:* éonisme *m*, transvestisme *m*.

eosin ['i(:)ousin], *s.* *Ch:* éosine *f.*

eosinophil(e) [i(:)ə'sinəfil, -fail], *a.* & *s.* *Physiol:* éosinophile (*m*).

eosinophilia [i(:)əsinou'filiə], *s.* *Med:* éosinophilie *f.*

eosinophilic [i(:)əsinou'filik], *a.* *Physiol:* éosinophile.

eosphorite [i(:)'ɔsfərait], *s.* *Miner:* éosphorite *f.*

Epacridaceae [epəkri'deisii:], *s.pl.* *Bot:* épacridacées *f.*

epacris ['epəkris, i'pækris], *s.* *Bot:* épacride *f.*

epact ['i:pækt], *s.* *Astr: Chr:* épacte *f.*

epanalepsis [epænə'lepsis], *s.* *Lit:* épanalepse *f.*

eparch ['epɑ:k], *s.* éparque *m* (gouverneur ou évêque d'une éparchie).

eparchy ['epɑ:ki], *s.* *Gr.Adm., Hist., & Ecc:* éparchie *f.*

epaulette [epɔ:'let], *s.* (*a*) *Mil:* épaulette *f*; (*b*) *Ent:* épaulette; (*c*) *Z:* **e. bat,** épomophore *f.*

épaulière [eipɔ:lieər], *s.* *A.Arm:* épaulière *f.*

epaulment [i'pɔ:lmənt], *s.* *Fort:* épaulement *m*.

épée ['eipei], *s.* *Fenc:* (*a*) épée *f*; (*b*) épéisme *m*.

épéeist ['eipeiist], *s.* *Fenc:* épéiste *m*.

epeirid [e'paiərid], *s.* *Arach:* épeire *f.*

epeirogenesis [epaiərou'dʒenəsis], *s.* *Geol:* ép(e)irogénèse *f.*

epirogenetic, epeirogenic [epaiəroudʒənetik, -'dʒenik], *a.* *Geol:* ép(e)irogénique.

epencephalon [epen'sefələn], *s.* *Anat:* arrière-cerveau *m*.

ependyma [e'pendimə], *s.* *Anat:* épendyme *m*.

ependymitis [ependi'maitis], *s.* *Med:* épendymite *f.*

epenthesis [e'penθisis], *s.* *Ling:* épenthèse *f.*

epenthetic [epen'θetik], *a.* *Ling:* (son *m*, lettre *f*) épenthétique.

epergne [i'pə:n], *s.* surtout *m* (de table).

epexegesis [epeksi'dʒi:sis], *s.* épexégèse *f.*

epexegetical [epeksi'dʒetikl], *a.* épexégétique.

ephah ['i:fə], *s.* *Jew.Meas: B:* épha *m*, éphi *m*.

ephebe [e'fi:b], *s.* *Gr.Ant:* éphèbe *m*.

ephectic [e'fektik], *a.* & *s.* *Phil:* éphectique (*mf*)

ephedra ['efidrə, e'fi:drə], *s.* *Bot:* éphèdre *f*; raisin *m* de mer.

ephedrine ['efidri(:)n], *s.* *Pharm:* éphédrine *f.*

ephelis, *pl.* **-ides** [i'fi:lis, -idi:z], *s.* *Med:* éphélide *f*; tache *f* de rousseur.

ephemera, *pl.* **-ae, -as** [i'femərə, -i:, -əz], *s.* **1.** *Ent:* éphémère *m*. **2.** chose *f* éphémère.

ephemeral [i'femərəl], *a.* (fièvre *f*, fleur *f*, insecte *m*) éphémère; **e. passion,** passion fugitive; **their beauty is e.,** leur beauté n'est que d'un jour, est passagère, éphémère.

ephemerid [e'femərid], *s.* *Ent:* éphémère *m*; éphéméride *m*.

Ephemeridae [efi'meridi:], *s.pl.* *Ent:* éphémérides *m*.

ephemeris, *pl.* **ephemerides** [i'feməris, efi'meridi:z], *s.* **1.** *Astr:* éphéméride *f*, almanach *m*, annuaire *m*. **2.** *Ent:* éphémère *m*.

ephemeron, *pl.* **-a, -ons** [i'femərən, -ə, -ənz], *s.* **1.** *Ent:* éphémère *m*. **2.** *pl.* **ephemera,** choses *f* éphémères.

Ephemeroptera [ifemə'rɔptərə], *s.pl.* *Ent:* éphéméroptères *m*.

ephemerous [i'femərəs], *a.* = EPHEMERAL.

Ephesian [i'fi:ʒ(ə)n]. *A.Geog:* (*a*) *a.* éphésien; (*b*) *s.* Éphésien, -ienne.

ephestia [e'festiə], *s.* *Ent:* ephestia *f*, *F:* teigne *f* de la farine.

Ephesus ['efesəs], *Pr.n.* *A.Geog:* Éphèse *f.*

ephialtes [efi'ælti:z], *s.* *Ent:* éphialtes *m*.

ephippiger [e'fipidʒər], *s.* *Ent:* **e. (provincialis),** éphippigère *f.*

ephippium [e'fipiəm], *s.* éphippie *f.*

ephod ['efɔd, 'i:fɔd], *s.* *Jew.Ant:* éphod *m*.

ephor ['efɔ:r], *s.* *Gr.Civ:* éphore *m*.

ephydrid ['efidrid], *a.* & *s.* *Ent:* éphydride (*m*).

ephydrogamous [efi'drɔgəməs], *a.* *Bot:* éphydrogame.

ephydrogamy [efi'drɔgəmi], *s.* *Bot:* éphydrogamie *f.*

epi- ['epi], *pref.* épi-.

epiblast ['epiblæst], *s.* *Biol:* épiblaste *m*.

epiblastic [epi'blæstik], *a.* *Biol:* épiblastique.

epiboly [i'pibəli], *s.* *Biol:* épibolie *f.*

epic ['epik]. **1.** *a.* épique; (combat *m*, etc.) légendaire. **2.** *s.* (*a*) poème *m* épique; épopée *f*; (*b*) film *m* à grand spectacle.

epical ['epik(ə)l], *a.* épique.

epicalyx [epi'keiliks], *s.* *Bot:* épicalice *m*.

epicanthic [epi'kænθik], *a.* *Anat:* **e. fold,** épicanthus *m*.

epicanthus [epi'kænθəs], *s.* *Anat:* épicanthus *m*.

epicardium [epi'kɑ:diəm], *s.* *Anat:* épicarde *m*.

epicarp ['epikɑ:p], *s.* *Bot:* épicarpe *m*.

epicarpanthous [epikɑ:'pænθəs], *a.* *Bot:* épicarpanthe.

epicauta [epi'kɔ:tə], *s.* *Ent:* épicaute *f.*

epicedium, *pl.* **-ia** [epi'si:diəm, -iə], *s.* épicédion *m*;

chant *m* funèbre.
epicene ['episi:n]. **1.** *a. Gram:* (mot *m*) épicène, de genre commun. **2.** *s.* hermaphrodite *m.*
epicentre ['episentər], **epicentrum** [epi'sentrəm], *s. Geol:* épicentre *m* (d'une séisme).
epichlorhydrin [epiklɔ:'haidrin], *s. Ch:* épichlorhydrine *f.*
epiclesis [epi'kli:sis], *s. Ecc:* épiclèse *f.*
epicomus [e'pikəməs], *s. Ter:* épicome *m.*
epicondyle [epi'kɔndil], *s. Anat:* épicondyle *m.*
epicondylian, epicondylic [epikɔn'diliən, -kɔn'dilik], *a. Anat:* épicondylien.
epicontinental [epikɔnti'nentl], *a. Oc:* épicontinental.
epicormic [epi'kɔ:mik], *a. For:* **e. branch,** branche gourmande.
epicotyl [epi'kɔtil], *s. Bot:* épicotyle *m,* axe épicotylé.
epicranial [epi'kreiniəl], *a. Anat:* épicranien.
epicranium [epi'kreiniəm], *s. Anat:* épicrâne *m.*
epicrisis [epi'kraisis], *s. Med:* épicrise *f.*
Epictetus [epik'ti:təs], *Pr.n.m. Gr.Phil:* Épictète.
epicure ['epikjuər], *s.* **1.** épicurien, -ienne. **2.** gourmet *m,* gastronome *m.*
epicurean [epikju'riən], *a. & s.* épicurien, -ienne.
epicureanism [epikju'riənizm], **epicurism** ['epikjurizm], *s.* épicurisme *m.*
Epicurus [epi'kju:rəs], *Pr.n.m. Gr.Phil:* Épicure.
epicycle ['episaikl], *s. Astr:* épicycle *m.*
epicyclic [epi'saiklik], *a. Mec.E:* (engrenage, train) épicycloïdal, -aux.
epicycloid [epi'saiklɔid], *s. Mth:* épicycloïde *f.*
epicycloidal [episai'klɔidl], *a. Mth: Mec.E:* épicycloïdal, -aux.
Epidaurus [epi'dɔ:rəs], *Pr.n. A.Geog:* Épidaure *f.*
epidemic [epi'demik]. **1.** *a.* (maladie *f*) épidémique. **2.** *s.* épidémie *f*; **animal e.,** épizootie *f*; **plant e.,** épiphytie *f.*
epidemical [epi'demikl], *a.* épidémique.
epidemically [epi'demik(ə)li], *adv.* épidémiquement.
epidemicity [epide'misiti], *s.* épidémicité *f.*
epidemiologic(al) [epidemiou'lɔdʒik(l)], *a.* épidémiologique.
epidemiology [epidemi'ɔlədʒi], *s.* épidémiologie *f.*
epidendron, epidendrum [epi'dendrən, -drəm], *s. Bot:* épidendron *m,* épidendrum *m.*
epiderm ['epidə:m], *s. Nat.Hist:* épiderme *m.*
epidermal, epidermic [epi'də:ml, -mik], *a.* épidermique.
epidermis [epi'də:mis], *s. Anat:* épiderme *m.*
epidermoid, epidermoidal [epi'də:mɔid, -də:'mɔidl], *a.* épidermoïde.
epidermolysis [epidə:'mɔlisis], *s. Med:* épidermolyse *f.*
epidermomycosis [epi'də:moumai'kousis], *s. Med:* épidermomycose *f.*
epidiascope [epi'daiəskoup], *s. Opt:* épidiascope *m.*
epidiascopic [epidaiə'skɔpik], *a.* épidiascopique.
epididymal [epidi'daim(ə)l], *a. Anat:* épididymaire.
epididymis [epidi'daimis], *s. Anat:* épididyme *m.*
epididymite [epi'didimait], *s. Miner:* épididymite *f.*
epididymitis [epididi'maitis], *s. Med:* épididymite *f.*
epidiorite [epi'daiərait], *s. Miner:* épidiorite *f.*
epidote ['epidout], *s. Miner:* épidote *m,* schorl vert.
epidotite ['epidoutait], *s. Miner:* épidotite *f.*
epidural [epi'dju:r(ə)l], *a. Anat:* épidural, -aux.
epifocal [epi'fouk(ə)l], *a. Meteor:* épifocal, -aux.
epigamous [e'pigəməs], *a. Biol:* épigamique.
epigastric [epi'gæstrik], *a. Anat:* épigastrique.
epigastrium [epi'gæstriəm], *s. Anat:* épigastre *m.*
epigeal [epi'dʒiəl], *a. Bot:* épigé.
epigene ['epidʒi:n], *a. Bot: Geol:* épigène.
epigenesis [epi'dʒenisis], *s. Biol:* épigénèse *f.*
epigenetic [epidʒə'netik], *a.* (*a*) *Biol:* épigénétique; (*b*) *Geol:* (*also* **epigenic** [epi'dʒenik]) épigénique; **e. river, valley,** cours *m* d'eau, vallée *f,* épigénique.
epigeous [epi'dʒiəs], *a. Bot:* (cotylédon, etc.) épigé.
epiglottic [epi'glɔtik], *a. Anat:* épiglottique.
epiglottis [epi'glɔtis], *s. Anat:* épiglotte *f.*
epignathous [epig'neiθəs], *a. Ter:* épignathe.
epignathus [epig'neiθəs], *s. Ter:* épignathe *m.*
epigone ['epigoun], **epigonium** [epi'gouniəm], *s. Bot:* épigone *m.*
Epigoni [e'pigənai], *s.pl. Gr.Myth: Lit:* Épigones *m.*
epigram ['epigræm], *s.* épigramme *f.*
epigrammatic [epigrə'mætik], *a.* épigrammatique.
epigrammatically [epigrə'mætik(ə)li], *adv.* épigrammatiquement.
epigrammatist [epi'græmətist], *s.* épigrammatiste *mf.*
epigrammatize [epi'græmətaiz], *v.i.* faire des épigrammes; épigrammatiser.
epigraph ['epigræf], *s.* épigraphe *f.*
epigraphic [epi'græfik], *a.* épigraphique.
epigraphist [i'pigrəfist], *s.* épigraphiste *mf.*
epigraphy [i'pigrəfi], *s.* épigraphie *f.*
epigyne ['epidʒain], **epigynum** [i'pidʒinəm], *s. Arch:* épigyne *m.*
epigynous [i'pidʒinəs], *a. Bot:* épigyne.
epigyny [i'pidʒini], *s. Bot:* épigynie *f.*
epiklesis [epi'kli:sis], *s. Ecc:* épiclèse *f.*
epilate ['epileit], *v.tr.* épiler.
epilation [epi'leiʃ(ə)n], *s.* épilation *f,* épilage *m.*
epilepsy ['epilepsi], *s.* épilepsie *f*; *F:* haut mal, mal caduc.
epileptic [epi'leptik], *a. & s.* épileptique (*mf*); **e. fit,** crise *f* d'épilepsie, accès *m* épileptique.
epileptiform [epi'leptifɔ:m], *a. Med:* épileptiforme.
epileptogenic [epileptou'dʒenik], *a. Med:* épileptogène.
epileptoid [epi'leptɔid], *a. Med:* épileptoïde.
epilimnion [epi'limniən], *s.* épilimnion *m.*
epilobium [epi'loubiəm], *s. Bot:* épilobe *m.*
epilogist [i'pilədʒist], *s.* **1.** auteur *m* de l'épilogue. **2.** acteur, -trice, qui dit l'épilogue.
epilogue ['epilɔg], *s.* épilogue *m.*
Epimenides [epi'menidi:z], *Pr.n.m. A.Hist:* Épiménide (de Cnosse).
epimer ['epimər], *s. Ch:* épimère *m.*
epimere ['epimiər], *s. Biol:* épimère *m.*
epimerization [epimərai'zeiʃ(ə)n], *s. Ch:* épimérisation *f.*
epimeron, *pl.* **-a** [i'pimərən, -ə], *s. Ent:* épimère *m.*
epimorphic [epi'mɔ:fik], *a. Z:* épimorphe.
epimorphosis [epi'mɔ:fəsis], *s. Biol:* épimorphose *f.*
epinasty ['epinæsti], *s. Bot:* épinastie *f,* courbure *f* de croissance.
epinephalus [epi'nefələs], *s. Ich:* épinéphèle *m.*
epipelagic [epipe'lædʒik], *a. Oc:* épipélagique.
epipetalous [epi'petələs], *a. Bot:* épipétale.
Epiphanes [i'pifəni:z], *Pr.n.m. A.Hist:* Épiphane.
Epiphanius [epi'feiniəs], *Pr.n.m. Rel.Hist:* Épiphane.
Epiphany [i'pifəni], *s. Ecc:* l'Épiphanie *f*; le jour, la fête, des Rois.
epipharynx [epi'færiŋks], *s. Ent:* épipharynx *m.*
epiphenomenalism [epifi'nɔminəlizm], *s. Phil: Psy:* épiphénoménisme *m.*
epiphenomenalist [epifi'nɔminəlist], *a. & s. Phil: Psy:* épiphénoméniste *mf.*
epiphenomenon, *pl.* **-mena** [epifi'nɔminən, -minə], *s. Phil: Psy:* épiphénomène *m.*
epiphloem [epi'flouəm], *s. Bot:* épiphléon *m*; enveloppe subéreuse.
epiphyllous [epi'filəs], *a. Bot:* épiphylle.
epiphyllum [epi'filəm], *s. Bot:* épiphylle *m.*
epiphysary [epi'fi:zəri], *a. Anat:* épiphysaire.
epiphyseal, epiphysial [epi'fiziəl], *a. Anat:* épiphysaire; **e. cartilage,** cartilage *m* épiphysaire; **e. closure,** soudure *f* des épiphyses; **e. separation,** décollement *m* épiphysaire.
epiphysis [i'pifisis], *s. Anat:* épiphyse *f.*
epiphytal [epi'faitl], *a. Bot:* épiphyte.
epiphyte ['epifait], *s. Bot:* épiphyte *m.*
epiphytic [epi'fitik], *a. Bot:* épiphytique; **e. disease,** maladie épiphytique; épiphytie *f.*
epiphytotic [epifai'tɔtik], *a. & s. Bot:* **e. (disease),** épiphytie *f.*
epiploic [epi'plouik], *a. Anat:* épiploïque.
epiploitis [epiplou'aitis], *s. Med:* épiploïte *f.*
epiploon [e'piplouən], *s. Anat:* épiploon *m.*
epipodium [epi'poudiəm], *s.* **1.** *Bot:* épipode *m.* **2.** *Z:* épipodium *m.*
Epipyropidae [epipi'rɔpidi:], *s.pl. Ent:* épipyropides *m.*
epirogenesis [ipairou'dʒenesis], *s. Geol:* ép(e)irogénèse *f.*
epirogenetic [ipairoudʒə'netik], *a. Geol:* ép(e)irogénique.
Epirote [e'paiərət]. *Geog:* (*a*) *a.* épirote; (*b*) *s.* Épirote *mf.*
Epirotic [epaiə'rɔtik], *a. Geog:* épirote.
epir(r)hizous [epi'raizəs], *a. Bot:* épirrhize.
Epirus [e'paiərəs], *Pr.n. Geog:* Épire *f.*
episcopacy [i'piskəpəsi], *s.* **1.** épiscopalisme *m,* gouvernement *m* de l'Église par les évêques. **2.** *coll.* **the e.,** l'épiscopat *m,* les évêques *m.*
episcopal [i'piskəp(ə)l], *a.* épiscopal, -aux; **e. palace,** évêché *m*; **e. ring,** anneau pastoral; (*in NAm: & Scot:*) **the E. Church,** l'Église épiscopale.
episcopalian [ipiskə'peiliən], *a. & s.* (*in NAm: & Scot:*) épiscopalien, -ienne; épiscopal, -e, -aux; (membre *m*) de l'Église épiscopale.
episcopate [i'piskəpeit], *s.* **1.** (*a*) (*office*) épiscopat *m*; (*b*) *coll.* **the E.,** l'Épiscopat; les évêques *m.* **2.** (*see*) évêché *m.*
episcope ['episkoup], *s. Opt:* épiscope *m.*
episiotomy [epi:zi'ɔtəmi], *s. Obst:* épisiotomie *f.*
episode ['episoud], *s.* épisode *m* (de la tragédie grecque, de la vie de qn); **one of the most horrible episodes of the Revolution,** un des plus horribles épisodes de la Révolution.
episodic(al) [epi'sɔdik(l)], *a.* épisodique; **e. novel,** roman *m* à tiroirs.
episodically [epi'sɔdik(ə)li], *adv.* épisodiquement.
episome ['episoum], *s. Biol:* épisome *m.*
epispastic [epi'spæstik], *a. & s. Med:* épispastique (*m*).
episperm ['epispə:m], *s. Bot:* épisperme *m.*
epispore ['epispɔ:r], *s. Bot:* (*a*) épisporange *m*; (*b*) épispore *f.*
epistasis [i'pistəsis], *s.* **1.** (*a*) *Med:* arrêt *m* (d'une sécrétion); (*b*) *Biol:* développement arrêté, arrêt de développement (d'un organisme). **2.** *Med:* épistase *f* (qui surnage dans l'urine).
epistatic [epi'stætik], *a. Biol:* épistatique.
epistaxis [epi'stæksis], *s. Med:* épistaxis *f,* saignement *m* du nez.
epistemological [ipistəmə'lɔdʒikl], *a. Phil:* épistémologique.
epistemology [ipistə'mɔlədʒi], *s. Phil:* épistémologie *f.*
episternum [epi'stə:nəm], *s. Anat:* épisterne *m,* episternum *m.*
epistle [i'pisl], *s.* (*a*) *Ecc:* épître *f*; **e. side (of altar),** côté *m* de l'épître; (*b*) épître, lettre *f*; *O: or Iron:* **to write a long e. home,** écrire une longue épître à ses parents.
epistolarian [ipistə'lɛəriən]. *Lit:* **1.** *a.* qui écrit beaucoup de lettres. **2.** *s.* épistolier, -ière.
epistolary [i'pistələri], *a. Lit:* (style, correspondance) épistolaire; **e. novel,** roman épistolaire.
epistoler [i'pistələr], *s. Ecc:* lecteur *m* de l'épître.
epistolographer [ipistə'lɔgrəfər], *s.* épistolographe *mf.*
epistolography [ipistə'lɔgrəfi], *s.* épistolographie *f.*
epistome ['epistoum], *s. Nat.Hist:* épistome *m.*
epistrophe [i'pistrəfi], *s. Rh:* épistrophe *f.*
epistyle ['epistail], *s. Arch:* épistyle *m,* architrave *f.*
epitaph ['epitæf], *s.* épitaphe *f.*
epitasis [i'pitəsis], *s. Gr.Drama:* épitase *f.*
epitaxial, epitaxic [epi'tæksiəl, -ik], *a. Cryst:* épitaxial, -aux.
epitaxy ['epitæksi], *s. Cryst:* épitaxie *f.*
epithalamium [epiθə'leimiəm], *s. Lit:* épithalame *m.*
epithelial [epi'θi:liəl], *a. Anat: Bot:* épithélial, -aux.
epithelialization [epi'θi:liəlai'zeiʃ(ə)n], *s. Biol:* épithélialisation *f.*
epithelioma [epiθi:li'oumə], *s. Med:* épithélioma *m.*
epithelium [epi'θi:liəm], *s. Anat:* épithélium *m.*
epithermal [epi'θə:m(ə)l], *a.* **1.** *Geol:* épithermal, -aux. **2.** *Atom.Ph:* épithermique.
epithet ['epiθet], *s.* épithète *f*; *Gram:* **e. adjective,** adjectif épithète, qualificatif; *F:* **she threw a lot of epithets at him,** elle l'a qualifié de nombreuses épithètes.
epithetic(al) [epi'θetik(l)], *a.* épithétique.
epitocous, epitokous [i'pitəkəs], *a. Ann:* épitoque; **e. reproduction,** épitoquie *f.*
epitome [i'pitəmi], *s.* **1.** épitomé *m,* abrégé *m,* résumé *m* (d'un livre, etc.); *O:* **e. of French history,** précis *m,* résumé, d'histoire de France. **2. to be the e. of sth.,** incarner qch.; **he is the e. of elegance,** il est l'élégance même; **the e. of Romanticism,** la quintessence *f* du Romantisme.
epitomize [i'pitəmaiz], *v.tr.* **1.** abréger, résumer (un discours, etc.); faire un précis (d'une correspondance, etc.). **2.** (*a*) **the tribe epitomizes the nation,** la tribu est la nation en raccourci, est une image en petit de la nation; (*b*) incarner (qch.).
epitrope [i'pitrəpi], *s. Rh:* épitrope *f.*
epizoanthus [epizou'ænθəs], *s. Bot:* épizoanthus *m.*
epizoic [epi'zouik], *a. Nat.Hist: Z:* épizoïque.
epizone ['epizoun], *s. Geol:* épizone *f.*
epizoon, *pl.* **-zoa** [epi'zouɔn, -'zouə], *s. Nat.Hist:* épizoaire *m.*
epizootic [epizou'ɔtik], *a. & s. Vet:* (maladie *f*) épizootique; épizootie *f.*
epizooty [epi'zouəti], *s. Vet:* épizootie *f.*
epoch ['i:pɔk], *s.* époque *f,* âge *m*; (*of events*) **to be, make, an e. (in s.o.'s life),** faire époque (dans la vie de qn); **to make, mark, an e.,** faire époque, faire date.
epochal ['i:pɔk(ə)l], *a.* **1.** historique. **2.** = EPOCH-MAKING.
epoche ['i:pɔki:], *s. Phil:* époché *f.*
epoch-making ['i:pɔkmeikiŋ], *a.* (découverte, événement) qui fait époque; inoubliable.
epode ['epoud], *s. Cl.Lit:* épode *f.*
epomophorus [i:pou'mɔfərəs], *s. Z:* épomophore *f.*
eponym ['epənim], *s.* éponyme *m.*
eponymic [epə'nimik], *a.* éponymique.
eponymous [i'pɔniməs], *a.* éponyme.
eponymy [i'pɔnimi], *s.* éponymie *f.*
epos ['epɔs], *s.* épopée *f.*
epoxy [i'pɔksi], *Ch:* **1.** *a.* époxyde; **e. resin,** résine *f* époxyde. **2.** *s.* époxyde *m.*
eprouvette [eipru:'vet], *s.* **1.** *Exp:* éprouvette *f*; **pistol e.,**

éprouvette à roue dentée; **vertical e.,** éprouvette à crémaillère. 2. *Metall:* cuiller *f* à fondants, à essais; éprouvette.

epsilon [ep'sailən], *s. Gr.Alph:* epsilon *m.*

Epsom ['epsəm], *Pr.n. Geog:* Epsom; *Pharm:* **E. salts,** sel *m* d'Epsom, sulfate *m* de magnésium hydraté; epsomite *f.*

epsomite ['epsəmait], *s. Miner:* epsomite *f.*

epulis, *pl.* **-lides** [i'pju:lis, -lidi:z], *s. Med:* épulide *f,* épulie *f,* épulis *f.*

epulo, *pl.* **epulones** ['epjulou, epju'louni:z], *s. Rom.Ant:* épulon *m.*

equability [ekwə'biliti, i:k-], *s.* uniformité *f,* égalité *f;* **e. of temper,** régularité *f* d'humeur; **e. of climate,** uniformité de climat.

equable ['ekwəbl, i:k-], *a.* uniforme, régulier; égal, -aux; **e. temperament,** humeur égale; **e. pulse,** pouls régulier.

equal[1] ['i:kwəl]. 1. *a.* (*a*) égal, -aux (**to, with,** à); **two and two are e. to four,** deux et deux égalent quatre; **a louis was e. to twenty francs,** un louis valait vingt francs; **on e. terms,** à conditions égales; **to fight on e. terms,** combattre à armes égales; **to be on e. terms, on an e. footing, with s.o.,** être sur un pied d'égalité avec qn; **with e. ease,** avec la même facilité; **e. distribution of taxes,** péréquation *f* de l'impôt; **to contribute e. shares to the expense,** contribuer pour une part égale à la dépense; **he gave each of them an e. sum of money,** il leur a donné à chacun une même somme d'argent; **cinema e. to any in London,** cinéma à l'instar de Londres; **all things being e.,** toutes choses pareilles; toutes choses égales (d'ailleurs); **e. pay for e. work,** à travail égal, salaire égal; *F:* **I'll get e. with you,** je prendrai ma revanche; (*b*) **to be e. to (doing) sth.,** être de force à, de taille à, à même de, capable de, faire qch.; **I don't feel e. to (doing) it,** je ne m'en sens pas le courage, la force; je ne suis pas à même de le faire; **to be e. to any emergency,** être à même de faire face à toutes les éventualités; **to be e. to the occasion, to a task,** être à la hauteur d'une situation, des circonstances, d'une tâche; **not to be e. to a task,** être au-dessous de la tâche; **to feel e. to the contest,** se sentir de force à soutenir la lutte; **he was not e. to the test,** il n'a pas supporté l'épreuve; **he's no longer e. to staying up late,** il ne supporte plus de se coucher tard; **he is no longer e. to the strain of business (life),** il ne peut plus soutenir le poids des affaires; (*c*) *A:* = EQUABLE. 2. *s.* (*a*) égal, -ale; pair *m;* **your equals,** vos pareils, vous égaux; **you won't find his e.,** vous ne trouverez pas son semblable, son pareil; **to treat s.o. as an e.,** traiter qn en égal, d'égal à égal; **as equals,** sur un pied d'égalité; en compagnons; (*b*) *pl. Mth:* **equals,** quantités égales.

equal[2], *v.tr.* (**equalled**) (*a*) égaler, être égal à (qn, qch.) (**in, en**); **there is nothing to e. it,** il n'y a rien de tel; **nothing can e. this splendour,** rien n'est égal à cette splendeur; rien ne saurait égaler cette splendeur; **not to be equalled,** sans égal; qui n'a pas son égal; (*b*) **four fives, four times five, equals twenty,** quatre fois cinq font vingt; **seventeen plus twenty-three equals forty,** dix-sept et vingt-trois égalent, font, quarante.

equalitarian [ikwɔli'tɛəriən], *a.* & *s.* égalitaire (*mf*).

equalitarianism [ikwɔli'tɛəriənizm], *s.* égalitarisme *m.*

equality [i(:)'kwɔliti], *s.* égalité *f* (*between two people,* entre deux personnes); **on a footing of e., on an e.,** sur un pied d'égalité (**with,** avec); de puissance à puissance; d'égal à égal (**with,** avec); **in case of e. of points . . .,** en cas d'égalité de points . . .; en cas d'ex æquo . . .; *Jur:* **creditors with e. of rights,** créanciers qui viennent en concurrence; *Typ:* **(sign of) e.,** égalité.

equalization [i:kwəlai'zeiʃ(ə)n], *s.* 1. égalisation *f;* *Fin:* régularisation *f* (de dividendes); *Adm:* péréquation *f* (de contributions, de traitements). 2. (*a*) compensation *f;* *Adm:* **e. fund,** (i) (*for family allowances, etc.*) caisse *f* de compensation; (ii) *Fin:* fonds *m* de régularisation; (*b*) *Civ.E:* compensation (de terrassements); *Mec.E:* équilibrage *m.*

equalize ['i:kwəlaiz]. 1. *v.tr.* (*a*) égaliser (**sth. with sth.,** qch. avec qch.); **to e. wages,** faire la péréquation des salaires; **to e. dividends,** régulariser les dividendes; **fortunes tend to become equalized through the breaking up of estates,** les fortunes tendent à se niveler par les partages; *Fb: etc:* **to e. (the score),** marquer égalité de points; égaliser (la marque); (*b*) compenser, équilibrer (des forces, etc.). 2. *v.i.* (*a*) s'égaliser; (*b*) se compenser, s'équilibrer.

equalizer ['i:kwəlaizər], *s.* 1. (*pers.*) égaliseur, -euse. 2. (*a*) *El:* égaliseur *m* de potentiel; compensatrice *f;* **pulse e.,** normalisateur *m;* (*b*) *Mec.E:* compensateur *m,* égalisateur *m;* équilibreur *m;* **e. spring,** ressort compensateur; (*c*) *Veh:* palonnier *m;* (*d*) *Sp:* (*Fb: etc:*) but égalisateur.

equalizing[1] ['i:kwəlaiziŋ], *a.* compensateur, -trice; *El:* **e. current,** courant compensateur; *Mec:* **e. pressure,** pression *f* de compensation.

equalizing[2], *s.* 1. égalisation *f;* péréquation *f* (des salaires); *Tls:* **e. file,** lime *f* à égaliser. 2. compensation *f,* équilibrage *m* (des forces); *Aut:* **e. gear,** différentiel *m;* *El:* **e. conductor,** fil *m* neutre, fil d'équilibre; *Mec.E:* **e. spring,** ressort compensateur.

equally ['i:kwəli], *adv.* également, pareillement; **e. responsible,** responsable au même degré; **e. exhausted,** tout aussi fatigué(s), éreinté(s); **time is e. precious,** le temps n'est pas moins précieux; **e. with s.o.,** à l'égal de qn; au même titre que qn; **e. divided opinions,** opinions mi-parties; **to contribute e. to the expenses,** contribuer pour une part égale à la dépense; *Jur:* **creditors who rank e.,** créanciers *m* qui viennent en concurrence.

equanimity [i:kwə'nimiti, ek-], *s.* égalité *f* d'âme, de caractère; sérénité *f;* tranquillité *f* d'esprit; équanimité *f;* **to disturb s.o.'s e.,** troubler la sérénité de qn; **to recover one's e.,** se ressaisir; retrouver son calme; se rasséréner; **with e.,** d'une âme égale.

equate [i'kweit], *v.tr.* 1. (*a*) égaler (**to, with,** à); **to e. the expenses with the income,** égaler les dépenses au revenu; égaliser les dépenses et le revenu; (*b*) *Mth:* mettre (deux expressions, etc.) en équation; **to e. an expression to, with, zero,** égaliser une expression à zéro. 2. **to e. Jupiter with Zeus,** établir un parallèle entre Jupiter et Zeus; donner Jupiter comme l'équivalent de Zeus.

equating [i'kweitiŋ], *s.* 1. égalisation *f.* 2. *Mth:* mise *f* en équation.

equation [i'kweiʒ(ə)n], *s.* 1. égalisation *f* des dépenses au revenu, etc.); *Com:* **e. of payments,** échéance commune (de billets de change). 2. *Mth:* équation *f;* **simple, quadratic, e.,** équation du premier, du deuxième, degré; **differential e.,** équation différentielle; **graph of an e.,** courbe représentative d'une équation; **to solve an e.,** résoudre une équation; **to find the e. of a problem,** mettre un problème en équation. 3. *Ch: etc:* équation; *Ph:* **e. of state,** équation d'état. 4. (*a*) *Astr:* **e. of time, of the centre,** équation du temps, du centre; (*b*) *Psy:* **personal e.,** équation personnelle.

equator [i'kweitər], *s.* équateur *m* (de la terre, etc.); **magnetic e.,** équateur magnétique; **at the e.,** sous, à, l'équateur; *Astr:* **celestial e.,** équateur céleste.

equatorial [ekwə'tɔ:riəl], *a.* équatorial, -aux; **e. doldrums,** calmes équatoriaux; *Mth:* **e. co-ordinates,** coordonnées équatoriales; **e. radius, e. semi-diameter,** rayon équatorial; *Astr:* **e. telescope,** équatorial *m;* *Biol:* **e. plate,** plaque équatoriale.

equatorially [ekwə'tɔ:riəli], *adv.* équatorialement.

equerry ['ekwəri, i'kweri], *s.m.* 1. écuyer. 2. officier de la maison du roi, de la reine.

equestrian [i'kwestriən]. 1. *a.* (*a*) (statue *f,* etc.) équestre; **e. performances,** exercices *m* d'équitation; (*b*) *Rom.Ant:* **the e. order,** l'ordre *m* équestre. 2. *s.* (*a*) (*f. occ.* **equestrienne**) cavalier, -ière; (*b*) écuyer, -ère (de cirque).

equestrianism [i'kwestriənizm], *s.* équitation *f.*

equi- ['i:kwi], *comb.fm.* équi-.

equiangular [i:kwi'æŋgjulər], *a. Mth:* équiangle.

equi-axed [i:kwi'ækst], *a.* équiaxe.

Equidae ['i:kwidi:], *s.pl. Z:* équidés *m.*

equidifferent [i:kwi'dif(ə)rənt], *a. Mth:* équidifférent.

equidistance [i:kwi'distəns], *s.* équidistance *f.*

equidistant [i:kwi'distənt], *a.* équidistant (**from,** de); **e. objects,** objets placés à écartement égal.

equidistribution ['i:kwidistri'bju:ʃ(ə)n], *s.* équirépartition *f.*

equilater ['i:kwilætər], *a. Mth:* équilatère.

equilateral [i:kwi'læt(ə)rəl], *a. Mth:* équilatéral, -aux.

equilenin [ekwi'lenin, i'kwilənin], *s. Biol:* équilénine *f.*

equilibrate [i:'kwilibreit]. 1. *v.tr.* (*a*) équilibrer; mettre en équilibre; (*b*) contre-balancer; faire contrepoids à (une force, etc.). 2. *v.i.* (*a*) s'équilibrer; être en équilibre; (*b*) (*of two forces, etc.*) se faire contrepoids.

equilibrating [i:'kwilibreitiŋ], *a.* (système, etc.) équilibreur, équilibrant.

equilibration [i:kwili'breiʃ(ə)n], *s.* équilibration *f* (**to, with,** avec); mise *f* en équilibre.

equilibrator [i:'kwilibreitər], *s.* équilibreur *m.*

equilibratory [i:kwi'librət(ə)ri], *a.* (poids, etc.) équilibreur, équilibrateur, -trice.

equilibrist [i:kwi'librist], *s.* équilibriste *mf;* danseur, -euse, de corde; funambule *mf.*

equilibrium [i:kwi'libriəm], *s.* 1. équilibre *m,* aplomb *m;* **e. of component forces,** équilibre des forces composantes; **e. point,** point *m* d'équilibre; **e. sense, sens** *m* de l'équilibre, sens de l'orientation; **neutral e.,** équilibre indifférent; **stable, unstable e.,** équilibre stable, instable; **to maintain, lose, one's e.,** garder, perdre, l'équilibre. 2. *Mch: Mec.E:* **e. curve,** courbe *f* d'équilibre; **e. ring,** bague compensatrice; *Ph:* **e. potential,** potentiel d'équilibre.

equimolecular [i:kwimɔ'lekjulər], *a. Ch:* équimoléculaire.

equimultiple [i:kwi'mʌltipl], *s. Mth:* équimultiple *m.*

equine ['i:kwain, 'ekwain], *a.* équin, caballin; de cheval; **e. race,** race chevaline; **the e. species,** les équidés *m;* *s.* **zebras are equines,** les zèbres sont des équidés; *Vet:* **e. variola,** variole équine.

equinoctial [i:kwi'nɔkʃ(ə)l, ek-]. 1. *a.* (*a*) équinoxial, -aux; *Astr:* **e. circle, line,** cercle équinoxial, ligne équinoxiale; équateur céleste; **e. year,** année équinoxiale; (*b*) **e. tides,** marées d'équinoxe, les grandes marées; **e. gale,** vent *m,* tempête *f,* d'équinoxe.

equinox ['i:kwinɔks, 'ek-], *s.* équinoxe *m;* **spring, vernal, March, e.,** équinoxe du printemps; point vernal; **autumn(al), September, e.,** équinoxe d'automne; **precession of the equinoxes,** précession *f* des équinoxes.

equip [i'kwip], *v.tr.* (**equipped**) (*a*) équiper, armer (un navire, un soldat); meubler, monter (une maison); installer, doter (une ferme, etc.); outiller, monter (une usine); **to e. s.o. with sth.,** munir, équiper, pourvoir, qn de qch.; **to e. a workman, a shop, with tools,** outiller un ouvrier, une usine; **to e. a works with new plant,** doter une usine d'un matériel neuf; (*b*) **he is well equipped to undertake the work,** il est bien équipé, bien préparé, pour faire ce travail; **more and more schools are equipped to give courses in Russian and Chinese,** il y a un nombre croissant de lycées équipés, capables, d'offrir des cours de russe et de chinois.

equipage ['ekwipidʒ], *s.* 1. équipement *m* (pour un voyage, etc.). 2. (*a*) (*vehicle*) équipage *m;* (*b*) *A:* équipage, suite *f* (d'un noble).

equipartition [i:kwipɑ:'tiʃ(ə)n], *s. Ph:* équipartition *f;* **e. of energy,** équipartition de l'énergie.

equipment [i'kwipmənt], *s.* 1. (*also* **equipping** [i'kwipiŋ]) équipement *m* (d'une expédition, d'une armée); aménagement *m* (d'une maison, etc.); armement *m,* équipement (d'un navire); outillage *m* (d'une usine, etc.); installation *f,* appareillage *m* (d'un laboratoire, etc.). 2. (objets *mpl* d') équipement; équipage *m,* appareils *mpl,* accessoires *mpl;* fournitures *fpl;* installations, matériel *m;* l'appareillage; **heavy e.,** matériel lourd; *Ind: etc:* **production e.,** matériel de série; **service, maintenance, e.,** appareillage, matériel, d'entretien; **standby, emergency, e.,** équipement, matériel, installations, de secours; **electrical e.,** équipement électrique; **radio e.,** appareillage, matériel, (de) radio; **modern radio, television and radar e. is highly sophisticated,** les appareils modernes de radio, de télévision et de radar sont extrêmement complexes; *W.Tel:* **monitoring e.,** appareillage, matériel, (i) de contrôle, (ii) d'écoute; *Phot: Typ: etc:* **reproduction, reproducing, e.,** matériel, appareils, de reproduction; *Cin:* **sound reproduction e.,** matériel de reproduction (cinématographique) sonore; *Pol.Ec:* **capital e.,** biens d'équipement, de production; outillage; capitaux *mpl* fixes; **technical e.,** capital *m* technique; *Sp:* **sports e.,** équipement sportif; **camping e.,** matériel de camping, de campement; *Mil: etc:* **regulation, standard, e.,** équipement, matériel, réglementaire; **special,** *U.S:* **project, e.,** équipement, matériel, spécial; **collective,** *U.S:* **organizational, e.,** équipement, matériel, collectif; **conventional e.,** matériel classique; **support e.,** matériel de soutien logistique; **ordnance, artillery, e., engineer e.,** matériel d'artillerie, du génie; **surplus e.,** matériel en excédent.

equipoise[1] ['i:kwipɔiz, 'ek-], *s.* (*a*) équilibre *m,* poids égal; **to preserve the e. of sth.,** maintenir qch. en équilibre; (*b*) contrepoids *m.*

equipoise[2], *v.tr.* 1. équilibrer, contre-balancer. 2. *A:* tenir (l'esprit) en suspens.

equipollence, equipollency [i:kwi'pɔləns, -'pɔlənsi; ek-], *s.* équipollence *f,* équivalence *f.*

equipollent [i:kwi'pɔlənt, ek-], *a.* équipollent, équivalent.

equiponderate [i:kwi'pɔndəreit, ek-], (*a*) *v.i.* être de poids égal; (*b*) *v.tr.* faire contrepoids à (qch.).

equipotential [i:kwipə'tenʃ(ə)l, ek-], *a. El:* équipotentiel; **e. surface,** (surface) équipotentielle *f.*

equipped [i'kwipt], *a.* **well-e.,** bien équipé; (laboratoire, etc.) bien installé, bien agencé; (ménage) bien monté, bien pourvu; (magasin) bien approvisionné.

Equisetales [i:kwise'teili:z, ek-], *s.pl. Bot:* équisétales *f.*

equisetum [ekwi'si:təm], *s. Bot:* equisetum *m.*

equitable ['ekwitəbl], *a.* équitable, juste; *Jur:* **e. claim,** réclamation *f* en accord avec les principes de l'équité.

equitableness ['ekwitəblnis], *s.* équité *f.*

equitably ['ekwitəbli], *adv.* équitablement; avec justice.

equitant ['ekwitənt], *a. Bot:* (*of leaves*) chevauchant, équitant; condupliqué.

equitation [ekwi'teiʃ(ə)n], *s.* équitation *f.*

equity ['ekwiti], *s.* **1.** équité *f*, justice *f*; **I cannot, in e., allow him to pay,** je ne peux pas, en toute justice, lui permettre de payer. **2.** *Jur:* équité; recours *m* aux principes mêmes de la justice (lorsque celle-ci se trouve en conflit avec le droit commun ou écrit); **e. of a statute,** esprit *m* d'une loi; *A:* **court of e.,** cour *f* d'équité. **3.** *Jur:* droit *m* (équitable); **e. of redemption,** droit de rachat, après forclusion, d'un bien hypothéqué. **4.** *U.S:* (*a*) *Jur:* part éventuelle à revenir au débiteur hypothécaire après forclusion; (*b*) *Fin:* masse des profits qui reste à être répartie entre les actionnaires (lors d'une liquidation) après paiement des obligations; part *f* résiduaire; *s.pl.* **equities,** actions *f* ordinaires. **5.** *Pr.n. Th: etc:* **E.,** le syndicat des artistes de la scène.

equivalence [i'kwivələns], *s.* **1.** équivalence *f*; égalité *f* (de valeur, de force); *Fin:* **equivalences of exchange,** parités *f* de change. **2.** *Ch: Ph:* équivalence; **e. ratio,** rapport stœchiométrique (mélange air-carburant).

equivalent [i'kwivələnt]. **1.** *a.* équivalent; **to be e. to sth.,** être équivalent, équivaloir, à qch.; **e. variation,** variation équivalente; **sum e. to £1000 sterling,** somme *f* qui atteint la contre-valeur de mille livres sterling. **2.** *s.* (*a*) équivalent *m*; **to drink the e. of one glass of wine,** boire la valeur d'un verre de vin; *Pol.Ec:* **man e.,** unité-travailleur *f*, *pl.* unités-travailleur; **coal e.,** équivalence *f* en charbon; **fuel oil e.,** équivalent fuel; *Ph:* **mechanical e. of heat, Joule's e.,** équivalent mécanique de la chaleur; équivalent calorifique; (*b*) *Atom.Ph:* épaisseur équivalente; **stopping e.,** épaisseur équivalente d'arrêt; **lead e.,** épaisseur équivalente de plomb.

equivalve ['i:kwivælv, 'ek-], *a. Moll:* équivalve.

equivocal [i'kwivək(ə)l], *a.* équivoque; (*a*) ambigu, -uë; (mot *m*) à double entente; **without e. phrases,** sans phrases équivoques, ambiguës; sans ambages; **to give an e. answer,** répondre d'une façon équivoque; *F:* répondre en Normand; (*b*) incertain, douteux; (*c*) suspect, douteux; **somewhat e. transactions,** affaires *f* un peu louches; affaires équivoques.

equivocality [ikwivə'kæliti], *s.* **1.** caractère *m* équivoque; équivoque *f*; **in order to avoid all e.,** pour parer à toute équivoque. **2.** (expression *f*) équivoque, expression à double entente.

equivocally [i'kwivəkəli], *adv.* d'une manière équivoque.

equivocalness [i'kwivəklnis], *s.* caractère *m* équivoque; équivoque *f.*

equivocate [i'kwivəkeit], *v.i.* user d'équivoque, tergiverser, jouer sur les mots.

equivocation [ikwivə'keiʃ(ə)n], *s.* **1.** tergiversation *f.* **2. to resort to equivocations,** user de faux-fuyants *m*; tergiverser.

equivocator [i'kwivəkeitər], *s.* tergiversateur, -trice.

equivoque ['ekwivouk], *s.* **1.** équivoque *f*; jeu *m* de mots; calembour *m*; *Rh:* dilogie *f.* **2.** = EQUIVOCALITY 2.

er [ə:r], *int.* (*in hesitating speech*) heu . . . heu . . ..

era ['iərə], *s.* ère *f*; **the Christian e.,** l'ère chrétienne; **to mark an e.,** faire époque; **geological e.,** ère géologique.

eradiate [i'reidieit], *v.i. Lit:* rayonner.

eradiation [ireidi'eiʃ(ə)n], *s. Lit:* radiation *f*, rayonnement *m.*

eradicable [i'rædikəbl], *a.* extirpable.

eradicate [i'rædikeit], *v.tr.* (*a*) *O:* déraciner (une plante); (*b*) **to e., prejudices,** extirper, déraciner, faire disparaître, des préjugés; (*c*) effacer (l'encre, etc.).

eradicated [i'rædikeitid], *a. Her:* **tree e. vert,** arbre arraché de sinople.

eradication [irædi'keiʃ(ə)n], *s.* (*a*) *O:* déracinement *m* (d'un arbre); (*b*) éradication *f*, extirpation *f* (d'un préjugé, etc.).

eradicator [i'rædikeitər], *s.* (*a*) extirpateur *m*; (*b*) produit *m* qui efface l'encre, etc., *R.t.m:* Corrector *m.*

eranthemum [i'rænθiməm], *s. Bot:* éranthème *m*, eranthemum *m.*

eranthis [i'rænθis], *s. Bot:* éranthe *f*, eranthis *m.*

erasability [ireizə'biliti], *s.* possibilité *f* d'effacement.

erasable [i'reizəbl], *a.* effaçable; *Cmptr:* **e. storage, store,** mémoire *f* effaçable.

erase [i'reiz], *v.tr.* **1.** effacer; raturer ou gommer (un mot, un chiffre); oblitérer (un souvenir); **to e. a word with a penknife,** gratter un mot avec un canif. **2.** *attrib. Cmptr:* **e. character, head,** caractère *m*, tête *f*, d'effacement; **e. count,** nombre *m* d'effacements.

erased [i'reizd], *a.* **1.** effacé. **2.** *Her:* arraché.

erasement [i'reizmənt], **erasion** [i'reiʒ(ə)n], *s.* = ERASURE.

eraser [i'reizər], *s.* **1.** effaceur, -euse. **2.** (*a*) grattoir *m*; (*b*) gomme *f* (à effacer); **ink e.,** gomme à encre; *Typewr:* **tape e.,** ruban *m* à effacer.

erasing [i'reiziŋ], *s.* effacement *m*; *Rec: Cmptr:* **e. head,** tête *f* d'effacement; **e. field,** champ *m* (magnétique) d'effacement.

Erasmus [i'ræzməs], *Pr.n.m.* Érasme.

Erastian [i'ræstiən], *a. & s. Rel.H:* érastien (*m*); disciple *m* d'Éraste.

Erastianism [i'ræstiənizm], *s. Rel.H:* érastianisme *m.*

Erastus [i'ræstəs], *Pr.n.m. Rel.H:* Éraste.

erasure [i'reiʒər], *s.* **1.** rature *f*; effaçure *f*; effacement *m*; grattage *m*; suppression *f*, effaçage *m*, oblitération *f.* **2.** mot, chiffre, effacé, gratté.

Erato [i'rɑ:tou]. *Pr.n.f. Gr.Myth:* Érato.

Eratosthenes [erə'tɔsθəni:z], *Pr.n.m.* Ératosthène.

erbium ['ə:biəm], *s. Ch:* erbium *m.*

erdvark ['ə:dvɑ:k], *s. Z:* oryctérope *m* (du Cap).

ere [ɛər]. *A: & Poet:* **1.** *prep.* avant; **e. night,** avant la nuit; **e. this,** déjà; **e. now,** auparavant, déjà; **e. long,** bientôt. **2.** *conj.* avant que + *sub.*

erebia [i'ri:biə], *s. Ent:* érébia *m.*

Erebus ['eribəs], *Pr.n.* **1.** *Myth:* Érèbe *m.* **2.** *Geog:* Érébus.

Erechtheion [i'rekθiən], *s. Gr.Arch:* Érechthéion *m.*

Erechtheus [i'rekθiəs], *Pr.n.m. Gr.Myth:* Érechthée.

erect[1] [i'rekt], *a.* (*of pers.*) droit, debout; (*of diameter*) vertical; (*of hair*) hérissé, dressé; **with tail e.,** la queue levée, dressée, en l'air; **with head e.,** la tête haute, relevée; le front haut, levé; **to stand e.,** se tenir droit; se redresser.

erect[2], *v.tr.* **1.** dresser (le corps, les oreilles, un mât); arborer (un mât, etc.). **2.** (*a*) ériger, construire (un édifice); bâtir (un immeuble); élever, ériger (une statue) (to, à); dresser (un échafaudage, un échafaud, un autel); monter, installer (une machine); imaginer, édifier (une théorie, un système); (*b*) **to e. a perpendicular on a line,** élever une perpendiculaire à une ligne; (*c*) *Jur:* instituer, ériger (un tribunal). **3.** *A:* **to e. a barony into a dukedom,** ériger une baronnie en duché. **4.** *Opt:* redresser (une image renversée).

erectile [i'rektail], *a. Physiol:* (tissu *m*) érectile.

erectility [irek'tiliti], *s. Physiol:* érectilité *f.*

erecting [i'rektiŋ], *s.* **1.** = ERECTION 1. **2.** *Opt:* redressement *m* (d'une image); **e. glass,** inverseur *m* (de télescope); **e. prism,** prisme redresseur; **e. eyepiece,** oculaire *m* à redressement.

erection [i'rekʃ(ə)n], *s.* **1.** (*a*) redressement *m* (du corps); dressage *m* (d'un mât, d'une colonne, des oreilles, etc.); (*b*) construction *f*, érection *f* (d'un édifice); érection (d'une statue); montage *m*, assemblage *m*, installation *f* (d'une machine); (*c*) érection (d'un tribunal); (*d*) *Physiol:* érection (d'un organe). **2.** bâtisse *f*, construction, édifice *m.*

erectly [i'rektli], *adv.* (marcher, etc.) (tout) droit.

erectness [i'rektnis], *s.* attitude droite; position *f* perpendiculaire.

erector [i'rektər], *s.* **1.** (*pers.*) constructeur *m* (de bâtiments), (ajusteur-)monteur *m* (de machines); *Const:* **steelwork e.,** monteur de charpentes métalliques. **2.** *Anat:* **e. (muscle),** muscle *m* érecteur; érecteur *m.* **3.** *Opt:* inverseur *m* (de télescope).

eremacausis [erimə'kousis], *s.* érémacausis *m.*

eremite ['erimait], *s. A: & Lit:* ermite *m.*

eremitic [eri'mitik], *a.* érémitique.

eremurus [eri'mju:rəs], *s. Bot:* érémure *f*, eremurus *m.*

erepsin [e'repsin], *s. Bio-Ch:* érepsine *f.*

erethism ['eriθizm], *s. Med:* éréthisme *m*, excitation anormale (d'un tissu érectile).

erethizon [eri'θi:zən], *s. Z:* éréthizon *m.*

Erethizontidae [eriθi:'zɔntidi:], *s.pl. Z:* éréthizontidés *m.*

ereuth(r)ophobia [eru:θ(r)ou'foubiə], **ereutrophobia** [eru:trou'foubiə], *s. Psy:* éreuth(r)ophobie *f.*

erewhile ['ɛə(h)wail], *adv. A: & Poet:* naguère; jadis.

erg[1] [ə:g], *s. Geog:* erg *m* (du Sahara).

erg[2], *s. Ph.Meas:* erg *m*; dyne *f* centimètre.

ergastoplasm [ə:'gæstouplæzm], *s. Biol:* ergastoplasme *m.*

ergastulum, *pl.* **-la** [ə:'gæstjuləm, -lə], *s. Rom.Ant:* ergastule *m.*

ergmeter ['ə:gmi:tər], *s. Ph:* ergmètre *m.*

ergo ['ə:gou, 'ɛəgou], *Lt.adv. Log:* ergo, donc, par conséquent.

ergograph ['ə:gougræf], *s.* ergographe *m.*

ergometer [ə:'gɔmitər], *s.* ergomètre *m.*

ergon ['ə:gɔn], *s. Ph:* = ERG[2].

ergonomics [ə:gou'nɔmiks], *s.pl.* (*sg. or pl. const.*) ergonomie *f.*

ergonomist [ə:'gɔnəmist], *s.* ergonomiste *mf.*

ergophobia [ə:gou'foubiə], *s.* aversion *f* pour le travail.

ergosterol [ə:'gɔstərɔl], *s. Ch:* ergostérol *m.*

ergot ['ə:gɔt], *s. Agr:* ergot *m* (des graminées); *Pharm:* ergot de seigle.

ergotamine [ə:'gɔtəmi:n], *s. Pharm:* ergotamine *f.*

ergoted ['ə:gətid], *a.* (blé, seigle) ergoté.

ergotherapy [ə:gou'θerəpi], *s. Med:* ergothérapie *f.*

ergotic [ə:'gɔtik], *a.* ergotique; *Med:* **e. poisoning,** ergotisme *m.*

ergotine ['ə:gɔti(:)n], *s.Pharm:* ergotine *f.*

ergotinine [ə:'gɔtini:n], *s. Pharm:* ergotinine *f.*

ergotism ['ə:gətizm], *s. Med:* ergotisme *m.*

ergotize ['ə:gətaiz], *v.tr.* attaquer de l'ergot (le blé, le seigle).

ergotized ['ə:gətaizd], *a. Agr:* ergoté.

erianthous [eri'ænθəs], *a. Bot:* érianthe.

erianthus [eri'ænθəs], *s. Bot:* érianthe *m.*

Erie ['erik], *Pr.n.m.* Érik; *Hist:* **E. the Red,** Érik le Rouge.

Ericaceae [eri'keisii:], *s.pl. Bot:* éricacées *f.*

ericaceous [eri'keiʃəs], *a. Bot:* éricacé.

Ericales [eri'keili:z], *s.pl. Bot:* éricales *f.*

ericeticolous [erisi'tikələs], *a. Bot:* éricicole.

Erie ['iəri], *Pr.n. Geog:* **Lake E.,** le lac Érié; **the E. Canal,** le canal Érié.

Erigena [i'ridʒinə], *Pr.n.m. Hist:* Érigène.

erigeron [i'ridʒərən], *s. Bot:* érigéron *m*, *F:* vergerette *f.*

Erin ['erin], *Pr.n.f. A: & Poet:* Irlande *f.*

Erinaceidae [erinə'si:idi:], *s.pl. Z:* érinacéidés *m.*

erineum [i'riniəm], *s. Hort:* érinéon *m*, érinose *f.*

erinite ['erinait], *s. Miner:* érinite *f.*

Erinnyes (the) [ði:i'rinii:z], *Pr.n.f.pl. Gr.Myth:* les Érinnyes, les Furies; les Euménides.

Eriocaulaceae [eriouko:'leisii:], *s.pl. Bot:* ériocaulacées *f.*

eriocaulon [eriou'kɔ:lɔn], *s. Bot:* ériocaule *m*, ériocaulon *m.*

Eriocraniidae [erioukræ'ni:idi:], *s.pl. Ent:* ériocraniides *m.*

Eriphyle [i'rifili], *Pr.n.f. Gr.Myth:* Ériphyle.

erismatura [irizmə'tju:rə], *s. Orn:* érismature *m.*

eristalis [i'ristəlis], *s. Ent:* éristale *m.*

eristic [i'ristik], *a. & s. Phil:* éristique (*f*); (école *f*) mégarique.

Eritrea [eri'triə], *Pr.n. Geog:* Érythrée *f.*

Eritrean [eri'triən]. *Geog:* (*a*) *a.* érythréen; (*b*) *s.* Érythréen, -enne.

eritrichium [eri'trikiəm], *s. Bot:* eritrichium *m.*

Erl-King (the) [ði'ə:rl'kiŋ], *s. Myth: Lit:* le Roi des Aulnes.

ermelin(e) ['ə:məlin], *s.* armeline *f.*

ermine ['ə:min], *s.* **1.** (*a*) *Z:* hermine *f*; (*b*) *Ent:* **e. moth,** yponomeute *f.* **2.** (*fur*) hermine, *Com:* roselet *m*; **e. tails,** mèches *f*, mouchetures *f*, d'hermine; *A:* **to rise to the e., to don the e.,** être nommé juge. **3.** *Her:* hermine.

ermined ['ə:mind], *a.* **1.** (*a*) fourré, garni, d'hermine; (*b*) (*of pers.*) revêtu d'hermine. **2.** *Her:* herminé.

ermines ['ə:minz], **erminees** ['ə:mini:z], *s. Her:* contre-hermine *f.*

erminois ['ə:minɔiz], *s. Her:* or semé d'hermines de sable.

erne [ə:n], *s. Orn:* pygargue *m* (à queue blanche), orfraie *f.*

erode [i'roud], *v.tr.* éroder; ronger; corroder (le fer, etc.).

eroded [i'roudid], *a.* érodé; rongé; (*of rock, etc.*) dénudé.

erodent [i'roudənt], *a. & s. Pharm:* érosif (*m*).

erodium [i'roudiəm], *s. Bot:* érodium *m.*

erogeneity [eroudʒə'ni:iti], *s.* érogénéité *f.*

erogenic [erou'dʒenik], **erogenous** [e'rɔdʒinəs], *a.* érogène.

Eros ['iərɔs]. **1.** *Pr.n. Gr.Myth:* Éros *m.* **2.** *Pr.n. Astr:* Éros. **3.** *s. Psy:* éros *m.*

erosion [i'rouʒən], *s.* (*a*) *Physiol:* érosion *f*; **dental e.,** érosion dentaire; (*b*) *Geol:* érosion; dénudation *f*; **differential e.,** érosion différentielle; **lateral e.,** érosion latérale; **marine e.,** érosion marine, abrasion *f*; **glacial e.,** érosion glaciaire; (*c*) **eolian, wind, e.,** érosion éolienne; **cycle of e.,** cycle *m* d'érosion; (*d*) détérioration *f*; **the e. of real earnings by inflation,** la diminution du salaire réel causée par l'inflation.

erosive [i'rousiv], *a.* érosif.

Erostratus [e'rɔstrətəs], *Pr.n.m. Gr.Hist:* Érostrate.

erotetic [erou'ti:tik], *a. Phil:* érotématique.

erotic [i'rɔtik]. **1.** *a.* érotique. **2.** *s.* poème *m* érotique.

erotically [i'rɔtik(ə)li], *adv.* érotiquement.

eroticism [i'rɔtisizm], *s.* érotisme *m.*

erotism ['erətizm], *s. Med:* érotisme *m.*

erotization [erətai'zeiʃ(ə)n], *s. Med:* érotisation *f.*

erotogenic [erətou'dʒenik], *a.* érotogène.

erotomania [eroutou'meiniə], *s.* érotomanie *f.*

erotomaniac [eroutou'meiniæk], *s.* érotomane *mf*; érotomaniaque *mf.*

erotylid [e'routilid], *s. Ent:* érotyle *m.*

Erotylidae [erou'tilidi:], *s.pl. Ent:* érotylidés *m.*

erotylus [e'routiləs], *s. Ent:* érotyle *m*; zonaire *m.*

err [ə:r], *v.i.* (*a*) s'égarer, s'écarter (**from,** de); **to e. from**

the straight path, s'égarer du droit chemin; (*b*) pécher; **he does not e. on the side of modesty,** il ne pèche pas par la modestie; **to e. out of ignorance,** pécher par ignorance; (*c*) errer; être dans l'erreur; faire erreur; se tromper; **to e. is human,** tout le monde peut se tromper; il est permis de se tromper.
errancy ['erənsi], *s. Lit:* état *m* d'erreur.
errand ['erənd], *s.* commission *f,* course *f;* **to go, run, (on) errands,** (aller) faire des commissions, des courses; **to run errands for s.o.,** faire les courses de qn; *Com:* **e. boy,** (i) garçon *m* de courses; (ii) garçon livreur.
errant ['erənt]. **1.** *a.* (*a*) errant; (*b*) tombé dans l'erreur; dévoyé. **2.** *a. & s. A:* (**knight**) **e.,** chevalier errant.
errantry ['erəntri], *s. A:* vie errante (des chevaliers); **knight e.,** chevalerie errante.
erratic [i'rætik], *a.* **1.** (*a*) *Med:* (douleur *f*) erratique; (*b*) *Geol:* **e. boulder,** *s.* **erratic,** bloc *m* erratique. **2.** (*a*) irrégulier; **e. working of a machine,** rendement inégal, irrégulier, d'une machine; fonctionnement intermittent; irrégularité *f* de marche; (*b*) *Aut: etc:* **e. driving,** conduite mal assurée. **3.** (*of pers.*) excentrique, fantasque, capricieux, bizarre, velléitaire; **e. opinions,** opinions extravagantes; **e. life,** vie désordonnée.
erratically [i'rætik(ə)li], *adv.* sans méthode, sans règle; excentriquement; capricieusement; **to work e.,** (i) (*of pers.*) travailler irrégulièrement, sans méthode, à bâtons rompus, par boutades; (ii) (*of machine*) fonctionner irrégulièrement, par à-coups; *Aut:* **to drive e.,** conduire d'une façon mal assurée, par à-coups.
erratum, *pl.* **-ta** [i'rɑːtəm, -tə], *s.* erratum *m, pl.* errata; **an errata slip,** un errata.
errhine ['erain], *a. Med:* errhin.
erring ['əːriŋ], *a.* dévoyé, égaré, tombé dans l'erreur.
erringly ['əːriŋli], *adv.* d'une manière erronée; à faux; mal.
erroneous [i'rouniəs], *a.* (calcul) erroné, faux; **e. doctrine, spelling,** doctrine, orthographe, fausse; **arguments resting on e. premises,** arguments *m* qui portent à faux.
erroneously [i'rouniəsli], *adv.* par erreur.
erroneousness [i'rouniəsnis], *s.* erreur *f,* fausseté *f* (d'une doctrine, d'une conclusion).
error ['erər], *s.* **1.** (*sth. wrong, incorrect, faulty*) (*a*) erreur *f,* faute *f,* méprise *f;* **e. of calculation,** erreur de calcul, faux calcul; **e. of judgement, of estimation,** erreur de jugement, d'évaluation; **printer's e.,** faute *f* d'impression, *F:* coquille; *Com:* **errors and omissions excepted,** sauf erreur ou omission; **sent by e.,** envoyé par erreur; **it is an e. to suppose that . . .,** c'est une erreur, on aurait tort, de croire que . . .; *F: O:* **he's a fool, and no e.!** c'est un imbécile, pas d'erreur! (*b*) *Jur:* erreur judiciaire; mal-jugé *m;* **writ of e.,** lettres *fpl.* renvoi *m,* de révision (d'un procès au criminel); (*c*) *Tchn:* erreur, écart *m,* aberration *f,* déviation *f;* **allowable e.,** erreur permise, tolérance *f;* (*of machine, instrument*) **e. of setting,** erreur de calage, de réglage; **zero e.,** déviation, déplacement *m,* du zéro (d'un appareil scientifique); **instrumental e.,** erreur instrumentale, due à l'instrument; **operational e.,** erreur de conduite, de manipulation, de pilotage (d'un appareil); **probable e.,** erreur, écart, probable; **quadrantal e.,** erreur quadrantale; *Artil: etc:* **e. in direction,** écart en direction, écart latéral; **e. in elevation, in range,** écart en portée; **e. of aim, sighting e.,** erreur de visée; **vertical e.,** écart en hauteur; *Nau: Av:* **e. of compass,** déviation du compas; **e. in dead reckoning,** erreur de l'estime; *Elcs: Rad:* **display e.,** erreur d'affichage, de présentation; **elevation e.,** erreur de site (d'antenne); *Cmptr:* **e. tape,** bande *f* recevant les erreurs; **e. routine,** sous-programme *m* de correction d'erreurs; *Surv:* **angular e.,** erreur angulaire; **e. of closure,** erreur de fermeture; **traverse e.,** erreur de cheminement; **personal e.,** équation personnelle; **triangle of e.,** chapeau *m* d'erreur. **2.** (*a*) (*condition of being wrong, etc.*) **to be in e.,** être dans l'erreur; avoir tort; **to lead s.o. into e.,** induire qn en erreur; **to fall into e.,** tomber dans l'erreur, se fourvoyer; **he has seen the e. of his ways,** il s'est rendu compte de son erreur, est revenu de ses égarements; (*b*) (*wrongdoing*) écart (de conduite); **errors of youth,** erreurs, écarts, de jeunesse.
ersatz [ɛəː'zæts, 'əːzæts], *a. & s.* succédané; **the coffee is e.,** le café n'est qu'un ersatz, un succédané.
Erse [əːs], *a. & s. Ling:* (*a*) erse (*m*), gaélique (*m*); (*b*) *F:* (*not used in Ireland*) irlandais (*m*).
erstwhile ['əːst(h)wail]. **1.** *adv. A: & Poet:* autrefois, jadis; *A:* naguère(s). **2.** *a.* **her e. lover,** son prétendu d'autrefois, d'antan.
erubescence [eru(:)'bes(ə)ns], *s.* érubescence *f.*
erubescent [eru(:)'bes(ə)nt], *a.* érubescent.
erubescite [e'ruːbisait], *s. Miner:* érubescite *f,* bornite *f.*
erucic [e'ruːsik], *a. Ch:* érucique.
eruciform [e'ruːsifɔːm], *a. Ent:* éruciforme.
eruct [i'rʌkt], **eructate** [i'rʌkteit], *v.tr. & i.* éructer, *F:* roter.
eructation [iːrʌk'teiʃ(ə)n], *s.* éructation *f,* renvoi *m, F:* rot *m.*
erudite ['eru(:)dait], *a.* érudit, savant.
eruditely ['eru(:)daitli], *adv.* d'une manière érudite, savante.
erudition [eru(:)'diʃ(ə)n], *s.* érudition *f;* **work of monumental e.,** vrai monument d'érudition; vrai travail de bénédictin.
erupt [i'rʌpt], *v.i.* **1.** (*of teeth*) percer. **2.** (*of volcano*) entrer en éruption; faire éruption. **3.** *Med:* **he erupted with measles,** il a eu une éruption de rougeole.
eruption [i'rʌpʃ(ə)n], *s.* **1.** (*a*) éruption *f* (d'un volcan, d'un geyser, des passions); **volcano in e.,** volcan en activité; (*b*) éclat *m,* accès *m* (de colère, de gaieté, etc.); (*c*) *A:* ruée *f* (de barbares, de hordes sauvages). **2.** (*a*) *Med:* éruption, poussée *f* (de boutons); efflorescence *f* (de la rougeole, etc.); (*b*) éruption (des dents).
eruptional [i'rʌpʃənl], *a.* (*of shock, tremor, etc.*) qui se rapporte à une éruption; dû à une éruption.
eruptive [i'rʌptiv], *a. Med: Geol:* (*of disease, rock, etc.*) éruptif.
Erycinidae [eri'sinidiː], *s.pl. Ent:* érycinides *m,* riodinides *m.*
Erymanthus [eri'mænθəs], *Pr.n. A.Geog:* Érymanthe *m.*
eryngium [e'rindʒiəm], *s. Bot:* érynge *m,* eryngium *m.*
eryon ['eriɔn], *s. Paleont:* éryon *m.*
erysimum [e'risiməm], *s. Bot:* érysimon *m,* erysimum *m.*
erysipelas [eri'sipiləs], *s. Med:* érysipèle *m,* érésipèle *m; Vet:* **swine e.,** rouget *m* (du porc).
erysipelatous [erisi'pelətəs], *a. Med:* érysipélateux.
erysipeloid [eri'sipəlɔid], *s. Med:* érysipéloïde *f.*
erysipelothrix [erisi'pelouθriks], *s. Bac:* érysipelothrix *m.*
Erysiphaceae [erisi'feisiiː], *s.pl. Fung:* érysiphacées *f.*
Erysiphe [eri'sifi], *s. Fung:* érysiphe *m.*
erythema [eri'θiːmə], *s. Med:* érythème *m.*
erythematous [eriθi'meitəs], *a. Med:* érythémateux.
erythraea [eri'θri(:)ə], *s. Bot:* érythrée *f, F:* petite centaurée.
Erythraean [eri'θri(:)ən], *a. Geog:* **the E. Sea,** la mer Érythrée.
erythr(a)emia [eri'θriːmiə], *s. Med:* érythrémie *f.*
erythrasma [eri'θræzmə], *s. Med:* érythrasma *m.*
erythrin [e'riθrin], *s. Ch:* érythrine *f.*
erythrina [eri'θrainə], *s. Bot:* érythrine *f.*
erythrinus [eri'θrainəs], *s. Ich:* érythrin *m.*
erythrism [e'riθrizm], *s. Anthr:* érythrisme *m.*
erythrite [e'riθrait], *s.* **1.** *Miner:* érythrine *f,* cobaltocre *m;* cobalt arséniaté. **2.** *Ch:* érythrite *f.*
erythroblast [e'riθroublæst], *s. Physiol:* erythroblaste *m.*
erythroblastic [eriθrou'blæstik], *a. Physiol:* érythroblastique.
erythroblastosis [eriθroublæs'tousis], *s. Med:* érythroblastose *f.*
erythrocarpous [eriθrou'kɑːpəs], *a. Bot:* érythrocarpe.
erythrocruorin [eriθroukruː'ɔːrin], *s. Biol:* érythrocruorine *f.*
erythrocyte [e'riθrousait], *s. Physiol:* érythrocyte *m,* hématie *f,* globule sanguin rouge.
erythrocytosis [eriθrousai'tousis], *s. Med:* érythrocytose *f.*
erythrodermia [eriθrou'dəːmiə], *s. Med:* érythrodermie *f.*
erythrol ['eriθrɔl], *s. Ch:* érythrol *m.*
erythrolysis [eriθ'rɔlisis], *s. Physiol:* érythrolyse *f.*
erythromelalgia [eriθroume'lældʒiə], *s. Med:* érythromélalgie *f.*
erythromycin [eriθrou'maisin], *s. Pharm:* érythromycine *f.*
erythronium [eri'θroniəm], *s. Bot:* érythrone *m;* erythronium *m.*
erythrophagocytosis [eriθrou'fægousai'tousis], *s. Physiol:* érythrophagocytose *f.*
erythrophilous [eriθ'rɔfiləs], *s. Biol:* érythrophile.
erythrophobia [eriθrou'foubiə], *s. Med:* érythrophobie *f.*
erythropia, erythropsia [eriθ'roupiə, -'rɔpsiə], *s. Med:* érythropsie *f.*
erythroplasia [eriθrou'pleisiə], *s. Med:* érythroplasie *f.*
erythropoiesis [eriθroupɔi'iːsis], *s. Med:* érythropoïèse *f.*
erythropsin [eriθ'rɔpsin], *s. Biol:* érythropsine *f.*
erythrose ['eriθrous], *s. Ch:* érythrose *m.*
erythrosiderite [eriθrou'sidərait], *s. Miner:* érythrosidérite *f.*
erythrosine [e'riθrousin], *s. Ch:* érythrosine *f.*
erythrosis [eriθ'rousis], *s. Med:* érythrose *f.*
erythrozincite [eriθrou'ziŋkait], *s. Miner:* érythrozincite *f.*
erythrulose [e'riθrulous], *s. Ch:* érythrulose *m.*
Erzerum ['ɛəzəruːm], *Pr.n. Geog:* Erzeroum *f.*
Esau ['iːsɔː], *Pr.n.m.* Ésaü.
esca ['eskə], *s. Bot:* (*disease of vine*) esca *m.*
escalade[1] [eskə'leid], *s.* escalade *f.*
escalade[2], *v.tr.* escalader.
escalate ['eskəleit], *v.i.* **1.** (*of prices, etc.*) (i) monter (en flèche); (ii) *occ.* dégringoler. **2.** *Mil: Pol:* **small incidents can easily e. into a world war,** de simples incidents (militaires) peuvent facilement mener à une guerre mondiale.
escalation [eskə'leiʃ(ə)n], *s.* **1.** *Pol.Ec:* augmentation *f* (rapide) (des prix, etc.); escalade *f;* **e. of interest rates,** escalade des taux d'intérêt. **2.** *Mil: Pol:* escalade, passage *m* de simples incidents (militaires) à des crises graves.
escalator ['eskəleitər], *s.* (*a*) escalier roulant, mécanique, mobile; escalator *m;* (*b*) *Pol.Ec:* **e. clause,** échelle *f* mobile.
escallop [es'kæləp], *s.* (*a*) *Her:* coquille *f;* (*b*) *Com: occ.* coquille Saint-Jacques.
escalope ['eskəlɔp], *s. Cu:* escalope *f* (de veau).
escapade ['eskəpeid], *s.* escapade *f,* frasque *f,* fredaine *f.*
escape[1] [is'keip], *s.* **1.** (*a*) fuite *f,* évasion *f;* (*from enemy, etc.*) dérobade *f;* **to make, effect, one's e.,** s'échapper, se sauver; **to invent a plan of e.,** inventer, imaginer, un moyen de s'échapper, un moyen d'évasion; **to make good one's e.,** réussir, parvenir, à s'échapper; **e. literature,** littérature *f* d'évasion; **alcohol may provide a means of e.,** l'alcool peut procurer un moyen d'évasion; *Jur:* **e. warrant,** mandat *m* d'arrestation d'un prisonnier échappé; (*b*) **to have a narrow e.,** l'échapper belle; en revenir d'une belle; (*of sick person*) revenir de loin; **he had a narrow e.,** il l'a eue chaude, il l'a échappé belle; **he had a narrow e. from falling,** il a failli tomber; il s'en est fallu de peu qu'il ne tombât, peu s'en faut, il s'en faut de peu, qu'il ne soit tombé; **to have a miraculous e.,** échapper comme par miracle; **I owe my e. to . . .,** je dois mon salut, ma délivrance, à . . .; **there is no (way of) e. from it,** il n'y a pas moyen d'y échapper, de s'y soustraire, il faut en passer par là; **way of e.,** issue *f;* **e. hatch,** trappe *f* de sortie, de secours; *Com: etc:* **e. clause,** clause *f* échappatoire; (*c*) échappement *m,* fuite, dégagement *m,* déperdition *f* (de gaz, d'eau, etc.); **e. of light,** filtrée *f* de lumière; (*d*) *Space:* libération *f* de l'attraction terrestre; **e. velocity,** vitesse *f* (i) de décrochage, (ii) de libération (d'un engin spatial). **2. fire e.,** échelle *f* de sauvetage. **3.** *Hyd.E:* déversoir *m; Mec.E. etc.* **e. valve,** soupape *f* d'échappement, de décharge, de trop plein; clapet *m* de sûreté; détendeur *m* (de pression, de vapeur); *Clockm:* **e. wheel,** roue *f* d'échappement. **4.** *Bot:* **garden e.,** plante cultivée qui s'est propagée hors des jardins.
escape[2]. **1.** *v.i.* (*a*) échapper, s'échapper, prendre la fuite; **to e. from, out of, prison,** s'échapper de prison; s'évader; **to e. from one's warders,** échapper à ses gardiens; **to e. to the mountains,** gagner les montagnes; **escaped prisoner,** évadé, -ée; **an escaped convict,** un forçat évadé; (*b*) **to e. by the skin of one's teeth,** échapper de bien près; échapper tout juste; s'en tirer tout juste; **to e. uninjured, with a broken arm,** s'en tirer sans aucun mal, avec un bras cassé; **he escaped with a fright,** il en a été quitte pour la peur; (*c*) (*of gases, fluids*) se dégager; s'échapper, fuir; se perdre. **2.** *v.tr.* (*a*) (*of pers.*) échapper à (un danger, sa destinée); **to e. pursuit,** échapper aux poursuites; se dérober aux poursuites; **he narrowly escaped death,** il a échappé tout juste à la mort; il a frisé la mort; il a été bien près de la mort; **to e. doing sth.,** éviter de, se dispenser de, faire qch.; **he just escaped being killed,** il s'en est fallu de bien peu qu'il ne fût tué; il a bien failli être tué; il a manqué (de) se faire tuer; **to e. observation,** se dérober aux regards; **doom that cannot be escaped,** sort inéluctable; sort auquel on ne peut échapper; (*b*) (*of thgs*) **to e. notice,** échapper à l'attention; passer inaperçu; **it will not have escaped the notice of anyone that . . .,** il n'aura échappé à personne que . . .; **fact that had hitherto escaped notice,** fait jusqu'alors inobservé; **that fact had escaped me,** ce fait m'avait échappé; (*c*) **an oath, a cry, escaped him, escaped his lips,** il laissa échapper un juron, un cri; **not a word escaped his lips,** pas un mot n'échappa, ne s'échappa, de ses lèvres; (*d*) **this word escaped me, I admit,** ce mot m'est échappé, j'en conviens.
escape[3], *s. Arch:* congé *m* (d'une colonne).
escapee [eskei'piː], *s.* évadé, -ée.
escapement [is'keipmənt], *s.* **1.** déversoir *m* (du tropplein d'énergie de qn, etc.). **2.** (*a*) *Clockm: etc:* échappement *m* (d'une pendule, d'un piano, etc.); *Clockm:*

hook e., échappement à ancre; (*b*) *Typewr:* espacement *m.*

escaper [is'keipər], *s.* fugitif, -ive.

escaping [is'keipiŋ], *s.* évasion *f* (d'un prisonnier); échappement *m* (de vapeur); dégagement *m* (de gaz).

escapism [is'keipizm], *s.* évasion *f* (de la réalité).

escapist [is'keipist], *s.* personne *f* qui cherche à fuir la réalité; *attrib.* **e. literature,** littérature *f* d'évasion.

escarbuncle [es'kɑːbʌŋkl], *s. Her:* escarboucle *f.*

escarp[1] [es'kɑːp], *s.* (*a*) *Fort:* escarpe *f;* (*b*) *O:* talus *m.*

escarp[2], *v.tr.* (*a*) *Fort:* escarper (un glacis, etc.); (*b*) escarper, taluter (un remblai, etc.).

escarpment [es'kɑːpmənt], *s.* escarpement *m.*

eschar ['eskɑːr], *s. Med:* escarre *f.*

eschara ['eskərə], *s. Nat.Hist:* eschare *m;* (*genus*) eschara *m.*

escharotic [eskə'rɔtik], *a. & s. Med:* esc(h)arotique (*m*).

eschatocol [e'skætəkɔl], *s.* protocole final, eschatocole *m* (d'une charte).

eschatological [eskətə'lɔdʒikl], *a. Theol:* eschatologique.

eschatology [eskə'tɔlədʒi], *s. Theol:* eschatologie *f.*

escheat[1] [is'tʃiːt], *s. Jur:* **1.** (*a*) déshérence *f;* dévolution *f* d'héritage à l'État; **right of e.,** (droit *m* d') aubaine *f;* (*of estate*) **to revert by e. to s.o.,** échoir, obvenir, à qn; (*b*) *Hist: Scot:* confiscation *f* de biens. **2.** bien (tombé) en déshérence; succession dévolue à l'État.

escheat[2]. **1.** *v.tr.* confisquer (une succession, etc.); **to e. an estate to s.o.,** faire échoir une succession à qn. **2.** *v.i. Jur:* (*a*) (*of estate, etc.*) tomber en déshérence; revenir à l'État, à la Couronne; **escheated succession,** succession dévolue à l'État; (*b*) échoir, obvenir (**to,** à).

escheatable [is'tʃiːtəbl], *a. Jur:* (*of estate, property*) susceptible de déshérence.

escheatment [is'tʃiːtmənt], *s. Jur:* déshérence *f;* dévolution *f* (d'un héritage) à l'État.

eschew [is'tʃuː], *v.tr. A: & Lit:* éviter (qch.); renoncer à (qch.); s'abstenir de (qch.); **e. evil!** ne faites point le mal!

eschscholtzia [es'kɔltʃə], *s. Bot:* eschscholzie *f;* (*genus*) eschscholtzia *f.*

eschynite ['eskinait], *s. Miner:* œschynite *f.*

escort[1] ['eskɔːt], *s.* **1.** (*pers.*) (*a*) (*group of pers.*) escorte *f;* suite *f* (d'attendants); **e. of honour,** escorte, piquet *m*, d'honneur; *Mil: etc:* **e. of the colours,** garde *f* du drapeau; (*b*) (*single pers.*) escorte; guide *m;* gardien *m*, garde du corps; (*to a woman*) cavalier *m.* **2.** (*fact of escorting*) escorte; **under the e. of. . .,** sous l'escorte, la conduite, de. . .; **to conduct a prisoner under e.,** conduire un prisonnier sous escorte. **3.** *Nau:* (*ship*) escorteur *m;* bâtiment *m* d'escorte; **coastal e.,** escorteur côtier; **destroyer e.,** escorteur rapide, d'escadre; **fleet e.,** escorteur d'escadre, de flotte; **e. (aircraft) carrier,** porte-avions *m* d'escorte; **radar-picket e.,** escorteur piquet radar; **sloop e.,** aviso *m* escorteur; **(coastal) hydrofoil e.,** escorteur (côtier) à aile portante; *Mil.Av:* **e. fighter,** chasseur *m* d'escorte.

escort[2] [is'kɔːt], *v.tr.* escorter, faire escorte à, servir d'escorte à (un général, un convoi); **to e. a lady,** servir de cavalier à une dame; **to e. a prisoner,** conduire un prisonnier sous escorte; **to e. s.o. on horseback,** suivre qn à cheval; **may I e. you home?** permettez-moi de vous raccompagner chez vous.

escribed [iː'skraibd], *a. Mth:* **e. circle,** cercle exinscrit.

escritoire [eskri(ː)'twɑːr], *s. Furn:* secrétaire *m;* bureau *m* (de salon).

escrow [es'krou], *s. Jur:* (*a*) engagement *m* sous seing-privé confié à un tiers pour être livré au destinataire lors de la réalisation de certaines conditions spécifiées; (*b*) *U.S:* retenue *f* de garantie.

escuage ['eskjuidʒ], *s. Hist:* écuage *m.*

escudo [es'kjuːdou], *s. Num:* escudo *m.*

esculent ['eskjulənt], *a. & s.* comestible (*m*); esculent (*m*).

esculetin [eskju'liːtin], *s. Bio-Ch:* esculétine *f.*

esculin ['eskjulin], *s. Ch:* esculine *f.*

escutcheon [es'kʌtʃ(ə)n], *s.* **1.** (*a*) *Her:* écu *m*, écusson *m;* (*b*) *N.Arch:* écusson (de la poupe); tableau *m.* **2.** *Tchn:* (*a*) écusson; entrée *f*, rondelle *f*, cache-entrée *m inv*, rouet *m* (de serrure); (*b*) (*on knife handle, etc.*) rosette *f;* (*c*) (*of scabbard*) bouterolle *f.* **3.** (*a*) **(milk) e.,** écusson (d'une vache); (*b*) *Ent:* écusson.

eserine ['eseriːn], *s. Pharm:* ésérine *f.*

esker ['eskər], *s. Geol:* esker *m.*

Eskimo, *pl.* **-o(e)s,** *also* **-o** ['eskimou, -ouz], *Ethn:* (*a*) *a.* esquimau, -aude, -aux (*occ. inv. in f.*); eskimo *inv;* **E. woman,** Esquimaude, femme esquimau; **E. dog,** chien *m* esquimau; **the E. civilization,** la civilisation esquimau(de); (*b*) *s.* Esquimau, -aude.

Esocidae [e'sɔsidiː], *s.pl. Ich:* ésocidés *m*, les brochets *m.*

esophag(o)- [i'sɔfəg(ou)], *pref. Anat:* œsophag(o)-.

esophagotomy [isɔfə'gɔtəmi], *s. Surg:* œsophagotomie *f.*

esophagus [i'sɔfəgəs], *s. Anat:* œsophage *m.*

esophoria [esə'fɔːriə], *s. Med:* ésophorie *f.*

esoteric [esou'terik], *a.* ésotérique; secret.

esoterically [esou'terik(ə)li], *adv.* d'une façon ésotérique; secrètement.

esotericism [esou'terisizm], **esoterism** [e'sɔtərizm], *s.* ésotérisme *m.*

espadrille [espæ'dril], *s. Bootm:* espadrille *f.*

espagnolette [espænjə'let], *s.* espagnolette *f;* targette *f* à l'espagnole; crémone *f*, bascule *f* (d'une fenêtre).

espalier[1] [es'pæliər, -iei], *s.* espalier *m* ((i) treillis, (ii) arbre); **on an e.,** en espalier.

espalier[2], *v.tr.* cultiver en espalier.

esparto [es'pɑːtou], *s.* **e. (grass),** sparte *m;* alfa *m;* lygée *f;* **e. grass products,** sparterie *f;* **e. paper,** papier *m* d'alfa.

especial [is'peʃ(ə)l], *a.* spécial, -aux; particulier; **of e. importance,** d'une importance toute particulière; *A:* **in e.,** surtout; en particulier.

especially [is'peʃ(ə)li], *adv.* surtout, particulièrement; **you ought to go for a long voyage, e. as you are well-to-do,** vous devriez faire un grand voyage, d'autant plus que, surtout que, vous êtes riche; **we were e. lucky with the weather,** le temps nous était particulièrement favorable.

Esperantist [espə'ræntist], *a. & s. Ling:* espérantiste (*mf*).

Esperanto [espə'ræntou], *s. Ling:* espéranto *m.*

espial [is'pai(ə)l], *s. A: & Lit:* **1.** espionnage *m* (par le trou de la serrure, etc.). **2.** action *f* d'apercevoir (qn au loin).

espionage ['espiənɑːʒ], *s.* espionnage *m.*

esplanade [esplə'neid], *s.* (*a*) *Fort: etc:* esplanade *f;* (*b*) (*in seaside town, etc.*) digue *f.*

espousal [es'pauz(ə)l], *s.* **1.** *A: usu. pl.* épousailles *f*, accordailles *f.* **2.** *Lit:* **e. of a cause,** adoption *f* d'une cause; adhésion *f* à une cause.

espouse [es'pauz], *v.tr.* **1.** *A: & Lit:* (*a*) épouser (une femme); (*b*) **espoused wife,** femme fiancée, promise. **2.** *A:* (*of parent*) **to e. one's daughter to s.o.,** marier sa fille à qn; donner sa fille en mariage à qn. **3.** épouser, embrasser (une cause, un parti, une opinion).

espresso [es'presou], *a. & s.* (*a*) **e. (coffee),** (café *m*) expresso (*m*), *F:* express (*m*); (*b*) **e. (machine),** cafetière *f* à pression, expresso.

esprit de corps ['espriːdə'kɔːr], *s.* esprit *m* de corps.

espy [es'pai], *v.tr. A: & Lit:* **1.** apercevoir, aviser, entrevoir, (qn, qch.) au loin, dans le lointain; **in the field he espied a mare,** dans le champ il avisa une jument. **2.** découvrir, remarquer (un défaut).

Esquiline ['eskwilain], *a. & s. Geog:* **the E. (Hill),** le mont Esquilin.

Esquimau ['eskimou], *a. & s.* = ESKIMO.

esquire [is'kwaiər], *s.* **1.** *A:* écuyer *m* (servant). **2.** *Corr:* (*titre honorifique d'un monsieur, abr.* **Esq.**) **David Thomas, Esq.** = Monsieur David Thomas.

ess, *pl.* **esses** [es, 'esiz], *s.* (*a*) (la lettre) s; (*b*) *Rac:* **the esses,** les virages *m* en s.

essay[1] ['esei], *s.* **1.** essai *m*, effort *m;* tentative *f* (**at,** de); *Lit:* **my first e. at authorship,** mes débuts comme écrivain. **2.** (*a*) *Lit:* essai; (*b*) *Sch:* dissertation *f;* composition *f* (littéraire). **3.** *Tchn:* essai.

essay[2] [e'sei], *v.tr. Lit:* **1.** mettre (qn, qch.) à l'épreuve. **2.** essayer (**sth., to do sth.,** qch., de faire qch.).

essayist ['eseiist], *s. Lit:* essayiste *mf;* auteur *m* d'essais.

essence ['esəns], *s.* **1.** *Phil: Theol: etc:* essence *f;* **metaphysics in conformity with the true e. of things,** métaphysique conforme à l'être, à l'essence, véritable des choses; **the e. of the matter,** le fond de l'affaire; **the e. of a book,** le suc, la moelle, d'un livre; **money is the e. of business,** l'argent est l'âme des affaires; **the very e. of authority,** l'autorité même; **the problem was in e. political,** le problème était essentiellement, surtout, politique; **time is of the e. of the contract,** le temps est de l'essence du contrat; il est important de faire vite; *Jur:* **e. of a crime,** qualité substantielle d'un crime. **2.** *Ch: Cu: etc:* essence, extrait *m;* **meat e.,** extrait de viande.

Essene ['esiːn], *s. B.Hist:* Essénien *m.*

Essenian [e'siːniən], *a. B.Hist:* essénien.

Essenism ['esənizm], *s. B.Hist:* essénisme *m.*

essential [i'senʃ(ə)l]. **1.** *a.* (*a*) (*of difference, etc.*) essentiel; (*b*) essentiel, indispensable; capital, -aux; **e. data,** données essentielles; **e. foodstuffs,** denrées *f* de première nécessité; **e. tool,** outil *m* de première utilité; **the e. point,** le point capital; **the e. part of a doctrine,** l'essence *f* d'une doctrine; **it is e. that. . .,** il est capital que, il importe (au premier chef) que, il est indispensable que + *sub.*; **it is e. to do that,** il est essentiel, absolument nécessaire, de toute nécessité, de faire cela; **the e. thing,** l'essentiel *m;* **prudence is e.,** la prudence est de commande; la prudence s'impose; **the e. influence of climate,** l'influence capitale du climat; **the e. feature of this policy. . .,** le fond de cette politique. . .; *Ecc:* **the e. vows,** les vœux *m* de la religion, les vœux monastiques, les trois vœux; (*c*) **e. oil,** huile essentielle. **2.** *s.usu. pl.* **reduced to its essentials,** dépouillé; **to concentrate on essentials,** s'attacher à l'essentiel; **one of the essentials of a business man,** une des qualités indispensables à un homme d'affaires.

essentiality [isenʃi'æliti], *s.* essentialité *f.*

essentially [i'senʃəli], *adv.* essentiellement.

essonite ['esənait], *s. Miner:* essonite *f.*

establish [is'tæbliʃ], *v.tr.* **1.** (*a*) affermir (sa foi); asseoir (des fondements, son crédit, son pouvoir); **to e. a reign of justice,** instaurer le règne de la justice; (*b*) *Cin: etc:* **to e. the scene,** placer, situer, la scène; (*c*) *Jur:* confirmer, ratifier (un testament); **to e. one's right,** faire apparoir son bon droit. **2.** établir (un gouvernement); édifier (un système); fonder (une maison de commerce); créer, instituer (une agence); constituer (une société, un tribunal); mettre sur pied (une paix); *Sch:* **to e. a new chair,** créer une nouvelle chaire; **to e. a tax on tobacco,** mettre un impôt sur le tabac; **to e. close relations with s.o.,** nouer des relations avec qn; **to e. a reputation for scholarship,** se faire une réputation de savant; **to e. s.o.'s reputation as an author,** faire la réputation de qn comme auteur; **to e. s.o., oneself, in business,** établir qn, s'établir, dans les affaires; **to e. oneself in a job,** s'établir dans un emploi; **to e. a custom,** établir, introduire, une coutume; **to e. a doctrine,** élever une doctrine; *O:* **to e. oneself in the country,** s'installer à la campagne; *Pej:* **to e. oneself in s.o.'s house,** s'établir, s'installer, s'ancrer, chez qn. **3.** établir, avérer (un fait); démontrer (la vérité d'une proposition, l'identité de qn); constater (la réalité d'un fait); **to e. a charge, s.o.'s innocence,** établir une accusation, l'innocence de qn; **it was established that the parcel contained nothing suspicious,** le paquet fut reconnu ne contenir rien de suspect; **the enquiry has enabled me to e. the following facts,** l'enquête m'a amené aux constations suivantes; **the facts established by the inquiry,** les faits qui résultent des informations; **the roll call establishes that 200 were present,** l'appel nominal constate deux cents présences. **4.** (*a*) ériger (une Église) en Église d'État; établir (une Église); (*b*) **to e. a city as a free city,** constituer une ville en ville libre.

established [is'tæbliʃt], *a.* établi; **e. reputation,** réputation solide, bien établie; **well-e. business, friendship,** maison *f*, amitié *f*, solide; **e. fact,** fait avéré; fait constant; fait acquis; **e. scientific fact,** fait acquis à la science; **e. bookseller, etc.,** libraire, etc., patenté; **well-e. fortune,** fortune bien assise; **man of e. position,** homme *m* solide, considérable; *Jur:* **witness of well-e. position,** témoin patenté (commerçant ou membre d'une profession libérale); **the E. Church,** (i) l'Église établie; (ii) la religion d'État; **the e. order,** l'ordre établi; *Adm:* **e. civil servants,** fonctionnaires titularisés; **non-e. civil servants,** fonctionnaires non titularisés, contractuels.

establishment [is'tæbliʃmənt], *s.* **1.** (*a*) affermissement *m* (de sa foi); confirmation *f*, ratification *f* (d'un testament); constatation *f* (d'un fait, etc.); (*b*) établissement *m* (d'un gouvernement, d'une industrie, d'une Église); création *f* (d'un système, d'un bureau); fondation *f* (d'une maison de commerce); constitution *f* (d'une société); assiette *f* (d'un impôt). **2.** établissement, maison *f;* **business e.,** maison de commerce; **e. charges,** frais généraux, dépenses *f* de la maison; **private e.,** maison particulière; **he keeps a separate e. (for a mistress),** il a un ménage en ville; **he has enlarged his e.,** il a augmenté sa maison; **to keep up an e.,** tenir maison; avoir un grand train de maison. **3.** (*a*) personnel *m* d'une maison; train *m* (de maison); **to be on the e.,** (i) faire partie du personnel; (ii) *Typ:* être en conscience; *Typ:* **e. hand,** ouvrier *m* en conscience; (*b*) *Mil: etc:* effectif *m* (d'une unité, etc.); **war e., peace e.,** effectifs de guerre; effectifs de paix, en temps de paix; **on a war, a peace, e.,** sur le pied de guerre, de paix; **to bring a division up to war e.,** porter une division à l'effectif de guerre. **4.** (*a*) **the (Church) E.,** l'Église établie; (*b*) **the E.,** (i) les institutions *f* (d'un pays); (ii) le monde traditionnel. **5.** *Adm:* titularisation *f* (d'un fonctionnaire). **6. e. of the port, vulgar, common, e.,** établissement du port, des marées dans un port.

estate [is'teit], *s.* **1.** état *m*, condition *f;* **man's e.,** l'âge viril; l'âge d'homme; **to have arrived at woman's e.,** être une femme faite; **the holy e. of matrimony,** le saint état de mariage. **2.** *usu. Lit:* rang *m*, condition; **of high,**

low, e., de haut rang, d'humble condition; **to fall from one's high e.,** déchoir du rang que l'on a occupé. **3.** *Fr.Hist:* **the Estates (of the Realm),** les états, les ordres (de l'ancien régime); **the Third E.,** le Tiers (État), la bourgeoisie; *F:* **the Fourth E.,** le journalisme, la Presse. **4.** *Jur:* (*a*) bien *m*, domaine *m*, immeuble *m*; **e. free from incumbrances,** immeuble sans servitudes, charges, ni hypothèques; **personal e.,** biens mobiliers, biens meubles; biens personnels; **real e.,** biens immobiliers; **landed e.,** propriété foncière; **joint e.,** biens en commun; **life e.,** biens en viager; (*b*) succession *f*, masse *f* des biens (d'un défunt); **e. duty,** droits *mpl* de succession; (*c*) actif *m* (d'un failli). **5.** (*a*) terre *f*, propriété *f*, bien; **country house and e. for sale,** à vendre château et domaine; (*b*) **housing e.,** (i) lotissement *m*; (ii) cité ouvrière; groupe *m* de H.L.M.; (*c*) **e. agent, agency,** agent immobilier, agence immobilière; (*d*) *Aut:* **e. car,** familiale *f*; commerciale *f*, break *m*.

esteem[1] [is'ti:m], *s.* estime *f*, considération *f*; **to hold s.o. in high, great, e.,** avoir qn en haute estime; estimer beaucoup qn; **to hold s.o. in low e.,** mésestimer qn; estimer peu qn; **to rise, fall, in s.o.'s e.,** monter, baisser, dans l'estime de qn.

esteem[2], *v.tr.* **1.** estimer (qn); priser (qch.); **much as I e. you,** si grande que soit pour vous mon estime; quelque estime que j'aie pour vous; **to e. sth. lightly,** faire peu de cas de qch.; **man highly esteemed,** homme fort estimé; homme considéré, bien vu; *Com: A:* **your esteemed favour,** votre honorée. **2.** estimer, regarder, considérer (**sth. as sth.,** qch. comme qch.); **to e. oneself happy,** s'estimer heureux.

ester ['estər], *s. Bio-Ch:* ester *m*.

esterase ['estəreis], *s. Bio-Ch:* estérase *f*.

esterification [esterifi'keiʃ(ə)n], *s. Ch:* estérification *f*.

esterify [es'terifai], *v.tr. Ch:* estérifier.

Estheria [es'θiəriə], *s. Crust:* estheria *f*.

estherian [es'θiəriən], *s. Crust:* esthérie *f*.

esthesi- [es'θi:zi], *pref.* (= aesthesi-) esthési-.

esthesia [es'θi:ziə], *s.* esthésie *f*.

esthesiogenic [esθi:ziou'dʒenik], *a.* esthésiogène.

esthesiology [esθi:zi'ɔlədʒi], *s.* esthésiologie *f*.

esthesiometer [esθi:zi'ɔmitər], *s.* esthésiomètre *m*.

esthiomene [es'θaioumi:n], *s. Med:* esthiomène *m*.

Esthonia [es'θouniə], *Pr.n.*, **Esthonian** [es'θouniən], *a.* & *s. O:* = ESTONIA, ESTONIAN.

estimable ['estiməbl], *a.* estimable, digne d'estine; **not a very e. person,** personne *f* peu recommandable.

estimate[1] ['estimət], *s.* **1.** appréciation *f*, évaluation *f*, calcul *m* (des pertes, du contenu de qch., de la force de qch.); **to form a correct e. of sth.,** se former, se faire, une idée exacte de qch.; **you have formed a wrong e. of my position,** vous vous êtes fait une idée fausse de ma situation; **rough e.,** évaluation en gros; approximation grossière; **these figures are only a rough e.,** ces chiffres sont très approximatifs; **on, at, a rough e.,** par aperçu; *F:* à vue de nez, à vue d'œil; **at the lowest e.,** au bas mot; *Mil: etc:* **intelligence e.,** synthèse *f* de renseignement. **2.** *Com:* devis (estimatif); état estimatif; état appréciatif; **building e.,** devis de construction; **printing e.,** devis d'imprimerie; **preliminary e., rough e.,** devis de prévision, devis approximatif; avant-projet *m*; **e. on demand,** devis sur demande; **to put in an e.,** donner un devis; soumissionner; **e. of expenditure,** chiffre prévu pour les dépenses; *Pol:* **the Estimates,** les prévisions *f* budgétaires; les crédits *m*; **naval, Navy, estimates,** budget *m* de la marine; **supplementary estimates,** crédits supplémentaires.

estimate[2] ['estimeit], *v.tr.* estimer, évaluer, apprécier (les frais); apprécier (une distance, etc.); évaluer (une forêt, la production d'un puits à pétrole, etc.); mesurer (une influence); **to e. a distance by eye,** mesurer une distance à la vue; **to e. sth. at so much,** estimer, calculer, qch. à tant; **his fortune is estimated at . . .,** on évalue sa fortune à . . .; **the phenomenon was estimated to have lasted five minutes,** la durée du phénomène a été évaluée à cinq minutes; **I e. that it will take three years,** j'estime que cela prendra trois ans, qu'il faudra trois ans; **a fortune impossible to e.,** une fortune impossible à évaluer.

estimated ['estimeitid], *a.* **e. cost,** coût estimatif; **e. value,** valeur estimée; **it is only an e. figure,** ce n'est qu'une estimation; **e. time of arrival,** heure prévue, probable, d'arrivée; **the e. death roll is 200,** on estime que 200 personnes ont été tuées; 200 personnes auraient été tuées.

estimation [esti'meiʃ(ə)n], *s.* **1.** (*also* **estimating** ['estimeitiŋ]) estimation *f*, appréciation *f*, évaluation *f*; calcul *m* (des frais, etc.); **e. of distance, of range,** appréciation des distances; **error of e.,** erreur *f* d'estimation. **2.** (*a*) jugement *m*; **in my e.,** d'après moi; à mon avis; à mon idée; (*b*) estime *f*, considération *f*; **to hold s.o. in e.,** tenir qn en grande estime; **he is rising in the e. of the public,** il remonte dans l'estime du public; **to fall in s.o.'s e.,** tomber dans l'estime de qn.

estimative ['estimətiv], *a.* estimatif.

estimator ['estimeitər], *s.* appréciateur, -trice; estimateur, -trice.

estival [es'taivəl], *a.* estival, -aux.

estocada [estə'ka:də], *s. Sp:* (*bullfighting*) estocade *f*.

Estonia [es'touniə], *Pr.n. Geog: Hist:* Estonie *f*.

Estonian [es'touniən], *a. Geog:* (*a*) *a.* estonien; **the E. Soviet Socialist Republic,** la République socialiste soviétique d'Estonie; (*b*) *s.* Estonien, -ienne.

estop [is'tɔp], *v.tr.* (**estopped**) (*usu. in passive*) *Jur:* opposer une exception, une fin de non-recevoir, à (qn); **to be estopped from sth., from doing sth.,** être exclus de qch.; être empêché de faire qch.

estoppage [is'tɔpidʒ], *s. Jur:* exclusion *f*, empêchement *m*.

estoppel [is'tɔp(ə)l], *s. Jur:* fin *f* de non-recevoir; exception *f*; non-recevabilité *f*, irrecevabilité *f*.

estovers [is'touvəz], *s. Jur:* **1.** bois *m* nécessaire pour l'entretien de la maison et pour les besoins domestiques; portion affouagère; **common of e.,** droit *m* de couper le taillis; affouage *m*; **section of forest conceded as e.,** portion affouagère; **wood that may be taken by e.,** bois affouagé; **allotment of e.,** affouagement *m*; **to grant s.o. e.,** afforester qn. **2.** pension *f* alimentaire d'une veuve, d'une femme séparée.

estrada [es'tra:də], *s.* sentier *m* (d'une plantation caoutchoutière).

estrade [es'tra:d], *s.* estrade (basse).

estradiol [estræ'daioul], *s. Bio-Ch:* œstradiol *m*.

estragol(e) ['estrægɔl], *s. Ch:* estragol(e) *m*.

estral ['i:strəl], *a. Biol:* œstral.

estrange [is'trein(d)ʒ], *v.tr.* (*a*) **to e. s.o.,** s'aliéner l'estime, l'affection, de qn; **he has estranged all his relations,** il s'est aliéné tous ses parents; **his conduct estranged him from his friends,** sa conduite lui aliéna l'estime de ses amis; **to become estranged from s.o., sth.,** se détacher de qn, qch.; **they have become estranged,** ils sont devenus des étrangers l'un pour l'autre; ils ne se connaissent plus; **to live estranged from the world,** vivre dans l'éloignement du monde, retiré du monde, dans la retraite; (*b*) **to e. s.o. from s.o.,** indisposer qn contre qn.

estranged [is'trein(d)ʒd], *a.* (cœur, etc.) aliéné; **e. friends,** amis brouillés.

estrangement [is'trein(d)ʒmənt], *s.* aliénation *f* (de qn); éloignement *m* (de deux personnes); brouille *f* (**between,** entre); **temporary e.,** brouille passagère.

estray [es'trei], *s. Jur:* animal domestique égaré, errant.

estreat [es'tri:t], *v.tr. Jur:* copier un extrait (d'amende, de condamnation pécuniaire) et l'adresser à la Cour de l'Échiquier.

Estremadura [estrəmə'duərə], *Pr.n. Geog:* Estrémadure *f*.

estriol ['i:straiɔl], *s. Bio-Ch:* œstriol *m*.

estrogen ['i:strədʒen], *s. Bio-Ch:* œstrogène *m*.

estrogenic [i:strə'dʒenik], *a. Bio-Ch:* œstrogène, œstrogénique.

estrone ['i:stroun], *s. Bio-Ch:* œstrone *f*.

estrous ['i:strəs], *a. Biol:* œstral.

estrus ['i:strəs], *s. Biol:* œstre *m*, œstrus *m*.

estuarine ['estjuərin], *a. Geog:* **e. culture,** culture dans les estuaires; *Rept:* **e. crocodile,** crocodile *m* des estuaires.

estuary ['estju(ə)ri], *s.* estuaire *m*.

esurience [e'sju:riəns], **esuriency** [e'sju:riənsi], *s. A:* & *Lit:* cupidité *f* famélique.

esurient [e'sju:riənt], *a. A:* & *Lit:* famélique et cupide.

eta ['i:tə], *s. Gr.Alph:* êta *m*.

etaerio [e'tiəriou], *s. Bot:* étairion *m*.

etatism [ei'tætizm], *s.* étatisme *m*.

etcetera [it'setrə]. **1.** *Lt.phr.* (*abbr.* **etc.**) et cætera. **2.** *s.* (*pl.* **etceteras**) et cætera *m inv*; extras *mpl*; **roast turkey with all the etceteras,** dinde rôtie avec tout ce qui s'ensuit.

etch [etʃ]. **1.** *v.tr.* graver (un dessin, etc.) à l'eau-forte; **to e. a plate,** mordre, faire mordre, une planche; graver une planche; **to e. a metal,** attaquer, ronger, un métal à l'acide; **to e. away the metal,** (i) enlever le métal à l'eau-forte; (ii) (*of acid*) attaquer le métal; **to e. off (a blemish, etc.) from a plate,** toucher une planche à l'eau-forte. **2.** *v.i.* faire de la gravure à l'eau-forte.

etcher ['etʃər], *s.* graveur *m* à l'eau-forte; graveur d'eaux fortes; aquafortiste *mf*; **line e.,** graveur de trait; **tone e.,** similiste *m*.

etching ['etʃiŋ], *s.* **1.** (*a*) art *m* de graver à l'eau-forte; (*b*) (i) attaque *f* à l'acide; corrosion *f*; décapage *m*; **e. solution,** réactif *m* d'attaque, solution *f* de morsure; **e. agent,** corrosif *m*; *Ind:* **e. test,** essai *m* par corrosion, *Cryst:* **e. figure,** figure *f* de corrosion; *Av:* **propeller e.,** macrographie *f* de l'hélice; (ii) gravure *f* à l'eau-forte; **deep e.,** grand-creux *m*; **dot e.,** retouche *f* par morsure du point; **fine e.,** remorsure *f*; **intaglio e.,** morsure en creux; **e. knife,** burin *m* de graveur; **e. needle,** pointe sèche (à graver); style *m*; **e. bath,** bain graveur; **e. ground,** enduit *m* à graver; **e. varnish,** vernis *m* de graveur; **e. machine,** machine *f* à graver. **2.** estampe gravée à l'eau-forte; gravure à l'eau-forte; gravure en creux; eau-forte *f*, *pl.* eaux-fortes.

Eteocles ['etiəkli:z], *Pr.n.m. Gr.Lit:* Étéocle.

Eteocretan [i:tiou'kri:tən]. *A.Hist:* (*a*) *a.* étéocrétois; (*b*) *s.* Étéocrétois, -oise.

eternal [i(:)'tə:n(ə)l]. **1.** *a.* (*a*) éternel; **the Father E.,** le Père éternel; **e. life,** la vie éternelle; (*b*) continuel, sans fin; sempiternel; **e. bickerings,** querelles sans fin, incessantes. **2.** *s.* **the E.,** l'Éternel *m*, Dieu *m*.

eternality [i:tə:'næliti], *s.* nature éternelle (d'une vérité).

eternalize [i(:)'tə:nəlaiz], *v.tr.* = ETERNIZE.

eternally [i(:)'tə:nəli], *adv.* éternellement; **I shall be e. grateful to you,** je vous en aurai une reconnaissance éternelle, je vous serai infiniment reconnaissant; **he is e. complaining,** il se plaint éternellement, sans cesse.

eternity [i(:)'tə:niti], *s.* (*a*) éternité *f*; l'éternité; *F:* **he kept me waiting for an e.,** il m'a fait attendre pendant une éternité, pendant des heures; (*b*) *pl.* **the eternities,** les vérités éternelles.

eternize [i:'tə:naiz], *v.tr.* éterniser; rendre éternel.

Etesian [i'ti:ʒiən], *a.* & *s. Meteor:* (vent) étésien (*m*).

ethal ['eθəl], *s. Ch:* éthal *m*.

ethanal ['eθənəl], *s. Ch:* éthanal *m*.

ethane ['eθein], *s. Ch:* éthane *m*.

ethanethiol [eθə'ni:θiɔl], *s. Ch:* éthanethiol *m*.

ethanoic [eθə'noik], *a. Ch:* **e. acid,** éthanoïque *m*.

ethanol ['eθənɔl], *s. Ch:* éthanol *m*.

ethanolamine [eθə'nɔləmi:n], *s. Ch:* éthanolamine *f*.

ethanolysis [eθə'nɔlisis], *s. Ch:* éthanolyse *f*.

ethene ['eθi:n], *s. Ch:* éthène *m*, éthylène *m*.

ether ['i:θər], *s.* éther *m*. **1.** (*a*) *Ch: Com:* **sulphuric e.,** éther sulfurique, ordinaire; **methyl e.,** éther méthylique; (*b*) *Med:* **e. mania,** éthéromanie *f*; **e. addict, maniac,** éthéromane *mf*. **2.** *Ph:* **waves in the e.,** ondes *f* de l'éther. **3.** *A.* & *Poet:* **the e.,** la voûte éthérée; la voûte céleste.

ethereal [i'θiəriəl], *a.* **1.** (*of regions, love, etc.*) éthéré; (*of form, vision*) léger, impalpable; qui n'est pas de ce monde. **2.** *Ch:* (*a*) (*of liquid*) éthéré, volatil; **e. oil,** huile essentielle; (*b*) **e. salt,** éther composé, ester *m*.

ethereality [iθiəri'æliti], *s.* légèreté éthérée (d'une vision, etc.).

etherealize [i'θiəriəlaiz], *v.tr.* donner à (qch.) la légèreté de l'éther; **to e. a passion,** élever une passion au-dessus des choses de ce monde.

ethereally [i'θiəriəli], *adv.* **e. beautiful,** d'une beauté éthérée.

Etheria [e'θi:riə], *s. Moll:* éthérie *f*.

Etheriidac [eθi'ri:idi:], *s.pl. Moll:* éthériidés *m*.

etherism ['i:θərizm], *s. Med:* éthérisme *m*.

etherization [i:θərai'zeiʃ(ə)n], *s. Med: Pharm:* éthérisation *f*; *Med: O:* anesthésie *f* (à l'éther).

etherize ['i:θəraiz], *v.tr. Med: Pharm:* éthériser (un malade, l'alcool).

etherizer ['i:θəraizər], *s. Med:* (*apparatus*) éthériseur *m*.

etheromania [i:θərou'meiniə], *s.* éthéromanie *f*.

ethic(al) ['eθik(əl)], *a.* **1.** moral, -aux; **denial of all e. principles,** amoralisme *m*; **ethical writer,** moraliste *m*. **2.** *Gram:* **ethic dative,** datif *m* éthique; **pronoun in the ethic dative,** pronom expressif d'intérêt atténué. **3.** *U.S: Pharm:* **ethical drug,** remède vendu uniquement sur l'ordonnance d'un médecin.

ethically ['eθik(ə)li], *adv.* d'après (les doctrines de) l'éthique.

ethics ['eθiks], *s.pl.* (*usu. with sg. const.*) éthique *f*, morale *f*.

ethionic [i:θi'ɔnik], *a. Ch:* (acide *m*) éthionique.

Ethiopia [i:θi'oupiə], *Pr.n. Geog:* Éthiopie *f*.

Ethiopian [i:θi'oupiən], *Geog:* (*a*) *a.* éthiopien; (*b*) *s.* Éthiopien, -ienne.

Ethiopic [i:θi'ɔpik], *a.* (langue *f*, église *f*) éthiopique.

ethmoid ['eθmɔid], *a. Anat:* (os) ethmoïde, spongieux, cribleux; **the e. (bone),** l'(os) ethmoïde *m*.

ethmoidal [eθ'mɔid(ə)l], *a. Anat:* ethmoïdal, -aux.

ethmoiditis [eθmɔi'daitis], *s. Med:* ethmoïdite *f*.

ethnarch ['eθna:k], *s.* ethnarque *m*.

ethnarchy ['eθna:ki], *s.* ethnarchie *f*.

ethnic(al) ['eθnik(l)], *a.* **1.** *Rel.H:* ethnique, gentil. **2.** ethnique, ethnologique.

ethnically ['eθnik(ə)li], *adv.* du point de vue ethnologique.

ethnicon ['eθnikɔn], *s.* ethnique *m*.

ethnocentric [eθnou'sentrik], *a.* ethnocentrique.

ethnocentrism [eθnou'sentrizm], *s.* ethnocentrisme *m.*
ethnocracy [eθ'nɔkrəsi], *s.* ethnocratie *f.*
ethnogeny [eθ'nɔdʒəni], *s.* ethnogénie *f.*
ethnographer [eθ'nɔgrəfər], *s.* ethnographe *mf.*
ethnographic(al) [eθnə'græfik(l)], *a.* ethnographique.
ethnography [eθ'nɔgrəfi], *s.* ethnographie *f.*
ethnological [eθnə'lɔdʒikl], *a.* ethnologique.
ethnologically [eθnə'lɔdʒik(ə)li], *adv.* ethnologiquement.
ethnologist [eθ'nɔlədʒist], *s.* ethnologue *mf.*
ethnology [eθ'nɔlədʒi], *s.* ethnologie *f.*
ethnos ['eθnɔs], *s.* ethnie *f.*
etholide ['eθoulaid], *s. Ch:* étholide *m.*
ethological [i:θə'lɔdʒik(ə)l], *a.* éthologique.
ethologist [i(:)'θɔlədʒist], *s.* éthologue *mf,* éthologiste *mf.*
ethology [i(:)'θɔlədʒi], *s.* éthologie *f.*
ethos ['i:θɔs], *s.* **1.** *Rh:* éthos *m*; **e. and pathos,** l'éthos et le pathos. **2.** génie *m* (d'un peuple, etc.).
ethoxide [e'θɔksaid], *s. Ch:* éthylate *m*; **sodium e.,** éthylate de sodium.
ethoxyl [e'θɔksil], *s. Ch:* éthoxyle *m.*
ethyl ['eθil], *s. Ch:* éthyle *m*; **e. oxide,** éther-oxyde *m,* éther *m* sulfurique, ordinaire; **e. alcohol,** alcool *m* éthylique; **e. acetate, bromide,** acétate *m,* bromure *m,* d'éthyle; **e. cellulose,** éthylcellulose *f*; **e. mercaptan,** éthylmercaptan *m.*
ethylamine ['eθiləmin], *s. Ch:* éthylamine *f.*
ethylate[1] ['eθileit], *s. Ch:* éthylate *m*; **vanadium e., sodium e.,** éthylate de vanadium, de sodium.
ethylate[2], *v.tr. Ch:* éthyler.
ethylation [eθi'leiʃ(ə)n], *s. Ch:* éthylation *f.*
ethylene ['eθili:n], *s. Ch:* éthène *m,* éthylène *m*; **e. hydrocarbons,** carbures *m* éthyléniques; **e. oxide,** oxyde *m* d'éthylène; **e. glycol,** éthylène glycol; **e. diamine,** éthylène diamine.
ethylenic [eθi'li:nik], *a. Ch:* éthylénique.
ethylic [e'θilik], *a. Ch:* éthylique.
ethylidene [e'θilidi:n], *s. Ch:* éthylidène *m*; **e. (di)chloride,** dichloréthane *f.*
ethylin ['eθilin], *s. Ch:* éthyline *f.*
ethylism ['eθilizm], *s.* éthylisme *m.*
ethylmorphine [eθil'mɔ:f(a)in], *s. Ch:* éthylmorphine *f.*
ethylsulphuric [eθilsʌl'fju:rik], *a. Ch:* éthylsulfurique.
ethylurethane [eθilju'ri:θein], *s. Ch:* éthyluréthane *m.*
etiolate ['i:tiouleit]. **1.** *v.tr.* étioler (une plante, une personne). **2.** *v.i.* (*of plants*) s'étioler.
etiolated ['i:tiouleitid], *a.* étiolé; (*of person*) anémié.
etiolation [i:tiou'leiʃ(ə)n], *s. Bot: etc:* étiolement *m,* chlorose *f.*
etiology [i:ti'ɔlədʒi], *s.* étiologie *f.*
etiquette ['etiket], *s.* (*a*) étiquette *f,* cérémonial *m,* formes cérémonieuses; (les) convenances *f*; (*in diplomatic service*) le protocole; **court e.,** le cérémonial de cour; **it is not e. to . . .,** il n'est pas d'étiquette, il n'est pas protocolaire, de . . .; **the exigencies of e.,** les exigences *f* du protocole; (*b*) **the e. of the Bar,** les règles *f* du Barreau, de l'Ordre des avocats.
Etna ['etnə]. **1.** *Pr.n. Geog:* **Mount E.,** le Mont Etna. **2.** *s. A:* réchaud *m* à alcool; lampe *f* à esprit de bois.
Etonian [i:tounian], *s.m.* élève (de l'école) d'Eton; **Old E.,** ancien élève d'Eton.
Etruria [i'truəriə], *Pr.n. A.Geog:* Étrurie *f*; *Hist:* **Kingdom of E.,** Royaume *m* d'Étrurie (1801–1808).
Etruscan [i'trʌskən], *A.Hist:* (*a*) *a.* étrusque; (*b*) *s.* Étrusque *mf.*
Etruscologist [i:trʌs'kɔlədʒist], *s.* étruscologue *mf.*
Etruscology [i:trʌs'kɔlədʒi], *s.* étruscologie *f.*
étude ['eitju:d], *s. Mus:* étude *f.*
etymological [etimə'lɔdʒikl], *a.* étymologique.
etymologically [etimə'lɔdʒik(ə)li], *adv.* étymologiquement.
etymologist [eti'mɔlədʒist], *s.* étymologiste *mf.*
etymologize [eti'mɔlədʒaiz]. **1.** *v.tr.* donner, rechercher, l'étymologie (d'un mot). **2.** *v.i.* faire de l'étymologie.
etymology [eti'mɔlədʒi], *s.* étymologie *f.*
etymon ['etimɔn], *s. Ling:* étymon *m*; racine *f*; mot *m* souche.
eu- [ju:], *pref.* eu-.
Euboea [ju'bi:ə], *Pr.n. Geog:* Eubée *f.*
Euboean [ju'bi:ən]. *Geog:* (*a*) *a.* eubéen; (*b*) *s.* Eubéen, -enne.
Euboic [ju'bouik], *a. Geog:* **the E. Sea,** la mer Euboïque.
eucaine ['ju:kein, ju'kein], *s. Pharm:* eucaïne *f.*
eucairite [ju'kairait], *s. Miner:* eucaïrite *f,* eukaïrite *f.*
eucalypt ['ju:kəlipt], *s. Bot:* eucalyptus *m.*
eucalyptol [jukə'liptɔl], *s. Ch:* eucalyptol *m.*
eucalyptus, *pl.* **-ti, -tuses** [jukə'liptəs; -tai, -ti:; -təsiz], *s.* **1.** *Bot:* eucalyptus *m.* **2.** *Pharm:* **e. oil,** essence *f* d'eucalyptus.
Eucarida [ju:kæridə], *s.pl. Crust:* eucarides *m.*
eucephalous [ju'sefələs], *a. Ent:* eucéphale.
eucharid ['ju:kərid], *s. Ent:* eucharis *m.*
eucharis ['ju:kəris], *s. Bot:* **e. (lily),** eucharis *m.*
eucharist (the) [ðə'ju:kərist], *s. Ecc:* l'eucharistie *f*; **to receive the e.,** recevoir l'eucharistie, le saint sacrement.
eucharistic(al) [jukə'ristik(l)], *a.* eucharistique.
euchologion [jukə'loudʒiən], **euchology** [ju'kɔlədʒi], *s. Ecc:* euc(h)ologe *m.*
euchre[1] ['ju:kər], *s. Cards:* euchre *m.*
euchre[2], *v.tr.* **1.** *Cards:* (*at euchre*) empêcher (son adversaire) de faire trois levées. **2.** *NAm: P:* **to e. s.o.,** mettre qn dans une impasse; enfoncer qn; **to be euchred,** être dans une impasse, dans le pétrin.
euchroite ['ju:krɔit], *s. Miner:* euchroïte *f.*
euchromatin [ju'kroumətin], *s. Biol:* euchromatine *f.*
Euchromiidae [jukrou'maiidi:], *s.pl. Ent:* euchromides *m,* syntomides *m.*
euchromosome [ju'kroumousoum], *s.* euchromosome *m.*
euclase ['ju:kleiz], *s. Miner:* euclase *f.*
eucleid ['ju:kli:d], *s. Ent:* eucléide *m.*
Eucleidae [ju'kli:idi:], *s.pl. Ent:* eucléides *m.*
Euclid ['ju:klid]. **1.** *Pr.n.m.* Euclide. **2.** *s. A:* géométrie (d'Euclide, euclidienne).
Euclidean [ju'klidiən], *a.* euclidien; (géométrie) euclidienne.
eucolite ['ju:koulait], *s. Miner:* eucolite *f.*
eucrasite ['ju:krəsait], *s. Miner:* eucrasite *f.*
eucryptite [ju'kriptait], *s. Miner:* eucryptite *f.*
eud(a)emonism [ju'di:mənizm], *s.* eudémonisme *m.*
eud(a)emonist [ju'di:mənist], *s.* eudémoniste *mf.*
eud(a)emonistic [judi:mə'nistik], *a.* eudémonique.
eudemis ['ju:dimis], *s. Ent:* **e. (moth),** eudémis *m.*
eudialyte ['ju:diəlait], *s. Miner:* eudialyte *f.*
eudidymite [ju'didimait], *s. Miner:* eudidymite *f.*
eudiometer [judi'ɔmitər], *s. Ch:* eudiomètre *m.*
eudiometric [judiou'metrik], *a.* eudiométrique.
eudiometry [judi'ɔmitri], *s.* eudiométrie *f.*
Eudist ['ju:dist], *s. R.C.Ch:* eudiste *m.*
eudromias [ju'droumiəs], *s. Orn:* eudromias *m.*
eugenate ['ju:dʒeneit], *s. Ch: Dent:* eugénate *m.*
Eugene [ju'dʒi:n], *Pr.n.m.* Eugène; *Hist:* **Prince E.,** le Prince Eugène.
eugenesis [ju'dʒenəsis], *s.* eugénésie *f.*
Eugenia [ju'dʒi:niə]. **1.** *Pr.n.f.* Eugénie. **2.** *s. Bot:* eugenia *m or f.*
eugenic [ju'dʒenik], *a.* eugénésique.
eugenics [ju'dʒeniks], *s.pl.* (*usu. with sg. const.*) eugénique *f,* eugénisme *m.*
eugenist [ju'dʒi:nist], *s.* eugéniste *mf.*
eugenol ['ju:dʒənɔl], *s. Ch:* eugénol *m.*
eugenolate [ju'dʒenouleit], *s. Ch: Dent:* eugénate *m.*
euglena [ju'gli:nə], *s. Prot:* euglène *f.*
Euglenidae [ju'glenidi:], **Euglenoidina** [juglenɔi'di:nə], *s.pl. Prot:* euglénidés *m.*
euglobulin [ju'glɔbjulin], *s. Bio-Ch:* euglobine *f,* euglobuline *f.*
Eugubine ['ju:gjubain], *a. Ant:* **E. tables,** tables eugubines.
euhedral [ju'hi:dr(ə)l], *a.* euhédral; automorphe.
Euhemerism [ju'hi:mərizm], *s. Gr.Phil:* évhémérisme *m.*
Euhemerist [ju'hi:mərist], *s. Gr.Phil:* évhémériste *mf.*
Euhemeristic [juhi:mə'ristik], *a. Gr.Phil:* évhémériste.
Euhemerus [ju'h:mərəs], *Pr.n.m. Gr.Phil:* Évhémère.
eukairite [ju'kaiərait], *s. Miner:* eukaïrite *f,* eucaïrite *f.*
eukolite, eukolyte ['ju:koulait], *s. Miner:* eucolite *f.*
Eulalia [ju'leiliə], *Pr.n.f.* Eulalie.
Eulerian [ɔi'liəriən], *a. Mth:* (constante, intégrante) d'Euler.
Eulimidae [ju'limidi:], *s.pl. Ent:* eulimidés *m.*
eulogia [ju'loudʒiə], *s. Ecc:* eulogie *f.*
eulogist ['ju:lədʒist], *s.* panégyriste *m.*
eulogistic [julə'dʒistik], *a.* élogieux.
eulogistically [julə'dʒistik(ə)li], *adv.* élogieusement.
eulogize ['ju:lədʒaiz], *v.tr.* (*a*) faire l'éloge, le panégyrique, de (qn, qch.); (*b*) adresser des éloges à (qn).
eulogy ['ju:lədʒi], *s.* éloge *m*; panégyrique *m*; **to pronounce a e. on s.o.,** faire l'éloge, le panégyrique, de qn.
eulytine ['ju:litain], **eulytite** ['ju:litait], *s. Miner:* eulytène *f,* eulytine *f,* eulytite *f.*
eumelanin [ju'melənin], *s. Bio-Ch:* eumélanine *f.*
eumenid ['ju:mənid, ju'menid], *s. Ent:* eumène *m.*
Eumenidae [ju'menidi:], *s.pl. Ent:* euménidés *m.*
Eumenides (the) [ðəju:'menidi:z], *Pr.n.f.pl. Gr.Myth:* les Euménides.
eumolpus [ju'mɔlpəs], *s. Ent:* eumolpe *m, F:* gribouri *m,* écrivain *m.*
Eumycetes [jumai'si:ti:z], *s.pl. Fung:* eumycètes *m.*
eunectes [ju'nekti:z], *s. Rept:* eunecte *m.*
eunician [ju'n(a)isiən], **eunicid** [ju'n(a)isid], *s. Ann:* eunice *f*; eunicidé *m.*
Eunicidae [ju'n(a)isidi:], *s.pl. Ann:* eunicidés *m.*
eunuch ['ju:nək], *s.* eunuque *m,* castrat *m.*
eunuchism ['ju:nəkizm], *s.* eunuchisme *m.*
eunuchoid ['ju:nəkɔid], *a.* eunuchoïde; *Med:* **e. voice,** voix *f* eunuchoïde.
euonymus [ju(:)'ɔniməs], *s. Bot:* euonymus *m,* évonymus *m*; fusain *m.*
euosmite ['ju:ɔzmait], *s. Miner:* euosmite *f.*
Eupalaeodictyoptera [jupælioudikti'ɔptərə], *s.pl. Ent: Paleont:* eupaléodictyoptères *m.*
eupatorium [jupə'tɔ:riəm], *s. Bot:* eupatoire *f.*
eupatrid, *pl.* **-ids, idae** [ju:'pætrid, -idz, -idi:], *s. Gr.Hist:* Eupatride *mf.*
eupepsia [ju'pepsiə], **eupepsy** [ju'pepsi], *s.* eupepsie *f.*
eupeptic [ju'peptik], *a.* eupeptique.
Euphausiacea [jufɔ:zi'eisiə], *s.pl. Crust:* euphausiacés *m.*
Euphemia [ju'fi:miə], *Pr.n.f.* Euphémie.
euphemism ['ju:fəmizm], *s.* euphémisme *m.*
euphemistic [jufə'mistik], *a.* euphémique.
euphemistically [jufə'mistik(ə)li], *adv.* euphémiquement; par euphémisme.
euphemize ['ju:fəmaiz], (*a*) *v.tr.* dire, exprimer, (qch.) par un euphémisme; (*b*) *v.i.* parler euphémiquement; avoir recours à un euphémisme.
euphonia [ju'founiə], *s. Orn:* euphone *m,* organiste *m.*
euphonic [ju'fɔnik], *a.* euphonique.
euphonically [ju'fɔnik(ə)li], *adv.* euphoniquement.
euphonious [ju'founiəs], *a.* agréable à l'oreille, mélodieux, euphonique.
euphonium [ju'founiəm], *s. Mus:* saxhorn *m* basse; basse *f* (des cuivres); **e. player,** bassiste *m.*
euphonize ['ju:fənaiz], *v.tr.* rendre (un mot, etc.) euphonique; donner de l'euphonie à (un mot, etc.).
euphony ['ju:fəni], *s.* euphonie *f*; **for the sake of e.,** par euphonie.
euphorbia [ju'fɔ:biə], *s. Bot:* euphorbe *f,* épurge *f*; *F:* cierge *m,* herbe *f* au lait; **tree e., arborescent e.,** euphorbe arborescente.
Euphorbiaceae [jufɔ:bi'eisii:], *s.pl. Bot:* euphorbiacées *f.*
euphorbium [ju'fɔ:biəm], *s.* **1.** *Bot:* = EUPHORBIA. **2.** *Pharm:* euphorbe *f.*
euphoria [ju'fɔ:riə], *s.* euphorie *f.*
euphoric [ju'fɔrik], *a.* euphorique.
euphrasy ['ju:frəsi], *s. Bot:* euphraise *f,* euphrasie *f*; *F:* casse-lunette(s) *m inv.*
Euphrates (the) [ðəju:'freiti:z], *Pr.n. Geog:* l'Euphrate *m.*
Euphrosyne [ju'frɔzini:], *Pr.n.f. Gr.Myth:* Euphrosyne.
euphuism ['ju:fjuizm], *s.* **1.** *Lit.Hist:* euphuïsme *m.* **2.** préciosité *f*; affectation *f* (de langage).
euphuist ['ju:fjuist], *s.* euphuïste *mf.*
euphuistic [jufju'istik], *a.* euphuïstique, euphuïste; (parler) précieux, affecté.
euphuistically [jufju'istik(ə)li], *adv.* euphuïstiquement; avec affectation.
euplectella [ju'plektələ], *s. Spong:* euplectelle *f.*
euplocomus [ju'plɔkəməs], *s. Orn:* euplocome *m*; *F:* houppifère *m.*
euploid ['ju:plɔid], *s. Biol:* euploïde *m.*
eupn(o)ea ['ju:pniə], *s. Med:* eupnée *f.*
eupn(o)eic ['ju:pniik], *a. Med:* eupnéique.
euquinine ['ju:kwini:n], *s. Pharm:* euquinine *f.*
Eurafrica [ju'ræfrikə], *Pr.n. Geog:* Eurafrique *f.*
Eurafrican [ju'ræfrik(ə)n]. **1.** *s.* Eurafricain, -aine. **2.** *a.* d'Europe et d'Afrique; (zone) eurafricaine; (oiseau, etc.) eurafricain.
Eurasia [ju'reiʃə, -ʒə], *Pr.n. Geog:* Eurasie *f.*
Eurasian [ju'reiʃən, -ʒən]. (*a*) *a. Ethn:* eurasien; *Nat.Hist:* (faune, etc.) eurasiatique; (*b*) *s. Ethn:* Eurasien, -ienne.
Eurasiatic [jureizi'ætik], *a.* eurasiatique.
Euratom [ju'rætɔm], *Pr.n.* Euratom *f.*
eurhythmic [ju'riθmik]. **1.** *a.* (*a*) eurythmique; (*b*) (*of building*) bien proportionné; (*c*) (*of pulse*) régulier. **2.** *s.pl.* (*usu. with sg. const.*) **eurhythmics,** gymnastique *f* rythmique.
eurhythmy [ju'riθmi], *s. Arch: Med: Mus:* eurythmie *f.*
Euripidean [juripi'di:ən], *a. Gr.Lit:* euripidien.
Euripides [ju'ripidi:z], *Pr.n.m. Gr.Lit:* Euripide.
Euripus [ju'raipəs], *Pr.n. Geog:* Euripe *m*; **the Strait of E.,** le Détroit, le Canal, de l'Euripe.
eurite ['ju:rait], *s. Miner:* eurite *f.*
Eurodollar ['ju:roudɔlər], *s. Fin:* Eurodollar *m.*
Europa [ju'roupə]. **1.** *Pr.n.f. Gr.Myth:* Europe. **2.** *Geog:* **E. Point,** la Pointe d'Europe.
Europe ['ju:rəp], *Pr.n. Geog:* Europe *f*; **Council of E.,** Conseil *m* de l'Europe; **to join E.,** devenir membre du

Marché commun.

European [jurə'pi:ən]. (*a*) *a.* européen; **E. Economic Community,** Communauté économique européenne; *NAm:* (*of hotel*) **E. plan,** location *f* des chambres (sans pension); (*b*) *s.* (i) Européen, -éenne; (ii) partisan, -ane, du Marché commun.

Europeanism [jurə'pi:ənizm], *s.* européanisme *m.*

Europeanization [jurəpiənai'zeiʃ(ə)n], *s.* européanisation *f*, européisation *f.*

Europeanize [jurə'pi:ənaiz], *v.tr.* européaniser, européiser; **to become Europeanized,** s'européaniser.

europic [ju'roupik], *a. Ch:* europique.

europium [ju'roupiəm], *s. Ch:* europium *m.*

europous [ju'roupəs], *a. Ch:* europeux.

eurotium [ju'routiəm], *s. Fung:* eurotium *m.*

Eurovision ['ju:rouviʒ(ə)n], *Pr.n.* Eurovision *f.*

Euryalida [juriæ'laidə], *s.pl. Echin:* euryales *m.*

Euryalus [ju'raiələs], *Pr.n.m. Lt.Lit:* Euryale.

Eurybiades [juri'baiədi:z], *Pr.n.m. Gr.Hist:* Eurybiade.

eurycephalic, eurycephalous [jurise'fælik, -'sefələs], *a. Anthr:* eurycéphale.

eurycephaly [juri'sefəli], *s. Anthr:* eurycéphalie *f.*

Eurycleia [juri'klaiə], *Pr.n.f. Gr.Lit:* Euryclée.

Eurydice [ju'ridisi(:)], *Pr.n.f. Gr.Myth: Astr:* Eurydice.

eurygnathous [jurig'neiθəs], *a. Anthr:* eurygnathe.

euryhaline [juri'heilain], *a. Nat.Hist:* euryhalin.

Eurylaimidae [juri'leimidi:], *s.pl. Orn:* eurylaimidés *m.*

eurylaimus [juri'leiməs], *s. Orn:* eurylaime *m.*

euryphagous [ju'rifigəs], *a. Nat.Hist:* euryphage.

eurypharynx [juri'færiŋks], *s. Ich:* eurypharynx *m.*

euryprosopia [juriprə'soupiə], *s. Anthr:* euryprosopie *f.*

euryprosopic [juriprə'soupik], *a. Anthr:* euryprosope.

Eurypterida [jurip'teridə], **Eurypteroidea** [juriptə'rɔidiə], *s.pl. Paleont:* euryptérides *m*, euryptéroïdea *m.*

Eurypygidae [juri'pidʒidi:], *s.pl. Orn:* eurypygidés *m.*

Eurystheus [ju'risθiəs], *Pr.n.m. Gr.Myth:* Eurysthée.

eurythermal, eurythermic, eurythermous [juri'θə:m(ə)l, -'θə:mik, -'θə:məs], *a. Biol:* eurytherme.

Eurytomidae [juri'tɔmidi:], *s.pl. Ent:* eurytomidés *m.*

Eusebius [ju'si:biəs], *Pr.n.m. Rel.H:* Eusèbe.

Euskarian [jus'kɛəriən]. **1.** *Geog:* (*a*) *a.* euscarien, euskarien, basque; (*b*) *s.* Euscarien, -ienne; Euskarien, -ienne; Basque *mf.* **2.** *s. Ling:* euscarien *m*, basque *m.*

Eustace ['ju:stəs], *Pr.n.m.* Eustache.

Eustachian [jus'teiʃən], *a. Anat:* **E. tube,** trompe *f* d'Eustache; **E. valve,** valvule *f* d'Eustache.

eustatic [ju'stætik], *a. Geol:* eustatique.

eustacy ['ju:stəsi], **eustatism** ['ju:stətizm], *s. Geol:* eustasie *f*, eustatisme *m.*

eustyle ['ju:stail], *s. Arch:* eustyle *m.*

eusynchite [ju'siŋkait], *s. Miner:* eusynchite *f.*

eutectic [ju'tektik], *a. & s. Ch:* eutectique (*m*).

eutectoid [ju'tektɔid], *a. & s. Metall:* **e. (alloy),** eutectoïde *m.*

Euterpe [ju'tə:pi]. **1.** *Pr.n.f. Gr.Myth:* Euterpe. **2.** *s. Bot:* Euterpe *f.*

eutexia [ju'teksiə], *s. Ch:* eutexie *f.*

euthanasia [juθə'neiziə], *s.* euthanasie *f.*

euthanasic [juθə'neizik], *a.* euthanasique.

Eutheria [ju'θiəriə], *s.pl. Z:* euthériens *m*; placentaires *m.*

eutocia [ju'tousiə], *s. Obst:* eutocie *f.*

eutrophic [ju'trɔfik], *a.* **1.** *Physiol:* eutrophique. **2.** (*of lake*) eutrophe.

eutrophy ['ju:trəfi], *s. Physiol:* eutrophie *f.*

Eutropius [ju'troupiəs], *Pr.n.m.* Eutrope.

Eutyches ['ju:tiki:z], *Pr.n.m. Rel.H:* Eutychès.

Eutychian [ju'tikiən], *a. & s. Rel.H:* eutychien, -ienne; eutychéen, -éenne.

Eutychianism [ju'tikiənizm], *s. Rel.H:* eutychianisme *m.*

euxenite ['ju:ksənait], *s. Miner:* euxénite *f.*

Euxine (the) [ðə'ju:ksain], *s. A.Geog:* le Pont-Euxin.

Eva ['i:və], *Pr.n.f.* Éva, Ève.

evacuant [i'vækjuənt], *a. & s. Med:* évacuant (*m*).

evacuate [i'vækjueit]. **1.** *v.tr.* (*a*) évacuer (un lieu); **all the houses threatened by the flood had been evacuated,** on avait évacué toutes les maisons menacées par l'inondation; (*b*) évacuer (des gens, des troupes); **to e. the population from a bombed town,** évacuer la population d'une ville bombardée; (*c*) *Physiol:* évacuer, décharger (le ventre); évacuer (les selles); (*d*) *Mch:* expulser, refouler (les gaz brûlés d'un moteur, etc.); *Ph:* raréfier (un gaz); *Ph:* **to e. a tube,** faire le vide dans un tube. **2.** *v.i.* (*of gas, etc.*) s'échapper, s'évacuer.

evacuation [ivækju'eiʃ(ə)n], *s.* **1.** (*a*) évacuation *f* (d'un lieu); (*b*) évacuation (des gens, des troupes); **e. of the population from a flooded area,** évacuation de la population d'un quartier inondé; (*c*) *Physiol:* évacuation, décharge *f* (du ventre); excrémentation *f*; (*d*) *Mch:* expulsion *f*, refoulement *m*, évacuation (des gaz brûlés d'un moteur, etc.); *Ph:* **e. of a tube,** production *f* du vide dans un tube. **2.** (*a*) rejet *m* (de l'eau, etc.); (*b*) *Physiol: usu. pl.* déjections *fpl*, selles *fpl.*

evacuative [i'vækjuətiv], *a. & s. Pharm:* évacuatif (*m*).

evacuee [ivækju:'i:], *s.* évacué, -ée.

evade [i'veid], *v.tr.* **1.** éviter (un coup, un danger); esquiver (un coup, ses créanciers); se soustraire à, se dérober à, éluder (un châtiment, la justice); éluder, tourner, contourner (un obstacle, une question, la loi); déjouer (la vigilance de qn); **to e. a duty,** se soustraire à un devoir. **2.** (*of thgs*) échapper à (l'intelligence).

evader [i'veidər], *s.* éludeur *m* (**of,** de); **tax e.,** fraudeur, -euse, du fisc.

evading [i'veidiŋ], *s.* évitement *m.*

evaginate [i'vædʒineit], *a. Bot:* évaginulé.

evagination [ivædʒi'neiʃ(ə)n], *s. Physiol:* évagination *f* (d'une partie engainée).

evaluable [i'væljuəbl], *a.* évaluable; **not e.,** inévaluable.

evaluate [i'væljueit], *v.tr.* évaluer (les dommages, *Mth:* une expression); estimer le montant (des dommages).

evaluation [ivælju'eiʃ(ə)n], *s.* évaluation *f* (du dommage, *Mth:* d'une expression); *Mil:* **e. of information,** critique *f* du renseignement.

Evander [i'vændər], *Pr.n.m. Rom.Myth:* Évandre.

evanesce [i:væ'nes], *v.i. Lit:* disparaître, s'effacer.

evanescence [i:væ'nesəns], *s.* évanescence *f*; nature *f* éphémère.

evanescent [i:væ'nesnt], *a.* **1.** (sentiment) évanescent; (gloire *f*, etc.) éphémère. **2.** *Mth: A:* (*of quantity*) évanouissant; infinitésimal, -aux.

evangelic [i:væn'dʒelik], *a. Ecc:* évangélique, conforme à l'Évangile.

evangelical [i:væn'dʒelik(ə)l]. **1.** *a.* = EVANGELIC. **2.** (*a*) *a.* qui appartient à la religion réformée; (*b*) *s.* membre *m* de la religion réformée; protestant *m* évangélique.

evangelicalism [i:væn'dʒelikəlizm], *s. Ecc:* évangélisme *m*; doctrine *f* de l'Église évangélique.

evangelically [i:væn'dʒelik(ə)li], *adv.* évangéliquement.

evangelism [i'vændʒilizm], *s. Ecc:* évangélisme *m*, prédication *f* de l'Évangile.

evangelist [i'væn(d)ʒilist], *s.* évangéliste *m.*

evangelization [ivæn(d)ʒilai'zeiʃ(ə)n], *s.* évangélisation *f.*

evangelize [i'væn(d)ʒilaiz]. **1.** *v.tr.* évangéliser; prêcher l'Évangile à (qn). **2.** *v.i.* prêcher l'Évangile.

evangelizer [i'væn(d)ʒilaizər], *s.* évangélisateur *m* (des races païennes, etc.).

evangelizing [i'væn(d)ʒilaiziŋ], *s.* évangélisation *f.*

Evaniidae [i:væ'naiidi:], *s.pl. Ent:* évaniidés *m.*

evansite ['evənzait], *s. Miner:* évansite *f.*

evaporable [i'væpərəbl], *a. Ph:* évaporable.

evaporate [i'væpəreit]. **1.** *v.tr.* (faire) évaporer (un liquide); **to e. down,** réduire par évaporation; **evaporated milk,** lait évaporé. **2.** *v.i.* (*a*) (*of liquids, perfumes, etc.*) s'évaporer, se vaporiser; (*of acid*) se volatiliser; (*b*) (*of thg*) s'évaporer; (*of pers. or thg*) disparaître comme par enchantement; (*of pers.*) filer; se défiler.

evaporating [i'væpəreitiŋ], *s.* évaporation *f*; **e. dish, basin,** vase évaporatoire, évaporateur; capsule *f* d'évaporation.

evaporation [ivæpə'reiʃ(ə)n], *s.* évaporation *f*, vaporisation *f* (d'un liquide, d'un parfum); volatilisation *f* (d'un acide, etc.); **vacuum e.,** évaporation sous vide; *Ch:* **batch e.,** évaporation discontinue; *Ph:* **e. point,** point *m* de vaporisation.

evaporative [i'væpəreitiv], *a.* (procédé) évaporatif; (pouvoir) vaporisateur (d'un combustible, etc.).

evaporativity [ivæpərə'tiviti], *s.* évaporativité *f.*

evaporator [i'væpəreitər], *s. Ind:* évaporateur *m*, bouilleur *m*; **vacuum e.,** évaporateur à vide.

evaporimeter, evaporometer [ivæpə'rimitər, -'rɔmitər], *s.* évaporimètre *m*, évaporomètre *m.*

evapotranspiration [ivæpoutrænspi'reiʃ(ə)n], *s.* évapotranspiration *f.*

evasion [i'veiʒ(ə)n], *s.* **1.** (*a*) évasion *f*, fuite *f*; escapade *f*; (*b*) dérobement *m*; **tax e.,** fraude fiscale; (*c*) *Psy:* évasion. **2.** subterfuge *m*, échappatoire *f*, faux-fuyant *m*, *pl.* faux-fuyants, biaisement *m*; **to resort to evasions, to use evasions,** user de détours *m*; biaiser; **without e.,** sans détours.

evasive [i'veisiv], *a.* évasif; **e. personality,** personnalité fuyante; **to give an e. answer,** faire une réponse évasive; répondre évasivement; *F:* répondre en Normand; *Mil: etc:* **to take e. action,** faire une manœuvre d'évitement, de dérobement.

evasively [i'veisivli], *adv.* évasivement.

evasiveness [i'veisivnis], *s.* caractère évasif (d'une réponse, etc.).

Eve[1] [i:v], *Pr.n.f. B.Hist:* Ève; *F:* **a daughter of E.,** une fille d'Ève; *Bot:* **Eve's needle,** yucca *m.*

eve[2], *s.* **1.** *A: & Poet:* soir *m*; **at e.,** le soir. **2.** (*a*) *Ecc:* vigile *f* (de fête); (*b*) veille *f*; **Christmas E.,** la veille de Noël; **New Year's E.,** la Saint-Sylvestre; **on the e. of . . .,** à la veille de . . .; **to be on the e. of success,** être à la veille du succès.

evection [i'vekʃ(ə)n], *s. Astr:* évection *f.*

even[1] ['i:v(ə)n], *s. Poet:* soir *m*; **at e.,** le soir.

even[2], *a.* **1.** (*a*) (*of surface, ground, etc.*) uni; plan; égal, -aux; uniforme, plat; (*b*) **to be e. with sth.,** être au niveau de, à fleur de, à ras de, qch.; affleurer qch.; (*c*) (*of spacing, weights, etc.*) égal; **to make e.,** araser (les assises d'une construction); aplanir (une surface); affleurer (les bords de deux planches, etc.); égaliser (des entre-deux, etc.); **to make the water level in two containers e.,** ramener l'eau dans deux vases au même niveau; *Typ:* **to make (the lines) e.,** espacer la composition, chasser (pour que la dernière ligne soit pleine); **making e.,** (i) arasement *m*, aplanissage *m*, aplanissement *m*, affleurement *m*; (ii) *Typ:* espacement *m* de la composition. **2.** (souffle, trot, pouls) égal, régulier, uniforme; **e. temperature,** température égale; **e. pace,** allure *f* uniforme; **e. colour,** couleur *f* uniforme; **e. temper,** caractère *m* calme; humeur égale; (*d*) **with an e. hand,** impartialement; équitablement. **3.** (*a*) **e. bet, e. money,** pari *m* avec enjeu égal; **to lay an e. wager, e. odds,** *s.* **to lay evens,** parier à égalité; **horse quoted at evens, at e. money,** cheval coté à égalité; *Fin:* **e. deal,** opération blanche; **to break e.,** ne faire ni pertes ni profits; (*b*) *Games:* **to be e.,** être but à but, manche à manche, tant à tant, point à point, *F:* point à; **e. match,** partie égale; **to get e. with s.o.,** (i) arriver, se mettre, à la hauteur de qn; (ii) rendre la pareille à qn, se venger de qn, prendre sa revanche sur qn; **to be e. with s.o.,** être quitte avec qn; **I'll be e. with him yet,** je lui revaudrai, rendrai; il ne perdra rien pour attendre; *F:* il ne le portera pas loin, il ne l'emportera pas en paradis; *P:* je le rechoperai dans un tournant; (*c*) **e. bargain,** marché *m* équitable, juste. **4.** (*a*) (nombre) pair; **odd or e.,** pair ou impair; (*b*) **e. money,** compte rond; **the debtor is bound to make up the e. money,** le débiteur est tenu de faire l'appoint. **5.** *Com: A:* **of e. date,** de même date; **your letter of e. date,** votre lettre *f* de ce jour.

even[3], *adv.* **1.** même; (*with comparative*) encore; (*with negative*) seulement, même; **or e. . . .,** ou même . . ., voire même . . .; **e. the cleverest,** même les plus habiles; **e. the children knew,** les enfants *m* mêmes le savaient; **e. discipline has its charm,** il n'y a pas jusqu'à la discipline qui n'ait ses charmes; **to love e. one's enemies,** aimer même ses ennemis; **to jest e. on the scaffold,** plaisanter jusque sur l'échafaud; **a grand and e. grandiloquent style,** un style grandiose jusqu'à l'emphase; **I never e. saw it,** je ne l'ai même pas vu; je ne l'ai pas seulement vu; **you suspect e. me of having done it!** vous me soupçonnez, moi, de l'avoir fait! **I have only one chisel, and e. that is a blunt one,** je n'ai qu'un ciseau, encore est-il émoussé; **e. supposing that . . .,** même en supposant que . . .; **that would be e. worse,** ce serait encore pis; **they know e. less about it than I do,** ils en savent encore moins que moi; **he seemed e. sadder than usual,** il paraissait encore plus triste que de coutume; **without e. speaking,** sans seulement parler; **he hasn't enough money e. to pay his fare,** il n'a pas seulement de quoi payer son voyage; **e. if, e. though, he failed,** même s'il échouait; alors même qu'il échouerait; quand même il échouerait; **e. though it were you,** quand ce serait vous, *Lit:* fût-ce même vous; **I'll do it, e. if I'm scolded,** je le ferai quitte à être grondé; **if e. one could speak to him,** encore, même, si on pouvait lui parler; **e. though I had known,** même si je l'avais su; **he always goes by bus, e. though he has a car,** il prend toujours l'autobus, bien qu'il ait une voiture; **e. so,** mais cependant, quand même, encore; **there are omissions; but, e. so, the book is a good one,** il y a des lacunes; mais le livre a quand même de la valeur; **e. then he wouldn't believe me,** même alors, quand même, il ne voulait pas me croire. **2.** (*a*) *A:* **e. as a shepherd guards his flocks, so . . .,** de même qu'un pasteur garde ses troupeaux, de même . . .; *B:* **e. so must the Son of Man be lifted up,** ainsi il faut que le Fils de l'homme soit élevé; **e. as,** précisément comme, tout comme; **it fell out e. as he had foretold,** les choses se sont passées précisément comme il l'avait annoncé; (*b*) **e. now,** à l'instant même; **e. then,** dès cette époque; déjà (à cette époque); **e. now, e. then, the sun was rising,** déjà le soleil se levait.

even[4], *v.tr.* **1.** aplanir, niveler, égaliser (une surface, etc.); affleurer (deux planches, etc.); araser (les assises d'un mur). **2.** *Lit:* (*a*) mettre (qn, qch.) de niveau (**to, avec**); égaler (qn, qch.) (**to, with,** à); (*b*) *A:* égaler; rivaliser avec (qn). **3.** (*a*) rendre égal; *Typ:* **to e. (out) the spacing,** égaliser l'espacement; **that will e. things up,** cela égalisera les choses; cela rétablira l'équilibre; (*b*) *F:* **to e. up on s.o.,** (i) s'acquitter envers qn; (ii) rendre la pareille à qn.

even-grained ['i:vən'greind], *a.* (bois *m*) à fibres régulières.

even-handed ['i:vən'hændid], *a.* (*of justice, etc.*) équitable; impartial, -aux.

even-handedly ['i:vən'hændidli], *adv.* équitablement; impartialement.

evening[1] ['i:vəniŋ], *s.* nivellement *m*; égalisation *f*.

evening[2] ['i:vniŋ], *s.* **1.** (*a*) soir *m*; (*duration of e.*) soirée *f*; **tomorrow e.,** demain (au) soir; **in the e.,** le soir, au soir; **at nine o'clock in the e.,** à neuf heures du soir; **(on) that e.,** ce soir-là; **(on) the e. before, (on) the previous e.,** la veille au soir; **the next e.,** le lendemain soir; **on the e. of the first of May,** le premier mai au soir; **one, on a, fine summer e.,** (par) un beau soir d'été; **every e.,** tous les soirs; **every Monday e.,** tous les lundis soir; **all the e.,** toute la soirée; **during the e.,** pendant la soirée; **long winter evenings,** longues veillées d'hiver; **to spend the e. at a friend's house,** passer la soirée chez un ami; **e. paper,** journal *m* du soir; *Ecc:* **e. prayer** = EVENSONG; *Th:* **e. performance,** représentation de soirée, donnée en soirée; **to go to an e. performance of Macbeth,** aller voir Macbeth en soirée; *Bot:* **e. campion,** compagnon blanc; **e. primrose,** œnothère *m*; *Astr:* **e. star,** étoile *f* du soir; (*b*) *Lit:* **the e. of life,** le déclin de la vie; **in the e. of life,** au soir, au déclin, de la vie. **2.** (*a*) (*evening party*) soirée; **musical e.,** soirée musicale; (*b*) **e. dress,** (i) (*for men*) tenue *f* de soirée; (ii) (*for women*) robe *f* de soirée, de bal; **in e. dress,** en tenue, en toilette, de soirée.

evenly ['i:vənli], *adv.* **1.** (étendre) uniment; **e. spun thread,** fil filé uniment. **2.** (*a*) (respirer, tourner) régulièrement; (diviser) également; (*b*) **e. matched,** de force égale. **3.** *A:* (agir) impartialement, équitablement.

evenness ['i:vənnis], *s.* **1.** égalité *f*; régularité *f* (de mouvement); *Mus:* **e. of execution,** égalité de jeu. **2.** sérénité *f*, calme *m* (d'esprit), égalité (d'humeur). **3.** *A:* impartialité *f*.

even-numbered ['i:vən'nʌmbəd], *a.* (portant un nombre) pair.

evensong ['i:vənsɔŋ], *s. Ecc: R.C.Ch:* vêpres *fpl* et salut *m*; *Ch. of Eng:* office *m* du soir.

event [i'vent], *s.* **1.** cas *m*; **in the e. of his refusing,** au cas, dans le cas, où il refuserait; pour le cas où il refuserait; **in the e. of his death,** en cas de décès; advenant son décès; **in that unfortunate e.,** au cas où malheureusement cet événement se produirait; **unforeseen e.,** occurrence imprévue; *Jur:* **fortuitous e.,** cas fortuit. **2.** (*a*) événement *m*; **it's quite an e.,** c'est un véritable événement; **big e.,** attraction principale; clou *m* (de la fête, etc.); *Com:* **great coat e.!** grandes soldes de manteaux! *F:* **to be expecting a happy e.,** attendre un heureux événement; **in the course of events,** au cours des événements; par la suite; (*b*) issue *f*, résultat *m*; **in either e.,** dans l'un ou l'autre cas; **wise after the e.,** sage après coup; **at all events,** dans tous les cas; en tout cas; du moins; quoi qu'il arrive; (*c*) *Ph:* événement, phénomène *m*. **3.** *Sp:* (*a*) réunion sportive; **sporting e.,** manifestation sportive; (*b*) (*athletics*) **field events,** concours *m*, épreuves *f*, sur terrain; **track events,** courses *f*, épreuves, sur piste; (*c*) rencontre *f* (de boxe, à l'épée, etc.); (*d*) **no horse can bring off the double e.,** la passe de deux ne peut se réaliser.

even-tempered ['i:vən'tempəd], *a.* d'humeur égale.

eventful [i'ventful], *a.* (*of story, life*) plein d'événements, d'incidents; mouvementé; (*of day*) mémorable, qui fait époque; **e. week,** semaine *f* fertile en événements; **e. year,** année *f* mémorable.

eventfulness [i'ventfulnis], *s.* abondance *f* d'événements, d'incidents, de faits remarquables (d'une journée, etc.).

eventide ['i:vəntaid], *s.* (*a*) *Poet:* soir *m*, *A:* vêpre *m*; la chute du jour; (*b*) (*usu. as Pr.n.*) **e. home,** hospice *m* pour vieillards.

eventless [i'ventlis], *a.* (période *f*, règne *m*) sans événements; (journée *f*, voyage *m*) sans incidents.

eventration [i:ven'treiʃ(ə)n], *s. Surg:* éventration *f*.

eventual [i'ventjuəl], *a.* **1.** éventuel; **he was reckoning on a share in the e. profits of this new business,** il comptait sur une part des profits éventuels de cette nouvelle affaire. **2.** définitif, final, -als; **his prodigality and his e. ruin,** sa prodigalité et sa ruine finale; **to leave out of account the e. injury caused by a prolonged strike,** laisser hors de compte le dommage qui résulte de toute grève prolongée; **he had foreseen these mistakes and the e. downfall of the government,** il avait prévu ces fautes, qui ne pouvaient aboutir qu'à la chute du ministère.

eventuality [iventju'æliti], *s.* éventualité *f*.

eventually [i'ventjuəli], *adv.* en fin de compte, par la suite, dans la suite; **he will e. be the gainer by it,** en définitive, en fin de compte, c'est à lui que cela profitera; **he will do it e.,** il le fera un jour ou l'autre; il finira bien par le faire; **he e. became a judge,** il finit par être nommé juge.

eventuate [i'ventjueit], *v.i. esp. U.S:* se terminer (**in,** par); aboutir (**in,** à); **the negotiations eventuated in a new treaty,** les négociations *f* ont eu pour résultat un nouveau traité, ont abouti à un nouveau traité; **as things eventuated,** comme il est arrivé.

ever ['evər], *adv.* **1.** (*a*) jamais; **the best mother that e. was,** la meilleure mère qui fût jamais; **I read seldom if e.,** je lis rarement, pour ne pas dire jamais; **now if e. is the time to . . .,** c'est maintenant ou jamais le moment de . . .; **if e. I catch him,** si jamais je l'attrape; **nothing e. happens,** il n'arrive jamais rien; **he hardly e., scarcely e., smokes,** il ne fume presque jamais; **do you e. miss the train?** vous arrive-t-il (jamais) de manquer le train? **he's a liar if e. there was one,** c'est un menteur s'il en fut jamais; **it started to rain faster than e.,** il s'est mis à pleuvoir de plus belle; **it's as warm as e.,** il fait toujours aussi chaud; **it is less than e. the time to . . .,** c'est moins que jamais le moment de . . .; **without e. having thought of it,** sans jamais y avoir pensé; **worst e., best e.,** sans précédent; *F:* **she's as dear a girl as e. was,** c'est une gentille fille s'il en fût; **next Sunday as e. is,** dimanche prochain, ni plus tôt ni plus tard; *P:* **did you e.!** a-t-on jamais vu? par exemple! c'est renversant! (*b*) **they lived happy, happily, e. after,** ils ont vécu heureux à tout jamais; depuis lors, à partir de ce jour, ils ont vécu toujours heureux; (*c*) **e. since (then),** dès lors, depuis (lors); **it has rained e. since,** depuis il n'a pas cessé de pleuvoir; **I have been here e. since lunch,** je suis là depuis le déjeuner; (*d*) *Lit:* **e. and anon, e. and again,** de temps en temps; de temps à autre. **2.** (*a*) toujours; **e-increasing influence,** influence toujours plus étendue; *Lit:* **the river grows e. wider,** le fleuve va s'élargissant; *Corr:* **yours e., e. yours,** bien cordialement à vous; tout(e) à vous; (*b*) **for e.,** pour toujours; à jamais; **to go away for e.,** partir sans retour; **for e. and e.,** à tout jamais; éternellement; jusqu'à la fin des siècles; **Scotland for e.!** vive l'Écosse! **to live for e.,** vivre éternellement; **he could talk for e. on this subject,** il est intarissable sur ce sujet; **he's for e. grumbling,** il ne cesse pas de se plaindre, il grogne sans cesse; **women who are for e. talking,** femmes qui ne font que bavarder; **to be for e. putting things off,** remettre les choses à l'infini; **to be for e. chopping and changing,** changer d'opinion à tout bout de champ; **if only we could make this hour last for e.!** si nous pouvions éterniser cette heure! **the mournful chant seemed to go on for e.,** le chant lugubre semblait s'éterniser. **3.** (*intensive*) (*a*) **as quickly as e. you can,** aussi vite que possible; du plus vite que vous pourrez; **as soon as e. he comes home,** aussitôt qu'il rentrera; **before e. the match began,** même avant le commencement du match; **we are the best friends e.,** nous sommes les meilleurs amis du monde; **it was the funniest sight e.,** c'était à se tordre; (*b*) *F:* **e. so pretty,** joli comme tout; **it was e. so long ago,** ça fait tellement longtemps; **it'll do you e. so much good,** ça vous fera un bien énorme; **e. so many times,** je ne sais combien de fois; *P:* **it's e. so kind of you,** c'est tellement gentil; **thank you e. so much,** merci mille fois; **I'm e. so pleased,** j'en suis tellement content; *Lit:* **be they e. so rich,** quelque riches, si riches, qu'ils soient; **no doctor, be he e. so skilful, can . . .,** aucun médecin, si habile soit-il, sait . . .; (*c*) (*intensive; ever always has the sentence emphasis; contrast* **however, whatever,** *etc.*); **how e. did you manage?** comment diable avez-vous fait? **how e. you manage I don't know,** je me demande comment vous faites; **what e. shall we do?** qu'est-ce que nous allons bien faire? **what ever's the matter with you?** mais qu'est-ce que vous avez donc? **what e. has happened to him?** que lui est-il donc arrivé? **what e. can it be?** qu'est-ce que ça peut bien être? **what e. do you mean?** que diable voulez-vous dire? **when e. will he come?** quand donc viendra-t-il? **where e. can he be?** où peut-il bien être? **where e. are you going?** où diable allez-vous? **where e. have you been?** mais d'où venez-vous? **who e. told you that?** qui est-ce qui a bien pu vous dire cela? qui donc vous a dit cela? **who e. can it be?** qui diable cela peut-il être? **why e. not?** mais pourquoi pas? pourquoi pas, grand Dieu!

Everglades (the) [ði:'evəgleidz], *Pr.n. Geog:* le marais des Everglades (de la Floride).

evergreen ['evəgri:n]. **1.** *a.* toujours vert; *Bot:* à feuilles persistantes; **e. oak,** chêne vert; **e. magnolia,** magnolia *m* grandiflora; **e. thorn,** pyracanthe *f*; *O:* **e. topic,** question *f* toujours à l'ordre du jour, toujours d'actualité. **2.** *s.* (*a*) arbre (toujours) vert, à feuilles persistantes; (*b*) *pl.* **evergreens,** plantes vertes.

everlasting [evə'lɑ:stiŋ]. **1.** *a.* (*a*) éternel; *B:* **the mighty God, the e. Father,** le Dieu tout-puissant, le Père éternel; (*b*) *Bot:* **e. flower,** immortelle *f*; **e. pea,** pois *m* vivace; pois de Chine; gesse *f* sauvage, à larges feuilles; (*c*) (*of material, etc.*) durable, inusable, solide; (*d*) perpétuel, continuel; sempiternel; **I am tired of her e. complaints,** je suis las de ses plaintes sans fin. **2.** *s.* (*a*) éternité *f*; *B:* **from e. to e.,** de toujours à toujours; (*b*) **the E.,** l'Éternel; (*c*) *Bot:* immortelle *f*; (*d*) *Tex:* lasting *m*, everlasting *m*.

everlastingly [evə'lɑ:stiŋli], *adv.* **1.** éternellement. **2.** sempiternellement; perpétuellement; **he's e. complaining,** il est toujours à se plaindre.

evermore [evə'mɔ:r], *adv.* toujours; **for e.,** à jamais, pour jamais, pour toujours; **their name liveth for e.,** leur nom vivra éternellement; **it will go on for e.,** cela va durer une éternité; **he would talk for e.,** il bavarderait jusqu'à demain.

eversion [i'və:ʃ(ə)n], *s. Surg:* éversion *f*, retournement *m* (d'un organe); **e. of the eyelid,** ectropion *m*; éraillement *m* de la paupière.

evert [i'və:t], *v.tr. Surg:* renverser, retourner (une paupière, etc.).

every ['evri], *a.* (*a*) chaque; tout; tous les . . .; **e. week,** toutes les semaines; chaque semaine; tous les huit jours; **e. word he says is false,** tout ce qu'il dit est mensonge; **I have copied e. word of it,** j'ai tout copié sans omettre un mot; je l'ai copié mot pour mot; **in e. Frenchman there is an idealist,** chez tout Français il y a un idéaliste; **he spends e. penny he earns,** il dépense tout ce qu'il gagne; il dépense jusqu'au dernier sou; autant il gagne, autant il dépense; **his desire to meet your e. wish,** son désir d'aller au-devant de chacun de vos désirs; **the task will take up e. spare moment,** cette tâche occupera tous ses loisirs; **e. action of his,** *Lit:* **his e. action, public and private, bears witness to . . .,** chacune de ses actions, tant publiques que privées, témoigne de . . .; **e. holiday I go to Scotland,** chaque fois que je prends des vacances, à toutes mes vacances, je vais en Écosse; **e. day,** chaque jour, tous les jours; **confidence is increasing e. day,** la confiance s'accroît de jour en jour; **I am here by myself all day and e. day,** je reste seul(e) ici toute la journée et tous les jours; **e. other day, e. second day,** tous les deux jours; un jour sur deux; de deux jours l'un; **e. other Sunday,** un dimanche sur deux; **e. second or third day,** tous les deux ou trois jours; **e. three days, e. third day,** tous les trois jours, un jour sur trois; **e. two or three minutes,** toutes les deux ou trois minutes; **e. third man was chosen,** on choisissait un homme sur trois; **for e. ten coupons you can get a gift,** on donne une prime pour dix bons, par dizaine de bons; **to do sth. e. quarter of an hour,** faire qch. tous les quarts d'heure; **at e. quarter past the hour,** toutes les heures, au quart; **e. few months he would come on a visit,** tous les deux ou trois mois il venait en visite; **e. few minutes,** toutes les cinq minutes; **e. other minute,** à tout bout de champ; **I expect him e. minute,** je l'attends d'un instant, d'un moment, à l'autre; **once in e. week,** une fois par semaine; **e. time he comes,** chaque fois qu'il vient; **you win e. time,** on gagne à tous les coups; à tous les coups l'on gagne; **perseverance wins e. time,** la persévérance l'emporte toujours; (*b*) (*intensive*) **he was e. inch, e. bit, a republican,** il était républicain jusqu'au bout des ongles, des doigts; c'était un républicain à tous crins; **he is e. inch a gentleman,** c'est un gentleman dans toute l'acception du terme; **he is e. bit of sixty,** il a soixante ans bien sonnés; **I have e. reason to believe that . . .,** j'ai toute raison, tout lieu, de croire que . . .; **e. bit as much . . .,** tout autant que . . .; **e. bit as good as . . .,** tout aussi bon que . . .; **he is e. bit as rich as you,** il est pour le moins aussi riche que vous; **I shall give you e. assistance,** je vous aiderai de tout mon pouvoir; **I wish you e. success,** (i) je vous souhaite une pleine réussite; (ii) tous mes souhaits pour l'avenir; **I look forward with e. confidence to the future,** j'envisage l'avenir avec une pleine confiance; (*c*) **e. one,** chacun, chacune; tout le monde; **e. one of us,** tous tant que nous sommes, tous sans exception; **e. one of us was there,** nous étions tous là, nous étions au grand complet; **they are my friends, e. one of them,** ils sont tous mes amis; **e. man for himself,** (i) chacun pour soi; (ii) (*in danger*) sauve qui peut! *Prov:* **let e. man stick to his trade,** chacun son métier; **e. person has this right,** chacun a ce droit; **e. man Jack of them,** tous sans exception; **e. man Jack, e. mother's son, perished,** ils ont péri jusqu'au dernier; **e. Jack had his Jill,** il n'y avait pas de jeune homme qui n'eût sa bonne amie, *F:* chacun avait sa chacune.

everybody ['evribɔdi], *indef.pron.* tout le monde; **e. has a way of his own,** chacun a sa manière à lui; **e. else,** tous les autres; **e. slanders e. else,** chacun médit du tiers et du quart; **e. knows that,** tout le monde, le premier venu, n'importe qui, sait cela; **it is being done, worn, by e.,** cela tombe dans le commun; **not e. can be a Milton,** il n'est pas donné à tout le monde d'être un Milton; **not e. can do it,** ce n'est pas tout le monde qui pourrait le faire.

everyday ['evridei], *a.* **1.** journalier, quotidien; **e. occurrence,** (i) fait journalier; (ii) fait banal; **e. life,** la vie quotidienne. **2.** de tous les jours; **my e. clothes,** mes vêtements *m* de la semaine, de tous les jours. **3.** usuel; banal, -aux; ordinaire, commun; **e. English,** l'anglais usuel; **e. expression,** expression courante; **words in e. use,** mots très usités, d'usage courant; **e. knowledge,** connaissances usuelles.

everyhow ['evrihau], *adv. U.S: F:* de toutes les façons.

Everyman ['evrimæn], *Pr.n.m. Lit: Hist:* Tout-homme (dans la Moralité du XVe siècle); *F:* **Mr E.,** monsieur Tout-le-monde.

everyone ['evriwʌn], *indef.pron.* chacun; tout le monde; tous; **e. has his hobby,** chacun a sa marotte; **as e. knows,** comme chacun, tout le monde, (le) sait; **he is known to e.,** tout le monde le connaît; **e. else knows it,** tous les autres le savent; **in a small town e. knows e. else,** dans une petite ville chacun se connaît; **e. we know is going,** tous nos amis et connaissances y vont; **e. seemed to be enjoying themselves very much,** tout le monde semblait beaucoup s'amuser.

everyplace ['evripleis], *adv. U.S: F:* partout.

everything ['evriθiŋ], *indef.pron.* (*a*) tout; **he has eaten up e.,** il a tout mangé; **(a place for e., and) e. in its place,** chaque chose *f* à sa place; **we must show him e.,** il faut tout lui montrer; il faut lui montrer tout; **e. good,** tout ce qu'il y a de bon; **e. in the way of games interests him,** tout ce qui est jeu l'intéresse; **they sell e.,** on y vend de tout; on peut y acheter n'importe quoi; *Com:* **e. for cyclists,** tout ce qui concerne le cyclisme; *Prov:* **there is mercy for e.,** à tout péché miséricorde; **he will give you e. and anything you want,** il vous donnera tout ce que vous pourrez désirer; *F:* (*vague addition*) **we're in a bad way with strikes and e.,** ça marche mal à cause des grèves et de tout ça; *U.S: F:* **he ran like e.,** il a couru comme un dératé; (*b*) de première importance; **money is e.,** l'argent *m* fait tout; **money is not e.,** l'argent n'est pas tout; **she is very pretty—beauty isn't e.,** elle est très jolie—il n'y a pas que la beauté (qui compte); **she's e. to me,** je ne vis que pour elle.

everyway ['evriwei], *adv.* de toutes les manières; sous tous les rapports.

everywhen ['evri(h)wen], *adv. U.S: F:* tout le temps.

everywhere ['evri(h)wɛər], **1.** *adv.* partout; en tout lieu; en tous lieux; **to look e. for s.o.,** chercher qn partout, de tous côtés; **e. you go,** partout où vous allez; **e. seemed quiet,** le calme régnait partout. **2.** *s.* **the e.,** l'infini *m.*

every which way ['evri'hwitʃ'wei], *adv.phr. U.S: F:* **they ran e. w. w.,** ils couraient de tous côtés.

evict [i'vikt], *v.tr.* **1.** évincer, expulser (un locataire) **(from,** de); jeter (des locataires) à la rue, sur le pavé; expulser (les fermiers); **evicted tenant,** locataire évincé. **2.** *Jur:* **to e. property, title of property, of, from, s.o.,** récupérer légalement une propriété, un titre de propriété, des mains de qn.

evicting [i'viktiŋ], *s.* évincement *m* (de locataires); expulsion *f.*

eviction [i'vikʃ(ə)n], *s. Jur:* **1.** éviction *f,* expulsion *f* (d'un locataire); dépossession *f;* **to threaten a tenant with e.,** menacer un locataire d'expulsion. **2.** rentrée légale en possession, prise légale de possession (d'une propriété).

evidence[1] ['evid(ə)ns], *s.* **1.** évidence *f;* (*a*) **to acknowledge the e. of the facts,** reconnaître l'évidence des faits; **to fly in the face of the e.,** se refuser à l'évidence; (*b*) (*of pers., etc.*) **to be in e.,** être en évidence; **his sister was not in e.,** sa sœur n'était pas là, n'était pas présente; **a man much in e. at present,** un homme très en vue actuellement. **2.** signe *m,* marque *f;* **to bear evidence(s) of, give e. of, sth.,** porter la marque, les marques, de qch.; **to give e. of intelligence,** (i) (*of action, etc.*) marquer l'intelligence; (ii) (*of pers.*) faire preuve d'intelligence; **land that bears, shows, e. of insufficient capital,** terre *f* où le manque de capitaux est manifeste; *Mec.E:* **there is e. of overheating,** il y a des traces *f* d'échauffement; **there was no e. of his stay in the house,** rien ne marquait qu'il eût séjourné dans la maison. **3.** (*a*) preuve *f;* **internal e.,** preuves intrinsèques, naturelles; **external e.,** preuves extrinsèques, artificielles; *Theol:* **the Evidences (of Christianity),** les preuves du christianisme; (*b*) *Jur:* preuve testimoniale; témoignage *m;* **oral e.,** preuve orale; **written e., documentary e., e. in writing,** document probant; preuve littérale, par écrit, documentaire; **to decide on documentary e.,** juger, décider, sur pièces; **prima facie e.,** commencement *m* de preuve; **to collect e.,** recueillir des témoignages; **to bear, give, e.,** témoigner, déposer (en justice); faire une déposition; porter témoignage; **to give e. in s.o.'s favour,** témoigner en faveur de qn; **to call s.o. in e.,** appeler qn en témoignage; **to take s.o.'s e.,** recueillir la déposition, les témoignages, de qn; **to get e.,** prendre des témoignages; **the hearing of e. of witnesses,** l'audition *f* des dépositions des témoins; **to put in e. that . . .,** invoquer à titre de preuve que . . .; **e. of indebtedness,** titre *m* de créance; **the e. was strongly against him,** les témoignages pesaient contre lui; **false e.,** faux témoignage; **to plant incriminating e. on s.o.,** substituer les preuves d'un délit sur un tiers; **common gossip is not e.,** les commérages *m* ne sont pas admissibles en preuve; **the e. of the senses,** le témoignage des sens; **if you can't believe the e. of your eyes!** si vous n'êtes pas convaincu par ce que vous voyez devant vous! **4.** *Jur:* (*pers.*) témoin(s) *m(pl);* **the e. for the prosecution, the defence,** les témoins à charge, à décharge; **King's, Queen's, e.,** *U.S: etc:* **State's e.,** témoin dénonciateur de ses complices; **to turn King's, Queen's, e.,** témoigner contre, dénoncer, ses complices (sous promesse de pardon).

evidence[2], **1.** *v.tr.* prouver, manifester, démontrer. **2.** *v.i. O:* porter témoignage; déposer (en justice) **(against,** contre).

evident ['evid(ə)nt], *a.* évident; **e. marks of smallpox,** marques évidentes de petite vérole; **e. fact, truth,** fait patent, vérité patente; **he had had too much, as was e. from the way he was walking,** il avait trop bu, et il y paraissait à sa démarche; **the truth become e. to him,** la vérité lui apparut.

evidential [evi'denʃ(ə)l], *a.* **1.** (christianisme) fondé sur les preuves. **2. e. of sth.,** indicateur, -trice, de qch.

evidently ['evidəntli], *adv.* évidemment, manifestement, sans aucun doute; **he was e. afraid,** il était évident, clair, qu'il avait peur.

evil ['i:v(i)l, 'i:v(ə)l]. **1.** *a.* (*a*) mauvais; **of e. repute,** de mauvaise réputation; **house of e. repute,** mauvais lieu; lieu mal famé; *Lit:* **e. tidings,** fâcheuses nouvelles; **measure attended by e. consequences,** mesure *f* néfaste; **e. omen,** présage *m* de malheur; **of e. omen,** de mauvais présage; sinistre; **of e. memory,** de sinistre mémoire; **to have e. forebodings,** avoir de noirs pressentiments; voir noir; **an e. day,** un jour malheureux; **in an e. moment,** dans un moment funeste; **to fall on e. days,** tomber dans l'infortune, dans la peine, dans le malheur, *F:* dans la débine; (*b*) méchant; **e. spirit,** esprit malfaisant, malin; **the E. One,** le Mauvais, l'Esprit malin, le Malin; **to play an e. part,** jouer un rôle malfaisant; **to look for an e. intention in everything,** chercher à tout de sinistres interprétations; voir le mal partout; **e. influence,** influence néfaste, malfaisante; **e. eye,** mauvais œil; **to cast an e. eye on s.o.,** jeter le mauvais œil sur qn; **e. tongue,** mauvaise langue; méchante langue; **to silence e. tongues,** faire taire la médisance; **to get into e. ways,** se dérégler. **2.** *s.* (*a*) mal *m, pl.* maux; **the e. wrought by typhus,** les ravages *m* du typhus; **a social e.,** une plaie sociale; **of two evils one must choose the less(er),** entre deux maux il faut choisir le moindre; **to put one's finger on the e.,** mettre le doigt sur la plaie; *Prov:* **e. be to him who e. thinks,** hon(n)i soit qui mal y pense; **to speak e. of s.o.,** dire du mal de qn; (*b*) *Med: A:* **the King's e.,** les écrouelles *f,* la scrofule. **3.** *adv.* mal; *B:* **wherefore hast thou so e. entreated this people?** pourquoi as-tu fait maltraiter ce peuple?

evil-boding ['i:vl'boudiŋ], *a. A: & Lit:* de mauvais présage, de mauvais augure.

evildoer ['i:vl'du:ər], *s. O:* malfaiteur, -trice; **evildoers,** les méchants *m.*

evildoing ['i:vl'du:iŋ], *s. O:* mauvaises actions, méfaits *m;* la méchanceté; le vice; le crime.

evil-eyed ['i:vl'aid], *a.* **to be e.-e.,** (i) avoir le mauvais œil; (ii) avoir l'air méchant.

evil-hearted ['i:vl'hɑ:tid], *a.* méchant; pervers.

evil-looking ['i:vllukiŋ], *a.* de mauvaise mine; qui ne dit rien de bon; (homme *m*) louche; (maison *f*) borgne; **he drew an e.-l. knife,** il tira un vilain couteau.

evilly ['i:vili], *adv.* **1. to live e.,** vivre dans le vice; **to eye s.o. e.,** regarder qn d'un mauvais œil, d'un air méchant. **2.** *U.S:* **e. disposed,** mal disposé; **e. reputed spot,** endroit mal famé.

evil-minded ['i:vl'maindid], *a.* porté au mal; malintentionné, malveillant; malin, -igne.

evil-smelling ['i:vl'smeliŋ], *a.* nauséabond.

evil-tongued ['i:vl'tʌŋd], *a.* **an e.-t. person,** une mauvaise langue, une langue de vipère.

evince [i'vins], *v.tr.* **1.** *A:* démontrer, prouver; **this evinces clearly that . . .,** cela démontre clairement que. . . . **2.** montrer, témoigner, manifester, annoncer, faire preuve de (qch.); **to e. curiosity,** manifester de la curiosité; **to e. intelligence,** faire paraître de l'intelligence; faire preuve d'intelligence; **to e. a taste for sth.,** témoigner d'un goût, montrer du goût, pour qch.

evincible [i'vinsibl], *a. A:* démontrable.

evincive [i'vinsiv], *a. A:* (*of action, etc.*) **to be e. of sth.,** témoigner de qch.

evirate ['evireit, 'i:v-], *v.tr. A: & Lit:* émasculer, châtrer, évirer.

eviration [evi'reiʃ(ə)n], *s. A: & Lit:* émasculation *f,* castration *f,* éviration *f.*

eviscerate [i'visəreit], *v.tr.* **1.** éviscérer, éventrer. **2.** émasculer (une loi, un ouvrage littéraire, etc.); vider (qch.) de sa substance.

evisceration [ivisə'reiʃ(ə)n], *s.* éviscération *f,* éventration *f.*

evitable ['evitəbl], *a.* évitable.

evocable ['evəkəbl], *a.* évocable.

evocation [evou'keiʃ(ə)n], *s.* évocation *f* ((i) d'un esprit, etc.; (ii) *Jur:* d'une affaire).

evocative [i'vɔkətiv], *a.* évocateur, -trice.

evocator ['evəkeitər], *s.* évocateur, -trice.

evocatory [i'vɔkət(ə)ri], *a.* évocatoire.

evoke [i'vouk], *v.tr.* **1.** (*a*) évoquer (les esprits, un souvenir); (*b*) **this remark evoked a smile,** cette observation a provoqué, suscité, un sourire. **2.** *Jur:* évoquer (une affaire) (d'un tribunal inférieur à un tribunal supérieur).

evolute[1] ['evəljut], *a. & s. Mth: etc:* **e. (curve),** développée *f;* **to describe the e. of a curve,** dérouler une courbe.

evolute[2] [i:və'ljut], *v.i. U.S:* se développer; évoluer.

evolution [i:və'l(j)u:ʃ(ə)n], *s.* **1.** (*a*) *Biol:* évolution *f,* développement *m* (d'une espèce, d'un projet, etc.); (*b*) **the e. of events,** le déroulement des événements. **2.** évolution (d'un acrobate, d'une flotte, de troupes, etc.); **to carry out an e.,** faire une évolution. **3.** *Mth:* (*a*) tracé *m* d'une développante (de courbe); déroulement *m* (d'une courbe); (*b*) extraction *f* de la racine. **4.** *Ch: Ph:* dégagement *m* (de chaleur, de lumière).

evolutionary [i:və'l(j)u:ʃən(ə)ri], *a. Biol:* évolutionnaire, évolutif.

evolutionism [i:və'l(j)u:ʃənizm], *s. Biol:* évolutionnisme *m.*

evolutionist [i:və'l(j)u:ʃənist], *s. Biol:* évolutionniste *mf.*

evolve [i'vɔlv]. **1.** *v.tr.* (*a*) dérouler, développer (des projets); **to e. a scheme from one's inner consciousness,** produire, élaborer, un projet dans son for intérieur; (*b*) développer, déduire (une théorie, une vérité) **(from,** de); (*c*) *Mth:* **to e. a surd,** extraire la racine d'une quantité irrationnelle; (*d*) *Ch:* dégager (de la chaleur, un gaz, etc.); (*e*) développer (par évolution). **2.** *v.i.* (*a*) (*of events, etc.*) se dérouler; (*b*) (*of gas, heat, etc.*) se dégager; (*c*) (*of race, etc.*) se développer, évoluer; **everything evolves from it,** tout le reste en découle.

evolvent [i'vɔlvənt], *s. Mth:* développante *f.*

evolving [i'vɔlviŋ], *s.* **1.** déroulement *m,* élaboration *f* (d'un projet); développement *m* (d'une théorie). **2.** dégagement *m* (d'un gaz, etc.).

evulse [i'vʌls], *v.tr.* arracher (une dent, etc.).

evulsion [i'vʌlʃ(ə)n], *s. Surg: etc:* évulsion *f.*

evzone ['evzoun], *s. Gr.Mil:* evzone *m.*

ewe [ju:], *s.* brebis *f;* **ewe's milk cheese,** fromage *m* de lait de brebis.

ewe-neck ['ju:nek], *s.* (*of horse*) encolure renversée, encolure de cerf.

ewe-necked ['ju:nekt], *a.* (cheval) à encolure de cerf, à encolure renversée.

ewer ['juər], *s. O:* pot *m* à eau; broc *m* de toilette; *Ecc:* aquamanile *m.*

ex[1] [eks], *prep.* **1.** *Com:* (*out of*) **ex store,** en magasin; **ex wharf, ex quay,** à prendre sur quai; **price ex works,** prix *m* départ usine, prix sortie d'usine. **2.** (*without*) *Fin:* **ex allotment,** ex répartition; **stock ex rights,** titre *m* ex-droit; **shares quoted ex dividend, ex coupon,** actions citées ex-dividende, sans intérêts, coupon détaché, ex coupon; **this stock goes ex coupon on the first of August,** le coupon de cette action se détache le premier août.

ex-[2] **1.** *pref.* (*formerly*) ancien; ex-; **ex-minister,** exministre; **he, she, is an ex-teacher,** c'est un ancien professeur; **ex-regular,** ancien militaire de carrière; **ex-**

wife, ex-femme. 2. *s. F:* **my ex,** mon ex.

exacerbate [eg'zæsəbeit], *v.tr.* exacerber, aggraver (une douleur, etc.); irriter, exaspérer (qn).

exacerbation [egzæsə'beiʃ(ə)n], *s.* exacerbation *f.*

exact[1] [eg'zækt], *a.* exact. **1.** (*a*) précis; **to give e. details,** donner des détails précis, des précisions *f*; préciser; **these are his e. words,** ce sont là ses propres paroles; **to be more e.,** pour mieux dire; **e. copy of a document,** copie conforme à un document, copie textuelle d'un document; **to make an e. replica of a drawing,** copier un dessin trait pour trait; **the e. sciences,** les sciences exactes; (*b*) juste; **the e. word,** le mot juste; **the e. fit of a screw,** la justesse d'une vis; **the public must tender the e. amount,** le public est tenu de faire l'appoint; (*c*) (*of discipline, etc.*) strict, rigoureux. **2. to be e. in one's payments,** être exact, ponctuel, dans ses paiements; **to be e. in carrying out one's duties,** être exact à s'acquitter de ses devoirs; **e. in business,** strict en affaires; **to be e. in one's actions,** être régulier dans ses actions.

exact[2], *v.tr.* **1.** (*a*) exiger (un impôt) (**from,** de); (*b*) extorquer (une rançon à qn). **2.** exiger, réclamer, requérir (l'obéissance, beaucoup de soins) (**from,** de).

exactable [eg'zæktəbl], *a.* (impôt *m*) exigible.

exacting [eg'zæktiŋ], *a.* (*of pers.*) exigeant; (*of work*) astreignant; **it would appear somewhat e. to demand . . .,** il y aurait quelque rigueur à exiger . . .; **to be too e.,** se montrer trop exigeant; **to be too e. with s.o.,** en demander trop à qn.

exaction [eg'zækʃ(ə)n], *s.* exaction *f.*

exactitude [eg'zæktitju:d], **exactness** [eg'zæktnis], *s.* **1.** exactitude *f*, précision *f*; justesse *f* (d'un raisonnement, d'un calcul); **to aim at e.,** viser à la précision; **e. of reasoning,** rigueur *f* de raisonnement. **2. e. in work,** exactitude dans le travail; **his e. in carrying out his duties,** son exactitude à s'acquitter de ses fonctions.

exactly [eg'zæktli], *adv.* (*a*) exactement, précisément, au juste, tout juste, justement; (*of time*) juste; **I know e. what you want,** je sais exactement ce qu'il vous faut; **I don't know e. what happened,** je ne sais pas au juste ce qui est arrivé; **e.!** précisément! parfaitement! **e. so!** c'est précisément cela; **timber cut e. (to shape),** pièce *f* de bois (allant) à la demande; **it is e. five,** il est cinq heures juste; **three months e.,** trois mois jour pour jour; **he is not e. a scholar,** ce n'est pas exactement, à vrai dire, un savant; (*b*) *O:* **to carry out one's duties e.,** s'acquitter de ses devoirs avec exactitude.

exactor [eg'zæktər], *s. A:* exacteur *m.*

exaggerate [eg'zædʒəreit], *v.tr.* exagérer; grossir anormalement, exagérément; agrandir, amplifier (les fautes de qn, les traits de qn, etc.); grandir (un incident); outrer (une mode, des éloges); charger (un récit); *v.i.* **let's not, don't, e.!** n'exagérons rien!

exaggerated [eg'zædʒəreitid], *a.* exagéré; **e. praise,** éloges outrés; **to have an e. opinion of oneself,** avoir une très haute opinion de soi-même; *F:* se gober; **to attach e. importance to sth.,** prêter une importance excessive à qch.; **e. style,** style outré.

exaggeratedly [eg'zædʒəreitidli], *adv.* exagérément.

exaggeration [egzædʒə'reiʃ(ə)n], *s.* **1.** exagération *f.* **2. that's an e.!** vous exagérez!

exaggerative [eg'zædʒərətiv], *a.* **1.** (langage) exagératif. **2.** (*of pers.*) porté à l'exagération; exagéré.

exaggerator [eg'zædʒəreitər], *s.* personne *f* qui exagère.

exalbuminous [eksæl'bju:minəs], *a. Bot:* exalbuminé.

exalt [eg'zɔ:lt], *v.tr.* **1.** élever, placer haut (qn en rang, en dignité, etc.); *Lit:* **to e. bribery to a system,** ériger la corruption en système. **2.** exalter, louer, vanter, relever (les vertus de qn); **to e. s.o. to the skies,** porter, élever, qn jusqu'aux nues. **3.** *A:* exciter, exalter, enflammer (l'imagination). **4.** *A: & Lit:* intensifier, rehausser (une couleur).

exaltation [egzɔl'teiʃ(ə)n], *s.* **1.** élévation *f* (**to a dignity,** à une dignité); exaltation *f* (d'un pape, de la Croix, du nom de Dieu). **2.** exaltation, surexcitation *f*; émotion passionnée. **3.** *A:* rehaussement *m* (d'une couleur, etc.). **4.** *Astrol: A:* **planet in e.,** planète *f* en exaltation.

exalted [eg'zɔ:ltid], *a.* **1.** (rang, sentiment) élevé; (personnage) haut placé. **2.** (*a*) exalté; (ton) élevé; (*b*) *A:* (*of imagination, etc.*) exalté, enflammé.

exam [eg'zæm], *s. F:* = EXAMINATION 2.

examinable [eg'zæminəbl], *a. Jur:* (*of case*) qui peut être instruit.

examination [egzæmi'neiʃ(ə)n], *s.* examen *m.* **1.** inspection *f*, visite *f* (des machines, etc.); vérification *f* (de comptes); dépouillement *m* (d'un rapport); *Jur:* compulsation *f* (de dossiers, etc.); **on e.,** après examen, examen fait; **on further e.,** après plus ample informé; après un examen plus approfondi; **this assertion will not bear e.,** cette assertion ne supporte pas l'examen; **under e.,** à l'examen; *Jur:* **the case is under e.,** l'affaire s'instruit, est soumise à vérification; **to undergo a medical e.,** passer une visite médicale; **the doctor gave me a thorough e.,** le médecin m'a examiné dans le plus grand détail, très minutieusement; *Nau:* **e. of the bill of health,** arraisonnement *m* de la patente de santé. **2.** *Sch: etc:* **entrance e.,** examen d'entrée; **competitive e.,** concours *m*; **competitive entrance e.,** concours d'admission; **admitted by competitive e.,** admis au concours, après concours; **written e.,** (i) épreuves écrites; (ii) épreuves d'admissibilité (à l'examen oral); **to pass (in) the written e.,** être admissible; **viva voce, oral, e.,** épreuves orales; examen oral; **end-of-year e.,** (i) compositions *fpl* de fin d'année; (ii) examen de passage; **state e.,** examen d'État; **eleven plus e.** = examen d'entrée en 6 · ; **to take, sit (for), an e.,** passer, subir, un examen; **to pass, fail, an e.,** être reçu, refusé, à un examen. **3.** *Jur:* (*a*) interrogatoire *m* (d'un accusé, etc.); audition *f* (de témoins); **e.-in-chief,** *U.S:* **direct e.,** interrogatoire d'un témoin par la partie qui l'a fait citer; **to undergo e., to be put under e.,** subir un interrogatoire; **to put s.o. through a searching e.,** faire subir à qn un interrogatoire serré, minutieux, rigoureux; (*b*) instruction *f* (d'une cause).

examine [eg'zæmin], *v.tr.* examiner. **1.** passer l'inspection de, inspecter (une machine); *Cust:* visiter (les bagages); vérifier (des comptes); contrôler, viser (un passeport); sonder (le terrain, la farine); scruter (les cœurs); compulser (des dossiers, etc.); dépouiller (un inventaire, un compte); **to e. oneself, one's conscience,** faire son examen de conscience; interroger son cœur; descendre en soi-même; **to e. a question thoroughly,** approfondir une question; examiner une question à fond; **to get examined,** se faire examiner par le médecin; *El:* **to e. the contacts,** vérifier les contacts; *Nau:* **to e. the bill of health,** arraisonner la patente de santé; **to stop and e. a ship,** arraisonner un navire. **2.** faire passer un examen à (qn); **to e. a candidate in Latin, on his knowledge of Latin,** examiner un candidat en latin; interroger un candidat en latin, sur le latin. **3.** *Jur: etc:* (*a*) interroger, faire subir un interrogatoire à (un prévenu, un témoin); **he was closely examined,** il a été interrogé minutieusement; (*b*) instruire (une cause).

examinee [egzæmi'ni:], *s. Sch:* candidat, -ate.

examiner eg'zæminər], *s.* **1.** inspecteur, -trice, visiteur, -euse (de machines, de bagages, etc.); compulseur *m* (de dossiers, etc.); *Ind:* repasseur, -euse; *Tex:* **skein e.,** repasseur, -euse, d'écheveaux. **2.** *Sch:* examinateur, -trice; **the examiners,** le jury (d'examen). **3.** *Jur:* **e. (in chancery)** = juge *m* d'instruction.

examining [eg'zæminiŋ], *a.* examinateur, -trice; **e. body,** jury *m* d'examen; **e. judge, magistrate** = juge *m* d'instruction.

example [eg'zɑ:mpl], *s.* exemple *m.* **1. to quote sth. as an e.,** citer qch. en exemple, à titre d'exemple; **examples from Livy,** exemples tirés de Tite-Live; **he showed me some examples of his work,** il m'a montré des spécimens *m* de son travail; **concrete, practical, e.,** cas concret; **for e., by way of e.,** par exemple; **large towns, as for e. London,** les grandes villes, telles que Londres (par exemple); *Sch:* **examples for practice,** exercices *m* d'application (d'un théorème, d'une règle). **2.** précédent *m*; **without e.,** sans exemple, sans précédent. **3. to give, set, an e., the e.,** donner l'exemple; **to make an e. of s.o.,** faire un exemple de qn; infliger à qn un châtiment exemplaire, punir qn pour l'exemple; **to hold s.o. up as an e.,** citer qn en exemple; **to take s.o. as an e.,** prendre exemple sur qn; prendre qn pour exemple, pour règle; se régler sur qn; **to follow s.o.'s e.,** suivre l'exemple de qn; **following the e., after the e., of. . .,** à l'exemple de . . .

exanimate [ek'sænimeit], *a. Lit:* **1.** inanimé, mort. **2.** *A:* abattu, découragé.

exanthema, *pl.* **-mata** [eksæn'θi:mə, -mətə], *s. Med:* exanthème *m.*

exanthematous [eksæn'θi:mətəs], *a. Med:* exanthémateux; exanthématique.

exarch ['eksɑ:k], *s. A.Hist: & Ecc:* exarque *m.*

exarchate ['eksɑ:keit], *s. A.Hist:* exarchat *m.*

exasperate [eg'zæspəreit, -'zɑ:-], *v.tr.* **1.** *A:* exaspérer, aggraver (la haine, une douleur, etc.). **2.** exaspérer, irriter; **the sound exasperated her,** ce bruit lui donnait, portait, *F:* tapait, sur les nerfs; **exasperated at, by, his insolence,** exaspéré de son insolence; poussé à bout par son insolence.

exasperating [eg'zæspəreitiŋ, -'zɑ:-], *a.* (ton, enfant) exaspérant, irritant.

exasperatingly [eg'zæspəreitiŋli, -zɑ:-], *adv.* (rire, agir) d'une manière exaspérante, irritante; **he is e. pessimistic,** il est d'un pessimisme exaspérant.

exasperation [egzæspə'reiʃ(ə)n], *s.* **1.** *A:* exaspération *f*, aggravation *f* (d'une douleur, etc.). **2.** (*of pers.*) exaspération, irritation *f*; **to drive s.o. to e.,** pousser qn à bout; **he threw it down in e.,** exaspéré, il l'a jeté par terre.

ex cathedra ['eks'kæθidrə, 'ekskə'θi:drə], *Lt.adv.phr.* ex cathedra; d'un ton doctoral.

excaudate [eks'kɔ:deit], *a. Z:* sans queue.

excavate ['ekskəveit], *v.tr.* excaver, creuser (un tunnel, le sol); déblayer (un terrain); fouiller (la terre); approfondir (un canal); déterrer (des ruines, etc.); **excavated road,** route *f* en déblai; *Archeol:* **to e. (a site),** faire des fouilles (dans un endroit).

excavating ['ekskəveitiŋ], *s.* excavation *f*, creusement *m*, déblaiement *m*, (travaux *mpl* de) déblai *m*, fouillement *m.*

excavation [ekskə'veiʃ(ə)n], *s.* excavation *f.* **1.** fouillement *m*, creusement *m* (de la terre, etc.); fouille *f*; déblaiement *m*, déblai *m*; approfondissement *m.* **2.** terrain excavé; fouille; **the excavations at Pompeii,** les fouilles de Pompéi.

excavator ['ekskəveitər], *s.* (*a*) *Civ.E:* excavateur, -trice, pelleteuse *f*; machine *f* à déblayer; piocheuse-défonceuse *f*, *pl.* piocheuses-défonceuses; (*b*) (*pers.*) fouilleur, -euse.

exceed [ek'si:d]. **1.** *v.tr.* (*a*) excéder, dépasser, outrepasser, aller au delà de (ses droits, etc.); **to e. a quantity by so much,** excéder une quantité de tant; **not exceeding ten pounds,** ne dépassant pas dix livres; jusqu'à concurrence de (la somme de) dix livres; *Post:* **not exceeding 250 gr.,** jusqu'à 250 gr.; **do not e. the stated dose,** ne pas dépasser la dose prescrite; **to e. one's instructions,** dépasser ses instructions; **to e. one's rights,** sortir des limites de son droit; outrepasser ses droits; **to e. one's powers,** sortir de sa compétence; *Aut:* **to e. the speed limit,** dépasser la limite de vitesse; **he was fined for exceeding the speed limit,** il a eu une contravention pour excès de vitesse; (*b*) surpasser (qn, qch.) (**in,** en); **the outcome exceeded all our hopes,** le résultat a dépassé toutes nos espérances. **2.** *v.i. A:* (*a*) prédominer, être prépondérant; **life that exceeds in pleasure,** vie *f* qui l'emporte en plaisirs; (*b*) manger, boire, à l'excès.

exceeding [ek'si:diŋ], *adv. A:* très, excessivement.

exceedingly [ek'si:diŋli], *adv.* très, extrêmement, excessivement; **I am e. grateful to you,** je vous en suis extrêmement reconnaissant; *O:* **to like s.o., sth., e.,** aimer beaucoup qn, qch.

excel [ek'sel], *v.* (**excelled**) **1.** *v.i.* exceller (**in doing sth.,** à faire qch.); **to e. in an art, in one's profession,** exceller dans un art, dans sa profession; **to e. at history,** exceller en histoire; **to e. at a game,** exceller à un jeu. **2.** *v.tr.* surpasser (qn); l'emporter sur (qn); **to e. s.o. in, at, tennis,** surpasser qn au tennis; **to e. all one's rivals,** surpasser tous ses rivaux; l'emporter sur tous ses rivaux; **to e. oneself,** se surpasser.

excellence ['eksələns], *s.* excellence *f.* **1.** perfection *f* (d'un ouvrage). **2.** mérite *m*, qualité *f*, supériorité *f* (de qn, de qch.).

excellency ['eksələnsi], *s.* **1.** *A:* = EXCELLENCE. **2.** (*title*) **Your E.,** votre Excellence *f*; **it is I, your E., who . . .,** c'est moi, Excellence, qui . . .; **his E. the French Ambassador,** son Excellence l'ambassadeur de France.

excellent ['eksələnt], *a.* excellent, parfait; **e. bargain, business,** marché *m*, affaire *f*, d'or.

excellently ['eksələntli], *adv.* admirablement, d'une manière excellente, *Lit:* excellemment.

excelsior [ek'selsiɔ:r]. **1.** *int.* excelsior. **2.** *s. U.S: R.t.m:* laine *f* de bois, copeaux *mpl* (d'emballage, de rembourrage).

except[1] [ek'sept]. **1.** *v.tr.* excepter, exclure (**from,** de); **present company excepted,** les présents exceptés; **errors and omissions excepted,** sauf erreur ou omission. **2.** *v.i. A:* **to e. against (s.o., sth.),** faire des objections à (qn, qch.); *Jur:* récuser (un témoin, un témoignage); décliner (la compétence d'un tribunal).

except[2]. **1.** *prep.* (*a*) excepté; à l'exception de; exception faite de; sauf; **everyone had arrived e. the bride,** tout le monde était arrivé, excepté la mariée; **he is everywhere e. where he ought to be,** il est partout si ce n'est où il devrait être; **nobody e. him,** personne excepté lui; **all e. the doctor,** tous, à l'exception du docteur; **he does nothing e. eat and drink,** il ne fait rien sinon manger et boire; **nobody heard it e. me,** il n'y a que moi qui l'aie entendu; **e. by agreement between the parties,** sauf accord entre les parties; **e. when,** sauf quand; **e. if,** sauf si; (*b*) **e. for,** à part, si ce n'est; **everything is correct e. for the omission of. . .,** tout est correct à part, si ce n'est, l'omission de . . .; **we had fine weather, e. for a little rain about midday,** nous avons eu beau temps, excepté qu'il a un peu plu vers midi; **the dress is ready e. for the buttons,** la robe est prête, à l'exception des boutons; **e.**

for this detail, à ce détail près; **I haven't done anything e. for writing some letters,** je n'ai rien fait, sauf d'écrire des lettres. **2.** (*a*) *conj. A: & Lit:* à moins que, si ce n'est que; **e. you told it, how could it have become known?** à moins que vous ne l'ayez raconté, comment cela se serait-il su? **e. a grain of wheat die . . .,** si le grain ne meurt . . .; **e. he be dead, he will return,** hors, hormis, qu'il soit mort, il reviendra; (*b*) *conj.phr.* **e. that,** excepté que, à cela près que, si ce n'est que, à la différence que, à la réserve que; **the cases are parallel e. that she is older than he is,** les cas sont semblables excepté qu'elle est plus âgée que lui; **he came out of it unscathed, e. that he lost his hat,** il en est sorti indemne, sauf qu'il a perdu son chapeau; **nothing was decided e. that peace was impossible,** rien n'y fut décidé sinon que la paix était impossible.

excepting [ek'septiŋ], *prep. & conj.* = EXCEPT². **not e., without e., my wife,** sans excepter ma femme.

exception [ek'sepʃ(ə)n], *s.* **1.** exception *f*; **to make an e. to a rule,** faire une exception à une règle; **to be an e. to a rule,** faire exception à une règle; **the e. proves the rule,** l'exception confirme la règle; **with that e. we are agreed,** à cela près nous sommes d'accord; **without e.,** sans (aucune) exception; **with the e. of . . .,** à l'exception de . . ., exception faite de . . ., sauf . . ., à part . . .; **with a few exceptions,** sauf de rares exceptions, à quelques exceptions près; **with certain exceptions,** sauf exceptions. **2.** objection *f*; **to take e. to sth.,** (i) trouver à redire à qch.; (ii) se formaliser, s'offenser, s'offusquer, se froisser, se choquer, de qch.; **they took e. to his youth,** on lui objecta sa jeunesse; *Jur:* **to take e. to a witness, to evidence,** récuser un témoin; reprocher un témoin, un témoignage; **witness to whom e. can be taken,** témoin reprochable; **the question was solved without anyone taking e. to the decision,** la question a été résolue sans soulever la moindre objection; **to take e. to s.o.'s doing sth.,** trouver mauvais que qn fasse qch.; **authority, etc., beyond e.,** autorité *f*, etc., irrécusable. **3.** *Jur:* exception, fin *f* de non-recevoir; **dilatory e.,** exception dilatoire; **bill of exceptions** = requête civile.

exceptionable [ek'sepʃ(ə)nəbl], *a.* (*usu. with a negative*) (rien de) blâmable, critiquable, répréhensible; **to find nothing e. in sth.,** ne rien trouver à redire à qch.

exceptional [ek'sepʃən(ə)l], *a.* exceptionnel. **1.** (*a*) (*constituting an exception*) **an e. favour,** une faveur exceptionnelle; (*b*) **jurisdiction of an e. court,** juridiction *f* d'exception. **2.** (*outstanding*) **e. talent,** talent *m* hors ligne, exceptionnel; **an e. man,** un homme exceptionnel, remarquable.

exceptionality [eksepʃə'næliti], *s.* caractère exceptionnel (de qch.).

exceptionally [ek'sepʃən(ə)li], *adv.* exceptionnellement. **1.** par exception. **2.** (*unusually*) extraordinairement; **e. cheap,** d'un bon marché exceptionnel; **e. gifted child,** enfant supérieurement, remarquablement, doué; **factors which make the crisis e. complex,** des éléments qui rendent exceptionnellement complexe la crise.

exceptive [ek'septiv], *a.* (*a*) exceptionnel; *esp. Jur:* **e. clause,** clause exceptionnelle; (*b*) *Log:* **e. proposition,** proposition exceptive.

excerpt¹ ['eksəːpt], *s.* (*a*) extrait *m*, citation *f*; **e. from a literary work,** emprunt *m* à une œuvre littéraire; (*b*) tirage *m* à part; (*c*) *Mus:* **excerpts from** *Carmen*, extraits de *Carmen*.

excerpt² [ek'səːpt], *v.tr.* extraire (un passage, etc.) (**from,** de).

excerption [ek'səːpʃ(ə)n], *s.* **1.** extraction *f*, citation *f* (de passages, etc.). **2.** = EXCERPT¹.

excess¹ [ek'ses], *s.* **1.** (*a*) excès *m* (de lumière, de zèle, etc.); **e. of precaution,** luxe *m* de précautions; **to e.,** (jusqu')à l'excès; **to eat, drink, to e.,** manger, boire, à l'excès, plus que de raison, outre mesure; **wisdom may be carried to e.,** on peut se montrer trop sage; **indulgence carried to e.,** indulgence outrée, poussée trop loin; **to act in e. of one's rights,** outrepasser ses droits; **if the subscriptions should be in e. of the sum required,** si les cotisations dépassent la somme requise; (*b*) **to commit excesses,** commettre des excès, des cruautés. **2.** excédent *m* (de poids, de dépenses, etc.); **e. of expenditure over revenue,** excédent des dépenses sur les recettes; **e. weight,** excédent de poids; surpoids *m*; *Num:* forçage *m* (d'une pièce de monnaie); **sum in e.,** somme *f* en excédent, en surplus, de surplus; *Ins:* **accidental damage e.,** franchise *f*; *Com:* **e. profits,** (i) surplus *m* des bénéfices; (ii) bénéfices extraordinaires; *Fin:* **e. profit tax,** impôt *m* sur les bénéfices exceptionnels; *Rail:* **e. fare,** supplément *m*; **to pay the e. (on one's ticket),** prendre un supplément; **e. luggage, luggage in e.,** excédent de bagages; bagages *mpl* en surpoids; **all luggage in e. of 50 kg to be paid for,** les bagages au-dessus de, excédant, 50 kg doivent payer la taxe; *Metalw:* **e. of metal,** surépaisseur *f* de métal; *El:* **e. current,** surintensité *f*; **e. voltage,** surtension *f*; *Mec:* **e. pressure,** excès de pression; surpression *f*.

excess², *v.tr. Rail:* percevoir un supplément sur (un billet).

excessive [ek'sesiv], *a.* (*of price, heat, etc.*) excessif; (*of zeal*) immodéré; (*of virtue, etc.*) outré, exagéré; (*of thirst*) extrême; (*of ambition*) démesuré; **e. rain,** pluie diluvienne; **to be an e. drinker, smoker,** boire, fumer, à l'excès; **e. expenses,** dépenses exagérées; **to make an e. display of force,** faire un emploi abusif de la force.

excessively [ek'sesivli], *adv.* (souffrir, etc.) excessivement, extrêmement; (ambitionner) démesurément; (manger) avec excès, à l'excès; **to be e. generous,** être par trop généreux.

excessiveness [ek'sesivnis], *s.* excessiveté *f*; manque *m* de modération, de mesure.

exchange¹ [eks'tʃeindʒ], *s.* **1.** (*a*) échange *m* (de marchandises, de prisonniers, de coups, etc.); *Sch: etc:* **we made an e. visit,** nous avons fait un échange; **e. and barter,** troc *m*; **e. of views between . . .,** échange de vues entre . . .; **in e. (for sth.),** en échange (de qch.); en retour (de qch.); **money of e.,** monnaie *f* de change; **fair, even-handed, e.,** troc pour troc; *Prov:* **e. is no robbery,** échange n'est pas vol; **car, etc., taken in part e.,** reprise *f*; *Chess:* **to win, lose, the e.,** gagner, perdre, l'échange; *Adm:* **e. of posts,** permutation *f* (de deux fonctionnaires); **civil servant seeking an e.,** fonctionnaire *m* cherchant un permutant; (*b*) **chemical e.,** échange chimique; *Atom.Ph:* **e. energy, e. force,** énergie *f*, force *f*, d'échange; **e. reaction,** réaction *f* d'échange. **2.** *Fin:* (*a*) **foreign e.,** change (extérieur, étranger); **operations in foreign e.,** opérations *f* de change; **e. bank,** banque *f* s'occupant d'opérations de change; **dollar e.,** change du dollar, en dollars; (**rate of**) **e.,** cours *m*, taux *m*, du change; **e. control,** contrôle *m* des changes; **fixed, direct, e.,** le certain; **at the current rate of e.,** au change du jour; **e. list,** bulletin *m* des changes; **e. premium, premium on e.,** agio *m*; prix *m* du change; (**foreign**) **e. broker,** cambiste *m*, agent *m* de change; **foreign e. office,** bureau *m* de change; **e. market,** marché *m* cambiste; (*at top of foreign bill*) **e. for £ . . .,** bon pour livres . . .; (*b*) **bill of e.,** effet *m*, traite *f*, lettre *f* de change; **foreign e.,** effet étranger; effet, devise *f*, traite, sur l'étranger; lettre de change à l'extérieur; devise étrangère; **short e.,** papier court; **first of e.,** première *f* de change; primata *m* de change; **second of e.,** seconde *f* de change; copie *f* de change; (*c*) *coll.* (*U.S: usu.* **exchanges**) devises, effets de commerce, lettres de change, traites. **3.** (*a*) bourse *f* (des valeurs); **Commodities E.,** (*in London*) **the Royal E.,** Bourse de commerce; **Corn E.,** bourse des céréales; halle *f* aux blés; (*b*) *U.S: Mil:* **post e.,** coopérative *f* militaire, économat *m* de l'armée; **e. officer,** officier gestionnaire d'une coopérative militaire, d'un économat de l'armée. **4.** *Tp:* (**telephone**) **e.,** central *m* téléphonique; **e. office,** bureau central (téléphonique), bureau (du téléphone); **local e. area** = réseau urbain; **e. flap,** volet *m* de standard.

exchange². **1.** *v.tr.* échanger (des marchandises, des coups, des paroles, des prisonniers); troquer (des denrées, etc.); **to e. sth. for sth.,** échanger, troquer, qch. pour, contre, qch., faire un échange de qch. pour, contre, qch.; **we e. (postage) stamps,** nous échangeons des timbres; **to e. glances,** échanger un regard; se consulter de l'œil; **they had exchanged hats,** ils avaient fait un échange de chapeaux; *Chess:* **to e. bishops,** faire un échange de fous; (*chess, draughts*) **to e. pawns, men,** pionner; *Fenc:* **exchanged hit,** coup fourré; *Adm:* **to e. (posts) with s.o.,** permuter avec qn. **2.** *v.i.* (*of coins*) s'échanger (**for,** contre).

exchangeability [ekstʃeindʒə'biliti], *s.* échangeabilité *f*.

exchangeable [eks'tʃeindʒəbl], *a.* **1.** échangeable (**for,** pour, contre). **2. e. value,** valeur *f* d'échange.

exchanger [eks'tʃeindʒər], *s.* **1.** échangeur, -euse; *Fin:* échangiste *m*. **2.** permutant, -ante (d'un poste). **3.** *Tchn:* **heat e.,** échangeur de température, thermique.

exchanging [eks'tʃeindʒiŋ], *s.* échange *m* (de marchandises, de prisonniers); troc *m* (de denrées); permutation *f* (de fonctionnaires).

exchequer [eks'tʃekər], *s.* **1.** *Jur: A:* **the Court of E.,** la Cour de l'Échiquier (une des trois Cours de droit commun). **2.** *Adm:* **the E.,** (i) la trésorerie, le fisc; (ii) le Trésor public; (iii) = le Ministère des Finances; **the Chancellor of the E.** = le Ministre des Finances; **e. bill,** bon *m* du trésor. **3.** *F:* budget *m*, finances *fpl* (d'un particulier); **the low, depleted, state of my e.,** l'appauvrissement *m* de mes finances; **my e. is empty,** je ne suis pas en fonds.

excipient [ek'sipiənt], *s. Pharm:* excipient *m*.

excisable [ek'saizəbl], *a. Adm:* imposable; (*of goods*) soumis aux droits de régie; (*of pers.*) sujet aux droits de régie.

excise¹ ['eksaiz], *s. Adm:* **1.** contributions indirectes; *Belg:* accise *f*. **2.** (*a*) service *m* des contributions indirectes; la régie; **Customs and E.,** la Régie; **E. Officer,** (i) receveur *m* des contributions indirectes; (ii) employé *m* de la régie; **e. duties,** droits *m* de régie; **e. tax,** impôt indirect; *Cust:* **e. bond,** acquit-à-caution *m*; passe-debout *m inv*; (*b*) *U.S:* **e. law,** loi *f* qui réglemente la vente des boissons alcooliques.

excise² ['eksaiz], *v.tr.* imposer (qn, une denrée, etc.); frapper (qch.) d'un droit de régie; soumettre (qn) à un droit de régie.

excise³ [ek'saiz], *v.tr.* **1.** (*a*) *Surg:* exciser, couper (un organe); (*b*) couper, retrancher (un passage d'un livre). **2.** encocher, entailler, inciser.

excised [ek'saizd], *a. Nat.Hist:* encoché, entaillé.

exciseman, *pl.* **-men** ['eksaizmən], *s.m.* employé de l'excise, de la régie.

excision [ek'siʒ(ə)n], *s.* **1.** excision *f*, coupure *f*; *Surg:* excision, abscission *f*, ablation *f*. **2.** incision *f*, entaille *f*, encoche *f*.

excitability [eksaitə'biliti], *s.* **1.** émotivité *f*. **2.** *El: Physiol:* excitabilité *f*.

excitable [ek'saitəbl], *a.* **1.** (*of pers., temperament*) émotionnable, surexcitable, prompt à s'émouvoir, à s'énerver; émotif; (*of population*) mobile; **to be terribly e.,** être vif comme la poudre. **2.** *El: Physiol:* excitable.

excitant ['eksitənt, ek'saitənt], *a. & s. Med:* (*a*) excitant (*m*), stimulant (*m*); (*b*) **coffee is an e.,** le café est agitant.

excitation [eksi'teiʃ(ə)n], *s.* (*a*) *Physiol:* excitation *f*; (*b*) *El:* excitation, amorçage *m* (d'une dynamo, etc.); **poor e.,** défaut *m* d'amorçage; **pole e.,** création *f* de pôles; (*c*) *Atom.Ph:* excitation.

excite [ek'sait], *v.tr.* **1.** (*a*) provoquer, exciter, soulever, faire naître (une révolte, un sentiment); inspirer, allumer (un sentiment); susciter (de l'intérêt); **to e. s.o.'s curiosity,** piquer, chatouiller, la curiosité de qn; *F:* aguicher qn; **his fortune excites envy,** sa fortune attire l'envie; **to e. a customer's interest,** intéresser un client; (*b*) *Physiol:* exciter, stimuler (un nerf); (*c*) *El:* exciter, amorcer (une dynamo, etc.); (*d*) *Phot. A:* sensibiliser (une plaque). **2.** (*a*) exciter, animer, aiguiser, enflammer (un sentiment, une passion); stimuler (l'appétit, l'émulation); **to e. interest to the highest pitch,** porter l'intérêt à son comble; **to e. s.o. to (do) sth.,** exciter, pousser, qn à (faire) qch.; (*b*) agiter, énerver, animer, émouvoir, troubler, surexciter, échauffer (qn); mettre (qn) en émoi; **to e. the mob,** passionner la foule; **easily excited,** surexcitable, émotionnable, prompt à s'émouvoir.

excited [ek'saitid], *a.* **1.** *El: Physiol:* excité; **e. state,** (i) *Atom.Ph:* état excité, d'excitation; (ii) *El:* état d'amorçage. **2.** (*of pers.*) (i) ému, troublé; (ii) impatient, fiévreux; (iii) agité, énervé, surexcité; **e. children,** enfants agités, excités; **e. voice,** voix (i) émue, (ii) animée; **e. crowd,** foule (i) surexcitée, en émoi, (ii) impatiente; **to get e.,** se monter la tête, perdre la tête, s'émotionner, s'énerver, s'animer; (*esp. with drink*) s'allumer; **don't get e.!** ne vous énervez pas! du calme! **he gets e. over nothing,** il s'emballe pour un rien; **to get e. over one's holidays,** être fiévreux, impatient, en songeant à ses vacances; **to be wildly e.,** être dans tous ses états.

excitedly [ek'saitidli], *adv.* d'une manière agitée; avec agitation.

excitement [ek'saitmənt], *s.* **1.** *Physiol:* surexcitation *f* (d'un organe). **2.** agitation *f*, vive émotion, animation *f*, trouble *m*, surexcitation; **the thirst for e.,** la soif des sensations fortes; **the e. of suspense,** la fièvre de l'attente; **the e. of departure,** l'émoi *m* du départ; **the pleasant excitements of a trip abroad,** les plaisirs excitants d'un voyage à l'étranger; **to cause great e.,** faire (grande) sensation; **to be in a state of e.,** être dans tous ses états; être très énervé; *F:* **what's all the e. about?** qu'est-ce qui se passe donc?

exciter [ek'saitər], *s.* **1.** (*pers.*) excitateur, -trice, instigateur, -trice, (de révolte, etc.). **2.** *El:* (*a*) **static, dynamic, e.,** excitateur *m*; (*b*) (dynamo) excitatrice *f*; **e. coil,** bobine inductrice; bobine de champ, d'inducteur; (*c*) *Elcs:* (i) étage *m* pilote; (ii) antenne active; *W.Tel:* **e. tube,** lampe excitatrice; *Cin:* **e. lamp,** lampe phonique, lampe d'excitation. **3.** *Med:* excitant *m*, stimulant *m*.

exciting [ek'saitiŋ], *a.* **1.** (*of subject, story, etc.*) passionnant, animant; captivant; (*of situation, scene*) sensationnel, émouvant, angoissant; **an e. novel,** un roman palpitant d'intérêt; un roman plein de suspense; *Sp:* **e. finish,** arrivée palpitante; **an e. game,** une partie mouvementée. **2.** (*a*) *Med:* **e. cause,** cause excitatrice; (*b*) *El:* **e. dynamo,** dynamo *f* d'excitation; (dynamo) excitatrice *f*; **e. battery,** batterie *f* d'excitation; **e. coil,** bobine inductrice; bobine de champ, d'inducteur; **e. voltage,** tension *f* d'excitation; **e. converter, e. transformer,** transformateur *m* d'excitation; **e. current,** courant *m* d'excitation; **e. rheostat,** rhéostat *m* d'excitation.

excitingly [ek'saitiŋli], *adv.* d'une manière sensationnelle, pleine d'intérêt.

excitomotor [ek'saitou'moutər], **excitomotory** [ek'saitou'moutəri], *a. Physiol:* excito-moteur, -trice.

exciton ['eksitɔn], *s. Elcs:* exciton *m*, molécule excitée.

excitosecretory [ek'saitousi'kri:təri], *a. Physiol:* excito-sécrétoire.

excitron ['eksitrɔn], *s. Elcs:* excitron *m*.

exclaim [eks'kleim]. **1.** *v.i.* s'écrier, s'exclamer; (*in indignation*) se récrier. **2.** *v.tr.* **"leave me alone," he exclaimed,** "laissez-moi," s'écria-t-il.

exclamation [eksklə'meiʃ(ə)n], *s.* exclamation *f*; **e. mark,** *U.S:* **e. point, note of e.,** point *m* d'exclamation.

exclamative [eks'klæmətiv], **exclamatory** [eks'klæmət(ə)ri], *a.* exclamatif.

exclamatively [eks'klæmətivli], **exclamatorily** [eks'klæmətrili], *adv.* exclamativement.

exclave ['ekskle:iv], *s.* partie détachée (d'un État).

exclosure [eks'klouʒjər], *s.* terrain *m* protégé par une clôture.

exclude [eks'klu:d], *v.tr.* (*a*) exclure (**from,** de); **to e. the sun, the air,** empêcher le soleil, l'air, d'entrer; **aliens are excluded from these posts,** les étrangers ne sont pas admis à ces emplois; **words excluded from polite conversation,** expressions proscrites de la conversation polie; **to e. s.o. from a society,** (i) bannir qn d'une société; (ii) refuser à qn l'entrée d'une société; *Ecc:* **to e. s.o. from the sacraments,** refuser les sacrements à qn; **excluding . . .,** à l'exclusion de . . .; (*b*) écarter (le doute, les soupçons); **this excludes all possibility of doubt,** le doute n'est plus permis, admis.

excluding [eks'klu:diŋ], *s.* exclusion *f*.

exclusion [eks'klu:ʒ(ə)n], *s.* **1.** exclusion *f* (**from,** de); **to the e. of . . .,** à l'exclusion de . . .; *Ph:* **e. principle,** principe *m* d'exclusion. **2.** refus *m* d'admission (**from,** à).

exclusive [eks'klu:siv], *a.* **1.** exclusif; **to have an e. voice in the election of the pope,** avoir voix exclusive dans l'élection du pape; **two qualities that are mutually e.,** deux qualités *f* qui s'excluent. **2.** (*a*) (droit, etc.) exclusif; **to have the e. rights of, e. rights in, a production,** avoir l'exclusivité *f* d'une production; *Journ:* **e. interview,** interview accordé exclusivement à un journal; *Com:* **e. models,** modèles exclusifs; *Cin:* **e. film,** film *m* en exclusivité; (*b*) seul, unique; **the e. work of . . .,** l'œuvre seule de . . .; **it has been his e. occupation for ten years,** ç'a été son occupation unique pendant dix ans; (*c*) élégant, à la mode; (*of dress, etc.*) (robe *f*, etc.) haute couture; (*d*) **e. profession,** profession très fermée; **very e. club, society,** cercle, monde, très fermé. **3.** *adv.* (*a*) exclusivement; **chapters one to twenty e.,** chapitres un à vingt exclusivement; (*b*) sans compter les extras; **rent (of a flat, etc.), £1000 a year e.,** loyer (d'un appartement, etc.) £1000 par an, contributions et charges en plus; (*c*) **e. of wrappings,** sans compter, non compris, l'emballage; **price of dinner e. of wine,** prix *m* du dîner, vin non compris. **4.** *s.* (*a*) personne exclusive; (*b*) *Journ:* article *m* en exclusivité; (*c*) *Com:* exclusivité *f*.

exclusively [eks'klu:sivli], *adv.* exclusivement; **sold e. in Great Britain by the X company,** agents exclusifs pour la Grande-Bretagne: Société X.

exclusiveness [eks'klu:sivnis], *s.* **1.** nature exclusive, caractère exclusif (de qch.). **2.** exclusivisme *m*.

exclusivism [eks'klu:sivizm], *s.* exclusivisme *m*.

exclusivist [eks'klu:sivist], *s.* exclusiviste *mf*.

excogitate [eks'kɔdʒiteit], *v.tr. Lit:* (*a*) imaginer, combiner (laborieusement) (un projet, etc.); (*b*) considérer, approfondir (une question).

excogitation [ekskɔdʒi'teiʃ(ə)n], *s. Lit:* excogitation *f*, résolution *f* (d'un problème, etc.); (longue) réflexion.

excommunicate[1] [ekskə'mju:nikət], *a. & s.* excommunié, -ée.

excommunicate[2] [ekskə'mju:nikeit], *v.tr.* excommunier.

excommunicating [ekskə'mju:nikeitiŋ], *s.* excommunication *f*.

excommunication [ekskəmju:ni'keiʃ(ə)n], *s.* excommunication *f*.

excommunicative [ekskə'mju:nikətiv], **excommunicatory** [ekskə'mju:nikətri], *a.* (décret, sentence) d'excommunication.

excoriate [eks'kɔ:rieit], *v.tr.* excorier, écorcher (la peau, le doigt, etc.).

excoriation [ekskɔ:ri'eiʃ(ə)n], *s.* excoriation *f*, écorchure *f*.

excrement ['ekskrimənt], *s.* excrément *m*.

excremental [ekskri'mentl], *a.* excrémentiel.

excrescence [eks'kres(ə)ns], *s.* excroissance *f*; *Bot:* (*round tree trunk*) bourrelet *m*, loupe *f*; **morbid e.,** production *f* morbide; **he considers unemployment as a morbid e. on the capitalist system,** il considère le chômage comme un développement morbide du capitalisme.

excrescent [eks'kres(ə)nt], *a.* **1.** qui forme une excroissance. **2.** superflu, inutile, redondant. **3.** *Ling:* (consonne *f*) épenthétique.

excreta [eks'kri:tə], *s.pl.* excréta *m*, excrétions *f*.

excrete [eks'kri:t], *v.tr.* excréter; (*of plant*) sécréter (un suc, etc.).

excretion [eks'kri:ʃ(ə)n], *s.* excrétion *f*; sécrétion *f* (d'une plante); **difficulties in e.,** troubles *m* excrétoires.

excretive [eks'kri:tiv], **excretory** [eks'kri:təri]. **1.** *a.* excréteur, -trice; excrétoire. **2.** *s.* **excretory,** organe excréteur.

excruciate [eks'kru:ʃieit], *v.tr. Lit:* mettre (qn) au supplice; torturer.

excruciating [eks'kru:ʃieitiŋ], *a.* (*of pain*) atroce, horrible; *F:* **e. music,** musique *f* atroce; *F:* **I find him e.,** je ne puis pas le sentir.

excruciatingly [eks'kru:ʃieitiŋli], *adv.* atrocement, cruellement, affreusement; *F:* **it's e. funny,** c'est à mourir, à crever, de rire; c'est à se tordre; **e. funny story,** histoire tordante, gondolante; **e. boring,** à en mourir d'ennui.

excruciation [ekskru:ʃi'eiʃ(ə)n], *s.* torture *f*, supplice *m*, tourment *m*.

exculpate ['ekskʌlpeit], *v.tr.* disculper, exonérer (**from,** de); justifier (qn).

exculpation [ekskʌl'peiʃ(ə)n], *s.* disculpation *f*, exonération *f* (**from,** de); justification *f* (de qn).

exculpatory [eks'kʌlpətəri], *a.* justificatif; qui disculpe.

excurrent [eks'kʌrənt], *a.* **1.** (sang) qui découle du cœur; (sang) artériel. **2.** (canal, etc.) de sortie. **3.** *Bot:* (*of stem, etc.*) excurrent.

excursion [eks'kə:ʃ(ə)n], *s.* **1.** excursion *f*; voyage *m* d'agrément; sortie *f*; *Aut: Cy: etc:* randonnée *f*; **school e.,** excursion, voyage *m* scolaire; **to make an e.,** faire une excursion; excursionner; *Rail:* **e. train,** (i) (*short distance*) train *m* de plaisir, à prix réduit; (ii) (*long distance*) train d'excursion; **e. ticket,** billet *m* d'excursion **2.** excursion, digression *f* (dans un discours, etc.); **e. into theory,** excursion dans la théorie. **3.** *Mil: A:* sortie *f*. **4.** *Astr:* excursion (d'une planète).

excursionist [eks'kə:ʃənist], *s.* excursionniste *mf*, touriste *mf*.

excursive [eks'kə:siv], *a.* **1.** (*of pers.*) enclin à s'écarter du sujet, aux digressions. **2.** (style) digressif, décousu. **3.** (imagination) vagabonde.

excursively [eks'kə:sivli], *adv.* sans suite; à bâtons rompus.

excursus, *pl.* **-uses** [eks'kə:səs, -əsiz], *s.* **1.** excursus *m*; dissertation *f* en forme de digression (ajoutée en appendice à l'ouvrage). **2.** digression *f*.

excurved [eks'kə:vd], *a.* (*of antennae, etc.*) excurvé.

excusable [eks'kju:zəbl], *a.* (erreur, etc.) excusable, pardonnable; **it's quite e. that you should have forgotten,** je comprends très bien que vous ayez oublié.

excusableness [eks'kju:zəblnis], **excusability** [ekskju:zə'biliti], *s.* excusabilité *f*.

excusably [eks'kju:zəbli], *adv.* excusablement.

excusal [eks'kju:z(ə)l], *s.* exemption *f* (des impôts locaux).

excuse[1] [eks'kju:s], *s.* **1.** excuse *f*; **in e. of his bad temper,** comme excuse de, pour excuser, sa mauvaise humeur; **there is no e. for him, for his behaviour,** il, sa conduite, est inexcusable; **that is no e. for (his, your) not writing,** cela ne l'excuse pas, ne t'excuse pas, de ne pas avoir écrit; **there was no e. for (doing) that,** il n'y avait aucun prétexte à (faire) cela; **ignorance of the law is no e.,** nul n'est censé ignorer la loi. **2.** (*a*) excuse, prétexte *m*; **poor, lame, e.,** mauvaise, faible, excuse; faux-fuyant *m, pl.* faux-fuyants; **to make excuses,** s'excuser; **to look for an e.,** (i) chercher des excuses; (ii) (*in order not to do sth.*) chercher des faux-fuyants, une échappatoire; **to find an e. for sth.,** trouver une excuse à qch.; **by way of e. he alleged that . . .,** en guise d'excuse il a prétendu que . . .; **to make sth. one's e.,** s'excuser sur qch.; prendre qch. comme excuse; donner qch. pour excuse; prétexter qch.; **to offer a reasonable e.,** donner, fournir, une excuse valable; **we have no valid e. for not accepting,** nous n'avons pas d'excuse valable pour ne pas accepter; (*b*) **a poor e. for a letter,** un semblant de lettre; **a poor e. for a car,** un vieux tacot délabré.

excuse[2] [eks'kju:z], *v.tr.* **1.** (*a*) excuser, pardonner; **to e. s.o.'s laziness, to e. s.o. for his laziness, to e. s.o. his laziness, to e. s.o.'s being lazy,** excuser la paresse de qn; **e. my being late,** excusez-moi d'être en retard; *F:* **e. me yawning,** je vous demande pardon, pardonnez-moi, si je bâille; **to e. oneself on the ground that . . .,** s'excuser en donnant pour raison que . . .; alléguer comme excuse que . . .; **to e. the absence of s.o.,** excuser l'absence de qn; excuser qn; **e. me for hurrying away, if I hurry away,** pardonnez-moi si je me sauve; **he may be excused for laughing,** il est excusable d'avoir ri; **if you will e. the expression,** si vous voulez me passer, me pardonner, l'expression; **e. me!** (i) excusez-moi! (ii) pardon! je vous demande pardon! pardonnez-moi! **e. my saying so,** pardonnez-moi ma hardiesse; (*expressing contradiction*) **e. me, it was yesterday that . . .,** pardon, c'était hier que . . .; (*b*) **to e. s.o. from doing sth.,** excuser, exempter, dispenser, qn de faire qch.; **to e. s.o. a fine,** faire remise, faire grâce, à qn d'une amende; **to e. s.o. from attendance,** excuser qn; **e. me from coming with you,** permettez-moi de ne pas vous accompagner; *F:* **e. me getting up,** pardonnez-moi si je ne me lève pas; **e.-me dance,** danse *f* où on change de partenaire; *Mil: Navy:* **to be excused a fatigue,** être exempté d'une corvée; **on the excused list, excused from duty,** exempt de service; *Sch:* **may I be excused?** est-ce que je peux sortir? **2. his youth excuses him,** sa jeunesse l'excuse, peut lui servir d'excuse.

exeat ['eksiæt], *s.* **1.** *Ecc:* exeat *m*. **2.** *Sch:* billet *m* de sortie, permission *f* de sortir.

execrable ['eksikrəbl], *a.* exécrable, abominable, détestable.

execrably ['eksikrəbli], *adv.* exécrablement, abominablement.

execrate ['eksikreit], *v.tr.* **1.** exécrer, détester. **2.** maudire; anathématiser.

execration [eksi'kreiʃ(ə)n], *s.* exécration *f*. **1.** détestation *f* (**of,** de). **2.** malédiction *f*; **to hold s.o. up to public e.,** vouer qn à la malédiction publique.

execratory ['eksikreitəri], *a.* (discours *m*, etc.) exécratoire.

executable ['eksikju:təbl], *a.* exécutable.

executant [eg'zekjutənt], *s. Mus:* exécutant, -ante, *esp.* exécutant(e) accompli(e).

execute ['eksikju:t], *v.tr.* **1.** (*a*) exécuter (un travail); mettre à exécution (un projet); s'acquitter (d'une tâche); accomplir (une opération); donner suite à, exécuter (un ordre); *Fin:* effectuer (une transfert); *Jur:* **to e. a judgment,** exécuter un jugement; **to e. a deed,** souscrire, signer, un acte; **to e. a will,** exécuter un testament; (*b*) *Mus:* exécuter, jouer (un morceau). **2.** exécuter (un criminel); **the executed criminals are buried at . . .,** on enterre les suppliciés à . . ..

executer ['eksikju:tər], *s.* = EXECUTOR 1.

execution [eksi'kju:ʃ(ə)n], *s.* **1.** (*a*) exécution *f* (d'un projet, d'un contrat, d'un ordre); accomplissement *m* (d'un dessein, etc.); **to put, carry, a plan into e.,** mettre un projet à exécution; **the order was not carried into full e.,** l'ordre n'a pas été complètement exécuté; **in the e. of one's duty,** dans l'exercice de ses fonctions; (*b*) *Jur:* souscription *f*, validation *f* (d'un acte, etc.); **e. of a will,** exécution d'un testament; (*c*) (i) exécution (d'un morceau de musique); (ii) jeu *m* (d'un musicien); (*of picture, etc.*) **elegant e.,** facture élégante. **2.** *Jur:* saisie-exécution *f*, *pl.* saisies-exécutions; **e. by sale of debtor's chattels,** saisie *f* des meubles d'un débiteur; **to put in an e. and levy (on s.o.'s goods),** faire, pratiquer, une saisie, faire une exécution (sur les biens de qn); **writ of e.,** (titre) exécutoire *m*; **to issue e. for the amount of the costs,** délivrer un exécutoire pour le montant des dépens. **3.** (*of artillery*) **to do e.,** causer des ravages; **every shot did e.,** tous les coups portaient; **to do great e. among the partridges,** massacrer les perdrix. **4.** (*a*) exécution (d'un criminel); exécution capitale; (*b*) **military e.,** exécution militaire; dévastation punitive (d'une ville, etc.).

executioner [eksi'kju:ʃənər], *s.* bourreau *m*; exécuteur *m* des hautes œuvres.

executive [eg'zekjutiv]. **1.** *a.* (*a*) exécutif; **the Commission has e. powers,** la Commission a des pouvoirs exécutifs; les décisions *f* de la Commission sont exécutoires; **e. secretary,** secrétaire *mf* de direction; *Furn:* **e. suite,** mobilier du directeur; *Cost:* **e. suit,** complet de ville; *Cin:* **e. producer,** producteur délégué; *U.S:* **e. order,** décret-loi *m, pl.* décrets-lois; *Mil: etc:* **e. duties,** service *m* de détail; *Mil:* **e. word of command,** commandement *m* d'exécution; (*b*) *Pol: etc: U.S:* **e. session,** séance *f* à huis clos. **2.** *s.* (*a*) pouvoir exécutif, exécutif *m* (d'un gouvernement); direction *f*; (*b*) agents exécutifs; (*c*) agent exécutif; directeur, -trice; cadre *m*; chef *m* de service; **sales e.,** directeur commercial; *Adm:* **e. (officer)** = rédacteur, -trice (de ministère).

executor, *s.* **1.** [ˈeksikju:tər], exécuteur *m* (d'un ordre, d'un plan, etc.). **2.** [egˈzekjutər], *Jur:* exécuteur, -trice, testamentaire (d'un testateur); ayant cause *m, pl.* ayants cause; **literary e.,** exécuteur littéraire.

executory [ekˈsekjutəri, egˈz-], *a. Jur:* **1.** (*a*) (jugement *m*, etc.) exécutoire; (loi, etc.) en vigueur; **e. formula,** formule *f* exécutoire; (*b*) **e. details,** détails *m* d'exécution; (*c*) = EXECUTIVE 1 (*a*). **2.** non encore exécuté; **e. trust,** trust *m* sous forme de simples recommandations (en attendant la rédaction de l'acte définitif).

executrix, *pl.* **-trices** [egˈzekjutriks, -trisi:z], *s.f. Jur:* exécutrice testamentaire.

exedra, *pl.* **-ae** [ˈeksidrə, ekˈsi:dri:], *s. Arch:* exèdre *f.*

exegesis [eksiˈdʒi:sis], *s.* exégèse *f.*

exegete [ˈeksidʒi:t], *s.* exégète *m.*

exegetic(al) [eksiˈdʒetik(əl)]. **1.** *a.* exégétique. **2.** *s.pl.* **exegetics,** théologie *f* exégétique.

exegetist [eksiˈdʒi:tist], *s.* exégète *m.*

exemplar [egˈzemplər], *s. Lit:* (*a*) exemplaire *m*; archétype *m*; (*b*) exemple *m.*

exemplarily [egˈzemplərili], *adv.* exemplairement, d'une manière exemplaire.

exemplariness [egˈzemplərinis], *Lit:* **exemplarity** [egzemˈplæriti], *s.* qualité *f* exemplaire, *Lit:* exemplarité *f.*

exemplary [egˈzempləri], *a.* exemplaire. **1. e. life,** conduite *f* exemplaire; **an e. husband,** un époux modèle. **2.** (*of punishment*) infligé pour l'exemple; *Jur:* **e. damages,** dommages-intérêts *m* exemplaires. **3.** qui fournit un exemple de qch.; typique.

exemplification [egzemplifiˈkeiʃ(ə)n], *s.* **1.** démonstration *f*, explication *f*, au moyen d'exemples; exemplification *f.* **2.** exemple *m.* **3.** *Jur:* ampliation *f*, copie *f* authentique (d'un acte).

exemplify [egˈzemplifai], *v.tr.* **1.** expliquer, démontrer, par des exemples; exemplifier; **to e. a rule,** donner un exemple d'une règle. **2.** servir d'exemple à (une règle, etc.). **3.** *Jur: A:* faire une ampliation (d'un acte); **exemplified copy,** copie *f* authentique; copie conforme.

exempt[1] [egˈzem(p)t]. **1.** *a.* exempt, dispensé, exempte (**from,** de); **e. from taxation,** franc, *f.* franche, d'impôts; *Mil:* **to be e. from fatigues,** être dispensé des corvées. **2.** *s.* exempté, -ée.

exempt[2], *v.tr.* **to e. s.o. (from sth.),** exempter, dispenser, qn (d'un impôt, du service militaire); exonérer qn (d'un impôt); affranchir qn (d'une autorité); **to e. s.o. from doing sth.,** exempter qn de faire qch.; *Mil:* **conscript provisionally exempted,** conscrit *m* en sursis; sursitaire *m*; **exempted from military service,** dispensé du service militaire.

exemption [egˈzem(p)ʃ(ə)n], *s.* **e. from sth.,** exemption *f*, dispense *f* (d'un impôt, du service militaire); exonération *f* (d'un impôt); affranchissement *m* (d'une autorité).

exencephalia [eksenseˈfeiliə], *s. Ter:* exencéphalie *f.*

exencephalic [eksenseˈfælik], **exencephalous** [eksenˈsefələs], *a. Ter:* exencéphale.

exencephalus [eksenˈsefələs], *s. Ter:* exencéphale *m.*

exenteration [eksentəˈreiʃ(ə)n], *s. Surg:* exentération *f.*

exequatur [eksiˈkweitər], *s. Jur:* exequatur *m.*

exequies [ˈeksikwiz], *s.pl. Lit:* convoi *m* funèbre; obsèques *fpl*; enterrement *m.*

exercisable [ˈeksəsaizəbl], *a.* (droit) dont on peut user; (autorité) que l'on peut exercer.

exercise[1] [ˈeksəsaiz], *s.* **1.** exercice *m* (d'une faculté, d'un privilège, de ses fonctions); **the e. of this right created some surprise,** on le, les, vit avec surprise se prévaloir de ce droit; **in the e. of one's duties,** dans l'exercice de ses fonctions; **free e. of one's religion,** libre pratique *f* de sa religion; *St.Exch:* **e. of an option,** levée *f* d'une prime. **2.** (*a*) **mental e.,** exercice de l'esprit; **outdoor e.,** exercice au grand air; **to take e.,** prendre de l'exercice; se donner du mouvement; **e. yard,** préau *m* (de prison); **lack of e.,** sédentarité *f*; (*b*) *Mil: Navy:* **tactical exercises,** évolutions *f* tactiques; **outdoor, field, e.,** exercice sur le terrain; **indoor e.,** exercice en salle; (*c*) **school e.,** exercice scolaire; **written e.,** exercice écrit; devoir *m*; **book of (grammatical, etc.) exercises,** exercices; (*notebook*) **e. book,** cahier *m*; **piano exercises,** exercices pour piano; *Gym:* **physical exercises,** exercices physiques; **limbering-up exercises,** exercices d'assouplissement; **breathing exercises,** gymnastique *f* respiratoire; **morning exercises,** gymnastique du matin; (*d*) **religious, devotional, exercises,** pratiques religieuses; dévotions; (*e*) *pl. U.S:* cérémonies *f*, célébrations *f* (scolaires, etc.).

exercise[2], *v.tr.* **1.** exercer (un droit, une influence, ses fonctions); exercer, pratiquer (un métier); **to e. a right,** user d'un droit; **to e. an influence (up)on s.o.,** agir sur qn; **to e. authority over s.o.,** exercer une autorité sur qn; **to e. one's will, one's authority,** faire acte de volonté, d'autorité; **to e. care in doing sth.,** apporter du soin à faire qch.; *Fin:* **to e. an option,** lever une prime, une option, l'option. **2.** (*a*) exercer (le corps, l'esprit); **to e. oneself,** prendre de l'exercice; **to e. oneself by doing sth.,** s'exercer, s'entraîner, à faire qch.; **to e. troops,** faire faire l'exercice à des troupes; **to e. a horse,** (i) exercer, (ii) promener, un cheval; **to e. one's wits in order to do sth., in order to please s.o.,** s'ingénier à faire qch., pour faire plaisir à qn; (*b*) *v.i.* (i) *A:* prendre de l'exercice; (ii) s'entraîner; *Mil:* faire l'exercice. **3.** tourmenter, tracasser; jeter (qn) dans la perplexité; **to e. s.o.'s patience,** mettre à l'épreuve la patience de qn; **the problem that is exercising our minds,** le problème qui nous préoccupe.

exerciser [ˈeksəsaizər], *s.* **1.** (*pers.*) exerçant *m* (d'un droit, etc.). **2.** (*device*) *Gym:* exerciseur *m.*

exercising [ˈeksəsaiziŋ], *s.* exercice *m* (d'un droit, d'une fonction, des membres); entraînement *m* (des troupes, etc.).

exercitant [ekˈsə:sitənt], *s. Ecc:* exercitant, -ante.

exercitation [egzə:siˈteiʃ(ə)n], *s.* **1.** exercice *m* (d'une faculté, etc.). **2.** *Lit:* dissertation *f* critique; exercice oratoire.

exeresis [ekˈserəsis], *s. Surg:* exérèse *f.*

exergue [egˈzə:g], *s. Num:* exergue *m.*

exert [egˈzə:t], *v.tr.* **1.** employer, faire usage de (la force); mettre en œuvre (la force, son talent); déployer (son talent); exercer (une influence, une pression); **the pressure exerted on . . .,** la pression qui s'exerce sur . . .. **2. to e. oneself,** se remuer, s'employer; se donner du mal; se donner du mouvement; **to e. oneself to do sth.,** s'efforcer de faire qch.; faire des efforts, travailler, pour faire qch.; **to e. oneself to the utmost to do sth.,** se dépenser, se mettre en quatre, pour faire qch.

exerting [egˈzə:tiŋ], *s.* emploi *m*, exercice *m*, usage *m* (de la force, de l'autorité).

exertion [egˈzə:ʃ(ə)n], *s.* **1.** usage *m*, emploi *m* (de la force, d'une faculté, d'un talent); **by a skilful e. of a minimum of strength . . .,** par l'emploi judicieux d'un minimum de force . . .. **2.** effort *m*, efforts; **to attain one's end without great e.,** arriver à ses fins sans grand effort; **the e. of travelling,** la fatigue d'un voyage; *A:* **I shall use every e. to help you,** je vais faire tous mes efforts, tout mon possible, pour vous aider.

exes [ˈeksiz], *s.pl. F:* (*abbr. of* **expenses**) dépenses *f*, frais *m.*

exeunt [ˈeksiənt]. *Lt.v.i. Th:* (*stage directions*) (un tel et un tel) sortent, exeunt (un tel et un tel); **exeunt omnes,** ils sortent tous; tous sortent; exeunt omnes.

exfoliate [eksˈfoulieit]. *Med: Bot: etc:* **1.** *v.tr.* exfolier (un os, une plante, une roche, etc.); déliter (une pierre). **2.** *v.i.* (*of bone, of rock, etc.*) s'exfolier.

exfoliation [eksfouliˈeiʃ(ə)n], *s.* **1.** *Med: Bot: Geol:* exfoliation *f*; desquamation *f* (en écailles); *Metalw:* affouillement *m* (du métal). **2.** squame *f* (d'un os).

exfoliative [eksˈfouliətiv], *a.* exfoliatif.

ex gratia [eksˈgrɑ:tiə, -ˈgreiʃiə]. **1.** *a.* **ex g. payment,** paiement *m* à titre de faveur. **2.** *adv.* **he wasn't eligible for a pension, but the firm gave him a lump sum ex. g.,** il n'avait pas droit à une retraite, mais la maison lui a donné un capital à titre de faveur.

exhalation [eks(h)əˈleiʃ(ə)n], *s.* **1.** (*a*) exhalation *f* (de vapeurs, d'odeurs); (*b*) expiration *f* (du souffle). **2.** effluve *m*, exhalaison *f.*

exhale [eksˈheil]. **1.** *v.tr.* (*a*) exhaler, émettre (un gaz, des vapeurs, des odeurs); **the flowers exhaled their fragrance,** les fleurs *f* répandaient leurs parfums; (*b*) exhaler (son dernier souffle, etc.). **2.** *v.i.* (*a*) (*of vapour, etc.*) s'exhaler; (*b*) expirer (l'air des poumons).

exhaling [eksˈheiliŋ], *s.* exhalation *f.*

exhaust[1] [egˈzɔ:st], *s.* **1.** *I.C.E: Mch: etc:* (*a*) (i) échappement *m*, évacuation *f* (de la vapeur, des gaz); **atmospheric e.,** échappement à l'air libre; **e. cut-out,** clapet *m* d'échappement (libre); **e. fumes,** gaz *m* d'échappement; **e. heat,** chaleur *f* d'échappement; **e. manifold,** collecteur *m* d'échappement; (*of radial engine*) **e. (collector) ring,** collecteur annulaire d'échappement; **e. pipe,** *I.C.E:* (tuyau *m* d')échappement; *Mch:* tuyau d'évacuation, de refoulement, de décharge; déchargeoir *m*; **e. port,** orifice *m* d'échappement; **e. valve,** soupape *f* d'échappement; **e. valve box, chest,** chapelle *f* de soupape d'échappement; **e. valve lifter,** décompresseur *m*; **e. valve spring, tappet,** ressort *m*, poussoir *m*, de soupape d'échappement; **e. stroke,** course *f* d'échappement, d'évacuation; **e. pressure,** pression *f* de l'échappement; **e. lag, lead,** retard *m*, avance *f*, à l'échappement; *Mch:* **e. lap,** recouvrement *m* de l'échappement, du tiroir; **e. waste gate,** volet *m* d'évacuation; (ii) (*of jet engine*) **e. system,** circuit *m* d'échappement; **e. nozzle,** tuyère *f* d'échappement; **fixed-area, variable-area, e. nozzle,** tuyère (d'échappement) à section invariable, variable; **e. cone,** cône *m* de fuite; **e. reheater,** réchauffeur *m* des gaz d'échappement, dispositif *m* de postcombustion; **e. augmentor,** augmentateur *m* de poussée; **e. stator blade,** aubage *m* fixe guide d'échappement; (*b*) gaz, etc., d'échappement. **2.** (*a*) (i) production *f* du vide (dans un cylindre, etc.); (ii) pompage *m* à vide, vidage *m* (des tubes électroniques); (*b*) **dust e.,** aspiration *f* des poussières; **e. draft,** tirage *m* par aspiration. **3.** (*a*) aspirateur *m*; **e. fan, blower,** ventilateur (aspirant), ventilateur négatif; (*b*) *I.C.E:* (tuyau d')échappement.

exhaust[2]. **1.** *v.tr.* (*a*) aspirer (l'air, un gaz, l'eau, la poussière); (*b*) épuiser (les ressources, les réserves, d'un pays; les forces de qn; un sujet de conversation); tarir (une source, ses ressources); **to have exhausted one's mandate,** être arrivé au terme de son mandat; (*c*) vider (**sth. of sth.,** qch. de qch.); **to e. a bulb, a tube (of air),** faire le vide dans une ampoule, dans un tube; (*d*) *I.C.E:* **to e. the burned gases,** balayer, refouler, expulser, les gaz brûlés; (*e*) épuiser, éreinter, exténuer (qn); **to e. oneself in useless efforts,** se consumer en efforts inutiles. **2.** *v.i. Mch: I.C.E:* (*of steam, etc.*) s'échapper (**into,** dans).

exhausted [egˈzɔ:stid], *a.* **1.** (*of bulb, etc.*) vide d'air. **2.** (*a*) épuisé; **e. land,** terre usée, fatiguée, effritée; (*b*) (*of pers., animal*) épuisé, exténué, rendu (de fatigue); recru de fatigue; *F:* éreinté, fourbu; à bout de forces; **I'm e.,** je n'en peux plus.

exhauster [egˈzɔ:stər], *s.* aspirateur *m*; **gas e.,** extracteur *m*, exhausteur *m*, de gaz; **brake e.,** pompe *f* à vide (pour le freinage).

exhaustible [egˈzɔ:stəbl], *a.* épuisable.

exhausting[1] [egˈzɔ:stiŋ], *a.* (effort, travail, climat) épuisant; *F:* (travail) éreintant.

exhausting[2], *s.* **1.** aspiration *f* (d'air, de gaz); épuisement *m* (d'une galerie de mine); **e. pipe,** tuyau *m* d'épuisement; **e. power of a chimney,** tirage *m* d'une cheminée. **2.** épuisement (de ressources, de forces, du sol).

exhaustion [egˈzɔ:stʃ(ə)n], *s.* **1.** *Ph:* aspiration *f*, exhaustion *f* (d'un gaz); **to carry e. to the utmost,** pousser le vide à ses dernières limites. **2.** épuisement *m* (du sol, des ressources); **gradual e. of mineral oils,** raréfaction *f* des pétroles bruts. **3. (state of) e.,** épuisement; **to be in a state of complete e.,** être complètement à bout de forces; **I was ready to drop with e.,** je tombais de fatigue, de faiblesse. **4.** *Mth: Log:* éliminations successives (d'hypothèses); **method of exhaustions,** méthode *f* d'exhaustion.

exhaustive [egˈzɔ:stiv], *a.* **1.** qui épuise toutes les hypothèses, toute la question; exhaustif; complet, -ète; **e. inquiry,** enquête approfondie; **to make an e. study of a subject,** traiter un sujet à fond; approfondir un sujet. **2.** *Log: Mth:* **e. method,** méthode *f* d'exhaustion.

exhaustively [egˈzɔ:stivli], *adv.* exhaustivement; **to treat a subject e.,** traiter un sujet à fond; épuiser un sujet; **to study a question e.,** étudier mûrement, longuement, une question; **to question s.o. e.,** interroger qn à fond.

exhedra, *pl.* **-ae** [ˈeksidrə, ikˈsi:drə, -i:], *s. Arch:* exèdre *f.*

exheredate [eksˈherideit], *v.tr. Jur:* exhéréder, déshériter.

exheredation [eksheriˈdeiʃ(ə)n], *s.* exhérédation *f*, déshéritement *m.*

exhibit[1] [egˈzibit], *s.* **1.** *Jur:* pièce *f* à conviction (en procédure criminelle); pièce ou document *m* à l'appui. **2.** objet, animal, etc., exposé (à une exposition, en vitrine); **there are several interesting exhibits,** il y a plusieurs pièces intéressantes; *P.N:* **do not touch the exhibits,** ne pas toucher aux objets exposés. **3.** = EXHIBITING; **e. engineer,** (ingénieur) démonstrateur *m*; **e. prototype,** prototype *m* de démonstration.

exhibit[2], *v.tr.* **1.** exhiber, montrer, faire voir (un objet); faire preuve (de courage, d'ignorance, de mauvaise volonté); *Adm:* **to e. one's passport,** présenter, exhiber, son passeport; **to e. large profits,** faire ressortir de gros bénéfices. **2.** offrir, présenter (qch. à la vue). **3. to e. pictures, etc.,** exposer des tableaux, etc.; *v.i.* **I am not exhibiting this year,** je n'expose pas cette année; **to e. goods in shop windows,** mettre, exposer, des marchandises à l'étalage, en vitrine; **to e. performing animals,** exhiber des animaux savants. **4.** *Jur:* (*a*) exhiber, produire (des pièces à l'appui); (*b*) soumettre (une requête); intenter (une action). **5.** *Med: A:* administrer (un médicament).

exhibiting [egˈzibitiŋ], *s.* exposition *f*, étalage *m* (d'objets, de marchandises); *Jur:* exhibition *f* (de pièces à l'appui).

exhibition [eksi'biʃ(ə)n], *s.* **1.** (*a*) exposition *f*, étalage *m* (de marchandises, etc.); manifestation *f* (d'un talent); *F:* **to make an e. of oneself,** se donner en spectacle; faire spectacle; se conduire d'une façon inepte; (*b*) démonstration *f* (d'un procédé, etc.); (*c*) *Jur:* **e. of documents,** exhibition *f*, production *f*, représentation *f*, des pièces. **2.** (*a*) exposition; **great international e.,** grande exposition internationale; **the Great E.,** l'exposition de Londres de 1851; **Ideal Home E.** = Salon *m* des Arts ménagers; (*b*) *Com:* **e. room,** salon d'exposition (d'automobiles, etc.); (*c*) *Sch: U.S:* séance (musicale, etc.) donnée par les élèves, et à laquelle sont invités les parents; (*d*) *Cin:* présentation *f* (d'un film). **3.** *Sch:* bourse *f*. **4.** *Med: A:* administration *f* (d'un médicament).

exhibitioner [eksi'biʃ(ə)nər], *s. Sch:* boursier, -ière (à une université).

exhibitionism [eksi'biʃənizm], *s.* (*a*) *Psy:* exhibitionnisme *m*; (*b*) désir *m* de se faire remarquer.

exhibitionist [eksi'biʃənist], *s.* (*a*) *Psy:* exhibitionniste *mf*; (*b*) m'as-tu-vu *m inv*; **he's an e.,** il aime se faire remarquer.

exhibitionistic [eksibiʃə'nistik], *a.* exhibitionniste.

exhibitive [eg'zibitiv], *a.* **e. of sth.,** qui montre qch.; représentatif de qch.

exhibitor [eg'zibitər], *s.* **1.** exhibiteur, -trice. **2.** (*at exhibition*) exposant, -ante. **3.** *Cin:* exploitant *m* d'une salle.

exhilarant [eg'zilərənt]. **1.** *a.* = EXHILARATING. **2.** *s. A:* (médicament) exhilarant *m*.

exhilarate [eg'zilәreit], *v.tr.* vivifier, ranimer, ragaillardir; émoustiller.

exhilarated [eg'zilәreitid], *a.* ragaillardi, émoustillé.

exhilarating [eg'zilәreitiŋ], *a.* vivifiant, émoustillant; **e. wine,** vin capiteux; **e. news,** nouvelles *f* qui vous remontent le cœur; nouvelles réjouissantes.

exhilaration [egzilә'reiʃ(ə)n], *s.* gaieté *f* de cœur, joie *f* de vivre.

exhilarative [eg'zilәrәtiv], *a.* = EXHILARATING.

exhort [eg'zɔ:t], *v.tr.* **1.** exhorter, encourager (**s.o. to (do) sth.,** qn à (faire) qch.). **2.** recommander ardemment, préconiser (une réforme, etc.).

exhortation [egzɔ:'teiʃ(ə)n], *s.* exhortation *f* (**to sth., to do sth.,** à qch., à faire qch.).

exhortative [eg'zɔ:tәtiv], **exhortatory** [eg'zɔ:tәtri], *a.* exhortatif, exhortatoire.

exhumation [eks(h)ju:'meiʃ(ə)n], *s.* exhumation *f*.

exhume [eks'hju:m], *v.tr.* exhumer, désensevelir, désenterrer, déterrer.

exhumer [eks'hju:mәr], *s.* déterreur *m*.

exigence ['eksidʒәns], **exigency** ['eksidʒәnsi], *s.* **1.** exigence *f*, nécessité *f*, besoin *m*; **to meet the exigencies of the time,** répondre aux exigences de l'époque. **2.** (*a*) situation *f* critique; crise *f*; cas pressant; **in this e.,** dans cette situation critique, urgente; dans cette extrémité; (*b*) *A:* **to be reduced to e.,** être dans le besoin.

exigent ['eksidʒәnt], *a. Lit:* **1.** urgent, pressant. **2.** exigeant; **e. of praise,** qui exige, demande, les éloges.

exigible ['eksidʒәbl], *a.* exigible (**from,** de).

exiguity [eksi'gjuiti], **exiguousness** [eg'zigjuәsnis], *s.* exiguïté *f* (d'un logement, etc.); modicité *f* (d'un revenu, d'un résultat).

exiguous [eg'zigjuәs], *a.* exigu, -uë; fort petit; (revenu *m*) modique.

exile[1] ['eksail], *s.* exil *m*, bannissement *m*; **to send s.o. into e.,** envoyer qn en exil; bannir qn; **to go into e.,** s'en aller en exil; partir en exil, pour l'exil; s'exiler; **to sentence s.o. to temporary e.,** frapper qn d'un exil temporaire.

exile[2], *s.* exilé, -ée; banni, -ie.

exile[3], *v.tr.* exiler, bannir (**from,** de).

exilic [ek'silik], *a. Jew.Hist:* exilien, exilique.

exility [eg'ziliti], *s. Lit:* ténuité *f*; subtilité *f*.

exine ['eksain], *s. Bot:* exine *f*.

exist [eg'zist], *v.i.* exister. **1.** être; **I think, therefore I e.,** je pense, donc je suis; **to cease to e.,** cesser d'exister; (*of pers.*) cesser de vivre; **to continue to e.,** subsister; **wherever these conditions e.,** partout où règnent ces conditions. **2.** se maintenir en vie; **I can't e. on that,** cela ne me suffit pas pour vivre.

existence [eg'zistәns], *s.* **1.** existence *f*; **to be in e.,** exister; être existant; **the oldest manuscript in e.,** le plus ancien manuscrit existant; **the firm has been in e. for fifty years,** la maison existe depuis cinquante ans; **to come into e.,** naître; **to call into e.,** faire naître; **to put out of e.,** anéantir; **to spring into e.,** naître soudainement. **2.** existence, vie *f*; **to lead a pleasant e.,** mener une existence agréable. **3.** *Phil:* être *m*, entité *f*.

existent [eg'zistәnt], *a.* **1.** existant. **2.** d'aujourd'hui; actuel.

existential [egzis'tenʃ(ə)l], *a.* existentiel, -elle.

existentialism [egzis'tenʃәlizm], *s. Phil:* existentialisme *m*.

existentialist [egzis'tenʃәlist], *a. & s. Phil:* existentialiste *mf*.

existing [eg'zistiŋ], *a.* existant; actuel, présent, du moment; **in e. circumstances,** dans les circonstances actuelles, présentes.

exit[1] ['eksit], *s.* sortie *f*. **1.** (*act of going out*) (*a*) *Th:* **sham e.,** fausse sortie; **to make one's e.,** (i) sortir; quitter la scène; (ii) *F:* mourir, quitter ce monde; (*b*) **the audience must have free e. at all times,** le public doit pouvoir sortir librement à tout moment; **e. staircase,** escalier *m* de sortie; (*c*) *Tchn:* **e. cone** (*of wind tunnel*), cône *m* de sortie; **e. velocity,** vitesse *f* à la sortie; **e. tube,** barillet (d'un four de cokerie). **2.** (*way out*) sortie, issue *f*, (porte *f*, couloir *m*, de) dégagement *m* (d'un théâtre, d'une gare, etc.); voie *f* de dégagement; **to provide for exits,** ménager des issues; **emergency e.,** sortie, issue, de secours; **e. only,** (passage, etc.) strictement réservé à la sortie.

exit[2], *v.i.* (**exited**) **1.** *Th:* (*stage direction*) **e. Macbeth,** Macbeth sort, exit Macbeth. **2.** *F:* (*a*) sortir; faire sa sortie; (*b*) quitter ce monde; mourir.

ex-libris [eks'l(a)ibris], *s.* (*also used as pl.*) ex-libris *m*.

ex-librist [eks'l(a)ibrist], *s.* collectionneur, -euse, d'ex-libris.

exmeridian [eksmә'ridiәn], *s. Nau: Surv:* **to take several exmeridians,** prendre plusieurs circumméridiennes *f*.

exo- ['ekso], *pref.* exo-.

Exoascaceae [eksouә'skeisii:], *s.pl. Fung:* exoascacées *f*.

exoascales [eksoue'skeili:z], *s.pl. Fung:* cloque *f* (du pêcher, etc.).

exoascus [eksou'æskәs], *s. Fung:* exoascus *m*.

Exobasidiaceae [eksoubeisidi'eisii:], *s.pl. Fung:* exobasidiacées *f*.

exobasidium [eksoubә'zidiәm], *s. Fung:* exobaside *m*.

exocardiac [eksou'kɑ:diæk], *a. Med:* exocardiaque.

exocarp ['eksoukɑ:p], *s. Bot:* épicarpe *m*.

exocoetus [eksou'si:tәs], *s. Ich:* exocet *m*, gabot *m*.

exocrine ['eksoukrain], *a. Physiol:* (glande *f*) exocrine, à sécrétion externe.

exode ['eksoud], **exodium** [ek'soudiәm], *s. Gr.Lit:* exode *m*.

exoderm ['eksoudә:m], *s.* exoderme *m*.

exodus ['eksәdәs], *s.* (*a*) exode *m* (des Hébreux, etc.); *B:* **(the Book of) Exodus,** l'Exode; (*b*) départ *m*, sortie *f* (d'un groupe de gens, etc.); *Fr.Hist:* **the e. of 1940,** l'exode de 1940; **after the Chairman's speech there was a general e.,** après le discours du président il y eut une sortie générale; **e. of capital,** évasion *f* des capitaux.

ex(-)officio ['eksә'fiʃiou], *adv.phr.* **to act ex(-)o.,** agir d'office; **ex(-)o. member,** membre *m* de droit, à titre d'office; **he is ex-o. responsible for . . .,** il est, de par ses fonctions, responsable de . . . .

exogamic [eksou'gæmik], **exogamous** [ek'sɔgәmәs], *a. Anthr:* exogame.

exogamy [ek'sɔgәmi], *s. Anthr:* exogamie *f*.

exogen ['eksoudʒen], *s. Bot:* plante *f* exogène; exogène *m*.

exogenic [eksou'dʒenik], **exogenous** [ek'sɔdʒenәs], *a. Bot: Geol:* exogène.

exognathia [eksɔg'neiθiә], **exognathism** [ek'sɔgnәθizm], *s. Anat:* exognathie *f*, exognathisme *m*.

exogonium [eksou'gouniәm], *s. Bot:* exogonium *m*.

exogynous [ek'sɔdʒinәs], *a. Bot:* exogyne.

exogyra [eksou'dʒairә], *s. Paleont:* exogyre *mf*

exomorphic [eksou'mɔ:fik], *a. Geol:* exomorphe.

exomorphism [eksou'mɔ:fizm], *s. Geol:* exomorphisme *m*.

exomphalos [ek'sɔmfәlɔs], *s. Med:* exomphale *f*; hernie ombilicale.

exon ['eksɔn], *s. Hist:* exempt *m*; (titre des quatre officiers des *Yeomen* qui appartenaient à la garde personnelle du souverain).

exonerate [eg'zɔnәreit], *v.tr.* **1.** exonérer, dispenser, décharger (**s.o. from an obligation,** qn d'une obligation). **2. to e. s.o. (from blame),** disculper, justifier, absoudre, qn; **evidence that exonerates you,** témoignage *m* à votre décharge.

exoneration [egzɔnә'reiʃ(ə)n], *s.* **1.** exonération *f*, décharge *f*, dispense *f* (**from,** de). **2. e. from blame,** disculpation *f*, justification *f*.

exonerative [eg'zɔnәrәtiv], *a.* qui exonère, qui décharge.

Exonian [ek'sonjәn], *a. & s.* (originaire, habitant, -ante) d'Exeter.

exophoria [eksou'fɔ:riә], *s. Med:* exophorie *f*.

exophthalmia [eksɔf'θælmiә], *s. Med:* exophthalmie *f*.

exophthalmic [eksɔf'θælmik], *a. Med:* (goître *m*, etc.) exophtalmique.

exophthalmos, exophthalmus [eksɔf'θælmәs], *s. Med:* exophtalmie *f*.

exoplasmic [eksou'plæzmik], *a. Biol:* (substance *f*) exoplasmique.

exopodite [ek'sɔpәdait], *s. Crust:* exopodite *m*.

Exopterygota [eksɔpteri'goutә], *s.pl. Ent:* exoptérygotes *m*.

exopterygotic [eksɔpteri'gɔtik], *a. Ent:* exoptérygote.

exorable ['eks(ә)rәbl], *a.* exorable; accessible à la pitié.

exorbitance [eg'zɔ:bit(ә)ns], *s.* exorbitance *f*, énormité *f*, extravagance *f*.

exorbitant [eg'zɔ:bit(ә)nt], *a.* exorbitant, exagéré, excessif, extravagant; (intérêt *m*) usuraire; **e. price,** prix exorbitant; *F:* prix salé; **to cost an e. price,** *F:* coûter les yeux de la tête.

exorbitantly [eg'zɔ:bit(ә)ntli], *adv.* d'une manière exorbitante, exorbitamment; excessivement, extravagamment.

exorcism ['eksɔ:sizm], *s.* exorcisme *m*.

exorcist ['eksɔ:sist], *s.* (*a*) exorciste *m*; exorciseur, -euse; (*b*) *Rel.H:* exorciste.

exorcize ['eksɔ:saiz], *v.tr.* exorciser (un démon, un possédé, etc.); conjurer (un esprit).

exorcizer ['eksɔ:saizәr], *s.* exorciseur, -euse, exorciste *m*.

exorcizing ['eksɔ:saiziŋ], *s.* exorcisation *f*, exorcisme *m*.

exordial [ek'sɔ:diәl], *a.* (discours *m*, etc.) d'introduction, liminaire, préliminaire.

exordium, *pl.* **-iums, -ia** [ek'sɔ:diәm, -iәmz, -iә], *s. Rh:* exorde *m*.

exoreic [eksɔ'reiik], *a. Geol:* exoréique.

exoreism [ekɔ'reiizm], *s. Geol:* exoréisme *m*.

exor(r)hiza [eksou'raizә], *s. Bot:* plante *f* exor(r)hize.

exor(r)hizal [eksou'raizәl], *a. Bot:* exor(r)hize.

exoskeleton [eksou'skelitәn], *s. Z:* exosquelette *m*.

exosmose ['eksɔsmous], **exosmosis** [eksɔs'mousis], *s. Ph:* exosmose *f*.

exosmotic [eksɔs'mɔtik], *a. Ph:* exosmotique.

exosphere ['eksousfiәr], *s.* exosphère *f*.

exospore ['eksouspɔ:r], *s. Bot:* exospore *m*.

exosporous [eksou'spɔ:rәs], *a. Bot:* exosporé.

exostome ['eksoustoum], *s. Bot:* exostome *m*.

exostosis [eksou'stousis], *s. Med: Bot:* exostose *f*.

exoteric [eksou'terik], *a.* (doctrine *f*, disciple *m*) exotérique.

exotericism [eksou'terisizm], *s.* exotérisme *m*.

exothecium [eksou'θi:siәm], *s. Bot:* exothèque *f*.

exothermic [eksou'θә:mik], *a. Ch:* (réaction *f*, etc.) exothermique.

exothermicity [eksouθә:'misiti], *s.* thermicité positive.

exotic [eg'zɔtik]. **1.** *a.* exotique; **a taste for the e.,** le goût de l'exotique. **2.** *s. Bot:* plante *f* exotique.

exotically [eg'zɔtikli], *adv.* exotiquement.

exoticism [eg'zɔtisizm], **exotism** ['eksәtizm], *s.* exotisme *m*.

exotoxin [eksou'tɔksin], *s. Bac:* exotoxine *f*.

expand [eks'pænd]. **1.** *v.tr.* (*a*) dilater (un gaz, l'air, un solide); étendre (les limites d'un empire); gonfler (un ballon); mandriner, renfler, dudgeonner (un tube de chaudière); développer (un abrégé, une formule algébrique, le corps, la poitrine); développer, amplifier (une idée); élargir (l'esprit); faire épanouir (l'âme, le cœur); *Mch:* détendre (la vapeur); **to e. a short story into a full-length novel,** transformer une nouvelle en grand roman; (*b*) déployer (les ailes, etc.); *Metalw:* **to e. sheet metal,** déployer la tôle; (*c*) *Veh:* **to e. the brake shoes,** écarter les segments de frein. **2.** *v.i.* (*a*) (*of solid, air, gas*) se dilater; (*of balloon*) se gonfler; (*of steam*) se détendre; (*of chest*) se développer; (*of quicklime*) foisonner; **as the Empire expanded,** à mesure que l'Empire grandissait, s'étendait; **his mind is expanding,** son esprit, son intelligence, se développe, s'épanouit; (*b*) (*of sail, etc.*) s'étendre, se déployer; (*of flower*) s'épanouir, s'ouvrir; (*c*) *Mec.E:* (*of belt*) s'allonger; (*d*) *F:* (*of pers.*) devenir expansif.

expandable [eks'pændәbl], *a.* dilatable, extensible.

expanded [eks'pændid], *a.* **1.** allongé; étendu; expansé; **e. polystyrene,** polystyrène expansé; *Metalw:* **e. metal,** métal déployé; *Rad:* **e. scope,** image (d'écran radar) agrandie. **2.** évasé. **3. e. at the end,** renflé au bout.

expander, expandor [eks'pændәr], *s.* **1.** *Gym:* **(chest) e.,** extenseur *m*, sandow *m* (*R.t.m.*). **2.** mécanisme *m* d'expansion; *W.Tel: etc:* expanseur *m*; **wedge e.,** mécanisme à coins; *Tls:* **tube e.,** expanseur; *Aut:* **rim e.,** ouvre-jante *m*, *pl.* ouvre-jantes; *Mec.E:* **e.-tube brake,** frein *m* à vessie.

expanding [eks'pændiŋ], *a.* **1.** en expansion; (gaz) qui se dilate; (ballon, vessie, etc.) qui se gonfle, qui enfle; (commerce) qui se développe, qui prend de l'extension; **the e. universe,** l'univers *m* en expansion. **2. e. bracelet,** bracelet *m* extensible; **e. suitcase,** valise *f* à soufflets; **e. bullet,** balle *f* dum-dum, balle à expansion; **e. bit,** mèche universelle; *Mec.E:* **e. borer,** foreuse *f* à mèche extensible; **e. (diameter) brake,** frein *m* à extension; **e. cone,** cône *m* extensible; **e. press,** presse *f* à mandriner, à dudgeonner; **e. tube of brake,** vessie *f* de frein; *Av:* **e. pitch of propeller,** pas *m* croissant de l'hélice; *Elcs:* **e. channel,** canal *m*, sélectivité *f*, variable.

expanse [eks'pæns], *s.* étendue *f* (de pays, d'eau, etc.); **a vast e. of desert,** une vastitude de désert; **vaste e. of sand,** mer *f* de sable; *Poet:* **the e.,** le firmament.

expansibility [eks'pænsibiliti], *s.* expansibilité *f*; *Ph:* dilatabilité *f*.

expansible [eks'pænsibl], *a.* expansible; *Ph:* dilatable.

expansion [eks'pænʃ(ə)n], *s.* **1.** (*making larger*) dilatation *f* (d'un gaz, d'un métal); mandrinage *m* (d'un tube de chaudière); développement *m* (d'un abrégé, de la poitrine, etc.); amplification *f* (d'un sujet); *Pol.Ec:* **currency e.,** expansion *f* monétaire. **2.** (*becoming larger*) (*a*) expansion *f* (d'un solide, d'un liquide, d'une activité, d'un commerce, etc.); dilatation *f* (d'un gaz, d'un métal, d'un corps, etc.); foisonnement *m* (de la chaux vive, de la terre extraite d'une fouille, etc.); évasement *m* (d'un orifice); **colonial e.,** expansion coloniale; *Ph:* **coefficient of e.,** coefficient *m* de dilatation; **cubic e.,** dilatation cubique; **linear e.,** dilatation linéaire; **heat e.,** dilatation thermique; **e. ratio,** rapport *m* d'évasement (d'une tuyère, d'un diffuseur, etc.); *Aedcs:* **e. wave,** onde *f* d'expansion; (*b*) épanouissement *m* (d'une fleur, du cœur); (*c*) *Pol.Ec:* relance *f*. **3.** (*a*) *Mec.E:* **e. clutch, e. coupling,** embrayage *m* à segments extensibles; accouplement *m* à mouvement longitudinal; **e. joint,** (i) fourreau compensateur; (joint) compensateur *m*; manchon *m* de dilatation (of pipe, etc.); (ii) (*in concrete work*); joint de dilatation; (iii) (*of coupling*) crabot *m*, clabot *m*; **e. pipe, e. tube,** (i) tuyau *m*, tube *m*, dilatable, extensible; (ii) tuyau, tube, compensateur, de compensation; **e. reamer,** alésoir *m* extensible; **e. shim,** cale *f* à joints; **e. tank,** bac *m*, réservoir *m*, à expansion; *Tls:* **e. bit,** foret *m*, mèche *f*, extensible; *Rail:* **e. gauge,** cale *f* à joints; **e. slide,** chariot *m* de dilatation, **e. space (of rails),** jeu *m* de dilatation au joint; (*b*) *Atom.Ph:* **(Wilson's) e. chamber,** chambre *f* à condensation, de Wilson; **e. orbit,** orbite *f* d'expansion; (*c*) *Mch: etc:* détente *f*, expansion (de la vapeur, des gaz, etc.); **e. cooling,** refroidissement *m* par détente; **e. curve,** courbe *f*, diagramme *m*, de détente; **e. damper,** papillon *m* de détente; **e. engine,** machine *f* à détente; **double-, triple-, quadruple-e. engine,** machine à double, triple, quadruple, expansion ou détente; **e. gear,** (mécanisme de) détente; **e. valve,** (i) soupape *f* de détente; (ii) vanne *f* de réglage (de frigorifère); **adiabatic e.,** détente adiabatique; **isothermal e.,** détente isotherme; *I.C.E:* **e. stroke,** course *f* de détente (du piston).

expansionary [eks'pænʃ(ə)nəri], *a.* qui tend vers, vise à, l'expansion.

expansionism [iks'pænʃ(ə)nizm], *s. Pol.Ec:* expansionnisme *m*.

expansionist [eks'pænʃ(ə)nist], *a. & s.* **1.** *Pol.Ec:* expansionniste (*mf*). **2. Colonial e.,** expansionniste colonial.

expansive [eks'pænsiv], *a.* **1.** (*a*) (*of force, etc.*) expansif; (*b*) (*of gas, etc.*) expansible, expansif, dilatable; *Mch:* **e. working,** marche *f* à la détente. **2.** (*of pers.*) expansif, démonstratif; qui aime à communiquer ses sentiments; **in an e. mood,** en veine d'épanchement; **to become e.,** s'ouvrir. **3.** (*extensive*) large, étendu.

expansiveness [eks'pænsivnis], *s.* **1.** expansibilité *f*; dilatabilité *f* (d'un gaz, etc.). **2.** expansivité *f*, nature expansive (de qn).

expansivity [ekspæn'sivəti], *s.* **1.** expansivité *f*. **2.** coefficient *m* de dilatation.

ex parte [eks'pɑːti]. *Lt.adv. & a.phr.* (*a*) *Jur:* (attestation, déclaration, témoignage) émanant d'une seule partie; unilatéral, -aux; (*b*) partial(ement).

expatiate [eks'peiʃieit], *v.i.* **1.** *A:* errer (sans contrainte); aller à son gré. **2.** discourir (longuement), s'étendre, disserter **(on, upon,** sur); **to be for ever expatiating on . . .,** ne pas tarir sur . . ..

expatiater, expatiator [eks'peiʃieitər], *s.* discoureur, -euse **(upon,** sur).

expatiation [ekspeiʃi'eiʃ(ə)n], *s.* **1.** dissertation *f*, long discours; *F:* laïus *m*. **2.** prolixité *f*.

expatriate[1] [eks'pætrieit], *v.tr.* expatrier, exiler, bannir (qn); **to e. oneself,** (i) s'expatrier; (ii) renoncer à sa nationalité.

expatriate[2] [eks'pætriət], *a. & s.* expatrié, -iée.

expatriation [ekspætri'eiʃ(ə)n], *s.* **1.** expatriation *f*. **2.** renonciation *f* à sa nationalité.

expect [iks'pekt], *v.tr.* **1.** attendre (qn, qch.); s'attendre à (un événement); compter sur (l'arrivée de qn, etc.); **to e. s.o. to dinner,** attendre qn à dîner; **she expects to be dismissed today,** elle s'attend à être renvoyée aujourd'hui; **I expected as much,** je m'y attendais; **I knew what to e.,** je savais à quoi m'attendre, à quoi m'en tenir; **if I knew what to e.,** si je savais sur quoi compter; **to e. the worst,** s'attendre au pire; **as one might e., as might be expected,** comme on doit s'y attendre; comme de bien entendu; comme de raison; **that is not the result I expected,** ce n'est pas là le résultat auquel je m'attendais; **it is not as difficult as I expected (it to be),** ce n'est pas aussi difficile que je le croyais; **he little expected that,** il ne s'attendait guère à cela; **I didn't e. that of him,** je n'attendais pas cela de lui; je ne m'attendais pas à ce qu'il fasse cela; **to e. that s.o. will do sth., that sth. will happen,** s'attendre à ce que qn fasse qch., à ce que qch. arrive; **it is to be expected that . . .,** il est vraisemblable que + *ind.*; **it is hardly to be expected that . . .,** il y a peu de chances (pour) que + *sub.*; **I expected him to refuse,** je m'attendais à un refus de sa part; je m'attendais à ce qu'il refusât; **I expected him to be waiting for me,** je comptais qu'il serait à m'attendre; **I e. her to come tomorrow,** je l'attends demain; **I did not e. things to turn out so badly,** je ne m'attendais pas à ce que les choses tournent si mal; **I do not e. him to answer me,** je ne m'attends pas à ce qu'il me réponde; **to e. to do sth.,** compter, espérer, penser, faire qch.; **he is expected to arrive next week,** on l'attend la semaine prochaine; **don't e. me till you see me,** vous me verrez quand j'arriverai; ne m'attendez pas à heure fixe; **he is not expected to recover,** on ne compte pas le sauver; **she was expected to outlive him,** on pensait qu'elle lui survivrait; **I hope and e. that . . .,** j'espère avec confiance que . . .; **she's expecting a baby,** *F:* **she's expecting,** elle attend un bébé. **2. to e. sth. from s.o.,** attendre, exiger, qch. de qn; **to e. from s.o. more than he can do,** demander à qn plus qu'il ne peut faire; **I e. you to be punctual,** je vous demanderai d'arriver à l'heure; je tiens à ce que vous arriviez à l'heure; **what do you e. me to do?** qu'attendez-vous de moi? **how do you e. me to do it?** comment voulez-vous que je le fasse? **am I expected to dress for dinner?** faut-il me mettre en smoking pour dîner? **it is not expected of you,** vous n'êtes pas tenu de le faire; **it's too much to e. of a child,** c'est trop attendre d'un enfant; (*to child*) **I shall e. you to pass round the biscuits,** ce sera à toi d'offrir les gâteaux (aux invités); **I know what is expected of me,** je sais ce qu'on attend de moi. **3.** penser, croire (que); **I e. he'll pay,** je pense qu'il payera; sans doute qu'il payera; **I e. so,** je pense, je crois, que oui.

expectancy [eks'pektənsi], *s.* **1.** expectance *f*, attente *f*; **eager e.,** vive impatience. **2.** *Jur:* expectative *f*, attente *f*, (d'un héritage, etc.); **estate, heir, in e.,** héritage *m*, héritier *m*, en expectative; héritage en espérance *f*; **life e.,** espérance de vie.

expectant [eks'pekt(ə)nt]. **1.** *a.* (*a*) qui attend; (qui est) dans l'attente **(of sth.,** de qch.); **e.-mother,** femme enceinte, future mère; (*b*) *Med:* **e. method (of treatment),** méthode *f* d'expectation *f*; (*c*) *Jur:* (bien, etc.) en expectative; **e. heir,** celui qui a un héritage en perspective; héritier en expectative. **2.** *s.* (*a*) *A:* candidat *m*, aspirant *m* (à un poste); (*b*) = **expectant heir.**

expectantly [eks'pekt(ə)ntli], *adv.* dans l'expectative, dans l'attente; **to gaze at s.o. e.,** regarder qn avec l'air d'attendre qch.

expectation [ekspek'teiʃ(ə)n], *s.* **1.** (*a*) attente *f*, espérance *f*, prévision *f*; **to come up to, fall short of, s.o.'s expectations,** remplir, répondre à, tromper, l'attente de qn; **if my expectations are fulfilled,** si mes prévisions sont exactes; **to succeed beyond one's expectations,** réussir au delà de ses espérances; **contrary to all expectations,** contrairement à toute attente; contre toute attente; contre toute prévision; **in (the) e. of,** dans l'attente de; en prévision de; **e. value,** valeur *f* d'attente (d'une récolte, etc.); (*b*) (*expectancy*) **with eager e.,** avec une vive impatience; **to live in e.,** vivre dans l'expectative. **2.** (*a*) *Jur:* expectative *f* d'héritage; **possessions in e.,** biens en expectative; (*b*) *pl.* **expectations,** espérances; **uncle, aunt, from whom one has expectations,** oncle *m*, tante *f*, à héritage; **to live up to one's expectations,** régler sa dépense sur ses espérances. **3.** probabilité *f* (d'un événement); *Ins:* **e. of life,** probabilités de la vie; vie moyenne, vie probable; espérance de vie; **e. of life tables,** tables *f* de survie.

expectative [eks'pektətiv]. *Ecc: Jur:* **1.** *a.* expectatif, -ive; *Theol:* **e. grace,** grâce expectative. **2.** *s.* (*a*) expectative *f*; (*b*) *Theol:* grâce expectative.

expected [eks'pektid], *a.* attendu, espéré.

expectorant [eks'pektərənt], *a. & s. Med:* expectorant (*m*); fluidifiant (*m*).

expectorate [eks'pektəreit], *v.tr.* expectorer (des mucosités, etc.); *v.i.* cracher.

expectoration [ekspektə'reiʃ(ə)n], *s.* expectoration *f*; (i) crachement *m*; (ii) crachat *m*.

expedance [eks'piːdəns], *s. El: Elcs:* impédance négative.

expedience [eks'piːdiəns], **expediency** [eks'piːdiənsi], *s.* **1.** convenance *f*, opportunité *f*, à-propos *m* (d'une mesure, etc.); **on grounds of expediency,** pour des raisons de convenance. **2.** *Pej:* **(doctrine of) expedience,** opportunisme *m*.

expedient [eks'piːdiənt]. **1.** *a.* expédient, convenable, opportun, à propos, pratique; **the only e. method by which it may be done,** le seul moyen commode, pratique, de le faire; **do what you think e.,** faites ce que vous jugerez à propos; **it is e. to . . .,** il est expédient, opportun, de . . ; *A:* **it is e. that you should stay,** il est expédient, convenable, que vous restiez. **2.** *s.* expédient *m*, moyen *m*; ressource *f*; *Pej:* artifice *m*; **to resort to expedients,** user d'expédients.

expediently [eks'piːdiəntli], *adv.* convenablement; avantageusement.

expedite ['ekspidait], *v.tr.* **1.** activer, pousser, hâter (une mesure); accélérer (un procédé). **2.** expédier, accomplir, avec diligence, dépêcher (une affaire).

expediter ['ekspidaitər], *s.* **1.** celui qui active ou a activé (une mesure), qui a accéléré (un procédé). **2.** celui qui a expédié, dépêché (une affaire).

expedition [ekspə'diʃ(ə)n], *s.* **1.** *Mil: Navy: etc:* expédition *f*; **e. to the South Pole,** expédition au pôle sud; **to be on an e.,** être en expédition; *Fr.Hist:* **the E. to Egypt,** l'Expédition d'Égypte. **2.** *O:* célérité *f*, promptitude *f*, diligence *f*; **to do sth. with (all) e., to use e. in doing sth.,** faire qch. avec célérité, avec promptitude, en toute diligence; **for the sake of e.,** pour aller plus vite.

expeditionary [ekspə'diʃ(ə)nəri], *a. Mil: Navy:* (corps *m*, armée *f*) expéditionnaire.

expeditious [ekspə'diʃəs], *a.* (procédé) expéditif; (trajet *m*) rapide; (réponse) prompte; **to be e. in business,** être expéditif, prompte, en affaires; **he is always e.,** il va toujours vite en besogne.

expeditiously [ekspə'diʃəsli], *adv.* expéditivement; rapidement; promptement.

expeditiousness [ekspə'diʃəsnis], *s.* célérité *f*, promptitude *f*.

expel [eks'pel], *v.tr.* **(expelled; expelling)** (*a*) expulser (un locataire); chasser, expulser (un corps étranger, l'ennemi, etc.); faire sortir (une balle d'une blessure); chasser, refouler (un liquide, un gaz); **to e. s.o. from a society,** bannir qn d'une société; **to e. a boy from school,** renvoyer, chasser, un élève (de l'école); **to e. a poison from the body,** éliminer un poison du corps; (*b*) *Adm:* **to e. an alien,** expulser, refouler, un étranger.

expeller [eks'pelər], *s.* **1.** pressoir *m* à huile. **2.** *Com:* tourteau *m* de graines oléagineuses; **e. seeds,** graines oléagineuses.

expelling[1] [eks'peliŋ], *a.* (*a*) expulsif; (*b*) *Physiol: Med:* expulseur, (*rare*) *f.* expultrice.

expelling[2], *s.* expulsion *f*.

expend [eks'pend], *v.tr.* **1.** (*a*) **to e. money (on sth., on doing sth.),** dépenser de l'argent (pour qch., à faire qch.); (*b*) **to e. care, time, on sth., in doing sth.,** consacrer, employer, du soin, du temps, à qch., à faire qch. **2.** (*a*) épuiser (ses ressources, ses forces); (*b*) **to e. too much ammunition,** consommer trop de munitions; **you are expending too much strength,** vous y mettez trop de force; vous vous dépensez trop.

expendable [eks'pendəbl]. **1.** *a.* consommable, dépensable; non récupérable, non réutilisable; *Mil:* sacrifiable; **e. equipment,** matériel *m* de consommation courante, matériel consommable; **e. radio sonobuoy,** bouée radio sacrifiée, non récupérable. **2.** *s.* **expendables,** (i) troupes sacrifiables sacrifiées; (ii) (*thgs*) pertes sèches; matériel non récupérable, non réutilisable.

expenditure [iks'penditʃər], *s.* **1.** (*spending*) dépense *f* (d'argent, de chaleur, etc.); consommation *f* (de munitions, etc.); **a useless e. of time,** une dépense inutile de temps. **2.** (*amount spent*) dépense(s); **it entails heavy e.,** cela entraîne une forte dépense, de fortes dépenses; **national e.,** les dépenses de l'État; **public e.,** dépenses publiques; **e. credit,** crédit *m* d'engagement de dépenses.

expense [iks'pens], *s.* **1.** (*a*) dépense *f*, frais *mpl*; **regardless of e.,** sans regarder à la dépense; **free of e.,** sans frais, franco; **book published at author's e.,** livre édité à compte d'auteur; **the postage will be at our e.,** le port sera à notre charge; **to go to e.,** se mettre en dépense; se mettre en frais; **to go to great e.,** faire beaucoup de dépense; **to put s.o. to e.,** faire faire des dépenses à qn; occasionner des frais à qn; *Jur:* constituer qn en frais, en dépenses; **don't go, run, to any e., don't put yourself to any e., over the dinner,** ne faites pas de frais pour le dîner; **I cannot go to that e.,** je ne peux pas faire cette dépense; **I cannot go to the e. of keeping a gardener,** je n'ai pas les moyens d'avoir un jardinier; *F:* **at the e. of his life,** au prix de sa vie; (*b*) *pl.* **expenses,** dépenses, débours *mpl*, frais; *Com:* sorties *f*; **travelling expenses,** frais de déplacement; **living expenses,** frais de séjour; *Com: Ind:* **petty expenses,** menus frais; **general expenses,** frais généraux; **incidental expenses,** faux frais; **household expenses,** dépenses du ménage; **running expenses (of a car),** frais d'entretien (d'une voiture); **preliminary expenses of a company,** frais de constitution d'une société; **legal expenses,** frais légaux; **to incur expenses,** faire des dépenses; **total expenses incurred,** total *m* des frais effectués; **to increase one's expenses,** augmenter ses dépenses; charger, grever, son budget; **I'll pay the expenses,** je me charge des frais; je règle les dépenses; **to have all expenses paid,** être défrayé de tout; **I have been, have gone, to considerable e.,** j'ai fait des dépenses, des frais, considérables; **dividing (the) expenses,** à frais communs; *Com:* **no expenses,** exempt de frais; (*on bill*) (retour) sans frais, sans protêt. **2.** dépens *m*; **a laugh at my e.,** un éclat de rire à mes dépens; **to raise a laugh at s.o.'s e.,** faire rire aux dépens de qn; **to live at the e. of others,** vivre aux dépens des autres; vivre sur le commun; **to get rich at s.o.'s e.,** s'enrichir aux dépens, au détriment, de qn; *F:* s'enrichir des dépouilles de qn. **3. to be a great e. to s.o.,** être une grande charge pour qn. **4.** (*allowance*) **expenses,** indemnité *f* (pour débours); **travelling expenses,** indemnité de voyage; **to allow s.o. his expenses,** rembourser les débours de qn; **to offer s.o. £100 and expenses,** offrir à qn £100, tous frais payés; **e. account,** indemnité pour frais professionnels.

expensive [eks'pensiv], *a.* (objet) coûteux, cher, de prix; (procédé, procès) dispendieux; *F:* (marchand) cher; **e. dress,** robe chère; **e. hobby,** passe-temps onéreux; **e. wife,** femme qui coûte cher à son mari; **a very e. builder,** un entrepreneur qui prend cher; **to be e.,** coûter cher *inv*; **that comes e.,** cela revient cher *inv*; **little places that are not too e.,** petits trous pas chers; **not too e.,** dans les prix doux; **travelling is e.,** les voyages coûtent cher.

expensively [eks'pensivli], *adv.* (s'habiller) coûteusement; (construire) à grands frais, dispendieusement; **to live e.,** dépenser beaucoup d'argent; mener la vie large.

expensiveness [eks'pensivnis], *s.* cherté *f* (d'une denrée, etc.); nature coûteuse (d'une guerre, etc.); prix élevé (de qch.).

experience[1] [eks'piəriəns], *s.* expérience *f*. **1.** (*a*) épreuve personnelle; **to go through painful experiences,** passer par de rudes épreuves; **terrifying e.,** aventure effrayante; **(varied) experiences,** avatars *m*; **to have a nasty e.,** (i) passer par un mauvais moment, *F:* un mauvais quart d'heure; (ii) faire une mauvaise rencontre; **it was a delightful e.,** ce fut un moment délicieux, une sensation délicieuse; **it was a new e. for them,** ce fut une nouveauté pour eux; **it was his first e. of love,** c'était la première fois qu'il est tombé amoureux; **to relate one's experiences,** raconter ce que l'on a vu et ressenti; raconter ses aventures; (*b*) *usu.pl.* expériences religieuses. **2. he learnt by e.,** l'expérience l'a rendu sage; **to gain e. of life,** faire l'apprentissage de la vie; **practical e.,** la pratique; **to have much e.,** avoir beaucoup d'expérience, d'acquis *m*; **e. in driving, driving e.,** expérience de la route; expérience routière; habitude *f* de conduire; **he still lacks e.,** il manque encore de métier, de pratique; **facts within my e.,** faits *m* dont j'ai été témoin; faits dont j'ai connaissance; **long personal e. allows me to . . .,** une longue pratique me permet de . . .; **a man of e.,** un homme d'expérience; **e. shows that . . .,** l'expérience démontre que . . .; **to know sth. from e.,** savoir qch. par expérience, pour l'avoir éprouvé, d'après son expérience personnelle; **I know from bitter e. that . . .,** je sais, pour l'avoir éprouvé cruellement, que . . .; **as far as my e. goes,** autant que je puisse dire (d'après mon expérience personnelle); **theatrical e.,** pratique du théâtre; **to have e. of teaching,** avoir (acquis) l'expérience de l'enseignement, avoir déjà enseigné; **have you had any previous e.?** avez-vous déjà travaillé dans ce métier? avez-vous déjà enseigné, pratiqué, etc.? **he has no e. of love,** il ne connaît pas l'amour; *F:* **she is not without e.,** elle n'est pas innocente; **he has a wide e. of men,** il a une grande pratique des hommes; **I have enough business e. to . . .,** j'ai assez de pratique des affaires pour . . .; *Ins:* **e. tables,** tables *f* d'expérience (de mortalité).

experience[2], *v.tr.* **1.** éprouver; faire l'expérience de (qch.); **to e. a sensation of warmth,** éprouver une sensation de chaleur; **to e. difficult times, heavy trials,** passer par des temps difficiles, par de rudes épreuves; **these shares have experienced a fresh decline,** ces actions ont éprouvé une nouvelle baisse; *U.S:* **to e. religion,** se convertir. **2.** apprendre (par expérience) **(that,** que).

experienced [eks'piəriənst], *a.* **1.** (effet) éprouvé, senti, subi. **2.** qui a de l'expérience, du métier; (général) expérimenté; (observateur) averti; (conducteur) exercé, expérimenté; (œil) exercé **(in,** à); **to be e. in sth.,** avoir l'expérience de, avoir l'usage de, être rompu à, qch.; s'y connaître à qch.; **e. in business,** rompu aux affaires.

experiential [ekspiəri'enʃəl], *a.* fondé sur l'expérience; (philosophie *f*) empirique.

experiment[1] [eks'perimənt], *s.* expérience *f*; essai *m*, épreuve *f*; **chemical e.,** expérience de chimie; **to make, try, carry out, an e.,** faire, tenter, procéder à, une expérience; **experiments on animals,** expériences sur des animaux; **model experiments,** *Ind:* essais sur modèles; *N.Arch:* essais au bassin des carènes; **this is proved by e.,** la preuve en a été établie par des expériences; **as an e., by way of e.,** à titre d'essai, d'expérience.

experiment[2] [eks'periment], *v.i.* expérimenter, faire une expérience, des expériences **(on, with,** sur, avec); **to e. (up)on dogs,** expérimenter sur les chiens; **this new reactor is being experimented with,** ce nouveau réacteur est à l'essai, à l'étude, en cours d'expérimentation.

experimental [eksperi'ment(ə)l], *a.* **1.** (savoir) expérimental, -aux; fondé sur l'expérience. **2.** (sujet) d'expérience; **e. laboratory,** laboratoire *m* d'expériences; **e. physics,** physique expérimentale; **e. research,** recherche (expérimentale); **e. determination of melting point,** détermination expérimentale du point de fusion; **e. rocket,** fusée expérimentale; **e. target,** cible *f* d'épreuve; *Ind:* **e. department,** service *m* des essais; **e. design(s),** conduite *f*, orientation *f*, de la recherche; **e. run of a new engine,** marche *f* d'essai d'une nouvelle machine, d'un nouveau moteur; *Agr: etc:* **e. plot,** champ *m*, terrain *m*, d'essai; **e. forestry,** expérimentation forestière; *Civ.E:* **e. road,** route *f* laboratoire.

experimentalism [eksperi'mentəlizm], *s.* expérimentalisme *m*.

experimentalist [eksperi'mentəlist], *s.* expérimentaliste *mf*.

experimentalize [eksperi'mentəlaiz], *v.i.* expérimenter.

experimentally [eksperi'mentəli], *adv.* **1.** (savoir qch.) par expérience. **2.** (découvrir, trouver) expérimentalement. **3.** pour essayer; à titre d'essai.

experimentation [eksperimen'teiʃ(ə)n], *s.* expérimentation *f*.

experimenter [eks'perimentər], *s.* expérimentateur, -trice.

experimenting [eks'perimentiŋ], *s.* expérimentation *f*.

expert ['ekspə:t]. **1.** *a.* expert, habile; **to be e. in, at, sth.,** être expert, connaisseur, en qch.; connaître à fond qch.; *Jur:* être idoine en qch. **2.** *s.* expert *m*; spécialiste *mf*; *Jur:* **medical e.,** médecin légiste; **the experts,** les gens *m* du métier; les spécialistes; **to be an e. on, in, economics,** connaître à fond l'économie politique; **he is an e. in this field,** il est expert dans la matière; il s'y connaît; **to pose as an e.,** se donner pour expert; **the eye of an e.,** un œil expert; **expert's report,** expertise *f*; rapport *m* d'expert; **e. advice,** avis autorisé; **according to the experts,** à dire d'experts; **according to e. opinion this picture is a copy,** l'expertise a établi que ce tableau est une copie.

expertise [ekspə:'ti:z], *s.* **1.** expertise *f*. **2.** = EXPERTNESS.

expertly ['ekspə:tli], *adv.* habilement, adroitement; en expert.

expertness ['ekspə:tnis], *s.* adresse *f*, habileté *f* **(in,** à); connaissances *f* techniques.

expiable ['ekspiəbl], *a.* expiable.

expiate ['ekspieit], *v.tr.* expier (un péché, une faute).

expiation [ekspi'eiʃ(ə)n], *s.* expiation *f*; **in e. of his crime,** pour expier, en expiation de, son crime; *Jew.Rel:* **Day of E.,** Fête *f* de l'Expiation, du Grand Pardon.

expiatory ['ekspiətəri, 'ekspieitəri], *a.* expiatoire; **e. of a sin,** qui sert à expier un péché.

expiration [ekspi'reiʃ(ə)n, -pai-], *s.* expiration *f*. **1. e. of air from the lungs,** expiration de l'air des poumons. **2.** cessation *f*, expiration (d'un bail, d'une concession); échéance *f* (d'un marché à prime); fin *f*, terminaison *f* (d'un terme); **date of e.,** date *f* d'expiration (d'une garantie, etc.); *Ins:* **e. of a policy,** expiration, déchéance *f* d'une police; **to repay before the e. of the period,** rembourser par anticipation.

expiratory [eks'pairət(ə)ri], *a.* (muscle) expirateur.

expire [eks'paiər]. **1.** *v.tr.* expirer, exhaler (l'air des poumons). **2.** *v.i.* (*a*) expirer, mourir, rendre l'âme; (*of lamp, fire*) s'éteindre; (*of hope*) s'évanouir; (*b*) (*of term, law, treaty, etc.*) expirer, cesser, prendre fin, se trouver épuisé; venir à expiration; **my lease has expired; it expired yesterday,** mon bail est expiré; il a expiré hier; *Com:* **expired bill,** effet périmé; *Ins:* **expired policy,** police déchue; *Bank:* **this letter of credit has expired,** cette lettre de crédit est expirée, périmée, ne reste plus en vigueur; **the validity of this passport expires on . . .,** ce passeport expire le . . ..

expiring[1] [eks'paiəriŋ], *a.* **1.** expirant, qui se meurt; (feu, lampe) qui s'éteint; (espoir) qui s'évanouit; **his e. words,** ses dernières paroles; **with an e. voice,** d'une voix mourante. **2.** (*of term, lease, contract*) qui expire; qui prend fin; qui est à son terme.

expiring[2], *s.* expiration *f*.

expiry [eks'paiəri], *s.* expiration *f*, fin *f*, terminaison *f* (d'un terme); terme *m* (d'une période).

explain [eks'plein]. **1.** *v.tr.* (*a*) expliquer, éclaircir, élucider (une règle de grammaire, une énigme, etc.); **I explained to them how I was placed, how I stood,** je leur ai exposé ma situation; **that explains everything,** voilà qui explique tout; **that is easily explained,** cela s'explique facilement; **to e. sth. away,** expliquer qch.; donner une explication satisfaisante de qch.; **to e. a passage to s.o.,** expliquer un passage à qn; **"it is a local custom," explained the guide,** "c'est une coutume du pays," dit le guide en explication; (*b*) justifier (sa conduite, etc.). **2. to e. (oneself),** (i) s'expliquer; (ii) se justifier, rendre raison de sa conduite; **you'd better e.,** allons, expliquez-vous. **3.** *v.i.* donner des explications; **that will e. to your father,** cela en donnera l'explication à votre père.

explainable [eks'pleinəbl], *a.* (phénomène *m*, conduite *f*) explicable; (conduite) justifiable.

explainer [eks'pleinər], *s.* explicateur, -trice; expliqueur, -euse (de songes).

explanation [eksplə'neiʃ(ə)n], *s.* explication *f*, éclaircissement *m*; **to give explanations,** fournir des explications; **to give an e. of one's behaviour,** justifier sa conduite; **to enter into long explanations,** entrer dans de longues explications.

explanative [eks'plænətiv], *a.* = EXPLANATORY.

explanatively [eks'plænətivli], **explanatorily** [eks'plænət(ə)rili], *adv.* (dit) en explication.

explanatory [eks'plænət(ə)ri], *a.* explicatif; explicateur, -trice; **e. note,** notice interprétative; **e. statement,** éclaircissement *m*; *Jur:* (*given in writing*) soutènement *m*.

expletive [eks'pli:tiv]. **1.** *a. Gram: etc:* explétif. **2.** *s.* (*a*) *Gram: etc:* particule explétive; explétif *m*; (*b*) juron *m*.

expletively [eks'pli:tivli], *adv.* explétivement.

explicable [eks'plikəbl], *a.* explicable.

explicableness ['eksplikəblnis], *s.* explicabilité *f*.

explicand [ekspli'kænd], *s.* chose *f* qu'il faut expliquer.

explicate ['eksplikeit], *v.tr. Log:* développer (une notion, un principe, etc.).

explication [ekspli'keiʃ(ə)n], *s. Log:* développement *m*, interprétation *f* (d'un principe, d'une notion).

explicative ['eksplikeitiv, eks'plikətiv]. **1.** *a.* (*a*) explicatif; (*b*) *Log:* essentiel. **2.** *s.* mot explicatif.

explicatory ['eksplikətəri, eks'plikət(ə)ri], *a.* explicateur, -trice.

explicit [eks'plisit], *a.* (*a*) explicite; formel, clair; **e. declaration,** déclaration formelle, catégorique; **to give more e. promises,** préciser ses promesses; **to be more e. (in one's statements),** préciser (ses affirmations); *Mth:* **e. function,** fonction explicite; *Theol:* **e. faith,** croyance *f* explicite; (*b*) (*of pers.*) qui a son franc parler; **to be e.,** s'expliciter.

explicitly [eks'plisitli], *adv.* explicitement; catégoriquement; **tell me more e.,** dites-le moi en termes plus clairs.

explicitness [eks'plisitnəs], *s.* clarté *f*, netteté *f* (de langage).

explode [eks'ploud]. **1.** *v.tr.* (*a*) démontrer la fausseté de (qch.); discréditer (une théorie, une opinion); (*b*) faire éclater (un obus); faire sauter (une mine); faire exploser (un gaz, une poudre). **2.** *v.i.* faire explosion; (*a*) (*of boiler, shell, etc.*) éclater; (*of powder magazine, mine, boiler*) sauter; (*of mine*) jouer; *F:* (*of pers.*) **to e. with laughter,** éclater de rire; *F:* **if he finds out he'll e.,** s'il découvre ça, il explosera, il va sortir de ses gonds, il va faire une de ces scènes; (*b*) (*of gas, dynamite, gunpowder, etc.*) exploser, détoner; (*c*) *Golf:* **to e. out of a bunker,** faire sauter la balle d'un bunker.

exploded [eks'ploudid], *a.* **1. e. theory,** théorie abandonnée, reconnue pour fausse; **e. opinion,** opinion discréditée. **2.** (obus) éclaté; (mine) qui a sauté. **3.** *Draw: Tchn:* **e. view,** (vue) éclatée (*f*).

explodent [eks'ploud(ə)nt], *s. Ling:* (consonne) explosive *f.*

exploder [eks'ploudər], *s.* **1. e. of a theory,** celui qui a le premier démontré la fausseté d'une théorie. **2.** (*device*) *Min:* (*a*) amorce *f,* détonateur *m;* (*b*) exploseur *m* (électrique); (*c*) *Agr:* (*against birds, etc.*) détonateur.

exploit[1] ['eksplɔit], *s.* exploit *m;* haut fait.

exploit[2] [eks'plɔit], *v.tr.* (*a*) exploiter (une mine, une forêt, etc.); (*b*) exploiter (qn, les talents de qn).

exploitable [eks'plɔitəbl], *a.* exploitable.

exploitation [eksplɔi'teiʃ(ə)n], *s.* exploitation *f* (d'une mine, de qn, *Mil:* du succès).

exploiter [eks'plɔitər], *s.* exploiteur, -euse.

exploiting [eks'plɔitiŋ], *s.* exploitation *f.*

exploration [eksplə'reiʃ(ə)n], *s.* **1.** (*a*) exploration *f;* **voyage of e.,** voyage *m* de découverte; *Mil:* **e. patrol,** patrouille *f* de découverte; (*b*) **e. of the ground,** reconnaissance *f* du terrain; **e. work,** travaux *m* de recherches. **2.** *Med:* exploration (d'une plaie, etc.).

explorative [eks'plɔrətiv], *a.* exploratif; explorateur, -trice.

exploratory [eks'plɔrət(ə)ri], *a.* **1.** (puits, sondage) d'exploration, de recherches. **2.** (voyage) exploratif, de découverte. **3. e. talks,** conversations *f* préliminaires; **e. surgery,** opération exploratoire.

explore [eks'plɔːr], *v.tr.* (*a*) explorer (une région); aller à la découverte dans (un continent, une mer); **to e. a country,** faire l'exploration d'un pays; **to e. the country,** *F:* battre le pays; **to e. the ground,** fouiller, reconnaître, tâter, le terrain; **to e. the archives of the town,** explorer, fouiller, les archives de la ville; *v.i.* **to e. for coal,** rechercher un filon houiller; (*b*) *Med:* **to e. an organ, a wound,** explorer un organe; explorer, sonder, une plaie; **to e. the human heart,** fouiller dans le cœur humain.

explorer [eks'plɔrər], *s.* **1.** (*pers.*) explorateur, -trice; voyageur, -euse. **2.** (*apparatus*) instrument explorateur, instrument de recherches; *esp. Med:* sonde *f.*

exploring [eks'plɔːriŋ], *s.* = EXPLORATION; *Surg:* **e. needle, e. trocar,** explorateur *m;* *El:* **e. coil,** bobine *f* exploratrice, d'exploration.

explosible [eks'plouzibl], *a.* explosible.

explosion [eks'plouʒ(ə)n], *s.* **1.** explosion *f* (d'un mélange gazeux, d'un obus, etc.); déflagration *f* (d'un gaz); *Min:* **firedamp e.,** coup *m* de feu; coup de grisou; **to cause an e.,** provoquer une explosion; *I.C.E:* **e. engine,** moteur *m* à explosion; **e. stroke,** détente *f;* **e. chamber,** chambre *f* d'explosion (du cylindre); *Ph:* **e. bomb,** bombe *f* calorimétrique; **e.-proof,** antidéflagrant. **2.** (*resulting noise*) détonation. **3.** *F:* débordement *m* (de fureur); explosion (de rires).

explosive [ek'splousiv]. **1.** *a.* (*a*) explosif, détonant; **e. bolt,** goupille explosive; **e. bullet,** balle explosive; **e. mixture,** (i) *Exp:* mélange explosif, détonant; (ii) *I.C.E:* mélange tonnant, gaz tonnant; **e. mixture of air and dust,** mélange explosif d'air et de poussière; **e. train,** circuit explosif, traînée explosive; **e. wave,** onde explosive; *Atom.Ph:* **e. material,** matière explosive; **e. fission,** fission explosive; (*b*) *Golf:* **e. shot,** coup explosif (pour faire sauter la balle d'un bunker, etc.); (*c*) *Ling:* **e. consonant,** consonne explosive; (*d*) **e. situation,** situation explosive. **2.** *s.* (*a*) *Exp:* explosif *m;* poudre *f;* **high e.,** explosif brisant, détonant; explosif à grande puissance; **high-e. shell,** obus explosif, obus (à explosif) brisant; **high-e. grenade,** grenade explosive; **low e.,** explosif déflagrant; **moulded e.,** poudre moulée; **progressive e.,** explosif progressif; **propellent e.,** explosif propulsif; **booster e.,** (explosif de) relais; **cartridge e.,** explosif en cartouche, en gargousse; **e. store,** dépôt *m* d'explosifs; (*b*) *Ling:* (consonne) explosive *f.*

explosiveness [eks'plousivnis], *s.* nature explosive, tendance explosive (d'un gaz, d'une matière); explosibilité *f.*

exponent [eks'pounənt], *s.* **1.** interprète *mf,* explicateur, -trice (d'un système, etc.); *Mus:* interprète, exécutant, -ante (d'une œuvre); **e. of a sport,** protagoniste *mf* d'un sport; **the leading e. of this art,** le chef de file et principal représentant de cet art. **2.** *Mth:* exposant *m* (d'une quantité).

exponential [ekspou'nenʃ(ə)l], *a.* exponentiel; *Mth:* **e. curve,** courbe exponentielle; **e. equation, function,** équation, fonction, exponentielle; **e. theorem,** théorème exponentiel; *Elcs:* **e. horn,** pavillon exponentiel (d'un haut parleur); **e. loudspeaker,** haut-parleur *m* (à pavillon) exponentiel; **e. tube,** tube *m* à pente variable; *Atom.Ph:* **e. pile,** pile exponentielle.

exponentiation [ekspounenʃi'eiʃ(ə)n], *s. Mth:* exponentiation *f.*

export[1] ['ekspɔːt], *s.* **1.** marchandise exportée; *pl.* **exports,** (i) articles *m* d'exportation; (ii) exportations *f* (d'un pays); **visible, invisible, exports,** exportations visibles, invisibles; **France is increasing her exports to Great Britain,** la France augmente ses exportations vers la Grande-Bretagne. **2.** exportation *f,* sortie *f;* **e. trade,** commerce *m* d'exportation; **a flourishing e. trade,** une exportation florissante; **e. duty,** droit(s) de sortie; **prohibition of exports,** prohibitions *fpl* de sortie; *Pol.Ec:* **gold e. point,** gold-point *m* de sortie.

export[2] [eks'pɔːt], *v.tr.* exporter (des marchandises) (**from,** de).

exportable [eks'pɔːtəbl], *a.* exportable.

exportation [ekspɔː'teiʃ(ə)n], *s.* exportation *f;* sortie *f* (de marchandises).

exporter [eks'pɔːtər], *s.* exportateur, -trice.

exporting[1] [eks'pɔːtiŋ], *a.* (marchand, etc.) exportateur, -trice.

exporting[2], *s.* exportation *f.*

expose [eks'pouz], *v.tr.* exposer. **1.** (*a*) laisser sans abri (une personne, une plante, etc.); **to e. a new-born child,** exposer, abandonner, un nouveau-né; **to e. sth. to the rain,** exposer qch. à la pluie; **not to be exposed to the air,** ne pas laisser à l'air; (*b*) **to e. s.o., oneself,** to **danger,** exposer qn, s'exposer, s'offrir, au danger; courir au-devant du danger; **to e. one's flank to the enemy,** prêter le flanc à l'ennemi; **to e. oneself to ridicule,** s'exposer à la risée publique; se rendre ridicule; (*c*) *Phot:* exposer (un film). **2.** (*a*) mettre (qch.) à découvert, à nu, à jour, en évidence; déchausser (des racines, des roches); **to e. one's ignorance,** afficher son ignorance; **to be exposed to view,** être exposé aux regards, à la vue de tous; (*b*) étaler (des marchandises à vendre); (*c*) *Ecc:* exposer (le saint Sacrement, une relique); (*d*) **to e. oneself, one's person,** faire de l'exhibitionnisme; *Jur:* commettre un outrage public à la pudeur. **3.** éventer (un secret); démasquer (un hypocrite); dévoiler (un crime); dénoncer (qn, un abus, un vice); livrer au ridicule (une manie, etc.).

exposé [eks'pouzei], *s.* (*a*) exposé *m;* (*b*) révélation *f* (d'un scandale, etc.).

exposed [eks'pouzd], *a.* **1.** (*a*) exposé (à la vue, aux éléments); **e. goods,** marchandises étalées, en montre; **not e. to east winds,** abrité contre les vents de l'est; **e. gearing,** engrenages à découvert; **the e. parts of the engine,** les organes apparents de la machine; *Mil:* **e. position,** endroit exposé; (*of troops*) **to be e.,** être en l'air; (*b*) (*laid bare*) à nu; (*of root, etc.*) déchaussé. **2.** *Phot:* (film, etc.) exposé, impressionné.

exposition [ekspə'ziʃ(ə)n], *s.* **1.** exposition *f* (d'un enfant, *Ecc:* du saint Sacrement, d'une relique). **2.** exposition, exposé *m,* interprétation *f,* commentaire *m* (d'une œuvre littéraire); *Mus: etc:* exposition. **3.** *U.S:* exposition (de peinture, etc.).

expositive [eks'pɔzitiv], *a.* (article, mot) d'exposition, expositoire, expositif.

expositor [eks'pɔzitər], *s.* interprète *mf,* commentateur, -trice (d'une doctrine, d'un texte, etc.).

ex post facto ['ekspoust'fæktou], *Lt.adj.phr. Jur:* (*of law, etc.*) rétroactif.

expostulate [eks'pɔstjuleit], *v.i.* **to e. with s.o.,** faire des remontrances à qn (**about,** sur, au sujet de; **for doing sth.,** de faire qch., d'avoir fait qch.).

expostulation [ekspɔstju'leiʃ(ə)n], *s.* remontrance(s) *f*(*pl*); **e. proved useless,** j'ai eu beau le raisonner.

expostulatory [eks'pɔstjulətəri, -leitəri], *a.* (lettre, discours) de remontrance.

exposure [eks'pouʒər], *s.* **1.** (*a*) exposition *f* (à l'air, au froid, à un danger); **to die of e.,** mourir de froid; **inured to e.,** endurci aux rigueurs des saisons; *Mil:* **e. suit,** combinaison *f* insubmersible; (*b*) *Phot:* prise *f* de vue; **instantaneous e.,** pose instantanée; instantané *m;* **time e.,** pose *f;* **e. time,** temps *m* de pose; **under e.,** manque *m* de pose; **e. meter,** posemètre *m,* exposemètre *m;* cellule *f* photo(-)électrique; **e. counter,** compteur *m* de prises de vue; (*c*) *Atom.Ph:* **e. (to radiation),** irradiation *f;* **acute e.,** irradiation aiguë; **permissible e.,** irradiation admissible. **2.** exposition, abandon *m* (d'un nouveau-né). **3.** (*a*) *Min: etc:* mise *f* à nu, à découvert (du minerai, etc.); (*b*) exposition, étalage *m* (de marchandises à vendre); (*c*) *Jur:* **indecent e.,** délit puni par la loi sur les mœurs; outrage public à la pudeur; (*d*) dévoilement *m* (d'un crime, etc.); dénonciation *f* (d'un escroc); **the fear of e.,** la crainte d'un éclat, d'un scandale; **to threaten s.o. with e.,** menacer qn d'un éclat. **4.** exposition, orientation *f* (d'un lieu, d'un bâtiment); **southerly, northerly, e.,** exposition au midi, au nord; **house with southerly e.,** maison exposée au sud.

expound [eks'paund], *v.tr.* **1.** exposer (une doctrine, ses principes). **2.** expliquer, interpréter (les Écritures saintes).

expounder [eks'paundər], *s.* = EXPOSITOR.

expounding [eks'paundiŋ], *s.* exposition *f,* explication *f,* interprétation *f.*

express[1] [eks'pres]. **1.** *a.* (*a*) **e. image,** image exacte, fidèle (**of,** de); (*b*) (*of law, stipulation, etc.*) exprès, *f.* expresse; (*of order*) exprès, formel, explicite; **for this e. purpose,** dans ce but même, pour cela même; (*c*) **e. train,** (train) express *m,* rapide *m;* **e. delivery,** envoi *m* par exprès; **e. letter,** lettre *f* exprès; **e. messenger,** messager *m* exprès; *Mil:* estafette *f;* **e. rifle,** fusil *m* express; fusil à tir rapide; *Post:* **by e. messenger,** par exprès; (*d*) *U.S:* **e. company,** *s. F:* **the e.,** compagnie *f* de messageries. **2.** *adv.* (*a*) **to go, send, e.,** aller, envoyer, en toute hâte; (*b*) sans arrêt; **lift that goes e. to the twentieth floor,** ascenseur *m* qui monte sans arrêt au vingtième étage. **3.** *s. Rail:* express *m,* rapide *m;* **pullman-car e.,** train *m* de luxe; *U.S:* **e. agent,** agent *m* de messageries; **e. car,** wagon *m* pour messageries.

express[2], *v.tr.* **1.** exprimer (le jus, l'huile) (**out of, from,** de); (*of nursing mother*) exprimer (du lait). **2.** énoncer (un principe); exprimer, rendre (ses sentiments, une pensée); dire (son sentiment); manifester (sa volonté); **to e. an opinion, a conclusion, a wish,** émettre une opinion; formuler une conclusion, un souhait; **terms expressing a principle,** termes énonciateurs d'un principe; **to e. one's gratitude,** témoigner sa reconnaissance; **to e. one's heartfelt thanks to s.o.,** exprimer, présenter, ses remerciements sincères à qn; **to e. the author's meaning,** rendre le sens de l'auteur; **to e. one's thoughts on paper,** traduire ses pensées sur le papier; **well, badly, expressed,** bien, mal, rendu; **the word is not expressed,** on sous entend ce mot; **face that expresses nothing,** visage qui ne dit rien; *Mth:* **to e. one quantity in terms of another,** exprimer une quantité en termes d'une autre. **3. he has difficulty in expressing himself,** il a du mal à s'exprimer; **he expressed himself strongly on this subject,** il s'est exprimé très carrément à ce sujet; **how do you e. it in French?** comment dit-on cela en français?

express[3], *v.tr.* **1.** *U.S:* envoyer, expédier (un colis, etc.) par les messageries. **2.** envoyer (une lettre, etc.) par exprès.

expressage [eks'presidʒ], *s. U.S:* (*a*) envoi *m* d'un colis par les messageries; (*b*) droit perçu pour un envoi par les messageries.

expressible [eks'presibl], *a.* (pensée *f,* etc.) exprimable; *Mth:* **x is easily e. in terms of y,** *x* s'exprime facilement en fonction de *y.*

expressing[1] [eks'presiŋ], *s.* expression *f.*

expressing[2], *s.* envoi *m* (d'une lettre) par exprès.

expression [eks'preʃ(ə)n], *s.* **1.** expression *f* (du jus d'une orange, etc.). **2.** expression, manifestation *f* (d'une pensée, de la joie, etc.); **beyond e., past e.,** au delà de toute expression; inexprimable; **his grief found e. in tears,** sa douleur se traduisit par des larmes; **to give e. to one's will,** manifester sa volonté; **to give eloquent e. to one's feelings,** prêter à ses sentiments une expression éloquente; **to give e. to one's gratitude to s.o.,** témoigner sa reconnaissance à qn; **freedom of e.,** liberté *f* d'expression. **3.** (*a*) expression, locution *f;* **exaggerated expressions,** grands mots; (*b*) **algebraical e.,** expression, formule *f,* algébrique; **to reduce a polynomial to the simplest e.,** réduire un polynome à sa plus simple expression. **4.** (*a*) expression (du visage, des yeux); **face that has much e.,** figure qui a beaucoup d'expression; **to listen with a delighted e.,** écouter avec un air charmé, d'un air ravi; (*b*) *Mus:* **to sing, play, with e.,** chanter, jouer, avec expression; **e. mark,** signe *m* d'expression; (*of harmonium*) **e. stop,** jeu *m* de l'expression.

expressionism [eks'preʃənizm], *s. Art: etc:* expressionnisme *m.*

expressionist [eks'preʃənist], *a. & s.* expressionniste (*mf*).

expressionless [eks'preʃ(ə)nlis], *a.* (figure, voix, regard, musique) sans expression; (visage *m*) impassible; **to be e.,** manquer d'expression.

expressive [eks'presiv], *s.* (*a*) expressif, plein d'expression; **to give s.o. an e. look,** regarder qn d'une manière significative, d'un air significatif; **e. gesture,** silence éloquent; (*b*) **a speech e. of his admiration,** un discours où il exprimait son admiration; **attitude e. of disdain,** attitude *f* qui exprime le dédain.

expressively [eks'presivli], *adv.* avec expression.

expressiveness [eks'presivnis], *s.* caractère expressif, force *f* d'expression (d'un visage, d'une langue, d'un mot).

expressivity [ekspre'siviti], *s.* **1.** *Biol:* expressivité *f.* **2.** force *f* d'expression.

expressly [eks'presli], *adv.* **1.** expressément, formellement (défendu, etc.); **I told him e. that. . .,** je lui ai dit en termes exprès que . . .. **2. here is a present which I bought e. for you,** voici un cadeau que j'ai acheté à votre intention; **I did it e. to please you,** je l'ai fait dans le seul but, à seule fin, de vous plaire.
expressman [eks'presmən, -mæn], *s. U.S:* employé *m* des messageries.
expressway [eks'preswei], *s.* (*a*) *U.S:* autoroute *f*; (*b*) chaussée *f*, voie *f*, rapide de raccordement.
expromission [eksprou'miʃ(ə)n], *s.* expromission *f*.
expropriate [eks'prouprieit], *v.tr.* exproprier (un propriétaire, une propriété); **to e. s.o. from sth.,** exproprier qn de qch.
expropriating [eks'prouprieitiŋ], *a.* expropriateur, -trice.
expropriation [eksproupri'eiʃ(ə)n], *s.* expropriation *f* (d'un propriétaire, d'une propriété); dépossession *f* (de qn).
expropriator [eks'prouprieitər], *s.* expropriateur, -trice.
expuition [ekspju'iʃ(ə)n], *s. Med:* expuition *f*.
expulsion [eks'pʌlʃ(ə)n], *s.* expulsion *f* (d'un étranger, des matières fécales, etc.); renvoi *m* (d'un élève); *Adm:* **e. order,** arrêté *m*, décret *m*, d'expulsion; interdiction *f* de séjour.
expulsive [eks'pʌlsiv], *a.* (*of force, etc.*) expulsif, -ive.
expunction [eks'pʌŋkʃ(ə)n], *s. Pal:* exponction *f*, exponctuation *f*.
expunge [eks'pʌndʒ], *v.tr.* **1.** effacer, omettre, rayer (un nom d'une liste, un passage dans un livre). **2. to e. an offence,** purger une offense.
expunging [eks'pʌndʒiŋ], *s.* effaçage *m*, omission *f*; radiation *f* (d'un nom).
expurgate ['ekspəːgeit], *v.tr.* (*a*) expurger (un livre); épurer (un texte); *F:* châtrer (une pièce de théâtre, etc.); **expurgated edition,** édition expurgée; (*b*) supprimer (un passage, etc.).
expurgation [ekspəː'geiʃ(ə)n], *s.* (*a*) expurgation *f* (d'un livre); épuration *f* (d'un texte, d'une association); (*b*) suppression *f* (d'un passage).
expurgator ['ekspəgeitər], *s.* celui, celle, qui expurge (un livre), qui épure (un texte).
expurgatory [eks'pəːgətəri], *a. R.C.Ch:* (index *m*) expurgatoire.
exquisite ['ekskwizit]. **1.** *a.* (*a*) (plat, vin, travail) exquis; **woman with an e. figure,** femme d'une taille ravissante; (*b*) (*of pleasure, pain, etc.*) vif; **e. torture,** supplice raffiné; tourment *m* atroce; **e. enjoyment,** jouissance délicieuse; **e. malice,** malice consommée; (*c*) très sensible, délicat, subtil. **2.** *s. A:* élégant *m*; petit-maître *m*, *pl.* petits-maîtres; dandy *m*, *pl.* dandys.
exquisitely ['ekskwizitli], *adv.* **1.** d'une manière exquise; (*of needlework, musical execution, etc.*) **e. done,** perlé; **e. polite,** d'une politesse exquise. **2.** excessivement, extrêmement; **e. minute, sensitive,** extrêmement petit, sensible.
exquisiteness ['ekskwizitnis], *s.* **1.** perfection délicate (d'une œuvre d'art). **2. the e. of his torments, of the pain,** ses tourments *m* atroces, l'acuité *f* de la douleur; **the e. of his pleasure,** son plaisir indicible; son vif plaisir. **3.** finesse *f* (de l'oreille, etc.).
exsanguination [eks(s)æŋgwi'neiʃ(ə)n], *s. Med:* exsanguination *f*.
exsanguine [eks'sæŋgwin], *a.* exsangue, anémique.
exsanguinotransfusion [eks(s)æŋwinoutrænz'fjuːʒ(ə)n], *s. Med:* exsanguino-transfusion *f*, *pl.* exsanguino-transfusions.
exscind [ek'sind], *v.tr.* exciser (une tumeur); *A:* extirper (de mauvaises habitudes, etc.).
exsert [ek(s)'səːt], **exserted** [ek(s)'səːtid], *a. Biol:* (aiguillon, etc.) ex(s)ert.
exsertile [ek(s)'səːtail], *a. Biol:* ex(s)ertile.
ex-serviceman, *pl.* **-men** [eks'səːvismən], *s.m.* ancien combattant, ancien mobilisé, ancien militaire.
exsiccate ['eksikeit], *v.tr.* assécher, mettre à sec (un terrain); dessécher (la végétation); faire évaporer (une solution).
exsiccation [eksi'keiʃ(ə)n], *s.* assèchement *m*, mise *f* à sec (d'un pays); exsiccation *f*, dessèchement *m* (des foins, etc.); évaporation *f* (d'une solution).
exsiccator ['eksikeitər], *s. Ch:* exsiccateur *m*.
exstipulate [ek'stipjulət], *a. Bot:* sans stipules.
exstrophy ['ekstrəfi], *s. Med:* exstrophie *f*.
exsuction [eks'sʌkʃ(ə)n], *s.* exsuccion *f*.
extant [ek'stænt], *a.* existant; qui existe encore; **still e.,** subsistant; **the earliest document e.,** le plus ancien document existant.
extemporaneous [ekstempə'reinjəs], *a.* **1.** (*of prayer, speech*) improvisé, impromptu. **2.** *Pharm:* (médicament) extemporané.
extemporaneously [ekstempə'reinjəsli], *adv.* = EXTEMPORE 1.
extemporary [eks'temp(ə)rəri], *a.* = EXTEMPORE 2.
extempore [eks'tempəri]. **1.** *adv.* **to speak, pray, e.,** parler, prier, d'abondance, impromptu, sans préparation; **to speak e.,** improviser (un discours). **2.** *a.* (*a*) improvisé, impromptu; **e. speech,** discours improvisé, impromptu; **to make an e. speech,** improviser un discours; (*b*) **e. speaker,** orateur qui parle volontiers d'abondance.
extemporization [ekstempərai'zeiʃ(ə)n], *s.* improvisation *f*.
extemporize [eks'temporaiz]. **1.** *v.tr.* improviser (un discours); faire (une prière) à l'impromptu. **2.** *v.i.* (*a*) improviser, parler à l'impromptu; parler d'abondance; (*b*) *Mus:* **to e. on the organ,** improviser à l'orgue.
extemporizer [eks'tempəraizər], *s.* improvisateur, -trice.
extend [eks'tend], *v.*
I. *v.tr.* **1.** (*a*) étendre, allonger (le corps, les membres); prolonger (une ligne); **to e. one's arm horizontally,** étendre le bras horizontalement; (*b*) *A:* **to e. shorthand,** transcrire de la sténographie; *Jur: Scot:* **to e. a deed,** grossoyer un acte; *Com:* **to e. an invoice,** donner les totaux partiels d'une facture; **to e. a balance,** transporter, reporter, une balance; (*c*) étendre, déployer (des troupes); (*d*) *Sp: etc:* **to e. a horse, a runner, etc.,** faire rendre son maximum à, pousser, un cheval, un coureur, etc.; (*of pers.*) **he does not e. himself,** il ne s'emploie pas. **2.** prolonger (une période de temps, *Rail:* un billet); *Com:* proroger (l'échéance d'un billet); continuer (des recherches); *Mil:* **to e. a man's leave for three more days,** prolonger de trois jours la permission d'un homme; accorder à un homme une prolongation de trois jours; *Bank:* **to e. the validity of a credit to . . .,** proroger jusqu'à . . . la durée d'un accréditif. **3.** étendre, porter plus loin (les limites, les dimensions); étendre (la signification d'un mot); accroître (des connaissances, un commerce); agrandir, augmenter (son pouvoir, ses terres); **to e. the frontiers of a state,** reculer les frontières d'un État; **we are going to e. our premises,** nous allons nous agrandir. **4.** (*a*) tendre (la main); (*b*) **to e. indulgence, kindness, to, towards, s.o.,** étendre son indulgence, sa bonté, sur qn; **to e. a welcome to s.o.,** souhaiter la bienvenue à qn; (*c*) *Jur:* **to e. a protest,** dresser un protêt. **5.** *Jur:* (*a*) évaluer (des biens, en vue d'une saisie); (*b*) saisir (les biens de qn).
II. *v.i.* **1.** s'étendre, s'allonger (**to, over, across,** jusqu'à, au delà de); **estate that extends to the sea,** propriété qui s'étend, qui va, qui continue, jusqu'à la mer; **the tapestry extends to nearly 20 m.,** la tapisserie mesure près de 20 m.; **wound extending to the lungs,** blessure qui a gagné le poumon, qui intéresse le poumon; **a long passage extends from the door to the garden,** un long corridor règne de la porte jusqu'au jardin; **to e. beyond the wall, etc.,** saillir, faire saillie, au delà du mur, etc.; déborder le mur; s'avancer en dehors du mur. **2.** (*of period of time*) se prolonger, continuer; **enquiries extending over a number of years,** demandes de renseignements prolongées pendant un grand nombre d'années.
extended [eks'tendid], *a.* **1.** (*a*) (corps, bras) étendu, allongé; *Typ:* **e. letter,** lettre allongée; **e. spring,** ressort *m* lège, déchargé; *Equit:* **e. trot,** trot allongé; (*b*) *Mil:* **e. troops,** troupes déployées; **in e. order,** en ordre dispersé; en tirailleurs; **horsemen in e. order,** cavaliers dispersés en fourrageurs; **charge in e. order,** charge *f* en fourrageurs. **2.** (*a*) (bail, etc.) prolongé; (*b*) long, prolongé; **to take an e. trip to Europe,** faire en Europe un voyage prolongé, un voyage de quelque durée; **an e. list of repairs,** une longue liste de réparations; *Rec:* **an e. play record,** un super 45 tours; (*c*) *Mec.E:* **e. (piston) rod,** contre-tige *f* (de piston), *pl.* contre-tiges. **3.** augmenté, agrandi; (commerce) accru; *Gram: Log:* **e. meaning (of a word),** extension *f* (d'un mot). **4.** *Jur:* **e. land,** (i) terre évaluée; (ii) terre saisie (pour dettes).
extender [eks'tendər], *s. Paint:* blanc *m* de charge (d'une couleur), charge *f*, extendeur *m*.
extendible [eks'tendəbl], *a. Jur:* (bien) sujet à saisie.
extending[1] [eks'tendiŋ], *a.* (table) à rallonges; (échelle) à coulisse.
extending[2], *s.* extension *f*, allongement *m*, prolongation *f*, augmentation *f*.
extensibility [ekstensi'biliti], *s.* extensibilité *f*.
extensible [eks'tensibl], *a.* extensible, allongeable.
extensile [eks'tensail], *a. Nat.Hist:* extensile; **with an e. tongue,** extensilingue.
extension [eks'tenʃ(ə)n], *s.* **1.** (*a*) (*extending*) extension *f* (du bras, des muscles); prolongement *m*, allongement *m* (d'un canal, d'un chemin de fer, etc.); agrandissement *m*, extension (d'une usine, etc.); *Surg:* **e. of a broken leg,** extension d'une jambe cassée; *Mec:* **elastic e.,** allongement unitaire élastique; **e. piece,** pièce *f* formant prolongement; (r)allonge *f* (de table, d'établi, de cric, etc.); clef *f* de rallonge (d'une clef en tube); **e. ladder,** échelle *f* à coulisse; **e. tripod,** trépied *m* extensible; (*b*) *Av:* sortie *f* (du train d'atterrissage, d'un volet, etc.); **e. flap,** volet type Fowler; (*c*) *Phot:* tirage *m* (du soufflet, d'un appareil); **double-e. camera,** chambre *f* à double tirage; **fixed e.,** tirage constant; (*d*) *Book-k:* transport *m*, report *m* (d'une balance); (*e*) *Jur:* dressement *m* (d'un protêt); (*f*) *U.S:* **e. services,** services *m* de vulgarisation. **2.** (*growing*) extension, accroissement *m* (des affaires, etc.); **there has been a considerable e. of his business,** son commerce a pris une extension considérable; **e. of a forest by natural seeding,** accrue *f* d'une forêt. **3.** (*a*) (r)allonge (de table, etc.); allonge (de câble); *Tp:* poste *m* supplémentaire; **e. 35,** poste 35; *El:* **e. light,** baladeuse *f*; *Elcs:* **e. loudspeaker,** haut-parleur séparé; *Tls:* **e. bit,** mèche *f* extensible, à rallonge; *Rail:* **line with extensions to . . .,** ligne *f* avec prolongements jusqu'à . . .; (*b*) annexe *f* (d'un bâtiment); (*c*) *Gram:* complément *m* (du sujet, de l'attribut). **4.** (*temporal*) prolongation *f* (de congé, d'échéance, d'un billet de chemin de fer); **to get an e. of time,** obtenir un délai; **to arrange with one's creditors for an e. of time,** s'atermoyer avec ses créanciers; **arrangement for an e. of time,** atermoiement *m*; *Bank:* **e. of credit,** prolongation d'un accréditif. **5.** *Phil:* étendue *f*, extension (de la matière); *Log:* **terms must not be given a wider e. in the conclusion than in the premises,** les termes ne doivent pas être pris plus universellement dans la conclusion qu'ils ne l'ont été dans les prémisses.
extensive [eks'tensiv], *a.* **1.** étendu, vaste, ample, considérable; **an e. sheet of water,** une nappe d'eau très étendue; une vaste nappe d'eau; **e. knowledge,** connaissances étendues; vastes connaissances; **e. researches,** travaux approfondis; **e. memory,** mémoire étendue; **criminal of fairly e. activities,** criminel *m* d'une certaine envergure; **to make e. use of sth.,** faire un usage considérable de qch. **2. e. agriculture,** agriculture extensive.
extensively [eks'tensivli], *adv.* **to use sth. e.,** se servir beaucoup, largement, considérablement, de qch.; faire un usage considérable de qch.
extensiveness [eks'tensivnis], *s.* étendue *f*.
extensometer [eksten'səmitər], *s. Mec.E:* indicateur *m* d'extension; extensomètre *m*.
extensor [eks'tensər], *s. Anat:* (muscle) extenseur *m*; *Med:* **e. plantar response,** réflexe *m* plantaire en extension.
extent [eks'tent], *s.* **1.** (*a*) *Hist:* estimation *f* de biens-fonds; (*b*) *Jur:* (i) évaluation *f*; (ii) saisie *f* (des biens d'un débiteur); **e. in chief,** saisie des biens d'un débiteur de la Couronne; **e. in aid,** saisie des biens d'un débiteur par un créancier qui lui-même est un débiteur de la Couronne. **2.** étendue *f*; **vast e. of ground,** grande superficie, grande étendue, de terrain; **what is the e. of the park?** jusqu'où va le parc? **track six kilometres in e.,** piste d'un développement de six kilomètres; **e. of the damage,** importance *f* du dommage; **e. of a wound,** importance d'une blessure; **the e. of tax relief,** la quotité du dégrèvement fiscal; **credit to the e. of £50,** crédit jusqu'à concurrence de cinquante livres sterling; **to a certain e., to some e.,** jusqu'à un certain point; dans une certaine mesure; **to be important to a certain e.,** avoir une certaine importance; **to a great e., to a large e.,** considérablement; en grande partie; dans une large mesure; **if orders should go down to any great e.,** si les commandes diminuent dans de sérieuses proportions; **to such an e. that . . .,** à tel point que . . .; **to some slight e.,** quelque peu; **to the full e. of his power,** de tout son pouvoir; (*of workmen*) **to work to the full e. of their powers,** travailler à plein rendement; **to what e.?** dans quelle mesure?
extenuate [eks'tenjueit], *v.tr.* **1.** *A:* exténuer, amaigrir, affaiblir. **2. to e. an offence, the guilt of s.o.,** atténuer, amoindrir, la faute, la culpabilité, de qn.
extenuating [eks'tenjueitiŋ], *a.* **e. circumstance,** circonstance atténuante.
extenuation [ekstenju'eiʃ(ə)n], *s.* **1.** exténuation *f*, affaiblissement *m* extrême (du corps). **2.** atténuation *f* (d'une faute, d'un crime); **to plead sth. in e. of a crime,** alléguer qch. pour atténuer un crime; **circumstances in e. of his fault,** circonstances *f* qui atténuent sa faute; circonstances atténuantes.
extenuatory [eks'tenjuət(ə)ri], *a.* atténuant.
exterior [eks'tiəriər]. **1.** *a.* extérieur (**to,** à), en dehors (**to,** de); *Mth:* **e. angle** (i) (*of polygon*) angle extérieur; (ii) (*between parallel lines and intersecting line*) angle externe; **we manufacture these articles without e. help,**

nous fabriquons ces articles sans aide du dehors. 2. *s.* (*a*) extérieur *m*, dehors *mpl*; **on the e.,** à l'extérieur; **house with an imposing e.,** maison aux dehors imposants; **despite his stern e. he is very likeable,** malgré un extérieur sévère il est très sympathique; (*b*) *Th: Cin:* extérieur.

exterioration [ekstiəriə'reiʃ(ə)n], *s. Physiol:* extérioration *f* (d'une sensation).

exteriority [ekstiəri'ɔriti], *s. Phil: etc:* extériorité *f*.

exteriorization [ekstiəriərai'zeiʃ(ə)n], *s. Phil: Psy:* extériorisation *f* (d'un état de conscience).

exteriorize [eks'tiəriəraiz], *v.tr.* extérioriser.

exteriorly [eks'tiəriəli], *adv.* à l'extérieur, extérieurement.

exterminate [eks'tə:mineit], *v.tr.* exterminer (des insectes, une population, etc.); **they were exterminated off the face of the earth,** ils furent exterminés de la face de la terre.

exterminating[1] [eks'tə:mineitiŋ], *a.* exterminateur, -trice.

exterminating[2], **extermination** [ekstə:mi'neiʃ(ə)n], *s.* extermination *f* (d'une population, etc.); extirpation *f* (d'une hérésie).

exterminative [eks'tə:mineitiv], *a.* qui tend à exterminer, exterminateur.

exterminator [eks'tə:mineitər], *s.* 1. (*pers.*) exterminateur, -trice; extirpateur, -trice. 2. **beetle e., ant e.,** tue-cafards *m inv*, tue-fourmis *m inv*.

extern [eks'tə:n], *s. Sch: Med:* externe *mf*.

external [eks'tə:nəl]. 1. *a.* (*a*) (médicament *m*, angle *m*) externe; *Med:* **for e. use only,** pour l'usage externe; *Anat:* **e. saphenous vein,** veine *f* saphène externe; (*b*) extérieur; du dehors; **e. walls,** murs extérieurs; **e. events,** affaires du dehors, de l'extérieur; (*c*) (*of trade, etc.*) extérieur; étranger, -ère; (*d*) **e. student,** étudiant, -ante, libre. 2. *s.* (*usu. in pl.*) (*a*) extérieur *m*, formes extérieures, dehors *m*; **to judge by externals,** juger les choses selon les apparences; **she was hardly conscious of externals,** elle avait à peine conscience du monde extérieur; (*b*) choses pas essentielles, secondaires.

externality [ekstə:'næliti], *s. Phil: Psy: etc:* extériorité *f*.

externalization [ekstə:nəlai'zeiʃ(ə)n], *s.* extériorisation *f*.

externalize [eks'tə:nəlaiz], *v.tr. Phil: Psy:* extérioriser.

externalizing [eks'tə:nəlaiziŋ], *s.* extériorisation *f*.

externally [eks'tə:nəli], *adv.* extérieurement; à l'extérieur; au dehors; d'après les dehors.

exteroceptive [ekstərou'septiv], *a. Physiol:* extéroceptif.

exteroceptor [ekstərou'septər], *s. Z: Anat:* extérocepteur *m*.

exterritorial [eksteri'tɔ:riəl], *a.* ex(tra)territorial, -aux.

exterritoriality [eksteritɔ:ri'æliti], *s.* ex(tra)territorialité *f*.

extinct [eks'tiŋ(k)t], *a.* (*a*) (*of fire, volcano, hope, passion*) éteint; (*b*) (*of race, of animals, plants*) disparu, qui n'existe plus; (*of office, title*) aboli, tombé en désuétude; (*of race, etc.*) **to become e.,** s'évanouir, s'éteindre.

extinction [eks'tiŋ(k)ʃ(ə)n], *s.* extinction *f* (d'un incendie, de la chaux, d'une race, d'une dette); anéantissement *m* (d'une espérance); amortissement *m* (d'une pension, etc.); **race threatened with e.,** race *f* en passe de disparaître; *Opt:* **two crossed nicols giving e.,** deux nicols à l'extinction; *Jur:* **e. of an action** (*no step having been taken within the statutory time*), péremption *f* d'instance.

extinctive [eks'tiŋ(k)tiv], *a.* extinctif.

extine ['ekstain], *s. Bot:* exine *f*.

extinguish [eks'tiŋgwiʃ], *v.tr.* éteindre (le feu, un incendie, la lampe, la chaux, les passions); souffler (la chandelle); anéantir, mettre fin à, éteindre (une espérance); abolir (une institution, une loi, un droit); exterminer, éteindre (un peuple, une race); amortir, éteindre (une dette, etc.); *Jur:* **to allow an easement to be extinguished,** laisser s'éteindre une servitude; **to be extinguished by s.o.,** (i) être surpassé, éclipsé, excellé, par qn; (ii) être réduit au silence par qn.

extinguishable [eks'tiŋgwiʃəbl], *a.* extinguible; que l'on peut éteindre.

extinguisher [eks'tiŋgwiʃər], *s.* 1. (*pers.*) éteigneur, -euse. 2. (*a*) appareil *m* d'extinction; (appareil) extincteur *m* (d'incendie); **foam e.,** extincteur à mousse; **hand e.,** extincteur à main; **spark e.,** souffleur *m* d'étincelles; (*b*) (*for candle, etc.*) éteignoir *m*.

extinguishing[1] [eks'tiŋgwiʃiŋ], *a.* extincteur, -trice.

extinguishing[2], *s.* extinction *f* ((i) d'un incendie, (ii) d'un droit, d'une dette); suppression *f* (d'un emploi); abolition *f*, abolissement *m* (d'une loi).

extirpate ['ekstə:peit], *v.tr.* extirper, déraciner (un arbre, une tumeur, un abus); exterminer, détruire entière ment (un peuple, etc.).

extirpation [ekstə:'peiʃ(ə)n], *s.* extirpation *f*, éradication *f* (d'un arbre, d'une tumeur, d'un vice); extermination *f*, destruction entière (d'un peuple, etc.).

extirpator ['ekstə:peitər], *s.* 1. (*pers.*) extirpateur, -trice (de cors, d'abus). 2. (*machine*) *Agr:* extirpateur *m*.

extol [eks'toul], *v.tr.* (**extolled**) exalter, vanter, louer (à dents, etc.). 2. (*a*) *Tls:* pince *f*; *Artil:* extracteur; *Dent:* de qn; **to e. s.o. to the skies,** porter qn aux nues; **to e. the beauty of sth.,** célébrer, chanter, la beauté de qch.

extoller [eks'toulər], *s.* panégyriste *m*, prôneur, -euse.

extolling [eks'touliŋ], **extolment** [eks'toulmənt], *s.* louange *f*, panégyrique *m*.

extort [eks'tɔ:t], *v.tr.* extorquer (une signature, etc.) (**from s.o.,** à qn); **to e. money from s.o.,** extorquer de l'argent à qn; pressurer qn; **to e. a promise, a confession, from s.o.,** arracher une promesse, des aveux, à qn.

extorter [eks'tɔ:tər], *s.* exacteur *m* (**of,** de).

extorting [eks'tɔ:tiŋ], **extortion** [eks'tɔ:ʃ(ə)n], *s.* extorsion *f*, exaction *f* (d'impôts, etc.); arrachement *m* (d'une promesse, d'un aveu).

extortionary [eks'tɔ:ʃnəri], *a.* (*of pers.*) extorsionnaire.

extortionate [eks'tɔ:ʃənət], *a.* 1. (*of pers.*) extorsionnaire, rapace. 2. **e. price,** prix exorbitant.

extortioner [eks'tɔ:ʃənər], **extortionist** [eks'tɔ:ʃənist], *s.* extorqueur, -euse; exacteur *m*.

extortive [eks'tɔ:tiv], *a.* (moyens, talents) d'extorsion.

extra ['ekstrə]. 1. *a.* (*a*) en sus, de plus; supplémentaire; d'extra; **e. dish,** plat *m* d'extra; **e. charge,** prix *m* en sus; supplément *m* de prix; **to make an e. charge,** percevoir un supplément; **e. weight,** surcharge *f*; **e. pay,** prime *f*, supplément *m* de salaire, sursalaire *m*; *Mil: Navy:* haute paie, accessoire *m*, supplément, de solde; *Mil: Navy:* **e. duty,** service *m* supplémentaire, hors tout (prescrit par mesure disciplinaire); **e. fatigue,** corvée *f* supplémentaire; **e. drill,** exercice *m* des punis, *F:* la pelote; **e. postage,** surtaxe postale; **e. work,** (i) heures *f* supplémentaires; (ii) surcroît *m* de travail; **e. horse, engine,** cheval *m*, locomotive *f*, de renfort; *Rail:* **to put on an e. coach,** rajouter une voiture; **e. fare,** supplément (de billet); **e. luggage,** excédent *m*, supplément, de bagages; **as an e. precaution,** pour plus de précaution; *Ins:* **e. premium,** surprime *f*; *Sch:* **e. subject,** matière facultative; **to make an e. effort,** faire un surcroît d'effort; **to work an e. half-day,** travailler une demi-journée supplémentaire; *Typ:* **e. sheets (of print),** main *f* de passe; simple passe *f*; (*b*) de réserve, de rechange; (*c*) (*of paper*) **e. foolscap octavo,** pot in-8 extra grand; (*d*) de qualité supérieure; extra-fin, superfin, exceptionnel; **e. binding,** reliure *f* de luxe; **rope of e. strength,** corde *f* d'une solidité exceptionnelle; corde extra-solide. 2. *adv.* (*a*) plus que d'ordinaire; extra-; **e. strong binding,** reliure extra-solide; **e. white,** extra-blanc; **e. superfine,** extra-fin; **e. smart,** ultra-chic; (*b*) en plus; **meals taken in the bedroom are charged (for) e.,** il y a un supplément pour les repas servis dans la chambre; **the wine is e.,** le vin est en plus; **this edition contains three maps e.,** cette édition a trois cartes en plus; **packing e.,** emballage compté à part, non compris. 3. *s.* (*a*) supplément (de menu); édition spéciale (d'un journal); numéro *m* supplémentaire (d'un programme varié); *Cr:* point supplémentaire; (*b*) (*pers.*) extra *m*; *Th: Cin:* figurant, -ante; **to be, work as, an e.,** faire de la figuration; (*c*) *pl.* **extras,** frais *m*, dépenses *f*, supplémentaires, extraordinaires; suppléments; *Sch:* arts *m* d'agrément; *Typ:* surcharge *f*; **little extras,** les petits à-côtés.

extra- ['ekstrə], *pref.* extra-.

extra-atmospheric ['ekstrəætməs'ferik], *a.* extra-atmosphérique, en dehors de notre atmosphère.

extra-axillary [ekstrəæk'siləri], *a. Bot:* extra-axillaire.

extrabudgetary ['ekstrə'bʌdʒit(ə)ri], *a.* extrabudgétaire.

extracardial ['ekstrə'ka:diəl], *a. Med:* extra(-)cardiaque.

extracellular ['ekstrə'seljulər], *a. Biol:* extra(-)cellulaire.

extraconjugal ['ekstrə'kɔn(d)ʒug(ə)l], *a.* extra-conjugal, -aux.

extracranial ['ekstrə'kreiniəl], *a. Anat:* extra(-)crânien.

extract[1] ['ekstrækt], *s.* 1. (*a*) extrait *m*; concentré *m*; **malt e.,** extrait de malt; **meat e.,** concentré de viande; **beef e.,** extrait de bœuf; (*b*) *Lit: Sch:* **extracts,** morceaux choisis; **to make extracts from an author,** faire des extraits d'un auteur. 2. *Jur: Scot:* copie *f* authentique.

extract[2] [eks'trækt], *v.tr.* extraire; (*a*) **to e. oil from shale,** extraire, (re)tirer, de l'huile du schiste; **extracted honey,** miel extrait des rayons (par centrifugeuse); **to e. sounds from a musical instrument,** tirer des sons d'un instrument de musique; **to e. pleasure from sth.,** retirer du plaisir de qch.; prendre, trouver, plaisir à qch.; (*b*) **to e. a passage from a book,** extraire un passage d'un livre; **to e. a tooth,** extraire, arracher, une dent; **to e. a bullet from a wound,** retirer une balle d'une plaie; **to e. money, a confession, from s.o.,** arracher de l'argent, un aveu, à qn; tirer de l'argent, un aveu, de qn; (*c*) *Mth:* **to e. the roots of an equation,** extraire les racines d'une équation.

extractable [eks'træktəbl], *a.* extractible.

extractant [eks'træktənt], *s. Ch: Atom.Ph:* solvant *m*, réactif *m*.

extracting [eks'træktiŋ], *s.* = EXTRACTION 1.

extraction [eks'trækʃ(ə)n], *s.* 1. (*a*) expression *f*, extraction *f* (du jus d'un citron); **e. of gasolene (from natural gas),** dégazolinage *m*; *Mill: etc:* **e. rate (of flour),** taux *m* de blutage (de la farine); *Mec.E:* **power e.,** prélèvement *m* de puissance; **e. turbine,** turbine *f* à extraction; **double e. turbine,** turbine à double extraction; *Ch: Atom.Ph:* **absorption e.,** extraction par absorption; **e. coefficient,** coefficient *m* d'extraction; **e. liquor,** solvant *m*; **solvent e.,** extraction par solvant, par dissolvant; (*b*) **e. of stone from a quarry,** extraction, tirage *m*, de la pierre d'une carrière; (*c*) arrachage *m* (d'un clou); extraction (d'une dent); (*d*) *Sm.a:* extraction (de l'étui de la cartouche); (*e*) *Mth:* extraction (d'une racine). 2. origine *f*; **of humble e.,** de basse extraction.

extractive ['eks'træktiv]. 1. *a. Pol.Ec: Ch: Pharm:* extractif. 2. *s. Ch: Pharm:* extractif *m*.

extractor [eks'træktər], *s.* 1. (*pers.*) extracteur *m* (de dents, etc.). 2. *Tls:* pince *f*; *Artil:* extracteur; *Dent:* davier *m*; *Surg:* extracteur (de calculs, etc.); **vacuum e.,** ventouse obstétricale; *Sm.a:* **(cartridge) e.,** arrache-cartouche *m*, *pl.* arrache-cartouches; arrache-douille *m*, *pl.* arrache-douilles; **e. plunger,** poussoir *m* de l'extracteur; **bullet e.,** tire-balle *m*, *pl.* tire-balles; *Tls:* **padding e.,** débourroir *m*; **valve e.,** démonte-soupape *m*; *pl.* démonte-soupapes; **e. hook,** griffe *f* de l'extracteur; (*b*) *Tchn:* extracteur, récupérateur *m*; **e. fan,** aérateur *m*, aspirateur *m* de buées; **centrifugal e.,** centrifugeur *m*, centrifugeuse *f*; **oil, grease, e.,** récupérateur d'huile, essoreuse *f* à huile, déshuileur *m*; **solvent e.,** extracteur de solvant; *Min:* **core e.,** extracteur de carotte; (*c*) **(juice) e.,** presse-fruit *m*, *pl.* presse-fruits; *Ap:* **(honey) e.,** extracteur (de miel); **wax e.,** cérificateur *m*.

extra-current ['ekstrə'kʌr(ə)nt], *s. El:* extra-courant *m*.

extra-curricular ['ekstrəkə'rikjulər], *a. Sch:* hors-programme *inv*; **e.-c. activities,** activités *f* périscolaires.

extraditable [ekstrə'daitəbl], *a.* 1. (*of pers.*) passible d'extradition. 2. **e. crime,** crime qui justifie l'extradition.

extradite ['ekstrədait], *v.tr. Jur:* 1. extrader (un criminel). 2. obtenir l'extradition (d'un criminel).

extradition [ekstrə'diʃ(ə)n], *s.* extradition *f*.

extrados [eks'treidɔs], *s. Arch:* extrados *m*.

extradosed [eks'treidɔst], *a. Arch:* extradossé.

extragalactic ['ekstrəgə'læktik], *a.* extragalactique.

extrahuman ['ekstrə'hju:mən], *a.* extra-humain.

extra-illustrate ['ekstrə'iləstreit], *v.tr.* truffer (un exemplaire d'un livre).

extrajudicial ['ekstrədʒu(:)'diʃ(ə)l], *a.* 1. extrajudiciaire; officieux; en dehors des débats. 2. extra-légal, -aux; injustifiable.

extrajudicially ['ekstrədʒu:'diʃ(ə)li], *adv.* extrajudiciairement.

extra-legal ['ekstrə'li:g(ə)l], *a.* extra-légal, -aux.

extra-marital ['ekstrə'mærit(ə)l], *a.* extra-conjugal, -aux.

extra-metropolitan ['ekstrəmetrə'pɔlit(ə)n], *a.* situé en dehors de la métropole.

extramundane ['ekstrə'mʌndein], *a.* situé en dehors, au delà, du monde matériel; extra-terrestre; qui appartient au monde de l'au-delà.

extramural ['ekstrə'mju:r(ə)l], *a.* 1. (quartier, enterrement, etc.) extra-muros *inv*. 2. *Sch:* **e. lecturer,** conférencier en dehors de la Faculté accrédité pour certains cours; **e. course,** cours *m* supplémentaire (pour adultes).

extraneous [eks'treiniəs], *a.* étranger (**to,** à); **to be e. to the matter in hand,** n'avoir rien à voir avec, ne pas se rapporter à, l'affaire; **e. considerations,** considérations *f* en dehors de la question, qui n'entrent pas en ligne de compte; *Mus:* **e. modulation,** modulation *f* dans les tons éloignés.

extraneousness [eks'treiniəsnis], *s.* manque *m* de rapport (**to,** avec).

extranuclear ['ekstrə'nju:kliər], *a.* extranucléaire.

extraordinarily [eks'trɔ:dinərili, ekstrə'ɔ:dənrili], *adv.*

extraordinairement.

extraordinariness [eks'trɔːdənrinis, ekstrə'ɔːdənrinis], *s.* caractère *m*, nature *f*, extraordinaire; singularité *f*.

extraordinary [eks'trɔːdənri, ekstrə'ɔːd(ə)nri]. **1.** *a.* extraordinaire; (*a*) **ambassador e.,** ambassadeur *m* extraordinaire; **to take e. care over sth.,** faire qch. avec un soin particulier; **to have e. ability,** avoir des talents *m* remarquables, extraordinaires; **to call an e. meeting of the shareholders,** convoquer d'urgence les sociétaires, convoquer une assemblée générale extraordinaire; (*b*) **e. conduct,** conduite *f* extraordinaire; **the e. thing is that . . .,** ce qu'il y a d'étrange, de singulier, de surprenant, c'est que . . .; (*c*) *F:* phénoménal, -aux; prodigieux; inouï; (*d*) *Opt:* **e. ray,** rayon *m* extraordinaire. **2.** *s.pl. Mil:* **extraordinaries,** rations *f* ou dépenses *f* extraordinaires.

extra-organic [ekstrəɔː'gænik], *a.* extra-organique.

extra-parliamentary ['ekstrəpɑːlə'ment(ə)ri], *a. Pol:* extra-parlementaire.

extra-parochial ['ekstrəpə'roukiəl], *a.* qui n'est pas de la paroisse; en dehors de la paroisse.

extraperiosteal ['ekstrəperi'ɔstiəl], *a. Anat:* extra(-)périosté.

extrapolate [ek'stræpəleit], *v.tr.* extrapoler.

extrapolation [èkstræpə'leiʃ(ə)n], *s.* extrapolation *f*.

extraprofessional ['ekstrəprə'feʃənəl], *a.* extra-professionnel.

extraregular ['ekstrə'regjulər], *a.* extra-réglementaire.

extra-retinal ['ekstrə'retinəl], *a.* extra-rétinien.

extrasensible ['ekstrə'sensibl], *a.* extra-sensible.

extrasensory ['ekstrə'sensəri], *a.* extra-sensoriel; **e. perception,** la perception extra-sensorielle.

extra-special ['ekstrə'speʃ(ə)l]. **1.** *a. & s. Journ:* **e.-s. (edition),** deuxième édition spéciale (d'un journal du soir). **2.** *a. F:* **e.-s. wine,** du vin extra; **I have e.-s. reasons for wishing it,** j'ai des raisons toutes particulières pour le souhaiter; **suit for e.-s. occasions,** costume *m* pour les grandes occasions; **sth. e.-s.,** de l'extra.

extra-spectral ['ekstrə'spektr(ə)l], *a. Ph:* en dehors du spectre solaire.

extra-statutory ['ekstrə'stætjut(ə)ri], *a.* extra(-)statutaire.

extrasystole ['ekstrə'sistəli], *s. Physiol:* extrasystole *f*.

extrasystolic ['ekstrəsis'tɔlik], *a. Physiol:* extrasystolique.

extratension ['ekstrə'tenʃ(ə)n], *s. Psy:* extratension *f*.

extratensive ['ekstrə'tensiv], *a. Psy:* extratensif.

extraterrestrial ['ekstrəte'restriəl], *a.* extra-terrestre.

extraterritorial ['ekstrəteri'tɔːriəl], *a.* (privilège) d'exterritorialité.

extraterritoriality ['ekstrəteritɔːri'æliti], *s.* ex(tra)territorialité *f*.

extra-uterine ['ekstrə'juːtərain], *a.* extra-utérin.

extravagance [iks'trævəgəns], *s.* **1.** extravagance *f*, exagération *f*. **2.** folles dépenses *f*, prodigalités *fpl*, gaspillage *m*; **a piece of e., an e.,** une dépense inutile.

extravagant [iks'trævəgənt], *a.* **1.** extravagant; **e. claims,** prétentions exagérées, déraisonnables; **e. praise,** éloges outrés; **e. style,** style exagéré. **2.** (*of pers.*) dépensier, prodigue, gaspilleur; **e. tastes,** goûts dispendieux; **e. recipe,** recette *f* (de cuisine) qui coûte cher; **don't be so e. with the butter,** ne gaspillez pas le beurre. **3.** (*of price*) exorbitant, prohibitif; **furs at e. prices,** fourrures *f* hors de prix.

extravagantly [iks'trævəgəntli], *adv.* **1.** d'une façon extravagante; **to talk, act, e.,** dire, faire, des folies, des extravagances. **2.** excessivement, à l'excès; **house e. furnished,** maison meublée avec un luxe exagéré.

extravaganza [ekstrævə'gænzə], *s.* **1.** *Lit: Mus:* œuvre (musicale, littéraire) d'une extravagance bouffonne; œuvre fantaisiste. **2.** histoire abracadabrante. **3.** (*of conduct*) folle équipée; folie *f*.

extravagate [eks'trævəgeit], *v.i. A:* **1.** vaguer loin, s'écarter (**from,** de); s'égarer, divaguer (**into,** dans). **2.** extravaguer; dépasser toutes les bornes.

extravasate [eks'trævəseit]. **1.** *v.tr.* extravaser, épancher (le sang). **2.** *v.i.* s'extravaser, s'épancher.

extravasation [ekstrævə'seiʃ(ə)n], *s.* extravas(at)ion *f*, épanchement *m*.

extravehicular ['ekstrəvi'hikjulər], *a.* extravéhiculaire.

extraversion [ekstrə'vəːʃ(ə)n], *s. Psy:* extraversion *f*.

extraversive ['ekstrə'vəːsiv], *a. Psy:* extraversif.

extravert[1] ['ekstrəvəːt], *a. & s. Psy:* extraverti, -ie.

extravert[2], *v.tr.* extravertir.

extreme [eks'triːm]. **1.** *a.* extrême; (*a*) (*farthest*) **e. boundary,** frontière *f* extrême; **mountains in the e. distance,** montagnes *f* dans l'extrême lointain; **at the e. end of the pier,** tout au bout du quai; **the e. penalty,** le dernier supplice; *R.C.Ch:* **e. unction,** extrême-onction *f*; *Pol:* **the e. left,** l'extrême gauche *f*; (*b*) **e. heat,** chaleur *f* extrême; **e. nationalism,** nationalisme outrancier; **to be in e. peril,** être en (très) grand danger; **they are in e. poverty,** ils sont dans une extrême misère; **to be e. in one's views, to hold e. opinions,** avoir des opinions extrémistes; **to behave with e. awkwardness,** se conduire avec la dernière gaucherie; **e. old age,** extrême vieillesse *f*; **e. youth,** grande jeunesse; **an e. case,** un cas exceptionnel; **the question is one of e. delicacy,** le problème est délicat entre tous. **2.** *s.* (*a*) extrême *m*; **to go from one e. to the other,** passer d'un extrême à l'autre; aller de la cave au grenier, du grenier à la cave; aller du blanc au noir; **in the e.,** à l'excès, au dernier degré, à l'extrême; **extremes meet,** les extrêmes se touchent; **to carry matters, to go, to extremes,** pousser les choses à l'extrême; se porter aux dernières extrémités; **to drive s.o. to extremes,** pousser qn à bout; **to be reduced to extremes,** être aux abois; (*b*) *Mth:* **the product of the means equals the product of the extremes,** le produit des moyens est égal au produit des extrêmes.

extremely [eks'triːmli], *adv.* extrêmement; au dernier degré, au dernier point; **to be e. witty,** avoir énormément d'esprit; **he's e. snobbish,** il est on ne peut plus snob.

extremism [eks'triːmizm], *s. Pol: etc:* extrémisme *m*.

extremist [eks'triːmist], *s. Pol: etc:* extrémiste *mf*; outrancier, -ière.

extremity [eks'tremiti], *s.* **1.** (*a*) extrémité *f*; point *m* extrême; bout *m* (d'une corde, d'une rue); sommité *f* (d'une plante, d'une branche); (*b*) **to drive s.o. to extremities,** pousser qn à bout, aux extrémités; **to push matters to the e. of a civil war,** aller jusqu'à la guerre civile; (*c*) *A:* **the e. of the weather,** la rigueur du temps. **2.** *pl.* **the extremities,** les extrémités (du corps). **3.** extrémité, gêne *f*; **they are in great e.,** ils sont dans une grande gêne; **to be reduced to the last e.,** en être réduit à la dernière extrémité; être aux abois.

extremum, *pl.* **-a** [eks'triːməm, -ə], *s. Mth:* extrémum *m*.

extricable ['ekstrikəbl], *a.* que l'on peut dégager.

extricate ['ekstrikeit], *v.tr.* **1.** dégager, tirer (**s.o. from a critical position,** qn d'un mauvais pas); **to e. a vehicle from the mud,** désembourber une voiture; **to e. oneself from a danger,** se tirer, sortir, d'un danger; **to e. oneself from difficulties,** se débrouiller; se tirer d'affaire. **2.** *Ch: A:* **to e. a gas,** libérer un gaz.

extrication [ekstri'keiʃ(ə)n], *s.* **1.** dégagement *m*, délivrance *f*. **2.** *Ch: A:* libération *f* (d'un gaz).

extrinsic [eks'trinsik], *a.* extrinsèque; **questions e. to the subject under consideration,** questions *f* en dehors du sujet.

extrinsically [eks'trinsikli], *adv.* extrinsèquement.

extrorse [eks'trɔːs], *a. Bot:* (anthère *f*) extrorse.

extrospection [ekstrous'pekʃ(ə)n], *s. Psy:* extrospection *f*.

extroversion [ekstrə'vəːʃ(ə)n], *s.* **1.** *Med:* extroversion *f* (de la vessie, de la paupière). **2.** *Psy:* extroversion, extraversion *f*.

extrovert[1] ['ekstrəvəːt], *a. & s. Psy:* extroverti, -ie.

extrovert[2], *v.tr.* extrovertir, extravertir.

extrude [eks'truːd]. **1.** *v.tr.* (*a*) expulser, faire jaillir (**from,** de) (en pressant, en se contractant); émettre (une sécrétion); (*b*) *Metalw:* filer, refouler, profiler; **extruded metal,** métal refoulé, tréfilé, flué; métal venu par refoulement; métal propulsé en barres; **extruded section, shape,** profilé *m*; (*c*) *Ind:* (*plastics*) boudiner (à chaud); (*d*) faire saillir; (*of insect, etc.*) sortir (son dard, etc.). **2.** *v.i. Geol:* (*of volcanic rock, etc.*) s'épancher.

extruding [eks'truːdiŋ], *s.* **1.** = EXTRUSION. **2.** **e. machine, press,** (i) *Metalw:* machine *f*, presse *f* à refouler, à boudiner, à filer; presse de filage; (ii) *Ind:* (*plastics*) boudineuse *f*; machine, presse, à boudiner.

extrusion [eks'truːʒ(ə)n], *s.* (*a*) expulsion *f* (de qn, de qch.); éjaculation *f*, émission *f* (d'une sécrétion); (*b*) *Geol:* extrusion *f*, épanchement *m* (volcanique); (*c*) *Metalw:* extrusion *f*; filage *m* (à chaud); fluage *m*; refoulage *m*, refoulement *m*; profilé *m*; **backward e.,** filage inverse; **forward e.,** filage direct; **rotary e.,** fluotournage *m*; repoussage *m* au tour; **cold e.,** filage à froid; (*d*) *Ind:* (*plastics*) boudinage *m*, extrusion; (*e*) saillie *f*, sortie *f* (d'un dard, d'une aspérité, etc.).

extrusive [eks'truːsiv], *a. Geol:* **e. rock,** roche extrusive.

exuberance [eg'zjuːb(ə)r(ə)ns], *s.* (*a*) exubérance *f*; richesse *f* (de végétation); surabondance *f* (d'idées); (*b*) (*of pers.*) joie *f* de vivre, gaieté débordante.

exuberant [eg'zjuːb(ə)r(ə)nt], *a.* exubérant; (*a*) (*of vegetation*) riche; (*of health, vitality*) débordant; **in e. health,** débordant de santé; (*b*) (*of pers.*) débordant de vie.

exuberantly [eg'zjuːb(ə)r(ə)ntli], *adv.* avec exubérance; **e. healthy,** débordant de santé.

exuberate ['eg'zjuːbəreit], *v.i. A:* abonder; déborder.

exudate ['eksjudeit], *s. Med:* exsudat *m*.

exudation [eksju'deiʃ(ə)n], *s.* exsudation *f*; *Arb:* **e. of sap,** écoulement *m* de la sève.

exudative [ek'sjuːdətiv], *a.* exsudatif.

exude [ek'sjuːd]. **1.** *v.tr.* exsuder. **2.** *v.i.* exsuder, suinter; (*of sap*) couler, s'écouler.

exulcerate [eg'zʌlsəreit]. **1.** *v.tr.* (*a*) *Med: A:* exulcérer; (*b*) ulcérer (qn, le cœur). **2.** *v.i.* (*a*) *A:* s'exulcérer; (*b*) (*of the feelings, etc.*) s'ulcérer.

exulceration [egzʌlsə'reiʃ(ə)n], *s.* **1.** *A:* exulcération *f*. **2.** ulcération *f* (du cœur, etc.).

exult [eg'zʌlt], *v.i.* **1.** exulter, se réjouir (**at, in,** de). **2.** **to e. over s.o.,** triompher de qn; chanter victoire.

exultancy [eg'zʌltənsi], *s.* = exultation *f*; joie triomphante.

exultant [eg'zʌltənt], *a.* (sentiment) joyeux; (cri) triomphant, exultant; **to be e.,** exulter.

exultantly [eg'zʌltəntli], *adv.* (parler, sourire) avec une joie triomphante, d'un air de triomphe; **he spoke e.,** il exultait.

exultation [egzʌl'teiʃ(ə)n], *s.* exultation *f*; joie triomphante.

exultet [eks'ultet], *s. Ecc:* exultet *m*.

exutory [eg'zjuːtəri], *s. Med:* exutoire *m*.

exuviable [eg'zjuːviəbl], *a. Nat.Hist:* exuviable.

exuviae [eg'zjuːviiː], *s.pl. Nat.Hist:* dépouille(s) *f*(*pl*) (de serpent, d'insecte, etc.).

exuvial [eg'zjuːviəl], *a. Nat.Hist:* exuvial.

exuviate [eg'zjuːvieit]. *Nat.Hist:* **1.** *v.i.* changer de peau, de carapace; se dépouiller. **2.** *v.tr.* dépouiller (sa peau, etc.).

exuviation [egzjuːvi'eiʃ(ə)n], *s. Nat.Hist:* exuviation *f*; (*of insects, etc.*) mue *f*.

ex-voto [eks'voutou], *s. Ecc:* (*also* **ex-voto offering**) ex-voto *m inv*.

eyas ['aiəs], *s. Orn:* jeune faucon *m*; *A:* niais *m*.

eye[1] [ai], *s.* **1.** (*a*) œil *m*, *pl.* yeux; *Anat:* **e.-ear plane,** plan horizontal de Francfort; *Z:* **simple e.,** ocelle *m*, stemmate *m*; **e. hospital,** hôpital *m* ophtalmologique, pour les maladies des yeux; **e. ward,** salle *f* (d'hôpital) pour les maladies des yeux; **e. bank,** banque *f* des yeux; **to have blue eyes,** avoir les yeux bleus; **black eyes,** yeux noirs; *F:* **black e.,** œil poché; **to give s.o. a black e., to black s.o.'s e.,** pocher l'œil, un œil, à qn; coller à qn un œil au beurre noir; **to lose an e.,** perdre un œil; devenir borgne; **to put out s.o.'s eyes,** crever les yeux à qn; aveugler qn; **glass e.,** (i) œil artificiel, œil de verre; (ii) *F: A:* monocle *m*; carreau *m*; *B:* **an e. for an e., a tooth for a tooth,** œil pour œil, dent pour dent; **to open, close, one's eyes,** ouvrir, fermer, les yeux; **to close one's eyes in death,** fermer la paupière; **to close s.o.'s eyes** (*as a last duty*), fermer les paupières à qn; **to open one's eyes wide,** ouvrir de grands yeux; ouvrir ses yeux tout grands; écarquiller les yeux; **that made him open his eyes,** ç'a été pour lui une révélation, une véritable surprise; **they look on, with their eyes starting out of their heads,** ils regardent, les yeux exorbités; **to screw up one's eyes,** faire les petits yeux; **to do sth. with one's eyes open,** faire qch. les yeux ouverts, en connaissance de cause; **to keep one's eyes and ears open,** avoir l'œil et l'oreille au guet; **to have all one's eyes about one, to keep one's eyes open,** *F:* **peeled, skinned,** avoir l'œil ouvert, les yeux ouverts; ouvrir l'œil (et le bon); être vigilant; être aux aguets; *F:* **he keeps his eyes skinned,** il n'a pas les yeux dans sa poche; **(he was so sleepy that) he could not keep his eyes open,** il dormait debout; **to open s.o.'s eyes (to sth.),** éclairer, désabuser, qn; débrider, ouvrir, les yeux à qn; arracher le bandeau des yeux de qn; dessiller les yeux à qn; **that opened his eyes to your motives,** cela lui a dessillé les yeux sur vos mobiles; **I have had my eyes opened,** je me suis rendu compte de la vérité; je suis revenu de mes illusions; **to shut, close, one's eyes to the evidence, to s.o.'s faults,** se refuser à l'évidence; être aveugle, s'aveugler, fermer les yeux, sur les défauts de qn; **to shut one's eyes to the truth,** se dissimuler la vérité; **one cannot shut one's eyes to the fact that . . .,** on ne se dissimule pas que . . .; on est bien obligé d'admettre que . . .; **to do sth. with one's eyes shut,** faire qch. les yeux fermés; **to look s.o. straight, squarely, in the e.,** regarder qn dans le blanc des yeux, entre les deux yeux; regarder qn bien en face; **to have the sun, the light, in one's eyes,** avoir le soleil, la lumière, dans les yeux; être ébloui par le soleil, par la lumière; **at e. level,** à la hauteur des yeux; (*on cooker*) **e.-level grill,** gril *m* à hauteur des yeux; **to be up to the eyes in work, in debt,** avoir du travail, des dettes, par-dessus la tête; être accablé de travail, de dettes; être dans les dettes jusqu'au cou; **to show the whites of one's eyes,** avoir, faire, des yeux de carpe pâmée; faire les yeux blancs; **with tears**

in one's eyes, les larmes aux yeux; **there was not a dry e.,** tout le monde avait la larme à l'œil; **to look on with dry eyes,** regarder d'un œil sec; **dry your eyes,** essuyez vos larmes; *F:* **that's one in the e. for him!** ça lui fait les pieds! *F:* **my e.!** mon œil! *F:* **that's all my e. (and Betty Martin),** tout ça c'est de la blague, des histoires, de la poudre aux yeux, des excuses à la noix (de coco); *P:* **in a pig's e.!** y a pas mèche! des clous! *Poet:* **the e. of day,** le soleil, l'astre *m* du jour; (*b*) (*of thg*) **to strike, catch, draw, the e.,** frapper, attirer, l'œil, les regards; donner dans la vue; (*of pers., thg*) **to catch s.o.'s e.,** attirer l'attention de qn; se signaler à l'attention de qn; (*in Parliament*) **to catch the Speaker's e.,** obtenir la parole; **it leaps to the e.,** cela saute aux yeux; **it pleases, delights, the e.,** cela charme, réjouit, les yeux, les regards; cela flatte le regard; **he has eyes at the back of his head,** il a des yeux d'Argus; **he has eyes for nobody but her,** il n'a d'yeux que pour elle; **to set eyes on sth.,** apercevoir, voir, qch.; **as soon as I set eyes on him,** dès que je l'ai vu; **to see sth. with one's own eyes,** voir qch. de ses propres yeux; **it took place before my (very) eyes,** cela s'est passé sous mes yeux; **to see sth. in one's mind's e.,** voir qch. en imagination, en idée; s'imaginer très bien qch.; évoquer qch.; **I see the scene in my mind's e. at this moment,** je vois encore la scène en ce moment; **where are your eyes?** êtes-vous aveugle? est-ce que vous avez les yeux dans votre poche? **to judge distance by (the) e.,** mesurer la distance à la vue; *Prov:* **no e. like the e. of the master,** il n'est pour voir que l'œil du maître; tant vaut l'homme, tant vaut la terre; (*c*) **with jealous eyes,** d'un œil jaloux; **to keep a jealous e. on s.o.,** observer qn d'un œil jaloux; **to cast a covetous e. on sth.,** regarder qch. d'un œil d'envie; *F:* reluquer qch.; **to make eyes at s.o.,** *F:* **to give s.o. the (glad) e.,** lancer des œillades, faire de l'œil, à qn; aguicher qn; jouer de la prunelle; *F:* **to make sheep's eyes at s.o.,** regarder qn tendrement; lancer des œillades amoureuses à qn; faire les yeux doux à qn; **to see e. to e. with s.o.,** voir les choses du même œil, juger de la même façon, que qn; **she does not see e. to e. with me,** elle ne voit pas les choses comme moi; **we see e. to e.,** nous avons les mêmes vues *f*, les mêmes opinions *f*; **I look upon the problem with a different e.,** j'envisage le problème d'un autre œil; **to see sth. with half an e.,** voir qch. au premier coup d'œil; **you can see that with half an e.,** cela saute aux yeux; c'est évident, **if you had half an e.,** si vous étiez tant soit peu observateur; **anyone can see with half an e. that she is in love with him,** il est de toute évidence qu'elle l'aime; **to run, cast, one's e. over sth.,** jeter un coup d'œil sur qch.; parcourir qch. des yeux; **he ran his e. anxiously over the telegram,** il a parcouru le télégramme d'un œil inquiet; **to cast one's eyes round the room,** promener son regard autour de la pièce; **to cast one's eyes up to heaven,** lever les yeux au ciel; *Mil:* **eyes right, left!** tête (à) droite, (à) gauche! **eyes front!** fixe! (*d*) **to keep an e. on sth., on s.o., to give an e. to sth.,** surveiller qch., qn; veiller à qch.; **to have one's e., to keep a sharp, a strict, e., on s.o.,** avoir l'œil sur qn; surveiller qn de près; exercer un contrôle sévère sur qn; **keep your e. on him!** ne le quittez pas des yeux! *Games:* **to keep one's e. on the ball,** suivre, *Golf:* fixer, la balle; **to have one's e. well in,** (i) (*billiards, shooting, etc.*) avoir l'œil exercé; (ii) (*tennis, etc.*) avoir la balle dans l'œil; **under the e. of. . .,** sous la surveillance de . . .; **he went on working with one e. on the stranger,** il continua son travail sans quitter l'étranger de l'œil; **to have an e. to everything,** avoir l'œil à tout; *F:* être très sur l'œil; **he always has an e. to his own interest,** il ne perd jamais de vue son propre intérêt; il est toujours à la recherche de son propre intérêt; **with an e. to . . .,** en vue de . . .; **to marry s.o. with an e. to her fortune,** épouser qn en vue de sa fortune; **to work with an e. to the future,** travailler en vue de l'avenir; **to be all eyes,** être tout yeux ; (*e*) **to have an e. for a horse,** s'y connaître en chevaux; être bon juge des chevaux; **to have an e. for landscape,** apprécier les paysages; **with the e. of a painter,** d'un œil de peintre; en peintre; (*f*) **equal in the eye(s) of the law,** égaux aux yeux de la loi; égaux devant la loi; **in the eyes of all he is guilty,** aux yeux de tous il est coupable; **to be very much in the public e.,** occuper une position très en vue; être à la cote; **people most in the public e.,** personnes *f* les plus en vue; (*g*) **private e.,** détective, enquêteur, privé. **2.** (*a*) **eyes in a peacock's tail,** yeux, miroirs *m*, de la queue d'un paon; (*in mahogany, etc.*) **bird's eyes,** tourbillons *m*; (*b*) *Hort:* (i) œil, bourgeon *m*; germe *m* (de pomme de terre); (ii) (*in grafting*) œilleton *m*. **3.** (*a*) œil (*pl.* œils) (d'un outil); œil, trou *m*, chas *m* (d'une aiguille); ancrure *f* (d'un tirant); emmanchure *f* (d'un marteau, etc.); toyère *f* (de fer de hache, etc.); œil, boucle *f*, cosse *f* (d'un cordage); collet *m*, œillet *m*, boucle (d'un étai); anneau *m* (pour tringle, etc.); œil (de meule, de roue); **e. of the loop, of the strop,** cosse de l'estrope; **e. splice,** épissure *f* à œil, à œillet; **to pass through the e. of a needle,** passer par le trou d'une aiguille; (*b*) piton *m*; **e. end,** œil, piton (de câble); **lifting e.,** piton de levage; **rudder e.,** piton de cervelle; **screw e.,** piton à vis; (*c*) *Veh:* **spring e.,** rouleau *m* de ressort. **4.** (*a*) *Ind:* orifice *m* d'évacuation (d'un tambour laveur, etc.); *Metall:* regard *m* (d'un fourneau, d'un cubilot); **impeller e.,** entrée *f* du rouet (d'une turbine centrifuge); (*b*) (orifice d'une) source; entrée *f*, orifice (d'un puits de mine); (*c*) *Phot:* œilleton *m* (de viseur iconomètre); (*d*) *Elcs:* **electric e., magic e.,** cellule *f* photoélectrique, œil magique; **tuning e.,** trèfle *m* cathodique. **5.** (*a*) *Meteor:* œil (d'un typhon); (*b*) *Nau:* **in the wind's e.,** dans le lit, dans l'épi *m*, du vent; contre le vent; dans l'œil de la tempête. **6. the eyes of a ship,** l'avant *m*, les joues *f*, d'un navire.

eye[2], *v.tr.* (**eyed; eyeing**) regarder, observer (d'un œil jaloux, soupçonneux, avec dégoût); mesurer (qn, un obstacle, etc.) des yeux; *F:* reluquer (qn); **to e. s.o. up and down, from head to foot,** toiser qn (de haut en bas); mesurer qn des yeux; **to e. sth. greedily,** avaler qch. des yeux.

eyeball ['aibɔ:l], *s.* **1.** bulbe *m*, globe *m*, de l'œil; globe oculaire. **2.** *A:* pupille *f* de l'œil.

eyebar ['aibɑ:r], *s. Tchn:* barre-tirant *f*, *pl.* barre-tirant(s).

eyebath ['aibɑ:θ], *s. Med:* œillère *f*; bassin *m* oculaire; bain *m* d'œil; gondole *f*.

eyebolt ['aiboult], *s.* **1.** boulon *m* à œil, à bout percé; tire-fond *m inv*. **2.** piton *m* à tige taraudée; anneau *m* à fiche, à piton; ficheron *m*.

eyebright ['aibrait], *s. Bot:* eufraise *f*, euphraise *f*, *F:* luminet *m*, casse-lunette(s) *m inv*.

eyebrow ['aibrau], *s.* **1.** sourcil *m*; **to knit one's eyebrows,** froncer, serrer, le(s) sourcil(s); *F:* **he never raised an e.,** il n'a pas sourcillé; *F:* **he's hanging on by his eyebrows,** il se maintient tout juste (dans son poste, etc.); il tient à un fil; il est dans une position périlleuse. **2.** (*a*) *Nau:* gouttière *f* (de hublot); *Av:* (*at leading edge of wing*) **e. (slat),** bec *m* de sécurité; (*b*) **e. window,** lucarne *f* à la capucine; *Av:* lunette *f* de virage.

eye-catcher ['aikætʃər], *s. F:* tire-l'œil *m inv*.

eye-catching ['aikætʃiŋ], *a. F:* accrocheur, -euse; **an e.-c. title,** un titre accrocheur; **e.-c. publicity,** publicité tapageuse.

eyecup ['aikʌp], *s.* = EYEBATH.

eyed [aid], *a.* **1. -eyed** (*with adj. or numeral prefixed, e.g.*) **a brown-e. boy,** un garçon aux yeux bruns; **big-e.,** aux grands yeux; **bird-e.,** à la vue perçante; **bleary-e.,** aux yeux troubles, larmoyants; **fierce-e.,** aux yeux féroces, farouches; **one-e.,** (vision) monoculaire; **one-e. (man),** borgne (*m*). **2.** (poinçon, bouterolle, tige) à œil. **3.** (*of feather*) ocellé; (*of insect's wing, etc.*) ocellé, moucheté, tacheté.

eyeful ['aiful], *s.* **to get an e.,** (i) recevoir une giclée dans l'œil; (ii) *F:* s'en mettre, en avoir, plein les yeux; se rincer l'œil; *F:* **what an e.!** quel coup d'œil! on se rince l'œil! **she's quite an e.,** elle vaut le coup d'œil; c'est un beau brin de fille.

eyeglass ['aiglɑ:s], *s.* monocle *m*; **watchmaker's e.,** loupe *f* d'horloger; *O:* **(pair of) eyeglasses,** binocle *m*, pince-nez *m inv*; lorgnon *m*.

eyehole ['aihoul], *s.* **1.** cavité *f* de l'œil; orbite *m* de l'œil. **2.** (*a*) (*of mask, etc.*) **eyeholes,** ouvertures *f* pour les yeux; (*b*) petite ouverture; judas *m* (d'une porte, etc.); *Tchn:* trou *m* de regard, de visite. **3.** œillet *m*; petit trou.

eyelash ['ailæʃ], *s.* cil *m*.

eyeless ['ailis], *a.* (i) sans yeux; (ii) aveugle; **e. sight,** vision *f* paroptique.

eyelet ['ailit], *s.* **1.** œillet *m*; petit trou. **2.** œillet (métallique); *Bootm:* œillet, garant *m*; *Nau:* (*in rope*) cosse *f*; (*in sail*) œil-de-pie *m*, *pl.* œils-de-pie. **3.** ocelle *m* (d'aile de papillon, etc.).

eyelid ['ailid], *s.* **1.** paupière *f*; *Med:* **dropped e.,** chute *f* de la paupière; ptosis *f*. **2.** *Av:* volet *m* mobile (de tuyère d'éjection de réacteur).

eye-minded ['ai'maindid], *a.* sensible aux impressions oculaires.

eye-opener ['aioup(ə)nər], *s. F:* révélation *f*; surprise *f*; **that was an e.-o. for him,** cela lui a ouvert, dessillé, les yeux; ç'a été une révélation pour lui.

eyepiece ['aipi:s], *s.* **1.** *Opt:* (*a*) oculaire *m* (de microscope, télescope, etc.); **e. cap,** couvercle *m*, bouchon *m*, obturateur *m*, d'oculaire; **e. micrometer,** micromètre *m* oculaire; **e. with cross wires, cross-hair e.,** oculaire à réticule, à fils; **focussing e.,** loupe *f* de mise au point; **hinged e.,** oculaire à charnière; **reading e.,** oculaire de lecture; **sighting e.,** oculaire de visée; (*b*) viseur *m* (de théodolite, etc.); (*c*) œilleton *m* (de viseur iconomètre, etc.). **2.** (*a*) *Metall:* lunette *f* de regard (d'un fourneau, d'un cubilot); (*b*) lunette (d'appareil respiratoire, de masque à gaz).

eyesalve ['aisɑ:v], *s.* onguent *m* pour les yeux; collyre mou.

eyeshade ['aisheid], *s.* visière *f*.

eye-shaped ['aiʃeipt], *a. Biol:* oculiforme.

eyeshot ['aiʃɔt], *s. used only in* **within, out of, e.,** à portée, hors de portée, de la vue; **to come within e. (of s.o.),** venir à portée de vue (de qn); devenir visible; apparaître.

eyesight ['aisait], *s.* **1.** vue *f*; acuité visuelle; **to have good e.,** avoir la vue bonne, une bonne vue, de bons yeux; **my e. is failing,** ma vue baisse. **2.** portée *f* de la vue.

eyesore ['aisɔ:r], *s.* ce qui blesse la vue, qui offense les regards; **one of the eyesores of London,** une des horreurs de Londres.

eyespot ['aispɔt], *s.* ocelle *m* (de mollusque, etc.).

eyespotted ['aispɔtid], *a. Nat.Hist:* ocellé.

eyestalk ['aistɔ:k], *s. Crust:* pédoncule *m* de l'œil.

eyestrain ['aistrein], *s.* **to suffer from e.,** avoir les yeux fatigués.

eyestrings ['aistriŋz], *s.pl. Anat: A:* fibres *f* de l'œil.

eyetooth, *pl.* **-teeth** ['aitu:θ, -ti:θ], *s.* dent œillère; dent canine; **to cut one's eyeteeth,** (i) faire ses œillères; (ii) *F:* sortir de sa première enfance, acquérir la sagesse que donne l'expérience; *F:* **he's cut his eyeteeth,** ce n'est plus un blanc-bec; c'est un malin.

eyewash ['aiwɔʃ], *s.* **1.** *Pharm:* collyre *m* liquide. **2.** *F:* **that's all e.,** tout ça c'est du boniment, de la poudre aux yeux, du bourrage de crâne, de la frime.

eyewater ['aiwɔ:tər], *s. A:* **1.** *Anat:* (i) humeur aqueuse, (ii) humeur vitrée (de l'œil). **2.** *Pharm:* = EYEWASH 1.

eyewitness ['aiwitnis], *s.* témoin *m* oculaire.

eyewort ['aiwə:t], *s. Bot:* = EYEBRIGHT.

eyot [eit], *s.* îlot *m*.

eyra ['eirə], *s. Z:* eyra *m*.

eyrie, eyry ['aiəri], *s.* aire *f* (d'un aigle).

Ezekiel [i'zi:kiəl], *Pr.n.m. B.Hist:* Ézéchiel.

Ezra ['ezrə], *Pr.n.m. B.Hist:* Esdras.

F

F, f [ef], *s.* **1.** (la lettre) F, *f f*; *Tp:* **F for Frederick,** *F* comme François; *I.C.E:* **F-head cylinder,** cylindre *m* à culasse en F; *Mus:* **f hole,** esse *f* (de violon). **2.** *Mus:* fa *m*; **F clef,** clef *f* de fa.

fa [fɑː], *s. Mus:* **1.** (*fixed* **fa**) fa *m*. **2.** (*movable* **fa** *in tonic solfa*) la sous-dominante.

Fabian ['feibiən]. **1.** *Rom.Hist:* (*a*) *a.* fabien; (*b*) *s.* Fabien, -ienne. **2.** *a.* (politique, etc.) de temporisation; **F. socialism,** socialisme fabien; **the F. Society,** l'Association fabienne.

Fabianism ['feibiənizm], *s.* fabianisme *m*.

fable ['feibl], *s.* **1.** fable *f*, conte *m*, histoire *f*; **the realm of f.,** le domaine de la légende; **to sort out fact from f.,** séparer le réel de l'imaginaire; **is commercial honesty only a f.?** est-ce que la loyauté dans les affaires n'est qu'un mythe? **that story's a mere f.,** cette histoire est de pure invention. **2.** *Lit:* fable, apologue *m* (d'Ésope, etc.). **3.** *Lit: A:* argument *m*, résumé *m*, sujet *m* (d'une pièce de théâtre, etc.).

fabled ['feibld], *a. Lit:* **1.** célèbre dans la fable. **2.** légendaire, fabuleux.

fabric ['fæbrik], *s.* **1.** (*a*) édifice *m*, bâtiment *m*; **the f. of society,** l'édifice social; (*b*) *Ecc:* fabrique *f*; **upkeep of the f.,** entretien *m* de la fabrique. **2.** *Tex: etc:* tissu *m*; étoffe *f*; toile *f*; drap *m*; **dress fabrics,** tissus pour robes; **silk, woollen and cotton fabrics,** soieries *f*, lainages *m* et cotonnades *f*; **f. gloves,** gants *m* en tissu; **biased f.,** étoffe croisée, tissu en fil biais; **rubberized f.,** tissu caoutchouté, toile caoutchoutée; **oiled f.,** toile huilée, tissu huilé; **impregnated f.,** toile imperméabilisée; **aircraft f.,** toile d'avion; **balloon f.,** tissu, étoffe, à ballon; tissu d'enveloppe; **doped f.,** tissu enduit. **3.** structure *f*, fabrique (d'un édifice, d'un système); gros œuvre (d'un bâtiment); contexture *f* (d'un roman, etc.); texture *f* (d'un tissu); **the f. of law,** l'ensemble *m* du système légal; **the nervous f. of the retina,** l'appareil nerveux de la rétine.

fabricate ['fæbrikeit], *v.tr.* **1.** *A:* fabriquer (des marchandises, etc.); construire (un système, etc.). **2.** inventer, controuver, fabriquer, forger (une nouvelle, un mensonge); fabriquer, contrefaire, forger (un document).

fabrication [fæbri'keiʃ(ə)n], *s.* **1.** *A:* fabrication *f* (de marchandises, etc.); construction *f* (d'un gouvernement, etc.). **2.** invention *f* (d'une nouvelle, etc.); fabrication (d'un passeport, etc.); contrefaçon *f* (d'un document); **it's pure f.,** c'est de la pure fabrication. **3.** (*a*) **a pure f.,** une histoire inventée de toute pièce; une pure invention; (*b*) supercherie *f* (littéraire); (*c*) pièce contrefaite; contrefaçon; (*d*) *Med:* fabulation *f*.

fabricator ['fæbrikeitər], *s.* **1.** *A:* constructeur *m*, faiseur *m* (**of,** de). **2.** inventeur, -trice, fabricateur, -trice (de calomnies); forgeur *m* (d'une histoire, d'un mensonge); contrefacteur *m* (d'un document).

fabulation [fæbju'leiʃ(ə)n], *s. Lit:* fabulation *f*.

fabulist ['fæbjulist], *s.* fabuliste *m*.

fabulous ['fæbjuləs], *a.* **1.** (conte, monstre, etc.) fabuleux; (personnage *m*) légendaire, mythique; **the f. ages,** les temps fabuleux. **2.** *F:* prodigieux, excessif; **a. f. price,** un prix fabuleux, fou; **we had a f. time,** on s'est bien amusé(s).

fabulously ['fæbjuləsli], *adv. F:* fabuleusement; prodigieusement (riche, etc.).

façade [fæ'sɑːd], *s.* (*a*) *Arch:* façade *f*; (*between pavilions*) courtine *f*; (*b*) **it's all f., nothing but f.,** ce n'est que façade, que décor.

face[1] [feis], *s.* **1.** (*a*) figure *f*, visage *m*; face *f*; **handsome f.,** beau visage; **a pretty little f.,** une jolie petite figure, *F:* une jolie petite frimousse; **I know that (man's) f.,** je connais cette tête; *F:* **to feed one's f.,** manger; bouffer; *P:* **he's messed his f. up,** il s'est abîmé le portrait; *P:* **what a f.!** quelle gueule! *P:* **shut your f.!** ta gueule! la ferme! **to strike s.o. in the f.,** frapper qn au visage, en pleine figure; donner un soufflet à qn; **he threw the inkpot in my f.,** il m'a jeté l'encrier au nez; **I shall never be able to look him in the f. again,** je ne pourrai jamais plus le regarder dans les yeux; je me sentirai toujours honteux devant lui; **he won't show his f. here again!** il ne se risquera pas à remettre les pieds ici! **full-f. portrait,** portrait *m* de face; **f. to the enemy,** face à l'ennemi; **f. to f.,** face à face; **to bring the two parties f. to f.,** mettre les deux parties face à face, en présence; **to bring s.o. f. to f. with s.o.,** confronter qn avec qn; **to meet s.o. f. to f., to come f. to f. with s.o.,** se trouver vis-à-vis, nez à nez, cap à cap, avec qn; **to fall on one's f.,** tomber à plat; tomber, se jeter, à plat ventre; **to set one's f. against sth.,** s'opposer résolument, se refuser, à qch.; s'élever contre qch.; **to set one's f. against doing sth.,** se refuser à faire qch.; *Lit:* **we shall set our faces to the south,** nous ferons route vers le sud; **the rain was beating full in our faces,** la pluie nous battait en plein visage; **in the f. of danger,** devant le danger, en présence du danger; **to succeed in the f. of many difficulties,** réussir malgré de nombreuses difficultés; **to fly in the f. of providence,** aller contre, porter un défi à, la providence; **to act in the f. of direct orders,** agir en dépit d'ordres formels; **I told him so to his f.,** je le lui ai dit au nez, à sa barbe; je ne le lui ai pas envoyé dire; **he did it in front of my very f.,** il l'a fait sous mes yeux; (*b*) *attrib.* **f. cream,** crème *f* de beauté; **f. pack,** masque (anti-rides, hydratant, etc.); **f. flannel** = gant *m* de toilette; **f. towel,** serviette *f* de toilette; *Ind:* **f. guard, f. shield,** masque protecteur, de protection; masque de soudeur; **f. piece,** masque (d'un appareil respiratoire); **f. glass, f. plate,** glace *f* du milieu, hublot *m* (de scaphandre); *Cards: N.Am:* **f. card,** figure *f*; (*c*) *Bot: F:* **f. and hood, three faces under a hood,** pensée *f* sauvage. **2.** (*a*) mine *f*, physionomie *f*; **to be a good judge of faces,** être physionomiste; **to make, pull, faces (at s.o.),** faire des grimaces (à qn); grimacer; **to keep a straight f.,** garder, tenir, son sérieux; **to put on a f. to suit the occasion,** faire une tête de circonstance; **to put a good f. on it,** faire contre mauvaise fortune bon cœur; (*b*) *F:* aplomb *m*, audace *f*, front *m*, effronterie *f*, impudence *f*, toupet *m*, culot *m*; **he had the f. to tell me so,** il a eu l'aplomb, le toupet, le culot, de me le dire; **how can you have the f. to come here?** comment osez-vous mettre les pieds ici? **3.** apparence *f*, aspect *m* (de qch.); **on the f. of it, of things,** au premier aspect, à première vue; **f. value,** valeur nominale; valeur faciale (d'une monnaie, d'un timbre-poste); **I took him at his f. value,** je l'ai jugé sur les apparences; **to save (one's) f.,** (i) se faire une contenance; (ii) sauver la face, les apparences; s'épargner une humiliation; **in order to save his f.,** (i) pour se garantir contre la critique; (ii) pour sauver les apparences; **to lose f.,** (i) perdre la face; perdre contenance; (ii) essuyer une humiliation; **loss of f.,** (i) décontenancement *m*; (ii) humiliation; perte *f* de réputation. **4.** surface *f* (de la terre); **they disappeared from the f. of the earth,** ils ont disparu de la surface du globe; **the f. of the waters,** la face des eaux. **5.** (*a*) face (d'une pièce de monnaie); endroit *m* (d'un tissu); recto *m* (d'un document); **f. up, f. down,** face en dessus, en dessous; **to lay the cards f. down on the table,** poser les cartes la face tournée vers la table; (*b*) devant *m*, façade *f* (d'un immeuble); face, pan *m* (d'un ouvrage en maçonnerie); pan, parement *m* (d'un mur); face (d'une falaise); parement (d'un talus, d'une pierre); *Min:* **coal f., working f.,** front *m* de taille (du charbon); **f. under attack,** front d'attaque, d'abattage; (*c*) face (d'un polyèdre, d'un prisme, etc.); pan (d'un écrou); face, facette *f*, plan *m* (d'un cristal); *Cryst:* **f. of cleavage,** plan de clivage; **f.-centred,** à face(s) centrée(s); **f.-centred cubic lattice,** réseau *m* face centrée; (*d*) tête *f*, face, aire *f*, plat *m* (d'un marteau); table *f*, aire (d'une enclume); face, tranche *f* (d'une meule); semelle *f* (d'un rabot); *Mch:* glace *f*, table (du tiroir); *Artil: Sm.a:* tranche (de la bouche, de la culasse mobile); *Sp:* face (d'une crosse de golf); *Av:* **propeller f.,** intrados *m* de pale; **f. pitch,** pas *m* angulaire de pale; *Mec.E:* **f. milling,** fraisage *m* de face; **f.(-milling) cutter, f. mill,** fraise axiale, fraise de face; (*e*) *Mec.E:* plateau *m* (de tour); **tail-stock f.,** contre-plateau *m*, *pl.* contre-plateaux; plateau de la contre-pointe; (*f*) *Civ.E: Mec.E:* surface; **bearing f.,** (sur)face portante, (sur)face d'appui; **guiding f.,** face de guidage; **plane f.,** (sur)face plane; (*g*) *Atom.Ph:* **load f., unload f.,** face de chargement, de déchargement (d'un réacteur); (*h*) cadran *m* (d'une horloge, d'une montre); (*i*) *Typ:* œil (d'un caractère); **bold f.,** (caractère) gras *m*; **light f.,** (caractère) maigre *m*; **small f.,** petit œil.

face[2], *v.*

I. *v.tr. & i.* **1.** *v.tr.* affronter, braver, faire face à, faire front à (un danger, un ennemi); envisager (les faits, la possibilité, etc.); **to f. facts,** regarder les choses en face; **let's f. it,** voyons les choses comme elles sont; **the problem that faces us,** le problème qui se pose (à nous); **to be faced with a difficulty,** se heurter à une difficulté; **to be faced with bankruptcy,** être acculé à la faillite; **I was faced with a lawsuit,** je me voyais menacé d'un procès; **he dared not f. me,** il n'a pas osé me rencontrer face à face; *F:* **to f. the music,** tenir tête à l'orage; affronter la critique, la tempête; faire front. **2.** (*a*) *v.tr.* faire face à, se tenir devant (qn, qch.); se présenter de face devant (qn); **sunflowers always f. the sun,** le tournesol regarde toujours le soleil; **window that faces the garden,** fenêtre *f* qui donne sur le jardin, qui regarde sur le jardin; **hotel facing the square,** hôtel *m* en façade sur la place; **house facing the church,** maison *f* qui fait face à l'église; **the picture facing page 10,** la gravure en regard de la page 10; **facing each other,** l'un en face de l'autre; vis-à-vis l'un de l'autre; **seats facing each other,** places *f*, sièges *m*, en vis-à-vis; *Rail:* **seat facing the engine,** place face à la route, dans le sens de la marche; **stand facing the light,** tenez-vous en face de la lumière; (*b*) *v.i.* **the house faces north,** la maison est exposée au nord, regarde le nord; **terrace facing south,** terrasse orientée au sud; **f. this way!** tournez-vous de ce côté! **to f. both ways,** (i) faire face des deux côtés; (ii) ménager la chèvre et le chou; *Mil:* **right f.!** face à droite! **left f.!** face à gauche! **3.** *v.tr. Cards:* retourner (une carte). **4.** *v.tr. Tchn:* (*a*) *Metalw: etc:* dresser, planer, surfacer, usiner; *Metall:* saupoudrer (un moule); **faced surface,** surface dressée, planée, usinée; *Tex:* **faced cloth,** drap fin; (*b*) revêtir, parer, parementer (un mur, etc.); **deal faced with oak,** bois de sapin contre-plaqué de chêne; (*c*) mettre les revers, les parements, à (un habit); parer (un habit, etc.); **coat faced with silk, silk-faced coat,** habit *m* à revers de soie.

II. (*compound verbs*) **1. face about.** (*a*) *v.i. Mil:* faire volte-face; faire face en arrière; faire demi-tour; (*b*) *v.tr.* **to f. a company about,** faire faire demi-tour à une compagnie.

2. face out, *v.tr.* (*a*) **to f. out a situation,** surmonter par soi-même les difficultés d'une situation; (*b*) soutenir effrontément (un mensonge); **to f. it out,** payer, d'audace; ne pas broncher; soutenir ce qu'on a dit.

3. face round, *v.i.* se retourner (vivement).

4. face up. (*a*) *v.i.* affronter la tempête; faire front; **to f. up to s.o., to a danger,** affronter qn, un danger; (*b*) *v.tr.* dresser (une surface plane).

face-about ['feisəbaut], *s.* volte-face *f.inv*; demi-tour *m*, *pl.* demi-tours.

faceache ['feiseik], *s.* névralgie faciale.

facecloth ['feisklɔθ], *s.* **1.** = gant *m* de toilette. **2.** *Tex:* drap fin.

face-harden ['feishɑ:d(ə)n], *v.tr. Metall:* aciérer, cémenter.

face hardening ['feishɑ:d(ə)niŋ], *s. Metall:* trempe superficielle.

faceless ['feislis], *a.* (*a*) sans visage; (*b*) anonyme; non-identifiable; **a f. mob,** une foule anonyme; **f. men in government offices,** fonctionnaires *m* anonymes.

facelift[1] ['feislift], **facelifting** ['feisliftiŋ], *s.* (*a*) lifting *m*, chirurgie *f* esthétique (du visage); (*b*) *F:* restauration *f* (de la façade d'un bâtiment); embellissement *m*, rénovation *f*, retapage *m*; **this year's model is really only last year's that has been given a facelift,** le modèle courant n'est que celui de l'année dernière avec quelques petits embellissements.

facelift[2], *v.tr. F:* restaurer (la façade d'un bâtiment, etc.); remettre (qch.) au goût du jour; faire des retouches à (un modèle antérieur, etc.).

face-off ['feisɔf], *s. Games:* (*lacrosse, etc.*) engagement *m* du jeu.

faceplate ['feispleit], *s.* **1.** *Mec.E:* plateau *m* (de tour); **f. jaw,** poupée *f* à griffes (de tour); **f. mounting,** montage *m* en l'air (d'un tour). **2.** *Tchn:* tas *m* à planer; marbre *m* à dresser, marbre d'atelier. **3.** *Elcs:* fond *m* (d'un tube cathodique).

facer ['feisər], *s. F:* **1.** gifle *f*, coup *m*, au visage. **2.** difficulté soudaine (à laquelle il faut parer d'urgence); obstacle inopiné; **that's a f.!** comment allons-nous nous tirer de là? quelle tuile!

facet[1] ['fæsit], *s.* **1.** facette *f* (d'un diamant, *Ent:* de l'œil, etc.); *Lap:* **star f.,** étoile *f*; **corner f.,** haléfis *m*; **main f.,** coin *m* de table; **cut in facets,** taillé à facettes. **2.** *Arch:* listel *m*, côte *f* (de colonne). **3.** aspect *m* (d'une situation, etc.).

facet[2], *v.tr.* (**facet(t)ed**) facetter (une pierre précieuse).

facet(t)ed ['fæsitid], *a.* (pierre) à facettes.

facetiae [fə'si:ʃii:], *s.pl.* **1.** facéties *f.* **2.** (*in booksellers' catalogues*) livres curieux (c.-à-d. drolatiques ou graveleux).

facet(t)ing ['fæsitiŋ], *s.* facettage *m.*

facetious [fə'si:ʃəs], *a.* facétieux, plaisant, gouailleur; **f. style,** style bouffon.

facetiously [fə'si:ʃəsli], *adv.* facétieusement.

facetiousness [fə'si:ʃəsnis], *s.* caractère facétieux (d'un discours, etc.); bouffonnerie *f* (de conduite); plaisanterie *f*; humeur facétieuse.

facework ['feiswə:k], *s. Const:* façade *f.*

facia ['fæʃiə], *s.* = FASCIA 1 (*b*).

facial ['feiʃ(ə)l], *a.* (nerf, etc.) facial, -aux; **f. expression, outline,** expression *f*, contour *m*, du visage; *Anthr:* **f. angle,** angle facial; **f. massage,** massage facial; *s.* **facial,** (i) massage facial; (ii) traitement *m* esthétique (pour le visage).

facies ['feiʃii:z], *s.* facies *m* (d'une plante, d'un groupe de strates); *Med:* **f. hippocratica,** facies hippocratique; facies grippé.

facile ['fæsail, -il], *a. usu. Pej:* (*of work, wit, etc.*) facile, qui a coûté peu d'efforts; **to have a f. pen,** avoir la plume facile; **to be a f. liar,** être habile à controuver des mensonges; avoir du talent pour le mensonge; avoir le mensonge facile. **2.** (*of pers.*) accommodant, complaisant; **f. morals,** morale large, facile.

facilely ['fæsailli], *adv. usu. Pej:* avec trop de facilité, d'une façon trop facile.

facilitate [fə'siliteit], *v.tr.* faciliter (une action, le progrès de qch., etc.); **a vacuum cleaner facilitates housework,** on fait le ménage plus facilement si on a un aspirateur.

facilitation [fəsili'teiʃ(ə)n], *s.* assouplissement *m.*

facility [fə'siliti], *s.* **1.** (*a*) facilité *f*; **f. in speaking, in writing,** facilité à parler, à écrire; **to speak with f.,** parler avec facilité; **f. with the pen,** souplesse *f* de plume; **to do sth. with great f.,** faire qch. avec une grande facilité; (*b*) **facilities for payment,** facilités de paiement; **overdraft facilities,** facilités de caisse; **to have, enjoy, facilities for doing sth.,** avoir la facilité de faire qch.; **they are given every f. for improving their French,** on leur accorde toutes facilités de se perfectionner en français. **2.** *usu. pl.* (*a*) aménagements *mpl*, installations *fpl*; **storage facilities,** installations de stockage; **alternative facilities,** installations de remplacement; **cooking facilities,** installations de cuisine; possibilité *f* de faire la cuisine; **there are no bathing facilities,** il n'existe aucune installation balnéaire; il n'y a pas de piscine; **we have no facilities for it,** nous ne sommes pas équipés, outillés, pour cela; **transport facilities,** moyens *m* de transport; *Av:* **ground facilities,** installations au sol; infrastructure aérienne; *Nau:* **harbour, docking, discharge, facilities,** installations portuaires, de carénage, de déchargement; **mooring facilities,** mouillages *mpl*; *Trans:* **loading and unloading facilities,** installations de chargement et de déchargement; **UNESCO has facilities for the supply of information,** l'UNESCO est en mesure de fournir des renseignements. **3.** caractère *m* traitable; souplesse *f* de caractère; complaisance *f.*

facing ['feisiŋ], *s.* **1.** (*a*) *Mil: etc:* mouvement *m* de front, conversion *f* (à droite, à gauche, etc.); **f. about,** volte-face *f*; (*b*) *Rail:* **f. points,** aiguilles (prises) de face; **f. point signal,** indicateur *m* de direction. **2.** *Join: Metalw: etc:* dressage *m* (d'une surface); lamage *m*, planage *m*, surfaçage *m*, usinage *m*; **rough f.,** dressage d'ébauche; **f. machine, tool,** machine *f*, outil *m*, à surfacer, à dresser; **f. lathe,** tour *m* en l'air, à plateau; tour à facer; **f. mill,** fraise axiale, fraise de face. **3.** (*a*) revers *m*, parement *m* (d'un habit, etc.); *Mil:* **regimental facings,** parements (de la manche ou du col) servant à distinguer les différents corps; (*b*) *Const:* revêtement *m*, parement, chemise *f* (d'un mur, etc.); placage *m*; perré *m* (d'un talus, d'une tranchée); **f. brick,** brique *f* de parement; **slag f.,** revêtement en laitier; **to apply a f. of marble, etc., to a wall,** appliquer un placage de marbre, etc., sur une paroi; (*c*) *Metalw: etc:* revêtement, dépôt *m* électrolytique; **chromium f.,** chromage *m*; **nickel f.,** nickelage *m*; **silver f.,** argenture *f*; **steel f.,** aciérage *m*; (*d*) *Civ.E: Mec.E:* surface *f* de portée; *Mch:* glace *f* (de tiroir); (*e*) garniture *f* (de frein, d'embrayage). **4.** *Metall:* poncif *m*, poncis *m* (du moule); **f. sand,** poussier *m* de moulage.

facsimile[1] [fæk'simili], *s.* (*a*) fac-similé *m*, *pl.* fac-similés; *Jur:* copie figurée (d'un testament, etc.); **copy in f.,** copie fac-similaire; **to reproduce sth. in f., to make a f. of sth.,** fac-similer qch.; *Typ:* **to set up a f. of the original,** composer 'chou pour chou'; *attrib.* **f. signature,** signature autographiée; (*b*) *Elcs: Tg:* (i) fac-similé, bélinogramme *m*; (ii) système *m* de facsimilé, procédé *m* bélinographique; téléphotographie *f*; **f. equipment,** appareillage *m*, équipement *m*, matériel *m*, bélinographique, pour la transmission d'images fixes; **f. broadcast station,** station *f* bélinographique; **f. photography,** téléphotographie *f*, phototélégraphie *f*; **f. receiver,** récepteur *m* bélinographique; récepteur d'images fixes; **f. telegraphy,** bélinographie *f*; **f. transmission,** transmission *f* d'images fixes.

facsimile[2], *v.tr.* fac-similer (un document, une signature).

fact [fækt], *s.* **1.** fait *m*, action *f*; (*in a few phrs., esp.*) **an accomplished f.,** un fait accompli; *Jur:* **taken in the f.,** pris sur le fait; pris en flagrant délit. **2.** (*a*) fait; **to bow before the facts,** s'incliner devant les faits; se rendre à l'évidence *f*; **to look facts in the face,** voir les choses telles qu'elles sont; **the ideal and the f.,** l'idéal *m* et la réalité; **f. and fiction,** le réel et l'imaginaire *m*; **scientific facts,** les vérités *f* scientifiques; **to stick to facts,** s'en tenir aux faits, aux réalités; **he is sure of his facts,** il parle en connaissance de cause; il est bien documenté; **the facts of a case,** les faits d'une cause; **I told him the facts of the case,** je lui ai dit ce qui en était; **if the f. be true,** si la chose est vraie; **by, owing to, the f. that . . .,** du fait que . . .; **to state sth. as a f.,** poser qch. en fait; **it's a f., an actual f.,** c'est un fait; c'est réel, c'est exact, c'est la vérité; **it's a f. that . . .,** il est de fait que . . .; **to know for a f. that . . .,** savoir pertinemment que . . .; **by the mere f. of, that, . . .,** par le, du seul, fait de, que . . .; **to tell s.o. the facts of life,** enseigner que les enfants ne se font pas par l'oreille, **the f. remains that you threatened him,** il reste constant que vous l'avez menacé; **it is not a f. that he was put through the third degree,** il est inexact qu'il ait été cuisiné; **to accept a statement as f.,** ajouter foi à une déclaration; **apart from the f. that . . .,** hormis que . . .; **the f. is, I have no money,** c'est que je n'ai pas d'argent; **in f.,** de fait; **king in name rather than in f.,** roi de nom plutôt que de fait; **I think so, in f. I am sure,** je le pense, et même j'en suis sûr; **in point of f.,** par le fait, au fait, en fait, en vérité; **as a matter of f.,** (i) à la vérité, en réalité, à vrai dire; (ii) en effet, aussi bien; **as a matter of f. I read it in the paper,** en fait, je l'ai lu dans le journal; **as a matter of f., I didn't see him come in,** de fait, le fait est que, je ne l'ai pas vu entrer; **the f. of the matter is that . . .,** cela revient à dire que . . .; (*b*) *Jur:* **the jury only decides issues of f.,** les jurés *m* ne sont juges que du fait.

fact-finding ['fæktfaindiŋ], *a.* (mission *f*, etc.) d'information; (agence *f*) de (recherche de) renseignements.

faction ['fækʃ(ə)n], *s.* **1.** *Pol: etc:* faction *f*, cabale *f.* **2.** (esprit *m* de) discorde *f*, (esprit de) dissension *f.*

factional ['fækʃən(ə)l], *a.* ayant rapport à une faction; factieux.

factionalism ['fækʃənəlizm], *s.* esprit *m* de discorde, de dissension.

factionary ['fækʃənəri], **factionist** ['fækʃənist], *s.* factieux, -ieuse; partisan *m.*

factious ['fækʃəs], *a.* factieux.

factiously ['fækʃəsli], *adv.* factieusement.

factiousness ['fækʃəsnis], *s.* esprit factieux, de faction.

factitious [fæk'tiʃəs], *a.* factice, artificiel, contrefait; faux, *f.* fausse; **f. enthusiasm,** enthousiasme factice, simulé, contrefait; **f. value,** valeur factice; fausse valeur.

factitiously [fæk'tiʃəsli], *adv.* facticement; d'une manière factice.

factitive ['fæktitiv], *a. Gram:* (verbe, etc.) factitif; **the f. object,** le régime du verbe factitif.

factor ['fæktər], *s.* **1.** (*pers.*) (*a*) *Com:* agent *m* (dépositaire); consignataire *m*; courtier *m* de marchandises, commissionnaire *m* en gros; (*b*) *Scot:* régisseur *m*; intendant *m* (d'un domaine); (*c*) *Jur: U.S:* (i) tiers appelé en justice; (ii) tiers-saisi *m*, *pl.* tiers-saisis. **2.** (*a*) *Mth: etc:* diviseur *m*, facteur *m*; coefficient *m*; **prime f.,** facteur, diviseur, premier; **the highest, greatest, common f.,** le plus grand commun diviseur; **correction f.,** coefficient de correction; **form f.,** facteur de forme; *Sch: U.S:* **regularizing f.,** coefficient (à un examen); (*b*) *El: Elcs:* (coefficient d')amplification *f*; *Atom.Ph: etc:* (coefficient de) dissipation *f*; **damping f.,** coefficient d'amortissement; **reduction f.,** facteur, coefficient, de réduction; **transfer f.,** facteur, coefficient, de transmission, de propagation; **demand f.,** (i) coefficient d'utilisation; (ii) facteur de consommation; (*c*) **safety f.,** coefficient, facteur, marge *f*, de sécurité; *Av: etc:* **range f.,** coefficient d'autonomie; **load f.,** coefficient de charge; **gust alleviation f.,** coefficient d'atténuation de rafales; (*d*) *Pol.Ec:* **f. price,** prix *m* de facteur; **f. income,** revenu *m* de facteur; **national income at f. cost,** revenu national au coût des facteurs; (*e*) *Phot:* **development f.,** facteur de développement; **Watkins f.,** coefficient de Watkins. **3.** facteur (concourant à un résultat); considération *f*; **f. of evolution,** facteur d'évolution; *Bot:* **growth f.,** facteur de croissance; **water is an important f. in geology,** le rôle de l'eau, en géologie, est considérable; **an important f. in the life of a nation,** un facteur important, une considération importante, dans la vie d'une nation; **the human f.,** l'élément humain.

factorage ['fæktəridʒ], *s. Com:* (*a*) courtage *m* (en marchandises); commission *f*; (*b*) droits *mpl* de commission.

factorial [fæk'tɔ:riəl]. *Mth:* **1.** *s.* factorielle *f.* **2.** *a.* **factorial x,** la factorielle de x.

factorization [fæktərai'zeiʃ(ə)n], *s. Mth:* factorisation *f.*

factorize ['fæktəraiz], *v.tr. Mth:* décomposer (une quantité) en facteurs; factoriser.

factorizing ['fæktəraiziŋ], *s.* factorisation *f.*

factorship ['fæktəʃip], *s.* **1.** *Com:* office *m* de facteur, de courtier. **2.** *Scot:* charge *f* de régisseur; intendance *f* (d'un domaine).

factory ['fækt(ə)ri], *s.* **1.** *Com: A:* factorerie *f*, comptoir *m* (aux Indes, etc.). **2.** *Ind:* usine *f*, fabrique *f*; **car f.,** usine d'automobiles; **munitions f.,** usine, fabrique, de munitions; **shoe f.,** fabrique de chaussures; **biscuit f.,** biscuiterie *f*; **canning f.,** conserverie *f* (de produits alimentaires); *Fish: etc:* **f. ship, floating f.,** navire-usine *m*, *pl.* navires-usines; usine flottante; **f. unit,** unité *f* de fabrication; **f.-installed component,** pièce *f* d'origine; **f. hand, worker,** ouvrier, -ière, d'usine; **f. inspector,** inspection, inspecteur *m*, inspection *f*, du travail; **the F. Acts,** la législation du travail; la loi sur les accidents du travail; *Pol:* **f. committee,** comité *m* d'usine.

factotum [fæk'toutəm], *s.* factotum *m*; homme *m* à tout faire; *F:* maître Jacques; **to be a general f.,** vaquer à toutes les besognes.

factual ['fæktjuəl], *a.* effectif, réel, positif; **f. knowledge,** connaissance *f* des faits; **f. history,** histoire événementielle; **f. considerations,** considérations *f* pratiques; **f. data,** données *f* de l'expérience; données, résultats *mpl*, pratiques.

factuality [fæktju'æliti], *s.* positivité *f*.

factum ['fæktəm], *s. Jur:* factum *m*; exposé *m* des faits.

facula, *pl* **-ae** ['fækjulə, -i:], *s. Astr:* facule *f*.

facultative ['fæk(ə)ltətiv], *a.* **1.** (*optional*) facultatif, -ive. **2.** qui peut arriver ou ne pas arriver; contingent, casuel. **3.** (activité, etc.) des facultés (physiques ou morales).

faculty ['fæk(ə)lti], *s.* **1.** (*a*) faculté *f*, pouvoir *m*; **mental faculties,** facultés morales, de l'esprit, de l'âme; **the f. of speech,** la faculté de parler; le don de la parole; **he was not in full possession of all his faculties,** il ne jouissait pas de la plénitude de ses facultés (mentales); **to be in possession of all one's faculties,** jouir de toutes ses facultés; (*b*) facilité *f*, talent *m*; **to have a great f. for doing sth.,** avoir une grande facilité à faire qch., un grand talent pour faire qch.; **to have the f. of observation,** savoir bien observer. **2.** *Sch: etc:* (*a*) faculté (des lettres, de droit, etc.); (*b*) (i) *NAm:* professorat *m*, corps enseignant (d'une université, d'un collège); (ii) **the medical f.,** les physiciens et les chirurgiens; (*c*) *Scot:* **the f. of advocates,** le corps du barreau. **3.** (*a*) faculté, liberté *f*, droit *m* (**to do sth.,** de faire qch.); (*b*) *Ecc:* **faculties,** approbation *f*, autorisation *f*, permission *f*.

facundity [fæ'kʌnditi], *s.* faconde *f*.

fad [fæd], *s.* marotte *f*, manie *f*, lubie *f*, dada *m*; **all his fads,** toutes ses manies; **to be full of fads,** *F:* avoir un tas de marottes; **he has his little fads,** il a ses petites manies; **it's a f. with him to . . .,** c'est une manie chez lui de . . .; **it's only a passing f.,** c'est un caprice dont on reviendra.

faddiness ['fædinis], *s.* caractère capricieux; maniaquerie *f*.

faddish ['fædiʃ], *a.* = FADDY.

faddist ['fædist], *s. F:* maniaque *mf*; homme, femme, à marottes; **food f.,** (i) maniaque en fait de nourriture; (ii) partisan, -ane d'un (certain) régime alimentaire.

faddy ['fædi], *a.* capricieux, maniaque; **he's f. about his food,** il est difficile sur la nourriture.

fade[1], *v.*

I. *v.i. & tr.* **1.** *v.i.* (*a*) (*of flowers, colour, etc.*) se faner, se flétrir, se défraîchir; (*of colour*) (se) passer son éclat; s'altérer; (*of pigment*) travailler; (*of material*) se décolorer, déteindre, blanchir; **guaranteed not to f.,** garanti bon teint; résistance au soleil garantie; **his glory has faded,** sa gloire a perdu de son lustre, s'est délustrée; (*b*) (*of light*) **to f. (away, out),** s'évanouir, s'affaiblir; **the (day)light is fading,** le jour s'éteint; **her smile faded (away),** son sourire s'est éteint; **hope was fading from his eyes,** l'espoir s'éteignait dans ses yeux; **colours that f. into each other,** couleurs dégradées, qui se fondent; **day is fading into night,** le jour baisse et la nuit se fait; **summer fades into autumn,** peu à peu l'automne succède à l'été; **the coast was fading from sight,** la côte s'estompait, disparaissait aux regards, se perdait de vue; **to f. from memory,** s'effacer de la mémoire; **impressions that f. away,** impressions qui se volatilisent; **she was fading away,** elle dépérissait; *F:* **when the police arrived he had faded away,** lorsque la police arriva il avait disparu, avait filé; *P:* **(you just) f. away!** fiche le camp! (*c*) (*of sound*) s'évanouir, s'amortir; s'en aller en mourant; **the sound faded away in the distance,** le son alla se perdre dans le lointain. **2.** *v.tr.* (*a*) faner; décolorer; **curtains faded by the sun,** rideaux décolorés par le soleil; (*b*) *Cin:* **to f. one scene into another,** opérer la fusion de deux scènes; enchaîner deux scènes; (*c*) *Golf:* faire dévier (la balle) légèrement à droite.

II. (*compound verbs*) **1. fade in.** *Cin: etc:* (*a*) *v.i.* arriver dans un fondu; apparaître progressivement; s'ouvrir; (*b*) *v.tr.* faire arriver (une scène) dans un fondu.

2. fade out. *Cin: etc:* (*a*) *v.i.* (*of scene*) s'effacer dans un fondu; disparaître progressivement; se fermer; (*b*) *v.tr.* faire partir (une scène) dans un fondu; *W.Tel: etc:* diminuer l'intensité de (la musique, etc.).

fade[2], *s.* **1.** *Cin:* fondu *m*; **cross f., f. over,** fondu enchaîné; **f. grey,** fondu au gris; **f. under,** fondu soutenu. **2.** *Golf:* coup *m* qui fait dévier la balle légèrement à droite.

faded ['feidid], *a.* (*of flower, colour, etc.*) fané, flétri; (*of material*) décoloré, passé de couleur; **f. curtains,** rideaux fanés; **f. beauty,** beauté défraîchie, passée, qui a perdu de son éclat; **f. face,** visage éteint; **f. photograph,** photographie jaunie.

fade-in ['feidin], **fading in** ['feidiŋin], *s. Cin:* (ouverture *f* en) fondu *m*; passage progressif de l'obscurité à la pleine lumière.

fade-out ['feidaut], **fading out** ['feidiŋaut], *s.* (*a*) *Cin: W.Tel: etc:* (fermeture *f* en) fondu *m*; (*b*) *W.Tel:* disparition totale (d'un signal radio-électrique).

fader ['feidər], *s. Cin: W.Tel: etc:* (*a*) affaiblisseur *m*, atténuateur *m* (du son); (*b*) contrôleur *m* de volume (du son).

fading[1] ['feidiŋ], *a.* (fleur) qui se fane; **f. light,** jour pâlissant, lumière pâlissante; **f. memory, glory,** souvenir, gloire, qui va en s'amoindrissant, qui s'efface; **the f. outline could still be seen,** on distinguait encore le contour de plus en plus estompé.

fading[2], *s.* **1.** (*a*) flétrissure *f* (d'une plante); décoloration *f* (d'une étoffe); altération *f* (d'une couleur); affaiblissement *m* (de la lumière, d'une photographie); (*b*) *W.Tel: etc:* fading *m*, atténuation *f* (du son); (*c*) *Aut:* fading (des freins). **2.** *Cin: etc:* (fermeture *f* en) fondu *m*.

faecal ['fi:k(ə)l], *a.* fécal, -aux; **f. matter,** matières fécales; déjections *fpl*.

faecaloid ['fi:kəlɔid], *a.* fécaloïde.

faecaloma [fi:kə'loumə], *s. Med:* fécalome *m*.

faecaluria [fi:kə'lju:riə], *s. Med:* fécalurie *f*.

faeces ['fi:si:z], *s.pl.* **1.** *Ch:* fèces *f*. **2.** *Physiol:* fèces; matières fécales.

faerie, faery ['fɛəri]. *A: & Poet:* **1.** *s.* féerie *f*, le monde des fées. **2.** *a.* (être *m*, pays *m*, etc.) féerique; **the F. Queene,** la Reine des fées.

fag[1] [fæg], *s.* **1.** *F:* (*a*) fatigue *f*, peine *f*, travail *m* pénible, corvée *f*; **what a f.!** quelle corvée! quelle barbe! ce que c'est rasoir! **it's too much f.,** ça prend trop de peine; c'est trop embêtant; (*b*) **brain f.,** surmenage *m*. **2.** *Sch:* petit attaché au service d'un grand. **3.** *F:* cigarette *f*, sèche *f*, sibiche *f*, cibiche *f*. **4.** *attrib.* **f. end,** (i) bout *m* (d'un morceau d'étoffe, etc.); bout décommis (d'un cordage); témoin *m* (d'un cordage neuf); (*cut off rope*) mouchure *f*; *F:* restes *mpl* (d'un gigot, etc.); (ii) queue *f* (de l'hiver, d'une affaire, etc.); bribes *fpl* (d'une conversation); (iii) *F:* mégot *m* (d'un cigare, d'une cigarette). **5.** *P:* pédé(raste) *m*.

fag[2], *v.* **(fagged) 1.** *F:* (*a*) *v.i. & pron. O:* **to f. (oneself),** travailler dur, trimer, s'échiner; **to f. (away) at sth.,** se fatiguer, s'échiner, à (faire) qch.; (*b*) *v.tr.* (*of work, etc.*) éreinter (qn); **fagged out,** épuisé, éreinté. **2.** *Sch:* (*a*) *v.i.* (*of young pupil*) **to f. for a senior,** être au service d'un grand; faire les corvées d'un grand; *Cr:* **to f. out,** tenir le champ pour renvoyer les balles; (*b*) *v.tr.* (*of senior boy*) **to f. a junior,** se faire servir par un petit. **3.** *v.i. Nau:* (*of rope*) **to f. (out), to become fagged,** se décommettre, s'étriper.

Fagaceae [fæ'geisii:], *s.pl. Bot:* fagacées *f*.

fagged [fægd], *a.* **1.** *F: O:* (*of pers.*) fatigué, éreinté. **2.** (*of rope*) étripé.

fagging[1] ['fægiŋ], *a. F: O:* (travail) éreintant, épuisant, échinant.

fagging[2], *s.* **1.** *F: A:* dur travail; turbin *m*. **2.** *Sch:* système d'après lequel les jeunes élèves font le service des grands.

faggot[1] ['fægət], *s.* **1.** (*a*) fagot *m*; bourrée *f* (de bois); (*large*) falourde *f* (de menu bois, de bois de chauffage); *Fort:* fascine *f*; **f. wood,** bois *m* à fagots; fagotage *m*; **f. maker, f. tier,** fagoteur, -euse; (*b*) *A:* supplice *m* du bûcher. **2.** *Metall:* paquet *m*, lopin *m*, faisceau *m*, trousse *f* (de fer en barres); **f. iron,** fer *m* de faisceau. **3.** *Cu:* boulette *f* (de viande). **4.** *Needlew:* **f. stitch(ing),** (i) (*with drawn threads*) faisceaux *mpl*; (ii) couture de raccord ajourée. **5.** *A:* nom fictif sur la liste des électeurs, des effectifs militaires, etc.; *Mil:* passe-volant *m*, *pl.* passe-volants; *Hist:* **f. vote,** vote *m* d'un électeur qualifié ad hoc comme censitaire. **6.** *P:* (*a*) pédé(raste) *m*, fagot; (*b*) **old f.,** vieille chipie.

faggot[2], *v.tr.* **(faggoted) 1.** fagoter, mettre en fagots (du bois à brûler, etc.); lier ensemble; *Metall:* paqueter, mettre en faisceaux, en lopins (le fer, l'acier); *v.i.* faire des fagots. **2.** *Needlew:* **to f. a hem,** faire des faisceaux dans un ouvrage ajouré; **to f. on a strip of material,** ajouter une bande d'étoffe par raccord ajouré.

faggoting ['fægətiŋ], *s.* **1.** fagotage *m* (de menu bois); *Metall:* paquetage *m*. **2.** *Needlew:* (i) faisceaux *mpl*; (ii) couture de raccord ajourée.

fagine ['feidʒi:n], *s. Bio-Ch:* fagine *f*.

fagmaster ['fægmɑ:stər], *s. Sch:* grand qui a un petit à son service.

fagopyrism(us) [fægou'paiərizm, -paiə'rizməs], *s. Vet:* fagopyrisme *m*.

fah [fɑ:], *s. Mus:* la sous-dominante.

faham ['fɑ:həm], *s. Bot:* thé *m* de Bourbon.

Fahlband ['fɑ:lbænd], *s. Miner:* fahlbande *f*.

fahler(t)z ['fɑ:lə:ts], *s. Miner:* cuivre gris, panabase *f*.

Fahrenheit ['færənhait], *a. Ph.Meas:* (échelle *f*, thermomètre *m*) fahrenheit; (degrés F. $-32 \times \frac{5}{9} =$ degrés centigrades).

faience [fa'jɑ̃:s], *s.* faïence *f*; poterie vernissée.

fail[1] [feil], *s.* manque *m*; (*used esp. in*) *adv.phr.* **without f.,** (i) sans faute, sans manque; (ii) immanquablement, à coup sûr.

fail[2]. **1.** *v.i.* (*a*) manquer, faillir, faire défaut, faire faute; **water often fails in the dry season,** l'eau manque souvent pendant la sécheresse; **when all else failed,** en désespoir de cause; **to f. in one's duty,** manquer, faillir, à son devoir; **to f. in respect for s.o.,** manquer de respect envers qn; **to f. to do sth.,** manquer, négliger, de faire qch.; **I shall not f. to do it,** je n'y manquerai pas; **he did not f. to accomplish his destiny,** il n'a pas manqué à sa destinée; **he failed to come, to answer the invitation,** il n'est pas venu; il n'a pas répondu à l'invitation; **owing to the government's having failed to carry out the conditions,** faute par le gouvernement d'avoir rempli les conditions; **I failed to hear the remark,** ce propos m'a échappé; **he failed to mention that . . .,** il a omis de faire remarquer que . . .; **we cannot f. to be conscious of it,** nous ne pouvons manquer d'en avoir conscience; **I had failed to notice it,** cela m'avait échappé; **things that cannot f. to be seen,** choses qu'on ne peut manquer de voir, qui ne sauraient échapper aux regards; **to f. s.o.,** manquer à ses engagements envers qn; **he failed me at the last minute,** au dernier moment il m'a fait faux bond, il a manqué à sa promesse; **my strength is failing me,** mes forces m'abandonnent, me trahissent; **his heart failed him,** le cœur lui manqua; **his memory often fails him,** sa mémoire lui fait souvent défaut; **your memory has failed you,** vos souvenirs vous ont mal servi; (*b*) **the engine failed to start,** le moteur a refusé de démarrer; **the brakes failed,** les freins ont lâché; (*c*) baisser, défaillir, déchoir; **the light is failing,** le jour baisse, s'éteint; **he, his health, is failing,** sa santé baisse, devient chancelante; **the patient is failing visibly,** le malade décline à vue d'œil; **his faculties are beginning to f.,** ses facultés *f* commencent à déchoir, à défaillir; **his sight is failing, is beginning to f.,** sa vue commence à baisser, à s'affaiblir, à faiblir; **his memory is failing,** sa mémoire baisse; **her looks are failing,** sa beauté décline; **my breath was beginning to f.,** la respiration commençait à me manquer; (*d*) ne pas réussir; échouer; manquer son coup; (*of chemical experiment, etc.*) ne pas aboutir; *F:* rater; (*of play*) être un four, faire fiasco, chuter; (*of negotiations*) ne pas aboutir; **his visit had failed to achieve its purpose,** sa visite avait manqué son but, n'avait abouti à rien; **if our hopes should f.,** si nos espérances ne se réalisent pas; **enterprise which failed,** entreprise qui a échoué, qui a avorté; **to f. in one's undertakings,** échouer dans ses entreprises; **to f. with one's goal in sight,** faire naufrage au port; **he failed for want of foresight,** *F:* il s'est trouvé au pied du mur sans échelle; **to f. to win s.o. over,** échouer dans une tentative auprès de qn; **I f. to see why . . .,** je ne vois pas pourquoi . . .; **I failed to convince him,** je n'ai pas réussi à le convaincre; *Jur:* **to f. in a suit,** perdre un procès; *Sch:* **to f. in an examination,** être refusé, être ajourné, subir un échec, échouer, être recalé, à un examen; (*e*) *Com:* faire faillite; tomber en faillite; **to f. for a million,** faire une faillite d'un million. **2.** *v.tr.* (*a*) *Sch:* refuser, recaler (un candidat); être refusé à (un examen); (*b*) **words f. me to express my thanks,** je ne sais comment vous exprimer mes remerciements; (*c*) **I won't f. you,** vous pouvez compter sur moi.

failed [feild], *a. U.S:* **f. firm,** maison *f* en faillite; *Sch: etc:* **f. candidate,** candidat refusé, recalé, échoué.

failing[1] ['feiliŋ], *a.* (*of sight, health, memory, etc.*) faiblissant, défaillant, baissant; **he has been in f. health for some time,** depuis longtemps sa santé s'affaiblit; (*of oil well, etc.*) **f. yield,** débit *m* qui baisse.

failing[2], *s.* **1.** (*a*) manquement *m*; **his f. in respect towards . . .,** son manque de respect envers . . .; **his f. to report the accident,** son silence sur l'accident; (*b*) affaiblissement *m*, défaillance *f* (de forces, etc.); baisse *f* (de la vue, etc.); (*c*) non-réussite *f*; échec *m*; (*d*) *Com:* faillite *f*. **2.** faible *m*, faiblesse *f*, défaut *m*; **with all his failings,** avec toutes ses faiblesses, tous ses défauts; **f. in s.o.,** faiblesse, défaut, chez qn; **his f. is his excessive shyness,** il pèche par trop de timidité; **drink is a f. of his,** la boisson est son faible.

failing[3], *prep.* à, au, défaut de; **f. payment within thirty days,** à défaut de paiement dans les trente jours; **f. a satisfactory reply,** faute de réponse satisfaisante; **f.**

which, faute de quoi; à défaut de quoi; **the chairman, f. whom the secretary, shall sign,** le président, en son absence le secrétaire, signera; **f. your advice to the contrary,** sauf avis contraire de votre part; **f. all else,** en désespoir de cause.

fail-safe ['feilseif], *a. Rail: etc:* **f. s. device, system,** dispositif *m* de sécurité positive, anti-rupture; *Mil.Av:* **f.-s. point,** zone *f* que les bombardiers ne peuvent survoler sans instructions spéciales.

failure ['feiljər], *s.* **1.** (*a*) manque *m*, manquement *m*, défaut *m*; **f. of justice,** manque de justice; **f. to answer the roll call,** manquement à l'appel; **f. to observe a bye-law, to keep a promise,** inobservation *f* d'un règlement de police, d'une promesse; manquement à une promesse; **f. to pay a bill,** défaut de paiement d'un effet; **alarm was felt at his f. to appear again,** on s'alarmait de ce qu'il ne reparaissait pas; (*b*) non-fonctionnement *m*; panne *f*; désamorçage *m* (d'un injecteur, d'une pompe, d'une dynamo); *I.C.E:* non-production *f* (de l'étincelle); ratés *mpl* (d'allumage); *El:* **power f.,** panne de courant; **partial f. of current,** fléchissement *m* d'un courant; *Med:* **heart f.,** arrêt *m* du cœur; syncope (mortelle); (*c*) = FAILING[2] 1 (*b*). **2.** (*a*) insuccès *m*, non-réussite *f*; avortement *m* (d'un projet, etc.); échec *m* (à un examen, dans une entreprise); *Th:* four *m*, fiasco *m*; chute *f* (d'une pièce); **f. of a prophecy,** non-réalisation *f* d'une prophétie; **to bring about the f. of a plan,** faire échouer un projet; **it's a f.,** c'est raté; **to court f.,** aller au-devant d'une défaite, d'un échec; (*b*) *Com:* faillite *f*. **3.** (*a*) (*of pers.*) raté, -ée; **as a doctor, he's a f.,** comme médecin il est nul, c'est un raté; **he was a f. as a barrister,** il n'a pas réussi comme avocat; il a fait un mauvais avocat; **to be a social f.,** ne pas briller dans le monde; *Sch:* **there are too many failures,** (i) (*at examination*) trop de candidats ont été refusés, recalés; (ii) (*in more general sense*) trop d'élèves ont fait de mauvaises études, n'ont pas profité de leurs études; **I don't say he's a f.,** je ne dis pas que ce soit un raté; (*b*) **the play was a f.,** la pièce est tombée à plat, a été un four; **a dead f.,** un four noir, un fiasco complet; **the experiment was, proved, turned out, a f.,** l'expérience *f* a manqué, n'a pas réussi, *F:* a raté; **his whole life was a f.,** ce fut une vie ratée; **apples are a complete f. this year,** cette année les pommes font absolument défaut.

fain[1] [fein], *A: & Lit:* **1.** *a.* (*a*) trop heureux, contraint par la nécessité (**to do sth.,** de faire qch.); **men were f. to eat horse-flesh,** on était trop heureux de manger de la viande de cheval; (*b*) bien disposé; accueillant. **2.** *adv.* volontiers, avec plaisir; **I f. would be, I would f. be, a father to your children,** je serais trop heureux d'être un père pour vos enfants; je voudrais bien être, je serais volontiers, un père pour vos enfants; **I would f. have stayed at home,** j'aurais bien voulu rester à la maison.

fain[2], **fains** [feinz], **fainits** ['feinitz], *int. Sch: F:* **1.** pouce! **2.** (*claiming exemption*) **fains I fielding!** c'est pas moi qui vais ramasser les balles!

faint[1] [feint], *a.* **1.** *A: & Lit:* timide; **f. heart,** cœur *m* lâche, pusillanime; *Prov:* **f. heart never won fair lady,** jamais honteux n'eut belle amie. **2.** (*a*) (*of spirit, intention, etc.*) faible, affaibli, alangui; **f. hope,** faible espoir *m*; **a. f. attempt,** une faible tentative; **f. praise,** éloges *m* tièdes; **to give a f. smile,** sourire du bout des lèvres; **to speak in a f. voice,** parler d'une voix faible, affaiblie, éteinte; (*b*) (*of colour*) pâle, délavé; (*of sound, breeze, touch, etc.*) léger, à peine perceptible; (*of smell, etc.*) faible, léger, peu prononcé; (*of idea, etc.*) vague, peu précis; (*of mark, colour, etc.*) à peine visible, peu apparent; **a f. tinge of blue,** une légère nuance bleuâtre; **f. inscription,** inscription indistincte; **he hasn't the faintest chance of success,** il n'a pas la moindre chance de réussir; **I haven't the faintest idea,** je n'en ai pas la moindre idée; **f. action,** action *f* peu efficace, à peine sensible; **sound that is growing fainter,** son *m* qui décroît; **the sound of the footsteps grew fainter,** le bruit des pas s'assourdit, s'affaiblit, s'éteignit; *Mus:* **growing fainter,** en s'éloignant. **3.** (*a*) = FEINT[3]; (*b*) *Jur:* **f. action, pleading,** cause fictive. **4. to feel f.,** se sentir mal; être pris d'une défaillance; avoir un malaise; *Lit:* **my heart felt f. within me,** mon cœur défaillait; le cœur me manquait.

faint[2], *s.* évanouissement *m*, syncope *f*, défaillance *f*; **to be in a (dead) f.,** être évanoui, être sans connaissance, être tombé en syncope; **to fall down in a f.,** tomber évanoui; tomber en faiblesse, en défaillance; avoir une syncope.

faint[3], *v.i.* **to f. (away),** s'évanouir, défaillir; tomber en syncope, en faiblesse; se trouver mal; **she nearly fainted,** il lui a pris une faiblesse; elle était sur le point de s'évanouir; **I was fainting with hunger,** je défaillais, je mourais, de faim.

faint(-)hearted ['feint'hɑ:tid], *a.* pusillanime, timide, peureux, lâche, sans courage.

faint(-)heartedly ['feint'hɑ:tidli], *adv.* avec pusillanimité; timidement, lâchement.

faint(-)heartedness ['feint'hɑ:tidnis], *s.* pusillanimité *f*, timidité *f*, lâcheté *f*.

fainting[1] ['feintiŋ], *a.* (*of courage, voice, etc.*) défaillant.

fainting[2], *s.* évanouissement *m*, défaillance *f*; **f. fit,** évanouissement, syncope *f*.

faintly ['feintli], *adv.* **1.** (*a*) timidement; sans courage; (*b*) faiblement, d'une manière languissante; mollement; **she answered f.,** elle répondit d'une voix éteinte. **2.** légèrement, un peu; **I can hear it f.,** je l'entends faiblement; **she smiled f.,** elle esquissa un sourire; **f. reminiscent of . . .,** qui rappelle vaguement . . .; **f. sarcastic tone,** ton *m* légèrement sarcastique; **f. visible,** à peine visible; **the coast could be seen f. through the mist,** la terre s'estompait dans la brume.

faintness ['feintnis], *s.* **1.** (*of voice, smile, etc.*) faiblesse *f*; (*of breeze, sound, etc.*) légèreté *f*; **the f. of the inscription,** le manque de lisibilité de l'inscription. **2.** malaise *m*, faiblesse; **a feeling of f. came over her,** elle sentait qu'elle allait s'évanouir.

faints [feints], *s.pl. Dist:* alcools *m* de tête, de queue; repasse *f*.

fair[1] [fɛər], *s.* **1.** foire *f*; grand marché; **horse f.,** foire aux chevaux; **world f.,** exposition universelle; **fun f.** = fête foraine. **2. (church, etc.) f.,** vente *f* de charité; kermesse *f*.

fair[2], *a. & adv.*

I. *a.* **1.** beau, *f.* belle; **the f. sex,** le beau sexe; *A:* **my f. readers,** mes (aimables) lectrices *f*; *s. A: & Poet:* **a fair,** une belle; *Hist:* **Charles the F.,** Charles le Bel; **Philip the F.,** Philippe le Bel. **2.** (*of speech, promise, etc.*) spécieux, plausible; *Lit:* **a f. tongue,** une langue mielleuse; **to put s.o. off with f. words, f. promises,** faire patienter qn avec de belles paroles, de belles promesses. **3.** (*of pers., hair*) blond; (*of skin, complexion*) blanc, *f.* blanche. **4.** (*a*) net, sans tache; *Lit:* **a f. name,** un nom sans tache; (*b*) (*intensive*) *P:* **it's a f. swindle, a f. do,** c'est une pure, une véritable, escroquerie; (*c*) juste, équitable; loyal, -aux; **you're not being f. to yourself,** vous n'êtes pas juste vis-à-vis de vous-même; **to win in a f. fight,** vaincre après une lutte loyale; *Lit:* **all I ask is a f. field and no favour,** je ne demande que la justice, sans faveur; **f. play,** (i) jeu loyal, franc jeu, fair-play *m inv*; (ii) traitement *m* juste; **the umpire will see f. play,** l'arbitre *m* veillera à ce que tout se passe selon les règles; **that's f. play,** c'est de bonne lutte, de bon jeu, de bonne guerre; **fair's f.,** il faut être juste; **that's only f.,** ce n'est que juste; **it's not f.,** ce n'est pas bien, ce n'est pas de jeu, cela passe le jeu; ce n'est pas juste; **f. enough!** ça va! d'accord! **as is, was, only f.,** comme de juste; **nothing can be fairer,** rien de plus juste; **it's all f. and above board, all f. and square,** c'est de la bonne guerre; c'est parfaitement juste; il n'y a rien de louche là-dedans; **to have a reputation for f. and square dealing,** avoir une réputation de loyauté en affaires; **he is strict but f.,** il est sévère mais sans parti pris; **to charge a f. price,** prendre un prix convenable, raisonnable; **to make f. profits,** réaliser des bénéfices normaux; *Com:* **f. trade,** libre échange basé sur des conditions de réciprocité; *Ind:* **f. wages,** salaire *m* équitable; **he got his f. share of praise,** il a reçu sa bonne part d'éloges; **it is only f. to say that . . .,** il faut dire que . . .; il n'est que juste d'ajouter que . . .; **it is only f. to give him a hearing,** ce n'est que justice, il est de toute justice, de l'entendre; **if it's a f. question, why . . .?** sans indiscrétion, pourquoi . . .? **by f. means,** par des moyens *m* licites; par des voies *f* honnêtes; **by f. means or foul,** d'une manière ou d'une autre; de gré ou de force; par tous les moyens, bons ou mauvais; *Jur:* **f. and accurate report,** compte rendu loyal et exact; (*in libel case*) **to plead f. comment,** invoquer en défense le droit de commenter loyalement un fait d'intérêt général; *Prov:* **all's f. in love and war,** en amour la ruse est de bonne guerre. **5.** passable, assez bon; **f. handwriting,** écriture *f* passable; **in f. condition,** acceptable; **f. accuracy,** assez grande précision; **a f. number of . . .,** un nombre respectable de . . .; **of f. size,** raisonnablement grand; **to have a f. amount of sense,** avoir assez de bon sens; **he has a f. chance of success,** il a des chances de réussir; (*in an examination*) **to obtain a f. mark,** obtenir une note passable; *F:* **f. to middling,** passable; pas mal; entre les deux; **how are you?—f. to middling,** comment ça va?—comme ci comme ça; pas mal; **I paid a f. price for it,** je l'ai payé assez cher. **6.** (*a*) (*of wind, etc.*) propice, favorable; *Nau:* **f. channel,** chenal sain; **f. wind,** bon vent, vent portant; (*b*) **f. weather,** beau temps; **set f.,** beau (temps) fixe; **the barometer is at set f.,** le baromètre est au beau fixe. **7.** *Nau:* caréné; *Av: Aut:* profilé.

II. *adv.* **1.** *A:* **to speak (s.o.) f.,** (i) parler courtoisement, poliment (à qn); (ii) *F:* faire patte de velours; (iii) faire (à qn) de belles promesses; **f. and softly,** tout doucement. **2.** *F:* (*honourably*) (agir) loyalement, de bonne foi; **to play f.,** jouer loyalement; jouer beau jeu; **to fight f.,** faire la bonne guerre. **3.** *F:* (*a*) complètement; (*b*) **struck f. (and square) on the chin,** frappé en plein menton. **4.** *O:* (écrit) au net, au propre, bien lisiblement. **5. to promise f. to do sth.,** avoir de grandes chances de faire qch.

fair[3], *v.tr.* **1.** *N.Arch:* effiler, finir, donner du fini à (la coque); *Av:* caréner, profiler (le fuselage); fuseler (le corps); *Aut:* profiler (la carrosserie). **2.** *Av: Aut: etc:* **to f. sth. into the fuselage, the bodywork,** intégrer, incorporer, qch. aérodynamiquement dans le fuselage, dans la carrosserie.

faired [fɛəd], *a.* (*a*) fuselé; caréné; profilé; (*b*) dans le prolongement d'un plan.

fair-faced ['fɛə'feist], *a. A:* (*a*) au teint clair; (*b*) beau, belle; gentil, gentille; (*c*) hypocrite; à deux visages.

fairfieldite ['fɛəfi:ldait], *s. Miner:* fairfieldite *f*.

fairground ['fɛəgraund], *s.* champ *m* de foire; *F:* **the place looks like a f.,** il y a du désordre partout.

fair-haired ['fɛə'hɛəd], *a.* blond; aux cheveux blonds.

fairing[1] ['fɛəriŋ], *s.* **1.** (*streamlining of structure*) *N.Arch:* effilement *m*; *Av: Aut:* profilage *m*; carénage *m*; capotage *m*. **2.** (*streamlined structure*) *Av: Aut: etc:* carénage; gaine profilée; capot profilé; *Civ.E:* éperon *m* (de la pile d'un pont).

fairing[2], *s. A:* cadeau acheté à la foire; **to give s.o. sth. as a f.,** donner sa foire à qn.

fairish ['fɛəriʃ], *a.* **1.** (*of hair, etc.*) plutôt blond. **2.** (*moderate*) passable, assez bon; comme ci comme ça; pas mal.

Fair Isle ['fɛərail], *Pr.n. Geog:* Fair Isle (une des îles Shetland); **F. I. woollen goods,** bonneterie et tricots décorés de motifs en couleurs vives.

fairlead ['fɛəli:d], *s.* **1.** *Nau:* (*a*) conduit *m* de drisse, margouillet *m*; (*b*) chaumard *m*, galoche *f*. **2.** *Av: Mec.E:* guide-câble *m*, *pl.* guide-câbles; supportguide *m* (de tuyau, etc.).

fairleader ['fɛəli:dər], *s. Nau:* = FAIRLEAD 1, 2.

fairlight ['fɛəlait], *s.* vasistas *m*; imposte (vitrée).

fairly ['fɛəli], *adv.* **1.** (juger, etc.) impartialement, équitablement, avec justice; **to treat s.o. f.,** traiter qn avec impartialité. **2.** (agir, jouer, etc.) honnêtement, loyalement, franchement; **to come by sth. f.,** obtenir qch. par des moyens honnêtes, à bon titre, à juste titre; **f. drawn sample,** échantillon prélevé consciencieusement; **I'll tell you f. (and squarely) how matters stand,** je vais vous dire franchement, carrément, sans détours, ce qui en est. **3.** (*a*) bien; **once the ship was f. under way,** une fois le navire en bonne route; (*b*) *F:* complètement, absolument; **we were f. caught in the trap,** nous étions bel et bien pris; **they dance and their feet f. talk,** ils dansent et c'est tout juste si leurs pieds ne parlent pas; **they f. screamed with delight,** ce fut une véritable explosion de cris de joie. **4.** moyennement, passablement; assez (riche, habile, etc.); **f. good wine,** vin passablement bon, qui se laisse boire; **it is f. certain that . . .,** il est à peu près certain que . . .; **to do sth. f. well,** faire qch. d'une façon passable.

fair-maid ['fɛəmeid], *s.* **1.** *Bot: F: & Lit:* **February fair-maids,** perce-neige *m or f inv*; **fair-maid-of-France,** renoncule *f* à feuilles d'aconit. **2.** *Fish:* pilchard fumé.

fair-minded ['fɛə'maindid], *a.* équitable, juste, impartial, -iaux.

fair-mindedness ['fɛə'maindidnis], *s.* impartialité *f*.

fairness ['fɛənis], *s.* **1.** *A: & Poet:* beauté *f*. **2.** couleur blonde (des cheveux); fraîcheur *f* (du teint, de la peau). **3.** équité *f*, honnêteté *f*, impartialité *f*; **f. in trade,** loyauté *f* dans les affaires; **in all f.,** en bonne conscience, en bonne justice, en toute justice, en toute impartialité.

fair-sized ['fɛə'saizd], *a.* assez grand; d'une grandeur raisonnable.

fair-spoken ['fɛə'spouk(ə)n], *a. A:* **1.** (*a*) qui parle courtoisement, doucement, poliment; à la parole courtoise; (*b*) à la parole mielleuse. **2.** qui fait de belles promesses; **a f.-s. man,** un beau parleur.

fairway ['fɛəwei], *s.* **1.** *Nau:* chenal *m*, passe *f*, passage *m*; **depth of water in the f.,** profondeur *f* d'eau dans le passage. **2.** (*a*) *Golf:* partie du parcours gazonnée, bien entretenue, et sans accident de terrain (où doivent tomber toutes les balles bien jouées); parcours normal; (*b*) *Ten: F:* milieu *m* du court.

fair-weather ['fɛə'weðər], *a.* (*a*) *Nau: etc:* (*of craft, etc.*) qui convient seulement pour le beau temps; (*b*) **f.-w. friends,** amis *m* des beaux jours, amis jusqu'à la bourse.

fairy ['fɛəri]. **1.** *s.* (*a*) fée *f*; **the wicked f.,** la fée Carabosse; *Th:* **f. play,** féerie *f*; (*b*) *Pej: P: A:* vieille mégère; vieille fée; (*c*) *P:* pédé (raste) *m*, tapette *f*, tante *f*. **2.** *a.* (*a*) féerique; **f. forest,** forêt *f* de féerie; **f. key,** clef *f* magique; **f. fingers,** doigts *m* de fée; **f. footsteps,** pas légers; **she was a f. figure in her shimmering dress,** elle avait l'air d'une sylphide dans sa robe chatoyante; **f. queen,** reine *f* des fées; **f. godmother,** (i) marraine *f* fée; (ii) *F:* marraine gâteau; **f. ring,** cercle *m*, rond *m*, de sorcières (dans les prés); **f.-ring mushroom,** mousseron *m*; **f. story, tale,** (i) conte *m* de fées; (ii) conte invraisemblable; (iii) mensonge *m*; **what's this f. story, tale, you're telling me?** qu'est-ce que tu me chantes là? **that's nothing but a f. story, tale,** tout ça c'est de la blague; **f. light, lamp,** lampion *m* (pour décorations); (*b*) *Bot:* **f. rose,** rose *f* pompon; (*c*) **f. cycle,** bicyclette *f* d'enfant.

fairyland ['fɛərilænd], *s.* (*a*) le pays, le royaume, des fées; (*b*) féerie *f*; **at night the garden became a f.,** le soir, le jardin se transforma en pays enchanté.

fairylike ['fɛərilaik], *a.* féerique; comme une fée; **f. work,** ouvrage *m* de fée.

fait accompli ['feitækɔmpli:], *s.* fait accompli; **to present s.o. with a f. a.,** mettre qn devant un fait accompli.

faith [feiθ], *s.* **1.** (*a*) foi *f*; confiance *f*, croyance *f*; **f. is everything,** il n'y a que la foi qui sauve; **to have f. in s.o., in sth.,** avoir confiance en qn, en qch.; **to have f. in God,** avoir foi en Dieu; **I have no f. in his promises,** je ne crois pas à ses promesses; je n'ajoute aucune foi à ses promesses; **to pin one's f. on s.o., sth.; to put one's f. in s.o.,** accorder toute sa confiance à qn; s'en rapporter à qn; mettre ses espérances, tout son espoir, en qch.; se fier aveuglément à qn, à qch.; **they had pinned their f. on this letter,** cette lettre était devenue leur évangile *m*; **f. cure,** guérison *f* (i) par la prière faite avec foi, (i) par (auto)suggestion; **f. healer,** guérisseur *m* qui pratique la thérapeutique fondée sur la prière et la suggestion; **f. healing,** thérapeutique fondée sur la prière et la suggestion; (*b*) religion *f*, croyance; **the Christian f.,** la croyance des chrétiens; la foi chrétienne; **it is of f. that Jesus Christ became man,** il est de foi que Jésus-Christ s'est fait homme; **to belong to the same f.,** appartenir à la même communion; **to die in the f., professing the f.,** mourir en religion; faire une bonne mort; bien mourir; **political f.,** credo *m* politique. **2.** (*a*) fidélité *f* à ses engagements ; **to keep f. with s.o.,** tenir ses engagements envers qn; **to break f. with s.o.,** manquer de foi, de parole, à qn; abuser de la confiance de qn; **to give, pledge, one's f.,** engager sa foi; (*b*) **good f.,** bonne foi, loyauté *f*; **to say sth. in good f.,** dire qch. en toute bonne foi, en (bonne) conscience; **to do sth. in all good f.,** faire qch. en tout honneur; **bad f.,** perfidie *f*, déloyauté *f*; **Punic f.,** la foi punique; *Com:* **purchaser in good f.,** acquéreur *m* de bonne foi. **3.** *int. A:* **(in) f.! i' f.!** ma foi!

faithful ['feiθful]. **1.** *a.* fidèle; (*a*) (*of friend, discharge of duty, etc.*) loyal, -aux; **to remain f. to s.o., to one's opinions,** rester fidèle à qn, à ses opinions; **f. promise,** promesse formelle; **f. memory,** mémoire *f* fidèle; **f. in the observance of . . .,** fidèle à observer . . .; (*b*) (*of report, copy, likeness, etc.*) exact, juste, vrai; **f. translation,** traduction *f* fidèle; **f. in every detail,** exact jusqu'au moindre détail. **2.** *s.pl. Ecc:* **the f.,** les fidèles *m*; (*Islam*) les croyants *m*; **the Father of the F.,** le Père des croyants; **the Commander of the F.,** le Père, le Commandeur, des croyants; le calife.

faithfully ['feiθfuli], *adv.* **1.** fidèlement, loyalement; *Corr:* **we remain yours f.,** agréez nos meilleures salutations; recevez l'expression de nos sentiments distingués; **to deal f. with s.o.,** régler son compte à qn; **he promised f. to come tomorrow,** il a promis formellement de venir demain; il a promis de venir demain sans faute; il (nous) a donné sa parole qu'il viendrait demain. **2.** (traduire, copier, etc.) exactement, fidèlement.

faithfulness ['feiθfulnis], *s.* **1.** fidélité *f*, loyauté *f* (to, envers). **2.** fidélité, exactitude *f* (d'un récit, d'un portrait, etc.).

faithless ['feiθlis], *a.* **1.** infidèle, sans foi. **2.** infidèle (**to,** à). **3.** déloyal, -aux; perfide.

faithlessly ['feiθlisli], *adv.* déloyalement, perfidement.

faithlessness ['feiθlisnis], *s.* **1.** infidélité *f* (to, à). **2.** déloyauté *f*; manque *m* de foi.

fake[1] [feik], *s. Nau:* plet *m*, glène *f* (de manœuvre).

fake[2], *v.tr. Nau:* lover (un cordage).

fake[3], *s.* article faux, truqué, maquillé, camouflé; maquillage *m*; **it's a f.,** c'est du chiqué, du trucage, du toc; **f. interview,** interview monté d'avance; interview imaginaire.

fake[4], *v.tr.* truquer (des calculs); maquiller (un meuble, etc.); altérer, adultérer (le vin, un texte, etc.); frelater (le vin); dissimuler les défauts (d'un chien, etc.); maquignonner (un cheval); cuisiner (des nouvelles); **faked balance sheet,** bilan truqué; **faked cards,** cartes biseautées; **to f. (up) a story,** inventer une histoire.

faker ['feikər], *s.* truqueur, -euse; maquilleur *m*; altérateur, -trice; faussaire *mf*.

faking ['feikiŋ], *s.* trucage *m*, maquillage *m*; altération *f*, adultération *f*; maquignonnage *m* (de chevaux); biseautage *m* (des cartes).

fakir [fæ'kiər, 'feikiər], *s.* fakir *m*.

falanaka [fælə'nɑ:kə], **falanouc** [fælə'nu:k], *s. Z:* euplère *m*.

falcate ['fælkeit], *a. Nat.Hist:* falciforme, falqué.

falchion ['fɔ:lʃ(ə)n], *s.* **1.** *A.Arms:* fauchon *m*. **2.** (*a*) *A:* cimeterre *m*, badelaire *m*; (*b*) *Poet:* glaive *m*.

falciform ['fælsifɔ:m], *a. Anat:* falciforme.

falcon ['fɔ:(l)kən], *s.* **1.** (*a*) *Orn:* faucon *m*; **young f.,** fauconneau *m*; **red-footed f.,** faucon kobez, faucon à pattes rouges; **Eleonora's f.,** faucon d'Éléonore; **Greenland f.,** gerfaut blanc; **Iceland f.,** gerfaut d'Islande; **lanner f.,** faucon lanier; **saker f.,** faucon sacre; **sooty f.,** faucon *m* concolore; **prairie f.,** *Fr.C:* faucon des prairies; **gyr f.,** gerfaut, faucon gerfaut; **peregrine f.,** faucon pèlerin; (*b*) *Ven:* faucon femelle; **f. house,** fauconnerie *f*. **2.** *Artil:* faucon.

falconer ['fɔ:kənər], *s.* fauconnier *m*.

falconet ['fɔ:kənet], *s.* **1.** *Artil: A:* fauconneau *m*. **2.** *Orn:* fauconnet *m*, falconelle *f*, faucon-moineau *m*, *pl.* faucons-moineaux.

Falconidae [fæl'kɔnidi:], *s.pl. Orn:* falconidés *m*.

Falconiformes [fælkɔni'fɔ:mi:z], *s.pl.* falconiformes *m*.

falconry ['fɔ:(l)kənri], *s.* fauconnerie *f*.

falderal ['fældəræl], **falderol** ['fɔldərɔl]. **1.** (*refrain*) lanlaire. **2.** *s. A:* babiole *f*; colifichet *m*.

faldstool ['fɔ:ldstu:l], *s. Ecc:* **1.** siège *m* d'évêque (sans accoudoirs). **2.** prie-dieu *m inv* (d'un souverain, lors du sacre).

Falerii [fə'liəriai], *Pr.n. A.Geog:* Faléries.

Falernian [fə'lə:niən], *a.* (*a*) *A.Geog:* de Falerne; (*b*) **F. (wine),** falerne *m*.

Faliscan [fə'liskən], *A.Geog:* (*a*) *a.* falisque; (*b*) *s.* Falisque *mf*.

Falkland ['fɔ:klənd], *Pr.n. Geog:* **the F. Islands,** les (îles) Malouines *f*, les îles Falkland; **the F. Sea,** la mer des Malouines.

fall[1] [fɔ:l], *s.* **1.** (*a*) chute *f* (d'un corps, etc.); descente *f* (d'un marteau, etc.); *Th:* chute, baisser *m* (du rideau); **free f.,** chute libre; **to have a f.,** faire une chute; tomber; **to ride for a f.,** (i) aller en casse-cou; (ii) courir à un échec; (*of ministry, etc.*) aller au-devant de la défaite; ne demander qu'à tomber; (*b*) *Wr:* tomber *m*; *F: O:* **to try a f. with s.o.,** lutter avec qn; rompre une lance avec qn; (*c*) **(place of) f.,** point *m* de chute; (*d*) quantité tombée (de neige, de pluie); **there has been a heavy f. of snow, of rain,** il est tombé beaucoup de neige, de pluie; (*e*) *Husb:* (i) agnelage *m*, agnèlement *m*, mise *f* bas (d'agneaux); (ii) agnelée *f*, ventrée *f*, portée *f*. **2.** (*a*) *Lit:* **the f. of day,** la chute du jour; **at f. of day,** à la tombée, au tomber, du jour; **the f. of the year,** le déclin de l'année; *Poet:* la chute des feuilles; (*b*) *NAm:* **the f.,** l'automne *m or f*. **3.** (*a*) *usu. pl.* chute (d'eau); cascade *f*, cataracte *f*; **the Victoria Falls,** les Chutes Victoria; **the Niagara Falls,** les Chutes du Niagara; (*b*) *Hyd.E:* colonne *f* d'eau; hauteur *f* de chute (d'un barrage); **f. between the leat and the water wheel,** saut *m* du moulin. **4.** (*a*) décrue *f*, baisse *f* (des eaux); reflux *m*, jusant *m* (de la marée); pente *f*, inclinaison *f* (d'une route, etc.); diminution *f* (de poids, de pouvoir, etc.); baisse, descente *f*, chute (du baromètre, etc.); baisse, abaissement *m* (de la température); cadence *f* (de la voix); *El:* **f. of potential,** baisse de potentiel (perte de charge ou chute de tension); (*b*) dénivellation *f*; *N.Arch:* **f. of the deck,** ravalement *m* du pont; (*c*) *Com: Fin:* baisse (des prix, des actions); **heavy f.,** forte baisse; débâcle *f*; **f. of the currency,** dépréciation *f* de la monnaie; **f. in wheat, in the bank rate,** baisse des blés, du taux officiel (d'escompte); **f. in prices,** abaissement, chute, de prix; *St.Exch:* **dealing for a f.,** opération *f* à la baisse; **to buy on a f.,** acheter à la baisse; (*d*) *Med:* **f. in resistance of the organism,** fléchissement *m* de l'organisme. **5.** perte *f*, ruine *f* (de qn); **f. from grace,** déchéance *f*; **the F.,** la chute de l'homme. **6.** chute (d'une place forte); déchéance (d'un empire, etc.); renversement *m* (d'un gouvernement, etc.); **the f. of Troy,** la chute de Troie; **the f. of the Bastille,** la prise de la Bastille. **7.** éboulement *m*, éboulis *m*, écroulement *m*, tombée *f* (de terre, de rocher). **8.** (*a*) *Cost:* (i) *A:* voile *m*, voilette *f*; (ii) tombant *m* (du col); (*b*) *Furn: A:* frange *f* en cuir (de rayon de bibliothèque). **9.** *Nau:* garant *m*; **boat f.,** garant d'embarcation; **f. block,** poulie *f* mobile (de palan). **10.** *For:* (*a*) abattis *m*; nombre *m* d'arbres à abattre; (*b*) **f. (notch),** entaille *f* de direction (désignant un arbre à abattre).

fall[2], *v.* (**fell** [fel]; **fallen** ['fɔ:l(ə)n])

I. *v.i.* **1.** (*a*) tomber; **to f. to the ground,** tomber à terre; **to f. under a bus,** être écrasé par un autobus; *F:* **if I f. under a bus tomorrow,** si je meurs demain; **to f. off a ladder, to f. (down) from a ladder,** tomber d'une échelle, de sur une échelle, à bas d'une échelle; **to f. down a precipice,** tomber du haut d'un précipice; **to f. down a well,** tomber dans un puits; **to f. out of the window,** tomber par la fenêtre; **to f. on one's feet,** (i) (re)tomber sur ses pieds; tomber d'aplomb; (ii) *F:* avoir de la chance, de la veine; (iii) trouver un emploi solide et durable; **to f. into a trap,** donner dans un piège; **to f. into s.o.'s hands,** tomber entre les mains de qn; **be careful you don't f. again,** prends garde de ne pas retomber; **to let f. a tear, a word,** laisser échapper une larme, un mot; **night is falling,** la nuit tombe; il se fait nuit; le jour baisse; **when night had fallen,** à la nuit tombée; *Typ:* **proof that falls well,** épreuve *f* qui repère bien; (*of type*) **to f. out of place,** chevaucher; (*b*) *Astr:* (*of star*) filer; (*c*) (*hang down*) **his fair fell to his shoulders,** ses cheveux *m* lui pendaient, lui descendaient, jusqu'aux épaules; **collar that falls on the shoulders,** col *m* qui se rabat sur les épaules; **dress that falls freely,** robe *f* à lignes tombantes; (*d*) *Husb:* (*of lambs, calves*) naître; (*e*) **Christmas falls on a Thursday,** Noël tombe un jeudi. **2.** (*from standing or perpendicular position*) (*a*) **to f. to the ground,** tomber par terre; (*of horse*) s'abattre; **to f. full length,** tomber de tout son long, de toute sa hauteur; s'aplatir par terre; se plaquer par terre, s'étaler; **to f. in a heap,** s'affaisser; **to f. on one's knees,** tomber à genoux; **he fell at my feet,** il est tombé à mes pieds; **to f. in a fit,** tomber en convulsions; **to f. on one's sword,** se jeter sur son épée; **to fall by the sword,** périr par l'épée; **those who fell at Agincourt,** ceux qui tombèrent à Azincourt; **two elephants fell to my gun,** j'ai abattu deux éléphants; **to f. (to temptation),** succomber à la tentation; (*b*) (*of building*) crouler, s'écrouler, s'effondrer; **to f. to pieces,** tomber en morceaux; *Cr:* **the first wicket fell at ten,** le premier guichet fut renversé à dix points; (*c*) **when Liège fell,** lorsque Liège capitula; **the government has fallen,** le Ministère est tombé, a été renversé; **Rome fell to the Goths,** Rome tomba entre les mains des Goths. **3.** (*to sink or subside*) (*a*) (*of tide, barometer, etc.*) descendre, baisser; (*of wind*) tomber, s'apaiser, s'abattre; (*of sea*) (se) calmer, *Nau:* calmir; (*of flames, price, weight, etc.*) diminuer; (*of price, exchange, etc.*) baisser, se déprécier, subir une baisse; (*of value*) s'avilir; *Fig:* **his stock is falling,** son crédit est en baisse; ses actions baissent; **his temperature is falling,** sa température baisse; **the thermometer has fallen ten degrees,** le thermomètre a baissé de dix degrés; (*b*) (*of ground*) aller en pente; s'incliner; *Mth:* (*of curve*) décroître; **the ground falls towards the river,** le terrain descend, s'abaisse, vers le fleuve; **her eyes fell,** elle a baissé les yeux, les paupières; **his face fell,** sa figure s'allongea; **my spirits fell,** je perdis tout courage; (*c*) *Nau:* (*of ship*) **to f. to leeward,** tomber sous le vent; (*d*) **to f. from one's position,** déchoir de sa position; **to f. from a high position,** retomber du faîte; **to f. in esteem,** déchoir dans l'estime (du public); **to f. in s.o.'s estimation,** perdre dans l'estime de qn; *B:* **how are the mighty fallen!** comment sont tombés les hommes forts! **4.** (*a*) **a shadow fell on the wall,** une ombre se projeta sur le mur; **the light fell on his face,** il avait le visage au jour, à la lumière; **the sunlight falls on the peaks,** le soleil donne sur les cimes; **a sound fell (up)on my ear,** un son frappa mon oreille; **the accent falls on the last syllable,** l'accent tombe sur, frappe, la dernière syllabe; (*b*) **to f. on s.o.'s neck, on one's food,** se jeter au cou de qn, sur la nourriture; **to f. (up)on the enemy,** fondre sur, attaquer, l'ennemi; (*c*) **vengeance fell upon them,** la vengeance est tombée sur eux; **suspicion fell on him,** les soupçons retombèrent sur lui; **his death will f. heavy upon his family,** sa mort sera un rude coup pour sa famille. **5.** (*to come by right, design, or chance*) (*a*) **to f. to s.o.'s share,** échoir (en partage) à qn; **share that falls to the heirs on the father's side,** part dévolue à la ligne paternelle; **charges falling on a legatee,** charges imposées à un légataire; **honour that falls to me (by right),** honneur *m* qui me revient (de droit); **the blame falls on . . .,** le blâme retombe sur . . .; la faute doit en être imputée à . . .; **the responsibility falls on me,** toute la responsabilité retombe sur moi; **duties that f. on s.o.,** devoirs *m* qui incombent à qn; **the duties that f. to the Court,** les fonctions *f* dont la cour est investie; **it falls to me to . . .,** c'est à moi qu'incombe la tâche de . . .; **it does not f. to me to . . .,** il ne m'appartient pas de . . .; **it fell to me to break the news to him,** c'est moi qui ai dû lui apprendre la nouvelle; **the most thankless task that can f. to s.o.,** la tâche la plus ingrate qui puisse échoir à qn; **these facts f. under another category,** ces faits entrent, se classent, se rangent, dans une autre catégorie; **the question falls naturally into four sections,** la question se divise en quatre parties; **this does not f. within my province,** ceci n'est pas de mon domaine, ne rentre pas dans mes fonctions; **that does not f. within our agreement,** cela n'entre pas, n'est pas compris, dans notre contrat; **it falls within article 10,** cela rentre dans, relève de, l'article 10; **credits falling into the budget,** crédits afférents au budget; (*b*) (*of pers.*) **to f. under s.o.'s displeasure,** encourir le déplaisir de qn; **to f. under s.o.'s power,** (i) tomber au pouvoir de qn; (ii) être assujetti au pouvoir de qn; **to f. under suspicion,** se trouver, devenir, l'objet des soupçons; devenir suspect; **to f. in with s.o.,** *O: & NAm:* **to f. across s.o.,** rencontrer qn par hasard; **to f. in with a request,** accéder à une requête, à une demande; **to f. in with a plan,** accepter une proposition, un projet; **to f. in with an arrangement,** se prêter à un accommodement; **to f. on, across, a means of doing sth.,** trouver un moyen de faire qch.; **to f. into conversation with s.o.,** entrer en, lier, conversation avec qn; **to f. on evil days,** connaître de mauvais jours; *B:* **he fell among thieves,** il tomba entre les mains des voleurs; (*c*) **I soon fell into their ways,** (i) je me suis vite accoutumé à leur manière de faire, à leurs habitudes; (ii) j'ai bientôt appris la routine; j'ai eu vite fait de prendre le courant, de me mettre à la page; **to f. into a habit,** contracter une habitude; **to f. into error,** être induit en erreur; **the custom fell into abuse,** la coutume dégénéra en abus. **6.** (*a*) (*with adj. complement*) **to f. ill, sick,** tomber malade; **to f. asleep,** s'endormir; (*of post*) **to f. vacant,** se trouver vacant; (*b*) **to f. a victim to . . .,** être victime de . . . . **7.** (*to begin*) **to f. to sth., to doing sth.,** se mettre à qch., à faire qch.; **they fell to work (again),** ils se (re)mirent au travail, à l'œuvre; **he fell to abusing me,** il se mit à m'injurier; *Lit:* **one night I fell (to) thinking of the past,** une nuit je me suis mis à réfléchir sur le passé, mes pensées se tournèrent vers le passé. **8.** *Tan:* (*of hides*) s'assouplir.

II. (*compound verbs*) **1. fall about,** *v.i.* tomber de côté et d'autre.

2. fall apart, *v.i.* se désintégrer; tomber en morceaux.

3. fall away, *v.i.* (*a*) (*of ground, etc.*) s'affaisser brusquement, s'abaisser; (*b*) (*of follower, etc.*) déserter; faire défection; *Theol:* apostasier; (*of prejudices, etc.*) disparaître; (*c*) **his face has fallen away,** son visage s'est émacié; ses joues se sont creusées.

4. fall back, *v.i.* (*a*) tomber à la renverse, en arrière; **to f. back on the cushions,** retomber sur les coussins; (*b*) *Mil: etc:* (*of troops*) se replier, reculer; **to f. back towards the south,** se rabattre vers le sud; **to f. back a pace,** reculer d'un pas; (*c*) *St.Exch: Fin:* se replier; (*d*) avoir recours (à qch.); **to have some money (put by) to f. back on,** avoir de l'argent en réserve comme en-cas; **failing meat we fell back on vegetables,** faute de viande il nous a fallu nous rabattre, nous rattraper, sur les légumes; **you can always f. back on me,** en dernière ressource vous pouvez compter sur moi.

5. fall behind, *v.i.* s'arriérer; rester en arrière; se laisser distancer, dépasser, devancer; **to f. behind with the rent,** être en retard pour payer son loyer.

6. fall down, *v.i.* (*a*) tomber à terre, par terre; se prosterner (devant qn); (*b*) (*of building, etc.*) crouler, s'écrouler, s'effondrer; (*c*) *F:* **to f. down on the job,** échouer dans une entreprise, louper le travail, faire un four.

7. fall for, *v. F:* (*a*) tomber amoureux de (qn); **he always falls for a pretty face,** il succombe toujours à l'attrait d'une jolie figure; (*b*) **to f. for a trick,** s'y laisser prendre.

8. fall in, *v.i.* (*a*) (i) (*of building, roof, etc.*) s'écrouler, s'effondrer; (*of trench, etc.*) s'ébouler; (ii) (*of mouth*) s'affaisser, rentrer; (*of cheeks*) se creuser; (iii) (*of plan, etc.*) tomber à l'eau; (*b*) *Mil:* former les rangs; se mettre en rangs; s'aligner; se rassembler; **f. in!** rassemblement! (*of single soldier*) **to f. in again,** rentrer dans les rangs; (*c*) (*of lease, etc.*) expirer; (*of debt*) arriver à échéance.

9. fall off, *v.i.* (*a*) (*of thg*) tomber; (*b*) *Nau:* abattre sous le vent; faire une abattée; arriver; **to f. off (the wind),** tomber en travers du vent; **let her f. off!** laissez arriver! (*c*) (*of followers, etc.*) lâcher; faire défection; (*d*) (*of profits, attendance*) diminuer; (*of speed*) ralentir, décroître; (*of zeal*) se relâcher; **the takings are falling off,** les recettes *f* diminuent; (*e*) (*deteriorate*) décliner; (*of skill, talent*) baisser; (*of flowers, colours, beauty*) passer; **his talent is falling off,** son talent fléchit; **his popularity is falling off,** sa popularité baisse.

10. fall out, *v.i.* (*a*) tomber dehors; (*b*) (*of hair*) tomber; (*c*) *Mil:* (i) quitter les rangs, quitter son rang; (ii) rompre les rangs; **f. out!** rompez (les rangs)! (*d*) *Navy:* rompre les postes (de combat, etc.); (*e*) se brouiller, se fâcher (**with,** avec); **to have fallen out with s.o.,** être brouillé avec qn; **they have fallen out,** ils sont mal ensemble; ils sont fâchés; (*f*) *Lit:* se passer; advenir; **it so fell out that . . .,** il advint, arriva, que . . ..

11. fall over, *v.i.* (*a*) (*of pers.*) tomber (par terre); (*of thg*) se renverser, être renversé; tomber; (*b*) *v.tr. & pron.* trébucher sur (un obstacle); *F:* **people were falling over each other to try to help him,** c'était à qui lui viendrait en aide; **publishers were falling over each other for his new book,** les éditeurs se disputaient avec acharnement son prochain livre; **he was falling over himself in his anxiety to please her,** il faisait tant et plus, il se mettait en quatre, pour lui plaire.

12. fall through, *v.i.* (*of scheme, etc.*) ne pas aboutir; échouer, avorter; n'arriver à rien; s'effondrer; *F:* tomber à, dans, l'eau.

13. fall to, *v.i.* (*a*) (*of door, etc.*) se (re)fermer; (*b*) (i) *O:* se mettre à l'œuvre, au travail; (ii) entamer la lutte; s'y mettre (c.-à-d. à se battre); (iii) *F: O:* s'attaquer au repas.

fallacious [fə'leiʃəs], *a.* (*of argument, promise, etc.*) fallacieux, trompeur, -euse; (espoir *m*, paix *f*) illusoire; **f. deduction,** déduction erronée.

fallaciously [fə'leiʃəsli], *adv.* fallacieusement, erronément, trompeusement.

fallaciousness [fə'leiʃəsnis], *s.* = FALLACY 2.

fallacy ['fæləsi], *s.* **1.** (*a*) *Log:* sophisme *m*, paralogisme *m*; faux raisonnement; (*b*) **a current f.,** une erreur courante; *Lit:* **the pathetic f.,** interprétation sentimentale de la nature. **2.** fausseté *f*, caractère erroné, illusoire (d'un argument, etc.).

fal-lals ['fæ'lælz], *s.pl. F:* falbalas *m*, colifichets *m*.

fallen ['fɔ:lən]. **1.** *a.* (*a*) **f. leaves,** feuilles tombées; (*b*) **f. angel,** ange déchu; **f. humanity,** l'humanité déchue; **f. woman,** femme déchue, fille perdue; (*c*) **the f. king,** le roi déchu; (*d*) *Algae:* **f. star,** nostoc *m*. **2.** *s.* **the f.,** les morts *m* (sur le champ de bataille).

faller ['fɔ:lər], *s.* (*a*) *Tex:* **f. (wire),** baguette *f* (d'un métier à filer); (*b*) *pl. Min:* **fallers,** taquets *m* à abaissement (de cage).

fall guy ['fɔ:l'gai], *s. NAm: F:* bouc *m* émissaire; souffre-douleur *m inv*.

fallibility [fæli'biliti], *s.* faillibilité *f*.

fallible ['fælibl], *a.* faillible.

fall-in ['fɔ:l'in], *s. Mil:* rassemblement *m*; **to beat, sound, the f.-in (call),** battre, sonner, l'appel, le rassemblement.

falling[1] ['fɔ:liŋ], *a.* (*of darkness, lines of garment, etc.*) tombant, *Ph:* **f. body,** corps *m* en chute; **f. temperature,** température *f* en baisse; *Com:* **f. market,** marché orienté à la baisse, avec tendance à la baisse; *Av:* **f.-leaf roll, drop,** descente *f* en feuille morte.

falling[2], *s.* **1.** (*a*) chute *f*; descente *f* (d'un marteau, etc.); (*b*) abaissement *m* (de prix); baisse *f* (de prix, des eaux, du baromètre, etc.); avilissement *m* (de la valeur de qch.). **2.** *Med:* descente (de la matrice). **3.** (*a*) **f. away,** (i) affaissement *m* brusque (du terrain); (ii) défection *f* (de partisans); *Theol:* apostasie *f*; (*b*) *Mil: etc:* **f. back,** repli *m*, repliement *m*, reculade *f*, retraite *f*; (*c*) **f. in,** (i) éboulement *m*, écroulement *m*, effondrement *m* (d'un bâtiment, d'une tranchée); (ii) *Mil:* rassemblement *m*; formation *f* des rangs; (iii) expiration *f* (d'un bail, etc.); échéance *f* (d'une dette, etc.); (iv) acquiescement *m* (à qch.); acceptation *f* (de qch.); (*d*) **f. off,** (i) défection *f* (de partisans); (ii) diminution *f*, décroissement (de chiffres, de taux, etc.); ralentissement *m*, décroissance *f* (de vitesse); fléchissement *m* (de talent); déchéance *f*, déclin *m* (de pouvoir, de popularité); ralentissement, relâchement *m* (de zèle); dépérissement *m* (d'une industrie); ralentissement (de commandes, des affaires).

Fallopian [fə'loupiən], *a. Anat:* (ligament, trompe, etc.) de Fallope.

fallout ['fɔ:laut], *s.* retombées (radioactives); **f. pattern,** diagramme *m*, graphique *m*, des retombées (radioactives); **initial f.,** retombées instantanées; **residual f.,** retombées résiduelles.

fallow[1] ['fælou], *Agr:* **1.** *s.* jachère *f*, friche *f*. **2.** *a.* (*of land*) affriché; en friche; en jachère, en repos; **f. break,** sole *f* en jachère; **to lie f.,** être en jachère; être, rester, en friche; **to become f.,** s'affricher; **to let a field lie f.,** affricher, laisser reposer, un champ; **to lay land f.,** mettre la terre en jachère; (*of land*) **to be laid f.,** retomber en friche; **to plough (up) f. land,** jachérer un champ; **f. mind,** esprit inculte.

fallow[2], *v.tr. Agr:* écroûter, jachérer, défricher (un terrain).

fallow[3], *a.* (*a*) *A:* (*of colour*) fauve; (*b*) **f. deer,** daim *m*.

fallowing ['fælouiŋ], *s. Agr:* écroûtage *m*, défrichage *m*, mise *f* en jachère (d'un terrain).

fallowness ['fælounis], *s. Agr:* inculture *f*.

fall trap ['fɔ:ltræp], *s. Ven: etc:* assommoir *m*.

fallway ['fɔ:lwei], *s.* trou *m* de levage (dans un plancher).

false [fɔ:ls], *a.* **1.** (*incorrect*) faux, *f.* fausse; **f. idea,** fausse, erronée; **f. report,** fausse nouvelle, *F:* canard *m*; **f. judg(e)ment,** jugement faux; **f. modesty,** (i) fausse pudeur; (ii) fausse modestie; **f. shame,** fausse honte; **to take a f. step,** faire un faux pas; **f. weight,** faux poids; **f. manœuvre,** fausse manœuvre; **f. stroke,** coup manqué, raté; *Turf: etc:* **f. start,** faux départ; **to be in a f. position,** se trouver dans une position fausse; **to put a f. interpretation on sth.,** interpréter qch. à faux; donner une fausse interprétation à qch.; *Arb:* **f. (annual) ring,** anneau incomplet; *Mus:* **f. note,** fausse note. **2.** faux; perfide; infidèle; (*of promise, etc.*) mensonger; **f. to the core,** faux comme un jeton; **f. to honour,** traître à l'honneur; **f. lover,** amant perfide; **f. balance sheet,** faux bilan; **to be f. to one's vows,** rompre ses vœux; **f. witness,** faux témoin; **to bear f. witness.** rendre faux témoignage; **f. accusation,** dénonciation calomnieuse; **that's as f. as can be,** c'est faux et archifaux; *adv.* **to play s.o. f.,** trahir qn; faire une perfidie à qn; commettre une déloyauté; **his memory played him f.,** sa mémoire l'a mal servi; **my memory never plays me f.,** j'ai la mémoire sûre. **3.** (*sham*) (*of hair, etc.*) artificiel, postiche; (*of action, tears, etc.*) feint, prétendu, simulé; (*of appearance*) menteur; (*of document, etc.*) forgé; (*of coin, seal, etc.*) faux, contrefait; *Mil:* **f. attack,** fausse attaque; **f. gods,** faux dieux; **f. teeth, hair,** fausses dents, faux cheveux; **piece of f. hair,** chichi *m*; **f. edge (of sword),** contre-pointe *f* (d'un sabre); **f. bottom,** double fond (d'une boîte, etc.); faux fond; fond intermédiaire; *Civ.E:* **f. works,** étaiement *m*, échafaudages *mpl*. **4.** (*a*) *Bot:* **f. cedar,** cédrel(a) odorant; **f. cypress,** chamæcyparis *m*; **f. dragon's head,** physostegia *m*; **f. flax;** caméline *f*; **f. hellebore,** vératre *m*; **f. sandalwood,** ximénie *f*; **f. willow,** baccharis *m*; *Fung:* **f. blusher,** amanite *f* panthère; (*b*) *Ich: F:* **f. cod,** fausse morue.

false-hearted ['fɔls'hɑ:tid], *a. O.* perfide; traître, *f.* traîtresse.

falsehood ['fɔ(:)lshud], *s.* **1.** (*a*) fausseté *f* (d'un bruit, etc.); (*b*) le faux; **to distinguish truth from f.,** distinguer le vrai d'avec le faux; distinguer le vrai du faux. **2.** mensonge *m*; **to tell a f.,** faire un mensonge; mentir.

falsely ['fɔ(:)lsli], *adv.* faussement; à faux.

falseness ['fɔ(:)lsnis], *s.* **1.** fausseté *f* (d'un rapport, etc.). **2.** (*a*) *O:* infidélité *f* (d'un amant, etc.); (*b*) fourberie *f*.

falsetto ['fɔ(:)l'setou]. **1.** *s. & a. Mus:* **f. (voice),** (voix *f*) de tête, de fausset; **to laugh in a high f.,** rire d'une voix de fausset. **2.** *s.* (*singer*) fausset *m*.

falsies ['fɔ(:)lsiz], *s.pl. F:* faux seins, faux nichons, roberts *m* de chez Michelin.

falsification [fɔlsifi'keiʃ(ə)n], *s.* falsification *f* (des faits, des comptes); altération *f* (d'un texte).

falsifier ['fɔ(:)lsifaiər], *s.* falsificateur, -trice (de comptes, etc.).

falsify ['fɔ(:)lsifai], *v.tr.* (**falsified; falsifying**) **1.** falsifier (un document); fausser (un bilan); adultérer, altérer (un texte, etc.); dénaturer (des faits, etc.). **2.** (*a*) prouver la fausseté de (qch.); (*b*) tromper (un espoir); **to f. a prophecy,** rendre une prédiction vaine.

falsity ['fɔ(:)lsiti], *s.* fausseté *f* (d'une doctrine, etc.); **to plead the f. of a police report,** s'inscrire en faux contre un procès-verbal.

falter ['fɔltər]. **1.** *v.i.* (*a*) (*of voice*) hésiter, trembler, se troubler, s'altérer; **he faltered in his speech,** sa voix se troubla; il eut un moment d'hésitation; (*b*) (*of pers.*) vaciller, chanceler; (*c*) (*of pers. or courage*) défaillir; flancher; **once he had made up his mind he never faltered,** une fois sa décision prise il n'hésita plus. **2.** *v.tr.* dire (qch.) d'une voix hésitante, tremblante; **to falter out (an excuse, etc.),** balbutier (une excuse, etc.); **yes, he faltered,** oui, balbutia-t-il, dit-il d'une voix tremblante.

faltering[1] ['fɔlt(ə)riŋ], *a.* **1.** (*of voice, etc.*) hésitant, tremblant, troublé; **to speak in a f. voice,** parler d'une voix tremblante, mal assurée. **2.** (*of legs*) vacillant, chancelant, flageolant; **he came forward with f. steps,** il s'avança à pas chancelants, d'un pas mal assuré. **3.** (*of courage, memory, etc.*) défaillant.

faltering[2], *s.* **1.** altération *f* (de la voix); hésitation *f*. **2.** vacillation *f*.

falteringly ['fɔlt(ə)riŋli], *adv.* **1.** (parler, etc.) d'une voix tremblante, troublée; en hésitant. **2.** (marcher, etc.) d'un pas vacillant, chancelant, mal assuré.

Famagusta [fæmə'gustə], *Pr.n. Geog:* Famagouste.

famatinite [fæmə'ti:nait], *s. Miner:* famatinite *f.*

fame [feim], *s.* **1.** (*a*) renom *m*, renommée *f*, réputation *f*; **love of f.,** amour *m* de la célébrité; **the f. of his deeds,** le bruit de ses exploits; **to win f.,** se faire un grand nom; atteindre la gloire; **titles to f.,** titres *m* de gloire; **ill f.,** mauvaise réputation; **of good, ill, f.,** bien, mal, famé; **house of ill f.,** maison mal famée; lieu mal famé; mauvais lieu; (*b*) *Myth:* la Renommée; *Lit:* **the House of F.,** le Temple de Mémoire. **2.** *A: & Lit:* la rumeur publique.

familial [fə'miliəl], *a. Med:* (*of complaint*) familial, -aux; de famille.

familiar [fə'miliər]. **1.** *a.* (*a*) familier, intime; **to be f., on f. terms, with s.o.,** être familier, vivre familièrement, en user familièrement, avoir des rapports d'intimité, avec qn; **to be on very f. terms with s.o.,** être à tu et à toi avec qn; **you are rather too f.,** vous prenez trop de privautés; (*b*) **f. spirit,** démon familier; (*c*) (*of thg*) familier, bien connu; de connaissance; **f. face,** figure *f* de connaissance; **in f. surroundings,** en pays de connaissance; **it strikes one as f.,** cela fait l'effet du déjà vu, du déjà entendu; **experiment f. to engineers,** expérience familière aux ingénieurs, bien connue des ingénieurs; **f. phrase,** expression bien connue; **to be on f. ground,** être sur son terrain; **his voice sounded f. to me,** il me sembla reconnaître sa voix; (*d*) (*of pers.*) **to be f. with sth.,** être familier avec qch.; bien connaître qch.; **I am not f. with this tool,** je n'ai pas l'habitude de cet outil; **I use books with which I am f.,** j'ai recours aux livres qui me sont familiers; **this author has made us f. with them,** cet auteur nous les a rendus familiers; **to grow f. with sth.,** s'habituer à qch.; s'accoutumer à qch.; se familiariser avec qch.; **to make oneself f. with a language,** se familiariser avec une langue; **to be f. with the customs,** être au fait, au courant, des usages; (*e*) *A:* (cercle, etc.) familial, -aux, de (la) famille. **2.** *s.* (*a*) *Rel.H:* familier *m* (de l'Inquisition); (*b*) familier; ami, amie, intime; **one of his familiars,** une personne de son entourage; (*c*) démon familier.

familiarity [fəmili'æriti], *s.* **1.** familiarité *f*; intimité *f*; **to treat s.o. with great f.,** traiter qn de pair à compagnon; **to be guilty of too much f. with s.o.,** prendre des libertés, des privautés, avec qn; **to be annoyed by s.o.'s f.,** être fâché des familiarités de qn; *Prov:* **f. breeds contempt,** la familiarité engendre, fait naître, le mépris. **2.** connaissance *f* (**with,** de); **his f. with French,** sa connaissance du français.

familiarization [fəmiliərai'zeiʃ(ə)n], *s.* accoutumance *f* (**with,** à); habitude *f* (**with,** de).

familiarize [fə'miliəraiz], *v.tr.* **1.** familiariser (qch.); rendre (qch.) familier. **2. to f. s.o. with sth.,** faire connaître qch. à qn; habituer qn à qch.; **to f. oneself with a language, with danger,** se familiariser avec une langue, avec le danger.

familiarly [fə'miliəli], *adv.* familièrement; intimement.

family ['fæm(i)li], *s.* **1.** (*a*) famille *f*; **large f.,** famille nombreuse; **my wife's, my husband's, f.,** ma belle-famille; **how are, is, the f.?** comment va la famille? *F:* comment ça va chez vous? **the f. all live together,** ils vivent en famille; **the Martin f.,** la famille Martin; **a friend of the f.,** un ami, un familier, de la maison; **to be one of the f.,** être de la maison; **man of good f.,** homme *m* de bonne famille; *A:* **people of no f.,** personnes *fpl* sans naissance; **it runs in the f.,** cela vient, cela tient, de famille; c'est de famille; **this talent runs in the f.,** il, elle, tient ce talent de la famille; **courage runs in the f.,** ils sont tous courageux dans la famille; **disease that runs in the f.,** maladie *f* héréditaire; (*b*) *attrib.* **a f. dinner,** un dîner en famille; **f. tree,** arbre *m* généalogique; **f. portraits,** portraits *m* d'ancêtres; **f. hotel,** hôtel *m* de famille; **in a f.-size(d) jar,** en pot familial; **f. likeness,** air *m* de famille; **f. quarrels,** disputes *f* de famille; **the f. circle,** le cercle de (la) famille; **f. living,** bénéfice *m* ecclésiastique dont la collation est la prérogative d'une certaine famille; **f. butcher,** boucher *m* qui livre à domicile; **f. life,** vie familiale; **f. man,** (i) père *m* de famille; (ii) homme d'intérieur; *Adm:* **f. allowance,** allocation familiale; indemnité *f* pour charges de famille; **f. planning,** limitation *f* des naissances, planning familial; *P:* **she's in the f. way,** elle est enceinte, dans une situation intéressante. **2.** famille (de plantes, de mots, etc.).

famine ['fæmin], *s.* (*a*) famine *f*; *A:* **to die of f.,** mourir de faim; (*b*) disette *f*; **water f.,** disette d'eau; **copper f.,** disette de cuivre; **produce at f. prices,** denrées *f* à des prix *m* inabordables, à des prix de famine.

famish ['fæmiʃ]. **1.** *v.tr.* (*a*) affamer (qn); faire souffrir (qn) de la faim; (*b*) réduire (une famille, un pays) à la famine. **2.** *v.i.* être affamé, souffrir de la faim, avoir grand-faim.

famished ['fæmiʃt], *a.* affamé; **f.-looking,** (à l'aspect) famélique; **I feel f.,** je meurs de faim.

famishing ['fæmiʃiŋ], *a.* affamé; **to be f.,** être affamé; avoir une faim de loup; **I was f.,** je mourais de faim.

Fammenian [fæ'mi:niən], *a. & s. Geol:* famennien (*m*).

famous ['feiməs], *a.* **1.** célèbre, renommé, illustre, mémorable (**for,** pour, par); **f. in history,** renommé, célèbre, dans l'histoire; **to make oneself f.,** se rendre célèbre; **town f. for its monuments,** ville *f* célèbre par ses monuments. **2.** *F: O:* **that's f.!** c'est parfait, fameux! à la bonne heure!

famously ['feiməsli], *adv. F:* fameusement, à merveille; **we're getting on f.,** ça va comme sur des roulettes; ça avance à grand train; **I get on f. with him,** on s'entend à merveille.

famulus, *pl.* **-i** ['fæmjuləs, -ai], *s. A:* assistant *m*, aide *m*, famulus *m* (d'un savant, d'un magicien).

fan[1] [fæn], *s.* **1.** *Agr:* (*a*) *A:* van *m*; (*b*) tarare *m*, cribleur *m*; van mécanique. **2.** (*a*) éventail *m*; **f. maker,** éventailliste *mf*; **f. painter,** éventailliste; *Geog:* **alluvial f.,** cône *m* d'alluvions, de déjection; *Arch:* **f. vaulting,** voûte(s) *f* en éventail; **f. tracery,** nervures *fpl* en éventail; *Elcs:* **f. beam,** faisceau *m* en éventail; **f. aerial,** antenne *f* en éventail; *Av:* **f. marker,** radiobalise *f* à faisceau en éventail; *Navy:* **to arrange the fleet in f. order,** disposer la flotte en éventail; (*b*) *Z:* nageoires *fpl* de la queue (d'une baleine); (*c*) *Bot:* **f. palm,** palmier-éventail; **dwarf f. palm,** palmier nain; palmette *f*; (*d*) *Moll:* **f. mussel,** pinne *f* (marine), *F:* jambonneau *m*; *Ann: F:* **f. worm,** spirographe *m*. **3.** ventilateur (rotatif, à ailes, soufflant); *Ind:* soufflet *m*; **ceiling f.,** ventilateur de plafond; **extractor f.,** aérateur *m*, aspirateur *m* de buées; **suction f., vacuum f.,** ventilateur aspirant, négatif; **suction f., rotary f. (of vacuum cleaner),** turbine *f* (d'aspirateur); **forced-draught f., induced-draught f.,** ventilateur à tirage forcé, induit; *Civ.E: Min:* **ventilation f.,** ventilateur d'aérage; *Aut:* **radiator f.,** ventilateur; *Dom.Ec:* **f. heater,** radiateur soufflant; **f. draught,** soufflage *m* par ventilateur; **f.-cooled,** refroidi par ventilateur; *Mec.E:* **force f.,** ventilateur foulant, soufflant; *Metalw:* **f. blower,** ventilateur, soufflerie *f*, de forge; **f. brake,** (i) *Mec.E:* frein *m* à palette; (ii) *Av:* moulinet *m*; *Mec.E:* **f. wheel,** roue *f* à ailettes; tourniquet *m* de ventilateur; **f. spindle,** axe *m* de ventilateur; **f. straighteners,** aubages redresseurs de flux (de ventilateur); **f. drive,** commande *f* de ventilateur; *Av:* **f. jet,** (i) réacteur *m*, moteur *m*, à double flux; (ii) appareil équipé d'un réacteur à double flux. **4.** (i) aile *f*, pale *f*, d'hélice; (ii) hélice *f* (d'une torpille, etc.). **5.** gouvernail *m* (d'un moulin à vent).

fan[2], *v.* (**fanned**)

I. *v.tr.* **1.** *Agr:* vanner (le grain). **2.** (*a*) éventer (qn); **terraces fanned by cool sea breezes,** terrasses rafraîchies par les brises de mer, sur lesquelles soufflent les vents frais de la mer; *Lit:* **fortune fans his sails,** il a le vent en poupe; (*b*) **to f. away the dust on sth.,** chasser la poussière de qch. avec un éventail, avec un journal, etc.; (*c*) **to f. (up) the fire,** souffler le feu; **to f. the passions,** attiser, aviver, exciter, les passions; **to f. a quarrel,** attiser, envenimer, une querelle. **3.** (*of punkah, etc.*) agiter (l'air).

II. (*compound verb*) **fan out,** (*a*) *v.i.* se déployer, s'étaler en éventail; (*b*) *v.tr.* étaler (qch.) en éventail.

fan[3], *s. F:* passionné, -ée, enragé, -ée, fanatique *mf*, fan *m*, fana *m* (de la télévision, du sport, etc.); **football f.,** fana de football; **record f.,** discophile *mf*; **f. club,** club *m* des fanas.

fanatic [fə'nætik], *a. & s.* fanatique (*mf*); **he's a f.!** c'est un cerveau brûlé!

fanatical [fə'nætikl], *a.* fanatique.

fanatically [fə'nætik(ə)li], *adv.* fanatiquement; en fanatique; avec fanatisme.

fanaticize [fə'nætisaiz], *v.tr.* fanatiser; **fanaticized mob,** foule fanatisée.

fanaticism [fə'nætisizm], *s.* fanatisme *m*.

fancied ['fænsid], *a.* imaginaire, imaginé.

fancier ['fænsiər], *s.* amateur, -trice (de chiens, de fleurs, etc.); connaisseur, -euse (en chiens, etc.); **dog f.,** (i) amateur de chiens; cynophile *mf*; (ii) éleveur, -euse, de chiens; (iii) marchand, -ande, de chiens.

fancification [fænsifi'keiʃ(ə)n], *s. F: esp. U.S:* embellissement *m*; enjolivement *m*.

fanciful ['fænsiful], *a.* **1.** (*a*) (*of pers.*) capricieux, fantasque; (*b*) (travail *m*, etc.) fantaisiste, fantastique; **f. portrait,** portrait *m* de fantaisie. **2.** (projet *m*) chimérique; (conte *m*) imaginaire; (revendications *f*) fantaisistes, de pure fantaisie; **I'm not a f. person, and I'm sure I really saw it,** je n'ai pas grande imagination et pourtant je vous assure que je l'ai vu.

fancifully ['fænsif(u)li], *adv.* (*a*) capricieusement; (*b*) d'une manière fantasque, fantaisiste.

fancifulness ['fænsifulnis], *s.* (*a*) caractère capricieux (de qn); (*b*) fantastique *m*, fantasque *m* (de qch.); caractère *m* fantaisiste (d'un costume, etc.).

fancify ['fænsifai], *v.tr. F: esp. U.S:* enjoliver.

fancily ['fænsili], *adv.* (décoré, etc.) d'un style orné, compliqué.

fancy[1] ['fænsi], *s. & a.*

I. *s.* **1.** (*a*) imagination *f*, fantaisie *f*; **the realm, world, of f.,** le pays des chimères, des idées; *Lit:* **in f. I saw . . .,** en esprit, en imagination, je voyais . . .; je voyais en idée . . .; (*b*) chose *f* imaginaire; **it's only f.!** c'est pure imagination! idées que tout cela! c'est une idée que vous vous faites! (*c*) idée *f*; **I have a f. that . . .,** j'ai idée que . . .; **idle fancies,** vaines imaginations; chimères *f*; idées creuses; **to be full of fancies,** rêver tout éveillé. **2.** (*a*) fantaisie *f*, caprice *m*; **he has strange fancies,** il a des lubies *f*; **to amuse oneself as the f. takes one,** s'amuser à sa fantaisie; **just as the f. takes me,** comme l'idée me prend, *F:* comme ça me chante; (*b*) fantaisie, goût *m*; **to take a f. to sth.,** prendre goût à qch.; **to take a f. to s.o.,** (i) prendre qn en affection; (ii) s'éprendre, s'enticher, se coiffer, se toquer, de qn; **he has taken your f.,** il a (eu) l'heur de vous plaire; **it took my f. at once,** cela m'a séduit du premier coup; **what takes your f. most?** qu'est-ce qui vous attire le plus? *O:* **to please s.o.'s f.,** séduire qn; **to be f. free,** avoir le cœur libre; **we must let her marry according to her f.,** il faut la laisser se marier à son idée; **it's only a passing f.,** ce n'est qu'une amourette; **when he was five, it was his f. to become an engine driver,** à cinq ans il rêvait de devenir conducteur de locomotive; *P: O:* **that suits my f., strikes my f.,** cela me va, me plaît. **3. the f.,** (i) *A:* les amateurs *m* de la boxe; (ii) *A:* la boxe; (iii) les éleveurs d'animaux, d'oiseaux, d'agrément. **4.** *P: A:* (*a*) amant *m* de cœur, gigolo *m*; (*b*) (i) prostituée *f*, poule *f*; (ii) maîtresse *f*.

II. *a.* **1.** (*a*) de fantaisie; **f. biscuits,** biscuits assortis; *O:* **f. cakes,** *s.* **fancies,** pâtisseries *f* (à la crème); *Pej:* **I don't want any of those f. loaves,** je ne veux pas de ces pains de fantaisie; **box lined with f. silk,** boîte *f* avec intérieur de soie de fantaisie; **f. waistcoats,** gilets *m* de fantaisie; **f. goods,** nouveautés *f*; objets *m* de fantaisie, de luxe; **f. dress,** travesti *m*, déguisement *m*; **f.-dress ball,** bal travesti; *Pej:* **of course, they had to give the child a f. name,** bien sûr, ils ont donné à l'enfant un nom fantaisiste, de fantaisie; *F:* **to cut out the f. stuff,** déblayer, élaguer; (*b*) **f. price,** prix trop élevé, fantaisiste; (*c*) *P:* **f. man,** (i) amant *m* de cœur, gigolo *m*; (ii) souteneur *m*; **f. woman, f. piece,** (i) prostituée *f*, poule *f*; (ii) maîtresse *f*. **2.** fantaisiste; d'imagination; **a f. portrait of an unknown benefactor,** portrait *m* de pure imagination d'un bienfaiteur inconnu.

fancy[2], *v.tr.* **1.** (*a*) s'imaginer, se figurer (qch.); **to f. all kinds of things,** s'imaginer toutes sortes de choses; se perdre en conjectures; se faire des idées; **he fancies he knows everything,** il se figure tout savoir; *F:* **f. now! just f.! f. (that)!** qui l'aurait dit? figurez-vous ça! comme ça se trouve! **just f. his astonishment,** imaginez un peu son étonnement! **f. meeting you!** je ne m'attendais guère à vous rencontrer! **f. anyone doing such a thing!** on n'a pas idée de faire une chose pareille! **f. her marrying him!** qui se serait attendu à ce qu'elle l'épouse, lui! **can you f. him risking his neck?** concevez-vous qu'il risque jamais sa peau? (*b*) croire, penser; **that won't last long, I f.,** cela ne durera pas, à ce qu'il me semble; **I f. he is out,** je crois bien, j'ai (l')idée, qu'il est sorti; **I f. I have seen him before,** j'ai l'impression de l'avoir déjà vu; **he fancied he heard footsteps,** il a cru entendre des pas. **2.** (*a*) **to f. sth.,** se sentir attiré vers qch.; **I don't f. his looks,** sa figure ne me revient pas, n'est pas à mon goût; **I don't f. his offer,** son offre *f* ne me dit rien; **I f. a bit of chicken,** je mangerais volontiers un morceau de poulet; **let him eat anything he fancies,** il peut manger tout ce qui lui dit; *Turf:* **strongly fancied horse,** cheval très coté; (*b*) **to f. s.o.,** se sentir attiré vers qn; être épris, entiché, de qn; (*c*) **to f. oneself,** être fort content, être infatué, de sa petite personne; se gober; **he fancies himself a bit,** (i) il se croit quelqu'un; (ii) il est un peu poseur; il s'en croit; **he fancies himself as a speaker,** il se croit orateur; **he fancies himself at tennis,** il se croit de première force au tennis; il se croit fin joueur. **3.** faire de l'élevage (d'oiseaux, de chiens de salon, etc.); faire de la culture de (plantes de fantaisie).

fancywork ['fænsiwə:k], *s. Needlew:* ouvrage(s) *m(pl)* d'agrément; broderie *f*; travaux *mpl* pour dames; ouvrages *mpl* pour dames.

fandangle [fæn'dæŋgl], *s. F:* **1.** oripeaux *mpl*, clinquant *m*. **2.** sottises *fpl*.

fandango [fæn'dæŋgou], *s. Danc:* fandango *m*.

fane [fein], *s. A: & Poet:* temple *m*.

fanfare [ˈfænfɛər], *s.* **1.** (*a*) fanfare (exécutée par des cors de chasse, des trompettes); sonnerie *f* (de trompettes); (*b*) *A:* = FANFARONADE. **2.** *Bookb:* **f. binding,** reliure *f* à la fanfare.

fanfaronade [fænfærəˈneid], *s.* fanfaronnade *f*, vanterie *f.*

fanfold [ˈfænfould], *a.* à pliage accordéon, à pliage paravent; *Cmptr:* **f. cards, paper,** cartes *f*, papier *m*, en continu à pliage paravent.

fang[1] [fæŋ], *s.* **1.** (*a*) croc *m* (de chien, etc.); défense *f* (de sanglier, etc.); (*b*) crochet *m* (de vipère); dent *f* à venin. **2.** *Tls:* soie *f* (d'un couteau, d'un outil); *Mec.E:* **f. bolt,** boulon *m* avec écrou à ergots. **3.** *Anat:* (pointe *f*, prolongement *m*, de) racine *f* (d'une dent).

fang[2], *v.tr.* amorcer (une pompe).

fanged [fæŋd], *a.* **1.** (animal) pourvu de crocs, de défenses, de crochets. **2.** (outil) muni d'une soie; (couteau *m*) à soie. **3.** *Dent:* **three-f. molar,** molaire *f* à racine avec trois prolongements.

fangless [ˈfæŋlis], *a.* **1.** (animal) sans crocs, sans défenses; (serpent) sans crochets; **old f. lion,** vieux lion édenté. **2.** (outil) sans soie. **3.** (dent) sans racine.

fango [ˈfæŋgou], *s. Med:* boue *f* des sources de Battaglia.

fanlight [ˈfænlait], *s.* imposte *f* (au-dessus d'une porte).

fanmail [ˈfænmeil], *s. F:* courrier *m* des admirateurs et admiratrices (d'une vedette, etc.).

fanner [ˈfænər], *s.* **1.** *Agr:* van *m* mécanique; tarare *m.* **2.** ventilateur (soufflant, à ailes) (pour forges, etc.); soufflet *m.*

fanning [ˈfæniŋ], *s.* **1.** *Agr:* vannage *m*, ventage *m* (du grain). **2.** soufflement *m* (du feu); attisage *m*, attisement *m* (d'une querelle).

Fanny [ˈfæni]. **1.** *Pr.n.f. F:* (*dim. of* **Frances**) Fanchon; *P: O:* **sweet F. Adams,** rien du tout, nib de nib; *Nau: P:* **F. Adams,** (i) gamelle *f*; (ii) viande *f* de conserve, singe *m.* **2.** *s.* (*a*) *P:* derrière *m*, fesses *fpl*; **not on your f.,** pour rien au monde; (*b*) *P:* **a load of f.,** un tas de foutaises; (*c*) *V:* vagin *m*, minou *m.*

fanon [ˈfænən], *s. Ecc.Cost:* fanon *m*, manipule *m.*

fan-shaped [ˈfænʃeipt], *a.* en éventail.

fantad [ˈfæntæd], *s.* = FANTOD.

fantail [ˈfænteil], *s.* **1.** *Orn:* (*a*) pigeon *m* paon; (*b*) rhipidure *f*, gobe-mouches *m inv* à queue en éventail. **2.** *Carp: etc:* queue-d'aronde *f.* **3.** bec *m* (de gaz) en éventail. **4.** gouvernail *m* (de moulin à vent).

fantailed [ˈfænteild], *a.* **1.** *Orn:* **f. pigeon,** pigeon *m* paon. **2.** *Carp:* (assemblage, etc.) à queue-d'aronde.

fantasia [fænˈteiziə], *s.* **1.** (*a*) *Mus:* fantaisie *f*; (*b*) *Lit:* fantasia *f.* **2.** (*Arab display*) fantasia.

fantasist [ˈfæntəzist], *s. Art: Lit:* fantaisiste *mf.*

fantastic [fænˈtæstik], *a.* (*of pers., thg*) fantasque, bizarre, excentrique, extraordinaire, extravagant; (*of pers.*) original, -aux; capricieux; (*of thg*) fantastique, grotesque; *Lit:* **on the light f. toe,** d'un pas léger et fantasque; **f. as a woman's mood,** aussi fantasque, aussi capricieux, que l'humeur d'une femme; *Com:* **f. reductions,** baisses phénoménales; **any sort of house fetches a f. price,** n'importe quelle maison coûte les yeux de la tête.

fantastically [fænˈtæstik(ə)li], *adv.* capricieusement; d'une manière fantasque, fantastique, bizarre, *F:* **f. beautiful, rich,** incroyablement beau, belle, riche.

fantasy [ˈfæntəzi], *s.* **1.** fantaisie *f*; (*a*) imagination capricieuse; (*b*) caprice *m.* **2.** (*a*) vision *f*, idée *f*, bizarre, fantastique; (*b*) idée fantasque; *Lit:* **a thousand fantasies begin to throng into my memory,** mille visions se pressent dans ma mémoire. **3.** (*a*) œuvre *f*, édifice *m*, etc., fantastique; (*b*) *Mus:* fantaisie *f*; *Lit:* fantasia *f.*

fantee, Fanti [ˈfænti]. **1.** *Ethn:* (*a*) *a.* fanti; (*b*) *s.* Fanti, -ie. **2.** *s. Ling:* fanti *m.*

fantod [ˈfæntəd], *s. F: O: esp. U.S:* **to have the fantods,** (i) être de mauvaise humeur; (ii) avoir ses nerfs; **it gives me the fantods just to see it,** rien que de le voir, ça me donne sur les nerfs; **don't get into a f. about it!** ne te monte pas la tête!

far[1] [fɑːr], *adv.* (**farther, -est** [ˈfɑːðər, -ist], **further, -est** [ˈfəːðər, -ist]). **1.** (*of place*) loin; (*a*) to **go f.,** aller loin; faire du chemin; **this young man will go f.,** ce jeune homme ira loin; **to go f. into Africa,** pénétrer très avant dans l'Afrique; **as f. south, east, as Paris,** aussi loin au sud, à l'est, que Paris; **to go too f.,** aller trop loin; s'avancer trop; **is it f. from here?** est-ce loin d'ici? **how f. is it from . . . to . . .?** combien y a-t-il de . . . à . . .? **how f. did he follow them?** jusqu'où les a-t-il suivis? **so f. and no farther,** jusque-là et pas plus loin; **thus f.,** jusqu'ici; jusque-là; **as f. as the eye can reach,** à perte de vue; **I cannot see as f. as that,** ma vue n'atteint pas jusque-là; **to live f. away, f. off,** demeurer au loin; **I saw them f. off,** je les ai vus dans le lointain; **his thoughts were f. away,** sa pensée était ailleurs; son esprit était absent; **f. and wide,** de tous côtés; partout; jusqu'au bout du monde; **f. and near,** partout; **do you come from f.?** est-ce que vous venez de loin? **people came from f. and near,** on venait des quatre coins du monde; **a stake driven f. into the ground,** un pieu enfoncé profondément dans la terre; **f. from . . .,** loin de . . .; *Lit:* **f. from the madding crowd,** loin de la foule en délire; **not f. from . . .,** à peu de distance de . . .; non loin de . . .; **we are too f. from the shore,** nous sommes trop au large; **the reasons for this hostility are not very f. to seek,** il ne faut pas chercher bien loin les raisons de cette hostilité; *Journ:* **the story so f.** = résumé *m* des chapitres précédents; (*b*) **these facts go f. to explain how . . .,** ces faits *m* expliquent dans une large mesure comment . . .; **that will go f. towards making up for our loss,** cela aidera beaucoup, contribuera beaucoup, à nous dédommager de notre perte; **a pound does not go very f. nowadays,** on ne va pas loin avec une livre de nos jours; **to make one's money go f.,** faire bon usage de son argent; **modesty won't carry you f.,** la modestie ne vous mènera pas loin; **to go so f. as to do sth., as doing sth.,** aller jusqu'à faire qch.; **I'll go so f. as to say that . . .,** je vais jusqu'à dire que . . .; **they went so f. as to claim . . .,** on a été jusqu'à prétendre . . .; **he went so f. as to laugh,** il se laissa aller à rire; **things went so f. that . . .,** les choses sont allées si loin que . . .; tant il y a eu que . . .; **he has gone too f. to withdraw,** il est trop engagé pour reculer; il s'est trop avancé pour reculer; **to let a disease go too f.,** laisser s'invétérer une maladie; **that is going too f.,** cela passe la mesure, les bornes; **to carry a joke too f.,** pousser trop loin une plaisanterie; **you are carrying things too f.,** vous allez trop loin; **to carry modesty too f.,** pousser trop loin la modestie; être modeste à l'excès; **how f. is he sincere?** dans quelle mesure, jusqu'à quel point, est-il sincère? **how f. have you got (in your reading, etc.)?** où en êtes-vous (de votre lecture, etc.)? **we haven't got as f. as you,** nous n'en sommes pas aussi loin que vous; **we had got so f. in our job,** nous en étions là de notre tâche; **as f. as I can judge . . .,** autant que je puis en juger . . .; à ce qu'il me paraît . . .; **as f. as I know,** autant que je sache; **as f. as feelings go . . .,** en matière de sentiment . . .; **as f. as that goes,** pour ce qui est de cela; **I will help you as f. as I can, as f. as possible, as f. as lies within my power,** je vous aiderai dans la mesure de mes forces, de mes moyens, du possible; je vous aiderai dans la mesure où cela me sera possible; **as f. as circumstances allow, permit,** autant que le permettront les circonstances; **so f. so good,** c'est fort bien jusque-là; jusqu'ici ça va bien; **in so f. . . .,** dans cette mesure . . .; **in so f. as . . .,** dans la mesure où . . .; pour autant que . . .; **I am a Russian in so f. as I was born in Russia,** je suis Russe en tant que (je suis) né en Russie; **account f. from the truth,** récit bien éloigné de la vérité; **to be far from believing sth.,** être à cent lieues de croire qch.; **f. from admiring him I loathe him,** bien loin de l'admirer je le déteste; **f. from diminishing, crime increases,** loin de diminuer les crimes augmentent; loin que les crimes diminuent ils augmentent; **so f. from his having finished . . .,** tant s'en faut qu'il ait achevé, que. . .; **he is f. from (being) happy,** il s'en faut de beaucoup qu'il soit heureux; **f. from it,** tant s'en faut; loin de là; il s'en faut! **not f. from it,** peu s'en faut; **if he is not dead, he is not f. from it,** s'il n'est pas mort, il n'en vaut guère mieux; **I am not dissatisfied, f. from it, but . . .,** je ne suis pas mécontent, bien loin de là, mais . . .; **f. be it from me to put pressure on you!** loin de moi l'idée de vous influencer! à Dieu ne plaise que je veuille vous influencer! **f. from us such a thought!** Dieu nous préserve (*sub.*) d'une telle pensée! **he is not f. off sixty,** il approche de la soixantaine; **by f.,** de loin; **by f. the best,** de beaucoup le meilleur; **by f. the best equipped,** le mieux équipé à beaucoup près. **2.** (*of time*) **so f.,** jusqu'ici; **have you seen him?—not so f.,** l'avez-vous vu?—pas jusqu'ici; pas encore; **I am only a student so f.,** je ne suis encore qu'étudiant; **as f. back as I can remember,** aussi loin, du plus loin, que je puisse me rappeler; du plus loin qu'il me souvienne; d'aussi loin qu'il me souvienne; **as f. back as 1900,** déjà en 1900; dès 1900; **as f. as I can see,** autant que je puisse prévoir; **f. back in the Middle Ages,** à une période reculée du moyen âge; **he did not look so f. into the future,** il ne regardait pas si avant (dans l'avenir); **to work f. into the night,** travailler bien avant dans la nuit. **3.** (*with qualifying adjectives, adverbs, etc.*) beaucoup, bien, fort; **it is f. better,** c'est beaucoup mieux, bien préférable; **it is f. more serious,** c'est bien autrement sérieux; **she looks far smarter than you,** elle est autrement chic que vous; **f. and away the best,** de beaucoup le meilleur; **this is f. and away better,** cela vaut infiniment mieux; **he is f. and away above the others,** il est bien au-dessus des autres; **f. and away beyond anything else,** bien supérieur à tout autre; **the night was f. advanced, f. spent,** la nuit était fort avancée.

far[2], *a.* (**farther, -est** [ˈfɑːðər, -ist]), **further, -est** [ˈfəːðər, -ist]) **1.** lointain, éloigné, reculé; **a f. country,** un pays lointain, un pays très loin; **in the f. distance,** tout au loin; *Geog:* **the F. East,** l'Extrême-Orient *m*; **F.-Eastern,** extrême-oriental, -aux. **2. the f. end (of a plank, etc.),** le bout le plus éloigné (d'une planche, etc.); **I caught sight of him at the f. end of the street,** je l'aperçus à l'autre bout de la rue; **the f. bank of the river,** la rive opposée de la rivière; **the f. side of the street,** l'autre côté *m* de la rue.

farad [ˈfæræd], *s. El.Meas:* farad *m.*

faradaic [færəˈdeiik], **faradic** [fæˈrædik], *a. El:* (courant, etc.) faradique.

faraday [ˈfærədei], *s. El:* **f. (constant),** faraday *m.*

faradimeter [færæˈdimitər], *s.* = FARADMETER.

faradism [ˈfærædizm], **faradization** [færædaiˈzeiʃ(ə)n], *s. Med:* faradisation *f.*

faradmeter [ˈfærædmiːtər], **faradometer** [færæˈdɔmitər], *s. El:* capacimètre *m*, faradmètre *m.*

farandole [ˈfærændoul], *s. Danc:* farandole *f.*

faraway [ˈfɑːrəwei]. **1.** *a.* (*of land, period, etc.*) lointain, éloigné, reculé; **his eyes had a f. look,** il avait le regard vague, abstrait, distrait, perdu dans le vague, plongé dans le lointain; son regard nageait dans le vague; **f. voice,** voix éteinte. **2.** *s. Cin:* vue prise de loin; lointain *m.*

farce[1] [fɑːs], *s.* **1.** *Th:* farce *f*; **knockabout f.,** grosse farce; **the trial was a f.,** le procès a été une dérision, une pure farce, une pure comédie. **2.** *Cu: A:* farce *f.*

farce[2], *v.tr.* **1.** *Cu: A:* farcir (du veau, etc.). **2.** *A: & Lit:* **book farced with Latin tags,** livre farci de bribes de latin.

farcical [ˈfɑːsikl], *a.* (*a*) *Th:* tenant de la farce; bouffon, burlesque; **a f. play,** une farce; (*b*) (*of incident*) risible, absurde, bouffon, grotesque; **this accusation is f.,** cette accusation est grotesque; **a f. examination,** un examen pour rire; **f. figures,** chiffres ridiculement bas.

farcically [ˈfɑːsik(ə)li], *adv.* d'une manière risible, absurde, ridicule, grotesque; **f. low figures,** chiffres ridiculement bas.

farcied [ˈfɑːsid], *a. Vet:* (cheval) farcineux.

farcy [ˈfɑːsi], *s. Vet:* (*a*) farcin *m* (du cheval); **f. bud, button,** bouton farcineux, de farcin; (*b*) **bovine f., cattle f.,** farcin des bovidés.

fardel [ˈfɑːd(ə)l], *s.* **1.** *A:* fardeau *m.* **2.** *Z:* feuillet *m*, troisième estomac *m* (des ruminants).

fare[1] [fɛər], *s.* **1.** (*a*) *Rail: etc:* prix *m* du voyage, de la place; (*in taxi*) prix de la course; **adult f., full f.,** plein tarif, place entière; **half f.,** demi-place *f, pl.* demi-places; **half-f. ticket,** billet *m* à demi-tarif; **single f.,** (prix du) billet simple, (prix d')aller *m*; **return f.,** aller et retour *m*, *F:* aller-retour *m*; **minimum f.,** minimum *m* de perception; **excess f.,** supplément *m*; **to pay one's f.,** payer son billet, sa course; **how much is the f.?** c'est combien le billet? (*in taxi*) je vous dois combien? (*in bus*) **fares, please!** les places, s'il vous plaît! **any more fares, please?** tout le monde est servi? (*b*) (*in taxi*) client, -ente; voyageur, -euse. **2.** chère *f*, manger *m*; **good f.,** bonne chère; **ordinary f., everyday f.,** manger de tous les jours; l'ordinaire *m*; **prison f.,** régime *m* de prison; **lenten f.,** viandes *fpl* de carême; **scanty f., poor f.,** maigre nourriture *f*, maigre chère; **to be fond of good f.,** aimer la table, la bonne chère.

fare[2], *v.i.* **1.** *A: & Lit:* voyager; **they fared through unknown seas,** ils naviguaient sur des mers inconnues; **to f. forth,** partir. **2.** (*a*) **to f. well, badly,** aller bien, mal; se trouver dans une bonne, mauvaise, situation; **in spite of his efforts he is faring no better,** malgré ses efforts ses affaires ne vont pas mieux; **he went out in the snow to see how the lambs were faring,** il est sorti sous la neige pour voir ce que devenaient les agneaux; **it is hard to guess how minorities will f. at the hands of the new government,** il est difficile de deviner quelle sera la situation des minorités sous le nouveau gouvernement; **to f. alike,** partager le même sort; *F:* **you could go further and f. worse,** ce n'est pas si mal ici; *A:* **f. well!** *A: & Poet:* **f. you well! f. thee well!** adieu! (*b*) *impers. A:* **how did it fare with him?** (i) est-ce que la Fortune lui a été propice? (ii) qu'est-il advenu de lui? **how fares it (with you)?** est-ce que ça marche? comment vous trouvez-vous? comment allez-vous? **3.** manger, vivre, se nourrir; **to f. well, badly,** faire bonne, maigre, chère.

farewell [fɛəˈwel], *int. & s.* adieu (*m*); **to bid s.o. f., to take a, one's f. of s.o.,** dire adieu, faire ses adieux, à qn;

Lit: **I have said f. to all that,** j'ai dit adieu à tout cela; j'en ai fini avec tout cela; **a f. call, dinner,** une visite, un dîner, d'adieu.

far-famed ['fɑː'feimd], *a. Lit:* dont la renommée s'est étendue au loin; célèbre.

far(-)fetched ['fɑː'fetʃt], *a.* (*of example, comparison, argument, etc.*) forcé, outré; tiré par les cheveux, amené de bien loin; **the story is too f.-f. to be credible,** l'histoire est trop tirée par les cheveux pour que l'on puisse y ajouter foi.

far-flung ['fɑːflʌŋ], *a. Lit:* (*of empire, etc.*) très étendu, vaste.

farinaceous [færi'neiʃəs], *a.* farineux, farinacé; **f. food,** (aliment) farineux *m.*

farinose ['færinous], *a. Nat.Hist:* farineux.

farm[1] [fɑːm], *s.* **1.** (*a*) ferme *f*, exploitation *f* agricole; (*rented on sharecropping lease*) métairie *f*; **sheep f.,** élevage *m* de moutons; **trout f.,** élevage de truites; **dairy f.,** ferme laitière; **poultry f.,** exploitation avicole, élevage de volailles; **ostrich f.,** autrucherie *f*; **stud f.,** haras *m*; **home f.,** ferme attachée à un domaine; **he was brought up on a f.,** il a été élevé dans une ferme; (*b*) = FARMHOUSE; (*c*) *attrib.* **f. equipment,** matériel *m* agricole; **f. machinery,** machines *f* agricoles; **f. butter,** beurre fermier; **f. labourer,** ouvrier *m* agricole; **f. horse,** cheval *m* de ferme, de labour; **f. buildings,** dépendances *f* (d'une ferme); **f. road,** chemin *m* de terre (menant à une ferme). **2.** (*a*) **sewage f.,** champs *mpl* d'épandage; (*b*) *Petr:* **tank f.,** parc *m* de stockage, à réservoirs.

farm[2], *v.*

I. *v.tr. & i.* **1.** *v.tr.* (*a*) *Hist:* prendre à ferme, affermer (des impôts); (*b*) cultiver, exploiter (une propriété, des terres); **to f. 400 acres** = exploiter 160 hectares. **2.** *v.i.* être cultivateur, agriculteur.

II. (*compound verb*) **farm out,** *v.tr.* (*a*) *Hist:* donner à ferme, affermer (des impôts); (*b*) mettre (des enfants) en nourrice; (*c*) *F:* **to f. o. work,** sous-traiter; faire appel à des collaborations extérieures.

farmer ['fɑːmər], *s.* **1.** *Hist:* **f. of revenues,** fermier *m* des impôts; **f. (of taxes),** financier *m*; *coll.* **the f. of taxes,** la finance; **f.-general,** fermier-général *m, pl.* fermiers-généraux. **2.** agriculteur *m*; cultivateur, -trice; exploitant, -ante, agricole; **(tenant) f.,** fermier, -ière; **the farmer's wife,** la fermière; **stock f.,** éleveur, -euse; **sheep f.,** éleveur de moutons; **poultry f.,** aviculteur, -trice; éleveur, -euse, de volailles; *NAm:* **dirt f.,** (i) cultivateur qui travaille la terre de ses propres mains; (ii) agriculteur (par opposition à éleveur).

farmhand ['fɑːmhænd], *s.* ouvrier *m* agricole.

farmhouse ['fɑːmhaus], *s.* (maison *f* de) ferme *f.*

farming[1] ['fɑːmiŋ], *a.* **f. communities,** (i) peuples cultivateurs; (ii) agglomérations rurales.

farming[2], *s.* **1.** *Hist:* affermage *m* (d'une propriété, des impôts). **2.** exploitation *f* agricole; culture *f*, agriculture *f*; **large-scale, small-scale, f.,** grande, petite, exploitation; **mixed f.,** polyculture *f*; **single-crop f.,** monoculture *f*; **dry f.,** culture sèche, à sec; dry farming *m*; **stock f.,** élevage *m*; **sheep f.,** élevage de moutons; **poultry f.,** aviculture *f*, élevage de volailles; **f. lease,** bail *m* à ferme.

farmstead ['fɑːmsted], *s.* ferme *f* (et ses dépendances).

farmyard ['fɑːmjɑːd], *s.* cour *f* de ferme; basse-cour *f*, *pl.* basses-cours.

Farnese [fɑː'neizei], *Pr.n. Hist:* Farnèse.

farnesol ['fɑːnəsɔl], *s. Bio-Ch:* farnésol *m.*

faro ['fɛərou], *s. Cards:* pharaon *m.*

Faroe ['fɛərou], *Pr.n. Geog:* **the F. Islands, the Faroes,** les îles *f* Féroé.

Faroeish ['fɛərouiʃ], *a. & s. Ling:* féroïen (*m*).

Faroese [fɛərou'iːz], *a. & s. Geog:* (natif, -ive, originaire) des îles Féroé.

far-off ['fɑːrɔf], *a.* (*of place, time, etc.*) lointain, éloigné, reculé; **a. f.-o. city,** une ville éloignée.

farrago [fə'rɑːgou], *s. Pej:* farrago *m*, méli-mélo *m, pl.* mélis-mélos; **f. of useless knowledge,** fatras *m* de connaissances.

far-reaching ['fɑː'riːtʃiŋ], *a.* de grande envergure, d'une grande portée; **to have a f.-r. influence,** être très influent; (*of event, etc.*) avoir une grande portée; (*of pers.*) *F:* avoir les mains longues, le bras long; **statement of f.-r. effect,** affirmation *f* d'une grande portée; **f.-r. consequences,** conséquences *f* d'une portée incalculable.

farrier ['færiər], *s.* **1.** maréchal(-ferrant) *m* (*pl.* maréchaux(-ferrants); *Mil: A:* **sergeant f.,** maître *m* maréchal-ferrant. **2.** *A:* vétérinaire *m.*

farriery ['færiəri], *s.* **1.** maréchalerie *f.* **2.** *A:* art *m* vétérinaire.

farrow[1] ['færou], *s.* portée *f* de cochons; cochonnée *f*; **sow in, with, f.,** truie pleine; **sow that has had fifteen pigs at one f.,** truie qui a mis bas quinze petits en une cochonnée.

farrow[2]. **1.** *v.tr.* mettre bas (des cochons). **2.** *v.i.* (*of sow*) **to f. (down),** faire des petits; cochonner; mettre bas.

far-seeing ['fɑː'siːiŋ], *a.* prévoyant, avisé, clairvoyant, perspicace; prescient; prudent; **to be f.-s.,** voir loin; *F:* avoir bon nez; avoir le nez fin.

far-sighted ['fɑː'saitid], *a.* **1.** = FAR-SEEING. **2.** (*a*) presbyte; (*b*) hypermétrope.

far-sightedly ['fɑː'saitidli], *adv.* d'une manière prévoyante, avisée, prudente, presciente; avec clairvoyance; avec prescience.

far-sightedness ['fɑː'saitidnis], *s.* **1.** prévoyance *f*; prescience *f*; perspicacité *f.* **2.** (*a*) presbytie *f*; (*b*) hypermétropie *f.*

fart[1] [fɑːt], *s. P:* pet *m*, prout *m.*

fart[2], *v.i. P:* (*a*) péter; faire un pet; lâcher un pet; prouter; (*b*) **to f. around, about,** (i) traîner son cul; (ii) faire le con.

farther ['fɑːðər]. (*comp. of* **far**) **1.** *adv.* (*a*) plus loin **(than,** que); **f. off,** plus éloigné; plus loin; **f. on,** (i) plus en avant; plus loin; (ii) plus en avance; **f. on we shall see that . . .,** plus loin nous verrons que . . .; **he is f. on than you,** il est plus avancé que vous; **to penetrate f. into the country,** pénétrer plus avant dans le pays; **I can go no f.,** (i) je ne saurais aller plus loin; (ii) je n'en peux plus! **anything he is told goes no f.,** ce qu'on lui dit ne va pas plus loin; **nothing is f. from my thoughts,** rien n'est plus éloigné de ma pensée; **f. than a certain point,** au delà d'un certain point; *F: O:* **to wish s.o. f.,** envoyer qn au diable; **I'll see you f. first!** plus souvent! va-t'en voir si j'y suis! (*b*) **f. (back),** plus en arrière; **f. back than 1500,** antérieurement à 1500; (*c*) davantage, de plus, aussi, encore. **2.** *a.* (*a*) plus lointain, plus éloigné; **at the f. end of the room,** à l'autre bout de la salle; au fond de la salle; **on the f. bank of the river,** sur la rive opposée de la rivière; (*b*) **f. back,** antérieur **(than,** à); (*c*) en plus, de plus; (**further** *is more usual in this sense*).

farthermost ['fɑːðəmoust], *a.* (*of place*) le plus lointain, le plus éloigné, le plus reculé; **to the f. ends of the earth,** jusqu'aux extrémités *f* de la terre.

farthest ['fɑːðist]. (*sup. of* **far**) **1.** *a.* (*a*) **f. (off),** le plus lointain, le plus éloigné, le plus reculé; **at (the) f.,** (*of place*) au plus loin; (*of time*) au plus tard; **in f. Siberia,** au fin fond de la Sibérie; (*b*) (*of way, distance, etc.*) le plus long; **it was the f. distance that we went,** c'est le plus loin que nous ayons pénétré. **2.** *adv.* le plus loin.

farthing ['fɑːðiŋ], *s. A.Num:* quart *m* d'un penny; *F:* **not to have a f.,** n'avoir pas le sou; n'avoir pas un sou vaillant; ne pas avoir un rond, un radis; **to pay to the uttermost, to the last, f.,** payer jusqu'au dernier sou; payer ric-à-rac; payer rubis sur l'ongle; **to stake one's last f.,** jouer son va-tout; **to take s.o.'s last f.,** sucer qn jusqu'au dernier sou, jusqu'à la moelle des os; **I would have given my last f. to help him,** j'aurais donné mon dernier sou pour l'aider; **not a f.!** pas un centime! **not to be worth a brass f.,** ne pas valoir un centime, un rouge liard; **I don't care a brass f.,** je m'en moque absolument; je m'en moque comme d'une guigne, comme de Colin-Tampon.

farthingale ['fɑːðiŋgeil], *s. A.Cost:* vertugadin *m*, bouffante *f.*

fascia, *pl.* **-iae** ['fæʃiə, -iiː], *s.* **1.** (*a*) *Arch:* fasce *f*, bandelette *f*, bande *f*; (*b*) *Com:* enseigne *f* en forme d'entablement; **f. writer,** peintre *m* en lettres. **2.** *Anat:* fascia *m*, aponévrose *f.* **3.** *Nat.Hist:* fascie *f*, bande de couleur.

fascial ['fæʃiəl], *a. Anat:* fascial, -iaux, aponévrotique.

fasciated ['fæʃieitid], *a.* (*a*) *Nat.Hist:* rayé; (*b*) *Bot:* fascié; **f. stem,** tige fasciée; fascie *f*; (*c*) *Bot:* (feuilles) fasciculées.

fasciation [fæʃi'eiʃ(ə)n], *s. Nat.Hist:* fasciation *f.*

fascicle ['fæsikl], **fascicule** ['fæsikjuːl], *s. Nat.Hist: Bookb: etc:* fascicule *m.*

fascicled ['fæsikld], **fascicular** [fæ'sikjulər], **fasciculate(d)** [fæ'sikjuleit(id)], *a. Nat.Hist:* fasciculé.

fasciculus [fæ'sikjuləs], *s. Anat:* trousseau *m* (de vaisseaux sanguins, etc.).

fascinate ['fæsineit], *v.tr.* (*a*) (*of serpent, etc.*) fasciner (sa proie); (*b*) fasciner, charmer, séduire (qn); **to be fascinated by sth.,** être fasciné par qch.

fascinating ['fæsineitiŋ], *a.* fascinateur, -trice; enchanteur, -eresse; attachant; attrayant, séduisant; (enfant) prenant; **f. piece of work to undertake,** œuvre passionnante à entreprendre; **his voice is as f. as ever,** sa voix est aussi prenante que jamais.

fascination [fæsi'neiʃ(ə)n], *s.* **1.** fascination *f* (d'une proie). **2.** fascination, charme *m*, attrait *m*, séduction *f*, attirance *f.*

fascinator ['fæsineitər], *s.* **1.** fascinateur, -trice. **2.** *Cost: A:* fichu *m* de laine légère.

fascine[1] [fæ'siːn], *s. Fort: Hyd.E:* fascine *f*; (*small*) faguette *f*; *Fort:* fagot *m* de sape; **f. work,** fascinage *m.*

fascine[2], *v.tr.* fasciner (un fossé, etc.).

fasciola [fæsi'oulə], *s. Ann:* fasciola *f*, fasciole *f.*

fasciolaria [fæsiou'lɛəriə], *s. Moll:* fasciolaria *f*, fasciolaire *f.*

Fasciolariidae [fæsioulæ'raiidiː], *s.pl. Moll:* fasciolariidés *m.*

fasciole ['feisioul], *s. Echin:* fasciole *f.*

fascism ['fæʃizm], *s. Pol:* fascisme *m.*

fascist ['fæʃist], *a. & s. Pol:* fasciste (*mf*).

fash[1] [fæʃ], *s. Metalw:* bavure *f.*

fash[2], *s. Scot:* tracas *m*, ennui *m.*

fash[3], *v.tr. Scot:* agacer, ennuyer (qn); **to f. oneself,** se tracasser, se tourmenter, se faire de la bile **(about,** à propos de).

fashion[1] ['fæʃ(ə)n], *s.* **1.** (*a*) *O:* façon *f* (d'un habit, etc.); forme *f* (d'un objet); (*b*) manière *f* (de faire qch.); **to do sth. in a leisurely f.,** faire qch. sans se presser, en prenant (tout) son temps; **crabs walk in a peculiar f.,** les crabes marchent d'une façon étrange; **after a f.,** tant bien que mal; **he's kind after a f.,** il est bon à sa manière; **she plays the piano after a f.,** elle joue du piano si vous voulez, tant bien que mal; *F:* elle tapote. **2.** *A:* habitude *f*, coutume *f*; **he rose at six, as was his f.,** il se leva à six heures, selon sa coutume. **3.** (*of clothes, customs, etc.*) mode *f*, vogue *f*; **in (the) f.,** à la mode, de mode, en vogue; **out of f.,** passé de mode; démodé; **it is no longer the f., in f.,** cela n'est plus de mode; **in the latest f.,** à la dernière mode; *F:* dernier cri; **in the reigning f., in the f. of the day,** au goût du jour; à la mode en vogue; **to bring sth. into f.,** mettre qch. à la mode; lancer la mode de qch.; **to set the f.,** faire école; lancer la mode; **to become the f., come into f.,** devenir la mode; **it's all the f. (now),** c'est la grande vogue (à l'heure actuelle); **to lead, set, the f.,** donner la note, le ton; fixer, mener, la mode; **a man, woman, of f.,** un élégant, une élégante; **f. plate,** (i) gravure *f* de modes; (ii) *F:* élégant, -ante; *Com:* **f. house,** maison *f* de haute couture; **f. show,** présentation *f* de collections; **f. magazine,** journal *m* (*pl.* -aux) de modes.

fashion[2], *v.tr.* **1.** (*a*) façonner, former, configurer (une poterie, un bloc de marbre, etc.); confectionner (une robe, etc.); élaborer (une matière brute); *B:* **God fashioned man in His likeness,** Dieu a formé l'homme à son image; (*b*) *Knit:* **to f. a stocking,** faire les diminutions *f* d'un bas. **2.** *A:* adapter **(to,** à).

fashionable ['fæʃ(ə)nəbl]. **1.** *a.* à la mode, élégant, en vogue; **blue is very f. this year,** le bleu se porte beaucoup cette année; **the f. world,** la société, le beau monde; *F:* le monde chic; **a f. resort,** un endroit mondain; **a f. man,** un élégant; **f. dinner,** dîner mondain; **a f. jacket,** une veste à la mode. **2.** *s.pl. A:* **our fashionables,** nos élégants; **our fair fashionables,** nos élégantes.

fashionably ['fæʃənəbli], *adv.* élégamment, à la mode.

fashioned ['fæʃənd], *a.* (*a*) (*of wood, marble, etc.*) façonné, travaillé, ouvré; (*b*) (*of knit goods*) **fully f.,** (entièrement) diminué, proportionné.

fashioning ['fæʃəniŋ], *s.* façonnement *m*, façonnage *m*, confectionnement *m*; *Lit:* **she would take refuge in a dream of her own f.,** elle cherchait un refuge dans un rêve qu'elle s'était forgé elle-même.

Fashoda [fæ'ʃoudə], *Pr.n. Geog: Hist:* Fachoda.

fassaite ['fæsəait], *s. Miner:* fassaïte *f.*

fast[1] [fɑːst], *s.* **1.** jeûne *m*; *Ecc:* **f. day,** jour *m* de jeûne; **the Lenten f.,** le jeûne du Carême; **to break one's f.,** (i) rompre le jeûne; (ii) déjeuner; **I have not yet broken my f.,** je suis encore à jeun; **to observe a rigorous f.,** observer un jeûne rigoureux. **2.** *Med:* diète *f.*

fast[2], *v.i.* **1.** (*a*) jeûner; s'infliger des jeûnes, des privations; s'abstenir **(from,** de); (*b*) *Ecc:* jeûner. **2.** *Med: etc:* être à la diète.

fast[3], *a., adv. & s.*

I. *a.* **1.** (*a*) (*of stake, etc.*) ferme, fixe, stable, solide; (*of grip, etc.*) tenace; **f. pulley,** poulie *f* fixe; **f. headstock (of lathe),** poupée *f* fixe (du tour); **f. wheel,** roue (i) fixe, (ii) calée, bloquée; **feet f. in the mud,** pieds embourbés, collés dans la boue; **to make (a post, etc.) f.,** assurer (un pieu, etc.); *Nau: etc:* **to make a rope f.,** tourner, amarrer, un cordage; **to make a rope f. to a cable,** frapper un cordage sur un câble; **to have f. hold of sth.,** tenir qch. serré; **to hold a prisoner f.,** (i) tenir ferme un prisonnier; (ii) tenir un prisonnier à l'étroit; *O:* **f. friends,** des amis sûrs, solides, fidèles; (*b*) *Nau:* **to make a boat f. to the shore,** amarrer un bateau à terre; **to make f. (to a buoy),** prendre le corps-mort; **to make f. (alongside),** s'amarrer; **to make f. with two warps,** s'amarrer avec deux grelins; **to make f. with four**

warps, s'amarrer à quatre; (c) (*of door, window, lid, etc.*) (bien) assujetti; bien fermé; *A:* **to make f. the doors,** fermer les portes; (d) *Dy:* (*of colour*) solide, résistant; bon teint *inv*; grand teint *inv*; **these colours are not f.,** ces couleurs ne résistent pas; (e) *Bac:* (microbe) qui possède une grande résistance vitale. **2.** (a) (*of horse, vehicle, journey, etc.*) rapide; *Nau:* **f. sailer,** fin voilier, bon marcheur; **f. runner, car, team,** coureur *m*, voiture *f*, équipe *f*, rapide; *Fb:* **f. forwards,** avants *m* très rapides; **you're a f. walker,** vous marchez vite; *Rail:* **f. train,** rapide *m*; express *m*; (b) *Games: etc:* **f. billiard table, tennis court,** billard *m*, court *m*, qui rend bien; (c) *Phot:* **f. lens,** objectif lumineux; (d) *F:* **that's a f. one!** en voilà une roublardise! **he pulled a f. one on me,** il m'a joué un mauvais tour. **3.** (a) (*of clock, watch*) en avance; **f. by Greenwich,** en avance sur l'heure de Greenwich; **my watch is five minutes f.,** ma montre avance de cinq minutes; (b) *U.S:* (balance *f*) qui exagère le poids, qui marque trop. **4.** *F: O:* (*of pers.*) (trop) émancipé; dévergondé; d'allures très libres; **the f. set,** les viveurs *m*; **f. life,** vie *f* de plaisirs; **to lead a f. life,** mener une vie de bâton de chaise; rôtir le balai.

II. *adv.* **1.** (a) ferme, solidement, fortement, bien; **to hold f.,** tenir ferme; tenir bon; **stake fixed f. in the ground,** pieu solidement fixé, bien assujetti, dans la terre; **to stand f.,** faire front, tenir bon; rester inébranlable; ne pas bouger; **he sat f. in his chair,** il restait collé sur sa chaise; il ne bougeait pas de sa chaise; **to stick f.,** (i) bien tenir; (ii) rester pris, rester collé; **to stick f. to sth.,** (i) bien adhérer à qch.; (ii) ne pas lâcher qch.; **the net got f. to a rock,** le filet s'est trouvé engagé par une roche; *Tex:* **f. dyed,** grand teint *inv*; **eyes f. closed,** yeux bien fermés; **to sleep f.,** dormir d'un profond sommeil, à poings fermés; *Prov:* **f. bind f. find,** méfiance est mère de sûreté; *F:* **to play f. and loose,** agir avec inconstance; manquer de droiture; jouer double jeu (**with s.o.,** avec qn); **to play f. and loose with s.o.'s affections,** se jouer, abuser, de l'affection de qn; trahir (une jeune fille); (b) *O:* **f. beside, fast by (sth.),** tout près (de qch.). **2.** vite, rapidement, **to run f.,** courir vite; **f.-moving car,** (i) voiture lancée à toute vitesse; (ii) voiture rapide; **not so f.!** pas si vite! doucement! (*to an interrupter*) permettez! **bad news travels f.,** les mauvaises nouvelles courent vite, ont des ailes; **it is raining f.,** il pleut à verse; **it is snowing f.,** il neige dru; **he ran off as f. as he could, as f. as his legs could carry him,** il s'est enfui à toute vitesse; il a pris ses jambes à son cou; il s'est sauvé à toutes jambes; **he went up as f. as he could,** il est monté du plus vite qu'il a pu; **he drew back as f. as I advanced,** (au fur et) à mesure que j'avançais il reculait; *F:* **he'll do it f. enough if you pay him well,** il le fera promptement, il ne se fera pas prier, si vous le payez bien.

III. *s. Nau:* amarre *f.*

fastback ['fɑːstbæk], *a. & s. Aut:* (à) arrière profilé.

fasten ['fɑːsn], *v.*

I. 1. *v.tr.* (a) (*attach*) attacher (**to, on,** à); **to f. papers together with a clip,** attacher des papiers (ensemble) avec une agrafe; **to f. a beam with dowels,** assujettir une poutre avec des chevilles de bois; **to f. a stay,** ancrer un tirant; **to f. a boat to a post,** amarrer un bateau à un pieu; **to f. one's eyes on s.o.,** attacher, fixer, le regard sur qn; fixer qn; **to f. a crime on s.o.,** imputer un crime à qn; **to f. a quarrel upon s.o.,** forcer qn à se quereller; **to f. the responsibility on s.o.,** mettre, rejeter, la responsabilité sur le dos de qn; (b) (*hold securely*) fixer, assurer, assujettir; **to f. a banging shutter,** fixer, arrêter, un volet qui bat; **to f. a door with a bolt,** fermer une porte au verrou; (c) cheviller (le bordé d'une embarcation, etc.). **2.** *v.i.* s'attacher, se fixer; (a) (*with passive force*) (*of garment*) s'agrafer, se boutonner; (*of door, etc.*) se fermer; **door that fastens with a bolt,** porte qui se ferme au verrou; **the tool fastens into the socket,** l'outil se fixe dans la douille; (b) **the crab fastened on to his leg,** le crabe s'accrocha à sa jambe; **his opponent fastened on to his leg,** son adversaire s'agrippa, se cramponna, à sa jambe; *O:* **he fastened on me as an easy prey,** il s'attacha à moi, flairant un jobard; **to f. on a pretext,** saisir un prétexte.

II. (*compound verbs*) **1. fasten down,** *v.tr.* assujettir (qch. à terre, le couvercle d'une boîte); fixer (qch.) à terre ou en place.

2. fasten off, *v.tr. & i. Needlew:* **to f. off (the stitches),** arrêter le fil.

3. fasten up, *v.tr.* attacher (solidement); **to f. up a dog,** mettre un chien à la chaîne; **to f. up one's dress, etc.,** agrafer, boutonner, sa robe, etc.

fastener ['fɑːsnər], *s.* **1.** attache *f*; (*of garment*) agrafe *f*; (*of book, purse*) fermoir *m*; (*of window, etc.*) fermeture *f*; (*of French window*) espagnolette *f*, patte *f*; **door f.,** targette *f*; *Aut: O:* **bonnet f.,** attache-capot *m inv*; attache de capot; crochet *m*, tirette *f*, de fermeture; **zip f.,** fermeture à glissière, à crémaillère; *R.t.m:* fermeture éclair; **snap f.,** bouton (fermoir) à pression. **2.** *A:* mandat *m* d'arrêt (d'un débiteur).

fastening ['fɑːsniŋ], *s.* **1.** attache *f*; fixage *m*, fixation *f* (de qch. sur qch., d'un outil dans une douille, etc.); assujettissement *m* (d'une porte, etc.); liaison *f*, chevillage *m* (de pièces d'assemblage, etc.); ancrage *m* (d'un tirant, etc.); amarrage *m* (d'un bateau à un pieu, etc.); agrafage *m* (d'un vêtement, etc.); (*with bolts*) boulonnage *m*. **2.** = FASTENER 1; **fastenings,** attaches; *Mec.E: etc:* pièces *f* d'assemblage.

faster ['fɑːstər], *s.* jeûneur, -euse.

fasti ['fæstiː], *s.pl. Rom.Ant:* fastes *m*.

fastidious [fæ'stidiəs], *a.* difficile, délicat, exigeant (**about sth.,** sur qch.); dégoûté, difficile à contenter; **to be f.,** être difficile à contenter; faire le difficile, le délicat; **to be very f. in, about, one's dress,** être d'une coquetterie méticuleuse, avoir de la coquetterie (pour sa tenue); **to be f. about grammar,** être à cheval sur la grammaire.

fastidiously [fæs'tidiəsli], *adv.* d'un air de dégoût; avec une délicatesse exagérée; dédaigneusement.

fastidiousness [fæs'tidiəsnis], *s.* goût *m* difficile; délicatesse exagérée.

fastigiate [fæs'tidʒieit], *a. Bot:* fastigié.

fastigium [fæs'tidʒiəm], *s. Arch:* fastigium *m*.

fasting[1] ['fɑːstiŋ], *a.* (*of pers.*) à jeun; *Med:* **to be taken f.,** à prendre le matin à jeun.

fasting[2], *s.* **1.** jeûne *m*. **2.** diète *f*.

fast-moving ['fɑːst'muːviŋ], *a.* rapide; **f.-m. narrative,** récit *m* rapide, dont les événements se suivent de près.

fastness ['fɑːstnis], *s.* **1.** (a) fermeté *f*, stabilité *f* (d'un pieu, d'un nœud, etc.); solidité *f* (d'une couleur, etc.); (b) rapidité *f*, vitesse *f*; (c) liberté *f* d'allures, légèreté *f* de conduite (d'une jeune fille, etc.). **2.** *Lit:* forteresse *f*, place forte; repaire *m* (de voleurs, etc.).

fast-paced ['fɑːst'peist], *a. esp. U.S:* rapide.

fat[1] [fæt], *a.* (**fatter; fattest**) **1.** (a) (*of pers.*) gros, *f.* grosse; gras, *f.* grasse; corpulent; (*of animal, meat*) gras; (*of tissue*) adipeux; *F:* **as f. as a pig,** *O:* **as a monk,** gras à lard; gras comme un moine; **to get, grow, f.,** engraisser; devenir corpulent; prendre de l'embonpoint; **to grow f. at the expense of others,** s'engraisser aux dépens d'autrui; **f. laugh,** rire gras; **he gave a f. laugh,** il a ri gras; **f. volume,** gros tome; **f. wallet,** portefeuille bien garni; *U.S: Pol: P:* **f. cat,** richard *m* (qui donne beaucoup d'argent au parti); *P: A:* **to cut it fat,** (i) exagérer; (ii) faire de l'épate; (b) **f. stroke,** plein *m* (d'une lettre); *Typ:* **f. type,** caractères gras; *Paint:* **f. edge,** excès de couleur laissé sur une arête; *Aut:* **f. spark,** étincelle nourrie; (c) (*of clay, lime, etc.*) gras; **f. coal,** houille grasse, bitumineuse; (d) *Z:* **f. dormouse,** loir gris. **2.** (*of land*) riche, fertile, gras; *F:* **f. salary,** de gros appointements; **f. living,** prébende *f* qui rapporte gros; grasse prébende; *F:* **a f. lot of good that'll do you!** cela vous fera une belle jambe! **a f. lot of difference it makes to you!** pour ce que ça vous coûte! **a. f. lot you know about it!** comme si vous en saviez quelque chose!

fat[2], *s.* **1.** (a) graisse *f*; *Com:* **fats,** matières grasses; **animal, vegetable, f.,** graisse animale, végétale; **mutton f.,** suif *m* de mouton; *Cu:* **frying f.,** friture *f*; **leaf f.,** panne *f*; **to smell of burnt f.,** sentir le graillon; *F:* **the fat's in the fire!** le feu est aux poudres, au pot! le torchon brûle! (b) **f. metabolism,** métabolisme *m* lipidique, des lipides; (*of pers.*) **to put on f.,** engraisser; prendre de l'embonpoint. **2.** gras *m* (de viande); **green f.,** parties gélatineuses (d'une tortue); **to live off, on, the f. of the land,** vivre comme un coq en pâte, de tout ce qu'il y a de meilleur; vivre grassement; mener la vie de château; *P: A:* **a bit of f.,** une affaire pépère; un coup de chance; un peu de beurre dans les épinards.

fat[3], *v.tr. & i. Husb:* = FATTEN.

fatal ['feit(ə)l], *a.* **1.** fatal, -als; (a) (*of occurrence, necessity, etc.*) inévitable; **the f. hour,** l'heure fatale; l'heure de la mort; (b) (*of omen*) sinistre; **during that f. night,** pendant cette nuit fatale; (c) *Myth:* **the f. Sisters,** les déesses fatales; les Parques *f*; **the f. thread,** le fil de la vie; **the f. shears,** les fatals ciseaux; les ciseaux de la Parque; (d) (*of resolution, etc.*) **when the f. moment came,** au moment fatal. **2.** (a) mortel; **f. blow,** coup fatal, mortel; **f. accident,** accident mortel, fatalité *f*; **f. disease,** maladie mortelle, qui ne pardonne pas; (b) funeste (**to,** à); **f. decision,** décision *f* funeste; décision de malheur; **reef f. to navigation,** écueil fatal, funeste, à la navigation; **to have a f. effect on s.o.,** exercer une influence néfaste sur qn; **that was a f. mistake of yours,** vous avez commis là une faute capitale.

fatalism ['feitəlizm], *s.* fatalisme *m*.

fatalist ['feitəlist], *a. & s.* fataliste (*mf*).

fatalistic [feitə'listik], *a.* fataliste.

fatalistically [feitə'listik(ə)li], *adv.* avec fatalisme.

fatality [fə'tæliti], *s.* **1.** (*fate*) fatalité *f*; (i) destinée *f* inévitable; (ii) destin *m*. **2.** caractère *m* funeste, influence *f* néfaste (**of,** de). **3.** accident mortel; sinistre *m*; **there were no fatalities,** il n'y a pas eu de mort *f*; **bathing fatalities,** baignades tragiques.

fatally ['feitəli], *adv.* **1.** fatalement, inévitablement. **2.** mortellement (blessé, etc.).

fatback ['fætbæk], *s. Ich:* menhaden *m*.

fate [feit], *s.* destin *m*, sort *m*; fatalité *f*; (a) **stroke of f.,** coup *m* du destin, du sort; **pursued by f.,** poursuivi par la fatalité; *Lit:* **there is no striving against f.,** on ne lutte pas contre le sort, contre le destin; **f. wills it,** ainsi le veut le sort; *Myth;* **the Fates,** les Parques *f*; les Sœurs filandières; (b) **to leave s.o. to his f.,** abandonner qn à son sort; **his f. was already decided,** on avait déjà décidé de son sort; (c) **he went to his f. like a hero,** il alla à la mort en héros; **he met his f. in 1915,** il trouva la mort en 1915; *Hum: O:* **he has found his f.,** il a trouvé l'âme sœur.

fated ['feitid], *a.* **1.** (*of day, occurrence, etc.*) fatal, -als; inévitable. **2.** destiné, condamné (**to do sth.,** à faire qch.); **f. to fail,** voué à l'échec; **I'm f. not to get there,** il est écrit que je ne peux pas y aller. **3.** voué à la destruction; condamné.

fateful ['feitful], *a.* **1.** (voix *f*, etc.) prophétique; **f. word,** parole *f* fatidique; **to pronounce the f. words,** prononcer les paroles sacramentelles. **2.** (jour, etc.) décisif, fatal, -als; **every minute was f.,** chaque minute était capable de décider de notre sort. **3.** (événement, etc.) fatal, inévitable.

fathead ['fæthed], *s. F:* imbécile *mf*; gourde *f*, citrouille *f*, cruche *f*, buse *f*, andouille *f*; bêta *m*; (**you**) **f.!** espèce d'imbécile! **what a f.!** quelle andouille!

fatheaded ['fæt'hedid], *a.* **1.** *Z:* à grosse tête. **2.** *F:* imbécile; à l'esprit bouché; sot, sotte; bête; **that f. idiot,** cette espèce d'imbécile.

father[1] ['fɑːðər], *s.* **1.** père *m*; **he is the f. of a family,** il est père de famille; c'est un père de famille; **from f. to son,** de père en fils; **they have been directors of the concern, f. and son, for a hundred years,** ils dirigent l'entreprise de père en fils depuis un siècle; **he's his father's son,** c'est bien le fils de son père; **on the father's side,** du côté paternel; **like a f.,** paternellement, en père; *F:* **to talk to s.o. like a f.,** sermonner qn; **yes, F.,** oui, (mon) père; oui, papa; **Father's day,** fête *f* des pères; *Th:* **heavy f.,** père noble; **to play heavy fathers,** tenir l'emploi de père noble; **heavy f. tone, air,** ton *m*, air *m*, paterne; *Prov:* **the child is f. of the man,** l'homme est en germe dans l'enfant; **like f. like son,** tel père tel fils; bon chien chasse de race; **F. Tiber,** le dieu Tibre; **F. Christmas,** le père Noël; *F:* **we had the f. and mother of a row,** nous avons eu une de ces empoignades! **he had the f. and mother of a cold,** il a eu un de ces rhumes! **2.** *pl.* **our fathers,** nos ancêtres *m*, nos aïeux *m*, nos pères. **3.** (a) père, fondateur *m*, créateur *m* (d'une science, d'un art, etc.); *Lit:* **the F. of Lies,** le père du mensonge; (b) **the Fathers of the Church,** les Pères de l'Église. **4.** *Theol:* **God the F.,** Dieu le Père; **Our F. which, who, art in Heaven,** notre Père qui es aux cieux; **the F., the Son, and the Holy Ghost,** le Père, le Fils et le Saint-Esprit. **5.** *Ecc:* (a) **the Holy F., the F. of the Faithful,** le Saint-Père, le père des fidèles; **F. confessor,** père spirituel, directeur *m* (de conscience); (b) **Father Martin,** (i) (*belonging to a monastic order*) le Père Martin; (ii) (*a priest*) l'abbé Martin; (*in address*) **Yes, F.,** (i) oui, mon Père; (ii) oui, monsieur l'Abbé; **a Carmelite f.,** un père carme; **the Capuchin fathers,** les pères capucins. **6.** doyen *m* (d'une société, de la Chambre, etc.); **the City Fathers,** (i) *Rom.Hist:* les Édiles *m*; (ii) *Hist: & NAm:* le conseil municipal; *Typ: etc:* **f. of the chapel,** chef *m* de l'atelier. **7.** (*in translation from Russian*) **little f.,** petit-père *m*.

father[2], *v.tr.* **1.** engendrer (un enfant); inventer, produire (qch.); concevoir (un projet). **2.** adopter (un enfant); servir de père à (un enfant, une tribu, etc.). **3.** avouer la paternité (d'un enfant, d'un livre, etc.). **4. to f. a child, a book, etc. on s.o.,** attribuer à qn la paternité d'un enfant, d'un livre, etc.

fatherhood ['fɑːðəhud], *s.* **1.** paternité *f*. **2.** doyenneté *f*.

fathering ['fɑːðəriŋ], *s.* **1.** engendrement *m* (d'un enfant). **2.** adoption *f* (d'un enfant).

father-in-law, *pl.* **fathers-in-law** ['fɑːðərinlɔː, 'fɑːðəzinlɔː], *s.m.* beau-père, *pl.* beaux-pères.

fatherland ['fɑːðəlænd], *s.* patrie *f*; **the f.,** la terre des ancêtres.

fatherless ['fɑːðəlis], *a.* sans père; *Adm: Jur:* orphelin, -ine, de père.

fatherlike ['fɑːðəlaik], *a.* paternel.

fatherly ['fɑːðəli]. **1.** *a.* (*of pers., tone, manner, etc.*) paternel; **to behave in a f. fashion towards s.o., to treat s.o. in a f. way,** se montrer paternel pour qn; être un père pour qn. **2.** *adv.* comme un père; en père.

fathership ['fɑːðəʃip], *s. esp. Parl:* doyenneté *f.*

fathogram ['fæðougræm], *s.* fathogramme *m.*

fathom[1] ['fæðəm], *s. Meas:* **1.** *Nau:* brasse *f* (= 6 feet = 1 m. 829); **depth in fathoms,** brassiage *m*; sondage *m*; (*often inv. in expressing measurements*) **harbour 4 f. deep,** port *m* avec un brassiage de 7 mètres. **2.** *Com:* (*in timber trade*) mesure *f* de 216 pieds cubes (6′ × 6′ × 6′). **3.** *Min:* unité *f* de face de taille de 6 × 6 pieds carrés; toise *f.*

fathom[2], *v.tr.* **1.** *Nau:* sonder; **to f. a chasm,** trouver le fond d'un abîme; **to f. the mystery,** approfondir, pénétrer, sonder, le mystère; **I can't f. him,** je ne le comprends pas. **2.** *A:* entourer (qch.) avec les bras; embrasser, étreindre.

fathoming ['fæðəmiŋ], *s.* **1.** *Nau:* brassiage *m*, sondage *m.* **2.** approfondissement *m* (d'un problème); pénétration *f* (d'un mystère).

fathomless ['fæðəmlis], *a.* **1.** (abîme *m*) sans fond, insondable; (gouffre) abismal, -aux. **2.** (*of mystery, etc.*) incompréhensible, impénétrable.

fatidic(al) [fei'tidik(l)], *a.* fatidique.

fatigability [fætigə'biliti], *s.* fatigabilité *f.*

fatigue[1] [fə'tiːg], *s.* **1.** (*a*) fatigue *f*; **nervous, mental, f.,** fatigue nerveuse, cérébrale; *Med:* **f. syndrome, combat f.,** psychose *f* traumatique; **to have reached f. limit,** être à la limite d'endurance; **to be dropping with f.,** tomber de fatigue, de lassitude; (*b*) *Tchn:* **metal f.,** fatigue des métaux; fragilisation *f*; **f. failure,** défaillance due à la fatigue, rupture *f* par fatigue; **acoustic f.,** fatigue acoustique; *Rail:* **track f.,** fatigue de la voie. **2.** *Mil:* **f. (duty),** corvée *f*; **barrack f.,** corvée de casernement, de quartier; **cookhouse f.,** corvée de cuisine(s), d'ordinaire; **extra f.,** fatigue supplémentaire; **to detail, tell off, a man for f. duty,** désigner un homme de corvée; **to have extra f.,** être puni de corvée; **f. man,** homme *m* de corvée; **f. party,** (détachement *m* de) fatigue; **f. dress,** tenue *f* de corvée; (jeu *m* de) treillis *m*; *A:* **f. coat,** bourgeron *m*; *A:* **f. cap,** bonnet *m* de police.

fatigue[2], *v.tr.* **1.** fatiguer, lasser (qn); travailler (un cheval); **to f. oneself doing sth.,** se fatiguer à faire qch. **2.** *Tchn:* fatiguer (un métal, un mât, etc.); *Rail:* **traffic that fatigues the track,** circulation *f* qui fatigue la voie.

fatiguing [fə'tiːgiŋ], *a.* fatigant, épuisant.

Fatima ['fætimə], *Pr.n.f. Hist:* Fatime, Fatima, Fathma.

Fatimid ['fætimid], **Fatimite** ['fætimait], *a. & s. Hist:* Fatimite (*m*), Fatimide (*m*).

fatless ['fætlis], *a.* (*of meat*) maigre; sans gras.

fatling ['fætliŋ], *s. Husb:* jeune bête à l'engrais.

fatness ['fætnis], *s.* **1.** adiposité *f* (de la chair, etc.); embonpoint *m*, corpulence *f* (de qn). **2.** *A:* graisse *f*, fertilité *f* (de la terre). **3.** onctuosité *f* (d'un corps gras, de l'argile).

fat-reducing ['fætri'djuːsiŋ], *a.* (régime, etc.) amaigrissant, obésifuge.

fat-soluble ['fæt'sɔljubl], *a.* lipsosoluble.

fatted ['fætid], *a.* (*a*) *A:* engraissé; (*b*) **to kill the f. calf,** tuer le veau gras; faire fête à qn.

fatten ['fæt(ə)n]. **1.** *v.tr.* (*a*) **to f. (up),** engraisser (des moutons, des veaux, etc.); empâter (de la volaille); (*b*) engraisser, fertiliser, enrichir (le sol). **2.** *v.i.* engraisser; devenir gras; **to put calves, etc., to f.,** mettre des veaux, etc., à l'engrais; **to f. on sth.,** s'engraisser, s'enrichir, de qch.

fattener ['fæt(ə)nər], *s.* **1.** (*pers.*) *Husb:* engraisseur, -euse (d'animaux). **2.** aliment engraissant.

fattening[1] ['fæt(ə)niŋ], *a.* (*of food, etc.*) qui fait grossir.

fattening[2], *s. Husb:* engraissement *m*, engraissage *m*; empâtement *m.*

fattish ['fætiʃ], *a.* grassouillet; un peu gras; dodu.

fatty ['fæti]. **1.** *a.* (*a*) (*of matter, deposit, etc.*) graisseux, onctueux, oléagineux; **f. foods,** aliments gras; (*b*) (*of soil, etc.*) gras; **f. clay,** argile grasse, plastique; **f. oil,** huile *f* fixe; *Ch:* **f. acid,** acide gras; **f. series,** série grasse; (*c*) (*of tissue, membrane, etc.*) adipeux; *Med: F:* **f. heart, kidneys,** dégénérescence graisseuse du cœur, des reins. **2.** *s. F:* gros enfant; grosse personne; gros bonhomme, patapouf *m*; **hi, f.!** ohé, mon gros!

fatuity [fæ'tjuːiti], *s.* sottise *f*; imbécillité *f* (d'une observation); **the f. of youth,** l'aveuglement *m* de la jeunesse.

fatuous ['fætjuəs], *a.* sot, imbécile, idiot; **f. smile,** sourire béat.

fatuously ['fætjuəsli], *adv.* sottement; d'un air imbécile, idiot.

fatuousness ['fætjuəsnis], *s.* = FATUITY.

faucal ['fɔːk(ə)l]. *Ling:* **1.** *a.* (son) guttural vélaire, *pl.* gutturaux vélaires. **2.** *s.* (une) gutturale vélaire.

fauces ['fɔːsiːz], *s.pl. Anat:* fosse gutturale; gosier *m.*

faucet ['fɔːsit], *s.* **1.** (*a*) *Brew:* fausset *m*, cannelle *f*, cannette *f* (de tonneau); (*b*) *NAm:* robinet *m.* **2.** *NAm:* douille *f* (d'un tuyau); **f. joint,** assemblage *m* à emboîtement; joint *m* à douille, à emboîture; **f. pipe,** boisseau *m.*

fauchard ['fouʃɑː], *s. A.Arms:* fauchard *m.*

faucre ['foukər], *s. A.Arms:* faucre *m*, fautre *m.*

faugh [fɔː], *int.* pouah!

faujasite ['fauʒəsait, -zait], *s. Miner:* faujasite *f.*

fault[1] [fɔːlt], *s.* **1.** (*a*) défaut *m*, travers *m* (de qn); imperfection *f*; défectuosité *f*; **to shut one's eyes to s.o.'s faults,** fermer les yeux sur les défauts de qn; **in spite of all his faults,** malgré tous ses travers; **his f. is excessive shyness,** il pèche par trop de timidité; **scrupulous to a f.,** scrupuleux à l'excès; **to buy a horse, a car, with all its faults,** acheter un cheval sans garantie de vices; acheter une voiture telle quelle; **to find a f. in sth.,** trouver un défaut à qch.; **to find f. with s.o.,** trouver à redire contre qn; reprendre, critiquer, qn; faire des observations à qn; se plaindre de qn; **to find f. with sth.,** trouver à redire à qch.; se plaindre de qch.; *F:* épiloguer, gloser, sur (la conduite de qn, etc.); **I have no f. to find with him; I can find no f. with him,** je ne trouve rien, je n'ai rien, à lui reprocher; **she is always finding f.,** elle trouve toujours à redire; elle n'est jamais contente; **people are always finding f. with me,** on me cherche noise à tout propos; (*b*) *Tchn:* défaut, imperfection; incident *m* technique, panne *f*; vice *f* (de construction); *Lap:* crapaud *m*, défaut; *Metall:* paille *f*; **f. in the construction of a machine,** défaut, vice, de construction d'une machine; **f. current,** (i) *El:* fuites *f*; à la terre; (ii) *Tg:* courant *m* de fuite, de défaut; **to look for a f. in the insulation of a cable,** chercher un défaut d'isolement dans un câble; *El: Mec.E:* **f. tracing, locating, localizing, localization,** (i) dépannage *m*; (ii) recherche *f*, localisation *f*, des défauts, des dérangements, des fuites, des pannes; **f.-locating bridge,** pont *m* de dépannage; **f. detector,** (i) déceleur *m*, détecteur *m*, de fuites; indicateur *m* des pertes à la terre; (ii) (*pers.*) (*also* **f. tracer**) dépanneur *m.* **2.** (*a*) faute *f*; **to commit a f.,** commettre une faute; **to be in f., at f.,** être en défaut; être fautif, coupable; **to find, catch, s.o. at f.,** trouver, prendre, qn en faute; *Jur:* **the party at f. in an accident,** l'auteur *m* d'un accident; **the argument is at f.,** l'argument pèche; **whose f. is it?** à qui la faute? **it is her f.,** c'est de sa faute, c'est elle qui en est cause; **it is your own f. that you do not succeed,** c'est de votre faute si vous ne réussissez pas; **I am afraid it was my f.,** je crains bien que ce ne soit de ma faute; **it is nobody's f. but your own,** il ne faut vous en prendre qu'à vous-même; **through no f. of mine,** sans que je sois en cause; **that is the f. of his education,** cela tient à son éducation; (*b*) **spelling f.,** faute d'orthographe. **3.** *Ten:* faute; **double f.,** double faute; **foot f.,** faute de pied. **4.** *Ven:* (*of hounds*) **to bark at f.,** aboyer à faux; **to be at f.,** être en défaut; **their instinct is never at f.,** leur instinct n'est jamais en défaut; **to be at f. for an answer,** être embarrassé pour répondre. **5.** *Geol:* faille *f*; géoclase *f*; paraclase *f*; *Min:* barle *f*; **step f.,** faille à gradins; **trough f.,** fosse *f* d'effondrement; **distributive f.,** faille en gradins, en escalier; **transverse f.,** décrochement *m*; **pivotal f.,** faille à charnière; **reverse(d), overlap, f.,** faille inverse; **dip f.,** faille de plongement; **upthrow f., thrust f.,** faille de chevauchement; **downthrow f.,** faille d'effondrement; **strike lip f.,** faille horizontale de décrochement; **lateral shearing f.,** faille à rejet horizontale; **collapsed f.,** faille serrée; **rejuvenated f.,** faille rajeunie; **f. line,** ligne *f* de faille; **f. plane,** plan *m* de faille; **f. scarp,** escarpement *m* de faille.

fault[2]. **1.** *v.tr.* (*a*) prendre (qn) en défaut; trouver un défaut dans (qch.); (*b*) *Geol:* disloquer (les couches); **faulted monocline,** flexure faillée; **faulted anticline,** pli-faille *m.* **2.** *v.i. Geol:* (*of strata*) se disloquer.

faulted ['fɔːltid], *a. Geol:* faillé.

faultfinder ['fɔːltfaindər], *s.* **1.** (*pers.*) (*a*) critiqueur, -euse; censeur, -euse; mécontent, -ente; sermonneur, -euse; (*b*) *El: Mec.E: etc:* dépanneur *m.* **2.** *El: etc:* (*device*) décleur *m*, détecteur *m*, de fuites, etc.; indicateur *m* de pertes à la terre.

faultfinding[1] ['fɔːltfaindiŋ], *a.* censeur, -euse; grondeur, -euse; chicanier, -ière; sermonneur, -euse; **f. attitude,** attitude critique.

faultfinding[2], *s.* **1.** disposition *f* à critiquer, à se plaindre; critique *f*; censure *f.* **2.** *El: Mec.E: etc:* (i) dépannage *m*; (ii) recherche *f*, localisation *f*, des défauts, des fuites, des pannes, des erreurs.

faultily ['fɔːltili], *adv.* fautivement, défectueusement, incorrectement.

faultiness ['fɔːltinis], *s.* incorrection *f* (de style, etc.); défectuosité *f*, imperfection *f* (d'un travail, etc.).

faultless ['fɔːltlis], *a.* (*of work, etc.*) sans défaut, sans faute; parfait; (*of dress, conduct, etc.*) impeccable, irréprochable; **to be f.,** avoir toutes les perfections.

faultlessly ['fɔːltlisli], *adv.* parfaitement, irréprochablement; d'une manière impeccable; **f. dressed,** d'une mise impeccable.

faultlessness ['fɔːltlisnis], *s.* perfection *f*; impeccabilité *f.*

faulty ['fɔːlti], *a.* (*of work, etc.*) défectueux, imparfait; (*of style, etc.*) incorrect; (*of reasoning, etc.*) erroné, inexact; **f. plumbing,** installation sanitaire défectueuse; **f. workmanship,** mauvaise construction; mauvaise façon, vice *m* de construction; défaut *m* d'exécution; malfaçon *f*; **f. article,** article mal fait, défectueux; **f. expression,** locution vicieuse; **f. articulation,** défaut *m*, vice *m*, de prononciation; *Gram:* **f. construction of a sentence,** construction vicieuse d'une phrase; **f. drafting (of document),** rédaction vicieuse; **the insulation, etc., is f.,** il y a un défaut (d'isolement, etc.); *El:* **f. circuit, f. line,** circuit *m*, ligne *f*, en dérangement; *Elcs:* **f. selection,** sélection déformée.

faun [fɔːn], *s. Myth:* faune *m.*

fauna ['fɔːnə], *s.* faune *f* (d'une région, d'un pays).

faunal ['fɔːn(ə)l], **faunistic** [fɔː'nistik], *a.* faunistique.

faunist ['fɔːnist], *s.* zoogéographe *mf.*

Faustina [fɔːs'tainə], *Pr.n.f. Rom.Hist:* Faustine.

Fauve [fouv], *s. Art:* fauve *m.*

Fauvism ['fouvizm], *s. Art:* fauvisme *m.*

Fauvist ['fouvist], *s. Art:* fauve *m.*

faux pas ['fou'pɑː], *s.* faux pas, gaffe *f.*

favella [fæ'velə], *s. Algae:* favelle *f.*

favellidium [fæve'lidiəm], *s. Algae:* favellidie *f.*

faveolate [fə'viəleit], *a. Nat.Hist:* favéolé; en nid d'abeilles.

faveolus, *pl.* **-li** [fævi'ouləs, -lai], *s. Nat.Hist:* favéole *f*; alvéole *m or f.*

faverolle ['fævərəl], *s. Husb:* coq *m*, poule *f*, de Faverolles; un, une, faverolles.

faviform ['feivifɔːm, 'fævi-], *a. Nat.Hist:* faviforme.

favism ['feivizm], *s. Med:* favisme *m.*

favose ['feivous], *a. Med:* faveux.

favosite ['fævousait], *s. Paleont:* favosite *f.*

Favositidae [fævou'saitidiː], *s.pl. Paleont:* favositidés *m.*

favour[1] ['feivər], *s.* **1.** faveur *f*, approbation *f*, bonnes grâces; **to find f. with s.o., in s.o.'s eyes; to gain s.o.'s f.,** gagner la faveur de qn; se faire aimer de qn; se faire bien voir de qn; trouver grâce auprès de qn, devant qn, aux yeux de qn; **to be in f. with s.o.,** être en faveur auprès de qn; jouir de la faveur de qn; être dans les bonnes grâces de qn; **to be in high f. with s.o., to stand high in s.o.'s f.,** être bien vu, bien vue, de qn; **to be in high f. at court,** être en grande faveur à la cour; **to rise, grow, in f. with s.o.,** monter en faveur auprès de qn; **to be restored, to return, to f.,** rentrer en grâce; **to be out of f.,** être disgracié; être mal en cour; **to fall out of f. with s.o.,** perdre les bonnes grâces de qn; **this fashion is out of f.,** cette mode est passée; **the government has fallen out of f.,** le gouvernement a perdu la faveur du public; **to look with f. on sth.,** approuver qch.; **to bring sth. into f.,** mettre qch. à la mode. **2.** grâce *f*, bonté *f*; **to ask a f. of s.o.,** solliciter une grâce, une faveur, de qn; demander une faveur à qn; **I ask you as a special f. to . . .,** je vous demande en grâce de . . .; **I should consider it a f. if you would . . .,** je considérerais comme une faveur que vous vouliez bien . . .; **to do s.o. a f.,** faire une faveur, une grâce, une gracieuseté, à qn; obliger qn; **they request the f. of your company to dinner,** ils vous prient de leur faire le plaisir de dîner avec eux; **will you do me a f.?** voulez-vous me faire plaisir? **do me the f. of . . .,** faites-moi le plaisir de, l'amitié de . . .; **will you do me a great f.?** voulez-vous me rendre un grand service? *Journ: A:* **for f. of publication in your columns,** prière d'insérer; **to lavish one's favours on s.o., to load s.o. with favours,** être prodigue de ses faveurs envers qn; combler qn de faveurs; *A:* (*of woman*) **to bestow her favours upon a man,** accorder ses faveurs à un homme; **as a f.,** à titre gracieux; *A:* **by your f., under f.,** avec votre permission, ne vous en déplaise; *Com: A:* **your f. of the 15th,** votre lettre, votre honorée, votre estimée, du 15; **thank you for your past favours,** nous vous remercions des marques de confiance dont vous nous avez honorés, de la confiance que vous avez bien voulu nous accorder. **3.** (*a*) partialité *f*, préférence *f*; traitement *m* de faveur; **to show f. towards s.o.,** favoriser qn; accorder une préférence à qn; accorder à qn un traitement de faveur; **to administer justice without fear or f.,** rendre la justice sans distinction de personnes; *Prov:* **kissing goes by f.,** (i) n'embrasse pas qui veut; (ii) aux jolis minois les baisers; (*b*) *A: & Lit:* appui *m*, protection *f*; **under f. of the night,** à la faveur de la nuit. **4.** *prep.phr.* **in f. of. . .,** en faveur de . . .; à l'avantage de . . .; **to write out a cheque in s.o.'s f.,** souscrire un chèque en faveur, au profit, de qn; **to speak in s.o.'s f.,** parler en faveur de qn, pour qn, à l'avantage de qn; **the tide has set in his f.,** ses actions remontent; **the business turned in my f.,** l'affaire a tourné à mon avantage; **to have everything in one's f.,** avoir tout pour soi; avoir vent et marée; **to decide in f. of s.o., in s.o.'s f.,** donner gain de cause à qn; donner raison à qn; **to be in f. of sth.,** être partisan de qch.; tenir pour qch.; préconiser qch.; **I am in f. of the proposal,** je suis pour la proposition; **I'm in f. of it!** moi, je suis pour! **5.** faveur *f*, cocarde *f*; nœud *m* de ruban. **6.** *A:* traits *mpl*, visage *m*.

favour[2], *v.tr.* **1.** approuver, préférer, aimer (qch.); accorder une préférence à (qn); **which colour do you f.?** quelle couleur préférez-vous? **to f. a scheme,** se prêter à un projet; approuver un projet; être pour un projet; **I don't f. the idea,** l'idée ne me plaît pas, ne me sourit pas. **2.** gratifier, obliger, favoriser (qn); accorder une grâce à (qn); **to f. s.o. with an interview,** accorder un rendez-vous à qn; **to f. s.o. with a smile,** gratifier, favoriser, qn d'un sourire; *Com: O: Lit:* **to be favoured with an order,** être honoré d'une commande; **he favoured us with his company,** il nous fit l'honneur de nous accompagner, de se joindre à nous, d'être des nôtres. **3.** (*a*) avantager (qn); montrer de la partialité pour (qn); **you are favouring him too much, unduly,** vous lui faites la part trop belle; **you are already greatly favoured,** vous êtes déjà fort avantagé; (*b*) faciliter (qch.); **the weather favoured our departure,** le temps a favorisé, facilité, notre départ; **favoured by fortune,** secondé par le sort; **to be favoured by circumstances,** avoir les circonstances en sa faveur; avoir vent et marée; avoir le vent en poupe. **4.** (*a*) (*of fact, etc.*) confirmer (un rapport); soutenir (une théorie, etc.); (*b*) *O:* **every indication favoured rain,** toutes les indications étaient à la pluie. **5.** *O:* ressembler à (qn); **he favours his father,** il tient de, ressemble à, son père. **6.** *F: & Dial:* ménager, épargner; *Vet:* **horse that favours one leg,** cheval *m* qui ménage un pied, qui y va doucement d'un pied, qui feint d'un pied.

favourable ['feivərəbl], *a.* favorable; (*of weather, wind, etc.*) propice; (*of reception, etc.*) bienveillant; (*of terms, circumstances, etc.*) bon, avantageux; (*of a report, etc.*) bon, rassurant; **to look on s.o. with a f. eye,** regarder qn d'un œil favorable; **in a f. light,** sous un jour favorable; **a f. star,** un astre favorable, bénin; une bonne étoile; **f. winds,** vents favorables, amis; *Com:* **on f. terms,** à bon compte; **the patient's condition is f.,** la condition du malade est satisfaisante.

favourableness ['feivərəblnis], *s.* caractère *m* favorable (du temps, d'un rapport, etc.).

favourably ['feivərəbli], *adv.* favorablement, avantageusement; **to look f. on s.o.,** regarder qn d'un œil favorable; **he spoke very f. of you,** il m'a parlé de vous en très bons termes; **to progress f.,** faire des progrès satisfaisants.

favoured ['feivəd], *a.* (*of pers.*) **1.** favorisé, avantagé; **the most-f.-nation clause,** la clause de la nation la plus favorisée; **the f. few,** les élus (du patron, etc.). **2.** *O:* (*of pers.*) **well-f.,** beau, *f.* belle; de bonne mine, bien fait; **ill-f.,** laid, de mauvaise mine.

favouring ['feivəriŋ], *a.* (*of wind, circumstance*) favorable.

favourite ['feiv(ə)rit]. **1.** *s.* favori, *f.* favorite; (*a*) **to be a f. with, of, s.o.; to be s.o.'s f.,** être aimé de qn; être bien vu(e) de qn; **the youngest daughter is his f.,** c'est la plus jeune qui est sa préférée; **you are a great f. with the public,** vous êtes dans les bonnes grâces du public; vous êtes l'enfant gâté du public; **as a speaker he is a great f.,** comme orateur il est très couru; **he is a universal f.,** tout le monde l'aime; **everybody's f.,** le chéri de tout le monde; *Rac:* **to back the f.,** jouer le favori; **the favourites and the second favourites,** les favoris et les sous-favoris; (*b*) **the favourites of the prince,** les favoris, les favorites, du prince. **2.** *a.* (fils, auteur, etc.) favori, préféré; **my f. opera,** mon opéra de prédilection; **f. event,** réunion (sportive) très courue.

favouritism ['feiv(ə)ritizm], *s.* favoritisme *m*, *F:* la cote d'amour; **he owes his promotion to f.,** il doit son avancement à la faveur, *F:* au piston; *F:* il a été pistonné.

favus ['feivəs], *s. Med: Vet:* favus *m*; teigne faveuse; teigne des oiseaux.

fawn[1] [fɔːn], *s.* **1.** *Z:* faon *m*; daneau, -eaux; **doe in f.,** daine pleine; daine grosse de son faon. **2. f. (colour),** couleur *f* fauve; *a.* **f.(-coloured),** fauve.

fawn[2]. **1.** *v.tr.* (*of doe*) mettre bas (un faon). **2.** *v.i.* (*of doe*) faonner; mettre bas.

fawn[3], *v.ind.tr.* **to f. on s.o.,** (i) (*of dog*) caresser qn. faire des caresses à qn; se coucher devant qn; (ii) (*of pers.*) aduler qn; faire le chien couchant, le plat valet, auprès de qn; lécher les bottes à qn; ramper, courber l'échine, devant qn; *F:* chatouiller l'épiderme à qn; **to f. and cringe,** faire des platitudes.

fawner ['fɔːnər], *s.* adulateur, -trice; flagorneur, -euse; **fawners upon the great,** les adulateurs des grands.

fawning[1] ['fɔːniŋ], *s. Z:* mise *f* bas (d'un faon).

fawning[2], *a.* (*of dog*) caressant; qui fait des caresses (à son maître, etc.); (*of pers.*) adulateur, -trice; servile; flagorneur, -euse.

fawning[3], *s.* adulation *f*; flagornerie *f*; servilité *f*.

fawningly ['fɔːniŋli], *adv.* (*of dog*) d'une manière caressante; (*of pers.*) servilement.

fay[1] [fei], *s. A: & Lit:* fée *f*.

fay[2]. **1.** *v.tr. N.Arch: etc:* affleurer (deux planches, etc.). **2.** *v.i.* (*of planks, etc.*) affleurer; *U.S:* (*of thg*) **to f. in with sth.,** s'accorder avec qch.

fayalite ['feiəlait], *s. Miner:* fayalite *f*.

faying ['feiiŋ], *s. N.Arch:* affleurement *m*.

Fayum [fa'juːm], *Pr.n. Geog:* le Fayoum.

faze [feiz], *v.tr. NAm: F:* (*usu. in neg.*) agiter, bouleverser (qn); **nothing fazes him,** rien ne le bouleverse, ne le dérange.

fealty ['fiəlti], *s. Hist:* féauté *f*; fidélité *f*; **taking of oath of f. accompanied by act of homage,** prestation *f* de foi et hommage.

fear[1] ['fiər], *s.* **1.** crainte *f*, peur *f*; appréhension *f*; **a sudden f.,** une frayeur, une alarme; **deadly f.,** effroi *m*; *Lit:* **have no f.,** ne craignez rien! n'ayez pas peur! **to be overcome by, with, f.,** être en proie à la frayeur, à la terreur; **wild with f.,** fou de terreur; **overcome by f. he ran and hid,** effrayé il courut se cacher; **to do sth. through f.,** faire qch. par peur; **to be, stand, go, in f. of s.o., of sth.,** avoir peur de, redouter, craindre, qn, qch.; trembler devant qn; **to stand in great f. of dismissal,** avoir grand-peur d'être renvoyé; **she was in deadly f. of being discovered,** elle tremblait qu'on (ne) la découvrît; **to go in f. of one's life,** craindre pour sa vie; se sentir sous le coup d'une menace perpétuelle; **for f. of making a mistake,** de crainte d'erreur, de crainte de se tromper; **for f. we should forget,** de peur que nous (n') oubliions; **I dare not speak for f. he may hear,** je n'ose pas parler de crainte, de peur, qu'il n'entende; **to have fears for s.o., for s.o.'s safety, future,** craindre pour qn; avoir des inquiétudes au sujet de qn; **there is no f. of losing it,** il n'y a pas de danger de le perdre; **there is no f. that he will come back, of his coming back,** il n'y a pas de danger, il n'y a pas à craindre, qu'il revienne; *F:* **no f.!** pas de danger (que je le fasse, etc.)! jamais de la vie! **no f. of my going!** plus souvent que j'irais! **2.** respect *m*, crainte (de Dieu, des lois, etc.); **he had a wholesome f. of punishment,** le châtiment lui inspirait une crainte salutaire; *F:* **to put the f. of God into s.o.,** faire à qn une semonce dont il se souviendra longtemps; faire trembler qn dans ses bottes; **he had had the f. of God put into him,** il n'en menait pas large.

fear[2], *v.tr.* **1.** craindre, avoir peur de, redouter (qn, qch.); **he is a man to be feared,** c'est un homme à redouter; **these animals are not greatly to be feared,** ces animaux ne sont pas autrement formidables; **I f. to speak in his presence,** j'ai peur, je crains, de parler en sa présence. **2.** (*a*) appréhender, craindre (un événement); **to f. for s.o., sth.,** s'inquiéter au sujet de qn, de qch.; **I f.,** *A:* **I f. me, it is too late,** j'ai peur, je crains, qu'il ne soit trop tard; **it is to be feared that . . .,** il est à craindre que (+ ne) + *sub.*; **she feared she would be discovered,** elle craignait d'être découverte; **I f. he will not come,** je crains qu'il ne vienne pas; **we need not f. that anything will go wrong,** nous n'avons pas à craindre que tout n'aille pas bien; *O:* **never f.! don't f.!** pas de danger! soyez tranquille! soyez sans crainte! n'ayez pas peur! (*b*) **I f. he's out,** je crois qu'il n'y est pas; **I f. I'm late,** je crois bien être en retard; **I f. I don't know,** je le regrette, mais je ne sais pas. **3.** respecter, craindre (Dieu, la loi, etc.); révérer (Dieu).

feared ['fiəd], *a.* (*of pers., event, etc.*) redouté.

fearful ['fiəful], *a.* **1.** (*of spectacle, noise, etc.*) affreux, effrayant, redoutable; **consequences f. to contemplate,** conséquences *f* formidables, terribles, à envisager; *F:* **a f. mess,** un désordre effrayant, formidable; une pagaïe terrible; **we're in a f. muddle,** nous ne savons où donner de la tête. **2.** (*of pers.*) (*a*) peureux, craintif, timide; (*b*) **f. of . . .,** qui craint de . . .; **I was f. of waking him up,** je tremblais de le réveiller; (*c*) inspiré par une crainte salutaire, respectueuse.

fearfully ['fiəfuli], *adv.* **1.** affreusement, terriblement; **it's f. hot!** il fait terriblement chaud! **2.** peureusement, craintivement, timidement.

fearfulness ['fiəfulnis], *s.* **1.** caractère épouvantable, terrifiant, terrible (de qch.). **2.** crainte *f*, timidité *f*; appréhension *f*.

fearless ['fiəlis], *a.* intrépide, courageux; sans peur (**of,** de); **he was f. of danger,** il ne reculait devant aucun danger; **he is f. of the future,** il est sans appréhensions pour l'avenir.

fearlessly ['fiəlisli], *adv.* intrépidement, courageusement; avec intrépidité; **to do sth. f.,** faire qch. sans peur, sans hésitation.

fearlessness ['fiəlisnis], *s.* intrépidité *f*, courage *m*; **his f. in attack,** son intrépidité à attaquer; sa bravoure dans l'attaque.

fearnought ['fiənɔːt], *s. Tex: Nau:* frise *f*.

fearsome ['fiəsəm], *a.* **1.** effrayant, redoutable, terrifiant. **2.** *Dial:* craintif, timide.

fearsomeness ['fiəsəmnis], *s.* = FEARFULNESS 1.

feasant ['fiːz(ə)nt], *a. Jur:* **cattle damage f.,** bétail trouvé en dommage.

feasibility [fiːzə'biliti], **feasibleness** ['fiːzəbəlnis], *s.* **1.** praticabilité *f*, possibilité *f* (d'une théorie, etc.). **2.** plausibilité *f*, vraisemblance *f* (d'une histoire, etc.). **3.** faisabilité *f* (d'un projet, etc.).

feasible ['fiːzəbl], *a.* **1.** (*of design, etc.*) faisable, possible, réalisable, exécutable, entreprenable, praticable. **2.** (*of story, theory, etc.*) vraisemblable, probable.

feast[1] [fiːst], *s.* **1.** *Ecc: etc:* **f. (day),** (jour *m* de) fête *f*; **movable f.,** fête mobile; **immovable f.,** fête fixe. **2.** festin *m*, banquet *m*, régal *m*, -als; **to make a f.,** donner un festin; **to make a f. of sth.,** se régaler de qch.

feast[2], **1.** *v.i.* faire festin; festoyer, banqueter, se régaler; faire bonne chère; **to f. (up)on sth.,** se régaler de qch. **2.** *v.tr.* (*a*) régaler, fêter (qn); **to f. one's eyes on sth.,** repaître ses yeux de qch.; regarder qch. avec délice; rassasier son regard à contempler qch.; **I feasted my eyes on the landscape,** je contemplais ce paysage avec délice(s); (*b*) **to f. the night away,** passer la nuit à festoyer.

feasting ['fiːstiŋ], *s.* festoiement *m*, bonne chère.

feat[1] [fiːt], *s.* **1.** exploit *m*, haut fait; **f. of arms,** fait d'armes; **brilliant f. of arms,** action *f* d'éclat; **to perform feats of valour,** faire des prouesses *f*; **a fine f., indeed!** voilà une belle prouesse! **2.** (*a*) tour *m* de force; **feats of engineering,** triomphes *m* de l'ingénieur; (*b*) **f. of skill,** tour d'adresse.

feat[2], *a. A:* **1.** (*of action, movement, etc.*) adroit, habile. **2.** (*of dress*) élégant, bien ajusté; seyant, coquet.

feather[1] ['feðər], *s.* **1.** (*a*) plume *f*; (*of tail, wing*) penne *f*; (*of bird*) **to grow new feathers,** se remplumer; **feathers of an arrow,** plumes, ailes *f*, (em)pennes *f*, pennons *m*, d'une flèche; *F:* **to show the white f.,** laisser voir qu'on a la frousse; manquer de courage; *F:* caner, caler; *A:* **to crop s.o.'s feathers,** remettre qn à sa place; **you could have knocked me down with a f.,** j'ai pensé tomber de mon haut; *Prov:* **fine feathers make fine birds,** la belle plume fait le bel oiseau; c'est la plume qui fait l'oiseau; *U.S:* **red f. campaign,** collecte *f* d'œuvres de charité; (*b*) *attrib.* **f. bed,** (i) lit *m* de plume; (ii) *F:* sinécure *f*; **f. broom, brush, duster,** plumeau *m*, houssoir *m*; *Carp:* **f. joint,** assemblage *m* à rainure et languette; *Sm.a:* **f. spring,** ressort *m* de gâchette, petit ressort; *Miner:* **f. ore,** jamesonite *f*; *Bot:* **f. grass,** stipe (plumeuse); **f. foil,** hottonie *f* des marais, plumeau *m*, plume d'eau, mille feuille *f* aquatique; *Orn: F:* **f. poke,** (i) pouillot *m*; (ii) mésange *f*; *Ich: F:* **f. fish, f.-back,** notoptère *m*; *Echin: F:* **f. star,** comatule *f*, antédon *m*; *Ent:* **f.-winged moth,** ornéode *m*. **2.** (*a*) plumage *m*; **to be in full f.,** (i) (*of bird*) avoir tout son plumage; (ii) *F:* (*of pers.*) être en grande toilette; être sur son trente et un; (iii) *F:* (*of pers.*) être en fonds; **to be in high f.,** être tout joyeux, gai et dispos, d'excellente humeur, plein d'entrain; **they are birds of a f.,** ce sont gens du même acabit; *Prov:* **birds of a f. flock together,** qui se ressemble s'assemble; (*b*) *Ven:* gibier *m* à plume(s). **3.** *Mil: Cost:* plumet *m*; *F:* **that's a f. in his cap,** c'est tout à son honneur; il peut en être fier. **4.** (*a*) (*of hair*) épi *m*; (*b*) (*in gem*) paillette *f*, crapaud *m*; (*c*) crête *f* (de vague). **5.** *Mec.E: etc:* (*a*) languette *f*; clavette plate, linguiforme; ergot *m*; **crankshaft f.,** clavette de vilebrequin; **sliding f.,** clavette coulissante; (*b*) (*spline*) nervure *f*, saillie *f*; (*c*) *Min:* (i) coin demi-rond; (ii) plat-coin *m*. **6.** *Row:* nage plate.

feather[2]. **1.** *v.tr.* (*a*) empenner (une flèche); emplumer (un chapeau, etc.); **to tar and f. s.o.,** emplumer qn; *Fig.* **to f. one's nest,** faire sa pelote, son beurre, ses choux gras; faire ses affaires; s'arrondir, mettre du foin dans ses bottes; amasser du bien; (*b*) *Ven:* faire voler quelques plumes à (un faisan, etc.); plumer (le gibier); (*c*) (i) tailler (une planche, etc.) en biseau; (ii) assembler (des planches) à rainure et à languette; (*d*) *Mec.E:* (i) claveter; (ii) canneler (un arbre); (*e*) *Row:* ramener (l'aviron) à plat; *v.i.* dévirer la rame; nager plat; **f. (your oars)!** avirons à plat! **to f. along the water,** plumer; (*f*) *Ven:* **to f. the hounds,** mettre les chiens sur la piste; (*g*) *Av:* **to f. a propeller,** mettre une hélice en drapeau. **2.** *v.i.* (*a*) (*of young bird*) **to f. (out),** s'emplumer; (*b*) (*of corn*) onduler au vent (comme des plumets); (*of waves*) se couvrir de crêtes blanches; **the snow came feathering down,** la neige tombait en flocons légers; (*c*) *Ven:* (*of dogs*) frétiller (sur la piste).

featherbed ['feðə'bed], *F:* **1.** *v.tr.* (*a*) subventionner (excessivement); **to f. weak branches of the economy,** subventionner les, venir en aide aux, secteurs faibles de l'économie générale; (*b*) **he's featherbedded by his wife,** il est gâté par sa femme. **2.** *v.i.* gonfler les besoins de main-d'œuvre.

featherbedding ['feðə'bediŋ], *s. F:* réduction *f* de la productivité des ouvriers pour éviter le chômage.

featherbrain ['feðəbrein], *s. F:* **she's a f.,** c'est une évaporée, une tête de linotte; **he's a f.,** c'est un hurluberlu.

featherbrained ['feðəbreind], *a. F:* écervelé, étourdi; sans cervelle; (*of woman*) à tête de linotte.

feathered ['feðəd], *a.* **1.** (*of hat, etc.*) emplumé, garni de plumes; (*of arrow*) empenné; *Lit: O:* **the f. tribe,** la race ailée, la gent ailée. **2.** (*of shaft, etc.*) cannelé, à nervures.

featheredge ['feðəredʒ], *s.* **1.** *Carp: etc:* biseau *m*, chanfrein *m*; bord *m* en biseau. **2.** (*on tool*) morfil *m*, bavure *f*.

featheredged ['feðəredʒd], *a.* (*of board, etc.*) taillé en biseau; à chanfrein; (*of file*) à losange, à dossière; (*of brick*) à couteau; **f. board,** planche *f* à clin.

feathering[1] ['feðəriŋ], *a.* **1.** (*of branches, foliage, etc.*) plumeux. **2.** *Nau:* (*of propeller blades*) mobile, articulé; **f. screw,** hélice *f* à ailes articulées.

feathering[2], *s.* **1.** (*a*) (i) (*of birds*) plumage *m*; (ii) (*of growing feathers*) emplumement *m*; (*b*) panachure *f* (d'une tulipe). **2.** *Arch:* foliation *f*, lobes *mpl* (d'un arc). **3.** empennage *m* (d'une flèche). **4.** (i) biseautage *m* (d'une planche, etc.); (ii) assemblage *m* (des planches) à rainure et à languette. **5.** *Row:* nage plate. **6.** *Av:* mise *f* en drapeau (de l'hélice, des pales); **full f. propeller,** hélice *f* à mise en drapeau complète, totale; **quick f. propeller,** hélice à mise en drapeau rapide; **f. override,** commande *f*, dispositif *m*, de mise en drapeau.

featherless ['feðəlis], *a.* **1.** sans plumes. **2.** déplumé.

featherlet ['feðəlet], *s.* plumule *f*.

featherstitch ['feðəstitʃ], *s. Needlew:* point *m* d'épines.

featherweight ['feðəweit]. **1.** *s.* (*a*) *Box:* poids *m* plume; (*b*) *Turf:* feather-weight *m*. **2.** *a.* **f. paper,** papier bouffant.

feathery ['feðəri], *a.* **1.** (*of snow, corn, grass, etc.*) plumeux; (*of dog's tail, etc.*) épié. **2.** (*of tissue, etc.*) doux et léger (comme la plume).

featly ['fi:tli], *adv. A:* **1.** adroitement; (*of dancing*) légèrement, avec agilité. **2.** (vêtue) coquettement, avec élégance, avec soin.

feature[1] ['fi:tjər], *s.* **1.** (*a*) trait *m* (du visage); **the features,** la physionomie; **pronounced, prominent, features,** traits accusés; **classical features,** visage sculptural; **cast of features,** le masque; **he has mobile features,** il a le masque mobile; (*b*) trait (de caractère, etc.); **they had no f. in common,** ils ne se ressemblaient en rien. **2.** (*a*) trait, caractéristique *f*, particularité *f* (d'un paysage, d'un édifice, etc.); **main features,** grands traits; fond *m* (d'une politique, etc.); **features of a work,** caractère *m* d'une œuvre; **physical features of a country,** topographie *f* d'un pays; **special f.,** trait caractéristique; particularité; **striking f.,** trait frappant; singularité *f*; **prominent f.,** trait saillant; **the redeeming f.,** le beau côté (de qch.); ce qui rachète les défauts; **the main f. of this machine,** le principal avantage de cette machine; (*b*) **paper that makes a f. of sports,** journal qui se spécialise dans les sports, qui fait une large place aux sports; **shop that makes a f. of its China tea,** boutique *f* qui a pour spécialité les thés de Chine; (*c*) *Cin:* **f. (film),** long métrage, *F:* grand film; **double-f. programme,** programme double, à deux longs métrages; (*d*) *Journ:* article *m* vedette, grand reportage; *W.Tel: etc:* numéro *m* vedette; *Com:* article *m* réclame.

feature[2], *v.tr.* **1.** caractériser, marquer, distinguer (qch.); **the small hills which f. the landscape,** les petites collines qui caractérisent, marquent, le paysage. **2.** (*a*) dépeindre, décrire (qn, qch.); (*b*) *Cin:* (i) représenter (qn); tourner (un rôle); (ii) **film featuring X,** film avec X en vedette. **3.** *Journ:* **to f. a piece of news,** mettre une nouvelle en manchette; *Journ:* **this new material is being featured in the London stores,** on expose actuellement ce nouveau tissu dans les grands magasins de Londres.

featureless ['fi:tʃəlis], *a.* sans traits bien marqués; sans caractère; peu intéressant; **a f. performance,** spectacle *m*, représentation *f*, audition *f*, assez terne.

febricant ['febrikənt], *a. Med:* fébrigène.

febricity [fe'brisiti], *s. Med:* fébrilité *f*.

febricula [fe'brikjulə], *s. Med:* fébricule *f*.

febrific [f'ebrifik], *a. Med:* fébrigène.

febrifugal [fe'brifjugəl], *a.* (médicament *m*, etc.) fébrifuge.

febrifuge ['febrifju:dʒ], *a.* & *s. Med:* fébrifuge (*m*).

febrile ['fi:brail], *a.* (pouls, etc.) fébrile, fiévreux.

febrility [fe'briliti], *s. Med:* fébrilité *f*.

Febronian [fe'brouniən], *a.* & *s. Ecc:* fébronien, -ienne.

Febronianism [fe'brouniənizm], *s. Ecc:* fébronianisme *m*.

February ['februəri], *s.* (*a*) février *m*; **in F.,** au mois de février, en février; **(on) the first, the seventh, of F.,** le premier, le sept, février; (*b*) *Bot:* **F. daphne,** mézéréon *m*.

fecal ['fi:k(ə)l], **feces** ['fi:si:z], etc. = FAECAL, FAECES, *etc.*

feckless ['feklis], *a.* **1.** veule; mou, *f.* molle; sans énergie. **2.** propre à rien; incapable; étourdi, irréfléchi.

fecklessly ['feklisli], *adv.* **1.** sans énergie; mollement. **2.** malhabilement, gauchement; d'une manière étourdie.

fecklessness ['feklisnis], *s.* **1.** veulerie *f*; manque *m* d'énergie. **2.** incapacité *f*; étourderie *f*, irréflexion *f*.

fecula ['fekjulə], *s.* fécule *f*, amidon *m*.

feculence ['fekjuləns], *s.* **1.** féculence *f*; manque *m* de limpidité. **2.** (*a*) fétidité *f*; (*b*) saleté *f*, crasse *f*.

feculent ['fekjulənt], *a.* **1.** féculent; chargé de lie, de sédiment, d'impuretés. **2.** sale, fétide, répugnant.

fecund ['fekənd], *a. Lit:* **1.** fécond; **f. era in literature,** époque *f* fertile de la littérature. **2.** fécondant, fertilisant.

fecundate ['fekəndeit], *v.tr. Lit:* & *Biol:* féconder.

fecundation [fekən'deiʃ(ə)n], *s.* fécondation *f*.

fecundity [fi'kʌnditi], *s.* fécondité *f*, productivité *f*.

federal ['fedərəl]. **1.** *a.* (*of government, etc.*) fédéral, -aux; *U.S:* **the F. City,** Washington. **2.** *s. U.S.Hist:* fédéral *m*, nordiste *m* (guerre civile de 1861–65).

federalism ['fedərəlizm], *s.* fédéralisme *m*.

federalist ['fedərəlist], *s.* fédéraliste *mf*.

federalization ['fedərəlai'zeiʃ(ə)n], *s.* union *f* (d'États, etc.) en fédération; fédération *f*.

federalize ['fedərəlaiz], *v.tr.* **1.** fédéraliser. **2.** *U.S:* charger le gouvernement fédéral du contrôle de (qch.).

federate[1] ['fedərət]. **1.** *a.* (*of states, etc.*) fédéré(s), allié(s). **2.** *s. Fr.Hist:* fédéré *m*.

federate[2] ['fedəreit]. **1.** *v.tr.* fédérer. **2.** *v.i.* se fédérer.

federation [fedə'reiʃ(ə)n], *s.* fédération *f*; **Federations of Employers,** syndicats patronaux; **the International Sporting F.,** la Fédération sportive internationale.

federationist [fedə'reiʃənist], *s.* partisan, -ane, de la fédération; fédéraliste *mf*.

federative ['fedərətiv], *a.* fédératif.

fedia ['fediə], *s. Bot:* fédie *f*, fedia *f*.

fedora [fi'dɔ:rə], *s. NAm:* chapeau mou.

fed up ['fed ʌp], *a. F:* dégoûté; **he, it, makes me f. up,** j'en ai plein le dos, j'en ai marre.

fee[1] [fi:], *s.* **1.** (*a*) *Hist:* fief *m*; (*b*) *Jur:* propriété *f* héréditaire (relevant de la Couronne). **2.** (*a*) honoraires *mpl* (d'un médecin consultant, d'un avocat, etc.); cachet *m* (d'un précepteur, d'un acteur); jeton *m* de présence (d'un administrateur); vacations *fpl* (d'un avoué); redevance *f*; **to draw one's fees,** toucher ses honoraires, ses cachets; (*of director*) toucher ses jetons; (*of lawyer, etc.*) **to pocket large fees,** toucher de fortes vacations; **extra fees,** honoraires supplémentaires; (*of lawyer*) vacations supplémentaires; **f. splitting,** partage *m* des honoraires; (*b*) *Jur:* **property held in f. simple,** propriété *f* sans conditions, libre, affectable; bien *m* immeuble *m*, en toute propriété; **to grant in f. simple,** céder avec tous droits de jouissance et de possession; **property held in f. tail,** propriété objet d'un fidéicommis; bien substitué; (*c*) gratification *f*, pourboire *m* (à un domestique, etc.); (*d*) droit *m* (de chancellerie, etc.); **school fees,** rétribution *f* scolaire; frais de scolarité; **boarding-school fees,** pension *f*; **examination f.,** droit d'examen; **entrance f.,** droit d'entrée; **patent f.,** taxe *f* de droits de brevet; *Post:* **registration f.,** taxe de recommandation; droit d'inscription; **late f.,** taxe supplémentaire; **late-f. post,** levée exceptionnelle; **for a small f.,** moyennant une légère redevance; **employment agencies charging a fee,** bureaux de placement payants.

fee[2], *v.tr.* **(feed, fee'd; feeing)** *A:* **1.** payer un cachet, des honoraires, à (qn); **to f. a lawyer,** retenir un avocat. **2.** (*a*) donner une gratification, un pourboire, à (qn); (*b*) *F:* graisser la patte à (qn).

feeble ['fi:bl], *a.* (*a*) (*of pers.*) faible, infirme, débile; (*of action, etc.*) faible; mou, *f.* molle; **f. pulse,** pouls déprimé, rare; **f. argument,** argument *m* faible, sans force; **f. light,** clarté douteuse; *F:* **that's pretty f.,** ça, c'est bien médiocre; (*b*) *F:* (*of pers.*) mou, sans caractère, peu capable.

feeble-minded ['fi:bl'maindid], (*a*) *a.* d'esprit faible; arriéré; (*b*) *s. coll.* **the f.-m.,** les faibles *mf* d'esprit; les débiles mentaux.

feeble-mindedness ['fi:bl'maindidnis], *s.* faiblesse *f* d'esprit; arriération *f*.

feebleness ['fi:blnis], (*of pers.*) faiblesse *f*, débilité *f*, infirmité *f*; (*of will, argument, etc.*) faiblesse; (*of novel, etc.*) médiocrité *f*.

feebly ['fi:bli], *adv.* faiblement; mollement.

feed[1] [fi:d], *s.* **1.** (*a*) alimentation *f* (d'un animal, etc.); pâturage *m*, broutement *m* (des moutons, des vaches, etc.); **out at f.,** mis au vert; (*b*) nourriture *f*, pâture *f* (pour les animaux); fourrage *m* (pour les chevaux, etc.); **to give the horse a f.,** donner à manger au cheval; **horse off his f.,** cheval *m* qui boude, renifle, sur son avoine; **it's time for baby's f.,** il faut donner à manger au bébé; *F:* (*of pers.*) **to be off one's f.,** bouder sur la nourriture; avoir perdu l'appétit; (*c*) mesure *f*, ration *f* (de nourriture pour les animaux); **f. of oats,** picotin *m* d'avoine; (*d*) *F:* repas *m*, festin *m*; **to have a good f.,** bien manger; faire bonne chère; (*e*) *Th: etc:* acteur, -trice, qui donne la réplique; **f. (line),** réplique *f*. **2.** *Tchn:* (*a*) alimentation *f* (d'une machine, etc., en combustible, etc.); **gravity f., suction f., vacuum f.,** alimentation par gravité, par aspiration, par dépression; **pressure f.,** alimentation sous pression; **pump f.,** alimentation par pompe; **f. pump,** pompe *f* d'alimentation; nourrice *f*; **f. pipe,** tuyau *m* d'alimentation, de prise d'eau; nourrice; **perforated f. pipe,** distributeur *m* alimentaire; **the f. pipes,** le circuit d'alimentation; **f. roll,** nourrisseur *m*; rouleau entraîneur (d'un laminoir); *Mec.E: etc:* **f. arm,** levier *m* d'alimentation; **f. chute,** (i) goulotte *f*, goulette *f*, (ii) canal *m*, d'alimentation; **f. compressor,** compresseur *m* d'alimentation; **f. valve,** valve *f*, soupape *f*, d'alimentation; **f. gear,** mécanisme *m*, engrenage *m*, (i) *Mec.E:* d'alimentation, (ii) *Mch.Tls:* d'avance; **f. screw,** (i) *Mec.E:* vis *f* de commande, vis-mère *f*; (ii) *Typ:* vis encreuse; **f. motion,** mouvement *m* de pression, d'avancement, d'entraînement; *I.C.E:* **f. shaft,** arbre *m* de commande; **f. tank,** (i) *Mch:* bâche *f* d'alimentation; réservoir *m* alimentaire; (ii) *I.C.E:* réservoir-nourrice *m*, *pl.* réservoirs-nourrices; nourrice (d'alimentation d'essence); *Mch: etc:* **f. cock,** robinet *m* d'alimentation, de refoulement, de remplissage; **f. donkey,** petit cheval alimentaire; **f. engine,** machine *f* auxiliaire; *Mch.Tls:* **f. bar, f. lever, f. rod,** barre *f*, levier *m*, de chariotage; **f. limiter,** limiteur *m* d'avance; **f. rack,** crémaillère *f* d'avance; **f. box,** (i) *Mec.E: etc:* boîte *f* d'alimentation; (ii) *Mch.Tls:* boîte d'avance; *Artil: Sm.a:* **belt f.,** alimentation par bande(-chargeur) souple; **f. block,** chambre *f* d'alimentation (d'une mitrailleuse); **f. trough,** auget *m* (de fusil à magasin); **f. pawl,** cliquet *m* d'alimentation; **f. jam,** défaut *m* d'alimentation, enrayage *m* du mécanisme d'alimentation; *Cin: etc:* **f. reel, spool,** bobine dérouleuse, débitrice; **f. magazine,** magasin débiteur; **f. sprocket,** tambour dérouleur; *Cmptr:* **card f.,** mécanisme *m* d'alimentation de cartes; alimentation en cartes; **tape f.,** mécanisme d'entraînement de bande; **f. alert,** incident *m* d'alimentation; *El:* **f. wire,** artère *f* d'alimentation; fil *m* d'amenée; (*b*) appareil *m*, système *m*, d'alimentation; conduit *m* d'alimentation; (*carrying material towards tool*) amenage *m*, avancement *m*; entraînement *m*; (*carrying tool towards material*) avance *f*; **traverse f.,** avance longitudinale; **cross f.,** avance transversale; **in f.,** avance en plongée; **f. lines, piping,** circuit(s), tuyauterie(s) *f*, d'alimentation; (*c*) (*thing fed in*) *Atom.Ph:* liqueur-mère *f*, alimentation; **f. makeup, preparation,** préparation *f* des liqueurs-mères; **oil f.,** arrivée *f* d'huile; *Hyd.E: etc:* **f. (water),** éclusée *f*; eau *f* d'alimentation; *Typ:* **f. board,** table *f* de marge; **twin-sheet f.,** marge *f* en double, à deux feuilles.

feed[2], *v.* **(fed [fed]; fed)**

I. *v.tr.* **1.** (*a*) nourrir; donner à manger à (qn); alimenter (une famille, etc.); approvisionner (un pays, etc.); ravitailler (une armée, des prisonniers); faire manger (un chien); faire paître (des vaches, des moutons, etc.); affourrager (des bestiaux); repaître (des animaux); allaiter (un enfant); (*of mother bird*) embecquer, abecquer, donner la becquée à (ses petits); **to f. a bird forcibly,** gaver un oiseau; **too helpless to f. himself,** trop faible pour se nourrir lui-même; **to f. a cold,** nourrir un rhume; *F:* **to f. one's face,** manger, se caler les joues; **to f. s.o. on hopes,** nourrir qn d'espérances; **to f. oats to the horses,** donner de l'avoine aux chevaux; (*b*) nourrir, servir à la nutrition de (qn, etc.); **field that feeds three cows,** champ *m* qui nourrit trois vaches; (*c*) **manure feeds the ground,** le fumier nourrit la terre; **to f. the mind,** nourrir l'esprit. **2.** (*a*) alimenter (une machine, une chaudière, le feu, le marché, etc.); charger (un fourneau, etc.); *Cmptr:* faire avancer, alimenter (une carte perforée); faire avancer, débiter (de la bande); *Tchn:* **to f. gas to the burner,** amener du gaz au brûleur; **to f. a machine with raw materials,** introduire les matières premières dans une machine; *Mill:* **to f. a threshing machine, the hopper, with fresh corn,** rengrener une batteuse, la trémie; *Mec.E:* **to f. the tool to the work,** (faire) avancer l'outil à la pièce; (*b*) *Fb: etc:* **to f. the forwards,** alimenter les avants; (*c*) *Th:* **to f. an actor,** donner la réplique à un acteur; soutenir un acteur. **3.** (*of cattle*) **to f. down, f. off, a meadow; to f. a meadow bare,** pâturer un pré; brouter l'herbe d'un pré.

II. *v.i.* manger; (*of cattle, sheep*) paître, brouter; (*of deer*) viander; (*of boar*) herbeiller; **I am expected to f. with the servants,** on veut que je mange, que je prenne mes repas, avec les domestiques; **to f. (up)on sth.,** se nourrir, s'alimenter, se repaître, vivre, de qch.; **to f. on s.o.,** (i) vivre aux dépens de qn; mettre qn en coupe réglée; (ii) faire sa proie de qn; (*of animal*) **to f. out of s.o.'s hand,** manger dans la main de qn.

III. (*compound verbs*) **1. feed back,** *v.tr. Cmptr:* réintroduire, réinjecter (des cartes).

2. feed in, into, *v.tr.* injecter; faire pénétrer (qch. dans qch.); *Cmptr:* introduire (des cartes) en machine, en mémoire.

3. feed up, (*a*) *v.tr.* **to f. up animals,** engraisser les animaux; **to f. s.o. up,** (i) *Med:* suralimenter qn; (ii) *F:* rassasier qn de qch.; *F:* **to be fed up,** en avoir assez; en avoir soupé; en avoir plein le dos; en avoir par-dessus la tête; en avoir marre; en être empoisonné; **I'm fed up with your friends!** j'en ai plein le dos, de vos amis! **I am fed up with it,** j'en ai une indigestion, j'en ai marre; (*b*) *v.i.* **to f. up (after illness),** se restaurer.

feedback ['fi:dbæk], *s. Tchn:* action *f*, alimentation *f*, en retour; *Mec: Ph:* renvoi *m*, retour *m* (de force); *Elcs: etc:* réaction *f*, rétroaction *f*, *F:* feed-back *m inv*; *Cmptr:* réaction, rétroaction, réinjection *f*, retour d'information; **degenerative, inverse, negative, reverse, f.,** contreréaction *f*; **f. amplifier,** amplificateur *m* à réaction; **f. circuit,** circuit *m* à réaction, à rétroaction, à action en retour; **f. oscillator,** oscillateur *m* à réaction; **f. coupling,** couplage réactif.

feeder ['fi:dər], *s.* **1.** (*pers.*) (*a*) nourrisseur *m* (de bestiaux); (*b*) *Ind:* alimenteur, -euse (d'une machine à carder, etc.); chargeur, -euse (d'un fourneau de forge, etc.); *Typ:* margeur, -euse; (*c*) mangeur, -euse; **heavy f.,** gros mangeur; **to be a dirty f.,** manger salement; (*d*) *Th:* acteur, -trice, qui donne la réplique; **he's a bad f.,** il ne sait pas donner la réplique. **2.** (*a*) bavette *f*, bavoir *m*; serviette *f* d'enfant; (*b*) biberon *m*. **3.** (*a*) *Geog:* affluent *m* (d'un cours d'eau); *Hyd.E:* canal *m* d'alimentation, d'amenée, de dérivation, de prise; nourricière *f*; *Agr:* fossé collecteur; *Trans:* route *f*, bretelle *f*, de raccordement; artère *f* de pénétration; *Rail:* embranchement *m*; **network of feeders (to the main roads),** réseau *m* capillaire (convergeant sur les grandes artères); *Av:* **f. line,** ligne *f* d'apport; **f. aircraft,** appareil *m* (utilisé sur les lignes) d'apport; *Navy:* **f. convoy,** bretelle de convoi; (*b*) *Av:* guidage *m* préliminaire; **f. system,** dispositif *m*, système *m*, de guidage préliminaire; (*c*) canalisation *f*, conduite *f* (de gaz, etc.); (*d*) *El:* câble *m*, ligne *f*, d'alimentation; artère, canalisation; feeder *m*; *W.Tel: etc:* descente *f* d'antenne; **radical f.,** feeder de sous-station. **4.** (*a*) *Mch: Mec.E: etc:* alimenteur *m*; **mechanical f.,** chargeur *m* mécanique; **air f.,** manche *f* à air; (*b*) *Artil:* transporteur *m* (d'obus); (*c*) *Tex: etc:* cylindre nourrisseur, alimentaire; (*d*) *Metall:* (i) pompe *f*; (ii) masselotte *f* (de pièce coulée); (*e*) *Typ:* margeur *m*; **automatic f.,** margeur automatique; **stream f.,** margeur à nappe; **friction-type, suction-type, f.,** margeur à friction, à succion; (*f*) *Atom.Ph:* **rotating f.,** distributeur rotatif; (*g*) *Cmptr:* **f. bin,** magasin *m* d'alimentation.

feedhead ['fi:dhed], *s. Metall:* masselotte *f*.

feeding[1] ['fi:diŋ], *a.* **1.** *Nau:* (*of storm, gale, etc.*) nourri. **2.** (*of cistern, etc.*) alimentaire; (*of cylinder*) nourrisseur.

feeding[2], *s.* **1.** (*a*) alimentation *f* (de qn, d'une machine, etc.); affourragement *m* (des bestiaux); abecquement *m* (de leurs petits par les oiseaux); **force, forced, forcible, f.,** gavage *m*; **f. bottle,** biberon *m* (de bébé); *Med:* **f. cup,** biberon, canard *m*; **f. time,** l'heure *f* de la pâtée, de l'affourragement (des animaux); *F:* l'heure du repas (des gens); *U.S:* **demand f.,** alimentation au rythme demandé par l'enfant; (*b*) *Ind:* **f. mechanism,** mécanisme alimentateur; **f. pipe,** tuyau *m* d'alimentation, de prise d'eau; nourrisseur *m*; (*c*) *Metall:* pompage *m*; **f. rod,** pompe *f*; **f. head,** masselotte *f*; (*d*) *Cmptr:* **form f.,** alimentation en papier. **2.** *Mec.E: etc:* amenage *m*, avance *f*, avancement *m* (du travail à l'outil, de l'outil au travail, etc.); (*of arc lamp*) **f. of the carbons,** avance des charbons; *Cin:* **f. claws,** griffes *f* de transport (du film).

feedout ['fi:daut], *s. Cmptr:* **form f.,** éjection *f* du papier.

feedstock ['fi:dstɔk], *s. Ind:* (*a*) stock *m*, charge *f*, d'alimentation; charge de départ; (*b*) alimentation *f*, produit *m* de base; base *f*, matière première.

feel[1] [fi:l], *s.* **1.** *Physiol:* toucher *m*, tact *m*; **rough to the f.,** rude au toucher. **2.** (*a*) toucher, manier *m*, main *f* (du papier, etc.); **material with a soft f.,** tissu *m* au manier doux; **to recognize sth. by the f.,** reconnaître qch. au toucher; (*b*) sensation *f*; **the f. of a collar round my neck,** la sensation d'un faux-col autour de mon cou; **I don't like the f. of his clammy hand,** je n'aime pas la sensation de sa main froide et moite; (*c*) **he has the f. of his car,** il a sa voiture bien en main; *Equit:* **to get the right f. of the reins,** ajuster les rênes; **you'll soon get the f. of the work,** vous allez bientôt vous habituer au travail.

feel[2], *v.* (felt [felt]; felt)

I. *v.tr. & i.* **1.** (*a*) *v.tr.* toucher (qch. avec la main, un bâton, etc.); promener les doigts sur (qch.); tâter (le pouls, une étoffe, etc.); palper (un membre cassé, etc.); manier (une étoffe, etc.); **the blind recognize objects by feeling them,** les aveugles reconnaissent les objets au toucher, en les palpant; **to f. whether, if, there are any bones broken,** tâter pour savoir s'il y a des os cassés; *Mil:* **to f. the enemy,** tâter l'ennemi; **f. your right!** appuyez à droite! (*b*) *v.tr. & i.* **to f. (about) for sth.,** chercher qch. à tâtons, en tâtant; tâter pour trouver qch.; **the blind man was feeling for his stick,** l'aveugle cherchait sa canne; **to f. about in the dark,** tâtonner dans l'obscurité; **to f. one's way,** (i) avancer, aller, marcher, à tâtons; (ii) sonder, explorer, le terrain; y aller doucement, avec précaution; (*of artist, writer, etc.*) se chercher; **to f. one's way towards sth.,** avancer vers qch. à tâtons, à l'aveuglette; **we shall have to f. our way,** il faudra agir avec beaucoup de circonspection; il ne faut rien brusquer; **to f. for the right word,** chercher le mot juste; **to f. in one's pockets for sth.,** chercher qch. dans ses poches. **2.** (*a*) *v.tr.* sentir (qch.); **to f. sth. under one's foot,** sentir qch. sous le pied; **I felt the floor trembling,** je sentais trembler le plancher; **I felt her trembling,** je la sentais qui tremblait; **she felt his arms around her,** elle se sentait pressée dans ses bras; **I can f. winter coming,** je sens l'hiver qui vient; (*b*) *v.tr. & i.* (res)sentir, éprouver (de la douleur, etc.); ressentir (une injure); **to f. the effects of an accident,** se ressentir d'un accident; **the effect will be felt,** l'effet se fera sentir; **you should f. the heat in there!** il fait un chaud là-dedans! **to f. the heat,** être incommodé par la chaleur; **to f. the cold,** être sensible au froid; être frileux; **we have felt the cold this winter,** le froid a été sensible cet hiver; **to make one's authority felt,** affirmer son autorité; *Nau:* (*of ship*) **to f. the rudder,** sentir la barre; obéir à la barre; **the lack of certain commodities made itself increasingly felt,** le manque de certaines denrées se faisait sentir de plus en plus; on ressentait de plus en plus le manque de certaines denrées; **she felt no pleasure when he came back,** elle n'a éprouvé aucune joie à son retour; **I felt it a great deal,** cela m'a fait quelque chose; **to f. great interest for s.o.,** éprouver de la sympathie pour qn; **to f. for, with, s.o. in his sorrow,** prendre part à, compatir à, partager, la douleur de qn; **to f. for the underdog,** se pencher sur les souffrances du peuple; **I f. for him,** je le comprends; il a toute ma sympathie; **some people cannot f.,** il y a des gens qui ne sentent rien; **how did you f.?** quels sentiments avez-vous éprouvés? **he feels very strongly,** il est très sensible; (*c*) *v.tr.* avoir conscience de (qch.); **he felt his hopes fading away,** il sentit son espoir s'envoler; **I f. it in my bones that I shall succeed,** quelque chose me dit que je réussirai; **I felt that I had come at the wrong moment,** j'avais conscience d'être arrivé mal à propos; **I felt it necessary to intervene,** j'ai jugé nécessaire d'intervenir; **what I f. about your brother is . . .,** mon sentiment sur votre frère, c'est que . . .. **3.** *v.i.* (*of pers.*) (*a*) **to f. hot, cold,** avoir chaud, froid; **to f. ill, tired,** se sentir malade, fatigué; **my foot feels better,** mon pied va mieux; **to f. all the better for it,** s'en trouver mieux; **I f. ten years younger,** je me sens dix ans de moins; **to f. in high spirits,** se sentir plein d'entrain; **he doesn't f. quite himself,** il ne se sent pas très bien; il n'est pas dans son assiette; **I f. quite myself again,** je me sens tout à fait rétabli; **to f. up to sth., to doing sth.,** se sentir (i) assez bien pour faire qch., (ii) de taille à faire qch.; **to f. certain that . . .,** être certain que . . .; (*b*) **I f. as if . . .,** j'ai l'impression que . . ., il me semble que . . .; **to f. like doing sth.,** se sentir d'humeur, d'inclination, à faire qch.; être en humeur de faire qch.; **I felt like crying,** j'avais envie de pleurer; **I don't f. like laughing,** je ne me sens pas en train de rire; **it makes me f. like . . .,** cela me donne envie de . . .; **if you f. like it,** si le cœur vous en dit; **I don't f. like it,** ça ne me dit rien; **do you f. like cheese?** un peu de fromage vous dirait-il? **I f. like a cup of tea,** je prendrais bien, je boirais bien, une tasse de thé. **4.** *v.i.* (*of thgs, with passive force*) **to f. hard, soft,** être dur, doux, au toucher; **the wall felt hot,** le mur était chaud au toucher; **the load feels heavy to me,** le fardeau me semble lourd; **the room feels damp,** la pièce (me) paraît humide; la pièce donne une impression d'humidité; **this chair feels very comfortable,** ce fauteuil me paraît, me semble, très confortable; **how does it f., what does it f. like, to** + *inf*. . .? quel effet cela produit-il de + *inf* . . .? **it feels like . . .,** cela donne la sensation de . . ..

II. (*compound verb*) **feel out.** (*a*) *v.tr. NAm:* **to f. out a new idea,** faire des sondages au sujet d'une nouvelle idée; **to f. out one's colleagues about a new project,** chercher (discrètement) l'avis de ses collègues au sujet d'un nouveau projet; (*b*) *v.i. Artil:* allonger le tir par coups successifs.

feeler ['fi:lər], *s.* **1.** (*a*) personne qui manie (une étoffe, etc.), qui tâte (le pouls, etc.); (*b*) personne sensible; (*c*) *Mil:* éclaireur *m*. **2.** (*a*) *Biol:* antenne *f*, palpe *f* (d'un insecte, etc.); corne *f* (d'escargot); moustache *f* (d'un chat, etc.); tentacule *m* (d'un mollusque etc.); (*b*) *Aut:* repère *m* d'aile; témoin *m* d'aile. **3.** ballon *m* d'essai; **to throw out a f.,** (i) lancer un ballon d'essai; (ii) tâter le terrain, faire des sondages *m*; **peace feelers,** sondages de paix. **4.** *Mec.E:* feuille *f* d'épaisseur, pige *f*, palpeur *m*; **set of feelers,** calibre *m* d'épaisseur (à lames); jeu *m* de cales, de calibres.

feeling[1] ['fi:liŋ], *a.* **1.** (*of pers.*) sensible. **2.** (*of language, manner, etc.*) ému.

feeling[2], *s.* **1.** tâtage *m*, palpation *f* (de qch. avec les mains); maniement *m* (du drap). **2.** *Physiol:* **(sense of) f.,** toucher *m*, tact *m*; **capable of physical f.,** sensible au toucher; **to have no f. in one's arm,** avoir le bras mort. **3.** sensation (douloureuse, de froid, etc.); *F:* **I've got that sinking f.,** (i) j'ai le coup de pompe (de onze heures); (ii) j'ai le trac; (iii) je me sens découragé. **4.** sentiment *m*; (*a*) **his feelings towards me,** ses sentiments envers moi, vis-à-vis de moi; **to have kindly feelings towards s.o.,** éprouver de la sympathie pour qn; **what were my feelings when I heard it!** jugez de mes sentiments lorsque je l'ai appris! **what is the f. of the meeting on this subject?** quelle est l'opinion, quel est le sentiment, de l'assemblée sur ce sujet? **public f. ran high against the proposal,** le sentiment populaire s'élevait contre cette proposition; **f. is running very high,** les esprits sont très montés; **class f.,** esprit *m* de classe; **no hard feelings!** sans rancune! (*b*) **I had a f. of danger,** j'avais le sentiment d'être en danger; je me sentais en danger; **I had a f. that I had arrived at the wrong moment,** j'avais conscience d'être arrivé mal à propos; **there is a general f. that . . .,** l'impression règne (dans le public) que . . .; (*c*) sensibilité *f*; émotion *f*; **a f. for nature,** le sentiment de la nature; **to have a f. for music,** être sensible à la musique; **to have no feelings,** (i) être dépourvu de toute sensibilité; (ii) n'avoir point de cœur; être sans pitié; **have you no feelings!** vous n'avez donc pas d'âme! **a man of f.,** un homme sensible; **to suppress one's feelings,** se contenir; **to do sth. with f.,** mettre de l'âme à faire qch.; **to speak with f.,** parler (i) avec enthousiasme, (ii) avec émotion, (iii) avec chaleur; **to play the piano with f.,** jouer du piano avec sentiment, avec âme.

feelingly ['fi:liŋli], *adv.* d'un air ému, avec émotion; **to speak f. of sth.,** parler (i) d'une voix émue, (ii) avec sympathie, (iii) avec chaleur, de qch.; **to sing f.,** chanter avec âme.

feign [fein]. **1.** (*a*) *v.tr.* feindre, simuler (une maladie, la folie , etc.); **to f. surprise,** affecter, jouer, la surprise; **to f. death,** faire le mort; *A:* **to f. to do sth.,** feindre, faire semblant, de faire qch.; **to f. that . . .,** feindre que + *ind.*; (*b*) *v.i.* **to f. sick,** faire semblant d'être malade; **to cease feigning,** cesser de feindre. **2.** *v.tr. A:* (*a*) inventer (une excuse, etc.); (*b*) contrefaire (un document, une écriture).

feigned [feind], *a.* (*of sorrow, illness, etc.*) feint, simulé; (*of voice, writing, etc.*) déguisé; **f. smile,** sourire *m* de commande; **to write in a f. hand,** déguiser son écriture; *Jur:* **f. action,** cause fictive.

feigning ['feiniŋ], *s.* feinte *f*; (dis)simulation *f*.

feint[1] [feint], *s.* (*a*) *Mil:* fausse attaque; **f. sortie,** fausse sortie; (*b*) *Box: Fenc: etc:* feinte *f*; coup *m* de temps; **a f. with the left,** une feinte du gauche; (*c*) **to make a f. of doing sth.,** feindre, faire semblant, de faire qch.; **his anger is only a f.,** sa colère n'est qu'une simulation.

feint[2], *v.i.* (*a*) *Mil:* faire une fausse attaque; (*b*) *Box: Fenc: etc:* feinter; **to f. with the right,** feinter du droit.

feint[3], *a. & adv. A:* = FAINT[1]; *still used in Com:* **f.-ruled paper, paper with f. lines,** papier réglé (en bleu clair).

feinter ['feintər], *s. Fb: etc:* feinteur *m*.

feldspar ['feldspɑːr], **feldspath** ['feldspæθ], *s. Miner:* feldspath *m*; **glassy f.,** sanidine *f*; **triclinic f.,** plagioclase *f*; **white f.,** albite *f*; **lime soda f.,** feldspath calcosodique.

feldspathic [feld'spæθik], *a.* (*of rocks, etc.*) feldspathique; à feldspath.

feldspathization [feldspæθai'zeiʃ(ə)n], *s. Miner:* feldspathisation *f*.

feldspathoid ['feldspæθɔid], *s. Miner:* feldspathoïde *m*, feldspathide *m*.

Felicia [fi'lisiə]. **1.** *Pr.n.f.* Félicie. **2.** *s. Bot:* félicie *f*, felicia *f*.

felicitate [fi'lisiteit], *v.tr.* **1.** *esp. Lit:* **to f. s.o. (up)on sth.,** féliciter qn de, sur, qch.; complimenter qn sur qch. **2.** *A:* rendre (qn) heureux.

felicitation [filisi'teiʃ(ə)n], *s. esp. Lit:* félicitation *f*, compliment(s) *m(pl)*; **to offer s.o. one's felicitations,** offrir ses félicitations à qn.

felicitous [fi'lisitəs], *a.* heureux. **1.** (*a*) (*of word, speech, etc.*) bien trouvé, à propos; **to introduce s.o. in a few f. words,** présenter qn en quelques mots appropriés, bien choisis; **to have a f. style of writing,** écrire avec bonheur; (*b*) (*of pers.*) **f. in his choice of words, in his descriptions,** heureux dans le choix de ses mots, dans ses descriptions. **2.** *A:* (bien)heureux; joyeux.

felicitously [fi'lisitəsli], *adv.* heureusement.

felicity [fi'lisiti], *s.* **1.** félicité *f*, bonheur *m*, joie *f*. **2.** (*a*) à-propos *m*, bien-trouvé *m*, bonheur (d'une observation, etc.); (*b*) phrase bien trouvée; mot bien trouvé; trouvaille *f*.

felid ['fiːlid], *s. Z:* félidé *m*.

Felidae ['fiːlidiː], *s.pl. Z:* félidés *m*, félins *m*, chats *m*.

feline ['fiːlain]. **1.** *a.* (*a*) *Z:* (animal, etc.) félin; (*b*) **f. grace,** grâce féline; grâce de chat; *Pej:* **f. amenities,** politesses aigres-douces. **2.** *s. Z:* félin *m*.

felinity [fi'liniti], *s.* félinité *f*.

Felix ['fiːliks], *Pr.n.m.* Félix.

fell[1] [fel], *s.* **1.** fourrure *f*; peau *f* (de bête). **2.** (*a*) toison *f*; (*b*) *A:* (*of pers.*) **a f. of hair,** une tignasse.

fell[2], *s.* (*N. of Eng.*) colline, montagne, rocheuse.

fell[3], *s.* **1.** *For:* nombre *m* d'arbres abattus (en une fois); coupe *f* d'arbres; abattis *m*. **2.** *Needlew:* (*a*) rabattage *m* (d'une couture); (*b*) couture rabattue, plate; **run and f. seam,** couture rabattue.

fell[4], *v.tr.* **1.** (*a*) abattre, terrasser (un adversaire, etc.); assommer (un bœuf, etc.); **to f. s.o. to the ground,** étendre qn à terre (d'un coup de poing, etc.); (*b*) abattre, couper (un arbre); **to f. a tree with an axe,** abattre un arbre à coups de cognée; **felled wood, timber,** abattis *m*, bois gisant, vente *f*. **2.** *Needlew:* rabattre (une couture).

fell[5], *a. A: & Lit:* **1.** (*of pers., animal, etc.*) féroce, cruel, sauvage. **2.** (*of thg*) funeste, désolant; **f. disease,** maladie *f* terrible, impitoyable, redoutable; **f. necessity,** nécessité *f* tragique; **f. design,** projet *m* sinistre; **f. silence,** silence lugubre, lourd de menaces.

fellagha ['feləgə], *s.* fellagha *m*.

fellah, *pl.* **fellaheen, fellahs** ['felə, 'feləhiːn, 'feləz], *s.* fellah *m*; paysan *m* (d'Égypte).

Fellatahs [fe'lɑːtəz], *s.pl. Ethn:* Fellatas *m*, Foulahs *m*.

feller[1] ['felər], *s.* **1.** abatteur *m* (d'arbres, de bœufs); *Min:* **granite f.,** piqueur *m* de granit. **2.** dispositif *m* de rabattage (d'une machine à coudre).

felling ['feliŋ], *s.* abattage *m* (d'un bœuf); abattage, coupe *f*, vente *f* (de bois); rabattage *m* (d'une couture); *For:* **the f. season,** la saison d'abattage; **strip f.,** coupe par bandes; **clear f.,** coupe blanche, à blanc; **after f.,** coupe secondaire; **f. saw,** (scie *f*) passe-partout (*m inv*).

fellmonger[1] ['felmʌŋgər], *s.* peaussier *m*, pelletier *m*.

fellmonger[2], *v.tr.* délainer (les peaux).

fellmongering ['felmʌŋgəriŋ], *s.* délainage *m*.

felloe ['felou], *s.* **1.** jante *f*, circonférence *f*, chanteau *m* (de roue). **2.** section *f* de la jante (d'une roue).

fellow[1] ['felou], *s.* **1.** camarade *m*, compagnon *m*, confrère *m*, collègue *m*; *attrib.* **f. servant, passenger, sufferer,** compagnon de service, de voyage, de misère; **f. being, creature,** semblable *mf*; **f. citizen,** concitoyen, -enne; **f. countryman, -woman,** compatriote *mf*, concitoyen, -enne, *F:* pays, payse; **f. worker,** (i) compagnon *m* (d'un ouvrier); (ii) collaborateur, -trice; confrère *m*; **f. soldier,** compagnon *m*, frère *m*, d'armes; camarade *m* de régiment; **f. student,** camarade *mf* d'études, condisciple *m*; **f. traveller,** (i) *O:* compagnon *m* de voyage, de route; (ii) *Pol:* communisant, -ante; **communists and f. travellers,** les communistes et leurs sympathisants; *Pol: etc:* **f. candidate,** colistier *m*; **f. feeling,** sympathie *f*; **to have a f. feeling for s.o.,** avoir, ressentir, de la sympathie pour qn; *Jur:* **f. delinquent,** coïnculpé *m*; **f. prisoner,** (i) compagnon de captivité; (ii) *Jur:* codétenu *m*. **2.** (*of pers., etc.*) semblable *m*, pareil *m*; (*of thg*) pendant *m*; **in his art he has no f.,** dans son art il n'a pas de rival, pas son pareil; **a vase and its f.,** un vase et son pendant; *O:* **a good glove, but I have lost its f.,** un beau gant, mais j'ai perdu celui qui fait la paire, qui va avec, mais j'ai perdu l'autre. **3.** (*a*) (*at university*) (i) professeur chargé de fonctions administratives; (ii) boursier chargé de cours; (*b*) membre, associé, -ée (d'une société savante); **F. of the Royal Society,** membre de la Société royale (de Londres). **4.** *F:* (*a*) *O:* homme *m*, garçon *m*; **a good f.,** un brave garçon, un bon diable, un bon, chic, type; **a jolly f.,** un bon compagnon, un joyeux compère; **a decent f.,** un bon gars; **he's a queer f.,** c'est un drôle de type; **the poor little f.,** le pauvre petit; **a great strapping f.,** un grand gaillard; **he's a stout f.,** c'est un hardi compagnon; **old f.,** mon vieux; (*slightly pej.*) **a young f.,** *F:* **a young f.-me-lad,** un petit jeune homme; (*b*) *Pej:* individu *m*; **good-for-nothing f.,** mauvais sujet; propre *m* à rien; *O:* **tell that f. to go away,** dites à cet individu-là de s'en aller; (*c*) (*indefinite*) *A:* **why can't you let a f. alone?** laissez-moi donc tranquille! **a f. must eat,** il faut bien manger; **a f. doesn't like to be treated like that,** on n'aime pas à être traité comme ça.

fellow[2], *v.tr. A:* appareiller, apparier (des gants, etc.); trouver un pendant à (un vase, etc.).

fellowship ['felouʃip], *s.* **1.** communion *f*, communauté *f*, participation *f*, solidarité *f*; **to live in intellectual f. with s.o.,** vivre en communion d'idées avec qn; *Ecc:* **the F. of the Holy Ghost,** la communion du Saint-Esprit. **2.** **(good) f.,** amitié *f*, camaraderie *f*; **long-standing f.,** camaraderie de longue date. **3.** association *f*, corporation *f*, société *f*, (con)fraternité *f*; **a f. banquet,** un banquet confraternel; **the f. of man,** la fraternité des hommes. **4.** (*a*) *Sch:* (i) dignité *f* de professeur chargé de fonctions administratives; (ii) bourse *f* universitaire (avec obligation de faire un cours, des recherches); (*b*) titre *m* de membre, d'associé (d'une société savante). **5.** *A:* association *f*; *Mth:* **(rule of) f.,** règle *f* de société.

felo-de-se ['fiːloudi'siː], *s. Jur:* **1.** (*of pers.*) (*pl.* **felones-de-se**) suicidé, -ée (de propos délibéré), ou celui, celle, qui a commis une tentative de suicide (en possession de toutes ses facultés). **2.** suicide *m*; homicide *m* de soi-même.

Feloidea [fiː'lɔidiə], *s.pl. Z:* féloïdes *m*.

felon[1] ['felən]. **1.** *a.* (*a*) *Poet:* cruel, vil, perfide, mauvais; (*b*) *Jur:* criminel. **2.** *s. Jur:* criminel, -elle.

felon[2], *s. Med:* panaris *m*.

felonious [fe'louniəs], *a.* **1.** *Poet:* = FELON[1] 1 (*a*). **2.** *Jur:* criminel; **f. act,** action *f* qui constitue un crime; **accused of loitering with f. intent,** accusé de vagabondage délictueux; **murder with f. intent,** meurtre *m* par guet-apens.

feloniously [fe'louniəsli], *adv.* criminellement.

felonry ['felənri], *s. Hist:* le monde criminel; *esp.* la population d'une colonie pénitentiaire.

felony ['feləni], *s.* **1.** *Hist:* félonie *f*. **2.** *Jur:* crime *m* (p. ex. meurtre, incendie volontaire, vol à main armée, faux); **to compound a f.,** pactiser avec un crime.

felsite ['felsait], *s. Miner:* felsite *f*, pétrosilex *m*.

felsobanyite ['felsou'bænjait], *s. Miner:* felsobanyite *f*.

felspar, *etc.* ['felspɑːr], *s.* = FELDSPAR, *etc.*

felstone ['felstoun], *s. Miner:* feldspath *m* amorphe.

felt[1] [felt], *s. Tex: etc:* feutre *m*; **hair f.,** feutre de poil; **carpet f.,** papier *m* feutre; carton *m* sous-tapis; **table f.,** molleton *m*; **imitation f.,** feutrine *f*; **asbestos f.,** feutre d'amiante; **roofing f., tarred f.,** feutre bitumé; **f. pad, ring, washer,** tampon *m*, bague *f*, rondelle *f*, de feutre; **f. side (of paper),** côté *m* feutre (du papier); **f. wiper,** racleur *m* à, en, feutre; **f. pen,** crayon *m* feutre.

felt[2]. **1.** *v.tr.* (*a*) *Tex:* feutrer (de la laine, des poils); (*b*) couvrir (un toit, etc.) de feutre bitumé. **2.** *v.i.* (*of wool, hair, etc.*) se feutrer, se coller, s'agglutiner.

felting ['feltiŋ], *s.* **1.** feutrage *m* (du poil, etc.). **2.** *coll.* (i) du feutrage, du feutre; (ii) du feutre bitumé.

felty ['felti], *a.* feutré; semblable au feutre.

felucca [fə'lʌkə], *s. Nau:* felouque *f*.

female ['fiːmeil]. **1.** *a.* (*a*) (*of pers.*) féminin; (de) femme; **f. child,** enfant *m* du sexe féminin; **my f. relations,** mes parentes *f*; **I have f. cousins,** j'ai des cousines *f*; **male and f. candidates,** candidats et candidates; **male and f. patients,** malades hommes et femmes; **f. voice,** voix féminine, de femme; **the f. sex,** le sexe féminin; *A:* **f. education,** l'éducation *f* des filles; **f. catheter,** cathéter *m* de femme; *Jur:* **male and f. heirs,** héritiers *m* mâles et femelles; (*b*) (*of animals, plants, etc.*) femelle; *Bot:* **bearing f. flowers,** fémininflore; (*c*) *Tchn:* femelle; **f. screw,** écrou *m*; **f. cal(l)iper gauge,** calibre *m* femelle, calibre simple; *Lap:* **f. sapphire,** saphir *m* femelle. **2.** *s.f.* (*a*) *Jur:* (*of pers.*) femme; *P:* femelle; **a young f.,** une jeune personne, une jeune fille, une jeune femme; (*b*) (*of animals, plants*) femelle.

femaleness ['fiːmeilnis], *s.* féminité *f*.

femcee ['fem'siː], *s.f. NAm: T.V: etc: F:* animatrice; maîtresse des cérémonies.

feme [fem], *s.f. Jur:* femme; **f. covert,** femme en puissance de mari; **f. sole,** femme non mariée, célibataire ou veuve.

feminality [femi'næliti], *s.* **1.** (*a*) *A:* = FEMININITY; (*b*) caractéristique féminine. **2.** colifichet *m* de femme.

femineity [femi'niːiti], *s.* = FEMININITY.

feminine ['feminin], *a.* féminin; **f. occupations,** occupations *f* de femme; *Lit: s.* **she is the embodiment of the eternal f.,** elle incarne l'éternel féminin; *Gram:* **in the f. gender,** *s.* **in the f.,** au féminin; **this word is f.,** ce mot est du féminin; *Pros:* **f. ending,** terminaison féminine.

feminineness ['femininnis], *s.* = FEMININITY.

femininity [femi'niniti], *s.* féminéité *f*, féminité *f*; caractère féminin (de qch.).

feminism ['feminizm], *s.* féminisme *m*.

feminist ['feminist], *a. & s.* féministe (*mf*).

feminity [fe'miniti], *s.* = FEMININITY.

feminization [feminai'zeiʃ(ə)n], *s.* féminisation *f*.

feminize ['feminaiz]. **1.** *v.tr.* féminiser (un garçon, une écriture, etc.); rendre (un garçon) efféminé. **2.** *v.i.* se féminiser.

femoral ['femərəl], *a. Anat:* fémoral, -aux.

femorotibial ['femərou'tibiəl], *a. Anat:* fémoro-tibial, -iaux.

femto ['femtou], *pref. Mth:* femto.

femur, *pl.* **femurs, femora** ['fiːmər, -əz, 'femərə], *s. Anat: etc:* fémur *m*.

fen [fen], *s.* marais *m*, marécage *m*; *Geog:* **the Fens,** les plaines marécageuses de l'Angleterre de l'est; **f. reeve,** intendant *m* des travaux hydrauliques des *Fens*.

fence[1] [fens], *s.* **1.** l'escrime *f*; **master of f.,** (i) fine lame; (ii) maître argumentateur. **2.** (*a*) clôture *f*, barrière *f*, palis *m*, palissade *f*; claie *f* (d'un champ, d'un pâturage); **lath f.,** clôture en lattes, en échalas, à claire-voie; lattis *m*; **wire f.,** clôture en fil métallique; **electric f.,** clôture électrique; **sunk f.,** saut *m* de loup; *Sp:* **to put a horse over the fences,** mettre un cheval sur les obstacles; *Turf:* (*of horse*) **never defeated over fences,** jamais vaincu dans un steeple; (*of jockey*) **first-class over fences,** de premier ordre pour les steeple-chases; **to sit on the f.,** ménager la chèvre et le chou; attendre voir d'où vient le vent; se réserver; **he always comes down on the right side of the f.,** il se trouve toujours du bon côté; **to come down on the wrong side of the f.,** faire la gaffe de se mettre du mauvais côté; **to be on the other side of the f.,** être (i) de l'autre côté de la barricade, (ii) *Pol:* du parti opposé; *U.S:* **he was building his fences for election as governor,** il ménageait ses électeurs dans l'espoir d'être élu gouverneur; *U.S:* **the tricky art of diplomatic f. mending,** l'art délicat de la conciliation diplomatique; *Austr: F:* **it's over the f.!** ça c'est un peu fort! **3.** *Tchn:* (*a*) guide *m*, réglette *f* (d'une scie circulaire, etc.); épaulement *m* (d'un rabot); (*b*) garde *f* (d'une machine-outil, etc.); garde-corps *m inv*; (*c*) mentonnet *m* (d'une serrure); (*d*) *Av:* arête *f*, guide (de la couche limite). **4.** *F:* (*a*) receleur, -euse (d'objets volés); (*b*) repaire *m* de receleurs.

fence[2]. **1.** *v.i.* faire de l'escrime, des armes; tirer des armes; **to f. with a question,** parer, éviter, une question; **to f. with a counsel,** répondre en éludant les questions d'un avocat. **2.** *v.tr.* (*a*) protéger, défendre (son corps, etc.); **to f. one's head from, against, blows,** protéger sa tête contre les coups; défendre sa tête des coups; **building fenced from the wind,** bâtiment abrité du vent; (*b*) **to f. (off) (an attack, etc.),** parer, éviter (une attaque, etc.). **3.** *v.tr.* **to f. (in) (a piece of ground, etc.),** clôturer, enclore, enceindre, palissader (un terrain, etc.); **to f. off one corner of a field,** séparer un coin d'un champ par une clôture; *A:* **to f. a town (about, round) with walls,** enceindre une ville de murailles; fortifier une ville; *B:* **fenced cities,** villes murées; **to f. (in) machinery,** munir des machines de gardes *f*, d'un garde-corps; **to f. in belting,** encoffrer des courroies. **4.** *v.tr. Jur: Ecc: Scot:* défendre (le tribunal, la Sainte-Table) contre toute intrusion ou abus (par une admonestation). **5.** (*a*) *v.tr.* recéler (des objets volés); (*b*) *v.i.* faire le recel. **6.** *v.i.* (*of horse*) sauter les haies.

fenceless ['fenslis], *a.* **1.** (*of land*) ouvert, sans clôture. **2.** *Lit:* (*of pers.*) sans défense; *Hist:* (*of city*) non-fortifié.

fencer ['fensər], *s.* **1.** escrimeur *m*, tireur *m* (d'armes); **he is a fine f.,** il manie superbement le fleuret, l'épée, les armes; il est bon tireur; c'est une fine lame. **2.** cheval sauteur de haies; **a good f.,** un bon sauteur de haies; un cheval bon aux barrières.

fenchene ['fen(t)ʃi:n], *s. Ch:* fenchène *m.*

fenchone ['fen(t)ʃoun], *s. Ch:* fenchone *f.*

fenchyl ['fen(t)ʃil], *s. Ch:* fenchyle *m*; **f. alcohol,** fenchol *m*, alcool *m* fenchylique.

fencible ['fensibl]. **1.** *s. Hist:* milicien *m*; soldat *m* de la garde nationale, de la garde territoriale. **2.** *a. Mil: Scot:* (homme *m*) valide.

fencing ['fensiŋ], *s.* **1.** escrime *f*; **f. with swords, with the epee,** escrime à l'épée; escrime de l'épée; **f. bout, f. match,** assaut *m* d'armes; **f. school,** école *f* d'escrime; salle *f* d'armes; **f. master,** maître *m* d'escrime, d'armes; **f. gloves,** gants *m* d'escrime; **he is impatient of forensic f.,** il n'aime pas les arguties, la chicane, du Palais. **2. f. (in) (of a piece of ground, etc.),** clôture *f*, palissadement *m* (d'un terrain, etc.). **3.** (*a*) clôture, barrière *f*, palissade *f*, enceinte *f*; **iron f.,** clôture en fer; **wire f.,** treillage *m* métallique, en fil de fer; (*b*) matériaux *mpl* pour clôture. **4.** *Ind:* (*a*) garde-corps *m inv* (de machine); garde *f*; (*b*) coffrage *m* (des courroies, etc.). **5.** *F:* recel *m*, recèlement *m.*

fend [fend]. **1.** *v.tr.* (*a*) *Poet:* **to f. s.o., sth., from sth.,** défendre qn, qch., de qch.; (*b*) **to f. off (a blow, etc.),** parer, détourner (un coup, etc.); *Nau:* **to f. off a collision,** parer un abordage; **f. off!** déficz! **2.** *v.i.* (*a*) *O:* **to f. for s.o.,** pourvoir aux besoins de qn; (*b*) **to f. for oneself,** se débrouiller; voler de ses propres ailes; **he can f. for himself,** il est débrouillard; il peut se suffire.

fender[1] ['fendər], *s.* (*a*) (i) *NAm:* pare-choc(s) *m inv* (de locomotive, de tramway); (ii) chasse-pierres *m inv*; chasse-bestiaux *m inv*; chasse-corps *m inv*; (*b*) *Nau:* ballon *m*, bourrelet *m*, de défense; **rope f.,** défense en filin, en cordage; **permanent f.,** ceinture *f* d'accostage; (*c*) *NAm: Aut:* garde-boue *m inv*; (*d*) (*protecting wall, door post, etc.*) bouteroue *f*, chasse-roue(s) *m inv*, borne *f*; *Civ.E:* éperon *m* (de pile de pont); **f. pile,** repoussoir *m*; (*e*) *Furn:* galerie *f* de foyer; garde-cendre *m inv.*

fender[2], *v.tr. Nau:* protéger (le bordage) avec des défenses; *Hyd.E:* protéger (les bords d'une rivière) avec un pilotis, etc.

fenestella[1] [fenes'telə], *s. Arch.* fenestella *f.*

fenestella[2], *s. Paleont:* fénestella *f.*

Fenestellidae [fenes'telidi:], *s.pl. Paleont:* fénestellidés *m.*

fenestra [fe'nestrə], *s. Anat:* **f. ovalis, f. vestibuli,** fenêtre ovale; **f. rotunda, f. cochleae,** fenêtre ronde.

fenestrate ['fenistreit], *v.tr. Med:* fenêtrer (un pansement).

fenestrate(d) ['fenistreit(id)], *a. Nat.Hist:* fenestré, fenêtré; *Med:* **fenestrated bandage,** bandage fenêtré.

fenestration [fenis'treiʃ(ə)n], *s.* **1.** *Arch:* fenêtrage *m*, fenestration *f.* **2.** *Nat.Hist:* état fenestré. **3.** *Med:* fenestration.

Fenian ['fi:niən], *s. Pol.Hist:* fénian *m.*

Fenianism ['fi:niənizm], *s. Pol.Hist:* fénianisme *m.*

fenland ['fenlænd], *s.* pays marécageux.

fenman, *pl.* **-men** ['fenmən], *s.m.* habitant des *Fens.*

fennec ['fenik], *s. Z:* fennec *m.*

fennel ['fenl], *s. Bot:* **1.** fenouil *m*; anet(h) doux; **sweet f.,** fenouil officinal; **hog's f., sow's f.,** fenouil de porc; **f. apple,** fenouillet *m*, fenouillette *f*; *Pharm:* **f. oil,** essence *f* de fenouil; **f. water,** fenouillette. **2. giant f.,** férule *f*; pamelier *m.* **3. sea f.,** crithme *m*; fenouil marin, de mer; perce-pierre *m*, *pl.* perce-pierres; casse-pierre(s) *m inv*; passe-pierre *m*, *pl.* passe-pierre(s), criste-marine *f*, *pl.* cristes-marines. **4. f. flower,** nigelle *f*, *F:* cheveux *mpl* de Vénus, quatre-épices *f.*

fent [fent], *s. Tex:* coupon *m* de drap.

fenugreek ['fenjugri:k], *s. Bot:* trigonelle *f*, fenugrec *m*; *F:* sénegré *m.*

feoff[1] [fi:f], *s. Hist:* fief *m.*

feoff[2], *v.tr. Jur:* (*a*) *A:* fieffer (qn); investir (qn) d'un fief; (*b*) **to f. out an estate,** fieffer une terre.

feoffee [fi:'fi:], *s. Jur:* (*a*) *A:* fieffataire *mf*; (*b*) **f. in, of, trust,** héritier *m* fidéicommissaire.

feoffer, feoffor ['fi:fər], *s. Jur: A:* fieffant, -e.

feoffment ['fifmənt], *s. Jur:* (*a*) *A:* inféodation *f*, investiture *f*; (*b*) don *m* en fief.

feracious [fe'reiʃəs], *a.* fertile, fécond.

feral[1] ['fiərəl, 'ferəl], *a.* **1.** *Nat.Hist:* (*a*) sauvage; (*b*) qui est retourné à l'état sauvage; **f. cat,** chat haret. **2.** *Lit:* brutal, -aux; sauvage.

feral[2], *a. Lit:* funeste.

feralia [fe'reiliə], *s.pl. Rom.Ant:* féralies *f.*

ferberite ['fə:bərait], *s. Miner:* ferbérite *f.*

fer-de-lance [fɛədə'lɑ:ns], *s. Rept:* fer-de-lance; *m.*, *pl* fers-de-lance.

fer-de-moline, -moulin [fɛədə'mouli:n, -mulɛ̃], *s. Her:* fer-de-moulin *m.*

Ferdinand ['fə:dinənd], *Pr.n.m.* Ferdinand, Fernand.

feretory ['feritəri], *s. Ecc:* châsse *f.*

ferg(h)anite ['fə:gənait], *s. Miner:* ferghanite *f.*

fergusonite ['fə:gəsənait], *s. Miner:* fergusonite *f.*

feria ['fiəriə], *s. Ecc:* férie *f*; jour non férié.

ferial ['fiəriəl], *a. Ecc:* **1.** (*weekday*) férial, -aux. **2.** (*holiday*) férié.

ferine ['fiərain], *a.* férin; sauvage; *Med:* **f. cough,** toux férine.

Feringhee [fə'riŋgi], *s.* (*in India*) **1.** *A:* Européen, -enne. **2.** *Pej:* Portugais, -aise, né(e) aux Indes; métis, métisse, de Portugais.

fermata [fə:'mɑ:tə], *s. Mus:* point *m* d'orgue.

ferment[1] ['fə:ment], *s.* **1.** ferment *m.* **2.** (*a*) fermentation *f* (des liquides); (*b*) agitation populaire, ouvrière; agitation (des esprits); **the whole town was in a (state of) f.,** toute la ville était agitée, en effervescence, dans un état d'agitation; **his mind is in a f.,** son esprit travaille.

ferment[2] [fə'ment]. **1.** *v.i.* (*a*) (*of liquids, etc.*) fermenter; (*of wine*) travailler; (*of beer*) guiller; (*of cereals*) s'échauffer; (*b*) *Dy:* venir en adoux; (*c*) (*of sedition, etc.*) fermenter; (*of the people*) être en effervescence. **2.** *v.tr.* (*a*) faire fermenter (un liquide, etc.); **to f. wine,** cuver le vin; **when youth ferments the blood,** lorsque la jeunesse échauffe le sang; (*b*) (*of the sun, damp, etc.*) échauffer (les céréales).

fermentable [fə'mentəbl], *a.* (*of liquor, etc.*) fermentable, fermentescible.

fermentation [fə:men'teiʃ(ə)n], *s.* (*a*) fermentation *f* (d'un liquide, etc.); guillage *m* (de la bière); travail *m* (du vin); échauffement *m* (des céréales); **cereals that smell of f.,** céréales *f* qui sentent l'échauffé; **to cause f. in wheat, hay,** échauffer le blé, le foin; *Wine-m:* **f. sheds,** vinée *f*; *Paperm:* **f. of rags,** pourrissage *m*; (*b*) *Fig:* agitation *f.*

fermentative [fə'mentətiv], *a.* fermentatif.

fermented [fə:'mentid], *a.* **1.** (*of liquor*) (qui a) fermenté. **2.** (pain) levé.

fermentescible [fəmen'tesibl], *a.* fermentescible.

fermenting [fə'mentiŋ], *s.* = FERMENTATION.

fermentor [fə'mentər], *s.* fermenteur *m.*

fermentum [fə'mentəm], *s. Ecc Hist:* ferment *m.*

Fermi ['fə:mi]. **1.** *Pr.n.* Fermi; *Atom.Ph:* **F. age, F. constant,** âge *m*, constante *f*, de Fermi; **F. plot,** droite *f* de Fermi; **F. Dirac statistics,** statistique *f* de Fermi-Dirac. **2.** *s. Ph.Meas:* fermi *m* (un cent-millième d'angström).

fermion ['fə:miən], *s. Atom.Ph:* fermion *m.*

fermium ['fə:miəm], *s. Ch:* fermium *m.*

fermorite ['fə:mərait], *s. Miner:* fermorite *f.*

fern [fə:n], *s. Bot:* fougère *f*; (*a*) **flowering, royal, f.,** osmonde royale; **wall f.,** polypode *m* vulgaire; polypode du chêne; **finger f., scale f.,** cétérac(h) *m*; **shield f.,** aspidie *f*, aspidium *m*; **bristle f.,** trichomanes *m*; *Pharm:* **f. oil,** essence *f* de fougère; **sweet f. oil,** essence de comptonia; (*b*) *coll.* **hillside covered with f.,** coteau couvert de fougères; (*c*) *Orn:* **f. owl,** engoulevent *m* (d'Europe).

fernery ['fə:nəri], *s.* fougeraie *f.*

ferny ['fə:ni], *a.* abondant en fougères; couvert de fougères.

ferocious [fə'rouʃəs], *a.* (*of animal, pers., look, etc.*) féroce.

ferociously [fə'rouʃəsli], *adv.* férocement, avec férocité; **he looked f. at me,** il avait l'air de vouloir me manger.

ferocity [fə'rɔsiti], *s.* férocité *f.*

Feronia [fə'rouniə], *Pr.n.f. Myth:* Féronie.

ferox ['ferɔks], *s. Ich:* truite *f* des lacs.

Ferrara [fe'rɑ:rə], *Pr.n. Geog:* Ferrare *f.*

Ferrarese [ferɑ:'ri:z], *Geog:* (*a*) *a.* ferrarais; (*b*) *s.* Ferrarais, -aise.

ferrate ['fereit], *s. Ch:* ferrate *m.*

ferreous ['feriəs], *a.* (corps, etc.) ferreux.

ferret[1] ['ferit], *s.* **1.** *Z:* furet *m*; **young f.,** furon *m*; (*b*) **f. badger,** blaireau-furet *m*, *pl.* blaireaux-furets; (*c*) *F: Pej:* **f. eyes,** yeux *m* de fouine. **2.** *F: Pej:* (*pers.*) (*a*) fureteur, -euse; furet; (*b*) espion *m* (dans un camp de prisonniers).

ferret[2], *v.* (**ferreted; ferreting**) **1.** *v.i.* fureter; chasser au furet; *Pej:* **to f. about,** fureter, fouiner, partout; **to f. (about) in one's pockets,** fureter, fouiller, dans ses poches (**for sth.,** pour trouver qch.). **2.** *v.tr.* fureter (un terrier, etc.); chasser, prendre, (les lapins, etc.) au furet; **to f. out (s.o., sth.),** dénicher (qn, qch.); découvrir (la vérité, un objet perdu); surprendre, déterrer (un secret).

ferret[3], *s. Tex:* padou *m*, fleuret *m*, filoselle *f.*

ferret[4], *s. Glassm: A:* ferret *m.*

ferreter ['feritər], *s. Ven. & F:* fureteur, -euse.

ferreting ['feritiŋ], *s.* **1.** furetage *m*; chasse *f* au furet. **2. f. out,** dénichement *m* (d'un objet perdu, etc.); mise *f* au jour (d'un secret).

ferrety ['feriti], *a.* **1.** de furet; *Pej:* **f. eyes,** yeux *m* de furet, de fouine. **2.** (*of pers.*) fureteur, -euse; fouineur, -euse; *F:* fouinard.

ferri- ['feri-], *comb.fm. Ch: Miner:* ferri-.

ferriage ['feriidʒ], *s.* **1.** passage *m* en bac; transport *m* par bac. **2.** droits *mpl* de passage.

ferric ['ferik], *a. Ch:* ferrique; **f. ammonium salt,** sel *m* ferrico-ammonique.

ferri(hydro)cyanic [feri(haidrou)sai'ænik], **ferricyanhydric** [ferisaiæn'haidrik], *a. Ch:* (acide *m*) ferricyanhydrique.

ferricyanide [feri'saiənaid], *s. Ch:* ferricyanure *m*; **potassium f.,** prussiate *m* rouge.

ferricyanogen [ferisai'ænoudʒen], *s. Ch:* ferricyanogène *m.*

ferriferous [fe'rifərəs], *a.* (roche *f*, etc.) ferrifère.

ferrimagnetic [ferimæg'netik], *a.* ferrimagnétique.

ferrimagnetism [feri'mægnitizm], *s.* ferrimagnétisme *m.*

Ferris wheel ['feris(h)wi:l], *s.* la grande roue (dans les parcs d'attractions).

ferrite ['ferait], *s.* ferrite *m*; *Cmptr:* **f. core,** tore *f* de ferrite; **f. core store, memory,** mémoire *f* à tores de ferrite.

ferritin(e) ['ferit(a)in], *s. Physiol:* ferritine *f.*

ferro- ['ferou], *pref. Ch: Miner:* ferro-.

ferro-alloy ['ferou'ælɔi], *s. Metall:* ferro-alliage *m*, *pl.* ferro-alliages; alliage ferreux.

ferro-aluminium ['ferouælju'miniəm], *s.* ferro-aluminium *m.*

ferroboron ['ferou'bɔ:rɔn], *s. Metall:* ferrobore *m.*

ferrocalcite ['ferou'kælsait], *s. Miner:* ferrocalcite *f.*

ferrocerium ['ferou'siəriəm], *s.* ferrocérium *m* (pour pierre à briquet).

ferrochrome, ferrochromium, ['ferou'kroum, -'kroumiəm], *s.* ferrochrome *m.*

ferroconcrete ['ferou'kɔŋkri:t], *s.* béton armé.

ferrocyanic ['ferousai'ænik], **ferrocyanhydric** ['ferousaiæn'haidrik], *a. Ch:* (acide *m*) ferrocyanhydrique.

ferrocyanide ['ferou'saiənaid], *s. Ch:* ferrocyanure *m*; **potassium f.,** prussiate *m* jaune.

ferrocyanogen ['ferousai'ænoudʒen], *s. Ch:* ferrocyanogène *m.*

ferroelectric ['feroui'lektrik], *a.* ferroélectrique.

ferrogallic ['ferou'gælik], *a. Phot:* (papier *m*) ferrogallique.

ferroglass ['ferouglɑ:s], *s. Ind:* cristal armé.

ferromagnesian ['feroumæg'ni:ziən], *a. Miner:* ferromagnésien.

ferromagnetic ['feroumæg'netik], *a.* ferromagnétique.

ferromagnetics ['feroumæg'netiks], *s.pl.* (*usu. with sg. const.*) ferromagnétisme *m.*

ferromagnetism ['ferou'mægnitizm], *s. El:* ferromagnétisme *m.*

ferromanganese ['ferou'mæŋgəni:z], *s. Miner:* ferromanganèse *m.*

ferromolybdenum ['feroumɔ'libdənəm], *s.* ferromolybdène *m.*

ferronickel ['ferou'nikl], *s.* ferronickel *m*; **f. alloys,** alliages *m* fer-nickel; **f. accumulator,** accumulateur *m* au fer-nickel.

ferroporphyrin ['ferou'pɔ:firin], *s. Bio-Ch:* ferroporphyrine *f.*

ferroprint ['ferouprint], *s. Phot:* épreuve *f* aux sels de fer.

ferroprussiate ['ferou'prʌʃieit], *s. Ch:* ferroprussiate *m.*

ferrosilicon ['ferou'silikɔn], *s. Metall:* ferrosilicium *m.*

ferrosoferric ['ferousou'ferik], *a. Ch:* ferrosoferrique; **f. oxide,** ferroferrite *f.*

ferrotitanium ['ferouti'teiniəm], *s. Metall:* ferrotitane *m.*

ferrotungsten ['ferou'tʌŋstən], *s. Miner:* ferrotungstène *m.*

ferrotype ['feroutaip]. *Phot:* (*a*) *s.* ferrotypie *f*; *A:* **f. photography,** photographie foraine; (*b*) *a.* ferrotypique.

ferrous ['ferəs], *a. Ch:* (oxyde, carbonate, etc.) ferreux; **f. sulphide,** pyrite *f* de fer.

ferrovanadium ['ferouvə'neidiəm], *s. Metall:* ferrovanadium *m.*

ferruginous [fi'ru:dʒinəs], *a. Miner: etc:* (quartz, etc.)

ferrugineux.
ferrugo [fe'ru:gou], *s. Agr:* rouille *f.*
ferrule[1] ['ferəl, 'ferju:l], *s.* virole *f,* bague *f,* frette *f* (d'un manche d'outil, d'une canne à pêche, etc.); bout ferré, embout *m* (de canne, de parapluie); sabot *m* (de piquet); croisière *f* (de sabre-baïonnette); bobine *f* (de foret à archet); embrassure *f* (d'une poutre); **f. of a pile,** frette, couronne *f,* d'un pieu; **wire f.,** coulant *m* de fil métallique; **transfer f.,** manchon *m* de raccordement, raccord *m* tubulaire; *Num:* **coining f.,** virole.
ferrule[2], *v.tr.* viroler, fretter, baguer (le manche d'un outil, etc.); ferrer, embouter (une canne, etc.); couronner (un pieu).
ferruled ['ferəld, 'ferju:ld], *a.* (*of tube, etc.*) bagué; (*of handle, etc.*) fretté; (*of stick, etc.*) embouté.
ferry[1] ['feri], *s.* (*a*) (endroit *m* de) passage *m* (d'un cours d'eau en bac); *F:* le bac; **to cross the f.,** passer le bac; (**air**) **f.,** service *m* de livraison d'avions; (*b*) bac *m*; **chain f.,** bac à chaine; **trail f.,** (bac à) traille *f,* va-et-vient *m*; **passenger, car, f.,** bac à piétons, à voitures; **train f.,** transbordeur *m* de trains; bac transbordeur; ferry-boat, *m, pl.* ferry-boats; **air f.,** avion transbordeur; **to take the f.,** prendre le bac; **f. bridge,** pont transbordeur; *Lit:* **Charon's f.,** la barque de Charon; (*c*) *Jur:* **f. (right),** droit *m* de bac.
ferry[2]. **1.** *v.i.* **to f. across a river,** passer une rivière en bac; traverser une rivière par le bac. **2.** *v.tr.* (*a*) **to f. s.o., a car, across a river,** passer qn, une voiture, en bac, dans le bac; transborder qn, une voiture; **will you f. me across?** voulez-vous me passer? **to f. troops,** transporter des troupes; **he spent the day ferrying voters to the poll,** il a passé la journée à véhiculer, transporter, des électeurs aux urnes; (*b*) **to f. a boat across a river,** faire traverser une rivière à un bateau; **to f. an aircraft,** livrer un avion (par air).
ferryboat ['feribout], *s.* bac *m*; bachot *m* de passeur.
ferrying ['feriiŋ], *s.* **1.** transport *m* en bac, par bac. **2. f. across,** passage *m* en bac; transbordement *m.*
ferryman, *pl.* **-men** ['ferimən], *s.m.* passeur; *Lit:* **the F. of the Styx,** le nocher du Styx, le nautonier des enfers.
ferrywoman, *pl.* **-women** ['feriwumən, -wimin], *s.f.* passeuse.
fertile ['fə:tail], *a.* **1.** (*a*) (sol, etc.) fertile, fécond (**in,** en); productif (**of,** de); généreux (en); (*of soil*) **to become more f.,** s'amender; *Geog:* **the F. Crescent,** le Croissant fertile; *Atom.Ph:* **f. material,** matière *f,* substance *f,* fertile; **f. imagination,** imagination *f* fertile; (*b*) (œuf) fécondé, coché. **2.** fécondant.
fertilisin [fə:'tilizin], *s. Biol:* fertilisine *f.*
fertility [fə:'tiliti], *s.* fertilité *f,* fécondité *f* (du sol, de l'imagination de qn, etc.); productivité *f* (du sol); **f. of mind, of invention,** fertilité d'esprit, d'invention; *Pol.Ec:* **f. rate,** taux *m* de fécondabilité.
fertilizable ['fə:tilaizəbl], *a.* **1.** fertilisable; (sol *m*) amendable. **2.** fécondable.
fertilization [fə:tilai'zeiʃ(ə)n], *s.* **1.** fertilisation *f,* fécondation *f* (d'un œuf, etc.); *Bot:* pollinisation *f*; **cross f.,** fécondation, pollinisation, croisée; **double f.,** double fécondation; **self f.,** (i) *Biol:* autofécondation *f*; (ii) *Bot:* pollinisation directe. **2.** fertilisation (du sol); amendement *m* (du sol avec des engrais).
fertilize ['fə:tilaiz], *v.tr.* **1.** fertiliser, féconder (un œuf, une plante, etc.); **fertilized fruit,** fruit noué; *Husb:* **to f. (a cow, etc.) artificially,** inséminer (une vache, etc.); *Bot:* **to cross f.,** hybrider (deux espèces). **2.** fertiliser (le sol).
fertilizer ['fə:tilaizər], *s.* **1.** agent fécondant. **2.** *Agr:* engrais *m,* fertilisant *m,* fertiliseur *m*; **artificial fertilizers,** engrais chimiques.
fertilizin ['fə:tilizin], *s. Biol:* fertilisine *f.*
fertilizing ['fə:tilaiziŋ], *a.* fécondateur, -trice.
ferula, *pl.* **-ae** ['ferjulə, -i:], *s. Bot:* férule *f.*
ferule ['ferju:l], *s.* **1.** *Sch: A:* férule *f.* **2.** *Bot:* = FERULA.
ferulic [fe'ru:lik], *a. Ch:* férulique.
fervanite ['fə:vənait], *s. Miner:* fervanite *f.*
fervency ['fə:vənsi], *s.* ardeur *f,* empressement *m,* fougue *f*; ferveur *f* (d'une prière, etc.).
fervent ['fə:vənt], *a.* **1.** (*of heat, etc.*) ardent. **2.** (*of pers., zeal, etc.*) vif, ardent, fervent; **f. prayer,** prière ardente, fervente.
fervently ['fə:vəntli], *adv.* (prier, etc.) avec ferveur; (désirer, etc.) ardemment, passionnément, avec ardeur.
fervid ['fə:vid], *a.* (*of preacher, imagination, etc.*) fervent, ardent, passionné.
fervidly ['fə:vidli], *adv.* ardemment, avec ferveur.
fervour ['fə:vər], *s.* **1.** *A: & Lit:* ardeur *f,* chaleur *f* (du soleil, etc.). **2.** passion *f,* ferveur *f,* ardeur, zèle *m.*
fescennine ['fesinain], *a. Lt.Lit:* (*of verse, etc.*) fescennin.
fescue ['feskju:], *s.* **1.** *Sch: O:* baguette *f* (pour démonstration au tableau noir). **2.** *Bot:* **f. (grass),** fétuque *f*; seigle bâtard; **sheep's f.,** fétuque ovine, coquioule *f.*
fess(e) [fes], *s. Her:* fasce *f*; **f.-point,** abîme *m*; **party per f.,** coupé.
fessey ['fesi], *a. Her:* fascé.
festal ['festəl], *a.* **1.** (jour, air, etc.) de fête. **2.** (gens) en fête.
fester[1] ['festər], *s.* **1.** *A:* ulcère *m,* pustule *f.* **2.** *Med:* plaie suppurante.
fester[2]. **1.** *v.i.* (*a*) (*of wound, etc.*) suppurer, s'ulcérer, s'envenimer; (*b*) (*of carrion, etc.*) se putréfier, pourrir; se corrompre; (*c*) (*of resentment, etc.*) couver. **2.** *v.tr.* (*a*) envenimer (une plaie); (*b*) putréfier, faire pourrir (de la charogne, etc.); (*c*) laisser couver, nourrir (la haine, etc.).
festering[1] ['festəriŋ], *a.* (*a*) (*of wound, etc.*) ulcéreux, suppurant; (*b*) putrescent, pourrissant.
festering[2], *s.* (*a*) suppuration *f,* ulcération *f* (d'une blessure, etc.); (*b*) putréfaction *f.*
festination [festi'neiʃ(ə)n], *s. Med:* festination *f.*
festival ['festiv(ə)l]. **1.** *s.* (*a*) fête (nationale, de la moisson, etc.); *Ecc:* **harvest f.,** office d'action de grâces (célébré après la rentrée des récoltes); (*b*) *Mus: etc:* festival *m,* -als; **the Shakespeare F.,** le festival shakespearien; **film f.,** festival du film. **2.** *a.* (*a*) (habits, etc.) de fête; (*b*) (musique) de festival.
festive ['festiv], *a.* **1.** (jour, air, etc.) de fête; (table, etc.) du festin; **the f. season,** l'époque *f* des réjouissances, des festins (Noël); *Lit:* **to gather round the f. board,** se rassembler à table pour le festin. **2.** (*of pers.*) (*a*) en humeur de se réjouir; gai, joyeux; jovial, -aux; **to be in f. mood,** avoir le cœur en fête; (*b*) *F: O:* un peu parti (après boire); éméché.
festively ['festivli], *adv.* d'une manière gaie, joyeuse; joyeusement.
festivity [fes'tiviti], *s.* fête *f,* réjouissance *f,* festivité *f*; **nothing marred the festivities,** rien ne troubla les festivités, la fête.
festoon[1] [fes'tu:n], *s.* **1.** *Arch: etc:* feston *m,* bouillon *m,* guirlande *f.* **2.** *El:* **f. lamp,** lampe *f* forme navette; navette *f.* **3.** *Anat:* **f. (of the gum),** feston gingival.
festoon[2]. **1.** *v.tr.* (*a*) festonner (qch.) (**with,** de) (*b*) disposer (des fleurs, etc.) en festons. **2.** *v.i.* pendre en festons.
festoonery [fes'tu:nəri], *s.* décoration *f* en festons.
fetal ['fi:tl], *etc. See* FOETAL, etc.
fetch[1] [fetʃ], *s.* **1.** *A:* effort *m*; **to take a f.,** faire un grand effort. **2.** *A:* ruse *f,* stratagème *m,* tour *m*; **to cast a f.,** tendre un piège. **3.** *Nau:* (*a*) chemin *m* à faire, distance *f* à parcourir; (*b*) *Oc:* fetch *m* (des vagues); (*c*) ouvert *m,* étendue *f* (d'une baie, etc.).
fetch[2], *v.*
I. *v.tr. & i.* **1.** *v.tr.* (*a*) aller chercher (qn, qch.); **come and f. me,** venez me chercher; venez me prendre (chez moi, etc.); **to f. water from the river,** aller puiser de l'eau dans la rivière; (*b*) apporter (qch.); amener (qn); *F:* **f. it here!** amenez-le-moi! (*to dog*) **f. (it)!** va chercher! (*of pers.*) **to f. and carry for s.o.,** être aux ordres de qn; faire les commissions de qn; **I seem to do nothing but fetch(ing) and carry(ing),** je ne fais rien que les petites besognes. **2.** *v.tr.* (*a*) *O:* tirer, faire venir (du sang, des larmes, etc.); (*b*) faire agglomérer (le beurre); (*c*) amorcer, allumer, charger (une pompe). **3.** *v.tr. Com: etc:* (i) rapporter, (ii) atteindre (un certain prix); **it fetched a high price,** cela s'est vendu cher; **it won't f. much,** cela ne rapportera pas beaucoup; **it will f. about £100,** cela va chercher dans les £100. **4.** *v.tr. F: O:* (i) faire appel à (l'imagination); faire de l'effet sur (qn); se gagner (qn); (ii) mettre (qn) en colère; *F:* **that'll f. him!** voilà qui le séduira, qui l'allumera! **5.** *v.tr.* **to f. one's breath,** prendre haleine; **to f. a sigh, a groan,** pousser un soupir, un gémissement. **6.** *v.tr. P:* **to f. s.o. a blow,** flanquer un coup à qn; **to f. s.o. a box on the ear,** envoyer, appliquer, une torgn(i)ole, une claque, à qn. **7.** *v.tr. A:* **to f. a compass, a circuit,** faire un circuit, un détour, un tour. **8.** *v.tr. Nau:* (*a*) gagner, atteindre (le rivage, un navire, etc.); **to f. headway,** prendre de l'erre; (*b*) **to f. a vessel to the quay,** aborder un navire au quai.
II. (*compound verbs*) **1. fetch about,** *v.i.* faire une bordée.
2. fetch away, *v.tr.* emmener (qn); emporter (qch.).
3. fetch back, *v.tr.* ramener (qn); rapporter (qch.).
4. fetch down, *v.tr.* (*a*) faire descendre (qn); descendre (qch.); (*b*) **to f. down a partridge, one's opponent,** abattre une perdrix, son adversaire.
5. fetch in, *v.tr.* faire entrer (qn); rentrer (qch.); **to f. in the washing,** rentrer la lessive.
6. fetch out, *v.tr.* faire sortir (qn, qch.).
7. fetch through, *v.i. Nau:* parvenir au port (malgré des avaries, le gros temps, etc.).
8. fetch up. (*a*) *v.tr.* (i) faire monter (qn, qch.); (ii) *P: O:* vomir (des aliments); (iii) *U.S: Dial:* élever (des enfants); (*b*) *v.i.* (i) *Nau:* **to f. up at a port,** parvenir, arriver, à un port; *F:* **they finally fetched up at our house,** ils ont finalement abouti chez nous; (ii) *F:* s'arrêter; **the car fetched up against a wall,** la voiture s'est (finalement) arrêtée en heurtant un mur; **he was fetched up short at a traffic light,** il a dû s'arrêter net à un feu rouge; (iii) *esp. NAm: F:* aboutir, finir; **she went out to buy a dress and fetched up with three,** elle est sortie acheter une robe et elle est rentrée avec trois.
fetch[3], *s. A: & U.S:* revenant *m*; fantôme *m,* apparition *f*; **f. candle,** lumière qui annonce la mort.
fetcher ['fetʃər], *s.* **f. and carrier,** garçon *m,* enfant *m,* qui fait les courses.
fetching ['fetʃiŋ], *a. F:* (sourire, air) séduisant, attrayant, attirant, aguichant; **there's something f. about her,** elle a de ça; **her paleness is rather f.,** sa pâleur lui donne un air intéressant.
fetchingly ['fetʃiŋli], *adv.* d'un air séduisant; (vêtue) à ravir.
fête[1] [feit], *s.* fête *f*; **village f.,** fête communale, du pays; **f. day,** (jour *m* de) la fête (de qn).
fête[2], *v.tr.* fêter (qn, un événement, etc.); faire fête à (qn).
fetial ['fi:ʃ(ə)l], *a. & s. RomAnt:* fécial (*m*), -aux.
fetid ['fetid, 'fi:tid], *a.* fétide, puant.
fetidity [fe'tiditi, fi:'tiditi], **fetidness** ['fetidnis, 'fi:tidnis], *s.* fétidité *f,* puanteur *f.*
fetish ['fi:tiʃ, 'fe-], *s.* fétiche *m*; **f. bird,** oiseau *m* fétiche; **to make a f. of the past,** avoir le culte du passé.
fetishism ['fi:tiʃizm, 'fe-], *s.* fétichisme *m.*
fetishist ['fi:tiʃist, 'fe-], *s.* fétichiste *mf.*
fetishistic [fi:ti'ʃistik, fe-], *a.* fétichiste.
fetlock ['fetlɔk], *s.* fanon *m* (du cheval); **f. joint,** boulet *m*; **overshot f.,** bouleture *f*; **horse with overshot f.,** cheval bouleté.
fetor ['fi:tɔ:r], *s. Med: etc:* mauvaise odeur; puanteur *f.*
fetter[1] ['fetər], *s. usu. in pl.* lien *m*; *pl.* chaines *f,* fers *m* (d'un prisonnier, etc.); entrave *f* (d'un cheval); **in fetters,** enchaîné; dans les fers; **to burst one's fetters,** rompre ses liens, ses fers; **to cast off the fetters,** s'affranchir de ses entraves, de ses liens.
fetter[2], *v.tr.* enchainer (qn); charger (qn) de fers, de chaines; entraver (un cheval).
fettered ['fetəd], *a.* (*of prisoner, etc.*) enchainé, dans les fers; (*of horse*) entravé.
fetterless ['fetəlis], *a.* sans fers, sans entraves; libre, indépendant.
fetterlock ['fetəlɔk], *s. Her:* entrave *f* de cheval.
fettle[1] ['fetl], *s.* **1.** (bonne) condition, forme *f* (de qn, d'un cheval, etc.); **to be in fine, in good, in high, f.,** être en condition, en forme, en bon état, en train, en haleine; être frais et dispos; être dans ses bons jours. **2.** *Metall:* garniture *f* (de fond de four à puddler).
fettle[2]. **1.** *Dial:* (*a*) *v.tr.* ajuster, ranger (qch.); mettre (qch.) en ordre; (*b*) *v.i.* faire l'affairé. **2.** *v.tr. Metalw:* (*a*) ébarber; ébavurer; (*b*) décaper; épiler (des pièces d'étain fondues); (*c*) retorcher (les parties érodées d'un fourneau).
fettler ['fetlər], *s. Metalw:* ébarbeur *m.*
fettling ['fetliŋ], *s.* **1.** *Dial:* travaux *mpl* de ménage, de mise en ordre. **2.** *Metalw:* (*a*) ébarbage *m,* ébavurage *m*; **f. machine,** ébarbeuse *f,* machine *f* à ébarber; (*b*) décapement *m,* décapage *m*; (*c*) remise *f* en état (d'un four à puddler).
fetus ['fi:təs], *s.* = FOETUS.
feu[1] [fju:], *s.* **1.** *Hist:* fief *m.* **2.** *Jur: Scot:* (*a*) bail perpétuel moyennant une redevance fixe; (*b*) petite propriété concédée à perpétuité mais assujettie à une redevance.
feu[2], *v.tr. Jur: Scot:* **to f. a piece of land,** concéder un terrain à perpétuité, moyennant redevance; **to f. out an estate,** morceler une propriété (moyennant redevances).
feud[1] [fju:d], *s.* inimitié *f* (entre familles, clans, etc.); **a deadly f., a death f., a blood f.,** une guerre à mort; **family blood f.,** vendetta *f*; **there is a blood f. between them,** il y a du sang versé entre eux; **family feuds,** dissensions *f* domestiques; **to be at f. with s.o.,** être à couteaux tirés avec qn; **families at open f.,** familles *f* en querelle ouverte.
feud[2], *v.i.* **they feuded over the will for years,** ils se sont querellés au sujet du testament pendant des années.
feud[3], *s. Hist:* fief *m.*
feudal ['fju:d(ə)l], *a. Hist:* (régime, service, etc.) féodal, -aux.
feudalism ['fju:dəlizm], *s.* le système féodal; le régime féodal; la féodalité.
feudalist ['fju:dəlist], *s.* **1.** partisan *m* du régime féodal. **2.** feudiste (versé dans la matière des fiefs).

feudality [fju:'dæliti], *s.* **1.** féodalité *f.* **2.** fief *m.*

feudalize ['fju:dəlaiz], *v.tr.* féodaliser (un peuple, etc.).

feudally ['fju:dəli], *adv.* féodalement.

feudatory ['fju:dətəri]. **1.** *a.* feudataire (**to, de**); vassal, -aux (**to, de**). **2.** *s.* **the great feudatories of the Crown,** les grands feudataires de la Couronne; les grands vassaux.

feutre ['fju:tər], *s. A.Arms:* faucre *m,* fautre *m.*

fever[1] ['fi:vər], *s.* (*a*) *Med:* (*high temperature*) fièvre *f*; **slight f.,** fièvre lente; **high f.,** forte fièvre; *F:* **raging f.,** fièvre de cheval; **f. heat,** température *f* de fièvre; (*b*) *Med:* (*disease*) fièvre; **malarial f.,** *U.S:* **f. and ague,** *O:* **marsh f.,** malaria *f,* paludisme *m*; **yellow f.,** vomito(-negro) *m*; fièvre jaune; **jungle f.,** fièvre des jungles; **hay f.,** rhume *m,* fièvre, des foins; *F:* **scarlet f.,** scarlatine *f*; **spotted f.,** (i) méningite cérébro-spinale; (ii) typhus *m*; *Med: Vet:* **canicola f.,** leptospirose *f*; *Vet:* **swine f.,** rouget *m* du porce; **f. blister, sore,** herpès *m* (qui apparaît au cours d'une fièvre); **it's a f. trap,** c'est un endroit malsain, où on attrape la typhoïde, la malaria, etc.; *O:* **f. swamp,** marécage *m* à fièvre, où règne la malaria; *A:* **f. hospital,** hôpital *m* des maladies contagieuses, de, pour, contagieux; *A:* **f. ward,** salle *f* des fiévreux (dans un hôpital); (*c*) *Bot:* **f. tree,** arbre *m* à fièvre; (*d*) *Fig:* fièvre; **f. of joy, of excitement,** joie, excitation, fébrile, fiévreuse; **expectation was f. high, had reached f. heat,** l'attente *f* était fiévreuse, fébrile; *Hist:* **gold f.,** fièvre de l'or.

fever[2], *v.tr.* enfiévrer; donner la fièvre à (qn).

fevered ['fi:vəd], *a.* enfiévré, fiévreux.

feverfew ['fi:vəfju:], *s. Bot:* chrysanthème *m* matricaire; matricaire *f*; pyrèthre *m*; *F:* pied *m* d'Alexandre.

feverish ['fi:v(ə)riʃ], *a.* **1.** *Med:* (état, etc.) fiévreux, fébrile, pyrexique; **to make s.o. f.,** donner la fièvre à qn, rendre qn fiévreux; *Fig:* **f. activity,** activité fébrile, fiévreuse. **2.** *O:* (*of climate, etc.*) fiévreux, malsain.

feverishly ['fi:v(ə)riʃli], *adv.* fiévreusement, fébrilement; **he threw himself f. into his work,** il s'est appliqué fiévreusement à son travail; il s'est jeté dans le travail à corps perdu.

feverishness ['fi:v(ə)riʃnis], *s.* état fiévreux; *Med:* fébrilité *f,* pyrexie *f.*

feverroot ['fi:vəru:t], *s. Bot:* triostée *m.*

feverwort ['fi:vəwə:t], *s. Bot:* (*a*) triostée *m*; (*b*) eupatoire *f.*

few [fju:], *a.* **1.** (*a*) peu de (personnes, choses); **very f. people,** très peu de gens; un très petit nombre de gens; **he has f. friends,** il a peu d'amis; il n'a guère d'amis; **the last f. years of his life,** les toutes dernières années de sa vie; **one of the f. people who . . .,** une des rares personnes qui . . .; **during the last** (*or* **next**) **f. days,** ces jours-ci; **with f. exceptions,** à de rares exceptions près; **his f. hundred pounds of state pension,** ses quelques centaines de livres *f* de retraite de l'État; **he wanted to save the f. thousands that he had left,** il voulait épargner les quelques mille livres qui lui restaient; **trains every f. minutes,** trains *m* à quelques minutes d'intervalle; **every f. days,** tous les deux ou trois jours; à quelques jours d'intervalle; **these f. minutes of conversation,** ces quelques minutes *f* d'entretien; (*b*) **a f.,** quelques; **I know a f. people who . . .,** je connais des gens qui . . .; **I have only a f. pounds,** je n'ai que quelques livres *f*; **a f. more,** encore quelques-uns, encore un peu; **he had a good f. enemies,** il avait pas mal d'ennemis, un nombre considérable d'ennemis; **in a f. minutes,** dans quelques minutes; **a. f. minutes after six,** à six heures et quelques minutes; (*c*) peu nombreux, rares; **we are very f., still fewer than yesterday,** nous sommes peu nombreux, encore moins (nombreux) qu'hier; **our days are f.,** nos jours sont comptés; **such occasions are f. (and far between),** de telles occasions sont rares, rarissimes; **his visits are f. and far between,** ses visites sont rarissimes, rares et espacées; il vient nous voir (si) peu souvent; **area where the houses are f. and far between,** région *f* où les maisons sont rares et espacées. **2.** (*with noun function*) (*a*) peu (de gens, etc.); *B:* **many are called, but f. are chosen,** il y a beaucoup d'appelés, mais peu d'élus; **f. of them had travelled,** peu d'entre eux avaient voyagé; **there are very f. of us,** nous sommes peu nombreux; **there are very f. of us who can remember it,** nous sommes peu à nous en souvenir; **f. are of this opinion,** peu de gens sont de cet avis; il y en a peu, de cet avis; **the fortunate f.,** une minorité de gens heureux; **the thinking f.,** le nombre très restreint de gens qui pensent; (*b*) quelques-uns, -unes; **I want a f. of these cakes, of these oranges,** je voudrais quelques-uns de ces gâteaux, quelques-unes de ces oranges; **a faithful f. remain,** il reste encore quelques fidèles *m*; **a f. thought otherwise,** quelques-uns pensaient autrement; **a f. of the survivors,** quelques-uns des survivants; **a f. of us remained to chat,** nous sommes restés quelques-uns, -unes, à causer; **I know a f. of them,** j'en connais quelques-uns; **we shall only be a f.,** nous serons en petit comité; **a f. of us,** quelques-uns, un petit nombre, d'entre nous; **there were a good f. of them,** il y en avait pas mal.

fewer ['fju:ər], *a.* (*comp. of* FEW) **1.** moins (de); **he has f. debts (than you),** il a moins de dettes (que vous); **there are f. (of them) than I thought,** il y en a moins que je n'avais pensé; **20% f. visitors (than last year),** 20 % de visiteurs en moins (que l'année dernière). **2.** plus rares, moins nombreux; **the houses became f. (and farther between),** les maisons s'espaçaient, s'éclaircissent, devenaient plus rares.

fewest ['fju:ist], *a.* (*sup. of* FEW) **1.** le moins (de); **the f. people possible,** le moins de gens possible; *Sch:* **he passed, but with the f. number of marks possible,** il a été reçu, mais avec la note minimum. **2.** les plus rares, les moins nombreux; **the area where there are the f. houses,** la région où les maisons sont les moins nombreuses, les plus rares.

fewter ['fju:tər], *s. A.Arms:* faucre *m,* fautre *m.*

fey [fei], *a. Scot:* **1.** (*a*) destiné à mourir; qui a des pressentiments de mort, des visions de l'au-delà; (*b*) sur le point de mourir; mourant; (*c*) qui a un air de venir d'un autre monde, un air de revenant; (*d*) qui est doué de seconde vue. **2.** fou, *f.* folle; **he's gone f.,** il a perdu l'esprit.

feyness ['feinis], *s.* **1.** *A:* gracilité *f* de fée (d'une actrice, etc.). **2.** *Scot:* don *m* de seconde vue.

fez [fez], *s. Cost:* fez *m.*

fiancé, *f.* **-ée** [fi'ɑ̃:nsei], *s.* fiancé, -ée.

Fiann [fi:n], *s. Irish Hist:* Fénian *m.*

fiasco [fi'æskou], *s.* fiasco *m, F:* four *m*; (*of play, ceremony, etc.*) **to be a f.,** faire fiasco; faire four.

fiat[1] ['faiæt], *s.* **1.** (*a*) consentement *m,* autorisation *f*; **to give one's f. to sth.,** donner son consentement à qch.; (*b*) *Jur:* autorisation donnée par le *Home Secretary* de poursuivre une action contre la Couronne. **2.** (*a*) décret *m,* commandement *m,* ordre *m*; **paternal f.,** (o)ukase paternel; (*b*) *Fin: U.S:* **f. money,** monnaie fiduciaire, fictive; papier-monnaie *m* inconvertible. **3.** *Psy:* fiat *m inv.*

fiat[2], *v.tr.* (*used only in inf. & pr.t.*) **1.** autoriser, sanctionner (qch.); consentir à (qch.). **2.** décréter (qch.).

fib[1] [fib], *s. F:* petit mensonge; conte *m,* blague *f.*

fib[2], *v.i.* (**fibbed**) *F:* mentir; blaguer; en conter (à qn); (*to child*) **you're fibbing!** ton nez remue!

fib[3], *s. Box: A:* coup *m* (de poing).

fib[4], *v.tr. F: A:* battre, frapper, (qn) à coups redoublés; malmener (qn).

fibber ['fibər], *s. F:* menteur, -euse; blagueur *m,* craqueur *m*; conteur *m* (de craques).

fibration [fai'breiʃ(ə)n], *s. Physiol:* fibration *f.*

fibre ['faibər], *s.* **1.** fibre *f*; filament *m*; (*a*) **muscle f.,** fibre musculaire; **f. cell,** fibre-cellule *f, pl.* fibres-cellules; **every f. of his being revolted at the idea,** chaque fibre de son être se révoltait à cette idée; (*b*) *Lit:* **our moral f.,** notre nature *f*; *O:* **a man of coarse f.,** un homme d'une trempe grossière, vulgaire; (*c*) *Metall:* fibre, nerf *m* (de l'acier); *Mec:* **f. stress,** effort *m* dans la matière. **2.** *Com:* **vegetable f., dwarf-palm f.,** crin végétal; **f. trunk,** malle *f* en fibre; **f. washer,** rondelle *f* en fibre; **wood f.,** fibre, laine *f,* de bois; *Tex:* **staple f.,** fibran(n)e *f*; **glass f.,** fibre de verre. **3.** *Bot:* radicelle *f.*

fibre board ['faibəbɔ:d], *s.* panneau *m* de fibres agglomérées.

fibreglass ['faibəglɑ:s], *s.* fibre *f,* laine *f,* soie *f,* ouate *f,* de verre; **f. insulation,** isolation *f* au moyen de laine de verre.

fibreless ['faibəlis], *a.* **1.** sans fibres. **2.** *F: O:* (*of pers.*) sans caractère, sans énergie; mou, *f.* molle.

fibriform ['faibrifɔ:m], *a.* en forme de fibres; fibreux.

fibril ['faibril], **fibrilla,** *pl.* **-ae** [fai'brilə, -i:], *s. Anat: Bot:* fibrille *f.*

fibrillar ['faibrilər], **fibrillary** ['faibriləri], **fibrillate(d)** ['faibrileit(id)], *a. Anat: Bot:* fibrillaire.

fibrillation [faibri'leiʃ(ə)n], *s. Physiol:* fibrillation *f.*

fibrilliform [fai'brilifɔ:m], *a.* en forme de fibrilles; fibrilleux.

fibrillose ['faibrilous], **fibrillous** ['faibriləs], *a.* (tissu, etc.) fibrilleux.

fibrin ['faibrin], *s. Ch: Physiol:* fibrine *f*; **f. ferment,** fibrin-ferment *m.*

fibrin(a)emia [faibri'ni:miə], *s. Med:* fibrinémie *f.*

fibrino- ['faibrinou], *comb.fm.* fibrino-.

fibrinogen [fai'brinoudʒen], *s. Ch:* fibrinogène *m.*

fibrinolytic ['faibrinou'litik], *a.* fibrinolytique.

fibrinoplastic ['faibrinou'plæstik], *a.* fibrino-plastique.

fibrinous ['faibrinəs], *a.* fibrineux.

fibrinuria [faibri'njuriə], *s. Med:* fibrinurie *f.*

fibro- ['faibrou], *comb.fm.* fibro-.

fibroblast ['faibroublæst], *s. Biol:* fibroblaste *m.*

fibrocartilage ['faibrou'kɑ:tilidʒ], *s. Anat:* fibrocartilage *m.*

fibrocartilaginous ['faibroukɑ:ti'lædʒinəs], *a. Anat:* (tissu, etc.) fibrocartilagineux.

Fibrocement ['faibrousi'ment], *s. Civ.E: etc: R.t.m:* Fibrociment *m.*

fibrochondroma ['faibroukən'droumə], *s. Med:* fibrochondrome *m.*

fibrocyst ['faibrousist], *s. Med:* fibrokyste *m.*

fibrocystic ['faibrou'sistik], *a. Med:* fibrokystique.

fibrocyte ['faibrousait], *s. Biol:* fibrocyte *m.*

fibroferrite ['faibrou'ferait], *s. Miner:* fibroferrite *f.*

fibroid ['faibrɔid]. **1.** *a.* (tumeur *f,* etc.) fibroïde; **f. degeneration,** dégénérescence fibreuse. **2.** *s. Med:* fibrome *m.*

fibroin ['faibrouin], *s. Ch:* fibroïne *f.*

fibrolite ['faibroulait], *s. Miner:* fibrolite *f.*

fibroma, *pl.* **-mata** [fai'broumə(tə)], *s. Med:* fibrome *m.*

fibromatosis ['faibroumə'tousis], *s. Med:* fibromatose *f.*

fibromatous [fai'brɔmətəs], *a. Med:* fibromateux.

fibromyoma ['faibroumai'oumə], *s. Med:* fibromyome *m.*

fibroserous ['faibrou'siərəs], *s. Med:* fibroséreux.

fibrosis [fai'brousis], *s. Med:* fibrose *f.*

fibrositis [faibrə'saitis], *s. Med:* fibrosite *f.*

fibrous ['faibrəs], *a.* **1.** (tissu, etc.) fibreux; *Bot:* **f. root,** racine fasciculée, fibreuse. **2.** *Metall:* (fer) nerveux; **f. fracture,** cassure nerveuse.

fibrousness ['faibrəsnis], *s.* qualité fibreuse (d'un tissu, etc.).

fibrovascular ['faibrou'væskjulər], *a. Bot:* (faisceau *m,* etc.) fibro(-)vasculaire.

fibula, *pl.* **-as, -ae** ['fibjulə(z), -i:], *s.* **1.** *Rom.Ant:* fibule *f.* **2.** *Anat:* fibula *f,* péroné *m.*

fiche ['fi:ʃ], *s. Cmptr: etc:* (*microfilm*) microfiche *f.*

fichu ['fiʃu:], *s. Cost:* fichu *m.*

fickle ['fikl], *a.* inconstant, volage, capricieux, mobile, muable; **f. disposition,** caractère changeant, versatile; **f. minded,** d'humeur volage.

fickleness ['fiklnis], *s.* inconstance *f*; humeur *f* volage; caractère capricieux; instabilité *f* de caractère.

fictile ['fiktail], *a.* **1.** (art *m,* etc.) céramique, plastique. **2.** **f. clay,** argile figuline.

fiction ['fikʃ(ə)n], *s.* **1.** fiction *f,* création *f* de l'imagination; *Jur:* **legal f., f. of law,** fiction légale, de droit; **these tales are pure f.,** tous ces contes sont de pure invention; tout cela, ce n'est que des contes. **2.** *Lit:* **(works of) f.,** romans *m*; ouvrages *m* d'imagination; littérature *f* d'imagination; **light f.,** romans de lecture facile; **science f.,** science-fiction *f*; **he writes only f.,** il n'écrit que des romans; *P.N:* (*in library, bookshop*) **fiction,** romans; **he has a good f. library,** il a une bonne collection de romans.

fictional ['fikʃənəl], *a.* fictif.

fictionalize ['fikʃənəlaiz], **fictionize** ['fikʃənaiz], *v.tr.* romancer; **fictionalized life of Napoleon,** biographie romancée de Napoléon.

fictitious [fik'tiʃəs], *a.* **1.** (*a*) fictif; **f. being,** être *m* imaginaire; *Com:* **f. assets,** actif fictif; *Fin:* **f. bill,** traite *f* en l'air; *Book-k:* **f. accounts,** comptes *m* de résultats; (*b*) (*of fight, treaty, etc.*) simulé, feint. **2.** **f. narrative,** récit inventé. **3.** *A:* (*of gem, coin*) factice; contrefait.

fictitiously [fik'tiʃəsli], *adv.* fictivement.

fictitiousness [fik'tiʃəsnis], *s.* **1.** caractère fictif, imaginaire (d'une histoire, etc.). **2.** *A:* fausseté *f,* caractère *m* factice (d'une pierre précieuse, etc.).

fictive ['fiktiv], *a.* fictif, imaginaire; *El:* **f. layers,** charges *f* de surface (d'un diélectrique).

ficus ['fikəs], *s.* **1.** *Bot:* ficus *m.* **2.** *Moll:* ficus.

fid [fid], *s.* **1.** *Nau:* clef *f* (de mât). **2.** *Nau:* **splicing f.,** épissoir *m*; burin *m* de gabier. **3.** (*a*) cale *f,* coin *m* (pour caler ou obturer qch.); (*b*) *F: A:* amas *m,* tas *m*; **there were fids of them,** il y en avait des mille et des cents.

fidate ['faideit], *v.tr. Chess:* rendre (une pièce) inattaquable.

fiddle[1] ['fidl], *s.* **1.** *F:* (*a*) violon *m*; **bass f.,** contrebasse *f*; *U.S: P:* **bull f.,** violoncelle *m*; *Prov:* **there's many a good tune played on an old f.,** c'est dans les vieux pots, les vieilles marmites, qu'on fait la bonne soupe; (*b*) (joueur, -euse, de) violon; violoniste *mf*; **first f.,** premier violon; **to play first f.,** (i) faire la partie de premier violon; occuper le pupitre des premiers violons; (ii) *Fig:* occuper la première place; avoir le premier rôle; **second f.,** (i) second violon; (ii) *Fig:* sous-fifre *m, pl.* sous-fifres; **to play second f. (to s.o.),** jouer un rôle secondaire (auprès de qn); jouer les utilités. **2.** *Nau:* violon de mer; fiche *f* de roulis, **f. block,** (poulie *f* à) violon. **3.** *Cer:* égouttoir *m* (pour pièces venant du bain de vernis). **4.** *F:* combine *f*; **to be on the f.,** faire du fricotage; **it's nothing but a f.,** ce n'est que du tripotage.

fiddle[2], *v. F:* **1.** (*a*) *v.i.* (i) jouer du violon; (ii) *Pej:* violoner; racler du violon; **Nero fiddled while Rome burned,** Néron jouait de la lyre pendant que Rome brûlait; *Fig:* **to f. while Rome burns,** s'occuper de choses futiles au lieu de lutter contre une calamité; (*b*) *v.tr.* jouer (un air) sur le violon. **2.** (*a*) *v.i.* s'amuser à des niaiseries, tripoter, bricoler, fignoler; **to f. with one's watch,** tourmenter, tripoter, jouer avec, taquiner du pouce, manier nerveusement, sa montre; **don't f. with the mechanism,** laissez le mécanisme tranquille; ne trifouillez pas le mécanisme; **he was fiddling (about) with his car,** il bricolait sur sa voiture; **I've spent the whole morning fiddling (about),** j'ai passé toute la matinée à bricoler; j'ai perdu toute ma matinée (à bricoler); **to f. away one's time,** perdre, gâcher, son temps; (*b*) *v.i.* **to f. for a bookmaker,** racoler pour un bookmaker; (*c*) (i) *v.i.* combiner, fricoter; (ii) *v.tr.* **to f. a meter,** bricoler un compteur; **to f. the accounts,** fricoter, truquer, tripatouiller, les comptes; maquiller la comptabilité; **to f. the expenses,** ratiboiser sur les notes de frais; **he fiddled a week's leave,** il a carotté huit jours de permission.

fiddlededee ['fidldi'di:], *int. F: O:* bah! turlututu! turlurette! quelle blague! chansons (que tout cela)!

fiddlefaddle[1] ['fidlfædl], *F:* **1.** *s.* bagatelles *fpl,* balivernes *fpl,* fadaises *fpl,* niaiseries *fpl,* chipoterie *f.* **2.** *a.* chipotier, musard. **3.** *int.* = FIDDLEDEDEE.

fiddlefaddle[2], *v.i.* muser, musarder, chipoter, baguenauder, fignoler.

fiddlefaddler ['fidlfædlər], *s.* baguenaudier *m,* fignoleur, -euse.

fiddlefaddling ['fidlfædliŋ], *s.* musarderie *f,* chipotage *m,* baguenauderie *f,* fignolage *m.*

fiddlehead ['fidlhed], *s. Nau:* violon *m* (de beaupré).

fiddle-headed ['fidl'hedid], *a.* **1.** *Nau:* (*of ship*) avec violon de beaupré. **2.** (*of spoon, fork*) à filet, à violon; avec manche *m* forme violon.

fiddler ['fidlər], *s.* **1.** *F:* (*a*) violoneur *m;* joueur *m* de violon; (*b*) **strolling f.,** ménétrier *m,* violoneux *m.* **2.** *F:* (*a*) bricoleur, -euse; (*b*) *Turf:* racoleur *m;* (*c*) combinard, -arde; chevalier *m* d'industrie; **he's an awful f.,** c'est un fameux combinard. **3.** *Crust:* **f. (crab),** crabe appelant.

fiddlestick ['fidlstik]. *F: O:* **1.** *s.* (*a*) archet *m* (de violon); *F:* baguette *f* (de violon); **fiddle and f.,** violon *m* et baguette; (*b*) rien *m,* bagatelle *f,* bêtise *f;* **I don't care a f. about it,** je m'en moque comme d'une guigne; **she died of a broken heart—broken fiddlesticks!** elle est morte le cœur brisé—ah, la bonne blague! **2.** *int.* **fiddlesticks!** sornettes!

fiddlewood ['fidlwud], *s. Bot: F:* citharexylon *m,* bois *m* de guitare.

fiddling[1] ['fidliŋ], *a. F:* (*a*) (*of pers.*) musard; qui s'amuse à des futilités; qui passe son temps à baguenauder, à muser; (*b*) (*of thg*) futile, insignifiant, sans importance; (*c*) **a f. job,** une besogne agaçante, un jeu de patience; **f. criticism,** critique tatillonne.

fiddling[2], *s. F:* **1.** raclage *m* (de violon). **2.** (*a*) **f. about,** tripotage *m,* baguenaudage *m;* perte *f* de temps; (*b*) combine(s) *f(pl);* **f. can be very profitable,** on peut faire beaucoup d'argent avec les combines.

fiddly ['fidli], *a.* (travail) délicat, minutieux.

fidei-commissary ['faidiai'kɔmisəri], *s. Jur:* fidéicommissaire *m.*

fidei-commissum ['faidiaikɔ'misəm], *s. Jur:* fidéicommis *m.*

fideism ['faidiizm], *s. Phil:* fidéisme *m.*

fideist ['faidiist], *s. Phil:* fidéiste *mf.*

fideistic ['faidiistik], *a. Phil:* fidéiste.

fidejussion ['faidi'ju:siən], *s. Jur:* fidéjussion *f.*

fidejussionary ['faidi'ju:siənəri], *a. Jur:* fidéjussoire.

fidejussor [faidi'ju:sɔ:r], *s. Jur:* fidéjusseur *m.*

fidejussory [faidi'ju:səri], *a. Jur:* fidéjussoire.

fidelity [fai'deliti, fi-], *s.* **1.** fidélité *f* (d'un ami, de la mémoire, etc.); loyauté *f* (de qn); **f. of s.o. to, towards, s.o.,** loyauté, fidélité, de qn à, envers, qn; **f. of a dog to his master,** la fidélité d'un chien pour son maître. **2. the f. of a translation,** la fidélité, l'exactitude *f,* d'une traduction; *Rec:* **high f.,** haute fidélité.

fidget[1] ['fidʒit], *s. F:* **1.** *usu. pl.* **the fidgets,** agitation nerveuse; inquiétudes *f,* énervement *m,* nervosité *f;* **to have the fidgets, to be in a f.,** ne pas tenir en place; se trémousser (sur sa chaise, etc.); avoir des impatiences dans les jambes; **it gives me the fidgets,** cela m'impatiente, m'énerve. **2.** (*of pers.*) **he's a f.,** c'est un énervé; il ne tient pas en place; il ne peut pas rester en place; **what a f. you are!** mais tiens-toi donc tranquille!

fidget[2], *v.* (**fidgeted**) **1.** *v.i.* (*a*) **to f. (about),** remuer continuellement; ne pas tenir en place; s'agiter, se trémousser; avoir la bougeotte; (*to child*) **don't f.!** tiens-toi tranquille! ne remue pas tout le temps! **to f. with one's keys,** tripoter ses clefs; (*b*) s'inquiéter, se tourmenter, s'énerver; **hurry up, your father is fidgeting!** dépêche-toi, ton père s'impatiente! **2.** *v.tr. F:* agacer, énerver, tourmenter (qn).

fidgetiness ['fidʒitinis], *s.* agitation nerveuse; nervosité *f.*

fidgeting[1] ['fidʒitiŋ], *a.* **1.** (*of pers.*) = FIDGETY. **2.** *F:* (*of thg*) énervant; (*of work*) minutieux.

fidgeting[2], *s.* = FIDGETINESS.

fidgety ['fidʒiti], *a. F:* **1.** qui ne reste pas, ne tient pas, en place; qui remue continuellement; agité. **2.** nerveux, impatient; **f. horse,** cheval incertain.

fidibus ['faidibəs], *s.* fidibus *m;* allumette *f* de papier; papillote *f.*

fiducial [fai'dju:ʃ(ə)l, fi-], *a. Surv: Astr: etc:* fiduciel; **f. line,** ligne *f* de foi; **f. mark,** marque *f* repère.

fiduciary [fai'dju:ʃiəri, fi-]. **1.** *a. Jur: Fin:* (prêt *m,* monnaie *f,* etc.) fiduciaire. **2.** *s. Jur:* (*a*) héritier *m* fiduciaire; héritière *f* fiduciaire; (*b*) (= TRUSTEE) dépositaire *mf.*

fidus Achates ['faidəsə'keiti:z], *Pr.n.m. Lit:* le fidèle Achate (de qn).

fie [fai], *int. A:* **f. (upon you)!** fi (donc)! vous devriez avoir honte!

fief [fi:f], *s. Hist:* fief *m.*

field [fi:ld], *s.* **1.** (*a*) *Agr: etc:* champ *m;* (*under pasture*) pré *m;* **f. of wheat,** champ de blé; **strawberry f.,** plantation *f* de fraisiers; **in the fields,** aux champs; **in the open f.,** en plein champ; **f. hand,** ouvrier, -ière, agricole; *Lit:* **our fields ran with blood,** le sang inonda nos champs, nos sillons; **the beasts of the f.,** les bêtes sauvages; **the lilies of the f.,** les lis *m* des champs; *Hist:* **the F. of the Cloth of Gold,** le Camp, le Champ, du drap d'or; (*b*) *attrib. Bot:* **f. flower,** fleur *f* des prés; **f. madder,** shérardie *f,* shérarde *f,* des champs; **f. ash,** sorbier *m* des oiseaux; *Orn:* **f. duck,** canepetière *f;* **f. lark,** alouette *f* des champs; **f. martin,** tyran *m;* *Ent:* **f. bee,** butineuse *f;* **f. cricket,** grillon *m* des champs; *Z:* **f. vole,** campagnol *m;* (*c*) *Agr:* (*in crop rotation*) sole *f;* (*d*) district *m,* région *f;* (*in comb.fm.*) champ (pétrolifère, etc.); gisement (houiller, pétrolifère); **diamond f.,** champ diamantifère; **tile f.,** tuilerie *f;* (*e*) *Mil:* **f. (of battle),** champ de bataille; **to take the f.,** entrer, se mettre, en campagne; **in the f.,** (i) en campagne; (ii) (lettre datée) aux armées; **in the open f.,** en rase campagne; **to bring three armies into the f.,** mettre trois armées en campagne; **to hold the f.,** (i) *Mil:* (*of army*) se maintenir sur ses positions; (ii) (*of theory, etc.*) être toujours en faveur; faire autorité; **to drive the enemy from the f.,** chasser l'ennemi du champ de bataille; **to withdraw from the f.,** se retirer de la lutte; **to be left in possession of the f.,** rester maître du champ de bataille; **f. of honour,** champ d'honneur; *attrib.* **f. force,** (i) corps *m* de bataille; (ii) armée *f,* troupes *fpl,* en campagne; **f. service,** service *m* en campagne; **f. (service) manual,** règlement *m,* manuel *m,* du service en campagne; **f. officer,** officier supérieur; **f. engineer,** sapeur-mineur *m, pl.* sapeurs-mineurs; sapeur *m* du génie de combat; **f. company,** compagnie *f* de sapeurs-mineurs, du génie de combat; **f. surgeon,** chirurgien d'ambulance; **f. hospital,** ambulance *f* divisionnaire; hôpital *m* de campagne; **f. dressing,** (i) paquet (individuel) de pansement; (ii) pansement *m* sommaire; **f. dress,** tenue *f* de campagne; **f. fortification,** fortification *f,* ouvrage *m,* de campagne; organisation *f* du terrain; **f. artillery,** artillerie *f* de campagne; *Navy:* artillerie navale; **corps, division(al), f. artillery,** artillerie de campagne de corps d'armée, divisionnaire; **(guided) missile f. artillery,** artillerie guidée; **f. battery,** groupe *m,* batterie *f* (d'artillerie) de campagne; **f. gun, piece,** pièce *f,* canon *m,* de campagne; **f. telegraph,** télégraphe *m* militaire, de campagne; **f. exercise,** exercice *m* en campagne; manœuvre *f;* **f. manœuvre,** manœuvre à double action; **f. day,** (i) jour *m* de grandes manœuvres, de revue; (ii) *esp. NAm:* réunion *f* athlétique; (iii) journée *f* de chasse, d'expédition aux champs, en pleine campagne; (iv) journée de grands débats, de grands événements, etc.; grande occasion; grand jour; *F:* **I'm going to have a f. day on my study,** je vais nettoyer mon bureau de fond en comble; **f. colours,** (i) *Mil:* fanion(s) *m* (de jalonnement); (ii) *Surv:* jalon(s) *m;* **f. rations,** ration *f* de guerre, de campagne; *Hist:* **f. grey,** gris *m* de l'uniforme des troupes allemandes; (*f*) *Av:* **landing f.,** terrain *m* d'atterrissage. **2.** (*a*) *Fb: Cr: etc:* terrain; (*baseball*) champ; *Cr:* **to be in the f.,** tenir le champ; (*b*) *Cr:* l'équipe du bôleur (répandue sur le terrain pour arrêter la balle); **to place the f.,** disposer l'équipe; placer le champ; (*c*) **f. events,** épreuves *f pl* d'athlétisme; *s.a.* **f. day,** 1(*e*). **3.** (*a*) *Turf:* (i) **the f.,** le champ; les partants; les chevaux courants (à l'exception du favori); **big f. (of starters),** champ fourni; **to bet against the f.,** parier contre le champ; *Fig:* **there are three candidates in the f.,** il y a trois candidatures de déposées; **I was told that there was already someone in the f.,** j'ai appris qu'il y avait déjà quelqu'un sur les rangs; **there are already several books in the f. on this subject,** plusieurs livres ont déjà paru sur ce sujet; (ii) **the f. (of runners),** le peloton; **to lead the f.,** mener le peloton; (*b*) *Ven:* **the f.,** les veneurs *m;* **were you among the f.?** étiez-vous de la chasse? **his father was killed on the hunting f.,** son père a été tué, s'est tué, à la chasse. **4.** (*a*) étendue *f,* espace *m* (de mer, de ciel, etc.); (*b*) *Her:* table *f* d'attente; champ, sol *m;* (*c*) *Art: etc:* champ, fond *m* (d'un tableau, d'une broderie, etc.); *Num:* champ (d'une médaille). **5.** (*a*) théâtre *m,* champ (d'opération, etc.); étendue, domaine *m* (d'une science); **this is a f. of action in which I may be of use,** voilà un domaine où je puis être utile; **the f. of conjecture,** le champ des hypothèses; **in the political f.,** sur le plan politique; **to have a clear f.,** avoir le champ libre; *Mil:* **f. of fire,** champ de tir; (*of fixed gun*) battage *m;* (*b*) *Com:* marché *m* (pour un produit); (*c*) **f. work,** (i) travaux *mpl,* recherches *fpl,* sur le terrain, sur les lieux; (ii) *Min: etc:* exploration *f;* (iii) *Com:* démarchage *m* auprès de la clientèle; (iv) *Mil:* ouvrage *m* de campagne; retranchement *m* provisoire; **f. survey, f. study,** étude *f* sur le terrain, sur les lieux; **f. botany, geology,** botanique *f,* géologie *f,* sur le terrain; **f. test,** essais *mpl,* épreuve(s) *f(pl),* sur le terrain; essais pratiques; **f. engineer,** ingénieur *m* de chantier, sur le terrain; **f. supervisor,** inspecteur *m,* surveillant *m,* itinérant; inspecteur des chantiers; *T.V: etc:* **f. broadcast,** radioreportage *m;* **f. equipment, gear,** matériel *m* de reportage. **6.** (*a*) *Opt: Phot: etc:* champ; **f. of view, of vision,** champ visuel; **focal f.,** champ de netteté; **flat f.,** champ corrigé; **f. glass,** verre *m* de champ (d'un microscope, etc.); **f. glasses,** jumelles *f;* **f. emission microscope,** microscope à champ émissif; **dark f. microscope,** microscope en lumière noire; (*b*) *Ph:* **differential f.,** champ différentiel; **f. of force,** champ de force; **magnetic f., f. of magnetic force,** champ magnétique; **gravitational f.,** champ de gravitation; **scalar f.,** champ scalaire; **vector f.,** champ vectoriel; *El: Elcs:* **electromagnetic, electrostatic, f.,** champ électromagnétique, électrostatique; **oscillating f., pulsating f.,** champ oscillant, pulsant; **rotary, rotating f.,** champ tournant; **f. current,** courant inducteur; **f. circuit,** circuit *m* d'excitation; **f. circuit breaker, f. breakup switch,** disjoncteur *m* de circuit d'excitation, commutateur *m* de champ; **f. distribution,** répartition *f* du champ; **f. emission,** émission *f* par champ électrique; **f. control,** réglage *m* de l'excitation; **f. regulator, rheostat,** rhéostat *m* de champ; **f. coil,** bobine *f,* bobinage *m,* d'excitation, d'inducteur; bobine inductrice; inducteur *m;* **f. magnet,** inducteur; électro-aimant *m* de champ; **f.-magnet coil,** bobine d'induction; **f. spider,** croisillon inducteur; **f. strength, intensity,** intensité *f* de champ; *Elcs:* **f. tube,** tube *m* de flux; (*c*) *El:* enroulement inducteur, bobine inductrice, bobine de champ; **f. winding,** enroulement, bobinage, inducteur; **burned-out f.,** enroulement inducteur brûlé, grillé.

field[2]. **1.** *v.i.* (*a*) *Turf:* parier pour, sur, le champ (contre le favori); (*b*) *Cr:* tenir le champ (pour relancer la balle). **2.** *v.tr.* (*a*) *Cr:* **to f. a ball,** arrêter (et relancer) une balle (dans le champ); *F:* **a passer-by fielded one of the missiles,** un passant attrapa un des projectiles; (*b*) *Sp:* **to f. a team,** réunir une équipe; (*c*) *Mil:* **to be able to f. 50,000 men,** pouvoir mettre 50.000 hommes en ligne; *Pol:* **to f. 500 candidates,** présenter 500 candidats.

fieldcraft ['fi:ldkrɑ:ft], *s. Mil:* engin *m,* véhicule *m,* de combat.

fielder ['fi:ldər], *s. Sp:* **1.** *Turf:* celui qui joue le champ. **2.** *Cr: etc:* chasseur *m;* membre *m* de l'équipe du lanceur, homme *m* de champ.

fieldfare ['fi:ldfɛər], *s. Orn:* grive *f* litorne, jocasse *f;* **red-tailed f.,** grive de Naumann.

fieldmouse, *pl.* **-mice** ['fi:ldmaus, -mais], *s. Z:* mulot *m;* rat *m* des champs; souris *f* de terre.

fiend [fi:nd], *s.* **1.** (*a*) démon *m,* diable *m,* esprit malin; **the F.,** Satan *m;* (*b*) monstre *m* (de méchanceté, de cruauté); *F:* **he's a perfect f.,** c'est un vrai suppôt de Satan. **2.** *F:* (*a*) peste *f;* **autograph f.,** coureur, -euse, d'autographes; (*b*) **cigarette f.,** fumeur, -euse, (de cigarettes) enragé(e); **examination f.,** bête *f* à concours.

fiendish ['fi:ndiʃ], *a.* démoniaque, diabolique; infernal, -aux; satanique; **to take a f. pleasure in sth.,** prendre un plaisir diabolique à qch.

fiendishly ['fi:ndiʃli], *adv.* **1.** diaboliquement, infernalement. 2. *F:* diablement; **it was f. cold,** il faisait un froid de tous les diables.

fiendishness [ˈfiːndiʃnis], *s.* méchanceté *f*, cruauté *f*, diabolique.

fiendlike [ˈfiːndlaik], *a.* = FIENDISH.

fierce [ˈfiəs], *a.* (*a*) (*of pers.*) violent; brutal, -aux; (*of animal*) sauvage, cruel, féroce; (*of fire, desire, etc.*) ardent; (*of battle, hatred, etc.*) acharné; (*of wind, etc.*) furieux, violent, impétueux; **f. eyes,** yeux *m* farouches, féroces; **f. encounter,** rencontre violente; **f. speech,** discours plein de menaces; **animals f. for blood,** animaux assoiffés de sang; **when the argument waxed fiercest,** au fort de la dispute; (*b*) *Aut: etc:* **f. brake,** frein brutal; **f. clutch,** embrayage brutal, dur, brusque; (*of clutch, etc.*) **to be f.,** agir brutalement; (*c*) *NAm: F:* désagréable; insupportable; douloureux; **the weather has been f.,** il a fait un temps de chien.

fiercely [ˈfiəsli], *adv.* violemment, véhémentement, impétueusement; avec fureur; âprement; avec acharnement.

fierceness [ˈfiəsnis], *s.* violence *f*, véhémence *f*, impétuosité *f*, virulence *f* (de qn); férocité *f* (d'un animal); ardeur *f* (du feu, du désir, etc.); acharnement *m* (de la bataille); impétuosité *f*, fureur *f* (du vent, etc.); *Aut: etc:* brutalité *f*, brusquerie *f* (de l'embrayage, des freins).

fieri facias [ˈfaiəraiˈfeiʃiəs], *s. Jur:* ordre *m* de saisie.

fierily [ˈfaiərili], *adv.* ardemment, passionnément, impétueusement; avec feu.

fieriness [ˈfaiərinis], *s.* **1.** (*a*) ardeur *f* (du soleil); (*b*) saveur cuisante (d'une boisson spiritueuse). **2.** ardeur, fougue *f*, impétuosité *f*, emportement *m*.

fiery [ˈfaiəri], *a.* **1.** (*of substance*) ardent, brûlant, de feu, enflammé; **f. furnace,** fournaise ardente; **f. red,** rouge ardent, rouge feu; **f. sky,** ciel embrasé; **f. sun,** soleil *m* de plomb; **the f. glow of the setting sun,** l'embrasement *m* du soleil couchant; **f. taste,** saveur cuisante; **f. glances,** regards ardents, brûlants; *Cr:* **f. pitch, wicket,** *Golf:* **f. green,** terrain très sec, élastique. **2.** (*of pers.*) (i) fougueux, emporté, impétueux; (ii) colérique, bouillant; (*passion f, imagination f*) volcanique; *Lit:* **f. steed,** coursier fougueux; **to make f. speeches against s.o.,** vomir feu et flamme contre qn. **3.** (*a*) (*of gas*) inflammable; (*of mine*) grisouteux, à grisou; (*b*) (*of steel*) sauvage.

Fiesco [fiˈeskou], *Pr.n. Hist:* Fiesque *m*; *pl.* **the Fieschi** [fiˈeskiː], les Fiesques.

Fiesole [fiˈeizoulei], *Pr.n. Geog:* Fiésole.

fi. fa. [ˈfai ˈfei], *s. Jur: F:* = FIERI FACIAS.

fife[1] [faif], *s. Mus:* fifre *m*.

fife[2], (*a*) *v.tr.* fifrer (une mélodie); (*b*) *v.i.* jouer du fifre.

fifer[1] [ˈfaifər], *s.* joueur *m* de fifre, fifre *m*.

Fifer[2], *a. & s. Geog:* (originaire, natif, ive) du comté de Fife.

fife rail [ˈfaifreil], *s. Nau:* râtelier *m* du grand mât.

fifteen [fifˈtiːn, ˈfiftiːn], *num.a. & s.* quinze (*m*); **she is f. (years old),** elle a quinze ans; **the train leaves at f. (hours) forty (15.40),** le train part à quinze heures quarante (15h.40); **the plane will land at f. thirty (15.30),** l'avion va atterrir à quinze heures trente (15h.30); *Rugby Fb:* **the French f.,** le quinze de France; *Hist:* **the F.,** l'insurrection *f* jacobite de 1715.

fifteenth [fifˈtiːnθ, ˈfiftiːnθ]. **1.** *num.a. & s.* quinzième; **Louis the F.,** Louis Quinze; **(on) the f. (of the month),** le quinze du mois. **2.** *s.* (*a*) (*fractional*) quinzième *m*; (*b*) *Mus:* quinzième *f*; octave redoublée.

fifteenthly [fifˈtiːnθli], *adv.* quinzièmement, en quinzième lieu.

fifth [fifθ]. **1.** *num.a. & s.* cinquième; **he arrived f. or sixth,** il est arrivé cinq ou sixième; **Henry the F.,** Henri Cinq; **(the Emperor) Charles the F.,** Charles-Quint; *Sch:* **f. form,** *approx.* = classe *f* de seconde; **f. wheel,** (i) *Veh:* cercle horizontal (de l'avant-train); (ii) *F:* quelqu'un, quelque chose, d'inutile; *Pol:* **f. column,** cinquième colonne; *Rel:* **the F. Monarchy,** l'avènement du royaume des cieux sur la terre; **F.-Monarchy men,** secte *f* du 17e siècle qui croyait au second avènement immédiat du Christ. **2.** *s.* (*a*) (*fractional*) cinquième *m*; **two fifths,** deux cinquièmes; (*b*) *Mus:* quinte *f*; **diminished f.,** fausse quinte; quinte diminuée.

fifthly [ˈfifθli], *adv.* cinquièmement, en cinquième lieu.

fifth-rate [ˈfifθreit], *a.* médiocre; de cinquième ordre.

fiftieth [ˈfiftiəθ], *num.a. & s.* cinquantième (*m*).

fifty [ˈfifti], *num.a. & s.* cinquante (*m*); **f.-one, -two,** cinquante et un, cinquante-deux; **doctor of f. years' standing,** docteur *m* jubilaire; **f.-f.,** moitié-moitié; **to go f.-f. with s.o., to do a deal on a f.-f. basis with s.o.,** être, se mettre, de moitié avec qn; mettre qn de compte à demi dans une affaire; **about f. books,** une cinquantaine de livres; **the fifties,** les années cinquante (1950–1959); **in the 1850s, in the fifties of the last century,** entre 1850 et 1860; **she is in her fifties,** elle a passé la cinquantaine; elle est quinquagénaire; *F:* (*intensive*) **I've f. things to tell you,** j'ai un tas de choses à vous dire; **I've told you f. times,** je vous l'ai dit et répété trente-six fois.

fig[1] [fig], *s.* **1.** (*a*) figue *f*; **wild f.,** figue sauvage; carique *f*; **green figs,** (i) figues blanches; (ii) figues fraîches; **dried figs,** figues sèches; *O:* **pulled figs,** figues de Turquie de premier choix; *F:* **a f. for him,** zut pour lui! **a f. for fame!** fi de de la célébrité! (*b*) **Hottentot's f.,** ficoïde *f* comestible; **keg f.,** figue caque; **f. marigold,** mésembryanthème *m*, ficoïde *f*; (*c*) *P: A:* **figs,** l'épicier *m*. **2. f. (tree),** figuier *m*; **wild f. (tree), goat f. (tree),** caprifiguier *m*; **Adam's f.,** figuier d'Adam; **sacred f. (tree),** arbre *m* des conseils. **3. Indian f.,** nopal *m*, -als; *F:* raquette *f*.

fig[2], *v.tr.* **(figged)** *A:* faire la figue à (qn).

fig[3], *s. F: O:* **1. in full f.,** en grande toilette; en grande tenue; en grand costume; en grand gala; sur son trente et un; en grand tralala. **2. in good f.,** en bonne forme; bien en train.

fig[4], *v.tr.* **(figged)** *O:* **1. to f. up, f. out, a horse,** faire fringuer un cheval. **2. to f. s.o. out, up,** attifer qn.

figbird [ˈfigbəːd], *s. Orn: Austr:* sphécothère *m*.

figeater [ˈfigiːtər], *s. Orn:* becfigue *m*.

fight[1] [fait], *s.* **1.** (*a*) *Mil: etc:* combat *m*, bataille *f*; engagement *m*, action *f*; **sea f.,** combat naval, sur mer; **sham f.,** (i) combat simulé, d'exercice; (ii) *Th: etc:* simulacre *m* de combat; (*b*) combat (entre deux personnes, deux animaux, etc.); *Box:* assaut *m* (de boxe), pugilat *m*; **hand to hand f.,** lutte *f* corps à corps; corps-à-corps *m*; **f. to the death,** lutte à mort; combat à outrance; **free f.,** (i) rixe *f*, bagarre *f*; (ii) mêlée, bataille, générale; *F: O:* **tea f., bun f.,** thé *m* (où l'on s'écrase); **to start the f.,** commencer les hostilités; **it was a good f.,** ils se sont bien battus; **they had a f.,** ils se sont battus. **2.** (*a*) lutte; **the f. for life,** la lutte pour la vie; **to have a hard f. to make (both) ends meet,** avoir à lutter pour joindre les deux bouts; **to carry on a stubborn f. against s.o.,** soutenir une lutte opiniâtre contre qn; (*b*) **to show f.,** résister; offrir de la résistance; *F:* montrer les cornes, les dents; sortir ses griffes; *Sp: etc:* **to put up a good f.,** bien se défendre; se bien acquitter; **to put up a poor f.,** se mal comporter; faire triste figure; **he put up a wonderful f.,** il a offert une résistance superbe; il s'est défendu vaillamment; **there was no f. left in him,** il n'avait plus de cœur à se battre; il était à bout de forces; **that piece of news took all the f. out of me,** cette nouvelle m'a cassé bras et jambes; **he had still some f. in him,** il n'était pas encore maté; **to put some f. into s.o.,** remettre du cœur au ventre à qn; **full of f.,** plein de mordant.

fight[2], *v.* **(fought [fɔːt]; fought)**

I. *v.i. & tr.* **1.** *v.i.* (*a*) se battre; combattre; lutter; **to f. against, with, the enemy,** combattre l'ennemi; se battre contre, avec, l'ennemi; **to f. against adversity,** lutter contre, se débattre contre, être aux prises avec, l'adversité; **to f. against disease,** combattre la maladie; **to f. against sleep,** lutter contre le sommeil; **to f. for s.o.,** se battre pour qn; **to f. for sth.,** (i) se battre pour une cause, etc.; (ii) se battre pour avoir qch.; **to f. for liberty,** se battre pour la liberté; **the porters fought for our luggage,** les porteurs *m* se sont disputé nos bagages; **two dogs fighting over a bone,** deux chiens *m* qui se disputent un os; **to f. like vultures over an inheritance,** se disputer une succession comme des corbeaux; **to f. with the gloves off,** (i) *Box:* se battre sans gants; (ii) *F:* ne pas ménager qn; **to f. fair,** faire la bonne guerre; se battre loyalement; **to f. desperately,** se battre à outrance; **she fought like a wild cat,** elle se débattait de toutes ses forces; **an army fights on its belly,** pour être d'attaque il faut que les troupes soient bien nourries; **they began to f.,** ils en vinrent aux mains; **to set cocks fighting,** faire jouter des coqs; (*b*) (*with cogn.acc.*) **to f. a battle,** livrer (une) bataille; **he fought a good fight,** il s'est bien battu; **to f. the good fight,** combattre pour la bonne cause; **a battle was fought near the frontier,** un combat a eu lieu près de la frontière; **the match was fought yesterday,** le match (de boxe, etc.) s'est disputé hier; **to f. s.o.'s battles,** prendre le parti de qn; **to f. one's battles over again,** (se) remémorer ses combats ou ses luttes de jadis; **to f. one's way (out),** se frayer un passage (pour sortir); **to f. an action (at law),** se défendre dans un procès; **to f. a point,** contester un fait, un principe, etc.; discuter sur un point (de droit, etc.). **2.** *v.tr.* (*a*) **to f. s.o.,** se battre avec, contre, qn; combattre qn; lutter contre qn; **to f. a fire,** combattre un incendie; (*b*) **to f. one's ships (in battle),** manœuvrer ses navires; **he fought his ship until she went down,** il continua à tirer jusqu'à ce que son navire sombrât; (*c*) faire battre (des coqs, des chiens, etc.); faire jouter (des coqs).

II. (*compound verbs*) **1. fight back,** (*a*) *v.tr.* **to f. back a disease,** résister (avec effort) à une maladie; **to f. one's way back again,** remonter le courant; (*b*) *v.i.* résister; se battre; *Pol:* se présenter à nouveau à une élection que l'on a perdue.

2. fight down, *v.tr.* vaincre (une passion, la résistance, etc.).

3. fight off, *v.tr.* (*a*) résister (avec effort) à (une maladie); **to f. off a cold with aspirin,** juguler un rhume à force d'aspirine; (*b*) **to f. off the enemy,** repousser l'ennemi.

4. fight out, *v.tr.* **to f. it out,** se battre jusqu'à une décision; vider une querelle, un différend; lutter jusqu'au bout; **to f. out the battle to the end,** se battre jusqu'au bout.

fighter [ˈfaitər], *s.* **1.** combattant *m*, guerroyeur *m*, *F:* batailleur *m*, ferrailleur *m*; **f. for an idea,** militant *m* d'une idée; **he is not a f.,** il n'a rien de combatif. **2.** *Mil.Av:* chasseur *m*, avion *m* de chasse; **day f., night f.,** chasseur de jour, de nuit; **f. controller,** contrôleur *m* de la chasse; **f. cover,** couverture *f* de chasse, protection assurée par la chasse; **f. reconnaissance aircraft,** chasseur de reconnaissance; **f. bomber,** chasseur-bombardier *m*, *pl.* chasseurs-bombardiers; avion d'assaut; **f. aviation, f. command, f. forces,** l'aviation *f* de chasse, la chasse.

fighting[1] [ˈfaitiŋ], *a.* militant, de combat; **f. men,** combattants *m*; *Mil:* hommes *m* disponibles; *Mil:* **f. forces,** effectifs *m* sous les armes; **f. wing of a party,** les militants *m* d'un parti.

fighting[2], *s.* combat *m*; *Box:* pugilat *m*, boxe *f*; **close f.,** lutte *f* corps à corps; **there will be some f.,** on va se battre; **I did not do any f.,** je n'ai pas combattu; **no f. here!** vous n'allez pas vous battre ici! **f. cock,** coq *m* de combat; *F:* **to live like a f. cock,** vivre, être, comme un coq en pâte; *Ich:* **f. fish,** poisson combattant; *Mil: etc:* **f. unit,** unité combattante; **f. strength,** effectif *m* de combat, de guerre; **f. range, line,** distance *f*, ligne *f*, de combat; *Navy:* **f. top,** hune *f* de combat; **f. efficiency,** valeur offensive et défensive, valeur tactique (d'une unité, d'un navire, etc.); **f. qualities,** qualités militaires, valeur guerrière, valeur au combat (d'une troupe); **f. spirit,** esprit combatif, agressivité *f*, ardeur guerrière, mordant *m*; **f. temper,** humeur belliqueuse; **f. policy,** politique militante; *F:* **to be on f. terms,** être à couteaux tirés; **I still have a f. chance,** j'ai encore une chance si je résiste jusqu'au bout; ça vaut la peine de lutter; **there's just a f. chance for his recovery,** il a une chance sur dix de s'en tirer; **f. drunk,** dans un état d'ivresse agressive.

figleaf [ˈfigliːf], *s.* **1.** feuille *f* de figuier. **2.** *Art:* feuille de vigne.

figment [ˈfigmənt], *s.* fiction *f*, invention *f*; **figments of the imagination,** imaginations *f*.

fig-shaped [ˈfigʃeipt], *a.* caricoïde.

figuline [ˈfigjuliːn]. *Cer:* **1.** *a.* figulin. **2.** *s.* (*a*) figuline *f*; vase *m* en terre cuite; poterie *f*; (*b*) argile figuline; terre *f* à poterie.

figurable [ˈfigjurəbl], *a.* figurable.

figurant, *f.* **-ante** [ˈfigjurənt], *s. Th:* (*esp. ballet*) figurant, -ante; **the figurants,** la figuration.

figuration [figjuˈreiʃ(ə)n], *s.* **1.** (*a*) figuration *f* (d'une idée, de la prononciation, etc.); (*b*) configuration *f*, contour *m*, silhouette *f* (d'un objet). **2.** représentation figurative; emblème *m*; allégorie *f*. **3.** (*a*) ornementation *f* (d'une broderie, etc.); (*b*) *Mus:* embellissement *m* (d'une mélodie, etc.); contrepoint fleuri.

figurative [ˈfigjurətiv], *a.* **1.** (*of ceremonial, etc.*) figuratif, symbolique, emblématique. **2.** (*of language, meaning, etc.*) figuré, métaphorique; **in the f. sense,** au figuré. **3.** (style, etc.) orné, plein de fioritures. **4.** en forme de tableau; *F.* **writing,** écriture *f* en images.

figuratively [ˈfigjurətivli], *adv.* **1.** figurativement, d'une manière figurative. **2.** au figuré; métaphoriquement; par métaphore.

figurativeness [ˈfigjurətivnis], *s.* caractère figuré, métaphorique (d'une expression, etc.).

figure[1] [ˈfigər, *NAm: also* ˈfigjər], *s.* **1.** (*a*) figure *f*, forme extérieure; (*b*) (*of pers.*) taille *f*, tournure *f*; silhouette *f*; **to have a good f.,** être bien bâti, bien fait de sa personne; avoir une jolie taille, une silhouette élégante; *F:* **what a f.!** ce qu'elle est bien roulée! **commanding f.,** port imposant; **to look after, keep, one's f.,** soigner, garder, sa ligne; **garment adjusted to the f.,** vêtement collant, qui moule le corps. **2.** (*a*) personne *f*, être *m*; forme humaine; **he could see two figures advancing,** il voyait deux silhouettes qui s'avançaient; **a fine f. of a man, of a woman,** un bel homme, une belle femme; **he's a magnificent f. of a man,** c'est un homme magnifique; il a un physique magnifique; **a f. of fun,** un grotesque, une caricature; (*b*) personnage *m*, personnalité *f*, figure; **the important figures in history,** les personnages remarquables, les grandes figures, de l'histoire; **a distinguished f.,** une personnalité, un personnage distingué; **the central f.,** le pivot de l'action; (*c*) figure, apparence *f*, air *m*; **to cut a brilliant, a sorry, f.,** faire belle, piètre, figure; **to make, cut, a f.,** faire (bonne) figure; briller (dans le monde); *A:* **a person of f.,** un personnage distingué. **3.** *Art: etc:* image *f*, représentation *f* (de la forme humaine); **anatomical f.,** pièce *f* d'anatomie; **the central f. of a painting,** le personnage principal d'un tableau; **a vase with Chinese figures,** un vase à personnages chinois; **he drew the f. of a cat,** il a dessiné l'image d'un chat; **to draw funny little figures,** dessiner de petits bonshommes comiques. **4.** (*a*) figure, illustration *f* (dans un livre); **geometrical f.,** figure géométrique; *Cryst:* **corrosion f.,** figure de corrosion; *Opt:* **interference f.,** figure d'interférence; (*b*) *Astrol: O:* horoscope *m*; **to cast a f.,** tirer un horoscope; (*c*) dessin *m*, brochure *f* (sur un tissu); (*d*) **the figures of a dance,** les figures d'une danse; **f. skating,** exécution *f* de figures sur glace; **to f. skate, to cut figures,** tracer des figures sur la glace; faire du patinage artistique; **f. skater,** patineur, -euse, artistique, qui trace des figures. **5.** (*a*) *Mth: etc:* chiffre *m*; **in round figures,** en chiffres ronds; **rounded figures,** chiffres arrondis; **to work out the figures,** faire les calculs; **to carry a f.,** retenir un chiffre; **I've found a mistake in the figures,** j'ai trouvé une erreur de calcul; **to be good at figures,** être bon calculateur, bon en calcul; **f. of merit,** coefficient *m*, facteur *m*, de qualité; facteur de mérite; **f. of eight,** (i) *Mth:* huit-de-chiffre(s) *m, pl.* huits-de-chiffres; figure en forme de huit, lemniscate *f*; (ii) (*knot*) nœud en forme de huit, nœud allemand; **f.-of-eight bandage,** (bandage *m* en) huit-de-chiffre(s); bandage croisé; **f.-of-eight calipers,** huit-de-chiffre(s); *Elcs:* **f.-of-eight reception,** réception *f* suivant un diagramme en huit; *Const:* **f.-of-eight stairs,** escalier *m* en huit; *Av:* **f.-of-eight turn,** huit horizontal; **f.-four trap,** quatre-de-chiffre *m inv*; *Com:* **sales figures,** chiffre d'affaires; chiffres de vente; **marked in plain figures,** marqué en chiffres connus; **to fetch a high f.,** se vendre cher, pour une grosse somme; **I bought it at a low f.,** je l'ai acheté à bas prix; *P:* **what's the f.?** ça fait combien? (*of score, etc.*) **to reach two, three, figures,** monter à, atteindre, dix, cent; **his income runs into five figures,** il a un revenu de plus de dix mille livres (par an); **our takings have reached four figures,** nous avons décroché les quatre chiffres; **we cannot allow you credit beyond this f.,** nous ne pouvons pas vous accorder un crédit plus important, un crédit au delà de ce chiffre; *Tchn:* **dimensional figures,** cotes *f* (d'une machine); (*b*) *pl.* **figures,** données *f* numériques, détails chiffrés (d'un projet, etc.); statistiques *f*; **the figures for 1975,** les statistiques de 1975. **6. f. of speech,** (i) figure de rhétorique, de mots; métaphore *f*; (ii) façon *f* de parler. **7.** *Mus:* (*a*) figure (de motif); (*b*) motif *m*. **8.** *Miner:* **f. stone,** pierre *f* à statuettes; agalmatolit(h)e *f*; bildstein *m*; pagodite *f*.

figure[2], *v.*

I. *v.tr. & i.* **1.** *v.tr.* (*a*) figurer, représenter (qn, un paysage, etc.); **f. to yourself a happy family,** imaginez, figurez-vous, une famille heureuse; (*b*) *NAm:* estimer, évaluer; penser, croire; **I f. that it will take three years,** j'estime que cela prendra trois ans; (*c*) brocher, gaufrer, ouvrager (la soie, le velours, etc.); imprimer (le coton, etc.); orner, ciseler (le métal, etc.); **blue figured in pink,** bleu imprimé rose; (*d*) marquer, écrire (une somme, etc.) en chiffres; *esp. U.S:* **a watch dial figured in green,** une montre aux chiffres verts; (*e*) *Mus:* chiffrer (la basse). **2.** *v.i.* (*a*) chiffrer, calculer; faire des chiffres; (*b*) (*appear*) figurer; **his name figures on the list,** son nom figure, se trouve, sur la liste; *Th:* **he does not f. until the last act,** il n'entre pas en scène avant le dernier acte; **he figures as both a servant and a policeman,** il joue les deux rôles de domestique et d'agent de police; (*c*) *NAm: F:* sembler logique, normal; **that figures,** ça colle.

II. (*compound verbs*) **1. figure on,** *v.tr. NAm: F:* (*a*) **I had figured on his staying for a week,** j'avais compté qu'il resterait huit jours; **I'm figuring on 50 dollars extra a month,** je compte sur 50 dollars de plus par mois; (*b*) **you can always f. on him to pay his debts,** vous pouvez être certain qu'il payera ses dettes; (*c*) **I f. on going over to town to buy some stores,** j'ai l'intention d'aller en ville faire des courses.

2. figure out. *F:* (*a*) *v.i.* **it will f. out at about £100,** cela coûtera, se chiffrera à, une centaine de livres; (*b*) *v.tr.* **she had soon figured out how much the new furniture would cost,** elle eut vite calculé le coût des nouveaux meubles; **to f. out a problem,** résoudre un problème; **he couldn't f. out what she meant,** il ne pouvait pas comprendre ce qu'elle voulait dire; **I can't f. it out,** ça me dépasse.

3. figure up, *v.tr. esp. U.S:* additionner, calculer (des comptes, etc.).

figured ['figəd, *NAm: also* 'figjəd], *a.* **1.** (*of material, metal, etc.*) façonné, ouvré, ouvragé; à dessins; à impressions; (*of silk, etc.*) broché. **2.** (bois) ronceux, à ramages, madré. **3.** *Mus:* (*a*) (contrepoint, etc.) fleuri, figuré; (*b*) **f. bass,** basse chiffrée, figurée, continue.

figurehead ['figəhed, *NAm: also* 'figjəhed], *s.* **1.** *N.Arch:* figure *f*, buste *m*, de proue guibre *f*. **2.** (*a*) homme *m* de paille; prête-nom *m, pl.* prête-noms; (*b*) personnage purement décoratif (siégeant à un conseil d'administration, etc.).

figurine ['figəri:n, *NAm: also* 'figjəri:n], *s.* figurine *f*, tanagréenne *f*.

figuring ['figəriŋ, *NAm: also* 'figjəriŋ], *s.* **1.** chiffrage *m* (des dépenses, etc.). **2.** *Mus:* chiffrage (de la basse).

figurism ['figjərizm], *s. Theol:* figurisme *m*.

figurist ['figjərist], *s. Theol:* figuriste *mf*.

figwort ['figwə:t], *s. Bot:* **1.** (renoncule *f*) ficaire *f*; *F:* petite éclaire; éclairette *f*; petite chélidoine. **2.** scrofulaire *f*; *F:* herbe *f* aux écrouelles.

Fiji ['fi:dʒi:], *Pr.n. Geog:* **the F. Islands,** les îles Fidji.

Fijian [fi:'dʒi:ən], *Geog:* (*a*) *a.* fidjien; (*b*) *s.* Fidjien, -ienne.

filagree ['filəgri:], *s.* = FILIGREE.

filament ['filəmənt], *s.* **1.** *Nat.Hist: etc:* filament *m*, filet *m*, cil *m*; *Bot:* filet (de l'étamine); **bamboo f.,** fibre *f* de bambou. **2.** *El:* fil *m*, filament (d'une lampe); **flat f.,** filament à ruban; **drawn f.,** filament étiré; **f. lamp,** lampe à incandescence; **metal f. lamp,** lampe à filaments métalliques; **heating f.,** filament chauffant; **f. (heating) circuit,** circuit *m* de chauffage; **f. current,** courant *m* de chauffage; **f. generator,** génératrice *f* du courant de chauffage; **f. voltage,** tension *f* de chauffage; **f. transformer,** transformateur *m* de chauffage; **f. resistance,** rhéostat, résistance *f* de chauffage; **f. winding,** bobinage *m*, enroulement *m*, de chauffage; **f. battery,** batterie *f* de chauffage. **3.** *Ph: etc:* filet (d'air, etc.).

filamentary [filə'ment(ə)ri], *a.* filamenteux.

filamented ['filəməntid], *a. Biol:* à filaments.

filamentous [filə'mentəs], *a.* filamenteux.

filao [fi'leiou], *s. Bot:* filao *m*.

filaria [fi'lɛəriə], *s. Ann:* filaire *m or f*; dragonneau *m*.

filariasis, filariosis [filɛəri'eisis, -'ousis], *s. Med:* filariose *f*.

Filarioidea [filɛəri'ɔidiə], *s.pl. Ann:* filarioïdés *m*.

filature ['filətjər], *s.* **1.** (*a*) filature *f* (de la soie); (*b*) dévidage *m* (des cocons). **2.** filature de soie; atelier *m* de dévidage.

filbert ['filbət], *s.* **1.** aveline *f*; grosse noisette. **2. f. (tree),** avelinier *m*.

filch [fil(t)ʃ], *v.tr.* chiper, barboter, chaparder, raboter (**sth. from s.o.,** qch. à qn); **to f. a book from a library,** chiper un livre dans une bibliothèque.

filcher ['fil(t)ʃər], *s.* chipeur, -euse; chapardeur, -euse.

filching ['fil(t)ʃiŋ], *s.* filoutage *m*; escamotage *m*, chapardage *m*.

file[1] [fail], *s. Tls:* lime *f*; **rough f., straw f., coarse f.,** grosse lime, lime grosse, lime d'Allemagne, lime en paquet; **rasp(ing) f., grater f.,** râpe *f* (à bois); **rough-cut f.,** lime à grosse taille, à taille rude; **smooth f.,** lime douce; **dead-smooth f.,** lime sourde; **single-cut, double-cut, f.,** lime à taille simple, à double taille; **middle-cut f.,** lime à taille moyenne; **second-cut f.,** lime à taille (de)mi-douce; **blunt f., parallel f.,** lime parallèle; **flat f.,** *U.S:* **mill f.,** lime plate; **hand f.,** lime plate à main; **square f.,** lime (à section) carrée, carreau *m*; (*small*) carrelet *m*; **three-square, three-cornered, triangular, f.,** lime triangulaire; tiers-point *m, pl.* tiers-points; **safe-edge f.,** lime à chants, à côtés, lisses; **rat-tailed f.,** lime queue de rat; **taper f.,** lime conique, pointue; **bundle f.,** lime en paquet; **knife f., slitting f.,** lime à couteau; **polishing f.,** brunissoir *m*; *Locksm:* carrelette *f*; **cotter f.,** carrelet plat; fendante *f*; **adjusting f.,** écouane *f*; **cabinet f., round-off f.,** lime à arrondir; **fretwork f.,** grelette *f*; *Toil:* **nail f.,** lime à ongles; **to touch a piece up with a f.,** donner un coup de lime à une pièce; **to cut a f.,** tailler une lime; **f. cutter,** tailleur *m*, fabricant *m*, de limes; **f. bench,** banc *m* à limer; banc d'ajusteur; **f. holder,** porte-lime *m, pl.* porte-limes; **f. carrier,** arbalète *f*; **f. dust,** limaille *f*, râpure *f*.

file[2], *v.tr.* limer (le métal, etc.); **to f. sth. again,** relimer qch.; **to f. down,** alléger (une plaque de métal, etc.); enlever (une saillie, etc.) à la lime; adoucir (une surface) à la lime; *Farr:* raboter (le sabot d'un cheval); **to f. away, off,** enlever (une saillie) à la lime; **to f. up,** (i) aiguiser (un outil) à la lime; (ii) raviver (une surface à souder) à la lime; **to f. over,** repasser à la lime; **to f. across,** limer en travers; *Toil:* **to f. one's nails,** se donner un coup de lime aux ongles.

file[3], *s.* **1.** (*a*) *A:* crochet *m* à papiers; **bill f., spike f.,** pique-notes *m inv*; (*b*) classeur *m*; casier *m*; **card-index f.,** fichier *m*; classeur à fiches, de fiches; **f. card,** fiche *f* (de classeur); **rotary f.,** rolling *m*; *Cmptr:* **card f., tape f., disc f.,** fichier sur cartes, sur bande, sur disque(s); **transaction f.,** fichier mouvement(s); **master f.,** fichier permanent; **f. store,** mémoire *f* fichier; **f. tape,** bande *f* sur bobine débitrice; **f. feed,** rampe *f* de chargement; **f. protection ring,** couronne *f* d'écriture; *esp. NAm:* **f. clerk,** archiviste *mf*, classier, -ière. **2.** collection *f*, liasse *f* (de papiers, de journaux); *pl.* **files,** archives *f*, *Jur: etc:* dossier *m*; **we have placed your report on our files,** nous avons ajouté votre rapport au dossier; **f. copy,** exemplaire *m*, pièce *f*, d'archives; **f. number,** cote *f* (d'un document dans un dossier); grebiche *f* (d'un manuscrit).

file[4], *v.tr.* **1.** classer (des fiches, etc.); archiver; ranger (des lettres, etc.); **to f. letters in alphabetical order,** classer des lettres par ordre alphabétique; **to f. documents,** mettre des documents en liasse; enliasser des documents. **2.** (*a*) *Jur:* **to f. a petition,** (i) enregistrer une requête; (ii) produire, déposer (une requête, un bilan); **to f. one's petition (in bankruptcy),** présenter une requête de mise en faillite; déposer son bilan; se mettre en faillite; **to f. an application for a patent,** déposer une demande de brevet; (*b*) *Adm: esp. U.S:* déposer (un document, une plainte); **applications for seats should be filed with the secretary,** les demandes de places devront être adressées au secrétaire.

file[5], *s.* **1.** (*a*) file *f*; **in single, Indian, f.,** en file indienne, *F:* à la queue leu leu; **to walk in single f.,** marcher à la file, en file indienne; *Mil:* **in f.,** (en colonne) par deux; **in single f., in column of files,** en colonne par un, en colonne de files; **in extended f.,** en colonne diluée, en colonne avec des distances entre les hommes; **blank, odd, f.,** colonne creuse; **without odd f.,** à files égales, sans file(s) creuse(s); **f. leader,** chef *m* de file; **f. closer,** serre-file *m inv*; (*b*) *Mil:* **a f. of men,** un petit groupe d'hommes, *usu.* deux hommes; (*c*) *Mil:* un homme (sur un rang); **connecting f.,** agent *m* de liaison, jalonneur *m* (le long d'une colonne). **2.** *Chess:* colonne *f* (de cases); **to command a f.,** battre une colonne.

file[6], **1.** *v.i.* marcher à la file, en ligne de file; **to f. off,** défiler; **to f. past a catafalque,** défiler devant un catafalque; **to f. in,** entrer à la file, un à un; **to f. out,** sortir à la file, en rangs, à la queue leu leu. **2.** *v.tr.* faire marcher (des troupes) à la file, en ligne de file; faire défiler (des troupes).

filefish ['failfiʃ], *s. Ich:* baliste *m*.

filemot ['filimɔt], *a. & s.* (couleur *f*) feuille-morte (*m*) *inv*.

filer[1] ['failər], *s. Ind:* limeur *m*, ajusteur *m*.

filer[2], *s.* **1.** (*pers.*) classier, -ière; archiviste *mf*. **2.** (*thg*) classeur *m*, fichier *m*.

filet ['filit], *s. Tex:* filet *m*; **f. lace,** dentelle *f* de filet.

filial ['filiəl], *a.* filial, -aux.

filially ['filiəli], *adv.* filialement.

filiation [fili'eiʃ(ə)n], *s.* **1.** filiation *f* (d'un enfant, des idées, etc.). **2.** filiale *f* (d'un parti, etc.); **languages that are all filiations of a common parent tongue,** langues qui sont toutes apparentées à une langue-mère.

Filibranchia(ta) [fili'bræŋkiə, -bræŋki'eitə], *s.pl. Moll:* filibranches *m*.

filibuster[1] ['filibʌstər], *s.* **1.** *Hist:* flibustier *m*. **2.** *Pol:* obstruction *f*.

filibuster[2], *v.i.* **1.** *Hist:* faire le flibustier; flibuster. **2.** *Pol:* faire de l'obstruction; **filibustering tactics,** manœuvres obstructives, obstructionnistes.

filibusterer ['filibʌstərər], *s. Pol:* obstructionniste *m*.

filibustering ['filibʌst(ə)riŋ], *s. Pol:* obstruction *f*.

Filicales [fili'keili:z], **Filices** ['filisi:z], *s.pl. Bot:* filicales *f*.

filicic [fi'lisik], *a. Ch:* filicique.

filicin ['filisin], *s. Pharm:* filicine *f*.

Filicinae [fili'saini:], *s.pl. Bot:* filicinées *f*.

filigree[1] ['filigri:], *s.* filigrane *m*; **f. earrings,** boucles *f* d'oreilles en filigrane; **f. work,** (travail *m* en) filigrane; **ornamented with f. work,** filigrané.

filigree[2], *v.tr.* filigraner.

filigreed ['filigri:d], *a.* (vase, etc.) filigrané; à filigrane; en filigrane.

filing[1] ['failiŋ], *s.* **1.** limage *m*, limure *f* (d'un métal, etc.); **f. down,** adoucissement *m*, adoucissage *m*, à la lime; rabotage *m* (des sabots de cheval); **f. machine,** machine *f* à limer; limeuse *f*. **2.** *pl.* **filings,** limaille *f*, râpure *f*; (*very fine*) sable *m* (de fer).

filing[2], *s.* **1.** classement *m* (de documents, de fiches, etc.); rangement *m*; archivage *m*; **f. system,** méthode *f* de classement; **f. cabinet,** fichier *m*, (meuble-)classeur *m*; **f. box,** boîte *f* à fiches; **f. tray, basket,** corbeille *f* pour correspondance, pour documents, à classer; **f. drawer,**

tiroir classeur; **f. clerk,** classier, -ière; archiviste *mf.* **2.** *Jur:* (*a*) enregistrement *m* (d'une requête); (*b*) dépôt *m* (d'une demande).

filipendula [fili'pendjulə], *s. Bot:* filipendule *f.*

Filipino, *f.* **-pina** [fili'pi:nou, -'pi:nə], *Geog:* (*a*) *a.* philippin; (*b*) *s.* Philippin, -ine.

fill[1] [fil], *s.* **1.** suffisance *f,* content *m, F:* soûl *m;* **to have one's f. of sth.,** avoir sa suffisance, son content, de qch.; **to eat one's f.,** manger à sa faim, à son appétit, à sa suffisance; manger jusqu'à satiété; manger tout son content; se repaître; **to have eaten one's f.,** être rassasié; *F:* avoir le ventre plein. **2.** (*a*) charge *f,* plein *m;* **a f. of tobacco,** une pipe de tabac; (*b*) *Tchn:* matériau *m,* matière *f,* de remplissage; *Civ.E:* remblai *m;* (*c*) *Cin: Phot:* **f. light,** lumière *f,* projecteur *m,* d'appoint.

fill[2], *v.*

I. *v.tr.* **1.** (*a*) remplir, emplir (une cruche, etc.) (**with,** de); **to f. a jug full to overflowing,** emplir un pot jusqu'au bord, jusqu'à le faire déborder; **to f. s.o.'s glass,** (i) servir, verser, à boire à qn; (ii) (*to the brim*) verser une rasade à qn; **to f. one's cup from the teapot,** remplir sa tasse avec la théière; **to f. a truck,** charger un wagon; **to f. a lamp,** garnir une lampe; **to f. one's pipe,** bourrer sa pipe; **well-filled pockets,** poches bien bourrées; **to f. sausages,** entonner des saucisses; *Phot:* **to f. a slide,** charger un châssis; **to f. a cylinder with compressed air,** charger un cylindre d'air comprimé; *Mch: etc:* **to f. (up) the boilers, the radiator, etc.,** faire le plein des chaudières, du radiateur, etc.; *Nau:* **to f. (away) the sails,** faire servir, faire porter, éventer, les voiles; mettre le vent dans les voiles; (*b*) **to f. the air with one's cries,** remplir l'air de ses cris; **an odour of cooking filled the house,** une odeur de cuisine envahissait la maison; **report filled with facts,** rapport nourri de faits; **to f. one's head with useless things,** se farcir la tête de choses inutiles; **to be filled with one's own importance,** être pénétré de son importance; **to be filled with admiration,** être rempli d'admiration; **he was filled with despair,** il était en proie au désespoir; (*c*) peupler, pourvoir (une ville d'habitants, un étang de poissons, etc.). **2.** (*a*) combler (une brèche, une lacune, etc.); **to f. old workings,** remblayer d'anciens chantiers; **to f. a tooth,** plomber, obturer, une dent; **to f. a tooth with gold,** aurifier une dent; **to f. woodwork (before painting),** mastiquer les boiseries avant de les peindre; masquer les trous; boucher les irrégularités de surface; *Cards:* (*poker*) **to f. a flush,** compléter une séquence; (*b*) **to f. a post, a vacancy,** suppléer, pourvoir, à une vacance; nommer qn à un poste; donner un titulaire à un poste; **two places remain to be filled,** deux postes restent à pourvoir. **3.** occuper; (*a*) **a post he has filled for some time,** un poste qu'il occupe depuis quelque temps; **to f. s.o.'s shoes,** (i) succéder à qn; (ii) prendre les fonctions de qn; *Th:* **to f. a part,** remplir, tenir, un rôle; (*b*) **the table fills the whole room,** la table occupe toute la pièce; **the thoughts that filled his mind,** les pensées qui occupaient son esprit; **to f. one's free time with sth., doing sth.,** occuper ses moments perdus, ses loisirs, à qch., à faire qch.; **reading fills my evenings,** la lecture remplit toutes mes soirées. **4.** satisfaire, assouvir (ses désirs, etc.); **to f. s.o. to repletion,** rassasier qn; **fruit does not f. a man,** les fruits ne rassasient pas. **5.** (*a*) (*fulfil*) **to f. every requirement,** répondre à tous les besoins; *Com:* **to f. an order,** exécuter une commande; (*b*) *Pharm:* **to f. a prescription,** exécuter une ordonnance. **6.** verser; **to f. concrete into a coffering,** verser du béton dans un coffrage; remplir un coffrage de béton. **7.** *N.Arch:* mailleter (la carène).

II. *v.i.* **1.** se remplir, s'emplir, se combler; **the lake is filling rapidly,** le lac se comble rapidement; **her eyes filled with tears,** ses yeux se remplissaient de larmes; **the empty space gradually filled with people,** l'espace s'est peuplé peu à peu; **the hall is beginning to f.,** la salle commence à se garnir. **2.** *Nau:* (*of sails*) se gonfler, s'enfler, porter.

III. (*compound verbs*) **1. fill in,** *v.tr.* (*a*) combler, boucher, remplir (un trou); condamner (une porte); remblayer (un fossé); *Tchn:* bouche-porer (du bois); (*b*) combler (des vides, des lacunes); compléter (une ébauche, etc.); remplir (un formulaire); **to f. in the date,** insérer la date; *F:* **to f. s.o. in on the details,** éclaircir qn sur les détails (d'une affaire); **f. me in!** mets-moi à la page!

2. fill out. (*a*) *v.tr.* (i) enfler, gonfler (un ballon, etc.); (ii) étoffer (un discours, etc.); **some of his conclusions need filling out,** quelques-unes de ses conclusions demandent à être établies avec plus d'ampleur; (iii) *NAm:* remplir (un formulaire); (*b*) *v.i.* s'enfler, se gonfler; s'arrondir; (*of pers.*) engraisser, grossir, prendre de l'embonpoint; s'étoffer; se remplumer; **her cheeks are filling out,** ses joues se remplissent; **that boy will be a big man when he fills out,** cet enfant aura de la carrure lorsqu'il aura pris du corps; *F:* **the children are filling out visibly,** les enfants profitent à vue d'œil.

3. fill up. (*a*) *v.tr.* (i) remplir (un verre) jusqu'au bord; combler (une mesure, etc.); regarnir (une forêt, etc.); *v.i.* **to f. up with petrol, with water,** faire le plein d'essence, d'eau; *Nau:* **to f. up (the freight) with coal,** faire le plein avec du charbon; *Typ:* **to f. up a page,** allonger la matière pour remplir la page; (ii) boucher (un trou avec du mastic, etc.); condamner (une porte); remblayer (un fossé, etc.); (iii) remplir (un formulaire); (*b*) *v.i.* se remplir, s'emplir, se combler; (*of gaps in woodland*) se regarnir.

filled [fild], *a.* **1.** (aliment, savon, etc.) qui contient un succédané; *Tex:* (tissu de coton, etc.) chargé d'empois. **2.** (*with sb. prefixed*) **water-f., gas-f.,** rempli d'eau, de gaz.

filler[1] ['filər], *s.* **1.** (*a*) (*pers.*) chargeur *m* (de haut fourneau); enfourneur *m* (de four); **f. (in),** remplisseur, -euse; *Civ.E:* **f. up,** remblayeur *m;* (*b*) (*thg*) (**bottle**) **f.,** remplisseuse *f;* **oil f.,** entonnoir *m;* **grease-gun f.,** remplisseur *m* de pompe. **2.** (*a*) (matière *f* de) remplissage *m;* tripe *f* (d'un cigare); *Rail:* entretoise *f;* **f. metal,** métal *m* d'apport; *Civ.E: Const:* **f. (block, slip),** (bois *m* de) remplissage; fourrure *f;* cale *f;* filler *m;* (*b*) charge *f* (de matière plastique, de caoutchouc, etc.); *Tchn:* bouche-pores *m inv* (de bois); *Paint:* (i) blanc *m* de charge; (ii) mastic *m;* (*c*) *Paperm:* âme *f* (du carton); (*d*) *Journ: F:* (chronique *f* des) chiens écrasés.

filler[2] ['fi:lər], *s. Num:* filler *m.*

fillet[1] ['filit], *s.* **1.** (*a*) *Cost:* filet *m,* bandelette *f* (pour maintenir les cheveux); (*b*) *Med:* bandelette, bandage *m,* bande *f;* (*c*) ruban *m,* bande (d'étoffe, de métal, etc.); *Num:* lame *f* (d'or, d'argent); *Tex:* ruban à carde. **2.** *pl.* **fillets,** reins *m,* lombes *m* (d'un cheval). **3.** *Cu:* (*a*) filet (de bœuf, de sole); (*b*) rouelle *f* (de veau). **4.** (*a*) *Arch: etc:* fasce *f;* bande; congé *m;* nervure *f,* nerf *m,* filet; **half-round f.,** angle arrondi; **outer f. (of dripping mould, label),** mouchette *f;* (*b*) *Join:* baguette *f,* listel *m* (de panneau); (*c*) *Mec.E:* collet *m,* bourrelet *m,* boudin *m* (sur un tuyau, etc.); arrondi *m* (à la base d'une dent); filet (d'une vis); *Metalw:* **f. (border) (of silver plate),** suage *m;* *I.C.E:* **piston ring f.,** congé de base de segment; (*d*) *Av:* **fin, wing, f.,** carénage *m* d'emplanture d'aile; (*e*) **f. weld,** soudure *f* (i) à clin, (ii) d'angle. **5.** (*a*) *Her:* filet; (*b*) *Bookb: Typ:* filet. **6.** *Bookb: Tls:* roulette *f.*

fillet[2], *v.tr.* (**filleted**) **1.** orner (qch.) d'un filet, d'un congé, d'une baguette. **2.** *Cu:* détacher, lever, les filets (d'un poisson); fileter, désosser (un poisson); **filleted sole,** filets *mpl* de sole.

filleting ['filitiŋ], *s.* **1.** (*a*) ornementation *f* (de qch.) avec des filets, des baguettes; (*b*) garniture *f* de filets, de baguettes. **2.** *Cu:* prélèvement *m* des filets (d'une sole, etc.).

fill-in ['filin], *s. F:* (*a*) (*pers.*) bouche-trou *m, pl.* bouche-trous; (*b*) *T.V: etc:* intermède *m;* bouche-trou; (*c*) mise *f* au courant, tuyautage *m;* (*d*) *attrib.* **f.-in light,** lumière *f* d'appoint.

filling[1] ['filiŋ], *a.* (*of food, etc.*) rassasiant.

filling[2], *s.* **1.** (*a*) (r)emplissage *m* (d'une mesure); chargement *m* (d'un wagon, etc.); bourrage *m* (d'une pipe à tabac); gonflement *m* (d'un ballon); mise *f* en eau (d'un réservoir); **f. point,** repère *m* de remplissage, de capacité; *Aer:* **f. neck,** raccordement *m* à manche (d'un ballon); *X Rays:* **f. defect,** image *f* lacunaire; *Aut:* **f. station,** poste *m* d'essence; station-service *f, pl.* stations-service; **f.-station attendant,** pompiste *mf;* *Nau:* **backing and f.,** vent dessus vent dedans; (*b*) peuplement *m* (d'un étang). **2.** (*a*) comblement *m* (d'un vide, d'un trou, d'un fossé); remblayage *m* (d'un fossé, etc.); *Civ.E: Const:* remplissage, remplage *m,* garnissage *m;* *Dent:* plombage *m,* obturation *f,* (*with gold*) aurification *f* (d'une dent); *Metalw:* **f. metal,** métal *m* d'appoint (pour souder); *Mil:* **f. of a gap,** colmatage *m* d'une brèche (dans une position, etc.); (*b*) **f. of a vacancy,** nomination *f* de quelqu'un à un poste. **3.** occupation *f* (d'un poste, de ses loisirs, etc.). **4.** *N.Arch:* mailletage *m* (de la carène). **5.** (matière *f* de) remplissage; fourrure *f;* tripe *f* (d'un cigare); *Tex:* charge *f;* charge (dans le savon, les matières plastiques, etc.); *Dent: Carp:* mastic *m;* *Civ.E: Const:* remplissage, matière inerte; (*rubble*) blocage *m;* (*liquid*) coulis *m;* *Cu:* garniture *f* (d'un sandwich); **cake with a chocolate f.,** gâteau fourré au chocolat; *Const:* **panel f.,** masque *m;* **beam f., plaster f. between joists,** solin *m;* *N.Arch:* **f. of the bows,** mouchoirs *m* des joues; *Tp:* **granular f.,** grenaille *f* (d'une capsule téléphonique); *Furn:* **hair f.,** rembourrage *m* de crin.

filling in ['filiŋ'in], *s.* **1.** comblement *m* (d'un trou); remplissage *m* (d'une broderie, etc.); remblayage *m* (d'un fossé); bouche-porage *m* (du bois). **2.** achèvement *m* (d'une ébauche, etc.); rédaction *f* (d'un formulaire).

filling out ['filiŋ'aut], *s.* **1.** enflement *m,* gonflement *m* (d'un ballon). **2.** élargissement *m* (de la taille).

filling up ['filiŋ'ʌp], *s.* (*a*) remplissage *m* (d'un tonneau); comblement *m* (d'une lacune, etc.); (*b*) bouchage *m* (d'un trou); remblayage *m* (d'un fossé); colmatage *m* (d'une brèche, etc.); (*c*) rédaction *f* (d'un formulaire, etc.); (*d*) *Mus:* **f.-up parts,** parties *f* de remplissage.

fillip[1] ['filip], *s.* **1.** (*a*) chiquenaude *f;* (*b*) *F:* vétille *f,* bagatelle *f;* **it's not worth a f.,** ça ne vaut pas un pet de lapin. **2.** stimulant *m,* encouragement *m;* coup de fouet (donné au sang, au système nerveux, etc.); **fresh f. to sales,** regain *m* de vente; **to give a f. to business,** stimuler les affaires; faire aller le commerce; **to give a f. to the appetite,** stimuler, raviver, activer, l'appétit.

fillip[2], *v.tr.* (**filliped**) **1.** donner une chiquenaude à (qn, une bille, etc.). **2.** stimuler, faire aller (les affaires, etc.); fouetter (le sang).

fillis ['filis], *s.* filasse *f* (de chanvre, etc.).

fillister ['filistər], *s.* **1.** *Tls:* (rabot *m* à) feuilleret *m;* bouvet *m* (à feuillures). **2.** *Const:* feuillure *f* (d'un châssis de fenêtre, etc.).

fillowite ['filouait], *s. Miner:* fillowite *f.*

fill-up ['filʌp], *s. W.Tel: etc: F:* remplissage *m.*

filly ['fili], *s.* **1.** pouliche *f.* **2.** *F:* jeune fille *f* (qui a de l'allant).

film[1] [film], *s.* **1.** (*a*) pellicule *f,* couche *f,* film *m* (de glace, d'huile); peau *f* (de lait bouilli); *Med:* **f. over the eye,** taie *f* sur l'œil; **grey f. (on the cornea),** opacité grise, voile *m* (de la cornée); (*b*) voile (de brume, de fumée, etc.). **2.** *Phot:* (*a*) pellicule, film; **cut f.,** *U.S:* **sheet f.,** pellicule rigide, plaque *f* souple, vitrose *f;* **roll f.,** pellicule, film, en bobine; **slow, fast, f.,** film lent, rapide; **panchromatic f.,** film panchromatique; **infra-red f.,** pellicule, film, sensible à l'infra rouge; **multilayer f.,** pellicule, film, à émulsions superposées; **process f.,** pellicule pour photomécanique; **colour f.,** film (en) couleur(s) ((i) (*reversal*) inversible; (ii) (*negative*) négatif); **raw f., unexpended f.,** pellicule, film, vierge; **f. cartridge, spool,** bobine *f* de pellicule, de film; **f. cassette,** cartouche *f* de pellicule, de film; **f. base,** support *m;* **f. layer,** émulsion *f* (de la pellicule, du film); **f. pack,** film(-)pack *m,* bloc-film *m, pl.* blocs-films; (*b*) couche *f* sensible (de la plaque, de la pellicule); (*c*) *Cmptr:* **f. card,** microfiche *f;* **f. file,** fichier *m* sur film. **3.** *Cin:* (*a*) film; bande *f;* **flat f.,** film plan; **lenticulated f.,** film gaufré; **reversal f.,** film réversible; **stereoscopic f.,** film en relief; **silent f.,** film muet; **sound f.,** film sonore, sonorisé, parlant; **full-length, short(-length) f.,** (film de) long métrage, court métrage; **supporting f.,** film supplémentaire; **news f.,** reportage filmé; actualités *fpl;* **f. pickup,** film télévisé; **f. recorder, reproducer,** lecteur *m* de son; **f. channel, track,** couloir *m,* chemin *m,* du film; **f. joint, splice,** collure *f;* **f. joiner, splicer,** colleuse *f;* **f. feeder spool,** bobine débitrice; dérouleuse *f;* **f. take-up spool,** bobine réceptrice; enrouleuse *f;* **f. script,** scénario *m,* script *m;* **to act, play in, a f.,** jouer dans un film; **to take, shoot, a f.,** tourner un film; **to have a f. test,** tourner une bande d'essai; (*b*) **the films,** le cinéma, l'écran *m;* **the f. industry,** l'industrie cinématographique, du cinéma; **f. actor, actress,** acteur, -trice, artiste *mf,* de cinéma; **f. rights,** droits *m* d'adaptation cinématographique, à l'écran; **f. library,** cinémathèque *f;* **f. club,** ciné-club *m;* **f. critic,** critique *m* du cinéma; **he's in films,** il fait du cinéma; **I've seen it on the films,** j'ai vu ça au cinéma. **4.** *Atom.Ph:* **f. badge,** détecteur, dosimètre, photographique individuel. **5.** *A: & Lit:* fil *m,* filament *m* (de gaze, de soie, etc.). **6.** *Typ:* typon *m;* **f. negative,** contre-typon *m, pl.* contre-typons.

film[2]. **1.** *v.tr.* (*a*) recouvrir (qch.) (i) d'une pellicule, (ii) d'un voile; *Phot:* filmer (une plaque); enduire (une plaque) d'une couche sensible; (*b*) *Cin:* filmer, enregistrer, cinématographier, tourner (une scène); filmer (un roman); présenter, mettre, porter, adapter, (un roman) à l'écran; (*with passive force*) **he films well,** il est photogénique. **2.** *v.i.* **to f. (over),** (i) (*of lake, etc.*) se couvrir d'une pellicule; (ii) (*of the eyes*) se couvrir d'une taie; (iii) (*of countryside, etc.*) se voiler.

filmable ['filməbl], *a.* (roman *m,* etc.) adaptable au cinéma.

film-building, -forming ['film'bildiŋ, -'fɔ:miŋ], *a. Paint:* filmogène.

filmic ['filmik], *a.* filmique.

filmslide ['filmslaid], *s. esp. U.S:* diapositif *m,* diapositive *f* (de projection).

filmstar ['filmstɑ:r], *s.* vedette *f* (de l'écran); étoile *f* de cinéma.

filmstrip ['filmstrip], *s.* film *m* fixe (d'enseignement).

filmy ['filmi], *a.* **1.** (*a*) (*of substance*) qui forme une pellicule; **a coating of f. ice,** une mince couche de glace; (*b*) (*of thg*) couvert d'une pellicule; (*of eye*) couvert d'une taie; (*c*) voilé (de brume, etc.); **the f. crescent of the moon,** le croissant embrumé de la lune. **2.** (*of lace, cloud, etc.*) léger, transparent.

filose ['failous], *a. Nat.Hist:* à terminaison filiforme.

filoselle ['filəsel], *s. Tex:* filoselle *f.*

filter[1] ['filtər], *s.* **1.** (*a*) filtre *m*; épurateur *m* (d'essence, etc.); **pressure f.,** filtre à, sous, pression; **vacuum f.,** filtre à vide; **suction f.,** filtre à aspiration; **rotary, rotating, f.,** filtre rotatif; **carbon, sand, f.,** filtre à charbon, à sable; **air f.,** filtre à air; épurateur d'air; tamis *m* anti-poussière; **coffee f.,** filtre à café; *Pharm: etc:* **cloth f.,** blanchet *m*; *Sug.-R:* **bone-black f.,** filtre à noir; **sewage f.,** filtre pour les eaux d'égout; **f. paper,** papier filtre; **f. tip (of cigarette),** bout filtrant, bout filtre (d'une cigarette); **f. cartridge,** cartouche filtrante; *Ind:* **f. press,** filtre-presse *m, pl.* filtres-presses; *Hyd.E:* **f. bed,** bassin filtrant, de filtration; lit *m* de filtrage; *Ch:* **f. pump,** trompe *f* à vide; *Miner:* **f. stone,** pierre *f* de liais; (*b*) *Med:* **f. passer, f.-passing bacillus,** bacille filtrant. **2.** *Opt: Phot:* **optical f.,** filtre optique; **colour f., light f.,** filtre de couleur; filtre, écran, coloré; écran *m* filtre; **white light f.,** filtre bleuté; **contrast f.,** filtre de contraste; **separation f.,** écran séparateur, sélectif; **compensation, correcting, f.,** filtre compensateur, correcteur; **neutral f.,** filtre neutre; **dummy f.,** filtre de mise au point; **f. screen,** écran filtre. **3.** *El: Elcs: etc:* **electric f., smoothing f.,** filtre électrique; filtre de courant, de tension; **frequency f.,** filtre de fréquences; **radio-frequency f.,** filtre haute fréquence; **f. frequency,** fréquence passante; **choke f.,** filtre à impédance; **f. choke,** self *f* de filtrage; **discrimination f.,** filtre discriminateur, sélecteur; **f. discrimination, selectivity of a f.,** rendement *m*, sélectivité *f*, d'un filtre; **duplexer f.,** filtre duplexeur; **rectifier f.,** filtre redresseur; **band f., wave f.,** filtre de bande; **wave-guide f.,** filtre de guide d'ondes; **band-stop, band-elimination, f.,** filtre éliminateur de bande; **band-pass f.,** filtre passe-bande; **f. pass band,** bande passante d'un filtre; **f. stop band,** bande d'atténuation d'un filtre; **band-rejection f.,** filtre de rejet de bande; **low-pass, high-pass, f.,** filtre passe-bas, passe-haut; **all-pass f.,** filtre passe-partout; **crystal f.,** filtre piézo-électrique, filtre à cristal; **f. circuit,** circuit *m* de filtrage; *W.Tel: T.V:* **tone f.,** filtre de tonalité; **interference f.,** filtre antiparasites; **directional f.,** aiguillage *m.*

filter[2]. **1.** *v.tr.* filtrer (l'eau); épurer, tamiser (l'air, etc.); **to f. out the impurities,** séparer, extraire, les impuretés par filtrage; *W.Tel:* **to f. out a station,** couper une station au moyen d'un filtre. **2.** *v.i.* (*a*) (*of water, etc.*) filtrer, s'infiltrer (**through,** à travers); (*seep*) suinter; **coffee must f. very slowly,** il faut que le café passe très lentement; **the light filtered through the branches,** la lumière filtrait à travers les branches; **the curtains allow only a faint light to f. through,** les rideaux ne laissent filtrer qu'un faible jour; **these new ideas were filtering into people's minds,** ces idées nouvelles s'infiltraient dans les esprits; **the news soon filtered through,** les nouvelles se divulguèrent bientôt; (*b*) *Aut: etc:* changer de file; couper la file; déboîter; **to f. to the right, to the left,** glisser à droite, à gauche.

filterable ['filtərəbl], *a.* filtrable; *Med:* **f. virus,** virus filtrant, infravirus *m.*

filterer ['filtərər], *s.* (*pers.*) tamiseur, -euse; filtreur *m.*

filtering ['filt(ə)riŋ], *s.* filtrage *m*, filtration *f*; *Hyd.E:* **f. tank,** purgeoir *m.*

filth [filθ], *s.* **1.** (*a*) ordure *f*; immondices *mpl*; (*b*) saleté *f*; **to live in (the midst of) f.,** vivre dans la saleté. **2.** (*a*) corruption morale; (*b*) propos orduriers, dégoûtants; **to talk f.,** dire des obscénités, des ordures, des saletés, des cochonneries; tenir des propos dégoûtants.

filthily ['filθili], *adv.* salement; d'une manière ordurière, immonde.

filthiness ['filθinis], *s.* **1.** grande malpropreté; saleté *f*; *F:* saloperie *f.* **2.** corruption morale, obscénité *f.*

filthy ['filθi], *a.* **1.** (*a*) sale, immonde, dégoûtant; **f. hovel,** taudis infect, d'une saleté dégoûtante; **a f. brat,** un gosse sale comme un peigne; **f. weather,** temps de chien, de cochon; **f. communist!** sale communiste! (*b*) **in a f. temper,** d'une humeur massacrante. **2.** (*of book, talk, etc.*) ordurier, crapuleux, obscène, infect; (*of pers.*) crapuleux.

filtrable ['filtrəbl], *a. Med:* (virus) filtrant, filtrable.

filtrate[1] ['filtreit], *s. Ch: etc:* filtrat *m*; *Pharm:* colature *f.*

filtrate[2], *v.* = FILTER[2].

filtration [fil'treiʃ(ə)n], *s.* filtration *f*, filtrage *m*, épuration *f*; *Pharm:* colature *f.*

fimbriate(d) ['fimbrieit(id)], *a.* **1.** *Nat.Hist:* fimbrié. **2.** *Her:* bordé.

fimbrillate, fimbrillose ['fimbrileit, -ous], *a. Bot:* à fimbrilles *f.*

fimbristylis [fimbri'stailis], *s. Bot:* fimbristyle *f*, fimbristylis *m.*

fin [fin], *s.* **1.** (*a*) *Nat.Hist:* nageoire *f* (d'un poisson, d'un pingouin, d'une baleine); battoir *m* (d'une baleine); aileron *m* (d'un requin); *Ich:* **abdominal, belly, f.,** nageoire abdominale; **anal f.,** nageoire anale; **caudal, tail, f.,** nageoire caudale; **pelvic f.,** pelvienne *f*; **breast, pectoral, f.,** nageoire pectorale; (*b*) *Swim:* **fins,** palmes *f*; (*c*) *P:* main *f*, pince *f*, patte *f*; *A:* **tip us your f.,** serre-moi la pince. **2.** (*a*) *N.Arch:* dérive *f*, dériveur *m*, aileron; **f. stabilizer,** stabilisateur *m* à ailerons; **stabilizer f.,** aileron stabilisateur; (*b*) *Av:* dérive, plan fixe vertical; empennage *m* (de dirigeable); **horizontal f.,** plan fixe horizontal; **stabilizer f.,** plan fixe stabilisateur; **twin f.,** double dérive; **dorsal, ventral, f.,** dérive dorsale, ventrale; **f. front, f. rear, spar,** poutrelle *f* avant, arrière, de dérive; **f. fuel tank,** réservoir *m* de dérive; (*c*) (*of bomb, grenade, etc.*) ailette *f*; **stabilizing fins,** ailettes stabilisatrices, empennage stabilisateur; (*d*) *Aut:* ailette (de radiateur, etc.); **cooling fins,** ailettes de refroidissement; **f.-cooled,** refroidi par ailettes, à refroidissement par ailettes.

finable ['fainəbl], *a.* passible d'(une) amende.

finagle [fi'neigl], *v.tr. & i. NAm: F:* resquiller, carotter.

finagler [fi'neiglər], *s. NAm: F:* resquilleur, -euse, carotteur, -euse, fricoteur, -euse.

final ['fain(ə)l]. **1.** *a.* final, -als; (*a*) dernier; **f. letter of a word,** dernière lettre, lettre finale, finale *f*, d'un mot; **f. preparations,** derniers préparatifs; **f. justification for sth.,** raison dernière de qch.; **the f. requests,** les dernières volontés (d'un mourant); **to make a f. effort,** faire un dernier effort; **to put the f. touches to sth.,** mettre la dernière main à qch.; *Com: Fin:* **f. date (for payment),** terme fatal, de rigueur; **f. instalment,** dernier versement; versement de libération; *Jur:* **f. process,** exécution *f*; **f. judgment,** jugement *m* exécutoire; *El: Elcs:* **f. amplifier,** amplificateur *m* de sortie; *Mil:* **f. protective line,** ligne *f* d'arrêt; (*b*) définitif, décisif; **f. text,** texte définitif; *Jur:* **f. judgment,** (i) jugement final de première instance; (ii) arrêt final (de la Cour d'Appel, de la Cour de Cassation); **the evidence is f.,** les témoignages sont concluants, ne laissent aucun doute; **the umpire's decision is f.,** la décision de l'arbitre est sans appel; **am I to consider that as f.?** c'est votre dernier mot? **take this as f.,** tenez-le-vous pour dit; (*c*) *Phil:* **f. cause,** cause finale; *Gram:* **f. clause,** proposition finale. **2.** *s.* (*a*) (lettre) finale *f* (d'un mot); (*b*) *Sp:* **the f.,** les (épreuves) finales; la finale; *Fb:* **cup f.,** finale de coupe; (*c*) *Sch:* **to sit, take, one's finals** = passer son dernier examen de licence; *Jur:* **the bar f.,** l'examen final pour être reçu avocat; (*d*) *Mus:* (*in plain song*) finale.

finale [fi'nɑːli], *s.* **1.** *Mus:* final(e) *m.* **2.** conclusion *f*; *Th:* **grand f.,** apothéose *f.*

finalism ['fainəlizm], *s. Phil:* finalisme *m.*

finalist ['fainəlist], *s.* **1.** *Phil:* finaliste *mf.* **2.** *Sp:* finaliste.

finality [fai'næliti], *s.* **1.** *Phil:* finalité *f.* **2.** caractère définitif (d'un jugement, etc.), irrévocabilité *f* (d'une décision); **there was a note of f. in his voice,** il a parlé avec décision, péremptoirement; **proposals in which there is no f.,** propositions *f* qui n'aboutissent à rien de décisif.

finalize ['fainəlaiz], *v.tr.* mener (qch.) à bonne fin; mettre la dernière main à (qch.).

finally ['fainəli], *adv.* finalement. **1.** enfin, à la fin; **f. justice triumphs,** la justice finit par triompher. **2.** définitivement, décisivement. **3.** en somme, en définitive.

finance[1] [fai'næns, fi-], *s.* **1.** finance *f*; **public f.,** finances publiques; **high f.,** (i) la haute finance; (ii) *coll.* la haute banque; **questions of f.,** la finance, les questions financières; *Pol:* **the F. Act (of 1935, etc.),** la loi de finances (de 1935, etc.); **f. company,** société *f* de crédits, de prêts; **f. development corporation,** fonds *m* de développement économique. **2. the finances of a state,** les finances d'un état; **his finances are low,** sa bourse est presque vide, ses fonds sont bas, en baisse.

finance[2], *v.tr.* financer, commanditer (qn, une entreprise, etc.); supporter tous les frais (d'une entreprise); **I want someone to f. the business,** il me faut un bailleur de fonds; **to f. the cost of the undertaking,** fournir les fonds nécessaires à l'entreprise.

financial [fai'nænʃ(ə)l, fi-], *a.* financier; **the f. world,** le monde de la finance; *Adm: Com:* **f. year,** exercice (financier); année *f* budgétaire; année d'exercice; **f. resources,** ressources fiscales, financières; **f. statement,** situation *f* de trésorerie; état *m* des finances; bilan *m.*

financially [fai'nænʃəli], *adv.* financièrement; **f. sound,** solvable, solide au point de vue financier.

financier[1] [fai'nænsiər, fi-], *s.* **1.** (*a*) financier *m*; homme *m* de finance; (*b*) *Fr.Hist:* financier (des droits du roi). **2.** bailleur *m* de fonds.

financier[2] [finæn'siər], *v.tr. & i. U.S: Pej:* **1.** faire de l'agiotage; agioter; **to f. one's money away,** gâcher son argent en mauvaises spéculations. **2. to f. money out of s.o.,** soutirer de l'argent à qn; filouter qn.

financing [fai'nænsiŋ, fi-], *s.* financement *m* (d'une entreprise, etc.); **compensatory official f.,** financement compensatoire officiel; **f. company,** compagnie *f*, société *f*, de financement.

finback ['finbæk], *s. Z:* baleinoptère *m*, rorqual *m*, -als; fausse baleine.

finch [fin(t)ʃ], *s. Orn:* fringille *f*; **ground f.,** (i) pinson *m* de Darwin; (ii) tohi *m*; **snow f.,** niverolle *f* des Alpes, pinson de neige; **citril f.,** venturon montagnard, alpin; **African f.,** grenadin *m*; **painted f.,** pape *m*; **parrot f.,** pape de Nouméa; **grey singing f.,** chanteur *m* d'Afrique; **green singing f.,** serin *m* de Mozambique; **bib f.,** spermète nain; **seed f.,** sporophile *m*; **grey f.,** sporophile bleuâtre; **fire-red f.,** sporophile nain; **plumbeous f.,** sporophile gris de plomb; **plum-capped f., cherry f.,** diamant *m* modeste; **Bicheno f.,** diamant de Bichenov; **Gouldian f.,** diamant de Gould; **ruficauda f., star f.,** diamant à queue rousse; **zebra f.,** diamant mandarin; **fire-tailed f.,** diamant à queue de feu; **parson f.,** diamant à bavette; **chestnut-breasted f.,** donacole commun; **pectoralis f.,** donacole à poitrine blanche; **yellow-rumped f.,** donacole à tête blanche; **lavender f.,** astrild *m* gris-bleu, queue-de-vinaigre; **quail f.,** astrild-caille *m* à lunettes; **red-headed f.,** amadine *f* à tête rouge; **melba f.,** beau-marquet *m*; **quelea f.,** quelea *m*, dioch *m*, *F:* travailleur; **saffron f.,** bouton *m* d'or ordinaire; **rose f.,** roselin *m* rose; **purple f.,** roselin pourpré; **Cassin's (purple) f.,** roselin de Cassin; **grey-crowned rosy f.,** roselin brun.

find[1] [faind], *s.* **1.** découverte *f*; *Ven:* découverte, vue *f*, de la bête. **2.** trouvaille *f.* **3. a sure f.,** (i) *Ven:* endroit *m* où on trouve toujours un renard; (ii) personne *f*, chose *f*, qu'on ne peut manquer de trouver.

find[2], *v.* (**found** [faund]; **found**)

I. *v.tr.* **1.** (*a*) trouver, rencontrer, découvrir; **to f. a treasure by accident,** trouver, découvrir, un trésor par hasard; **to f. misprints in a book,** trouver des fautes d'impression dans un livre; **you can f. them anywhere,** on les trouve partout; **such men are not often found,** de tels hommes ne se rencontrent pas souvent; **good domestic help is not easily found,** il est difficile de trouver une bonne femme de ménage; **to f. happiness with s.o.,** rencontrer le bonheur auprès de qn; **to f. a good friend in s.o.,** trouver en qn un bon ami; **to f. some difficulty in doing sth.,** éprouver quelque difficulté à faire qch.; **the bullet found its mark,** la balle a atteint son but; (*b*) **to f. s.o. at home, in,** trouver qn chez lui; **I found he was not at home, I found him out,** je ne l'ai pas trouvé chez lui; j'ai trouvé qu'il était sorti; **they found him dead,** on l'a trouvé mort; **we must leave everything as we find it,** il faut tout laisser tel quel; **I found her gathering flowers,** je l'ai trouvée en train de cueillir des fleurs; **I found him waiting in the hall,** je l'ai trouvé qui m'attendait dans le vestibule; **six months later we f. him saying the exact opposite,** six mois plus tard il se trouva dire tout le contraire; **I often f. myself smiling,** je me surprends souvent à sourire; **Christmas found him still looking for a job,** à Noël il n'avait pas encore trouvé d'emploi; **one of these days he will f. them stolen,** un de ces jours il se les verra enlever. **2.** (*discover by searching*) (*a*) **the (lost) key has been found,** la clef s'est retrouvée; **to try to f. sth.,** chercher qch.; **I managed to f. it, him,** je suis arrivé à le trouver, à le dénicher; **I ran to f. a doctor,** j'ai couru à la recherche d'un médecin; **he is not to be found (anywhere),** on ne le trouve, on ne peut le trouver, nulle part; il est introuvable; *B:* **seek and ye shall f.,** cherchez et vous trouverez; **to f. a job for s.o.,** trouver, procurer, un emploi à qn; **I have found what I want,** j'ai trouvé ce qu'il me faut; **to f. a leak in a main,** localiser une fuite dans une conduite; **I can't f. anything wrong with it,** je n'y trouve aucun défaut; **I can f. no reason for . . .,** je ne vois pas de raison pour . . .; **the child couldn't f. his way home,** l'enfant n'a pas pu retrouver le chemin pour rentrer chez lui; **to f. a way to do sth.,** trouver le moyen de faire qch.; **I can't f. time to . . .,** je n'ai pas le temps de . . .; **he found (the) courage to . . .,** il a eu le courage de . . .; **to f. it in one's heart to do sth.,** avoir le cœur de faire qch.; **to f. oneself,** (i) prendre conscience de soi-même, de ses talents, de ses capacités; (ii) trouver sa voie, sa vocation; (*b*) obtenir (une sûreté, une caution); **to f. favour with s.o.,** gagner la faveur de qn. **3.** (*a*) (*perceive, establish a fact*) constater; **I f. that I was mistaken,** je me rends compte, je suis arrivé à la conclusion, que je m'étais trompé; **you will f. that I am right,** vous verrez que j'ai raison; **it has been found that . . .,** on a constaté que . . .; **I was surprised to f. that . . .,** j'ai été surpris de constater que . . .; **I found that she had left the house,** j'ai appris qu'elle avait quitté la maison; **this letter, I f., arrived yesterday,** cette lettre, à ce que je vois, à ce que j'apprends, est arrivée hier; **you'll f. that it will do you good,** vous trouverez que cela vous fera du bien; **I f. that it pays to . . .,** je trouve qu'il vaut la peine de . . .; **I opened the case and found there was a pearl necklace in it,** en ouvrant la valise j'y ai trouvé un collier de perles; (*b*) **they will f. it easy, difficult,** cela leur sera facile, difficile; **we f. it very difficult to get (domestic) help,** nous avons beaucoup de peine à nous procurer une femme de ménage; **to f. it impossible, necessary, to do sth.,** se trouver dans l'impossibilité, dans la nécessité, de faire qch.; **how do you f. this wine?** comment trouvez-vous ce vin? **I f. his fits of temper very childish,** ses accès d'humeur me semblent bien puérils; **I f. them ridiculous,** je les juge ridicules; *O:* **how do you f. yourself?** comment vous trouvez-vous? comment allez-vous? (*c*) **they found an unexpected supporter in Mr X,** ils ont trouvé en M. X un partisan inattendu. **4.** *Jur:* (*a*) **to f. s.o. guilty,** déclarer qn coupable; (*b*) rendre (un verdict); **to f. for s.o.,** prononcer, rendre, un verdict en faveur de qn; **to f. for the plaintiff,** adjuger au demandeur ses conclusions; (*c*) **to f. a (true) bill against s.o.,** prononcer une mise en accusation contre qn. **5.** (*provide*) (*a*) procurer, fournir (qch.); **to f. the money for an undertaking,** procurer les capitaux, fournir l'argent, pour une entreprise; **X finds half the money,** X baille les fonds pour moitié, apporte la moitié des fonds; (*b*) (i) *A:* **to f. s.o. in food,** fournir, donner, la nourriture à qn; **to f. oneself,** se pourvoir soi-même; subvenir à son propre entretien; (ii) **wages £20, all found,** gages *m* £20, nourri, logé, chauffé et blanchi; gages £20, tout fourni.

II. (*compound verb*) **find out.** (*a*) (i) *v.tr.* se rendre compte (des faits); **to f. out the truth,** découvrir la vérité; **to f. out how to do sth.,** découvrir le moyen de faire qch.; (ii) *v.i.* **to f. out about sth.,** se renseigner sur qch.; **I have found out all about it,** j'ai pu établir tous les faits; **what have you done with it?—f. out!** qu'en avez vous fait?—à vous de trouver! **I'll f. out,** je le saurai; (*b*) *v.tr.* **to f. s.o. out,** (i) découvrir le vrai caractère de qn, démasquer qn; (ii) trouver, prendre, qn en défaut; **he has been found out,** (i) on a découvert son secret; (ii) on l'a pris en défaut; **your sins will f. you out,** on n'échappe pas aux conséquences de ses fautes.

findable ['faindəbl], *a.* trouvable.

finder ['faindər], *s.* **1.** (*pers.*) trouveur, -euse; *Jur:* inventeur, -trice (d'un objet perdu); *Jur:* **f. of a waif,** inventeur d'une épave. **2.** (*a*) (*of telescope*) chercheur *m*, trouveur *m*; lunette *f* de repère; (*b*) *El:* **short-circuit f.,** chercheur, détecteur, de courts-circuits; **pole f.,** indicateur *m* de pôles; cherche-pôle *m inv*; *Tp:* **line f.,** chercheur de lignes.

finding ['faindiŋ], *s.* (*a*) *usu.pl.* découverte(s) *f*; **he published his findings in a scientific journal,** il a fait publier les résultats de ses recherches dans un journal scientifique; (*b*) **findings,** trouvaille *f*; *Prov:* **findings (is) keepings,** ce qui tombe dans le fossé est pour le soldat; (*c*) *Jur:* conclusion *f* (du tribunal, du jury) sur un point de fait; **to bring in a f. for, against, s.o.,** rendre, prononcer, un verdict en faveur de, contre, qn; **inconsistent findings,** conclusions contradictoires; **his f. is that . . .,** il est arrivé à la conclusion que . . .; (*d*) *Ind: U.S:* **findings,** fournitures *f*, menues pièces et outils (d'un métier); crépins *m* (de cordonnier).

fine[1] [fain], *s.* **1.** *A:* fin *f*; *now used only in adv. phr.* **in fine,** enfin, finalement. **2.** *Jur:* (*a*) pas *m* de porte; (*b*) **right to annul a sale by paying a f.,** stipulation *f* d'arrhes; (*c*) amende *f*; peine *f* pécuniaire; **heavy f.,** amende élevée, lourde amende; **to impose a f. on s.o.,** infliger une amende à qn; **to pay the fines,** payer, acquitter, les condamnations.

fine[2]. **1.** *v.i. O:* payer des arrhes (pour obtenir un privilège). **2.** *v.tr.* condamner (qn) à une amende; mettre (qn) à l'amende; infliger une amende à (qn); frapper (qn) d'une amende; **to f. s.o. (in) £20 and costs,** frapper qn d'une amende de £20 plus les frais.

fine[3], *a.* **1.** (*a*) (*of metals, oil, etc.*) fin, pur; **f. gold,** or *m* de coupelle; **gold that is nine-tenths f.,** or qui contient neuf dixièmes de fin; **gold twenty-two carats f.,** or à vingt-deux carats de fin; (*b*) fin, subtil, raffiné; *Lit:* **the f. flower of chivalry,** la fine fleur de la chevalerie; **to dress with f. taste,** s'habiller avec un goût raffiné, exquis; **f. distinction,** distinction subtile; **a f. sense of the ridiculous,** un sens aigu, aiguisé, du ridicule. **2.** beau, bel, belle, beaux; (*a*) **a f. statue,** une belle statue; **f. woman,** belle femme, femme superbe; **it is a f. piece of writing,** c'est une belle page; **the f. arts,** les beaux-arts *m*; (*b*) **f. sentiments,** de beaux sentiments, des sentiments nobles; **to appeal to s.o.'s finer feelings,** faire appel aux sentiments élevés de qn; **it was very f. of him to take that attitude,** c'est très beau à lui d'avoir adopté cette attitude; **it is a f. thing to see . . .,** il fait beau voir . . .; (*c*) (*of manners*) affecté; **to call things by f. names,** appeler les choses par de grands noms. **3.** (*a*) **f. workman,** bon ouvrier; ouvrier accompli; **f. swordsman,** forte lame; fine lame; **f. example of Romanesque architecture,** bel exemple de l'architecture romane; **meat of the finest quality,** viande *f* surchoix, de premier choix; *Com:* **f. bills,** beau papier; **f. trade paper,** papier de haut commerce, de premier ordre; (*b*) excellent, magnifique; **it was a f. thing for him,** c'était une excellente affaire pour lui; **f. display,** étalage *m* superbe; **f. piece of business,** affaire magnifique, affaire d'or; **f. future,** bel avenir; **f. dinner,** dîner *m* de premier ordre; **we had a f. time,** nous nous sommes bien amusés; **that's f.!** voilà qui est parfait; (*c*) *Iron:* **you're a f. fellow, you are!** vous êtes joli, vous! **that's all very f., but . . .,** tout ça c'est bien joli; cela est bel et bon, fort beau, mais . . .; **one hears some f. things about you,** on en apprend de belles sur votre compte; **a f. thing indeed!** c'est du propre! **a f. service you have rendered me!** vous m'avez rendu là un drôle de service! **you're a f. one to talk!** c'est bien à vous de parler! vous êtes joliment qualifié pour parler! (*d*) *F:* (*intensive*) **he was in a f. (old) temper!** il était d'une humeur! ce qu'il rageait! *Dial:* **they'll be f. and vexed!** ils vont être joliment fâchés! **4.** (*of weather, day*) beau; **when the weather is f.,** quand il fait beau; **it looks as if it were going to be f.,** le temps a l'air d'être au beau; **a f. day,** une belle journée; **one of these f. days,** un de ces beaux jours; un de ces quatre matins; *s.* **in rain or f.,** par tous les temps. **5.** (*a*) (*of texture*) fin; (*of gravel, dust, etc.*) menu, subtil; **f. rain,** pluie fine; **to chop meat f.,** hacher menu la viande; (*b*) effilé; (*of writing, thread*) délié, mince; **fine shouldered horse,** cheval effilé; **f. print,** petits caractères; **f. needle,** aiguille fine; **f. edge,** tranchant affilé, aigu; **f. nib,** plume pointue; **not to put too f. a point on it,** pour dire la chose sans détours; pour parler franc, carrément; pour ne pas mâcher les mots, pour appeler les choses par leur nom; en termes crus. **6. to cut it f., to run it f.,** faire qch. tout juste; réussir tout juste; arriver de justesse; **he never misses his train, but he cuts it f.,** il ne manque jamais son train, mais c'est tout juste; **prices are cut very f.,** les prix sont au plus bas; **aren't you cutting your profits too f.?** est-ce que vous ne réduisez pas vos profits à rien? *Bill:* **to cut the ball too f.,** prendre la bille trop fin, trop fine; *Sp:* **to train an athlete, a horse, too f.,** pousser trop loin l'entraînement d'un athlète, d'un cheval. **7.** *s.pl. Min:* **fines,** minerai *m* de haute teneur; fins *m*.

fine[4], *int.* bon! entendu! d'accord! à la bonne heure! épatant!

fine[5]. **1.** *v.tr.* (*a*) **to f. (down),** clarifier, coller (la bière, le vin); clairer (le sucre); (*b*) affiner (l'or, etc.); (*c*) **to f. (away, down, off),** rendre (qch.) effilé; amincir (qch.); affiner, alléger (une planche, etc.); **to f. down a bas soon reed,** préler une anche de basson. **2.** *v.i.* (*a*) (*of liquid*) se clarifier, devenir clair; (*b*) **to f. (down, off),** devenir effilé; s'amincir.

fine-bore ['fain'bɔ:r], *v.tr. Metalw:* reforer; polir; repasser (à l'aléseuse).

fine borer ['fain'bɔ:rər], *s. Sm.a: Artil: etc:* adoucisseur *m*, polisseur *m*.

fine-cut ['fain'kʌt], *a.* **1.** finement ciselé; délicatement ciselé. **2.** (tabac) haché fin. **3.** coupé tout juste.

fine-darn ['fain'dɑ:n], *v.tr. O: Needlew:* stopper.

fine-draw ['fain'drɔ:], *v.tr.* (**fine-drew; fine-drawn**) *Needlew:* rentraire; faire une reprise perdue à (une déchirure).

fine-drawer ['fain'drɔ:ər], *s. Needlew:* rentrayeur, -euse.

fine drawing ['fain'drɔ:iŋ], *s. Needlew:* rentrayage *m*.

fine-drawn ['fain'drɔ:n], *a.* **1.** (*a*) *Needlew:* **f.-d. seam, mend,** reprise perdue; rentraiture *f*; (*b*) (*of wire*) finement étiré; (*of thread*) délié, ténu; (*c*) *Sp:* (athlète) amaigri, réduit à son poids minimum (par l'entraînement et le régime); (*d*) (*of features, etc.*) fin. **2.** subtil, fin, délié; **f.-d. arguments, distinctions,** arguments subtils, distinctions subtiles.

fine-grained ['fain'greind], *a.* (métal *m*, bois *m* etc.) à grain fin, serré, à petit grain.

fine-looking ['fain'lukiŋ], *a.* **a f.-l. man,** un bel homme; **I never saw a finer looking man, girl,** jamais je n'ai vu un plus bel homme, une plus belle fille.

finely ['fainli], *adv.* **1.** finement; (*a*) habilement, admirablement, artistement, on ne peut mieux; (*b*) délicatement, minutieusement, subtilement; (*c*) **f. powdered,** finement pulvérisé; **f. chopped,** haché fin, menu. **2.** admirablement, magnifiquement.

fineness ['fainnis], *s.* **1.** titre *m*, aloi *m*, fin *m* (de l'or, de l'argent); titre (des monnaies); pureté *f* (du vin, etc.); **coins of legal f.,** monnaies *f* au titre légal. **2.** qualité supérieure, excellence *f* (d'un article, d'un ouvrage, etc.). **3.** splendeur *f*, élégance *f*, magnificence *f* (d'un costume, d'un étalage, etc.); beauté *f* (du paysage, etc.). **4.** finesse *f* (des cheveux, d'un tissu, d'une poudre, etc.); ténuité *f* (d'un fil, d'un cheveu); délicatesse *f*, subtilité *f* (des sentiments, de l'esprit, etc.).

finer ['fainər], *s. Metalw:* (*pers.*) affineur *m*.

finery[1] ['fainəri], *s. Metall:* **1.** finerie *f*, affinerie *f*, mazerie *f*. **2.** affinage *m* (des métaux).

finery[2], *s.* parure *f*; fanfreluches *fpl*; **decked out in all her f.,** parée de ses plus beaux atours.

fine-spoken ['fain'spouk(ə)n], *a. O:* (*of pers.*) au beau parler.

fine-spun ['fain'spʌn], *a.* **1.** *Tex:* tissé serré; au fil ténu, délié. **2.** (raisonnement, etc.) subtil.

finesse[1] [fi'nes], *s.* **1.** *Lit: Art:* finesse *f*, délicatesse *f*, subtilité *f* (du style, etc.). **2.** finesse, artifice *m*; ruse *f*. **3.** *Cards:* finesse, impasse *f*.

finesse[2]. **1.** *v.i.* y aller d'une manière rusée; *Pej:* finasser; *Cards:* (i) faire une impasse; (ii) risquer l'impasse. **2.** *v.tr.* (*a*) *Cards:* **to f. sth. away,** prendre qch. par ruse; (*b*) **to f. the queen,** (i) faire une impasse à la dame; (ii) risquer l'impasse à la dame; **to f. a low trump (in ruffing),** faire la passacaille.

finessing [fi'nesiŋ], *s.* finesse *f*, ruse *f*, *Pej:* finasserie *f*.

fine-toothed ['fain'tu:θt], *a.* (peigne *m*) aux dents fines; (peigne) fin.

finfoot ['finfut], *s. Orn:* grébifoulque *m*.

Fingal ['fiŋgəl], *Pr.n. Geog:* **Fingal's Cave,** la grotte de Fingal.

finger[1] ['fiŋgər], *s.* **1.** (*a*) doigt *m* (de la main); **first f.,** index *m*; **middle f., second f.,** médius *m*, doigt du milieu, doigt majeur; **third f., ring f.,** annulaire *m*; **little f.,** petit doigt; auriculaire *m*; *F:* **to lift the little f.,** lever le coude; (trop) boire; **he's got a pain in his little f.,** il se croit malade (pour un rien); **to wear a ring on one's f.,** porter une bague au doigt; **to eat sth. with one's fingers,** manger qch. avec ses doigts; *F:* manger qch. avec la fourchette du père Adam; **the f. of Fate, of God,** le doigt du destin, de Dieu; **he can lay his f. right away on any passage in the Bible,** il met le doigt sans hésitation sur n'importe quel passage de la Bible; **to lay, put, one's f. on the source of the trouble,** mettre le doigt sur la source du mal; *F:* **don't you dare lay a f. on him,** je vous défends de le toucher; **he wouldn't stir, lift, a f. to help you,** il ne remuerait pas le petit doigt, il ne remuerait pas d'un doigt, pour vous aider; **move a f. and you are a dead man,** faites un geste et vous êtes mort; *P:* **to wet one's f.,** prêter serment avec un doigt mouillé (qu'on se passe autour du cou); **to point the f. of scorn at s.o.,** montrer qn au doigt; **to hold up a f. (in warning),** lever le doigt (pour avertir qn); **they could be counted on the fingers of one hand,** on pourrait les compter sur les doigts de la main; **to keep one's fingers crossed** = toucher du bois; *P:* **get, pull, take, your f. out! finger(s) out!** grouille-toi! secoue tes puces! *P:* **to put the f. on s.o.,** (i) balancer qn; (ii) dénoncer qn, donner qn (à la police); *F:* **to have a f. in the pie,** être mêlé à l'affaire; être pour quelque chose dans l'affaire; y être pour quelque chose; **he has a f. in every pie,** il est mêlé à tout; **f. tip,** (i) bout *m* du doigt; (ii) doigtier *m* (d'archer, etc.); **f.-tip control,** commande *f* au doigté; **with f.-tip control,** commandé, mû, par simple pression du doigt; **he is a Frenchman to the f. tips,** il est Français jusqu'au bout des ongles; **he's a gentleman to the f. tips,** c'est un parfait gentleman; **to have sth. at one's f. ends, at one's f. tips,** savoir qch. sur le bout du doigt; **he has the whole business at his fingers' ends,** il est au courant de toute l'affaire; *Mus:* **passage requiring light fingers,** passage qui demande un doigté léger; **f. board,** (i) touche *f* (de violon, etc.); (ii) clavier *m* (de piano, etc.); **f. work,** doigté *m*; exercices *mpl* de doigté; (*b*) (*as measure, etc.*) **f. of brandy,** doigt de cognac; **f. of bread,** mouillette *f*; **just a f. of bread!** un tout petit peu, un soupçon, de pain! **the dress is too short by the width of a f.,** la robe est trop courte d'un doigt, est d'un doigt trop courte; (*c*) doigt (d'un gant); (*d*) *Coel: F:* **dead man's fingers,** alcyon *m*; *Paleont:* **f. stone,** bélemnite *f*; (*e*) *Hort: F:* **f. and toe,** hernie *f* (des choux, des navets); (*f*) *attrib.* **f. alphabet,** alphabet *m* dactylologique, des sourds-muets; **f. plate,** plaque *f* de propreté (d'une porte); **f. post,** poteau *m* indicateur; *Dom.Ec:* **f. bowl,** rince-doigts *m inv*; *Cu:* **f. biscuit,** biscuit *m* à la cuiller; langue-de-chat *f, pl.* langues-de-chat; **f. guard,** garde *f*; pas-d'âne *m inv* (d'une épée). **2.** *Tchn:* (*a*) *Mec.E:* doigt (de guidage); touche guidée; **iron f. of a ratchet wheel,** doigt métallique d'une roue à rochet; *Tex:* **guide f.,** distributeur *m* du fil; *El:* **contact f.,** manette *f*, doigt, de contact; (*b*) index *m* (d'un instrument à cadran, etc.); *A:* aiguille *f* (d'une horloge, etc.); (*c*) *pl. Typ:* griffes *f* (d'une presse); (*d*) *Sm.a:* **f. (piece) of a trigger,** queue *f* de détente. **3.** *Com:* **bunch of bananas with two hundred fingers,** régime *m* de deux cents bananes.

finger², *v.tr.* **1.** manier, toucher, tâter, palper; *F:* tripoter (qch.); **to f. sth. over,** promener ses doigts sur qch.; *F:* **to finger s.o.'s money,** palper l'argent de qn. **2.** (*a*) **to f. the piano,** tapoter sur le piano; **to f. a guitar,** agacer les cordes d'une guitare; (*b*) *Mus:* doigter (un morceau, un passage).

fingered ['fiŋgə:d], *a. Bot:* (*of leaf, etc.*) digité; (*of fruit, root, etc.*) digitiforme.

finger-grip ['fiŋgəgrip], *a. Dom.Ec:* **f.-g. handle,** queue crantée.

fingerhold ['fiŋgəhould], *s.* prise *f* pour les doigts.

finger hole ['fiŋgəhoul], *s. Mus:* trou *m* (de flûte, etc.).

fingering¹ ['fiŋgəriŋ], *s.* **1.** (*a*) maniement *m*; (*b*) palpation *f*. **2.** *Mus:* doigté *m*; **f. exercises,** exercices *m* de doigté; (*for flute, etc.*) **f. chart,** tablature *f*.

fingering², *s.* laine *f* à tricoter.

fingerling ['fiŋgəliŋ], *s.* **1.** *F: A:* nain *m*; tom-pouce *m, pl.* tom-pouces. **2.** *Ich:* saumoneau *m*, parr *m*.

fingermark ['fiŋgəmɑ:k], *s.* empreinte *f* de doigt sale.

fingermarked ['fiŋgəmɑ:kt], *a.* (papier) maculé d'empreintes de doigts.

fingernail ['fiŋgəneil], *s.* **1.** ongle *m* (de la main). **2.** *Moll:* **f. clam, f. shell,** cyclade *f*.

fingerprint¹ ['fiŋgəprint], *s. Adm:* empreinte digitale; **f. identification,** dactyloscopie *f*; **examination of a prisoner's fingerprints,** examen *m* dactyloscopique d'un prévenu.

fingerprint², *v.tr.* prendre les empreintes digitales de (qn).

fingerstall ['fiŋgəstɔ:l], *s. Med:* doigtier *m*; **rubber f.,** doigtier en caoutchouc.

finial ['finiəl], *s. Arch:* fleuron *m*, épi *m* (de faîte); faîteau *m*.

finical ['finik(ə)l], **finikin** ['finikin], **finicking** ['finikiŋ], **finicky** ['finiki], *a.* (*of pers., style, etc.*) méticuleux, vétilleux; (*of picture, work, style*) trop léché; (*of style*) mièvre, précieux; (*of pers.*) fignoleur, -euse; **work with too much f. detail,** travail trop poussé.

finicality [fini'kæliti], **finicalness** ['finikəlnis], **finickiness** [fini'kinis], *s.* méticulosité *f*; maniaquerie *f*; (*of style*) mièvrerie *f*.

finick ['finik], *v.i. F:* fignoler; **to f. over a job,** fignoler un travail.

fining ['fainiŋ], *s.* **1.** collage *m*, clarification *f* (du vin, etc.). **2.** *Metall: etc:* affinage *m* (des métaux, d'une planche); **f. slag,** scorie *f* d'affinage; **f. forge, furnace,** forge *f*, four *m*, d'affinage; **f. pot,** creuset *m*.

finis ['finis], *s.* (*at end of book, story*) fin *f*.

finish¹ ['finiʃ], *s.* **1.** (*a*) fin *f* (de la vie, d'une représentation, etc.); *Sp:* arrivée *f* (d'une course); fin (d'un match); **to fight (it out) to a f.,** se battre à outrance, jusqu'à une décision; aller jusqu'au bout; *Box: A:* **fight to the f.,** match *m* au finish; *Sp:* **he has a fast f.,** il a un bon finish; *F:* **that was the f. of the scheme,** cela a mis fin au projet; **that was the f. (of him, of it),** ce fut la fin, le coup de grâce; *Ven:* **the f.,** la mise à mort (du renard); **to be in at the f.,** (i) *Ven:* assister à la mise à mort; (ii) *Sp: Turf:* voir la fin de la course; assister à l'arrivée; (iii) voir la fin de l'aventure; *Row:* **f. of the stroke,** le dégagé; (*b*) *Sp:* la ligne, le poteau, d'arrivée; l'arrivée. **2.** (*a*) fini *m*, achevé *m* (d'un travail); finesse *f* de l'exécution (d'un travail, etc.); (*b*) apprêt *m* (d'un drap, etc.); (*c*) *Tchn:* finition *f*.

finish². **1.** *v.tr.* finir; (*a*) terminer, achever; mettre fin à (une histoire, une affaire, etc.); compléter, accomplir (un ouvrage, etc.); **to f. doing sth.,** achever, finir, de faire qch.; **he had finished dressing,** il avait fini de s'habiller; **I haven't finished packing,** je n'ai pas fini de faire mes valises; **he soon finished fastening the straps,** il a eu bientôt fait d'attacher les courroies; **as I was finishing my dinner,** comme j'achevais de dîner; **to f. off a piece of work,** mener un travail à terme; **to f. off a wounded animal,** achever une bête blessée; donner le coup de grâce à une bête; *F:* **to f. s.o. off,** donner son reste à qn; **this last misfortune finished him (off),** ce dernier malheur l'a achevé, lui a coupé bras et jambes; **he's finished!** il est fini, achevé! *F:* il est flambé! **they finished (up) the beer,** ils ont bu ce qui restait de la bière; **f. (up) your soup!** finis ta soupe! **to f. up the evening at the theatre,** terminer, clore, la soirée au théâtre; **to f. one's military service,** terminer son service militaire; (*b*) perfectionner, donner du fini à, parachever, parfaire (un ouvrage, son éducation, etc.); confirmer (un cheval); *Tex:* apprêter (un tissu); *Metalw:* usiner (une pièce); **to f. off a picture,** donner le dernier coup de main, mettre la dernière main, à une peinture; *Needlew:* **to f. (off) a buttonhole,** brider une boutonnière. **2.** *v.i.* (*a*) finir, cesser, se terminer, s'achever; prendre fin; **his engagement finishes this week,** son engagement prend fin cette semaine; **the storm has finished,** l'orage a cessé; **I shall be, shall have, finished before you are, have,** j'aurai fini avant vous; **the meeting finished in a brawl,** le meeting s'acheva, se termina, par des coups; **he finished with a smile,** il a terminé avec un sourire; *Tp:* **have you finished?** terminé? (*b*) **to f. in a point,** se terminer, finir, en pointe; (*c*) **he finished by calling me a liar,** il a fini par me traiter de menteur; **he finished by admitting I was right,** à la fin il m'a donné raison; **you will f. by breaking your neck,** vous allez finir par vous casser le cou; (*d*) **I've finished with it,** je n'en ai plus besoin; *F:* **I'm finished with it,** j'en ai marre, je ne m'en occupe pas; *F:* **I've finished with you,** tout est fini entre nous; je ne veux plus vous revoir; (*e*) **wait until I've finished with him,** attendez que je lui aie réglé son compte! (*f*) **to f. fourth (in a race),** terminer, finir, arriver, quatrième (dans une course).

finished ['finiʃt], *a.* **1.** (article, etc.) fini, apprêté; (produit) ouvré; **machine f.,** apprêté à la machine; **highly f. article,** article d'un beau fini; **badly f. goods,** marchandises mal apprêtées; **f. iron,** fer marchand; *Ind:* **f. diameter of a shaft, etc.,** diamètre définitif d'un arbre de couche, etc. **2.** (*of pers., appearance, execution, etc.*) soigné, parfait; **a f. speaker,** un parfait orateur; un orateur accompli; **the f. gentleman,** le parfait gentleman; le gentleman accompli; **a f. portrait,** un portrait achevé; **work translated with f. skill,** œuvre traduite avec un talent consommé.

finisher ['finiʃər], *s.* **1.** *Ind:* (*pers.*) finisseur, -euse; apprêteur, -euse; repasseur, -euse; pareur, -euse; affineur, -euse; *Dressm:* retoucheuse *f*; *Sp:* finisseur, -euse; **he's a fast f.,** c'est un bon finisseur. **2.** (machine) finisseuse *f*; *Tex:* carde *f* en fin. **3.** *F:* coup *m* de grâce.

finishing¹ ['finiʃiŋ], *a.* dernier; qui finit; **f. sentence,** phrase finale; **the f. stroke,** le coup de grâce; **f. touches,** finitions *f*.

finishing², *s.* **1.** (*a*) achèvement *m*, parachèvement *m* (d'une tâche, etc.); **f. school,** école *f* d'arts d'agrément; école où l'on parachève l'éducation des jeunes filles; (*b*) *Tchn:* finition *f*, finissage *m* (d'un article de commerce); apprêtage *m* (des tissus, du cuir, du papier); **the f. takes as long as the construction,** les finitions demandent autant de temps que la construction; **f. coat,** dernière couche, couche finale (de peinture, etc.); dernier enduit (de plâtre, de chaux, etc.); *Ind:* **f. shop, room,** atelier *m*, salle *f*, de finissage, de finitions; **f. machine,** finisseuse *f*; machine *f* à apprêter (le cuir, le papier, les tissus); *Metalw:* **f. roll,** cylindre finisseur, de finissage; **f. rolls,** laminoir *m* de finissage; **f. pass,** passe *f* de finissage; **f. tool,** achevoir *m*, plane *f*; (*c*) *Const:* **finishings,** menuiserie *f* (d'une maison, etc.). **2.** *Sp:* **f. line,** ligne *f* d'arrivée.

finite ['fainait]. **1.** *a.* (*a*) (*of surface, nature, etc.*) fini, limité, borné; *Mth:* **f. magnitude,** grandeur finie; (*b*) *Gram:* **f. moods,** modes finis, définis; **f. verb,** verbe *m* à un mode fini. **2.** *s.* **the f. and the infinite,** le fini et l'infini.

finiteness ['fainaitnis], *s.* caractère fini, finitude *f* (d'une surface, etc.).

finitude ['finitju:d, 'fain-], **finity** ['finiti], *s. Phil:* finitude *f*.

Finland ['finlənd], *Pr.n. Geog:* Finlande *f*.

Finn [fin], *s. Geog:* Finlandais, -aise; Finnois, -oise.

finnan ['finən], *s. Cu:* **f. (haddock),** haddock (fumé); finnan haddock.

finned [find], *a.* **1.** *Ich:* à nageoires. **2.** *I.C.E:* **f. cylinder,** cylindre *m* à ailettes.

finnemanite ['finmənait], *s. Miner:* finnemanite *f*.

finner ['finər], *s. Z:* baleinoptère *m*, rorqual *m*, -als.

Finnic ['finik], *a. Ethn:* finnois.

Finnish ['finiʃ]. **1.** *a.* finlandais. **2.** *s. Ling:* finnois *m*.

finnoc(k) ['finək], *s. Ich:* (jeune) truite saumonée.

Finno-Ugrian, -Ugric ['finou'ju:griən, -'ju:grik]. *Ethn:* (*a*) *a.* finno-ougrien; (*b*) *s.* Finno-ougrien, -ienne.

finny ['fini], *a.* à nageoires.

Finsen ['finsən], *Pr.n. Med:* **F. (light) treatment,** finsenthérapie *f*.

fiord [fjɔ:d], *s. Geog:* fjord *m*, fiord *m*.

fiorin ['faiərin], *s. Bot:* fiorin *m*, traînasse *f*; agrostide traçante.

fiorite [fi'ɔ:rait], *s. Miner:* (opale) fiorite *f*.

fioritura, *pl.* **-e** [fiɔ:ri'tju:rə, -ei], *s. Mus:* fioriture *f*.

fir [fə:r], *s.* **1.** *Bot:* **f. (tree),** sapin *m*; **silver f.,** sapin blanc, argenté, pectiné; **silver f. of Canada, balsam f.,** sapin baumier; **Douglas f., red f.,** sapin de Douglas; **Scotch f., Scots f., common f.,** pin *m* sylvestre; pin rouge; pin d'Écosse; sapin du nord; **yellow f.,** (i) pin d'Écosse; (ii) sapin de Douglas; (iii) sapin du Canada; **f. cone,** pomme *f*, cône *m*, de pin; pigne *f*; **f. plantation,** sapinière *f*. **2.** *Com:* (bois *m* de) sapin; (bois de) pin; *Carp: etc:* **f. plank,** planche *f* de sapin, de pin.

fire¹ ['faiər], *s.* **1.** feu *m*; (*a*) (*element*) **to make f.,** faire du feu; **f. worship,** culte *m* du feu; pyrolâtrie *f*; **f. worshipper,** adorateur, -trice, du feu; ignicole *mf*, pyrolâtre *mf*; **I would go through f. and water for him, to serve him,** je me mettrais au feu, je me mettrais, jetterais, dans le feu, je me mettrais en quatre, pour le servir; **he has gone through the f. (of adversity),** il en a vu de dures; *Theol:* **the eternal f.,** les flammes éternelles; *Hist:* **ordeal by f.,** épreuve *f* du feu; (*b*) **open f.,** feu dans la cheminée, feu nu; **camp f.,** feu de camp; **wood f.,** feu de bois; **gas, electric, f.,** radiateur *m* à gaz, électrique; **to lay a f.,** préparer le feu; **to light a f.,** faire du feu; **the f. is catching,** le feu prend; **to make up the f.,** charger, arranger, le feu; **to throw sth. into the f.,** jeter qch. au feu; **a rousing, roaring, f.,** une belle flambée; **f. basket,** brasier *m*, brasero *m*; **f. screen,** (i) écran *m*, devant *m*, de cheminée; (ii) écran ignifuge; **f. irons,** garniture *f* de foyer; **he was sitting over the f.,** *F:* **keeping the f. warm,** il gardait le coin du feu; **to cook sth. on a slow f.,** faire cuire qch. à petit feu, à feu doux; (*of cooking utensils, etc.*) **to stand the f.,** aller au feu; **f. walker,** fakir *m* qui marche sur les charbons ardents; (*c*) feu, foyer *m* (d'une locomotive); **blacksmith's f.,** feu de forge; *Ch: Metall:* **oxidizing f.,** feu oxydant; **reducing f.,** feu de réduction; **f. box,** foyer, boîte *f* à feu, chambre *f* de combustion (d'une chaudière, d'une locomotive); **f. chamber,** (i) chambre à feu (d'une chaudière); (ii) *Metall:* (chambre de) chauffe *f* (d'un fourneau); **f. bar,** barreau *m* de grille (de foyer); *Mch: Metall:* **f. bridge,** autel *m*; *Mch: etc:* **f. door, f. hole,** porte *f* de foyer, de chargement, de chauffe; gueule *f*; (*of reverberating furnace*) taquerie *f*; **f.-door shield,** contre-porte *f* de foyer; **f. surface,** surface *f* de chauffe; **f. tube,** tube *m* de, à, fumée; tube de chaudière; **f.-tube boiler,** chaudière ignitubulaire; **f. iron,** ringard *m* (de fourneau); **f. rake, f. hook,** ratissette *f*; pique-feu *m inv*; rouable *m*, râble *m*, attisoir *m*, attisonnoir *m*; *Metall:* **f. crack,** crique *f*, criqûre *f*, de recuit; tapure *f* de chauffage; *Min:* **f. setting,** abattage *m*, travail *m*, au feu; *Cer: etc:* **f. sand,** sable *m* réfractaire; *Hist:* **f. balloon,** montgolfière *f*; (*d*) incendie *m*; sinistre *m*; **pit f.,** incendie de mine; **bush f.,** feu de brousse; **to cause, start, a f.,** provoquer, causer, un incendie; **to catch f.,** prendre feu; **the house, her dress, caught f.,** le feu a pris à la maison, à sa robe; **f. broke out, there was an outbreak of f.,** un incendie s'est déclaré; **fire!** (i) au feu! (ii) *Min:* gare la mine! **on f.,** en feu, en flammes; **chimney on f.,** feu de cheminée; **the house, the ship, is on f.,** la maison, le navire, brûle; *Navy: A:* **f. ship,** brûlot *m*; *F:* **to get on like a house on f.,** avancer à pas de géant; (*of work, etc.*) marcher rondement; (*with pers.*) s'entendre à merveille; **to save sth. from the f.,** arracher qch. au feu; **the victims of the f.,** les victimes *f* de l'incendie, les sinistrés *m*; **to add fuel to the f.,** jeter de l'huile sur le feu; alimenter la querelle; *Hist:* **by, with, f. and sword,** par le fer et par le feu; **to put a town to f. and sword,** mettre une ville à feu et à sang; *Prov:* **one f. burns out another's burning,** un clou chasse l'autre; **f. raiser,** incendiaire *mf*; *Jur:* **f. raising,** incendie volontaire, par malveillance; **f. fighting,** lutte *f*, précautions *fpl*, contre l'incendie; service *m* d'incendie; **f.-fighting equipment,** matériel *m* d'incendie; **f. fighter,** lutteur *m* contre l'incendie; *NAm:* (sapeur-)pompier *m*; **f. protection,** protection *f* contre l'incendie; **f. insurance,** assurance *f* contre l'incendie, assurance-incendie *f, pl.* assurances-incendie; **f.(-insurance) policy,** police *f* d'assurance contre l'incendie; police-incendie *f, pl.* polices-incendie; **f. risk,** (i) risque *m* d'assurance-incendie; (ii) chose assurée contre l'incendie; *Ins:* **f. department,** branche *f* assurance-incendie; **f. brigade,** *NAm:* **f. department,** (corps *m* de) sapeurs-pompiers *m*, *F:* les pompiers; **f. station,** poste *m* d'incendie; poste, caserne *f*, de (sapeurs-)pompiers; **f. hydrant,** *NAm:* **f. plug,** prise *f*, bouche *f*, d'eau; bouche d'incendie; **f. engine,** pompe *f* à incendie; **f. extinguisher,** extincteur *m* d'incendie; grenade extinctrice, ignifuge; (*trigger type*) pistolet extincteur; **f. bucket,** seau *m* à incendie; **f. hose,** tuyau *m* de pompe, lance *f*, manche *f*, à incendie; **f. escape,** (i) échelle *f* à incendie; (ii) escalier *m* de secours; **f. drill,** exercice *m* de lutte contre l'incendie, de sauvetage en cas d'incendie; *U.S:* **f. chief,** chef *m* des (sapeurs-)pompiers; **f. marshal,** commandant *m* en chef des (sapeurs-)pompiers; directeur *m* de la lutte contre l'incendie; **f. door,** porte *f* coupe-feu; **f. shutter,** volet *m* pare-feu; *Nau: Av:* **f. bulkhead,** cloison *f* pare-feu; **f. float,** ponton *m* d'incendie; bateau-pompe *m, pl.* bateaux-pompes; *Nau:* **f. quarters,** postes *m* d'incendie; *For:* **f. belt,** pare-feu *m inv*; **f. line,** tranchée *f* garde-feu; *U.S:* **f. warden,** *Can:* **f. ranger, f. spotter,** guetteur *m* (d'incendies); (*e*) *Pyr:* **blue f.,** feu de Bengale; *A:* **Greek f., wild f.,** feu grégeois; (*f*) lumière *f*, éclat *m*; feux (d'un diamant); **f. opal,** opale *f* de feu, à flammes; girasol *m*; **St. Elmo's f., dead f.,** feu de Saint-Elme; (*g*) *U.S: Ent: F:* **f. beetle,** pyrophore *m*, mouche *f* de feu. **2.** *Med: O:* fièvre *f*, inflammation *f*; *A:* **St. Anthony's f.,** feu céleste, feu Saint-Antoine. **3.** ardeur *f*, enthousiasme *m*; fougue *f*; **the f. of youth,** la chaleur, l'enthousiasme, de la jeunesse; *Th: O:* **to act with f.,** brûler les planches; *Lit:* **to be filled with the sacred f.,** avoir le feu sacré. **4.** *Mil: etc:* feu, tir *m*; fusillade *f*; coups *mpl* de feu; **individual f., f. at will,** tir à volonté; **oblique f.,** feu d'écharpe; *Navy:* **bow f.,** tir en chasse; *Navy:* **astern f.,** feu de retraite; **adjustment f., ranging f., registering f.,** tir de réglage; **well aimed f.,** tir ajusté; **close-range, long-range f.,** tir à courte, à grande, distance; **combing, raking, f.,** tir de ratissage; **direct, indirect, f.,** tir direct, indirect; **f. for effect,** tir d'efficacité; **f. from a defiladed position,** tir à défilement; **f. without sweeping,** tir sans fauchage; **occasional f.,** tir sporadique; **pre-arranged f., schedule f.,** tir programmé, suivant horaire; **brisk f., rolling f., running f.,** feu roulant; *Fig:* **f. of questions,** feu roulant, bombardement *m*, de questions; **(close) supporting f.,** tir d'appui (direct); **unaimed, visual, f.,** tir au jugé, à vue; **withering f.,** tir foudroyant; **zone f.,** tir sur zone; *Navy:* **f. at hull,** tir en belle; **f. control,** (préparation *f* et) direction *f*, commande *f*, du, de, tir; **f. control equipment,** appareillage *m*, appareils *mpl*, matériel *m*, de préparation et de direction du tir, de commande de tir; **f. control radar,** radar *m* de tir; **f. control building, f. direction centre,** poste central (de commande) de tir; *Navy:* **f. control room,** centrale *f* de tir; **f. control officer,** directeur *m* de tir; *Cmptr:* **f. control computer,** calculateur *m* de tir; *Mil:* (*apparatus*) **f. director,** télépointeur *m*; **f. trench,** tranchée *f* de première ligne, de tir; **f. step,** banquette *f*, gradin *m*, de tir (d'une tranchée); **f. discipline,** (i) discipline *f* du feu; (ii) consignes *fpl* de tir; **method of f.,** modalité *f* du tir; **rate of f.,** cadence *f*, régime *m*, du tir; **unit of f.,** unité *f* de feu; **to open f.,** ouvrir, commencer, déclencher, le feu; **to cease f.,** cesser le feu; **to bring f. (to bear) on (sth.),** prendre (qch.) sous son feu; **to go under, be under, f.,** aller au feu, essuyer le feu; **under enemy f.,** sous le feu de l'ennemi; **we are under f.,** on tire sur nous; **he had never (yet) been under f.,** il n'avait encore jamais vu le feu; **to be steady under f.,** être ferme au feu; *Fig:* **he has been under f. for his extremist views,** on lui a reproché ses opinions extrémistes; **to be between two fires,** être pris entre deux feux; **to lay f. on (sth.),** concentrer son feu, diriger son tir, sur (qch.); **to lift f.,** reporter le tir; **to register f.,** relever les éléments de tir (fournis par le réglage); repérer le tir.

fire², *v.*

I. *v.tr.* **1.** (*a*) mettre feu à, embraser (qch.); (*b*) mettre le feu à, incendier (une maison, etc.); (*c*) animer, enthousiasmer (qn); enflammer (les passions, le courage, etc.); exciter (l'imagination); **he fired me with his enthusiasm,** il m'a communiqué son enthousiasme; **to be fired with enthusiasm for sth.,** brûler d'enthousiasme pour qch. **2.** (*a*) cuire (de la poterie, des briques, etc.); (*b*) *Vet:* cautériser (un cheval); (*c*) exposer au feu (qch. d'humide). **3.** *Mch: etc:* chauffer, charger (une locomotive, un four, etc.); allumer (une chaudière); **oil fired central heating,** chauffage (central) à mazout. **4.** (*a*) *I.C.E:* **to f. the mixture,** enflammer le mélange; *A:* **to f. a blast, a mine,** allumer, mettre le feu à, un fourneau de mine; faire jouer, exploser, une mine; (*b*) **to f. a rocket, a torpedo,** lancer une fusée, une torpille; (*c*) (i) *v.i. Artil:* déboucher à zéro; **to f. over open sights** = faire feu presque à bout portant; **to f. at, on, s.o., sth.,** tirer sur qn, qch.; **to f. at s.o. with a revolver,** tirer un coup de revolver sur qn; **to f. standing, to f. direct,** tirer à bras francs, de but en blanc; **fire!** feu! (ii) **to f. a gun at s.o.,** lâcher un coup de fusil à qn; **to f. a gun,** tirer, faire partir, un canon; tirer un coup de canon; (*with passive force*) **guns were firing,** on tirait le canon; **without firing a shot,** sans tirer un coup (de canon, etc.); **we were fired on,** nous avons reçu des coups de feu; **to f. a salute,** tirer une salve; **to f. a question at s.o.,** poser une question à qn à brûle-pourpoint; (*d*) *Cmptr:* déclencher (les marteaux d'impression). **5.** *F:* renvoyer, congédier, saquer, mettre à la porte (un employé, etc.).

II. *v.i.* **1.** *A: & Lit:* prendre feu, s'enflammer, allumer. **2.** (*a*) (*of shot*) partir; **the revolver failed to f.,** le revolver a fait long feu; (*b*) *I.C.E:* (*of mixture*) exploser; **the engine is firing evenly, badly,** le moteur tourne régulièrement, mal; **the engine is firing on only three cylinders,** le moteur ne fonctionne, ne marche, qu'à trois cylindres.

III. (*compound verbs*) **1. fire away,** *v.i.* (*a*) **to f. away at the enemy,** tirer à l'ennemi à feu continu; (*b*) *F:* **f. away!** allez-y! commencez! allez, racontez!

2. fire off, *v.tr.* (*a*) tirer, faire partir (un coup de fusil, etc.); (*b*) poser (des questions) à brûle-pourpoint.

3. fire up. (*a*) *v.tr.* allumer, mettre en feu (une chaudière, un haut(-)fourneau, etc.); (*b*) *v.i. F:* (*of pers.*) s'emporter, s'emballer; monter comme une soupe au lait; **he fires up at the slightest thing,** il s'emporte, prend feu, pour la moindre chose.

firearm ['faiərɑːm], *s.* arme *f* à feu.

fireback ['faiəbæk], *s.* **1.** plaque *f* de cheminée; contre-feu *m*. **2.** *Orn:* houppifère *m* ignicolore; **f. (pheasant),** lophure *m*, faisan *m* pyronote.

fireball ['faiəbɔːl], *s.* **1.** *Meteor:* (*a*) aérolithe *m*, bolide *m*; (*b*) éclair *m* en boule, globe *m* de feu, globe fulminant. **2.** *Mil: Pyr:* balle *f*, pot *m*, à feu; pot d'artifice; carcasse *f*; bombe flamboyante.

firebird ['faiəbəːd], *s. Orn:* loriot *m* d'Amérique.

fireboat ['faiəbout], *s.* **1.** bateau-pompe *m*, *pl.* bateaux-pompes. **2.** *Navy: A:* brûlot *m*.

fire-bote ['faiəbout], *s. Jur: A:* affouage *m*, afforestage *m*; **to grant s.o. the privilege of f.-b.,** afforester qn.

firebrand ['faiəbrænd], *s.* **1.** tison *m*, brandon *m*. **2.** (*pers.*) brandon de discorde; tison, torche *f*, de discorde; boutefeu *m*; brûlot *m* (d'un parti).

firebreak ['faiəbreik], *s. For:* tranchée *f*, sentier *m*, garde-feu; pare-feu(x) *m inv*; coupe-feu *m inv*; essartement *m* de protection.

firebrick ['faiəbrik], *s.* brique *f* réfractaire.

firebug ['faiəbʌg], *s. F: esp. NAm:* **1.** *Ent:* (*a*) luciole *f*, ver luisant; (*b*) punaise *f* rouge des jardins. **2.** incendiaire *mf*, pyromane *mf*.

fireclay ['faiəklei], *s.* argile *f* réfractaire, apyre; chamotte *f*; terre *f* réfractaire; terre à poêle; terre à pipe; **plug of f.,** tampon *m* réfractaire.

firecrest ['faiəkrest], *s. Orn:* roitelet *m* à triple bandeau.

firedamp ['faiədæmp], *s. Min:* (feu) grisou *m*; méthane *m*; mofette *f* inflammable; **f. indicator, detector, warner,** grisoumètre *m*; détecteur *m* de grisou; **f. effluvia,** effluves grisouteux; **f. testing,** mesures *f* grisoumétriques.

firedog ['faiədɔg], *s. Furn:* chenet *m*, chevrette *f*; (*large*) landier *m*.

fire-eater ['faiəriːtər], *s.* **1.** (saltimbanque, etc.) avaleur *m* de feu. **2.** *F:* batailleur *m*, exalté *m*; brandon *m* de discorde; tranche-montagne *m*, *pl.* tranche-montagnes; matamore *m*; avaleur de gens. **3.** *U.S.Hist: F:* sudiste *m*.

fire-eating ['faiəriːtiŋ], *a.* pyrophage.

firefinch ['faiəfin(t)ʃ], *s. Orn:* astrild *m* amarante; **Peter's spotted f.,** amarante enflammée.

fireflair ['faiəflɛər], *s. Ich:* pastenague *f*.

firefly ['faiəflai], *s. Ent:* luciole *f*, lampyre *m*, phosphène *m*; *F:* mouche *f* à feu.

fireguard ['faiəgɑːd], *s.* **1.** pare-étincelles *m inv*; garde-feu *m inv*. **2.** (*pers.*) *For: U.S:* guetteur *m* (d'incendies).

fireless ['faiəlis], *a.* sans feu; *Mch:* **f. locomotive,** locomotive *f* sans foyer, sans feu, à provision de vapeur, à vapeur emmagasinée; *Dom.Ec:* **f. cooker,** marmite norvégienne.

firelight ['faiəlait], *s.* lumière *f* du feu; **by, in, the f.,** à la lumière du feu.

firelighter ['faiəlaitər], *s. Dom.Ec:* allume-feu *m inv*.

firelock ['faiəlɔk], *s. Sm.a: A:* (i) mousquet *m* à mèche; (ii) mousquet à rouet; (iii) fusil *m* à pierre.

fireman, *pl.* **-men** ['faiəmən], *s.m.* **1.** (*a*) chauffeur (d'une machine à vapeur, etc.); *Rail:* aide-conducteur, *pl.* aides-conducteurs; **assistant f.,** aide-chauffeur, *pl.* aides-chauffeurs; (*b*) cuiseur (de poterie, de briques, etc.). **2.** (sapeur-)pompier. **3.** *Min:* chercheur de grisou.

fireplace ['faiəpleis], *s.* cheminée *f*, âtre *m*, foyer *m*.

fireproof¹ ['faiəpruːf], *a.* (*a*) incombustible, imbrûlable, ininflammable, ignifuge, à l'épreuve du feu; **f. material,** ignifuge *m*; matière ignifugée; **f. vault,** salle blindée; **f. door,** porte *f* coupe-feu; **to make a door, etc., f.,** ignifuger une porte, etc.; *Cin:* **f. spool box,** boîte *f* pare-feu *inv*; (*b*) *Cer:* réfractaire, apyre; **f. dish,** plat *m* allant au feu, allant au four.

fireproof², *v.tr.* ignifuger (un tissu, etc.); rendre (qch.) ininflammable.

fireproofing ['faiəpruːfiŋ], *s.* ignifugation *f*, incombustibilisation *f* (de tissus, etc.).

firer ['faiərər], *s.* **1.** *Min: etc:* (*device*) exploseur *m*, déflagrateur *m*, boutefeu *m*. **2.** *Sm.a:* **single f., double f.,** fusil à un, deux, coups.

fireranger ['faiəreindʒər], *s.* guetteur *m* d'incendies (dans une forêt).

fire-resistant, -resisting ['faiəri'zistənt, -ri'zistiŋ], *a.* **1.** ignifuge. **2.** *Cer:* réfractaire.

fireside ['faiəsaid], *s.* cheminée *f*, foyer *m*; coin *m* du feu; **seated by the f., round the f.,** assis au coin du feu, autour de la cheminée, autour du foyer; **f. chair,** chaise *f* de coin du feu; (fauteuil *m*) coin de feu; chauffeuse *f*; **f. chat,** causerie *f* au coin du feu.

firestone ['faiəstoun], *s. Miner:* pierre *f* à feu.

firetrap ['faiətræp], *s.* **this building's a real f.,** ce bâtiment est une véritable souricière (en cas d'incendie).

firewall ['faiəwɔːl], *s.* cloison *f*, mur *m*, pare-feu; panneau *m* ignifuge.

firewarden ['faiəwɔːdən], *s.* guetteur *m* d'incendies.

firewatch ['faiəwɔtʃ], *v.i.* guetter les incendies.

firewatching ['faiəwɔtʃiŋ], surveillance *f* contre les incendies.

firewatcher ['faiəwɔtʃər], *s.* guetteur *m* (d'incendies).

firewater ['faiəwɔːtər], *s. F:* gnole *f*, gnôle *f*, gniole *f*, gniaule *f*.

firewood ['faiəwud], *s.* **1.** bois *m* de chauffage; bois à brûler; **bundle of f.,** margotin *m*, fagot *m*. **2.** *Orn:* **f. gatherer,** annumbi *m*.

firework ['faiəwəːk], *s.* **1.** pièce *f* d'artifice; **a spent f.,** (i) une pièce d'artifice qui a brûlé; (ii) un homme qui n'a plus rien dans son sac, qui n'a plus d'influence, plus de moyens, ou qui n'est plus à craindre; **f. manufacturer,** artificier *m*. **2.** *pl.* **fireworks,** (*a*) feu *m* d'artifice; **grand display of fireworks,** grand feu d'artifice; **to let off fireworks,** (i) tirer un feu d'artifice; (ii) *F:* faire des discours à grand effet (où il n'y a rien de solide); *F:* **whenever they get together there's fireworks,** quand ils se rencontrent il y a du pétard, du grabuge; **if you do that again there'll be fireworks,** si tu recommences ça va barder.

firing ['faiəriŋ], *s.* **1.** (*a*) *Brickm: Cer: etc:* cuite *f*, cuisson *f* (des briques, de la poterie, etc.); *Cer:* **reduction f.,** bleuissage *m*; (*b*) *Vet:* cautérisation *f* (d'un cheval). **2.** chauffage *m*, chauffe *f*, chargement *m*, mise *f* en feu (d'un four, d'une locomotive, etc.); **coal f., oil f.,** chauffe au charbon, au mazout; **hand f.,** chargement à la main; **control of the f.,** conduite *f* des feux. **3.** (*a*) *Min: Exp:* allumage *m*, mise à feu, tir *m* (d'un coup de mine); **f. switch,** commutateur *m* de tir, de mise à feu; **f. machine,** exploseur *m*; **f. mechanism, wire,** mécanisme *m*, fil *m*, de mise à feu; (*b*) *I.C.E:* allumage; **erratic, irregular, f.,** ratés *mpl* d'allumage; **f. order, sequence,** ordre *m* d'allumage (des cylindres); (*c*) *Mil: etc:* tir, mise à feu (d'un engin, d'une fusée); **f. chamber,** chambre *f* de combustion; **f. button, device,** bouton *m*, dispositif *m*, de mise à feu; (*d*) *Elcs:* **f. potential,** (i) (*of vacuum tube*) tension *f* d'amorçage; (ii) (*thermionic work function*) potentiel *m* d'ionisation; **f. pulse,** impulsion *f* d'amorçage; (*e*) *Cmptr:* déclenchement *m* (des marteaux d'impression). **4.** *Artil: Sm.a:* tir, feu *m*, fusillade *f*, exécution *f* des feux; **group f.,** tir collectif; **independent f.,** feu à volonté; **ball f.,** tir à balles; **dummy, blank, f.,** tir fictif, à blanc; **field f.,** tir de guerre, de combat; **f. area,** secteur *m* de tir; **f. bay,** emplacement *m* de tir(eur), tranchée *f* de tir; **f. point,** (i) (point *m*) origine *f* du tir; (ii) emplacement du tir; **f. position,** (i) (*of weapon*) position *f* de tir; (ii) position du tireur; **f. practice,** exercice *m* de tir, instruction *f*, pratique *f*, de tir; **f. data,** données *fpl*, éléments *mpl*, de, du, tir; **f. pin,** percuteur; **f.-pin channel, hole, vent, way,** canal *m* du percuteur *m*; **f.-pin stop,** butée *f* du percuteur; **f. key,** détente *f*; **f. range,** (i) distance *f* de tir; (ii) stand *m*, travée *f*, de tir; **f. support,** support *m*, béquille *f*, de tir; appui *m* (pour tireur); **f. manual,** (manuel *m*, règlement *m*, d') instruction du tir; **f. line,** (i) ligne *f* de feu; (ii) pas *m*, emplacement, de tir, des tireurs; **f. party, squad,** (i) peloton *m* d'exécution; (ii) peloton chargé de tirer la salve d'honneur; *Av:* **f. pass,** passe *f* de tir; *Navy:* **broadside f.,** feu de bordée; **heavy f. could be heard,** on entendait une vive fusillade; **to concentrate the f. on an objective,** concentrer le feu, le tir, sur un objectif; **to return a gun to (the) f. position,** remettre une pièce en batterie; (*of gun*) **to return to f. position,** revenir en batterie; **to cease, suspend, f.,** cesser le feu; faire halte au feu. **5.** combustible *m*, *esp.* bois (mort), petit bois.

firkin ['fəːkin], *s.* **1.** tonnelet *m*, barillet *m* (pour beurre, poisson, ou liquides). **2.** mesure *f* de capacité de 8 à 9 *gallons*; *approx.* = quartaut *m*.

firm¹ [fəːm], *s. Com:* **1.** raison sociale, nom social; firme *f.* 2. maison (sociale, de commerce); société commerciale; société en nom collectif; entreprise *f*; firme; **name, style, of the f.,** nom social; raison sociale; **a large f.,** une grosse entreprise, *F:* une grosse boîte; **f. of solicitors** = étude *f* de notaire; *F:* **long f. fraud,** carambouillage *m.*

firm[2], *a.* **1.** (*of substance, flesh, etc.*) ferme; consistant, compact; (*of post, nail, rock, etc.*) solide, fixe, stable; (*of touch, tread, etc.*) vigoureux, assuré; (*of outline*) soutenu; **a f. jelly,** une gelée ferme; **f. material,** tissu *m* qui a de la tenue; **as f. as a rock,** inébranlable; **to take a f. hold of sth.,** saisir qch. d'une main ferme; **to rule with a f. hand,** gouverner d'une main ferme; **to walk with a f. step,** marcher d'un pas assuré. **2.** (*of law, etc.*) immuable, établi; (*of friendship, etc.*) constant, inaltérable; (*of intention, etc.*) résolu, déterminé; (*of person, character, tone, etc.*) décidé, résolu; **f. chin,** menton *m* qui dénote la fermeté; menton volontaire; **to be f. about sth.,** tenir bon sur qch.; **to be very f. in maintaining one's authority,** être très ferme à maintenir, maintenir fermement, son autorité; **to have a f. belief, to be f. in the belief, that. . .,** être fermement convaincu, avoir la conviction inébranlable, la ferme conviction, que . . .. **3.** *Com: Fin:* (*of market, offer, sale*) ferme; (*of contango rates*) tendu; **f. stock,** valeur ferme, tenue; **these shares remain f. at . . .,** ces actions se maintiennent à . . .; *Com:* **article in f. demand,** article constamment demandé. **4.** *adv.* **to stand f.,** tenir bon; tenir ferme; tenir pied; **table that stands f.,** table *f* qui pose bien sur ses pieds; **to stand f. about sth.,** tenir bon sur qch.; **to hold f. to sth.,** se retenir solidement à qch.

firm[3]. **1.** *v.tr.* (*a*) **to f. the soil,** affermir, tasser, le sol; (*b*) **to f. up a post,** raffermir un poteau. **2.** *v.i.* (*of prices, etc.*) **to f. (up),** se raffermir.

firmament ['fəːməmənt], *s.* firmament *m.*

firmer ['fəːmər], *s. Tls:* **f. (chisel),** ciseau *m* à biseau; fermoir *m,* queue-de-renard *f*; **f. gouge,** ciseau à gouge.

Firmisternia [fəːmi'stəːniə], *s.pl. Amph:* firmisternes *m.*

firmly ['fəːmli], *adv.* **1.** fermement, solidement; **to lay a stone f.,** poser une pierre carrément; **to build f.,** bâtir, construire, solidement; **to hold the reins f.,** tenir les rênes d'une main ferme; **to walk f.,** marcher d'un pas assuré; **I f. believe that . . .,** je suis fermement convaincu, j'ai la ferme conviction, que . . .. **2.** d'un ton ferme.

firmness ['fəːmnis], *s.* fermeté *f*; consistance *f,* solidité *f* (d'une substance); stabilité *f* (d'une table, des idées, etc.); force *f* (de caractère, etc.); constance *f* (d'une amitié); *Com: Fin:* **f. of stocks, etc.,** fermeté, raffermissement *m,* tenue *f* (des valeurs, etc.).

firmware ['fəːmwɛər], *s. Cmptr:* microprogrammation *f,* micrologique *f,* firmware *m.*

firn [fəːn], *s.* névé *m.*

first [fəːst], *a., s. & adv.*

I. *a.* **1.** premier; (*a*) (*in time, order*) **the f. (day) of the month,** le premier (jour) du mois; **F. Day,** dimanche *m* (chez les Quakers); *Scot:* **Sunday f.,** dimanche prochain; *Post:* **f.-day cover,** (enveloppe *f* de) premier jour (d'émission); **the f. of April,** le premier avril; *Ven:* **the F.,** le premier septembre (ouverture de la chasse aux perdrix); **the f. three years,** les trois premières années; *Th:* **the f. two acts,** les deux premiers actes; **the f. house on the left,** la première maison à gauche; **the f. house but one,** la deuxième maison; **on the f. floor,** (i) au premier étage; (ii) *NAm:* au rez-de-chaussée; **Charles the F.,** Charles Premier; **at f. sight,** à première vue; **at the f. attempt, go,** au premier, de prime, abord; **at the f. opportunity,** dès que possible; à la prochaine occasion, au premier jour; **in the f. place,** d'abord, en premier lieu; **to succeed the f. time,** réussir du premier coup; **to wear a new dress for the f. time,** étrenner une robe; **it was my f. flight, my f. experience under fire,** c'était mon baptême de l'air, du feu; **to fall head f.,** tomber la tête la première; **to be the f. person to do sth.,** être le premier, la première, à faire qch.; **to come out f. in an examination,** être reçu premier à un examen; **f. name,** prénom *m*; **to be on f.-name terms with s.o.,** appeler qn par son prénom; **f. cousin,** cousin(e) germain(e); **I'll do it f. thing,** je le ferai tout de suite, sans tarder; **I'll do it f. thing tomorrow (morning),** je le ferai dès demain matin; **f. thing in the morning,** de grand matin; **wine from the f. pressing,** vin *m* de la mère goutte; *Th: etc:* **f. night, f. performance,** première *f*; **f. nighter,** habitué, -ée, des premières; *NAm:* **f. run,** (i) première récolte (d'eau d'érable); (ii) *Cin:* première (d'un film); *Med:* **f. aid,** secourisme *m*; premiers secours, soins, soins d'urgence (aux blessés, etc.); **f.-aid outfit, kit,** trousse *f* de secours, de première urgence; **f.-aid station, post,** poste *m* de (premiers) secours; **f.-aid worker, f. aider,** secouriste *mf*; *Mil:* **f.-aid dressing,** paquet individuel de pansement; *Gram:* **in the f. person,** à la première personne; *Const:* **f. step,** marche *f* de départ; *Min:* **f. working,** (travaux *mpl* de) traçage *m*; *Sch:* **f. form** = (classe *f* de) sixième *f*; *Aut:* **f. gear,** première vitesse; *Publ:* **f. edition,** édition princeps, originale; **the F. World War,** la première guerre mondiale; *Box:* **f. round,** round initial; *Sp:* (*baseball*) **f. base,** premier piquet; *NAm: F:* **it never even got to f. base,** cela a complètement échoué; *F:* **I haven't the f. idea,** je n'ai pas la moindre idée; (*b*) (*in importance, etc.*) **to put f. things f.,** mettre en avant les choses essentielles, les choses de première importance; **f. quality article,** article *m* de premier choix; **of f. importance,** d'importance primordiale; **to travel f. class,** voyager en première (classe); **f. lieutenant,** lieutenant *m* en premier; **f. engineer,** maître-mécanicien *m, pl.* maîtres-mécaniciens; **star of the f. magnitude,** étoile *f* de la première magnitude; *U.S:* **F. Lady,** la femme du Président; (*c*) **to have news at f. hand,** tenir une nouvelle de première main, d'original; **to buy sth. (at) f. hand,** acheter qch. de première main. **2.** unième; **twenty-f., thirty-f.,** vingt et unième, trente et unième; **seventy-f.,** soixante et onzième; *Sw.Fr: Fr.C: Belg:* septante et unième; **eighty-f.,** quatre-vingt-unième; *Sw.Fr: Fr.C:* octante et unième; *Belg: Sw.Fr:* huitante et unième; **ninety-f.,** quatre-vingt-onzième; *Sw.Fr: Fr.C: Belg:* nonante et unième; **one hundred and f.,** cent unième.

II. *s.* **1.** (le) premier, (la) première; **we were the very f. to arrive,** nous sommes arrivés les tout premiers, tout les premiers; **he was among the very f.,** il est arrivé dans les tout premiers; **the f. to arrive was Mrs X,** la première à venir, la première arrivée, fut Mme X; *Sp: etc:* **to come in an easy f.,** arriver bon, beau, premier; **f. come f. served,** les premiers vont devant; premier arrivé, premier servi; premier venu, premier moulu; **to be the f. to do sth.,** être le premier à faire qch.; **X was the f. to carry out this experiment,** X le premier a fait cette expérience; **I am the very f. to acknowledge that . . .,** je suis tout le premier à reconnaître que . . .; *Sch:* (*of degree*) **to get a f.** = avoir une mention (très) bien; (*at Cambridge*) **to get a double f.** = avoir une mention (très) bien dans chacune des deux parties de l'examen; **he got a double f. in French and geography** = il a eu une mention (très) bien en français et en géographie. **2.** commencement *m*; **from f. to last,** du commencement jusqu'à la fin; depuis le début jusqu'à la fin; **from the f.,** dès le commencement; dès le premier jour; **I distrusted him from the f.,** je me suis méfié de lui dès l'abord, dès le premier jour; **at f.,** au commencement; d'abord; **I come back to what I said at f.,** je reviens à mon début, à ce que j'ai dit d'abord. **3.** (*a*) *Com:* **firsts,** articles *m,* produits *m,* de première qualité, de surchoix; (*b*) *Fin:* **f. of exchange,** première, primata *m,* de change. **4. to travel f.,** voyager en première (classe); *Aut:* **to climb a hill in f.,** monter une côte en première (vitesse).

III. *adv.* premièrement, au commencement, au début, d'abord; **f. and foremost,** surtout et avant tout; avant toute autre chose; **f. of all,** pour commencer; au préalable; en premier lieu; auparavant; tout d'abord; avant tout; **f. of all, I must tell you that. . .,** pour commencer, je dois vous dire que . . .; *U.S:* **f. off,** au premier abord, de prime abord; **f. and last,** en tout et pour tout; **you will have to do it f. or last,** que vous tardiez ou non il faudra bien que vous y veniez; tôt ou tard il faudra en venir là; **to say f. one thing and then another,** dire tantôt blanc tantôt noir; **f. forget that . . .,** commencez par oublier que . . .; **when he f. went to war,** au début de ses campagnes; **when he f. grew up,** au sortir de l'enfance. **2.** pour la première fois; **when did you f. see him?** quand l'avez-vous vu pour la première fois? **3.** plutôt; **I'd die f.,** plutôt mourir; *F:* **I'll see him damned f.,** qu'il aille au diable. **4.** le premier, la première; **he arrived f.,** il arriva le premier; **to claim the right to speak f.,** réclamer la priorité; **who plays f.?** (i) *Cards:* à qui d'entamer? (ii) *Bowls:* à qui la boule? (iii) *Golf:* à qui l'honneur? **you go f.!** allez devant! **interest always comes f.,** l'intérêt prime tout; *adv. or s.* **f. come. f. served,** les premiers vont devant; premier arrivé premier servi; premier venu premier moulu; les premiers venus sont les premiers servis; **ladies f.!** place aux dames! **women and children f.!** les femmes et les enfants d'abord!

firstborn ['fəːstbɔːn], *a. & s.* (enfant) premier-né, *pl.* premiers-nés; (*the f.* premier-née *or* première-née *is hardly used*).

first(-)class ['fəːst(')klɑːs]. **1.** *a.* (*a*) (voyageur, wagon) de première classe; (marchandises, article) de première qualité, de (tout premier) choix; (hôtel, etc.) de premier ordre; **f.-c. dinner,** dîner soigné; **f.-c. player,** joueur, -euse, de premier ordre, de première force; *Nau:* **f.-c. vessel (according to Lloyd's Register)** = navire *m* de première cote (selon le Bureau Véritas); **he's a f.-c. liar,** c'est un menteur de premier ordre; *F:* **a f.-c. idiot,** un sombre imbécile; **that's really f.-c.!** ça c'est vraiment de premier ordre, *F:* extra! (*b*) *Post:* urgent; *NAm:* **f.-c. mail,** lettre close; paquet clos. **2.** *adv.* **to travel f.-c.,** voyager en première; *Post:* **to send a letter f.-c.,** expédier une lettre en urgence.

first-degree ['fəːstdi'griː], *a.* **f.-d. burn,** brûlure *f* au premier degré; **f.-d. murder,** assassinat *m.*

firstfooter ['fəːst'futər], *s. Scot: F:* la première personne à mettre les pieds chez vous après minuit sonné du dernier de l'an; première visite de l'année.

firstfooting ['fəːst'futiŋ], *s. Scot:* visites du premier de l'an (le plus souvent immédiatement après minuit, et copieusement arrosées de whisky).

firstfruits ['fəːstfruːts], *s.pl.* **1.** prémices *f* (de la moisson, d'un travail, etc.). **2.** *A.Jur: Ecc.Hist:* annates *f.*

firsthand ['fəːst(')hænd], *a.* (nouvelle *f*) de première main.

firstling ['fəːstliŋ], *s. Husb:* petit *m* de la première portée (d'une brebis, etc., ou de la saison); premier-né *m* (d'un troupeau), *pl.* premiers-nés.

firstly ['fəːstli], *adv.* premièrement; en premier lieu.

first(-)rate ['fəːst(')reit], *a.* excellent; de première classe; de première qualité; de première force; de premier ordre; **f.-r. firm,** maison *f* de premier rang, de premier ordre; **f.-r. workmanship,** façon *f* impeccable; facture *f* irréprochable; **of f.-r. quality,** de toute première qualité; **f.-r. dinner,** dîner soigné; *F:* dîner à la hauteur; **f.-r. idea,** fameuse idée; **he's a f.-r. man,** c'est un homme supérieur; *F:* **f.-r. deal,** affaire *f* superbe; *F:* **that's f.-r.!** (i) ça c'est extra! (ii) bon! excellent! à la bonne heure! *adv. F:* **it's doing, going, f.-r.,** ça marche à merveille, comme sur des roulettes.

first-rater ['fəːst'reitər], *s. F:* as *m.*

firth [fəːθ], *s. Geog: Scot:* estuaire *m,* firth *m,* golfe (formé par l'embouchure d'un fleuve); **the F. of Forth,** le golfe du Forth.

fisc [fisk], *s.* fisc *m.* **1.** *Rom.Ant:* le Trésor (de l'empereur). **2.** *Scot:* le Trésor public; la Couronne (à laquelle reviennent les biens en déshérence).

fiscal ['fisk(ə)l]. **1.** *a. Fin:* fiscal, -aux; **f. period,** exercice (financier); **f. year,** année *f* budgétaire; année d'exercice; **he is the f. agent of the government,** il assure le service de Trésorerie de l'État; *Mil: U.S:* **f. officer,** officier ordonnateur (des dépenses). **2.** *s.* (*a*) fonctionnaire *m* judiciaire (dans certains pays); (*b*) *Scot:* **(procurator) f.,** procureur général. **3.** *s. Orn:* **f. (shrike),** fiscal *m.*

fiscalism ['fiskəlizm], **fiscality** [fis'kæliti], *s. Pej:* fiscalité *f.*

fiscally ['fiskəli], *adv.* fiscalement.

fischerite ['fiʃərait], *s. Miner:* fischérite *f.*

fish[1], *pl.* **fishes,** *coll.* **fish** [fiʃ, 'fiʃiz], *s.* **1.** poisson *m*; **freshwater, salt-water, f.,** poisson d'eau douce, de mer; **white f.,** poisson à chair blanche; **f. skin,** peau *f* de poisson; *Med:* **f.-skin disease,** ichtyose *f*; **f. breeding, farming,** pisciculture *f*; **f. farm,** établissement *m* piscicole; **f. preserve,** (i) vivier *m*; (*in river*) congre *m*; (ii) pêche réservée; **f. tank,** réservoir *m* à poissons; vivier; **f. weir, garth,** avaloire *f*; (*in boat*) **f. well,** vivier; **f. spear,** foine *f,* foëne *f,* trident *m*; **f. basket,** (i) panier *m* de pêche; (ii) bourriche *f* à poissons; **f. train,** train *m* de marée; **f. packing,** conservation *f* du poisson; **f. market,** marché *m* au poisson; poissonnerie *f*; **f. salesman,** mareyeur *m*; poissonnier *m,* marchand *m* de poisson; **f. shop,** poissonnerie; *Cu:* **fried f.,** poisson frit; **f. and chips,** poisson frit en beignets servi avec des frites; *F:* poisson-frites; **f.-and-chip shop,** friterie *f*; *Comest:* **(frozen) f. fillets, fingers,** *NAm:* **sticks,** filets de poisson panés; **f. meal, f. flour,** farine *f* de poisson; *Dom.Ec:* **f. kettle,** poissonnière *f*; turbotière *f*; **f. knife,** couteau *m* à poisson; **f. knife and fork,** couvert *m* à poisson; **f. slice,** truelle *f* à poisson; *Agr:* **f. manure,** engrais *m* de poisson; *Ind:* **f. glue,** colle *f* de poisson; *El: etc:* **f. paper,** presspahn *m* (*R.t.m.*); *Prov:* **there's as good f. in the sea as ever came out of it,** il, elle, n'est pas unique au monde; **all is f. that comes to his net,** tout lui est bon; il fait feu de tout bois; **I've other f. to fry,** j'ai d'autres chats, d'autres chiens, à fouetter; **neither f., flesh nor fowl, neither f., flesh nor good red herring,** ni chair ni poisson; *Lit:* **to cry stinking f.,** se dénigrer; *F:* **to feed the fishes,** (i) se noyer, engraisser les poissons; (ii) avoir le mal de mer, donner à manger aux poissons; *F:* **he's a queer, an odd, f.,** c'est un drôle de type, un type à part, un original; *F:* **he's a poor f.,** c'est un pauvre type; *NAm:* **f. story,** hâblerie *f.* **2.** *Astr:* **the Fish(es),** les Poissons.

fish[2]. **1.** *v.i.* pêcher; **to f. for trout, for pearls,** pêcher la truite, des perles; **to f. with a fly, etc.,** pêcher à la mouche, etc.; *F:* **to f. for compliments,** quêter, chercher, des compliments; **don't f.!** trop de modestie! **you'll have to learn to f. for yourself,** il te faut apprendre à te débrouiller. **2.** *v.tr.* (a) (i) pêcher (un saumon, etc.); (ii) pêcher avec (une mouche, etc.) pour appât; (b) **to f. up, out, a dead body,** (re)pêcher un cadavre; **to f. up a mine,** relever une mine; *F:* **to f. s.o., sth., out of sth.,** tirer qn, qch., de qch.; **he fished a pencil out of his pocket,** il a fouillé dans sa poche et en a tiré un crayon; **to f. secrets out of s.o.,** tirer les vers du nez de qn; **he tried to f. out of me what I intended to do,** il a voulu me faire avouer mes intentions; (c) *Nau:* **to f. the anchor,** traverser l'ancre; (d) **to f. a river,** pêcher une rivière; **this lake has been fished out,** on a tant pêché dans ce lac qu'il n'y a plus de poisson.

fish[3], *pl.* **fishes,** *s.* **1.** *N.Arch:* jumelle *f*, fourrure *f* de renfort, armure *f*, clamp *m* (d'un mât); **f. front,** gaburon *m* (d'un mât). **2.** *Rail: Const:* éclisse *f*; **f. joint,** éclissage *m*.

fish[4], *v.tr.* **1.** *N.Arch:* jumeler, reclamper (un mât, une vergue, etc.); **fished beam,** poutre assemblée à jumelles. **2.** *Rail:* éclisser (les rails, la voie).

fish[5], *pl.* **fishes,** *s. Nau:* **f. (tackle),** traversière *f*; **f. davit,** bossoir *m* de traversière.

fish[6], *pl.* **fish,** *s. Games:* fiche *f*.

fishable ['fiʃəbl], *a.* (*of stream*) pêchable.

fishball ['fiʃbɔ:l], *s. Cu:* boulette *f* de poisson.

fish-bellied ['fiʃbelid], *a. Mec.E:* **f.-b. girder,** poutre *f* (en) ventre de poisson.

fishbolt ['fiʃboult], *s. Rail:* boulon *m* d'éclisse.

fishbone ['fiʃboun], *s.* **1.** arête *f* (de poisson). **2.** *attrib. Elcs:* **f. antenna,** antenne directionnelle en arête de poisson.

fishcake ['fiʃkeik], *s. Cu:* croquette *f* de poisson.

fish-eating ['fiʃi:tiŋ], *a.* ichtyophage.

fisher ['fiʃər], *s.* **1.** *A:* pêcheur *m*; *Ecc:* **fishers of men,** pêcheurs *m* d'hommes. **2.** animal pêcheur; **f. (cat),** pékan *m*.

fisherman, *pl.* **-men** ['fiʃəmən], *s.m.* pêcheur; *Ecc:* **the Fisherman's ring,** l'anneau *m* du pêcheur.

fisherwoman, *pl.* **-women** ['fiʃəwumən, -wimin], *s.f.* pêcheuse.

fishery ['fiʃəri], *s.* **1.** pêche *f*; **cod, whale, f.,** pêche à la morue, à la baleine; **coral f.,** la pêche du corail; **high-sea(s) f., deep-sea, f.,** la grande pêche; **coast f., inshore f.,** petite pêche, pêche côtière; **f.-protection vessel,** garde-pêche *m inv*; bâtiment *m* de surveillance des pêches. **2.** pêcherie *f*, lieu *m* de pêche.

fishgig ['fiʃgig], *s. Fish:* foène *f*, digon *m*.

fish-hawk ['fiʃhɔ:k], *s. Orn:* orfraie *f*.

fish-hook ['fiʃhuk], *s.* **1.** *Fish:* hameçon *m*; **double f.-h.,** bricole *f*; **to attach the f. h.,** empiler l'hameçon. **2.** *Nau:* croc *m* de traversière.

fishily ['fiʃili], *adv. F:* d'une manière louche.

fishiness ['fiʃinis], *s.* **1.** goût *m*, odeur *f*, de poisson. **2.** caractère louche, suspect (d'une affaire, etc.).

fishing[1] ['fiʃiŋ], *s.* (a) la pêche; **trout f.,** pêche à la truite; **sardine, cod, f.,** pêche à la morue, à la sardine; **oyster f., pearl f.,** pêche aux huîtres, des perles; **deep-sea f.,** la grande pêche; la pêche hauturière; **underwater f.,** chasse, pêche, sous-marine; **fly f.,** pêche à la mouche; **f. ground,** pêcherie *f*, lieu *m* de pêche; **f. preserve,** pêche réservée; (*in river*) **f. place, pool,** coup *m*; **f. stream,** cours d'eau poissonneux, rivière *f* pêchable; **f. tackle,** articles *mpl*, engins *mpl*, appareil *m*, attirail *m*, de pêche; **f. line,** ligne *f* (de pêche); **f. rod,** canne *f* à pêche; (*in one piece*) gaule *f*; **f. net,** filet *m* de pêche; (*for tunny fish*) combrière *f*; (*square*) échiquier *m*; **f. boat, smack,** bateau *m*, barque *f*, de pêche; **f. port,** port *m* de pêche; (b) *Petr:* **f. hook,** harpon *m*.

fishing[2], *s. Tchn:* **1.** jumelage *m*. **2.** éclissage *m*.

fishmonger ['fiʃmʌŋgər], *s.* poissonnier *m*, marchand *m* de poisson; **fishmonger's (shop),** poissonnerie *f*.

fish owl ['fiʃaul], *s. Orn:* hibou pêcheur; **brown, Asian, f. o.,** (hibou *m*) kétupa *m*.

fishplate ['fiʃpleit], *s. Carp:* couvre-joint *m*, *pl.* couvre-joints; fourrure *f*; *Mec.E:* ferrure *f* d'assemblage; *N.Arch:* jouet *m*; *Rail:* éclisse *f*; **angle f.,** éclisse cornière, éclisse d'équerre.

fishplating ['fiʃpleitiŋ], *s. Rail: etc:* éclissage *m*.

fishpond ['fiʃpɔnd], *s.* **1.** (a) vivier *m*; réservoir *m* (à poisson); (b) étang (plein de poissons). **2.** *F:* **the f.,** la mer, la grande tasse.

fishpot ['fiʃpɔt], *s. Fish:* casier *m*.

fishtail[1] ['fiʃteil], *s.* queue *f* de poisson; **f. gas burner,** bec *m* en queue de poisson.

fishtail[2], *v.i.* faire des queues *f* de poisson *f*.

fishway ['fiʃwei], *s.* couloir *m*, échelle *f*, à poissons.

fishwife, *pl.* **-wives** ['fiʃwaif, -waivz], *s.f.* marchande de poisson; *F:* poissarde; harengère; **she swears like a f.,** elle jure comme un charretier.

fishy ['fiʃi], *a.* **1.** (odeur *f*, goût *m*) de poisson; *F:* **f. eyes,** yeux ternes, vitreux. **2.** *F:* (*of pers., business, etc.*) douteux, louche, équivoque, véreux; **it looks f. to me,** ça ne me dit rien qui vaille; **f. story,** histoire *f* qui ne tient pas debout.

fissi- ['fisi], *comb.fm. Z: etc:* fissi-.

fissidactyl [fisi'dæktil], *a. Z:* fissidactyle.

fissile ['fisail], *a.* fissile, scissile.

fissilingual [fisi'liŋgwəl], *a. Rept:* fissilingue.

Fissilinguia [fisi'liŋgwiə], *s.pl. Rept:* fissilingues *m*.

fissility [fi'siliti], *s.* fissilité *f*.

fission ['fiʃ(ə)n], *s.* **1.** *Biol:* fissiparité *f*; scissiparité *f*; **binary f.,** fissiparité binaire; **f. fungus,** schizomycète *m*. **2.** *Ph:* fission *f*, division *f*; **nuclear f.,** fission nucléaire; **fast-neutron, slow-neutron, f.,** fission (provoquée) par neutrons rapides, lents; **f. neutron,** neutron de fission, neutron engendré, produit, par la fission; **chain f.,** fission en chaîne; **independent f.,** fission primaire; **thermal f.,** fission thermique; **f. products,** produits *m* de fission; **f. species,** espèces *f*, types *m*, de fission; **f. barrier, threshold,** barrière *f*, seuil *m*, de fission; **f. bomb,** bombe *f* (nucléaire) à fission.

fissionable ['fiʃənəbl], *a. Ph:* fissible; fissile; **f. material,** substance *f*, matière *f*, fissile, scissile; **f. nucleus,** noyau *m* fissile.

Fissipara [fi'sipərə], *s.pl. Biol:* fissipares *m*.

fissiparism [fi'sipərizm], *s. Biol:* fissiparité *f*.

fissiparity [fisi'pæriti], *s. Astr:* fissiparité *f*, scissiparité *f*.

fissiparous [fi'sipərəs], *a. Biol:* fissipare, scissipare.

fissiped ['fisiped], **fissipedal** [fi'sipidl], **fissipedate** [fi'sipideit], *a. Z:* fissipède.

Fissipeda [fi'sipidə], *s.pl. Z:* fissipèdes *m*.

fissirostral [fisi'rɔstrəl], *a. Orn:* fissirostre.

Fissirostres [fisi'rɔstri:z], *s.pl. Orn:* fissirostres *m*.

fissural ['fisjurəl], *a. Med:* fissuraire.

fissuration [fisju'reiʃ(ə)n], *s. Geol: etc:* fissuration *f*.

fissure[1] ['fiʃər], *s.* fissure *f*, fente *f*, crevasse *f* (dans un mur, une planche, une roche, etc.); bâillement *m* (entre deux planches, etc.); *Surg:* fissure (d'un os); *Tchn:* renard *m* (dans un barrage de rivière, une plaque de chaudière, etc.); **microscopic f.,** microfissure *f*; *Anat:* **sphenoidal f.,** fente sphénoïdale; **f. of Rolando,** scissure *f* de Rolando; **f. of Sylvius, Sylvian f.,** scissure de Sylvius; **Glaserian, petrotympanic, f.,** scissure de Glaser; **interhemispheric f.,** scissure interhémisphérique, grande scissure; **fissures of the liver,** sillons *m* du foie.

fissure[2]. **1.** *v.tr.* fissurer, fendre, crevasser (un rocher, etc.). **2.** *v.i.* (*of rock, etc.*) se fissurer, (se) crevasser, se fendre.

fissurella [fiʃə'relə], *s. Moll:* fissurelle *f*.

Fissurellidae [fiʃə'relidi:], *s.pl. Moll:* fissurellidés *m*.

fist[1] [fist], *s.* **1.** poing *m*; **to fight with one's fists,** se battre à coups de poing; **he went for them with his fists,** il tomba sur eux à coups de poing; **to clench the f.,** serrer le poing; **to use one's fists,** faire le coup de poing; **to shake one's f. at s.o.,** menacer qn du poing. **2.** *F: O:* **to make a good, a poor, f. of a job,** bien, mal, réussir une besogne. **3.** *F: A:* **he writes a first-class f.,** il a une jolie écriture; il écrit joliment bien. **4.** *P:* main *f*; **give us your f.!** donne ta pince, que je la serre! serre-moi la pince!

fist[2], *v.tr. Fb:* **to f. the ball clear,** éloigner le ballon avec un coup de poing.

fistful ['fistful], *s. F:* poignée *f* (d'argent, etc.).

fisticuffs ['fistikʌfs], *s.pl.* coups *m* de poing; *P:* cognage *m*; **to resort to f.,** se battre à coups de poing; faire le coup de poing; (*of two or more*) échanger des coups de poing; se cogner.

fistnote ['fistnout], *s. Typ:* main *f*.

fistula ['fistjulə], *s.* **1.** *Med:* fistule *f*, fusée *f*; *Vet:* **f. of the withers,** fistule du garrot. **2.** *Z:* évent *m* (d'une baleine).

fistulana [fistju'leinə], *s. Moll:* fistulane *f*.

fistular ['fistjulər], *a.* fistulaire.

fistularia [fistju'lɛəriə], *s. Ich:* fistulaire *f*.

fistulina [fistju'lainə], *s. Fung:* fistuline *f*, *F:* foie-de-bœuf *m*, foie-de-chêne *m*, langue-de-bœuf *f*.

fistulization [fistjulai'zeiʃ(ə)n], *s. Med:* fistulisation *f*.

fistulize ['fistjulaiz], *v.i. Med:* se fistuliser.

fistulous ['fistjuləs], *a.* fistuleux; *Vet:* **f. withers,** fistule *f* du garrot; *Bot:* **f. stem,** tige fistuleuse.

fit[1] [fit], *s.* **1.** (a) accès *m*, attaque *f* (de fièvre, de rhumatisme, etc.); **f. of madness,** accès de folie, de démence; **f. of coughing,** quinte *f* de toux; (b) (i) crise *f* épileptique; (ii) attaque d'apoplexie; **fainting f.,** évanouissement *m*, syncope *f*; **to fall into a f.,** *F:* **to throw a f.,** tomber en convulsions, *F:* piquer une crise; *F:* **he'll have a f. when he knows,** il en aura une congestion, cela lui donnera un coup de sang, ça le fera sauter, quand il le saura; **to send s.o. into a f.,** (i) provoquer une crise (épileptique), une congestion, chez qn; donner des convulsions à qn; (ii) *F:* transporter qn de colère, etc.; *F:* **it almost sent her into fits, she was almost in fits,** cela a failli lui donner une crise de nerfs; **to frighten s.o. into fits,** effrayer qn (jusqu') à lui donner des convulsions; **to beat s.o. into fits,** battre qn à plate couture; *P:* brosser (un concurrent); **to give s.o. fits,** (i) battre qn à plate couture; (ii) *U.S:* semoncer qn; tancer qn de la belle manière. **2.** accès, mouvement *m* (de mauvaise humeur, etc.); **to answer in a f. of temper,** répondre sous le coup de la colère, dans un mouvement de colère, dans un moment d'humeur; **f. of crying,** crise de larmes; **fits of jealousy,** transports *m* de jalousie; **f. of laughter,** accès de rire; **to be in fits of laughter,** avoir le fou rire; **to go into fits (of laughter),** être pris d'un fou rire; **he sent us into fits (of laughter),** il nous faisait tordre de rire; **to have a f. of laziness,** se laisser aller à la paresse; **in a f. of idleness, of industry,** dans un moment de paresse, de zèle; **to have sudden fits of energy,** avoir des élans d'énergie; **he has fits of silence, of abstraction,** il a des silences, des absences; **he composes when the f. is on him, when the f. takes him,** il compose de caprice; **to work by fits and starts,** travailler par à-coups, par accès, par foucades.

fit[2], *a.* **(fitter, fittest) 1.** bon, propre, convenable **(for sth.,** à qch.); **it is not a f. life for you,** ce n'est pas la vie qui vous convient; **f. to** + *inf.*, bon à, propre à + *inf.* **f. to eat,** bon à manger, mangeable; **f. to drink,** buvable, potable; **wine that is not yet f. to drink,** vin qui n'est pas encore en boite; **f. to wear,** mettable; **I've nothing fit to wear,** je n'ai rien à me mettre; **story that is not f. to be repeated,** histoire qu'il ne serait pas convenable de répéter; **materials not f. for the job,** matériaux *m* impropres à cet usage; *Com:* **goods in sound condition and f. for acceptance,** marchandises bonnes et recevables; **I'm not f. to be seen,** je ne suis pas présentable; **at a f. and proper time,** en temps et lieu; **at a fitter moment,** à un moment plus opportun; **to think f., see f., to do sth.,** juger convenable, juger à propos, trouver bon, de faire qch.; **do as you see, think, f.,** faites comme bon vous semble; faites à votre idée; **you will act as you think f.,** vous ferez ce que vous jugerez à propos; *Adm: Jur:* **as shall seem f.,** ainsi qu'il appartiendra; (*adverbial use*) **she cried f. to break her heart,** elle pleurait à gros sanglots; **it made us laugh f. to kill ourselves,** cela nous faisait mourir de rire; **a noise f. to bring the house down,** un bruit à tout casser; **he was f. to be tied,** il était dans une colère folle. **2.** (a) capable; **f. for sth.,** en état de faire qch.; apte à qch.; **f. for duty, for service,** bon pour le service; *Mil:* valide; **to be f. for one's job,** être à la hauteur de sa tâche; **to be just f. for sth.,** être mûr pour qch.; **f. to do sth.,** capable de, apte à, faire qch.; **f. to carry arms,** en état de porter les armes; **he is not f. to take your place,** il n'est pas capable de vous remplacer; **he is not f. to live,** il n'est pas digne de vivre; **he is f. for nothing,** il n'est propre à rien; c'est un propre à rien; **that's all he's f. for,** il n'est bon qu'à cela; (b) disposé, prêt (à faire qch.); **I felt f. to drop,** je me sentais prêt à tomber de fatigue; je tombais de fatigue; je n'en pouvais plus. **3.** *Med: Sp: etc:* (*of pers.*) **to be (fighting) fit,** avoir une bonne constitution; être en bonne santé, en forme; être dispos; *Mil:* (*of troops*) être d'attaque; **to keep f.,** rester en forme; se tenir en haleine; s'entretenir; **he is not yet f. to go back to work,** il n'est pas encore en état de reprendre son travail; *F:* **to be as f. as a fiddle,** être en parfaite santé; être frais et dispos; se porter comme un charme, comme le Pont-Neuf; **you don't look very f.,** vous n'avez pas bonne mine; vous avez mauvaise mine.

fit[3], *s.* (a) ajustement *m*, adaptation *f*; **your coat is a perfect f.,** votre pardessus vous va parfaitement, est juste à votre taille; **my dress is a tight f.,** ma robe est un peu serrée, un peu juste; **I like shoes that are an easy f.,** j'aime les chaussures larges; **it was a tight f.,** on tenait tout juste; on y était étroitement serré; (b) *Mec.E:* ajustage *m* (d'un assemblage, etc.); frottement *m* (d'organes mobiles); **easy f.,** ajustage lâche, à jeu; frottement doux; **tight f., exact f.,** ajustage serré; calage *m* juste; frottement dur, à refus; **pressed-on f.,** calage à la presse; **shrunk-on f.,** calage à retrait; **clearance f.,** ajustage à dépouille; **close f.,** ajustage précis; **drive f.,** ajustage légèrement dur; **press f.,** ajustage serré, pressé; **slide f.,** ajustage coulissant; **push f.,** ajustage coulissant juste; (c) *Cards:* (*bridge*) fit *m*.

fit[4], *v.* **(fitted)**

I. *v.tr.* **1.** s'accorder avec (qch.). **2.** (*of clothes, etc.*) aller à (qn); être à la taille de (qn); **these shoes don't f. me very well,** ces chaussures ne me vont pas très bien; **key that fits the lock,** clef qui va, qui s'ajuste, à la serrure, qui entre dans la serrure; **the pinion does not f. the shaft,** le pignon ne se rapporte pas avec l'arbre. **3.** (a) adapter, ajuster, accommoder (**sth. to sth.,** qch. à qch.); **to f. a nozzle on, to, the end of a pipe,** adapter un ajutage à l'extrémité d'un tuyau; **to f. a handle to a broom,** emmancher un balai; **to f. a lens on a camera,** monter un objectif sur un appareil; **to f. a key in the lock, a pipe into an opening,** engager une clef dans une serrure, un tube dans une ouverture; **to f. an axle into the nave,** emboîter un essieu dans le moyeu; **to f. one part into another,** emboîter une pièce dans une autre; **to f. two beams into each other,** enclaver deux poutres l'une dans l'autre; **to f. a garment on s.o.,** ajuster un vêtement à qn; **I'm going to be fitted for my new dress,** je vais faire l'essayage de ma nouvelle robe; **to make the punishment f. the crime,** proportionner les peines aux délits; (*b*) **to f. parts (together),** ajuster, monter, assembler, des pièces; **to f. a machine, a garment, together,** assembler une machine, un vêtement. **4.** (*a*) **to f. s.o. for sth., for doing sth.,** préparer qn à qch., à faire qch.; **nothing fits the body so well to stand fatigue,** rien ne dispose mieux le corps à supporter la fatigue; *U.S:* **to f. a boy for college,** préparer un jeune homme à entrer à l'université; (*b*) **to f. oneself for a job,** acquérir les connaissances nécessaires pour occuper une situation. **5. to f. sth. with sth.,** garnir, munir, pourvoir, qch. de qch.; **fitted with two propellers,** muni, pourvu, de deux hélices.

II. *v.i.* (*a*) **to f. (together),** s'ajuster, s'adapter, s'agencer, se raccorder, s'emmancher; **pieces that f. together,** pièces *f* rapportables; **pieces that f. freely,** pièces qui comportent du jeu; **to f. on sth.,** s'adapter sur qch.; **to f. into sth.,** s'emboîter, s'enclaver, dans qch.; **a pipe fits into the opening,** un tube s'engage dans l'ouverture; **piece that fits into another,** pièce qui entre dans une autre; **tubes that f. into one another,** tubes qui rentrent les uns dans les autres; **to f. exactly to sth.,** épouser la forme de qch.; (*b*) (*of sails*) **to f. well, badly,** bien, mal, établir; **your dress fits well, badly,** votre robe vous va, ne vous va pas, bien; *F:* **my face doesn't f.,** on ne m'accepte pas, je suis mal vu; (*c*) **you can't get there in three hours, the trains don't f.,** on ne peut pas faire le voyage en trois heures, les trains ne correspondent pas.

III. (*compound verbs*) **1. fit in.** (*a*) *v.tr.* (i) emboîter (des tubes, etc.); (ii) faire concorder, faire cadrer (des témoignages, etc.); (*b*) *v.i.* (i) **to f. in between two things,** s'emboîter entre deux choses; (ii) **to f. in with sth.,** être en harmonie avec qch.; **your plans don't f. in with mine,** vos projets ne s'accordent pas, ne cadrent pas, avec les miens; **he doesn't f. in,** il n'est pas adaptable, ne sait pas s'adapter.

2. fit out, *v.tr.* équiper (**sth. with sth.,** qch. de qch.); armer (un navire); équiper, aménager (un navire neuf); **to f. s.o. out (with clothing, etc.),** équiper qn (de vêtements, etc.).

3. fit up, *v.tr.* aménager (**sth. for sth.,** qch. pour qch.).

fitch [fitʃ], *s.* **1.** (*fur*) putois *m.* **2.** (*a*) (brosse *f* en) putois; (*b*) brosse en soies de porc.

fitchet ['fitʃit], **fitchew** ['fitʃu:], *s.* **1.** *Z:* putois *m.* **2.** = FITCH 1.

fitchy ['fitʃi], *a. Her:* fiché.

fitful ['fitf(u)l], *a.* (*of light, breeze, impulse, etc.*) irrégulier, capricieux; (*of pers.*) d'humeur changeante; (*of sleep, etc.*) troublé; *Med:* **f. cough,** toux quinteuse.

fitfully ['fitfuli], *adv.* irrégulièrement; par à-coups, par accès.

fitment ['fitmənt], *s.* **1.** meuble *m.* **2.** *Ind: etc:* montage *m*; support *m*; monture *f.*

fitness ['fitnis], *s.* **1.** (*of pers.*) aptitude *f* (**for,** à, pour); **f. to do sth., for doing sth.,** aptitude à faire qch., compétence *f* pour faire qch.; *Aut:* **f. to drive,** aptitude à conduire. **2.** (*a*) à-propos *m*, justesse *f* (d'une remarque); (*b*) convenance *f*, bienséance *f*; **to have a sense of the f. of things,** avoir le sentiment des convenances. **3. physical f.,** santé *f*, bon état, physique; *Sp:* bonne forme.

fit-out ['fitaut], *s. F: O:* (*a*) trousseau *m*; (*b*) équipement *m*; **what a f.-o.!** comme vous voilà équipé!

fitted ['fitid], *a.* **1.** (*a*) ajusté, monté; (*of case, chest, etc.*) **f. (up),** garni; (*b*) *Dressm:* ajusté, cintré; appuyé à la taille; (*c*) **f. carpet,** tapis cloué, ajusté; **f. sheet,** drap *m* housse. **2.** (*of pers., thg*) **to be f. for sth., to do sth.,** être fait pour qch.; être apte à faire qch.

fitter ['fitər], *s.* **1.** *Mec.E: Aut: etc:* ajusteur *m*, monteur *m*; assembleur, -euse; **metal f.,** ajusteur sur métaux; ajusteur mécanicien; **electrical f.,** appareilleur *m* d'installation électrique; installateur *m* d'appareils électriques. **2.** *Dressm: Tail:* essayeur, -euse. **3.** *Nau:* **f. out,** armateur *m* (d'un navire, d'une expédition).

fitting[1] ['fitiŋ], *a.* **1.** (*suitable*) convenable, bienséant; approprié (**to,** à); **f. comment,** remarque *f* à propos; observation *f* très juste; *O:* **it is not f.,** il ne convient pas. **2. f. coat,** manteau ajusté.

fitting[2], *s.* **1.** (*a*) ajustage *m*, ajustement *m* (d'une pièce, etc.); emboîtement *m* (d'un pignon, etc.); installation *f*, pose *f* (d'appareils); **f. (up, together) of a machine, etc.,** montage *m*, agencement *m*, adaptation *f*, d'une machine, etc.; **f. of sth. on sth.,** adaptation de qch. à qch.; montage de qch. sur qch.; **hand f.,** ajustage à la main; **f. on of a tyre,** montage d'un pneu; *Ind:* **f. shop,** atelier *m* d'ajustage ; (*b*) *Tail: etc:* essayage *m*, ajustage (de vêtements); **f. room,** salon *m* d'essayage; (*c*) *Com:* **made in three fittings,** fabriqué en trois tailles, (*of shoes*) en trois largeurs; (*d*) **f. out,** équipement *m* (d'un navire, d'une expédition, etc.); armement *m* (d'un navire); **f. up,** ameublement *m*, aménagement *m* (d'un magasin, etc.); armement (d'une machine). **2.** *usu. pl.* agencements, installations, ajustements (d'un bureau, d'un atelier, etc.); armature(s) *f* (d'une chaudière, etc.); garniture *f* (d'une chaudière, d'une chambre); agrès *m* (d'un gymnase); accessoires *m* (sanitaires, pour automobiles, etc.); appareillage *m* (pour lumière électrique, etc.); outillage *m* (d'une mallette de couture, etc.); gainerie *f* (de carrosserie); **metal fittings,** ferrages *m*, ferrures *f*; **gas fittings,** appareillage pour le gaz, appareils *m* à gaz; **roller blind fittings,** monture *f* de store à rouleau; **door fittings,** ferrures de porte; **brass fittings,** garnitures en cuivre; *El:* **ceiling f.,** plafonnier *m*; **wall f.,** applique *f*; *Sp:* **ski fittings,** fixation *f*, attaches *fpl*, de ski.

fittingly ['fitiŋli], *adv.* convenablement, à propos.

fit-up ['fitʌp], *s. Th: O:* accessoires *mpl*; scène *f* démontable (d'une troupe ambulante); **f.-up company,** troupe ambulante; *A:* **f.-up town,** ville *f* sans salle de théâtre.

five [faiv]. **1.** *num.a. & s.* cinq (*m*); **f. apples,** cinq pommes; **f. sixes are thirty, f. times six is thirty,** cinq fois six font trente; **thirty is f. times (as much as) six,** trente est le quintuple de six; **a f.-pound note,** un billet (de banque) de cinq livres; (*at dominoes, etc.*) **double f.,** double-cinq *m*, *pl.* doubles-cinq; **a badly written f.,** un cinq mal écrit; **he leaves his office at f.,** il quitte son bureau à cinq heures; *Hist:* **the Big F.,** les cinq grandes Puissances (d'après la Guerre de 1914–1918) (les États-Unis, la France, la Grande-Bretagne, l'Italie, le Japon); *Pol.Ec:* **the F. Year Plan,** le Plan quinquennal. **2.** *s.pl. P:* **a bunch of fives,** *A:* **fives,** la main, le poing; **he handles his fives very well,** il sait jouer des poings. **3.** *s. Games:* **fives** = balle *f* au mur; **fives court,** (i) cour *f* où l'on joue à la balle au mur; (ii) mur contre lequel on lance la balle; = fronton *m.*

five-barred ['faiv'bɑ:d], *a. Rac: etc:* (barrière *f*) à cinq planches, à cinq barres.

five-figure ['faiv'figər], *a. Mth:* **f.-f. number,** nombre *m* de cinq chiffres; **f.-f. logarithm tables,** table *f* de logarithmes à cinq décimales.

five-finger ['faiv'fiŋgər]. **1.** *s. Bot:* (*a*) quintefeuille *f*; (*b*) primevère élevée; (*c*) lotier corniculé. **2.** *a. Mus:* **f.-f. exercises,** exercices *m* de doigté.

fivefold ['faivfould]. **1.** *a.* quintuple. **2.** *adv.* cinq fois autant; au quintuple; **to repay s.o. f.,** rendre à qn cinq fois autant; **to increase f.,** quintupler.

five-master ['faiv'mɑ:stər], *s. Nau:* cinq-mâts *m inv.*

fivepence ['faifpəns], *s.* (somme *f*, pièce *f*, de) cinq pence.

fivepenny ['faifpəni], *a.* valant cinq pence; **f. stamp,** timbre *m* de cinq pence.

five-phase ['faiv'feiz], *a. El:* (courant) pentaphasé.

fiver ['faivər], *s. F:* billet *m*, somme *f*, de cinq livres, *U.S:* de cinq dollars.

fivesome ['faivsəm], *s.* groupe *m* de cinq personnes; *Golf:* partie *f* à cinq joueurs.

five-square ['faiv'skwɛər], *a.* (*of reamer, etc.*) pentagonal, -aux.

fix[1] [fiks], *s.* **1.** *F:* embarras *m*, difficulté *f*, mauvais pas; **to be in a f.,** être dans une situation embarrassante; être à l'accul; se trouver dans une impasse; être dans le pétrin, dans de beaux draps; **to get into a f.,** se mettre dans l'embarras, dans le pétrin; s'enfourner; **now I'm in a nice f.!** me voilà frais! **how are we to get out of this f.?** comment sortir de ce mauvais pas? **to put s.o. in a fix,** enfermer qn dans un dilemme, mettre qn dans l'embarras; **to get s.o. out of a f.,** tirer qn d'un mauvais pas, d'une impasse. **2.** *Nau: Av:* relèvement *m.* **3.** *P:* piqûre *f* de drogue, piquouse *f.*

fix[2], *v.*

I. *v.tr. & i.* **1.** *v.tr.* fixer; caler, monter (une roue sur l'essieu, une poulie, etc.); emmancher (une poulie); assujettir (une poutre, un monocle, etc.); ancrer (un tirant); arrêter, assurer (une planche avec des clous, etc.); attacher (un hameçon à une ligne, etc.); clouter (un fer à cheval); **to f. a stake into the ground,** ficher un pieu en terre; **to f. sth. in one's memory,** se graver qch. dans la mémoire; **to f. suspicion on s.o.,** faire peser le soupçon sur qn; **to f. one's attention on sth.,** fixer, arrêter, son attention sur qch.; **to f. one's eye(s) on s.o.,** fixer, arrêter, ses yeux sur qn; braquer, poser, les yeux sur qn; fixer qn (du regard). **2.** (*a*) *v.tr. Ch: Phot: etc:* fixer (le mercure, une plaque, une épreuve, un fusain, etc.); *Dy:* fixer (une teinture); (*b*) *v.tr. Med:* stériliser (une préparation microscopique) (à la formaline, etc.); (*c*) *v.i.* (*of fluid, etc.*) se prendre, se congeler, se concréter, se coaguler. **3.** *v.tr.* (*a*) établir; **to f. a camp,** établir un camp; **to f. one's residence in a place,** établir son domicile dans un endroit; (*b*) **to f. oneself somewhere,** s'installer, se placer, se mettre, se caser, quelque part. **4.** (*a*) *v.tr.* fixer, établir (le sens d'un mot, une limite, une indemnité, le taux de l'intérêt, etc.); arrêter, nommer, assigner, désigner (un jour, etc.); désigner, assigner (l'endroit pour un rendez-vous); régler (l'itinéraire d'un voyage, etc.); *Fin:* constater (les cours des valeurs, etc.); **to f. the budget,** déterminer le budget; **the government has fixed the income tax at . . .,** le gouvernement a fixé l'impôt sur le revenu à . . .; **to f. a meeting for three o'clock,** fixer une séance pour trois heures; **the date is not yet fixed,** la date n'est pas encore certaine, pas encore arrêtée; **on the date fixed,** à la date prescrite; **we'll f. the date afterwards,** nous conviendrons d'un jour par la suite; **his departure was fixed for Monday,** son départ a été fixé à lundi; **there's nothing fixed yet, nothing is fixed yet,** il n'y a encore rien de décidé; *F:* **how are you fixed tonight?** que faites-vous ce soir? **how are you fixed for money?** tu as de l'argent, assez d'argent? **I'm not very well fixed for time,** je n'ai pas beaucoup de temps (libre); *U.S: F:* **to be well fixed,** être riche, avoir du beurre à mettre dans les épinards; (*b*) *v.ind.tr.* **to f. on sth.,** se décider pour qch.; choisir qch.; **we've fixed on a holiday in Spain,** nous avons décidé de passer nos vacances en Espagne; (*c*) *v.tr. U.S:* **to be fixing to do sth.,** être décidé, déterminé, de faire qch.; avoir l'intention de faire qch.; **they are fixing to send off the goods next week,** ils ont l'intention d'expédier les marchandises la semaine prochaine; **it's fixing to rain,** le temps est à la pluie. **5.** *v.tr.* (*a*) **to f. sth. with s.o.,** arranger qch. avec qn; **I've fixed it with him,** je me suis arrangé avec lui; (*b*) *F:* réparer, retaper (qch.); **I think I can f. your radio,** je crois que je vais pouvoir réparer votre radio; **to f. a puncture,** réparer un pneu crevé; **just wait while I f. my hair,** attends que je me coiffe; (*c*) *F:* préparer (un repas, etc.). **6.** *v.tr. F:* (*a*) **I'll f. him!** je lui ferai son affaire! **I'll f. him yet!** je l'aurai au tournant! **I've fixed him!** il a son compte; (*b*) graisser la patte à (qn); suborner (un juré); (*c*) truquer (un match, etc.). **7.** *v.tr. P:* faire une piqûre (de drogue), une piquouse, à (qn); **to f. oneself,** se piquer, se faire une piquouse.

II. (*compound verb*) **fix up,** *v.tr.* (*a*) **to f. up a room as a study,** transformer une pièce en bureau; (*b*) arranger, régler, conclure (une affaire, etc.); **I've fixed it up,** j'ai conclu l'affaire; **it's all fixed up,** c'est une affaire réglée; **I can f. you up with a room,** je puis vous procurer une chambre; **I can f. you up for the night,** je puis vous héberger pour la nuit; *F:* **now she's fixed up for life,** la voilà casée; *F:* **they got fixed up,** (i) ils se sont casés; (ii) ils se sont fait mettre en règle; (*c*) *F:* réparer, retaper (qch.); mettre (qch.) en état; (*d*) *U.S: F:* **I fixed myself up as well as I could,** je me suis habillé(e) du mieux que j'ai pu.

fixate [fik'seit], *v.tr. Psy:* **1.** fixer les yeux, le regard, sur (qch.). **2.** (*of child*) **to f. the libido on a parent,** fixer la libido sur un des parents.

fixation [fik'seiʃ(ə)n], *s.* **1.** fixation *f* (de l'impôt, etc., *Ch: etc:* du mercure, de l'huile, etc.); *For:* **f. of drifting sands,** fixation des dunes; **f. abscess,** abcès *m* de fixation. **2.** *Psy:* (*a*) fixation des yeux (**on,** sur); (*b*) **f. of the libido,** fixation de la libido.

fixative ['fiksətiv]. **1.** *a.* fixatif. **2.** *s.* (*a*) *Art: Toil:* fixatif *m*; (*b*) *Biol:* fixateur *m.*

fixed [fikst], *a.* **1.** fixe, immobile, stationnaire; (boulon, etc.) prisonnier; (vitrage, etc.) dormant; **f. beam,** poutre encastrée; *Ind: etc:* **f. plant,** matériel *m* fixe; **f. boiler,** chaudière *f* fixe, stationnaire; **f. engine,** moteur *m* fixe; **f. pulley,** poulie *f* fixe; **f. wheel,** roue calée, fixe; *El:* **f. capacitor, condenser,** condensateur *m* fixe; **f. resistor,** résistance *f* fixe; *Jur:* **f. property,** (biens *mpl*) immeubles *mpl*; *Fish:* **f. net,** filet *m* fixe. **2.** (*a*) fixe, constant, invariable; **of f. length,** de longueur constante; **f. rule,** règle établie, immuable, absolue; *Opt:* **lenses with f. separation,** lentilles *f* à écartement invariable; **f.-focus camera,** appareil *m* à foyer fixe; *Com: Fin:* **f. charges,** frais fixes, frais généraux; **f. price,** prix *m* fixe, forfaitaire, fait, coté; **f. in advance,** forfaitaire, à forfait; **f. deposit,** dépôt *m* à terme (fixe), à échéance fixe; **f. income,** revenu *m* fixe; **f.-interest security,** valeur *f* à intérêt fixe; *Sp:* **f. odds bet,** pari *m* à la cote; *Meteor:* **f. wind,** vent fait; (*b*) **f. idea,** idée *f* fixe; **to have f. ideas,** avoir des idées (bien) arrêtées; **to have no f. plans,** ne pas avoir des projets bien déterminés; (*c*) **f. stare,** regard *m* fixe, qui appuie; **f. smile,** sourire figé, stéréotypé; (*d*) fixe, permanent; **f. point,** point *m* fixe, point de repère; *Mil:* **f. battery,** batterie *f* fixe; **f. gun,** pièce *f* fixe, statique; **f. ammunition, f. round,** munition *f* en cartouche; *Elcs:* **f. tuning,** accord *m* fixe; **f.-tuned,** à accord fixe; *Astr:* **f. star,** étoile *f* fixe; *Com:* **f. capital,** capital fixe, immobilisé; **f. assets,** immobilisations *f.* **3.** *Ch:* **f. oil, salt,** huile *f,* sel *m,* fixe. **4.** *F:* **f. match, etc.,** match, etc. truqué.

fixed-head [ˈfikstˈhed], *a. Aut:* **f.-h. coupé,** coupé *m* non décapotable.

fixedly [ˈfiksidli], *adv.* fixement.

fixedness [ˈfiksidnis], *s.* fixité *f;* (i) immobilité *f;* (ii) permanence *f* (de qch.); fermeté *f,* constance *f* (des opinions, etc.).

fixer [ˈfiksər], *s.* **1.** (*pers.*) (*a*) ouvrier *m* qui pose, qui monte (un appareil, etc.); monteur *m;* (*b*) *F:* complice *m* qui se charge d'acheter le silence des autorités; (*c*) *Th: U.S:* collaborateur *m* qui se charge de la mise en scène; (*d*) *P:* pourvoyeur *m* de drogues. **2.** (*a*) *Art: etc:* fixatif *m;* (*b*) *Phot: etc:* fixateur *m;* bain *m* de fixage.

fixing [ˈfiksiŋ], *s.* **1.** (*a*) fixation *f,* mise *f* en place (d'un appareil, etc.); fixage *m* (d'une épreuve photographique); fixation (de l'azote, d'une date, d'une indemnité); congélation *f* (de la fonte); calage *m* (d'une roue); encastrement *m* (d'une poutre); ancrage *m* (de tirants, de crampons, etc.); assujettissement *m* (d'une planche, etc.); pose *f* (d'une serrure); *Phot:* **f. solution, bath,** solution *f,* bain *m,* de fixage; fixateur *m;* (*b*) *Av: Nau:* relevé *m,* relèvement *m,* détermination *f* (d'un point, d'une position); **radar f.,** repérage *m* (par) radar; (*c*) *Com: etc:* fixation, établissement *m,* détermination (des prix, des droits, etc.). **2.** *pl. esp. NAm:* **fixings,** accessoires *m,* embellissements *m;* garniture *f; Cu: F:* **with all the fixings,** garni.

fixity [ˈfiksiti], *s.* (*a*) fixité *f* (d'un corps, d'un regard, etc.); immutabilité *f* (des lois, etc.); **f. of purpose,** détermination *f;* **I want f. of tenure,** il me faut un bail assuré; (*b*) fixité (d'une huile).

fixture [ˈfikstjər], *s.* **1.** (*a*) appareil fixe, fixé à demeure; meuble *m* à demeure; partie *f,* pièce *f,* fixe, à demeure (d'une machine, etc.); **to make sth. a f.,** fixer qch. (à demeure); sceller qch.; ancrer qch. en place; *F:* (*of pers.*) **after 20 years of service he is considered a f. in the factory,** au bout de 20 ans de travail on ne peut pas imaginer l'usine sans lui; **he's become a f. here,** il s'est bien ancré chez nous, il ne bouge plus d'ici; il fait partie des meubles; (*b*) *pl.* **fixtures,** choses fixées à demeure; meubles à demeure fixe; matériel *m* à attache; aménagements *m* (d'une maison, etc.); appareils (électriques, etc.); agencements *m* inamovibles; *Jur:* immeubles *m* par incorporation (d'une maison, etc.); **landlord's fixtures,** immeubles par destination; **£1000 for fixtures and fittings,** £1000 de reprise; **bathroom fixtures and fittings,** installations *f* et accessoires *m* de salles de bain; *Ind:* **small fixtures,** petit appareillage; *Jur:* **inventory of fixtures,** état *m* des lieux; (*c*) *Mec.E:* mandrin *m,* support *m.* **2.** *Sp:* rencontre (prévue); match (prévu); engagement *m;* **list of fixtures,** programme *m* (des rencontres); calendrier *m* (de la saison).

fix-up [ˈfiksʌp], *s.* (*a*) *F: A:* appareil *m,* truc *m,* machin *m;* (*b*) *P:* piqûre *f* (de drogue), piquouse *f.*

fizgig [ˈfizgig], *s. F:* **1.** *A:* (*pers.*) évaporée *f,* toupie *f.* **2.** (*toy*) toupie. **3.** *Pyr:* serpenteau *m.* **4.** *Fish:* foène *f,* digon *m.* **5.** *Austr: P:* mouchard *m.*

fizz[1] [fiz], *s.* **1.** pétillement *m,* effervescence *f* (du champagne, etc.); fusement *m* (des nitrates, etc.); *Mch:* crachement *m,* sifflement *m* (de la vapeur). **2.** *F:* champagne *m;* mousseux *m.*

fizz[2], *v.i.* (*of champagne, etc.*) pétiller, faire effervescence; (*of gunpowder*) fuser; (*of escape of steam*) cracher, siffler.

fizzing[1], *a.* **1.** (*of wine, etc.*) pétillant; (*of gunpowder*) fusant. **2.** *Sch: F: A:* épatant, bœuf *inv.*

fizzing[2], *s.* = FIZZ[1] 1.

fizzle[1] [ˈfizl], *s.* **1.** pétillement *m* (du champagne, etc.); sifflement *m* (d'un bec de gaz); grésillement *m* (de la graisse bouillante); fusement *m* (de la poudre). **2.** *F: O:* four *m,* fiasco *m.*

fizzle[2], *v.*

I. *v.i.* (*of wine, etc.*) pétiller; (*of gas burner, etc.*) siffler; (*of boiling fat, etc.*) grésiller; (*of gunpowder*) fuser.

II. (*compound verb*) **fizzle out,** *v.i. F:* (*of affair, plan, etc.*) ne pas aboutir; avorter; faire four; faire fiasco; finir en queue de poisson; s'en aller en eau de boudin; faire long feu.

fizzy [ˈfizi]. **1.** *a.* (*of mineral water, etc.*) gazeux, effervescent; (*of wine*) mousseux. **2.** *s. F: A:* champagne *m.*

fjeld [fiːˈeld], *s. Geog:* fjeld *m.*

fjord [ˈfiːɔːd], *s. Geog:* fjord *m,* fiord *m.*

flabbergast [ˈflæbəgɑːst], *v.tr. F:* épater, ébaubir, abasourdir, ahurir (qn); couper la respiration à (qn); **I was flabbergasted,** j'en étais sidéré; j'en suis resté éberlué; **we were flabbergasted at the news,** nous sommes restés abasourdis de la nouvelle; **he gazed at them flabbergasted,** il les regardait interdit et bouche bée.

flabbergasting [ˈflæbəgɑːstiŋ], *a.* ahurissant, abasourdissant, sidérant.

flabbily [ˈflæbili], *adv.* mollement.

flabbiness [ˈflæbinis], *s.* flaccidité *f,* manque *m* de fermeté (de la chair, etc.); mollesse *f,* inconsistance *f* (de qn, du caractère); mollesse (du style).

flabby [ˈflæbi], *a.* (*of muscles, etc.*) flasque; mou, *f.* molle; (*of cheeks*) avalé, pendant; (*of pers., character*) mollasse, avachi, amorphe; (*of style*) flasque, mou, amorphe; (*of wine*) mou; **to feel f.,** se sentir les jambes en pâte de guimauve; *F:* **he's a f. sort of person,** c'est une chique molle.

flabellate [fləˈbeleit], **flabelliform** [fləˈbelifɔːm], *a. Nat.Hist:* flabellé, flabelliforme.

flabellum, *pl.* **-a** [fləˈbeləm, -ə], *s.* **1.** *Ecc: A:* flabellum *m,* éventail cérémonial. **2.** *Nat.Hist:* flabellum.

flaccid [ˈflæksid], *a.* **1.** mou, *f.* molle; (*chair f*) flasque; **f. cheeks,** joues pendantes. **2.** (volonté *f*) flasque, mollasse. **3.** *Ser:* (*of silkworm*) flat.

flaccidity [flækˈsiditi], *s.* **1.** flaccidité *f.* **2.** *Ser:* (*also* **flacherie, flachery** [ˈflæʃəri]) flacherie *f* (des vers).

flack [flæk], *s. NAm: F:* agent *m* publicitaire.

flacourtia [flæˈkɔːtiə], *s. Bot:* flacourtia *m.*

Flacourtiaceae [flækɔːtiˈeisiiː], *s.pl. Bot:* flacourtiacées *f.*

flag[1] [flæg], *s. Bot:* **1.** (*a*) iris *m;* **water f., yellow f.,** iris des marais; iris jaune; glaïeul *m* des marais; *O:* **garden f.,** iris d'Allemagne, *F:* flambe *f;* **sweet(-smelling) f.,** acore *m;* lis *m* des marais; jonc odorant; roseau *m* aromatique; (*b*) canche gazonnante; (*c*) massette *f.* **2.** pampe *f* (de céréale, etc.).

flag[2], *v.tr.* **(flagged) 1.** mettre des feuilles de massette entre les douves (d'un tonneau). **2. to f. wheat,** couper les pampes du blé.

flag[3], *s. Const:* **(paving) f.,** carreau *m* (en pierre); dalle *f,* cadette *f;* pierre plate de pavage; pierre à paver; **room floored with stone flags,** pièce pavée de dalles; **f. pavement,** carrelage *m,* dallage *m* (de trottoir); trottoir carrelé, dallé.

flag[4], *v.tr.* daller, carreler (un trottoir, etc.); paver (un vestibule, etc.) de carreaux.

flag[5], *s.* penne *f* de l'aile (d'un oiseau); rémige *f.*

flag[6], *s.* **1.** (*a*) drapeau *m;* **red f., danger f.,** drapeau rouge, fanion *m* de sécurité, signalant un danger; *Sp:* **to drop the f.,** abaisser le drapeau (comme signal de départ); **f. day,** (i) jour *m* de vente d'insignes, jour de quête, pour une œuvre de bienfaisance; (ii) *U.S:* le 14 juin (anniversaire de l'adoption du drapeau national); *F: Pej:* **f. wagger, f. waver,** chauvin *m;* **f. wagging, waving,** chauvinisme *m,* esprit cocardier; (*b*) *Mil:* drapeau, fanion *m;* **battalion, company, f.,** fanion de bataillon, de compagnie; **general's f.,** fanion du général; **headquarters f.,** fanion de quartier général, de (poste de) commandement; **f. of truce,** drapeau parlementaire; **white f.,** drapeau blanc; **Red Cross f.,** drapeau de la Croix Rouge; fanion d'ambulance; **signalling f.,** fanion de signalisation; **f. signals,** signalisation *f* par fanions; *Fig:* **to keep the f. flying,** ne pas se laisser abattre, ne pas se décourager; **with flags flying,** enseignes déployées; (*c*) *Nau:* pavillon *m;* **yellow f.,** pavillon de quarantaine; **f. of distress,** pavillon de détresse; **pilot f.,** pavillon (de) pilote; **black f.,** pavillon noir, de pirate; **f. of convenience,** pavillon de complaisance; **vessel flying, sailing under, the Panamanian f.,** navire *m* sous (le) pavillon panamien; **the f. covers the goods,** le pavillon couvre la marchandise; *Navy:* **the Admiral's f.,** le pavillon de l'Amiral; **f. officer,** officier général; **f. captain,** commandant *m* du navire amiral; **f. lieutenant,** officier d'ordonnance; (*d*) *Ski:* **pair of flags,** porte *f;* (*e*) drapeau (de taximètre); **taxi with the f. up,** taxi *m* libre; (*f*) *Typ:* (*in proof correcting*) signe *m* qui indique un bourdon; (*g*) *Cmptr:* drapeau, indicateur *m;* **f. bit,** bit indicateur. **2.** *Ven:* queue *f* (de setter); fouet *m.*

flag[7], *v.tr.* **1.** pavoiser (un navire, un édifice). **2.** transmettre des signaux à (qn) au moyen de fanions; communiquer (un message) au moyen de fanions-signaux; **to f. a taxi,** arrêter un taxi; **to f. down a motorist, a car,** faire signe à un automobiliste de s'arrêter; arrêter, stopper, un automobiliste, une voiture. **3.** *Sp:* **to f. out a race course,** jalonner un champ de course.

flag[8], *v.i.* **1.** (*of thg*) pendre mollement; (*of sail*) battre, fouetter. **2.** (*of plant, etc.*) languir; (*of pers.*) s'alanguir; (*of conversation, etc.*) se ralentir, traîner, languir; (*of attention, etc.*) faiblir, fléchir; (*of zeal, courage*) se relâcher, s'amollir; **his strength was flagging,** il était à bout de force; **the interest does not f.,** l'intérêt *m* se soutient.

flagellant [flæˈdʒelənt], *s. Rel.H:* flagellant *m.*

flagellaria [flædʒəˈleəriə], *s. Bot:* flagellaire *f.*

Flagellata [flædʒəˈleitə], *s.pl. Prot:* flagellates *m.*

flagellate[1] [ˈflædʒəleit]. **1.** *a. Nat.Hist:* (*a*) flagellé; (*b*) flagellaire, flagelliforme. **2.** *s. Prot:* flagellate *m,* flagellé *m.*

flagellate[2], *v.tr.* flageller; fouetter.

flagellation [flædʒəˈleiʃ(ə)n], *s.* flagellation *f.*

flagellator [ˈflædʒəleitər], *s.* flagellateur, -trice.

flagelliferous [flædʒəˈlifərəs], *a. Bot:* flagellifère.

flagelliform [flæˈdʒelifɔːm], *a. Nat.Hist:* flagelliforme.

flagellum, *pl.* **-a** [flæˈdʒeləm, -ə], *s.* **1.** *A:* fouet *m.* **2.** *Bot:* stolon *m.* **3.** *Nat.Hist:* flagellum *m.*

flageolet[1] [ˈflædʒəlet, flædʒəˈlet], *s. Mus:* flageolet *m.*

flageolet[2], *s. Hort: Cu:* (haricot *m*) flageolet *m.*

flagged [flægd], *a.* (*of pavement, floor, etc.*) carrelé, dallé.

flagging[1] [ˈflægiŋ], *s.* carrelage *m,* dallage *m;* **concrete f.,** dallage en ciment.

flagging[2], *a.* **1.** (*of thg*) pendant; (*of sail*) battant. **2.** (*of conversation, interest, etc.*) languissant.

flagging[3], *s.* **1.** fouettement *m* (d'une voile). **2.** amollissement *m* (du courage); ralentissement *m* (du zèle).

flagitious [fləˈdʒiʃəs], *a. A:* infâme, abominable.

flagon [ˈflægən], *s.* **1.** flacon *m; Ecc:* burette *f.* **2.** grosse bouteille ventrue; fiasque *f;* **Burgundy f.,** bourguignonne *f.* **3.** pot *m* (à anse, pour vin, etc.).

flagpole [ˈflægpoul], *s.* mât *m* de drapeau.

flagrancy [ˈfleigrənsi], *s.* flagrance *f,* énormité *f,* caractère scandaleux (d'un crime, etc.).

flagrant [ˈfleigrənt], *a.* (*of offence*) flagrant, énorme, scandaleux; (*of offender*) notoire; **a f. injustice,** une injustice criante, flagrante; **a f. case,** un cas notoire.

flagrante delicto (in) [inflə'græntidiˈliktou], *Lt.adv.phr. Jur:* en flagrant délit.

flagrantly [ˈfleigrəntli], *adv.* scandaleusement, d'une manière flagrante.

flagship [ˈflægʃip], *s. Navy:* (navire *m*) amiral *m;* bâtiment commandant.

flagstaff [ˈflægstɑːf], *s.* **1.** (i) mât *m* de drapeau; (ii) hampe *f* de drapeau. **2.** *Nau:* (*a*) mât de pavillon; **the rear f.,** le bâton; (*b*) gaule *f* (d'enseigne); digon *m.*

flagstone [ˈflægstoun], *s.* dalle *f;* **f. pavement,** dallage *m* en pierre.

flail[1] [fleil], *s.* **1.** *Agr:* fléau *m.* **2.** *A. Arms:* fléau d'armes.

flail[2]. **1.** *v.tr.* (*a*) *Agr:* battre au fléau; (*b*) battre, flageller. **2.** *v.i.* **to f. around,** s'agiter; se débattre des mains et des pieds.

flair [ˈfleər], *s.* (*a*) flair *m,* perspicacité *f;* **to have a f. for bargains,** avoir du flair pour les occasions; (*b*) aptitude *f* (for, à); **to have a f. for languages,** avoir le don des langues.

flajolotite [flæˈdʒɔloutait], *s. Miner:* flajolotite *f.*

flak [flæk], *s.* (*a*) artillerie anti-aérienne; (*b*) tir *m* contre-avions; (*c*) **f. jacket,** gilet *m* de protection (contre les éclats d'obus, etc.); (*d*) *Fig:* critique (violente).

flake[1] [fleik], *s.* **1.** claie *f* (pour faire sécher le poisson, etc.); séchoir *m.* **2.** *Nau:* échafaud suspendu (de calfat, etc.).

flake[2], *s.* **1.** (*a*) flocon *m* (de neige, de laine, etc.); (*b*) étincelle *f,* flammèche *f* (de feu); (*c*) écaille *f,* éclat *m,* lamelle *f,* paillette *f* (de minéral, de métal, etc.); feuillette *f* (de pâte, etc.); coquille *f* (de beurre); paillette (de savon); **flakes of mica,** paillettes de mica; **picture that is coming off in flakes,** tableau *m* qui s'écaille; **f. white,** blanc *m* de céruse; céruse *f* en lamelles. **2.** *Bot:* œillet panaché.

flake[3]. **1.** *v.i.* (*a*) (*of snow, etc.*) tomber en flocons; (*b*) (*of metal, mineral, etc.*) **to f. (away, off),** s'écailler, se feuilleter; se diviser en lamelles, en paillettes; (*of stone*) s'épaufrer; **the paint is flaking off,** la peinture s'écaille, se détache par écailles; **picture that is flaking (off),** tableau *m* qui s'écaille; **the scales f. off,** les écailles *f* se détachent. **2.** *v.tr.* (*a*) couvrir, parsemer, de flocons (de neige, etc.); (*b*) écailler (la peinture, etc.).

flake[4], *v.i. P:* **to f. (out),** (i) s'évanouir, tomber dans les pommes; (ii) tomber de fatigue; s'endormir (après avoir trop bu, etc.); **to be flaked (out),** être vidé, vanné, crevé.

flake[5], *s. Ich: Com: F:* roussette *f.*

flake[6], *s. P:* cocaïne *f,* coco *f.*

flaked[1] [fleikt], *a.* en écailles; **f. soap,** savon *m* en paillettes.

flaked[2], *a. P:* (*also* **flakers** [ˈfleikəz]) vidé, vanné, crevé,

esquinté, claqué.
flaking ['fleikiŋ], *s.* écaillement *m* (de la peinture); craquelure *f.*
flaky ['fleiki], *a.* **1.** (*of snow, wool, etc.*) floconneux. **2.** (*of mineral, metal, etc.*) écailleux, lamellé, lamelleux, lamelliforme; (*of soap*) en paillettes; **f. pastry,** pâte feuilletée; feuilletage *m*; feuilleté *m.*
flam[1] [flæm], *s. F: O:* **1.** histoire *f*, blague *f.* **2.** *esp U.S:* escroquerie *f*, filouterie *f.*
flam[2], *v.tr. F: O: esp. U.S:* escroquer, refaire, rouler (qn).
flam[3], *s.* fla *m* (sur le tambour).
flambé ['flæmbei, 'flɑ̃bei]. **1.** *a. & s. Cer:* flammé (*m*). **2.** *a. Cu:* flambé.
flamberg(e) ['flæmbəːdʒ], *s. A.Arms:* flamberge *f.*
flamboyance, flamboyancy [flæm'bɔiəns, -'bɔiənsi], *s.* qualité flamboyante (du style, etc.).
flamboyant [flæm'bɔiənt]. **1.** *a.* (*a*) *Arch:* (style) flamboyant; (*b*) (*of pers. speech, etc.*) flamboyant. **2.** *s. Bot:* (*also* **flamboyante**) flamboyant *m.*
flame[1] [fleim], *s.* **1.** (*a*) flamme *f*; feu *m*, flamme (de chalumeau); **to commit s.o. to the flames,** condamner qn au feu; **to commit one's manuscripts to the flames,** faire un autodafé de ses manuscrits, brûler ses manuscrits; **in flames,** en flammes, en feu; **to burst, break, into flame(s), to go up in flames,** s'enflammer brusquement, se mettre à flamber; *Ch: Metall:* **oxidizing, reducing, f.,** flamme oxydante, réductrice; **carburizing f.,** flamme carburante; (*b*) *attrib.* **f. arrester, f. trap,** *Ind:* **f. guard,** pare-flamme *m, pl.* pare-flammes; *Metalw:* **f. cutter,** chalumeau *m* à découper; *El:* **f. arc,** arc *m* à flamme; **f. tube,** (i) tube brûleur (de lampe à souder); (ii) (*of jet engine*) chambre *f* de combustion (de réacteur); (*of jet engine*) **f. holder,** aubage *m* de tourbillonnement; brûleur *m*; *Ch: Metall:* **f. test,** essai *m* de coloration; *Ph:* **f. spectra (of metals),** spectres *m* (de vapeurs métalliques); (*c*) *a.* **f.(-coloured),** ponceau *inv*; couleur de feu *inv*; **f. (red),** rouge feu *inv*; (*d*) *Bot:* **f. flower,** tritome *m.* **2.** éclat *m* (d'une lumière, d'une couleur, d'une pierre précieuse). **3.** (*a*) *Lit:* passion *f*, ardeur *f*, flamme; **to fan the f.,** attiser les passions; (*b*) *F: O:* (*pers.*) béguin *m*, caprice *m*; **he, she, is an old f. of mine,** c'est une de mes anciennes amours, un de mes anciens béguins, un de mes anciens flirts.
flame[2], *v.*
I. *v.i. & tr.* **1.** *v.i.* (*a*) (*of fire, house, etc.*) flamber, flamboyer, jeter des flammes; *Lit:* (*of passions, etc.*) flamber, s'enflammer; (*b*) (*of diamond, gold, etc.*) briller, luire. **2.** *v.tr. Med: etc:* flamber (un instrument); passer (un instrument) à la flamme.
II. (*compound verbs*) **1. flame out,** *v.i.* (*a*) jeter des flammes; (*b*) (*of jet engine*) s'éteindre.
2. flame up, *v.i.* (*a*) s'enflammer; **to f. up again,** se renflammer; (*b*) *F:* (*of pers.*) s'enflammer de colère; s'emporter; (*c*) *F: O:* (*of pers.*) rougir comme une pivoine; devenir cramoisi.
flameless ['fleimlis], *a.* (feu, etc.) sans flamme; *Min:* **f. explosive,** explosif *m* de sûreté.
flamen ['fleimen], *s. Rom.Ant:* flamine *m.*
flamenco [flə'meŋkou], *s. Danc:* flamenca *f.*
flameout ['fleimaut], *s.* (*of jet engine*) extinction *f.*
flameproof ['fleimpruːf], **flame-resistant** ['fleimri'zistənt], *a.* (*a*) ignifugé; ininflammable, à l'épreuve des flammes; (*b*) antidéflagrant; *Atom.Ph:* **f. monitor,** détecteur *m* antidéflagrant.
flamethrower ['fleimθrouər], *s. Mil: Hort:* lance-flammes *m inv.*
flameware ['fleimwɛər], *s. coll. Com:* plats *mpl* allant au four, au feu.
flaming[1] ['fleimiŋ], *a.* **1.** (feu) flambant, flamboyant; (maison *f*, etc.) en flammes; *Lit:* (sabre) flamboyant; *El:* **f. arc,** arc *m* à flamme. **2. f. sun,** soleil ardent, flamboyant; **f. red,** rouge feu *inv*; **f. red tie,** cravate *f* d'un rouge flamboyant; *F:* **in a f. temper,** d'une humeur massacrante. **3.** *P:* sacré; **a f. idiot,** un sacré imbécile; *adv.* **he's so f. lazy!** il est tellement paresseux!
flaming[2], *s.* flamboiement *m*, embrasement *m*; *El:* **f. of the arc,** flamboiement de l'arc.
flamingo, *pl.* **-o(e)s** [flə'miŋgou, 'flæmiŋgou, -ouz]. **1.** *s. Orn:* flamant *m* (rose). **2.** *a. & s.* écarlate (*f*).
Flaminian [flə'miniən], *a. Rom.Ant:* **the F. Way,** la Voie flaminienne.
flammability [flæmə'biliti], *s. NAm:* inflammabilité *f.*
flammable ['flæməbl], *a. NAm:* inflammable.
flammulated ['flæmjuleitid], *a. Orn:* flammé; à taches couleur de flamme.
flan [flæn], *s.* **1.** *Num:* flan *m.* **2.** *Cu:* (sorte de) tarte *f*, gâteau *m*, aux fruits, etc.; tarte à la crème; **f. pastry,** pâte brisée.
flanch [flɑːnʃ], *s. Her:* flanc *m.*
flanched [flɑːnʃt], *a. Her:* flanqué.
flancon(n)ade [flæŋkə'neid], *s. Fenc:* flanconade *f.*
Flanders ['flɑːndəz], *Pr.n. Geog:* la Flandre; **West, East, F.,** la Flandre occidentale, orientale; **the battles of F.,** les batailles des Flandres; **the F. poppy,** le coquelicot des Flandres (vendu le 11 novembre dans toute la Grande-Bretagne au profit de l'œuvre des mutilés de guerre).
Flandrian ['flɑːndriən], *a. & s. Geol:* flandrien (*m*).
flange[1] [flændʒ], *s.* **1.** (*a*) bourrelet *m* (d'un tuyau, d'une cartouche, etc.); bride *f*, collerette *f* (d'un cylindre, d'un tube, d'un tuyau); collet *m*, rebord *m* (d'une feuille de métal, d'une tôle); saillie *f* (sur une pièce de métal, etc.); *Av:* bord relevé; **blank f., blind f.,** bride, joint, d'obturation, joint plein; **coupling f.,** collerette d'assemblage, de raccordement; *N.Arch:* **deck f.,** collerette *f* de pont, de bordé; **exhaust f.,** bride d'échappement; **f. assembly, connection, f. coupling, f. joint,** (i) joint, raccordement *m*, à bride; (ii) *I.C.E:* raccordement, manchon *m*, à plateaux; **loose f.,** bride mobile; **pressed f.,** bord embouti, épanoui, d'un tube; *I.C.E: etc:* **flywheel f.,** embase *f* pour la fixation du volant (sur le vilebrequin); *Mch: Tls:* **spindle f.,** collet de la broche; (*b*) boudin *m*, bourrelet, mentonnet *m*, rebord (d'une roue); joue *f* (d'un galet); mâchoire *f* (d'une poulie à gorge); (*c*) aile *f*, semelle *f*, panne *f*, table *f* (d'une poutre); membrure *f* (d'une poutre à âme pleine); *Rail:* patin *m* (de rail); *I.C.E: Mch:* **f. of connecting rod,** aile de bielle; *Av: etc:* **angle section f.,** aile de cornière; (*d*) chape *f* (d'une poulie, d'un rouleau); flasque *m* (d'assemblage, de moteur, etc.); joue (de tambour de treuil, de touret); **attaching f.,** flasque de fixation; *Aut:* **wing f.,** joue, bajoue *f*, d'aile; **brake f.,** flasque de frein; (*e*) taquet *m* (de châssis de moulage). **2.** *I.C.E: etc:* **cooling f.,** ailette *f*, nervure *f*, de refroidissement; **f.-cooled cylinder, engine,** cylindre *m* à refroidissement par ailettes; moteur *m* à ailettes.
flange[2], *v.tr. Tchn:* brider, faire une bride à (qch.); **to f. a pipe,** brider un tube; faire un collet à un tube; rabattre la collerette d'un tube; **to f. a plate,** border une tôle; rabattre un collet sur une tôle; rabattre, refouler, le bord d'une tôle; tomber le bord d'une tôle; **to f. a wheel,** bourreler une roue; **to f. an edge,** tomber un bord.
flanged [flændʒd], *a.* **1.** (tube, etc.) à bride(s); (roue, etc.) à boudin, à bourrelet, à mentonnet, à rebord; (engrenage, etc.) à joues; (rail) à patin; (poutre) à aile, à semelle; **f. plate,** tôle *f* à bord tombé. **2.** *Aut:* (radiateur *m*) à ailettes.
flanger ['flændʒər], *s.* machine *f* à border, à rabattre.
flanging ['flændʒiŋ], *s. Metalw: etc:* **1.** (i) façonnage *m*, (ii) rabattement *m*, des brides, des bords, des collerettes; tombage *m* des bords; bordage *m*; **f. machine, press,** machine *f*, presse *f*, à border, à rabattre. **2.** *Coll.* les collets, collerettes, brides, etc. (*See* FLANGE[1].)
flank[1] [flæŋk], *s.* **1.** (*a*) flanc *m* (d'une personne, d'un animal); (*b*) *Cu:* flanchet *m* (de bœuf); **thin f.,** grasset *m.* **2.** (*a*) côté *m*, flanc (d'une montagne, d'un édifice, etc.); berge *f* (d'une montagne); *Mec.E:* flanc (d'une dent d'engrenage); *Arch:* rein *m* (d'une voûte); (*b*) *Mil: Fort:* flanc (d'une armée, d'un bastion, etc.); **open f.,** flanc découvert; **protected f.,** flanc couvert, protégé; **pivoting, wheeling, f.,** aile pivotante, marchante; **to protect one's flanks,** se couvrir sur les flancs; **unit covered on both flanks,** unité encadrée; **to expose one's f.,** découvrir, exposer, son flanc; **to attack, take the enemy, on the f.,** attaquer, prendre l'ennemi, de flanc; **f. thrown forward, thrown back,** crochet offensif, défensif; **f. march, attack,** marche *f*, attaque *f*, de flanc; **f. spotting,** observation latérale.
flank[2], *v.tr.* **1.** flanquer; défendre, soutenir, (qch.) sur le flanc; **to f. sth. with, by, sth.,** flanquer qch. de qch.; **the battleships were flanked with destroyers,** les torpilleurs étaient échelonnés le long de la ligne de cuirassés. **2.** *Mil:* prendre (l'ennemi, etc.) de flanc; *Artil:* enfiler, prendre en enfilade (une tranchée, etc.). **3.** (*a*) être disposé à côté de (qch.); **mountains flanked us on either side,** les montagnes étaient de chaque côté de nous; nous avions des montagnes de chaque côté; **the accused is flanked by two policemen,** le prévenu est encadré de deux gendarmes; (*b*) passer à côté de, sur le flanc de (qch.).
flanker ['flæŋkər], *s.* **1.** *Fort:* flanquement *m*, ouvrage flanquant. **2.** *Mil:* (*pers.*) (*a*) flanqueur *m*; (*b*) flanc-garde *f, pl.* flancs-gardes; **mobile, stationary, f.,** flanc-garde mobile, fixe.
flanking ['flæŋkiŋ], *s.* flanquement *m*; *Mil:* **f. fire,** tir *m* de flanquement.
flannel[1] ['flænəl], *s.* **1.** (*a*) *Tex:* flanelle *f*; **cotton f., Canton f.,** flanelle de coton; flanellette *f*; pilou *m*; **to wear f.,** porter de la flanelle; **f. trousers,** un pantalon de flanelle; **a f. vest,** un gilet de flanelle; **f. jacket,** (i) gilet *m* de flanelle; (ii) *P: A:* terrassier *m*, piocheur *m*; homme *m* de peine; (*b*) *pl.* **flannels,** articles *m* de flanelle; flanelles; *Cost:* **to wear flannels,** (i) porter un costume en, de, flanelle, un pantalon de flanelle; (ii) *O:* porter un costume de cricket; (*c*) *F:* flatterie *f*, flagornerie *f.* **2.** *Dom.Ec:* **(floor) f.,** serpillière *f*; **(face) f.** = gant *m* de toilette. **3.** *Ent:* **f. moth,** mégalopygide *m.*
flannel[2], *v.tr. & v.i. F:* jeter de la poudre aux yeux (à qn).
flannelette [flænə'let], *s. Tex:* flanelle *f* de coton; flanellette *f*, pilou *m*, veloutine *f.*
flannelgraph ['flænəlgræf], *s. Sch:* tableau *m* de feutre, tableau-feutre *m, pl.* tableaux-feutre.
flannelly ['flænəli], *a.* semblable à la flanelle; pelucheux; lâche; sans consistance.
flanning ['flæniŋ], *s. Const:* embrasure *f* (de fenêtre, etc.).
flanque [flæŋk], *s. Her:* flanc *m.*
flap[1] [flæp], *s.* **1.** (*a*) battement *m*, coup *m* (d'aile, etc.); clapotement *m*, claquement *m* (d'une voile); flottement *m* (d'un pavillon); voltigement *m* (d'un rideau); *F:* affolement *m*; **to get into a f.,** s'agiter, s'affoler, être bouleversé; ne plus savoir où donner de la tête; (*b*) coup léger (de la main); tape *f*; (*c*) *Ling:* **f. (consonant),** consonne *f* à un seul battement (de la langue). **2.** (*a*) rabat *m*, patte gommée, patte de gommage (d'une enveloppe); patte (d'une poche); rabat (d'une caisse en carton, etc.); pan *m* (d'un vêtement); rabat (de la jaquette d'un livre); *Harn:* **saddle f.,** quartier *m* de selle; *Ich:* **(gill) f.,** opercule *m*; *Crust:* **terminal f.,** telson *m*; (*b*) *Mec.E: etc:* clapet *m* (à charnière); volet *m*; **cowl f.,** volet de capot (de moteur); *Hyd.E:* **valve f.,** clapet de soupape; **f. valve,** soupape *f* à clapet, à charnière; *Nau:* **porthole f.,** mantelet *m* de sabord; (*c*) abattant *m*, battant *m* (de table, etc.); trappe *f* (de cave, etc.); *Join:* **f. hinge,** briquet *m*; **desk with a writing f.,** bureau *m* en fruitier, secrétaire *m*; **f. table,** table *f* à abattant, à battant; **f. seat,** strapontin *m*; *Sm.a:* **back-sight f.,** planche *f*, lamelle *f*, de hausse; **f. sight,** hausse *f* à charnière; *Phot:* **f. shutter,** obturateur *m* à volet; (*d*) *Av:* volet; **camber f., plain f.,** volet de courbure; **fillet f.,** volet d'emplanture; **slotted f.,** volet à fente; **split f.,** volet d'intrados; **extension f., (high-)lift f., Fowler f.,** (volet) hypersustentateur *m*, volet Fowler; **extended f.,** volet sorti; **deflected f.,** volet braqué; **dive f.,** frein *m* de piqué; **landing f.,** volet d'atterrissage; **f. down, lowered f.,** volet baissé; **f. up, retracted f.,** volet rentré; **f. angle,** braquage *m* du, de, volet; **f. (position) indicator,** indicateur *m* de position de volet, des volets; (*e*) *Surg:* lambeau *m*, manchette *f*, volet; greffon *m*; **f., double-f., amputation,** amputation *f* à lambeau, à double lambeau; **sliding f.,** greffe *f* de Celse; **osteoplastic bone f.,** volet ostéoplastique.
flap[2], *v.* **(flapped) 1.** *v.tr.* (*a*) battre; **the bird flaps its wings,** l'oiseau bat des ailes, trémousse des ailes; **to f. one's arms about,** agiter les bras; *v.i.* **a heron came flapping up the creek,** un héron remontait l'estuaire en battant des ailes; *P: A:* **to f. one's mouth,** caqueter, bavarder; (*b*) frapper (qch.) légèrement; **to f. away the flies,** chasser les mouches. **2.** *v.i.* (*a*) (*of sail, etc.*) battre, fouetter, claquer; (*of curtain*) voltiger; (*of wings*) battre; (*of shutter*) ballotter; **the sails were flapping idly,** les voiles remuaient à peine; *Mec.E:* **the belt is flapping,** la courroie flotte; (*b*) *F:* s'agiter sans but; s'affoler.
flapdoodle [flæp'duːdl], *s. F:* bêtises *fpl*; blagues *fpl.*
flap-eared ['flæpiːəd], *a.* (chien, etc.) aux oreilles pendantes.
flapjack ['flæpdʒæk], *s.* **1.** *Cu:* matefaim *m inv.* **2.** *Toil: A:* poudrier *m.*
flapped [flæpt]. *a.* **1.** (*of cheek, ear*) pendant. **2.** (*of coat, etc.*) à pans; (*of pocket, etc.*) à patte; (*of cap, etc.*) à rabats.
flapper ['flæpər], *s.* **1.** (*a*) **(fly-)f.,** balai *m* tue-mouches; chasse-mouches *m inv*; tapette *f*; (*b*) battoir *m* (d'un fléau); (*c*) claquette *f*, claquoir *m*; (*d*) *P: O:* (i) oreille *f*; (ii) main *f*, pince *f*, patte *f.* **2.** (*a*) = FLIPPER; **1.** *Av:* **f. wings,** ailes articulées; (*b*) *Crust:* telson *m.* **3.** *Orn:* (i) halbran *m*; (ii) perdreau *m.* **4.** *F:* (*a*) *A:* gamine *f*; jeunesse *f*; *Pol.Hist:* **f. vote,** (i) le droit de vote accordé aux jeunes femmes âgées de 21 ans; (ii) le suffrage des jeunes femmes; (*b*) **he's, she's, an awful f.,** il, elle, s'agite, s'affole, pour des riens.
flapping ['flæpiŋ], *s.* (*a*) battement *m* (des ailes, etc.); clapotement *m*, claquement *m* (d'une voile); flottement *m* (d'un pavillon, etc.); voltigement *m* (d'un rideau); (*b*) *F:* affolement *m*; agitation *f.*
flare[1] ['flɛər], *s.* **1.** (*a*) flamboiement irrégulier, flamme vacillante (de gaz, etc.); (*of jet engine, etc.*) flammes *fpl*; (*b*) *Mil: Av: etc:* feu *m* de signal, artifice *m* de signalisation, signal *m* pyrotechnique; artifice éclairant, fusée éclairante; phare *m*; **f. bomb,** bombe

éclairante; **f. pistol,** pistolet *m* lance-fusée, à fusée, de signalisation; **f. parachute,** parachute *m* de fusée; **parachute f.,** fusée (éclairante) à parachute; **f. path,** piste (d'aérodrome) éclairée; **ground f., landing f.,** fusée, phare, d'atterrissage; (*c*) **f. fishing,** pêche *f* au pharillon, au lamparo; (*d*) *Phot:* **f. (spot),** tache centrale, par réflexion; spectre *m* secondaire; image *f* vague du diaphragme (sur le film, la plaque); (*d*) *Med:* flambée *f,* réaction érythémateuse, rougeurs *fpl.* **2.** (*a*) évasement *m* (d'un orifice); évasement,godet *m* (d'une jupe); épanouissement *m,* renflement *m* (d'un tube); pavillon *m* (d'un entonnoir); **f. of the root of a tree,** empattement *m* d'un arbre; *Elcs:* **f. factor (of loudspeaker),** ouverture *f* (d'un haut-parleur); (*b*) *Av:* évasement, galbe *m* (de la cellule d'un avion, de la coque d'un hydravion); *Nau:* évasement (des flancs d'un navire); devers *m,* renvoi *m.*

flare[2], *v.*

I. *v.i. & tr.* **1.** *v.i.* (*a*) (*of candle, lamp, etc.*) flamboyer, vaciller; brûler avec une lumière irrégulière; donner une lumière inégale; (*b*) *Tchn:* (*of tube, etc.*) s'évaser; (*of metal plate, etc.*) se dilater, se renfler; faire saillie; (*of skirt, of ship's sides*) s'évaser. **2.** *v.tr.* évaser (un tube, les hauts d'un navire, une jupe, une embrasure, etc.).

II. (*compound verbs*) **1. flare out,** *v.i.* (*a*) flamboyer; (*b*) *F:* **to f. out at s.o.,** faire une algarade à qn.

2. flare up, *v.i.* (*a*) (*of beacon, candle, etc.*) s'enflammer brusquement; lancer des flammes; **to f. up again,** se renflammer; (*b*) *F:* (*of pers.*) s'emporter, se mettre en colère; **he flares up at the least thing,** il se fâche pour un oui ou pour un non; il monte comme une soupe au lait.

flare[3], *s. Cu:* lard *m* (de porc).

flared ['flɛəd], *a.* **1.** (jupe, etc.) évasée, en forme. **2.** (tube, etc.) évasé, épanoui. **3.** *Av:* (atterrissage) avec arrondi, (contact de l'atterrisseur avec le sol) après arrondi.

flare-out ['flɛəraut], *s. Av:* arrondi *m* (avant d'atterrir); **f.-o. path,** trajectoire *f* de l'arrondi.

flarepot ['flɛəpɔt], *s.* (*a*) *Pyr:* pot *m* à feu, bengale *m;* (*b*) *Av:* brûlot *m.*

flare-up ['flɛərʌp], *s.* **1.** (*a*) flambée soudaine; (*b*) *F:* (i) altercation *f,* scène *f,* prise *f* de bec; (ii) bagarre *f;* (*c*) *F:* colère bleue. **2.** *Nau:* **flare-up (light),** feu *m* de fortune; flare up *m.*

flaring[1] ['flɛəriŋ], *a.* **1.** (*a*) (*of light, etc.*) flamboyant; (*b*) *F:* (*of colours, etc.*) voyant, éclatant, éblouissant. **2.** (*of ship's sides, shape, etc.*) évasé.

flaring[2], *s.* **1.** flamboiement *m* (d'une lumière, etc.). **2.** (*a*) évasement *m* (d'une jupe, etc.); (*b*) *N.Arch:* **f. of timbers,** dévoiement *m.*

flash[1] [flæʃ], *s.* **1.** (*a*) éclair *m;* lueur soudaine; effulguration *f;* éclat *m* (de flamme, d'étincelles); *El:* **f. across the terminals,** débordement *m,* jaillissement *m,* d'étincelles entre les bornes; **a f. of lightning,** un éclair; **f. of wit,** saillie *f* (d'esprit); **f. of genius,** éclair, étincelle *f,* de génie; **f. of hope,** rayon *m* d'espoir; **flashes of laughter,** (brefs) éclats de rire; **in a f.,** en un rien de temps, en un clin d'œil; **in a f. he recognized the spot,** tout brusquement, tout soudain, sans s'en rendre compte, il a reconnu l'endroit; **it all happened in a f.,** tout s'est passé en moins de rien; (*b*) *Artil: Sm.a:* lueur, éclair (d'une arme à feu); **f. of discharge, muzzle f.,** lueur de départ; **f. ranging,** repérage *m,* réglage *m* (du tir) aux lueurs; **f. spotting,** repérage (des pièces ennemies) aux lueurs; **f. concealer, f. eliminator, f. hider, f. screen,** cache-flamme *m,* cache-lueur *m, pl.* cache-flamme(s), lucur(s); *A:* **f. pan,** bassinet *m* (d'un fusil à pierre); *Fig:* **a f. in the pan,** un feu de paille; *Mil:* **f. hole,** évent *m* (d'une fusée); **f. bomb,** bombe éclairante; (*c*) *Petr:* détente *f;* **f. drum,** ballon *m* de détente; **f. tower,** tour *f,* colonne *f,* de détente; **f. evaporation,** évaporation *f* par détente; (*d*) *Mch:* **f. boiler, f. (steam) generator,** chaudière *f* à vaporisation instantanée; *Metalw:* **f. welding,** soudure *f* par étincelage; (*e*) *Atom.Ph:* **f. burn,** brûlure *f* par irradiation; **f.-dose indicator,** dosimètre *m* photosensible; (*f*) *Phot:* lampe-éclair *f, pl.* lampes-éclair; **(electronic) f.,** flash *m* (*pl.* flashes) (électronique); **f. cube,** flash cube; **f. factor,** nombre-guide *m, pl.* nombres-guides (pour lampe-éclair); **f. bulb,** ampoule *f* (de) flash; (*g*) *Journ:* flash; *Tp: etc:* **f. (service),** priorité absolue; **f. message,** (i) message immédiat, flash; (ii) message condensé; (*h*) *Cin:* scène de raccord (très courte). **2.** *A:* (*a*) *F:* faste *m,* ostentation *f,* épate *f,* esbrouffe *f;* (*b*) *P:* argot *m* de la basse pègre. **3.** *Metall:* bavure *f* (d'une pièce brute de fonderie); *Metalw:* (*in welding*) projection *f.* **4.** *Hyd.E:* (*a*) chasse *f* d'eau (pour déséchouer les bateaux envasés); (*b*) réservoir d'eau (ménagé dans une rivière). **5.** *Mil:* écusson *m.*

flash[2], *a. F:* **1.** = FLASHY. **2.** *A:* (*a*) bien éveillé, rusé, fin; (*b*) **f. gentry,** les filous *m,* les escrocs *m;* la haute pègre; **f. language,** argot *m* des voleurs.

flash[3], *v.*

I. *v.i.* (*a*) (*of fire, light, eyes, etc.*) jeter des éclairs; jeter une lueur; lancer des étincelles; flamboyer; (*of diamonds, etc.*) éclater, briller, étinceler; (*of lake, armour, etc.*) miroiter; (*of beacon, signal lamp, etc.*) **to f. in sequence,** émettre, jeter, des éclats successifs, des éclairs consécutifs; **his eyes flashed with anger,** ses yeux lançaient des éclairs de colère; ses yeux étincelaient, flamboyaient, de colère; la colère éclatait dans ses regards; *with cogn.acc.* **his eyes flashed fire,** ses yeux ont jeté des éclairs; *A:* (*of gun*) **to f. in the pan,** faire long feu; (*b*) **to f. past,** passer comme un éclair; **the thought flashed through my mind,** cette pensée traversa mon esprit comme un éclair; **it flashed across my mind that . . .,** l'idée m'est venue tout d'un coup que . . ..

II. *v.tr.* **1.** (*a*) faire flamboyer (un sabre, etc.); faire étinceler (ses bijoux); (*b*) projeter; **to f. a beam of light on sth.,** projeter un rayon de lumière sur qch.; **to f. a light in s.o.'s eyes,** diriger un jet de lumière dans les yeux de qn; *Cin:* **to f. a portrait, etc., on the screen,** projeter un portrait, etc., sur l'écran; **he flashed a glance of hatred at me,** il a dardé sur moi un regard chargé de haine; **to f. back defiance,** riposter par un défi; **"leave me alone," she flashed (out),** "laissez-moi," dit-elle brusquement; (*c*) **to f. a piece of news all over Europe,** répandre une nouvelle en éclair à travers l'Europe. **2.** *Glassm:* (*a*) plaquer; **flashed glass,** verre plaqué; (*b*) étendre (le verre) en feuilles. **3.** *El:* nourrir, carburer (le filament d'une lampe). **4.** *Hyd.E:* (*of water, pers.*) **to f. a river,** donner une chasse à une rivière.

III. (*compound verbs*) **1. flash back,** *v.i.* (*of gas stove, etc.*) avoir un retour de flamme.

2. flash over, *v.i. El:* (*of conductor, etc.*) cracher, faire jaillir, des étincelles.

flash[4], *v.tr. Const:* chaperonner (un assemblage).

flashback ['flæʃbæk], *s.* **1.** retour *m* de flamme; *El:* arc *m* en retour. **2.** *Cin: etc:* retour en arrière; scène rétrospective, flash-back *m;* **a f. to prewar days,** un coup d'œil rétrospectif sur les années d'avant-guerre.

flashboard ['flæʃbɔːd], *s. Hyd.E:* (*of dam, sluice gate, etc.*) hausse *f,* batardeau *m* mobile.

flashed [flæʃt], *a. Const:* (joint) chaperonné; (joint) à rejéteau.

flasher ['flæʃər], *s.* dispositif *m* d'éclairage intermittent; éclipseur *m;* signalisateur *m;* clignotant *m.*

flashgun ['flæʃgʌn], *s.* (*a*) projecteur *m* de signalisation à main; (*b*) *Phot:* flash *m, pl* flashes.

flashily ['flæʃili], *adv.* **f. dressed,** à toilette tapageuse.

flashiness ['flæʃinis], *s.* (*of speech*) éclat superficiel, faux brillant; (*of dress*) ton tapageur.

flashing[1] ['flæʃiŋ], *a.* (*of sword, torch, gem, etc.*) éclatant, flamboyant; (*of armour, etc.*) miroitant; **f. eyes,** yeux étincelants; **f. light,** feu *m,* signal *m,* clignotant, à éclats; phare *m* à éclats, à occultation, à feu tournant; **f. lamp,** lampe *f* à éclairs, projecteur *m* de signalisation; **f. beacon,** balise *f,* phare, à éclats, à occultation.

flashing[2], *s.* **1.** flamboiement *m* (du feu); éclat *m,* étincellement *m* (d'un diamant); miroitement *m* (d'un miroir à alouettes, etc.); clignotement *m* (d'un signal); **f. point** = FLASHPOINT. **2.** projection *f* (d'un rayon de lumière). **3.** *Glassm:* (*a*) placage *m;* (*b*) étalage *m* en feuilles. **4.** *El:* nourrissage *m,* carburation *f* (du filament). **5.** *Hyd.E:* ouverture *f* des écluses.

flashing[3], *s.* (*a*) *Const:* (i) pose *f* du chaperon; (ii) chaperon; bande *f* de solin; **f.-board, -moulding,** reverseau *m;* rejéteau *m,* rejetteau *m;* jet *m* d'eau; (*b*) *Plumb:* noquet *m;* noue *f.*

flashlamp ['flæʃlæmp], *s.* **1.** lanterne *f,* projecteur *m,* de signalisation. **2.** torche *f* (électrique); lampe *f* de poche.

flashlight ['flæʃlait], *s.* **1.** (*of lighthouse, etc.*) feu *m* à éclats. **2.** *Phot:* ampoule *f* de flash; **f. photography,** prise *f* de vues au flash. **3.** torche *f* (électrique); lampe *f* de poche.

flashover ['flæʃouvər], *s. El:* amorçage *m;* contournement *m* (de l'étincelle); étincelle *f* de rupture; court-circuit *m* (*pl.* courts-circuits) avec jaillissement d'étincelles; **f. voltage,** tension *f* (i) d'arc, (ii) de contournement.

flashpoint ['flæʃpɔint], *s.* **1.** (*of an oil fuel, etc.*) point *m* d'éclair, d'inflammabilité, d'inflammation; point de combustion, d'ignition. **2.** *Fig:* situation explosive, (extrêmement) critique.

flashtube ['flæʃtjuːb], *s. Phot:* flash *m* (*pl.* flashes) électronique.

flashy ['flæʃi], *a.* d'un faux brillant; voyant, éclatant, tapageur, -euse, clinquant; **f. young man, young woman,** jeune homme, jeune femme, à toilette tapageuse, d'un chic douteux; **it's very f.,** c'est du tape-à-l'œil.

flask [flɑːsk], *s.* **1.** (*a*) flacon *m;* gourde *f;* **brandy f.,** flacon à cognac; **vacuum f.,** bouteille isolante; **Florence f.,** fiasque *f;* (*b*) *Ch:* (i) fiole *f;* (ii) ballon *m;* **flat-bottomed f.,** ballon à fond plat; **volumetric f.,** fiole jaugée; **filter f.,** fiole à vide; **Dumas's f.,** ampoule *f* de Dumas. **2.** *Arm: A:* **(powder) f.,** poire *f,* flasque *f,* cornet *m,* à poudre. **3.** *Metall:* châssis *m* (de moulage).

flat[1] [flæt], *a., adv., & s.*

I. *a.* **1.** (*a*) plat; horizontal, -aux; posé à plat; **f. roof,** toit plat, toit en terrasse; **f. desk,** pupitre plat; *Golf:* **f. club,** crosse *f* à face très renversée; *Needlew:* **f. seam,** couture rabattue; *Med:* **f. feet,** pieds plats; (*b*) (*of curve, etc.*) aplati; *Arch:* **f. arch,** voûte plate; arc déprimé; *Ball:* **f. trajectory,** trajectoire rasante, tendue; *Av:* **f. approach,** approche basse; **f. dive, glide,** descente *f* en piqué, en plané, sous angle faible; **f. spin,** vrille *f* à plat; *Golf:* **f. swing,** ballant horizontal; (*c*) (*of surface*) plat, uni, plan, méplat; **f. country,** pays plat; pays de plaine; **f. coast,** côte basse; **f. side of a sword,** plat *m* d'un sabre; **f. iron,** fer méplat; **f. iron bar,** fer méplat, plat *m* de fer; **f. chest,** poitrine plate; **f. nose,** nez épaté, aplati, camus; **f. tyre,** pneu dégonflé, à plat; pneu crevé; **to wear a surface f.,** araser une surface; **to make, beat, sth. f.,** aplatir qch.; *Turf:* **f. racing,** le plat; **f. race,** course plate, de plat; *Bookb:* **f. sheets,** feuilles *f* à plat; **f. back,** (i) dos plat; (ii) livre *m* à dos plat; *Opt:* **f. field,** champ plan; *Mth:* **f. projection,** (plan) géométral *m;* *F:* **as f. as a pancake,** plat comme une galette, comme une punaise; (*d*) (*of picture*) sans relief; **f. tint,** teinte plate, *Engr:* aplat *m;* (*e*) *I.C.E:* **f. spot,** point mort, trou *m* (dans la carburation); (*f*) *Paint:* **f. surface, colour,** surface mate, couleur mate; **f. patch,** embu *m;* (*of paint*) **to become f.,** s'emboire. **2.** net, *f.* nette, positif; **f. denial,** dénégation formelle; démenti formel, absolu, direct; **f. refusal,** refus net, catégorique, absolu; **to give a f. refusal,** refuser net; **that is f. heresy,** c'est de l'hérésie pure; **rule that is in f. opposition to practice,** règle qui est nettement en opposition avec la pratique; *F:* **that's f.!** voilà qui est net! qui est clair! mettez ça dans votre poche! **3.** (*a*) (*of existence, etc.*) monotone, ennuyeux, veule; (*of style, conversation, etc.*) fade, terne, insipide; (*of pers.*) ennuyeux, stupide; **f. voice,** voix terne, blanche; **yesterday was a f. day,** la journée d'hier a été ennuyeuse; **I was feeling a bit f.,** je n'étais pas dans mon assiette; je me sentais un peu las; je me sentais déprimé, à plat; *Com:* **f. market,** marché calme, languissant; *Nau:* **f. calm,** calme plat; (*b*) (*of drink*) éventé, plat; qui a un goût d'évent, un goût évaporé; **f. wine,** vin mou; (*c*) **f. battery,** accumulateur à plat. **4.** invariable, uniforme; **f. rate,** taux *m,* tarif *m,* unique, uniforme; **f. rate of pay,** taux uniforme de salaires; **f.-rate subscription,** abonnement *m* à forfait; **f. price,** prix unique; *U.S:* **f. quotation,** cotation *f* sans intérêts. **5.** (*a*) (son, etc.) sourd; (*b*) *Mus:* (i) bémol *inv;* **symphony in D f.,** symphonie *f* en ré bémol; (ii) **you're f.,** vous chantez, jouez, en dessous du ton. **6.** *Gram:* **f. adverb,** adverbe *m* de la même forme que l'adjectif correspondant.

II. *adv.* **1.** à plat; dans une position horizontale; **to fall f. on one's face,** tomber, se jeter, à plat ventre; **to fall f. on one's back,** tomber sur le dos; **lying, stretched, f. on the ground,** couché, étendu, à plat sur le sol; **to place sth. f. against a wall,** mettre qch. à plat contre un mur; **stones laid f.,** pierres *f* à plat; **the blow laid him f.,** le coup l'a terrassé. **2.** (*a*) nettement, positivement; *F:* **he told me f. that. . .,** il m'a dit carrément que. . .; **to be f. broke,** être à sec, sans le sou; (*b*) **to work f. out,** travailler d'arrache-pied; *Aut: etc:* **to go f. out,** filer à toute allure. **3. to fall f.,** (i) (*of joke, etc.*) rater, manquer son effet; tomber à plat; (ii) (*of play, etc.*) faire four. **4.** *Mus:* (chanter, etc.) en dessous du ton.

III. *s.* **1.** (*a*) plat *m* (d'un sabre, etc.); **the f. of the hand,** l'avant-main *m;* **blow with the f. of the hand,** coup donné avec la main plate; **f. of an anvil,** aire *f* d'une enclume; *Const:* **f. of a roof,** plate-forme *f, pl.* plates-formes; **to wear a f. on a wheel,** aplatir par l'usage une section de la jante d'une roue; **screw-thread f.,** troncature *f* de filet; *Art:* **on the f.,** sur papier, sur toile; (*b*) **optical f.,** plan *m* optique. **2.** (*a*) plaine *f;* pays plat; bas-fond *m, pl.* bas-fonds; marécage *m;* (*b*) *Oc:* basse *f,* bas-fond; (*left exposed at low tide*) sèche *f,* platin *m.* **3.** (*horizontal*) (*a*) **to cast a pipe on the f.,** couler un tuyau horizontalement; *Rail:* **track on the f.,** voie *f* en palier; *Rac:* **on the f.,** sur le plat; (*b*) *Turf:* **the f.,** la saison du plat; (*c*) *Min:* plateure *f.* **4.** (*a*) *A:* étage *m* (d'une maison); (*b*) appartement *m;* **furnished, unfurnished, f.,** appartement meublé, non meublé; **service f.,** appartement avec service; **block of flats,** maison *f* de rapport, immeuble (divisé en appartements). **5.** (*a*) *Nau.* bateau plat; plate *f;* (*b*) (*basket*) calais *m;* (*c*) *Th:* châssis *m;*

ferme *f*; paroi *f* (d'une scène); **the flats,** les fermes; les coulisses *f*; **to join the flats of . . .,** raccorder les parties de . . .; (*d*) (*of cinema studio*) décor, panneau, insonorisé. **6.** (*a*) *Artil:* pan *m* de canon; (*b*) *Veh:* pan latéral (de carrosserie). **7.** *N.Arch:* varangue *f* de fond; **in the flats,** à fond de cale. **8.** *Mus:* bémol *m*. **9.** (*a*) *F:* pneu dégonflé, à plat; pneu crevé; (*b*) *P:* individu *m* bête; idiot, -ote; nouille *f*.

flat[3], *v.tr.* **(flatted) 1.** aplatir (une barre de métal, etc.); laminer, écacher (le fil de fer, etc.). **2.** amortir, amatir, rendre mat (une surface, une couleur, etc.); **to f. down the paint,** poncer les apprêts. **3.** *NAm: Mus:* bémoliser (une note).

flatbill ['flætbil], *s. Orn:* (*a*) todier *m* (des Antilles); (*b*) platyrhynque *m*.

flatboat ['flætbout], *s. Nau:* bateau plat; plate *f*.

flat-bottomed ['flæt'bɔtəmd], *a.* (bateau) ras, à fond plat; (rail *m*) à patin, à base plate.

flatcar ['flætkɑ:r], *s. NAm: Rail:* wagon *m* en plate-forme.

flat-coated ['flæt'koutid], *a.* (chien *m*, etc.) à poil ras.

flatfish ['flætfiʃ], *s. Ich:* pleuronecte *m*; poisson plat.

flatfoot ['flætfut], *s.* **1.** *Med:* pied plat. **2.** *F:* agent *m* de police, flic *m*, pied-plat *m*, *pl.* pieds-plats.

flat-footed ['flæt'futid], *a.* **1.** à pied plat, aux pieds plats. **2.** *NAm: F:* (*a*) (*of answer, etc.*) franc, *f.* franche; carré; brutal, -aux; **f.-f. refusal,** refus absolu, catégorique, brutal; (*b*) *adv.* **he refused f.-f.,** il a refusé catégoriquement, net. **3.** *F:* bête, stupide, lourdaud. **4.** *F:* **to catch s.o. f.-f.,** prendre qn en flagrant délit, la main dans le sac.

Flathead ['flæthed], *s.* **1.** *Ethn:* Tête-plate *m*, *pl.* Têtes-plates (de l'Amérique du Nord). **2.** *F:* individu *m* bête; idiot, -ote, nouille *f*.

flat-headed ['flæt'hedid], *a.* (*a*) (*of pers., nail, etc.*) à tête plate; *Z:* **f. cat,** chat *m* à tête plate; (*b*) *F:* (*of pers.*) bête, stupide, bas de plafond.

flatiron ['flætaiən], *s.* fer *m* à repasser.

flatlet ['flætlit], *s.* petit appartement; studio *m*.

flatly ['flætli], *adv.* **1.** (*a*) à plat; **f. arched,** à arc déprimé; (*b*) *Art:* **to paint f.,** peindre sans relief. **2.** nettement, carrément; **to deny sth. f.,** nier absolument qch.; **to refuse f.,** refuser carrément, tout sec, tout net; **he f. refused to fall in with my wishes,** il a opposé un refus absolu à mes désirs; **f. opposed,** en contradiction directe. **3.** d'une façon monotone, sans intérêt; platement; **she droned on f. about her misfortunes,** elle racontait ses malheurs d'une voix monotone.

flatmate ['flætmeit], *s.* colocataire *mf* (d'un appartement).

flatness ['flætnis], *s.* **1.** égalité *f*, nature plate (d'une surface, etc.); égalité de surface; *Art:* manque *m* de relief: *Opt: Phot:* **f. of the field,** absence *f* de distorsion du champ. **2.** aplatissement *m* (d'une courbe, etc.); *Ball:* tension *f* (de la trajectoire). **3.** netteté *f* (d'un refus). **4.** (*a*) monotonie *f* (de l'existence, etc.); engourdissement *m*, langueur *f* (du marché, etc.); platitude *f*, insipidité *f* (du style, etc.); (*b*) (*of beer, etc.*) évent *m*. **5.** (*of paint, painting*) embu *m*.

flat-nosed ['flætnouzd], *a.* au nez épaté, camard, camus.

flatted ['flætid], *a.* **1.** aplati, laminé, écaché. **2.** (*of pigment, surface*) mat.

flatten ['flætn], *v.* **(flattened) 1.** *v.tr.* (*a*) **to f. (down, out),** aplatir, aplanir (qch.); *Metalw:* laminer, écacher (le fil de fer, etc.); *Needlew:* **to f. out a seam,** aplatir un surjet; rabattre une couture; **to f. the end of a rod,** former des méplats *m* à l'extrémité d'une tige; **to f. a piece on one side,** pratiquer un plat sur un côté d'une pièce; **to f. the head of the needles,** palmer les aiguilles; **to f. curled prints,** redresser des épreuves gondolées; **to f. oneself against a wall,** se plaquer, se coller, contre un mur; *F:* **to f. s.o.,** aplatir, écraser, déconcerter qn; remettre qn à sa place; (*b*) *Nau:* **to f. (in) a sail,** border plat une voile; (*c*) rendre (qch.) fade, insipide; éventer (une boisson); (*d*) *Mus:* bémoliser (une note); (*e*) rendre mat; amatir, amortir (une couleur, une couche de peinture). **2.** *v.i.* (*a*) s'aplatir, s'aplanir; *Mec.E: etc:* **to f. under load,** s'affaisser, s'aplatir, s'écraser, en charge; (*b*) devenir fade, insipide; s'affadir; (*of wine, etc.*) s'éventer; (*c*) *Av:* **to f. out,** (i) se redresser (après un vol piqué); reprendre le vol horizontal; (ii) allonger le vol.

flattened ['flætənd], *a.* **1.** (*a*) aplati, aplani; **f. end (of rod, etc.),** méplat *m* (d'une tige, etc.); **f. nose,** nez épaté, écaché; (*b*) (pneu, etc.) mis à plat. **2.** déprimé; **f. arch,** voûte déprimée, surbaissée. **3.** *Mus:* **f. note,** note bémolisée.

flattener ['flætnər], *s.* **1.** aplatisseur, -euse. **2.** *Tls:* chasse *f* à parer. **3.** *F:* coup *m* d'assommoir, knock-out *m*.

flattening ['flæt(ə)niŋ], *s.* **1.** (*a*) aplatissement *m*, aplatissage *m* (d'une courbe, d'un pneu, etc.); affaissement *m*, écrasement *m* (en charge); laminage *m*, écachement *m* (du fil de fer, etc.); redressement *m* (d'une épreuve gondolée); (*b*) éventement (d'une boisson); (*c*) amortissement *m* (d'une couleur). **2.** *Av:* **f. out (after dive),** ressource *f*, redressement *m*.

flatter[1] ['flætər], *s. Tls:* chasse *f* à parer; paroir *m*, aplatissoir *m*; **counter f.,** sous-chasse *f*, *pl.* sous-chasses.

flatter[2], *v.tr.* **1.** flatter (qn); **to f. s.o.'s vanity,** flatter, caresser, la vanité de qn; **portrait that flatters the sitter,** portrait qui flatte le modèle; **to f. oneself on one's cleverness, on being clever,** se flatter de son habileté, d'être habile; **he flatters himself that he will succeed,** il se flatte de réussir; **he flatters himself that we shall need him,** il se flatte qu'on aura besoin de lui; **to f. oneself with hopes of success,** nourrir, se bercer de, l'espoir de réussir. **2.** *Lit:* charmer, flatter (les yeux, l'oreille); **music that flatters the ear,** musique qui flatte, chatouille, l'oreille.

flatterer ['flætərər], *s.* flatteur, -euse; adulateur, -trice; flagorneur, -euse.

flattering[1] ['flæt(ə)riŋ], *a.* (*of words, portrait, etc.*) flatteur, -euse; (*exaggerated*) adulatoire, flagorneur, -euse; **to speak in f. terms of s.o., to make f. remarks about s.o.,** parler de qn en termes flatteurs; faire l'éloge de qn; se montrer élogieux à l'égard de qn; **to draw a f. portrait of s.o.,** tracer un portrait flatté de qn; flatter le portrait de qn.

flattering[2], *s.* = FLATTERY.

flatteringly ['flæt(ə)riŋli], *adv.* flatteusement; en termes flatteurs; **to speak f. of s.o., of sth.,** faire l'éloge de qn, de qch.; parler de qn, de qch., en termes flatteurs, élogieux.

flattery ['flætəri], *s.* flatterie *f*; (*exaggerated*) adulation *f*, flagornerie *f*.

flattie ['flæti], *s. F:* agent *m* de police, flic *m*, pied-plat *m*, *pl.* pieds-plats.

flatting ['flætiŋ], *s.* **1.** (*a*) *Metalw:* aplatissement *m*, aplatissage *m*, laminage *m*; **f. hammer,** aplatissoir *m*; **f. mill,** laminoir *m*, aplatissoir; (*b*) (*in coachwork*) **f. down,** ponçage *m* des apprêts. **2.** (*a*) *Const:* couche *f* de mortier, de ciment; (*b*) vernis mat.

flat-top ['flæt'tɔp]. **1.** *a.* (*a*) *Ph: etc:* **f.-t. rays,** rayons *m* en nappe; *Elcs:* **f.-t. antenna,** antenne *f*, aérien *m*, en nappe; (*b*) *Civ.E:* **f.-t. culvert,** dalot *m*. **2.** *s. F:* (*a*) *U.S:* porte-avions *m inv*; (*b*) *NAm: Hairdr:* coupe *f* en brosse.

flat-twin ['flæt'twin], *a.* (*a*) *I.C.E:* (moteur *m*) à deux cylindres opposés; (*b*) *El:* (fil *m*) deux conducteurs avec enveloppe isolante commune méplate.

flatulence, flatulency ['flætjuləns, -lənsi], *s.* **1.** *Med:* flatulence *f*, flatuosité *f*, ventosité *f*; ballonnement *m* (de l'estomac); fermentation gastro-intestinale; météorisation *f*; **to suffer from f.,** avoir des vents. **2.** (*a*) prétention *f*, vanité *f*; (*b*) emphase *f*, boursouflure *f* (de style, etc.).

flatulent ['flætjulənt], *a.* **1.** *Med:* (*of disease, pers., etc.*) flatulent; (*of food*) flatueux; **to make f.,** météoriser (l'abdomen). **2.** (*a*) bouffi d'orgueil; (*b*) (style) emphatique, boursouflé.

flatus ['fleitəs], *s. Med:* flatuosité *f*.

flatware ['flætwɛər], *s.* (*a*) vaisselle plate; (*b*) coutellerie *f*.

flatways, flatwise ['flætweiz, -waiz], *adv.* à plat.

flatwoods ['flætwudz], *s.pl. U.S:* bas-fonds boisés.

flatworm ['flætwə:m], *s. Ann:* planaire *f*.

flat-wound ['flæt'waund], *a. El:* enroulé, bobiné, à plat.

flaunt [flɔ:nt]. **1.** *v.i.* (*a*) *O: & Lit:* (*of flag, plume, etc.*) flotter (fièrement); (*b*) (*of pers.*) parader, se pavaner, s'afficher. **2.** *v.tr.* étaler, afficher, faire parade de (sa richesse, une passion, etc.); **to f. one's wealth,** faire montre, faire étalage, de son opulence; étaler tout son luxe; *F:* éclabousser le monde de son luxe; **to f. advanced opinions,** arborer, afficher, des opinions avancées; **to f. an action,** faire qch. à la barbe des gens. **3.** *v.tr. U.S:* faire fi de (l'autorité de qn); se moquer (d'un ordre).

flaunting[1] ['flɔ:ntiŋ], *a.* **1.** *O:* (drapeau, etc.) flottant au vent. **2.** (*of pers., etc.*) ostentateur, -trice; (*of dress, etc.*) tapageur, -euse, voyant; **f. air,** air *m* de bravade.

flaunting[2], *s.* étalage *m*, affichage *m* (de richesses, d'opinions).

flautist ['flɔ:tist], *s. Mus:* flûtiste *mf*.

flavanone ['fleivənoun], *s. Ch:* flavanone *f*.

flavanthrene, flavanthrone ['fleivənθri:n, -θroun], *s. Ch:* flavanthrène *m*.

flavescence [flei'ves(ə)ns], *s. Vit: etc:* flavescence *f*.

flavescent [flei'ves(ə)nt], *a.* (blé, etc.) flavescent, qui tourne au jaune.

Flavian ['fleiviən], *Pr.n.m.* Flavien.

flavin ['fleivin], *s. Ch:* flavine *f*.

flavone ['fleivoun], *s. Ch:* flavone *f*.

flavonol ['fleivənɔl], *s. Ch:* flavonol *m*.

flavoprotein [fleivou'prouti:n], *s. Bio-Ch:* protéoflavine *f*.

flavopurpurin [fleivou'pə:pərin], *s. Ch:* flavopurpurine *f*.

flavour[1] ['fleivər], *s.* saveur *f*; goût *m*; (*of meat, etc.*) fumet *m*; (*of wine*) bouquet *m*; parfum *m*; (*of tea, etc.*) arôme *m*; (*of ice cream, etc.*) parfum; **the cinnamon has lost its f.,** la cannelle s'est affadie; **his stories have a f. of the sea,** ses histoires ont toute l'atmosphère de la mer; **his attitude has an unpleasant f.,** son attitude a une saveur désagréable.

flavour[2], *v.tr.* assaisonner, aromatiser, parfumer, donner du goût à (un mets, etc.); **flavoured with garlic,** assaisonné d'ail; **to f. a sauce with garlic,** relever une sauce avec de l'ail; **to f. a dish with lemon,** parfumer, relever, un plat d'un filet de citron; **vanilla flavoured,** (parfumé) à la vanille.

flavouring ['fleivəriŋ], *s.* **1.** assaisonnement *m* (d'un mets). **2.** assaisonnement, condiment *m*, parfum *m*; **flavourings for soups,** aromes *m* pour potages.

flavourless ['fleivəlis], *a.* (*of food, etc.*) sans saveur; fade, insipide; (*of wine*) plat.

flavoursome ['fleivəsəm], *a.* (*of food*) savoureux.

flaw[1] [flɔ:], *s.* rafale *f*; *Nau:* grain *m*.

flaw[2], *s.* **1.** (*a*) (*in article, material, etc.*) défaut *m*, défectuosité *f*, imperfection *f*; (*in timber*) flache *f*; (*in nap of cloth, etc.*) mâchure *f*; (*in garment*) claire *f*; (*in gem*) glaire *f*, glace *f*, jardinage *m*, paillette *f*, crapaud *m*, gendarme *m*; (*in mirror*) accroc *m*; (*in metal*) paille *f*, soufflure *f*, crique *f*; (*in reputation, etc.*) flétrissure *f*, tache *f*; **f. in a scheme,** point *m* faible d'un projet; (*b*) (*in glass, china, etc.*) fêlure *f*; (*in wood, etc.*) fissure *f*, fente *f*, crevasse *f*; (*in metal*) brisure *f*. **2.** *Jur:* (*in document, title, etc.*) vice *m* de forme (entraînant la nullité).

flaw[3]. **1.** *v.tr.* endommager, défigurer; fêler. **2.** *v.i.* se fêler; se fendre.

flawed [flɔ:d], *a.* (*of article, etc.*) défectueux; (*of timber*) gercé; (*of iron*) pailleux; **f. diamond,** diamant *m* qui a un crapaud.

flawless ['flɔ:lis], *a.* sans défaut, sans imperfection; parfait; **f. technique,** technique *f* impeccable.

flawlessly ['flɔ:lisli], *adv.* parfaitement; sans défauts, sans imperfections.

flawlessness ['flɔ:lisnis], *s.* perfection *f* (d'un article, etc.).

flawn [flɔ:n], *s. Cu: A:* (*a*) flan *m*; (*b*) crêpe *f*.

flawy ['flɔ:i], *a.* (*of article, material, etc.*) plein de défauts; (*of iron*) pailleux, paillé; (*of diamond*) gendarmeux; *Metall:* **f. steel,** acier cendreux.

flax [flæks], *s.* (*a*) *Bot:* lin *m*; **New Zealand f., f. lily,** phormium *m*; chanvre *m*, lin, de la Nouvelle-Zélande; **mountain f.,** (i) (*also* **purging f.**) lin purgatif; (ii) *Miner:* amiante *f*; liège *m*, cuir *m*, fossile, de montagne; **spurge f.,** sainbois *m*, garou *m*; **false f.,** lin bâtard, caméline *f*; **f. seed,** (i) graine *f* de lin; linette *f*; (ii) *U.S: Ent:* pupe *f* de la cécidomyie destructrice; **f. field,** linière *f*; **f. blue,** bleu de lin; (*b*) *Tex:* **f. trade,** commerce *m* du lin; **f. dressing,** préparation *f*, peignage *m*, affinage *m*, du lin; drégeage *m*; **f. dresser,** filassier, -ière; racleur, -euse, de lin; **f. dresser's knife,** racloir *m* à lin.

flax-coloured ['flækskʌləd], *a.* couleur de lin *inv*.

flaxcomb ['flækskoum], *s. Tex:* peigne *m* pour lin; drège *f*, séran *m*, sérançoir *m*.

flaxen ['flæks(ə)n], *a.* **1.** (toile *f*, etc.) de lin. **2.** (*of hair*) blond de lin *inv*; blond filasse *inv*; couleur de chanvre, d'étoupe *inv*.

flay [flei], *v.tr.* **1.** (*a*) écorcher (un animal, etc.); dépouiller (un animal); découenner (un porc); **to be flayed alive,** être écorché vif; (*b*) *F:* fouetter, rosser, étriller (qn); **the critics flayed him,** les critiques l'ont éreinté; (*c*) *F: O:* (*of shopkeeper*) écorcher, saler (un client). **2.** enlever (la peau, l'écorce d'un arbre, le gazon, etc.).

flayer ['fleiər], *s.* (*pers.*) écorcheur *m*.

flaying ['fleiiŋ], *s.* écorchement *m*, dépouillement *m*, découennage *m*.

flea [fli:], *s.* **1.** *Ent:* puce *f*; **water f.,** puce d'eau; **f. beetle,** puce terrestre, de terre; altise *f*, tiquet *m*; *Crust:* **sand f., beach f.,** crevettine *f*. **2.** *Av: F: A:* **flying f.,** pou *m* du ciel. **3.** *F:* **f. market,** marché *m* aux puces.

fleabag ['fli:bæg], *s. P:* (*a*) pucier *m* ((i) lit *m*; (ii) sac *m* de couchage); (*b*) (*pers.*) pouilleux, -euse; (*domestic animal*) sac *m* à puces; (*c*) *U.S:* chambre pouilleuse; hôtel pouilleux.

fleabane ['fli:bein], *s. Bot:* **1.** pulicaire *f*. **2.** érigéron *m*, *F:* vergerette *f*; **f. oil,** essence *f* d'érigéron. **3.** = FLEAWORT, 1, 2.

fleabite ['fli:bait], *s.* **1.** morsure *f* de puce. **2.** *F:* (*mere* *trifle*) vétille *f*, bagatelle *f*, rien *m*; dommage *m* sans importance; tâche *f* qui n'offre aucune difficulté **3.** (*on horse's coat*) moucheture *f*, truiture *f*.

fleabitten ['fli:bitn], *a.* **1.** (*of pers.*) mordu par les puces. **2.** (*of horse's coat*) moucheté, truité; **f. horse,** étourneau *m*; **f. grey,** gris truité, moucheté.

fleadock ['fli:dɔk], *s. Bot:* pétasite *m*; *F:* herbe *f* aux teigneux.

fleam [fli:m], *s. Vet:* flamme *f* (pour saignées).

fleapit ['fli:pit], *s. P:* cinéma, etc., pouilleux.

fleatrap ['fli:træp], *s. P:* (*a*) taudis pouilleux; nid *m*, trou *m*, à puces; (*b*) cinéma, etc., pouilleux.

fleawort ['fli:wə:t], *s. Bot:* **1.** plantain *m* pulicaire; herbe *f* aux puces; pucier *m*. **2.** conyse *f*, herbe aux puces. **3. marsh f.,** seneçon *m* des marais.

flèche [flɛʃ], *s. Games:* (*backgammon*) flèche *f*.

fleck[1] [flek], *s.* **1.** petite tache (de rousseur, de lumière, etc.); goutte *f*, moucheture *f* (de couleur). **2.** particule *f* (de poussière, etc.); **f. of cloud,** diablotin *m*.

fleck[2], *v.tr.* tacheter, moucheter (qch.) (**with,** de); **glass flecked with gold,** verre sablé d'or; **hair flecked with grey,** cheveux *m* qui commencent à grisonner; **sky flecked with clouds,** ciel pommelé; *Tex:* **flecked material,** tissu moucheté; **the meadow was flecked with daisies,** des pâquerettes *f* émaillaient le pré.

flecking ['flekiŋ], *s.* mouchetures *fpl* (d'une fourrure, etc.).

fledge [fledʒ]. **1.** *v.i. Orn:* (*of birds*) s'emplumer. **2.** *v.tr.* élever (les jeunes oiseaux) jusqu'à ce qu'ils soient en état de voler. **3.** *v.tr.* empenner (une flèche).

fledged [fledʒd], *a.* (oiseau) qui a toutes ses plumes; *F:* **he's a fully-f. doctor now,** il est docteur en titre; il a tous ses diplômes.

fledg(e)ling ['fledʒliŋ], *s.* **1.** oisillon *m*. **2.** novice *mf*; **f. poet,** poète *m* en herbe.

flee [fli:], *v.* (**fled** [fled]; **fled**) **1.** *v.i.* (*a*) (*of pers.*) fuir, s'enfuir, se sauver, prendre la fuite; **to f. from a place,** s'enfuir d'un endroit; **to f. to s.o., to America,** se sauver, se réfugier, auprès de qn, en Amérique; *Lit:* **leaves fleeing before the wind,** feuilles chassées par le vent; (*b*) fuir; **time was fleeing (away),** le temps passait, s'écoulait, vite; le temps fuyait. **2.** *v.tr.* s'enfuir de (qn, la ville, etc.); fuir, éviter (la tentation, etc.).

fleece[1] [fli:s], *s.* **1.** toison *f*; *Husb:* **f. washing,** lavage *m* (de la laine) à dos; **f.-washed wool,** laine lavée à dos; *Lit:* **the Golden F.,** la Toison d'or; *Hist:* **the Order of the Golden F.,** l'ordre de la Toison (d'or). **2.** nuages ouatés; moutonnement *m* de nuages. **3.** *Tex:* (*a*) (*carding*) nappe *f*; (*b*) molleton *m*; **f. lining,** doublure *f* de molleton.

fleece[2], *v.tr.* **1.** *occ:* tondre (les moutons). **2.** *F:* tondre, écorcher, gruger, estamper, ratiboiser, entôler, égorger, plumer (qn); faire le poil à (qn); avoir du poil de (qn); rançonner (un client); **I have been fleeced,** je me suis fait échauder; j'ai essuyé le coup de fusil; **to allow oneself to be fleeced,** se laisser tondre la laine sur le dos.

fleeced [fli:st], *a.* pourvu, couvert, d'une toison; **golden-f.,** à la toison d'or; *Lit:* **plain f. with snow,** plaine couverte d'un manteau de neige.

fleecer ['fli:sər], *s. F:* écorcheur, -euse.

fleecing ['fli:siŋ], *s. F:* écorcherie *f*, grugerie *f*, plumée *f*, estampage *m*; **grown rich by f.,** enrichi de, par, ses rapines.

fleecy ['fli:si], *a.* (*of wool*) floconneux; (*of hair, material, etc.*) laineux; (*of cloud*) moutonné, cotonneux, ouaté; **f. waves,** vagues moutonnantes, moutonnées.

fleed [fli:d], *s. Cu:* lard *m* (de porc).

fleeing[1] ['fli:iŋ], *a.* (*of army, years, etc.*) en fuite.

fleeing[2], *s.* fuite *f*.

fleer[1] [fliər], *s. A:* grimace (moqueuse); ricanement *m*.

fleer[2], *v.i. A:* railler, se moquer, ricaner; **to f. at s.o.,** faire la grimace à qn; se moquer de qn; railler qn.

fleet[1] [fli:t], *s.* **1.** (*a*) *Navy:* flotte *f*; (*a naval unit*) escadre *f*; **the F.,** la Flotte (de guerre), l'armée *f* de la mer; = la Marine nationale; **the Atlantic F.,** l'escadre de l'Atlantique; **the Home F.,** la flotte métropolitaine, les escadres métropolitaines; **f. destroyer, f. escort,** destroyer *m*, escorteur *m*, d'escadre; **battle f.,** flotte de ligne, de combat; **the F. Air Arm** = l'Aéronavale *f*; (*b*) **merchant f.,** flotte de commerce, flotte marchande; **a fishing f.,** une flottille de pêche; **the fishing f.,** la flotte de pêche; **river f.,** (i) (*barges, etc.*) batellerie fluviale; (ii) (*passenger craft*) flotte fluviale. **2.** (*a*) **air f.,** flotte aérienne; (*b*) parc *m* (d'autobus, de voitures, de locomotives); **a f. of coaches took the tourists to their hotel,** une caravane de cars a amené les touristes à leur hôtel.

fleet[2], *a. Lit:* vite, leste, rapide; **f. of foot,** léger à la course; aux pieds légers, agiles; au pied léger.

fleet[3]. **1.** *v.i.* (*of time, thought, etc.*) passer rapidement; s'enfuir. **2.** *v.tr. Nau:* reprendre (un palan).

fleet[4], *s.* **1.** *A: & Dial:* ruisseau *m*; crique *f*; petit bras de mer. **2. the F.,** (*a*) nom d'un affluent de la Tamise à Londres; (*b*) *Hist:* la prison pour dettes (située au bord du Fleet); *A:* **F. marriage,** mariage clandestin célébré dans la prison du Fleet; **F. parson,** ecclésiastique véreux qui hantait les abords de la prison dans l'espoir d'être embauché pour célébrer un mariage. **3.** *Journ:* **F. Street,** la presse (du nom de la rue de Londres qui est le centre principal du journalisme).

fleet[5], *A: & Dial:* **1.** *a.* peu profond. **2.** *adv.* à peu de profondeur, près de la surface.

fleet-footed ['fli:t'futid], *a. Lit:* au pied léger.

fleeting ['fli:tiŋ], *a.* (*of shadow, time, etc.*) fugitif, fugace; (*of beauty, etc.*) passager; (*of happiness, etc.*) éphémère; **the f. years,** les années qui passent, qui s'envolent; **to pay s.o. a f. visit,** faire une courte visite à qn; *Mil: Navy:* **f. target,** but fugitif.

fleetingly ['fli:tiŋli], *adv.* fugitivement, rapidement, à la hâte.

fleetly ['fli:tli], *adv. Lit:* vite, lestement, rapidement.

fleetness ['fli:tnis], *s.* **1.** vitesse *f*, rapidité *f* (à la course). **2.** *Lit:* qualité *f* éphémère (du bonheur, etc.).

Fleming ['flemiŋ], *s. Geog:* Flamand, -ande.

Flemish ['flemiʃ]. **1.** *a.* flamand; *Nau:* **F. eye,** œil *m* à la flamande; **to make a F. coil,** lover une manœuvre en galette. **2.** *s. Ling:* flamand *m*.

flench [flenʃ], **flense** [flenz], *v.tr.* **1.** dépecer (une baleine). **2.** dépouiller, écorcher (un phoque).

flencher ['flenʃər], **flenser** ['flenzər], *s.* **1.** charpentier *m*, dépeceur *m* (de baleines). **2.** écorcheur *m* (de phoques).

flenching ['flenʃiŋ], **flensing** ['flenziŋ], *s.* **1.** dépeçage *m* (d'une baleine). **2.** écorchement *m* (d'un phoque).

flesh[1] [fleʃ], *s.* chair *f*; (*as a whole*) charnure *f*. **1.** (*a*) **to make s.o.'s f. creep, crawl,** donner la chair de poule à qn; horripiler qn; **to have firm f.,** avoir une charnure ferme; (*of animal*) **to be in f.,** être en chair; **to put on f.,** (*of animal*) prendre chair; (*of pers.*) grossir, devenir adipeux, prendre de l'embonpoint, du corps; **to lose f.,** maigrir, s'amaigrir, perdre son embonpoint; **he is losing f. every day,** il fond à vue d'œil; **f. wound,** blessure légère, en séton, dans les chairs; *Toil: O:* **f. brush, f. glove,** brosse *f*, gant *m*, à friction; **he exacts his pound of f. from his debtors,** il traite ses débiteurs en usurier; (*b*) *occ:* viande *f*; **f. diet,** alimentation carnée; *Ecc:* **to eat f.,** faire gras; *Ent:* **f. fly,** sarcophage *f*; mouche *f* carnaire, à viande; (*c*) chair (d'une pêche, d'un melon, etc.); (*d*) **f. (side) of a hide,** (côté *m*) chair d'une peau. **2. to mortify the f.,** mortifier, châtier, son corps; **to be of the f.,** être de chair; **it was he in the f.,** in **f. and blood,** c'était lui en chair et en os, en personne; **his own f. and blood,** la chair de sa chair; son propre sang; ses parents, les siens; *Lit:* **to take up arms against one's own f. and blood,** s'armer contre ses propres entrailles; **it is more than f. and blood can stand, can bear,** c'est plus que la nature humaine, que l'homme, ne saurait endurer; **the spirit is willing but the f. is weak,** l'esprit est prompt, mais la chair est faible, infirme, fragile; **to go the way of all f.,** payer sa dette à la nature; aller où va toute chose; **the sins of the f.,** le péché de chair; **the world, the f. and the devil,** le monde, le démon et la chair. **3. f. colour,** couleur *f* (de) chair; **f.-coloured,** (couleur) chair, carné; **f. pink,** (rose) incarnat (*m inv*); carné (*m*); *Th: etc:* **f. tights,** maillot *m* chair; *Art:* **f. tints,** carnations *f*, chairs.

flesh[2], *v.tr.* **1.** (*a*) *Ven:* **to f. the dogs,** acharner les chiens; mettre les chiens en curée; faire curée; (*b*) donner le goût du sang à (un chien, etc.); (*c*) *Lit:* donner le baptême du sang à (des troupes, son épée); étrenner (son épée). **2.** *Lit:* assouvir, rassasier (sa vengeance, ses passions, etc.). **3.** (*a*) engraisser (un animal); (*b*) *v.i.* engraisser, prendre de l'embonpoint, du corps. **4.** *Leath:* écharner, drayer, trancher (les peaux).

flesher ['fleʃər], *s. Leath:* **1.** (*pers.*) écharneur *m*. **2.** *Tls:* cornette *f*.

fleshiness ['fleʃinis], *s.* état charnu (du corps, du nez, etc.); empâtement *m* des chairs; embonpoint *m*.

fleshing ['fleʃiŋ], *s.* **1.** *Leath:* écharnage *m*, drayage *m* (des peaux); **f. iron,** drayoire *f*; **f. knife,** écharnoir *m*, tranchant *m*; **f. machine,** écharneuse *f*, machine *f* à écharner. **2.** *pl.* **fleshings,** (*a*) *Leath:* chair *f* (d'une peau); (*b*) *Th: etc: O:* maillot *m* chair.

fleshless ['fleʃlis], *a.* (os, etc.) décharné.

fleshliness ['fleʃlinis], *s. A:* appétits charnels.

fleshly ['fleʃli], *a. A:* (*of lusts, etc.*) charnel, de la chair; (*of countenance*) sensuel.

fleshpots ['fleʃpɔts], *s.pl. B:* potées *f* de chair, les pots *m* de viande (d'Égypte); **the f. (of Egypt),** le luxe, la bonne chère; **to sigh for the f. of Egypt,** regretter les oignons d'Égypte.

flesh split ['fleʃsplit], *s. Leath:* croûte *f* (d'une peau fendue).

fleshy ['fleʃi], *a.* (*of limb, leaf, fruit, etc.*) charnu; (*of leaf*) succulent; **the f. part of the forearm,** la partie charnue de l'avant-bras; **man of f. build,** homme à la chair empâtée; **a fine, f., comfortable woman,** une belle matrone, bien en chair, avec qui il ferait bon vivre.

fletch [fletʃ], *v.tr.* empenner (une flèche).

fletcher ['fletʃər], *s.* fabricant *m* de flèches.

fletcherism ['fletʃərizm], *s. Med: A:* fletchérisme *m*.

fletcherize ['fletʃəraiz], *v.tr. A:* mastiquer très lentement (sa nourriture) (comme l'a préconisé le docteur H. Fletcher).

fletching ['fletʃiŋ], *s.* empennage *m* (d'une flèche).

fleur-de-lis, *pl.* **fleurs-de-lis** ['flə:də'li:], *s.* **1.** *Bot:* iris *m*. **2.** *Her:* fleur *f* de lis.

fleuret ['flə:rit], *s. Arch: etc:* fleurette *f*.

fleuron ['flə:rɔn], *s. Arch: Her: etc:* fleuron *m*.

fleury ['flə:ri], *a. Her:* fleurdelisé.

flews [flu:z], *s.pl.* babines *f* (d'un dogue, etc.).

flex[1] [fleks]. **1.** *v.tr.* fléchir (le bras, une articulation, etc.); **to f. one's muscles,** faire jouer ses muscles; *Equit:* **position flexed,** ramener *m*. **2.** *v.i.* (*of spring*) fléchir; (*of stratum*) se plier; (*of belt*) **to f. over the pulley,** épouser la forme de la poulie.

flex[2], *s. Mth:* point *m* d'inflexion (d'une courbe).

flex[3], *s. El:* cordon *m*, câble *m* (souple); conducteur *m* souple; flexible *m*.

flexibility [fleksi'biliti], *s.* flexibilité *f*; élasticité *f*; souplesse *f*; **f. of working,** souplesse, élasticité, de fonctionnement; *Aut:* **f. of the engine,** souplesse du moteur; **f. of the voice,** souplesse de la voix; **f. of character,** (i) souplesse de caractère; liant *m*; (ii) complaisance *f*.

flexible ['fleksibl], *a.* flexible, souple, pliant, pliable; *Aut:* **f. engine,** moteur souple; **f. language,** langue *f* maniable; **f. voice,** voix *f* flexible, souple; **f. character,** caractère (i) liant, souple, (ii) complaisant; *Mec.E: etc:* **f. connection,** accouplement *m*, raccordement *m*, flexible; liaison *f* souple; **metallic f. tubing,** tube *m* souple avec armature métallique; flexible *m* métallique; *El:* **f. wire,** flexible, cordon *m* souple; *Bookb:* **f. binding,** reliure *f* souple.

flexile ['fleksail], *a. A:* souple, flexible; (*of features*) mobile.

flexing ['fleksiŋ], *s.* fléchissement *m*; flexion *f*; flexure *f*.

flexion ['flekʃ(ə)n], *s.* **1.** flexion *f*, courbure *f* (d'un ressort, d'un membre, etc.); *Mec.E: etc:* **lateral f.,** flambement *m*, flambage *m*. **2.** courbe *f*. **3.** *Gram:* inflexion *f*, flexion. **4.** *Mth:* = FLEXURE 3.

flexional ['flekʃən(ə)l], *a. Ling: Gram:* flexionnel; **f. ending,** désinence *f*.

flexor ['fleksər], *s. Anat:* (muscle) fléchisseur *m*.

flextime ['flekstaim], *s. Ind: etc:* heures de travail flottantes.

flexuose ['fleksjuous], *a. Bot:* (*of stem, etc.*) flexueux.

flexuosity [fleksju'ɔsiti], *s.* flexuosité *f* (d'une tige, etc.).

flexuous ['fleksjuəs], *a. Nat.Hist:* flexueux.

flexure ['flekʃər], *s.* **1.** = FLEXION 1. **2.** = FLEXION 2. **3.** *Mth:* courbure *f* (d'un arc, d'une surface). **4.** *Geol:* flexure *f*, pli *m*, courbure (d'un seul versant); **f. fault,** pli-faille *m*, *pl.* plis-failles.

flibbertigibbet ['flibəti'dʒibit], *s. F:* écervelé, -ée; évaporé, -ée; hurluberlu *m*.

flick[1] [flik], *s.* **1.** petit coup (de fouet, de torchon, de queue, etc.); (*with finger*) chiquenaude *f*; **to give the horse a f. of one's whip,** toucher son cheval de la mèche de son fouet; **a f. of the wrist,** un tour de main; **at the f. of a switch,** juste en tournant, en appuyant sur, un bouton. **2.** petit bruit sec; flicflac *m*; claquement *m*. **3.** *F: A:* film *m*; **the flicks,** le cinéma.

flick[2]. **1.** *v.tr.* (*with whip, etc.*) effleurer (un cheval, etc.); (*with finger*) donner une chiquenaude à (qch.); **to f. sth. away, off, with a duster,** faire envoler qch. d'un coup de torchon; **to f. a duster over sth.,** donner un coup de torchon à qch.; **he flicked a fly off his sleeve,** d'une chiquenaude il a chassé une mouche de sa manche; *Aut:* **to f. on the lights,** allumer les phares. **2.** *v.i.* **he was flicking away at the mosquitoes,** il essayait de chasser les moustiques (d'un coup de main).

flicker[1] ['flikər], *s.* (*a*) petit mouvement vacillant; tremblotement *m*; **f. of the eyelids,** battement *m*, clignement *m*, de paupière; **a f. of amusement crossed his lips,** un petit sourire amusé a traversé ses lèvres; (*b*) **a f. of light,** une petite lueur tremblotante; (*c*) *Cin:* scintillement *m* (de la reproduction); *T.V:* papillotement *m*.

flicker[2], *v.i.* (*of flame, moving objects, etc.*) trembloter, vaciller; (*of light*) luire par intermittence; papilloter, clignoter; (*of snake's tongue*) onduler; (*of flag*) voltiger; (*of speedometer needle, etc.*) osciller; *Cin:* (*of* *reproduction*) scintiller; **the candle flickered out,** la bougie vacilla et s'éteignit; **his life is flickering out,** il n'a plus que le souffle; il n'y a plus d'huile dans la lampe; **a smile flickered on his lips,** un sourire voltigeait sur ses lèvres.

flicker[3], *s. Orn:* colapte doré; *Fr.C:* pic doré; **red-shafted f.,** colapte cuivré, *Fr.C:* pic rosé.

flickering[1] ['flikəriŋ], *a.* tremblotant, vacillant.

flickering[2], *s.* (*a*) tremblotement *m*, vacillement *m*, papillotement *m*, clignotement *m*; *El:* **f. of the arc,** soubresauts *mpl* de l'arc; (*b*) *Cin:* scintillement *m*; *T.V:* papillotement *m*.

flick-knife ['fliknaif], *s.* (*with folding blade*) couteau *m* à cran (d'arrêt); (*with retractable blade*) couteau à lame rentrable.

flier ['flaiər], *s.* = FLYER.

flight[1] [flait], *s.* **1.** (*act or manner of flying*) vol *m* (d'un oiseau, d'un insecte, d'un avion, etc.); course *f* (d'un projectile, d'un astre, etc., dans l'espace); (*a*) *Orn:* **flapping f. (of large bird),** vol ramé (d'un grand oiseau); **f. feather,** penne *f*, rémige *f*; (*of bird*) **to take its f.,** prendre son vol, son essor; s'envoler; (*b*) **f. time,** période *f* d'essaimage (des abeilles); (*c*) *Av:* **contact f.,** vol, navigation *f*, à vue; navigation observée; **blind f.,** vol sans visibilité; **instrument f.,** vol aux instruments; **altitude f.,** vol à haute altitude; **level f.,** vol horizontal, en palier; **soaring f.,** vol à voile, vol plané; **inverted f.,** vol renversé, vol sur le dos; **over-the-top f.,** vol au-dessus des nuages; **f. line,** ligne *f* de vol; **f. path,** trajectoire *f* de vol; **in-f. refuelling,** ravitaillement *m* en vol; **f. reliability,** sécurité *f* en vol; **f. trainer,** appareil *m* d'entraînement au vol; entraîneur *m*; **f. simulator,** simulateur *m* de vol; **f. personnel,** personnel navigant; **f. engineer,** (i) mécanicien navigant, de bord; (ii) ingénieur navigant, de bord; **f. deck,** (i) poste *m* de pilotage (d'un avion); (ii) pont *m* d'envol (d'un porte-avions); **angled f. deck,** pont d'envol à piste oblique; **they will start on their f. tomorrow,** ils s'envoleront demain; (*d*) **f. of fancy, of imagination,** élan *m*, essor *m*, de l'imagination; **it's just one of his usual flights of fancy,** c'est encore une de ses inventions; **f. of oratory, of eloquence,** envolée *f* d'éloquence; **in his wildest flights of frenzy,** au paroxysme de sa folie. **2.** (*distance covered*) (*a*) volée *f*, distance parcourue (par un oiseau, etc.); migration *f* (d'oiseaux, d'insectes, etc.); **long-f. bird,** oiseau voilier; (*b*) trajectoire *f* (d'un mobile, d'un projectile, dans l'espace); **ballistic f.,** vol balistique; **time of f.,** durée *f* du trajet (d'un projectile, etc.); (*c*) portée *f* (d'une flèche); (*d*) *Av:* **it's an hour's f. from London,** c'est à une heure de vol de Londres. **3.** (*specific trip of aircraft, spacecraft, etc.*) (*a*) *Av:* **initial f., maiden f.,** vol inaugural, premier vol (d'un avion); (*of pers.*) **first f.,** baptême *m* de l'air; **solo f.,** vol en solo; **endurance f.,** vol d'endurance; **practice f., training f.,** vol d'entraînement; **position f.,** vol de mise en place; **stunt f.,** vol d'acrobatie; **f. A to Brussels,** vol A pour Bruxelles; **acceptance f.,** vol de réception, de recette (d'un avion); **connecting f.,** (vol de) correspondance *f*; **holding f.,** vol d'attente; **holding f. path,** circuit *m* d'attente; **f. plan,** plan *m* de vol; **f. clearance,** autorisation *f* de vol; **f. profile,** profil *m* de vol; **f. recorder,** (appareil) enregistreur *m* de vol; **f. log,** carnet *m*, journal *m*, de vol; **f. control,** (i) conduite *f* (d'un avion, etc., en vol); (ii) contrôle *m* de la navigation aérienne; (iii) *Mil:* contrôle, direction *f*, des missions aériennes; **f. controller unit,** contrôleur *m* de vol; (*b*) *Mil.Av:* **operational f.,** vol opérationnel; **reconnaissance f.,** vol de reconnaissance; **group f.,** vol en groupe; **f. formation,** *U.S:* **f. pattern,** formation *f* de vol; **normal f. formation,** formation *f* de croisière; (*c*) *Mil.Av:* **f. lieutenant,** capitaine aviateur; **f. sergeant,** sergent-chef *m* (d'aviation) *pl.* sergents-chefs; (*d*) *Space:* **earth-orbital f.,** vol en orbite terrestre; **coasting f.,** vol inertiel, vol sur sa lancée; **pre-set f.,** vol programmé à l'avance; **parking f.,** vol (sur une orbite) d'attente; **transfer f. (from one orbit to another),** vol de transfert (d'une orbite à une autre). **4.** (*group flying together*) (*a*) bande *f*, troupe *f*, vol, volée (d'oiseaux, etc.); *Fig:* **in the top f.,** parmi les tout premiers; (*b*) escadrille *f* (d'avions); **the Queen's, King's, F.,** avions au service de la famille royale; (*c*) décharge *f* (de flèches, etc.). **5.** (*a*) *Const:* **f. of stairs,** volée d'escalier; escalier *m*; (*b*) série *f*; *Rac:* **f. of hurdles,** série de haies (dans une course d'obstacles); *Hyd.E:* **f. of locks,** suite *f* de biefs; *Fish:* **f. of hooks,** monture *f* d'hameçons.

flight[2]. **1.** *v.i.* (*of birds*) s'envoler (en bande). **2.** *v.tr.* (*a*) *Ven:* faire partir, faire lever (un canard sauvage, etc.); (*b*) empenner (une flèche).

flight[3], *s.* fuite *f*; **headlong f.,** sauve-qui-peut *m inv*, panique *f*; **to take to f., to find safety in f.,** prendre la fuite; se mettre en fuite; lâcher pied; **to put the enemy to f.,** mettre l'ennemi en fuite, en déroute; **in full f.,** en pleine déroute; *Fin:* **the f. of capital,** l'exode *m* des capitaux.

flightiness ['flaitinis], *s.* inconstance *f*; instabilité *f* (de caractère); légèreté *f*, étourderie *f*.

flighting ['flaitiŋ], *s. Ven:* chasse *f* à la passée.

flighty ['flaiti], *a.* (*a*) frivole, écervelé, léger, évaporé, étourdi; (*b*) volage; **f. behaviour,** écarts *mpl* de conduite; conduite inconstante, instable.

flimflam[1] ['flimflæm], *s. esp. NAm: F:* **1.** baliyernes *f*, fadaises *f*; **that's all f.,** tout ça, c'est du boniment. **2.** tromperie *f*, duperie *f*.

flimflam[2], *v.tr.* (**flimflammed**) *esp. NAm: F:* duper (qn); **to f. s.o. out of sth.,** filouter qch. à qn.

flimsiness ['flimzinis], *s.* manque *m* de solidité; (*a*) légèreté *f*; manque de consistance (d'un tissu, du papier, etc.); (*b*) futilité *f*, faiblesse *f* (d'une excuse, du style, etc.).

flimsy ['flimzi]. **1.** *a.* sans solidité; fragile; (*a*) (*of material, paper, etc.*) léger; peu résistant; peu solide; sans consistance; qui n'a pas de corps, de résistance; (*b*) (*of excuse, etc.*) pauvre; (*of style, etc.*) superficiel, faible, creux; (*of evidence, etc.*) peu convaincant; **to condemn s.o. on the flimsiest evidence,** condamner qn sur les indices les plus faibles. **2.** *s.* (*a*) papier *m* pellicule; papier pelure; (*b*) *P:* billet *m* de banque, fafiot *m*; (*c*) *Journ:* copie *f* (de reporter).

flinch [flin(t)ʃ], *v.i.* (*a*) reculer, fléchir, défaillir; **I flinched at the thought of it,** j'ai reculé en y pensant; (*b*) tressaillir, sursauter (de douleur); **to bear pain without flinching,** supporter la douleur sans broncher, sans sourciller, sans défaillir.

flinders[1] ['flindəz], *s.pl.* morceaux *m*, éclats *m*; **to break, fly, in(to) f.,** voler en éclats.

Flinders[2], *Pr.n. Nau:* **F. bar,** flinders *m*, aimant correcteur.

flindersia [flin'də:siə], *s. Bot:* flindersia *m*.

fling[1] [fliŋ], *s.* **1.** (*a*) jet *m*, coup *m*; (*of horse*) ruade *f*; **to have a f. at s.o.,** (i) (*of horse*) lancer un coup de pied à qn; (ii) *F:* (*of pers.*) envoyer, lancer, un trait à qn; lancer son mot à qn; donner un coup de patte à qn; égratigner qn; *F:* **that's a f. at you,** c'est un coup de patte à votre adresse, une pierre dans votre jardin; (*b*) *F:* essai *m*, tentative *f*; **I'll have a f. at it,** je vais essayer, je vais tenter la chance. **2.** *Danc:* **(highland) f.,** pas seul écossais. **3.** *F:* **to have one's f.,** faire la fête; faire des folies; s'en donner à cœur joie; jeter sa gourme; **youth will have its f.,** il faut que jeunesse se passe.

fling[2], *v.* (**flung** [flʌŋ]; **flung**)

I. *v.tr. & i.* **1.** *v.tr.* (*a*) jeter (qch.); lancer (une balle, une grenade, etc.); **he flung a stone into the pond,** il a jeté, lancé, une pierre dans la mare; **to f. a scarf over, round, one's shoulders,** jeter une écharpe sur ses épaules; **to f. s.o. into prison,** jeter qn en prison; **to f. troops into the fray,** jeter des troupes dans la bataille; **to f. one's arms round s.o.'s neck,** se jeter, sauter, au cou de qn; **to f. oneself into s.o.'s arms, into an armchair,** se jeter dans les bras de qn, dans un fauteuil; **to f. abuse at s.o.,** lancer des injures à qn; **to f. mud at s.o.,** médire de qn; éclabousser la réputation de qn; *F:* (*of woman*) **to f. herself at s.o.'s head,** se jeter à la tête de qn; (*b*) (*of horse*) désarçonner (son cavalier); *Wr:* jeter par terre, renverser (son adversaire). **2.** *v.i.* se précipiter, s'élancer; **he flung out of the house,** il est sorti brusquement, furieusement, en coup de vent, de la maison.

II. (*compound verbs*) **1. fling about,** *v.tr.* jeter (des objets) de côté et d'autre; **to f. one's arms about,** gesticuler violemment; **to f. oneself about like a madman,** se démener comme un possédé; **to f. one's money about,** gaspiller son argent.

2. fling aside, *v.tr.* rejeter (qch.); jeter (qch.) de côté.

3. fling away, *v.tr.* jeter (qch.) de côté; se défaire de (qch.); mettre (qch.) au rancart; **to f. away one's money,** prodiguer, gaspiller, son argent.

4. fling back, *v.tr.* repousser, renvoyer, violemment (qch.); ouvrir brusquement (la porte); repousser (l'ennemi); *Lit:* **to f. back defiance,** riposter par un défi.

5. fling down, *v.tr.* jeter (qch.) à terre; **he flung the books down on the table,** il a jeté les livres sur la table.

6. fling off. (*a*) *v.tr.* (i) secouer (le joug); (ii) retirer brusquement (son manteau, etc.) (et le jeter par terre, etc.); (*b*) *v.i.* partir brusquement, furieusement, en coup de vent.

7. fling open, *v.tr.* ouvrir toute grande (la fenêtre, etc.); ouvrir brusquement (un tiroir, etc.); **to f. open the door,** ouvrir la porte (i) d'un mouvement brusque, (ii) à deux battants.

8. fling out. (*a*) *v.tr.* (i) jeter (qch.) dehors; *F:* mettre (qch.) au rancart; *F:* **to f. s.o. out,** flanquer qn à la porte; (ii) **to f. out one's arm,** étendre le bras d'un grand geste; (*b*) *v.i.* (*of horse, etc.*) ruer, lancer une ruade; (*of cow*) ginguer; *F:* (*of pers.*) **to f. out at s.o.,** invectiver, injurier, qn; lancer des injures à qn.

9. fling to, *v.tr.* **to f. the door to,** faire claquer la porte.

10. fling up, *v.tr.* (*a*) jeter (qch.) en l'air; (*of horse*) **to f. up its heels,** ruer; (*b*) *F:* abandonner, renoncer à (un projet, une tâche); **to f. up one's job,** démissionner, lâcher son emploi.

flinkite ['fliŋkait], *s. Miner:* flinkite *f*.

flint [flint], *s.* (*a*) *Miner:* silex *m*; **horn f.,** silex corné; **rock f.,** silex noir; **f. clay,** argile *f* réfractaire, apyre; *Const:* **(knapped) f. work,** appareil *m* en silex; **to have a heart of f.,** avoir un cœur de pierre, de bronze, un cœur dur comme pierre; (*b*) caillou silicieux; pierre *f* à feu; (*for cigarette lighter*) pierre à briquet; *Prehist:* **f. implements,** outils *m* en pierre, silex taillés; *Sm.a: A:* **gun f.,** pierre à fusil; **f. gun,** fusil *m* à pierre; **f. and steel,** briquet *m* à silex; *F:* **he'd skin,** *O:* **flay, a f.,** il est d'une avarice incroyable; il tondrait, trouverait à tondre sur, un œuf; (*c*) **f. glass,** flint(-glass) *m*; verre *m* de plomb.

flinthearted ['flint'ha:tid], *a. F:* au cœur de pierre.

flintlock ['flintlɔk], *s. Sm.a: A:* **1.** platine *f* à pierre, à silex. **2.** fusil *m* à pierre.

flintware ['flintwɛər], *s. Cer:* grès fin; faïence fine; cailloutage *m*.

flinty ['flinti], *a.* **1.** (*a*) de silex; (*b*) caillouteux, rocailleux. **2.** (cœur) dur, sans pitié, insensible.

flip[1] [flip], *s.* (*drink*) flip *m*.

flip[2], *s.* **1.** chiquenaude *f*, pichenette *f*. **2.** (*a*) petite secousse vive; **f. of the tail,** coup *m* de queue; **f. of a gun,** déplacement horizontal d'un fusil au moment du tir; (*b*) *F:* **f. side (of a record),** revers *m* (d'un disque). **3.** *Av: F: O:* petit tour de vol.

flip[3], *v.tr.* (**flipped**) **1.** (*a*) donner une chiquenaude, une pichenette, à (une boulette de papier, etc.); **to f. s.o. on the ear, to f. (at) s.o.'s ear,** donner à qn une chiquenaude sur l'oreille; **to f. the ash off one's cigarette,** secouer la cendre de sa cigarette d'un petit coup de doigt; **to f. (at) the horse with the whip,** toucher le cheval avec le fouet; (*b*) *El:* (*of switch*) basculer. **2.** donner une secousse vive à (sa ligne en pêchant, etc.); claquer (son fouet). **3.** *v.i.* **to f. through a book,** feuilleter un livre. **4.** *v.tr. & v.i. P:* **to f. (one's lid),** (i) se mettre en boule; (ii) perdre le nord. **5.** *v.i. Av: F: O:* **to f. around,** faire un petit tour de vol.

flip[4], *a. P:* impudent, désinvolte, culotté, qui a du toupet.

flip-flap ['flipflæp]. **1.** *adv.* flicflac; **to go f.-f.,** flicflaquer; faire flicflac. **2.** *s.* (*a*) saut périlleux; (*b*) flip-flap *m inv* (des foires).

flip-flop ['flipflɔp]. **1.** *adv.* = FLIP-FLAP 1. **2.** *s.* saut périlleux. **3.** *a. & s. Elcs:* **f.-f. (circuit),** (circuit) basculeur *m* monostable.

flippancy ['flipənsi], *s.* légèreté *f*, irrévérence *f*, désinvolture *f* (de ton, de manière, etc.).

flippant ['flipənt], *a.* (*of behaviour, remark, etc.*) léger, désinvolte, irrévérencieux, cavalier.

flipped [flipt], *a. P:* **f. out,** flippé (par la drogue).

flippantly ['flipəntli], *adv.* légèrement, d'une manière désinvolte.

flipper ['flipər], *s.* **1.** (*a*) nageoire *f*, battoir *m* (de cétacé); nageoire, aile *f* (de manchot); (patte-)nageoire *f* (de phoque, de tortue); aileron *m* (de requin); (*b*) palme *f* (de nageur sous-marin, etc.). **2.** *P:* (*a*) main *f*, patte *f*, pince *f*; (*b*) bras *m*, nageoire.

flipperty-flopperty ['flipəti'flɔpəti], *F:* **1.** *a.* pendant, souple, qui traîne. **2.** *adv.* (marcher) en traînant ses pantoufles, etc.

flipping ['flipiŋ], *a. F:* satané, fichu; **a f. nuisance,** un fichu embêtement.

flirt[1] [flə:t], *s.* **1.** *O:* petit mouvement rapide (d'un éventail, des ailes, etc.). **2.** (*a*) (*pers.*) flirteur *m*; (*woman*) coquette *f*; (*b*) *O:* **he used to be a f. of mine,** c'est un de mes anciens flirts.

flirt[2]. **1.** *v.tr.* (*a*) jeter, lancer (qch.) (d'un mouvement sec); donner une chiquenaude à (qch.); (*b*) (*of bird*) agiter (les ailes, etc.); (*c*) **to f. a fan,** agiter un éventail; jouer de l'éventail. **2.** *v.i.* (*a*) se mouvoir par saccades, s'agiter; (*of bird, etc.*) se trémousser; papillonner; (*b*) flirter; **to f. with s.o.,** (*of woman*) coqueter, faire la coquette, avec qn; dire des coquetteries à qn; (*of man*) conter fleurette à (une jeune fille); faire le galant auprès (d'une femme); **every pretty girl likes to be flirted with,** toute jolie fille aime le flirt.

flirtation [flə:'teiʃ(ə)n], *s.* flirt *m*, flirtage *m*, coquetterie *f*; **to carry on a f. with a woman,** faire la cour à une femme.

flirtatious [flə:'teiʃəs], *a. F:* (*of man*) flirteur; (*of woman*) coquette.

flirting ['flə:tiŋ], *s.* **1.** agitation *f*, trémoussement *m* (des ailes, etc.); jeu *m* (d'éventail). **2.** flirt *m*, flirtage *m*.

flit[1] [flit], *s.* (*a*) *Scot:* déménagement *m*; (*b*) *F:* **moonlight f.,** déménagement à la cloche de bois; **to do a**

moonlight f., déménager à la cloche de bois; mettre la clef sous la porte; faire un trou à la lune; (*c*) *F:* fuite *f* (avec un amant, etc.).

flit[2], *v.i.* **(flitted) 1. to f. (away),** partir; **time was flitting away,** le temps passait rapidement. **2.** (*a*) *Scot:* déménager; (*b*) *F:* mettre la clef sous la porte; déménager à la cloche de bois; (*c*) *F:* s'enfuir (avec un amant, etc.). **3.** (*of pers., bird, etc.*) **to f. by,** passer légèrement, comme une ombre; **to f. about, to f. to and fro,** aller et venir d'un pas, d'un vol léger; aller et venir sans bruit; (*of bat*) zigzaguer; **to f. into a room,** se glisser (vivement) dans une pièce; (*of bird*) **to f. from tree to tree,** voleter d'arbre en arbre; **a smile flitted across his face,** un sourire fugitif a passé sur son visage.

flitch[1] [flitʃ], *s.* **1.** flèche *f* (de lard). **2.** dalle *f* (de baleine, de flétan). **3.** (*a*) dosse *f* (de bois); (*b*) *Const: etc:* **f.(-plate),** plaque rapportée; plaquette *f*, éclisse *f* de renfort; contre-plaque *f*, *pl.* contre-plaques; **f. (beam),** poutre *f* à plaques rapportées, poutrelle composée.

flitch[2], *v.tr.* **1.** débiter (un flétan) (en dalles). **2. to f. the trunk of a tree,** couper les dosses d'un tronc d'arbre.

flitter ['flitər], *v.i.* voleter, voltiger.

flittermouse ['flitəmaus], *s. Z:* chauve-souris *f*, *pl.* chauves-souris.

flitting[1] ['flitiŋ], *a.* (*of pers., shadow, etc.*) fugitif.

flitting[2], *s.* **1.** départ *m*. **2.** *Scot:* déménagement *m*. **3.** volettement *m*, voltigement *m*.

flivver ['flivər], *s. F:* **1.** *U.S:* four *m*, fiasco *m*; **he's a f.,** il porte (la) guigne. **2.** *esp. NAm:* (*a*) bagnole *f*; (vieux) tacot; (*b*) petit avion.

float[1] [flout], *s.* **1.** (*a*) masse flottante (d'algues, de glace, etc.); (*b*) flot *m*, train *m* (de bois); brelle *f*; (*c*) radeau *m*, ras *m*; **f. bridge,** pont *m* de radeaux. **2.** (*a*) *Mec.E: etc:* flotteur *m* (de chaudière, de carburateur, de cuve, etc.); **ball f.,** flotteur sphérique, à boule; **alarm f.,** flotteur avertisseur; **f. feed,** alimentation *f* à flotteur; **f.-operated valve, f. gauge,** niveau *m* à flotteur; **f. stop,** butée *f* de flotteur; *I.C.E:* **f. chamber,** *U.S:* **f. bowl,** chambre *f* du flotteur; pot *m*, cuve *f*, à niveau constant (du carburateur); **f. needle, f. spindle,** pointeau *m* (du carburateur); **f. valve,** soupape *f* à flotteur; **f. feed,** alimentation *f* par flotteur; **f.-controlled,** à commande par flotteur; **f.-type carburettor,** carburateur à flotteur; *El:* **f. switch,** commutateur *m*, interrupteur *m*, à flotteur; *Av:* **parallel, paired, twin, floats,** flotteurs (disposés) en catamaran; **wing-tip f.,** flotteur en bout d'aile; **detachable f.,** flotteur largable; **stabilizing f.,** flotteur stabilisateur; **outboard stabilizing f.,** flotteur stabilisateur d'aile; **f. strut,** jambe *f*, contrefiche *f*, de flotteur; **f. seaplane,** hydravion *m* à flotteur(s); **wing f.,** ballonnet *m* (d'hydravion); (*c*) *Fish:* flotteur, flotte *f*, bouchon *m*, lignage *m* (d'une ligne, d'un filet de pêche); galet *m* (de filet); (*d*) *Nat.Hist:* flotteur (de plante aquatique); vessie *f* natatoire (de poisson); *Bot:* **f. grass,** glycérie flottante. **3. f. (board) (of a hydraulic wheel),** aube *f*, palette *f*, pale *f*, aileron *m*, alichon *m*, volet *m* (de roue hydraulique). **4.** *Mec.E:* jeu *m*, flottement *m*, déplacement *m* (d'une pièce mécanique, d'une roue, d'un essieu). **5.** (*a*) *Th: Cin:* portant *m* mobile; (*b*) *Th:* (*lighting*) **the floats,** la rampe. **6.** (*a*) charrette basse à essieu brisé; (*b*) fourgon *m* (pour le transport du gros bétail); (*c*) (i) wagon *m* en plate-forme; (ii) char *m* de cavalcade, de cortège de carnaval; **milk f.,** voiture *f* de livraison du lait; (*d*) **floats of a cart,** fausses ridelles. **7.** *Tls:* (*a*) taloche *f* (de maçon, de plâtrier); (*b*) lime *f* à taille simple; **f. cut,** taille simple. **8.** *Min:* paillettes flottantes. **9.** *Com: Fin:* (*a*) petite caisse; monnaie *f*; (*b*) (fonds *mpl*) de roulement *m*.

float[2], *v.*

I. *v.i.* **1.** (*a*) flotter, nager (sur un liquide); surnager; (*of boat*) être à flot; **wreckage floating on the sea,** des débris qui flottent sur la mer; **cork floats on the surface of water,** le liège surnage à la surface de l'eau; **impurities that f. on the surface of a solution,** les impuretés qui surnagent une solution; **to f. down the stream,** descendre le courant; flotter au fil de l'eau; **the boat was floating out to sea,** le bateau flottait vers le large; (*b*) *Swim:* faire la planche. **2.** (*a*) **plankton floating in the water,** du plancton qui nage dans l'eau; **to f. to the surface,** revenir à la surface; **the corpse floated to the surface,** le cadavre est revenu sur l'eau, a reparu à la surface; (*b*) **to f. in the air,** planer dans l'air; **clouds floating in the sky,** des nuages qui flottent dans le ciel; **the flag was floating in the breeze,** le drapeau flottait dans la brise; **there were rumours floating about that . . .,** le bruit courait que . . .; **visions floated before his eyes,** des chimères *f* flottaient devant ses yeux; (*c*) (*of axle, etc.*) **to f. freely,** tourner librement. **3.** (*a*) *Mec.E:* (*of part of machine, etc.*) avoir du jeu, jouer, flotter; (*b*) *Metall:* (*of casting core, etc.*) se déplacer. **4.** (*a*) *esp. U.S: Pol:* (*of voter*) être indécis; (*b*) **she floated out of the room,** elle est sortie de la pièce d'un pas léger, flottant; (*c*) **to f. from job to job,** changer fréquemment d'emploi (sans but déterminé). **5.** *esp. U.S: Fish:* pêcher à la flotte.

II. *v.tr.* **1.** (*a*) flotter (des bois, un câble, etc.); **to f. timber downstream,** jeter du bois à flot perdu; (*b*) (i) mettre (un navire) à flot, à l'eau; (ii) déséchouer, renflouer (un navire); (*c*) *Const:* fonder (un immeuble, etc.) sur radier. **2.** (*a*) *Com:* créer, fonder, lancer (une compagnie, etc.); *Fin:* **to f. a loan,** émettre, lancer, un emprunt; (*b*) **to f. a rumour,** répandre, faire circuler, un bruit; lancer une rumeur. **3.** *Agr:* inonder, submerger (un terrain, etc.). **4.** *Const:* aplanir, lisser (le plâtre d'un plafond, etc.); crépir.

III. (*compound verbs*) **1. float off.** *Nau:* (*a*) *v.i.* (*of ship*) se déséchouer; (*b*) *v.tr.* faire flotter, mettre à flot (un navire, etc.); renflouer, afflouer, déséchouer (une épave); **the tide will f. the boat off,** la marée soulèvera le bateau.

2. float out, *v.tr.* **to f. out a ship,** sortir un navire des chantiers de construction.

floatable ['floutəbl], *a.* flottable.

floatage ['floutidʒ], *s.* **1.** (*a*) flottement *m* (d'un bateau, etc.); (*b*) flottage *m* (des bois). **2.** = FLOTSAM. **3.** tonnage *m* des navires à flot (sur une rivière). **4.** flottabilité *f*.

floatation [flou'teiʃ(ə)n], *s.* = FLOTATION.

floater ['floutər], *s.* **1.** (*pers.*) (*a*) *Swim:* baigneur, -euse, qui fait la planche; (*b*) *Fin:* lanceur *m* (d'une compagnie, etc.); (*c*) *esp. U.S:* (i) vagabond, -onde; (ii) personne *f* qui change souvent son domicile, son emploi; (iii) *Pol:* voteur indécis; électeur *m* accessible à l'influence, qui peut être acheté. **2.** (*thg*) (*a*) *Tchn:* flotteur *m*; (*b*) *Golf:* balle *f* insubmersible; (*c*) *St.Exch: F:* titre *m* de premier rang; (*d*) *Ins:* police flottante; (*e*) *F:* prêt *m*; argent emprunté; (*f*) *F:* faux pas, gaffe *f*, bourde *f*. **3.** *Rec:* **tone-arm f.,** coude *m* mobile.

floating[1] ['floutiŋ], *a.* **1.** (*a*) flottant, à flot; **f. bodies,** corps flottants; **f. light,** veilleuse *f* (à flotteur, à huile); **f. particles of dust,** poussières *f* en suspension; **f. bridge,** pont flottant; pont de bateaux, de radeaux; **f. crane,** ponton-grue *m*, *pl.* pontons-grues; **f. hotel,** hôtel flottant; **f.-dial compass,** compas *m* à liquide, à rose flottante, mobile; *Const:* **f. foundations,** fondations *f* en cuvelage, sur radier; **f. floor,** dalle flottante; *Nau:* **f. workshop,** navire-atelier *m*, *pl.* navires-ateliers; *F:* **f. coffin,** cercueil flottant; navire qui n'est pas en état de tenir la mer; *Navy:* **f. target,** cible flottante; *A:* **f. battery,** batterie (d'artillerie) flottante; (*b*) *Com:* **f. cargo,** cargaison *f* sur mer; (*c*) *esp. U.S:* (i) ivre, soûl; (ii) flippé par la drogue. **2.** libre, mobile; (*a*) **f. population,** population flottante, instable; *Fin:* **f. capital, assets,** capital circulant, flottant, mobile, disponible; fonds *mpl* de roulement, capitaux roulants; **f. debt,** dette flottante; **f. exchange rate,** taux de change flottant; *Ins:* **f. policy,** police flottante; (*b*) *Anat:* **f. ribs,** fausses côtes, côtes flottantes; *Med:* **f. kidney,** rein mobile, flottant; néphroptose *f*; (*c*) *Mec.E: etc:* **f. bearing,** coussinet flottant; **f. bushing,** bague flottante; **f. ring,** anneau *m* mobile; **f. piston pin,** axe de piston flottant; **f. control,** commande flottante; *Av:* **f. aileron,** aileron flottant, aileron entre plans; *Typ:* **f. platen (of press),** platine flottante (de presse); *Opt:* **f. reticle,** réticule *m* mobile, réglable; (*d*) *Pol:* **f. voter,** voteur indécis. **3.** *El:* **f. carrier system, modulation,** système *m*, modulation *f*, à porteuse variable; **f. grid,** grille *f* en l'air; **f. charge,** charge *f* d'entretien. **4.** *Bot:* **f. heart,** villarsia *m*, nymphoïde *m*.

floating[2], *s.* **1.** (*a*) flottement *m* (d'un bâtiment); (*b*) *Swim:* la planche; (*c*) *Metall:* déplacement *m* (de l'âme du moule). **2.** (*a*) mise *f* à flot (d'un navire); **f. (off),** renflouage *m*, renflouement *m*, afflouage *m*, déséchouage *m*, déséchouement *m* (d'une épave, etc.); (*b*) flottage *m* (à bûches perdues); écoulage *m* (des bois); (*c*) flottaison *f* sur bain de mercure (d'un système optique); (*d*) *Com:* lancement *m* (d'une société commerciale, etc.); *Fin:* émission *f*, lancement (d'un emprunt). **3.** *Agr:* submersion *f* (d'un pré, etc.). **4.** *Const:* aplanissage *m*, aplanissement *m* (du plâtre). **5.** *El:* marche *f* en tampon.

floccose ['flɔkous], *a. Bot:* floconneux.

flocculant ['flɔkjulənt], *s. Ph:* floculant *m*.

flocculate[1] ['flɔkjuleit], *Ph:* **1.** *a.* floconneux. **2.** *s.* floculé *m*; floculat *m*.

flocculate[2], *v.i.* (*a*) floconner, former des flocons; (*b*) *Ph:* floculer.

flocculation [flɔkju'leiʃ(ə)n], *s.* floculation *f*.

floccule ['flɔkjul], *s. Ch: etc:* flocon *m*, micelle *f* (de précipité).

flocculent ['flɔkjulənt], **flocculose** ['flɔkjulous], **flocculous** ['flɔkjuləs], *a.* floculeux; floconneux.

flocculus, *pl.* **-li** ['flɔkjuləs, -lai], *s.* **1.** *pl. Ch:* flocons *m*, précipité *m*. **2.** *Anat:* flocculus *m*, lobule *m* du pneumogastrique. **3.** *Astr:* **(solar) flocculi,** flocculi *mpl*.

floccus, *pl.* **-i** ['flɔkəs, 'flɔksai], *s.* **1.** *Bot:* (*a*) flocon *m* (de poils); (*b*) *pl.* hyphes *m* (d'un champignon). **2.** *Z:* duvet *m* (d'un oisillon encore sans plumes).

flock[1] [flɔk], *s.* **1.** (*a*) flocon *m* (de laine, de coton, etc.); **f. of wool,** bourre *f* de laine, bourre lanice; (*b*) **f. mattress,** matelas *m* en bourre de laine. **2.** *Tex: Paperm:* **(cropping) flock(s),** (bourre) tontisse *f*; tonture *f*; **f. paper,** papier soufflé, velouté, tontisse. **3.** *Ch:* *pl.* **flocks,** flocons, précipité *m*.

flock[2], *s.* bande *f*, troupe *f* (d'animaux); troupeau *m* (de moutons, de chèvres, d'oies); volée *f*, harde *f* (d'oiseaux); **flocks and herds,** le menu et le gros bétail; **f. book,** flock-book *m*; **a pastor and his f.,** un pasteur et ses ouailles *f*; *Ecc:* **those who have strayed from the f.,** ceux qui se sont écartés du bercail; **a f. of visitors,** une foule de visiteurs; **they arrived in flocks,** ils arrivaient par mille et par cents; ils arrivaient en bandes, en foule.

flock[3], *v.i.* **to f. (together),** s'attrouper, s'assembler; **everybody is flocking to see the exhibition,** tout le monde se précipite pour voir l'exposition; **children flocking (a)round the Christmas tree,** des enfants qui s'assemblent autour de l'arbre de Noël; **in summer people f. to the sea,** en été les gens affluent, vont en foule, se précipitent, au bord de la mer; **tourists were flocking in and out of the palace in their hundreds,** il y avait au palais un va-et-vient de centaines de touristes.

flocking ['flɔkiŋ], *s. Tex:* flocage *m*, floconnage *m*.

floe [flou], *s.* glaçon flottant; masse *f*, île *f*, de glaces flottantes; banc *m* de glace; banquise *f*; floe *m*.

flog [flɔg], *v.tr.* **(flogged) 1.** (*a*) flageller (qn); battre (qn) à coups de fouet, de cravache; **masters are not allowed to f. the boys,** il est défendu aux professeurs de fouetter les élèves; **I'll f. it into him,** je le lui ferai apprendre à coups de fouet; **to f. a horse,** (i) fouetter, (ii) cravacher, un cheval; *F:* **to f. a dead horse,** faire des efforts inutiles, se dépenser en pure perte; enfoncer des portes ouvertes; *F:* **to f. a car,** esquinter une voiture (en conduisant trop vite); *Cr:* **to f. the ball,** donner à la balle un coup violent; **to f. s.o. to death,** matraquer qn; **he's flogging himself to death,** il s'éreinte, se crève, à force de travailler; **to f. a subject to death,** ne pas savoir se taire sur une question; éreinter ses auditeurs (quand on parle de qch.); (*b*) *Fish:* **to f. a stream,** fouetter un cours d'eau; pêcher au fouetter. **2.** (*a*) *F:* bazarder, trafiquer, troquer, lessiver (qch.); (*b*) *P:* voler, barboter, chiper, faucher (qch.).

flogging ['flɔgiŋ], *s.* flagellation *f*; *Jur:* le châtiment du fouet; *Sch:* **to give s.o. a f.,** donner le fouet à qn.

flood[1] [flʌd], *s.* **1.** *Oc:* **f. (tide),** flot *m*, flux *m* (de la marée); marée montante; **ebb and f.,** flux et reflux; **half f.,** mi-flot *m*; **quarter f.,** (i) quart *m* de flot; (ii) trois quarts de flot; **f. current,** courant *m* de flot. **2.** (*a*) inondation *f*; déluge *m*; **the melting snow caused serious floods,** la fonte des neiges a causé de sérieuses inondations; **the river was in f.,** la rivière débordait; **crops ruined by the floods,** récoltes perdues à cause des inondations; **the victims of the f.,** les inondés; *P.N:* **floods!** route inondée; **after the heavy rain we found a f. in the cellar,** à la suite d'une pluie torrentielle l'eau a envahi notre cave; *B:* **the F.,** le Déluge; (*b*) crue *f* (d'une rivière); **the floods of the Nile,** les crues du Nil; **f. plain,** lit majeur (d'un fleuve); plaine *f* d'inondation; (*c*) (i) **a f. of light,** un flux lumineux; des flots de lumière; **floods of tears, of abuse,** un torrent, un déluge, de larmes; un torrent, un débordement, d'injures; **a f. of talk,** un flot de paroles; **a f. of oratory,** un déluge d'éloquence; (ii) *Phot:* (lampe *f*) flood (*f*); (*d*) *Mch: etc:* **full f. of lubricant,** plein jet de lubrifiant.

flood[2]. **1.** *v.tr.* (*a*) inonder, submerger, couvrir d'eau (un terrain, etc.); **the river overflowed its banks and flooded the fields,** la rivière a débordé et a inondé les champs; (*of house, ship, etc.*) **to be flooded,** être envahi par l'eau; **we were flooded out of the house,** l'eau nous a forcés à quitter la maison; *Navy:* **to f. the magazines,** noyer les soutes; (*b*) *Agr:* irriguer, noyer, submerger (un champ, etc.); *Mil:* **to f. a region,** tendre une inondation sur une région; faire des tendues d'eau dans une région; (*c*) *I.C.E:* **to f. the carburettor,** noyer le carburateur; **to f. the engine,** étouffer le moteur; **to f. a (cigarette) lighter,** noyer la mèche d'un briquet; (*d*) **the rays of the setting sun flooded the street,** la lumière du soleil couchant inondait la rue; **to f. the market with . . .,** inonder le marché de . . .; **to be flooded with letters,** être inondé, submergé, de lettres. **2.** *v.i.* (*a*) (*of river, etc.*) (i) déborder; (ii) être en crue; (*b*) **the sun's rays came flooding through the window,** les rayons du soleil entraient à flots par la fenêtre; (*c*) *Med:* (*of woman*) souffrir de métrorragie; avoir des pertes de sang.

floodable ['flʌdəbl], *a.* (terrain, etc.) inondable, submersible; *N.Arch:* **f. length,** longueur *f* envahissable.

flooded ['flʌdid], *a.* (*a*) (terrain, etc.) inondé; **they were using boats to get through the f. streets,** on circulait en bateau dans les rues inondées; (*b*) (carburateur) noyé.

floodgate ['flʌdgeit], *s.* vanne (plongeante, de décharge); porte *f* d'écluse; **to open, close, the floodgates,** lever, mettre, les vannes; **to open the floodgates of one's passions,** lâcher les écluses à ses passions; **and then the floodgates opened,** et alors, elle a fondu en larmes.

flooding ['flʌdiŋ], *s.* **1.** (*a*) inondation *f*, submersion *f* (d'un terrain, etc.); débordement *m* (d'une rivière, etc.); *P.N:* **road liable to f.,** route inondable, submersible; (*b*) *Agr:* irrigation *f* (d'un champ, etc.); *Nau: etc:* noyage *m* (des soutes, etc.); **f. cock,** robinet *m*, vanne *f*, de noyage; *Hyd.E:* **f. chamber,** sas *m*. **2.** *Med:* métrorragie *f*; perte *f* de sang.

floodlight[1] ['flʌdlait], *s.* (*a*) **f. (projector),** projecteur *m* (pour l'illumination des monuments, *Th:* de la scène); phare *m* d'éclairage; *Av:* **landing-area f.,** projecteur d'atterrissage; **runway f.,** projecteur de piste; (*b*) lumière *f* de grande intensité; (*c*) *Phot:* (lampe *f*) flood (*f*).

floodlight[2], *v.tr.* (*p.t. & p.p.* **floodlighted** *or* **floodlit**) illuminer (un monument, etc.) par projecteurs, *F:* embraser (un monument).

floodlighting ['flʌdlaitiŋ], *s.* illumination *f* (d'un monument, etc.) par projecteurs.

floodlit ['flʌdlit], *a.* (monument) illuminé (par des projecteurs).

floodmark ['flʌdmɑːk], *s.* (*a*) ligne *f* de la haute marée; (*b*) niveau *m* de la crue.

floodometer [flʌ'dɔmitər], *s. Hyd.E:* échelle *f* d'étiage.

floor[1] [flɔːr], *s.* **1.** (*a*) parquet *m*; plancher *m*; sol *m*; **oak f.,** parquet de chêne; **deal f.,** plancher en sapin; **parquet f.** = parquet à l'anglaise; **tiled f.,** carrelage *m*; dallage *m*; pavement *m*, sol, en céramique; **(wood) mosaic f.,** parquet en mosaïque; **tessellated f.,** pavement, sol, en mosaïque; **asphalt f.,** sol asphalté; **cement f., mud f.,** sol en ciment, en terre battue; **f. joist,** solive *f*, traverse *f*, de plancher; **f. plank,** lame *f* de parquet; **f. polish, f. wax,** encaustique *f*; cire *f* à parquet; **f. polisher,** (i) (*pers.*) cireur, -euse, de parquets; (ii) (*machine*) cireuse *f*; *Carp:* **f. dresser,** aplanisseur *m* de parquets; *Furn: esp. NAm:* **f. lamp,** lampadaire *m*; torchère *f*; **to throw sth. on the f.,** jeter qch. à terre, par terre; *F:* **to wipe the f. with s.o.,** battre qn à plate couture; éreinter qn; (*b*) parquet (à la Bourse); parquet, prétoire *m* (d'un tribunal); parquet, enceinte *f* (d'une assemblée législative); *Th:* plateau *m* (de la scène); **to take the f.,** prendre la parole; **to hold the f.,** accaparer la conversation; *U.S: Parl:* **f. leader,** chef *m* de parti (qui dirige les votes); (*c*) **dance f.,** piste *f* de danse; **to take the f.,** se joindre aux danseurs; **f. show,** spectacle *m* de cabaret; (*d*) **the factory f.,** l'atelier *m*; **he became a foreman after five years on the factory f.,** il est monté contremaître après cinq ans d'atelier; (*e*) *Box:* **the f. of the ring,** le canevas. **2.** étage *m*; palier *m*; **house on two floors,** maison *f* avec étage; **the ground f.,** le rez-de-chaussée; **mezzanine, intermediate, f.,** entresol *m*; demi-étage *m*, *pl.* demi-étages; **first f.,** (i) premier étage; (ii) *NAm:* rez-de-chaussée; **to live on the fifth f.,** habiter (i) au cinquième, (ii) *NAm:* au sixième, (étage); **on the top f.,** au dernier étage; **we live on the same f.,** nous habitons sur le même palier, nous sommes voisins de palier; *F:* **to get in on the ground f.,** (i) acheter des actions, etc., dès leur émission, au plus bas prix; s'assurer la primeur d'une bonne spéculation; (ii) s'assurer un avantage, une situation privilégiée; *attrib.* **f. waiter,** garçon *m* d'étage (dans un hôtel); **f. key,** clef *f* passe-partout (qui ouvre toutes les portes de l'étage); *NAm:* **f. manager,** (i) chef *m* d'étage (qui a la responsabilité administrative d'un étage); (*in shop*) chef de rayon; (ii) *T.V:* régisseur *m*. **3.** (*a*) fond *m* (de l'océan, d'un lac); (*b*) *Min:* sole *f* (d'une galerie de mine, d'un chantier); *Mil:* sol (de fossé, de caponnière); (*c*) (i) *Ind:* aire (de lavage, de séchage); **(threshing) f.,** aire *f* (d'une grange); (ii) *Agr:* airée *f* (de blé, etc.); (*d*) *Civ.E: etc:* platelage *m*, tablier *m* (d'un pont); radier *m* (d'un sas d'écluse, d'une voie souterraine); *Metall:* sol (d'une fonderie); **f. timber,** semelle *f* (d'un pont en bois); *Mec.E:* **vertical f. bearing,** boîtard *m*; (*e*) *N.Arch:* **f. timber,** varangue *f*; **main f., midship f.,** maîtresse varangue; **transom f.,** varangue d'arcasse; **rising f.,** varangue acculée; **deep f.,** haute varangue; **filling f.,** fausse varangue; **f. plate,** plaque *f* de varangue; **f. rider,** varangue de porque; **f. ceiling,** (i) plafond *m*, payol *m* (de la chambre d'une embarcation); (ii) vaigre *f* de fond; (*f*) *Anat:* plancher (de la bouche, d'une cavité, etc.). **4.** *Geol:* (*a*) mur *m*, éponte inférieure (d'une couche de houille); (*b*) couche *f*, lit *m* (d'étain, etc.).

floor[2], *v.tr.* **1.** *Const:* (i) planchéier, (ii) parqueter, (iii) carreler (une pièce). **2.** (*a*) terrasser, renverser, accabler (un adversaire); (*b*) *F:* mettre, réduire, (qn) à quia; clouer le bec à (qn); asseoir, aplatir (qn); *Sch:* coller (un candidat, etc.).

floorage ['flɔːridʒ], *s.* superficie *f*, surface *f* (des planchers, etc.).

floorboard ['flɔːbɔːd], *s.* **1.** planche *f* (du plancher, à planchéier). **2.** *N.Arch:* vaigre *f* de fond; lierne *f*. **3.** *Aut: Av:* plancher *m*; planche de fond.

floorcloth ['flɔːklɔθ], *s.* **1.** *O:* linoléum *m*. **2.** *Dom.Ec:* serpillière *f*.

floorer ['flɔːrər], *s. F:* **1.** coup *m* qui vous terrasse. **2.** (*a*) nouvelle déconcertante; (*b*) (*in an examination*) colle *f*; (*c*) argument *m* sans réplique; **that's a f. for you!** ça te la coupe!

flooring ['flɔːriŋ], *s.* **1.** planchéiage *m*, parquetage *m*; carrelage *m*, dallage *m*; *Carp:* **f. cramp,** étreignoir *m*. **2.** (*a*) plancher *m*; dallage; **cement(-block) f.,** dallage en ciment; **parquet f.** = parquet *m* à l'anglaise; (*b*) *Veh:* plancher (d'une voiture, d'un avion, etc.); (*c*) *Civ.E: etc:* platelage *m* (d'un pont, etc.). **3.** (*a*) *Wr: etc:* mise *f* au parquet, tombée *f*, renversement *m* (d'un adversaire); (*b*) *F:* mise à quia (d'un adversaire).

floorplate ['flɔːpleit], *s. N.Arch:* (*a*) tôle-varangue *f*, *pl.* tôles-varangues; (*b*) *pl.* **floorplates (of boiler room),** parquet *m* de chaufferie.

floorspace ['flɔːspeis], *s.* (*a*) surface (couverte), superficie *f* (d'une pièce, etc.); *Veh:* surface du plancher; **there isn't enough f. for dancing,** il n'y a pas assez de place pour danser; (*b*) encombrement *m* (d'un objet); **we shall need 100 sq.m. of f. to stock these goods,** nous aurons besoin de 100 m² (dans le hangar) pour stocker ces marchandises.

floorwalker ['flɔːwɔːkər], *s. Com:* (*in a store*) inspecteur, -trice; surveillant, -ante; chef *m* de rayon; (*in a bank*) surveillant, -ante.

floozie, floozy ['fluːzi], *s. P:* pouffiasse *f*.

flop[1] [flɔp], *s.* **1.** coup mat; bruit sourd (d'un rat qui plonge, etc.); **down he went with a f.,** il a fait plouf en tombant. **2.** *F:* (*a*) four *m*, fiasco *m*; (*b*) dégringolade *f* (du franc, etc.). **3.** *F:* (*pers.*) mollasse *mf*; raté, -ée; poule mouillée. **4.** *P:* lit *m*; pieu *m*, paddock *m*.

flop[2], *int. & adv.* **1.** plouf! patapouf! floc! **to fall f.,** tomber comme une masse; faire patapouf. **2. to go f.,** (i) (*of business, etc.*) dégringoler, aller à vau-l'eau, faire échec; (*of play, etc.*) faire four; *F:* être recalé (à un examen); (ii) (*of pers.*) s'effondrer (de fatigue, etc.).

flop[3], *v.i.* (**flopped**) **1.** (*a*) (*of stone, etc.*) faire plouf; faire floc; (*b*) (*of pers.*) **to f. (down),** se laisser tomber; s'affaler; **to f. down on to a seat,** s'asseoir tout d'une pièce; tomber mollement, lourdement, sur un siège; se laisser tomber comme un sac, comme un paquet, sur un siège; s'effondrer, s'écrouler, s'affaler, dans un fauteuil; (*c*) **to f. about,** faire des sauts de carpe; (*d*) **to f. along,** marcher lourdement, en faisant flic flac. **2.** *F:* échouer, faire faillite; (*of play, etc.*) faire four. **3.** *v.tr.* **he flopped the parcels down on the table,** il a posé lourdement les paquets sur la table. **4.** *v.i. Pol: U.S: F:* tourner casaque.

flophouse ['flɔphaus], *s. P:* (*a*) hôtel *m* borgne; (*b*) asile *m* de nuit.

floppy ['flɔpi], *a.* (*of hat, brim, etc.*) pendant, flasque, souple; (*of garment*) lâche, trop large; *F:* (*of pers.*) veule, avachi, mollasse; **with f. ears,** (chien) à oreilles pendantes.

Flora ['flɔːrə]. **1.** *Pr.n.f.* Flore. **2.** *s.* **the f. and fauna of a region,** la flore et la faune d'une région. **3.** *s. Med:* **intestinal, bacterial, f.,** flore intestinale, microbienne.

floral ['flɔːrəl], *a.* **1.** floral, -aux; **dress with a bold f. design,** robe *f* à grands ramages; *Bot:* **f. leaf,** feuille florale; *Lit: Hist:* **f. festival,** floralie(s) *f(pl)*; **f. games,** jeux floraux. **2. f. zone,** zone végétale.

floralia [flɔː'reiliə], *s.pl. Rom.Ant:* floralies *f*.

florencite ['flɔrənsait], *s. Miner:* florensite *f*.

Florentine ['flɔrəntain]. **1.** *Geog:* (*a*) *a.* florentin; (*b*) *s.* Florentin, -ine. **2.** *a. & s. Tex:* **F. (drill),** florentine *f*; **F. (satin),** florentine.

florescence [flɔː'res(ə)ns], *s.* fleuraison *f*, floraison *f*.

floret ['flɔːrit], *s. Bot:* fleuron *m*; **ligulate f.,** demi-fleuron *m*, *pl.* demi-fleurons; **florets of the disc,** fleurs non rayonnantes (d'une composée); **florets of the ray,** fleurs extérieures, rayonnantes (d'une composée).

floribunda [flɔri'bʌndə], *a. & s. Hort:* (rose *f*, rosier *m*) floribunda *inv.*

florican ['flɔrikæn], *s. Orn:* florican *m*.

floriculture ['flɔrikʌltjər], *s.* floriculture *f*.

floriculturist [flɔːri'kʌltjərist], *s.* horticulteur *m* fleuriste.

florid ['flɔrid], *a.* (*of style, speech, etc.*) fleuri; orné à l'excès; (*of dress, architecture, etc.*) flamboyant; (*of countenance*) coloré, rubicond, fleuri; **to have a f. complexion,** être haut en couleur; *Mus:* **f. counterpoint,** contrepoint fleuri, contrepoint figuré; figuré *m*.

Florida ['flɔridə], *Pr.n.* **1.** *Geog:* Floride *f*. **2. F. moss,** mousse *f* d'Espagne; barbe *f* de vieillard.

Florideae [flɔ'ridiiː], *s.pl. Algae:* floridées *f*, algues *f* rouges.

Floridian [flə'ridiən], *Geog:* (*a*) *a.* floridien; (*b*) *s.* Floridien, -ienne.

floridity [flɔ'riditi], **floridness** ['flɔridnis], *s.* style fleuri (d'un discours, etc.); flamboyant *m* (d'une toilette, etc.); rougeur *f*, hauteur *f* (du teint).

floridly ['flɔridli], *adv.* (parler, écrire) d'un style fleuri.

floriferous [flɔː'rifərəs], *a. Bot:* florifère.

floriken ['flɔrikin], *s. Orn:* florican *m*.

florilegium, *pl.* **-ia** [flɔri'liːdʒiəm, -iə], *s.* florilège *m*.

florin ['flɔrin], *s. Num:* **1.** *A:* florin *m*; pièce *f* de deux shillings. **2.** florin (de divers pays).

florist ['flɔrist], *s.* fleuriste *mf*.

floristic [flɔ'ristik], *a.* floristique.

floristry ['flɔristri], *s.* art *m* du fleuriste.

florula, florule ['flɔrjul(ə)], *s. Bot:* florule *f*.

floscular ['flɔskjulər], **flosculous** ['flɔskjuləs], *a. Bot:* flosculeux.

floscule ['flɔskjuːl], *s. Bot:* fleuron *m*.

flos ferri ['flɔs'feri], *s. Miner:* flos-ferri *m*.

floss[1] [flɔs], *s. Tex:* araignée *f*, rave *f*, bourrette *f*; **f. (silk),** bourre *f* de soie; frison *m*; filoselle *f*; soie *f* floche, fleuret *m*, strasse *f*.

floss[2], *s. Metall:* floss *m*; **f. hole,** trou *m* à laitier.

flossy ['flɔsi], *a.* (*a*) soyeux; duveté; (*b*) *F:* voyant, tape-à-l'œil.

flotation [flou'teiʃ(ə)n], *s.* **1.** (*a*) *Nau:* flottaison *f*; **plane, line, of f.,** ligne *f*, plan *m*, de flottaison; (*b*) *Av:* **f. gear,** dispositif *m* d'amerrissage (pour avion terrestre). **2.** (*a*) flottage *m* (du bois, etc); (*b*) (*for ores, etc.*) **f. (process),** flottation *f*. **3.** *Com:* lancement *m* (d'une compagnie, etc.); *Fin:* émission *f* (d'un emprunt, etc.).

flotilla [flə'tilə], *s.* (*a*) *Navy: Nau:* flottille *f*; escadrille *f*; **f. leader,** chef *m*, conducteur *m*, de flottille; (*b*) *Navy:* **destroyer f.,** escadrille de contre-torpilleurs.

flotsam ['flɔtsəm], *s.* **1.** *Jur:* épave(s) flottante(s); **f. and jetsam,** choses *f* de flot et de mer. **2.** naissain *m* (d'huîtres).

floturning ['floutəːniŋ], *s. Metalw:* fluotournage *m*, repoussage *m* au tour.

flounce[1] [flauns], *s.* **1.** (*of fish in water, etc.*) secousse *f* (de corps); coup *m* (de queue). **2.** (*of pers.*) mouvement vif (d'indignation, d'impatience).

flounce[2], *v.i.* **1.** (*of fish in water, etc.*) se débattre, se démener. **2.** (*of pers.*) s'élancer, se jeter (avec un mouvement d'indignation, d'impatience); **to f. in, out, off,** entrer, sortir, partir, brusquement, dans un mouvement d'indignation, de dignité blessée.

flounce[3], *s. Dressm:* volant *m*; *Laund:* **f. iron,** coq *m* (de blanchisseuse).

flounce[4], *v.tr.* garnir (une jupe, etc.) de volants; **flounced skirt,** jupe à volants, à falbalas.

flounder[1] ['flaundər], *s. Ich:* flet *m*, carrelet *m*; *F:* flaiteau *m*.

flounder[2], *s.* mouvements gauches, décousus (pour avancer, pour se relever, pour s'empêcher de tomber); (*of horse*) débattement *m* (par terre).

flounder[3], *v.i.* **1.** patauger, barboter, patouiller (dans la boue, etc.); *Sp:* (*of boxer, etc.*) cafouiller; **to f. about in the water,** se débattre dans l'eau; **floundering among the seaweed,** empêtré dans les algues; **to f. along,** avancer en trébuchant; **to f. in a speech, in an explanation,** patauger dans un discours; s'embourber, s'empêtrer, cafouiller, dans une explication; **to f. through a translation,** traduire avec force accrocs. **2.** (*of horse*) (*a*) se débattre (par terre); (*b*) faire feu des quatre fers (pour ne pas tomber).

flounderer ['flaundərər], *s.* pataugeur, -euse.

floundering[1] ['flaundriŋ], *a.* **1.** qui trébuche (pour ne pas tomber); qui patauge, barbote (dans la boue, etc.); **f. explanation,** explication confuse, dans laquelle on barbote, on s'embourbe. **2.** (cheval *m*) qui se débat (par terre).

floundering[2], *s.* **1.** barbotage *m*, débattement *m*, pataugeage *m*; *Sp: etc:* cafouillage *m*. **2.** (*of horse*) débattement (par terre).

flour[1] ['flauər], *s.* **1.** (*a*) farine *f*; *Mill:* **pure wheaten f.,** fleur *f* de farine; **f. for bread,** farine panifiable; **second f.,** recoupe *f*; **third f.,** recoupette *f*; **f. mill,** minoterie *f*; moulin *m* à farine; **f. milling,** minoterie *f*, meunerie *f*; **f. dredger,** saupoudroir *m* à farine; **f. dust,** folle farine; **to cover, dust, sth. with f.,** (en)fariner qch.; **to get covered with f.,** *F:* **to get all over f.,** s'enfariner; (*b*) *Ent:* **f. beetle, f. weevil,** ténébrion *m*; tribolium *m*, *F:* cafard *m*, meunier *m*, escarbot *m* de la farine; **f. moth,** ephestia *f*; *Arach:* **f. mite,** acarus *m*. **2.** (*a*) crème *f* (de riz, etc.); farine (de moutarde, etc.); **potato f.,** fécule *f* de pommes de terre; (*b*) fleur (de soufre); **f. emery,** fleur *f*, potée *f*, d'émeri; (*c*) **f. of gypsum,** plâtre *m* au sas. **3.** *Civ.E:* fleur (dans un filler).

flour[2]. **1.** *v.tr.* (*a*) (en)fariner (qn, qch.); saupoudrer (une pâte, etc.) de farine; *Cu:* **f. before frying,** passez-les dans la farine avant de les faire frire; (*b*) *NAm:* moudre (le grain). **2.** *v.i.* (*of mercury*) se réduire en farine.

flourbin ['flauəbin], *s.* farinière *f*, huche *f*, maie *f*.

flouring ['flauəriŋ], *s.* (*a*) *Cu:* saupoudrage *m*; (*b*) *NAm:* **f. mill,** minoterie *f*.

flourish[1] ['flʌriʃ], *s.* **1.** (*a*) trait *m* de plume, enjolivure *f*; (*after signature*) parafe *m*; (*b*) fleur *f* (de rhétorique); fioriture *f* (de style). **2.** grand geste; brandissement *m* (d'épée); *Fenc: etc:* moulinet *m*; **to take off one's hat with a f.,** saluer d'un geste élégant, d'un grand geste; **he showed us in with a f.,** d'un geste large il nous a fait entrer; **to carry things off with a f.,** y mettre du panache. **3.** *Mus:* (*a*) fanfare *f* (de trompettes, de clairons); **to proclaim sth. with a great f. (of trumpets),** proclamer qch. à son de trompe; (*b*) (i) fioriture(s), ornement *m*; (ii) *Mil:* sonnerie *f* en fantaisie; (iii) (*vocal*) roulade *f*.

flourish[2]. **1.** *v.i.* (*a*) (*of plant*) croître, se développer, bien venir; **to f. in a sandy soil,** se plaire dans un terrain sablonneux; **plant that does not f. in this climate,** plante qui se déplaît sous ce climat; (*b*) (*of pers., business, etc.*) être florissant, prospérer; (*of arts*) fleurir; **trade will f.,** le commerce prendra de l'extension, deviendra florissant; **trade is flourishing,** le commerce est prospère; (*c*) être dans sa fleur, dans tout son éclat; battre son plein; (*d*) *A:* faire des phrases, de belles phrases; user d'un style fleuri; (*e*) *Mus:* faire des fioritures, des roulades; (*f*) (*of trumpets*) sonner une fanfare. **2.** *v.tr.* (*a*) brandir (une épée, un bâton); **to f. one's arms (about),** battre l'air; agiter les bras; gesticuler; **to f. one's stick,** (i) agiter sa canne; (ii) faire des moulinets avec sa canne; (*b*) faire parade de (son savoir, etc.).

flourishing[1] ['flʌriʃiŋ], *a.* (*of plant, pers., industry, etc.*) florissant; **f. trade,** commerce *m* prospère; **how are you?—f.,** comment allez-vous?—à merveille.

flourishing[2], *s.* **1.** croissance *f*, développement *m* (de plantes); prospérité *f*, état florissant (de qn). **2.** brandissement *m* (d'épée). **3.** *Mus:* fanfare *f* (de trompettes). **4.** *Needlew:* **f. thread,** lin *m* floche.

flourishingly ['flʌriʃiŋli], *adv.* d'une manière florissante; à merveille.

flourometer [flau'rɔmitər], *s. Civ.E:* fleuromètre *m*.

floury ['flauəri], *a.* **1.** enfariné; couvert de farine. **2.** (*of potatoes, etc.*) farineux. **3.** *Ent: Austr:* **f. miller,** (espèce de) cigale *f*.

flout[1] [flaut], *s. O:* moquerie *f*, raillerie *f*, insulte *f*.

flout[2]. **1.** *v.tr.* (*a*) railler (qn); **to f. one's enemies,** narguer ses ennemis; *O:* **a flouted lover,** un amoureux bafoué; (*b*) faire fi de (l'autorité de qn); se moquer (d'un ordre). **2.** *v.i.* se railler, se moquer, se gausser (de qn); se payer la tête de (qn).

flow[1] [flou], *s.* **1.** (*act or manner of flowing*) (*a*) écoulement *m*, coulée *f* (d'un liquide); coulée (de métal en fusion, etc.); **laminar f.,** écoulement laminaire, continu; **gravity f.,** écoulement par gravité; **single, multiple, f.,** écoulement simple, multiple; **return f.,** écoulement inversé, renversé, de retour; **smooth f.,** écoulement uniforme; **metered f.,** écoulement dosé; **back f.,** refoulement *m* (de l'eau d'une chaudière, etc.); **f. pattern,** diagramme *m*, schéma *m*, figure *f*, d'écoulement; **field of f.,** champ *m* d'écoulement; (*b*) *Mch:* courant *m*, flux *m* (de vapeur); **double f.,** flux alternatif; (*c*) *Metall: etc:* fluage *m*; **cold f.,** fluage à froid; **f. point,** point *m* de fluage; limite *f* d'écoulement; (*d*) *Geog: Geol:* écoulement (d'un cours d'eau, d'une couche); **glacier f.,** écoulement glaciaire; **coefficient of f.,** coefficient *m*, quotient *m*, d'écoulement; **viscous, plastic, f.,** flux, écoulement, visqueux, plastique; **zone of plastic f.,** zone *f* de flux (du sima); (*e*) *El:* passage *m* (d'un courant); **parallel-f. condenser,** condensateur *m* à courants dans le même sens; **counter-f. condenser,** condensateur à contre-courant; (*f*) passage, arrivée *f* (d'air, d'essence, etc.); (*g*) **f. of the tide,** flot *m*, flux, de la marée; **ebb and f.,** flux et reflux; (*h*) crue *f* (du Nil, etc.); (*i*) *Med:* écoulement (du sang); **renal plasma f.,** flux plasmatique rénal; (*j*) *Fin:* **f. of capital,** mouvement *m* de capital; **f. of money,** flux monétaire; (*k*) *Cmptr:* circulation *f* (de l'information); déroulement *m* (des opérations); **f. path,** branche *f* de traitement; **f. diagram,** organigramme *m*, ordinogramme *m*; (*l*) **grain f.,** sens *m* de la fibre du bois; (*m*) **a steady f. of immigrants,** un courant ininterrompu d'immigration. **2.** (*quantity flowing at a certain time*) (*a*) volume *m* (de liquide débité); débit *m*, écoulement (d'une rivière, d'un lac); débit, refoulement (d'une pompe); débit (d'un courant électrique, d'un flux électronique, radioactif); **hourly f.,** débit horaire; **f. control,** (i) régulation *f*, (ii) régulateur *m*, de débit; **f. regulator,** régulateur de débit; **f. density,** débit spécifique; **the f. of traffic,** le débit de la circulation; **there was a heavy f. of traffic,** il y avait une grande circulation. **3.** (*sth. that flows*) (*a*) courant, cours *m* (d'eau); (*b*) coulée *f* (de lave); (*c*) flot, flux (de sang, de paroles, etc.); **what a f. of words!** quels flots d'éloquence! (*d*) *Physiol:* menstrues *fpl*, règles *fpl*; (*e*) lignes tombantes (d'une robe); drapé *m* (d'un vêtement); (*f*) *Cer:* flux; fondant *m*.

flow[2], *v.*

I. *v.i.* **1.** (*stream along*) (*a*) couler, s'écouler; **to f. by gravity,** s'écouler par gravité; (*of river*) **to f. into the sea,** se jeter, se verser, dans la mer; **river flowing into the Atlantic,** fleuve *m* tributaire de l'Atlantique; **river flowing beside, alongside, a meadow,** rivière qui baigne un pré; **lava that flows down the mountain,** lave *f* qui dévale de la montagne; (*b*) *Geol:* (*of stratum*) s'écouler; (*c*) (*of tide*) monter, remonter; (*d*) (*of babbit, etc.*) fondre; (*e*) (*of blood, electric current, etc.*) circuler; **blood flowing to the head,** sang *m* qui afflue à la tête; (*f*) (*of people*) aller, venir, en masse; (*of conversation, etc.*) aller son train; (*of literary style*) couler facilement, avec aisance; (*g*) (*of hair, drapery, etc.*) flotter; (*h*) *Cmptr:* (*of information*) circuler. **2.** (*stream forth*) (*of stream, blood, tears, etc.*) se répandre, jaillir; **to cease flowing,** se tarir. **3.** (*result*) dériver, découler, provenir (**from,** de); **God, from Whom all blessings f.,** Dieu, de qui découlent toutes les grâces. **4.** *Lit:* (*of wines, etc.*) abonder; **land flowing with milk and honey,** pays *m* où coulent le lait et le miel.

II. (*compound verbs*) **1. flow away,** *v.i.* (*of liquid*) s'écouler.

2. flow back, *v.i.* refluer; (*of water*) regorger (dans un tuyau, etc.).

3. flow in, *v.i.* (*a*) (*of liquid*) entrer; (*b*) (*of people, money*) affluer; (*c*) *Cmptr:* (*of information*) arriver.

4. flow out, *v.i.* (*a*) sortir, s'écouler; (*b*) *Cmptr:* (*of information*) sortir.

flowage ['flouidʒ], *s.* (*a*) *Geol:* écoulement *m* (des roches, de la glace d'un glacier, etc.); (*b*) *U.S:* inondation *f*.

flowchart[1] ['floutʃɑːt], *s.* (*a*) *Cmptr:* organigramme *m*; ordinogramme *m*; **logical f.,** organigramme logique; **programming f.,** organigramme de programmation; **f. template,** organigraphe *m*; (*b*) *Ind: etc:* diagramme *m* des débits, des opérations successives, etc.; schéma *m* (de principe).

flowchart[2], *v.tr. Cmptr:* établir, faire, un organigramme.

flowcharting ['floutʃɑːtiŋ], *s. Cmptr:* établissement *m* d'un organigramme.

flower[1] ['flauər], *s.* **1.** *Bot:* fleur *f*; **late f.,** fleur tardive; arrière-fleur *f*, *pl.* arrière-fleurs; **wild flowers,** fleurs sauvages, des champs; **f. cup,** calice *m*; **bunch of flowers,** bouquet *m* (de fleurs); **cut flowers,** fleurs coupées; **to put flowers on a grave,** fleurir une tombe; **no flowers by request,** ni fleurs ni couronnes; **the room was all decorated with flowers,** la pièce était toute fleurie; (*of pers., at carnival, etc.*) **decked, decorated, with flowers,** enguirlandé, fleuri; **to have a f. in one's buttonhole,** avoir la boutonnière fleurie; **f. garden,** jardin *m* de fleurs, jardin d'agrément; **f. bed,** parterre *m*; plate-bande *f*, *pl.* plates bandes; (*round*) corbeille *f*; **f. grower,** jardinier *m* fleuriste; **f. market,** marché *m* aux fleurs; **f. seller, f. girl,** marchande *f* de fleurs (dans la rue); bouquetière *f*; **I bought it at the f. shop,** je l'ai acheté chez le fleuriste; **f. basket,** corbeille *f* à fleurs; **f. box,** caisse *f*, bac *m*, à fleurs; **f. holder,** porte-fleurs *m inv*; porte-bouquet *m*, *pl.* porte-bouquets; **f. vase,** vase *m* à fleurs; **f. stand,** jardinière *f*; **f. show,** exposition *f* horticole, d'horticulture; floralies *fpl*; *Ent:* **f. beetle,** cétoine *f*. **2.** (*a*) *Ch: etc:* **flowers of antimony, of sulphur,** fleur d'antimoine, de soufre; **flowers of wine,** fleurs de vin; (*b*) *Fung:* **flowers of tan,** fleur du tan. **3.** (*ornament*) (*a*) *Typ:* fleuron *m*; (*b*) *Arch:* rose *f*; œil *m* (de l'abaque du chapiteau corinthien); (*c*) *Lit:* **flowers of speech,** fleurs de rhétorique. **4.** fine fleur, crème *f*, élite *f* (de la race, de l'armée, etc.). **5.** (*of plant*) floraison *f*; **in f.,** en fleur; **in full f.,** en plein épanouissement; **to burst into f.,** fleurir; **in the f. of one's age,** dans la fleur de l'âge; **in the f. of youth,** dans la première fleur de la jeunesse. **6.** *pl. Physiol: A:* **flowers,** règles *f*, menstrues *f*.

flower[2]. **1.** *v.i.* (*of plant*) fleurir, pousser des fleurs, être en fleur; **the scheme flowered into an epoch-making reform,** le projet aboutit à une réforme qui a fait époque. **2.** *v.tr.* (*a*) *Hort:* faire fleurir (des plantes); (*b*) fleurir (qch.); orner (un tissu, etc.) de fleurs, de ramages.

flower-de-luce [flauədi'luːs], *s. Her: A:* fleur *f* de lis.

flowered ['flauəd], *a.* (*a*) (jardin, talus, etc.) fleuri; (*b*) **white-f.,** à fleurs blanches; **many-f.,** multiflore; (*c*) *Tex:* **f. material,** tissu *m* à fleurs, à ramages; (*d*) *Her:* fleuri.

flowerer ['flauərər], *s.* plante *f* qui fleurit, qui porte des fleurs; **early f.,** plante hâtive; **prolific f.,** plante très florifère.

floweret ['flauəret], *s. Poet:* fleurette *f*, petite fleur.

flowerfly ['flauəflai], *s. Ent:* syrphe *m*; volucelle *m*.

flowerhead ['flauəhed], *s. Bot:* capitule *m*.

floweriness ['flauərinis], *s. usu. Pej:* style fleuri (d'un livre, etc.); fleurs *fpl* de rhétorique (d'un discours).

flowering[1] ['flauəriŋ], *a.* **1.** (*of garden, plant*) fleuri, en fleur; **f. meadow,** pré fleuri; prairie couverte de fleurs. **2. f. plant, shrub,** plante *f*, arbrisseau *m*, à fleurs.

flowering[2], *s.* **1.** fleuraison *f* (d'une plante). **2.** *Tex:* fleurage *m* (d'un tissu).

flower-pecker ['flauəpekər], *s. Orn:* dicée *m*; **orange-breasted f.-p.,** dicée à ventre orange.

flowerpiece ['flauəpiːs], *s.* (*a*) *Art:* étude *f* de fleurs; tableau *m* de fleurs; (*b*) vase, etc., de fleurs (arrangé avec goût).

flower-piercer ['flauəpiəsər], *s. Orn:* diglosse *m*.

flowerpot ['flauəpɔt], *s.* pot *m* à fleurs; (*ornamental*) cache-pot *m inv*.

flowery ['flauəri], *a.* **1.** (pré, etc.) fleuri, couvert de fleurs; (tapis, etc.) orné de fleurs, de ramages; **f. paths,** sentiers fleuris; *A:* **the F. Land, Kingdom, Empire,** la Chine. **2.** *Pej:* (*of speech, style, etc.*) fleuri, empanaché; **f. phrases,** fleurs *f* de rhétorique; **to speak in f. language,** faire des phrases; faire de grandes phrases.

flowing[1] ['flouiŋ], *a.* **1.** (*of stream, etc.*) coulant; (*of tide*) montant; (*of oil well*) coulant naturellement; *Cer:* (*of colours*) noyé, confus. **2.** (*of style, line, etc.*) coulant, fluide, facile; (*of movement*) gracieux, aisé. **3.** (*of draperies*) flottant; à lignes tombantes; (*of hair*) tombant (dans le cou); **f. beard,** barbe longue, fleurie, barbe de fleuve; *Nau:* **with f. sail, sheet,** les écoutes filées.

flowing[2], *s.* **1.** coulement *m*, affluence *f* (d'une rivière, etc.). **2.** écoulement *m* (de l'eau, du métal); **f. out,** écoulement, sortie *f*.

flowline, flow line ['floulain], *s.* (*a*) *Geol:* plan *m* d'écoulement; ligne *f* de flux (d'un glacier); (*b*) *Cmptr:* ligne de jonction de symboles (sur un organigramme); (*c*) *Ind:* **f. production,** travail *m* à la chaîne.

flowmeter ['floumiːtər], *s.* débitmètre *m*; indicateur *m* d'écoulement, de débit (des liquides, etc.); **fluid f.,** débitmètre de fluide.

flown[1] [floun], *a. A: & Lit:* enflé; **f. with pride,** bouffi d'orgueil.

flown[2], *a.* (*philately*) **f. cover,** enveloppe (timbrée) envoyée par poste aérienne.

flowoff ['flouɔf], *s. Geog:* ruissellement *m*.

flow pipe ['floupaip], *s.* conduite montante (d'une tuyauterie d'eau chaude de ménage).

flowstone ['floustoun], *s. Geol:* plancher *m* stalagmitique; (dépôt *m* de) travertin *m*.

flu [fluː], *s. Med: F:* grippe *f*; **Asian f.,** grippe asiatique.

fluate ['flueit], *s. Ch:* fluate *m*.

flub[1] [flʌb], *v.tr. & i.* (**flubbed**) *NAm: F:* faire une gaffe, une bévue, une bourde; **to f. (the dub),** rater (qch.).

flub[2], *s. NAm: F:* échec *m*; erreur *f*; gaffe *f*, bévue *f*, bourde *f*.

flubdub ['flʌbdʌb], **flubdubbery** [flʌb'dʌbəri], *s. NAm: F:* grandiloquence *f*, emphase *f*.

fluctuant ['flʌktjuənt], *a.* (*a*) fluctuant, instable, variable, oscillant; (*b*) *Med:* (*of tumour, etc.*) fluctuant.

fluctuate ['flʌktjueit], *v.i.* **1.** fluctuer; (*of conditions, etc.*) varier; (*of markets, values*) osciller; **income that fluctuates between £2000 and £2500,** revenu *m* qui varie, oscille, roule, entre £2000 et £2500; **prices f. between . . . and . . .,** les prix flottent entre . . . et . . . . **2.** (*of pers.*) flotter, balancer, vaciller, hésiter (dans ses opinions, etc.); **to f. between fear and hope,** flotter entre la crainte et l'espérance.

fluctuating ['flʌktjueitiŋ], *a.* (*of temperature, etc.*) variable; (*of prices, etc.*) oscillant.

fluctuation [flʌktju'eiʃ(ə)n], *s.* oscillation *f*; variations *fpl* (de température); **f. in exchange, of the franc,** fluctuation(s) *f*, variation(s), oscillation, du change, du (cours du) franc; **curve showing violent fluctuations,** courbe saccadée; *El: etc:* **service f., power f.,** fluctuation dans le fonctionnement; variation de la puissance, **f. of terrestrial magnetism,** variation du magnétisme terrestre; **cyclic(al) f.,** variation cyclique.

flue[1] [fluː], *s. Fish:* **f. (net),** tramail *m*.

flue[2], *s.* peluches *fpl*, duvet *m*.

flue[3], *s.* **1.** (*a*) *Const:* conduit *m*, tuyau *m*, de cheminée; conduit de fumée; gaine *f* (d'évacuation), cheminée *f* (d'une meule à charbon de bois, etc.); **f. pipe,** tuyau de poêle; (*b*) *Mch:* tube-foyer *m*, *pl.* tubes-foyers (de chaudière); **heating f.,** gaine *f* de chauffe; **f. boiler,** chaudière *f* à tubes-foyers; **f. surface,** surface *f* de chauffe; **f. plate, f. sheet,** plaque *f* tubulaire (de chaudière); (*c*) aspirail *m* (*pl.* -aux), carneau *m* (de four); échappement rampant (de four à réverbère); courant *m* de flammes; **down f., upper f.,** courant de flammes de haut en bas, de bas en haut; **flash f.,** courant de flammes longitudinal; (*d*) **f. brush,** torche-tubes *m inv*; écouvillon *m*, hérisson *m*; *Ind: Atom.Ph:* **f. gas,** gaz *m* de fumée, les fumées *f*; (*e*) *Tex:* **hot f.,** chambre chaude. **2.** *Mus:* bouche *f* (de tuyau d'orgue); **f. pipe,** tuyau à bouche; **f. stop,** (jeu *m* de) flûte *f* (d'un orgue).

flue[4]. **1.** *v.tr.* ébraser (une ouverture, etc.). **2.** *v.i.* (*of opening, etc.*) s'ébraser.

flueless ['flu:lis], *a.* (poêle *m*) sans gaine d'évacuation, sans tuyau.

fluellen [flu:'elin], *s. Bot:* véronique *f* femelle.

fluellite [flu:'elait], *s. Miner:* fluellite *f*.

fluency ['flu:ənsi], *s.* facilité *f* (de parole, de style).

fluent ['flu:ənt], *a.* **1.** (*of speech, style, etc.*) coulant, facile, fluide; **to be a f. speaker,** avoir la parole facile; parler facilement; **he is a f. speaker of French,** il parle le français couramment. **2.** (*of curve, outline*) coulant, fluide. **3.** *Mth:* **f. quantity,** grandeur *f* en mouvement.

fluently ['flu:əntli], *adv.* (parler, lire, etc.) couramment; (s'exprimer) avec facilité.

fluey ['flu:i], *a.* pelucheux.

fluff[1] [flʌf], *s.* **1.** (*a*) duvet *m* (d'étoffe); peluches *fpl*; coron *m* (de laine); *F:* minou *m*; (*of cloth*) **to lose, shed, its f.,** pelucher; jeter son coton; **a bit of f.,** une peluche; *F:* **a little bit of f.,** une petite femme, une jeunesse; (*b*) (*under bed, etc.*) **(pieces of) f.,** moutons *mpl*, minets *mpl*. **2.** fourrure douce (d'un jeune animal, d'un lapin, etc.). **3.** *Th: F:* loup *m*.

fluff[2], *v.tr.* **1.** (*a*) *Leath:* poncer (une peau); (*b*) (i) lainer (un drap, etc.); (ii) réduire (qch.) en peluches; **to f. old rope,** faire de l'étoupe avec de vieux cordages; (*c*) **to f. (out) one's hair,** faire bouffer ses cheveux; se retaper les cheveux; **bird that fluffs (up) its feathers,** oiseau *m* qui hérisse ses plumes. **2.** *Th: F:* **to f. one's entrance, one's part,** rater, louper, bouler, son entrée; bouler son rôle; **fluffed entrance,** loup *m*; *Sp:* **to f. a shot,** rater un coup.

fluffless ['flʌflis], *a.* (papier, etc.) non pelucheux.

fluffy ['flʌfi], *a.* (drap, papier) pelucheux; (poussin, etc.) duveteux; **f. hair,** cheveux flous; (*of worn material, etc.*) **to become f.,** pelucher; jeter son coton; *F:* **a f. little thing,** une petite frou-frou (*pl.* frou-frous).

flugelhorn ['flu:gəlhɔ:n], *s. Mus:* bugle *f*.

fluid ['flu:id]. **1.** *a.* (*a*) *Ph: Ch:* fluide, liquide; **f. substances,** corps *m* fluides; *Pharm:* **f. extract,** extrait *m* fluide; (*b*) *Mec.E:* **f. coupling, f. clutch,** accouplement *m*, embrayage *m*, hydraulique; **f. drive, f. transmission,** transmission *f* fluide; (*c*) (*of style, speech, etc.*) fluide, coulant, facile; (*of opinions, etc.*) changeant, inconstant; **industry in a f. state,** industrie *f* en voie de transformation rapide, qui n'a pas encore atteint son point d'équilibre; *Mil:* **f. front,** ligne de contact fluide, mouvante; **f. operations,** opérations fluides; **f. situation,** situation *f* fluide. **2.** *s.* (*a*) fluide *m*, liquide *m*, solution *f*; *Ph:* **f. measures,** mesures *fpl* pour les liquides; **f. mechanics,** mécanique *f* des fluides; **f. pressure,** pression exercée par un, des, fluide(s); **incompressible f.,** liquide incompressible; **(electric) f.,** fluide (électrique); *Metalw:* **soldering f.,** eau *f* à souder; *Aut:* **brake f.,** liquide pour freins; *El:* **single-f. cell,** élément *m* à un liquide; *Engr:* **etching f.,** solution pour graver; *Med:* **sterilizing f.,** solution stérilisante; *Nau:* **f. compass,** compas *m* à liquide; (*b*) *Physiol:* **body fluids,** sécrétions *f*; **cephalorachidian f.,** liquide céphalorachidien; **follicular f.,** liquide folliculaire.

fluidal ['flu:idl], *a.* fluidal, -aux; *Geol:* **f. texture,** texture fluidale.

fluidic [flu:'idik]. **1.** *a.* fluidique. **2.** *s.pl.* (*usu. with sg. const.*) **fluidics,** fluidique *f*.

fluidify [flu:'idifai], *v.tr.* fluidifier, liquéfier (un solide).

fluidity [flu:'iditi], *s.* **1.** fluidité *f* (de l'eau, etc.). **2.** (*a*) fluidité, facilité *f* (de style, etc.); (*b*) caractère changeant, inconstance *f* (des opinions de qn, etc.).

fluidization [flu:idai'zeiʃ(ə)n], *s. Tchn:* fluidisation *f*.

fluidize ['flu:idaiz], *v.tr. Tchn:* fluidiser, rendre fluide; *Atom.Ph:* **fluidized(-fuel) reactor,** réacteur *m* à combustible fluidisé.

fluke[1] [flu:k], *s.* **1.** *Ich:* flet *m*, carrelet *m*. **2.** *Vet:* **f. (worm),** trématode *m*; *esp.* douve *f* (du foie).

fluke[2], *s.* **1.** (*a*) *Nau:* patte *f*, aile *f* (d'ancre); **to foul the flukes,** surpatter; **mooring anchor with only one f.,** ancre *f* borgne; (*b*) *A.Arms:* fer *m* de lance à barbillons. **2.** *pl. Z:* (nageoires *f* de la) queue (d'une baleine).

fluke[3], *s.* (*a*) *Bill:* (coup *m* de) raccroc *m*; point volé; **to make flukes,** raccrocher; **by a f.,** par raccroc; (*b*) coup de veine, de hasard; chance *f*; **his success was due to a f.,** c'est un hasard qu'il ait réussi.

fluke[4]. **1.** *v.tr.* (*a*) *Bill:* raccrocher (la balle, un coup); (*b*) **to f. a win,** gagner par un coup de veine. **2.** *v.i.* (*a*) *Bill:* raccrocher; (*b*) avoir un coup de veine.

fluked [flu:kt], *a. Vet:* douvé.

flukiness ['flu:kinis], *s.* caractère incertain (du jeu, du vent, etc.).

fluky ['flu:ki], *a.* (coup, etc.) de raccroc; (jeu) hasardeux, incertain; *Nau:* **f. wind,** vent changeant, incertain.

flume[1] [flu:m], *s.* **1.** buse *f*, abée *f*, rayère *f*, reillère *f* (d'un moulin à eau); glissoir *m* à eau. **2.** (*for logs, etc.*) canal *m* d'amenée, de dérivation (en bois); canalisation *f* sur chevalets; auge *f*, flume *m*. **3.** *Geol: U.S:* (*a*) (*ravine*) auge, ravin *m*; (*b*) torrent *m* (de ravin).

flume[2], *v.tr. U.S:* transporter, amener (l'eau, du bois, etc.) dans une canalisation en bois.

flummery ['flʌməri], *s.* **1.** *Cu:* entremets *m* aux œufs et au lait; crème *f* aux œufs. **2.** *F:* (*a*) vétilles *fpl*; bêtises *fpl*; (*b*) flatterie *f*, boniment *m*; **that's all f.,** tout ça c'est de la blague.

flummox ['flʌməks], *v.tr. F:* réduire (qn) à quia; démonter (qn); **he isn't easily flummoxed,** il ne se laisse pas démonter; rien ne l'épate.

flump[1] [flʌmp], *F:* **1.** *int.* plouf! **2.** *s.* coup sourd (de qch. qui tombe); plouf *m*, floc *m*.

flump[2]. **1.** *v.i.* **to f. about,** marcher à pas lourds; **to f. down,** tomber plouf. **2.** *v.tr.* **to f. sth. down,** laisser tomber, jeter à terre, un objet (lourd).

flunk[1] [flʌŋk], *s. esp. NAm: F:* recalage *m*, collage *m* (à un examen).

flunk[2], *v. F:* **1.** *v.i.* (*a*) se faire recaler, se faire coller (à un examen); (*b*) y renoncer; flancher. **2.** *v.tr.* recaler, coller (qn à un examen).

flunkey ['flʌŋki], *s.* **1.** *A: or Pej:* laquais *m*, valet *m* de pied; *F:* larbin *m*. **2.** *F:* flagorneur *m*, sycophante *m*; *A:* pied plat.

fluoaluminate [flu:ouə'lju:mineit], *s.* fluoaluminate *m*.

fluoborate [flu:ou'bɔ:reit], *s.* fluoborate *m*.

fluoboric [flu:ou'bɔrik], *a.* fluoborique.

fluocerine, fluocerite [flu:ou'serain, -'serait], *s. Miner:* fluocérine *f*, fluocérite *f*, flucérine *f*.

fluophosphate [flu:ou'fɔsfeit], *s.* fluophosphate *m*.

fluor ['flu:ɔ:r], *s. Miner:* = FLUORSPAR.

fluoranthene [flu:ɔ'rænθi:n], *s. Ch:* fluoranthène *m*.

fluorene ['flu:ɔri:n], *s. Ch:* fluorène *m*.

fluoresce [flu:ə'res], *v.i. Ph:* (*of a body*) entrer en fluorescence.

fluorescein [flu:ə'resiin], *s. Ch:* fluorescéine *f*.

fluorescence [flu:ə'res(ə)ns], *s.* fluorescence *f*.

fluorescent [flu:ə'res(ə)nt], *a. Ph:* (corps, etc.) fluorescent; **f. screen,** écran fluorescent; **f. lighting,** éclairage fluorescent, par fluorescence.

fluoridation [flu:ɔri'deiʃ(ə)n], *s. Ch:* fluoration *f*, fluoruration *f*.

fluoride ['flu:əraid], *s. Ch:* fluorure *f*.

fluorimeter [flu:ɔ'rimitər], *s.* fluorimètre *m*.

fluorine ['flu:əri:n], *s. Ch:* fluor *m*.

fluorite ['flu:ərait], *s. Miner:* = FLUORSPAR.

fluoroform ['flu:əroufɔ:m], *a. Ch:* fluoroforme.

fluorography [flu(:)ə'rɔgrəfi], *s. Engr:* fluorographie *f*.

fluorometer [flu(:)ə'rɔmitər], *s. Ch:* fluoromètre *m*.

fluorophotometer ['flu(:)əroufou'tɔmitər], *s.* fluoromètre *m*.

fluoroscope ['flu(:)ərəskoup], *s.* fluoroscope *m*.

fluoroscopic [flu(:)ərə'skɔpik], *a.* **f. observation,** examen *m* radioscopique.

fluoroscopy [flu(:)ə'rɔskəpi], *s. X Rays:* fluoroscopie *f*.

fluorosis [flu(:)ə'rousis], *s. Vet:* fluorose *f*.

fluorspar ['flu:əspɑ:r], *s. Miner:* spath *m* fluor; chaux fluatée; fluorine *f*; **blue f.,** saphir *m* femelle.

fluosilicate [flu:ou'silikeit], *s. Ch:* fluosilicate *m*.

fluosilicic [flu:ousi'lisik], *a. Ch:* (acide *m*) fluosilicique.

fluosulphonic [flu:ousʌl'fɔnik], *a. Ch:* fluosulfonique.

flurry[1] ['flʌri], *s.* **1.** (*a*) *Nau:* risée *f*, grain *m* (de vent); brise folle; (*b*) rafale *f* (de neige); *NAm: occ.* averse *f*. **2.** agitation *f*, bouleversement *m*, émoi *m*; **all in a f.,** tout ébouriffé, tout effaré, tout étourdi, tout en émoi; **a f. on the stock exchange,** une panique, une crise, de bourse. **3. the death f.,** les derniers débattements, les dernières convulsions (de la baleine expirante, d'un chien écrasé, etc.).

flurry[2], *v.tr.* agiter, ébouriffer, étourdir, bouleverser, effarer (qn); **to get flurried,** perdre la tête; se troubler; **to be flurried,** être (tout) en émoi; (*of candidate*) être interdit.

flurry[3], *s. Dy:* fleurée *f* (du bleu indigo).

flush[1] [flʌʃ], *s. Ven:* envolée *f* (d'oiseaux).

flush[2]. **1.** *v.tr. Ven:* (faire) lever, faire partir (des perdrix, etc.); **to f. (and scatter) game,** égailler le gibier. **2.** *v.i.* (*of game*) s'envoler; s'égailler.

flush[3], *s.* **1.** (*a*) *Hyd.E:* chasse *f* (d'eau); **automatic f.,** chasse automatique; **f. tank,** réservoir *m* de chasse; **f. valve,** robinet *m*, soupape *f*, de vidange; **f. board,** hausse *f*; (*b*) curage *m* (d'un égout); (*c*) canal *m* de fuite (de moulin). **2.** (*a*) pousse *f* (des bourgeons, des feuilles, etc.); (*b*) accès *m*, élan *m* (d'émotion, de passion, etc.); **in the first f. of victory,** dans l'ivresse de la victoire; (*c*) abondance soudaine; **a f. of orders,** une poussée de commandes. **3.** (*a*) éclat *m* (de lumière, de couleur, de la beauté, etc.); **the first f. of dawn,** les premières lueurs de l'aube; **in the first f. of youth,** dans le premier éclat, la première fraîcheur, de la jeunesse; (*b*) rougeur *f*, afflux *m*, flot *m* de sang (au visage); *Med:* **(hot) f.,** suffusion *f*; bouffée *f* de chaleur; enchymose *f*; **the words brought a f. to his cheeks,** ces mots l'ont fait rougir.

flush[4], *v.* **1.** (*a*) *v.i.* (*of liquid, stream, etc.*) **to f. (out, up),** jaillir; **to f. over,** déborder; (*b*) *v.tr.* faire jaillir (l'eau); inonder (un pré); **to f. (out) a drain,** donner une chasse à un égout; balayer, débourber, un égout à grande eau; curer un égout; **to f. the lavatory,** tirer la chasse d'eau; **to f. away,** jeter à l'égout; *Aut:* **to f. (out) the radiator,** rincer le radiateur. **2.** (*a*) *v.i.* (*of plants, etc.*) pousser de nouvelles feuilles; (*b*) *v.tr.* (*of rain, etc.*) faire pousser (les plantes, etc.). **3.** *v.i.* (*a*) (*of light, colour, etc.*) éclater; (*of the sky*) rutiler, s'empourprer; (*b*) (*of pers.*) rougir; (*of blood*) monter (au visage); *Med:* éprouver des chaleurs; **he, his face, flushed,** il a rougi; le sang lui est monté au visage; **he flushed an angry red,** (i) son visage s'est empourpré; (ii) il a rougi de colère. **4.** *v.tr.* **the exercise had flushed their cheeks,** l'exercice leur avait fouetté le sang, leur avait fait monter le sang au visage.

flush[5], *s. Cards:* (*poker*) floch(e) *m*, flush *m*; longue couleur; **straight f.,** séquence *f* flush; séquence royale; quinte *f* flush; quinte de couleur.

flush[6], *a.* **1.** (*a*) (*of stream, etc.*) plein à déborder; débordant; (*b*) *F:* (*of pers.*) **to be f. (with money),** être en fonds, avoir de l'argent plein les poches. **2.** (*of surface, etc.*) ras; de niveau; affleurant; dans le même plan; (*of door lock, etc.*) encastré; entaillé; (*of screw, nail*) noyé; (*of bolt, rivet*) affleurant, à tête noyée, perdue, fraisée; **f. joint,** assemblage affleuré, à francs bords; aboutement *m*; joint *m* lisse; **f. riveting,** rivetage *m*, rivure *f*, à fleur, à franc bord; **f. welding,** soudure affleurée; **f. fitted,** assemblé à francs bords, à joint(s) lisse(s); **f. mounted,** monté à fleur; **f. countersunk,** fraisé à fleur; à tête noyée, perdue; **to cut sth. off, machine sth., f.,** araser qch.; **to make parts f.,** affleurer, araser, mettre à fleur, raccorder, des pièces; **to be f. with sth.,** être à fleur, au ras, de qch.; être à la même hauteur que qch.; être au niveau de, de niveau avec, qch.; affleurer, s'affleurer avec, qch.; **to drive a nail f. with the wood,** enfoncer un clou à fleur de bois; **f. with the ground,** de plein pied; à ras, à fleur, de terre; à ras de, au niveau du, sol; **houses built f. with the pavement,** maisons construites de plein pied avec le trottoir, au niveau du, de niveau avec le, trottoir; *W.Tel: etc:* **f. antenna,** antenne rase; *Bookb:* **f. binding,** cartonnage rogné à ras de page.

flush[7], *v.tr.* affleurer, affronter (deux surfaces, etc.).

flushed [flʌʃt], *a.* (visage) enfiévré, empourpré, congestionné; **to have a f. face,** avoir le visage en feu; **f. with anger,** rouge de colère; **face f. with drink,** visage allumé, enluminé, rougi, par la boisson; **f. with success,** ivre de succès, exalté par le succès.

flushing[1] ['flʌʃiŋ], *s.* **1.** curage *m*, chasse *f* (d'un égout); **f. chamber,** chambre *f* de chasse (d'un égout); **f. cistern,** réservoir *m* de chasse. **2.** pousse *f* (des feuilles, des bourgeons). **3.** rougeur *f* (au visage); *Med:* enchymose *f*, bouffée *f* de chaleur.

Flushing[2], *Pr.n. Geog:* Flessingue *f*.

fluster[1] ['flʌstər], *s.* agitation *f*, trouble *m*, bouleversement *m*; **in a f.,** tout en émoi, tout ébouriffé, tout déconcerté, bouleversé.

fluster[2]. **1.** *v.tr.* (*a*) *A:* griser (qn); (*b*) agiter, ébouriffer, bouleverser (qn); faire perdre la tête à (qn); rendre (qn) nerveux; **to be, get, flustered,** se troubler; être démonté, bouleversé; *F:* **as flustered as an old hen with one chick,** empêtré comme une poule qui n'a qu'un poussin. **2.** *v.i.* s'agiter, s'échauffer; s'énerver.

flustra, *pl.* **-ae, -as** ['flʌstrə, -i:, -əz], *s. Biol:* flustre *f*.

Flustridae ['flʌstridi:], *s.pl.* flustridés *m*.

flute[1] [flu:t], *s.* **1.** *Mus:* (*a*) flûte *f*; **transverse f., German f.,** flûte traversière; **concert f.,** grande flûte; **f. in E flat,** flûte tierce; *Th:* **the Magic F.,** la Flûte enchantée; (*b*) **fipple f.,** flûte à bec; (*c*) **f. (stop),** (jeu *m* de) flûte (de l'orgue); (*d*) **eunuch f.,** mirliton *m*. **2.** *Mus:* **f. (player),** (joueur, -euse, de) flûte. **3.** (*a*) (*in wood, etc.*) rainure *f*; cannelure *f* (de colonne, de carton ondulé); (*b*) *Laund:* tuyau *m*; (*c*) *Tex:* flûte; (*d*) **f. (glass),** flûte; (*e*) *Hort:* **f.**

grafting, greffe *f* en anneau.

flute². **1.** (*a*) *v.i.* (i) jouer de la flûte; (ii) (*of birds*) flûter; (*b*) *v.tr.* jouer (un air) sur la flûte. **2.** *v.tr.* (*a*) rainer, rainurer (une planche, un écrou, etc.); canneler, strier (une colonne); évider (un outil); **to f. a reamer,** tailler un alésoir; (*b*) *Laund:* tuyauter, cisailler, rucher, godronner (une coiffe, etc.); gaufrer (le linge) (à la paille).

flutebird ['flu:tbə:d], *s. Orn: F:* flûteur *m*.

fluted ['flu:tid], *a.* **1.** (*of notes, voice, etc.*) flûté. **2.** (*a*) (*of wood, tool, nut, etc.*) à rainure(s); à cannelures; (*of column*) cannelé, strié; *Furn:* **f. leg,** pied *m* en carquois; *Tls:* **f.-shank drill,** foret *m*, mèche *f*, à tige cannelée; (*b*) *Laund:* (linge) tuyauté, à godets.

flutelike ['flu:tlaik], *a. F:* (voix) flûtée.

fluting ['flu:tiŋ], *s.* **1.** (*a*) *Mus:* (i) (action de jouer de) la flûte; (ii) sons flûtés; (*b*) (i) façonnage *m* des rainures, des cannelures; évidage *m* (d'un outil); **f. machine,** machine *f* à canneler; **f. plane,** guillaume *m* à canneler; (ii) *Laund:* tuyautage *m*, cisaillage *m*, gaufrage *m* (du linge); **f. iron,** fer *m* à tuyauter. **2.** *coll.* (*a*) rainures *fpl*, cannelures *fpl*; (*b*) *Laund:* tuyaux *mpl*, tuyauté *m*, godrons *mpl*; *Dressm:* tuyaux d'orgue.

flutist ['flu:tist], *s.* (joueur, -euse, de) flûte *f*.

flutter¹ ['flʌtər], *s.* **1.** (*a*) volètement *m*, voltigement *m*, trémoussement *m* (d'un oiseau); battement *m* (des ailes, des paupières); palpitation *f* (du cœur); flottement *m*, voltigement (d'un rideau, d'un drapeau, etc.); jeu *m* rapide (d'un éventail); (*b*) *Av:* vibration *f* (d'un plan d'avion sous l'effet de forces aérodynamiques); (*c*) *Ac: Elcs:* pleurage *m*, pulsation *f* (du son); **f. echo,** écho *m* à battements, écho multiple; (*d*) *T.V:* scintillation *f*, sautillement lumineux. **2.** agitation *f*, trouble *m*, émoi *m*; excitation *f* fébrile; *Med:* **auricular f.,** tachysystolie *f* auriculaire; **f. of pleasure,** mouvement *m* de plaisir; **to be in a f. of excitement,** *F:* **all in a f.,** être tout en émoi, tout bouleversé; **that will cause a f. in the dovecotes,** cela portera l'alarme dans le camp. **3.** *Fin: F:* petite spéculation; *Cards: Turf:* **to have a little f.,** risquer de petites sommes au jeu; faire un ou deux petits paris.

flutter². **1.** *v.i.* (*a*) (*of birds, insects*) voleter, battre des ailes; (*of flag, ribbon, etc.*) flotter, s'agiter (au vent); (*of heart*) palpiter, battre; (*of pulse*) battre irrégulièrement; **to make s.o.'s heart f.,** faire tressaillir le cœur de qn; **to f. about,** voleter, voltiger, papillonner; **the letter fluttered to the ground,** la lettre a volé par terre; (*b*) (*of pers.*) trembler, frémir, s'exciter; **to f. with joy,** frémir de joie; (*c*) *I.C.E:* (*of valve*) **to f. on its seat,** battre sur le siège. **2.** *v.tr.* (*a*) agiter, faire flotter, secouer (un drapeau, son mouchoir, etc.); jouer de (l'éventail); (*of bird*) **to f. its wings,** battre des ailes; (*b*) *F:* agiter, troubler, ahurir (qn); **to f. the dovecotes,** porter l'alarme dans le camp; mettre l'alarme au quartier.

fluttering¹ ['flʌt(ə)riŋ], *a.* (oiseau, etc.) trémoussant, voltigeant, voletant; (drapeau, ruban) flottant; (ruban) qui badine; (cœur) palpitant.

fluttering², *s.* = FLUTTER¹ 1. (*a*).

fluty ['flu:ti], *a.* (*of voice, etc.*) flûté.

fluvial ['flu:viəl], *a.* fluvial, -aux.

fluviatile ['flu:viətail], *a.* fluviatile.

fluvioglacial [flu:viou'gleisiəl, -'gleiʃ(ə)l], *a. Geol:* (cailloutis *m*, etc.) fluvio(-)glaciaire.

fluviograph ['flu:viougræf], *s.* fluviographe *m*.

fluviomarine ['flu:vioumə'ri:n], *a. Geol:* (dépôt) fluvio(-)marin.

fluviometer [flu:vi'ɔmitər], *s.* fluviographe *m*, fluviomètre *m*.

fluviometric [flu:viou'metrik], *a.* fluviométrique.

flux¹ [flʌks], *s.* **1.** (*a*) *Med:* flux *m* (de sang, de pus, etc.); *A:* **the bloody f.,** la dysenterie; (*b*) *Oc:* flux, flot *m*, montant *m* (de la marée); **f. and reflux,** flot et jusant, flux et reflux; (*c*) flot, courant *m*, écoulement *m* (d'eau, etc.). **2.** (*a*) flux, changement continuel; **to be in a state of f.,** être sujet à des changements fréquents, à des vicissitudes; (*b*) *Ph: El: etc:* flux (magnétique, lumineux, etc.); **magnetic f.,** flux (d'induction) magnétique, de force (magnétique); **f. density,** (i) densité *f* de flux; (ii) densité, intensité *f*, du champ magnétique; **f. depression,** diminution *f* du flux; **f. gate, f. valve,** vanne *f* de flux; *Atom.Ph:* **radiation f.,** flux de rayonnement; **neutron f.,** flux de neutrons; *El:* **induction f.,** flux d'induction; **balancing f.,** flux compensateur, équilibreur; **leakage f., stray f.,** flux de dispersion; **f. linkage,** couplage inductif; (*c*) *Mth:* flux, déplacement, continuel (d'un point). **3.** (*a*) *Metall:* fondant *m*, flux; **casting f.,** fondant de coulée; **clay f.,** (h)erbue *f*; **limestone f.,** castine *f*; **f. chips,** écailles *f* de fondant; (*b*) *Cer:* rocaille *f*; **enamelling f.,** roquette *f*; (*c*) *Glassm:* **gold f.,** aventurine *f*; (*d*) *Metalw:* décapant *m*, fondant de brasage; **acid f.,** acide *m* à souder; **soldering, welding, f.,** décapant, fondant, pour souder; **salt f.,** flux, fondant, salin; **powdered f.,** fondant en poudre, poudre décapante.

flux². **1.** *v.i.* (*a*) (*of liquids*) jaillir, ruisseler; (*b*) (*of metal*) fondre; devenir liquide. **2.** *v.tr.* (*a*) *Metall:* fondre, mettre en fusion (un métal); (*b*) *Metall:* **to f. the ore,** ajouter le fondant au minerai; (*c*) *Metalw:* couvrir de fondant, rocher (le métal à braser); (*d*) *Civ.E: etc:* fluxer.

fluxing ['flʌksiŋ], *s.* **1.** *Tchn:* fluxage *m*; *Petr:* fluidification *f*. **2.** *Metalw:* rochage *m* (du métal à braser); **f. paste,** décapant *m* en pâte.

fluxion ['flʌkʃ(ə)n], *s.* **1.** *Med:* (*a*) fluxion *f* (de sang, etc.); (*b*) *A:* flux *m* (de sang, etc.). **2.** *Mth: A:* fluxion; différentielle *f* (d'une quantité); **the method of fluxions,** la méthode des fluxions.

fluxional ['flʌkʃən(ə)l], **fluxionary** ['flʌkʃənəri], *a. Mth: etc:* fluxionnaire.

fluxmeter ['flʌksmi:tər], *s. Ph:* fluxmètre *m*; *Atom.Ph:* **fast-neutron, slow-neutron, f.,** fluxmètre de neutrons rapides, de neutrons lents; **counter-tube f.,** fluxmètre à tube compteur.

fly¹, *pl.* **flies** [flai(z)], *s.* **1.** (*a*) *Ent:* mouche *f*; **house f.,** mouche commune; **Spanish f., blistering f.,** mouche d'Espagne, cantharide *f*; **bot f., horse f.,** taon *m*, mouche des chevaux; **tsetse f.,** (mouche) tsé-tsé *f*; **vinegar f.,** mouche du vinaigre; **f. fungus,** empuse *f* de la mouche; **f. speck,** chiure *f*, chiasse *f*, de mouche; **f. killer, f. poison,** mort *f* aux mouches; **f. powder,** poudre *f* anti-mouches; **f. swatter, f. whisk,** chasse-mouches *m inv*, tapette *f* à mouches; (*for horse, etc.*) **f. net,** chasse-mouches, émouchoir *m*, émouchette *f*, épissière *f*; **they were dying like flies,** on mourait comme des mouches; **he wouldn't hurt a f.,** il ne ferait pas de mal à une mouche; *F:* **a f. in the ointment,** une ombre au tableau, un cheveu (sur la soupe); **that's the f. in the ointment,** voilà le hic; **a f. in amber,** une curiosité; **to catch flies,** bayer aux corneilles; **there are, there's, no flies on him,** c'est un malin, il n'est pas bête, n'est pas né hier, n'est pas manchot; *Prov:* **you catch more flies with honey than with verjuice,** on prend plus de mouches avec du miel qu'avec du vinaigre; (*b*) *Ent:* **f. weevil,** charançon *m* du blé, *F:* botte *f*; (*c*) *Fish:* mouche (artificielle ou naturelle); **salmon f.,** mouche à saumon; **spent-gnat f.,** spent *f*; **sunk f.,** mouche noyée; **wet f.,** mouche mouillée, noyée; **to fish with f.,** pêcher à la mouche; **wet-f. fishing,** pêche à la mouche noyée; **dry-f. fishing,** pêche à la mouche sèche, flottante; **to rise to the f.,** (i) (*of fish*) mordre à l'appât; (ii) *F: O:* (*of pers.*) gober la mouche; (*d*) *Bot:* **f. orchis,** ophrys *f* mouche; *Fung:* **f. agaric, f. fungus,** tue-mouches *m inv*; (*e*) (*used for insects in general*) **crops damaged by the f.,** récoltes gâchées par les insectes. **2.** *Typ:* (*a*) receveur, -euse; (*b*) receveur mécanique.

fly², *s.* **1.** vol *m*; **to catch a ball on the f.,** attraper une balle au vol; *esp. U.S:* **I've been on the f. all day,** je n'ai pas pu me reposer toute la journée. **2.** *A:* (*pl. usu.* **flys**) fiacre *m*; voiture *f* de place. **3.** (*a*) patte *f* (de pardessus, etc.); braguette *f* (de pantalon); **zip f.,** braguette à glissière; **overcoat with a f. front, f.-fronted overcoat,** pardessus *m* à fermeture sous patte; (*b*) **f. of a flag,** battant *m* d'un drapeau, d'un pavillon; (*c*) (i) auvent *m*, (ii) toit *m* (de tente). **4.** *Th:* **the flies,** les cintres *m*, les dessus *m*; **the upper flies,** le gril; **f. system,** machinerie *f* des cintres. **5.** (*a*) *Tchn:* moulinet *m* (de radiomètre, d'anémomètre, etc.); balancier *m* (de presse monétaire, etc.); régulateur *m*, contrepoids *m*, volant *m* (de sonnerie d'horloge, etc.); *Tex:* ailette *f* (de banc à broches); **f. press,** presse *f* à vis et à balancier; *Num:* balancier *m* monétaire; **f. pulley,** poulie-volant *f*, *pl.* poulies-volants; **f. nut,** écrou ailé, à oreilles; papillon *m*; *Tex:* **f. frame,** banc *m* à broches; **f.-frame tenter,** bancbrocheur, -euse; (*b*) *Tex:* **f. (shuttle),** navette volante; (*c*) *Ind:* **f. ash,** escarbilles *fpl*. **6.** *Tex:* duvet *m* (de lin, de coton). **7.** *Nau:* rose *f* des vents.

fly³, *v.* (**flew** [flu:]; **flown** [floun])

I. *v.i.* **1.** (*a*) (*of bird, arrow, etc.*) voler; **to f. swiftly,** voler à tire d'aile; **to f. into a room,** entrer en volant dans une pièce; **to shoot a bird flying,** tirer un oiseau au vol, à la volée; *F:* **the bird has flown,** l'oiseau s'est envolé, a déniché; il a décampé; **to find the birds flown,** trouver buisson creux, le nid vide; *Ven:* (*of hawk, etc.*) **trained to f. at the heron, etc.,** dressé à voler le héron, etc.; **to f. high,** (i) voler haut; (ii) (*of pers.*) viser haut; avoir de l'ambition; **as the crow flies,** à vol d'oiseau; **there's some gossip flying around,** il y a des bruits qui courent; *F:* **it's flown,** (i) je l'ai perdu; je ne le retrouve pas; (ii) on me l'a chipé; (*b*) *Av:* voler; effectuer un vol; naviguer; **to f. by dead reckoning,** naviguer, voler, à l'estime; **to f. (by, on) instruments,** naviguer, voler, aux instruments; **to f. blind,** naviguer, voler, sans visibilité; **to f. the beam,** voler par radio-alignement; **to f. level,** voler au palier; **to f. against, in, the wind, up wind,** voler contre le vent, dans le vent, vent debout; **to f. down wind, with the wind,** voler vent arrière, dans le dos; **to f. upside down,** voler sur le dos; **to f. above the clouds,** voler au-dessus des nuages; **to f. across a desert,** voler au-dessus d'un désert, traverser un désert en avion; **to f. to Paris,** se rendre à Paris en avion; **to f. back to Paris,** retourner à Paris en avion; **I flew part of the way,** j'ai fait une partie du trajet en avion; **to f. over London,** survoler Londres; *Mil:* **to f. (on) cover, escort, reconnaissance, mission,** effectuer une mission de couverture, d'escorte, de reconnaissance. **2.** (*of hair, flag, garment, etc.*) flotter; (*of signal, flag*) être battant. **3.** (*a*) (*of pers., etc.*) courir, aller à toute vitesse; (*of time*) fuir, filer, passer rapidement; **he flew into, out of, the room,** il est entré (dans la pièce), il est sorti, en coup de vent; **to f. to s.o.'s help,** courir à l'aide de qn; **it's late, I must f.,** il se fait tard, il faut que je me sauve; **time is flying,** le temps s'envole; (*of wine, blood*) **to f. to the head,** monter à la tête; **to f. to arms,** courir aux armes; **to f. (out) at s.o.,** (i) s'élancer sur qn; (ii) lancer des injures à qn; **to f. at s.o.'s throat,** sauter à la gorge de qn; **to f. into a rage, a passion, a temper,** s'emporter; se mettre en colère; prendre la mouche; **he flies into a passion for the least thing,** il prend feu pour la moindre chose; **the door flew open,** la porte s'ouvrit brusquement, soudainement, en coup de vent; (*b*) (*of cork, etc.*) voler, sauter en l'air; (*of sparks*) jaillir; **the horse made the sparks f. from his hoofs,** le cheval a fait feu des quatre pieds; **to make the money f.,** prodiguer son argent; **to make the fur f., the sparks f.,** faire une scène; **to f. off the handle,** (i) (*of axe head, etc.*) se démancher, s'envoler; (ii) *F:* s'emporter, s'emballer; sortir de ses gonds; *F:* **to send s.o. flying,** envoyer rouler qn (sur le carreau); **to send a plate flying,** envoyer, lancer, une assiette à la volée; **he sent the book flying at me,** il m'a lancé le livre à la tête; **the shock sent everything flying,** la secousse a fait voler les objets de tous côtés; **the wheels sent the puddles flying,** les roues faisaient jaillir les flaques d'eau; (*c*) **to f. to pieces, to bits,** éclater; voler en éclats; (*of steel*) s'égrener; (*d*) *Nau:* (*of wind*) **to f. (about),** sauter, jouer; (*e*) (*of stair*) monter droit. **4.** **to let f.,** lancer (un projectile, une flèche); décocher (un trait, une épigramme); lâcher (une volée d'injures); **to let fly a volley of oaths,** se répandre en jurons; **to let f. at s.o.,** (i) décharger son fusil sur, contre, qn; tirer sur qn; (ii) *F:* flanquer un coup à qn; (*of horse*) détacher une ruade, un coup de sabot, à qn; (iii) s'en prendre à qn; **to let f. at s.o. with one's foot,** lâcher un coup de pied à qn; *Nau:* **to let f. a broadside,** lâcher une bordée. **5.** (= FLEE, *in pres. tenses only*) (*a*) fuir, s'enfuir, se sauver; **to send the enemy flying,** mettre l'ennemi en fuite; **to f. to Belgium,** se sauver en Belgique; **to f. to s.o. (for protection),** se réfugier auprès de qn; **to f. from sth.,** s'enfuir (d'un endroit); se dérober (au danger, au combat); **to f. from justice,** se soustraire à l'action de la justice; **to f. for one's life,** chercher son salut dans la fuite; (*b*) *v.tr.* **to f. the country,** s'enfuir du pays; émigrer; *A:* (*of tram, etc.*) **to f. the track,** sortir de la voie; quitter la voie; dérailler.

II. *v.tr.* **1.** *Nau:* **to f. a flag,** battre un pavillon. **2.** (*a*) *Ven:* lancer, (faire) voler (un faucon, etc.); (*b*) (*with a hawk*) **to f. partridges,** voler la perdrix. **3.** (*a*) **to f. pigeons,** faire un lancer de pigeons voyageurs; (*b*) **to f. a kite,** (i) lancer, faire voler, un cerf-volant; (ii) *Fig:* lancer un ballon d'essai. **4.** *Av:* piloter (un avion); emmener qn, qch., en avion; transporter qn, qch., par avion; **to f. s.o. to Paris,** transporter qn à Paris par avion; **to f. munitions to an army,** amener par avion du matériel de guerre à une armée; ravitailler par avion une armée en matériel de guerre; **to f. the Channel, the Atlantic,** survoler la Manche, l'Atlantique; traverser la Manche, l'Atlantique, en avion; **letters are flown to London,** le courrier est transporté à Londres par avion.

III. (*compound verbs*) **1. fly about,** *v.i.* (*of bird*) voler çà et là, voleter, voltiger; (*of butterfly, etc.*) voltiger.

2. fly along, *v.i.* avancer, passer, à toute vitesse.

3. fly away, *v.i.* (*a*) (*of bird, etc.*) s'envoler; prendre son vol; (*b*) (*of pers.*) s'enfuir; se sauver.

4. fly back, *v.i.* (*a*) revenir (i) en volant, (ii) au plus vite; (*b*) (*of steel rod, etc.*) faire ressort; revenir (soudain) en arrière.

5. fly by, *v.i.* (*a*) passer très rapidement, comme un éclair, à toute allure, à toute vitesse; **as the days flew by,** à mesure que les jours fuyaient, s'enfuyaient, s'écoulaient; (*b*) *Av:* (*of aircraft*) (i) passer; (ii) faire, effectuer, un défilé (aérien).

6. fly in, *v.i.* arriver en avion.

7. fly off, *v.i.* (*a*) (*of bird, etc.*) s'envoler; (*b*) (*of pers.*) s'en aller en coup de vent; (*c*) (*of button, etc.*) sauter.

8. fly past, *v.i. Mil.Av:* défiler (devant un général, etc.);

faire, effectuer, exécuter, un défilé (aérien). **9. fly up,** *v.i.* s'élever; se projeter en l'air.

fly[4], *a. F: O:* malin, -igne; astucieux; **he's very f.,** c'est un malin.

flyaway ['flaiəwei]. **1.** *a.* (*a*) (*of garment, bow, etc.*) flottant, négligé; (*b*) (*of pers.*) léger, écervelé, étourdi; (*c*) (*of idea, etc.*) fantasque; bizarre. **2.** *s.* (*a*) fuyard *m*; (*b*) personne *f*, chose *f*, difficile à saisir.

flyback ['flaibæk], *s. Elcs: T.V:* retour *m* du spot, du faisceau (électronique) (dans un tube à vide, dans un tube d'indicateur panoramique).

flyball ['flaibɔ:l], *s. Mch: etc:* boule *f* (du régulateur).

flybane ['flaibein], *s. Bot:* (*a*) silène *m* attrape-mouches; (*b*) conyse raboteuse; herbe *f* aux mouches; (*c*) *Fung:* amanite *f* tue-mouches.

flybill ['flaibil], *s.* **1.** feuille volante; prospectus *m*. **2.** (*poster*) papillon *m*.

flyblow ['flaiblou], *s.* (*a*) œufs *mpl* de mouche (dans la viande); souillures *fpl* (de la viande); (*b*) *F:* chiures *fpl* de mouche.

flyblown ['flaibloun], *a.* (*a*) plein, couvert, d'œufs de mouches; (viande) gâtée; *F:* (*of reputation, etc.*) souillé, entaché; (*b*) *F:* couvert de chiures de mouche.

fly(-)by ['flaibai], *s.* (*a*) *Av:* passage *m* (d'un avion); défilé aérien; (*b*) *Space:* passage rapide à proximité d'une planète.

fly-by-night ['flaibainait], *s. F:* **1.** (*a*) oiseau *m* de nuit; noctambule *mf*; coureur *m*; (*b*) fille *f* de trottoir; coureuse *f*, pierreuse *f*. **2.** déménageur *m* à la cloche de bois.

flycatcher ['flaikætʃər], *s.* **1.** (*a*) attrapeur, -euse, de mouches; (*b*) piège *m* à mouches; attrape-mouche(s) *m inv*. **2.** *Orn:* (*a*) (*old world*) gobe-mouches *m inv*; **paradise f.,** gobe-mouches de paradis, *F:* oiseau *m* de la Vierge; **spotted f.,** gobe-mouches gris; **pied f.,** gobe-mouches noir; **red-breasted f.,** gobe-mouches nain, rougeâtre; **brown f.,** gobe-mouches brun; **white-collared f.,** gobe-mouches à collier; (*b*) (*new world*) tyran *m*, moucherolle *f*; **royal f.,** roi *m* des gobe-mouches, moucherolle royale; **scissor-tailed f.,** moucherolle à longue queue, **vermilion f.,** tyran écarlate; *NAm:* **Acadian f.,** moucherolle verte; **Traill's f., alder f.,** moucherolle des aulnes; **(great) crested f.,** moucherolle huppée; **Hammond's f.,** moucherolle de Hammond; **least f.,** moucherolle tchébec; **olive-sided f.,** moucherolle à côtés olive; **western f.,** moucherolle du Pacifique; **Wright's f.,** moucherolle sombre; **yellow-bellied f.,** moucherolle à ventre jaune; (*c*) *Austr:* **restless f.,** seisure *m*, gobe-mouches turbulent. **3.** *Bot:* (*a*) dionée *f*; attrape-mouches; gobe-mouches; (*b*) apocyn *m*; gobe-mouches.

flycutter ['flaikʌtər], *s. Mch.Tls:* fraise rotative, outil de coupe rotatif.

flyer ['flaiər], *s.* **1.** (*a*) oiseau *m*, insecte *m*, qui vole; *Ven:* (*of hawk*) voleur *m*; (*b*) aviateur, -trice; (*c*) *F:* (*of horse, etc.*) bon coureur; (*d*) *U.S:* train *m* rapide; express *m*. **2.** (*a*) aile *f*, volant *m*, gouvernail *m* (de moulin à vent); (*b*) balancier *m* (de tournebroche, etc.); (*c*) *Tex:* ailette *f* (de banc à broches); (*d*) *Adm: Com:* note *f*, fiche volante. **3.** *Const:* marche (d'escalier) carrée; **flyers,** escalier droit, à rampe droite. **4.** saut *m* (au-dessus de qch.); *Cy:* **to take a f. over the handlebars,** se trouver lancé, projeté, par-dessus le guidon.

fly half ['flai'hɑ:f], *s. Rugby Fb:* demi *m* d'ouverture.

flying[1] ['flaiiŋ], *a.* **1.** (*a*) (oiseau, etc.) volant; **f. fish,** poisson volant; (i) dactyloptère *m*, *F:* landole *f*; (ii) exocet *m*, gabot *m*; **f. fox,** roussette *f*; **the flying foxes,** les mégachiroptères *m*; **f. squirrel,** écureuil volant; polatouche *m*; **Russian f. squirrel,** écureuil volant eurasiatique; **f. ant,** fourmi volante; (*b*) *Av: U.S:* **f. corps,** corps d'armée aérien; *A:* **Royal F. Corps** = l'Armée de l'Air; **f. personnel, f. staff,** personnel navigant; **f. test,** (i) essai *m* (d'un avion) en vol; (ii) épreuves *fpl* de pilotage; **unidentified f. object,** objet volant non identifié. **2.** (voile, ruban, etc.) volant, flottant, léger. **3.** (*a*) (*course f*, etc.) rapide; **f. camp,** camp volant, temporaire; **f. column,** (i) *Mil:* colonne *f* mobile, groupement *m* mobile; (ii) police *f* de la route; *Elcs:* **f. spot,** spot *m* mobile; *Navy:* **f. squadron,** escadre, division, volante; **to take a f. shot at sth.,** tirer (un oiseau, etc.) au vol; **to give s.o. a f. kiss,** embrasser qn en passant; (*b*) (*of visit, etc.*) court, passager; **to pay a f. visit to London,** faire une visite éclair à Londres; (*c*) **f. start,** départ foudroyant, en flèche; départ lancé; **we got off to a f. start,** nous nous sommes lancés (dans ce projet, etc.) sans anicroche; nous avons fait un départ foudroyant; *Fb:* **f. kick,** coup de pied donné en pleine course; **to take a f. leap over sth.,** franchir qch. d'un saut. **4.** *Civ.E: etc:* **f. scaffold(ing),** échafaudage volant, à bascule; **f. bridge,** pont volant; traille *f*, appontement *m*; *Nau:* passerelle volante. **5.** (*fleeing*) en fuite; **the F. Dutchman,** (i) *Lit: Mus:* le Vaisseau fantôme, le Hollandais volant; (ii) *Rail: A:* le rapide de Londres à Exeter.

flying[2], *s.* **1.** (*a*) vol *m* (d'un oiseau, d'une flèche, du temps, etc.); (*b*) *Av:* (i) aviation *f*; (ii) vol; navigation *f*; pilotage *m* (d'un avion); **contact f.,** vol à vue, navigation observée; **blind f.,** vol sans visibilité; **instrument f.,** vol, navigation, pilotage, aux instruments; **acceptance f.,** vol de réception; **trick f.,** acrobatie(s) aérienne(s); vol(s) d'acrobatie, de virtuosité; *attrib.* **f. surface,** voilure *f* (d'un avion); **f. controls,** commandes *f* de vol; **power-assisted f. control,** servocommande *f*; **power-operated f. control,** commande automatique; **f. boom,** perche *f* de ravitaillement en vol; *O:* **f. wing,** aile volante; **f. crew,** équipage *m* (d'avion, de vaisseau spatial); **f. club,** aéro-club, *pl.* aéro-clubs; **f. centre,** centre *m* d'aviation; **f. ground,** terrain *m*, champ *m*, d'aviation; **f. hours, f. time,** heures *f*, temps *m*, de vol; **f. school,** école *f* de pilotage; **f. range,** distance *f* franchissable; **f. angle,** angle *m* de vol; **f. speed (under load),** vitesse *f* de croisière; **maximum f. altitude,** (valeur *f* de) plafond *m*; **f. boat,** hydravion *m* à coque; (hydravion) monocoque *m*; *F:* **f. coffin,** cercueil volant; avion d'une fiabilité douteuse; **he is interested in anything connected with f.,** il s'intéresse à tous les aspects de l'aviation. **2.** sautage *m* (d'un rivet, d'un bouchon, etc.); jaillissement *m* (d'étincelles). **3.** fuite *f* (de qn). **4.** (*a*) lancement *m* (d'un faucon, des pigeons, d'un cerf-volant); (*b*) déploiement *m* (d'un drapeau).

flyleaf ['flaili:f], *s. Bookb:* (feuille *f* de) garde *f* (d'un livre broché).

flyman, *pl.* **-men** ['flaimən], *s.m.* **1.** *A:* cocher de fiacre. **2.** *Th:* machiniste.

flyover ['flaiouvər], *s.* **1.** *Civ.E:* enjambement *m*, passage supérieur, saut-de-mouton *m*, *pl.* sauts-de-mouton; **f. crossing,** croisement *m* à niveaux différents. **2.** *Av:* (*a*) survol *m*; (*b*) défilé aérien.

flypaper ['flaipeipər], *s.* (papier *m*) attrape-mouche(s) *m inv*; (papier) tue-mouches *m inv*.

flypast ['flaipa:st], *s. Mil.Av:* défilé aérien.

flypost [flaipoust], *v.tr.* coller des papillons, des affichettes.

flysch [fliʃ], *s. Geol:* flysch *m*.

flysheet ['flaishi:t], *s.* **1.** feuille volante; prospectus *m*. **2.** double toit *m* (d'une tente).

flytrap ['flaitræp], *s.* = FLYCATCHER.

flyweight ['flaiweit], *s.* **1.** *Box:* poids minime, poids mouche. **2.** *Mch: etc:* boule *f* (du régulateur); *Mec.E:* masselotte *f*.

flywheel ['flai(h)wi:l], *s. Mec.E: etc:* volant *m* (d'entraînement, de commande); **driving f., belt-pulley f.,** poulie-volant *f*, *pl.* poulies-volants; **heavy f.,** volant à grande masse; *Aut:* **fluid f.,** embrayage *m* hydraulique; **f. gear,** couronne *f* du volant; **f. housing,** carter *m* du volant; **to have a f. effect,** faire volant.

fly wing ['flaiwiŋ], *s. Bookb:* titre imprimé sur un morceau de cuir collé sur le dos du livre.

foal[1] [foul], *s.* poulain *m*, pouliche *f*; (*of donkey*) ânon *m*, bourriquet *m*; **mare in, with, f.,** jument pleine.

foal[2], *v.tr.* (*of mare, etc.*) mettre bas (un poulain); *abs.* pouliner.

foam[1] [foum], *s.* **1.** écume *f*; (*on beer*) mousse *f*; *Dy:* (*on indigo blue*) fleurée *f*; **sea f.,** écume de la mer; **sheet of f.,** nappe *f* d'écume; **waves white with f.,** vagues moutonneuses; (*of wave*) **to break into f.,** déferler; **his horse was in a f.,** son cheval écumait; **f.-flecked,** moucheté d'écume; *Toil:* **f. bath,** bain moussant. **2.** (*a*) (*slaver*) bave *f*; (*b*) écume (à la bouche). **3.** mousse; (*a*) **f. fire extinguisher,** extincteur *m* à mousse carbonique; **f. tender (of fire brigade),** remorque *f*, tender *m* à mousse carbonique; (*b*) **f. glass,** verre *m* mousse, multicellulaire; **f. rubber,** caoutchouc *m* mousse; **f. rubber back(ed) mat,** tapis *m* avec envers de caoutchouc mousse.

foam[2], *v.i.* (*of sea, etc.*) écumer, moutonner; (*of beer, etc.*) mousser; **to f. over,** déborder en moussant; **to f. at the mouth,** avoir l'écume aux lèvres; (*of dog, etc.*) baver; *F:* **to f. (at the mouth) (with rage),** écumer; être furieux.

foamed [foumd], *a.* **1.** couvert de mousse, d'écume. **2. f. glass, rubber,** verre *m*, caoutchouc *m*, mousse; **f. plastic,** mousse *f* plastique.

foamflower ['foumflauər], *s. Bot:* tiarella *m*.

foaming[1] ['foumiŋ], *a.* (*of sea, horse, etc.*) écumant; (*of sea*) moutonnant; (*of beer, etc.*) moussant; (*of blood, saliva*) spumeux; *Lit:* **the f. cup,** la coupe de vin mousseux.

foaming[2], *s.* **1.** écume *f* aux lèvres. **2.** écumage *m*, moussage *m* (dans une chaudière, etc.).

foamy ['foumi], *a.* (*of sea, etc.*) écumant; (*of drink, etc.*) mousseux.

fob[1] [fɔb], *s.* **f. (pocket),** gousset *m* (de pantalon); **f. chain,** régence *f*; **f. seal,** breloque *f*.

fob[2], *v.tr.* **(fobbed) to f. s.o. (off),** tromper, duper, qn; **to f. s.o. off with sth., to f. sth. off on s.o.,** *F:* refiler qch. à qn; *O:* **to f. s.o. out of sth.,** filouter qch. à qn.

focal ['fouk(ə)l], *a.* (*a*) *Ph: Opt: Mth:* focal, -aux; **f. point (of a mirror, etc.),** foyer *m* (d'un miroir, etc.); **f. length,** (i) distance, longueur, focale; focale *f*; (ii) *Phot:* tirage *m* de la chambre noire; **f. plane,** plan focal; *Phot:* **f.-plane shutter,** obturateur focal, de plaque; **f. line,** focale; *Elcs:* **f. spot,** foyer (optique), spot lumineux, tache focale (de tube focus); *Mth:* **f. transformation,** transformation arguésienne; (*b*) *Med:* **f. infection,** infection focale.

focalization [foukəlai'zeiʃ(ə)n], *s.* **1.** *Opt: Elcs:* mise *f* au point; focalisation *f*. **2.** *Med:* localisation *f* (d'une maladie) à son foyer.

focalize ['foukəlaiz], *v.tr.* **1.** = FOCUS[2] 1. **2.** mettre au point (l'œil). **3.** (*a*) localiser (une maladie) à son foyer; (*b*) *v.i.* (*of illness*) se localiser à son foyer.

focalizing ['foukəlaiziŋ], *s.* focalisation *f*.

focimeter [fou'simitər], *s. Phot:* focimètre *m*.

focometer [fou'kɔmitər], *s. Opt:* focomètre *m*.

fo'c'sle ['fouksl], *s. Nau:* **1.** gaillard *m* (d'avant); plage *f* avant; *A:* **topgallant f.,** (pont *m*) teugue *f*; teugue d'avant; **f. deck,** pont de gaillard. **2.** (*in merchant vessel*) poste *m* de l'équipage.

focus[1], *pl.* **foci, focuses** ['foukəs, 'fousai, 'foukəsiz], *s.* **1.** *Mth: Opt: etc:* foyer *m* (de lentille, de miroir, de courbe, etc.); *Opt:* **depth of f.,** (i) profondeur *f* de foyer; (ii) profondeur de champ; **in f.,** (i) (*of image*) au point; (ii) (*of instrument*) réglé; **out of f.,** (i) (*of image*) pas au point; brouillé; (ii) (*of instrument*) non réglé, déréglé; (iii) (*of headlamp bulb, etc.*) mal centré, mal réglé; *Fig:* **the question is out of f.,** la question demande une mise au point, a besoin d'être mise au point; **to bring sth. into f.,** mettre qch. au point; **the fieldglasses are not at the right f. for me,** les jumelles ne sont pas à ma vue; **to check the f.,** mettre au point; *Phot:* **fixed-f. camera,** appareil *m* à mise au point fixe; **diffused-f., soft-f., lens,** objectif *m* anachromatique, pour le flou; **soft-f. effect,** flou artistique. **2.** centre *m* (d'un tremblement de terre, d'un orage, etc.); *Med:* siège *m*, foyer (d'une maladie); **f. of infection,** foyer d'infection, infectieux.

focus[2], *v.tr.* **(focused;** *occ.* **focussed) 1.** concentrer (les rayons de lumière, les sons, l'observation, etc.) **(in, on,** dans, sur); faire converger (des rayons); *Opt: Elcs:* focaliser; *v.i.* (*of light, sound, etc.*) converger **(on,** sur); **all eyes were focused on him,** il était le point de mire de tous les yeux. **2.** (*a*) mettre au point (une image, un objectif, un microscope, etc.); **to f. opera glasses to suit one's sight,** mettre une jumelle à sa vue; **to f. a headlamp, a searchlight,** régler la lampe d'un phare, d'un projecteur; *v.i. Phot:* **to f. on an object,** mettre au point sur un objet; **to f. on, for, infinity,** mettre au point sur l'infini; régler, accrocher, à l'infini; (*b*) mettre au point (un objet).

focuser ['foukəsər], *s. Elcs:* focalisateur *m*.

focusing ['foukəsiŋ], *s.* **1.** concentration *f*, convergence *f* (de rayons, etc.). **2.** (*a*) mise *f* au point (d'une jumelle, etc.); *Aut: etc:* réglage *m* (d'un phare); **lens in f. mount,** objectif *m* à mise au point hélicoïdale; **f. ring,** anneau *m* de mise au point (de l'objectif); **f. cloth,** voile noir de mise au point; **f. scale,** échelle *f* des distances; échelle de mise au point; **f. screw,** vis *f* de mise au point; écrou *m* de réglage du foyer; **f. glass,** (i) loupe *f* de mise au point; (ii) (*also* **f. screen**), (châssis *m* à) glace dépolie; verre dépoli; **f. eyepiece,** loupe *f* de mise au point; **f. viewer,** viseur *m* focimétrique, focométrique; (*b*) *Opt:* focalisation *f*; *Elcs:* focalisation, concentration (du faisceau électronique); **f. coil,** bobine *f* de concentration, de focalisation; **f. tube,** tube *m* de concentration, de convergence; tube convergent.

fodder[1] ['fɔdər], *s.* fourrage *m*, affour(r)agement *m*; **green f.,** fourrage (en) vert; **dry f.,** fourrage (en) sec; **compressed f.,** biscuit *m* de fourrage; **f. straw,** paille fourrageuse; **field sown with a f. crop,** fourragère *f*; **to gather f.,** faire du fourrage (dans un champ); *F:* **cannon f.,** chair *f* à canon.

fodder[2], *v.tr.* affour(r)ager, affener, affenager (les bestiaux); donner le fourrage à (une bête).

foddering ['fɔdəriŋ], *s.* affour(r)agement *m*, affenage *m*.

foe [fou], *s. Lit:* ennemi *m*, adversaire *m*; **to be a f. of, to, sth.,** être l'ennemi de qch.

foehn [fə:n], *s. Meteor:* foehn *m*, föhn *m*.

foeman, *pl.* **-men** ['foumən], *s.m. A: & Lit:* ennemi, adversaire; **he has found a f. worthy of his steel,** il a trouvé un adversaire digne de lui.

foenus ['fi:nəs], *s. Ent:* fœne *m*.

foetal ['fi:t(ə)l], *a. Biol:* fœtal, -aux.

foetalization [fi:təlai'zeiʃ(ə)n], *s. Biol:* fœtalisation *f*.

foetation [fi:'teiʃ(ə)n], *s. Biol:* formation *f* du fœtus.

foeticidal [fi:ti'saidl], *a. Jur:* fœticide.

foeticide ['fi:tisaid], *s. Jur:* fœticide *m.*

foetus, *pl.* **-uses** ['fi:təs, -əsiz], *s. Biol:* fœtus *m.*

fog¹ [fɔg], *s.* **1.** *Agr:* (*a*) regain *m*; (*b*) regain laissé sur pied pendant l'hiver; (*c*) herbe folle; (*d*) *Bot:* **Yorkshire f.,** houlque laineuse. **2.** *Scot:* mousse *f* (des terrains de tourbe).

fog², *s.* **1.** (*a*) brouillard *m*; *Nau:* (*usu.*) brume *f*; **wet f.,** brouillasse *f*; **thick f., heavy f.,** fort brouillard, brouillard intense; *F:* **f. that could be cut with a knife,** brouillard à couper au couteau; **ice f.,** brouillard givrant; **radiation f.,** brouillard de rayonnement; *Mil: etc:* **artificial f.,** brouillard artificiel; **season of fogs,** saison brumeuse; **in the f.,** par le brouillard; *Fig:* **my mind is in a f.,** mon esprit est comme dans un brouillard; **I'm in a f.,** je ne sais plus où j'en suis; je n'y comprends rien; *Nau:* **f. bell,** cloche *f* de brume; *Av: etc:* **f. dispersal,** dénébulation *f*; **f. light,** (i) projecteur *m* pour le brouillard; (ii) *Aut:* (phare) antibrouillard; **f. signal,** (i) *Nau:* signal *m*, -aux, de brume, de brouillard; (ii) *Rail:* pétard *m*; **f. signal apparatus,** appareil *m* pour signaux de brume; **f. whistle,** sifflet *m* de brume; (*b*) *Phot:* (*on negative*) voile *m*; **chemical f.,** voile chimique; **red f., green f.,** voile dichroïque. **2.** buée *f* (sur les vitres, etc.).

fog³, *v.* (**fogged**) **1.** *v.tr.* (*a*) embrumer (un endroit); *F:* brouiller (les idées); embrouiller (qn); emmêler, obscurcir (la situation); **I am a bit fogged,** je ne sais plus où j'en suis; (*b*) embuer, ternir (une glace, etc.); (*c*) *Ind:* brumiser; (*d*) *Phot:* voiler (un cliché). **2.** *v.i.* (*a*) (*of spectacles, etc.*) **to f. (up),** se couvrir de buée; (*b*) *Phot:* (*of negative*) se voiler; **plate that does not f. easily,** plaque *f* avec une grande résistance au voile; (*c*) *Hort:* (*of plant*) **to f. off,** pourrir.

fogbank ['fɔgbæŋk], *s.* banc *m* de brume.

fogbound ['fɔgbaund], *a.* arrêté par le brouillard; pris dans le brouillard, dans la brume.

fogbow ['fɔgbou], *s.* arc-en-ciel, *pl.* arcs-en-ciel, vu dans le brouillard.

fogey ['fougi], *s. F:* **old f.,** vieille baderne, vieille galoche, vieille perruque, vieille barbe; **he's a bit of an old f.,** il est un peu vieux jeu.

fogged [fɔgd], *a.* **1.** couvert de buée; embué; terni. **2.** (cliché) voilé.

fogger ['fɔgər], *s.* **1.** *Rail:* poseur *m* de pétards (par temps de brouillard). **2.** *Ind:* brumiseur *m.*

foggily ['fɔgili], *adv.* confusément; comme dans un brouillard.

fogginess ['fɔginis], *s.* **1.** état brumeux (du temps). **2.** manque *m* de précision; confusion *f* (des idées de qn); *Phot:* manque de netteté; voile *m.*

fogging ['fɔgiŋ], *s.* **1.** ternissement *m* (d'une glace). **2.** *Phot:* voile *m.* **3.** *Rail:* signalisation *f* par temps de brouillard. **4.** *Ind:* brumisage *m.*

foggy ['fɔgi], *a.* **1.** brumeux; **f. weather,** temps *m* de brume; temps brumailleux, gris; *Nau:* temps gras; **on a f. day,** par un jour de brouillard; **it's f.,** il y a, il fait, du brouillard; *Nau:* il brume; *F:* il brouillasse; **it's turning f.,** le brouillard tombe. **2.** (*of photograph, vision, etc.*) voilé, brouillé; (esprit, etc.) confus; **to have only a f. idea of sth.,** n'avoir qu'une vague idée de qch.; *F:* **I haven't the foggiest (idea)!** je n'en ai pas la moindre idée.

foghorn ['fɔghɔ:n], *s. Nau:* corne *f* de brume; cornet *m* à bouquin; sirène *f*; *F:* **voice like a f.,** (i) voix *f* de taureau; (ii) voix enrouée.

foglamp ['fɔglæmp], *s. Aut:* (phare *m*) antibrouillard *m.*

fogman ['fɔgman], *s. Rail:* poseur *m* de pétards (par temps de brouillard).

fogy ['fougi], *s. F:* = FOGEY.

föhn [fɔ:n], *s. Meteor:* foehn *m*, föhn *m.*

foible ['fɔibl], *s.* (*a*) côté *m* faible, point *m* faible; faible *m* (de qn); **this is a f. of his,** c'est un de ses dadas *m*; *Prov:* **every man has his f.,** à chaque fou sa marotte; (*b*) *Fenc:* faible (de l'épée).

foie gras ['fwɑ:grɑ:], *s. Cu:* foie gras.

foil¹ [fɔil], *s.* **1.** *Arch:* lobe *m* (d'un arc, etc.). **2.** *Metalw:* (*a*) feuille *f*, lame *f* (d'or, d'argent, etc.); clinquant *m*; **brass f.,** oripeau *m*; **platinum f.,** lame de platine, platine laminé; **lead f.,** papier *m* de plomb; mince feuille de plomb; **silver f.,** argent battu, feuille d'argent; *Cu:* **household f., cooking f.,** feuille d'aluminium; *Elcs:* **reflective f.,** marque réfléchissante (de bande magnétique); (*b*) tain *m* (d'une glace); (*c*) *Needlew:* lame. **3.** patin *m*, aile *f* (d'un hydrofoil). **4.** (*a*) *Lap:* feuille, paillon *m* (de monture); (*b*) *F:* (*of pers., thg*) repoussoir *m*; *Th:* faire-valoir *m inv.*; **to serve as a f. to s.o.'s beauty,** servir de repoussoir à la beauté de qn.

foil², *v.tr.* **1.** couvrir, envelopper, (qch.) d'une feuille métallique. **2.** *Lap:* monter (un diamant) sur un paillon. **3.** faire ressortir (qch.); servir de repoussoir à (la beauté de qn, etc.).

foil³, *s. Fenc:* **1.** fleuret *m.* **2.** *pl.* **foils,** escrime *f* au fleuret.

foil⁴, *s.* **1.** *Ven:* foulée *f*, piste *f*; (*of quarry*) **to run (upon) the f.,** doubler la voie. **2.** *A:* échec *m.*

foil⁵, *v.tr.* **1.** *Ven:* (*of game*) **to f. the ground, the scent,** doubler la voie; dévoyer, dépister, la meute; mettre la meute en défaut. **2.** (*a*) *A:* vaincre (un adversaire); défaire (l'ennemi); l'emporter sur (l'ennemi); (*b*) faire échouer, faire manquer (une tentative, etc.); déjouer (qn, un complot); **to be foiled at all points,** échouer sur toute la ligne.

foiled [fɔild], *a. Arch:* (arc *m*, etc.) à lobes.

foilist ['fɔilist], **foilsman,** *pl.* **-men** ['fɔilzmən], *s. Fenc:* fleurettiste *m.*

foist [fɔist], *v.tr.* refiler, colloquer (**sth. on s.o.,** qch. à qn); **to have a difficult job foisted on one,** se voir chargé d'une tâche difficile; **to f. a bad coin on s.o.,** repasser une fausse pièce à qn; **to f. one's goods on the public,** imposer ses produits au public; **to f. oneself on s.o.,** s'implanter chez qn; s'imposer à qn, chez qn; **he had foisted her upon us,** il l'avait intronisée parmi nous; **to f. a book on an author,** attribuer, imputer, un livre à un auteur.

folacin, -ine ['fɔləsin, fou-, -si:n], *s. Bio-Ch:* acide *m* folique.

fold¹ [fould], *s.* **1.** *Husb:* **sheep f.,** parc *m* à moutons; bergerie *f*, bercail *m*; **goat f.,** chèvrerie *f*; **to drive the sheep into the f.,** parquer les moutons; **to turn the sheep out of the f.,** déparquer les moutons. **2.** sein *m* (i) de l'Église, (ii) de la famille; bercail; **to bring back a lost sheep to the f.,** ramener au bercail une brebis égarée; **to return to the f.,** (*of member of family*) revenir, rentrer, au bercail; (*of renegade politician, etc.*) revenir à son parti.

fold², *v.tr.* **1.** (em)parquer (les moutons). **2.** parquer les moutons sur (un terrain pour l'engraisser).

fold³, *s.* **1.** (*a*) pli *m*, repli *m* (du papier, d'une robe); pli, repli, ride *f*, accident *m* (de terrain); **curtain that falls in perfect folds,** rideau *m* qui (se) plisse parfaitement; *Dressm:* **flat folds,** plis couchés, plats; **box folds, inverted folds,** plis rentrés, creux; **folds of a serpent,** replis d'un serpent; (*in linen, etc.*) **f. mark,** cassure *f*; **folds of fat,** bourrelets *m* de graisse (autour du cou, etc.); (*b*) *Metalw:* repli, agrafe *f* (d'une tôle); (*c*) battant *m*, vantail, -aux *m* (d'une porte); châssis *m*, feuille *f* (de paravent); (*d*) *Geol:* pli, flexure *f*, plissement *m*; **drag f.,** pli étiré; **overthrust f.,** pli de chevauchement; **recumbent f.,** pli couché; **f. axis,** axe *m* du pli. **2.** *Anat:* (i) pli, repli; (ii) ligament *m*; (iii) valvule *f*; **umbilical f.,** repli ombilical; **gastro-pancreatic f.,** ligament gastro pancréatique. **3.** *Bookb:* pliure *f* (des feuilles).

fold⁴, *v.*

I. *v.tr.* **1.** plier (une feuille de papier, etc.); *Tex:* **to f. a piece of material lengthways,** fauder une pièce d'étoffe; **to f. sth. together, in two,** plier qch. en deux; doubler qch.; **to f. a sheet in three, in four,** plier une feuille en trois doubles, en quatre doubles. **2.** *Metalw:* agrafer, replier (des tôles). **3.** **to f. sth. (up) in paper,** envelopper, empaqueter, qch. dans du papier; *Lit:* **hills folded in mist,** collines enveloppées de brume, noyées dans la brume; **to f. s.o. in one's arms,** enlacer, serrer, qn dans ses bras; **to f. s.o. to one's heart,** presser qn sur son cœur, sur son sein. **4.** **to f. one's arms,** (se) croiser les bras; **with folded arms,** les bras croisés; **she folded her shawl over, across, her breast,** elle croisa son châle sur sa poitrine; **to f. one's hands,** (i) joindre les mains; (ii) rester oisif; se croiser les bras.

II. *v.i.* **1.** (*of screen*) se (re)plier, se briser. **2.** *F:* = FOLD UP (*b*) (ii).

III. (*compound verbs*) **1. fold back,** (*a*) *v.tr.* rabattre (un col, ses manchettes, etc.); retourner (les couvertures d'un lit); **door folded back to the wall,** porte rabattue contre la paroi; (*b*) *v.i.* (*of door, etc.*) se rabattre.

2. fold down, (*a*) *v.tr.* retourner (les couvertures d'un lit); (*b*) *v.i.* (*of seat, etc.*) se rabattre.

3. fold in, *v.tr.* (*a*) replier (les bords) en dedans; (*b*) **literary supplement folded in with each number,** supplément littéraire encarté dans chaque numéro; (*c*) *Cu:* **to f. in the white of the eggs, etc.,** incorporer le blanc des œufs, etc.

4. fold under, *v.tr.* replier (les bords) en dessous.

5. fold up, (*a*) *v.tr.* (re)plier (un siège, une table); **to f. sth. up again,** replier qch.; **to f. up a screen,** replier, fermer, un paravent; (*b*) *v.i.* (i) se replier; **seat that folds up,** siège pliant; (ii) *F:* (*of business, etc.*) cesser les affaires; *Th:* **the play folded up after a week,** la pièce a été retirée, abandonnée, au bout d'une semaine.

-fold⁵, *comb. fm.* -uple; **tenfold,** décuple; **a hundredfold,** centuple, cent fois.

foldable ['fouldəbl], *a.* pliable; **not f.,** impliable.

foldaway ['fouldəwei], *a.* repliable, escamotable; **f. seat,** siège pliant, rabattable; **f. bed,** lit *m* escamotable; meuble-lit *m*, *pl.* meubles-lits.

foldboat ['fouldbout], *s. Nau:* (canot *m*) Berthon.

folded ['fouldid], *a.* plié; *Geog:* **f. mountains,** montagnes *f* de structure plissée.

folder ['fouldər], *s.* **1.** (*pers.*) plieur, -euse (de journaux, etc.); *Tex:* faudeur *m.* **2.** *Tls: Bookb: etc:* plioir *m.* **3.** *Com:* prospectus (plié). **4.** (*jacket for papers, etc.*) chemise *f*, dossier *m.* **5.** *pl. A:* **folders,** pince-nez *inv* pliant; binocle *m.*

folderol ['fɔldərɔl], *s.* (*song refrain*) tralala; la faridondaine.

folding¹ ['fouldiŋ], *a.* (*a*) pliant, repliable, rabattable; (joint) brisé; **f. album, f. set of views,** dépliant *m*; **f. bed,** (i) lit pliant, à rabattement; (ii) lit-cage *m*, *pl.* lits-cages; (iii) lit de sangle; *Nau:* **f. boat,** canot *m* pliable; **f. bulwarks,** pavois *m* rabattables; **f. camera,** appareil *m* à soufflet; folding *m*; **f. chair,** chaise pliante; **f. door,** porte brisée, à brisures; **f. joint (of a ruler, etc.),** assemblage *m* à charnière; brisure *f*; **f. ladder,** échelle brisée; **f. screen,** paravent *m*; **f. shutters,** volets brisés; **f. stool,** pliant *m*; **f. table,** (i) table pliante; (ii) table qui se rabat, à battants; **car with a f. top,** voiture *f* décapotable; **f. tripod,** pied pliant, à brisures; *Av:* **f. wings,** ailes *f* repliables; (*b*) *NAm: P:* **f. (money),** billets *mpl* de banque, faffes *mpl.*

folding², *s.* **1.** (*a*) pliage *m* (de l'étoffe, du papier, etc.); *Bookb:* pliure *f* (de feuilles); **f. up, down,** repliage *m*, repliement *m*, rabattement *m*; **f. machine,** machine *f* de pliage; plieuse *f*; (*b*) enveloppement *m* (**of sth. in sth.,** de qch., dans, qch.); (*c*) croisement *m* (des bras); (*d*) *Metalw:* agrafage *m* (de tôles). **2.** *Geol:* plissement *m* (du terrain, d'une couche).

fold-out ['fouldaut], *s. Bookb:* dépliant *m.*

foliaceous [fouli'eiʃəs], *a.* **1.** *Bot:* (thalle, etc.) foliacé. **2.** (*of rock*) foliacé, feuilleté, à lames.

foliage ['fouliidʒ], *s.* feuillage *m*, frondaison *f*; **f. leaf,** feuille verte, normale; **f. plant,** plante *f* à feuillage; *Arch: Sculp:* **ornamental f.,** rinceau *m.*

foliaged ['fouliidʒd], *a.* **1.** feuillagé, feuillé; **light-f. tree,** arbre à couvert léger. **2.** *Arch:* à rinceaux.

foliar ['fouliər], *a. Bot:* foliaire.

foliate¹ ['fouliət], *a.* **1.** *Bot:* (*a*) (*of stalk, etc.*) feuillé, feuillu; (*b*) **five-f. leaf,** feuille *f* à cinq folioles. **2.** (*of shape*) folié; *Mth:* **f. curve,** folium *m.*

foliate² ['foulieit]. **1.** *v.i.* (*of stone, etc.*) s'écailler; se diviser en lames. **2.** *v.tr.* (*a*) étamer (une glace); (*b*) *Arch:* faire des lobes à (un arc, etc.); (*c*) folioter (les feuilles d'un livre, etc.).

foliated ['foulieitid], *a.* (*a*) *Geol: etc:* folié, feuilleté, lamellaire, lamellé, lamelleux; **f. coal,** houille schisteuse; **f. crystalline rocks,** roches cristallophylliennes; (*b*) *Arch:* **f. scroll,** rinceau *m.*

foliation [fouli'eiʃ(ə)n], *s.* **1.** (*a*) foliation *f*, feuillaison *f*, frondaison *f* (d'une plante); (*b*) *Arch:* ornementation *f* en rinceaux; rinceaux *mpl.* **2.** *Geol:* (*a*) écaillement *m*, foliation (d'une roche, etc.); schistosité *f* (d'une roche); **close f.,** fausse schistosité. **3.** (*a*) *A:* laminage *m* (d'un métal); (*b*) étamage *m* (des glaces). **4.** foliotage *m* (d'un livre); *Book-k:* pagination *f* à livre ouvert; *Pal:* foliotation *f.*

folic ['fɔlik], *a. Bio-Ch:* (acide *m*) folique.

foliicolous [fouli'ikələs], *a. Ent: Bot:* foliicole.

folinic [fou'linik], *a. Ch:* (acide *m*) folinique.

folio¹, *pl.* **-os** ['fouliou, -ouz], *s.* **1.** (*a*) *Bookb:* folio *m*, feuille *f*, feuillet *m* (de manuscrit, de registre); (*b*) *Typ: etc:* numéro *m* (d'une page); folio; *Book-k:* **posting f.,** rencontre *f.* **2.** *Jur:* feuille manuscrite ou dactylographiée, de soixante-douze mots. **3.** *s. & a. Bookb:* **(book in) f., f. book,** (livre *m*) in-folio *m.* **4.** chemise *f*; dossier *m.*

folio², *v.tr.* folioter (les feuilles d'un livre); *Book-k:* paginer (un registre, etc.) à livre ouvert.

foliolate ['fouliəleit], **foliolose** ['fouliəlous], *a. Bot:* foliolé.

foliot ['fouliət], *s. Hor:* foliot *m.*

foliole ['fouliou l], *s. Bot:* foliole *f.*

folium, *pl.* **-ia** ['fouliəm, -iə], *s.* **1.** *Geol:* feuillet *m* de schiste. **2.** *Mth:* folium *m* (de Descartes).

folk [fouk], *s.* **1.** *A:* race *f*, peuple *m*, nation *f.* **2.** (*pl.* **folk,** *occ., esp. NAm:* **folks**) gens *mf*, personnes *f*; *A:* **carriage f.** — les riches; **our neighbours are simple f.,** nos voisins sont des gens simples; **country f.,** campagnards *m*; **my f., your f.,** les miens, les vôtres; ma famille, votre famille; **the old f. (at home),** les parents; *F:* les vieux; *Scot:* **the F. of Peace,** les fées *f*; *esp. NAm: F:* **hello, folks!** salut, tout le monde! **3.** *attrib.* folklorique, traditionnel; **f. dance,** danse villageoise, rustique, folklorique; **f. dancer,** danseur, -euse, de danses folkloriques; **f. dancing,** danses villageoises, rustiques, folkloriques; **f. etymology,** étymologie *f* populaire; **f. music,** musique *f* folklorique; **f. singer,** (i) chanteur, -euse, de chansons traditionnelles, folkloriques; (ii) (*modern*) folk-singer *m, pl.* folk-singers; **f. song,** (i) chanson traditionnelle, folklorique; (ii) (*modern*) folk-song *m, pl.* folk-songs; **f. speech,** dialecte *m,* patois *m.*

folklore ['fouklɔ:r], *s.* folklore *m*; tradition *f.*

folkloric ['fouklɔ:rik], *a.* folklorique.

folklorist ['fouklɔ:rist], *s.* folkloriste *mf.*

folksy ['fouksi], *a. F:* **1.** (*a*) familier, liant, sociable; (*b*) *Pej:* finaud, démagogue. **2.** (village, etc.) folklorique.

follicle ['fɔlikl], *s.* **1.** *Anat: Bot: etc:* follicule *m*; *Physiol:* **f.-stimulating hormone,** folliculo-stimuline *f.* **2.** *Ent:* cocon *m.*

follicular [fɔ'likjulər], *a. Anat: Bot:* folliculeux, folliculaire.

folliculated [fɔ'likjuleitid], *a. Bot: Ent:* pourvu de follicules; folliculeux.

follicule ['fɔlikju:l], *s.* = FOLLICLE.

folliculin [fɔ'likjulin], *s. Physiol:* folliculine *f.*

folliculina [fɔlikju'lainə], *s. Prot:* folliculine *f.*

folliculitis [fɔlikju'laitis], *s. Med:* folliculite *f,* adénotrichie *f.*

folliculose [fɔ'likjulous], **folliculous** [fɔ'likjuləs], *a.* = FOLLICULAR.

follow[1] ['fɔlou], *s.* **1.** (*a*) *Bill:* **f. (stroke),** coulé *m*; **to play a f.,** couler (la bille); (*b*) *Phot: Cin:* **f. shot,** prise *f* de vues en poursuite. **2.** *F:* (*in restaurant*) portion *f* supplémentaire. **3.** *Mec.E:* **f. rest,** lunette *f* à suivre.

follow[2], *v.*

I. *v.tr.* **1.** suivre; (*a*) marcher derrière (qn, etc.); **to f. s.o. about,** suivre qn partout; *F:* être toujours pendu aux trousses de qn, aux jupes de (sa mère, etc.); **go on, I'll f. you,** partez, je vous suis; **to be followed by s.o., sth.,** être suivi de, par, qn, qch.; **a man followed by his dog,** un homme suivi de son chien; **trade follows the flag,** le commerce suit le pavillon; **to f. s.o. in, to f. s.o. out,** entrer, sortir, à la suite de, après, qn; **to f. s.o. to his grave, to the graveside,** suivre les obsèques de qn; *v.i. O:* **shall you f.?** est-ce que vous irez jusqu'au cimetière? **to f. the hounds,** chasser à courre; *F:* **to f. one's nose,** aller tout droit devant soi; **to f. s.o. with one's eyes,** suivre qn des yeux, du regard; **to f. a young man's progress,** suivre, observer, les progrès d'un jeune homme; *Turf:* **horses to f.,** chevaux *m* à suivre; *Nau:* **to f. a ship closely,** s'accrocher à un navire; (*b*) (*go along*) **to f. a road,** suivre un chemin; **boat that follows the coast,** bateau qui longe la côte; (*in reading*) **to f. the lines with one's finger,** suivre les lignes avec son doigt; *Rac:* **to f. the course,** suivre sa ligne; (*c*) (*succeed*) succéder à (qn, qch.); **night follows day,** la nuit succède au jour; **the years f. one another,** les années se succèdent, se suivent; **meat followed the soup,** au potage succéda la viande; **George IV was followed by William IV,** Guillaume IV succéda à Georges IV; **dinner followed by a dance,** dîner suivi d'un bal; **nervous debility following (on) influenza,** débilité nerveuse qui suit la grippe, causée par la grippe; (*of action*) **to be followed by consequences,** entraîner des conséquences; **following the decision arrived at,** à la suite de la décision prise; **following our correspondence,** comme suite à notre échange de lettres; **following the request made to us by Messrs . . .,** conformément à la demande que nous a adressée la Maison . . .. **2.** (*a*) *A:* accompagner, servir (un prince, etc.); faire partie de la suite (d'un prince); (*b*) être le disciple, le partisan, de (qn); **to f. the old masters,** imiter les anciens maîtres; **to f. the conservative party,** être du parti conservateur. **3.** poursuivre (l'ennemi, le plaisir, la renommée, etc.); **justice follows crime,** la justice poursuit le crime; **to f. (after) truth,** rechercher la vérité. **4.** suivre, se conformer à (la mode, etc.); **to f. a strict diet,** s'assujettir à un régime strict; **to f. s.o.'s advice, example,** suivre le conseil, l'exemple, de qn; **I have followed your instructions,** je me suis conformé à vos ordres. **5.** exercer, suivre (une profession); faire (un métier); s'attacher à, poursuivre (une carrière); **to f. one's father's profession,** suivre la profession de son père; **they f. the same profession,** ils sont de la même profession; **to f. the sea,** être marin; se faire marin; *O:* **to f. the drum, the plough,** être soldat, laboureur. **6.** (*a*) aller aussi vite que (qn); **he went too fast for me to f.,** il allait trop vite pour que je puisse le suivre; (*b*) suivre, comprendre (une explication, etc.); **I don't quite f. you,** je ne vous comprends pas très bien, je ne saisis pas votre pensée; j'ai peine à vous suivre, à suivre votre raisonnement; (*c*) prêter attention à, suivre (un discours, un sermon). **7.** **to f. a tragedy with a light comedy,** faire suivre une tragédie d'une comédie légère.

II. *v.i.* **1.** **to f. (after),** suivre; aller, venir, à la suite; s'ensuivre; **a spell of fine weather following after the rain,** une période de beau temps à la suite de la pluie; **a long silence followed,** il se fit, il s'ensuivit, un long silence; **as follows,** ainsi qu'il suit; **our method is as follows,** notre méthode est la suivante; **I answered as follows,** j'ai répondu comme suit; **he then spoke as follows,** il s'exprima ensuite en ces termes; *Com:* **all charges to f.,** sous suite de tous frais. **2.** **to f. in s.o.'s footsteps,** marcher sur les traces, les pas, de qn; suivre les brisées de qn; **to f. close behind s.o.,** emboîter le pas à qn; serrer qn de près; talonner qn. **3.** s'ensuivre, résulter, être la conséquence (**from,** de); **the conclusion follows from the premises,** la conclusion découle des prémisses; **the rule follows at once,** la règle découle d'elle-même; **granted this, the rest follows,** cela étant admis le reste s'ensuit, en découle; **it follows that . . .,** il s'ensuit que . . .; **from what I have said it follows that . . .,** de ce que j'ai dit il ressort que . . .; **it does not f. that . . .,** ce n'est pas à dire que, il n'en résulte pas que, + *sub.*; **that does not f.,** ce n'est pas là une déduction légitime; **just because I say nothing, it does not f. that I see nothing,** de ce que je ne dis rien il ne faut pas conclure que je ne vois rien.

III. (*compound verbs*) **1. follow on,** *v.i.* (*a*) continuer (dans la même direction); (*b*) *Bill:* couler; (*c*) *Cr:* reprendre la garde du guichet au commencement de la seconde partie du match (au lieu d'alterner avec l'autre équipe), faute d'avoir marqué le nombre de points requis.

2. follow out, *v.tr.* poursuivre (une idée, une entreprise, etc.) jusqu'à sa conclusion; exécuter (des ordres).

3. follow through, (*a*) *v.tr.* **to f. a project through (to the end),** poursuivre un projet jusqu'à sa conclusion; (*b*) *v.i. Cr: Ten: Golf:* suivre la balle (avec la batte, la raquette, la crosse, etc.); suivre le coup.

4. follow up, *v.tr.* (*a*) suivre (qn, qch.) de près; (*b*) (i) poursuivre (avec énergie); *Com:* suivre, *F:* chauffer (une affaire); faire suivre (une lettre) d'une seconde lettre; **to f. up a clue,** suivre une piste; **to f. up an advantage,** poursuivre un avantage; **to f. up a success,** exploiter un succès; (ii) donner suite immédiate à (une victoire, une menace, etc.); **he followed up his letter with a summons,** il fit suivre sa lettre aussitôt d'une citation en justice.

follower ['fɔlouər], *s.* **1.** (*pers.*) (*a*) serviteur *m,* satellite *m,* affidé, -ée (d'un prince, etc.); **the King and his followers,** le roi et sa suite, et son escorte *f*; (*b*) compagnon *m* d'armes; (*c*) partisan, -ane, disciple *mf,* sectateur, -trice; (*d*) *F: A:* amoureux *m,* admirateur *m* (d'une domestique). **2.** (*a*) *Mec.E:* (i) pièce, roue, commandée, conduite, par une autre; (ii) **f. rest, f. steady,** lunette *f* (de tour) à suivre; (*b*) plateau *m* mobile, platine *f* (d'une presse); (*c*) *Mch:* (i) plateau, couvercle *m* (de piston); (ii) chapeau *m,* gland *m* (de presse-étoupe); (*d*) *Civ.E:* allonge *f* (de pilot); (*e*) *Sm.a:* (i) piston *m* (de magasin tubulaire de fusil); (ii) (planchette *f* de l')élévateur *m* (de boîte-chargeur); (*f*) *Cmptr:* **curve f.,** lecteur *m* de courbes.

following[1] ['fɔlouiŋ], *a.* **1.** qui suit; *Nau:* **f. sea,** mer *f* de l'arrière; *N.Arch: Av:* **f. edge,** bord *m* de sortie (d'une hélice); *Mec.E:* **f. steady,** lunette *f* (de tour) à suivre. **2.** (*a*) suivant; **in the f. year,** l'année suivante; **on the f. day,** le jour suivant; le jour d'après; le lendemain; *St.Exch:* **f. settlement, f. account,** liquidation suivante; **in the f. chapter,** au chapitre suivant; (*b*) **the f. resolution,** la résolution énoncée ci-après, la résolution que voici; **I shall do it in the f. manner,** je le ferai et voici comment; **in the f. rules,** dans les règles ci-après; **the f. persons,** les personnes dont les noms suivent; **among the dishes served were the f.,** entre autres on a servi les plats suivants; **the f. are invited,** voici la liste des invités; **the f. is the full list,** voici la liste complète; (*c*) **two days f.,** deux jours de suite.

following[2], *s.* **1.** poursuite *f* (de qn, etc.). **2.** (*a*) suite *f* (d'un prince); (*b*) *Pol: etc:* parti *m* (d'un chef); **to have a numerous f.,** avoir un grand nombre de partisans, de disciples; **television programme that commands a wide f.,** programme de télévision très suivi.

follow-me-lads ['fɔloumilædz], *s. Cost: A:* suivez-moi-jeune-homme *m inv.*

follow-my-leader ['fɔloumi'li:dər], *s.* jeu *m* de la queue leu leu; *F:* **f.-my-l. policy,** politique *f* à la remorque.

follow-on ['fɔlou'ɔn], *s.* continuation *f,* suite *f*; *Com:* **f.-o. orders,** commandes *f* qui suivent, résultent de, la première; *Cr:* **to try to save the f.-o.,** s'efforcer de marquer le nombre de points requis pour ne pas avoir à reprendre la garde du guichet.

follow-through ['fɔlou'θru:], *s. Cr: Ten: Golf:* fin *f* du coup; *Bill:* coup allongé; coup à suivre; coulé *m.*

follow-up ['fɔlou'ʌp], *s.* (*a*) poursuite *f*; suite *f*; *Com: etc:* relance *f* (du client, de la publicité, etc.); **f.-up work,** travail *m* complémentaire, de continuation; **f.-up letter,** lettre *f* de rappel; (*b*) *Med:* examens *mpl* de contrôle à distance, à long terme; mise *f* à jour du dossier; contrôle *m* ambulatoire; **f.-up care,** soins post-hospitaliers; (*c*) *Mil:* soutien *m,* progression *f* en soutien; exploitation *f*; poursuite; **f.-up action,** action *f* de soutien, d'exploitation.

folly ['fɔli], *s.* **1.** folie *f,* sottise *f,* déraison *f*; **an act, a piece, of f., a f.,** une folie; **it would be a fatal act of f.,** ce serait une fatale sottise; **it would be the height of f. to . . .,** ce serait la plus grande folie, le comble de la sottise, de . . .; **to pay for one's f.,** être victime de sa propre folie; *F:* payer la folle enchère. **2.** édifice (surtout à la campagne) coûteux et inutile; folie. **3.** *A:* la Folie (avec marotte et grelots). **4.** *Th: pl.* **follies,** (i) **the Ziegfeld Follies,** la revue de Ziegfeld; (ii) (les) Girls (d'une revue).

foment [fou'ment], *v.tr.* **1.** *Med:* fomenter (une plaie, etc.). **2.** exciter, stimuler (les sentiments, etc.); fomenter (la discorde, des troubles).

fomentation [foumen'teiʃ(ə)n], *s.* **1.** *Med:* fomentation *f.* **2.** stimulation *f,* excitation *f* (des sentiments); fomentation (de la discorde, etc.).

fomenter [fou'mentər], *s.* fomentateur, -trice, fauteur, -trice (de troubles, etc.).

fomes, *pl.* **-mites** ['foumi:z, -'maiti:z], *s.* **1.** *Bot:* fomes *m.* **2.** *Med:* matière contaminée.

fond [fɔnd], *a.* **1.** *A:* crédule, naïf, simple. **2.** (*a*) (parent, etc.) follement dévoué, trop indulgent; **f. mother,** mère indulgente, trop bonne; (*b*) affectueux, tendre, aimant; **f. smile,** sourire caressant, attendri; (*c*) (sentiment, souvenir, etc.) doux, *f.* douce; **f. hope,** espoir *m* dont on se flatte, dont on se berce. **3.** (*a*) **to be f. of s.o., sth.,** aimer, affectionner, avoir de l'attachement pour, qn, qch., ressentir de l'affection pour qn; *F:* en tenir pour qn; **they are f. of each other,** ils s'aiment; **my mother is very f. of Paul,** Paul est fort sympathique à ma mère; **he was very f. of me,** il me portait beaucoup d'affection; *F:* il me portait dans son cœur; **to be rather f. of s.o.,** avoir un penchant pour qn; **to become f. of s.o.,** s'attacher à qn; (*b*) **to be f. of music, of novelty,** être amateur de musique, de nouveauté; prendre plaisir à la musique; **f. of sweets, of venison,** friand de sucreries, gourmand de chevreuil; **to be f. of the bottle,** aimer, caresser, la bouteille; **he is f. of a joke,** il est porté à la plaisanterie, il plaisante volontiers; il a toujours le mot pour rire; **to be f. of doing sth.,** aimer (à) faire qch., faire volontiers qch.; **he is passionately f. of reading,** il adore, il aime passionnément, la lecture; il raffole de la lecture; il a la passion de lire; **he is especially f. of hunting,** la chasse est son inclination dominante; **he is f. of hearing his own voice,** il aime (à) s'entendre parler.

fondant ['fɔndənt], *s.* fondant *m.*

fondle ['fɔndl], *v.tr.* caresser, câliner, *F:* chouchouter (qn); faire des mamours à (qn); **to f. s.o.'s hair, etc.,** caresser les cheveux à qn.

fondler ['fɔndlər], *s.* caresseur, -euse; câlin, -ine.

fondling[1] ['fɔndliŋ], *a.* (sourire, etc.) câlin, caressant.

fondling[2], *s.* câlinerie *f,* caresses *fpl.*

fondly ['fɔndli], *adv.* **1.** crédulement, naïvement; **I f. imagined that . . .,** je me figurais naïvement que . . .; **he f. hoped to . . .,** il se flattait de . . .. **2.** tendrement, affectueusement; **to look f. at s.o.,** couver qn des yeux; caresser qn du regard.

fondness ['fɔndnis], *s.* **1.** dévouement *m* aveugle, indulgence excessive (d'une mère, etc.). **2.** affection *f,* tendresse *f* (**for,** pour, envers); **to have a f. for s.o.,** avoir qn en affection; porter de l'affection à qn. **3.** penchant *m,* prédilection *f,* goût *m* (**for sth.,** pour qch.); **to have a f. for sth.,** affectionner qch.; avoir l'amour de qch.; **f. for study,** attachement *m* à l'étude; **a f. for drink,** un penchant à la boisson; **f. for talking,** loquacité *f.*

fondue ['fɔndju], *s. Cu:* fondue *f.*

fonduk ['fɔndək, -duk], *s.* (*in N.Africa*) fondouk *m.*

font[1] [fɔnt], *s.* **1.** fonts baptismaux; **at the f.,** sur les fonts baptismaux; **f. name,** nom *m* de baptême. **2.** bénitier *m.* **3.** réservoir *m* de lampe.

font[2], *s. Typ:* fonte *f*; assortiment complet d'un certain œil; **wrong f.,** lettre *f* d'un autre œil; **f. case,** casseau *m.*

fontal ['fɔnt(ə)l], *a.* **1.** qui coule de source; original, -aux; (*of truth*) fondamental, -aux. **2.** baptismal, -aux.

fontanel(le) [fɔntə'nel], *s. Anat:* fontanelle *f.*

fontange [fɔ̃tɑ̃:ʒ], *s. Cost: A:* fontange *f.*

fontinalis [fɔnti'neilis], *s. Moss:* fontinalis *m.*

food [fu:d], *s.* **1.** (*a*) nourriture *f*; aliments *mpl*; vivres *mpl*; provisions *fpl* de bouche; victuailles *fpl*; **to offer s.o. f.,** offrir à manger à qn; **he had brought f.,** il avait apporté à manger; **f. and clothing,** le vivre et le vêtement; **insufficient f.,** alimentation insuffisante; **plain f.,** aliments simples; **hotel where the f. is good,**

hôtel où la cuisine, la table, est bonne, où on fait de la bonne cuisine, où l'on mange bien; **to be off one's f.,** ne pas avoir d'appétit; **articles of f.,** articles *m* d'alimentation; comestibles *m*; denrées *fpl*; **f. counter,** (*in large store*) **f. hall, f. department, f. store,** rayon *m* d'alimentation; **f. material,** matière nutritive; aliment; **f. poisoning,** intoxication *f* alimentaire; **f. pack,** colis *m* de vivres; **f. products,** produits *m* alimentaires; **f. crops,** cultures vivrières; **the f. industry,** l'industrie *f* alimentaire; **f. manufacturer,** fabricant *m* de comestibles; **f. value,** valeur nutritive; nutritivité *f*; **alcohol has no f. value,** l'alcool n'est pas un aliment; *Adm:* **f. allowance,** allocation *f* pour nourriture; **f. control,** ravitaillement *m*; **f. controller,** organisateur *m* du ravitaillement; (*b*) aliment; **patent foods,** spécialités *f* alimentaires; **canned, tinned, foods,** conserves *f* alimentaires, vivres de conserve (en boîte, en boîtes métalliques), aliments conservés; **convenience foods,** aliments minute; **health foods,** produits *m* diététiques, de régime; **complete f.,** aliment complet; *Toil:* **skin f.,** aliment pour la peau; (*c*) *Husb:* pâture *f* (d'animaux); mangeaille *f* (de volaille); (*for poultry*) **soft f.,** pâtée *f*; **hard f.,** grain *m*; (*for cattle*) **green f.,** fourrages verts, coupage *m*; (*of animal*) **to hunt, search, for f.,** chercher sa nourriture, sa gueulée; **every day they gave the leopard a live rabbit for f.,** tous les jours on donnait au léopard un lapin vivant en pâture; *F:* **to be f. for worms,** être mort et enterré; être la proie des vers; **to become f. for fishes,** se noyer; (*d*) **plant f.,** (i) *Bot:* aliments des plantes; (ii) *Hort:* engrais *m*; (*e*) **f. for the mind,** nourriture de l'esprit; pâture intellectuelle; **book that provides f. for the mind,** livre *m* qui donne de la pâture à l'esprit; **to give s.o. f. for thought,** donner à penser, à réfléchir, à qn; fournir matière à réflexion; **f. for controversy,** matière à controverse. **2.** (*as opp. to drink*) manger *m*; **f. and drink,** le boire et le manger, à boire et à manger.

foodless ['fu:dlis], *a.* **1.** sans nourriture, sans vivres. **2.** (pays *m*) stérile.

foodstuff(s) ['fu:dstʌf(s)], *s.*(*pl.*) produits *m* alimentaires, d'alimentation; denrées *f* (alimentaires); comestibles *m*.

fool[1] [fu:l], *s.* **1.** imbécile *mf*; idiot, -ote; niais, -aise; sot, *f.* sotte; *F:* abruti *m*; *B:* **thou f., this night thy soul shall be required of thee,** insensé, en cette même nuit ton âme te sera redemandée; **born f., hopeless f.,** parfait idiot; **to play, act, the f.,** faire le sot, l'imbécile, l'idiot, le plaisant; faire la bête; faire des bêtises, des sottises; **try and not be a f., try not to be a f.,** tâchez de ne pas faire de sottises; **to make a f. of oneself,** se rendre ridicule; faire des âneries; **he'll be a f. as long as he lives,** il mourra dans la peau d'un imbécile; **I wasn't such a f.!** pas si bête! **he isn't such a f. as he looks,** il n'est pas si bête, si niais, qu'il en a l'air; *F:* **silly f.!** espèce d'idiot, de crétin! **what a f.!** quel idiot! quel nigaud! **more f. you (to have done it)!** quelle bêtise! **he's no f.,** il n'est pas bête; **more of a f. than a knave,** plus bête que méchant; **any f. could do it,** c'est le pont aux ânes; **any f. knows that,** le premier imbécile venu sait cela; **some f. (of a) politician,** quelque imbécile d'homme politique . . .; **no more of your f. ideas!** assez de vos idées stupides, de vos bêtes d'idées! **his f. carelessness,** sa négligence d'imbécile; *Prov:* **a fool's bolt is soon shot,** un sot a bientôt vidé son sac; de fou juge brève sentence; **one f. praises another,** l'âne frotte l'âne; **a f. among rogues,** un âne parmi les singes; **there's no f. like an old f.,** un vieux fou est le pire des fous. **2.** fou *m*, bouffon *m*; *Pej:* pitre *m*; **to play the f.,** faire le bouffon, le pitre (*cf.* *1.*); **fool's cap,** (i) bonnet *m* de fou; (ii) *Sch:* *A:* bonnet d'âne; (*cf.* FOOLSCAP). **3.** dupe *f*; **to make a f. of s.o.,** berner, mystifier, qn; se payer la tête, *P:* la fiole, de qn; *F:* mettre qn en boîte; **she made a f. of me,** elle s'est moquée, s'est fichue, de moi; **they made a f. of him,** on s'est moqué de lui; **he's a f. for his pains,** il en est pour sa peine; **he's nobody's f.,** il ne se laisse pas berner; c'est un malin, un rusé; **he's a f. for flattery,** il se laisse prendre aux flatteries; **to go on a fool's errand,** y aller pour des prunes, pour le roi de Prusse; se casser le nez; **to send s.o. on a fool's errand,** envoyer qn décrocher la lune, ferrer les oies; **All Fools' Day,** le premier avril. **4.** **fool's gold,** pyrite *f* de fer; *occ.* pyrite de cuivre; *Bot:* **fool's parsley,** petite ciguë; ciguë des jardins; æthuse *f*; *F:* persil des fous; faux persil; ache *f* des chiens. **5.** *Orn:* *NAm:* **f. duck,** érismature roux; **f. hen,** jeune tétras *m*.

fool[2], *v.*

I. *v.i. & tr.* **1.** *v.i.* (*a*) faire la bête; **stop fooling!** assez de bêtises! **who's been fooling with the radio?** qui est-ce qui a tripoté le poste (de radio)? **to f. with a gun,** jouer avec un fusil; (*b*) dire des blagues; blaguer; **I was only fooling,** je n'étais pas sérieux; je plaisantais. **2.** *v.tr.* berner, mystifier, duper (qn); *F:* se payer la tête de (qn); faire marcher (qn); (*of debtor*) payer (qn) en monnaie de singe; **you can't f. me,** on ne m'a pas comme ça; **you can't f. me with your excuses,** ces histoires-là, ça ne prend pas avec moi; **to (allow oneself to) be fooled,** se laisser tromper, duper; *F:* être le dindon de la farce; *O:* **I have been fooled out of my money,** on m'a escamoté mon argent; **to be fooled into doing sth.,** être amené par duperie à faire qch.; se laisser persuader bêtement de faire qch.

II. (*compound verbs*) **1. fool about, fool around,** *v.i.*, flâner; baguenauder; gâcher son temps; courir la ville **(with,** avec); **to be always fooling around with women,** rechercher toujours la compagnie des femmes; *F:* courir le cotillon; **to f. around with a girl,** lutiner une jeune fille.

2. fool away, *v.tr.* gaspiller, gâcher (son argent, son temps).

fool[3], *s.* *Cu:* marmelade *f* à la crème; **gooseberry f.,** marmelade de groseilles (à maquereau) à la crème.

foolery ['fu:ləri], *s.* **1. (piece of) f.,** sottise *f*, folie *f*, niaiserie *f*, bêtise *f*. **2.** bouffonnerie *f*; pitrerie *f*.

foolhardily ['fu:lhɑ:dili], *adv.* témérairement, imprudemment.

foolhardiness ['fu:lhɑ:dinis], *s.* témérité *f*, imprudence *f*.

foolhardy ['fu:lhɑ:di], *a.* (*of pers., action, etc.*) téméraire, imprudent; **f. person,** casse-cou *m inv*; **f. policy,** politique *f* de casse-cou.

fooling ['fu:liŋ], *s.* **1.** bouffonnerie *f*; (*in school, etc.*) dissipation *f*; **f. around, f. about,** baguenaudage *m*, baguenauderie *f*. **2.** bernement *m*, duperie *f*; **no f.?** sans blague?

foolish ['fu:liʃ], *a.* **1.** (*a*) (*of conduct, pers.*) insensé; fou, *f.* folle; étourdi; **it is f. of him to . . .,** c'est folie à lui, c'est fou de sa part, de . . .; **he was so f. as to . . .,** il a eu la folie de . . .; *B:* **the f. Virgins,** les vierges folles; **a f. hope,** un fol espoir; (*b*) sot, *f.* sotte; bête; **to do sth. f.,** faire une sottise, une bêtise. **2.** absurde, ridicule; **to look f.,** avoir l'air penaud; **this answer made him look f.,** cette réponse l'a décontenancé; **to feel f.,** rester tout sot; rester penaud.

foolishly ['fu:liʃli], *adv.* **1.** follement; étourdiment; d'une manière insensée. **2.** sottement, bêtement.

foolishness ['fu:liʃnis], *s.* **1.** folie *f*, étourderie *f*. **2.** sottise *f*, bêtise *f*.

foolproof ['fu:lpru:f], *a.* (mécanisme *m*) indéréglable, indétraquable, de sûreté, à toute épreuve, à l'épreuve des fausses manœuvres, empêchant toute fausse manœuvre.

foolscap ['fu:lskæp], *s.* papier *m* ministre; (papier) tellière *m*; (*cf.* **fool's cap** *under* FOOL[1] 2).

foot, *pl.* **feet** [fut, fi:t], *s.* **1.** pied (humain); (*a*) **he gets under your feet,** il se met dans vos jambes; **to put one's best f. foremost, forward,** (i) avancer vite, à toute allure; presser, allonger, le pas; (ii) pousser la besogne; faire de son mieux, consacrer, apporter, appliquer, toute son énergie à une tâche; (iii) se mettre à l'ouvrage; *A:* **to measure others' feet by one's own last,** mesurer les autres à son aune; *A:* **to know the length of s.o.'s f.,** connaître son homme; **I have found the length of his f.,** j'ai pris sa mesure; **to sit at s.o.'s feet,** (i) s'asseoir aux pieds de qn; (ii) être le disciple de qn; **to set f. on an island,** mettre pied sur une île; aborder dans, sur, une île; **I have never set f., put my f., inside his house,** je n'ai jamais mis les pieds chez lui; **I shall never set f. in his house again,** jamais je ne remettrai, ne replanterai, les pieds chez lui; **I haven't set f. outside all day,** je n'ai pas mis le pied dehors de toute la journée; **to put one's feet up,** (i) surélever les pieds; (ii) se reposer; se relâcher; **to knock s.o. off his feet,** faire tomber qn; renverser qn; **my illness has knocked me off my feet,** ma maladie m'a coupé les jambes, m'a terrassé; **a wave bore him off his feet,** une vague lui fit perdre pied; *F:* **to carry s.o. off his feet,** transporter qn d'admiration, d'enthousiasme, etc.; enthousiasmer qn; **this good news fairly took him off his feet,** cette bonne nouvelle le transporta; **to keep one's feet,** (i) rester debout; (ii) *F:* tenir bon, ferme; **to get on to, rise to, one's feet (again),** se (re)lever; se (re)mettre debout; se redresser; (*in debate*) **to rise to one's feet,** prendre la parole; **that brought him to his feet,** cela lui fit prendre la parole; **to jump, spring, to one's feet,** se lever d'un bond; **he sprang to his feet,** d'un bond il fut debout; **to be on one's feet,** se tenir debout; **once I am on my feet,** une fois que je suis debout; **she is on her feet all day,** elle est sur ses jambes du matin au soir; **he's on his feet again,** il est de nouveau sur pied; le voilà remis; **to set s.o. on his feet,** (i) (re)mettre qn sur pied, (r)établir qn; (ii) lancer qn (dans les affaires, etc.); **to set s.o. on his feet, a chair, horse, on its feet, again,** relever qn, une chaise, un cheval; **to get a business on its feet,** mettre une affaire sur pied; **to find one's feet,** trouver son équilibre; se débrouiller; **he's beginning to find his feet,** il commence à s'acclimater; **to have time to find one's feet,** avoir le temps de se retourner; **to find one's feet again (after a setback),** se réhabituer; **the market has found its feet again,** le marché a repris son aplomb; **to begin to feel one's feet,** commencer à s'y faire; (*of nation, etc.*) être en train de prendre conscience de soi-même; **to put one's f. down,** réprimer énergiquement (un abus); opposer un refus formel à (un projet, etc.); faire acte d'autorité; *F:* marquer le coup; **to get one's f. in (the door),** prendre pied, s'implanter (chez qn); *F:* **to put one's f. in it,** mettre les pieds dans le plat; faire une bourde; commettre un impair; gaffer; **idol with feet of clay,** statue *f* aux pieds d'argile; *F:* **to have, get, cold feet,** avoir la frousse, le trac, *P:* les foies; caner, caponner; **to have one's feet firmly on the ground,** avoir les pieds sur terre; **not to put a f. wrong,** ne faire aucune erreur; **to catch s.o. on the wrong f.,** (i) *Ten: etc:* prendre qn à contre-pied; (ii) prendre qn au dépourvu; **to start off on the wrong f.,** partir du pied gauche; **I know I shall leave this house feet first, foremost,** je sais que je ne quitterai cette maison que les pieds devant; *F:* **my f.!** mon œil! *Aut:* *F:* **put your f. down!** accélérez! mettez la gomme! écrasez le champignon! (*b*) marche *f*; **to have a light, heavy, f.,** avoir le pied léger, lourd; avoir une démarche légère, lourde; *O:* **swift of f.,** aux pieds agiles; léger à la course; leste; (*c*) *adv.phr.* **on f.,** à pied; **to go on f.,** aller à pied; **journey on f.,** voyage *m* à pied; **to set negotiations on f.,** ouvrir, mettre en train, des négociations; **under f.,** sous les pieds; **it has stopped raining but it is wet under f.,** il ne pleut plus mais il fait mouillé à marcher; **the hard snow crunches under f.,** la neige durcie craque sous les pieds; **to trample, tread, sth. under f.,** fouler qch. aux pieds. **2.** pied (d'animaux à sabot); patte *f* (de chien, de chat, d'insecte, d'oiseau); *Equit:* **the fore feet,** le bipède antérieur (du cheval); **the hind feet,** le bipède postérieur; **the near feet,** le bipède gauche; *Vet:* **f. and mouth disease,** fièvre aphteuse. **3.** *coll.* *Mil:* fantassins *mpl*; soldats *mpl* d'infanterie; **f. and horse,** infanterie *f* et cavalerie *f*; **the fifth regiment of f.,** le cinquième régiment d'infanterie. **4.** (*a*) pied, semelle *f* (d'un bas); (*b*) bas bout (d'une table); pied (d'un lit, d'une tombe); extrémité inférieure (d'un lac); (*c*) base *f* (de colonne, etc.); patin *m* (d'enclume); pied (de verre à boire), *Rull:* patin, semelle, appui *m* (d'un rail); *Rail:* **f. rail,** rail à patin; **to break off the f. of a wine-glass,** épater un verre à vin; (*d*) pied, bas (de montagne, d'échelle, de page); racine *f* (de montagne); départ *m* (d'un escalier); *Nau:* fond *m*, bordure *f* (de voile); *Typ:* pied (d'une lettre); **at the f. of the stairs,** au bas, en bas, de l'escalier; **at the f. of the page,** au bas de la page; en bas de page; **at the f. of the list, of the class,** à la queue de la liste, de la classe; **see at f.,** voir au bas de la page. **5.** *Ind:* (*pl.* **foots**) tourteau *m* (d'huile, de sucre, etc.). **6.** (*a*) *Pros:* pied; (*b*) *Meas:* pied anglais (de 30 cm 48); **running f., f. run,** pied courant, linéaire; **square, cubic, f.,** pied carré, pied cube; **to be five f., five feet, high,** avoir cinq pieds de haut(eur); **a room eight feet high with doors five foot seven,** une pièce haute de huit pieds avec des portes de cinq pieds sept pouces. **7.** *attrib.* (*a*) (*on foot*) **f. passenger,** voyageur *m* à pied; piéton *m*; **f. racing,** courses *fpl* à pied; **f. soldier,** soldat *m* d'infanterie; fantassin *m*; **the f. soldiers,** *F:* la piétaille; **the F. Guards,** les gardes *m* à pied; la garde à pied (comprenant cinq régiments de la Garde royale); (*b*) (*for, of, the feet*) **f. guard,** (i) botte *f*, bottine *f* (de cheval); (ii) *Rail:* garde-pied *m*, *pl.* garde pieds; **f. pan,** (i) bain *m* de pieds; (ii) *Rail: etc:* *A:* chaufferette *f*; **f. scraper,** gratte-pieds *m inv*; *Nau:* **f. spar,** marchepied *m* de nage; **f. warmer,** (i) *Rail:* *A:* bouillotte *f*; (ii) chaufferette; chauffe-pieds *m inv*; *Ecc:* **f. washing,** lavement *m* des pieds; *Aut:* **f. well,** cave *f* (pour les pieds); (*c*) (*worked by the foot*) **f. brake,** frein *m* à pédale, à pied, au pied; **f. control,** commande *f* au pied; **f. drill,** machine *f* à percer à (commande par) pédale; **f. lathe,** tour *m* à pédale; **f. pump,** pompe *f* à pied; **f. starter,** démarreur *m* à pédale (de motocyclette); (démarreur à) kick *m*; (*d*) (*at the foot*), *Nau:* **f. band,** bordure *f* de fond (d'une voile); *Civ.E:* **f. piece,** semelle, sole *f* (de poteau, etc.); **f. screw,** vis calante, vérin *m* (sous les pieds d'un meuble, d'un appareil, etc.); *Hyd.E:* **f. valve,** clapet *m*, soupape *f*, de pied.

foot[2], *v.tr.* **1.** (*a*) *A:* danser (un quadrille, etc.); (*b*) *F:* **to f. it,** (i) *A:* danser; (ii) marcher; faire le trajet à pied; *P:* prendre le train onze; (iii) (*of boat, etc.*) filer à grande vitesse. **2.** rempiéter, enter (un bas); mettre un pied, faire un pied, à (un bas). **3.** *F:* **to f. the bill,** payer la note, les dépenses; *P:* casquer. **4.** *NAm:* *F:* (*a*) **to f. (up) an account,** additionner un compte; (*b*) *v.i.* **his debts footed up to 2000 dollars,** ses dettes (se) montaient à deux mille dollars.

footage ['futidʒ], *s.* longueur *f* (en pieds); métrage *m* (d'un film, etc.); *Cin:* **f. indicator,** compteur *m* de film; métreuse *f.*

football ['futbɔ:l], *s.* **1.** ballon *m* (de football). **2.** (*a*) (i) (*soccer*) football *m*; *F:* foot *m*; (ii) **Rugby f.,** rugby *m*; **f. ground,** terrain *m* de football; (*b*) **pin table f.,** baby-foot *m*; p'tit foot.

footballer ['futbɔ:lər], *s.* footballe(u)r *m.*

footbath ['futbɑ:θ], *s.* bain *m* de pieds; lave-pieds *m inv.*

footboard ['futbɔ:d], *s.* **1.** repose-pied(s) *m inv*; (*a*) *Veh:* (planche *f*) marchepied *m*; (*in front of driver*) coquille *f*; (*b*) *Artil:* tablier *m* (d'avant-train). **2.** *NAm:* = FOOTPLATE. **3.** pédale *f* (d'un tour à pied, etc.). **4.** *Furn:* panneau *m* pied (d'un lit).

footboy ['futbɔi], *s. A:* petit laquais.

footbridge ['futbridʒ], *s.* passerelle *f*; pont *m* de service; pont pour piétons.

footcandle ['futkændl], *s. Ph.Meas:* unité *f* d'éclairement = 10,764 lux.

footcloth ['futklɔθ], *s.* **1.** *A:* housse *f.* **2.** *A:* tapis *m*; carpette *f.* **3.** *Mil: etc:* chaussette *f* russe.

foot drop ['futdrɔp], *s. Med:* paralysie *f* des fléchisseurs de la jambe.

footed ['futid], *a.* **1.** (animal, etc.) pourvu de pattes, de pieds. **2.** (*with adj. prefixed, e.g.*) **flat-f. child,** enfant aux pieds plats; **sure-f. donkey,** âne au pied sûr; **four-f.,** à quatre pattes; quadrupède.

footer ['futər], *s. F:* football *m*, foot *m.*

footfall ['futfɔ:l], *s.* (bruit *m* de) pas *m*; **I heard a light f.,** j'entendis un pas léger.

foot fault[1], **footfault**[1] ['futfɔ:lt], *s. Ten:* faute *f* de pied.

foot-fault[2], **footfault**[2]. *v. Ten:* **1.** *v.i.* faire une faute de pied. **2.** *v.tr.* (*of umpire*) **to f. a player,** décider qu'un joueur a fait une faute de pied.

footgear ['futgiər], *s.* chaussures *fpl.*

foothills ['futhilz], *s.pl.* collines basses, avancées (d'une chaîne); avant-monts *m*; contreforts *m* (d'un massif).

foothold ['futhould], *s.* prise *f*, assiette *f*, pour le pied; assiette de pied; **to get a f.,** prendre pied; **to keep one's f.,** préserver l'équilibre; se tenir debout; **to lose one's f.,** perdre pied; perdre l'équilibre; glisser; faire un faux pas.

footie ['futi], *s. P:* **to play f. (f.) with s.o.,** faire du pied à qn.

footing ['futiŋ], *s.* **1.** (*a*) *Fenc: Danc: etc:* pose *f* des pieds; (*b*) = FOOTHOLD; (*in bathing, etc.*) **to lose one's f.,** perdre pied, perdre terre; **to miss one's f.,** poser le pied à faux (en descendant, etc.); **I missed my f.,** le pied me manqua. **2.** (*a*) situation sûre; pied *m*; **to gain a f.,** s'implanter, prendre pied, s'impatroniser, s'ancrer (quelque part); **he has gained a f. among them,** il a pris pied dans leur entourage; (*b*) position *f*, condition *f*, posture *f* (d'une personne); condition, état *m* (d'une institution, etc.); **war f.,** effectif *m* de guerre; **on a war, a peace, f.,** sur le pied de guerre, de paix; en état de guerre; **to place (two people) on the same f.,** égaler (deux personnes); mettre (deux personnes) sur le même rang; assimiler (des fonctionnaires de catégories différentes); **to be on an equal f. (with . . .),** être de pair, sur un pied d'égalité (avec . . .); être sur le même pied; **on a good f.,** sur un bon pied; **to be on a good f. with s.o.,** être en bons termes, être fort bien, avec qn; **to be on a bad f. with s.o.,** être en mauvais termes avec qn; (*c*) entrée *f* (dans une société, etc.); admission *f* (à une société, etc.); **to pay one's f.,** payer sa bienvenue; graisser la marmite; *Mil:* arroser ses galons, *P:* arroser. **3.** rempiétage *m* (d'un bas). **4.** *Lacem:* bisette *f.* **5.** (*a*) *Const:* empattement *m* pied, (em)base *f*, socle *m* (d'un mur); **to give f. to a wall,** empatter un mur; **concrete f.,** base en béton; (*b*) *Mec.E:* encastrement *m*, emplanture *f* (des aubes d'une turbine). **6.** *F:* **f. the bill,** paiement *m* de l'addition. **7.** *NAm:* **f. (up),** addition *f* (d'une colonne de chiffres, etc.).

foot juggler ['futdʒʌglər], *s.* antipodiste *mf.*

foot juggling ['futdʒʌgliŋ], *s.* antipodisme *m*; **f.-j. exercises,** exercices *m* antipodistes.

foot lambert ['fut'læmbət], *s. Ph:* unité de luminance égale à celle d'une surface émettant un flux lumineux d'un lumen par pied carré.

footle ['fu:tl], *v.i. F:* **to f. about,** s'occuper à des bagatelles, à des futilités; faire, dire, des niaiseries; **to f. away one's time,** gâcher son temps; passer son temps à des futilités.

footless ['futlis], *a.* **1.** apode; sans pieds, sans pattes. **2.** *NAm: F:* futile, stupide.

footlet ['futlit], *s. Cost:* bout *m* de pied; protège-bas *m inv*; footlet *m.*

footlights ['futlaits], *s.pl. Th:* rampe *f*; **to come before the f.,** affronter les feux de la rampe; **the lure of the f.,** l'attrait *m* du théâtre.

footling ['fu:tliŋ], *a. F:* insignifiant, frivole, futile; **to busy oneself with f. jobs,** s'occuper à des futilités; **f. writer,** piètre écrivain *m.*

footloose ['futlu:s], *a.* (personne) (i) libre, sans entraves, (ii) qui a la bougeotte.

footman, *pl.* **-men** ['futmən], *s.m.* **1.** *Mil: A:* fantassin; soldat d'infanterie. **2.** valet de pied; laquais.

footmark ['futmɑ:k], *s.* empreinte *f* de pied, du pied, d'un pied; trace *f* de pas.

footmuff ['futmʌf], *s.* chancelière *f*; chaufferette *f.*

footnote ['futnout], *s.* apostille *f*; note *f*, renvoi *m*, au bas de la page; renvoi en bas de page; note infra-paginale; **a f. to history,** en marge de l'histoire.

footpace ['futpeis], *s.* **1.** (*of horse, etc.*) allure lente; pas *m*; **to go, ride, at a f.,** aller au pas. **2.** *A:* (*a*) estrade *f*, plate-forme *f*, *pl.* plates-formes; (*b*) palier *m* (d'escalier).

footpad ['futpæd], *s.* **1.** *A:* voleur *m* de grand chemin; détrousseur *m* de grand chemin. **2.** *Space:* semelle *f* (du pied d'un module).

footpage ['futpeidʒ], *s.* petit laquais.

footpath ['futpɑ:θ], *s.* (*a*) sentier *m* pour piétons; chemin *m* piéton; (*b*) (*by canal, highway, railway*) banquette *f*, accotement *m*, marchepied *m*; (*c*) (*in street*) trottoir *m.*

footplate ['futpleit], *s. Mch:* plate-forme *f*, *pl.* plates-formes, tablier *m* (de locomotive); poste *m* de conduite; **side f.,** trottoir *m.*

footplateman, *pl.* **-men** ['futpleitmən], *s.m. Rail:* mécanicien de locomotive; aide-conducteur, *pl.* aides-conducteurs.

foot-pound ['fut'paund], *s.* (*pl.* **foot-pounds**) *Mec.Meas:* pied-livre *m*, *pl.* pieds-livres; **f.-p.-second,** pied-livre-seconde *m.*

foot-poundal ['fut'paundl], *s.* (*pl.* **foot-poundals**) *Mec.Meas:* unité *f* de travail du système pied-livre-seconde.

footprint ['futprint], *s.* **1.** empreinte *f* de pas; **footprints on the sands,** pas (empreints) sur le sable; **to follow the footprints,** suivre la piste. **2.** *Space:* aire *f* d'atterrissement (d'un module).

footrace ['futreis], *s. Sp:* course *f* à pied.

footrest ['futrest], *s.* (*a*) *Veh:* coquille *f*; *Cy:* repose-pied(s) *m inv*; cale-pied(s) *m inv*; *Furn:* bout *m* de pied; *Med:* porte-pieds *m inv*; (*b*) sellette *f* (de décrotteur).

footrope ['futroup], *s. Nau:* **1.** ralingue *f* de fond, de bordure (d'une voile). **2.** marchepied *m* (de vergue, etc.).

footrot ['futrɔt], *s.* **1.** *Vet:* fourchet *m*, piétin *m.* **2.** *Agr:* piétin.

footrule ['futru:l], *s. Tls: Draw:* pied *m* (de roi); règle *f* (d'un pied); verge *f* de charpentier; **you can't measure men with a f.,** les hommes ne se mesurent pas à l'aune; **there's no f. for measuring morality,** il n'y a pas d'étalon des mœurs.

foot-second ['fut'sekənd], *s.* (*pl.* **foot-seconds**) *Mec.Meas:* pied *m* par seconde.

footsie ['futsi], *s. P:* **to play f. with s.o.,** faire du pied avec qn.

footslog ['futslɔg], *v.i.* (**footslogged**) *P:* marcher; faire la route à pied.

footslogger ['futslɔgər], *s. Mil: P:* pousse-cailloux *m inv*; *P:* biffin *m.*

footsore ['futsɔ:r], *a.* aux pieds endoloris; qui a mal aux pieds; qui a les pieds meurtris.

footstalk ['futstɔ:k], *s.* **1.** *Bot:* pétiole *m* (de feuille); pédoncule *m* (de fleur); *F:* queue *f* (de feuille, de fleur). **2.** *Z:* tige *f* (de crinoïde, d'anatife, etc.).

footstall ['futstɔ:l], *s. Arch:* piédestal *m*, -aux (de pilier); socle *m.*

footstep ['futstep], *s.* **1.** pas *m*; **I hear footsteps,** j'entends un bruit de pas; j'entends marcher; **quick footsteps,** un bruit de pas précipités. **2.** (empreinte *f* de) pied; **to follow, tread, walk, in s.o.'s footsteps,** marcher sur les traces, pas, de qn; suivre les brisées de qn; *F:* emboîter le pas à qn; **to follow in one's father's footsteps,** suivre les traces de son père. **3.** *Mec.E:* **f. (bearing),** (palier *m* de) butée *f*; palier de pied; crapaudine *f* (d'arbre vertical).

footstock ['futstɔk], *s. Mch.Tls:* poupée *f* mobile; contre-poupée *f*, *pl.* contre-poupées; contre-pointe *f*, *pl.* contre-pointes.

footstone ['futstoun], *s.* **1.** *Const:* première pierre. **2.** pierre tumulaire (au pied d'une tombe).

footstool ['futstu:l], *s.* **1.** tabouret *m* (pour poser les pieds). **2.** *U.S:* **God's f., the f.,** la Terre; ici-bas.

foot-ton ['fut'tʌn], *s.* (*pl.* **foot-tons**) *Mec.Meas:* pied-tonne *m*, *pl.* pieds-tonnes; pied-tonneau *m*, *pl.* pieds-tonneaux; tonne-pied *f*, *pl.* tonnes-pieds.

foot-up ['futʌp], *s. Rugby Fb:* infraction aux règles commise par un joueur qui quitte le sol du pied ou des pieds avant que le ballon ait été mis dans la mêlée.

footwalk ['futwɔ:k], *s.* **1.** sentier *m*; chemin *m* pour piétons. **2.** trottoir *m.*

footwarmer ['futwɔ:mər], *s.* chancelière *f*, chaufferette *f.*

footway ['futwei], *s.* **1.** chemin *m* pour piétons. **2.** *Min:* échelle *f* de puits.

footwear ['futwɛər], *s.* chaussures *fpl*; **f. specialist,** chausseur *m.*

footwork ['futwɔ:k], *s.* **1.** *Sp:* jeu *m* des pieds, des jambes. **2. job that requires a lot of f.,** emploi qui exige qu'on se déplace beaucoup.

footworn ['futwɔ:n], *a.* **1.** (escalier, trottoir) usé. **2.** = FOOTSORE.

footy ['futi], *s.* = FOOTIE.

foozle[1] ['fu:zl], *s.* (*a*) *Golf:* coup raté; (*b*) *F:* coup, travail, loupé, bousillé.

foozle[2], *v.tr. & abs.* **1.** *Golf:* **to f. (a shot),** rater, manquer, un coup. **2.** *F:* louper, bousiller (un coup, un travail).

fop [fɔp], *s. A:* bellâtre *m*, fat *m*, dameret *m*; petit-maître *m*, *pl.* petits-maîtres; dandy *m*; **old f.,** vieux coquard.

foppery ['fɔpəri], *s.* dandysme *m*; élégance affectée; fatuité *f.*

foppish ['fɔpiʃ], *a.* (*a*) (homme) bellâtre, fat; (*b*) qui apporte trop de recherche à sa toilette; (*c*) (*of clothes*) d'une élégance affectée; extravagant.

foppishly ['fɔpiʃli], *adv.* en bellâtre; en petit-maître; avec une élégance affectée.

foppishness ['fɔpiʃnis], *s.* = FOPPERY.

for [fɔ:r, *unstressed* fər], *prep. & conj.*

I. *prep.* pour. **1.** (*a*) (i) (*representing*) **member f. Liverpool,** député *m* de Liverpool; *Tp:* **A f. Andrew,** A comme André; (ii) (*instead of*) **to act f. s.o.,** agir pour qn, au nom de qn; **he is writing f. me,** il écrit à ma place, de ma part; **he took me f. my brother,** il m'a pris pour mon frère; **he was wearing a blanket f. a dressing gown,** il portait une couverture en guise de robe de chambre; (*b*) (*introducing predicative complement*) **he wants her f. his wife,** il la veut pour femme; **you are lucky to have her f. a daughter,** vous êtes heureux de l'avoir pour fille; **to have s.o. f. a teacher,** avoir qn comme, pour, professeur; **he was sold f. a slave,** il fut vendu comme esclave; **they left him f. dead,** on le laissa pour mort; **to hold sth. f. certain,** tenir qch. pour certain; **I despised him f. a coward,** sa lâcheté m'inspirait du mépris; *A:* **to be hanged f. a pirate,** être pendu pour piraterie; (*c*) (*in requital of*) **to be paid f. one's services,** recevoir des gages pour ses services; **claim f. loss of . . .,** réclamation *f* résultant de la perte de . . .; (*d*) (*in exchange for*) **you can hire a car f. five pounds a day,** on peut louer une voiture moyennant cinq livres par jour; **to exchange one thing f. another,** échanger une chose contre une autre; **to change one's car f. a larger one,** échanger sa voiture pour une autre plus grande; **I gave too much f. my house,** j'ai trop donné pour ma maison; **to sell sth. f. ten francs,** vendre qch. dix francs; **he'll do it f. a fiver,** il le fera pour cinq livres; **the manuscript was knocked down to him f. £50,** le manuscrit lui a été adjugé pour £50; (*e*) *NAm: F:* **to get sth. f. free,** obtenir qch. gratis, pour rien; **this time it's f. real,** cette fois c'est vrai; **a f.-real cowboy,** un vrai cowboy. **2.** (*a*) (*in favour of, in support of*) **he is f. free trade,** il est partisan du libre-échange; il est pour le libre-échange; **are you f. staying here?** (i) êtes-vous d'avis de rester ici? (ii) cela vous va-t-il de rester ici? **the exchange is f. us,** le change nous est favorable, est favorable à notre place; **judgment f. the plaintiff,** arrêt en faveur du demandeur; **hurrah f. France!** vive la France! (*b*) **it is not f. you to blame him,** ce n'est pas à vous de le critiquer; il ne vous appartient pas de le critiquer. **3.** (*a*) (*purpose*) **what f.?** pourquoi (faire)? **what's that gadget f.?** à quoi sert ce truc-là? **I don't know what he said that f.,** je ne sais pas pourquoi il a dit cela; **to intend s.o., sth., f. sth.,** destiner qn, qch., à qch.; **garments f. men,** vêtements pour hommes; **f. sale,** à vendre; **to ring f. the maid,** sonner la bonne; **she rang f. tea,** elle sonna pour commander le thé; **to play cards f. money,** jouer aux cartes pour de l'argent; **f. example,** par exemple; **a cure f. indigestion,** un remède contre l'indigestion; **it is f. your own good,** c'est pour votre bien; **I am saving f. my old age,** je mets de côté pour quand je serai vieux; **we have no room f. a piano,** nous n'avons pas de place pour mettre un piano; *Mth:* **conditions f. reality,** conditions *f* de réalité; *F:* **he's f. it** ['fɔ:rit], **he's in f. it** ['infərit], son affaire est bonne; je ne le vois pas blanc; qu'est-ce qu'il va prendre! (*b*) (*because of*) (i) **to marry s.o. f. his money,** épouser qn pour son argent; **to choose s.o. f. his ability,** choisir qn en raison de sa compétence; **to die f. one's country,** mourir pour la patrie; **art f. art's sake,** l'art pour l'art; **to jump f. joy,** sauter de joie; **he couldn't speak f. laughing,** il riait tellement qu'il ne pouvait pas parler; **she could hardly see f. tears,** les larmes lui voilaient la vue; **to criticize s.o. f. doing sth.,** critiquer qn d'avoir fait qch.; (ii) (*with comparative*) **I have slept all day and feel the better f. it,** j'ai dormi toute la journée et je m'en trouve mieux; **if you owned millions, would you be (any) the happier f. it?** si vous aviez des millions en seriez-vous plus heureux? (*c*) (*considering*) **f. all he's doing he may as well go and play,** pour ce qu'il fait il peut aussi bien aller jouer. **4.** (*direction*) (*a*) **ship (bound) f. America,** navire *m* à destination de l'Amérique, en partance pour l'Amérique; **the trains f. Orleans,** les trains pour, sur, Orléans; **the train f. London,** le train allant à Londres; *F:* le train de Londres; *P.N:* **trains f. London,** trains direction (de) Londres; **are you f. Brighton?** allez-vous à Brighton? **change here f. Bristol,** direction de Bristol changez de train; on change de train pour Bristol; **I'm leaving f. France,** je pars pour la France; **parcels f. the provinces,** colis à destination de la province; (*b*) **his feelings f. you,** ses sentiments envers vous, à votre égard. **5.** (*extent in space*) **we did not see a house f. six miles,** nous avons fait six milles sans voir une maison; **the road is lined with trees f. two miles,** la route est bordée d'arbres pendant deux milles; *P.N:* **bends f. one mile,** virages sur un mille. **6.** (*extent of time*) (*a*) (*future*) **I'm going away f. a fortnight,** je pars pour quinze jours; **he will be away f. a year,** il sera absent pendant un an; **he can't go out f. two or three days,** il ne pourra pas sortir avant deux ou trois jours; **we have food f. three days,** nous avons des vivres pour trois jours; **he won't be back f. a week,** il ne reviendra pas d'ici à huit jours; (*b*) (*past*) **he was away f. a fortnight,** il fut absent pendant quinze jours; **I lived there f. five years,** j'y ai vécu (pendant) cinq ans; **I have not seen him f. three years,** voilà, il y a, trois ans que je ne l'ai vu; je ne l'ai pas vu de trois ans; **I have not been there f. a long time,** voilà, il y a, longtemps que je n'y suis (pas) allé; (*c*) (*past extending to pres.*) **I have been here f. three days,** il y a trois jours que je suis ici; je suis ici depuis trois jours; **I had known him f. years,** je le connaissais depuis des années; il y avait des années que je le connaissais; **I have been living in Paris f. three months,** j'habite Paris depuis trois mois. **7.** (*intention, destination*) (*a*) **this box is f. you,** cette boîte est pour vous; **a cake had been set aside f. me,** on avait mis de côté un gâteau à mon intention; **any letter that may come f. me,** toute lettre qui arrivera à mon nom; **I'll come f. you tomorrow,** je viendrai vous prendre demain; **to make a name f. oneself,** se faire un nom; **here's news f. you,** voici une nouvelle qui vous intéressera; **to act f. the best,** agir pour le mieux; **to write f. the papers,** écrire dans les journaux; (*b*) **your task f. tomorrow,** votre devoir pour demain; **can you give him an appointment f. three o'clock?** pouvez-vous lui donner un rendez-vous pour trois heures? **dinner at seven f. seven thirty,** dîner à sept heures trente, réception à partir de sept heures. **8. to care f. s.o., sth.,** aimer qn, qch.; **you are the man f. me,** vous êtes mon homme; **that is just the thing f. you,** c'est juste ce qu'il vous faut; **eager f. praise,** avide d'éloges; **fit f. nothing,** bon à rien; **ready f. dinner,** prêt à dîner, prêt pour le dîner; **it's time f. school,** c'est l'heure de la classe; **too beautiful f. words,** d'une beauté ineffable; **too stupid f. words,** d'une bêtise indicible, insondable; **there's nobody like a Cockney f. giving you a pat answer,** il n'y a rien de tel que les Londoniens pour avoir de ces reparties; **oh, f. some peace and quiet!** que ne donnerais-je pour la paix! **oh, f. a glass of wine!** oh, donnez-moi un verre de vin! *Lit:* **oh, f. a muse of fire!** que n'ai-je une muse enflammée! **now f. a cup of tea!** maintenant une tasse de thé! **now f. it!** (i) allons-y! (ii) ça y est! **9.** (*to the amount of*) **to draw on s.o. f. £50,** fournir une traite de £50 sur qn; **put me down f. £1,** inscrivez-moi pour £1. **10.** (*a*) (*with regard to*) **he is big f. his age,** il est grand pour son âge; **he is clever f. a child,** pour un enfant il est adroit; **not bad f. a beginner!** pour un commençant ce n'est pas si mal! **as f. him,** quant à lui; pour ce qui est de lui; **as f. you, you may go,** quant à vous, vous pouvez vous en aller; **as f. that,** pour ce qui est de cela; **as f. handkerchiefs, I have plenty,** en fait de mouchoirs, j'en ai des quantités; **f. myself, f. my part, I shall do nothing of the sort,** pour moi, quant à moi, pour ma part, parlant pour ce qui me concerne, je n'en ferai rien; **speaking f. myself and in the name of my colleagues,** parlant en mon nom et au nom de mes collègues; (*pleonastic*) **I shall try to find out f. myself,** je chercherai à savoir par moi-même; **to examine sth. f. oneself,** examiner qch. par soi-même; **see f. yourself!** voyez par vous-même! (*b*) (*in spite of*) **f. all that,** malgré tout, malgré cela, tout de même, ce nonobstant, pourtant, néanmoins; **f. all that, you should have let me know,** encore vous aurait-il fallu me prévenir; **f. all you say, I shall stick to my purpose,** en dépit de ce que vous dites, quoi que vous en disiez, je resterai fidèle à mon dessein; **I don't believe it f. all you (may) say,** je n'en crois rien en dépit de vos affirmations; **she loved him, f. all his faults,** elle l'aimait malgré ses défauts; **f. all that he is so wealthy,** bien qu'il soit si riche; tout riche qu'il est; (*c*) (*owing to*) **were it not f. her, but f. her, except f. her, I should have died,** n'eût été elle, sans elle, je serais mort; (*d*) (*corresponding to, in opposition to*) **word f. word,** mot pour mot; **translate word f. word,** traduisez mot à mot; **line f. line translation,** traduction linéaire; **f. one enemy he has a hundred friends,** pour un ennemi il a cent amis; **death f. death, it is better to drown than to be hanged,** mourir pour mourir, mieux vaut être noyé que pendu.

II. *prep.*(*introducing an infinitive clause*) **1. it is easy, difficult, impossible, f. him to come,** il lui est facile, difficile, impossible, de venir; **it is easy f. you to talk,** cela vous est facile à dire; **it is too late f. us to start,** il est trop tard pour que nous partions; **it is too much f. me to do alone,** c'est trop pour que je puisse le faire tout seul; **there is no time f. us to see the church,** nous n'avons pas assez de temps pour visiter l'église; le temps manque pour que nous visitions l'église; **f. this to be feasible,** pour que cela se puisse. **2. they made way f. him to pass,** on se rangea pour le laisser passer; **I have brought it f. you to see,** je l'ai apporté pour que vous le voyiez; **they have bought a tent f. the children to play in,** ils ont acheté une tente où les enfants puissent jouer; **these conclusions are f. my readers to accept or not,** c'est à mes lecteurs d'admettre ou de rejeter ces conclusions; **it is f. you to see to it,** c'est à vous de vous en occuper; **it is not f. me to decide,** ce n'est pas à moi, il ne m'appartient pas, de décider; la question n'est pas de mon ressort; **it is not f. you to reproach me,** vous êtes mal venu à me faire des reproches. **3. it is usual f. the mother to accompany her daughter,** il est d'usage que la mère accompagne sa fille; **it's no use f. you to be angry,** ça ne vous avancera pas de vous fâcher; **it's no good f. Mr X to talk,** M. X a beau dire; **it would never do f. them to see me,** cela serait très embarrassant s'ils m'apercevaient; **would it annoy you f. me to come back tomorrow?** cela vous ennuierait-il que je revienne demain? **4. I am delighted f. Miss X to know,** je suis enchanté que Mlle X le sache; **she was glad f. him to take Mary out,** elle était contente qu'il sorte avec Marie. **5. he gave orders f. the trunks to be packed,** il donna l'ordre de faire les malles; **there is a tendency f. weak vowels to disappear,** les voyelles faibles tendent à disparaître. **6. to arrange f. s.o. to meet him,** prendre des dispositions pour que qn soit à l'attendre; **to arrange f. sth. to be done,** prendre des dispositions pour que qch. se fasse; **to wait f. s.o. to do it,** attendre que qn le fasse; **to wait f. sth. to be done,** attendre que qch. se fasse; **to long f. sth. to be done,** désirer ardemment que qch. se fasse. **7. it took an hour f. the taxi to get to the station,** le taxi a mis une heure pour aller jusqu'à la gare; *Dial: & F:* **I hadn't expected f. more callers to turn up,** je ne m'attendais pas à ce qu'il survienne encore des visites; **we agreed f. me to come,** il a été convenu que je viendrais. **8. the best plan will be f. you to go away for a time,** le mieux sera que vous vous absentiez pour quelque temps; **it would be remarkable f. John to have invented it,** ce serait remarquable que Jean l'ait inventé. **9. f. her not to go would look as if she were afraid of meeting him,** si elle n'y allait pas elle aurait l'air d'avoir peur de le rencontrer; **it would be a disgrace f. you to back out now,** vous retirer maintenant serait honteux.

III. *conj.* car; **wait a moment, f. I have something to tell you,** attendez un instant, car j'ai quelque chose à vous dire; *conj.phr. A: & Lit:* **f. that . . .,** car, parce que . . ..

forage[1] ['fɔridʒ], *s.* **1.** fourrage(s) *m*(*pl.*), affouragement *m*; **green f.,** fourrages verts; **pelleted f.,** fourrages agglomérés; **f. wagon,** fourragère *f.* **2.** fourrage, fourragement *m*; **to go on the f.,** aller au fourrage; *F:* **I found him on the f. in the kitchen,** je le trouvai en train de fourrager dans la cuisine; *Mil:* **f. cap,** bonnet *m* de police; calot *m.*

forage[2]. **1.** *v.i.* (*a*) fourrager, aller au fourrage; **to f. for hay, grass,** fourrager au sec, au vert; *F:* **to f. for sth.,** fouiller pour trouver qch.; **to f. in one's pockets,** fouiller dans ses poches; **to f. among papers,** fourrager dans des papiers; **to f. about, around, in a drawer,** fouiller dans un tiroir; **to f. for oneself,** (i) acheter soi-même ses petites provisions; (ii) trouver de quoi improviser un repas; **never mind me, I'll f. for myself,** ne t'occupe pas de moi, je me débrouillerai; (*b*) *A:* faire des ravages (en pays ennemi). **2.** *v.tr.* (*a*) **to f. corn,** fourrager pour le blé; (*b*) ravager, saccager, fourrager (un pays); (*c*) donner du fourrage à (un cheval, etc.).

forager ['fɔridʒər], *s.* **1.** fourrageur *m.* **2.** *Ent:* butineuse *f.*

foraging[1] ['fɔridʒiŋ], *a.* qui fourrage, au fourrage; *Ent:* **f. bee,** butineuse *f.*

foraging[2], *s.* fourragement *m*; **to go f.,** aller au fourrage.

foramen, *pl.* **-mina** [fə'reimən, fɔ'ræminə], *s. Anat: etc:* foramen *m*, orifice *m*, trou *m*; **mental f.,** trou mentonnier; **f. magnum,** trou occipital; **f. ovale,** trou de Botal.

foraminate [fə'ræminət], **foraminated** [fə'ræmineitid], *a. Anat: etc:* foraminé.

Foraminifera [fɔræmi'nifərə], *s. pl. Prot:* foraminifères *m.*

forasmuch [fɔrəz'mʌtʃ], *adv. A:* **f. as,** d'autant que, vu que, attendu que, puisque, eu égard à ce que.

foray[1] ['fɔrei], *s.* razzia *f*, incursion *f*, raid *m*; **to make a brief f. into the business world,** faire une courte incursion dans le monde des affaires.

foray[2]. **1.** *v.tr.* ravager, saccager, fourrager (un pays); faire une incursion, une razzia, dans (un pays). **2.** *v.i.* faire des incursions, des raids.

forb [fɔ:b], *s. Agr:* plante herbacée (à l'exception des graminées).

forbear[1] ['fɔ:bεər], *s.* aïeul *m*, -eux; ancêtre *m*; **our forbears,** nos pères.

forbear[2] [fɔ:'bεər], *v.* (**forbore** [fɔ:'bɔ:r]; **forborne** [fɔ:'bɔ:n]) *Lit:* **1.** *v.tr.* s'abstenir de (qch.); **I forbore reproaching them,** je me suis abstenu de leur faire des reproches; *A:* **to f. (to drink) wine,** s'abstenir de vin, de boire du vin. **2.** *v.i.* (*a*) s'abstenir; **to f. from doing sth.,** s'abstenir de, s'empêcher de, se garder de, faire qch.; **to f. from mentioning sth.,** se taire sur, de, qch.; **when in doubt, f.,** dans le doute, abstiens-toi; (*b*) montrer de la patience; **to f. with s.o.,** se montrer indulgent envers qn; **to f. with sth.,** prendre qch. en patience; **to bear and f.,** se montrer patient et indulgent.

forbearance [fɔ:'bεərəns], *s.* **1. f. from, of, sth., from doing sth., to do sth.,** abstention *f* de qch., de faire qch. **2.** patience *f*, longanimité *f*; **to show f. towards s.o.,** montrer de la patience, de l'indulgence, envers qn.

forbearing [fɔ:'bεəriŋ], *a.* patient, endurant, indulgent, clément.

forbearingly [fɔ:'bεəriŋli], *adv.* avec patience, avec longanimité.

forbesite ['fɔ:bzait], *s. Miner:* forbésite *f.*

forbid [fə'bid], *v.tr.* (**forbade** [fə'bæd, -'beid]; **forbidden** [fə'bidn]) **1.** défendre, interdire; proscrire (un usage, etc.); *Jur:* prohiber (qch.); **to f. bullfights,** prohiber, défendre, les combats de taureaux; **fishing is forbidden,** pêche interdite; **smoking forbidden,** défense de fumer; **to f. the use of a door, window,** condamner une porte, une fenêtre; **to f. s.o. sth.,** défendre, interdire, qch. à qn; **the doctor has forbidden him wine,** le médecin lui a défendu le vin; **I am forbidden (to drink) tea,** le thé m'est défendu; **to f. s.o. the house,** interdire, défendre, (l'entrée de) sa maison à qn; **to f. s.o. to do sth.,** défendre à qn, faire défense à qn, de faire qch.; défendre que qn fasse qch.; **the public are forbidden to smoke in the garage,** il est interdit au public de fumer dans le garage; **he had been forbidden to go out,** il lui avait été défendu de sortir, on lui avait défendu de sortir; **he was expelled and forbidden ever to return,** on l'expulsa avec défense expresse de jamais revenir; **they were bound to the soil which they were forbidden to leave,** ils étaient attachés au sol qu'il leur était défendu de quitter; **questions into which we are forbidden to enquire,** questions interdites à nos recherches. **2.** empêcher (qch.); *A:* **my health forbids my coming,** ma santé m'empêche de venir; **Heaven f. that I should do such a thing!** Dieu me préserve de faire une telle chose! **God f. (that . . .)!** à Dieu ne plaise (que + *sub.*)! Dieu m'en préserve!

forbiddance [fə'bid(ə)ns], *s. O: & Lit:* = FORBIDDING[2].

forbidden [fə'bidn], *a.* défendu, interdit; **f. fruit,** fruit défendu; **f. subjects of conversation,** sujets tabous; **to tread on f. ground,** (i) empiéter sur un terrain défendu; (ii) toucher à un sujet défendu, tabou; *Mil:* **f. arms,** armes prohibées; *Cmptr:* **f. combination,** combinaison prohibée; **f. combination check,** contrôle *m* de caractère invalide, par détection de code interdit; *Elcs:* **f. (energy) band,** bande interdite.

forbidding[1] [fə'bidiŋ], *a.* (visage, aspect) sinistre, rébarbatif; (caractère, etc.) mal avenant, désagréable; (ciel *m*, temps *m*) sombre; (rocher, etc.) menaçant; (travail) rebutant; **f. region,** région inhospitalière.

forbidding[2], défense *f*, interdiction *f*, prohibition *f.*

forbiddingly [fə'bidiŋli], *adv.* d'une manière sinistre, menaçante; d'un air rébarbatif.

forbiddingness [fə'bidiŋnis], *s.* caractère menaçant, sinistre (de qch.); aspect rébarbatif.

forbye [fɔr'bai], *prep. & adv. Scot:* d'ailleurs, en outre.

force[1] [fɔ:s], *s.* force *f.* **1.** (*a*) violence *f*, contrainte *f*; **to make s.o. do sth. by f.,** contraindre, obliger, qn de faire qch.; **by sheer, brute, main, f.,** de vive force; **by sheer f.**

of will, à force de volonté; **the f. of circumstances,** la force, la contrainte, des circonstances; **owing to the f. of circumstances,** par la force des choses; **to resort to f.,** (i) faire appel à la force; (ii) se porter à des voies de fait; **to yield to f.,** céder à la force; succomber sous le nombre; *U.S:* **f. bill,** mesure coercitive; (*b*) influence *f*, autorité *f*; **f. of example,** influence de l'exemple; **moral f.,** force morale; **today he is an international f.,** aujourd'hui il exerce une grande influence internationale; **former party leader who is now a spent f.,** ancien chef de parti qui est maintenant une force épuisée, qui n'a plus d'autorité. **2.** (*a*) énergie *f* (d'un coup, *Fig:* de l'âme, etc.); effort *m* (d'un choc, etc.); effort(s), intensité *f* (du vent); activité *f* (d'un poison, etc.); vigueur *f* (de l'imagination, etc.); **a blow with plenty of f. behind it,** un coup bien appuyé, bien asséné; **he argued with much f. that . . .,** il a représenté avec insistance que . . .; (*b*) *Mec.E:* **f. fit,** ajustage *m*, montage *m*, emmanchement *m*, à force; *Plumb:* **f. cup,** débouchoir *m* à ventouse; *Hyd.E:* **f. pipe,** tuyau *m* de refoulement; **f. pump,** refouleur *m*; pompe (re)foulante, à plongeur. **3.** *Mec:* force, effort; (*a*) **f. exerted by an engine,** effort d'une machine, d'un moteur; **f. of gravity,** (force de la) pesanteur; **accelerating, accelerative, f.,** force accélératrice, d'accélération; **deflecting f.,** (i) (*on indicator, etc.*) force déviante; (ii) (*on beam, etc.*) force fléchissante; **impulsive f.,** force d'impulsion; **Lorentz f.,** force de Lorentz; **motive, propelling, f.,** force motrice; **peripheral f.,** force tangentielle, appliquée à la circonférence; **repellent f., repelling f., repulsive f., f. of repulsion,** force répulsive, de répulsion; **restoring f.,** force de rappel; **retarding f.,** force de freinage; **tensor f.,** force tensorielle; (*b*) *Atom.Ph:* **nuclear f.,** force nucléaire; **disruptive f., fission-producing f.,** force disruptive; **exchange f.,** force d'échange; **central f.,** force (nucléaire) centrale; **non-central f.,** force non-centrale; **long-, short-range f.,** force à longue, courte, portée, à long, court, rayon d'action; **radial f.,** force radiale; **interatomic f.,** force interatomique; (*c*) *Meteor:* **f. ten on the Beaufort scale,** la force dix de l'échelle Beaufort; (*d*) *Civ.E: etc:* **f. piece, strut,** (jambe *f* de) force. **4.** (*a*) *Mil:* force, troupe *f*, élément(s) *m*(*pl.*); détachement *m*; armée *f*; *Navy:* force (navale); **an armed f.,** une force (armée); **an armoured f.,** des (éléments) blindés; **the armoured forces,** l'arme blindée; les blindés; **attacking f.,** troupe d'attaque; unités chargées de, lancées dans, l'attaque; **field forces,** corps *m* de bataille; forces d'intervention; **forces in the field,** forces, troupes, en campagne, sur le terrain; **ground forces,** éléments, forces, terrestres; unités à terre; **the land forces,** les forces terrestres, l'armée de terre; **main f.,** gros *m* (des forces, de l'armée); **striking force(s),** masse *f* de manœuvre; **strike f.,** *Av:* force de frappe; *Navy:* force d'intervention; **task f.,** *Mil:* groupement opérationnel, tactique; *Navy:* force (navale) opérationnelle, tactique; task force *f*; **to bring up heavy forces,** amener des effectifs considérables; (*b*) *pl.* **the (armed) forces,** les forces armées; **the naval forces,** les forces navales; l'armée de mer; la marine de guerre; *W.Tel:* **the Forces programme,** programme *m* de radio pour les forces armées (*esp.* 1939–45); (*c*) **the police f.,** *F:* **the F.,** les forces de police; la force publique; la Police; *A:* **the detective f.,** la police judiciaire; la sûreté; (*d*) **a strong f. of police,** de gros effectifs, un fort détachement, de police; *Ind:* **f. of men employed,** effectif *m* de la main-d'œuvre, du personnel; **to combine forces,** joindre ses forces; **to join forces with s.o. in doing sth.,** se joindre à, *F:* s'atteler avec, qn pour faire qch.; **we turned out in (full) f.,** nous étions là en masse, au grand complet, en force. **5.** (*a*) vertu *f*, valeur *f*, efficacité *f* (d'un remède, d'un argument, etc.); (*b*) signification *f* (d'un mot, d'un document, etc.); valeur *f* (d'un mot, d'une expression); **verb used with passive f.,** verbe employé avec la valeur d'un passif. **6.** (*of law, rule, etc.*) **to be in f.,** être en vigueur; **the methods in f.,** les méthodes appliquées actuellement; **rates in f.,** tarifs *m* en vigueur; **to put a law into f.,** mettre une loi en vigueur; **to put the law into f.,** appliquer la loi; **to bring a law into f. again,** rétablir une loi; **to come into f.,** entrer en vigueur.

force[2], *v.*

I. *v.tr.* **1.** (*a*) **to f. s.o.'s hand,** forcer la main à qn; **he tried to f. the hand of fortune,** il voulut brusquer la fortune; **to f. the pace,** forcer l'allure, les pas, la vitesse; **to f. one's voice,** forcer la voix; **she forced a smile,** elle eut un sourire contraint, elle grimaça un sourire; elle s'est forçée à sourire; **to f. (the meaning of) a word,** tordre, forcer, le sens d'un mot; *Cards:* **to f. an ace, to f. trumps,** forcer un as, les atouts; (*b*) prendre (qn, qch.) par force, de force; obtenir (qch.) par violence; violer (une femme); forcer (un camp); crocheter, desceller (un coffre-fort); **to f. one's way,** se frayer, s'ouvrir, un chemin de force; se faire jour (à travers la foule); **to f. one's way into s.o.'s house, to f. one's way in,** entrer, pénétrer, de force dans une maison; forcer la porte de qn; **he forced his way into the manager's office,** il a pénétré jusqu'au bureau du directeur; **to f. (open) a door,** forcer, enfoncer, une porte; **to try to f. open a door,** exercer des pesées sur une porte; **to f. a mountain pass,** parvenir à traverser un col; (*c*) pousser, faire avancer (qch.); **to f. sth. into sth.,** faire entrer qch. de force dans qch.; **he forced a tip into my hand,** il m'a forcé à accepter un pourboire; **to f. food down the throat of s.o., of a goose,** faire avaler des aliments à qn; gaver qn, une oie; *Ind:* **to f. (in) air over the fire,** insuffler de l'air par-dessus le feu; *I.C.E:* **to f. air into the carburettor,** refouler l'air dans le carburateur; (*d*) **to f. fruit, a plant,** forcer, hâter, la maturation des fruits; chauffer une plante; **to f. poultry,** stimuler la ponte de la volaille; **to f. a pupil,** (i) pousser, chauffer, un élève; (ii) surmener un élève; *Aut: etc:* **to f. the engine,** trop pousser le moteur. **2.** (*a*) **to f. s.o. to do sth., into doing sth.,** forcer, contraindre, obliger, qn à faire qch.; violenter qn pour lui faire faire qch., pour qu'il fasse qch.; **the town was forced to capitulate,** la ville fut obligée de capituler; **I am forced to conclude that . . .,** je suis forcé de conclure que . . .; **to be forced to pay a sum of money,** verser une somme par force; **to be forced to give way,** céder à la force; (*b*) **to f. s.o. into, out of, the room,** faire entrer, faire sortir, qn de force; **they forced her into a convent,** on la contraignit d'entrer au couvent; **to f. a nation into war,** forcer une nation à entrer en guerre; (*c*) **to f. sth. (up)on s.o.,** imposer qch. à qn; forcer qn à accepter qch.; **to f. drink on s.o.,** contraindre qn à boire; **to f. an action on the enemy,** contraindre l'ennemi à la bataille; **I don't want to f. a husband on you,** je ne veux pas forcer votre inclination; **to f. one's confidences on s.o.,** imposer ses confidences à qn; **to f. one's ideas on children,** inculquer de force ses idées aux enfants; **to f. one's attentions upon s.o.,** poursuivre qn de ses assiduités; **the conviction forced itself upon me that . . .,** la conviction s'imposa à mon esprit que . . .; (*d*) **to f. sth. from s.o.,** extorquer, arracher, (une promesse, etc.) à qn.

II. (*compound verbs*) **1. force back,** *v.tr.* (*a*) repousser, faire reculer (l'ennemi, etc.); **I was forced back upon the assumption of his guilt,** force me fut de conclure à sa culpabilité; (*b*) refouler (l'air, l'eau, etc.); **to f. back one's tears,** refouler, avaler, ses larmes.

2. force down, *v.tr.* faire descendre (qch.) de force; **to f. down the lid of a box,** fermer une boîte en forçant; **to f. air down into a mine shaft,** refouler de l'air dans un puits de mine; **to f. prices down,** faire baisser les prix; **to f. down a pill,** avaler une pilule avec un grand effort; *Av:* **the plane was forced down,** l'avion a dû faire un atterrissage forcé.

3. force in, *v.tr.* (*a*) enfoncer (une porte, etc.); (*b*) (i) faire entrer (qn) de force; (ii) *Mec.E: etc:* faire entrer (une pièce) à force.

4. force off, *v.tr.* (*a*) obliger (qn) à lâcher prise, à descendre, etc.; (*b*) obliger (le couvercle, etc.) à se décoller; décoller (une soupape, etc.).

5. force on, *v.tr.* (*a*) forcer (qn) à avancer; (*b*) embattre (un bandage de roue); *Mec.E:* **to f. on a collar in the press,** caler une frette à la presse.

6. force out, *v.tr.* pousser (qn, qch.) dehors; faire sortir (qn, qch.) de force; *I.C.E:* **to f. out the burnt gases,** refouler au dehors les gaz brûlés; **to f. out a few words of congratulation,** féliciter qn du bout des lèvres.

7. force up, *v.tr.* faire monter (qch.) de force; **to f. prices up,** surélever, surhausser, faire hausser, faire monter, les prix.

forced [fɔːst], *a.* **1.** forcé; obligatoire; **f. sale,** vente forcée; **f. labour,** travail forcé; *Fin:* **f. currency, f. loan,** cours, emprunt, forcé; *Av:* **f. landing,** atterrissage forcé. **2.** (*a*) forcé, contraint; **f. praise,** louanges *fpl* de commande; **f. laugh,** rire forcé, artificiel, faux; rire de commande; rire du bout des lèvres, du bout des dents; **to give a f. laugh,** rire faux, rire pointu; **his laughter is always f.,** son rire ne passe pas les lèvres; (*b*) *Mil:* **f. march,** marche forcée; **to advance by f. marches,** avancer à marches forcées; (*c*) *Mec.E: Mch:* **f. circulation,** circulation forcée (d'une chaudière); **f. draught,** tirage forcé; **f. feed (of oil),** graissage forcé, sous pression; **f. cooling,** refroidissement forcé, accéléré; *I.C.E:* **f.-induction engine,** moteur *m* à alimentation forcée; **f. fit,** ajustage *m*, montage *m*, emmanchement *m*, à force; *Mec:* **f. oscillations, f. vibrations,** oscillations, vibrations, forcées; (*d*) *Husb: etc:* **f. feeding,** gavage *m*. **3.** (*of crops, plants*) forcé; **f. vegetables, f. fruit,** légumes *m*, fruits *mpl*, de forcerie; primeurs *fpl*.

forcedly ['fɔːsidli], *adv.* forcément.

force-feed[1] ['fɔːs'fiːd], *a. Mec.E: etc:* **f.-f. oiler,** burette *f* à pompe, à piston; **f.-f. lubrication,** graissage *m* sous pression.

force-feed[2], *v.tr.* (-fed; -fed.) *Husb: etc:* gaver (qn, une oie).

forceful ['fɔːsful], *a.* (*of pers., speech, etc.*) (*a*) plein de force; énergique; (*b*) violent.

forcefully ['fɔːsfuli], *adv.* avec force; vigoureusement; puissamment.

force-land ['fɔːs'lænd], *v.i. Av:* faire un atterrissage forcé.

forcemeat ['fɔːsmiːt], *s. Cu:* farce *f*, hachis *m*, godiveau *m*; **f. ball,** boulette *f*.

forceps ['fɔːseps], *s. inv.* **1. a (pair of) f.,** une pince; (*a*) *Surg:* **dressing f.,** bec-de-corbeau *m*, *pl.* becs-de-corbeau; **bullet f.,** tire-balle *m*, *pl.* tire-balles; **artery f.,** pince à artère; pince hémostatique; presse-artère *m*, *pl.* presse-artères; artériodème *m*; clamp *m*; **suture f.,** serre-fine *f*, *pl.* serre-fines; (*b*) *Obst:* forceps *m*; *F:* fers *mpl*; (*c*) *Dent:* davier *m*, précelles *fpl*; **stump f., molar f.,** trivelin *m*, tire-racine(s) *m inv*; pied-de-biche *m*, *pl.* pieds-de-biche. **2.** *Ent:* pince, forceps (de forficule).

forcible ['fɔːsibl]. *a.* **1.** (entrée, etc.) de, par, force; *esp. Jur:* **f. detainer,** possession illégale obtenue par violence; **f. entry,** prise de possession illégale et par la violence. **2.** (langage, écrivain, etc.) énergique, vigoureux, plein de force.

forcibleness ['fɔːsiblnis], *s.* **1.** force *f*, violence *f*. **2.** énergie *f*, vigueur *f*.

forcibly ['fɔːsibli], *adv.* **1.** par force, de force; **to detain s.o. f.,** retenir qn de force. **2.** énergiquement, vigoureusement.

forcing ['fɔːsiŋ], *s.* **1.** (*a*) **f. (open),** forcement *m* (d'une serrure); descellement *m* (d'un coffre-fort); enfoncement *m* (d'une porte); (*b*) refoulement *m* (d'air dans un puits de mine); *Hyd.E:* **f. pump,** refouleur *m*; **f. valve,** (i) soupape *f* (d'un respirateur, etc.); (ii) *Mch:* robinet purgeur; (*c*) viol *m* (d'une femme); (*d*) embattage *m* (du bandage sur la roue); (*e*) *Cu:* **f. bag,** poche *f* à douille; (*f*) *Sm.a:* **f. cone,** cône *m* de forcement. **2.** (*a*) *Hort:* forçage *m*; culture forcée; culture sous châssis (de fruits, légumes); **f. bed,** forcerie *f*; couche *f* (de fumier); **f. frame,** châssis *m*; **f. house,** forcerie; (*b*) *Sch:* (i) chauffage *m*, (ii) surmenage *m* (d'un élève); (*c*) *Husb:* (*for poultry*) **f. mixture,** produit stimulant. **3.** *Cards: Sp:* forcing *m*.

forcipressure ['fɔːsipreʃər], *s. Surg:* forcipressure *f*.

ford[1] [fɔːd], *s.* gué *m*; **to pass, go, through a f.,** passer un gué.

ford[2], *v.tr.* guéer, traverser à gué (une rivière).

fordable ['fɔːdəbl], *a.* guéable, traversable.

fording ['fɔːdiŋ], *s.* passage *m* à gué.

fordone [fɔː'dʌn], *a. Lit:* épuisé, à bout de forces.

fore [fɔːr], *a., s., & int.*

I. *a.* (*a*) antérieur; de devant; **the f. side of sth.,** la partie antérieure, le devant, de qch.; *Surv:* **f. observation,** coup *m* avant; *Veh:* **f. axle,** essieu *m* avant (d'un wagon de chemin de fer, etc.); **f. body,** avant *m* de carrosserie; (*b*) *Nau:* (de l')avant; **the f. rigging,** le gréement de misaine; **f. hatch,** panneau *m* avant; (*c*) *Mch:* **f. eccentric,** excentrique *m* pour la marche avant.

II. *s.* (*a*) *Nau:* avant *m*; **at the f.,** au mât de misaine; (*b*) (*of pers., etc.*) **to the f.,** (i) en vue, en évidence, en vedette; (ii) présent; **to be always to the f. in a fight,** être toujours sur la brèche; **to come to the f.,** commencer à être connu; faire sa trouée; **this theory is once more to the f.,** cette théorie est de nouveau mise en avant; *A:* **to have money to the f.,** avoir de l'argent disponible; **to find oneself with nothing to the f.,** se trouver sans ressources.

III. *int. Golf:* attention devant! gare devant!

fore(-)and(-)aft ['fɔːrənd'ɑːft], *a. & adv.* **1.** de bout en bout; *Nau:* de l'avant à l'arrière; **f.-and-a. sail,** voile *f* aurique; **f.-and-a. (rigged) vessel,** navire *m* à voiles auriques; **f.-and-a. bulkhead,** cloison médiane; **f.-and-a. bridge,** passavant *m*; **f.-and-a. moorings,** embossage *m*. **2.** (dans le sens) longitudinal; parallèle à l'axe longitudinal (de la voiture, etc.); **f.-and-a. axis, line,** axe longitudinal; *Av:* **f.-and-a. inclinometer, level,** indicateur *m* de pente longitudinale; *Mil:* **f.-and-a. cap,** (sorte *f* de) calot (porté par les troupes anglaises, 1939–45).

fore-and-after ['fɔːrənd'ɑftər], *s. Nau:* **1.** bâtiment *m* à voiles auriques. **2.** *F: A:* chapeau bicorne porté en colonne.

forearm[1] ['fɔːrɑːm]. **1.** *s.* avant-bras *m inv*. **2.** *a. & s. Ten:* **f. stroke,** coup *m* d'avant-main; coup droit; **f. drive,** drive *m* de coup droit; **to take a ball on the f.,** jouer le coup droit.

forearm[2] [fɔːr'ɑːm], *v.tr.* prémunir (qn).

forebay ['fɔːbei], *s. Hyd.E:* chambre *f*, bassin *m*, de mise en charge; chambre d'eau.

forebear ['fɔːbɛər], *s.* = FORBEAR[1].

forebode [fɔː'boud], *v.tr.* **1.** (*of thg*) présager, augurer (le malheur, etc.); **policy that forebodes disaster,** politique qui laisse prévoir le désastre. **2.** (*of pers.*) pressentir (un malheur); avoir un pressentiment de (qch.).

foreboder [fɔː'boudər], *s.* **1.** augure *m*, présage *m* (**of,** de). **2.** (*pers.*) devin, -eresse; prophète *m*.

foreboding[1] [fɔː'boudiŋ], *a.* de mauvais augure; sinistre.

foreboding[2], *s.* **1.** mauvais augure; présage *m* (sinistre). **2.** (mauvais) pressentiment; **a f. of evil,** un pressentiment de malheur.

forebodingly [fɔː'boudiŋli], *adv.* sinistrement.

forebrain ['fɔːbrein], *s. Anat:* cerveau antérieur.

forebreast ['fɔːbrest], *s. Min:* front *m* de taille, des travaux.

forecabin ['fɔːkæbin], *s. Nau:* cabine *f* de l'avant; cabine d'avant (d'un paquebot).

forecaddie ['fɔːkædi], *s. Golf:* caddie *m* qui précède le joueur.

forecarriage ['fɔːkæridʒ], *s.* avant-train *m*, *pl.* avant-trains (d'une voiture).

forecast[1] ['fɔːkɑːst], *s.* prévision *f*, pronostication *f* (d'un malheur, etc.); **racing f., betting f.,** pronostic *m* des courses; **dual f.,** couple gagnant; pari jumelé; **f. of the first three horses in the right order, in any order,** (pari) tiercé dans l'ordre, dans le désordre; *Meteor:* **weather f.,** prévision météorologique; **daily f.,** prévision journalière; **long-range f.,** prévision à longue échéance; **extended f.,** prévision sur période prolongée; **short-range f.,** prévision sur période courte; **upper-air f.,** prévision en altitude; **surface f.,** prévision en surface.

forecast[2], *v.tr.* (*p.t. & p.p.* **forecast(ed)**) calculer, prévoir (les événements, etc.); **to f. the weather,** prévoir le temps; **to f. the future of . . .,** prédire quel sera l'avenir de . . .; **to f. the future according to the past,** augurer l'avenir d'après le passé; *Sp:* **to f. the result,** pronostiquer le résultat.

forecaster ['fɔːkɑːstər], *s.* pronostiqueur, -euse; **weather f.,** prévisionniste *mf*.

forecasting ['fɔːkɑːstiŋ], *s.* pronostication *f* (d'un résultat, etc.); prévision *f* (du temps).

forecastle ['fouksl], *s. A: Nau:* **1.** gaillard *m* (d'avant); plage *f* avant; **topgallant f.,** (pont *m*) teugue *f*; teugue d'avant; **f. deck,** pont de gaillard. **2.** (*in merchant vessel*) poste *m* de l'équipage.

forecheck ['fɔːtʃek], *v.tr. Sp:* (*ice hockey*) intercepter (un adversaire) dans sa zone de défense.

foreclose [fɔː'klouz], *v.tr.* **1.** *A:* exclure, *A:* forclore (qn); **to f. s.o. from sth.,** exclure qn de qch.; **to f. s.o. from doing sth., to do sth.,** empêcher qn de faire qch.; *Jur:* forclore qn (de produire une pièce en justice, etc.). **2.** *Jur:* **to f. the mortgagor (from, the equity of redemption), to f. the mortgage,** saisir, poursuivre la vente de, l'immeuble hypothéqué. **3. to f. an objection,** aller audevant d'une objection.

foreclosure [fɔː'klouʒər], *s. Jur:* forclusion *f*; saisie *f* (d'une hypothèque).

foreconscious [fɔː'kɒntʃəs], *s. Psy:* préconscient *m*.

forecourt ['fɔːkɔːt], *s.* avant-cour *f*, *pl.* avant-cours; **garage f.,** piste *f* de garage, de ravitaillement.

foredeck ['fɔːdek], *s. Nau:* (*of merchant ship*) pont *m* avant; gaillard *m* d'avant; *Navy:* avant-pont *m*, *pl.* avant-ponts.

foredeep ['fɔːdiːp], *s. Geol:* avant-fosse *f*, *pl.* avant-fosses (d'une guirlande insulaire).

foredoom [fɔː'duːm], *v.tr.* **1.** condamner (qn, qch.) d'avance. **2.** déterminer (la chute, etc., de qn) d'avance; **to f. s.o. to sth., to do sth.,** prédestiner qn à qch., à faire qch. **3.** présager, prédire (le sort de qn).

foredoomed [fɔː'duːmd], *a.* (*of pers., enterprise, etc.*) condamné d'avance (**to,** à); **plan f. to failure,** projet voué à l'insuccès, mort-né.

fore edge ['fɔːredʒ], *s. Bookb:* gouttière *f* (d'un livre).

fore-end ['fɔːrend], *a. Agr:* **f.-e. loader,** chargeur frontal.

forefather ['fɔːfɑːðər], *s.m.* aïeul, -eux; **our forefathers,** nos pères, nos devanciers, nos aïeux.

forefield ['fɔːfiːld], *s. Min:* front *m* de taille, des travaux.

forefinger ['fɔːfiŋgər], *s.* index *m*.

forefoot, *pl.* **-feet** ['fɔːfut, -fiːt], *s.* **1.** (*of animal*) pied antérieur; patte *f* de devant; **the forefeet of a horse,** le bipède antérieur d'un cheval. **2.** *Nau:* (*a*) brion *m* (d'un navire); **f. knee,** marsouin *m* (d'un navire); (*b*) étrave *f*.

forefront ['fɔːfrʌnt], *s.* **1.** (*a*) *A:* devant *m* (de qch.); façade *f* (d'une construction); (*b*) premier rang, premier plan; **this question is still in the f.,** cette question occupe toujours le premier plan. **2.** *Mil:* première ligne; le front.

foregather [fɔː'gæðər], *v.i.* = FORGATHER.

foregift ['fɔːgift], *s. Jur:* droit *m*, redevance *f*, au début d'un bail.

forego[1] [fɔː'gou], *v.tr.* (**forewent** [fɔː'went]; **foregone** [fɔː'gɒn]) *A: & Lit:* précéder; aller devant (qch.).

forego[2], *v.tr.* = FORGO.

foregoer [fɔː'gouər], *s.* prédécesseur *m*; devancier, -ière.

foregoing ['fɔːgouiŋ], *a.* précédent, antérieur; déjà cité; **the f.,** ce qui précède.

foregone ['fɔːgɒn], *a.* **1.** (*of time, event*) passé. **2.** (*of conclusion, intention, etc.*) décidé d'avance; prévu; déjà envisagé; déjà escompté; **it was a f. conclusion,** l'issue n'était pas douteuse.

foreground ['fɔːgraund], *s.* **1.** *Art: Phot: etc:* premier plan; avant-plan *m*, *pl.* avant-plans; *Art:* **strong piece of f.,** repoussoir *m* (pour éloigner le reste du tableau); **in the f.,** au premier plan; **to bring s.o., a question, into the f.,** mettre en avant qn, une question. **2.** *Mil:* avant-terrain *m*. **3.** *Cmptr:* **f. processing,** traitement *m* prioritaire (des programmes); **f. programme,** programme *m* prioritaire.

foregrounding ['fɔːgraundiŋ], *s. Cmptr:* traitement *m* prioritaire (des programmes).

forehand ['fɔːhænd]. **1.** *s.* (*of horse*) avant-main *m*. **2.** *Ten:* (*a*) *a.* **f. stroke,** coup *m* d'avant-main; coup droit; **f. drive,** drive *m* de coup droit; **f. court,** côté droit du court; (*b*) *s.* **to serve on to one's opponent's f.,** servir sur le coup droit adverse; **to take a ball on the f.,** jouer le coup droit. **3.** *a.* **f. welding,** soudure *f* à gauche.

forehanded ['fɔːhændid]. **1.** = FOREHAND 2 (*a*); **to take a ball f.,** jouer le coup droit. **2.** *NAm:* (*a*) prévoyant; (*b*) (*of pers.*) qui a fait des économies; qui est à l'aise; aisé.

forehandedness [fɔː'hændidnis], *s. NAm:* prévoyance *f*, prévision *f*.

forehander ['fɔːhændər], *s. Ten:* coup droit, d'avant-main.

forehead ['fɒrid, 'fɔːhed], *s. Anat:* front *m*; **wide f.,** front large; **receding f.,** front fuyant.

fore hearth ['fɔːhɑːθ], *s. Metall:* (*of furnace*) avant-foyer *m*, *pl.* avant-foyers; avant-creuset *m*, *pl.* avant-creusets.

forehock ['fɔːhɒk], *s. Cu:* jambonneau *m* avant, patte *f* de devant du porc.

forehold ['fɔːhould], *s. Nau:* cale *f* avant; avant-cale *f*, *pl.* avant-cales.

forehoof ['fɔːhuːf], *s.* sabot *m* de jambe antérieure.

forehook ['fɔːhuk], *s. N.Arch:* guirlande *f*.

foreign ['fɒrin], *a.* étranger. **1.** qui n'appartient pas à (qch.), qui n'a pas trait à (qch.), qui est en dehors de (la question); **f. to, from (sth.),** étranger à, éloigné de, sans rapport avec (qch.); **such feelings are f. to his nature,** de tels sentiments lui sont étrangers; *Med: etc:* **f. body,** corps étranger. **2.** qui n'est pas du pays; qui appartient à un autre pays; (*a*) (*situated abroad*) **f. countries, f. parts,** pays étrangers, l'étranger *m*, l'extérieur *m*; **he has been in f. parts,** il a été à l'étranger; **ship bound for f. countries,** navire *m* à destination de l'étranger; **our relations with f. countries,** nos rapports *m* avec l'extérieur; **f. travel,** voyages *mpl* à l'étranger; **the f. colony in Paris,** la colonie exotique de Paris; *Mil:* **f. service,** service *m* à l'étranger; *Dipl:* **the F. Service,** le corps diplomatique; *Nau:* **f. navigation,** navigation hauturière, au long cours, au large; (*b*) (*dealing with foreign countries*) **the F. Debt,** la Dette extérieure; **f. trade,** commerce extérieur; *Nau:* long cours; *Nau:* **to be in the f. trade,** naviguer au long cours; **f. correspondent,** (i) correspondant *m* pour les langues étrangères; commis correspondant; (ii) correspondant à l'étranger; **f. correspondence clerk,** correspondancier *m* pour l'étranger; **f. money order,** mandat international; *Pol:* **F. Affairs,** les Affaires étrangères; affaires extérieures; **the F. Office** = le Ministère des Affaires étrangères; **the F. Secretary** = le Ministre des Affaires étrangères. **3.** *U.S:* qui appartient à un autre État (de l'Union).

foreign-built ['fɒrin'bilt], *a.* (voiture, etc.) de marque étrangère; (navire, etc.) construit à l'étranger.

foreigner ['fɒrinər], *s.* **1.** étranger, -ère. **2.** *Dial:* homme, etc., qui n'est pas d'ici. **3.** *St.Exch:* **foreigners,** valeurs étrangères, fonds étrangers.

foreign-going ['fɒrin'gouiŋ], *a.* **f.-g. ship,** navire *m* au long cours; long-courrier *m*, *pl.* long-courriers; **master of a f.-g. ship,** capitaine au long cours.

foreign-grown ['fɒrin'groun], *a.* (fruit, etc.) de provenance étrangère, exotique.

foreignness ['fɒrinnis], *s.* air étranger; exotisme *m*.

forejudge [fɔː'dʒʌdʒ], *v.tr. & abs.* préjuger; juger (qn, qch.) par avance.

forejudgment [fɔː'dʒʌdʒmənt], *s.* préjugement *m*.

foreknow [fɔː'nou], *v.tr.* (**foreknew** [fɔː'njuː]; **foreknown** [fɔː'noun]) connaître d'avance.

foreknowing [fɔː'nouiŋ], *a.* préconnaissant; prescient.

foreknowingly [fɔː'nouiŋli], *adv.* avec préconnaissance.

foreknowledge [fɔː'nɒlidʒ], *s.* préconnaissance *f*; prescience *f*.

forel ['fɒrəl], *s. Bookb:* parchemin *m* de peau de mouton.

foreland ['fɔːlənd], *s.* **1.** cap *m*, promontoire *m*; pointe *f* (de terre); falaise *f* à pic. **2.** *Geol:* **tectonic f.,** avant-pays *m*. **3.** *Fort:* berme *f*.

foreleg ['fɔːleg], *s.* jambe antérieure, de devant (d'un cheval); patte *f* de devant (d'un chien).

foreloader ['fɔːloudər], *s. Agr: Civ.E:* chargeur frontal.

forelock[1] ['fɔːlɒk], *s.* (*of pers.*) mèche *f* (de cheveux) sur le front; (*of pers., horse*) toupet *m*; **to take time, the occasion, by the f.,** saisir l'occasion aux cheveux, par les cheveux; **to touch one's f.,** porter la moin à son front (en témoignant de la déférence à, envers, qn).

forelock[2], *s. Mec.E:* clavette *f*, goupille *f* (d'un boulon); **f. bolt,** boulon à clavette.

forelock[3], *v.tr. Mec.E:* clavet(t)er, goupiller (un boulon).

foreman, *pl.* **-men** ['fɔːmən], *s.m.* **1.** *Jur:* chef (du jury). **2.** (*a*) *Ind: etc:* contremaître; chasse-avant *inv*; (*in shop*) chef d'atelier; **f. of a gang of workmen,** chef d'équipe, de brigade; brigadier; caporal, -aux; **works f.,** conducteur des travaux; **mine f.,** premier mineur; **farm f.,** maître valet de ferme; *Nau:* **f. stevedore,** chef arrimeur; (*b*) *Typ:* **printer's f.,** prote *m*; **deputy f.,** sous-prote, *pl.* sous-protes; **working f.,** prote à tablier.

foremanship ['fɔːmənʃip], *s.* fonction *f* de (i) chef (du jury), (ii) contremaître (d'atelier).

foremast ['fɔːmɑːst], *s. Nau:* mât *m* de misaine; (arbre *m* de) trinquet *m*.

forementioned [fɔː'menʃənd], *a.* dont nous avons déjà parlé; dont il a déjà été fait mention; *Jur: Adm:* précité.

foremilk ['fɔːmilk], *s.* **1.** premier lait fourni (à une traite). **2.** colostrum *m*; *F:* amouille *f*.

foremost ['fɔːmoust]. **1.** *a.* premier; qui précède les autres; le plus avancé; le plus en avant; (tout) en tête; (position *f*) extrême avant; **in the f. rank,** au tout premier rang; **to hold the f. place among philosophers,** tenir le premier rang parmi les philosophes; **one of the f. citizens of the day,** un des premiers citoyens du jour; **to be among the f. to do sth.,** être parmi les premiers à faire qch.; **to come f.,** venir tout en tête; **to fall head f.,** tomber la tête la première, la tête en bas; **I know I shall only leave this room feet f.,** je sais que je ne quitterai cette chambre que les pieds devant. **2.** *adv.* **first and f.,** tout d'abord; en premier lieu; d'abord et avant tout.

forename ['fɔːneim], *s.* prénom *m*.

forenoon ['fɔːnuːn], *s.* (*esp. Scot. & Irish*) matinée *f*; **in the f.,** dans, pendant, la matinée.

forensic [fə'rensik, fɔ-]. **1.** *a.* (éloquence *f*, etc.) judiciaire, du Palais, du barreau; **f. term,** terme *m* de Palais, de pratique; **f. contests,** luttes *f* de la tribune, du Palais; **f. medicine, chemistry,** médecine, chimie, légale; **f. scientist,** expert *m* légiste. **2.** *s. NAm:* (*a*) leçon *f*, classe *f*, d'argumentation; (*b*) *pl.* (*usu. with sg. const.*) **forensics,** (art *m* de l')argumentation *f*.

foreordain [fɔːrɔː'dein], *v.tr.* **1.** prédestiner (**s.o. to sth., to do sth.,** qn à qch., à faire qch.); *B:* **who verily was foreordained before the foundation of the world,** déjà ordonné avant la fondation du monde. **2. what God hath foreordained,** ce que Dieu a préordonné.

foreordination ['fɔːrɔːdi'neiʃ(ə)n], *s.* prédestination *f*.

forepart ['fɔːpɑːt], *s.* **1.** avant *m*, devant *m*, partie la plus en avant (de qch.); avant-corps *m inv* (d'un bâtiment, etc.); tête *f* (d'un train, etc.); **the f. of the ship,** la partie avant du navire; **f. of a furnace,** avant d'un fourneau; face *f* de coulée. **2.** (*in time*) commencement *m* (de la journée, etc.).

forepaw ['fɔːpɔː], *s.* patte *f* de devant.

forepayment ['fɔːpeimənt], *s.* paiement *m* d'avance.

forepeak ['fɔːpiːk], *s.* **1.** *Nau:* coqueron *m* avant (d'un navire). **2.** batte *f* (d'une selle).

foreplan ['fɔːplæn], *v.tr.* (**foreplanned**) projeter (une entreprise, etc.).

foreplane ['fɔːplein], *s. Tls: Carp:* riflard *m*.

forepole ['fɔːpoul], *v.i. Min:* chasser par palplanches.

forepoling ['fɔːpouliŋ], *s. Min: etc:* soutènement *m* provisoire.

forequarter ['fɔːkwɔːtər], *s.* quartier *m* de devant (de bœuf, etc.); **forequarters of a horse,** avant-main *m*, avant-train *m*, train *m* de devant, d'un cheval.

forereach ['fɔːriːtʃ], *v. Nau:* **1.** *v.i.* gagner au vent. **2.** *v.tr. & i.* **to f. (on) a ship,** dépasser un navire; gagner l'avant d'un navire.

forerun [fɔː'rʌn], *v.tr.* (**foreran** [fɔː'ræn]; **forerun; forerunning** [fɔː'rʌniŋ]) précéder, devancer (un événement, l'aurore, etc.); **the calm that foreruns the storm,** le calme avant-coureur de la tempête.

forerunner ['fɔːrʌnər], *s.* **1.** avant-coureur *m pl.* avant-coureurs; avant-courrier, -ière, *pl.* avant-courriers, -ières; précurseur *m*; **the F. of our Lord,** le précurseur de Notre-Seigneur; **swallows, the forerunners of spring,** les hirondelles, messagères du printemps; **signs that are forerunners of a storm,** signes avant-coureurs d'une tempête. 2. *Ski:* ouvreur *m*. 3. *Nau:* houache *f* (d'un loch).

foresaid ['fɔːsed], *a.* précité; mentionné ci-dessus.

foresail ['fɔːseil, *Nau:* 'fɔːsl], *s. Nau:* (voile *f* de) misaine *f*; **balloon f.**, trinquette-ballon *f, pl.* trinquettes-ballons (de yacht).

foresee [fɔː'siː], *v.tr.* (**foresaw** [fɔː'sɔː]; **foreseen** [fɔː'siːn]) prévoir, entrevoir (un malheur, des difficultés, etc.); **to f. the future**, percer, augurer, l'avenir; **it was an accident which should have been foreseen**, c'était un accident à prévoir; **she foresaw enquiries being made**, elle prévoyait qu'on irait aux renseignements.

foreseeable [fɔː'siːəbl], *a.* (conséquence, etc.) que l'on peut prévoir; (l'avenir, etc.) prévisible.

foreseeing[1] [fɔː'siːiŋ], *a.* (*of pers.*) prévoyant.

foreseeing[2], *s.* prévoyance *f*.

foreshadow [fɔː'ʃædou], *v.tr.* présager, annoncer, préfigurer, faire prévoir, laisser prévoir, faire pressentir (un événement, etc.).

foreshaft ['fɔːʃɑːft], *s. Min:* avant-puits *m inv*.

foresheet ['fɔːʃiːt], *s. Nau:* 1. écoute *f* de misaine. 2. *pl.* **the foresheets**, le gaillard; la chambre du brigadier (d'un canot).

foreshock ['fɔːʃɔk], *s. Meteor:* (choc *m*) avant-coureur *m, pl.* (chocs) avant-coureurs (d'un séisme).

foreshore ['fɔːʃɔːr], *s.* 1. plage *f*. 2. laisse *f* de haute mer, de marée; *Jur:* lais *mpl* (et relais *mpl*) de la mer; laisse de mer.

foreshorten [fɔː'ʃɔːtn], *v.tr. Art:* dessiner, présenter, (un objet) en raccourci, en perspective.

foreshortened [fɔː'ʃɔːt(ə)nd], *a. Art:* raccourci, en raccourci, en perspective; **f. figure**, figure vue de raccourci.

foreshortening [fɔː'ʃɔːt(ə)niŋ], *s. Art:* raccourci *m*; effet *m* de perspective.

foreshow [fɔː'ʃou], *v.tr.* (*p.p.* **foreshown**) présager, annoncer, faire prévoir (un événement).

foreside ['fɔːsaid], *s.* devant *m*, partie antérieure.

foresight ['fɔːsait], *s.* 1. (*a*) prévision *f* (de l'avenir); (*b*) prévoyance *f*; **lack of f.**, imprévoyance *f*, imprévision *f*; **he failed for want of f.**, il a échoué par défaut de prévoyance; *F:* il s'est trouvé au pied du mur sans échelle; **to have f. and perspicacity**, voir de loin; voir bien loin. 2. (*a*) *Sm.a:* guidon *m*; bouton *m* de mire; (*b*) *Artil:* fronteau *m* de mire. 3. *Surv:* coup *m* avant.

foresighted ['fɔːsaitid], *a.* (*of pers.*) prévoyant.

foreskin ['fɔːskin], *s. Anat:* prépuce *m*.

forest[1] ['fɔrist], *s.* 1. (*a*) forêt *f*; **high f., matured f.**, (forêt de haute) futaie; **open f.**, forêt-parc *f, pl.* forêts-parcs; **gallery f.**, forêt-galerie *f, pl.* forêts-galeries; **deciduous f.**, forêt à feuilles caduques, forêt caducifoliée; **coniferous f.**, forêt de conifères; **broad-leaved f.**, forêt feuillue; **thorn f.**, forêt épineuse; **virgin, primaeval, f.**, forêt vierge; **equatorial f.**, forêt équatoriale; **tropical rain f.**, forêt tropicale humide; **sub-tropical f.**, forêt subtropicale; **monsoon f.**, forêt des moussons; **dry f.**, forêt sèche; **f.-covered hills**, collines boisées; **the national forests**, le domaine forestier; **state f.**, forêt domaniale; *Geog:* **the Black F.**, la Forêt Noire; *Fig:* **a f. of masts, of telegraph poles**, une forêt de mâts, de poteaux télégraphiques; (*b*) *attrib.* forestier; **f. administration**, administration forestière; **f. range**, cantonnement *m*; **f. ranger, guard**, garde forestier; **f. laws**, Code forestier; **f. officer**, agent forestier; **f. school**, école forestière; **f. tree**, arbre forestier, de haute futaie; forestier *m*; *Austr:* **f. oak**, casuarine *f*, filao *m*; *Ent:* **f. fly**, hippobosque *m*. 2. chasse royale; chasse seigneuriale; **deer f.**, chasse gardée pour le cerf.

forest[2], *v.tr.* boiser (une région).

forestage ['fɔːsteidʒ], *s.* 1. *Jur: Hist:* droit d'affouage. 2. *Th:* avant-scène *f, pl.* avant-scènes.

forestall [fɔː'stɔːl], *v.tr.* 1. *Hist: & NAm:* accaparer (un objet de commerce); *abs.* faire de l'accaparement. 2. anticiper, devancer, prévenir (qn, un événement); prendre les devants sur (un concurrent, etc.); couper l'herbe sous le pied à (qn); **to f. a plot**, aller au-devant d'un complot; **to f. s.o.'s desires**, prévenir les désirs de qn.

forestaller [fɔː'stɔːlər], *s.* 1. *Hist: & NAm:* accapareur, -euse (de denrées, etc.). 2. **my f.**, la personne qui m'a devancé, qui m'a coupé l'herbe sous le pied.

forestalling [fɔː'stɔːliŋ], *s.* 1. *Hist: & NAm:* accaparement *m* (de denrées). 2. anticipation *f* (des désirs de qn); devancement *m* (d'un concurrent, etc.).

fore starling ['fɔːstɑːliŋ], *s. Civ.E:* avant-bec *m, pl.* avant-becs (de ponton, etc.).

forestay ['fɔːstei], *s. Nau:* 1. étai *m* de misaine. 2. **f. (sail)**, trinquette *f*, tourmentin *m* (d'une goëlette, etc.).

forested ['fɔristid], *a.* (*of region, etc.*) couvert de forêts.

forester ['fɔːristər], *s.* 1. (*a*) garde forestier; forestier *m*; (*b*) brigadier forestier. 2. (*a*) forestier, -ière; habitant *m* d'une forêt; (*b*) **the Ancient Order of Foresters**, nom d'une société de secours mutuels. 3. oiseau *m*, animal *m*, -aux, des forêts. 4. (arbre *m* de haute) futaie; arbre forestier.

forestland ['fɔristlænd], *s.* terre forestière.

forestry ['fɔristri], *s.* 1. sylviculture *f*; **school of f.**, école forestière; *Adm:* **F. Commission**, service *m* des Eaux et Forêts. 2. *coll.* les forêts *f* (d'un pays).

foretack ['fɔːtæk], *s. Nau:* amure *f* de misaine.

foretaste[1] ['fɔːteist], *s.* avant-goût *m, pl.* avant-goûts.

foretaste[2] [fɔː'teist], *v.tr.* avoir un avant-goût de (qch.); goûter (qch.) par avance.

foretell [fɔː'tel], *v.tr.* (*p.t. & p.p.* **foretold** [fɔː'tould]) 1. (*of pers.*) prédire; annoncer (qch.) d'avance; pronostiquer (le temps, etc.). 2. présager; **the sky foretells fine weather**, le ciel annonce le beau temps.

foretellable [fɔː'teləbl], *a.* qui peut être prédit, pronostiqué.

foreteller [fɔː'telər], *s.* prophète, *f.* prophétesse; devin, *f.* devineresse; pronostiqueur, -euse (du temps, etc.).

foretelling[1] [fɔː'teliŋ], *a.* (signe, etc.) prophétique.

foretelling[2], *s.* prédiction *f*, prophétie *f*.

forethought[1] ['fɔːθɔːt], *a.* (crime, etc.) prémédité.

forethought[2], *s.* 1. (*a*) préméditation *f*; **crime of f.**, crime prémédité; (*b*) **to speak without f.**, parler sans réfléchir, sans réflexion. 2. prévoyance *f*, prudence *f*.

forethoughtful [fɔː'θɔːtful], *a. Lit:* prudent, prévoyant.

foretime ['fɔːtaim], *s. Lit:* le passé; l'autrefois *m*.

foretoken[1] ['fɔːtoukən], *s.* augure *m*, présage *m*, indice annonciateur, signe avant-coureur (**of**, de).

foretoken[2] [fɔː'toukən], *v.tr.* présager, annoncer (une tempête, etc.).

foretooth, *pl.* **-teeth** ['fɔːtuːθ, -tiːθ], *s.* (dent) incisive *f*; dent du devant.

foretop ['fɔːtɔp], *s.* 1. toupet *m* (d'un cheval). 2. *Nau:* hune *f* de misaine.

fore-topgallant ['fɔːtɔp'gælənt, *Nau:* -tə'gælənt], *a. Nau:* (mât, etc.) de petit perroquet.

foretopman, *pl.* **-men** [fɔː'tɔpmən], *s.m. Nau:* gabier de misaine.

foretopmast ['fɔːtɔpmɑːst, *Nau:* -təp-], *s. Nau:* petit mât de hune.

foretopsail ['fɔː'tɔpseil, *Nau:* -sl], *s. Nau:* petit hunier.

foretrysail ['fɔː'traisl], *s. Nau:* misaine *f* goëlette.

foretype ['fɔːtaip], *s.* prototype *m*.

forever [fər'evər]. 1. *adv.* (*a*) pour toujours, à jamais; (*b*) éternellement, sans cesse (*s.a.* EVER 2 (*b*)). 2. *s. NAm: F:* **to take f. to do sth.**, prendre une éternité à faire qch.

forevermore [fər'evə'mɔːr], *adv.* pour toujours, à jamais.

forewarn [fɔː'wɔːn], *v.tr.* prévenir, avertir; **to f. s.o. against sth.**, mettre qn en garde contre qch.; prémunir qn contre qch; *Prov:* **forewarned is forearmed**, un homme averti en vaut deux; qui dit averti dit muni; qui prévoit peut prévenir.

forewarning [fɔː'wɔːniŋ], *s.* avertissement *m*, pressentiment *m*.

forewoman, *pl.* **-women** ['fɔːwumən, -wimin], *s.f.* 1. *Jur:* porte-parole *m inv* (d'un jury). 2. *Ind: etc:* contremaîtresse; *F:* première.

foreword ['fɔːwəːd], *s.* (*to book*) avant-propos *m inv*, préface *f*; avis *m* au lecteur; avertissement *m*; épître *f* liminaire.

foreyard[1] ['fɔːjɑːd], *s. Nau:* mât *m* de misaine.

foreyard[2], *s.* avant-cour *f, pl.* avant-cours.

forfeit[1] ['fɔːfit], *a. Hist: Jur:* confisqué; perdu; **his lands and money were f.**, on confisqua ses terres et on le dépouilla de son argent.

forfeit[2], *s.* 1. (*a*) amende *f*; (*for non-performance of contract*) dédit *m*; *Sp: esp. Turf:* forfait *m*; *St.Exch:* **to relinquish the f.**, abandonner la prime; **f. clause (of a contract)**, clause *f* de dédit; **to have to pay a f.**, être mis à l'amende; **his life was the f. of his crime**, il paya son crime de sa vie; (*b*) *Games:* gage *m*, punition *f*; **to play (at) forfeits**, jouer aux gages. 2. = FORFEITURE.

forfeit[3], *v.tr.* 1. perdre (qch.) par confiscation; *Hist:* forfaire (un fief); **his land was forfeited to the State**, ses terres furent confisquées par l'État; **to f. one's driving licence**, se voir retirer son permis de conduire; **to f. a right**, être déchu d'un droit; laisser périmer un droit; *Jur:* **to f. a patent**, déchoir d'un brevet. 2. perdre (qch.); **to f. one's life**, payer de sa vie; se faire tuer; **to f. s.o.'s esteem**, démériter de qn; se perdre dans l'estime de qn; **to f. one's honour**, forfaire à l'honneur.

forfeitable ['fɔːfitəbl], *a.* confiscable.

forfeiting ['fɔːfitiŋ], *s.* = FORFEITURE 1.

forfeiture ['fɔːfitʃər], *s.* 1. perte *f* (de biens) par confiscation; perte (de la vie, de l'honneur, etc.); *Jur: Fin:* déchéance *f*, forfaiture *f* (de titres, d'un droit, etc.); **action for f. of patent**, action *f* en déchéance de brevet; **f. of one's driving licence**, retrait *m* du permis de conduire. 2. (i) amende *f*; (ii) bien(s) confisqué(s); chose perdue par confiscation.

forfend [fɔː'fend], *v.tr. A:* détourner, empêcher, écarter (un malheur, etc.); **God, Heaven, f.!** à Dieu ne plaise! Dieu m'en préserve!

forfex ['fɔːfeks], *s. Ent:* pince abdominale (de perce-oreille, etc.).

forficate ['fɔːfikət], **forficiform** [fɔː'fisifɔːm], *a. Nat.Hist:* en forme de pince.

forficula [fɔː'fikjulə], *s. Ent:* forficule *f*.

Forficulidae [fɔːfi'kjuːlidiː], *s.pl. Ent:* forficulidés *m*.

forgather [fɔː'gæðər], *v.i.* 1. s'assembler; se réunir. 2. *Pej:* **to f. with doubtful company**, fréquenter une compagnie louche. 3. **to f. with s.o.**, rencontrer qn.

forge[1] [fɔːdʒ], *s.* 1. forge *f*, chaufferie *f*; **portable f.**, forge volante, portative, de campagne; **blacksmith's f.**, forge à main, de maréchalerie; **fan f.**, forge à ventilateur; **Catalan f.**, forge (à la) catalane; **f. fire, f. hearth**, feu *m* de forge. 2. (*a*) atelier *m* de forgeron, de maréchal-ferrant, de maréchalerie; forge; (*b*) *Metall:* **f. (shop)**, atelier de forge; forge; usine *f* (métallurgique); **f. hammer**, (i) *Metalw:* marteau *m* à forger; (ii) *Metall:* marteau-pilon *m, pl.* marteaux-pilons; **f. roll**, cylindre forgeur; **f. roller**, lamineur *m*.

forge[2], *v.tr.* 1. (*a*) forger (un fer à cheval, etc.); **to f. hot, cold**, forger à chaud, à froid; (*with passive force*) **steel that forges well**, acier qui se forge bien; (*b*) *Metall:* forger, cingler, corroyer (le fer); (*c*) *v.i.* (*of horse*) forger, frapper les fers de devant avec ceux de derrière. 2. forger (une excuse, une histoire); contrefaire (une signature, des billets de banque); supposer (un testament); fabriquer, inventer (une calomnie, etc.); *v.i.* commettre, faire, un faux.

forge[3], *v.i.* 1. **to f. ahead**, (*a*) *Nau:* (*of ship*) courir sur son erre; courir de l'avant; **to f. ahead over the anchor**, courir sur son ancre; (*b*) (i) *Nau:* avancer à toute vitesse; détaler; voguer à pleines voiles; (ii) gagner les devants; (*of pers.*) dépasser tous ses concurrents; (*in business*) pousser de l'avant; *Rac:* foncer. 2. **to f. on**, (*a*) = *forge ahead* (*a*); (*b*) avancer, se frayer un chemin, à travers les obstacles.

forgeable ['fɔːdʒəbl], *a.* 1. *Metalw:* forgeable. 2. (signature, etc.) qui se laisse contrefaire.

forged ['fɔːdʒd], *a.* 1. *Metall:* (fer, etc.) forgé; **rough f.**, brut de forge; **f. in one piece with . . .**, venu de forge avec . . .. 2. (document, billet de banque, etc.) faux, contrefait, falsifié; **f. document**, forgerie *f*; *Jur:* **to present, produce, a f. will**, supposer un testament; **production of f. documents**, supposition *f*.

forgeman, *pl.* **-men** ['fɔːdʒmən], *s.m.* (*a*) *Metall:* forgeron; ouvrier forgeur; marteleur; (*b*) maréchal-ferrant, *pl.* maréchaux-ferrants.

forgemaster ['fɔːdʒmɑːstər], *s.* maître *m* de forges; métallurgiste *m*.

forger ['fɔːdʒər], *s.* 1. (*a*) *Metall:* forgeron *m*; ouvrier forgeur; marteleur *m*; (*b*) maréchal-ferrant *m, pl.* maréchaux-ferrants. 2. contrefacteur *m* (de billets de banque); (*of signature, document, etc.*) faussaire *mf*, falsificateur, -trice.

forgery ['fɔːdʒəri], *s.* 1. contrefaçon *f* (d'une signature, de billets de banque); falsification *f* (de documents); supposition *f* (de testament); altération *f* (d'une clef); *Jur:* **plea of f.**, inscription *f* de faux; **to put in a plea of f.**, arguer une pièce de faux; **to be guilty of f.**, être coupable de faux, d'un crime de faux. 2. document fabriqué; faux *m*; forgerie *f*; **the signature was a f.**, la signature était contrefaite.

forget[1] [fə'get], *v.tr.* (*p.t.* **forgot** [fə'gɔt]; *p.p.* **forgotten** [fə'gɔtn], *A:* **forgot**; *pr.p.* **forgetting**) oublier. 1. perdre le souvenir, la mémoire, la notion, de (qch.); **to f. a fact**, oublier un fait; **to f. one's Latin**, désapprendre son latin; **I shall not f. (this insult, etc.)**, je me souviendrai; **f. (about) it!** (i) n'y pensez plus! (ii) (*in reply to apology*) je vous en prie! il n'y a pas de quoi! **a story which he forgot he had already told**, un récit qu'il oubliait avoir déjà fait; **I forgot all about those books you asked me to buy**, j'ai tout à fait oublié ces livres que vous m'avez prié d'acheter; **he warned me of the danger but I forgot (all) about it**, il m'a averti du danger mais je n'y ai plus pensé, je n'y ai pas repensé; **I had forgotten that I already had an appointment**, je ne songeais pas que j'étais déjà pris; **I had forgotten it**, j'en avais perdu le souvenir; **don't f. that he is only ten years old**, faites attention qu'il n'a que dix ans; *F:* **and don't you f. it!** faites-y bien attention! **to f. how to do sth.**, oublier comment faire qch.; ne plus savoir faire qch.; **to f. how time goes**, perdre la notion de l'heure, du temps; **to be forgotten**, être oublié; tomber dans l'oubli; **that's easily forgotten**, cela s'oublie facilement; **it's best forgotten**, il vaut mieux ne plus en parler; **things best forgotten**, choses qu'il vaut autant ne pas rappeler; **I shall never f.**

seeing her fall over the cliff, je la verrai toujours tombant du haut de la falaise; **a beating is soon forgotten,** une raclée s'oublie vite; **poem deservedly forgotten,** poème voué à l'oubli; **he died forgotten by all,** il mourut oublié de tous; **never to be forgotten,** inoubliable; **the never-to-be-forgotten day of the great fire,** le jour mémorable du grand incendie. **2.** (*a*) omettre, oublier (un nom sur une liste, etc.); **to f. to do sth.,** oublier, omettre, de faire qch.; ne plus penser à faire qch.; **don't f. to . . .,** ne manquez pas de . . .; **ah! I was forgetting,** ah! j'oubliais; **don't f. yourself,** n'oubliez pas vos propres intérêts; songez à vous-même; (*b*) oublier (son mouchoir, ses gants, etc.); (*c*) négliger (son devoir, etc.); **to f. one's orders,** *F:* manger la consigne. **3.** *F:* **to f. oneself,** s'oublier; (*a*) manquer à soi-même, aux bienséances; **I think you are forgetting yourself!** vous vous oubliez, je pense! **to f. oneself so far as to do sth.,** s'oublier au point de faire qch.; (*b*) ne plus penser à ce qu'on fait; **I forgot myself!** ça m'a échappé! **he forgot himself and called the captain by his Christian name,** il lui échappa d'appeler le capitaine par son prénom.

forget[2] ['fɔːdʒit], *s.* = FORGETT.

forgetful [fə'getful], *a.* **1.** oublieux (**of,** de); **he is very f.,** il a très mauvaise mémoire; **f. of decorum, he sat down,** oubliant les convenances, il s'assit. **2.** négligent.

forgetfulness [fə'getfulnis], *s.* **1.** (*a*) manque (habituel) de mémoire; (*b*) **a moment of f.,** un moment d'oubli *m.* **2.** négligence *f.*

forget-me-not [fə'getminɔt], *s. Bot:* myosotis *m*; *F:* ne m'oubliez pas *m inv*; oreille-de-souris *f, pl.* oreilles-de-souris; **f.-m.-n. eyes,** yeux *m* de pervenche.

forgett ['fɔːdʒit], *s.* fourchette *f* (de gant).

forgetting [fə'getiŋ], *s.* oubli *m.*

forging ['fɔːdʒiŋ], *s.* **1.** *Metalw:* forgeage *m,* travail *m* de forge; **compression f.,** forgeage par compression; **cored f.,** matriçage *m* extrusion; **die f.,** forgeage par matriçage; **impact f.,** forgeage par choc; **hammer f.,** forgeage par martelage; **roll f.,** forgeage par roulage; **upset f.,** forgeage par refoulement; **f. machine,** forgeuse *f*; **f. mill,** forge *f*; **f. press,** presse *f* à forger, à matricer; marteau-pilon *m, pl.* marteaux-pilons. **2.** (*a*) pièce forgée; pièce (venue) de forge; **heavy f., light f.,** grosse, petite, pièce de forge; **rough f.,** pièce brute de forge; (*b*) pièce estampée; ébauche matricée. **3.** contrefaçon *f,* falsification *f* (de documents, billets de banque, etc.).

forgivable [fə'givəbl], *a.* (péché, etc.) pardonnable.

forgivableness [fə'givəblnis], *s.* excusabilité *f.*

forgivably [fə'givəbli], *adv.* excusablement; **he's f. proud of what he has achieved,** on lui pardonnera d'être fier de ce qu'il a accompli.

forgive [fə'giv], *v.tr.* (**forgave** [fə'geiv], **forgiven** [fə'giv(ə)n]). **1.** (*a*) pardonner (une injure, une faute); *A: & Ecc:* remettre (une faute, une injure); **f. this whim of mine,** passez-moi ce caprice; **to f. s.o. sth.,** pardonner qch. à qn; *Lit:* absoudre qn de qch.; (*b*) **to f. s.o. a debt,** faire grâce, faire remise, d'une dette à qn. **2. to f. s.o.,** pardonner à qn; **he asked me to f. him,** (i) il m'a demandé pardon; (ii) il m'a demandé grâce; **I have never been forgiven for this joke,** on ne m'a jamais pardonné cette plaisanterie; on me tient rigueur de cette plaisanterie; on me fait grief de cette plaisanterie; **one might perhaps be forgiven for thinking that. . .,** on est excusable, il n'est pas interdit, de penser que . . .; **(we must) f. and forget,** il faut oublier et pardonner; à tout péché miséricorde.

forgiveness [fə'givnis], *s.* **1.** (*a*) pardon *m,* rémission *f* (d'une faute, d'un péché, etc.); pardon (d'une injure); **to ask s.o.'s f.,** (i) demander pardon à qn; (ii) demander grâce à qn; (*b*) remise *f* (d'une dette). **2.** indulgence *f,* clémence *f*; absence *f* de rancune.

forgiver [fə'givər], *s.* pardonneur, -euse.

forgiving [fə'giviŋ], *a.* (*of pers., disposition*) indulgent, clément; peu rancunier.

forgivingly [fə'giviŋli], *adv.* avec indulgence, clémence.

forgivingness [fə'giviŋnis], *s.* indulgence *f,* clémence *f.*

forgo [fɔː'gou], *v.tr.* (**forwent** [fɔː'went]; **forgone** [fɔː'gɔn]) renoncer à (qch.); s'abstenir de (qch.); **to f. wine,** s'interdire le vin; se passer de vin; **to f. one's rights,** renoncer à, délaisser, ses droits; **I cannot f. mentioning it,** je ne peux pas m'abstenir d'en parler.

forgoing [fɔː'gouiŋ], *s.* renoncement *m* (**of sth.,** à qch.); abstention *f* (**of,** de).

forint ['fɔrint], *s. Num:* forint *m.*

fork[1] [fɔːk], *s.* **1.** *Agr: Hort:* fourche *f*; **two-pronged f.,** fourchet *m*; **three-pronged f.,** fourche à trois dents, fourchons; **garden f.,** fourche à bêcher; fourche de jardinier; **hand f.,** fourche à main. **2.** fourchette *f* (de table); **carving f.,** fourchette à découper; bident *m*; *F:* **f. meal, f. buffet,** repas *m* à la fourchette. **3.** (*a*) (*for vine, branch, etc.*) poteau fourchu; (*of gas mantle*) potence *f*; porte-manchon *m inv*; (*b*) (*of water diviner*) baguette *f* divinatoire; (*c*) branche fourchue, bifurquée (d'un arbre); (*d*) *Hist:* **the Caudine Forks,** les Fourches Caudines. **4.** (*a*) *Tchn:* **shifter f.,** fourchette, fourche, de baladeur; **belt f., strap f.,** fourche, fourchette (de débrayage) de courroie; **cardan f.,** chape *f,* fourche, de cardan; **f. joint, f. link,** articulation *f* à fourche; étrier *m,* enfourchement *m*; *Aut:* **gear-change selector f.,** fourchette de commande de changement de vitesse, de baladage; **clutch throw-out f.,** fourchette de débrayage; *Cy:* **front fork(s),** fourche avant, de direction; **spring f.,** fourche élastique; *Av:* **f. end,** chape; **hinge f.,** fourche d'articulation (du train avant); *Tex:* **weft f.,** (fourchette) casse-trame *m inv*; (*b*) *Mus:* **tuning f.,** diapason *m.* **5.** (*a*) (i) bifurcation *f,* jonction *f*; carrefour *m*; fourche (de routes); bivoie *f*; (ii) **take the left f.,** prenez le chemin, la route, le sentier, à gauche; (*b*) (en)fourchure *f,* fourchement *m,* fourchon *m,* fourchet *m* (de branches, etc.); enfourchure (des jambes); fourche, fourchet (de pantalon); (*c*) **f. of lightning,** zigzag *m* (d'éclair). **6.** *Min:* fond *m* du puisard; (*of pump*) **to be in f., to have the water in f.,** renifler; **the mine is in f.,** la mine est à sec. **7.** *Artil:* **f. fire,** tir *m* à fourchette, de l'encadrement; **to reduce the f.,** resserrer la fourchette. **8.** *Cards:* fourchette.

fork[2]. **1.** *v.i.* (*of tree, etc.*) fourcher; (*of road*) fourcher, faire la fourche, (se) bifurquer; *P.N:* **f. right for York,** prenez à droite pour York. **2.** *v.tr.* (*a*) **to f. (up),** fourcher (le sol); remuer, retourner (le sol, le foin) à la fourche; **to f. in manure,** enfouir du fumier en fourchant; **to f. out weeds,** déraciner les mauvaises herbes à la fourche; **to f. over a bed,** retourner légèrement un parterre à la fourche; (*b*) *Chess:* fourcher (deux pièces avec un cavalier, etc.); (*c*) *Min:* assécher, épuiser (une mine); (*d*) *NAm:* enfourcher (un cheval). **3.** (*a*) *v.tr. F:* **to f. out,** *NAm:* **f. over, f. up, money,** allonger, abouler, de l'argent; **I've had to f. out a lot this year,** j'ai eu beaucoup de frais cette année; j'ai fait beaucoup de débours cette année; (*b*) *v.i.* **he had to f. out,** il a dû s'exécuter, *P:* casquer, cracher.

fork chuck ['fɔːk'tʃʌk], *s. Mec.E:* mandrin *m* (de tour) à trois pointes.

forked [fɔːkt], *a.* **1.** (*of branch, pipe, etc.*) fourchu, bifurqué, en fourche; (*of road*) bifurqué, à bifurcation; **f. tongue,** langue fourchue; **f. reamer,** alésoir *m* à fourche; **f. lever,** levier coudé, fourché. **2.** (*with numeral prefixed*) **two-f., three-f.,** (i) à deux, trois, branches; (ii) (fourche, etc.) à trois dents.

forkful ['fɔːkful], *s.* **1.** fourchée *f* (de foin, etc.). **2.** (**table-**) **f.,** fourchetée *f.*

forking ['fɔːkiŋ], *s.* **1.** bifurcation *f,* fourchement *m* (d'un arbre, d'une route, etc.). **2.** assèchement *m* (d'une mine); épuisement *m* de l'eau.

fork(lift) truck ['fɔːk(lift)'trʌk], *s.* chariot (élévateur) à fourche; chariot gerbeur; gerbeuse *f.*

forktail ['fɔːkteil], *s. Orn:* énicure *m.*

forlana [fɔː'lɑːnə], *s. Danc:* forlane *f.*

forlorn [fə'lɔːn], *a. Lit:* **1.** (*of undertaking, etc.*) désespéré, perdu. **2.** (*a*) (*of pers., place, etc.*) abandonné, délaissé, solitaire; (*b*) **f. appearance,** mine triste, pitoyable, désolée; (*c*) *NAm:* **f. of hope,** privé de tout espoir.

forlorn hope [fə'lɔːn'houp], *s.* (i) *Mil:* troupe sacrifiée; (ii) aventure désespérée; (iii) (*erroneously*) rayon *m* d'espoir.

forlornly [fə'lɔːnli], *adv.* d'un air morne; tristement; d'un air désolé.

forlornness [fə'lɔːnnis], *s.* **1.** état désespéré (d'une entreprise, etc.). **2.** solitude *f,* abandon *m* (d'une personne, d'un endroit, etc.); **in a state of utter f.,** dans un abandon général; **the f. of his appearance,** son air désolé, pitoyable; sa mine piteuse.

form[1] [fɔːm], *s.* **1.** (*a*) forme *f,* conformation *f,* configuration *f* (d'un objet); *Cryst:* **crystal f.,** forme cristalline; **to take f.,** prendre forme; se former; **statistics in tabular f.,** statistique *f* sous forme de tableau; *Av:* **f. drag,** traînée *f* de forme; *Surv:* **f. line,** ligne *f* intercalaire (entre courbes de niveau); **f. lines (of ground),** lignes de forme (du terrain); (*b*) figure *f,* silhouette *f* (d'un homme, d'un animal, etc.); **the devil appeared before him in the f. of a dog,** le diable lui apparut sous la forme d'un chien. **2.** (*a*) forme, nature *f*; manière *f* d'être; **tonic taken in the f. of pills,** remontant pris sous la forme de pilules; **his liberality takes a practical f.,** sa libéralité prend une forme pratique, s'exerce dans l'ordre pratique; **to alter the f. of government,** changer la forme de gouvernement, le régime; **poverty in every f.,** la misère sous toutes ses formes; (*b*) (i) *Biol:* forme (spéciale) (d'une variété); (ii) sorte *f,* espèce *f,* façon *f*; **it's a f. of disease,** c'est une forme spéciale de maladie; **the different forms of worship,** les différentes façons d'adorer Dieu; (*c*) *Phil:* forme, principe substantiel (du concept, etc.); (*d*) *Gram: Lit: Mus:* forme; **work that lacks f.,** œuvre qui manque de forme; **the f. and the substance,** la forme et le fond; *Mus:* **binary f., ternary f.,** forme binaire, ternaire. **3.** forme, formalité *f*; (*a*) *Jur: etc:* **in (due, proper) f., in common f.,** en bonne (et due) forme; dans les formes; **receipt in due f.,** quittance régulière; **to prove a will in common f.,** homologuer un testament sur simple attestation de l'exécuteur testamentaire; **to go through the f. of refusing,** faire la simagrée de refuser; **for form's sake, as a matter of f.,** pour la forme; par manière d'acquit; pour la bonne règle; **it is a mere matter of f.,** c'est une pure formalité; **to do sth. for form's sake,** faire qch. par acquit de conscience, pour la forme; *F:* **to know the f.,** savoir ce qu'il faut faire; **what's the f.?** qu'est ce qu'il faut faire? comment s'y prend-on? que se passe-t-il? **when it comes to handling the civil service he knows the f.,** lorsqu'il s'agit de ménager l'Administration il sait bien ce qu'il faut faire; **she was all hysterical, you know the f.,** elle était dans tous ses états, vous savez ce que cela veut dire; (*b*) les convenances *f*; l'étiquette *f*; **the rules of good f.,** les règles du savoir-vivre; **it is good f.,** c'est de bon ton; **good f. demands that. . .,** la politesse exige que . . .; **it is not good f., it's bad f.,** c'est de mauvais ton, de mauvais genre, de mauvais goût; cela ne se fait pas, ne se dit pas; c'est un manque de politesse, de savoir-vivre; **it's bad f. to . . .,** c'est contraire à l'étiquette de . . .; c'est le fait d'un malappris de . . .. **4.** (*a*) formule *f,* forme (d'un acte, de prière, de politesse, etc.); **correct f. of words,** tournure correcte de phrase; **forms of address,** titres *m* de politesse; **it's only a f. of speech,** ce n'est qu'une façon de parler; (*b*) formule; **printed f.,** imprimé *m*; **printed f. of receipt,** formule de quittance(s); **f. for bill of exchange,** formule d'effet de commerce; **f. 20,** modèle *m* numéro 20; **f. of tender,** modèle de soumission; **inquiry f.,** bulletin *m* de demande de renseignements; **application f.,** (i) bulletin de demande; (ii) (*for shares*) bulletin de souscription; **order f.,** bulletin de commande; *Bank:* **listing forms,** bordereaux *m* en blanc; **f. of return,** feuille *f* de déclaration (de revenu, etc.); **cheque f.,** (i) formule, (ii) volant *m,* de chèque; *Cmptr:* **coding f.,** feuille, imprimé, de programmation; **continuous f.,** imprimé, papier, (en) continu; **f. feed(ing),** alimentation *f* en papier; **to fill in, up, a f.,** remplir une formule, un formulaire, un bordereau. **5.** (*a*) *Sp:* (*of horse, athlete, etc.*) forme; état *m,* condition *f* (d'entraînement); **to be in f., out of f.,** être, ne pas être, en forme; **racehorse in f.,** cheval de course affûté; **to be in good f.,** être en haleine, dans ses bons jours; **to be in poor f.,** être en petite forme, en méforme; **return to f.,** retour *m* en forme; (*b*) (*of pers.*) verve *f*; **to be in excellent f.,** être en train, dans une forme excellente, fort en verve; **he felt in good f.,** il se sentait gaillard; (*c*) *Turf:* (i) performances *fpl* (d'un cheval); (ii) tableau *m* des performances (des chevaux). **6.** *Sch:* classe *f*; **first f.** = *approx.* (classe de) sixième *f*; **sixth f.** = *approx.* (classe de) première; **f. master,** professeur principal; **f. room,** salle *f* de classe; la classe. **7.** banc *m,* banquette *f*; (*in amphitheatre*) gradin *m*; (*in class room*) banc. **8.** (*a*) *Metall: etc:* forme, moule *m*; **f. factor,** facteur *m* de forme; *Mec.E:* **f. block,** bloc *m* d'emboutissage; **f. milling,** fraisage *m* de forme; (*b*) *Civ.E: etc:* coffrage *m,* coffre *m,* banche *f* (pour béton armé); **arch f.,** coffrage en voûte; **ceiling f.,** coffrage de toit; **concrete moulded with forms,** béton banché; (*c*) *Typ:* forme; **inner f.,** côté *m* de deux; **outer f.,** côté de première; **to lock up a f.,** serrer une forme; **f. man, f. setter,** imposeur *m.* **9.** gîte *m,* lit *m,* forme (du lièvre); **hare in its f.,** lièvre en forme.

form[2], *v.tr. & i.*

I. *v.tr.* **1.** (*a*) former, faire, façonner; **to f. sth. after, from, (up)on, the model of sth.,** former qch. sur (le modèle de) qch., à l'image de qch.; **to f. sth. from, out of, sth.,** faire qch. de qch.; **to have difficulty in forming certain words,** avoir de la difficulté à prononcer, à énoncer, certains mots; **to f. a child's mind,** développer, façonner, l'esprit d'un enfant; **to f. one's style on . . .,** former son style sur . . .; **men formed to command,** hommes formés au commandement; (*b*) *Metalw:* former, emboutir, profiler (une pièce). **2.** (*a*) former, organiser, constituer (une société, etc.); instituer, établir (une république, etc.); **to invite s.o. to f. a ministry,** inviter qn à former, à choisir, un ministère; **they formed themselves into a committee,** ils se constituèrent en comité; (*b*) former, faire, composer (un nouveau mot, etc.); **the past tense is formed by the addition of -*ed*,** le passé se forme par l'addition de *-ed*; (*c*) se former, se faire (une idée, une opinion, etc.); **to f. doubts regarding . . .,** concevoir des doutes sur . . .; (*d*) former, contracter (une liaison, une habitude, une alliance, etc.); (*e*) former, arrêter (un plan); **he had formed a plan to . . .,** il avait projeté de . . .. **3.** (*a*) former, faire; **the rain formed large puddles on the lawn,** la pluie formait, faisait, de grandes flaques d'eau sur la pelouse; **the coastline forms a series of curves,** le littoral dessine une série de courbes; **the walls f. a square,** les murs forment un carré; *Mil: A:* **to f. fours,** se mettre par quatre; **f. fours!** en colonne par quatre! **f. fours—right!** à droite par quatre—droite! **to f. a column,** se mettre en colonne; (*b*) **to f. part of sth.,** faire partie de qch.; **the ministers who f. the cabinet,** les ministres qui composent, constituent, le gouvernement. **4.** *El:* **to f. accumulator plates,** former les plaques d'un accumulateur.

II. *v.i.* **1.** prendre forme, se former, se produire; **his style is forming,** son style se fait. **2.** *Mil:* **to f. (up),** se former en rangs; se ranger; **to f. into line,** se mettre en ligne; **to f. (into a)square,** se former en carré; former le carré.

formal[1] ['fɔːm(ə)l], *a.* **1.** *Log: Theol: etc:* (*of reason, cause, sin, etc.*) formel. **2.** (*of procedure, etc.*) formel, en règle; (*of order, etc.*) positif, explicite, défini; **f. denial,** démenti formel; **f. contract,** contrat *m* en due forme; *Dipl:* **f. provisions of agreement,** clauses *f* protocolaires d'accord; *Jur:* **f. summons,** citation libellée; **to give s.o. a f. warning,** avertir qn dans les formes; **to make a f. speech,** prononcer quelques mots; **the invitation is entirely f.,** l'invitation est de pure forme; **f. politeness,** politesse formelle. **3.** (*a*) cérémonieux, solennel; **f. dress,** tenue *f* de (i) cérémonie, (ii) soirée; **f. bow,** salut cérémonieux; **f. dinner,** dîner prié; **f. style,** style empesé; **f. prize distribution,** distribution solennelle des prix; (*b*) *s. NAm:* (i) (*for men*) complet *m* de cérémonie, de soirée; (*for women*) robe *f* de soirée; (ii) soirée formelle; bal formel. **4.** (*a*) (*of pers.*) pointilleux, formaliste, cérémonieux; guindé; **he's always very f.,** il est toujours très compassé; **she's very f.,** *F:* elle est très collet monté; (*b*) (art, style) conventionnel; **he had no f. schooling,** il n'a pas fait des études conventionnelles; il n'est jamais allé à l'école; (*c*) (jardin) régulier, tiré au cordeau.

formal[2] [fɔː'mæl], *s. Ch:* formal *m.*

formaldehyde [fɔː'mældihaid], *s. Ch:* formaldéhyde *m*; aldéhyde *m* formique; *Leath:* **f. tanning,** tannage *m* au formol.

formalin ['fɔːməlin], *s. Ch:* (solution aqueuse de) formol *m.*

formalism ['fɔːməlizm], *s.* (*a*) *Phil: Mth:* formalisme *m*; (*b*) conformisme *m*; traditionalisme *m*; formalisme.

formalist ['fɔːməlist], *s.* (*a*) *Phil:* formaliste *mf*; (*b*) conformiste *mf*; traditionaliste *mf*; formaliste.

formalistic [fɔːmə'listik], *a.* formalistique.

formality [fɔː'mæliti], *s.* **1.** formalité *f*; **legal formalities,** formes *f* juridiques; **to comply with all the necessary formalities,** accomplir, remplir, toutes les formalités requises; **a mere f.,** une pure formalité. **2.** (*a*) raideur *f* (de maintien); compassement *m*, style guindé (d'un discours); **he received them with frozen f.,** il les reçut avec une raideur glacée, glaciale; (*b*) cérémonie *f*, formalité(s), formes *fpl*, étiquette *f*; **house where a certain amount of f. is retained,** maison où l'on a encore quelques usages.

formalization [fɔːməlai'zeiʃ(ə)n], *s.* formalisation *f.*

formalize ['fɔːməlaiz], *v.tr.* **1.** donner une forme exacte, précise, à (un récit, etc.). **2.** (*a*) donner une forme conventionnelle à (son art, etc.); (*b*) guinder (son style); mettre du formalisme à (une cérémonie, une réception, etc.). **3.** *Log:* formaliser.

formally ['fɔːməli], *adv.* **1.** formellement; à titre officiel. **2.** cérémonieusement, avec formalité. **3.** quant à la forme; **f. correct but materially false,** correct quant à la forme mais faux quant au fond.

formamide ['fɔːməmaid], *s. Ch:* form(i)amide *m.*

formant ['fɔːmənt], *s. Ac: Ling:* formant *m*, formante *f.*

format[1] ['fɔːmæt], *s.* **1.** format *m* (d'un livre, etc.). **2.** *Cmptr:* (*a*) dessin *m* (d'une carte); (*b*) format; **address f.,** format d'adresse; **f. control,** contrôle *m* de format; **f. effector,** caractère *m* de mise en page.

format[2], *v.tr.* **(formatting)** *Cmptr:* composer (un message); préparer (une ligne à imprimer).

formate ['fɔːmeit], *s. Ch:* formiate *m.*

formation [fɔː'meiʃ(ə)n], *s.* **1.** (*a*) formation *f* (du pluriel, d'un objet, de la houille, etc.); génération *f* (d'un métal); **the f. of a child's mind,** le développement de l'esprit d'un enfant; *For:* **f. of woods,** création *f* de peuplements; (*b*) formation (d'une alliance, etc.); constitution *f* (d'une société, etc.); établissement *m* (d'une république, etc.); (*c*) *El:* formation (des plaques d'un accumulateur). **2.** *Mil: etc:* (*a*) formation, dispositif *m*, ordre *m*, disposition *f* (des troupes, des parties d'un tout, etc.); **approach f.,** dispositif, formation, d'approche; **attack f.,** formation d'attaque; **battle f.,** *U.S:* **combat f.,** dispositif, formation, de combat; **close f.,** dispositif serré, formation serrée; **dense f.,** formation dense, groupée; **flexible f.,** formation articulée; **f. in depth,** formation en profondeur; **loose f.,** dispositif fluide; formation fluide, diluée; **march f., road f., route f.,** formation de route, de marche; **march-past f.,** formation de défilé; *Av:* **aircraft in triangular f.,** avions en formation triangulaire; **f. flying,** vol *m* de groupe; **to break f.,** décrocher; (*b*) formation, unité *f*; **higher f., lower f.,** grande, petite, unité; **armoured f.,** formation blindée; **to run into enemy formations,** se heurter à des formations ennemies. **3.** (*a*) **pathological f. on a bone,** formation pathologique sur un os; *Geol:* **granite f.,** formation, terrain *m*, granitique; (*b*) *Civ.E: Rail:* **f. (level),** plate-forme *f*, *pl.* plates-formes, des terrassements; niveau *m* des remblais. **4.** *Bot:* formation (végétale).

formative ['fɔːmətiv]. **1.** *a.* formatif, formateur, -trice; **the f. years,** les années *f* de formation; **the f. arts,** les arts *m* plastiques; *Bot:* **f. region,** zone *f* d'accroissement; méristème *m*. **2.** *s. Ling:* formative *f*; élément formatif, formateur.

formazyl ['fɔːməzil], *s. Ch:* formazyle *m.*

forme [fɔːm], *s. Typ:* = FORM[1] 8 (*c*).

formed [fɔːmd], *a.* **1.** formé; **badly f. letters,** lettres mal formées. **2.** *Metalw:* (*of casting*) profilé.

formene ['fɔːmiːn], *s. Ch: A:* formène *m*, méthane *m.*

former[1] ['fɔːmər], *a.* **1.** antérieur, -eure, précédent, ancien; **f. mayor,** ancien maire; **my f. pupils,** mes anciens élèves; **a f. convict,** un repris de justice; **his f. letters,** ses lettres précédentes; **f. times,** le passé; **in f. times,** autrefois; **f. customs, customs of f. days,** coutumes *f* d'autrefois; **f. events prove that . . .,** les événements antérieurs démontrent que . . .; **he is a mere shadow of his f. self,** c'est un pâle reflet de l'homme qu'il fut autrefois; il n'est plus que l'ombre de lui-même. **2.** (*as opposed to the latter*) **I prefer the f. alternative to the latter,** je préfère la première alternative à la dernière; (*b*) *pron.* celui-là, celle-là, ceux-là, celles-là; **of the two methods I prefer the f.,** des deux méthodes je préfère celle-là; **the former's victory over the latter,** la victoire du premier sur le dernier; la victoire de celui-là sur celui-ci.

former[2], *s.* **1.** (*pers.*) façonneur, -euse; fondateur, -trice (d'une alliance, etc.). **2.** *Mec.E:* gabarit *m*, calibre *m* (de forme); forme *f*, matrice *f*, moule *m*; *El:* **winding f.,** gabarit de bobinage, d'enroulement; **f. winding,** enroulement *m* sur gabarit; **f. wound,** enroulé sur gabarit; **f. of a galvanometer coil,** cadre *m* de la bobine d'un galvanomètre.

-former[3], *s.* (*with numeral prefixed*) *Sch:* **first-f.** = élève *mf* de sixième; **sixth-f.** = élève de première.

formeret ['fɔːməret], *s. Arch:* (arc *m*) formeret (*m*).

formerly ['fɔːməli], *adv.* **1.** autrefois, jadis; précédemment; dans le temps; **I knew him f.,** je l'ai connu autrefois; **Mr Martin, f. a liberal,** M. Martin, ci-devant libéral; **Mrs Thomas, f. Mrs Gainsborough,** Madame Thomas, auparavant Madame Gainsborough. **2.** *A:* auparavant.

formfitting ['fɔːmfitiŋ], *a.* (vêtement) qui épouse les formes; collant.

formic ['fɔːmik], *a. Ch:* (acide *m*) formique.

Formica [fɔː'maikə], *s. R.t.m:* Formica *m.*

formicant ['fɔːmikənt], *a. Med:* (pouls) formicant.

Formicariidae [fɔːmikə'riːidiː], *s.pl. Orn:* formicariidés *m.*

formicary ['fɔːmikəri], *s.* fourmilière *f.*

formication [fɔːmi'keiʃ(ə)n], *s. Med:* formication *f*; *F:* fourmillement *m.*

Formicidae [fɔː'misidiː], *s.pl. Ent:* formicidés *m.*

formidable ['fɔːmidəbl], *a.* formidable, redoutable; **a f. adversary,** un rude adversaire; **a f.-looking mastiff,** un molosse à l'aspect redoutable.

formidableness ['fɔːmidəblnis], *s.* nature *f*, aspect *m*, formidable (de qn, qch.).

formidably ['fɔːmidəbli], *adv.* formidablement.

forming ['fɔːmiŋ], *s.* **1.** (*a*) formation *f* (d'une lettre, etc.); formation, développement *m* (du caractère, etc.); *T.V:* **image f.,** formation de l'image; (*b*) *Metalw:* formage *m*, façonnage *m*, emboutissage *m*, mise *f* en forme, profilage *m* (d'une pièce); **cold f., hot f.,** formage à froid, à chaud; **f. block,** forme *f*; **f. die,** matrice *f* de forme; **f. press,** presse *f* à former, rectifier; (*c*) *El:* formation (de plaques d'accumulateur). **2.** constitution *f* (d'une société, etc.). **3.** *Mil:* **f. up,** rassemblement *m.*

formless ['fɔːmlis], *a.* informe, sans forme.

formlessness ['fɔːmlisnis], *s.* absence *f* de forme.

formol ['fɔːmɔl], *s. Ch: Com:* formol *m.*

formolize ['fɔːməlaiz], *v.tr. Ch: Med:* formoler.

formolizing ['fɔːməlaiziŋ], *s. Ch:* formolage *m.*

Formosa [fɔː'mousə], *Pr.n. Geog:* Formose *f.*

Formosan [fɔː'mous(ə)n]. **1.** *Geog:* (*a*) *a.* formosan; (*b*) *s.* Formosan, -ane. **2.** *s. Ling:* les parlers formosans.

formula, *pl.* **-as, -ae** ['fɔːmjulə, -əz, -iː], *s.* formule *f.* **1.** **the baptismal f.,** la formule de baptême; **hackneyed formulas,** formules stéréotypées; clichés *m*; *Pol: etc:* **to find a f. acceptable to all parties,** découvrir une formule qui soit acceptable à tous les partis. **2.** (*pl. usu.* **formulae**) *Ch: Mth: etc:* formule; **dental f.,** formule dentaire; *Ch:* **empiric f.,** formule empirique, brute; **structural f., constitutional f., graphic f., rational f.,** formule de constitution, rationnelle, développée; *I.C.E:* **horsepower f.,** formule de puissance. **3.** (*a*) *Cu:* recette *f*; (*b*) *Pharm:* formule, ordonnance *f.*

formul(at)able ['fɔːmjuləbl, fɔːmju'leitəbl], *a.* formulable.

formulary ['fɔːmjuləri]. **1.** *s.* formulaire *m*. **2.** *a.* qui tient de la formule; qui appartient à la formule; rituel; prescrit.

formulate ['fɔːmjuleit], *v.tr.* **1.** formuler (une loi, une doctrine, etc.); élaborer (un projet). **2.** formuler, exprimer (son opinion, etc.); former (des objections).

formulation [fɔːmju'leiʃ(ə)n], *s.* **1.** formulation *f*, élaboration *f* (d'un projet). **2.** formulation, expression *f* (d'une opinion, etc.). **3.** produit préparé d'après une formule.

formulism ['fɔːmjulizm], *s. Art: Lit:* attachement *m* aux formules de l'art; formalisme *m*; *F:* poncif *m*, pompiérisme *m.*

formulist ['fɔːmjulist], *s.* formuliste *mf*, *F:* pompier *m.*

form word ['fɔːmwəːd], *s. Ling:* mot-outil *m*, *pl.* mots-outils; mot *m* faisant fonction de désinence.

formwork ['fɔːmwəːk], *s. Const: Civ.E:* coffrage *m* (pour béton armé).

formyl ['fɔːmil], *s. Ch:* formyle *m.*

fornicate[1] ['fɔːnikeit], *v.i.* forniquer.

fornicate[2], *a. Bot:* arqué.

fornication [fɔːni'keiʃ(ə)n], *s.* fornication *f.*

fornicator ['fɔːnikeitər], *s.m.* fornicateur.

fornicatress ['fɔːnikeitris], **fornicatrix,** *pl.* **-ices** ['fɔːnikeitriks, -isiːz], *s.f.* fornicatrice.

fornix, *pl.* **-ices** ['fɔːniks, -isiːz], *s.* **1.** *Anat:* trigone cérébral; fornix *m*. **2.** *Bot:* fornice *f.*

forrader ['fɔrədər], *adv. F:* plus en avant; **we're no f.,** on n'est pas plus avancé pour ça; **I can't get any f.,** je ne peux plus avancer; je suis dans une impasse.

forrard ['fɔrəd], *adv. & a. Nau:* (de l')avant; sur l'avant.

for(r)el ['fɔrəl], *s. Bookb:* parchemin *m* de peau de mouton.

forsake [fə'seik], *v.tr.* **(forsook** [fə'suk]; **forsaken** [fə'seik(ə)n]**)** **1.** abandonner, délaisser (qn); **to be forsaken by all,** (i) être abandonné de tous; (ii) (*of place, etc.*) être dans un abandon général; **his friends are forsaking him,** ses amis l'abandonnent; **his confidence forsook him,** la confiance lui fit défaut. **2.** renoncer à, abandonner (une habitude, une croyance, etc.); **to f. one's religion,** apostasier.

forsaking [fə'seikiŋ], *s.* **1.** abandon(nement) *m*, délaissement *m* (de qn). **2.** renoncement *m* (of, à); **f. of one's religion,** apostasie *f.*

forsooth [fə'suːθ], *adv. A: & Lit:* **1.** en vérité. **2.** *Iron:* par exemple! ma foi!

forspent [fɔː'spent], *a. A:* épuisé, à bout de forces.

forsterite ['fɔːstərait], *s. Miner:* forstérite *f.*

forswear [fɔː'sweər], *v.tr.* **(forswore** [fɔː'swɔːr]; **forsworn** [fɔː'swɔːn]**)** **1.** abjurer, renier, répudier (qch.); renoncer à (qch.). **2.** **to f. oneself,** se parjurer; commettre un parjure.

forswearer [fɔː'sweərər], *s.* parjure *mf.*

forswearing [fɔː'sweəriŋ], *s.* **1.** abjuration *f*, répudiation *f* (of, de). **2.** parjure *m.*

forsworn [fɔː'swɔːn], *a.* (*of pers.*) parjure.

forsythia [fɔː'saiθiə], *s. Bot:* forsythia *m.*

fort [fɔːt], *s. Mil:* **1.** fort *m*; **coastal-defence f.,** fort maritime; **barrier f.,** fort d'arrêt; **small f.,** fortin *m*. **2.** place fortifiée; forteresse *f*; *F:* **to hold the f.,** gérer la maison, assurer la permanence (en l'absence des chefs).

fortalice ['fɔːtəlis], *s.* **1.** *A: & Poet:* forteresse *f*. **2.** fortin *m.*

forte[1] [fɔːt], *s.* **1.** fort *m*; **singing is not his f.,** le chant n'est pas son fort. **2.** fort (d'une lame d'épée, de sabre).

forte[2] ['fɔːti], *a., adv. & s. Mus:* forte (*m inv*).

forte-piano ['fɔːtipi'ænou], *s. Mus:* forte-piano *m*, *pl.* forte-pianos.

forth [fɔːθ], *adv.* **1.** (*place*) en avant; *A:* **to go, sally, f.,** sortir, se mettre en route; **to stretch f. one's hand,** avancer la main; *NAm:* **to walk back and f.,** marcher de long en large; **back-and-f. movement,** mouvement *m* de va-et-vient, d'avance et de recul. **2.** (*time*) **from this time f.,** dès maintenant; désormais, dorénavant; d'ores et déjà; à partir de ce moment; **from this day f.,**

de ce jour en avant; partir de ce jour. **3. and so f.,** et ainsi de suite; et cætera.

forthcoming [fɔːθ'kʌmiŋ], *a.* **1.** (*a*) qui arrive, qui va se présenter; **help is f.,** des secours sont en route; (*b*) **(of events, etc.)** prochain, futur, à venir; **the f. session,** la prochaine session. **2.** *Publ:* (livre) en préparation; *Jur:* prêt à comparaître. **3. to be f.,** ne pas se faire attendre; **the things were immediately f.,** les objets furent promptement apportés; **the money will be f.,** on trouvera l'argent nécessaire; **the answer is always f.,** la réponse ne se fait jamais attendre; **at last the truth is f.,** enfin la vérité se dégage; **the promised help was not f.,** les secours promis ont fait défaut. **4.** (*of pers.*) (*a*) sociable, expansif; (*b*) ouvert, franc, franche; **the Minister was not f. on the government's intentions,** le Ministre était réservé, renfermé, au sujet des intentions du Gouvernement.

forthright ['fɔːθrait]. **1.** *adv. A: & Lit:* (*a*) tout droit; carrément; nettement; (*b*) tout de suite, immédiatement. **2.** *a.* (*of pers.*) franc, franche; carré.

forthrightness ['fɔːθraitnis], *s.* franchise *f.*

forthwith [fɔːθ'wið], *adv.* sur-le-champ; tout de suite, immédiatement, aussitôt, sans délai, incontinent; séance tenante; **ask him to come to my office f.,** priez-le de passer à mon cabinet sur-le-champ, toute affaire cessante; **the Council must be summoned f.,** il faut convoquer le Conseil immédiatement, d'urgence.

fortieth ['fɔːtiiθ], *num.a. & s.* quarantième (*m*).

fortifiable ['fɔːtifaiəbl], *a.* fortifiable.

fortification [fɔːtifi'keiʃ(ə)n], *s.* **1.** (*a*) fortification *f* (d'une ville, etc.); renforcement *m* (d'une barricade, etc.); (*b*) fortification, affermissement *m* (du courage, etc.); (*c*) *Winem:* vinage *m,* alcoolisage *m;* (*d*) augmentation *f* de la valeur nutritive (d'un aliment). **2.** *pl.* **fortifications,** fortifications (d'une ville); **field fortifications,** fortifications de campagne; **hasty field fortifications,** fortifications improvisées, de fortune, provisoires, passagères; **permanent fortifications,** fortifications permanentes; **coastal fortifications,** fortifications maritimes; **low-level fortifications,** fortifications rasantes.

fortifier ['fɔːtifaiər], *s.* **1. the f. of a city, etc.,** le constructeur des fortifications, *A:* le fortificateur, d'une ville, etc. **2.** (*drug, drink, etc.*) fortifiant *m.*

fortify ['fɔːtifai], *v.tr.* **1.** (*a*) renforcer, fortifier (un navire, etc.); (*b*) fortifier (qn, l'estomac, etc.); affermir, fortifier, encourager (qn, la résolution de qn); **fortified by your valuable help . . .,** fort de votre aide précieuse . . .; **fortified with the rites of the Church,** muni des sacrements de l'Église; **to f. oneself against the cold,** (i) se garantir contre le froid; (ii) *P:* boire une goutte; prendre une goutte; **courage fortified against dangers,** courage armé contre les dangers; (*c*) *Vet:* immuniser (le bétail); (*d*) corroborer (un rapport, etc.); renforcer (son dire, etc.). **2.** (*a*) *Winem.* remonter (un vin) en alcool; viner, alcooliser (un vin); (*b*) **to f. a food,** augmenter la valeur nutritive d'un aliment. **3.** *Mil:* fortifier (une place); **fortified area,** zone, position, fortifiée; **fortified town,** ville fortifiée; place *f* de guerre; place forte.

fortifying[1] ['fɔːtifaiiŋ], *a.* fortifiant; (*of drink, etc.*) remontant.

fortifying[2], *s.* **1.** (*a*) renforcement *m* (d'un navire, etc.); (*b*) affermissement *m* (de la santé, du courage, de qn). **2.** (*a*) *Winem:* vinage *m,* alcoolisage *m,* remontage *m;* (*b*) augmentation *f* de la valeur nutritive (d'un aliment). **3.** fortification *f* (d'une place).

fortin[1] ['fɔːtin], *s.* fortin *m,* petit fort.

Fortin[2], *Pr.n. Meteor:* **Fortin('s) barometer,** baromètre *m* de Fortin.

Fortisan ['fɔːtisæn], *s. R.t.m: Tex:* Fortisan *m.*

fortissimo [fɔː'tisimou], *adv. & s. Mus:* fortissimo (*m inv*).

fortitude ['fɔːtitjuːd], *s.* force morale; force d'âme; courage *m;* fermeté *f; Lit:* fortitude *f.*

fortlet ['fɔːtlit], *s.* petit fort; fortin *m.*

fortnight ['fɔːtnait], *s.* quinzaine *f;* quinze jours *m;* deux semaines *f;* **today f.,** (d')aujourd'hui en quinze; **a f. from tomorrow,** de demain en quinze; **a f. ago,** il y a quinze jours; **to adjourn a case for a f.,** remettre une cause à quinzaine; **to take a fortnight's rest,** prendre quinze jours de repos.

fortnightly ['fɔːtnaitli]. **1.** *a.* bimensuel, semi-mensuel; *Ind:* **f. payroll,** feuille *f* de quinzaine. **2.** *adv.* bimensuellement; tous les quinze jours.

Fortran, FORTRAN ['fɔːtræn], *s. Cmptr:* Fortran *m.*

fortress ['fɔːtris], *s.* forteresse *f;* place forte; camp retranché; *Av: A:* **flying f.,** forteresse volante.

fortuitous [fɔː'tju(ː)itəs], *a.* fortuit, imprévu; *Jur:* **f. event,** cas imprévu.

fortuitously [fɔː'tju(ː)itəsli], *adv.* fortuitement; par hasard.

fortuitousness [fɔː'tju(ː)itəsnis], *s.* casualité *f,* fortuité *f.*

fortuity [fɔː'tju(ː)iti], *s.* **1.** = FORTUITOUSNESS. **2.** accident fortuit; cas fortuit; fortuité *f.*

fortunate ['fɔːtʃənət, -tʃ-], *a.* **1.** (*of pers., etc.*) heureux, fortuné; **to be f.,** avoir de la chance; **I was f. in my teacher,** j'eus à me louer de mon professeur; **I have been singularly f. in my advisers,** je n'ai qu'à me féliciter de mes conseillers; **to be f. enough to . . ., to be so f. as to . . .,** avoir la chance de . . .; *Gr.Myth:* **the F. Islands,** les îles Fortunées. **2.** (*of occasion, etc.*) propice, favorable, heureux; **f. omen,** bon augure; **what a f. circumstance!** *F:* comme cela se trouve! **how f.!** quel bonheur! quelle chance!

fortunately ['fɔːtʃənətli, -tʃ-], *adv.* **1.** heureusement. **2.** par bonheur.

fortune ['fɔːtjən, -tʃən], *s.* fortune *f.* **1.** (*a*) hasard *m,* chance *f;* **ill f.,** mauvaise chance; **piece of good f.,** coup *m* de bonheur; **by good f.,** par bonheur; **I had the good f., it was my good f., to succeed,** j'eus le bonheur, la chance, de réussir; **to try one's f.,** tenter (la) fortune; tenter la chance; **f. favours him,** la fortune lui sourit; **what in the name of f. are you doing?** que diable faites-vous là? (*b*) *Myth:* le Sort, le Destin; **the goddess F.,** la Fortune; **F. is blind,** le Sort est aveugle; (*c*) destinée *f,* sort; **if it were my f. to . . .,** si c'était ma destinée de . . .; **the f. of war,** le sort des armes; **to tell fortunes,** dire la bonne aventure; **to tell s.o.'s f. by cards,** tirer les cartes à qn. **2.** (*a*) bonne chance; bonheur *m;* **bits of f. which do not come my way,** de bonnes chances qui ne m'arrivent jamais; **stroke of f.,** coup *m* de fortune, de veine; (*b*) prospérité *f,* richesse *f;* **a man of f.,** un homme riche; **born to f.,** né coiffé; (*c*) richesses *fpl,* avoir *m,* biens *mpl;* **to make a, one's, f.,** faire fortune; *F:* faire son beurre; **she had made a small f.,** *F:* elle avait fait sa petite pelote; **to come into a f.,** hériter une fortune; faire un gros héritage; **to waste the family f.,** gaspiller la fortune, les richesses, de la famille; **he has doubled his f.,** il a doublé son avoir; **a young man without a f.,** un jeune homme pauvre, sans fortune; **her jewels are worth a f.,** ses bijoux valent une fortune; *F:* **it cost me a (small) f.,** cela m'a coûté énormément d'argent, un argent fou; **he spent a f. over this business,** il a dépensé des sommes folles dans cette affaire; (*d*) (*marriage portion*) dot *f;* **to marry a f.,** épouser une grosse dot; faire un riche mariage; *F:* trouver la nappe mise; **her face is her f.,** jolie fille porte sur son front sa dot.

fortune-hunter ['fɔːtjənhʌntər], *s.* chercheur *m* de richesses, de fortune; *esp.* coureur *m* de dots.

fortuneless ['fɔːtjənlis], *a.* sans fortune.

fortune-seeker ['fɔːtjənsiːkər], *s.* chercheur *m* de fortune, de richesses.

fortune-teller ['fɔːtjəntelər], *s.* diseur, -euse, de bonne aventure; marchand, -ande, de bonheur; (*with cards*) tireur, -euse, de cartes; cartomancien, -ienne.

fortune-telling ['fɔːtjənteliŋ], *s.* la bonne aventure; (*with cards*) cartomancie *f.*

forty ['fɔːti], *num.a. & s.* quarante (*m*); **f.-one, f.-two,** quarante et un; quarante-deux; **about f. guests,** une quarantaine d'invités; **to be f. (years old),** avoir quarante ans; **when one has turned f.,** quand on a franchi le cap de la quarantaine; **she'll never see f. again,** elle a passé la quarantaine; *F:* elle est d'âge canonique; **she is in the forties,** elle a une quarantaine d'années; elle a passé la quarantaine; **he was somewhere in the late forties,** il frisait la cinquantaine; **the forties,** les années quarante (1940–50); **the 1840's, the forties of last century,** les années entre 1840 et 1850, de 1840 à 1850; *R.C.Ch:* **the f. hours (devotion),** les (prières *f* des) quarante heures *f;* *Meteor:* **the roaring forties,** les parages océaniques situés entre les 40ᵉ et 50ᵉ degrés de latitude nord; *F:* **to have f. winks,** piquer, faire, un petit somme; faire une courte sieste.

forty-eight ['fɔːti'eit]. **1.** *num.a. & s.* quarante-huit (*m*); *Mil:* **f.-e. hours' leave,** *s.* **f.-e.,** permission *f* de quarante-huit heures (surtout le samedi et le dimanche). **2.** *s.pl. Typ:* **f.-eights,** in-quarante-huit *m inv.*

forty-eightmo ['fɔːti'eitmou], *a. & s. Typ:* in-quarante-huit (*m inv*).

forty-eleven ['fɔːtii'levən], *a. U.S: P:* je ne sais combien de, trente-six (fois, etc.).

forty-five ['fɔːti'faiv]. **1.** *num.a. & s.* quarante-cinq (*m*). **2.** *s.* (*a*) *Eng.Hist:* **the F.-five,** l'insurrection *f* jacobite de 1745; (*b*) *Rec:* disque *m* quarante cinq tours.

fortyish ['fɔːtiiʃ], *a.* d'une quarantaine d'années.

forty-niner ['fɔːti'nainər], *s. U.S:* un de ceux qui prirent part à la première course à l'or en 1849.

forum ['fɔːrəm], *s.* **1.** *Rom.Ant:* forum *m; Fig:* **tried in the f. of public opinion,** jugé devant le tribunal de l'opinion publique. **2.** tribune *f* libre, forum.

forward[1] ['fɔːwəd, *Nau:* 'fɔrəd], *a., adv., & s.*

I. *a.* **1.** (*a*) de devant, d'avant, situé en avant; *Nau:* (de l')avant, sur l'avant; *Navy:* **f. turret,** tourelle *f* avant; *Mec.E:* **f. axle,** essieu antérieur, d'avant; (*b*) (mouvement, etc.) progressif, en avant; **f. motion,** marche *f* (en) avant; **the f. journey,** l'aller *m;* **f. and backward movement,** mouvement *m* d'avance et de recul; (mouvement de) va-et-vient (*m*); *Mch:* **f. eccentric,** excentrique *m* de marche avant; **f. stroke (of piston, etc.),** aller, course directe (du piston, etc.); *Fb:* **f. pass,** passe *f* en avant; en-avant *m inv;* *El:* **f. shift, f. lead,** (dé)calage *m* en avant (des balais). **2.** (*of plants, season, child, etc.*) avancé; précoce. **3.** (*of opinions, school of thought, etc.*) avancé. **4.** effronté, hardi, indiscret, émancipé; **f. tone,** ton cavalier, présomptueux. **5.** empressé, impatient **(to do sth.,** de faire qch.). **6.** *Com:* (*of price, delivery, etc.*) à terme; *St.Exch:* **f. deals,** opérations *f* à terme. **7.** *El:* (*of current, voltage, etc.*) direct. **8.** *Cmptr:* **f. sort,** tri croissant.

II. *adv.* (*occ.* **forwards** ['fɔːwədz]) **1.** (*a*) (*of extent of time*) **from that day f.,** à partir de ce jour-là; **to look f. to sth., to doing sth.,** attendre qch. avec plaisir, avec impatience; se faire une fête de faire qch.; (*b*) *Com:* **to date f. a cheque, etc.,** postdater un chèque, etc.; **carriage f.,** (en) port dû; **charges f.,** frais *m* à percevoir à la livraison; (*c*) *Com: Fin:* **to sell f.,** vendre à terme; *Bank:* **f. rates,** taux *m* pour les opérations à terme. **2.** (*a*) (*direction*) en avant; **to go, move, get, f.,** (s')avancer; **moving f., putting f.,** avancement *m;* **the inquiry is going f.,** l'enquête suit son cours; *A:* **something is going f. here,** il se passe quelque chose ici; **to go straight f.,** aller tout droit; **to rush f.,** avancer à grande vitesse, se précipiter (en avant); **to come, step, f.,** se détacher (des autres); faire un pas en avant; **odd numbers, one pace f.!** numéros impairs, un pas en avant! **to send s.o. f.,** envoyer qn en avant; faire prendre les devants à qn; *O:* (*in shop*) **Miss X. f.!, f. please!** mademoiselle, à la vente! **to move f.,** avancer; **f.!** en avant! **we can't get any forwarder,** on ne peut pas avancer, progresser; **a stocking heel is worked forwards plain and backwards purl,** un talon de bas se fait en allers à l'endroit, et en retours à l'envers; *Row:* **to get f.,** retourner sur l'avant; **f.!** sur l'avant! (*b*) (*position*) à l'avant; **the seat is too far f.,** la banquette est trop avancée; *Fb:* **to play f.,** jouer comme avant; *Nau:* **f. of the beam,** sur l'avant du travers; à l'avant du travers; **the crew's quarters are f.,** le logement de l'équipage est à l'avant; **look out f.!** ouvre l'œil devant! (*c*) *Com: Book-k:* **to carry the balance f.,** reporter le solde à nouveau; **(carried) f.,** à reporter; report *m.* **3.** en évidence; en vue; **new doctrines were put f., brought f.,** on mit en avant de nouvelles doctrines; **to come f.,** se proposer, s'offrir (pour un emploi, etc.); **to thrust, push, oneself f.,** (i) se mettre en évidence, se faire valoir, (ii) s'imposer. **4.** en avance; **I want to get f. with tomorrow's work,** je veux m'avancer pour demain.

III. *s. Fb: etc:* (*player*) avant *m; Rugby Fb:* **the back row forwards,** les embusqués *m.*

forward[2], *v.tr.* **1.** (*a*) avancer, favoriser (les intérêts de qn, etc.); seconder (un projet, des vues, etc.); (*b*) *Bot:* hâter, forcer, avancer (la croissance d'une plante, etc.); pousser (une plante); (*c*) *Bookb:* coller et endosser (un livre). **2.** (*a*) expédier, envoyer, *Com:* transiter (des marchandises, etc.); **to f. sth. to s.o.,** faire parvenir qch. à qn; **to f. goods to Paris,** diriger des marchandises sur Paris; acheminer des marchandises sur, vers, Paris; **we are forwarding our account to you,** nous vous faisons tenir notre compte; (*b*) transmettre, faire suivre (une lettre); faire passer (une lettre) à son adresse; **to be forwarded, please f.,** prière de faire suivre; à faire suivre; **f. my letters to this address,** adressez, faites suivre, mes lettres à cet endroit.

forwarder[1] ['fɔːwədər], *s.* **1.** promoteur, -trice (d'une affaire). **2.** (*a*) expéditeur, -trice (d'un colis, etc.); envoyeur, -euse (d'un paquet, etc.); (*b*) = *forwarding agent, q.v. under* FORWARDING 2.

forwarder[2] ['fɔːwədər, *F:* 'fɔrədər], *adv. see* FORWARD[1] II 2 (*a*).

forwarding ['fɔːwədiŋ], *s.* **1.** (*a*) avancement *m* (d'une affaire, etc.); (*b*) forçage *m* (de jeunes plantes, etc.); (*c*) *Bookb:* collage *m* et endossage *m.* **2.** (*a*) expédition *f,* envoi *m;* acheminement *m* (d'un colis); **f. time,** durée *f* d'acheminement; **International f.,** transport international; **f. instructions,** indications *f* concernant l'expédition; **f. agent,** entrepreneur *m* de transports; (agent) expéditeur *m;* expéditionnaire *m;* commissionnaire(-expéditeur); commissaire *m* de transport; transporteur *m;* transitaire *m;* *Nau:* chargeur *m;* **f. agency,** maison *f* de transit; **f. house,** maison d'expédition; (*b*) transmission *f* (d'une lettre).

forward-looking ['fɔːwədlukiŋ], *a.* progressiste.

forwardly [ˈfɔːwədli], *adv.* hardiment, effrontément.

forwardness [ˈfɔːwədnis], *s.* **1.** avancement *m*, progrès *m* (d'un travail, etc.). **2.** état avancé, précocité *f* (de la récolte, de la saison, d'un élève, etc.). **3.** empressement *m*, ardeur *f*. **4.** hardiesse *f*, présomption *f*, effronterie *f*.

forwards [ˈfɔːwədz], *adv. see* FORWARD[1] II.

fossa[1], *pl.* **-ae** [ˈfɔsə, -iː], *s. Anat:* fosse (nasale, iliaque, etc.); **canine f.,** fosse canine; **f. ovalis,** fosse ovale; **submaxillary f.,** fossette *f* sous-maxillaire.

fossa[2], *pl.* **-as** [ˈfɔsə, -əz], *s. Z:* fosa *m*, cryptoprocte *m* féroce.

fossane [ˈfɔsein], *s. Z:* fossane *f*.

fosse [fɔs], *s.* **1.** *Fort: etc:* fossé *m*; **advanced f.,** contre-fossé *m*, *pl.* contre-fossés. **2.** *Anat:* = FOSSA[1].

fossette [ˈfɔset], *s. Nat.Hist:* fossette *f*.

fosse way [ˈfɔswei], *s. Hist:* voie romaine (flanquée de fossés).

fossick [ˈfɔsik], *v.i.* **1.** *Austr: & N.Z:* marauder dans les mines d'or. **2.** *P:* fureter, fouiller (pour trouver qch.).

fossicker [ˈfɔsikər], *s. Austr: N.Z:* maraudeur *m* dans les mines d'or.

fossicking [ˈfɔsikiŋ], *s. Austr: N.Z:* maraudage *m* dans les mines d'or.

fossil [ˈfɔs(i)l]. **1.** *s.* fossile *m*; *F:* **an old f.,** une vieille baderne, un vieux fossile, une croûte. **2.** *a.* fossile; **f. flora,** flore *f* fossile; **f. fuels,** combustibles *m* fossiles; **f. man,** l'homme fossile; **f. soil,** paléosol *m*.

fossilation [fɔsiˈleiʃ(ə)n], **fossilization** [fɔsilaiˈzeiʃ(ə)n], *s.* fossilisation *f*.

fossiliferous [fɔsiˈlifərəs], *a.* fossilifère.

fossilize [ˈfɔsilaiz]. **1.** *v.tr.* fossiliser. **2.** *v.i.* (*a*) se fossiliser; *F:* (*of pers.*) prendre des idées arriérées; devenir encroûté; s'encroûter; se fossiliser; (*b*) aller à la recherche des fossiles.

fossilized [ˈfɔsilaizd], *a.* (*a*) fossilisé; (*b*) (*of ideas, etc.*) fossile.

fossilizing [ˈfɔsilaiziŋ], *a. Geol:* (*of soil constituents*) fossilateur, -trice.

fossorial [fɔˈsɔːriəl], *a. Nat.Hist:* (animal, insecte) fouisseur, fossoyeur; (membre, etc.) destiné à creuser le sol.

foster [ˈfɔstər], *v.tr.* **1.** (*a*) *A:* prendre (un enfant) en nourrice; (*b*) élever, nourrir (un enfant, etc.). **2.** entretenir, nourrir (une idée, un sentiment, etc.); encourager, favoriser (les plans, les opinions, de qn); développer, encourager (les vices); protéger (les arts, etc.); fomenter (la sédition); entretenir (une agitation); **to f. friendship between peoples,** développer, stimuler, l'amitié entre les peuples; **literature that fosters licence,** littérature éducatrice de la licence; **times that fostered the growth of heavy industries,** époque *f* favorable à la croissance des grandes industries.

fosterage [ˈfɔstəridʒ], *s.* **1.** mise *f* en nourrice (d'un enfant); **during his f.,** pendant qu'il était en nourrice. **2.** (*a*) fonctions *fpl* de nourrice; (*b*) (i) gages *mpl* de la nourrice; (ii) pension *f* de nourrice. **3.** placement familial (d'un enfant).

fosterbrother [ˈfɔstəbrʌðər], *s.m.* **1.** frère de lait. **2.** frère adoptif.

fosterchild [ˈfɔstətʃaild], *s.* **1.** nourrisson, -onne; enfant en nourrice, confié à une nourrice. **2.** enfant confié à une famille qui n'est pas la sienne; *occ.* enfant adopté.

fosterer [ˈfɔstərər], *s.* **1.** (*a*) parent nourricier; (*b*) parent adoptif. **2.** patron, -onne, protecteur, -trice, promoteur, -trice (d'une œuvre, d'une affaire, etc.); fomentateur, -trice (de sédition).

fosterfather [ˈfɔstəfɑːðər], *s.m.* **1.** père nourricier. **2.** père adoptif.

fosterhome [ˈfɔstəhoum], *s.* foyer *m* des parents (i) nourriciers, (ii) adoptifs; **placing of children in fosterhomes,** placement familial des enfants.

fostering[1] [ˈfɔstəriŋ], *a.* (*of pers.*) protecteur, -trice, promoteur, -trice, bienfaisant; (*of circumstances, etc.*) favorable, propice; **f. care,** tendres soins *m*.

fostering[2], *s.* **1.** prise *f* (d'un enfant) en nourrice. **2.** entretien *m* (d'une idée, etc.); protection *f*, patronage *m*, encouragement *m* (des arts, etc.); fomentation *f* (de la sédition).

fosterling [ˈfɔstəliŋ], *s.* = FOSTERCHILD.

fostermother [ˈfɔstəmʌðər], *s.f.* **1.** (*a*) (mère) nourricière; (mère) nourrice; (*b*) *Husb:* **artificial f.,** couveuse artificielle; éleveuse artificielle. **2.** mère adoptive.

fosterparents [ˈfɔstəpeər(ə)nts], *s.pl.* **1.** parents nourriciers. **2.** parents adoptifs.

fostersister [ˈfɔstəsistər], *s.f.* **1.** sœur de lait. **2.** sœur adoptive.

Foucault [ˈfuːkou], *Pr.n.* Foucault; *Ph:* **F. current,** courant *m* de Foucault; **Foucault('s) pendulum,** pendule *m* de Foucault; **F. prism,** prisme *m* de Foucault.

fouetté [ˈfwetei], *s. Danc:* fouetté *m*.

fougade [fuːˈgæd], **fougasse** [fuːˈgæs], *s. Mil: A:* fougasse *f*.

foul[1] [faul], *a., s., & adv.*

I. *a.* **1.** (*a*) (*loathsome*) infect, fétide; puant, nauséabond; repoussant, répugnant, dégoûtant; méphitique; **f. breath,** mauvaise haleine; haleine fétide; **f. air,** air vicié, malsain, infect; **to make the air f.,** méphitiser l'air, infecter l'air; **f. gas,** gaz *m* toxique; (*b*) (*gross*) (*of thoughts, etc.*) immonde, impur, corrompu; (*of language*) grossier, ordurier; **f. word,** gros mot; **f. lie,** mensonge puant, infect; (*c*) (*abominable*) (*of deed, motive, etc.*) noir, atroce, infâme, odieux; **f. deed,** infamie *f*; *F:* **a f. trick,** une crapulerie, un coup crapule; (*d*) *F:* infect, horrible; **to have a f. cold,** être affreusement enrhumé; **what f. weather!** quel sale temps! quel temps infect! **2.** (*a*) (*dirty*) (linge, etc.) sale, malpropre, souillé; **f. water,** eau trouble, bourbeuse, croupie; (*b*) (*clogged*) (*of gun, chimney, pen, sparking-plug, etc.*) encrassé; (*of pump*) engorgé; (*of machine, etc.*) cambouisé; (*of tongue*) chargé; **to have a f. mouth,** (i) avoir mauvaise bouche; avoir la bouche mauvaise; (*after drinking*) avoir la gueule de bois; (ii) dire (habituellement) des ordures; *Nau:* (*of ship*) **f. bottom,** carène *f* sale; (*c*) *Typ:* **f. copy,** copie peu claire, illisible; **f. proof,** (i) mauvaise épreuve; (ii) épreuve en première. **3.** *Nau:* (*a*) engagé; (*of anchor*) surjalé, surpatté; **f. cable,** tour *m* de chaîne; tour dans les chaînes; **to run f. of another ship,** aborder, heurter, rencontrer, s'engager dans, entrer en collision avec, un autre navire; **two ships ran f. of each other in the fog,** il y a eu un abordage causé par le brouillard; *F:* **to run f. of a car,** accrocher une voiture; **to fall f. of s.o., of the law,** se brouiller avec qn, avec la justice; se prendre de querelle avec qn; tomber sous le coup de la loi; (*b*) **f. weather,** gros temps, *F:* un temps de bran; **f. wind,** vent *m* contraire; (*c*) **f. bottom,** mauvais fond (pour mouiller); (*d*) **f. bill of health,** patente brute; **f. bill of lading,** connaissement *m* avec réserves. **4.** *Sp: etc:* déloyal, -aux, illicite; **f. play,** (i) *Sp:* jeu déloyal; tricherie *f*; (ii) perfidie *f*, trahison *f*; intrigue déloyale; malveillance *f*; **to meet with f. play,** être victime d'un guet-apens; être attaqué lâchement; **f. play is not suspected,** on ne croit pas à un crime.

II. *s.* **1.** *Nau:* collision *f*, entrechoquement *m*. **2.** *Sp:* faute *f*; coup illicite, déloyal; *Fb:* poussée irrégulière; *Box:* coup bas; **to claim a f.,** réclamer contre un coup déloyal, contre une poussée, etc.

III. *adv.* irrégulièrement; déloyalement; **to fight f.,** se battre déloyalement, contre les règles; **to play s.o. f.,** faire une crasse à qn.

foul[2], *v.tr. & i.*

I. *v.tr.* **1.** (*a*) salir, souiller (un endroit, sa réputation, etc.); (*b*) encrasser (un canon de fusil, *I.C.E:* les bougies); (*of water, etc.*) **to f. up the boiler tubes,** entartrer les tubes de la chaudière. **2.** (*a*) embarrasser, obstruer (une ligne de chemin de fer, etc.); *Nau:* surjaler, surpatter, engager (une ancre); engager (un cordage, etc.); (*b*) *F:* **to f. up a machine,** déranger, dérégler, une machine; mettre une machine en panne; **to f. up a scheme,** embrouiller, gâcher, un projet; **to get fouled up,** (i) (*of machine*) se dérégler, se déranger; tomber en panne; (ii) (*of plan*) échouer; (iii) (*of pers.*) s'embrouiller; (*c*) *Nau: etc:* (*of ship, etc.*) entrer en collision avec, (se) heurter contre, tomber sur, aborder, s'engager dans (un autre navire, etc.). **3.** (*a*) *Sp:* commettre une faute contre (qn); *Fb:* gêner ou plaquer (l'adversaire) en dehors des règles; *Turf:* couper (un cheval); (*b*) *Nau:* **to f. a ship's course,** venir en travers de la route d'un navire; (*c*) *v.i. Mec.E: etc:* (*of moving part*) toucher.

II. *v.i.* **1. to f. (up),** (*of gun barrel, etc.*) s'encrasser; (*of pump*) s'engorger, prendre. **2.** *Nau:* (*of anchor, propeller, rope, etc.*) s'engager; (*of anchor*) surjaler, surpatter.

Foulahs [ˈfuːlɑːz], *s.pl. Ethn:* Fellatas *m*, Foulahs *m*.

foulard [ˈfuːlɑː(d)], *s. Tex: Cost:* foulard *m*.

foulbrood [ˈfaulbruːd], *s. Ap:* loque *f*; pourriture *f* du couvain.

foul-hook [ˈfaulhuk], *v.tr. Fish:* ferrer (le poisson) par le corps.

fouling [ˈfauliŋ], *s.* **1.** encrassement *m* (d'un fusil, *I.C.E:* des bougies); engorgement *m* (d'une pompe); *Sm.a:* **f. shot,** coup *m* de décrassement. **2.** (*a*) engagement *m* (d'une ancre, d'une hélice, etc.); (*b*) abordage *m* (de deux navires, etc.). **3.** *Artil: Sm.a:* crasse *f*.

foully [ˈfauli], *adv.* **1.** salement; d'une manière dégoûtante, infecte. **2.** (plaisanter, parler, etc.) grossièrement, d'une manière obscène. **3.** abominablement, méchamment, ignoblement, bassement; **he was f. murdered,** il fut ignoblement assassiné; **he has been f. slandered,** on l'a lâchement calomnié; on a publié sur son compte des calomnies ignobles.

foul-mouth [ˈfaulmauθ], *s.* personne *f* au langage ordurier.

foul-mouthed [ˈfaulˈmauðd], *a.* (*of pers.*) au langage ordurier.

foulness [ˈfaulnis], *s.* **1.** (*a*) impureté *f*, fétidité *f* (de l'air, etc.); (*b*) saleté *f*, malpropreté *f*; (*c*) encrassement *m* (d'une arme à feu, etc.). **2.** grossièreté *f*, obscénité *f* (de langage, etc.). **3.** infamie *f*, noirceur *f*, turpitude *f* (d'un acte).

foul-spoken [ˈfaulˈspouk(ə)n], *a. O:* (*of pers.*) au langage ordurier.

foul-up [ˈfaulʌp], *s. F:* (*a*) dérèglement *m*, dérangement *m* (d'un instrument, etc.); (*b*) embrouillement *m*; *P:* cafouillage *m*; **there's been a f.-up somewhere,** il y a eu (i) un contretemps, (ii) un malentendu, quelque part.

foumart [ˈfuːmɑːt], *s. Z:* putois *m*.

found[1] [faund]. **1.** *v.tr.* (*a*) fonder (un édifice, une ville); poser, établir, les fondations (d'un édifice); (*b*) fonder, créer (un collège, un empire, etc.); établir, instituer (une maison de commerce, etc.); **to f. a family,** fonder une famille; faire souche; faire tige; **to f. a fortune,** (i) établir les bases d'une fortune; (ii) élever, édifier, une fortune (**on,** sur); *Sch:* **to f. a scholarship,** fonder une bourse; **to f. a chair,** créer une chaire; (*in art, etc.*) **to f. a school,** faire école; *Jur:* **to f. an entail,** instituer un majorat; faire une substitution; (*c*) baser, fonder, appuyer (ses soupçons, etc.) (**on,** *Lit:* **in,** sur); **to f. one's opinion on the fact that . . .,** asseoir son opinion sur le fait que . . .; (*of novel, etc.*) **founded on fact,** reposant sur des faits véridiques; pris sur le vif; vécu; **code of morals founded on pleasure,** morale qui ramène tout au plaisir; **well founded,** (*of belief, etc.*) bien fondé, établi; (*of fear, etc.*) légitime; **ill-founded,** (bruit, etc.) mal fondé, sans fondement. **2.** *v.pr. & v.i.* **to f. (oneself) on, upon, sth., s.o.,** se fonder sur qch.; appuyer ses opinions, son dire, sur qch.; s'appuyer de l'autorité de qn; **to f. upon a statement,** prendre texte d'une affirmation; **to f. upon justice,** prendre la justice pour base.

found[2], *a.* (*with adverb prefixed*) **well f., fully f.,** (bateau, etc.) bien équipé, bien établi (**in,** de); **house well f. in plate and linen,** maison bien fournie d'argenterie et de linge, bien montée en argenterie et en linge; **ill-f.,** (navire, etc.) mal équipé, mal fourni, mal pourvu.

found[3], *v.tr. Metall:* fondre (les métaux); mouler (la fonte).

found[4], *s. Glassm:* fusion *f* (des matières premières).

foundation [faunˈdeiʃ(ə)n], *s.* **1.** (*a*) fondation *f* (d'un édifice, d'une ville, etc.); établissement *m*, institution *f*, création *f* (d'une académie, d'un empire, d'une maison de commerce); **f. member,** membre *m* originaire (d'une société, etc.); (*b*) fondation et dotation *f* (d'un hôpital, d'une œuvre, d'un monastère). **2.** (*a*) massif *m* de base, soubassement *m*; fondement *m*, fondation, substruction *f* (d'un édifice); assiette *f*, hérisson *m* (d'une chaussée); assise *f* (d'une machine, etc.); **the foundations of a building,** les fondements, le gros œuvre, d'un édifice; **to dig the foundations,** creuser les fondations; **to lay the foundations of a building, of a business,** établir les fondations, les fondements, d'un édifice, d'un commerce; fonder un commerce; **to lay the f. of an alliance,** jeter les bases d'une alliance; **house shaken to its foundations,** maison ébranlée jusque dans ses fondements; *Const:* **f. block,** massif de base, de fondation; **f. mass,** soubassement; **f. pier,** abloc *m*; **f. stone,** pierre *f* de fondation, fondamentale; **to lay the f. stone,** poser la première pierre; *Fig:* **the f. stone of a philosophy,** le fondement d'une philosophie; **f. wall,** jambage *m*, substruction *f*; *Civ.E: etc:* **f. bolt,** boulon *m* de fondation; tire-fond *m inv*; *Mec.E: etc:* **f. plate,** plaque *f* de fond, de fondation, d'assise, de base; plaque-semelle *f*, *pl.* plaques-semelles; contre-plaque *f*, *pl.* contre-plaques; *Mch:* **f. ring,** cadre *m* du foyer (d'une machine à vapeur); (*b*) **the foundations of music,** les bases *f* de la musique; *Mus:* (*organ*) **f. stop,** jeu *m* de fond; fond *m* d'orgue; *Fig:* **the foundations of modern society,** les assises de la société moderne. **3.** (*a*) fond (d'une robe, etc.); *Lacem:* toilage *m*; **embroidery on a silk f.,** broderie *f* sur fond de soie; **f. muslin, f. net,** mousseline forte; (*crochet, etc:*) **f. chain,** base de mailles en l'air; premier rang de mailles; (*b*) *Dressm:* bougran *m*; (*c*) *Furn:* doublure *f*, remplissage *m* (pour garniture de sièges, etc.); (*d*) *Paint:* fond de teint (d'une toile); *Th: Toil:* **make-up f.,** base de maquillage, fond de teint; (*e*) *Cost:* **f. (garment),** gaine *f*; combiné *m*; (*f*) *Ap:* **wax comb f.,** gaufre *f* de cire. **4.** fondement, base, appui *m*, principal *m* (d'une théorie, etc.); motif *m*, cause *f* (d'un doute); **rumour without f.,** bruit dénué de fondement; **statement wholly devoid of f.,** assertion *f* de pure imagination. **5.** (*a*) institution dotée; fondation; **f. school,** école dotée; *Sch:* **f. scholar,** élève boursier; **to**

put s.o. on the f., donner une bourse à qn; (*b*) capital légué pour œuvres de bienfaisance; fondation.

foundational [faun'deiʃən(ə)l], *a.* (*of doctrine, etc.*) fondamental, -aux.

foundationer [faun'deiʃənər], *s. Sch:* boursier, -ière.

founder[1] ['faundər], *s.* fondateur *m* (d'un hôpital, etc.); auteur *m* (d'une race); souche *f* (d'une famille); **f. member,** membre fondateur; *Fin:* **founder's shares,** parts *f* bénéficiaires, de fondateur.

founder[2], *s. Vet:* **foot f.,** fourbure *f*, sole battue; **chest f., body f.,** courbature (générale); fortraiture *f*.

founder[3], *s. Metall:* fondeur *m*.

founder[4]. **1.** *v.i.* (*a*) (*of building, cliff, etc.*) s'effondrer, s'écrouler; (*b*) (*of horse*) (i) s'effondrer; (ii) **to f. in the mire,** s'enfoncer dans la boue, s'embourber; (iii) se mettre à boiter; devenir fourbu; (*c*) *Nau:* (*of ship*) sombrer; couler; **to f. head down, by the bows,** sombrer par l'avant. **2.** *v.tr.* (*a*) (i) outrer, courbaturer (un cheval); (ii) faire boiter, éclopcr (un cheval); (*b*) couler (un navire).

foundered ['faundəd], *a. Vet:* (cheval) (i) fourbu, (ii) courbatu, fortrait.

foundering ['faundəriŋ], *s.* effondrement *m* (i) du sol, d'un édifice, (ii) d'un cheval.

founding[1] ['faundiŋ], *a.* (*of member, etc.*) fondateur, -trice; *U.S: Hist:* **F. Father,** membre de la Convention constituante de 1787.

founding[2], *s.* = FOUNDATION 1.

founding[3], *s. Metall:* fonderie *f*, moulage *m*.

foundling ['faundliŋ], *s.* enfant trouvé, -ée; *Adm: A:* **foundlings,** enfants assistés; *Hist:* **f. hospital,** hospice *m* des enfants trouvés; **to send a child to the f. hospital,** envoyer un enfant aux enfants trouvés, à l'Assistance publique.

foundress ['faundris], *s.f.* fondatrice.

foundry ['faundri], *s.* **1.** *Metall:* fonderie *f* (de fer, cuivre, etc.); **f. iron, f. pig,** fonte *f* de moulage; **f. pit,** fosse *f* de moulage; **f. sand,** sable *m* de moulage; **f. scrap,** débris *mpl,* déchets *mpl,* de fonte; **f. work,** fonderie. **2.** *Typ:* clicherie *f*.

fount[1] [faunt], *s.* **1.** *Poet: Lit:* source *f* (d'eau); source, cause *f*, principe *m* (du bonheur, etc.); **f. of all knowledge,** source de toute science; **he is a f. of knowledge,** c'est un puits de science. **2.** réservoir *m* (d'huile dans une lampe, d'encre dans un stylo).

fount[2] [faunt, *among printers* fɔnt], *s. Typ:* fonte *f*; assortiment complet (d'un certain œil); **wrong f.,** lettre *f* d'un autre œil; **f. case,** casseau *m*.

fountain[1] ['fauntin], *s.* **1.** fontaine *f*; (*a*) *A: & Lit:* source *f* (d'eau); **f. of wisdom,** source de sagesse; **God is the f. of all goodness,** toute bonté dérive de Dieu; (*b*) **drinking f.,** (i) borne-fontaine *f, pl.* bornes-fontaines; fontaine publique; (ii) *Ind: etc:* poste *m* d'eau potable; **soda f.,** (i) distributeur *m* d'eau de Seltz; (ii) bar *m* pour glaces et rafraîchissements non alcooliques; (*c*) jet *m* d'eau (de jardin public, etc.). **2.** réservoir *m* (d'une lampe, etc.); *Typ:* **(ink) f.,** distributeur (d'encre), encrier *m*; **water f.,** bassine *f* de mouillage; **f. solution,** eau *f* de mouillage.

fountain[2]. **1.** *v.i.* (*of water, etc.*) **to f. (up),** jaillir, s'élancer; sortir (de la terre, etc.) à flots. **2.** *v.tr.* verser (de l'eau) à flots.

fountainhead ['fauntinhed], *s.* source *f* (d'une rivière, etc.); **the f. of all knowledge,** la source de toute science; **to go to the f.,** puiser à la source, aux sources.

fountain pen ['fauntinpen], *s.* stylo *m* à encre; **self-filling f. p.,** stylo à remplissage automatique; **f. p. ink,** encre *f* à stylo.

fountain shell ['fauntinʃel], *s. Moll:* strombe géant.

four [fɔ:*r*], *num.a. & s.* **1.** quatre (*m*); **twenty-f.,** *A:* **f. and twenty,** vingt-quatre; **f. fives, five fours, are twenty, f. times five is twenty,** quatre fois cinq, cinq fois quatre, font vingt; **twenty is f. times (as much as) five,** vingt est le quadruple de cinq; *A:* **f. and six(pence),** quatre shillings six pence; **we have tea at f. thirty,** nous prenons le thé à quatre heures et demie; **the f. thirty train,** le train de (i) quatre heures trente, (ii) seize heures trente; **the plane will arrive at f. (hours) thirty,** l'avion arrivera à quatre heures trente; **to be f. (years old),** avoir quatre ans; **f. of my pupils,** quatre d'entre mes élèves; **carriage and f.,** voiture *f* à quatre chevaux; *Cards:* **sequence of f.,** quatrième *f*; (*at poker*) **f. of a kind,** carré *m*; *F:* **he came down f. steps at a time,** il est descendu quatre à quatre; **house exposed to the f. winds of heaven,** maison exposée aux quatre vents du ciel; **scattered to the f. corners of the earth,** éparpillés aux quatre coins du monde; **nowhere within the f. corners of the pact,** nullement dans les termes du pacte; *Mil: A:* **(move) to the right in fours!** à droite par quatre! **to run on all fours,** courir à quatre pattes, *O:* **to be on all fours with . . .,** aller de pair avec . . .; **the two cases are not on all fours,** il n'y a pas de parité entre les deux cas; les deux cas ne sont pas analogues; **his account is on all fours with mine,** son récit s'accorde (entièrement) avec le mien; **decision on all fours with that of another case,** décision analogue à celle d'un autre cas. **2.** *Sp:* (*a*) *Row:* **a f.,** un quatre; (*b*) *Cr:* **to hit a f.,** marquer quatre points; (*c*) *Golf:* **a f.-ball (match),** une partie à quatre joueurs et quatre balles.

four-address ['fɔ:rədres], *a. Cmptr:* **f.-a. instruction,** instruction *f* à quatre adresses.

fourail ['fuəreil], *s. Ven:* fouaille *f*.

four-ale ['fɔ:reil], *s. A:* bière vendue à quatre pence la pinte; **f.-a. bar,** bar *m* où l'on vendait les boissons les moins chères.

four-angled ['fɔ:ræŋgld], *a.* quadrangulaire.

four-by-two ['fɔ:bi'tu:], *s. Sm.a:* chiffon *m* de flanelle (pour décrassage).

four-centred ['fɔ:'sentəd], *a. Arch:* **f.-c. arch,** arc *m* en accolade.

fourchette [fuə'ʃet], *s.* **1.** *also* ['fɔ:ʃet], fourchette *f* (de gant). **2.** *Anat:* fourchette vulvaire. **3.** *Orn:* fourchette, lunette *f*. **4.** *Cards:* tenace *f*, fourchette.

four-cleft ['fɔ:kleft], *a. Bot:* quadrifide, quadriparti, -ite.

four-colour ['fɔ:'kʌlər], *a. Engr: etc:* à quatre couleurs; quadricolore; **f.-c. process, work,** travail *m* à quatre couleurs; quadrichromie *f*.

four-cornered ['fɔ:'kɔ:nəd], *a.* à quatre coins; carré, quadrangulaire.

four-coupled ['fɔ:'kʌpld], *a. Rail:* (locomotive) à quatre roues accouplées, à deux essieux couplés.

four-cycle ['fɔ:'saikl], *a. I.C.E:* (moteur) à quatre temps.

four-dimensional ['fɔ:dai'menʃənəl], *a.* quadridimensionnel.

four-electrode ['fɔ:ri'lektroud], *a. Elcs:* **f.-e. valve,** tube *m* électronique tétrode, à quatre électrodes; tétrode *f*.

four-engined ['fɔ:r'endʒind], *a. Av:* **f.-e. aircraft,** (avion) quadrimoteur (*m*); **f.-e. jet aircraft,** (avion) quadriréacteur (*m*).

four-eyes ['fɔ:raiz], *s.* **1.** *Ich:* (*also* **four-eyed fish**) anableps *m*; gros-œil *m, pl.* gros-œils. **2.** *P:* binoclard, -arde.

four-figure ['fɔ:'figər], *a. Mth:* (nombre) à quatre chiffres; (logarithme) à quatre décimales.

four flush ['fɔ:flʌʃ]. **1.** *s. Cards:* flush *m* de quatre cartes. **2.** *a. U.S: F:* **f.-f.,** faux, fausse; postiche.

four flusher ['fɔ:flʌʃər], *s. NAm: F:* épateur, -euse; bluffeur, -euse.

four-flushing[1] ['fɔ:'flʌʃiŋ], *a. NAm: F:* hâbleur.

four-flushing[2], *s. NAm: F:* bluff *m*, hâblerie *f*.

fourfold ['fɔ:fould]. **1.** *a.* (*a*) quadruple; (*b*) **f. (draught) screen,** paravent *m* à quatre feuilles; **f. tripod stand,** pied *m* (d'appareil) à trois brisures. **2.** *adv.* quatre fois autant; au quadruple; **to repay s.o. f.,** rendre à qn quatre fois autant; **to return a service f.,** rendre un bienfait au quadruple; **to increase f.,** quadrupler.

four-foot ['fɔ:fut], *a.* de quatre pieds; *Rail:* **f.-f. way,** entre-rail *m* (de la voie normale).

four-footed ['fɔ:'futid], *a.* (animal) quadrupède; à quatre pattes.

four-handed ['fɔ:'hændid], *a.* **1.** (singe *m*) à quatre mains, quadrumane. **2.** (*a*) (jeu *m*) à quatre (personnes); (*b*) *occ.Mus:* (morceau *m*) à quatre mains.

four-horned ['fɔ:'hɔ:nd], *a.* tétracère; à quatre cornes; **f.-h. antelope,** tétracère *m*.

four-horse(d) ['fɔ:'hɔ:s(t)], *a.* (véhicule) à quatre chevaux.

Fourier ['furiər], *Pr.n. Mth:* **F. series,** séries *fpl* de Fourier; séries trigonométriques.

Fourierism ['fuəriərizm], *s. Social Hist:* fouriérisme *m*.

Fourierist ['fuəriərist], *s. Social Hist:* fouriériste *m*.

four-in-hand ['fɔ:in'hænd]. **1.** *s.* (*a*) véhicule *m* à quatre chevaux; attelage *m* à quatre; mail-coach *m, pl.* mail-coaches; (*b*) *NAm: Cost:* **f.-in-h. (tie),** cravate-plastron *f, pl.* cravates-plastrons. **2.** *adv.* **to drive f.-in-h.,** conduire à grandes guides, à quatre (chevaux).

four-leaved ['fɔ:'li:vd], *a. Bot:* quadrifolié.

four-legged ['fɔ:'legid], *a.* (*a*) (table) à quatre pieds; (*b*) (animal) quadrupède.

four-letter ['fɔ:'letər], *a. F:* **f.-l. word,** obscénité *f*; *P: O:* **f.-l. man,** (i) (*c.-à-d.* s h i t) merdeux; (ii) (*c.-à-d.* h o m o) homosexuel; (iii) (*c.-à-d.* d u m b) sot, imbécile.

fourmarierite [fuə'mæriərait], *s. Miner:* fourmariérite *f*.

four-master ['fɔ:'mɑ:stər], *s. Nau:* quatre-mâts *m inv.*

four-oar ['fɔ:rɔ:*r*], *s.* canot *m* à quatre avirons.

four-oared ['fɔ:rɔ:d], *a.* (canot) à quatre avirons.

four-o'clock [fɔ:rə'klɔk], *s. Bot: F:* nyctage *m*, belle-de-nuit *f, pl.* belles-de-nuit.

four-part ['fɔ:'pɑ:t], *a. Mus:* à quatre parties; à quatre voix.

fourpence ['fɔ:p(ə)ns, -pens], *s.* somme *f* de quatre pence.

fourpenny ['fɔ:p(ə)ni], *a.* qui vaut quatre pence; **10 f. stamps,** 10 timbres à quatre pence; *P:* **to give s.o. a f. one,** flanquer un gnon, une beigne, à qn.

four-phase ['fɔ:'feiz], *a. El:* (système) tétraphasé.

four-place ['fɔ:'pleis], *a. Mth:* (logarithme) à quatre décimales.

four-ply ['fɔ:plai], *a.* (*of fabric, veneer, etc.*) à, en, quatre épaisseurs; quadruple; **f.-p. wool,** laine *f* quatre fils; *Mec.E:* **f.-p. belt,** courroie *f* à quatre épaisseurs, à quatre plis.

four-pole ['fɔ:'poul], *a. El:* (dynamo, etc.) à quatre pôles, quadripôle, tétrapolaire.

four-poster ['fɔ:'poustər]. **1.** *a. & s.* (lit *m*) à colonnes. **2.** *s. Nau: F:* quatre-mâts *m inv.*

fourscore ['fɔ:skɔ:*r*], *a. A: & Lit:* quatre-vingts; **at the age of f. years and ten,** à l'âge de quatre-vingt-dix ans.

foursome ['fɔ:səm]. **1.** *a.* à quatre; *Danc:* **f. reel,** "reel" dansé à quatre. **2.** *s.* partie *f*, groupe *m*, de quatre personnes; (*with two of each sex*) partie carrée; *Golf:* partie (de) double, à deux contre deux.

four-speed ['fɔ:'spi:d], *a. Aut:* à quatre vitesses.

foursquare ['fɔ:'skwɛər], *a. & adv.* (i) carré(ment); (ii) solide(ment); **we have stood f. to every storm,** nous avons tenu tête à toutes les tempêtes, à tous les vents.

four-stroke ['fɔ:'strouk], *a. & s. I.C.E:* (moteur *m*) à quatre temps; *Aut:* **f.-s. (motor cycle),** motocyclette *f* avec moteur à quatre temps.

fourteen ['fɔ:ti:n; fɔ:'ti:n], *num.a. & s.* quatorze (*m*); **she is f.,** elle a quatorze ans; **two fourteens are, twice f. is, twenty-eight,** deux fois quatorze font vingt-huit; **the plane will arrive at fourteen (hours) thirty,** l'avion arrivera à quatorze heures trente; **f. houses,** quatorze maisons.

fourteenth [fɔ:'ti:nθ]. **1.** *num.a. & s.* quatorzième; **Louis the F.,** Louis Quatorze; **the f.** ['fɔ:ti:nθ] **house,** la quatorzième maison; **he's f. in his class,** il est le quatorzième de sa classe; **(on) the f. (of May),** le quatorze (mai). **2.** *s.* (*a*) (*fractional*) quatorzième *m*; (*b*) *Mus:* quatorzième *f*; réplique *f*, octave *f*, de la septième.

fourteenthly [fɔ:'ti:nθli], *adv.* quatorzièmement; en quatorzième lieu.

fourth [fɔ:θ]. **1.** *num.a. & s.* quatrième; **Henry the F.,** Henri Quatre; **he arrived f. or fifth,** il est arrivé quatre ou cinquième; **he's f. in his class,** il est le quatrième de sa classe; *Aut:* **in f. (gear),** en quatrième (vitesse); **the f. of January, January the f.,** le quatre janvier; *U.S:* **the (glorious) F.,** le quatre juillet (fête nationale); *Sch:* **the f. form,** *approx.* = la classe de troisième; *Cards: etc:* **to make a f.,** faire le quatrième. **2.** *s.* (*a*) (*fractional*) quart *m*; **three-fourths of the globe,** les trois quarts du globe; (*b*) *Mus:* quarte *f*; **augmented f.,** quarte augmentée; triton *m*.

fourthly ['fɔ:θli], *adv.* quatrièmement, en quatrième lieu.

fourthrate ['fɔ:θreit], *a.* de quatrième ordre.

four-toed ['fɔ:'toud], *a. Z:* tétradactyle.

four-walled ['fɔ:'wɔ:ld], *a.* (cour, etc.) à quatre murs; (vie, etc.) entre quatre murs.

four-way ['fɔ:wei], *a.* (robinet) à quatre voies.

four-went-way ['fɔ:'went'wei], *s. Dial:* carrefour *m* (de routes).

four-wheel ['fɔ:'(h)wi:l], *a.* **1.** (*also* **four-wheeled** ['fɔ:'(h)wi:ld]) (véhicule) à quatre roues. **2.** *Aut:* **f.-w. brakes,** freins *m*, freinage *m*, sur les quatre roues; freinage intégral; **tractor with a f.-w. drive,** tracteur *m* à quatre roues motrices.

four-wheeler ['fɔ:'(h)wi:lər], *s.* voiture *f* à quatre roues; *esp. A:* fiacre *m*, voiture de place (par opposition au *hansom cab*).

four-wire ['fɔ:'waiər], *a. El:* (système de distribution, etc.) à quatre fils; **f.-w. circuit,** circuit *m* bifilaire double.

foussa ['fusə], *s. Z:* fosa *m*; cryptoprocte *m* féroce.

fovea, *pl.* **-eae** ['fouviə, -ii:], *s. Anat: etc:* fovéa *f*, fosse *f*.

foveal ['fouviəl], *a. Anat: etc:* fovéal, -aux.

foveola, *pl.* **-as, -ae** [fou'vi:ələ, -əz, -i:], *s. Anat: etc:* fovéole *f*.

foveolar [fou'vi:ələr], *a. Anat: etc:* fovéolaire.

foveolate ['fouviəleit], *a. Biol: Bot:* fovéolé.

fowl[1] [faul], *s.* **1.** (*a*) *Lit:* oiseau *m*; volatile *m*; **all the fowl(s) of the air,** tous les oiseaux des cieux; (*b*) *coll.* oiseaux; **wild f.,** gibier *m* d'eau. **2.** (*a*) poule *f*, coq *m*, volaille *f*, oiseau de basse-cour; **to keep fowls,** élever des poules, de la volaille; **f. house,** poulailler *m*; **f. run,** parcours *m* de poulailler; *Vet:* **f. cholera,** choléra *m* des poules, choléra aviaire; peste *f* aviaire; pasteurellose *f* des volailles; **f. paralysis,** paralysie *f* aviaire; maladie *f* de Marek; **f. pest,** (i) (*also* **f. plague**) peste aviaire, des poules; (ii) peste de Newcastle; pseudopeste *f*; **f. pox,** diphtérie *f* aviaire, des volailles; (*b*) *Cu:* volaille; **boiling**

f., poule (au pot).

fowl[2], *v.i.* **1.** faire la chasse au gibier ailé. **2.** oiseler (au filet).

fowler[1] ['faulər], *s.* oiseleur *m.*

Fowler[2], *Pr.n. Av:* **F. flap,** volet *m* de Fowler; *Pharm:* **Fowler's solution,** liqueur *f* de Fowler.

fowlerite ['faulərait], *s. Miner:* fowlérite *f.*

fowling ['fauliŋ], *s.* chasse *f* aux oiseaux; **night f.,** *A:* **bat f.,** fouée *f*; **f. piece,** fusil *m* de chasse (à petit plomb).

fox[1] [fɔks], *s.* **1.** (*a*) renard *m*; **she f., f. bitch** (*usu.* VIXEN), renarde *f*; **young f., f. cub,** renardeau *m*; **red f.,** renard commun; **white f., Arctic f.,** renard polaire; renard bleu; **long-eared f., big-eared f.,** otocyon *m*; **sand f.,** renard famélique; **American grey f.,** urocyon *m*; **silver f.,** renard argenté; **f. brush,** queue *f* de renard; **fox's hole, burrow, earth,** renardière *f*; terrier *m* de renard; **f. trap,** piège *m* à renards; **f. skin,** peau *f*, fourrure *f*, de renard; *Cost:* **f. fur,** (fourrure en) renard; **f. collar,** renard; *F:* **to set the f. to keep the geese,** enfermer le loup dans la bergerie; (*b*) *F:* **an old f.,** un vieux renard, un vieux madré; un vieux malin; **a sly, cunning, f.,** un madré; un fin renard; un roublard; un fin matois; un finaud; **to play the f.,** renarder; (*c*) *Z:* **flying f., f. bat,** roussette *f*; *Ich:* **sea f., f. shark,** renard (marin), renard de mer. **2.** *Astr:* **the F.,** le Renard. **3.** *U.S: P:* jolie femme, jolie pépée. **4.** *Mec.E:* **f. (wedge),** contre-clavette *f, pl.* contre-clavettes; **f. bolt, f. key,** goupille fendue pour contre-clavette.

fox[2]. **1.** *v.tr.* (*a*) tacher de roux, piquer, décolorer (les feuilles d'un livre); maculer, piquer (une gravure); (*b*) *Bootm:* mettre une bande de renfort, une baguette, à (un soulier); (*c*) *P:* mystifier, tromper (qn). **2.** *v.i.* (*a*) *F:* feindre; ruser; user de feintes; renarder; (*b*) **to f. about, to go foxing round,** fureter partout; (*c*) *Brew:* (*of beer*) s'acidifier, se piquer; (*d*) (*of paper*) se piquer.

foxaline ['fɔksəli:n], *s.* (fourrure *f*) similirenard *m inv.*

foxbane ['fɔksbein], *s. Bot:* aconit *m* tue-loup *inv.*

foxberry ['fɔksberi], *s. Bot:* (i) busserole *f*; raisin *m* d'ours; (ii) myrtille *f* rouge; airelle ponctuée.

foxed [fɔkst], *a.* **1.** (*of paper, etc.*) maculé. **2.** (*of pers.*) (i) *F:* mystifié; (ii) *P: A:* ivre, gris, soûl.

fox evil ['fɔksi:vl], *s. Med: F:* pelade *f.*

fox fire ['fɔksfaiər], *s. U.S:* phosphorescence *f* (du bois pourri, etc.).

foxfish ['fɔksfiʃ], *s. Ich:* **1.** callionyme *m.* **2.** renard (marin).

foxglove ['fɔksglʌv], *s. Bot:* digitale (pourprée); *F:* gantelée *f*; gant *m* de bergère; gant de Notre-Dame; doigtier *m*; doigt *m* de la Vierge.

foxhole ['fɔkshoul], *s.* **1.** renardière *f*; terrier *m* de renard. **2.** *Mil:* trou *m* de tirailleur; abri individuel.

foxhound ['fɔkshaund], *s.* chien courant (pour la chasse au renard); fox-hound *m, pl.* fox-hounds.

foxhunt ['fɔkshʌnt], *s.* chasse *f* au renard.

foxhunter ['fɔkshʌntər], *s.* chasseur *m* de renards.

foxhunting ['fɔkshʌntiŋ], *s.* chasse *f* au renard.

foxiness ['fɔksinis], *s.* **1.** astuce *f*; roublardise *f.* **2.** état maculé (des pages d'un livre). **3.** goût foxé (du vin); goût aigri (de la bière).

foxing ['fɔksiŋ], *s.* **1.** *F:* feinte *f*, finasserie *f.* **2.** (*a*) acidification *f* (de la bière); (*b*) décoloration *f*, piqûre *f* (du papier). **3.** (*on paper, books*) piqûres *fpl*; macules *fpl* (d'une estampe). **4.** *Bootm:* bande *f* de renfort; baguette *f.*

foxlike ['fɔkslaik], *a.* **1.** qui ressemble à un renard. **2.** *F:* rusé, astucieux, malin, madré, roublard.

fox mange ['fɔksmeindʒ], *s. Med:* alopécie *f.*

foxmark ['fɔksma:k], *s.* tache *f* de roux (sur une feuille d'un livre).

fox squirrel ['fɔks'skwir(ə)l], *s. Z:* écureuil *m* de la Caroline.

foxtail ['fɔksteil], *s.* **1.** queue *f* de renard. **2.** *Bot:* (*a*) **f. (grass),** vulpin *m*, queue-de-renard *f, pl.* queues-de-renard; **meadow f.,** vulpin des prés; vulpine *f*; (*b*) lycopode *m* en massue; soufre végétal; mousse *f* terrestre; pied-de-loup *m, pl.* pieds-de-loup; (*c*) **f. lily,** eremurus *f*; **f. millet,** millet *m* à grappes. **3.** (*a*) *Carp:* **f. joint,** mortaise *f* à queue de renard; **f. saw,** scie *f* d'encadreur; (*b*) *Mec.E:* **f. wedging,** assemblage *m* à contre-clavette.

fox terrier ['fɔks'teriər], *s.* fox-terrier *m, pl.* fox-terriers; *F:* fox *m*; **smooth-haired, wire-haired, f. t.,** fox-terrier à poil lisse, à poil dur.

foxtrot[1] ['fɔkstrɔt], *s.* **1.** petit trot (de renard). **2.** *Danc:* fox-trot *m inv.*

foxtrot[2], *v.i.* (**fox-trotted**) danser le fox-trot.

fox wood ['fɔkswud], *s.* bois vermoulu.

foxy ['fɔksi], *a.* **1.** (*a*) (visage, etc.) qui ressemble à un renard; au nez pointu; **f. smell,** odeur *f* de renard, infecte, fétide; (*b*) rusé, astuce; **to play f.,** finasser. **2.** (*a*) (*of hair, complexion*) roux, *f.* rousse; (*b*) *Art:* tirant sur le rouge; à tons de brique. **3.** (*a*) (bois) pouilleux; (*b*) (livre, papier) piqué; (*of print*) maculé (de taches de rouille). **4.** (*of wine, beer*) foxé; **f. taste,** fox *m*; **to turn f.,** s'acidifier, aigrir. **5.** *U.S: P:* (*of girl*) attirant, appétissant.

foyaite ['fɔi(j)əait], *s. Geol:* foyaïte *f.*

foyer ['fɔiei, 'fwajei], *s. Th:* foyer *m* du public; *Cin:* (hall *m* d')entrée *f.*

fracted ['fræktid], *a. Her:* (*of fesse*) brisé.

fraction ['frækʃ(ə)n], *s.* **1.** *Ecc:* fraction *f* (du pain). **2.** petite portion, petite partie (de qch.); fragment *m*; **there was not a f. left,** il n'en restait pas le moindre petit morceau. **3.** (*a*) *Mth:* fraction; nombre *m* fractionnaire; **vulgar f., common f.,** fraction ordinaire; **decimal f.,** fraction décimale; **improper f.,** expression *f* fractionnaire; **compound f., complex f.,** fraction de fraction; **f. in its lowest terms,** fraction irréductible; (*in calculus*) **partial fractions, part fractions,** petites parties d'une fraction; *Com:* **fractions of a franc are charged as a franc,** l'addition, etc., est arrondie au franc supérieur; **he escaped death by a f. of a second, by the f. of an inch,** il a été à deux doigts de la mort; **move it a f.,** déplacez-le un tout petit peu; (*b*) *Fin:* fraction, rompu *m* (d'action, d'obligation); (*c*) *Mapm:* **representative f.,** échelle *f* (numérique). **4.** *Ch:* fraction (de distillation). **5.** *Atom.Ph:* **mole f.,** fraction molaire; **packing f.,** fraction de tassement. **6.** *Pol:* fraction; groupe *m* fractionnaire (d'un parti).

fractional ['frækʃən(ə)l], *a.* **1.** *Mth: etc:* fractionnaire; **f. part,** fraction *f*; **f. coins,** monnaie *f* divisionnaire, d'appoint; *NAm:* **f. note,** (billet *m* de banque de) petite coupure; *Mec.E:* **f. horsepower engine,** moteur inférieur à un cheval, de moins d'un cheval, à fraction de cheval; *F:* **the difference is only f.,** la différence est minime. **2.** *Ch:* (*of crystallization, etc.*) fractionné; **f. distillation,** distillation fractionnée; fractionnement *m.*

fractionally ['frækʃənəli], *adv.* **1. f. larger,** plus grand d'un tout petit peu. **2.** *Ch:* (distiller) par fractionnement.

fractionary ['frækʃənəri], *a.* fractionnel.

fractionate ['frækʃəneit], *v.tr. Ch: Ind:* fractionner (le pétrole, etc.).

fractionating ['frækʃəneitiŋ], *s. Ch: Ind:* fractionnement *m*; **f. column, tower,** tour *f* de fractionnement; fractionnateur *m.*

fractionation [frækʃə'neiʃ(ə)n], *s. Ch: Ind:* fractionnement *m.*

fractionator ['frækʃəneitər], *s. Ch: Ind:* appareil *m* de fractionnement; fractionnateur *m.*

fractionism ['frækʃənizm], *s. Pol:* fractionnisme *m.*

fractionist ['frækʃənist], *s. Pol:* fractionniste *mf.*

fractionize ['frækʃənaiz], *v.tr. Mth: etc:* fractionner (une expression).

fractious ['frækʃəs], *a.* (*a*) difficile de caractère; revêche; (*b*) de mauvaise humeur; maussade; **a f. baby,** un bébé pleurnicheur; **the baby was f.,** le bébé ne cessait pas de pleurer, ne voulait pas s'endormir; (*c*) (cheval) difficile, rétif; (vache *f*) indocile.

fractiously ['frækʃəsli], *adv.* **1.** d'un air, d'un ton de mauvaise humeur. **2.** indocilement.

fractiousness ['frækʃəsnis], *s.* (*a*) mauvaise humeur; humeur hargneuse, querelleuse; (*of a baby*) pleurnicherie *f*, pleurnichage *m*; (*b*) rétivité *f* (d'un animal); indocilité *f.*

fractocumulus ['fræktou'kju:mjuləs], *s. Meteor:* fractocumulus *m.*

fractonimbus ['fræktou'nimbəs], *s. Meteor:* fractonimbus *m.*

fractostratus ['fræktou'streitəs], *s. Meteor:* fractostratus *m.*

fracture[1] ['fræktʃər], *s.* **1.** (*a*) fracture *f*, rupture *f* (d'un essieu, etc.); (*b*) fracture (d'un os, etc.); **simple f.,** fracture simple, fermée; **compound f., open f.,** fracture compliquée, ouverte; **fissure f., fissured f.,** fêlure *f*; **spontaneous f., pathologic f.,** fracture spontanée; **Colles('s) f.,** fracture de Colles, par retour de manivelle; **suspected f.,** fracture présumée; **to set a f.,** réduire une fracture; (*c*) *Metalw:* crique *f* (dans le métal). **2.** *Miner: Geol:* cassure *f*, fracture; **f. plane,** plan *m* de fracture, de cassure; **rock f.,** lithoclase *f.* **3.** *Ling:* fracture (d'une voyelle).

fracture[2]. **1.** *v.tr.* (*a*) casser, briser (qch.); (*b*) fracturer (un os); **fractured skull,** crâne fracturé; **fractured ribs,** côtes enfoncées; (*c*) *U.S:* enfreindre (la loi, un traité, etc.); (*d*) *U.S: P:* **to f. s.o.,** faire pouffer qn de rire. **2.** *v.i.* (*a*) se casser, se briser; (*b*) (*of rock, limb*) se fracturer.

fraenum ['fri:nəm], *s. Anat:* frein *m*, filet *m* (de la langue, etc.).

fragile ['frædʒail], *a.* **1.** (*of thg*) fragile. **2.** (*of pers.*) faible; mièvre, chétif; *F:* **I'm feeling a bit f. this morning,** (i) je ne me sens pas bien d'aplomb, (ii) j'ai mal aux cheveux, ce matin.

fragilely ['frædʒailli], *adv.* fragilement.

fragility [frə'dʒiliti], *s.* **1.** (*of thg*) fragilité *f*; *Metall: etc:* frangibilité *f.* **2.** (*of pers.*) faiblesse *f*; délicatesse *f.*

fragment[1] ['frægmənt], *s.* **1.** fragment *m*, morceau *m* (de porcelaine, de papier, etc.); éclat *m*, brisure *f* (d'obus, etc.); brin *m* (de papier, etc.); **smashed to fragments,** réduit en fragments, en miettes; brisé en mille morceaux; *Lit:* **the fragments of a meal,** les bribes *f*, les miettes *f*, d'un repas. **2.** *Lit:* fragment; (*a*) œuvre inachevée (d'un auteur); (*b*) extrait *m* (d'un livre).

fragment[2] [fræg'ment], *v.tr.* réduire en fragments; briser en morceaux.

fragmental [fræg'mentl], *a. Geol:* clastique, détritique; **f. deposition,** fragmentation *f.*

fragmentary ['frægmənt(ə)ri], *a.* **1.** fragmentaire. **2.** *Geol:* = FRAGMENTAL.

fragmentation [frægmən'teiʃ(ə)n], *s.* fragmentation *f*; *Biol:* **f. of chromosomes,** fragmentation chromosomique; *Mil:* **f. bomb, grenade, shell,** bombe *f*, grenade *f*, obus *m*, à fragmentation.

fragrance ['freigrəns], *s.* parfum *m*; bonne odeur, odeur suave; *Lit:* fragrance *f.*

fragrant ['freigrənt], *a.* parfumé, odorant, odoriférant, fragrant; **f. smell,** odeur embaumée; bonne odeur (de cuisine, etc.); **her room was f. of violets,** sa chambre embaumait la violette; les violettes embaumaient sa chambre; **woods f. with wild strawberries,** bois parfumés de fraises sauvages.

fraid(y) ['freid(i)], *a. P:* (*schoolchild's word*) **f. cat,** peureux, -euse; poltron, -onne.

frail[1] [freil], *a.* **1.** (*a*) (*easily broken*) peu solide; fragile; frêle; (*b*) (*transient*) (bonheur, etc.) transitoire; éphémère, fugitif. **2.** (*weak*) (*a*) (*of pers., health*) faible, frêle, débile, délicat; **she's getting very f.,** elle commence à se casser; (*b*) *O:* (*morally weak*) **a f. woman,** une faible femme, une femme de petite vertu. **3.** *s.f. NAm: P:* femme; *P:* frangine.

frail[2], *s. Com:* cabas *m*, panier *m* de jonc (pour l'emballage des figues, raisins secs).

frailness ['freilnis], *s.* **1.** (*a*) fragilité *f* (du verre, etc.); (*b*) fugacité *f*, fragilité (du bonheur); caractère éphémère, transitoire (de la beauté, etc.). **2.** (*a*) (*of pers., health*) faiblesse *f*, débilité *f*, fragilité; *esp.* faiblesse de l'âge; (*b*) faiblesse morale; faiblesse contre les tentations; facilité *f* à pécher; fragilité humaine.

frailty ['freilti], *s.* **1.** = FRAILNESS 2 (*b*). **2.** (*a*) faible *m*; défaut *m*; (*b*) péché *m*, faux pas.

fraise[1] [freiz], *s.* **1.** *Fort:* fraise *f.* **2.** *A.Cost:* fraise (à godrons).

fraise[2], *s. Tls:* fraise *f.*

framboesia [fræm'bi:ziə], *s. Med:* pian *m.*

frame[1] [freim], *s.* **1.** (*a*) construction *f*, structure *f*, disposition *f*, forme *f*; **f. of mind,** état *m*, disposition, d'esprit; **he is in a bad f. of mind,** il est de mauvaise humeur; il est mal disposé; (*b*) système *m*, forme (de gouvernement); ordre *m* (de la société, etc.); plan *m* (de l'univers). **2.** (*a*) ossature *f* (d'une personne, d'un animal); **man of gigantic f.,** homme d'une taille, d'une stature, colossale; **sobs shook her f.,** des sanglots lui secouaient le corps; (*b*) *Const: Min:* charpente *f*, monture *f* (d'un bâtiment, d'un comble, d'un pont, etc.); colombage *m*, pan *m* (de cloison, de mur); *Min:* **timbering f.,** cadre *m*, châssis *m*, de mine; **head f.,** chevalement *m*, chevalet *m* (d'extraction); *Civ.E:* **f. bridge,** pont *m* en charpente; *NAm:* **f. house,** maison *f* en bois; (*c*) ossature *f* (de l'aile d'un avion); cadre (d'une bicyclette, etc.); carcasse *f* (d'un moteur électrique); châssis *m* (d'une locomotive, d'une automobile, d'un canon, etc.); caisse *f*, train *m* (d'une voiture); bâti *m* (d'une machine, d'une dynamo, d'un métier, etc.); soucherie *f* (d'un marteau à bascule); affût *m* (d'une fusée, d'un canon, etc.); monture (d'un parapluie, d'un sac à main, etc.); carcasse (d'un parapluie); armature *f* (d'une raquette); cerce *f* (d'un tamis, etc.); corps *m* (d'un filtre); monture, châsse *f* (d'une paire de lunettes); **f. of an armchair,** bois *m* d'un fauteuil; **f. of a bed,** châlit *m*; bois de lit; **saw f.,** châssis, monture, affût, arçon *m*, de scie; porte-scie *m inv*; **fret-saw f., piercing saw f.,** bocfil *m*; **f. saw,** scie montée, à châssis; **poster f., bill f.,** tableau *m* d'affichage; *Ap:* **f. of a hive,** cadre d'une ruche; *Av:* **air f.,** (i) fuselage *m*; (ii) appareil *m* de sustentation (d'un avion); *Turb:* **governor f.,** corbeille *f* de régulateur; *Veh:* (*half-round*) **f. of a cart tilt,** cerceau *m* d'une bâche; **f. to support the squab(s),** banquette *f*, parclose *f*, à coussin; (*d*) *N.Arch:* (i) membrure, carcasse (d'un navire); (ii) membre *m*, couple *m*; **web f.,** porque *f*; **floor f.,** varangue *f*; **filling f.,** couple de remplissage; **the midship f.,** le maître couple; **stern f.,** arcasse *f*; **f. spacing,** écartement *m* des membrures; (*e*) *Mth:* **f. of**

reference, reference f., système *m* de coordonnées; référentiel *m*. **3.** (*a*) cadre, encadrement *m* (d'un tableau, miroir, etc.); **gilded f.**, cadre doré; *Phot:* **printing f.**, châssis positif; châssis-presse *m*, *pl.* châssis-presses; (*b*) **f. of a window**, chambranle *m*, dormant *m*, châssis dormant, armature *f*, d'une fenêtre; **door f.**, dormant de porte; *N.Arch:* **f. of a port-hole**, dormant d'un hublot; *Ch:* (*of a fume cupboard*) **sliding f.**, châssis coulissant; (*c*) *N.Arch:* cadre (de l'hélice); (*d*) *Cin:* image *f* (de film); *T.V:* (i) trame *f* (double), (ii) image; *Cin:* **f. line**, ligne *f* de séparation de deux images; *T.V:* **f. frequency**, fréquence *f* des trames, d'exploration; *U.S:* fréquence des images; **emission at 25 frames per second**, émission *f* de 25 images par seconde; **f. output transformer**, transformateur *m* de balayage. **4.** (*a*) *Needlew:* métier *m* (à broder, à dentelle, tapisserie, etc.); tambour *m* (à broder); carreau *m* (de dentellière); **f. work**, travail *m*, -aux, au métier (à broder, etc.) (*cf.* FRAMEWORK); (*b*) *Tex:* métier (à filer); **stocking f.**, métier à bas; **drawing f.**, banc *m* d'étirage (des rubans cardés); **flyer f.**, banc à broches. **5.** (*a*) *Elcs: Tp:* **distribution f.**, répartiteur *m*; **main distribution f.**, répartiteur d'entrée; (*b*) *Cmptr:* unité *f* d'information; **main f.**, unité centrale (de traitement). **6.** *Farr: Vet:* travail, *pl.* travails (pour cheval). **7.** *Hort:* châssis (de couches); bâche; **hot f.**, **cold f.**, châssis chaud, froid. **8.** *Min:* (*for ore dressing*) table dormante, à toile inclinée. **9.** *Sp:* (*bowling*) reprise *f*, coup *m* (de jeu de quilles). **10.** *F:* coup monté (contre qn).

frame[2], *v.tr.* **1.** former, régler (ses pensées, ses actions, etc.); **to f. s.o. for, to, sth.**, former, façonner, disposer, qn à qch.; **to f. sth. to, into, sth.**, ajuster, adapter, qch. à qch.; *v.i.* **he is framing well**, il montre des dispositions; il donne de grandes espérances. **2.** (*a*) **to f. a roof**, faire la charpente d'un toit; **to f. a ship**, construire la carcasse d'un navire; (*b*) projeter (un dessein); charpenter (un roman, etc.); composer (un poème, une réponse, etc.); **to f. a speech**, établir, arrêter, disposer, le plan d'un discours; *Jur:* **to f. a law**, rédiger une loi; (*c*) articuler, prononcer (un mot, etc.). **3.** (*a*) imaginer, concevoir (une idée, etc.); se faire (une opinion); (*b*) fabriquer (une histoire, etc.); ourdir (un complot); **to f. an accusation against s.o.**, monter une accusation contre qn; *F:* **to f. s.o.**, monter une accusation, un coup, contre qn; **I've been framed**, c'est un coup monté (contre moi); **to f. (up) a contest, a result**, truquer un concours, un résultat; **try to f. up something**, tâchez de manigancer quelque chose. **4.** (*a*) encadrer (un tableau, etc.); **black hair framed her pale face**, des cheveux noirs encadraient son pâle visage; **she stood framed in the doorway**, elle se tenait dans l'encadrement de la porte; (*b*) *T.V:* cadrer, centrer (l'image).

framed [freimd], *a.* *Const:* **1.** (bâtiment) à structure discontinue; squeletté; (*of picture*) encadré. **2.** *NAm:* (maison) de bois.

framemaker ['freimmeikər], *s.* carcassier *m* (de parapluies, etc.).

framer ['freimər], *s.* **1.** auteur *m* (d'un projet); rédacteur *m* (d'un traité, etc.). **2.** (**picture**) **f.**, encadreur *m*.

frame-up ['freimʌp], *s.* *F:* coup monté.

framework ['freimwəːk], *s.* (*cf.* **frame work** *under* FRAME[1] 4 (*a*)) **1.** (*a*) charpente *f*, bâti *m*, ossature *f*, carcasse *f*, squelette *m*; *Av:* **wing with a wooden f.**, aile ossaturée de longerons et nervures en bois; **f. of a novel**, charpente d'un roman; **it comes within the f. of U.N.O.**, cela rentre dans le cadre de l'O.N.U.; *Th:* **f. of a flat**, portant *m* de décor; (*b*) construction *f* en cloisonnage; revêtement *m* (de boisage); boisage *m* (d'un puits); système articulé (d'un pont); coffrage *m* (de travaux en béton); **open f.**, treillis *m*; (*c*) *Geol:* armature *f* (d'un volcan). **2.** fabrication *f* de cadres. **3.** *Mapm:* canevas *m*; **f. of triangles**, canevas de triangles géodésiques.

framing ['freimiŋ], *s.* **1.** (*a*) construction *f*, formation *f*, façonnement *m* (de qch.); **f. of sth. to sth.**, ajustage *m*, adaptation *f*, de qch. à qch.; (*b*) composition *f* (d'un poème, etc.); conception *f* (d'une idée; *Jur:* rédaction *f* (d'une loi); (*c*) articulation *f* (d'un mot, etc.); (*d*) invention *f*, fabrication *f* (d'une accusation, etc.); (*e*) *F:* accusation à tort; trucage *m* (d'un concours, d'un résultat); (*f*) encadrement *m* (d'un tableau, etc.); **f. strip (for parquet flooring)**, frise *f* de parquet; (*g*) *T.V:* cadrage *m*, centrage *m* (de l'image); **f. coil**, bobine *f* de cadrage, centrage; (*h*) *Min:* concentration faite sur la table dormante. **2.** = FRAME[1] 2. **metal f. (for windows)**, vitrière *f*.

franc [fræŋk], *s.* *Num:* franc *m*.

France [frɑːns], *Pr.n.* *Geog:* France *f*; **in F.**, en France; **the wines of F.**, les vins de France; *Hist:* **Free F.**, la France libre; **Fighting F.**, la France combattante.

Frances ['frɑːnsis], *Pr.n.f.* Françoise.

franchise ['fræn(t)ʃaiz], *s.* **1.** *Hist: Jur:* franchise *f*, immunité *f*, privilège *m*. **2.** (*a*) concession (octroyée à une compagnie d'utilité publique); (*b*) *Com:* **to have the f., a f., for sth. in a given territory**, avoir le droit (exclusif) de vendre qch. dans un territoire déterminé. **3.** droit *m* de cité, de bourgeoisie; droits civils; *Pol:* droit de vote; électorat *m*; **f. for all**, suffrage universel. **4.** *Ins:* minimum d'avaries au-dessous duquel l'assureur est libéré de toute responsabilité.

franchisee [fræn(t)ʃai'ziː], *s.* *Com:* concessionnaire *mf* (d'une marque de marchandise).

franchiser ['fræn(t)ʃaizər], *s.* **1.** = FRANCHISEE. **2.** = FRANCHISOR.

franchisor ['fræn(t)ʃaizər], *s.* *Com:* personne *f*, société *f*, qui donne le droit de vente à un concessionnaire.

Francien ['frænsiən], *s.* *Ling:* francien *m*.

Francis ['frɑːnsis], *Pr.n.m.* François.

Franciscan [fræn'siskən], *s.* & *a.* *Ecc:* franciscain (*m*); **F. nun**, franciscaine.

francium ['frænsiəm], *s.* *Ch:* francium *m*.

francization [frænsi'zeiʃ(ə)n], *s.* francisation *f* (d'un mot).

francize ['frænsaiz], *v.tr.* franciser.

Franco-American ['fræŋkouə'merikən], (*a*) *a.* franco-américain, -aine; *pl.* franco-américain(c)s; (*b*) *s.* Franco-Américain, -aine.

Franco-Canadian ['fræŋkoukə'neidiən], *a.* & *s.* franco-canadien, -ienne; *pl.* franco-canadiens, -iennes.

Francoism ['fræŋkouizm], *s.* *Pol:* franquisme *m*.

francolin ['fræŋkoulin], *s.* *Orn:* francolin *m*.

francolite ['fræŋkəlait], *s.* *Miner:* francolite *f*.

francomania [fræŋkou'meiniə], *s.* gallomanie *f*.

Franconia [fræŋ'kouniə], *Pr.n.* *Hist:* Franconie *f*.

Franconian [fræŋ'kouniən], *a.* & *s.* **1.** *Hist:* franconien, -ienne. **2.** *Geol:* (étage) franconien (*m*).

francophil ['fræŋkoufil], **francophile** ['fræŋkoufail], *a.* & *s.* francophile.

francophilia [fræŋkou'filiə], *s.* francophilie *f*.

francophobe ['fræŋkoufoub], *a.* & *s.* francophobe (*mf*).

francophobia [fræŋkou'foubiə], *s.* francophobie *f*, misogallisme *m*.

Franco-Prussian ['fræŋkou'prʌʃ(ə)n], *a.* franco-prussien, -ienne; **the F.-P. War**, la guerre franco-allemande (de 1870).

franc-tireur ['frɑ̃tirœːr], *s.* franc-tireur *m*, *pl.* francs-tireurs.

frangibility [frændʒi'biliti], *s.* frangibilité *f*.

frangible ['frændʒibl], *a.* frangible, cassant, fragile.

frangipane ['frændʒipein, frændʒi'pæni], *s.* **1.** *Cu:* frangipane *f*. **2.** = FRANGIPAN(N)I.

frangipan(n)i [frændʒi'pæni], *s.* **1.** *Bot:* frangipanier *m*. **2.** *Toil:* frangipane *f*. **3.** *Cu:* = FRANGIPANE.

franglais ['frɑ̃glei], *s.* franglais *m*.

frangula ['fræŋgjulə], *s.* *Pharm:* écorce *f* de bourdaine.

frangulin ['fræŋgjulin], *s.* *Ch:* franguline *f*.

Frank[1] [fræŋk], *s.* **1.** *Hist:* franc, *f*; Franque. **2.** (*in the Levant*) Franc *m*; Européen, -enne.

frank[2], *a.* **1.** (*of pers., feelings*) franc, *f.* franche; sincère; (*of speech, action*) direct, ouvert; **f. as a child**, d'une candeur d'enfant; **to be quite f.**, parler franchement, à cœur ouvert. **2.** *A:* libre; *Jur:* **f.-fee**, franc-fief *m*, *pl.* francs-fiefs; **f. tenement** = FREEHOLD. **3.** *Med:* qui ne laisse place à aucun doute diagnostique.

frank[3], *s.* *Post:* **1.** *A:* (*a*) contreseing *m*; (*b*) lettre contresignée, envoyée en franchise. **2.** marque *f* d'affranchissement.

frank[4], *v.tr.* **1.** *Post:* (*a*) *A:* contresigner (une lettre); (*b*) affranchir (une lettre, un paquet) (*esp.* à la machine). **2.** *esp. U.S:* faciliter le passage de, laisser passer (qn, qch.).

Frank[5], *Pr.n.m.* (*dim. of Francis*) François.

frank[6], *s.* *NAm: Cu: F:* saucisse *f* de Francfort.

frankenia [fræŋ'kiːniə], *s.* *Bot:* frankénie *f*.

Frankeniaceae [fræŋkiːni'eisiiː], *s.pl.* *Bot:* frankéniacées *f*.

Frankenstein ['fræŋkənstain], *s.m.* homme qui est ruiné, perdu, par ses propres œuvres (comme l'étudiant Frankenstein dans le roman de Mary Shelley); **to raise a Frankenstein's monster,** (*incorrectly*) **to raise a veritable F.**, créer un monstre dont on ne peut plus se défaire.

franker ['fræŋkər], *s.* *Post:* machine *f* à affranchir (les lettres).

Frankfurt ['fræŋkfəːt], *Pr.n.* *Geog:* Francfort *m*; *Anthr:* **F. horizontal, F. plane**, plan *m* de Francfort; *Art:* **F. black**, noir *m* d'Allemagne; *Cu:* **F. sausage**, saucisse *f* de Francfort.

Frankfurter ['fræŋkfəːtər]. **1.** *Geog:* (*a*) *a.* francfortois; (*b*) *s.* Francfortois, -oise. **2.** *s.* *Cu:* saucisse *f* de Francfort.

frankincense ['fræŋkinsens], *s.* encens *m* (mâle); oliban *m*; **f. oil**, essence *f* d'encens.

franking ['fræŋkiŋ], *s.* *Post:* affranchissement *m* (*esp.* à la machine); **f. privilege**, franchise *f* de port; **f. machine**, machine *f* à affranchir (les lettres).

Frankish ['fræŋkiʃ]. **1.** *a.* *Hist:* (*also in the Levant*) franc, *f.* franque. **2.** *A.Ling:* la langue franque, le francique.

franklin ['fræŋklin], *s.* *Hist:* franc-tenancier *m*, *pl.* francs-tenanciers.

franklinite ['fræŋklinait], *s.* *Miner:* franklinite *f*.

Franklinization [fræŋklinai'zeiʃ(ə)n], *s.* *Med:* franklinisation *f*.

frankly ['fræŋkli], *adv.* franchement, avec franchise; sincèrement; à visage découvert; ouvertement; **f. incredible**, tout bonnement incroyable; **to speak f.**, parler sans ambages, sans détours; parler franc, à cœur ouvert; **I tell you f. that. . .**, je vous dis carrément que . . .; **to confess quite f. that . . .**, avouer en toute franchise que . . .; (**quite**) **f. no!** franchement, non!

frankness ['fræŋknis], *s.* franchise *f*, sincérité *f*; ouverture *f* de cœur.

frantic ['fræntik], *a.* **1.** frénétique, forcené; fou, *f.* folle; **f. applause**, applaudissements *m* frénétiques; **f. joy**, joie délirante; **f. efforts**, efforts effrénés, prodigieux; **f. with joy, with pain**, fou de joie, de douleur; **he was in a f. rage**, il était dans une colère à tout casser; **it drives him f.**, cela le met hors de lui. **2.** *P:* **f. toothache**, mal de dents affreux; **I have a f. amount of things to do**, j'ai un tas de choses à faire; je ne sais où donner de la tête; **to spend a f. amount of money**, dépenser un argent fou.

frantically ['fræntik(ə)li], *adv.* **1.** frénétiquement, follement, avec frénésie; **to applaud f.**, applaudir avec furie, à tout rompre, à tout casser; **to rush f. around**, courir çà et là comme un affolé. **2.** *F:* affreusement, terriblement; **I'm f. busy**, (j'ai tellement à faire que) je ne sais où donner de la tête.

Franz Josef Land [frænts'dʒouziflænd], *Pr.n.* *Geog:* l'archipel *m* François Joseph.

frap [fræp], *v.tr.* (**frapped**) *Nau:* **1.** brider, genoper, aiguilleter (un cordage). **2.** *A:* ceintrer (un navire).

frapping ['fræpiŋ], *s.* **1.** (*a*) bridage *m*, bridure *f*, aiguilletage *m* (de cordages); (*b*) *A:* ceintrage *m* (d'un navire). **2.** genope *f*, bridure *f*, liure *f*.

Frasch [fræʃ], *Pr.n.* *Min:* **F. process**, procédé *m* Frasch.

Frasnian ['fræzniən], *a.* & *s.* *Geol:* frasnien (*m*).

frass [fræs], *s.* poudre *f* de bois (piqué des vers).

frat[1] [fræt], *s.* *NAm: F:* **1.** = FRATERNITY 3. **2.** membre *m* d'une association de camarades de classe, d'anciens élèves, d'étudiants.

frat[2], *v.i.* *Mil: F:* fraterniser (**with**, avec).

frater[1] ['freitər], *s.* *Hist:* réfectoire *m*.

frater[2] ['frɑːtər], *s.* **1.** *Ecc:* frère *m*. **2.** *NAm: F:* = FRAT[1] 2.

fraternal [frə'təːn(ə)l], *a.* fraternel; *Biol:* **f. twins**, jumeaux dizygotes, faux jumeaux.

fraternally [frə'təːnəli], *adv.* fraternellement.

fraternity [frə'təːniti], *s.* **1.** fraternité *f*. **2.** confrérie *f*. **3.** *NAm:* association *f* de camarades de classe, d'anciens élèves, d'étudiants.

fraternization [frætənai'zeiʃ(ə)n], *s.* fraternisation *f* (**with**, avec).

fraternize ['frætənaiz], *v.i.* fraterniser (**with**, avec).

fraternizing ['frætənaiziŋ], *s.* fraternisation *f* (**with**, avec).

fratricidal [frætri'said(ə)l], *a.* (guerre *f*, etc.) fratricide.

fratricide[1] ['frætrisaid], *s.* fratricide *mf*.

fratricide[2], *s.* (crime *m* de) fratricide *m*.

fratting ['frætiŋ], *s.* *Mil: F:* fraternisation *f* (avec l'ennemi, etc.).

fraud [frɔːd], *s.* **1.** (*a*) *Jur:* fraude *f*, dol *m*; **in f. of s.o., to the f. of s.o.**, (agissements) dans le but de frauder qn, en fraude de qn; **to obtain sth. by f.**, obtenir qch. par fraude, frauduleusement; **guilty of f.**, coupable de manœuvres frauduleuses; **frauds relating to goods**, tromperie *f* sur la marchandise; **the f. squad**, la brigade de la police chargée de la répression des fraudes; (*b*) supercherie *f*, tromperie *f*. **2.** *F:* (*a*) (*pers.*) truqueur, -euse; charlatan *m*, imposteur *m*, empileur *m*; **he's a f.**, c'est un imposteur; il est faux comme un jeton; (*b*) (*pers.*) *Hum:* blagueur *m*, farceur *m*; (*c*) attrape *f*; attrape-nigaud *m*, *pl.* attrape-nigauds; (*d*) chose *f* qui ne répond pas à l'attente; **this place is a f.**, cet endroit ne répond pas à la réputation qu'on lui a faite; **the match was a complete f.**, ç'a été un match pour rire.

fraudulence ['frɔːdjuləns], **fraudulency** ['frɔːdjulənsi], *s.* (*a*) caractère frauduleux (d'une transaction, etc.); (*b*) infidélité *f* (d'un dépositaire, etc.).

fraudulent ['frɔːdjulənt], *a.* *Jur:* frauduleux; dolosif; **f. balance sheet**, faux bilan; **f. transaction**, transaction entachée de fraude; **f. clause (in a contract)**, clause dolosive; **f. bankrupt,** banqueroutier frauduleux.

fraudulently ['frɔ:djuləntli], *adv.* frauduleusement, par fraude; **goods imported f.,** marchandises passées en fraude.

fraught [frɔ:t], *a.* **1.** *A:* (*a*) **ship f. with goods,** navire chargé de marchandises; (*b*) pourvu, muni, fourni (**with,** de). **2.** *Lit:* fertile (**with,** en); gros (**with,** de); **f. with danger,** qui entraîne des conséquences funestes. **3.** (*of thg*) désolant, pénible; (*of pers.*) désolé.

Fraunhofer ['fraunhoufər], *Pr.n. Ph:* **Fraunhofer's lines,** les raies noires du spectre; les raies de Fraunhofer.

fraxinella [fræksi'nelə], *s. Bot:* fraxinelle *f,* dictame *m.*

fray[1] [frei], *s.* **1.** (*a*) bagarre *f,* échauffourée *f,* mêlée *f;* **in the thick of the f.,** au plus épais de la mêlée; (*b*) rixe *f.* **2.** *Lit:* combat *m,* lutte *f,* conflit *m;* **who began this bloody f.?** qui a commencé cette lutte sanglante? **always ready for the f.,** toujours prêt à se battre; qui ne rêve que plaies et bosses; **to enter the f.,** *F:* descendre dans l'arène; **to return to the f.,** rentrer en lice.

fray[2], *s.* éraillure *f,* effilochure *f* (d'une étoffe, des manchettes, etc.).

fray[3]. **1.** *v.tr.* (*a*) *Ven:* (*of deer*) **to f. (its head),** frayer sa tête; (*b*) érailler, effiler, effilocher (un tissu, etc.); **the constant noise frays my nerves,** le bruit continuel me met les nerfs à vif; **my nerves are frayed,** je suis à bout de nerfs. **2.** *v.i.* (*of material*) s'érailler, s'effiler, s'effilocher, s'effranger; (*of rope*) s'étriper, foirer; **my collar is fraying,** mon col s'effrange au bord.

frayed [freid], *a.* **1.** (*of cloth, garment, etc.*) éraillé, frangé; (*of rope*) étripé, usé; **shirt f. at the cuffs,** chemise élimée aux manchettes. **2.** (*of nerves*) à vif; **tempers were getting a little f.,** on commençait à perdre patience, à se fâcher.

fraying ['freiiŋ], *s.* **1.** éraillage *m,* effilochage *m,* frangeage *m* (d'un tissu). **2.** *pl.* **frayings,** éraillures *f,* effilochures *f.*

frazil ['fræzil], *s. Geog: Can:* glaces *fpl* de fond (surtout attachées aux rives d'un cours d'eau); *Fr.C:* frasil *m.*

frazzle[1] ['fræzl]. **1.** *Dial:* (*a*) *v.tr.* érailler, effiler, effilocher (un tissu); (*b*) *v.i.* s'effiler, s'effilocher. **2.** *v.tr. F:* épuiser, éreinter (qn).

frazzle[2], *s.* **1.** état usé, éraillé, élimé (d'un vêtement, etc.). **2.** *adv.phr.* **to a f.,** complètement, entièrement; **to beat s.o. to a f.,** battre qn à plate(s) couture(s); aplatir qn; **I'm done to a f.,** je suis éreinté, à plat; **a joint cooked to a f.,** un rôti calciné.

frazzled ['fræzld], *a.* **1.** (*of shirt cuff, etc.*) éraillé, élimé. **2.** *U.S: P:* ivre, soûl.

freak[1] [fri:k], *s.* **1.** caprice *m,* fantaisie *f, F:* lubie *f;* **freaks of fashion,** caprices de la mode; **f. of fortune, of chance,** jeu *m* de la fortune, du hasard; **mere f. of humour,** simple lubie. **2.** *O:* tour *m,* farce *f,* fredaine *f,* frasque *f.* **3. f. (of nature),** (i) *Nat.Hist:* variation sportive; jeu *m* de la nature; (ii) *F:* monstre *m,* phénomène *m,* avorton *m;* **f. showman,** montreur *m* de phénomènes; **he's a f.,** (i) c'est un grotesque, un type à part, *F:* un drôle de numéro; (ii) c'est un toxicomane; (iii) c'est un homosexuel. **4.** *attrib.* **f. car, f. ship,** voiture *f,* navire *m,* de forme spéciale, de construction fantaisiste; *Mil: F:* **f. religion,** religion *f* de fantaisie (non prévue dans les règlements concernant les offices du dimanche); **f. weather,** temps inouï; **f. accident,** accident *m* invraisemblable, incroyable.

freak[2], *s.* bigarrure *f.*

freak[3], *v.tr.* barioler, bigarrer, rayer.

freak[4], **to f. out,** *v.i.* être sous l'effet du L.S.D., être du voyage.

freakish ['fri:kiʃ], *a.* **1.** capricieux, fantasque, bizarre; **f. imagination,** imagination libertine; **f. notion,** fantaisie *f.* **2.** monstrueux; phénoménal, -aux.

freakishly ['fri:kiʃli], *adv.* capricieusement, bizarrement; d'une manière fantasque, baroque.

freakishness ['fri:kiʃnis], *s.* caractère *m* fantasque, baroque, bizarre (de qch.); nature capricieuse (d'un cheval, etc.); **to do sth. out of f.,** faire qch. par caprice, pour se singulariser.

freaky ['fri:ki], *a.* = FREAKISH.

freckle[1] ['frekl], *s.* éphélide *f;* tache *f* de rousseur; *F:* tache de son; **freckles,** taches de rousseur; *Med:* lentigo *m;* **lotion to remove freckles,** lotion *f* antéphélique.

freckle[2]. **1.** *v.tr.* (*of the sun, etc.*) marquer (qn, la peau) de taches de rousseur. **2.** *v.i.* (*of the skin, of pers.*) se couvrir de taches de rousseur.

freckled ['frekld], *a.* **1.** couvert de taches de rousseur; taché de rousseur; *F:* taché de son. **2.** (*of animal's coat*) tacheté, tavelé; truité.

freckly ['frekli], *a.* = FRECKLED 1.

Fred [fred], **Freddy** ['fredi], *Pr.n.m. F:* (*dim. of Frederick*) Frédéric.

Frederica [fredə'ri:kə], *Pr.n.f.* Frédérique.

Frederic(k) ['fred(ə)rik], *Pr.n.m.* Frédéric.

free[1] [fri:], *a. & adv.*

I. *a. & adv.* **1.** (*a*) libre; **f. country, f. state,** état *m* libre; **state that has become f.,** état qui s'est affranchi; *Hist:* **the F. City of Danzig,** la Ville libre de Dantzig; **F. France,** la France libre; *Nau:* **f. port,** port franc; **f. house,** débit *m* de boissons qui est libre de vendre les produits de n'importe quelle brasserie, qui est libre de choisir ses fournisseurs; *Ind:* **f. labour,** travail *m* libre; **thought is f.,** on ne saurait entraver la pensée; **man is a f. agent,** l'homme est libre; *F:* **it's a f. country,** *U.S:* **you're f., white and (over) twenty-one,** vous avez (le droit d'agir selon) votre libre arbitre; (*b*) en liberté; (*of bird, etc.*) **to get f. from a snare,** se déprendre d'un piège; **to set s.o. f.,** mettre qn en liberté; *F:* briser les fers de qn; **to set a slave f.,** affranchir un esclave; **to set a bird f.,** laisser échapper, laisser envoler, un oiseau; **to set f. a prisoner,** délivrer, élargir, libérer, un prisonnier; *O:* **she offered to set him f.,** elle lui proposa de lui rendre sa parole; *Fin:* **to set money f.,** mobiliser de l'argent; **setting f.,** mise *f* en liberté, affranchissement *m,* élargissement *m;* mobilisation *f* (de l'argent); **to break f.,** (i) se dégager de ses liens; (ii) s'évader, s'échapper; **to wrench oneself f.,** se dégager d'un effort violent; **to shake oneself f. from s.o.'s embrace,** se dégager de l'étreinte de qn; **to be allowed to go f.,** être mis en liberté; être relâché; **why is he allowed to go f.?** pourquoi est-il en liberté? **2.** (*unoccupied*) libre; **is this table f.?** est-ce que cette table est libre? *Tg: Tp:* **f. line,** ligne dégagée; **f. time, f. moment,** temps *m,* moment *m,* libre; moment de loisir; **to have some time f.,** avoir du temps de libre; **have you any time f. during the week?** avez-vous des libertés pendant la semaine? **tomorrow is my f. day, I am f. tomorrow,** c'est demain mon jour de liberté; je suis libre demain. **3.** (*unrestricted*) (*a*) libre, sans entraves, sans empêchement; **f. love,** amour *m* libre; **f. speech,** libre parole *f;* **right of f. entry,** droit *m* de passer librement les frontières; **to have f. play, a f. hand,** avoir pleine liberté d'action, avoir ses coudées franches (**to, pour**); **to give, allow, s.o. a f. hand, a f. rein,** laisser qn libre d'agir, donner carte blanche à qn; *F:* lâcher la gourmette à qn; **as f. as the air,** libre comme l'air; **to be (entirely) f. to do sth.,** être (entièrement) libre de faire qch., être maître absolu de faire qch.; **you are f. to do so,** libre à vous de le faire; il vous est libre, permis, loisible, de le faire; **I am f. to do what I please,** je suis libre de mes mouvements; **he is not f. to act,** il a les mains liées; **to be f. to roam,** *F:* avoir la clef des champs; **fishing is f.,** la pêche est autorisée; *Geog:* **f. meander,** méandre *m* libre; (*of rock*) **f. face,** face *f* libre; (*b*) (*of touch, style, etc.*) franc, *f.* franche; sans raideur; hardi; aisé; (*of bearing, gait*) souple, désinvolte; **she's f. and graceful in all her actions,** elle fait tout avec aisance et grâce; *Th:* **his acting is f.,** il a un jeu rond; (*c*) **he grasped the cord with his f. hand,** il saisit la corde avec sa main libre; **f. end,** brin libre, dégagé, détaché (d'un cordage); *Mec.E:* **f. motion of a piece,** jeu *m* d'une pièce; **pulley mounted f., f. to move,** poulie folle; (*of part*) **to work f.,** prendre du jeu; se dégager; *Ph: Sp:* **f. fall,** chute *f* libre (d'un poids, d'un parachutiste); (*d*) **f. from, of, sth.,** débarrassé, exempt, indemne, pur, de qch.; **he's never f. from pain,** ses douleurs ne lui laissent pas un moment de répit; **to be f. from care, anxiety,** être exempt d'inquiétude, sans souci; **if I were f. from care,** si j'avais l'esprit libre; **f. from all preoccupations,** affranchi de toute préoccupation; **place f. from dust,** endroit exempt de poussière; **ship f. of water,** navire franc d'eau; **mine that is f. from water,** mine qui est débarrassée d'eau, qui est à sec; **wood f. from knots,** bois exempt de nœuds; **wound f. from any morbid germ,** plaie *f* indemne de tout germe morbide; **style f. from affectation,** style dénué de toute recherche; **district f. from labour troubles,** district non-affecté par les crises ouvrières; **f. from illusions,** exempt d'illusions; **f. from all ambition,** exempt de toute ambition; **f. from partiality,** exempt de partialité; **f. from prepossessions,** exempt, libre, de préjugés; **at last I am f. of him,** enfin je suis débarrassé de lui; **to break f. from an influence,** s'affranchir d'une influence; (*e*) franc (**of, de**); **interest f. of tax,** intérêts nets, libres d'impôt, exempts d'impôt, franco d'impôt; *Cust:* **f. of duty,** exempt de droits d'entrée; **to import sth. f. of duty,** faire entrer qch. en franchise; **f. import of . . .,** entrée *f* en franchise de . . .; **f. list,** liste *f* d'exemptions; **you are allowed to bring in half a litre f.,** il y a une tolérance d'un demi-litre; **f. zone,** zone franche; **f. food,** aliments non grevés d'impôts. **4.** (*a*) *Ch: etc:* (*of gas, acid, etc.*) (à l'état) libre, non-combiné; **f. gold,** or *m* à l'état natif; (*b*) (*of power, energy*) libre, disponible; (*c*) (*of material*) peu résistant; malléable. **5.** (*a*) (*of action, etc.*) libre, spontané, volontaire; **f. offer,** offre spontanée; **f. choice,** choix *m* arbitraire; **as a f. gift,** en pur don; **f. translation,** traduction *f* libre; *Pros:* **f. verse,** vers *m* libres; *Sch:* **f. composition,** composition *f* libre (en langue étrangère); **I am f. to confess that . . .,** je veux bien avouer que . . .; **you are very f. in blaming others,** vous êtes très enclin à blâmer les autres; vous blâmez volontiers les autres; (*b*) (*of pers.*) libéral, généreux; **to be f. in business,** être large en affaires; **to be f. with sth.,** donner libéralement de qch.; **to be f. with one's money,** ne pas regarder à l'argent; être prodigue de son argent; dépenser sans compter; être trop généreux; **to be f. with one's hands, with one's fists,** avoir la main leste; **he was very f. with his advice,** il a été très libéral de conseils; **f. horse, f. goer,** cheval franc du collier; (*c*) (*of supply, etc.*) abondant, copieux; (*d*) (*of pers., manner, speech*) franc, ouvert, sans réserve, aisé; **f. and easy,** désinvolte; sans gêne; sans façon; sans cérémonie; **to be f. and easy,** prendre ses aises; **f. and easy bearing,** tournure cavalière; **f. and easy tone,** ton dégagé; **f. and easy talk,** propos libres; **to lead a f. and easy life,** mener une vie de bohème; **f. and easy holiday,** vacances *f* libres et sans contrainte; (*e*) libre de contrainte; **to make f. with s.o.,** prendre des libertés avec qn; traiter qn sans façon(s); **to make f. with the office girls,** lutiner les employées du bureau; **to make f. with sth.,** se servir de qch. sans se gêner, sans façons; user librement de qch.; **he made very f. with my whisky,** il ne se gênait pas pour boire mon whisky; il se versait de généreuses rasades de mon whisky; **to make too f. a use of sth.,** faire abus de qch.; (*f*) (*of language*) libre, licencieux; **to be f. of speech,** être libre, peu gêné, dans ses discours; **to be rather f. in one's conversation,** tenir des propos peu convenables. **6. to be f. of a city,** avoir le droit de cité; **to make s.o. f. of sth.,** mettre qch. à la disposition de qn; **to be f. of s.o.'s house,** avoir ses entrées libres chez qn; **I was f. of the whole house,** j'étais libre d'aller partout dans la maison; *F:* **feel f.,** faites comme chez vous. **7.** (*without charge*) gratuit, franco; **f. concert,** concert gratuit; **admission f., f. admission,** entrée gratuite, gratis; admission *f* en franchise; **f. sample, trial,** échantillon, essai, gratuit; **we send you the machine for f. trial,** nous vous envoyons la machine gratuitement à l'essai; **f. demonstration in the home,** démonstration gracieuse à domicile; *Th: etc:* **f. ticket,** billet *m* de faveur; **the f. list is suspended,** pas de billets de faveur; **no f. seats,** toutes les places sont payantes; **fruit f. to all comers,** fruits *m* à la discrétion des promeneurs; *Publ:* **f. copy,** spécimen *m;* **f. (allowance of) luggage,** bagage(s) *m* en franchise; *Com: etc:* **delivery f.,** livré franco *inv;* **post f.,** franco de port; **f. on rail,** franco gare; **f. alongside ship, f. at quay, on wharf,** franco (à) quai; **f. over side,** franco allège; **f. on board,** franco à bord; sur pont. **8.** *adv.* (*a*) franco, gratuitement; **catalogue sent f. on request,** catalogue franco sur demande; **the gallery is open f. on Saturdays,** l'entrée du musée est gratuite le samedi; (*b*) *Nau:* **running f.,** le largue; **vessel running f.,** navire *m* courant largue; **to sail f.,** avoir du largue, naviguer vent largue, naviguer à l'allure du largue; (*c*) *adv.phrs. F:* **for f., f., gratis and for nothing,** gratis; **to get sth. for f.,** obtenir qch. gratis, pour rien; (*d*) (*followed by a present participle*) = FREELY; **f. flowing,** qui coule abondamment, copieusement; **f. flowering,** qui fleurit abondamment; (*of plant, shrub*) **f. growing,** vigoureux; **f. cutting metal,** métal qui se coupe facilement; **f. working,** (terre) facile à travailler.

II. -free (*with noun prefixed*); **knot-f. timber,** bois sans, exempt de, nœuds; **accident-f. driving record,** passé *m* de chauffeur vierge d'accidents; **acid-f. paper,** papier exempt d'acide.

free[2], *v.* (**freed; freeing**) **1.** *v.tr.* (*a*) affranchir (un peuple, un esclave, etc.); libérer, délivrer, élargir (un prisonnier, etc.); **to f. s.o. from a life of servitude,** affranchir qn d'une vie de servitude; **mind freed from all influence,** esprit émancipé de toute influence; **to f. oneself from s.o.'s grasp,** se dégager des mains de qn, de l'étreinte de qn; **I couldn't f. my foot,** je ne pouvais pas dégager mon pied; **to f. s.o. from a burden,** délivrer qn d'un fardeau; **to f. s.o. from an obligation,** libérer, exempter, qn d'une obligation; **to f. oneself from one's commitments,** se délier de tous ses engagements; **to f. one's estate of debt,** purger ses terres de dettes; (*b*) débarrasser (**from, of, de**); dégager (un sentier, etc.); déblayer (le terrain); **to f. a room (from encumbrance),** désencombrer une pièce; (*c*) *Mec.E: etc:* dégager (une pièce); donner du jeu à (une pièce); *I.C.E:* **valve-freeing tool,** outil *m* pour dégager les soupapes; (*d*) décolmater, désobstruer (un filtre, un tuyau engorgé); **to f. a pump,** dégorger, franchir, une pompe; (*e*) **to f. a property (from mortgage),** déshypothéquer, dégrever, une propriété; (*f*) *Adm:* (i) mettre (des denrées réglementées) en vente libre; détaxer (des denrées taxées). **2.** *v.i. Nau:* (*of wind*) fraîchir.

free-and-easiness ['fri:ənd'i:zinis], *s.* désinvolture *f*, laisser-aller *m*; sans-façon *m*, sans-gêne *m*; débraillé *m*.

free-and-easy ['fri:ənd'i:zi]. **1.** *a.* (réunion, etc.) sans cérémonie. **2.** *s. F: O:* soirée amicale (passée à chanter, fumer, boire, etc.).

freebee, freebie ['fri:bi], *s. U.S: P:* (i) repas gratuit; (ii) billet *m* de faveur.

freeboard ['fri:bɔ:d], *s.* **1.** *Nau:* (franc-)bord *m*, *pl.* (francs-)bords; accastillage *m*; **vessel of high f.,** navire haut sur l'eau; **adequate f.,** battant *m*; **freshwater f.,** franc-bord en eau douce; **f. depth,** creux *m* de franc-bord; **f. deck,** (i) pont *m* de franc-bord; (ii) *Navy:* plage *f.* **2.** *NAm: Aut:* hauteur *f* du châssis au-dessus du sol.

freebooter ['fri:bu:tər], *s.* **1.** *Hist:* flibustier *m*. **2.** *F:* maraudeur *m*, pillard *m*.

freebooting ['fri:bu:tiŋ], *s.* **1.** *Hist:* flibuste *f.* **2.** *F:* maraude *f*; pillage *m*.

freeborn ['fri:bɔ:n], *a.* libre de naissance; né libre.

free diver ['fri:'daivər], *s.* plongeur, -euse, autonome.

free diving ['fri:'daiviŋ], *s.* plongée sous-marine autonome.

freedman, *pl.* **-men** ['fri:dmən], *s.m. Hist:* affranchi.

freedom ['fri:dəm], *s.* **1.** (*a*) liberté *f*, indépendance *f* (d'une personne, d'un état, etc.); **to give a slave his f.,** rendre la liberté à, affranchir, un esclave; **animals in f.,** animaux *m* en liberté; (*b*) liberté d'action; liberté d'agir, de penser; **f. of speech,** le franc-parler, la liberté d'expression; **f. of religion,** liberté religieuse; **f. to do sth.,** liberté de faire qch. **2.** (*a*) franchise *f*, aisance *f*, familiarité *f* (d'une conversation, du style, etc.); **to speak with f.,** parler franchement, sans gêne; (*b*) hardiesse *f*; sans-gêne *m*. **3.** (*of action, movement, etc.*) facilité *f*, liberté, souplesse *f*. **4.** (*a*) exemption *f*, immunité *f*, franchise; **f. from tax,** exemption, immunité, d'impôts; **f. from dust,** absence *f* de poussière; **f. (of members of Parliament, etc.) from arrest,** immunité (parlementaire); **f. from hunger campaign,** campagne *f* contre la faim; (*b*) **f. of a city,** (i) droit *m* de cité, de bourgeoisie; (ii) citoyenneté *f* d'honneur d'une ville; **to receive the f. of a town,** être nommé citoyen, -enne, honoraire, d'honneur, d'une ville; **f. of a livery company,** maîtrise *f* d'une Corporation. **5.** (*a*) jouissance *f*, libre usage *m* (de qch.); **the f. of the seas,** la liberté de la haute mer; **to give s.o. the f. of one's library,** mettre sa bibliothèque à la disposition de qn; (*b*) entrée *f* (libre) (dans un théâtre, etc.).

Freedomites ['fri:dəmaits], *s.pl. Can:* secte *f* des Doukhobors.

free drop[1] ['fri:'drɔp], *s. Av.* (*a*) largage *m*; (*b*) vivres, etc. largués d'un avion.

free drop[2], *v.tr.* (**free-dropped**) *Av:* larguer (qch.) d'un avion.

free-for-all ['fri:fər'ɔ:l], *a.* & *s. F:* **f.-f.-a. (race, competition),** concours auquel tout le monde peut participer; **f.-f.-a. (fight),** rixe *f*, bagarre *f*, mêlée *f*.

freehand ['fri:hænd], *s.* (*usu. attrib.*) & *adv.* **f. (drawing),** dessin *m* à main levée, à vue; **drawn (by) f.,** dessiné à main levée.

freehanded ['fri:'hændid], *a.* généreux; libéral, -aux.

freehandedness [fri:'hændidnis], *s.* générosité *f*; libéralité *f*.

freehearted ['fri:'hɑ:tid], *a.* **1.** (*of pers.*) (*a*) franc, *f.* franche; sincère; (*b*) jovial, -aux; gai, enjoué; (*c*) généreux; libéral, -aux. **2.** spontané.

freehold ['fri:hould]. **1.** *a.* (*a*) *Hist:* tenu en franc-alleu; allodial, -aux; (*b*) tenu en propriété perpétuelle et libre. **2.** *s.* (*a*) *Hist:* franc-alleu *m*, franc-fief *m*, *pl.* francs-alleux, francs-fiefs; (*b*) propriété foncière perpétuelle et libre.

freeholder ['fri:houldər], *s.* **1.** *Hist:* franc-tenancier *m*, *pl.* francs-tenanciers. **2.** propriétaire foncier (à perpétuité).

freeing ['fri:iŋ], *s.* **1.** libération *f*, délivrance *f* (d'un prisonnier); affranchissement *m* (d'un esclave); exemption *f* (de qn d'un impôt). **2.** dégagement *m* (d'un cordage); débarrassement *m* (d'un passage, etc.); dégorgement *m* (d'un tuyau, etc.).

freelance[1] ['fri:lɑ:ns]. **1.** *s.* (*a*) *Hist:* soldat *m* mercenaire; (*b*) (i) journaliste indépendant(e); pigiste *mf*; (ii) politicien, représentant, etc., indépendant. **2.** *a.* (journaliste, etc.) indépendant; *Journ:* **f. work,** travail *m* à la pige.

freelance[2], *v.i.* être un journaliste, acteur, etc., indépendant, sans contrat; *Journ:* travailler à la pige.

freelancer ['fri:lɑ:nsər], *s.* = FREELANCE[1] 1(*b*).

free-liver ['fri:'livər], *s.* viveur *m*.

free-living ['fri:'liviŋ], *a.* **1.** (*of pers.*) intempérant. **2.** *Nat.Hist:* (animal, etc.) indépendant.

freeload ['fri:loud], *v.i. NAm: F:* écornifler, faire le parasite.

freeloader [fri:'loudər], *s. NAm: F:* pique-assiette *mf inv*; écornifleur, -euse.

freely ['fri:li], *adv.* **1.** (donner, faire, qch.) librement, volontairement, spontanément, aisément; **to give f. to s.o.,** faire des libéralités à qn. **2.** (parler, agir, etc.) franchement, sans contrainte, en toute liberté; **to speak perfectly f. to s.o.,** parler à qn en toute confiance, à cœur ouvert. **3.** (*a*) (couler, etc.) abondamment, copieusement; (*b*) **to see that a mechanism works f.,** s'assurer du bon fonctionnement d'un mécanisme.

freeman, *pl.* **-men** ['fri:mən], *s.m.* **1.** homme libre. **2.** (i) citoyen; (ii) citoyen d'honneur. **3.** maître (d'une Corporation).

freemartin ['fri:mɑ:tin], *s. Husb:* vache-bœuf *f*, *pl.* vaches-bœufs.

freemason ['fri:meisn], *s.m.* franc-maçon, *pl.* francs-maçons.

freemasonry ['fri:meisnri], *s.* franc-maçonnerie *f*; *F:* **the f. of writers,** la camaraderie des écrivains.

free-range ['fri:'reindʒ], *a.* **f.-r. eggs, chicken,** œufs *m*, poulet *m*, de ferme.

free rider ['fri:'raidər], *s.* (ouvrier, -ière) non-syndiqué(e) (qui profite des avantages gagnés par les syndicats).

freesia ['fri:ziə], *s. Bot:* freesia *m*, freesie *f*.

free-spoken ['fri:'spouk(ə)n], *a.* (*of pers.*) franc, *f.* franche; qui parle ouvertement; qui a son franc-parler.

free-spokenness ['fri:'spoukənnis], *s.* franchise *f*; franc-parler *m*.

freestanding ['fri:'stændiŋ], *a.* (mur, etc.) auto-supportant, *pl.* auto-supportants; *Arch:* **f. column,** colonne isolée.

freestone ['fri:stoun], *s.* **1.** pierre *f* de taille; grès *m* à bâtir. **2.** *Hort:* **f. (peach),** pêche *f* dont la chair n'adhère pas au noyau.

freestyle ['fri:stail], *s. Swim:* nage *f* libre; **the 200 metres f.,** le 200 mètres nage libre.

freethinker ['fri:θiŋkər], *s.* libre penseur, -euse; esprit fort.

freethinking[1] ['fri:'θiŋkiŋ], *a.* de libre penseur.

freethinking[2], **freethought** ['fri:'θɔ:t], *s.* libre pensée *f*.

free trade ['fri:'treid], *s.* libre-échange *m*; **f.-t. policy,** politique *f* antiprotection(n)iste, libre-échangiste (*pl.* libre-échangistes).

free trader ['fri:'treidər], *s.* **1.** libre-échangiste *mf*, *pl.* libre-échangistes; antiprotection(n)iste *mf.* **2.** *U.S:* commerçant indépendant des consortiums.

freeway ['fri:wei], *s.* (*a*) route *f* à grande circulation avec interdiction de stationner; (*b*) *NAm:* autoroute *f*.

free(-)wheel[1] ['fri:'(h)wi:l], *s. Cy: Aut:* roue *f* libre; **f. bicycle,** bicyclette *f* à roue libre.

free(-)wheel[2], *v.i.* **1.** (*a*) *Cy:* faire roue libre; **to f. down a hill,** descendre une côte en roue libre; (*b*) *Aut:* marcher, rouler, en roue libre; (*c*) *Av:* **freewheeling airscrew,** hélice tournant en moulinet. **2.** (*of pers.*) aller son petit bonhomme de chemin; ne pas se fouler la rate; (*of government, etc.*) suivre une politique de laisser-faire.

free-wheeling ['fri:'(h)wi:liŋ], *a.* **1.** (cycliste) qui fait roue libre. **2.** *F:* (représentant, etc.) indépendant.

freewill [fri:wil], *s.* libre arbitre *m*; franc arbitre; **of one's own f.,** de (son) propre gré; de (son) plein gré; de bonne volonté; *attrib.* **f. offering,** don gratuit, volontaire; don fait de plein gré.

freewoman, *pl.* **-women** ['fri:wumən, -wimin], *s.f.* (i) citoyenne; (ii) citoyenne d'honneur.

freeze[1] [fri:z], *s.* **1.** gel *m*, gelée *f*; **the big winter freezes,** les grandes gelées d'hiver. **2. price and wage f.,** blocage *m* des prix et des salaires. **3.** *Cmptr:* **f. mode,** (i) état *m* d'interruption; (ii) état figé.

freeze[2], *v.* (**froze** [frouz]; **frozen** [frouzn])

I. *v.i.* **1.** *impers.* **it's freezing,** il gèle; **it's freezing hard,** il gèle ferme, à pierre fendre. **2.** (*of liquid*) (se) geler; se congeler; prendre; **the river is, has, frozen,** la rivière est prise; **the river has frozen (up) again,** la rivière a repris; **the radiator froze,** le radiateur a gelé; **the oil is freezing,** l'huile se fige; **oil that freezes easily,** huile gélive; *F:* **till Hell freezes (over),** jusqu'à la Saint-Glinglin; *F:* **I'm freezing,** j'ai très froid, je gèle; **the wheels were frozen fast in the mud,** les roues étaient prises dans la boue glacée; **his fingers froze on to his rifle,** ses doigts collaient à son fusil; *F:* **to f. on to s.o.,** (i) se coller, se cramponner, à qn; (ii) s'attacher à qn; **the smile froze on his lips,** le sourire se figea sur ses lèvres; **at this request his face froze,** à cette demande son visage se ferma. **3. to f. to death,** mourir de froid; périr gelé. **4.** (*of pers.*) (i) rester figé, cloué, sur place; se figer; (ii) se raidir; se guinder; **f.!** ne bougez pas!

II. *v.tr.* **1.** geler, congeler (qch.); congeler, frigorifier (la viande); **to f. the blood (in one's veins),** glacer le sang, le cœur; **to be frozen to death,** périr gelé; mourir de froid. **2. to f. credits, currencies,** geler des crédits, des devises; **to f. wages,** bloquer les salaires; **the skilled operatives in the heavy industries are frozen,** les ouvriers spécialisés des industries lourdes ont été figés. **3.** *Med:* insensibiliser (les gencives, etc.) avec une anesthésie locale.

III. (*compound verbs*) **1. freeze in,** *v.tr.* **the vessel was frozen in,** le vaisseau était retenu, bloqué, pris, par les glaces, dans les glaces.

2. freeze out, *v.tr.* (*a*) évincer (qn); supplanter (un rival); étrangler (une maison de commerce qui vous fait concurrence); (*b*) mettre (qn) en quarantaine; boycotter (qn).

3. freeze over, (*a*) *v.i.* **the pond has, is, frozen over,** l'étang a, est, gelé d'un bout à l'autre; (*b*) *v.tr.* **to f. over a liquid,** couvrir un liquide de glace.

4. freeze up, *v.i.* **the river has frozen up,** la rivière est prise; **the radiator froze up,** le radiateur a gelé.

freeze-dry ['fri:z'drai], *v.tr.* lyophiliser (un sérum, etc.).

freeze-drying ['fri:z'draiiŋ], *s.* lyophilisation *f*.

freeze-out ['fri:zaut], *s. NAm:* **1.** *Cards:* poker *m* de famille. **2.** boycottage *m* (de qn).

freezer ['fri:zər], *s.* **1.** (appareil) congélateur (*m*); sorbetière *f.* **2. f. (compartment),** compartiment *m* de congélation; congélateur; *F:* freezer *m* (d'un réfrigérateur). **3.** réfrigérateur; **f. trawler,** chalutier *m* frigorifique.

freeze-up ['fri:zʌp], *s.* **1.** gelée *f*; gel *m*; **the f.-up was early this winter,** la gelée est arrivée tôt cet hiver. **2.** *Aut: F:* congélation *f* (du radiateur).

freezing[1] ['fri:ziŋ], *a.* réfrigérant, congelant; (temps, vent, etc.) glaçant; glacial, -als; **f. mixture,** mélange réfrigérant, mixture *f* frigorifique; *Fig:* **f. politeness,** politesse glacée, glaciale.

freezing[2], *s.* **1.** (*becoming frozen*) congélation *f*, prise *f* (d'une rivière, etc.); gel *m*; *Ph:* **f. point,** point *m* de congélation; point de froid; **f. point of water,** température *f* de la glace fondante; **the thermometer is at f. point,** le thermomètre est à glace, (*if centigrade*) à zéro. **2.** (*making frozen*) (*a*) réfrigération *f* (d'un liquide, etc.); congélation, frigorification *f* (de la viande, etc.); **f. apparatus,** (i) appareil *m* frigorifique; (ii) congélateur *m*; (iii) sorbetière *f*; **f. chamber,** chambre *f* de congélation; **f. compartment (of refrigerator),** compartiment *m* de congélation; congélateur *m*; *F:* freezer *m*; **f. mixture,** mélange réfrigérant, mixture *f* frigorifique; *Austr:* & *N.Z:* **f. works,** abattoir *m* et entrepôt *m* frigorifique; usine *f* frigorifique; (*b*) *Min:* **f. process,** procédé *m* de creusement de tunnel dans les sols friables par congélation préalable du sol. **3.** blocage *m* (des salaires, d'une dette, etc.).

freezingly ['fri:ziŋli], *adv.* d'un ton, d'un air, glacé, glacial.

Freiburg ['fraibɔ:g], *Pr.n. Geog:* Fribourg

freight[1] [freit], *s.* **1.** (*a*) fret *m*; (*b*) transport *m* (de marchandises) par voie d'eau, *NAm:* par voie de terre; **air f.,** transport par air; **sent by air f.,** envoyé par air, par avion. **2.** (*a*) fret, cargaison *f*, chargement *m* (d'un navire); **to take in f.,** prendre du fret; **dead f.,** (i) faux fret; (ii) dédit *m* pour défaut de chargement; **home f., onward f.,** fret de retour, de sortie; (*b*) marchandises (transportées); **f. train,** train *m* de marchandises; convoi *m* à marchandises; **f. engine,** locomotive *f* de train de marchandises; *Av:* **f. plane,** avion-cargo *m*, *pl.* avions-cargos; cargo aérien; *NAm:* **f. car,** wagon *m* à, de, marchandises; wagon à caisse; **f. depot,** gare *f* de marchandises; **f. elevator,** monte-charge *m inv.* **3.** fret; prix *m* de louage d'un bâtiment, du transport de marchandises; **f. by weight,** fret au poids; **amount of f. on a package,** montant *m* du fret afférent à un colis; **to pay the f.,** payer le fret.

freight[2], *v.tr.* **1.** (af)fréter (un navire). **2. to f. (out) a ship,** donner un navire à fret. **3.** charger (un vaisseau). **4.** (*a*) transporter, (*b*) faire transporter, envoyer (des marchandises) (i) par voie d'eau, (ii) par avion, (iii) *NAm:* par voie de terre.

freightage ['freitidʒ], *s.* **1.** (af)frètement *m* (d'un vaisseau). **2.** fret *m*, cargaison *f*. **3.** transport *m* des marchandises (i) par voie d'eau, (ii) par avion, (iii) *NAm:* par voie de terre.

freighter ['freitər], *s.* **1.** affréteur *m* (d'un vaisseau). **2.** *NAm:* (*a*) consignateur, -trice (de marchandises pour transport par voie de terre); (*b*) conducteur *m* de train de marchandises. **3.** entrepreneur *m* de transports; exportateur *m*. **4.** (*a*) cargo *m*; vapeur *m* de charge, navire *m* de charge, (*b*) *Rail: NAm:* wagon *m* de marchandises; (*c*) *Av:* avion-cargo *m*, *pl.* avions-cargos; cargo aérien.

freighting ['freitiŋ], *s.* = FREIGHTAGE 1, 3.

freightliner ['freitlainər], *s.* train *m* de marchandises en conteneurs.

fremitus ['fremitəs], *s. Med:* tremissement *m*; **hydatic f.,** frôlement *m* hydatique.

French [fren(t)ʃ], *a. & s.* I. *a.* 1. (*a*) français; **the F. character,** le caractère français; **F. king,** roi *m* de France; **F. emperor,** empereur *m* des Français; **the F. Ambassador,** l'ambassadeur de France; **the F. delegate,** le délégué de la France; **of F. make,** de fabrication française; **the F. form of "London" is "Londres",** "London" francisé donne "Londres"; *Nau:* **the F. line,** la Compagnie générale transatlantique; (*b*) (*of dish, fashion, etc.*) à la française; *Cu:* **F. dressing,** vinaigrette *f*; *Const:* **F. window,** porte-fenêtre *f*, *pl.* portes-fenêtres; *NAm:* **F. door,** porte vitrée (entre deux pièces); *Furn: NAm:* **F. bed,** lit *m* en portefeuille; **F. polish,** vernis *m* au tampon, à l'alcool; **F. polisher,** vernisseur *m* au tampon; **F. polishing,** vernissage *m* au tampon; *P:* **F. letter,** capote anglaise; (*c*) *Sch:* **F. master, mistress,** professeur *m* de français; **F. lesson,** leçon *f* de français; (*d*) *Pej: O:* (*of farce, novel, etc.*) licencieux. 2. **F. Canadian, Canadian F.,** *Can:* **French,** canadien français; du Canada français; **F. Canada,** le Canada français. II. *s.* 1. le français; la langue française; **to speak F.,** parler français; **to learn, know, F.,** apprendre, connaître, le français; **say it in F.,** dites-le en français; **he's a good F. speaker,** il parle bien français; *P:* **pardon my F.,** excusez la grossièreté de mon langage. 2. (*a*) *pl.* **the F.,** les Français; (*b*) **F. Canadian,** Canadien, -ienne, français(e), francophone; *Ling:* **F. Canadian, Canadian F.,** le français canadien, du Canada.

Frenchie ['fren(t)ʃi], *s.m. F: Pej:* Français.

Frenchified ['fren(t)ʃifaid], *a.* francisé, à la française.

Frenchify ['fren(t)ʃifai]. 1. *v.tr.* franciser (son style, etc.). 2. *v.i.* se franciser.

Frenchman, *pl.* **-men** ['fren(t)ʃmən], *s.* 1. Français *m.* 2. *Nau: O:* vaisseau français. 3. *Orn:* perdrix *f* rouge.

French-polish ['fren(t)ʃ'pɔliʃ], *v.tr.* vernir (un meuble, etc.) au tampon; *F:* tamponner (un meuble); **F.-polished walnut,** noyer verni.

French-speaking ['fren(t)ʃ'spi:kiŋ], *a.* francophone.

Frenchwoman, *pl.* **-women** ['fren(t)ʃwumən, -wimin], *s.f.* Française.

Frenchy ['fren(t)ʃi]. *F: Pej:* 1. *a.* à la française. 2. *s.* Français *m.*

frenetic [frə'netik], *a.* (*of pers., action, etc.*) frénétique; fou, *f.* folle.

frenetically [frə'netik(ə)li], *adv.* frénétiquement.

frenulum, *pl.* **-a** ['frenjuləm, -ə], *s. Anat:* frein *m*, filet *m* (de la langue, etc.); *Ent:* frein.

frenum, *pl.* **-a** ['fri:nəm, -ə], *s. Anat:* frein *m*, filet *m* (de la langue, etc.).

frenzied ['frenzid], *a.* (*a*) (*of pers.*) affolé, forcené; (*b*) (*of rage, etc.*) fou, *f.* folle; (*of joy, applause, etc.*) frénétique, délirant.

frenziedly ['frenzidli], *adv.* frénétiquement, follement.

frenzy ['frenzi], *s.* 1. frénésie *f*, folie *f* (du désespoir, de la colère); **f. of joy,** transport *m* de joie; **poetic f.,** fureur *f* poétique, ivresse *f* poétique. 2. *Med:* délire *m* (d'un accès de folie); **to fall into a f.,** avoir le délire, un accès de délire.

Freon ['friɔn], *s. R.t.m: Ch:* Fréon *m.*

frequence ['fri:kwəns], *s.* = FREQUENCY 1.

frequency ['fri:kwənsi], *s.* 1. (*of letters, visits, etc.*) fréquence *f*, répétition *f*; **f. of the pulse,** fréquence du pouls; *Mth:* **f. of errors,** répartition *f* des erreurs. 2. (*a*) *Ph: etc:* fréquence (d'un mouvement ondulatoire); *Ac:* **bass, base, frequencies,** basses fréquences; *F:* **I'm not on your f.,** je ne suis pas sur la même longueur d'onde que vous; (*b*) *El: Elcs:* **high f., low f.,** haute, basse, fréquence; **ultra-high f.,** fréquence ultra-haute, ultra-haute fréquence; **very high f.,** très haute fréquence; **intermediate f., medium f.,** fréquence intermédiaire, moyenne; **centre f., mid-band f.,** fréquence centrale; **beat f.,** fréquence de battement, de récurrence; **carrier f.,** fréquence porteuse, de courant porteur; **common f.,** fréquence commune; **effective f.,** fréquence utile; **filter f.,** fréquence passante; **fundamental f.,** fréquence fondamentale; **natural f.,** fréquence propre, naturelle; **operating f.,** fréquence de fonctionnement; **recurrence f., repetition f.,** fréquence de récurrence, de répétition (des impulsions); **spot f.,** fréquence unique, ponctuelle; **threshold f., top f.,** fréquence limite; (*c*) *T.V: Rad:* **radio f.,** fréquence radio(électrique); **line f.,** fréquence de ligne; **field f., vertical f.,** fréquence d'exploration; **frame f.,** fréquence de trame; **picture f., vision f.,** fréquence d'image; **scanning f., sweep f.,** fréquence de balayage; **video f.,** fréquence vidéo; vidéofréquence *f*; (*d*) *attrib.* **f. allotment,** répartition *f* des fréquences; **f. band,** bande *f* de fréquences; **f. block,** lot *m* de fréquences; **f. change,** changement *m* de fréquence; **f. changer, f. converter,** changeur *m*, convertisseur *m*, de fréquence; **f. clearing,** libération *f* de fréquences; **f. complement,** jeu *m* de fréquences; **f. controller,** contrôleur *m* de fréquence; **f. curve,** graphique *m* des fréquences; **f. distribution,** distribution *f* des fréquences; **f. diversity,** diversité *f* de, en, fréquence; **f. divider, f. multiplier,** diviseur *m*, multiplicateur *m*, de fréquence; **f. drift,** dérive *f*, glissement *m*, de fréquence; **f. indicator,** indicateur *m* de fréquences; **f. meter,** fréquencemètre *m*; **f. modulation,** modulation *f* de fréquence; **f. range,** gamme *f* de fréquences; **f. rate,** taux *m* de fréquence; **f. shift,** déplacement *m* de fréquence; **f. spacing,** intervalle *m* de fréquence; **f. spectrum,** spectre *m* de fréquence; **f. standard,** étalon *m*, standard *m*, de fréquence; **f. table,** table *f* des fréquences.

frequent[1] ['fri:kwənt], *a.* 1. (*a*) très répandu; nombreux, abondant; **plant that is very f. in the south of England,** plante très répandue dans le sud de l'Angleterre; **it's quite a f. practice,** c'est une coutume assez répandue; (*b*) *Med:* **f. pulse,** pouls *m* rapide. 2. (*of visits, letters, etc.*) fréquent; qui arrive souvent; **f. attendance on s.o.,** assiduité *f* auprès de qn; **f. visits to the theatre,** fréquentation du théâtre. 3. (*of visitor*) familier; (*of customer, etc.*) habituel.

frequent[2] [fri'kwent], *v.tr.* 1. fréquenter, hanter, courir (les théâtres, les cafés, etc.); **a much frequented road,** une route très passante; **ill-frequented street,** rue mal fréquentée; **to f. s.o.,** fréquenter qn; fréquenter avec, chez, qn. 2. **to f. the sacraments,** fréquenter les sacrements.

frequentation [fri:kwen'teiʃ(ə)n], *s.* fréquentation *f* (de qn, d'un endroit, des sacrements, etc.).

frequentative [fri'kwentətiv], *a. & s. Gram:* (verbe) fréquentatif (*m*); verbe itératif.

frequenter [fri'kwentər], *s.* habitué *m*, familier *m* (d'une maison, etc.); *Pej: F:* pilier *m* (de cabaret, etc.); **he is an assiduous f. of political circles,** il est très répandu dans les milieux politiques.

frequently ['fri:kwəntli], *adv.* fréquemment, souvent.

fresco[1], *pl.* **-o(e)s** ['freskou(z)], *s. Art:* 1. fresque *f*; **to paint in f.,** peindre à fresque; **f. painting,** (peinture *f* à) fresque; **f. painter,** (peintre *m*) fresquiste. 2. (peinture à) fresque; **the frescoes of Raphael,** les fresques de Raphaël.

fresco[2], *v.tr. Art:* peindre (une paroi) à fresque.

fresh [freʃ], *a., adv., & s.* I. *a.* 1. (*a*) nouveau, -el, -elle; **to meet f. faces,** rencontrer de nouveaux visages; **f. idea,** idée originale; **f. paragraph,** nouveau paragraphe; **the authorities will have to set f. papers,** il sera nécessaire de faire recommencer l'examen; **that blade is blunt; take a f. one,** cette lame est émoussée; prenez-en une neuve; **f. horses,** (i) chevaux frais; (ii) *A:* chevaux de relais; **to put f. courage into s.o.,** ranimer le courage de qn; **to let f. air into a room,** renouveler l'air d'une pièce; **he has had a f. attack of gout,** la goutte l'a repris; **f. outbreak of fire, of an epidemic,** recrudescence *f* du feu, d'une épidémie; **a f. day is dawning,** le jour renaît; (*b*) (*of news, traces, etc.*) frais, *f.* fraîche; récent; **it is still f. in my memory,** je l'ai encore frais à la mémoire; j'en ai le souvenir tout frais; **f. from London,** nouvellement arrivé de Londres; **she is f. from the country,** c'est une nouvelle débarquée à Londres; **a young man f. from college,** un jeune homme frais émoulu de l'université; **the bread was f. from the oven,** le pain sortait du four; **f. from the wash,** qui revient de la lessive, (linge) blanc de lessive. 2. (*of pers.*) (*a*) inexpérimenté, novice; **to be a f. hand at sth.,** être novice dans qch.; (*b*) *P:* (*of girl*) pucelle. 3. (*a*) **f. or tinned peas,** pois frais ou en boîte; **f. or salt pork,** porc frais ou salé; **f. vegetables,** légumes verts; (*b*) (air) frais, pur; **in the f. air,** au grand air, en plein air; **to enjoy the f. air,** prendre l'air, le frais; *F:* **f.-air fiend,** maniaque *mf*, fanatique *mf*, du plein air; **f. water,** (i) (*newly drawn*) eau fraîche; (ii) (*not salt*) eau douce; (*c*) (*colours, garments, etc.*) frais. 4. (*a*) (teint) frais, fleuri; **as f. as a daisy, as a rose, as paint,** frais comme une rose; (*b*) (*of pers.*) vigoureux, alerte; dispos; (*of horse, etc.*) fougueux, animé; **f. troops,** troupes fraîches; **the ponies are very f. today,** les poneys sont très en l'air aujourd'hui; (*c*) *F:* outrecuidant, effronté; **don't (you) get f.!** ne faites pas le malin! **to get f. with a girl,** prendre des libertés avec, lutiner, une jeune fille. 5. *Nau:* **f. breeze,** bonne brise; brise fraîche; **it blows, the wind's, f.,** il vente frais. 6. *F:* (*of pers.*) éméché, pompette; un peu gris; gai. 7. *Husb:* (vache) en train de donner du lait après le vêlage. II. *adv.* fraîchement, nouvellement, récemment (arrivé, peint, etc.); **f.-cut flowers,** fleurs nouvellement cueillies; **f.-killed poultry,** volaille fraîchement tuée, du jour; **f.-shaven,** rasé de frais. III. *s.* 1. fraîcheur *f* (du matin, etc.); fraîche *f* (du soir). 2. (*a*) crue *f*; (*b*) descente *f* d'eau (de fonte des neiges, etc.); sous-berme *f*, *pl.* sous-bermes.

fresh-coloured ['freʃkʌləd], *a.* (visage) au teint frais; (visage) poupin; (teint) frais.

fresh-complexioned ['freʃkəm'plekʃ(ə)nd], *a.* au teint frais.

freshen ['freʃ(ə)n]. 1. *v.i.* (*a*) (*of temperature*) (se) rafraîchir; (*b*) (*of wind, weather*) fraîchir; (*c*) (*of salt water*) se dessaler; (*d*) (*of pers.*) **to f. (up),** faire un bout de toilette; (*e*) *Husb:* (*of cow*) commencer à donner du lait. 2. *v.tr.* (*a*) rafraîchir (l'air, un tableau, la mémoire, etc.); **sleep freshens the complexion,** le sommeil repose le teint; **to f. up paint,** (r)aviver la couleur; *F:* **to f. s.o. up,** (i) ragaillardir qn; (ii) requinquer qn; (*b*) dessaler (l'eau de mer, etc.); (*c*) *Nau:* rafraîchir (une amarre, les remorques).

freshener ['freʃ(ə)nər], *s.* chose *f* qui rafraîchit, qui ravive, qui remet en train; *esp.* petit verre (qui ravigote); **to take the dog for a f.,** faire prendre l'air au chien.

freshening ['freʃ(ə)niŋ], *s.* 1. rafraîchissement *m* (de l'atmosphère, etc.); ravivage *m* (d'une couleur, etc.). 2. dessalure *f*, dessalement *m* (de l'eau de mer).

fresher ['freʃər], *s. F:* = FRESHMAN.

freshet ['freʃit], *s.* 1. courant *m* d'eau douce (dans la mer); queue *f* (d'un fleuve). 2. crue *f*, inondation *f*, avalaison *f*.

freshly ['freʃli], *adv.* 1. (*with p.p. only*) fraîchement, de frais, nouvellement, récemment; **f. gathered peaches,** des pêches fraîches cueillies. 2. vigoureusement, vivement. 3. avec une apparence, une odeur, fraîche.

freshman, *pl.* **-men** ['freʃmən], *s.m. & f.* (*at a university*) étudiant, -ante, de première année; *F:* bizut(h) *m.*

freshness ['freʃnis], *s.* 1. caractère récent (d'un événement). 2. (*a*) fraîcheur *f* (de l'air, d'une fleur, d'un visage, d'une impression, etc.); **the f. of youth,** la fraîcheur, l'éclat *m*, de la jeunesse; (*of young woman*) la beauté du diable; (*b*) fraîcheur, froideur *f* (du vent, etc.). 3. (*of pers.*) (*a*) vigueur *f*, vivacité *f*; (*b*) naïveté *f*, inexpérience *f*; (*c*) *F:* outrecuidance *f*; hardiesse *f*; effronterie *f*, toupet *m.*

fresh-run ['freʃ'rʌn], *a.* (saumon, etc.) nouvellement remonté de la mer.

freshwater ['freʃwɔ:tər], *a.* 1. (poisson, etc.) d'eau douce; *Biol:* (poisson, plante) dulcaquicole; *F:* **f. sailor,** marin d'eau douce. 2. *U.S: F:* **f. college,** petit collège universitaire de province.

Fresnel ['frein(ə)l], *Pr.n. Ph:* Fresnel; **F. biprism,** biprisme *m* de Fresnel; **Fresnel's integrals,** intégrales *f* de Fresnel; **Fresnel('s) mirror(s),** miroirs *mpl* de Fresnel; **F. lens,** lentille *f* à échelons (de phare, etc.).

fret[1] [fret], *s.* 1. *Arch:* **(Greek) f.,** grecque *f*; frette *f*. 2. *Her:* frette. 3. *Tls:* **f.-cutting machine,** machine *f* à chantourner, à découper.

fret[2], *v.tr.* (**fretted**) 1. diaprer, bigarrer (qch.). 2. *Arch:* sculpter, orner (un plafond, etc.).

fret[3], *s. Mus:* touchette *f*, touche *f* (de guitare, etc.).

fret[4], *v.tr.* (**fretted**) fournir (une guitare) de touchettes.

fret[5], *s.* 1. (*a*) agitation *f*, inquiétude *f*, de l'âme; (*b*) irritation *f*; état *m* d'agacement; mauvaise humeur; **to be in a f., on the f.,** se faire du mauvais sang, de la bile; se tracasser. 2. **sea f.,** brume légère de mer.

fret[6], *v.* (**fretted**) 1. *v.tr.* (*a*) (*of mice, moths, etc.*) ronger (qch.); **horse that frets its bit,** cheval qui ronge son mors; **to f. a rope,** érailler un cordage; **fretted rope,** cordage mâché; **rust has fretted the iron (away),** la rouille a rongé, corrodé, érodé, le fer; **rocks fretted by the river,** rochers usés par le frottement de l'eau; **the stream has fretted a channel through the rock,** le ruisseau a creusé un chenal dans le roc; (*b*) inquiéter, tracasser, irriter, tourmenter (qn); **to f. one's horse,** tourmenter son cheval; (*c*) agiter, faire bouillonner (un ruisseau). 2. *v.pr. & i.* (*a*) **to f. (oneself),** se chagriner, se tourmenter, s'inquiéter; se ronger (le cœur); se faire du mauvais sang, se manger le(s) sang(s); **don't f.!** (i) ne vous faites pas de bile! ne vous faites pas de mauvais sang; (ii) ne vous inquiétez pas! **child fretting for his mother,** enfant qui réclame sa mère (en pleurnichant); **she has fretted a lot over this disappointment,** cette déception l'a beaucoup chagrinée; **he fretted away the rest of his life in banishment,** il passa le reste de sa vie à se ronger le cœur dans l'exil; **to f. in idleness,** se ronger dans l'inactivité; **to f. over, about, trifles,** s'irriter pour des sujets futiles; **he fretted himself into a fever,** à force de se faire de la bile il se donna la fièvre; **to f. and fume,** se ronger d'impatience; rager, enrager, *F:* endiabler; (se) faire une pinte de mauvais sang; se faire du mauvais sang; (*b*) (*of stream, etc.*) s'agiter, bouillonner; (*c*) *Brew:* (*of stored beer*) fermenter.

fretful ['fretful], *a.* 1. (*of pers.*) chagrin; qui se ronge le cœur; qui se fait du mauvais sang; irritable; maussade; **f. old age,** vieillesse chagrine; **f. baby,** bébé agité. 2. *Lit:* (*of water*) agité, tourmenté; (*of wind*) qui souffle par rafales.

fretfully [ˈfretfuli], *adv.* **1.** d'un air chagrin, contrarié; avec irritation; d'un ton maussade. **2.** (*of wind*) (souffler) par rafales.

fretfulness [ˈfretfulnis], *s.* **1.** irritabilité *f.* **2.** agitation *f* (de la mer).

fretsaw[1] [ˈfretsɔː], *s.* scie *f* à découper; bocfil *m.*

fretsaw[2], *v.i.* découper (le bois).

frettage [ˈfretidʒ], *s. Mec.E:* usure *f* (entre les surfaces d'un joint sec).

fretted [ˈfretid], *a.* **1.** (*of ceiling, etc.*) orné, sculpté. **2.** *Her:* fretté.

fretter [ˈfretər], *s.* insecte rongeur.

fretting[1] [ˈfretiŋ], *a.* (*of bottled, barrelled, beer*) qui fermente.

fretting[2], *s.* ornementation *f* (d'un plafond).

fretting[3], *s.* **1.** érosion *f,* corrosion *f,* usure *f; Mec.E:* usure entre les surfaces d'un joint sec. **2.** rongement *m* d'esprit; chagrin *m,* inquiétude *f.*

fretty[1] [ˈfreti], *a. Her:* fretté; **f. cloué,** treillissé.

fretty[2], *a.* **1.** (enfant) maussade, pleurnicheur. **2.** *Brew:* (bière) qui fermente en bouteille, en barrique.

fretwork [ˈfretwəːk], *s.* **1.** (*of ceilings, etc.*) ornementation *f,* sculpture *f.* **2.** *Woodw:* découpage *m;* ouvrage *m* à claire-voie; travail ajouré; bois découpé.

Freudian [ˈfrɔidiən], *a. Psy:* freudien.

Freud(ian)ism [ˈfrɔid(iən)izm], *s. Psy:* freudisme *m.*

friability [fraiəˈbiliti], **friableness** [ˈfraiəblnis], *s.* friabilité *f.*

friable [ˈfraiəbl], *a.* friable; **f. soil,** terre friable, grumeleuse.

friagem [ˈfraiədʒem], *s. Meteor:* coup *m* de froid (au campos du Brésil).

friar [ˈfraiər], *s.* **1.** *R.C.Ch:* moine *m,* frère *m,* religieux *m;* **Grey Friars,** frères mineurs, Franciscains *m;* **Black Friars,** Dominicains *m,* frères prêcheurs; **White Friars,** Carmes *m; F:* **friar's lantern,** feu follet; *Bot:* **friar's cap,** tue-loup *m inv;* **friar's cowl,** arum maculé; gouet *m.* **2.** *Typ:* moine, feinte *f.*

friarbird [ˈfraiəbəːd], *s. Orn:* philémon *m,* philédon *m.*

friar's balsam [ˈfraiəzˈbɔːlsəm], *s. Pharm:* baume *m* de benjoin.

friary [ˈfraiəri], *s.* monastère *m;* couvent *m* (de moines); maison *f* de religieux; *F:* moinerie *f,* capucinière *f.*

fribble[1] [ˈfribl], *s. F: O:* **1.** (*pers.*) baguenaudier, -ière. **2.** frivolité *f,* sottise *f.*

fribble[2], *v.i. & tr. F: O:* baguenauder; s'amuser à des niaiseries, à des choses frivoles; **to f. away one's money,** gaspiller son argent.

fribbler [ˈfriblər], *s. F: O:* baguenaudier, -ière.

fricassee[1] [frikəˈsiː], *s. Cu:* fricassée *f;* (*of rabbit or hare*) gibelotte *f;* (*of fowl*) grenadin *m*

fricassee[2], *v.tr. Cu:* fricasser.

fricative [ˈfrikətiv], *Ling:* **1.** *a.* (*of consonant, etc.*) fricatif, sifflant, soufflant. **2.** *s.* fricative *f,* sifflante *f;* **voiceless f.,** fricative sourde; **voiced f.,** fricative sonore.

friction [ˈfrikʃ(ə)n], *s.* **1.** *Med: Hairdr:* friction *f;* **f. gloves,** gants *m* de crin, à friction. **2.** frottement *m,* attrition *f* (de deux corps); **f. surface,** frottoir *m* (d'une boîte d'allumettes); *Geol:* **f. breccia,** brèche *f* de friction. **3.** *Mec: Ph:* frottement, friction; **f. coefficient,** coefficient *m,* indice *m,* de frottement; module *m* de glissement; **force of f.,** force *f* de frottement; *Mec:* **boundary f.,** frottement onctueux; **dry f.,** frottement à sec; **fluid f.,** frottement visqueux; **skidding f.,** frottement de dérapage; **f. of, from, rest, of repose, at starting,** frottement au départ; **f. of motion,** frottement en mouvement; *Aedcs; Av:* **air f.,** frottement de l'air; *Aut:* **marginal f.,** ralentissement marginal; *attrib.* **f. band,** frein *m* (de gouvernail, etc.); **f. block, f. shoe,** sabot *m,* semelle *f,* de frottement; **f. brake,** frein à friction; **f. damper,** amortisseur *m* à friction; **f. disk,** plateau *m* à friction; **f.-disk brake,** frein à disque (de friction); **f. drive,** entraînement *m* par friction; **f. gear(ing),** transmission *f* à friction, par frottement; *Hyd.E:* **f. head,** perte frictionnelle; **f. layer,** (i) *Meteor:* couche turbulente; (ii) *Aedcs:* couche *f* de frottement; *Exp:* **f. primer (tube), f. tube,** étoupille *f,* amorce *f,* à friction; *Paperm:* **f. roller,** cylindre frictionneur; *El:* **f. tape,** chatterton *m;* ruban isolant. **4.** friction, désaccord *m; Dipl:* points *mpl* de friction; **there's f. between them,** il y a du tirage entre eux.

frictional [ˈfrikʃən(ə)l], *a. Mec: Ph: etc:* à, de, frottement; à, de, friction; **f. coefficient,** coefficient *m,* indice *m,* de frottement; **f. contact,** contact *m* à, par, frottement; **f.-geared device,** appareil *m,* dispositif *m,* à embrayage à friction; **f. loss,** perte *f* par frottement; *Aedcs: Hyd: Nau:* **f. drag, f. force, f. resistance,** (résistance *f* de, par) frottement; **f. wake,** sillage *m* de frottement.

frictionally [ˈfrikʃənəli], *adv.* (commandé, actionné) par friction.

friction-glaze [ˈfrikʃ(ə)nˈgleiz], *v.tr. Paperm:* frictionner (du papier).

friction-proof [ˈfrikʃ(ə)npruːf], *a.* antifriction *inv.*

Friday [ˈfraidi], *s.* vendredi *m;* **he's coming (on) F.,** il viendra vendredi; **he comes on Fridays,** il vient le vendredi, *occ.* les vendredis; **he comes every F.,** il vient tous les vendredis; *F: O:* **F. face,** face *f* de carême; **Good F.,** (le) Vendredi saint; **Black F.,** vendredi néfaste, de sinistre mémoire; **Man F.,** (i) *Lit:* Vendredi (le domestique de Robinson Crusoé); (ii) *F:* factotum *m;* homme à tout faire; *F:* **Girl F.,** super-secrétaire *f.*

fridge [fridʒ], *s. F:* réfrigérateur *m; F:* frigo *m.*

Friedel-Crafts [ˈfriːdəkrɑːfts], *Pr.n. Ch:* **F.-C. reaction,** réaction *f* de Friedel et Crafts.

friedelite [ˈfriːdəlait], *s. Miner:* friedélite *f.*

Friedrich [ˈfriːdriχ], *Pr.n. Med:* **Friedrich's ataxia,** maladie *f* de Friedrich; **Friedrich's foot,** pied bot symptomatique de la maladie de Friedrich.

friend [frend], *s.* **1.** (*a*) ami, *f.* amie; **I am speaking to you as a f.,** je vous parle en ami(e); **man f., boy f.,** ami; **woman f., girl f.,** amie; **bosom f.,** ami(e) intime; intime *mf;* **they are bosom friends,** ils sont étroitement liés; **we're just good friends,** nous sommes de bons amis, sans plus; **to be friends with s.o.,** être lié (d'amitié) avec qn; être ami avec qn; **I am friends with Smith,** Smith et moi sommes amis; je suis lié d'amitié avec Smith; **not to be friends with s.o.,** bouder qn; battre froid à qn; **they became great friends,** ils se sont pris d'amitié l'un pour l'autre; **to become friends with s.o. again,** se raccommoder avec qn; **to make a f.,** se faire un ami; **to make friends with s.o.,** se prendre d'amitié pour qn; se lier d'amitié avec qn; **I have made great friends with him,** nous sommes devenus de grands amis; **he tries to make friends with everybody,** il est liant avec tout le monde; **nature quick to make friends,** caractère liant; **to have friends to stay,** avoir des amis en visite; **one of his friends, a f. of his,** un de ses amis, *F:* un ami à lui; **a soldier f. of his,** un militaire de ses amis; *Provs:* **everybody's f. is nobody's f., a f. to all is a f. to none,** ami de chacun, ami d'aucun; **the best of friends must part,** il n'est si bonne compagnie qui ne se sépare; **a f. in need is a f. indeed,** au besoin on connaît l'ami; (*b*) (*not an enemy*) **I don't care much for him but we are quite good friends,** je ne l'aime pas beaucoup mais nous ne sommes pas en mauvais termes; *F:* **you'd better be, keep, friends with them,** vous ferez bien de ne pas vous brouiller avec eux; **let us part friends,** séparons-nous (en) bons amis; **he's no f. of mine,** (i) il n'est nullement mon ami; (ii) il ne me veut pas de bien; **he was no f. to me,** il n'a pas agi en ami envers moi. **2.** (*a*) (*in duel*) témoin *m;* (*b*) connaissance *f;* **train f.,** connaissance que l'on s'est faite en voyageant régulièrement dans le train; **to make friends with s.o.,** faire connaissance avec qn; **he has influential friends,** il a des amis influents; il a de belles relations; *F:* **a f. at court,** un ami en haut lieu, bien placé; **to have friends at court,** avoir des protections; être protégé en haut lieu; *P:* avoir du piston; *Com:* **he has a large circle of friends,** il a une grande clientèle; **to be far from all one's friends,** être éloigné de toutes ses relations; **to dine with a few friends,** dîner en petit comité; **f. Robinson,** notre ami Robinson; *F:* **our f. with the nagging wife,** notre ami qui a une femme grondeuse, difficile; *Com:* **our f. in Scotland,** notre accrédité en Écosse; *Parl:* **my honourable f.,** *Jur:* **my learned f.,** mon (cher) confrère; (*c*) *pl. Scot:* parents *m;* **his friends are well off,** sa famille est riche. **3.** (*a*) **f. of the poor,** bienfaiteur, -trice, des pauvres; **a public f.,** un bienfaiteur public; (*b*) ami, partisan *m* (de l'ordre, etc.); (*c*) patron, -onne (des arts, etc.); **the Friends of Canterbury Cathedral,** la Société des Amis, les Amis, de la Cathédrale de Cantorbéry. **4.** *Rel:* Quaker, -eresse; Ami, -ie; **the Society of Friends,** la Société des Amis; les Quakers.

friendless [ˈfrendlis], *a.* délaissé, abandonné, sans amis, sans appui; **to be completely f.,** être seul au monde.

friendlessness [ˈfrendlisnis], *s.* délaissement *m,* abandon *m,* solitude *f.*

friendliness [ˈfrendlinis], *s.* bienveillance *f,* bonté *f,* dispositions amicales (**to, towards,** envers).

friendly [ˈfrendli], *a. & s.*

I. *a.* **1.** (*a*) (ton, sentiment) amical, -aux; sympathique, d'ami; **do me a f. turn,** rendez-moi un service d'ami; **a f. curiosity,** une curiosité amie; **piece of f. advice,** avis amical; **f. gathering,** réunion *f* d'amis; **to be f. with s.o.,** être ami avec qn; **they became very f.,** ils se sont pris d'amitié l'un pour l'autre; **they are no longer f.,** ils ne sont plus amis; *F:* leurs chiens ne chassent plus ensemble; **in a f. manner,** amicalement; **to be looked upon in a f. way by s.o.,** être sympathiquement connu à qn; (*b*) (*not hostile*) **to be on f. terms with s.o.,** être en bons termes, en bons rapports, en relations d'amitié, avec qn; **we are on f. terms with the new tenants,** nous voisinons avec les nouveaux locataires; **f. nation,** pays ami; *Mil:* **f. troops,** troupes amies; *Sp:* **f. match,** match amical. **2.** (*of pers.*) bienveillant, favorablement disposé; (*of thg, circumstance, etc.*) favorable, propice; **f. winds,** vents *m* propices; **he proved very f.,** il s'est montré très gentil; **to give s.o. a f. reception,** recevoir favorablement qn; faire bon accueil à qn. **3. f. society,** association *f* de bienfaisance; société *f* de secours mutuels, de mutualité.

II. *s.* **1.** *Hist:* indigène ami; *pl.* **friendlies,** tribus amies. **2.** *Sp:* match amical.

Friendly Islands (the) [ðəˈfrendliailəndz], *Pr.n.pl. Geog:* l'archipel *m* de Tonga; les îles *f* des Amis.

friendship [ˈfrendʃip], *s.* amitié *f;* **to form a f. with s.o.,** se lier (d'amitié) avec qn; nouer amitié avec qn; **to conceive a great f. for s.o.,** se prendre d'une vive amitié pour qn; **I did it out of f.,** je l'ai fait par amitié; **tribes living in f.,** tribus qui vivent en bonne intelligence.

fries [fraiz], *s.pl. F:* **French f.,** pommes de terre frites; *F:* des frites *f.*

Friesian [ˈfriːziən]. **1.** *a. & s. Geog: Ling:* = FRISIAN. **2.** *a. & s. Husb:* **F. (cow),** vache frisonne; *pl.* **Friesians,** la race frisonne.

Friesland [ˈfriːzlənd], *Pr.n. Geog:* la Frise.

frieze[1] [friːz], *s. Tex:* frise *f;* ratine *f.*

frieze[2], *v.tr. Tex:* ratiner (le drap).

frieze[3], *s.* **1.** *Arch:* frise *f;* (*of Tuscan, Doric, column*) colarin *m.* **2.** bordure *f* (de papier peint de tenture).

friezing [ˈfriːziŋ], *s. Tex:* ratinage *m;* **f. machine,** ratineuse *f,* frise *f.*

frig[1] [fridʒ], *s. F:* réfrigérateur *m, F:* frigo *m.*

frig[2] [frig], *v.i. & tr. V:* (*not in decent use*) **1.** (*a*) *v.i.* forniquer, faire l'amour; (*b*) *v.tr.* baiser, aiguiller (une femme). **2.** *v.i.* **to f. about, around,** tripoter, trifouiller; **to f. about with sth.,** jouer avec qch., tripoter qch.; **f. off!** fous-moi le camp (d'ici)! **3.** *v.tr.* **f. him!** que le diable l'emporte! **what about the cost? —f. the cost!** et le coût?—je m'en fiche, je m'en fous!

frigate [ˈfrigət], *s.* **1.** *Navy:* (*a*) *Hist:* (*sailing ship*) frégate *f;* (*b*) frégate, escorteur *m;* **anti-aircraft f.,** frégate antiaérienne; **utility f.,** escorteur polyvalent. **2.** *Orn:* **f. (bird),** frégate; **magnificent f. bird,** frégate superbe; **f. petrel,** pétrel *m* frégate.

frigger [ˈfrigər], *s. Glassm:* petit ornement de verre; *pl.* **friggers,** verroterie *f.*

fright[1] [frait], *s.* **1.** peur *f,* effroi *m, P:* trac *m;* **he was seized with f.,** l'effroi l'a saisi; *P:* il a eu le trac; **to take f.,** prendre peur; s'effrayer, s'effarer (**at, de**); **to give s.o. a f.,** faire peur à qn, *F:* donner le trac à qn; **to be in a deadly f., half dead with f.,** (i) *Lit:* être saisi d'épouvante; (ii) *F:* avoir un trac formidable; **she was in such a f. that . . .,** elle avait tellement peur que . . .; *F:* **I got an awful f.,** j'ai eu une peur bleue, une belle peur. **2.** *F:* (*esp. of woman*) personne *f* laide, grotesque; épouvantail *m, pl.* épouvantails; **what a f. that woman is!** quelle horreur, quelle caricature, quel épouvantail, que cette femme! **what a f. you look!** comme vous voilà fagotée! **she's a perfect f.,** *F:* c'est un remède d'amour.

fright[2], *v.tr. A: & Lit:* = FRIGHTEN.

frighten [ˈfraitn], *v.*

I. *v.tr.* effrayer (qn); faire peur à (qn); *Lit:* épouvanter (qn); **it frightens him, her,** cela lui fait peur; **these animals are easily frightened,** ces animaux s'effarouchent d'un rien; **you f. me to death,** vous me faites mourir de peur; **to f. s.o. out of his wits,** (i) rendre qn fou de terreur; (ii) *F:* faire une peur bleue à qn; **to f. s.o. into doing sth.,** faire faire qch. à qn sous le coup de la peur; **I'm not going to be frightened into apologizing,** on ne m'arrachera pas des excuses en essayant de m'intimider.

II. (*compound verb*) **frighten away, off,** *v.tr.* faire sauver (qn) (en lui faisant peur); **the dog frightened the thieves away,** le chien a fait décamper les voleurs; **don't f. away the birds,** n'effarouchez pas les oiseaux; **he frightened away all the birds,** il a égaillé, fait sauver, tous les oiseaux.

frightened [ˈfraitnd], *a.* (*of pers., etc.*) apeuré, épeuré; **easily f.,** peureux, poltron; **f. child,** enfant apeuré; **I wasn't as f. as you were,** je n'avais pas aussi peur que vous; je n'avais pas peur (au) tant que vous; **to feel f.,** avoir peur; ressentir de la peur; **f. out of one's wits,** terrifié; **f. to death,** en proie à une frayeur mortelle; **he is, was, more f. than hurt,** il a eu plus de peur que de mal.

frightener [ˈfraitnər], *s. P:* homme fort (employé par un gangster); **to put the frighteners on s.o.,** tâcher d'intimider qn.

frightening [ˈfraitniŋ], *a.* effrayant, épouvantable.

frighteningly [ˈfraitniŋli], *adv.* épouvantablement, à

faire peur.

frightful ['fraitful], *a.* terrible, effroyable, affreux, épouvantable; **he was in a f. passion,** il était dans une colère terrible; *F:* **to have a f. headache,** avoir un mal de tête affreux; **he has a f. amount of work,** il a énormément à faire.

frightfully ['fraitfuli], *adv.* terriblement, épouvantablement, effroyablement, affreusement; à faire peur; **he is f. ugly,** il est affreusement laid, laid à faire peur; **f. badly dressed,** terriblement mal habillé; *F:* **I am f. sorry,** je regrette énormément, infiniment; **he is f. vain,** il est excessivement vaniteux; **f. rich,** colossalement riche; **he is f. pleased,** il est joliment content; **that's f. nice of you,** c'est vraiment chic de ta part.

frightfulness ['fraitfulnis], *s.* **1.** horreur *f,* caractère hideux, atrocité *f* (d'un crime, etc.). **2.** *Hist:* (1914–18) **policy of f.,** politique *f* de feu et de sang, politique de terrorisme.

frigid ['fridʒid], *a.* **1.** *(a)* glacial, -als; (très) froid; **the f. zones,** les zones glaciales; *(b)* *(of pers.)* froid; **f. style,** style glacial, ennuyeux; **f. politeness,** politesse glaciale, glacée; **f. answer,** réponse glacée; **f. welcome,** accueil *m* frigide. **2.** *Med:* (femme) frigide.

frigidarium [fridʒi'dɑ:riəm], *s. Rom.Ant:* frigidarium *m.*

frigidity [fri'dʒiditi], *s.* **1.** frigidité *f;* grande froideur, caractère glacial (d'un climat, d'un accueil, etc.); **f. of style,** froideur de style. **2.** froideur (sexuelle); frigidité.

frigidly ['fridʒidli], *adv.* glacialement, très froidement; **to be f. polite,** être d'une politesse glaciale.

frigidness ['fridʒidnis], *s.* = FRIGIDITY 1.

frigorific [frigə'rifik], *a.* frigorifique.

frigorifico [frigə'rifikou], *s.* usine *f* frigorifique (d'Argentine).

frigorimeter [frigə'rimitər], *s. Meteor:* frigorimètre *m.*

frigotherapy [frigou'θerəpi], *s. Med:* frigothérapie *f,* cryothérapie *f.*

frill[1] [fril], *s.* **1.** *Cost: etc:* *(a)* volant *m,* ruche *f,* tuyauté *m,* tuyautage *m;* **pleated f.,** plissé *m;* **toby f.,** collerette plissée; fraise *f;* **shirt f.,** jabot *m;* *Cu:* **(cutlet, ham) f.,** papillote *f;* *F:* **Newgate f.,** barbe *f* en collier; collier *m* de barbe; *(b)* *pl. F:* **frills,** affectation *f,* façons *f;* **to put on frills,** faire des façons; poser; **to write without frills,** écrire sans apprêt; **a plain meal without frills,** un repas simple sans présentation compliquée; *(c)* *Orn:* (i) cravate *f* (de pigeon); (ii) pigeon *m* à cravate; *(d)* *Fung:* armille *f.* **2.** mésentère *m;* *Cu:* fraise (de veau, etc.). **3.** *Phot:* partie décollée de la gélatine (au bord d'une plaque); plissement *m.*

frill[2]. **1.** *v.tr.* plisser, froncer, tuyauter, rucher (le linge, etc.). **2.** *v.i. Phot:* *(of emulsion)* se décoller; se plisser.

frilled [frild], *a.* **1.** *(a)* *(of ribbon, etc.)* froncé, ruché; *(of skirt)* à volants; *(of coif)* godronné, tuyauté; *(of shirt)* à jabots; *(of elastic)* frisé; *(b)* *Orn:* **f. pigeon,** pigeon *m* à cravate; *(c)* *Rept:* **f. lizard,** chlamydosaure *m;* iguane australien. **2.** *Phot:* *(of emulsion)* décollé au bord; plissé.

frilliness ['frilinis], *s.* **1.** tuyauté *m* (d'une robe, etc.). **2.** affectation *f* (de style).

frilling ['friliŋ], *s.* **1.** *(a)* plissage *m,* froncement *m,* tuyautage *m* (d'une bande, etc.); *(b)* *Phot:* décollement *m,* détachement *m,* plissement *m* (au bord de la plaque). **2.** ruché *m,* rabat *m,* plissé *m,* tuyauté *m.*

frilly ['frili]. **1.** *a.* froncé, ruché. **2.** *s.pl. F:* **frillies,** vêtements de dessous ruchés; falbalas *m.*

fringe[1] [frindʒ], *s.* **1.** *Tex:* frange *f;* *(on upholstered furniture)* crépine *f;* *(of ends left loose)* effilé *m,* effiloche *f,* effiloque *f;* tombant *m,* bouillon *m* (d'épaulette). **2.** *(a)* bordure *f,* bord *m;* **f. of trees,** bordure d'arbres; **the f. of the forest,** la lisière de la forêt; **the outer fringe(s) of London,** la banlieue excentrique de Londres; *Can:* **f. land,** terres (au Nord) éloignées du chemin de fer; **you have only touched the f. of the question,** vous n'avez fait qu'effleurer la question; **to live on the f. of society,** vivre en marge de la société; **f. benefits,** avantages *m* accessoires; *(for employees)* compléments *m* de salaire en nature; **f. theatre,** petit théâtre expérimental de banlieue, de province; *Opt:* **chromatic f.,** frange chromatique; *T.V:* **f. area,** zone *f* limitrophe; *(b)* *Hairdr:* frange; devant *m* de cheveux; cheveux *mpl* à la chien; **to wear a f.,** être coiffée à la chien; **f. net,** réseau *m;* filet *m* à cheveux; *F:* **Newgate f.,** barbe *f* en collier; collier *m* de barbe. **3.** *Z:* cirres *mpl;* *Bot:* cils *mpl,* fimbrilles *fpl.*

fringe[2]. **1.** *v.tr.* franger (un tapis, etc.); garnir (un meuble, etc.) d'une crépine; **the oaks that f. the forest,** les chênes en bordure de la forêt, qui forment la lisière de la forêt; **eyes fringed with black lashes,** yeux bordés, frangés, de cils noirs. **2.** *v.i.* *(a)* *(of material)* s'effiler, s'effilocher; former des franges; *(b)* **to f. upon sth.,** border, franger, qch.; **boldness that fringes on insolence,** hardiesse *f* qui frise l'insolence.

fringe bush, tree ['frindʒbuʃ, tri:], *s. Bot:* chionanthe *m,* chionanthus *m,* arbre *m* de neige.

fringed [frindʒd], *a.* *(a)* *Tex:* frangé, effilé, à frange; *Furn:* garni, orné, d'une crépine; *(b)* *Nat.Hist:* fimbrié.

Fringillidae [frin'dʒilidi:], *s.pl. Orn:* fringillidés *m.*

fringing[1] ['frindʒiŋ], *a.* marginal, -aux; (récif) en bordure, frangeant; **f. forest,** forêt *f* en bordure d'une rivière.

fringing[2], *s.* **1.** *(of tissue)* frangeage *m,* effilochage *m.* **2.** *(a)* *Opt:* iridescence *f;* *(b)* *Phot:* flou *m;* image floue. **3.** *El: etc:* dispersion *f* électromagnétique (d'entrefer); **f. coefficient,** coefficient *m* de dispersion électromagnétique.

frippery ['fripəri], *s.* **1.** *A:* friperie *f.* **2.** parure *f* sans valeur; camelote *f;* *(of speech, style, etc.)* étalage *m,* faste *m,* clinquant *m.* **3.** *usu. pl.* **fripperies,** (i) colifichets *m,* brimborions *m;* (ii) babioles *f,* bagatelles *f.*

frippet ['fripit], *s.f. P:* femme volage; *P:* poule.

Frisco ['friskou], *Pr.n. Geog: F:* *(dim. of)* San Francisco.

Frisian ['friziən]. **1.** *a. & s.* *(a)* *Geog:* frison, -onne; *(b)* *Husb:* = FRIESIAN. **2.** *s. Ling:* le frison.

frisk[1] [frisk], *s.* **1.** gambade *f,* cabriole *f.* **2. with a f. of its tail,** (i) *(of horse)* en donnant un coup de queue; (ii) *(of dog)* avec un frétillement de queue.

frisk[2]. **1.** *v.i.* **to f. (about),** *(of lambs, etc.)* s'ébattre; faire des cabrioles; gambader, folâtrer; *(of horse)* fringuer, caracoler, cabrioler, faire des caracoles; *(of dog, etc.)* **to come frisking in, up,** entrer, arriver, en gambadant. **2.** *v.tr.* *(of dog, etc.)* **to f. its tail,** frétiller de la queue. **3.** *v.tr. F:* *(a)* (i) palper, (ii) fouiller (un suspect, etc.); *(b)* prendre quelque chose à (qn) dans sa poche; voler (une montre, etc.) à la tire.

frisket ['friskit], *s. Typ:* *(a)* cache *m;* *(b)* frisquette *f* (d'une presse à bras).

friskily ['friskili], *adv.* folâtrement; d'un air fringant.

friskiness ['friskinis], *s.* folâtrerie *f;* vivacité *f.*

frisking ['friskiŋ], *s. F:* **1.** palpation *f* (d'un suspect, voyageur, etc.). **2.** vol *m* à la tire.

frisky ['friski], *a.* vif, folâtre; (cheval) fringant, animé, en l'air, qui a du feu, qui fait des cabrioles *(of pers.)* **to feel f.,** se sentir plein d'entrain.

frit[1] [frit], *s. Glassm: Cer:* fritte *f.*

frit[2], *v.tr.* **(fritted)** *Glassm:* fritter (les matières premières).

frit fly ['fritflai], *s. Ent:* oscine *f.*

frith[1] [friθ], *s.* **1.** *Dial:* *(a)* pays boisé, buissonneux; *(b)* taillis *m.* **2.** haie *f,* claie *f.*

frith[2], *s. Geog: Scot:* estuaire *m,* firth *m;* golfe (formé par l'embouchure d'un fleuve).

fritillaria [friti'lɛəriə], *s. Bot:* fritillaire *f.*

fritillary [fri'tiləri], *s.* **1.** *Bot:* fritillaire *f* (méléagride); damier *m;* *F:* pintade *f,* œuf-de-vanneau *m, pl.* œufs-de-vanneau. **2.** *Ent:* damier; **pearl-bordered f.,** collier argenté; **greasy f.,** mélitée *f* artémise; **Phoebe f.,** mélitée phœbe; **Queen of Spain f.,** petit nacré; **silver-washed f.,** argynne *m* tabac d'Espagne; empereur *m.*

fritter[1] ['fritər], *s. Cu:* beignet *m,* roussette *f;* **apple f.,** beignet de, aux, pommes.

fritter[2], *v.tr.* **to f. (sth.) away, down,** morceler (qch.); réduire (qch.) à rien; dissiper, émietter, éparpiller (sa fortune); **to f. time away,** perdre le temps, son temps; muser; **to f. away one's money,** dépenser tout son argent en bêtises; gaspiller son argent.

fritting ['fritiŋ], *s. Glassm:* frittage *m.*

Fritz[1] [frits], *Pr.n.m.* Fritz; *Hist:* *(1914–18)* *F:* **the Fritzes, F.,** les Allemands, *F:* les boches.

fritz[2], *s. NAm: P:* *(of machine, etc.)* **to be on the f.,** être hors service, en panne; **to go on the f.,** avoir une panne; *F:* flancher; **to put the f. on sth.,** mettre fin à, supprimer, qch.

Friuli [fri'u:li], *Pr.n. Geog:* le Frioul.

Friulian [fri'u:liən]. **1.** *Geog:* *(a)* *a.* frioulien; *(b)* *s.* Frioulien, -ienne. **2.** *s. Ling:* le frioulan.

frivol ['friv(ə)l], *v.* **(frivolled)** *F:* **1.** *v.i.* baguenauder, muser, lanterner; s'amuser (à des frivolités, à faire la cour aux femmes). **2.** *v.tr.* **to f. away one's time, one's money,** gaspiller son temps, son argent.

frivolity [fri'vɔliti], *s.* **1.** frivolité *f,* baguenauderie *f;* légèreté *f* d'esprit. **2. to talk frivolities,** (i) s'entretenir de frivolités; (ii) parler pour ne rien dire.

frivoller ['frivələr], *s.* personne *f* frivole; évaporé, -e.

frivolling[1] ['frivəliŋ], *a.* *(of pers.)* frivole; baguenaudier.

frivolling[2], *s.* baguenauderie *f.*

frivolous ['frivələs], *a.* frivole; *(of claim, complaint, objection)* vain, futile, injustifié; *(of pers.)* baguenaudier, évaporé.

frivolously ['frivələsli], *adv.* frivolement, futilement.

frivolousness ['frivələsnis], *s.* **1.** frivolité *f;* légèreté *f* d'esprit. **2.** futilité *f* (d'une objection, etc.).

frizz[1] [friz], *s.* *(a)* crêpelure *f,* crêpage *m* (des cheveux); *(b)* cheveux crêpelés.

frizz[2], *v.tr.* **1.** *(a)* crêper, frisotter, moutonner, bichonner (les cheveux); *(b)* *v.i.* *(of hair)* frisotter. **2.** *Leath:* poncer (les peaux). **3.** *Tex:* ratiner (le drap).

frizz[3], *v.i.* = FRIZZLE[3] 1.

frizziness ['frizinis], *s.* crêpelure *f* (des cheveux).

frizzle[1] [frizl], *s.* **1.** cheveux crêpelés, crêpelus, frisottés, moutonnés. **2.** *Husb:* **f. fowl,** poule frisée.

frizzle[2], *v.tr. & i.* = FRIZZ[2] 1.

frizzle[3]. **1.** *v.i.* *(a)* grésiller, chanter (dans la poêle); *(b)* crépiter. **2.** *v.tr.* *Cu:* *(a)* faire frire (le lard, etc.); *(b)* griller (le lard, etc.).

frizzy ['frizi], *a.* *(of hair)* crêpelé, crêpelu, frisotté, moutonné.

fro [frou], *adv.* en s'éloignant; **to go to and f.,** aller et venir.

froing ['frouiŋ], *s. F:* **toing and froing,** va-et-vient *m.*

frock [frɔk], *s. Cost:* **1.** robe *f* (d'enfant, de femme); **to wear short frocks,** porter des robes courtes. **2.** *(a)* froc *m,* bure *f* (de moine); **to wear the f.,** être prêtre, porter le froc; *(b)* blouse *f,* sarrau *m, A:* souquenille *f* (de paysan, d'ouvrier); *(c)* *Nau:* chemise *f,* jersey *m,* tricot *m,* maillot *m* (de marin); *(d)* *Mil:* tunique *f* de petite tenue. **3.** *Mil: P: A:* **the frocks,** les politiciens *m;* *O:* les pékins *m* de l'Administration.

frock coat ['frɔk'kout], *s. Cost:* redingote *f;* **clerical f. c.,** soutanelle *f.*

frocked [frɔkt], *a.* (femme) qui porte une robe; **short-f.,** en robe courte; **f. priests,** prêtres revêtus de leurs frocs.

Froebel(ian)ism [frə:'bi:liənizm, 'frə:bəlizm], *s.* système *m* de Froebel sur l'éducation des tout-petits.

frog[1] [frɔg], *s.* **1.** *Amph:* *(a)* grenouille *f;* **agile f.,** grenouille agile; **bush f.,** rhacophore *m;* **common f., grass f.,** grenouille rousse; **Darwin's f.,** rhinoderme *m* du Chili; **edible f.,** grenouille verte; **goliath f.,** grenouille géante du Cameroun; **hairy f.,** grenouille poilue; **horned f.,** crapaud cornu; **Indo-Malayan flying f.,** grenouille volante indo-malaise; **Javan flying f.,** grenouille arboricole de Java; **(South American) leaf f.,** rainette *f* maki; **leopard f.,** grenouille léopard; **moor f.,** grenouille oxyrhine; **nurse f.,** alyte *m,* crapaud accoucheur; **parsley f.,** grenouille persillée; **Siberian f.,** grenouille de Sibérie; **strawberry f.,** grenouille des fraises; **tree f.,** rainette (verte), grenouille d'arbre, grasset *m;* **water reservoir f.,** grenouille fouilleuse australienne; **(American) wood f.,** grenouille des bois; *(b)* *attrib. F:* **f. eater, Frog,** mangeur, -euse, de grenouilles; Français, -aise; **f. pond,** grenouillère *f;* *Civ.E:* **f. rammer,** grenouille; **f. spit(tle),** (i) crachat *m* de coucou, de grenouille; (ii) œufs *mpl* de grenouille; (iii) *NAm:* algue verte d'eau douce; **frog('s) spawn,** (i) œufs de grenouille; (ii) *P:* tapioca *m* au lait; *Med: F:* **f. tongue,** grenouillette *f,* ranule *f.* **2.** *Ich:* **fishing f.,** (i) poisson-grenouille *m, pl.* poissons-grenouilles, baudroie *f,* lophie pêcheuse; (ii) antennaire *m,* bouffon *m* des mers; crapaud, grenouille, de mer. **3.** *Med:* aphte *m;* *F:* **to have a f. in one's throat,** avoir un chat dans la gorge, le gosier. **4.** porte-fleurs *m inv* (dans un vase). **5.** *Mus:* hausse *f* (d'archet).

frog[2], *s. Farr:* fourchette *f* (du sabot); **f. pad,** bourrelet *m.*

frog[3], *s. Mil: etc:* **1.** porte-épée *m inv;* porte-baïonnette *m inv;* pendant *m,* bélière *f,* de ceinturon; passant *m* (de baudrier). **2.** *Cost:* soutache *f,* olive *f;* **frogs and loops,** brandebourgs *m.*

frog[4], *s. Rail:* (cœur *m* de) croisement *m;* **f. point,** cœur de croisement; pointe *f* de cœur; **aerial f.,** aiguillage aérien.

frogbit ['frɔgbit], *s. Bot:* grenouillette *f,* mors *m* de grenouille, grâce *f* des eaux, mor(r)ène *f.*

frogfish ['frɔgfiʃ], *s. Ich:* = **fishing frog,** *q.v. under* FROG[1] 2.

frogged [frɔgd], *a. Cost:* orné de brandebourgs.

froggery ['frɔgəri], *s.* grenouillère *f.*

froggy ['frɔgi]. **1.** *s.* *(a)* *(child's word)* grenouille *f;* *(b)* *P:* mangeur, -euse, de grenouilles; Français, -aise. **2.** *a. F:* *(a)* qui tient de la grenouille; *(b)* (endroit) plein de grenouilles; *(c)* français.

froghopper ['frɔghɔpər], *s. Ent:* cercope *f.*

froglet ['frɔglit], *s.* grenouillette *f.*

frog-like ['frɔglaik], *a.* ranin.

frogman, *pl.* **-men** ['frɔgmən], *s.* homme-grenouille *m, pl.* hommes-grenouilles; **frogman's mask,** masque sous-marin.

frogmarch[1] ['frɔgmɑ:tʃ], *s.* transport *m* d'un récalcitrant, le derrière en l'air, par quatre agents, etc., dont chacun tient un de ses membres.

frogmarch[2], *v.tr.* porter (qn) à quatre, le derrière en l'air.

frogmouth ['frɔgmauθ], *s. Orn:* podarge *m.*

Fröhlich ['frə:liχ], *Pr.n. Med:* **Fröhlich's syndrome,** le syndrome adiposo-génital.

frolic[1] ['frɔlik]. **1.** *s.* *(a)* ébats *mpl,* gambades *fpl;* *(b)* fredaine *f*, divertissement *m*. **2.** *a. A: & Lit:* lutin, folâtre.

frolic², *v.i.* (**frolicked**) se divertir, s'ébattre, folâtrer, gambader, batifoler; lutiner.

frolicker ['frɔlikər], *s.* **1.** fêtard, -arde; batifoleur, -euse. **2.** gambadeur, -euse.

frolicking¹ ['frɔlikiŋ], *a.* gai, joyeux, folâtre.

frolicking², *s.* divertissement *m*, ébats *mpl*, folâtrerie *f*, batifolage *m*.

frolicky ['frɔliki], *a.* folâtre, folichon, -onne.

frolicsome ['frɔliksəm], *a.* (*of pers., manner, etc.*) gai, joyeux, folâtre, folichon, -onne, espiègle, lutin.

from [frɔm, *unstressed,* frəm], *prep.* de. **1.** (*a*) (*indicating departure from a place*) de; **he returned f. London,** il est revenu de Londres; **to jump f. the train,** sauter du train; **he flung himself f. the cliff,** il se jeta du haut de la falaise; **f. Paris to London,** de Paris à Londres; depuis Paris jusqu'à Londres; **f. town to town,** de ville en ville; **f. flower to flower,** de fleur en fleur; **f. side to side,** d'un côté à l'autre; (*b*) (*indicating lower limit*) **the bird lays f. four to six eggs,** l'oiseau pond de quatre à six œufs; **f. seventeen to twenty sail of the line,** de dix-sept à vingt vaisseaux de ligne; **the fleet consisted of f. seventeen to twenty sail of the line,** la flotte comprenait entre dix-sept et vingt vaisseaux de ligne; **wines, f. four francs a bottle,** vins depuis, à partir de, quatre francs la bouteille. **2.** (*indicating starting point in time*) depuis, dès, à partir de; **f. that day,** depuis, dès, ce jour; à partir de, à dater de, ce jour; **f. tomorrow on,** à partir de demain; **reckoning f. yesterday,** comptant à partir d'hier; **f. the earliest records onward,** à partir des plus anciens documents; **I lived in Paris f. 1970,** j'ai vécu à Paris à partir de 1970; **the agreement begins as f. January 1st,** le contrat est valable à partir du premier janvier; **house let f. June 1st,** maison louée à compter du premier juin; **I knew him f. a boy,** je l'ai connu alors qu'il était petit; **he had known the farm f. a boy,** il connaissait la ferme depuis son enfance; **f. his childhood, f. a child,** depuis, dès, son enfance; **he has been sickly f. (his) childhood, f. a child,** il a été maladif dès sa jeunesse; **f. morning to, till, night,** depuis le matin jusqu'au soir; **f. time to time,** de temps en temps. **3.** (*denoting distance, absence*) **he is (away, absent) f. home,** il est absent, sorti, en voyage; **not far f. . . .,** pas loin de . . .; **ten kilometres f. Paris,** à dix kilomètres de Paris. **I am far f. saying that . . .,** je suis loin d'affirmer que . . .. **4.** (*a*) (*denoting separation, removal, freedom*) de, à; **separation f. s.o.,** séparation d'avec qn; **take that knife f. that child,** ôtez ce couteau à cet enfant; **he stole a pound f. her,** il lui a volé une livre; **to tear the bandage f. s.o.'s eyes,** arracher le bandeau de dessus les yeux de qn; **to dissuade s.o. f. doing sth.,** dissuader qn de faire qch.; **I cannot refrain f. laughing,** je ne peux pas m'empêcher de rire; (*b*) (*denoting protection*) contre; **to shelter f. the rain,** s'abriter contre la pluie; **protection of buildings f. lightning,** protection des bâtiments contre la foudre. **5.** (*a*) (*indicating change of state*) **f. bad to worse,** de mal en pis; **f. (being an) office boy he became director,** de saute-ruisseau (qu'il était) il est devenu directeur; **f. being attacked he became the aggressor,** d'attaqué il devint l'agresseur; **the price has been increased f. five pence to ten pence,** on a augmenté le prix de cinq pence à dix pence; (*b*) (*signifying distinction, difference*) d'avec, de; **he can't distinguish the good f. the bad,** il ne sait pas distinguer le bon d'avec le mauvais, **this bird differs f., is distinct f., other birds in . . .,** cet oiseau diffère, se distingue, des autres oiseaux par . . .; (*c*) **to pick s.o. out f. the crowd,** démêler qn parmi la foule; **to glean f. one and another,** glaner chez les uns et les autres; **he grabbed a revolver f. the table,** il saisit un revolver sur la table; **to draw water f. the river,** puiser de l'eau à la rivière; **to drink f. the stream,** boire au ruisseau; **to drink f. the bottle, a glass,** boire à même la bouteille, dans un verre; **to read sth. (aloud) f. a book,** lire qch. dans un livre; **to take sth. f. one's pocket,** prendre qch. dans sa poche. **6.** (*a*) (*indicating origin, source*) **he is, comes, f. Manchester,** il est natif, originaire, de Manchester; **a train f. the North,** un train en provenance du nord; **airlines to and f. the Continent,** lignes aériennes à destination ou en provenance du Continent; **wheat f. Russia,** blé venant de Russie; **broadcast commentary (on the Derby) f. Epsom,** radio-reportage émanant d'Epsom, à partir d'Epsom, depuis Epsom; **a quotation f. Shakespeare,** une citation empruntée à Shakespeare, tirée de Shakespeare; **tales f. oral tradition,** contes recueillis dans la tradition orale; **words f. the heart,** langage qui part du cœur; **I heard it f. him,** je l'ai appris de lui; **fuels manufactured f. coal,** combustibles à base de charbon; **to draw a conclusion f. sth.,** tirer une conclusion de qch.; **to write f. s.o.'s dictation,** écrire sous la dictée de qn; **f. your point of view,** à votre point de vue; (*b*) (*indicating giver, sender*) **a letter f. my father,** une lettre de mon père; **petition f. a group,** pétition émanant d'un groupe; **the petition is f. . . .,** la pétition émane de . . .; **I have brought it to you f. a friend,** je vous l'apporte de la part d'un ami; **a dispatch f. the colonel,** une dépêche de la part du colonel; **you will obtain the same indulgence f. them,** vous obtiendrez la même indulgence de leur part; **the services required f. me,** les services que l'on attend de moi; **tell him that f. me,** dites-lui cela de ma part; (*on parcel*) **f. . . .,** envoi de . . .; expéditeur, -trice . . .; (*c*) (*indicating model, copy*) d'après; **painted f. life, f. nature,** peint d'après nature; **the house was so named f. the owner,** la maison portait le nom de son propriétaire. **7.** (*indicating cause, motive, reason, ground*) **to act f. conviction,** agir par conviction; **it happened f. carelessness,** cela arriva par négligence; **he grew shy f. being laughed at,** il est devenu timide parce qu'on se moquait de lui; **I know him f. seeing him at the club,** je le reconnais pour l'avoir vu au cercle; **to die f. fatigue,** mourir de fatigue; **not f. any fault of his own,** sans qu'il y ait de sa faute; **f. his looks you might suppose that . . .,** à le voir on dirait que . . .; **f. his staggering I took him to be drunk,** de ce qu'il titubait je l'ai cru ivre; **f. what I heard . . .,** d'après ce que j'ai entendu dire . . .; **f. what I can see . . .,** à ce que je vois . . .. **8.** (*a*) (*with adv., prep.*) **f. above,** d'en haut; **I saw him f. a long way off,** je l'ai vu de loin; *Lit:* **he went f. hence, f. thence,** il est parti d'ici, de là; **f. henceforth,** à partir d'aujourd'hui; **f. among . . ., f. amidst . . .,** de parmi . . .; **he came f. amongst the crowd,** il se détacha de la foule; **to look at s.o. f. under, f. over, one's spectacles,** regarder qn par-dessous, par-dessus, ses lunettes; **to come out f. under the ground,** sortir de dessous terre; *NAm:* **to get f. under,** se tirer d'affaire; *P:* **take that thing f. off the table,** enlevez cela de sur la table, de dessus la table; **f. of old,** du temps jadis, du vieux temps; *F:* de dans le temps; **I know it f. of old,** je le sais de longue date; (*b*) (*after adv.*) **to come down f. one's room,** descendre de sa chambre; **to move away f. s.o.,** s'éloigner de qn; **to come out f. a house,** sortir d'une maison.

frond [frɔnd], *s. Bot:* **1.** fronde *f* (de fougère, d'algue). **2.** *F:* feuille *f* (de palmier).

frondage ['frɔndidʒ], *s. Bot:* ensemble *m* des frondes.

fronded ['frɔndid], *a.* (plante) à frondes.

frondescence [frɔn'des(ə)ns], *s.* frondaison *f*, (i) feuillaison *f*; (ii) feuillage *m*.

frondescent [frɔn'des(ə)nt], *a. Bot:* frondescent.

frondiferous [frɔn'difərəs], *a. Bot:* frondifère.

frondose ['frɔndous], **frondous** ['frɔndəs], *a. Bot:* feuillu.

frons [frɔnz], *s. Nat.Hist:* front *m* (de tête).

front¹ [frʌnt], *s. & a.*

I. *s.* **1.** (*a*) *A:* (= FOREHEAD) front *m*; (*b*) *F:* front, contenance *f*, face *f*; maintien *m*; **f. to f.,** face à face; **to show a bold f., to put a bold f. on it,** faire bonne contenance; payer d'audace; (*c*) **to have the f. to do sth.,** avoir l'effronterie, le toupet, le front, de faire qch.; (*d*) **his profession is only a f.,** son métier n'est qu'une couverture; **it's only a f. on his part,** ce n'est qu'une façade de sa part; (*e*) *NAm: P:* prête-nom *m*, *pl.* prête-noms. **2.** (*a*) *Mil:* front; (i) **to pass down the f. of the troops (on parade),** passer sur le front des troupes; (ii) (**battle**) **f.,** ligne *f* de contact, de feu; *A:* front de bataille; **fluid f.,** front fluide; **stabilized f.,** front stabilisé; **operations on wide fronts,** opérations *f* sur de grands fronts; **to present an unbroken f.,** présenter un front continu, inentamé; **to be sent to the f.,** être envoyé au front, au feu, en première ligne; **the home f.,** l'arrière *m*, les civils *m*; **all's quiet on the home f.,** (i) pour ce qui est des civils le calme règne; (ii) tout va bien chez nous; (*b*) *Pol:* **common f., united f.,** front commun; **popular f.,** front populaire; (*c*) *F:* **to make progress on all fronts,** faire des progrès de tous côtés; **on the kitchen f.,** dans le domaine de la cuisine; (*d*) *Meteor:* **warm f., cold f.,** front chaud, froid. **3.** (*a*) devant *m*, partie antérieure (de qch.); façade *f*, face (d'un bâtiment); *Arch.Draw:* élévation *f*; devanture *f* (d'un magasin, d'une chaudière); étalage *m* (de boutique); avant *m* (d'une voiture); montre *f* (d'un orgue); corps *m* (d')avant (d'un appareil photographique); (faux) toupet (de cheveux); frange *f* (de faux cheveux); devant (de chemise, de robe); **carriage in the f. of the train,** voiture *f* en tête du train; voiture de tête; **to look at the f. of sth.,** regarder qch. de face; *Ph:* **wave f.,** front d'onde; *Nau:* **bridge f.,** façade du château; *Aut:* **false f. of the radiator,** grillage *m*, grille *f*, de radiateur; protège-radiateur *m inv*; *Furn:* **drop f., fall f. (of desk),** abattant *m* (de secrétaire); *Bootm:* **plain f. shoe,** chaussure *f* sans bout rapporté; *Fenc:* **to show less f.,** s'effacer; (*b*) *Lit: & Poet:* **in the f. of summer, of March,** au seuil de l'été, au début de mars; (*c*) (*at seaside*) **the f.,** la promenade, le front de mer; **house on the f.,** maison *f* faisant face à la mer. **4.** premier rang; **to push one's way to the f.,** se frayer un chemin jusqu'au premier rang; se pousser (en avant); (*of pers.*) **to come to the f.,** arriver au premier rang; se révéler; se faire connaître; **author who is beginning to come to the f.,** auteur qui commence à percer; **idea that is coming to the f.,** idée *f* qui se fait jour; (*of topic*) **to come to the f. again,** revenir sur l'eau. **5.** *adv.phr.* **in f.,** devant, en avant; **stand further in f.,** mettez-vous plus en avant; **to send s.o. on in f.,** envoyer qn devant, en avant; **attacked in f. and in the rear, in f. and rear,** attaqué par devant et par derrière; *Th:* **out f.,** dans la salle; *prep.phr.* **in f. of,** *U.S:* **f. of,** (i) en face de, vis-à-vis de; (ii) devant, au devant de; **a terrace in f. of the house,** une terrasse devant la maison; **he stood right in f. of me,** (i) il se trouvait juste en face de moi, (ii) il s'est mis juste devant moi; **look in f. of you,** regardez devant vous; **my office is in f. of the church,** mon bureau est en face de l'église, fait face à l'église; *Mec.E:* **eccentric in f. of the crank,** excentrique avance sur la manivelle.

II. *a.* (*a*) antérieur, de devant, d'avant, de face; **f. seat,** siège *m* d'avant; *F:* **to have a f. seat,** être aux premières loges; **f. door,** porte *f* d'entrée (principale); porte de devant; porte sur la rue, sur la façade; **f. room,** chambre *f* sur le devant, sur la rue; **f. wall,** mur *m* de façade; **f. carriage,** (i) (*of train*) voiture *f* de tête; (ii) *Veh:* avant-train *m*, *pl.* avant-trains; **I was in the f. part of the train,** je me trouvais en tête de train; **f. rank,** premier rang; **artists in the f. rank,** artistes *mf* de premier plan; **f.-rank actors,** acteurs *m* les plus en vue; **f. view,** vue *f* de face, de front; *Arch:* élévation *f*; *Artil: Sm.a:* **f. sight,** guidon *m* de mire; bouton *m* de mire; *Bookb:* **f. board,** recto *m*, plat supérieur (d'un livre); *Cy: Aut:* **f. brake,** frein *m* avant; **f. wheel,** (i) *Veh:* roue *f* (d')avant; *Cy:* roue directrice; *Aut:* **f.-wheel drive,** traction *f* avant; **car with a f.-wheel drive,** voiture *f* à avant-train moteur, à roues avant motrices; *Journ:* **f. page,** première page; *F:* la une; **f.-page advertisement,** annonce *f* en première page; **f.-page news,** nouvelles sensationnelles; *Laund:* **f.-loading washing machine,** machine *f* à laver avec chargement en façade; *Ling:* **f. vowel, f. consonant,** voyelle, consonne, palatale, antérieure, d'avant; palatale *f*; *Mch:* **f. plate,** plaque *f* de devanture (de chaudière, fourneau); *Mec.E:* **f. tool,** outil *m* (de tour) de face; *Mil:* **f. line,** ligne *f* de contact, de feu; *A:* ligne de bataille; **f.-line troops,** troupes *f* du front; *Mus:* **f. pipe,** tuyau *m* de montre (d'un orgue); *Phot:* **f. lens,** lentille frontale (d'un objectif); **f. lighting,** éclairage frontal; *Th:* **f. cloth,** toile *f*; rideau *m*; *Veh:* **f.-end loader,** chargeur frontal; (*b*) *NAm:* **f. man,** (i) prête-nom *m*, *pl.* prête-noms; (ii) représentant *m* (d'une société), porte-parole *m inv* (d'une délégation); *Mus:* **the f. men,** les joueurs d'instruments à cordes ou à vent (d'un orchestre de jazz); **f. name,** prénom *m*; **f. office,** (i) bureau(x) *m(pl)* de l'administration; (ii) commissariat (central) de police; **f. runner,** concurrent principal; *Publ:* **f. matter,** feuilles *f* liminaires.

front². **1.** *v.tr. & i.* (*a*) **to f. (sth.); to f. (up)on, to(wards), (sth.),** faire face à (qch.); être tourné vers (qch.); **the house fronts north,** la maison est exposée, orientée, au nord; la maison fait face au nord; la maison regarde le nord; **windows that f. (on to) the street,** fenêtres qui donnent sur la rue; **the river and the houses fronting on it,** le fleuve et les maisons donnant dessus; (*b*) *NAm:* diriger (un orchestre de jazz). **2.** *v.tr.* (*a*) affronter, braver (l'ennemi, une accusation, etc.); (*b*) **to f. s.o. with s.o.,** confronter qn avec qn. **3.** *v.tr.* donner une (nouvelle) façade à (un édifice); **house fronted with stone,** maison avec façade en pierre; **wide-fronted house,** maison à large façade. **4.** *Mil:* (*a*) *v.i.* faire front; **left f.!** à gauche front! à gauche, gauche! (*b*) *v.tr.* établir le front de (l'armée, etc.). **5.** *v.tr. Ling:* palataliser (une consonne). **6.** *v.i. P:* **to f. for s.o.,** servir de couverture à qn.

frontage ['frʌntidʒ], *s.* **1.** terrain *m* en bordure (d'un fleuve, d'une chaussée, etc.). **2.** longueur *f* de façade (d'un édifice); devanture *f* (d'un magasin); **premises with a good f.,** local *m* avec une belle devanture. **3.** (*a*) façade *f*; **premises with frontages on two streets,** local avec façades sur deux rues; **to buy land at so much per metre of f.,** acheter un terrain à tant le mètre courant sur la rue, à tant le mètre de façade; **f. line,** alignement *m* (d'une rue); (*b*) *Jur:* droit *m* de façade. **4.** *Mil:* front *m*; étendue *f*, largeur *f*, du front; **f. to be covered by fire,** front à battre. **5.** orientation *f*, vue *f*, perspective *f*.

frontager ['frʌntidʒər], *s.* **1.** (propriétaire) riverain *m*. **2.** propriétaire ayant maison sur une rue, ayant villa vis-à-vis la mer.

frontal[1] [ˈfrʌnt(ə)l], *s.* **1.** *Cost:* fronteau *m*, bandeau *m*. **2.** (*a*) *Anat:* os frontal, os coronal; le frontal; (*b*) *Archeol:* frontail *m*, fronteau (de cheval). **3.** *Ecc:* devant *m* d'autel; frontel *m*, fronteau *m*, frontier *m*. **4.** façade *f* (d'un bâtiment).

frontal[2], *a.* **1.** (*a*) *Anat:* (*of bone, vein, etc.*) frontal, -aux; (*b*) *Arch:* (vue, etc.) de face; *Art:* **f. nudity,** nu(e) vu(e) de face. **2.** *Tls:* **f. hammer,** (marteau) frontal *m*. **3.** *Mil:* (attaque, etc.) de front; *Av: etc:* **f. resistance,** résistance *f* à l'avancement.

frontality [frʌnˈtæliti], *s. Art:* frontalité *f*.

frontally [ˈfrʌntəli], *adv.* (attaquer, etc.) de front.

front-bencher [ˈfrʌntˈben(t)ʃər], *s. Parl:* membre *m* de la Chambre siégeant aux premières banquettes (occupées d'un côté par les ministres et de l'autre par les ex-ministres et "ministrables" de l'opposition).

frontier [ˈfrʌntiər], *s.* **1.** frontière *f*; **to extend the frontiers of a state,** reculer les frontières d'un état; **natural frontiers,** barrières naturelles; **the frontiers of human knowledge,** les frontières, bornes *f*, des connaissances humaines; *attrib.* **f. guard,** garde-frontière *m*, *pl.* gardes-frontière; **f. station,** gare *f* frontière; **f. town,** ville *f* frontière; **f. districts,** régions frontalières, de la frontière; **f. post,** poteau-frontière *m*, *pl.* poteaux-frontière; **the inhabitants of the f. zone,** les habitants de la frontière; **North-West f.,** la frontière entre le Pakistan et l'Afghanistan. **2.** *U.S: Hist: Can:* ligne *f* de séparation entre les régions en exploitation et les régions encore vierges.

frontier(s)man, *pl.* **-men** [ˈfrʌntiə(z)mən], *s.m.* **1.** habitant de la frontière; frontalier. **2.** *U.S:* broussard.

fronting [ˈfrʌntiŋ], *s.* **1.** (*a*) exposition *f*, orientation *f* (d'un édifice); (*b*) affrontement *m* (de l'ennemi, etc.); (*c*) confrontation *f* (de deux personnes); (*d*) *Mil:* établissement *m* d'un front. **2.** façade *f* (d'un édifice).

frontispiece [ˈfrʌntispiːs], *s.* **1.** *Arch:* façade principale; *A:* frontispice *m* (d'un édifice); fronton *m*. **2.** *Typ:* frontispice. **3.** *P: A:* figure *f*, visage *m*, devanture *f*.

frontispieced [ˈfrʌntispiːst], *a.* garni d'un frontispice; **f. with a portrait of the author,** avec, en frontispice, un portrait de l'auteur.

frontlet [ˈfrʌntlit], *s.* **1.** *Cost:* (*a*) bandeau *m*, filet *m*; *Ecc:* fronteau *m* (de nonne); (*b*) *Jew.Civ:* fronteau, phylactère *m*. **2.** front *m* (d'un animal). **3.** parement *m* (d'un autel).

frontogenesis [frʌntouˈdʒenisis], *s. Meteor:* frontogénèse *f*.

frontolysis [frʌnˈtɔlisis], *s. Meteor:* frontolyse *f*.

fronton [ˈfrʌntən], *s. Arch:* fronton *m*.

fronto-parietal [ˈfrʌntoupəˈraiitəl], *a. Anat:* fronto-pariétal, *pl.* fronto-pariétaux.

front-ranker [ˈfrʌntˈræŋkər], *s. F:* artiste *mf*, etc., de premier plan.

frontwards [ˈfrʌntwədz], *adv.* (au) devant; en devant (**of,** de).

frontwise [ˈfrʌntwaiz], *adv.* de face.

frore [frɔːr], *a. Poet: A:* gelé, glacé.

frost[1] [frɔst], *s.* **1.** (*a*) *Meteor:* gelée *f*, gel *m*; **early f.,** gelée automnale; **late f., spring f.,** gelée printanière; **hard f.,** forte gelée; **ground f., white f.,** gelée blanche; **there has been a white f.,** il a gelé (à) blanc; **black f.,** verglas *m*; *F:* **Jack F.,** le bonhomme Hiver; la gelée; **ten degrees of f.,** dix degrés *m* de froid; **the f. was hardening the roads,** le gel durcissait les routes; **we are going to have f.,** le temps est à la gelée; **the f. was still in the meat,** la viande n'était pas encore dégelée; (*b*) **hoar f.,** givre *m*; *Lit:* frimas *m*; **glazed f.,** verglas; **winter had already covered the trees with (white) f.,** l'hiver avait déjà givré les arbres; (*c*) *attrib.* **f. flowers,** fleurs *f* de givre; **f. heave, f. heaving,** *NAm:* **f. boil,** gonflement *m*, boursouflement *m*, de la terre occasionné par le gel; *Farr:* **f. nail,** crampon *m*; clou *m* à glace; **f. nip,** brûlure *f* (des plantes) par la gelée; gelure *f*, brouissure *f*; **f. precautions,** précautions *f* contre le gel; **the F. Saints,** les saints de glace (*i.e.* Mamert, Pancrace, Servais, dont les fêtes sont les onze, douze, treize, mai); *Farr:* **f. shoe,** fer *m* à glace, à crampons; *Geol:* **f. thrust, thrusting,** soulèvement (de blocs de roche) engendré par le gel; (*d*) *Fig: A:* **there was a f. in his manner,** il y avait une froideur dans sa manière. **2.** (*a*) *F: O:* (*of play, book, etc.*) four *m*, fiasco *m*, déception *f*; **the play was a dead f., a perfect f.,** la pièce a fait four; ç'a été un four noir; (*b*) **the whole thing turned out a f.,** toute l'affaire s'en est allée en eau de boudin.

frost[2], *v.tr.* **1.** (*a*) geler, attaquer de champelure, griller (un arbre, fruitier, etc.); (*b*) *Dom.Ec:* surgeler (des comestibles). **2.** (*a*) givrer (les vitres, l'herbe, etc.); (*b*) *v.i.* (*of windscreen, etc.*) **to f. (over, up),** se givrer, se couvrir de givre. **3.** (*a*) blanchir (les cheveux); (*b*) saupoudrer (qch.) de sucre, etc.; glacer (un gâteau); givrer (un gâteau, un arbre de Noël, etc.). **4.** (*a*) glacer (un métal); (*b*) dépolir (le verre); mater (l'or). **5.** mettre des crampons à (un fer à cheval); ferrer (un cheval) à glace.

frostbite [ˈfrɔstbait], *s.* **1.** *Med:* (*of feet, etc.*) gelure *f*, froidure *f*, congélation *f*. **2.** *Agr: Hort:* (*of plants*) brûlure *f* par la gelée; gelure, brouissure *f*; (*of fruit-trees*) champelure *f*, champlure *f*.

frostbitten [ˈfrɔstbitn], *a.* **1.** (*of nose, etc.*) gelé. **2.** (*of plants*) brûlé par le froid; grillé (par la gelée); (*of fruit-trees, etc.*) champlé.

frostbound [ˈfrɔstbaund], *a.* (vaisseau, etc.) retenu par les glaces.

frostcleft[1] [ˈfrɔstkleft], **frostcrack** [ˈfrɔstkræk], *s. Arb:* gélivure *f* (du bois).

frostcleft[2], **frostcracked** [ˈfrɔstkrækt], *a.* (*of wood, stone*) gélif.

frosted [ˈfrɔstid], *a.* **1.** (*a*) = FROSTBITTEN; (*b*) (*of food*) surgelé. **2.** (*of trees, window panes, etc.*) givré. **3.** (*a*) (*of hair*) blanc; (*b*) saupoudré (**with,** de); **f. cake,** gâteau glacé. **4.** (*of glass*) dépoli; (*of gold, etc.*) mat; *El:* **f. bulb,** lampe dépolie (intérieurement). **5. f. gelatine,** gélatine cristallisée, à surface chagrinée; **f. enamel,** émail cristallisé.

frostfish [ˈfrɔstfiʃ], *s. Ich:* **1.** gade *m*. **2.** lépidope *m*, jarretière *f*.

frost-hardy [ˈfrɔsthɑːdi], *a. Hort:* résistant au froid.

frostily [ˈfrɔstili], *adv.* (répondre, etc.) glacialement; d'une manière très froide, glacée.

frostiness [ˈfrɔstinis], *s.* **1.** froid glacial (du temps); **f. of the air,** froidure *f*. **2.** manière glaciale (de qn); **the f. of my reception,** l'accueil glacial qui m'a été fait.

frosting [ˈfrɔstiŋ], *s.* **1.** (*a*) givrage *m*; (*b*) glaçage *m* (d'un métal); (*c*) dépolissage *m* (du verre). **2.** *Cu:* sucre pilé (pour glaçage).

frost-nailed [ˈfrɔstneild], *a.* (cheval) ferré à glace.

frost-nipped [ˈfrɔstnipt], *a.* = FROSTBITTEN.

frostproof [ˈfrɔstpruːf], *a.* résistant à la gelée; ingélif.

frost-shoe [ˈfrɔstʃuː], *v.tr.* (**frost-shoeing; frost-shod** [-ʃɔd]) ferrer (un cheval, etc.) à glace.

frost-tender [ˈfrɔs(t)tendər], *a. Hort:* sensible au froid.

frostweed [ˈfrɔstwiːd], *s. Bot:* hélianthème *m*, ciste *m*.

frostwork [ˈfrɔstwəːk], *s.* (*on windows, etc.*) gelée *f*; fleurs *fpl* de givre.

frosty [ˈfrɔsti], *a.* **1.** gelé, glacial, -als; **f. weather,** temps *m* de gelée; temps à la gelée. **2. f. reception,** accueil glacial; **f. answer,** réponse glacée. **3.** (*of window*) couvert de givre; (arbre) givré.

froth[1] [frɔθ], *s.* **1.** écume *f* (du bouillon, aux lèvres); mousse *f* (du savon, de la bière, etc.); faux col (d'un verre de bière); **sea f.,** écume de la mer; **f. flotation,** flotation *f*. **2.** *F:* futilités *fpl*; paroles creuses; **his speech was all f.,** son discours ne contenait rien de solide.

froth[2]. **1.** *v.i.* écumer, mousser; (*of waves*) moutonner, bouillonner; **to f. up,** mousser fortement; **to f. over,** déborder (en moussant); **he was frothing at the mouth,** sa bouche écumait. **2.** *v.tr.* faire mousser (le savon, les œufs, etc.).

froth-blower [ˈfrɔθblouər], *s. P: O:* buveur *m* de bière.

frother [ˈfrɔθər], *s. Ch:* moussant *m*.

froth-hopper [ˈfrɔθhɔpər], *s. Ent:* cercope *f*.

frothiness [ˈfrɔθinis], *s.* **1.** état écumeux (de la mer, etc.); état mousseux (d'une boisson, etc.); état moutonneux (des vagues). **2.** *F:* futilité *f*, manque *m* de substance (d'un discours, etc.).

frothy [ˈfrɔθi], *a.* **1.** (*a*) écumeux, écumant; mousseux; (sang, etc.) spumeux; (*of sea, waves*) moutonneux, moutonné; (*b*) (tissu) léger, bouffant. **2.** *F:* (*of speech, etc.*) vide, creux.

frottage [ˈfrɔtɑːʒ], *s. Art:* frottis *m*.

frotton [ˈfrɔtən], *s. Typ:* frotton *m*.

Froude [fruːd], *Pr.n. Mec.E:* **F. brake,** frein *m* de Froude.

frouzy [ˈfrauzi], *a.* = FROWZY.

froward [ˈfrouəd], *a. A:* (*of pers.*) obstiné, entêté, rebelle, mutin, indocile.

frowardly [ˈfrouədli], *adv. A:* obstinément, indocilement, en rebelle.

frowardness [ˈfrouədnis], *s. A:* indocilité *f*, obstination *f*, entêtement *m*, humeur *f* revêche.

frown[1] [fraun], *s.* **1.** froncement *m* de sourcils; regard courroucé, sévère; regard de colère; regard soucieux; **to look at s.o. with a f.,** regarder qn en fronçant les sourcils; **a f. had settled on his brow,** son visage s'était embruni. **2.** air désapprobateur; désapprobation *f*. **3.** *Lit:* **the frowns of fortune,** les rigueurs *f* du sort.

frown[2], *v.i. & tr.* (*a*) (*of pers.*) froncer les sourcils; se renfrogner, renfrogner sa mine; **to f. at, (up)on, s.o.,** regarder qn de travers, en fronçant les sourcils; faire mauvais visage à qn; *F:* faire la tête à qn; **fortune frowned on him,** le sort lui a été sévère; **to f. upon a suggestion,** désapprouver une suggestion; **to f. defiance on the crowd,** regarder la foule d'un air de menace et de défi; **to f. s.o. into silence, to f. s.o. down,** imposer le silence à qn d'un regard sévère; **to f. s.o. away,** écarter qn d'un regard sévère; (*b*) (*of thgs*) avoir l'air sombre, menaçant; être contraire (**on,** à).

frowning[1] [ˈfrauniŋ], *a.* (*of looks, face, etc.*) renfrogné, rechigné; (*of brow*) sourcilleux; (*of thgs*) sombre, menaçant.

frowning[2], *s.* froncement *m* de sourcils; renfrognement *m*.

frowningly [ˈfrauniŋli], *adv.* en fronçant les sourcils; d'un air sombre, menaçant.

frowst[1] [fraust], *s. F:* atmosphère *f* qui sent le renfermé; odeur *f* de renfermé.

frowst[2], *v.i. F:* rester enfermé au coin du feu.

frowstiness [ˈfraustinis], *s. F:* manque *m* d'air; odeur *f* de renfermé.

frowsty [ˈfrausti], *a. F:* qui sent le renfermé.

frowy [ˈfraui], *a.* (bois) cassant.

frowzy [ˈfrauzi], *a.* **1.** (salle) qui sent le renfermé. **2.** (*a*) (*of pers., hair, clothes, etc.*) sale, mal tenu, peu soigné; (*b*) **f. complexion,** teint couperosé.

frozen [ˈfrouzn], *a.* **1.** (*a*) gelé, glacé; **the f. North,** le grand nord; **f. foods,** (produits) surgelés (*m*), congelés (*m*); **f. meat,** viande congelée, frigorifiée; *F:* frigo *m*; *Fin:* **f. assets,** fonds *m* non liquides; fonds gelés; **f. credits,** créances gelées; **my hands are f.,** j'ai les mains gelées, glacées; **I am f. to death,** je meurs de froid; **you'll be f.,** vous allez mourir de froid; (*b*) *F:* **I have got f. waiting for you,** je me suis gelé à vous attendre; (*b*) *F:* **he received them with f. formality,** il les a reçus avec une raideur glacée, glaciale; (*c*) *NAm: F:* (*of pers.*) **to be f.,** être transi de peur. **2.** *Mec.E:* (écrou, boulon) rouillé, qui ne veut pas bouger; **f. bearings,** coussinets coincés. **3.** *Bill:* (*of ball*) collé sous bande. **4.** *Med:* **f. shoulder,** épaule ankylosée.

fructan [ˈfrʌktæn], *s. Ch:* fructosane *m*.

fructed [ˈfrʌktid], *a. Her:* fruité.

fructescent [frʌkˈtes(ə)nt], *a.* fructescent.

fructiferous [frʌkˈtifərəs], *a.* frugifère, fructifère.

fructification [frʌktifiˈkeiʃ(ə)n], *s.* fructification *f*; (i) production *f* de fruits; (ii) *Bot:* organes reproducteurs (des cryptogames).

fructiform [ˈfrʌktifɔːm], *a.* fructiforme, carpomorphe.

fructify [ˈfrʌktifai]. **1.** *v.i.* fructifier; (i) produire du fruit; (ii) *F:* rapporter; produire des bénéfices. **2.** *v.tr.* faire fructifier; féconder.

fructifying [ˈfrʌktifaiiŋ], *s.* fructification *f*.

fructivorous [frʌkˈtivərəs], *a. Nat.Hist:* frugivore.

fructosan [ˈfrʌktəsæn], *s. Ch:* fructosane *m*.

fructose [ˈfrʌktous], *s. Ch:* fructose *m*; lévulose *usu. m*; sucre *m* de fruit.

fructule [ˈfrʌktjuːl], *s. Bot:* fructule *m*.

fructuous [ˈfrʌktjuəs], *a.* fructueux; (sol) fertile, fécond.

fructus [ˈfrʌktəs], *s. Jur:* croît *m* (du cheptel, etc.).

frugal [ˈfruːg(ə)l], *a.* **1.** (*of pers., life, mind*) frugal, -aux; économe; **f. woman,** femme *f* économe; **to be f. of sth.,** ménager qch. **2.** (*of meal, board, etc.*) frugal, sobre, simple, modeste; **f. meal,** repas *m* d'anachorète; **f. eater,** homme *m* sobre.

frugality [fruˈgæliti], *s.* frugalité *f*; (i) économie *f*; (ii) sobriété *f*.

frugally [ˈfruːgəli], *adv.* frugalement; (i) économiquement; (ii) sobrement.

frugiferous [fruˈdʒifərəs], *a. Bot:* frugifère, fructifère.

frugivorous [fruˈdʒivərəs], *a. Nat.Hist:* frugivore.

fruit[1] [fruːt], *s.* fruit *m*. **1.** (*a*) **bananas, apples and other fruit(s),** les bananes, les pommes et autres fruits; **a stone f.,** un fruit à noyau; *B:* **by their fruits ye shall know them,** (i) *B:* vous les connaîtrez à leurs fruits; (ii) *Prov:* à la laine on connaît la brebis; (*b*) *coll:* **eat more f.,** mangez plus de fruits; **to strip a tree, an orchard, of f.,** effruiter un arbre, un verger; **tree in f.,** arbre portant des fruits; **soft f.,** *NAm:* **small f.,** petits fruits; **dried f.,** fruits secs; **stewed f.,** compote *f* de fruits; (*at table*) **to serve the f.,** servir le fruit; **to bear f.,** (i) (*of tree*) fruiter; rapporter, donner des fruits; porter fruit; (ii) *Fig:* (*of labour, etc.*) porter fruit, fructifier; **my enquiries bore f.,** mes recherches furent couronnées de succès; (*c*) *Bot:* **the f. of the rose-tree, of the larkspur,** le fruit du rosier, du pied-d'alouette; (*d*) *attrib.* **f. basket,** cueilloir *m*; *Ent:* **f. bark beetle, f. tree (bark) beetle,** scolyte *m*; *Z:* **f. bats,** chauves-souris *f* frugivores; *Bac:* **f. body,** corps *m* fructifère; *Bot:* **f. bud,** bourgeon *m* à fruit; **f. business,** fruiterie *f*; **f. cocktail,** macédoine de fruits (avec ou sans alcool) servie dans un verre à pied; **f. cup,** boisson glacée avec fruits; **f. dish,** (i) compotier *m*; (ii) corbeille *f* à fruits; **f. drop,** pastille parfumée de fruits; **f. farmer, f. grower,** fructiculteur *m*, pomiculteur *m*; producteur *m* de fruits; **f. farming,** fructiculture *f*; *Ent:* **f. fly,** drosophile *f*; mouche *f* à fruits; **f. gatherer, f.**

picker, (i) (*pers.*) cueilleur, -euse, de fruits; (ii) *Tls:* cueille-fruits *m inv,* cueilloir *m*; **f. house,** fruitier *m,* fruiterie *f*; **f. juice,** jus *m* de fruits; **f. knife,** couteau *m* à fruit(s); pèle-fruits *m inv*; **f. machine,** machine *f* à sous; *P:* tire-pognon *m, pl.* tire-pognons; *Art:* **f. piece,** tableau *m* de fruits; *Orn:* **f. pigeon,** carpophage *m*; **f. salad,** (i) macédoine *f,* salade *f,* de fruits; (ii) *Mil: P:* décorations *fpl* militaires; *P:* batterie *f* de cuisine; *Arb:* **f. shoot,** lambourde *f*; **f. stalk,** pédoncule *m*; **f. stand,** fruitier *m,* compotier *m*; **f. stoner,** énucloir *m,* dénoyauteur *m*; **f. sugar,** fructose *m,* lévulose *usu. m*; sucre *m* de fruit; **f. tree,** arbre fruitier, à fruit; **f. wall,** mur *m* à espaliers. **2.** (*a*) **the fruits of the earth,** les fruits, les biens *m,* de la terre; **the f. of her womb,** le fruit de ses entrailles; (*b*) **the fruits of the hunt, of industry, of peace,** les fruits, les produits *m,* de la chasse, de l'industrie; les fruits, les biens, de la paix; (*c*) fruit, résultat *m*; **his knowledge is the f. of much study,** son savoir est le fruit de longues études; **his downfall was the f. of his extravagance, of his hasty marriage,** il doit sa ruine à sa prodigalité, à son mariage irréfléchi. **3.** *U.S: P:* homosexuel *m*; *P:* tante *f.*

fruit². **1.** *v.i.* fruiter; porter des fruits; **to f. well,** saisonner. **2.** *v.tr.* faire fruiter (un arbre, etc.).

fruitage ['fru:tidʒ], *s.* **1.** fructification *f.* **2.** *coll.* fruits *mpl.*

fruitarian [fru:'tɛəriən], *a. & s.* fruitarien, -ienne.

fruit-bearing¹ ['fru:tbɛəriŋ], *a.* frugifère, fructifère; (arbre) fruitier.

fruit-bearing², *s.* fructification *f.*

fruit(-)crow ['fru:tkrou], *s. Orn:* coracine *f,* piauhau *m.*

fruit-eater ['fru:ti:tər], *s.* **1.** (*pers.*) mangeur, -euse, de fruits. **2.** *Nat.Hist:* frugivore *m.*

fruit-eating ['fru:ti:tiŋ], *a. Nat.Hist:* frugivore, carpophage.

fruited ['fru:tid], *a.* (arbre) portant des fruits, chargé de fruits.

fruiter ['fru:tər], *s.* **1.** *Nau:* navire transporteur de fruits; cargo fruitier. **2.** arbre fruitier; **a sure f.,** arbre fruitier à rendement assuré. **3.** (*pers.*) fructiculteur *m.*

fruiterer ['fru:tərər], *s.* fruitier, -ière; **fruiterer's shop,** fruiterie *f.*

fruiteress ['fru:təris], *s.f.* fruitière.

fruitful ['fru:tful], *a.* **1.** (*of tree, etc.*) fructueux, productif; (*of soil, etc.*) fertile, fécond; **the f. rain,** la pluie féconde; la pluie fécondante. **2.** (*a*) (*of marriage*) fécond; (*b*) (*of animals, etc.*) prolifique; *Fig:* **action f. of, in, consequences,** action *f* fertile en conséquences; **a budget f. of discontent,** un budget qui n'a engendré que du mécontentement. **3.** (*of work*) fructueux, profitable.

fruitfully ['fru:tfuli], *adv.* fructueusement, utilement, d'une manière profitable.

fruitfulness ['fru:tfulnis], *s.* productivité *f* (d'un arbre, etc.); fertilité *f* (du sol, etc.); fécondité *f* (d'une femelle, *F:* d'un écrivain, etc.); caractère fructueux, utilité *f* (d'un travail, etc.).

fruiting ['fru:tiŋ], *a.* (*of tree, stem, etc.*) frugifère, fructifère; *Bac:* **f. body,** corps *m* fructifère.

fruition [fru(:)'iʃ(ə)n], *s.* **1.** jouissance *f* (d'un bien). **2.** réalisation *f* (d'un projet, d'un espoir); fructification *f* (d'une idée, etc.); **results long of f.,** résultats *m* à longue échéance; **to come to f.,** fructifier; porter fruit; se réaliser.

fruitless ['fru:tlis], *a.* (*of plant, tree, work, etc.*) sans fruit, stérile, infructueux; **f. efforts,** vains efforts; efforts sans résultat; *F:* coups *m* d'épée dans l'eau.

fruitlessly ['fru:tlisli], *adv.* infructueusement, sans fruit; vainement, inutilement.

fruitlet ['fru:tlit], *s.* drupéole *m,* fructule *m* (d'une framboise, etc.).

fruitwood ['fru:twud], *s. Furn:* bois fruitier.

fruity ['fru:ti], *a.* **1.** (*a*) (goût, etc.) de fruit; (*b*) (vin) fruité, fruiteux. **2.** *F:* (*a*) **f. voice,** voix (trop) étoffée; (*b*) (roman, scandale, etc.) corsé.

frumentaceous [frumen'teiʃəs], *a. Bot:* frumentacé.

frumenty ['fru:mənti], *s. Cu:* fromentée *f*; bouillie *f* de froment.

frump [frʌmp], *s. F:* femme mal attifée, en retard sur la mode; **old f.,** vieille caricature, vieille toupie, vieux tableau, vieille fée; **isn't she a f.!** regardez-moi ce paquet! **she's an awful f.,** elle est affreusement fagotée.

frumpily ['frʌmpili], *adv.* = FRUMPISHLY.

frumpiness ['frʌmpinis] *s.* manque *m* d'élégance (dans la toilette d'une femme).

frumpish ['frʌmpiʃ], **frumpy** ['frʌmpi], *a.* (*a*) (femme) fagotée, mal attifée; (chapeau, robe) informe; (*b*) *A:* revêche, acariâtre.

frumpishly ['frʌmpiʃli], *adv.* (*a*) (habillée) sans goût, sans élégance; (*b*) *A:* d'un ton, d'un air, revêche.

frustrate¹ ['frʌstreit], *a. A: & Poet:* (espoir, dessein) frustré, déjoué.

frustrate² [frʌs'treit], *v.tr.* (*a*) faire échouer, faire avorter (un projet, etc.); **to f. a plot,** déjouer un complot; **to f. s.o.'s hopes,** frustrer qn dans son espoir; frustrer, désappointer, l'espoir de qn; **the wind frustrated our efforts,** le vent a rendu vains nos efforts; (*b*) contrecarrer (qn).

frustrated [frʌs'treitid], *a.* **1.** frustré; **to feel f.,** avoir un sentiment de frustration. **2.** *Com:* **f. exports,** produits destinés à l'exportation en souffrance.

frustrating [frʌs'treitiŋ], *a.* frustrant.

frustration [frʌs'treiʃ(ə)n], *s.* **1.** anéantissement *m* (des projets de qn); frustration *f* (d'un espoir). **2.** *Psy:* frustration.

frustrative [frʌs'treitiv], *a.* frustratif, frustratoire.

frustule ['frʌstju:l], *s. Biol:* frustule *m* (d'une diatomée).

frustum, *pl.* **-ta, -tums** ['frʌstəm, -tə, -təmz], *s. Mth:* tronc *m* (de cône, de prisme, etc.); **f. of pyramid,** tronc de pyramide; pyramide tronquée; *Arch:* **f. of a column,** tronçon *m* d'une colonne; colonne tronquée.

frutescent [fru:'tes(ə)nt], *a. Bot:* frutescent.

frutex, *pl.* **-ices** ['fru:teks, -isi:z], *s. Bot:* arbrisseau *m.*

fruticetum, *pl.* **-ta** [fru:ti'si:təm, -tə], *s.* fruticetum *m.*

fruticose ['fru:tikous], **fruticulose** [fru'tikjulous], *a. Bot:* fruticuleux; **fruticose lichens,** lichens fruticuleux.

fry¹ [frai], *s. coll.* **1.** *Ich:* (*a*) frai *m,* fretin *m,* alevin *m,* nourrain *m,* poissonnaille *f*; **small f.,** menu fretin; menuisaille *f*; (*b*) **salmon f.,** tacons *mpl*; alevins *mpl* de saumon; saumoneaux *mpl* dans la deuxième année; (*c*) (*of frogs, bees, etc.*) jeunes *mpl.* **2.** *F:* **the small f.,** (i) le menu fretin, le menu peuple, les gens insignifiants, les petites gens; les balayeurs *m* (de la littérature, etc.); (ii) les gosses *m,* les loupiots *m.*

fry², *v.* (**fried**) **1.** *v.tr.* (*a*) **to (deep-)f.,** (faire) frire, (faire) cuire en friteuse (du poisson, etc.); **(French) fried potatoes,** pommes (de terre) frites; frites *fpl*; (*b*) (faire) sauter (de la viande, etc.); **to f. up the remains of the joint,** (faire) sauter les restes du rôti; **fried potatoes,** pommes (de terre) sautées; **fried eggs,** œufs sur le plat; **to f. an egg,** faire cuire un œuf sur le plat. **2.** *v.i.* (*of food*) frire; *F:* **to f. in one's own grease,** mijoter dans son jus; **to f. with impatience,** griller d'impatience. **3.** *P:* **to be fried,** être soûl, ivre; avoir sa cuite.

fry³, *s.* **1.** *Cu:* (*a*) plat *m* de viande frite; friture *f*; (*b*) sauté *m.* **2.** issues *fpl*; fressure *f* (d'agneau, de porc). **3.** *W.Tel: etc:* crachements *mpl,* friture.

fryer ['fraiər], *s.* **1.** (*pers.*) friturier, -ière. **2.** *Dom.Ec:* casserole *f,* bassine *f* à friture; poêle *f* à frire; **deep f.,** friteuse *f.* **3.** *NAm:* poulet *m* à frire.

frying ['fraiiŋ], *s.* **1.** friture *f*; **f. basket,** panier *m* à friture, (panier) égouttoir *m*; **f. pan,** poêle *f* à frire; *F:* **to jump out of the f. pan into the fire,** tomber d'un mal dans un pire; tomber de Charybde en Scylla. **2.** (*a*) *El:* sifflement *m* (d'un arc); (*b*) *W.Tel: etc:* crachements *mpl,* friture.

frypan ['fraipæn], *s. NAm:* poêle *f* à frire.

fubsy ['fʌbzi], *a. F:* (*of pers.*) courtaud.

Fucaceae [fju'keisii:], *s.pl. Algae:* fucacées *f.*

Fucales [fju'keili:z], *s.pl. Algae:* fucales *f.*

fuchsia ['fju:ʃə], *s. Bot:* fuchsia *m.*

Fuchsian ['fuksiən], *a. Mth:* **F. group,** fonctions, relations, fuchsiennes.

fuchsine ['fuksi:n], *s. Dy:* fuchsine *f*; rouge *m* Solférino; rouge de Magenta.

fuchsite ['fuksait], *s. Miner:* fuchsite *f.*

fuchsone ['fuksoun], *s. Dy:* fuchsone *f.*

fucidin ['fju:sidin], *s. Pharm:* fucidine *f.*

fucivorous [fju'sivərəs], *a.* qui se nourrit d'algues.

fuck¹ [fʌk], *s. V:* (*not in decent use*) copulation *f,* coït *m.*

fuck², *v.tr. & i. V:* (*not in decent use*) **1.** *v.tr.* foutre, baiser (une femme). **2.** *v.i. & tr.* **to f. about,** lambiner; **f. off!** fous le camp! **all fucked up,** foutu.

fucoid ['fju:kɔid], *Algae:* **1.** *a.* fucoïde, fucoïdé, fucacé. **2.** *s.* fucoïde *m,* fucacée *f.*

Fucoideae [fju'kɔidii:], *s.pl. Algae:* fucoïdées *f.*

fucose ['fju:kous], *s. Ch:* fucose *m.*

fucosterol [fju'kɔstərɔl], *s. Ch:* fucostérol *m.*

fucoxanthin [fjukou'zænθin], *s. Ch:* fucoxanthine *f.*

fucus, *pl.* **-ci, -cuses** ['fju:kəs, -sai, -kəsiz], *s. Algae:* fucus *m,* varech *m*; goémon *m* jaune; **f. zone,** niveau *m* des goémons jaunes.

fuddle¹ ['fʌdl], *s. F:* **1.** *A:* ribote *f*; **to go on the f.,** faire (la) ribote. **2. to be in a f.,** (i) être un peu parti; être dans les vignes du Seigneur; (ii) avoir le cerveau brouillé.

fuddle², *F:* **1.** *v.i. A:* riboter; se pocharder. **2.** *v.tr.* (*a*) soûler, griser, *P:* pocharder (qn); **the wine had fuddled his brain,** le vin lui avait enfumé le cerveau; (*b*) brouiller les idées de (qn); hébéter (qn).

fuddled ['fʌdld], *a. F:* **1.** soûl; pris de vin; gris; **to get f.,** s'enivrer; s'enfumer le cerveau; **they were slightly f.,** ils étaient un peu partis, un peu gris. **2.** brouillé (dans ses idées); hébété.

fuddling ['fʌdliŋ], *a. A:* buveur, riboteur.

fuddy-duddy ['fʌdidʌdi], *s. F:* vieil encroûté.

fudge¹ [fʌdʒ]. **1.** *int. O:* bah! quelle(s) bêtise(s)! quelle blague! **2.** *s.* (*a*) bâclage *m,* rafistolage *m,* bousillage *m*; (*b*) (i) bêtise(s) *f,* sottise(s) *f,* baliverne(s) *f,* (ii) bourde *f,* blague *f,* craque *f*; (iii) pathos ampoulé; (*c*) *Typ: Journ:* (i) dernières nouvelles; (ii) rouleau *m* auxiliaire pour l'impression en manchette des dernières nouvelles; (*d*) *Cu:* espèce de fondant américain.

fudge². **1.** *v.tr.* (*a*) bâcher, saveter, bousiller (un travail, etc.); (*b*) cuisiner, faire cadrer (des comptes, etc.); donner le coup de pouce à (un compte, etc.); (*c*) *U.S:* **to f. an issue,** éluder, escamoter, une question; (*d*) *U.S:* **to f. (up) a story,** inventer une histoire de toutes pièces. **2.** *v.i.* (*a*) faire de la mauvaise besogne; *U.S:* **to f. on an exam,** tricher à un examen; (*b*) *U.S:* chercher des faux-fuyants, des échappatoires; éviter de se compromettre.

Fuegian [fu'i:dʒiən]. *Geog:* **1.** *a.* fuégien. **2.** *s.* Fuégien, -ienne.

fuel¹ ['fjuəl], *s.* combustible *m*; (*a*) **domestic f., household f.,** combustible de ménage; **liquid f., solid f.,** combustible liquide, solide; **patent f., compressed f.,** aggloméré(s) *m(pl.)*; briquettes *fpl* de charbon; **powdered f., pulverized f.,** combustible pulvérulent; **wood for f.,** bois *m* de chauffage; **f. bunker,** soute *f* à combustible; **f. consumption,** consommation *f* de, dépense *f* en, combustible; **f.-saving heating system,** système *m* de chauffage économique; *Adm:* **f. allowance,** allocation *f,* indemnité *f,* de chauffage; **the fire had burnt out for lack of f.,** le feu s'était éteint faute de combustible; **to stock up with f., to get in one's f. supplies,** s'alimenter en combustible; *Fig:* **to add f. to the flames,** jeter de l'huile sur le feu; (*b*) *I.C.E:* carburant *m,* essence *f*; **heavy f., light f.,** carburant lourd, léger; **jet f.,** carburéacteur *m*; **f. system, f. circuit,** circuit *m,* système *m,* d'alimentation (en carburant); **f.-air mixture,** mélange *m* air-carburant; **f. dump, f. depot,** dépôt d'essence, de carburant; *NAm:* **f. truck,** camion-citerne *m, pl.* camions-citernes; **f. tank,** réservoir *m* à, de, carburant, à essence, d'essence; (*c*) **atomic f., nuclear f.,** combustible atomique, nucléaire; **f. accumulator,** accumulateur *m* de départ; **f. element,** élément *m,* cartouche *f,* de combustible; **f. rod,** barre *f,* barreau *m,* cartouche, de combustible; **f. slug,** bloc *m,* pièce *f,* de combustible.

fuel², *v.* (**fuelled**) **1.** *v.tr.* (*a*) alimenter, charger (un fourneau, etc.); (*b*) ravitailler, alimenter, pourvoir (un véhicule, une machine, la flotte, etc.) en combustible, en carburant, en essence. **2.** *v.i.* **to f. (up),** se ravitailler, s'alimenter, se pourvoir, en combustible, en carburant, en essence; faire le plein.

fuel(l)er ['fjuələr], *s. NAm:* **1.** (*pers.*) (*a*) marchand *m* de combustible, de carburant; (*b*) chargeur *m* (d'un foyer). **2.** (*a*) camion-citerne *m, pl.* camions-citernes; ravitailleur *m* en combustible, en carburant; (*b*) poste *m* de remplissage.

fuelling ['fjuəliŋ], *s.* **1.** approvisionnement *m,* ravitaillement *m,* alimentation *f,* en combustible, en carburant, en essence; remplissage *m.* **2.** combustibles *mpl.*

fuel-oil ['fjuəlɔil], *s.* fuel(-oil) *m*; huile *f* combustible; mazout *m*; **domestic f.-o.,** fuel-oil domestique, fluide, léger.

fug¹ [fʌg], *s. F:* **1.** (*a*) forte odeur de renfermé; odeur confinée; touffeur *f*; air empesté de tabac; (*b*) poussière *f,* balayures *fpl* (dans une salle mal nettoyée). **2.** individu casanier.

fug², *v.i.* **to f. at home,** rester enfermé chez soi.

fugacious [fju'geiʃəs], *a.* **1.** (*of colour, perfume, etc.*) fugace. **2.** *Nat.Hist:* éphémère; caduc, *f.* caduque; *Bot:* fugace.

fugacity [fju'gæsiti], *s.* **1.** *Lit:* fugacité *f* (d'une couleur, etc.). **2.** *Nat.Hist:* caducité *f.*

fugal ['fjug(ə)l], *a. Mus:* (style, etc.) fugué.

fugato [fju'gɑ:tou], *Mus:* **1.** *adv.* en style fugué. **2.** *s.* fugato *m.*

fugginess ['fʌginis], *s. F:* touffeur *f* de l'air.

fuggy ['fʌgi], *a. F:* **1.** (salle, etc.) qui sent le renfermé, qui empeste le tabac; **this place smells f.,** ça sent le renfermé ici. **2.** (*of pers.*) qui n'aime pas l'air frais; **they're a f. lot,** ils ne détestent pas l'odeur de renfermé.

fughetta [fju'getə], *s. Mus:* fuguette *f.*

fugitive ['fju:dʒitiv]. **1.** *a.* (*a*) (*of prisoner, slave, etc.*) fugitif, fuyard; (*b*) (*of happiness, impression, etc.*) fugitif, fugace, éphémère, transitoire; de courte durée; **f. colour,** couleur fugitive; *Lit:* **f. works,** œuvres *f* éphémères, d'intérêt transitoire, fugitives. **2.** *s.* (*a*) fugitif, -ive; fuyard *m*; **a f. from justice,** un fugitif poursuivi, recherché, par la justice; (*b*) exilé, -ée; réfugié, -ée; (*c*) *A:* déserteur *m.*

fugitively ['fju:dʒitivli], *adv.* fugitivement.

fugleman, *pl.* **-men** ['fju:glmən], *s.m.* **1.** *Mil: A:* chef de file. **2.** *F:* (*a*) celui qui donne le ton aux autres; le meneur; le chef; (*b*) porte-parole *m inv.*

fugue [fju:g], *s. Mus: Psy:* fugue *f.*

fugued [fju:gd], *a. Mus:* (mouvement, etc.) fugué.

fuguist ['fju:gist], *s. Mus:* compositeur *m* de fugues.

führer ['fjurər], *s.m. Pol:* führer.

Fula(h), *pl.* **Fula(h)(s)** ['fulɑ:, -ɑ:z]. **1.** *s. & a. Ethn:* Fellata *m*, Foulah *m*, Foulbé *m*. **2.** *s. Ling:* le peu(h)l.

Fulani, *pl.* **Fulani(s)** [fu'lɑ:ni, 'fuləni, -i:z]. **1.** *s. & a. Ethn:* Fulani *inv.* **2.** *s. Ling:* le peu(h)l.

Fulbe, *pl.* **Fulbe(s)** ['fulbi, -i:z], *a. & s.* = FULA.

fulcrum[1], *pl.* **-cra, -crums** ['fʌlkrəm, -krə, -krəmz], *s.* **1.** *Mec:* (point *m*, axe *m*, d')appui *m*, centre *m*, pivot *m* (d'un levier); couteau *m* (d'un fléau de balance); **pedal f.,** axe de pédale; **give me a f. and I will lift the world,** qu'on me donne un point d'appui et je soulèverai le monde. **2.** *Bot: Ich: Z:* fulcre *m*, fulcrum *m.*

fulcrum[2], *v.i.* pivoter (**on,** sur).

fulfil [ful'fil], *v.tr.* (**fulfilled**) **1.** (*a*) accomplir (une prophétie); répondre à, remplir (l'attente de qn); *B:* **that it might be fulfilled which was spoken by the prophets,** afin que fût accompli ce qui avait été dit par les prophètes; **to f. oneself,** trouver sa vocation; remplir sa destinée; donner toute sa mesure; (*b*) satisfaire (un désir); exaucer (une prière); (*c*) accomplir (une tâche); **to f. an obligation, a duty,** s'acquitter d'une obligation, d'un devoir, acquitter, remplir, une obligation, un devoir; **to f. one's trust,** s'acquitter de sa charge; (*d*) remplir (les conditions requises, etc.); **to f. the purpose in view,** répondre au but envisagé; (*e*) obéir à (un commandement); **to f. s.o.'s instructions,** remplir les instructions de qn. **2.** achever, compléter; *B:* **for my days are fulfilled,** car mon temps est accompli.

fulfiller [ful'filər], *s.* personne *f* qui accomplit (une prophétie, etc.), qui remplit (une obligation, etc.), qui satisfait (un désir, etc.).

fulfilling [ful'filiŋ], **fulfilment** [ful'filmənt], *s.* **1.** (*a*) accomplissement *m* (d'une prophétie, d'un vœu, devoir, etc.); (*b*) exaucement *m* (d'une prière); accomplissement (d'un désir); **to have a feeling of fulfilment,** sentir qu'on a réussi, qu'on a atteint son but; (*c*) exécution *f* (d'un projet, contrat); **f. of a condition,** exécution, *Jur:* accomplissement, d'une condition. **2.** achèvement *m* (d'une période de temps, etc.).

fulgent ['fʌldʒənt], *a. Poet:* éclatant, resplendissant.

fulgora ['fʌlgərə], *s. Ent:* fulgore *m.*

fulgorid ['fʌlgərid], *a. & s. Ent:* fulgoride (*m*); **the fulgorids,** les fulgores *m.*

Fulgoridae [fʌl'gɔridi:], *s.pl. Ent:* fulgoridés *m.*

fulgurant ['fʌlgjurənt], *a.* fulgurant.

fulgurate ['fʌlgjureit], *v.i.* fulgurer; (*of metals*) éclairer.

fulguration [fʌlgju'reiʃ(ə)n], *s.* **1.** (*of silver, etc.*) fulguration *f*, éclair *m*. **2.** *Med:* fulguration; action *f* de la foudre.

fulgurite ['fʌlgjurait], *s. Geol: Exp:* fulgurite *f.*

fulham ['fuləm], *s. P: O:* dé pipé, chargé.

fuliginous ['fju'lidʒinəs], *a.* fuligineux.

full[1] [ful], *a., s., & adv.*

I. *a.* **1.** (*a*) (*of receptacle*) plein, rempli, comble; **f. to the brim,** *F:* **f. up,** entièrement plein; rempli jusqu'au bord; *Nau:* **to be f. up with coal or oil,** avoir le grand plein des soutes; *F:* **to be f. up with business,** être accablé d'affaires; avoir beaucoup de travail; **f. as an egg,** plein comme un œuf; **f. to overflowing,** plein à déborder; **f. day,** jour chargé; **don't speak with your mouth f.,** ne parle pas la bouche pleine; *Fig:* **his heart was f.,** il avait le cœur gros, gonflé; (*b*) **to be f. of sth.,** être plein, comblé, de qch.; **to have one's pockets f. of money,** avoir ses poches pleines d'argent; avoir de l'argent plein les poches; **she had her hands f. of them,** elle en avait les mains pleines, elle en avait plein les mains; **her eyes were f. of tears,** elle avait les yeux pleins de larmes; elle avait des larmes plein les yeux; **exercise f. of mistakes,** devoir plein de fautes; **f. of holes,** tout troué; plein de trous; **glance f. of sadness,** regard imprégné de tristesse; **look f. of gratitude, of hatred,** regard chargé de reconnaissance, animé de haine; **his eyes are f. of admiration,** l'admiration éclate dans ses yeux; **face f. of terror,** visage empreint de terreur; **to be f. of hope,** être rempli d'espoir; avoir bon espoir; **to be f. of praise of s.o.,** se répandre en éloges sur qn; **to be f. of ideas,** remuer beaucoup d'idées; **the papers are f. of the murder,** les journaux ne parlent que de l'assassinat; (*c*) (truie, etc.) pleine; portant des petits. **2.** (*of room, bus, etc.*) plein, complet; **f. house,** (i) salle *f* comble, (ii) *Cards:* (*poker*) main pleine; **house f. to overflowing,** salle pleine à crouler, à craquer; **f. session (of a committee, etc.),** réunion, assemblée, plénière; **to be f. up,** avoir son plein; **the bus is f. up,** l'autobus *m* est au complet; **f. up!** complet! **room f. of company,** salle garnie de monde; *Cards:* (*poker*) **f. hand,** main pleine. **3.** (*of pers.*) (*a*) **to be f. of sth.,** être pénétré de qch.; *P:* en avoir plein la bouche; **to be f. of one's own importance,** être pénétré de sa propre importance; **f. of oneself,** plein de soi-même; **to be f. of the news,** être impatient de répandre la nouvelle; **he was f. of his subject,** il était plein de son sujet; (*b*) (*of pers.*) (i) **to be f. (up),** être repu, rassasié; (ii) *F:* **to be f.,** être soûl; *P:* **to be f. as a tick,** être soûl comme un porc; (*c*) *B:* **to die f. of years,** mourir chargé d'ans, plein de jours. **4.** (*of facts, notes, etc.*) ample, abondant, copieux; **she received her f. share of the money,** elle a eu sa bonne part de l'argent; **in the fullest detail,** dans le plus grand détail; **for fuller information apply to . . .,** pour renseignements *m* complémentaires s'adresser à . . .; **until fuller information is available . . .,** jusqu'à plus ample informé; **to ask for fuller information,** demander des précisions sur qch.; **a book that is rather fuller on this point,** un livre qui traite plus amplement ce sujet. **5.** complet, entier; (*a*) **f. meal,** repas complet; **f.-cream milk,** lait non écrémé, intégral, intact, entier; **in f. retreat,** en pleine retraite; **f. pay,** paie entière; paie de présence, d'activité; solde entière; **leave on f. pay, f.-pay leave,** congé *m* à solde entière; **f. price,** prix fort; *Th:* **to pay f. price,** *Rail:* **to pay f. fare,** payer place entière; **f. payment,** remboursement intégral; *Mil: etc:* **f. discharge,** congé définitif; **f. weight, f. measure,** poids *m* juste, mesure *f* juste; mesure comble; **we were under f. sail,** nous avions toutes voiles dehors; **f. cargo,** plein chargement; *El.E:* **f. circuit,** circuit total; **f. leather binding,** reliure *f* pleine peau; **f. statement,** exposé complet; **f. text,** texte intégral; **f. force of men,** personnel *m* au complet; (*b*) **to come to f. maturity,** arriver en pleine maturité; **in f. flower,** en pleine fleur; **roses in f. bloom,** roses larges épanouies; **in f. uniform,** en grande tenue; en grand uniforme; **the f. enjoyment of . . .,** la jouissance intégrale de . . .; **to give f. scope to s.o.,** donner libre carrière à qn, laisser à qn les coudées franches; **I give you f. liberty to act,** je vous donne toute liberté d'agir; **in f. flight,** en pleine déroute; (*c*) **I waited two f. hours,** j'ai attendu deux bonnes heures, deux grandes heures; **it takes three f. hours to go,** il faut trois bonnes heures, *P:* trois heures bien tassées, pour y aller; **it is a f. five miles from here,** c'est à au moins deux lieues d'ici; (*d*) **f. brother, f. sister,** frère germain, sœur germaine; *Sch:* **f. professor,** professeur *m* titulaire; **f. member,** membre *m* titulaire. **6.** (*a*) (*of face*) plein; (*of figure*) rond, replet; (*of chin*) renflé; **f. lips,** lèvres grosses, fortes; **the f. curves of her bosom,** les rondeurs *f* de sa gorge; **ship with f. lines,** navire *m* aux formes lourdes; (*b*) (*of dress, sleeve, etc.*) ample, large, froncé, bouffant; **too f.,** trop large; *Dressm:* **f. sleeve,** manche étoffée; (*c*) **f. voice,** voix pleine, ronde, étoffée; **f. note,** son nourri; (*d*) *Bill:* **to strike the ball f., half-f.,** prendre la bille pleine, demi-pleine. **7.** *Nau:* (*of sail*) plein, gonflé; **we were sailing f.,** nous voguions à pleines voiles; **the sails are f.,** les voiles portent bien; **to keep her f.,** porter plein; **f. and by,** près et plein; *F:* **taking it f. and by . . .,** à tout prendre . . . .

II. *s.* **1.** cœur *m*, fort *m* (de la saison, etc.); apogée *f* (de la gloire, etc.); **the moon is at the f.,** la lune est dans son plein; **the f. of the moon,** la pleine lune. **2.** banc *m* de galets, de sable (laissé par la marée). **3.** *adv.phr.* (*a*) **in f.:** **to publish a letter in f.,** publier une lettre intégralement; **account given in f.,** compte rendu in extenso; **money refunded in f.,** on rembourse intégralement l'argent, l'argent en entier, en totalité; *Fin:* **capital paid in f.,** capital entièrement versé; *Com:* **in f. of all demands,** pour fin de compte; pour solde de tout compte; **acceptance in f. of the conditions,** acceptation intégrale des conditions; **name in f.,** (i) nom *m* et prénoms; (ii) nom en toutes lettres; **to write out a word in f.,** écrire un mot en toutes lettres; (*b*) **to the f.,** complètement, tout à fait, dans toute son étendue; **to indulge one's tastes to the f.,** donner libre carrière à ses goûts.

III. *adv.* **1.** *A: & Lit:* **f. many a time,** bien des fois; **I know it f. well,** je le sais bien, parfaitement; **it is f. five miles from here,** c'est à au moins deux lieues d'ici. **2.** (*a*) précisément, justement, en plein; **lying f. in the sun,** couché en plein (au) soleil; **f. in the middle,** au beau milieu; **f. in the centre,** en plein dans le centre; **f. in the beams of the searchlights,** en plein dans le faisceau des projecteurs; **hit f. in the face, in the chest,** atteint en pleine figure, en pleine poitrine; (*b*) **to turn a tap f. on,** ouvrir un robinet en grand; **to turn the wireless f. on,** mettre la radio au plus fort de sa puissance; **to drive a car f. out,** conduire une voiture à pleins gaz; **the factory was running f. out,** l'usine travaillait à plein rendement, en pleine activité; **to make a f.-out effort to do sth.,** faire l'effort maximum pour faire qch.

full[2]. **1.** *v.tr. Dressm:* froncer (une jupe, etc.); faire bouffer (une manche, etc.). **2.** *v.i. NAm:* (*of moon*) passer par son plein.

full[3], *v.tr. Tex: Tan:* (re)fouler, terrer (l'étoffe, le cuir).

fullback ['fulbæk], *s. Fb:* arrière *m.*

full-blood ['ful'blʌd]. **1.** *a.* = FULL-BLOODED 1. **2.** *s.* (*a*) personne *f* de race pure; (*b*) *Breed:* pur-sang *m inv.*

full-blooded ['ful'blʌdid], *a.* **1.** (*a*) (*of brother, sister*) germain; (*b*) de race pure; (cheval) de sang, pur-sang *inv.*; **f.-b. Indians,** Indiens *m* pur sang. **2.** vigoureux; robuste; **f.-b. interpretation of a part,** interprétation *f* robuste d'un rôle. **3.** (tempérament) sanguin.

fullblown ['ful'bloun], *a.* **1.** (*of rose, etc.*) épanoui; en pleine fleur. **2.** *F:* **he is a f. doctor, lawyer, etc.,** il a (obtenu) tous ses diplômes; **you are a f. doctor now!** vous voilà docteur pour de bon!

fullbodied ['ful'bɔdid], *a.* **1.** (*of pers.*) replet, corpulent. **2.** **f. wine,** vin corsé, qui a du corps.

full-bottom ['ful'bɔtəm], *s.* **full-bottomed** ['ful'bɔtəmd], *a. A. & Jur:* **f.-bottom, f.-bottomed wig,** perruque carrée.

fullbred ['ful'bred], *a.* de race pure; **f.-b. horse,** (cheval *m*) pur-sang *m inv.*

full-cheeked ['ful'tʃi:kt], *a.* aux grosses joues.

full-chested ['ful'tʃestid], *a.* à forte poitrine; **f.-c. jacket,** veston *m* à poitrine bombée.

full-choke ['ful'tʃouk], *s. Sp:* **f.-c. gun,** full-choke, *m.*

full-dress ['ful'dres], *a.* **f.-d. clothes,** habits *m*, tenue *f*, de cérémonie, de parade; *Mil: Navy:* **f.-d. uniform,** tenue numéro un; *Th:* **f.-d. rehearsal,** répétition générale, en costume; **f.-d. dinner,** dîner *m* d'apparat; *F:* **f.-d. debate,** débat solennel; **the argument developed into a f.-d. row,** la discussion tourna en vraie querelle.

full-edged ['ful'edʒd], *a.* (bois) équarri à vives arêtes.

fuller[1] ['fulər], *s. Tex:* fouleur, -euse; foulon *m*; **fuller's earth,** terre *f* savonneuse; terre à détacher, à foulon; marne *f* à foulon; glaise *f* à dégraisser; argile *f* smectique; smectite *f*; *Bot:* **fuller's grass,** saponaire commune; herbe *f* à foulon; **fuller's teasel, thistle, weed,** cardère *f* à foulon; chardon bonnetier; chardon à foulon.

fuller[2], *s.* **1.** *Tls: Metalw:* (*a*) (*for grooving*) dégorgeoir *m*; matrice *f*; **(top) f.,** chasse ronde; **bottom f.,** tranchet *m* à dégorger; (*b*) (*for caulking*) matoir *m*; **hand f.,** matoir à main; **anvil f.,** matoir pour enclume. **2.** (*on bayonet, etc.*) cannelure *f*, gouttière *f*; onglet *m* (d'épée).

fuller[3], *v.tr. Metalw:* **1.** dégorger (le fer). **2.** mater, refouler (le bord d'une tôle).

fullering ['fuləriŋ], *s.* **1.** matage *m*, refoulement *m* (du bord d'une tôle). **2.** (*on bayonet, etc.*) cannelure *f*, gouttière *f*; onglet *m* (d'épée).

full-face ['ful'feis]. **1.** *a.* = FULL-FACED 2, 3. **2.** *s. Typ:* caractère gras.

full-faced ['ful'feist], *a.* **1.** (*of pers.*) à la figure ronde; au visage plein. **2.** (*of portrait*) de face. **3.** *Typ:* **f.-f. type,** caractères gras.

full-fall ['ful'fɔ:l], *a. Cost: O:* **f.-f. trousers,** culotte *f* à pont.

full-flavoured ['ful'fleivəd], *a.* **1.** (tabac, etc.) qui a du corps; (vin) savoureux, fruité, qui a du bouquet; **f.-f. olive oil,** huile d'olive fruitée. **2.** (*of story, joke, etc.*) épicé, corsé.

full-fledged ['ful'fledʒd], *a.* (*of bird*) qui a toutes ses plumes; *F:* (*of artist, etc.*) qualifié, achevé, en possession de tous ses moyens, pourvu de tous ses grades.

full-grown ['ful'groun], *a.* (*a*) (arbre *m*, plante *f*) qui a atteint son développement complet, toute sa croissance; (arbre) fait, adulte, de haute futaie; (*b*) (*of pers.*) adulte.

fulling ['fuliŋ], *s.* (re)foulage *m*, (re)foulement *m*, foulure *f* (des draps, du cuir); **f. mill,** (moulin *m* à) foulon *m.*

fullish ['fuliʃ], *a.* assez plein; (*of lips*) assez gros; (*of sleeves, etc.*) assez ample, assez bouffant.

full-length ['ful'leŋθ], *a.* (*a*) (portrait) en pied; **f.-l. mirror,** miroir qui permet de se voir en pied; **f.-l. window,** fenêtre *f* qui descend du plafond au parquet; **f.-l. evening dress,** robe (de soirée) longue; (*b*) **f.-l. film,** grand film; long métrage.

full-line ['ful'lain], *a. Draw:* (courbe, etc.) en trait plein.

full-mouthed ['ful'mauðd], *a.* **1.** (*of horse, etc.*) qui a toutes ses dents. **2.** (*a*) (chien) à la voix profonde; (*b*) (*of pers.*) (i) à la voix pleine, ronde; (ii) *P:* gueulard; (*c*) (style *m*) sonore.

ful(l)ness ['fulnis], *s.* **1.** (*a*) état plein (d'un récipient); plénitude *f* (de l'estomac); **out of the f. of his heart he told us . . .,** comme son cœur débordait il nous raconta . . .; (*b*) **the earth and its f.,** la terre et tout ce qu'elle renferme. **2.** plénitude, perfection *f*, totalité *f* (de la force, etc.); **in the f. of time,** quand les temps furent, seront, révolus; *B:* en la consommation des temps. **3.** (*a*) ampleur *f* (d'un vêtement); (*b*) ampleur (d'un compte rendu, etc.); abondance *f* (de détail); **to treat a subject with the f. due to it,** traiter un sujet avec l'ampleur qu'il mérite; (*c*) rondeur *f* (de la forme); (*d*) richesse *f* (du style, d'une couleur, etc.); **to give f. to a sentence,** arrondir une période; **to give f. to the voice, to the tone,** étoffer la voix, nourrir le son.

full-page ['ful'peidʒ], *a.* **f.-p. illustration,** illustration *f* hors texte.

full-rigged ['ful'rigd], *a. Nau:* gréé en trois-mâts carré; **f.-r. ship,** trois-mâts carré.

full-scale ['ful'skeil], *a.* **1.** = FULL-SIZE(D). **2.** (*of reform, etc.*) complet, intégral, total; (*of attack, etc.*) de grande envergure, de grand style.

full-size(d) ['ful'saiz(d)], *a.* (dessin, etc.) (i) grandeur nature, de grandeur naturelle, en vraie grandeur, en grand, (ii) *Ind:* à la dimension exacte; à la cote.

full stop ['ful'stɔp], *s.* (*in punctuation*) point (final); *F:* **things came to a f. s.,** tout s'arrêta net, court; **he came to a f. s.,** il est resté court (dans son discours).

full-throated ['ful'θroutid], *a.* (chant, etc.) à plein gosier, à pleine gorge.

full time ['ful'taim]. **1.** *adv.* **to work f. t.,** travailler à plein temps. **2.** *a.* **f.-t. employment,** emploi *m* à temps complet, à plein temps; *F:* **looking after the baby is a f.-t. job,** soigner le bébé occupe toute la journée.

full-timer ['ful'taimər], *s.* **1.** employé, -ée, qui travaille à plein temps. **2.** *Sch: A:* élève *mf* qui assistait à tous les cours (au lieu de faire une demi-journée à l'usine ou à l'atelier).

fully ['fuli], *adv.* **1.** (*a*) pleinement, entièrement, complètement, amplement; **to be f. satisfied,** être pleinement satisfait; **f. armed,** armé de toutes pièces; **f. paid,** payé intégralement; **until f. paid,** jusqu'à parfait paiement; **capital f. paid (up),** capital entièrement versé; **f. paid shares,** actions entièrement libérées; **f. charged battery,** accumulateur chargé à fond, à refus; *Aut:* **to depress the pedal f.,** appuyer à fond sur la pédale; (*b*) **to treat a subject, develop a negative, f.,** traiter un sujet, développer un cliché, à fond; **I will write you more f.,** je vous écrirai plus longuement; **you must go more f. into details,** il faut entrer plus longuement dans les détails. **2.** bien, au moins; **it takes f. two hours,** cela prend bien, au moins, deux heures; **it is f. ten miles,** il y a largement, au moins, dix milles.

fully-fashioned ['fuli'fæʃ(ə)nd], *a.* (*of stockings*) entièrement diminué; proportionné.

fully fledged ['fuli'fledʒd], *a.* = FULL-FLEDGED.

fulmar ['fulmər], *s. Orn:* **f. (petrel),** fulmar *m*; pétrel glacial; *Fr.C:* fulmar boréal; **giant f.,** ossifrage *m*.

fulminant ['fʌlminənt], *a.* **1.** fulminant. **2.** *Med:* (*of disease*) qui se développe subitement; foudroyant.

fulminate[1] ['fʌlmineit], *s. Ch:* fulminate *m* (de mercure, etc.).

fulminate[2]. **1.** *v.i.* (*a*) fulminer, faire explosion; (*b*) *Metall: A:* (*of gold, etc.*) éclairer. **2.** *v.tr. & i. Ecc:* fulminer (une excommunication, des imprécations) **(against,** contre); *F:* **to f. against s.o., an abuse,** fulminer contre qn, un abus.

fulminating ['fʌlmineitiŋ], *a.* **1.** fulminant; *Ch:* **f. powder,** poudre fulminante. **2.** *Med:* = FULMINANT 2.

fulmination [fʌlmi'neiʃ(ə)n], *s. Ch: Ecc:* fulmination *f*; *F:* **I am not afraid of his fulminations,** je ne crains pas ses foudres; sa grosse voix ne m'effraie pas.

fulminatory ['fʌlminətəri], *a.* fulminatoire.

fulminic [fʌl'minik], *a. Ch:* (acide *m*) fulminique.

fulminous ['fʌlminəs], *a.* fulminaire.

fulness ['fulnis], *s.* = FULLNESS.

fulsome ['fulsəm], *a.* (*of praise, style, etc.*) écœurant, excessif; **f. flattery,** flagornerie *f*, adulation *f*; **f. compliments,** compliments plats, fastidieux, écœurants.

fulsomely ['fulsəmli], *adv.* à l'excès, excessivement; d'une façon écœurante.

fulsomeness ['fulsəmnis], *s.* bassesse *f*, platitude *f* (des louanges, etc.).

fulvene ['fʌlvi:n], *s. Ch:* fulvène *m*.

fulvous ['fʌlvəs], *a.* fauve.

fumagillin [fju:mə'dʒilin], *s. Bio-Ch:* fumagilline *f*.

fumagine ['fju:mədʒi:n], *s. Arb:* fumagine *f*, noir *m*, suie *f*.

fumago [fju:'meigou], *s. Fung:* fumago *m*.

Fumariaceae [fju:məri'eisii:], *s.pl. Bot:* fumariacées *f*.

fumaric ['fju:mərik], *a. Ch:* (acide *m*) fumarique.

fumarolle ['fju:məroul], *s. Geol:* fumerol(l)e *f*.

fumaroyl ['fju:mərɔil], **fumaryl** ['fju:məril, rail], *s. Ch:* fumaryle *m*.

fumatorium [fju:mə'tɔ:riəm], **fumatory** ['fju:mətəri], *s. Hort:* chambre *f* pour fumigations.

fumble[1] ['fʌmbl], *s.* maniement maladroit; gaucherie *f*; tâtonnement *m*.

fumble[2]. **1.** *v.i.* fouiller (au hasard); farfouiller, tâtonner; **to f. in a drawer for sth.,** farfouiller dans un tiroir pour trouver qch.; **to f. in a dark room for sth.,** chercher qch. à tâtons dans une chambre obscure; **to f. for words,** chercher ses mots; **to f. with sth.,** manier qch. maladroitement; **to f. with the key at the keyhole,** tâtonner avec sa clé pour trouver le trou de la serrure; **to f. about in the dark,** chercher son chemin dans l'obscurité. **2.** *v.tr.* manier (qch.) maladroitement, gauchement; tripoter (qch.); **to f. one's way along,** chercher son chemin à tâtons; *Sp:* **to f. the ball,** arrêter, attraper, la balle maladroitement. **3.** *v.i.* commettre des gaucheries.

fumble-fisted ['fʌmblfistid], *a.* aux mains maladroites; maladroit, gauche.

fumbler ['fʌmblər], *s.* lourdaud, -e; maladroit, -e.

fumbling[1] ['fʌmbliŋ], *a.* lourdaud, maladroit, gauche.

fumbling[2], *s.* **1.** tripotage maladroit; maniement maladroit. **2.** tâtonnement *m*.

fumblingly ['fʌmbliŋli], *adv.* **1.** maladroitement, gauchement. **2.** à tâtons.

fume[1] [fju:m], *s.* **1.** fumée *f*, vapeur *f*, exhalaison *f*, exhalation *f*, gaz *m*; **fumes of sulphur, of petrol,** vapeurs de soufre, d'essence; **fumes of an explosive,** gaz, fumée, provenant d'un explosif; *Ind:* **factory fumes,** fumée d'usine; *I.C.E:* **exhaust fumes,** gaz d'échappement; *Ch:* **f. chamber, f. cupboard,** sorbonne *f* (de laboratoire); **f. hood,** hotte *f*, auvent *m*, de laboratoire; **the fumes from the roast,** la vapeur du rôti; **fumes of wine,** fumées de vin; *Lit:* **judgment clouded with the fumes of passion, of enthusiasm,** jugement obnubilé par la passion, par l'exaltation. **2.** *F: O:* accès *m* de colère.

fume[2]. **1.** *v.tr.* (*a*) exposer (qch.) à la fumée, à une vapeur, à un gaz; *Phot:* renforcer (une plaque); **fumed oak,** chêne patiné; (*b*) encenser (l'autel, etc.). **2.** *v.i.* (*a*) fumer; émettre de la fumée, des vapeurs; (*b*) (*of smoke, vapour*) monter, s'exhaler; (*c*) *F:* (*of pers.*) rager; se faire du mauvais sang; *F:* fumer (de colère); râler (de colère); **he was fuming with vexation,** il se rongeait les poings de dépit; **I was fuming,** j'étais exaspéré **(at,** de); **he's still fuming at having missed the chance,** il ne décolère pas d'avoir raté l'occasion; **"It's outrageous", he fumed,** "cela dépasse toutes les bornes", grommela-t-il.

fumerole ['fju:məroul], *s. Geog:* fumerol(l)e *f*.

fumet[1] ['fju:mit], *s. Cu:* fumet *m*.

fumet[2], *s. Ven:* fumée *f* (de daim).

fumigant ['fju:migænt], *s.* fumigant *m*.

fumigate ['fju:migeit], *v.tr.* exposer (qch.) à la fumée; fumiger (qch.); désinfecter (un appartement, etc.) par fumigation; mécher (un baril, etc.); **to f. with sulphur,** faire des fumigations de soufre.

fumigating[1] ['fju:migeitiŋ], *a.* (appareil, etc.) fumigatoire.

fumigating[2], **fumigation** [fjumi'geiʃ(ə)n], *s.* fumigation *f*; désinfection *f* (d'une chambre); méchage *m* (d'un baril, etc.).

fumigator ['fju:migeitər], *s.* **1.** (*pers.*) fumigateur. **2.** appareil *m* fumigatoire.

fumigatorium [fju:migə'tɔ:riəm], *s. Hort: NAm:* chambre *f* étanche pour fumigations.

fumigatory [fju:mi'geitəri], *a.* fumigatoire.

fuming[1] ['fju:miŋ], *a.* **1.** fumant; qui émet de la fumée, de la vapeur; *Ch:* **f. sulphuric, nitric, acid,** acide sulfurique, nitrique, fumant. **2.** (*of pers.*) qui rage; bouillonnant de colère; qui ne décolère pas.

fuming[2], *s.* **1.** fumage *m*; patinage *m* (du chêne); *Phot:* renforcement *m* (d'une plaque); encensement *m* (de l'autel). **2.** *F:* emportement *m*, rage *f*, irritation *f*.

fumitory ['fju:mitəri], *s. Bot:* fumeterre *f*; *F:* lait battu; fiel *m* de terre; **climbing f.,** adlumie *f*.

fumy ['fju:mi], *a.* fumeux.

fun[1] [fʌn], *s.* amusement *m*, gaieté *f*; plaisanterie *f*; *P:* rigolade *f*; **to make f. of, poke f. at, s.o., sth.,** se moquer, se railler, de qn, de qch.; rire de qn; tourner qn, qch., en ridicule, en dérision; se payer la tête de qn; s'amuser de qch., aux dépens de qn; *P:* charrier, chiner, qn; **they poke f. at him for always carrying an umbrella,** on le raille de ce qu'il porte toujours un parapluie; **for f., in f.,** (i) pour rire; pour jouer; en blaguant; par plaisanterie; (ii) pour se distraire; par amusement; pour son amusement; **I was only in f.,** je voulais rire; je voulais seulement plaisanter; **I did it for the f. of the thing, of it,** je l'ai fait pour le plaisir, histoire de rire; **are you doing that for the f. of the thing?** c'est par plaisir que vous faites cela? **he is great f., full of f.,** il est très gai, très drôle, très farceur; il a toujours le mot pour rire; c'est un boute-en-train; **it was great f.,** c'était fort amusant, très gai; **it will be great f. bathing in the sea,** ce sera très amusant de se baigner dans la mer; **it's poor f. to . . .,** ce n'est guère amusant de . . .; **I don't see the f. of waiting, there's no f. in waiting,** je ne trouve pas drôle d'attendre, ce n'est pas amusant d'attendre; **it's no f. working a sixteen-hour day,** ce n'est pas drôle de travailler seize heures par jour; **to have f.,** s'amuser, se divertir; **we shall have (some) f.,** nous allons rire; **we had great f.,** *F:* **a lot of f. and games,** on s'est bien amusé; **we had lots of f. and games with the customs,** nous avons eu bien des ennuis avec la douane; **we shall get some f. out of him,** on va rire à ses dépens; **it's good clean f.,** (i) c'est d'un comique sain; (ii) *Iron:* c'est plutôt risqué; **it was only my f.,** c'était pour rire; **he likes his bit of f.,** c'est un loustic; **let them come to us and they will see some f.,** qu'ils viennent chez nous et ils verront du sport; **to take the f. out of sth.,** gâter le plaisir de qch.; (*of battle, etc.*) **now the f. is beginning!** voilà la danse qui va commencer! **that's when the f. began,** c'est là que ça a commencé à barder; **that's where the f. comes in,** c'est là que cela commence à devenir drôle; **all the f. of the fair,** toutes les attractions de la foire; **what f.!** (i) quel bonheur! (ii) la bonne blague! **everything went like f.,** tout marchait comme sur des roulettes; **he went at it like f.,** il s'y est mis énergiquement, vigoureusement; **to laugh like f.,** rire comme tout; **the engine was roaring away like f.,** le moteur ronflait à tout casser; **how are things going?—like f.,** comment ça marche?—(i) à merveille; (ii) *Iron:* pas du tout.

fun[2], *v.i.* **(funned)** plaisanter, badiner.

funambulatory [fju'næmbjulət(ə)ri], *a.* funambulesque.

funambulist [fju'næmbjulist], *s.* funambule *mf*; danseur, -euse, de corde.

function[1] ['fʌŋ(k)ʃ(ə)n], *s.* **1.** fonction *f*; (*a*) *Physiol:* **the functions of the stomach, heart,** les fonctions de l'estomac, du cœur; **the f. of respiration,** la fonction respiratoire; **vital functions,** fonctions vitales; (*b*) **the recoil spring performs the f. of a shock absorber,** le ressort récupérateur joue le rôle d'(un) amortisseur; **the f. of society is the protection of the individual,** la société a pour fonction de protéger l'individu; (*c*) *Cmptr:* **f. chart,** diagramme fonctionnel, de fonction; **f. generator,** générateur *m* de fonctions; **f. key,** touche *f* de fonction, de service. **2.** (*a*) (*of office holder, etc.*) fonction, charge *f*; **it was my f. as minister . . .,** c'était mon devoir comme ministre . . .; **in his f. as a magistrate,** en sa qualité de magistrat; **he combines the functions of servant and gardener,** il tient le double emploi de domestique et de jardinier; (*b*) *pl.* **to discharge one's functions,** s'acquitter de ses fonctions; **it is part of my functions to . . .,** c'est à moi qu'il appartient de . . .. **3.** (*a*) cérémonie (religieuse); (*b*) réception *f*, soirée *f*, réunion *f*; **society f.,** réception, réunion, mondaine; (*c*) cérémonie *f* publique; solennité *f*; **the prizegiving is one of my yearly functions,** la distribution des prix est une solennité à laquelle je prends part tous les ans. **4.** *Mth: etc:* fonction; **trigonometric f.,** fonction trigonométrique; **sine f.,** fonction de sinus; **inverse f.,** fonction inverse; **the resistance is a f. of the pressure,** la résistance est fonction de la pression; **to express a quantity as a f. of another,** exprimer une quantité en fonction d'une autre.

function[2], *v.i.* **1.** fonctionner, marcher, agir; **the carburetter functions well,** le carburateur marche, débite, bien; *F:* **this gadget won't f.,** ce truc ne marche pas. **2. adjective that functions as an adverb,** adjectif qui fait fonction d'adverbe.

functional ['fʌŋ(k)ʃən(ə)l], *a.* (*a*) *Physiol: Mth: Cmptr: etc:* fonctionnel; *Cmptr:* **f. character,** caractère *m* de fonction, de commande, de service; **f. diagram,** schéma fonctionnel, de fonctionnement; (*b*) **f. furniture,** mobilier fonctionnel, utilitaire; **primitive yet f. stoves,** fours primitifs mais qui fonctionnent; (*c*) *Mil:* **f. bombing,** bombardement *m* des installations et des centres vitaux.

functionalism ['fʌŋ(k)ʃənəlizm], *s.* fonctionnalisme *m*.

functionalist ['fʌŋ(k)ʃənəlist], *s.* fonctionnaliste *mf*.

functionally ['fʌŋ(k)ʃənəli], *adv.* fonctionnellement.

functionarism ['fʌŋ(k)ʃənərizm], *s.* fonctionnarisme *m*.

functionary ['fʌŋ(k)ʃənəri], *s.* fonctionnaire *m*.

functionate ['fʌŋ(k)ʃəneit], *v.i.* = FUNCTION[2].

fund[1] [fʌnd], *s.* **1.** fonds *m*, capacité *f* (d'esprit, d'érudition, etc.); **unfailing f. of humour,** fonds d'humour intarissable; **he has a great f. of wit,** il a de l'esprit jusqu'au bout des doigts; **he has a perfect f. of anecdotes,** c'est un vrai répertoire d'anecdotes. **2.** *Fin: etc:* (*a*) fonds *m*, caisse *f*; **International Monetary F.,** Fonds Monétaire International; **common f.,** caisse commune; **old-age pension f., retirement f.,** caisse des retraites pour la vieillesse; **fighting f.,** caisse de défense (d'une association, etc.); **bribery f.,** caisse noire; **to start a f.,** lancer une souscription; **f.-raising scheme,** projet *m* pour se procurer des fonds; (*b*) *pl.* **funds,** fonds, masse *f*; ressources *f* pécuniaires; **funds of a**

company, fonds social; masse sociale; (*of company*) **to make a call for funds,** faire un appel de capital; **funds on which an annuity is secured,** assiette *f* d'une rente; **to be in funds,** être en fonds; *F:* **when he's in funds he's generous,** lorsqu'il a de l'argent il est généreux; **at the moment I am out of funds,** à ce moment je n'ai pas d'argent; **funds are low,** les fonds sont bas; **to have funds with a banker,** avoir une provision chez un banquier; *Bank:* **"no funds",** "défaut *m* de provision," "manque *m* de fonds"; "pas d'encaisse"; **insufficient funds, not sufficient funds,** insuffisance *f* de provision; **these societies have ample funds,** ces sociétés ont un budget bien garni; **to misappropriate public funds,** détourner les deniers de l'État, les deniers publics; *Mil:* **regimental funds,** masse régimentaire; (*c*) *pl.* **funds,** la dette publique; les fonds publics; la rente sur l'état; **to buy funds,** acheter de la rente; **f.-holder,** rentier, -ière.

fund², *v.tr. Fin:* **1.** consolider (une dette publique). **2. to f. money,** placer de l'argent dans les fonds publics; acheter de la rente. **3.** pourvoir (une société, etc.) de fonds.

fundable [ˈfʌndəbl], *a.* (dette, etc.) consolidable.

fundament [ˈfʌndəmənt], *s. Anat:* fondement *m*; (i) *F:* le derrière; (ii) l'anus *m*.

fundamental [fʌndəˈment(ə)l], *a. & s.*

I. *a.* **1.** (*a*) (*of reason, change, rule, principle, etc.*) fondamental, -aux; essentiel; **f. question,** question principale; question de fond; **f. qualities of s.o.,** qualités foncières de qn; **condition of f. importance,** condition essentielle, d'une importance capitale; **these theories were f. to all his political teaching,** ces théories servaient de base à tout son enseignement politique; (*b*) (*of colours, form, etc.*) primitif; original, -aux. **2.** *Ph: etc:* fondamental; **f. constants,** constantes fondamentales; **f. units,** unités fondamentales; *Mth:* **f. component,** composante *f* harmonique; *Mus:* **f. note,** note fondamentale; **f. tone,** son générateur (d'un harmonique).

II. *s.* **1.** *pl.* **fundamentals,** principe(s) *m*; notions fondamentales, fondements *mpl* (d'une science, théorie, etc.); partie essentielle (d'un système, etc.); articles fondamentaux (d'une religion, etc.); **fundamentals of arithmetic,** notions fondamentales d'arithmétique; **fundamentals of target practice,** principes du tir à la cible; *Mil:* mécanisme du tir à la cible; **to reach agreement on fundamentals,** aboutir à un accord de principe; réaliser un accord sur les points essentiels. **2.** *Mus:* son fondamental; (note) fondamentale (*f*).

fundamentalism [fʌndəˈmentəlizm], *s. Theol:* fondamentalisme *m*.

fundamentally [fʌndəˈmentəli], *adv.* fondamentalement; **science is f. ontological,** la science en son fin fond est ontologique; **his argument is f. wrong,** son raisonnement pèche par la base.

funded [ˈfʌndid], *a.* **f. property,** biens *mpl* en rentes; **f. capital,** capitaux investis; **long-term f. capital,** capitaux consolidés à long terme; **f. debt,** dette consolidée, fonds consolidés.

funding [ˈfʌndiŋ], *s.* consolidation *f* (d'une dette); assiette *f* (d'une rente); **f. loan,** emprunt *m* de consolidation.

fundus [ˈfʌndəs], *s. Anat:* fond *m* (d'un sac, de l'utérus).

Fünen [ˈfjuːnən], *Pr.n. Geog:* la Fionie.

funeral [ˈfjuːnərəl], *s.* **1.** (*a*) funérailles *fpl*; obsèques *fpl*; enterrement *m*; **to give s.o. a military, a state, f.,** faire des funérailles militaires, nationales, à qn; **to attend s.o.'s f.,** assister à l'enterrement de qn; suivre le cortège de qn; accompagner qn à sa dernière demeure; *F:* **that's your f.!** ça c'est votre affaire! **that's not my f.,** ce n'est pas moi que ça regarde; ce n'est pas moi qui en pâtirai; (*b*) convoi *m* funèbre; cortège *m* funèbre. **2.** *attrib.* **f. ceremony, oration,** cérémonie *f*, oraison *f*, funèbre; **the f. procession,** le convoi (funèbre); **f. expenses,** frais *m* funéraires; **f. service, bell,** office *m*, cloche *f*, des morts; **f. director,** entrepreneur de pompes funèbres; *NAm:* **f. home, f. parlour,** établissement *m* de pompes funèbres; *F:* **to proceed at a f. pace,** avancer à un pas d'enterrement.

funerary [ˈfjuːnərəri], *a.* (urne, etc.) funéraire.

funereal [fjuˈniəriəl], *a.* **1.** *Poet:* funèbre, funéraire. **2.** *F:* (*of surroundings, meeting, etc.*), lugubre, funèbre, triste; (*of voice*) lugubre, sépulcral, -aux; (*of pace*) lent, mesuré; **a f. face,** une figure d'enterrement.

funereally [fjuˈniəriəli], *adv.* funèbrement, lugubrement.

fun fair [ˈfʌnˈfɛər], *s.* (*a*) fête foraine; foire *f*; (*b*) parc *m* d'attractions.

fungal [ˈfʌŋg(ə)l], *a. Bot:* fongique.

fungia [ˈfʌndʒiə], *s. Coel:* fongia *f*, fongie *f*; fungia *f*, fungie *f*.

fungible [ˈfʌndʒibl], *a. Jur:* fongible.

fungicidal [fʌndʒiˈsaidl], *a.* fongicide.

fungicide [ˈfʌndʒisaid], *s.* fongicide *m*.

fungiform [ˈfʌndʒifɔːm], *a.* fongiforme.

fungistatic [fʌndʒiˈstætik], *a. Med:* fongostatique.

fungivorous [fʌnˈdʒivərəs], *a.* fongivore.

fungoid [ˈfʌŋgɔid], *a.* **1.** *Bot:* fongoïde. **2.** *Med:* fongueux.

fungosity [fʌŋˈgɔsiti], *s. Med:* fongosité *f*; (i) état fongueux; (ii) tumeur fongueuse; végétation spongieuse.

fungous [ˈfʌŋgəs], *a. Bot: Med:* fongueux, fongoïde; **f. growth,** (i) excroissance fongueuse; (ii) *F:* chose qui est venue en une nuit comme un champignon.

fungus, *pl.* **-uses, -i** [ˈfʌŋgəs, -əsiz, -gai; ˈfʌndʒai], *s.* **1.** (*a*) *Bot:* mycète *m*; champignon *m*; **edible f.,** champignon comestible; **house f.,** mérule *f*; **smut, brand, fungi,** ustilaginales *f*; *Ent:* **f. beetle,** zonaire *m*; **f. gnat, f. midge,** mycétophile *m*; (*b*) *F:* chose *f* qui pousse en une nuit; **f. towns,** villes *f* champignons. **2.** *Med:* fongus *m*.

fungus-dwelling [ˈfʌŋgəsdweliŋ], *a. Nat.Hist:* fongicole.

fungus-proof [ˈfʌŋgəspruːf], *a.* protégé contre les moisissures.

funicle [ˈfjuːnikl], *s. Bot: Ent:* funicule *m*, cordon *m*.

funicular [fjuˈnikjulər], *a. & s.* **1.** (machine, etc.) funiculaire; *Mth:* **f. (polygon),** (polygone *m*) funiculaire *m*; **f. curve,** (courbe) funiculaire *f*; **f. (railway),** funiculaire *m*. **2.** *Anat: Med:* (hernie, etc.) funiculaire.

funiculate [fjuˈnikjulət], *a. Bot:* funiculé.

funiculitis [fjuːnikjuˈlaitis], *s. Med:* funiculite *f*.

funiculus, *pl.* **-i** [fjuˈnikjuləs, -ai], *s.* **1.** *Bot: Ent:* funicule *m*, cordon *m*. **2.** *Anat:* cordon; **funiculi of a nerve,** cordons nerveux.

funiform [ˈfjuːnifɔːm], *a. Miner: Bot:* funiforme.

funk¹ [fʌŋk], *s. P:* **1.** frousse *f*, trac *m*; **to be in a (blue) f.,** avoir une peur bleue; avoir la peur au ventre; avoir une frousse de tous les diables; avoir le trac, la frousse, la trouille, la colique, les foies, les grelots; les avoir à la retourne; saigner du nez; caner, foirer; **it put me in a blue f.,** ça m'a donné une peur bleue; **to get into a f.,** caner; se dégonfler. **2.** (*pers.*) froussard, -arde; caneur, -euse; chiasseur, -euse, capon, -onne; trouillard, -arde; flanchard, -arde; péteux, -euse.

funk², *v.tr. & i. P:* **to f. (it),** caner, foirer; saigner du nez; avoir les foies (blancs); **to f. s.o., sth., to f. doing sth., to f. at sth.,** avoir peur de qn, de qch.; avoir peur de faire qch.

funk hole [ˈfʌŋkhoul], *s. F: esp. Mil:* planque *f*.

funkiness [ˈfʌŋkinis], *s. F:* couardise *f*, timidité *f*; poltronnerie *f*.

funky [ˈfʌŋki], *a. P:* (*of pers.*) froussard, foireux, capon; **to feel f.,** avoir la frousse, le trac.

funnel¹ [ˈfʌnl], *s.* **1.** (*a*) entonnoir *m*; **straining f.,** entonnoir à grille; **wine f.** (*with holes*), chantepleure *f*; *Ch:* **separating f., separatory f.,** ampoule *f*, ballon *m*, entonnoir, à décanter, de décantation; **f. tube,** tube *m* à entonnoir; *Elcs: W.Tel:* **f. aerial,** antenne *f* en pyramide renversée; (*b*) *Metall:* (trou *m* de) coulée *f*; (*c*) *Ind:* **(charging, loading) f.,** trémie *f*, hotte *f*; *Metall:* **sand f.,** trémie à sable; (*d*) embouchure *f* (de tube). **2.** (*a*) évent *m*, tuyau *m*, cheminée *f*, d'aération, d'aérage; **air f.,** manche *f* à air; (*b*) cheminée (d'une locomotive, d'un bateau à vapeur, d'une meule de charbon de bois); *Nau: etc:* **f. cap, hood,** parapluie *m* de cheminée; **f. casing,** enveloppe *f* de cheminée; **f. head,** chapeau *m* de cheminée; **f. guy, shroud, stay,** hauban *m* de cheminée; **hinged, lowering, f.,** cheminée à rabattement, à charnière; **telescopic f.,** cheminée télescopique.

funnel², *v.* (**funnelled**) **1.** *v.i.* (*a*) (*of valley, etc.*) se rétrécir; (*b*) **the crowd, the wind, funnelled into a narrow passage,** la foule, le vent, s'engouffra dans un passage étroit. **2.** *v.tr.* (*a*) **to f. one's hands,** mettre les mains en porte-voix; (*b*) canaliser (la foule, etc.); **complaints are funnelled to a central office,** les réclamations sont canalisées, dirigées, vers un bureau central.

funnelled [ˈfʌnld], *a.* **1.** en forme d'entonnoir. **2.** (*with numeral prefixed*) **two-f. steamer,** bateau à vapeur à deux cheminées.

funnel-shaped [ˈfʌnlʃeipt], *a.* en (forme d')entonnoir; *Anat: Bot:* infundibuliforme.

funnily [ˈfʌnili], *adv.* drôlement; (i) comiquement, d'une manière amusante, facétieuse; (ii) curieusement, bizarrement; **f. enough . . .,** chose curieuse . . ..

funniness [ˈfʌninis], *s.* **1.** drôlerie *f*; caractère amusant, comique, facétieux (de qch.). **2.** bizarrerie *f*, caractère curieux.

funning [ˈfʌniŋ], *s. A:* plaisanterie *f*, badinage *m*.

funny¹ [ˈfʌni], *a. & s.*

I. *a.* drôle. **1.** comique, amusant, facétieux; **it was the funniest sight,** c'était très amusant à voir; c'était à se tordre; **it was really too f.! it was too f. for words!** c'était vraiment trop drôle! *F:* c'était d'un rigolo! c'était tordant; **he looked too f. for words!** il était à peindre! **none of your f. tricks! I don't want any f. business!** pas de vos farces! pas de vos supercheries! je ne veux pas d'histoires! **the f. thing about it is . . .,** le comique de la chose c'est que . . .; **he is trying to be f.,** il veut faire de l'esprit; **it isn't at all f.,** je la trouve mauvaise; *Cin:* **f. film,** film *m* comique; *Th:* **f. man,** bouffon *m*; (*in circus*) Auguste *m*, Gugusse *m*; **he's the f. man of the show,** c'est lui l'Auguste, le comique. **2.** curieux, bizarre; **he is a f. person,** c'est un drôle d'homme; **he was f. that way,** il était comme ça; **f. shapes,** formes *f* bizarres; **a f. idea,** une drôle d'idée; **how f. he should have forgotten it!** comme c'est drôle qu'il l'ait oublié! **well, that's f.!** tiens! voilà qui est curieux, étrange, bizarre; comme c'est drôle! **there's something f. in this business,** il y a quelque chose de louche dans cette affaire; *F:* **no f. business!** (i) pas de blagues! (ii) pas d'histoires! (iii) à bas les pattes! *P:* **f. money,** monnaie contrefaite; **this butter tastes f.,** ce beurre a un drôle de goût; *F:* **do you mean f. peculiar or f. ha-ha?** par drôle voulez-vous dire rigolo ou bizarre? **he's a f.-tempered fellow,** il a un drôle de caractère; il est mauvais coucheur; c'est un bâton épineux. **3.** *P:* **he looks very f.,** il a l'air tout chose; **I came over all f.,** je me suis senti(e) tout(e) chose; **he went a bit f. in his old age,** il devint un peu fou, un peu bizarre, dans sa vieillesse.

II. *s.* **1.** *Th: Cin: etc:* (*a*) (*pers.*) bouffon *m*; (*at circus, etc.*) Auguste *m*, Gugusse *m*; **they're the funnies of the show,** ils sont les comiques du spectacle; (*b*) film *m* comique; (*c*) *F:* plaisanterie *f*, blague *f*. **2.** *NAm:* (*a*) dessin *m* humoristique; bande dessinée; (*b*) *usu.pl.* **funnies,** bandes dessinées, pages *f* comiques (d'un périodique).

funny², *s.* skiff *m* à un rameur.

funnybone [ˈfʌniboun], *s. F:* le petit Juif (à l'articulation du coude).

fur¹ [fəːr], *s.* **1.** (*a*) fourrure *f*, pelleterie *f*; **to coat, line, a garment with f.,** fourrer un vêtement; **to put on one's fur(s),** mettre sa fourrure, ses fourrures; **f.-clad,** habillé en, de, fourrures; **f. coat,** manteau *m* de fourrure; **f.-dresser,** fourreur *m*; pelletier, -ière; **f. fabric,** fourrure synthétique; **f. farm,** élevage *m* d'animaux à fourrure; **f. farming,** élevage des animaux à fourrure; **f. felt,** velours *m* de feutre; **f.-lined coat,** manteau doublé de fourrure; manteau fourré; pelisse *f*; **f. making,** pelleterie *f*; **f. skins,** pelleterie; **f. trade,** commerce *m* de fourrures; pelleterie; **f.-trader,** pelletier, -ière; fourreur; **f.-trimmed,** (manteau, etc.) garni de fourrure; *Ent:* **f. moth,** teigne *f* des fourrures; *Z:* **f. seal,** loutre *f* d'Europe; (*b*) poil *m*, pelage *m* (de lapin, de loutre, etc.); **the tiger has a striped f.,** le tigre a un pelage rayé; *F:* **to make the f. fly,** se battre avec acharnement; faire les cent coups; **then the f. began to fly,** alors on s'est attaqué du bec et des ongles; (*c*) *Ven:* gibier *m* à poil; **f. and feather,** gibier à poil et à plume; **dog trained to f. and feather,** chien dressé au poil et à la plume; (*d*) *pl.* **furs,** peaux *fpl* (d'animaux). **2.** *Her:* fourrure. **3.** (*a*) (*in wine bottles, etc.*) dépôts *mpl*; (*in boiler, radiator, etc.*) incrustations *fpl*, tartre *m*, calcin *m*, crasse(s) *f(pl)*, entartrage *m*; (*b*) *Med:* (*on tongue*) enduit *m* (blanchâtre, noirâtre). **4.** *Const:* fourrure (de poutre).

fur², *v.tr. & i.* (**furred**)

I. *v.tr.* **1.** fourrer (un manteau, etc.); garnir, doubler (un manteau, etc.) de fourrure. **2.** entartrer, incruster (une chaudière, etc.); *Med:* charger (la langue). **3.** désincruster, détartrer, décrasser, piquer (une chaudière). **4.** *Const:* fourrer (une poutre).

II. *v.i.* **to f. (up),** (*of boiler, etc.*) s'incruster, s'entartrer; (*of the tongue*) se charger, s'empâter.

furan [ˈfjuəræn], **furane** [ˈfjuərein], *s. Ch:* furan(n)e *m*, furfurane *m*.

furanose [ˈfjuərənouz], *s. Bio-Ch:* furannose *m*.

furbearer [ˈfəːbɛərər], *s.* animal *m* à fourrure.

furbelow [ˈfəːbilou], *s.* **1.** *Dressm: A:* falbala *m*. **2.** *pl. Pej:* **furbelows,** parure *f*, fanfreluches *f*. **3.** *Algae:* baudrier *m* de Neptune.

furbelowed [ˈfəːbiloud], *a. Dressm: A:* falbalassé.

furbish [ˈfəːbiʃ], *v.tr.* **1. to f. (up),** fourbir, polir, nettoyer, astiquer (une pièce de métal, *Mil:* son fourniment, etc.). **2. to f. up,** (re)mettre à neuf (une robe, des meubles, etc.); **to f. up one's Latin,** se remettre au latin, lire du latin pour se dérouiller; **to f. up an old tale,** recrépir, replâtrer, retaper, un vieux conte.

furbisher [ˈfəːbiʃər], *s.* fourbisseur *m*; **sword f.,** polisseur *m* d'armes blanches.

furbishing [ˈfəːbiʃiŋ], *s.* **1. f. (up),** fourbissage *m*, fourbissement *m*, fourbissure *f*, astiquage *m*. **2. f. up,** remise *f* à neuf.

furcate¹ [ˈfəːkeit], *a.* (*of road, etc.*) en bifurcation;

fourché; (*of hoof*) fourchu; *Nat.Hist:* bifurqué.

furcate², *v.i.* (*of road, etc.*) bifurquer, fourcher; faire la fourche.

furcation [fəː'keiʃ(ə)n], *s.* bifurcation *f* (d'une branche, d'un chemin, etc.).

furcraea [fəː'kriːə], *s. Bot:* furcraea *f*, fourcroya *f*.

furcula, *pl.* **-ae** ['fəːkjulə, -iː], *s. Orn:* furcula *f*, fourchette *f*, lunette *f* (d'oiseau).

furfur, *pl.* **-ures** ['fəːfər, 'fəːfjuriːz], *s. Med:* furfur *m*, furfure *f*.

furfuraceous [fəːfju'reiʃəs], *a. Med: etc:* furfuracé.

furfural ['fəːfjurəl], **furfuraldehyde** [fəːfju'rældihaid], *s. Ch:* furfural *m*.

furfuran ['fəːfjuræn], *s. Ch:* furan(n)e *m*, furfurane *m*.

furfuryl ['fəːfjuril], *s. Ch:* furfuryle *m*.

furfurylidene [fəːfju'rilidiːn], *s. Ch:* furfurylidène *m*.

furil(e) ['fjuəril], *s. Ch:* furile *m*.

furilic [fju'rilik], *a. Ch:* (acide *m*) furilique.

furioso [fjuri'ousou], *adv. & a. Mus:* furioso.

furious ['fjuəriəs], *a.* (*of pers., animal, look, etc.*) furieux; (*of look*) furibond; *Lit:* courroucé; (*of battle, zeal, etc.*) acharné, forcené; (*of wind*) furieux, violent, impétueux; **to be in a f. hurry,** être très pressé; **to go at a f. pace,** courir à toute bride, à bride abattue; **to drive at a f. speed,** conduire à tombeau ouvert, comme un fou; **f. at having failed,** furieux d'avoir manqué son coup; **he was f. at having been outwitted,** il était furieux qu'on l'eût mis dedans; **to get f.,** entrer en fureur; **to be f. with s.o.,** être furieux contre, *F:* après, qn; **the fun grew fast and f.,** la gaieté devenait folle et bruyante; *adv.* **he was going at it fast and f.,** il y allait frénétiquement; *Jur: A:* **f. driving,** excès *m* de vitesse.

furiously ['fjuəriəsli], *adv.* (parler, regarder, etc.) furieusement; (combattre, etc.) avec acharnement, avec furie; (conduire) à une allure folle; (*of horseman*) (courir) à bride abattue; **the fire was blazing f.,** l'incendie *m* faisait rage.

furiousness ['fjuəriəsnis], *s.* fureur *f* (de qn); acharnement *m* (d'un combat, etc.); fureur, furie *f*, violence *f*, impétuosité *f* (du vent, etc.).

furl¹ [fəːl], *s.* **1.** rouleau *m* (de papier, etc.). **2.** *Nau:* serrage *m* (d'une voile).

furl², **1.** *v.tr.* (*a*) *Nau:* serrer, ferler (une voile); **with all sail furled,** toutes voiles dedans; (*b*) rouler (un parapluie, etc.); serrer (une tente); fermer (un éventail); replier (les ailes, etc.); *Mil: etc:* **flag furled and craped,** drapeau *m* en berne. **2.** *v.i.* (*a*) **to f. (up),** s'enrouler, se rouler; (*b*) (*of clouds*) **to f. away,** se replier à l'horizon; se dissiper.

Furlanian [fəː'leiniən], *a. & s. Geog:* frioulien, -ienne.

furling ['fəːliŋ], *s.* **1.** *Nau:* serrage *m*, ferlage *m* (des voiles); **f. gasket,** chambrière *f*; **f. line,** raban *m* de ferlage. **2.** enroulage *m*, enroulement *m* (d'un parapluie, etc.); serrage *m* (d'une tente); pliage *m* (des ailes).

furlong ['fəːlɔŋ], *s. A. Meas:* furlong *m* (= 201 mètres).

furlough¹ ['fəːlou], *s. Mil: etc:* congé *m*, permission *f*; **to be, go, on f.,** être, aller, en permission; **the men on f.,** les permissionnaires *m*.

furlough², *v.tr. NAm:* accorder un congé à (qn); *Mil:* envoyer (un homme) en permission.

furmety ['fəːmiti], *s.* fromentée *f*; bouillie *f* de froment.

furnace ['fəːnis], *s.* **1.** (*a*) *Metall: Glassm: Ch: etc:* fourneau *m*, four *m*; **reverberatory f.,** fourneau à réverbère; **Catalan f.,** feu catalan; **bar-heating f.,** four à réchauffer les barres; **batch f.,** four individuel, discontinu; **forging f.,** fourneau de forge; **cementation f., cementing f.,** four(neau) de cémentation; **cupel f., cupellation f., cupelling f.,** four à coupellation, à coupelles; **glass f.,** four de verrerie; **electric f.,** four électrique; **air f.,** four à vent; **oil f.,** four à huile lourde; (*b*) *Fig:* fournaise *f*; **this room is like a f.,** cette chambre est une (vraie) fournaise; **he has been tried in the f.,** il s'est retrempé dans l'adversité. **2.** (*a*) **(house-heating) f.,** calorifère *m*; (*b*) foyer *m* (de chaudière); (*c*) *Min:* foyer d'aérage.

Furnariidae [fəːnə'riːidiː], *s.pl. Orn:* furnariidés *m*.

furnish¹ ['fəːniʃ], *s. Paperm:* matières premières.

furnish², *v.tr.* **1.** (*a*) fournir, donner (des renseignements, des preuves, etc.); pourvoir (les fonds nécessaires, etc.); produire, alléguer (des raisons, etc.); offrir, présenter, fournir (une occasion, etc.); **this vegetable furnishes a wholesome food,** ce légume constitue une nourriture saine; (*b*) **to f. s.o., sth., with sth.,** fournir, pourvoir, munir, qn, qch., de qch.; garnir qch. de qch.; procurer qch. à qn; **to f. an army with supplies,** fournir une armée de vivres; approvisionner, ravitailler, une armée; **to f. s.o. with what he needs,** pourvoir aux besoins de qn; **to f. s.o. with information,** fournir des renseignements à qn; **we wish to be furnished with proof that . . .,** nous désirons être mis en possession de preuves (de ce) que . . .; **to f. a fort with guns,** garnir un fort de canons; **to f. a turbine wheel with blades,** garnir d'aubes une roue turbine; *El:* **to f. a factory with current,** alimenter une usine de courant. **2.** meubler, garnir (une maison, etc.); **to f. a house, a flat, etc., for s.o.,** mettre qn dans ses meubles; **to f. one's room, one's home,** se meubler; **knick-knacks that help to f.,** bibelots *m* qui meublent. **3.** *v.i.* (*of dog, horse, etc.*) prendre du corps; forcir.

furnished ['fəːniʃt], *a.* **1.** pourvu, fourni, équipé (**with,** de); **report well f. with facts,** rapport nourri de faits; **well f. purse, shop,** bourse bien garnie, magasin bien assorti, bien achalandé. **2. f. flat, rooms,** appartement meublé; chambres meublées; **to live in f. apartments,** loger en garni, en meublé, dans une maison meublée; **to let f. apartments,** louer des garnis; tenir un meublé, un hôtel garni; **well f., badly f., house,** maison bien montée, bien meublée; maison mal meublée, pauvrement meublée.

furnisher ['fəːniʃər], *s.* **1.** fournisseur *m* (**of,** de); *esp.* marchand *m* d'ameublement; **you will find that at a (house) furnisher's,** vous trouverez cela dans une maison d'ameublement. **2.** *Tex:* rouleau fournisseur (de machine à imprimer); **brush f.,** brosse fournisseuse.

furnishing ['fəːniʃiŋ], *s.* **1.** (*a*) fourniture *f*, provision *f* (des choses nécessaires, etc.); prestation *f* (de capitaux); allégation *f* (d'une raison, etc.); (*b*) fourniture, apport *m*, de meubles pour (une maison, etc.); action de meubler (une maison, etc.); **house-f. firm,** maison *f* d'ameublement; **f. fabrics,** tissus *m* d'ameublement. **2.** (*thg furnished*) (*a*) garniture *f*; (*b*) *pl.* **furnishings,** ameublement *m* (d'une maison).

furniture ['fəːnitʃər], *s.* **1.** meubles *mpl*, ameublement *m*, mobilier *m* (d'une maison, etc.); *Jur:* meubles meublants; **piece of f.,** meuble; **suite, set, of f.,** mobilier; *Com:* meuble (de salon, etc.); **set of dining-room f.,** mobilier, meuble, de salle à manger; **to have one's own f.,** *F:* être dans ses meubles; **school f.,** matériel scolaire; *attrib. Ent:* **f. beetle,** vrillette *f* domestique; **f. dealer,** brocanteur, -euse (de vieux meubles); **f. polish,** encaustique *f* pour les meubles; **f. remover,** déménageur *m*; entrepreneur *m* de déménagements; **f. shop,** maison *f* d'ameublement; **f. van,** camion *m*, fourgon *m*, de déménagement; **f. warehouse,** (i) garde-meuble *m*, *pl.* garde-meubles; (ii) maison d'ameublement en gros. **2.** (*a*) ferrures *fpl* (d'une porte, d'un cercueil, etc.); *Sm.a.:* garniture *f* (de fusil); (*b*) *Nau:* matériel *m*, gréement *m*; (*c*) *Typ:* garniture. **3.** *Publ:* livres *mpl* de fond. **4.** *Mus:* (*of organ*) **f. (stop),** (jeu *m* de) fourniture *f*; jeu de mixture.

furoin ['fjuərouin], *s. Ch:* furoïne *f*.

furor ['fjuərɔːr], *s.* **1.** *esp. Med: & Poet:* fureur *f* (prophétique, poétique); folie *f* frénétique. **2.** *A:* = FURORE.

furore [fju(ə)'rɔːri], *s. F:* fureur *f*; enthousiasme démesuré; **to create a f.,** (i) (*in popularity*) faire fureur; (ii) provoquer un tumulte.

furphy ['fəːfi], *s. Austr: P:* fausse nouvelle, canard *m*.

furred [fəːd], *a.* **1.** (*a*) (manteau, etc) fourré; (*b*) (*of pers.*) habillé de fourrures; **to be f. to the eyes,** être emmitouflé de fourrures jusqu'aux yeux; être enfoui dans ses fourrures; (*c*) (animal) à poil. **2.** (*of boiler, etc.*) entartré, incrusté; revêtu d'incrustations; *Med:* **f. tongue,** langue chargée.

furrier¹ ['fʌriər], *s.* pelletier, -ière; fourreur *m*.

furrier², *v.tr.* apprêter (une fourrure).

furriery ['fʌriəri], *s.* pelleterie *f*.

furring ['fəːriŋ], *s.* **1.** (*a*) garnissage *m* (d'un manteau, etc.) avec une fourrure; (*b*) entartrage *m*, incrustation *f* (d'une chaudière, etc.); *Med:* chargement *m* (de la langue); (*c*) détartrage *m*, décrassage *m* (des chaudières). **2.** (*a*) (*in boiler, etc.*) calcin *m*, tartre *m*, crasse(s) *f(pl)*; (*b*) *Const:* fourrure *f*; *N.Arch:* soufflage *m*; **f.(-piece) of a roof,** coyau *m* d'un toit.

furrow¹ ['fʌrou], *s.* **1.** (*a*) *Agr:* (i) **(open) f.,** sillon *m*; (ii) billon *m*; tranche *f* (de terre) retournée par la charrue; **boundary f., water f.,** dérayure *f*; **to cut the boundary f., the last f., of a field,** dérayer un champ; **to plough a straight f.,** mener droit son sillon; *Fig:* **to plough a lonely f.,** poursuivre seul une idée; faire bande à part; **to plough one's own f.,** faire, creuser, son sillon; (*b*) *Lit:* sillage *m* (d'un navire). **2.** *Carp: Metalw: etc:* cannelure *f*, rainure *f*; rayure *f* (de canon de fusil); gorge *f* (de filet de vis). **3.** (*on face, etc.*) ride profonde; sillon.

furrow², *v.tr.* **1.** labourer (la terre); creuser des sillons dans (la terre); rayonner (un champ); *F:* (*of ship*) sillonner (les mers, etc.); **mountainside furrowed by, with, deep ravines,** flanc de montagne sillonné, creusé, de profonds ravins. **2.** *Carp: Metalw: etc:* canneler, rainer (une planche, un ciseau, etc.). **3.** (*a*) rider profondément (le front, etc.); **age has furrowed his face,** l'âge a sillonné, labouré, son visage; **his brow is furrowed with wrinkles,** des rides profondes lui creusent, lui sillonnent, le front; (*b*) *v.i.* (*of brow, etc.*) se rider, se sillonner.

furrowed ['fʌroud], *a.* **1.** (champ) coupé de sillons; sillonné (**with,** de). **2.** cannelé; (fusil) rayé. **3.** (front, visage) creusé, coupé, de rides profondes.

furrowy ['fʌroui], *a.* **1.** (champ, etc.) coupé de sillons. **2.** (visage) ridé, haché, rugueux.

furry ['fəːri], *a.* **1.** (animal) à poil; (insecte, etc.) velu; (mousse, etc.) qui ressemble à (de) la fourrure. **2.** (*of boiler, etc.*) entartré, incrusté, tartreux, revêtu d'incrustations; **f. tongue,** langue chargée.

further¹ ['fəːðər]. **1.** *adv.* (*a*) plus loin (**than,** que); **we did not go on any f. after dark,** nous ne sommes pas allés plus loin à la nuit; **to penetrate f. into the country,** pénétrer plus avant dans le pays; **I can go no f.,** (i) je ne saurais aller plus loin; (ii) je n'en peux plus; **anything I'm told goes no f.,** ce qu'on me dit ne va pas plus loin; **to draw f. back,** se reculer davantage; **the people (standing) f. away, off,** ceux qui se trouvent plus loin, plus éloignés; **to move f. away,** s'éloigner; **I went f. on,** je suis allé plus loin; **f. on we shall see that . . .,** plus loin nous verrons que . . .; **he's f. on than his class,** il est en avance sur, plus avancé que, sa classe; **to go f. and fare worse,** tomber d'un mal dans un pire; **you might go f. and fare worse,** vous pourriez trouver pis; ce n'est déjà pas si mal; *P:* **I'll see you f. first!** plus souvent! va-t'en voir si j'y suis! tu peux te fouiller! (*b*) davantage, plus; **I don't know any f.,** je n'en sais pas davantage; **I didn't question him any f.,** je ne l'ai pas interrogé davantage; **without troubling any f.,** sans plus se tracasser; **until you hear f.,** jusqu'à nouvel avis; (*c*) **to go f. into sth.,** entrer plus avant dans qch.; **to go no f. in the matter,** en rester là; **to go f. than s.o.,** renchérir sur qn.; **to add water to the wine to make it go f.,** allonger le vin d'eau; **that doesn't get us much f.,** cela ne nous avance pas beaucoup; (*d*) (*in time*) **f. back,** à une période plus reculée; **to go f. back,** remonter plus haut, plus en arrière; **f. back than the last century,** antérieurement au siècle dernier; (*e*) d'ailleurs, en outre, de plus, aussi, du reste; **and, f., I think it expedient to . . .,** qui plus est, d'ailleurs, du reste, je trouve opportun de . . .; **we would f. add that . . .,** nous nous permettons d'ajouter en outre que . . .. **2.** *a.* (*a*) plus lointain; plus éloigné; **at the f. end of the room,** à l'autre bout, au fond, de la salle; **on the f. bank of the river,** sur la rive opposée de la rivière; (*b*) nouveau, additionnel, supplémentaire, ultérieur, en plus, de plus; **to remand a case for f. enquiry,** remettre une affaire pour plus ample informé; renvoyer une cause à plus ample informé; **the f. recommendations of . . .,** les autres recommandations *f* de . . .; **without f. loss of time,** sans autre perte de temps; sans perdre plus de temps; **without f. ado,** sans plus de cérémonie; sans plus . . .; **a f. reason,** une nouvelle raison; une autre raison; une raison de plus; **upon f. consideration,** après plus ample(s) réflexion(s); après un examen plus approfondi, attentif; **to postpone a matter for f. consideration,** ajourner une question pour supplément d'examen; **one or two f. details,** encore un ou deux détails; quelques détails complémentaires; quelques indications *f* supplémentaires; quelques précisions; **to go into f. details,** entrer dans de plus amples détails; **I wish to hear no f. details,** n'entrez pas plus avant dans le détail; je ne veux pas entendre d'autres détails; **f. information,** renseignements *m* complémentaires (**about,** au sujet de); **to await f. news,** attendre de plus amples nouvelles; *Com:* **f. orders,** commandes ultérieures; nouvelles commandes; **with f. reference to, f. to, my letter of the 15th,** comme suite de, à, ma lettre du 15; **a f. £50 on account,** un nouvel acompte de £50; **to ask for a f. credit,** demander un crédit supplémentaire; **f. education,** enseignement *m* postscolaire; formation continue.

further², *v.tr.* avancer, favoriser, servir (les intérêts de qn, etc.); faciliter (un système d'éducation, etc.); seconder (un dessein); aider (au succès); **this does not f. our object,** cela ne nous avance pas beaucoup.

furtherance ['fəːðərəns], *s.* avancement *m* (d'un travail, etc.); **for the f. of, in f. of (sth.),** pour avancer, pour servir (qch.); pour aider à l'avancement, au progrès, de (qch.).

furtherer ['fəːðərər], *s.* personne *f* qui avance, qui aide à l'avancement de (qch.); **a meeting of all the furtherers of the scheme,** une réunion de tous ceux qui s'emploient à faire aboutir ce projet, de tous ceux qui ont ce projet à cœur.

furthermore [fəːðə'mɔːr], *adv.* en outre, outre cela, au surplus, de plus, du reste, d'autre part, par ailleurs, qui plus est . . ..

furthermost ['fəːðəmoust], *a.* (endroit, etc.) le plus lointain, le plus reculé, le plus éloigné; **to the f. ends of the**

earth, jusqu'aux extrémités *f* de la terre.

furthest ['fə:ðist], *adv. & a.* **he went f.,** il est allé le plus loin; **the f. part of the cave,** la partie la plus reculée de la caverne; **his house was f. off, away,** sa maison était la plus éloignée.

furtive ['fə:tiv], *a.* (*a*) (*of manner, pers.*) sournois, cachottier; (*b*) (*of glance, smile, etc.*) furtif, dérobé, à la dérobée; en cachette.

furtively ['fə:tivli], *adv.* (*a*) sournoisement; (*b*) furtivement, à la dérobée; **to watch s.o. f.,** regarder qn en dessous, à la dérobée.

furuncle ['fjuərʌŋkl], *s. Med:* furoncle *m.*

furuncular [fjuə'rʌŋkjulər], **furunculous** [fjuə'rʌŋkjuləs], *a. Med:* furonculeux.

furunculosis [fjuərʌŋkju'lousis], *s. Med:* furonculose *f.*

fury ['fjuəri], *s.* **1.** furie *f*, fureur *f*, emportement *m* (de qn); acharnement *m* (d'un combat, etc.); déchaînement *m*, violence *f* (du vent, etc.); **the f. of the storm,** la fureur, la furie, de la tempête; **with the f. of despair,** avec la fureur du désespoir; **to get into a f.,** entrer en fureur, en furie, *F:* se mettre dans une colère bleue; s'emporter; **he was beside himself with f.,** il était hors de lui; *F:* **to work like f.,** travailler avec acharnement, comme quatre; **it was raining like f.,** il pleuvait à seaux. **2.** (*a*) *pl. Myth:* **the Furies,** les Furies *f*; les Érinnyes *f*; (*b*) *F:* mégère *f*, furie.

furyl ['fjuəril], *s. Ch:* furyle *m.*

furze [fə:z], *s. Bot:* ajonc *m*; jonc marin; genêt épineux; ulex *m*; *F:* vignon *m*, landier *m*; **ground f.,** bugrane *f*, arrête-bœuf *m inv*; **f. bush,** touffe *f* d'ajonc.

furzy ['fə:zi], *a.* couvert d'ajoncs.

fusain ['fju:zein], *s.* **1.** *Art:* fusain *m.* **2.** *Min: Geol:* fusain, charbon *m* fossile.

fusariose [fju'zɛərious], **fusariosis** [fjuzɛəri'ousis], *s. Med:* fusariose *f.*

fusarol(e) ['fju:zəroul], *s. Arch:* fusarol(l)e *f*, fuserolle *f.*

fuscous ['fʌskəs], *a. Nat.Hist:* brun foncé; noirâtre, bistre; sombre.

fuse[1] [fju:z], *s.* **1.** *Artil: Pyr: etc:* fusée *f* (d'obus, etc.); amorce *f*; **base f.,** fusée de culot; **nose f., point f.,** fusée d'ogive; **combination f., double-action f., time and percussion f.,** fusée à double effet; **concussion f., impact f., percussion f.,** fusée percutante, à percussion; **percussion-f. shell,** obus percutant; **detonating f., explosive f.,** fusée-détonateur *f*, *pl.* fusées-détonateurs; **inertia f.,** fusée à inertie; **delay(ed-action) f., time f.,** fusée à retard(ement), retardée, à effet retardé; **mechanical time f.,** fusée à mouvement d'horlogerie; **non-delay(ed action) f.,** fusée sans retard; **direct-action f., instantaneous f.,** fusée instantanée; **disk f.,** fusée à plateau; **proximity f.,** fusée de proximité, à influence, fonctionnant par influence; **self-destroying f.,** fusée autodestructrice; *attrib.* **f. body, f. case,** corps *m* de fusée; **f. cap, f. cover,** chapeau *m*, coiffe *f*, de fusée; **f. hole,** lumière *f*, œil *m* (d'obus); trou *m* d'amorce, de fusée; **f. mallet,** chassoir *m*; **f. puncher, f. setter, f. borer,** débouchoir *m*; **f. setting,** réglage *m* de la fusée; **to set a f.,** régler une fusée; **to range for f.,** régler la hauteur d'éclatement (d'un obus). **2.** *Min: etc:* **(safety) f., common f., Bickford f.,** cordeau *m* (bickford); étoupille *f*, mèche *f*; corde *f* à feu; **electric f.,** amorce électrique; **f. composition,** composition fusante.

fuse[2], *v.tr.* pourvoir (un projectile) d'une fusée; insérer une fusée dans (un projectile); amorcer (une bombe); *Min: etc:* étoupiller (un trou de mine).

fuse[3], *s. El:* **(safety) f.,** fusible *m* (de sécurité); (*in private house*) plomb *m*; **house service f.,** fusible de compteur; **bridge f.,** fusible à pont; **cartridge f.,** fusible à cartouche; **horn f.,** coupe-circuit *m inv* à antennes; **plug f.,** fusible à bouchon; **strip f.,** fusible à lame; **f. block, f. holder,** porte-fusible *m*, *pl.* porte-fusibles; **f. box,** boîte *f* à fusibles; brise-circuit *m inv*; **six-way f. box,** boîte à six fusibles; **f. cutout,** coupe-circuit à fusible; **f. (disconnecting) switch,** disjoncteur *m* à fusible; **f. panel,** panneau *m* de fusibles; **f. tube,** (corps *m* de) fusible; **f. wire,** fil *m* à fusible; **to blow a f.,** faire sauter un plomb.

fuse[4], *v.tr.* protéger (un circuit, etc.) par un fusible.

fuse[5]. **1.** *v.tr.* (*a*) fondre, mettre en fusion (un métal, etc.); **to f. two pieces together, apart,** réunir, séparer, deux pièces par fusion; **to f. two wires together,** fondre deux fils ensemble; (*b*) (i) vitrifier (l'émail) par fusion; (ii) parfondre (les couleurs dans l'émail); (*c*) *Fig:* fusionner, amalgamer, réunir (deux partis, etc.); (*d*) *El:* **to f. a circuit,** faire sauter les plombs d'un circuit. **2.** *v.i.* (*a*) (*of metals, etc.*) fondre; (*b*) (*of two bones*) se souder; (*c*) *Fig:* (*of parties, motives, etc.*) fusionner; s'amalgamer; s'unir par la fusion; (*d*) *El:* **the lights have fused,** les plombs ont sauté.

fused[1] [fju:zd], *a.* (obus, etc.) pourvu d'une fusée; amorcé.

fused[2], *a.* **1.** (*of metals, etc.*) fondu. **2.** (*of parties, languages, etc.*) fusionné.

fused[3], *a. El:* (circuit) protégé par un fusible.

fusee [fju:'zi:], *s.* **1.** (*a*) *Clockm:* fusée *f* (d'une montre, etc.); (*b*) *Mec.E:* tambour *m*, poulie *f*, conique. **2.** *Vet:* suros *m*; exostose *f* du canon. **3.** allumette-tison *f*, *pl.* allumettes-tisons. **4.** *Rail: NAm:* feu *m* de signal.

fuselage ['fju:zəlɑ:ʒ], *s. Av:* fuselage *m.*

fusel oil ['fju:z(ə)lɔil], *s. Ch: Dist:* huile *f* de fusel, de pomme de terre; alcool *m* amylique.

fusibility [fju:zi'biliti], *s.* fusibilité *f* (d'un métal, etc.).

fusible ['fju:zibl], *a.* fusible.

fusiform ['fju:zifɔ:m], *a. Nat.Hist:* fusiforme; en forme de fuseau; *Av:* fuselé.

fusil ['fju:zil], *s. Her:* fusée *f.*

fusilier [fju:zi'liər], *s. Mil:* fusilier *m*; *pl.* **Fusiliers,** nom que portent encore certains régiments.

fusillade[1] [fju:zi'leid], *s. Mil:* fusillade *f.*

fusillade[2], *v.tr. O:* **1.** soumettre (une position) à une fusillade. **2.** passer (une compagnie, les habitants d'un village, etc.) par les armes; fusiller (les habitants).

fusilly ['fju:zili], *a. Her:* fuselé.

fusing ['fju:ziŋ], *s.* **1.** fusion *f*, fonte *f*. **2.** vitrification *f* par fusion.

fusinist ['fju:zinist], *s. Art:* fus(a)iniste *mf.*

fusion ['fju:ʒ(ə)n], *s.* fusion *f*. **1.** (*a*) fondage *m*, fonte *f* (d'un métal); **f. welding,** soudure *f* par fusion; (*b*) *Atom.Ph:* **f. energy,** énergie *f* de fusion; **f. reactor,** réacteur *m* à fusion, thermonucléaire; **controlled f.,** fusion contrôlée, ménagée; *Mil:* **f. bomb,** bombe *f* à fusion, thermonucléaire. **2.** fusionnement *m* (de plusieurs banques, etc.); *Pol:* fusion (de deux partis, etc.); *F:* brassement *m* (de deux nations, etc.); *Psy:* fusion (de plusieurs sensations); *Biol:* fusion (de deux cellules).

fusionist ['fju:ʒənist], *s. Pol: etc:* fusionniste *mf.*

fusocellular [fju:zou'seljulər], *a. Med:* (tumeur *f*) fusocellulaire.

fuss[1] [fʌs], *s.* **1.** bruit exagéré; potin *m*; **what's all this f. about?** (i) qu'est-ce que c'est que toutes ces histoires? (ii) qu'est-ce qui cloche? **without any f.,** sans bruit; **a lot of f. over a trifle, about nothing,** bien du tapage pour peu de chose; beaucoup de bruit pour rien; **to make,** *F:* **kick up, a f.,** faire un tas d'histoires; faire des chichis; **to make a great f. (about sth.),** faire toutes sortes d'histoires (au sujet de qch.); en faire tout un plat; **he'll make an awful f.,** il va en faire des histoires! **why make all that f.?** pourquoi tant d'histoires? **you're making all this f. for a beggarly twenty pence!** vous m'en faites des histoires pour vingt malheureux pence! **there's nothing to make a f. about,** (i) il n'y pas de quoi se récrier, s'exclamer; (ii) il n'y a pas là de quoi fouetter un chat; *O:* **to be in a fine f.,** être dans tous ses états. **2.** embarras *mpl*; façons *fpl*; **a great f.,** bien des cérémonies; **the presentation took place without (any) f.,** la présentation se fit sans cérémonies, très simplement; **after a great deal of f. he accepted,** après avoir fait toutes sortes de manières il a accepté; **to make a f.,** faire des cérémonies, des embarras; **don't make such a f. about it,** ne faites pas tant de simagrées, tant d'embarras; **to make a f. of s.o.,** (i) être aux petits soins pour qn; (ii) mettre qn en avant; **he likes to be made a f. of,** (*of pers.*) il aime qu'on fasse grand cas de lui; (*of dog, etc.*) il aime qu'on le caresse; **style free from f.,** style *m* simple; *A:* **f. and feathers,** de l'esbrouf(f)e.

fuss[2]. **1.** *v.i.* tatillonner; faire de l'embarras; faire des embarras; faire des histoires; se tracasser; **to f. about, to f. round,** faire l'affairé, s'affairer; **she never fussed,** elle restait toujours calme; **people fussing about trifles,** gens affairés de riens; **to f. over, around, s.o.,** être aux petits soins pour qn, avec qn; faire l'empressé auprès de qn; **she never stops fussing with her hair,** elle ne cesse pas d'arranger nerveusement ses cheveux. **2.** *v.tr.* (*a*) tracasser, agiter (qn); (*b*) *NAm:* être aux petits soins auprès de (qn).

fussed [fʌst], *a. NAm: F:* **f. up,** (i) embarrassé, mis en émoi; **he was f. up,** il avait la tête montée; (ii) (*of woman*) attifée; parée de tous ses atours.

fussily ['fʌsili], *adv.* **1.** (*a*) d'une manière tatillonne; (*b*) d'un air important; en faisant des embarras. **2. f. dressed,** vêtu avec trop de recherche; trop pomponné.

fussiness ['fʌsinis], *s.* **1.** (*of pers.*) (i) tatillonnage *m*; façons *fpl*, embarras *mpl*; (ii) esprit tracassier. **2.** manque *m* de simplicité; style pomponné (d'une robe, etc.).

fussing ['fʌsiŋ], *s.* **1.** tatillonnage *m.* **2.** embarras *mpl*; cérémonie *f*; *F:* chichis *mpl.*

fusspot ['fʌspɔt], *s. P:* (i) tatillon, -onne; (ii) faiseur, -euse, d'embarras; chichiteux, -euse.

fussy ['fʌsi], *a.* **1.** (*of pers.*) tatillon, -onne; tracassier, méticuleux, difficultueux; **to be f.,** (i) faire des difficultés à propos de rien; (ii) *F:* faire des embarras; **to be f. about one's food,** être difficile sur la nourriture; **to be too f. about one's health,** s'occuper trop de sa santé. **2.** (*of dress, etc.*) qui a trop de façon; trop pomponné; (style) recherché, qui manque de simplicité.

fust [fʌst], *s. Arch:* fût *m* (d'une colonne).

fustanella [fʌstə'nelə], **fustanelle** ['fʌstənel], *s. Cost:* fustanelle *f.*

fustet ['fʌstit], *s. Bot:* fustet *m*; sumac *m* (à perruque); arbre *m* à perruque.

fustian ['fʌstjən]. **1.** *s.* (*a*) *Tex:* futaine *f*; (*b*) grandiloquence *f*, emphase *f*. **2.** *a.* (*a*) (manteau, etc.) de futaine; (*b*) (style) ampoulé, boursouflé, extravagant.

fustibal ['fʌstibəl], *s. Arm:* fustibale *f.*

fustic ['fʌstik], *s.* bois *m* jaune; (*a*) *Dy:* **young f.,** sumac *m* (fustet), *F:* fustet *m*; **(old) f.,** maclure *f*; (*b*) *Bot:* **young f. (tree), Zante f.,** fustet, sumac (à perruque); arbre *m* à perruque; **(old) f.,** maclure (des teinturiers), mûrier tinctorial.

fustigate ['fʌstigeit], *v.tr. Hum:* fustiger (qn).

fustigation [fʌsti'geiʃ(ə)n], *s. Hum:* fustigation *f.*

fustigator ['fʌstigeitər], *s. Hum:* fustigeur, -euse.

fustiness ['fʌstinis], *s.* **1.** odeur *f* de renfermé, de moisi (dans une chambre, etc.). **2.** caractère suranné, démodé (d'une science, d'une théorie, des connaissances de qn).

fusty ['fʌsti], *a.* **1.** (pain, etc.) qui sent le moisi; (maison, vêtement) qui sent le renfermé; **f. smell,** odeur *f* de renfermé. **2. f. ideas,** idées surannées, démodées; idées vieux jeu.

fusula, *pl.* **-ae** ['fʌzjulə, -i:], *s. Arach:* fusule *f.*

fusulina [fju:zu'lainə], *s. Paleont:* fusuline *f.*

Fusulinidae [fju:zu'linidi], *s.pl. Paleont:* fusulinidés *m.*

futchel ['fʌtʃəl], *s. Veh:* armon *m*, fourchette *f.*

futile ['fju:tail], *a.* **1.** vain; **f. attempt,** vaine tentative; tentative inefficace, platonique. **2.** (prétexte, etc.) puéril, futile; **f. ideas,** idées creuses.

futilely ['fju:tailli], *adv.* **1.** vainement. **2.** futilement.

futility [fju:'tiliti], *s.* **1.** futilité *f*; **to waste one's efforts in sheer f.,** se dépenser en pure perte; **the f. of his efforts,** l'impuissance *f* de ses efforts. **2. he uttered a lot of futilities,** il nous a sorti des futilités, des boniments à la graisse d'oie.

futtock ['fʌtək], *s. N.Arch:* genou-allonge *m*, *pl.* genoux-allonges; allonge *f*; **f. plate,** latte *f* de hune; **f. shroud,** gambe *f* (de revers); jambe *f* de hune; **f. staff,** bastet *m*; quenouillette *f* de trélingage.

future ['fju:tʃər]. **1.** *a.* (*a*) (*of life, etc.*) futur; (*of events*) à venir; (*of prospects, etc.*) d'avenir; **my f. wife,** ma future; **at some f. date,** dans l'avenir; *Jur:* **f. estates,** biens *m* à venir; *Com:* **your f. orders,** vos nouvelles commandes; **f. delivery,** livraison *f* à terme; **goods for f. delivery,** marchandises *f* livrables ultérieurement, à terme; *Fin:* **exchange for f. delivery,** opérations *f* de change à terme; **to sell for f. delivery,** vendre livrable à terme; **the hope of a f. life,** l'espoir d'une vie future; (*b*) *Gram:* **f. tense,** temps futur. **2.** *s.* (*a*) avenir *m*; **in (the) f., for the f.,** à l'avenir; **in the near f.,** dans un proche avenir, sous peu; à brève échéance; **we shall act in the near f.,** nous agirons à bref délai; **in the distant f.,** dans un avenir lointain; **speculation with a view to the f.,** spéculation *f* à retardement; **it lies with the f. whether . . .,** le temps décidera si . . .; **what has the f. in store for us?** qu'est-ce que demain, l'avenir, nous réserve? **to think of the f.,** songer au lendemain; *Phil:* **f. contingent,** futur contingent; **future(s) study, research,** prospective *f*; (*b*) *Gram:* (temps) futur; **f. perfect,** futur antérieur; **verb in the f.,** verbe *m* au futur; (*c*) avenir (de qn); **job with no f.,** situation *f* sans avenir; **job with a (good) f.,** situation d'avenir; **to ruin one's f.,** briser son avenir; **to settle the f. of one's children,** assurer le sort de ses enfants; faire un sort à ses enfants; **he has a (brilliant) f. before him,** il a de l'avenir; il a devant lui un bel avenir; (*d*) *pl. Fin:* **(quotations for) futures,** cotations *f*, livraisons *f*, à terme; **selling of futures, sale for futures,** vente *f* à forfait, à découvert.

futurism ['fju:tʃərizm], *s. Art:* futurisme *m.*

futurist ['fju:tʃərist], *a. & s. Art:* futuriste (*mf*).

futuristic ['fju:tʃə'ristik], *a. Art:* futuriste.

futurition [fju:tʃə'riʃ(ə)n], *s. Phil:* futurition *f*, futur *m.*

futurity [fju:'tjuəriti], *s.* **1.** (*a*) l'avenir *m*; **f. alone can judge the value of it,** l'avenir seul pourra juger de sa valeur; (*b*) *Phil:* futurition *f*, futur *m*; (*c*) **the hope of a f.,** l'espoir d'une vie future; **to endanger one's f.,** mettre en danger son salut éternel. **2.** *pl. O:* **futurities,** événements *m* à venir.

futurologist [fju:tjə'rɔlədʒist], *s.* personne *f* qui étudie la prospective; pronostiqueur, -euse.

futurology [fju:tjə'rɔlədʒi], *s.* prospective *f.*

fuze [fju:z], *s.* = FUSE[1].

fuzee [fju:ˈzi:], *s.* = FUSEE.

fuzz[1] [fʌz], *s.* **1.** (*on blankets, etc.*) peluches *fpl*, bourre *f*, duvet *m*; **a f. of hair,** cheveux bouffants, frisottés, crêpelus. **2.** *Phot:* flou *m*. **3.** *W.Tel: Rec: etc:* bruissements *mpl*.

fuzz[2], *v.* **to f. (out). 1.** *v.i.* (*a*) (*of hair, etc.*) bouffer, frisotter; (*b*) (*of silk, etc.*) s'érailler. **2.** *v.tr.* faire bouffer, crêper, frisotter, moutonner (les cheveux).

fuzz[3], *s. P:* (*a*) (i) agent *m* de la Sûreté; flic *m*; (ii) *coll.* **the f.,** les flics; (*b*) geôlier *m*; gardien *m* de prison.

fuzz ball [ˈfʌzbɔ:l], *s. Fung:* vesse-de-loup *f*, *pl.* vesses-de-loup.

fuzzily [ˈfʌzili], *adv.* (peindre, etc.) flou.

fuzziness [ˈfʌzinis], *s.* **1.** crêpelure *f* (des cheveux). **2.** manque *m* de netteté (d'un contour, *W.Tel: etc:* d'un enregistrement); *Art: Phot:* flou *m* (d'un tableau, cliché, etc.).

fuzzy [ˈfʌzi], *a.* **1.** (*a*) (*of hair*) (i) bouffant, flou; (ii) crêpelu, frisotté, moutonné; (*of cloth, etc.*) floconneux; (*b*) (*of silk, etc.*) éraillé. **2.** (*of outline, etc.*) sans netteté; *Art: Phot:* flou; **everything looks f. to me,** j'ai une vue confuse, trouble, de tout; *W.Tel: Rec:* **f. recording,** enregistrement *m* qui manque de netteté. **3.** *F:* un peu ivre; gris; éméché.

fuzzy(-wuzzy) [ˈfʌziwʌzi], *s.* **1.** *A:* guerrier soudanais. **2.** indigène *m* (des îles Fidji, etc.) aux cheveux crêpelus.

fylfot [ˈfilfɔt], *s.* croix cramponnée; *esp.* croix gammée, svastika *m*.

Fyn [fju:n], *Pr.n. Geog:* la Fionie.

G

G, g [dʒi:], *s.* **1.** (la lettre) G, g *m*; *Tp:* **G for George,** G comme Gaston; *Tls:* **G. cramp, clamp,** happe *f*; serre-joint(s) *m inv*; bride *f* à capote; presse *f* à vis. **2.** *Mus:* sol *m*; **G clef,** clef *f* de sol; **in G minor,** en sol mineur; **G string,** (i) corde *f* de sol; (ii) *Cost:* cache-sexe *m inv*.

gab[1] [gæb], *s. F:* caquet *m*; faconde *f*; jactage *m*; **to have the gift of the g.,** (i) avoir la langue bien pendue; avoir de la faconde; avoir bon bec; (ii) avoir du bagout; bien débiter sa marchandise; savoir vendre sa salade; *P:* **stow your g.!** la ferme!

gab[2], *v.i.* **(gabbed)** *F:* jaser; caqueter; bavarder; tenir le crachoir.

gab[3], *s. Mec.E:* enclenche *f*, encoche *f*.

gabardine [gæbə'di:n, 'gæbədi:n], *s.* = GABERDINE.

gabble[1] ['gæbl], *s.* **1.** bredouillement *m* (de paroles prononcées trop vite). **2.** (*a*) caquet *m*, jacasserie *f* (des femmes, etc.); (*b*) caquet (des oies).

gabble[2]. **1.** *v.i.* (*a*) bredouiller, manger ses mots; **don't g.!** ne parlez pas si vite! (*b*) (*of pers., birds, etc.*) caqueter, jacasser; (*of goose*) cacarder. **2.** *v.tr.* (*a*) *Th:* **to g. one's part,** débiter son rôle trop vite et sans intelligence; (*b*) **to g. (out) a speech,** débiter un discours à toute vitesse; **to g. through a poem,** réciter un poème avec autant d'intelligence qu'une oie; **to g. off a mass,** dire sa messe au galop; expédier une messe.

gabbler ['gæblər], *s.* **1.** bredouilleur, -euse. **2.** caqueteur, -euse; jacasse *f*; bavard, -arde.

gabbling ['gæbliŋ], *s.* = GABBLE[1].

gabbro ['gæbrou], *s. Geol: Art:* gabbro *m*.

gabby ['gæbi], *a. F:* bavard; **to be g.,** avoir la langue bien pendue.

gabelle [gæ'bel], *s. Hist:* gabelle *f*.

gaberdine [gæbə'di:n, 'gæbədi:n], *s.* **1.** *Tex:* gabardine *f*; **g. suit,** complet *m* en gabardine. **2.** *Cost:* (*a*) *A:* ga(l)vardine *f*; (*b*) gabardine.

Gabes ['geibi:z], *Pr.n. Geog:* Gabès.

gabfest ['gæbfest], *s. esp. U.S: F:* congrès *m*, réunion *f*, où on parle beaucoup.

gabion[1] ['geibiən], *s. Fort:* gabion *m*; corbeille (défensive); **to protect a trench with gabions,** gabionner une tranchée; **g. entrenching,** gabionnage *m*; **wicker g.,** gabion clayonné.

gabion[2], *v.tr. Fort:* gabionner; **gabioned parapet,** gabionnage *m*.

gabionade [geibiə'neid], *s. Fort:* gabionnade *f*.

gabionage ['geibiənidʒ], *s. Fort:* gabionnage *m*.

gable ['geibl], *s. Arch: Const:* **g. (end),** pignon *m*; **g. roof,** comble *m* sur pignon(s); comble à, en, dos d'âne; **stepped g.,** pignon à redans; **g. window,** lucarne faîtière; **g.-topped,** à comble sur pignons; (*over door, etc.*) **ornamental g.,** gable, gâble *m*; **small g.,** gablet *m*.

gabled ['geibld], *a.* (*of house*) à pignon(s); (*of wall*) en pignon; (*of roof*) sur pignon(s); en dos d'âne; (*of dormer window, etc.*) à gable.

gablet ['geiblit], *s. Arch:* gablet *m*.

Gabon ['gæbən], *Pr.n. Geog:* le Gabon.

Gabonese [gæbə'ni:z]. *Geog:* (*a*) *a.* gabonais; (*b*) *s.* Gabonais, -aise.

Gaboon [gə'bu:n]. **1.** *Pr.n. Geog: A:* le Gabon. **2.** *s. Com:* bois *m* d'okoumé. **3.** *attrib. Rept:* **G. adder, viper,** vipère *f* du Gabon.

Gabriel ['geibriəl], *Pr.n.m.* Gabriel.

gaby ['geibi], *s. F: esp. NAm:* benêt *m*, nigaud *m*, idiot, -ote.

gad[1] [gæd], *s.* **1.** *A:* (*a*) pointe *f* (de lance, de flèche); (*b*) aiguillon *m*. **2.** *Dial:* bâton *m*. **3.** *Min:* (*a*) coin *m* (de fer); (*b*) pince *f* (de mineur).

gad[2], *s. A:* **to be on the g.,** courir (le monde); *F:* être en vadrouille.

gad[3], *v.i.* **(gadded)** (*a*) **to g. (about),** courir le monde, la ville, les rues; *F:* courailler, vadrouiller; courir la pretentaine; **she's always gadding about,** elle est toujours à courir, toujours par voie et par chemin, toujours en visite, en voyage; (*b*) *Lit:* **the gadding vine,** la vigne vagabonde.

Gad[4], *int.* (= GOD) *A:* **(by) G.!** ma foi! parbleu! sapristi! **by G., you're right!** mais c'est que vous avez raison!

gadabout ['gædəbaut], *s.* personne qui est toujours sortie, toujours en voyage d'agrément; coureur, -euse.

Gadarene ['gædəri:n]. *B.Hist:* (*a*) *a.* gadarénien; (*b*) *s.* Gadarénien, -ienne.

gadder ['gædər], *s.* = GADABOUT.

gade [geid], *s. Ich:* gade *m*.

gadfly ['gædflai], *s. Ent:* (*a*) taon *m*; (*b*) œstre *m*.

gadget ['gædʒit], *s. F:* (*a*) accessoire *m* (de machine); dispositif *m*; **car with a lot of gadgets,** voiture *f* avec un tas de petites inventions; (*b*) chose *m*, machin *m*, truc *m*, gadget *m*; **what d'you call this g.?** comment appelez-vous ce truc-là?

gadgetry ['gædʒitri], *s. F:* (*a*) accessoires *mpl*, dispositifs *mpl*; (*b*) trucs *mpl*.

Gadhelic [gə'delik], *a. Ling:* gaélique.

Gadidae ['gædidi:], *s.pl. Ich:* gadidés *m*.

Gadiformes [gædi'fɔ:mi:z], *s.pl. Ich:* gadiformes *m*.

gadoid ['geidɔid]. *Ich:* **1.** *a.* gadoïde. **2.** *s.* gadoïde *m*, gade *m*.

gadolinite ['gædəlinait], *s. Miner:* gadolinite *f*.

gadolinium [gædə'liniəm], *s. Ch:* gadolinium *m*.

gadroon[1] [gə'dru:n], *s. Arch: Dressm: etc:* godron *m*; *Arch:* canneau *m*.

gadroon[2], *v.tr. Arch:* godronner.

gadrooning [gæ'dru:niŋ], *s. Arch:* godronnage *m*.

gadwall ['gædwɔ:l], *s. Orn:* canard chipeau, ridenne *f*.

gadzooks [gæd'zu:ks], *int. A:* ventrebleu!

Gaea ['gi:ə], *Pr.n.f. Gr.Myth:* Gé, Géa.

Gael [geil], *s. Ethn:* Gaël *m*.

Gaelic ['geilik]. **1.** *a.* (*a*) *Ethn: Ling:* gaélique; (*b*) *Hist:* **G. League,** Ligue *f* gaélique; (*c*) **G. coffee,** café crème arrosé de whiskey (irlandais). **2.** *s. Ling:* gaélique *m*.

Gaeta [gɑ'eitə], *Pr.n. Geog:* Gaète.

Gaetulia [gi:'tju:liə], *Pr.n. A.Hist:* Gétulie *f*.

Gaetulian [gi:'tju:liən], *s. A.Hist:* Gétule *mf*.

gaff[1] [gæf], *s.* **1.** *Fish:* (*a*) gaffe *f*; **to bring a fish to g.,** ramener un poisson pour le gaffer; **g. hook,** gaffeau *m*; (*b*) harpon *m*. **2.** *Nau:* corne *f*; **g. sail,** voile *f* à corne; **g. sail,** voile goélette; **g. topsail,** voile de flèche; flèche *f* en cul. **3.** *A:* éperon *m* (pour coq de combat).

gaff[2], *v.tr.* gaffer (un saumon, etc.).

gaff[3], *s. F:* **1. to blow the g.,** vendre la mèche; se mettre à table, manger le morceau; **to blow the g. on s.o.,** dénoncer qn; vendre qn. **2.** *NAm:* **to stand the g.,** (i) subir en silence les conséquences d'une injustice; ne pas broncher; (ii) payer les pots cassés; **I shall have to stand the g.,** tout ça retombera sur moi.

gaff[4], *s. P: A:* **(penny-)g.,** théâtre *m* de bas étage; bouiboui *m*, *pl.* bouis-bouis; beuglant *m*.

gaff[5], *v.i. P: A:* (*a*) jouer pour de l'argent; **to g. for a pound,** jouer une livre; (*b*) jouer à pile ou face.

gaffe [gæf], *s.* gaffe *f*, bourde *f*.

gaffer ['gæfər], *s.* **1.** *F: A:* l'ancien *m*; vieux bonhomme; **G. Jones,** le (vieux) père Jones. **2.** *F:* (*a*) contremaître *m*, chef *m* d'équipe; (*b*) *Turf:* commissaire *m*; (*c*) le patron, le singe.

gag[1] [gæg], *s.* **1.** bâillon *m*; *Med:* ouvre-bouche *m inv*; *Vet:* (*for horse, dog, etc.*) pas *m* d'âne; *Fish:* pince *f* à dégorger; *Harn:* **g. bit,** mors rude, de force. **2.** *F:* (*in Parliament*) clôture *f* (des débats). **3.** *Th: Cin: F:* interpolation faite par l'acteur; trouvaille *f*; idée *f* drôle; *F:* gag *m*. **4.** *F: O:* mystification *f*, blague *f*, bobard *m*.

gag[2], *v.tr.* **(gagged) 1.** bâillonner (qn); mettre un bâillon à (qn); **to g. the press,** museler, bâillonner, la presse. **2.** *Pol: F:* clôturer (un débat). **3.** *Th: F:* **to g. (one's part),** prendre son rôle à la cascade; cascader; faire des gags; (*when memory is at fault*) enchaîner. **4.** *F: O:* mystifier; en imposer à (qn); *v.i.* faire de la mystification, blaguer. **5.** *v.i. P:* avoir des haut-le-cœur.

gaga ['gɑ:gɑ:, 'gægə], *a. F:* gaga, gâteux; **to go g.,** (i) retomber en enfance, devenir gâteux; (ii) perdre la boussole.

gage[1] [geidʒ], *s.* **1.** gage *m*, garantie *f*; *Jur:* nantissement *m*; **to give sth. in g., to lay sth. to g.,** donner qch. en gage; **to leave sth. in g.,** laisser qch. pour gage; **to lie to g., to be at g.,** être en gage. **2.** *A:* **g. (of battle),** gage de bataille, de combat; **to throw down the g. to s.o.,** (i) jeter devant qn le gage de combat; (ii) lancer un défi à qn; jeter le gant à qn.

gage[2], *v.tr. A:* mettre, donner, (qch.) en gage; engager (sa vie, etc.).

gage[3], *s. & v.tr.* = GAUGE[1,2]; *esp. Nau:* = GAUGE[1] 5.

gage[4], *s. F: Hort:* reine-claude *f*, *pl.* reines-claudes.

gagger ['gægər], *s.* **1.** *O:* bâillonneur *m*; *F:* museleur *m* (de la presse, etc.). **2.** *Th: Cin: F:* cascadeur, -euse. **3.** *Metall:* crochet *m* de fonderie.

gagging ['gægiŋ], *s.* **1.** bâillonnement *m*; *F:* musellement *m* (de la presse, etc.). **2.** *Pol: F:* clôture *f* (d'un débat). **3.** *Th: etc:* interpolations *fpl* (le plus souvent comiques) dans un rôle. **4.** *F: O:* mystification *f* (de qn).

gaggle[1] ['gægl], *s.* **1.** (*a*) troupeau *m* (d'oies); (*b*) *F:* troupe *f* (de femmes bavardes). **2.** caquet *m*, bavardage *m*.

gaggle[2], *v.i.* (*of goose*) cacarder.

gahnite ['gɑ:nait], *s. Miner:* gahnite *f*.

gaiety ['geiəti], *s.* **1.** gaieté *f*; enjouement *m*, allégresse *f*; *F:* **to add to the g. of nations,** donner la comédie aux gens; faire rire. **2.** *usu.pl.* amusement *m*, fête *f*, réjouissances *fpl*. **3. these costumes add to the g. of the scene,** ces costumes contribuent à donner du brillant, de l'éclat, au spectacle.

gaillardia [gei'lɑ:diə], *s. Bot:* gaillarde *f*; gaillardie *f*.

gaily ['geili], *adv.* **1.** gaiement, allègrement, guillerettement. **2. g. dressed,** habillé de couleurs gaies; **g. coloured,** aux couleurs vives.

gain[1] [gein], *s.* **1.** gain *m*, profit *m*, avantage *m*, bénéfice *m*; **eager for g.,** âpre au gain; **love of g.,** amour *m* du gain; *Prov:* **no gains without pains,** on n'a rien sans mal; **ill-gotten gains seldom prosper,** bien mal acquis ne profite jamais; **my g. is your loss,** le profit de l'un est le dommage de l'autre. **2.** (*a*) accroissement *m*, augmentation *f*; **g. in weight,** accroissement de poids; **g. of the waters,** crue *f* des eaux; (*b*) *El: Elcs: etc:* **current g.,** gain en courant; **power g.,** gain de puissance; **g. control,** réglage *m* de puissance; **g. amplifier,** pré-amplificateur *m*, *F:* pré-ampli *m*; *Atom.Ph:* **breeding g.,** gain de régénération; (*c*) avance *f* (d'une pendule, etc.).

gain[2], *v.tr. & i.* gagner. **1.** acquérir (une réputation, des faveurs, etc.); **to g. time,** gagner du temps; **to g. strength,** (re)prendre des forces; **to g. information,** obtenir des renseignements; **to g. a hearing,** (i) obtenir une audience; (ii) se faire écouter; **you will g. nothing by it,** vous n'y gagnerez rien; **there is nothing to be gained by waiting,** nous ne gagnerons rien à attendre; **he gained nothing but ridicule,** il ne remporta que du ridicule; **to g. by the change,** gagner au change; **to g. by doing sth.,** gagner à faire qch.; **I shall g. by it,** j'y gagnerai; *Nau:* **to g. the wind,** gagner au vent, s'élever dans le vent. **2. to g. adherents to a cause,** gagner des adhérents à une cause; **to g. s.o.'s sympathy,** s'acquérir la sympathie de qn; faire la conquête de qn; **to g. s.o.'s esteem, s.o.'s heart,** conquérir, gagner, l'estime, le cœur, de qn; **to g. s.o.'s affection,** s'affectionner qn; **his conduct gained him many friends, much praise,** sa conduite lui a gagné beaucoup d'amis, lui a valu beaucoup d'éloges. **3. to g. weight,** prendre du poids; **to g. (in) popularity,** gagner de la popularité; **he has gained prestige through this action,** cette action a rehaussé son prestige; **this work gains from being compared with . . .,** cette œuvre gagne à être comparée avec . . .. **4.** (*a*) **to g. a battle, the day,** gagner une bataille; remporter la victoire; **to g. the upper hand,** prendre le dessus; **to g. one's cause,** avoir gain de cause; **to g. one's liberty,** conquérir, se faire accorder, sa liberté; **lands gained from the sea,** terrains (re)conquis sur la mer; (*b*) (*of sea*) **to g. (ground) on the land,** empiéter sur la terre; **to g. (ground) on s.o.,** gagner (du terrain) sur qn; *Sp:* **to g. on a competitor,** prendre de l'avance sur un concurrent; **a bad habit gains on one,** une mauvaise habitude s'impose, s'enracine, peu à peu; **to g. on a ship,** se rapprocher d'un navire, gagner un navire de vitesse; **music that gains on the listener,** musique que l'on apprécie d'au tant plus qu'on l'entend plus souvent; (*c*) *Lit:* **to g. the further shore,** gagner, atteindre, parvenir à, l'autre rive. **5.** (*of clock*) avancer, prendre de l'avance; **to g. five minutes a day,** avancer de cinq minutes par jour.

gainer ['geinər], *s.* **1.** gagneur, -euse (d'argent, etc.). **2.** gagnant, -ante (d'une victoire, etc.). **3. to be the g. by sth.,** gagner à qch.

gainful ['geinful], *a.* **1.** (*of trade, etc.*) profitable, avantageux; rémunérateur, -trice; lucratif. **2.** *A:* (homme) âpre au gain.

gainfully ['geinfuli], *adv. Pol.Ec:* **the g. employed population,** la population active.

gaining[1] ['geiniŋ], *a. Sm.a:* **g. twist,** pas progressif (de canon rayé).

gaining[2], *s.* **1.** gain *m* (d'un avantage, d'une bataille, etc.); **g. of contact,** prise *f* de contact. **2.** *usu.pl.* **gainings,** gain, gains; profit *m*.

gainsay [gein'sei], *v.tr.* (*p.p. & p.t.* **gainsaid** [gein'sed, -'seid]) *usu. Lit:* contredire, démentir (qn, qch.); nier (un fait, etc.); **to g. a statement,** contredire une affirmation; **I don't g. it,** je n'en disconviens pas; **facts that cannot be gainsaid,** faits *m* indéniables; **evidence that cannot be gainsaid,** témoignages *m* irrécusables; **argument that cannot be gainsaid,** argument *m* irréfutable.

gainsayer [gein'seiər], *s.* contradicteur *m*.

gainsaying [gein'seiiŋ], *s.* contradiction *f*, démenti *m*.

Gainsborough ['geinzbərə], *Pr.n. Cost:* **g. hat,** chapeau *m* Gainsborough; gainsborough *m*.

'gainst [geinst], *prep. Poet:* contre.

gait [geit], *s.* (*a*) *O: & Lit:* allure *f*, démarche *f*; **unsteady g.,** pas chancelant, mal assuré; **to have a graceful g.,** avoir une démarche gracieuse; **to know s.o. by his g.,** reconnaître qn à son allure; **I knew him by his awkward g.,** je l'ai reconnu à sa dégaine; (*b*) allures, train *m* (d'un cheval); **to break up, ruin, a horse's g.,** détraquer un cheval.

gaiter ['geitər], *s.* **1.** *Cost:* guêtre *f*; **short gaiters,** guêtrons *m*; **strapped gaiters,** guêtres à bandes; jambières *f*; **to put on one's gaiters,** mettre ses guêtres; se guêtrer; *F:* **he's all gas and gaiters,** il prêche pour ne rien dire. **2.** (*a*) *Aut: Cy:* guêtre, emplâtre *m* (pour réparation de pneu); (*b*) *Aut: A:* **spring g.,** gaine *f* de ressort.

gaitered ['geitəd], *a.* guêtré.

gaize [geiz], *s. Miner:* gaize *f*.

gal[1] [gæl], *s. Ph:* gal *m*.

gal[2] [gæl, *O:* gel], *s.f. F:* (jeune) fille.

gala ['gɑ:lə], *s.* fête *f*, réjouissances *fpl*, gala *m*; **swimming g.,** grand concours de natation; *attrib.* **g. day,** jour *m* de gala, de fête; **in g. (dress),** en habits de gala; **g. week,** la grande semaine (dans une station balnéaire, etc.); *Th: etc:* **g. performance,** représentation *f* de gala; *a. NAm:* **the whole thing will be very g.,** ce sera un véritable gala.

galactan [gæ'læktæn], *s. Bio-Ch:* galactane *f*.

galactase [gæ'lækteis], *s. Bio-Ch:* galactase *f*.

Galactia [gæ'læktiə], *s.pl. Bot:* galactites *f*.

galactic [gæ'læktik], *a. Astr:* galactique; **g. coordinates,** coordonnées *f* galactiques; **g. pole,** pôle *m* galactique.

galactite ['gælæktait], *s. Miner:* galactite *f*.

galactocele [gæ'læktousi:l], *s. Obst:* galactocèle *m*.

galactogogue [gæ'læktougɔg], *a. & s. Biol:* galactogogue (*m*), galactogène (*m*).

galactometer [gælæk'tɔmitər], *s.* galactomètre *m*, pèse-lait *m inv*, lacto-densimètre *m*, *pl.* lacto-densimètres.

galactonic [gælæk'tɔnik], *a.* (acide) galactonique.

galactophagous [gælæktou'feigəs], *a. Biol:* galactophage.

galactophore [gæ'læktoufɔ:ər], *s. Biol:* vaisseau *m* galactophore.

galactophoritis [gælæktoufə'raitis], *s. Med:* galactophorite *f*.

galactophorous [gælæktou'fɔ:rəs], *a. Biol:* galactophore.

galactophorus [gælæktou'fɔ:rəs], *s. Med:* galactophore *m*.

galactopoiesis, galactopoieses [gælæktoupɔi'i:sis], *s. Biol:* galactopoïèse *f*.

galactopoietic [gælæktoupɔi'i:tik], *a. Biol:* galactopoïétique.

galactorrh(o)ea [gælæktɔ'ri:ə], *s. Med:* galactorrhée *f*.

galactose [gæ'læktous], *s. Bio-Ch:* galactose *f*.

galactos(a)emia [gælæktou'si:miə], *s. Med:* galactosémie *f*.

galactosuria [gælæktou'sju:riə], *s. Med:* galactosurie *f*.

galactozyme [gæ'læktouzaim], *s. Med:* galactozyme *m*, galazyme *m*.

galago [gə'leigou], *s. Z:* galago *m*.

galah [gə'lɑ:], *s.* **1.** *Orn:* cacatoès *m* rosalbin. **2.** *Austr: F:* idiot, -ote.

Galahad ['gæləhæd], *Pr.n.m. Lit:* Galaad.

Galalith ['gæləliθ], *s. R.t.m:* Galalithe *f*.

Galam ['gælæm], *Pr.n. Geog:* Galam *m*; **G. butter,** beurre *m* de Galam.

galanga [gə'læŋgə], **galangal** ['gæləŋgæl], **galangale** ['gæləŋgeil], *s.* = GALINGALE.

galantine ['gælənti:n], *s. Cu:* galantine *f*.

Galapagos [gə'læpəgɔs], *Pr.n. Geog:* **G. Islands,** Iles *f* Galapagos.

Galatea [gælə'tiə]. **1.** *Pr.n.f. Myth:* Galatée. **2.** *s. Tex:* coutil blanc à raies.

Galatia [gə'leiʃə], *Pr.n. A.Geog:* la Galatie.

Galatian [gə'leiʃ(ə)n], *s. B.Hist:* Galate *mf*; **Epistle to the Galatians,** Épître aux Galates.

Galaxiidae [gælæk'si:idi:], *s.pl. Ich:* galaxiidés *m*.

galaxite ['gæləksait], *s. Miner:* galaxite *f*.

galaxy ['gæləksi], *s.* **1.** *Astr:* **the G.,** la Voie lactée; la Galaxie. **2.** assemblée brillante (de belles femmes, etc.); constellation *f* (d'hommes illustres, etc.); **g. of beauty,** groupe *m* de femmes d'une beauté éclatante.

galbanum ['gælbənəm], *s. Bot: Pharm:* galbanum *m*.

Galbulidae [gæl'bju:lidi:], *s.pl. Orn:* galbulidés *m*.

galbulus ['gælbjuləs], *s. Bot:* galbule *m* (de cyprès).

gale[1] [geil], *s.* (*a*) (*non-technical use*) grand (coup de) vent, vent fort; **it's blowing a g.,** le vent souffle en tempête, fait rage; il fait un vent carabiné; *Meteor: Nau:* (*force*) **near g.,** vents forts; (*force 8*) **gale,** coups *m* de vent; (*force 9*) **strong g.,** fort coup de vent; **g. warning,** avis *m*, signal *m*, de tempête; (*b*) *A: & Poet:* brise *f*, zéphyr *m*; (*c*) **g. of laughter,** accès *m* de rires.

gale[2], *s. Bot:* **(sweet) g.,** galé *m*; myrte bâtard, des marais; myrte écossais; poivre *m* de Brabant; piment royal; bois-sent-bon *m inv*.

gale[3], *s. Jur:* (*a*) loyer *m*; **hanging g.,** arrérages *mpl* de loyer; (*b*) *A:* droit *m* d'exploitation (d'une mine).

galea ['geiliə], *s. Bot: Orn:* casque *m*; *Ent:* galea *f*.

galeate(d) ['gælieit(id)], *a. Nat.Hist:* (*a*) à casque; casqué; (*b*) en casque; galéiforme.

galeiform ['gæliifɔ:m], *a. Bot:* galéiforme.

Galen ['geilən]. **1.** *Pr.n.m. Hist:* Galien. **2.** *s. F: A:* médecin *m*.

galena [gə'li:nə], *s. Miner:* galène *f*; plomb sulfuré; **false g.,** blende *f*, sphalérite *f*; **silver-bearing g.,** galène argentifère; **g. detector,** détecteur *m* à galène.

Galenic(al)[1] [gə'lenik(l)], *a. Hist. of Med:* galénique.

galenic(al)[2], *a. Miner:* qui contient de la galène.

Galenism ['geilənizm], *s. Hist. of Med:* galénisme *m*.

Galenist ['geilənist], *s. Hist. of Med:* galéniste *m*.

galenobismutite [gəli:nou'bizmətait], *s. Miner:* galénobismuthite *f*.

galeocerdo [gæliou'sə:dou], *s. Ich:* galéocerdo *m*.

galeopithecus [gælioupi'θi:kəs, -'piθikəs], *s. Z:* galéopithèque *m*.

Galerucidae [gælə'ru:sidi:], *s.pl. Ent:* galérucinés *m*.

Galicia [gə'lisiə, -ʃiə], *Pr.n. Geog:* **1.** (*in Poland*) Galicie *f*. **2.** (*in Spain*) Galice *f*.

Galician [gəlisiən, -ʃiən], *a. & s. Geog:* (originaire, habitant, -ante) (i) de la Galicie, (ii) de la Galice.

galidia [gə'lidiə], *s. Z:* galidie *f*, galidia *f*.

Galilean[1] [gæli'li:ən]. *B.Hist:* (*a*) *a.* galiléen; (*b*) *s.* Galiléen, -éenne.

Galilean[2], *a. Opt:* (lunette, etc.) de Galilée.

Galilee ['gælili:]. **1.** *Pr.n. Geog:* Galilée *f*; **the Sea of G.,** la mer, le lac, de Galilée. **2.** *s. Arch:* galilée *m*, porche *m* (d'une église).

Galileo [gæli'leiou], *Pr.n.m. Hist. of Astr:* Galilée.

galingale ['gæliŋgeil], *s.* **1.** *Bot:* **(sweet, English) g.,** souchet long; souchet odorant. **2.** *Pharm: A:* galanga *m*.

galipot ['gælipɔt], *s.* galipot *m*; térébenthine *f* de Bordeaux.

gall[1] [gɔ:l], *s.* **1.** (*a*) fiel *m*, bile *f*, amer *m* (d'animal); **ox g.,** fiel de bœuf; **g. duct,** conduit *m* biliaire; *Vet:* **g. sickness,** anaplasmose *f*; *Fig:* **to vent one's g. on s.o.,** épancher sa bile contre qn; **the g. of life,** l'amertume *f* de la vie; *Lit:* **pen dipped in g.,** plume trempée dans le fiel; (*b*) **g. (bladder),** vésicule *f* biliaire; (*c*) *F:* effronterie *f*, toupet *m*, culot *m*. **2.** *Glassm:* **(glass) g.,** fiel de verre; suint *m* (du verre). **3.** *Bot:* **earth g., g. of the earth,** fiel de terre; petite centaurée.

gall[2], *s.* (*a*) *Bot:* galle *f*, cécidie *f*; **g. oak,** chêne *m* à la noix de galle; *Dy: etc:* **g. nut,** noix *f* de galle; (*b*) *Ent:* **g. gnat,** cécidomyie *f*; **g. insect,** pemphigus *m*; **g.-producing insect,** insecte *m* cécidogène; **g. wasp,** cynips *m*.

gall[3], *s.* **1.** (*a*) écorchure, blessure, excoriation (causée par le frottement); (*b*) froissement *m*, humiliation *f*; blessure (faite à l'amour-propre). **2.** défaut *m*, imperfection *f*; éraillure *f* (d'une étoffe). **3.** endroit dénudé (dans une prairie, etc.). **4.** *Glassm:* **glass g.,** suint *m* du verre.

gall[4]. **1.** *v.tr.* (*a*) écorcher (par le frottement); excorier; mettre (le talon, etc.) à vif; *Vet:* (*of saddle, etc.*) frayer, fouler (le cheval); (*b*) irriter, exaspérer, vexer (qn); froisser, blesser, humilier (qn); (*c*) *Mil:* harceler (l'ennemi). **2.** *v.i.* (*of horse*) se frayer.

gallant[1] ['gælənt], *a. & s.*

I. *a.* **1.** (*a*) brave, vaillant; chevaleresque; *Lit:* valeureux; **g. deed,** acte *m* de bravoure; action *f* d'éclat; **his g. bearing in the field,** sa belle conduite sur le champ de bataille; **he made a g. defence,** il se défendit bravement; (*in Parliament*) **the honourable and g. member for . . .,** l'honorable et vaillant représentant de . . . (formule consacrée lorsque le député est un officier des armées de terre, de mer, (ou de l'air); (*b*) (*of ship, horse, etc.*) beau, *f.* belle; noble, fier, superbe; *A:* (*of dress*) galant, élégant; **g. display,** étalage *m* superbe (of, de). **2.** (*usu.* [gə'lænt]) galant (auprès des femmes).

II. *s. A:* **1.** galant *m*, élégant *m*; amadis *m*. **2.** (*usu.* [gə'lænt]) (*a*) (homme) galant; (*b*) *Pej:* amant *m*, galant.

gallant[2] [gə'lænt]. **1.** *v.i. & tr. Lit:* **to g. (with) the ladies,** faire le galant, être assidu, auprès des dames. **2.** *v.tr. A:* accompagner, escorter (une femme).

gallantly, *adv.* **1.** ['gæləntli] (*a*) galamment, bravement, vaillamment; avec valeur; en galant homme; (*b*) élégamment, magnifiquement. **2.** [gə'læntli, 'gæləntli] en homme galant; avec empressement (auprès d'une femme).

gallantry ['gæləntri], *s.* **1.** vaillance *f*, valeur *f*, bravoure *f*, courage *m*; belle conduite (d'un soldat). **2.** (*a*) galanterie *f* (auprès des femmes); (*b*) *A:* intrigue (amoureuse).

gallate ['gæleit], *s. Ch:* gallate *m*.

galleass ['gæliəs], *s.* = GALLIASS.

galled [gɔ:ld], *a.* **1.** (*a*) écorché; mis à vif; *Vet:* frayé; (*b*) **g. rope,** cordage mâché. **2.** irrité, exaspéré, humilié, blessé. **3.** (endroit) dénudé (dans un pré, etc.).

gallein [gɔ:'li:in], *s. Ch:* galléine *f*.

galleon ['gæliən], *s. A.Nau:* galion *m*.

galleried ['gælərid], *a. Arch:* (salle, maison) à galerie.

gallery ['gæləri], *s.* **1.** (*a*) galerie *f* (d'une salle, etc.); (*in Houses of Parliament*) **strangers' g., public g.,** tribune réservée au public, tribune publique; **press g.,** tribune de la presse, des journalistes; (*b*) **the g.,** (i) *Th:* la (troisième) galerie, l'amphithéâtre *m*; *F:* le poulailler, le paradis; (ii) *Cards: Sp: etc:* l'ensemble *m* des spectateurs; la galerie; **to play to the g.,** jouer pour la galerie; *Sp:* **g. play,** jeu *m* à effet, à épate; (*c*) *Nau: A:* **stern g.,** galerie de poupe; **quarter g.,** bouteille *f*; balcon *m* arrière; (*d*) *NAm:* (i) balcon *m*; (ii) véranda *f*; (*e*) estrade *f* (d'un temple de la Société des Amis, sur laquelle se trouvent les chaises des anciens); **g. friend,** ancien *m* (de la Société des Amis); (*f*) *Prehist:* **g. tomb, g. grave,** allée couverte. **2.** (**art**) **g.,** (i) galerie; (ii) musée *m* (d'art); **the galleries of the Louvre,** les galeries, les salles, du Louvre; **portrait g.,** galerie, musée, de portraits. **3.** (*a*) *Min:* galerie; **blind g.,** beurtia(t) *m*; **drainage g.,** galerie d'exhaure; **evacuation g.,** galerie de vidange; (*b*) *Fort: Civ.E: etc:* **arched g.,** galerie voûtée; **counter-arched g.,** galerie en décharge; **lined g.,** galerie coffrée; (*c*) *Mil: etc:* **shooting g.,** stand *m* de tir; **g. practice,** tir réduit, de stand; (*d*) **g. forest,** forêt-galerie *f*, *pl.* forêts-galeries. **4.** (*a*) galerie (autour d'un meuble); (*b*) griffe *f* (de lampe à pétrole).

galley ['gæli], *s.* **1.** *Nau:* (*a*) *A:* galère *f*; **to be sent to the galleys,** être condamné aux galères, à la chaîne; **g. slave,** galérien *m*; *F:* **I'm nothing but a g. slave,** c'est à moi de faire toutes les sales besognes; (*b*) yole *f* (d'amiral). **2.** *Nau:* cuisine *f*, coquerie *f*; *Av:* cuisine, office *m*. **3.** *Typ:* (*a*) galée *f*; **slice g.,** galée à coulisses; (*b*) **g. press,** presse *f* à épreuves; **g. proof,** (épreuve *f* en) placard *m*. **4.** *Myr:* **g. worm,** iule *m*, mille-pattes *m inv*; mille-pieds *m inv*.

gallfly ['gɔ:lflai], *s. Ent:* cynips *m*.

galliambic [gæli'æmbik], *a. Pros:* galliambe.

galliard ['gæliəd], *s. Danc: Mus:* gaillarde *f*.

galliass ['gæliæs], *s. A.Nau:* galéasse *f*.

Gallic[1] ['gælik], *a.* (*a*) *Hist:* gaulois; (*b*) français.

gallic[2], *a. Ch:* (acide *m*) gallique.

Gallican ['gælikən], *a. & s. Ecc:* gallican, -ane.

Gallicanism ['gælikənizm], *s. Ecc:* gallicanisme *m*.

Gallicanist ['gælikənist], *s. Ecc:* gallican, -ane; gallicaniste *mf*.

gallicism ['gælisizm], *s. Ling:* gallicisme *m*.

gallicize ['gælisaiz]. **1.** *v.i.* se franciser. **2.** *v.tr.* franciser.

gallicola [gɔ:'likələ], *s. Ent:* gallicole *m*.

gallicolous [gɔ:'likələs], *a. Ent:* gallicole.

Galliformes [gæli'fɔ:mi:z], *s.pl. Orn:* galliformes *m*.

galligaskins ['gæli'gæskinz], *s.pl.* **1.** (*a*) *F:* pantalon *m*, culotte *f*, (*b*) *Dial:* guêtres *fpl*. **2.** *Bot:* coucou *m*.

gallimaufry [gæli'mɔ:fri], *s. A:* salmigondis *m*; galimafrée *f*.

Gallinaceae [gæli'neisii:], *s.pl. Orn:* gallinacés *m*.

gallinacean [gæli'neiʃ(ə)n], *a. & s. Orn:* gallinacé (*m*).

gallinaceous [gæli'neiʃəs], *a. Orn:* gallinacé.

Gallinae [gæ'laini:], *s.* = GALLINACEAE.

galling[1] ['gɔ:liŋ], *a.* (*a*) qui écorche; (*b*) (*of restrictions, etc.*) irritant, exaspérant, vexatoire; (*of remark, etc.*) blessant, humiliant; *Mil:* **g. fire,** feu meurtrier, bien nourri; **g. experience,** expérience amère.

galling[2], *s.* **1.** écorchure *f*; mise *f* à vif; excoriation *f*; *Harn:* **g. leather,** pièce *f* de frottement. **2.** froissement *m* (de qn); humiliation *f*.

gallinule ['gælinjul], *s. Orn:* gallinule *f*; **common, Florida, g.,** poule *f* d'eau, *Fr.C:* gallinule commune; **purple g.,** poule sultane, *Fr.C:* gallinule pourprée; **Allen's g.,** talève *f* d'Allen; **green-backed g.,** talève bleue.

Gallio ['gæliou]. **1.** *Pr.n.m. B.Hist:* Gallion. **2.** *s. A:* gallioniste *m*; indifférent *m* (en matière de religion).

gal(l)iot ['gæljət], *s. A.Nau:* galiote *f*.

gallipot ['gælipɔt], *s.* **1.** *Pharm:* petit pot (pour pommade, etc.). **2.** *F: A:* apothicaire *m*.

gallium ['gæliəm], *s. Ch:* gallium *m*.

gallivant ['gælivænt], *v.i.* (*a*) fréquenter la société des femmes; courailler, être toujours par monts et par vaux (avec des compagnons de l'autre sexe); courir la prétentaine; (*b*) être toujours en voyage, en visite; être toujours à la recherche de distractions.

Gallo- ['gælou], *comb.fm.* gallo-.

Gallo-Belgian ['gælou'beldʒən], *a.* gallo-belge, *pl.* gallo-belges.

Gallo-German ['gælou'dʒə:mən], *a.* franco-allemand, *pl.* franco-allemands.

gallomania [gælou'meiniə], *s.* gallomanie *f*.

gallomaniac [gælou'meiniæk], *a. & s.* gallomane (*mf*).

gallon ['gælən], *s.* gallon *m* (= 4 lit. 54; *U.S:* = 3 lit. 78); *Aut:* **miles per g.,** = consommation *f* d'essence aux cent kilomètres; *F:* **they drink gallons of beer,** ils boivent de la bière à tire-larigot.

galloon [gə'lu:n], *s.* galon *m*.

gallop[1] ['gæləp], *s.* **1.** galop *m*; **extended g.,** galop allongé; **at a g.,** au galop (allongé); **full g.,** grand galop; (**at**) **full g.,** au grand galop; à fond de train; (*of horse*) ventre à terre; (*of rider*) à bride abattue, à franc étrier; **to break into a g.,** se mettre à galoper; prendre le galop; faire prendre le galop à son cheval. **2.** galopade *f*; **to have, go for, a g.,** faire une galopade. **3.** *Med:* **g. rhythm,** bruit *m* de galop.

gallop[2], *v.* (**galloped**) **1.** *v.i.* (*a*) (*of horse*) galoper; aller au galop; (*b*) (*of rider*) aller au galop, à bride abattue; **to g. off,** piquer des deux; **to g. away,** (i) partir, s'éloigner, au galop; (ii) *F:* parler vite; **to g. back,** revenir au galop; **to g. up,** accourir au galop, à bride abattue; *F:* **to g. through a book,** lire un livre au galop; **to g. through prayers,** réciter les prières au grand galop. **2.** *v.tr.* faire aller (un cheval) au (grand) galop; galoper (un cheval).

galloper ['gæləpər], *s.* **1.** (*a*) cheval *m*, cavalier *m*, qui va au galop; (*b*) personne *f* qui y va d'un train d'enfer; (*c*) *Mil: A:* officier *m* d'ordonnance; aide *m* de camp *m*. **2.** *Artil: A:* **g. carriage,** affût *m* à limonière; **g. gun,** canon *m* à affût à limonière.

gallophile ['gæloufail], *a. & s.* gallophile (*mf*).

gallophobe ['gæloufoub], *a. & s.* gallophobe *mf*.

gallophobia [gælou'foubiə], *s.* gallophobie *f*.

galloping[1] ['gæləpiŋ], *a.* **1.** (*of horse, etc.*) au galop. **2.** *Med:* galopant; *O:* **g. consumption,** phtisie galopante.

galloping[2], *s.* galop *m*.

Gallo-Roman ['gælou'roumən], *a.* gallo-romain, *pl.* gallo-romains.

Gallovidian [gælou'vidiən], *a. & s.* (originaire, habitant, -ante) du Galloway (en Écosse).

gallows ['gælouz], *s.* (*often with sg. const.*) **1.** potence *f*, gibet *m*; **to hang s.o. on the g.,** mettre, attacher, qn à la potence; **to have a g. look, to have the g. in one's face,** avoir une mine patibulaire; sentir la potence; **crime worthy of the g.,** crime *m* qui mérite l'échafaud; **he will come to the g., he is heading straight for the g.,** il se fera pendre; **to miss the g. by a hair's breadth,** friser la corde; *F:* **g. bird,** gibier *m*, réchappé *m*, de potence; pendard *m*. **2.** portique *m* (de gymnastique). **3.** *Min:* **g. frame,** chevalement *m*.

gallstone ['gɔ:lstoun], *s. Med:* calcul *m* biliaire.

Gallup ['gæləp], *Pr.n.* **G. poll,** sondage *m* Gallup.

galoot [gə'lu:t], *s. P:* (*a*) lourdaud *m*, empoté *m*; (*b*) individu *m*, type *m*, client *m*.

galop ['gæləp], *s. Danc:* galop *m*.

galore [gə'lɔ:r], *adv. F:* en abondance, à profusion; à gogo; en veux-tu; **cousins g.,** une foule de cousins; **children g.,** une ribambelle d'enfants; **books g.,** des livres en masse; **money g.,** de l'argent à gogo.

galosh [gə'lɔʃ], *s.* **1.** *A:* galoche *f*. **2.** caoutchouc *m*; couvre-chaussure *m*, *pl.* couvre-chaussures. **3.** *Bootm:* quartier *m*, claque *f*.

galoshed [gə'lɔʃt], *a. Bootm:* **g. with calf,** à quartiers de veau.

galumph [gə'lʌmf], *v.i. F:* avancer dans un galop triomphal; caracoler; galoper lourdement.

galvanic [gæl'vænik], *a. El:* galvanique.

galvanism ['gælvənizm], *s.* galvanisme *m*.

galvanization [gælvənai'zeiʃ(ə)n], *s.* **1.** galvanisation *f* (du corps humain, etc.). **2.** *Metalw:* galvanisation; galvanisage *m*; (i) métallisation *f* électrique; (ii) zingage *m* au trempé, étamage *m*.

galvanize ['gælvənaiz], *v.tr.* **1.** galvaniser (un cadavre, etc.); **to g. sth. into life,** insuffler à qch. un instant de vie; donner à qch. une animation passagère; galvaniser qch. **2.** *Metalw:* galvaniser; (i) plaquer par galvanoplastie; (ii) zinguer, étamer (le fer, etc.).

galvanized ['gælvənaizd], *a.* **1.** galvanisé. **2.** *Metalw:* galvanisé; (i) plaqué (par galvanoplastie); (ii) zingué, étamé; **g. (sheet) iron,** fer galvanisé; tôle galvanisée.

galvanizer ['gælvənaizər], *s. Metalw:* galvanis(at)eur *m*.

galvanizing ['gælvənaiziŋ], *s.* = GALVANIZATION.

galvano- ['gælvənou, gælvə'nɔ], *comb.fm.* galvano-.

galvanocaustic ['gælvənou'kɔ:stik], *a.* galvanocaustique.

galvanocautery ['gælvənou'kɔ:təri], *s. Med:* galvanocautère *m*.

galvanofaradization ['gælvənoufærədi'zeiʃ(ə)n], *s.* galvanofaradisation *f*.

galvanography [gælvə'nɔgrəfi], *s.* galvanographie *f*.

galvanomagnetic ['gælvənoumæg'netik], *a.* galvanomagnétique.

galvanometer [gælvə'nɔmitər], *s. El:* galvanomètre *m*; **dead-beat, aperiodic, g.,** galvanomètre apériodique; **astatic g.,** galvanomètre astatique; **torsion g.,** galvanomètre à torsion; **mirror, reflexion, reflecting, g.,** galvanomètre à miroir, à réflexion; **ballistic g.,** galvanomètre balistique; **hot-wire g.,** galvanomètre thermique, à fil chaud; **shunted g.,** galvanomètre en dérivation, à résistance shunt; **loop g.,** galvanomètre à cadre; **string g.,** galvanomètre à corde; **moving coil g.,** galvanomètre à cadre mobile; **sine g., tangent g.,** boussole *f* des sinus, des tangentes.

galvanometric ['gælvənou'metrik], *a. El:* galvanométrique.

galvanoplastic ['gælvənou'plæstik], *a.* galvanoplastique.

galvanoplasty ['gælvənou'plæsti], *s.* galvanoplastie *f*.

galvanopuncture ['gælvənou'pʌŋktjər], *s. Med:* galvanoponcture *f*.

galvanoscope ['gælvənouskoup], *s. El:* galvanoscope *m*.

Galwegian [gæl'wi:dʒən], *a. & s.* (originaire, habitant, -ante) (i) du Galloway (en Écosse), (ii) de Galway (en Irlande).

gam[1] [gæm], *s. Nau:* **1.** troupe *f* (de baleines). **2.** réunion *f* (en mer), soirée *f* en commun, des pêcheurs de baleine de différents bateaux.

gam[2], *v.i.* (**gammed**) **1.** (*of whales*) s'attrouper, s'assembler. **2.** *esp. U.S:* (*of pers.*) se réunir pour causer et pour se distraire.

gam[3], *s. P:* jambe *f*, guibolle *f*.

gamb [gæm], *s. Her:* **lion's g.,** membre *m* de lion.

gamba ['gæmbə], *s. Mus:* **1.** *A:* **g. (viol), viola da g.,** viole *f* de gambe. **2.** (*of organ*) **g. (bass),** gambe *f*.

gambade [gæm'beid], *s.* **1.** *Equit:* gambade *f*, bond *m*. **2.** *A:* escapade *f*, frasque *f*.

gambet ['gæmbit], **gambetta** [gæm'betə], *s. Orn:* **1.** chevalier *m*, gambette *m*. **2.** combattant *m*.

Gambia (the) [ðə'gæmbiə], *Pr.n. Geog:* la Gambie.

gambier ['gæmbiər], *s.* **1.** *Bot:* gambier *m*. **2.** *Pharm: Dy:* gambir *m*, cachou *m* pâle.

gambit ['gæmbit], *s.* (*a*) *Chess:* gambit *m*; **g. pawn,** (pion *m* de) gambit; (*b*) *Fig:* tour *m*, manœuvre *f*; **opening g.,** manœuvre d'approche.

gamble[1] ['gæmbl], *s.* (*a*) jeu *m* de hasard; *O:* **to go on the g.,** s'adonner au jeu; (*b*) affaire *f* où l'on risque fort de perdre; **pure g.,** pure spéculation, affaire de chance; **everything's a g.,** tout est coup de dé, tout est affaire de chance, dans ce monde.

gamble[2]. **1.** *v.i.* jouer de l'argent; **to g. on a throw of the dice,** miser sur un coup de dé(s); **to g. on the Stock Exchange,** agioter; **to g. on a rise in prices,** jouer à la hausse; **to g. in wheat,** tripoter sur les blés; **you can g. on that,** vous pouvez compter là-dessus; **to g. with one's health,** jouer avec sa santé. **2.** *v.ind.tr.* **to g. away** (**one's fortune, etc.**), perdre (sa fortune, etc.) au jeu; *v.tr.* **to g. one's money on horses,** jouer aux courses.

gambler ['gæmblər], *s.* joueur, -euse (pour de l'argent); **g. on the Stock Exchange,** joueur à la Bourse; spéculateur, -trice; agioteur, -euse; *Prov:* **once a g. always a g.,** qui a joué jouera.

gambling ['gæmbliŋ], *s.* le jeu; jeux d'argent; **g. on the Stock Exchange,** agiotage *m*; **g. debts,** dettes *f* de jeu; **g. den, g. house,** *U.S:* **g. joint,** maison *f* de jeu; tripot *m*, brelan *m*, claque(dent) *m*; **g. table,** table *f* de jeu.

gamboge [gæm'boudʒ, -'bu:ʒ], *s. Bot: Paint:* gomme-gutte *f*; **g. tree,** guttier *m*.

gambol[1] ['gæmb(ə)l], *s.* (*a*) gambade *f*, cabriole *f*; (*b*) *pl.* ébats *m*, divertissements *m*.

gambol[2], *v.i.* (**gambolled**) (*a*) gambader, cabrioler; faire des gambades; (*b*) s'ébattre, se divertir.

gambrel ['gæmbrəl], *s.* **1.** tinet *m*, jambier *m* (de boucherie). **2.** *Arch:* **g. roof,** toit *m* en croupe.

gambusia [gæm'bju:ziə], *s. Ich:* gambusie *f*.

game[1] [geim], *s.* **1.** (*a*) amusement *m*, divertissement *m*, jeu *m*; **to make g. of s.o.,** se moquer, se jouer, de qn; *F:* **what a g.!** quelle farce! (*b*) jeu; **g. of skill, of chance,** jeu d'adresse, de hasard; **card games,** jeux de cartes; **ball g.,** (i) jeu à la balle, au ballon; (ii) *NAm:* le baseball; **round g.,** jeu à un nombre indéfini de joueurs; jeu en commun; **square g.,** jeu, partie *f*, à quatre; **outdoor games,** jeux de plein air; *Tchn:* **g. theory,** théories *f* des jeux rectangulaires; (*c*) **Olympic games,** jeux olympiques; *Sch:* **games,** sports *mpl*; **games master, mistress,** maître, maîtresse, d'éducation sportive; (*d*) **to play a good g.,** être bon joueur; **he plays a good g. of cards, of billiards,** il joue bien aux cartes, au billard; **he plays a remarkable g.,** il a un jeu remarquable; *Fb:* **to play a rough g.,** jouer un football dur; **to play the g.,** jouer franc jeu; jouer, agir, loyalement; agir dans les règles, jouer selon les règles; **that's not playing the g.,** ce n'est pas loyal; ce n'est pas de jeu; **to play a dangerous g.,** jouer un jeu dangereux; **to play s.o.'s g.,** faire le jeu de qn; **to beat s.o. at his own g.,** battre qn avec ses propres armes; **two can play at that g.,** à bon chat bon rat; à voleur voleur et demi; je vous revaudrai cela, on sera deux; **to be on one's g.,** être (bien) en forme; **to be off one's g.,** jouer mal, moins bien que d'habitude; *Ten:* ne pas être en raquette; **to go off one's g.,** se dérégler; (*e*) *F:* **what's his g.?** où veut-il en venir? quel but poursuit-il? **I know your (little) g.!** je sais bien où vous voulez en venir! **so that's your g.!** voilà donc ce que vous manigancez! **I was watching their (little) g.,** j'observais leur manège; **I can see through your g.!** je vous vois venir! **he's at his old games again,** voilà qu'il refait des siennes; **that's a dirty g. you're playing!** vous faites là un vilain métier; (*of prostitute, etc.*) **to be**

on the g., travailler, turbiner; faire le turbin; **none of your games (with me)!** à bas les pattes! pas de ça, Lisette! **to spoil s.o.'s g.,** déjouer les plans de qn; **the game's up,** l'affaire est dans l'eau; il n'y a plus rien à faire; **his (little) game's up,** il est grillé; (*f*) partie *f* (de cartes, de billard, d'échecs, etc.); manche *f* (d'une partie de cartes); **to have, play, a g. of cricket,** faire une partie de cricket; **did you have a good g.?** vous avez fait une bonne partie? **five points are g.,** la partie se joue en cinq; **the g. is three (to) two,** la partie en est à trois à deux; **how's the g. going?** (i) comment marche, (ii) où en est, la partie? **to be g.,** avoir gagné la partie; **to be g. all, g. and g.,** être à égalité; *Cards:* être manche à manche; **the odd g., the deciding g.,** la belle; **to get, have, the best of the g.,** dominer la partie; *Ten:* **g., set, and match,** jeu, set, et partie; *Chess: etc:* **opening g.,** début *m* de partie; **middle g.,** milieu *m* de partie; **end g.,** fin *f* de partie; **to have, hold, the g. in one's hands,** tenir le succès entre ses mains. **2.** (*a*) gibier *m*; **good g. country,** pays giboyeux; **big g.,** (i) gros gibier; (ii) les grands, fauves; **big-g. hunting,** la chasse aux grands fauves; **small g.,** menu gibier; **furred g.,** gibier à poil; **winged g., g. birds,** gibier à plumes, gibier ailé; **black g.,** lyrure *m*; petit coq de bruyère; **g. fowl,** combattant *m*; **g. preserve,** parc *m* à gibier; **g. bag,** carnassière *f*, carnier *m*, gibecière *f*; **g. licence,** permis *m* de chasse; **g. laws,** lois *f* sur la chasse; **he's fair g.,** c'est une bonne proie, un gibier de bonne prise; on a bien le droit de se moquer de lui; **to fly at too high g.,** viser trop haut; (*b*) *Cu:* gibier; **g. pie,** pâté de gibier en croûte. **3.** troupeau *m* (de cygnes).

game². **1.** *v.i.* jouer (de l'argent); **to g. deep,** jouer gros jeu. **2.** *v.ind.tr.* **to g. away one's money, a fortune,** perdre son argent au jeu; dissiper une fortune au jeu.

game³, *a.* courageux, résolu, *F:* crâne; **to be g.,** (i) avoir du cran, de l'estomac; avoir le cœur bien attaché; (ii) être d'attaque; (iii) (*of dog*) être de bonne race; **are you g. for a twenty-kilometre walk?** vous sentez-vous de force à faire vingt kilomètres à pied? **he wasn't g. enough to take on a really big job,** il n'avait pas le cran nécessaire pour se charger d'une grosse besogne; **I'm g.!** d'accord! j'en suis! **he's g. for anything,** il est prêt à tout, capable de tout; il a du cœur au ventre; **to die g.,** mourir crânement, avec crânerie, en héros.

game⁴, *a.* **g. arm,** bras estropié; **g. leg,** jambe boiteuse, perclus(e); **to have a g. right leg,** boiter, être estropié, de la jambe droite.

gamecock ['geimkɔk], *s.* (*a*) coq *m* de combat; combattant *m*; (*b*) **a fierce little g. of a man,** un petit homme fier et courageux.

gamekeeper ['geimki:pər], *s.* garde-chasse *m*, *pl.* gardes-chasse(s), garde forestier; *Cost:* **gamekeeper's pocket,** poche *f* à soufflet.

game-legged ['geim'legid], *a.* estropié, boiteux.

gameness ['geimnis], *s.* courage *m*, *F:* crânerie *f*.

gamesmanship ['geimzmənʃip], *s.* l'art *m* de gagner sans enfreindre les règles du jeu.

gamesome ['geimsəm], *a.* *O:* enjoué, folâtre.

gamester ['geimstər], *s.* *O:* joueur, -euse (pour de l'argent).

gametangium, *pl.* **-ia** [gæmi'tændʒiəm, -iə], *s.* *Biol:* gamétange *m*.

gamete ['gæmi:t, gæ'mi:t], *s.* *Biol:* gamète *m*.

gametocide [gæ'mi:tousaid], *s.* gamétocide *m*.

gametocyte [gæ'mi:tousait], *s.* *Biol:* gamétocyte *m*.

gametogenesis ['gæmitou'dʒenisis], *s.* *Biol:* gamétogénèse *f*.

gametophyte [gæ'mi:toufait], *s.* *Bot:* gamétophyte *m*.

gaming ['geimiŋ], *s.* jeu *m*; **g. debt,** dette *f* de jeu; *Jur:* **g. and wagering,** jeu-pari *m*; **to plead the G. Act,** invoquer l'exception de jeu; **g. table,** table *f* de jeu; **g. room,** salle *f* de jeu; **g. house,** maison *f* de jeu; **g. losses,** pertes *f* au jeu.

gamma ['gæmə], *s.* (*a*) *Gr.Alph:* gamma *m*; (*b*) *Phot:* **g. infinity,** gamma infini; (*c*) *Metall:* **g. iron,** fer *m* gamma; **g. uranium,** uranium *m* gamma; (*d*) *Atom.Ph:* **g. particle,** particule *f* gamma; **g. rays,** rayons *m* gamma; **g. radiation,** radiation *f*, rayonnement *m*, gamma; **g.-ray energy,** énergie *f* du rayonnement gamma; **g. cascade,** cascade *f* de rayons gamma, émission *f* gamma en cascade; **g. flux,** flux *m* de rayons gamma; **g.(-ray) shield,** écran *m* de protection (contre les rayons) gamma; **capture g.,** (rayon) gamma de capture; **prompt g.,** (rayon) gamma immédiat, instantané; **g. monitor,** détecteur *m* (de rayons) gamma; **g. (radiation) meter,** gammamètre *m*; **g.(-ray) spectrometer,** spectromètre *m* (de rayons) gamma; **g.-ray pasteurization,** pasteurisation *f* par irradiation gamma; **g.-ray therapy,** gammathérapie *f*; **g. radiography,** gammagraphie *f*; (*e*) **g. globulin,** gammaglobuline *f*; (*f*) *Ent:* **g. (moth),** plusie *f*.

gammacism ['gæməsizm], *s.* *Med:* gammacisme *m*.

gammadion [gæ'meidiən], *s.* croix gammée, cramponnée.

gammagraphy [gæ'mægrəfi], *s.* gammagraphie *f*; **industrial g.,** gammagraphie industrielle.

gammarid ['gæmərid], *s.* *Crust:* gammare *m*, gammaridé *m*, *F:* puce *f* de mer, d'eau.

Gammaridae [gæ'mɑ:ridi:], *s.pl.* *Crust:* gammaridés *m*.

gammatherapy [gæmə'θerəpi], *s.* *Med:* gammathérapie *f*.

gammer ['gæmər], *s.* *F:* *A:* vieille (bonne) femme; **g. Martin,** la mère Martin.

gammexane [gæ'meksein], *s.* *Ch:* gammexane *m*.

gammon¹ ['gæmən], *s.* (*a*) quartier *m* (du porc); (*b*) quartier de lard fumé; (*c*) *A:* jambon *m*; (*d*) jambon fumé.

gammon², *v.tr.* saler et fumer (le lard).

gammon³, *s.* *Games:* (*backgammon*) bredouille *f*; **to win the g.,** gagner la partie bredouille.

gammon⁴, *s.* *P:* blague *f*; bourrage *m* de crâne, baliverne(s) *f*(*pl.*); boniment(s) *m*(*pl.*); bobard(s) *m*(*pl.*).

gammon⁵. *P:* **1.** *v.i.* (*a*) blaguer, baliverner; **to g. well,** avoir du bagout; (*b*) feindre, faire semblant (**to do sth.,** de faire qch.). **2.** *v.tr.* blaguer (qn); duper (qn); monter un bateau, raconter des balivernes, à (qn); **to g. s.o. into doing sth.,** monter le coup à qn pour lui faire faire qch.; **to g. s.o. out of sth.,** détourner qn de qch. à force de bluff.

gammy ['gæmi], *a.* *F:* = GAME⁴.

gamo- ['gæmou], *comb.fm.* gamo-.

gamogenesis [gæmou'dʒenisis], *s.* *Biol:* gamogénèse *f*.

gamogenetic [gæmoudʒə'netik], *a.* *Biol:* gamogénétique.

gamolepis [gæmou'lepis], *s.* *Bot:* gamolépis *m*.

gamomania [gæmou'meiniə], *s.* gamomanie *f*.

gamone ['gæmoun], *s.* *Biol:* gamone *f*.

gamont ['gæmənt], *s.* *Biol:* gamonte *m*.

gamopetalous [gæmou'petələs], *a.* *Bot:* gamopétale.

gamophobia [gæmou'foubiə], *s.* *Med:* gamophobie *f*.

gamophyllous [gæmou'filəs], *a.* *Bot:* gamophylle.

gamosepalous [gæmou'sepələs], *a.* *Bot:* gamosépale.

gamotropism [gæmou'troupizm], *s.* *Z:* gamotropisme *m*.

gamp [gæmp], *s.* *F:* (grand) parapluie (mal roulé); pépin *m*.

gamut ['gæmət], *s.* **1.** *Mus:* (*a*) gamme *f*; (*b*) étendue *f* (de la voix); clavier *m* (de la clarinette). **2.** gamme (de couleurs, etc.); **the whole g. of pleasurable sensations,** toute la gamme des voluptés; **he has the whole g. of business at his fingertips,** il connaît les affaires depuis A jusqu'à Z.

gamy ['geimi], *a.* **1.** (bois, etc.) giboyeux. **2.** *Cu:* faisandé, avancé; (goût) de gibier.

gander ['gændər], *s.* **1.** jars *m*. **2.** *F:* idiot, -ote; imbécile *mf*. **3.** *P:* coup *m* d'œil; **just take a g.!** mate-moi ça!

gand(o)ura [gæn'duərə], *s.* *Cost:* gandoura *f*; tunique portée sous le burnous.

gang¹ [gæŋ], *s.* **1.** *Dial:* chemin *m*; passage *m*. **2.** (*a*) groupe *m*, troupe *f* (de personnes); *Ind: etc:* équipe *f*; *Min:* coupe *f* (d'ouvriers); **erection g.,** équipe de montage; **g. of convicts,** convoi *m* de prisonniers; (*b*) bande *f*, *F:* gang *m* (de voleurs, etc.); **the whole g.,** toute la bande; **g. war(fare),** guerre *f*, lutte *f*, entre bandes rivales. **3.** (*a*) série *f* (d'outils qui vont ensemble); **g. driller,** perceuse *f* à forets multiples; **g. plough,** (charrue *f*) polysoc *m*; **g. saw,** scie *f* multiple, scie alternative à plusieurs lames; **g. mill,** fraise *f* à lames multiples; **g. tool,** outil multiple, sérié; **g. control,** *W.Tel:* **two-g. condenser,** condensateur *m* à deux blocs; (*b*) *Com:* **g. labels,** étiquettes pliées en zigzag.

gang², *v.*

I. *v.tr.* monter (des scies, des forets, etc.) ensemble, en série.

II. (*compound verb*) **gang up,** *v.i.* s'allier (**with,** avec); **to g. up on s.o.,** se liguer contre qn; attaquer qn de concert.

gang³, *v.i.* *Dial:* *Scot:* *A:* (*a*) aller; (*b*) marcher.

gang⁴, *s.* = GANGUE.

gangava [gæŋ'gɑ:və], *s.* *Nau:* gangave *f*.

gangboard ['gæŋbɔ:d], *s.* = GANGPLANK.

ganged [gæŋd], *a.* *Tchn:* à commande unique; (outils) multiples, montés ensemble; *W.Tel:* **g. condensers,** condensateurs *m* à blocs combinés; *El:* **g. circuits,** circuits *m* à commande unique; *Elcs:* **g. tuning,** accord *m* à commande unique.

ganger ['gæŋər], *s.* **(boss) g.,** *Rail:* chef *m* d'équipe; cantonnier *m* chef; chef cantonnier; *Civ.E:* brigadier *m* cantonnier.

Ganges (the) [ðə'gæn(d)ʒi:z], *Pr.n.* *Geog:* le Gange.

Gangetic [gæn'dʒetik], *a.* gangétique; (delta *m*, etc.) du Gange.

gangland ['gæŋlænd], *s.* (*a*) la zone des bandits, des gangsters (dans une grande ville); (*b*) le monde criminel, le milieu.

gangliated ['gæŋglieitid], *a.* *Anat:* ganglionné.

gangliectomy [gæŋgli'ektəmi], *s.* *Surg:* gangliectomie *f*.

gangliform ['gæŋglifɔ:m], *a.* *Anat:* gangliforme.

gangling ['gæŋgliŋ], *a.* dégingandé.

ganglion, -ia ['gæŋgliən, -iə], *s.* **1.** (*a*) *Anat:* ganglion *m*; **g. cell,** ganglion nerveux; (*b*) *Fig:* centre *m*, foyer *m*, d'activité. **2.** *Med:* ganglion synovial, -aux; kyste synovial.

ganglionary ['gæŋgliənəri], *a.* *Anat:* ganglionnaire.

ganglionated ['gæŋgliəneitid], *a.* = GANGLIATED.

ganglionectomy [gæŋgliə'nektəmi], *s.* *Surg:* gangliectomie *f*.

ganglionic [gæŋgli'ɔnik], *a.* *Anat:* ganglionnaire.

gangly ['gæŋgli], *a.* dégingandé.

gangplank ['gæŋplæŋk], *s.* *Nau:* planche *f* à débarquer, de débarquement; planche d'embarquement; appontement *m*; (*between two ships*) traversine *f*.

gangrene¹ ['gæŋgri:n], *s.* (*a*) *Med:* gangrène *f*, mortification *f*, sphacèle *m*; **dry, humid, senile, g.,** gangrène sèche, humide, sénile; **gas g.,** gangrène gazeuse; *A:* **hospital g.,** ulcère rongeant; ulcère rongeur; pourriture *f* d'hôpital; (*b*) *Fig:* pourriture.

gangrene². **1.** *v.tr.* gangrener, mortifier. **2.** *v.i.* se gangrener.

gangrened ['gæŋgri:nd], *a.* gangrené.

gangrenous ['gæŋgrinəs], *a.* gangreneux, gangrené, sphacélé.

gangster ['gæŋstər], *s.* **1.** gangster *m*; bandit *m*. **2.** *Pol:* *A:* **an old g.,** un membre de la vieille bande; un des vieux routiers. **3.** *Civ.E:* équipier *m*; membre d'une équipe de cantonniers.

gangsterism ['gæŋstərizm], *s.* gangstérisme *m*.

gangue [gæŋ], *s.* *Miner:* *Geol:* gangue *f*, gaine *f*; roche *f* mère; **to separate the ore from the g.,** dérocher le minerai.

gangway ['gæŋwei], *s.* **1.** passage *m*; couloir central (d'autobus, etc.) **central g.,** allée centrale; *Pol:* **members above, below, the g.,** membres influents, peu influents, du parti; **g. please!** dégagez, s'il vous plaît! laissez passer) s'il vous plaît! **2.** *Nau:* (*a*) passerelle *f* de service (pour débarquement, etc.); (*b*) (*opening or port*) coupée *f* (dans la muraille); **to come up the g.,** monter la coupée; (*c*) **(fore-and-aft) g.,** passavant *m* (entre gaillards).

ganister ['gænistər], *s.* *Miner:* gannister *m*; *Metall: etc:* **g. mud,** boue *f* réfractaire.

gannet ['gænit], *s.* *Orn:* fou *m* (de Bassan).

ganoid ['gænɔid], *a.* & *s.* *Ich:* ganoïde (*m*).

Ganoidei [gæ'nɔidi:ai], *s.pl.* *Ich:* ganoïdes *m*.

ganomalite [gə'nɔməlait], *s.* *Miner:* ganomalite *f*.

ganophyllite [gænou'filait], *s.* *Miner:* ganophyllite *f*.

gantline ['gæntlain], *s.* *Nau:* (*a*) cartahu *m* (simple); (*b*) ceinture *f* de hamac.

gantry ['gæntri], *s.* **1.** chantier *m* (pour fûts); porte-fût(s) *m inv.* **2.** *Ind:* (*a*) portique *m*; pont roulant (pour grue mobile); *Nau:* beffroi *m* (de drague); *Rail:* **signal g.,** pont à signaux; **g. (crane),** grue *f* à portique; **travelling g.,** portique roulant; (*b*) chevalet *m* de levage; (*c*) *Av:* portique de lancement; (*for missiles*) portique de service.

Ganymede ['gænimi:d]. **1.** *Pr.n.m.* *Myth:* Ganymède. **2.** *s.m.* *A:* *Lit:* échanson, verseur.

gaol¹ [dʒeil], *s.* prison *f*; maison *f* d'arrêt; **the County g.** = la maison centrale; **six months' g.,** six mois de prison; **to be in g.,** être en prison; être sous les verrous; **g. delivery,** (i) levée *f* d'écrou (de prisonniers); (ii) ordre *m* de mise en jugement (des prisonniers); (iii) session *f* de cour d'assises; *Med:* *A:* **g. fever,** typhus *m*.

gaol², *v.tr.* mettre (qn) en prison; écrouer (qn).

gaolbird ['dʒeilbə:d], *s.* échappé, -ée, de prison; gibier *m* de potence.

gaoler ['dʒeilər], *s.* gardien *m* de prison.

gap¹ [gæp], *s.* **1.** (*a*) trou *m*; trouée *f*, ouverture *f*, vide *m* (dans une haie, etc.); brèche *f* (dans un mur, etc.); discontinuité *f*, solution *f* de continuité (d'une surface); *Tchn:* renard *m* (dans une tôle, un barrage, etc.); **wide clearings that make gaps in the forest,** de larges clairières qui trouent la forêt, font des vides dans la forêt; **to fill (in, up), a g., to stop a g.,** boucher, colmater, un trou, une brèche; combler un vide; (*b*) *Geog:* trouée *f*; *esp. U.S:* col *m*; ravin *m*; **water g.,** cluse (vive); percée *f*; **wind g.,** cluse sèche, morte; **g. town,** ville *f*, centre *m* de communications, qui commande une trouée; **the Belfort G., the Saverne G.,** la Trouée de Belfort, de Saverne; (*c*) interstice *m*; intervalle *m*; écartement *m*, écart *m*; créneau *m*, distance *f* (entre deux convois, deux formations militaires); **there are gaps between the planks,** il y a des jours *m* entre les planches; **gaps between the teeth of a pinion,** vides, creux *m*, entre les dents d'un pignon; **there's a g. in the curtains,** les rideaux bâillent; *El:* **g. between contacts,** écartement des contacts; **g. between electrodes,** distance, intervalle, entre les électrodes; **armature g.,** ouverture, entrefer *m*, d'induit; *I.C.E:* **g. type distributor,** distributeur *m* à étincelles sautantes; **g. width,** écartement des électrodes (d'une bougie); **g. arrester,** parafoudre *m* à étincelles; **g. gauge,** calibre *m* à mâchoires; **starter g.,** intervalle d'allumage; (*d*) *Av:* écartement (des plans); (*e*) trou, lacune *f*, vide (dans des souvenirs, etc.); **a noticeable g.,** un vide sensible; **his death leaves, makes, a g. in the family circle,** sa mort laisse un vide dans la famille; **to fill the gaps in one's education,** combler les lacunes de son éducation; **to bridge the g.,** combler le fossé, le déficit; faire, effectuer, la soudure; **the g. between two generations,** le fossé entre deux générations; **the g. that separates him from his colleagues,** l'abîme qui le sépare de ses collègues; *Pol.Ec: etc:* **trade g.,** déficit commercial; découvert *m* de la balance commerciale; **the dollar g.,** le déficit en dollars; *Mil:* **the missile g.,** le retard dans le domaine des missiles; **credibility g.,** manque de crédit (accordé à un gouvernement, etc.); crise *f* de confiance (envers qn); **communicating g.,** manque de compréhension; **there's a complete communications g. between them,** ils n'arrivent pas à se comprendre, à s'expliquer entre eux; (*f*) *Rec:* blanc *m* sonore; (*in recorded tape*) plage *f* de silence; (*g*) (*in time*) **age g.,** écart d'âge; **a g. of over twenty years,** un intervalle de plus de vingt ans. **2.** *Mec.E:* coupure *f*, rompu *m* (d'un banc de tour); **g. bed,** banc rompu; **g.(-bed) lathe,** tour *m* à banc rompu. **3.** *Typ:* colombier *m* (entre les mots).

gap[2], *v.tr.* échancrer, entailler (une plaque, etc.).

gape[1] [geip], *s.* **1.** bâillement *m*; *Vet:* **the gapes,** le bâillement, la syngamose (de la volaille); *F:* **to give s.o. the gapes,** faire bâiller qn. **2.** contemplation *f* bouche bée.

gape[2], *v.i.* **1.** (*a*) (*of pers.*) (i) ouvrir la bouche toute grande; (ii) bâiller (d'ennui); (*b*) (*of bird*) ouvrir un large bec; (*c*) (*of thg*) **to g. (open),** s'ouvrir (tout grand); (*of hole*) être béant; (*of seam, etc.*) bâiller; **these boards g.,** ces planches ne joignent pas; **coat that gapes at every seam,** habit *m* qui rit par toutes les coutures. **2.** (*of pers.*) être, rester, bouche bée; bayer aux corneilles; *F:* gober des mouches; **he stood there gaping,** il restait planté là comme un ahuri; **to g. at s.o., sth.,** regarder qn, qch., bouche bée, d'un air hébété; *A:* **to g. after sth., for sth.,** désirer ardemment qch.; soupirer après qch.

gaper ['geipər], *s.* **1.** (*a*) bayeur, -euse; badaud, -aude; *F:* gobe-mouches *m inv*; (*b*) bâilleur, -euse. **2.** (*a*) *Orn:* bec-ouvert *m*, *pl.* becs-ouverts; (*b*) *Moll:* **g. (shell),** mye *f*.

gapeseed ['geipsi:d], *s. F: O:* (*a*) chose *f*, spectacle *m*, qui attire les badauds; attrape-nigaud *m*, *pl.* attrape-nigauds; (*b*) badaud, -aude; gobe-mouches *m inv.*

gapeworm ['geipwə:m], *s. Ann:* syngame trachéal; bâille-bec *m inv*; ver rouge, ver fourchu.

gaping[1] ['geipiŋ], *a.* béant; **g. wound,** blessure béante; **g. astonishment,** étonnement muet; **g. oyster,** huître grande ouverte; **g. chasm,** abîme béant.

gaping[2], *s.* **1.** contemplation *f* bouche bée. **2.** bâillement *m*.

gap-toothed ['gæptu:θt], *a.* aux dents écartées.

gapy ['geipi], *a.* **1.** *F:* bâilleur, -euse. **2.** (*of poultry*) atteint de bâillement.

gar [gɑ:r], *s. Ich:* = GARFISH.

gara ['gærə], *pl.* **gour** [guər], *s. Geol: Geog:* gour *mpl* (*generally used for the sg.*).

garage[1] ['gærɑ:ʒ], *s. Aut:* garage *m*; **locking g.,** box *m*, *pl.* boxes; **g. proprietor, owner,** garagiste *m*; **g. mechanic,** mécanicien *m* de garage, *F:* garagiste; **I'll put the car (back) in the g.,** je vais garer, remiser, la voiture.

garage[2], *v.tr.* (i) garer, (ii) remiser (une voiture).

garageman, *pl.* **-men** ['gærɑ:ʒmæn, -men], *s.m.* mécanicien de garage, *F:* garagiste.

garb[1] [gɑ:b], *s. O: & Lit:* vêtement *m*, costume *m*, habit *m*; **clerical g.,** costume, habit, ecclésiastique; **in such a g.,** dans, sous, un tel accoutrement; *A:* **in nature's g.,** en état de pure nature; nu; (*of man*) dans le costume d'Adam; **his usual g. of indifference,** ses dehors habituels d'indifférence.

garb[2], *v.tr. A: & Lit:* habiller, vêtir (**in,** de); **garbed all in black,** tout de noir vêtu.

garb[3], *s. Her:* gerbe *f*.

garbage ['gɑ:bidʒ], *s.* **1.** *A:* tripaille *f*, entrailles *fpl*; issues *fpl* (de boucherie); **to feed on g.,** se nourrir de rebuts *mpl*. **2.** (*a*) immondices *fpl*, détritus *mpl*; déchets *mpl*; **literary g.,** rebut *m* de la littérature; (*b*) *esp. NAm:* ordures ménagères; **g. heap,** tas *m* d'ordures; **g. can,** poubelle *f*; boîte *f* à ordures; **g. disposal unit,** broyeur *m* à ordures; **g. chute,** manche *f* à ordures; **g. man, g. collector,** boueur *m*; *Nau:* **g. lighter,** bette *f* à saletés.

garble ['gɑ:bl], *v.tr.* **1.** tronquer, fausser (des nouvelles, une citation, des comptes, etc.); dénaturer (les faits); mutiler, altérer (un texte); altérer (l'histoire); **garbled account,** compte rendu trompeur, mensonger; faux rapport; **garbled edition,** édition tronquée; **to g. s.o.'s words,** mal interpréter, fausser, les paroles de qn. **2.** *A:* trier (des pièces de monnaie).

garbler ['gɑ:blər], *s.* mutilateur, -trice (d'un texte, etc.); faussaire *m* (de faits, etc.).

garbling ['gɑ:bliŋ], *s.* mutilation *f*, altération *f* (d'un texte, d'une citation).

garboard ['gɑ:bɔ:d], *s. N.Arch:* ga(l)bord *m*; **g. strake,** virure *f* de gabord.

garden[1] ['gɑ:dn], *s.* (*a*) jardin *m*; **small g.,** jardinet *m*; **flower g.,** jardin d'agrément, jardin de fleurs; **kitchen g., vegetable g.,** (jardin) potager *m*; **market g.,** *NAm:* **truck g.,** jardin maraîcher; **(market-)g. produce,** produits maraîchers; fruits et légumes; **nursery g.,** pépinière *f*; **landscape g.,** jardin à l'anglaise; **rock g.,** jardin alpin; jardin de rocaille; **sunken g.,** jardin encaissé; **hanging g.,** jardin suspendu; **window g.,** balcon fleuri; **g. of remembrance** = cimetière *m* d'un crématorium; **botanical g.,** jardin botanique; jardin des plantes; **zoological gardens,** jardin zoologique; **winter g.,** (i) jardin d'hiver; grande serre; (ii) *O:* (*in hotel, etc.*) hall vitré; **tea g.,** (i) plantation *f* de thé; (ii) jardin (d'hôtel, de restaurant) où on sert le thé; **beer g.** = café *m* en plein air; *F:* **to lead s.o. up the g. (path),** duper, faire marcher, qn; *attrib.* **g. plants,** plantes *f* de jardin; **g. tools,** outils *m*, instruments *m*, de jardinage; **g. furniture,** meubles *mpl* de jardin; **g. chair,** chaise *f* de jardin; **g. seat,** banc *m*, siège *m*, de jardin; **g. shed,** abri *m* de jardin; **g. hose,** tuyau *m* d'arrosage; **g. frame,** châssis *m*; **g. room,** (i) pièce *f* avec porte qui donne sur le jardin; (ii) (*separate from house*) cabanon *m* de jardin; **g. party,** réception *f* en plein air; garden-party *f*, *pl.* garden-parties; **g. suburb, g. city,** cité-jardin *f*, *pl.* cités-jardins; *Orn:* **g. warbler,** fauvette *f* des jardins; *Ent:* **g. white,** piéride *f* du chou; *a.phr. F:* **common or g.,** (i) ordinaire; commun; (ii) banal; (*b*) **(public) garden(s),** jardin public; parc *m*; (*c*) *pl.* (*as Pr.n.*) rue *f* (avec jardins ou qui avait autrefois des jardins); (*d*) *Gr.Phil:* **the G.,** les Jardins d'Épicure; **the G. (Sect),** les disciples *m* d'Épicure.

garden[2]. **1.** *v.i.* (*a*) jardiner; faire du jardinage; (*b*) *Cr: F:* aplatir les inégalités du terrain avec sa batte. **2.** *v.tr.* entretenir (un parterre, etc.).

Gardenal ['gɑ:dnəl], *s. R.t.m:* Gardénal *m*.

gardener ['gɑ:dnər], *s.* **1.** jardinier *m*; **landscape g.,** jardinier paysagiste; **market g.,** *NAm:* **truck g.,** maraîcher, -ère; **nursery g.,** pépiniériste *mf*. **2.** *Bot:* **gardener's delight,** coquelourde *f*; **gardener's garters,** alpiste panaché; ruban *m* de bergère. **3. g. bird,** amblyornis *m*, oiseau-jardinier *m*, *pl.* oiseaux-jardiniers.

gardenia [gɑ:'di:niə], *s. Bot:* gardénia *m*, gardénie *f*.

gardening ['gɑ:dniŋ], *s.* jardinage *m*; horticulture *f*; **landscape g.,** l'art *m* de dessiner les jardins; **market g.,** *NAm:* **truck g.,** maraîchage *m*; l'industrie maraîchère; **g. tools,** outils *m*, instruments *m*, de jardinage; **soilless g.,** culture *f* hydroponique.

garderobe ['gɑ:droub], *s. A:* garde-robe *f* (la chambre ou les vêtements).

garefowl ['gɛəfaul], *s. Orn:* grand pingouin.

garfish ['gɑ:fiʃ], *s. Ich:* aiguille *f* (des pêcheurs); aiguille de mer; orphie *f*; lépidostée *m*.

garganey ['gɑ:gəni], *s. Orn:* **g. (duck),** sarcelle *f* d'été.

gargantuan [gɑ:'gæntjuən], *a.* gargantuesque.

gargle[1] ['gɑ:gl], *s. Med:* gargarisme *m*.

gargle[2]. **1.** *v.i.* se gargariser. **2.** *v.tr.* **to g. one's throat,** se gargariser la gorge.

gargling ['gɑ:gliŋ], *s.* gargarisme *m*.

gargoyle ['gɑ:gɔil], *s. Arch: etc:* gargouille *f*.

gargoylism ['gɑ:gɔilizm], *s. Med:* gargoylisme *m*.

Garibaldi [gæri'bɔ:ldi], *Pr.n.* Garibaldi; *Cost: A:* **G. (shirt), G. (blouse),** garibaldi *m*; **G. (cap),** garibaldi; *Cu:* **G. biscuit,** biscuit fourré aux raisins de Corinthe.

Garibaldian [gæri'bɔ:ldiən], *a. & s. Hist:* garibaldien (*m*).

garish ['gɛəriʃ], *a.* **1.** (*of dress, decoration, etc.*) voyant; d'un luxe criard; d'un faste de mauvais goût. **2. g. light,** lumière crue, aveuglante.

garishly ['gɛəriʃli], *adv.* **1.** (meublé, etc.) avec un luxe criard. **2.** (éclairé) avec une crudité qui blesse les yeux.

garishness ['gɛəriʃnis], *s.* **1.** luxe criard; faste *m*. **2.** éclat excessif; crudité *f* (d'une couleur, de l'éclairage).

garland[1] ['gɑ:lənd], *s.* **1.** guirlande *f*; couronne *f* (de fleurs); **to hang sth. with garlands,** orner, parer, qch. de guirlandes; *Lit:* **to win, carry away, the g.,** remporter la palme, la couronne. **2.** *A:* anthologie *f*, chrestomathie *f*; guirlande (de ballades, etc.). **3.** *A.Nau:* grosse erse. **4.** *Bot:* **g. flower,** hedychium *m*.

garland[2], *v.tr.* (en)guirlander; **garlanded with flowers,** paré de guirlandes de fleurs.

garlic ['gɑ:lik], *s. Bot:* **1.** ail *m*, *pl.* ails *or* aulx; **clove of g.,** gousse *f* d'ail; caïeu *m* d'ail; **head of g.,** tête *f* d'ail. **2. wild g.,** moly *m*, ail doré; **hedge g., g. mustard,** alliaire *f*; **Spanish g.,** rocambole *f*; **g. pear,** cratæra gynandra.

garment ['gɑ:mənt], *s.* vêtement *m*.

garn [gɑ:n], *int. P:* (= **go on!**) et ta sœur!

garner[1] ['gɑ:nər], *s.* **1.** *NAm: & Lit:* grenier *m* (pour la récolte). **2.** *A:* recueil *m* (de poésies, etc.).

garner[2], *v.tr. NAm: & Lit:* mettre (le grain) en grenier, en grange; engranger, rentrer (le blé, etc.); **to g. the fruits of the earth,** recueillir les fruits de la terre; **memories garnered up in the heart,** souvenirs amassés, accumulés, dans le cœur.

garnering ['gɑ:nəriŋ], *s.* engrangement *m* (du blé, etc.).

garnet[1] ['gɑ:nit], *s. Miner:* grenat *m*; **g. rock,** grenatite *f*; *attrib.* **g. (red) silk,** soie *f* grenat *inv*; *Hort:* **g. berry,** groseillier *m* rouge.

garnet[2], *s. Nau:* palan *m* de charge, bredindin *m*.

garnierite ['gɑ:niərait], *s. Miner:* garniérite *f*.

garnish[1] ['gɑ:niʃ], *s.* **1.** *Cu: etc:* garniture *f*. **2.** *A:* bienvenue (payée par un nouveau détenu à ses compagnons de prison).

garnish[2], *v.tr.* **1.** garnir, orner, embellir (**with,** de); *Cu:* **to g. a dish,** garnir un plat. **2.** *Jur:* (*a*) appeler (un tiers) en justice; (*b*) saisir-arrêter.

garnishee [gɑ:ni'ʃi:], *s. Jur:* (*a*) tiers appelé en justice; (*b*) tiers-saisi *m*, *pl.* tiers-saisis; **g. order,** ordonnance *f* de saisie-arrêt.

garnisher ['gɑ:niʃər], *s.* **1.** garnisseur, -euse. **2.** *Jur:* (*a*) partie *f* qui appelle un tiers en justice; (*b*) saisissant *m* (dans une saisie-arrêt).

garnishing ['gɑ:niʃiŋ], *s.* **1.** garnissage *m*, garnissement *m*, embellissement *m*. **2.** garniture *f* (d'un plat); ornement *m*, fioriture *f* (de style).

garnishment ['gɑ:niʃmənt], *s.* **1.** = GARNISHING. **2.** *Jur:* (*a*) appel *m* en justice d'un tiers; assignation *f* en intervention forcée; (*b*) saisie-arrêt *f*, *pl.* saisies-arrêts; opposition *f*.

garniture ['gɑ:nitjər], *s.* **1.** garniture *f*, accessoires *mpl*. **2.** garniture (d'un plat, d'une robe, etc.); ornement *m*, fioriture *f* (de style).

garpike ['gɑ:paik], *s. Ich:* = GARFISH.

garret[1] ['gærət], *s.* mansarde *f*, galetas *m*, soupente *f*; grenier *m*; **to live in a g.,** demeurer sous les toits, sous les combles; **g. window,** (fenêtre *f* en) mansarde.

garret[2], *v.tr. Const:* garnir, caler (une assise de pierres).

garreting ['gærətiŋ], *s. Const:* calage *m*.

garrison[1] ['gærisn], *s.* garnison *f*; **to be in g., keep g., in a town,** être en garnison, tenir garnison, dans une ville; *attrib.* **g. duty,** service *m* de place, de garnison; **g. troops,** troupes *f* sédentaires; **g. life,** vie *f* de garnison; **g. artillery,** artillerie *f* de place; **g. soldier,** soldat *m* en garnison; **g. town,** ville *f* de garnison, place *f*; **g. adjutant,** major *m* de garnison; **g. order,** consigne *f* de place; ordre *m* du commandement de la garnison, de la place; **g. ration,** ration *f* du temps de paix, ration d'ordinaire.

garrison[2], *v.tr.* **1. to g. a town,** (i) placer, mettre, une garnison dans une ville; (ii) (*of troops*) être en garnison dans une ville; **to g. a stronghold,** garnir une place de guerre. **2.** mettre (des troupes) en garnison; **troops garrisoned at Lille,** troupes *f* en garnison à Lille.

garrot[1] ['gærət], *s. Med:* garrot *m*, tourniquet *m*.

garrot[2], *s. Orn:* garrot *m*.

gar(r)otte[1] [gə'rɔt], *s.* **1.** garrotte *f*; supplice *m* du garrot. **2.** strangulation *f*; *F:* coup *m* du père François.

gar(r)otte[2], *v.tr.* **(ga(r)rotted) 1.** faire subir le supplice du garrot à (qn); faire périr (qn) par la garrotte; garrotter (qn). **2.** étrangler (qn); *F:* faire le coup du père François à (qn).

gar(r)otter [gə'rɔtər], *s.* **1.** (*in Spain*) le bourreau. **2.** étrangleur *m*.

gar(r)otting [gə'rɔtiŋ], *s.* **1.** garrottage *m*, garrotte *f*; supplice *m* du garrot. **2.** strangulation *f*; *F:* coup *m* du père François.

garrulity [gæ'ru:liti], **garrulousness** ['gæruləsnis], *s.* **1.** loquacité *f*; garrulité *f*. **2.** verbosité *f* (de style).

garrulous ['gæruləs], *a.* **1.** loquace, bavard; **g. old age,** la vieillesse causeuse, conteuse, raconteuse. **2.** (discours, style) verbeux. **3.** *A: & Lit:* (oiseau, ruisseau) babillard.

garrulously ['gæruləsli], *adv.* avec volubilité; verbeusement.

garter[1] ['gɑ:tər], *s.* (*a*) jarretière *f*; **the Order of the G.,** l'Ordre *m* de la Jarretière; **Knight of the G.,** chevalier *m* de l'Ordre de la Jarretière; (*b*) *NAm:* jarretelle *f*; (*for socks*) fixe-chaussettes *mpl*; **g. belt,** porte-jarretelles *m* *inv*; (*c*) **arm g.,** bracelet *m* (pour retenir les manches de chemise); (*d*) *Bot: F:* **lady's garters,** phalaris *m*; (*e*) *Ich:* **g. fish,** lépidope *m*, *F:* jarretière.

garter[2], *v.tr.* jarreter (sa jambe, ses bas); attacher (ses bas) avec (i) des jarretières, (ii) *NAm:* des jarretelles.

garth [gɑːθ], *s.* **1.** *A: & Dial:* clos *m*, courtil *m*. **2.** (**cloister**) **g.,** cour *f*, gazon *m* (entouré par les cloîtres).

gas[1], *pl.* **gases** [gæs, 'gæsiz], *s.* **1.** gaz *m*; (*a*) *Ch: etc:* **natural g.,** gaz naturel; **g. field, deposit of (natural) g.,** gisement *m* de gaz (naturel); **degenerate, non-degenerate, g.,** gaz dégénéré, non-dégénéré; **deleterious g.,** gaz délétère; **foul, poisonous, g.,** gaz toxique, intoxicant; **detonating, electrolytic, g.,** gaz détonant; **occluded g.,** gaz occlus; **ideal, inert, noble, rare, g.,** gaz parfait, inerte, noble, rare; **marsh g.,** gaz des marais, méthane *m*; **sewage g.,** gaz de gadoue; **g. sand,** sable *m* à gaz; **g. spring,** mofette *f*; (*b*) *Ind: etc:* **the g. industry,** l'industrie gazière, du gaz; **g. furnace,** four *m*, fourneau *m*, à gaz; **blast-furnace g.,** gaz de haut-fourneau; **coke-oven g.,** gaz de four à coke; **fuel g.,** gaz combustible; **oil, petroleum, g.,** gaz de pétrole; **residual g.,** gaz résiduel; **producer g.,** gaz pauvre, de gazogène; **g. producer,** gazogène *m*; (appareil) gazifère *m*; **g. generator,** générateur *m* de gaz; gazogène; **g. condenser,** condensateur *m* à gaz; **g. holder, g. tank,** gazomètre *m*; réservoir *m* à gaz; **g. cylinder,** émetteur *m* de gaz; bouteille *f* à gaz; tube *m* de gaz comprimé; **g. liquor,** eau ammoniacale; **g. carbon,** charbon *m* de cornue; **g. cleaner, scrubber,** épurateur *m* de gaz; barboteur *m* à gaz; **g. washer,** laveur *m* de gaz; **g. cleaning,** épuration *f* du gaz; *Metall: I.C.E:* **burnt g., exhaust g., escape g.,** gaz d'échappement (de haut-fourneau, de moteur, etc.); **exhaust-g. engine,** moteur à gaz (de haut-fourneau); *Mec.E:* **g. turbine,** turbine *f* à gaz; *Metalw:* **g. cutting,** oxycoupage *m*, découpage *m* au chalumeau; **g. welding,** soudure *f* oxyacétylénique, au gaz; (*c*) *Dom.Ec: etc:* **lighting g.,** gaz d'éclairage; (**town**) **g.,** gaz de ville; **there's no g. laid on in this village,** ce village n'a pas le gaz de ville; **g. main, g. pipe,** tuyau *m* à gaz; conduite *f* de, du, gaz; **to lay g. mains in a street,** canaliser une rue pour le gaz; poser la canalisation du gaz dans une rue; **g. burner,** bec *m* de gaz; **g. mantle,** manchon *m* (de bec de gaz à incandescence); **g. bracket,** applique *f* à gaz; (*in street*) **g. lamp,** réverbère *m*; bec de gaz; **to cook by g.,** faire la cuisine au gaz; **to turn on, off, the g.,** ouvrir, fermer, le gaz; **to turn up, down, the g.,** lever, baisser, le gaz; **g. cooker, g. stove,** cuisinière *f* à gaz; **g. oven,** four *m* à gaz; *F:* **to put one's head in the g. oven,** s'asphyxier, se suicider, au gaz; **g. ring,** (i) réchaud *m* à gaz (à un feu); (ii) brûleur *m* à couronne; (iii) *I.C.E:* segment *m* d'étanchéité; **g. fire,** radiateur *m* à gaz; **g. lighter,** (i) allume-gaz *m inv*; (ii) briquet *m* (à gaz); **g. fitter,** gazier *m*; poseur *m*, ajusteur *m*, d'appareils à gaz; **g. fitting,** pose *f* des appareils à gaz; **g. fittings,** appareillage *m* pour le gaz; (*d*) *Elcs:* **electron g.,** gaz électronique; **g. discharge,** décharge gazeuse; **g.-discharge tube, lamp,** tube *m*, lampe *f*, à décharge (gazeuse); (*e*) *Med:* (i) **g. bacillus,** vibrion *m* septique; (ii) *F:* **to feel, be, full of g.,** avoir des gaz; (iii) *A:* **laughing g.,** gaz hilarant; *Dent: F:* **to have g.,** se faire anesthésier (pour l'extraction d'une dent); (*f*) *Mil: etc:* gaz de combat; **g. warfare,** guerre chimique, guerre des gaz; **tear g.,** gaz lacrymogène; **mustard g.,** ypérite *f*; **asphyxiating g.,** *F:* **poison g.,** gaz asphyxiant, gaz toxique; **lethal g.,** gaz mortel, toxique; **persistent, non-persistent, g.,** gaz persistant, fugace; **g. with delayed effect,** gaz insidieux; **blister g.,** gaz vésicant; **choking g., lung-irritant g.,** gaz suffocant; **irritant g.,** gaz irritant, gaz toxique spécialisé; **sneeze g., nose-irritant g.,** gaz sternutatoire; **g. bomb,** bombe asphyxiante, à gaz; **g. chamber,** chambre *f* à gaz; **g.-chamber exercise, test,** passage *m* à la chambre à gaz; *A:* **g. shell,** obus asphyxiant, toxique; obus à gaz (de combat); **g. shelter,** abri-filtre *m*, *pl.* abris-filtres; **g. sentry, g. officer,** éclaireur *m*, officier *m*, Z; **g. alarm, g. attack warning,** alerte *f* aux gaz; **g. attack,** attaque *f* par gaz; **g. clear,** fin *f* d'alerte (aux gaz); **g. discipline,** consignes *f* relatives aux gaz; **to release g.,** lâcher, lancer, projeter, des gaz (asphyxiants); **defence against g.,** défense *f* contre les gaz; **g. equipment,** matériel *m* antigaz, matériel de protection contre les gaz; **g. cape,** cape *f* antigaz; **g. curtain,** rideau *m* antigaz, rideau de protection contre les gaz; **g. freeing,** dégazage *m*; (*for oil tanker*) **g.-freeing certificate,** certificat *m* de dégazage; (*g*) *Min:* (**pit**) **g.,** grisou *m*; **g. detector,** détecteur *m*, indicateur *m*, de grisou; grisoumètre *m*. **2.** *F:* (*a*) *NAm:* essence *f*; **to fill up with g.,** faire le plein d'essence; (*b*) **to step on the g.,** marcher à plein gaz. **3.** *F:* bavardage *m*; verbiage *m*. **4.** *Bot: F:* **g. plant,** fraxinelle *f*.

gas[2], *v.* (**gassed**) **1.** *v.tr.* (*a*) *Ch: Ind:* passer (un produit) au gaz; *Tex:* gazer, flamber (la toile); (*b*) asphyxier, intoxiquer (par un gaz); *Mil:* gazer; **to g. oneself,** s'asphyxier; **gassed,** atteint par les gaz asphyxiants; gazé; **to be fatally gassed,** (i) succomber à une intoxication par le gaz; (ii) *Mil:* être gazé; (*c*) *U.S: P:* embobiner (qn) à force de belles paroles. **2.** *v.i.* (*a*) (*of liquid, accumulator, etc.*) dégager des gaz; gazer; (*of accumulator*) bouillonner; (*b*) *F:* jaser, bavarder; pérorer; se vanter.

gasbag ['gæsbæg], *s.* **1.** (*a*) ballon *m* à gaz (pour oxygène, etc.); (*b*) *F:* grand parleur; bavard, -arde; vantard *m*. **2.** *Aer:* (*a*) enveloppe *f* (à gaz); (*b*) (*also* **gas cell**) ballonnet *m* (de dirigeable, etc.).

Gascon ['gæskən]. *Geog:* (*a*) *a.* gascon; (*b*) *s.* Gascon, -onne.

gasconade[1] [gæskə'neid], *s.* gasconnade *f*.

gasconade[2], *v.i.* se vanter comme un Gascon; raconter des gasconnades; gasconner.

Gascony ['gæskəni], *Pr.n. Geog:* la Gascogne.

gaselier [gæsə'liər], *s. A:* lustre *m* (à gaz); suspension *f* à gaz.

gaseous ['gæsiəs, 'geisiəs], *a.* gazeux; **g. exchanges,** échanges gazeux; **g. conduction,** conductibilité dans les gaz.

gas-filled ['gæsfild], *a. El:* (lampe) gazeuse, à atmosphère gazeuse; **g.-f. rectifier,** (i) soupape *f* ionique, soupape à gaz; (ii) tube redresseur à gaz; **g.-f. relay, g.-f. triode,** triode *f* à gaz.

gash[1] [gæʃ], *s.* **1.** coupure *f*, entaille *f* (faite dans la chair); estafilade *f*, taillade *f*; (*on face*) balafre *f*; (*caused by horns or tusks of animal*) décousure *f*. **2.** coup *m* de couteau, de sabre. **3.** *a. & s. P:* (en) rabiot *m*.

gash[2], *v.tr.* entailler, couper; balafrer (le visage); **to g. one's chin, one's cheek,** se faire une entaille, une estafilade, au menton, à la joue; *F:* se charcuter le menton; s'écharper la joue; **his forehead was gashed with a deep cut,** une profonde entaille lui ouvrait le front.

gasholder ['gæshouldər], *s.* réservoir *m* à gaz.

gasifiable ['gæsifaiəbl], *a.* gazéifiable.

gasification [gæsifi'keiʃ(ə)n], *s.* gazéification *f*.

gasifier ['gæsifaiər], *s.* générateur *m* à gaz.

gasiform ['gæsifɔːm], *a.* gazéiforme.

gasify ['gæsifai]. **1.** *v.tr.* gazéifier. **2.** *v.i.* se gazéifier.

gasket ['gæskit], *s.* **1.** *Nau:* garcette *f*, jarretière *f*, ruban *m* (de ris, de ferlage); sangle *f*. **2.** *Mec.E:* joint *m* d'étanchéité; garniture *f* (de joint); **rubber g.,** joint caoutchouté, garniture en caoutchouc; **packing g.,** baderne *f*; joint de presse-étoupe; tresse de garniture; **copper-asbestos g.,** joint métalloplastique; *I.C.E:* **cylinder-head g.,** joint de culasse; *Elcs:* **wave-guide g.,** joint de guide d'ondes; **g. leakage,** fuite *f*, perte *f*, au(x) joint(s).

gaslight ['gæslait], *s.* lumière *f* du gaz; **to work by g.,** travailler au gaz, à la lumière du gaz; *A.Phot:* **g. paper,** papier *m* au gélatino-chlorure (d'argent); papier pour épreuves à la lumière.

gasman, *pl.* **-men** ['gæsmæn, -men], *s.m. F:* (*a*) gazier; (*b*) contrôleur, employé, du gaz.

gasmask ['gæsmɑːsk], *s.* masque *m* à gaz, antigaz; appareil *m* respiratoire; **g. with oxygen container,** appareil isolant; **filter-type g.,** appareil filtrant; **diaphragm g.,** appareil permettant la conversation.

gasmeter ['gæsmiːtər], *s.* compteur *m* (à gaz).

gasogene ['gæsədʒiːn], *s.* gazogène *m* (pour eaux gazeuses de table); seltzogène *m*; **g. powder,** carbogène *m*.

gas-oil ['gæsɔil], *s.* gas-oil *m*, gaz-oil *m*.

gasolene, gasoline ['gæsəliːn], *s.* (*a*) gazoline *f*; (*b*) *Aut: NAm:* essence *f*.

gasolier [gæsə'liər], *s. A:* = GASELIER.

gasometer [gæ'sɔmitər], *s.* gazomètre *m*; réservoir *m* à gaz.

gasometry [gæ'sɔmitri], *s.* gazométrie *f*.

gasoscope ['gæsouskoup], *s. Min:* gazoscope *m*.

gasp[1] [gɑːsp], *s.* hoquet *m*, sursaut *m* (de surprise, de terreur, etc.); **he gave a g. on hearing a knock,** il sursauta en entendant frapper; **to breathe in painful gasps,** respirer par secousses pénibles; haleter; **her voice came in hoarse gasps,** sa voix n'était qu'un râle; **to be at one's last g.,** agoniser; être à l'agonie, à la dernière extrémité, sur le point d'expirer; n'avoir plus que le souffle; **to defend sth. to the last g.,** défendre qch. jusqu'à son dernier souffle; **to give one's last g.,** rendre le dernier soupir.

gasp[2], *v.i. & tr.* (*a*) avoir un hoquet (de surprise, etc.); **to g. with fright, with astonishment,** sursauter; **to make s.o. g.,** couper la respiration, le souffle, à qn; **the news made me g.,** cette nouvelle m'a coupé le souffle, *F:* m'a estomaqué; **to g. out sth.,** dire qch. d'une voix entrecoupée; (*b*) **to g. for breath, for air,** haleter, suffoquer; **the gassed men were gasping their lives out,** les asphyxiés râlaient; *F:* **I'm gasping for a drink,** je meurs de soif.

gasper ['gɑːspər], *s. P: O:* cigarette *f*, sèche *f*.

gasping ['gɑːspiŋ], *s.* halètement *m*; respiration pénible, entrecoupée, saccadée.

gas-producing ['gæsprə'djuːsiŋ], *a.* gazogène.

gasproof ['gæspruːf], *a. Mil:* (abri *m*, etc.) à l'épreuve des gaz.

gassing ['gæsiŋ], *s.* **1.** (*a*) *Ch: Ind:* passage *m* au gaz; (*b*) asphyxie *f*, intoxication *f*, (i) par les gaz de combat, (ii) par le gaz d'éclairage. **2.** (*a*) dégagement gazeux; bouillonnement *m* (d'un accumulateur); (*b*) *F:* verbiage *m*; bavardage *m*, jaserie *f*.

gassy ['gæsi], *a.* **1.** (*a*) gazeux; (*of wine*) mousseux, crémant; (*b*) *Min:* grisouteux. **2.** *F:* verbeux, bavard.

gasteria [gæs'tiəriə], *s. Bot:* gastéria *m*.

Gasteromycetae, Gasteromycetes ['gæstəroumai'siːtiː, -mai'siːtiːz], *s.pl. Fung:* gastéromycètes *f*.

Gasterophilidae ['gæstərou'filidiː], *s.pl. Ent:* gastérophiles *m*, les œstres *m*.

gasteropod ['gæstərəpɔd], *a. & s. Moll:* gastéropode (*m*).

Gasteropoda [gæstə'rɔpədə], *s.pl. Moll:* gastéropodes *m*.

gasteropodous [gæstə'rɔpədəs], *a. Moll:* gastéropode.

Gasterosteidae ['gæstərou'stiːidiː], *s.pl. Ich:* gastérostéidés *m*.

gas-tight ['gæstait], *a.* étanche, imperméable, au gaz.

gastralgia [gæs'trældʒiə], *s. Med:* gastralgie *f*, gastrodynie *f*.

gastralgic [gæs'trældʒik], *a. Med:* gastralgique.

gastrectomy [gæs'trektəmi], *s. Surg:* gastrectomie *f*.

gastric ['gæstrik], *a.* gastrique; **g. juice,** suc *m* gastrique; **g. gland,** glande *f* gastrique; **g. contents,** contenu *m* de l'estomac; bol *m* alimentaire; **g. troubles,** embarras *m* gastrique; **g. ulcer,** ulcère *m* simple de l'estomac; gastrite ulcéreuse; **g. influenza,** grippe gastro-intestinale.

gastrin ['gæstrin], *s. Physiol:* gastrine *f*.

gastritis [gæs'traitis], *s. Med:* gastrite *f*.

gastro- ['gæstrou], *comb.fm.* gastro-.

gastrochaena [gæstrou'kiːnə], *s. Moll:* gastrochaena *m*.

gastrocnemius, *pl.* **-ii** ['gæstrou'niːmiəs, -iai], *s. Anat:* gastrocnémien *m*.

gastrocele ['gæstrousiːl], *s. Med:* gastrocèle *f*, hernie *f* de l'estomac.

gastrocolic [gæstrou'kɔlik], *a.* gastro-colique.

gastrocolitis [gæstroukə'laitis], *s. Med:* gastro-colite *f*.

gastroduodenal ['gæstroudjuou'diːnl], *a. Med:* gastro-duodénal, -aux.

gastroduodenitis ['gæstroudjuoudi'naitis], *s. Med:* gastro-duodénite *f*.

gastroduodenostomy ['gæstroudjuoudi'nɔstəmi], *s. Surg:* gastro-duodénostomie *f*.

gastrodynia [gæstrou'dainiə], *s. Med:* gastrodynie *f*.

gastro-enteric ['gæstrouen'terik], *a. Med:* gastro-entérique, *pl.* gastro-entériques.

gastro-enteritis ['gæstrouentə'raitis], *s. Med:* gastro-entérite *f*; *Vet:* **feline g.-e.,** typhus *m* du chat.

gastro-enterocolitis ['gæstrou'entəroukə'laitis], *s. Med:* gastro-enterocolite *f*.

gastro(-)enterologist ['gæstrouentə'rɔlədʒist], *s. Med:* gastro-entérologue *m*.

gastro(-)enterology ['gæstrouentə'rɔlədʒi], *s. Med:* gastro-entérologie *f*.

gastro(-)enteroptosis ['gæstrouentərɔp'tousis], *s. Med:* gastro-entéroptôse *f*.

gastro(-)enterostomy ['gæstrouentə'rɔstəmi], *s. Surg:* gastro-entérostomie *f*.

gastro(-)epiploic ['gæstrouepip'loik], *a. Anat:* gastro-épiploïque.

gastro(-)hepatitis ['gæstrouhepə'taitis], *s. Med:* gastro-hépatite *f*.

gastro(-)intestinal ['gæstrouin'testinl, -tes'tainl], *a. Med:* gastro-intestinal, -aux.

gastro(-)jejunal ['gæstroudʒi'dʒuːnl], *a. Anat:* gastro-jéjunal, -aux.

gastro(-)jejunostomy ['gæstroudʒidʒu'nɔtəmi], *s. Surg:* gastro-jéjunostomie *f*.

gastrolith ['gæstrəliθ], *s.* **1.** *Crust:* gastrolithe *m*. **2.** *Med:* calcul *m* gastrique.

gastrological [gæstrə'lɔdʒikl], *a.* gastrologique.

gastrology [gæs'trɔlədʒi], *s.* gastrologie *f*.

gastrolysis [gæs'trɔlisis], *s. Surg:* gastrolyse *f*.

Gastromycetes [gæstroumai'siːtiːz], *s. etc:* = GASTEROMYCETES.

gastronome ['gæstrənoum], **gastronomer** [gæs'trɔnəmər], **gastronomist** [gæs'trɔnəmist], *s.* gastronome *m*.

gastronomic(al) [gæstrə'nɔmik(l)], *a.* gastronomique.

gastronomy [gæs'trɔnəmi], *s.* gastronomie *f*.

gastropexy ['gæstroupeksi], *s. Surg:* gastropexie *f*.

gastropod ['gæstroupɔd], *s. etc:* = GASTEROPOD.
gastroptosis [gæstrɔp'tousis], *s. Med:* gastroptôse *f.*
gastrorrhagia [gæstrou'reidʒiə], *s. Med:* gastrorragie *f.*
gastrorrhea [gæstrou'ri:ə], *s. Med:* gastrorrhée *f.*
gastroscope ['gæstrouskoup], *s. Med:* gastroscope *m.*
gastroscopy ['gæstrəskoupi], *s. Med:* gastroscopie *f.*
gastrospasm ['gæstrouspæzm], *s.* gastrospasme *m.*
gastrostomy [gæs'trɔstəmi], *s. Surg:* gastrostomie *f.*
gastrotomy [gæs'trɔtəmi], *s. Surg:* gastrotomie *f.*
Gastrotricha [gæs'trɔtrikə], *s.pl. Ann:* gastrotriches *m.*
gastro(-)vascular ['gæstrou'væskjulər], *a. Anat:* gastro-vasculaire, *pl.* gastro-vasculaires.
gastrula ['gæstrulə], *s. Biol:* gastrula *f.*
gastrulation [gæstru'leiʃ(ə)n], *s. Biol:* gastrulation *f.*
gasworks ['gæswə:ks], *s.pl.* (*usu. with sg.const.*) usine *f* à gaz.
gat[1] [gæt], *s.* **1.** chenal *m*, -aux; détroit *m*; *Nau:* passe *f* (entre bancs de sable). **2.** (dans le Kent) échancrure *f* (des falaises).
gat[2], *s. P:* revolver *m*, calibre *m.*
gate[1] [geit], *s.* **1.** (*a*) porte *f* (d'une ville, d'un château fort, etc.); **the gate(s) of heaven, of hell,** les portes du paradis, de l'enfer; *Myth:* **the ivory g.,** la porte d'ivoire; *Fort:* **second g.,** contre-porte *f*; **the g. to the Continent, to the East,** la porte du Continent, de l'Orient; *Sch: O:* (*esp. Oxford, Cambridge*) **to break gates,** ne pas être rentré à l'heure prescrite; découcher; **g. fine,** amende *f* pour rentrée tardive; *NAm: P:* **to give s.o. the g.,** congédier qn; **to get the g.,** être congédié, renvoyé, mis à la porte; (*b*) *Geog:* pas *m* (de montagne); chenal (encaissé); passe *f*; **the Iron Gates,** les Portes de Fer (du Danube); (*c*) (*giving admission to exhibition, sports meeting, etc.*) entrée *f*; **to pay at the g.,** payer à l'entrée; *Sp:* **g. meeting,** réunion sportive à entrée payante; **the g.,** (i) le public (à un match); (ii) (*also* **g. money**) la recette; les entrées. **2.** (*a*) barrière *f*, porte à claire-voie; (*iron, etc.*) grille *f* (d'entrée); **five-barred g.,** barrière à cinq planches; **swing g.,** barrière battante, tournante, pivotante; **sliding g.,** barrière roulante; **sliding lattice g.,** fermeture *f* à grille extensible; **level-crossing,** *NAm:* **grade-crossing, g.,** barrière du passage à niveau; **toll g.,** (barrière de) péage *m*; (*b*) *Rac:* **starting g.,** barrière; (*c*) *Ski:* porte. **3.** (*a*) *Hyd.E:* **(lock) g.,** vanne *f* (d'écluse), porte d'écluse; **bottom g., undersluice g.,** vanne de fond; **crown g., head g.,** porte d'amont (d'écluse); **crest g.,** vanne de retenue; **turbine g.,** vanne de turbine; **water-wheel g.,** vanne lancière; **g. valve,** robinet-vanne *m, pl.* robinets-vannes; **g. gear,** dispositif *m*, mécanisme *m*, de vannage; (*b*) *Metall: Min:* **air g.,** porte d'aérage. **4.** *Aut:* **g. (quadrant),** grille (de changement de vitesse); **visible g.,** secteur *m* à grille; **g. change-speed lever,** changement *m* de vitesse à grille. **5.** *Cin:* **film g. (of projector),** (i) fenêtre *f* de projection; (ii) porte de la fenêtre. **6.** *Tls:* châssis *m*, cadre *m* (d'une scie); **g. saw,** scie *f* à châssis, à cadre. **7.** (*a*) *Telecom:* absorbeur *m*; (*b*) *Elcs:* (i) déclencheur *m* d'entrée périodique; gâchette *f*, grille *f*, gate *f*; (ii) circuit *m* à déclenchement périodique; **g. tube,** tube *m* à seuil; *Cmptr:* **AND g.,** circuit ET; **OR g.,** mélangeur *m*, circuit OU.
gate[2], *v.tr.* **1.** *Sch:* consigner (un étudiant); **to be gated,** se faire consigner. **2.** *Hyd.E:* vanner (une écluse, une turbine). **3.** *Elcs:* déclencher périodiquement; **gated amplifier,** amplificateur *m* à déclenchement périodique.
gate[3], *s. Metall:* (*a*) **g. (channel),** trou *m*, jet *m*, de coulée; échenal *m*; (*b*) coulée (attenante à la pièce).
gate[4], *s.* **1.** *Scot:* chemin *m*; **to take the g.,** se mettre en route; **to let s.o. gang his own g.,** laisser qn se débrouiller. **2.** *Min:* galerie *f*; **mother g.,** galerie principale; **inclined mother g.,** vallée *f*; **wind g.,** voie *f* d'aérage. **3.** *Hyd.E:* **way g.,** canal *m* (*pl.* -aux) de décharge, de fuite.
gâteau ['gætou], *s.* gros gâteau à la crème.
gatecrash ['geitkræʃ], *v.tr. & i. F:* resquiller; faire l'intrus.
gatecrasher ['geitkræʃər], *s. F:* resquilleur, -euse; passe-volant *m, pl.* passe-volants; intrus, -use; *Th:* hirondelle *f.*
gatecrashing ['geitkræʃiŋ], *s. F:* resquillage *m.*
gatehouse ['geithaus], *s.* **1.** loge *f* de garde (à l'entrée d'un parc). **2.** (*a*) corps-de-garde *m inv* (d'un château fort, d'une porte de ville); (*b*) cachot *m* du corps-de-garde.
gatekeeper ['geitki:pər], *s.* **1.** portier, -ière. **2.** *Rail:* garde-barrière *mf, pl.* gardes-barrière(s).
gatelegged ['geitlegd], *a.* (table) à abattants.
gatepost ['geitpoust], *s.* montant *m* (de barrière, de porte).
gate(s)man, *pl.* **-men** ['geit(s)mən], *s.m. Rail: etc:* garde-barrière, *pl.* gardes-barrière(s).
gateway ['geitwei], *s.* **1.** porte *f*, entrée *f*, passage *m*; *A:* **carriage g.,** porte cochère; porte charretière; **the g. to the East, to the Continent,** la porte de l'Orient, du Continent. **2.** porte monumentale; voûte *f* d'entrée; portail *m.*
Gath [gæθ], *Pr.n. B:* Gath; **tell it not in G.,** ne l'annoncez point dans Gath; n'allez pas crier cela sur les toits; n'allez pas le répéter au premier venu.
gather ['gæðər], *v.*
I. *v.tr.* **1.** (*a*) assembler, rassembler (des personnes); rassembler, recueillir (des choses); **to g. one's friends together,** rassembler ses amis; **to g. troops, etc., together,** amasser des troupes, etc.; **to g. what remains of an army,** recueillir les restes d'une armée; **to g. one's thoughts,** se recueillir; **to g. all one's strength (in order) to . . .,** recueillir, rassembler, ramasser, toutes ses forces pour . . .; *Lit:* **to be gathered to one's fathers,** être recueilli auprès de ses pères; aller rejoindre ses ancêtres; *Nau:* **to g. the boats,** bâcler les bateaux; (*b*) ramasser; **to g. up the cards, the dominoes,** ramasser les cartes, les dominos; **to g. up the crumbs,** recueillir les miettes; **he gathered up, together, his papers and left,** ayant ramassé ses papiers il est parti; **to g. (up) one's hair into a knot,** tordre ses cheveux en chignon; **to g. up one's skirts,** retrousser ses jupes; *Bookb:* **to g. the pages of a book,** rassembler les feuilles d'un livre; *Glassm:* **to g. the glass,** cueillir le verre; *Rugby Fb:* **to g. the ball,** cueillir le ballon; (*c*) cueillir (des fleurs); recueillir (du blé); **to g. (in) the crops, the harvest,** rentrer la récolte, la moisson; récolter le blé; **to g. strawberries, etc.,** faire la cueillette des fraises, etc.; **to g. sticks (for firewood),** ramasser du bois; (*of bees*) **to g. honey from the flowers,** butiner les fleurs; **to g. taxes, rents, etc.,** percevoir les contributions, les loyers; **to g. information,** recueillir des renseignements; (*d*) **to g. (oneself) together for a spring,** se ramasser, ramasser son corps, se replier sur soi-même, pour sauter; **tiger gathered for a spring,** tigre ramassé, accroupi, avant de sauter; **to g. (up) one's legs under one,** se ramasser (sur soi-même); (*e*) *Equit:* **to g. a horse,** rassembler, avertir, un cheval; (*f*) *Cmptr:* rassembler, (re)grouper; **to g. write,** écrire en regroupant. **2.** **to g. speed,** acquérir, prendre, de la vitesse; (*of pers.*) **to g. strength,** reprendre des forces; **to g. volume,** croître en volume; **to g. one's breath,** reprendre haleine; **to g. rust,** s'enrouiller; **to g. dirt,** s'encrasser. **3.** (*a*) serrer; **to g. the blankets round one,** se serrer dans les couvertures; **he gathered her (up) in his arms,** il l'a serrée dans ses bras; (*b*) *Needlew:* **to g. a skirt, etc.,** froncer une jupe, etc. **4.** conclure; **I g. from the papers that he has . . .,** à en croire les journaux il aurait . . .; **so far as I can g.,** à ce que je comprends; à ce que j'ai cru comprendre; **I can't g. what he's talking about,** je ne puis rien démêler, je ne comprends rien, à ce qu'il dit; **as will be gathered from the enclosed letter,** comme il ressort de la lettre ci-jointe; **I g. from the evidence that . . .,** j'infère, je déduis, de ces témoignages que . . .
II. *v.i.* **1.** (*of pers.*) (*a*) se réunir, s'assembler, se rassembler; **to g. round the fire, round s.o.,** se grouper autour du feu; se rassembler autour de qn; **gather round!** approchez-vous! faites cercle! (*b*) affluer, s'attrouper (en foule); **a crowd gathered,** une foule se forma, il se forma un (grand) attroupement; **to g. in groups in the streets,** former des groupes dans les rues. **2.** (*of thgs*) s'accumuler, s'amonceler, s'amasser; (*a*) **the boats are gathered together in a corner of the harbour,** les bateaux se tassent dans un coin du port; **the clouds are gathering,** les nuages s'amoncellent, s'amassent, se forment; **a storm is gathering,** un orage se prépare; **tears gathered in her eyes,** ses yeux se mouillèrent; ses yeux se remplirent de larmes; (*b*) **the river, the news, gathers on its way,** la rivière, la nouvelle, grossit en chemin; **in the gathering darkness,** dans la nuit grandissante; **with gathering force,** avec une force croissante; **the story gathered like a snowball,** l'histoire faisait boule de neige. **3.** *Med:* (*of wound*) abcéder; (*of abscess*) **to g. to a head,** aboutir, mûrir; **the pus gathers,** le pus se collecte; **to have a gathered finger,** avoir un abcès, *F:* un bobo, au doigt.
gathered ['gæðəd], *a.* (*a*) (front) sourcilleux; (*b*) *Needlew:* (volant, etc.) froncé, à fronces; (*c*) *Bookb:* **g. sheets,** feuilles assemblées.
gatherer ['gæðərər], *s.* **1.** (*pers.*) (*a*) (r)amasseur, -euse; *Bookb:* assembleur, -euse (de feuilles); *Glassm:* cueilleur *m* (de verre); (*b*) cueilleur, -euse (de fruits, etc.); *A:* **tax g.,** percepteur *m* des contributions. **2.** (*device*) (*a*) (*for fruit*) cueilloir *m*; (*for flowers*) cueille-fleurs *m inv*; (*b*) fronceur *m* (d'une machine à coudre).
gathering ['gæð(ə)riŋ], *s.* **1.** (*a*) rassemblement *m*, attroupement *m*, ameutement *m* (d'une foule); conciliabule *m*, rassemblement (des hirondelles); **g. cry,** cri *m* de ralliement; (*b*) accumulation *f* (de choses); *Nau:* bâclage *m* (de bateaux dans un port); *Bookb:* assemblage *m* (des feuilles); (*c*) cueillette *f* (des fruits, etc.); **g. (in) of the crop,** (rentrage *m* de la) récolte *f*; (*d*) **g. of speed,** gain *m*, augmentation *f*, de vitesse; **g. of strength,** reprise *f* de forces; (*e*) froncement *m* (des sourcils); *Needlew:* fronçure *f* (d'une robe, etc.); (*f*) accumulation *f*, amoncellement *m* (de nuages); (*g*) *Med:* collection *f* (du pus); abcédation *f*; (*h*) *Cmptr:* rassemblement, (re)groupement *m*, groupage *m*; **data g.,** collecte *f*, rassemblement, de données. **2.** (*a*) assemblée *f*, réunion *f*, compagnie *f* (dans une salle); assemblage, rassemblement, attroupement (dans les rues); amas *m* (de personnes); **family g.,** assemblée, réunion, de famille; **friendly g.,** réunion d'amis; **industrial g.,** comice industriel; **we were a large g.,** nous étions nombreux; (*b*) *Needlew:* froncis *m*, fronces *fpl*; (*c*) *Med:* abcès *m*; (*d*) *Bookb:* cahier *m.*
gathers ['gæðəz], *s.pl. Needlew:* fronces *f*, fronçures *f*, froncis *m sg*; **to take out, undo, the g. (of a skirt, etc.),** défroncer (une jupe, etc.).
gating ['geitiŋ], *s.* **1.** *Sch:* consigne *f*; privation *f* de sortie. **2.** *Hyd.E:* vannage *m.* **3.** *Elcs:* déclenchement *m* périodique, cyclique; **g. switch,** interrupteur *m* périodique, cyclique; **g. pulse,** impulsion sélectrice, de déclenchement.
Gatling ['gætliŋ], *Pr.n. Mil:* **G. (gun),** mitrailleuse *f* Gatling.
gauche [gouʃ], *a.* gauche, maladroit.
gauchely ['gouʃli], *adv.* gauchement, maladroitement.
gaucheness ['gouʃnis], *s.* gaucherie *f*, maladresse *f.*
gaucherie ['gouʃəri], *s.* gaucherie *f*, maladresse *f.*
gaucho ['gautʃou], *s.* gaucho *m.*
gaud [gɔ:d], *s. A: & Lit:* **1.** (*a*) ornement criard; parure *f* de mauvais goût; (*b*) babiole *f.* **2.** *pl.* **gauds,** pompes *f*, fastes *m.*
gaudery ['gɔ:dəri], *s. O:* oripeaux *mpl*, clinquant *m*, *F:* tape-à-l'œil *m.*
gaudete [gɔ:'deite], *attrib. R.C.Ch:* **G. Sunday,** le troisième dimanche de l'avent.
gaudily ['gɔ:dili], *adv.* d'une manière voyante; avec du clinquant; fastueusement; (peint, etc.) en couleurs criardes.
gaudiness ['gɔ:dinis], *s.* éclat criard (d'une couleur); ostentation *f*; clinquant *m*; *F:* tape-à-l'œil *m* (d'un étalage, etc.).
gaudy[1] ['gɔ:di], *s. Sch:* banquet *m* anniversaire des anciens étudiants (d'un collège d'université).
gaudy[2], *a.* (*of colours, etc.*) voyant, criard, éclatant; (*of crowd*) panaché; (*of display, etc.*) fastueux, de mauvais goût.
gauffer[1,2] ['goufər, 'gɔfər], *s. v.tr.* = GOFFER[1,2].
gauge[1] [geidʒ], *s.* **1.** (*a*) calibre *m* (d'un écrou, d'un fusil de chasse, etc.); jauge *f* (d'une futaille, etc.); **8-g. gun,** fusil calibre 8; **fine g., heavy g., stockings,** bas *m* de jauge fine, de grosse jauge; (*b*) *Veh:* voie *f*, espacement *m* (des roues); *Rail:* écartement *m*, largeur *f* (de la voie); entre-rail *m, pl.* entre-rails; **standard-g., normal-g., track,** voie normale; **narrow-g., broad-g., track,** voie étroite; voie large, à grand écartement; **increase, slacking, of g.,** surécartement *m* (de la voie); **narrowing, tightening, of g.,** resserrement *m* (de la voie); (*c*) *Stonew:* **g. saw,** sciotte *f*; (*d*) *Cin:* **frame g.,** pas *m* de l'image; **perforation g.,** pas de la perforation; **standard g.,** pas normal; format *m* standard; (*e*) *Const:* pureau *m* (d'une tuile, d'une ardoise). **2.** (*a*) *Tchn:* (appareil *m*) vérificateur *m*; calibre, jauge (pour mesurer qch.); **master g.,** calibre mère; **reference g., standard g.,** calibre de référence; calibre, jauge, étalon; gabarit *m*; **adjustable g.,** calibre réglable; **limit g., clearance g.,** calibre de tolérance, à limite; **go g.,** jauge, calibre, entre; **no-go g.,** jauge, calibre, n'entre pas; **feeler g.,** calibre à lames, d'épaisseur; **thickness g.,** calibre, jauge, cale *f*, d'épaisseur; **depth g.,** calibre de profondeur; **ring g.,** (i) baguier *m*; (ii) jauge annulaire; **plug g.,** calibre à bouchon; **dial g.,** calibre a cadran; **strain g.,** jauge de contrainte, tensiomètre *m*, extensomètre *m*; **cylindrical g.,** cylindre, tampon, vérificateur; tampon-calibre *m, pl.* tampons-calibres; tampon-jauge *m, pl.* tampons-jauges; **cal(l)iper g.,** jauge à coulisse; calibre mâchoire, de précision; **female cal(l)iper g.,** calibre femelle; **slide, sliding, g.,** calibre coulant, à courseur; pied *m*, compas *m*, à coulisse; **plate g.,** calibre pour tôles (épaisses); **sheet(-metal) g.,** calibre pour tôles (minces); **screw(-pitch) g.,** calibre, jauge, de pas; calibre à, pour, vis; **thread g.,** calibre, jauge, de filetage; **wire g.,** calibre, jauge, à fil(s), pour fils métalliques; **English standard wire g., Birmingham g.,** jauge anglaise standard, jauge de Birmingham; **American wire g., Brown and Sharpe g.,** jauge américaine, jauge Brown et Sharpe; **French wire g.,** jauge de Paris; *Rail:* **rail g., track g., g. template,**

gabarit d'écartement (des voies); **track-laying g.,** gabarit (de pose) de voie; **loading g., tunnel g.,** gabarit de chargement; **curve g.,** gabarit de courbe; **wear and tear g.,** gabarit d'usure des rails; *Aut: Av: etc:* **assembling g.,** montage *m*; gabarit d'assemblage; *Typ:* **line g.,** typomètre *m*; *Typewr:* **line-space g.,** pointeau *m* d'interligne; *Surv: etc:* **angle g.,** goniomètre *m*; **wheelwright's g.,** cintre *m* de charron; (*b*) *Carp:* **(marking, shifting) g.,** trusquin *m*; (*on timber*) **g. mark, notch,** coche *f*; *Mec.E:* **surface g.,** trusquin à marbre; **drilling g.,** gabarit de perçage; **g. lathe,** tour *m* à gabarit. **3.** indicateur *m*, contrôleur *m*; (*a*) *Ph: etc:* **vacuum g.,** indicateur, jauge, du vide; vacuomètre *m*; **acetylene g.,** manomètre *m* à acétylène; **ionization g.,** jauge thermionique, à ionisation; **beta-absorption g.,** jauge bêta; *Metall:* **draught g., blast g.,** indicateur du tirage; manomètre de vent; (*b*) *Mch: etc:* **water g., oil g.,** (indicateur de) niveau *m* d'eau, d'huile; **pressure g.,** manomètre *m*; jauge de pression; **oil-pressure g.,** manomètre de pression d'huile; **g. glass,** tube *m* de niveau; indicateur du niveau (d'eau, etc.); **g. cock,** robinet *m* de jauge, de hauteur d'eau; **flow g.,** jaugeur *m*, indicateur, de débit; *Aut:* **petrol g., fuel g.,** jauge à essence; **tyre g.,** manomètre (pour pneus); contrôleur, vérificateur, de pression (pour pneus). **4.** *Const: etc:* dose *f*, proportion *f* (de ciment dans le béton, etc.). **5.** *Nau:* (*a*) tirant *m* d'eau (d'un navire); (*b*) **weather g.,** avantage *m* du vent; dessus *m* du vent; **to have the weather g. of a ship,** être au vent d'un navire, avoir l'avantage du vent sur un navire; **lee g.,** désavantage *m* du vent; dessous *m* du vent; **to have the lee g. of a ship,** être sous le vent d'un navire.

gauge[2], *v.tr.* **1.** calibrer, étalonner (un écrou, etc.); jauger, mesurer (le vent, etc.); jauger, velter (un tonneau); compasser (le canon d'une arme à feu, etc.); gabarier, standardiser (une pièce); **to g. sth. by the eye,** mesurer qch. à l'œil, à la vue; (*of car driver, etc.*) **to g. the clearance,** apprécier l'espace libre; **to g. s.o.'s capacities,** estimer, jauger, les capacités de qn; **to g. events, the future,** prévoir les événements, l'avenir. **2.** (*a*) *Carp:* trusquiner (le bois); (*b*) tailler (des briques) aux dimensions voulues; (*c*) *Num:* ajuster. **3.** *Const:* doser (le ciment). **4.** *Dressm:* bouillonner (une jupe, etc.).

gaugeable ['geidʒəbl], *a.* **1.** susceptible d'être mesuré. **2.** *Cust:* soumis aux droits.

gauged [geidʒd], *a.* **1.** calibré; étalonné; standardisé. **2.** *Const:* (*of bricks, etc.*) conforme à l'échantillon. **3.** (*of plaster, etc.*) dosé. **4.** *Cost: O:* **g. sleeves,** manches *f* à bouillons.

gauger ['geidʒər], *s.* (*pers.*) jaugeur *m*, mesureur *m*; *Num:* ajusteur *m*.

gauging ['geidʒiŋ], *s.* **1.** calibrage *m*; étalonnage *m*; standardisation *f*; jaugeage *m*; vérification *f*, mesurage *m*; veltage *m* (des tonneaux), compassage *m* (d'un canon, etc.); *Num:* ajustage *m*; **g. rod, stick,** jauge *f*, velte *f*; **g. line,** échelle *f*. **2.** dosage *m* (du ciment). **3.** *Dressm:* bouillon *m*.

Gaul [gɔːl], **1.** *Pr.n.A.Geog:* Gaule *f*. **2.** *s.* Gaulois, -oise.

gauleiter ['gaulaitər], *s. German Hist:* gauleiter *m*.

Gaulish ['gɔːliʃ]. **1.** *a. Hist:* gaulois. **2.** *s. Ling:* gaulois *m*.

gaullism ['goulizm], *s. Hist: Pol:* gaullisme *m*.

gaullist ['goulist], *a.* & *s. Pol:* gaulliste (*mf*).

gault [gɔːlt], *s. Geol:* gault *m*; étage albien; albien *m*; argile *f* téguline.

gaultheria [gɔːl'θiəriə], *s. Bot:* gaulthérie *f*; *Pharm:* **g. oil,** gaulthérilène *f*.

gaumless ['gɔːmlis], *a. F: Dial:* stupide, bête.

gaunt [gɔːnt], *a.* **1.** maigre, décharné, étique; **g. face,** visage décharné, évidé, hâve, aux joues creuses; **his cheeks are growing g.,** ses joues se creusent. **2.** (*a*) d'aspect redoutable, farouche; (*b*) lugubre, désolé.

gauntlet[1] ['gɔːntlit], *s.* **1.** (*a*) *Arm:* gantelet *m*, gant *m*; **to throw down, fling down, the g. to s.o.,** jeter le gant à qn; **to take up the g.,** relever le gant; (*b*) *Her:* gantelet. **2.** gant à crispins, à manchette; crispin *m*; **riding gauntlets,** gants de buffle; **g. gloves,** gants à la mousquetaire. **3.** *Fenc: etc:* crispin, manchette *f*, rebras *m* (de gant).

gauntlet[2], *s.* **to run the g.,** *Mil:* passer par les bretelles, par les baguettes; *Nau:* courir la bouline; **to run the g. of adverse criticism,** soutenir un feu roulant de critiques adverses.

gauntness ['gɔːntnis], *s.* maigreur *f*; aspect *m* hâve (de qn, des joues de qn).

gaur ['gauər], *s. Z:* gaur *m*.

gauss [gaus], *s. Magn.Meas:* gauss *m*.

gaussage ['gausidʒ], *s. Magn:* intensité *f* (du champ) en gauss.

Gaussian ['gausiən], *a. Mth:* gaussien; (logarithmes *m*, etc.) de Gauss; **G. distribution,** distribution *f* de Gauss, loi de Gauss.

gaussmeter ['gausmiːtər], *s.* gaussmètre *m*.

gauze [gɔːz], *s.* **1.** (*a*) gaze *f*; *Med:* **sterilized, antiseptic, g.,** gaze aseptique, stérilisée; **iodoform g.,** gaze iodoformée; (*b*) **wire g.,** toile *f*, tissu *m*, gaze, tamis *m*, métallique; crépine *f* (de pompe à huile, etc.); **g. strainer,** tamis métallique; **plastic g.,** tamis, treillis, en matière plastique. **2.** vapeur légère, voile *m* (de fumée).

gauziness ['gɔːzinis], *s.* légèreté *f*, inconsistance *f* (d'un voile, etc.).

gauzy ['gɔːzi], *a.* diaphane; léger.

gavel[1] ['gævl], *s. Agr:* javelle *f*; (*of corn*) **to lie on the g.,** rester en javelles.

gavel[2], *s.* marteau *m* (de commissaire-priseur, *NAm:* de juge).

gavelkind ['gævlkaind], *s.* **1.** *Hist:* tenure *f* de terres dont les fils du tenancier devaient hériter par portions égales. **2.** partage égal (de terres) entre les fils du défunt.

gavial ['geiviəl], *s. Rept:* gavial *m*, -als.

Gavin ['gævin], *Pr.n.m.* Gauvain.

gavotte [gə'vɔt], *s. Danc: Mus:* gavotte *f*.

Gawain ['gæwein], *Pr.n.m. Lit:* Gauvain.

gawk[1] [gɔːk], *s. F:* (*a*) personne *f* gauche; *F:* empoté, -ée; godiche *mf*; godichon, -onne; (*b*) **g. of a man,** escogriffe *m*, grand flandrin; grand dadais; **g. of a woman,** grande godiche; grande jument; grande bique; grande bringue; grande calebasse; asperge montée.

gawk[2], *v.i. F:* = GAPE[2], 2.

gawkily ['gɔːkili], *adv.* gauchement.

gawkiness ['gɔːkinis], *s.* gaucherie *f*; air empoté.

gawky ['gɔːki]. **1.** *a.* dégingandé, gauche; *F:* empoté, godiche; **a long-legged g. young woman,** une grande gigue. **2.** *s. F:* = GAWK[1].

gawp [gɔːp], *v.i. F:* = GAPE[2], 2.

gay [gei], *a.* **(gayer, gayest) 1.** (*a*) gai, réjoui, allègre, guilleret; **as g. as a lark,** gai comme un pinson; **g. laugh,** rire enjoué; (*b*) **to lead a g. life,** mener une vie de plaisir(s); s'amuser, sortir, beaucoup; (*c*) *A:* **g. deceiver,** libertin *m*; **g. woman,** femme galante; **to go g.,** se dévergonder; mal tourner; (*d*) *P:* **g. deceivers,** nénés *m* de chez Michelin; (*e*) *P:* homosexuel; (*f*) *U.S: O:* outrecuidant, effronté. **2.** gai, splendide, brillant; **g. colours,** couleurs vives, gaies; **room g. with flowers,** pièce égayée de fleurs.

gayal ['geijəl], *s. Z:* gayal *m*, -als; bœuf *m* des jungles.

gaylussite ['geilusait], *s. Miner:* gay-lussite *f*.

gaze[1] [geiz], *s.* regard *m* fixe; **exposed to the public g.,** exposé aux regards inquisiteurs de tous; **a horrible sight met his g.,** un spectacle horrible s'offrait à ses yeux, à sa vue; *Her:* **at g.,** la tête de face.

gaze[2], *v.i.* regarder fixement; **to g. into space,** regarder dans le vide; **to g. at, on, s.o.,** fixer, contempler, considérer, qn; envelopper qn d'un regard; **he was gazing at a shop window,** il était en contemplation devant une vitrine.

gazebo [gə'ziːbou], *s.* belvédère *m*.

gazelle [gə'zel], *s. Z:* gazelle *f*; **Tibetan g.,** gazelle du Tibet; **dorcas g.,** gazelle africaine.

gazer ['geizər], *s.* contemplateur, -trice (**at,** de); curieux, -euse.

gazette[1] [gə'zet], *s.* **1.** *A:* gazette *f*; journal *m*; **g. writer,** gazetier *m*. **2.** journal officiel, *esp.* la *London Gazette*; **to appear in the G.,** figurer à la *Gazette*; **the Police G.,** la Gazette des tribunaux; **the Diplomatic G.,** le Mémorial diplomatique.

gazette[2], *v.tr.* annoncer, publier (une faillite, une nomination, etc.) dans un journal officiel; (*of officer, etc.*) **to be gazetted,** être à la *London Gazette*, = à l'Officiel; **he was gazetted last week,** sa nomination a paru la semaine dernière.

gazetteer [gæzi'tiər], *s.* **1.** (*pers.*) *A:* (*a*) gazetier (officiel); (*b*) nouvelliste *m*. **2.** répertoire *m* géographique; dictionnaire *m* géographique; **g. index,** index *m* géographique.

gazing ['geiziŋ], *s.* contemplation *f*.

gazogene ['gæzədʒiːn], *s.* = GASOGENE.

gean [giːn], *s. Bot:* **1.** cerise *f* sauvage; merise *f*; guigne *f*. **2. g. (tree),** cerisier *m* sauvage; merisier *m*; guignier *m*.

geanticlinal [dʒiːænti'klainl], *a. Geol:* géanticlinal, -aux.

geanticline [dʒiː'æntiklain], *s. Geol:* géanticlinal *m*, -aux.

gear[1] [giər], *s.* **1.** (*a*) *A:* accoutrement *m*; (*b*) harnais *m*, harnachement *m* (de cheval de trait); (*c*) attirail *m*, équipement *m*, appareil *m*; *Nau:* apparaux *mpl*; **fishing g.,** attirail de pêche; engin(s) *m(pl.)*, harnais, de pêche; **boat g.,** armement *m*, gréement *m*, accessoires *mpl*, agrès *mpl*, d'un canot; **spare g.,** la drome; **anchor g.,** garniture *f* d'ancre; **camping g.,** matériel *m* de camping, de campement; **photographic g.,** équipement, matériel, photographique; *Journ: T.V:* **field g.,** matériel de reportage; *Civ.E: etc:* **hoisting g., lifting g.,** matériel de levage; appareil(s), engin(s), de levage, de hissage; *Mec.E:* **g. of a crane,** agrès d'une grue; **screw(-cutting) g.,** appareil(lage) *m*, outillage *m*, de filetage; **pump g.,** garniture, gréement, d'une pompe; *F:* **just wait while I get my g.,** attends que je cherche mes effets, mes bagages; **he arrived with all his g.,** il est arrivé avec tout son attirail, tous ses bagages, tout son barda. **2.** *Mec.E:* (*a*) appareil, mécanisme *m*; **control g.,** appareils, organes, de commande; *Av:* dispositif, organe(s), de manœuvre; **operating g., working g.,** organes de fonctionnement, de manœuvre; mécanisme; **running g.,** organes de roulement; **engaging g.,** (mécanisme d')enclenchement; **steering g.,** mécanisme de direction; **distribution g.,** mécanisme de distribution; **safety g.,** mécanisme de sécurité; *Artil: etc:* **loading g.,** appareil, mécanisme, de chargement; **sighting g.,** appareils de pointage; **elevating g.,** appareils, mécanisme, de pointage en hauteur; **traversing g.,** appareils, mécanisme, de pointage en direction; **deflection g.,** appareils, mécanisme, de correction but; **firing g.,** dispositif de mise à, de feu; mécanisme de détente, de percussion; *Av:* **landing g.,** train *m* d'atterrissage; **trim g.,** réducteur *m* de trim; (*b*) **(driving, transmission) g.,** transmission *f*, commande *f*; organes, engrenage(s) *m(pl.)* de transmission; **wheel g.,** transmission, commande, par engrenage; **belt g.,** transmission, commande, par courroie(s); **chain g.,** transmission, commande, par chaîne(s); **crank g.,** (i) transmission, commande, par manivelle, par bielle, par coulisseau; (ii) pédalier *m* (de bicyclette); **counter g.,** transmission intermédiaire; **g. drive,** transmission (de mouvement), commande, par engrenages; **g.-driven,** commandé, à entraînement, par engrenages; **bevel g.,** engrenage conique, à biseau, d'angle; **face g.,** engrenage conique plat; **helical g.,** engrenage hélicoïdal; **herringbone g., double helical g.,** engrenage à chevrons; **spur g.,** engrenage cylindrique, droit; **annular, internal, g.,** engrenage (à dents) intérieur(es); **involute g.,** engrenage à développante; **step-tooth g.,** engrenage à denture croisée; **straight(-tooth) g.,** engrenage à denture droite; **step-up, stepdown, g.,** engrenage multiplicateur, démultiplicateur; **pick-off g.,** engrenage sélectif; **timing g.,** engrenage de distribution; **sliding g., throw-over g.,** (pignon, train) bal(l)adeur *m*; **train of gears,** harnais d'engrenage; train d'engrenages; **in g.,** (i) embrayé, engagé, enclenché, en prise; (ii) (*of machine, of mechanism*) en action, en marche; **to throw, put, (sth.) into g. again,** (i) rembrayer, rengréner, renclencher (des rouages, un élément de mécanisme); (ii) remettre (une machine, un mécanisme) en action, en marche; **out of g.,** (i) débrayé, désengrené, déclenché, hors de prise; (ii) (*of machine, of mechanism*) au repos; (iii) dérangé, détraqué, hors d'action, hors de service; (iv) *Fig:* (*of organization, etc.*) désorganisé, perturbé; **to throw, put, (sth.) out of g.,** (i) débrayer, désengrener, déclencher (des rouages, un élément de mécanisme); (ii) mettre (une machine, un mécanisme) au repos; (iii) déranger, détraquer; mettre (qch.) hors d'action, hors de service; (iv) *Fig:* désorganiser, perturber (une organisation, les plans de qn, etc.); **this has put me completely out of g.,** cela m'a complètement désorienté, désaxé; *attrib.* **g. cutting, milling,** taille *f* d'engrenages; **g. withdrawer,** arrache-pignon *m*, *pl.* arrache-pignons; (*c*) **g. ratio,** rapport *m* d'engrenages, des dentures; multiplication *f*; **reduction g. ratio,** démultiplication *f*; (rapport de) réduction *f*; **to reduce the g. ratio,** démultiplier; **bicycle with a 66 inch g.,** bicyclette *f* avec un développement de 5 m 25, qui développe 5 m 25; (*d*) *Aut:* vitesse *f*; **neutral g.,** point mort; **first, bottom, g.,** première vitesse; **top g.,** prise (directe); **to climb a hill in top g.,** monter une côte en prise; **reverse, reversing, g.,** (i) *Aut:* marche arrière; (ii) *Mec.E:* (appareil de) changement *m* de marche; (pignon *m* de) marche arrière; embrayage *m*, mécanisme, de renversement, de renvoi; **change(-speed) g.,** (i) *Aut:* (boîte *f* de) changement de vitesse; (ii) *Mec.E:* mécanisme de changement de vitesse, de renversement de marche; (iii) *Mch.Tls:* engrenage, pignon, de rechange; **g. changes,** changements de vitesse; **to change g.,** changer (i) *Aut:* de vitesse, (ii) *Cy:* de braquet; **to change to a higher, a lower, g.,** passer à la vitesse supérieure, inférieure; **to run through the gears,** passer les vitesses; **to run in neutral g.,** tourner à vide; **I can't get (the car) into g.,** je n'arrive pas à passer les vitesses; *Aut:* **g. pinion,** pignon de boîte de vitesse; **g. lever,** levier (i) *Aut:* de changement, (ii) *Mec.E:* de commande, des vitesses.

gear[2]. **1.** *v.tr.* (*a*) harnacher (une bête de trait, etc.); (*b*) équiper (une machine); (*c*) embrayer, enclencher, engrener (un pignon dans une roue, etc.). **2.** *v.i.* s'embrayer, s'enclencher, s'engrener; **wheels, cogs, that g. with each other,** roues, dents, qui s'engrènent l'une dans l'autre. **3.** *v.tr.* (*a*) **to g. up, down,** multiplier, démultiplier (la vitesse de révolution); **to g. up a bicycle,** pourvoir une bicyclette d'un grand développement; **geared down engine,** moteur démultiplié; moteur à démultiplicateur; (*b*) **wages geared to the cost of living,** salaires indexés au coût de la vie; **this book is geared to the needs of students,** ce livre est spécialement adapté aux besoins des étudiants.

gearbox ['giəbɔks], *s.* (i) *Aut:* boîte *f* de changement de vitesse, boîte de vitesses; (ii) *Mec.E:* boîte, carter *m*, d'engrenage, de transmission; boîte, carter, de démultiplication; **auxiliary g., accessory g., subsidiary g.,** (i) *Aut:* boîte de vitesses auxiliaire; (ii) *Mec.E:* boîte, carter, d'engrenage secondaire, intermédiaire.

gearcase ['giəkeis], *s.* (*a*) *Aut:* carter *m* de boîte de vitesses; (*b*) *Mec.E:* carter d'engrenage.

geared ['giəd], *a. Mec.E:* (tour *m*, etc.) à engrenage(s); **g. engine,** moteur démultiplié.

gearing ['giəriŋ], *s.* **1.** (*a*) engrenage *m*, embrayage *m*, enclenchement *m*; **g. of five to one,** engrenage de rapport cinq à un; (*b*) **g. up,** multiplication *f*; *Cy:* développement *m*; **g. down,** démultiplication *f*, réduction *f* (des rapports de rotation); **g.-down device,** organe démultiplicateur. **2.** transmission *f*, commande *f*; **(train of) g.,** harnais *m*, équipage *m*, d'engrenage(s); système *m*, jeu *m*, train *m*, d'engrenages; **rope g.,** transmission par câble; **back g.,** engrenage intermédiaire.

gearless ['giəlis], *a. Mec.E:* (moteur, etc.) sans engrenages, sans (dé)multiplication, à prise directe.

gearshaft ['giəʃɑ:ft], *s. Mec.E:* arbre *m* (i) porte-pignon(s), (ii) secondaire, intermédiaire.

gearshift ['giəʃift], *s. Aut: NAm:* changement *m* de vitesse; **automatic g.,** changement de vitesse automatique; **vacuum g.,** changement de vitesse à dépression, à vide; **g. lever,** levier *m* de changement de vitesse; levier (de commande) des vitesses; **g. bar,** coulisseau *m*.

gearwheel ['giə(h)wi:l], *s.* (*a*) *Mec.E:* (roue *f* d')engrenage *m*; roue dentée; rouage *m*; **set of gearwheels,** jeu *m* d'engrenages; (*b*) *Cy:* pignon *m*.

geaster, geastrum [dʒi'æstər, -'æstrəm], *s. Fung:* géaster *m*, géastre *m*.

gecko, *pl.* **-os, -oes** ['gekou, -ouz], *s. Rept:* gecko *m*, margouillat *m*; **wall g.,** gecko des murs, des murailles; **Turkish g.,** gecko verruqueux, à doigts en disques; **Madagascar, green g.,** gecko diurne de Madagascar; **(South-West African) rock g.,** gecko des rochers (sud-ouest africain); **(Australian) spiny-tailed g.,** gecko à queue épineuse.

Geckonidae [ge'kɔnidi:], *s.pl. Rept:* geckonidés *m*.

gedacktwork [gə'dæktwə:k], *s. Mus:* tuyaux fermés (d'un orgue).

gedanite ['gedənait], *s. Miner:* gédanite *f*.

Gedinnian [gə'diniən], *a. & s. Geol:* gédinnien (*m*).

gedrite ['gedrait], *s. Miner:* gédrite *f*.

gee[1] [dʒi:]. **1.** *int.* (*to horse*) **g.-up! gee-ho!** hue! huhau! **2.** *s. F: Turf:* **the gees,** les chevaux.

gee[2], *int. esp. NAm:* **(g. whiz(z))** bon Dieu! ça alors! mince alors!

gee-gee ['dʒi:dʒi:], *s. F:* (*child's language*) cheval *m*; dada *m*; *Turf:* **the gee-gees,** les chevaux.

geezer ['gi:zər], *s. F:* **old g.,** vieux type; (*woman*) vieille toupie; **funny old g.,** drôle *m* de bonhomme.

gefuffle [gi'fʌfl], *s. F:* commotion *f*, agitation *f*.

Gehenna [gi'henə]. **1.** *Pr.n. B.Hist:* (*a*) la Géhenne; la vallée de Hinnom; (*b*) la Géhenne, l'Enfer. **2.** *s. Lit:* **their prison was a g.,** leur prison était une (véritable) géhenne.

gehlenite ['geilənait], *s. Miner:* gehlénite *f*.

geic ['dʒi:ik], *a. Ch: Agr:* (acide *m*) géique.

Geiger ['gaigər], *Pr.n. Atom.Ph:* **G.(-Müller) counter,** compteur *m* de Geiger(-Müller).

geikielite ['gi:kilait], *s. Miner:* geikielite *f*.

geisha ['geiʃə], *s.* geisha *f*, ghesha *f*.

geitonogamy [gi:tə'nɔgəmi], *s. Bot:* gitonogamie *f*.

Gekkonidae [ge'kɔnidi:], *s.pl. Rept:* geckonidés *m*.

gel[1] [dʒel], *s. Ch:* colloïde (coagulé); gel *m*; **reversible g.,** colloïde soluble; **irreversible g.,** colloïde insoluble.

gel[2], *v.i.* **(gelled)** (*of colloid*) se coaguler, se gélifier.

gelatinate [dʒi'lætineit], *v.tr.* = GELATINIZE.

gelatine [dʒelə'ti:n], *s.* (*a*) gélatine *f*; *Phot:* **to coat a plate with g.,** gélatiniser une plaque; **g. solution,** solution gélatineuse; *Phot:* **g. paper,** papier gélatiné; *Com:* **sheet g.,** papier gélatine; papier glacé; **g. printing,** impression *f* à la gélatine; (*b*) *Exp:* **explosive g.,** plastic *m*; **blasting g.,** gélatine détonante, explosive.

gelatiniform [dʒelə'tinifɔ:m], *a.* gélatiniforme.

gelatinization [dʒilætinai'zeiʃ(ə)n], *s.* gélatinisation *f*.

gelatinize [dʒi'lætinaiz]. **1.** *v.tr.* gélatiniser. **2.** *v.i.* se gélatiniser.

gelatinized [dʒi'lætinaizd], *a.* gélatiné.

gelatino-bromide [dʒi'lætinou'broumaid], *s. Ch: Phot:* gélatino-bromure *m*.

gelatino-chloride [dʒi'lætinou'klɔ:raid], *s. Ch: Phot:* gélatino-chlorure *m*.

gelatinoid [dʒi'lætinɔid], *a.* gélatineux, gélatiniforme.

gelatinous [dʒi'lætinəs], *a.* gélatineux.

gelation [dʒe'leiʃ(ə)n], *s.* **1.** *Ch:* gélification *f*. **2.** (*of soil*) gélation *f*.

geld [geld], *v.tr.* (*a*) châtrer, *F:* couper (un animal); (*b*) hongrer (un cheval).

gelder ['geldər], *s.* (*a*) châtreur *m*; (*b*) hongreur *m* (de chevaux).

Gelderland ['geldəlænd], *Pr.n. Geog:* la Gueldre.

Geldern ['geldə(:)n], *Pr.n. Geog:* Gueldre, Geldern (ville d'Allemagne).

gelding[1] ['geldiŋ], *s.* castration *f*.

gelding[2], *s.* **1.** *A:* eunuque *m*. **2.** (*a*) animal châtré; (*b*) cheval *m* hongre; hongre *m*.

gelechiid [dʒe'leki(:)id], *s. Ent:* géléchie *f*; géléchiidé *m*.

Gelechiidae [dʒeli'kaiidi:], *s.pl. Ent:* géléchiidés *m*.

gelid ['dʒelid], *a.* (*a*) glacé; glacial, -als; (*b*) froid; frais, *f.* fraîche.

Gelidiales [dʒelidi'eili:z], *s.pl. Algae:* gélidiales *f*.

gelidium [dʒe'lidiəm], *s. Algae:* gélidium *m*.

gelification [dʒelifi'keiʃ(ə)n], *s.* gélification *f*.

gelignite ['dʒelignait], *s. Exp:* gélignite *f*.

gelivity [dʒe'liviti], *s. Geol:* gélivité *f*.

gelling[1] ['dʒeliŋ], *a. Ch:* gélifiant; **g. power,** pouvoir gélifiant.

gelling[2], *s. Ch:* gélification *f*.

Gelo ['gi:lou], *Pr.n.m. Gr.Hist:* Gélon.

gelose [dʒe'lous], *s. Ch:* gélose *f*.

gelsemine ['dʒelsəmi:n], *s. Ch:* gelsémine *f*.

gem [dʒem], *s.* **1.** (*a*) pierre précieuse; gemme *f*, joyau *m*; **g. stone,** pierre gemme; (*b*) **the g. of the collection,** le joyau de la collection; *F:* **he's a g. of a husband,** c'est la perle, la crème, des maris; **a. g. of a child,** un bijou d'enfant; (*c*) *Sch: F:* (= *mistake*) perle *f*; (*d*) *Typ:* diamant *m*. **2.** pierre gravée; intaille *f*, camée *m*; **collection of carved gems,** glyptothèque *f*.

Gemara (the) [ðəge'mɑ:rə], *s. Rel.Lit:* la Gémara.

Gemaric [ge'mɑ:rik], *a. Rel.Lit:* gémarique.

gematria [ge'mætriə], *s.* gématrie *f*.

gemel ['dʒeml], *a.* **g. ring,** bagues jumelées; **g. windows,** fenêtres géminées; **g. hinge,** gond *m* à piton; *Her:* **(bar) g.,** jumelle *f*.

gemellary [dʒe'meləri], *a.* gémellaire.

gemelliparous [dʒemə'lipərəs], *a.* gémellipare.

gemellus [dʒe'meləs], *s. Anat:* **g. (muscle),** jumeau *m*.

geminate[1] ['dʒemineit]. **1.** *a.* (*a*) (*of leaves, columns, etc.*) géminé, accouplé; (*b*) *Gram:* (*of letter*) géminé, double. **2.** *s.* consonne, voyelle, géminée, double.

geminate[2], *v.tr.* **1.** *Arch: Art:* géminer; disposer (des motifs) par paires; accoupler (des colonnes, etc.). **2.** doubler (une consonne, etc.).

gemination [dʒemi'neiʃ(ə)n], *s.* **1.** *Biol: Dent:* gémination *f*. **2.** *Gram:* redoublement *m*, gémination (d'une lettre).

Gemini ['dʒeminai]. **1.** *Pr.n.pl. Astr:* les Gémeaux *m*. **2.** *int. P: A:* **o g.** ['dʒimini]! mon Dieu, mon Dieu! grand Dieu!

gemma, *pl.* **-ae** ['dʒemə, -i:], *s.* **1.** *Bot:* (*a*) bourgeon *m* (à feuilles); gemme *f*; (*b*) gemme, cellule *f* (d'une mousse). **2.** *Biol:* bourgeon, gemme.

gemmate[1] ['dʒemeit], *a. Biol: Bot:* **1.** couvert de bourgeons, de gemmes. **2.** qui se reproduit par gemmation, par bourgeonnement.

gemmate[2], *v.i. Biol:* (*a*) bourgeonner, gemmer; (*b*) se reproduire par bourgeonnement, par gemmation.

gemmation [dʒe'meiʃ(ə)n], *s. Nat.Hist:* gemmation *f*.

gemmed [dʒemd], *a.* orné de pierres précieuses, de pierreries; gemmé.

gemmiferous [dʒe'mifərəs], *a. Miner: Biol:* gemmifère.

gemmiflorate [dʒemi'flɔ:reit], *a. Bot:* gemmiflore.

gemmiform ['dʒemifɔ:m], *a.* gemmiforme.

gemmiparous [dʒe'mipərəs], *a. Biol:* gemmipare; **g. reproduction,** gemmiparité *f*.

gemmologist [dʒe'mɔlədʒist], *s.* gemmologiste *mf*.

gemmology [dʒe'mɔlədʒi], *s.* gemmologie *f*.

gemmule ['dʒemju:l], *s. Nat.Hist:* gemmule *f*.

Gemonies (the) [ðə'dʒeməniz], *s.pl. Rom.Ant:* les Gémonies *f*.

Gempylidae [dʒem'pilidi:], *s.pl. Ich:* gempylidés *m*, les maquereaux-serpents *m*.

gemsbok ['gemzbɔk], *s. Z:* gemsbok *m*; oryx *m* gazelle; oryx, chamois *m*, du Cap; pasan *m*.

gen [dʒen], *s. F:* renseignements *mpl*, tuyaux *mpl*.

genal ['dʒi:nl], *a. Anat:* génal, -aux.

genappe [dʒe'næp], *s. Tex:* génappe *m*.

gendarme ['ʒɔndɑ:m], *s. Geol:* gendarme *m*.

gender ['dʒendər], *s.* **1.** *Gram:* genre *m*; **common g.,** genre commun; **words of common g.,** mots *m* des deux genres; mots épicènes. **2.** *F:* sexe *m*.

genderless ['dʒendəlis], *a. Gram:* (mot, etc.) qui ne fait pas de distinction de genres.

gene [dʒi:n], *s. Biol:* gène *m*; facteur *m* (d'hérédité); **dominant g.,** gène, facteur, dominant; **recessive g.,** gène, facteur, récessif.

genealogical [dʒi:niə'lɔdʒik(ə)l], *a.* généalogique; **g. table, tree,** tableau *m*, arbre *m*, généalogique.

genealogist [dʒi:ni'ælədʒist], *s.* généalogiste *mf*.

genealogy [dʒi:ni'ælədʒi], *s.* généalogie *f*.

genecology [dʒi:ni'kɔlədʒi], *s. Biol:* génécologie *f*.

genera ['dʒenərə]. *See* GENUS.

general ['dʒen(ə)rəl], *a. & s.*

I. *a.* général, -aux. **1. g. paralysis,** paralysie générale; **the rain has been pretty g.,** il a plu un peu partout; **g. enquiry,** enquête *f* d'ensemble; **g. drawing, sketch,** dessin *m* d'ensemble (d'une machine, etc.); *Nau:* **g. chart,** carte *f* à petit point; **g. effect,** effet *m* d'ensemble (d'un tableau, etc.); *Pol: U.S:* **g. ticket,** scrutin *m* de liste. **2.** (*a*) **g. meeting,** assemblée générale; (*in agenda of meeting*) **g. business,** questions diverses; **g. mathematics,** éléments *m* de mathématiques; *Ecc:* **g. council,** concile général; *Pol:* **g. election,** élections générales; *Adm:* **g. holiday,** fête publique; jour férié; *Navy:* **g. signal,** signal *m* à tous; *Ecc:* **g. confession,** confession *f* en commun; (*b*) **word in g. use,** mot généralement employé, couramment employé; mot répandu, d'un usage général; mot courant; **to bring sth. into g. use,** rendre général l'usage de qch.; **to come into g. use,** se généraliser; **this article has come into g. use,** l'usage de cet article s'est répandu; **as a g. rule,** en règle générale; **speaking in a g. way, as a g. thing,** parlant d'une manière générale; **the g. opinion,** l'opinion *f* vulgaire; **he is a g. favourite,** tout le monde l'aime; **the g. public,** le grand public, le gros public; **the g. reader,** le commun des lecteurs; les lecteurs *m*; le public (qui lit); (*c*) **g. knowledge,** connaissances générales; **g. store(s), shop,** épicerie-droguerie *f*; magasin *m* de village, *F:* alimentation générale; **g. maid,** *s. O:* **general,** bonne *f* à tout faire; *Publ:* **g. books,** livres *m* pour le grand public; (*d*) **g. resemblance,** ressemblance générale, vague; **g. terms,** termes généraux; (*e*) *Cmptr:* **g. program(me), routine,** programme général, banalisé; **g. register,** registre banalisé; **g. storage, store,** mémoire banale. **3.** (*a*) **inspector g.,** inspecteur général, en chef; (*Fr.Hist: & Channel Is.*) **States G.,** États généraux; (*b*) *Mil:* **g. officer,** officier général. **4.** *adv.phr.* **in g.,** en général, généralement; **she complained of everything in g. and of the cooking in particular,** elle se plaignait de tout en général et de la cuisine en particulier.

II. *s.* **1. to argue from the g. to the particular,** arguer du général au particulier. **2.** *A:* **the g.,** le gros public. **3.** (*a*) *Mil:* (i) (= **general officer**) général *m*; (ii) (*rank*) général d'armée; **G. Martin,** le Général Martin; **lieutenant g.,** général de corps d'armée; **major g.,** général de division; *U.S:* **brigadier g.,** général de brigade; **g. in chief,** général en chef; **the general's wife,** la générale; **one of the greatest generals in history,** l'un des plus grands généraux de l'histoire; **he's no g.,** il n'est pas grand stratège; (*b*) *Ecc:* général (d'un ordre religieux); **our abbess is the g. of our order,** notre abbesse est générale de tout l'ordre.

generalate ['dʒen(ə)rəleit], *s. Mil: Ecc:* généralat *m*.

generalissimo [dʒen(ə)rə'lisimou], *s. Mil:* généralissime *m*.

generality [dʒenə'ræliti], *s.* généralité *f*; (*a*) caractère général; **g. of a statement,** portée générale d'une affirmation; **g. of an appeal,** ampleur *f* d'un appel; (*b*) considération générale; **to confine oneself to generalities,** s'en tenir aux généralités; (*c*) **the g. of mankind,** la généralité, la plupart, des hommes; la grande masse du genre humain.

generalizable [dʒen(ə)rə'laizəbl], *a.* généralisable.

generalization [dʒen(ə)rəlai'zeiʃ(ə)n], *s.* généralisation *f*; **to avoid too hasty generalizations,** éviter les généralisations trop hâtives; **to make (rash) generalizations,** conclure du particulier au général.

generalize ['dʒen(ə)rəlaiz]. **1.** *v.tr.* (*a*) généraliser (des faits, etc.); (*b*) répandre, populariser (un usage, etc.). **2.** *v.i.* généraliser, faire des généralisations.

generalized ['dʒen(ə)rəlaizd], *a.* généralisé; *Cmptr:* **g. routine,** programme général.

generalizer ['dʒen(ə)rəlaizər], *s.* généralisateur, -trice.

generalizing[1] ['dʒen(ə)rəlaiziŋ], *a.* généralisateur, -trice; généralisant.

generalizing[2], *s.* généralisation *f*.

generally ['dʒen(ə)rəli], *adv.* **1.** généralement, universellement; **man g. esteemed,** homme généralement estimé. **2.** généralement, en général; **to help g. in the house, in the business, to make oneself g. useful,** aider un peu à tout dans la maison; se rendre généralement utile; **g. speaking,** (parlant) d'une manière générale; en général; généralement parlant. **3.** le plus souvent; **he g. comes on Thursday,** en règle générale il vient le jeudi; il vient généralement le jeudi.

general-purpose ['dʒen(ə)rəl'pə:pəs], *a* (à) toutes fins, (pour) tous usages; (d'usage) universel, polyvalent, banalisé; *Cmptr:* **g.-p. computer,** calculateur universel; **g.-p. storage,** mémoire banale.

generalship ['dʒen(ə)rəlʃip], *s.* **1.** généralat *m.* **2.** stratégie *f,* tactique *f;* **to give proofs of great g.,** se montrer grand général, grand capitaine.

generant ['dʒenərənt], *s. Mth:* génératrice *f.*

generate ['dʒenəreit], *v.tr.* **1.** *A:* engendrer (des êtres vivants, des plantes, etc.). **2.** générer, produire (de la vapeur, un courant électrique); produire, engendrer (de la chaleur, etc.). **3.** *Mth:* engendrer (une surface, etc.); **volume generated by a curve,** volume engendré par une courbe. **4.** amener, produire (un résultat); provoquer, faire naître (un sentiment); **environment that generates crime,** ambiance génératrice de crime. **5.** *Cmptr:* créer, générer; **generated address,** adresse calculée.

generating[1] ['dʒenəreitiŋ], *a.* générateur, -trice; *Ch: etc:* **g. apparatus,** appareil producteur; générateur *m* (de gaz, etc.); *El:* **g. set, unit,** (groupe) générateur; groupe électrogène; **g. station,** centrale *f* électrique; station, usine, génératrice, électrique; **main g. station,** supercentrale *f;* **steam g. station,** centrale thermique; *Mch:* **steam-g. heat,** chaleur *f* de vaporisation; *Mth:* **g. function,** fonction génératrice; **g. line,** génératrice *f;* *Cmptr:* **g. program(me), routine,** programme générateur.

generating[2], *s.* génération *f;* *Cmptr:* création *f,* génération.

generation [dʒenə'reiʃ(ə)n], *s.* **1.** (*a*) *Biol:* **equivocal g., spontaneous g.,** génération spontanée; (*b*) génération, production *f* (de la chaleur, etc.); (*c*) *Mth:* génération, engendrement *m* (d'une surface, etc.); (*d*) génération, formation *f* (des idées, etc.); (*e*) *Cmptr:* création *f,* génération; **data g.,** élaboration *f* des données. **2.** (*a*) **descendant six generations removed,** descendant *m* à la sixième génération; **family of three generations,** famille *f* qui comprend trois générations; **to live through, see, three generations,** vivre, voir, trois âges d'homme; **from g. to g.,** de génération en génération; d'âge en âge; de père en fils; **for generations there had always been a doctor in the family,** ils étaient médecins de père en fils, *F. O:* **it's generations since anybody did such a thing,** on n'a pas fait une telle chose depuis des siècles; *F:* **all that happened a g. ago,** il y a trente ans de tout cela; (*b*) **the rising g.,** la jeune, la nouvelle, génération; la génération qui monte; **the present g.,** la génération actuelle; **the g. gap,** le fossé des générations.

generative ['dʒenərətiv, -eitiv], *a.* génératif; générateur, -trice; producteur, -trice.

generator ['dʒenəreitər], *s.* **1.** (*pers.*) générateur, -trice (d'une idée, d'une erreur, etc.). **2.** (*a*) *Tchn:* générateur, appareil producteur (de gaz, de chaleur, de son(s), etc.); **acetylene g.,** générateur d'acétylène; *Mch:* **steam g.,** chaudière *f* à vapeur; **gas g.,** générateur de gaz; gazogène *m;* **g. gas,** gaz *m* pauvre; (*b*) *El:* génératrice, générateur, dynamo (génératrice); **electric, thermoelectric, electrostatic, g.,** générateur électrique, thermoélectrique, électrostatique; *Ch: Ind:* **electrolytic g.,** générateur pour électrolyse; **lighting g.,** dynamo *f* d'éclairage; **alternating current g., A.C. g.,** génératrice de courant alternatif; **direct current g., D.C. g.,** génératrice de courant continu; **homopolar g.,** génératrice homopolaire; **heteropolar g.,** génératrice hétéropolaire; **single-phase g.,** génératrice monophasée; **two-phase g.,** génératrice diphasée; **multiphase g., polyphase g.,** génératrice polyphasée; **multicurrent g., multiple-current g.,** génératrice polymorphique; **engine-driven g.,** génératrice couplée au moteur; *Rail:* **axle g.,** génératrice couplée aux essieux; **hand-driven g.,** génératrice à main; **steam-driven g.,** génératrice à vapeur; **wind-driven g.,** génératrice actionnée par le vent, entraînée par la vitesse (d'un avion, etc.); *Elcs:* **audio-frequency, low-frequency, g.,** générateur basse fréquence; **radio-frequency, high-frequency, g.,** générateur haute fréquence; **pulse g.,** générateur d'impulsion; **signal(ling) g.,** générateur de signaux; **sweep g.,** générateur de balayage; générateur à balayage ou à exploration de fréquence; **X-ray g.,** générateur de rayons X; (*c*) *Cmptr:* (programme) générateur; **program(me) g.,** générateur de programme; **sort g.,** générateur de programme de tri; **random number g.,** générateur de nombres pseudo-aléatoires. **3.** *Mth:* génératrice (d'une surface, etc.). **4.** *Mus:* son fondamental, générateur, basse fondamentale (d'un accord).

generatrix, *pl.* **-ices** ['dʒenəreitriks, -isi:z], *s. Mth:* génératrice *f* (d'une surface, etc.).

generic [dʒi'nerik], *a.* générique; *Nat.Hist:* **g. name,** nom *m* générique.

generically [dʒi'nerik(ə)li], *adv.* génériquement. **1.** par rapport au genre. **2.** par rapport à l'ensemble.

generosity [dʒenə'rɔsiti], *s.* **1.** (*a*) générosité *f,* magnanimité *f;* **to act in a spirit of g.,** agir par, avec, générosité; (*b*) générosité, libéralité *f;* **this gift was an example of his g.,** ce don montrait, faisait preuve de, sa générosité; **the library was founded thanks to the g. of Mr X,** la fondation de la bibliothèque a été due à la libéralité, au don généreux, de M. X. **2.** *A:* noblesse *f* (de naissance).

generous ['dʒen(ə)rəs], *a.* **1.** (*a*) généreux, magnanime; **he has a g. nature,** c'est une âme généreuse; (*b*) généreux, libéral, -aux; **g. gift,** don généreux; **he's g. with his money,** il n'est pas avare de son argent, il ne regarde pas à la dépense; *F:* il n'est pas près de ses sous; (*c*) **g. soil,** sol généreux, fertile; **g. wine,** vin généreux, chaud; (*d*) **he took a g. helping of the stew,** il s'est servi amplement du ragoût; *F:* **she's built on g. lines,** elle a des formes généreuses. **2.** *A:* (*a*) généreux, de haute naissance; (*b*) (*of horse, etc.*) de bonne race; racé.

generously ['dʒen(ə)rəsli], *adv.* (*a*) généreusement, magnanimement; (*b*) généreusement, libéralement; (*c*) **he helped himself g. to the stew,** il s'est servi amplement, libéralement, du ragoût.

genesiac(al) [dʒeni:si'æk(l)], *a.* génésiaque.

genesis ['dʒenisis], *s.* **1.** genèse *f,* origine *f.* **2.** *B:* **(the Book of) G.,** la Genèse.

genesitic [dʒeni'sitik], *a.* génésiaque.

genet ['dʒenit], *s. Z:* genette *f.*

genethliacal [dʒeneθ'laiəkl], *a. Astrol: Lit:* généthliaque.

genethliacon [dʒeneθ'laiəkɔn], *s. Poet:* généthliaque *m.*

genetic [dʒi'netik], *a.* **1.** *Phil:* génétique. **2.** *Biol:* génétique; (instinct *m*) génésique.

genetically [dʒi'netik(ə)li], *adv. Biol:* génétiquement.

geneticist [dʒi'netisist], *s.* généticien, -ienne, génétiste *mf.*

genetics [dʒi'netiks], *s.pl.* (*usu. with sg. const.*) génétique *f.*

genetism ['dʒenitizm], *s. Psy:* génétisme *m.*

genetrix, *pl* **-ices** ['dʒenitriks, -isi:z], *s.f.* génitrice.

Geneva [dʒi'ni:və], *Pr.n. Geog:* Genève *f;* **the Lake of G.,** le lac de Genève; le lac Léman; *attrib.* **the G. Cross,** la croix de Genève; *Mec:* **G. wheel, G. gear,** croix de Malte; **G.(-cross) movement, G. motion,** mouvement *m* de Genève; entraînement *m* par croix de Malte; *Hist:* **the G. Convention,** la Convention de Genève; *Ecc:* **G. bands,** rabat *m* ecclésiastique; **G. gown,** robe noire (des prédicateurs calvinistes).

Genevan [dʒi'ni:vən], **Genevese** [dʒenə'vi:z], *Geog:* (*a*) *a.* genevois; (*b*) *s.* Genevois, -oise.

Genevieve ['dʒenəvi:v], *Pr.n.f.* Geneviève; *Ecc:* **canonici of St G.,** religieux génovéfains; **daughter of St G.,** génovéfine *f.*

genial[1] ['dʒi:niəl], *a.* **1.** (*a*) (*of climate, etc.*) doux, *f.* douce; clément; (*of fire, warmth, etc.*) réconfortant; **g. wine,** vin généreux; **soil g. to the seed,** sol *m* propice à la semence; (*b*) plein de bienveillance; plein de bonne humeur; jovial, -aux; cordial, -aux; plein d'entrain; sympathique. **2.** (*of talent, etc.*) génial, -aux; de génie.

genial[2] [dʒi'naiəl], *a. Anat:* mentonnier, du menton; **g. process, tubercle,** apophyse génienne, apophyse géni.

geniality [dʒi:ni'æliti], *s.* (*a*) douceur *f,* clémence *f* (d'un climat); (*b*) bienveillance *f;* bonne humeur; jovialité *f;* cordialité *f;* entrain *m.*

genially ['dʒi:niəli], *adv.* affablement, cordialement; d'un air engageant.

genialness ['dʒi:niəlnis], *s.* = GENIALITY.

geniculate(d) [dʒe'nikjuleit(id)], *a. Nat.Hist:* géniculé.

geniculation [dʒenikju'leiʃ(ə)n], *s. Nat.Hist:* géniculation *f.*

genie, *pl. usu.* **genii** [dʒi:ni, 'dʒi:niai], *s. Myth:* djinn *m,* génie *m;* **the genii of the Arabian Nights,** les génies des contes arabes.

genioglossal [dʒe'naiou'glɔsl], *a. Anat:* génio(-)glosse.

genioglossus [dʒe'naiou'glɔsəs], *s. Anat:* génio(-)glosse *m.*

genio-hyoid [dʒe'naiou'haiɔid], *a. & s. Anat:* génio-hyoïdien (*m*), *pl.* génio-hyoïdiens.

genioplasty [dʒe'naiou'plæsti], *s. Surg:* génioplastie *f.*

genip ['dʒenip], *s. Bot:* **g. (tree),** génipayer *m.*

genipi ['dʒenipi], *s. Bot:* génépi (musqué).

genista [dʒi'nistə], *s. Bot:* genêt *m;* genista *m.*

genistein ['dʒenistain], *s. Ch:* genistéine *f.*

genital ['dʒenitl]. **1.** *a.* génital, -aux. **2.** *s.pl.* **genitals,** organes génitaux externes; parties génitales; parties naturelles; parties sexuelles; *F:* les parties; **(male) genitals,** virilités *fpl,* parties viriles.

genitival [dʒeni'taivl], *a. Gram:* du génitif.

genitive ['dʒenitiv], *a. & s. Gram:* génitif (*m*); **in the g.,** au génitif; *Gr.Gram:* **g. absolute,** génitif absolu.

genito-crural ['dʒenitou'kruərəl], *a. Anat:* génito-crural, -aux.

genitor ['dʒenitər], *s.m.* géniteur *m.*

genito-urinary ['dʒenitou'juərinəri], *a. Anat:* génito-urinaire, *pl.* génito-urinaires.

genitrix, *pl.* **-ices** ['dʒenitriks, -isi:z], *s.f.* génitrice.

genius ['dʒi:niəs], *s.* **1.** (*a*) (*only in sg.*) génie *m,* esprit *m* tutélaire (d'un lieu, etc.); **to invoke the g. of Liberty,** invoquer le génie de la liberté; **she is his good g., his bad, evil, g.,** c'est son bon, son mauvais, génie; (*b*) (*with pl.* **genii** ['dʒi:niai]) génie, démon *m,* esprit, djinn *m.* **2.** (*no pl.*) (*a*) génie particulier, esprit (d'une époque, d'une nation, d'une langue, etc.); (*b*) *Lit:* **g. of a place,** (i) souvenirs (historiques, littéraires, etc.) associés avec un endroit; (ii) pouvoir *m* d'évocation d'un endroit. **3.** (*no pl.*) (*ability*) (*a*) aptitudes naturelles; **to have a g. for mathematics,** avoir un génie marqué pour les mathématiques; avoir le don, *F:* la bosse, des mathématiques; **to have a g. for business,** avoir le génie des affaires; **to have a g. for doing sth.,** avoir le don de faire qch.; **his g. for extricating himself from difficulties,** son génie, son habileté géniale, à se tirer d'affaire; (*b*) **man of g.,** homme *m* de génie; **work of g.,** œuvre géniale, de génie; **to show g.,** faire preuve de génie; **to show g. in war,** avoir le génie de la guerre. **4.** (*pers.*) (*pl.* **geniuses** ['dʒi:niəsiz]) **to be a g.,** être un génie; **he's no g.,** ce n'est pas un aigle; **you haven't got to be a g. to see that,** il n'y a pas besoin d'être sorcier, d'être bien malin, pour s'en apercevoir.

Gennesaret(h) [ge'nezərit, -riθ], *Pr.n. B:* **Lake of G.,** lac *m* de Génésareth.

Genoa ['dʒenouə], *Pr.n.* (*a*) *Geog:* Gênes *f;* (*b*) *Cu:* **G. cake,** cake aux fruits recouvert d'amandes.

genocide ['dʒenəsaid], *s.* génocide *m.*

genodermatosis [dʒi:noudəmə'tousis], *s. Med:* génodermatose *f.*

Genoese [dʒenou'i:z], (*a*) *a. Geog:* génois; *Cu:* **G. pastry,** génoise *f,* mille-feuille *f;* (*b*) *s. Geog:* Génois, -oise.

genoid ['dʒi:nɔid], *s. Biol:* génoïde *m.*

genome ['dʒi:noum], *s. Biol:* génome *m.*

genomere ['dʒi:noumiər], *s. Biol:* génomère *m.*

genotype ['dʒi:noutaip], *s. Biol:* génotype *m.*

genotypical [dʒi:nou'tipikl], *a. Biol:* génotypique.

genouillère [ʒə'noujɛər], *s.* (*a*) *N.Arm:* genouillère *f;* (*b*) *Fort:* genouillère.

genre ['ʒɔnrə], *s.* genre *m;* **g. painting,** peinture *f* de genre.

gent [dʒent], *s.* (*a*) *P:* monsieur *m;* **flashy g.,** épateur *m;* **he's ever such a g.,** il est de la haute; c'est un type bien; **he's no g.,** il est plutôt commun; (*b*) *Com:* **gents' footwear,** chaussures *fpl* pour hommes; (*c*) *P.N:* (*on public convenience*) **gents,** hommes; *P:* **where's the gents?** où sont les W.C.?

genteel [dʒen'ti:l], *a.* (*a*) *A:* de bon ton; comme il faut; distingué; (*b*) **g. poverty,** pauvreté *f* qui s'efforce de sauver les apparences; (*c*) *Pej:* maniéré; qui affecte la distinction; qui imite l'aristocratie; *P:* **she always tries to be so g.,** elle veut vous faire croire qu'elle est de la haute.

genteelly [dʒen'ti:lli], *adv.* (*a*) *A:* comme il faut; (*b*) *Pej:* d'un ton maniéré, d'une façon maniérée; en affectant une soi-disant distinction.

genteelness [dʒen'ti:lnis] *s.* = GENTILITY.

genthite ['dʒenθait], *s. Miner:* genthite *f.*

gentian ['dʒenʃiən], *s. Bot:* gentiane *f;* **horse g.,** triostéc *m;* **g. bitter,** (amer *m* de) gentiane; *Pharm:* **g. root,** racine *f* de gentiane.

Gentianaceae [dʒenʃiə'neisii:], *s.pl. Bot:* gentian(ac)ées *f.*

Gentianales [dʒenʃiə'neili:z], *s.pl. Bot:* gentianales *f.*

gentianella [dʒenʃiə'nelə], *s. Bot:* gentianelle *f;* gentiane *f* acaule.

gentianin ['dʒenʃiənin], *s. Ch:* gentianine *f.*

Gentile ['dʒentail], *a. & s.* **1.** (*a*) gentil, -ile ((i) non-juif, -juive; (ii) *A:* (*as used by early Christians*) païen, -enne); **the Gentiles,** les Gentils, la gentilité; *B:* **to preach to the Gentiles,** prêcher la foi aux Gentils; (*b*) *U.S:* non-Mormon. **2.** *Gram: A:* **g. (noun),** gentilé *m.*

gentilitial [dʒenti'liʃ(ə)l], *a. A:* **1. g. name,** (i) nom *m* générique, de famille; (ii) gentilé *m.* **2. g. family,** famille *f* de vieille noblesse.

gentility [dʒen'tiliti], *s.* **1.** (*a*) *A:* distinction *f*; bon ton; manières distinguées; **family of undoubted g.,** famille (i) bien posée dans le monde, (ii) dont la descendance est bien établie; (*b*) **shabby g.,** la misère en habit noir; (*c*) *Pej:* prétention *f* à la distinction, au bon ton; ton maniéré; manières affectées. **2.** *coll. A:* **the g.,** la haute bourgeoisie.

gentiobiose [dʒenʃiou'baious], *s. Bio-Ch:* gentiobiose *m.*

gentiopicrin [dʒenʃiou'pikrin], *s. Bio-Ch:* gentiopicrine *f.*

gentisate ['dʒentiseit], *s. Ch:* gentisate *m.*

gentisic [dʒen'tisik], *a. Ch:* (acide) gentisique.

gentisin ['dʒentisin], *s. Ch:* gentisine *f.*

gentle[1] ['dʒentl], *a.* & *s.*

I. *a.* (**gentler, gentlest**) **1.** (*a*) *A:* bien né, *A:* gentil; **of g. birth,** de bonne naissance; de bonne extraction; **g. family,** bonne famille; **g. pursuits,** passe-temps *m*, professions *f*, dignes de la noblesse; professions distinguées; **the g. and simple classes,** les classes privilégiées et les roturiers *m*; (*b*) *Her:* ayant droit au blason; (*c*) *Lit:* **the g. art, craft,** la pêche à la ligne; *Iron:* **the g. art of smuggling,** le noble art de la contrebande; (*d*) *A:* **g. reader,** cher, noble, lecteur; aimable lectrice. **2.** (*of pers., animal, wind, heat, sound, etc.*) doux, *f.* douce; **g. as a lamb,** doux comme un agneau; **g. disposition,** caractère doux; **to be g. with one's hands,** avoir la main légère; **the gentle(r) sex,** le sexe faible; **g. rebuke,** réprimande *f* peu sévère; **g. tap,** tape légère; **g. exercise,** exercice physique modéré; **g. slope,** pente douce, faible; **gentler slopes,** pentes moins raides; **g. breeze,** brise molle, *Nau:* petite brise; *F:* (*pers.*) **a g. creature,** un doux, une douce.

II. *s.* **1.** *A:* **gentles** = GENTLEFOLK. **2.** *Fish:* asticot *m*, achée *f.*

gentle[2], *v.tr.* flatter (un cheval).

gentlefolk ['dʒentl'fouk], *s.pl.* (*a*) *A:* gens *m* comme il faut, bien élevés, de bonne société; (*b*) personnes *fpl* de bonne famille, de la meilleure bourgeoisie; **distressed g.** = les économiquement faibles, les nouveaux pauvres.

gentleman, *pl.* **-men** ['dʒentlmən], *s.m.* **1.** *A:* gentilhomme, *pl.* gentilshommes; *still so used in* **G. in waiting,** gentilhomme servant, de service (près du roi); **G.-at-arms,** gentilhomme de la garde; *A:* **G. at large,** (i) gentilhomme attaché à la Cour sans fonctions spéciales; (ii) *Hum:* personne *f* qui se trouve sans emploi; *Sch: A:* (*at Oxford*) **g. commoner,** (i) étudiant privilégié; (ii) *F:* (*empty bottle*) cadavre *m.* **2.** homme bien élevé; homme comme il faut; gentleman; **g. by birth,** homme bien né, gentleman de naissance; **one of Nature's gentlemen,** un gentleman né; un homme d'un naturel foncièrement courtois et loyal; **a fine old English g.,** un gentleman de la vieille roche; **gentleman's agreement,** convention verbale, où n'est engagée que la parole d'honneur entre les deux parties; **to act, behave, like a g.,** se conduire en homme bien élevé; *Pej:* **he's quite a g.,** il est très convenable; **he's no g.,** il est mal élevé, il manque de savoir-vivre. **3.** (*a*) *Jur:* **g. (of independent means),** homme sans profession; rentier; **to be a g. of leisure, to lead a gentleman's life,** vivre de ses rentes; **g. farmer,** gentleman-farmer, *pl.* gentlemen-farmers; (*b*) *Sp:* amateur; *Hist. of Cr:* **Players v. Gentlemen,** (match de) professionnels contre amateurs. **4.** monsieur, homme; (*to audience*) **Ladies and Gentlemen!** mesdames et messieurs! **the g. on my right,** le monsieur qui est à ma droite; **there's a g. to see you, sir,** il y a un monsieur qui voudrait vous parler, monsieur; *O:* **young g.,** jeune homme; (*to child*) **tell the g. your name,** dis ton nom au monsieur; *F:* **the old g. (in black),** le diable; *Hist: F:* **the little g. in black velvet,** (chez les Jacobites) une taupe (Guillaume III mourut des suites d'une chute, son cheval ayant buté contre une taupinière); *Com:* **gentlemen's hairdresser,** coiffeur *m* pour hommes; d'hommes; **gentlemen's suitings,** tissus *m* pour hommes; *P.N:* (*on public convenience*) **gentlemen,** messieurs; **gentleman's g.,** valet de chambre; *A:* **g. of fortune,** boucanier, pirate; **g. of the road,** voleur *m* de grand chemin; *P:* **her g. friend,** son ami. **5.** *Danc:* cavalier; (*of a lady*) **to dance, take, g.,** remplacer un cavalier; faire le cavalier; conduire.

gentlemanlike ['dʒentlmənlaik], *a. A:* = GENTLEMANLY.

gentlemanliness ['dʒentlmənlinis], *s.* bonnes manières; savoir-vivre *m*; tenue parfaite.

gentlemanly ['dʒentlmənli], *a.* bien élevé; distingué; **g. appearance,** air distingué; **it would have been more g. to say nothing,** un homme bien élevé n'aurait rien dit.

gentleness ['dʒentlnis], *s.* **1.** *A:* bonne naissance. **2.** douceur *f*; **g. achieves more than violence,** plus fait douceur que violence.

gentlewoman, *pl.* **-women** ['dʒentlwumən, -wimin], *s.f.* **1.** (*a*) dame, demoiselle (i) bien née, de bonne famille, (ii) distinguée, bien élevée; (*b*) *Jur:* dame sans profession, qui vit de ses rentes. **2.** *A:* dame d'honneur; dame de compagnie (à la Cour); suivante (d'une princesse, etc.).

gently ['dʒentli], *adv.* **1.** *A:* **g. born,** bien né; de bonne naissance. **2.** doucement; **to speak g.,** parler d'un ton doux, avec douceur; **g. (does it)!** allez-y doucement, en douceur; tout beau! **to deal g. with s.o.,** traiter qn avec indulgence; ménager qn; ne pas être trop dur avec qn.

gentry ['dʒentri], *s. coll.* **1.** petite noblesse; gentry *f*; **the nobility and g.,** la haute et la petite noblesse; **the g. of the county,** les familles territoriales du comté; **landed g.,** aristocratie terrienne. **2.** *Pej:* gens *mpl*, individus *mpl*; **the light-fingered g.,** les voleurs *m* à la tire.

genuflect ['dʒenjuflekt], *v.i.* faire des génuflexions; faire une génuflexion.

genuflection, genuflexion [dʒenju'flekʃ(ə)n], *s.* génuflexion *f.*

genuine ['dʒenjuin], *a.* **1.** (personne) de pure race; (cheval) pur sang; (chien) de race. **2.** (*a*) (manuscrit *m*, antique *f*, etc.) authentique, véritable; **g. coin,** pièce *f* de bon aloi; **g. old nobility,** noblesse *f* de bon aloi; *Com:* **g. article,** article garanti d'origine; (*of car, etc.*) **g. part,** pièce *f* d'origine; **g. burgundy,** bourgogne *m* authentique; **a g. diamond,** un diamant véritable; **there are few g. Liberals left,** il reste peu de véritables libéraux, de libéraux à proprement parler; (*b*) véritable, sincère; franc, *f.* franche; **to display one's g. character,** montrer son véritable caractère; **g. simplicity,** simplicité vraie, franche simplicité; **g. surprise,** véritable surprise *f*; **g. truth,** pure vérité; **g. belief,** croyance *f* sincère; **g. friend,** ami loyal, sans hypocrisie; **g. person,** personne *f* sans détours, sans affectation; *Com:* **g. purchaser,** acheteur sérieux; **g. tears,** larmes *f* véritables; **his laughter is never g.,** il ne rit jamais franchement; son rire ne passe pas les lèvres.

genuinely ['dʒenjuinli], *adv.* **1.** authentiquement. **2.** franchement, véritablement, sincèrement.

genuineness ['dʒenjuinnis], *s.* **1.** authenticité *f* (d'un manuscrit, d'une marque de fabrique, etc.); historicité *f* (d'un événement). **2.** sincérité *f*, loyauté *f* (d'une personne); sincérité (d'un sentiment, d'une excuse).

genus, *pl.* **genera** ['dʒi:nəs, 'dʒenərə], *s.* **1.** *Log:* genre *m*; **the highest g.,** l'idée *f* d'être en général; *A:* le genre suprême; **subaltern g.,** genre intermédiaire; **the g. and differentia,** le genre et la différence. **2.** (*a*) *Nat.Hist:* genre; **the g. Homo,** le genre humain; (*b*) genre, espèce *f.*

geo- [dʒiə, [(')]dʒiou, dʒi:'ɔ], *comb.fm.* géo-.

geobiology [dʒioubai'ɔlədʒi], *s.* géobiologie *f.*

geobionts [dʒiou'baiənts], *s.pl. Biol:* géobiontes *m.*

geoblast ['dʒioublæst], *s. Bot:* géoblaste *m.*

geobotany [dʒiou'bɔtəni], *s.* géobotanique *f.*

geocentric [dʒiou'sentrik], *a. Astr:* géocentrique.

geocerite [dʒi:'ɔsərait], *s. Miner:* géocérite *f.*

geochemical [dʒiou'kemikl], *a.* géochimique.

geochemist [dʒiou'kemist], *s.* géochimiste *mf.*

geochemistry [dʒiou'kemistri], *s.* géochimie *f.*

geochronology [dʒioukrə'nɔlədʒi], *s.* géochronologie *f.*

geocratic [dʒiou'krætik], *a.* géocratique.

geocronite [dʒiou'krounait], *s. Miner:* géocronite *f.*

geocyclic [dʒiou'saiklik], *a.* géocyclique.

geode ['dʒi:oud], *s. Geol:* (*a*) géode *f*; four *m*, poche *f*, à cristaux; (*b*) craque *f*, druse *f* (dans une géode).

geodesic [dʒiou'desik]. **1.** *a.* géodésique. **2.** *s.* (ligne *f*) géodésique *m.*

geodesist [dʒi:'ɔdisist], *s.* géodésien *m*, géodésiste *m.*

geodesy [dʒi:'ɔdisi], *s.* géodésie *f.*

geodetic [dʒiou'detik]. **1.** *a.* (*a*) géodésique; **g. arc, line, point,** arc *m*, ligne *f*, point *m*, géodésique; **g. levelling,** nivellement *m* géodésique; **g. survey,** levé *m* géodésique, opérations *fpl* géodésiques; (*b*) *Av:* **g. construction,** construction *f* géodésique. **2.** *s.* (ligne *f*) géodésique *m.*

geodetics [dʒiou'detiks], *s.pl.* (*usu. with sg. const.*) géodésie *f.*

geodic [dʒi:'ɔdik], *a. Geol:* géodique.

geodimeter [dʒi:'ɔdimi:tər], *s.* géodimètre *m.*

geoduck ['dʒi:oudʌk], *s. Moll:* glycimère *f.*

geodynamic [dʒioudai'næmik]. **1.** *a.* géodynamique. **2.** *s.pl.* (*usu. with sg. const.*) **geodynamics,** géodynamie *f.*

Geoffrey ['dʒefri], *Pr.n.m.* Geoffroi.

geogeny [dʒi:'ɔdʒəni], *s.* géogénie *f.*

geognosy [dʒi:ɔgnəsi], *s.* géognosie *f.*

geographer [dʒi'ɔgrəfər], *s.* géographe *mf.*

geographic(al) [dʒiə'græfik(l)], *a.* géographique; **g. coordinates,** coordonnées *fpl* géographiques; **g. latitude,** latitude *f* géographique, latitude terrestre; **g. engineer,** ingénieur *m* géographe; **g. survey,** levé *m* géographique; *Nau:* **g. range,** portée lumineuse, portée géographique (d'une lumière).

geography [dʒi'ɔgrəfi], *s.* (*a*) géographie *f*; **economic, human, g.,** géographie économique, humaine; **physical g.,** géographie physique; *F:* **I'll show you the g. of the house,** je vais vous montrer la toilette; (*b*) **g. (book),** (traité *m* de) géographie.

geoid ['dʒi:ɔid], *s.* géoïde *m.*

geoidal [dʒi'ɔidl], *a.* géoïdique.

geologic(al) [dʒiə'lɔdʒik(l)], *a.* géologique; **g. epoch, era, period, time,** époque *f*, ère *f*, période *f*, temps *m*, géologique; **g. structure,** structure *f* géologique; **g. map,** carte *f* géologique; **g. survey,** levé *m*, étude *f*, géologique; travaux *mpl* géologiques; **g. section,** coupe *f* géologique.

geologically [dʒiə'lɔdʒik(ə)li], *adv.* géologiquement.

geologist [dʒi'ɔlədʒist], *s.* géologue *mf.*

geologize [dʒi'ɔlədʒaiz], *v.i.* faire de la géologie.

geology [dʒi'ɔlədʒi], *s.* géologie *f.*

geomagnetic [dʒioumæg'netik], *a.* géomagnétique.

geomagnetism [dʒiou'mægnitizm], *s.* géomagnétisme *m.*

geomancy ['dʒioumænsi], *s.* géomancie *f.*

geometer [dʒi:'ɔmitər], *s.* **1.** géomètre *m.* **2.** *Ent:* (*a*) (chenille) arpenteuse *f*; (*b*) (*moth*) géomètre *f.*

geometric(al) [dʒiə'metrik(l)], *a.* géométrique; **g. drawing,** dessin *m* géométrique, linéaire; **g. mean,** moyenne *f* géométrique; **g. progression, series,** progression *f* géométrique; *Av:* **g. pitch (of propeller),** pas *m* géométrique (d'hélice).

geometrician [dʒiəme'triʃ(ə)n], *s.* géomètre *m.*

geometrid [dʒi:'ɔmitrid], *a. Ent:* **g. moth,** géomètre *f.*

Geometridae [dʒiə'metridi:], *s.pl. Ent:* géométrides *m.*

geometrization [dʒiəmetrai'zeiʃ(ə)n], *s.* géométrisation *f.*

geometrize [dʒi:'ɔmitraiz], *v.tr.* & *i.* géométriser.

geometry [dʒi'ɔmitri], *s.* géométrie *f*; (*a*) **Euclidian g.,** géométrie ancienne; **plane g.,** géométrie plane; **analytical, co-ordinate, g.,** géométrie analytique; **solid, three-dimensional, g.,** géométrie dans l'espace, à trois dimensions; **descriptive g.,** géométrie descriptive; (*b*) *Mec.E: etc:* géométrie; configuration *f*, dessin *m*, forme *f*, tracé *m*, géométrique; *Aut:* **steering g.,** géométrie de la direction; *Av:* **fixed-g., variable-g., aircraft,** avion *m* à géométrie fixe, variable; *Atom.Ph:* (*of reactor, irradiation, etc.*) **good, poor, standard, g.,** bonne, mauvaise, géométrie; géométrie normale.

geomorphic [dʒiə'mɔ:fik], *a.* géomorphique.

geomorphogenesis [dʒioumɔ:fou'dʒenəsis], *s.* géomorphogénèse *f.*

geomorphogeny [dʒioumɔ:'fɔdʒəni], *s.* géomorphogénie *f.*

geomorphologic(al) [dʒioumɔ:fə'lɔdʒik(l)], *a.* géomorphologique.

geomorphologist [dʒioumɔ:'fɔlədʒist], *s.* géomorphologue *mf.*

geomorphology [dʒioumɔ:'fɔlədʒi], *s.* géomorphologie *f.*

Geomyidae [dʒiou'maiidi:], *s.pl. Z:* géomyidés *m.*

geonoma [dʒiou'noumə], *s. Bot:* géonoma *m.*

geophagist [dʒi:'ɔfədʒist], *s.* géophage *mf.*

geophagous [dʒi:'ɔfəgəs], *a.* géophage.

geophagy [dʒi:'ɔfədʒi], *s.* géophagie *f.*

geophilus [dʒi:'ɔfiləs], *s. Ent:* géophile *m.*

geophone ['dʒi:əfoun], *s.* géophone *m.*

geophysical [dʒiou'fizikl], *a.* géophysique; **g. engineer,** ingénieur géophysicien; **g. engineering,** sciences *fpl* géophysiques; **g. prospecting,** prospection *f*, exploration *f*, géophysique; **g. satellite,** satellite *m* géophysique.

geophysicist [dʒiou'fizisist], *s.* géophysicien, -ienne.

geophysics [dʒiou'fiziks], *s.* (*usu. with sg. const.*) géophysique *f*; physique *f* du globe.

geophyte ['dʒioufait], *s. Bot:* géophyte *f.*

geopolitician [dʒioupɔli'tiʃ(ə)n], *s.* géopoliticien.

geopolitics [dʒiou'pɔlitiks], *s.pl.* (*usu. with sg. const.*) géopolitique *f.*

geoponic(al) [dʒiou'pɔnik(l)], *a.* géoponique.

geoponics [dʒiou'pɔniks], *s.pl.* (*usu. with sg. const.*) géoponique *f.*

geopotential [dʒioupə'tenʃ(ə)l], *s.* cote géopotentielle (d'un point).

georama [dʒi:ə'rɑ:mə], *s.* géorama *m.*

Geordie ['dʒɔ:di]. **1.** *Pr.n.m. Scot: F:* (*dim. of* **George**) Georges. **2.** *s. esp. Scot: F:* mineur *m*, houilleur *m.* **3.** *s. F:* habitant, -ante, originaire *mf*, du Tyneside.

George [dʒɔ:dʒ]. **1.** *Pr.n.m.* Georges; **Saint G.,** saint Georges (patron de l'Angleterre); *F: O:* **by G.!** sapristi! **St George's Cross,** la croix de St-Georges (la croix rouge de l'Union Jack); **St George's day,** le 23 avril. **2.** *s.* (*a*) médaillon *m* de saint Georges (insigne de l'Ordre de la Jarretière); (*b*) (*decorations*) **G. Cross,** Croix de Georges; **G. Medal,** Médaille de Georges; (*c*) *Num: A:* **yellow G.,** guinée *f*. **3.** *s. Av:* pilote *m* automatique, *F:* George *m*.

georgette [dʒɔː'dʒet], *s. Tex:* crêpe *m* georgette; georgette *f*.

Georgia ['dʒɔːdʒiə], *Pr.n. Geog:* Géorgie *f* ((i) en Russie, (ii) aux États-Unis); **South G.,** Géorgie du Sud.

Georgian[1] ['dʒɔːdʒiən], *a. Eng.Hist:* (i) du règne des quatre rois Georges; (ii) du règne de Georges V.

Georgian[2]. *Geog:* (*a*) *a.* géorgien; (*b*) *s.* Géorgien, -ienne.

Georgic ['dʒɔːdʒik], *s. Lt.Lit:* **the Georgics,** les Géorgiques *f* (de Virgile); **the first G.,** la première Géorgique.

geospiza [dʒiou'spaizə], *s. Orn:* pinson *m* de Darwin.

geostatic [dʒiou'stætik], *a.* géostatique.

geostatics [dʒiou'stætiks], *s.pl.* (*usu. with sg. const.*) géostatique *f*.

geostationary [dʒiou'steiʃən(ə)ri], *a. Space:* (*of orbit, satellite, etc.*) géostationnaire.

geostrophic [dʒiou'strɔfik], *a. Meteor:* géostrophique.

geosynclinal [dʒiousin'klainl], *a. Geol:* géosynclinal, -aux.

geosyncline [dʒiou'sinklain], *s. Geol:* géosynclinal *m*, -aux.

geotaxis, geotaxy [dʒiou'tæksis, -'tæksi], *s. Biol:* géotaxie *f*.

geothermal [dʒiou'θəːm(ə)l], *a.* géothermal, -aux.

geothermic [dʒiou'θəːmik], *a.* géothermique; **g. energy,** énergie *f* géothermique; houille *f* rouge.

geothermics [dʒiou'θəːmiks], *s.pl.* (*usu. with sg. const.*) géothermie *f*.

geothermometer [dʒiouθə'mɔmitər], *s.* géothermomètre *m*.

geotrichosis [dʒioutri'kousis], *s. Med:* géotrichose *f*.

geotropic [dʒiou'trɔpik], *a. Bot:* géotropique.

geotropism [dʒi'ɔtrəpizm], *s. Bot:* géotropisme *m*.

geotrupes [dʒiou'truːpiːz], *s. Ent:* géotrupe *m*.

Gerald ['dʒerəld], *Pr.n.m.* Gérard.

Geraniaceae [dʒəreini'eisii], *s.pl. Bot:* géraniacées *f*.

geraniol [dʒə'reiniɔl], *s. Ch:* géraniol *m*.

geranium [dʒə'reiniəm], *s.* **1.** *Bot:* géranium *m*; *F:* bec-de-grue *m*, *pl.* becs-de-grue. **2.** (*a*) *Hort:* pélargonium *m*; géranium; **rose g.,** géranium rosat; (*b*) *P: O:* nez fleuri; nez rubicond. **3.** *a.* **g. (red),** vermeil, -eille.

geranyl ['dʒerənil], *s. Ch:* géranyle *m*.

gerb(e) [dʒəːb], *s. Pyr:* gerbe *f*.

gerbil(le) ['dʒəːbil], *s. Z:* gerbille *f*.

gerenuk ['gərənuk], *s. Z:* gerenuk *m*, gazelle-girafe *f*, *pl.* gazelles-girafes.

gerfalcon ['dʒəːfɔː(l)kən], *s. Orn:* gerfaut *m*.

gerhardtite [gə'hɑːtait], *s. Miner:* gerhardtite *f*.

geriatrician [dʒeriə'triʃ(ə)n], **geriatrist** [dʒeri'ætrist], *s. Med:* gériatre *mf*.

geriatrics [dʒeri'ætriks], *s.pl. Med:* (*usu. with sg. const.*) gériatrie *f*.

germ[1] [dʒəːm], *s.* **1.** *Biol:* germe *m* (d'un organisme); **g. cell,** cellule *f*; (i) spermatozoïde *m*; (ii) ovule *m*; **g. plasm,** plasma germinatif; *Fig:* **the g. of an idea,** le germe d'une idée; **to kill a rebellion in its g.,** étouffer une révolte dans le germe. **2.** *Med:* germe, microbe *m* (d'une maladie), bacille *m*; **g. warfare,** guerre *f* bactériologique; **g. carrier,** porteur, -euse, de bacilles; **g.-destroying,** germicide; **g.-free,** stérile.

germ[2], *v.i.* germer.

german[1] ['dʒəːmən], *a.* germain; (apparenté) au premier degré; **cousin g.,** cousin(e) germain(e).

German[2]. **1.** *a. Geog:* allemand; **West-G., East-G.,** ouest-allemand, est-allemand; **the G. Democratic Republic,** la République démocratique allemande; *Hist:* **the G. Empire,** l'Empire *m* d'Allemagne; l'Empire germanique. **2.** *s.* (*a*) Allemand, -ande; (*b*) *A.Hist:* Germain, -aine. **3.** *s. Ling:* allemand *m*; **High G., Low G.,** haut, bas, allemand; **G. scholar,** germaniste *mf*; germanisant *m*; **G. phrase, idiom,** germanisme *m*. **4.** *a. Typ:* **G. text,** caractères *m* gothiques.

germander [dʒəː'mændər], *s. Bot:* germandrée *f*; **wall g.,** germandrée petit chêne; chêneau *m*, chênette *f*.

germane [dʒəː'mein], *a.* **1.** *A:* = GERMAN[1]. **2.** approprié (to, à), en rapport (to, avec); se rapportant (to, à); **questions g. to the subject,** questions *f* se rapportant au sujet.

Germania [dʒəː'meiniə], *Pr.n. Hist:* Germanie *f*.

Germanic[1] [dʒəː'mænik], *a.* **1.** allemand. **2.** *Hist:* germanique, germain; **the G. Confederation,** la Confédération germanique. **3.** *s. Ling:* germanique *m*.

germanic[2], *a. Ch:* (sel *m*, etc.) de germanium.

Germanism ['dʒəːmənizm], *s.* **1.** *Ling:* germanisme *m*. **2.** germanophilie *f*, teutomanie *f*.

Germanist ['dʒəːmənist], *s.* **1.** *Ling:* germanisant, -ante; germaniste *mf*. **2.** germanophile *mf*, teutomane *mf*.

germanite ['dʒəːmənait], *s. Miner:* germanite *f*.

germanium [dʒəː'meiniəm], *s. Ch:* germanium *m*; **g. flake, g. pellet,** pastille *f* de germanium; **g. diode,** diode *f* au germanium.

Germanization [dʒəːmənai'zeiʃ(ə)n], *s.* germanisation *f*.

Germanize ['dʒəːmənaiz], *v.tr.* germaniser (son nom, etc.).

Germanizing[1] ['dʒəːmənaiziŋ], *a.* germanisant.

Germanizing[2], *s.* germanisation *f*.

Germanomania [dʒəːmənou'meiniə], *s.* teutomanie *f*.

Germanophile [dʒəː'mænoufail], *s.* germanophile *mf*, teutomane *mf*.

Germanophobe [dʒəː'mænoufoub], *s.* germanophobe *mf*.

Germanophobia [dʒəːmənou'foubiə], *s.* germanophobie *f*.

Germanophobic [dʒəːmənou'foubik], *a.* germanophobe.

Germany ['dʒəːməni], *Pr.n. Geog:* Allemagne *f*; **the Federal Republic of G.,** la République fédérale de l'Allemagne occidentale; **West G., East G.,** l'Allemagne de l'ouest, de l'est.

germen ['dʒəːmen], *s. Biol:* germen *m*.

germicidal [dʒəːmi'saidl], *a.* germicide.

germicide ['dʒəːmisaid], *s.* germicide *m*.

germinal ['dʒəːminl], *a.* **1.** *Biol:* (*of vesicle, etc.*) germinal, -aux; germinatif. **2.** (*of ideas, etc.*) en germe.

germinate ['dʒəːmineit]. **1.** *v.i.* germer; **the idea germinated in the mind of a poet,** cette idée a germé dans l'esprit d'un poète. **2.** *v.tr.* faire germer (des graines, etc.).

germinating ['dʒəːmineitiŋ], *s.* germination *f*.

germination [dʒəːmi'neiʃ(ə)n], *s.* germination *f*; *Hort:* **g. test,** essai *m* des graines.

germinative ['dʒəːmineitiv], *a. Biol:* germinateur, -trice; germinatif.

gerodontia [dʒerou'dɔntiə], *s. Dent:* odontogérontologie *f*.

Gerona [dʒe'rounə], *Pr.n. Geog:* Gérone.

gerontocracy [dʒerɔn'tɔkrəsi], *s.* gérontocratie *f*.

gerontocratic [dʒerɔntou'krætik], *a.* gérontocratique.

gerontologist [dʒerɔn'tɔlədʒist], *s. Med:* gérontologue *mf*.

gerontology [dʒerɔn'tɔlədʒi], *s.* gérontologie *f*.

gerontophilia [dʒerɔntou'filiə], *s.* gérontophilie *f*.

Gerrhosauridae [dʒerou'sɔːridiː], *s.pl. Rept:* gerrhosaurinés *m*.

gerrymander[1] ['gerimændər], *s.* découpage *m* arbitraire de circonscriptions électorales dans un but politique.

gerrymander[2], *v.tr.* **to g. constituencies,** découper ou remanier arbitrairement les circonscriptions électorales (dans un but politique).

gerrymandering [dʒeri'mændəriŋ], *s.* truquage électoral.

gersdorffite ['gəːzdɔfait], *s. Miner:* gersdorffite *f*.

gerund ['dʒerənd], *s. Gram:* gérondif *m*; substantif verbal; **in the g.,** au gérondif; *F: A:* **g.-grinder,** pédant *m*, pédagogue *m*, marchand *m* de participes.

gerundial [dʒi'rʌndiəl], **gerundival** [dʒerən'daivl], *a. Gram:* du gérondif.

gerundive [dʒi'rʌndiv], *Gram:* **1.** *a.* du gérondif. **2.** *s. Lt.Gram:* (gérondif employé comme) adjectif verbal (de la voix passive).

Gervase ['dʒəːvəs], *Pr.n.m.* Gervais.

Gerydinae [dʒe'ridiniː], *s.pl. Ent:* gérydines *f*.

Gesneriaceae [gesnəri'eisiː], *s.pl. Bot:* gesnér(i)acées *f*.

gesso ['dʒesou], *s.* **1.** plâtre *m* de Paris; gypse *m*. **2.** *Art:* enduit de plâtre (destiné à recevoir une fresque).

gestaltism [gə'stæltizm], *s. Phil:* gestaltisme *m*.

gestaltist [gə'stæltist], *a. & s. Phil:* gestaltiste (*mf*).

Gestapo [ge'stɑːpou], *s.* Gestapo *f* (from German *Geheime Staatspolizei*).

gestation [dʒes'teiʃ(ə)n], *s. Physiol:* gestation *f*.

gestatorial [dʒestə'tɔːriəl], *a. Ecc:* **g. chair,** chaise *f* gestatoire.

gesticulate [dʒes'tikjuleit], *v.i.* gesticuler.

gesticulation [dʒestikju'leiʃ(ə)n], *s.* gesticulation *f*.

gesticulatory [dʒes'tikjuleitəri], *a.* gesticulatoire.

gesture[1] ['dʒestjər], *s.* **1.** geste *m*, signe *m*; mouvement *m*; **to make a g.,** faire un geste; **with a sweeping g.,** d'un geste large; **g. of defiance,** geste de défi; **oratorical gestures,** action *f* oratoire; **by gestures,** par gestes, à la muette; *Dipl: etc:* **handsome g., sympathetic g. (by a neighbouring state, etc.),** beau geste, geste de sympathie (de la part d'un État voisin, etc.); **as a g. of friendship,** en témoignage d'amitié. **2.** le geste; **the language of g.,** le langage des gestes; **to signal by g.,** mimer un signal; **he is a master of g.,** il est passé maître en fait de gestes.

gesture[2]. **1.** *v.i.* faire des gestes. **2.** *v.tr.* exprimer (qch.) par gestes.

get[1] [get], *s.* **1.** (*a*) progéniture *f*; (*b*) portée *f* (d'un animal); (*c*) *F:* enfant, *esp.* enfant bâtard. **2.** *Min:* rendement *m* (d'une mine, d'un piqueur). **3.** *Ten:* renvoi *m* (de la balle).

get[2], *v.* (*p.t.* **got** [gɔt]; *p.p.* **got,** *A: & NAm: also* **gotten** ['gɔtn]; *pr.p.* **getting** ['getiŋ])

I. *v.tr.* **1.** (*a*) procurer, obtenir; **to g. sth. for s.o.,** procurer qch. à qn; acheter qch. pour qn; **where did you g. that?** où avez-vous trouvé, acheté, cela? **to g. sth. to eat,** (i) trouver de quoi manger; (ii) manger qch. (au restaurant, etc.); **you (just) can't g. it,** c'est introuvable; il est impossible d'en trouver, de s'en procurer; **where can I g. them?** où puis-je en trouver, en acheter? **I must g. a new hat,** il faut que je m'achète un nouveau chapeau; **I'll g. one for you,** je vais vous en procurer, vous en acheter, un; **I g. my meat from the local butcher,** j'achète ma viande chez le boucher du coin; **England gets all her tea from abroad,** l'Angleterre achète tout son thé à l'étranger, fait venir tout son thé de l'étranger; **I got this car cheap,** j'ai eu, j'ai acheté, cette voiture (à) bon marché; **he wasn't long in getting his corporal's stripes,** il eut tôt fait de décrocher ses galons de caporal; (*b*) acquérir, gagner; **to g. power, a fortune,** acquérir de la puissance, une fortune; **to g. a name (for oneself),** se faire un nom; **to g. a wife,** prendre femme; **to g. the prize,** gagner, remporter, le prix; **to g. one's living,** gagner sa vie; **to g. £5,000 a year,** gagner £5,000 par an; **to g. 10% interest,** recevoir 10 % d'intérêt; **I'll see what I can g. for it,** je verrai ce qu'on m'en donnera; **I g. only a small profit,** il ne me revient, je n'en retire, qu'un léger bénéfice; **to g. nothing by it, out of it, from it,** n'y rien gagner; **a good master gets good results,** un bon maître obtient de bons résultats; *Mth:* **what answer have you got?** quelle est votre solution? **I don't think I've got the answer right,** j'ai dû faire une erreur de calcul; **I don't think I've got the right answer,** je n'ai pas encore trouvé la solution; *F: A:* **don't you wish you may g. it!** je vous en souhaite! (*c*) **to g. mercy (from s.o.),** obtenir miséricorde (de qn); **to g. s.o.'s permission to do sth.,** obtenir la permission de qn de faire qch.; **you can't g. admission to the palace without a permit,** il vous faut un permis (spécial) pour visiter, entrer dans, le château; **to g. one's own way,** faire valoir sa volonté; **to g. a little sleep,** dormir un peu; **I'll do it if I g. the time,** je le ferai si j'ai le temps, si je trouve un moment; **you g. a fine view from the top of the mountain,** il y a une vue magnifique du sommet de la montagne; (*d*) *W.Tel:* **we can't g. Moscow,** nous ne pouvons pas avoir Moscou; *Tp:* **I had a job to g. you,** j'ai eu du mal à vous joindre. **2.** (*a*) recevoir (un cadeau, une lettre, etc.); **I got his answer this morning,** j'ai eu, j'ai reçu, sa réponse ce matin; **room that gets no sun,** pièce où le soleil ne donne pas; **he gets his shyness from his mother,** il tient sa timidité de sa mère; (*b*) attraper (un rhume, une maladie); **you'll g. a chill,** vous allez prendre froid; **he got a severe blow on the head,** il a reçu, attrapé, un coup violent sur la tête; **he got a bullet in his shoulder,** il a reçu une balle dans l'épaule; **to g. a splinter in one's finger,** avoir une écharde dans le doigt; *F:* **to g. religion,** se convertir; *F:* **to g. ten years,** attraper dix ans de prison; *F:* **to g. the sack,** *U.S:* **the hook,** être congédié, mis à la porte; **that's what you g. for talking too much,** voilà ce que c'est que de trop parler; *F:* **to g. it (hot), g. it in the neck,** en prendre pour son compte. **3.** (*a*) prendre, attraper (une bête fauve, etc.); **I got him first shot,** je l'ai atteint, je l'ai eu, au premier coup; **I've got my man,** (i) je tiens mon homme; (ii) *F:* j'ai tué mon homme; *F:* **we'll g. them yet!** on les aura! **you've got me this time,** (i) cette fois-ci vous m'avez eu; (ii) je donne ma langue au chat; *F:* **that's got him!** ça c'est envoyé; *F:* **I'll g. you for that!** j'aurai ta peau, je t'aurai au tournant! **rheumatism that gets me in the back,** des rhumatismes qui me tiennent dans le dos; (*b*) *F:* émouvoir (qn); **it always gets me to see a woman crying,** ça me fait toujours quelque chose de voir pleurer une femme; **the play didn't really g. me,** la pièce ne m'a pas dit grand chose, ne m'a pas emballé; **it gets me how he can be so stupid,** ça m'énerve de le voir si bête; **what's got him?** qu'est-ce qu'il a? qu'est-ce qui lui prend? **that gets me, gets my goat,** ça m'énerve, me met en boule; (*c*) *F:* comprendre; **I don't g. you, your meaning,** je ne vous comprends pas; je ne pige pas; **g. me?** tu y es? tu saisis? **4.** aller chercher; (*to secretary*) **would you g. me my letters, please,** voulez-vous aller me chercher, m'apporter, le courrier, s'il vous plaît; **he went and got a book from the library,** il est allé chercher un livre dans la bibliothèque; **he got his hat and went out,** il a pris, a mis, son chapeau et il est sorti; **go and g. a doctor,** allez chercher un médecin. **5.** (*a*) faire parvenir; **to g. sth. somewhere,** faire transporter qch. quelque part; **how can I g. it to you?** comment vous le faire parvenir? **how am I to g. this parcel home?** comment vais-je faire transporter ce paquet chez moi? **don't worry! I'll g. you to the station,** ne vous inquiétez pas! je vais vous conduire à la gare; **to g. s.o. upstairs,** aider qn à monter l'escalier; **I don't know how you'll ever g. it upstairs,** je ne sais pas comment vous ferez pour le monter (au premier, jusqu'en haut); **to g. the children to bed,** faire coucher les enfants; **to g. s.o. on (to) a subject,** amener qn à parler de qch.; **when you g. him on the Common Market there's no stopping him,** quand il parle du Marché commun il est impossible de l'arrêter; (*b*) **to g. the answer right,** trouver la réponse juste, la bonne solution; *A:* **to g. sth. (off) by heart,** apprendre qch. par cœur; **to g. lunch (ready),** préparer le déjeuner; **to g. s.o. into trouble,** attirer des histoires à qn; *F:* **to g. a woman into trouble,** mettre une femme à mal; *O:* **to g. a woman with child,** faire un enfant à une femme; *F:* **it gets me down,** ça me décourage, me donne le cafard. **6.** (*a*) **to g. sth. done by s.o., to g. s.o. to do sth. (for one),** (se) faire faire qch. à, par, qn; **to g. sth. mended,** faire raccommoder qch.; **the difficulty is not to tell the truth but to g. oneself believed,** le difficile ce n'est pas de dire la vérité mais de se faire croire; **he got himself appointed chairman,** il s'est fait nommer président; **to g. oneself noticed,** attirer l'attention (sur soi); se faire remarquer; (*b*) **g. him to read,** faites-le lire; **g. him to read it,** faites-le-lui lire; **to g. s.o. to agree,** décider qn à consentir; **can I g. you to help me?** puis-je vous demander de m'aider? **we must g. him to come and see us,** il faut le persuader de venir nous voir; **I can never g. him to go to bed,** je n'arrive pas à le faire coucher; **I can't g. the door to shut,** je n'arrive pas, je ne réussis pas, à fermer la porte; **can you g. roses to grow in your garden?** est-ce que vous arrivez à cultiver des roses chez vous? (*c*) **to g. one's work finished,** finir, venir à bout de, son travail; **I must g. my work finished before this evening,** il faut que je termine mon travail avant ce soir; **to g. one's arm broken,** se casser le bras; **to g. one's dress torn,** déchirer sa robe; (*d*) *Aut:* **to g. the engine running,** mettre le moteur en marche; *F:* **that got him guessing,** ça l'a intrigué, lui a mis la puce à l'oreille. **7. have got;** (*a*) avoir; (i) **what have you got there?** qu'avez-vous là? **what's that got to do with it?** qu'est-ce que cela y fait? **he's got measles,** il a la rougeole; **you haven't got the meaning right,** vous n'avez pas bien saisi le sens; vous vous êtes trompé de sens; *F:* **you've got it!** vous avez deviné! vous y êtes! (ii) (**got** *is redundant, and would be omitted in formal style*) **have you got any children?** avez-vous des enfants? **I haven't got any,** je n'en ai pas; **have you got a light?** *P:* **got a light?** avez-vous du feu? (*b*) être obligé (de faire qch.); **you've got to do it,** il faut absolument que vous le fassiez; **it has got to be done,** il faut que cela se fasse; **we've got to get down to it quickly,** il s'agit de faire vite; **have you really got to work on Sundays?** est-ce que vous êtes vraiment obligé de travailler le dimanche? **8.** *Min: O:* exploiter, extraire (du charbon, etc.). **9.** (*of animals, A: of men*) engendrer; *Breed:* **Gladiator got by Monarch out of Gladia,** Gladiator par Monarch et Gladia. **10.** *v.pr. A:* **g. thee gone!** allez-vous-en! **g. thee behind me, Satan,** éloigne-toi de moi, Satan!

II. *v.i.* **1.** (*a*) (*with adj. complement*) devenir (riche, etc.); **to g. old,** devenir, se faire, vieux; vieillir; **to g. grey,** grisonner; **I'm getting used to it,** je commence à m'y habituer, à m'y accoutumer, à m'y faire; **to g. angry,** se mettre en colère; **to g. better,** (i) s'améliorer; (ii) (*after illness*) se remettre; **flowers are getting scarce,** les fleurs se font rares; **it's getting late,** il se fait tard; **it's getting dark,** il commence à faire nuit; (*b*) (*usu. classified v.i.; either virtually v.pr.* (**get dressed**) *or used with passive force* (**got dismissed**)) **to g. dressed,** s'habiller; **to g. married,** se marier; **to g. shaved,** (i) se raser; (ii) se faire raser; **to g. killed,** se faire tuer; **to g. drowned,** se noyer; **to g. caught,** se laisser prendre (par la police, etc.); se trouver pris (dans une machine, etc.); être surpris (par une averse, etc.); **Henry is getting called Old Henry now,** Henri est en voie d'être appelé le vieil Henri; **that vase will g. broken,** ce vase-là va être cassé; **he got dismissed,** il a reçu son congé; **everything gets known,** tout se sait; (*c*) **to g. going,** (i) partir, se mettre en route; (ii) se mettre au travail; (iii) se dépêcher; **let's g. going,** *F:* **g. cracking,** allons-y! en route! **to g. talking with s.o.,** entrer en conversation avec qn; **when we g. talking about the future,** quand nous venons à parler de l'avenir. **2.** (*a*) aller, arriver, se rendre (à un endroit, etc.); **I expect he'll g. here tomorrow,** je pense qu'il arrivera demain; **how does one g. there?** comment fait-on pour y aller? (*asking one's way*) **how do I g. to the station?** le chemin de la gare, s'il vous plaît? **at last the rescuers got to him,** enfin les sauveteurs sont parvenus jusqu'à lui; **we shall soon g. there,** nous y arriverons bientôt; **shall we g. there in time?** arriverons-nous à temps? *F:* **to g. there,** (i) comprendre, y être; (ii) arriver, réussir; **he's well known today, but it took him a long time to g. there,** il est célèbre aujourd'hui, mais il lui a fallu du temps; *F:* **(have you) got there (yet)?** tu saisis ? tu piges? **we're not getting anywhere, we're getting nowhere,** nous n'aboutissons à rien; **to g. to the top of a tree, of a ladder,** monter jusqu'au haut d'un arbre, d'une échelle; **to g. to the top of the tree, the ladder,** réussir; devenir célèbre; se faire un nom; **where have you got to (in your work, etc.)?** où en êtes-vous (dans votre travail, etc.)? **where on earth has my book got to?** où diable est mon livre? **where has he got to?** qu'est-ce qu'il est devenu? *P:* **g. to, the, hell out of here!** *esp. U.S:* **get!** fiche(-moi) le camp! **I had got so far when . . .,** j'en étais (arrivé) là lorsque . . .; **he got as far as saying . . .,** il a été jusqu'à dire . . .; **we got on to (the subject of) divorce,** nous en sommes venus à parler du divorce; **he gets on my nerves,** il m'agace; (*of aircraft*) **to g. above the clouds,** s'élever au-dessus des nuages; **once one gets above, beyond, the tree line,** dès qu'on a dépassé la limite supérieure des arbres; **this has got beyond me,** cela me dépasse; *F:* **it's getting beyond a joke,** ça dépasse la plaisanterie; ça c'est le comble! *F:* **he's getting a bit above himself,** il se croit; (*b*) se mettre; **to g. within s.o.'s reach,** se mettre à la portée de qn; **to g. behind a tree,** se mettre derrière un arbre; *F:* **if you don't g. behind him he doesn't work,** si vous n'êtes pas toujours derrière lui, à ses trousses, il ne travaille pas; **to g. under a table,** se mettre, se glisser, sous une table; **to g. to work,** (i) se mettre au travail; (ii) arriver à son (lieu de) travail; **to g. to bed,** (aller) se coucher; (*c*) **to g. to do sth.,** finir par, en arriver à, faire qch.; **you'll g. to like him,** vous arriverez à l'aimer, vous finirez par l'aimer; **to g. to know sth.,** apprendre qch.; **when you g. to know him,** quand on le connaît mieux; **they got to be friends,** ils sont devenus amis.

III. (*compound verbs*) **1. get about,** *v.i.* (*a*) (*of pers.*) circuler; **you can g. about quickly if you have a car,** si on a une voiture on circule vite; **he gets about a great deal,** il voyage, se déplace, beaucoup; il sort beaucoup; (*of invalid*) **to g. about again,** être de nouveau sur pied; **he can't g. about yet,** il ne peut pas encore sortir; (*b*) (*of news*) se répandre, circuler, s'ébruiter.

2. get across. (*a*) *v.i.* (arriver à) traverser (une rue, une rivière), passer (une rivière); **he got across by swimming,** il a traversé la rivière à la nage; *Th: F:* **the play failed to g. across,** la pièce n'a pas passé la rampe; *F:* **to g. across to s.o.,** se faire comprendre par qn; **the idea didn't g. across,** l'idée n'a pas pénétré; (*b*) *v.tr.* faire passer, faire traverser; **I can't g. you across the river because of the floods,** je ne puis pas vous faire passer la rivière à cause des inondations; *Com:* **I'll g. the goods across to you tomorrow,** je vais vous faire livrer les marchandises demain; *Th: F:* **they couldn't g. the play across,** ils ont fait four, la pièce n'a pas passé la rampe; *F:* **I couldn't g. it across to him,** je n'ai pas réussi à le lui faire comprendre.

3. get along, *v.i.* (*a*) s'avancer (dans son chemin); **it's time for me to be getting along,** il est temps que je parte; *F:* **g. along with you!** (i) allez-vous-en! filez! (ii) allons donc! vous plaisantez! (*b*) (= GET ON) faire des progrès (dans son travail, etc.); (*c*) (= GET ON) s'entendre, s'accorder (avec qn).

4. get around, *v.i.* (*a*) circuler, voyager; rouler sa bosse; **she gets around a great deal,** elle voyage, sort, beaucoup; elle est toujours par ci, par là; (*b*) **to g. around to doing sth.,** arriver à faire qch.; trouver le temps de faire qch.; (*c*) circonvenir, surmonter (des difficultés, etc.).

5. get at, *v.tr. & i.* (*a*) parvenir à, atteindre (un endroit); accéder jusqu'à, atteindre (qn); **the village is difficult to g. at,** le village est peu accessible, difficile à atteindre, d'un accès difficile; **he's so busy (that) you can never g. at him,** il est tellement occupé qu'on ne peut jamais le voir, l'atteindre; **we've got the painters in the study and I can't g. at my books,** les peintres occupent le bureau et je ne puis pas prendre, atteindre, mes livres; **to g. at the root of the trouble,** trouver la racine du mal; **to g. at the truth,** découvrir la vérité; **that's what I'm trying to g. at,** c'est là que je veux en venir; **you're trying to g. at something and there's nothing to g. at,** vous voulez pénétrer le secret; or, il n'y a pas de secret; **the dog couldn't g. at me,** le chien ne pouvait pas arriver jusqu'à moi; *F:* **just let me g. at him!** si jamais il me tombe sous la patte! (*b*) *F:* acheter (qn); graisser la patte à (qn); suborner, travailler (un témoin); (*c*) *F:* attaquer (qn), faire des insinuations contre (qn); **who are you getting at?** (i) à qui, après qui, en avez-vous? (ii) c'est pour moi, ça? **she's always getting at her husband,** elle est toujours à dénigrer son mari.

6. get away. (*a*) *v.i.* (i) partir; (*of prisoner, etc.*) s'échapper, se sauver; **to g. away early from the office,** quitter le bureau de bonne heure; **we didn't g. away until midnight,** nous n'avons pas pu partir avant minuit; **to g. away for a few days,** (parvenir à) s'absenter pendant quelques jours; **they got away to the mountains,** ils sont partis (en vacances) à la montagne; **to g. away from one's surroundings,** échapper, se soustraire, à son entourage; **how wonderful to g. away from it all!** quel plaisir de tout quitter! **g. away (from here)!** allez-vous-en! filez! *F:* fiche-moi la paix! *P:* **g. away (with you)!** tu plaisantes! ça ne prend pas! **there's no getting away from him,** (α) on ne peut pas s'en débarrasser; il vous suit partout; (β) il vous retient d'une façon impossible; **there's no getting away from it,** il n'y a pas à sortir de là; il faut bien l'admettre; (ii) *Aut:* démarrer; **car that gets away quickly,** voiture qui a une bonne reprise; (iii) **the burglars got away with £10,000,** les cambrioleurs ont raflé £10,000; *F:* **to g. away with it,** faire accepter quelque chose; s'en tirer à bon compte; **it was an extraordinary plan but he got away with it,** le projet paraissait extraordinaire mais il a réussi à le faire accepter; **he won't g. away with it,** il ne l'emportera pas au paradis; **you won't g. away with that excuse,** vous ne vous en tirerez pas avec cette excuse-là; (*b*) *v.tr.* arracher (qch. à qn); éloigner (qn); **I managed to g. her away at eleven,** j'ai réussi à l'emmener à onze heures; **they got him away to Australia,** ils l'ont envoyé, expédié, en Australie.

7. get back. (*a*) *v.i.* (i) reculer; (ii) revenir, retourner; **to g. back home,** rentrer chez soi; **he got back into his car,** il est remonté dans sa voiture; **to g. back into bed,** se recoucher; **to g. back to nature,** retourner à la nature; (*b*) *v.tr.* (i) se faire rendre (qch.); rentrer en possession de (qn); retrouver (un objet perdu); recouvrer (ses biens); reprendre (ses forces); **try to g. that letter back,** tâchez de ravoir cette lettre; **to g. one's money back,** (α) rentrer dans ses fonds; (β) se faire rembourser; **now that I've got you back,** maintenant que vous êtes de retour, que vous m'êtes revenu; *F:* **to g. one's own back,** *v.i. NAm:* **to g. back at s.o.,** prendre sa revanche (sur qn); rendre la pareille (à qn); **I'll g. my own back on you!** vous ne perdrez pas pour attendre! (ii) faire revenir (qn); (iii) **I've got it off, out, and now I can't g. it back,** je l'ai ôté, sorti, et maintenant je n'arrive pas à le remettre; **to g. sth. back into its box,** faire rentrer qch. dans sa boîte; **we must g. the trunk back to the attic, to London,** il faut remonter la malle au grenier; il faut (trouver moyen de) renvoyer la malle à Londres.

8. get by, *v.i.* (*a*) passer; **there wasn't enough room to g. by,** il n'y avait pas assez de place pour passer; (*b*) *F:* se débrouiller; **we just g. by,** on s'en tire, voilà tout.

9. get down. (*a*) *v.i.* (i) descendre (**from, off,** de); **please may I g. down, Mummy?** est-ce que je puis quitter la table, s'il te plaît maman? **to g. down on one's knees,** se mettre à genoux; (*to dog, etc.*) **g. down!** (à) bas les pattes! (ii) **to g. down to work,** se mettre au travail; **once you g. down to it,** quand on s'y met; **we'd better g. down to the facts,** il faut en venir aux faits; (*b*) *v.tr.* (i) descendre (un livre d'un rayon, etc.); décrocher (son chapeau d'une patère); *Nau:* amener (une voile, une vergue); (ii) **to g. sth. down (in writing, on paper),** noter qch. (par écrit); **I couldn't g. it all down,** je n'ai pas pu tout noter; (iii) avaler (une bouchée, etc.); **I couldn't g. it down,** je n'ai pas pu l'avaler, le faire passer.

10. get in. (*a*) *v.i.* (i) entrer; **we got in at about eleven,** nous sommes rentrés (chez nous) vers onze heures; **he got in through the window,** il est entré par la fenêtre; **to g. in a train,** monter dans un train; *Aut:* **g. in, I'm starting,** monte, je démarre; **water had got in everywhere,** l'eau avait pénétré, s'était introduite, partout; **if the train gets in on time,** si le train arrive à l'heure; **I could only just g. in,** c'est à peine si j'ai pu m'y glisser, m'y introduire; **to g. in between two people,** s'introduire, se glisser, se mettre, entre deux personnes; (ii) *F:* **to g. in with s.o.,** s'insinuer dans les bonnes grâces de qn; se mettre sur un bon pied avec qn; (iii) *Pol:* **to g. in (for a constituency),** être élu député (pour une circonscription); **he's sure to g. in,** il sera certainement élu; **the Conservatives got in,** le parti conservateur a accédé au pouvoir; (*b*) *v.tr.* (i) rentrer (la moisson, etc.); *Nau:* **to g. a boat in,** rentrer une embarcation; **to g. coal in for the winter,** faire une provision de charbon, acheter du charbon, pour l'hiver; *Com:* **to g. one's Christmas goods in,** s'approvisionner pour Noël; **it's often difficult to g. one's money in,** il est souvent difficile de se faire payer; **to g. a man in to mend a window,** faire venir un homme pour réparer une fenêtre; (ii) **to g. a**

blow in, donner, placer, un coup; **I can't g. a word in (edgeways),** je n'arrive pas à placer un mot; **I'll do it if I can possibly g. it in,** je le ferai si toutefois j'en trouve le temps; (iii) **to g. one's hand in,** se faire la main; *Games: etc:* **to g. one's eye in,** assurer son coup d'œil; (iv) planter, semer (des graines, etc.).

11. get into, *v.tr. & i.* (*a*) (*mainly prepositional*) entrer dans (une maison, etc.); pénétrer dans (un bois, etc.); monter dans (une voiture, un train, etc.); **the burglars got into the kitchen,** les cambrioleurs se sont introduits dans la cuisine; **to g. into a club,** se faire élire, être élu, membre d'un club; **to g. into parliament,** être élu député; **to g. into a university,** entrer en faculté; **to g. into bad company,** faire de mauvaises connaissances; (*b*) mettre (ses vêtements); endosser (un pardessus, etc.); enfiler (ses bas, etc.); **I can't g. into this dress any more,** je n'entre plus dans cette robe; **to g. into a rage,** se mettre en rage; **to g. into a bad habit,** acquérir, prendre, une mauvaise habitude; **to g. into the way of doing sth.,** (i) apprendre à faire qch.; (ii) prendre l'habitude de faire qch.; **you'll soon g. into (the way of) it,** on s'y met, s'y fait, vite; (*c*) **to g. sth. into sth.,** (faire) (r)entrer, enfoncer, qch. dans qch.; **to g. the key into the lock,** mettre, entrer, introduire, la clef dans la serrure; **to g. an article into a paper,** faire accepter un article par un journal.

12. get off. (*a*) *v.i.* (i) descendre (d'un autobus, etc.); **the conductor will tell you where to g. off,** le receveur vous dira où descendre; *P:* **I told him where to g. off,** je lui ai dit ses quatre vérités; *P:* **g. off!** fous-moi la paix! (ii) se faire exempter (d'une corvée, etc.); (iii) se tirer d'affaire; être acquitté; **to g. off easily, lightly,** s'en tirer facilement, à bon compte; **to g. off with a fine,** en être quitte pour une amende; (iv) partir; *Av:* décoller; **we got off at eleven,** nous sommes partis à onze heures; **to g. off to sleep,** s'endormir; (v) *P:* **to g. off with s.o.,** faire une touche; (*b*) *v.tr.* (i) ôter (ses vêtements); enlever (des vêtements, une bague, etc.); **to g. a nut off,** desserrer un écrou; **to g. stains off (sth.),** ôter, enlever, faire partir, faire disparaître, des taches (de qch.); (ii) *Sp:* **to g. off a round (of a tournament),** jouer une épreuve; *F:* **to g. a speech off,** faire un discours; (iii) expédier (un colis, une lettre); **we managed to g. him off on time,** nous avons réussi à le faire partir à l'heure; (iv) **to g. sth. off one's hands,** se débarrasser de qch.; *F:* **he's got his daughter off his hands,** il a marié, casé, sa fille; (v) faire acquitter (un prévenu); tirer (qn) d'affaire; (vi) *Nau:* renflouer, déséchouer (un navire); **to g. the crew off,** débarquer l'équipage (d'un navire naufragé); (vii) *A:* **to g. off fifty lines of Latin,** apprendre par cœur cinquante vers latins.

13. get on. (*a*) *v.tr.* mettre (ses chaussures, etc.), enfiler (ses bas, etc.); **I can't g. these trousers on any more,** je n'entre plus dans ce pantalon; (*b*) *v.i.* (i) **to g. on (to) a ladder, a train, etc.,** monter sur une échelle, dans un train, etc.; (ii) s'avancer (vers un endroit); **we must be getting on now,** il est temps de nous remettre en route; **to be getting on (in years),** prendre de l'âge; avancer en âge; être d'un certain âge; ne pas être de première jeunesse; **to be getting on for forty,** approcher de, aller sur, friser, la quarantaine; **time's getting on,** l'heure s'avance; le temps passe; il se fait tard; **it's getting on for midnight,** il est presque minuit, il n'est pas loin de minuit; **there are getting on for 300 pupils,** il n'y a pas loin de, il y a presque, 300 élèves; **it's getting on for three months since we had any news,** ça va bientôt faire trois mois que nous sommes sans nouvelles; (ii) faire des progrès; réussir (dans la vie); faire son chemin (dans le monde); **he is determined to g. on (at all costs),** il est résolu à réussir, à faire son chemin; *Pej:* c'est un arriviste; **the way to g. on,** le moyen de réussir; **to g. on with one's work,** continuer son travail; **how are you getting on?** comment allez-vous? comment vont les affaires? comment va votre travail? *F:* ça marche? **how did you g. on in your exam(ination)?** comment votre examen a-t-il marché? *F:* et votre examen? **I'll let you know how he's getting on,** je vous donnerai de ses nouvelles; **to g. on without s.o., sth.,** se passer de qn, de qch.; **I can't g. on without him, without his help,** je ne puis pas me passer de lui, de ses services; (iii) **to g. on (well) with s.o.,** s'entendre, s'accorder, avec qn; vivre en bonne intelligence avec qn; faire bon ménage avec qn; **we don't g. on very well (together),** nous ne nous entendons pas très bien; nous sommes en froid; **easy to g. on with,** commode à vivre; (iv) *F:* **g. on with you!** (α) tu crois? pour qui me prends-tu? (β) va te promener! (v) *F:* **to g. on to sth.,** découvrir qch.; découvrir le truc; **to g. on to s.o.,** (α) contacter qn; (β) découvrir le vrai caractère de qn.

14. get out. (*a*) *v.tr.* (i) arracher (un clou, etc.); tirer, retirer (un bouchon); enlever, faire disparaître (une tache); **to g. sth. out of sth.,** faire sortir, tirer, qch. de qch.; **I can't g. the idea out of my mind,** je ne puis pas me débarrasser de l'idée; **to g. a secret out of s.o.,** arracher un secret à qn; **I'll g. the truth out of him,** je me charge de lui faire dire la vérité; **I can't g. anything out of him,** je ne peux rien tirer de lui; **to g. money out of s.o.,** tirer de l'argent de qn, *Pej:* soutirer de l'argent à qn; **I didn't g. much out of the transaction,** je n'ai pas retiré grand-chose de la transaction; **I wonder whether we shall g. anything out of it,** je me demande si nous allons y gagner quelque chose; **to g. nothing out of it,** n'y rien gagner; **to g. s.o. out of a difficulty,** tirer qn d'une difficulté, d'un mauvais pas; **I can't g. (myself) out of the habit,** je ne puis pas me défaire de l'habitude; (ii) sortir (ses outils, etc.); **to g. out one's car,** sortir sa voiture; **to g. out a boat,** mettre une embarcation à la mer; **I got out a pencil to write the address,** j'ai sorti, j'ai pris, un crayon pour écrire l'adresse; (*of publisher*) **to g. out a book,** publier un livre; **to g. out a book from the library,** emprunter un livre à la bibliothèque; **to g. out a list,** rédiger une liste; *Com:* **to g. out a balance sheet,** établir, dresser, un bilan; **he could hardly g. a word out,** c'est à peine s'il a pu sortir un mot; (*b*) *v.i.* (i) **to g. out of sth.,** sortir de qch.; **to g. out of the train, etc.,** descendre du train, etc.; **the lion got out of its cage,** le lion s'est échappé de sa cage; **the secret got out,** le secret s'est fait jour, fut percé à jour; **to g. out of s.o.'s clutches,** se dérober à l'étreinte, aux griffes, de qn; **to g. out of s.o.'s way,** faire place à qn; se ranger (pour laisser passer qn); **to g. out of bed,** se lever; *F:* **g. out (of here)!** allez-vous-en! fiche(-moi) le camp! **you'll do it or g. out!** il faut passer par là ou par la porte; (ii) **to g. out of a difficulty,** se soustraire à une difficulté; se tirer d'une position difficile; **we've got to g. out of this,** il nous faut nous tirer de ça, nous débrouiller; **he was lucky to g. out of it,** il a eu de la chance de s'en tirer; **to g. out of a duty, of doing sth.,** se faire exempter, se faire dispenser, d'une corvée, de faire qch.; **there's no getting out of it,** il n'y a pas à sortir de là; il faut passer par là; **to g. out of the habit of doing sth.,** perdre l'habitude de faire qch.; **to g. out without (a) loss,** couvrir ses frais.

15. get over, *v.tr. & i.* (*a*) franchir, escalader, passer par-dessus (un mur, etc.); **to g. sth. over a wall,** passer qch. par-dessus un mur; **to g. over a great deal of ground,** parcourir beaucoup de terrain; *Th:* **the play didn't g. over,** la pièce n'a pas passé la rampe; **to g. a play over,** gagner la salle; (*b*) **to g. sth. over (and done with),** en finir avec qch.; **it's best to g. it over,** il vaut mieux en finir; **to g. s.o. over (to one's side),** gagner qn à sa cause; (*c*) **to g. over an illness,** se remettre, guérir, revenir, d'une maladie; **to g. over one's losses,** se consoler de ses pertes; **she can't g. over it,** (i) (*of illness*) elle ne guérit pas, ne se remet pas; (ii) (*of surprise, shock, etc.*) elle n'en revient pas; (iii) (*of loss*) elle est inconsolable; **it will take her a long time to g. over it,** elle s'en ressentira longtemps; **to g. over one's shyness,** vaincre sa timidité; **to g. over one's difficulties,** surmonter, venir à bout de, ses difficultés; **to g. over one's surprise,** revenir de sa surprise; **I can't g. over his having failed,** je ne reviens pas qu'il ait échoué.

16. get round, *v.i. & tr.* (*a*) tourner (un coin, un obstacle); tourner, contourner (une difficulté); contourner, tromper (la loi); **to g. round s.o.,** persuader, enjôler, qn; **I know how to g. round her,** je sais comment la prendre; **I got round them at last,** j'ai fini par les persuader; (*b*) **to g. round to doing sth.,** trouver le temps de faire qch.; **I shall never g. round to (seeing) all my patients today,** je n'aurai jamais le temps de voir tous mes malades aujourd'hui; (*c*) *F:* circuler, voyager; **she gets round a great deal,** elle est toujours à circuler, à voyager, en visite.

17. get through, *v.tr. & i.* (*a*) (*prepositional*) (i) passer par (un trou, une fenêtre); se frayer un chemin à travers (la foule, etc.); **to g. through a hedge,** traverser, passer à travers, une haie; (ii) accomplir, achever, arriver au bout de (son travail, etc.); **to g. through a lot of work,** abattre du travail; **I'll soon have got through the washing,** j'aurai bientôt terminé la lessive; **to g. through the day,** faire passer la journée; **we shall never g. through all this food,** nous ne viendrons jamais à bout de toute cette nourriture; **to g. through a fortune,** manger toute une fortune; **to g. through (an exam(ination)),** être reçu (à un examen); (*b*) (*adverbial*) parvenir à franchir un obstacle; **they got through to the injured men,** ils ont réussi à parvenir jusqu'aux blessés; **the news got through to them,** la nouvelle leur est parvenue; **to g. through (to s.o.),** (i) *Tp:* obtenir la communication (avec qn); *F:* contacter qn (au téléphone); (ii) *F:* faire comprendre (qn); (*c*) **to g. through with sth.,** en finir avec qch.; terminer (un travail, un livre); (*d*) **to g. a bill through (parliament),** faire adopter un projet de loi; **bill that will never g. through,** projet de loi qui ne passera jamais; **to g. sth. through the customs,** (faire) passer qch. à la douane.

18. get together. (*a*) *v.i.* (*of people*) (i) se réunir, se rassembler; (ii) se mettre d'accord; (*b*) *v.tr.* rassembler, ramasser (des objets); rassembler, réunir (des amis, etc.); **let me g. my thoughts together,** laissez-moi rassembler mes idées.

19. get under, *v.tr.* **to g. one's opponent under,** maîtriser son adversaire, mettre son adversaire dessous; **to g. a fire under,** se rendre maître d'un incendie.

20. get up. (*a*) *v.tr. & i.* (i) **to g. up a ladder, etc.,** monter à une échelle, etc.; **to g. s.o. up a ladder,** faire monter qn à une échelle; **to g. s.o. up the stairs,** aider qn à monter l'escalier; (ii) **to g. up to s.o.,** arriver à la hauteur de qn; **to g. up to Chapter 5,** arriver au chapitre 5; **where have you got up to?** où en êtes-vous? **to g. a trunk up to the attic,** monter une malle au grenier; *Equit:* **to g. up behind s.o.,** monter en croupe derrière qn; (iii) *Nau:* **to g. up a mast,** gréer un mât; **to g. up a sunken vessel,** relever un navire coulé; (iv) *Aut: etc:* **to g. up speed,** donner de la vitesse; (*b*) *v.i.* (i) se lever, se mettre debout; **g. up!** levez vous! **to g. up from a chair, from (the) table,** se lever de sa chaise, de table; **to g. up (from the ground),** se relever; (ii) se lever (du lit); **I g. up at seven,** je me lève à sept heures; *v.tr.* **g. me up early,** réveillez-moi de bonne heure; (iii) (*of wind*) se lever, s'élever; (*of sea*) grossir; *Nau:* **the sea is getting up,** la mer se fait; (*c*) *v.tr.* (i) organiser, arranger (une fête, etc.); monter (une pièce de théâtre); (ii) *Com:* apprêter, habiller, présenter (un article pour la vente); **the book is well got up,** le livre est bien présenté; *Laund:* **to g. up a shirt,** blanchir, apprêter, une chemise; (iii) préparer, travailler (un sujet d'examen); **to g. up a lecture,** préparer une conférence; (iv) *F:* **to g. oneself up,** (α) se faire beau, belle; (β) se maquiller; (γ) se déguiser; **to g. oneself up (ready) for a dance,** s'habiller, se faire belle, pour aller à un bal, **to g. oneself up as a sailor,** se déguiser en marin; *O:* **got up like a duchess,** *P:* **to the nines, to kill, regardless,** parée comme une duchesse; endimanché(e); dans ses plus beaux atours.

Getae ['dʒi:ti:], *s.pl. A.Hist:* Gètes *m.*

getatable, get-at-able [get'ætəbl], *a. F:* accessible; d'accès facile.

getaway ['getəwei], *s.* **1.** fuite *f*; évasion *f*; **g. car,** voiture *f* de fuite; **to make one's g.,** s'enfuir, s'évader. **2.** (*a*) *Rac:* (i) départ *m* (d'un concurrent); démarrage *m* (d'un coureur); (ii) échappée *f*; (*b*) *Aut:* démarrage; **smart g.,** départ nerveux; bonne accélération; **a motor cycle has a smarter g. than a car,** une motocyclette a plus de nervosité qu'une voiture, démarre plus vite qu'une voiture. **3.** *Ven:* débucher *m.*

Gethsemane [geθ'seməni], *Pr.n. B.Hist:* Gethsémani *m.*

get-out [get'aut], *s. F:* échappatoire *f.*

get-rich-quick ['get'ritʃ'kwik], *a. F:* (projet) qui promet la lune, qui promet monts et merveilles; (homme) qui ne songe qu'à la fortune; **a deal of the g.-r.-q. kind,** une affaire du genre enrichissez-vous-vite.

gettable ['getəbl], *a.* **1.** procurable. **2.** *Min: O:* (houille *f*) exploitable.

getter[1] ['getər], *s.* **1.** (*a*) acquéreur *m*; (*b*) *Min:* piqueur *m*; ouvrier *m* à la veine; (*c*) *Breed:* père *m.* **2.** **g.-up,** (*a*) organisateur, -trice (d'une fête); promoteur, -trice (d'une entreprise); (*b*) compilateur, -trice (d'un livre, etc.).

getter[2], *s. Elcs:* dégazeur *m* (de tube à vide, de lampe radio); getter *m.*

getter[3], *v.tr. Elcs:* dégazer (un tube à vide, une lampe radio); **to g. gases,** dégazer au moyen d'un getter.

get-there ['getðeər], *a. F:* **g.-t. policy,** (i) politique *f* qui ne considère que le but à atteindre; (ii) politique d'arrivisme.

getting up ['getiŋ'ʌp], *s.* lever *m*; **the g.-up bell,** la cloche du lever.

get-together ['get(t)əgeðər], *s. F:* rassemblement *m*, réunion *f*; **you and I must have a little g. t.,** il faut qu'on discute la chose ensemble.

Getulia [dʒi'tju:ljə], *Pr.n. A.Hist:* la Gétulie.

Getulian [dʒi'tju:ljən], *s. A.Hist:* Gétule *mf.*

getup, get-up ['getʌp], *s.* **1.** (*a*) habillement *m*, tenue *f*, toilette *f*; *Pej:* affublement *m*, attifement *m* accoutrement *m*; **what a g.!** quel costume! s'il, si elle, se croit bien habillé(e)! (*b*) (*fancy dress*) déguisement *m*; (*c*) *Com:* façon *f*, présentation *f*, habillage *m* (des marchandises); présentation (d'un livre). **2.** *NAm:* (*also* **get-up-and-go, get-up-and-get**) entrain *m*, allant *m.*

geum ['dʒi:əm], *s. Bot:* benoîte *f.*

gewgaw ['gju:gɔ:], *s. O:* **1.** colifichet *m*, fanfreluche *f*, brimborion *m*, affûtiau *m*, affiquet *m*. **2.** bagatelle *f*,

babiole *f*; *pl.* **gewgaws,** affèteries *f*.
geyser ['gi:zər, 'gaizər], *s.* **1.** *Geol:* geyser *m*. **2.** chauffe-bain(s) *m, pl.* chauffe-bains; chauffe-eau *m inv* à gaz.
geyserite ['gaizərait], *s. Miner:* geysérite *f*.
Ghana ['gɑ:nə], *Pr.n. Geog:* Ghana *m*.
Ghanaian, Ghanian [gɑ:'neiən, 'gɑ:niən]. *Geog:* (*a*) *a.* ghanéen; (*b*) *s.* Ghanéen, -enne.
gharial ['gɑ:riəl], *s. Rept:* garial *m*, -als.
Ghassulian [gə'su:liən], *a. Prehist:* ghassoulien.
ghastliness ['gɑ:stlinis], *s.* **1.** horreur *f* (d'un crime); aspect *m* horrible, sinistre (de qch.). **2.** pâleur mortelle.
ghastly ['gɑ:stli]. **1.** *a.* (*a*) horrible, effroyable, effrayant, affreux, épouvantable; **g. accident,** accident affreux; (*b*) *F:* **what g. weather!** quel temps abominable! **a g. mistake,** une erreur monstrueuse; *F:* **what a g. nuisance!** c'est bigrement embêtant! (*c*) blême; **g. paleness,** pâleur mortelle; **g. light,** lumière spectrale, blafarde; **he looked g.,** il avait l'air d'un déterré; il avait une mine de déterré; **g. smile,** sourire affreux à voir. **2.** *adv.* (*a*) horriblement, effroyablement, affreusement; *F:* **she has g. bad taste,** elle est absolument dépourvue de goût; (*b*) **g. pale,** pâle comme un mort; blême.
gha(u)t [gɔ:t, gæt]. **1.** *s.* (*in India*) ghât *m*; **burning g.,** palier *m* de crémation. **2.** *Pr.n.pl. Geog:* **the Gha(u)ts,** les Ghâtes *f*.
Gheber ['geibər], *s. Rel.Hist:* Guèbre *mf*.
ghee [gi:], *s. Comest:* ghee *m*, ghy *m*.
Ghent [gent], *Pr.n. Geog:* Gand *m*.
gherkin ['gə:kin], *s.* cornichon *m*; *Comest:* **pickled gherkins,** cornichons confits (au vinaigre).
ghetto ['getou], *s.* ghetto *m*.
Ghibelline ['gibəlain, -li:n]. *Hist:* (*a*) *a.* gibelin; (*b*) *s.* Gibelin, -ine.
ghost[1] [goust], *s.* **1.** *A:* âme *f*; (*still so used in*) **to give up the g.,** rendre l'âme; expirer. **2. the Holy G.,** l'Esprit Saint, le Saint-Esprit. **3.** (*a*) fantôme *m*, spectre *m*, revenant *m*, ombre *f*, apparition *f*; **to believe in ghosts,** croire aux revenants; **there are ghosts in the red room,** il y a des revenants dans la chambre rouge; **I've seen a g.,** un spectre m'est apparu; **you look as if you'd seen a g.,** vous avez l'air d'un déterré; **to raise a g.,** évoquer un esprit; **to lay a g.,** conjurer, exorciser, un esprit; *Th: F:* **the g. walks,** on touche les appointements; c'est aujourd'hui la Sainte-Touche; *attrib.* **g. ship,** vaisseau *m* fantôme; **g. story,** histoire *f* de revenants; (*b*) **to be the mere g. of one's former self,** n'être plus que l'ombre de soi-même; **not the g. of a chance, of a doubt,** pas la moindre chance; pas l'ombre d'un doute; **I haven't the g. of a notion,** je n'en ai pas la moindre idée; **g. of a smile,** sourire *m* vague. **4.** *F:* collaborateur, -trice, anonyme; nègre *m* (d'un auteur, etc.); hétéronyme *m*. **5.** (*a*) *Opt:* spectre *m* secondaire; image blanche; (*b*) *T.V:* écho *m*; *Rad: T.V:* **g. image,** image fantôme. **6.** *Ent:* **g. moth,** hépiale *m* du houblon.
ghost[2], *v.i.* **1.** servir de nègre (**for an author, etc.,** à un écrivain, etc.). **2.** prêter sa plume à qn qui n'a pas l'habitude d'écrire; prêter à qn une collaboration anonyme; *v.tr.* **his memoirs have been very ably ghosted,** pour la rédaction de ses mémoires il s'est assuré la collaboration d'un excellent écrivain; **ghosted work,** hétéronyme *m*.
ghosting ['goustiŋ], *s. T.V:* écho *m*.
ghostlike ['goustlaik]. **1.** *a.* spectral, -aux; de spectre. **2.** *adv.* comme un spectre.
ghostly ['goustli], *a.* **1.** *A:* (conseil, directeur) spirituel; *Ecc:* **g. father,** confesseur *m*; **our g. enemy,** l'ennemi *m* du genre humain. **2.** spectral, -aux; de fantôme; **g. shadows across the path,** des ombres spectrales qui se projettent en travers du chemin.
ghoul [gu:l], *s.* **1.** *Myth:* goule *f*, strige *f*, vampire *m*. **2.** *F:* (*a*) (*body snatcher*) déterreur *m* de cadavres; corbeau *m*; (*b*) amateur, -trice, du macabre.
ghoulish ['gu:liʃ], *a.* de goule; vampirique; **g. humour,** esprit *m* macabre.
ghoulishness ['gu:liʃnis], *s.* appétits *mpl* de goule; férocité *f* vampirique, macabre.
ghyll [gil], *s. Geog: A:* = GILL[3]; *as Pr.n.* **Gaping G.** = gouffre béant.
giant ['dʒaiənt]. **1.** *s.* (*a*) géant *m*; colosse *m*; *Geog:* **the Giant's Causeway,** la Chaussée des Géants; (*b*) *Civ.E:* monitor *m*. **2.** *a.* (chêne, etc.) géant, gigantesque; (*at fair*) **g. woman,** femme colosse; **with g. strides,** à pas de géant; *Gym:* **g. stride,** vindas *m*, pas-de-géant *m inv*; *Com:* **g. packet,** carton géant; *Exp:* **g. powder,** poudre géante.
giantess ['dʒaiəntes], *s.f.* géante.
giantism ['dʒaiəntizm], *s. Med:* gigantisme *m*.
giantlike ['dʒaiəntlaik], *a.* gigantesque; de géant.
giaour ['dʒauər], *s.* giaour *m*.
gib[1] [dʒib], *s.* **1.** (*a*) *Mec.E:* contre-clavette *f*, *pl.* contre-clavettes; **g. and cotter, g. and key,** clavette *f* et contre-clavette; **g.-head(ed) key,** clavette à tête, à mentonnet, à talon; **g.-heel key,** clavette à talon; (*b*) *Mch: I.C.E:* semelle *f* (de tête de piston); **g. and cotter end,** tête *f* de bielle avec chape. **2.** *Carp:* **mitre-box g.,** lardon *m* de guidage de la boîte à onglets.
gib[2], *v.tr.* (**gibbed**) clavet(t)er.
gibber[1] ['dʒibər], *s.* (*a*) sons inarticulés (du singe, etc.); cris inarticulés; (*b*) baragouin *m*.
gibber[2], *v.i.* (*a*) produire des sons inarticulés (comme un singe, un idiot); **he was gibbering with rage,** il bégayait de rage; (*b*) baragouiner.
gibberella [dʒibə'relə], *s. Fung:* gibberella *m*.
gibberellin [dʒibə'relin], *s.* gibbérelline *f*.
gibbering[1] ['dʒibəriŋ], *a.* (singe *m*, etc.) qui pousse des cris, qui produit des sons imitant la parole; **g. idiot,** (i) idiot aphasique; (ii) *F:* espèce *m* d'idiot, sacré idiot.
gibbering[2], *s.* baragouinage *m*.
gibberish ['dʒibəriʃ], *s.* baragouin *m*, charabia *m*; galimatias *m*.
gibbet[1] ['dʒibit], *s.* gibet *m*, potence *f*; fourche *f* patibulaire; **he'll end up on the g.,** il finira par être pendu.
gibbet[2], *v.tr.* (*a*) pendre (un criminel); (*b*) attacher, pendre, (un cadavre) au gibet; (*c*) *Fig: O:* **to g. a man,** clouer un homme au pilori.
gibbon ['gibən], *s. Z:* gibbon *m*; **whitehanded g., lar g.,** gibbon aux mains blanches.
gibbose [gi'bous], **gibbous** ['gibəs], *a.* **1.** gibbeux, convexe; **the g. portions of the moon,** les parties gibbeuses de la lune. **2.** (*of pers.*) gibbeux, bossu.
gibbosity [gi'bɔsiti], *s.* gibbosité *f*, bosse *f*; **gibbosities of the moon,** parties gibbeuses de la lune.
gibbsite ['gibzait], *s. Miner:* gibbsite *f*.
gibbus ['gibəs], *s. Med:* gibbosité *f*.
gibe[1] [dʒaib], *s.* raillerie *f*; plaisanterie acérée; moquerie *f*; sarcasme *m*; quolibet *m*, brocard *m*; trait *m* de médisance, de satire.
gibe[2], *v.tr. & i.* **to g. (at) s.o.,** railler qn; se moquer de qn; lancer des brocards à qn; brocarder qn; poursuivre qn de quolibets, de railleries.
Gibeon ['gibiən], *Pr.n.m. Geog:* Gabaon.
Gibeonite ['gibiənait], *s.* (*a*) *B.Hist:* Gabaonite *mf*; (*b*) *A:* être *m* voué aux plus viles tâches; esclave *mf*; ilote *m*.
gib-headed ['dʒib'hedid], *a.* (clavette *f*) à mentonnet.
gibing[1] ['dʒaibiŋ], *a.* railleur, -euse; moqueur, -euse.
gibing[2], *s.* raillerie *f*.
giblets ['dʒiblits], *s.pl.* abat(t)is *m* (de volaille).
Gibraltar [dʒi'brɔ:ltər], *Pr.n. Geog:* Gibraltar; **the Straits of G.,** le Détroit de Gibraltar.
Gibraltarian [dʒibrɔ:l'tɛəriən], *s. Geog:* habitant, -ante, originaire *mf*, de Gibraltar.
gibus ['dʒaibəs], *s. Cost:* gibus *m*, claque *m*.
gid [gid], *s. Vet:* tournis *m* (des moutons).
giddily ['gidili], *adv.* **1.** d'une manière vertigineuse; à une hauteur vertigineuse. **2.** étourdiment, à l'étourdie.
giddiness ['gidinis], *s.* **1.** étourdissement *m*, vertige *m*; tournement *m* de tête; **to have fits of g.,** avoir des étourdissements, des vertiges, des éblouissements. **2.** (*a*) étourderie *f*; (*b*) frivolité *f* (de caractère); légèreté *f*.
giddy[1] ['gidi], *a.* **1.** (*a*) étourdi; **to be, feel, turn, g.,** *F:* **to come over g.,** être tout étourdi; être pris de vertige; avoir un éblouissement, un étourdissement; **I feel g.,** la tête me tourne; tout tourne autour de moi; **it makes me (feel) g.,** cela me donne le vertige; (*b*) vertigineux, qui donne le vertige; **at this g. height,** à cette hauteur vertigineuse; **g. round of pleasures,** tourbillon *m* de plaisirs; **the g. whirl of modern life,** le tourbillon étourdissant de la vie d'aujourd'hui. **2.** frivole, insouciant, volage, étourdi, écervelé; *F: O:* **to play the g. goat,** faire le fou, l'imbécile, l'idiot, le zouave; batifoler, folâtrer, folichonner; mener une vie de patachon; *A:* **g. pate,** étourneau *m*; écervelé, -ée; hurluberlu *m*; tête *f* de linotte; *O:* **she's a g. young thing,** c'est une évaporée. **3.** *F:* (*intensive*) **that's the g. limit,** ça c'est un peu fort de café.
giddy[2], *v.tr. O:* étourdir (qn); donner le vertige à (qn); **at a giddying speed,** à une vitesse vertigineuse.
Gideon ['gidiən], *Pr.n.m. B.Hist:* Gédéon.
Giffard ['dʒifəd, 'gifəd], *Pr.n.* Giffard; *Mch:* **G. injector,** giffard *m*.
gift[1] [gift], *s.* (*a*) don *m*; donation *f*; *Jur:* avantage *m*; **to make a g. of sth. to s.o.,** faire don de qch. à qn; **the appointment is in the g. of the minister,** la nomination est à la discrétion du ministre; *Jur:* **as a g.,** à titre d'avantage; **deed of g.,** (acte *m* de) donation entre vifs; **to acquire sth. by free g.,** acquérir qch. à titre gratuit; *F:* **he thinks he's God's g. to mankind,** il se prend pour le nombril du monde; (*b*) cadeau *m*; *Com:* **gifts,** pour offrir; **Christmas g.,** cadeau de Noël; **it was a g.,** (i) on me l'a offert; c'était un cadeau; (ii) (*sth. bought cheaply*) c'était donné; **g. shop,** magasin *m* de nouveautés; **I wouldn't have it, take it, (even) as a g.,** je n'en voudrais pas quand (bien) même on me le donnerait; *Prov:* **never look a g. horse in the mouth,** à cheval donné on ne regarde pas à la bride; (*c*) *Com:* (*on presentation of coupons*) prime *f*; (*d*) talent *m*; **g. of tongues,** don des langues; **to have a g. for mathematics,** avoir le don, le génie, *F:* la bosse, des mathématiques; être doué pour les mathématiques; **he has the g. of amusing people,** il sait amuser les gens.
gift[2], *v.tr.* **1.** (*a*) douer (**with,** de); (*b*) gratifier (**s.o. with sth.,** qn de qch.). **2.** *esp. Scot:* donner (**sth. to s.o.,** qch. à qn); **to g. sth. away,** donner qch. en présent.
giftbook ['giftbuk], *s.* livre *m* de luxe pour cadeau; livre d'étrennes.
gifted ['giftid], *a.* bien doué; (artiste) de valeur, de talent; **g. child,** enfant doué; **poorly g.,** peu apte, peu doué.
gig[1] [gig], *s.* **1.** *Veh:* cabriolet *m*. **2.** *Nau:* petit canot, yole *f*, youyou *m*, guigue *f*.
gig[2], *s. Fish:* foëne *f*, foene *f*.
gig[3], *v.tr. Fish:* foëner, foéner.
gig[4], *s. Tex:* **g. (mill),** laineuse *f*, échardonneuse *f*.
gigahertz ['dʒigəhə:ts], *s. Meas:* gigahertz *m*.
gigantic [dʒai'gæntik], *a.* géant, gigantesque; (bâtiment, etc.) colossal, -aux, (travail) de Titan.
gigantically [dʒai'gæntik(ə)li], *adv.* gigantesquement; colossalement.
gigantism ['dʒaigæntizm], *s. Med:* gigantisme *m*.
gigantoblast [dʒai'gæntoublæst], *s.* gigantoblaste *m*.
gigantolite [dʒai'gæntoulait], *s. Miner:* gigantolite *f*.
gigantopithecus [dʒai'gæntoupi'θeikəs], *s. Paleont:* gigantopithèque *m*.
Gigantostraca [dʒaigæn'tɔstrəkə], *s.pl. Paleont:* gigantostracés *m*.
Gigartinales [dʒiga:ti'neili:z], *s.pl. Algae:* gigartinales *f*.
giggle[1] ['gigl], *s.* petit rire nerveux; rire bébête; petit rire affecté; petit gloussement; *P:* **to do sth. for a g.,** faire qch. pour rire, pour s'amuser; **it's a g.!** c'est marrant!
giggle[2], *v.i.* rire nerveusement, bêtement, avec affectation; glousser; pousser des petits rires.
giggling[1] ['gigliŋ], **giggly** ['gigli], *a.* qui rit nerveusement, bêtement.
giggling[2], *s.* rires nerveux, bébêtes; petits rires bêtes.
giglamp ['giglæmp], *s.* **1.** *A.Veh:* lanterne *f* de cabriolet. **2.** *pl. F: O:* **giglamps,** lunettes *f*, besicles *f*.
gigolo ['dʒigəlou], *s.m. Pej:* gigolo.
gigot [dʒigət], *s. Scot: NAm:* gigot *m*.
gigsman, *pl.* **-men** ['gigzmən], *s.m. Nau:* yoleur *m*.
Gila ['hi:lə, 'dʒi:lə], *Pr.n. Geog:* **the G. (River),** la rivière Gila; *Rept:* **G. monster,** héloderme *m*.
Gilbert ['gilbət]. **1.** *Pr.n.m.* Gilbert. **2.** *s. El.Meas:* gilbert *m*.
Gilbertian [gil'bə:tiən], *a.* = vaudevillesque; (situation, etc.) d'opéra-comique (telles les situations cocasses dont sont remplies les opérettes de Gilbert et Sullivan).
Gilboa [gil'bouə], *Pr.n. B.Geog:* Guilboa *m*.
gild[1] [gild], *v.tr.* (*p.t.* **gilded;** *p.p.* **gilded,** *occ.* **gilt** [gilt]) dorer; **the sun gilded the hilltops,** le soleil dorait les cimes; **to g. sth. over,** couvrir qch. d'une couche de dorure; **to g. the lily,** faire œuvre de superfétation; orner la beauté même; **to g. the pill,** dorer la pilule.
gild[2], *s.* = GUILD.
gilded ['gildid], *a.* doré; *Hist:* **the G. Chamber,** la Chambre Dorée; la Chambre des Lords; *Lit:* **g. youth,** la jeunesse dorée.
gilder ['gildər], *s. Ind:* doreur, -euse.
gilding ['gildiŋ], *s.* dorure *f*; **leaf g.,** dorure à la feuille; *Metalw:* **cold g.,** dorure à froid.
Gilead ['giliæd], *Pr.n. B.Geog:* Galaad *m*; *Bot:* **balm of G.,** baume *m* de la Mecque, térébenthine *f* de Judée.
Giles [dʒailz], *Pr.n.m.* Gilles.
gill[1] [gil], *s.* **1.** *usu.pl.* ouïe(s) *f*, branchie(s) *f* (de poisson); **g. cover,** opercule (branchial); *Fish:* **g. net,** araignée *f*, sanglon *m*, manet *m*. **2.** *pl.* **gills,** (*a*) caroncules *f*, fanons *m* (d'un oiseau); (*b*) lames *f*, lamelles *f* (d'un champignon); (*c*) *F:* bajoues *f* (de qn); **to be rosy about the gills,** avoir le teint frais et rose; **to be, look, green (blue, yellow) about the gills,** avoir le teint vert; avoir l'air malade; **to turn red about the gills,** rougir de colère; **to look white about the gills,** avoir mauvaise mine. **3.** *Mch: Ind:* (*flange, rib*) ailette *f* (de cylindre, de radiateur, etc.); **flat g.,** ailette plate; *Mec.E:* **cowl g., cooling g.,** volet *m* de capot.
gill[2] [gil], *v.tr.* **1.** vider (un poisson). **2.** éplucher (un champignon); ôter les lamelles. **3.** prendre (un poisson) au filet par les ouïes.
gill[3] [gil], *s. Geog:* (*esp. in N.Eng:*) (*a*) gorge boisée, ravin boisé; (*b*) ruisseau *m*, ruisselet *m* (coulant dans un ravin).
gill[4] [gil], *s. Tex:* peigne *m*, gill *m* (à lin, à chanvre).
gill[5] [gil], *v.tr. Tex:* peigner (le lin, le chanvre, la laine).

gill[6] [dʒil], *s. Meas:* gill *m* = canon *m* (d'eau-de-vie).

gilled [gild], *a.* **1.** (*a*) *Biol:* pourvu de branchies, de caroncules, de lames; (*b*) *F: A:* (*of pers.*) **rosy-g.,** au teint frais et rose. **2.** *Mch: etc:* **g. tube, radiator,** tube *m*, radiateur *m*, à ailettes; *Mec.E:* **g. cowl,** capot *m* à volet(s), à ouïe(s).

Gillian ['dʒiliən], *Pr.n.f.* Julienne.

gillie[1] ['gili], *s. Scot:* **1.** *Hist:* suivant *m* (d'un chef de clan). **2.** *Ven: Fish:* serviteur *m* (d'un chasseur, d'un pêcheur); porte-carnier *m inv*; rameur *m* du bateau, etc.

gillie[2], *v.i. Scot:* **to g. for s.o.,** accompagner qn à la chasse, à la pêche (en qualité de serviteur).

gilling ['giliŋ], *s. Tex:* gillsage *m*.

gillyflower ['dʒiliflauər], *s. Bot:* **1.** (**clove**) **g.,** œillet *m* giroflée; œillet des fleuristes. **2.** *F:* (*a*) giroflée *f* jaune, des murailles; ravenelle *f*; (*b*) **stock g.,** quarantaine *f*.

Gilsonite ['gilsənait], *s. R.t.m:* Gilsonite *f*.

gilt[1] [gilt], *a.* doré; **g. frames, furniture,** cadres de tableaux, meubles, dorés.

gilt[2], *s.* dorure *f*; doré *m*; **g. bronze,** bronze doré; **imitation g.,** similor *m*; *Bookb: etc:* **g.-edged,** doré sur tranche; **g.-topped,** doré en tête; **g.-lettered,** avec titre en lettres d'or; *St.Exch:* **g.-edge(d) stock(s),** *spl.* **gilts,** fonds *m* d'État; valeurs *f* de tout repos, de premier ordre, *F:* de père de famille; *F:* **that takes the g. off the gingerbread,** voilà qui enlève le charme, l'attrait, qui nuit au charme, qui gâte le plaisir.

gilt[3], *s. Z:* cochette *f*, jeune truie *f*.

gilthead ['gilthed], *s. Ich:* dorade (méditerranéenne).

gimbal ['dʒimb(ə)l], *s.* (*a*) *Av: Nau: etc:* **gimbals,** (suspension *f* à la) cardan *m*; balancier(s) *m*; **g. bearing, mounting,** suspension à la cardan; **hung, mounted, on gimbals,** suspendu(e) à la cardan; **g.-mounted chronometer,** chronomètre monté sur cardan; **g. ring,** anneau *m*, cercle *m*, de suspension à la cardan; *Space: Ball:* **four-g. inertial platform,** plateforme *f* à inertie à quatre axes de cardan; (*b*) *Mec.E:* **g. joint,** joint *m*, rotule *f*, de, à la, cardan.

gimcrack ['dʒimkræk]. **1.** *a.* (meubles, etc.) de pacotille, de camelote, boiteux; (maison) de carton; (bijoux) en toc; **to buy g. furniture,** se meubler avec de la camelote. **2.** *s.* article *m* de pacotille, en toc.

gimcrackery ['dʒimkrækəri], *s.* pacotille *f*, camelote *f*, toc *m*, tape-à-l'œil *m*.

gimlet[1] ['gimlit], *s. Tls: Carp:* vrille *f*, avant-clou, *pl.* avant-clous; foret *m* à bois; perçoir *m*; queue-de-cochon *f*, *pl.* queues-de-cochon; **shell g.,** vrille en cuiller, à gouge; **twist g.,** vrille torse, en spirale, à mèche hélicoïdale; **g. bit,** foret hélicoïdal fraiseur; **g. eyes,** yeux perçants, en trou de vrille.

gimlet[2], *v.tr.* vriller (une planche, etc.).

gimlet[3], *s.* mélange *m* de gin ou de vodka avec du jus de citron.

gimmal ['giməl], *s.* = GEMEL.

gimmick ['gimik], *s. F:* machin *m*, combinaison *f*, combine *f*, truc *m*, astuce *f*, bidule *m*; **advertising g.,** artifice *m*, trouvaille *f*, astuce, truc, publicitaire.

gimmick(e)ry ['gimikri], *s. F:* astuces *fpl*; combinaisons *fpl* (pour attirer l'attention du public); truquage *m*.

gimmicky ['gimiki], *a. F:* plein de trucs, d'astuces; conçu pour attirer l'attention (du public).

gimp[1] [gimp], *s.* **1.** *Furn:* ganse *f*, galon *m*, lézarde *f*, guimpe *f*, passement *m*; *Dressm:* milanaise *f*; **g. pin,** petite pointe pour ganse. **2.** *Lacem:* gros fil pour contours. **3.** *Fish:* corde *f* à guitare.

gimp[2], *v.tr.* **1.** passementer (un meuble, etc.); garnir (un fauteuil) d'une ganse. **2.** *Tex:* guimper.

gimping ['gimpiŋ], *s. Tex:* guimpage *m*.

gin[1] [dʒin], *s.* **1.** *Ven:* piège *m*, trébuchet *m*, lacet *m*, attrape *f*. **2.** (*a*) *Civ.E: Mec.E:* chèvre *f*, engin *m* de levage; **g. pulley,** poulie *f* de chèvre; **g. tackle,** agrès *mpl*, palan *m*, de chèvre; (*b*) *Min:* treuil *m* à manège, cabestan *m* à cheval; (*c*) *Nau:* chape *f* (de mât de charge), rouet *m*; **g. tackle,** caliorne *f* de braguet; **g. block,** poulie *f* avec chape et crochet; palan *m* de chèvre. **3.** *Tex:* (**cotton**) **g.,** égreneuse *f* de coton; machine *f* à égrener.

gin[2], *v.tr.* (**ginned**) **1.** prendre (un animal) au piège, au trébuchet. **2.** *Tex:* égrener (le coton).

gin[3], *s.* gin *m*; (*made in Holland, N.Fr.*) genièvre *m*; (*in bar*) **g. and French, g. and Italian,** gin au vermouth blanc sec, au vermouth rouge; *F: O:* **g. palace,** *U.S:* **g. mill,** bar *m* (de basse classe).

gin[4], *s.f. Austr: F:* (*a*) femme aborigène; (*b*) femme mariée.

ginger[1] ['dʒindʒər]. **1.** *s.* (*a*) gingembre *m*; **black g., white g.,** gingembre gris, blanc; **preserved g.,** gingembre confit; **g. race,** racine *f* de gingembre; **g. wine,** vin *m* de gingembre; **g. ale, g. beer, g. pop,** boisson gazeuse au gingembre; *Bot:* **g. lily,** hedychium *m*; (*b*) *F:* entrain *m*, énergie *f*, vitalité *f*; **to put some g. into it,** y mettre de l'énergie; *Pol: etc:* **g. group,** groupe *m* de pression; les militants *m* (d'un parti). **2.** *a. F:* (*of hair*) roux, *f.* rousse; rouquin, carotte; *s.* **hi, g.!** ohé, poil de carotte!

ginger[2], *v.tr.* **1.** aromatiser (une boisson, etc.) au gingembre. **2. to g. up a horse,** chauffer, émoustiller, un cheval; *F:* **to g. s.o. up,** mettre du cœur au ventre de qn; secouer, remonter, exciter, qn; émoustiller qn; **to g. up the production,** pousser, activer, la production; *Th:* **to g. up a scene,** chauffer une scène.

gingerbread ['dʒindʒəbred], *s.* **1.** *s.* pain *m* d'épice; *attrib.* **g. man,** bonhomme *m* de, en, pain d'épice. **2.** *attrib. F:* clinquant; de mauvais goût; **g. architecture,** architecture prétentieuse et sans solidité.

gingerly ['dʒindʒəli], *adv.* & *a.* **in a g. fashion, g.,** délicatement, doucement, avec précaution; **to proceed, to go about it, g.,** y aller doucement, avec le dos de la cuiller.

gingernut, gingersnap ['dʒindʒənʌt, -snæp], *s.* biscuit *m* au gingembre.

gingery ['dʒindʒəri], *a.* **1.** (*a*) qui a un goût de gingembre; (*b*) *O:* (*of book, etc.*) poivré; (*c*) (*of temperament*) irascible, coléreux. **2.** *F:* (*of hair*) roux, *f.* rousse; rouquin.

gingham ['giŋəm], *s.* **1.** *Tex:* guingan *m*. **2.** *F: A:* parapluie *m* (de coton); riflard *m*, pépin *m*.

gingili ['dʒindʒili], *s. Bot:* sésame *m* d'Orient, de l'Inde; *Com:* **g. oil,** huile *f* de sésame.

gingiva, *pl.* **-ae** [dʒin'dʒaivə, -iː], *s. Anat:* gencive *f*; **attached g.,** gencive adhérente; **free g.,** gencive libre.

gingival [dʒin'dʒaiv(ə)l], *a. Anat:* gingival, -aux.

gingivectomy [dʒindʒi'vektəmi], *s. Surg:* gingivectomie *f*.

gingivitis [dʒindʒi'vaitis], *s. Med:* gingivite *f*.

gingko, ginkgo ['giŋkou], *s. Bot:* gin(g)ko *m*; arbre *m* aux quarante écus.

ginglymus, *pl.* **-mi** ['giŋglimәs, 'dʒiŋ-, -mai], *s. Anat:* ginglyme *m*.

gink [giŋk], *s. P:* type *m*, individu *m*.

Ginkgoales [giŋkou'eiliːz], *s.pl. Bot:* ginkgoales *f*.

ginnery ['dʒinəri], *s. Tex:* ginnerie *f*.

ginning ['dʒiniŋ], *s.* **1.** chasse *f* au trébuchet. **2.** égrenage *m* (du coton).

ginpole, gin pole ['dʒinpoul], *s. Civ.E: etc:* flèche *f* de levage.

ginseng ['dʒinseŋ], *s. Bot:* ginseng *m*, panax *m*, panacée *m*.

giobertite [dʒiou'bəːtait], *s. Miner:* giobertite *f*.

Gioconda (la) [lɑːdʒ(i)ə'kɔndə], *Pr.n.f. Hist. of Art:* la Joconde; **a G. smile,** un sourire de Joconde.

gip [dʒip], *s. F:* **it's giving me g.,** ça me fait un mal de tous les diables.

gipper ['dʒipər], **gippo**[1] ['dʒipou], *s. Dial:* sauce *f*, graisse *f* (d'un rôti).

gippo[2], *s. P: Pej:* **1.** *O:* arabe natif d'Égypte. **2.** = GIPSY.

gipsy ['dʒipsi], *s.* **1.** bohémien, -ienne; nomade *mf*; romanichel, -elle; zingaro *m*; (*Spanish*) gitane *mf*; gitano *m*, gitana *f*. **2.** (*a*) *Ent:* **g. moth,** zigzag *m*; (*b*) *Bot:* **g. rose,** scabieuse *f*.

gipsyish, gipsylike ['dʒipsiiʃ, -laik], *a.* (*a*) comme un bohémien, un romanichel; (*b*) noiraud.

gipsyweed, gipsywort ['dʒipsiwiːd, -wəːt], *s. Bot:* lycope *m*; chanvre *m* d'eau; pied-de-loup *m*, *pl.* pieds-de-loup; marrube *m* aquatique, lance *f* de Christ; patte-de-loup *f*, *pl.* pattes-de-loup.

giraffe [dʒi'ræf, *occ.* -'rɑːf], *s.* **1.** *Z:* girafe *f*; **baby g.,** girafeau *m*, girafon *m*. **2.** *Cin: T.V: F:* girafe (perche de microphone).

Giraffidae [dʒi'ræfidiː], *s.pl. Z:* giraffidés *m*.

girandole ['dʒirəndoul], *s.* **1.** (*a*) (*chandelier*) girandole *f*, lustre *m*; (*b*) *Pyr: Hyd.E:* girandole, girande *f*. **2.** (*earring or pendant*) girandole.

girasol(e) ['dʒirəsɔl, -soul], *s. Miner:* girasol *m*.

gird[1] [gəːd], *v.tr.* (*p.t.* & *p.p.* **girded, girt**) *A:* & *Lit:* **1.** ceindre; (*a*) **to g. up one's loins,** se ceindre les reins; ceindre ses reins; **to g. oneself for the fray, for a task,** se préparer à la lutte, à une tâche; (*b*) **to g. s.o. with sth., to g. sth. on s.o.,** ceindre qn de qch.; ceindre qch. à qn; **to g. (on) one's sword, one's armour,** ceindre son épée; revêtir son armure; *Hist:* **to g. a knight,** ceindre l'épée à un chevalier; **to g. s.o. with authority,** revêtir qn d'autorité. **2.** entourer, encercler, ceindre (**with,** de); **sea-girt Britain,** la Grande-Bretagne, encerclée par les mers.

gird[2], *s. A:* = GIBE[1].

gird[3], *v.i. A:* **to g. at s.o.,** railler qn, se moquer de qn.

girded ['gəːdid], *a. Lit:* (*of pers.*) **with g. loins,** les reins ceints; **with g. sword,** ceint d'une épée.

girder ['gəːdər], *s.* (*a*) *Carp: Const:* solive *f*, long(ue)rine *f* (de plancher); (**small**) **g.,** soliveau *m*; (*b*) *Const: Metalw:* poutre *f* (métallique); (**small**) **g.,** poutrelle *f*; **anchored g., fixed g., g. with fixed ends,** poutre encastrée; **arched g.,** ferme ceintrée, ferme en arc; **articulated g., hinged g.,** poutre articulée; **cantilever g., overhung g.,** poutre en console, en encorbellement; **compound g., built-up g.,** poutre d'assemblage; poutre composée, rapportée; **intermediate g.,** poutre intermédiaire; **through g.,** poutre continue; **plate g., web g.,** poutre (à âme) pleine; **truss(ed) g.,** poutre armée, renforcée; ferme (métallique); **twin girders,** poutres jumelles; **g. pass,** cannelure *f* à poutrelles; *Civ.E: etc:* **longitudinal g., side g.,** longeron *m*, longrine *f*, (de pont, etc.); **independent g.,** travée *f* (de pont métallique); **auxiliary g.,** sous-longeron *m*, *pl.* sous-longerons; **g. bridge,** pont *m* à longerons, à poutres; **box g.,** poutre à caisson, en caisson; poutre-caisson *f*, *pl.* poutres-caissons; poutre tubulaire; poutres accouplées, jumelées; (*c*) *N.Arch:* poutre, support *m*; **centre g.,** support central; **side g.,** support latéral; **deck g.,** entremise *f* sous barrots; **g. between deckhouses,** longis *m*; **hull g.,** poutre-navire *f*, *pl.* poutres-navires.

girderage ['gəːdəridʒ], *s. Const:* (*a*) solivage *m*; (*b*) poutrage *m*, empoutrerie *f*.

girdle[1] ['gəːdl], *s.* **1.** (*a*) ceinture *f*; *Rom.Ant:* ceste *m* (de Vénus, de Junon); *A.Cost: Lit:* zone *f*; **dressing-gown g.,** cordelière *f* de robe de chambre; *Lit:* **g. of walls,** ceinture de murailles; (*b*) *Cost:* gaine *f*; (*c*) *Anat:* **pelvic g., pectoral g.,** ceinture pelvienne, scapulaire. **2.** *Arb:* incision *f* annulaire. **3.** *Lap:* feuilletis *m* (de diamant); rondis *m*.

girdle[2], *v.tr.* **1.** ceinturer, ceindre, encercler; *Lit:* **the hills that g. the town,** les collines *f* qui entourent, qui ceignent, la ville. **2.** *Arb:* faire une incision annulaire à (un arbre); anneler, cerner (un arbre).

girdle[3], *s.* tôle (sur laquelle on cuit des galettes); **g. cake** = galette *f*.

girdling ['gəːdliŋ], *s. Arb:* incision *f* annulaire; cernement *m*.

girella [dʒi'relə], *s. Ich:* girelle *f*.

girl [gəːl], *s.f.* (*a*) fille; **little g.,** petite fille, fillette; **when I was a g.,** quand j'étais petite; **girl's name,** prénom féminin; **the three (little) Martin girls,** les trois petites Martin; **girls' school,** école *f* de filles; **school of 500 girls,** école de cinq cents élèves; **old g.,** ancienne élève; (*b*) **a French g., an Indian g.,** une jeune Française, une jeune Indienne; **a blind g.,** une jeune aveugle; (*c*) jeune fille, jeune femme; **the Martin girls,** les demoiselles Martin; **his fiancée is a charming g.,** sa fiancée est charmante; **his g. wife,** sa toute jeune femme; *F:* (*said by woman*) **I'm going out with some g. friends, some of the girls,** je sors avec des amies; *F:* **his g. friend,** son amie, sa petite amie; **my dear g.!** ma chère (amie)! *F: O:* **old g.!** ma vieille! *F:* **the old girls (of the village),** les vieilles demoiselles (du village); *P:* **the old g.,** (i) ma femme, la bourgeoise; (ii) ma mère; (iii) la patronne; (iv) *F:* ma vieille voiture, bagnole; *F:* **a nice old g.,** une vieille dame charmante; (*to dog*) **come on, old g.!** viens, ma vieille! (*d*) **my eldest, youngest, g.,** ma fille aînée, cadette; (*e*) **chorus g.,** girl; *F:* **glamour g.,** ensorceleuse; beau morceau; *O:* **shop g.,** vendeuse, employée de magasin; *A:* **servant g.,** *U.S:* **hired g.,** domestique, bonne; **I've found a g. to look after the children,** j'ai trouvé quelqu'un pour s'occuper des enfants; *F:* **I'm not that kind of g.,** je ne suis pas celle que vous croyez.

girlhood ['gəːlhud], *s.* jeunesse *f* (d'une femme); **in her g.,** quand elle était (i) petite fille, (ii) jeune fille; **from her g.,** dès son enfance, dès sa jeunesse.

girlie ['gəːli], *s.f. F:* (*a*) *O:* fillette, petite; (*b*) *attrib.* **g. magazines,** revues *f* qui contiennent de nombreuses photos de femmes nues.

girlish ['gəːliʃ], *a.* **1.** (*of behaviour, figure, etc.*) de petite fille, de jeune fille; de la jeunesse. **2.** (*of boy, etc.*) mou, efféminé; **g. air,** air mignard.

girlishly ['gəːliʃli], *adv.* **1.** en jeune fille, en petite fille. **2.** comme une petite fille.

girlishness ['gəːliʃnis], *s.* manières *fpl*, air *m*, de petite fille.

Giro ['dʒairou], *s. Post: Bank:* **G. (bank) system** = service *m* de chèques postaux.

Girondist [dʒi'rɔndist], *a.* & *s. Fr.Hist:* Girondin, -ine; **the G. Party,** la Gironde.

girt [gəːt], *a.* **1.** *Lit:* entouré, ceint (**with,** de). **2.** *Nau:* (navire) affourché trop raide.

girth[1] [gəːθ], *s.* **1.** *Harn:* sangle *f*; sous-ventrière *f* (de harnais de trait); **saddle g.,** sangle de selle; **to slacken girths,** desserrer les sangles; dessangler; **g. leather, strap,** contre-sanglon *m*, *pl.* contre-sanglons. **2.** (*a*) circonférence *f* (d'un arbre, etc.); tour *m* (de poitrine, de taille); contour *m* (d'une forêt, etc.); périphérie *f* (d'un colis, etc.); **100 cm. in g.,** 100 cm. de tour, de circonférence; (*of pers.*) **of considerable g.,** d'une belle corpulence; (*b*) *N.Arch:* périmètre *m*, développement *m*; **g. of frame,** développement des couples.

girth[2]. **1.** *v.tr.* (*a*) sangler (un cheval); (*b*) **the saddle was insecurely girthed,** la sangle était lâche. **2.** *v.tr. Post:* **to g. a parcel,** mesurer au cordeau la périphérie d'un colis. **3.** *v.i.* **to g. ten metres,** avoir, mesurer, dix mètres de tour.

Girtonian [gəː'touniən], *s.f. Sch:* étudiante du collège de Girton (Cambridge).

gismo ['gizmou], *s.* = GIZMO.

gismondine, gismondite [dʒiz'mɔndain, -dait], *s. Miner:* gismondine *f*, gismondite *f*.

gist [dʒist], *s.* **1.** *Jur:* principal motif (d'une action). **2.** fond *m*, substance *f*, essence *f* (d'une conversation, etc.); point essentiel (d'une question); **to get to the g. of the matter,** entrer dans le vif de la question.

gith [giθ], *s. Bot:* **1.** nigelle *f*. **2.** nielle *f* des champs, des blés.

gitter ['gitər], *s. Opt:* réseau *m*.

gittern ['gitəːn], *s. A.Mus:* cistre *m*.

give[1] [giv], *s.* **1.** élasticité *f*; **shoes with no g. in them,** chaussures qui ne prêtent pas. **2. g. and take,** (i) accommodement *m*; concessions mutuelles; (ii) jeu *m* (dans un mécanisme, etc.); **there's room for g. and take,** il y a lieu de transiger, de faire des concessions de part et d'autre; **it's a case of g. and take,** c'est donnant donnant; **the g. and take of conversation,** le feu croisé de la conversation; *attrib.* **g.-and-take policy,** politique *f* de concessions mutuelles.

give[2], *v.* (**gave** [geiv]; **given** ['givn])

I. *v.tr.* donner. **1.** (*a*) **to g. sth. to s.o., to g. s.o. sth.,** donner qch. à qn; **he was given a book,** on lui a donné un livre; **to g. s.o. a present,** faire, donner, un cadeau à qn; **it was given (to) me,** c'était un cadeau; on me l'a offert, donné; **to g. alms,** faire l'aumône; **to g. to the poor,** donner aux pauvres; **to g. one's daughter in marriage,** donner sa fille en mariage; **to g. a dinner,** donner un dîner; inviter des amis à dîner; **to g. s.o. lunch,** offrir un déjeuner à qn; inviter qn à déjeuner; **to g. a luncheon for s.o., to g. s.o. a luncheon,** offrir un déjeuner en l'honneur de qn; **God g. me courage!** que Dieu me donne du courage! *F:* **God g. me strength!** nom de Dieu! quel(s) imbécile(s)! **it is not given to all to succeed,** il n'appartient pas, il n'est pas donné, à tous de réussir; **given health and youth it can be done,** avec la santé et la jeunesse on peut en venir à bout; **g. me the good old days!** parlez-moi du bon vieux temps! *F:* **g. me a pint of beer any time!** il n'y a rien de tel qu'un grand verre de bière! (*b*) *Tp:* **g. me Mr X,** passez-moi, donnez-moi, M. X; (*c*) **to g. and take,** faire des concessions mutuelles; y mettre chacun du sien; **we'll get there in two hours, g. or take a few minutes,** on fera le trajet en deux heures, ou à quelques minutes près, ou plus ou moins en quelques minutes. **2.** (*a*) **to g. a patient his medicine,** donner son médicament à un malade; **to g. s.o. sth. to eat, to drink,** donner à manger, à boire, à qn; **to g. s.o. six months' imprisonment,** condamner qn à six mois de prison; *F:* **they gave him six months,** (i) *Med:* on lui a donné six mois à vivre; (ii) il a eu six mois de prison, de tôle; **to g. a child a name,** donner un nom à un enfant; **he was given the name (of) David,** il a reçu le nom de David; on l'a baptisé David; **to g. s.o. a job to do,** assigner une tâche, un rôle, à qn; **to g. s.o. a book to read,** donner un livre à lire à qn; **to g. the children sth. to do,** donner aux enfants qch. à faire; occuper les enfants; **g. me your letters to post,** si vous me donnez votre courrier je le mettrai à la poste; (*b*) **to g. sth. into s.o.'s hands,** remettre qch. entre les mains de qn; **to g. s.o. a note from s.o.,** remettre à qn un petit mot de qn; **to g. s.o. into custody,** remettre qn aux mains de la police; faire arrêter qn; (*c*) **g. him our congratulations,** félicitez-le de notre part; présentez-lui nos félicitations; **g. her my love,** embrasse-la pour moi; **to g. s.o. one's support,** prêter son appui à qn; (*d*) engager (son honneur, etc.); **to g. one's word,** donner sa parole. **3.** (*a*) **to g. sth. in exchange for sth.,** donner qch. pour, contre, qch.; **to g. a good price for sth.,** donner, payer, un bon prix pour qch.; **what did you g. for it?** combien l'avez-vous payé? **I'll g. you £10 for it,** je vous en donnerai £10; **what will you g. me for it?** combien m'en offrez-vous? **I would g. a great deal to know . . .,** je donnerais beaucoup pour savoir. . .; **I'd g. my life for it,** j'en donnerais tout, ma vie; **I wouldn't g. him anything, a penny, for it,** je ne lui en donnerais pas un sou; (*b*) *St.Exch:* **to g. for the call,** acheter la prime à livrer; **to g. for the put,** acheter la prime à recevoir. **4.** (*a*) **to g. oneself to prayer,** se consacrer à la prière; **to g. one's mind, oneself, to one's studies,** s'adonner, s'appliquer, à ses études; (*b*) (*of woman*) **to g. herself,** se donner. **5.** (*a*) **to g. a jump,** (i) sauter, faire un saut; (ii) tressauter; **to g. a laugh,** rire; laisser échapper un rire; **to g. a sigh,** soupirer, pousser un soupir; **to g. a cry of astonishment,** pousser un cri d'étonnement; **to g. s.o. a blow,** porter, donner, un coup à qn; **to g. s.o.'s hand a squeeze,** serrer la main à qn; **to g. one's hat a brush,** donner un coup de brosse à son chapeau; **to g. the furniture a dust,** épousseter les meubles; donner un coup de torchon aux meubles; **to g. s.o. a smile,** adresser un sourire à qn; **he gave me an odd look,** il m'a lancé un regard singulier; (*b*) **to g. an answer,** faire une réponse; **he gave his age as twenty,** il a déclaré avoir vingt ans; **to g. orders,** donner des ordres; (*at shop*) **to g. an order,** faire une commande; **to g. s.o. one's blessing,** donner sa bénédiction à qn; **to g. s.o. the lie,** accuser qn de mentir; *A:* **to g. s.o. good-day,** souhaiter le bonjour à qn. **6.** (*a*) **to g. s.o. one's hand,** donner, tendre, la main à qn; **she gave him her hand (in marriage),** elle lui a accordé sa main; (*b*) **to g. one's attention to s.o.,** faire attention à qn; **I will g. the matter careful attention,** j'y mettrai tous mes soins; **he gave it considerable thought,** il l'a considéré avec beaucoup de soin. **7.** (*a*) **to g. one's opinion,** donner son avis; **to g. particulars,** donner, fournir, des détails; **to g. a description of sth.,** faire, donner, une description de qch.; décrire qch.; **to g. a decision,** (i) donner, faire connaître, sa décision; (ii) *Jur:* prononcer, rendre, un arrêt; *Jur:* **to g. the case for s.o., against s.o.,** décider en faveur de qn, contre qn; **to g. damages,** adjuger, accorder, des dommages-intérêts; **given this fourth day of March,** délivré ce jour d'hui quatre mars; *Cr:* **to g. s.o. out,** déclarer qn hors jeu; *F: O:* **I'll g. you best,** je reconnais que vous êtes plus fort que moi; je vous donne gagné; (*b*) **to g. no sign of life,** ne donner aucun signe de vie; **to g. an average of . . .,** rendre une moyenne de . . .; **further analysis gives . . .,** une analyse plus approfondie fait ressortir . . .; (*c*) **to g. an example,** donner un exemple; **facts given as a hypothesis,** faits donnés comme hypothèse; **given these facts, explain why . . .,** à partir de ces données, expliquez pourquoi . . .; **given a triangle ABC,** soit un triangle ABC; **given (any) two points,** soient deux points; (*d*) **to g. a recitation,** réciter, dire des vers; **Mrs X will now g. us a song,** nous allons maintenant entendre chanter Mme X; *Th:* **they're giving** *Macbeth* **this week,** on donne, on joue, *Macbeth* cette semaine; (*e*) **to g. a toast,** boire à la santé de qn; proposer un toast; **I g. you our host,** je bois à la santé de notre hôte. **8.** (*a*) **he gave me his cold,** il m'a donné, passé, son rhume; **that gave me the idea of travelling,** cela m'a donné l'idée de voyager; **the river gives its name to the province,** la rivière donne son nom à la province; (*b*) **to g. pain, pleasure,** faire, causer, de la peine, du plaisir; **to g. oneself trouble,** se donner du mal; **to g. oneself time to do sth.,** se réserver le temps de faire qch.; (*c*) **to g. s.o. to believe that. . .,** faire croire à qn que. . .; **to g. s.o. to understand that. . .,** donner à entendre à qn que . . .; (*d*) rendre; **investment that gives 10%,** placement *m* qui rend, rapporte, 10%; **this lamp gives a poor light,** cette lampe éclaire mal. **9.** (*a*) *F:* **to g. it (to) s.o.,** (i) semoncer qn, laver la tête à qn; (ii) rosser qn; **g. it them!** allez-y! ne les ménagez pas! **I'll g. you something to cry for!** je t'apprendrai à pleurer! *P:* **I gave him what for!** je l'ai arrangé de la belle façon! je lui ai flanqué un fameux coup! (*b*) *F:* **to g. as good as one gets,** rendre coup pour coup; **g. it all you've got!** faites le maximum! donnez un bon coup de collier! **10.** (*a*) **to g. way,** céder, fléchir, succomber; (*of ladder, etc.*) se casser, se rompre; (*of cable*) partir; **the ground gave way under our feet,** le sol s'est affaissé, s'est dérobé, sous nos pieds; **ground that gives way under the feet,** terrain *m* qui cède, se dérobe, sous les pas; **the floor gave way under the weight of the wardrobe,** le plancher s'est effondré sous le poids de l'armoire; **the building has given way at the base,** le bâtiment a cédé par la base; **the foundations (of the house) were giving way,** la maison commençait à faiblir par les fondations; **my legs are giving way (under me),** mes jambes fléchissent, mollissent, se dérobent, sous moi; j'ai les jambes rompues; mes jambes me rentrent dans le corps; **his strength is giving way,** les forces lui manquent; **his health is giving way,** sa santé s'affaiblit; *Mil:* **the line gave way,** la ligne s'effondra; (*b*) **to g. way to s.o.,** céder à qn; **to g. way to s.o.'s whims,** se prêter aux caprices de qn; **if she cries, don't g. way,** si elle pleure, ne vous laissez pas attendrir; **to g. way to despair, to grief,** s'abandonner au désespoir, à la douleur; **to g. way to temptation,** céder à la tentation; **to g. way to anger,** se laisser emporter par la colère; **to g. way to tears, to one's emotions,** se laisser aller aux larmes, à ses émotions; **don't g. way like that!** ne vous laissez pas aller comme ça! (*c*) **to g. way to s.o., to a car,** céder la place à qn, le passage à une voiture; *P.N: Aut:* **g. way,** cédez le passage; *Nau:* **to g. way to a ship,** céder la place à, se déranger pour, un naivre; (*d*) *Nau:* **to g. way,** souquer sur les avirons; **g. way!** souquez partout! nagez partout!

II. *v.i.* **1.** (*a*) (*of cloth, elastic, etc.*) prêter, donner; **the rope has given,** le cordage a donné, s'est relâché; **the springs don't g. enough,** les ressorts manquent de souplesse; (*b*) céder, fléchir; **the door will g. if you push hard enough,** la porte cédera si vous la poussez assez fort; **the beam is giving under the weight,** la poutre plie sous le poids; (*c*) **the frost is beginning to g.,** il commence à dégeler; **the ice was giving,** la glace commençait à fondre. **2. the window gives on (to) the garden,** la fenêtre donne sur le jardin; **this door gives into the yard,** cette porte donne accès à la cour, donne dans la cour. **3.** *F:* (*from German* **was gibt's**) **what gives?** (i) salut! (ii) qu'est-ce qui se passe, se fricote? (iii) quoi de neuf? **4.** *P:* **g.!** vide ton sac!

III. (*compound verbs*) **1. give away,** *v.tr.* (*a*) donner (qch. à qn); se dénantir de (ses possessions); **I would rather g. it away,** je préférerais en faire cadeau; **it's given away, that's giving it away,** c'est donné; **to g. away the prizes,** distribuer les prix; (*b*) **to g. away the bride,** conduire, accompagner, la mariée à l'autel; **the bride was given away by her father,** la mariée est entrée dans l'église au bras de son père; (*c*) **to g. s.o. away,** trahir, vendre, dénoncer, qn; **to g. oneself away,** se révéler; se trahir; se contredire; **she can talk without giving herself, her background, away,** elle sait parler sans trahir son origine; **to g. the show, the game, away,** lâcher le secret; vendre la mèche; **he's not giving anything away,** il garde bien ses secrets.

2. give back, *v.tr.* (*a*) rendre, restituer; **have you given back the books you borrowed?** est-ce que vous avez rendu les livres que vous avez empruntés? **to g. s.o. back his liberty,** rendre la liberté à qn; (*b*) renvoyer (un écho); refléter (une image).

3. give in. (*a*) *v.tr.* **to g. in one's name,** donner son nom; **to g. in a parcel (at the door),** livrer, remettre, un paquet (à la porte); **to g. in one's examination paper,** remettre sa copie d'examen; **please g. in your essays by Thursday,** donnez-moi vos dissertations jeudi au plus tard; (*b*) *v.i.* céder; se rendre, se soumettre; **to g. in to s.o.,** céder à qn; **to g. in with a smile,** se soumettre en souriant.

4. give off, *v.tr.* (*a*) dégager, émettre, répandre, exhaler (une odeur, etc.); répandre (la chaleur); *Ch:* dégager (un gaz); **oxygen is given off,** il se dégage de l'oxygène; (*b*) (*of plants*) **to g. off shoots,** faire des pousses.

5. give on, *v.tr. St.Exch:* faire reporter (des titres).

6. give out. (*a*) *v.tr.* (i) distribuer (du ravitaillement, des livres, etc.); (ii) dégager (une odeur, etc.); répandre (la chaleur); (iii) **to g. out a notice,** lire une communication; *Ecc:* **to g. out a hymn,** annoncer un cantique; **it was given out that . . .,** on a annoncé, proclamé, dit, que . . .; **it was given out that he was dead,** on le disait mort; (*b*) *v.i.* manquer, faire défaut; (*of supplies*) s'épuiser; **our supplies are giving out,** nos provisions s'épuisent, tirent à leur fin, commencent à manquer; **my strength was giving out,** j'étais à bout de forces, la force me manquait; **my patience was giving out,** j'étais à bout de patience, je perdais patience; **patience gives out in the end,** la patience échappe à la longue; **his luck gave out,** sa chance l'a abandonné; **my brakes gave out,** mes freins ont lâché.

7. give over, *v.tr.* (*a*) **to g. sth. over to s.o.,** remettre qch. entre les mains de qn; abandonner qch. à qn; **she gave the old man over to his housekeeper,** elle a remis le vieillard aux soins de sa gouvernante; (*b*) **given over to despair,** abandonné, en proie, au désespoir; (*c*) *P:* cesser, finir; renoncer à (qch.); **g. over crying!** mais cessez donc de pleurer! **g. over, will you?** ça c'est vraiment assez! est-ce fini, par exemple! laisse tomber!

8. give up, *v.tr.* (*a*) rendre (sa proie); abandonner (ses biens, ses prétentions); **to g. up all one's possessions,** se dénantir, se démunir, de tout ce qu'on possède; **to g. up one's seat to s.o.,** céder sa place à qn; **g. up your ticket when leaving the station,** remettez votre billet au contrôleur à la sortie (de la gare); (*b*) renoncer à (un projet, etc.); **to g. up sth. for sth. else,** renoncer à qch. pour autre chose; **to g. up the idea of doing sth.,** renoncer à faire qch.; **I haven't completely given up the idea of going to Greece,** je n'ai pas complètement abandonné, renoncé à, l'idée d'un voyage en Grèce; **he refuses to g. up his point of view,** il ne veut pas en démordre; **I gave her up,** j'ai renoncé à elle; **to g. up smoking,** cesser de, renoncer à, fumer; **to g. up a newspaper,** cesser son abonnement, se désabonner, à un journal; **to g. up business,** se retirer des affaires; **the firm had to g. up,** la maison a dû fermer; **to g. up the stage,** quitter le théâtre; **to g. up one's job,** résigner son emploi, ses fonctions; **to g. up the game, the struggle,** abandonner la partie; donner partie gagnée (à qn); renoncer à la lutte; **don't g. up!** tenez bon! **to g. up, to g. it up as a bad job,** y renoncer; (*of riddle*) **I g. (it) up,** je donne ma langue au chat; (*c*) **to g. s.o. up (for lost),** considérer qn comme perdu; **the doctors have given him up,** les médecins l'ont condamné, le considèrent comme perdu; **I'd given you up!** je ne vous attendais plus! je ne vous espérais plus! (*d*) (i) livrer (qn à la justice, etc.); faire arrêter (qn); **to g. oneself up,** se dénoncer, se constituer prisonnier; (ii) **to g. oneself up to sth.,** se livrer à qch.; s'absorber dans la lecture, etc.; s'appliquer, s'adonner, à l'étude, etc.; s'abandonner à ses méditations, etc.; se prêter au plaisir, etc.; **his mornings were given up to business,** ses matinées étaient consacrées aux affaires; **to g. up one's life to study,** se vouer, vouer sa vie, à l'étude.

giveaway ['givəwei], *s. F:* (*a*) trahison *f*; révélation *f* involontaire; **it was a dead, a real, g.,** c'était un geste, un mot, etc., qui en disait long; (*b*) *Com:* **g. (price),** (prix) défiant toute concurrence; **it was a g.!** c'était donné! (*c*) *T.V: W.Tel: NAm:* **g. (show),** concours télévisé, radiophonique (où les gagnants reçoivent des prix).

given ['givn], *a.* (*a*) donné; **in a g. time,** dans un délai donné, convenu, déterminé; **at a g. point,** à un point donné; **g. number of revolutions,** nombre déterminé de tours; *Mth:* **in a g. triangle,** dans un triangle donné; (*b*) *esp. NAm:* **g. name,** prénom *m*; nom *m* de baptême.

giver ['givər], *s.* donneur, -euse; donateur, -trice; *Com: Jur:* **g. of a trade order,** auteur *m* d'une commande; *St.Exch:* **g. of option money,** acheteur *m* de primes; **g. of stock,** reporté *m*; **the market is all givers,** la place est chargée; **there are no givers on this stock,** personne ne veut se reporter sur cette valeur.

Givetian [dʒi'veiʃən], *a. & s. Geol:* givétien (*m*).

giving[1] ['giviŋ], *a.* (*of pers.*) donnant; **of a g. nature,** généreux.

giving[2], *s.* (*a*) don *m*, donation *f*; *esp. NAm: F:* **givings totalled . . .,** les donations ont atteint un chiffre de . . .; *Sch:* **prize g.,** distribution *f* des prix; **g. is sometimes better than receiving,** il est parfois plus agréable de donner que de recevoir; (*b*) *Med: F:* **g. set,** appareil *m* à faire des transfusions de sang.

gizmo ['gizmou], *s. U.S: F:* machin *m*, truc *m*, bidule *m*.

gizzard ['gizəd], *s.* gésier *m*; *F:* **that sticks in my g.,** je ne peux pas avaler, digérer, ça; **this refusal still sticks in his g.,** il n'a pas digéré ce refus; *A:* **to fret one's g.,** se tourmenter; se faire du mauvais sang, de la bile.

glabella [glə'belə], *s. Anat:* glabelle *f*.

glabrous ['gleibrəs], *a.* **1.** *Nat.Hist:* glabre. **2.** *A:* (visage *m*, menton *m*) imberbe, glabre.

glabrousness ['gleibrəsnis], *s. Nat.Hist:* glabrisme *m*.

glacé ['glæs(e)i], *a.* (*a*) (cuir, etc.) glacé; **g. kid,** chevreau glacé; (*b*) *Cu:* **g. fruits,** fruits glacés.

glacial ['gleisiəl, -ʃəl], *a.* **1.** *Geol:* glaciaire; **g. erosion,** érosion *f* glaciaire; **g. drift,** apport *m* des glaciers; **g. valley,** vallée *f* glaciaire; **g. epoch, period,** époque *f*, période *f*, glaciaire; glaciaire *m*. **2.** (vent, etc.) glacial, -als; **g. reception,** accueil glacial. **3.** *Ch:* cristallisé; en cristaux; **g. acetic acid,** acide acétique concentré.

glacially ['gleisiəli, -ʃəli], *adv.* glacialement.

glaciate ['gleisieit, -ʃieit], *v.tr.* (*a*) couvrir de glaciers; transformer en champ de glace; **the whole valley was glaciated,** la vallée entière (i) était remplie d'un glacier, (ii) a subi l'érosion glaciaire; (*b*) geler.

glaciated ['gleisieitid, -ʃi-], *a.* glacié; **g. valley,** vallée glaciée.

glaciation [gleisi'eiʃ(ə)n, -ʃi'ei-], *s.* glaciation *f*.

glacier ['glæsiər], *s.* glacier *m*; **high-polar, subpolar, temperate, g.,** glacier polaire, sub-polaire, tempéré; **valley g. (Alpine type),** glacier encaissé, glacier de vallée (du type alpin); **cirque, corrie, g.,** glacier de cirque; **hanging g.,** glacier suspendu; **piedmont g.,** glacier de piémont.

glaciered ['glæsiəd], *a.* couvert de glaciers; glacié.

glacieret ['glæsiəret, -ʃəret], *s.* petit glacier.

glaciofluvial ['gleisiou'flu:viəl, 'glæs-], *a.* fluvio-glaciaire.

glaciolacustrine ['gleisioulæ'kʌstrain, 'glæs-], *a.* glaciolacustre.

glaciological [gleisiou'lɔdʒikl, glæs-], *a.* glaciologique.

glaciologist [gleisi'ɔlədʒist, glæs-], *s.* glaciologue *mf*, glaciologiste *mf*.

glaciology [gleisi'ɔlədʒi], *s.* glaciologie *f*.

glacis ['glæsis], *s.* (*a*) *Fort:* glacis *m*; (*b*) *Geol:* glacis, pente douce.

glad [glæd], *a.* **(gladder, gladdest) 1.** (*of pers.*) heureux; joyeux; bien aise; content; **to be g. to hear sth.,** apprendre qch. avec plaisir; être heureux, bien content, d'apprendre qch.; **I'm g. to hear it, I'm very g. about it,** j'en suis bien aise; tant mieux; je l'apprends avec plaisir; **to be g. that sth. has happened,** être heureux, joyeux, que qch. soit arrivé, de ce que qch. est arrivé; **we have no reason to be g.,** nous n'avons pas sujet à nous réjouir; **I'm g. you like him,** je suis très heureux, cela me fait (grand) plaisir, que vous l'aimiez; **he is only too g. to help you,** il ne demande pas mieux que de vous aider; **how g. she was!** comme elle était contente! **I should be g. to know whether . . .,** je serais bien heureux de savoir si . . .; **they would be g. of your help,** ils seraient bien heureux d'avoir votre aide; votre aide leur ferait plaisir; **we should be g. if you would accept,** nous serions heureux que vous acceptiez; **it makes my heart g. to hear him,** cela me réjouit le cœur de l'entendre; *Lit:* **wine maketh g. the heart of man,** le vin réjouit le cœur. **2.** (*a*) **a g. shout,** un cri de plaisir; **a g. smile,** un sourire de contentement; (*b*) **g. news,** *Lit:* **g. tidings,** bonne, heureuse, nouvelle; (*c*) **on a g. spring morning,** par une gaie matinée de printemps; (*d*) *U.S: F:* **g. hand,** accueil chaleureux, empressé (pas toujours désintéressé); (*e*) *F:* **to put on one's g. rags,** (i) mettre ses plus beaux habits; s'endimancher; (ii) (*of woman*) mettre une robe de soirée; (*of man*) mettre un smoking, une queue-de-morue.

gladden ['glædn], *v.tr.* réjouir; rendre (qn) bien aise, bien heureux; **it gladdens my heart to see them,** cela me réjouit le cœur de les voir.

gladdon ['glædən], *s. Bot: F:* iris *m* fétide; iris-gigot *m*.

glade [gleid], *s.* clairière *f*, sommière *f*, percée *f*, éclaircie *f* (dans une forêt).

glad-hand ['glædhænd], *v.tr. & i. U.S: F:* accueillir (qn) chaleureusement, faire un accueil chaleureux (à qn), serrer la main à tout le monde (souvent pour arriver à ses propres fins).

glad-hander ['glædhændər], *s. U.S: F:* personne chaleureuse, accueillante, liante (qui agit souvent dans son propre intérêt).

gladiate ['gleidieit], *a. Bot:* gladié; (feuille) en glaive.

gladiator ['glædieitər], *s.* gladiateur *m*.

gladiatorial [glædiə'tɔ:riəl], *a.* gladiatorial, -aux; **g. combats,** combats *m* de gladiateurs.

gladiolus, *pl.* **-luses, -li** [glædi'ouləs, -ləsiz, -lai], *s. Bot:* glaïeul *m*.

gladite ['glædait], *s. Miner:* gladite *f*.

gladly ['glædli], *adv.* avec plaisir, volontiers, de bon cœur, de grand cœur; heureusement; joyeusement, avec joie, **I'll g. help him,** je ne demande pas mieux que de l'aider; **I accept g.,** j'accepte volontiers, avec grand plaisir.

gladness ['glædnis], *s.* joie *f*, allégresse *f*.

gladsome ['glædsəm], *a. A: & Lit:* **1.** heureux, joyeux; **g. tidings,** bonne nouvelle; **g. countenances,** mines réjouies. **2. the g. sunshine,** le soleil réjouissant.

Gladstone ['glædstən], *Pr.n.* **G. bag,** sac-jumelle *m*, *pl.* sacs jumelles; sac américain.

glair[1] [glɛər], *s.* **1.** *Bookb:* glairure *f*, glaire *f*; blanc *m* d'œuf. **2.** *Med:* glaire.

glair[2], *v.tr. Bookb:* glairer.

glaireous ['glɛəriəs], **glairy** ['glɛəri], *a. Med:* glaireux.

glairin ['glɛərin], *s. Ch:* glairine *f*, barégine *f*.

glairing ['glɛəriŋ], *s. Bookb:* glairage *m*.

glaive [gleiv], *s. A: & Poet:* glaive *m*.

glamorize ['glæməraiz], *v.tr.* donner une beauté factice (comme à une star de cinéma); *Com:* améliorer la présentation de (qch.), donner du cachet à (des marchandises); **to g. war,** peindre la guerre sous de belles couleurs; *F:* **you've been glamorizing yourself!** tu t'es fait une beauté!

glamorous ['glæmərəs], *a.* enchanteur, -eresse, charmeur, -euse, fascinateur, -trice; ensorcelant; prestigieux, -euse.

glamour ['glæmər], *s.* **1.** *Lit:* enchantement *m*, charme *m*; **to cast a g. over s.o.,** exercer un charme sur qn; ensorceler qn. **2.** (*a*) fascination *f*; prestige *m* (d'un nom, etc.); éclat *m*; **g. of glory,** prestige de la gloire; **the false g. of war,** le faux éclat de la guerre; **to lend a g. to . . ., throw a g. over . . .,** prêter de l'éclat à . . .; (*b*) *F:* **g. boy,** séducteur *m*; beau mâle; cupidon *m*; **g. girl,** ensorceleuse *f*; beau morceau; *P:* **g. puss,** ensorceleuse; minette *f*.

glance[1] [glɑ:ns], *s.* **1.** coup *m* qui ricoche; coup en biais; ricochet *m*. **2.** regard *m*, coup d'œil; **at a g.,** d'un coup d'œil; **at the first g.,** à première vue; au premier coup d'œil; au premier aspect; **angry g.,** regard irrité; regard de travers. **3.** trait *m* de lumière; éclat *m*, éclair *m*; lueur soudaine.

glance[2], *v.i.* **1.** (*a*) (*of bullet, etc.*) **to g. aside, g. off,** dévier, ricocher; **the sword glanced off his ribs,** l'épée *f* lui glissa sur les côtes; **to g. off, from, a subject,** glisser sur un sujet; ne faire qu'effleurer un sujet; (*b*) *v.tr.* **to g. back rays of light,** réfléchir, refléter, les rayons de lumière. **2. to g. at s.o., at sth.,** jeter un regard sur qn, sur qch.; lancer un coup d'œil à qn; **to g. up, down,** jeter un coup d'œil en haut, en bas; **to g. around,** jeter un regard autour de soi; **to g. aside,** détourner le regard; **to g. through, over, sth.,** examiner rapidement qch.; jeter un regard sur qch.; parcourir, feuilleter (un livre); **he glanced down the list,** il a parcouru la liste. **3.** *A:* **to g. at s.o.,** faire une allusion ironique, désobligeante, à qn. **4.** (*of steel, weapons, etc.*) étinceler; jeter des lueurs.

glance[3], *s. A:* minerai lustré, métallifère; (*still occ. used in compounds*) *O:* **g. coal,** anthracite *m*; **cobalt g., g. cobalt,** cobalt gris; cobaltine *f*; **copper g., g. copper,** cuivre éclatant, chalcocite *f*, sulfure cuivreux.

glancing ['glɑ:nsiŋ], *a.* **1.** (*of blow, etc.*) oblique. **2.** étincelant.

gland[1] [glænd], *s. Biol:* glande *f*; **g. cell,** cellule *f* glandulaire; *Anat:* **lachrymal g.,** glande lacrimale; *Anat: Med:* **lymphatic glands,** ganglions *m* lymphatiques; **swollen glands,** (i) glandes engorgées; (ii) (*in childhood*) états *m* ganglionnaires de l'enfance; *F:* **to have swollen glands,** avoir des glandes au cou; *Rept:* **poison g.,** glande à venin.

gland[2], *s. Mec.E: Mch:* serre-garniture *m*, *pl.* serre-garnitures; bague *f* d'emboîtement; couronne *f*, gland *m*, chapeau *m*; **stuffing(-box) g., packing g.,** bague, couronne, chapeau, de presse-étoupe; gland; **stuffing box and g.,** presse-étoupe *m inv*; **expansion g.,** boite *f* de joint glissant; **bearing g.,** douille *f* palier; **thrust g.,** manchon *m* de butée; **grease g.,** graisseur *m* automatique; **g. nut,** écrou *m* de presse-étoupe; **g. ring,** bague *f* de presse-étoupe, d'étanchéité; **g. housing,** porte-garnitures *m inv*; **g. support,** support *m* de presse-étoupe; **pump g.,** presse-étoupe de pompe; *N.Arch:* **stern g.,** presse-étoupe arrière, presse-étoupe d'étambot.

glandered ['glændəd], *a. Vet:* (cheval) morveux, glandé.

glanders ['glændəz], *s.pl.* (*with sg. const.*) *Vet: Med:* morve *f* (chez le cheval ou l'homme).

glandiferous [glæn'difərəs], *a. Bot:* glandifère.

glandiform ['glændifɔ:m], *a.* glandiforme.

glandless ['glændlis], *a. Mec.E:* sans garniture, sans presse-étoupe; *Biol:* sans glande(s).

glandular ['glændjulər], *a. Physiol: Med:* glandulaire; adénoïde; *Med:* **g. fever,** mononucléose infectieuse.

glandule ['glændju:l], *s. Bot: Anat:* glandule *f*.

glanduliferous [glændju'lifərəs], *a. Bot: Anat:* glandulifère.

glandulous ['glændjuləs], *a. Bot: Anat:* glanduleux, -euse.

glans [glænz], *s.* **1.** *Anat:* gland *m* (du pénis). **2.** *Bot:* gland (du chêne, etc.).

glare[1] ['glɛər], *s.* **1.** (*a*) éclat *m*, clarté *f*, rayonnement *m*, éblouissement *m*, lumière crue, éblouissante (du soleil, des projecteurs, etc.); **in the full g. of the sun,** à la grande clarté du soleil; au grand soleil; **in the full g. of publicity,** sous les feux de la rampe; (*b*) éblouissement *m*, aveuglement *m* (d'un phare, etc.); *Aut:* **non-g. goggles,** lunettes anti-éblouissantes. **2.** clinquant *m*; faux éclat; fausse splendeur (de cirque forain, etc.). **3.** regard fixe et irrité; **he looked at me with a g.,** il a fixé sur moi un regard irrité.

glare[2], *v.i.* **1.** (*of sun, etc.*) briller d'un éclat éblouissant. **2.** (*a*) **to g. at s.o.,** lancer un regard furieux, furibond, à qn; regarder qn d'un œil indigné; **they were glaring at one another,** ils se regardaient en chiens de faïence; (*b*) *Lit: with cogn. acc.* **to g. defiance, anger, at s.o.,** lancer un regard plein de défi, de colère, à qn.

glare[3], *a. & s. NAm:* **g. (ice),** nappe *f* de glace; (glace) lisse et transparente.

glareole ['glɛərioul], *s. Orn:* glaréole *f*.

Glareolidae [glæri'ɔlidi:], *s.pl. Orn:* glaréolidés *m*, glaréoles *f*.

glaring ['glɛəriŋ], *a.* **1.** (*a*) (*of light, etc.*) éblouissant, éclatant; (soleil) aveuglant; (*b*) (*of costume, colour, etc.*) voyant, éclatant; (*of colour*) cru. **2.** (*of fact, etc.*) manifeste, patent, qui saute aux yeux, qui crève les yeux; (*of injustice, etc.*) flagrant; **g. lie,** mensonge *m* manifeste; **g. abuses,** abus scandaleux, choquants; **g. blunder,** faute grossière. **3. with g. eyes,** (i) d'un œil furieux; (ii) aux yeux menaçants.

glaringly ['glɛəriŋli], *adv.* **1.** avec un faux éclat; avec trop d'éclat. **2.** manifestement; d'une manière patente, flagrante.

glaringness ['glɛəriŋnis], *s.* **1.** éclat éblouissant, clarté crue (de la lumière). **2.** évidence *f*, clarté; flagrance *f*; **the g. of the falsehood,** l'évidence du mensonge.

glass[1] [glɑ:s], *s.* **1.** verre *m*; (*a*) **the g. industry,** l'industrie *f* du verre, la verrerie; **lead g.,** verre de plomb; **quartz g.,** verre quartzeux; **soda g.,** verre à base de soude; **annealed g.,** verre recuit; **unannealed g.,** verre non recuit; **blown g.,** verre soufflé; **cut g.,** verre taillé, cristal taillé; **drawn g.,** verre étiré; **flashed g.,**

verre doublé; **three-ply flashed g.,** verre triplex; **foam g.,** verre mousse, verre cellulaire; **hardened g., tempered g., toughened g.,** verre dur(ci), verre trempé; **soft g.,** verre tendre; **pressed g.,** verre moulé, pressé; **rolled g.,** verre laminé; **flat g.,** verre plat; **plate g.,** glace *f* sans tain, glace de vitrage; verre à glaces; verre laminé, cylindré, blanc; **laminated plate g.,** verre stratifié; **fibrous g., spun g.,** fibre de verre, verre filé; **g.-fibre reinforced plastic,** stratifié *m* en tissu de verre; **a g. fibre,** une fibre de verre; **g. silk,** soie *f* de verre; **g. wool,** laine *f* de verre; **g. paper,** papier *m* de verre; **g. thread, g. yarn,** fil *m* de verre; **g. plate,** plaque *f* de verre; **square, plate, of g.,** plat *m* de verre; **powdered g., g. dust,** verre en poudre, poudre *f* de verre; **broken g.,** éclats *mpl* de verre; **flying g.,** éclats de verre (qui volent); (*b*) **Bohemian g.,** verre de Bohême; verre à gobeleterie; **Jena g.,** verre d'Iéna; **crown g., soda-lime g.,** semi-cristal *m*; **optical g.,** verre d'optique; **bottle g., green g.,** verre à bouteilles; chambourin *m*; **white g.,** verre blanc; **clear g.,** verre clair (non dépoli); **frosted g., ground g.,** verre dépoli; **crackle g.,** verre givré; **ribbed g., rippled g.,** verre strié; **cathedral g.,** verre cathédrale, verre brut coulé; **coloured g., stained g.,** verre de couleur, verre coloré, verre teinté; **stained-g. window,** vitrail *m, pl.* vitraux; verrière *f*; **the stained g. of a church,** les vitraux, les verrières, d'une église; **artist in stained g.,** peintre *m* sur verre, peintre verrier; **decorated g.,** verre décoré; (*c*) vitre *f* (de fenêtre); glace *f* (de voiture); verre (de montre, de lampe); **pane of g.,** vitre, glace; carreau *m* (de verre); **pane g., window g., sheet g.,** verre à vitres; **g.-holding frame,** châssis *m* porte-glace; **bevelled g.,** glace biseautée, verre biseauté; **curved g.,** glace galbée, verre galbé; **plane g.,** glace plane, verre plan; **safety g., splinter-proof g., unbreakable g.,** glace, verre, de sécurité; glace, verre, incassable; **bullet-proof g.,** glace, verre, à l'épreuve des balles; glace blindée, verre blindé; **armoured g., reinforced g., gauze g., wire g.,** glace armée, grillagée; verre armé, grillagé; glace, verre, à fil de fer noyé; (*d*) **g. cutting,** (i) taillage *m* de glaces; (ii) taille *f* du verre; cristallerie *f*; **g. cutter,** (i) (*pers.*) coupeur *m* de verre, vitrier *m*; tailleur *m* de verre, cristallier *m*; (ii) *Tls:* diamant *m* (de vitrier); coupe-verre *m inv*; **circular g. cutter,** tournette *f*; **wheel g. cutter,** coupe-verre à molette; **g. blowing,** soufflage *m* du verre; **g. blower,** souffleur *m* de verre; bossetier *m*; **power g. blower,** souffleur de verre industriel; **g. engraver,** tailleur de verre, cristallier; **g. grinding,** façonnage *m* de glaces; **g. making, manufacture,** verrerie *f*. **2.** (*a*) **(drinking) g.,** verre (à boire); **wine g.,** verre à vin; **g. of wine,** verre de vin; **champagne g.,** flûte *f*, coupe *f*, à champagne; **claret g.,** verre à Bordeaux; **hock g.,** verre à vin du Rhin; **liqueur g.,** verre à liqueur; **stem, stemmed, g.,** verre à pied; **graduated g., measuring g.,** verre gradué; **g. rack, stand,** verrier *m*; **to have had a g. too much, too many,** avoir bu (un coup de) trop; *F:* **let's have a g. together,** allons trinquer, boire un coup, ensemble; **to call for glasses all round,** commander une tournée générale; (*b*) *coll.* **table g.,** verrerie de table; **oven g.,** verrerie allant au four; **hollow g.,** verres creux; gobeleterie *f*; **hollow g. factory, trade,** gobeleterie; **g. and china shop,** magasin *m* de verrerie et porcelaine; *Post: etc:* **g. with care,** fragile. **3.** (*a*) lentille *f* (d'un instrument d'optique); (*b*) **magnifying g.,** loupe *f*; verre grossissant; **weaver's g.,** loupe de tisserand; (*c*) **(field) g.,** lunette *f* d'approche; longue-vue *f, pl.* longues-vues; **field glasses,** jumelles *f*; **opera glasses,** jumelles de théâtre; (*d*) *pl.* **glasses,** lunettes, verres; **dark glasses, sun glasses,** lunettes de soleil; **snow glasses,** lunettes d'alpiniste; **to wear glasses,** porter des lunettes; **to put on one's glasses,** mettre ses lunettes. **4. (looking) g.,** glace, miroir *m*; **shaving g.,** miroir à barbe; **to do one's hair in front of the g.,** se coiffer devant la glace, le miroir. **5.** baromètre *m* (à cadran); **the g. is falling,** le baromètre baisse. **6.** *Hort:* (i) châssis *m*; (ii) serre(s) *f(pl.)*; **grown under g.,** cultivé sous verre, en serre, sous châssis. **7. musical glasses,** harmonica *m*. **8.** *Ch:* **g. of antimony,** verre d'antimoine; **uranium g.,** verre d'urane; **volcanic g.,** verre volcanique; obsidiane *f*, obsidienne *f*. **9.** *attrib.* de, en, verre; **g. bottle,** bouteille *f* de, en, verre; **g. door,** porte vitrée; porte de, en, verre; **g. window,** fenêtre vitrée; **g. partition,** cloison *m* de, en, verre; **g. wall,** paroi *f* de, en, verre; **g. roof,** verrière *f* (de gare, etc.); **g. roofing,** vitrerie de toit; **g. paving,** pavé *m* en verre; **g. (stirring) rod,** agitateur *m*, baguette *f*, en verre; **g. stopper,** bouchon *m*, de, en, verre; **g. case, g.-fronted cabinet,** vitrine *f*; **to keep, display, sth. in a g. case, under g.,** garder, exposer, qch. sous verre; *F:* **he ought to be kept in a g. case,** il est à mettre sous verre; *Prov:* **people who live in g. houses shouldn't throw stones,** il faut être sans défauts pour critiquer autrui. **10.** (*a*) *Ich:* **g. eel,** civelle *f*, piballe *f*; (*b*) *Rept:* **g. snake,** (i) ophisaure *m*; serpent *m* de verre; (ii) pseudope *m*; (*c*) *Moll:* **g. snail,** vitrine transparente; **g. shell,** hyale *f*.

glass², *v.tr.* **1. to g. in a balcony, etc.,** vitrer un balcon, etc. **2.** mettre (une statuette, etc.) sous verre. **3.** *P:* taillader (qn) avec du verre cassé (dans une rixe).

glasscloth ['glɑːsklɔθ], *s.* **1.** torchon *m* essuie-verres *inv.* **2.** toile verrée.

glassful ['glɑːsful], *s.* (plein) verre; *occ.* verrée *f* (d'eau, etc.); **that really is a good g.,** ça c'est une rasade.

glasshouse ['glɑːshaus], *s.* **1.** (*a*) *Hort:* serre *f*; (*b*) atelier vitré (pour la photographie). **2.** *Tchn:* verrerie *f*. **3.** *F:* prison *f* militaire, ours *m*.

glassine [glæ'siːn], *s. Com:* papier *m* cristal.

glass-lined ['glɑːs'laind], *a. Ind:* **g.-l. tank,** cuve verrée.

glassware ['glɑːswɛər], *s.* articles *mpl* de verre; cristaux *mpl*; verrerie *f*; **small g.,** verroterie *f*, verraille *f*.

glasswork ['glɑːswəːk], *s.* **1.** (*a*) verrerie *f*; (*b*) (*in church*) vitraux *mpl*, vitrage *m*. **2.** *pl.* (*usu. with sg. const.*) **glassworks,** verrerie *f*, glacerie *f*; (*for crystal*) cristallerie *f*.

glasswort ['glɑːswəːt], *s. Bot:* (*a*) **jointed g.,** salicorne *f*; (*b*) **prickly g.,** kali *m*, soude *f*.

glassy ['glɑːsi], *a.* vitreux; *Nat.Hist: Miner:* hyalin; **g. eye,** œil vitreux; **g. sea,** mer unie comme un miroir; **the g. depths of the lake,** les profondeurs transparentes du lac.

Glaswegian [glæs'wiːdʒiən], *a. & s.* (originaire *mf*, habitant, -ante) de Glasgow.

Glauber ['glaubər], *Pr.n. Pharm:* **Glauber('s) salt(s),** sel *m* (admirable) de Glauber; sulfate *m* de soude.

glauberite ['glaubərait], *s. Miner:* glaubérite *f*.

glaucescence [glɔː'ses(ə)ns], *s. Bot:* glaucescence *f*.

glaucescent [glɔː'ses(ə)nt], *a. Bot:* glaucescent.

glaucium ['glɔːsiəm], *s. Bot:* glaucière *f*, glaucienne *f*.

glaucochroite [gloukə'krouait], *s. Miner:* glaucochroïte *f*.

glaucodot ['gloukədɔt], *s. Miner:* glaucodote *m*.

glaucoma [glɔː'koumə], *s. Med:* glaucome *m*.

glaucomatous [glɔː'koumətəs], *a. Med:* glaucomateux.

glaucomys ['gloukəmis], *s. Z:* glaucomys *m*.

glauconiferous [gloukə'nifərəs], *a. Miner:* glauconifère.

glauconite ['glɔːkənait], *s. Miner:* glauconie *f*.

glauconitic [gloukə'nitik], *a. Miner:* glauconieux.

glaucophane ['gloukəfein], *s. Miner:* glaucophane *f*.

glaucous ['glɔːkəs], *a.* **1.** glauque. **2.** *Bot:* pruiné; pruineux, -euse. **3.** *Orn:* **g. gull,** goéland *m* bourgmestre; **g.-winged gull,** goéland à ailes glauques.

glaze¹ [gleiz], *s.* **1.** (*a*) glace *f*, lustre *m*, glacé *m*, vernissure *f* (du drap, du cuir, etc.); (*b*) aspect vitreux (de l'œil). **2.** *Cer:* glaçure *f*, glaçage *m*, vernis (luisant), enduit *m*, couverte *f*, émail *m*, **tin g.,** glaçure stannifère; **transmutation g.,** lustre (irisé). **3.** *Cu:* glace ((i) de jus de viande, (ii) de blanc d'œuf); dorure *f*. **4.** *Paint:* glacis *m*, jus *m*. **5.** *U.S:* verglas *m*; givre limpide, transparent.

glaze², *v.*

I. *v.tr.* **1.** vitrer (une fenêtre, une maison, etc.); **to g. in a window,** garnir une fenêtre de vitres; poser les vitres (d'une fenêtre). **2.** (*a*) glacer, lustrer, satiner (un tissu); vernir, vernisser, glacer (le cuir); lisser, surglacer (le papier, etc.); (*b*) **to g. the eye,** embuer l'œil; (*c*) *Cer:* glacer, vernir, vernisser, émailler (la poterie); plomber (la vaisselle de terre); vitrifier (les tuiles, etc.); (*d*) *Cu:* glacer, dorer; (*e*) *Paint:* glacer (un tableau), passer (un tableau) au jus; (*f*) *Phot:* émailler (une épreuve).

II. *v.i.* **to g. (over),** se glacer; (*of eye*) devenir vitreux.

glazed [gleizd], *a.* **1.** (*of roof, door*) vitré; (*of picture*) **framed and g.,** encadré et sous verre; **g.-in light,** verrine *f*. **2.** (*a*) (tissu) glacé, lustré, satiné; (cuir) glacé, verni, vernissé; (papier) brillant, satiné; **g. lining,** garniture *f* lisse; **g. surface,** glacis *m*; (*b*) *Cer:* glacé, émaillé; (*of brick*) vitrifié; (*c*) *Cu:* glacé, doré.

glazer ['gleizər], *s.* **1.** (*pers.*) glaceur *m*; lustreur, -euse; vernisseur *m*; satineur, -euse. **2.** *Phot:* (*instrument*) glaceur, satineur.

glazier ['gleiziər], *s.* vitrier *m*; *F:* **is your father a g.?** tu n'es pas transparent, tu sais!

glaziery ['gleiziəri], *s.* vitrerie *f*.

glazing ['gleiziŋ], *s.* **1.** (*a*) pose *f* des vitres; (*b*) glaçage *m*, lustrage *m*, vernissage *m*, satinage *m*; *Cer: Phot:* émaillage *m*; *Mch: I.C.E:* **g. of the cylinders,** glaçage des cylindres; **g. machine,** glaceur *m*, satineuse *f*; **g. roll,** cylindre *m* à satiner; **g. wheel,** meule *f* d'émeri. **2.** vitrerie *f*; **double g.,** double vitrage *m*, survitrage *m*.

gleam¹ [gliːm], *s.* (*a*) rayon *m*, lueur *f*, trait *m*, filtrée *f* (de lumière); **a long g. of light,** une longue traînée de lumière; **the first gleams of the sun,** les premières clartés du soleil; **g. of hope,** lueur d'espoir; rayon d'espérance; **there was a dangerous g. in his eye,** il y avait dans son regard une lueur inquiétante; (*b*) reflet *m* (d'un couteau, des eaux, etc.); miroitement *m* (d'un lac, etc.).

gleam², *v.i.* luire, reluire, rayonner; (*of water*) miroiter, brasiller; **his knife gleamed in the dark,** (i) son couteau luisait dans l'ombre; (ii) son couteau jeta un éclair dans l'ombre; **fury gleams in his eyes,** la fureur étincelle dans ses yeux; **a cat's eyes g. in the dark,** les yeux du chat éclairent dans l'obscurité.

gleaming¹ ['gliːmiŋ], *a.* rayonnant, luisant, miroitant; **g. eyes,** yeux luisants.

gleaming², *s.* rayonnement *m*, miroitement *m*.

glean [gliːn], *v.tr.* **1.** glaner (du blé, des renseignements, etc.); *v.i.* faire la glane; **to g. a field,** glaner dans un champ; **to g. from one person and another,** glaner chez les uns et les autres; **there is something to be gleaned from everyone,** il y a à prendre chez tout le monde. **2.** *Vit:* grappiller.

gleaner ['gliːnər], *s.* **1.** glaneur, -euse. **2.** *Vit:* **grappilleur,** -euse.

gleaning ['gliːniŋ], *s.* **1.** (*a*) glanage *m*, glane *f*; (*b*) *Vit:* grappillage *m*. **2.** *pl.* **gleanings,** (*a*) glanure *f*, glanes *fpl*; (*b*) *Lit:* analectes *m*; **gleanings from the newspapers,** glanures prises dans les journaux.

glebe [gliːb], *s.* **1.** *Poet: A:* terre *f*, terrain *m*, glèbe *f*. **2.** *Ecc:* terre assignée à un bénéfice.

glee [gliː], *s.* **1.** joie *f*, gaieté *f*, allégresse *f*; **in high g.,** au comble de la joie; jubilant; tout joyeux; plein de joie. **2.** *Mus:* petit chant à trois ou quatre parties pour voix d'hommes solo, sans accompagnement; **g. club,** chorale *f*.

gleeful ['gliːful], *a.* joyeux, allègre; plein de joie.

gleefully ['gliːfuli], *adv.* joyeusement, avec joie, allègrement; **she g. pointed out his mistake,** elle lui a indiqué son erreur avec un petit air de triomphe.

gleeman, *pl.* **-men** ['gliːmən], *s. A:* ménestrel *m*, jongleur *m*.

gleet [gliːt], *s.* **1.** *Med:* (*a*) écoulement *m* (de l'urètre); goutte *f* militaire; (*b*) *A:* pus *m*, écoulement. **2.** *Vet:* jetage *m*.

Gleichenia [glai'kiːniə], *s. Bot:* gleichenia *m*.

glen [glen], *s.* vallée étroite; vallon *m*, ravin *m*; gorge *f* (de montagne).

glene ['gliːni], *s. Anat:* **1.** glène *f*; cavité glénoïdale. **2.** orbite *f* de l'œil.

glengarry [glen'gæri], *s.* (coiffure écossaise du genre) calot *m*; toque (haute sur le devant); glengarry *m*.

glenoid ['gliːnɔid], **glenoidal** [gle'nɔidl], *a. Anat:* glénoïde; glénoïdal, -aux; **g. cavity,** glénoïde *f*; cavité glénoïdale.

gley [glei], *s. Geol:* gley *m*.

gliadin ['glaiədin], *s. Bio-Ch:* gliadine *f*.

glial ['glaiəl], *a. Anat:* glial; **g. tissue,** tissu glial.

glib [glib], *a.* **1.** *A:* (*of surface*) lisse, glissant. **2.** *Pej:* (*a*) (*of answer, excuse*) spécieux, patelin; (*of lie*) fait de sang-froid; (*b*) (*of speaker*) qui a de la faconde; beau parleur; **to have a g. tongue,** avoir la langue affilée, déliée, bien pendue; avoir le débit facile; *A:* **to be as g. as a bagman,** avoir un bagout de commis-voyageur.

glibly ['glibli], *adv.* (*a*) spécieusement; d'un ton patelin; (*b*) (parler) avec aisance, avec volubilité; (répondre) sans hésiter.

glibness ['glibnis], *s.* **1.** spéciosité *f* (d'une excuse, etc.). **2.** faconde *f*; facilité *f* (de parole); volubilité *f*, bagout *m*.

glide¹ [glaid], *s.* **1.** (*a*) glissement *m*; *Cryst:* **g. face,** face *f* de glissement; **g. plane,** plan *m* de glissement; (*b*) *Danc:* glissade *f*, glissé *m*; *Sp:* (*skating*) **forward g.,** en-avant *m inv*; **backward g.,** en-arrière *m inv.* **2.** *Av:* (i) vol plané; (ii) descente *f* en (vol) plané, descente planée, descente avec moteur(s) réduit(s); **spiral g.,** descente en spirale; **g. path,** (i) trajectoire *f* de (vol) plané; (ii) (*also* **g. slope**) trajectoire, axe *m*, de descente, d'atterrissage; **g. path transmitter,** émetteur *m* d'axe(s) de descente, d'atterrissage; *Mil.Av:* **g. bomb,** bombe planante, volante; **g. bomber,** bombardier *m* en plané; **g. bombing,** bombardement *m* (i) avec des bombes volantes, (ii) en (vol) plané. **3.** *Mus:* port *m* de voix; glissade. **4.** *Ling:* son *m* transitoire; **on g.,** arrivée *f*; **off g.,** détente *f*.

glide². **1.** *v.i.* (*a*) (se) glisser, couler; **to g. (along) over the water,** glisser sur l'eau; **to g. past, out,** passer, sortir, doucement, légèrement, à pas feutrés, comme une ombre; **the years are gliding past, by,** les années coulent; **a boat was gliding past, by,** un bateau passait; **to g. over the difficult passages,** passer légèrement sur les endroits difficiles; (*b*) (*of birds*) planer (dans l'air); (*c*) *Av:* (i) planer; effectuer, faire, un vol plané; (ii) faire du vol à voile; **to g. down,** descendre en (vol) plané; effectuer, faire, une descente, un atterrissage, en (vol) plané, avec moteur(s) réduit(s); **to g. in for a landing,** atterrir en vol plané. **2.** *v.tr.* (*a*) **the wind glides the boat over the**

water, le vent fait glisser le bateau sur l'eau; (*b*) *Cr:* **to g. the ball to leg,** détourner la balle vers la gauche (avec la batte).

glide-bomb ['glaidbɔm], *v.tr. Mil.Av:* bombarder (un objectif) (i) avec des bombes volantes, (ii) en (vol) plané.

glider ['glaidər], *s. Av:* (*a*) (*pers.*) spécialiste *mf* du vol à voile; (*b*) (*machine*) planeur *m*; **towed g.,** planeur remorqué; **train of gliders,** train *m* de planeurs; **powered g.,** planeur à moteur; *Mil.Av:* **g. bomb,** bombe planante, volante; (*c*) *Sp:* **hang g.,** deltaplane *m*.

gliding ['glaidiŋ], *s.* (*a*) glissement *m*; *Cryst:* **g. face,** face *f* de glissement; **g. plane,** plan *m* de glissement; (*b*) *Av:* (i) (vol *m*) plané *m*; (ii) vol à voile; **g. range,** distance *f* franchissable en vol plané; **g. ratio,** finesse *f*; **g. club,** club *m* de vol à voile; (*c*) *Sp:* **hang g.,** vol libre.

glim [glim], *s. P:* (*a*) *O:* lumière *f*, bougie *f*, *F:* camoufle *f*; (*b*) *A:* **chuck us a g.,** passe-moi une allumette.

glimmer[1] ['glimər], *s.* **1.** faible lueur *f* (d'une chandelle, etc.); reflet *m*, miroitement *m* (de l'eau, etc.); **the first g. of dawn,** les premières lueurs de l'aube; **g. of hope,** rayon *m*, lueur, d'espoir; **not the slightest g. of intelligence,** pas la moindre trace, pas une lueur, d'intelligence. **2.** *P: A:* (*in police language*) mendiant *m*.

glimmer[2], *v.i.* jeter une faible lueur; brillot(t)er; entreluire; (*of water*) miroiter; (*of sea*) brasiller; **a light was glimmering through the curtains,** une lumière filtrait à travers les rideaux.

glimmering[1] ['glimәriŋ], *a.* (*of light*) faible, douteux, vacillant; qui brillotte.

glimmering[2], *s.* **1.** émission *f* d'une faible lueur; miroitement *m* (d'un lac, etc.). **2.** = GLIMMER[1] 1.

glimpse[1] [glim(p)s], *s.* vision momentanée (de qch.); **g. of a subject,** aperçu *m* sur un sujet; **to catch a g. of sth.,** entrevoir, aviser, apercevoir, qch.; **I caught only a g. of him,** je n'ai fait que l'entrevoir; *Lit:* **through attitude and gesture one gets a g. of the soul,** l'âme transparaît dans l'attitude et le geste; **a g. of the moon revealed to us . . .,** une courte échappée de clair de lune, une courte apparition de la lune, nous fit apparaître . . ., nous découvrit . . .; *F:* **a g. of the obvious,** une vérité de La Palisse.

glimpse[2], *v.tr.* **to g. sth.,** avoir la vision fugitive de qch.; entrevoir qch.; jeter un rapide coup d'œil sur qch.; *Lit:* **he had glimpsed death,** il avait entrevu la mort.

glint[1] [glint], *s.* trait *m*, lueur *f*, éclair *m* (de lumière); reflet *m* (d'un couteau, etc.); **hair with glints of gold,** chevelure *f* à, aux, reflets d'or.

glint[2], *v.i.* entreluire, étinceler; briller par moments, çà et là; **the lights were glinting in the water,** les lumières *f* miroitaient dans l'eau; **his eyes were glinting with fury,** ses yeux étincelaient de fureur.

glioma, *pl.* **-ata** [glai'oumə, -ətə], *s. Med:* gliôme *m*.

gliosis [glai'ousis], *s. Med:* gliose *f*.

Gliridae ['gliridi:], *s.m.pl. Z:* glíridés *m*, les loirs *m*.

glissade[1] [gli'sɑ:d, -'seid], *s.* **1.** *Danc:* glissade *f*, glissé *m*. **2.** *Mount:* glissade; **standing g.,** glissade debout; **sitting g.,** glissade assise.

glissade[2], *v.i.* **1.** *Danc:* faire une glissade. **2.** *Mount:* **to g. (down),** filer en ramasse.

glissando [gli'sændou], *adv. & s. Mus:* glissando (*m*).

glissette [gli'set], *s. Math:* glissette *f*.

glisten[1] ['glisn], *s.* étincellement *m*, scintillement *m*; miroitement *m*, chatoiement *m*.

glisten[2], *v.i.* étinceler, reluire, scintiller, briller; (*of sea*) miroiter, brasiller, chatoyer; **his forehead was glistening with perspiration,** la sueur perlait sur son front.

glistening[1] ['glis(ə)niŋ], *a.* étincelant, luisant, scintillant; chatoyant; (*of armour, etc.*) miroitant; **the wet and g. streets,** les rues mouillées et miroitantes.

glistening[2], *s.* = GLISTEN[1].

glitter[1] ['glitər], *s.* étincellement *m*, scintillement *m*, éclat *m*, brillant *m*; **life's noise and g.,** le bruit et le clinquant de la vie.

glitter[2], *v.i.* scintiller, étinceler, (re)luire, papilloter, chatoyer; (*of sea*) brasiller; *Prov:* **all is not gold that glitters,** tout ce qui reluit, tout ce qui brille, n'est pas or.

glittering[1] ['glitəriŋ], *a.* brillant, étincelant, éclatant, reluisant, resplendissant; **g. silver,** argenterie reluisante; **g. jewels,** bijoux *m* qui lancent des éclairs.

glittering[2], *s.* étincellement *m*, scintillement *m*.

gloaming ['gloumiŋ], *s.* crépuscule *m* (du soir); *Lit:* l'heure *f* du berger; **in the g.,** entre chien et loup; à la brune; *Sm.a:* **g. sight,** mire *f* de nuit.

gloat[1] [glout], *s.* (*a*) regard *m* d'exultation; (*b*) **to enjoy a g. over sth.,** se réjouir (méchamment) de qch.

gloat[2], *v.i.* **to g. over, on, sth.,** (i) couver, dévorer, qch. des yeux, du regard; (ii) contempler qch. avec un plaisir mauvais, méchant, repaître ses yeux de qch.; savourer (un livre, un spectacle, sa vengeance); **to g. over one's victim,** couver du regard sa victime; **to g. over the sight of (victim, etc.),** boire (qn) des yeux; **to g. over the news,** se réjouir (méchamment) de la nouvelle; **to g. over s.o.'s misfortune,** triompher du malheur de qn.

gloating ['gloutiŋ], *a.* (œil *m*) avide; (sourire *m*) d'exultation méchante.

gloatingly ['gloutiŋli], *adv.* avec un sourire d'exultation méchante; avec une satisfaction méchante; **to look g. at one's victim,** dévorer sa victime des yeux.

global ['gloubl], *a.* **1.** (poids, etc.) global, -aux. **2.** mondial, -aux; planétaire; **g. war(fare),** guerre mondiale.

globalization [gloubəlai'zeiʃ(ə)n], *s.* planétisation *f*.

globe [gloub], *s.* globe *m*; (*a*) sphère *f*; (*b*) (la) terre; la boule terrestre; **to go round the g.,** faire le tour du globe; (*c*) *Sch:* **terrestrial g., celestial g.,** globe terrestre, céleste; *A:* **use of the globes,** étude *f* de la sphère; (*d*) globe (de lampe); cloche *f*, coupe *f*; **electric light g.,** globe électrique; tulipe *f*; (*e*) bocal *m*, -aux (pour poissons rouges); (*f*) *Anat:* globe (de l'œil); (*g*) *attrib.* (i) *Hort:* **g. artichoke,** artichaut *m*; *Bot:* **g. daisy,** globulaire *f*; **g. thistle,** échinope *m*, échinops *m*; (ii) *Mec.E:* **g. joint,** joint *m* à rotule (sphérique); **g. valve,** robinet *m* d'arrêt sphérique; soupape *f* à boulet; (iii) *Meteor:* **g. lightning,** globe fulminant, de feu; éclair *m* en boule.

globed [gloubd], *a.* globulaire, sphérique.

globefish ['gloubfiʃ], *s. Ich:* **1.** diodon *m*; orbe épineux; poisson-boule *m*, *pl.* poissons-boules. **2.** tétrodon *m*. **3.** triodon *m*. **4.** môle *f*.

globeflower ['gloubflauər], *s. Bot:* trolle *m*, boule-d'or *f*, *pl.* boules-d'or.

globe-shaped ['gloubʃeipt], *a.* sphérique; en forme de sphère.

globetrot ['gloubtrɔt], *v.i. F:* faire le tour du monde; voyager partout.

globetrotter ['gloubtrɔtər], *s. F:* touriste *mf* qui court le monde; globe-trotter *m*.

globetrotting ['gloubtrɔtiŋ], *s. F:* parcours *m* du monde (en globe-trotter); tourisme *m* à l'échelle mondiale; vie *f* de voyages.

globicephala [gloubi'sefələ], *s. Z:* globicéphale *m*.

globigerina [gloubidʒə'rainə], *s. Prot:* globigérine *f*; *Geol:* **g. ooze,** boue *f* à globigérines.

Globigerinae [gloubidʒə'raini:], *s.pl. Prot:* Globigérines *f*.

Globigerinidae [gloubidʒə'rinidi:], *s.pl. Prot:* globigerindés *m*.

globin ['gloubin], *s. Bio-Ch:* globine *f*.

globose ['gloubous], *a. Bot. etc:* globeux.

globular ['glɔbjulər], *a.* globulaire, globuleux; sphérique; **g. lightning,** éclair *m* en boule.

globularia [glɔbju'lɛəriə], *s. Bot:* globulaire *f*.

Globulariaceae ['glɔbjuləri'eisii:], *s.pl. Bot:* globulariacées *f*.

globule ['glɔbju:l], *s.* (*a*) globule *m*, gouttelette *f* (d'eau, etc.); (*b*) *Pharm:* globule.

globulin ['glɔbjulin], *s. Bio-Ch:* globuline *f*; **gamma g.,** gamma-globuline *f*.

globulose ['glɔbjulous], **globulous** ['glɔbjuləs], *a.* globuleux.

globus ['gloubəs], *s. Med:* **g. hystericus,** boule *f* hystérique, globe *m* hystérique; **g. pallidus,** globus pallidus *m*, pallidium *m*.

glochidiate [glɔ'kidieit], *a. Bot:* glochidié.

glockenspiel ['glɔkənʃpi:l], *s. Mus:* glockenspiel *m*.

glome [gloum], *s. Z:* (*of horse*) glome *m*.

glomerate ['glɔməreit], *a. Bot:* glomérulé; *Anat:* congloméré.

glomerule ['glɔməru:l], *s. Bot: Anat:* glomérule *m*.

glomerulonephritis [glɔmə'ru:louni'fraitis], *s. Med:* glomérulonéphrite *f*.

glomus, *pl.* **glomera** ['gloumәs, 'glɔmərə], *s. Anat:* glomus *m*.

gloom[1] [glu:m], *s.* **1.** obscurité *f*, ténèbres *fpl*; **dismal pictures shrouded in g.,** tableaux tristes et enténébrés. **2.** assombrissement *m*, mélancolie *f*; tristesse *f* pessimiste; **to cast, throw, a g. over, on, the company,** jeter une ombre sur, jeter un voile de tristesse sur, assombrir, attrister, l'assemblée; rembrunir l'assemblée; **this news cast a g. over the town,** cette nouvelle répandit la tristesse dans la ville; **there is g. in the City,** la Bourse est pessimiste; **Byronic g.,** mélancolie byronienne; mal *m* du siècle; **cypresses strike a note of g. in the foreground,** des cyprès endeuillent le premier plan du tableau.

gloom[2]. *O: & Lit:* **1.** *v.i.* (*a*) se renfrogner; **to g. at, on, s.o.,** regarder qn d'un mauvais œil; (*b*) (*of sky*) s'obscurcir, s'assombrir, se couvrir; (*of pers.*) s'attrister, s'assombrir. **2.** *v.tr.* assombrir (le ciel, qn); obscurcir (qch.); attrister (qn).

gloomily ['glu:mili], *adv.* sombrement, lugubrement, mélancoliquement; d'un air sombre, pessimiste.

gloominess ['glu:minis], *s.* assombrissement *m*; (*a*) obscurité *f*, noirceur *f* (du temps, etc.); (*b*) tristesse *f*, air *m* sombre (de qn).

gloomy ['glu:mi], *a.* **1.** sombre, obscur, ténébreux. **2.** lugubre, morne, sombre, attristant; (pensées) noires; (front) ténébreux; **g. weather,** temps *m* sombre; **the weather is g.,** il fait sombre; **g. poet,** poète mélancolique; **g. picture,** tableau poussé au noir; **to have a g. outlook; to take a g. view of things,** voir tout en noir; noircir le tableau; **to see the g. side of things, to feel g.,** voir noir; avoir du sombre dans l'âme; broyer du noir; **to give sth. a g. appearance,** assombrir, attrister, qch; (*of pers.*) **to become g.,** se rembrunir.

gloria ['glɔ:riə], *s. Ecc:* **1.** gloria *m*. **2.** = GLORY[1] 3.

glorification [glɔ:rifi'keiʃ(ə)n], *s.* **1.** glorification *f* (des élus, d'un grand homme, du travail, etc.). **2.** *F: O:* réjouissance *f*, partie *f* de plaisir.

glorified, *a.* **1.** *Theol:* glorifié; **g. body,** corps glorieux. **2.** (*a*) (*of thg*) en plus grand, en mieux; **their chapel is a sort of g. barn,** leur temple n'est guère qu'une grange, rappelle une grange; (*b*) (*of pers.*) avec la gloriole en plus, paré d'un peu de dignité.

glorifier ['glɔ:rifaiər], *s.* glorificateur, -trice; louangeur, -euse.

glorify ['glɔ:rifai], *v.tr.* (*a*) glorifier; rendre gloire à (Dieu, un saint, etc.); **to g. s.o.'s memory,** auréoler la mémoire de qn; (*b*) exalter, célébrer; chanter les louanges de (qn).

glorifying ['glɔ:rifaiiŋ], *s.* glorification *f*.

gloriole ['glɔ:rioul], *s.* gloire *f*, auréole *f*, nimbe *m*, (d'un saint).

glorious ['glɔ:riəs], *a.* **1.** (règne, soldat, martyr) glorieux; **g. deed,** action éclatante; action d'éclat. **2.** (*a*) resplendissant, radieux; **the heavens were g. with stars,** les cieux resplendissaient d'étoiles; **g. in her youth and beauty,** resplendissante de jeunesse et de beauté; (*b*) *O:* magnifique, superbe, splendide; **to have a g. time,** s'amuser follement, épatamment; **what g. weather!** quel temps superbe! *Iron;* **a g. mess,** un joli gâchis. **3.** *F: O:* éméché; parti (pour la gloire); **to be a little g.,** avoir son panache, son pompon.

gloriously ['glɔ:riəsli], *adv.* **1.** glorieusement; avec gloire. **2.** *F: O:* **g. drunk,** complètement ivre.

glory[1] ['glɔ:ri], *s.* gloire *f*. **1.** (*a*) honneur *m*, renommée *f*; **to cover oneself with g.,** se couvrir de gloire; **to do sth. for the sake of g.,** faire qch. pour la gloire, pour la gloriole; *Lit:* **to crown s.o. with g.,** glorifier qn; **to take the g. for sth.,** s'attribuer la gloire de qch.; (*b*) **to give g. to God,** rendre gloire à Dieu; **to the greater g. of God,** pour la plus grande gloire de Dieu; **g. (be) to God!** gloire à Dieu! *F: O:* **g. (be)!** grand Dieu! (*c*) sujet *m* de gloire; **to be the g. of the age,** faire la gloire du siècle; (*d*) **eternal g.,** gloire éternelle; **the saints in g.,** les glorieux; *F:* **to go to g.,** (i) mourir; (ii) (*of thg*) aller à la ruine; aller à vau-l'eau; *F:* **to send s.o. to g.,** envoyer qn dans l'autre monde. **2.** splendeur *f*, éclat *m* (d'un spectacle, etc.); **Solomon in all his g.,** Salomon dans toute sa gloire; **to be in one's g.,** être à l'apogée de sa gloire; *F: O:* **in all her g.,** sur son trente-et-un, parée de ses plus beaux atours; **Spain, in the days of her g.,** l'Espagne, aux jours de sa splendeur. **3.** (*a*) gloire, auréole *f*, nimbe *m* (d'un saint); (*b*) *Opt:* anthélie *f*. **4.** *U.S: F:* **Old G.,** la bannière étoilée (des États-Unis). **5.** *Bot:* **g. bush,** tibouchina *m*; **g. flower, pea,** clianthe *m*.

glory[2], *v.i.* **to g. in sth.,** se glorifier de qch.; mettre sa gloire à, en, qch.; se faire gloire de qch.; être fier de qch.; **to g. in doing sth.,** se glorifier, se faire gloire, se faire un mérite, de faire qch.

gloryhole ['glɔ:rihoul], *s. F:* **1.** (*a*) capharnaüm *m*, (chambre *f* de) débarras *m*; (*b*) *Nau:* poste *m* (i) des chauffeurs, (ii) des garçons de cabine. **2.** *Ind:* regard *m* (de fourneau). **3.** (*a*) *Min:* excavation *f* à ciel ouvert; (*b*) *Mil:* abri-caverne *m*, *pl.* abris-cavernes.

gloss[1] [glɔs], *s.* **1.** (*a*) glose *f*; (*b*) glossaire *m*, commentaire *m*; (*c*) traduction *f* interlinéaire. **2.** fausse interprétation, faux rapport; glose.

gloss[2]. **1.** (*a*) *v.tr.* gloser sur, annoter (un texte); **the words glossed in this dictionary,** les mots expliqués dans ce dictionnaire; (*b*) *v.i. A:* **to g. on, upon, s.o.'s conduct,** trouver à redire à, éplucher sur, *A:* gloser (sur), la conduite de qn. **2.** *v.tr.* fausser le sens (d'une observation); donner une explication spécieuse (d'une action).

gloss[3], *s.* **1.** lustre *m*, glacé *m*, vernis *m*, poli *m*, satiné *m*, brillant *m*, éclat *m*, luisance *f*; *Tex:* cati *m*; **to give a new g. to sth.,** relustrer qch.; **to take the g. off sth.,** délustrer qch.; *Tex:* décatir (une étoffe); **to lose its g.,** se délustrer; *attrib.* **g. paint,** peinture *f* vernis. **2. to put a g. on the truth,** farder la vérité; **to cover one's actions with a g. of legality,** couvrir ses actions sous un vernis de légalité.

gloss[4], *v.tr.* **1.** lustrer, glacer; *Tex:* catir (l'étoffe); brillanter (le fil). **2. to g. the truth,** farder, gazer, la vérité; **to g. over the facts,** farder les faits; **to g. over s.o.'s faults,** glisser sur, vernir, les défauts de qn; **to g. over a point,** passer un fait sous silence.

glossa, *pl.* **-ae, -as** ['glɔsə, -i:, -əz], *s. Ent:* glosse *f.*

glossal ['glɔs(ə)l], *a. Anat:* glossien.

glossalgia [glɔs'ældʒiə], *s. Med:* glossalgie *f*, glossodynie *f.*

glossarist ['glɔsərist], *s.* **1.** glossateur *m*; auteur *m* d'une glose. **2.** auteur d'un glossaire.

glossary ['glɔsəri], *s.* glossaire *m*, lexique *m.*

glossator [glɔ'seitər], *s.* =GLOSSARIST.

glossematics [glɔsi'mætiks], *s.* (*usu. with sg. const.*) *Ling:* glossématique *f.*

glosseme ['glɔsi:m], *s. Ling:* glossème *m.*

glosser[1] ['glɔsər], *s.* = GLOSSARIST.

glosser[2], *s. Tex:* catisseur, -euse.

glossette [glɔ'set], *s. Pharm:* glossette *f.*

glossina [glɔ'si:nə], *s. Ent:* glossine *f*, tsé-tsé *f.*

glossiness ['glɔsinis], *s.* glacé *m*, lustre *m*, vernis *m*; aspect brillant ou luisant; éclat soyeux (des cheveux).

glossing ['glɔsiŋ], *s.* lustrage *m*, glaçage *m*; *Tex:* catissage *m.*

Glossinidae [glɔ'sinidi:], *s.pl. Ent:* glossinidés *m.*

glossist ['glɔsist], *s.* = GLOSSARIST.

glossitis [glɔ'saitis], *s. Med:* glossite *f.*

glossodynia [glɔsou'diniə], *s. Med:* glossodynie *f.*

glossographer [glɔ'sɔgrəfər], *s.* glossographe *mf.*

glossography [glɔ'sɔgrəfi], *s.* glossographie *f.*

glossoid ['glɔsɔid], *a.* glossoïde.

glossolalia [glɔsou'leiliə], *s.* glossolalie *f.*

glossology [glɔ'sɔlədʒi], *s.* glossologie *f.*

glossopalatine [glɔsou'pælətain], *a. Anat:* glosso-palatin, *pl.* glosso-palatins.

glossophaga [glɔ'sɔfədʒə], *s. Z:* glossophage *m.*

glossopharyngeal [glɔsoufærin'dʒi:əl], *a. Anat:* glosso-pharyngien, *pl.* glosso-pharyngiens.

glossoplegia [glɔsou'pli:dʒiə], *s. Med:* glossoplégie *f.*

glossotomy [glɔ'sɔtəmi], *s. Surg:* glossotomie *f.*

glossy ['glɔsi], *a.* lustré, glacé, brillant; (poil) lustré, (re)luisant, poli; (feuille) vernissée; (métal) décapé; *Phot:* **g. paper,** papier brillant; **g. print,** épreuve glacée; **g. magazine,** *s.* **glossy** (*pl.* **glossies**), revue *f* illustrée.

glottal ['glɔtl], *a.* (*a*) *Anat: Ling:* glottal, -aux, glottique; *Anat:* glossien; *Ling:* **g. stop, catch,** coup *m* de glotte.

glottic ['glɔtik], *a.* glottique.

glottis ['glɔtis], *s. Anat:* glotte *f.*

glove[1] [glʌv], *s.* (*a*) gant *m*; **doeskin gloves,** gants en (peau de) daim; **chamois-leather gloves,** gants en chamois; **leather, fabric, gloves,** gants de, en cuir, en tissu; **suède gloves,** gants de suède; **knitted gloves,** gants en tricot; **long gloves, elbow-length gloves,** gants longs; **kid gloves,** gants (en peau) de chevreau; **you have to handle him with kid gloves (on),** il faut prendre des gants pour l'approcher; **riding gloves,** gants de bufle; **driving gloves,** gants de chauffeur; **lined gloves,** gants fourrés; **rubber gloves,** gants en caoutchouc; **oven g.,** gant isolant; *Toil:* **flesh g., friction g.,** gant de crin; **to put on one's gloves,** mettre ses gants, se ganter; **to take off one's gloves,** se déganter; **where do you buy your gloves?** chez qui vous gantez-vous? *Lit:* **to show the velvet g.,** faire patte de velours; (*b*) *Sp:* **fencing gloves,** gants d'escrime; **boxing gloves,** *F:* **the gloves,** gants de boxe; **to put on the gloves,** mettre les gants, les mitaines; **to handle s.o. without gloves, with the gloves off,** traiter qn durement, sans mettre les gants, sans ménagement; **to take the gloves off,** attaquer (qn) carrément, à poings nus; **the gloves were off,** on y allait carrément, sans ménagement; (*c*) *attrib.* **g. fastener,** bouton *m* fermoir; *Dom.Ec: Atom.Ph:* **g. box,** boîte à gants; *Aut:* **g. box, compartment,** boîte à gants; **g. factory, g. manufacture, g. trade,** ganterie *f*; **g. maker, manufacturer,** gantier, -ière; **g. cutter,** dépeceur, -euse, de gants; **g. stitcher,** piqueuse *f* en ganterie de peau; **g. shop,** (*in large store*) **g. counter, department,** ganterie; **g. stretcher,** baguette(s) *f* à gants; tourne-gants *m inv*, ouvre-gants *m inv*, demoiselle *f*, quille *f*; *A:* **g. money,** pourboire *m*, *A:* gants; (*d*) *Spong:* **g. sponge,** gant de Neptune.

glove[2], *v.tr.* ganter; **she is always well gloved,** elle est toujours bien gantée; elle se gante toujours bien.

gloveless ['glʌvlis], *a.* **1.** sans gants. **2.** déganté.

glover ['glʌvər], *s.* gantier, -ière; *Surg:* **glover's suture,** suture *f* à points passés.

glovewear ['glʌvwɛər], *s. Com:* ganterie *f.*

glow[1] [glou], *s.* **1.** (*a*) lueur *f* (rouge); incandescence *f*; **the g. of the setting sun,** les feux *m*, l'embrasement *m*, du soleil couchant; **a lurid g.,** un rougement sinistre; **in a g.,** (i) incandescent, chauffé au rouge; (ii) (*of coal, etc.*) embrasé; (*b*) *El: Elcs:* lueur, luminescence *f*, incandescence; **anode g.,** lueur anodique; **blue g.,** tension *f*, voltage *m*, de luminescence (d'une cellule photoélectrique); **g. potential,** potentiel *m*, tension *f*, d'allumage, d'amorçage; **g. discharge,** effluve(s) *m*(*pl.*); décharge luminescente, à lueur; **g.-discharge cathode,** cathode *f* à décharge (luminescente); **g.-discharge microphone,** microphone *m* à décharge; **g.-discharge rectifier,** redresseur *m* à décharge (luminescente); soupape *f*, valve *f*, (de redressement) à décharge (luminescente); **g. tube,** tube luminescent; tube redresseur (à gaz) à cathode froide; **g.-discharge tube,** tube à décharge, à lueurs; **g.-discharge voltage regulator,** tube à décharge régulateur de tension; **g. switch,** commutateur *m* (d'allumage) d'un tube luminescent; *I.C.E:* **g. plug,** bougie incandescente (d'un moteur Diesel). **2.** (*a*) *Physiol:* sensation *f* de douce chaleur; réaction *f* (après un bain, etc.); **the exercise had given me a g.,** *F:* **had made me all of a g.,** l'exercice m'avait fouetté le sang; (*b*) ardeur *f*, chaleur *f* (d'une passion); **in the first g. of enthusiasm,** dans les premiers transports d'enthousiasme. **3.** teint *m* rouge (de qn); cramoisi *m*, vermeil *m* (des joues, etc.); **g. of health,** éclat *m* du teint dû à la santé.

glow[2], *v.i.* **1.** luire rouge, rougeoyer; **to (begin to) g.,** (i) (*of metal*) rougir; être porté au rouge; (ii) (*of coal, etc.*) s'embraser; (iii) *El:* (*of lamp*) s'allumer. **2.** (*a*) rayonner; **her face was glowing with pleasure,** son visage rayonnait de plaisir; **his eyes were glowing with anger,** ses yeux flamboyaient de colère; (*of painting, etc.*) **to g. with colour,** rayonner de couleur; (*b*) **to be glowing with health,** éclater de santé; (*c*) **his cheeks were glowing,** il avait les joues en feu. **3.** sentir une douce chaleur (dans le corps); **to make s.o. g.,** fouetter le sang à qn; **to g. with enthusiasm,** brûler d'enthousiasme.

glower ['glauər], *v.i.* **1.** faire la mine; **to g. at s.o.,** faire grise mine à qn, regarder qn de travers. **2.** braquer, fixer, les yeux **(at s.o.,** sur qn) (d'un air maussade, menaçant).

glowering ['glauəriŋ], *a.* maussade; (œil *m*, regard *m*) farouche, torve.

gloweringly ['glauəriŋli], *adv.* d'un air maussade, menaçant.

glowing[1] ['glouiŋ], *a.* **1.** (chauffé au) rouge; incandescent, rougeoyant; *Lit:* rutilant. **2.** (*of coal, etc.*) embrasé; **g. sky,** ciel rouge, embrasé, en feu; **g. eyes,** yeux *m* de braise. **3.** rayonnant; **g. cheeks,** joues rouges, vermeilles. **4.** (*of colours, words*) chaleureux; (*of pers.*) ardent, enthousiaste; **g. description,** description *f* en termes chaleureux; **to paint sth. in g. colours,** présenter qch. sous un jour des plus favorables; **to speak in g. terms of s.o.,** dire merveille de qn.

glowing[2], *s.* **1.** incandescence *f* (du fer, etc.); embrasement *m* (du charbon, etc.); échauffement *m* au rouge. **2.** rayonnement *m*; lueur *f.*

glowingly ['glouiŋli], *adv.* en termes chaleureux; avec enthousiasme.

glowlamp ['gloulæmp], *s. El: Elcs:* lampe *f* à incandescence, à lueurs, à décharge (luminescente).

glow-worm ['glouwə:m], *s. Ent:* (*a*) ver luisant; lampyre *m*; (*b*) luciole *f.*

gloxinia [glɔk'siniə], *s. Bot:* gloxinie *f*, gloxinia *m.*

gloze [glouz]. **1.** *v.tr. A:* = GLOSS[2] 1. **2.** *v.i.* **to g. over (sth.),** glisser sur, pallier (les défauts, etc.).

glucagon ['glu:kəgɔn], *s. Ch:* glucagon *m.*

glucamine ['glu:kəmain], *s. Ch:* glucamine *f.*

glucide ['glu:said], *s. Ch:* glucide *m.*

glucinium, glucinum [glu:'siniəm, -'sainəm], *s. Ch:* glucinium *m*, béryllium *m.*

glucitol ['glu:sitɔl], *s.* glucite *f*, glucitol *m.*

glucocorticoid ['glu:kou'kɔ:tikɔid], *s. Bio-Ch:* glucocorticoïde *m.*

glucoh(a)emia [glu:kou'hi:miə], *s. Med:* hyperglycémie *f.*

glucometer [glu:'kɔmitər], *s. Brew:* glucomètre *m.*

gluconate ['glu:kəneit], *s.* gluconate *m.*

gluconic [glu:'kɔnik], *a. Ch:* (acide) gluconique.

glucoprotein ['glu:kou'prouti:n], *s.* glucoprotéine *m*, glucoprotéide *m*, glycoprotéine *m.*

glucopyranose [glu:kou'paiərənous], *s. Ch:* glucopyrannose *m.*

glucosamine [glu:'kousəmain], *s. Ch:* glucosamine *f.*

glucosan ['glu:kousæn], *s. Ch:* glucosan(n)e *m.*

glucose ['glu:kous], *s.* glucose *m or f.*

glucoside ['glu:kousaid], *s. Ch:* glucoside *m.*

glucosuria [glu:kou'sju:riə], *s. Med:* glucosurie *f.*

glue[1] [glu:], *s.* colle (forte); **animal g.,** colle animale; **gelatine g.,** colle à la gélatine; **casein g.,** colle caséine; **fish g.,** colle de poisson, ichtyocolle *f*; **wood g.,** colle à bois; **marine g.,** glu marine; **g. boiler,** fabricant *m* de colle forte; **g. heater,** chauffe-colle *m inv*; **g. stock,** carnasse *f*; *Algae:* **g. plant,** plocaire *f*; *F:* **he sticks to me like g.,** il me suit partout, il ne me quitte pas d'une semelle.

glue[2], *v.tr.* **(glued; gluing)** (*a*) coller (à la colle forte); **he glued the wings on (to) the model aircraft,** il a collé les ailes sur la maquette; **to g. on a broken piece,** recoller un morceau cassé; **he glued up the broken box,** il a recollé, raccommodé (à la colle), la boîte cassée; **my fingers are all glued up,** mes doigts sont remplis de colle; (*b*) **he walked slowly, his eyes glued on the road,** il marchait lentement, sans quitter la route des yeux; **she watched the crowds passing, her face glued to the window,** son visage collé à la fenêtre, elle regardait passer la foule; *F:* **she always seems glued to her mother's skirts,** elle ne quitte pas sa mère d'une semelle; (*c*) *v.i.* **wood that glues well,** bois *m* qui prend bien la colle.

gluepot ['glu:pɔt], *s.* pot *m* à colle.

gluer ['glu(:)ər], *s.* colleur, -euse.

gluey ['glu:i], *a.* gluant, poisseux.

glug[1] [glʌg], *s.* **g. (g.),** glouglou *m.*

glug[2], *v.i.* **(glugged)** faire glouglou.

gluing ['glu:iŋ], *s.* **1.** collage *m* (à la colle forte). **2.** *Bookb:* collure *f.*

glum [glʌm], *a.* (visage) renfrogné, maussade; (air *m*) triste, sombre, morne; (*of disposition*) noir; **to look g.,** se renfrogner, *F:* faire une tête.

Glumaceae [glu:'meisii:], *s.pl. Bot:* glumacées *f.*

glumaceous [glu:'meiʃəs], *a. Bot:* glumacé.

glume [glu:m], *s. Bot:* glume *f*, balle *f.*

glumella [glu:'melə], *s. Bot:* glumelle *f.*

Glumiflorae [glu:mi'flɔ:ri:], *s.pl. Bot:* glumiflores *f.*

glumly ['glʌmli], *adv.* d'un air maussade; (regarder qch.) d'un œil morne.

glumness ['glʌmnis], *s.* air *m* sombre; air maussade; tristesse *f.*

glumose [glu(:)'mous], **glumous** ['glu:məs], *a. Bot:* (*of flower*) glumé.

glut[1] [glʌt], *s.* **1.** (*a*) assouvissement *m*, rassasiement *m* (de l'appétit, etc.); (*b*) excès *m* (de nourriture, etc.). **2.** *Com:* (*a*) encombrement *m*, pléthore *f* (du marché); **it's a g. in the market,** c'est un article dont tout le monde est pourvu, dont personne ne veut plus; (*b*) surabondance *f* (d'une denrée, etc.); **there is a g. of pears (in the market),** le marché surabonde en poires, regorge de poires; *Fin:* **g. of money,** pléthore de capitaux.

glut[2], *v.tr.* **(glutted)** (*a*) rassasier, assouvir (qn, sa faim, sa curiosité, etc.); gorger (un enfant); surcharger (son estomac); **to g. oneself,** se rassasier, se gorger, se soûler (on, de); **glutted with food, with drink,** soûl de manger, de boisson; **glutted with pleasure,** gorgé, rassasié, de plaisirs; (*b*) *Com:* encombrer, inonder, écraser, surcharger (le marché); créer une pléthore sur (le marché); **the market is glutted with this article,** le marché regorge de cet article, surabonde de, en, cet article.

glutamic [glu:'tæmik], *a. Ch:* (acide *m*) glutamique.

glutamine ['glu:təmain], *s. Ch:* glutamine *f.*

glutaric [glu:'tærik], *a. Ch:* glutarique.

glutathione [glu:tə'θaioun], *s. Ch:* glutathion *m.*

gluteal ['glu:tiəl, glu:'ti:əl], *a. Anat:* (muscle) fessier.

gluten ['glu:tən], *s.* gluten *m*; **g. bread,** pain *m* de gluten; **devitalized g.,** gluten dénaturé.

gluteus ['glu:tiəs, glu:'ti:əs], *s. Anat:* (muscle) fessier *m*; **g. maximus,** le grand fessier.

glutinize ['glu:tinaiz], *v.tr.* rendre glutineux.

glutinosity [glu:ti'nɔsiti], **glutinousness** ['glu:tinəsnis], *s.* glutinosité *f.*

glutinous ['glu:tinəs], *a.* glutineux.

glutting ['glʌtiŋ], *s. Pol.Ec:* **g. of the markets,** engorgement *m* des marchés.

glutton ['glʌt(ə)n], *s.* **1.** (*a*) gastromane *m*; gourmand, -ande; glouton, -onne; goulu, -e, *F:* goinfre *m*, avaletout *m inv*; bâfreur, -euse; (*b*) **he's a g. for work,** c'est un cheval à l'ouvrage, un bœuf pour le travail; c'est un bourreau de travail; **he's a g. for books,** c'est un dévoreur de livres; *Box:* **g. for punishment,** encaisseur *m.* **2.** *Z:* glouton, goulu.

gluttonize ['glʌtənaiz], *v.i.* manger gloutonnement; *F:* goinfrer.

gluttonous ['glʌtənəs], *a.* gourmand, glouton, goulu, vorace.

gluttonously ['glʌtənəsli], *adv.* gloutonnement, goulûment, voracement; avec voracité.

gluttony ['glʌtəni], *s.* gloutonnerie *f*, gourmandise *f*; *F:* goinfrerie *f.*

glycaemia [glai'si:miə], *s.* glycémie *f.*

glycera ['glisərə], *s. Ann:* glycère *f.*

glyceria [gli'siəriə], *s. Bot:* glycérie *f.*

glyceric [gli'serik], *a. Ch:* glycérique.

glyceride ['glisəraid], *s. Ch:* glycéride *f.*

glycerinate [ˈglisərineit], *v.tr. Bac:* glycériner (une lymphe).
glycerin(e) [ˈglisərin, -iːn], *s. Ch: etc:* glycérine *f*; **to rub sth. over, treat sth., with g.,** glycériner qch.: **solution in g.,** glycéré *m*, glycérat *m*, glycérolé *m*; *Pharm:* **g. of tannic acid,** *F:* **g. and tannin,** glycéré de tannin.
glycerite [ˈglisərait], *s. Pharm:* glycéré *m*, glycérat *m*, glycérolé *m*.
glycerized [ˈglisəraizd], *a. Pharm: etc:* glycériné.
glycerol [ˈglisərɔl], *s. Ch:* glycérol *m*.
glycerole [ˈglisəroul], *s. Pharm:* glycérolé *m*, glycéré *m*, glycérat *m*.
glycerophosphate [ˈglisərouˈfɔsfeit], *s. Ch: Pharm:* glycérophosphate *m*.
glycerophosphoric [ˈglisəroufɔsˈfɔrik], *a. Ch:* (acide) glycérophosphorique.
glyceryl [ˈglisəril], *s. Ch:* glycéryle *m*.
glycidic [gliˈsidik], *a. Ch:* (acide) glycidique.
glycin [ˈglisin], *s. Ch:* glycine *f*, glycocolle *m*; sucre *m* de gélatine.
glyco- [(ˈ)glaikou, (ˈ)glikou], *comb.fm.* glyco-; NOTE: *as the pronunciation* [glai-] *appears to be the more usual, the alternative has not been listed in the words given below.*
glycocoll [ˈglaikəkɔl], *s. Ch:* glycocolle *m*, glycine *f*.
glycogen [ˈglaikədʒin], *s. Ch:* glycogène *m*.
glycogenesis [glaikouˈdʒenəsis], *s. Physiol:* glycogénèse *f*, glycogénie *f*.
glycogenic [glaikouˈdʒenik], *a. Physiol:* glycogénique.
glycoh(a)emia [glaikouˈhiːmiə], *s. Med:* glycémie *f*.
glycol [ˈglaikɔl], *s. Ch:* glycol *m*.
glycolic [glaiˈkɔlik], *a. Ch:* (acide) glycolique.
glycoline [ˈglaikəl(a)in], *s. Ch:* glycoline *f*.
glycolysis [glaiˈkɔlisis], *s. Physiol:* glycolyse *f*.
glycolytic [glaikəˈlitik], *a.* glycolitique.
glyconic [glaiˈkɔnik], *a. & s. Gr.Pros:* (vers *m*) glyconique.
glycoproteid [glaikouˈproutiːd], *s.* glycoprotéine *m*, glucoprotéine *m*.
glycose [ˈglaikous], *s. Ch:* ose *m*.
glycoside [ˈglaikousaid], *s. Ch:* glycoside *f*; oside *m*; hétéroside *m*; **flavonolic g.,** hétéroside flavonolique.
glycosuria [glaikouˈsjuːriə], *s. Med:* glycosurie *f*, glucosurie *f*.
glycosuric [glaikouˈsjuːrik], *a.* glycosurique.
glycuresis [glaikjuˈriːsis], *s. Med:* glycuronurie *f*.
glycuronic [glaikjuˈrɔnik], *a. Ch:* (acide) glycuronique.
glycylglycine [ˈglaisilˈglaisiːn], *s. Ch:* glycyglycine *f*.
Glycymeridae [glisiˈmeridiː], *s.pl. Moll:* glycymérides *m*.
glycyphagus [glaiˈsifəgəs], *s. Ent:* glycyphage *m*.
glycyrrhizin [glisiˈraizin], *s.* glycyrrhizine *f*.
glyoxal [glaiˈɔksəl], *s. Ch:* glyoxal *m*.
glyoxaline [glaiˈɔksəlain], *s. Ch:* glyoxaline *f*.
glyoxime [glaiˈɔksaim], *s. Ch:* glyoxime *f*.
glyoxylic [glaiɔkˈsilik], *a. Ch:* (acide) glyoxilique.
glyph [glif], *s. Arch:* glyphe *m*.
glyptics [ˈgliptiks], *s.pl. (usu. with sg. const.)* glyptique *f*.
glyptodon [ˈgliptədɔn], *s. Paleont:* glyptodon(te) *m*.
glyptogenesis [gliptouˈdʒenəsis], *s. Geol:* glyptogénèse *f*.
glyptography [glipˈtɔgrəfi], *s.* glyptographie *f*.
gmelina [g(ə)ˈmelinə], *s. Bot:* gmelina *m*.
gmelinite [g(ə)ˈmelinait], *s. Miner:* gmélinite *f*.
gnarl [nɑːl], *s.* loupe *f*, nœud *m*, broussin *m*, rugosité *f* (d'un arbre).
gnarled [nɑːld], *a.* **1.** *(of tree)* *(a)* noueux, loupeux, broussiné, rugueux; *(b)* tortu, tordu. **2.** *(of hands, fingers)* noueux, déformé.
gnash [næʃ], *v.tr.* **to g. one's teeth,** grincer des dents.
gnashing [ˈnæʃiŋ], *s.* grincement *m* (des dents); *B:* **weeping and g. of teeth,** des pleurs et des grincements de dents.
gnat [næt], *s. Ent:* *(a)* moucheron *m*; moustique *m*; *F:* cousin *m*; *B:* **to strain at a g. and swallow a camel,** rejeter le moucheron et avaler le chameau; **to strain at a g.,** attacher de l'importance à des vétilles; *(b) U.S:* simulie *f*.
gnatcatcher [ˈnætkætʃər], *s. Orn:* polioptile *m*; **blue-grey g.,** *Fr.C:* gobe-mouches *m* gris-bleu.
gnathic [ˈneiθik], *a. Anthr:* gnathique; **g. index,** indice *m* gnathique.
gnathion [ˈneiθiən], *s. Anat:* gnathion *m*.
Gnathobdellida [neiθəbˈdelidə], *s.pl. Ent:* gnathobdellidés *m*.
gnathology [neiˈθɔlədʒi], *s. Dent:* gnatologie *f*.
gnathopod [ˈneiθoupɔd], *s. Crust:* gnathopode *m*.
Gnathostomata [neiθouˈstoumətə], *s.pl. Z:* gnathostomes *m*.
gnaw [nɔː], *v.tr. & i.* (*p.t.* **gnawed;** *p.p.* **gnawed, gnawn**) *(a)* *(of rodent, etc.)* **to g. (at, into) sth.,** ronger qch. *(of dog)* **to g. a bone,** ronger un os; *(of acid, etc.)* **to g. into a metal,** ronger, corroder, mordre, un métal; **to g. away, off,** enlever (qch.) (en le rongeant); **to g. one's fingers with impatience,** se mordre, se ronger, les poings d'impatience; *(b)* **gnawed by hunger, by remorse,** tenaillé par la faim, par le remords; rongé par le remords.
gnawing[1] [ˈnɔːiŋ], *a.* *(a)* *(of animal)* rongeur, -euse; *(b)* *(of hunger)* dévorant; tenaillant; *(of anxiety, etc.)* rongeant; **to feel the g. pains of hunger,** sentir les tiraillements de la faim; avoir des crampes d'estomac; **g. care,** soucis dévorants.
gnawing[2], *s.* *(a)* rongement; *(b)* **g. at, of, the stomach,** tiraillements *mpl* d'estomac; **g. of hunger,** tiraillement de la faim.
gneiss [nais], *s. Geol:* gneiss *m*.
gneissic [ˈnaisik], *a. Geol:* gneissique.
Gnetaceae [neˈteisiiː], *s.pl. Bot:* gnétacées *f*.
Gnetales [neˈteiliːz], *s.pl. Bot:* gnétales *f*.
gnetum [ˈniːtəm], *s. Bot:* gnète *m*.
gnocchi [ˈnɔki], *s.pl. Cu:* gnocchi *m*.
gnome[1] [noum], *s.* **1.** *(a) Myth:* gnome *m*; gobelin *m*; *F:* **the gnomes of Zürich,** les banquiers internationaux de Zürich. **2.** *Orn:* *(a) U.S:* oiseau-mouche patagon; *(b)* **g. owl,** chevêchette *f*.
gnome[2] [ˈnoum(i)], *s. Gr.Lit:* sentence *f*, aphorisme *m*, maxime *f*.
gnomic [ˈnoumik], *a.* (poète *m*, aoriste *m*) gnomique.
gnomide [ˈnoumid], *s.f. Myth:* gnomide.
gnomish [ˈnoumiʃ], *a.* de gnome; de gnomide.
gnomon [ˈnoumɔn], *s.* **1.** *Astr:* gnomon *m*. **2.** *Hor:* gnomon, aiguille *f*, style *m* (de cadran solaire).
gnomonic [nouˈmɔnik], *a.* gnomonique; *Mapm:* **g. projection,** projection *f* gnomonique, centrale; **g. chart,** carte *f* gnomonique.
gnomonics [nouˈmɔniks], *s.pl.* *(usu. with sg. const.)* gnomonique *f*.
gnoseology [nousiˈɔlədʒi], *s. Phil:* gnoséologie *f*.
gnosis [ˈnousis], *s.* **1.** *Theol:* gnose *f*. **2.** *Phil:* gnosie *f*.
gnostic [ˈnɔstik], *a. & s.* gnostique *(mf)*.
gnosticism [ˈnɔstisizm], *s. Rel.H.:* gnosticisme *m*.
gnu [nuː], *s. Z:* gnou *m*; **brindled g.,** gnou gorgon, taurin, rayé, bleu; **whitetailed g.,** gnou à queue blanche; **g. goat,** takin *m*.
go[1] [gou], *s.* (*pl.* **goes**) *F:* **1.** *(a)* aller *m*; **to be always on the go,** être toujours à trotter, à courir; être remuant; avoir toujours un pied en l'air; ne faire qu'aller et venir; ne pas avoir le temps de se moucher; **to keep s.o. on the go,** faire trimer qn; faire tourner qn comme un toton; *(b)* **it's all go,** on n'a pas une minute à soi. **2.** entrain *m*, allant *m*; **to be full of go, to have plenty of go,** être plein d'entrain; avoir de l'allant; être plein d'énergie; **music full of go,** musique pleine de vie, de brio. **3.** *(a)* coup *m*, essai *m*; **to make a go of it,** y réussir; *Games: etc:* **(it's) your go!** à vous de jouer! **to have a go at sth.,** (i) tenter l'aventure; essayer (de faire qch.); (ii) s'attaquer à (un rôti, un pâté, etc.); **let's have a go!** essayons le coup! allons-y! essayons un peu! voyons (voir) si ça peut se faire! tentez la chance! **to have a good go at sth.,** faire tous ses efforts pour faire qch.; **to have another go (at sth.),** (i) faire une nouvelle tentative; (ii) reprendre (du pâté, etc.); en reprendre; **to have several goes at sth. (before succeeding),** s'y reprendre à plusieurs reprises (pour faire qch.); faire qch. par épaulées; **at one go,** d'un (seul) coup; d'un (seul) trait; tout d'une haleine; *Typew:* **she can do six copies at one go,** elle peut faire six exemplaires en une seule frappe; *(b)* *(at fair, etc.)* tour *m*; **two goes on the roundabouts,** deux tours de manège; *(c)* accès *m* (de fièvre, etc.); **to have a bad go of flu,** avoir une forte attaque de grippe. **4. that's a poor,** *O:* **rum, pretty, go!** (i) quelle affaire! (ii) nous voilà propres, dans de beaux draps! **that was a near go!** nous l'avons échappé belle! il s'en est fallu de peu! **no go!** ça ne marche, ne prend, pas! rien à faire! **5.** *O:* **it's all the go,** ça fait fureur, rage; ça c'est la mode. **6.** *a. Space:* *F:* **all systems are go,** tout est paré et en ordre de marche (pour le départ).
go[2], *v.* **(he goes** (*A:* **thou goest** [ˈgouist]); **went** [went]; **gone** [gɔn]) *(the aux. is usu.* **have,** *occ.* **be)**
I. *v.i.* **1.** aller; **to go to a place,** aller, se rendre, à un endroit; *F:* **to go places,** (i) sortir (beaucoup); (ii) voyager; (iii) réussir; **where do we go from here?** et quoi ensuite? **to go to Paris, to the country, abroad,** aller à Paris, à la campagne, à l'étranger; **to go to France, to Japan,** aller en France, au Japon; **to go to church, to mass,** aller à l'église, à la messe; **to go to a funeral,** aller à un enterrement; **to go to a party,** aller à une réunion, une soirée; **what shall I go in?** qu'est-ce que je vais mettre? comment vais-je m'habiller? **to go to the doctor's,** aller consulter, aller chez, le médecin; **to go to prison,** être mis en prison; **to go to the window,** aller, se mettre, à la fenêtre; **to go to the lavatory,** aller à la toilette; *F:* **I can't go,** je ne peux pas aller; *F:* **I've been wanting to go for ten minutes,** voilà dix minutes que j'ai envie de faire pipi! **to come and go,** aller et venir; **I always go to the local butcher('s) for my meat,** j'achète, je prends, toujours ma viande chez le boucher du coin; **if I can't buy it here I shall have to go somewhere else,** si je ne peux pas l'acheter ici il me faudra le chercher ailleurs; **to go to s.o.'s house,** aller chez qn; **to go on a journey,** faire un voyage; aller en voyage; **to go for a walk,** aller se promener; faire une promenade; **to go on a world tour, to go round the world,** faire le tour du monde; **to go on foot, on horseback, by train, by car, by plane,** aller à pied, à cheval, par le train, en voiture, par avion; **we can talk about it as we go,** nous pourrons en parler en chemin; **there he goes!** le voilà qui passe! **who goes there?** qui va là? qui vive? **to go the shortest way,** prendre par le plus court; **to go at a good pace,** aller bon train; **to go at 100 km an hour,** faire 100 km, du cent, à l'heure; *Nau:* **to go at 10 knots,** faire, filer, 10 nœuds; **to go at full speed,** se lancer à toute vitesse; **to go like the wind,** filer comme le vent; **we had already gone more than half the distance,** nous avions déjà fait plus que la moitié du chemin; **you go first!** (i) partez en tête, le premier; (ii) à vous d'abord; **you go next!** à vous ensuite; à votre tour; **I'll go after, later,** je vais y aller plus tard; **I wish I had gone before,** je regrette de ne pas y être allé plus tôt; *(b)* *(s.a. the relevant prepositions and the compound verbs* **go up, go down,** *etc.)* **to go up, down, across, along, a street,** monter, descendre, traverser, passer par, une rue; **to go through a hedge, a country,** passer par une haie; traverser un pays; **to go into a room,** entrer dans une pièce; **to go behind a tree,** (aller) se cacher derrière un arbre; **to go behind s.o.'s back,** faire qch. derrière le dos de qn; faire qch. en évitant qn et en s'adressant à son supérieur; **to go over, across, a bridge,** traverser un pont; **to go under a bridge,** passer sous un pont; **the ball went over the wall,** la balle a passé par-dessus le mur; **the dog went under the table to escape from the cat,** le chien s'est caché, s'est réfugié, sous la table pour échapper au chat; **he was going towards the station,** il s'acheminait vers la gare; **to go by, in front of, a house,** passer devant une maison; *P:* **to go after the girls,** courir après les femmes, les filles; **if you go beyond the last houses you will find a footpath across the fields,** si vous allez au delà des dernières maisons vous trouverez un chemin à travers champs; **that's going beyond a joke, beyond the limits of common sense,** cela dépasse la plaisanterie, les limites du bon sens; **to go forward,** avancer; **to go ahead of s.o.,** devancer qn; **you go ahead and I'll catch you up,** partez d'abord; je vais vous rattraper; **to go against the tide, the current,** prendre le contresens de la marée, du courant; nager, voguer, contre la marée, le courant; **it goes against me, against my conscience, against the grain, to . . .,** il me répugne de . . .; *(c)* **which road goes to London?** quel est le chemin qui va, mène, à Londres? **the road goes across a broad plain,** la route traverse une vaste plaine; **does the road go over or under the railway?** est-ce que la route passe par-dessus ou en dessous du chemin de fer? *Rail:* **the line goes north from Paris,** à partir de Paris la ligne va vers le nord; *(d)* **to go to school,** (i) aller à, (ii) fréquenter, l'école; **to go on the stage,** se faire acteur; monter sur les planches; **to go to sea,** se faire marin; **to go into the army,** *A:* **to go for a soldier,** (i) se faire soldat; s'engager (dans l'armée); (ii) *(conscription)* partir au régiment; *(e)* **to go hungry, thirsty,** souffrir de la faim, de la soif; **wine that goes to the head,** vin qui monte à la tête; *(f) O:* *(of animal)* **to go with young,** porter; *F:* *(of woman)* **to be six months gone,** être enceinte de six mois; *(g)* **to go one's own way,** faire à sa guise; *F:* **anything goes,** on fait ce qu'on veut, s'habille comme on veut, etc.; **to go with the crowd,** aller avec, suivre, la foule; se laisser entraîner par la foule; **to go one better (than s.o.),** surenchérir (sur qn); *(h)* **the names go in alphabetical order,** les noms sont rangés par ordre alphabétique; **promotion goes by seniority,** l'avancement se fait, a lieu, à l'ancienneté. **2.** marcher; *(a)* **to set, get, a piece of machinery going,** mettre une machine en marche, en mouvement; lancer une machine; embrayer, enclencher, engrener, un mécanisme; **we must get the engine going again,** il faut remettre la machine en marche; **we must get some French classes going,** il faut organiser des cours de français; *F:* **get going!** file! vas-y! **my watch won't go,** ma montre ne marche pas; **to keep industry going,** maintenir l'activité de, faire marcher, l'industrie; **enough timber to keep three sawmills going,** assez de bois pour alimenter trois scieries;

we've enough coal to keep us going this winter, nous avons assez de charbon pour tout l'hiver; **to keep the conversation going,** entretenir la conversation; faire les frais de la conversation; **to keep a patient going,** soutenir un malade; (*b*) **everything's going well,** tout marche bien; **things are going badly,** cela ne marche pas; **how are things going (with you)?** comment ça va? **if all goes well (with us),** si tout va bien; si la fortune nous est propice; **the business is going well,** l'affaire marche bien, est en bonne voie; **the rehearsal went well, badly,** la répétition a bien, mal, marché; **to make things go,** (i) faire marcher rondement les choses; (ii) mettre de l'entrain dans la réunion, dans la conversation; **the way things are going,** au train où vont les choses; *F:* **when he gets going he never stops,** quand il est lancé, une fois lancé, il ne sait pas s'arrêter; **what he says goes,** c'est lui qui commande; tout le monde fait ce qu'il veut; (*c*) **the bell is going,** la cloche sonne; **it has just gone eight,** huit heures viennent de sonner; **it has gone four,** il est passé quatre heures; **it has already gone six,** il est déjà six heures passées; **he's gone forty,** il a dépassé la quarantaine; il a quarante ans sonnés; *F: O:* **to be going (on for) fifteen,** avoir près de quinze ans; (*d*) **to go crack, bang,** faire crac, pan; **go like this with your left foot,** faites comme ça du pied gauche; (*e*) **I forget how the tune goes,** l'air m'échappe; **the tune goes like this,** je vais vous chantonner, jouer, l'air; **how does the chorus go?** quelles sont les paroles du refrain? *F: vendre* **goes like** *descendre, vendre* se conjuge comme *descendre;* (*f*) **there was no doubt about which way the war would go,** il n'y avait pas de doute sur le résultat de la guerre; **which way will the decision go?** comment décidera-t-on? **I don't know how things will go,** je ne sais pas comment cela tournera; je ne sais pas quelle sera l'issue de l'affaire; **judgement went for, against the plaintiff,** l'arrêt fut prononcé en faveur du, contre le, demandeur; **the damages go to the injured party,** les dommages-intérêts vont, sont applicables, à la partie lésée; (*g*) **these colours don't go (together),** ces couleurs jurent; **the carpet doesn't go with the furniture,** le tapis n'est pas assorti aux meubles. **3.** (*a*) (*of time*) passer; **the time will soon go,** le temps passera vite; **time goes very quickly when I am with you,** le temps passe vite, ne paraît pas long, quand je suis avec vous; **ten minutes gone and nothing done,** dix minutes de passées et rien de fait; **there were only five minutes to go before . . .,** il ne restait que cinq minutes avant . . .; **how's the time going?** combien de temps nous reste-t-il? *F: O:* **how goes the enemy?** quelle heure est-il? (*b*) **the story goes that . . .,** à ce que l'on raconte; **as the saying goes,** selon l'adage, le dicton; **she isn't a bad cook as cooks go these days,** étant donné la médiocrité des cuisinières d'aujourd'hui elle n'est pas mauvaise; **as things go today,** par le temps qui court; **that's not dear as things go,** ce n'est pas cher au prix où sont les choses, au prix où est le beurre; (*c*) **to go by, under, a false name,** être connu sous un faux nom; (*d*) **it goes without saying that . . .,** il va de soi que . . .; on n'a pas besoin de dire, de préciser, que . . .; **that goes without saying,** cela va sans (le) dire. **4.** (*a*) partir; s'en aller; **the guests have all gone,** les invités sont tous partis; **after I have gone,** après mon départ; **don't go yet,** ne partez pas encore; **we must go, must be going,** il nous faut partir; il est temps de partir; **let me go,** laissez-moi partir; **go!** (i) allez-vous-en! (ii) *Sp:* partez! **from the word go,** dès le commencement; (*b*) **a hundred employees will have to go,** il va falloir mettre cent employés à la porte, congédier cent employés; (*c*) disparaître; **my hat has gone,** mon chapeau a disparu; **it's all gone,** il n'y en a plus; **that's the way the money goes,** voilà comme l'argent file; **a hundred pounds went in gambling debts,** cent livres ont filé en dettes de jeu; **the big car will have to be the first luxury to go,** la première grosse dépense à supprimer sera la grosse voiture; **whatever isn't finished must go,** pour ce qui n'est pas fini, tant pis! **the day of individualism has gone,** les jours de l'individualisme sont révolus; **the old hatreds are not all gone,** les anciennes rancunes ne sont pas entièrement dissipées; **my strength is going,** mes forces s'affaiblissent, s'en vont; **her sight is going,** elle est en train de perdre la vue; **his teeth are all gone,** il a perdu toutes ses dents; (*d*) se casser; (*of cable, etc.*) partir; **the spring went,** le ressort s'est cassé; *El:* **a fuse went,** un plomb a sauté; **two lamps have gone,** deux lampes ont grillé; **my dress is going at the seams,** ma robe se déchire, part, aux coutures; (*e*) **to be going cheap,** se vendre (à) bon marché; **they are going at ten francs each,** ils sont en vente, en solde, à dix francs pièce; **the lot went for £20,** le lot fut adjugé à £20; **going! going! gone!** une fois! deux fois! adjugé! (*f*) **if I hear of a job going that would suit you,** si j'entends parler d'un emploi qui vous conviendrait; **let's see if there's any lunch going,** allons voir si le déjeuner est prêt; **there are drinks going in the drawing room,** on sert l'apéritif dans le salon; (*g*) mourir; **his wife went first,** sa femme est morte la première, avant lui; **when I am gone, after I have gone,** après ma mort; *O:* **she is gone,** elle n'est plus, elle est partie; (*on tombstone, etc.*) **not lost but gone before,** il n'est pas à jamais perdu, mais nous a précédés; *Lit:* **to go the way of all flesh, to go to a better world,** mourir, aller où va toute chose; **to go west,** (i) *P:* mourir; (ii) *F:* (*of thg*) se casser; être fichu; (iii) *F:* (*of business, etc.*) faire faillite; *F:* **that's another £10 gone west,** voilà encore £10 de dépensés, de claqués. **5.** (*a*) **to go and do sth.,** aller faire qch.; **to go and dine, to go to dinner, with s.o.,** aller dîner avec qn, chez qn; **to go to see, and see, s.o.,** aller voir qn; **go and shut the door!** allez fermer la porte! **to go and fetch s.o., to go for s.o.,** aller chercher qn; **to go and look for sth.,** aller chercher qch.; **he went and fetched, got, his hat,** il est allé prendre son chapeau; *F:* **and then he went and got married!** et puis il a eu l'idée de se marier! il a fait la bêtise de se marier! *P:* **now you've (been and) gone and done it!** vous avez fait là un beau coup! vous en avez fait une belle! ça y est cette fois-ci! (*b*) **he went (forward) to help her, but . . .,** il est allé pour l'aider, il a fait un mouvement pour l'aider, mais . . .; (*c*) **I'm going to have my own way,** je veux faire à ma tête; **I'm not going to be cheated,** je ne me laisserai pas abuser; (*d*) (*expressing intention*) **I was going to walk,** j'avais l'intention d'y aller, de faire le trajet, à pied; **we are going to be at home in any case,** de toute façon nous comptons rester à la maison; **I'm going to France for my holiday,** je compte passer mes vacances en France; (*e*) (*aux. forming an immediate future*) **I'm going to tell you a story,** je vais vous raconter une histoire; **he thought he was going to be ill,** il sentait qu'il allait être malade; **the shortage is not going to last,** la disette ne durera pas; (*f*) **to go motoring, riding,** (aller) se promener en voiture, à cheval; **to go hunting, fishing,** aller à la chasse, à la pêche; **to go looking for sth.,** partir à la recherche de qch.; **you just go looking for trouble!** tu cherches des ennuis! **there you go again!** vous voilà reparti! *P:* **don't go doing that!** ne fais pas ça! **6.** (*a*) **to go to law,** avoir recours à la justice; **to go to war,** se mettre en guerre; entrer en guerre; **to go to press,** mettre sous presse; **to go to great lengths to do sth.,** se donner beaucoup de peine pour faire qch.; **he won't even go to the trouble of . . .,** il ne veut même pas prendre, se donner, la peine de . . .; **I will go as far as saying that . . .,** j'irai jusqu'à dire que . . .; **I will go up to £100,** je veux bien y mettre, payer, jusqu'à £100; (*b*) *Gaming:* **to go £10,** risquer, miser, £10; (*c*) *Cards:* **to go two, three, no trumps,** annoncer deux, trois, sans atout; **to go one better,** renchérir. **7.** (*a*) **too big to go into the basket,** trop grand pour aller, entrer, dans le panier; **I can't get everything to go in, to go into my case,** je n'arrive pas à mettre toutes mes affaires dans ma valise; **the key won't go in(to) the lock,** la clef n'entre pas dans la serrure; **trunk that will go under the bed,** malle qui entre, qui se case, sous le lit; (*b*) **where does this book go?** où faut-il mettre, où est la place de, ce livre? (*c*) *Mth: F:* **six into twelve goes two,** douze divisé par six fait deux; **four into three won't go,** trois n'est pas divisible par quatre; **three into seven goes two and one over,** sept divisé par trois fait deux et il reste un. **8.** **the proceeds will go to charity,** les bénéfices seront distribués, iront, à des œuvres charitables; **the prize went to the youngest,** le prix fut adjugé au plus jeune; c'est le plus jeune qui a reçu le prix; **his estate will go to his eldest son,** son fils aîné va hériter de la propriété. **9.** contribuer (à qch.); **much thought had gone (in)to making everybody comfortable,** on s'était étudié à, s'était donné beaucoup de peine pour, mettre tout le monde à l'aise; **the qualities that go to make a great man,** les qualités qui constituent un grand homme; **ingredients that go to make a good dish,** ingrédients qui contribuent à faire un bon plat; **to go to prove sth.,** servir à prouver qch.; **it only goes to show that you can't be too careful,** cela montre qu'on ne peut jamais prendre trop de précautions; **that just goes to show!** tu vois! **10.** s'étendre; **the garden goes down to the river,** le jardin s'étend jusqu'à la rivière; **wound that does not go very deep,** blessure qui n'est pas très profonde; **the difference goes deep,** il y a une profonde différence; **as far as the style goes,** quant au style; pour ce qui est du style; **the report is exact as far as it goes,** le rapport est exact mais il omet beaucoup de choses. **11.** (*a*) devenir; **to go mad,** devenir fou; **to go Communist,** se faire, devenir, communiste; **the town went Labour,** la ville a fait volte-face et a voté socialiste; **he went cold all over,** son sang s'est glacé; **to go white, red, etc.,** rougir, blanchir, etc.; **my hair is going grey,** mes cheveux grisonnent, deviennent gris; **she went as pale as death,** une pâleur mortelle s'est répandue sur son visage; (*b*) (*of pers.*) **to go to the bad,** mal tourner; (*c*) *F:* **let the rest of them go hang!** tant pis pour les autres! **12.** (*a*) **to let go,** lâcher prise; **to let go one's hold of sth.,** lâcher, laisser échapper, une corde, etc.; **let me go!** lâchez-moi! *Nau:* **to let a rope go,** laisser aller, lâcher, filer, un cordage; larguer une amarre; **all gone!** tout est largué! **let go forward!** larguez devant! (*b*) **to let oneself go,** (i) s'abandonner; se laisser aller; (ii) donner carrière à ses sentiments, etc.; s'abandonner à sa fureur, etc.; **to let oneself go on a subject,** s'étendre sur un sujet; (*c*) **we'll let it go at that,** tenons-nous-en là; cela ira comme ça; **well, let it go at that!** passons! **13.** *F:* (*a*) **to go it,** aller grand train; se lancer; **go it!** vas-y! allez-y! (*b*) **to go it alone,** agir tout seul; être seul contre tous.

II. (*compound verbs*) **1. go about,** *v.i.* (*a*) (i) circuler; aller çà et là; **to go about a great deal,** sortir beaucoup; **to go about in gangs,** aller par bandes; **there is a rumour going about,** un bruit court; (ii) *Nau:* virer de bord; envoyer vent devant; (iii) *Mil: etc:* faire demi-tour; (*b*) (*with cogn. acc.*) (i) **to go about the country,** parcourir le pays; **to go about the streets,** circuler dans les rues; (ii) **to go about one's work,** se mettre à, vaquer à, son travail; **how to go about it,** comment s'y prendre; *F:* **you'd better go about your business!** occupez-vous de ce qui vous regarde!

2. go along, *v.i.* (*a*) suivre son chemin; **I check the figures as I go along,** je vérifie les chiffres à mesure; (*b*) **to go along with s.o.,** coopérer, être d'accord, avec qn; **to go along with sth.,** approuver, accepter, qch. (en tout et pour tout); (*c*) *F:* **go along with you!** allons donc! dites cela à d'autres!

3. go around, *v.i.* circuler; voyager; **she goes around a lot,** elle sort, voyage, beaucoup; (*b*) *Av; etc: F:* faire un tour, des tours, de piste; (*c*) *esp. NAm:* **there isn't enough to go around,** il n'y en a pas assez pour tout le monde.

4. go at, *v.* s'attaquer à (qn, qch.); **to go at it hard, for all one's worth,** ne pas y aller de main morte, y aller de toutes ses forces.

5. go away, *v.i.* s'en aller, partir; s'absenter; **to go away on business, for the weekend,** s'absenter pour affaires, pour le week-end; *Ven:* (*horn signal*) **gone away,** le débucher; (*b*) **to go away with sth.,** emporter qch.; (*c*) *F:* **go away!** va te promener!

6. go back, *v.i.* (*a*) (i) s'en retourner; **to go back to one's native country,** retourner dans sa patrie; **to go back home,** rentrer chez soi; (ii) retourner en arrière; rebrousser chemin; **to go back on one's steps,** revenir sur ses pas; **to go back the same way,** revenir, retourner, par le même chemin; (iii) reculer; **to go back two paces,** reculer de deux pas; faire deux pas en arrière; (iv) **to go back to a subject,** revenir sur un sujet; **to go back to the beginning,** recommencer; **he went back to his reading,** il a repris, s'est replongé dans, sa lecture; **to go back to sleep,** se rendormir; **to go back to the last lesson,** revenir à la dernière leçon; **to go back to one's old ways,** retomber dans ses anciennes habitudes; **I've gone back to my winter overcoat,** j'ai repris mon pardessus d'hiver; **we're going back to long skirts,** on (en) revient aux jupes longues; (*b*) remonter (à l'origine de qch.); **to go back to the Flood,** remonter (jusqu') au déluge; **to go back to the past,** se reporter au passé; remonter dans le passé; revenir sur le passé; **his family goes back to the Crusades,** sa famille descend des Croisés; (*c*) **to go back on a promise,** revenir sur sa promesse; **to go back on one's word,** revenir sur sa parole; se dédire; manquer à sa parole; **to go back on a friend,** trahir, abandonner, lâcher, un ami.

7. go by, *v.i.* (*a*) passer; (*of time*) s'écouler; **as the years go by,** à mesure que les années passent; **to watch people going by,** regarder passer les gens; **to let an opportunity go by,** laisser passer, manquer, une occasion; (*b*) **to go by s.o., sth.,** se régler sur qn, sur qch.; **to go by appearances,** juger d'après les apparences; **that's nothing to go by,** on ne peut pas se fonder là-dessus; **the only thing to go by,** la seule chose qui puisse nous guider.

8. go down, *v.i.* (*a*) descendre; **to go down to dinner,** descendre dîner; **go down and open the door,** descends ouvrir la porte; (*in lift*) **going down!** on descend! pour descendre! *Sch:* **to go down (from the university),** (i) quitter l'université (à la fin de ses études); (ii) partir en vacances (à la fin du trimestre); *Th:* **when the curtain goes down,** à la chute du rideau; (*b*) (*of sun*) se coucher; (*c*) (i) (*of ship*) sombrer, couler à fond; (*of pers.*) se noyer; (*of ship*) **to go down by the bows,** piquer de l'avant; (ii) *F:* tomber malade; **to go down**

with flu, attraper la grippe; (*d*) **to go down in s.o.'s estimation,** baisser dans l'estime de qn; **to go down well,** (i) (*of drink*) se laisser boire; (*of food*) se laisser manger; (ii) (*of entertainment, speech, etc.*) plaire; être bien reçu; *F:* (*of idea, etc.*) **it didn't go down too well with them,** ils ont eu du mal à l'avaler; **a crumb went down the wrong way,** j'ai avalé une miette de travers; (*e*) **he went down with a thud,** il est tombé lourdement; **to go down on one's knees,** se mettre, se jeter, à genoux; **to go down before the enemy,** tomber devant l'ennemi; (*f*) *Cards:* (*bridge*) perdre le coup; ne pas faire autant de levées qu'on en a annoncé; (*g*) (*of floods, temperature, etc.*) baisser, s'abaisser; (*of wind*) baisser, tomber; (*of prices, value*) baisser; **district that has gone down,** quartier qui a déchu; **he's gone down in the world,** il a connu des jours meilleurs; (*h*) (*of swelling, etc.*) se désenfler, se dégonfler; (*of tyre, balloon, etc.*) se dégonfler; (*i*) continuer (jusqu'à la fin de la page, etc.); **to go down to posterity,** passer à la postérité.
9. go for, *v. F:* (*a*) (i) attaquer, tomber sur, s'élancer sur (qn); (*to dog*) **go for him!** pille! pille! (ii) attaquer (qn), chercher noise à (qn); **to go for s.o. in the papers,** attaquer qn dans les journaux; **they went for each other in court,** ils se sont empoignés, engueulés, devant le tribunal; (*b*) **I don't go for him much,** il ne me plaît guère, ne me dit pas grand-chose; **I don't go for that,** cela ne m'emballe pas beaucoup.
10. go forth, *v.i. A: & Lit:* (*a*) (*of pers.*) sortir; (*b*) (*of decree, etc.*) paraître.
11. go in, *v.i.* (*a*) entrer; rentrer; **let's go in!** entrons! allons-y! **shall we go in?** on y va? **I must go in and cook the dinner,** il faut que je rentre préparer le dîner; *O:* **the theatres were just going in,** c'était l'heure de l'ouverture des théâtres; (*b*) (*of sun*) se cacher; (*c*) *Cr:* prendre son tour au guichet; (*d*) **to go in for sth.,** faire qch.; s'occuper de, se mêler de, qch.; **to go in for painting,** faire de la peinture; **to go in for politics,** se lancer dans la politique; faire de la politique; **to go in for golf,** faire du golf; jouer au golf; **to go in for teaching,** entrer dans l'enseignement; se faire professeur, instituteur; **to go in for an examination,** préparer un examen; se présenter à un examen; **to go in for a competition,** prendre part à un concours; (*e*) **to go in with s.o.,** se joindre à qn (dans une entreprise, etc.); (*f*) *Mil: etc: F:* attaquer.
12. go into, *v.* (*a*) **to go into a lengthy explanation,** entrer dans de longues explications; **to go into details,** entrer dans des détails; (*b*) **to go into mourning,** prendre le deuil; **to go into hysterics,** avoir une attaque, une crise, de nerfs; **to go into fits of laughter,** éclater de rire; (*c*) examiner, étudier (une question); mettre (une question) à l'étude; **I shall go into the matter,** je vais m'occuper de l'affaire; **your proposal will be carefully gone into,** votre proposition sera l'objet d'un examen approfondi.
13. go off, *v.i.* (*a*) partir, s'en aller, s'éloigner; *Th:* quitter la scène; *F:* **she's gone off and left him,** elle l'a quitté; **to go off in pursuit of s.o.,** se mettre à la poursuite de qn; **to go off with sth.,** emporter, enlever, qch.; (*b*) (*of gun*) partir, se décharger; **the pistol didn't go off,** le pistolet a raté; (*c*) *F:* (i) s'endormir; (ii) *O:* perdre connaissance; *F:* tomber dans les pommes; (*d*) *F:* (*of feeling, etc.*) passer; (*of tennis player, etc.*) perdre de sa forme; baisser; (*of woman*) perdre de sa beauté; (*e*) *F:* (*of food, etc.*) se détériorer; (*of wine*) perdre de son arôme; s'éventer; (*of milk*) tourner; (*of butter*) rancir; (*of fish, meat*) se gâter; (*f*) **everything went off well,** tout a bien marché, s'est bien passé; (*g*) perdre le goût de (qch.); **I've gone off cheese,** je ne mange plus de fromage; je n'aime plus le fromage; **I've completely gone off him,** j'ai commencé à le prendre en grippe.
14. go on, *v.i.* (*a*) continuer; **time goes on,** le temps marche; **I must go on with my work,** il me faut continuer mon travail; **go on looking!** cherchez toujours! **he went on again after a moment,** il a repris après un instant; **the war went on until 1945,** la guerre s'est prolongée jusqu'en 1945; **I have enough to go on with,** j'en ai assez pour le moment; j'ai de quoi marcher, continuer; **that's enough to be going on with,** (i) voilà du pain sur la planche; (ii) j'en ai vraiment assez (de vos histoires); **how he goes on!** impossible de l'arrêter! *F:* **he's going on for forty,** il va sur, frise, la quarantaine; **it's going on for three (o'clock),** il est près de trois heures; (*b*) **to go on to another question,** passer à une autre question; **he went on to give me the details,** puis il m'a donné les détails; *P:* **go on (with you)!** allons donc! à d'autres! (*c*) marcher; **this has been going on for years,** cela dure depuis des années; **how are things going on?** comment ça marche-t-il? comment allez-vous? **what's going on here?** qu'est-ce qui se passe ici? (*d*) *F:* se conduire; **you mustn't go on like that,** il ne faut pas vous laisser aller comme ça; **I don't like her way of going on,** je n'aime pas ses manières, sa façon de se conduire; (*e*) *P:* faire une scène; **he's always going on at me,** il est toujours à me gronder; (*f*) *Th:* monter en scène; entrer en scène.
15. go out, *v.i.* (*a*) (i) sortir; **out you go!** va-t-en! sors! file! **she was dressed to go out,** elle était en tenue de ville; **to go out riding,** sortir, se promener, à cheval; **to go out for a walk,** faire une promenade (à pied); **to go out to dinner with friends,** (aller) dîner chez des amis; **he doesn't go out much,** il sort peu; il est casanier; **the lifeboats went out fifty times last year,** l'année dernière les canots de sauvetage ont fait cinquante sorties; **to go out (on strike),** se mettre en grève; *F:* **he was going out with her for two years before they got married,** il l'a fréquentée pendant deux ans avant de l'épouser; (ii) **my heart went out to him,** (α) je l'ai trouvé tout de suite sympathique; (β) j'ai ressenti de la pitié pour lui; (*b*) passer de mode; se démoder; **short skirts have gone out,** les jupes courtes ne sont plus à la mode, ont passé de mode; (*c*) (*of fire, etc.*) s'éteindre; (*d*) *F:* (*of pers.*) mourir; **he went out like a light,** (i) il est mort subitement; (ii) il s'est évanoui, *F:* est tombé dans les pommes; (*e*) (*of tide*) baisser, se retirer.
16. go over, *v.* (*a*) examiner, vérifier, revoir (un compte, un rapport, etc.); passer (des papiers, etc.) en revue; relire (un document); repasser, revoir (une leçon, etc.); **to go over the ground,** reconnaître le terrain; **to go over sth. in one's mind,** repasser qch. dans son esprit; (*b*) **to go over to the enemy, to the other camp,** passer à l'ennemi, dans l'autre camp; se joindre à l'ennemi; **to go over to the other side,** changer de parti; (*c*) faire son petit effet, passer la rampe.
17. go round, *v.i.* (*a*) faire un détour, un circuit; **to go a long way round,** faire un grand détour; (*b*) (*of wheel, etc.*) tourner; **a child likes to see the wheels go round,** un enfant aime à voir tourner les roues; **my head's going round,** la tête me tourne; (*c*) (*of rumour, etc.*) circuler, courir; (*of bottle, etc.*) circuler; (*d*) **to make the food go round,** ménager la nourriture; **there isn't enough to go round,** il n'y en a pas assez pour tout le monde.
18. go through, (*a*) *v.tr.* remplir, accomplir (des formalités), subir, essuyer, souffrir, passer par (de rudes épreuves, etc.); **if you knew all that I have gone through!** si vous saviez tout ce que j'ai enduré, souffert! *F:* **I really went through it!** j'ai passé un mauvais quart d'heure; **he's gone through a lot,** il en a vu des vertes et des pas mûres; (*b*) *v.tr.* examiner (des documents, etc.); repasser (une leçon, des comptes); trier (sa garde-robe, etc.); *Cust:* visiter, fouiller (des valises); **to go through s.o.'s pockets,** fouiller dans les poches de qn; **to go through all one's money,** dépenser tout son argent; (*c*) *v.i.* **the bill has gone through,** la loi a passé; **the deal didn't go through,** le marché n'a pas été conclu; l'affaire a raté; **to go through with a divorce,** divorcer; **I mean to go through with it,** j'irai jusqu'au bout.
19. go to, *v.i. A:* (*a*) se mettre à l'œuvre; s'y mettre; (*b*) **go to!** (i) allons! (ii) en voilà assez!
20. go under, *v.i.* (*a*) (*of drowning man*) couler, enfoncer; (*b*) succomber, sombrer; faire faillite.
21. go up, *v.i.* (*a*) monter; **to go up to bed,** monter se coucher; **to go up in an aircraft,** monter en avion; (*in lift*) **going up!** on monte! pour monter! *Th:* **before the curtain goes up,** avant le lever du rideau; **a shout went up from the crowd,** un cri s'éleva de la foule; **to go up in s.o.'s estimation,** monter dans l'estime de qn; (*b*) **to go up to Town, to London,** aller à Londres; *Sch:* **to go up (to Oxford, etc.),** entrer à l'université; (*c*) (*of prices, barometer, temperature, etc.*) monter; hausser; **bread is going up,** le pain renchérit; **the bidding went up to £200,** les enchères ont monté à £200; (*d*) (*of mine*) sauter; **to go up in flames,** se mettre à flamber.
22. go with, *v.i.* (*a*) marcher, aller, de pair avec (qch.); (*b*) s'accorder avec (qch.); (*of colours*) se marier avec (une teinte); s'assortir, (*c*) *P:* **he went with her a long time before they got married,** il l'a fréquentée longtemps avant de l'épouser.
23. go without, *v.i.* (*a*) se passer de (qch.); (*b*) manquer de (qch.), être privé de (qch.).
goa[1] ['gouə], *s. Z:* antilope *f* du Tibet; gazelle *f* du Tibet.
Goa[2], *Pr.n. Geog:* Goa; *Pharm:* **G. powder,** araroba pulvérisé; poudre *f* de Goa.
goad[1] [goud], *s.* aiguillon *m*; pique-bœuf *m, pl.* pique-bœufs.
goad[2], *v.tr.* aiguillonner, piquer, toucher (les bœufs); **to g. s.o.'s curiosity,** piquer, stimuler, la curiosité de qn; **to g. s.o. on,** aiguillonner, inciter, qn; **to g. s.o. on to, into, doing sth.,** talonner qn jusqu'à ce qu'il fasse qch.; **to g. s.o. into a fury,** mettre qn en furie, en rage.
goadsman, *pl.* **-men** ['goudzmən], *s.m.* toucheur (de bœufs); pique-bœuf, *pl.* pique-bœufs.
goaf [gouf], *s. Min: Dial:* remblai *m*.
go-ahead ['gouəhed]. *F:* **1.** *a.* (*a*) plein d'allant; actif; entreprenant; **g.-a. business man,** homme d'affaires entreprenant; brasseur *m*, remueur *m*, d'affaires; **g.-a. times,** époque *f* de progrès; (*b*) **go-a. signal,** feu vert. **2.** *s.* **to give s.o. the go-a.,** donner à qn le feu vert.
go-aheadness [gouə'hednis], *s. F:* allant *m*; nature entreprenante.
goal [goul], *s.* **1.** but *m*; (*a*) **my g. is in sight,** j'approche de mon but, du but; (*b*) *Sp:* (*Fb: hockey, etc.*) **to score a g.,** marquer, réussir, un but; (*rugby*) **g. from a try, converted g.,** but de transformation; **g. from a free kick,** but sur coup franc; **dropped goal,** drop-goal *m, pl.* drop-goals; **to keep g.,** garder le but; **g. line,** ligne *f* de but; **g. mouth,** portique *m*, entrée *f*, du but; **to score from the g. mouth,** marquer un but à bout portant; *F:* **to play g.,** être gardien *m* du but. **2.** *Rom.Ant:* borne *f* (du cirque).
goaler ['goulər], *s. Sp: NAm:* gardien *m* de but.
goalkeeper ['goulki:pər], *F:* **goalie** ['gouli], *s. Sp:* gardien *m* de but, *F:* le goal.
goalless ['goullis], *a. Sp:* **g. draw,** match *m* sans but marqué; match nul.
goalpost ['goulpoust], *s.* montant *m* de but; poteau *m* de but.
Goan ['gouən], **Goanese** [gouə'ni:z], *a. & s. Geog:* (habitant, -ante, originaire) de Goa.
go-around ['gouəraund], *s. Av: etc: F:* tour *m* de piste.
go-ashore ['gouəʃɔ:ər], *a. Nau:* **go-a. clothes,** *s. F:* **go-ashores,** tenue *f* de débarquement; tenue portée à terre.
go-as-you-please ['gouəzju:'pli:z], *a. F:* **1.** *Sp:* (course *f*) à volonté. **2.** (vie *f*) libre, sans entraves. **3.** (travail *m*) sans discipline, sans méthode.
goat [gout], *s.* **1.** (*a*) chèvre *f*; **she g.,** bique *f*, chèvre; **he g.,** bouc *m*; **old (he) g.,** (i) bouquin *m*; (ii) *F:* (*pers.*) vieux satyre; vieux birbe; *F:* **to stink like an old g.,** puer le bouc, puer comme un bouc; **young g.,** chevreau, *f.* chevrette; **wild g.,** chèvre égagre; **mountain g.,** chèvre des neiges; **the g. family, the goats,** les caprinés *m*; **g. fold,** chèvrerie *f*; **goat's milk,** lait *m* de chèvre; **g. cheese, goat's milk cheese,** fromage *m* de chèvre; *F:* **don't be a g., don't act, play, the g.,** ne fais pas l'imbécile; **that gets my g.,** ça me met en boule, me tape sur les nerfs; **he gets my g.,** il m'exaspère, me tape sur les nerfs, me sort par les narines; (*b*) *Bookb:* peau *f* de bouc; (*c*) *Bot:* **g. willow, g. sallow,** marceau *m*; **goat's rue,** galéga *m*; **goat's beard,** (i) ulmaire *f*, reine *f* des prés; (ii) salsifis *m* sauvage, barbe-de-bouc *f, pl.* barbes-de-bouc; (*d*) *Ent:* **g. moth,** (cossus *m*) gâte-bois *m inv.* **2.** *Astr:* **the G.,** le Capricorne. **3.** *NAm: F:* (*pers.*) bouc émissaire.
goatee [gou'ti:], *s.* barbiche *f* (sous le menton); bouc *m*; **to wear a g.,** porter le bouc.
goatherd ['goutha:d], *s.* chevrier, -ière.
goatlike ['goutlaik], *a.* semblable à un bouc.
goatling ['goutliŋ], *s.* chevreau *m, f.* chevrette.
goatskin ['goutskin], *s.* **1.** peau *f* de chèvre; peau de bique. **2.** (*bottle*) outre *f* (en peau de bouc); bouc *m* (de vin, d'huile).
goatsucker ['goutsʌkər], *s. Orn:* engoulevent *m* (d'Europe), *F:* crapaud volant, tête-chèvre *m, pl.* tête-chèvres.
goatweed ['goutwi:d], *s. Bot:* **1.** capraire *f.* **2.** égopode *m*.
goaty ['gouti], *a.* (odeur) de bouc.
gob[1] [gɔb], *s.* **1.** *F:* gros morceau (de qch.). **2.** *P:* crachat *m*; graillon *m*, glaviot *m*, gluau *m*, molard *m*.
gob[2], *v.i.* (**gobbed**) *P:* cracher, molarder.
gob[3], *s. P:* bouche *f*, gueule *f*; **shut your g.!** ferme-la! ta gueule!
gob[4], *s. Min:* remblai *m*; **g. fire,** feu *m* dans les remblais.
gob[5], *s. U.S: F:* marin *m*, mathurin *m*.
gobbet ['gɔbit], *s. F:* (*a*) gros morceau (de qch.); grosse bouchée (de viande, etc.); (*b*) *Sch:* extrait *m* à commenter (d'un livre au programme).
gobbie ['gɔbi], *s. Nau: F: A:* garde-côte *m, pl.* garde-côtes.
gobble[1] ['gɔbl], *v.tr. & i.* **to g. sth. (up),** avaler qch. goulûment, gloutonnement; dévorer, bâfrer, engloutir, *F:* bouffer, qch.; **to g. up a chicken in no time,** croquer un poulet en moins de rien; (*to child*) **don't g.!** mange plus lentement!
gobble[2], *s.* (*of turkey*) glouglou *m*.
gobble[3], *v.i.* (*of turkey*) glouglouter.
gobble[4], *s. Golf:* coup roulé qui va droit au trou.
gobbledegook, gobbledygook ['gɔb(ə)ldigu:k], *s. F:* jargon *m*, charabia *m*, *esp.* jargon administratif.
gobbler[1] ['gɔblər], *s.* avaleur, -euse; goinfre *m*; bâfreur, -euse.
gobbler[2], *s. F:* dindon *m*.
go-between ['goubitwi:n], *s.* intermédiaire *mf*; en-

tremetteur, -euse; truchement *m*; agent *m* d'intrigues; **to act, serve, as a go-b.,** servir d'intermédiaire (to, à).

Gobiesocidae [goub(a)iə'sɔsidiː], *s.pl. Ich:* gobiesocidés *m*.

gobiesox ['goub(a)isɔks], *s. Ich:* gobiesox *m*.

Gobiidae [gou'baiidiː], *s.pl. Ich:* gobiidés *m*.

goblet ['gɔblit], *s.* **1.** *A:* (*a*) gobelet *m*; (*b*) *Lit:* coupe *f*. **2.** *Com:* verre *m* à pied.

goblin ['gɔblin], *s.* **1.** gobelin *m*, lutin *m*. **2.** *P: A:* livre *f* (sterling).

gobo [goubou], *s. Cin: T.V:* (*a*) (écran *m*) pare-lumière *m inv*; (*b*) (écran) pare-son *m inv*; (*c*) (décor *m*) intercalaire *m*.

gobstick ['gɔbstik], *s. Fish:* dégorgeoir *m*.

gobstopper ['gɔbstɔpər], *s. F:* gros bonbon en boule.

goby ['goubi], *s. Ich:* **(common, sand) g.,** gobie *m*; **rock g.,** gobie brun; **black g.,** goujon *m* de mer.

go-by ['goubai], *s. F:* **to give s.o., sth., the go-by,** (i) dépasser, devancer (un concurrent); (ii) se dérober à (ses ennemis, etc.); esquiver (qn, une difficulté); (iii) oublier (qn, qch.); passer (le nom de qn) sur une liste, à l'avancement; **he gave me the go-by yesterday,** hier il a fait semblant de ne pas me reconnaître.

gocart, go-cart ['goukaːt], *s.* **1.** chariot *m*, parachute *m*, trotteuse *f* (pour apprendre à marcher aux bébés); (*of wicker*) panier roulant. **2.** (*a*) chaise pliante, charrette pliante (pour enfants); poussette *f*; (*b*) charrette à bras. **3.** kart *m*.

god [gɔd], *s.* **1.** (*a*) dieu *m*; **the gods of Egypt,** les dieux d'Égypte; **the g. of war,** le dieu des combats; **feast (fit) for the gods,** festin *m* digne des dieux; **to worship false gods,** adorer des idoles *f*, de faux dieux; *F:* **little tin g.,** petit dieu en toc; petit dieu de camelote; **to make a (little tin) g. of s.o.,** se faire un dieu de qn; faire une idole de qn; dresser des autels à qn; **to make a g. of money,** se faire un dieu de l'argent; déifier l'argent; *F: O:* **ye gods (and little fishes)!** grands dieux! (*b*) *Th: F:* **the gods,** le poulailler, le paradis. **2. God,** Dieu; **I'm sure G. will forgive you,** bien sûr que le bon Dieu te pardonnera; *A:* **God's acre,** le cimetière, le champ de repos; *O:* **God's word, book,** la Bible; **the voice of G.,** la voix de Dieu; **to be with G.,** être au ciel; **trusting in G., we must trust in G.,** à la grâce de Dieu; **G. willing,** s'il plaît à Dieu; **would to G. . . ., I wish to G. . . .,** plût à Dieu . . .; **G. (above only) knows what he wants,** Dieu seul sait ce qu'il veut; **G. knows how much I loved you!** Dieu m'est témoin si je vous ai aimé! **in God's name, in the name of G.,** au nom de Dieu; pour l'amour de Dieu; *F:* **what in God's name are you doing?** que faites-vous là, grand Dieu! **by the living G.!** par le Dieu vivant! **G. Almighty!** Dieu tout-puissant! **thank G.!** Dieu merci! grâce au ciel! *P:* **oh G.! my G.! good G.!** oh! mon Dieu! grand Dieu!

god-awful ['gɔdɔːful], *a. P:* répugnant, dégueulasse, infect.

godchild, *pl.* **-children** ['gɔdtʃaild, -tʃildrən], *s.* filleul, *f.* filleule.

God-damn ['gɔd(d)æm]. **1.** *int. A:* sapristi! nom de Dieu! *A:* Dieu me damne! **2.** *a.* (*more often* **goddam(ed)** *P:* sacré; **it's no g. use!** ça ne sert à rien de rien! **this g. idiot,** ce sacré imbécile.

god(-)daughter ['gɔddɔːtər], *s.f.* filleule.

goddess ['gɔdis], *s.f.* (*a*) déesse; (*b*) **she's a real g.!** c'est une véritable déesse! ce qu'elle est belle!

godet ['gɔdit], *s. Dressm:* godet *m*; **g. skirt,** jupe *f* à godets.

godetia [gou'diːʃiə], *s. Bot:* godétia *f*, godétie *f*.

godfather[1] ['gɔdfaːðər], *s.m.* parrain; **to stand g. to a child,** tenir un enfant sur les fonts (baptismaux).

godfather[2], *v.tr.* tenir (un enfant) sur les fonts baptismaux; **to g. sth.,** être le parrain de qch.; donner son nom à qch.

God-fearing, *a.* (homme) craignant Dieu, élevé dans la crainte de Dieu.

godforsaken ['gɔdfəseik(ə)n], *a.* abandonné de Dieu; misérable, *F:* **g. place,** endroit perdu; **a g. job,** un chien de métier; **what a g. country!** quel fichu pays! quel bled!

Godfrey ['gɔdfri], *Pr.n.m.* Godefroi, Godefroy.

godhead ['gɔdhed], *s.* divinité *f*; **the Godhead,** Dieu *m*.

godille [gɔ'diː], *s. Ski:* godille *f*.

godless ['gɔdlis], *a.* (*of pers.*) athée, impie, sans Dieu; qui n'a ni foi ni loi; (*of action, etc.*) impie.

godlessness ['gɔdlisnis], *s.* impiété *f*.

godlike ['gɔdlaik], *a.* de Dieu; d'un dieu; divin; **g. head,** tête olympienne; **g. Ulysses,** le divin Ulysse.

godliness ['gɔdlinis], *s.* piété *f*.

godly ['gɔdli], *a.* dévot, pieux, saint; tout en Dieu; **to lead a g. life,** vivre pieusement, saintement.

godmamma ['gɔdməmaː], *s.f. F: O:* marraine.

God(-)man (the) [ðə'gɔdmæn], *s. Theol:* l'Homme-Dieu *m*.

godmother ['gɔdmʌðər], *s.f.* marraine; **to stand g. to a child,** tenir un enfant sur les fonts (baptismaux).

godown ['goudaun], *s. Com: A:* comptoir *m*, entrepôt *m* (aux Indes).

godpapa ['gɔdpəpaː], *s.m. F: O:* parrain.

godparent ['gɔdpeərənt], *s.* parent spirituel; **my godparents,** mon parrain et ma marraine.

godroon [gə'druːn], *s.* = GADROON.

godsend ['gɔdsend], *s.* aubaine *f*, bénédiction *f*, bienfait *m* du ciel; **it's a g. (to me, to us),** cela (m')arrive, cela (nous) arrive, comme marée en carême; **this money is a g. to him,** cet argent lui tombe du ciel.

godship ['gɔdʃip], *s.* divinité *f*.

godson ['gɔdsʌn], *s.m.* filleul.

Godspeed ['gɔd'spiːd], *int. & s. O:* bon voyage! adieu! **to bid, wish, s.o. G.,** souhaiter bon voyage, bonne chance, à qn.

godwit ['gɔdwit], *s. Orn:* barge *f*; **bar-tailed g.,** barge rousse, *Fr.C:* barge de Laponie; **Hudsonian g.,** *Fr.C:* barge hudsonienne; **marbled g.,** *Fr.C:* barge marbrée; **black-tailed g.,** barge égocéphale, à queue noire.

goer ['gouər], *s.* (*a*) **comers and goers,** allants *m* et venants *m*; entrants *m* et sortants *m*; (*b*) (*of horse, vehicle, etc.*) **good g., bad g.,** bon, mauvais, marcheur; (*c*) **cinema g.,** habitué, -ée, du cinéma; (*d*) *F:* expert, -erte; calé, -ée; (*d*) *P:* **she's a g.,** c'est une chaude lapine; elle en veut.

gofer ['goufər], *s. Cu:* gaufre *f*.

goffer[1] ['gɔfər, 'goufər], *s.* **1.** *Cost:* godron *m*, tuyauté *m*, tuyautage *m*, tuyau *m*, plissé *m*. **2.** fer *m* à tuyauter, à gaufrer; canon *m* de repasseuse; godron *m*.

goffer[2], *v.tr.* (*a*) *Laund:* gaufrer à la paille; godronner, tuyauter; cisailler, plisser; (*b*) *Bookb: etc:* gaufrer (le papier, le cuir); (*c*) frapper (des papiers peints, etc.).

goffered ['gɔfəd, 'gou-], *a.* (*a*) *Laund:* gaufré, tuyauté, plissé; (*b*) *Bookb:* (papier, etc.) gaufré; (*c*) (*of wallpaper, etc.*) frappé.

gofferer ['gɔfərər, 'gou-], *s.* (*a*) *Laund: Bookb: etc:* gaufreur, -euse; (*b*) frappeur *m* (de papiers peints).

goffering ['gɔfəriŋ, 'gou-], *s.* **1.** (*a*) *Laund:* gaufrage *m* à la paille; tuyautage *m*; plissage *m*; **g. tongs, g. iron(s),** fer *m* à tuyauter, à gaufrer; canon *m* de repasseuse; godron *m*; (*b*) *Bookb:* gaufrage. **2.** *coll.* gaufrure *f*; tuyauté *m*, tuyautage *m*; plissés *mpl*.

go-getter ['gougetər], *s. F:* arriviste *mf*.

go-getting ['gougetiŋ], *s. F:* arrivisme *m*.

goggle[1] ['gɔgl]. **1.** *v.tr.* **to g. one's eyes,** rouler de gros yeux. **2.** *v.i.* (*a*) rouler de gros yeux; **to g. at s.o.,** regarder qn en roulant de gros yeux; (*b*) (*of the eyes*) être saillants; **the frog's large eyes were goggling out of its head,** les gros yeux de la grenouille lui sortaient de la tête.

goggle[2], *a. F:* (yeux) à fleur de tête, en boules de loto.

gogglebox ['gɔglbɔks], *s. F:* la télé.

goggle-eyed, ['gɔglaid], *a. F:* qui a des yeux à fleur de tête, en boules de loto.

goggles ['gɔglz], *s.pl.* **1.** *Ind: Aut: etc:* lunettes (protectrices); *Ind:* lunettes de travail; **welding g.,** lunettes de soudeur; **snow g.,** lunettes d'alpiniste. **2.** *Vet:* tournis *m*.

goglet ['gɔglit], *s. Cer:* gargoulette *f*, gargouillette *f*, alcarazas *m*.

Goidel ['gɔidl], *s. Ethn:* Gaël *mf*.

Goidelic [gɔi'delik]. **1.** *a. Ethn:* gaélique. **2.** *a. & s. Ling:* gaélique (*m*).

going[1] ['gouiŋ], *a.* **1.** qui marche; **g. concern,** affaire *f* qui marche; **the business is a g. concern,** la maison est en pleine activité. **2. the g. price,** le prix courant, actuel. **3.** (*in compounds*) **slow-g., fast-g.,** qui marche lentement, vite; **theatre-g.,** qui fréquente les théâtres.

going[2], *s.* **1.** (*a*) aller *m*; **comings and goings,** allées *f* et venues *f*; (*b*) marche *f* (de qn, d'une machine); **that's very good g.!** c'est bien marché! c'est une bonne allure! (*c*) *Typ:* **g. to press,** mise *f* sous presse; *Fin:* **g. to press prices,** dernières cotes; (*d*) **g. to law, to war,** recours *m* à la justice, à la guerre; (*e*) **theatre g.,** visites *fpl* au théâtre. **2.** départ *m*. **3.** état *m* du sol; **the g. is rough,** le chemin est rude; la route est mauvaise; *Rac:* **good, heavy, g.,** terrain bon, lourd; **to go, get out, while the going's good,** partir pendant que la voie est libre; battre le fer pendant qu'il est chaud; **the g. was poor,** nous n'avons pas fait beaucoup de progrès; **it's heavy g. getting him to talk,** on a du mal à le faire parler. **4.** (*compound nouns*) (*a*) *Nau:* **g. about,** virage *m* de bord; virement *m*; (*b*) *A: & Lit:* **the g. down of the sun,** le coucher du soleil; (*c*) **g. back,** (i) retour *m*; (ii) recul *m*; **g. back on one's word,** manque *m* de parole; (*d*) **g. out,** sortie(s) *f(pl)*; (*e*) *F:* **to give s.o. a g. over,** (i) fouiller qn; (ii) battre, rosser, qn; (*f*) *F:* **goings on,** manège *m*; **I can't stand such goings on,** je ne supporte pas de telles allures, de tels manèges; (*g*) *attrib.* **going-away dress,** robe *f* de voyage de noces.

goitre ['gɔitər], *s. Med:* goitre *m*.

goitred ['gɔitəd], *a. Med:* goitreux.

goitrous ['gɔitrəs], *a. Med:* goitreux; **a g. person,** un goitreux, une goitreuse.

go-kart ['goukaːt], *s.* kart *m*; **go-k. racing,** karting *m*.

Golconda [gɔl'kɔndə], *Pr.n. A.Geog:* Golconde *f*.

gold [gould], *s.* or *m*; (*a*) *Min:* **placer g.,** or alluvionnaire; **native, virgin, g.,** or natif, vierge; **vein g.,** or filonien; **g. in nuggets,** or brut; **g. quartz,** quartz *m* aurifère; **g. sand,** sable *m* aurifère; **g.-bearing vein,** filon *m* aurifère; **g. digger,** (i) chercheur *m* d'or; (ii) *F:* (*woman*) exploiteuse *f* d'hommes riches; croqueuse *f* de diamants; **g. digging,** exploitation *f* (i) de quartz aurifère, (ii) *F:* des richards (par les femmes); **g. diggings,** placer *m*; *F:* **fool's g.,** (i) pyrite *f* de fer; (ii) chalcopyrite *f*; *Hist:* **the g. rush,** la ruée vers l'or; (*b*) *Metall:* **fine g.,** or fin; **refined g.,** or affiné; **ingot g.,** or en barres; **scrap g.,** déchets *mpl*, débris *mpl*, d'or; **pure g.,** or pur; **g. alloy,** alliage *m* d'or; **g. content,** teneur *f* en or; **standard g.,** or au titre; **red g.,** or rouge; **white g.,** or blanc; **Dutch g.,** simili *m* or, or de Mannheim, oripeau *m*; **mat g.,** or mat; **mosaic g.,** or mussif; **platinized g.,** or platiné; **argental g.,** or argental, électrum *m*; **g.-copper alloy,** alliage d'or et de cuivre; **powdered g.,** or en poudre; **g. dust,** (i) poudre *f* d'or; (ii) *Bot: F:* alysse *m*, alysson *m*, saxatile; corbeille *f* d'or; (*c*) *Metalw: Jewel:* (*as opposed to gold-plated*) or massif; **g. plate,** vaisselle *f* d'or, or orfévré; **to eat off g. plate,** manger dans l'or; **g. plating,** dorage *m*, dorure *f*; **g. plater,** doreur *m*; **g.-plated, g.-filled, g.-cased,** doublé d'or; plaqué (d')or; **g. leaf, g. foil,** feuille *f* d'or; or battu, en feuille; **shell g.,** or de coquille; **g. size,** vernis *m* d'apprêt; mixtion *f*, mordant *m*; or (de) couleur; **g. washing,** orpaillage *m*; **g. washer,** (i) (*pers.*) pailleteur *m*, orpailleur *m*, laveur *m* d'or; (ii) (*appliance*) lavoir *m* d'or; **g.-washed,** doré au trempé; **wrought g.,** or ouvragé, travaillé; **g. brooch, g. necklace,** broche *f*, collier *m*, d'or, en or; **g. medal,** (*at Olympic Games, etc.*) *s.* **gold,** médaille d'or; **g. fillet,** filet *m* d'or; *Cost:* **g. lace,** galon *m* d'or; **laced with g., g.-laced,** galonné d'or; **g-faced, faced with g.,** à parements d'or, à revers de dorures; **g. lamé dress,** robe lamée d'or; **g.-rimmed spectacles,** lunettes *f* à monture d'or; *Hist:* **g. stick,** bâton doré (que porte le colonel du corps des cavaliers du souverain dans les cérémonies de la Cour); **the G. Stick,** l'officier *m* qui porte le bâton d'or; (*d*) *Geog: Hist:* **the G. Coast,** la Côte de l'Or; *Hist:* **the Field of the Cloth of G.,** le camp du Drap d'or; (*e*) *Dent:* **to fill, stop, a tooth with g.,** obturer une dent avec de l'or; aurifier une dent; **g. filling, stopping,** obturation *f* à l'or, en or; aurification *f* d'une dent, des dents; **g. crown,** couronne *f*, coiffe *f*, en or; (*f*) *Pharm:* **g. salt,** sel *m* d'or; *Med:* **g. therapy,** chrysothérapie *f*, aurothérapie *f*, thérapeutique *f* par les sels d'or; (*g*) *Fin:* **g. currency, money,** monnaie *f* d'or; pièces *fpl* d'or, en or; **g. coin,** pièce d'or; **g. specie,** or monnayé; **g. bullion,** or en barres, en lingots; **g. coin and bullion,** encaisse *f* or; **to pay s.o. in g.,** payer qn en or; **g. franc,** franc *m* or; **g. reserve,** réserve *f* d'or; **the bank's g. reserve,** le stock d'or de la banque; **the g. standard,** l'étalon *m* d'or, l'étalon-or *m*; **g. ratio,** rapport *m* de l'encaisse en or à la monnaie en circulation; **g. point,** gold-point *m*, point *m* d'or; **export, outgoing, g. point,** point de sortie de l'or, gold-point de sortie; **import, incoming, g. point,** point d'entrée de l'or, gold-point d'entrée; **to maintain the exchange above the g. point,** maintenir le change au-dessus du gold-point; *St.Exch:* **g. bond,** obligation *f* or; **g. shares,** *F:* **golds,** valeurs *f* aurifères; (*h*) *Phot:* **g. toning,** virage *m* à l'or; (*i*) *Sp:* (*archery*) centre *m* de la cible; (*j*) *a. & s.* (couleur *f* de l')or; **g. dress,** robe *f* couleur de l'or; **the reds and golds of autumn,** les rouges *m* et les ors de l'automne; **old g.,** vieil or *inv*; **old-g. curtains, drapes,** rideaux vieil or.

goldbeater ['gouldbiːtər], *s.* batteur, -euse, d'or; **goldbeater's skin,** baudruche *f*.

goldbeating ['gouldbiːtiŋ], *s.* battage *m* d'or.

goldbrick[1] ['gouldbrik], *s. NAm: P:* (*a*) attrape-nigaud, *pl.* attrape-nigauds; (*b*) paresseux, -euse, tire-au-flanc *m inv*.

goldbrick[2], *NAm: P:* (*a*) *v.tr.* duper, filouter (qn); (*b*) *v.i.* paresser, tirer au flanc.

goldbricker ['gouldbrikər], *s. NAm: P:* (*a*) paresseux, -euse, tire-au-flanc *m inv*; (*b*) cscroc *m*.

goldcrest ['gouldkrest], *s. Orn:* roitelet huppé.

golden ['gould(ə)n], *a.* (*a*) d'or; **the G. Fleece,** la Toison d'or; **to worship the g. calf,** adorer le veau d'or; (*b*) **g. hair,** cheveux *mpl* d'or, d'un blond doré; *Geog:* **the G. Horn,** la Corne d'Or; *A.Geog:* **the G. Chersonese,** la Chersonèse d'Or; *Orn:* **g. eagle,** aigle royal, doré; **g. pheasant,** faisan doré; **g.-crested, wren,** *U.S:* **kinglet,**

roitelet huppé; *Z:* **g. cat,** chat doré; *Ent: Dial:* **g. knop,** coccinelle *f*, bête *f* à bon Dieu; *Bot:* **g. rod,** solidage *m*, verge *f* d'or; **g. bell,** forsythia *m*; **g. rain,** cytise *f*; (*c*) **the g. age,** l'âge d'or; *U.S:* **g. ager,** personne âgée; **an illness common among g. agers,** une maladie propre au troisième âge; **g. rule,** règle *f* d'or; **g. opportunity,** occasion *f* magnifique; affaire *f* d'or; **the g. mean,** le juste milieu; Ecc: **g. number,** nombre *m* d'or; **the G. Bible,** le Livre de Mormon; (*d*) **g. wedding,** noces *fpl* d'or; (*e*) **g. smile,** sourire radieux, accueillant; *Mus:* **g. note,** son doux, harmonieux.

goldeneye ['gouldənai], *s.* **1.** *Orn:* **(common, American) g.,** garrot *m* à œil d'or, canard *m* garrot, *Fr.C:* garrot commun; **Barrow's g.,** garrot d'Islande, *Fr.C:* garrot de Barrow. **2.** *Ent:* (*also* **golden-eyed fly**) chrysope *f*, œil *m* d'or.

goldfield ['gouldfi:ld], *s.* champ *m*, district *m*, région *f*, aurifère.

goldfinch ['gouldfin(t)ʃ], *s. Orn:* chardonneret *m*; **American g., common g.,** tarin *m* d'Amérique, *Fr.C:* chardonneret jaune.

goldfish ['gouldfiʃ], *s. Ich:* poisson *m* rouge; dorade *f* (de la Chine); cyprin doré.

goldilocks ['gouldilɔks], *s. F:* **1.** *O:* jeune fille aux cheveux d'or. **2.** *Bot:* renoncule *f* tête d'or, *pl.* renoncules tête d'or.

goldmine ['gouldmain], *s.* mine *f* d'or; *F:* **a regular g.,** une vraie mine d'or; une affaire d'or.

gold-nibbed ['gould'nibd], *a.* (style *m*) avec plume en or.

gold-of-pleasure ['gouldəv'pleʒər], *s. Bot:* cameline *f*, caméline *f*.

goldsmith ['gouldsmiθ], *s.* **1.** orfèvre *m*; **goldsmith's work,** orfèvrerie *f*. **2.** *Ent:* **g. beetle,** cétoine dorée.

gold-tipped ['gould'tipt], *a.* à bout doré.

golf[1] [gɔlf], *s.* golf *m*; **clock g.,** jeu *m* de l'horloge; **miniature g.,** golf miniature; **g. ball,** balle *f* de golf; **g. club,** (i) crosse *f* de golf, club *m*; (ii) club de golf; **to join a g. club,** devenir membre d'un club de golf; **g. course, links,** terrain *m*, parcours *m*, de golf; un golf.

golf[2], *v.i.* jouer au golf; **I went golfing yesterday,** hier j'ai fait du golf.

golfer ['gɔlfər], *s.* golfeur, -euse; joueur, -euse, de golf.

Golgotha ['gɔlgəθə], *Pr.n. B.Hist:* Golgotha *m*.

Goliath [gə'laiəθ]. **1.** *Pr.n.m. B.Hist:* Goliath. **2.** *s.* (*a*) *Mec.E:* **g. crane,** grue *f* chevalet; (*b*) *Orn:* **g. heron,** héron Goliath; (*c*) *Ent:* **g. beetle,** goliath géant.

golliwog ['gɔliwɔg], *s.* poupée *f* grotesque en étoffe représentant un nègre.

gollop ['gɔləp], *v.tr. P:* avaler goulûment (sa nourriture, de la bière, etc.).

golly[1] ['gɔli], *int. F: O:* fichtre! mince (alors)!

gollywog ['gɔliwɔg], **golly**[2] *s.* = GOLLIWOG.

golosh [gə'lɔʃ], *s.* = GALOSH.

golp(e) [gɔlp], *s. Her:* gulpe *m*; tourteau *m* de pourpre.

Gomorrha(h) [gə'mɔrə], *Pr.n. A.Geog:* Gomorrhe *f*.

gomphosis [gɔm'fousis], *s. Anat:* gomphose *f*.

gonad ['gɔnæd, 'gou-], *s. Anat: etc:* gonade *f*.

gonadal ['gɔnədæl, 'gou-], *a. Anat: etc:* gonadique.

gonadotrop(h)ic ['gɔnədou'trɔfik, -'troufik; -'trɔpik, -'troupik; 'gou-], *a. Physiol:* gonadotrope.

gonadotrop(h)in ['gɔnədou'troufin, -pin], *s.* gonadostimuline *f*.

gondola ['gɔndələ], *s.* **1.** *Nau:* gondole *f*. **2.** (*a*) gondole, nacelle *f* (d'un ballon, etc.); (*b*) *NAm:* nacelle, cabine *f*, téléphérique. **3.** *NAm:* (*a*) bachot *m* (pour navigation fluviale); plate *f*; (*b*) *Rail:* **g. (car),** wagon plat, à hausscttes. **4.** *Com:* (*in supermarket, etc.*) gondole. **5.** *NAm: Furn:* **g. (chair),** fauteuil *m* en gondole.

gondolier [gɔndə'liər], *s.* gondolier *m*.

Gondwanaland [gɔn'dwɑ:nəlænd], *Pr.n. Geol:* le continent du Gondvana.

gone [gɔn], *a.* (*s.a.* GO[2], *v.*) (*a*) *F:* **he's a g. man, a g. guy,** c'en est fait de lui; il est fichu, foutu; (*b*) *F:* dans un état avancé (d'ivresse, etc.); (*c*) *P:* **g. on s.o.,** amoureux, épris, toqué, de qn; emballé sur qn.

goner ['gɔnər], *s. F:* (*a*) mort, morte; **I thought he was a g.,** je pensais qu'il allait mourir, crever; (*b*) type fini, fichu; **he's a g.,** il est fichu, foutu; c'en est fait de lui; (*c*) chose perdue, qui ne vaut plus rien.

gonfalon ['gɔnfælən], **gonfanon** ['gɔnfænɔn], *s. A:* gonfalon *m*, gonfanon *m*.

gonfalonier [gɔnfælə'niər], *s. A:* gonfalonier *m*, gonfanonier *m*.

gong[1] [gɔŋ], *s.* (*a*) gong *m*; **to sound the g. (for dinner),** faire retentir le gong; (*b*) timbre *m* (de pendule); **stroke on the g.,** coup *m* de timbre; (*c*) *Ind: Nau: etc:* **electric g.,** timbre électrique; **alarm g.,** timbre avertisseur; *Nau:* **the fire g.,** la cloche "feu"; (*d*) *F:* décoration *f*, médaille *f*, banane *f*; **he was wearing all his gongs,** il exhibait tous ses crachats.

gong[2], *v.tr. Aut: F: O:* **to be gonged,** se faire siffler (par la police).

Gongorism ['gɔŋgərizm], *s. Lit:* gongorisme *m*.

goniatite ['gouniətait], *s. Paleont:* goniatite *f*.

gonidial [gou'nidiəl], *a. Bot:* gonidial, -aux; **g. layer,** couche gonidiale.

gonidium, *pl.* **-ia** [gou'nidiəm, -iə], *s. Bot:* gonidie *f*.

goniocotes [gouniou'kouti:z], *s. Ent:* goniocote *m*, goniocotes *m*.

Goniodes [gouni'oudi:z], *s. Ent:* goniodes *m*.

goniometer [gouni'ɔmitər], *s.* **1.** goniomètre *m*; *Surv:* cercle *m* de visée; *Cryst:* **contact g.,** goniomètre d'application; **reflecting g.,** goniomètre à réflexion; **panoramic g.,** goniomètre panoramique; **periscopic g.,** *Mil:* **trench g.,** goniomètre périscopique. **2.** *W.Tel:* radiogoniomètre *m*.

goniometric(al) [gouniou'metrik(l)], *a.* goniométrique.

goniometry [gouni'ɔmitri], *s.* goniométrie *f*.

gonion ['gouniən], *s. Anat:* gonion *m*, gonium *m*.

goniopholis [gouni'ɔfəlis], *s. Paleont:* goniopholis *m*.

gonioscopy [gouni'ɔskəpi], *s. Med:* gonioscopie *f*.

goniosight ['gouniousait], *s. Artil: Av:* collimateur *m*.

gonk [gɔŋk], *s. F:* poupée *f* comique (en étoffe).

gono- [(ᵒ)gɔnou, (ᵒ)gɔnə], *comb.fm.* gono-.

gonochorism [gɔnou'kɔ:rizm], *s. Biol:* gonochrisme *m*, gonochorie *f*.

gonochorismal, gonochorismic [gɔnoukɔ'rizm(ə)l, -mik], *a. Biol:* gonochorique.

gonococcus, *pl.* **-cocci** [gɔnou'kɔkəs, -'kɔksai], *s. Bac: Med:* gonocoque *m*.

gonophore ['gɔnoufɔ:r], *s. Bot: Z:* gonophore *m*.

gonoplax ['gɔnəplæks], *s. Crust:* gonoplax *m*.

gonorrhoea [gɔnə'riə], *s.* gonorrhée *f*.

gonorrhoeal [gɔnə'riəl], *a.* gonorrhéique.

gonosome ['gɔnəsoum], *s. Nat.Hist:* gonosome *m*.

gonotome ['gɔnətoum], *s. Biol:* gonotome *m*.

gonozooid [gɔnou'zouoid], *s. Nat.Hist:* gonozoïde *m*.

gony ['gouni], *s. Orn:* albatros *m*.

gonys ['gounis], *s. Orn:* gonys *m*.

Gonzaga [gɔn'zɑ:gə], *Pr n. Hist:* Gonzague *m*.

goo [gu:], *s. F:* **1.** substance collante. **2.** sentimentalité excessive, à l'eau de rose.

goober ['gu:bər], *s. U.S: Dial:* cacahuète *f*.

good [gud], *a. & s.*

I. *a.* **(better, best)** bon. **1.** (*a*) **g. wine,** bon vin; vin de bonne qualité; **g. book,** bon livre; *O:* **the G. Book,** la (sainte) Bible; **g. handwriting,** belle écriture; **g. weather,** beau temps; **g. story,** bonne histoire; *F:* **that's a g. one!** en voilà une bonne! **g. to eat,** bon à manger; **to like what is g., to like g. things,** (i) aimer la bonne qualité; (ii) aimer les bons morceaux, les bonnes choses; **give me something g.,** donnez-moi quelque chose de bien, de bon; **this looks g.,** cela a l'air bon, bon air; (*of food*) cela a l'air appétissant; **that smells g.,** cela sent bon; **this is g. enough for me,** cela me suffit, me suffira; cela fera mon affaire; **this isn't g. enough,** (i) cela ne suffit pas; je n'accepte pas cela; (ii) ça, c'est un peu fort! (iii) cela n'est pas d'une assez bonne qualité, n'est pas assez solide, ne tiendra pas le coup; **to have a g. time,** s'amuser (bien); **I've had a g. life,** j'ai eu une vie agréable; j'ai bien rempli ma vie; *Pol: F:* **you've never had it so g.,** le pays n'a jamais été si prospère; **he's too g. for that job,** il mérite une meilleure situation; **a g. business man,** un excellent homme d'affaires; **a g. doctor,** un médecin de premier ordre; **in g. (plain) English,** en bon anglais; **to have g. sight,** avoir une bonne vue, de bons yeux; **g. feeling,** (i) bonne entente; (ii) sympathie *f*; **g. fellowship,** camaraderie *f*, confraternité *f*; **g. nature,** bon naturel; bonhomie *f*; bonté *f* de cœur; **he's very g.-natured,** il est d'un bon naturel; **g. living,** (i) bonnes mœurs; (ii) bonne chère; **g. neighbour,** bon voisin; **g. neighbourliness, g. neighbourship, g. neighbourhood,** rapports *mpl* de bon voisinage; (*b*) (*of food, etc.*) bon (à manger), en bon état; **is the meat still g.?** est-ce que la viande est encore bonne? **it won't be g. tomorrow if you don't put it in the fridge,** cela ne se conservera pas jusqu'à demain si vous ne le mettez pas au frigo; (*c*) **g. reason,** bonne raison, raison valable; **g. banknote,** bon billet de banque; **g. debt,** bonne créance; **g. receipt,** quittance *f* valable; (*for subscription, etc.*) **how much are you g. for?** je peux compter sur vous pour combien? **he, his credit, is g. for £25,000,** il peut payer jusqu'à £25,000, il est bon pour £25,000; **ticket g. for two months,** billet valable, bon, pour deux mois; **this car ought to be g. for another five years,** cette voiture devrait me faire encore cinq ans; *F:* **he's g. for another ten years,** il en a encore bien pour dix ans à vivre; **are you g. for a long walk?** (i) vous sentez-vous de force à faire un long trajet à pied? (ii) est-ce que cela vous dirait de faire une longue promenade (à pied)? (*d*) avantageux; **g. marriage,** mariage avantageux; **g. opportunity,** bonne occasion; **to live at a g. address,** habiter dans un quartier chic; **people of, in a, g. position,** des gens bien placés; **to be in a g. position to do sth.,** être bien placé pour faire qch.; **it is not always g. to . . .,** il n'est pas toujours bon de . . .; **I thought it would be a g. idea to do this,** il m'a semblé bon, avantageux, de le faire; *Rac: etc:* **a g. day,** un jour de veine; **to make a g. thing out of sth.,** tirer bon parti de qch.; **to earn g. money,** gagner largement sa vie; (*e*) heureux; **g. news,** bonnes, heureuses, nouvelles; **too g. to be believed, to be true,** trop beau pour y croire, pour être vrai; **g. for you! g. show!** *Austr:* **g. on you!** tant pour toi, pour vous! à la bonne heure! **(that's) g.! that's a g. thing!** bon! tant mieux! **very g.!** (i) très bien! parfait! (ii) très bien, je m'en occupe, m'en charge; **it's a g. thing that you can do it,** il est bien heureux que vous puissiez le faire; **it's g. to be alive!** il fait bon vivre! **it's g. to be home again,** cela fait plaisir de rentrer chez soi; (*f*) **g. morning! g. day! g. afternoon!** bonjour (monsieur, etc.)! **to say g. morning to s.o.,** dire bonjour à qn; **to wish s.o. a g. night,** souhaiter une bonne nuit à qn; (*g*) **this climate is not g. for the health,** ce climat est insalubre, contraire à la santé; **this medicine is very g. for a cough,** ce remède est très bon pour la toux; **it is g. for him to spend plenty of time out of doors,** il lui est salutaire de passer beaucoup de temps en plein air; **beer is not g. for me,** la bière ne me vaut rien; **to drink more than is g. for one,** boire plus que de raison, plus qu'on n'en peut supporter; (*h*) **to be g. with one's hands,** être adroit, habile, de ses mains; **g. for nothing, no g. for anything,** bon à rien; propre à rien; **to be g. at maths,** être bon, fort, en math; **he's g. at games,** c'est un sportif; **he was g. at nothing except tennis,** il ne brillait en rien sauf au tennis; **to be g. at dancing,** être bon danseur, bonne danseuse; **to be g. at carving,** savoir, être expert à, découper un rôti; **he's not g. enough to play first violin,** il n'est pas à même de faire une partie de premier violon; (*i*) *F:* **to feel g.,** se sentir en bonne forme, bien en train; **I don't feel too g.,** je ne suis pas dans mon assiette; **I don't feel too g. about it,** cela ne m'enchante pas, ne me dit rien, me donne de l'inquiétude; (*j*) *Bot: F:* **G. King Henry,** toute-bonne *f*. **2.** (*a*) **g. Christian,** bon chrétien, bonne chrétienne; **g. citizen,** bon citoyen, bonne citoyenne; **g. man,** homme *m* de bien; **to lead a g. life,** vivre en homme de bien; mener une vie exemplaire; **g. conduct, behaviour,** bonne conduite; **he proved to be a g. friend,** il s'est montré un véritable ami; **he's a g. husband (to her),** c'est un bon mari; *Lit: Jur:* **g. men and true,** hommes bons et braves; **the g. and the bad,** les bons et les méchants; *O: & Lit:* **the g. people,** les fées *f*; **my g. sir!** mon bon monsieur! *O:* (*with patronizing tone*) **my g. man!** mon brave! **g. old John!** bravo Jean! *esp. Lit:* **the g. ship Arethusa,** l'Aréthuse; (*b*) (*of child*) sage; **be g.!** sois sage! **as g. as gold, as g. as g.,** sage comme une image, sage au possible; (*c*) *O:* **her g. man, his g. lady,** son mari, sa femme; (*d*) aimable; **that's very g. of you,** c'est bien aimable, gentil, bon, de votre part; **it's very g. of you to invite me,** vous êtes bien aimable, gentil, de m'inviter; **would you be g. enough to . . .?** auriez-vous l'amabilité, la gentillesse, de . . .? **will you be g. enough to do it immediately!** je vous prie de bien vouloir le faire tout de suite; **to be g. to animals,** être bon pour les animaux; **he has always been g. to me,** il s'est toujours montré bon pour moi; **he's a g. sort,** *O:* **a g. chap,** c'est un bon garçon, un bon type; il est bien gentil; **she's a g. sort,** elle est bien gentille, bien aimable; (*e*) **g. Lord, deliver us!** Seigneur, délivrez-nous! *F:* **g. Lord! g. heavens! g. gracious!** grand Dieu! par exemple! ciel! ça alors! **g. grief!** fichtre alors! **3.** (*a*) **a g. half,** une bonne moitié; **a g. two hours,** deux bonnes heures; **it will take me a g. hour,** je n'aurai pas trop d'une heure pour le faire; **a g. while, a g. time,** pas mal de temps; **you still have a g. way to go,** vous avez encore un bon bout de chemin à faire; **a g. ten kilometres,** dix bons kilomètres; **a g. round sum,** une somme rondelette; **a g. twenty years ago,** il y a bien vingt ans, vingt ans bien comptés; **a g. deal, a g. many,** beaucoup; **a g. few,** pas mal; **I've a g. many books,** j'ai beaucoup, pas mal, de livres; **after a g. cry,** après avoir bien pleuré; après une crise de larmes; **take g. care not to fall,** prenez bien soin de ne pas tomber; **to come in a g. third,** arriver bon troisième; (*b*) *adv. F:* **to tell s.o. off g. and proper,** dire à qn son fait; **they beat us g. and proper,** ils nous ont battus à plates coutures; **he was g. and mad,** il était furieux; **he was g. and sorry,** il le regrettait amèrement. **4.** (*a*) *F: O:* **we had as g. stay here,** autant vaut rester ici; (*b*) **my family is as g. as his,** ma famille vaut bien la sienne; **his example is as g. as a sermon,** il prêche d'exemple; **it's as g. a way as any other,** c'est une façon qui en vaut une autre; **drink water, it's just as g.,** buvez de l'eau, cela vous fera autant de bien; **to expect as g. as one gives,** s'attendre à la pareille; **to give s.o. as g. as one gets,** rendre à qn la monnaie de sa pièce; rendre la pareille à qn; rendre coup pour coup; **it's as g. as new,** c'est pour ainsi dire neuf; c'est comme neuf, quasi neuf; **to make sth. as g. as new,** remettre qch. à neuf; **it's as g. as done, settled,** c'est une affaire faite ou autant vaut; *F:* l'affaire est dans le sac; **the battle was as g. as lost,** la bataille était autant dire perdue; **he is as g. as dead,** c'est tout comme s'il était mort; il est mort ou peu s'en faut; **as g. as cured,** quasiment guéri; **it is as g. as saying that . . .,** autant vaut dire que . . .; **it's as g. as a play,** c'est une vraie comédie; c'est à payer sa place! *F:* **he's as g. as got the job,** s'il n'est pas encore nommé, c'est tout comme. **5. to make g.,** (i) se rattraper de (ses pertes, etc.); remédier à (l'usure); réparer (une injustice, des dégâts); pourvoir à, combler (un déficit); combler (une perte; *Mil:* les vides dans les rangs); (ii) justifier (une affirmation); remplir, dégager (sa promesse); (iii) accomplir, opérer, effectuer (sa retraite, etc.); (iv) assurer (sa position); faire prévaloir (ses droits); prouver, établir (le bien fondé de sa réclamation); (v) (*of pers.*) prospérer, faire son chemin; (vi) se refaire une vie; racheter son passé; **to make g. one's escape,** parvenir à s'échapper, à s'évader.

II. *s.* **1.** bien *m*; (*a*) **to return g. for evil,** rendre le bien pour le mal; **to do g.,** faire du, le, bien; **he will never do any more g.,** il ne fera plus jamais rien de bon; **that will do more harm than g.,** cela fera plus de mal que de bien; **it will do neither g. nor harm,** cela n'y fera ni chaud ni froid; **to become a power for g.** exercer une influence salutaire; **he's up to no g.,** il prépare quelque mauvais coup; il machine quelque chose; **there's some g. in him,** il a du bon; **for g. or ill we have . . .,** que ce soit un bien ou un mal, nous avons . . .; **to extract all the g. out of sth.,** tirer tout le suc de qch.; (*b*) **I did it for your g.,** je l'ai fait pour votre bien; **for the g. of one's health,** en vue de sa santé; **for the g. of the house,** pour le plus grand bien de la maison; **to act for the common g.,** agir dans l'intérêt commun; **to work for the common g.,** travailler pour le bien public; **it will do you g. to spend a week in the country,** cela vous fera du bien de passer une semaine à la campagne; **much g. may it do you!** grand bien vous fasse! **much g. that will do you!** la belle avance! **what g. will that do you? what g. will it be to you?** à quoi cela vous avancera t-il? *F:* **a (fat) lot of g. that will do you!** c'est ça qui vous fera une belle jambe! la belle avance! **a lot of g. that's done you!** vous voilà bien avancé! **that won't be much g.,** ça ne servira pas à grand-chose; **what's the g. of that?** en quoi cela vous avancera-t-il? à quoi bon (faire) cela? **it's not a bit of g.,** ça n'avance (à) rien; **it's not a bit of g. your apologizing,** des excuses de votre part n'y feront rien; **it's no g.,** (i) cela ne donne aucun résultat; (ii) ce sont des efforts perdus; **it is no g. saying . . .,** rien ne sert de dire . . .; **it was no g. being insistent,** il était inutile d'insister; **no g. talking about it,** inutile d'en parler; vous ferez mieux de n'en rien dire; **that's no g.,** (i) cela est inutile, ne sert à rien; (ii) cela ne vaut rien; **it's no g. their saying they are sorry,** cela ne les avance pas de faire des excuses; **he will come to no g.,** il ne fera jamais rien de bon; il tournera mal; **he's no g.,** il est nul; il n'a rien dans le ventre; c'est une non-valeur; (*c*) **to be five pounds to the g.,** avoir cinq livres de gagné, de profit; **it is all to the g.,** c'est autant de gagné; tant mieux; **that's so much to the g.,** c'est autant de gagné sur l'ennemi, de pris sur l'ennemi; (*d*) *adv.phr.* **for g.: he is gone for g. (and all),** il est parti définitivement, pour (tout) de bon, pour ne jamais revenir, à tout jamais; **to settle down for g.,** se fixer définitivement; **I'm here for g.,** je suis ici à demeure; **for g. and all,** une bonne fois pour toutes. **2.** *pl.* **goods;** (*a*) *Jur:* biens, effets *m*, meubles *m*; (*b*) *Com: Pol.Ec:* (*comme singulier on emploie le mot* COMMODITY) marchandises *f*; denrées *f*; objets *m*, articles *m*; **capital goods,** biens d'équipement; biens capitaux; **manufactured goods,** produits fabriqués; **canned, tinned, goods,** conserves *f* en boîte; **leather goods,** articles en cuir; maroquinerie *f*; **knit(ted) goods,** bonneterie *f*; **consumer goods,** biens de consommation; **perishable goods,** denrées périssables; **saleable, unsaleable, goods,** marchandises vendables, invendables; *esp. U.S:* **soft goods,** articles de nouveauté; **hard goods,** biens d'équipement; **wet goods,** liquides *m*; **damaged goods,** marchandise avariée; **stolen goods,** objets volés; **to deliver the goods,** (i) livrer la marchandise, les marchandises; (ii) *F:* remplir ses engagements; tenir parole; *F:* **to catch s.o. with the goods,** prendre qn la main dans le sac; *F:* **to have the goods,** être capable, avoir de ça, de quoi; *P:* **to have the goods on s.o.,** tenir le bon bout contre qn; *F:* **it's, that's, the goods!** ça tombe pile! (*c*) *Rail:* **goods train,** train *m* de marchandises; **goods station, depot,** gare *f*, dépôt *m*, de marchandises; **to send sth. by goods train, service,** *F:* **by goods,** expédier qch. par train de marchandises; (*d*) *P:* **a nice bit of goods,** un beau morceau, brin, de fille; une jolie poupée.

goodbye [gud'bai], *int. & s.* au revoir; (*with finality or Dial: as int.*) adieu (*m*); **g. for the moment, for now!** à bientôt! **to say g. to s.o.,** dire au revoir à qn; faire ses adieux à qn; **I must say g. now,** il faut que je vous dise au revoir, que je vous quitte, maintenant; **when all the goodbyes had been said,** après tous les adieux; *F:* **I can say g. to the Legion of Honour,** je peux faire mon deuil de la Légion d'Honneur.

good-for-nothing ['gudfənʌθiŋ]. **1.** *a.* (*of pers.*) qui n'est bon à rien; (*of thg*) sans valeur. **2.** *s.* (*a*) propre *mf* à rien; bon *m* à rien, bonne à rien; (*b*) vaurien, -ienne.

good-hearted [gud'hɑːtid], *a.* (personne) qui a bon cœur; compatissant; bon, bonne.

good-heartedness [gud'hɑːtidnis], *s.* bonté *f* de cœur.

good-humoured [gud'hjuːməd], *a.* (personne) d'un caractère facile; (sourire, etc.) de bonne humeur, plein de bonhomie; (air *m*) bon enfant *inv*; (plaisanterie, etc.) sans malice; **he is always g.-h.,** il a bon caractère, il est facile à vivre.

good-humouredly [gud'hjuːmədli], *adv.* avec bonhomie; **to laugh g.-h.,** rire avec bonne humeur; **to grumble at s.o. g.-h.,** bougonner après qn d'un ton pas méchant.

goodies ['gudiz], *s.pl. F:* bonbons *m*, sucreries *f*; gâteries *f*.

goodish ['gudiʃ], *a.* **1.** assez bon, passable. **2.** assez grand (nombre, etc.); **it's a g. step from here,** c'est à un bon bout de chemin d'ici.

goodliness ['gudlinis], *s. A:* beauté *f*; belle apparence (de qn).

good-looker [gud'lukər], *s.* **1.** *F:* bel homme, belle femme. **2.** cheval *m* de belle allure.

good-looking [gud'lukiŋ], *a.* beau, *f.* belle; **he's very g.-l.,** il est beau garçon; **she's quite g.-l.,** elle n'est pas mal.

goodly ['gudli], *a.* **1.** *A: & Lit:* d'une belle apparence; de belle taille; beau, *f.* belle. **2.** large, ample (portion, etc.); *O:* **g. heritage,** bel héritage; **g. number,** nombre *m* considérable.

goodman, *pl.* **-men** ['gudmæn, -men], *s.m.* **1.** *A: & Lit:* maître (de la maison). **2.** *Scot: O:* **the g.,** mon mari.

good-natured [gud'neitjəd], *a.* (*of pers.*) au bon naturel, accommodant, de bon caractère; **g.-n. smile,** bon sourire, sourire bon enfant; **g.-n. laugh,** rire jovial; **to look g.-n.,** avoir l'air bon; **how g.-n. they are!** comme ils ont bon caractère!

good-naturedly [gud'neitjədli], *adv.* aimablement; avec bonhomie.

goodness ['gudnis], *s.* **1.** (*a*) bonté *f* (de cœur, etc.); (*b*) bonne qualité (d'un article, etc.). **2. to extract all the g. out of sth.,** extraire de qch. tout ce qu'il y a de bon; **don't boil all the g. out of the meat,** ne faites pas bouillir la viande au point d'en retirer tout le suc, tout ce qu'elle contient de fortifiant. **3. g. gracious!** bonté divine! miséricorde! **my g.!** mon Dieu! **thank g.!** Dieu merci! **for goodness' sake, stop!** taisez-vous, pour l'amour de Dieu! **I wish to g. you had told me that before!** si seulement vous me l'aviez dit plus tôt! **g. (only) knows what I must do,** Dieu seul sait ce que je dois faire.

goodnight [gud'nait]. **1.** *int.* (*a*) bonsoir! (*b*) bonne nuit! **2.** *s.* **after they had said their goodnights,** après s'être dit bonsoir.

good-oh ['gudou], *int. esp. Austr: F:* parfait! épatant! chic alors!

good-tempered [gud'tempəd], *a.* de caractère facile, égal; facile à vivre; placide; qui a bon caractère; **he's always g.-t.,** il a bon caractère.

good-temperedly [gud'tempədli], *adv.* aimablement; sans se fâcher.

good-time [gud'taim], *a. P:* **g.-t. girl,** fille rigolote; **g.-t. Charley,** viveur *m*.

goodwife, *pl.* **-wives** ['gudwaif, -waivz], *s.f. A: & Scot:* **1.** maîtresse (de la maison). **2. the g.,** ma femme.

goodwill ['gud'wil], *s.* **1.** bonne volonté; bienveillance *f*; bon vouloir (**towards,** pour, envers); **to gain s.o.'s g.,** se faire bien voir de qn; **to retain s.o.'s g.,** conserver les bonnes grâces de qn. **2.** bon cœur; **to set to work with g.,** se mettre à l'œuvre de bon cœur. **3.** *Com:* clientèle *f*; achalandage *m*; pas *m* de porte; **to give up the g.,** céder le pas de porte; **the g. is to be sold with the business,** l'achalandage se vend avec l'établissement; *Publ:* **books belonging to the publisher's g.,** livres *m* de fonds.

goody[1] ['gudi], *s.f. A:* commère, bonne femme; **G. So-and-so,** la mère une telle.

goody[2], *int. F: O:* tant mieux! chouette!

goody(-goody) ['gudi(gudi)], *a. & s. F:* (*a*) *Pej:* (personne *f*) d'une piété affectée; **she's awfully g.-g.,** elle fait la prude, la sainte nitouche; **he's just a g.-g.,** c'est un petit saint de bois; (*b*) **the goodies and the baddies,** les bons types et les vauriens.

gooey ['guːi], *a. F:* **1.** gluant, collant. **2.** (sentimentalité) à l'eau de rose.

goof[1] [guːf], *s.* **1.** (*a*) *F:* idiot, -ote; sot, sotte; timbré *m*; (*b*) *NAm: P:* drogué *m*, toxico *m*. **2.** *NAm: F:* gaffe *f*, bévue *f*.

goof[2], *v.i. esp. NAm:* **1.** *F:* gaffer, faire une gaffe. **2.** *F:* **to g. (off),** paresser; être dans les nuages; traînasser, flemmarder. **3.** *P:* se droguer, se camer; **goofed up,** sous l'influence d'un narcotique, d'un barbiturique; bourré, chargé.

goofball ['guːfbɔːl], *s. NAm: P:* **1.** drôle *m* de type, d'oiseau. **2.** barbiturique *m*; dose *f* de narcotique.

goofy ['guːfi], *a. F:* loufoque.

googly[1] ['guːgli], *s. Cr:* balle *f* qui a de l'effet à droite du batteur.

googly[2], *a.* **1.** (yeux) en boules de loto. **2.** = GOO-GOO.

googol ['guːgɔl], *s. Mth:* googol *m* (10^{100}).

goo-goo ['guːguː], *a. F:* **to make g.-g. eyes at s.o.,** faire les yeux doux à qn.

goon [guːn], *s. P:* **1.** crétin *m*. **2.** *esp. NAm:* gorille *m*, cogneur *m*, casseur *m* de gueules.

goony ['guːni], *s. Orn:* albatros *m*.

goop[1] [guːp], *s. P:* **1.** = GOOF. **2.** rustre *m*.

goop[2], *s. U.S:* = GOO 1.

goopy ['guːpi], *a. P:* renchéri, fat; *O:* **to feel g. about a girl,** être entiché d'une petite.

goora ['guːrə], *s.* **g. nut,** noix *f* de kola.

gooral ['guːrəl], *s. Z:* = GORAL.

goosander [guː'sændər], *s. Orn:* harle bièvre, grand harle.

goose, *pl.* **geese** [guːs, giːs], *s.* **1.** *Orn:* (*a*) (*female of species*) oie *f*; (*b*) (*generic*) oie; **wild g.,** oie sauvage; **greylag g.,** oie cendrée; **Egyptian g.,** oie d'Égypte; **Cape Barren g.,** oie *f* céréopse; **kelp g.,** oie hybride; **knob-billed g., nutka g.,** oie caronculée, oie à crête; **maned g.,** oie à crinière; **pigmy g.,** sarcelle *f* à oreillons, sarcelle de Coromandel; **spurwing g.,** oie de Gambie; **upland g.,** oie de Magellan; **brent g.,** bernache *f* cravant; **Canada g.,** bernache *f* du Canada, *Fr.C:* bernache canadienne; **barnacle g.,** bernache nonnette; **blue g.,** oie bleue; **emperor g.,** oie empereur; **Ross's g.,** oie de Ross; **snow g.,** oie des neiges, *Fr.C:* oie blanche; **bean g.,** oie des moissons; **Sushkin's g.,** oie des moissons de Russie; **bar-headed g.,** oie barrée; **lesser white-fronted g.,** oie naine; **white-fronted g.,** oie rieuse, oie à front blanc; **pink-footed g.,** oie à bec court; **red-breasted g.,** bernache à cou roux; **flock of geese,** troupeau *m* d'oies; *A:* **g. girl,** gardeuse *f* d'oies; **g. egg,** (i) œuf *m* d'oie; (ii) *Sp: U.S:* zéro *m*; **g. fat, grease,** graisse *f* d'oie; *Cu:* **green g.,** oison *m* (de moins de quatre mois); *Fig:* **all his geese are swans,** tous ses enfants sont des prodiges; tout ce qu'il fait tient du prodige; il n'y a de beau que ce qui lui appartient; *F: O:* **to beat the g.,** se brasser; battre des bras (pour se réchauffer); (*c*) (i) *Z:* **sea g.,** oie-de-mer *f*, *pl.* oies-de-mer, dauphin *m*; (ii) *Moll:* **g. barnacle, g. mussel,** anatife *m*, lépas *m*, bernache *f*, bernacle *f*; (*d*) *Bot:* **g. grass,** (i) grateron *m*, gaillet accrochant; (ii) potentille *f* ansérine; argentine *f*; (*e*) *A:* **the game of g.,** le jeu de l'oie; (*f*) *F:* (*pers.*) niais, *f.* niaise; bébête *f*; *O:* **I'm not such a g.,** je ne suis pas si bête que ça. **2.** *Mus: F:* **g. (note),** couac *m* (sur la clarinette, etc.). **3.** *Tail:* (*pl.* **gooses**) carreau *m* (à repasser).

gooseberry ['guzb(ə)ri], *s.* **1.** groseille *f* à maquereau, groseille verte; **g. (bush),** groseillier *m* (à maquereau); *Cu:* **g. fool,** crème *f* de groseilles (à maquereau); purée *f* de groseilles à la crème; **g. wine,** vin *m* de groseilles vertes; *F:* **to play g.,** (i) faire le chaperon; (ii) se trouver en tiers (avec deux amoureux); *P: A:* **to play old g.,** faire les cent coups; *Journ: A:* **the big g. season,** la morte-saison (où les journaux en sont réduits à publier des canards). **2.** *Bot:* **Cape g.,** coqueret *m* du Pérou; **Coromandel g.,** carambolier *m*; **Barbados g.,** groseillier d'Amérique; **Chinese g.,** souris végétale.

gooseflesh ['guːsfleʃ], *s.* **1.** chair *f* d'oie. **2.** *F:* chair de poule; *Med:* peau ansérine.

goosefoot ['guːsfut], *s.* **1.** *Bot:* (*pl.* **goosefoots**) chénopode *m*; ansérine *f*; patte-d'oie *f*, *pl.* pattes-d'oie; **stinking g.,** vulvaire *f*; arroche puante. **2.** (*a*) *Mec.E: Aer: etc:* (*pl.* **goosefeet**) patte-d'oie; (*b*) (*diverging roads*) patte-d'oie.

goosegog ['guzgɔg], *s. F:* = GOOSEBERRY 1.

gooseherd ['guːs(h)əːd], *s.* gardeur, -euse, d'oies.

gooseneck ['guːsnek], *s.* **1.** *Tls:* col *m* de cygne; bec *m* de cygne; bec d'oie; **g. lamp,** lampe *f* à monture flexible. **2.** *Metall:* coude *m* porte-vent. **3.** *Nau:* vit *m* de mulet; col, cou *m*, de cygne; aiguillot *m* de gui, ferrure *f* (de

bout de gui); **g. band,** cercle *m* de vit de mulet.
goosenecked ['gu:snekt], *a. Mec.E: etc:* (applique *f*, etc.) en col de cygne, en col d'oie.
gooseskin ['gu:sskin], *s.* = GOOSEFLESH 2.
goosestep ['gu:sstep], *s. Mil:* pas *m* de l'oie.
goosewing ['gu:swiŋ], *s. Nau:* voile *f* en ciseaux; fanon *m* (de voile).
goos(e)y ['gu:si], *a. F:* **to go g.,** avoir la chair de poule.
gopher[1] ['goufər], *s.* **1.** *Z:* **(pocket) g.,** géomyidé *m*; thomomys *m*; saccophore *m*. **2.** *Z:* spermophile *m*. **3. g. (snake),** serpent noir des États-Unis. **4.** *Min:* **g. (drift),** galerie irrégulière. **5.** *F:* habitant, -ante, du Minnesota.
gopher[2], *v.i.* **1.** creuser une galerie souterraine. **2.** *Min:* exploiter une mine, un filon, sans méthode.
gopher[3,4], *s. & v.tr.* = GOFFER[1,2].
gopher[5], *s. B:* **g. wood,** bois *m* de gopher.
goral ['gourəl, go'rɑ:l], *s. Z:* goral *m*.
gorblim(e)y [gɔ:'blaimi], *int. P:* bon Dieu!
Gordiacea [gɔ:di'eisiə], *s.pl. Ann:* gordiacés *m*, gordiens *m*.
Gordian ['gɔ:diən], *a. A.Hist:* gordien; **to cut the G. knot,** trancher le nœud gordien.
gordonite ['gɔ:dənait], *s. Miner:* gordonite *f*.
gore[1] [gɔ:r], *s.* **1.** (*a*) *Tail: Dressm:* chanteau *m*, élargissure *f*; (*b*) *Dressm:* (i) soufflet *m*, (ii) godet *m*; (iii) lé *m* (d'une jupe, etc.); (*c*) *Nau:* pointe *f*, langue *f* (de voile); **small g.,** chiquet *m*. **2.** *Arch:* pan *m* (d'un dôme). **3.** langue de terre; enclave *f*. **4.** (*a*) *N.Arch:* grain-d'orge *m*, *pl.* grains-d'orge; (*b*) *Mapm: Aer:* fuseau *m* (d'un globe terrestre, d'un ballon, d'un parachute).
gore[2], *v.tr.* **1.** tailler (un tissu) en pointe; *Nau:* **goring cloth,** laize *f* de pointe (de voile). **2.** *Dressm:* (i) faire, mettre, des soufflets à (une robe, etc.); (ii) faire goder (une robe, etc.); (iii) mettre des lés à (une jupe, etc.); **gored skirt,** jupe à lés, à godets; **four-gored skirt,** jupe à quatre lés.
gore[3], *s. Lit:* **1.** sang coagulé. **2.** sang versé; **he lay in his g.,** il baignait dans son sang.
gore[4], *v.tr.* (*of horned animal*) blesser (qn) avec les cornes, encorner (qn); découdre (qn); **the bull gored him in the stomach,** le taureau lui a décousu le ventre; **gored to death,** tué d'un coup de corne.
gorge[1] [gɔ:dʒ], *s.* **1.** *A: & Lit:* (*a*) gorge *f*, gosier *m*; (*b*) (*what has been swallowed*) **it makes my g. rise,** cela me soulève le cœur; j'en ai des nausées, des haut-le-cœur; *A:* **to cast (up) the g.,** vomir de dégoût. **2.** *Geog:* gorge, défilé *m*. **3.** *Fort:* gorge (d'un bastion, etc.). **4.** *Mec.E:* gorge (de poulie). **5.** *Arch:* gorge, gorgerin *m* (d'une moulure).
gorge[2], *s. F: O:* repas plantureux; gueuleton *m*, ripaille *f*, empiffrerie *f*.
gorge[3]. **1.** *v.i.* **to g. (oneself),** se gorger, se repaître **(on,** de); se rassasier; s'assouvir; *F:* se gaver de nourriture; s'empiffrer **(on,** de); manger à ventre déboutonné, s'en fourrer jusque-là. **2.** *v.tr.* (*a*) assouvir, gorger, rassasier (qn); (*b*) avaler, engloutir (sa nourriture); (*c*) engaver, gaver (une oie, etc.).
gorged [gɔ:dʒd], *a.* **1.** rassasié, repu, gorgé, gavé **(with,** de). **2.** *Med:* (rein, etc.) engorgé.
gorgeous ['gɔ:ddʒəs], *a.* (*a*) magnifique, fastueux, splendide; **he was a g. figure in his new uniform,** il était tout flambant dans son uniforme neuf; **a g. sunset,** un coucher de soleil splendide; (*b*) *F:* épatant, superbe; **a g. meal,** un repas somptueux; (to girl) **hello g.!** bonjour ma belle!
gorgeously ['gojqdʒəsli], *adv.* magnifiquement, splendidement; somptueusement.
gorgeousness ['gɔ:dʒəsnis], *s.* somptuosité *f*, splendeur *f* magnificence *f*, faste *m*.
gorgerin ['gɔ:dʒərin], *s. Arm: Arch:* gorgerin *m*.
gorget[1] ['gɔ:dʒit], *s.* **1.** *Arm:* gorgerin *m*. **2.** *Cost: A:* gorgerette *f*. **3.** *Mil: A:* hausse-col *m*, *pl.* hausse-col(s).
gorget[2], *s. Surg:* gorgeret *m* (pour la taille).
gorging ['gɔ:dʒiŋ], *s.* **1.** rassasiement *m*. **2.** *F:* bâfrerie *f*; empiffrerie *f*; gavage *m*.
gorgon ['gɔ:gən], *s. Gr.Myth:* gorgone *f*.
Gorgonacea [gɔ:gə'neisiə], *s.pl. Coel:* gorgonaires *m*.
gorgonia, *pl.* **-iae, -ias** [gɔ:'gouniə, -ii:, -iəz], *s. Z:* gorgonie *f*.
gorgonian [gɔ:'gouniən], *a.* de gorgone.
Gorgoniidae [gɔ:gə'naiidi], *s.pl. Coel:* gorgonidés *m*.
gorgonize ['gɔ:gənaiz], *v.tr.* (*a*) pétrifier (qn); glacer (qn) d'effroi; (*b*) méduser (qn) du regard.
gorilla [gə'rilə], *s. Z:* gorille *m*.
goring ['gɔ:riŋ], *s.* (*in bullfighting*) cornade *f*.
gormandism ['gɔ:məndizm], *s.* gloutonnerie *f*.
gormandize[1] ['gɔ:məndaiz], *s.* goinfrerie *f*, gloutonnerie *f*.
gormandize[2]. **1.** *v.tr.* bâfrer, manger goulûment. **2.** *v.i.* goinfrer; *P:* s'empiffrer.
gormandizer ['gɔ:məndaizər], *s.* glouton, -onne, goulu, -ue; *F:* bâfreur, -euse; goinfre *m*.
gormandizing ['gɔ:məndaiziŋ], *s.* goinfrerie *f*.
gormless ['gɔ:mlis], *a. F:* mollasse, bouché; **he's g.,** c'est une nouille.
gorse [gɔ:s], *s.* (*a*) *Bot:* ajonc(s) *m*(*pl*); vignon *m*, ulex *m*; *F:* landier *m*; **(needle) g.,** genêt épineux; (*b*) *Ent:* **g. weevil,** apion *m*.
gorsy ['gɔ:si], *a.* **1.** (plateau, etc.) couvert d'ajoncs. **2.** (odeur, etc.) d'ajonc.
gory ['gɔ:ri], *a.* sanglant, ensanglanté.
gosh [gɔʃ], *int. F:* sapristi! mince (alors)!
goshawk ['gɔshɔ:k], *s. Orn:* autour *m* (des palombes); **chanting g.,** melierax *m*, faucon chanteur.
Goshen ['gouʃ(ə)n], *Pr.n. B.Hist:* Gos(c)en *m*, Gessen *m*.
goslarite ['gɔslərait], *s. Miner:* goslarite *f*.
gosling ['gɔzliŋ], *s.* oison *m*; **g. green,** (couleur *f*) caca *m* d'oie (*inv.*).
go-slow ['gou'slou], *a. & s.* flânerie *f* systématique; **go-s. (strike),** grève perlée; travail *m* au ralenti; **go-s. policy,** politique *f* d'attente.
gospel ['gɔsp(ə)l], *s.* évangile *m*; (*a*) **St Mark's G., the G. according to St Mark,** l'Évangile selon saint Marc; **g. oath,** serment prêté sur l'évangile; *F:* **to take sth. for g.,** accepter qch. comme parole d'évangile, pour argent comptant; **it's g. truth,** c'est (vrai comme) parole d'évangile; **he takes it all for g.,** il croit que c'est arrivé; (*b*) *Ecc:* **the g. for the day,** l'évangile du jour; *Ecc.Arch:* **the g. side (of the altar),** le côté de l'évangile (à l'autel); (*c*) **to preach the g.,** prêcher l'évangile; **Ministry of the G.,** ministère *m* de la prédication, de la parole; **Minister of the G.,** ministre *m* de l'évangile; **to preach the g. of economy,** prêcher l'économie.
gospeller ['gɔspələr], *s.* **1.** *A:* protestant, -ante, puritain, -aine; *F:* **hot g.,** protestant outré, à tous crins. **2.** *Ecc:* officiant *m* qui lit l'Évangile. **3.** évangélisateur *m*.
gossamer ['gɔsəmər]. **1.** *s.* (*a*) fils *mpl* de la Vierge; filandres *fpl*; **g. thread,** freluche *f*, filandre *f*; (*b*) *Tex:* gaze légère; (*c*) *NAm:* imperméable léger. **2.** *a.* (*a*) (tissu) très léger, arachnéen; (*b*) *F: A:* (discours *m*) frivole.
gossan ['gɔsæn, 'gɔzn], *s. Geol:* chapeau *m* de fer; chapeau ferrugineux (d'une couche métallifère).
gossip[1] ['gɔsip], *s.* **1.** (*pers.*) (*a*) *A:* commère *f*, marraine *f* (à un baptême); (*b*) *A:* ami, -ie; compère *m*, commère *f*; (*c*) causeur, -euse; caqueteur, -euse; bavard, -arde; (*d*) (*ill-natured*) commère; potinier, -ière; cancanier, -ière; clabaudeur, -euse. **2.** (*a*) causerie *f*, caquet(age) *m*; bavardage *m*; commérage(s) *m* (*pl.*); **endless g.,** des jacasseries *f* sans fin; *Journ:* **g. (column),** chronique mondaine; échos *mpl*; **g. writer,** échotier *m*; *F:* **they settled down to a good old g.,** et puis c'était un bon bavardage, des racontars sans fin; (*b*) (*ill-natured*) cancans *mpl*; potins *mpl*, ragots *mpl*.
gossip[2], *v.i.* (*a*) bavarder, caqueter, papoter; (*b*) (*ill-naturedly*) cancaner, potiner, commérer; **to g. about s.o.,** faire des cancans, des commérages, sur qn; ragoter sur le compte de qn.
gossiper ['gɔsipər], *s.* = GOSSIP[1] 1 (*c*), (*d*).
gossiping[1] ['gɔsipiŋ], *a.* (*a*) bavard, causeur, caqueteur, papoteur; (*b*) = GOSSIPY.
gossiping[2], *s.* (*a*) bavardage *m*, caquetage *m*, papotage *m*; (*b*) potinage *m*, commérage *m*, racontage *m*.
gossipy ['gɔsipi], *a.* (style) anecdotique; (article) familier; **g. letter,** lettre pleine de racontars; **g. old woman,** vieille bavarde, caqueteuse.
gossypium [gɔ'sipiəm], *s. Bot:* gossypium *m*, cotonnier *m*.
Goth [gɔθ], *s.* **1.** *Hist:* Goth *m*. **2.** *Geog:* habitant, -ante, de la Gothic. **3.** *Fig:* goth, vandale *m*, barbare *m*.
gotha ['gouθə, 'goutə], *s. Av:* (1914–1918) avion de bombardement allemand; gotha *m*.
Gotham ['gɔtəm], *Pr.n.* **wise man of G.,** gribouille *m*, nigaud *m*.
Gothic ['gɔθik]. **1.** *a.* (*a*) (race, etc.) gothique; (*b*) *Arch:* gothique; (*c*) *Typ:* **g. type, characters,** caractères *m* gothiques; (*d*) *F:* barbare. **2.** *s. Art: etc:* gothique *m*; *Ling:* gothique, gotique *m*.
Gothick ['gɔθik], *s.* gothique *m* troubadour.
Gothish ['gɔθiʃ], *a. A:* gothique, barbare.
Gothland ['gɔθlənd], **Gotland** ['gɔtlænd], *Pr.n. Geog:* Gothie *f*.
gotten ['gɔtn]. *See* GET[2].
gouache [gu'ɑ:ʃ], *s. Art:* gouache *f*; **to paint in g.,** peindre à la gouache.
gouge[1] [gaudʒ], *s.* **1.** *Tls:* (*a*) *Carp:* gouge *f*; **turning g.,** gouge à ébaucher; **spoon g., entering g.,** gouge à nez rond, à cuiller; **bent g.,** gouge à bec de corbin; (*b*) *Surg:* gouge. **2.** rainure *f*; *For:* **g. blaze,** griffe (faite à un arbre). **3.** *NAm: F:* filouterie *f*, escroquerie *f*.
gouge[2], *v.tr.* **1.** gouger (le bois). **2. to g. out,** creuser (une cannelure, etc.) à la gouge; *Engr:* échopper; **to g. out s.o.'s eye,** faire sauter un œil à qn. **3.** *NAm: F:* (*a*) duper, enjôler, refaire (qn); (*b*) **to g. sth. out of s.o., to g. s.o. out of sth.,** extorquer qch. à qn.
gouger ['gaudʒər], *s. NAm: F:* filou *m*, escroc *m*.
gouging ['gaudʒiŋ], *s.* **1.** travail *m* à la gouge. **2. g. out,** creusage *m* à la gouge.
Goulard [gu:'lɑ:d], *Pr.n. Pharm: A:* **G. water, Goulard's extract,** eau *f* de Goulard; extrait *m* de Saturne.
goulash ['gu:læʃ], *s. Cu:* goulache *f*.
gouldia ['gu:ldiə], *s. Orn:* gouldie *f*.
goura ['gu:rə], *s. Orn:* goura *m*.
gourami [gu:'rɑ:mi], *s. Ich:* gourami *m*.
gourd ['guəd], *s.* **1.** *Bot:* courge *f*, gourde *f*; **red and yellow g.,** courge potiron; **the g. family,** les cucurbitacées *f*; **g. melon,** bénincase *f*; **g. tree,** calebassier *m*; **dishcloth g., dishrag g., sponge g.,** luffa *m*, torchon végétal. **2.** (*bottle*) gourde, calebasse *f*.
gourmand ['guəmənd]. **1.** *a.* (*a*) glouton; (*b*) gourmand. **2.** *s.* (*a*) glouton *m*; (*b*) gourmet *m*.
gourmandism ['guəməndizm], *s.* gourmandise *f*.
gourmet ['guəmei], *s.* gourmet *m*; gastronome *m*.
gout [gaut], *s.* **1.** *Med:* goutte *f*; *A:* **rheumatic g.,** rhumatisme goutteux; goutte rhumatismale; **chronic g.,** goutte nouée. **2.** *Agr:* goutte (du blé); *Ent:* **g. fly,** chlorops *m*. **3.** *A: & Lit:* (*a*) goutte, caillot *m* (de sang); (*b*) large tache *f* (de couleur).
goutweed ['gautwi:d], *s. Bot:* égopode *m*; *F:* herbe *f* aux goutteux; petite angélique; podagraire *f*.
gouty ['gauti]. **1.** *a.* (*a*) (*of pers., joint, etc.*) goutteux; (*b*) (vin *m*, etc.) qui tend à donner la goutte. **2.** *s. usu.pl. F: O:* **gouties,** couvre-chaussures montants.
govern ['gʌvən], *v.tr.* **1.** (*a*) gouverner, régir (un État, etc.); administrer (une entreprise, une province, etc.); régir, diriger (une maison); *v.i.* **to g.,** gouverner; (*b*) **laws that g. chemical reactions,** lois *f* qui régissent les réactions chimiques; **considerations that governed the choice of a representative,** considérations *f* qui ont influencé le choix d'un représentant, qui nous ont guidés dans le choix d'un représentant; (*c*) *Gram:* **to g. the accusative,** se construire avec, gouverner, régir, l'accusatif. **2.** maîtriser, gouverner, contenir, assujettir (ses passions, etc.); *A:* **to g. one's tongue,** mettre un frein à sa langue; **to g. one's temper,** se maîtriser. **3.** *A:* régler (une machine); *Tchn:* **movement governed by a pendulum,** mouvement gouverné par un pendule.
governable ['gʌv(ə)nəbl], *a.* gouvernable.
governance ['gʌvənəns], *s.* **1.** gouvernement *m*, gouvernance *f* (d'une province, etc.). **2.** maîtrise *f*, empire *m*; *Ecc:* **the hearts of kings are in Thy rule and g.,** les cœurs des rois sont sous ta domination et ta conduite.
governess ['gʌvənis], *s.f.* (*a*) institutrice; **resident g.,** institutrice à demeure; **visiting g., daily g.,** institutrice à domicile; (*b*) *A.Veh:* **g. cart,** tonneau *m*; (*of wicker*) panier *m*.
governing[1] ['gʌvəniŋ], *a.* (*a*) gouvernant; **g. commission,** commission *f* de gouvernement; **g. body,** conseil *m* d'administration (d'une église, d'une société, d'un orphelinat); (*b*) **g. ideas,** idées maîtresses, dominantes, directives *f*, (d'un projet).
governing[2], *s.* **1.** (*a*) gouvernement *m*; (*b*) maîtrise *f* (des passions, etc.). **2.** *A:* réglage *m* (d'une machine, etc.).
government ['gʌv(ə)nmənt], *s.* **1.** gouvernement *m*; (*a*) **form of g.,** régime *m*; **monarchical g.,** régime monarchique; **local g.,** gouvernement local; **self g.,** autonomie *f* (d'un État); (*b*) **the British G.,** le Gouvernement anglais; **g. offices,** bureaux *m* du Gouvernement, ministères *m*; **g. stock,** fonds *mpl* d'État, fonds publics; **g. loan,** emprunt public; (*c*) ministère *m*; **to form a g.,** former, constituer, un ministère, un gouvernement; **the G. party,** le parti gouvernemental; **newspaper that supports the G.,** journal ministériel. **2.** (*province or district administered by a governor*) gouvernement. **3.** *U.S:* (*a*) conseil *m* d'administration (d'un collège); (*b*) conseil municipal. **4. G. house,** résidence (officielle) (du gouverneur).
governmental [gʌvən'mentl], *a.* gouvernemental, -aux.
governmentalism [gʌvən'mentəlizm], *s. Pol:* gouvernementalisme *m*.
governor ['gʌv(ə)nər], *s.* **1.** gouvernant *m*; **the governors and the governed,** les gouvernants et les gouvernés. **2.** (*a*) gouverneur *m* (d'une colonie, d'une forteresse, d'une banque, d'une prison); **the wife of the g.,** madame la Gouvernante; **lieutenant g.,** *Fr.C:* lieutenant gouverneur; **g. general,** gouverneur général; (*b*) directeur *m* (d'une école de réforme, etc.); (*c*) membre *m* du conseil d'administration (d'une école, etc.); (*d*) *F:* **the g.,** (i) le patron, le singe. **3.** (*device*) (*a*) *Mec.E:* régulateur *m*; modérateur *m* (de vitesse); **(fly) ball g.,** régulateur à boules; **g. flyballs, weights,** masselottes *f* de régulateur; **inertia g.,** régulateur à inertie; **hydraulic**

g., régulateur hydraulique; **oil-relay g.**, régulateur à relais d'huile; **pendulum g.**, régulateur à pendule, pendule *m* à boules; **spring g.**, régulateur à ressort; *I.C.E:* (*of Diesel engine*) **centrifugal and vacuum g.**, régulateur à force centrifuge et à dépression; **g. drive, g. link**, commande *f* de régulateur; **double-drive g.**, régulateur à double effet; **g. head**, pendule *m*, tachymètre *m*, de régulateur; (*b*) *Mch:* **pressure g.**, régulateur de pression; **steam g.**, régulateur de vapeur; (*c*) *Av:* **fuel g.**, régulateur de pompe d'injection (of jet engine); (*d*) *Nau:* **log g.**, régulateur de loch; (*e*) *Hyd.E: etc:* **water-turbine g.**, régulateur de turbine hydraulique; **g. pump**, pompe régulatrice; **g. valve**, soupape, vanne, régulatrice.

governorate ['gʌvənəreit], *s.* gouvernorat *m.*

governorship ['gʌvənəʃip], *s.* **1.** gouvernorat *m.* **2.** durée *f* des fonctions; temps *m* de gouvernement.

gowan ['gauən], *s. Bot: Scot:* pâquerette *f*; petite marguerite.

gowk [gauk], *s.* **1.** *Orn: F: Dial:* coucou *m.* **2.** *F:* idiot, -ote; sot, sotte.

gown[1] [gaun], *s.* **1.** *Com:* robe *f* (de femme); **dinner g.**, robe de soirée. **2.** (*a*) robe, toge *f* (de magistrat, universitaire, etc.); **judge in his g.**, juge *m* en robe; *Surg:* **operating g.**, blouse *f* de chirurgien; (*b*) *A: & Lit:* toge romaine (emblème de la vie civile); *Lit:* **to give up the g. for the sword**, quitter la robe pour l'épée.

gown[2]. **1.** *v.tr.* revêtir (qn) d'une robe, d'une toge; habiller (qn); **gowned solicitor**, avoué *m* en robe. **2.** *v.i.* (*of judge, etc.*) revêtir sa robe.

gownsman, *pl.* **-men** ['gaunzmən], *s.m.* **1.** (*a*) *Rom.Ant:* Romain adulte (portant la robe virile); (*b*) *A:* civil. **2.** *O:* (*a*) membre d'une université; (*b*) étudiant.

goy, *pl.* **goyim, goys** [gɔi, gɔiəm, gɔiz], *s.* goy(e) *m*, goï *m*, *pl.* goyim, goïm.

goyazite ['gɔiəzait], *s. Miner:* goyasite *f.*

Graafian ['grɑːfiən], *a. Anat:* **G. vesicles**, vésicules *f* de Graaf.

grab[1] [græb], *s.* **1.** (*a*) mouvement vif de la main pour saisir qch.; **to make a g. at sth.**, faire un mouvement, avancer vivement la main, la patte, pour saisir qch.; *F:* **policy of g.**, politique *f* (de) rapace, de la foire d'empoigne; *NAm:* **g. bag**, baquet rempli de son (où l'on plonge la main pour retirer une surprise); (*of bath, etc.*) **g. bar**, poignée *f* de sécurité; (*b*) **g. iron**, (i) *Rail:* (*of wagon, locomotive*) poignée montoire; (ii) *Tls: Min:* accrocheur *m* (de sonde); harpon *m* (de repêchage); *Min:* **tool g.**, grappin *m* de repêchage; **g. rod**, (i) *Nau:* main *f* de fer; (ii) *Rail:* poignée montoire; *Nau:* **g. rope**, faux-bras *m inv* de ceinture. **2.** *Civ.E: etc:* **g. (bucket)**, benne preneuse, piocheuse; pelle *f* mécanique; **earth g.**, cuiller *f* d'excavation, pelleteuse *f*, pelle mécanique; **g. crane**, (i) grue *f* à benne preneuse; (ii) grue à grappin; *Hyd.E: etc:* **g. (dredge(r))**, drague *f* à benne preneuse, piocheuse. **3.** *Mec.E:* broutage *m* (d'un frein).

grab[2], *v.tr. & i.* **(grabbed) 1. to g. (hold of) sth., s.o.**, saisir qch. (d'un geste brusque); prendre qch. d'un geste sec; se saisir de qch., empoigner qn; harper, qn, qch.; mettre la main sur qch.; **he grabbed a revolver from the table**, il a saisi un revolver sur la table; **to save oneself by grabbing a rope**, se rattraper, se raccrocher, se reprendre, à un cordage; **to g. at sth., for sth.**, faire un mouvement, avancer vivement la main, la patte, pour saisir qch; to g. at s.o., s'agripper à qn. **2.** *v.i. Mec.E:* (*of brake, etc.*) brouter.

grabber ['græbər], *s.* personne *f* âpre au gain; accapareur, -euse; *F:* agrippeur, -euse; attrapeur, -euse.

grabbing ['græbiŋ], *s.* **1.** empoigne *f*; **money g.**, mercantilisme *m.* **2.** *Mec.E:* broutage *m* (d'un frein).

grabble ['græbl], *v.i.* **1. to g. for sth.**, chercher qch. à tâtons, à quatre pattes; **the boys grabbled for the pennies**, les garçons se battaient pour ramasser les sous. **2.** *A:* s'étendre par terre, se traîner à quatre pattes.

graben ['grɑːbən], *s. Geol:* graben *m*, fossé *m.*

grabhook ['græbhuk], *s.* croc *m*, grappin *m*; crochet *m* de levage; crochet grappin.

Gracchi (the) [ðə'grækai, -kiː], *Pr.n.pl. Rom.Hist:* les Gracques *m.*

grace[1] [greis], *s.* **1.** grâce *f*; (*a*) grâce *f*, élégance *f* (d'un mouvement, etc.); (*b*) **to do sth. with a good, a bad, g.**, faire qch de bonne, mauvaise, grâce; montrer de la bonne, mauvaise, volonté; **to have the g. to apologize**, avoir la bonne grâce, la politesse, la délicatesse, de faire des excuses; **he had the g. to be ashamed**, il faut dire à son honneur qu'il se montra confus; **you cannot refuse with any g.**, vous ne pouvez refuser sans mauvaise grâce; vous ne pouvez pas décemment refuser; (*c*) *Gr.Myth:* **the Graces**, les Grâces. **2.** (*a*) faveur *f*, gracieuseté *f*; **act of g.**, gracieuseté, faveur; **it would be an act of g. on your part to . . .**, ce serait une gracieuseté de votre part de . . .; **to be in s.o.'s good graces**, être dans les bonnes grâces de qn, en odeur de sainteté auprès de qn; **to get into s.o.'s good graces**, se mettre dans, entrer dans, obtenir, les bonnes grâces de qn; se faire bien venir de qn; **to fall out of g. with s.o.**, perdre les bonnes grâces de qn; **by God's g.**, grâce à Dieu; **g.-and-favour house**, maison appartenant à la Couronne mise gratuitement à la disposition de certaines personnes; (*b*) *Sch: A:* autorisation (délivrée à un candidat par son Collège) de se présenter à l'examen pour obtenir un diplôme; (*c*) *Theol:* **the g. of God**, la grâce de Dieu; **in a state of g.**, en état de grâce; **to fall from g.**, perdre la grâce; **the means of g.**, les sacrements *m*; **sign of g.**, signe *m* de grâce; **sufficient g.**, grâce suffisante; **efficacious g.**, grâce efficace; **saving g.**, grâce sanctifiante; **it has the saving g. that . . .**, cela a au moins ce mérite que . . .; **in the year of g. 1066**, en l'an de grâce 1066. **3.** (*a*) *A:* grâce, pardon *m*; (*still so used in*) **act of g.**, (i) lettres *fpl* de grâce; (ii) loi *f* d'amnistie; (*b*) **measure of g.**, mesure gracieuse; (*c*) **days of g.**, (i) *Com:* délai (accordé pour le paiement d'un effet); (ii) *Ins:* délai (accordé pour le paiement des primes d'assurances sur la vie); **to give a creditor seven days' g.**, accorder à un créancier sept jours de grâce, de répit, de faveur; **last day of g.**, terme fatal; **he never gives me a moment's g.**, il ne me donne jamais un moment de répit. **4.** (*a*) **grace**, (i) (*before meal*) bénédicité *m*, prière *f* avant le repas; (ii) (*after meal*) grâces, prière après le repas; (*b*) **now for the g. cup!** passons la coupe pour le dernier toast! **5. His G. the Duke of Rutland**, Monsieur le duc de Rutland; **His G. the Archbishop of Canterbury**, Monseigneur, sa Grandeur, l'archevêque de Cantorbéry; **Her G. (the Duchess of . . .)**, Madame la duchesse (de . . .); **Your G.**, votre Grandeur; Monsieur le Duc; Monseigneur. **6.** *Mus:* (*a*) **g. note**, note *f* d'agrément, de goût; fioriture *f*, ornement *m*, agrément *m*; **g. notes**, notes de passage; (*b*) *pl. A:* **graces**, broderies *f*, agréments. **7.** *Games: A:* **the graces**, jeu *m* de grâces.

grace[2], *v.tr.* **1.** (*a*) honorer (**with**, de); faire honneur à (qn); **to g. a meeting with one's presence**, honorer une réunion de sa présence; **she graced me with a smile**, elle m'a fait l'aumône d'un sourire; (*b*) embellir, orner; *Mus:* orner (un morceau de musique) de fioritures. **2.** *A:* qualifier (qn) de "votre Grandeur."

graceful ['greisf(u)l], *a.* **1.** gracieux, élégant; **g. figure**, taille élégante; **g. architecture**, architecture élégante; **she is a g. dancer**, elle danse avec grâce; **the g. movements of a Siamese cat**, l'élégance d'un chat siamois; **these birds are g. in flight**, ces oiseaux ont un vol gracieux. **2. a g. speech**, un discours gracieux, poli, bien tourné; **it would be a g. act on your part**, ce serait une gracieuseté de votre part. **3.** *Cmptr:* **g. degradation**, fonctionnement *m* en mode dégradé.

gracefully ['greisfuli], *adv.* **1.** avec grâce; avec élégance; **to dance g.**, danser avec grâce; **she does everything g.**, elle met de la grâce dans tout. **2. we cannot very g. decline**, on ne peut pas refuser sans mauvaise grâce; on ne peut pas décemment refuser.

gracefulness ['greisf(u)lnis], *s.* grâce *f*, élégance *f*, aise *f*, désinvolture *f* (d'un mouvement, etc.).

graceless ['greislis], *a.* **1.** *A:* sans grâce, inélégant, gauche. **2.** (*a*) *Theol:* qui n'est pas en état de grâce; (*b*) perdu sans rémission, impie, dépravé; (*c*) *F:* effronté; mauvais sujet; **how's that g. nephew of yours getting on?** que devient votre garnement *m* de neveu?

gracelessness ['greislisnis], *s.* **1.** *A:* inélégance *f*, gaucherie *f.* **2.** impiété *f*, dépravation *f.*

gracilariid [græsi'lɑːriid], *s. Ent:* **g. (moth)**, gracilaire *m.*

Gracil(l)ariidae [græsilɑː'riːidiː], *s.pl. Ent:* gracillariidés *m*, gracilaridés *m.*

gracile ['græsail], *a.* gracile, grêle.

gracilis ['græsilis], *s. Anat:* (muscle) droit interne (de la cuisse).

gracious ['greiʃəs], *a.* **1.** *A:* aimable; (*of thg*) agréable. **2.** (*a*) gracieux, indulgent, bienveillant; **to be g. to s.o.**, faire des gracieusetés, faire bon visage, à qn; être gracieux pour, envers, qn; être affable à, avec, envers, qn; **the most g. of hosts**, le plus accueillant des hôtes; **by the g. consent of . . .**, par la grâce de . . .; (*b*) **our g. King, Queen**, notre gracieux souverain. **3.** (*of God*) miséricordieux, bon, bienveillant (to, envers); plein de grâce, de compassion, de charité (to, envers); **Lord, be g. unto him**, Seigneur, soyez-lui miséricordieux. **4. g. (me)! good(ness) g.! my g.!** miséricorde! bonté divine! mon Dieu! **good g. no!** jamais de la vie!

graciously ['greiʃəsli], *adv.* **1.** avec bienveillance; **to be g. pleased to do sth.**, daigner faire qch.; vouloir bien faire qch.; **to be g. pleased to accept a present**, agréer un présent; **His, Her, Majesty has g. consented to . . .**, sa Majesté a gracieusement consenti à . . .. **2.** miséricordieusement, avec clémence.

graciousness ['greiʃəsnis], *s.* **1.** grâce *f*; aménité *f* (de style). **2.** (*a*) *A:* amabilité *f*, affabilité *f* (**to, towards**, avec, envers); (*b*) gracieuseté *f*, condescendance *f*, bienveillance *f* (**to, towards**, envers). **3.** bonté *f*, bienveillance *f*, miséricorde *f* (de Dieu).

grackle ['grækl], *s. Orn:* (*a*) (*Asia*) mainate *m*, *F:* merle-mandarin *m*; (*b*) (*America*) quiscale *m*, *Fr.C:* mainate; **common g., bronzed g.**, mainate bronzé.

grad[1] [græd], *s. Mth:* grade *m.*

grad[2], *s. Sch: F: O:* = licencié, -ée.

gradate [grə'deit]. **1.** *v.i.* (*of colours*) se dégrader, se fondre. **2.** *v.tr.* dégrader, fondre (des teintes, etc.).

gradated [grə'deitid], *a.* disposé en gradins.

gradation [grə'deiʃ(ə)n], *s.* **1.** (*a*) gradation *f*, progression *f*; *Aut:* **g. of speeds**, échelonnement *m* des vitesses; (*b*) **g. by degree of imperfection**, classification *f* par degrés d'imperfection; (*c*) *Art:* (dé)gradation *f* (des teintes). **2.** degré *m*; **to advance by easy gradations**, avancer par gradations insensibles, petit à petit, graduellement. **3.** *Ling:* **(vowel) g.**, mutation *f* vocalique; alternance *f* de voyelles; apophonie *f.*

gradational [grə'deiʃənl], *a.* graduel; *Biol:* **g. forms**, formes *f* impliquant une gradation.

grade[1] [greid], *s.* **1.** *Mth:* grade *m.* **2.** (*a*) grade, rang *m*, degré *m* (d'une hiérarchie, etc.); **the various grades of the Civil Service**, les divers échelons de l'administration; (*b*) qualité *f*; classe *f*; (*of lubricating oil, etc.*) grade; *Min:* teneur *f* (du minerai); *Com: etc:* **high-g., top-g., choice-g.**, de qualité supérieure, de (tout) premier choix, *F:* (de qualité) extra; **low-g., below g.**, de qualité inférieure; **leaf grades (of tea)**, qualités de thé; **different grades of coffee**, de différentes qualités de café; **prime-g. beef**, bœuf *m* de premier choix; *Aut:* **high-g. petrol** = supercarburant *m*, *F:* super *m*; *Min:* **high-g. ore**, minerai *m* à, de, haute teneur, d'un haut titre; **low-g. ore**, mineral pauvre, à, de, faible teneur, à bas titre; (*c*) *Med:* degré d'intensité (d'une fièvre); état *m* (d'une maladie); (*d*) *Sch: NAm:* **to get high grades** = avoir de bonnes notes. **3.** *Breed:* **g. cattle, grades**, bétail amélioré par le croisement; **high-g. cattle**, bétail métis de premier croisement. **4.** (*a*) *Civ.E: U.S:* (*gradient*) pente *f*, rampe *f*; montée *f* ou descente *f* (d'une voie ferrée, d'une route, etc.); **g. level**, ligne *f* de pente; **to make the g.**, (i) parvenir au sommet; arriver en palier; (ii) (*also Eng.*) *Fig:* surmonter ses difficultés; (*b*) *Civ.E: Const: NAm:* niveau *m*; **g. level**, palier *m*; **at g.**, à niveau; **under, over, g.**, à un niveau inférieur, supérieur; **below g.**, en sous-sol; **below-g. entrance**, entrée *f* en sous-sol; **to make up ground to the required g.**, amener le terrain au niveau requis; *Rail:* **g. crossing**, passage *m* à niveau; (*of roads*) **g. separation**, croisement étagé, à des niveaux différents; (*c*) *Sch:* (i) *NAm:* classe *f* (*esp.* dans une école primaire); (ii) *U.S:* **g. school, the grades** = école primaire; **g. teacher**, instituteur, -trice. **5.** *Geol:* profil *m* d'équilibre, profil du lit (d'un cours d'eau).

grade[2], *v.tr. & i.* **1.** (*a*) classer, trier (des marchandises, etc., selon leurs qualités); calibrer; *Phot:* étalonner (des clichés); (*b*) *Sch: NAm:* **to g. essays** = corriger des dissertations (et leur donner une note). **2.** *Breed:* (*a*) **to g. (up)**, améliorer (une race, etc.) par le métissage; (*b*) *v.i.* **to g. down to a lower type**, passer par degrés à un type inférieur; **to g. up to a higher type**, passer par degrés à un type supérieur; *U.S: F:* **to g. up to s.o.**, parvenir à la hauteur de qn; se mettre de pair avec qn. **3.** (*a*) graduer (des exercices, etc.); **graded tax**, impôt (i) progressif, (ii) dégressif; **graded advertising rates**, tarif d'annonces dégressif; (*b*) *Art:* dégrader, fondre (des teintes); *v.i.* **red and yellow g. into orange**, les rouges et les jaunes se dégradent et passent à l'orange. **4.** *NAm:* (*a*) *Civ.E: Rail:* (*a*) ménager, régulariser, la pente de (la voie, etc.); (*b*) *Civ.E:* niveler (un terrain). **5.** *Ling:* (*of vowel*) s'altérer par mutation (vocalique), par apophonie.

grader ['greidər], *s.* **1.** (*pers.*) classeur *m*, trieur *m* (de minerai, etc.). **2.** *Civ.E:* (*machine*) niveleuse *f*, grader *m.* **3.** *Sch: NAm:* **first g.** = élève de onzième.

gradient ['greidiənt], *s.* **1.** *Civ.E: etc:* inclinaison *f*; dénivellation *f*; **downward g.**, pente *f*, déclivité *f*; **upward, rising, g.**, rampe *f*, côte *f*, montée *f*; **uncompensated g.**, rampe brute; **g. compensated for curves**, rampe nette; *Rail:* **the gradients**, les pentes et les rampes; **along the g.**, suivant la pente; **angle of g.**, angle *m* de gradient; **steep, low, g.**, forte, faible, pente, rampe; rampe à fort, à faible, pourcentage; **road with gradients of 1 in 10, of 10%**, route *f* avec des rampes de 10%; **g. post**, poteau (indicateur) de pente; *Aut: etc:* **speed on a g.**, vitesse *f* en côte; *Aut: Av:* **g. indicator, meter**, indicateur *m* de pente; clinomètre *m.* **2.** (*a*) *Mth: Ph: etc:* gradient *m*; **temperature g., thermal g.**, gradient de température; **speed, velocity, g.**, gradient de vitesse; **potential g.**, gradient de potentiel; **pressure**

g., gradient de pression; *El:* **voltage g.,** gradient de tension; *Meteor:* **g. wind,** vent *m* du gradient; **geothermal g.,** gradient géothermique; (*b*) *Biol:* gradient (physiologique).
gradin ['greidin], **gradine**[1] [grə'di:n], *s.* gradin *m* (d'amphithéâtre, d'autel, etc.).
gradine[2], *s. Tls: Sculp:* gradine *f.*
grading ['greidiŋ], *s.* **1.** (*a*) classement *m*, gradation *f*; calibrage *m*; triage *m* (du minerai, etc.); étalonnage *m* (des clichés); (*b*) *Sch: NAm:* correction *f* (des dissertations, etc., avec notes). **2.** *Breed:* amélioration *f* par le métissage. **3.** (dé)gradation *f* (des teintes). **4.** (a)ménagement *m* (d'une pente). **5.** mutation *f* vocalique; apophonie *f.*
gradual ['grædju(ə)l]. **1.** *a.* (*a*) graduel; progressif; **g. slope,** pente douce; **g. transition,** transition ménagée (**from . . . to . . .,** de . . . à . . .); **g. process,** gradation *f*; *Phot:* **g. sky filter,** écran de ciel dégradé, nuancé; (*b*) *Ecc:* **g. psalms,** psaumes graduels. **2.** *s. Ecc:* graduel *m.*
gradually ['grædjuəli], *adv.* graduellement; par degrés, par gradations; petit à petit; peu à peu.
gradualness ['grædju(ə)lnis], *s.* gradualité *f.*
graduand [grædju'ænd], *s.* candidate, -e, à un diplôme.
graduate[1] ['grædjuət], *s.* **1.** (*a*) *Sch:* diplômé, -ée; = licencié, -ée; (*b*) *attrib. NAm:* **g. nurse,** infirmier, -ière diplômé(e); **he's in g. school** = il prépare une maîtrise, un doctorat, etc. **2.** *Pharm: NAm:* verre gradué.
graduate[2] ['grædjueit]. **1.** *v.i.* (*a*) *Sch:* (i) recevoir ses diplômes; =être reçu licencié(e); **he graduated from Oxford, at Harvard,** il a fait ses études à Oxford, à Harvard; **he graduated in a hard school,** il est parti de rien; (ii) *NAm:* **to g. from high school,** terminer ses études au lycée; (*b*) **to g. into sth.,** se changer graduellement en . . .; passer graduellement à . . .. **2.** *v.tr. Sch: NAm:* conférer un diplôme à (un étudiant, etc.). **3.** *v.tr.* (*a*) graduer (une échelle, un thermomètre, etc.); **graduated in centimetres,** gradué en centimètres; (*b*) graduer (des exercices, etc.); **to g. a tax according to the taxpayer's income,** établir un impôt proportionnellement au revenu du contribuable; **graduated taxation,** taxes imposées par paliers; **graduated income tax,** impôt progressif; impôt proportionnel au revenu du contribuable; (*c*) dégrader (des teintes); (*d*) graduer, concentrer (une solution, l'eau de mer, etc.).
graduating ['grædjueitiŋ], *s.* = GRADUATION.
graduation [grædju'eiʃ(ə)n], *s.* **1.** *Sch:* (*a*) remise *f* des diplômes (= de licence, *NAm:* de fin d'études secondaires); **g. ceremony, day,** cérémonie *f* de la remise des diplômes (aux étudiants); (*b*) (*by student*) réception *f* d'un diplôme. **2.** (*a*) graduation *f* (d'un thermomètre, etc.); (*b*) *pl.* **graduations,** degrés *m*, grades *m*. **3.** gradation *f* (d'exercices, de paiements, etc.). **4.** (dé)gradation *f* (des teintes). **5.** concentration *f*, graduation (d'une solution). **6.** *Mapm:* **g. tick,** amorce *f* de graticule.
graduator ['grædjueitər], *s.* (*device*) **1.** graduateur *m* (de thermomètre). **2.** concentrateur *m* (d'eau de mer, de solutions). **3.** *Mec.E:* machine *f* à diviser, diviseuse *f.*
graduette [grædju'et], *s.f. F: O:* (*not used in university milieu*) = licenciée.
gradus ['greidəs, 'grædəs], *s. Sch: A:* **g. (ad Parnassum),** gradus *m* (ad Parnassum); Parnasse *m.*
Graecism ['gri:sizm], *s.* hellénisme *m*; (i) esprit *m* hellénique; grécité *f*; (ii) locution grecque.
Graecize ['gri:saiz], *v.tr. & i.* gréciser, helléniser.
Graeco- ['gri:kou], *comb.fm.* gréco-; helléno-.
Graeco-Buddhist ['gri:kou'budist], *a.* **G.-B. art,** art *m* gréco-bouddhique.
Graeco-Latin ['gri:kou'lætin], *a.* gréco-latin, *f.* gréco-latine, *pl.* gréco-latin(e)s.
Graecomania [gri:kou'meiniə], *s.* grécomanie *f.*
Graecophile ['gri:koufail], *s.* hellénophile *mf.*
Graeco-Roman ['gri:kou'roumən], *a.* gréco-romain, *f.* gréco-romaine, *pl.* gréco-romain(e)s.
Graeco-Slavonic ['gri:kouslə'vonik], *a.* gréco-slave, *pl.* gréco-slaves.
graffito, *pl.* **-i** [græ'fi:tou, -i:], *s.* **1.** *Archeol: Art:* graffite *m*; graffito *m*, *pl.* graffiti; *Art:* **g. style,** manière égratignée; graffito; **g. artist,** égratigneur, -euse; *F:* **obscene graffiti on the wall,** graffiti obscènes sur le mur; *U.S:* **maxi-graffiti,** inscriptions *f* de mauvais goût faites à l'aide d'un pistolet à peinture. **2.** *Art:* (*painting*) sgraffite *m.*
graft[1] [grɑ:ft], *s.* **1.** (*a*) *Arb: Hort:* greffon *m*, greffe *f*, ente *f*; (*b*) *Surg:* (i) greffe, implantation *f*; (ii) greffon; **autoplastic g.,** greffe, greffon, autoplastique; **heteroplastic g.,** greffe, greffon, hétéroplastique; **bone g.,** greffe osseuse; greffon osseux; **epidermal, epidermic, g.,** greffe, greffon, épidermique; **skin g.,** greffe cutanée; greffon cutané; **g. rejection,** rejet *m* de greffon. **2.** (*a*) = GRAFTING[1]; (*b*) (*place where plant is grafted*) greffe.
graft[2], *v.tr.* **1.** (*a*) *Arb:* greffer, enter (un greffon, une souche); **to g. one variety on, upon, in, into, another,** greffer une variété sur une autre; **to g. on a seedling stock,** greffer sur franc; (*b*) *Surg:* greffer, implanter. **2.** (*a*) *Carp:* enter (deux pièces de bois); (*b*) *Knit:* **to g. a new foot on a sock,** enter un bas; **to g. a patch into a stocking,** re(m)mailler un bas. **3.** *Nau:* garnir (un anneau, etc.) de bitord.
graft[3], *s.* (profondeur *f* de) fer *m* de bêche; **to dig a graft('s) depth,** bêcher à un fer de bêche.
graft[4], *s. F:* **1.** gratte *f*, graissage *m* de patte, pots-de-vin *mpl.* **2. hard g.,** travail *m*, boulot *m.*
graft[5], *v.i. F:* rabioter, gratter; faire de la gratte; donner ou recevoir des pots-de-vin.
graftage ['grɑ:ftidʒ], *s.* = GRAFTING.
grafter[1] ['grɑ:ftər], *s. Arb: Hort:* **1.** (*pers.*) greffeur *m*; écussonneur *m*. **2.** *Tls:* greffoir *m.*
grafter[2], *s. F:* fonctionnaire, politicien, véreux, qui fait de la gratte, politicard *m*; tripoteur *m.*
grafting ['grɑ:ftiŋ], *s.* **1.** (*a*) *Arb:* greffe *f*, greffage *m*; **ordinary g.,** greffe par rameau détaché; **g. by approach,** greffe par approche; **cleft g.,** greffe en fente simple; **saddle g.,** greffe en fente à cheval; **whip g.,** greffe en fente anglaise; **crown g.,** greffe en couronne; **flute g.,** greffe en anneau; **shield g.,** greffe en écusson, écussonnage *m*; **double g.,** contre-greffe *f*; surgreffage *m*; **g. knife,** greffoir *m*, entoir *m*; **g. wax,** engluement *m*; mastic *m* à greffer; (*b*) *Surg:* greffe (humaine); implantation *f*; **skin g.,** greffe épidermique. **2.** *Carp: Knit:* entement *m*; *Knit:* **g. of a patch** (*into a piece of knitting*), rem(m)aillage *m* (des parties d'un tricot). **3.** *Nau:* garnissage *m* (d'un anneau, etc.) de liure, de bitord.
Grail[1] [greil], *s. Lit:* **the Holy G.,** le Saint-Graal, le Graal.
grail[2], *s. Ind:* (*comb making*) grêle *f.*
grail[3], *v.tr. Ind:* (*comb making*) grêler.
grailing ['greiliŋ], *s. Ind:* (*comb making*) grêlage *m.*
grain[1] [grein], *s.* **1.** (*a*) grain *m* (de blé); (*b*) *coll.* **g. crop,** récolte *f* de grains, de céréales; **refuse g.,** grenaille *f*; petit blé; **ears full of g.,** épis grenus; **g.-producing lands,** terres *f* à blé; **g. market,** marché *m* aux grains; **g. carrier,** céréalier *m*; (navire) transporteur *m* de blé; (*c*) **(brewers') grains,** drêche *f*, drague *f*. **2.** (*a*) grain (de poivre, etc.); *Bot:* **grains of Paradise, Guinea grains,** poivre *m* de Guinée; graine *f* de paradis; malaguette *f*; (*b*) grain (de sel, de sable, de soudure, etc.); (*in stone*) **hard g.,** durillon *m*; (*in goldsmith's work*) **g. of solder,** paillon *m*; paillette *f* de soudure; *Exp:* **large g. powder, small g. powder,** poudre *f* à gros grains, à grains fins; **g. of consolation,** brin *m* de consolation; **not a g. of common sense, of malice,** pas un grain, pas un brin, pas une once, pas l'ombre, de bon sens, de méchanceté; (*c*) *Meas:* grain (= 0 gramme 0648). **3.** (*a*) grain (du bois, de la pierre, du fer, etc.); texture *f* (de la fonte, etc.); **close g.,** grain fin, dense; **cleaving g. (of stone),** lit *m* de la pierre; *Phot:* **coarse g.,** gros grain; **fine g.,** grain fin; **man of coarse g.,** homme *m* sans délicatesse; (*b*) fil *m* (du bois, de la viande); **to work wood with the g.,** travailler le bois dans le sens du fil; **to saw with the g.,** scier de long; **to cut wood with, along, the g.,** couper le bois de droit fil; **against, across , the g.,** contre le fil; à contre-fil; à rebours; **it goes against the g. for me to do it,** c'est à contrecœur que je le fais; (*c*) *Leath:* (i) grain, grenure *f* (du cuir); **g. side of leather,** fleur *f*, côté *m* cuir, de la peau; côté poil du cuir; **g. split,** fleur (du cuir fendu); (ii) **g. (leather),** chagrin *m*; (*d*) *Com:* **g. tin,** étain en larmes. **4.** (*a*) *Dy: A:* graine *f* d'écarlate; cochenille *f*; **to dye sth. in g.,** (i) *A:* teindre qch. en rouge de cochenille, *A:* en graine; (ii) teindre qch. grand teint; (*b*) *A: & Lit:* **in g.,** indélébile, invétéré; **a rogue in g.,** un coquin fieffé, invétéré.
grain[2], *v.tr.* **1.** grener (le sel, etc.); granuler (la poudre); *v.i.* (*of salt, etc.*) se grener, se granuler. **2.** *A:* teindre grand teint. **3.** greneler, chagriner, crépir, grainer (le cuir, le papier, etc.). **4.** *Paint:* (*a*) veiner (une surface) façon bois; (*b*) marbrer (une surface). **5.** *Tan:* dépiler, rebrousser (le cuir).
grain[3], *v.tr.* foéner (un poisson).
graine [grein], *s. Ser:* graines *fpl* (des vers à soie).
grained [greind], *a.* **1.** (*a*) granulé, granuleux; grenu; **g. leather,** cuir grenu, crépi; chagrin *m*; (*b*) *Dy: A:* (étoffe *f*) grand teint; (*c*) *Paint:* (i) veiné; (ii) marbré. **2.** (*with a prefixed*) **close-g.,** (i) (*of wood*) à grain(s) fin(s), serré(s); (ii) *Miner:* à grains fins, à fine cristallisation; **coarse-g.,** (i) (*of wood*) à gros fil; (ii) (*of metal, etc.*) à gros grain(s), à grain grossier; (*of metal, wood*) **fine-g.,** à grain fin, serré; à petit grain.
grainer ['greinər], *s.* **1.** (*pers.*) (*a*) peintre spécialisé dans le veinage; marbrier *m*; (*b*) *Leath:* chagrineur, -euse, crêpeur *m*. **2.** (*a*) peigne *m* de peintre, à décor; (*b*) *Leath:* (i) couteau *m* à dépiler; crépisseuse *f*; (ii) marguerite *f*, paumelle *f.*
graining ['greiniŋ], *s.* **1.** grenage *m* (de la poudre à canon, etc.). **2.** *A:* teinture *f* (de qch.) grand teint. **3.** *Leath:* (i) crépissage *m*, grenure *f*; (ii) dépilage *m*, rebroussement *m*; **g. board,** marguerite *f*, paumelle *f*. **4.** veinage *m* (de la peinture); décor *m* imitant le bois, le marbre; décor en bois, en marbre; **g. comb,** peigne *m* de peintre, à décor; **g. brush,** spalter *m*, veinette *f*. **5.** *Num:* grènetis *m*, crénelage *m.*
grains [greinz], *s. Fish:* foène *f*; harpon *m* à trois branches.
grainsick ['greinsik], *s. Vet:* (*also* **grain founder**) empansement *m*, ballonnement *m*, météorisme *m* (des ruminants).
grainy ['greini], *a.* **1.** (épi) grenu. **2.** *Miner:* granulaire; (marbre) grenu.
Grallae ['græli:], **Grallatores** [grælə'tɔ:ri:z], *s.pl. Orn:* échassiers *m.*
grallatorial [grælə'tɔ:riəl], *a.* qui appartient aux échassiers.
grallatory ['grælət(ə)ri], *a.* **g. bird,** échassier *m.*
gralloch[1] ['grælɔχ], *s. Ven: Scot:* entrailles *fpl* (du cerf).
gralloch[2], *v.tr. Ven: Scot:* éviscérer (le cerf).
gram[1] [græm], *s. Meas:* = GRAMME[1].
gram[2], *s.* pois *m* chiche.
Gram[3], *Pr.n. Bac:* **Gram's solution,** liqueur *f* de Gram, gram *m*; **g. positive, negative,** gram positif, négatif.
grama ['grɑ:mə], *s. Bot:* **g. (grass),** bouteloue *m.*
gramarye ['græməri], *s. A:* magie *f.*
gramenite ['græmənait], *s. Miner:* graménite *f.*
gramercy [grə'mə:si], *int. A:* grand merci (**for,** de).
gramicidin [græmi'saidin], *s. Bac:* gramicidine *f.*
Graminaceae [græmi'neisii:], *s.pl. Bot:* graminacées *f*, graminées *f.*
graminaceous [græmi'neiʃəs], *a. Bot:* graminé; **g. plants,** graminées *f.*
Gramineae [grə'minii:], *s.pl. Bot:* graminées *f.*
graminiferous [græmi'nifərəs], *a.* (plaine, etc.) où croissent les graminées; (terrain) herbeux.
graminiform [grə'minifɔ:m], *a. Bot:* graminiforme.
graminivorous [græmi'niv(ə)rəs], *a.* qui mange des graminées; herbivore.
graminology [græmi'nɔlədʒi], *s. Bot:* graminologie *f.*
gramma ['græmə], *s. Bot:* = GRAMA.
grammalogue ['græməlɔg], *s.* (*in shorthand*) sténogramme *m.*
grammar ['græmər], *s.* (*a*) grammaire *f*; **to speak, write, bad g.,** faire de fréquentes entorses aux règles de la grammaire; parler, écrire, peu grammaticalement; **that's not (good) g.,** ce que vous dites là n'est pas grammatical; *A:* **to learn the g. of a subject,** apprendre la grammaire, les rudiments, d'un sujet; (*b*) (livre *m*, traité *m*, de) grammaire; **a French g.,** une grammaire française; (*c*) **g. school** = lycée *m.*
grammarian [grə'mɛəriən], *s.* grammairien, -ienne.
grammatical [grə'mætikl], *a.* grammatical, -aux.
grammaticalization [grəmætikəlai'zeiʃ(ə)n], *s.* grammaticalisation *f.*
grammaticalize [grə'mætikəlaiz], *v.tr.* grammaticaliser.
grammatically [grə'mætik(ə)li], *adv.* grammaticalement.
grammaticalness [grə'mætik(ə)lnis], *s.* grammaticalité *f.*
grammaticize [grə'mætisaiz]. **1.** *v.tr.* rendre (un langage, un passage) grammatical. **2.** *v.i.* discourir sur des points de grammaire.
grammatist ['græmətist], *s.* grammatiste *m.*
grammatite ['græmətait], *s. Miner:* trémolite *f*; grammatite *f.*
gramme[1] [græm], *s. Meas:* gramme *m*; *Mec:* **g. centimetre,** centimètre-gramme *m*, *pl.* centimètres-grammes; *Ph:* **g. weight,** gramme-force *m*, *pl.* grammes-force; gramme-poids *m*, *pl.* grammes-poids; *Ch:* **g. atom, g.-atomic weight,** atome-gramme *m*, *pl.* atomes-grammes; **g. ion, ion g.,** ion gramme *m*, *pl.* ions-grammes; **g. molecule, g.-molecular weight,** molécule-gramme *f*, *pl.* molécules-grammes; **g. calorie, calory,** calorie-gramme *f*, *pl.* calories-grammes; petite calorie; **g. equivalent,** gramme-équivalent *m*, *pl.* gramme-équivalents.
Gramme[2], *Pr.n.m. El:* **G. dynamo,** gramme-dynamo *f*; **G. ring,** anneau *m* de Gramme.
gramophone ['græməfoun], *s.* phonographe *m*, tourne-disque *m*, *pl.* tourne-disques.
gramophonic [græmə'fɔnik], *a.* phonographique.
grampus ['græmpəs], *s.* **1.** *Z:* épaulard *m*, orque *f*. **2.** *F:* gros bonhomme poussif.
gran[1] [græn], *s.f. F:* grand-maman, mamé.

gran², *s. Com: F:* sucre cristallisé.
Granada [grə'nɑːdə], *Pr.n. Geog:* Grenade; **native, inhabitant, of G.,** Grenadin, -ine.
granadilla [grænə'dilə], *s. Bot:* grenadille *f.*
granary ['grænəri], *s. (a)* grenier *m; Com:* entrepôt *m* de grain; *Hist:* **public granaries,** greniers d'abondance; *(b)* **Egypt was the g. of the ancient world,** l'Égypte était le grenier de l'ancien monde.
grand [grænd], *a.* **1.** grand; **the G. Turk,** le grand Turc; **the G. Vizier,** le grand vizir; **g. duke,** grand-duc *m, pl.* grands-ducs; **g. duchess,** grande-duchesse *f, pl.* grandes-duchesses; **g. duchy,** grand-duché *m, pl.* grands-duchés; **g.-ducal,** grand-ducal, -aux. **2.** *(a)* grand, principal, -aux; **the G. Fleet,** la Grande Flotte; **g. staircase,** escalier *m* d'honneur; **G. Hotel,** le Grand Hôtel; **G. Cross,** grand-croix *f inv;* **Knight G. Cross,** grand-croix *m, pl.* grands-croix; **g. master,** (i) grand maître (d'un ordre de chevalerie, etc.); (ii) vénérable *m* (d'une loge de francs-maçons); (iii) champion *m* (aux échecs, au bridge); *Geog:* **the G. Banks,** le Grand Banc (de Terre-Neuve); **the G. Canyon,** le Grand Canyon; **the G. Canal,** le Grand Canal (de Venise); *Turf:* **the G. National,** la course classique de steeple (qui se court à Aintree, Liverpool); *(b)* **g. total,** total global, général. **3.** *(full-sized, complete in form) (a)* **g. concert,** grand concert; **g. concerto,** concerto *m* grosso; **g. display of fireworks,** grand feu d'artifice; *(b)* **g. piano,** *s.* **grand,** piano *m* à queue; **upright g.,** piano droit grand modèle, à cordes obliques; **concert g.,** piano à queue de concert; **drawing-room g.,** piano à queue de salon; **boudoir g., half g.,** (piano à) demi-queue *m inv;* **miniature, small, baby, g.,** (piano) quart de queue. **4.** *(a)* grandiose, imposant, magnifique, impressionnant; **g. style,** style grandiose, grand style; **the g. manner,** la grande manière; **the G. Old Man,** surnom de W. E. Gladstone; **the g. old man of the village,** le (vénérable) vieillard respecté de tout le village; **g. old man of trade unionism,** vétéran *m* du syndicalisme; *(b)* **a g. lady,** une grande dame; **she thinks herself too much of a g. lady to do this,** elle est trop grande dame pour faire cela; **I don't like g. company,** je n'aime pas la belle société, les réunions mondaines; *s. A:* **they love to do the g.,** ils aiment à paraître, à faire de l'épate, les importants, les grands seigneurs. **5.** *F: (a)* excellent, splendide, fameux, épatant; **g. dinner,** grand dîner, dîner magnifique; **he's g.,** c'est un type épatant; *(b)* **I'm not feeling too g.,** ça ne va qu'à moitié, je ne suis pas dans mon assiette. **6.** *NAm: F:* mille dollars *m; U.K:* £1000.
grandad ['grændæd], *s.m.* = GRAND-DAD.
grandala ['grændələ], *s. Orn:* rossignol bleu.
grandam ['grændæm], **grandame** ['grændeim], *s.f. A:* grand-mère, *pl.* grand-mères; aïeule.
grand(-)aunt ['grænd'ɑːnt], *s.f. O:* grand-tante, *pl.* grand-tantes.
grandchild, *pl.* **-children** ['græn(d)tʃaild, -tʃildrən], *s.* petit-fils *m* ou petite-fille *f, pl.* petits-enfants *m.*
grand-dad ['græn(d)dæd], *s.m. F:* grand-papa, *pl.* grands-papas; pépé *m.*
grand-daughter ['græn(d)dɔːtər], *s.f.* petite-fille, *pl.* petites-filles.
grandee [græn'diː], *s. (a)* grand *m* (d'Espagne); *(b) F:* grand personnage.
grandeeship [græn'diːʃip], *s.* grandesse *f* (d'Espagne).
grandeur ['grændjər], *s.* grandeur *f; (a)* noblesse *f,* éminence *f;* **at the summit of human g.,** au faîte de la grandeur humaine; *(b)* splendeur *f,* magnificence *f;* **the g. of the landscape,** le caractère sublime, imposant, du paysage; la majesté du paysage; *(c)* pompe *f,* éclat *m* (d'une cérémonie, d'un train de vie).
grandfather ['græn(d)fɑːðər], *s.m.* **1.** grand-père, *pl.* grands-pères; aïeul. **2.** *Cmptr:* **g. tape,** bande *f* première génération; **g. cycle,** période *f* de conservation portant sur trois générations de fichiers.
grandfatherly ['græn(d)fɑːðəli], *a.* de grand-père; **g. advice,** avis paternel.
gran(d)fer ['grænfər], *s. Dial:* = GRANDFATHER.
grandiloquence [græn'diləkwəns], *s.* grandiloquence *f;* emphase *f.*
grandiloquent [græn'diləkwənt], *a.* grandiloquent, grandiloque; (ton) magnifique, doctoral, -aux, pompeux; (style) emphatique, ampoulé.
grandiloquently [græn'diləkwəntli], *adv.* d'un ton, dans un style, grandiloquent, emphatique; avec emphase.
grandiose ['grændious, -ouz], *a. (a)* grandiose, magnifique, splendide; *(b)* pompeux; qui affiche la grandeur; qui vise à la majesté.
grandiosely ['grændiouzli, -sli], *adv. (a)* grandiosement; *(b)* pompeusement.
grandiosity [grændi'ɔsiti], *s. (a)* magnificence *f,* grandiose *m; (b)* caractère pompeux.
grandly ['grændli], *adv. (a)* grandement, magnifiquement, splendidement; à merveille; *(b)* grandiosement.
grandma ['græn(d)mɑː], **grandmam(m)a** [græn(d)məmɑː], *s.f. F:* grand-maman, *pl.* grand-mamans; mamé, mémé.
grandmother ['græn(d)mʌðər], *s.f.* grand-mère, *pl.* grand-mères; aïeule; *F:* **he'd murder his own g.,** il est méchant comme un âne rouge.
grandmotherly ['græn(d)mʌðəli], *a.* de grand-mère; tatillon.
grand nephew ['grænd 'nefju], *s.m.* petit-neveu, *pl.* petits-neveux.
grandness ['grændnis], *s.* **1.** grandeur *f;* grandiose *m* (d'un spectacle). **2.** *Pej:* affectation *f* de grandeur; air important.
grand niece ['grænd 'niːs], *s.f.* petite-nièce, *pl.* petites-nièces.
grandpa ['grænpɑː], **grandpapa** ['græn(d)pəpɑː], *s.m. F:* grand-papa, *pl.* grands-papas; pépé.
grandparent ['græn(d)peər(ə)nt], *s.* grand-père *m,* aïeul *m;* grand-mère *f,* aïeule; *pl.* grands-parents *m.*
grandparental [græn(d)pə'rentl], *a.* (influence, etc.) des grands-parents.
Grand Prix ['grɑ̃'priː], *s. Rac:* Grand Prix.
grandsire ['græn(d)saiər], *s.m. (a) Lit:* grand-père, *pl.* grands-pères; *(b) Lit:* aïeul, *pl.* aïeux; ancêtre *m; (c) Breed:* père au second degré (d'un animal).
grandson ['græn(d)sʌn], *s.m.* petit-fils, *pl.* petits-fils.
grandstand ['grændstænd], *s. Sp:* tribune *f* (d'honneur), grande tribune; *F:* **g. play,** jeu *m* pour s'attirer les applaudissements de la tribune; *Rac:* **g. finish,** arrivée palpitante.
grand uncle ['grænd'ʌŋkl], *s.m. O:* grand-oncle, *pl.* grands-oncles.
grange [greindʒ], *s.* **1.** grange *f.* **2.** manoir *m* (avec ferme); château *m.* **3.** *Hist:* ferme *f* (d'un monastère, etc.). **4.** *U.S:* syndicat *m* d'agriculteurs.
granger ['greindʒər], *s.* **1.** régisseur *m* d'une ferme. **2.** *U.S:* membre *m* d'un syndicat d'agriculteurs.
grangerite ['greindʒərait], *s.* truffeur *m* (de livres).
grangerize ['greindʒəraiz], *v.tr. Bookb:* **to g. a book,** truffer un exemplaire d'un livre.
grangerizing ['greindʒəraiziŋ], *s.* truffage *m* (d'un livre).
Granicus [græ'naikəs], *Pr.n. A.Geog:* le Granique.
graniferous [græ'nifərəs], *a. Bot:* granifère.
graniform ['grænifɔːm], *a. Bot: Anat:* graniforme.
granite ['grænit], *s.* granit(e) *m;* **binary g.,** granit à deux micas; **g. formation,** formation graniteuse, granitique.
granitic [græ'nitik], *a.* granitique, graniteux.
granitization [grænitai'zeiʃ(ə)n], *s. Geol:* granitisation *f.*
granitoid ['grænitɔid], *a. Geol:* granitaire, granitoïde.
granivore ['grænivɔːr], *s. Nat.Hist:* granivore *m.*
granivorous [græ'nivərəs], *a. Nat.Hist:* granivore.
grannie, granny ['græni], *s. F: (a)* grand-maman *f, pl.* grand(s)mamans; mémé *f,* mamé *f; (b)* **an old g.,** une vieille commère; *(c)* **g. (knot),** nœud mal fait, de ménagère, de soldat.
granodiorite [grænoudi'ɔːrait], *s. Miner:* granodiorite *f.*
granolithic [grænou'liθik], *a. Civ.E:* **g. paving stone,** dalle *f* en ciment à parement de granit concassé.
grant¹ [grɑːnt], *s.* **1.** *(a)* concession *f,* octroi *m* (d'une permission, etc.); délivrance *f* (d'un brevet); *(b) Jur:* don *m,* cession *f* (d'un bien, etc.); **post in s.o.'s g.,** poste *m* en la disposition de qn; *(c) Jur:* acte *m* de donation; acte de transfert. **2.** aide *f* pécuniaire; subvention *f,* allocation *f,* prime *f; Sch:* allocation d'études; **capital g.,** subvention à fonds perdu; **g. in aid,** subvention; **g.-aided,** subventionné (par l'État); **to make a g. to s.o.,** accorder une subvention, une allocation, à qn; doter (un général); **to receive a State g.,** être subventionné, doté, par l'État; **to put in a claim for a g.,** demander une allocation. **3.** *esp. NAm:* concession (de terrain).
grant², *v.tr.* **1.** *(a)* accorder, concéder, octroyer, conférer (une permission, une grâce, etc.); délivrer (une autorisation, un brevet; **the rights granted to them,** les droits à eux cédés; **the king granted the prisoner his freedom,** le roi accorda la mise en liberté du prisonnier; **he was granted permission to . . .,** il reçut la permission de . . .; **the countries that have been granted autonomy,** les pays qui se sont vu accorder l'autonomie; *Lit:* **heaven g. that . . .,** fasse le ciel que . . .; **God g. it!** Dieu le veuille; **God g. that . . .,** Dieu veuille que . . .; *P:* **I beg your pardon—granted!** je vous demande pardon—il n'y a pas de quoi; mais comment donc! *(b)* **to take sth. for granted,** considérer qch. comme admis, comme accordé, comme convenu, comme allant de soi; **you take too much for granted,** vous présumez trop; vous allez trop vite; **to take success for granted,** escompter un succès; **he takes it for granted that he can borrow my books,** il se croit permis d', il ne se gêne pas pour, emprunter mes livres; **we take all this for granted,** tout cela nous semble normal; *(c)* exaucer (une prière); accéder à (une requête); satisfaire (le désir de qn); *(d) Jur:* faire cession de (qch.). **2.** accorder, allouer (une subvention à qn); **to g. a loan,** consentir un prêt (to, à). **3.** admettre, concéder (un argument, etc.); **it must be granted that . . .,** il faut reconnaître que . . .; **granting, granted, that this story is true,** si l'on admet la vérité de cette histoire; **I g. you that he is lazy,** il est paresseux, je le veux bien; **I g. you that,** pour ça, vous avez bien raison; **granted!** soit! d'accord!
grantable ['grɑːntəbl], *a.* accordable, allouable, concessible.
grantee [grɑːn'tiː], *s. Jur:* (con)cessionnaire *mf,* donataire *mf;* impétrant, -ante (d'un brevet, etc.).
grantia ['grɑːnt(ʃ)iə], *s. Spong:* grantia *m.*
grantor [grɑːn'tɔːr], *s. Jur:* donateur *m,* concesseur *m,* (con)cédant *m;* constituant *m,* constituteur *m* (d'une annuité, etc.).
granular ['grænjulər], *a. (a) (of surface, texture)* granulaire, granuleux; *(b) (of fracture)* grenu, à grains; *(of tumour)* granuleux; *F:* **g. lids,** conjonctivite granuleuse.
granularity [grænju'læriti], *s. (a)* grenu *m* (du marbre, etc.); *(b) Phot:* granularité *f.*
granulate ['grænjuleit]. **1.** *v.tr. (a)* granuler; grener, grainer (la poudre, un métal, etc.); cristalliser (le sucre); grenailler (un métal, la cire, etc.); *(b)* greneter, greneler (une surface). **2.** *v.i. (a)* se former en grains; se grenailler; *(of sugar, etc.)* se cristalliser; *(b) Med: (of wound)* bourgeonner.
granulated ['grænjuleitid], *a.* **1.** *(a)* granulé, grené; (métaux, etc.) en grains, en grenaille; (sucre) cristallisé; *Tp: etc:* **g. carbon,** grenaille *f* de charbon; *(b) (of surface)* grenu; *(of paper)* chagriné. **2.** *Med: (of tumour)* granuleux.
granulating ['grænjuleitiŋ], *s.* = GRANULATION 1; **g. machine** = GRANULATOR.
granulation [grænju'leiʃ(ə)n], *s.* **1.** granulation *f;* granulage *m* (de la poudre, etc.); grenaillement *m* (d'un métal, de la cire). **2.** grenetage *m,* grainetage *m* (d'une surface); *Astr:* **(solar) g.,** grains *mpl* de riz. **3.** *pl. Med:* **granulations,** granulations, bourgeonnement *m.*
granulator ['grænjuleitər], *s. Metall:* granulatoire *m; Ch: Exp:* grenoir *m,* granulateur *m.*
granule ['grænjul], *s.* granule *m; Tp: etc:* **carbon granules,** grenaille *f* de charbon; *Biol:* **g. cell,** cellule granuleuse.
granulite ['grænjulait], *s. Miner:* granulite *f.*
granulitic [grænju'litik], *a.* granulitique.
granulitis [grænju'laitis], *s. Med:* granulite *f.*
granulo-adipose ['grænjulou'ædipouz], *a. Med:* granulo-graisseux.
granulocyte ['grænjulousait], *s. Physiol:* granulocyte *m.*
granulocytopenia ['grænjulousaitou'piːniə], *s. Med:* granulopénie *f,* granulocytopénie *f.*
granuloma [grænju'loumə], *s. Med:* granulome *m.*
granulomatosis [grænjuloumə'tousis], *s. Med:* granulomatose *f.*
granulometric [grænjulou'metrik], *a.* granulométrique.
granulometry [grænju'lɔmitri], *s.* granulométrie *f.*
granulopenia [grænjulou'piːniə], *s. Med:* granulopénie *f.*
granulose ['grænjulous]. **1.** *s. Ch: Physiol:* granulose *f.* **2.** *a.* = GRANULAR.
granulous ['grænjuləs], *a.* granuleux, granulaire.
grape [greip], *s.* **1.** *(a)* (grain *m* de) raisin *m; (b) Hort:* **a (variety of) g.,** un raisin; **table g., dessert g.,** raisin de table, de treille; *(c)* **bunch of grapes,** grappe *f* de raisin; **dessert grapes,** raisin(s) de table; **for dessert I'll have grapes,** comme dessert je prendrai un raisin, du raisin; **to gather the grapes,** vendanger; faire la vendange; **to glean grapes,** grappiller; *Lit:* **the juice of the g.,** le jus de la treille; *F:* **sour grapes!** ils sont trop verts! *(d) attrib.* **g. basket,** vendangeoir *m;* hotte *f* (de vendangeur); **g. gatherer, picker,** vendangeur, -euse; **g. gathering, picking, g. harvest,** vendange *f;* **g. sugar,** sucre *m* de raisin, glucose *f; Med:* **g. cure,** cure uvale; *Bot:* **g. hyacinth,** muscari *m; (e) Bot:* **Oregon g.,** mahonia *m* (à feuilles de houx). **2.** *Mil: A:* = GRAPESHOT. **3.** *pl. Vet:* **grapes,** la grappe.
grapefruit ['greipfruːt], *s.* pamplemousse *m;* **g. tree,** pamplemoussier *m.*
grapehouse ['greiphaus], *s.* serre *f* à raisins; grapperie *f.*
grapejuice ['greipdʒuːs], *s.* jus *m* de raisin.
grapery ['greipəri], *s. (a)* serre *f* à raisin(s); grapperie *f; (b)* vignoble *m.*
grapeshot ['greipʃɔt], *s.* mitraille *f; A:* **to fire g. on troops, to pepper troops with g.,** mitrailler les troupes; **discharge of g.,** mitraillade *f.*
grapestone ['greipstoun], *s.* pépin *m* de raisin.

grapevine ['greipvain], *s.* 1. *NAm:* vigne *f*, treille *f*. 2. *F:* téléphone *m* arabe; **I heard on the g. that . . .**, on m'a dit que . . .; la rumeur publique voudrait que . . . . 3. *Wr:* clef *f* de pied, de bras.

graph[1] [græf], *s.* 1. graphique *m*, graphe *m*, diagramme *m*; courbe *f*, tracé *m* (d'une équation, etc.); **directed, undirected, g.**, graphique, graphe, orienté, non orienté; **flow g.**, graphique, graphe, de débit, d'écoulement, de transfert; **g. paper**, papier *m* pour graphique, papier millimétré, millimétrique. 2. abaque *m*, nomogramme *m*; barème *m* graphique.

graph[2], *v.tr.* 1. graphiquer (une courbe); tracer (une courbe) graphiquement. 2. abaquarrer (la table de Pythagore, etc.).

grapheme ['græfi:m], *s. Ling:* graphème *m*.

graphic ['græfik], *a.* 1. (*a*) *Mth: etc:* (*also* **graphical**) (représentation *f*, solution *f*, etc.) graphique; (*b*) *Miner:* **g. granite**, pegmatite *f* graphique. 2. (*of description, etc.*) pittoresque, vivant; **g. artist**, graphiste *mf*; **g. art**, art *m* graphique.

graphically ['græfik(ə)li], *adv.* 1. (résoudre un problème) graphiquement. 2. (décrire) d'une manière pittoresque.

graphics ['græfiks], *s.pl.* (*usu. with sg. const.*) la graphique.

graphiola [græfi'oulə], *s. Fung:* graphiola *m*.

graphite ['græfait], *s.* graphite *m*; mine *f* de plomb; plombagine *f*; **retort g.**, graphite de cornue; **colloidal g.**, graphite colloïdal; **g. flake**, écaille *f*, flocon *m*, de graphite; **flaky g.**, graphite écailleux, graphite en lamelles; **g. oil**, huile graphitée; **to coat with g.**, graphiter, plombaginer; *Mec.E:* **lubricating g.**, graphite de graissage; **non-freezing g.**, bouillie *f* de graphite; *Atom.Ph:* **g.-moderated pile, reactor**, réacteur modéré au graphite, utilisant le graphite comme ralentisseur; **g. moderator**, modérateur *m* en graphite.

graphited ['græfaitid], *a.* graphité.

graphitic [grə'fitik], *a.* graphitique.

graphitization [græfitai'zeiʃ(ə)n], *s.* graphitisation *f*.

graphitize ['græfitaiz], *v.tr.* graphiter.

graphiure ['græfijuər], *s. Z:* graphiure *m*.

graphological [græfə'lɔdʒikl], *a.* graphologique.

graphologist [græ'fɔlədʒist], *s.* graphologue *mf*.

graphology [græ'fɔlədʒi], *s.* graphologie *f*.

graphomania [græfou'meiniə], *s. Med:* graphomanie *f*, *F:* scribomanie *f*.

graphometer [græ'fɔmitər], *s. Surv:* graphomètre *m*; demi-cercle *m*, *pl.* demi-cercles.

graphometric [græfou'metrik], *a.* graphométrique.

graphometry [græ'fɔmitri], *s.* graphométrie *f*.

graphoscope ['græfouskoup], *s.* graphoscope *m*.

graphotype ['græfoutaip], *s. Engr:* graphotypie *f*.

graphy ['græfi], *s. Ling:* graphie *f*.

grapnel ['græpnəl], *s. Nau:* grappin *m*, crochet *m*, drague *f*, harpeau *m*; *Hyd.E:* araignée *f*; *Aer:* ancre *f* (de ballon).

grapple[1] ['græpl], *s.* 1. (*a*) = GRAPNEL; (*b*) *Petr:* harpon *m*. 2. lutte *f* corps à corps.

grapple[2]. 1. *v.tr.* (*a*) *A:* grappiner; jeter le grappin sur (un bateau, etc.); (*b*) accrocher, agripper (qn, qch.). 2. *v.i.* (*a*) *Nau: A:* **to g. with a ship**, aborder un navire; (*b*) **to g. with s.o.**, en venir aux prises avec qn; saisir qn à bras le corps; **to g. with a difficulty**, en venir aux prises avec, s'attaquer à, une difficulté; (*c*) **to g. on to sth.**, s'accrocher à qch.

grappler ['græplər], *s.* 1. = GRAPNEL. 2. personne *f* qui vient aux prises avec qn.

grappling ['græpliŋ], *s.* 1. accrochage *m*. 2. (*a*) (i) *NAm: A:* abordage *m*; (ii) **g. iron, hook**, grappin *m*, crochet *m*; (*b*) lutte *f* corps à corps, corps-à-corps *m* (**with**, avec); colletage *m*.

graptolite ['græptoulait], *s. Paleont:* graptolit(h)e *m*.

Graptolitoidea [græptouli'tɔidiə], *s.pl. Paleont:* graptolit(h)es *m*.

grapy ['greipi], *a.* (goût, etc.) de raisin.

grasp[1] [grɑ:sp], *s.* 1. (*a*) poigne *f*; **to have a strong g.**, avoir de la poigne; (*b*) prise *f*; étreinte *f*; **to lose one's g.**, lâcher prise; **to wrest sth. from s.o.'s g.**, arracher qch. à l'étreinte de qn, des mains de qn; **to escape from s.o.'s g.**, échapper à l'étreinte de qn; **to have sth. within one's g.**, avoir qch. à sa portée; **to have s.o. within one's g.**, avoir qn en son pouvoir, entre ses griffes; **to have success within one's g.**, tenir le succès entre ses mains; **beyond one's g.**, hors d'atteinte; (*c*) compréhension *f*; **to have a good g. of modern history**, avoir une bonne connaissance de l'histoire moderne. 2. poignée *f* (d'un aviron, d'une épée).

grasp[2]. 1. *v.tr.* (*a*) saisir; empoigner (un outil, etc.); prendre (qch.); serrer (qch.) dans sa main; étreindre (qch.); **to g. s.o.'s hand**, serrer la main à qn; **I grasped his arm**, je lui ai saisi le bras; (*b*) s'emparer de (qch.); saisir (la couronne); se saisir de (qch.); **to g. the opportunity**, saisir l'occasion au vol; saisir l'occasion (de faire qch.). 2. *v.tr.* comprendre (une difficulté, etc.); **I did not quite g. what he said**, je n'ai pas tout à fait saisi ce qu'il disait; **argument difficult to g.**, raisonnement *m* difficile à saisir; **to g. the importance of sth.**, se rendre compte de l'importance de qch. 3. *v.i.* **to g. at sth.**, (i) tâcher de saisir, d'atteindre, qch.; chercher à saisir qch.; (ii) saisir avidement (une occasion, une offre).

grasper ['grɑ:spər], *s. F:* personne *f* âpre au gain; accapareur, -euse; agrippeur, -euse; attrapeur, -euse.

grasping[1] ['grɑ:spiŋ], *a.* 1. (*of claws, etc.*) tenace. 2. avide, cupide, intéressé; pingre; âpre au gain; **to be g.**, avoir les dents longues.

grasping[2], *s.* 1. prise *f*, empoignement *m*; étreinte *f* (dans la main). 2. compréhension *f*.

grass[1] [grɑ:s], *s.* 1. (*a*) herbe *f*; **blade of g.**, brin *m* d'herbe; **to cut g. (for fodder)**, faire de l'herbe; **to cut the g. from under s.o.'s feet**, couper l'herbe sous le pied de qn; **he doesn't let the g. grow under his feet**, il ne perd pas son temps; *attrib.* **g. seed**, (i) graine fourragère; (ii) graine pour gazon; **g. hook**, faucille *f*; *F:* **g. widow**, femme délaissée; femme dont le mari est absent, en voyage; veuve *f* à titre temporaire; demi-veuve *f*; **g. widower**, mari *m* dont la femme est absente; veuf *m* à titre temporaire; *Dom.Ec:* **g. brush**, brosse *f* en chiendent; (*b*) *Bot:* **beach g.**, roseau *m* des sables; **ribbon g.**, roseau panaché; **bent g.**, (i) jonc *m*; (ii) agrostide *m*; **lemon g.**, schénanthe *m*; jonc odorant; **meadow g.**, *U.S:* **spear g.**, pâturin *m*; **deer g.**, rhexia *f*; **hard g.**, rottboellia *m*; **quaking g.**, (i) briza *f*; (ii) (*also* **rattlesnake g.**), glycérie *f*; **China g.**, ortie *f* utile; ramie blanche; **feather g.**, stipe (plumeuse); **rye g.**, ivraie *f* vivace; fausse ivraie; faux seigle; **g. of Parnassus**, parnassie *f* des marais, gazon *m* du Parnasse; **g. tree**, xanthorrhée *f*; *Algae:* **g. wrack**, zostère *f*, *F:* baugue *f*, bauque *f*; (*c*) *Amph:* **g. frog**, grenouille rousse; *Rept:* **g. snake**, couleuvre *f* à collier, serpent *m* d'eau; *F:* **he's a snake in the g.**, c'est un perfide. 2. (*a*) herbage *m*, pâture *f*, fourrage *m* en vert; **to put, turn, send, a horse out to g.**, mettre un cheval à l'herbe, au vert, en pâture; mettre paître, herbager, un cheval; **to be at g.**, **(put) out to g.**, (i) (*of animal*) être au vert; (ii) *F:* (*of pers.*) être à la retraite; être mis au vert; aller planter ses choux; **to take a horse off g.**, remettre un cheval à sec, au sec; **to put land under g.**, enherber une terre; mettre un terrain en pré; convertir un champ en herbe; (*b*) gazon *m*; *P.N:* **do not walk on the g.**, **(please) keep off the g.**, défense de marcher sur le gazon, sur les pelouses; *F:* **keep off the g.!** n'empiétez pas sur mes plates-bandes, sur mes prérogatives; *Turf:* **three riders were on the g.**, trois jockeys avaient vidé les arçons, étaient par terre; *F: A:* **to send s.o. to g.**, étendre qn par terre; **to go to g.**, s'étaler par terre, mordre la poussière; (*c*) *Min:* surface *f*, jour *m*; **to bring ore to g.**, remonter le minerai. 3. *Rad: F:* parasites *mpl*. 4. *esp. U.S: F:* (i) asperges *fpl*; (ii) salade *f*, laitue *f*. 5. *F:* marijuana *f*, thé (vert). 6. *P:* = GRASSER.

grass[2], *v.tr.* 1. mettre en herbe, enherber (un champ); gazonner (un terrain). 2. *Tex:* blanchir sur pré, herber, curer (le lin). 3. (*a*) *F:* étendre (un adversaire) par terre; désarçonner (un cavalier); (*b*) *Fish:* amener (un poisson) à terre; (*c*) *Ven:* abattre, descendre (un oiseau). 4. *Min:* remonter (le minerai). 5. *v.i. P:* chanter; cafarder; **to g. on s.o.**, dénoncer qn.

grass-bleached ['grɑ:sbli:tʃt], *a. Tex:* blanchi sur l'herbe, sur pré.

grassbox ['grɑ:sbɔks], *s.* panier *m* à herbes (d'une tondeuse de gazon).

grasscloth ['grɑ:sklɔθ], *s.* 1. *Tex:* (toile *f* de) ramie *f*. 2. *Bot:* **g. plant**, ramie.

grassed [grɑ:st], *a. Golf:* (club) à face légèrement inclinée.

grasser ['grɑ:sər], *s. P:* chanteur, -euse; dénonciateur, -trice; cafardeur, -euse.

grass-feed ['grɑ:sfi:d], *v.tr.* mettre (le bétail) à pâturer.

grassfinch ['grɑ:sfin(t)ʃ], *s. Orn:* **long-tailed g.**, diamant *m* à longue queue; **masked g.**, diamant à masque; **white-eared g.**, diamant à oreilles blanches.

grass(-)green ['grɑ:s'gri:n], *a.* & *s.* vert pré (*m*) *inv*.

grass-grown ['grɑ:sgroun], *a.* herbu, herbeux, enherbé.

grasshopper ['grɑ:shɔpər], *s. Ent:* sauterelle *f*; **water g.**, cigale *f* de rivière; **the longhorned grasshoppers**, les ensifères *m*; **to have a g. mind**, avoir une tête de linotte.

grassing ['grɑ:siŋ], *s.* 1. mise *f* en herbe, en gazon (d'un terrain). 2. *Tex:* blanchissage *m*, blanchiment *m*, sur pré; curage *m* (du lin). 3. (*a*) désarçonnage *m* (d'un cavalier); (*b*) abattage *m* (d'un oiseau). 4. remontage *m* (du minerai). 5. *P:* dénonciation *f* (de ses complices).

grassland ['grɑ:slænd], *s.* prairies *fpl*, prés *mpl*, herbages *mpl*; *Geog:* **tropical g.**, savane *f*; **temperate g.**, prairie; steppe (tempérée).

grassquit ['grɑ:skwit], *s. Orn:* tiaris *m*; chanteur *m* de Cuba, jacarini *m*; **Cuban g.**, petit chanteur de Cuba; **glossy g.**, jacarini *m*; **yellow-faced g.**, grand chanteur de Cuba.

grassroots ['grɑ:sru:ts], *s.pl.* (*with sg. or pl. const.*) 1. couche supérieure du sol. 2. (*a*) région *f* agricole; les communes rurales et la campagne; (*b*) la population rurale; **g. democracy**, le populisme. 3. fondation *f*, source *f*, base *f*; **to attack a problem at the g.**, remonter à la source d'un problème.

grassy ['grɑ:si], *a.* herbu, herbeux; (*of pasture land*) herbageux; **g. path**, chemin vert; **g. plains**, plaines verdoyantes.

grate[1] [greit], *s.* (*a*) grille *f* (de foyer, *Mch:* de foyer de chaudière); *Mch:* **dump(ing) g.**, grille basculante; **revolving g.**, grille tournante; **rocking g.**, **shaking g.**, **jigging g.**, grille oscillante, à secousses; **steep g.**, grille inclinée; **g. area, surface**, surface *f*, aire *f*, de grille; **g. bar**, barreau *m* de grille; **g. (-bar), (fire-) g., bearer**, sommier *m*, châssis *m*, de grille; (*b*) foyer *m*, âtre *m*; **let's have a fire in the g.!** faisons un feu dans la cheminée, une flambée! (*c*) *Min:* grille, tamis *m* (de bocard).

grate[2], *v.tr.* griller (une fenêtre, etc.).

grate[3]. 1. *v.tr.* râper (du fromage, de la muscade); **grated cheese**, fromage râpé. 2. (*a*) *v.tr.* **to g. one's teeth**, grincer des dents; (*b*) **to g. sth. on sth.**, frotter qch. contre qch. (avec un grincement). 3. *v.i.* (*a*) (*of machinery, etc.*) grincer; (*of chalk on blackboard, etc.*) crisser; **the brake grated on the wheel**, le frein frottait, grinçait, contre la roue; **the door grated on its hinges**, la porte grinçait, criait, sur ses gonds; (*b*) **to g. on the ear**, choquer, écorcher, déchirer, affliger, blesser, l'oreille; **word that grates on the ear**, mot dissonant; mot désagréable à l'oreille; **to g. on the nerves**, taper sur les nerfs; agacer les nerfs.

grated ['greitid], *a.* grillé, à grille.

grateful ['greitf(u)l], *a.* 1. (*of pers.*) reconnaissant (**to, towards, s.o. for sth.**, à, envers, qn de qch.); **to be g. to s.o. for sth., for having done sth.**, savoir (bon) gré à qn de qch., d'avoir fait qch.; **to have reason to be g. to s.o.**, devoir de la reconnaissance à qn; **I am g. to you for giving me a warning**, je vous suis très reconnaissant de m'avoir prévenu. 2. *A:* & *Lit:* (*of thg*) agréable; (repos) réconfortant, bienfaisant; à propos.

gratefully ['greitfuli], *adv.* avec reconnaissance.

gratefulness ['greitf(u)lnis], *s.* reconnaissance *f*, gratitude *f*.

grater ['greitər], *s. Dom.Ec:* râpe *f*.

Gratian ['greiʃiən], *Pr.n.m. Rom.Hist:* Gratien.

graticulate [grə'tikjuleit], *v.tr. Draw:* graticuler (un dessin).

graticulation [grətikju'leiʃ(ə)n], *s. Draw: Mapm:* graticulation *f*.

graticule ['grætikju:l], *s.* 1. *Draw: Mapm:* graticule *m*; *Mapm:* carroyage *m* (de méridiens et parallèles). 2. *Opt: Tchn:* (i) réticule *m*; (ii) micromètre *m*.

gratification [grætifi'keiʃ(ə)n], *s.* 1. satisfaction *f*, plaisir *m*; **to do sth. for one's own g.**, faire qch. pour son propre contentement; **it is a real g. to learn that . . .**, c'est un réel plaisir d'apprendre que . . . . 2. satisfaction, assouvissement *m* (des passions). 3. *A:* (*a*) gratification *f*, récompense *f*; (*b*) pot-de-vin *m*, *pl.* pots-de-vin.

gratified ['grætifaid], *a.* satisfait, content (**with**, de); **g. smile**, sourire *m* de satisfaction; **in his heart of hearts he was very much g.**, au fond il était très flatté, il était enchanté.

gratify ['grætifai], *v.tr.* 1. *A:* donner une gratification, une récompense, à (qn). 2. faire plaisir, être agréable, à (qn). 3. satisfaire, contenter (une passion, le désir de qn, etc.); **to g. s.o.'s whims**, satisfaire aux caprices de qn; flatter les caprices de qn.

gratifying ['grætifaiiŋ], *a.* agréable; flatteur, -euse; (perspective *f*, etc.) qui donne de la satisfaction; **it is very g. to learn that . . .**, c'est un réel plaisir d'apprendre que . . ..

gratinate ['grætineit], *v.tr. Cu:* gratiner.

gratiné ['grætinei], *a. Cu:* gratiné.

grating[1] ['greitiŋ], *s.* 1. (*a*) grille *f*, grillage *m* (de fenêtre, etc.); treillis *m*, lattis *m*; claire-voie *f*, *pl.* claires-voies; *Pisc:* écrille *f* (d'un étang); *Hyd.E: etc:* gril *m* (en amont d'une vanne); grille, pommelle *f* (d'égout, de tuyau, etc.); crapaudine *f* (de débouché); *Ind: etc:* **g. floor**, plancher *m* en lattis; *Nau:* **boiler-room g.**, plancher de la chaufferie; *Navy:* **armoured g.**, grillage blindé; (*b*) *Nau:* caillebot(t)is *m*. 2. *Elcs: Opt:* **diffraction g.**, réseau *m* (de diffraction); **g. constant**, constante *f*, équidistance *f*, des raies (d'un réseau de diffraction);

Elcs: **g. converter,** transformateur *m* (de guide d'ondes).

grating², *a.* **1.** (*of noise, etc.*) discordant, râpeux, grinçant; qui écorche, déchire, l'oreille; **g. sound,** grincement *m*, crissement *m*; **g. laugh,** ricanement *m*; **g. laughter,** ricanements; **g. voice,** voix *f* rude. **2.** choquant, désagréable.

grating³, *s.* **1.** (*a*) râpage *m*; (*b*) *pl.* **gratings,** râpure(s) *f*(*pl*). **2.** grincement *m*, crissement *m* (d'un gond, etc.); frottement *m* (d'une roue, etc.).

gratingly ['greitiŋli], *adv.* **1.** avec un son râpeux; d'un ton discordant. **2.** désagréablement.

gratiola [græ'taiələ], *s. Bot:* gratiole *f*.

gratis ['greitis]. **1.** *a.* gratis, gratuit. **2.** *adv.* gratis, gratuitement, à titre gratuit.

gratitude ['grætitju:d], *s.* gratitude *f*, reconnaissance *f* (to, envers).

gratuitous [grə'tju(:)itəs], *a.* **1.** gratuit; (service *m*, etc.) bénévole; **g. contract,** contrat *m* à titre gratuit; contrat de bienfaisance. **2. g. insult,** insulte injustifiée, gratuite, sans motif; **g. lie,** mensonge sans motif; mensonge gratuit.

gratuitously [grə'tju(:)itəsli], *adv.* **1.** gratuitement; à titre bénévole, gratuit; bénévolement, gracieusement. **2.** sans motif; gratuitement.

gratuitousness [grə'tju(:)itəsnis], *s.* gratuité *f*; (*of a remark, etc.*) manque *m* d'à-propos, inopportunité *f*.

gratuity [grə'tju(:)iti], *s.* **1.** gratification *f*, pourboire *m*; *P.N:* **no gratuities,** défense de donner des pourboires. **2.** (*given to retiring employee*) prime *f*; *Mil: etc:* prime de démobilisation, pécule *m*; *Adm:* (*given to convict on discharge*) pécule.

gravamen, *pl.* **-mina** [grə'veimen, -minə], *s.* **1.** (*a*) plainte *f*, grief *m*; (*b*) *Ecc:* mémoire présenté par la Chambre Basse de la Convocation à la Haute Chambre, ayant rapport à des désordres ou à des sujets de plainte dans l'Église. **2.** *Jur:* fond *m*, fondement *m* (d'une accusation); **g. of a charge,** matière *f* d'un crime.

grave¹ [greiv], *s.* (*a*) tombe *f*, tombeau *m*, fosse *f*; **family g.,** tombeau de famille; *A:* **the paupers' g.,** la fosse commune; **mass g.,** tombe collective; **open g.,** tombe qui attend son cercueil; **Imperial War Graves Commission** = Comité impérial des Sépultures de Guerre; *F:* Service des Sépultures Militaires; **to be in one's g.,** être enterré, sous terre, en terre, dans la tombe; *Lit:* **he just escaped a watery g.,** il a failli être enseveli sous les ondes; *F:* **he must have turned in his g.,** il a dû frémir dans sa tombe; **someone's walking over my g.,** j'ai des frissons; j'ai le frisson; **to have one foot in the g., to be on the brink of the g.,** avoir un pied dans la tombe; être au bord de la tombe, de la fosse; être aux portes du tombeau; **to be brought to an early g.,** avoir une fin prématurée; (*b*) **from beyond the g.,** d'outre-tombe; **never on this side of the g.,** jamais de la vie; *B:* **O g., where is thy victory?** où est, ô sépulcre, ta victoire?

grave², *v.tr.* (*p.t.* **graved;** *p.p.* **graven, graved**) **1.** *A:* creuser (une fosse). **2.** graver, ciseler, tailler, échopper (une inscription, etc.); *Lit:* **graven on his memory,** gravé dans sa mémoire.

grave³, *a.* (*a*) grave, sérieux; **to look g.,** avoir l'air sévère; **as g. as a judge,** sérieux comme un juge, comme un pape; **g. tone,** ton grave; ton solennel; **g. colours,** couleurs *f* sobres, sévères; **to pass from g. to gay,** passer du grave au doux; **matters g. and gay,** le grave et le plaisant; (*b*) **g. news,** de graves nouvelles; **g. accusation,** accusation grave, importante; **g. mistake,** lourde erreur; **to make a g. mistake,** se tromper lourdement; *Med: etc:* **g. symptoms,** symptômes *m* graves, inquiétants.

grave⁴ [grɑ:v, *occ.* greiv], *a. Ling:* **g. accent,** accent *m* grave.

grave⁵ [greiv], *v.tr. Nau:* **to g. a ship,** radouber, espalmer, un navire; gratter le fond d'un navire.

gravecloth ['greivklɔθ], *s.* **graveclothes** ['greivklouðz], *s.pl.* linceul *m*, suaire *m*.

gravedigger ['greivdigər], *s.* **1.** fossoyeur *m*. **2.** *Ent: F:* nécrophore *m*.

gravedigging¹ ['greivdigiŋ], *a. Ent:* **g. insect,** nécrophore *m*.

gravedigging², *s.* fossoyage *m*.

gravel¹ ['græv(ə)l], *s.* **1.** gravier *m*, gravelage *m*; **fine g.,** gravier fin; gravillon *m*; **coarse g.,** gros gravier; *Const: Civ.E: etc:* **sea g.,** arène marine; *Min:* (*gold*) **pay g.,** gravier rémunérateur, payant; **g. pit,** gravière *f*, cailloutière *f*, ballastière *f*; *attrib.* **g. path,** allée gravelée, sablée; *P.N: Aut: NAm:* **gravel!** gravillons! *Fr.C:* gravelle! *Belg:* pierres errantes! **2.** *Med:* gravelle *f*, *F:* graviers, sable *m*; **suffering from g.,** graveleux.

gravel², *v.tr.* (**gravelled**) **1.** graveler; **to g. a path,** recouvrir un chemin de gravier; sabler un chemin; **gravelled path,** allée gravelée, sablée. **2.** *esp. NAm: F:* embarrasser (qn); mettre, réduire, (qn) à quia; coller (qn); **to be gravelled,** être à quia; **to get gravelled,** s'embourber.

gravel-blind ['grævlblaind], *a.* presque aveugle.

graveless ['greivlis], *a.* sans tombe, sans tombeau, sans sépulture.

gravelling ['grævəliŋ], *s.* gravelage *m*; **fine g.,** gravillonnage *m*.

gravelly ['grævəli], *a.* **1.** mêlé de gravier; graveleux; (lit de rivière, etc.) pierreux; (chemin) sablonneux; **g. soil,** terrain *m* de gravier. **2.** *Med:* (*of urine, etc.*) graveleux.

gravely ['greivli], *adv.* gravement, sérieusement; sévèrement; solennellement.

graven ['greiv(ə)n], *a.* gravé, taillé, échoppé; *esp. B:* **g. image,** image taillée.

graveness ['greivnis], *s.* gravité *f*, sévérité *f*.

graver¹ ['greivər], *s.* **1.** (*pers.*) graveur *m*. **2.** *Tls:* échoppe *f*, burin *m*, gravoir *m*, ciselet *m*, onglette *f*, style *m*.

graver², *s.m. Nau:* radoubeur, espalmeur.

Graves [greivz], *Pr.n. Med:* **Graves's disease,** goitre *m* exophtalmique; maladie *f* de Graves.

gravestone ['greivstoun], *s.* pierre *f* tumulaire; pierre funéraire; pierre tombale.

Gravettian [grə'vetiən], *a. Prehist:* gravétien, gravettien.

graveyard ['greivjɑ:d], *s.* (*a*) cimetière *m*; *Lit:* **g. school (of poetry, etc.),** école *f* de la nuit et des tombeaux; *U.S: F:* **g. vote,** vote frauduleux (fait au nom d'un mort); (*b*) cimetière (de vieilles voitures, etc.); **this firm is the g. of personal initiative,** cette maison est le tombeau, la fin, de toute initiative individuelle; (*c*) *NAm: F: Ind:* **g. shift,** (i) shift *m*, (ii) équipe *f*, de nuit; *Nau:* **g. watch,** quart *m* de minuit à quatre heures.

gravid ['grævid], *a. Lit:* (*of woman*) gravide, grosse, enceinte; (*of animal*) pleine; *Lit:* **g. with ideas,** lourd d'idées.

gravidity [grə'viditi], *s.* gravidité *f*.

gravidocardiac ['grævidou'kɑ:diæk], *a. Med:* gravidocardiaque.

gravimeter [grə'vimitər], *s. Ph:* gravimètre *m*, aréomètre *m*.

gravimetric [grævi'metrik], *a.* gravimétrique.

gravimetry [grə'vimitri], *s.* gravimétrie *f*.

graving¹ ['greiviŋ], *s.* échoppage *m*, taille *f*; **g. tool,** échoppe *f*, burin *m*, gravoir *m*.

graving², *s. Nau:* radoub *m*; **g. dock,** bassin *m* de radoub; **g. beach,** (cale *f* d')échouage *m*; **g. piece,** romaillet *m*; *Carp:* limande *f*.

gravitate ['græviteit], *v.i.* graviter (**towards,** vers; **round,** autour de); **the larger stones g. to the bottom,** les gros cailloux descendent au fond par gravitation; **most of the guests had gravitated to the bar,** la plupart des invités la plupart des invités s'étaient dinges vers le bar, s'étaient dirigés vers le bar.

gravitation [grævi'teiʃ(ə)n], *s.* gravitation *f*; attraction universelle; **law of g.,** la loi de la pesanteur; *Min:* **g. stamp,** pilon *m* à chute libre.

gravitational [grævi'teiʃən(ə)l], *a.* gravitationnel, de gravitation, gravifique; **g. acceleration,** accélération *f* terrestre, accélération due à la pesanteur; **g. field,** champ *m* de gravitation; **g. system,** système *m* de gravitation; **g. force,** force *f* de gravitation; **g. pull,** gravitation *f*.

gravity ['græviti], *s.* **1.** gravité *f*; (*a*) sérieux *m*; **to preserve, lose, one's g.,** garder, perdre, son sérieux, sa gravité; **that upset his g.,** cela lui fit perdre son sérieux; il ne put se retenir de rire; (*b*) **g. of a situation, etc.,** gravité d'une situation, etc.; **g. of a decision,** gravité, importance *f*, d'une décision; **g. of a wound,** gravité d'une blessure. **2.** (*a*) *Ph:* gravité, pesanteur *f*; *Astr:* (force *f* de) gravitation *f*; **centre of g.,** centre *m* de gravité; **force of g.,** force gravifique; **specific g.,** poids *m* spécifique, gravité spécifique; densité *f*; **specific g. bottle, flask,** flacon *m* à densité; **high-g. liquid,** liquide *m* de poids spécifique élevé; **g. acceleration,** accélération *f* terrestre, accélération due à la pesanteur; (*b*) *Hyd.E:* **g. wave,** onde *f* de gravité; **g. irrigation,** irrigation *f* au fil de l'eau; (*c*) *Mec.E: Tchn:* **g. feed,** alimentation *f* en charge, par gravité; **g.-fed,** alimenté en charge, par gravité; **g. tank,** réservoir *m* en charge; *Civ.E:* **g. dam,** barrage *m* poids; **g. spillway dam,** barrage poids déversoir; *Ind: Min:* **separation, sorting, by g.,** séparation *f*, triage *m*, par gravité; *Nau:* **g. davit,** bossoir *m* à gravité, bossoir automatique; (*d*) *Geol:* **g. fault,** faille *f* normale.

gravy ['greivi], *s.* **1.** *Cu:* (*a*) jus *m* (qui sort de la viande); (*b*) sauce *f* (au jus); **g. boat,** saucière *f*. **2.** *esp. NAm: P:* gros bénéfice; profit *m* illicite; gratte *f*; **the g. train, boat,** l'assiette *f* au beurre; un bon filon; **to ride the g. train,** (i) taper dans l'assiette au beurre; (ii) se la couler douce.

gray [grei], *a. & s.* = GREY.

grayling ['greiliŋ], *s.* **1.** *Ich:* ombre *m* (de rivière). **2.** *Ent:* (papillon *m*) agreste *m*.

graywacke ['greiwækə], *s. Miner:* grauwacke *f*.

graze¹ [greiz]. **1.** *v.i.* paître, brouter, pâturer; *Ven:* (*of deer*) viander; **to g. on a field,** pâturer un champ. **2.** *v.tr.* (*a*) paître, faire paître, mener paître (un troupeau); (*b*) pacager, mettre en pacage (un champ); (*c*) (*of cattle, etc.*) pâturer (un champ); paître (l'herbe); **to g. down grass,** tondre l'herbe.

graze², *s.* **1.** effleurage *m*, effleurement *m*, frisage *m*, frôlement *m*. **2.** (*a*) écorchure *f*, éraflure *f*; (*b*) *Arb:* talure *f*.

graze³, *v.tr.* **1.** écorcher, érafler (ses genoux, etc.). **2.** effleurer, raser, friser, frôler; **the bullet grazed his shoulder,** la balle lui rasa, lui fraya, l'épaule; **the bullet only grazed him,** la balle ne l'a touché que superficiellement; **the sword grazed his ribs,** l'épée *f* lui a glissé sur les côtes; *Ten:* **ball that just grazes the net,** balle *f* à fleur de corde; *Nau:* (*of ship*) **to g. the bottom,** labourer le fond; toucher.

grazier ['greiziər], *s. Husb:* herbager, -ère; cheptelier *m*; éleveur *m*.

grazing¹ ['greiziŋ], *s.* **1.** pâturage *m* (de troupeaux, etc.); élevage *m* (de moutons); **g. rights,** droit *m* de pâturage, de pacage. **2. g. (land, ground),** pâture *f*, pacage *m*, pâtis *m*, dépaissance *f*; (*for deer*) viandis *m*; **g. forest,** pré-bois *m*, *pl.* prés-bois.

grazing², *a.* (coup) qui effleure le but.

grazing³, *s.* effleurement *m*; accrochage *m* (d'une voiture).

grease¹ [gri:s], *s.* **1.** (*a*) graisse *f* (d'un animal; *used in the phr.* **deer in prime, pride, of g.,** cerf gras); (*b*) **wool g.,** suint *m*; graisse de laine; **wool in (the) g.,** laine *f* en suint. **2.** (*a*) *Mec.E: etc:* graisse; (*when dirty from use*) cambouis *m*; **non-freezing g., anti-freeze g.,** graisse anti-gel, incongelable; **graphite g.,** graisse graphitée; **hard, solid, thick, g.,** graisse consistante, épaisse; **high melting-point g.,** graisse à température de fluage élevée; **cup g.,** graisse à godet; **g. cup,** godet *m* à graisse, de graissage; (godet) graisseur *m*; **belt g.,** enduit *m*, graisse, à courroies; **axle g.,** graisse pour essieux; *Mil: etc:* **g. for arms,** graisse d'arme; **rifle g.,** axonge *f*; **g. channel,** rainure *f*, gorge *f*, de graissage; patte *f* d'araignée (de coussinet); *Mch:* **g. box,** boîte *f* à graisse, de graissage; boîte d'essieu; **caulker's g. box,** escarbit *m*; **g. cock,** robinet graisseur; **g. gun, g. injector,** pompe *f* à graisse; injecteur *m*, pistolet *m*, à graisse; pistolet graisseur; **g. spot,** tache *f* de graisse, d'huile; *F:* **I feel like a g. spot,** je suis en train de fondre (de chaleur); **g. remover,** (i) *Ind:* dégraisseur *m*; (ii) *Mch:* déshuileur *m* (d'eau); (iii) *Leath:* dégraisseuse *f*; *Hyd.E:* **g. trap,** siphon *m* de dépôt de graisse (des eaux vannes, etc.); **g.-tight, g.-sealed,** étanche à la graisse; **to clean off the g., to extract the g., from sth.,** dégraisser qch.; **to get g. on one's clothes,** tacher ses vêtements de graisse; (*b*) *Ind: Ch:* corps gras; **g.-receptive,** acceptant les corps gras; **g.-repellent, g.-resisting,** refusant les corps gras. **3.** *Arb:* glu *f* horticole; colle *f* à chenilles; **g. band,** bande enduite de glu horticole. **4.** *Vet:* crapaud *m*, crapaudine *f* (du cheval). **5.** *P:* boniments *mpl* à la graisse d'oie.

grease² [gri:s, *occ.* gri:z], *v.tr.* **1.** graisser, encrasser (ses habits). **2.** (*a*) graisser, lubrifier (une machine, etc.); suiffer (un mât); **to keep one's tools slightly greased,** avoir toujours ses outils légèrement graissés; **to keep a mechanism well greased,** entretenir un mécanisme au gras; *Fig:* **that will g. the wheels,** cela graissera les roues; (*b*) *Tex:* ensimer (la laine); (*c*) *Cu:* **g. the tin,** beurrer un moule (à gâteau, etc.). **3.** *Vet:* ulcérer le sabot d'(un cheval); donner le crapaud à (un cheval). **4.** *P:* acheter (qn).

grease-band ['gri:sbænd], *v.tr.* cercler (un arbre) de glu horticole.

greasepaint ['gri:speint], *s.* fard *m*; *Th:* **stick of g.,** crayon gras (de maquillage); **white g.,** blanc gras.

greaseproof ['gri:spru:f], *a.* (papier) imperméable à la graisse, à l'épreuve de la graisse; (papier) parcheminé; *F:* (papier) jambon, (papier) beurre.

greaser ['gri:sər, *occ.* 'gri:zər], *s.* **1.** (*pers.*) (*a*) graisseur *m*; (*b*) *Nau: F:* chef *m* de chauffe; mécanicien *m*, graisseur; (*c*) *U.S: P: Pej:* Hispano-américain *m*, Mexicain *m*; (*d*) *P:* soudoyeur *m*, graisseur, chien couchant. **2.** (*instrument*) *Mec.E: etc:* graisseur; godet à graisse, de graissage.

greasiness ['gri:sinis, *occ.* 'gri:zinis], *s.* **1.** état graisseux, gras; onctuosité *f*. **2.** *F:* onctuosité (de langage, etc.).

greasing ['gri:siŋ], *s.* **1.** graissage *m*; lubrification *f*; *I.C.E: etc:* **pressure g.,** graissage sous pression. **2.** ensimage *m* (de la laine).

greasy ['gri:si, *occ.* 'gri:zi], *a.* **1.** (*a*) graisseux, huileux, onctueux; **to taste g.,** sentir le graillon; (*b*) taché d'huile, de graisse; **to make one's clothes g.,** graisser ses habits; (*c*) (laine) en suint. **2.** (*a*) gras, *f.* grasse, glissant; **g. road,** chemin gras, pâteux, glissant; **g. pole,** mât *m* de cocagne, mât de beaupré (de fête villageoise, etc.); *Nau:* **g. weather,** temps gras; (*b*) (*of manner*) onctueux, patelin; (*c*) *Vet:* **g. heel,** crapaud *m*, crapaudine *f.*

great [greit], *a.* grand; (*a*) **a g. crowd,** une grande foule, une foule énorme; **a g. big man,** un homme de grande taille; **one of those g. lorries,** un de ces énormes poids-lourds; **to grow greater (and greater),** augmenter, s'agrandir, grandir (de plus en plus); *Geog:* **the G. Lakes,** les Grands Lacs; **Greater London,** le grand Londres, l'agglomération londonienne; *Fish:* **g. line,** ligne *f* de mer; *Nav:* **g. circle,** grand cercle; *A:* **g. with child,** enceinte, grosse d'un enfant; (*b*) **a g. deal,** beaucoup (of, de); une grande quantité; une quantité considérable (of, de); **I heard a g. deal of what was said,** j'ai entendu beaucoup de ce qui se disait; **a g. many,** beaucoup (de + *pl.*); **he has a g. many friends,** il a beaucoup d'amis; **a g. many people,** beaucoup de gens; beaucoup de monde; **there were not a g. many people there,** il n'y avait pas grand monde; **the g. majority, the greater part,** la plupart, la majeure partie (of, de); **to a g. extent, in g. measure,** en grande partie, considérablement; **a g. while ago,** il y a bien longtemps; **to reach a g. age,** parvenir à un âge avancé; **of g. antiquity,** de haute antiquité; **at a g. pace,** à une allure rapide, à grand train; (*c*) **his greatest fault,** son plus grand défaut; son défaut capital; **there was a g. bustle,** ce fut un grand remue-ménage; **to take g. care,** prendre grand soin (of, de); prendre beaucoup de soin; **to pay still greater attention,** redoubler d'attention; **greater and greater leniency was shown to them,** on les traitait avec de plus en plus d'indulgence; **g. difference,** grande, forte, différence; **of greater difficulty,** plus difficile; **with g. pleasure, with the greatest of pleasure,** avec grand plaisir, avec le plus grand plaisir; **the G. War,** la Grande Guerre; (*d*) **g. artist,** grand artiste; **the g. men (of the age),** les grands hommes, les célébrités *f* de (l'époque); *s.* **the g. of the earth,** les grands de la terre; **g. thoughts,** grandes, nobles, pensées; *F:* **G. God! G. Scott!** grands dieux! **Alexander the G.,** Alexandre le Grand; **James the Greater,** Jacques le Majeur; *Ecc:* **the greater orders,** les ordres majeurs; (*e*) **g. eater,** grand, gros, mangeur; **g. scoundrel,** grand fripon; **they are g. friends,** ils sont grands amis; *F:* **to be g. at tennis,** être fort au tennis; **he's g. on dates,** il est très ferré, très calé, sur les dates; (*f*) **it is no g. matter,** ce n'est pas une grosse affaire; **to have no g. opinion of s.o.,** tenir qn en médiocre estime; **it is a g. thing to have a knowledge of French,** c'est un grand avantage de savoir le français; **the g. thing is that he is already on the spot,** le grand avantage, le principal, c'est qu'il est déjà sur les lieux; *F:* **wouldn't it be g. if . . .,** comme on serait content si . . .; **to have a g. time,** s'amuser follement; **it was a g. joke,** ça nous a joliment amusés; **(that's) g!** fameux! magnifique! **isn't he g.!** quel homme!

great-aunt ['greit'ɑ:nt], *s.f.* grand-tante, *pl.* grand(s)-tantes.

greatcoat ['greitkout], *s.* **1.** (*a*) pardessus *m*; (*b*) houppelande *f* (de berger, etc.). **2.** *Mil:* (*a*) manteau *m* (de cavalerie); (*b*) capote *f* (d'infanterie); (*c*) *Mil: Navy:* **hooded g.,** capot *m.*

greaten ['greit(ə)n], *v.tr.* & *i. A:* grandir; (s')agrandir.

great-grandchild, *pl.* **-children** ['greit'græn(d)tʃaild, -tʃildrən], *s.* arrière-petit-fils *m*, arrière petite-fille *f*, *pl.* arrière-petits-enfants *m.*

great-granddaughter ['greit'græn(d)dɔ:tər], *s.f.* arrière-petite-fille, *pl.* arrière-petites-filles.

great-grandfather ['greit'græn(d)fɑ:ðər], *s.m.* arrière-grand-père, *pl.* arrière-grands-pères; bisaïeul, *pl.* bisaïeuls.

great-grandmother ['greit'græn(d)mʌðər], *s.f.* arrière-grand-mère, *pl.* arrière-grand-mères; bisaïeule.

great-grandparents ['greit'græn(d)pɛərənts], *s.pl.* arrière-grands-parents *m.*

great grandson ['greit'græn(d)sʌn], *s.m.* arrière-petit-fils, *pl.* arrière-petits-fils.

great-great-grandfather ['greit'greit'græn(d)fɑ:ðər], *s.m.* trisaïeul, *pl.* trisaïeuls.

great-great-grandmother ['greitgreit'græn(d)mʌðər], *s.f.* trisaïeule.

great-hearted ['greit'hɑ:tid], *a.* au grand cœur; généreux, magnanime.

great-heartedness ['greit'hɑ:tidnis], *s.* générosité *f* de cœur; magnanimité *f.*

greatly ['greitli], *adv.* grandement; (*a*) beaucoup; **he is g. superior to me,** il m'est de beaucoup supérieur; **we were g. amused,** cela nous a beaucoup amusés; **g. irritated,** très irrité; fortement irrité; **I would g. prefer . . .,** je préférerais (de) beaucoup . . .; **it is g. to be feared that . . .,** il est fort à craindre que . . .; **to contribute g. to a result,** contribuer puissamment à un résultat; (*b*) *Lit:* avec grandeur; noblement.

great-nephew ['greit'nefju:], *s.m.* petit-neveu, *pl.* petits-neveux.

greatness ['greitnis], *s.* grandeur *f*; (*a*) énormité *f* (de l'éléphant, de la baleine, etc.); (*b*) élévation *f*, noblesse *f* (de pensée); **g. of soul,** grandeur d'âme; (*c*) importance *f*, étendue *f*, intensité *f*; **the g. of his crime,** la grandeur de son crime.

great-niece ['greit'ni:s], *s.f.* petite-nièce, *pl.* petites-nièces.

greats [greits], *s.pl. Sch:* examen définitif, final (langues classiques et philosophie) (à l'université d'Oxford).

great-uncle ['greit'ʌŋkl], *s.m.* grand-oncle, *pl.* grands-oncles.

greave [gri:v], *s.* (*a*) *A.Arm:* jambart *m* (de l'armure); jambière *f*; (*b*) *Gr.Ant:* cnémide *f.*

greaved [gri:vd], *a. A.Arm:* jambardé.

greaves [gri:vz], *s.pl. Cu:* cretons *m*, fritons *m*, rillons *m.*

grebe [gri:b], *s. Orn:* grèbe *m*; **great crested g.,** grèbe huppé, grand grèbe; **little g.,** grèbe castagneux, petit grèbe; **sun g.,** grébifoulque *m*; **black-necked g.,** *NAm:* **eared g.,** grèbe *m* à cou noir; **Slavonian g.,** *NAm:* **horned g.,** grèbe esclavon, grèbe oreillard, *Fr.C:* grèbe cornu; **pied-billed g.,** grèbe à bec bigarré; **red-necked g., Holboell's g.,** grèbe à joues grises, *Fr.C:* grèbe jougris; **western g.,** grèbe de l'ouest.

Grecian ['gri:ʃ(ə)n]. **1.** *a.* grec, *f.* grecque; **in the G. style,** dans le style grec; à la grecque; **G. knot,** coiffure *f* à la grecque; **G. gift,** présent *m* dont il y a lieu de se méfier. **2.** *s.* hellénisant *m*, helléniste *m.*

Grecism, Grecize, Greco-, *etc.* = GRAECISM, GRAECIZE, GRAECO-, etc.

grecque [grek], *s. Arch: Art:* grecque *f.*

Greece [gri:s], *Pr.n. Geog:* Grèce *f.*

greed [gri:d], *s.* (*a*) avidité *f*, cupidité *f*; **his g. for power,** son avidité de s'emparer du pouvoir; (*b*) gourmandise *f*, lècherie *f*; (*c*) âpreté *f* au gain.

greedily ['gri:dili], *adv.* **1.** avidement, cupidement. **2.** avec gourmandise, gloutonnement; **to eat g.,** manger à belles dents, goulûment, avec avidité.

greediness ['gri:dinis], *s.* **1.** avidité *f*, cupidité *f*; âpreté *f* au gain. **2.** gourmandise *f*, gloutonnerie *f.*

greedy ['gri:di], *a.* **1.** avide; âpre (au gain); cupide, avaricieux. **2.** gourmand; glouton, -onne; vorace, goulu; **to be g.,** avoir les dents longues.

greedyguts ['gri:digʌts], *s. P:* goinfre *m*, bâfreur *m*, glouton *m*, goulu *m*; bouffe-la-balle *m inv.*

Greek [gri:k]. **1.** *a.* (*a*) grec, *f.* grecque; **to use G. phrases, to give a G. turn to a phrase,** gréciser; **G. spirit,** grécité *f*; *Arch: Art:* **G. key pattern, G. border,** grecque *f*; (*b*) **the G. church,** l'Église grecque; l'Église orthodoxe. **2.** *s.* (*a*) *Geog:* Grec, Grecque; **when G. meets G. then comes the tug of war,** c'est lorsqu'on rencontre un adversaire digne de soi que la lutte devient sérieuse; **it's a case of G. meeting G.,** la lutte est égale; (*b*) *s.m. F: A:* fripon, escroc, grec. **3.** *s. Ling:* grec *m*; **modern G.,** le grec moderne; le romaïque; *F:* **it's all G. to me,** c'est du latin, de l'hébreu, de l'algèbre pour moi.

green[1] [gri:n], *a.* & *s.* **1.** *a.* vert; (*a*) **as g. as grass,** vert comme pré; **to grow g.,** verdir; (*of grass, etc.*) verdoyer; **the moss forms a g. mantle on the old walls,** la mousse verdit les vieux murs; **g. table,** table *f* de jeu; le tapis vert; **the G. Cloth,** l'Intendance *f* de la Maison du Souverain; (*b*) **g. arbour,** tonnelle *f* de verdure; **g. winter,** hiver doux, clément; **we shall have a g. Christmas,** nous aurons un Noël sans neige; *Husb:* **g. food, g. meat,** fourrages verts, frais; coupage *m*; **g. crop,** récolte *f* de fourrages verts; (*c*) **g. old age,** verte vieillesse; **enjoying a g. old age,** encore vert, verdelet; **to keep s.o.'s memory g.,** entretenir, chérir, la mémoire de qn; **memories still g.,** souvenirs *m* encore vivaces; *A:* & *Lit:* **g. wound,** plaie ouverte; blessure encore fraîche; (*d*) **g. fruit,** fruits verts; **the grapes are too g.,** les raisins sont trop verts; **g. corn,** (i) blé *m* en herbe; (ii) *Cu: U.S:* épis de maïs encore verts; *Tan:* **g. hide,** peau verte; peau crue; carbatine *f*; **g. meat,** viande crue; **g. bacon,** lard salé et non fumé; **g. ivory,** ivoire vert; (*fresh from the quarry*) **g. stone,** pierre verte; **g. cigar,** cigare encore humide, qui n'est pas fait; (*e*) (*of complexion*) blême; **to go, turn, g.,** blêmir; verdir; **to make s.o. g. with jealousy, with envy,** faire pâlir qn de jalousie, d'envie; (*f*) (i) jeune, inexpérimenté; **g. workman,** novice *m*, bleu *m*; *O:* **she was g. from her village,** elle arrivait de son village; elle était fraîche débarquée de son village; (ii) naïf, serin; **rather g.,** simplet; **he's g.!** il est bien de son pays, de son village! **he's not so g.,** il n'est pas né d'hier; **he's not so g. as he looks,** il n'est pas si niais qu'il en a l'air; **to be so g. as to imagine that . . .,** avoir la naïveté de, être assez simple pour, s'imaginer que . . .; (*g*) **she has g. fingers,** *NAm:* **a g. thumb,** en jardinage, tout lui sourit, elle a la main heureuse, le pouce vert; (*h*) (i) *Ich: F:* **g. bone,** orphie *f*; lotte *f* vivipare; *Crust:* **g. crab,** carcin enragé; *Ent:* **g. louse,** puceron; (ii) *Miner:* **g. earth,** glauconie *f.* **2.** *s.* vert *m*; (*a*) **the greens of a picture,** les verts d'un tableau; *F:* **do you see any g. in my eye?** me prenez-vous pour une poire, pour un bleu? *F:* **they are still in the g.,** ils sont encore jeunes, dans leur première jeunesse; (*b*) verdure *f*, feuillage *m*; (*c*) *pl.* **greens,** légumes verts; (*d*) pelouse *f*, gazon *m*; **village g.,** pelouse communale, pré communal; = place *f* du village; **to dance on the g.,** danser sur le gazon, sur la pelouse; *Turf:* **the g.,** la pelouse; *Golf:* **through the g.,** à travers le parcours; **putting g.,** pelouse du trou, d'arrivée; le vert; **bowling g.,** (terrain *m* pour) jeu *m* de boules. **3.** *s.* & *a.* (*in Fr. a.inv.*) **chrome(-)g.,** vert de chrome; **grass(-)g.,** vert pré; **sea(-)g.,** vert de mer, d'eau; *a.* glauque; **bottle(-)g.,** vert bouteille; **olive(-)g.,** (couleur *f* d')olive (*m*); **emerald(-)g., viridian(-)g.,** vert émeraude; **parrot(-)g.,** céladon (*m*); **Paris g., Schweinfurt g.,** vert de Schweinfurt.

green[2]. 1. *v.i.* verdir, verdoyer. **2.** *v.tr.* (*a*) verdir; faire verdoyer (les champs); recouvrir de vert; (*b*) *esp. U.S: F:* mystifier (qn); monter un bateau à (qn).

greenback ['gri:nbæk], *s. F:* billet *m* de banque; greenback *m.*

green-blind ['gri:nblaind], *a. Med:* atteint d'achloropsie.

green-blindness ['gri:nblaindnis], *s.* achloropsie *f.*

greenbottle ['gri:nbɔtl], *s. Ent:* **g. (fly),** mouche verte, dorée; lucilie *f.*

greenbul ['gri:nbul], *s. Orn:* bulbul vert.

greener ['gri:nər], *s. esp. U.S: F:* novice *mf*; ouvrier inexpérimenté; débutant, -ante.

greenery ['gri:nəri], *s.* **1.** verdure *f*, feuillage *m.* **2.** *Hort:* serre *f.*

green-eyed ['gri:naid], *a.* aux yeux verts; *Lit:* **the g.-e. monster,** la sombre jalousie.

greenfinch ['gri:nfinʃ], *s. Orn:* verdier *m.*

green-flowered ['gri:n'flauəd], *a.* à fleurs vertes; *Bot:* viridiflore.

greenfly ['gri:nflai], *s. Ent:* **1.** puceron *m* (du rosier); aphis *m.* **2.** *coll.* aphidés *mpl*, aphidiens *mpl.*

greengage ['gri:ngeidʒ, gri:n'geidʒ], *s.* reine-claude *f*, *pl.* reines claudes.

greengrocer ['gri:ngrousər], *s.* marchand, -ande, de légumes; fruitier, -ière; **greengrocer's (shop),** magasin *m* de marchand de légumes; fruiterie *f.*

greengrocery ['gri:ngrousəri], *s.* **1.** commerce *m* de légumes; fruiterie *f.* **2.** *pl.* **greengroceries,** légumes *mpl* et fruits *mpl.*

greenhead ['gri:nhed], *s. Orn: U.S:* **g. (duck),** malard *m.*

greenheart ['gri:nhɑ:t], *s. Bot:* greenheart *m*; ébène vert.

greenhorn ['gri:nhɔ:n], *s. F:* blanc-bec *m*, *pl.* blancs-becs; bleu *m*, cornichon *m*, béjaune *m*; serin, -ine.

greenhouse ['gri:nhaus], *s. Hort:* serre *f.*

greening[1] ['gri:niŋ], *s.* pomme verte (à l'état mûr).

greening[2], *s.* verdissement *m* (des huîtres).

greenish ['gri:niʃ], *a.* verdâtre; tirant sur le vert.

greenkeeper ['gri:nki:pər], *s. Golf:* entreteneur *m* du parcours.

Greenland ['gri:nlənd], *Pr.n. Geog:* Groenland *m*; **in G.,** au Groenland.

Greenlander ['gri:nləndər], *s. Geog:* Groenlandais, -aise.

Greenlandic [gri:n'lændik]. **1.** *a.* groenlandais. **2.** *s. Ling:* groenlandais *m.*

green-leaved ['gri:n'li:vd], *a.* à feuilles vertes; *Bot:* viridifolié.

greenlet ['gri:nlit], *s. Orn:* viréo *m.*

greenness ['gri:nnis], *s.* **1.** verdeur *f*; (*a*) couleur verte, viridité *f*; (*b*) immaturité *f* (d'un fruit, d'un projet, etc.); *Turf:* manque *m* d'entraînement (d'un cheval); (*c*) (i) inexpérience *f*; (ii) naïveté *f*, simplicité *f*; (*d*) *A:* jeunesse *f*, verdeur, vigueur *f* (d'un vieillard). **2.** verdure *f* (du paysage, des arbres, etc.).

greenockite ['gri:nəkait], *s. Miner:* greenockite *f.*

greenovite ['gri:nouvait], *s. Miner:* greenovite *f.*

greenroom ['gri:nru:m], *s. Th:* foyer *m* des artistes.

greensand ['gri:nsænd], *s.* **1.** *Miner:* sable glauconieux; sable vert; grès vert. **2.** *Metall:* sable vert; sable maigre; **g. mould,** moule *m* à vert; **to cast in g.,** couler à vert.

greenshank ['gri:nʃæŋk], *s. Orn:* chevalier *m* à pattes vertes.

greensickness ['gri:nsiknis], *s. Med:* chlorose *f.*

greenstick ['gri:nstik], *s. Med:* **g. (fracture),** fracture incomplète.

greenstone ['gri:nstoun], *s. Miner:* **1.** roche verte. **2.** néphrite *f*; *F:* pierre divine.
greenstuff ['gri:nstʌf], *s.* (*a*) verdure *f*; herbages *mpl*; (*b*) fourrage *m*; foin *m*; (*c*) jardinage *m*.
greensward ['gri:nswɔ:d], *s. Lit:* pelouse *f*; gazonnée *f*; (tapis *m* de) gazon *m*; tapis de verdure; prairies gazonnées.
greenweed ['gri:nwi:d], *s. Bot:* **dyer's g.,** genêt *m* des teinturiers, *F:* cornéole *f*.
Greenwich ['grinidʒ], *Pr.n. Geog:* Greenwich; (*a*) *Hor:* **G. apparent midnight, apparent noon,** minuit, midi, apparent de Greenwich; **G. mean time,** temps moyen de Greenwich; **G. sidereal time,** temps sidéral de Greenwich; *Astr:* **G. hour angle (of star),** angle *m* horaire de Greenwich (d'une étoile); (*b*) **G. Hospital** = Hôtel des Invalides de la Marine.
green-winged ['gri:n'wiŋd], *a.* à ailes vertes; à élytres verts; *Ent: Orn:* viridipenne.
greenwood ['gri:nwud], *s.* bois *m*, forêt *f* (en été); taillis *m* en verdure; **under the g. tree,** sous la verte ramée; *A:* **to go to the g.** = se réfugier dans le maquis; prendre le maquis; vivre en bandit hors la loi.
greenyard ['gri:njɑ:d], *s.* fourrière *f*.
greet[1] [gri:t], *v.tr.* (*a*) saluer, aborder, accueillir (qn) avec quelques paroles aimables; **to g. s.o. with a nod,** saluer qn d'un signe de tête; **to g. a speech with cheers,** acclamer un discours; saluer un discours d'acclamations; (*b*) **to g. the ear,** frapper l'oreille; **to g. the eyes,** s'offrir à l'œil.
greet[2], *v.i. Scot:* pleurer.
greeting[1] ['gri:tiŋ], *s.* salutation *f*, salut *m*; **greetings card,** carte *f* de vœux; **to send (one's) greetings to s.o.,** envoyer le bonjour, ses salutations, à qn; **new-year greetings,** compliments *m* du jour de l'an; **greetings to all!** salut à tous! rappelez-moi au bon souvenir de tous; *Jur:* **to all whom these presents may concern, g.,** à tous ceux qui ces présents verront, salut.
greeting[2], *s. Scot:* pleurs *mpl*.
Gregarinida [gregə'rinidə], *s.pl. Prot:* grégarines *f*.
gregarious [gri'gɛəriəs], *a.* **1.** *Z:* grégaire, grégarien; vivant par bandes; (animal *m*) sociétaire; **these animals are g.,** ces animaux vivent en troupe; **the g. instinct,** l'instinct *m* grégaire; **men are g.,** les hommes aiment à vivre en société. **2. g. plants,** plantes *f* grégaires.
gregariously [gri'gɛəriəsli], *adv.* **1.** *Z:* (vivre) en troupes, par bandes. **2.** *Bot:* (croître) en touffes.
gregariousness [gri'gɛəriəsnis], *s.* grégarisme *m*.
Gregorian [gri'gɔ:riən], *a. Ecc:* (chant, etc.) grégorien.
Gregory ['gregəri], *Pr.n.m.* **1.** Grégoire. **2.** *Pharm: A:* **Gregory's powder,** rhubarbe *f* en poudre; poudre *f* de rhubarbe.
greisen ['graizən], *s. Geol:* greisen *m*.
gremial ['gri:miəl], *s. Ecc:* grémial, -aux.
gremlin ['gremlin], *s. F:* lutin *m*.
Grenada [grə'nɑ:də], *Pr.n. Geog:* la Grenade.
grenade [grə'neid], *s.* **1.** *Mil:* (*a*) grenade *f*; **hand g.,** grenade à main; **stick g.,** grenade à manche; **sticky g.,** grenade adhésive; **rifle g.,** grenade à fusil; **(rifle) g., discharger, launcher,** lance-grenade *m* (à fusil), *pl.* lance-grenades; **g. thrower,** grenadier *m* lanceur; **g. pouch,** porte-grenades *inv.*, grenadière *f*; **fragmentation g.,** grenade à fragmentation, grenade défensive; **offensive g.,** grenade offensive; **asphyxiating g.,** grenade asphyxiante, suffocante; **chemical g.,** grenade chimique; **incendiary g.,** grenade incendiaire; **illuminating g., light g.,** grenade éclairante; **smoke g.,** grenade fumigène; **drill g., training g., practice g.,** grenade d'exercice; **blank g.,** grenade à blanc; **dummy g.,** grenade inerte, fausse grenade; (*b*) (*on uniform, etc.*) **g. ornament,** grenade. **2. (fire) g.,** grenade extinctrice.
grenadier [grenə'diər], *s. Mil:* grenadier *m*.
grenadin ['grenədin], *s. Hort:* grenadin *m*; œillet *m* à ratafia.
grenadine[1] ['grenədi:n], *s. Cu:* grenadin *m* (de veau, etc.).
grenadine[2], *s.* **1.** *Tex:* grenadine *f*. **2.** (*syrup*) grenadine; *Pharm:* sirop grenadin. **3.** *Exp:* grenadine.
gressorial [gre'sɔ:riəl], *a. Orn: Z:* (patte *f*, etc.) ambulatoire.
Gretna Green ['gretnə'gri:n], *Pr.n. Geog:* premier village d'Écosse après la frontière d'Angleterre, où se célébraient au pied levé les mariages par enlèvement; (le droit coutumier d'Écosse n'imposait aucune condition de domicile ni de publicité); **G. G. marriage,** mariage *m* par enlèvement; mariage clandestin (célébré par le "forgeron" de Gretna Green).
grevillea [gre'viliə], *s. Bot:* grevillea *m*.
grey[1] [grei], *a. & s.* **1.** *a.* gris; (*a*) **g. sky, day,** ciel gris, journée grise; **painted g.,** peint en gris; *Engr:* **g. tint, g. wash,** gris *m*; **at sunset the room fills with g. shadows,** au soleil couchant la salle se remplit de grisailles *f*; *Anat:* **g. matter,** substance grise (du cerveau); **work done without much expenditure of g. matter,** travail fait sans grand effort cérébral; (*b*) (*of hair*) gris; **to turn, go, g.,** grisonner; **hair turning g.,** cheveux grisonnants; **he is turning g.,** il commence à blanchir; **at thirty she was quite g.,** à trente ans elle était toute grise; **to worry oneself g.,** se faire des cheveux blancs; **grown g. in the service, in harness,** blanchi sous le harnais; (*c*) (*of complexion, etc.*) **(ashen) g.,** blême; **to turn (ashen) g.,** blêmir; (*d*) (*of outlook, prospect, etc.*) sombre, mélancolique, morne; (*e*) *Tex:* (coton) écru. **2.** *s.* (*a*) gris *m*; **to paint, tint, with g.,** griser; **hair touched with g.,** cheveux grisonnants; **his hair is touched with g.,** ses cheveux grisonnent; **the g. of the morning,** l'aube *f* du jour; *Tex:* **goods in the g.; greys,** tissus écrus; *U.S: Hist:* **to wear the g.,** porter l'uniforme des Sudistes; (*b*) cheval gris; *Mil:* **the (Scots) Greys,** le deuxième régiment de dragons; (*c*) *Orn:* ridenne *f*, chipeau *m*; (*d*) *pl. Cost: F: O:* **greys,** pantalon *m* de flanelle grise. **3.** *s. & a.* (*Fr. a.inv.*) **dull g.,** gris mat; **charcoal g.,** gris anthracite; **dapple(-)g.,** (cheval) gris pommelé; **iron(-)g.,** gris (de) fer; **iron-g. beard,** barbe *f* poivre et sel; **mouse(-)g.,** gris (de) souris; **pearl(-)g.,** gris (de) perle; **silver(-)g.,** gris argenté; **slate(-)g.,** gris ardoise; **steel(-)g.,** gris d'acier.
grey[2], *v.tr. & i.* grisailler; (*of hair*) grisonner; *Art:* **to g. (over) the whites,** engrisailler les blancs (d'une eau-forte).
greyback ['greibæk], *s.* **1.** *U.S: Hist: F:* = GREYCOAT. **2.** *Orn:* corneille cendrée, mantelée. **3.** *P:* pou *m*, *pl.* poux; toto *m*. **4.** *Mil: P: A:* chemise *f* (de flanelle grise).
greybeard ['greibiəd], *s.* **1.** grison *m*; vieille barbe; vieux barbon. **2.** *Cer:* cruche *f*, cruchon *m*.
grey-bearded [grei'biədid], *a.* à barbe grise.
greycoat ['greikout], *s. U.S: Hist:* soldat *m* des États confédérés.
grey-eyed ['grei'aid], *a.* aux yeux gris; *Lit:* **g.-e. Minerva,** Minerve aux yeux pers.
grey-haired, -headed ['grei'hɛəd, 'hedid], *a.* aux cheveux gris; grisonnant; *Orn:* **grey-headed woodpecker,** pic cendré.
greyhen ['grei'hen], *s. Orn:* femelle du lyrure des bouleaux, du tétras lyre; poule *f* des bouleaux, petite poule de bruyère.
greyhound ['greihaund], *s.* lévrier *m*; **g. bitch,** levrette *f*; **Italian g.,** levron *m*; levrette de salon; **g. racing,** courses *fpl* de lévriers; **g.(-racing) track,** cynodrome *m*; **g. belly,** ventre levretté (d'un cheval).
greying[1] ['greiiŋ], *a.* grisonnant.
greying[2], *s.* grisonnement *m*.
greyish ['greiiʃ], *a.* grisâtre.
greylag ['greilæg], *s. Orn:* **g. (goose),** oie sauvage, cendrée.
greymalkin [grei'mɔ:lkin], *s. F: O:* = GRIMALKIN.
greyness ['greinis], *s.* **1.** teinte grise; **the g. of London,** la grisaille de Londres; la tonalité grise de Londres; **the g. of the evening over the estuary,** les grisailles du soir sur l'estuaire. **2.** caractère *m* morne, sombre; tristesse *f*.
greywacke ['greiwækə], *s. Miner:* grauwacke *f*.
gribble ['gribl], *s. Crust:* limnorie *f*.
grice [grais], *s.* cochonnet *m*; marcassin *m*.
grid[1] [grid], *s.* **1.** (*a*) grille *f*, grillage *m*; *Hyd.E:* gril *m*, grille, claie *f*; *Mch:* grillage (de foyer de chaudière); *El:* grille, grillage (d'accumulateur); *Hyd.E:* **(protective) g.,** grille de finition; (*b*) *El: Elcs: W.Tel: etc:* grille (d'un tube électronique, etc.); **g. valve,** tube à grille; **multi-g. valve,** tube à grilles multiples; **double-g. valve,** lampe bigrille; **three-g. tube,** penthode *f*; lampe trigrille, à cinq électrodes; **suppressor g.,** grille d'arrêt, grille suppresseuse; **shield g.,** grille d'arrêt, de protection; **heating g.,** grille chauffante; **g. potential, voltage,** potentiel *m*, tension *f*, de grille; **g. leak,** résistance *f* de fuite de la grille; **g. condenser,** condensateur *m* de la grille; **g. battery,** pile *f* de polarisation; **g. bias,** polarisation *f* de grille; **g. current,** courant *m* de grille; **g. circuit,** circuit *m* de grille; **g. swing,** amplitude *f* de tension de grille; **g. control,** commande *f* de grille; **g. mesh,** (i) maille *f* de grille; (ii) maillage *m* (d'un réseau); *Ball:* **g. guidance,** guidage *m* (d'un missile) par radio-maillage. **2.** = GRIDIRON. **3.** (*a*) *Mapm:* quadrillage *m*, carroyage *m* (d'une carte); graticule *m*; **standard g.,** quadrillage, carroyage, international; **kilometric g.,** quadrillage, carroyage, kilométrique; **perspective g.,** quadrillage kilométrique perspectif; **g. system,** réseau *m*, système *m*, de quadrillage; **g. north,** nord *m* du quadrillage; **g. azimuth, g. bearing,** azimut *m*, gisement *m*, par rapport au nord du quadrillage; **g. declination,** déclinaison *f* de la ligne nord-sud du quadrillage; **g. lines,** droites *f* du quadrillage; *Av:* **g. course,** cap *m*, route *f*, calculé(e) par rapport au (nord du) quadrillage; **g. data,** éléments *m* numériques du quadrillage; **g. letters, g. numbers, g. reference,** lettres *f*, chiffres *m*, du quadrillage; (*b*) **the g.,** le réseau électrique national; (*c*) *Town P:* **g. layout,** quadrillage, damier *m*, plan orthogonal; *Can:* **g. road,** route municipale qui suit un plan orthogonal. **4.** *Opt:* (*of sighting instrument*) micromètre *m*. **5.** *Mil:* (*secret code for listing members of an association*) **personnel g., members g.,** grille d'effectifs.
grid[2], *v.tr.* **(gridded)** quadriller (une carte, etc.).
griddle[1] ['gridl], *s.* **1.** *Cu:* = GIRDLE[3]. **2.** *Min:* crible *m*.
griddle[2], *v.tr.* **1.** *Cu:* griller. **2.** *Min:* **to g. out ore,** cribler le minerai.
gride[1] [graid], *s.* crissement *m*, grincement *m* (d'une roue, etc.).
gride[2], *v.i.* **to g. along, against, sth.,** grincer sur qch.
gridiron ['gridaiən], *s.* **1.** (*a*) *Cu:* gril *m*; *Fig:* **to be on the g.,** être sur des charbons ardents; (*b*) *Ph:* **g. pendulum,** balancier *m* à gril; *Cy:* **g. carrier,** porte-bagages *m inv* en tubes d'acier; *Rail:* **g. (track),** gril; *Mch:* **g. valve,** tiroir *m* à grille, à lanterne; (*c*) *Nau:* gril de carénage; (*d*) *Th:* gril (pour la manœuvre des décors). **2.** *NAm:* terrain *m* de football.
grief [gri:f], *s.* chagrin *m*, douleur *f*, peine *f*; **to give way to g.,** s'abandonner à la douleur; **to die of g.,** mourir de chagrin; **plunged in g.,** plongé dans la désolation, dans l'affliction *f*; **to come to g.,** (i) se voir accablé de malheurs; faire de mauvaises affaires; sombrer; (ii) (*of plan, etc.*) échouer, faire fiasco, mal tourner; (iii) avoir un accident; (*of rider*) faire une chute (de cheval, de bicyclette, etc.); **to come to g. when all was going well,** verser en beau chemin; **drive more slowly or you'll come to g.,** allez moins vite ou vous allez avoir un accident; **if you don't work you will come to g.,** si vous ne travaillez pas, vous allez échouer; **to bring s.o., sth., to g.,** faire échouer qn, qch.; *F:* **good g.!** mon Dieu!
grief-stricken ['gri:fstrikn], *a.* pénétré, accablé, de douleur; en proie à la douleur; en proie aux remords; **g.-s. heart,** cœur percé de douleur; cœur navré.
grievance ['gri:v(ə)ns], *s.* **1.** grief *m*; **to have a g. against s.o.,** avoir un grief contre qn; **to air, state, one's grievances,** conter, exprimer, ses doléances; exposer ses griefs personnels; **people with a g.,** les gens *m* qui ont à se plaindre; **to hold sth. as a g. against s.o.,** faire grief à qn de qch.; **people with a g.,** les aigris *m*. **2.** injustice *f*; **to redress a g.,** réparer un tort fait à qn; réformer un abus.
grieve [gri:v]. **1.** *v.tr.* chagriner, attrister, affliger, peiner (qn); faire de la peine à (qn); **it grieves me to see him so changed,** cela me fait de la peine de le voir si changé; **we are grieved to learn. . .,** nous apprenons avec peine . . .. **2.** *v.i.* se chagriner, s'affliger, s'attrister, se désoler **(over, about, sth.,** de qch.); **do not g. so,** ne vous désolez pas comme ça; **I g. to see them in such poverty,** cela me fait de la peine de les voir dans la misère; **the whole nation grieved at his death,** la nation entière pleura sa mort.
grieved [gri:vd], *a.* chagriné, attristé, affligé, désolé, peiné **(at,** de); **deeply g.,** navré **(at,** de).
grieving[1] ['gri:viŋ], *a.* **1.** chagrinant, affligeant, attristant. **2.** chagriné, affligé, attristé, désolé.
grieving[2], *s.* chagrin *m*, douleur *f*.
grievous ['gri:vəs], *a.* **1.** douloureux, pénible; **g. loss,** perte cruelle. **2.** (blessure *f*, faute *f*, etc.) grave; **g. mistake,** erreur *f* grave, lamentable; *Jur:* **to cause g. bodily harm,** causer de graves blessures. **3.** (*of news, etc.*) triste, affligeant, douloureux.
grievously ['gri:vəsli], *adv.* **1.** douloureusement, Péniblement, cruellement. **2.** gravement; grièvement (blessé).
grievousness ['gri:vəsnis], *s.* **1.** caractère pénible, affligeant (d'un événement, d'une perte). **2.** gravité *f* (d'une blessure, etc.).
griff[1], **griffe** [grif], *s. U.S: Pej:* griffe *mf*; mulâtre *mf, f. occ.* mulâtresse.
griff[2], *s. Tex:* griffe *f* (de métier).
griffin[1] ['grifin], *s.* **1.** *Myth:* griffon *m*. **2.** *F: A:* vieille duègne; dragon *m*.
griffin[2], *s.* **1.** *O:* (*in Far East*) nouveau venu, nouveau débarqué; *F:* bleu *m*, béjaune *m*. **2.** poney *m* qui n'a jamais participé aux courses.
griffin[3], *s. U.S:* = GRIFF[1].
griffin[4], *s. Turf: etc: A:* tuyau *m*.
griffon[1] ['grifən], *s.* (chien) griffon *m*.
griffon[2], *s.* **1.** *Myth:* griffon *m*. **2.** *Orn:* **g. (vulture),** vautour *m* fauve, vautour griffon.
grig [grig], *s.* **1.** *Ich:* (*a*) équille *f*, lançon *m*; anguille *f* de sable; anguille plat-bec; (*b*) petite anguille. **2.** *Ent:* grillon *m*.
grike [graik], *s. Geol:* fente *f*, crevasse *f*.
grill[1] [gril], *s.* **1.** *Cu:* grillade *f*. **2. g. (room),** grill-room *m* (de restaurant); rôtisserie *f*.
grill[2], *s. Cu:* gril *m*; grilloir *m*; *F:* **to put a prisoner on the**

g., cuisiner un prisonnier, un détenu.

grill[3], **1.** *v.tr.* griller, brasiller (la viande); faire cuire (qch.) sur le gril; *F:* **to g. a prisoner,** cuisiner un détenu. **2.** *v.i.* griller, être grillé; cuire sur le gril.

grill[4], *s.* = GRILLE[1].

grill[5], *v.tr.* = GRILLE[2].

grillage ['grilidʒ], *s. Civ.E: Const:* grillage *m*, treillis *m* (en sous-œuvre); racinaux *mpl*; **to lay down a g. for a building, etc.,** grillager les fondements d'un édifice, etc.

grille[1] [gril], *s.* **1.** grille *f* (de couvent, de porte, de radiateur); judas *m* (de porte); **(counter) g.,** grille de comptoir (d'un bureau de banque, etc.); **to fit a g. on to a window, etc.,** grillager une fenêtre, etc.; *Hyd.E:* **(protective) g.,** grille de finition; *Aut:* **radiator g.,** calandre *f*. **2.** *Pisc:* incubateur *m*.

grille[2], *v.tr.* grillager, griller.

grilled[1] ['grild], *a.* grillé; **g. meat,** viande grillée; grillade *f*; carbonnade *f*; **g. steak,** bifteck *m* sur le gril; charbonnée *f*.

grilled[2], *a.* grillagé, grillé, à grille.

griller ['grilər], *s.* **1.** *(pers.)* grilleur, -euse. **2.** gril *m* (de fourneau); grilloir *m*.

grilse [grils], *s. Fish:* saumon *m* de quatre ans; saumoneau *m*, grilse *m*.

grim [grim], *a.* menaçant, sinistre; **g. and ghostly figures,** formes spectrales et menaçantes; **g. landscape,** paysage lugubre, menaçant; **g. laugh,** ricanement *m* de mauvais augure; **g. smile,** sourire *m* sardonique; **g. humour,** humour *m* macabre; **g. face,** visage sévère, rébarbatif; **to keep a g. silence,** garder un silence sévère, de mauvais augure; *Lit:* **g. Death,** la Mort inexorable; **to hold on like g. death,** se cramponner en désespéré, avec acharnement; **g. necessity compelled him to . . .,** la dure et sévère nécessité le força à . . .; **to do sth. out of g. necessity,** être dans la nécessité cruelle de faire qch.; **g. truth,** la vérité brutale, poignante; **g. battle,** bataille acharnée; **g. determination,** volonté *f* inflexible; *(of pers.)* **to look g.,** avoir une mine sévère; *F:* **he was looking pretty g.,** il avait l'air (i) furieux, (ii) malade; **how do you feel?—pretty g.!** comment ça va?—plutôt mal; **it's a g. prospect, things are looking g.,** ça marque mal, s'annonce mal.

grimace[1] [gri'meis], *s.* **1.** grimace *f*; **to make a g.,** faire la grimace. **2.** *A:* affectation *f*; **to make grimaces,** faire des simagrées, des façons.

grimace[2], *v.i.* **1.** grimacer; faire la grimace. **2.** *A:* faire des mines, des simagrées, des façons.

grimalkin [gri'mɔːlkin], *s. F: O:* **1.** *(cat)* mistigri *m*. **2.** *(woman)* mégère *f*; vieille taupe; vieille sorcière.

grime[1] [graim], *s.* saleté *f*; poussière *f* de charbon, de suie (qui vous entre dans la peau).

grime[2], *v.tr.* *(of coal dust, etc.)* salir, noircir (le visage, les mains).

griminess ['graiminis], *s.* saleté *f*, noirceur *f* (du visage, des mains, des manchettes).

grimly ['grimli], *adv.* sinistrement; d'une façon menaçante; sévèrement; **he looked at me g.,** il m'a regardé d'un air (i) sévère, (ii) lugubre; **to fight g.,** se battre avec acharnement.

Grimm [grim], *Pr.n. Ling:* **Grimm's law,** la loi *f* de Grimm; la loi de la substitution consonantique.

grimness ['grimnis], *s.* caractère *m* sinistre, aspect *m* redoutable (de qch.); sévérité *f* (de visage); acharnement *m* (d'un combat); inflexibilité *f* (d'une volonté).

grimy ['graimi], *a.* sale, encrassé, noirci; noir (de suie, de charbon, de poussier); **g. hands, linen,** mains noires; linge noir, crasseux; **g. face,** visage noir, barbouillé.

grin[1] [grin], *s.* **1.** grimace *f* qui découvre les dents; rictus grimaçant. **2.** large sourire; sourire épanoui; **to give a broad g.,** se fendre la bouche en un large sourire; sourire à belles dents.

grin[2], *v.i.* **(grinned) 1.** grimacer en montrant les dents; avoir un sourire forcé. **2.** rire, sourire, d'une oreille à l'autre; to **g. at s.o.,** (i) adresser à qn un sourire de grosse gaieté; (ii) regarder qn avec un sourire narquois, moqueur; **he grinned broadly,** son visage s'est épanoui en un large sourire; **to g. and bear it,** (tâcher de) garder le sourire; faire contre mauvaise fortune bon cœur; *F:* encaisser (sans broncher); **to g. like a Cheshire cat,** sourire jusqu'aux oreilles; *F:* **you'll g. on the other side of your face if you have to pay for the damage,** ça te coupera le sourire si tu as à payer les dégâts. **3.** *Paint: esp. U.S:* **the undercoat is grinning through in places,** la première couche se laisse voir par endroits.

grind[1] [graind], *s.* **1.** grincement *m*, crissement *m* (de roues, etc.). **2.** *F:* *(a)* labeur *m* monotone et continu; turbin *m*; **the daily g.,** le boulot journalier; le train-train quotidien; **what a g.!** quelle corvée! **it's a constant g.,** il faut tout le temps bûcher, piocher; **to go back to the old g.,** reprendre le collier, se remettre au turbin; **the g. of a teacher's life,** la vie ingrate de l'instituteur. **3.** *F:* *(a)* course *f* difficile; *(b)* steeple *m*. **4.** *Sch: NAm: F:* bûcheur, -euse; piocheur, -euse. **5.** mouture *f* (du blé, etc.).

grind[2], *v.* **(ground [graund]; ground) 1.** *v.tr.* *(a)* moudre (du blé, du café); moudre, concasser (du poivre); râper (le tabac à priser); broyer (des couleurs); piler (qch. dans un mortier); réduire (qch.) en grains; **to g. sth. (down) to dust,** pulvériser qch.; réduire qch. en poudre; **to g. sth. between one's teeth,** broyer qch. entre ses dents; **to g. sth. under one's heel,** écraser qch. sous ses pieds; **to g. sth. into the earth with one's heel,** enfoncer qch. dans la terre en le broyant du talon; **I had mathematics ground into me,** on m'a fait entrer de force les mathématiques dans la tête; **to g. (down) the poor, to g. the faces of the poor,** pressurer, opprimer, les pauvres; **people ground down with taxes,** peuple écrasé d'impôts; *(b)* meuler (une pièce coulée); rectifier (une pièce) à la meule; roder (une lentille, etc.); dépolir (le verre, un bouchon); égriser (une pierre précieuse); doucir (le verre à glaces); *Mec.E:* **to g. true,** rectifier; **to g. (in) a valve,** roder une soupape; **to g. in the piston,** roder le piston dans le cylindre; **to g. (down) a lens, etc.,** meuler une lentille, etc.; **to g. dry, wet,** meuler à sec, à l'eau; *(c)* aiguiser, émoudre, affûter (un outil); passer (un couteau, etc.) à la meule; repasser (un couteau, un outil, etc.) (sur la meule); mettre le tranchant à (une lame); *(d)* **to g. one's teeth,** grincer des dents; grincer les dents; crisser des dents; **to g. out an oath,** jurer entre ses dents; *(e)* tourner (une manivelle); **to g. a barrel organ,** jouer d'un orgue de Barbarie; **to g. (out) a tune,** tourner, seriner, un air; *(f) F: O:* faire travailler (ses élèves) sans relâche; chauffer (un élève) pour un examen; **to g. him in Greek,** lui faire travailler le grec. **2.** *(with passive force)* *(of corn)* se moudre; *(of colours)* se broyer; *(of almonds, etc., in a mortar)* se piler. **3.** *v.i.* *(a)* *(of wheels, etc.)* grincer, crisser; **I could hear the keel grinding on the rocks,** j'entendais grincer la quille sur les roches; **a cart came grinding past,** une charrette passa en faisant crier ses roues; *(b) F:* bûcher, turbiner; *Sch:* bachoter; **to g. for an exam,** potasser un examen; **to g. (away) at Latin,** piocher, potasser, son latin.

grinder ['graindər], *s.* **1.** *(a)* pileur, -euse; broyeur, -euse; **organ g.,** joueur, -euse, d'orgue de Barbarie; *(b) Cer:* useur, -euse; *(c)* rémouleur *m* (de couteaux, de ciseaux); **itinerant g.,** repasseur ambulant; *(d) Opt:* lapideur *m* (de verre optique); *(e) Sch: F: A:* chauffeur *m*, répétiteur *m*. **2.** *(a)* (dent) molaire *f*, (dent) mâchelière *f*; *Z:* grès *m*, canine supérieure (du sanglier); *(b) pl. F: O:* **grinders,** dents *f*, croquantes *f*. **3.** *(a)* appareil broyeur; broyeuse *f*; **coffee g.,** moulin *m* à café; **colour g.,** moulin à couleurs; *(b)* meule courante (d'un moulin); *(c) Mec.E:* rectifieuse *f*; meuleuse *f*; machine *f* à rectifier; *(polisher)* rodoir *m*; **face g.,** rectifieuse à meuler à 90°; *(d)* machine *f* à aiguiser, à affûter; affûteuse *f*; *(e) F:* **to put s.o. through the g.,** faire passer un mauvais quart d'heure à qn. **4.** *Orn: Austr:* **g. (bird),** seisure *m*, gobe-mouches *inv* turbulent.

grindery ['graindəri], *s.* **1.** *Bootm: F:* crépins *mpl*; saint-crépin *m*. **2.** *Ind:* atelier *m* de meulage; aiguiserie *f*, affilerie *f*.

grinding[1] ['graindiŋ], *a.* **1.** (dent *f*) molaire. **2. g. sound,** grincement *m*, crissement *m*. **3.** *(of pain)* douloureux, déchirant; **g. care,** soucis rongeurs, rongeants; **g. poverty,** la misère écrasante.

grinding[2], *s.* **1.** mouture *f* (du blé); broyage *m*, broiement *m* (des couleurs); pilage *m* (dans un mortier); **g. to dust,** pulvérisation *f*, réduction *f* en poudre; **wet g.,** broyage à l'eau, par voie humide; **dry g.,** broyage à sec, par voie sèche; **fine, medium, coarse, g.,** broyage fin, moyen, grossier; *Ind:* **g. mill,** broyeur *m*, malaxeur *m*. **2.** oppression *f*, écrasement *m* (du peuple). **3.** *(a)* meulage *m*; rectification *f* à la meule; rodage *m*; adoucissage *m*; polissage *m* à la meule; **machine g.,** meulage à la machine; **off-hand g.,** meulage à la main; **g. wheel,** roue *f* à meuler; meule *f* de rectification; **g. powder,** poudre *f* à roder; **g. compound, paste,** pâte *f* à roder; **g. machine,** (i) machine *f* à meuler; (ii) machine à ébarber, ébarbeuse *f*; (iii) machine à rectifier, rectifieuse *f*; (iv) *Glassm: etc:* polisseuse *f*; *(b)* aiguisage *m*, affûtage *m*, émoulage *m*, repassage *m*; **g. shop,** affilerie *f*; **g. machine,** machine à affûter, affûteuse *f*. **4.** *(a)* grincement *m*, crissement *m*; *(b) Dent:* **g. (habit),** grincement (des dents).

grindstone ['graindstoun], *s.* meule *f* (en grès) à aiguiser; *(small)* mallard *m*, meuleton *m*; *(medium-sized)* meul(l)arde *f*; *(large)* meulard *m*; **(tool grinder's) g.,** meul(l)ardeau *m*; **fine g.,** meule douce; **medium g.,** meule demi-douce; **rough g.,** meule à gros grains; *Geol:* **g. grit,** (pierre) meulière *f*; **g. factory,** meulerie *f*; **g. maker,** meulier *m*; *F:* **to keep one's nose to the g.,** travailler sans relâche, sans désemparer; être assujetti à son travail; **he keeps our noses to the g.,** il exige qu'on soit tout à la besogne; il ne nous laisse aucun répit.

gringo ['griŋgou], *s. usu. Pej:* *(in Latin America)* Anglo-américain, -aine; Anglais, -aise.

gringolée ['griŋgəlei], **gringoly** ['griŋgəli], *a. Her:* gringolé.

grinning[1] ['griniŋ], *a.* grimacier, grimaçant.

grinning[2], *s.* grimacerie *f*.

griotte [gri'ɔt], *s. Miner:* **g. (marble),** griotte *f*.

grip[1] [grip], *s.* **1.** prise *f*, serrage *m*; serrement *m* (d'un outil, des mains); étreinte *f* (des mains); **masonic g.,** attouchement *m* maçonnique; **to have a strong g.,** avoir une bonne poigne; **to be at grips with the enemy,** être aux prises, lutter corps à corps, avec l'ennemi; **to come to grips,** en venir aux mains, aux prises **(with,** avec); *F:* se colleter; **g. of the wheels,** adhérence *f*, accrochage *m*, des roues sur la route; **to get a g. on sth.,** prendre prise à qch.; **to lose one's g.,** (i) lâcher prise; (ii) *F:* baisser (du point de vue mental); *Equit:* **to keep a tight g. on one's horse,** serrer les côtes à son cheval, bien embrasser son cheval; **the g. of poverty,** l'étreinte de la misère; **in the g. of a disease,** sous l'étreinte d'une maladie; en proie à une maladie; **the fever has him in its g.,** la fièvre le tient; *(in handwriting)* **correct g.,** position correcte des doigts; **to have a firm g. (on sth.),** tenir (qch.) bien en main; **to get, take, keep, a g. on oneself,** se maîtriser; se contrôler; **g. of a play on the audience,** effet poignant, impression poignante, d'une pièce sur la salle; **to have, get, a good g. of the situation,** avoir, prendre, la situation bien en main; **to have a good g. of a subject,** connaître un sujet à fond; bien posséder un sujet; manier facilement (les mathématiques, etc.); **he lacks g.,** il manque de poigne. **2.** *(a)* poignée *f* (d'aviron, etc.); poignée, crosse *f* (de pistolet); **ball g.,** boule-poignée *f*, *pl.* boules-poignées; *(b) Ten:* manchon *m*, couvre-manche *m*, *pl.* couvre-manches (pour raquette); *Cy:* manchon, poignée (de guidon). **3.** *(a) Mec.E: etc:* douille *f* de serrage; pince *f*; griffe *f*; *(b) pl.* **grips,** mâchoires *f*, mordaches *f* (d'un étau, etc.); *(c) Hairdr:* **(hair) g.,** pince (à cheveux). **4.** *NAm:* valise *f*; mallette *f*.

grip[2], *v.tr.* **(gripped)** *(a)* saisir, prendre (qch.); serrer, étreindre, (qch.) dans la main; empoigner, agriffer, agripper, (qch.); **to g. hold of s.o.,** s'agripper à qn; **to g. sth. in a vice,** serrer, pincer, qch. dans un étau; *Equit:* **to g. a horse close,** serrer les bottes; envelopper un cheval; *(b) v.i.* **the wheels are not gripping,** les roues *f* n'adhèrent pas (sur la route); *(c)* **fear gripped him,** la peur le saisit; **play that grips the audience,** pièce *f* qui tient, passionne, les spectateurs; **story that grips you,** histoire passionnante.

grip[3], *s.* fossé *m*, rigole *f*.

gripe[1] [graip], *s.* **1.** *A:* saisissement *m*, étreinte *f*. **2.** *A: & U.S:* poignée *f* (de manche, d'outil, etc.). **3.** *pl.* **gripes,** (i) *F:* colique *f*; (ii) *Vet:* tranchées *f* rouges (d'un cheval). **4.** *pl. Nau:* **gripes,** saisines *f*, sangles *f* (de canot). **5.** *F:* ronchonnerie *f*, rouspétance *f*.

gripe[2], *v.* **1.** *v.tr. A:* saisir, empoigner, étreindre. **2.** *v.tr. A:* opprimer (les pauvres, etc.). **3.** *v.tr. F:* *(a)* affliger (qn); *(b)* donner la colique à (qn). **4.** *v.tr. Nau:* saisir (un canot à bord); amarrer (un canot) avec les saisines. **5.** *v.i. Nau:* *(of ship)* venir au vent; être ardent; passer sur sa barre. **6.** *v.i. F:* râler, ronchonner, grogner, rouspéter.

griper ['graipər], *s.* rouspéteur, -euse.

griphite ['grifait], *s. Miner:* griphite *f*.

griping[1] ['graipiŋ], *a.* **1.** *A:* rapace, avare. **2.** *F:* (aliment, etc.) coliqueux; **g. pains,** colique *f*. **3.** *F:* rouspéteur, -euse.

griping[2], *s. F:* rouspétance *f*.

grippe [grip], *s. NAm: Med:* grippe *f*.

gripper ['gripər], *s.* pince *f*, griffe *f*; *Typ: Engr: Mapm:* **g. allowance, g. margin,** blanc *m* de pince, marge *f* de pince; **g. bite,** prise *f* de pince; **g. block, g. post,** appui-pince *m*, *pl.* appuis-pince; **g. guide,** taquet *m* de pince; **g. mark,** repère *m* en pinces.

gripping[1] ['gripiŋ], *a.* passionnant, captivant.

gripping[2], *s.* prise *f*, étreinte *f*, serrement *m*; **g. device,** appareil *m* de préhension; *Mec.E:* mâchoire *f*.

gripsack ['gripsæk], *s. U.S:* valise *f*.

grisaille [gri(:)'zaijl], *s. Art:* grisaille *f*; **to paint sth. in g.,** grisailler qch.; peindre qch. en grisaille.

Griselda [gri'zeldə], *Pr.n.f. Lit:* Grisélidis.

griseofulvin [griziou'fulvin], *s.* griséofulvine *f*.

griseous ['griziəs], *a. Nat.Hist:* gris perlé.

gris-gris ['gri:gri:], *s.* **1.** *Anthr:* gris-gris *m inv.*; amulette *f*; **g.-g. man,** sorcier *m*. **2.** *Bot:* mancône *m*.

griskin ['griskin], *s. Cu:* échinée *f* (de porc); grillade *f* (de porc).

grisliness ['grizlinis], *s. Lit:* (*a*) aspect *m* horrible, effroyable; (*b*) aspect sinistre, macabre.

grisly ['grizli], *a. Lit:* (*a*) affreux, horrible, effroyable, épouvantable; (*b*) effrayant, sinistre, macabre; **g. shadow,** ombre monstrueuse.

grison ['griz(ə)n], *s. Z:* grison *m*.

grisounite ['grizu:nait], *s. Min: Exp:* grisou-naphtalite *f*.

grisoutine ['grizu:tain], *s. Min: Exp:* grisou-dynamite *f*.

grist[1] [grist], *s.* **1.** blé *m* à moudre; **g. mill,** moulin *m* à blé; **g. miller,** meunier *m*; **that brings g. to the mill,** c'est du blé en grenier, ça fait venir l'eau au moulin; ça met du beurre dans les épinards; c'est lucratif; **all is g. that comes to his mill,** tout lui est bon; il fait profit de tout. **2.** blé moulu. **3.** *Brew:* malt broyé; brai *m*. **4.** *U.S: F:* grand nombre, grande quantité, tas *m* (de choses).

grist[2], *s. Tex:* titre *m* (du fil); épaisseur *f* (d'un cordage).

gristle ['grisl], *s.* cartilage *m*, croquant *m*.

gristly ['grisli], *a.* cartilagineux; plein de croquant.

grit[1] [grit], *s.* **1.** (*a*) grès *m*, sable *m*; (*b*) *Mec.E: etc:* corps étrangers; impuretés *fpl*; **to put, throw, g. in the bearings,** entraver la marche des affaires; mettre des bâtons dans les roues. **2.** (*gritstone*) grès (dur); **millstone g., grindstone g.,** grès meulier, grès à meule(s); silex meulier; (pierre) meulière *f*; **sandstone g.,** grès grossier. **3.** grain *m* (d'une pierre). **4.** carrière *f* (d'une poire). **5.** *F:* (*a*) cran *m*, courage *m*, endurance *f*; **man of g., who has plenty of g.,** homme *m* qui a du cran, de l'étoffe, du caractère, du mordant; (*b*) *Pol: Can:* **the Grits,** les membres du parti libéral.

grit[2], *v.* (**gritted**) **1.** *v.i.* grincer, crisser; **the sanded floor grits under our feet,** le plancher sablé nous crépite sous les pieds. **2.** *v.tr.* **to g. one's teeth,** grincer des dents. **3.** *v.tr.* sabler (un pavé glissant, etc.).

grits [grits], *s.pl.* gruau *m* d'avoine; grosse farine d'avoine.

gritstone ['gritstoun], *s.* grès (dur); pierre *f* de grès.

grittiness ['gritinis], *s.* toucher graveleux.

gritty ['griti], *a.* **1.** (*a*) (sol) gréseux, sablonneux, cendreux; (crayon, etc.) graveleux; **g. pear,** poire graveleuse, pierreuse, lapilleuse; (*b*) abrasif. **2.** *NAm: F:* qui a du cran; résolu.

grivet ['grivit], *s. Z:* grivet *m*, singe vert.

grizzle[1] ['grizl], *a.* gris, grison, grisonnant.

grizzle[2], *v.tr. & i.* grisonner.

grizzle[3], *s.* **1.** épanchement *m* d'humeur, de bile; **to have a good g.,** raconter ses griefs; ronchonner tout son soûl. **2.** pleurnicherie *f*.

grizzle[4], *v.i.* **1.** se faire de la bile; ronchonner; grognonner. **2.** pleurnicher, geindre.

grizzled ['grizld], *a.* **1.** (*of hair*) gris, grisonnant; **g. beard,** barbe *f* poivre et sel; **g. wig,** grisaille *f*; perruque *f* en grisaille. **2.** (*of pers.*) aux cheveux gris; grisonnant.

grizzler ['grizlər], *s.* **1.** ronchonneur, -euse; ronchonnot *m*; ronchon *m*. **2.** pleurnicheur, -euse; geignard, -arde; geigneur, -euse.

grizzling[1] ['grizliŋ], *s.* grisonnement *m*.

grizzling[2], *s.* **1.** grognonnerie *f*. **2.** pleurnicherie *f*, pleurnichement *m*.

grizzly ['grizli], *a.* **1.** (*a*) (*of hair*) grisâtre, grisonnant; poivre et sel; (*b*) (*of pers.*) grisonnant; aux cheveux gris. **2.** *Z:* **g. (bear),** ours gris d'Amérique; ours grizzlé, grizzli *m*, grizzly *m*.

groan[1] [groun], *s.* **1.** gémissement *m*, plainte *f*; **to give, utter, a deep g.,** pousser un profond gémissement. **2.** *pl.* (*at public meeting, etc.*) **groans,** murmures *m* (de désapprobation).

groan[2]. **1.** *v.i.* gémir; pousser un gémissement; **to g. with pain,** gémir de douleur; **to g. with fatigue,** ahaner de fatigue; **to g. inwardly,** étouffer une plainte, un gémissement; **to g. under the yoke of tyranny,** gémir sous le joug de la tyrannie; **the cart is groaning under the load,** la charrette gémit sous le fardeau; **the door groans on its hinges,** la porte crie sur ses gonds; *A: & Lit:* **to g. for sth.,** languir après qch. **2.** *v.tr.* **he groaned out the whole story,** il a raconté entre ses gémissements ce qui était arrivé.

groaning ['grouniŋ], *s.* **1.** gémissement(s) *m(pl)*. **2.** (*at meeting, etc.*) murmures *mpl*.

groat [grout], *s. Num: A:* pièce *f* de quatre pence; groat *m*; **not worth a g.,** qui ne vaut pas un liard.

groats [grouts], *s.pl.* gruau *m* d'avoine, de froment, d'orge.

grocer ['grousər], *s.* épicier, -ière; **the grocer's wife,** l'épicière; **you can get it at the grocer's,** vous aurez cela chez l'épicier, dans une épicerie; **the grocer's will be closed,** l'épicerie sera fermée; **grocer's port,** porto *m* de qualité inférieure; *F:* **grocer's itch,** eczéma *m*.

grocery ['grousəri], *s.* **1.** épicerie *f*; **to be in the g. business,** être dans l'épicerie. **2.** (*a*) *esp. NAm:* (*shop*) épicerie; (*b*) *U.S: F: Dial:* débit *m* de boissons. **3.** *pl.* **groceries,** (articles *m* d')épicerie.

grœnendael [gru:nəndæl], *s. Z:* grœnendael *m*.

grog[1] [grɔg], *s.* (*a*) grog *m*; (*b*) *NAm: Austr:* boisson *f* alcoolique; (*c*) *F:* (i) *Nau:* rhum *m*; (ii) **g. blossom,** bourgeon *m*, bouton *m* (au nez d'un ivrogne).

grog[2], *v.* (**grogged**) **1.** *v.i. F: O:* boire des grogs; être adonné à la boisson. **2.** *v.tr.* ébouillanter (un tonneau) (pour en extraire l'alcool qui imprègne le bois).

grog[3], *s. Cer: etc:* chamotte *f*, charmot *m*.

groggily ['grɔgili], *adv. F:* (avancer, etc.) en chancelant, en titubant.

grogginess ['grɔginis], *s. F:* (*a*) faiblesse *f* (des jambes); titubation *f*; (*b*) état branlant, peu solide (du mobilier, etc.).

groggy ['grɔgi], *a. F:* **1.** (*a*) *A:* gris, soûl; (*b*) pochard. **2.** chancelant, titubant, vacillant; (boxeur) groggy, sonné; **to be a bit g. about the legs, to feel g.,** être un peu faible des jambes; avoir des jambes de laine, en coton, en flanelle, en pâte de guimauve; être peu solide, vaciller, sur ses jambes; **g. horse,** (i) cheval fatigué; (ii) cheval boiteux, faible des jambes de devant; **g. old table,** vieille table bancale; (*c*) **I'm feeling a bit g.,** je ne suis pas dans mon assiette; (*d*) *F:* **the business is a bit g.,** l'affaire marche cahin-caha.

grogram ['grɔgrəm], *s. Tex:* gros-grain *m*; ottoman *m*.

grogshop ['grɔgʃɔp], *s. F: O:* cabaret *m*; bistro *m*.

groin[1] [grɔin], *s.* **1.** *Anat:* aine *f*; **wounded in the g.,** blessé à l'aine. **2.** *Arch:* (*a*) **g. (rib),** arête *f* (de voûte); (*b*) nervure *f* (d'arête); (*c*) **g. vault,** voûte *f* d'arêtes.

groin[2], *v.tr. Arch:* (*a*) fournir (une voûte) d'arêtes; (*b*) tailler les nervures sur (les arêtes).

groin[3,4], *s. & v.* = GROYNE[1,2].

groined [grɔind], *a. Arch:* **g. vault,** voûte *f* d'arêtes.

gromia ['groumiə], *s. Prot:* gromie *f*.

grommet ['grʌmit], *s.* **1.** *Nau:* erseau *m*, erse *f*, estrope *f*. **2.** *Mec.E: etc:* (*a*) bague *f* d'étoupe; (*b*) virole *f*, rondelle *f* (en caoutchouc, etc.).

gromwell ['grɔmwəl], *s. Bot:* grémil *m*; **common g.,** herbe *f* aux perles.

Groningen ['grouniŋən], *Pr.n. Geog:* Groningue.

groom[1] [gru:m], *s.m.* **1.** gentilhomme, valet (de la Chambre du Roi, etc.); **g. in waiting,** gentilhomme de service; **g. of the bedchamber,** gentilhomme de la chambre. **2.** (*a*) palefrenier; garçon d'écurie; harnacheur; (*b*) jockey, laquais (dont on se fait suivre à cheval). **3.** (*at wedding*) le marié.

groom[2], *v.tr.* **1.** panser (un cheval). **2. to g. a man for office,** (i) dresser un candidat (en vue d'un poste, d'une fonction dans la politique); (ii) préparer les voies à un candidat.

groomed [gru:md], *a.* **well-g.,** (i) (cheval) bien entretenu, bien pansé; (ii) (homme, etc.) bien soigné, bien astiqué, bien peigné; habillé de façon soignée; soigné de sa personne; dans une tenue très soignée; **ill-g.,** (homme, etc.) peu soigné dans sa mise.

grooming ['gru:miŋ], *s.* pansage *m* (d'un cheval).

groomsman, *pl.* **-men** ['gru:mzmən], *s.m.* garçon d'honneur (à un mariage).

groove[1] [gru:v], *s.* **1.** (*a*) rainure *f*; rayure *f* (d'un canon, etc.); cannelure *f* (d'une colonne, d'une pièce mécanique, etc.); gouttière *f* (d'une épée, etc.); *Anat:* sillon *m*, gouttière, rainure (d'un os); (*of penknife, etc.*) **thumbnail g.,** onglet *m*; (*b*) *Carp: Mec.E:* **dovetail g.,** rainure trapézoïdale, rainure en queue d'aronde; **rectangular g.,** rainure rectangulaire; **half-round g., semicircular g.,** rainure semi-circulaire, *Carp:* noix *f*; **V(ee) g.,** rainure en V; (*c*) *Carp:* goujure *f*; (*notch*) encoche *f*; (*rabbet*) râblure *f*, feuillure *f*; **to cut grooves,** mortaiser, rainer; **rounded g.,** gueule-de-loup *f*, *pl.* gueules-de-loup; **g. and tongue joint,** assemblage *m* à rainure et languette; **to join two pieces by g. and tongue,** affourcher deux pièces; (*d*) *Mec.E:* creux *m* (d'une vis); (*for a sliding part, shutter, etc.*) coulisse *f*, glissière *f*; **pulley-wheel g.,** gorge *f*, cannelure, d'une poulie, d'un réa; **ball g.,** cuvette *f* de roulement; *Mch:* **cruciform grooves,** pattes *f* d'araignée; *Metalw:* **box g.,** cannelure fermée (de laminoir); *I.C.E:* **piston-ring g.,** gorge de piston, de segment; rainure annulaire, cannelure, de piston; (*e*) *Rec:* **(sound) g.,** sillon sonore; (*f*) *Mount:* dièdre *m*. **2.** *F:* routine *f*; **to get into a g.,** s'encroûter; devenir routinier; **to get out of the g.,** sortir de l'ornière. **3.** *F:* (*a*) **it's a g.,** c'est chic, épatant; (*b*) **in the g.,** en pleine forme, en plein boum.

groove[2], *v.tr.* rainer; rayer (un canon, etc.); canneler (une colonne); **mountainside grooved by torrents,** flanc de montagne sillonné, strié, creusé, par les torrents; *Carp:* **to g. a board,** bouveter, feuiller, une planche; **to g. and tongue,** assembler à rainure et languette; embrever; *Mec.E:* **to g. the bearings,** faire les pattes d'araignée dans les paliers; **to g. out a piece of metal, etc.,** chever une pièce métallique, etc.

grooved [gru:vd], *a.* rayé, rainé, cannelé; à rayures, à rainures, à cannelures; **g. column,** colonne cannelée, striée; **g. tyre,** pneu cannelé; **g. rubber matting,** tapis *m* en caoutchouc à côtes; **g. wheel,** roue *f* à gorge, réa *m*; **g. rail,** rail *m* à gorge, à rigole, à ornière; **g. bearing,** coussinet *m* à gorges, à pattes d'araignée; *Mch:* **g. block,** bossage cannelé; **g. shaft,** arbre cannelé; *Phot: etc:* **g. trough,** cuve *f* à rainures; *Carp:* **g. board,** planche bouvetée; **g. panel,** panneau tarabiscoté.

grooving ['gru:viŋ], *s.* **1.** (*a*) rayage *m*, rainurage *m*; creusage *m*; **g. machine,** machine *f* à rainer, à canneler; (*b*) *Carp:* **(tonguing and) g.,** bouvetage *m*; **tonguing and g. irons,** fers *m* à bouveter; **tonguing and g. machine,** machine *f* à faire les rainures et languettes; **g. plane,** bouvet *m* femelle, à rainure; rabot *m* à languette; guillaume *m*; feuilleret *m*, guimbarde *f*. **2.** *coll.* rainures *fpl*, cannelures *fpl*; rayures *fpl* (de canon, etc.).

groovy ['gru:vi], *a. F:* **1.** *O:* (*of pers.*) routinier, -ière. **2.** magnifique, de premier ordre.

grope [group], *v.i.* tâtonner; aller, marcher, à tâtons; **to g. for, after, sth.,** chercher qch. à tâtons, à l'aveuglette, en colin-maillard; tâtonner en cherchant qch.; **to g. in one's pocket for a handkerchief,** chercher un mouchoir dans sa poche; **to g. one's way,** avancer à tâtons, à l'aveugle, à l'aveuglette; se diriger en tâtonnant **(towards sth.,** vers qch.); **to g. one's way in, out,** entrer, sortir, à tâtons.

groper ['groupər], *s.* tâtonneur, -euse; **the gropers after truth,** ceux qui, à l'aveuglette, cherchent à découvrir la vérité.

groping[1] ['groupiŋ], *a.* tâtonnant.

groping[2], *s.* tâtonnement *m*.

grosbeak ['grousbi:k], *s. Orn:* gros-bec *m*, *pl.* gros-becs; **republican g.,** républicain *m*; **black-headed g.,** *Fr.C:* gros-bec à tête noire; **blue g.,** évêque bleu à épaulettes brunes, *Fr.C:* gros-bec bleu; **evening g.,** *Fr.C:* gros-bec errant; **pine g.,** dur-bec *m* (*pl.* durs-becs) des sapins, *Fr.C:* gros-bec des pins; **rose-breasted g.,** *Fr.C:* gros-bec à poitrine rose; **scarlet g.,** roselin cramoisi.

grosgrain ['grougrɛ̃, 'grousgrein], *s. Tex:* gros-grain *m*, *pl.* gros-grains.

gros point [grou'pwɛ̃, -'pɔint], *s. Needlew:* gros point.

gross[1] [grous], *s. inv. in pl.* douze douzaines *f*; grosse *f*; **six g. of pens,** six grosses de plumes; **great g.,** douze grosses.

gross[2], *a.* **1.** gras, *f.* grasse; gros, *f.* grosse; bouffi; tout en chair. **2.** grossier; (*a*) **g. ignorance,** ignorance crasse, grossière; **g. injustice,** injustice flagrante; **g. abuse,** abus choquant; **g. carelessness,** manque de soins avéré; **g. mistake,** grosse faute, faute grossière, lourde faute; **g. imposture,** grossière imposture; (*b*) **g. world,** monde grossier; **g. pleasures,** plaisirs grossiers; **g. feeder,** goulu, -ue; glouton, -onne; gros mangeur d'aliments grossiers; (*c*) (*of story, joke, etc.*) grivois, gaulois, graveleux, indécent; **book full of g. passages,** livre plein de crudités, de grossièretés. **3.** (*of growth, shoot, etc.*) trop fort; exubérant. **4.** (*a*) *Com: Fin:* brut; **g. amount,** montant brut (d'une facture, etc.); **g. cost,** prix de revient brut; **g. profit,** bénéfice brut; **g. proceeds,** produit brut (d'une opération commerciale ou financière); **g. loss,** perte brute; **g. receipts, g. revenue,** recette(s) brute(s), revenu brut; *Pol.Ec:* **g. national income,** revenu national brut; (*b*) *Com: etc:* **g. weight,** poids brut; brut *m*; (*c*) *Nau:* **g. displacement,** déplacement global, total; **g. (register) ton,** tonneau *m* de jauge brute; **g. (register) tonnage,** (tonnage *m* de) jauge brute, tonnage brut; (*d*) *M.Ins:* **g. average,** grosse(s) avarie(s), avarie(s) commune(s).

gross[3], *v.tr. Com: etc:* produire (tant de francs) brut; donner des recettes brutes de (tant de francs); **they grossed £10 million,** cela leur a rapporté brut 10 millions de livres.

grossly ['grousli], *adv.* grossièrement; **g. insulted,** grossièrement insulté; **g. exaggerated,** exagéré énormément, outre mesure; **g. ignorant,** d'une ignorance crasse; **to be g. mistaken,** se tromper grossièrement.

grossness ['grousnis], *s.* **1.** grossièreté *f*; flagrance *f*, énormité *f* (d'un abus, etc.). **2.** grossièreté, crudité *f*; indécence *f* (d'une histoire, etc.).

grossularite ['grɔsjulərait], *s. Miner:* grenat *m* calcifère.

grot [grɔt], *s. Poet:* grotte *f*.

grotesque[1] [grou'tesk]. **1.** *a. & s.* grotesque (*m*). **2.** *a.* absurde; bizarre; saugrenu.

grotesque[2], *v.tr.* caricaturer.

grotesquely [grou'teskli], *adv.* grotesquement.

grotesqueness [grou'tesknis], *s.* caractère *m* grotesque (de qch., d'une physionomie).

grothite ['grouθait], *s. Miner:* grothite *f*.

grotto, *pl.* **-oes, -os** ['grɔtou, -ouz], *s.* grotte *f* (pittoresque); **g. work,** rocaille *f*.

grotty ['grɔti], *s. P:* moche; dégueulasse.

grouch[1] [grautʃ], *s.* **1.** maussaderie *f*; **to have a g.,** être de mauvaise humeur; être en rogne; **to have a g. against s.o.,** en vouloir à qn. **2.** = GROUCHER.

grouch[2], *v.i.* grogner, grommeler, ronchonner; être de mauvaise humeur.

groucher ['grautʃər], *s.* grogneur, -euse; ronchonneur, -euse.

grouchy ['grautʃi], *a.* maussade, grognon.

ground[1] [graund], *a.* **1.** moulu, broyé, pilé; **g. coffee,** café moulu; **g. rice,** semoule *f* de riz. **2. g. steel,** acier meulé; **g. glass,** verre dépoli; **g. (glass) stopper,** bouchon *m* à l'émeri. **3.** aiguisé, affûté, émoulu.

ground[2], *s.* **1.** (*a*) fond *m* (de la mer); *Nau:* (*of ship*) **to take (the) g.,** échouer; **to touch g.,** (i) talonner; (ii) *Fig:* en venir aux faits, au solide; **to strike g.,** trouver le fond en sondant; (*b*) *attrib. Nau:* **g. swell,** houle *f,* lame *f,* de fond; mer *f* du fond; **g. sea,** grosses lames déferlant à la côte (par temps calme); **g. tackle,** apparaux *mpl* de mouillage, d'ancrage; amarre *f* de fond; **g. mine,** torpille *f* de fond; *Ich:* **g. fish,** poisson *m* de fond; **g. gudgeon,** loche *f;* **g. fishing,** pêche *f* de fond; *Fish:* **g. line,** ligne *f* de fond; traînée *f;* **g. bait,** amorce *f* de fond; **g.-bait fishing,** pêche *f* au coup; **to g.-bait,** amorcer (un coup, etc.); **g. baiting,** amorçage *m.* **2.** *pl.* **grounds,** marc *m* (du café, etc.); sédiment *m* (du bouillon, etc.); lie *f* (du vin). **3.** (*a*) fond, champ *m* (d'un tableau, d'une tapisserie); **light colour on a dark g.,** couleur claire sur un fond sombre; **flowered g.,** fond à bouquets; *Lacem:* **g. (net),** toilé *m,* toilage *m; Paint: etc:* **g. coat, colour,** (i) première couche de peinture; (ii) fond (de papier peint, etc.); *Cin:* **g. noise** (*accompanying sound film*), bruit *m* de fond; (*b*) *Art:* **the middle g.,** le second plan (d'un tableau). **4.** (*a*) raison *f,* cause *f,* sujet *m,* motif *m;* base *f* (de soupçons, etc.); **grounds for litigation,** matière *f* à procès, sujet de procès; **g. for complaint,** grief *m;* **what is the g. of his complaint?** sur quoi porte sa plainte? **grounds for hope,** raisons d'espérer; **there are grounds for supposing that . . .,** il y a lieu de supposer que . . .; **what grounds have you for saying that?** sur quoi vous fondez-vous pour affirmer cela? **what are his grounds for denying that . . .?** sur quoi se fonde-t-il pour nier que . . .? **what grounds are there for these reports?** qu'est-ce qu'il y a de fondé dans ces bruits qui courent? **I acted on good grounds,** j'ai agi en connaissance de cause; c'est à bon escient que j'ai agi; **on what grounds?** à quel titre? **on both these grounds,** à ce double titre; **to excuse oneself on the ground(s) of illness,** s'excuser pour raison de santé, sous prétexte de maladie; **on grounds of expediency,** pour des raisons de convenance; **on legal grounds,** pour des raisons de droit; **on personal grounds,** pour des raisons personnelles; (*b*) *Jur:* **grounds for divorce,** motifs de divorce; **grounds for a judgment,** considérants *m* d'un jugement; **grounds for appeal (to superior court),** voies *f* de recours; moyens *m* d'appel. **5.** (*a*) sol *m,* terre *f;* **sitting on the g.,** assis par terre; **to sleep on the (bare) g.,** coucher sur la dure, sur le carreau; **to put one's ear to the g.,** appuyer son oreille contre terre; **to fall to the g.,** (i) tomber à, par, terre; (ii) (*of scheme*) tomber à l'eau; ne pas aboutir; avorter; **he threw it on the g.,** il l'a jeté par, à, terre, sur le sol; **to dash s.o.'s hopes to the g.,** anéantir, ruiner, les espérances de qn; *Veh:* **g. clearance,** garde *f* (au sol); hauteur *f* du châssis au-dessus du sol; **rear axle g. clearance,** liberté *f* au-dessous du pont; **above g.,** (i) sur terre; sortant, sorti, de terre; *Min:* au jour, à la surface; (ii) *F:* (*of pers.*) pas encore enterré; *F:* **is he still above g.?** est-il toujours sur terre, toujours de ce monde? **under g.,** sous terre; **at g. level,** au niveau du sol, de la terre; **curtains down to the g.,** rideaux *m* qui pendent jusqu'à terre; **burnt (down) to the g.,** brûlé de fond en comble; **to cut a tree to the g.,** (i) couper un arbre au ras du sol; (ii) ravaler un arbre; *F:* **that suits me down to the g.,** *U.S:* **from the g. up,** (i) cela me va à merveille; (ii) ça m'arrange le mieux du monde, ça fait mon compte, mon beurre; **that dress suits her down to the g.,** cette robe lui va à merveille; *U.S:* **to begin again from the g. up,** recommencer à zéro; **to study a case from the g. up,** étudier un problème de A à Z; *Games:* **off g.,** chat perché; *Jur:* **g. underneath a building,** tréfonds *mpl* d'un immeuble; **g. plan,** (i) *Const: etc:* plan *m* de fondation; plan horizontal; projection horizontale; (ii) *Fort: etc:* tracé *m* (d'une œuvre); **firm g.,** terre compacte, bien assise; (*of building*) **to rest on firm g.,** reposer sur un terrain solide; **to be on sure, firm, g., to be sure of one's g.,** connaître le terrain; être sûr de son fait; aller à coup sûr; **to feel the g.,** sonder, tâter, le terrain; **to cut the g. from under s.o.'s feet,** couper l'herbe sous le pied à qn; (*b*) *Av:* **g. crew, g. personnel, g. staff,** personnel *m* au sol, personnel non navigant, *F:* les rampants *m;* **g. environment, g. installations, g. organization,** infrastructure *f;* **g. handling,** manœuvre(s) *f(pl)* (des appareils) au sol; **g. light,** balise *f;* **g. marking(s),** balisage *m;* **g. position,** position *f* (par rapport au) sol; **g. position indicator,** indicateur *m* de position (par rapport au) sol; **g. speed,** vitesse *f* par rapport au sol; **g. speed indicator,** indicateur de vitesse par rapport au sol; *Mil.Av:* **g. control approach,** station(s) *f(pl)* de contrôle d'approche; **g. control interception,** station(s) de direction des interceptions; *Mil:* **g. observer,** guetteur *m* à vue, guetteur d'avions; **g. observer team,** poste *m* de guetteurs d'avions; **g.-guided missile,** missile guidé à partir du sol; (*of atom bomb*) **g. zero,** point *m* zéro; **desired g. zero,** point visé; *Aedcs:* **g. effect,** effet *m* de sol, effet d'interaction au sol; **g. cushion,** coussin *m* d'air (résultant de l'effet de sol); *Elcs:* **g. return,** écho *m* de sol (d'un radar); *W.Tel:* **g. wave,** onde *f* de sol, de surface; (*c*) *Ven:* (*of fox*) **to run, go, to g.,** se terrer; **to run a fox to g.,** poursuivre un renard jusqu'à son terrier; (*d*) *Z:* **g. squirrel,** (i) tamias *m;* (ii) spermophile *m;* **g. pig,** thryonomys *m; Orn:* **g. dove,** géopélie *f;* **g. thrush,** (i) géocichle *m;* geocichla *m;* (ii) brève *f,* grive *f* superbe; **(Indian) orange-headed g. thrush,** merle *m* orange; *Ent:* **g. beetle,** carabique *m,* carabidé *m, F:* jardinière *f,* sergent *m; Bot:* **g. ash,** (i) plant *m* de frêne; (ii) angélique *f* sauvage; (iii) = GOUTWEED; **g. box,** buis commun, des forêts, buis pour bordure; **g. cherry,** physalis *m;* **g. cypress,** santoline *f* cyprès; **g. ivy,** lierre terrestre, rampant; *F:* herbe *f* de Saint-Jean; **g. pine,** (i) ive *f,* ivette *f;* (ii) lycopode *m* en massue; mousse *f* terrestre; **g. leaf,** feuille *f* (de tabac) qui pousse au niveau du sol: (*e*) terrain *m;* (i) **undulating g.,** terrain vallonné, onduleux; **rocky, rough, g.,** terrain rocheux, raboteux; *Mil:* **g. study,** étude *f* (tactique) du terrain; **to have an eye for g.,** avoir le sens du terrain; **close, open, g.,** terrain couvert, découvert; **commanding, dominating, g.,** les hauteurs dominantes; les points du terrain offrant des vues, constituant des observatoires; **dead g.,** les angles morts; **vantage g.,** terrain favorable, avantageux; (ii) **building g.,** terrain à bâtir; **grounds and buildings,** propriétés *f* et bâtiments *m;* **country house with extensive grounds,** château *m* avec domaine; **g. landlord,** propriétaire foncier; le propriétaire du sol; **g. rent,** loyer *m* de la terre; redevance *f* emphytéotique; (*as source of income*) rente foncière; (iii) **camping g.,** terrain de camping; **football g.,** terrain de football; *Mil:* **drill g., parade g., training g.,** terrain d'exercice, de manœuvre; champ *m* de manœuvre; *Fig:* **to find a common g. for negotiations,** trouver un terrain d'entente en vue de négocier; **to meet one's opponents on their own g.,** se placer sur le même terrain que ses adversaires; **to change, shift, one's g.,** changer ses batteries, changer d'arguments, déplacer la question; **to tread on forbidden g.,** (α) empiéter sur un terrain défendu; (β) toucher à un sujet interdit, à un sujet tabou; **to cover a lot of g.,** (α) faire beaucoup de chemin; (β) parcourir un champ très vaste; aborder, traiter, un très grand nombre de sujets; **we have a lot of g. to cover,** (α) nous avons beaucoup de chemin à faire; (β) nous avons un vaste programme à parcourir; *Aut:* **to cover the g.,** faire de la route; **to dispute the g.,** disputer le terrain; **to gain g.,** gagner du terrain, progresser; (*of idea*) faire son chemin, prendre pied; (*of news*) se répandre, s'accréditer; *Nau:* **to gain g. on the tack,** gagner à la bordée; **to give, lose, g.,** céder, perdre, du terrain; faire marche arrière, lâcher pied; (*of troops*) se replier, mollir; **to hold, stand, one's g.,** tenir bon, tenir ferme, tenir pied, tenir tête; ne pas lâcher pied; *Cr:* (*of batsman*) **to be out of one's g.,** avoir franchi les limites du guichet. **6.** *El: NAm:* (i) terre; (ii) masse *f* (d'un châssis de voiture, etc.); **to connect to g.,** mettre (un pôle) à la masse; **g. connection,** prise *f* de terre; retour *m* à la terre, à la masse; **g. mat,** prise de terre multiple; **g. rod,** piquet *m* de prise de terre; **g. terminal,** borne *f* de mise à la terre; **g. wire,** fil *m* de terre; **g. leak,** perte *f* à la terre; **g. return circuit,** circuit *m* de retour par la terre. **7.** *attrib.* fondamental, -aux; *Mus:* **g. note,** son fondamental; **g. bass,** basse contrainte, obstinée.

ground[3]. **1.** *v.tr.* (*a*) fonder, baser, appuyer (**on, in, sth.,** sur qch.); **to g. one's belief on certain facts,** asseoir sa conviction sur certains faits; (*b*) **to g. a pupil in Latin,** enseigner à fond les rudiments du latin à un élève; donner à un élève de bons éléments du latin, une bonne base en latin; (*c*) (i) préparer le fond (d'un tableau, d'une tapisserie); (ii) donner la première couche de peinture à (une surface); (*d*) mettre (qch.) à terre; *Golf:* **to g. one's club,** asseoir sa crosse sur le sol; *Mil:* **g. arms!** l'arme au pied! reposez armes! (*e*) *El: NAm:* mettre (le courant) à la terre, à la masse; (*f*) *Nau:* jeter (un navire) à la côte; (*g*) *Av:* **to g. an aircraft,** interdire de vol un avion. **2.** *v.i.* (*a*) *Nau:* (*of ship*) (i) échouer, s'échouer (**on,** sur); (ii) talonner; (*b*) (*of balloon, etc.*) atterrir.

groundage ['graundidʒ], *s. Nau:* droits *mpl* de mouillage, d'ancrage.

grounded ['graundid], *a.* **1. well g., ill g., belief,** croyance bien, mal, fondée; **well g. rumour,** bruit consistant. **2.** (*a*) (*of mains, etc.*) au sol, enterré; (*b*) *El: NAm:* (mis) à la terre, à la masse; **g. circuit,** circuit *m* à la terre; **g. grid,** grille *f* à la masse.

grounder ['graundər], *s. Games:* coup *m* qui fait rouler la balle sur le sol; balle qui roule sur le sol.

groundhog ['graundhɔg], *s. Z:* marmotte *f* d'Amérique.

grounding ['graundiŋ], *s.* **1.** (*a*) assise *f* (d'un argument sur qch.); (*b*) *El: NAm:* mise *f* (du courant) à la terre, à la masse; (*c*) *Nau:* (i) échouage *m;* (ii) talonnement *m;* (*d*) atterrissage *m* (d'un ballon, etc.). **2.** (*a*) **to have a good g. in Latin,** avoir une connaissance solide des rudiments du latin; **he has a good g.,** il connaît bien ses éléments; il a une bonne base; (*b*) fond *m* (de tapisserie); (*c*) *Paint: etc:* première couche; couche d'impression.

groundless ['graundlis], *a.* (soupçon, bruit, etc.) mal fondé, sans raison, sans fondement, immotivé; **g. report,** bruit sans fondement, qui ne repose sur rien; **g. assumption,** supposition gratuite; **my suspicions were g.,** mes soupçons n'étaient pas fondés, étaient sans motif.

groundlessly ['graundlisli], *adv.* (s'alarmer) sans cause, sans raison.

groundling ['graundliŋ], *s.* **1.** *Ich:* (*a*) loche épineuse de rivière; (*b*) gobie noir; (*c*) (*more widely*) poisson *m* de fond. **2.** *Bot:* (*a*) plante rampante; (*b*) plante naine. **3.** (*a*) *Th: A:* spectateur *m* du parterre; (*b*) *Lit: A:* **the groundlings,** les gens *m* sans culture; les bourgeois *m;* les philistins *m.*

groundman, *pl.* **-men** ['graundmæn, -mən], *s.m. esp. U.S:* **1.** terrassier. **2.** préposé à l'entretien d'un terrain de jeux.

groundnut ['graundnʌt], *s. Bot:* arachide *f.*

groundsel[1] ['graun(d)səl], *s. Bot:* seneçon *m,* séneçon *m;* **g. tree,** seneçon en arbre; **arborescent g., tree g.,** seneçon arborescent.

groundsel[2], *s. Const: etc:* sole *f,* semelle *f,* sablière basse (de cadre); seuil *m* (de dormant de porte).

groundsheet ['graundʃiːt], *s.* bâche *f* de campement, tapis *m* de sol.

groundsman, *pl.* **-men** ['graundzmən], *s.m.* préposé à l'entretien d'un terrain de jeux.

groundwork ['graundwəːk], *s.* **1.** fond *m* (de tapisserie, etc.); couleur *f* de fond (d'un tableau, etc.). **2.** (*a*) fondement *m,* fond; base *f;* (*b*) plan *m,* canevas *m* (d'un roman, etc.); (*c*) **to do the g.,** préparer le terrain.

group[1] [gruːp], *s.* groupe *m* (de personnes); *Ind: etc:* groupe, groupement *m,* société *f;* **to go about in a g., in groups,** se promener en groupe, par groupes; **to form a g.,** se grouper; **little groups were forming to discuss the news,** de petits apartés, de petits groupes, se formaient pour discuter la nouvelle; **social groups,** groupes sociaux; **g. action, g. decision,** action, décision, collective; *Mil:* **g. training,** instruction collective; *Pol: etc:* **parliamentary g.,** groupe parlementaire; **political g.,** groupe(ment) politique; **ultra-conservative g.,** groupe d'extrême droite; **pressure g.,** groupe de pression; **study g.,** groupe de travail, d'étude; *Physiol:* **blood g.,** groupe sanguin; *Med: etc:* **control g.,** groupe témoin (dans une étude, une expérience, etc.); *Psy:* **g. therapy,** sociatrie *f;* **literary g.,** cercle *m* littéraire; *Art:* **g. of figures,** groupe(ment) de personnages; **a bronze g. representing a mother and child,** un groupe en bronze représentant la mère et l'enfant; *Mus:* **(pop) g.,** formation *f,* groupe, pop; (*b*) *Mil.Av:* (i) commandement aérien tactique; (ii) zone *f* de défense aérienne; (iii) *U.S:* escadre aérienne; **g. captain,** colonel *m; Mil:* **army g.,** groupe d'armées; **artillery g.,** groupement d'artillerie; **brigade g.,** *U.S:* **battle g.,** groupement d'infanterie; **battalion g.,** sous-groupement *m* d'infanterie; **g. operations centre,** centre *m* d'opérations de zone; (*c*) groupe, ensemble *m* (de choses); *Mec.E:* ensemble (structural ou mécanique); **arrangement in groups,** groupement, groupage *m;* **lamps arranged in groups of three,** lampes disposées en groupes de trois; **to arrange articles in groups,** grouper des articles; **harmonious g. of colours,** ensemble harmonieux de couleurs; *Mth: etc:* **g. theory,** théorie *f* des ensembles; *W.Tel:* **g. velocity,** vitesse *f* de groupe (d'ondes); *Tg: etc:* **g. of figures, of letters, of words,** groupe de chiffres, de lettres, de mots; **g. count,** (i) *Tg:* indication *f* du nombre de mots; (ii) (*in cipher*) compte *m* de groupes; *Mus:* **g. of notes,** groupe de notes; *Geol:* **g. of faults,** faisceau *m* de failles; *Rail:* **g. of sidings,** faisceau de voies; *Tp:* **g. of lines,** faisceau de lignes; *Av:* **tail g.,** empennage *m;* (*d*) *Tp:* groupe (de jonctions); **g.**

centre, (i) centre de distribution, de groupement; (ii) centrale régionale; **g.-occupancy time meter,** enregistreur *m* des durées de communications (d'un groupe de jonctions); **g. selector,** sélecteur *m* de groupe; chercheur *m*; (*e*) *Ch:* radical *m*; groupe; groupement; **hydroxy g., ketone g.,** groupe hydroxyle, cétone.

group[2]. **1.** *v.tr.* grouper, disposer en groupes, répartir par groupes (des articles, des faits, etc.); allotir (des provisions, etc.); combiner (des idées); *El:* grouper, (ac)coupler, associer (des piles); *Art:* **the figures are well grouped,** les figures sont bien agencées, heureusement disposées. **2.** *v.i.* se grouper (**round,** autour de); **figures that g. well,** figures qui groupent bien.

groupage ['gru:pidʒ], *s.* = GROUPING.

grouped [gru:pt], *a.* groupé; **g. columns,** colonnes groupées.

grouper ['gru:pər], *s. Ich:* épinéphèle *m*, mérou *m*.

grouping ['gru:piŋ], *s.* (*a*) groupage *m* (de colis, de marchandises, etc.); groupement *m* (de figures, etc.); combinaison *f* (de couleurs); allotissement *m* (de provisions); **age g. of the population,** répartition *f* de la population par groupes d'âge; **blood g.,** groupage sanguin; **the g. of the figures in a picture,** l'agencement *m* des figures d'un tableau; *El:* **g. of cells,** association *f* des piles; (*b*) *Ball:* groupement *m* (d'impacts de projectiles); **g. (of shots) on a horizontal target,** groupement horizontal; **g. (of shots) on a vertical target,** groupement vertical; *Mil:* **g. (of shots) by a single man,** groupement individuel; **g. by a body of men,** groupement collectif; **g. practice,** tir de groupement.

grouse[1] [graus], *s. inv. in pl. Orn:* tétras *m*, grouse *m* or *f*; faisan bruyant; **wood g., great g.,** grand tétras; coq *m* de bruyère; **red g.,** lagopède *m* (rouge) d'Écosse; **black g.,** tétras lyre; coq des bouleaux; **willow g.,** lagopède des saules; **pinnated g.,** gelinotte *f* des prairies; tétras cupidon (de l'Amérique du Nord); **dusky g.,** tétras obscur, *Fr.C:* tétras sombre; **ruffed g.,** tétras à fraise, *Fr.C:* gelinotte huppée; **sharp-tailed g.,** tétras à longue queue, *Fr.C:* gelinotte à queue fine; **spruce g.,** *Fr.C:* tétras des savanes; **sage g.,** tétras centrocerque, *Fr.C:* gelinotte des armoises.

grouse[2], *s.* **1.** grogne *f*; **he enjoys a good g.,** il aime à grogner; il aime ronchonner. **2. to have a g. against s.o.,** avoir un grief contre qn; **to have a good g., a real g.,** (i) avoir bonne raison de se plaindre; (ii) donner vent à sa mauvaise humeur; vider son sac.

grouse[3], *v.i.* ronchonner, grogner, grincher, groller, bougonner, maugréer (**at, about,** contre).

grouser ['grausər], *s.* grognon *mf*; ronchonneur, -euse; grincheux, -euse; bougon, -onne.

grousing ['grausiŋ], *s.* grognonnerie *f*; bougonnage *m*.

grout[1] [graut], *s.* (*a*) *Const: etc:* coulis *m*; mortier clair, liquide; **cement g.,** lait *m*, laitance *f*, de ciment; **bituminous g.,** enduit bitumineux; **g. hole,** trou *m* d'injection; (*b*) **coffee grouts,** fond *m* du café.

grout[2], *v.tr. Const:* **to g. (in) stones,** couler des pierres; liaisonner, jointoyer, des pierres (avec du mortier liquide); sceller des pierres au ciment.

grout[3]. **1.** *v.i.* (*of pig*) fouiller (avec le groin). **2.** *v.tr.* (*of pig*) **to g. out truffles,** découvrir les truffes (en fouillant la terre).

grouting ['grautiŋ], *s. Const:* **1.** jointoiement *m* au mortier liquide; injection *f*. **2.** = GROUT[1] (*a*).

grove [grouv], *s.* bocage *m*, futaie *f*, bosquet *m*; bouquet *m* de bois; plantation *f* (d'arbres); **beech g.,** hêtraie *f*; **orange g.,** orangeraie *f*; **olive g.,** oliveraie *f*; **palm g.,** palmeraie *f*.

grovel ['grɔv(ə)l], *v.i.* (**grovelled**) ramper; **to g. in the dirt,** se vautrer, se traîner, dans la boue, dans la fange; **to g. to, before, s.o.,** ramper, se prosterner, s'aplatir, se mettre à plat ventre, devant qn; lécher les bottes de qn, à qn.

groveller ['grɔvələr], *s.* sycophante *m*, flagorneur *m*; *F:* chien couchant.

grovelling[1] ['grɔvəliŋ], *a.* rampant; bas, vil, abject; **g. toadies,** sycophantes rampants.

grovelling[2], *s.* **1.** rampement *m*; vautrement *m*. **2.** prosternation *f*, aplatissement *m* (devant la richesse, etc.).

grow [grou], *v.* (**grew** [gru:]; **grown** [groun])

I. *v.i.* **1.** (*a*) (*of plants*) croître, pousser; **to g. again,** recroître, repousser; (*of plants, hair*) revenir; (*of plant*) **to g. down,** pousser vers le bas; (*of nail*) **to g. in,** s'incarner; *Prov:* **ill weeds g. apace,** mauvaise herbe croît toujours; (*b*) (*of seeds*) germer; **a feeling of hate gradually grew (up) between the two friends,** un sentiment de haine naissait peu à peu entre les deux amis; **the custom has grown up,** la coutume s'est établie; **this state grew out of a few small towns,** cet état est né de quelques bourgades, doit son origine à quelques bourgades; **institutions out of which the Constitution of England grew,** institutions *f* qui ont servi à former la Constitution de l'Angleterre, qui sont à la base de la Constitution de l'Angleterre; (*c*) **olives do not g. in England,** l'olivier ne pousse pas en Angleterre; *F:* (*esp. of money*) **it doesn't g. on trees,** ça ne pousse pas sur les arbres. **2.** (*of pers.*) grandir; **to g. tall,** devenir grand; se faire grand; grandir; **how your youngster has grown!** comme votre petit a grandi! **to g. into boyhood,** devenir adolescent; **to g. into a woman,** passer femme; **he had grown into a man,** il était devenu homme; **she had grown into a fine girl,** elle était devenue une belle fille; **to stop growing,** finir de pousser, cesser de grandir, achever sa croissance; **to g. up,** grandir; devenir grand; atteindre l'âge adulte; **she is growing up,** elle se fait grande; **all these children are growing up,** tous ces enfants poussent; **to g. out of one's clothes,** devenir trop grand pour ses vêtements; **he's mischievous, but he will g. out of it,** s'il est espiègle, cela passera avec l'âge. **3.** (*a*) s'accroître, croître, augmenter, grandir; **the crowd grew,** la foule s'accroissait, augmentait, grossissait; **the firm has grown very considerably,** la maison a pris une extension considérable; **his influence grew,** son influence a grandi, s'est accrue; **the rumour was growing,** la rumeur grandissait; **astonishment grew and grew,** l'étonnement *m* allait toujours croissant; **to g. in favour,** monter en faveur; **to g. in wisdom, in beauty,** croître, augmenter, en sagesse, en beauté; avancer, profiter, en sagesse; (*b*) **habit that grows on one,** habitude *f* qui vous gagne; (*c*) *F:* **that picture grows on me,** plus je regarde ce tableau plus il me plaît, plus il me dit; **it grows on you,** on ne l'apprécie pas tout d'abord. **4.** (*a*) devenir; **to g. old,** devenir vieux; se faire vieux; vieillir; **his parents had grown old,** ses parents *m* avaient vieilli, étaient vieux; **to g. young again, to g. younger,** rajeunir; **to g. big, bigger,** (i) grandir; (ii) grossir; (iii) augmenter; **to g. smaller,** (i) rapetisser; (ii) diminuer; **to g. alarmed, excited,** s'alarmer, s'exciter; **to g. angry,** se fâcher, se mettre en colère; **to g. rarer,** se faire plus rare; **to g. less,** diminuer; **it is growing dark,** il commence à faire sombre; la nuit se fait; (*b*) **he grew to be more obedient,** il en arriva peu à peu à se montrer plus obéissant; **I have grown to think that . . .,** j'en suis venu à penser que . . ..

II. *v.tr.* **1.** cultiver (des roses, etc.); planter (des choux, etc.); faire venir (du blé); **farm that grows beetroot,** ferme *f* où on fait de la betterave; **soil that will not g. asparagus,** sol *m* qui se refuse aux asperges. **2.** laisser pousser (sa barbe, etc.); **the stag grows fresh antlers every year,** le cerf renouvelle ses andouillers chaque année.

growable ['grouəbl], *a.* cultivable.

grower ['grouər], *s.* **1.** (*of plant*) **fast g., slow g.,** plante *f* qui croît vite, lentement. **2.** (*pers.*) cultivateur, -trice (de légumes, etc.); exploitant *m* (d'une forêt); **potato g.,** planteur *m* de pommes de terre; **vine g.,** viticulteur *m*; vigneron *m*; **rose g.,** rosiériste *mf*.

growing[1] ['grouiŋ], *a.* **1.** croissant; qui pousse; **g. crops,** récoltes *f* sur pied; *Jur:* récoltes pendantes par (les) racines. **2.** grandissant; (*a*) **g. child,** enfant *mf* en cours de croissance; (*b*) **g. debt,** dette grossissante, qui augmente; **ever-g. sympathy,** sympathie toujours grandissante; **g. opinion,** opinion de plus en plus répandue; **there was a g. fear that . . .,** on craignait de plus en plus que . . .. **3. wheat-g., potato-g., district,** région *f* qui produit du blé, des pommes de terre; région à blé, à pommes de terre.

growing[2], *s.* **1.** croissance *f*; **plants that have no g. space,** plantes *f* qui manquent d'espace pour se développer; **the g. age,** l'âge *m* de la croissance; *Med: F:* **g. pains,** douleurs *f* de croissance; **g. weather,** temps *m* qui fait croître les plantes; temps propice à la croissance des plantes. **2.** culture *f* (de plantes).

growl[1] [graul], *s.* grondement *m*, gognement *m* (d'un chien, etc.); **the low g. of the distant traffic,** la rumeur sourde de la circulation dans le lointain.

growl[2], *v.i. & tr.* **1.** (*of animal*) grogner; (*of cat*) feuler; gronder (**at,** contre); **the dog growled at me,** le chien m'a reçu avec un grognement. **2.** (*of pers.*) gronder, grogner, grommeler, *F:* maronner, ronchonner; **to g. (out) a refusal,** grogner un refus.

growler ['graulər], *s.* **1.** (*pers.*) grogneur, -euse; grognon *mf*; ronchonneur, -euse. **2.** *El: U.S:* vibreur *m* (pour vérification des induits). **3.** *A.Veh: F:* fiacre *m*. **4.** glaçon (détaché d'un iceberg). **5.** *U.S:* cruche *f* à bière.

growling[1] ['grauliŋ], *a.* **1.** grondant, grognant. **2.** ronchonneur, grognon.

growling[2], *s.* grognement *m*, grondement *m*; (*of cat*) feulement *m*.

grown [groun], *a.* (**full-**)**g.,** grand; qui a fini sa croissance; **g. man,** homme fait; **to be g. up,** être adulte; **when you are g. up,** quand tu seras grand; **children are all g. up nowadays,** il n'y a plus d'enfants; *s.* **the g.-ups,** les grands; les grandes personnes; les adultes *m*.

growth [grouθ], *s.* **1.** croissance *f*, venue *f*; **to attain full g.,** (i) avoir entièrement fini sa croissance; atteindre l'âge adulte; (ii) (*of plant, etc.*) arriver à maturité; **trees in full g.,** arbres *m* en pleine végétation, en pleine croissance; **plant of quick g.,** plante *f* qui pousse vite. **2.** accroissement *m*; augmentation *f* (en quantité), développement *m* (des affaires); extension *f* (des affaires, d'une maison de commerce); **economic g.,** développement, croissance, économique; **rate of g.,** taux *m* d'expansion, de croissance; **g. point,** pôle *m* de croissance; **the rapid g. of urban population,** l'expansion *f* rapide de la population urbaine. **3.** (*a*) **yearly g.,** pousse annuelle; **second g.,** regain *m*; *For:* **new g.,** revenue *f*; **wine of the first g.,** vin *m* de première cuvée; **wine of the grand first g.,** vin de tête de cuvée; première ligne; (*b*) poussée *f* (de cheveux, etc.); **a week's g. on his chin,** le menton couvert d'une barbe de huit jours. **4.** *Med:* grosseur *f*, tumeur *f*, excroissance *f*; **benign, malignant, g.,** tumeur bénigne, maligne; **morbid g.,** excroissance morbide.

groyne[1] [grɔin], *s. Hyd.E:* épi *m* à dent (d'une plage); brise-lames *m inv*, éperon *m* (brise-lames); estacade *f* (perpendiculaire au rivage).

groyne[2], *v.tr.* établir des épis, des brise-lames, des éperons, en travers de (la plage).

groyning ['grɔiniŋ], *s.* **1.** construction *f* d'épis, d'estacades, de brise-lames. **2.** *coll.* (ensemble *m* des) épis *m*, estacades *f*, brise-lames.

grub[1] [grʌb], *s.* **1.** *Ent:* (*a*) larve *f*; (*b*) *F:* ver (blanc); asticot *m*. **2.** *F:* (*pers.*) (*a*) *A:* gratte-papier *m inv*; (*b*) indésirable *m*; individu *m* de mauvaise mine; (*c*) enfant sale, petit morveux. **3.** *Cr:* balle bôlée à ras de sol. **4.** *Civ.E:* excavateur *m*, excavatrice *f*. **5.** *P:* mangeaille *f*, boustifaille *f*; **grub's up!** à la soupe!

grub[2], *v.*

I. *v.tr. & i.* **1.** *v.tr.* (*a*) fouir, travailler superficiellement (la terre); (*b*) défricher (un terrain). **2.** *v.i.* fouiller (dans la terre); **she was grubbing among the flower beds to find her ring,** elle fouillait dans les parterres pour retrouver sa bague. **3.** *v.i. P: O:* manger, bouffer.

II. (*compound verbs*) **1. grub about,** *v.i.* fouiller, farfouiller; **to g. about in a library,** fouiller, bouquiner, dans une bibliothèque.

2. grub along, *v.i. F:* vivoter.

3. grub away, *v.i.* bûcher, trimer.

4. grub out, *v.tr.* extirper (des racines, etc.).

5. grub up, *v.tr.* (i) essoucher (une vigne, un terrain); extirper (une racine); déraciner (une plante); (ii) essarter, défricher (un terrain).

grubber ['grʌbər], *s.* **1.** (*pers.*) (*a*) fouilleur, -euse (dans la terre, etc.); (*b*) *Sch: F: O:* bûcheur, -euse; piocheur, -euse. **2.** *Agr:* (*implement*) (*a*) extirpateur *m*; déchaumeur *m*, déchaumeuse *f*; machine *f* à essarter; (*b*) hoyau *m*; pioche *f* à pic; (*c*) arrachoir *m*, arracheur *m*, arracheuse *f*.

grubbily ['grʌbili], *adv.* salement, malproprement.

grubbiness ['grʌbinis], *s.* saleté *f*; malpropreté *f*.

grubbing ['grʌbiŋ], *s.* (*a*) fouillage *m*; (*b*) **g. up,** essouchement *m* (d'un terrain); extirpation *f* (des racines); essartage *m*, essartement *m*, défrichage *m*, défrichement *m* (d'un terrain); **g. hoe, hook, mattock,** hoyau *m*; pioche *f* à pic; **g. plough,** arrachoir *m*, arracheur *m*, arracheuse *f*.

grubby ['grʌbi], *a.* **1.** (arbre) véreux, mangé des vers. **2.** sale, crasseux, malpropre; **g. hands,** mains douteuses.

grubstake[1] ['grʌbsteik], *s.* **1.** *NAm:* (*a*) *Min:* provisions *fpl*, argent *m*, donné(es) à un prospecteur (contre un pourcentage de ses profits); (*b*) prêt *m* ou subvention *f* (fait(e) à qn qui se trouve dans des circonstances difficiles). **2.** *Can:* stock *m* de provisions, de denrées alimentaires.

grubstake[2], *v.tr. NAm:* donner un *grubstake* à (qn).

Grub Street ['grʌbstri:t], *Pr.n.* **1.** rue *f* de Londres où demeuraient les écrivassiers du dix-huitième siècle; *F:* **G.-S. hack, journalist,** gratte-papier *m inv*. **2.** *coll. F:* la bohème littéraire.

grudge[1] [grʌdʒ], *s.* rancune *f*; **to bear, owe, s.o. a g.; to have, nurse, keep up, a g. against s.o.,** garder rancune à qn; garder de l'animosité contre qn; en vouloir à qn, tenir rigueur à qn; *F:* avoir une dent contre qn; en avoir à, contre, qn (**for having done sth.,** d'avoir fait qch.); **to cherish a secret g. against s.o.,** ressentir un dépit secret contre qn; **to pay off old grudges,** satisfaire de vieilles rancunes.

grudge[2], *v.tr.* **1.** donner, accorder, (qch. à qn) à contrecœur à regret; **to g. s.o. the food he eats,** lésiner sur la nourriture de qn; mesurer la nourriture à qn; **he does**

not g. his efforts, il ne marchande pas sa peine. **2. to g. s.o. his pleasures,** voir d'un mauvais œil les plaisirs de qn; trouver mauvais que qn s'amuse.

grudging[1] ['grʌdʒiŋ], *a.* **1.** (*of praise, gift, etc.*) fait, donné, accordé, à contrecœur, de mauvaise grâce, en rechignant. **2.** (*of pers.*) lésineur, -euse.

grudging[2], *s.* **1.** lésinerie *f*; **given without g.,** donné à pleines mains. **2.** mauvaise volonté.

grudgingly ['grʌdʒiŋli], *adv.* (faire qch.) comme pour l'amour de Dieu, à contrecœur, à son corps défendant, en rechignant, de mauvaise grâce; **to praise s.o. g.,** marchander ses éloges à qn; louer qn du bout des lèvres.

gruel[1] ['gru(:)əl], *s.* **1.** *Cu:* gruau *m* (d'avoine, à l'eau ou au lait); (*thin*) brouet *m*. **2.** *F: O:* **to give s.o. his g.,** (i) battre qn comme plâtre, flanquer une bonne raclée à qn; (ii) échiner, éreinter, qn; **to take, get, one's g.,** avaler sa médecine; encaisser; **he's had his g.,** il a écopé; il a reçu son compte.

gruel[2], *v.tr. F: A:* échiner, éreinter (un adversaire).

gruelling[1] ['gru(:)əliŋ], *a.* éreintant, épuisant; (match, etc.) âprement disputé; **to give s.o. a g. time,** faire passer un mauvais quart d'heure à qn; **we had a g. time,** ç'a été tout ce qu'il y a de plus dur.

gruelling[2], *s. F:* raclée *f*; épreuve éreintante; **he gave me a g.,** il m'a fait passer un mauvais quart d'heure.

gruesome ['gru:səm], *a.* horrible, macabre, affreux; qui vous donne la chair de poule; qui donne le frisson; **a g. story,** une histoire macabre; *s.* **the gruesome,** le macabre.

gruesomely ['gru:səmli], *adv.* horriblement, affreusement, macabrement; à vous donner le frisson.

gruesomeness ['gru:səmnis], *s.* caractère *m* horrible (d'une apparition, d'un récit, etc.); **the g. of the situation,** l'horreur *f* de la situation.

gruff [grʌf], *a.* (ton) bourru, bougon, revêche, rébarbatif, rude, brusque; **g. voice,** grosse voix; **he's somewhat, a bit, g.,** il est un peu ours.

gruffly ['grʌfli], *adv.* d'un ton bourru, rébarbatif; avec brusquerie.

gruffness ['grʌfnis], *s.* ton bourru, rébarbatif; *F:* ourserie *f*; **the g. of his greeting,** la brusquerie de son accueil.

Gruidae ['gru:idi:], *s.pl. Orn:* gruidés *m*, les grues *f*.

Gruiformes [gru:i'fɔ:mi:z], *s.pl. Orn:* gruiformes *m*, ralliformes *m*.

grumble[1] ['grʌmbl], *s.* (*a*) grommellement *m*, grognement *m*, grondement *m*, grognonnerie *f*; (*b*) murmure *m* (de mécontentement); **to obey without a g.,** obéir sans murmurer; (*c*) *F:* **to have a good old g.,** donner vent à sa mauvaise humeur; rouspéter.

grumble[2], *v.i.* grommeler, grogner, grognonner, murmurer; *F:* ronchonner, bougonner, rouspéter; **the troops were grumbling,** les troupes *f* murmuraient; **to g. about, over, the food,** se plaindre de la nourriture; trouver à redire à la nourriture; **you needn't g.,** vous n'avez pas à vous plaindre; il n'y a pas de quoi vous plaindre; **to g. at s.o.,** grommeler, gronder, rouspéter, contre qn.

grumbler ['grʌmblər], *s.* **1.** grognard, -arde, grognon *m*, grommeleur, -euse, bougon, -onne, rouspéteur, -euse; **an old g.,** un vieux ronchon. **2.** mécontent, -ente; **they arrested all the grumblers,** on arrêta tous les mécontents, tous ceux qui faisaient preuve d'un mauvais esprit.

grumbling[1], ['grʌmbliŋ], *a.* (*a*) grommelant, grognon, bougon; grondeur, -euse; (*b*) (*of pain*) sourd; **g. appendix,** appendicite *f* chronique.

grumbling[2], *s.* **1.** grognonnerie *f*; *F:* rouspétance *m*. **2.** mécontentement *m*.

grumblingly ['grʌmbliŋli], *adv.* en grommelant; d'un ton grognon; en murmurant.

grume [gru:m], *s. esp. Med:* caillot *m* (de sang); grumeau *m* (de pus).

grummet ['grʌmit], *s.* = GROMMET.

grumous ['gru:məs], *a. esp. Med:* grumeleux; à demi coagulé.

grumpily ['grʌmpili], *adv.* maussadement; d'un ton, d'un air, maussade, renfrogné; en ronchonnant, en rouspétant.

grumpiness ['grʌmpinis], *s.* mauvaise humeur; maussaderie *f*; caractère *m* désagréable.

grumpy ['grʌmpi], *a.* maussade, renfrogné, grincheux, grognon, bougon; peu abordable; **how g. you are today!** comme vous êtes désagréable aujourd'hui! **a g. old man,** un vieux grincheux.

Grundy ['grʌndi], *Pr.n. O:* **Mrs G.,** personnification *f* du qu'en-dira-t-on, d'un certain code de bienséance (dans *Speed the Plough*, de Morton (1798), Mrs Grundy est la voisine dont l'opinion fait loi en matière de bienséance); **I don't care what Mrs G. says,** je me moque du qu'en-dira-t-on.

Grundyism ['grʌndiizm], *s. O:* pruderie *f*, bégueulerie *f*, bégueulisme *m*, pudibonderie *f*.

grünerite ['gru:nərait], *s. Miner:* grünérite *f*.

grunt[1] [grʌnt], *s.* **1.** grognement *m* (de porc, de qn); **to give a g.,** pousser, faire entendre, un grognement. **2.** *Ich:* grogneur *m*.

grunt[2], *v.* (*a*) *v.i.* (*of pig, of pers.*) grogner, grognonner; pousser, faire entendre, un grognement; (*b*) *v.tr.* **to g. (out) an answer,** grogner une réponse; **he grunted (out) his consent,** il fit entendre un grognement pour nous dire qu'il consentait.

grunter ['grʌntər], *s.* **1.** grogneur, -euse. **2.** *F:* porc *m*.

grunting[1] ['grʌntiŋ], *a.* grognant; qui grogne; grogneur, -euse; *Z:* **g. ox,** ya(c)k *m*.

grunting[2], *s.* grognement(s) *m*(*pl*).

gruntling ['grʌntliŋ], *s.* cochonnet *m*, porcelet *m*.

gryllid ['grilid], *s. Ent:* gryllidé *m*.

Gryllidae ['grilidi:], *s.pl. Ent:* gryllidés *m*.

Grylloblattodea [griloublæ'toudiə], *s.pl. Ent:* grylloblattides *m*.

gryllos ['grilɔs], *s.* grylle *m*.

gryphaea [gri'fi:ə], *s. Moll: Paleont:* gryphée *f*.

gryphon ['grifən], *s. Myth:* griffon *m*.

gryposis [gri'pousis, grai-], *s. Med:* grypose *f*.

grysbok ['graisbɔk, 'greis-], *s. Z:* grisbock *m*.

guacharo, *pl.* **-os** ['gwɑ:(t)ʃərou, -ouz], *s. Orn:* guacharo *m*.

guadalcazarite [gwædəl'kæzərait], *s. Miner:* guadalcazarite *f*.

Guadeloupe ['gwɑ:dəlu:p], *Pr.n. Geog:* Guadeloupe *f*.

guaiacol ['gwaiəkɔl], *s. Ch:* gaïacol *m*.

guaiaconic [gwaiə'kɔnik], *a. Ch:* (acide *m*) gaïaconique.

guaiacum ['gwaiəkəm], *s.* **1.** *Bot:* (bois *m* de) gaïac *m*. **2.** *Pharm:* **(gum) g.,** résine *f* de gaïac.

guaiaretic [gwaiə'retik], *a. Ch:* (acide *m*) gaïarétique.

guan [gwɑ:n], *s. Orn:* pénélope *f*, yacou *m*.

guanaco, *pl.* **-os** [gwə'nɑ:kou, -ouz], *s. Z:* guanaco *m*.

Guanches ['gwæntʃiz], *s.pl. Ethn:* Guanches *m*.

guanidine ['gwænidi:n], *s. Ch:* guanidine *f*.

guanine ['gwæni:n], *s. Ch:* guanine *f*.

guano[1] ['gwɑ:nou], *s.* guano *m*; **fish g.,** guano de poissons.

guano[2], *v.tr.* guaner (un champ); fumer (un champ) au guano.

guanyl ['gwænil], *s. Ch:* guanyle *m*.

Guarani ['gwærəni], *s.* (*a*) *Ethn:* Guarani, -ie; (*b*) *Ling:* guarani *m*.

guarantee[1] [gærən'ti:], *s.* **1.** (*pers.*) (*a*) (*guarantor*) garant, -ante; caution *f*; **to go g. for s.o.,** se rendre, se porter, garant pour qn; se porter caution pour qn; (*b*) créancier *m* à qui est donné caution; garanti, -ie. **2.** (*guaranty*) garantie *f* (**against,** contre); **clock with g. for two years,** pendule *f* avec une garantie de deux ans; **I bought it secondhand, without g.,** je l'ai acheté d'occasion, et tel quel, et sans garantie; *Com:* **g. of bill of exchange,** aval *m* d'une lettre de change; **g. fund,** fonds *m* de garantie; **g. company, society,** société *f* de sécurité; **g. commission,** ducroire *m*; *Jur:* **g. given (in lieu of bail) for an individual,** acte *m* de soumission. **3.** (*security*) garantie, caution, gage *m*; **to leave sth. as a g.,** donner qch. pour caution; laisser qch. en gage; **for a more secure g.,** pour plus de garantie; **to secure all guarantees,** prendre toutes ses sûretés; s'assurer toutes les garanties nécessaires; **his interest is the best g. of his discretion,** son intérêt est le garant de sa discrétion.

guarantee[2], *v.tr.* **1.** garantir, cautionner (qn, qch.); se porter garant, caution, pour (qn, qch.); répondre de la bonne foi de (qn); répondre pour (qn); **to g. a debt,** garantir une dette; **watch guaranteed for two years,** montre garantie pour deux ans; **to g. a horse free from vice,** garantir un cheval de tout défaut; **I g. his obedience,** je réponds de son obéissance; **he'll come, I g.,** il viendra, je vous en réponds, je vous le garantis; *Com:* **to g. an endorsement,** avaliser la signature (sur une traite); **to g. a bill of exchange,** avaliser une lettre de change. **2. to g. s.o. from loss, against loss,** garantir les pertes à qn.

guaranteed [gærən'ti:d], *a.* (*a*) garanti; **g. bonds, stocks,** obligations, valeurs, garanties; **minimum g. wage, g. wage plan, g. hourly rate,** salaire minimum garanti, *F:* smig *m*; (*b*) (*of bill*) signé pour aval, avalisé; **g. by,** bon pour aval.

guaranteeing[1] [gærən'ti:iŋ], *a.* **g. Power,** Puissance garante.

guaranteeing[2], *s.* cautionnement *m*; garantie *f*.

guarantor [gærən'tɔ:r], *s.* garant, -ante; caution *f*, répondant *m*; donneur *m* de garantie, de caution; *Com:* avaliste *m*; donneur d'aval (d'une lettre de change); **to stand as g. for s.o.,** appuyer qn de sa garantie; cautionner qn.

guaranty ['gærənti], *s.* = GUARANTEE[1] 2, 3.

guard[1] [gɑ:d], *s.* **1.** garde *f*; (*a*) posture *f* de défense; *Fenc: Box:* **to take one's g.,** se mettre en garde; **to break g.,** se découvrir; **on g.!** en garde! *Box:* **left-arm g.,** garde à gauche; **g. arm,** bras *m* de garde; (*b*) **to be, stand, on one's g.,** être, se tenir, sur ses gardes; se tenir pour averti; s'observer, se surveiller, se tenir sur la réserve, se méfier; **to be on one's g. against sth.,** être sur ses gardes contre qch.; se méfier de qch.; se prémunir contre qch.; **to put s.o. on (his) g. (against a danger),** mettre qn en garde, prémunir qn (contre un danger); donner l'éveil à qn; **to throw, put, s.o. off his g.,** tromper la surveillance de qn; endormir la vigilance de qn; **to attack s.o. when off his g.,** prendre qn en traître; **to be caught, taken, off one's g.,** être pris au dépourvu; (*c*) (*of sentry, etc.*) **to be on g. (duty),** être en, de, faction; être de garde; monter la garde; **soldier on g. at the door,** soldat *m* de garde à la porte, en faction à la porte; factionnaire *m*; **to go on g.,** to **mount g.,** monter la garde; **to come off g.,** descendre de garde; **to mount g. over s.o., sth.,** monter la garde auprès de qn, de qch.; **to keep g.,** faire la garde, être de garde; *Navy:* **officer of the g.,** officier *m* de garde; **to keep a prisoner under g.,** garder un prisonnier à vue; **he was marched off under g.,** il fut emmené sous escorte. **2.** *coll.* (*a*) *Mil:* garde *f*; **main g.,** gros *m* d'avant-garde; **quarter g.,** garde du camp; **new g., relieving g.,** garde montante; **old g.,** garde descendante; **mounting of the g.,** parade *f*; faction *f*; **the sergeant in charge of the quarter g., the g. commander,** le sergent de garde, le chef de poste; **one of the old g.,** un vieux de la vieille; **g. of honour,** garde d'honneur; **to form a g. of honour,** faire, former, la haie; (*b*) **to set a g. on a house, on a bridge,** faire surveiller une maison, un pont; **to set a g. on one's passions,** surveiller ses passions. **3.** (*pers.*) (*a*) *A:* courrier *m*, postillon *m* (de diligence); *Rail:* chef *m* de train; **frontier g.,** garde-frontière *m*, *pl.* gardes-frontière; (*b*) *Mil:* **the Guards,** les Gardes *m* du corps; les soldats de la Garde; **Home G.** = milice *f*; (*c*) *U.S:* **(prison) g.,** geôlier *m*, gardien *m* de prison. **4.** (*a*) dispositif protecteur; protecteur *m* (d'une machine); carter *m* (d'engrenages, etc.); garde-fou *m*, *pl.* garde-fous; garde-corps *m inv* (de passerelle, etc.); **flywheel g.,** garde *f* du volant; **wire g. (of lamp),** corbeille *f* de protection (d'une lampe); **(fire) g.,** garde-feu *m inv*, pare-étincelles *m inv*; **(trigger) g.,** pontet *m* (de fusil); sous-garde *f*, *pl.* sous-gardes; **keyhole g.,** cache-entrée *m inv*; **tree g.,** armure *f* d'un arbre; *Artil:* **band g.,** cache-ceinture *m inv* (d'un obus); *Mch:* **water-level g.,** protecteur de niveau d'eau; *N.Arch:* **rat g.,** garde-rats *m inv*; **g. rail,** (i) garde-corps, garde-fou; *N.Arch:* (filière *f* de) rambarde *f*; (ii) *Rail:* contre-rail *m*, *pl.* contre-rails; contrecœur *m*; (*of crossover*) joue *f* de croisement; rail *m* contre-aiguilles; (iii) balustrade *f*; bouteroue *f* (de chaussée, etc.); *Rail:* **g. iron,** chasse-bestiaux *m inv*; cow-catcher *m*; **g. pile,** (i) pilotis *m* (pour protéger les piles d'un pont, etc.); (ii) bouteroue (de chaussée); **g. post,** bouteroue, *Fr.C:* borne *f* de protection (des piétons); **g. stone,** bouteroue, chasse-roues *m inv* (de tablier de pont, etc.); **g. plate,** (i) *Mec.E: Civ.E: etc:* contre-plaque *f*, *pl.* contre-plaques; (ii) *Rail: etc:* plaque *f* de garde; **g. lock,** sas *m* de sûreté (d'avant-port); *Navy:* **g. boat,** canot *m* de ronde; embarcation *f* de garde; (bateau) patrouilleur *m*; **g. ship,** (i) (navire *m*) stationnaire *m*; (ii) bâtiment *m* de veille, de garde; *El:* **g. net,** filet *m* de protection (de câble aérien); **g. ring,** anneau *m* de garde (d'un électromètre absolu); (*b*) **(hand) g. of a foil, of a sword,** garde *f*, coquille *f*, d'un fleuret, d'une épée; **cross g.,** quillon *m*, croisée *f* (d'épée); (*c*) *O:* cordon *m*, laisse *f* (de chapeau); **g. chain,** chaîne *f* de garde (d'une montre); sautoir *m*; **g. ring,** bague *f* de sûreté (portée au doigt); (*d*) *Furs:* **g. hair,** jarre *m*; (*e*) *Bookb:* onglet *m*; (*f*) *Fb: etc:* **abdominal g.,** ceinture protectrice abdominale. **5.** *Med:* correctif *m* (d'un médicament). **6.** *Paleont:* rostre *m* (d'une bélemnite).

guard[2], *v.* **1.** *v.tr.* (*a*) garder; **to g. s.o. from, against, a danger,** garder, défendre, protéger, parer, qn d'un danger; **to g. oneself,** se tenir sur ses gardes; **angels g. thee!** que les anges te gardent! que les anges veillent sur toi! **to g. the gates,** garder les portes; **she is well guarded,** elle est très surveillée; *A:* **to g. a prisoner,** escorter, garder, un prisonnier; *A:* **to g. s.o. to his house,** escorter qn jusque chez lui; (*b*) **to g. one's tongue, one's words,** surveiller sa langue; mesurer ses paroles; (*c*) *Bookb:* fournir (un livre) d'onglets; (*d*) *Ind:* protéger (une courroie, un engrenage, etc.); grillager (une machine-outil); mettre un carter à (un mécanisme); (*e*) *Cards:* **to g. one's clubs,** se garder à trèfle; **my king is guarded,** j'ai la garde au roi; **my queen is not guarded,** ma reine n'est pas gardée; (*f*) *Med:* mêler un correctif à (un narcotique). **2.** *v.i.* **to g. against sth.,** se garder, se mettre à l'abri, de qch.; se prémunir, se précautionner, contre qch.; parer à qch.; **to g. against an error,** se méfier d'une erreur.

guarded ['gɑ:did], *a.* **1.** (*of speech, etc.*) prudent, mesuré, circonspect; **g. answer,** réponse *f* qui n'engage à rien. **2.**

(*a*) *Ind: etc:* (mécanisme etc.) protégé, grillagé, muni d'un carter; (*b*) *Cards:* **g. king,** roi second; **g. queen,** dame troisième; **g. Jack,** valet quatrième. **3.** (prisonnier) gardé à vue.

guardedly ['gɑːdidli], *adv.* avec réserve, avec circonspection, avec précaution.

guardhouse ['gɑːdhaus], *s. Mil:* (*a*) corps-de-garde *m inv*; (*b*) poste *m* de police.

guardian ['gɑːdiən], *s.* **1.** (*a*) gardien, -ienne; **g. of the public interests,** gardien, défenseur *m*, des intérêts publics; (*b*) conservateur, -trice (d'un musée, etc.); (*c*) *Ecc:* père gardien (d'un couvent de franciscains). **2.** tuteur, -trice, curateur, -trice (de mineur, etc.); conseil *m* judiciaire (d'un prodigue); **acting g.,** protecteur, -trice; **deputy g.,** subrogé tuteur. **3.** *A:* **G. of the Poor,** administrateur, -trice, de l'Assistance publique; **the Board of Guardians,** *F:* **the Guardians,** le comité d'administration de l'Assistance publique. **4.** *attrib.* gardien, tutélaire; **g. angel,** ange gardien; **the g. principle of equality,** le principe tutélaire de l'égalité.

guardianship ['gɑːdiənʃip], *s.* **1.** garde *f*; **under the g. of the laws,** sous la garde des lois. **2.** *Jur:* gestion *f* tutélaire; tutelle *f*, curatelle *f*; **under g.,** pourvu d'un conseil judiciaire; **child under g.,** enfant *mf* en tutelle; **to give an account of one's g.,** rendre sa tutelle.

guarding ['gɑːdiŋ], *s.* (*a*) garde *f*; (*b*) gardiennage *m* (de chemins de fer, etc., en temps de guerre, de marchandises à quai).

guardroom ['gɑːdruːm], *s. Mil:* **1.** corps-de-garde *m inv*. **2.** salle *f*, poste *m*, de police; salle de discipline; *F:* bloc *m*, tôle *f*.

guardsman, *pl.* **-men** ['gɑːdzmən], *s.m.* **1.** officier de la Garde. **2.** soldat de la Garde.

guarinite ['gwɑːrinait], *s. Miner:* guarinite *f*.

Guatemala [gwæti'mɑːlə], *Pr.n. Geog:* Guatemala *m*.

Guatemalan [gwæti'mɑːlən], *Geog:* (*a*) *a.* guatémaltèque; (*b*) *s.* Guatémaltèque *mf*.

guava ['gwɑːvə], *s. Bot:* **1.** goyave *f*; *Cu:* **g. jelly,** confiture *f* de goyave. **2. g. (tree),** goyavier *m*.

gubbins ['gʌbinz], *s.pl.* (*with sg. or pl. const.*) *F:* (*a*) déchets *m*; saletés *f*; (*b*) gadget *m*, truc *m*, machin *m*; (*c*) (*pers.*) **you silly g.!** espèce d'idiot!

gubernatorial [g(j)uːbənə'tɔːriəl], *a. U.S:* **1.** du gouverneur, du gouvernement. **2.** paternel.

guck [gʌk], *s. NAm: P:* chose sale, désagréable, répugnante, *esp.* substance vaseuse, fangeuse; **g. from the sewers,** la fange des égouts; **I spew rice pudding and all that g.!** je dégobille le gâteau de riz et toutes ces saletés!

guddle ['gʌdl], *v.tr. & i.* pêcher (les truites) à la main.

guddling ['gʌdliŋ], *s.* pêche *f* (de la truite) à la main.

gudgeon[1] ['gʌdʒən], *s.* **1.** *Ich:* goujon *m*; *Fish:* **g. trap,** carafe *f*; *O:* **to swallow a g.,** avaler un goujon; gober l'appât, le morceau, la mouche. **2.** *F: O:* benêt *m*, jocrisse *m*, jobard *m*; gogo *m*.

gudgeon[2], *s.* **1.** *Mec.E:* goujon *m*, tourillon *m*, broche *f*, axe *m*; **g. pin,** (i) *I.C.E:* axe de pied de bielle, de piston; (ii) *Mch:* tourillon de la crosse; **floating g. pin,** axe mobile; **g.-pin bosses,** bossages *m* du piston. **2.** (*a*) penture *f* (de gond); (*b*) *Nau:* femelot *m* (de gouvernail). **3.** *Const:* goujon (pour pierres).

Guebre ['giːbər, 'geibər], *s. Rel.H:* Guèbre *mf*.

Guelderland ['geldəlænd], *Pr.n. Geog:* Gueldre *f*.

guelder rose ['geldə'rouz], *s. Bot:* boule-de-neige *f*, *pl.* boules-de-neige; rose *f* de Gueldre; obier *m*, caillebot *m*; **wild g. r.,** aubour *m*; sureau *m* aquatique, d'eau.

Guelph [gwelf], *s. Hist:* Guelfe *mf*.

Guelphism ['gwelfizm], *s. Hist:* guelfisme *m*.

guemal ['gweiməl], *s. Z:* huemal *m*, cerf andin.

guenon ['genɔ̃(ŋ)], *s. Z:* cercopithèque *m*.

Guercino [gweə'tʃiːnou], *Pr.n. Hist. of Art:* le Guerchin.

guerdon[1] ['gəːd(ə)n], *s. A: & Poet:* récompense *f*.

guerdon[2], *v.tr. A: & Poet:* récompenser.

guereza [gə'rezə], *s. Z:* guéréza *m*, colobe *m* à manteau blanc.

Guernsey ['gəːnzi]. **1.** *Pr.n. Geog:* Guernesey. **2.** *s.* (*a*) (vareuse *f* en) tricot *m*; jersey *m*; (*b*) vache *f* de Guernesey.

guer(r)illa [gə'rilə], *s. Mil:* guérillero *m*; franc-tireur *m*, *pl.* francs-tireurs; **troop, band, of guer(r)illas,** guérilla *f*; **g. warfare,** guérilla; guerre *f* de guérillas, de partisans; guerre d'embuscades.

guess[1] [ges], *s.* conjecture *f*, estimation *f*; **to give, have, make, a g.,** (i) hasarder une conjecture, une solution; (ii) tâcher de deviner; **that's a good g.,** vous avez bien deviné; **that was an easy g.,** c'était facile à deviner; **you've made a lucky g.,** vous êtes bien tombé; vous avez rencontré juste; **to make a g. at what happened, at what will happen,** hasarder une hypothèse sur la marche probable des événements; **your g. is as good as mine,** j'en sais autant que toi; **it's anybody's g.,** qui sait? Dieu seul le sait; **I give you three guesses,** (i) tu as droit à trois réponses; je te le donne en mille; (ii) d'après toi? tu devines? **at a g.,** au jugé, au juger, à l'estime, à vue de nez; *Nau:* **to steer by g. and by God,** gouverner à la grâce de Dieu.

guess[2], *v.tr. & i.* **1. to g. at sth.,** (tâcher de) deviner, conjecturer, qch.; **to g. the length of sth.,** estimer la longueur de qch.; **g. who did it!** devinez qui l'a fait! **I can g. your answer,** je devine ce que vous allez répondre; **I guessed him to be twenty-five,** je lui ai donné vingt-cinq ans; **to have, keep, an opponent guessing,** mystifier un adversaire; *F:* **that got him guessing,** ça l'a intrigué; ça lui a mis la puce à l'oreille. **2. to g. right, wrong,** bien, mal, deviner; **to g. a riddle,** trouver le mot d'une énigme; **you've guessed it! you've guessed right!** vous l'avez deviné! vous y êtes! vous êtes bien tombé! vous avez rencontré juste! vous avez mis le doigt dessus! **to g. sth. from s.o.'s manner,** juger qch. d'après l'attitude de qn. **3.** *esp. NAm:* croire, penser; **I g.,** à ce que je pense; m'est avis; **I g. you're right,** m'est avis que vous avez raison; vous avez joliment raison; **I g. so!** sans doute!

guessable ['gesəbl], *a.* devinable.

guesser ['gesər], *s.* devineur, -euse (d'une énigme, etc.).

guessing ['gesiŋ], *s.* conjecture *f*, estimation *f*; **g. games,** devinettes *f*; **I'm no good at g. games!** mon Dieu! dis-le-moi tout carrément.

guesstimate[1] ['gestimət], *s. F:* conjecture *f*, estimation (bien pesée); **to make a g. at sth.,** estimer qch. au pifomètre.

guesstimate[2] ['gestimeit], *v.tr. F:* estimer (qch.) au pifomètre.

guesswork ['geswəːk], *s.* estime *f*, conjecture *f*; **it's pure g.,** c'est pure conjecture; **by g.,** à l'estime; au jugé; à vue de nez; au sentiment.

guest [gest], *s.* **1.** convive *mf*; invité, -ée; hôte, -esse; **habitual g.,** habitué, -ée; **g. chamber,** (i) chambre *f* des hôtes, hôtellerie *f* (d'un monastère); (ii) *A:* chambre d'ami(s); **g. night,** soirée *f* des invités (d'un club, etc.); *Iron:* **be my g.!** c'est à vous! faites comme chez vous! **2.** client, -ente (d'un hôtel); **the landlord and his guests,** l'hôtelier *m* et ses hôtes; **paying g.,** pensionnaire *mf*. **3.** *Ent: etc:* commensal *m*.

guesthouse ['gesthaus], *s.* **1.** hôtellerie *f* (d'un monastère, etc.). **2.** pension *f* de famille.

guestmaster ['gestmɑːstər], *s.* hôtelier *m* (d'un monastère).

guestroom ['gestruːm], *s.* chambre *f* d'ami(s).

guestrope ['gestroup], *s. Nau:* **1.** faux-bras *m inv* de ceinture. **2.** faux-bras de touée.

guff [gʌf], *s. F:* blague *f*, bêtises *fpl*.

guffaw[1] [gʌ'fɔː], *s.* (éclat *m* de) rire *m*; gros rire (bruyant); pouffement *m*.

guffaw[2], *v.i.* pouffer, éclater, de rire; s'esclaffer; rire bruyamment; partir d'un gros rire.

guffawing [gʌ'fɔːiŋ], *s.* pouffement *m* (de rire).

guggle ['gʌgl], *v.i. F:* glousser (en riant).

gugglet ['gʌglit], *s.* = GOGLET.

Guiana [gi'ɑːnə], *Pr.n. Geog: Hist:* Guyane *f*.

Guianese [giə'niːz]. *Geog: Hist:* (*a*) *a.* guyanais; (*b*) *s.* Guyanais, -aise.

guib(a) [(ʷ)gib(ə)], *s. Z:* guib *m*.

guidance ['gaid(ə)ns], *s.* **1.** direction *f*, gouverne *f*, conduite *f*; **I owe much to his g.,** je dois beaucoup à ses conseils; **under the g. of. . .,** sous la direction de . . ., sous la conduite de . . .; **to steer by the g. of the stars,** gouverner sur les étoiles; **this is for your g.,** ceci est à titre d'indication, à titre d'information; ceci est pour votre gouverne; **sent for your g.,** envoyé à titre d'indication; *Sch:* **vocational g.,** orientation professionnelle. **2.** *Ball: Space:* guidage *m*; **beam rider g.,** guidage par faisceau directeur, par faisceau électro-magnétique; guidage sur faisceau; **command g.,** guidage par télécommande (électronique), téléguidage *m* électronique; **homing g.,** autoguidage *m*; **active, passive, homing g.,** autoguidage actif, passif; **direct, indirect, homing g.,** autoguidage direct, indirect; **inertial g.,** guidage par inertie; **infra-red g.,** guidage par infrarouges; **radio g.,** radioguidage *m*; **stellar, celestial, g.,** guidage astronomique; **radio-stellar, radio-celestial, g.,** guidage radio-astronomique; **stellar-inertial g.,** guidage mixte par inertie et visée astronomique; **vectoring g.,** guidage sur vecteur; **mid-course g.,** guidage à mi-course; **terminal g.,** guidage terminal; **preset g.,** guidage programmé; **g. operator's console,** pupitre *m* de servant de guidage.

guide[1] [gaid], *s.* **1.** (*pers.*) (*a*) guide *m*; **Alpine g.,** guide alpin; **museum g.,** guide de musée; *Lit:* **g., philosopher and friend,** directeur *m* de conscience; philosophe *m* et ami; mentor *m*; **to take sth. as a g.,** prendre qch. pour règle; **to take reason as one's g.,** prendre la raison pour guide; **let reason be your g.,** laissez-vous guider par la raison; (*b*) *Scout:* **(girl) g.,** éclaireuse *f*; *R.C.Ch:* guide de France; (*c*) *Mil:* guide (de la compagnie); **the right, left, g.,** le guide à droite, à gauche; (*d*) *Navy:* (*vessel*) régulateur *m* (de la flotte). **2.** (*book*) guide; itinéraire *m*; **g. to Switzerland,** guide de la Suisse; **museum g.,** livret *m* de musée; **railway g.,** indicateur *m* des chemins de fer; **g. to photography,** introduction *f*, initiation *f*, à la photographie. **3.** (*a*) indication *f*, exemple *m*; **as a g.,** à titre indicatif; **let this be a g. to you,** que ceci vous serve d'exemple; **it was a g. to the state of his feelings,** c'était une indication de ses sentiments; (*b*) *Mec.E: etc:* guide (d'ascenseur, etc.); **guides of a mine shaft, of a pile driver monkey,** guidage *m*, guidonnage *m*, glissières *f*, d'un puits de mine, d'un mouton de sonnette; **belt g., g. roller,** guide de courroie, guide-courroie *m*, *pl.* guide-courroie(s); galet *m* de guidage (de courroie); **g. rope,** (i) câble *m* de guidage; (ii) *Aer:* guide-rope *m*, *pl.* guide-ropes; **g. pulley,** galet *m* (guide); galet de renvoi; **g. post,** guide, montant *m* (de sonnette); **g. path,** chemin *m* de glissement; *Mec.E:* **g. screw,** vis mère *f*, *pl.* vis-mères (d'une taraudeuse, d'un tour); *Rail:* **g. rail,** contre-rail *m*, *pl.* contre-rails; **g. plate,** rampe *f* de remise, plaque *f* guide; *Mch:* **(slipper) g.,** glissière; **cross-head g., g. bar, g. rod,** guide, glissière, de la crosse du piston; **g. blade,** aube directrice; *Hyd.E:* **g. channel,** coursier *m*; *Hyd.E: El:* **g. vane,** guideau *m*; directrice *f* (de turbine); *Veh:* **window guides,** glissières de la glace; *Tex:* **thread g., g. finger,** distributeur *m* de fil; (*in calico printing*) **g. pin,** repère *m*; (*c*) **g. line,** ligne *f* pour guider la main (en écrivant); **g. lines,** (i) transparent (rayé); (ii) directives *fpl*; (*of card index, etc.*) **g. cards, guides,** intercalaires *m*.

guide[2], *v.tr.* guider, conduire, diriger; **to g. a child's first steps,** guider les premiers pas d'un enfant; **to g. the way for s.o.,** guider qn; **to g. the plough,** conduire, guider, la charrue; **circumstances that g. s.o.'s judgment,** circonstances *f* qui gouvernent les décisions de qn; **I will be guided by your advice,** je suivrai vos conseils; **all are guided by him,** tous se règlent sur lui.

guided ['gaidid], *a.* (*a*) (excursion *f*, visite *f* de musée, etc.) sous la conduite d'un guide; (*b*) *Ball: Space:* (missile *m*, etc.) guidé; **command-g. missile,** missile téléguidé (par commande électronique); **radio-g.,** radioguidé; *Av:* **g. aircraft-missile,** engin *m* guidé aéroporté.

guideline ['gaidlain], *s. Pol: etc:* directive *f*; indication *f* d'une politique à suivre.

guideway ['gaidwei], *s. Mec.E:* coulisse *f*; guide *m*.

guiding[1] ['gaidiŋ], *a.* **1.** qui sert de guide; directeur, -trice; **g. principle,** principe directeur; **the g. principles of his life,** les principes sur lesquels se guide sa vie; **to serve as a g. principle for you,** pour vous servir de gouverne, pour votre gouverne; **g. star,** guide *m*. **2.** *Mec.E: etc:* (dispositif *m*) de guidage.

guiding[2], *s.* guidage *m*, conduite *f*, direction *f*.

Guido ['giːdou], *Pr.n.m.* **1.** *Hist. of Art:* **Guido Reni,** le Guide. **2.** *Hist. of Mus:* **G. d'Arezzo,** Guido, Gui, d'Arezzo.

guidon ['gaidən], *s. Mil:* guidon *m*; étendard *m* de cavalerie.

Guienne [gi'en], *Pr.n. Hist:* la Guyenne.

guilandina [gwilæn'dainə], *s. Bot:* guilandine *f*.

guild [gild], *s.* **1.** *Hist:* corporation *f*; **merchant g.,** g(u)ilde *f* de commerçants; **trade g.,** corps *m* de métier. **2.** association *f*, confrérie *f*; **church g.,** cercle *m* (catholique, etc.); *Ecc:* **the (Head) G. of the Virgin,** l'archiconfrérie *f* de la Vierge.

guilder ['gildər], *s. Num:* guld(en) *m*; florin *m*.

guildhall ['gildhɔːl], *s.* **1.** salle *f* de réunion d'une guilde. **2.** hôtel *m* de ville.

guile [gail], *s.* artifice *m*, ruse *f*, astuce *f*, fourberie *f*, perfidie *f*; **to get sth. by g.,** obtenir qch. par ruse, par artifice; **she uses the g. of her sex,** elle use de la finesse de son sexe; *B:* **in him was no g.,** en lui il n'y avait point de fraude.

guileful ['gailful], *a.* astucieux, artificieux, rusé; finassier, -ière; trompeur, -euse; fourbe, perfide.

guilefully ['gailfuli], *adv.* astucieusement, artificieusement, trompeusement, perfidement.

guileless ['gaillis], *a.* **1.** franc, *f.* franche; sincère, loyal; sans malice. **2.** candide, naïf, simple, innocent; **she is as g. as a newborn babe,** elle est d'une candeur de nouveau-né.

guilelessly ['gaillisli], *adv.* **1.** franchement, sincèrement, loyalement. **2.** candidement, naïvement, simplement, innocemment.

guilelessness ['gaillisnis], *s.* **1.** franchise *f*, sincérité *f*. **2.** candeur *f*, naïveté *f*, simplicité *f*, innocence *f*.

guillemot ['gilimɔt], *s. Orn:* **g.** (*uria aalge*), guillemot *m* de Troïl, guillemot à capuchon, *Fr.C:* marmette commune; **Brünnich's g.,** guillemot, *Fr.C:* marmette, de Brünnich; **black g.,** guillemot à miroir blanc, *Fr.C:* guillemot noir; **pigeon g.,** *Fr.C:* guillemot du Pacifique;

bridled g., guillemot bridé.

guilloche[1] [gi'louʃ], *s.* guillochis *m*; **g. ornamentation,** ornementation *f* de, en, guillochis.

guilloche[2], *v.tr.* guillocher.

guillotine[1] ['gilətiːn], *s.* **1.** guillotine *f*; bois *m* de justice; **g. window,** fenêtre *f* à guillotine. **2.** (*a*) *Bookb:* guillotine, cisaille *f* (à carton), massicot *m*, massiquot *m*; presse *f* à rogner; (*b*) *Mec.E:* **g. shears,** cisailles à guillotine. **3.** *Surg:* **(tonsil) g.,** amygdalotome *m*. **4.** *Parl:* clôture *f* par tranches.

guillotine[2], *v.tr.* **1.** guillotiner, décapiter (qn); **to be guillotined,** être guillotiné; *F:* épouser la veuve. **2.** *Bookb:* guillotiner, massicoter (les tranches d'un livre, etc.). **3.** *Parl:* appliquer la clôture par tranches à (un projet de loi).

guillotiner [gilə'tiːnər], *s.* guillotineur *m*.

guillotining [gilə'tiːniŋ], *s.* guillotinement *m*; exécution *f*.

guilt [gilt], *s.* **1.** culpabilité *f*; **the g. does not lie with him alone,** il n'y a pas que lui de coupable. **2.** *A:* crime *m*, offense *f*.

guiltily ['giltili], *adv.* coupablement; comme un coupable; d'un air coupable.

guiltiness ['giltinis], *s.* culpabilité *f*.

guiltless ['giltlis], *a.* innocent (**of sth.,** de qch.); **to hold s.o. g.,** tenir qn pour innocent.

guiltlessly ['giltlisli], *adv.* innocemment.

guiltlessness ['giltlisnis], *s.* innocence *f*.

guilty ['gilti], *a.* coupable; (*a*) **g. of theft,** coupable de vol; **g. of an offence against God,** coupable envers Dieu; **g. person,** coupable *mf*; **he is not only g. party,** il n'y a pas que lui de coupable; **g. or innocent, he is to be pitied,** coupable ou non, noir ou blanc, il est digne de pitié; *Jur:* **to plead g., not g.,** s'avouer coupable; se déclarer innocent, nier sa culpabilité; **the accused pleads not g.,** l'accusé nie; **to declare s.o. not g.,** innocenter qn; **to find s.o. g., not g.,** prononcer, déclarer, qn coupable, innocent; **he was found g.,** il fut reconnu coupable; **verdict of g., not g.,** verdict *m*, déclaration *f*, de culpabilité, d'acquittement; **g. in fact and in law,** atteint et convaincu; (*b*) qui se sent coupable; **g. conscience,** mauvaise conscience; conscience chargée, pas tranquille; **g. look,** regard confus; (*c*) **g. act,** acte coupable.

guimp [gimp], *s.* = GIMP[1].

Guinea ['gini]. **1.** *Pr.n. Geog:* Guinée *f*; *attrib. Tex:* **G. cloth, cotton,** guinée; *Orn:* **G. goose,** jabotière *f*; *Bot:* **g. grass,** herbe *f* de Guinée; **G. grains, G. pepper,** graines *f* de paradis, de Guinée; malaguette *f*; *Ann:* **G. worm,** ver *m* de Guinée, ver de Médine, filaire *m or f*; dragonneau *m*. **2.** *s. A:* (*a*) (pièce *f* d'or d'une) guinée (= 21 shillings); (*b*) guinée (monnaie de compte d'usage courant dans les professions libérales, pour les souscriptions aux œuvres de bienfaisance, etc.); **his fee is five guineas,** ses honoraires *m* sont de cinq guinées; **put me down for half a guinea,** inscrivez-moi pour une demi-guinée (10 sh. 6 pence).

guinea cock ['ginikɔk], *s.m. Orn:* pintade *f* mâle.

guineafowl ['ginifaul], *s.* (*a*) *Orn:* pintade *f*; **crested g.,** pintade huppée; **helmet g.,** pintade à casque; **vulturine g.,** pintade vulturine; **young g.,** pintadeau *m*; **g. breeder,** méléagriculteur *m*; (*b*) *Cu:* pintadon *m*.

guinea hen ['ginihen], *s.f.* **1.** *Orn:* pintade *f*. **2.** *Bot:* **g. h. weed,** petiveria *m*.

Guinean ['giniən]. *Geog:* (*a*) *a.* guinéen; (*b*) *s.* Guinéen, -éenne.

guineapig ['ginipig], *s.* **1.** *Z:* cobaye *m*; cochon *m* d'Inde; rat *m* d'Amérique. **2.** (*in experiments, etc.*) **to be a g.,** servir de cobaye.

guinea poult ['ginipoult], *s. Orn:* pintadeau *m*.

Guinevere ['gwiniviər], *Pr.n.f. Lit:* Guenièvre.

Guinness ['ginis], *s. R.t.m.* bière *f* de la brasserie Guinness; (*in bar*) **two Guinesses, please,** deux verres de Guinness, s'il vous plaît.

guisarme [giːzɑːm], *s. A.Arm:* guisarme *m*.

guise [gaiz], *s.* **1.** *A:* vêtements *mpl*, habits *mpl*, costume *m*; *Lit:* **in lowly g.,** modestement vêtu; **in the g. of a pilgrim,** vêtu, travesti, en pèlerin. **2.** dehors *m*, apparence *f*; **she appeared in the g. of a nymph,** elle apparut sous la forme d'une nymphe; **under, in, the g. of friendship,** sous l'apparence, sous le masque, de l'amitié; sous un semblant, sous de faux semblants, d'amitié; **under the g. of religion,** sous le manteau, le couvert, de la religion.

guiser ['gaizər], *s. Scot:* masque *m* (qui prend part à une mascarade); **the guisers,** gamins *m* au visage charbonné qui à certaines fêtes viennent vous jouer une piécette et quémander des sous.

guising ['gaiziŋ], *s. Scot:* mascarade *f* (d'enfants).

guitar [gi'tɑːr], *s.* **1.** *Mus:* guitare *f*; **electric g.,** guitare électrique; **to play the g.,** jouer, pincer, de la guitare. **2.** *Ich:* **g. fish,** guitare.

guitarist [gi'tɑːrist], *s. Mus:* guitariste *mf*.

guitguit ['gwitgwit], *s. Orn:* guit-guit *m*.

Gujarat [guːdʒə'rɑːt], *Pr.n. Geog:* le Goudjerat, Gujrat.

Gujarati [guːdʒə'rɑːti], *s. Ling:* gujrati *m*.

gular ['gjuːlər], *a.* (*in amphibians, etc.*) **g. pouch, sac,** poche *f*, sac *m*, gulaire.

gulch [gʌltʃ], *s. U.S:* ravin *m* (aurifère).

gules [gjuːlz], *Her:* **1.** *s.* gueules *m*. **2.** *a.* **or a lion g.,** d'or à un lion de gueules.

gulf [gʌlf], *s.* **1.** *Geog:* golfe *m*; **the G. of Lions,** le golfe du Lion; **the G. Stream,** le Courant du Golfe; le Gulfstream. **2.** (*a*) gouffre *m*, abîme *m*; abysse *m* (de la mer); **there is a g. between the two ideologies,** un abîme sépare les deux idéologies; (*b*) gouffre, tourbillon *m*; **the g. that swallowed all his fortune,** le gouffre qui a englouti toute sa fortune. **3.** *Sch:* *F:* *A:* (*at Oxford and Cambridge*) **to be put in the g., to get a g.,** se voir refuser un grade avec '*honours*' (*q.v.*) pour cause d'insuffisance; passer tout juste.

gulfweed ['gʌlfwiːd], *s. Algae:* sargasse *f* baccifère.

gull[1] [gʌl], *s. Orn:* mouette *f*, goéland *m*; **black-headed g.,** mouette rieuse; **lesser black-backed g.,** goéland brun; **common g.,** *NAm:* **short-billed g.,** goéland cendré; **California g.,** goéland de Californie; **glaucous g.,** goéland bourgmestre; **glaucous-winged g.,** goéland à ailes glauques; **great black-backed g.,** goéland à manteau noir, goéland marin; **herring g.,** goéland argenté, goéland à manteau bleu; **Iceland g.,** goéland leucoptère, goéland à ailes blanches, *Fr.C:* goéland arctique; **ring-billed g.,** goéland à bec cerclé; **slaty-backed g.,** goéland à manteau ardoisé; **western g.,** goéland occidental; **Bonaparte's g.,** mouette *f* de Bonaparte; **Franklin's g.,** mouette de Franklin; **Heermann's g.,** mouette de Heerman; **ivory g.,** mouette sénateur, goéland sénateur, pagophile *f* blanche; *Fr.C:* mouette blanche; **laughing g.,** goéland atricille, *Fr.C:* mouette rieuse; **Ross's g.,** mouette de Ross, *Fr.C:* mouette rosée; **Sabine's g.,** mouette de Sabine; **Audouin's g.,** goéland d'Audouin; **great black-headed g.,** goéland à tête noire; **little g.,** mouette pygmée; **Mediterranean g.,** mouette mélanocéphale, **slender-billed g.,** goéland railleur, à bec grêle; **dominican g., southern black-backed g.,** goéland dominicain; **dusky g.,** mouette fuligineuse; **grey-headed g.,** mouette à tête grise; **Magellan g.,** goéland de Scoresby; **Red Sea black-headed g.,** goéland à iris blanc; **swallow-tailed g.,** mouette à queue fourchue; **g. rookery,** roche *f* à mouettes.

gull[2], *s.* **1.** *O:* gogo *m*, jobard *m*, dupe *f*, gobeur *m*, gobe-mouches *m inv*, gobe-la-lune *m inv*, poire *f*. **2.** *A:* duperie *f*. **3.** *A:* escroc *m*.

gull[3], *v.tr. O:* jobarder, duper, tromper, mystifier, flouer, rouler (qn); en conter de belles, de fortes, à (qn); **he is easily gulled,** il se laisse facilement rouler; c'est un jobard.

gullet ['gʌlit], *s.* **1.** *Anat:* œsophage *m*, *F:* gosier *m*; *P:* **to put sth. down one's g.,** se coller qch. dans le cornet. **2.** (*a*) *Dial:* passe *f*, goulet *m*, chenal *m*; (*b*) *A:* défilé *m* (de montagne); ravin *m*. **3.** *Tls:* **g. tooth,** dent-de-loup *f*, *pl.* dents-de-loup.

gullibility [gʌli'biliti], *s.* crédulité *f*, jobarderie *f*, jobardise *f*.

gullible ['gʌlibl], *a.* facile à duper, à jobarder; crédule; jobard; qui s'en laisse conter; mystifiable.

gullied ['gʌlid], *a.* raviné; creusé.

gully[1] ['gʌli], *s.* **1.** *Geol:* (petit) ravin, ravinée *f*; ravine *f*, couloir *m*. **2.** *Civ.E:* *etc:* caniveau *m*; rigole *f*; **g. drain,** raccord *m* d'égout; **g. hole,** bouche *f* d'égout. **3.** (*stream*) ru *m*.

gully[2], *v.tr.* raviner; creuser; **to g. out a hole,** creuser un trou.

gully[3], *s. Scot:* **g. (knife),** grand couteau.

gullying ['gʌliiŋ], *s.* ravinement *m*; creusement *m*.

gulonic [g(j)uː'lɔnik], *a. Ch:* (acide) gulonique.

gulose ['g(j)uːlous], *s. Ch:* gulose *m*.

gulp[1] [gʌlp], *s.* **1.** coup *m* de gosier; **to swallow sth. at one g.,** avaler qch. d'un coup, *F:* tout de go; **to empty a glass at one g.,** vider un verre d'un (seul) trait, d'une lampée, d'un seul coup. **2.** grosse bouchée; *F:* goulée *f*.

gulp[2], *v.* **1.** *v.tr.* (*a*) **to g. sth. down,** avaler qch. à grosses bouchées; engloutir, ingurgiter, gober (une huître, un morceau); avaler (un verre de vin) à grandes gorgées, à pleine gorge; lamper, boire d'un trait (un verre de vin); **he gulped it down,** il n'en fit qu'une bouchée; (*of drink*) il n'en fit qu'une gorgée; (*b*) **to g. down, back, one's tears,** avaler, refouler, ses larmes; **to g. down a sob,** ravaler un sanglot; **to g. down one's rage,** étouffer sa rage. **2.** *v.i.* essayer d'avaler; avoir un brusque serrement de gorge; **he gulped,** sa gorge se serra.

gulper ['gʌlpər], *s.* gobeur, -euse (d'huîtres, etc.).

gum[1] [gʌm], *s.* **1.** (*a*) gomme *f* (soluble à l'eau); *Com:* **British g.,** dextrine *f*; **g. dextrine,** colle *f* à la dextrine; *Phot:* **g. bichromate, dichromate, process,** procédé *m* à la gomme bichromatée; (*b*) (*adhesive*) gomme, colle; (*c*) *Ser:* **to remove the g. from raw silk,** dégommer, décruser, la soie grège; **g. silk,** soie non décrusée. **2.** (*a*) **g. arabic, g. acacia,** gomme arabique; (suc *m* d')acacia *m*; **g. arabic tree,** acacia d'Arabie; **g. ammoniac,** gomme-ammoniaque *f*, *pl.* gommes-ammoniaques; **g. animé,** gomme animé; courbaril *m*, courbarine *f*; animé occidental; copal *m* tendre; **g. dragon, g. tragacanth,** gomme adragante; **g. lac,** gomme laque; **g. resin,** gomme-résine *f*, *pl.* gommes-résines; **red g.,** gomme-résine rouge; **g. juniper, g. sandarac,** gomme de genévrier; sandaraque *f*; vernis sec; (*b*) **g. elastic,** gomme élastique, caoutchouc *m*; (*c*) *Exp:* **g. dynamite,** dynamite *f* gomme; gélatine explosive, détonante. **3.** *Comest:* (*a*) chewing-gum *m*; (*b*) boule *f* de gomme. **4.** (*of eye*) chassie *f*. **5.** (*disease of fruit trees*) gomme. **6.** *Bot:* **g. (tree),** gommier *m*; eucalyptus *m*; **blue g. (tree),** eucalyptus, gommier, bleu; **red g. (tree),** eucalyptus résineux; **sweet g. (tree),** liquidambar *m* styraciflua, gommier doux, copalme *m*; **Botany Bay g.,** acroïde *f* jaune; *F:* **to be up a g. tree,** être dans l'embarras, dans le pétrin.

gum[2], *v.* **(gummed) 1.** *v.tr.* (*a*) gommer, engommer (un tissu, etc.); *Bookb:* *etc:* encoller (le papier, la toile); (*b*) coller (une page dans un livre, etc.); **to g. two pages together,** réunir deux feuilles avec de la colle; (*c*) **to g. (up),** (i) *I.C.E:* gommer (un piston); (ii) encrasser (une lime). **2.** *v.i.* (*a*) (*of oil*) goudronner; (*b*) **to g. (up),** (i) (*of piston, etc.*) (se) gommer; (ii) (*of file, etc.*) s'encrasser.

gum[3], *s.* gencive *f*; **swollen gums,** gencives enflées; *Box:* **g. shield,** protège-dents *m inv*.

gum[4], *int. F:* *O:* (*euphemism for* GOD) **by g.!** fichtre! mazette! **good g.! what's that?** qu'est-ce que c'est que ça, grand Dieu!

gumbo ['gʌmbou], *s. Bot:* ketmie *f* comestible; gombo *m*.

gumboil ['gʌmbɔil], *s.* abcès *m* à la gencive; fluxion *f* de la gencive; fluxion à la joue; *Med:* parulie *f*.

gumboot ['gʌmbuːt], *s.* botte *f* de caoutchouc.

gumdrop ['gʌmdrɔp], *s. Comest:* boule *f* de gomme.

gum-lac ['gʌmlæk], *v.tr.* **(-lacked)** gommelaquer.

gumma ['gʌmə], *s. Med:* gomme *f*; *esp.* gomme syphilitique.

gummatous ['gʌmətəs], *a. Med:* (tumeur) gommeuse.

gummed [gʌmd], *a.* **1.** (*of label, etc.*) gommé. **2. g. (up) piston,** piston gommé; **g. oil,** huile goudronnée; *F:* **all g. up,** (projet) qui ne marche plus.

gummer ['gʌmər], *s. Bookb:* *etc:* encolleur, -euse.

gummiferous [gʌ'mifərəs], *a. Bot:* gommifère, gummifère.

gumminess ['gʌminis], *s.* viscosité *f*; toucher gluant.

gumming ['gʌmiŋ], *s.* **1.** (en)gommage *m*; gommement *m*. **2.** collage *m* (à la gomme). **3. g. (up),** (i) gommage (d'un piston); (ii) encrassement *m* (d'une lime).

gummite ['gʌmait], *s. Miner:* gummite *f*.

gummosis [gʌ'mousis], *s. Arb:* gommose *f*; gomme *f*.

gummy ['gʌmi], *a.* **1.** gommeux, gluant, visqueux; **g. oil,** huile goudronneuse. **2.** (*of trees, etc.*) gommeux, goudronneux. **3.** (*of eyes*) chassieux. **4.** (*of ankle, etc.*) enflé, bouffi.

gump [gʌmp], *s. F:* idiot, -ote; imbécile *mf*.

gumption ['gʌm(p)ʃ(ə)n], *s.* **1.** *F:* jugeotte *f*, sens *m* pratique; **he's got plenty of g.,** c'est un débrouillard; il est débrouillard; **he hasn't any g.,** il n'est pas débrouillard pour deux sous. **2.** *Paint:* véhicule *m*.

gum-resinous ['gʌm'rezinəs], *a.* gommo-résineux.

gumshoe[1] ['gʌmʃuː], *s. U.S:* **1.** (*rubber overshoe*) caoutchouc *m*. **2.** *F:* (*also* **gumshoer**) détective *m*, flic *m*.

gumshoe[2], *v.tr. U.S:* *F:* espionner, filer, pister (qn).

gum-yielding ['gʌmjiːldiŋ], *a.* gommifère, gummifère; **g.-y. plant,** plante gommeuse.

gun[1] [gʌn], *s.* **1.** (*a*) *Artil:* canon *m*, bouche *f* à feu, pièce *f* (d'artillerie); **heavy g., large-calibre g.,** canon lourd, grosse pièce; canon, pièce, de gros calibre; **light g., small-calibre g.,** canon, pièce, de petit calibre; **medium g.,** canon, pièce, de moyen calibre; **superheavy g.,** canon lourd; pièce lourde, à grande puissance; **105-mm g.,** canon de 105 (millimètres); **the guns,** l'artillerie *f*, le canon; **the big guns,** la grosse artillerie, les grosses pièces; *F:* **g. fodder,** chair *f* à canon; **guns in pair,** canons jumelés, pièces jumelées; **long-range g.,** canon, pièce, à longue portée; **short-range g.,** canon, pièce, à courte portée; **short-barrelled g.,** canon court; **flat-trajectory g.,** canon, pièce, à tir tendu; **high-angle g.,** canon, pièce, à tir courbe; obusier *m*; **automatic g.,** canon automatique; **recoilless g.,** canon sans recul; **revolving g.,** canon-revolver *m*, *pl.* canons-revolvers; **self-propelled g.,** canon automoteur, automouvant; autocanon *m*; **motorized g., tractor-drawn g.,** canon tracté; **g. on railway mounting, railway g.,** canon, pièce, sur voie ferrée; **accompanying g.,** canon d'accompagnement; **assault g.,** canon d'assaut; **antitank g.,** canon, pièce, antichar; **coastal defence g.,** canon de côte; canon, pièce, de défense côtière; **atomic g.,** canon atomique; **service of the g.,** service *m* de la pièce; **to serve the g.,** servir la pièce; **g. commander,** chef *m* de pièce; **g. detachment,** peloton *m*, équipe *f*, de pièce; **g. number,** servant *m*; **g. emplacement, g. position,** emplacement *m* de pièce; **g.-position officer,** lieutenant *m* de tir; **directing g., pivot g.,** *U.S:* **base g.,** pièce directrice; **g. in observation,** pièce en observation; **g. in firing position, g. ready for action,** pièce en batterie; **firing g.,** pièce en action; **to bring a g. into action, into firing position,** mettre une pièce en batterie; **to bring guns into play,** faire donner, tirer, l'artillerie; tirer au, le, canon; **guns were being fired,** l'artillerie tirait; on tirait au, le, canon; **do you hear the guns?** entendez-vous le canon? **antiaircraft g.,** canon antiaérien, pièce antiaérienne; **automatically-aimed g.,** canon à pointage automatique; **power-operated g.,** canon à pointage et à chargement automatiques; **g. defended area,** zone *f* d'artillerie (antiaérienne); **guns free,** tir *m* libre (sur avions); **guns tight,** tir interdit; *Mil.Av:* **air g., aerial g.,** canon d'avion, de bord; *Navy:* **naval g.,** canon, pièce, de marine, de bord; **after g.,** pièce de retraite; **foremost g.,** pièce de chasse; **broadside g.,** pièce de batterie; **surface g.,** pièce de surface; **g. firing all round,** (i) *Navy:* pièce axiale, pièce tirant des deux bords; (ii) *Mil:* canon, pièce, (tirant) tous azimuts; **ship carrying 15 ten-inch guns,** navire *m* portant quinze canons de 240 mm; **g. direction,** direction *f* de tir; **g.-direction officer,** officier directeur du tir; *Nau:* **distress g.,** canon de détresse; **line-throwing g.,** canon porte-amarre; *attrib.* **g. foundry,** fonderie *f* de canons; canonnerie *f*; **g. pit,** alvéole *f*; **g. sponge,** écouvillon *m*; **g. cover,** bagnolette *f*; **g. carriage,** affût *m* de canon; (*at military funeral*) prolonge *f* d'artillerie; **g. layer,** pointeur *m*; *Fort:* **g. bank,** épaulement *m*; **g. ring,** tourelle *f* (de mitrailleuse); **g. spotter,** avion *m* de repérage d'artillerie; (*b*) **(machine) g.,** mitrailleuse *f*; *Av: etc:* **camera g.,** mitrailleuse photographique; (*c*) coup *m* de canon; **saluting g.,** salve *f* d'honneur; **salute of six guns,** salve (d'honneur) de six coups de canon; **to return a salute g. for g.,** rendre un salut coup pour coup; *Navy:* **morning, evening, g.,** coup de canon de la diane, de la retraite; (*d*) *Elcs:* **electron g.,** canon à électrons, canon électronique; **ion g.,** canon ionique; (*e*) *F:* (*pers.*) **big g.,** gros manitou, grosse légume; **it was blowing great guns,** il faisait un vent à décorner les bœufs; **to be going great guns,** marcher tambour battant; **he's going great guns,** il est (i) en pleine forme, (ii) en plein succès; *O:* **son of a g.,** coquin *m*, loustic *m*. **2.** (*a*) fusil *m*, *esp.* fusil de chasse non rayé; **single-barrelled, double-barrelled, g.,** fusil à un coup, à deux coups; **drop-down g.,** fusil à bascule; **cane g.,** canne-fusil *f*, *pl.* cannes-fusils; **sporting g.,** fusil de chasse; **air g.,** fusil, carabine *f*, à air comprimé; **harpoon g.,** fusil harpon; *Mil:* **service g.,** fusil réglementaire; **automatic g.,** fusil mitrailleur automatique; *Sp:* **starter's g.,** pistolet *m* de starter; *F:* **to jump, beat, the g.,** brûler le feu, marcher avant les violons; **to stick to one's guns,** tenir bon; ne pas en démordre; *attrib.* **g. barrel,** canon de fusil; **g. case,** boîte *f*, étui *m*, fourreau *m*, à fusil; **g. rack,** râtelier *m* d'armes; **g. runner,** contrebandier *m* d'armes; flibustier *m*; **g. running,** contrebande *f* d'armes; (*b*) (*pers.*) chasseur *m*; **a party of six guns,** une bande de six chasseurs. **3.** revolver *m*; pistolet *m*. **4.** (*a*) *Mec.E:* seringue *f*, injecteur *m* (à graisse); *I.C.E:* injecteur (à carburant); *Petr:* **jet g.,** éjecteur *m* pour boues; **to cut the g.,** fermer la manette des gaz, couper les gaz; **to give the g.,** ouvrir la manette des gaz, mettre les gaz; *Mec.E:* **oil g.,** pistolet graisseur; seringue (à huile); (*b*) *Paint:* **spray g.,** pistolet (à peinture, de vernissage); *Const:* **cartridge g., rivet g.,** pistolet de scellement; *Hort:* **flame g.,** agriflamme *m*.

gun[2], *v.* **(gunned) 1.** *v.i.* (*a*) **to g. for, after, game,** chasser le gibier au tir; (*b*) *F:* **to g. for sth., s.o.,** pourchasser qch., qn; **he's gunning for us,** c'est à nous qu'il en veut. **2.** *v.tr. F:* **to g. s.o. (down),** tuer (qn) d'un coup de revolver; fusiller, descendre, flinguer, qn. **3.** *v.tr. & i. Aut: etc:* (faire) emballer (son moteur); **he gunned into the road,** il s'est lancé à toute vitesse sur la route.

gunboat ['gʌnbout], *s.* aviso-torpilleur *m*, *pl.* avisos-torpilleurs.

guncotton ['gʌnkɔtn], *s. Exp:* coton *m* azotique, coton fulminant, fulmicoton *m*, nitrocellulose *f*, coton-poudre *m*; *F:* coton; *Ch:* pyroxyle *m*, pyroxyline *f*.

gundeck ['gʌndek], *s. Navy:* batterie *f*.

gundog ['gʌndɔg], *s.* chien *m* d'arrêt.

gunfight ['gʌnfait], *s.* bagarre *f* entre bandits armés.

gunfire ['gʌnfaiər], *s.* **1.** *Artil:* (*a*) canonnade *f*; feu *m* (des pièces); (*b*) tir *m* rapide. **2.** *Mil: Navy:* (*a*) (coup *m* de canon de) diane *f*; (*b*) (coup de canon de) retraite *f*.

gunite[1] ['gʌnait], *s. Const:* gunite *f*.

gunite[2], *v.tr. Const:* guniter.

guniting ['gʌnaitiŋ], *s. Const:* gunitage *m*.

gunkhole ['gʌŋkhoul], *s.* **1.** *U.S: Nau:* chenal peu profond et à peine navigable. **2.** *Can:* petite anse entourée de rochers (où la pêche est bonne).

gunmaker ['gʌnmeikər], *s.* fabricant *m* d'armes; armurier *m*.

gunman, *pl.* **-men** ['gʌnmən], *s.m.* **1.** (*a*) partisan armé; (*b*) voleur armé; bandit *m*; terroriste *m*. **2.** = GUNSMITH.

gunmetal ['gʌnmetl], *s.* **1.** (*a*) bronze *m* à canon; (*b*) bronze industriel; fonte verte. **2.** *Com: F:* métal oxydé. **3. g. (grey),** gris acier (foncé).

gunnel[1] ['gʌnl], *s.* = GUNWALE.

gunnel[2], *s. Ich:* gon(n)elle *f*, papillon *m* de mer.

gunner ['gʌnər], *s.* **1.** (*a*) artilleur *m*, canonnier *m*; (*b*) **machine g.,** mitrailleur *m*; **g. observer,** mitrailleur guetteur; (*c*) *Navy:* (*warrant officer*) canonnier. **2.** chasseur *m* (au tir).

gunnera ['gʌnərə], *s. Bot:* gunnère *f*.

gunnery ['gʌnəri], *s.* artillerie *f*; tir *m* au canon; canonnage *m*; balistique *f*; **to have a thorough knowledge of g.,** connaître parfaitement l'artillerie; *Navy:* **g. ship,** école *f* de canonnage; **g. records,** les feuilles *f* de tir.

gunning ['gʌniŋ], *s.* tir *m*, chasse *f*.

gunny ['gʌni], *s.* **1.** toile *f* de jute; toile de chanvre des Indes; toile à sac. **2.** sac *m* en jute.

gunplay ['gʌnplei], *s.* coups *mpl* de revolver.

gunport ['gʌnpɔːt], *s. Navy:* sabord *m* de batterie; embrasure *f*.

gunpowder ['gʌnpaudər], *s.* **1.** poudre *f* (à canon); **g. works,** poudrerie *f*; *Hist:* **the G. Plot,** la Conspiration des Poudres. **2. g. (tea),** thé *m* poudre à canon.

gunroom ['gʌnruːm], *s.* **1.** *Navy:* poste *m* des aspirants. **2.** salle *f* aux fusils, armurerie *f* (d'un chasseur).

gunshot ['gʌnʃɔt], *s.* **1.** coup *m* de fusil, de canon; coup de feu; **g. wound,** blessure *f* de balle, de boulet; **to receive a g. wound,** recevoir un coup de feu. **2. within g.,** à (une) portée de fusil; **out of g.,** hors de portée de fusil.

gunshy ['gʌnʃai], *a.* (chien) qui a peur du coup de fusil.

gunslinger ['gʌnsliŋər], *s. F:* vaurien armé, porte-flingue *m*.

gunsmith ['gʌnsmiθ], *s.* armurier *m*; **gunsmith's shop,** armurerie *f*.

gunstick ['gʌnstik], *s.* baguette *f* (de fusil).

gunstock ['gʌnstɔk], *s.* fût *m* (de fusil).

Gunter ['gʌntər], *Pr.n.m.* **1.** *Mth:* **Gunter's scale,** échelle *f* de Gunter. **2.** *s.* (*a*) *Nau:* **sliding G. sail,** (voile *f* à) houari *m*; **G. iron,** rocambeau *m*; (*b*) *Surv:* **Gunter('s chain),** chaîne *f* d'arpentage.

gunwale ['gʌn(ə)l], *s. Nau:* (*a*) plat-bord *m*, *pl.* plats-bords; **g. under,** le plat-bord dans l'eau; (bateau) engagé; (*of ship*) **to roll g. under,** engager; rouler bord sur bord; **to roll g. to g.,** rouler panne sur panne; (*b*) *pl.* **gunwales,** fargues *f* (de canot).

gup [gʌp], *s. P:* sottises *fpl*, bêtises *fpl*, foutaises *fpl*.

guppy ['gʌpi], *s. Ich:* guppy *m*.

gurgitation [gəːdʒi'teiʃ(ə)n], *s. Lit:* bouillonnement *m* (des vagues, etc.).

gurgle[1] ['gəːgl], *s.* (*a*) (*of liquid*) glouglou *m*; gargouillis *m* (de l'eau qui tombe); murmure *m* (d'un ruisseau); (*b*) (*of pers.*) gloussement *m*, roucoulement *m*; **gurgles of laughter,** des roucoulements de rire.

gurgle[2]. **1.** *v.i.* (*of liquid*) (*a*) glouglouter; faire glouglou (en sortant de la bouteille); (*b*) gargouiller (en tombant); (*c*) (*of stream*) murmurer. **2.** *v.i. & tr.* (*of pers.*) glousser, roucouler; **he gurgled with laughter,** il a gloussé de rire.

gurgling[1] ['gəːgliŋ], *a.* **1.** (*a*) (*of liquid in bottle*) glougloutant; qui fait glouglou; (*b*) (ruisseau) murmurant. **2. a loud g. laugh,** un gloussement de rire; **a low g. laugh,** un petit rire roucoulant, perlé; un rire doux comme un murmure de source.

gurgling[2], *s.* **1.** (*a*) glouglou *m*; (*b*) gargouillement *m*. **2.** roucoulement *m*.

Gurian ['guəriən], *Geog:* (*a*) *a.* gourien; (*b*) *s.* Gourien, -ienne.

gurjun ['gəːdʒən], *s.* **g. (balsam),** baume *m* de gurjun, de gurju, de Copahu.

Gurkha ['gəːkə], *s. Ethn:* Go(u)rkha *m*.

gurlet ['gəːlit], *s. Tls:* grelet *m* (de maçon).

gurnard ['gəːnəd], **gurnet** ['gəːnit], *s. Ich:* **red g.,** grondin *m* rouge; milan *m*; trigle *m* pin; caraman *m*; **grey g.,** grondin gris; gournaud *m*; **piper g.,** trigle lyre, trigle cardinal; **sapphirine g.,** trigle hirondelle; **yellow g.,** callionyme *m* lyre; doucet *m*; **armed g.,** malarmat *m*; **flying g.,** dactyloptère *m*; rouget volant; **long-finned g.,** morrude *m*.

guru ['guruː], *s.m. Hindu Rel:* gourou.

gush[1] [gʌʃ], *s.* **1.** jaillissement *m*, effusion *f* (d'une source, de larmes); bouillonnement *m* (d'un torrent). **2.** jet *m*, flot *m* (de sang). **3.** épanchement *m* de sentiments; débordement sentimental; sensiblerie *f*.

gush[2], *v.* **1.** *v.i.* (*a*) **to g. (forth, out),** jaillir, saillir, couler à flots; ruisseler; (*of torrent*) bouillonner; **spring that gushes from the earth,** source *f* qui sort à flots de la terre; **the blood was gushing out,** le sang sortait à gros bouillons; **tears gushed from her eyes,** des pleurs jaillirent de ses yeux; **the tears gushed into her eyes,** un flot de larmes lui monta aux yeux; (*b*) **his nose gushed, was gushing, with blood,** le sang lui jaillissait du nez; (*c*) faire de longs discours sentimentaux; faire de la sensiblerie; *F:* la faire au sentiment; **she gushed over their baby,** elle s'attendrissait sur leur bébé. **2.** *v.tr.* **to g. water, oil,** lancer des jets d'eau, un jet de pétrole.

gusher ['gʌʃər], *s.* **1.** personne exubérante, expansive. **2.** *Petr:* source (de pétrole) jaillissante; puits jaillissant.

gushing[1] ['gʌʃiŋ], *a.* **1.** (*of water*) jaillissant, vif; (*of torrent*) bouillonnant; **g. spring,** source *f* d'eau vive. **2.** (*of pers.*) exubérant, expansif; **g. compliments,** compliments chaleureux; débordement *m* de compliments; **she's rather g.,** elle se jette à votre tête.

gushing[2], *s.* = GUSH[1].

gushingly ['gʌʃiŋli], *adv.* avec effusion; avec exubérance.

gushy ['gʌʃi], *a. F:* = GUSHING[1] 2.

gusla, gusle [gu(ː)slə], *s. Mus:* guzla *f*.

gusset ['gʌsit], *s.* **1.** gousset *m* (d'armure). **2.** (*a*) pièce *f* triangulaire (d'étoffe, etc.); *Dressm: Tail:* élargissure *f*, soufflet *m*; gousset (de manche, etc.); (*b*) *Her:* gousset. **3.** *Mec.E:* **g. (plate, stay),** gousset, éclisse *f*; plaque *f* de jonction, d'éclissage; **g. girder,** poutre *f* à gousset; **integral g.,** gousset venu d'emboutissage.

gusseted ['gʌsitid], *a.* **1.** *Dressm: Tail:* à élargissure(s), à soufflet(s). **2.** *Mec.E:* renforcé de goussets; éclissé.

gust [gʌst], *s.* **1.** bouffée *f* (de fumée, d'éloquence, de colère, etc.). **2.** (*a*) **g. of rain,** ondée *f*, giboulée *f*; (*b*) **g. of wind,** (i) risée *f*; coup *m* de vent; rafale *f*, bourrasque *f*, *Nau:* grain *m*; (ii) remous *m* d'air.

gustation [gʌs'teiʃ(ə)n], *s. A:* gustation *f*; goût *m*.

gustative ['gʌstətiv], *a.* gustatif.

gustatory ['gʌstətəri], *a.* (nerf, etc.) gustatif.

Gustavus [gʌs'teivəs], *Pr.n.m.* Gustave; *Hist:* **G. Adolphus,** Gustave-Adolphe.

gustiness ['gʌstinis], *s.* **1. the g. of the weather,** les rafales qui soufflent par moments. **2.** *Meteor:* coefficient *m* d'intensité des rafales.

gusto ['gʌstou], *s.* délectation *f*, goût *m*; **to eat sth. with g.,** manger qch. savoureusement, en savourant; *F:* **to do sth. with g.,** faire qch. (i) avec plaisir, (ii) avec élan, avec entrain, avec brio.

gusty ['gʌsti], *a.* (temps, lieu) venteux; **g. wind,** vent *m* à rafales, qui souffle par rafales, par bourrasques; **g. day,** journée *f* de grand vent.

gut[1] [gʌt], *s.* **1.** *Anat:* boyau *m*, intestin *m*; **small g.,** intestin grêle; **blind g.,** (i) cæcum *m*, (ii) *F:* cul-de-sac *m*; *Ind:* **g.-dresser,** boyaudier *m*; **g.(-dressing) works,** boyauderie *f*. **2.** *pl.* **guts,** (*a*) boyaux, intestins, entrailles *f*; vidure *f* (de volaille); *F:* **I can take, tear, the guts out of a book in half an hour,** en une demi-heure je peux extraire d'un livre tout l'essentiel; **they were tearing each other's guts out,** ils s'étripaient; (*b*) *P:* (*of pers.*) **to have guts,** avoir du cran, du cœur au ventre; **put some guts into it!** mettez-en un (bon) coup! **he hasn't any guts, hasn't the guts of a louse,** il manque de cran; il n'a rien dans le ventre; c'est une nouille; **to sweat one's guts out,** en foutre un coup, se casser les reins. **3.** corde *f* à, de, boyau (pour violons, etc.). **4.** *Fish:* **silkworm g., silk g.,** crin *m* de Florence; florence *f*; racine (anglaise). **5.** (*a*) goulet *m* (dans un cours d'eau, dans un port, etc.); (*b*) passage étroit, défilé *m*; (*of street*) boyau, étranglement *m*.

gut[2], *v.tr.* **(gutted) 1.** (*a*) étriper (un animal); vider (un poisson, une volaille); (*b*) **the fire gutted the house,** le feu n'a laissé que les quatre murs, que la carcasse, de la maison. **2.** résumer (un livre); extraire l'essentiel, la moelle (d'un livre).

gutless ['gʌtlis], *a. P:* mou, *f.* molle; mollasse; sans énergie, sans nerf; qui manque de cran.

gutsy ['gʌtsi], *P:* **1.** (*a*) *a.* goinfre, goulu; (*b*) *s.* bâfreur *m*. **2.** *a.* qui a du cran.

gutta ['gʌtə], *s.* **1.** *Arch:* goutte *f*. **2.** *Ent:* goutte, tache *f* (de couleur). **3.** *Her:* goutte.

gutta-milk ['gʌtəmilk], *s.* latex *m* de la gutta.

gutta-percha ['gʌtə'pəːtʃə], *s.* gutta-percha *f*; gutta *f*.

guttate ['gʌteit], *a.* **1.** guttiforme. **2.** tacheté, moucheté.

guttation [gʌ'teiʃ(ə)n], *s. Bot:* guttation *f*.

gutter[1] ['gʌtər], *s.* **1.** gouttière *f*, chéneau *m* (de toit); **wooden g.,** échenal *m*, -aux; busard *m*; **g. pipe,** tuyau *m* de descente; **g. overhang,** larmier *m*; **g. lead** [led], noue *f*, noquet *m*; **g. tile,** tuile creuse, tuile gouttière; **g. bracket,** crochet *m* de gouttière. **2.** ruisseau *m* (de rue); caniveau *m*, cunette *f* (de chaussée); **open g.,** cassis *m*; **g. stone,** culière *f*, caniveau, évier *m*; **g. child,** gamin, -ine, des rues; **g. bred, brought up in the g.,** bercé dans la fange; **to rise from the g.,** sortir de la fange; partir de rien, de zéro; **to end up in the g.,** tomber, rouler, dans le ruisseau; tomber très bas; **to pick up a living in the g.,** gratter le pavé; **g. language,** langage *m* des rues; parler *m* voyou; **g. wit,** esprit gouailleur; *Journ: F:* **g. paper,** feuille *f* de chou; **g. press,** bas-fonds *mpl* du journalisme. **3.** (*a*) rigole *f*; sillon (creusé par la pluie, etc.); (*b*) cannelure *f*, rainure *f* (dans une tôle, etc.); (*c*) *Anat:* **jugular gutters,** gouttières des jugulaires; (*d*) *Typ: Bookb:* les petits fonds (de deux pages en vis-à-vis); (*e*) *Ven:* gouttière.

gutter[2], *v.* **1.** *v.tr.* (*a*) fournir (une maison) de gouttières; fournir (une rue) de caniveaux; (*b*) sillonner, raviner (la terre, etc.); rainer (une tôle, etc.). **2.** *v.i.* (*a*) (*of water*) couler en ruisseau(x); (*b*) (*of candle*) couler.

gutter[3], *s.* videur, -euse (de morues).

guttering ['gʌtəriŋ], *s.* **1.** (*a*) sillonnage *m*, ravinement *m* (de la terre par la pluie, etc.); (*b*) coulage *m* (d'une bougie). **2.** *coll.* (*a*) *Const:* gouttières *fpl* (d'une maison); (*b*) *Civ.E:* caniveaux *mpl* (d'une rue).

guttersnipe ['gʌtəsnaip], *s.* gamin, -ine, des rues; *O:* gavroche *m*; petit voyou, petite voyoute.

Guttiferae [gʌ'tifəri:], *s.pl. Bot:* guttiféracées *f*, guttifères *m*, clusiacées *f*.

guttiferous [gʌ'tifərəs], *a. Bot:* guttifère.

guttiform ['gʌtifɔ:m], *a.* guttiforme.

gutting ['gʌtiŋ], *s.* étripage *m*; vidage *m* (d'un poisson).

guttural ['gʌtərəl]. **1.** *a.* guttural, -aux. **2.** *s. Ling:* gutturale *f*.

gutturally ['gʌtərəli], *adv.* gutturalement; d'un ton guttural.

gutturality [gʌtə'ræliti], **gutturalness** ['gʌtərəlnis], *s.* ton guttural; accent guttural (d'une langue).

gutturalize ['gʌtərəlaiz], *v.tr.* **1.** prononcer (un son) d'un ton guttural, de la gorge. **2.** *Ling:* rendre (un son) guttural.

gutty ['gʌti], *s. Golf: A:* balle pleine en gutta-percha.

guv [gʌv], **guv'nor** ['gʌv'nər], *s. P:* **the g.,** (i) le patron, le singe; (ii) le vieux, le paternel.

Guy[1] [gai]. **1.** *Pr.n.m.* Gui, Guy. **2.** *s.* (*a*) effigie *f* burlesque de Guy Fawkes, le chef de la Conspiration des Poudres (1605); (les gamins la portent en procession et la brûlent le 5 novembre); (*b*) épouvantail *m*; chienlit *mf*, chie-en-lit *mf inv*; paquet *m*; **she's a regular g.,** elle est ficelée comme quatre sous; **what a g.!** comme la voilà fagotée, attifée, affublée! *F:* quelle touche elle a! quel paquet! **dressed like a g.,** fichu(e) comme l'as de pique. **3.** *F:* type *m*, individu *m*; **who's that g.?** qu'est-ce que c'est que ce type-là? **a great g.,** un bon garçon; un chic type; **a big g.,** (i) un gros bonnet; (ii) un criminel de marque; **a tough g.,** un dur; **a wise g.,** un donneur de conseils; un je-sais-tout; *esp. U.S:* **fall g.,** (i) bouc *m* émissaire; (ii) dupe *f*, pigeon *m*. **4.** *P:* **to do a g.,** se sauver, filer, se cavaler; **to give s.o. the g.,** échapper à qn; donner le change à qn; brûler la politesse à qn.

guy[2], *v.* (**guyed; guying**) **1.** *v.tr.* (*a*) faire, exhiber une effigie de (qn); (*b*) se moquer de (qn); *F:* charrier (qn); mettre (qn) en boîte; (*c*) *Th:* charger, travestir, cascader (un rôle); prendre (un rôle) à la cascade. **2.** *v.i. P:* se sauver, filer.

guy[3], *s.* (*a*) *Tchn:* corde *f* de tension, de traction; étai *m*; *Const:* verboquet *m*, vireboquet *m*, vingtaine *f*; *esp. U.S:* hauban *m* (d'antenne, etc.); **chimney g.,** hauban de cheminée (de navire, etc.); *U.S:* **g. wire,** fil *m* de hauban; *Civ.E:* **guys of shears,** étais de bigue; *Mil: etc:* **storm g.,** grande corde de tente; (*b*) *Nau:* (i) (câble *m*, chaîne *f*, amarre *f*, de) retenue *f*; (ii) gui *m*; **derrick g.,** retenue de mât de charge, palan *m* de garde; **g. span,** entremise *f* (de mât de charge); **flying guys,** haubans de clinfoc; **lazy g.,** *U.S:* **boom g.,** retenue de gui.

guy[4], *v.tr.* assujettir avec des haubans, des retenues; hauban(n)er.

Guyana [gai'ænə], *Pr.n. Geog:* Guyane *f*.

Guyanese [gaiə'ni:z], *Geog:* (*a*) *a.* guyanais; (*b*) *s.* Guyanais, -aise.

guyed [gaid], *a. Nau:* hauban(n)é.

guying[1] ['gaiiŋ], *s. Th:* charge *f* (d'un rôle).

guying[2], *s. Nau:* étayage *m*; hauban(n)age *m*.

guyot ['gi:ou], *s. Geol:* guyot *m*.

guyrope ['gairoup], *s.* (*a*) cordon *m* (de tente); (*b*) *Ten: O:* corde *f* de contre-appui (de poteau de filet); (*c*) *Aer:* corde de manœuvre; (manœuvre *f* de) retenue *f* (d'un dirigeable).

guze [gju:z], *s. Her:* guse *f*.

guzzle[1] ['gʌzl], *s. F:* godaille *f*, bâfre *f*.

guzzle[2], *v.tr. & i. F:* (*a*) (*eating*) bâfrer, bouffer, chiquer (la nourriture); s'empiffrer, goinfrer, godailler; (*b*) (*drinking*) boire avidement, lamper (la boisson).

guzzler ['gʌzlər], *s. F:* (*a*) bâfreur, -euse; goinfre *m*; godailleur, -euse; grand gosier; avaleur *m* (de viande); (*b*) buveur, -euse; pochard, -arde; sac *m* à vin.

guzzling[1] ['gʌzliŋ], *a. F:* (*a*) glouton, goulu; (*b*) biberon, pochard.

guzzling[2], *s. F:* (*a*) bâfrée *f*, bâfre *f*, empiffrerie *f*, goinfrerie *f*; (*b*) buverie *f*, pocharderie *f*.

gybe[1] [dʒaib], *s. Nau:* empannage *m*.

gybe[2], *v. tr. & i. Nau:* coiffer, gambier, gambiller, gambeyer (une voile); (*of ship*) empanner, s'empanner.

gybing ['dʒaibiŋ], *s.* empannage *m*.

Gyges ['gaidʒi:z], *Pr.n.m. A.Hist:* Gygès.

gyle [gail], *s. Brew:* **1.** brassin *m*. **2.** moût *m* en fermentation. **3.** cuve *f* de fermentation; brassin.

gym [dʒim], *s. F:* **1.** = GYMNASIUM 1. **2.** = GYMNASTICS.

gymkhana [dʒim'kɑ:nə], *s.* gymkana *m*.

gymnasiarch [dʒim'neiziɑ:k], *s. Gr.Ant:* gymnasiarque *m*.

gymnasium, *pl.* **-iums, -ia** [dʒim'neiziəm, -iəmz, -iə], *s.* **1.** gymnase *m*; **g. exercises,** gymnastique *f* aux agrès. **2.** (*occ.* [gim'nɑ:zium]) *Sch:* (*in Germany*) gymnase, lycée *m*.

gymnast ['dʒimnæst], *s.* gymnaste *mf*.

gymnastic [dʒim'næstik]. **1.** *a.* gymnastique. **2.** *s.pl.* (*usu. with sg. const.*) **gymnastics,** gymnastique *f*; **medical gymnastics,** gymnastique médicale; **slack-rope gymnastics,** voltige *f*; **to do gymnastics, to go in for gymnastics,** faire de la gymnastique; *Equit:* **mounted gymnastics,** voltige; **mental gymnastics,** gymnastique intellectuelle.

gymnic ['dʒimnik], *a.* gymnique.

gymnite ['dʒimnait], *s. Miner:* gymnite *f*.

Gymnoblastea [dʒimnou'blæstiə], *s.pl. Nat.Hist:* gymnoblastiques *m*.

gymnoblastic [dʒimnou'blæstik], *a. Nat.Hist:* gymnoblaste.

gymnocarpous [dʒimnou'kɑ:pəs], *a. Bot:* gymnocarpe.

gymnodactylus [dʒimnou'dæktiləs], *s. Rept:* gymnodactyle *m*.

gymnodont ['dʒimnoudɔnt], *a. & s. Ich:* gymnodonte (*m*).

gymnoglossate [dʒimnou'glɔseit], *a. Moll:* gymnoglosse.

gymnogynous [dʒim'nɔdʒinəs], *a. Bot:* gymnogyne.

Gymnolaemata [dʒimnouli:'mɑ:tə], *s.pl. Nat.Hist:* gymnolémates *m*.

Gymnophiona [dʒimnou'faiənə], *s.pl. Amph:* gymnosophiste *mf*.

gymnorhina [dʒimnou'rainə], *s. Orn:* gymnorhine *m*.

gymnosomate [dʒimnou'soumeit], **gymnosom(at)ous** [dʒimnou'soum(ət)əs], *a. Moll:* gymnosome.

gymnosophist [dʒim'nɔsəfist], *s. A.Phil:* gymnosophiste *mf*.

gymnosophy [dʒim'nɔsəfi], *s. A.Phil:* gymnosophie *f*.

gymnosperm ['dʒimnouspə:m], *s. Bot:* gymnosperme *m*.

gymnospermous [dʒimnou'spə:məs], *a. Bot:* gymnosperme, gymnospermé.

gymnospermy ['dʒimnouspə:mi], *s. Bot:* gymnospermie *f*.

Gymnostomata [dʒimnou'stoumətə], *s.pl. Nat.Hist:* gymnostomes *m*.

gymnostom(at)ous [dʒimnou'stoum(ət)əs], *a. Bot:* gymnostome.

gymnotus, *pl.* **-i** [dʒim'noutəs, -ai], *s. Ich:* gymnote *m*.

gynaeceum [dʒaini'siəm], *s.* **1.** *Cl.Ant:* gynécée *m*. **2.** *Bot:* = GYNOECIUM.

gynaeco- ['gainikou, gaini'kɔ, dʒai-], *comb.fm.* gynéco-.

gynaecocracy [gaini'kɔkrəsi, dʒai-], *s.* gynécocratie *f*.

gynaecologic(al) [gainikɔ'lɔdʒik(l), dʒai-], *a.* gynécologique.

gynaecologist [gaini'kɔlədʒist, dʒai-], *s.* gynécologiste *mf*, gynécologue *mf*.

gynaecology [gaini'kɔlədʒi, dʒai-], *s.* gynécologie *f*.

gynaecomastia, gynaecomasty [gainikou'mæstiə, -'mæsti; dʒai-], *s. Med:* gynécomastie *f*.

gynaecopathy [gaini'kɔpəθi, dʒai-], *s. Med:* gynécopathie *f*.

gynaecophore ['gainikoufɔ:r, 'dʒai-], *a.* gynécophore.

gynandroid [gai'nændrɔid, dʒai-], *a. & s. Med:* gynandroïde (*f*).

gynandromorph [gai'nændroumɔ:f, dʒai-], *s.* gynandromorphe *m*.

gynandromorphism [gainændrou'mɔ:fizm, dʒai-], *s.* gynandromorphisme *m*.

gynandromorphous [gainændrou'mɔ:fəs, dʒai-], *a.* gynandromorphe.

gynandrous [gai'nændrəs, dʒai-], *a. Bot:* gynandre, épistaminé.

gynandry [gai'nændri, dʒai-], *s. Bot:* gynandrie *f*.

gyneco- ['gainikou, gaini'kɔ, dʒai-], *comb.fm.* = GYNAECO-.

gynerium [dʒi'niəriəm], *s. Bot:* gynérion *m*.

gyno- [gainou, dʒainou], *comb.fm.* gyno-.

gynobase ['gainoubeis, 'dʒai-], *s. Bot:* gynobase.

gynobasic [gainou'beisik, dʒai-], *a. Bot:* gynobasique.

gynocardic [gainou'kɑ:dik], *a. Ch:* (acide) gynocardique.

gynodioecious [gainoudai'i:ʃəs, dʒai-], *a. Bot:* gynodioïque.

gynoecium, *pl.* **-ia** [gai'ni:siəm, dʒai-; -iə], *s. Bot:* gynécée *m*.

gynogenesis [gainou'dʒenəsis, dʒai-], *s. Biol:* gynogénèse *f*.

gynogenetic [gainoudʒe'netik, dʒai-], *a.* gynogénétique.

gynomonoecious [gainoumɔ'ni:ʃəs, dʒai-], *a. Bot:* gynomonoïque.

gynophore ['gainoufɔ:r, 'dʒai-], *s. Bot:* gynophore *m*.

gynostemium, *pl.* **-ia** [gainou'sti:miəm, -iə; dʒai-], *s. Bot:* gynostème *m* (des orchidées).

gyp[1] [dʒip], *s.* (*Cambridge and Durham Univ.*) domestique (attaché au service des étudiants).

gyp[2], *s. F:* **to give s.o. g.,** (i) flanquer une raclée à qn; (ii) (*of aching tooth, etc.*) faire souffrir qn.

gyp[3], *s. NAm: F:* escroquerie *f*.

gyp[4], *v.i.* (**gypped**) *NAm: F:* escroquer.

gypaetus [dʒi'peiətəs], *s. Orn:* gypaète *m*.

gypoun [gi'pu:n], *s. A.Mil.Cost:* cotte *f* d'armes.

gypseous ['dʒipsiəs], *a.* gypseux, plâtreux.

gypsiferous [dʒip'sifərəs], *a.* gypsifère.

gypsography [dʒip'sɔgrəfi], *s. Engr:* gypsographie *f*.

gypsophila [dʒip'sɔfilə], *s. Bot:* gypsophile *f*.

gypsum[1] ['dʒipsəm], *s. Miner:* gypse *m*; chaux sulfatée; pierre *f* à plâtre; **burnt, unburnt, g.,** plâtre cuit, cru; **satin g.,** spath satiné; **crystalline, foliated, g.,** sélénite *f*; **g. quarry,** plâtrière *f*; **g. kiln,** plâtrière, four *m* à plâtre.

gypsum[2], *v.tr. Agr:* plâtrer (une terre).

gyrate[1] ['dʒaireit], *a. Bot:* circinal, -aux.

gyrate[2] [dʒai'reit], *v.i.* tourner; tournoyer.

gyration [dʒai'reiʃ(ə)n], *s.* giration *f*, gyration *f*, révolution *f*; *Mec:* **centre of g.,** centre *m* des masses centrifuges, excentriques.

gyratory ['dʒaiərət(ə)ri, dʒai'reitəri], *a.* giratoire, gyratoire; *Adm:* **g. traffic-system,** système *m* de circulation giratoire.

gyrfalcon ['dʒə:fɔ:(l)kən], *s. Orn:* (faucon *m*) gerfaut (*m*).

gyrinid ['dʒirinid], *s. Ent:* gyrin *m*.

Gyrinidae [dʒi'rinidi:], *s.pl. Ent:* gyrinidés *m*.

gyro ['dʒairou]. **1.** *comb.fm.* gyro-. **2.** *attrib.* gyroscopique, équipé d'un ou plusieurs gyroscopes; **gyro control,** commande *f* gyroscopique; **gyro instruments,** appareils *m* gyroscopiques; **gyro platform,** plate-forme *f* gyroscopique; **gyro (gun)sight,** appareil de visée gyroscopique, viseur *m* gyroscopique, **g. horizon,** gyrohorizon *m*; horizon artificiel. **3.** (*a*) = GYROSCOPE; (*b*) = GYROCOMPASS.

gyroaviation ['dʒairoueivi'eiʃ(ə)n], *s.* gyraviation *f*.

gyrocar ['dʒairoukɑ:r], *s. Rail:* monorail *m* gyroscopique.

gyrocompass ['dʒairou'kʌmpəs], *s. Nau.* gyrocompas *m*; compas *m* gyroscopique.

gyro-controlled ['dʒairoukən'trould], *a.* à commande *f* gyroscopique, commandé par gyroscope.

gyrodyne ['dʒairoudain], *s. Av:* gyrodyne *m*.

gyrofrequency ['dʒairou'fri:kwənsi], *s. Atom.Ph:* fréquence *f* de rotation (des particules).

gyrolite ['dʒairoulait], *s. Miner:* gyrolite *f*.

gyromagnetic ['dʒairoumæg'netik], *a.* gyromagnétique; **g. compass,** compas *m* gyromagnétique; **g. ratio,** rapport *m* gyromagnétique.

gyromancy ['dʒairoumænsi], *s.* gyromancie *f*.

gyrometer [dʒai'rɔmitər], *s.* gyromètre *m*.

gyromitra [dʒai'rɔmitrə], *s. Fung:* gyromitre *m*.

gyron ['dʒairən], *s. Her:* giron *m*.

gyronny [dʒai'rɔni], *a. Her:* gironné.

gyropilot ['dʒairou'pailət], *s.* (*a*) *Av:* pilote *m* automatique, gyropilote *m*; (*b*) *Nau:* (i) auto-gouvernail *m*, *pl.* auto-gouvernails; commande *f* gyroscopique de barre; (ii) (*compass*) gyropilote.

gyroplane ['dʒairəplein], *s. Av:* giravion *m*; autogyre *m*.

gyroscope ['dʒairəskoup], *s.* gyroscope *m*, gyro *m*; **g. top,** toupie *f* gyroscopique; *Av:* **directional g., flight g.,** gyroscope directionnel; indicateur *m* gyroscopique de cap, de direction; **trim g.,** gyroscope d'assiette; **vibratory g.,** gyroscope à vibrations.

gyroscopic [dʒairə'skɔpik], *a.* (mouvement *m*) gyroscopique; *Mec:* **g. effect,** effet *m* de toupie; **g. torque,** couple *m* gyroscopique.

gyroscopics [dʒairə'skɔpiks], *s.pl.* (*usu. with sg. const.*) gyroscopie *f*.

gyrostabilization ['dʒairousteibilai'zeiʃ(ə)n], *s.* gyrostabilisation *f*, stabilisation *f* gyroscopique.

gyrostabilized ['dʒairou'steibilaizd], *a.* gyrostabilisé.

gyrostabilizer ['dʒairou'steibilaizər], *s.* (i) *Av: Ball:* gyrostabilisateur *m*; (ii) *Nau:* stabilisateur *m* gyroscopique.

gyrostat ['dʒairəstæt], *s. Dyn:* gyrostat *m*.

gyrostatic [dʒairə'stætik], *a. Dyn:* gyrostatique.

gyrovague ['dʒairouveig], *s. Ecc.Hist:* gyrovague *m*.

gyve [dʒaiv], *v.tr. A. & Poet:* enchaîner (qn); mettre les fers à (qn).

gyves [dʒaivz], *s.pl. A. & Poet:* fers *m*, chaînes *f*.

H

H, h [eitʃ], *s.* **1.** (la lettre) H, h *mf*; **silent h,** h muette; **aspirate h,** h aspirée; **to drop one's h's** ['eitʃiz], ne pas aspirer les h; *Tp:* **H for Harry,** H comme Henri. **2.** *Const: etc:* **H beam, H girder,** poutre *f* en H, en double T; *El:* **H armature,** induit *m* Siemens. **3.** *Mil:* **H bomb,** bombe *f* H, bombe à (l')hydrogène.

ha [hɑ:], *int.* ha! ah!

haar [hɑ:r], *s. Dial:* brouillard *m*, brume *f* (de mer); *esp. Scot:* brume glaciale qu'apporte le vent d'est.

Habakkuk ['hæbəkʌk], *Pr.n.m. B.Hist:* Habacuc.

habeas corpus ['heibiəs'kɔ:pəs], *s. Jur:* habeas corpus *m* (assignation à un fonctionnaire, ayant sous sa garde un prisonnier, de l'amener devant la Cour; garantit les citoyens contre l'emprisonnement sans cause démontrée).

habenaria [hæbə'nɛəriə], *s. Bot:* habenaria *m.*

haberdasher ['hæbədæʃər], *s. Com:* **1.** chemisier *m.* **2.** mercier *m.*

haberdashery ['hæbədæʃəri], *s. Com:* **1.** chemiserie *f.* **2.** mercerie *f.*

habergeon ['hæbədʒən], *s. A.Arm:* haubergeon *m.*

habiliment [hə'bilimənt], *s.* **1.** *A:* attirail *m.* **2.** *pl.* **habiliments,** *(a)* vêtements *m* de cérémonie, de parade; *(b)* habillement *m*, vêtements.

habilitate [hə'biliteit]. **1.** *v.tr. Min: U.S:* fournir à (qn) des fonds pour l'exploitation. **2.** *v.i.* (*of German university professor*) se faire habiliter.

habilitation [həbili'teiʃ(ə)n], *s.* **1.** *Min: U.S:* avance *f* de fonds (pour l'exploitation). **2.** (*in German universities*) habilitation *f.*

habilitator [hə'biliteitər], *s. Min: U.S:* bailleur *m* de fonds.

habit[1] ['hæbit], *s.* **1.** *(a)* habitude *f*, coutume *f*; **to be in the h., to make a h., of doing sth.,** avoir coutume, avoir l'habitude, avoir pour habitude, être dans l'habitude, de faire qch.; **he is in the h., makes a h., of doing it,** il a la coutume de le faire; **I don't make a h. of it,** ce n'est pas une habitude chez moi; **once does not make a h.,** une fois n'est pas coutume; **he has a h. of scratching his nose,** il a la manie de se gratter le nez; **it's a h. with him,** c'est une habitude chez lui; c'est un de ses tics; **to form, fall into, get into, the h. of doing sth.,** prendre, contracter, l'habitude de faire qch.; **to grow into a h.,** (i) (*of pers.*) contracter une habitude; (ii) (*of vice, etc.*) devenir une habitude; tourner en habitude; **to get into bad habits,** prendre de mauvaises habitudes, *F:* prendre un mauvais pli; **to fall out, get out, of a h.,** perdre une habitude; se défaire d'une habitude; **to grow out of a h.,** perdre une habitude en grandissant, en vieillissant, avec le temps; se défaire d'une habitude; **the force of h.,** la force, la puissance, de l'habitude; **from force of h.,** poussé par l'habitude; **out of (sheer) h.,** par habitude, par routine; **to do sth. by sheer force of h.,** faire qch. par pure habitude; **friendship that time and h. have strengthened,** amitié que le temps et l'user *m* ont affermie; *(b) F:* (i) **the h.,** l'usage *m* des drogues; **off the h.,** décamé, désintoxiqué; (ii) dose habituelle de drogues. **2.** *(a)* **h. (of body),** manière *f* d'être; tempérament *m*; habitude du corps; constitution *f* physique; **man of portly h.,** homme corpulent; *(b)* **h. of mind,** tournure *f* d'esprit; disposition *f*; *(c) Bot:* manière de croître, port *m*, habitus *m* (d'un arbre, d'une plante). **3.** *Cost:* *(a)* habit *m* (de religieuse); *(b)* **riding h.,** amazone *f*; habit de cheval.

habit[2], *v.tr.* vêtir; **habited in white,** vêtu de blanc.

habitability [hæbitə'biliti], **habitableness** ['hæbitəbəlnis], *s.* habitabilité *f.*

habitable ['hæbitəbl], *a.* habitable; (maison *f*) tenable; *Jur:* **to keep one's tenant's house in h. repair,** tenir son locataire clos et couvert.

habitant ['hæbitənt], *s.* **1.** *A: & Lit:* habitant, -ante. **2.** *NAm:* (*in Can. also* [abitɑ̃]) habitant, -ante, exploitant, -ante, agricole de langue française; *attrib.* **h. style,** style habitant; **h. song,** chanson habitant.

habitat ['hæbitæt], *s.* **1.** habitat *m.* **2.** *Nat.Hist:* aire *f* d'habitation (d'une espèce); biotope *m.*

habitation [hæbi'teiʃ(ə)n], *s.* **1.** habitation *f* (d'une maison); **fit for h.,** en état d'être habité. **2.** habitation, demeure *f*; lieu *m* de séjour.

habit-forming ['hæbitfɔ:miŋ], *a.* (*of drug*) qui cause, crée, accoutumance; **non h.-f. drug,** drogue qui ne cause pas accoutumance.

habitual [hə'bitjuəl], *a.* **1.** (*customary*) habituel, d'usage, d'habitude. **2.** (menteur, ivrogne) invétéré; **h. offender,** récidiviste *mf.*

habitually [hə'bitjuəli], *adv.* habituellement, d'habitude; par habitude.

habituate [hə'bitjueit], *v.tr.* **to h. s.o. to sth., to doing sth.,** habituer, accoutumer, qn à qch., à faire qch.; faire prendre à qn l'habitude de qch., de faire qch.; **to h. oneself to sth., to doing sth.,** s'habituer, s'accoutumer, à qch.; prendre l'habitude de faire qch.

habituation [həbitju'eiʃ(ə)n], *s.* accoutumance *f* (to, à).

habitude ['hæbitju:d], *s. Lit:* **1.** disposition *f*, tempérament *m*; habitude *f* du corps ou de l'esprit. **2.** habitude, coutume *f.*

habitué [hæ'bitjuei], *s.* habitué, -ée.

habitus ['hæbitəs], *s. Nat.Hist: Physiol:* habitus *m.*

haboob [hæ'bu:b], *s. Meteor:* haboob *m.*

habromania [hæbrou'meiniə], *s. Psy:* habromanie *f.*

habronema [hæbrou'ni:mə], *s. Ann:* habronème *m.*

habronemiasis [hæbrouni'maiəsis], **habronemosis** [hæbrouni'mousis], *s. Vet:* habronémose *f.*

hachure[1] ['hæʃjər, hæ'ʃju:ər], *s. Mapm:* hachure *f*; **h. lines,** hachures.

hachure[2], *v.tr.* hachurer; **hachured map,** carte *f* en hachures.

hack[1] [hæk], *s.* **1.** pic *m*, pioche *f* (de mineur, etc.). **2.** *(a)* taillade *f*, entaille *f*; *(b) Fb:* coup *m* de pied (sur le tibia). **3.** (*on tree*) blanchis *m*, griffe *f*, encoche *f.*

hack[2]. **1.** *v.tr. & i.* *(a)* hacher; ébrécher (une épée, etc.); *Surg: F:* charcuter (un malade); **to h. one's chin in shaving,** se taillader, s'écharper, le menton en se rasant; **hacked chin,** menton haché de coupures; **to h. sth. to pieces,** couper, tailler, qch. en pièces; **to h. sth. away, down,** démolir, abattre, qch. à coups de pioche; **to h. (away) at a tree,** entailler un arbre à coups de hache; s'escrimer contre un arbre avec la hache; **to h. a figure out of the rock,** tailler une image dans le roc; **to h. out a figure,** tailler une image à coups de pic, à coups de pioche; **hacked out,** fait, taillé, à la serpe, à coups de serpe, à coups de hache; **to h. up the joint,** massacrer le rôti; **to h. one's way through,** se frayer un chemin du tranchant et de la pointe; **to h. at s.o. with one's sword,** écharper qn à coups de sabre; *(b) Fb: etc:* **to h. s.o.'s shins,** donner déloyalement à un adversaire un coup de pied sur le tibia. **2.** *v.i.* émettre une toux sèche.

hack[3], *s.* **1.** *(a)* cheval *m*, -aux, de louage; *(b) F:* canasson *m*, rosse *f*, haridelle *f*; *(c)* cheval de selle à toutes fins. **2.** *NAm:* *(a) A:* voiture *f* de place, de louage; *(b)* (i) *F:* taxi *m*; (ii) *F:* chauffeur *m* de taxi; (iii) *P:* corbillard *m*. **3.** *(a)* homme *m* de peine; **literary h.,** écrivain *m* à la tâche; nègre *m*; **h. writer,** écrivain besogneux; barbouilleur *m* de papier; **to be a h. reporter,** faire la chronique des chiens écrasés; *(b) U.S: F:* gardien *m* de prison. **4.** *F: A:* **garrison h.,** coquette *f* qui court après les militaires; femme *f* à soldats. **5.** *Nau:* **h. (watch),** montre *f* d'habitacle, compteur *m.*

hack[4]. **1.** *v.tr.* *(a)* banaliser (qch.); **to h. an argument to death,** ressasser un argument; *(b)* louer (des chevaux). **2.** *v.i.* *(a)* **to h. along the road,** cheminer à cheval; **to h. home after the hunt,** rentrer au petit trot après une journée de chasse au renard; *(b)* (i) monter des chevaux de louage; (ii) *NAm: F:* être chauffeur de taxi; (iii) *NAm:* aller en taxi; *(c)* **to h. for s.o.,** être le nègre de qn.

hack[5], *s.* **1.** *Ven:* mangeoire *f* (de faucon); **hawk at h.,** faucon *m* en cours de dressage. **2.** *Brickm:* claie *f* de séchage.

hackberry ['hækbəri], *s. Bot:* **1.** cerisier *m* à grappes. **2.** *(a)* micocoule *f* (de l'Amérique du Nord); *(b)* **h. (tree),** micocoulier (occidental).

hackbut ['hækbʌt], *s. A.Arms:* haquebute *f.*

hackbuteer [hækbʌ'tiər], **hackbutter** ['hækbʌtər], *s. A.Mil:* haquebutier *m.*

hacker ['hækər], *s.* **1.** (*pers.*) piocheur *m.* **2.** *Tls:* hache *f*, pioche *f.*

hacking[1] ['hækiŋ], *a.* **h. cough,** toux sèche et pénible.

hacking[2], *s.* **1.** hachage *m*, hachement *m*; coups *mpl* de hache, de pioche; *Med:* (*in massage*) hachement; **h. knife,** couteau *m* à démastiquer; hachette *f* de vitrier. **2.** *Fb: etc:* coups de pied (sur le tibia).

hacking[3], *s.* promenade(s) *f* à cheval; **h. coat, jacket,** jaquette *f* de cheval.

hackle[1] ['hækl], *s.* **1.** *Tex:* peigne *m*, séran *m*, sérançoir *m*, regayoir *m*, drège *f*, échanvroir *m*. **2.** *(a) Orn:* plume *f* de cou ou de dos (des gallinacés); *pl.* **hackles,** camail *m*; *F:* (*of pers.*) **when his hackles are up,** quand il monte sur ses ergots; quand il lève la crête; **dog with its hackles up,** chien hérissé de colère; *(b) Mil:* plume (de bonnet à poil). **3.** *Fish:* mouche artificielle.

hackle[2], *v.tr. Tex:* peigner, sérancer, affiner, émoucheter (le lin, le chanvre); échanvrer, regayer (le chanvre).

hackler ['hæklər], *s. Tex:* peigneur, -euse, séranceur *m*; affineur, -euse.

hackling ['hækliŋ], *s.* peignage *m*, sérançage *m*, affinage *m*, émouchetage *m*; **h. machine,** peigneuse *f.*

hackly ['hækli], *a.* (*of rock, outline, etc.*) haché, dentelé, rugueux; **h. fracture,** cassure hachée, crochue, inégale.

hackmatack ['hækmətæk], *s. Bot:* mélèze *m* d'Amérique; épinette *f* rouge.

hackney[1] ['hækni], *s.* **1.** *(a)* cheval *m*, -aux, de louage; *(b)* cheval de route; bidet *m*; *(c)* (cheval) trotteur *m* (de course). **2.** *attrib.* **h. carriage,** (i) *A.Veh:* (*also* **h. coach**) voiture *f* de place, de louage; (ii) *Adm:* = taxi *m.*

hackney[2], *v.tr.* banaliser (un sujet, etc.).

hackneyed ['hæknid], *a.* (discours) rebattu, usé, banal; **h. phrase,** expression devenue banale; formule stéréotypée; cliché *m*.

hacksaw ['hæksɔ:], *s.* scie *f* à métaux.

hackwork ['hækwə:k], *s.* **1.** travail *m* d'écrivain à gages. **2.** travail (de plume) bâclé au jour le jour, à titre de gagne-pain; besogne *f* alimentaire.

haddock ['hædək], *s. Ich:* aiglefin *m*, eglefin *m*, aigrefin *m*; **Norway h.,** sébaste *m*, cherre *m*; *Cu:* **smoked h., finnan h.,** haddock (fumé).

hade[1] [heid], *s. Geol: Min:* pendage *m*, pente *f* (d'un filon, d'une faille); écart *m* de la verticale.

hade[2], *v.i. Geol: Min:* (*of shaft, vein, fault, etc.*) s'incliner (par rapport à la verticale).

Hades ['heidi:z], *s. Gr.Myth:* **1.** (*a*) Hadès *m*, les Enfers *m*, *Poet:* l'Averne *m*; (*b*) *F: O:* (*euphemism for hell*) **to send s.o. to H.,** envoyer dinguer qn; **what the H. do you think you're doing?** que diable faites-vous? **2.** *Pr.n.m.* Pluton.

hading ['heidiŋ], *s.* = HADE[1].

hadj [hædʒ], *s.* hadj *m* (pèlerinage de la Mecque).

hadji ['hædʒi], *s.* hadji *m*, hadj *m* (Musulman qui a fait le pèlerinage de la Mecque).

Hadrian ['heidriən], *Pr.n.m. Rom.Hist:* Adrien, Hadrien; **Hadrian's Wall,** le Mur d'Adrien.

hadrome ['hædroum], *s. Bot:* hadrome *m*.

Hadromerina ['hædroumə'rainə], *s.pl. Spong:* hadromérides *m*.

haemal ['hi:m(ə)l], *a. Physiol:* hémal, -aux.

haemangiectasia [hi:mandʒek'təsiə], **haemangiectasis** [hi:mændʒiek'teisis], *s. Med:* hémangiectasie *f*.

haemangioma [hi:mændʒi'oumə], *s. Med:* hémangiome *m*; **capillary, cavernous, h.,** hémangiome capillaire, caverneux.

haemangiomatosis [hi:'mændʒioumæ'tousis], *s. Med:* hémangiomatose *f*.

haemanthus [hi'mænθəs], *s. Bot:* haemanthus *m*.

haemarthrosis [hi:mɑ:'θrousis], *s. Med:* hémarthrose *f*.

haematemesis [hi:mətə'məsis], *s. Med:* hématémèse *f*.

haematic [hi'mætik], *a. Physiol:* hématique.

haematidrosis [hi:mæti'drousis], *s. Med:* hématidrose *f*.

haematimetry [hi:mæ'timitri], *s. Med:* hématimétrie *f*.

haematin(e) ['hi:mətin, -tain], *s. Ch: Physiol:* hématine *f*.

haematite ['hemətait, 'hi:-], *s. Miner:* hématite *f*; (fer) oligiste *m*; ferret *m* d'Espagne; **red h., earthy h.,** sanguine *f*; **brown h.,** hématite brune; ocre *f* jaune; terre *f* jaune; limonite *f*.

haemato- ['hi:mətou, hi:mə'tɔ], *comb.fm.* hémato-.

haematoblast ['hi:mətoublæst], *s. Physiol:* hématoblaste *m*.

haematocele ['hi:mətousi:l], *s. Med:* hématocèle *f*.

haematocolpos [hi:mətou'kɔlpɔs], *s. Med:* hématocolpos *m*.

haematocrit ['hi:mætoukrit], *s.* hématocrite *m*.

haematogenous [hi:mə'tɔdʒənəs], *a. Physiol:* hématogène.

haematography [hi:mə'tɔgrəfi], *s.* hématographie *f*.

haematolite [hi:'mætoulait], *s. Miner:* hématolite *f*.

haematologic(al) [hi:mætə'lɔdʒik(l)], *a. Med:* hématologique.

haematologist [hi:mə'tɔlədʒist], *s. Med:* hématologue *mf*.

haematology [hi:mə'tɔlədʒi], *s. Physiol:* hématologie *f*.

haematoma [hi:mə'toumə], *s. Med:* hématome *m*; **h. auri,** hématome auriculaire.

haematometra [hi:mə'tɔmitrə], *s. Med:* hématomètre *m*.

haematomyelia [hi:mətoumai'i:liə], *s. Med:* hématomyélie *f*.

haematopoiesis [hi:mətoupɔi'i:sis], *s. Med:* hématopoïèse *f*.

haematoporphyrin [hi:mətou'pɔ:fərin], *s. Bio-Ch:* hématoporphyrine *f*.

haematoscope ['hi:mətouskoup], *s. Med:* hématoscope *m*.

haematose ['hi:mətous], *a. Med:* hémateux.

haematosis [hi:mə'tousis], *s. Physiol:* hématose *f*.

haematoxylon [hi:mə'tɔksilɔn], *s. Bot:* haematoxylon *m*.

haematozoon, *pl.* **-zoa** [hi:mətou'zouɔn, -zouə], *s.* hématozoaire *m*.

haematuria [hi:mə'tjuriə], *s. Med:* hématurie *f*.

haemo- ['hi:mou], *comb.fm.* hémo-.

haemochromatosis [hi:moukroumə'tousis], *s. Med:* hémochromatose *f*.

haemoconcentration [hi:moukɔnsən'treiʃ(ə)n], *s. Med:* hémoconcentration *f*.

haemocyanin [hi:mou'saiənin], *s. Moll: etc:* hémocyanine *f*.

haemodiagnosis [hi:moudaiə'gnousis], *s. Med:* hémodiagnostic *m*.

haemodynamics [hi:moudai'næmiks], *s.pl.* (*usu. with sg. const.*) hémodynamique *f*.

haemogenia [hi:mou'dʒi:niə], *s. Med:* hémogénie *f*.

haemogenic [hi:mou'dʒenik], *a. Med:* hémogénique.

haemoglobin [hi:mou'gloubin], *s. Physiol:* hémoglobine *f*.

haemoglobinuria [hi:mougloubin'ju:riə], *s. Med:* hémoglobinurie *f*.

haemogram(me) ['hi:mougræm], *s. Med:* hémogramme *m*.

haemolysin [hi:'mɔlisin], *s. Ch: Med:* hémolysine *f*; hémotoxine *f*.

haemolysis [hi:'mɔlisis], *s. Med:* hémolyse *f*.

haemolytic [hi:mou'litik], *a. Med:* hémolytique.

haemopathy [hi:'mɔpəθi], *s. Med:* hémopathie *f*.

haemophile ['hi:moufil], *a. Med:* hémophile.

haemophilia [hi:mou'filiə], *s. Med:* hémophilie *f*.

haemophiliac [hi:mou'filiæk]. *Med:* **1.** *a.* (*also* **haemophilic**) hémophile. **2.** *s.* hémophile *mf*.

haemophthalmia [hi:mɔf'θælmiə], *s. Med:* hémophtalmie *f*.

Haemoprotidae [hi:mou'proutidi:], *s.pl. Ent:* hémoprotidés *m*.

haemoptysical [hi:mɔp'tizik(ə)l], *a. Med:* hémoptysique.

haemoptysis [hi:'mɔptisis], *s. Med:* hémoptysie *f*; crachement *m* de sang.

haemorrhage ['hemərid3], *s. Med:* hémorragie *f*; **h. of the lungs,** pneumorragie *f*; **cerebral h.,** hémorragie cérébrale; apoplexie *f*; **post-operative h.,** hémorragie post-opératoire.

haemorrhagic [hemə'rædʒik], *a. Med:* hémorragique; **h. diathesis,** hémophilie *f*.

haemorrhoidal ['hemərɔid(ə)l], *a. Med:* hémorroïdal, -aux; **h. tumour,** marisque *f*.

haemorrhoids ['hemərɔidz], *s.pl. Med:* hémorroïdes *f*.

haemostasia, haemostasis [hi:mou'steiziə, -'steisis], *s. Physiol:* hémostase *f*.

haemostat ['hi:məstæt], *s.* **1.** *Surg:* pince *f* hémostatique. **2.** *Med:* hémostatique *m*, antihémorragique *m*.

haemostatic [hi:mə'stætik], *a. Med:* hémostatique; *Surg:* **h. forceps,** pince *f* hémostatique.

haemothorax [hi:mou'θɔ:ræks], *s. Med:* hémothorax *m*.

haemotoxin [hi:mou'tɔksin], *s.* hémotoxine *f*.

hafnium ['hæfniəm], *s. Ch:* hafnium *m*.

haft[1] [hɑ:ft], *s.* manche *m*, poignée *f* (d'un poignard, d'un outil, etc.).

haft[2], *v.tr.* emmancher, mettre un manche à (un outil, etc.).

hafting ['hɑ:ftiŋ], *s.* emmanchement *m* (d'un outil, etc.).

hag[1] [hæg], *s.* **1.** (vieille) sorcière; *F:* **she's an old h.,** c'est la fée Carabosse, c'est une vieille fée, une vieille taupe, une vieille peau, une vieille roupie. **2.** *Ich:* gastrobranche *m* aveugle; myxine *f*.

hag[2], *v.tr.* (**hagged**) *A: Dial:* fatiguer, éreinter.

hag[3], *s. Scot:* (**moss**) **h.,** fondrière *f*; tourbière défoncée.

Hagar ['heigɑ:r], *Pr.n.f. B:* Agar.

hagberry ['hægbəri], *s. Bot:* cerisier *m* à grappes.

hagfish ['hægfiʃ], *s. Ich:* myxine *f*, gastrobranche *m* aveugle.

haggard ['hægəd]. **1.** *a.* (*a*) hâve; (visage) décharné; (*b*) (visage) égaré, hagard, décomposé, défait, altéré. **2.** *a. & s. Ven:* (faucon) hagard (*m*).

haggis ['hægis], *s. Cu:* estomac *m* de mouton bourré d'un hachis d'abats et de farine d'avoine, le tout très épicé (mets national écossais).

haggish ['hægiʃ], *a.* (femme) vieille et hideuse; (apparence) de vieille sorcière; *F:* **she looks pretty h.,** elle a l'air bien moche.

haggle ['hægl], *v.i.* marchander, *F:* lésiner, liarder, chipoter, chicoter; **to h. about, over, the price of sth.,** chicaner sur le prix de qch., marchander qch.; **I didn't h. about the price,** je n'ai pas débattu le prix.

haggler ['hæglər], *s.* marchandeur, -euse, *F:* liardeur, -euse.

haggling ['hægliŋ], *s.* marchandage *m*.

Hagiographa (the) [ðəhægi'ɔgrəfə], *s.pl. B.Lit:* les livres *m* hagiographes.

hagiographal [hægi'ɔgrəf(ə)l], *a.* hagiographe.

hagiographer [hægi'ɔgrəfər], *s.* hagiographe *mf*.

hagiographic(al) [hægiə'græfik(l)], *a.* hagiographe, hagiographique.

hagiography [hægi'ɔgrəfi], *s.* hagiographie *f*.

hagiolatry [hægi'ɔlətri], *s.* hagiolâtrie *f*.

hagiologic(al) [hægiə'lɔdʒik(l)], *a.* hagiologique.

hagiologist [hægi'ɔlədʒist], *s.* hagiographe *mf*.

hagiology [hægi'ɔlədʒi], *s.* hagiologie *f*.

hagridden ['hægridn], *a.* (*a*) tourmenté de cauchemars; en proie aux cauchemars; (*b*) obsédé (par une idée, etc.), (*c*) (*of man*) tourmenté par sa femme.

hagtaper ['hægteipər], *s. Bot: F:* bouillon-blanc *m*, *pl.* bouillons-blancs.

Hague (the) [ðə'heig], *Pr.n. Geog:* la Haye; *Hist:* **the H. Conventions,** les Actes *m*, les Conventions *f*, de la Haye; **the H. Conference,** la Conférence de la Haye.

hah [hɑ:], *int.* ah! ha!

ha-ha[1] ['hɑ:'hɑ:], *int.* ha, ha!

ha-ha[2], *s.* saut *m* de loup; haha *m*.

hai(c)k [haik], *s.* haïk *m*.

haidingerite [hai'diŋgərait], *s. Miner:* haidingérite *f*.

hail[1] [heil], *s.* **1.** grêle *f*. **2.** grêle, volée *f* (de coups, de pierres).

hail[2], *v.i. & tr.* grêler; (*a*) *impers.* **it's hailing,** il grêle; (*b*) **bullets were hailing down on us,** les balles nous pleuvaient dru comme grêle; **to h. down curses, blows, on s.o.,** faire pleuvoir des malédictions, des coups, sur qn.

hail[3]. **1.** *int.* salut! *R.C.Ch:* **hail, Mary, full of grace!** je vous salue, Marie, pleine de grâce! *s.* **the H. Mary,** l'Ave Maria *m inv*, la salutation angélique. **2.** *s.* appel *m*; **within h.,** à portée de (la) voix; **keep within h.,** ne vous éloignez pas.

hail[4]. **1.** *v.tr.* (*a*) saluer (qn); **to h. s.o. (as) king,** acclamer, saluer, qn roi; **his appearance was hailed with long applause,** son entrée fut saluée par de longs applaudissements; (*b*) héler (qn, un navire); *Nau:* arraisonner (un navire); **to h. a taxi,** (i) appeler, héler, un taxi (qui passe); (ii) faire avancer un taxi; **within hailing distance,** à portée de (la) voix. **2.** *v.i. Nau:* (*of ship*) **to h. from a port,** (i) dépendre d'un port; (ii) venir d'un port; **ship hailing from London,** (i) navire *m* ayant Londres pour port d'attache; **where does he h. from?** d'où vient-il? d'où est-il originaire?

hail-fellow-well-met ['heilfelouwel'met], *a.* **to be h.-f.-w.-m. with everyone,** traiter les gens de pair à compagnon; être à tu et à toi avec tout le monde; se lier avec Pierre et Paul.

hailing ['heiliŋ], *a.* arraisonneur; *Nau:* **the h. ship,** le navire arraisonneur.

hailstone ['heilstoun], *s.* grêlon *m*.

hailstorm ['heilstɔ:m], *s.* abat *m* de grêle; orage accompagné de grêle.

Hainault ['heinɔlt], *Pr.n. Geog: Hist:* le Hainaut.

hair[1] ['hɛər], *s.* **1.** (*of human head*) (*a*) cheveu *m*; **exact to a h.,** exact à un cheveu près, (*in metal*) **h. crack,** gerçure *f*; *Typ:* **h. lead** [led], interligne *f* très mince; **h. space,** espace *f* d'un point; **h. stroke,** (i) empattement *m* (de lettre); (ii) (*in handwriting*) délié *m*; **to split hairs,** couper les cheveux en quatre; *F:* **to have s.o. by the short hairs,** avoir qn à sa merci; (*b*) *coll.* **the h.,** les cheveux, la chevelure; **long fair h.,** de longs cheveux blonds; **magnificent head of h.,** chevelure luxuriante; **h. tonic, lotion,** lotion *f* capillaire; **h. cream,** crème coiffante; **h. oil,** brillantine *f*; **h. spray,** laque *f*; **h. band,** bandeau *m*; **h. grip,** pince *f* (à cheveux); **to comb one's h.,** se peigner; **to curl one's h.,** se friser; **to have, get, one's h. cut,** se faire couper les cheveux; **to do one's h.,** se coiffer, se peigner; s'arranger les cheveux; **to wash one's h.,** se laver la tête; **to set one's h.,** se faire une mise en plis; **to have one's h. set,** *F:* **done,** se faire faire une mise en plis; **back h.,** cheveux de l'arrière de la tête, *esp.* chignon *m*; **to put up one's h., to put one's h. up,** se faire un chignon, se coiffer en chignon; **to let down one's h.,** défaire, laisser tomber, ses cheveux; *F:* **to let one's h. down,** (i) se mettre à son aise; (ii) se raconter (réciproquement) ses secrets intimes; (iii) s'amuser follement; **to tear one's h.,** s'arracher les cheveux; **to tear each other's h.,** se prendre aux cheveux; (*of women*) se crêper le chignon; **it was enough to make your h. stand on end,** c'était à faire dresser les cheveux (sur la tête); **to lose one's h.,** (i) perdre ses cheveux; *F:* se déplumer; (ii) *F:* se mettre en rage; se fâcher tout rouge; *F:* **keep your h. on!** calmez-vous! ne t'emballe pas! t'en fais pas! *F:* **to get in s.o.'s h.,** (i) taper sur les nerfs à qn; (ii) enquiquiner qn. **2.** (*a*) (*of human face & body, animals, plants*) (*coll. sg. more usual than pl.*) poil *m*; **to remove s.o.'s superfluous h.,** épiler, dépiler, qn; **removal of superfluous h.,** épilation *f*, dépilation *f*; (*b*) *coll.* (*of animal*) poil, pelage; **the cat was losing, shedding, its h.,** le chat perdait ses poils; **to stroke a cat against the h.,** caresser un chat à contre-poil, à rebrousse-poil; (*c*) crin *m* (de cheval); soie *f* (de porc); *Furn: etc:* **curled h.,** crin frisé; **h. mattress,** matelas *m* de crin; **h. shirt,** haire *f*, cilice *m*; **h. sieve,** tamis *m* de crin; *Mus:* **bow h.,** mèche *f* d'archet. **3.** *Opt:* cheveu, fil *m* (de réticule d'appareil de visée); **cross hairs,** réticule *m*. **4.** (*press cloth*) étendelle *f* (de pressoir à huile).

hair[2], *v.tr.* **1.** *Mus:* garnir (un archet) de sa mèche. **2.** *Tan:* dépiler (une peau).

hairball ['hɛəbɔ:l], *s.* **1.** trichobézoard *m*. **2.** phytobézoard *m*.

hair-brained ['hɛəbreind], *a.* = HAREBRAINED.

hairbreadth ['hɛəbredθ]. **1.** *s.* = HAIR'S BREADTH. **2.** *attrib.* **to have a h. escape,** l'échapper belle; échapper comme par miracle.

hairbrush ['hɛəbrʌʃ], *s.* brosse *f* à cheveux.

haircloth ['hɛəklɔθ], *s.* **1.** *A:* (*for penitents*) cilice *m*, haire *f*. **2.** (*for furniture*) tissu *m* de crin; étamine *f* de crin; (*for* *friction*) lanière *f* en crin; **cow h., coarse h.,** thibaude *f*.

haircut ['hɛəkʌt], *s.* (*a*) taille *f* de cheveux; coupe *f* de cheveux; **to have a h.,** se faire couper, se faire tailler, les cheveux; (*b*) (style *m* de) coiffure *f*.

hairdo ['hɛədu:], *s. F:* coiffure *f*.

hairdresser ['hɛədresər], *s.* coiffeur, -euse.

hairdressing ['hɛədresiŋ], *s.* coiffure *f*; **style of h.,** coiffure.

hairdrier, hairdryer ['hɛədraiər], *s.* (casque *m*) sèche-cheveux *m inv.*

haired ['hɛəd], *a.* (*with sb. or adj. prefixed, e.g.*) **long-h., black-h.,** (*of pers.*) aux cheveux longs, noirs; (*of animal*) à long pelage, à pelage noir.

hair grass ['hɛəgrɑ:s], *s. Bot:* canche *f*.

hairiness ['hɛərinis], *s.* **1.** aspect *m* hirsute (du corps); épaisseur *f*, longueur *f* de poil (d'un chimpanzé, etc.). **2.** *Bot:* pubescence *f*.

hairless ['hɛəlis], *a.* (*of pers.*) sans cheveux; chauve; (*of animal*) sans poils; **h. face,** visage *m* glabre, nu; **h. horse,** cheval nu; **h. skin, hide,** peau pelée.

hairlike ['hɛəlaik], *a.* (fil *m*, plumage *m*) criniforme, qui ressemble à un cheveu; aussi mince qu'un cheveu.

hairline ['hɛəlain], *s.* **1.** délié *m*; **h. distinction,** distinction subtile; **to make a h. distinction,** couper un cheveu en quatre. **2.** *Typ:* **h. type,** capillaires *fpl.* **3.** *Tchn:* (*in metal*) gerçure *f*. **4.** *Opt:* cheveu *m*, fil *m* (de réticule d'appareil de visée); *pl.* **hairlines,** réticule *m*. **5.** naissance *f* des cheveux; **his h. is receding,** il commence à se déplumer.

hairnet ['hɛənet], *s.* filet *m* (pour cheveux).

hairpad ['hɛəpæd], *s.* crépon *m*.

hairpiece ['hɛəpi:s], *s.* mèche *f* postiche.

hairpin ['hɛəpin], *s.* épingle *f* à cheveux; (*on road*) **h. bend,** lacet *m*; virage *m* en épingle à cheveux; **there is a dangerous h. bend at . . .,** la route fait un lacet dangereux à. . . .

hair-raiser ['hɛəreizər], *s.* histoire *f*, pièce *f* de théâtre, etc., à gros effets à vous faire dresser les cheveux sur la tête.

hair-raising ['hɛəreiziŋ], *a.* effrayant; **h.-r. adventure,** aventure *f* effroyable; **h.-r. story,** récit *m* horrifique, à vous faire dresser les cheveux sur la tête.

hair's breadth ['hɛəzbredθ], *s.* épaisseur *f* d'un cheveu; **he escaped death by a h. b.,** il a été à deux doigts de la mort, il a échappé à la mort comme par miracle, il a frisé la mort; **accurate to a h. b.,** d'une exactitude rigoureuse; **he didn't depart by a h. b. from his instructions,** il ne s'est pas écarté d'un iota de ses instructions; **to be within a h. b. of disaster,** être à un cheveu de la ruine.

hair-splitter ['hɛəsplitər], *s.* ergoteur *m*, chicaneur *m*.

hair-splitting ['hɛəsplitiŋ]. **1.** *s.* ergotage *m*, ergoterie *f*; chicane(rie) *f*; distinctions subtiles; subtilités *f*. **2.** *a.* (*of argument, etc.*) (trop) subtil.

hairspring ['hɛəspriŋ], *s. Clockm:* ressort spiral, spiral *m* (d'une montre).

hairstreak ['hɛəstri:k], *s. Ent:* **h. butterfly,** thecla *m*, thècle *m*; **the h. butterflies,** les théclines *m*.

hairstyle ['hɛəstail], *s.* coiffure *f*.

hairtail ['hɛəteil], *s. Ich:* ceinture *f* d'argent, trichiure *m*.

hair-trigger ['hɛətrigər], *s.* (*a*) *Sm.a:* déclic *m* (de détente); **h.-t. lock,** platine *f* à double détente; (*b*) *attrib.* nerveux; **h.-t. reaction,** réflexe instantané; **h.-t. situation,** situation *f* d'un équilibre délicat.

hairwash ['hɛəwɔʃ], *s. F:* shampooing *m*.

hairworm ['hɛəwə:m], *s. Ann:* **1.** crin *m* de fontaine, de mer. **2.** ver *m* de Guinée, filaire *f*.

hairy ['hɛəri], *a.* **1.** (*a*) (*of hands, chest, etc.*) velu, poilu; (*of scalp*) chevelu; (*of pers.*) hirsute; (*b*) *P:* périlleux, épineux, difficultueux. **2.** (*a*) *Bot:* velu; **h.-stemmed,** à tige velue; trichocaule; (*b*) *Orn:* **h. woodpecker,** pic chevelu.

Haiti ['heiti, 'hai-]. *Pr.n. Geog:* Haïti *m or f*; **to live in H.,** vivre en Haïti.

Haitian ['heitiən, 'hai-, heiʃ(ə)n], *Geog:* (*a*) *a.* haïtien; (*b*) *s.* Haïtien, -ienne.

hajji ['hædʒi], *s.* = HADJI.

hake [heik], *s. Ich:* merluche *f*, *F:* colin *m*.

Hal [hæl]. *Pr.n.m.* (*dim. of Henry*) *Hist: F:* **Prince H.,** le prince Henri.

halated [hæ'leitid, hə-], *a. Phot:* (cliché *m*) qui présente du halo.

halation [hæ'leiʃ(ə)n, hə-], *s. Phot:* halo *m*, irradiation *f*, auréole *f*; **anti-h.,** antihalo.

halberd ['hælbəd], **halbert** ['hælbət], *s. Mil: A:* hallebarde *f*.

halberdier [hælbə'di:ər], *s.m.* hallebardier.

halcyon ['hælsiən]. **1.** *s.* (*a*) *Myth:* alcyon *m*; (*b*) *Orn:* halcyon *m*; martin-chasseur *m*, *pl.* martins-chasseurs. **2.** *attrib.* **h. days,** jours alcyoniens; jours de calme, de bonheur paisible.

hale[1] [heil], *a.* (vieillard) vigoureux, robuste, encore gaillard; **to be h. and hearty,** être frais et gaillard; avoir bon pied bon œil; être solide; être d'une santé florissante; se porter comme un charme.

hale[2], *v.tr. A:* (*haul*) haler.

halesia [hæ'li:ziə], *s. Bot:* halesia *m*.

half, *pl.* **halves** [hɑ:f, hɑ:vz]. **1.** *s.* (*a*) moitié *f*; **h. (of) his men,** la moitié de ses hommes; **a good h., fully a h., of his employees are ill,** une bonne moitié de ses employés est malade, sont malades; **what is h. (of) twelve?** quelle est la moitié de douze? **she has lost h. her money,** elle a perdu la moitié de son argent; **I have forgotten h. of it,** j'en ai oublié la moitié; **I can do it in h. the time,** je peux le faire en deux fois moins de temps; **h. the time he isn't there,** la moitié du temps, il n'est pas là; **more than h. the time,** les trois quarts du temps; **the first h. of the year,** la première moitié de l'année; **to fold, cut, sth. in h., in halves,** plier, couper, qch. en deux; **divided into two halves,** partagé en deux moitiés; **to go halves with s.o.,** partager avec qn; se mettre de moitié, de compte à demi, avec qn; **he offered to go halves with me,** il a proposé de faire de moitié avec moi; **to go halves in the expense of hiring a car,** louer une voiture à mi-frais; **to cry halves,** réclamer sa part; demander à partager; **bigger by h.,** plus grand de moitié; **too much by h.,** trop de moitié; *F:* **he is too clever by h.,** il est beaucoup trop malin; **reduced by h.,** réduit de moitié; **to do things by halves,** faire les choses à moitié, à demi; (*b*) demi *m*, demie *f*; **two halves,** (i) deux demis; (ii) *Rail: etc:* deux demi-places; (iii) deux bières, = deux demis; **three and a h.,** trois et demi; **I waited for two hours and a h., two and a h. hours,** j'ai attendu pendant deux heures et demie (*cp.* 3 (*b*)); (*c*) (*pers.*) *F:* **my better h.,** ma (chère) moitié; **where's your other h.?** où est ton alter ego? **the other h.,** les autres; (*d*) *Rail:* (*of ticket*) **outward h., return h.,** coupon *m* d'aller; coupon de retour; (*e*) *F:* (*of drink*) **how about the other h.?** on remet ça? *Fb: etc.* (i) **the first h. (of the game),** la première mi-temps; **the second h.,** la seconde mi-temps; la reprise; **in the second h.,** en seconde mi-temps; (ii) **in our h. (of the ground),** dans notre camp; (iii) (*pers.*) demi; **wing halves,** demis aile; **scrum h.,** demi de mêlée; **fly h., stand-off h.,** demi d'ouverture; **centre h.,** demi centre; (*f*) *Sch:* trimestre *m*; (*g*) *Com: F:* **have you the odd h.?** est-ce que vous auriez un demi-penny? **2.** *a.* demi; (*a*) **h. an hour,** une demi-heure; **the interval sometimes runs to as much as h. an hour,** l'entr'acte pousse parfois jusqu'à la demi-heure; *F:* **go and put on your hat and don't be h. an hour about it!** allez mettre votre chapeau et que ça ne traîne pas! **h. a second,** une demi-seconde; **I'll be with you in h. a second,** je reviens en moins d'un instant, en moins de rien; **a h. dollar, h. a dollar,** un demi-dollar, 50 cents; *A:* **it costs h. a crown,** *F:* **h. a dollar,** cela coûte deux shillings six pence; **h. a dozen,** une demi-douzaine; *F:* **to be in h. a dozen places at once,** se multiplier; **h. a cup,** une demi-tasse; *Arb:* **h. standard,** demi-tige *f*; *Danc:* **on h. toe,** sur (la) demi-pointe; *Atom.Ph:* **h. thickness,** demi-épaisseur *f*; *Mth:* **h. line, h. ray,** demi-droite *f*; *El:* **h. cell,** demi-cellule *f*; **at h. price,** à moitié prix; **h.-partition,** cloison *f* à mi-hauteur; *Mil:* **h. right,** demi-à-droite *m*; **h. left,** demi-à-gauche *m*; **h. day,** demi-journée *f*; **I have a h. day tomorrow,** demain je travaille le matin, j'ai un après-midi de congé; **to work h. days,** faire des demi-journées, travailler à la demi-journée; **h. time,** (i) *Adm: Ind: etc:* travail *m* à mi-temps, à la demi-journée; (ii) *Fb: etc:* (la) mi-temps; **h.-time worker,** travailleur, -euse, à mi-temps, à la demi-journée; **to work h. time,** travailler à mi-temps, à la demi-journée; *Sch: A:* **the h.-time system,** régime sous lequel, dans les villes industrielles, l'enfant passait une moitié de la journée à l'école, et l'autre à l'usine ou à la fabrique; **on h. profits,** de compte à demi; *St.Exch:* **h. commission,** remise *f*; **h. commission man,** remisier *m*; **h. one thing and h. another,** moitié figue, moitié raisin; mélangé; (*b*) (*rendered by* mi-); **h. quadruped, h. fish,** mi-quadrupède, mi-poisson. **3.** *adv.* à moitié, à demi; mi; (*a*) **he only h. understands,** il ne comprend qu'à moitié; **she h. got up,** elle se releva à demi; **he h. opened, h. closed, the door,** il entrouvrit, entreferma, la porte; **the door h. opened,** la porte s'entrouvrit; **h.-closed,** entreclos; **h.-open,** entrouvert; **turn h. right, h. left,** tournez légèrement à droite, à gauche; **the bottle was h. full, h. empty,** la bouteille était à moitié; **we h. emptied the bottle,** nous avons vidé la moitié de la bouteille; **h. dressed,** à moitié vêtu; à demi vêtu; **h. naked,** à moitié nu; **he was h. undressed,** il était à demi dévêtu; **h. asleep,** à moitié endormi; **h. dead, (only) h. alive,** à moitié mort; **more than h. dead,** aux trois quarts mort; **h. dead with fright,** plus mort que vif; **women h. dead with hunger,** femmes demi-mortes de faim; **h. done,** (i) (ouvrage, etc.) à moitié fait; (ii) (rôti, etc.) à moitié cuit; **h. finished,** (travail) (i) à moitié fait, (ii) bâclé, imparfait; **h. frozen,** à moitié gelé; *F:* **more than h. frozen,** aux trois quarts gelé; **to be leaning h. out of the window,** être penché à mi-corps à la fenêtre; **h. laughing, h. crying,** moitié riant, moitié pleurant; **dress h. black and h. white,** robe mi-partie de blanc et de noir; **to do sth. h. willingly, h. under compulsion,** faire qch. mi de gré mi de force; **only h. joking,** ne plaisantant qu'à moitié; **I was h. afraid that you wouldn't come,** j'avais quelque crainte que vous ne veniez pas; **my leave is h. up,** voilà déjà la moitié de mon congé de passé; *F:* **it isn't h. bad,** ce n'est pas mauvais du tout; c'est très mangeable, très buvable; ce n'est pas si mal; *P:* (*intensive use*) **she isn't h. smart!** elle est rien chic! **he isn't h. a liar!** comme menteur il est un peu là! **he didn't h. swear,** ce qu'il a juré! **it isn't h. cold!** il fait rien froid! **there wasn't h. a crowd!** qu'est-ce qu'il y avait comme populo! **not h.!** un peu! tu parles! beaucoup! et comment! (*b*) **it is h. past two,** *F:* **h. two,** il est deux heures et demie; **h. past twelve,** midi, minuit, et demi; **is it six o'clock?—it's h. past,** est-il six heures?—il est la demie; (*c*) **h. as big,** moitié aussi grand; **he is not h. so formidable as people think,** il n'est pas de moitié si redoutable qu'on le pense; **I got h. as much,** j'en ai reçu la moitié autant, la moitié moins; **he gets h. as much money as you,** il reçoit moitié moins d'argent que vous; **there are h. as many people,** il y a moitié moins de monde; **the station is h. as far,** (i) la gare est moitié aussi loin; (ii) la gare est à mi-chemin; **h. as big again,** plus grand de moitié; **he is h. as old again as I am,** il est de moitié plus âgé que moi; **I got h. as much again as you,** j'en ai reçu (la) moitié plus que vous; **the station is h. as far again,** la gare est moitié plus loin.

halfa ['hælfə], *s. Bot:* alfa *m*.

half-and-half ['hɑ:fənd'hɑ:f]. **1.** (*a*) *adv.* moitié l'un moitié l'autre, *F:* moitié-moitié; (*b*) *a. & adv.* **h.-and-h. mixture of oil and vinegar,** mélange *m* d'huile et de vinaigre à doses égales; **how shall I mix them?—h.-and-h.,** comment faut-il les mélanger?—à doses égales; **how do you like your coffee?—h.-and-h.,** comment prenez-vous le café?—moitié café, moitié lait. **2.** *s.* mélange *m* *esp. A:* de bière et de porter.

half axle ['hɑ:f'æksl], *s. Veh:* demi-essieu *m*, *pl.* demi-essieux.

halfback ['hɑ:fbæk], *s. Fb:* demi-arrière *m*, *pl.* demi-arrières; demi *m*.

half-baked ['hɑ:f'beikt], *a.* **1.** (*of meat, etc.*) à moitié cuit. **2.** *F:* (*a*) (*of pers.*) (i) inexpérimenté, mal dégrossi, mal léché; (ii) niais; (*b*) insuffisamment étudié; incomplet; **h.-b. measures,** mesures qui n'ont pas été mises au point; **h.-b. scheme,** projet bâclé, qui ne tient pas debout.

halfbeak ['hɑ:fbi:k], *s. Ich:* demi-bec *m*, *pl.* demi-becs.

half-beam ['hɑ:fbi:m], *s. N.Arch:* barrotin *m*.

half binding ['hɑ:f'baindiŋ], *s. Bookb:* demi-reliure *f*, *pl.* demi-reliures, à (petits) coins.

half-blood ['hɑ:fblʌd], *s.* **1.** parenté *f* d'un seul côté. **2.** (*a*) parent, -ente, d'un seul côté; (*b*) = HALFBREED.

half-blooded ['hɑ:f'blʌdid], *a.* = HALF-BRED.

half boot ['hɑ:fbu:t], *s.* demi-botte *f*, *pl.* demi-bottes.

half-bound ['hɑ:f'baund], *a. Bookb:* en demi-reliure à (petits) coins.

half-bred ['hɑ:f'bred], *a. & s.* **1.** métis, -isse. **2. h.-b. (horse),** cheval *m* demi-sang, demi-sang *m inv.*

halfbreed ['hɑ:fbri:d], *s.* **1.** métis, -isse. **2.** cheval *m* demi-sang, *pl.* chevaux demi-sang.

half brother ['hɑ:fbrʌðər], *s.m.* demi-frère, *pl.* demi-frères; (*through mother*) frère utérin, de mère; (*through father*) frère consanguin, de père.

half cadence ['hɑ:f'keidəns], *s. Mus:* demi-cadence *f*, *pl.* demi-cadences.

halfcaste ['hɑ:fkɑ:st], *a. & s.* métis, -isse.

half-circle ['hɑ:f'sə:kl], *s.* demi-cercle *m*, *pl.* demi-cercles; *Nau:* **to turn a h.-c.,** faire demi-tour; *Fenc:* **h.-c. parry,** demi-cercle.

halfcloth ['hɑ:f'klɔθ], *s. Bookb:* mi-toile *f* à coins; cartonnage *m* bradel.

half cock[1] ['hɑ:f'kɔk], *s. Sm.a.* **(gun) at h. c.,** (fusil etc.) au demi-armé; **h.-c. notch,** cran *m* de repos; *F:* **to go off at h. c.,** mal partir, mal démarrer.

half-cock[2], *v.tr.* mettre (un fusil, etc.) au demi-armé.

half-cocked ['hɑ:f'kɔkt], *a.* (fusil) au demi-armé; *U.S: F:* **to go off h.-c.,** agir avec trop de hâte.

halfcrown ['hɑ:f'kraun], *s. Num:* demi-couronne *f*; **three new halfcrowns,** trois demi-couronnes neuves.

half deck ['hɑ:fdek], *s.* **1.** *Nau:* demi-pont *m*, *pl.* demi-ponts; demi-tillac *m*, *pl.* demi-tillacs. **2.** *Moll:* crepidula *f*.

half-decked ['hɑ:f'dekt], *a.* (bateau) à moitié couvert, mi-ponté.

half dome ['hɑ:fdoum], *s. Arch:* cul-de-four *m*, *pl.* culs-de-four.

half dozen ['hɑ:f'dʌzn], *s.* demi-douzaine *f*, *pl.* demi-douzaines.

half-duplex ['hɑ:f'dju:pleks], *a. Cmptr:* semi-duplex; **h.-d. operation,** exploitation *f* en semi-duplex.

half floor ['hɑːfflɔːr], *s. N.Arch:* demi-varangue *f, pl.* demi-varangues.
half frame ['hɑːffreim], *s. N.Arch:* demi-membrure *f, pl.* demi-membrures.
halfhearted ['hɑːf'hɑːtid], *a.* tiède, sans enthousiasme; (effort) timide, hésitant.
halfheartedly ['hɑːf'hɑːtidli], *adv.* sans enthousiasme, sans entrain; **to do sth. h.,** montrer peu d'empressement à faire qch.; **he agreed h.,** il dit oui du bout des lèvres.
halfheartedness ['hɑːf'hɑːtidnis], *s.* tiédeur *f,* manque *m* d'enthousiasme.
half hitch ['hɑːfhitʃ], *s. Nau:* (*knot*) demi-clef *f, pl.* demi-clefs.
half holiday ['hɑːf'hɔlidei], *s.* après-midi *m or f* de congé.
half hose ['hɑːf'houz], *s. Com:* chaussettes *fpl* (d'hommes), demi-bas *m inv.*
half hour ['hɑːf'auər], *s.* demi-heure *f, pl.* demi-heures; **clock that strikes the half hours,** pendule *f* qui sonne les demies *f*; **the h. h. is striking,** la demie sonne; **a spoonful to be taken every h. h.,** prendre une cuillerée de demi-heure en demi-heure, toutes les demi-heures.
half-hourly ['hɑːf'auəli]. **1.** *adv.* toutes les demi-heures; de demi-heure en demi-heure. **2.** *a.* de toutes les demi-heures.
half landing ['hɑːflændiŋ], *s. Arch:* demi-palier *m, pl.* demi-paliers.
half-lap(ped) ['hɑːflæp(t)], *a. Carp:* **h.-l. joint,** *s.* **half-lap,** assemblage *m* à mi-bois.
half-leather ['hɑːf'leðər], *s. Bookb:* demi-reliure *f, pl.* demi-reliures, à (petits) coins.
half-length ['hɑːf'leŋθ], *s.* demi-longueur *f, pl.* demi-longueurs; *attrib.* **h.-l. portrait,** portrait *m* en buste; *Phon:* **h.-l. sign,** demi-longueur.
half-life ['hɑːflaif], *s. Atom.Ph:* demi-vie *f* (d'un isotope, etc.), *pl.* demi-vies; **h.-l. period,** période *f* de demi-valeur; **biological h.-l.,** demi-vie biologique; **effective h.-l.,** demi-vie effective, résultante.
half light ['hɑːf'lait], *s.* demi-jour *m, pl.* demi-jours; pénombre *f.*
half-lined ['hɑːf'laind], *a.* (*of clothes*) doublé mi-corps.
half mast[1] ['hɑːf'mɑːst], *s. in the adv. phr.* **at h. m., h. m. high,** à mi-mât; **flag at h. m.,** pavillon *m* en berne.
half-mast[2], *v.tr.* mettre (un pavillon) en berne, à mi-mât.
half measure ['hɑːf'meʒər], *s.* demi-mesure *f, pl.* demi-mesures; **half measures are no use,** les demi-mesures ne servent à rien, il faut trancher dans le vif; *F:* **there are no half measures with him,** avec lui il n'y a pas de demi-mesure.
half-monthly ['hɑːf'mʌnθli], *a.* semi-mensuel.
half moon ['hɑːf'muːn], *s.* **1.** demi-lune *f, pl.* demi-lunes. **2.** lunule *f* (des ongles).
half-mourning ['hɑːf'mɔːniŋ], *s.* demi-deuil *m, pl.* demi-deuils.
half Nelson ['hɑːf'nelsn], *s. Wr:* simple prise *f* de tête à terre; **to put a h. N. on s.o.,** (i) porter une simple prise de tête à terre à qn; (ii) *F:* paralyser les efforts de qn; tenir qn à sa merci.
half-note ['hɑːfnout], *s. Mus:* blanche *f.*
half-pace ['hɑːf'peis], *s.* **1.** *Mil:* (*when changing step*) contre-pas *m inv.* **2.** *Const: Arch:* demi-palier *m, pl.* demi-paliers; palier *m* de repos.
half pay ['hɑːf'pei], *s.* demi-solde *f*; solde *f* de non-activité; **on h. p.,** en demi-solde, en disponibilité; **h.-p. officer,** officier *m* en disponibilité, en demi-solde; *F:* demi-solde *m inv*; **to put an officer on h. p.,** mettre un officier en non-activité.
halfpenny ['heipni, 'hɑːfpeni], *s.* demi-penny *m*; *F:* = sou *m.* **1.** (*pl.* **halfpence,** *F:* **ha'pence** ['heipəns]) **it will cost you three halfpence,** cela vous coûtera trois sous; *F:* **he is not a h. the worse for it,** il n'en a pas souffert le moindre mal. **2.** (*pl.* **halfpennies**) pièce *f* d'un sou; **he gave me the change in halfpennies,** il m'a rendu la monnaie en petites pièces; *F:* **bad h.,** vaurien *m.*
halfpennyworth ['heip(ə)niwəːθ, *F:* 'heipəθ], *s. A:* **to buy a h. of bread,** acheter (pour) un sou de pain.
half roll ['hɑːf'roul], *s. Av:* demi-tonneau, *pl.* demi-tonneaux.
half round ['hɑːf'raund]. **1.** *a.* demi-rond; demi-circulaire; *Tls:* **h.-r. file,** demi-ronde *f, pl.* demi-rondes. **2.** *s.* demi-cercle *m, pl.* demi-cercles.
half-seas-over ['hɑːfsiːz'ouvər], *a. F:* **to be h.-s.-o.,** être gris, ivre, soûl; avoir du vent dans les voiles.
halfshaft ['hɑːfʃɑːft], *s. Aut:* demi-arbre *m, pl.* demi-arbres.
half sister ['hɑːfsistər], *s.f.* demi-sœur, *pl.* demi sœurs; (*through the father*) sœur consanguine, de père; (*through the mother*) sœur utérine, de mère.
half sovereign ['hɑːf'sɔvrin], *s. Num: A:* demi-souverain *m, pl.* demi-souverains.
half staff ['hɑːfstɑːf], *s. & v.tr. U.S:* = HALF MAST[1,2].
half-stuff ['hɑːfstʌf], *s. Paperm:* défilé *m.*
half term ['hɑːf'təːm], *s. Sch:* congé *m* de mi-trimestre.
half tide ['hɑːf'taid], *s. Nau:* mi-marée *f*; **h.-t. basin,** bassin *m* de, accessible à, mi-marée.
half-timbered ['hɑːf'timbəd], *a.* **h.-t. house,** maison *f* en colombage, à poutres apparentes.
half timbering ['hɑːf'timbəriŋ], *s.* colombage *m.*
halftimer ['hɑːf'taimər], *s.* **1.** employé, -ée, (qui travaille) à mi-temps, à la demi-journée. **2.** *Sch: A:* écolier, -ière, qui partageait sa journée entre l'école et la fabrique ou l'atelier.
half-title ['hɑːf'taitl], *s. Typ:* faux titre *m*; avant-titre *m* (d'un livre), *pl.* avant-titres.
half-tone ['hɑːf'toun], *s.* **1.** *Art:* demi-teinte *f, pl.* demi-teintes; *Phot.Engr:* similigravure (tramée); *F:* simili *m*; **h.-t. block,** *F:* simili; **h.-t. engraver,** similiste *m*; **h.-t. work,** gravure *f* en relief, en simili; **h.-t. reproduction,** reproduction *f* photographique; phototypographie *f.* **2.** *Mus:* demi-ton *m, pl.* demi-tons.
halftrack ['hɑːftræk], *s. Veh:* (auto)chenille *f,* half-track *m*; **h.-t. (vehicle),** (véhicule) semi-chenillé, autochenille, half-track.
half value ['hɑːf'væljuː], *s.* **1.** *Mth:* demi-valeur *f, pl.* demi-valeurs; valeur moyenne. **2.** *Atom.Ph:* demi-atténuation *f, pl.* demi-atténuations; **h.-v. layer,** couche *f* de demi-atténuation.
half volley ['hɑːf'vɔli], *s. Ten:* demi-volée *f, pl.* demi-volées.
half watt ['hɑːf'wɔt], *s. El:* demi-watt *m, pl.* demi-watts; **h.-w. lamp,** lampe *f* demi-watt *inv,* demi-watt *f.*
half wave ['hɑːf'weiv], *s. Ph:* (i) demi-onde *f, pl.* demi-ondes; (ii) demi-alternance *f, pl.* demi-alternances; demi-période *f, pl.* demi-périodes; *Elcs:* **h.-w. aerial,** antenne *f* demi-onde; **h.-w. dipole,** dipôle *m* demi-onde; **h.-w. rectifier,** (i) redresseur *m* à une demi-onde; (ii) valve *f* simple.
halfway ['hɑːf'wei]. **1.** *adv.* à moitié chemin; à mi-chemin; (*of piston*) à mi-course; **h. between the two towns,** à mi-chemin entre les deux villes, à égale distance des deux villes; **h. to Paris,** à mi-chemin de Paris; **we are h. there, h. across,** nous sommes à moitié de la route, du chemin; nous sommes à moitié chemin, à mi-chemin; **h. up, h. down, the hill,** à mi-côte, à mi-pente; **the shell must have fallen h. up, down, along, the street,** l'obus avait dû tomber à la moitié de la rue; **I was h. up, down, the stairs,** j'étais à mi-hauteur de l'escalier; **she walked h. along the path,** elle marcha jusqu'à mi-chemin de l'allée; **h. up the legs,** à mi-jambe; **h. through (a period of time),** à mi-terme; **to meet s.o. h.,** (i) rencontrer qn à mi-distance; (ii) *F:* faire la moitié des avances; partager le différend, la différence, par la moitié; couper la poire en deux; venir à composition avec qn; composer avec qn. **2.** *attrib.* **h. house,** maison *f,* auberge *f,* à mi-chemin (*A:* entre relais), à demi-étape; *Fb:* **h. line,** ligne des cinquante mètres, ligne médiane. **3.** *s.* **there's no h. with him,** avec lui il n'y a pas de demi-mesures.
half wheel ['hɑːf'(h)wiːl], *s.* **1.** *Av:* volant *m* (de pilotage). **2.** *Mil:* **right h. w.,** demi-à-droite *m, pl.* demis-à-droite; **left h. w.,** demi-à gauche *m, pl.* demis-à-gauche.
half-wing ['hɑːf'wiŋ], *s. Av:* demi-aile *f, pl.* demi-ailes.
halfwit ['hɑːfwit], *s.* (*a*) faible *mf* d'esprit; simple *mf*; (*b*) *F:* **you h.!** espèce d'idiot!
halfwitted ['hɑːf'witid], *a.* faible d'esprit, simple, *F:* à moitié idiot.
half year ['hɑːf'jiər], *s.* semestre *m*; **first h. y.,** semestre de janvier, d'hiver; **second h. y.,** semestre de juillet, d'été.
half-yearly ['hɑːf'jiəli]. **1.** *a.* semestriel; **h.-y. meeting,** assemblée semestrielle; **h.-y. dividend, payment,** semestre *m.* **2.** *adv.* semestriellement; par semestre; tous les six mois.
halibut ['hælibət], *s. Ich:* flétan *m*; halibut *m.*
Halicarnassus [hælikɑː'næsəs], *Pr.n. A.Geog:* Halicarnasse *m.*
halicondria [hæli'kɔndriə], *s. Spong:* halichondrie *f.*
Halictidae [hæ'liktidiː], *s.pl. Ent:* halictes *m.*
halictus [hæ'liktəs], *s. Ent:* halicte *m.*
halid(e) ['hælid, -aid], *Ch:* **1.** *s.* halogénure *m*; sel *m* halogène; **silver h.,** halogénure d'argent; **alkali h.,** halogénure alcalin; **vinyl h.,** halogénure vinylique. **2.** *a.* haloïde.
halidom ['hælidəm], *s. A:* relique *f,* chose sainte; **by my h.!** sur mes reliques! par ma foi!
halieutic [hæli'juːtik], *a.* halieutique.
halieutics [hæli'juːtiks], *s.pl.* (*usu. with sg. const.*) halieutique *f.*
Haliotidae [hæli'outidiː], *s.pl. Moll:* halioti(di)dés *m.*
haliotis [hæli'outis], *s. Moll:* haliotide *f*; oreille *f* de mer; ormier *m,* ormeau *m.*
halite ['hælait], *s. Miner:* halite *f*; sel *m* gemme.
halitherium [hæli'θiəriəm], *s. Paleont:* halitherium *m.*
halitosis [hæli'tousis], *s. Med:* mauvaise haleine.
halituous [hæ'litjuəs], *a.* halitueux.
hall [hɔːl], *s.* **1.** (grande) salle; (*a*) **(dining) h.,** (i) salle à manger (d'un château, etc.); (ii) *Sch:* (*of college, etc.*) réfectoire *m*; (*at university*) **to dine in h.,** dîner (en commun) au réfectoire; **in h.,** pendant le dîner; **the students were rather rowdy in h.,** au réfectoire les étudiants faisaient pas mal de tapage; (*b*) **the servants' h.,** l'office *f*; la salle commune (des domestiques); (*c*) **lecture h.,** salle de conférences; **school h., assembly h.,** salle d'assemblée; **concert h.,** salle de concert; **dance h.,** salle de danse, de bal; dancing *m*; **music h.,** (i) music-hall *m*; (ii) *NAm:* salle de concert; **to be, appear, on the halls,** faire du music-hall; (*d*) **parish h., parochial h.,** salle d'œuvres de la paroisse. **2.** (*a*) (*usu. as Pr.n.*) = manoir *m*; **there are a lot of guests at the H.,** il y a beaucoup d'invités au manoir, au château; (*b*) maison *f* (d'un corps de métier, etc.); **town h.,** hôtel *m* de ville; (*c*) *Hist:* **Westminster H.,** le Palais de justice de Westminster; (*d*) *Sch:* (i) fondation *f* universitaire (à Oxford et Cambridge); (ii) = maison d'étudiants. **3.** (*a*) **(entrance) h.,** vestibule *m,* entrée *f* (d'une maison); hall *m* (d'un grand hôtel); **h. porter,** concierge *m*; (*b*) *NAm:* couloir *m,* corridor *m*; **h. bedroom,** petite chambre aménagée au bout d'un corridor.
hallelujah [hæli'luːjə], *int. & s.* alléluia *m*; *F: A:* **h. lasses,** salutistes *f.*
halliard ['hæljəd], *s.* = HALYARD.
hallmark[1] ['hɔːlmɑːk], *s.* (cachet *m* de) contrôle *m* (sur les objets d'orfèvrerie, apposé primitivement au *Goldsmiths' Hall*); **h. stamp,** poinçon *m* de contrôle; **the h. of genius,** le cachet, l'empreinte *f,* du génie; **work bearing the h. of genius,** ouvrage marqué au coin du génie.
hallmark[2], *v.tr.* contrôler, poinçonner (l'orfèvrerie); **hallmarked silver,** argenterie contrôlée.
hallo[1] [hə'lou], *int. & s.* (*a*) holà! ohé! (*b*) *Tp:* allo!
hallo[2], *v.i.* crier; lancer des ohés.
halloo[1] [hə'luː]. **1.** *s.* cri *m* d'appel; *Ven:* huée *f.* **2.** *int. Ven:* taïaut!
halloo[2], *v.i.* (*a*) crier, appeler; **to h. to s.o.,** appeler qn (à grands cris); (*b*) *Ven:* huer; crier taïaut; *Prov:* **don't h. till you are out of the wood,** il ne faut pas se moquer des chiens qu'on ne soit hors du village; il ne faut pas trop tôt chanter victoire.
hallooing [hə'luːiŋ], *s.* **1.** cris *mpl* d'appel. **2.** *Ven:* huée *f.*
hallow[1] ['hælou], *s. A:* saint, sainte; *Ecc:* **All Hallows' (Day),** (le jour de) la Toussaint.
hallow[2], *v.tr.* sanctifier, consacrer; **hallowed** [hæloud *occ.* 'hælouid] **be Thy name,** que Ton nom soit sanctifié; **hallowed ground,** terre sainte.
hallow[3]. **1.** *v.i.* huer; crier taïaut. **2.** *v.tr.* exciter (la meute, par des cris de taïaut).
Hallowe'en [hælou'iːn], *s.* veille *f* de la Toussaint.
Hallowmas ['hæloumæs], *s.* (le jour de) la Toussaint.
halloysite [hæ'lɔisait], *s. Miner:* halloysite *f.*
hallstand ['hɔːl'stænd], *s.* porte-habit(s) *m.*
Hallstatt(ian) [hæl'stæt(iən), -'ʃtæt-], *a. Paleont:* (homme, etc.) hallstattien.
hallucinate [hə'l(j)uːsineit], *v.tr.* halluciner.
hallucination [həl(j)uːsi'neiʃ(ə)n], *s.* hallucination *f,* illusion *f*; **to be under a h.,** être en proie à une hallucination.
hallucinatory [hə'l(j)uːsinət(ə)ri], *a.* hallucinatoire.
hallucinogen [hæl(j)u'sinoudʒen], *s.* hallucinogène *m.*
hallucinogenic [hæli(j)usinou'dʒenik], *a.* hallucinogène.
hallucinosis [hæl(j)usi'nousis], *s. Psy:* hallucinose *f.*
hallux, *pl.* **halluces** ['hæləks, hæ'l(j)uːsiz], *s.* (*a*) *Anat:* orteil *m*; *Med:* **h. valgus,** hallux valgus *m*; **h. varus,** hallux varus *m*; **h. valgus and varus,** hallux valgus varus; (*b*) avillon *m* (d'un oiseau de proie).
hallway ['hɔːlwei], *s.* **1.** vestibule *m,* entrée *f.* **2.** *NAm:* corridor *m* d'étage.
halm [hɑːm], *s.* = HAULM.
halma ['hælmə], *s.* (jeu *m* de) halma *m.*
halo[1], *pl.* **-os, -oes** ['heilou, -ouz], *s.* **1.** *Astr: Opt:* halo *m*; cercle lumineux; auréole *f,* aréole *f* (de la lune). **2.** auréole, nimbe *m* (d'un saint); **the h. of glory,** l'auréole de la gloire. **3.** *Phot:* halo. **4.** *Anat:* aréole, halo (du mamelon).
halo[2], *v.tr.* auréoler, nimber.
halobates [hə'lɔbətiːz], *s. Ent:* halobate *m.*
haloed ['heiloud], *a.* auréolé, nimbé.
halogen ['hælədʒən], *s. Ch:* halogène *m.*
halogenation [hælədʒə'neiʃ(ə)n], *s. Ch:* halogénation *f.*
halogenide ['hælədʒənaid, hæ'lɔdʒ-], *s. Ch:* halogénure *m.*
halogenous [hæ'lɔdʒənəs], *a. Ch:* (composé *m*) halogène; (dérivé) halogéné; (résidu *m*) halogénique.
halography [hæ'lɔgrəfi], *s. Ch:* halographie *f.*
haloid ['hælɔid], *Ch:* **1.** *a.* haloïde. **2.** *s.* halosel *m,* haloïde *m,* halogénure *m.*
halology [hæ'lɔlədʒi], *s. Ch:* halochimie *f.*

halometer [hə'lɔmitər], *s. Ch: Cryst:* halomètre *m.*
halometry [hə'lɔmitri], *s. Ch: Cryst:* halométrie *f.*
halophilous [hə'lɔfiləs], *a. Bot:* halophile.
halophyte ['hæloufait], *s. Bot:* halophyte *f.*
halophytic [hælou'fitik], *a. Bot:* halophyte.
Haloragaceae [hælərə'geisii:], **Halor(h)agidaceae** [hælərædʒi'deisii:], *s.pl. Bot:* halorrhagidacées *f*, halorragacées *f.*
halosaur ['hælousɔ:r], *s. Ich:* halosaure *m.*
halotechny ['hæloutekni], *s. Ch:* halotechnie *f.*
halotrichite [hæ'lɔtrikait], *s. Miner:* halotrichite *f*; alun *m* de fer.
halt¹ [hɔlt], *s.* **1.** arrêt *m*, temps *m* d'arrêt; interruption (momentanée); halte *f*, pause *f*; *(a) (of machine, vehicle)* **at the h.**, à l'arrêt; **dead h.**, arrêt instantané; **to bring to a h.**, faire marquer un temps d'arrêt, une pause (à un processus, à une progression, etc.); provoquer l'interruption momentanée (d'un mouvement, d'une action); arrêter, faire stopper (un véhicule, une foule ou une troupe en marche, etc.); **to come to a h.**, (i) marquer un temps d'arrêt, s'interrompre momentanément; s'arrêter, stopper; (ii) *(on journey)* faire halte; (iii) *(in a speech)* rester sans pouvoir rien dire; *Aut:* **h. sign**, stop *m*; **h. sign ahead sign**, pré-stop *m*, *pl.* pré-stops; *(b) Mil:* **at the h.**, de pied ferme, sur place; **clock-hour h.**, halte horaire; **long h.**, **principal h.**, grande halte. **2.** stationnement *m* (d'un véhicule, d'un train, d'une troupe, etc.); *Mil:* **h. area**, zone *f* de stationnement; **during halts**, (i) au stationnement; (ii) pendant les haltes; *U.S:* **security during halts**, sûreté *f* en station. **3.** *Rail: (small station)* halte.
halt². **1.** *v.i.* faire halte; s'arrêter; **to h. at. . .**, faire un arrêt, s'arrêter, à . . .; *F:* **to h. in one's tracks**, s'arrêter net; **halting place**, étape *f*; *Mil:* **squad h.! platoon h.! party h.!** section halte! **company h.!** compagnie halte! **2.** *v.tr.* faire faire halte à (qn).
halt³, *s. (a)* boitement *m*; **to walk with a h.**, boiter (en marchant); *(b)* hésitation *f* (de parole); **to speak with a h.**, hésiter en parlant.
halt⁴, *a. A: & B:* boiteux; *s.pl.* **the h. and the blind**, les estropiés et les aveugles.
halt⁵, *v.i. A: & Lit: (of pers., verse, argument)* boiter, clocher; **to h. between two opinions**, hésiter, balancer, entre deux opinions.
halter¹ ['hɔ:ltər], *s.* **1.** *(a)* licou *m*, licol *m* (pour chevaux); **h. rope**, longe *f*; *Vet:* **h. cast**, enchevêtrure *f*. **2.** corde *f* (de pendaison); **to put a h. round one's own neck**, se mettre la corde au cou. **3.** *Cost: (a)* **h. (neck)**, encolure *f* bain-de-soleil; col-bretelle *m,pl.* cols-bretelles; bretelle *f* tour de cou; *(b) NAm:* corsage *m*, haut *m*, bain-de-soleil.
halter², *v.tr.* **1. to h. (up) a horse**, mettre un licou à un cheval; attacher un cheval avec un licou. **2.** *(a)* mettre la corde au cou à (qn); *(b)* pendre (un malfaiteur).
halter-break ['hɔ(:)ltəbreik], *v.tr.* accoutumer (un poulain) au licou.
halteres [hæl'tiəri:z], *s.pl. Ent:* haltères *m.*
halting¹ ['hɔ:ltiŋ], *a. (of words, policy, etc.)* hésitant; **h. speech**, (i) discours hésitant; (ii) débit hésitant; **h. verse**, vers *m* qui boitent; **h. style**, style heurté, hésitant; **to read sth. in a h. manner**, ânonner qch.
halting², *s. A: & Lit:* **1.** boitement *m*, clochement *m*, claudication *f*. **2.** hésitation *f*; débit hésitant.
haltingly ['hɔ:ltiŋli], *adv.* en hésitant.
halve [hɑ:v], *v.tr.* **1.** *(a)* diviser en deux; couper en deux moitiés, par (la) moitié; **halved votes**, suffrages mipartis; *(b)* partager (qch. en deux); **we will h. the winnings**, nous partagerons le bénéfice; *Golf:* **halved hole**, trou partagé; *(c)* réduire (les dépenses, etc.) de moitié, à la moitié. **2.** *Carp: Metalw:* **to h. and lap**, assembler à mi-bois, à mi-fer; **halved joint**, assemblage *m* à mi-bois, à mi-fer; paume *f*.
halving ['hɑ:viŋ], *s.* **1.** partage *m* en deux, division *f* en deux, mi-partition *f*. **2.** *Carp:* **h. and lapping**, assemblage *m* à mi-bois, à mi-fer.
halyard ['hæljəd], *s. Nau:* drisse *f*; **the signal h.**, la drisse des signaux, de pavillon.
ham¹ [hæm], *s.* **1.** *(a) A:* jarret *m*; *(b) pl. F:* **the hams**, les fesses *f*, le derrière; **he fell on his hams**, il est tombé sur son séant, sur le derrière. **2.** *Cu:* jambon *m*; **h. and eggs**, des œufs au jambon; **foreleg h.**, jambonneau *m*. **3.** *F: (a) Th: (of play)* navet *m*; **h. actor**, cabotin *m*; **he's a real h.**, il joue comme un pied; *(b)* **(radio) h.**, amateur *m* de radio.
ham². *Th: F: (a) v.i.* jouer comme un pied; *(b) v.tr.* **he hams all his parts**, il joue tous ses rôles en charge.
Ham³, *Pr.n.m. B:* Cham.
ham⁴, *s. A: & Hist:* bourg *m*, village *m*, manoir *m.*
hamada [hə'mɑ:də], *s. Geog:* hamada *f.*
hamadryad [hæmə'draiæd], *s.* **1.** *Gr.Myth:* hamadryade *f*. **2.** *Z:* hamadryas *m*, (singe *m*) cynocéphale *m*. **3.** *Rept:* hamadryade.
hamadryas [hæmə'draiəs], *s.* **1.** *Rept:* hamadryade *f*. **2.** *Z:* hamadryas *m*, (singe *m*) cynocéphale *m.*
Hamamelidaceae ['hæməmi:li'deisii:], *s.pl. Bot:* hamamélidacées *f.*
hamamelis [hæmə'mi:lis], *s. Bot:* hamamélis *m.*
Haman ['heimæn], *Pr.n.m. B.Hist:* Aman.
hambergite ['hæmbə:gait], *s. Miner:* hambergite *f.*
Hamburg ['hæmbə:g], *Pr.n. Geog:* Hambourg; *Husb:* **H. fowls**, poules *f* race de Hambourg; *Vit:* **H. grape**, frankenthal *m*; *Cu:* **H. steak** = HAMBURGER. **2.** *(b).*
Hamburger ['hæmbə:gər], *s.* **1.** *Geog:* Hambourgeois, -oise. **2.** *s.m. Cu:* *(a)* (sorte de) saucisse allemande; *(b)* boulette *f* de bœuf haché; *(c)* boulette de bifteck haché entre deux morceaux de pain, hamburger *m.*
hame [heim], *s. Harn:* attelle *f*; **h. rein**, fausse rêne.
hamelia [hæ'mi:liə], *s. Bot:* hamelia *m.*
hamesucken ['heimsʌk(ə)n], *s. Jur: Scot:* délit *m* de voies et faits commis dans le domicile de la victime; trouble *m* de jouissance.
hamfisted ['hæm'fistid], *a.* **1.** (personne) avec des mains comme des battoirs. **2.** maladroit, brutal (dans sa façon de manier un outil, etc.). **3.** *Fig:* cafouilleur, -euse.
Hamilcar ['hæmilkɑ:r], *Pr.n.m. A.Hist:* Amilcar.
Hamiltonian [hæmil'tounian], *a. Phil: Mth:* hamiltonien.
hamiltonism ['hæmiltənizm], *s. Phil:* philosophie *f* de Hamilton.
haminoea [hæmi'ni:ə], *s. Moll:* haminée *f.*
Hamite¹ ['hæmait], *s. B.Hist:* chamite *mf.*
hamites [hə'maiti:z], *s. Paleont:* hamite *m.*
Hamitic [hə'mitik], *a.* (langue *f*, etc.) chamitique.
Hamito-Semitic ['hæmitousi'mitik], *a.* chamito-sémitique.
hamlet ['hæmlit], *s.* hameau *m.*
hamlinite ['hæmlinait], *s. Miner:* hamlinite *f.*
hammada [hə'mɑ:də], *s. Geog:* = HAMADA.
hammer¹ ['hæmər], *s.* **1.** *Tls:* marteau *m*; *(heavy)* masse *f*, massette *f*; *(a)* (i) **wooden h.**, maillet *m*; *Join:* **veneering h.**, marteau à plaquer; **glazier's h.**, besaiguë *f*, marteau de vitrier; *Farr:* **shoeing h.**, brochoir *m*, marteau à ferrer (les chevaux); **shoeing smith's h.**, ferratier *m*, ferretier *m*, fertier *m*; **fitter's h.**, marteau d'adjusteur; **h. axe**, malebête *f* (de calfat); **h. block**, panne *f* (de marteau mécanique); **h. claw**, panne à pied de biche (d'un marteau); **caster's h.**, robine *f*; **claw h.**, marteau à panne fendue, à dent; *F: O:* **claw-h. coat**, habit *m* à queue de morue, à queue de pie, *F:* queue *f* de morue; (ii) *Stonew:* **quarryman's h.**, marteau de carrier; **stone-cutter's h.**, **stone-mason's h.**, polka *f*, marteau de tailleur de pierres; **granite h.**, têtu *m*; **slater's h.**, marteau à ardoise, marteau de couvreur; **h.-dressed stone**, pierre dressée au marteau; *Civ.E:* **bush h.**, boucharde *f*, marteau à boucharder; (iii) *Metalw:* **chasing h.**, marteau à emboutir; **repoussé h.**, marteau à gouges, à repousser; **forging h.**, marteau à forger; **riveting h.**, marteau à river, (marteau) rivoir *m*; **holding-up h.**, mandrin *m* d'abattage (pour river); **half-round h.**, marteau à panne sphérique; **sharp-faced h.**, fonçoir *m*; **soft-faced h.**, marteau doux; **h.-forged**, forgé au marteau; **h.-hardening**, écrouissage *m*, battage *m*, à froid, au marteau; **h.-riveting**, rivetage *m* au marteau; (iv) *Bookb:* marteau à endosser; *(b) Civ.E: Min:* **air h.**, **pneumatic h.**, marteau pneumatique; **single-shot (pneumatic) h.**, marteau (pneumatique) coup par coup; **multiple-shot h.**, marteau (pneumatique) multifrappe; *(c) F:* **to go at it h. and tongs**, y aller de bon cœur, ne pas y aller de main morte, ne pas y aller avec le dos de la cuiller; *(of swordsmen)* ferrailler; **h.-and-tongs fighting**, ferraillement *m*; **last night our neighbours were at it h. and tongs**, hier soir, on se disputait ferme, le torchon brûlait, chez les voisins; on se bagarrait dur chez les voisins; *(d) Moll:* **h. oyster**, **h. shell**, marteau. **2.** marteau (de commissaire-priseur); **to come under the h.**, être mis aux enchères, passer sous le marteau, être vendu aux enchères. **3.** *(a) Mus:* marteau (de piano, de xylophone); *(b) Mus:* **tuning h.**, accordoir *m*; marteau, clef *f*, d'accordage, d'accordeur; *(c) Clockm: El:* marteau (de sonnerie *f* d'horloge, de sonnette électrique); *(d) Anat:* marteau (de l'oreille interne). **4.** *Sm.a:* chien *m*, percuteur *m* (d'un arme à feu); **h. gun**, fusil *m* (à percussion centrale) à chien(s) extérieur(s). **5.** *Sp:* **throwing the h.**, lancement *m* du marteau. **6.** *Med:* **h. toe**, orteil *m* en marteau, hallux flexus. **7.** *Hyd.E:* coup *m* d'eau, coup de bélier (dans une tuyauterie).
hammer², *v.*
I. *v.tr. & i.* **1.** *v.tr. (a)* marteler; battre au marteau; **to h. iron**, forger, battre, le fer; travailler le fer au marteau; **to h. a scythe (sharp)**, battre une faux; **to h. sth. into shape**, (i) façonner (un pot, etc.) à coups de marteau; (ii) *F:* perfectionner (un projet, etc.); mettre (un projet, etc.) au point; *F:* **to h. sth. into s.o.**, faire entrer qch. dans la tête à qn; *(of boxer, etc.)* **to h. one's opponent**, cogner dur sur son adversaire; *Mil:* **to h. the enemy**, (i) s'acharner sur, (ii) pilonner, l'ennemi; *(b) St.Exch:* **to h. a defaulter**, proclamer la déconfiture d'un agent en défaut; exécuter un agent; *(c) F:* **to h. prices**, faire baisser les prix; *(d) U.S: F:* critiquer, éreinter (qn, un livre). **2.** *v.i. (a)* travailler avec le marteau; *F:* **to h. at, on, the door**, heurter à la porte à coups redoublés; **to h. (away) at sth.**, travailler d'arrache-pied à qch.; s'acharner à (un travail); **to h. away at s.o.**, harceler qn; *P:* **to h. into s.o.**, rentrer dedans à qn; *(b) (of machine part, etc.)* tambouriner, cogner, marteler.
II. *(compound verbs)* **1. hammer down**, *v.tr.* **to h. down a rivet**, aplatir un rivet; **to h. down an irregularity**, rabattre une inégalité.
2. hammer in, *v.tr.* **to h. in a nail**, enfoncer un clou à coups de marteau.
3. hammer out, *v.tr.* **to h. out (gold, etc.)**, étendre l'or, etc.) sous le marteau; gironner, écolleter (l'or, etc.); panner (le cuivre); *F:* **to h. out lines of verse**, (i) *(of reciter)* marteler des vers; (ii) *(of poet)* forger des vers; **to h. out an excuse**, se forger une excuse; inventer une excuse; **to h. out the facts**, démêler les faits.
hammerbeam ['hæməbi:m], *s. Arch:* blochet *m* à mi-bois; **h. roof** = charpente *f* à blochets.
hammercloth ['hæməklɔθ], *s. Veh:* housse *f* (de siège de cocher, pour grandes occasions).
hammer-dressed ['hæmədrest], *a. (of stone, etc.)* dressé au marteau.
hammered ['hæməd], *a. O:* **1.** *(of metal, etc.)* martelé, battu; **h. ironwork**, fer ouvré. **2.** *P: O:* marié.
hammerer ['hæmərər], *s.* **1.** manieur *m* d'un marteau; *(a) Ind:* marteleur *m*, *esp.* riveur *m*; *(b) F: O:* minéralogiste *m*, géologue *m*. **2.** *Box: F:* cogneur *m.*
hammer-harden ['hæməhɑ:d(ə)n], *v.tr. Metalw:* écrouir (l'acier); marteler à froid; battre à froid, au marteau.
hammerhead ['hæməhed], *s.* **1.** *(a)* tête *f* de marteau; **h. of a power hammer**, mouton *m*, pilon *m*, d'un marteau-pilon; *(b) attrib.* en forme de marteau; **h. crane**, grue *f* marteau. **2.** *Ich:* **h. (shark)**, marteau *m*, maillet *m*, demoiselle *f*. **3.** *Orn: (also* **hammerheaded stork***)* ombrette *f* (du Sénégal).
hammering ['hæməriŋ], *s.* **1.** *(a)* martelage *m*, martèlement *m*; battage *m* (du fer); **h. (down)**, aplatissage *m* (d'un rivet, etc.); **bush h.**, bouchardage *m*; *(b) F:* dégelée *f (de coups)*; **to give s.o. a good h.**, cogner dur sur qn; bourrer qn de coups; rosser qn d'importance; *(c) Artil:* pilonnage *m*. **2.** *(a) Mec.E: Mch:* tambourinage *m*, cognement *m*, martèlement *m*, battement *m*; choc *m* (d'un coussinet, etc.); *Hyd.E:* **(water) h. in a pipe**, coup(s) *m(pl)* de bélier dans une conduite; *(b) Rail:* martèlement (de la voie par une locomotive mal équilibrée); mouvement *m* de lacet.
hammerkop ['hæməkɔp], *s. Orn:* ombrette *f* (du Sénégal).
hammerless ['hæmələs], *a.* (fusil *m*) hammerless, à chien caché.
hammer-lock¹ ['hæməlɔk], *s. Wr:* retournement *m* de bras.
hammer-lock², *v.tr. Wr:* retourner le bras à (l'adversaire).
hammerman, *pl.* **-men** ['hæmәmәn], **hammersmith** ['hæməsmiθ], *s.* marteleur *m*; frappeur *m*; *Metall:* martineur *m*; *Metalw:* **smith's hammerman**, daubeur *m.*
hammock ['hæmək], *s.* hamac *m*; *Nau:* branle *m*, hamac (de matelot); **h.-seat**, siège *m* en hamac; **h.-chair**, chaise-longue *f* de jardin (à fond de toile), *pl.* chaises-longues; transatlantique *m*, *F:* transat *m*; **garden h.**, balancelle *f*; *Nau: A:* **h. cloth**, toiles *fpl* de bastingage.
hammy ['hæmi], *a. F:* **1.** qui a un goût de jambon. **2.** *Th: etc:* (acteur) cabotin *inv.*; (style, discours) pompier *inv.*
hamper¹ ['hæmpər], *s.* manne *f*, mannequin *m*, panier *m*, banne *f*; calais *m* (à provisions, etc.); bourriche *f* (d'huîtres, etc.); *(small)* banneau *m*, bannette *f*; **Christmas h.**, panier de Noël.
hamper², *s. Nau:* accessoires lourds, encombrants ou gênants.
hamper³, *v.tr.* **1.** embarrasser, gêner, empêtrer (qn); empêcher les mouvements de (qn, etc.); **to h. the progress of business**, entraver la marche des affaires; **nothing hampered our march**, rien ne gêna notre marche; **to h. oneself with luggage**, s'empêtrer de colis; **she was hampered by her long cloak**, elle était empêtrée dans, par, son grand manteau; **I must not be hampered in my work**, il me faut mes coudées franches. **2.** brouiller, mêler (une serrure, etc.).
hampered ['hæmpəd], *a. (of style, movements, etc.)* embarrassé.
hamster ['hæmstər], *s. Z:* hamster *m*, **golden h.**, hamster roux, doré; **h.-rat of Gambia**, rat *m* de Gambie.
hamstring¹ ['hæmstriŋ], *s. Anat:* tendon *m* du jarret; *F:* corde *f* du jarret.
hamstring², *v.tr. (p.t. & p.p.* **hamstringed** *or* **-strung***)* **1.**

couper le(s) jarret(s) à (qn, une vache, un cheval). **2.** couper les moyens à (qn); donner un coup de Jarnac à (qn).

hamular ['hæmjulər], **hamulate** ['hæmjuleit], **hamulose** ['hæmjulous], *a. Bot:* hamuleux.

hamulus, *pl.* **-li** ['hæmjuləs, -lai], *s. Biol:* hamule *m.*

hanap ['hænæp], *s. A:* hanap *m.*

hanaper ['hænəpər], *s. A:* hanapier *m.*

hand[1] [hænd], *s.* **1.** main *f;* (*a*) **to hurt one's h.,** se faire mal à la main; **he writes with his left h.,** il écrit de la main gauche; **the cold h. of death,** la froide main de la mort; **the h. of God,** le doigt de Dieu; **to go on one's hands and knees,** aller, marcher, à quatre pattes; **to raise one's hands to heaven,** lever les bras au ciel; **to vote by show of hands,** voter à main levée; **not to move h. or foot,** ne remuer ni bras ni jambe; ne remuer ni pied ni patte; **to have one's hands tied,** (i) avoir les mains liées; (ii) être lié par ses engagements; se trouver dans l'impossibilité d'agir; **to hold (sth.) in one's h.,** tenir, avoir, (une épée, son chapeau) à la main, (des graines) dans la main, (le succès) entre les mains; **who put weapons into their hands?** qui leur a mis des armes aux mains? **to take s.o. by the h.,** prendre qn par la main; **to take s.o.'s h., to lead s.o. by the h.,** donner la main à qn; **give me your h.,** donnez-moi la main; *O:* (*of woman*) **to give her h. to a suitor,** donner, accorder, sa main à un prétendant; **to take sth. with both hands,** prendre qch. à deux mains; **to spend money with both hands,** prodiguer l'argent; dépenser l'argent sans compter; *F:* **to put, dip, one's h. in the till,** puiser dans la caisse; **to receive sth. from s.o.'s hands,** recevoir qch. des mains de qn; **I can't put my h. on it,** je ne peux pas le retrouver, y mettre la main; **here's my h. on it!** d'accord! *F:* tope là! **to lay hands on sth.,** mettre la main sur qch.; se saisir, s'emparer, de qch.; *F:* mettre le grappin sur qch.; **to lay (violent) hands on s.o.,** faire violence à qn; *Ecc:* **to lay hands on s.o.,** imposer les mains à qn; **if anyone should lay a h. on you,** si quelqu'un vous touchait, portait la main sur vous; **hands off!** (i) on ne touche pas! n'y touchez pas! (ii) bas les mains! *F:* à bas les pattes! **hands off China!** la Chine aux Chinois! **hands up!** haut les mains! rendez-vous! **to fight for one's own h.,** travailler pour soi, à son propre avancement; soigner ses intérêts; **to act with a high h.,** agir en despote, de haute main, avec intransigeance, tyranniquement; **to carry it off with a high h.,** trancher du grand; le prendre de haut; **to rule s.o. with a high h.,** mener qn tambour battant, le bâton haut; gouverner qn en despote; **to rule with a firm h.,** gouverner d'une main ferme; **believers in the strong h.,** partisans *m* de la manière forte; **to have a light h.,** avoir la main légère; *Fb:* **hands,** faute *f* de mains; **the birds come and eat out of my h.,** les oiseaux viennent manger dans ma main; *F:* **I'll soon have him eating out of my h.,** je l'amènerai bientôt à faire exactement ce que je veux; (*b*) **to try one's h. at sth.,** essayer (de faire) qch., y mettre la main; **to put one's h. to a job,** entreprendre, commencer, un travail; **to put one's h. to the plough,** mettre la main à la charrue, à l'œuvre; **I don't know what to put my h. to first,** (i) je ne sais pas où commencer; (ii) je ne sais pas où donner de la tête; **to get one's h. in,** se faire la main, prendre le tour de main; **I've got my h. in,** je suis bien en train, j'ai pris le tour de main; **he can turn his h. to anything,** c'est un homme qui peut tout faire, qui peut s'adapter à tout; **can you turn your h. to this?** est-ce que vous pouvez faire, vous mettre à, cela? **he never does a hand's turn,** il ne fait jamais rien, ne fait jamais œuvre de ses dix doigts; **to have a h. in sth.,** y être pour quelque chose; se mêler de qch.; *Pej:* tremper dans (un crime); **to have no h. in it,** ne pas avoir de part, n'y être pour rien; **I had no h. in it,** je n'y suis pour rien; **to take a h. in sth.,** se mêler de qch.; se mettre du jeu, de la partie; y aller de sa personne; **I thought it was time for me to take a h.,** j'ai jugé qu'il était temps d'intervenir, d'y mettre la main; **to give, lend, s.o. a (helping) h.,** aider qn; donner un coup de main à qn; prêter la main à qn; **to lend a h.,** mettre la main à la pâte; **I got a friend to give me a h.,** je me suis fait aider par un ami; **give me a h. with my overcoat,** aidez-moi à mettre mon pardessus; **everyone's h. is against me,** tout le monde est contre moi; (*c*) **to have one's hands full,** avoir fort à faire, avoir beaucoup de besogne sur les bras; **to have s.o., sth., on one's hands,** avoir qn, qch., à sa charge, sur les bras; **to have an hour on one's hands,** avoir une heure à tuer; **to get s.o., sth., off one's hands,** se décharger de qn, de qch.; **to take sth. off s.o.'s hands,** débarrasser qn de qch.; *F:* **I've got my daughter off my hands,** j'ai marié ma fille; *Com:* **goods left on one's hands,** marchandises invendues, laissées pour compte; **to change hands,** (i) passer (qch.) à l'autre main; (ii) (*of goods, etc.*) passer en d'autres mains; (iii) (*of business, etc.*) changer de propriétaire; **to fall into enemy hands, into the enemy's hands,** tomber entre les mains, au pouvoir, de l'ennemi; **to be in the hands of s.o., in s.o.'s hands,** (i) (*of thg*) être entre les mains de qn; (ii) (*of pers.*) être aux mains de qn; s'en remettre complètement à qn; **to be in good hands,** (i) être en bonnes mains; (ii) être à bonne école; **to put oneself in s.o.'s hands,** se confier, s'en remettre, à qn; **my fate is in your hands,** mon sort est entre vos mains; **to have s.o. in the hollow of one's h.,** tenir qn dans le creux de la main; avoir qn sous sa coupe, à sa merci; *Jur:* **to put a matter in the hands of a lawyer,** confier une affaire à un homme de loi; (*d*) applaudissement(s) *m(pl)*; *F:* **to give s.o. a big h.,** applaudir vivement qn. **2.** *phrs.* (*a*) **at h.: to be (near) at h.,** (i) (*of object, etc.*) être sous la main, à portée de la main; (ii) (*of event, etc.*) approcher, être prochain; **spring is at h.,** voici venir le printemps; nous touchons au printemps; **the day will soon be at h. when . . .,** le jour approche où . . .; **the hour is at h.,** l'heure est proche; voici l'heure; **there is always a doctor at h.,** il y a toujours un médecin de service; (*b*) **by h.: made, done, by h.,** fait à la main; **to bring up a lamb, a calf,** *A:* **a child, by h.,** nourrir, élever, un agneau, un veau, un enfant, au biberon; **to send a letter by h.,** envoyer une lettre par porteur; (*c*) **in h.,** (i) **sword, revolver, in h.,** sabre, revolver, au poing; **hat, cap, in h.,** chapeau bas; en quêtant, en quémandant; (ii) **to have so much money in h.,** avoir tant d'argent disponible; *Com:* **cash in h.,** espèces *fpl* en caisse; **stock in h.,** marchandises *fpl* en magasin; **to catch a train with five minutes in h.,** prendre un train avec cinq minutes d'avance, de bon; **I've five minutes in h.,** j'ai encore cinq minutes; (iii) **the matter in h.,** la chose en question, dont il s'agit; la question en discussion; **work in h.,** travail *m* en cours, en chantier, sur le chantier, sur le métier; **the business is in h.,** l'affaire est à l'étude, en préparation; on s'occupe de l'affaire; **I'll take it in h.,** je m'en charge; (iv) **horse light in h.,** cheval *m* facile à mener; *Equit:* **position in h.,** ramener *m;* **to have one's horse, one's car, well in h.,** être maître de son cheval, de sa voiture; **to have oneself well in h.,** être maître de soi, se contenir; **the situation is well in h.,** la situation est bien en main; (v) *Bill:* **to be in h.,** être obligé de remettre sa bille dans le demi-cercle de départ; (*d*) **on h.:** (i) **work on h.,** travail en cours; travail à faire; *Com:* **goods left on h.,** marchandises non vendues, laissées pour compte; (ii) **I'm on h. if you need me,** je suis tout près, à votre disposition, si vous avez besoin de moi; (iii) **on every h., on all hands,** partout; de toutes parts; **fact admitted on all hands,** fait universellement reconnu; **on (the) one h.,** d'une part; **on the other h.,** d'autre part; en revanche; par contre; **weak in maths, but on the other h. good at French,** faible en math mais en revanche fort en français; (*e*) **out of h.:** (i) **to do sth. out of h.,** faire qch. sur-le-champ; **to shoot s.o. out of h.,** abattre qn sans autre forme de procès, (ii) (*of troops, children, etc.*) **to get out of h.,** s'indiscipliner; perdre toute discipline; **these children are quite out of h.,** on ne peut plus tenir ces enfants; (*f*) **to h.:** (i) (*of letter, etc.*) **to come to h.,** arriver à destination; **your parcel came to h. this morning,** votre paquet m'est parvenu, m'est arrivé, ce matin; j'ai bien reçu votre paquet ce matin; (ii) **the first excuse to h.,** le premier prétexte venu; (*g*) **h. in glove,** *occ.* **h. and glove: to be h. in glove with s.o.,** être d'intelligence, *Pej:* de mèche, avec qn; **they're h. in glove,** ils sont comme les doigts de la main; ce sont deux têtes sous un même bonnet; ils ne font qu'un; (*h*) **h. and foot: to wait on s.o. h. and foot,** être aux petits soins pour, avec, qn; (*i*) **h. in h.: to go h. in h. with s.o.,** (i) marcher avec qn la main dans la main; (ii) agir de concert, d'intelligence, avec qn; **here stock raising goes h. in h. with the cultivation of cereals,** ici l'élevage marche de pair avec la culture des céréales; (*j*) **h. over h., h. over fist,** main sur main (en grimpant, etc.); **to make up on a ship h. over h.,** gagner un navire main sur main; (*of ship*) **to come up h. over h.,** approcher à toute vitesse; *Nau:* **to climb h. over fist,** se paumoyer; *F:* **to make money h. over fist,** s'enrichir rapidement, faire des affaires d'or; (*k*) **h. to h.:** (i) **to fight h. to h.,** combattre corps à corps; **h.-to-h. fight,** corps-à-corps *m inv.*; (ii) **to pass sth. from h. to h.,** passer qch. de main en main; **money given from h. to h.,** argent donné de la main à la main; (*l*) **h. to mouth: to be living from h. to mouth, to lead a h.-to-mouth existence,** vivre au jour le jour; pouvoir à peine joindre les deux bouts; (*m*) **hands down:** *Rac: etc:* **to win hands down,** gagner haut la main, facilement, aisément, sans cravache; *F:* arriver dans un fauteuil; **to beat s.o. hands down,** battre qn à plate(s) couture(s). **3.** (*a*) (*pers.*) ouvrier, -ière; manœuvre *m;* *Nau:* matelot *m;* *pl.* **(the ship's) hands,** l'équipage *m;* *Ind: etc:* **to take on hands,** embaucher de la main-d'œuvre; **hands wanted,** on embauche; on demande de la main-d'œuvre; *Nau:* **all hands on deck!** tout le monde sur le pont! en haut tout le monde! (*of ship*) **to be lost with all hands,** périr corps et biens; (*b*) **to be a good, a great, h. at sth., at doing sth.,** être adroit, avoir de l'habileté, à qch., à faire qch.; avoir le talent de faire qch.; **to be a great h. at tennis,** être fort au tennis; être un très bon joueur de tennis; **I'm a poor h. at billiards,** je suis un piètre joueur de billard; **I'm no great h. at poetry,** la poésie n'est pas mon fort; **to be a new h. at sth.,** être novice dans qch.; **he is no new h. at it,** il n'en est pas à son premier essai; **an old China h.,** un spécialiste des affaires chinoises. **4.** (*a*) écriture *f;* **round h., running h.,** écriture ronde, cursive; **to write (in) a small h.,** écrire en petits caractères; écrire fin; **he writes a very good h.,** il a une belle main, une belle écriture; **to write a letter in one's own h.,** écrire une lettre de sa propre main; **letters in the h. of the emperor,** lettres de la main de l'empereur; (*b*) signature *f;* *Jur:* **to set one's h. to a deed,** apposer sa signature à un acte; **under your h. and seal,** signé et scellé de votre propre main; **ordinance under the h. of. . .,** ordonnance signée par . . .; **note of h.,** billet *m* à ordre. **5.** *Cards:* (*a*) jeu *m;* **to have a good h.,** avoir beau jeu; avoir du jeu; **I'm holding my h.,** je me réserve; (*b*) la main, le coup; **to win the h.,** gagner la main; (*c*) joueur, -euse; **besique for three hands,** bésigue *m* à trois; **first h., fourth h.,** premier, dernier, en cartes; (*d*) partie *f;* **let's have a h. at bridge,** faisons une partie de bridge; si on faisait un bridge? **to finish the h.,** finir le coup. **6.** *Meas: Farr:* paume *f,* paumée *f;* **horse fifteen hands high,** cheval de quinze paumes. **7.** (*a*) *Typ:* index *m,* ☞; (*b*) (*of signpost*) indicateur *m;* (*c*) indicateur (de baromètre, etc.); aiguille *f* (de montre). **8.** (*a*) *Cu:* **h. of pork,** jambonneau *m;* (*b*) **h. of bananas,** paquet *m,* régime *m,* de bananes; (*c*) **h. of tobacco,** manoque *f* de feuilles de tabac. **9.** *Dom.Ec:* **Scotch hands,** palettes *f* à beurre. **10.** *Tex:* main (d'un tissu). **11.** *Z:* main; **the monkey has four hands,** le singe a quatre mains; **the hands of a parrot, of a hawk,** les mains d'un perroquet, d'un faucon. **12.** *attrib.* **h. luggage,** bagages *mpl* à main; **h. tool,** outil *m* à main; **h. lamp,** lampe portative, à main; baladeuse *f;* **(wash) h. basin,** lavabo *m;* cuvette *f;* **h. guard,** protège-main *m inv;* **h. pump,** pompe *f* à main; **h. sewn, h. stitched,** cousu (à la) main; **h. knitted,** tricoté à la main; **h. loom,** métier *m* (à tisser) à la main; métier à domicile; **h.-loom weaving,** tissage *m* à la main, à domicile; **h. sorting,** triage *m* à la main; *Min:* **scheidage, to h.-sort,** trier (qch.) à la main; *Min:* scheider (le minerai); **h. press,** (i) presse *f* à main; (ii) *Typ:* presse à bras; imprimeuse *f;* **h. lever,** manette *f;* levier *m* de manœuvre; *Aut: etc:* **h. brake,** frein *m* à main, à levier; *Mch: etc:* **h. feeding, firing, stoking,** alimentation *f,* chargement *m,* à la main; *Equit:* **h. gallop,** petit galop, galop de manège; *Ski:* **h. strap,** dragonne *f.*

hand[2], *v.*

I. *v.tr.* **1. he handed her into, out of, the car,** il lui a donné la main pour l'aider à monter dans la voiture, à sortir de la voiture. **2.** (*a*) passer, remettre, donner (qch. à qn); **to h. one's card to s.o.,** tendre sa carte à qn; **he handed her the letter to read,** il lui a donné la lettre à lire; (*b*) *F:* **to h. a boy a punishment,** coller une punition à un élève; **don't h. me that!** ne me raconte pas cela! (*c*) *F:* **to h. it to s.o.,** reconnaître la supériorité de qn; présenter le bouquet à qn; **you've got to h. it to him,** devant lui, chapeau! **for cheek, I must h. it to you,** pour ce qui est de toupet, il n'y a que vous. **3.** *Nau:* **to h. a sail,** serrer une voile.

II. (*compound verbs*) **1. hand down,** *v.tr.* (*a*) donner la main à (qn) pour l'aider à descendre; (*b*) descendre (qch.) (et le remettre à qn); (*c*) transmettre (une tradition, une coutume).

2. hand in, *v.tr.* (*a*) remettre, déposer (un paquet, un télégramme); **to h. in one's resignation,** démissionner; **to h. in one's checks,** (i) toucher ses jetons; (ii) *P:* mourir; (*b*) *Nau:* **to h. in the sail,** crocher dans la toile.

3. hand off, *v.tr. Rugby Fb:* écarter (un adversaire) avec le plat de la main.

4. hand on, *v.tr.* transmettre (une coutume, une tradition); **to h. on news,** passer une nouvelle (**to,** à).

5. hand out, *v.tr.* (*a*) tendre, remettre (qch. à qn); (*b*) **to h. out the wages,** distribuer la paie.

6. hand over, *v.tr.* remettre (qch. à qn); **to h. over the money,** remettre, *F:* allonger, l'argent; **to h. over a draft to a bank for collection,** confier à une banque le soin d'encaisser une traite; **you will h. it over to him personally,** vous le lui remettrez de la main à la main; **to h. over the money direct,** payer de la main à la main; **to h. s.o. over to justice,** livrer, remettre, qn aux mains de la justice; **to h. over the command to. . .,** remettre le commandement à . . .; **to h. over one's authority,** transmettre ses pouvoirs (**to,** à); **to h. over one's property to s.o.,** céder son bien à qn.

7. hand round, *v.tr.* passer, faire passer, (la bouteille, les gâteaux, etc.) à la ronde; faire circuler (la bouteille, etc.); **to hand around the box, the hat,** faire la quête.

handbag ['hændbæg], *s.* sac *m* à main.

handball ['hændbɔ:l], *s.* (*a*) balle *f* (pour jeux); (*b*) *Games:* hand-ball *m*; **indoor h.,** hand-ball à sept; **field h.,** hand-ball à onze.

handbell ['hændbel], *s.* sonnette *f*, clochette *f*.

handbill ['hændbil], *s.* prospectus *m*; programme *m* (de spectacle); affiche *f* à la main; **to give out handbills,** distribuer des prospectus.

handbook ['hændbuk], *s.* **1.** *Sch: etc:* manuel *m* (de sciences, etc.). **2.** guide *m* (du voyageur, du touriste); livret *m* (d'un musée, etc.). **3.** *Turf: NAm:* livre *m* de paris.

handbookman, *pl.* **-men** ['hændbukmən], *s. Turf: NAm:* bookmaker *m*, *F:* book *m*.

handcart ['hændkɑ:t], *s.* voiture *f* à bras, charrette *f* à bras; baladeuse *f*; diable *m*.

hand-controlled ['hændkən'trould], *a.* commandé à la main.

handcraft ['hændkrɑ:ft], *s.* = HANDICRAFT.

handcuff ['hændkʌf], *v.tr.* mettre les menottes à (qn), menotter (qn); **handcuffed,** emmenotté, menottes *f* aux mains.

handcuffs ['hændkʌfs], *s.pl.* menottes *f*.

-handed ['hændid], *a. with num. or adj. prefixed, e.g.* **two-h., four-h.,** à deux, à quatre, mains; **long-h.,** aux mains longues; *Z:* longimane.

Handel ['hænd(ə)l], *Pr.n. Mus. Hist:* Hændel.

Handelian [hæn'di:liən], *a. Mus:* de Hændel; à la manière de Hændel.

hand-feed ['hændfi:d], *s.* **1.** *Mch:* alimentation manuelle, à la main; *Mch.Tls:* avance *f* (d'un outil) à la main. **2.** *Typ:* marge *f* à main.

hand-fed ['hændfed], *a. Mch:* alimenté à la main, manuellement; (*of gun, computer, etc., magazine*) garni, rempli, à la main; (*of contents of magazine*) introduit à la main, manuellement.

handful ['hændful], *s.* **1.** poignée *f* (de sable, de noisettes, etc.); **to throw away handfuls of money, to throw money away by the h., in handfuls,** jeter l'argent à pleines mains, à poignées; **there was only a h. there,** il n'y avait là que quelques personnes. **2.** *F:* **that child is a h.,** cet enfant-là me donne du fil à retordre; c'est un enfant terrible. **3.** *Cards:* **to have a h. of trumps,** avoir de l'atout plein les mains.

handglass ['hændglɑ:s], *s.* **1.** loupe *f* à main (pour la lecture). **2.** miroir *m* à main. **3.** *Hort:* cloche *f*.

handgrip ['hændgrip], *s.* **1.** prise *f*; **to come to handgrips,** en venir aux prises, aux mains; **to be at handgrips with s.o.,** être aux prises avec qn. **2.** poignée *f* de main. **3.** *Cy:* poignée.

handhold ['hændhould], *s.* **1.** prise *f*; **crag with no h.,** varappe *f* où la main ne trouve pas de prise. **2.** (*of implement*) poignée *f* (de canne à pêche, etc.); main *f* de fer.

handicap[1] ['hændikæp], *s.* **1.** (*a*) *Sp:* handicap *m*; (*of racehorse*) **weight h.,** surcharge *f*; **time h., distance h.,** rendement *m* de temps, de distance; (*b*) *Turf:* (*race*) handicap; (*c*) désavantage *m*; **to overcome the h.,** (i) combler le handicap; (ii) compenser le désavantage; **he used to stammer, but he managed to overcome this h.,** il bégayait, mais il a réussi à vaincre ce handicap; **to have a severe h.,** être fort handicapé, désavantagé. **2.** rendement (accordé à un concurrent); *Golf:* nombre de coups concédé à un joueur en plus de la normale du parcours.

handicap[2], *v.tr.* (**handicapped**) **1.** *Sp:* handicaper. **2. he is handicapped by his poor health,** il est handicapé, désavantagé, par sa mauvaise santé.

handicapped ['hændikæpt], (*a*) *a.* handicapé; désavantagé; (*b*) *s.* **the h.,** les handicapés; **the physically h.,** les diminués physiques; **the mentally h.,** les déficients mentaux.

handicapper ['hændikæpər], *s.* **1.** *Sp:* handicapeur *m*. **2.** *Turf:* cheval *m* qui participe à des handicaps.

handicapping ['hændikæpiŋ], *s. Sp:* handicapage *m*; *Y:* allégeance *f*.

handicraft ['hændikrɑ:ft], *s.* **1.** travail manuel; habileté manuelle. **2.** (*a*) (*trade*) métier manuel; **productions of the local handicrafts,** produits *m* d'artisanat régional; (*b*) artisanat *m* d'expression.

handicraftsman, *pl.* **-men** ['hændikrɑ:ftsmən], *s.m.* artisan, ouvrier; homme de métier.

handily ['hændili], *adv.* **1.** adroitement, habilement. **2.** (placé) commodément, sous la main.

handiness ['hændinis], *s.* **1.** adresse *f*, dextérité *f*; habileté (manuelle). **2.** (*a*) commodité *f* (d'un outil, etc.); (*b*) maniabilité *f* (d'un navire, etc.).

handing ['hændiŋ], *s.* remise *f* (de qch. à qn); **h. down, on,** transmission *f* (d'une tradition, etc.); **h. over,** (i) remise *f* (de qch.) entre les mains de qn; (ii) cession *f*, délivrance *f* (de biens); transmission *f* (de pouvoirs); résignation *f* (d'un bénéfice, etc.).

handiwork ['hændiwə:k], *s.* (*a*) travail manuel; (*b*) ouvrage *m*, travail *m*, œuvre *f*; **his h.,** le travail de ses mains; son ouvrage; *F:* **that's some of his h.!** voilà encore de son ouvrage! c'est encore lui qui a fait des siennes!

handkerchief ['hæŋkətʃi:f], *s.* **1.** (**pocket**) **h.,** mouchoir *m* (de poche); **fancy h.,** pochette *f*; **silk h.,** mouchoir de soie; **garden the size of a pocket h.,** jardin grand comme un mouchoir de poche. **2.** (*for the head*) fanchon *f*, marmotte *f*, carré *m*.

handle[1] ['hændl], *s.* **1.** (*a*) manche *m* (de balai, etc.); bras *m*, balancier *m*, brimbale *f* (de pompe); branloire *f* (de soufflet de forge); brancard *m* (de civière); bras (de brouette); (*of shovel, etc.*) **crutch h.,** manche à poignée en croisillon; **stirrup h., D h.,** manche à poignée en étrier; *Cr: F:* **to use the long h.,** frapper dur; (*b*) (*grip*) manche (de couteau, d'outil); queue *f* (de poêle); poignée *f* (d'épée, de levier, d'aviron, de bicyclette, etc.); clef *f* (de robinet); (*of crank handle, etc.*); **loose h.,** nille *f*, giron *m*, maneton *m*; **bow h. of a file,** arbalète *f* d'une lime; *El:* **switch h.,** manette *f* d'interrupteur; **to fix a new h. on a tool,** (r)emmancher un outil; **to remove the h. of a tool,** démancher un outil; (*of tool*) **to lose its h.,** se démancher; *F:* **to have a h. to one's name,** (i) avoir un titre (de noblesse); (ii) avoir un nom à particule; avoir la particule; **you're giving him a h. against you,** vous lui donnez des armes, un avantage, contre vous; (*c*) anse *f* (de broc, de corbeille, de seau, etc.); portant *m* (de boîte, de valise); happe *f* (de chaudière); (*d*) (*crank handle*) manivelle *f*; menotte *f* (de treuil); *Aut:* (**starting**) **h.,** manivelle (de mise en marche). **2.** *Com:* panier *m* (de fruits).

handle[2], *v.tr.* **1.** tâter des mains; **to h. a material,** tâter un tissu; (*with passive force*) **paper that handles easily,** papier *m* qui a de la main. **2.** (*a*) manier, manipuler (qch.); **tool easy to h.,** outil *m* facile à manier, bien en main(s), à la main; **how to h. a gun,** comment se servir d'un fusil; **to learn to h. sth.,** se faire la main; *Post:* **h. with care** = fragile; *Ind: etc:* **to h. heavy pieces,** manutentionner des pièces lourdes; *Nau:* **to h. a ship, the sails,** manœuvrer, manier, un navire, les voiles; gouverner un navire; *A:* **to h. the ribbons,** tenir les guides; (*b*) manier (qn, une affaire); manipuler (une affaire); **he is hard to h.,** il n'est pas commode; il est peu traitable; **to h. s.o. roughly,** malmener, rudoyer, qn; **to h. a subject delicately,** traiter un sujet, s'y prendre, avec ménagement; **to h. a situation,** prendre en main une situation; **he handled the situation in a masterly manner,** il s'est montré à la hauteur de la situation; (*c*) **to h. a lot of business,** brasser beaucoup d'affaires; **to h. large orders,** s'occuper de grandes commandes; **to h. a lot of money,** remuer beaucoup d'argent, avoir un maniement considérable; **we don't h. these goods,** nous ne tenons pas ces articles; **we are in a position to h. any sort of business,** nous sommes à même d'exécuter n'importe quelle opération; **the firm that will h. our move,** la maison qui assurera notre déménagement. **3.** *Fb:* **to h. the ball,** toucher le ballon.

handle[3], *v.tr.* emmancher (un outil).

handlebar ['hændlbɑ:r], *s.* **1.** guidon *m* (de bicyclette); **racing type h.,** guidon course; **bent h.,** guidon cintré; *F:* **h. moustache,** moustaches *f* raides, en guidon (de bicyclette). **2.** poignée *f* de direction.

handled[1] ['hændld], *a. Fb:* **h. ball,** ballon manié.

handled[2], *a.* **1.** (outil, etc.) emmanché, à manche. **2.** *with adj. or sb. prefixed;* **ivory-h.,** à manche d'ivoire; **short-h.,** à manche court; **crutch-h. umbrella,** parapluie *m* à béquille; **crutch-h. walking stick,** béquillon *m*.

handler ['hændlər], *s.* manipulateur, -trice; *Com:* manutentionnaire *mf*.

handline ['hændlain], *s. Fish:* ligne *f*; cordeau *m* à main.

handling[1] ['hændliŋ], *s.* (*a*) maniement *m* (d'un outil, etc.); manipulation *f* (des explosifs, etc.); manutention *f* (de bagages, de marchandises, etc.); manœuvre *f* (d'un navire); **industrial h.,** manutention industrielle; *Ind:* **h. capacity,** capacité *f* de traitement; *Cmptr: Rad:* **data h.,** exploitation *f* de l'information; **to understand the h. of a car,** s'entendre au maniement, à la conduite, d'une voiture; **skill in h.,** dextérité manœuvrière; *Aer:* **h. guy,** corde *f* de manœuvre; (*b*) traitement *m* (de qn, d'un sujet, etc.); *F:* **he takes some h.,** il n'est pas commode; **rough h.,** traitement brutal; **the enquiry will call for delicate h.,** l'enquête sera délicate; (*c*) maniement (de fonds); (*d*) *Com:* distribution *f*.

handling[2], *s.* emmanchement *m* (d'un outil).

handmade ['hænd'meid], *a.* fait, fabriqué, à la main.

handmaid(en) ['hændmeid(n)], *s. A:* servante *f*.

hand-me-downs ['hændmidaunz], *s.pl. esp. NAm: F:* vêtements usagés, d'occasion; frusques *fpl*; décrochez-moi-ça *m*.

hand-operated ['hænd'ɔpəreitid], *a.* à commande manuelle; commandé, actionné, à la main.

handout ['hændaut], *s. F:* **1.** (i) aumône *f*; (ii) nourriture distribuée aux mendiants; **to live on handouts,** vivre d'aumône. **2.** (*a*) *Journ:* compte rendu communiqué à la presse; (*b*) *Sch: etc:* notes (polycopiées) (données aux élèves). **3.** *Com:* (*a*) prospectus *m*, circulaire *m* publicitaire; (*b*) cadeau *m* publicitaire.

handover ['hændouvər], *s. Com: etc:* passation *f*.

hand-pick ['hændpik], *v.tr.* trier (le charbon, etc.) à la main; éplucher (la laine, etc.) à la main; *F:* **hand-picked gathering,** réunion triée sur le volet, très sélecte; *Mil:* **hand-picked troops,** troupes d'élite, triées sur le volet.

hand-picking ['hændpikiŋ], *s.* ramassage *m* à la main, cueillette *f*.

handrail ['hændreil], *s.* garde-fou *m*, *pl.* garde-fous; garde-corps *m inv*; balustrade *f*; lisse *f*, barre *f* d'appui (de pont); rampe *f*, main courante, main coulante (d'escalier, de locomotive, etc.); (*on wall side of staircase*) écuyer *m*; *Nau:* rambarde *f*.

handsaw ['hændsɔ:], *s.* scie *f* à main; (*small*) égohine *f*, égoïne *f*; *Stonew:* sciotte *f*.

handsel[1] ['hænsl], *s.* **1.** (*a*) étrenne *f*; (*b*) *Com:* première vente (de la journée). **2.** arrhes *fpl*.

handsel[2], *v.tr.* (**handselled**) **1.** (*a*) donner des étrennes à (qn); (*b*) **to h. a dealer,** donner des arrhes à un marchand. **2.** (*a*) (*use for the first time*) étrenner, avoir l'étrenne de (qch.).

handset ['hændset], *s. Tp:* combiné *m*.

handshake ['hændʃeik], *s.* (*a*) poignée *f* de main; serrement *m* de main; *F:* **golden h.,** indemnité *f* de départ, cadeau *m* d'adieu, pont *m* d'or; **to give s.o. the golden h.,** remercier qn en le dédommageant grassement; (*b*) *Cmptr:* **h. message,** message *m* d'établissement de liaison, de colloque.

handshaker ['hændʃeikər], *s. esp. U.S: F:* homme *m* à l'accueil expansif, qui a la poignée de main facile.

handshaking ['hændʃeikiŋ], *s.* (*a*) poignées *f* de main; **I'm on h. terms with him,** je le connais assez pour lui serrer la main; (*b*) *Cmptr:* établissement *m* d'une liaison, d'une colloque.

handsome ['hænsəm], *a.* (*a*) beau, *f.* belle; **a h. man,** un bel homme, un homme bien fait; **h. young man,** jeune homme bien tourné, de belle mine; **as h. as a (young) Greek god,** beau comme l'Amour; **to grow h.,** embellir; **at sixty she was still a h. woman,** à soixante ans elle était toujours belle; **a h. wardrobe,** une belle armoire; une armoire élégante; **h. house,** belle demeure; (*b*) (*of conduct, etc.*) gracieux, généreux; **he received very h. treatment (in spite of . . .),** (en dépit de . . .) on l'a traité d'une façon généreuse; *F:* **to do the h. (thing) by s.o.,** être généreux, se montrer chic, envers qn; *Prov:* **h. is that, as, h. does,** beau est qui bien fait; la naissance ne fait pas la noblesse; noblesse vient de vertu; (*c*) (*considerable*) **h. fortune,** belle fortune; **h. price,** bon prix; **h. gift,** cadeau généreux; **to make a h. profit,** faire, réaliser, de beaux bénéfices; (*d*) *adv. F:* **to come down h.,** ouvrir largement sa bourse; se montrer généreux.

handsomely ['hænsəmli], *adv.* **1.** (agir) généreusement; (payer) libéralement, sans regarder à la dépense; **they acted very h. towards him,** ils l'ont traité d'une façon très généreuse; *F:* **to come down h.,** ouvrir largement sa bourse; payer sans se faire tirer l'oreille; se montrer généreux. **2.** *Nau:* doucement, en douceur, à la demande.

handsomeness ['hænsəmnis], *s.* (*a*) beauté *f*, élégance *f*, grâce *f* (d'une personne, d'un monument, etc.); (*b*) générosité *f* (d'une action); libéralité *f* (d'une récompense).

handspike ['hændspaik], *s.* **1.** (*a*) *Nau:* barre *f* d'anspect; levier *m* (en bois); barre de guindeau; (*b*) **carrying h.,** brancard *m*; (*c*) *Artil:* levier de manœuvre. **2. claw h.,** pince *f* à pied de biche.

handstand ['hændstænd], *s. Gym:* **to do a h.,** faire l'arbre fourchu, l'arbre droit, le poirier.

hand-tool ['hændtu:l], *v.tr. Bookb:* dorer (une couverture) à la main.

hand-tooling ['hændtu:liŋ], *s.* **1.** *Ind:* travail *m* à la main (sur le tour, etc.). **2.** *Bookb:* dorure à froid faite à la main.

handwork ['hændwə:k], *s.* travail *m* à la main, travail manuel.

handworker ['hændwə:kər], *s.* ouvrier, -ière.

handwriting ['hændraitiŋ], *s.* écriture *f*; **English style of h.,** écriture anglaise; **h. expert,** expert *m* en écritures; **this letter is in the h. of. . . ,** cette lettre a été écrite par . . ., est de la main de . . ..

handwritten ['hændrit(ə)n], *a.* (*of letter, etc.*) manuscrit.

handy ['hændi], *a.* **1.** (*of pers.*) adroit (de ses mains); habile; qui peut mettre la main à tout; débrouillard; **he's very h.,** il sait se servir de ses dix doigts; **he's very h. about the house,** (i) il aide bien au ménage; (ii) il sait bien faire les petites réparations (à la maison); c'est un bon bricoleur; **h. at sth., at doing sth.,** adroit à qch., à faire qch.; **to be h. with a tool, with one's fists,** savoir se servir d'un outil, de ses poings; *Dressm: O:* **h. girl,** petite main. **2.** (*of tool, etc.*) maniable, bien en main(s); **h. ship,** navire maniable, manœuvrier. **3.** commode; **h. size,** format *m* commode; *Com:* **with h. grip,** avec nervures de préhension; **a small car would be very h.,** une petite voiture serait bien commode, ferait bien notre affaire; **that would come in very h.,** cela serait très utile, ferait bien l'affaire. **4.** (*ready to hand*) à portée (de la main); sous la main; **I always keep my tools h.,** j'ai toujours mes outils sous la main.

handyman, *pl.* **-men** ['hændimæn, -men], *s.m.* homme à tout faire, à toute main; bricoleur, factotum.

hang[1] [hæŋ], *s.* **1.** (*a*) pente *f*, inclinaison *f* (d'une falaise, etc.); (*b*) ajustement *m* (d'un vêtement); drapé *m* (d'un tissu); (*c*) *F:* **to get the h. of sth.,** (i) attraper le coup, saisir le truc, de qch., pour faire qch.; (ii) comprendre, piger, qch.; saisir le sens de qch.; **I couldn't get the h. of what he was saying,** je n'ai pas pu suivre ce qu'il disait; je me demande bien ce qu'il voulait dire; **when you've got the h. of things,** quand vous serez au courant. **2.** *Metall:* accrochage *m* (du minerai dans le haut fourneau). **3.** *F:* **I don't give, care, a h.,** je m'en moque, m'en fiche; *O:* **it's not worth a h.,** ça ne vaut pas deux sous, ne vaut pas tripette.

hang[2], *v.* (**hung** [hʌŋ]; **hung**)

I. *v.tr.* **1.** pendre, accrocher, suspendre (**on, from,** à); **to h. one's hat on a peg,** accrocher son chapeau à une patère; **to h. a lamp from the ceiling,** pendre une lampe au plafond; **to h. a bell,** poser une sonnette; **to h. sth. on the wall,** pendre qch. au mur; **to h. a picture,** (i) suspendre un tableau; (ii) exposer un tableau (au salon, etc.); **to h. a door,** monter, poser, accrocher, une porte; mettre une porte sur ses gonds; garnir une porte de gonds; *Nau:* **to h. the rudder,** monter le gouvernail; *Veh: etc:* **hung on springs,** monté sur ressorts; *Aut: etc:* **low-hung (axle, etc.),** (essieu, etc.) surbaissé. **2.** (*droop*) **to h. one's head,** baisser la tête; **the old dog hung its ears,** le vieux chien laissait pendre ses oreilles. **3.** *Cu:* faire faisander, mortifier, faire vener (la viande, le gibier); attendre (la viande). **4.** (*a*) **to h. a room with tapestries,** tendre une salle de tapisseries; **windows hung with lace curtains,** fenêtres garnies de rideaux en dentelle; **hall hung with flags,** salle ornée de drapeaux; (*b*) **to h. wallpaper,** coller du papier à tapisser. **5. to h. fire,** (i) (*of firearms*) faire long feu; (ii) (*of undertaking, etc.*) traîner (en longueur); *Artil:* **fuse that hangs fire,** fusée *f* qui foire; **the business is hanging fire,** l'affaire est mal emmanchée, l'affaire fait long feu. **6.** (*p.t. & p.p.* **hanged**) (*a*) pendre (un criminel); **to be hanged for a pirate,** être pendu pour piraterie; **he hanged himself out of despair,** il s'est pendu par désespoir; *F:* **h. him!** que le diable l'emporte! **you be hanged!** va te faire pendre! **I'm hanged if I know!** je n'en sais fichtre rien! **h. it!** zut! mince alors! **h. the expense!** tant pis pour la dépense! **that be hanged!** si tu crois que je vais avaler ça! *Prov:* **as well be hanged for a sheep as for a lamb,** autant vaut être pendu pour un mouton que pour un agneau; pendu pour pendu, autant vaut être pendu pour quelque chose; *F:* puisqu'on est sûrs d'être punis, autant vaut en avoir pour sa punition; (*b*) *NAm:* **to h. a jury,** faire avorter les délibérations d'un jury, (i) (*of lawyer*) en faisant refuser, (ii) (*of juror*) en refusant de se conformer à, l'avis de la majorité.

II. *v.i.* **1.** pendre, être suspendu; *Cu:* (*of game*) se faisander; (*of monkey*) **to h. by the tail,** pendre, être suspendu, par la queue; **picture hanging on the wall,** tableau pendu, accroché, au mur; **fruit hanging on a tree,** fruits *m* qui pendent à un arbre; **goat hanging on to a rock,** chèvre suspendue au flanc d'une roche; **aqueduct hanging over a torrent,** aqueduc suspendu sur un torrent; **to h. out of the window,** (*of pers.*) se pencher par la fenêtre, (*of thg*) pendre à la fenêtre. **2. a thick fog hangs over the town,** un épais brouillard plane, pèse, sur la ville; **a great danger is hanging over you, over your head,** un grand danger vous menace, plane au-dessus de vous; vous êtes sous le coup d'un grand danger; **the danger hanging over our heads,** le danger suspendu sur nos têtes; **the threat hanging over this country,** la menace suspendue sur notre pays; **a heavy silence hung over the meeting,** un silence pesait sur l'assemblée. **3.** (*a*) **to h. on s.o.'s arm,** (*of thg*) pendre au bras de qn; (*of pers.*) se pendre au bras de qn; s'appuyer sur le bras de qn; se cramponner au bras de qn; **to h. round s.o.'s neck,** se (sus)pendre au cou de qn; **to h. on s.o.'s lips, words,** être suspendu aux lèvres de qn; boire les paroles de qn; **the children hung on his every word,** les enfants l'écoutaient avidement; (*b*) (*depend*) **everything hangs on his answer,** tout dépend de sa réponse; **the whole of human life hangs on probabilities,** toute la vie humaine roule sur des probabilités; **everything hangs on this essential point,** ce point essentiel emporte tout le reste; **the whole thing hangs on that,** cela c'est, c'est là, le nœud de l'affaire, l'affaire tourne là-dessus. **4. horse that hangs on the bit,** cheval *m* qui appuie sur le mors; **responsibility hangs heavy upon him,** la responsabilité pèse sur lui; **time hangs heavy (on my hands),** le temps me pèse, me dure, me semble long; les heures traînent, sont bien lentes; les heures se traînent lourdement. **5.** (*a*) fainéanter, flâner; **he's always hanging about, around, here,** il est toujours à rôder par ici; **to h. about, around, the house doing nothing,** traîner à la maison sans rien faire; **to keep s.o. hanging about, around,** faire poireauter qn; **to h. round a woman,** tourner autour d'une femme; (*b*) **their cavalry was hanging about our flanks,** leur cavalerie s'attachait à nos flancs, nous harcelait de part et d'autre. **6.** (*a*) (*of drapery, clothes, etc.*) tomber, se draper; **to h. loose,** pendiller, flotter; **to h. limply,** pendouiller; **his clothes h. loosely on him,** il flotte dans ses vêtements; **her hair was hanging round her neck, down her back,** ses cheveux lui flottaient autour du cou, lui descendaient dans le dos; (*b*) **this door hangs badly,** cette porte est mal suspendue (sur ses gonds); (*c*) **that steeple hangs,** ce clocher penche. **7.** (*of criminal*) être pendu; *A:* **to h. as high as Haman,** être pendu haut et court; **you shall h. for it,** je te ferai pendre! *F:* **if he doesn't like it he can go h.,** si ça ne lui plaît pas, qu'il aille au diable, qu'il aille se faire pendre, se faire fiche. **8.** (*to be slow, delay*) *Nau:* **to h. in the wind,** rester dans le vent; **the ship is hanging,** le navire est engourdi; *Metall:* **the furnace hangs,** le haut fourneau s'accroche.

III. (*compound verbs*) **1. hang back,** *v.i.* (*a*) rester en arrière; (*b*) hésiter; faire le réservé; montrer peu d'empressement; renâcler.

2. hang behind, *v.i.* rester en arrière; traîner derrière.

3. hang down, *v.i.* (*a*) pendre; **your hair's hanging down,** vos cheveux pendent; (*b*) pencher (sous le poids de qch.).

4. hang on, *v.i.* se cramponner, s'accrocher; **you'll have to h. on to your job,** il ne faut pas que vous lâchiez votre emploi; *Tp:* **h. on!** ne quittez pas (l'écoute)! **h. on for a moment,** attendez un moment; **we must h. on until reinforcements arrive,** il faut tenir bon jusqu'à l'arrivée des renforts; **he's always hanging on to his mother's apron strings,** il est toujours dans les jupons de sa mère; **he's hung on to me all day,** il a été à mes talons toute la journée; *Nau:* **to h. on to a ship,** s'accrocher à un navire; suivre un navire de près; **to h. on by the skin of one's teeth, like grim death,** se cramponner; tenir tout juste.

5. hang out. (*a*) *v.tr.* pendre, mettre, (qch.) au dehors; étendre (le linge); arborer (un pavillon); (*of thg*) **to h. out its tongue,** tirer la langue; *NAm:* (*of lawyer, doctor, dentist*) **to h. out one's shingle,** ouvrir une étude, un cabinet; (*b*) *v.i.* (i) pendre (au dehors); **his trousers were torn and his shirt was hanging out,** son pantalon était déchiré et sa chemise passait; *F:* **where do you h. out?** où nichez-vous? où perchez-vous? où juchez-vous? (ii) **the rocks h. out over the gully,** les rochers surplombent le ravin; (iii) *Ind: etc:* **to h. out for better terms,** s'obstiner à obtenir de meilleures conditions.

6. hang over, *v.i.* (*a*) (*of rock, etc.*) surplomber; (*b*) *NAm:* (*of belief, etc.*) survivre.

7. hang together, *v.i.* (*a*) (*of pers.*) se sentir les coudes, rester unis; (*b*) (*of statements, etc.*) s'accorder, se tenir, *F:* tenir debout.

8. hang up, *v.tr.* (*a*) (i) accrocher, pendre (son chapeau, un vêtement, un tableau, etc.); **to h. up one's sword,** pendre, mettre, son épée au croc; (ii) *Tp:* raccrocher (l'appareil); *F:* **to h. up on s.o.,** couper la communication avec qn; (*b*) **to h. up a plan,** ajourner un projet; remettre un projet à plus tard; **the work is hung up,** le travail est arrêté, suspendu; **parcels hung up in transit,** les colis *m* en souffrance; **all my plans are hung up pending decision of this lawsuit,** ce procès a mis mes projets en souffrance, a arrêté tous mes projets; **we were hung up with a puncture,** nous avons été retardés par une crevaison.

hangar ['hæŋər], *s. esp. Av:* hangar *m*; **revolving h.,** hangar orientable; **portable h.,** hangar démontable; **h. floor,** aire *f* de hangar.

hangarage ['hæŋəridʒ], *s.* hangars *mpl* (pour avions).

hangbird ['hæŋbəːd], *s. Orn: NAm:* loriot *m.*

hangdog ['hæŋdɔg], *a.* **h. look,** air *m* de chien battu.

hanger[1] ['hæŋər], *s.* **1.** (*pers.*) (*a*) poseur *m* (de tapisseries, etc.); **bell h.,** poseur *m* de sonnettes; (*b*) *A:* = HANGMAN. **2.** (*device*) (*a*) crochet *m* (de suspension); croc *m*; **(coat) h.,** cintre *m*; porte-vêtements *m inv*; *A:* **pothooks and hangers,** bâtons *m* et jambages *m* (de la première leçon d'écriture); (*b*) *U.S:* pancarte *f*; (*c*) *Mec.E:* suspenseur *m*; **bearing h.,** chaise suspendue, chaise pendante; **bracket h.,** palier *m* à potence, de suspension; **pipe h.,** étrier *m* de suspension (de canalisations); **h. pin,** boulon *m* de suspension; *Veh:* **h. of a spring,** main *f* de fer d'un ressort. **3.** pente boisée, coteau boisé; petit bois à flanc de coteau. **4.** (*pers.*) **h.-back,** *pl.* **hangers-back,** renâcleur *m.* **5.** (*pers.*) **h.-on,** *pl.* **hangers-on,** (i) dépendant *m*; (*of minister, etc.*) pilier *m* d'antichambre; (ii) parasite *m*, *F:* écumeur *m* de marmites, pique-assiette *m inv*, écornifleur *m*; (iii) *A:* non-combattant *m* à la suite de l'armée.

hanger[2], *s. A:* (*a*) coutelas *m*; (*b*) couteau *m* de chasse.

hanging[1] ['hæŋiŋ], *a.* **1.** (pont) suspendu; (crochet, lustre) pendant; (échafaudage) volant; *Arch:* en pendentif; **h. stair,** escalier *m* en encorbellement; **h. sleeves,** manches tombantes; (*under cart*) **h. box,** branloire *f*; **h. compass,** compas renversé; **h. door,** porte battante; **h. cupboard,** armoire murale; **h. flower-pot,** suspension *f* porte-pot; **the h. gardens of Babylon,** les jardins suspendus de Babylone; **h. valley,** vallée suspendue; *Arch:* **h. keystone,** clef pendante. **2.** *F:* **h. judge,** juge *m* féroce, qui condamne tous les accusés à la potence.

hanging[2], *s.* **1.** (*a*) suspension *f* (d'une lampe, d'un tableau, etc.); pose *f* (d'une sonnette, etc.); montage *m*, accrochage *m* (d'une porte); *Cu:* mortification *f* (du gibier); attendrissement *m* (de la viande); (*b*) tenture *f* (d'une tapisserie); (*c*) pendaison *f* (d'un criminel); **it's a h. matter,** c'est un cas pendable; il y va de la corde; *F:* **hanging's too good for him,** il ne vaut pas la corde pour le pendre; il n'est pas bon à jeter aux chiens; (*d*) **h. wardrobe, closet, press,** penderie *f*; **h. committee,** comité *m* de réception, jury *m* d'admission, des tableaux au Salon (à Paris), à la *Royal Academy* (à Londres); **h. post (of lock gate, entrance-gate, etc.),** chardonnet *m* (de sas d'écluse, de porte cochère, etc.). **2.** *pl.* **hangings,** tenture *f*; tapisserie *f*; **window hangings,** décor *m* de fenêtre; **bed hangings,** rideaux *m* de lit; **funeral hangings (in church),** ceinture *f* de deuil, ceinture funèbre.

hangman, *pl.* **-men** ['hæŋmən], *s.m.* bourreau.

hangnail ['hæŋneil], *s.* envie *f* (filet de peau qui s'est détaché de l'ongle).

hangout ['hæŋaut], *s. F:* (*a*) logement *m*, chez soi *m*; (*b*) repaire *m*, nid *m* (de criminels, etc.).

hangover ['hæŋouvər], *s. F:* **1.** reliquat *m*, reste *m* (de superstition, d'une habitude, etc.). **2.** obnubilation matinale; **to have a h.,** avoir la gueule de bois, avoir mal aux cheveux.

hang-up ['hæŋʌp], *s.* (*a*) *Cmptr:* arrêt imprévu (de la machine, du programme); (*b*) *F:* trouble *m* psychique.

hank [hæŋk], *s.* **1.** écheveau *m* (de laine, etc.); torchette *f*, poignée *f* (de fil); matteau *m* (de soie grège); manoque *f* (de filin); **to bundle yarn into hanks,** torcher le fil; **h. knotter,** torcheuse *f.* **2.** *Nau:* rocambeau *m*, cosse *f*, bague *f*, manoque *f.*

hanker ['hæŋkər], *v.i.* **to h. after sth.,** désirer vivement, ardemment, qch.; avoir bien envie de, soupirer après, convoiter, qch.; être talonné par le désir de qch.; **to h. after praise,** être affamé, assoiffé, de louanges; avoir soif de louanges.

hankering ['hæŋkəriŋ], *s.* vif désir, grande envie (**after, for,** de); **to have a h. for sth.,** soupirer après qch.; **h. after power,** soif *f*, ambition *f*, du pouvoir; **h. after the stage,** aspirations *fpl* à la scène; **he had hankerings after the sea,** (i) il avait la nostalgie de la mer; (ii) il avait des envies de se faire marin.

Hankow ['hæŋ'kau], *Pr.n. Geog:* Hankéou *m*, Hang-Kéou *m.*

hanky ['hæŋki], *s. F.* mouchoir *m.*

hanky-panky ['hæŋki'pæŋki], *s.* **1.** tour *m* de passe-passe. **2.** *F:* supercherie *f*; finasseries *fpl*; **that's all h.-p.,** tout ça c'est du boniment; **to play h.-p. with s.o.,** (i) se jouer de qn, mettre qn dedans, tendre un panneau à qn; (ii) finasser avec qn.

Hannah ['hænə], *Pr.n.f.* Anne, Anna.

Hannibal ['hænib(ə)l], *Pr.n.m. A.Hist:* Annibal.

Hanno ['hænou], *Pr.n.m. A.Hist:* Hannon.

Hanoi [hæ'nɔi], *Pr.n. Geog:* Hanoï.

Hanover ['hænəvər], *Pr.n. Geog:* Hanovre *m.*

Hanoverian [hænə'viəriən]. **1.** *Geog:* (*a*) *s.* Hanovrien, -ienne; (*b*) *a.* hanovrien. **2.** *s. Hist:* **the Hanoverians,** la dynastie de Hanovre.

Hansard ['hænsɑːd], *s.* compte rendu officiel des débats parlementaires (longtemps rédigé par M. Hansard).

hanse [hæns], *s. Hist:* hanse *f*; **the H.,** la Hanse, la Ligue hanséatique.

Hanseatic [hænsi'ætik], *a. Hist:* (ville *f*) hanséatique; **the H. League,** la Ligue hanséatique; la Hanse.

hansel[1,2] ['hænsl], *s.* & *v.tr.* = HANDSEL[1,2].

hansom ['hænsəm], *s. A.Veh:* **h. (cab),** hansom *m.*

Hanuman ['hænjumən]. **1.** *Pr.n.m. Indian Myth:*

Hanouman. **2.** *s. Z:* entelle *m.*

hap[1] [hæp], *s. A:* **1.** hasard *m*, sort *m*, destin *m*. **2.** événement fortuit et malheureux; hasard malencontreux.

hap[2], *v.i.* **(happed)** *A:* **1.** arriver par hasard. **2.** *(of pers.)* **to h. on sth.,** trouver, rencontrer, qch. par hasard; **to h. to do sth.,** faire qch. par hasard.

hap[3], *v.tr.* **(happed,** *Scot:* **happit)** *Dial:* couvrir, envelopper **(s.o. with sth.,** qn de qch.); **to h. a child in bed,** border un enfant dans son lit.

Hapalidae [hæ'pælidi:], *s.pl. Z:* hapalidés *m.*

ha'penny, *pl.* **ha'pence** ['heipəni, -pəns], *s. F:* = HALFPENNY; **more kicks than ha'pence,** plus de peine que de profit.

haphazard [hæp'hæzəd]. **1.** *adv.* par, au, hasard; au petit bonheur, à l'aventure. **2.** *a.* **h. attempt,** tentative *f* au petit bonheur; **h. arrangement,** disposition fortuite; **to act, choose, in a h. way,** agir, choisir, à l'aveuglette.

haphazardly [hæp'hæzədli], *adv.* au petit bonheur; à l'aveuglette; aventureusement, à l'aventure.

hapless ['hæplis], *a. A: & Lit:* infortuné, malheureux.

haplite ['hæplait], *s. Miner:* aplite *f.*

haplobiont [hæplou'baiɔnt], *s. Biol:* haplobionte *m.*

haplobiontic [hæploubai'ɔntik], *a. Biol:* haplobiontique.

haplography [hæp'lɔgrəfi], *s.* haplographie *f.*

haploid ['hæplɔid], *a. Biol:* haploïde.

haploidy ['hæplɔidi], *s. Biol:* haploïdie *f.*

haplology [hæp'lɔlədʒi], *s. Gram: Ling:* haplologie *f.*

haploma [hæp'loumə], *s. Ecc:* haplome *f.*

Haplomi ['hæploumai], *s.pl. Ich:* haplomes *m.*

haplomitosis [hæploumi'tousis], *s. Biol:* haplomitose *f.*

haplont ['hæplɔnt], *s. Biol:* haplonte *m.*

haplopetalous ['hæplou'petələs], *a. Bot:* haplopétale.

haplophase ['hæploufeiz], *s. Biol:* haplophase *f.*

haply ['hæpli], *adv. A:* **1.** peut-être; il se peut que + *sub.* **2.** par hasard.

ha'p'orth ['heipəθ], *s. F:* (= HALFPENNYWORTH) **give me a h.,** donnez-m'en pour un sou; **he hasn't a h. of courage,** il n'a pas pour deux sous de courage.

happen ['hæp(ə)n], *v.i.* **1.** *(take place)* *(a)* arriver, se passer; advenir, survenir, se produire; **it happened ten years ago,** cela s'est passé il y a dix ans; **it can never h. here,** cela ne nous arrivera pas; **accidents will h.,** les accidents arrivent; *F:* **worse things h. at sea,** il y a pire; **to h. again,** se reproduire, se renouveler; **thing that happens over and over again,** chose qui se répète souvent; **don't let it h. again!** que cela n'arrive plus! que cela ne vous arrive plus! **fortunately nothing of the kind happened,** par bonheur il n'en fut rien; **just as if nothing had happened,** comme si de rien n'était; sans faire semblant de rien; **to relate the facts as they actually happened,** raconter les faits historiquement; **I don't (quite) know how it happened,** je ne sais pas (trop) comment cela s'est fait; **whatever happens,** quoi qu'il advienne; quoi qu'il arrive; dans tous les cas; **h. what may,** advienne que pourra; **how does it h. that . . .?** d'où vient que . . .? **it might h. that . . .,** il pourrait se faire que . . .; **it so happened that . . .,** le hasard a voulu que . . .; il se trouva que . . .; il arriva que . . .; **it so happens that I have an hour to spare,** il se trouve que j'ai une heure de libre; **as it happens, happened,** justement, précisément; **should it so h.,** le cas échéant; **this seldom happens,** ce fait est rare; **as often happens,** comme il est fréquent; **how things h.!** comme cela se rencontre! *(b)* **what has happened to him?** (i) qu'est-ce qui lui est arrivé? (ii) qu'est-ce qu'il est devenu? **if anything happened to you,** (i) s'il vous arrivait quelque chose; (ii) si vous veniez à mourir; **something's happened to him,** il lui est arrivé quelque malheur; **what's happened to my pen?** qu'est-ce qu'on a fait de mon stylo? **something's happened to the radio,** la radio ne marche plus. **2.** *(chance)* **to h. to do sth.,** faire qch. accidentellement; **he happened to pass that way,** il s'est trouvé passer par là; **a taxi happened to be passing,** par hasard, par bonheur, un taxi passait; **the house happened to be empty,** la maison se trouvait vide; **I happened to be there,** je me trouvais là; **I h. to know that . . .,** je me trouve savoir que . . .; **do you h. to know whether . . .?** sauriez-vous par hasard si . . .? **how do you h. to know?** comment se fait-il que vous le sachiez? **if I do sometimes h. to forget,** s'il m'advient, m'arrive, quelquefois d'oublier; **if you h. to find it,** s'il arrive que vous le trouviez. **3. to h. on sth., on s.o.,** tomber sur qch., qn; trouver, rencontrer, qch., qn, par hasard; *F:* **to h. in on s.o., to h. along,** entrer chez qn en passant.

happenchance, happenstance ['hæp(ə)ntʃæns, -stæns], *s. U.S: F:* événement fortuit.

happening ['hæp(ə)niŋ], *s.* **1.** *(a)* événement *m*; **important happenings,** événements importants; *(b) F:* spectacle improvisé. **2.** *F:* **happenings,** drogues *fpl*, narcotiques *mpl.*

happily ['hæpili], *adv.* *(a)* heureusement; (i) dans le bonheur; (ii) par bonheur; **to live h.,** vivre heureux; **he did not die h.,** sa mort ne fut pas heureuse; **h., he did not die,** par bonheur il ne mourut pas; **to live, get on, h. together,** faire bon ménage (ensemble); **she smiled h.,** elle eut un sourire de contentement; *(b)* **h. expressed,** heureusement, bien, exprimé.

happiness ['hæpinis], *s.* bonheur *m*, félicité *f*; **life of h. and prosperity,** vie heureuse et prospère.

happy ['hæpi], *a.* heureux. **1.** *(a)* **h. circumstance,** circonstance heureuse; **in happier circumstances,** dans des circonstances plus favorables; **in a h. hour,** dans un heureux moment; à un moment propice; *(b)* **h. life,** vie heureuse; **to be as h. as the day is long, as a king, as a sandboy,** *Austr:* **as Larry,** être heureux et sans soucis; être heureux comme un roi; être heureux comme un poisson dans l'eau; **those were h. days!** c'était le bon temps! *F:* *(as toast)* **h. days!** à votre santé! **h. group of children,** bande joyeuse d'enfants; **h. family,** famille heureuse; *Games:* **h. families,** jeu *m* des métiers; **I am extremely h. that you agree,** je suis infiniment heureux que vous consentiez; **I'm very h. with his work,** je suis très satisfait, content, de son travail; **I'm not at all h. about it,** cela ne me plaît pas, ne me dit rien; il y a là quelque chose qui ne va pas; **I was h. to have, in having, a son,** j'avais le bonheur de (i) posséder, (ii) donner naissance à, un fils; **to make s.o. h.,** (i) rendre qn heureux; (ii) faire la joie de qn; **you have made one man h.,** vous avez fait un heureux; **to be h. to do sth.,** être heureux, bien aise, content, de faire qch.; *(c) F: O:* **to be h.,** être un peu gris, un peu gai, un peu parti. **2. h. phrase,** expression heureuse, bien choisie, à propos; **he is h. at repartee,** il a la repartie heureuse; **h. thought!** (c'est) bien trouvé! bonne inspiration!

happy-go-lucky ['hæpigou'lʌki], *a.* sans souci, insouciant; **a h.-go-l. man,** un insouciant; **to do sth. in a h.-go-l. fashion,** faire qch. au petit bonheur, à vue de nez, à la flan, à la va-comme-je-te-pousse; **to live in a h.-go-l. way,** vivre à l'aventure; **h.-go-l. housewife,** ménagère peu méthodique.

Hapsburg ['hæpsbə:g], *Pr.n. Hist:* *(a)* **the House of H.,** la maison de Habsbourg; *(b) attrib.* Habsbourgeois.

hapten ['hæpten], **haptene** ['hæptin], *Bio-Ch:* haptène *m*, haptine *f.*

haptere ['hæptiər], **hapteron** ['hæptərɔn], *s. Bot:* haptère *m.*

haptic(al) ['hæptik(l)], *a.* haptique.

haptoglobin [hæptou'gloubin], *s. Bio-Ch:* haptoglobine *f.*

haptometer [hæp'tɔmitər], *s. Med:* haptomètre *m.*

haptophore ['hæptəfɔ:r], *a. Biol: Ch:* haptophore.

Haptopoda [hæp'tɔpədə], *s.pl. Paleont:* haptopoda *m.*

haptotropism [hæptou'troupizm], *s. Bot:* haptotropisme *m.*

haqueton ['hæktən], *s. A.Arm:* hoqueton *m.*

hara-kiri ['hɑ:rə'kiəri], *s.* hara-kiri *m.*

harangue[1] [hə'ræŋ], *s.* harangue *f.*

harangue[2]. **1.** *v.tr.* haranguer (la foule, etc.). **2.** *v.i.* prononcer, faire, une harangue; discourir (en public).

haranguer [hə'ræŋər], *s.* harangueur, -euse.

harass ['hærəs], *v.tr.* **1.** *Mil:* harceler, fatiguer, inquiéter, tenir en alerte (l'ennemi); **the enemy harassed their march,** l'ennemi ne leur laissait aucun répit au cours de leur marche. **2.** harasser, vexer, tracasser, tourmenter (qn); **harassed with debts,** accablé de dettes.

harassing[1] ['hærəsiŋ], *a.* harassant, harcelant, fatigant; *Mil:* **h. fire,** tir *m* de harcèlement.

harassing[2], *s.* = HARASSMENT.

harassment ['hærəsmənt], *s.* **1.** harcèlement *m.* **2.** harassement *m*, vexation *f*, tracasserie *f*, tourment *m.*

Harbin ['hɑ:bin], *Pr.n. Geog:* Kharbin(e) *m.*

harbinger[1] ['hɑ:bindʒər], *s. Lit:* avant-coureur *m*, *pl.* avant-coureurs; messager, -ère; annonciateur, -trice; précurseur *m*; **the swallow, h. of spring,** l'hirondelle, avant-courrière du printemps, messagère du printemps.

harbinger[2], *v.tr. Lit:* annoncer l'approche de (qn); annoncer (le printemps).

harbour[1] ['hɑ:bər], *s.* **1.** *(a) A: & Lit:* gîte *m*, abri *m*, asile *m*, refuge *m*; **to give h. to a criminal,** donner asile à un criminel; *(b) Ven:* lit *m* (d'un cerf). **2.** *Nau:* port *m*; **inner h.,** arrière-port *m*, *pl.* arrière-ports; **outer h.,** avant-port *m*, *pl.* avant-ports; rade *f*; **artificial h.,** port artificiel; **natural h.,** port naturel; **dry h., stranding h.,** port d'échouage; **tidal h.,** port à, de, marée; **deep-water h.,** port de toute marée; **open h.,** port non abrité; **safe h.,** port abrité; **commercial h.,** port commercial; **fishing h.,** port de pêche; **h. of refuge,** port de refuge, de relâche forcée; **h. authorities,** autorités *f* portuaires, direction *f* de port; **h. master,** capitaine *m*, officier *m*, de port; *(of small port)* lieutenant *m* de port; **h. dues,** droits *m* de port, de mouillage; **h. capacity,** capacité *f* portuaire; **h. equipment,** équipement *m* portuaire; **h. installations, h. facilities, h. works,** installations *f* portuaires; **h. boat service,** service *m* maritime portuaire; **h. (service) craft,** bâtiment *m* de direction de port, bâtiment de servitude; **h. patrol craft,** bâtiment de surveillance de port; **h. tug,** remorqueur *m* de port; **h. light,** feu *m* de port; **h. signals,** signaux *m* de port; *Mil:* **h. defences,** défenses *f* portuaires (côté mer); **h.-mouth barrier,** barrière *f* d'entrée, de sortie, de port; **to enter h.,** entrer au, dans le, port; **to leave h.,** sortir du port; **to clear the h.,** quitter le port; *(of ship)* **to remain off the h.,** rester en rade. **3.** *A:* **cold h.,** reposoir *m*, logement *m*, asile *m* de nuit (sans feu ni hôtellerie).

harbour[2]. **1.** *v.tr.* héberger; donner asile à (qn); **to h. a criminal,** receler un criminel; **the woods h. much game,** les bois abritent beaucoup de gibier; **to h. dirt,** retenir la saleté; **to h. a grudge against s.o.,** garder rancune à qn; **to h. suspicions,** entretenir, nourrir, des soupçons; **to h. fears,** avoir des appréhensions. **2.** *v.i.* *(a)* chercher asile, se réfugier, se mettre à l'abri **(in,** dans); *(b) Ven:* *(of stag)* avoir son lit **(in,** dans).

harbourage ['hɑ:bəridʒ], *s.* **1.** refuge *m*, abri *m*, asile *m*; **to offer h. to s.o.,** accueillir qn. **2.** *Nau:* **to give good h.,** offrir un bon mouillage, une rade sûre.

harbourer ['hɑ:bərər], *s.* **1.** *(a)* receleur, -euse (de malfaiteurs, etc.); *(b)* **h. of evil thoughts,** celui qui nourrit de mauvaises pensées. **2.** *Ven:* valet *m* de limier (qui surveille le cerf).

harbouring ['hɑ:bəriŋ], *s.* hébergement *m*; **h. of criminals,** recel *m* de malfaiteurs.

harbourless ['hɑ:bəlis], *a.* **1.** *A: & Lit:* (personne) sans asile. **2.** (côte) sans ports, sans rades.

hard [hɑ:d], *a., adv. & s.*

I. *a.* **1.** *(firm)* dur; *(a)* **h. substance,** substance dure; **h. wheat,** blé dur; **as h. as adamant,** dur comme le diamant; *(of cement, etc.)* **to become, get, h.,** durcir; **to make sth. harder,** rendurcir qch.; **to become harder,** se rendurcir; **h. snow,** neige durcie; *Metall:* **h. metal,** métal écroui; **h. iron,** fer *m* de roche; **h. lead,** plomb *m* aigre; **h. soldering,** brasure *f*, brasage *m*; soudure *f* au cuivre; **h. muscles,** muscles *m* fermes; **h. as a bone, as iron,** dur comme pierre; **to be as h. as nails,** (i) être en bonne forme, en bonne condition; (ii) être sans pitié, impitoyable; *Med:* **h. tissues,** tissus scléreux; *Equit:* **horse with a h. mouth,** cheval *m* à la bouche insensible; *(b) Fin:* *(of stock, rates, etc.)* tendu, tenu, soutenu, raffermi; *(c)* *(of ship)* **h. and fast,** à sec; bien pris; **h. and fast rule,** règle absolue, immuable, rigoureuse. **2.** *(difficult)* difficile; (tâche *f*, chemin *m*) pénible; **to be h. to please,** être exigeant, difficile à contenter; être par trop difficile; faire le difficile; **a h. man to satisfy,** un homme difficile à contenter; **she wants a boss who isn't too h. to please,** il lui faut un patron pas trop difficile; **h. to deal with,** peu commode; **to be h. to wake,** avoir le sommeil dur; **to be h. of hearing,** être dur d'oreille; entendre dur; avoir l'oreille dure; **article that is h. to sell,** article dur à la vente, peu vendable, d'écoulement difficile; *esp. NAm:* **the h. sell,** publicité poussée à fond; battage *m* publicitaire; *esp. Can:* **it's h. sledding,** le chemin est difficile; il n'y a rien pour nous aider; *I.C.E:* **the engine is h. to start,** le moteur est dur à lancer; **to find it a h. matter to do sth.,** avoir de la difficulté à faire qch.; **I find it h. to believe that . . .,** j'ai peine à croire que + *sub.*; **it is h. to understand,** c'est difficile à comprendre; **the hardest part of the job is done,** le plus dur est fait; **book that is h. reading,** livre *m* d'une lecture difficile. **3.** *(severe; harsh)* *(a)* *(of pers., manner, etc.)* dur, sévère, sans pitié, rigoureux **(to, towards,** envers); **h. master,** maître sévère, exigeant; **h. heart,** cœur dur; *(of heart)* **to grow h.,** s'endurcir; **to be as h. as flint,** (i) avoir un cœur de pierre; (ii) être intraitable (en affaires); **to be h. on s.o.,** être sévère, user de rigueur, envers qn; **don't be so h. on him,** (i) ne le jugez pas si sévèrement; (ii) ne vous montrez pas aussi sévère; **to be h. on one's clothes,** user rapidement ses vêtements; *(b)* **to say h. things to s.o.,** dire des duretés à qn; **to call s.o. h. names,** injurier qn; qualifier durement qn; **h. common sense,** bon sens brutal; **h. fact,** fait brutal, indiscutable; **times are h.,** les temps sont rudes, durs, difficiles, pleins de misère; **to have a h. time of it,** en voir de dures; faire son purgatoire en ce monde, de son vivant; **to lead a h. life,** mener une vie dure; **he was brought up in a h. school,** il a été formé à une rude école; **h. fate,** sort cruel, rigoureux; **he's had h. luck,** il a eu de la malchance; **h. luck! h. lines!** pas de chance! quelle guigne! *(c)* rude; **h. to the touch,** rude au toucher; **h. water,** eau calcaire; *Mch: Ind:* eau incrustante; **h. wine,** vin vert; **h. liquor,** spiritueux *mpl*; *F:* **a drop of the h. stuff,** une goutte d'alcool, d'eau-de-vie; un petit coup de gnole; **h. drugs,** toxiques majeurs (opiacés et cocaïne); **h. light,** lumière crue, qui donne des ombres à contours nets; **h. silk,** soie *f* grège; **h. voice,** voix dure; *Ling:* **h. consonants,** consonnes dures; **to paint with a h. touch,** peindre sèchement; *Phot:* **h. print,** épreuve heurtée, contrastée; **h. paper,** papier *m* à contrastes; **h.-contrast picture,** image dure, heurtée. **4.** (*strenuous*) **h. work,** (i) travail assidu; (ii) travail ingrat; **desperately h. work,** travail acharné; **to make money by sheer h. work,** gagner de l'argent à la force du poignet; **to take the h. work out of cleaning,** faciliter le nettoyage; **it was h. work to convince him,** j'ai eu fort à faire pour le convaincre; **it is h. work for me to . . ., I find it h. work to . . .,** j'ai beaucoup de peine à . . .; j'ai bien du mal à . . .; **h. rider,** cavalier *m* infatigable; **h. gallop,** galop soutenu; **h. drinker,** grand buveur; **h. drinking,** abus *m* des boissons alcooliques; **h. fight,** rude combat *m*; **h. match,** match vivement disputé; **to strike s.o. a h. blow,** porter un coup rude à qn; **it's a h. blow for him,** c'est un rude coup pour lui; **to try one's hardest,** faire tout son possible, faire l'impossible; **all worked their hardest,** tous travaillaient à qui mieux mieux; **h. labour,** travaux forcés; *s. F:* **fifteen years' h.,** quinze longes *f* des durs. **5.** (*extreme*) (*a*) **h. frost,** forte gelée; gelée à pierre fendre; **h. winter,** hiver rigoureux; (*b*) *W.Tel:* **h. valve,** valve *f* à vide très poussé.

II. *adv.* **1.** (*a*) (*vigorously*) fort; **pull the bell h.,** tirez fort la sonnette; **as h. as one can,** de toutes ses forces; **he was running as h. as ever he could,** il courait à perdre haleine; *Ten:* **to drive the ball h.,** jouer la balle raide; **to ride h.,** chevaucher à toute vitesse; **to row, pull, h.,** faire force de rames; **to throw a stone h.,** lancer une pierre avec raideur; **to hit h., strike h.,** cogner dur; frapper raide; frapper à main fermée; **he goes at it h., he hits h.,** il n'y va pas de main morte; **to jam on the brakes h.,** serrer les freins à bloc; **to swear h.,** jurer comme un charretier; **to bite h.,** mordre serré; **to beg h.,** prier instamment; **to look, gaze, stare, h. at s.o.,** regarder fixement qn; **to think h.,** réfléchir profondément; **to work h.,** travailler dur, ferme; **to work desperately h.,** travailler avec acharnement; y mettre de l'acharnement; **to work h. at sth.,** travailler ferme à qch.; s'appliquer à qch.; **to work h. for one's living,** gagner laborieusement sa vie; **he works too h.,** il se surmène; **to be h. at work,** être en plein travail; **he is h. at work on it,** il y travaille assidûment; **he is always h. at it,** il est toujours attelé à son travail, à la besogne; il est toujours à peiner; **it was a h. run business,** (i) c'était très serré; (ii) *F:* c'était moins une; **he is kept h. at it, at work,** (i) on le fait trimer; (ii) il a fort à faire; **he studies h.,** il étudie sans relâche; **it's raining h.,** il pleut fort; il pleut à verse; **the rain is coming down harder,** la pluie tombe plus fort; **to freeze h.,** geler dur, vif, serré; **to snow h.,** neiger dru; (*b*) **it will go h. with him if . . .,** cela sera sérieux (pour lui) si . . .; **if you fail, it will go h. with you,** si vous échouez, vous en verrez de dures; *A: & Lit:* **it shall go h. but I will find them,** je me fais fort de les trouver; à moins de difficultés insurmontables je les trouverai bien; **it comes, bears, h. on him,** (i) c'est dur pour lui; (ii) c'est pour lui une lourde charge; (*c*) **valve h. closed,** robinet fermé à refus; *Nau:* **h. over!** la barre toute! **h. a-port!** babord toute! **h. a-lee!** lofe tout! **h. a-weather!** toute au vent! *Bill:* **to be h. (against the cushion),** être collé sous bande; **to be h. up (for money), to be h. pushed,** être dans la gêne; être à court (d'argent); **I'm not so h. up as all that,** je ne suis pas à cela près; **to be h. up for sth.,** être à sec de qch.; avoir grand besoin de qch.; **to be h. up for an excuse,** (i) éprouver de la difficulté à trouver une excuse, à se dérober; (ii) être à court d'excuses; **to be h. up for something to do,** ne savoir à quoi employer son temps. **2.** (*with difficulty*) difficilement, avec peine; **h. bought experience,** expérience chèrement achetée; **h.-earned wages,** salaire péniblement gagné; **h.-got fortune,** fortune acquise à grand-peine. **3.** (*near*) **h. by,** tout près, tout contre, (tout) auprès; **he lives h. by,** il demeure tout près, tout à côté; **to run s.o. h., to be h. upon s.o.,** serrer qn de près; **to follow h. (up)on, after, behind, s.o.,** suivre qn de près; **to be h. on fifty,** friser la cinquantaine; aller sur ses cinquante ans; **it was h. on twelve,** il était bientôt midi, minuit.

III. *s.* **1.** tabac *m* en carotte, en barre. **2.** *Nau:* cale *f* (de débarquement). **3.** *pl.* **hards,** déchets *m* de chanvre, de lin; étoupe blanche. **4.** *P:* (*not in decent use*) **to have a h. on,** bander.

hardback ['hɑ:dbæk], *s.* livre cartonné.

hardbake ['hɑ:dbeik], *s. Cu:* caramel dur aux amandes.

hardbaked ['hɑ:dbeikt], *a. F:* (*of pers.*) dur, endurci.

hard-bitten ['hɑ:dbitn], *a.* **1.** (*of dog, etc.*) qui a la mor sure tenace; qui ne lâche pas. **2.** *F:* (*of pers.*) tenace, boucané, dur à cuire.

hardboard ['hɑ:dbɔ:d], *s. Const:* carton dur, Isorel *m* (*R.t.m.*).

hard( )boil ['hɑ:d'bɔil], *v.tr.* durcir (un œuf).

hardboiled ['hɑ:dbɔild], *a.* (*a*) (œuf) dur; (*b*) *F:* = HARD-BITTEN 2.

hardcore ['hɑ:dkɔ:r], *s. Const:* blocaille *f*.

hard-drawn ['hɑ:d'drɔ:n], *a.* (métal *m*) de haute résistance.

harden ['hɑ:dn]. **1.** *v.tr.* (*a*) durcir, (r)endurcir (qch.); tremper (l'acier, etc.); *Med:* indurer, scléroser (les muscles, etc.); **alcohol hardens the blood vessels,** l'alcool sclérose les vaisseaux sanguins; **the fire has hardened the leather,** le feu a racorni le cuir; **to h. s.o. to fatigue,** aguerrir qn à, contre, la fatigue; **to h. oneself to the cold,** s'endurcir au froid; s'aguerrir au froid, contre le froid; **to h. s.o.'s heart,** endurcir le cœur de qn; **selfishness has hardened his heart,** l'égoïsme lui a bronzé le cœur; (*b*) *Hort:* **to h. (off) seedlings,** fortifier de jeunes plants; (*c*) *Metall:* **to (case-)harden,** cémenter (l'acier); (*d*) *Phot:* durcir, aluner (une émulsion). **2.** *v.i.* (*a*) (*of substance*) (se) durcir, s'endurcir, s'affermir; (*of tissue*) s'ossifier; (*of leather, etc.*) se racornir; **his voice hardened,** sa voix devint dure; (*b*) *Fin:* (*of shares, etc.*) **to h. (up),** se tendre, se raffermir; **prices are hardening,** les prix sont en hausse; (*c*) (*of the constitution*) s'endurcir; s'aguerrir; (*d*) **scientific opinion has hardened to the view that . . .,** le monde savant est de plus en plus d'avis que . . ..

hardened ['hɑ:dnd], *a.* (*of substance*) durci, endurci; (*of steel, glass*) trempé; **h. athlete,** athlète des mieux trempés; **h. criminal,** criminel endurci; **h. old sinner,** vieux dur à cuire; **h. conscience,** conscience cautérisée, calleuse; **constitution h. to fatigue,** tempérament dur à la fatigue.

hardener ['hɑ:dnər], *s.* **1.** durcisseur *m*; **habit is a great h.,** l'habitude vous endurcit. **2.** *Phot:* bain durcissant; liquide durcissant.

hardening ['hɑ:dniŋ], *s.* (*a*) durcissement *m*, (r)endurcissement *m*, affermissement *m*; *Metall:* trempe *f*; **air h.,** (i) prise *f*, durcissement, (du ciment, etc.) à l'air; (ii) *Metall:* trempe à l'air; **h. steel,** acier *m* de trempe; *Metall:* **age h.,** durcissement par l'âge, par vieillissement; durcissement structural; **contour h.,** durcissement périphérique; **h. of the voice,** durcissement de la voix; **one is aware of a certain h. of attitude,** on se rend compte d'un certain durcissement d'attitude; (*b*) *Metall:* **(case) h.,** cémentation *f* (de l'acier); (*c*) *Phot:* durcissement, tannage *m* (de clichés); **alum h.,** alunage *m*; **h.-fixing bath,** bain *m* de fixage aluné; fixateur aluné; (*d*) durcissement (des artères).

hard-faced, -featured [hɑ:d'feist, -'fi:tʃəd], *a.* (personne) aux traits durs, sévères; au masque dur.

hardfisted ['hɑ:d'fistid], *a. F:* (*a*) aux mains fortes; (*b*) (homme) dur à la détente; (*c*) avare.

hard-fought ['hɑ:d'fɔ:t], *a.* vivement contesté; chaudement contesté; âprement disputé.

hardhanded ['hɑ:d'hændid], *a.* **1.** aux mains calleuses. **2.** à la main de fer.

hardhead ['hɑ:dhed], *s.* **1.** homme positif, pratique; dur à cuire *m*. **2.** *Ich:* (*a*) cotte-scorpion *m*, *pl.* cottes-scorpions; (*b*) grondin gris.

hard-headed ['hɑ:d'hedid], *a.* (*of pers.*) (*a*) positif, pratique; **h.-h. business man,** homme d'affaires dur (à cuire); (*b*) obstiné, têtu.

hardhearted ['hɑ:d'hɑ:tid], *a.* (*of pers.*) insensible, inflexible, impitoyable, au cœur dur; **h. father,** père dénaturé.

hardheartedly ['hɑ:d'hɑ:tidli], *adv.* impitoyablement; sans pitié.

hardheartedness ['hɑ:d'hɑ:tidnis], *s.* insensibilité *f*; dureté *f* de cœur.

hard-hitting ['hɑ:d'hitiŋ], *a.* qui frappe dur; *Box: etc:* **h.-h. opponent,** adversaire cogneur.

hardihood ['hɑ:dihud], *s.* hardiesse *f*; (i) intrépidité *f*, courage *m*; (ii) audace *f*, effronterie *f*; **you have the h. to deny that . . .!** vous avez l'audace de nier que . . .!

hardily ['hɑ:dili], *adv.* **1.** hardiment, audacieusement, intrépidement, avec intrépidité. **2.** vigoureusement, robustement.

hardiness ['hɑ:dinis], *s.* **1.** robustesse *f*, vigueur *f*. **2.** *A:* = HARDIHOOD.

hard-laid ['hɑ:d'leid], *a.* (fil) à torsion forte; (cordage) commis serré.

hardly ['hɑ:dli], *adv.* **1.** (*a*) sévèrement; **to use s.o. h., to deal h. with s.o.,** user de rigueur envers qn; **don't think so h. of him,** ne le jugez pas si sévèrement; *F:* **to be h. done by,** être mal traité; (*b*) **h. contested,** vivement, chaudement, contesté; **the battle was h. contested,** la lutte a été chaude; (*c*) péniblement; **h. acquired knowledge,** savoir péniblement acquis. **2.** (*a*) à peine; ne . . . guère; **there is h. time,** nous avons à peine le temps; **she can h. read,** (c'est) à peine si elle sait lire; **it can h. be doubted that . . .,** il n'est guère douteux que . . .; **he had h. escaped when he was recaptured,** à peine s'était-il échappé qu'on le repinça; **we had h. gone out when the rain began,** à peine étions-nous sortis qu'il se mit à pleuvoir; **they think of selling their shares and h. of anything else,** ils songent à vendre leurs actions et guère à autre chose; **you'll h. believe it,** vous aurez (de la) peine, du mal, à le croire; **I h. know,** je n'en sais trop rien; **I h. know why,** je ne sais trop pourquoi; **I need h. say . . .,** point besoin de dire . . .; il va sans dire . . .; **h. pronounceable,** difficilement prononçable; **h. anyone,** presque personne; **h. anything,** presque rien; **h. ever,** presque jamais; (*b*) sûrement pas; **he could h. have said that,** il n'aurait sûrement pas dit cela.

hardmouthed ['hɑ:dmauðd], *a.* (cheval) dur de bouche, fort en bouche, sans bouche, qui n'a pas de bouche, qui a la bouche insensible; (cheval) pesant à la main, qui a l'appui lourd; *F:* (cheval) gueulard.

hard-natured ['hɑ:d'neitjəd], *a.* (homme) dur de caractère.

hardness ['hɑ:dnis], *s.* **1.** (*a*) dureté *f* (d'une substance); (*b*) trempe *f* (de l'acier, d'un outil); (*c*) tons heurtés (d'un cliché, d'un tableau); dureté (de style); (*d*) crudité *f* (de l'eau). **2.** *Fin:* tension *f*, raffermissement *m* (du marché, des actions). **3.** (*a*) difficulté *f* (d'une démarche, d'un travail, d'un problème, etc.); (*b*) **h. of hearing,** dureté d'oreille. **4.** (*a*) sévérité *f*, rigueur *f* (d'une règle, etc.); (*b*) caractère *m* insensible (de qn); dureté, brutalité *f*. **5.** robustesse *f*, vigueur *f*.

hardpan ['hɑ:dpæn], *s.* (*a*) *Geol:* croûte concrétionnée; croûte, carapace *f* (calcaire, ferrugineuse, etc.); (*b*) terrain *m* solide; (*c*) *U.S:* **the h. of the question,** l'essentiel *m* du problème.

hard-pressed, -pushed ['hɑ:d'prest, -'pʌʃt], *a.* (*of debtor, etc.*) aux abois, fort embarrassé.

hard-set ['hɑ:d'set], *a.* **1.** (*of pers.*) fort embarrassé, aux abois; **to be h.-s. to find money,** être fort embarrassé pour trouver de l'argent; être très gêné. **2.** (*a*) qui a durci; dur; **when the cement is h.-s.,** lorsque le ciment a bien pris, a durci; (*b*) **h.-s. egg,** œuf couvé.

hard-shell(ed) ['hɑ:d'ʃel(d)], *a.* **1.** (*a*) (mollusque) à carapace dure; (*b*) *Hort:* (amande) à coque dure. **2.** *NAm: F:* = HARD BITTEN 2.

hardship ['hɑ:dʃip], *s.* privation *f*, fatigue *f*; (dure) épreuve; tribulation *f*; **he has suffered great hardships,** il en a vu de dures; **early rising is not a h. in summer,** en été ce n'est pas dur de se lever tôt.

hard-solder ['hɑ:d'souldər, -'sɔl-], *v.tr. Metalw:* braser; souder au cuivre.

hardstand ['hɑ:dstænd], *Av: Civ. E:* aire *f* en dur.

hardtack ['hɑ:dtæk], *s. Nau:* biscuit *m* de mer; *F:* galette *f*.

hardtop ['hɑ:dtɔp], *s.* **1.** *Aut:* hard-top *m*. **2.** *Civ: E: etc:* route *f*, aire *f*, en dur.

hardware ['hɑ:dwɛər], *s.* **1.** (*a*) quincaillerie *f*, ferronnerie *f*, grosserie *f*; **builders' h.,** serrurerie *f* de bâtiments; **h. dealer,** quincaillier *m*; **h. shop, store,** quincaillerie *f*; **builders' h. merchant,** serrurier *m* en bâtiments; (*b*) *F:* armes *fpl*. **2.** (*a*) éléments *m*, parties *f*, métalliques (d'un appareil, d'une installation); ferrures *f*; (*b*) *Cmptr:* ensemble *m* des éléments matériels d'un ordinateur; matériel *m*; *F:* hardware *m*; **h. configuration, environment,** composition *f* de l'ordinateur, les différentes machines composant l'ensemble; **h. device,** dispositif câblé; **h. failure,** incident *m* (de) machine; **h. engineer,** ingénieur constructeur, logicien; **h. register,** registre *m* interne.

hardwareman, *pl.* **-men** ['hɑ:dwɛəmən], *s. O:* quincaillier *m*, ferronnier *m*.

hard-wearing ['hɑ:d'wɛəriŋ], *a.* (vêtements, etc.) de bon usage, de bon service; (tissu *m*) durable.

hardwire [hɑ:d'waiər], *v.tr. Cmptr:* câbler (une fonction).

hard-won ['hɑ:d'wʌn], *a.* **h.-w. trophy,** trophée chaudement disputé, remporté de haute lutte; **my hardest-won prizes,** les prix qui m'ont coûté le plus d'efforts.

hardwood ['hɑ:dwud], *s.* bois dur; **h. forest,** forêt *f* d'arbres feuillus.

hard-working ['hɑ:d'wə:kiŋ], *a.* laborieux, travailleur, -euse, assidu.

hardy[1] ['hɑ:di], *a.* **1.** hardi, courageux, audacieux, intrépide. **2.** (*a*) robuste; endurci (à la fatigue, etc.); (*b*) *Bot:* résistant; rustique; (arbuste *m*) vivace; (plante *f*) de pleine terre; **h. fruit tree,** arbre fruitier plein-vent; **h. annual,** (i) *Bot:* plante annuelle de pleine terre; (ii) *F:* question *f* qui revient régulièrement sur le tapis.

hardy[2], *s. Tls: Metalw:* tasseau *m*, tranche *f*, tranchet *m* (d'enclume); casse-fer *m inv*; **h.-hole,** trou carré de tasseau (dans l'enclume).

hare[1] ['hɛər], *s.* **1.** lièvre *m*; **buck h.,** bouquin *m*; **doe h.,** hase *f*; **Arctic, polar, h.,** lièvre arctique, des neiges; **Patagonian h.,** lièvre patagon, mara *m*; **snowshoe h.,** lièvre américain; **varying h.,** lièvre variable; **Himalayan woolly h.,** lièvre de l'Himalaya; **Filchner's tolai h.,** lièvre de Filchner; **brown h.,** lièvre brun; *Cu:* **stewed h., jugged h.,** civet *m* de lièvre; **to run with the h. and hunt with the hounds, to hold with the h. and run with the hounds,** ménager la chèvre et le chou; jouer double jeu; nager entre deux eaux; donner une chandelle à Dieu et une au diable; **to start a h.,** (i) *Ven:* lever un lièvre; (ii) donner un nouveau tour à la conversation; **first catch your h.,** assurez-vous d'abord de l'essentiel; pour faire un civet, prenez un lièvre; *Sp:* **h. and hounds,** rallye-paper *m* (à pied), *pl.* rallye-papers; rallie-papier *m, pl.* rallie-papiers. **2.** *Z:* (*a*) **Belgian h.,** léporide *m*; (*b*) **jumping h.,** lièvre sauteur, lièvre du Cap, pédète *f*, hélamys *m*. **3.** *Bot:* **hare's ear,** buplèvre *m*, oreille-de-lièvre *f*, *pl.* oreilles-de-lièvre; perce-feuille *f, pl.* perce-feuilles; **hare's foot,** (i) *Bot:* pied-de-lièvre *m, pl.* pieds-de-lièvre; (ii) *Th:* (houppe *f* en) patte *f* de lapin (pour maquillage).

hare[2], *v.i. F:* (*of pers.*) courir comme un lièvre, à toutes jambes; **to h. back home,** regagner la maison à toutes jambes; **to h. off, to h. it,** se sauver à toutes jambes; **h. off after him and tell him to come back,** courez vite après lui et dites-lui de revenir.

harebell ['hɛəbel], *s. Bot:* (*a*) jacinthe *f* des prés; (*b*) campanule *f* à feuilles rondes.

harebrained ['hɛəbreind], *a.* écervelé, étourdi; **to be h.,** avoir une cervelle de moineau, une tête de linotte; **h. scheme,** projet insensé.

harelip ['hɛəlip], *s.* bec-de-lièvre *m, pl.* becs-de-lièvre.

harelipped ['hɛəlipt], *a.* (personne) à bec-de-lièvre.

harem [hɑː'riːm], *s.* harem *m.*

harewood ['hɛəwud], *s. Com: Join:* érable *m.*

haricot ['hærikou], *s.* **1.** *Cu:* **h. mutton,** haricot *m* de mouton. **2. h. (bean),** *Bot:* haricot *m*; *Cu:* haricot sec.

hark [hɑːk], *v.i.* **1.** prêter l'oreille à, écouter (un son, etc.); **h.!** écoutez! **h. at him!** ta, ta, ta, comme il y va! **2.** *Ven:* **h. away!** taïaut! (*of hounds*) **to h. back,** prendre le contre-pied; revenir sur leurs pas; (*of pers.*) **to h. back to sth.,** ramener la conversation sur un sujet; en revenir à un sujet; **to h. back to the past,** ressasser de vieux griefs; **he's always harking back to that,** il y revient toujours; c'est sa turlutaine; **to h. after s.o.,** s'élancer à la poursuite de qn.

harkback ['hɑːkbæk], *s.* retour *m* en arrière; **h. to the past,** retour sur le passé.

harken ['hɑːk(ə)n], *v. A:* = HEARKEN.

harl [hɑːl], *s.* **1.** *Tex:* tille *f*, teille *f*, filament *m* (du chanvre, du lin). **2.** *Fish: etc:* barbe *f* de plume (d'autruche, etc.).

harlequin ['hɑːlikwin], *s.* **1.** *Th:* arlequin *m*; *attrib.* **h. coat,** habit bigarré ou mi-parti. **2.** chien danois arlequin; arlequin. **3.** *Ent:* **h. beetle,** arlequin de Cayenne.

harlequinade [hɑːlikwi'neid], *s.* arlequinade *f.*

harlot[1] ['hɑːlət], *s.* prostituée *f*; fille *f* de joie; *A:* **to play the h.,** se prostituer.

harlot[2], *v.i.* se prostituer.

harlotry ['hɑːlətri], *s.* prostitution *f.*

harm[1] [hɑːm], *s.* mal *m*, tort *m*; **to do h. to s.o.,** faire du tort à qn; **what h. can it do you?** quel tort cela peut-il vous faire? en quoi cela peut-il vous nuire? **he's used to this climate, it won't do him any h.,** il est fait à notre climat, il n'attrapera pas de mal; **you are doing yourself h. by your lack of . . .,** vous vous faites du tort par votre manque de . . .; **to see no h. in sth.,** ne pas voir de mal, de malice, à qch.; **I see no h. in his coming,** je ne vois pas d'inconvénient à ce qu'il vienne; **he saw no great h. in that,** il n'y trouvait pas grand mal; **you will come to h.,** il vous arrivera malheur; **out of harm's way,** (i) à l'abri du danger, en sûreté, en lieu sûr; (ii) mis dans l'impossibilité de nuire à personne; **it will do more h. than good,** cela fera plus de mal que de bien; **it will do no h. to . . .,** cela ne fera pas de mal de . . .; **that won't do any h.,** cela ne gâtera rien; cela ne nuira en rien; **there's no h. in saying so,** il n'y a pas de mal à le dire; **there's no h. in trying,** on peut toujours essayer; **what h. is there in warning him?** quel danger y a-t-il à l'avertir? **there's no h. in him,** ce n'est pas un méchant homme; il n'est pas méchant.

harm[2]. **1.** *v.tr.* faire du mal, du tort, à (qn); causer du tort à (qn); nuire à (qn); léser (les intérêts de qn). **2.** *v.i. O:* **he will not h. for a little privation,** un peu de privation ne lui fera pas de mal.

harmattan [hɑː'mæt(ə)n], *s. Meteor:* harmattan *m.*

harmful ['hɑːmful], *a.* malfaisant, pernicieux; nocif, nuisible (**to,** à); **h. step,** démarche *f* préjudiciable.

harmfully ['hɑːmfuli], *adv.* nuisiblement.

harmfulness ['hɑːmfulnis], *s.* nocivité *f*; nature *f* nuisible préjudiciable (**of,** de).

harmless ['hɑːmlis], *a.* **1.** *A:* sain et sauf; *Jur:* **to save s.o. h.,** mettre qn à couvert (**from any claim,** d'aucune réclamation). **2.** (animal) inoffensif; (animal, homme) pas méchant; (homme) sans malice; (passe-temps) innocent; (médicament) anodin; **h. talk,** conversation anodine.

harmlessly ['hɑːmlisli], *adv.* sans (faire de) mal; (s'amuser) innocemment.

harmlessness ['hɑːmlisnis], *s.* innocuité *f* (d'un breuvage, etc.); innocence *f* (d'un passe-temps).

harmonic [hɑː'mɔnik]. **1.** *a.* (*a*) *Ac: Mus:* harmonique; *Mth: Ph:* harmonique, sinusoïdal; **h. tone,** son harmonique; **h. series,** (i) *Mus:* échelle *f* harmonique; (ii) *Mth:* série *f* harmonique; *Mth: Ph:* **h. component, h. constituent,** composante *f* harmonique; partiel *m*, partielle *f*; **h. curve,** courbe *f* sinusoïdale; sinusoïde *f*; **h. motion** mouvement sinusoïdal; **h. oscillation,** oscillation sinusoïdale; **h. analysis,** analyse *f* harmonique; **h. conjugates,** conjugués *m* harmoniques; **h. division,** division *f* harmonique; **h. mean,** moyenne *f* harmonique; **h. pencil,** faisceau *m* harmonique; **h. content,** résidu *m*; *El:* **h. current,** courant *m* harmonique; *Elcs:* **h. aerial,** antenne *f* fonctionnant sur un harmonique de sa fréquence propre; **h. distortion,** distorsion *f* harmonique, non linéaire; (*b*) *Anat:* **h. suture,** suture *f* harmonique. **2.** *s.* (*a*) *Mus:* harmonique *m* (d'un son fondamental); (*on stringed instrument*) harmonique, son flûté; **harmonics,** sons harmoniques; **artificial, natural, harmonics,** harmoniques artificiels, naturels; (*b*) *Mth: Ph:* harmonique (d'un mouvement ondulatoire); **h. analyser,** analyseur *m* d'harmoniques; **h. range, h. row,** rang *m* de l'harmonique; *El:* **first-h. current,** courant de l'harmonique supérieur; *Elcs: W.Tel:* **h. detector,** détecteur *m* d'harmoniques; **h. filter,** filtre *m* d'harmoniques; **h. suppression,** filtrage *m* d'harmoniques; **h. generator,** générateur *m* d'harmoniques.

harmonica [hɑː'mɔnikə], *s.* harmonica *m.*

harmonically [hɑː'mɔnik(ə)li], *adv.* harmoniquement.

harmonichord [hɑː'mɔnikɔːd], *s. A.Mus:* harmonicorde *m.*

harmonicon [hɑː'mɔnikən], *s.* harmonica *m.*

harmonious [hɑː'mouniəs], *a.* harmonieux. **1.** accordant, en bon accord. **2.** mélodieux.

harmoniously [hɑː'mouniəsli], *adv.* harmonieusement; **colours h. blended,** couleurs harmonieusement mêlées; **they work h. together,** ils travaillent en harmonie, en bon accord, de bon accord.

harmoniphon(e) [hɑː'mɔnifɔn, -foun], *s. A.Mus:* harmoniphon(e) *m.*

harmonist ['hɑːmənist], *s.* harmoniste *mf.*

harmonistic [hɑːmə'nistik]. **1.** *a. Mus:* harmonisateur, -trice. **2.** *s. Theol: A:* **harmonistic(s),** harmonistique *f.*

harmonium [hɑː'mouniəm], *s.* harmonium *m*, orgue *m* de salon.

harmonization [hɑːmənai'zeiʃ(ə)n], *s. Mus:* harmonisation *f.*

harmonize ['hɑːmənaiz]. **1.** *v.tr.* (*a*) harmoniser (des idées, etc.); concilier, faire accorder (des textes, etc.); allier, harmoniser (des couleurs, etc.) (**with,** avec); (*b*) *Mus:* harmoniser (une mélodie). **2.** *v.i.* (*of sounds, colours, etc.*) s'harmoniser, s'allier, s'assortir; (*of facts, thgs*) s'accorder; (*of pers., ideas, etc.*) se mettre en harmonie, s'accorder; **colours that h. well,** couleurs qui vont bien ensemble; **these colours do not h.,** ces couleurs jurent ensemble; **to h. with sth.,** s'adapter harmonieusement à qch.; être en harmonie, être d'accord, s'accorder, se marier, avec qch.

harmonizer ['hɑːmənaizər], *s. Mus:* harmonisateur, -trice.

harmonizing ['hɑːmənaiziŋ], *s.* harmonisation *f.*

harmony ['hɑːməni], *s.* **1.** *Mus:* harmonie *f*; (*a*) **to study h.,** étudier l'harmonie; (*b*) **songs full of h.,** chants mélodieux. **2.** (*a*) (*of pers., thgs, ideas, etc.*) harmonie *f*, accord *m*; (*of voices, instruments*) concert *m*; **colours in perfect h.,** assortiment parfait de couleurs; **to live in perfect h.,** vivre en parfaite intelligence; vivre en, de, bon accord; **h. reigns everywhere,** partout règne l'accord; **in h. with . . .,** en rapport avec . . .; qui s'harmonise avec . . .; qui s'accorde avec . . .; **to be in h. with public opinion,** être d'accord avec l'esprit public; **his tastes are in h. with mine,** ses goûts sont conformes aux miens; (*b*) concordance *f* (de textes); **to bring one text into h. with another,** mettre un texte en harmonie avec un autre; faire concorder un texte avec un autre.

harmotome ['hɑːmətoum], *s. Miner:* harmotome *m.*

harness[1] ['hɑːnis], *s.* **1.** (*a*) harnais *m*, harnachement *m* (d'un cheval); harnais (d'un chien); **h. horse,** cheval d'attelage; **horse fit for h.,** cheval attelable; **draught h.,** harnais d'attelage; **light h.,** harnais agricole; **collar h.,** harnais à collier; **h. pad,** sellette *f*; **h. room,** sellerie *f*; **h. maker,** bourrelier *m*, harnacheur *m*; sellier-bourrelier *m, pl.* selliers-bourreliers; **h. making,** bourrellerie *f*, harnacherie *f*; **h. race,** course *f* sous harnais; **to go, run, in single h.,** (i) (*of horse*) être dressé à l'attelage par un; être attelé par un; (ii) (*of pers.*) être célibataire; (*of pers.*) **to get back into h. (again),** reprendre le collier; **to die in h.,** mourir à la besogne, à la tâche; mourir debout; **now that I'm out of h.,** maintenant que je suis à la retraite; (*b*) *A.Arm:* harnais, harnois *m*; (*c*) équipement (professionnel); **soldier's h.,** équipement, harnachement, militaire; **parachute h.,** ceinture *f*, harnais, de parachutiste; *Ind: Aut: etc:* **safety h.,** harnais de sécurité. **2.** *Tex:* harnais (de métier à tisser); (*of pers.*) **h. fixer,** lamier *m*. **3.** (*a*) *Mec.E:* appareillage *m*, harnais; (*b*) *El:* rampe *f* (d'une bougie d'allumage); *I.C.E:* **ignition h.,** rampe d'allumage. **4.** *Nau:* **h. cask,** charnier *m* pour les salaisons.

harness[2], *v.tr.* **1.** harnacher (un cheval); **to h. a horse to a cart,** atteler un cheval à une charrette. **2.** *Arm: A:* barder (un chevalier). **3.** aménager (une chute d'eau, etc.); domestiquer (l'énergie atomique, etc.); **to h. atomic energy for industrial purposes,** mettre l'énergie atomique au service de l'industrie.

harnessing ['hɑːnisiŋ], *s.* **1.** harnachement *m*; **h. to a cart,** attelage *m* à une charrette. **2.** aménagement *m*, mise *f* en valeur (d'une chute d'eau, etc.).

harp[1] [hɑːp], *s.* **1.** (*a*) *Mus:* harpe *f*; **to strike, play, the h.,** pincer de la harpe, jouer de la harpe; (*b*) **Jew's h.,** (i) *Mus:* guimbarde *f*; (ii) *Nau:* manille *f*, cigale *f* (de chaîne d'ancre); (iii) *Bot:* (espèce de) trillie *f*. **2.** claie *f* (à sable, à charbon).

harp[2], *v.i.* jouer de la harpe; *F:* **to be always harping on the same string, on the same note,** rabâcher toujours la même chose; réciter toujours la même litanie; chanter toujours la même rengaine, le même refrain, la même antienne; rengainer toujours la même histoire; **he's always harping on about that,** c'est toujours la même guitare, la même ritournelle, la même antienne; il y revient toujours.

harpa ['hɑːpə], *s. Moll:* harpe *f.*

harper ['hɑːpər], *s.* (*a*) *A:* ménestrel *m* (s'accompagnant sur la harpe); (*b*) joueur, -euse, de harpe.

Harpidae ['hɑːpidiː], *s.pl. Moll:* harpidés *m.*

harpings ['hɑːpiŋz], *s.pl. Nau:* lisses *f* de l'avant.

harpist ['hɑːpist], *s. Mus:* harpiste *mf.*

harpoon[1] [hɑː'puːn], *s.* harpon *m*, lance *f*; **pronged h.,** foëne *f*; **h. head,** harpoise *f*; **h. line,** harpoire *f*; **h. gun,** canon *m* lance-harpon; fusil *m* à harpon.

harpoon[2], *v.tr.* harponner.

harpooner [hɑː'puːnər], *s.* harponneur *m.*

harpooning [hɑː'puːniŋ], *s.* harponnage *m*, harponnement *m.*

harpsichord ['hɑːpsikɔːd], *s. Mus:* clavecin *m.*

harpsichordist ['hɑːpsikɔːdist], *s.* claveciniste *mf.*

harpy ['hɑːpi], *s.* **1.** *Myth:* harpie *f*; *F:* **old h.,** vieille mégère, vieille harpie. **2.** (*a*) *Z:* **h. (bat),** harpie; (*b*) *Orn:* **h. (eagle),** harpie (féroce).

harquebus ['hɑːkwibʌs], *s. A.Arms:* arquebuse *f.*

harquebusade [hɑːkwibʌ'seid], *s. A:* arquebusade *f.*

harquebusier [hɑːkwibə'siər], *s. A.Mil:* arquebusier *m.*

harridan ['hærid(ə)n], *s. F:* vieille sorcière; vieille mégère; vieille chipie; **a frightful h.,** une horrible mégère.

harrier[1] ['hæriər], *s.* **1.** dévastateur *m*, pilleur *m*, pillard *m*. **2.** *Orn:* busard *m*; **hen h.,** busard Saint-Martin; **marsh h.,** busard des roseaux, busard harpaye; **pallid h.,** busard pâle, blafard; **Montagu's h.,** busard de Montagu, busard cendré.

harrier[2], *s.* **1.** (*a*) *Ven:* (*dog*) harrier *m*; (*b*) *Sp:* (*pers.*) harrier, coureur *m*. **2.** *pl.* **harriers,** (*a*) *Ven:* meute *f*, équipage *m* (de chiens pour la chasse au lièvre); (*b*) *Sp:* club *m* de coureurs, de cross.

Harriet ['hæriət], *Pr.n.f.* Henriette.

Harrovian [hə'rouviən], *a. & s.* (élève *m*, ancien élève) de l'école de Harrow.

harrow[1] ['hærou], *s.* **1.** *Agr:* herse *f*; **revolving h.,** herse roulante; **chain h.,** herse à chaînons; **brake h.,** grosse herse, brise-mottes *m inv*, broie *f*; **bush h.,** herse d'épines; balayeuse *f*; traînoir *m*; **disk h.,** pulvérisateur *m*; **drill h.,** herse à semer; *Lit:* **to be under the h.,** subir des tribulations, de dures épreuves. **2.** (*a*) *Mil:* formation *f* en échelon; (*b*) vol *m* d'oies en échelon.

harrow[2], *v.tr. Agr:* herser (un terrain); *Fig:* **to h. s.o.'s feelings, to h. s.o.,** agir sur la sensibilité de qn, raconter des choses navrantes à qn; déchirer le cœur à qn.

harrow[3], *v.tr.* = HARRY[2].

harrower ['hærouər], *s. Agr:* herseur *m.*

harrowing ['hærouiŋ], *a.* (conte, etc.) lamentable, poignant, navrant; (cri) déchirant.

Harry¹ ['hæri], *Pr.n.m.* **1.** (*dim.*) = Henri; *F:* **any, every, Tom, Dick and H.,** tout le monde; le premier venu. **2.** *F:* **old H.,** le diable; **to play old H. with s.o.,** en faire voir de grises, de bleues, à qn; **the climate has played old H. with his health, with his nerves,** le climat lui a détraqué la santé, les nerfs.

harry², *v.tr.* **1.** dévaster, ravager, piller, mettre à sac (un pays). **2.** harceler, tourmenter (qn); **to h. the enemy,** ne laisser à l'ennemi aucun répit; **to h. a debtor,** pourchasser, harceler, un débiteur.

harsh [hɑːʃ], *a.* **1.** dur, rêche, rude (au toucher); âpre (au goût); discordant, aigre, strident (à l'oreille); **h. material,** tissu *m* rêche; **h. noise,** bruit râpeux, désagréable; **h. voice,** voix rude, rauque, éraillée; **to give a h. laugh,** rire sec; ricaner; **the h. throbbing note of the boilers,** le ronflement rêche des chaudières; **h. wine,** vin *m* âpre, râpeux; **h. style,** style dur; *Engr:* **h. lines,** tailles *f* aigres; aigreurs *f.* **2.** (caractère) bourru; (traitement) dur; (maître, réponse) rude; **to say h. things to s.o.,** en dire de dures à qn; **to exchange h. words,** échanger des propos durs; **too h. a reprimand,** réprimande trop crue.

harshly ['hɑːʃli], *adv.* (répondre, etc.) durement, avec dureté, rudement, avec rudesse, âprement, brusquement, d'un ton bourru; (traiter qn) sévèrement, avec rigueur.

harshness ['hɑːʃnis], *s.* **1.** dureté *f,* rudesse *f* (au toucher); âpreté *f* (d'un fruit); discordance *f,* aigreur *f* (d'un son); aspérité *f* (du style, du caractère, de la voix); *Engr:* aigreur (des tailles). **2.** sévérité *f,* dureté, rudesse *f* (d'une punition, d'une loi); rigueur *f* (du destin).

hart [hɑːt], *s.* **1.** cerf *m*; *Ven:* cerf âgé de plus de cinq ans; **h. of ten,** cerf dix cors. **2.** *Bot:* **hart's tongue,** langue-de-cerf *f, pl.* langues-de cerf; scolopendre *f*; herbe *f* à la rate.

hart(e)beest ['hɑːt(i)biːst], *s. Z:* bubale *m,* caama *m.*

hartite ['hɑːtait], *s. Miner:* hartite *f.*

hartshorn ['hɑːtshɔːn], *s.* corne *f* de cerf (râpée); *Ch: A:* **spirit of h.,** essence *f,* esprit *m,* de corne de cerf; (solution aqueuse d')ammoniaque *f.*

harum-scarum ['hɛərəm'skɛərəm], *a.* & *s. F:* étourdi (comme un hanneton); écervelé; hurluberlu *m,* étourneau *m*; **he's a h.-s.,** c'est un écervelé, il a le cerveau brûlé, il n'a pas de plomb dans la tête; **she's a h.-s.,** c'est une évaporée, une éventée; **to do sth. in a h.-s. way,** faire qch. à la diable, par-dessous la jambe, à la six-quatre-deux.

haruspex, *pl.* **-spices** [(ˈh)æruspeks, (h)æ'ruspisiːz], *s. Rom.Ant:* (h)aruspice *m.*

haruspication [hærʌspi'keiʃ(ə)n], **haruspicy** [hæ'rʌspisi], *Rom.Ant:* haruspication *f.*

harvest¹ ['hɑːvist], *s.* **1.** moisson *f* (du blé); récolte *f* (des fruits); fenaison *f* (du foin); vendange *f* (du vin); **to get in the h.,** faire la moisson; **research that has yielded a rich h. of information,** recherches *f* qui ont donné une riche moisson de renseignements; **he reaped a bitter h. of misery,** il n'en a récolté que d'amers déboires. **2.** (temps *m,* époque *f,* de) la moisson. **3.** *attrib.* **h. thanksgiving, festival,** action *f* de grâces (après la rentrée des récoltes); **h. home,** fête *f* de la moisson; fin *f* de la moisson; **h. moon,** lune *f* de la moisson; lune de septembre; *Z:* **h. mouse,** (i) souris *f* des moissons; (ii) (*American*) reithrodontomys *m*; *Ent:* **h. fly,** cigale *f*; *Arach:* **h. bug, louse, mite, tick,** lepte automnal, *F:* aoûtat *m,* rouget *m,* vendangeon *m*; **h. spider,** faucheur *m,* faucheux *m.*

harvest². (*a*) *v.tr.* moissonner (les blés); récolter (les fruits); (*b*) *v.i.* rentrer, faire, la moisson.

harvester ['hɑːvistər], *s.* **1.** (*pers.*) moissonneur, -euse. **2.** (*machine*) moissonneuse *f*; *esp.* moissonneuse-lieuse *f, pl.* moissonneuses-lieuses; **combine h.,** moissonneuse-batteuse *f, pl.* moissonneuses-batteuses. **3.** *Arach:* lepte automnal, *F:* aoûtat *m,* rouget *m,* vendangeon *m.*

harvesting ['hɑːvistiŋ], *s.* moissonnage *m*; rentrée *f* de la moisson.

harvestman, *pl.* **-men** ['hɑːvistmən], *s.* **1.** (*pers.*) moissonneur *m.* **2.** *Arach:* faucheur *m.*

has-been ['hæzbiːn], *s. F:* (*a*) homme *m* vieux jeu; vieux ramolli; *Mil:* (vieux) ramollot, vieille culotte de peau; **he's a h.-b.,** c'est une (vieille) croûte; **she's one of the has-beens,** c'est une beauté d'antan; (*b*) homme dont la carrière est finie; homme fini.

hash¹ [hæʃ], *s.* **1.** *Cu:* (*a*) hachis *m,* émincé *m*; (*b*) *F:* nourriture *f,* boustifaille *f.* **2.** *F:* **to make a h. of sth.,** gâcher, gâter, un travail; faire un joli gâchis, un beau gâchis, de qch.; gaspiller (sa vie); **to make a h. of it,** bousiller l'affaire; **to settle s.o.'s h.,** (i) régler son compte à qn; faire son affaire à qn; (ii) dire son fait à qn; rabattre le caquet à qn; (iii) bouleverser les projets de qn; **I'll settle his h., I've settled his h.,** son compte est bon. **3.** *F:* **h.(-up),** réchauffé *m,* ripopée *f* (de vieux contes, etc.); compilation *f* (de l'œuvre d'autrui). **4.** *Rad:* signaux *mpl* parasites.

hash², *v.tr.* (*a*) **to h. (up) meat,** hacher de la viande (en petits morceaux); (*b*) *F:* **we've hashed and rehashed this question long enough,** on a déjà mis assez de temps à considérer et reconsidérer cette question; (*c*) *F:* **he hashed the whole thing completely,** il a tout bousillé.

Hashemite, -imite ['hæʃimait], *s. Rel:* Hachémite *mf.*

hashish, *occ.* **hasheesh** ['hæʃiːʃ], *s.* hachisch *m.*

Hasid, *pl.* **Hasidim** ['hæsid(im), χæ'siːd(im)], *s. Jew.Rel:* Has(s)idim *m.*

Hasidism ['hæsidizm, 'χæ-], *s. Jew.Rel:* has(s)idisme *m.*

haslet ['hæzlit, 'heiz-], *s.* fressure *f* (de porc, etc.).

Hasmonean [hæzmə'niən], *s. Jew.Hist:* Asmonéen *m.*

hasp¹ [hæsp], *s.* **1.** (*for padlocking*) (**staple**) **h.,** moraillon *m.* **2.** (*a*) loquet *m* (de porte); (*b*) espagnolette *f* (de porte-fenêtre); (*c*) fermoir *m,* agrafe *f* (d'album, etc.). **3.** *Tex:* écheveau *m.*

hasp², *v.tr.* fermer (une porte) au loquet; cadenasser (une porte, un couvercle).

hassle¹ ['hæsl], *s. F:* (*a*) chamaillerie *f,* bagarre *f*; (*b*) lutte *f*; (*c*) pagaïe *f,* pagaille *f.*

hassle². *F:* **1.** *v.tr.* embêter (qn). **2.** *v.i.* se chamailler, se bagarrer; lutter (avec qn).

hassock ['hæsək], *s.* **1.** agenouilloir *m*; carreau *m,* coussin *m* (pour les pieds). **2.** touffe *f* d'herbe.

hastate ['hæsteit], *a. Bot:* hasté, hastifolié, hastiforme.

haste¹ [heist], *s.* hâte *f,* diligence *f,* célérité *f*; **to do sth. in h.,** (i) faire qch. à la hâte; (ii) faire qch. à l'étourdie; *esp. Lit:* **I am in h. to leave,** j'ai hâte de partir; **he rose in h.,** il se leva avec précipitation *f*; **to make h.,** se hâter, se dépêcher, faire diligence; **to make h. to do sth.,** se hâter, se presser, se dépêcher, de faire qch.; **make h.!** dépêchez-vous! *Prov:* **more h. less speed,** plus on se hâte moins on avance; plus on se presse moins on arrive; plus on se dépêche moins on réussit; hâtez-vous lentement; ne confondons pas vitesse et précipitation; qui trop se hâte reste en chemin.

haste², *v.tr.* & *i. A:* & *Lit:* = HASTEN.

hasten ['heisn]. *esp. Lit:* (*in everyday speech* **hurry** *is used*) **1.** *v.tr.* (*a*) accélérer, hâter, presser (le pas, etc.); hâter (qn); presser, avancer (le départ de qn); **to h. dinner,** avancer le dîner, l'heure du dîner; **to h. the climax,** brusquer le dénouement; **this action hastened his fall,** cette action précipita sa chute; **to h. s.o.'s death,** avancer la mort de qn; (*b*) activer (la combustion, une réaction). **2.** *v.i.* se hâter, se dépêcher, se presser (**to do sth.,** de faire qch.); **I hastened to reassure him,** je me suis empressé de le rassurer; **we h. to assure you that . . .,** nous nous empressons de vous assurer que . . .; **to h. back,** revenir en tout hâte; **they hastened forward towards us,** ils s'avancèrent vers nous rapidement, à pas précipités.

hastening ['heisniŋ], *s. esp. Lit:* avancement *m* (d'un événement).

hastily ['heistili], *adv.* **1.** à la hâte, précipitamment; **h. planned,** sommairement organisé. **2. to speak h.,** parler sans réfléchir; **to judge sth. h.,** juger qch. à la légère. **3.** brusquement, avec vivacité; **to reply h.,** répondre brusquement, avec brusquerie.

hastiness ['heistinis], *s.* **1.** précipitation *f,* hâte *f.* **2.** (*of temper*) emportement *m,* vivacité *f,* brusquerie *f.*

hasting ['heistiŋ], *a. Dial:* (fruit) hâtif; *Hort:* **h. pear,** hâtiveau *m.*

hasty ['heisti], *a.* **1.** (départ, adieu) précipité; (croquis) fait à la hâte; (repas *m*) sommaire; **I sent him a h. note,** je lui ai envoyé un billet écrit à la hâte; **to be too h. in doing sth.,** mettre trop de hâte à faire qch.; *Cu:* **h. pudding,** bouilli *f* au lait; tôt-fait *m, pl.* tôt-faits; *U.S:* bouillie de maïs au lait. **2.** (aveu) irréfléchi; **to jump to a h. conclusion,** conclure à la légère; **people h. in their decisions,** gens précipités dans leurs décisions. **3.** (*a*) emporté, vif; **to be h. tempered,** être vif, d'humeur prompte; (*b*) *Exp: O:* **h. powder,** poudre vive. **4.** (*of growth, etc.*) rapide.

hat¹ [hæt], *s.* chapeau *m*; **top h., silk h.,** chapeau haut de forme; (**soft**) **felt h.,** chapeau mou, souple; **opera h.,** chapeau claque, chapeau Gibus; **straw h.,** chapeau de paille; **paper h.,** chapeau de papier, coiffure *f* de cotillon; **picture h., Gainsborough h.,** chapeau Gainsborough; *Ecc:* **Cardinal's h., red h.,** chapeau de cardinal, chapeau rouge; **he was aiming at the red h.,** il visait au cardinalat; **h. block,** forme de chapeau, à chapeaux; **h. lining,** coiffe *f*; **h. maker,** chapelier, -ière; **h. making,** chapellerie *f,* l'industrie chapelière; **h. brush,** brosse *f* à chapeaux; **h. rack, rail,** *U.S:* **h. tree,** porte-chapeaux *m inv*; **h. trick,** (i) (*conjuring*) tour *m,* coup *m,* du chapeau; (ii) *Cr:* mise *f* hors jeu de trois batteurs avec trois balles de suite; *Fb:* *etc:* trois buts marqués par le même joueur; (iii) trois réussites de suite; **h. in hand,** chapeau bas; **to put on, take off, one's h.,** mettre, enlever, son chapeau; **to keep one's h. on,** garder son chapeau; **to raise, take off, one's h. to s.o.,** saluer qn d'un coup de chapeau, donner un coup de chapeau à qn, ôter son chapeau à qn; **I take my h. off to him, you!** chapeau! **hats off!** chapeaux bas! *F:* **to pass the h. round, to go round with the h. (for s.o., sth.),** faire passer le chapeau, faire la quête, une collecte (pour qn, qch.); *F:* **he wants to hang up his h.,** il veut se marier; *F:* **my h.!** mon Dieu! mince alors! pas possible! *F:* **to talk through one's h.,** parler à tort et à travers; radoter; *F:* **to keep sth. under one's h.,** garder qch. pour soi; *F:* **if that comes off I'll eat my h.,** si ça, réussit, je l'irai dire à Rome; *F:* **that's old h.,** ça, c'est vieux jeu, démodé, déjà vu, vieux comme le monde; *F:* **he's wearing his other hat,** il considère les choses sous un aspect différent; *F:* **he's a bad h.,** c'est un vaurien; *NAm: F:* **to throw, toss, one's h. into the ring,** se faire inscrire pour un concours; poser sa candidature.

hat², *v.tr.* **1.** fournir un chapeau, des chapeaux, à (qn); *F:* chapeauter (qn). **2.** conférer à (un ecclésiastique) le chapeau de cardinal.

hatband ['hætbænd], *s.* ruban *m* de chapeau.

hatbox ['hætbɔks], *s.* boîte *f,* carton *m,* étui *m,* à chapeau.

hatch¹ [hætʃ], *s.* **1.** partie basse d'une porte coupée; demi-porte *f, pl.* demi-portes. **2.** *Nau:* (*a*) **h. (way),** descente *f,* écoutille *f*; (entrée *f,* ouverture *f* de) panneau *m*; **ventilation h.,** panneau d'aération; **cargo h.,** panneau de chargement, de déchargement; (*b*) **h. (cover),** panneau de descente, panneau (d'écoutille); opercule *m*; capot *m*; **h. coaming,** hiloires *fpl,* surbau *m*; **close h.,** panneau plein, panneau de mer; **grated h.,** panneau à claire-voie, panneau grillagé; **flush-deck h.,** panneau à plat pont; **ceiling h.,** panneau de vaigrage; **sliding h.,** panneau à glissière; **steel h. cover,** opercule *m* d'acier; **h. bars, battens,** tringles *f* de panneaux; **under hatches,** (i) dans la cale; (ii) *F:* mort et enterré; **to clap a mutineer under hatches,** mettre un mutin dans la cale; **to batten down the hatches,** condamner les descentes, les panneaux; (*c*) *F:* **down the h.!** (i) à la vôtre! (ii) videz vos verres! cul sec! **3.** (*a*) trappe *f*; panneau d'accès; **service h., buttery h.,** passe-plats *m inv*; guichet *m* de dépense; (*b*) *Av: etc:* **escape h.,** panneau d'évacuation, de secours; **landing-gear h.,** trappe de l'atterrisseur; **ejection and maintenance h.,** trappe d'entretien et d'éjection. **4.** *Hyd.E:* vanne *f* d'écluse.

hatch², *s. Husb:* **1.** éclosion *f* (d'un œuf, d'une couvée). **2.** couvée *f.*

hatch³. **1.** *v.tr.* (*a*) faire éclore (des poussins); **to h. out eggs,** incuber, (faire) couver, des œufs; **to h. a plot,** ourdir, tramer, monter, couver, mijoter, un complot; brasser une intrigue; (*b*) *Pisc:* incuber (les œufs). **2.** *v.i.* (*of young birds or eggs*) **to h. (out),** éclore; **newly hatched chickens,** poussins *m* qui sortent de la coquille; **to be only just hatched,** être à peine sorti de sa coquille; **a plot is hatching,** il se trame quelque chose.

hatch⁴, *s.* **1.** *Engr:* hachure *f.* **2.** bretteIure *f* (d'une pièce d'orfèvrerie).

hatch⁵, *v.tr.* **1.** *Engr:* *Her:* hacher, hachurer (un dessin). **2.** bretteler (une pièce d'orfèvrerie).

hatchability [hætʃə'biliti], *s.* éclosabilité *f* (d'un œuf).

hatchback ['hætʃbæk], *s.* (voiture *f* à) hayon *m* arrière (relevable).

hatchel¹·² ['hætʃ(ə)l], *s.* & *v.tr.* = HACKLE¹ 1,².

hatcher ['hætʃər], *s.* **1.** *Husb:* (*a*) (poule) couveuse *f*; (*b*) couveuse artificielle. **2.** machinateur *m* (d'intrigues).

hatchery ['hætʃəri], *s. Husb:* couvoir *m,* poussinière *f,* couveuse *f*; **h. operator,** accouveur, -euse; *Pisc:* établissement *m* de pisciculture; **trout h.,** alevinier *m* à truites.

hatchet ['hætʃit], *s.* (*a*) hachette *f,* cognée *f*; hache *f* à main; **hammer-head h.,** hache à marteau; **to bury the h.,** enterrer la hache de guerre; faire la paix; se réconcilier; **to take up the h.,** entrer en guerre; **to dig up the h.,** déterrer la hache de guerre, recommencer la guerre; *F: A:* **to throw, heave, sling, the h.,** hâbler, exagérer; (*b*) **to have a h. face,** avoir le visage en lame de couteau; **h.-faced,** au visage en lame de couteau; (*c*) *Ich:* **h. fish,** poisson-hache *m, pl.* poissons-haches.

hatchettine ['hætʃitiːn], **hatchettite** ['hætʃitait], *s. Miner:* hatchettine *f,* hatchettite *f*; suif minéral; adipocérite *f.*

hatching¹ ['hætʃiŋ], *s.* **1.** (*a*) éclosion *f* (d'une couvée); *Pisc:* incubation *f* (des œufs); **hatching box,** auge *f* d'incubation; (*b*) machination *f* (d'un complot). **2.** couvée *f.*

hatching², *s. Engr: Mapm: Her:* hachure(s) *f(pl)*; **cross h., counter h.,** hachure(s) croisée(s).

hatchling ['hætʃliŋ], *s.* oiseau *m* qui vient d'éclore;

poisson *m* qui vient de naître.

hatchment ['hætʃmənt], *s. Her:* **1.** écusson *m* funéraire; armoiries *f* funéraires (tendues sur la façade de la demeure du défunt). **2.** *A:* écusson; armoiries.

hatchway ['hætʃwei], *s. Nau:* descente *f*, écoutille *f*; entrée *f* des panneaux.

hate[1] [heit], *s.* **1.** (*a*) antipathie *f* (pour, contre, qn, qch.); aversion *f* (pour, contre, qn); **he had developed a h. for such things,** il était venu à détester de telles choses; (*b*) **full of bigotry and h.,** rempli de bigoterie et de haine; **his life is dominated by h.,** sa vie entière est tournée vers la haine, est une manifestation de la haine; (*c*) *F:* **I've got a h. (on) against him,** je l'ai pris en grippe. **2.** objet *m* d'aversion; **his greatest h. was big business,** ce qu'il détestait surtout c'était les grosses affaires.

hate[2], *v.tr.* **1.** haïr, détester, exécrer (qn, qch.), avoir (qn) en aversion, en haine, en horreur; **I h. him,** il m'est odieux; **to h. s.o. like poison, like the plague,** haïr qn comme la peste, à l'égal de la peste; **to h. s.o. for doing sth.,** haïr qn d'avoir fait qch.; **I h. myself for consenting,** je m'en veux d'avoir consenti. **2. to h. to do sth.,** détester (de) faire qch.; **she hates to be contradicted,** elle ne peut pas souffrir qu'on la contredise; **I h. being bothered,** je déteste être dérangé; **I h. to bother you,** je suis désolé de vous déranger; **I h. being cheated,** je déteste qu'on me dupe; **she hates being kissed,** elle a (en) horreur qu'on l'embrasse; **I should h. to be late,** cela m'ennuierait fort d'être en retard; **I h. complaining, I h. to complain,** je déteste d'avoir à me plaindre; **I h. his going so far away,** cela me chagrine, me fait de la peine, qu'il s'en aille si loin; **I h. you to talk about it,** je n'aime pas que vous en parliez.

hateable ['heitəbl], *a.* haïssable.

hateful ['heitful], *a.* (*of pers., thg*) odieux, détestable; **the h. part of the business is that . . .,** l'odieux *m* de la chose c'est que . . .

hatefully ['heitfuli], *adv.* odieusement, détestablement.

hatefulness ['heitfulnis], *s.* odieux *m*, nature *f* détestable (de qch.).

hater ['heitər], *s.* haïsseur, -euse; **a h. of all display,** un ennemi de tout apparat.

hatful ['hætful], *s.* plein chapeau (de fruits, etc.).

Hathor ['hɑːθɔːr], *Pr.n.f. Myth:* Hathor.

hatless ['hætlis], *a.* (homme, etc.) sans chapeau, tête nue; (femme) en cheveux.

hatpeg ['hætpeg], *s.* patère *f*; porte-chapeau *m*, *pl.* porte-chapeaux.

hatpin ['hætpin], *s.* épingle *f* à chapeau; fixe-chapeau *m*, *pl.* fixe-chapeaux.

hatred ['heitrid], *s.* haine *f* (**of s.o.,** de, contre, qn); **to incur s.o.'s h.,** s'attirer la haine de qn; **to excite universal h.,** soulever la haine universelle; **his h. of you,** la haine qu'il vous porte; **they persecute him out of h. for his father,** on le persécute en haine de son père.

hatshop ['hætʃɔp], *s.* **1.** (*for men*) chapellerie *f*. **2.** (*for women*) boutique *f* de modiste; **at the h.,** chez la modiste.

hatstand ['hætstænd], *s.* porte-chapeaux *m inv.*

hatter ['hætər], *s.* chapelier, -ière.

hauberk ['hɔːbəːk], *s. A.Mil: Cost:* haubert *m.*

haugh [hɑːχ, hɑːf], *s. Scot:* prairie *f* irrigable; noue *f*.

haughtily ['hɔːtili], *adv.* hautainement; d'une manière hautaine, arrogante; altièrement; **to speak h.,** parler avec hauteur.

haughtiness ['hɔːtinis], *s.* arrogance *f*, hauteur *f*, morgue *f*.

haughty ['hɔːti], *a.* hautain, arrogant, altier, sourcilleux.

haul[1] [hɔːl], *s.* **1.** amenée *f*; effort *m* (pour tirer, haler, ou amener qch.). **2.** *Fish:* (*a*) **at one h. (of the net),** d'un seul coup de filet; *F:* **the police made a h. (of them),** la police les a ramassés d'un seul coup de filet; (*b*) prise *f*, pêche *f*; **to make, get, a good h.,** (i) ramener un fameux coup de filet; faire (une) bonne pêche; (ii) *F:* (*of financier*) faire son butin; **the burglars didn't get much of a h.,** les cambrioleurs *m* n'ont pas trouvé grand-chose à rafler. **3.** (i) chemin parcouru par un objet traîné; (ii) parcours *m*, trajet *m*; (iii) transport *m*; **length of h.,** distance *f* de transport; **short h.,** transport à, sur, courte distance; **medium h.,** transport à, sur, moyenne distance; **long h.,** transport sur longue, à grande, distance; *Av: etc:* **short-h., medium-h., long-h., route,** étape courte, moyenne, longue; **short-h. transport aircraft,** avion *m* de transport sur petite(s) distance(s); **short-h. jet liner,** court courrier à réaction; **medium-h. jet liner,** moyen courrier à réaction; **long-h. jet liner,** long courrier à réaction; **there's still a long h. ahead,** il y a encore toute une tirée.

haul[2], *v.*

I. *v.tr. & i.* **1.** *v.tr.* (*a*) tirer; traîner, transporter (une charge); remorquer (un bateau, un train); **the engine was hauling 25 trucks,** la locomotive traînait 25 wagons; **car hauling a trailer,** voiture suivie d'une remorque; *Min:* **to h. the trucks,** rouler les wagons; hercher; (*b*) transporter (des marchandises) par camions; camionner; (*c*) *Nau:* **to h. the wind,** serrer le vent (de près); repiquer dans le vent. **2.** *v.i. Nau:* (*a*) **to h. on a rope,** haler sur une manœuvre; (*b*) **to h. alongside,** accoster; (*c*) **to h. upon, to, the wind,** serrer, rallier, le vent; haler le vent, se haler dans le vent; **to h. to starboard,** venir sur tribord; (*d*) (*of wind*) haler; **to h. aft, on the beam,** haler l'arrière, le travers; **the wind is hauling,** la brise refuse.

II. (*compound verbs*) **1. haul down,** *v.tr. Nau:* haler bas, rentrer, affaler (les voiles, etc.); rentrer (un pavillon); **to h. down a signal,** amener un signal; **the ship hauled down her colours,** le vaisseau amena.

2. haul in. *Nau:* (*a*) *v.tr.* haler en dedans; **to h. in a rope,** haler, rentrer, virer, une manœuvre; **h. in the ropes!** embraquez les amarres! **to h. in the sheets,** choquer les écoutes; **to h. in a bit of the towing rope,** embraquer un peu la remorque; **to h. in the log,** rentrer le loch; **to h. in the line,** relever la sonde; *Mil:* **to h. in each half of a pontoon bridge to the bank,** replier un pont; (*b*) *v.i.* rallier la terre.

3. haul off. *v.i. Nau:* s'élever au large.

4. haul out. *v.i.* (*a*) *Navy:* **to h. out of the line,** sortir, déboîter, de la ligne; quitter la ligne; (*b*) (*of male seal*) aller à terre.

5. haul up. (*a*) *v.tr.* (i) *Nau:* hisser (un pavillon); **to h. up a boat** (*aboard ship*) rentrer une embarcation; (*on the beach*) haler une embarcation à sec; (ii) *F:* **to h. s.o. up (for sth., for doing sth.),** demander une explication à qn; demander compte à qn (de qch.); prendre qn à partie (d'avoir fait qch.); **to be hauled up before the beak,** être sommé de comparaître (devant le juge); (*b*) *v.i. Nau:* remonter dans le vent.

haulage ['hɔːlidʒ], *s.* **1.** (*a*) (transport *m* par) roulage *m*, charriage *m*, camionnage *m*; **road h.,** transports routiers; **road h. depot,** gare routière (de marchandises); **h. contractor,** entrepreneur *m* de transports; (*b*) traction *f*, remorquage *m*, halage *m*; *Min:* traînage *m* (des wagons); herchage *m*; **man h.,** traction à bras; **h. rope,** câble *m* de traînage; *Min:* **h. man,** rouleur *m*, hercheur *m*. **2.** (*costs*) frais *mpl* de roulage, de transport.

hauler ['hɔːlər], *s.* **1.** (*pers.*) (*a*) haleur, -euse; (*b*) *Min:* = HAULIER 2. **2.** *Trans:* (véhicule) transporteur *m*; *Av:* **short, medium, long, h.,** avion *m* de transport à courte, moyenne, grande, distance.

haulier ['hɔːliər], *s.m.* **1.** camionneur; routier; entrepreneur de transports. **2.** *Min:* hercheur, rouleur, traineur de wagonnets.

hauling ['hɔːliŋ], *s.* (*a*) traction *f*, remorquage *m*; *Min:* herchage *m*; **h. engine,** moteur *m* de roulage; *Rail:* **h. stock,** matériel remorqueur, de traction; (*b*) *Nau:* halage *m*; **h. rope,** câble *m* de halage; **h. line,** va-et-vient *m inv*; **h. slip,** cale *f* à halage; **h. end of a tackle,** garant *m* d'un palan.

haulm [hɔːm, hɑːm], *s. Bot:* **1.** fane *f* (de légume). **2.** *coll.* fanes, fanage *m*; chaume *m*.

haulmy ['hɔːmi, 'hɑːmi], *a.* fanu.

haunch [hɔːn(t)ʃ], *s.* **1.** (*a*) *Anat:* hanche *f*; **h. bone,** os *m* iliaque, coxal; (*b*) *Cu:* cuissot *m*, quartier *m*, cimier *m* (de venaison, de chevreuil); (*c*) *pl.* **haunches,** arrière-train *m*; **to pull a horse up on its haunches,** arrêter un cheval sur cul *m*; **dog sitting on his haunches,** chien assis sur son derrière. **2.** (*a*) *Arch:* rein *m*, aisselle *f* (d'une voûte); (*b*) *Carp:* renfort *m*; **bevelled h.,** mordâne *m*.

haunched [hɔːnʃt], *a. Carp:* (tenon *m*) à mordâne.

haunt[1] [hɔːnt], *s.* lieu fréquenté (par une personne, un animal); retraite *f*; repaire *m* (de bêtes féroces, de voleurs, etc.); rendez-vous *m* (de bons compagnons); **an evil, a low, h.,** un mauvais lieu; **he wanted to see the haunts of his youth,** il voulait revoir les lieux où s'était passée sa jeunesse; **to go back to one's old haunts,** revenir à ses anciennes fréquentations; *Lit:* **the busy haunts of men,** les lieux où se porte la foule; les lieux fréquentés par la foule.

haunt[2]. **1.** *v.tr.* (*a*) (*of pers., animal*) fréquenter, hanter (un endroit, qn); **haunted by robbers,** fréquenté par les voleurs, infesté de voleurs; (*b*) (*of ghost*) hanter (une maison); **the red room is haunted,** il y des revenants dans la chambre rouge; (*c*) (*of thoughts, ideas, dreams*) obséder, poursuivre (qn), troubler, hanter (l'esprit, le sommeil); **to be haunted by memories,** être assiégé, obsédé, par des souvenirs. **2.** *v.i.* (*usu. of animal*) **to h. in, about, a place,** fréquenter un endroit.

haunted ['hɔːntid], *a.* (*a*) **h. house,** maison hantée (par des revenants); (*b*) **h. eyes,** yeux hagards, fous; **he has a h. look,** il a l'air d'un halluciné.

haunter ['hɔːntər], *s.* habitué, -ée (de théâtres, etc.); *F:* **pub h.,** pilier *m* de cabaret.

haunting[1] ['hɔːntiŋ], *a.* (mélodie, etc.) qui vous hante, qui vous trotte dans la mémoire, qui revient constamment à la mémoire; (souvenir, doute) obsédant; **h. thought,** pensée hallucinante; **h. memory,** hantise *f*.

haunting[2], *s.* fréquentation *f*, hantement *m*.

Hausa ['hausə], *s.* **1.** *Ethn:* Haous(s)a *mf.* **2.** *Ling:* haous(s)a *m*.

Hausaland ['hausəlænd], *Pr.n. Geog:* Haous(s)a *m*.

hausmannite ['hausmənait], *s. Miner:* hausmannite *f*.

haustellate [hɔː'steleit], *a. Nat.Hist:* haustellé.

haustellum, *pl.* **-a** [hɔː'steləm, -lə], *s. Nat.Hist:* haustellum *m*, suçoir *m*, trompe *f* (d'insecte, de crustacé).

haustorial [hɔː'stɔːriəl], *a. Bot:* haustellé.

haustorium, *pl.* **-ia** [hɔːs'tɔːriəm, -iə], *s. Bot:* haustoire *f*, haustorium *m*, suçoir *m*.

haustration [hɔː'streiʃ(ə)n], *s. Med:* haustration *f*.

haustrum, *pl.* **-ra** ['hɔːstrəm, -rə], *s. Anat:* saccule *m* du côlon.

hautbois, hautboy ['houbɔi], *s.* **1.** *Mus: A:* hautbois *m*. **2.** *Bot:* **h. (strawberry),** (i) capron *m*, (ii) (*plant*) capronnier *m*; fraisier élevé.

haute couture ['outku'tjuːər], *s.* haute couture.

haute école ['outei'kɔl], *s. Equit:* haute école.

hauyne [ɔː'win], **hauynite** [ɔː'wiːnait], *s. Miner:* haüyne *f*.

Havana [hə'vænə, -'vɑː-]. **1.** *Pr.n. Geog:* la Havane. **2. a H. (cigar),** un havane.

Havanan [hə'vænən, -'vɑː-], **Havanese** [hævə'niːz]. *Geog:* (*a*) *a.* havanais; (*b*) *s.* Havanais, -aise.

have[1] [hæv], *s.* **1.** *pl. F:* **the haves and the h.-nots,** les riches *m* et les pauvres *m*; les propriétaires *m* et les prolétaires *m*. **2.** *F:* (*a*) (*swindle*) attrape *f*; escroquerie *f*; (*b*) (*joke*) attrape, bateau *m*; **it's a h.!** on a été refaits!

have[2], *v.* (*pr. ind.* **have**; *A: 2nd pers. sing.* **hast**; *3rd pers.* **has**, *A: & B:* **hath**, *pl.* **have**; *pr. sub. sg. & pl.* **have**; *past ind. & sub.* **had, hadst, had**, *pl.* **had**; *pr.p.* **having**; *p.p.* **had**; *have not, has not, had not, are frequently shortened into* **haven't, hasn't, hadn't**; *I have, he has, we have, you have, they have, into* **I've, he's, we've, you've, they've**; *I had, etc., into* **I'd**, *etc*).

I. *v.tr.* **1.** (*a*) avoir, posséder; **a week has seven days,** une semaine a sept jours; **he had no friends,** il n'avait pas d'amis; **would you like to h. such a man for a friend?** cela vous plairait-il d'avoir un pareil homme pour ami? **to h. ten thousand pounds a year,** avoir dix mille livres de rente(s); **all I h.,** tout ce que je possède, tout mon avoir; **pens, pencils, and what h. you,** des stylos, des crayons et tout ce qui s'ensuit; **he has a shop,** il tient une boutique; **I h. the key of the riddle,** je tiens la clef de l'énigme; **the purse had nothing in it,** il n'y avait rien dans la bourse; la bourse était vide; **my bag has no name on it,** ma valise ne porte pas de nom; **the door has no key to it,** la porte n'a pas de clef; **I don't know whether you still h. apples for sale; if you h., send me a case,** je ne sais si vous avez encore des pommes à vendre; dans l'affirmative, expédiez-m'en une caisse; **I h. nothing to do,** je n'ai rien à faire; **I h. work to do,** j'ai à travailler; **the work I h. for you to do,** le travail que je vous réserve; **to h. s.o. to deal with,** avoir affaire à qn; **you h. my sympathy, my apologies,** je vous plains; je vous demande pardon; **to h. a right,** jouir d'un droit; **I h. no words to express . . .,** les mots me manquent pour exprimer . . .; **he has no Latin or Greek,** il ne sait ni latin ni grec; **ah! I h. it!** ah! j'y suis! *F:* **you h. me?** vous me comprenez? *F:* **to h. it in for s.o.,** garder à qn un chien de sa chienne; **to h. it on s.o.,** l'emporter sur qn; **to h. nothing on s.o.,** ne l'emporter sur qn en quoi que ce soit; *B:* **he that hath, to him shall be given,** à celui qui a il sera donné; (*b*) **we don't h. many visitors,** nous ne recevons pas beaucoup de visites; **we're having visitors tomorrow,** nous attendons des invités demain; **Caroline's having her sisters over on Sunday,** Caroline va avoir ses sœurs chez elle dimanche; **we h. friends staying with us,** nous avons des amis en visite; **to h. friends (in) to dinner,** avoir des amis à dîner; **we really must h. them back,** il nous faut absolument rendre leur invitation; **we're having them down for the weekend,** nous les avons invités à passer le week-end chez nous; **I'm having my cousin up to do some shopping,** j'ai invité ma cousine à venir à Londres faire des courses; **we shall h. the painters in next week,** la semaine prochaine nous aurons les peintres; **we had to h. the doctor in,** nous avons dû appeler le médecin. **2.** (*a*) (*give birth to*) avoir, faire; **how many children has she had?** combien d'enfants a-t-elle eus? **our cat has had kittens,** notre chatte a fait des petits; (*b*) (*beget*) **he had had two children by her,** il avait eu d'elle deux enfants. **3.** (*obtain*) (*a*) **there was no work to be had,** on ne pouvait pas obtenir, se procurer, de travail; **it's to be** had at the chemist's, at all the bookshops, cela se trouve chez le pharmacien; c'est en vente chez tous les libraires; to h. one's wish, obtenir, avoir obtenu, ce que l'on désire; *P:* to h. a woman, avoir une femme; (*b*) to h. news from s.o., recevoir des nouvelles de qn; I had it from my neighbour, je tiens ce renseignement de mon voisin; je le tiens de mon voisin; I h. it on good authority, je l'ai appris de bonne source; (*c*) I must h. them by tomorrow, il me les faut pour demain; I will let you h. it, you may h. it, for £5, je vous le céderai, je vous le laisserai, pour cinq livres; let me h. the money tomorrow, envoyez-moi l'argent demain; let me h. your keys, donnez-moi, laissez-moi, vos clefs; let me h. it back, rendez-le-moi; vous me le rendrez, n'est-ce pas? you shall h. it back tomorrow, je vous le rendrai demain; let me h. an early reply, répondez-moi sans retard; *Com:* let me h. your order as soon as possible, transmettez-moi votre commande au plus tôt; let him h. his sleep out, laissez-le dormir, finir son somme; *F:* to h. it out with s.o., vider une querelle avec qn; s'expliquer avec qn; now we'll h. it out, à nous deux maintenant; *F:* I let him h. it, (i) je lui ai dit son fait; (ii) je lui ai flanqué une raclée, une tripotée; je lui ai réglé son compte; *P:* you've had it, chum! (i) tu es fait, mon vieux! tu peux te mettre la ceinture, mon vieux! (ii) tu es foutu, mon vieux! *P:* don't get het up, you've had it, pas besoin de s'en faire, c'est loupé; *F:* I've had it, me voilà frais; *P:* (= *dead, dying*) he's had it, il a sa dose. 4. (*take*) prendre (de la nourriture); to h. tea with s.o., prendre le thé avec qn; will you h. tea? voulez-vous du thé? where do you h. your meals? où prenez-vous vos repas? what will you h., sir?—I'll h. a chop, que prendra monsieur?—donnez-moi une côtelette; he is having his dinner, il est en train de dîner; she hasn't had anything for three days, elle n'a rien mangé, rien pris, depuis trois jours; I had some more, j'en ai repris; to h. a cigar, a cigarette, fumer un cigare, une cigarette; *F:* I'm not having any! on ne me la fait pas! ça ne prend pas! très peu pour moi! I've had some, thank you! je sors d'en prendre! 5. (*in numerous verbal phrases; e.g.*) (*a*) to h. measles, avoir la rougeole; to h. a cold, être enrhumé; to h. a fit of coughing, avoir une quinte de toux; to h. dealings with s.o., avoir affaire à qn; to h. the choice, avoir le choix; to h. faith in s.o., avoir foi en qn; to h. an idea, avoir une idée; to h. no idea, no notion, of . . ., n'avoir aucune idée de . . ., to h. need of sth., avoir besoin de qch.; to h. recourse to s.o., sth., avoir recours à qn, qch.; to h. a talk, a word, with s.o., avoir un entretien avec qn; to h. a taste for sth., avoir le goût de qch.; to h. a right to sth., avoir droit à qch.; (*b*) to h. a dream, faire un rêve; to h. a walk, a drive, faire une promenade; to h. a game, faire une partie; to h. a fall, faire une chute; (*c*) to h. a lesson, prendre une leçon; to h. a bath, a shower, prendre un bain, une douche; to h. a wash, se laver; to h. a shave, (i) se raser, (ii) se faire raser; (*d*) to h. a pleasant evening, passer une soirée agréable; to h. a joke with s.o., plaisanter avec qn; I didn't h. any trouble at all, cela ne m'a donné, coûté, aucune peine; I didn't h. any trouble in finding it, je n'ai eu aucune peine à le trouver; if you're not careful we shall h. the police here, si vous ne prenez pas garde, nous allons avoir une descente de la police; we had a rather strange adventure, il nous est arrivé une aventure assez étrange; the only thing I ever had happen to me was . . ., la seule chose qui me soit jamais arrivée, c'est . . .; (*e*) to h. fine, wet, weather, avoir du beau temps, de la pluie; we had snow at Easter, à Pâques il a neigé. 6. (*a*) (*assert*) prétendre, soutenir, affirmer; he *will* h. it that Hamlet is mad, il soutient, il affirme à tout venant, que Hamlet est fou; il veut à toute force que Hamlet soit fou; *O:* they are not so old as you would h. them, ils n'ont pas l'âge que vous leur prêtez, que vous leur donnez; rumour has it that . . ., le bruit court que . . .; (*b*) as Plato has it, comme dit Platon; (*c*) (*admit*) he will not h. it that she is delicate, il n'admet pas qu'elle soit de santé délicate. 7. (*a*) to h. s.o. in one's power, avoir qn en son pouvoir; *F:* to h. s.o. on the end of a piece of string, tenir qn où on le veut; *F:* to h. s.o. on, monter un coup à qn; faire marcher qn; I h. him beaten, je l'ai à ma merci; le voilà enfoncé; je le tiens, *F:* je l'ai; he had me by the throat, il me tenait à la gorge; (*b*) you h. me there! voilà où vous me prenez en défaut! à cela je ne sais que répondre! that's where I h. him! c'est là que je l'attends! (*c*) *F:* (*outwit*) avoir, attraper (qn); mettre (qn) dedans; to be had, donner dans le piège, dans le panneau; *F:* donner dedans; you've been had! on vous a eu! on vous a acheté! vous avez été refait! (*for a purchase*) on vous a passé un rossignol; I've been properly had! on m'a bien attrapé! I had him properly, je lui ai joué un tour de mon métier; I've been had by a swindler, j'ai été la victime d'un escroc; j'ai été refait par un escroc; I'm not to be had, on ne me la fait pas; ça ne prend pas. 8. (*a*) (*causative*) to h. sth. done, faire faire qch.; to h. s.o. do sth., faire faire qch. à qn; to h. one's hair cut, se faire couper les cheveux; h. it repaired, faites-le réparer; I had it built on purpose, je l'ai fait bâtir exprès; the proposals that I should like to h. considered, les propositions *f* que je voudrais voir étudier; he *would* h. me come in, il a voulu à toute force me faire entrer; (*b*) he had his leg broken, il s'est cassé la jambe; three houses had their windows shattered, trois maisons ont eu leurs fenêtres brisées; I had my watch stolen, je me suis fait, laissé, voler ma montre; to h. a tooth out, se faire arracher une dent; she had had a story accepted by a weekly, un de ses contes avait été accepté par une publication hebdomadaire; we h. had a double task imposed on us, nous nous sommes vu imposer une double tâche; he likes to h. people come to see him, il aime qu'on vienne le voir; I like to h. my garden look its best, j'aime que mon jardin ait bonne apparence; (*c*) I shall h. everything ready, je veillerai à ce que tout soit prêt; I shall h. the water boiling, je ferai en sorte qu'il y ait de l'eau bouillante; (*d*) to h. one's hands full, one's pockets empty, one's eyes open, avoir les mains pleines, les poches vides, les yeux ouverts. 9. (*a*) which one will you h.? lequel voulez-vous? she won't h. him, elle ne veut pas de lui; will you h. me to help you? voulez-vous de moi pour vous aider? what more would you h.? que vous faut-il de plus? as luck would h. it he arrived too late, la malchance voulut qu'il arrivât trop tard; (*b*) what would you h. me do? que voulez-vous que je fasse? I would h. you know that. . ., sachez que . . .; he would h. had her suppose that . . ., il aurait voulu lui faire supposer que . . .; (*c*) (*allow*) I will not h. such conduct, je ne supporterai pas une pareille conduite; I won't h. him teased, je ne veux pas, je ne souffre pas, qu'on le taquine; I won't h. you coming in here, je ne veux pas que vous entriez ici; I can't h. Rosie know about it, ça ne m'irait pas du tout que Rosie l'apprenne. 10. (*a*) (*of pers.*) (*be compelled*) to h. to do sth., devoir faire qch.; être obligé, forcé, de faire qch.; I had to go away, j'ai dû m'en aller; we shall h. to walk more quickly, il nous faudra marcher plus vite; il faudra que nous marchions plus vite (que ça); he has to walk five miles, il lui faut faire cinq milles à pied; I don't h. to work, moi je n'ai pas besoin de travailler; *Iron:* of course you *had* to go and tell him about that! dire qu'il te fallait lui parler de ça! (*b*) my shirt will h. to be ironed, ma chemise a besoin d'être repassée; il va falloir me repasser ma chemise; the clock will h. to be mended, la pendule a besoin d'être réparée. 11. to h. sth. on a horse, faire un pari, miser, sur un cheval. 12. (*as auxiliary*) (*a*) to h. been, to h. given, to h. done, avoir été, avoir donné, avoir fait; to h. come, to h. hurt oneself, être venu, s'être blessé; when I had dined, I went out, (i) quand j'avais dîné, je sortais; (ii) quand j'eus dîné, je sortis; (iii) quand j'ai eu dîné, je suis sorti; I h. lived in London for three years, voilà trois ans que j'habite Londres; (*emphatic*) well, you *have* grown! ce que tu as grandi! *had* I seen him? si je l'avais vu! (*b*) he went to the office, as his father had before him, il allait au bureau, comme l'avait fait son père avant lui; you h. forgotten your gloves—so I h.! vous avez oublié vos gants—en effet! tiens, c'est vrai! you haven't swept the room—I h.! vous n'avez pas balayé la pièce—si! mais si! si fait! you h. been in prison before—I haven't! vous avez déjà fait de la prison—c'est faux! 13. (*past sub.* had = *would have*) I had better say nothing, je ferais mieux, ferai mieux, de ne rien dire; *Lit:* I had as soon, as lief, stay here, j'aimerais autant rester ici; I'd much rather start at once, j'aimerais bien mieux partir tout de suite.

II. (*compound verb*) **have up**, *v.tr. F:* (*a*) faire assigner (qn) (en justice); citer (qn) en justice; she says she'll h. him up for breach of promise, elle dit qu'elle va le poursuivre pour violation de promesse de mariage; (*b*) (*of magistrate*) assigner, citer, (qn) en justice; sommer (qn) de comparaître; to be had up for an offence, être cité devant les tribunaux pour un délit; *F:* avoir, ramasser, une contravention (pour excès de vitesse, etc.).

haven ['heiv(ə)n], *s.* (*a*) havre *m*, port *m*; (*b*) abri *m*, asile *m*, refuge *m*, retraite *f*; h. of refuge, port de salut.

have-on ['hævɔn], *s. F:* attrape *f*, bateau *m*, blague *f*.

haver ['heivər], *v.i. Scot:* (*a*) dire des balivernes, des niaiseries, des sottises, des bêtises; (*b*) hésiter.

haverite ['heivərait], *s. Miner:* havérite *f*.

havers ['heivəz], *s.pl. Scot:* sottises *f*, bêtises *f*.

haversack ['hævəsæk], *s.* 1. *Mil:* musette *f*. 2. havresac *m* (de tourisme, de camping).

Haversian [hæ'vəːsiən], *a. Anat:* (canaux, etc.) de Havers.

havoc[1] ['hævək], *s.* ravage *m*, dégâts *mpl*, dévastation *f*, destruction *f*; to make h., play h. (in the streets, among the pheasants, etc.), faire de grands dégâts, de grands ravages (dans les rues, etc.); massacrer (les faisans); to make h. of a town, saccager une ville; the frosts have wrought h. in, made h. of, played h. among, the vineyards, les gelées ont fait de grands dégâts dans les vignobles, ont fait beaucoup de tort aux propriétaires des vignobles.

havoc[2], *v.tr.* (havocked) ravager, saccager, dévaster.

haw[1] [hɔː], *s.* 1. *Bot:* (*a*) cenelle *f*; (*b*) = HAWTHORN. 2. *A:* (*a*) haie *f*, clôture *f*; (*b*) enclos *m*.

haw[2], *s. Z:* 1. paupière nictitante, membrane clignotante, membrane nictitante (d'un cheval, d'un chien, d'un oiseau). 2. *pl.* haws of a bloodhound, caroncules *f* d'un limier.

haw[3], *s.* bégaiement *m*.

haw[4], *v.i.* bégayer; to hum and h., hem and h., (i) bégayer; (ii) se montrer indécis, hésiter (en parlant).

haw[5], *int. NAm:* (*to horse*) dia!

haw[6], *v.i. NAm:* (*of horse*) tourner à gauche; aller à dia.

Hawaii [hə'waiiː], *Pr.n. Geog:* Hawaï.

Hawaiian [hə'waiən]. *Geog:* (*a*) *a.* hawaïen; the H., islands, les îles Hawaï; *Geol:* H. eruption, éruption hawaïenne; *Mus:* H. guitar, guitare hawaïenne; (*b*) *s.* Hawaïen, -ïenne.

hawfinch ['hɔːfinʃ], *s. Orn:* gros-bec *m* (*pl.* gros-becs) casse-noyaux.

haw-haw[1] ['hɔː'hɔː]. 1. *s.* rire bruyant; rire bête; gros rire. 2. *a. O:* (prononciation) affectée.

haw-haw[2], *v.i.* rire bruyamment, bêtement; faire des ho, ho, ho.

hawk[1] [hɔːk], *s.* 1. *Orn:* (*a*) faucon *m*; bat h., buse *f* des chauves-souris; carrion h., caracara *m*; crested h., baza *m*, *F:* huppard *m*; chanting h., melierax *m*, faucon chanteur; red h., faucon saure; (American) rough-legged h., buse pattue; broad-winged h., *Fr.C:* petite buse; Cooper's h., *Fr.C:* épervier *m* de Cooper; marsh h., busard *m* Saint-Martin, *Fr.C:* busard des marais; red-shouldered h., buse à manteau rouge, *Fr.C:* buse à épaulettes rousses; red-tailed h., *Fr.C:* buse à queue rousse; sharp-shinned h., *Fr.C:* épervier brun; Swainson's h., *Fr.C:* buse de Swainson; duck h., faucon pèlerin; pigeon h., faucon émerillon; (American) sparrow h., faucon des moineaux, *Fr.C:* crécerelle américaine; (*b*) h. eagle, aigle-autour *m*, spizaëte *m*; common h. cuckoo, coucou épervier *m*; h. owl, chouette épervière; to have eyes like a h., avoir des yeux d'aigle, *Lit:* he doesn't know a h. from a handsaw, il n'y connaît absolument rien. 2. *F:* (*pers.*) (*a*) vautour *m*, homme *m* rapace; (*b*) *Pol: etc:* belliciste *m*, faucon, épervier. 3. *Bot:* hawk's beard, crépide *f*.

hawk[2], *v.i. Ven:* 1. chasser au faucon. 2. (*of bird, insect*) to h. at the prey, fondre sur la proie.

hawk[3], *s. F:* graillement *m*, expectoration *f*.

hawk[4], *v.i. & tr. F:* graillonner; to h. up phlegm, expectorer des mucosités; graillonner.

hawk[5], *s. Tls:* taloche *f* (de plâtrier).

hawk[6], *v.tr.* colporter, cameloter (qch.); crier (des marchandises) dans les rues.

hawkbill ['hɔːkbil], *s.* 1. *Rept:* tortue *f* à écaille. 2. *Tls:* pincette *f* à souder; tenaille *f* à souder.

hawkbit ['hɔːkbit], *s. Bot:* léontodon *m*, liondent *m*; (common) h., liondent à tige nue; rough h., liondent hispide; smooth h., liondent d'automne.

hawker[1] ['hɔːkər], *s.* fauconnier *m*.

hawker[2], *s.* (*a*) colporteur *m*, marchand ambulant, camelot *m*; (*b*) (*of fruit, vegetables*) marchand des quatre saisons.

hawk-eyed ['hɔːkaid], *a.* (personne) aux yeux d'aigle, au regard d'aigle, qui a la vue perçante.

hawking[1] ['hɔːkiŋ], *s.* chasse *f* au faucon; fauconnerie *f*; chasse au vol; to go h., faire la chasse au faucon.

hawking[2], *s.* graillonnement *m*; expectoration *f* (de mucosités).

hawking[3], *s.* colportage *m*.

hawkish ['hɔːkiʃ], **hawklike** ['hɔːklaik], *a.* qui ressemble à un faucon; de faucon; with a h. swoop, comme un aigle qui fond sur sa proie.

hawkmoth ['hɔːkmɔθ], *s. Ent:* sphinx *m*; crépusculaire *m*, smérinthe *m*; the hawkmoths, les sphingidés *m*; hummingbird h., moro-sphinx *m inv*; sphinx moineau *m*; macroglosse *m* du caille-lait; sphinx du caille-lait; privet h., sphinx du troène; death's-head h., sphinx tête de mort.

hawknose ['hɔːknouz], *s.* nez aquilin, en bec d'aigle, recourbé.

hawknosed ['hɔːknouzd], *a.* (personne) au nez recourbé, au nez aquilin, en bec d'aigle; to be h., avoir le nez aquilin.

hawksbill ['hɔːksbil], *s. Rept:* **h. (turtle),** tortue *f* à écaille.

hawkweed ['hɔːkwiːd], *s. Bot:* épervière *f.*

haworthia [hə'wəːθiə], *s. Bot:* haworthia *m.*

hawse [hɔːz, hɔːs], *s.inv. Nau:* **1.** (*a*) = HAWSEHOLE; (*b*) *pl.* **the h.,** les écubiers *m.* **2.** (*a*) affourchage *m*, évitage *m*; **to anchor in a ship's h.,** mouiller dans les ancres d'un navire; (*b*) **clear, open, h.,** chaînes claires; **foul h.,** tours *mpl* de chaînes, câble engagé.

hawsehole ['hɔːzhoul', hɔːs-], *s. Nau:* écubier *m.*

hawsepipe ['hɔːzpaip, 'hɔːs-], *s. Nau:* manchon *m* d'écubier.

hawser ['hɔːzər, 'hɔːs-], *s. Nau:* (*a*) aussière *f*, grelin *m*; (*b*) amarre *f*; **steel h.,** amarre, aussière, en fil d'acier; (*c*) câble *m* de remorque; (*d*) **h. bend,** nœud *m* de plein poing.

hawser-laid ['hɔːzəleid, 'hɔːs-], *a.* **h.-l. rope,** cordage commis en aussière.

hawthorn ['hɔːθɔːn], *s. Bot:* aubépine *f*, aubépin *m*, épine blanche, noble-épine *f.*

hay[1] [hei], *s.* foin *m*; *Husb:* fourrage *m* en sec; **h. knife,** coupe-foin *m inv*, couteau *m* à foin; **h. press,** presse *f* à fourrages; **h. waggon,** *A:* **h. wain,** fourragère *f*; **h. rake,** râteau *m*, fauchet *m*; **to make h.,** faire le(s) foin(s); faner; *Prov:* **to make h. while the sun shines,** battre le fer tant qu'il est chaud, pendant qu'il est chaud; mettre l'occasion à profit; *F:* **to make h. of sth.,** embrouiller qch.; mettre qch. en désordre, sens dessus dessous; faire un gâchis de qch.; **to make h. of an argument,** réduire un argument à rien; démolir un argument; *F:* **to hit the h.,** se coucher, se pieuter.

hay[2], *v.i.* faire les foins.

hay[3], *s. A.Danc:* contre-danse *f*, *pl.* contre-danses (espèce de farandole).

haybox ['heibɔks], *s. Dom.Ec:* marmite suédoise, norvégienne.

haycart ['heikaːt], *s.* fourragère *f.*

haycock ['heikɔk], *s.* tas *m*, meulon *m*, meulette *f*, de foin; buirette *f*; **to make haycocks,** rucher le foin.

hayfork ['heifɔːk], *s.* fourche *f* à foin.

haying ['heiiŋ], *s.* fenaison *f*; **h. time,** époque *f* de la fenaison.

hayloft ['heilɔft], *s.* (*U.S: also* **haymow** ['heimou]) fenil *m*; grenier *m*, grange *f*, à foin.

haymaker ['heimeikər], *s.* **1.** (*pers.*) faneur, -euse. **2.** (*machine*) faneuse *f*, tourne-foin *m inv.* **3.** *P:* coup de poing balancé.

haymaking ['heimeikiŋ], *s.* fenaison *f.*

hayrack ['heiræk], *s.* **1.** râtelier *m* d'écurie. **2.** (*on cart*) fausse ridelle.

hayrick ['heirik], **haystack** ['heistæk], *s.* meule *f* de foin; (*small*) meulette *f*; (*square*) barge *f.*

hayseed ['heisiːd], *s.* **1.** graine *f* de foin (recueillie au grenier). **2.** *U.S: F:* paysan *m*, rustaud *m.*

haywire ['heiwaiər], *a. F:* (*a*) confus, embrouillé; (*of plan*) **to go h.,** être loupé, finir en queue de poisson; (*b*) (*of pers.*) emballé, excité, cinglé; **he's gone h.,** il ne tourne plus rond, il déraille, il déménage; (*c*) *esp. NAm:* (*of job, etc.*) bousillé.

hazard[1] ['hæzəd], *s.* **1.** (*a*) hasard *m*; **game of h.,** jeu *m* de hasard; (*b*) risque *m*, péril *m*; *Aut: etc:* point dangereux; **at the h. of his life,** au risque de sa vie; **the hazards of war,** les hasards, les périls, les risques, de la guerre; **to run the h.,** courir le risque. **2.** *Bill:* coup *m* qui fait entrer une des billes dans la blouse; **to play a winning h.,** blouser la bille sur laquelle on vise; **to play a losing h.,** se blouser. **3.** *Golf:* accident *m* de terrain. **4.** trou gagnant (au jeu de paume). **5.** *Paperm:* **h. machine,** tambour culbuteur.

hazard[2], *v.tr.* hasarder, risquer, aventurer (sa vie, sa fortune); hasarder (une opinion); **to h. a battle,** risquer une bataille.

hazardous ['hæzədəs], *a.* (coup, commerce) hasardeux, chanceux, hasardé, risqué, périlleux; (profit, etc.) aléatoire; **h. plan,** projet aventureux; **the business is too h.,** l'affaire présente trop d'aléas.

hazardously ['hæzədəsli], *adv.* hasardeusement, aventureusement.

haze[1] [heiz], *s.* (*a*) brume légère; brumasse *f*; **morning h.,** vapeurs *fpl* du matin; **there is a h. over the hills,** une brume voile les collines; (*b*) obscurité *f*, incertitude *f* (de l'esprit).

haze[2]. **1.** *v.tr.* rendre brumeux, embrumer (l'horizon, etc.). **2.** *v.i. A: Dial:* bruiner.

haze[3], *v.tr.* (*a*) *Dial:* (i) effaroucher, (ii) gronder, (iii) rosser (qn); (*b*) *Nau:* harasser (qn) de corvées; (*c*) *U.S:* brimer (un nouvel étudiant).

hazel ['heizl], *s.* **1.** (*a*) **h. (tree),** noisetier *m*, coudrier *m*, avelinier *m*, avellanier *m*; **h. grove, wood,** coudraie *f*; (*b*) noisette *f*, aveline *f.* **2.** *attrib.* **h. eyes,** yeux *m* couleur (de) noisette. **3.** *Orn:* **h. grouse, hen,** gelinotte *f* des bois.

hazelnut ['heizlnʌt], *s. Bot:* noisette *f*, aveline *f*; **h. plantation,** noiseraie *f.*

hazily ['heizili], *adv.* vaguement, obscurément, indistinctement.

haziness ['heizinis], *s.* état brumeux, nébuleux (du temps, de l'esprit); **the h. of his knowledge,** le vague, l'imprécision *f*, l'incertitude *f*, de son savoir.

hazy ['heizi], *a.* **1.** (*of weather*) brumeux, embrumé, gris; **h. horizon,** horizon embrumé; **it's rather h.,** il fait une légère brume. **2.** (*a*) (contour, etc.) flou, estompé; (*b*) (*of ideas, etc.*) vaporeux, nébuleux, fumeux; **h. recollection, h. knowledge,** souvenir *m* vague; vague souvenir; connaissance *f* vague; **to be h. about sth.,** n'avoir qu'une connaissance imprécise de qch.; n'avoir qu'un souvenir vague, imprécis, d'un événement; (*c*) *F: O:* un peu gris, un peu ivre; enfumé par la boisson.

he [hiː, *unstressed* hi; *in rapid speech often* i(ː)], *pers. pron. nom. m.* **1.** (*unstressed*) il; (*a*) (*of pers., male animal, Lit: of certain things personified*) **he loves her,** il l'aime; **he didn't see me,** il ne m'a pas vu; **what is he saying?** que dit-il? **what did he say?** qu'a-t-il dit? **when the dog heard the doorbell he barked,** quand le chien a entendu sonner à la porte, il a aboyé; *Lit:* **when Death comes he comes unannounced,** quand la Mort vient elle entre sans prévenir; (*b*) **here he comes,** le voici qui vient; **he's a strange man,** c'est un homme étrange; (*c*) *F:* (*to baby boy*) **did he hurt himself then!** tu t'es fait mal, mon petit? **2.** (*stressed*) (*a*) lui; **he and I,** lui et moi; **I am as tall as he (is),** je suis aussi grand que lui; **it was he who said so,** c'était lui qui l'a dit; *Lit:* **I am he,** c'est moi; **if I were he,** (si j'étais) à sa place; **I guessed (that it was) he (who) was the father,** j'ai deviné que c'était lui le père; **he at any rate knows nothing about it,** quant à lui, il n'en sait rien; (*b*) *esp. Lit:* (*antecedent to a rel.pron.*) celui; **he who believes,** celui qui croit; **he whom you saw,** celui que vous avez vu; **he of whom you speak,** celui dont vous parlez; (*c*) *Lit:* **he of the red robe,** l'homme à la robe rouge; **and if only one remains, I shall be he,** et s'il n'en reste qu'un, je serai celui-là. **3.** (*as substantive*) (*a*) *F:* mâle; **it's a he,** (i) (*of newborn child*) c'est un (petit) garçon; (ii) (*of animal*) c'est un mâle; **a litter of three pups, one he and two she's,** une portée de trois chiots, un mâle et deux femelles; **she's always thinking about a he,** elle a toujours un homme en tête; (*b*) *attrib.* **he bear,** ours mâle; **he goat** bouc; (*c*) *Games:* (jeu *m* de) chat *m*; **to play at he,** jouer à, au, chat; **I'm he!** c'est moi le chat!

head[1] [hed], *s.* **1.** tête *f*; (*a*) **bald h.,** tête chauve; **bullet h.,** tête ronde; **from h. to foot,** de la tête aux pieds, des pieds à la tête; (armé) de pied en cap; **he put his h. in at the door,** il a mis la tête à la porte; **to walk with one's h. in the air,** marcher le front haut; **with his h. bent over his work,** le front courbé sur son travail; **to sell a house over s.o.'s h.,** vendre une maison sans donner au locataire l'occasion de l'acheter; **he gave orders over my h.,** il a donné des ordres sans me consulter; **he was promoted over my h.,** on m'a fait une injustice pour lui donner de l'avancement; **h. down,** la tête baissée; **h. downwards,** la tête en bas; **h. first, foremost,** la tête la première; **to stand on one's h.,** se tenir sur sa tête; faire le poirier; **I don't know whether I'm standing on my h. or my heels,** j'ai la tête à l'envers; je ne sais pas à quel saint me vouer; **I could do it (standing) on my h.,** c'est simple comme bonjour; **to go, turn, h. over heels,** faire la culbute; faire une cabriole; tomber à la renverse; **to knock s.o. h. over heels,** culbuter qn; **to fall h. over heels in love with s.o.,** devenir éperdument amoureux de qn; **he is taller than his brother by a h.,** il dépasse son frère de la tête; *Turf:* (*of horse*) **to win by a h.,** gagner d'une tête; **his horse won only by a h.,** son cheval ne l'a emporté que d'une tête; **to win by a short h.,** gagner de justesse; **to give a horse its h.,** lâcher la bride, la gourmette, à un cheval; donner carrière, rendre la main, à un cheval; écouter un cheval; lâcher les rênes; **to let s.o. have his h.,** lâcher les rênes à qn; donner (libre) carrière à qn; **ruin is hanging over your h.,** la ruine vous menace; votre ruine est imminente; **his guilt be on his own h.,** puisse son crime retomber sur lui; **his blood will be upon your h.,** son sang retombera sur votre tête; **to cut off s.o.'s h.,** décapiter qn; **to lose one's h.,** (i) être décapité; (ii) perdre la tête; être pris de panique; **it will cost him his h.,** cela lui coûtera la tête, la vie; *F:* **to talk s.o.'s h. off,** étourdir qn; parler à qn avec une volubilité extraordinaire; rompre les oreilles à qn; **a fine h. of hair,** une belle chevelure; *Mus:* **h. voice, h. register,** voix *f* de tête; (voix de) fausset *m*; (*b*) *Anthr:* **h. hunting,** chasse *f* aux têtes; **h. hunter,** chasseur *m* de têtes; **h. shrinker,** (i) (Indien) réducteur *m* de têtes; (ii) *F:* psychiatre *mf*; **h. feast,** festin *m* de chasseurs de têtes; (*c*) (*pers.*) **crowned h.,** tête couronnée; (*d*) *Art: etc:* **fine h. by an unknown artist,** belle tête exécutée par un artiste inconnu; **coinage bearing the h. of George III,** monnaie (frappée) à l'effigie de Georges III; *Ecc:* **h. reliquary,** chef *m* reliquaire; (*e*) *Cu:* **sheep's h., calf's h.,** tête de mouton, de veau; **boar's h.,** hure *f* de sanglier; **potted h.,** *NAm:* **h. cheese,** fromage *m* de tête; hure; (*f*) *Ven:* (*antlers*) bois *m*, tête (de cerf); **deer of the first, second, h.,** cerf *m* à la première, deuxième, tête. **2.** (*a*) (*intellect, mind*) **he has a good h. on his shoulders, his h. is screwed on the right way,** c'est une forte tête, un homme de tête, de bon sens; il a de la tête, il a la tête solide; **to have a good h. for business,** avoir l'entente, l'entendement, des affaires; s'entendre aux affaires; **he has no h. (for business, etc.),** il n'a pas de tête (pour les affaires, etc.); **it does more credit to his heart than (to) his h.,** cela indique chez lui plus de cœur que d'intelligence; **idea running through my h.,** idée *f* qui me trotte dans la cervelle; **to reckon in one's h.,** calculer de tête; **to get sth. into one's h.,** se mettre qch. dans la tête, en tête, dans l'esprit; s'imaginer qch.; **I can't get that into his h.,** je ne peux pas lui enfoncer ça dans la tête, dans la cervelle; **he has got, taken, it into his h. that . . .,** il s'est mis dans la tête, en tête, que . . .; **to take it into one's h. to do sth.,** s'aviser, se mettre en tête, de faire qch.; **the thought came into my h. that . . .,** l'idée m'est venue que . . .; **it never entered my h. that . . .,** je n'aurais jamais pensé que . . .; **I can't get it out of my h. that. . .,** je ne peux pas m'ôter de l'idée que . . .; **what put that into your h.?** où avez-vous pris cette idée-là? où avez-vous trouvé cela? **to put ideas into s.o.'s h.,** donner des idées à qn; **to put an idea out of one's h.,** se défaire d'une idée; **his name has gone out of my h.,** son nom m'est sorti de la mémoire; son nom m'échappe; **it sent my appointment clean out of my h.,** cela m'a fait complètement oublier mon rendez-vous; **we laid, put, our heads together,** nous avons conféré ensemble; nous nous sommes entendus, consultés, concertés; *Prov:* **two heads are better than one,** deux conseils, deux avis, valent mieux qu'un; **he gave an answer out of his own h.,** il a donné une réponse de son cru; **I think he made it up out of his own h.,** je crois que c'est lui qui a inventé ça; je crois que c'est une histoire de son cru; **to have a strong, good, h. for drink,** avoir la tête solide, bien porter le vin; **wine that goes to one's h.,** vin *m* qui coiffe; vin qui porte, tape, à la tête; **wine goes to his h.,** le vin lui monte au cerveau, à la tête, le prend à la tête; (*of speech, lecture, etc.*) **to be over the heads of the audience,** dépasser l'entendement de l'auditoire; **you shouldn't talk over the heads of your audience,** il faut rester à la portée de votre auditoire; mettez-vous au niveau de votre auditoire; **to keep one's h.,** conserver sa tête; **to lose one's h.,** perdre la tête, *F:* la boule, la boussole; perdre le nord; **he's off his h.,** *U.S:* **out of his h.,** il est timbré, il déménage; il n'a plus sa tête à lui; **to go off one's h.,** devenir fou; tomber en démence; **he's not quite right in his h., a bit weak in the h.,** il est faible d'esprit, un peu timbré; (*b*) *F:* **I've got a bad h., an awful h.,** j'ai mal à la tête, un de ces maux de tête; (*after drinking*) j'ai mal aux cheveux; **to have a thick h.,** avoir des lourdeurs de tête; (*after drinking*) avoir mal aux cheveux. **3.** (*a*) tête (d'arbre, de fleur, de chou, de laitue); pomme *f* (de chou); pointe *f* (d'asperge); pied *m* (de céleri); épi *m* (de blé); **fine heads of cabbage,** choux bien pommés; (*b*) (*knob-shaped end*) tête (de violon, d'épingle, de clou, *Anat:* de l'humérus); pomme (de canne); champignon *m* (de rail); **rivet h.,** rivure *f*; **battered h.,** rivure écrasée; (*c*) (*detachable end*) tête *f* (de marteau); mouton *m* (de mailloche); fer *m* (de lance, etc.); couronne *f* (de pieu); *Rec:* **pick-up h.,** tête de lecture; *Ball:* **homing h.,** tête chercheuse; (*d*) (*top section*) tête (de volcan, etc.); haut *m* (de page); chapiteau *m* (de colonne, etc.); cuvette *f*, hotte *f* (de gouttière); chef *m* (d'une ardoise); *Nau:* **h. of a sail,** (i) têtière *f*, (ii) envergure *f*, d'une voile; **h. yards,** phare *m* de misaine; (*e*) haut (de l'escalier, etc.); *Min:* (i) carreau *m* (de carrière, de mine); (ii) bouche *f*, gueule *f* (de puits de mine); (*f*) (*rounded end, cover*) tête, culasse *f*, fond *m* (de cylindre); chapiteau (d'alambic, de fusée, etc.); *I.C.E:* **combustion h.,** culasse, calotte *f*; **engine with a detachable h.,** moteur *m* à culasse rapportée; *Mch:* **h. end,** avant *m* (d'un piston de locomotive); *Aut:* **body h.,** capote *f* (de coupé, etc.); **sliding h.,** toit ouvrant; **car with a folding h.,** voiture *f* décapotable; *Navy:* **torpedo h.,** cône *m* (de charge) de torpille; **practice h., dummy h.,** cône d'exercice(s); (*g*) (*flat end*) tête (de piston, de livre); fond (de barrique, etc.); fonçaille *f* (de barrique); peau *f* (de tambour); (*h*) **(poppet) h. of a lathe,** poupée *f* de tour; **loose h.,** contre-pointe *f* (de tour); **ball h.,** pendule *m*, tachymètre *m*, à boule; (*i*) chevet *m*, tête (de lit); haut bout (de la table);

source *f* (d'une rivière); **at the h. of the lake,** à l'amont du lac; au fond, à l'extrémité, du lac; *Hyd.E:* **h. water,** eau *f* d'amont; **h. race,** canal *m* de prise, d'amenée, de dérivation; bief *m* d'amont (d'un moulin à eau); rayère *f* (d'une roue à auges); **h. gate,** porte *f* d'amont (d'une écluse); **h. bay,** bief d'amont; arrière-bief *m*; *Min:* **h. of a level,** avancée *f*, (galerie *f* d')avancement *m*; **h. frame,** chevalement *m*; chevalet *m* d'extraction; *Metalw:* **h. seam,** soudure *f* de fond; (*j*) *Med:* **h. of a boil, of an abscess,** tête d'un furoncle, d'un clou; **to bring an abscess to a h.,** faire mûrir, faire aboutir, un abcès; (*of abscess, etc.*) **to come to a h., to gather to a h.,** mûrir, aboutir; **to bring a matter to a h.,** faire aboutir une affaire; **to bring matters to a h.,** forcer une décision, amener une crise; **things are coming to a h.,** une crise est proche; (*k*) *Ch: Brew:* (*on fermenting liquid*) chapeau *m*; **h. on beer,** mousse *f*, *F:* faux-col *m*, *pl.* faux-cols; **beer with no h.,** bière éventée; (*l*) = HEADING 3; (*m*) *Ten:* tête (d'une raquette); (*n*) *Mth:* (*of vector*) extrémité *f*. **4.** (*category*) **on this h.,** sur ce chapitre, sur ce point, sur cet article; **she reassured me on this h.,** elle me rassura sur ce point; **under separate heads,** articulairement, sous des rubriques différentes; **under the same h.,** dans la même catégorie; **the subject falls under the h. of rhetoric,** ce sujet ressortit à la rhétorique; *Jur:* **heads of a charge,** chefs *m* d'accusation. **5.** (*projecting part*) (*a*) nez *m*, avant *m*, cap *m* (de navire); poulaine *f* (de navire); *N.Arch:* **h. rail,** lisse *f*, herpe *f*, de poulaine; **h. of a jetty, a pier,** musoir *m*; *Nau:* (*of ship*) **to collide with a ship h. on,** aborder un navire par l'avant; **to be h. to the sea,** présenter l'avant à la lame; naviguer debout à la lame; **h. on to the wind,** cap au vent; **ship down by the h.,** navire sur le nez; **how is her h.?** où a-t-on le cap? où est le cap? *Nau: F:* (*latrines*) **the heads,** (*for officers*) les bouteilles *f*; (*for crew*) les poulaines, les corneaux *m*; (*b*) *Cy:* colonne *f* de direction (du cadre); (*c*) = HEADLAND 2. **6.** (*a*) (*front or chief place*) **at the h. of a column (of troops), of a procession,** à la tête d'une colonne, d'un cortège; **to march at the h. of the troops,** marcher en tête des troupes; **to be at the h. of the list,** venir en tête de liste; **to be at the h. of a party, of affairs,** être à la tête d'un parti, des affaires; mener la barque; **those at the h. of affairs,** nos dirigeants *m*; *Row:* (*at Oxford and Cambridge*) **h. of the river,** canot qui dans les *'bumping races,' q.v.* n'a pas été heurté par ses concurrents, et a monté jusqu'à la première place; *A:* **the h. and front of an undertaking,** l'initiateur *m* et le chef d'une entreprise; (*b*) (*pers.*) chef (de la famille, de l'Église, d'une entreprise); directeur, -trice (d'une école, d'une entreprise); **h. of state,** chef d'État; **h. of department, departmental h.,** chef de service; (*in store*) chef de rayon; *Sch:* **h. boy, girl,** élève choisi(e) parmi les grand(e)s pour maintenir la discipline, etc.; (*c*) (*in genealogy*) souche *f* (d'une famille); (*d*) *attrib.* **h. clerk,** premier commis; commis principal; chef de bureau; **h. agent,** agent principal; **h. gardener,** jardinier *m* en chef; **h. foreman,** chef d'atelier; **h. saleswoman,** première *f*; **h. post office,** bureau central (des postes); *Jur:* **h. lessee,** principal locataire. **7.** (*a*) (*unit*) *inv.* **six h. of cattle,** six têtes, pièces *f*, de bétail; **thirty h. of deer, of oxen,** trente cerfs *m*, trente bœufs *m*; **the park feeds about forty h. of deer,** la réserve nourrit une quarantaine de cerfs; **ten h. of game,** dix pièces de gibier; (*b*) **to pay so much per h., so much a h.,** payer tant par tête, par personne; (*c*) **h. money,** (i) *Hist:* capitation *f*; taille capitale; (ii) prix mis sur la tête de qn. **8.** nombre global; **forest with a large h. of deer,** réserve avec bon nombre de cerfs; **large h. of rabbits,** garenne bien peuplée. **9. h. of a coin,** face *f*; **to toss heads or tails,** jouer à pile ou face; *F:* **heads I win, tails you lose,** je gagne de toutes les façons; *F:* **I can't make h. or tail of this, I can make neither h. nor tail of this,** je n'y comprends rien; ma tête s'y perd; je m'y perds; **story one can't make h. or tail of,** histoire *f* sans queue ni tête. **10.** *Metall:* masselotte *f* (d'une pièce coulée). **11.** *Ph: Hyd.E: Mec.E:* charge *f*, pression *f* (d'un fluide, gaz, liquide, etc.); **h. of water,** (i) charge, pression, d'eau; (ii) chute *f* (d'eau); hauteur *f* de chute, hauteur d'eau, hauteur manométrique; **hydraulic h.,** pression en colonne d'eau, en colonne de liquide; **the waters are gathering h.,** le niveau, la pression, des eaux monte; **h. of oil on a filter,** huile *f* en charge sur un filtre; *Mch:* **h. of steam,** charge, pression, volant *m*, de vapeur; *Ph:* **static h.,** charge statique; **velocity h.,** charge dynamique; **total h.,** pression totale; **loss of h.,** perte *f* de pression; *Fig:* **discontent is gathering h.,** le mécontentement augmente, ne cesse de croître. **12.** = HEADWAY.

head², *v.*

I. *v.tr. & i.* **1.** *Arb:* **to h. (down) a tree, a branch,** étêter, écimer, un arbre, une branche. **2.** (*put a head on*) (*a*) entêter, brocher, mettre une tête à (une épingle, un clou, etc.); (*b*) **to h. (up) a barrel,** mettre un fond à, foncer, fermer, enjabler, un tonneau; (*c*) **to h. a chapter, a letter, with certain words,** mettre certains mots en tête d'un chapitre, d'une lettre; **these words h. the charge,** ces mots sont en tête de l'accusation; **the article is headed . . .,** l'article est intitulé . . .; **headed with these words,** portant cet intitulé; portant ces mots en tête. **3.** (*a*) conduire, mener (un cortège, un parti); être à la tête (d'un parti); venir en tête (d'un cortège); **to h. the column,** marcher en tête de la colonne; **the procession was headed by the band,** le cortège était précédé de la musique; **to h. the poll,** venir en tête du scrutin; **to h. the list,** (i) s'inscrire en tête de la liste (de souscriptions, etc.); (ii) être, venir, en tête de (la) liste; venir en première ligne; ouvrir la liste; **to h. one's class,** être à la tête de la classe; (*b*) (*of thg*) surmonter, couronner, coiffer; (*c*) *Cards:* **to h. the trick,** (i) jouer, (ii) avoir joué, la plus forte carte de la levée. **4.** (*oppose*) s'opposer à, affronter (un danger); *Nau:* **to h. the sea,** faire tête à la lame; prendre la mer debout. **5.** *Mch:* **to h. the engine,** mettre la machine en avant; *Nau:* **to h. the ship for Southampton,** mettre le cap sur Southampton; **to h. one's horse for home,** faire prendre à son cheval le chemin de la maison. **6.** contourner (un lac) par l'amont, (une rivière) par sa source. **7.** *Fb:* **to h. the ball,** jouer le ballon de la tête; renvoyer d'un coup de tête; **he headed a goal to equalize, he headed the equalizer,** d'un coup de tête il égalisa. **8.** *v.i.* (*a*) (*move forward*) **to h. for a place,** (i) *Nau:* piquer, gouverner, avoir le cap, mettre le cap, sur un endroit; (ii) (s')avancer, se diriger, vers un endroit; **we were heading for . . .,** nous étions en route pour . . .; (*of ship*) **to h. (to the) East,** faire de l'Est; **how does she h.?** où est le cap? **the country is heading for ruin,** le pays va tout droit vers la ruine, marche à la ruine; (*b*) *Min:* avancer. **9.** *v.i.* (*form a head*) (*of cabbage, etc.*) pommer; (*of grain*) épier; (*of abscess*) aboutir, mûrir. **10.** *v.i. U.S:* (*of stream*) prendre sa source (**at,** à).

II. (*compound verbs*) **1. head back,** *v.tr.* rabattre (le gibier); couper la retraite à (l'ennemi).

2. head off, *v.tr.* (*a*) barrer la route à (qn); détourner, intercepter (des fugitifs); rabattre (le gibier, l'ennemi); faire rebrousser chemin à (qn); couper la retraite à (l'ennemi); (*b*) **I headed him off from making a speech,** je l'ai détourné de l'idée de faire un discours; **to h. off an awkward question,** parer à une question embarrassante.

3. head up, *U.S:* (*a*) *v.i.* (*of cabbage*) pommer; (*of grain*) épier; (*b*) *v.tr.* **to h. up a drive (for a good cause),** être à la tête d'une campagne au profit d'une œuvre.

headache ['hedeik], *s.* (*a*) mal *m* de tête, *pl.* maux de tête; **sick h.,** migraine *f*; *Med:* encéphalalgie *f*; **to have a h.,** avoir mal à la tête; **to have a splitting h.,** avoir un mal de tête fou, tuant, affreux; *F:* avoir la tête en quatre; *F:* **you give me a h.,** vous me rompez le cerveau; vous me cassez la tête; (*b*) *F:* embêtement *m*, casse-tête *m*; **this job's an awful h.,** ça c'est un travail à vous rendre fou; **that's his h.,** ça c'est son affaire; *P:* c'est pas mes oignons.

headband ['hedbænd], *s.* **1.** (*a*) bandeau *m*; (*b*) *Tp:* **headbands of headphones,** bandes *f* élastiques, casque *m*, de serre-tête téléphonique. **2.** *Bookb:* tranchefile *f*, comète *f*.

headboard ['hedbɔ:d], *s.* **1.** *N.Arch:* pavois *m* de poulaine, herpe *f* de guibre. **2.** *Furn:* dosseret *m* (d'un lit).

head-down ['heddaun], *a.* *Av:* **h.-d. display, instrument,** affichage *m*, instrument *m*, à lecture tête basse.

head-dress ['heddres], *s.* **1.** *Hairdr:* coiffure *f*. **2.** *Cost:* coiffure; coiffe *f* (de paysanne).

headed ['hedid], *a.* **1.** muni (i) d'une tête, (ii) d'un en-tête; **h. cabbage,** chou pommé, cabus; **h. (note) paper,** papier *m* à en-tête. **2.** (*with noun or adj. prefixed*) (*a*) (*of pers., animal, etc.*) **double-h. monster,** monstre *m* à deux têtes; **black-h.,** (i) (personne) aux cheveux noirs, à la chevelure noire, (ii) (oiseau, etc.) à tête noire; (*b*) (*of thg*) **gold-h. cane,** canne *f* à pomme d'or.

header ['hedər], *s.* **1.** (*pers.*) (*a*) entêteur *m*, têtier *m* (d'épingles); (*b*) *Coop:* assembleur *m* de fonds. **2.** *Min:* (*a*) (*pers.*) coupeur *m* au front de taille; (*b*) (*machine*) coupeuse *f*, excavateur *m*. **3.** (*a*) **to take a h.,** (i) plonger (dans l'eau) la tête la première; faire le plongeon; piquer une tête; (ii) *F:* tomber (par terre) la tête la première; piquer une tête; faire panache; (*b*) *Fb:* coup *m* de tête; **to get in a h.,** réussir une crâne. **4.** *Const:* boutisse *f*; **h. work,** appareil *m* en boutisses. **5.** (*a*) *Civ.E: etc:* chapeau *m* (de pilotis, etc.); (*b*) *Mch:* collecteur *m* (de surchauffeur); **discharge h.,** collecteur de refoulement; **suction h.,** collecteur d'aspiration. **6.** *Metall:* jet *m* de coulée *f*; masselotte *f*.

headfast ['hedfɑ:st], *s.* *Nau:* amarre *f*; cordage *m*, chaîne *f*, d'amarrage.

headgear ['hedgi:ər], *s.* **1.** garniture *f* de tête; coiffure *f*; chapeau *m*; coiffe *f* (de paysanne). **2.** *Min:* (*a*) chevalement *m* (d'un puits de mine); (*b*) machine *f* à molettes.

headiness ['hedinis], *s.* **1.** (*a*) emportement *m*, impétuosité *f*; (*b*) *A:* entêtement *m*. **2.** qualité capiteuse (d'un vin).

heading ['hediŋ], *s.* **1.** (*a*) écimage *m* (d'un arbre, d'une branche); fonçage *m* (d'un baril); *Ind:* **h. machine,** machine *f* à étêter (des poissons); (*b*) façonnement *m* des têtes (de clous, etc.); **nail-h. tool,** clouière *f*, cloutière *f*. **2.** *Fb:* (jeu *m* de) tête *f*; **to practise h.,** s'exercer aux coups de tête. **3.** vocable *m*; tête, intitulé *m* (d'un chapitre, d'un article); rubrique *f* (d'un article); chapeau *m* (de passage cité, d'une requête, d'un rapport); en-tête *m*, *pl.* en-têtes (d'une page, d'une lettre, d'une facture); *Book-k:* poste *m*, rubrique; **under the same h. you may read . . .,** sous la même rubrique vous lirez . . .; **this subject comes under the h. of rhetoric,** ce sujet ressortit à la rhétorique. **4.** *Min:* (i) avancée *f*, avancement *m*; (ii) galerie *f* d'avancement; **diagonal h.,** thierne *f*. **5.** *Coop:* fond *m*, fonçailles *fpl* (de tonneau). **6.** *Const:* **h. (course),** assise *f* de boutisses. **7.** *Tex:* **h. of a web,** chef *m* d'une pièce de drap. **8.** *Av: Ball:* cap *m*; **collision h.,** cap de collision; **h. information,** information *f* de cap.

headlamp ['hedlæmp], *s.* = HEADLIGHT.

headland ['hedlənd], *s.* **1.** *Agr:* tournière *f*, capvirade *f*, fourrière *f*; chaintre *m or f*. **2.** *Geog:* cap *m*, promontoire *m*; pointe *f* de terre.

headledge ['hedledʒ], *s.* *N.Arch:* fronteau *m* d'écoutille; surbau transversal.

headless ['hedlis], *a.* **1.** (*a*) (corps, clou, etc.) sans tête; **we found his h. body,** nous avons trouvé son corps décapité; (*b*) *Nat.Hist:* (animal, etc.) acéphale. **2.** (parti *m*, assemblée *f*, etc.) sans chef.

headlight ['hedlait], *s.* phare *m*, projecteur *m* (d'automobile, de locomotive); fanal *m*, -aux, de tête; feu *m* d'avant (de locomotive); *Aut:* feu *m* de route; **to dip the headlights,** se mettre en code; **dipped h.,** feu de croisement; phare code.

headline¹ ['hedlain], *s.* **1.** *Nau:* amarre *f* d'avant. **2.** *Typ:* en-tête *m*, *pl.* en-têtes; ligne *f* de tête; *Journ:* titre, sous-titre *m* (de rubrique, etc.); titre en vedette; manchette *f*; **running h.,** titre courant; **large,** *F:* **banner, headlines,** gros titres; **to get into,** *F:* **hit, the headlines,** tenir la manchette (des journaux); **h. writer,** titreur *m*.

headline², *v.tr.* (*a*) mettre en vedette, en première page; (*b*) faire une grande campagne publicitaire pour (qch.).

headlock ['hedlɔk], *s.* *Wr:* collier *m* de force; cravate *f*.

headlong ['hedlɔŋ]. **1.** *adv.* **to fall h.,** tomber la tête la première; **to fall h. into a trap,** donner tête baissée dans un piège; **to rush h. into the fight,** se jeter tête baissée dans la mêlée; **to rush h. to one's ruin,** courir à bride abattue, à corps perdu, à sa ruine; **to plunge h. into a description of . . .,** se lancer à fond dans une description de . . .. **2.** *a.* (*a*) **h. fall,** chute *f* la tête la première; **to take a h. dive,** piquer une tête; (*b*) (*of pers., action*) précipité, irréfléchi, impétueux; **h. flight,** sauve-qui-peut *m inv*; panique *f*.

headman, *pl.* **-men** ['hedmən], *s.m.* chef (d'une tribu, etc.).

headmaster [hed'mɑ:stər], *s.m.* directeur (d'une école); principal (d'un collège); proviseur (d'un lycée).

headmastership [hed'mɑ:stəʃip], *s.* *Sch:* directorat *m*; direction *f*; (*in Fr.*) provisorat *m*, principalat *m*.

headmistress [hed'mistris], *s.f.* directrice (d'une école).

headmistress-ship [hed'mistrisʃip], *s.* *Sch:* directorat *m*, direction *f*.

headmost ['hedmoust], *a.* (navire, etc.) de tête, au premier rang, le plus en avant.

head-on ['hed'ɔn], *a. & adv.* de front; **h.-on collision,** collision frontale, de plein fouet; **they met h.-on,** ils se sont abordés de front.

headphone ['hedfoun], *s.* *Tp: W.Tel:* écouteur *m*; **headphones,** casque *m* (téléphonique, d'écoute).

headpiece ['hedpi:s], *s.* **1.** (*helmet*) casque *m*; *A:* armure *f* de tête; armet *m*. **2.** *A:* (*intellect*) tête *f*. **3.** *Typ:* vignette *f*, fleuron *m* de tête; tête *f* de page; en-tête *m*, *pl.* en-têtes.

headquarter [hed'kwɔ:tər], *v.i.* *U.S:* établir son état-major (à); siéger (à).

headquarters [hed'kwɔ:təz], *s.pl.* (*often with sg. const.*) **1.** *Mil:* (*a*) (*lower units*) poste *m* de commandement; **battalion, company, platoon, h.,** poste de commandement de bataillon, de compagnie, de section; **dug-in h.,** poste de commandement enterré; (*b*) (*higher units*) quartier général; **army, corps, division, h.,** quartier général d'armée, de corps d'armée, de division; **general**

h., grand quartier général; **forward h., tactical h., battle h.**, quartier général avancé, tactique; **rear h.**, quartier général arrière; **main h.**, quartier général principal; **h. commandant**, commandant *m* de quartier général; (*c*) état-major *m, pl.* états-majors; organe *m*, élément *m*, de commandement; **h. staff**, état-major du commandant, du général, en chef; **battalion h.**, section *f* de commandement du bataillon; **company h., platoon h.**, groupe *m* de commandement de la compagnie, de la section; **h. company, h. squadron, h. battery**, compagnie *f*, escadron *m*, batterie *f*, de commandement et des services; *A:* **h. wing**, compagnie hors rang. **2.** *Adm: Com: etc:* centre *m*, siège social, résidence (administrative), bureau principal (d'une administration, d'une banque, etc.); **administration centrale** (de l'O.N.U., etc.); **to have its h. at . . .**, siéger, avoir son siège, à . . ..

headrest ['hedrest], *s.* appui-tête *m, pl.* appuis-tête; support *m* de tête; *Aut:* repose-tête *m inv*; **h. cover**, têtière *f*.

headroom ['hedru:m], *s.* **1.** encombrement vertical; tirant *m* d'air; échappée *f* (d'un arc). **2.** *Mec.E: Mch: etc:* hauteur *f* libre (pour le soulèvement des pistons; etc.).

headrope ['hedroup], *s.* **1.** *Harn:* longe *f*, licou *m*, licol *m*, attache *f* (de cheval). **2.** *Nau:* (*a*) envergure *f*; (*b*) amarre *f* d'avant; amarre de bout.

headsail ['hedseil], *s. Nau:* foc *m*.

headscarf ['hedskɑ:f], *s.* foulard *m* de tête, fanchon *f*.

headset ['hedset], *s.* casque *m* (radio, téléphonique).

headship ['hedʃip], *s.* direction *f* (d'un collège, etc.); première place (dans une administration, une classe); primauté *f* (du Saint-Siège).

headsman, *pl.* **-men** ['hedzmən], *s.m.* **1.** *A:* bourreau; *A:* exécuteur des hautes œuvres. **2.** (*a*) *Ind: etc: A:* chef d'équipe; (*b*) *Nau:* patron (de baleinière).

head-splitting ['hedsplitiŋ], *a.* (bruit *m*) qui casse la tête; **h. job**, casse-tête *m inv*.

headspring ['hedspriŋ], *s. Lit:* source *f* (d'une rivière, etc.).

headstall ['hedstɔ:l], *s. Harn:* têtière *f*, licou *m*, licol *m*.

headstock ['hedstɔk], *s.* **1.** *Mec.E:* (*a*) poupée *f* (d'un tour, d'une machine-outil); **fast h.**, poupée fixe; **loose h.**, contre-pointe *f, pl.* contre-pointes; (*b*) (chariot *m*) porte-broche *m, pl.*, porte-broches. **2.** *Min:* chevalement *m*, chevalet *m* d'extraction; châssis *m* à molettes (d'un puits de mine). **3.** (*a*) *Tex:* traverse *f*, chapeau *m* (d'un métier); (*b*) *Rail:* traverse (de châssis de wagon).

headstone ['hedstoun], *s.* **1.** pierre *f* tumulaire; pierre tombale. **2.** *Arch: Const:* (*a*) clef *f* de voûte; (*b*) pierre angulaire.

headstream ['hedstri:m], *s.* ruisseau *m*, torren *m* d'amont (à origine d'une rivière).

headstrong ['hedstrɔŋ], *a.* volontaire, têtu, entêté, obstiné.

headstrongness ['hedstrɔŋnis], *s.* entêtement irréfléchi; obstination *f*.

head-up ['hedʌp], *a. Av:* **h.-u. display, instrument**, affichage *m*, instrument *m*, à lecture tête haute.

headwater ['hedwɔ:tər], (*a*) *s.pl.* **the headwaters of a stream**, la partie d'un cours d'eau le plus près de la source; (*b*) *attrib.* **h. erosion**, érosion régressive.

headway ['hedwei], *s.* **1.** progrès *m*; *Nau:* erre *f*; marche *f* avant; sillage *m*; **to make h.**, avancer; faire des progrès; (*of ship*) faire de la route; siller; avancer; aller de l'avant; **the ship is making good h.**, le navire saille de l'avant; **these opinions had made h.**, ces opinions avaient fait du chemin; **to make no h.**, ne pas avancer; **the enquiry is making no h.**, l'enquête piétine; **to make h. against . . .**, faire tête à . . .; **to gather, fetch, h.** prendre de l'erre; **to get under h.**, se mettre en route. **2.** *Civ.E:* hauteur *f* libre, échappée *f* (d'une voûte). **3.** intervalle *m* (entre autobus, etc.); **six minutes' h.**, intervalle de six minutes.

headwear ['hedwɛər], *s.* = HEADGEAR 1.

headwind ['hedwind], *s. Nau:* vent *m* contraire; vent debout.

headword ['hedwə:d], *s.* (mot *m*) en-tête *m, pl.* en-têtes; premier mot (d'un chapitre, d'un document); article *m*, mot *m* (qui figure dans un dictionnaire).

headwork ['hedwə:k], *s.* **1.** travail *m* de tête; travail intellectuel. **2.** *Fb:* jeu *m* de tête. **3.** *pl. Hyd.E:* **headworks**, travaux *m* d'art. **4.** plate-forme *f*; radeau *m* (d'où l'on manœuvre les bois flottés).

heady ['hedi], *a.* **1.** (*of pers., action*) impétueux, emporté, violent. **2.** (*a*) (parfum, etc.) capiteux, entêtant, qui monte au cerveau; (parfum) troublant; **h. wine**, vin capiteux; (*b*) (*of height, etc.*) vertigineux.

heal [hi:l]. **1.** *v.tr.* guérir (**s.o. of a disease, of a wound**, qn d'une maladie, d'une blessure); guérir, cicatriser (une blessure); **time heals all sorrows**, le temps cicatrise toutes les douleurs; **to h. the breach (between two people)**, amener une réconciliation (entre deux personnes), raccommoder deux personnes. **2.** *v.i.* (*of wounds*) **to h. (up)**, (se) guérir, se cicatriser, se refermer, se consolider, se recoller; **to h. up again**, reprendre; **the wound has not healed yet**, la blessure n'est pas encore fermée; **to h. over**, se recouvrir.

heal-all ['hi:lɔ:l], *s.* **1.** panacée *f*. **2.** *Bot:* valériane *f*.

heald [hi:ld], *s. Tex:* remisse *m*, bâton *m* d'encroix (du métier); **h. eye**, maillon *m*.

healder ['hi:ldər], *s. Tex:* (*pers.*) garnisseuse *f* de maillons.

healding ['hi:ldiŋ], *s. Tex:* garnissage *m* des maillons (du harnais).

healer ['hi:lər], *s.* guérisseur, -euse; (*of nature, etc.*) médicateur, -trice; **time, the great h.**, le temps, médecin *m* de tous les maux.

healing[1] ['hi:liŋ], *a.* **1.** (remède, etc.) curatif, sanatoire; (onguent) cicatrisant; (plante, remède) vulnéraire; (conseil, discours, etc.) apaisant, calmant, salutaire, conciliateur. **2. h. sore**, plaie *f* qui se cicatrise, qui est en train de se refermer.

healing[2], *s.* **1.** guérison *f*; *Hist:* guérison des écrouelles par attouchement. **2.** cicatrisation *f*, consolidation *f* (d'une plaie).

health [helθ], *s.* santé *f*; (*a*) **to restore s.o. to h.**, rendre la santé à qn; guérir qn; **to regain one's h.**, recouvrer la santé; se guérir; se remonter; **sunshine and fresh air are good for the h.**, rien de plus salubre, de plus sanitaire, que le soleil et le grand air; **he looks the picture of h.**, son visage respire la santé; il respire la santé par tous les pores; *Prov:* **h. before wealth**, santé passe richesse; (*b*) **good h.**, bonne santé; **ill h., poor h.**, mauvaise santé; manque *m* de santé; **chronic ill h.**, invalidité *f*; **for reasons of (ill) h.**, pour raison de santé; **to be in good h.**, être en bonne santé, bien portant; se porter bien; **to be in the best of h., in radiant h.**, se porter à merveille, comme un charme; être en parfaite santé; avoir une santé florissante; **to be in bad, poor, h.**, se porter mal, être mal portant; **public h.**, santé publique; hygiène publique; **public h. officer, inspector**, officier *m*, inspecteur *m*, de la santé publique; **medical officer of h.** = médecin *m* de la santé publique; **the Department of H. and Social Security** = le Ministère de la Santé publique; **the H. Service**, le Service de Santé de la Sécurité sociale; **h. insurance**, assurance *f* maladie; **h. certificate**, certificat médical; *F:* **businessmen don't work (just) for the good of their h.**, les hommes d'affaires ne travaillent pas pour leur bon plaisir; (*c*) **to drink to s.o.'s h.**, boire à la santé de qn; **(your very) good h.!** (à votre) santé!

healthful ['helθful], *a.* (air) salubre; (exercice *m*, effet *m*) salutaire.

health-giving [helθgiviŋ], *a.* assainissant; (air, etc.) fortifiant, vivifiant.

healthily ['helθili], *adv.* **1.** sainement. **2.** salubrement, salutairement.

healthiness ['helθinis], *s.* salubrité *f* (d'un endroit, d'un climat).

healthy ['helθi], *a.* **1.** (*a*) (*of pers.*) sain; en bonne santé; robuste, bien portant; **to have a h. look, a h. colour**, avoir un air de santé; avoir l'air bien portant, avoir un teint florissant; **h. skin**, peau saine; (*b*) (*of climate, food, air, etc.*) salubre; **to make (sth.) healthier**, assainir (qch.); **to put the finances of a country on a h. footing**, assainir les finances d'un pays; **it is not a h. place for arthritic people**, l'endroit ne vaut rien aux arthritiques. **2. h. appetite**, appétit *m* d'homme bien portant; appétit robuste; **he showed a h. interest in sports**, il manifestait pour les sports un intérêt tout viril; **h. criticism**, critique vivifiante; **it is a h. sign that . . .**, il est encourageant que + *sub*.

heap[1] [hi:p], *s.* (*a*) tas *m*, monceau *m*, amas *m*, amoncellement *m* (de bois, de pierres, de boue); amassage *m* (de châtaignes, etc.); **sand h.**, tas de sable; moie *f*; **h. of junk**, tas de ferraille; *hence U.S: P:* **h.**, (i) vieille auto de rebut; (ii) bagnole *f*, tacot *m*; *P:* **you h.!** espèce de nouille, d'andouille! **in a h.**, en tas; (*of pers.*) **to fall in a h.**, s'affaisser (sur soi-même); tomber comme une masse (inerte); *F:* **to strike, knock, s.o. all of a h.**, estomaquer, épater, qn; couper les jambes à qn; **to be struck all of a h.**, en rester abasourdi, stupéfait, tout ébaubi, tout pantois, baba; en rester assis tout pantois; (en) être comme deux ronds de flan; **I was struck all of a h.**, les bras m'en sont tombés, ça m'a coupé bras et jambes; (*b*) *F:* (*large number*) **she had heaps of children**, elle avait une ribambelle d'enfants; **there were heaps (and heaps) of them**, il y en avait des mille et des cents; **I've got heaps of things to do**, j'ai un tas de choses à faire; **there are heaps of it**, il y en a des tas, des monceaux; **heaps of times**, bien des fois; très souvent; **I have told you so heaps of times**, je vous l'ai dit vingt fois, mille fois; **you've got heaps of time**, vous avez largement le temps; **she felt heaps, a h., better already**, déjà elle se sentait beaucoup mieux, infiniment mieux, cent fois mieux.

heap[2], *v.tr.* **1.** (*a*) **to h. (up)**, entasser, amonceler, mettre en tas, en pile (des pierres, du bois); amasser (des richesses); **to h. up a mound**, faire un tas, un monceau; **to h. sth. up again**, rentasser qch.; (*b*) **to h. praises, insults, on s.o.**, combler qn d'éloges; accabler, charger, abreuver, agonir, qn d'injures. **2. to h. sth., s.o., with sth.**, combler qch., qn, de qch.; **she heaped my plate with cherries**, elle a rempli mon assiette de cerises.

heaped ['hi:pt], *a.* **1.** entassé, amoncelé. **2. h.** (*U.S: occ.* **heaping) measure**, mesure *f* comble; **h. spoonful**, cuillère bien pleine, arrondie.

hear [hiər], *v.tr.* (**heard** [hə:d]; **heard**) **1.** entendre; **I h. you**, je vous entends; **I h. the bells**, j'entends les cloches; **I heard a ring**, j'ai entendu sonner; **a groan was heard**, un gémissement se fit entendre; **there was nothing to be heard but the dry rustle of the leaves**, on ne percevait, ne distinguait, rien ne se distinguait, que le bruissement sec des feuilles; **let me h. the story**, racontez-moi l'histoire; **let's h. it**, dites (donc); *B:* **he that hath ears to h., let him h.**, qui a des oreilles pour ouïr, qu'il entende; **I heard my name (mentioned)**, j'ai entendu dire mon nom; **to h. s.o. speak**, entendre parler qn; **I heard, could h., him laugh(ing)**, je l'ai entendu rire; je l'entendais rire; **I could hardly make myself heard**, je pouvais à peine me faire entendre; **one cannot h. oneself speak here**, on ne s'entend pas ici; **he likes to h. himself talk**, il aime à s'entendre parler; il s'écoute volontiers parler; c'est un grand discoureur; **I heard a clock striking**, j'ai entendu sonner une horloge; j'ai entendu une horloge qui sonnait l'heure; **I heard the dog bark**, j'ai entendu le chien pousser un aboiement; j'ai entendu aboyer le chien; **to h. sth. said, told, to s.o.**, entendre dire qch. à qn; **to h. s.o. say sth.**, entendre dire qch. à qn, par qn; **I heard him say he would come**, je lui ai entendu dire qu'il viendrait; **I have heard it said, I have heard tell, that . . .**, j'ai entendu dire que . . .; **I have heard of the matter**, j'ai entendu parler de cela; **I remember hearing that . . .**, je me rappelle avoir entendu dire que . . .; **I have heard that song sung already**, j'ai déjà entendu chanter cette chanson; **I have heard her sing that song**, je l'ai entendue chanter cette chanson; je lui ai entendu chanter cette chanson; **I have heard her described as a beauty**, je l'ai entendu citer comme une beauté; *F:* **I've heard that one before!** connu! *F:* **you heard!** ne faites pas le sourd! *F:* **I heard that!** je ne suis pas dur d'oreille, moi! **2.** (*listen to*) (*a*) écouter; **they refused to h. me**, on n'a pas voulu m'entendre, m'écouter; **h. me out**, écoutez-moi, entendez-moi, jusqu'au bout; **to h. a deputation**, recevoir (et entendre) une députation; (*at meeting*) **h.! h.!** très bien! très bien! **your petition will be heard**, votre requête sera entendue; *Ecc:* **to h. mass**, assister à la messe; *Jur:* **to h. a case**, (i) connaître d'un différend; (ii) entendre une cause; **to h. the witnesses**, entendre les témoins; **the case will be heard in January**, l'affaire passera, se plaidera, en janvier; (*b*) *Sch: A:* **to h. a lesson**, écouter une leçon; **to h. a child his lesson**, faire réciter, faire répéter, sa leçon à un enfant; (*c*) **to h. a prayer**, exaucer, écouter, une prière; **h. my prayer!** (i) ayez égard à ma supplique! (ii) (Seigneur,) exaucez ma prière! **3.** (*learn*) **to h. a piece of news**, apprendre une nouvelle; **to h. the truth**, apprendre, savoir, la vérité; **I have heard that . . .**, j'ai entendu dire, j'ai appris, on m'a appris, que . . .; **have you heard the news?** connaissez-vous la nouvelle? **4.** (*a*) **to h. from s.o.**, recevoir des nouvelles, une lettre, de qn; **you will h. from me**, je vous écrirai; **we shall h. from him in good time**, on aura de ses nouvelles en temps utile; **let me h. from you**, écrivez-moi un mot; **let me h. how you get on**, donnez-moi de vos nouvelles; **to h. regularly from one another**, être en relations suivies; (*as a threat*) **you will h. from me!** vous aurez de mes nouvelles! *Corr:* **hoping to h., looking forward to hearing, from you soon**, en espérant recevoir bientôt de vos nouvelles; (*b*) **to h. of, about, s.o., sth.**, avoir des nouvelles de qn, entendre parler de qn, de qch.; **he has not been heard of since**, depuis on n'en a plus entendu parler; on n'eut plus jamais de ses nouvelles; **they were not heard of for a long time**, on fut longtemps sans entendre parler d'eux; **the explorers were never heard of again**, on n'a plus retrouvé trace des explorateurs; **this is the first I have heard of it**, c'est la première fois que j'en entends parler; en voici la première nouvelle; **having heard of my misfortune he offered to help me**, ayant entendu parler de mon malheur il m'a offert son aide; **I only heard of it yesterday**, je n'en ai eu connaissance qu'hier; **nobody let me h. of it,** personne ne m'en a donné connaissance; **we first h. of this disease in the sixth century,** la première mention de cette maladie date du sixième siècle; **I have heard a great deal about . . .,** on m'a beaucoup parlé de . . .; **I never heard of such a thing!** a-t-on jamais entendu une chose pareille! je n'ai jamais vu une chose pareille! c'est inouï! c'est inadmissible! **who ever heard of going to bed at ten!** il est inouï de se coucher à dix heures; **I h. of nothing else,** j'en ai les oreilles rebattues; **father won't h. of it,** mon père ne veut pas en entendre parler, n'en veut rien savoir, s'y oppose absolument; *F:* **you'll h. of it!** il vous en cuira!

hearer ['hiərər], *s.* auditeur, -trice; *pl.* **hearers,** auditoire *m.*

hearing ['hiəriŋ], *s.* **1.** (*a*) audition *f* (d'un son); **to judge an opera at the first h.,** juger d'un opéra à la première audition; (*b*) audition, audience *f*; **trial h. of a singer,** audition d'un chanteur; **this witness was immediately given a h.,** ce témoin fut entendu aussitôt; **give me a h.!** veuillez m'entendre! **he was refused a h.,** on refusa de l'entendre; **to gain a h.,** (i) se faire écouter; (ii) obtenir une audience; **to condemn s.o. without a h.,** condamner qn sans connaissance de cause, sans entendre sa défense; **to dismiss s.o. without a h.,** congédier qn sans l'entendre; (*c*) *Jur:* **h. of witnesses,** audition des témoins; témoignages *mpl*; **h. of the case,** (i) l'audience; (ii) l'audition de la cause par le juge (sans jury); **to put a case down for h.,** audiencer une cause; **the case comes up for hearing tomorrow,** la cause sera entendue demain; **the defence is given a full h.,** les débats sont contradictoires. **2.** ouïe *f*; **the organ of h.,** l'organe *m* de l'ouïe; **to be quick of h., to have a keen sense of h.,** avoir l'oreille, l'ouïe, fine; avoir l'oreille sensible; *Med:* **h. aid,** appareil *m* de correction auditive, appareil contre la surdité; *Psy* **coloured h.,** audition colorée; **within h.,** à portée d'oreille, de la voix; **if I had been within h.,** si j'avais été assez près pour entendre; **out of h.,** hors de portée de la voix; **it was said in my h.,** on l'a dit devant moi, en ma présence; **it came to my h.,** cela m'est parvenu aux oreilles. **3. that's good h.!** voilà une bonne nouvelle! je suis bien aise d'apprendre ça!

hearken ['hɑːk(ə)n], *v.i. A: & Lit:* écouter; **to h. to s.o., to sth.,** écouter qn, qch.; prêter l'oreille à qn, à qch.

hearsay ['hiəsei], *s.* ouï-dire *m inv*; **I know it, have it, only from h.,** je ne le sais que par ouï-dire; **to take sth. on h.,** accepter qch. d'ouï-dire; *Jur:* **h. evidence,** (i) déposition *f* sur la foi d'autrui; (ii) (preuve *f* par) commune renommée; (iii) simples ouï dire (non admissibles).

hearse [həːs], *s.* **1.** *Ecc:* (*a*) **(taper) h.,** if *m*, herse *f* (d'église); (*b*) *A:* chapelle ardente (de catafalque); (*c*) *A:* catafalque *m.* **2.** corbillard *m*, char *m* funèbre; **motor h.,** corbillard automobile; **h. cloth,** drap *m* mortuaire; *A.* **the pauper's h.,** le char des pauvres.

hearst [həːst], *s. Ven:* biche *f* de deux ou trois ans.

heart[1] [hɑːt], *s.* **1.** (*a*) cœur *m*; *Med:* **h. disease,** maladie *f* de cœur; **to have h. trouble, a weak h.,** être cardiaque; **h. attack,** crise *f* cardiaque; **h. failure,** asystolie *f*, insuffisance *f* mécanique du cœur; **h. block,** syndrome *m* d'Adams-Stokes; pouls lent permanent; **fatty h.,** cœur gras, adipeux; **h. transplant,** greffe *f* de, du, cœur; **open-h. surgery,** opération *f* à cœur ouvert; **h.-lung machine,** cœur-poumon artificiel; *F:* **hole in the h.,** communication *f* (i) inter-ventriculaire, (ii) inter-auriculaire; *F:* trou *m* dans le cœur; **killed by a bullet in the h.,** tué d'une balle au cœur; *F:* **to have one's h. in one's mouth,** avoir un serrement de cœur; être angoissé; *F:* **it made my h. leap into my mouth, my h. leapt into my mouth,** mon sang n'a fait qu'un tour; j'ai eu un serrement de cœur; cela m'a bouleversé; *F:* **to have one's h. in one's boots,** avoir une peur bleue, terrible, un trac formidable; **to press, clasp, s.o. to one's h.,** serrer, presser, qn sur son cœur; étreindre qn; **to cry, sob, one's h. out,** pleurer à chaudes larmes, à gros sanglots; **to break s.o.'s h.,** briser le cœur à qn; **he died of a broken h.,** il est mort de chagrin, le cœur brisé; **to break one's h. over sth.,** se ronger le cœur au sujet de qch.; **it broke his h. to leave her,** il lui a fendu le cœur de la quitter; **it was enough to break your h.,** c'était à fendre le cœur, l'âme; **to cry fit to break one's h.,** pleurer à gros sanglots; (*b*) *R.C.Ch:* **the Sacred H.,** le Sacré-Cœur; **Convent of the Sacred H.,** couvent *m* du Sacré-Cœur; **the (Immaculate) H. of Mary,** le Cœur (Immaculé) de Marie. **2.** (*a*) **h. of gold,** cœur d'or; **h. of steel,** cœur de fer; cœur impénétrable; **h. of stone,** cœur de pierre, de granit; *Prov:* **kind hearts are more than coronets,** un cœur chaud vaut mieux que des lettres de noblesse; **have a h.!** ayez un peu de cœur! **he is a man of no h., he has no h.,** c'est un homme sans cœur, sans conscience; **his h. is in the right place,** il a le cœur bien placé; il est plein de cœur; son cœur ne se trompe pas; **to wear one's h. on one's sleeve,** manquer de réserve; ne pas être réservé; se montrer trop expansif; ne savoir rien garder pour soi; agir et parler à cœur ouvert; (*of thg*) **to do one's h. good, to rejoice one's h.,** réjouir, réchauffer, le cœur; **set your h. at rest,** ne vous inquiétez pas; tranquillisez-vous; soyez tranquille; **his h. was full, heavy,** il avait le cœur gros; **with a heavy h.,** le cœur serré, navré; **to do sth. with a light h., with a heavy h.,** faire qch. le cœur léger, le cœur joyeux, d'un cœur léger, avec insouciance; faire qch. à contre cœur; **bless my, your, h.!** mon Dieu! par exemple! (*term of endearment*) **dear h.!** m'amour! mon (cher, petit) cœur! mon chéri! ma chérie! (*b*) (*innermost being, core*) **sight that goes to one's h., cuts one to the h., makes one's h. ache,** spectacle *m* qui vous fend, perce, crève, le cœur, qui vous blesse au cœur; spectacle navrant, qui vous navre; **this news cut him to the h.,** cette nouvelle lui fut un coup de poignard; **it cuts me to the h. to think . . .,** cela me fend le cœur, j'ai le cœur navré, de penser . . .; **they were cut to the h.,** ils étaient navrés; **in my h. of hearts,** au plus profond de mon cœur; dans le tréfonds de mon cœur; dans le for de ma conscience; en mon for intérieur, en mon âme et conscience; **in his h. (of hearts) he did not believe the explanation,** au fond de son cœur il ne croyait pas à l'explication; **h. to h. talk,** conversation *f* intime; **to have a h. to h. talk with s.o.,** parler avec qn à cœur ouvert; **I congratulate you from the bottom of my h.,** je vous félicite de tout mon cœur; **he's not bad at h.,** au fond ce n'est pas un mauvais garçon; **at h. he felt very glad,** il éprouvait une grande joie intérieure; **to be sad, sick, at h.,** avoir le cœur gros, navré, serré; être abattu; **with open h.,** à cœur ouvert; **h. searchings,** inquiétudes *f* de l'âme; **to learn sth. by h.,** apprendre qch. par cœur; **I know it by h.,** je le sais par cœur; (*c*) **to love s.o. with all one's h.,** aimer qn de tout son cœur; **to give, lose, one's h. to s.o.,** donner son cœur à qn; s'éprendre de qn; **to win s.o.'s h.,** gagner le cœur de qn; faire la conquête de qn; **he knows how to find his way into people's hearts,** il sait se rendre cher à tous, il sait éveiller la sympathie; **cause nearest one's h.,** cause *f* qu'on a le plus à cœur, qui vous tient le plus au cœur; **to have s.o.'s welfare at h.,** avoir à cœur le bonheur de qn; **to take sth. to h.,** prendre qch. à cœur; **don't take it so much to h.,** ne vous affligez pas ainsi, ne le prenez pas au tragique; **he has taken it to h.,** il l'a sur le cœur; **take that to h.,** faites-en votre profit; (*d*) (*desire*) **to have set one's h. on sth., on doing sth.,** avoir qch. à cœur; avoir, prendre, à cœur de faire qch.; vouloir absolument avoir qch.; être déterminé à posséder qch., à faire qch.; **the thing he has set his h. on,** la chose qui lui tient au cœur; l'objet de ses désirs; **I have set my h. on it,** j'y tiens; **he's a man after my own h.,** c'est mon homme; c'est un homme selon mon cœur, un homme comme je les aime; il m'est très sympathique; **it goes against my h. to . . .,** c'est à contre cœur que je . . .; **to one's heart's content,** à cœur joie, à souhait; **to indulge oneself to one's heart's content,** s'en donner à cœur joie; **to eat, drink, to one's heart's content,** manger, boire, tout son soûl, tout son content; **everything has succeeded to our heart's content,** tout a réussi au gré de nos désirs; (*e*) (*enthusiasm, interest*) **to put (all) one's h. into sth.,** y aller de tout son cœur; mettre son zèle à qch.; mettre toute son énergie à faire qch.; **to have one's h. in one's work,** avoir le cœur à l'ouvrage; **his, my, h. isn't in it,** le cœur n'y est pas; **with all my h.,** du meilleur de mon cœur, de tout mon cœur; **to desire sth. with all one's h.,** désirer qch. de toute son âme; **with h. and soul,** de cœur et d'âme, de tout cœur; **to put one's h. and soul, to throw oneself h. and soul, into sth.,** se jeter, entrer, de tout son cœur dans une affaire; se donner corps et âme à une affaire; (*f*) (*courage*) **to put new h. into s.o.; to put s.o. in good h.,** donner du courage, du cœur, à qn; réchauffer le cœur à qn; relever le cœur de qn; ragaillardir qn; réconforter le cœur à qn; remettre du cœur au ventre de qn; encourager qn; **this speech put fresh h. into the troops,** ce discours ranima les troupes; **to pluck up, take, h.,** *A:* **h. of grace,** (re)prendre courage; prendre confiance; **to take h. again,** renaître à l'espérance; **to be of good h.,** avoir bon courage; **they were in better h.,** ils avaient repris courage; **be of good h.! keep a good h.!** ne vous laissez pas abattre! ne perdez pas courage! du courage! ayez confiance! **to take the h. out of s.o.,** décourager, abattre, rebuter, qn; **to lose h.,** perdre courage; se laisser aller au découragement; se décourager, se rebuter; **my h. sank (into my boots),** *Lit:* **died within me, at the news,** à cette nouvelle mon courage s'évanouit; **not to find it in one's h., not to have the h., to do sth.,** ne pas avoir le cœur, le courage, de faire qch.; ne pouvoir se décider à faire qch.; **to be in (good, strong) h.,** (i) (*of pers.*) être de bonne humeur; être gaillard, en train; (ii) *Agr:* (*of soil*) être bien entretenu, productif, d'un bon rapport; **out of h.,** (i) (*of pers.*) abattu, découragé; (ii) *Agr:* (*of land*) amaigri, effrité, épuisé. **3.** cœur (d'un chou); cœur, vif *m* (d'un arbre); *Arb:* **h. shake,** fente *f* de cœur; gélivure *f* (dans le bois); cadran(n)ure *f*; **h. of oak,** homme courageux; cœur de chêne; *A:* **the (British) Hearts of Oak,** (i) les vaisseaux, (ii) les marins, de la Marine anglaise; **h. of a cable,** âme *f*, mèche *f*, d'un câble; **the h. of the matter,** le vif de l'affaire; **to come to the h. of the matter,** entrer dans le vif de la question; **the h. of a forest,** le fond, le fort, d'une forêt; **to make for the h. of the woods,** s'enfoncer dans les taillis; **in the h. of . . .,** au cœur (d'une ville), au (beau) milieu (d'une forêt), au (fin) fond (d'un désert); au cœur (d'un pays); **in the h. of winter,** en plein hiver; au cœur de l'hiver; **in the h. of summer,** au fort de l'été; *Hist:* **the H. of Midlothian,** la prison d'Édimbourg. **4.** *Cards:* **heart(s),** cœur; **to play a h., hearts,** jouer (du) cœur; **have you any hearts?** avez-vous du cœur? **king, queen, of hearts,** roi, dame, de cœur. **5.** *Her:* **h. (point),** cœur, abîme *m* (de l'écu). **6.** (*a*) *Mec.E:* came *f*, excentrique *m*, en cœur; **h.-shaped driver, carrier,** cœur de tour; (*b*) *Nau:* moque *f* (pour cordage). **7.** (*a*) *Bot:* **h. cherry,** guigne *f*; cerise *f* en cœur; **h. clover,** médicago maculé; (*b*) *Echin:* **h. urchin,** spatangue *m.*

heart[2]. **1.** *v.i.* (*of cabbage, lettuce*) **to h. (up),** pommer. **2.** *v.tr. Const:* **to h. (in),** remplir (un espace entre deux parements, etc.).

heartache ['hɑːteik], *s.* chagrin *m*, peine *f* de cœur, douleur *f*; **to have h.,** avoir le cœur endolori.

heartbeat ['hɑːtbiːt], *s.* battement *m*, pulsation *f*, du cœur.

heartbreak ['hɑːtbreik], *s.* déchirement *m* de cœur; chagrin poignant.

heartbreaker ['hɑːtbreikər], *s.* bourreau *m* des cœurs.

heartbreaking ['hɑːtbreikiŋ], *a.* navrant, accablant, déchirant; **h. disappointment,** crève cœur *m inv*; **it was h.,** c'était à fendre l'âme; **it's h. work,** c'est un travail tout ce qu'il y a de plus rebutant.

heartbroken ['hɑːtbrouk(ə)n], *a.* **to be h.,** avoir le cœur brisé; **I am h. that he has failed,** je suis navré qu'il ait échoué.

heartburn ['hɑːtbəːn], *s.* **1.** *Med:* aigreurs *fpl* (d'estomac); ardeur(s) *fpl*, brûlures *fpl*, d'estomac; pyrosis *m*; cardialgie *f*; *F: A:* fer-chaud *m.* **2.** = HEARTBURNING.

heartburning ['hɑːtbəːniŋ], *s.* irritation mêlée de dépit; jalousie *f*; **to cause much h.,** exciter bien des rancunes.

hearten ['hɑːtn]. **1.** *v.tr.* **to h. s.o. (on),** encourager qn; **to h. s.o. (up),** ranimer, relever, le courage de qn; rendre le courage à qn; mettre du baume au cœur de qn; ragaillardir qn; donner du cœur à qn; **this speech heartened the troops,** ce discours ranima le courage des troupes, ranima les troupes. **2.** *v.i.* **to h. (up),** reprendre courage.

heartener ['hɑːtnər], *s.* personne *f*, nouvelle *f*, qui encourage, qui rend le courage (à qn); rameneur, -euse, de courage.

heartening ['hɑːtniŋ], *a.* (conseil, mot) encourageant, qui rend le courage, qui ragaillardit; **h. news,** nouvelles rameneuses d'espoir.

heartfelt ['hɑːtfelt], *a.* (émotion *f*, vœu *m*) sincère; qui vient, part, du cœur; **h. words,** paroles bien senties; **to make a h. appeal,** mettre tout son cœur dans son plaidoyer; **to express one's h. thanks to s.o.,** exprimer ses remerciements sincères à qn.

heart-free ['hɑːtfriː], *a.* qui a le cœur libre; qui n'a pas d'amour en tête.

hearth, *pl.* **hearths** [hɑːθ, hɑːðz], *s.* **1.** foyer *m*, âtre *m*; **fire blazing in the h.,** feu *m* qui flambe dans le foyer, dans l'âtre; **cinders on the h.,** la cendre du foyer; **without h. or home,** sans feu ni lieu; *Hist:* **h. tax, money,** fouage *m.* **2.** (*a*) *Metall:* aire *f*, foyer, sole *f*, laboratoire *m* (de four à réverbère); creuset *m* (de haut-fourneau); **low h.,** bas-foyer *m*, *pl.* bas-foyers; **open-h. furnace,** four *m* à sole; four Martin; (*b*) **smith's h.,** âtre, foyer, de forge; forge *f*; **h. back, plate,** plaque *f* de contre-feu (de forge).

hearthrug ['hɑːθrʌg], *s.* tapis *m*, carpette *f*, de foyer; devant *m* de foyer; (tapis-)foyer *m.*

hearthstone ['hɑːθstoun], *s.* **1.** pierre *f* de la cheminée; (marbre *m* du) foyer; sous-âtre *m*, *pl.* sous âtres. **2.** *Dom.Ec:* *O:* blanc *m* d'Espagne.

heartily ['hɑːtili], *adv.* **1.** (saluer) cordialement; (accueillir qn, applaudir) chaleureusement; (travailler, rire) de bon cœur; (rire) à belles dents; (se réjouir) sincèrement; **to go at it h.,** y aller de tout son cœur; *F:* **to be h. sick of sth.,** être profondément, franchement, dégoûté de qch. **2.** (dîner) copieusement; (manger) de bon appétit, avec appétit; **to eat more h. than ever,** redoubler d'appétit.

heartiness ['hɑːtinis], *s.* cordialité *f*, chaleur *f* (d'un accueil); sincérité *f* (d'un consentement); vigueur *f* (de l'appétit); ardeur *f*, empressement *m*.

heartland ['hɑːtlænd], *s. Pol: Pol.Ec:* centre (i) important, (ii) stratégique; **the main German industrial h. of the Ruhr,** le principal centre industriel allemand de la Ruhr.

heartless ['hɑːtlis], *a.* (personne *f*) sans cœur, insensible, sans pitié, sans entrailles; (traitement, mot) dur, cruel; **you will not be so h. as to do that,** vous n'aurez pas le cœur de faire cela.

heartlessly ['hɑːtlisli], *adv.* sans cœur, sans pitié; (traiter qn) cruellement, durement.

heartlessness ['hɑːtlisnis], *s.* manque *m* de cœur; cruauté *f*; insensibilité *f*.

heart-piercing ['hɑːtpiːəsiŋ], *a.* (cri, spectacle, etc.) déchirant, qui perce le cœur, qui fend le cœur.

heartrending ['hɑːtrendiŋ], *a.* (soupir *m*, nouvelle *f*) à fendre le cœur, qui fend l'âme; (spectacle) navrant; **h. cries,** cris déchirants.

heartrot ['hɑːtrɔt], *s. Arb:* pourriture *f* du cœur.

heartsearching ['hɑːtsəːtʃiŋ]. **1.** *a.* (question, regard) qui sonde le(s) cœur(s). **2.** *s.* examen *m* de conscience; scrupule *m*; **after many heartsearchings, I accepted,** après m'être longtemps tâté, j'ai accepté.

heartsease ['hɑːtsiːz], *s. Bot:* pensée *f* sauvage.

heartseed ['hɑːtsiːd], *s. Bot:* cardiosperme *m*.

heart-shaped ['hɑːtʃeipt], *a.* cordiforme; en (forme de) cœur.

heartsick ['hɑːtsik], *a.* **1.** écœuré; **h. consciousness of failure,** sentiment poignant, morne, d'avoir échoué; **to be, feel, h.,** être, se sentir, découragé; avoir la mort dans l'âme; avoir le cœur navré. **2. h. lover,** soupirant désolé, éploré; amoureux transi.

heartsickness ['hɑːtsiknis], *s.* écœurement *m*; découragement *m*.

heartsinking ['hɑːtsiŋkiŋ], *s.* serrement *m* de cœur; sentiment accablant de découragement; désespérance *f*; affaissement *m* de l'âme.

heartsome ['hɑːtsəm], *a. A: & Lit:* joyeux, gai, enjoué.

heartsore ['hɑːtsɔːər], *a.* blessé au cœur; chagriné, affligé.

heart-stirring ['hɑːtstəːriŋ], *a.* (discours) entraînant, qui vous remue le cœur; (musique) entraînante.

heartstrain ['hɑːtstrein], *s. Med:* cœur forcé.

heartstricken, heartstruck ['hɑːtstrikn, -strʌk], *a.* frappé au cœur; navré.

heartstrings ['hɑːtstriŋz], *s.pl.* **1.** *Anat: A:* fibres *f*, tendons *m*, du cœur. **2. to tug at s.o.'s h.,** serrer le cœur de qn; **to play on s.o.'s h.,** agir sur les affections de qn, sur la sensibilité de qn; toucher le cœur de qn.

heartthrob ['hɑːtθrɔb], *s.* (*a*) battement *m* de cœur; palpitation *f*; (*b*) *F:* objet *m* de l'amour, béguin *m*.

heartwhole ['hɑːthoul], *a.* **1.** qui a le cœur libre; qui n'est pas amoureux; qui n'a pas d'amour en tête. **2. h. affection,** affection sincère, vraie. **3.** qui a conservé tout son courage; qui ne s'est pas laissé abattre.

heartwood ['hɑːtwud], *s. Arb:* bois *m* de cœur; cœur *m* du bois; bois parfait; duramen *m*.

hearty ['hɑːti], *a.* **1.** cordial, *pl.* -aux; (sentiment *m*) sincère, qui part du cœur; **my heartiest congratulations,** mes cordiales félicitations; mes félicitations les plus chaleureuses; **good h. laugh,** rire jovial; rire bon enfant; **h. supporter of . . .,** partisan convaincu de . . .; **the heartiest of welcomes awaited us,** nous avons été accueillis avec la plus grande cordialité; **h. cheers,** acclamations nourries, chaleureuses. **2.** (*a*) vigoureux, robuste, bien portant; **he is still (hale and) h.,** il est encore gaillard; (*b*) (repas) copieux, abondant, solide; **h. appetite,** fort, gros, rude, excellent, appétit; **he's a h. eater,** il mange ferme; c'est un gros mangeur, une bonne fourchette; (*c*) (*of land*) productif, d'un bon rapport. **3.** *s. A:* (*a*) *Nau:* **now then, my hearties!** allons, mes braves! (*b*) *Sch:* (*at universities*) sportif (brillant et borné).

heat[1] [hiːt], *s.* **1.** (*a*) chaleur *f*; ardeur *f* (du soleil, d'un foyer); **the great h. of summer,** les grandes chaleurs de l'été; **in the h. of the day,** au plus chaud de la journée; **the h. of the day was over,** le chaud du jour était passé; **h. haze,** brume due à la chaleur; **h. lightning,** éclairs *mpl* de chaleur; **excessive h. and cold should be avoided,** le chaud et le froid excessifs sont à éviter; **to generate h. (by fermentation),** produire l'échauffement; *Hort:* **to sow in h.,** semer sur couche; **bottom h.,** couche chaude; (*b*) *Ph: Ch: etc:* chaleur; **h. of combustion,** chaleur de combustion; **h. of condensation, of vaporization,** chaleur de condensation, d'évaporation; **h. of decomposition, of formation,** chaleur de décomposition, de formation; **h. of radioactivity,** chaleur de désintégration radioactive; *Ch:* **h. of reaction,** chaleur de réaction; **specific h.,** chaleur spécifique; **latent h.,** chaleur latente; **radiant h.,** chaleur radiante, rayonnante; **dark h.,** chaleur obscure; **h. generation,** production *f* de chaleur; **h. capacity,** capacité *f* calorifique; **h. constant,** constante *f* calorifique; **h. efficiency,** rendement *m* calorifique; **h. energy,** énergie *f* thermique; **h. value,** valeur *f* calorique, calorifique; **h. conduction,** conduction *f* de chaleur; **h. conductivity,** conductibilité *f* calorifique, thermique; thermoconductibilité *f*; **h. conduction losses,** pertes *f* de chaleur par conductibilité; **h. conductor,** conducteur *m* thermique, de chaleur; **h. dissipation,** dispersion *f*, dissipation *f*, de chaleur; **h. exchange,** échange *m* de chaleur; **h. transfer,** transmission *f* de chaleur; **h. insulation,** calorifugeage *m*; **h. insulator,** calorifuge *m*; *Ph:* **h. spectrum,** spectre *m* calorifique; *Av: Ball:* **h. barrier,** mur de la chaleur, mur thermique; (*c*) *Tchn:* **h. engine,** machine *f*, moteur *m*, thermique; **h. exchanger,** échangeur *m* de chaleur; **h. pump,** thermopompe *f*; **h. screen,** écran *m* thermique; **h. shield,** *Mec.E:* bouclier *m* thermique (d'un véhicule spatial, etc.), *Elcs:* écran thermique (d'un tube cathodique); **h-shield material,** matériau *m* pour bouclier thermique; **h. sensing element,** sonde *f* thermique; *Ind:* **h. treatment,** traitement *m* thermique; (*d*) **blood h.,** température *f* du sang; *Med: Vet:* **h. treatment, h. cure,** thermothérapie *f*; (*e*) *Metall:* (i) (*temperature*) chaleur, chaude *f*; **red h.,** chaude rouge, chaleur rouge; **dark red h.,** chaude sombre; **white h.,** chaleur d'incandescence; chaude blanche, grasse; chaleur blanche; blanc suant, soudant; **welding h.,** chaleur suante; chaude blanc-soudant; **to raise iron to a white, red, h.,** chauffer le fer à blanc, au rouge; porter le fer au rouge-blanc; **bright white h. of wire,** chaleur blanche, incandescence *f*, du fil; **h. balance,** bilan *m* thermique, calorifique (d'un haut fourneau, etc.); **h. sealing,** thermocollage *m*; (ii) (*heating*) chaude; **horseshoe that requires two heats,** fer *m* à cheval qui exige deux chaudes; **rolling that requires several heats,** laminage *m* qui nécessite plusieurs chaudes; (*f*) *Cu:* intensité *f* de chauffe; température. **2.** (*a*) (*passion*) **to get into a h.,** s'échauffer, s'emporter; **to work oneself up into a white h.,** entrer dans un état de violente surexcitation; **to reply with some h.,** répondre avec une certaine vivacité; **h. of a discussion,** feu *m*, vivacité, d'une discussion; **h. of youth,** fougue *f* de la jeunesse; **the h. of passion,** la fougue des passions; **in the h. of the moment,** dans la chaleur du moment; **you must forgive what was said in the h. of the moment,** pardonnez quelques vivacités; **in the h. of the debate,** dans la chaleur, l'emportement, de la dispute; **in the first h. of his resentment,** dans le premier feu de sa colère; **in the h. of the battle,** dans la fièvre de la mêlée, dans la chaleur du combat; *F:* **to turn on the h.,** (i) s'enflammer, s'échauffer; (ii) faire pression sur qn, mettre le feu au derrière (de qn). **3.** (*of animal*) rut *m*, œstrus *m*, chaleur; **to be in, on, h.,** être en chaleur, en rut. **4.** *Med:* rougeur *f* (sur la peau); **prickly h.,** miliaire *f*, sudamina *mpl*; **h. rash,** échauffaison *f*, échauffure *f*. **5.** *Sp: Rac:* (*a*) épreuve *f*, manche *f*; **qualifying, eliminating, h.,** (épreuve *f*, série *f*) éliminatoire *f*; (*b*) **dead h.,** course *f* à égalité.

heat[2], *v.*

I. *v.tr. & i.* **1.** *v.tr.* (*a*) chauffer (l'eau, le métal, une maison, etc.); **to h. sth. to (a temperature of) 80°,** porter qch. à 80°; **to h. a house with coal, gas, oil,** chauffer une maison au charbon, au gaz, au mazout; (*b*) (*abnormally*) échauffer (le sang, etc.); enflammer (l'esprit); **to h. oneself, get heated, running,** s'échauffer à courir; **to h. the imagination, the passions,** échauffer, enflammer, l'imagination, les passions; (*c*) (*ferment*) échauffer (le foin, le grain, le bois). **2.** *v.i.* (*a*) (*of water, etc.*) chauffer; (*b*) (*of bearing, etc.*) **to h. (up),** chauffer, s'échauffer; (*c*) (*of hay, etc.*) s'échauffer, fermenter.

II. (*compound verb*) **heat up,** *v.tr.* (faire) réchauffer (un plat, etc.).

heat-absorbing ['hiːtəbsɔːbiŋ], *a.* (vapeur, etc.) qui absorbe la chaleur.

heat-conducting ['hiːtkən'dʌktiŋ], *a.* (thermo)conductible; **h.-c. bond,** liaison *f* thermique, thermoconductible.

heated ['hiːtid], *a.* **1.** chaud, chauffé; **h. air,** air chaud; **electrically h. mat,** tapis chauffant; *Av: etc:* **h. flying suit,** combinaison *f* de vol chauffante; **h. space suit,** combinaison spatiale chauffante. **2.** (*a*) **h. bearing,** palier échauffé, qui chauffe; (*b*) **h. debate,** discussion chaude, animée; **h. words,** paroles prononcées sous l'empire de la colère; **to make a h. reply,** répondre avec emportement.

heatedly ['hiːtidli], *adv.* avec chaleur, avec emportement.

heater ['hiːtər], *s.* **1.** (*a*) **(space) h.,** radiateur *m*; **electric h.,** radiateur électrique; **convection h.,** radiateur à convection; **fan h.,** radiateur soufflant; **infra-red h.,** radiateur à infrarouge; **oil-filled electric h.,** radiateur à circulation d'huile; **oil-h.,** calorifère *m*, poêle *f*, à mazout, à pétrole; *Aut:* **(car) h.,** appareil *m* de chauffage (d'une voiture); **if you're cold put on the h.,** si vous avez froid mettez le chauffage; (*b*) **(electric, gas) water h.,** chauffe-eau *m inv* (électrique, à gaz); **(electric) immersion h.,** thermoplongeur *m*; (*c*) *I.C.E: etc:* réchauffeur *m*; **intake h.,** réchauffeur d'admission; **h. barrel,** enveloppe *f*, manchon *m*, de réchauffeur; **oil h.,** (i) *Mch:* réchauffeur d'huile; (ii) *Agr:* réchauffeur au pétrole; **oil-h. jacket,** chemise *f* de réchauffeur d'huile; (*d*) réchaud *m*; **soldering-iron h.,** réchaud à souder; (*e*) *Mch:* (tube) bouilleur *m* (de chaudière); (*f*) *U.S: P:* revolver *m*. **2.** (*pers.*) **rivet h.,** chauffeur *m* de rivets.

heath [hiːθ], *s.* **1.** (*a*) (*tract of land*) bruyère *f*, lande *f*, brande *f*; (*b*) *Orn:* **h. cock, game, fowl,** petit coq de bruyère; tétras *m*; **h. hen,** petite poule de bruyère. **2.** *Bot:* bruyère, brande; **fine-leaved h.,** bruyère cendrée; **cross-leaved h.,** bruyère des marais, clarin *m*.

heathbell ['hiːθbel], *s. Bot:* **1.** fleur *f* de la bruyère; cloche *f* de bruyère. **2.** campanule *f*, clochette *f*; jacinthe *f* des prés.

heathberry ['hiːθberi], *s. Bot:* camarine *f*.

heathen ['hiːð(ə)n], *a. & s.* **1.** païen, -ienne; **the natives were heathens,** les indigènes étaient des païens; *coll.* **the h.,** les païens; *B:* les gentils *m*. **2.** *F:* d'une simplicité primitive; barbare; plongé dans l'ignorance. **3.** *F:* **these youngsters are regular heathens,** ces gamins-là ne respectent rien.

heathendom ['hiːðəndəm], *s.* le monde païen, le paganisme; *B:* la gentilité.

heathenism ['hiːðənizm], *s.* **1.** paganisme *m*, idolâtrie *f*. **2.** barbarie *f*.

heathenize ['hiːðənaiz], *v.tr.* paganiser.

heather ['heðər], *s.* (*a*) *Bot:* bruyère *f*, brande *f*; **ling h., common h.,** callune (commune); bruyère commune; **Scotch h., bell h.,** bruyère cendrée; **h. country,** un pays de brandes; **to take to the h.,** se réfugier dans la lande, = prendre le maquis; (*b*) *Tex:* **h. mixture,** drap chiné bruyère.

heatherbell ['heðəbel], *s.* = HEATHBELL 1.

heathy ['hiːθi], *a.* (*of region, etc.*) couvert de landes.

heating[1] ['hiːtiŋ], *a.* (*a*) de chauffage, de réchauffage; chauffant, réchauffant; **h. power,** puissance *f*, pouvoir *m*, calorifique; rendement *m* calorique; *El:* puissance de chauffage; **h. action of the sun,** action calorifiante du soleil; *Tchn:* **h. apparatus,** appareil *m* de chauffage, calorifère *m* (d'immeuble); **h. plant,** installation *f* de chauffage; **h. pipe,** conduit *m* de chaleur; *Ind:* **h. furnace,** four *m* de réchauffage; **h. oven,** four calorifère; *Metall:* **bar-h. furnace,** four à réchauffer les barres; *Mec.E: etc:* **h. coil,** serpentin *m* de chauffage, réchauffeur *m*; **h. fabric,** tissu chauffant; **h. panel,** panneau chauffant; *El: etc:* **h. circuit,** circuit *m* de chauffage; **h. element, h. unit,** élément *m* de chauffage, élément chauffant; **h. resistor,** résistance *f* de chauffage; **h. filament,** filament chauffant; **h. wire,** fil chauffant; **h. grid,** grille chauffante; **h. plate,** plaque chauffante; **h. effect,** effet *m* thermique; (*b*) échauffant; **h. food,** nourriture échauffante.

heating[2], *s.* **1.** (*making hot*) (*a*) chauffage *m*; **conductive h.,** chauffage par conduction; **convective h.,** chauffage par convection; **radiant h.,** chauffage par rayonnement; **electric h.,** chauffage électrique; **oil h.,** chauffage au pétrole, au mazout; **steam h.,** chauffage à la vapeur; **floating h.,** chauffage par zone flottante; **central h.,** chauffage central; **district h.,** chauffage urbain; **hot-air h.,** chauffage à, par, l'air chaud; **h. expenses,** frais de chauffage; *Rail:* **to turn on, off, the h.,** ouvrir, fermer, le chauffage (des chaudières); *Mch:* **h. surface,** surface *f* de chauffe (d'une chaudière); *Metalw:* **arc h.,** chauffage par arc électrique; **white, red, h.,** chauffage au blanc, au rouge; (*b*) réchauffage *m* (d'un plat, d'une barre de métal, etc.); *I.C.E: etc:* **fuel h.,** réchauffage du combustible. **2.** (*becoming hot*) (*a*) échauffement *m* (d'une pièce de machine, d'un outil, etc.); *Rail:* **h. of axles,** échauffement de l'essieu; *Av: Ball:* **ram h.,** échauffement aérodynamique; *Ph:* **friction h.,** échauffement par friction; (*b*) échauffement, fermentation *f* (du fourrage, du grain, etc.); *Miner:* **h. of shales,** fermentation des schistes.

heat-producing ['hiːtprədjusiŋ], *a. Physiol:* (aliment *m*) thermogène.

heatproof ['hiːtpruːf], *a.* (vernis, etc.) allant au feu, qui va au feu, calorifuge.

heat-resistant, -resisting ['hiːtri'zistənt, -ri'zistiŋ], *a.* **1.** anti-calorique, calorifuge, résistant à la chaleur,

thermorésistant. 2. *Metall:* (métal *m*) indétrempable.
heat-setting ['hi:tsetiŋ], *a.* (résine) thermodurcissable.
heatstroke ['hi:tstrouk], *s. Med: Vet:* coup *m* de chaleur.
heat-treat ['hi:tri:t], *v.tr. Metall: etc:* traiter thermiquement, par la chaleur; **heat-treated metal,** métal traité, revenu.
heatwave ['hi:tweiv], *s.* (*a*) *Ph:* onde *f* calorifique; (*b*) *Meteor:* vague *f* de chaleur.
heaume [houm], *s. A.Arm:* heaume *m.*
heave[1] [hi:v], *s.* soulèvement *m.* **1.** (*a*) effort *m* (pour soulever); **with a mighty h.,** d'un effort puissant; (*b*) *Wr:* tour *m* de bras; (*c*) *Gym:* **to do heaves,** faire des tractions *f.* **2.** (*a*) haut-le-cœur *m inv*; nausée *f*; effort *m* pour vomir; (*b*) haut-le-corps *m inv* (de surprise, etc.); palpitation *f* (du sein). **3.** (*a*) *Nau:* **h. of the sea,** poussée *f,* entraînement *m,* ondulation *f,* des lames; houle *f*; (*b*) *Geol:* déplacement latéral (d'une couche); rejet horizontal (d'une faille); recouvrement horizontal (d'une faille de chevauchement); (*c*) *Min: etc:* gonflement *m,* boursouflement *m* (de la sole d'une galerie, etc.). **4.** *pl.* (*with sing. const.*) *Vet:* **the heaves,** la pousse; **the horse had the heaves,** le cheval était poussif.
heave[2], *v.* (*p.t. & p.p.* **heaved** *or* (*esp. Nau:*) **hove** [houv]) **I.** *v.tr.* **1.** (*a*) (*lift*) lever, soulever (un fardeau); **the wind heaves the waves,** le vent soulève les vagues; *Nau:* **to h. (up) the anchor,** déraper; lever l'ancre; (*b*) *Geol:* (*of stratum*) déplacer latéralement (une autre couche). **2.** (*utter*) pousser, laisser échapper (un soupir, etc.). **3.** (*a*) (*pull, haul*) **to h. coal,** (i) porter, (ii) décharger, le charbon; (*b*) *Nau:* **to h. the ship ahead, astern,** virer le navire de l'avant, de l'arrière. **4.** (*throw*) lancer, jeter (**sth. at s.o., sth.,** qch. contre qn, qch.); *F:* balancer (des pierres, etc.); *Nau:* **to h. the lead,** jeter la sonde, le plomb; sonder. **5.** *Sp:* **to h. oneself up,** faire un rétablissement.
II. *v.i.* **1.** (*a*) (*swell*) (se) gonfler, se soulever; (*of sea*) s'agiter, se soulever; (*of ship*) se soulever sur la lame; (*of bosom*) palpiter; *Min:* (*of floor*) se boursoufler; **her bosom heaved (with a sigh),** un soupir lui souleva la poitrine; *F:* **to h. with laughter,** se tenir les côtes de rire; se gondoler; (*b*) (*retch*) (*of pers.*) avoir des haut-le-cœur, faire des efforts pour vomir; (*of the stomach*) se soulever, se retourner; **my stomach heaved at the sight,** le spectacle m'a tourné l'estomac, m'a donné des nausées; (*c*) (*of horse*) battre du flanc. **2.** *Nau:* **to h. (away) at the capstan,** virer au cabestan; **h. a long pull!** halez à grands coups! **3.** *Nau:* (*of land, ship*) **to h. in sight,** paraître (à l'horizon); poindre, hausser.
III. (*compound verbs*) **1. heave down,** *v.tr. Nau:* caréner (un navire); abattre (un navire) en carène.
2. heave in, *v.tr. & i.* virer, rentrer (un cordage).
3. heave off, *v.tr. Nau:* déhaler, renflouer (un navire).
4. heave out, *v.tr. Nau:* déferler (une voile d'étai).
5. heave over, *v.tr.* = HEAVE DOWN.
6. heave to, *v.tr. & i. Nau:* (se) mettre en panne, à la cape; prendre la panne; (*in gale*) capeyer; **to be hove to,** être en panne, à la cape.
heave-ho ['hi:v'hou]. **1.** *int. Nau:* ohé! ô hisse! **2.** *s. P:* **to get the h.-ho,** être congédié, flanqué à la porte.
heaven ['hev(ə)n], *s.* **1.** ciel *m, pl.* cieux; **in h.,** au ciel; dans le ciel; **to go to h.,** aller au ciel, en paradis; **it's h. on earth,** c'est le paradis sur terre; **to move h. and earth to do sth.,** faire des efforts inouïs, remuer ciel et terre, faire des pieds et des mains, pour faire qch.; **blessings that come from h.,** grâces *f* qui viennent d'en haut; **the heavens opened,** il a commencé à pleuvoir à torrents; **it's sheer h. to be able to relax,** il est magnifique de pouvoir se reposer; *F:* **it stinks to high h.,** ça pue; **and h. knows we need it!** Dieu sait si nous en avons besoin! **h. only knows!** qui sait? Dieu seul le sait! **and h. knows what,** et je ne sais quoi encore; **(good) heavens! heavens above!** juste ciel! bonté divine! mon Dieu! **thank h. (for that)!** Dieu merci! **for heaven's sake!** pour l'amour de Dieu! **who in the name of h. told you to do that?** qui diable vous a dit de faire cela? **what in (the name of) h. made him do it?** que diable lui a donné l'idée de faire cela? **where in the name of h. is he?** où diable est-il? **2.** *Bot:* **tree of h., h. tree,** ailante *m.*
heaven-born ['hevnbɔ:n], *a.* **1.** (de naissance) céleste; divin. **2.** *A:* (professeur, etc.) particulièrement doué.
heavenliness ['hev(ə)nlinis], *s.* caractère *m* céleste; perfection *f*; beauté divine.
heavenly ['hevnli]. **1.** *a.* (musique *f,* etc.) céleste; (don) du ciel; **h. body,** astre *m*; **our h. Father,** notre Père céleste; *F:* **what h. peaches!** quelles pêches délicieuses! **it's just h. to . . .,** il est magnifique de . . . . **2.** *adv. Lit:* (*in combination with adj., e.g.*) **h. fair,** divinement belle.
heavenly-minded ['hevənli'maindid], *a.* dévot; pieux.
heaven-sent ['hev(ə)nsent], *a.* providentiel.
heavenward(s) ['hevnwəd(z)], *adv.* vers le ciel.
heaver ['hi:vər], *s.* **1.** (*pers.*) chargeur *m,* porteur *m* (de charbon, etc.); déchargeur *m* (de charbon, etc.); débardeur *m*; **ballast h.,** délesteur *m.* **2.** (*a*) levier *m* de manœuvre; brimbale *f,* bringuebale *f* (de pompe); (*b*) *Nau:* trésillon *m*; (*c*) *Tls:* épinglette *f* (d'ouvrier voilier).
heavier-than-air ['heviəðən'eər], *a. Av:* plus lourd que l'air.
heavily ['hevili], *adv.* **1.** (marcher, tomber) lourdement; **h. armed knights,** chevaliers pesamment armés; **time hangs h. on his hands,** le temps lui pèse, lui dure; **he walked h.,** il avançait d'un pas pesant, à pas pesants; *Av:* **to land too h.,** atterrir trop durement; faire un atterrissage trop dur. **2.** fortement, fort; **h. underlined,** fortement souligné; **h. booted feet,** pieds chaussés de grosses bottes, de forts brodequins; *Rail:* **h. travelled line,** ligne *f* à trafic intense, à fort trafic; **h. mineralized quartz,** quartz hautement minéralisé; **to drink h.,** boire beaucoup; **to lose h.,** perdre une forte somme; perdre gros; **to be h. hit,** être gravement atteint (par ses pertes, etc.); **to be h. fined,** être frappé d'une lourde amende; **to be h. taxed,** être fortement imposé. **3. to sigh h.,** soupirer profondément; **to sleep h.,** dormir profondément; dormir d'un sommeil lourd, d'un sommeil de plomb; dormir à poings fermés. **4.** (respirer, se mouvoir) péniblement; (se mouvoir) avec difficulté.
heaviness ['hevinis], *s.* **1.** (*a*) lourdeur *f,* pesanteur *f* (d'un corps, de l'allure); poids *m* (d'un fardeau); lourdeur (d'un aliment); *Av:* (*of aircraft*) **tail h.,** tendance *f* à cabrer; **nose h.,** tendance à piquer; (*b*) caractère oppressif (des impôts, etc.); poids (des impôts); (*c*) engourdissement *m,* lassitude *f,* langueur *f,* abattement *m* (des membres, du corps, de l'esprit); **growing h.,** alourdissement *m,* appesantissement *m*; **h. in the head,** lourdeur de tête; **h. of heart,** serrement *m* de cœur; tristesse *f.* **2.** nature grasse (du sol); (*b*) mauvais état, état peu roulant (des routes).
heaving[1] ['hi:viŋ], *a.* **h. waves,** vagues agitées; **h. flanks,** flancs haletants; **h. bosom,** poitrine palpitante; *Lit:* sein bondissant.
heaving[2], *s.* **1.** soulèvement *m* (des flots, du cœur); *Min:* boursouflement *m* (de la sole). **2.** *Nau:* virage *m* (d'un navire); **h. down,** abattage *m* en carène; **h. off,** renflouage *m*; **h. line,** ligne *f* d'attrape, lance-amarre *m, pl.* lance-amarres.
Heaviside ['hevisaid], *Pr.n.* **H. layer,** (i) *Ph:* couche *f* de Heaviside; ionosphère *f*; (ii) *Av:* zone *f* d'inflexion.
heavy[1] ['hevi], *a.* **1.** lourd; (*a*) **h. weights,** poids lourds; **h. parcel,** paquet lourd, pesant; **to weigh h.,** peser lourd; **burden heavier than I can bear,** (i) fardeau plus lourd que je ne puis porter; (ii) tâche qui dépasse la mesure de mes forces; **to make a burden heavier,** alourdir, appesantir, un fardeau; **in time the lightest burden becomes, gets, h.,** à la longue le plus léger fardeau pèse, s'appesantit; **beam carrying a h. load,** poutre *f* qui peine beaucoup; **h. blow,** (i) coup violent; (ii) rude coup (du sort, etc.); **h. dough,** pâte lourde, mate, trop compacte; **food that lies h. on the stomach, h. food,** nourriture lourde, indigeste, qui pèse sur l'estomac; **h. wine,** vin à forte teneur d'alcool; **h. in hand,** (i) (cheval) pesant à la main; (ii) *F:* (personne) de conversation difficile, difficile à amuser; (*b*) **h. tread,** pas pesant, lourd, alourdi; **h. style,** style lourd, monotone; **to have a h. hand,** être gauche, maladroit; **the market is h.,** le marché est lourd; (*c*) (*of animal*) **h. with young,** gravide; (*d*) *Ph:* **h. bodies,** corps *m* graves; *Atom.Ph:* **h. atom,** atome lourd; **h. nucleus,** noyau lourd; **h. particle,** particule lourde; **h. hydrogen,** hydrogène lourd; **h. water,** eau lourde; **h.-water moderator,** modérateur *m* en eau lourde, eau lourde servant de modérateur; **h.-water reactor,** réacteur *m* à eau lourde. **2.** (*a*) gros, *f.* grosse; **h. luggage,** gros bagages; **h. flywheel,** volant *m* à grande masse; **h. lathe,** gros tour; **h. motor,** gros moteur; **h. wire,** fil *m* (de) grosse épaisseur; *For:* **h. timber,** gros bois; *Metall:* **h. castings,** grosses pièces; **h. forging,** grosse pièce de forge; *Mil:* **h. metal,** artillerie lourde; *F:* **he's h. metal,** c'est un homme de poids; **h. cavalry,** grosse cavalerie; *s.pl.* **the Heavies,** (i) les dragons lourds (de l'armée anglaise), les Dragons de la Garde; (ii) la grosse artillerie, l'artillerie lourde; *Navy:* **h. armament,** artillerie de gros calibre; **ship with h. ordnance,** navire fort en artillerie; (*b*) **h. features,** gros traits; physionomie dépourvue de finesse, de vivacité; **h. line,** gros trait, trait gras; *Typ:* **h.(-faced) type, type with a h. face,** caractères gras; (*c*) fort; **h. beard,** forte barbe; **h. crop,** grosse récolte, récolte abondante; **there is a h. crop of wheat,** les blés sont forts; **h. meal,** (i) repas copieux; (ii) repas lourd à digérer; *Mil:* **h. fire,** feu nourri; feu vif; feu intense; **h. rain,** pluie battante; grande, grosse, forte, pluie; **h. shower,** grosse averse; **the rain is getting heavier,** la pluie augmente; **h. fog,** brouillard épais; **there was a h. dew,** il y avait une forte rosée; **h. expenditure,** dépenses *f* considérables; grosses dépenses; **h. losses,** lourdes, fortes, pertes; *Com:* **h. sales,** ventes massives; **h. percentage,** pourcentage élevé; **contangoes are h.,** les reports sont chers; **h. pressure,** haute pression; *El:* **h. current,** courant intensif, intense; **h. cold,** gros rhume; **to have a h. cold,** être fortement enrhumé; (*d*) profond; **h. silence,** silence profond; **h. sleep,** profond sommeil; sommeil de plomb, de mort. **3.** (*oppressive*) **h. odour,** odeur lourde; **air h. with scent,** air chargé de parfums; **h. responsibility,** lourde responsabilité; **h. tax,** lourd impôt; **h. fine,** lourde amende; **h. charge on the budget,** charge onéreuse pour le budget; **to rule with a h. hand,** gouverner d'une main rude, sévère; **these old engines are very h. on petrol,** ces vieilles machines mangent beaucoup d'essence; **h. sky,** temps couvert; ciel sombre, morne, menaçant. **4. h. eyes,** yeux battus; **h. with sleep,** appesanti par le sommeil, accablé de sommeil; **h. with wine,** alourdi par le vin; pris de vin; (*of weather, etc.*) **to make s.o. feel h.,** assoupir qn. **5.** (*a*) (travail) pénible, difficile, dur, laborieux; **h. task,** lourde tâche; **he did the h. work,** c'est lui qui a fait le gros de la besogne; **this book is h. reading,** ce livre est indigeste, touffu, est ardu à la lecture, de lecture malaisée; **h. day,** journée chargée; **to find it h. going,** avancer avec difficulté; **h. soil, h., ground,** terrain lourd; sol gras; sol fort; **h. breathing,** respiration *f* pénible; (*b*) **h. weather,** gros temps; **h. sea,** forte mer, grosse mer; **a h. sea was running,** il faisait une mer houleuse; **to ship a h. sea,** embarquer un coup de mer. **6.** *Th:* **h. parts,** rôles sombres, sérieux, tragiques; **he plays the h. uncle,** il a un rôle d'oncle aux tirades emphatiques; *P: A:* **to do, play, come, the h. (swell),** faire le gros monsieur, le type huppé; faire du volume; faire l'important. **7. h. eater,** gros mangeur; **h. drinker,** franc buveur; **to be a h. sleeper,** avoir le sommeil dur.
heavy[2] ['hi:vi], *a. Vet:* (cheval) poussif.
heavy-duty ['hevi'djuti], *a.* (machine) à grand, à fort, rendement, à fort débit, de grande puissance; (appareil) soumis à un travail très dur; **h.-d. tyres,** pneus *m* tous-terrains; **h.-d. jack,** cric *m* pour poids lourds; **h.-d. oil,** huile *f* à haute tenue.
heavy-eyed ['hevi'aid], *a.* aux yeux battus; aux yeux remplis de sommeil.
heavy-handed ['hevi'hændid], *a.* **1.** (*a*) à la main lourde; (*b*) oppressif, cruel. **2.** maladroit, gauche.
heavy-headed ['hevi'hedid], *a.* **1.** (*a*) à grosse tête; (cheval) chargé de ganache; (*b*) (blé, etc.) à épis pleins. **2. to feel h.-h.,** (i) se sentir la tête lourde; (ii) avoir envie de dormir. **3.** *A:* stupide, bête, lourdaud.
heavy-hearted ['hevi'hɑ:tid], *a.* abattu; qui a le cœur lourd, gros.
heavy-laden ['hevi'leid(ə)n], *a.* **1.** lourdement chargé. **2.** abattu (par le chagrin, le malheur); chargé de soucis; *B:* **all ye that labour and are h.-l.,** vous tous qui êtes fatigués et chargés.
heavyweight ['heviweit]. **1.** *s. Box:* poids lourd; **light h.,** poids mi-lourd. **2.** *a.* lourd; **h. materials,** étoffes lourdes, tissus lourds.
hebdomadal [heb'dɔməd(ə)l], *a.* hebdomadaire.
hebdomadary [heb'dɔmədəri]. **1.** *a.* = HEBDOMADAL. **2.** *s. R.C.Ch:* (*pers.*) semainier, -ière, hebdomadier, -ière; **a. h. canon,** chanoine hebdomadier.
Hebe ['hi:bi]. **1.** *Pr.n.f. Gr.Myth:* Hébé. **2.** *s.f. F: A:* serveuse (de café, etc.). **3.** *s. Bot:* véronique *f.*
hebeostcotomy [hi:biɔsti'ɔtəmi], *s. Surg:* hébotomie *f,* pubiotomie *f.*
hebephrenia [hi:bi'fri:niə], *s. Psy:* hébéphrénie *f.*
hebephrenic [hi:bi'fri:nik], *a. & s. Psy:* hébéphrénique (*mf*).
hebetate ['hebiteit]. *A: & Lit:* **1.** *v.tr.* hébéter, abrutir. **2.** *v.i.* s'hébéter, s'abrutir.
hebetude ['hebitju:d], *s. A: & Lit:* hébètement *m,* hébétude *f,* abrutissement *m.*
Hebraic [hi'breiik], *a.* hébraïque.
Hebraism ['hi:breiizm], *s.* hébraïsme *m.*
Hebraist ['hi:breiist], *s.* hébraïsant, -ante, hébraïste *mf.*
Hebraistic [hi:brei'istik], *a.* hébraïque; qui se rapporte à, ressemble à, l'hébreu.
Hebraize ['hi:breiaiz], *v.i. & tr.* hébraïser.
Hebrew ['hi:bru:]. **1.** *B.Hist:* (*a*) *a.* hébreu, *f.* hébraïque; (*b*) *s.* Hébreu, *esp.* Israélite *mf*; *B:* **the Epistle to the Hebrews,** l'Épître *f* aux Hébreux. **2.** *s. Ling:* l'hébreu *m*; la langue hébraïque; **H. alphabet,** alphabet hébraïque; **H. scholar,** hébraïste *mf,* hébraïsant, -ante.
Hebridean [hebri'di:ən], *Geog:* (*a*) *a.* hébridais; (*b*) *s.* Hébridais, -aise.
Hebrides (the) [ðə'hebridi:z], *Pr.n.pl. Geog:* les Hébrides *f.*
Hebron ['hi:brɔn, 'heb-], *Pr.n. Geog:* Hébron *m.*

Hebrus ['hi:brəs], *Pr.n. A.Geog:* l'Hèbre *m*, l'Hébros *m*.
Hecate ['hekəti], *Pr.n.f. Gr.Myth:* Hécate.
hecatomb ['hekətu:m], *s.* hécatombe *f*.
hecatonstylon ['hekətən'stailən], *s. Arch:* hécatonstyle *m*.
hechtia ['hektiə], *s. Bot:* hechtia *m*.
heck[1] [hek], *s.* **1.** estacade *f* à claire-voie (pour retenir les poissons). **2.** *Scot:* râtelier *m* à fourrage. **3.** *Tex: Dial:* grille *f* (de chaîne).
heck[2]. *F:* (*a*) *int.* sapristi! mon Dieu! (*b*) *s.* **what the h. are you doing there?** que diable fais-tu là? **how the h. can one . . .?** comment diable peut-on . . .? **a, the, h. of a lot,** une grande quantité, tout un tas (de).
heckle[1] ['hekl], *s. Tex:* = HACKLE[1].
heckle[2], *v.tr.* **1.** *Tex:* = HACKLE[2]. **2.** (*at public meetings*) interpeller; chahuter.
heckler ['heklər], *s.* **1.** *Tex:* = HACKLER. **2.** *Pol: etc:* interpellateur, -trice; adversaire *m* qui cherche à embarrasser le candidat; chahuteur, -euse.
heckling ['hekliŋ], *s.* **1.** *Tex:* = HACKLING. **2.** *Pol: etc:* interpellation *f*; chahut *m*.
hectare ['hekta:r], *s. Meas:* hectare *m*.
hectic ['hektik], *a.* **1.** *Med:* (*a*) (fièvre *f*, rougeur *f*) hectique; (*b*) **h. cough,** toux *f* de phtisique. **2.** agité, fiévreux; **h. life,** existence trépidante; **h. morning,** matinée mouvementée; **we had a h. time,** (i) nous ne savions où donner de la tête; (ii) on a fait une de ces noces!
hectically ['hektikli], *adv.* fiévreusement.
hecticity [hek'tisiti], *s. Med:* hecticité *f*, hectisie *f*.
hecto- ['hektə, -tou], *comb.fm.* hecto-.
hectocotylus [hektou'kɔtiləs], *s. Moll:* hectocotyle *m*, bras copulateur.
hectogram(me) ['hektəgræm], *s.* hectogramme *m*, *F:* hecto *m*.
hectograph[1] ['hektəgræf], *s. O:* **1.** (*instrument*) autocopiste *m*; hectographe *m*; appareil *m* à polycopier. **2.** (*process*) autocopie *f*.
hectograph[2], *v.tr. O:* autocopier, hectographier, polycopier; tirer (une circulaire, etc.) à la pâte à copier.
hectolitre ['hektəli:tər], *s.* hectolitre *m*; *F:* hecto *m*.
hectometre ['hektəmi:tər], *s.* hectomètre *m*.
Hector[1] ['hektər]. **1.** *Pr.n.m. Gr.Lit:* Hector. **2.** *s. F: A:* bravache *m*, matamore *m*, fendant *m*, fanfaron *m*; *A:* fier-à-bras *m inv*.
hector[2], *v.tr. & i.* faire de l'esbroufe; faire le fendant; prendre un ton autoritaire avec (qn); intimider, rudoyer, dragonner (qn); **she was hectored into marrying her cousin,** on l'a sermonnée, dragonnée, jusqu'à ce qu'elle épouse son cousin.
hectoring ['hektəriŋ], *a.* (ton, etc.) autoritaire, impérieux.
hectoringly ['hektəriŋli], *adv.* impérieusement, d'un ton, d'une manière, autoritaire.
hectowatt ['hektəwɔt], *s. El:* hectowatt *m*.
Hecuba ['hekjubə], *Pr.n.f. Lit:* Hécube.
heddle ['hedl], *s. Tex:* lisse *f*, lice *f* (d'un métier); **h. bar,** liais *m*; **h. hook,** passette *f*; **h. eye,** œillet *m* (d'une lice); **h. maker,** lamier *m*.
hedenbergite ['hedənbə:gait], *s. Miner:* hédenbergite *f*.
hederaceous [hedə'reiʃəs], *a. Bot:* hédéracé, hédéré.
hederagenin [hedræ'dʒenin, hedə'rædʒənin], *s. Ch:* hédéragénine *f*.
hederiform ['hedərifɔ:m], *a. Bot:* hédériforme.
hederin ['hedərin], *s. Ch:* hédérine *f*.
hedge[1] [hedʒ], *s.* **1.** haie *f*; **quickset h.,** haie vive; **dead h.,** haie morte, sèche; **h. clippers, h. shears,** taille-buissons *m inv*; cisaille *f* à haies; **h. bill, h. hook,** serpe *f*, croissant *m*, vouge *m*; **to sit on the h.,** se réserver; ménager la chèvre et le chou; attendre voir de quel côté vient le vent; **to come down on the wrong side of the h.,** se mettre du mauvais côté de la barricade; **it doesn't grow on the hedges, on every h.,** ça ne se trouve pas partout, sous les pas, le pied, d'un cheval. **2.** haie (d'agents de police, de troupes, etc.). **3.** *St.Exch:* arbitrage *m* (de portefeuille); couverture *f*; **to buy, sell, for the account as a h.,** acheter, vendre, à terme comme couverture; *Com: etc:* **h. clause,** clause de sauvegarde (insérée dans un contrat). **4.** *attrib. Pej: O:* de bas étage; interlope; **h. preacher,** prédicateur *m* de carrefour; **h. priest, h. parson,** prêtre (i) ignorant, (ii) interlope; **h. lawyer,** avocat marron; *Publ:* **h. press,** presse interlope; **h. writer,** écrivassier *m*, écrivailleur *m*; **h. wine,** piquette *f*; vin fabriqué; *A:* **h. tavern,** cabaret *m* de bas étage; *A:* (*in Ireland*) **h. school,** (i) école buissonnière; école en plein air; (ii) petite école de rien du tout.
hedge[2]. **1.** *v.tr.* **to h. in a piece of ground,** mettre une haie autour d'un terrain; enfermer, enclore, un terrain; entourer, clore, un terrain d'une haie; **hedged in, hedged about, with difficulties,** entouré de difficultés; enserré par des difficultés; **to h. off a piece of ground,** séparer un terrain par une haie (**from,** de). **2.** *v.i.* (*a*) *Turf:* parier pour et contre; (*b*) *St.Exch:* arbitrer, se couvrir; **to h. one stock against another,** arbitrer arbitrager, une valeur contre une autre; **to h. by a sale for the account,** se couvrir par une vente à terme; (*c*) (*in discussion*) chercher des échappatoires; se réserver; éviter de se compromettre; ne pas répondre franchement; chercher des faux-fuyants; s'échapper par la tangente; *Pol:* tendre les voiles du côté que vient le vent.
hedgehog ['hedʒhɔg], *s.* **1.** (*a*) hérisson *m*; **to curl up like a h.,** se hérisser; se mettre en boule; (*b*) *Mil:* hérisson; (*c*) *Ich: F:* **h. fish,** hérisson de mer; *Echin:* **sea h.,** oursin *m*; *Moll:* **h. shell,** murex *m*; (*d*) *Bot:* **h. cactus,** échinocactus *m*, *F:* coussin *m* de belle-mère. **2.** *NAm:* porc-épic *m*, *pl.* porcs-épics.
hedgehop ['hedʒhɔp], *v.i.* (**hedgehopped**) *Av: F:* voler en rase-mottes, *F:* faire du rase-mottes.
hedgehopper ['hedʒhɔpər], *s. Av: F:* (*a*) aviateur, -trice, qui vole en rase-mottes; (*b*) avion *m* qui fait du rase-mottes.
hedgehopping ['hedʒhɔpiŋ], *s. Av: F:* (*a*) vol *m* en rase-mottes; (*b*) rase-mottes *m inv*.
hedger ['hedʒər], *s.* **1.** (*a*) jardinier planteur de haies; (*b*) rénovateur *m*, réparateur *m*, de haies. **2.** (*a*) *St.Exch:* arbitragiste *m*; (*b*) *Turf:* parieur, -euse, pour et contre; (*c*) personne *f* qui se réserve, qui évite de se décider.
hedgerow ['hedʒrou], *s.* bordure *f* de haies, d'arbres, d'arbustes, formant une haie.
hedging ['hedʒiŋ], *s.* **1.** entretien *m* des haies. **2.** bordure *f*. **3.** (*a*) *Turf:* pari *m* pour et contre; (*b*) *St.Exch:* arbitrage *m*; *U.S:* contrepartie *f*; (*c*) hésitation *f* à prendre des décisions.
hedonic [hi:'dɔnik], *a.* = HEDONISTIC.
hedonics [hi:'dɔniks], *s.pl.* (*usu. with sg. const.*) *Phil:* l'hédonistique *f*.
hedonism ['hi:dənizm], *s. Phil:* hédonisme *m*.
hedonist ['hi:dənist], *s. Phil:* hédoniste *mf*.
hedonistic [hi:də'nistik], *a. Phil:* hédonistique.
hedrocele ['hi:drousi:l], *s. Med:* hédrocèle *f*.
hedychium [hi:ə'dikiəm], *s. Bot:* hedychium *m*.
heebie-jeebies ['hi:bi'dʒi:biz], *s.pl. P:* **to have the h.-j.,** (i) avoir le cafard; (ii) avoir ses nerfs.
heed[1] [hi:d], *s. esp. Lit:* attention *f*, garde *f*, soin *m*; **to give, pay, h. to sth., to s.o.,** faire attention à qch.; prêter (son) attention à qn; **to take h.,** prendre garde; **to take h. of sth.,** tenir compte de qch.; **pay h. to my words,** prenez note de mes paroles; soyez attentif à mes paroles, à ce que je vous dis; **pay no h. to them,** ne faites pas attention à eux; **he takes little h. of your criticisms,** il ne se soucie guère de vos critiques; il ne fait pas grand cas de vos critiques; **to take no h. of sth.,** ne tenir aucun compte de qch.
heed[2], *v.tr. esp. Lit:* faire attention à, prendre garde à, observer, écouter, tenir compte de (qch.); **horse that heeds neither bit nor spur,** cheval *m* qui n'obéit ni au mors ni à l'éperon; **his advice was not heeded,** on n'a tenu aucun compte de ses conseils.
heedful ['hi:dful], *a. Lit:* vigilant, prudent, circonspect; **h. of advice,** attentif aux conseils; **to be h. to do sth., of doing sth.,** être attentif à faire qch.; avoir soin de faire qch.; **we must be h. of the future,** il faut songer à l'avenir.
heedfully ['hi:dfuli], *adv. Lit:* attentivement, avec attention, soigneusement, avec vigilance, prudemment.
heedfulness ['hi:dfulnis], *s. Lit:* attention *f* (**of,** à); soin *m* (**of,** de); vigilance *f*, prudence *f*.
heedless ['hi:dlis], *a.* **1.** étourdi, insouciant, imprudent. **2. to be h. of (sth.),** être inattentif à (ce qui se passe); être sourd à (la plainte de qn); être peu soucieux de (l'avenir, etc.); **h. of public opinion, he went ahead,** sans se soucier de l'opinion il alla de l'avant; **he was always h. of advice,** jamais il n'a écouté les conseils.
heedlessly ['hi:dlisli], *adv.* (agir) étourdiment, à l'étourdie, avec insouciance, imprudemment.
heedlessness ['hi:dlisnis], *s.* inattention *f* (**of,** à); étourderie *f*, insouciance *f*.
hee-haw[1] ['hi:hɔ:], *s.* **1.** hi-han *m*; braiment *m*. **2.** gros rire (bruyant).
hee-haw[2], *v.i.* **1.** braire; faire hi-han. **2.** pouffer de rire.
hee hee ['hi:'hi:], *int.* (*sound of laughter*) hi, hi, hi!
heel[1] [hi:l], *s.* **1.** (*a*) talon *m* (du pied); **h. bone,** calcanéum *m*; **to be under the h. of the invader,** être sous la botte de l'envahisseur; **to have the police at one's heels,** avoir la police à ses trousses; **to tread on, be at, on, s.o.'s heels,** marcher, être, sur les talons de qn; talonner qn; être aux trousses de qn; **to follow close, fast, on s.o.'s heels, to tread on s.o.'s heels,** suivre qn de près; emboîter le pas à qn; **the events tread on each other's heels,** les événements se suivent de près, se précipitent; **famine followed on the heels of war,** la guerre fut suivie de près par la famine; **to show a clean pair of heels, to take to one's heels,** prendre la fuite; tourner les talons; se sauver à toutes jambes; prendre ses jambes à son cou; **he showed us a clean pair of heels,** il nous a échappé; *Ven:* (*of hounds*) **to run h.,** suivre, prendre, le contre-pied; **to lay, clap, s.o. by the heels,** arrêter qn; *F:* pincer qn; mettre qn au bloc; **to be laid by the heels,** être coffré; *Nau: F:* **to have the heels of another ship,** dépasser, enganter, un autre navire; **to turn on one's h.,** pivoter sur ses talons; faire demi-tour; *F:* tourner les talons (sans plus de cérémonie); *F:* **to kick, cool, one's heels,** croquer le marmot; faire le pied de grue; faire le poireau; poireauter; *Mil: P:* astiquer la grille du quartier; **to kick, cool, one's heels in the hall,** se morfondre dans l'antichambre; **he was left to cool his heels for half an hour,** on l'a laissé poireauter pendant une demi-heure; **to kick up one's heels,** sauter de joie; **to come to h.,** (*of dog*) venir derrière à l'ordre; obéir à l'appel; *F:* (*of pers.*) se soumettre; **to bring s.o. to h.,** mater qn; mettre qn au pas; (*b*) talon (d'une chaussure, d'un bas); **high heels, low, heels,** talons hauts, bas; **medium heels,** talons bottier; **stiletto heels,** *U.S:* **spike heels,** talons aiguille; **Louis h.,** talon Louis XV; **rubber h.,** talonnette *f* en caoutchouc; **h. plate,** fer *m* de botte; plaque de talon (de patin); **out at heels,** (bas) troués aux talons; *F:* (*of pers.*) **to be out at heels,** (i) porter des bas percés; être loqueteux; (ii) être dans la dèche; **down at h.,** (soulier) éculé; *F:* (*of pers.*) **to be down at h.,** (i) porter des souliers éculés; traîner la savate; (ii) être dans la dèche; *Geog: F:* **the h. of Italy,** la Terre d'Otrante; le talon de la botte; *Arch:* **h. moulding,** (moulure *f* en) talon droit; (*c*) croûton *m* (de pain); (*d*) *P:* (*pers.*) non-valeur *f*, gouape *f*; **he's a bit of a h.,** c'est une canaille. **2.** *Tchn:* talon (d'outil, d'archet de violon, de crosse de golf, d'un pain, *Nau:* de carène, *Rail:* d'aiguille); queue *f* (du dos d'un livre); pied *m*, caisse *f* (de mât); battement *m* (de couteau genre eustache); diamant *m* (de pince); *Nau:* **h. of the rudder, keel,** talon du gouvernail, de la quille; **h. of a rifle butt,** talon d'une crosse de fusil; **h. plate,** plaque *f* de couche (d'un fusil). **3.** (*a*) *Orn:* éperon *m*, ergot *m* (de coq); (*b*) derrière *m* du sabot (d'un cheval, etc.); (*of horse*) **to fling out its heels,** ruer.
heel[2]. **1.** *v.i.* danser en frappant du talon; taper du talon. **2.** *v.tr.* (*a*) (i) mettre un talon à (un soulier, un bas); (ii) réparer le talon (d'un soulier); refaire le talon (d'un bas); (*b*) *Sp:* armer, éperonner (un coq); (*c*) *Rugby Fb:* talonner (le ballon) pour le sortir de la mêlée; (*d*) suivre (qn) de près, emboîter le pas à (qn); (*e*) (*to dog*) **h.!** au pied! (*f*) *For: Agr:* **to h. in,** mettre en jauge (les jeunes plants).
heel[3], *s. Nau:* bande *f*, gîte *f*, inclinaison *f* (d'un navire); **on the h.,** à la bande; **h. rope,** hale-breu *m inv* (d'un mât, d'une bigue).
heel[4] **(over)** ['hi:l('ouvər)], *v.* **1.** *v.i.* (*a*) (*of ship*) avoir, donner, de la bande; se coucher sur le flanc; pencher sur le côté; prendre de la gîte; gîter; s'incliner; renvoyer; (*b*) (*of aircraft*) s'incliner sur l'aile, donner de la bande. **2.** *v.tr.* mettre (un navire) à la bande; faire coucher (un navire); charger (un navire).
heel-and-toe[1] ['hi:lənd'tou], *a.* **1. a h.-a.-t. dance,** une gigue. **2.** *Sp:* **h.-a.-t. walking,** marche *f* réglementaire (de concours athlétiques).
heel-and-toe[2], *v.tr. F: O:* **to h.-a.-t. it,** faire la route à pied.
heelball ['hi:lbɔ:l], *s. Bootm:* cire *f* à déformer.
heelcap ['hi:lkæp], *s. Bootm:* contrefort *m* du talon (d'un soulier).
heeled ['hi:ld], *a.* **1. h. shoes,** chaussures *f* à talons; (*with adj. prefixed*) **high-h. shoes,** chaussures à hauts talons; **low-h. shoes,** chaussures à talons bas, plats. **2.** (coq) éperonné. **3.** *esp. U.S: P:* (*a*) (**well**) **h.,** riche, plein aux as; (*b*) armé d'un revolver, flingué.
heeler ['hi:lər], *s.* **1.** *Bootm:* poseur *m* de talons. **2.** *U.S: F:* (**ward**) **h.,** homme *m* de confiance, âme damnée (d'un chef de parti).
heeling[1] ['hi:liŋ], *s.* **1.** (*a*) pose *f* du talon (à un soulier, etc.); (*b*) réparation *f* du talon; **soling and h., £2.50,** semelles et talons, ressemelage complet, £2.50. **2.** *Rugby Fb:* talonnage *m*.
heeling[2], *s. Nau:* = HEEL[3]; **h. error** (*of compass*), erreur due à la bande.
heelmaker ['hi:lmeikər], *s. Bootm:* talonnier *m*.
heelpiece ['hi:lpi:s], *s.* **1.** talonnette *f* (d'un bas). **2.** *El:* culasse *f* (d'électro-aimant).
heelpost ['hi:lpoust], *s.* **1.** *Const:* montant (auquel est accrochée une porte ou une barrière). **2.** *Hyd.E:* poteau *m* tourillon (de porte d'écluse).
heeltap ['hi:ltæp], *s.* **1.** *Bootm:* rondelle *f* en cuir (pour talon); hausse *f*; sous-bout *m*, *pl.* sous-bouts. **2.** *pl. F:* **heeltaps,** fonds *m* de verre; **to leave no heeltaps,** faire rubis sur l'ongle; faire cul sec; **no heeltaps!** videz vos

verres! vidons bien les verres! cul sec!

heft[1] [heft], *s. NAm: F:* **1.** poids *m.* **2.** soulèvement *m,* effort *m.* **3. the h. of the crop,** le gros de la récolte.

heft[2], *v.tr. NAm: F:* soupeser (qch.); soulever (qch.) (pour en juger le poids).

hefty ['hefti], *a. F:* **1.** (homme) fort, solide, costaud. **2.** lourd, pesant; **a h. book,** un gros bouquin bien lourd. **3.** gros, important; **a h. bill,** une note de taille; **a h. chunk,** un morceau imposant; **that's a h. job!** comme besogne, ça c'est vraiment quelque chose!

Hegelian [he'gi:liən], *a. & s. Phil:* hégélien, -ienne.

Hegelianism [he'gi:liənizm], *s. Phil:* hégélianisme *m.*

hegemony [hi'geməni], *s.* hégémonie *f.*

hegira [hi'dʒairə], *s.* hégire *f.*

he he ['hi: 'hi:], *int.* (*sound of tittering*) hi, hi, hi!

Heidelberg ['haidlbə:g], *Pr.n. Geog:* Heidelberg; *Paleont:* **H. man,** l'homme *m* d'Heidelberg, de Mauer.

heifer ['hefər], *s.* **1.** génisse *f,* taure *f.* **2.** *P:* (jeune) femme *f.*

heigh [hei], *int.* **1.** hé! **2.** hé, là-bas!

heigh-ho ['hei'hou], *int.* (*a*) ce que c'est que de nous! (*b*) allons-y!

height [hait], *s.* **1.** (*a*) hauteur *f,* élévation *f;* **wall two metres in h.,** mur *m* qui a deux mètres de haut; *Const:* **h. of a stone,** appareil *m* d'une pierre; *Typ:* (*of type*) **h. to paper,** hauteur en papier; (*of vehicle*) **overall h., h. overall,** hauteur totale; (*b*) **h. of an arch,** flèche *f,* montée *f,* d'un arc; **available h., maximum h.** (**of bridge**), hauteur libre (d'un pont); **running h.,** hauteur d'encombrement; *Mec.E:* (*of gears*) **h. above pitch line,** hauteur au-dessus du primitif; (*c*) taille *f,* grandeur *f,* stature *f* (de qn); **full h.,** taille debout; **of average h.,** de taille moyenne; **her heels add to her h.,** ses talons la grandissent. **2.** altitude *f;* **h. above sea level,** altitude au-dessus du niveau de la mer; **situated at a h. of 500 metres,** situé à une altitude de 500 mètres; **barometric h.,** hauteur barométrique; **hypsometric h.,** hauteur hypsométrique; **true h.,** altitude géométrique; *Av:* **cruising h.,** altitude de croisière; **critical h.,** altitude de rétablissement; **h. indicator, finder,** altimètre *m;* **h. factor, figure,** indice *m* d'altitude; **h.-finder radar,** radar *m* d'altimétrie, de site; *Mapm:* **spot h.,** point coté; **h. of burst,** (i) *Artil:* hauteur d'éclatement; (ii) (*of atom bomb*) hauteur d'explosion; **to have a fear of heights, a bad head for heights,** avoir facilement le vertige; **to have a good head for heights,** ne pas avoir le vertige. **3.** (*hill, mountain*) hauteur; éminence *f* (de terrain); **up on the heights,** sur les hauteurs; sur le haut du plateau; en haut sur les collines, sur l'arête. **4.** (*highest point*) apogée *m* (de la fortune, de la gloire); faîte *m* (des grandeurs); comble *m* (de la folie, de l'effronterie); sommet *m* (de l'éloquence); **this is the h. of insolence!** c'est de la plus haute insolence! **it would be the h. of folly to . . .,** ce serait la plus grande folie, le comble de la folie, de . . .; **at the h. of the storm,** au (plus) fort de l'orage; **when the battle was at its h.,** au plus fort de la bataille; **at the h. of her beauty,** dans tout l'éclat de sa beauté; **in the h. of summer,** au cœur, au milieu, de l'été; en plein été; **the season is at its h.,** la saison bat son plein; **prices are higher in the h. of the season,** les prix sont plus élevés en pleine saison; **it's the h. of fashion,** c'est la dernière mode, le dernier cri; **it's the h. of vulgarity,** c'est du dernier vulgaire; **it's the h. of absurdity,** c'est d'un ridicule achevé.

height-adjustable ['haitə'dʒʌstəbl], *a.* réglable en hauteur.

heighten ['haitn]. **1.** *v.tr.* (*a*) surélever, surhausser, rehausser (un mur, un immeuble); augmenter (un prix); (*b*) accroître, augmenter (un plaisir), rendre (un plaisir) plus grand; aggraver (un mal); accentuer (un contraste); relever, faire ressortir (une couleur, la beauté de qch.); renchérir sur (une histoire); **to h. the interest in sth.,** augmenter l'intérêt pour qch.; **illness heightened by anxiety,** maladie aggravée par l'anxiété; **her heightened colour,** l'animation *f* de son teint, son teint animé; *Art:* **sepia drawing heightened with white,** dessin à la sépia rehaussé de blanc. **2.** *v.i.* s'élever; se rehausser; augmenter.

heightening ['haitniŋ], *s.* **1.** surélévation *f,* surhaussement *m* (d'un mur, des prix). **2.** accroissement *m* (d'un plaisir); aggravation *f* (d'un mal); rehaussement *m* (d'une couleur, du teint).

heinous ['heinəs], *a.* (crime) odieux, atroce, abominable; (accusation) odieuse; **to render an offence more h.,** aggraver une offense.

heinously ['heinəsli], *adv.* odieusement, atrocement, abominablement.

heinousness ['heinəsnis], *s.* énormité *f* (d'une action, d'un crime, d'un péché); atrocité *f* (d'un crime).

heir ['ɛər], *s.* héritier *m;* **to be h. to a relative, to an estate,** être l'héritier, le légataire, d'un parent, le légataire d'une propriété; **the sole h. of his body,** son unique héritier; **to fall h. to a property,** hériter d'un bien; *Lit:* **flesh is h. to many ills,** l'humanité a hérité de bien des maux; **h. apparent,** (i) *Jur:* héritier présomptif (dont le droit de succession ne peut être compromis par la naissance d'aucun autre héritier); (ii) *F:* dauphin *m* (d'un homme politique, etc.); **h. presumptive,** héritier présomptif (sauf naissance d'un héritier en ligne directe); **h.-at-law,** *pl.* **heirs-at-law, rightful h.,** héritier légitime.

heirdom ['ɛədəm], *s.* **1.** droit *m* de succession. **2.** *A: & Lit:* héritage *m.*

heiress ['ɛəres], *s.f.* héritière.

heirless ['ɛəlis], *a.* sans héritier.

heirloom ['ɛəlu:m], *s.* meuble *m,* bijou *m,* de famille.

heirship ['ɛəʃip], *s.* qualité *f,* droit *m,* d'héritier.

hejira [hi'dʒairə], *s.* = HEGIRA.

Helen ['helin], *Pr.n.f.* Hélène; *Myth:* **H. of Troy,** Hélène de Troie.

Helena ['helinə], *Pr.n.f.* Hélène.

helenin ['helənin], *s. Pharm:* hélénine *f.*

helenium [hi'li:niəm], *s. Bot:* helenium *m.*

heliacal [hi'laiəkl], *a. Astr:* héliaque.

helianthemum [hi:li'ænθiməm], *s. Bot:* hélianthème *m.*

helianthin(e) [hi:li'ænθin, -θain], *s. Ch:* hélianthine *f.*

helianthus [hi:li'ænθəs], *s. Bot:* hélianthe *m,* tournesol *m.*

heliborne ['helibɔ:n], *a. Av:* héliporté.

helical ['helik(ə)l], *a.* **1.** *Conch:* **h. shell,** hélice *f,* coquille contournée. **2.** *Mec.E:* (*of gear, etc.*) hélicoïdal, -aux; (*of spring*) hélicoïde, en hélice, en spirale, spiralé; **double h. gear,** engrenage *m* à chevrons.

helically ['helikəli], *adv.* en spirale, en hélice.

Helicidae [he'lisidi:], *s.pl. Moll:* hélicidés *m.*

heliciform [he'lisifɔ:m], *a. Nat.Hist:* héliciforme.

helicina [he'lisinə], *s. Moll:* hélicine *f.*

helicoid ['helikɔid]. **1.** *a. Nat.Hist: Mth:* (*also* **helicoidal**) hélicoïde; hélicoïdal, -aux; **h. motion,** mouvement *m* hélicoïdal. **2.** *s. Mth:* hélicoïde *m.*

Helicon ['helikɔn]. **1.** *Pr.n. A.Geog:* l'Hélicon *m.* **2.** *s. Mus:* hélicon (contrebasse *f* des musiciens montés).

Heliconiidae [helikɔ'ni:idi:], *s.pl. Ent:* hélicon(i)ides *m.*

helicopter ['helikɔptər], *s. Av:* hélicoptère *m;* **single-rotor h., tandem-rotor h.,** hélicoptère à un rotor, à deux rotors en tandem; **pressure-jet h.,** hélicoptère à éjection d'air comprimé en bout de pales; **heavy-lift h.,** hélicoptère-grue *m, pl.* hélicoptères-grues.

helicotrema [helikou'tri:mə], *s. Anat:* hélicotrème *m.*

Heligoland ['heligoulænd], *Pr.n. Geog:* Héligoland *m.*

hello[1,2] ['hi:liou], *s. & v.tr. F: O:* = HELIOGRAPH[1,2].

helio-[3] ['hi:liou, hi:li'ɔ], *comb.fm.* hélio-.

heliocentric [hi:liou'sentrik], *a. Astr:* héliocentrique.

heliochromy ['hi:lioukroumi], *s. Phot:* héliochromie *f;* photographie *f* en couleurs.

Heliodinidae [hi:liou'dinidi:], *s.pl. Ent:* héliodinides *m.*

heliodor ['hi:lioudɔ:r], *s. Miner:* héliodore *m.*

Heliodorus [hi:liou'dɔ:rəs], *Pr.n.m. Gr.Lit:* Héliodore.

helio-electric ['hi:lioui'lektrik], *a.* hélio-électrique, *pl.* hélio-électriques.

Heliogabalus [hi:liou'gæbələs], *Pr.n.m. Rom.Hist:* Héliogabale, Élagabale.

heliogram ['hi:liougræm], *s.* héliogramme *m.*

heliograph[1] ['hi:liəgræf], *s.* **1.** (*a*) héliographe *m* (de signalisation); héliostat *m;* (*b*) message envoyé par héliographe. **2.** *Phot: O:* héliographe. **3.** *Phot.Engr:* héliogravure *f.*

heliograph[2], *v.tr.* **1.** *Mil:* communiquer (un message) par héliographe. **2.** *Phot: O:* photographier (le soleil) au moyen de l'héliographe. **3.** *O:* reproduire (un dessin, etc.) par héliogravure.

heliographic [hi:liə'græfik], *a. O:* héliographique.

heliography [hi:li'ɔgrəfi], *s. O:* **1.** *Phot:* héliographie *f.* **2.** *Phot.Engr:* héliogravure *f.*

heliogravure [hi:liougrə'vju(ə)r], *s. O:* héliogravure *f;* phototypogravure *f;* photogravure *f.*

heliolite ['hi:lioulait], *s. Miner:* héliolite *f.*

heliometer [hi:li'ɔmitər], *s. Astr:* héliomètre *m.*

heliometric(al) [hi:liou'metrik(l)], *a. Astr:* héliométrique.

heliophilic, heliophilous [hi:li'ɔfilik, 'ɔfiləs], *a.* héliophile.

helioscope ['hi:liəskoup], *s. Astr:* hélioscope *m.*

heliostat ['hi:liəstæt], *s. Astr: Surv:* héliostat *m.*

heliotherapy [hi:liou'θerəpi], *s.* héliothérapie *f.*

heliotrope ['hi:liətroup]. **1.** *s.* (*a*) *Bot:* héliotrope *m;* **winter h.,** héliotrope d'hiver; (*b*) *Miner:* héliotrope, jaspe sanguin, sanguine *f.* **2.** *a.* héliotrope *inv.*

heliotropic [hi:liə'trɔpik], *a. Bot:* héliotropique.

heliotropin [hi:li'ɔtrəpin], *s. Ch:* héliotropine *f.*

heliotropism [hi:li'ɔtrəpizm], *s. Bot:* héliotropisme *m.*

heliotype ['hi:lioutaip], *s. Phot.Engr: O:* **1.** héliotypie *f.* **2.** héliotype *m.*

Heliozoa [hi:liou'zouə], *s.pl. Prot:* héliozoaires *m.*

heliport ['helipɔ:t], *s.* héliport *m.*

helium ['hi:liəm], *s. Ch:* hélium *m;* **h. spectrum,** spectre *m* de l'hélium; **h. nucleus,** noyau *m* d'hélium; hélion *m.*

helix, *pl.* **helices** ['hi:liks, 'heliks; 'helisi:z], *s.* **1.** (*a*) *Mth:* hélice *f;* (*b*) *Arch: etc:* spirale *f;* volute *f;* hélice; (*c*) *El:* spire *f* (de bobine). **2.** *Anat:* hélix *m,* rebord *m,* aile *f,* ourlet *m* (de l'oreille). **3.** *Moll:* (*snail*) hélice, escargot *m,* colimaçon *m.*

hell [hel], *s.* **1.** *Myth:* les enfers *m.* **2.** (*a*) enfer *m;* **in heaven and h.,** au ciel et en enfer; **h. is let loose,** les diables sont déchaînés; *F:* **it was (all) h. let loose,** ce fut le sabbat déchaîné; c'était infernal; *F:* **this place is a h. on earth, just plain h.,** cet endroit est un vrai enfer; **to make s.o.'s life h., a h. on earth,** faire un enfer de la vie de qn; *F:* **it's as cold as h.,** il fait un froid de canard, de loup; (*b*) (i) *F:* **(oh) h.!** zut alors! *P:* (*not in polite use*) **(oh) bloody h.!** merde! *F:* **hell's bells (and buckets of blood)!** (sacré) nom de nom! *P:* **go to h.!** va(-t-en) au diable! **to h. with it!** au diable que tout cela! **to h. with him!** qu'il aille au diable! **get the h., get to h., out of here!** fiche-moi le camp d'ici! *F:* **h., I don't know,** diable, je n'en sais rien; *P:* **would he go? would he h.!** partir? le bougre ne bougeait pas! *P:* **like h. I will!** jamais de la vie! *F:* **I feel like h.,** je me sens au cent mille dessous; *F:* **to give s.o. h., a h. of a time,** faire passer un mauvais quart d'heure à qn; *P:* **there'll be h. to pay,** on va être engueulé(s); ça va barder; *F:* **to do sth. for the h. of it,** faire qch. histoire de rire, pour se payer une tranche; *F:* **come h. or high water,** advienne que pourra; *F:* **to work, run, like h.,** travailler, courir, comme un dératé; *F:* **to go h. for leather, at the h. of a speed, a lick,** galoper à toute bride, ventre à terre; courir avec le feu au derrière; conduire comme si le diable était à ses trousses; **like a bat out of h.,** à une vitesse vertigineuse; *P:* **to knock h. out of s.o.,** battre qn comme plâtre; bourrer qn de coups; (ii) *F:* **a h. of a price,** un prix salé; *P:* **it's a, the, h. of a** (*occ. written* **helluva**) **bind,** c'est rudement embêtant; *P:* **you've got a, the, h. of a (helluva) nerve!** tu as un culot du diable! **a h. of a row,** (α) un bruit d'enfer, de tous les diables; un vacarme infernal; (β) une engueulade maison; **he'll make a h. of a good sailor,** il fera un marin du tonnerre (de Dieu); (iii) *P:* **what the h. do you think you're doing?** que diable es-tu en train de fabriquer? **what in hell's name is that?** qu'est-ce que c'est que ce sacré truc? **what the h. (does it matter, do I care)?** diable si ça me regarde! **who the h. are you?** mais qui diable êtes vous? **who the h. d'you think you are anyway?** tu te prends pour qui, nom du diable? **why the h. doesn't he belt up?** pourquoi diable ne la ferme-t-il pas? **3.** (*gambling den*) tripot *m.*

helladic [he'lædik], *a. Gr.Hist:* helladique.

helladotherium [helədou'θiəriəm], *s. Paleont:* helladothérium *m.*

hellandite ['heləndait], *s. Miner:* hellandite *f.*

hellanodic [helə'noudik], *s. Gr.Ant:* hellanodice *m,* hellanodique *m.*

Hellas ['helæs], *Pr.n. A.Geog:* l'Hellade *f.*

hellbender ['helbendər], *s.* **1.** *U.S: Amph:* ménopome *m.* **2.** *P:* (*a*) ribote *f;* (*b*) riboteur *m,* noceur *m,* débauché *m.*

hellbent ['helbent], *F:* **1.** *a.* (*a*) d'une détermination féroce, têtue; **to be h. on doing sth.,** vouloir à tout prix faire qch.; (*b*) (allure) infernale. **2.** *adv.* (conduire, etc.) à une allure infernale, diabolique.

hellborn ['helbɔ:n], *a.* sorti de l'enfer; infernal, -aux.

hellbox ['helbɔks], *s. F: Typ:* boîte *f* à défets.

hellbroth ['helbrɔθ], *s. F:* brouet *m* de sorcières.

hellcat ['helkæt], *s. F:* (*a*) sorcière *f,* mégère *f;* (*b*) femme cruelle, mesquine; mégère.

helleboraster [helibɔ:'ræstər], *s. Bot:* ellébore *m* fétide.

hellebore ['helibɔ:r], *s. Bot:* ellébore *m,* varaire *m or f;* **stinking h.,** ellébore fétide; pied-de-griffon *m, pl.* pieds-de-griffon; patte-de-griffon *f, pl.* pattes-de-griffon; **black h.,** ellébore noir; rose *f* de Noël; **white h., false h.,** vératre *m;* **green h.,** herbe *f* à sétons.

helleborine ['helibɔ'ri:n], *s. Bot:* helléborine *f,* sérapias *m.*

Hellene ['heli:n], *s.* Hellène *mf;* **King of the Hellenes,** roi *m* de Grèce.

Hellenic [he'li:nik]. **1.** *a.* (race *f*) hellène; (langue *f,* histoire *f*) hellénique. **2.** *s.pl.* **hellenics,** histoire grecque; littérature grecque.

Hellenica (the) [ðəhe'li:nikə], *s.pl. Gr.Lit:* les Helléniques *f* (de Xénophon).

Hellenism ['helinizm], *s.* hellénisme *m.*

Hellenist ['helinist], *s.* helléniste *mf.*

Hellenistic [heli'nistik], *a.* (langue *f,* période *f*) hellénistique.

Hellenization [helinai'zeiʃ(ə)n], *s.* hellénisation *f.*

Hellenize ['helinaiz]. **1.** *v.tr.* helléniser. **2.** *v.i.* (*a*) helléniser; (*b*) s'helléniser.

Hellenized ['helinaizd], *a. Hist:* **H. Jew,** helléniste *m*; juif hellénisant.

heller[1] ['helər], *s. Num:* heller *m.*

heller[2], *s. NAm: P:* = HELLION.

Hellespont (the) [ðə'helispɔnt], *Pr.n. A.Geog:* l'Hellespont *m.*

hellfire ['hel'faiər], *s.* feu *m*, tourments *mpl*, de l'enfer.

hellhole ['helhoul], *s.* **1.** l'abîme *m* de l'enfer. **2.** *F:* endroit mal famé, coupe-gorge *m inv.*

hellhound ['helhaund], *s.* chien *m* de l'enfer, suppôt *m* de Satan.

hellion ['heliən], *s. NAm: F:* (*a*) vaurien *m*, sale type *m*, fripouille *f*; (*b*) enfant terrible, petit diable.

hellish ['heliʃ], *a.* (*a*) infernal, -aux; d'enfer; diabolique; (*b*) *F:* **h. weather,** un temps du diable, infernal; **it was (simply) h.,** c'était infernal.

hellishly ['heliʃli], *adv. F:* infernalement, diaboliquement; **h. cold,** diaboliquement froid.

hellishness ['heliʃnis], *s.* méchanceté *f* diabolique; **the h. of war,** l'horreur *f* de la guerre.

hello [he'lou], *int.* (*a*) bonjour! (*b*) (*calling attention*) **h. there, wake up!** holà! debout! hé, là-bas, debout! (*c*) (*indicating surprise*) **h., is that you?** tiens! c'est vous! (*d*) *Tp:* allô! *U.S: F:* **h. girl,** téléphoniste *f.*

helluva ['heləvə], *adj.phr. P:* see HELL 2(*b*).

hellweed ['helwi:d], *s. Bot: F:* (*a*) cuscute *f*; (*b*) liseron *m* (des haies).

helm[1] [helm], *s.* (*a*) *A:* heaume *m*; (*b*) *Meteor: Dial:* **h. cloud,** nuage *m* qui coiffe un pic (*esp.* dans la région des Lacs).

helm[2], *s. Nau:* barre *f* (du gouvernail); gouvernail *m*, timon *m*; **the man at the h.,** (i) l'homme de barre; (ii) l'homme qui tient le gouvernail, qui dirige l'entreprise; **to be at the h.,** être à la barre; tenir la barre; **to shift the h.,** changer la barre; **to put the h. hand over,** mettre la barre en grand; **steady the h.!** droite la barre! **down (with the) h.!** la barre dessous! **up (with the) h.!** la barre au vent! **h. (angle) indicator,** axiomètre *m*; **h. hole, port,** jaumière *f*; **the h. of the State,** le timon de l'État; **to take the h.,** prendre la direction des affaires; prendre l'affaire en main.

helmet ['helmit], *s.* **1.** (*a*) casque *m* (de soldat, de pompier, etc.); *Mil:* **steel h. (1914–18),** casque de tranchées; *F:* bourguignotte *f*; **tropical h.,** casque colonial; couvre-nuque *m inv*; **crash h.,** casque protecteur, de protection; *F:* **Blue helmets,** Casques bleus (troupes de l'O.N.U.); (*b*) *A.Arm: Her:* heaume *m*; **close h.,** armet *m.* **2.** *Bot: Conch:* casque (de la corolle, etc.).

helmeted ['helmitid], *a. Mil: etc:* portant un casque; casqué.

helmetflower ['helmitflauər], *s. Bot:* aconit napel *m*; *F:* char *m* de Vénus.

helminth ['helminθ], *s. Ann:* helminthe *m*; ver intestinal.

helminthagogic [helminθə'gɔdʒik], *a.*, **helminthagogue** [hel'minθəgɔg], **helminthic** [hel'minθik], *a.* & *s. Pharm:* (remède *m*) helminthagogue (*m*); anthelminthique (*m*); vermifuge (*m*).

helminthiasis [helmin'θaiəsis], *s. Med: Vet:* helminthiase *f.*

helminthoid [hel'minθɔid], *a.* helminthoïde, vermiforme.

helminthologist [helmin'θɔlədʒist], *s. Med: etc:* helminthologiste *m.*

helminthology [helmin'θɔlədʒi], *s. Med: etc:* helminthologie *f.*

helmsman, *pl.* **-men** ['helmzmən], *s.m. Nau:* homme de barre; timonier.

Helobiae [hi'loubii:], *s.pl. Bot:* hélobiées *f*, hélobiales *m.*

helobious [hi'loubiəs], *a. Bot:* hélobié.

Helodermatidae [hiloudə'mætidi:], *s.pl. Rept:* hélodermatidés *m.*

helopeltis [helou'peltis], *s. Ent:* hélopeltis *m.*

helophyte ['heloufait], *s. Bot:* hélophyte *f.*

helot ['helət, 'hi:-], *s.* **1.** *Gr.Ant:* ilote *m.* **2.** serf, serve; esclave *m.*

helotism ['helətizm], *s.* **1.** *Gr.Ant:* ilotisme *m.* **2.** servage *m.* **3.** *Nat.Hist:* hélotisme *m.*

help[1] [help], *s.* **1.** aide *f*, assistance *f*, secours *m*; **mutual h.,** entraide *f*, secours réciproque; **with the h. of a friend,** avec l'aide d'un ami; **with God's h.,** Dieu aidant; grâce à Dieu; **with the h. of time,** le temps aidant; **to shout for h.,** crier au secours; appeler à l'aide; **we shall have to get h.,** il nous faut nous faire aider; *Aut:* (*for breakdown*) il faut appeler le garage, le service de dépannage; **it's very difficult to get h. these days,** il est très difficile de nos jours (i) de se faire aider, (ii) de trouver une femme de ménage; **to be without h., (in the house),** ne pas avoir de femme de ménage; **past h.,** perdu; **can I be of (any) h.?** puis-je vous aider, vous être d'aucun secours? **he always tries to be of h.,** il veut toujours essayer d'aider les gens; **to promise one's h.,** promettre son concours, son aide; **he was elected with h. from the left,** il a été élu avec des appoints de la gauche. **2. to come to s.o.'s h.,** venir au secours de qn, porter secours à qn; donner un coup de main à qn. **3. there's no h. for it,** il n'y a pas de remède, la chose est sans remède; c'est irrémédiable; il n'y a rien à faire. **4.** (*a*) **to be a h. to s.o.,** être d'un grand secours à qn; rendre service à qn; **he was a great h. to me,** il m'a beaucoup aidé; **the medicine was a great h.,** le remède m'a beaucoup soulagé, aidé; (*b*) (*pers.*) (i) aide *mf*; (**domestic, daily**) **h.,** femme *f* de ménage; **home h.,** aide ménagère; **mother's h.,** aide familiale; (ii) *esp. NAm:* (*pl.* **help**) ouvrier, -ière; employé, -ée; **he treats his h. well,** il traite bien ses employés, ses ouvriers.

help[2], *v.*

I. *v.tr.* **1.** (*a*) aider, secourir, assister; venir en aide à (qn); donner son appui, prêter son concours, à (qn); seconder (qn); **that won't h. you,** cela ne vous servira à rien, ne vous sera d'aucun secours; **can I, may I, h. you?** puis-je vous aider? **nobody can h. you,** personne ne peut vous aider; **God h. you!** (que) Dieu vous aide! **so h. me God!** que Dieu me juge si je ne dis pas la vérité! en mon âme et conscience! **he never tries to h.,** il ne fait jamais rien pour aider (qui que ce soit); **come and h. me,** venez m'aider, me donner un coup de main; **I got a friend to h. me,** je me suis fait aider par un ami; **I'll h. you with the luggage,** je vais vous aider à porter les bagages; **to h. s.o. to do sth.,** aider qn à faire qch.; **h. me to find the answer,** aidez-moi à trouver la solution, la réponse; **he helped the blind man to cross, across, the street,** il a aidé l'aveugle à traverser la rue; **to h. s.o. into, out of, a car, on (to), out of, off, a train,** aider qn à monter dans une voiture, un train, à descendre d'une voiture, d'un train; **he helped the old lady up, down, the stairs,** il a aidé la vieille dame à monter, à descendre, l'escalier; **he helped me on, off, with my coat,** il m'a aidé à mettre, à enlever, mon manteau; **h. me over the wall,** aide-moi à franchir le mur; **she fell and he ran to h. her up,** elle est tombée et il s'est précipité pour l'aider à se relever; **to h. one another,** s'entraider; *F:* **he knows how to h. himself,** il sait se tirer d'affaire; *Prov:* **God helps him who helps himself,** aide-toi et le ciel t'aidera; **to h. wash up,** aider à faire la vaisselle; **h.!** au secours! **h.! I'm late!** mon Dieu! je suis en retard! (*b*) faciliter (la digestion, le progrès); **it helped us to finish the job quickly,** cela nous a aidés à, nous a permis de, terminer rapidement le travail; **all this helps towards increasing prices,** tout cela aide à, contribue à, l'augmentation des prix; **that doesn't h. the situation, doesn't h. much,** cela ne guérit rien, ne nous avance pas; *Iron:* **to h. matters, we had a puncture,** ce qui n'était pas pour arranger les choses, nous avons eu une crevaison. **2.** (*at table*) servir (qn); **to h. s.o. to soup, to wine,** servir du potage, verser du vin, à qn; **h. yourself,** servez-vous; **I helped myself to mustard,** j'ai pris de la moutarde; **he helped himself to a good quarter of the tart,** il s'est servi d'un bon quart de la tarte; **h.-yourself store,** magasin *m* libre-service; *F:* **to h. oneself to sth.,** voler, prendre, chiper, qch. **3.** (*with negation expressed or implied*) (*a*) empêcher; **things we cannot h. (happening),** choses qu'on ne saurait empêcher; **I can't h. the rain,** ce n'est pas (de) ma faute s'il pleut; je ne peux pas empêcher la pluie; **I can't h. it,** je n'y peux rien; **I can't h. it if he's annoyed,** ce n'est pas (de) ma faute s'il se fâche; **one can't h. one's nature,** on ne peut pas changer son caractère; **it can't be helped!** tant pis! on n'y peut rien! il n'y rien à faire; **how can I h. it?** que voulez-vous que j'y fasse? qu'y faire? on ne peut pas faire autrement; (*b*) s'empêcher, se défendre (de faire qch.); **I can't h. laughing,** je ne peux pas m'empêcher de rire; **I can't h. it,** c'est plus fort que moi; **I can't very well h. accepting,** il m'est impossible de ne pas accepter; **one can't h. loving her,** on ne peut pas se défendre de l'aimer; **I can't h. wishing you had told me before,** si seulement vous me l'aviez dit plus tôt! (*c*) **don't be away longer than you can h.,** tâchez d'être absent le moins de temps possible; **he doesn't do more than he can h.,** il ne fait que le strict nécessaire, *F:* il ne se foule pas outre mesure.

II. (*compound verb*) **help out,** *v.tr.* aider (qn) à sortir d'une difficulté; tirer (qn) d'embarras; dépanner (qn); suppléer à (des approvisionnements insuffisants); parer à l'insuffisance de (qch.); **these imports will h. us out until the new crop is ready,** ces importations vont nous dépanner jusqu'à la moisson; **last Sunday she ran out of butter but I was able to h. her out,** dimanche dernier elle était sans beurre mais j'ai pu la dépanner.

helper ['helpər], *s.* **1.** aide *mf*; assistant, -ante; auxiliaire *mf*; **God being my h.,** Dieu aidant; avec l'aide de Dieu. **2.** *Rail:* **h. (engine),** machine *f* de secours.

helpful ['helpful], *a.* **1.** (personne *f*) secourable, serviable; **he always tries to be h.,** il essaie toujours de rendre service. **2.** (livre *m*, etc.) utile; (remède *m*) salutaire; (avis *m*) utile, salutaire; **be a little more h.,** donnez-vous la peine de nous aider; **the dictionary is not a bit h.,** le dictionnaire ne sert pas à grand-chose.

helpfully ['helpfuli], *adv.* utilement; **he said h., not very h., that . . .,** il a dit, ce qui nous aidait, ce qui ne nous aidait guère, que . . .

helpfulness ['helpfulnis], *s.* **1.** serviabilité *f.* **2.** utilité *f*, aide *f.*

helping[1] ['helpiŋ], *a.* **to lend a h. hand,** prêter son aide; donner un coup d'épaule; pousser à la roue; **to give a h. hand to s.o.,** prêter son aide à qn; donner un coup de main à qn; prêter la main à qn; tendre une main secourable à qn.

helping[2], *s.* portion *f* (de nourriture); **two helpings of soup,** deux assiettées *f* de soupe; **I had two helpings, a second h.,** j'en ai redemandé; j'en ai repris; (*in restaurant*) **second h.,** portion supplémentaire.

helpless ['helplis], *a.* **1.** (orphelin, etc.) sans ressource, sans appui, délaissé; **h. and hopeless,** sans ressource et sans espoir. **2.** (*a*) faible, impuissant; réduit à l'impuissance; **I am h. in the matter,** je n'y puis rien; il n'y a rien à faire; **h. and speechless (with astonishment),** bras ballants et bouche bée; *F:* **he's one of the h. sort,** il n'a aucune initiative; il manque d'initiative, de ressource; (*b*) **h. ship,** navire désemparé.

helplessly ['helplisli], *adv.* **1.** sans ressource. **2.** faiblement; sans faire preuve d'aucune initiative, d'aucune ressource.

helplessness ['helplisnis], *s.* **1.** abandon *m*, délaissement *m.* **2.** faiblesse *f*, impuissance *f*; manque *m* d'énergie, de force; manque d'initiative, de ressource.

helpmate ['helpmeit], *s.* **1.** *O:* aide *mf*, collaborateur, -trice. **2.** *A:* = HELPMEET.

helpmeet ['helpmi:t], *s. A:* compagnon *m*, compagne *f*; *esp.* épouse *f.*

helter(-)skelter ['heltər'skeltər]. **1.** *adv.* (courir, fuir) pêle-mêle, en désordre, à la débandade; (*of one pers.*) **to run h. s.,** courir par bonds désordonnés. **2.** *a.* **h.-sk. flight,** fuite désordonnée; débandade *f*; sauve-qui-peut *m inv.* **3.** *s.* (*a*) tohu-bohu *m*, pêle-mêle *m inv*, débandade *f*; (*b*) toboggan *m* (dans une foire).

helve[1] [helv], *s.* manche *m* (d'une hache, d'un marteau); **h. ring,** bague *f* (de marteau de forge); hurasse *m* (de pioche, etc.).

helve[2], *v.tr.* emmancher, monter (une hache, etc.).

Helvetia [hel'vi:ʃə], *Pr.n. Hist: Geog:* l'Helvétie *f.*

Helvetian [hel'vi:ʃ(ə)n]. **1.** *Hist: Geog:* (*a*) *a.* helvétien; *A.Hist:* helvète; (*b*) *s.* Helvétien, -ienne. **2.** *a.* & *s. Geol:* helvétien (*m*).

Helvetic [hel'vetik], *a.* (canton *m*, *Hist:* république *f*) helvétique.

Helvetii [hel'vi:ʃiai], *s.pl. A.Hist:* **the H.,** les Helvètes *m.*

helvin(e) ['helvin, -vain], **helvite** ['helvait], *s. Miner:* helvine *f.*

hem[1] [hem], *s.* **1.** bord *m* (d'un vêtement). **2.** ourlet *m* (d'un mouchoir, etc.); **false h.,** faux ourlet; **plain h.,** ourlet simple; **stitched h.,** ourlet piqué; **openwork h.,** ourlet à jour.

hem[2], *v.tr.* **1.** (*a*) border, mettre un bord à (un vêtement); (*b*) *Nau:* gainer (une voile). **2.** ourler (un mouchoir, du drap). **3. to h. in,** entourer, cerner (l'ennemi); investir (une place); **mountains that h. in the valley,** montagnes *f* qui enferment la vallée; **mansion hemmed in by small houses,** château entouré de maisonnettes; **garden hemmed in by walls,** jardin enclavé entre des murs; **hemmed in by high mountains,** enserré entre de hautes montagnes.

hem[3], *int.* hem!

hem[4], *v.i.* **1.** faire hem, hum; tousser un coup; toussoter. **2. to h. and haw,** (i) toussoter; bredouiller, bafouiller; (ii) hésiter (à prendre une décision, etc.).

hem(a)- ['hi:m(ə)], **hemato-** ['hi:mətou], *comb.fm.* = HAEM(A)-, HAEMATO-.

he-man, *pl.* **-men** ['hi:mæn, -men], *s.m. F:* homme dominateur, homme viril; **a real he-m.,** un beau mâle.

hemelytral [he'melitr(ə)l], *a. Ent:* (aile) hémélytre.

hemelytron, *pl.* **-tra** [he'melitrɔn, -trə], *s. Ent:* hémélytre *f.*

hemeralope ['hemərəloup], *s. Med:* nyctalope *mf.*

hemeralopia [hemərə'loupiə], *s. Med:* nyctalopie *f.*

hemeralopic [hemərə'loupik], *a. Med:* nyctalope, nyctalopique.

hemeraphonia [hemərə'founiə], *s. Med:* émérophonie *f.*

hemerobius [hemə'roubiəs], *s. Ent:* hémérobe *m.*

hemerocallis [hemərou'kælis], *s. Bot:* hémérocalle *f*, hémérocallis *m*.

hemerology [hemə'rɔlədʒi], *s.* hémérologie *f*.

hemerotemperature [hemərou'temp(ə)rətjər], *s. Bot:* hémérotempérature *f*.

hemi- ['hemi], *pref.* hémi-.

hemi-acetal [hemi'æsit(ə)l], *s. Ch:* hémiacétal *m*.

hemiageusia [hemiæ'gju:ziə], *s. Med:* hémiagueusie *f*.

hemialgia [hemi'ældʒiə], *s. Med:* hémialgie *f*.

hemianaesthesia [hemiænis'θi:ziə], *s. Med:* hémianesthésie *f*.

hemianopsia, hemianopia [hemiə'nɔpsiə, -'noupiə], *s. Med:* hémianop(s)ie *f*.

hemiatrophy [hemi'ætrəfi], *s. Med:* hémiatrophie *f*.

hemiballismus [hemibæ'lizməs], *s. Med:* hémichorée *f*, hémiballisme *m*.

hemicellulose [hemi'seljulouz], *s. Bio-Ch:* hémicellulose *f*.

hemicephalic, hemicephalous [hemise'fælik, -'sefələs], *a.* hemicéphalique.

Hemichorda(ta) [hemi'kɔ:də, -kɔ:'deitə], *s.pl. Nat.Hist:* hémic(h)ordés *m*.

hemicrania [hemi'kreiniə], *s. Med:* hémicranie *f*, migraine *f*.

hemicryptophyte [hemi'kriptoufait], *s. Bot:* hémicryptophyte *f*.

hemicrystalline [hemi'kristəlain], *a.* hémicristallin, semi-cristallin.

hemicycle ['hemisaikl], *s. Arch:* hémicycle *m*.

hemicyclic [hemi'saiklik], *a.* hémicyclique.

hemicylindrical [hemisi'lindrik(ə)l], *a.* hémicylindrique.

hemidemisemiquaver ['hemi'demi'semikweivər], *s. Mus:* quadruple croche *f*.

hemidrosis [hemi'drousis], *s. Med:* hémidrose *f*.

hemihedral [hemi'hi:drəl], *a. Cryst:* hémièdre, hémiédrique, défectif.

hemihedric [hemi'hi:drik], *a. Cryst:* hémiédrique.

hemihedrism [hemi'hi:drizm], *s. Cryst:* hémiédrie *f*.

hemihedron [hemi'hi:drən], *s. Cryst:* hémièdre *m*.

Hemimetabola [hemime'tæbələ], *s.pl. Ent:* hémimétaboles *m*.

hemimetabolic, hemimetabolous [hemime'tæbəlik, -'tæbələs], *a. Ent:* hémimétabole.

hemin ['hi:min], *s. Bio-Ch:* hémine *f*.

hemione ['hemioun], *s. Z:* hémione *m*.

hemiopia [hemi'oupiə], *s. Med:* hémiopie *f*.

hemiparasite [hemi'pærəsait], *s. Biol:* hémiparasite *m*.

hemiparesis [hemi'pærisis], *s. Med:* hémiparésie *f*.

hemiplegia [hemi'pli:dʒiə], *s. Med:* hémiplégie *f*.

hemiplegic [hemi'pli:dʒik], *a. & s. Med:* hémiplégique (*mf*).

hemipode ['hemipoud], *s. Orn:* **(Andalusian) h.,** turnix *m*, (d'Andalousie).

Hemiptera [he'miptərə], *s.pl. Ent:* hémiptères *m*, hémiptéroïdes *m*.

hemipteral [he'miptərəl], *a. Ent:* hémiptère.

hemipteran [he'miptərən], *a. & s. Ent:* hémiptère (*m*).

hemipterous [he'miptərəs], *a. Ent:* hémiptère.

hemisphere ['hemisfiər], *s.* hémisphère *m*; *Geog:* **the northern, southern, h.,** l'hémisphère nord, boréal; l'hémisphère sud, austral; *Anat:* **the cerebral hemispheres,** les hémisphères du cerveau.

hemispherectomy [hemisfə'rektəmi], *s. Surg:* hémisphérectomie *f*.

hemispheric(al) [hemi'sferik(l)], *a.* hémisphérique.

hemispheroid [hemi'sferɔid], *s.* hémisphéroïde *m*.

hemispheroïdal [hemisfe'rɔidl], *a.* hémisphéroïde.

hemistich ['hemistik], *s. Pros:* hémistiche *m*.

hemitrope ['hemitroup], **hemitropic** [hemi'trɔpik], *a. Cryst:* (feldspath) hémitrope, maclé.

hemitropism [he'mitroupizm], *s. Cryst:* hémitropie *f*.

hemixis [hi:'miksis], *s. Biol:* hémixie *f*.

hemline ['hemlain], *s. Dressm:* hauteur *f* de l'ourlet.

hemlock ['hemlɔk], *s. Bot:* **1.** ciguë *f*; *F:* fenouil *m* sauvage; **water h.,** ciguë aquatique, ciguë vireuse, cicutaire *f* aquatique; *Pharm:* **containing h.,** cicuté. **2. h. fir, h. spruce,** sapin *m* du Canada; sapin-ciguë *m*, *pl.* sapins-ciguë; tsuga *m*; **ground h.,** if *m* du Canada; **h. pitch,** exsudat *m*, résine *f*, du tsuga.

hemmer ['hemər], *s.* **1.** (*device*) (*a*) ourleur *m* (de machine à coudre); (*b*) *Metalw:* ourleur. **2.** (*pers.*) ourleuse *f*.

hemming, *s. Needlew:* point *m* d'ourlet.

hemo- ['hi:mou], *comb.fm. See* HAEMO-.

hemp [hemp], *s.* **1.** (*a*) *Bot:* chanvre *m*; **h. field,** chènevière *f*; (*b*) *Tex:* chanvre, filasse *f*; **h. (cloth),** tissu *m* de chanvre; **rope made of the finest h.,** cordage *m* de premier brin; **h. brake, breaker,** broie *f*; **h. comb,** échanvroir *m*; **h. kiln,** haloir *m*, hâloir *m*; **h. dresser,** chanvrier, -ière; *F: A:* **to stretch the h.,** être pendu. **2.** *Bot:* **Bengal h.,** crotalaire *f*, chanvre du Bengale; **African h.,** (i) (*also* **bowstring h.**) chanvre d'Afrique, sansevière *f*; (ii) sparmannie *f*; **Canada h., Indian h., h. dogbane,** apocyn chanvrin, chanvre du Canada; **brown Indian h.,** ketmie *f* à chanvre; **water h.,** bident *m* à calice feuillé; chanvre aquatique; **bastard h.,** (i) (*also* **Cretan h.**) chanvre de Crète, datisque *m*; (ii) (*also* **h. agrimony**) eupatoire *f* à feuilles de chanvre; (iii) (*also* **h. nettle**) galéopsis *m*, ortie *f* rouge, chanvre bâtard, chanvrin *m*; **h. palm,** trachycarpus *m*. **3.** *Pharm: etc:* **Indian h.,** chanvre indien, hachisch *m*.

hempen ['hempən], *a.* (tissu *m*, corde *f*, fil *m*) de chanvre; *A:* **h. collar,** corde de potence; cravate *f* de chanvre; *F: A:* **h. widow,** veuve *f* d'un pendu.

hempseed ['hempsi:d], *s.* chènevis *m*.

hemstitch[1] ['hemstitʃ], *s. Needlew:* ourlet *m* à jour; rivière *f*.

hemstitch[2], *v.tr.* faire les ajours (d'un mouchoir, etc.); ourler (un mouchoir) à jour.

hemstitched ['hemstitʃt], *a.* (mouchoir, etc.) à ourlets à jour; **h. hem,** ourlet *m* à jour.

hen [hen], *s.* **1.** (*a*) poule *f*; *Cu:* **boiling h.,** poule à mettre au pot; *F:* **old h.,** vieille femme, vieille dinde; **h. party,** réunion féminine, de femmes seules; (*b*) *Orn:* **Cape h.,** pétrel équinoxial; *NAm:* **sage h.,** tétras *m* centrocerque, *Fr.C:* gelinotte *f* des armoises. **2.** femelle *f* (d'oiseau, etc.); **h. bird,** oiseau *m* femelle; **h. pigeon,** pigeon *m* femelle; **h. canary,** serin *m* femelle; serine *f*; **h. blackbird,** merlette *f*; **h. lobster,** homard *m* femelle.

henbane ['henbein], *s. Bot:* jusquiame *f*; *F:* mort *f* aux poules; hanebane *f*.

hence [hens], *adv.* **1.** *A: & Lit:* (*a*) (*of place*) **(from) h.,** d'ici; **five miles h.,** à deux lieues d'ici; *A:* **(get thee) h.!** hors d'ici! va-t'en d'ici! **h. with this!** emportez cela! (*b*) (sortir) de ce monde, de cette vie; **to go from h. into the other world,** quitter cette vie pour l'autre. **2.** (*of time*) dorénavant, désormais; à partir d'aujourd'hui; **five years h.,** dans cinq ans (d'ici). **3.** (*of issue, consequence*) de là; en conséquence, d'où il découle; **h. his anger,** de là sa fureur; **h. it is that . . .,** de là vient que . . ..

henceforth [hens'fɔ:θ], **henceforward** [hens'fɔ:wəd], *adv.* désormais, dorénavant, à l'avenir.

henchman, *pl.* **-men** ['henʃmən], *s.m.* (*a*) *Hist:* écuyer; homme de confiance (d'un chef); (*b*) *Pol: etc:* partisan, acolyte, satellite, séide.

hencoop ['henku:p], *s.* cage *f* à poules.

hendeca- [hen'dekə, hende'kæ], *comb.fm.* hendéca-.

hendecachord [hen'dekəkɔ:d], *s. A.Mus:* gamme *f* de onze notes.

hendecagon [hen'dekəgən], *s.* hendécagone *m*.

hendecagonal [hende'kægən(ə)l], *a.* hendécagone.

hendecahedron [hendekə'hi:drən, -'hedrən], *s.* hendécaèdre *m*.

hendecandrous [hende'kændrəs], *a.* hendécandre.

hendecasyllabic [hendekəsi'læbik], *a. Pros:* hendécasyllabique, hendécasyllabe.

hendecasyllable [hendekə'siləbl], *s. Pros:* hendécasyllabe *m*.

hendiadys [hen'daiədis], *s. Rhet:* hendiadys *m*.

henhouse ['henhaus], *s.* poulailler *m*.

henna[1] ['henə], *s. Bot: etc:* henné *m*.

henna[2], *v.tr.* teindre au henné.

hennery ['henəri], *s.* **1.** poulailler *m*, basse-cour *f*, *pl.* basses-cours. **2.** ferme *f* d'élevage (de volailles).

henpeck ['henpek], *v.tr. F:* (*of wife*) gouverner (son mari); mener (son mari) par le bout du nez.

henpecked ['henpekt], *a. F:* **h. husband,** mari *m* dont la femme porte la culotte, que sa femme mène par le bout du nez; mari mené par sa femme.

Henrician [hen'riʃ(ə)n], *a. Hist:* de Henri VIII.

Henrietta [henri'etə], *Pr.n.f.* Henriette; *Hist:* **H. Maria,** Henriette-Marie (de France).

henroost ['henru:st], *s.* (*a*) juchoir *m*, perchoir *m*; (*b*) *F:* poulailler *m*.

Henry[1] ['henri], *Pr.n.m.* Henri; *Hist:* **H. the Navigator,** Henri le Navigateur; *Bot:* **good King H.,** épinard *m* sauvage.

Henry[2], *pl.* **henries** ['henriz], *s. El.Meas:* Henry *m*, *pl.* henrys.

hep[1] [hep], *s. Bot:* cynorrhodon *m*, fruit *m* du rosier.

hep[2], *a. F:* (*a*) qui apprécie la musique swing; (*b*) qui est dans le vent; **a h. guy,** un affranchi; **to put s.o. h.,** mettre qn à la page, affranchir qn.

heparin ['hepərin], *s. Bio-Ch:* héparine *f*.

hepatalgia [hepə'tældʒiə], *s. Med:* hépatalgie *f*.

hepatectomy [hepə'tektəmi], *s. Surg:* hépatectomie *f*.

hepatic [he'pætik], *a. Anat: etc:* hépatique.

hepatica [he'pætikə], *s. Bot:* (anémone *f*) hépatique *f*, *F:* herbe *f* de la Trinité.

hepatism ['hepətizm], *s. Med:* hépatisme *m*.

hepatite ['hepətait], *s. Miner:* hepatite *f*.

hepatitis [hepə'taitis], *s. Med:* hépatite *f*.

hepatization ['hepətai'zeiʃ(ə)n], *s. Med:* hépatisation *f* (du poumon).

hepatize ['hepətaiz], *v.tr.* (*of lungs, etc.*) **to become hepatized,** s'hépatiser.

hepato- ['hepətou], *comb.fm. Anat: Med:* hépato-.

hepatocele ['hepətousi:l], *s. Med:* hépatocèle *f*, hernie *f* du foie.

hepatogastritis ['hepətougæs'traitis], *s. Med:* hépatogastrite *f*.

hepato-intestinal ['hepətouintes'tainl], *a.* hépato-intestinal, -aux.

hepatolith ['hepətouliθ], *s. Med:* hépatolithe *f*, calcul *m* biliaire.

hepatology [hepə'tɔlədʒi], *s. Med:* hépatologie *f*.

hepatomegaly ['hepətou'megəli], *s. Med:* hépatomégalie *f*.

hepatonephritis ['hepətoune'fraitis], *s. Med:* hépatonéphrite *f*.

hepatopexy ['hepətou'peksi], *s. Surg:* hépatopexie *f*.

hepatorrhagia ['hepətou'reidʒiə], *s. Med:* hépatorragie *f*.

hepatorrhaphy ['hepətou'ræfi], *s.* hépatorraphie *f*.

hepatorrhexis ['hepətou'reksis], *s. Med:* hépatorrhexie *f*.

hepatoscopy [hepə'tɔskəpi], *s. Ant:* hépatoscopie *f*.

hepcat ['hepkæt], *s. P:* **1.** (*a*) musicien *m* faisant partie d'un orchestre swing; (*b*) fanatique *mf* de la musique swing; (*c*) danseur, -euse, swing. **2.** individu *m* nouvelle vague, dans le vent.

hepialid [he'paiəlid]. *Ent:* **1.** *a.* hépiale. **2.** *s.* hépiale *m*, hépialide *m*.

Hepialidae [hepi'ælidi:], *s.pl. Ent:* hépialides *m*.

hepialus [he'paiələs], *s. Ent:* hépiale *m*.

hepta- ['heptə, hep'tæ], *comb.fm.* hepta-.

heptachord ['heptəkɔ:d], *a. & s. Mus:* heptacorde (*m*).

heptad ['heptæd], *s. Phil: Ch: etc:* heptade *f*.

heptagon ['heptəgən], *s.* heptagone *m*.

heptagonal [hep'tægən(ə)l], *a.* heptagone; heptagonal, -aux.

heptahedral [heptə'hi:drəl, -'hed-], *a.* heptaédrique.

heptahedron [heptə'hi:drən, -'hed-], *s.* heptaèdre *m*.

Heptameron (the) [ðə hep'tæmərən], *s. Lit.Hist:* l'Heptaméron *m*.

heptameter [hep'tæmitər], *s. Pros:* heptamètre *m*.

heptane ['heptein], *s. Ch:* heptane *m*.

heptaphyllous [heptə'filəs], *a. Bot:* heptaphylle.

heptarch ['heptɑ:k], *s. Hist:* heptarque *m*.

heptarchic(al) [hep'tɑ:kik(l)], *a. Hist:* heptarchique.

heptarchy ['heptɑ:ki], *s. Hist:* heptarchie *f*.

heptasyllabic [heptəsi'læbik], *a. Pros:* heptasyllabe.

Heptateuch (the) [ðə'heptətju:k], *s. B.Hist:* l'Heptateuque *m*.

heptavalent [heptə'veilənt], *a. Ch:* septivalent, heptavalent.

heptene ['hepti:n], *s. Ch:* heptène *m*.

heptode ['heptoud], *s. Elcs:* heptode *f*.

heptose ['heptous], *s. Ch:* heptose *m*.

heptyl ['heptil], *s. Ch:* heptyle *m*.

heptylene ['heptili:n], *s. Ch:* heptylène *m*.

heptylic ['heptilik], *a. Ch:* heptylique.

heptyne ['heptain], *s. Ch:* heptyne *m*.

her[1] [*unstressed* hər; *stressed* hə:r], *pers. pron. f; objective case.* **1.** (*unstressed*) (*a*) (*direct*) la, (*before a vowel sound*) l'; (*indirect*) lui; **I hate h.,** je la déteste, je la hais; **have you seen h.?** l'avez-vous vue? **I obey h.,** je lui obéis; **I shall tell h. so,** je le lui dirai; **look at h.,** regardez-la; **tell h.,** dites lui; **give it (to) h.,** donnez-le-lui; **send h. a present,** envoyez-lui un cadeau; (*b*) **I am thinking of h.,** je pense à elle; je ne l'oublie pas; **I remember h.,** je me souviens d'elle; (*c*) (*refl.*) elle; **she took her parcel away with h.,** elle emporta son paquet avec elle; **she closed the door behind h.,** elle referma la porte derrière elle; **she dragged her broken doll behind h.,** elle traînait derrière elle, derrière soi, sa poupée cassée; (*d*) (*refl.*) *A: & Poet:* **she bethought h. of the consequences,** elle s'avisa des conséquences; **she laid h. down to sleep,** elle se coucha pour dormir. **2.** (*stressed*) (*a*) elle; **I can forgive her parents but not *her*,** je puis pardonner à ses parents, mais pas à elle; **I don't want to go with *her*,** je n'ai pas envie d'y aller avec elle; **there were a lot of people at the station but I didn't see *her*,** il y avait beaucoup de monde à la gare mais elle, je ne l'ai pas vue; (*b*) (*with dem.force*) *Lit:* celle; **to h. who should take offence at this I would say . . .,** à celle qui s'en offenserait je dirais. . . .. **3.** (*complement of verb to be*) **it's h.!** c'est elle! **that's h.!** la voilà! **it's h. I'm thinking of,** c'est à elle que je pense.

her[2], *poss.a.* (*denoting a f, possessor*) **1.** (*a*) son, *f.* sa, *pl.* ses; **h. hat,** son chapeau; **h. dress, h. dresses,** sa robe, ses robes; **h. friend, h. friends,** son ami, *f.* son amie; ses amis, *f.* ses amies; **h. father and mother,** son père et sa mère; *Adm:* ses père et mère; **h. own sons,** ses propres fils; **h. eyes are blue,** elle a les yeux bleus; **she has hurt h. hand,** elle s'est fait mal à la main; (*emphatic*) *her* **idea would be to . . .,** son idée *f* à elle serait de . . .; (*b*) **H. Ladyship,** madame (la comtesse, etc.); **H. Majesty,** sa Majesté. **2. she knew h. Homer from beginning to end,** elle savait son Homère d'un bout à l'autre.

Heracleia [herə'klaiə], *Pr.n. A.Geog:* Héraclée *f.*

Heracles ['herəkli:z], *Pr.n.m. Gr.Myth:* Héraklès.

Heraclid, *pl.* **-idae** ['herəklid, herə'klaidi:], *s. Myth:* héraclide *m.*

Heraclitean [heroklai'tiən]. *Gr.Phil:* **1.** *a.* héraclitéen. **2.** *s.* disciple *m* d'Héraclite.

Heraclitus [herə'klaitəs], *Pr.n.m. Gr.Phil:* Héraclite.

herald[1] ['herəld], *s.* (*a*) héraut *m*; **the Heralds' College,** le Collège héraldique (à Londres); **the Heralds' Office,** le bureau des armoiries; l'armorial *m*; (*b*) avant-coureur, *pl.* avant-coureurs; précurseur *m*; avant-courrier, -ière, *pl.* avant-courriers, -ières; messager, -ère; *Lit:* **the lark, h. of the morn,** l'alouette, avant-courrière du matin.

herald[2], *v.tr.* annoncer, proclamer (l'arrivée, etc., de qn, de qch.); **event that heralds a new era,** événement *m* qui annonce une époque nouvelle; **to h. (in) the dawn,** annoncer l'aube du jour.

heraldic [hi'rældik], *a.* héraldique; **h. bearing,** armoirie *f*, blason *m*; **to decorate a panel with h. bearings,** armorier un panneau; **h. designer, engraver,** armoriste *m.*

heraldically [hi'rældik(ə)li], *adv.* en blason.

heraldist ['herəldist], *s.* héraldiste *mf.*

heraldry ['herəldri], *s.* **1.** l'art *m*, la science, héraldique; l'héraldique *f*; le blason; **canting h.,** armes parlantes; **book of h.,** armorial *m*, *pl.* -aux. **2.** pompe *f* héraldique.

herapathite [herə'pæθait], *s. Miner:* hérapathite *f.*

herb [hə:b], *s. Bot:* **1.** (*a*) herbe *f*; (*b*) (*for seasoning*) (sweet) **herbs,** (fines) herbes; **medicinal herbs,** plantes médicinales; simples *m*; **h. beer, h. tea,** infusion *f*, tisane *f*, d'herbes; **h. shop,** boutique *f* d'herboriste; herboristerie *f*; *O:* **h. woman,** herbière; **h. trade,** herboristerie *f*. **2.** (*in names of plants*) **h. bennet,** benoîte commune; galliote *f*; **h. Paris,** herbe à Paris; parisette *f*; raisin *m* de renard; **h. Robert,** herbe à Robert; herbe à l'esquinancie; géranium robertin; **h. twopence,** lysimaque *f*; lysimachie *f*, nummulaire *f*; **h. (of) grace,** rue *f*, rhue *f*; **h. ivy,** ive *f*, ivette *f*, **h. patience,** grande patience, patience officinale.

herbaceous [hə:'beiʃəs], *a. Bot:* herbacé; **h. plant,** plante herbacée; **h. border,** bordure herbacée.

herbage ['hə:bidʒ], *s.* **1.** herbes *fpl*; herbage(s) *m.* **2.** *Jur:* droit(s) *m* de pacage.

herbal ['hə:b(ə)l]. **1.** *s.* herbier *m.* **2.** *a.* (breuvage) fait avec des herbes; (infusion *f*, tisane *f*) d'herbes; **h. medicines,** remèdes *m* galéniques.

herbalist ['hə:bəlist], *s.* **1.** *Hist:* (*botanizer*) herborisateur, -trice; botaniste *mf.* **2.** (*herb seller*) herboriste *mf.* **3.** guérisseur *m* (par les plantes).

herbarium [hə:'bɛəriəm], *s.* herbier *m*; jardin sec.

Herbivora [hə:'bivərə], *s.pl. Z:* herbivores *m.*

herbivore ['hə:bivɔ:r], *s. Z:* herbivore *m.*

herbivorous [hə:'bivərəs], *a. Z:* herbivore.

herborize ['hə:bəraiz], *v.i.* herboriser.

herbous ['hə:bəs], *a.* (*of flower, vegetation*) herbeux.

hercogamy [hə:'kɔgəmi], *s. Bot:* hercogamie *f.*

Herculaneum [hə:kju'leiniəm], *Pr.n. Hist: Geog:* Herculanum *m.*

Herculean [hə:kju'liən], *a.* (travail, effort) herculéen; (taille) d'Hercule; **of H. strength,** d'une force d'Hercule.

Hercules ['hə:kjuli:z]. **1.** *Pr.n.m. Myth: Astr:* Hercule. **2.** *s.* (*a*) homme *m* d'une grande force; hercule *m*; (*b*) *Ent:* **H. beetle,** hercule des Antilles; (*c*) *Bot:* **Hercules' club,** xanthoxylum *m.*

Herculid ['hə:kjulid], *s. Astr:* étoile *f* de la constellation d'Hercule.

Hercynian [hə:'siniən], *a. Geol:* hercynien.

hercynite ['hə:sinait], *s. Miner:* hercynite *f.*

herd[1] [hə:d], *s.* (*a*) troupeau *m* (de gros bétail, de porcs); harde *f* (de cerfs); troupe *f*, bande *f* (de chevaux, de baleines, etc.); bande (de buffles); troupe, compagnie *f* (de chevreuils); harpail *m* (de biches et de jeunes cerfs); **the h. instinct,** (i) l'instinct *m* grégaire; (ii) l'instinct qui gouverne le troupeau; **h. book,** herd-book *m*; livre *m* généalogique des races bovines; (*b*) troupeau, foule *f* (de gens); *O:* **the common, vulgar, h.,** la foule; le populaire, le peuple; le commun des hommes.

herd[2]. **1.** *v.i.* (*a*) (*of animals*) **to h. together,** (i) vivre en troupeaux; (ii) s'assembler en troupeau; **these animals h. together,** ces animaux *m* vivent en troupe, sont grégaires; (*b*) (*of pers.*) s'associer, se déplacer, en grands groupes, *F:* en troupeau; **the tourists were herding into the cathedral,** les touristes entraient en foule dans la cathédrale. **2.** *v.tr.* (*a*) (r)assembler (le bétail, etc.) en troupeau; (*b*) **the candidates were all herded into the waiting room,** on avait entassé les candidats dans l'antichambre.

herd[3], *s. O:* pâtre *m*; bouvier *m*; gardien *m* (de bêtes).

herd[4], *v.tr.* garder, surveiller, soigner (le bétail, les moutons, les oies, etc.); *F:* diriger (un groupe de touristes).

herdboy ['hə:dbɔi], *s.m.* jeune bouvier, aide-bouvier.

herderite ['hə:dərait], *s. Miner:* herdérite *f.*

herdsman, *pl.* **-men** ['hə:dzmən], *s.m.* **1.** bouvier; *occ.* pâtre. **2.** *Astr:* **the H.,** le Bouvier; Bootès.

here [hi:ər], *adv.* **1.** (*a*) ici; là; **I'd prefer to stay h.,** je préférerais rester ici, ne pas bouger; **come h.!** (venez) ici! **in h.,** ici; **in h., please,** par ici, s'il vous plaît; **do you belong, live, h.?** êtes-vous d'ici? **up to, down to, h.,** jusqu'ici; **about h.,** par ici; **what's he doing h.?** qu'est-ce qu'il fait dans ces parages? **near h.,** près d'ici; **from h. to there,** d'ici là; **between h. and London,** d'ici à Londres; **Christmas is h.!** voici Noël! (*of fashion, etc.*) **it's h. to stay,** cela restera; **he doesn't know you're h.,** il ne sait pas que vous êtes ici, là, que vous êtes arrivé; **h. she began to laugh,** arrivée à ce point elle a commencé à rire; **h. words will not help,** ici, dans pareille circonstance, les paroles ne sont d'aucun secours; **h. and now,** immédiatement, tout de suite, dès maintenant, sur-le-champ; **h. goes!** allons-y! (*b*) (*on tombstone*) **h. lies . . .,** ci-gît . . .; (*c*) (*at roll call*) présent! (*d*) *esp. Lit:* (*on this earth*) **h. below,** ici-bas. **2. here's your hat!** voici, voilà, votre chapeau! **here's one!** en voilà un; **h. you are!** (i) vous voici! vous voilà! (ii) tenez! voici, voilà, votre affaire! **cigarettes? h. you are, sir!** des cigarettes? voilà, monsieur! **h. she comes!** la voici (qui vient)! **h. I am!** me voici! me voilà! **h.! take it! take it away!** tenez! prenez-le! débarrassez-moi, de ça! **h.! I want you!** hé! venez ici! écoutez un peu! **h. comes the procession,** voici venir le cortège; **here's where I leave you,** (i) voici l'endroit où je vous quitte; (ii) maintenant il me faut vous quitter. **3.** (*esp. over aperitif, etc.*) **here's to you! here's all the best!** à votre santé! bonne chance! **4. my friend h. will tell you,** mon ami que voilà, que voici, vous le dira; *P:* **this h.** ['ðisiə] **thing,** ce truc-là. **5. h. and there,** par-ci, par-là; çà et là; de part et d'autre; **h., there and everywhere,** (un peu) partout; **I can't be h., there and everywhere,** je ne peux pas être partout à la fois, à la ville et à la campagne, au four et au moulin; **neither h. nor there,** ni ici ni ailleurs; **that's neither h. nor there,** cela est en dehors de la question, n'entre pas en ligne de compte, n'a aucune importance; ce n'est pas de cela qu'il s'agit.

hereabout(s) ['hiərəbaut(s)], *adv. F:* près d'ici, par ici, dans ces parages, dans les environs; **he doesn't belong h.,** il n'est pas de par ici.

hereafter [hiər'ɑ:ftər]. **1.** *adv.* (*a*) (*of position*) (*in book, writings, etc.*) ci-après, ci-dessous; (*b*) *esp. Jur:* (*of time*) dorénavant, à l'avenir, désormais; **any convention h. agreed to,** toute convention qui sera ultérieurement conclue; (*c*) *Lit: O:* dans la vie à venir; dans l'autre monde; au delà de la tombe. **2.** *s. Lit:* l'au-delà *m*; la vie future; la vie à venir; **in the h.,** dans l'autre monde.

hereat [hiər'æt], *adv. A:* là-dessus.

hereby [hiə'bai, 'hiəbai], *adv.* **1.** (*a*) par ceci, par ce moyen, par là; (*b*) *Jur:* par ces présentes; **the council h. declares that . . .,** le conseil déclare par le présent acte que . . .. **2.** *A: & Dial:* tout près d'ici.

hereditable [hi'reditəbl], *a.* (*of property*) dont on peut hériter.

hereditament [heri'ditəmənt], *s. Jur:* **1.** tout bien transmissible par héritage; *esp. pl.* **hereditaments,** biens composant la succession; terres *f* et immeubles *m.* **2.** succession.

hereditary [hi'redit(ə)ri], *a.* héréditaire.

hereditism [hi'reditizm], *s. Biol:* héréditarisme *m.*

heredito-syphilitic [hi'reditousifi'litik], **heredosyphilitic** [hi'redousifi'litik], *a. Med:* hérédosyphilitique.

heredity [hi'rediti], *s.* hérédité *f.*

herein [hiər'in], *adv. Lit: & Jur:* **1.** (*of place, position*) ici, dans ce livre, dans ce lieu; **the letter enclosed h.,** la lettre ci-incluse; *Jur:* **h. above, h. before,** ci-dessus, ci-devant; **h. after, h. under,** ci-dessous; **the event to be related h. after,** l'événement *m* dont il sera rendu compte ci-après. **2.** (*in this matter*) en ceci, sur ce point.

hereof [hiər'ɔv], *adv. A:* de ceci; **upon the receipt h.,** au reçu de cette lettre.

heresiarch [he'ri:ziɑ:k], *s.* hérésiarque *m.*

heresy ['herəsi], *s.* hérésie *f*; (*of opinion*) **to smack, savour, of h.,** sentir l'hérésie, le roussi, le brûlé, le fagot.

heretic ['herətik], *s.* hérétique *mf*; **relapsed h.,** relaps, *f.* relapse.

heretical [hi'retikl], *a.* hérétique.

hereto [hiə'tu:, 'hiətu:], *adv.* **1.** *Jur:* **annexed h., h. annexed,** ci-joint. **2.** *A:* = HITHERTO.

heretofore ['hiətu:'fɔ:r]. *adv. A: & Lit:* jadis, autrefois; jusqu'ici; **as h.,** comme par le passé; comme auparavant.

hereunder [hiə'rʌndər], *adv. Jur: etc:* ci-dessous.

hereupon ['hiərəpɔn], *adv.* (*a*) *Jur: etc:* là-dessus; **we are not in agreement h.,** nous ne sommes pas d'accord là-dessus; (*b*) *Lit:* sur ce; **h. he left us,** sur ce il nous quitta.

herewith [hiə'wið], *adv.* avec ceci; *Com:* **I am sending you h. . . .,** je vous envoie ci-joint, sous ce pli . . .; **price list h. enclosed,** prix-courant ci-inclus, sous ce pli.

heriot ['heriət], *s. Jur: A:* droit *m* de meilleur cheptel, *A:* de meilleur chatel.

heritable ['heritəbl], *a.* **1.** *Biol:* (maladie *f*, vice *m*) héréditaire. **2.** *Jur:* (*a*) (droit *m*) héréditaire; (propriété *f*) héritable, dont on peut hériter (par droit de descendance); (*b*) (*of pers.*) capable d'hériter; apte à hériter.

heritage ['heritidʒ], *s.* **1.** (*a*) héritage *m*, patrimoine *m*; **each nation has its h. of folk songs,** chaque nation a son fonds de chansons populaires; (*b*) *Jur: Scot:* biens immobiliers. **2.** (*a*) *B:* le peuple d'Israël; le peuple élu; (*b*) *Ecc:* l'Église *f*; **O Lord, bless thine h.,** Seigneur, bénis ton Église, ton peuple.

heritor ['heritər], *s. Jur:* **1.** héritier, -ière. **2.** *Ecc.Adm: Scot:* censitaire *m.*

herl [hə:l], *s. Fish:* barbe des grandes plumes d'autruche, de paon, etc., utilisée pour la confection de certaines mouches artificielles.

herling ['hə:liŋ], *s. Ich:* jeune truite de mer, truite saumonée.

hermaphrodism [hə:'mæfrədizm], *s.* = HERMAPHRODITISM.

hermaphrodite [hə:'mæfrədait]. **1.** *a. & s. Z: Bot:* hermaphrodite (*m*); *a. Bot:* stamino-pistillé. **2.** *s. Nau:* brick-goëlette *m*, *pl.* bricks-goëlettes.

hermaphroditic [hə:mæfrə'daitik], *a.* (fleur *f*, caractère *m*) hermaphrodite.

hermaphroditism [hə:'mæfrə'daitizm], *s.* hermaphrodisme *m.*

hermeneut ['hə:minjut], *s. Ecc:* herméneute *m.*

hermeneutic(al) [hə:mi'nju:tik(l)], *a.* herméneutique.

hermeneutics [hə:mi'nju:tiks], *s.pl.* (*usu. with sg. const.*) herméneutique *f.*

Hermes ['hə:mi:z], *Pr.n.m.* **1.** *Gr.Myth:* Hermès. **2.** *Gr.Phil:* **H. Trismegistus,** Hermès Trismégiste.

hermetic [hə:'metik], *a.* **1. h. philosophy, art, science,** la philosophie hermétique; l'alchimie *f*; **h. sealing,** scellement *m* hermétique; bouchage *m* hermétique. **2.** *Arch:* **h. column,** colonne *f* hermétique; gaine *f*; hermès *m.*

hermetically [hə:'metik(ə)li], *adv.* (scellé) hermétiquement.

hermeticism [hə:'metisizm], *s.* hermétisme *m.*

hermetics [hə:'metiks], **hermetism** ['hə:mitizm], *s. Alch:* hermétisme *m*; l'alchimie *f.*

hermetist ['hə:mitist], *s. Alch:* hermétiste *m.*

hermit ['hə:mit], *s.* **1.** ermite *m*; **to live like a h.,** vivre en solitaire, en ermite. **2.** *Crust:* **h. crab,** pagure *m*; bernard-l'ermite *m.* **3.** *Orn:* colibri *m* ermite.

hermitage ['hə:mitidʒ], *s.* ermitage *m.*

hermodactyl(us) [hə:mou'dæktil(əs)], *s. Bot:* *hermodactylus m.*

hernia ['hə:niə], *s. Med:* (*a*) hernie *f*; descente *f* (de boyau); **inguinal h., femoral h.,** hernie inguinale; hernie crurale, mérocèle *f*; **umbilical h.,** hernie ombilicale; omphalocèle *f*, entéromphale *f*, exomphale *f*; **strangulated h.,** hernie étranglée; (*b*) **cerebral h.,** hernie du cerveau; **h. of the lung,** hernie du poumon.

hernial ['hə:niəl], **herniary** ['hə:niəri], *a.* herniaire.

herniated ['hə:nieitid], *a. Med:* (intestin, etc.) hernié.

herniation [hə:ni'eiʃ(ə)n], *s. Med:* formation *f* d'une hernie.

herniotomy [hə:ni'ɔtəmi], *s. Surg:* herniotomie *f.*

hero[1], *pl.* **-oes** ['hiərou, -ouz], *s.m.* héros; **to die like a h.,** se faire tuer en héros; **to become the h. of the hour,** devenir le héros du jour; **h. worship,** culte *m* des héros; *Prov:* **no man is a h. to his valet,** il n'y a pas de grand homme pour son valet *m* de chambre.

Hero[2]. **1.** *Pr.n.f. Gr.Myth:* Héro. **2.** *Pr.n.m. Gr.Hist:* **H. of Alexandria,** Héron l'Ancien.

Herod ['herəd], *Pr.n.m. Hist:* Hérode.

Herodian [hi'roudiən]. **1.** *a.* hérodien; *Med:* **H. disease,** maladie *f* pédiculaire. **2.** *s.pl. Jew.Hist:* **Herodians,** hérodiens *m.*

Herodias [he'roudiæs], *Pr.n.f. Hist:* Hérodiade.

Herodotus [he'rɔdətəs], *Pr.n.m. Gr.Lit:* Hérodote.

heroic(al) [hi'rouik(l)]. **1.** *a.* héroïque; **h. deed,** action *f* d'éclat; **h. remedy,** remède *m* héroïque; **h. tales,** romans *m* de cape et d'épée; **h. poem,** poème *m* épique; **h. verse, couplet,** vers *m* décasyllabe, vers héroïque;

distique *m* héroïque; **mock h.,** héroï-comique. **2.** *s.* (*usu. pl.*) **heroics,** (*a*) vers héroïques; (*b*) déclamation *f* de sentiments outrés; grandiloquence *f*; emphase *f*; **to indulge in heroics,** monter sur ses grands chevaux.

heroically [hi'rouik(ə)li], *adv.* héroïquement.

heroin ['herouin], *s. Ch:* héroïne *f*, *F:* blanche *f*.

heroine ['herouin], *s.f.* héroïne.

heroinism ['herouinizm], *s. Med:* héroïnomanie *f*.

heroism ['herouizm], *s.* héroïsme *m*.

heroize ['hiərouaiz]. **1.** *v.tr.* faire un héros de (qn), héroïser (qn). **2.** *v.i.* faire le héros, l'héroïne; se poser en héros, en héroïne.

heron ['herən], *s. Orn:* héron *m*; **young h.,** héronneau *m*; **dusky-grey h., great-billed h.,** héron *m* de Sumatra; **Louisiana h.,** héron à ventre blanc; **great white h.,** aigrette blanche, *Fr.C:* grande aigrette; **great blue h.,** grand héron; **little blue h.,** petit héron bleu; **buff-backed h.,** (héron *m*) garde-bœuf *m*, *pl.* gardes-bœufs; **common h.,** héron cendré; **night h.,** héron bihoreau; **black-crowned night h.,** *Fr.Cr:* bihoreau *m* à couronne noire; **yellow-crowned night h.,** bihoreau violacé; **purple h.,** héron pourpré; **squacco h.,** héron crabier; **African black h.,** héron ardoisé.

heronry ['herənri], *s.* héronnière *f*.

heronshaw ['herənʃɔ:], *s. Orn: A:* **1.** héronneau *m*. **2.** héron *m*.

hero-worship ['hiərouwə:ʃip], *v.tr.* idolâtrer (qn); mettre (qn) sur un piédestal.

herpes ['hə:pi:z], *s. Med:* herpès *m*; dartres *fpl*.

herpetic [hə:'petik], *a. Med:* herpétique; dartreux.

herpetiform [hə:'petifɔ:m], *a. Med:* herpétiforme.

herpetism ['hə:petizm], *s. Med.* herpétisme *m*.

herpetofauna [hə:petou'fɔ:nə], *s.* faune *f* (h)erpétologique.

herpetological [hə:petə'lɔdʒikl], *a. Z:* (h)erpétologique.

herpetologist [hə:pi'tɔlədʒist], *s. Z:* (h)erpétologiste *m*.

herpetology [hə:pi'tɔlədʒi], *s. Z:* (h)erpétologie *f*.

herring ['heriŋ], *s. Ich:* hareng *m*; *Com:* **fat h.,** hareng marchais; **salted h.,** hareng salé, braillé; **freshly salted h.,** hareng pec; **red h.,** (i) hareng saur; (ii) diversion *f*; **h. boat, trawler,** harenguier *m*, trinquart *m*; **h. net,** harenguière *f*; **h. catch,** harengaison *f*; **h. market,** harengerie *f*; **h. fisher,** harenguier *m*; *F: O:* **the H. Pond,** l'Atlantique *m*; la Mare aux harengs.

herringbone[1] ['heriŋboun], *s.* (*a*) arête *f* de hareng; **h. pattern,** dessin *m*, tracé *m*, en arête de poisson, en chevrons, à chevrons, à brin de fougère; **h. flooring,** parquet *m* à bâtons rompus; *Arch:* **h. work,** appareil *m* en épi, en feuille de fougère, en arête de poisson; *Needlew:* **h. (stitch),** point croisé; point de chausson; point russe; point d'épine; *Mec.E:* **h. teeth,** dents chevronnées; denture *f* à chevrons; (*b*) *Ski:* montée *f* en ciseaux, en pas de canard.

herringbone[2], *v.tr. Needlew:* faire (un ouvrage) au point de chausson.

hers [hə:z], *poss. pron.f.* le sien, la sienne, les siens, les siennes; **she took my pen and h.,** elle a pris mon stylo et le sien; **this book is h.,** ce livre est à elle, lui appartient; c'est son livre; **my shoes are too large, h. are too small,** mes souliers sont trop grands, les siens sont trop petits; **a friend of h.,** un(e) de ses ami(e)s; un(e) ami(e) à elle; **it's no business of h.,** ce n'est pas son affaire; **no effort of h.,** aucun effort de sa part; **that pride of h.,** cet orgueil dont elle ne peut se défaire.

herschelite ['hə:ʃəlait], *s. Miner:* herschélite *f*.

herse [hə:s], *s. A. Fort:* herse *f*, sarrasine *f*.

herself [hə(:)'self], *pers. pron.* (*a*) (*emphatic*) elle-même; **I saw Louise h.,** j'ai vu Louise elle-même, en personne; **she doesn't drive the car h.,** elle ne sait pas conduire; (*after illness*) **she's looking (quite) h. again,** elle parait complètement remise; (*b*) (*reflexive*) **she hurt h.,** elle s'est fait mal; **she doesn't take care of h.,** elle se soigne mal; **she keeps h. to h.,** elle vit retirée, est très casanière; elle est peu accueillante; **she was living by h.,** elle vivait seule.

hertz [hə:ts], *s. El. Meas:* hertz.

Hertzian ['hə:tsiən], *a. El:* hertzien; **h. waves,** ondes hertziennes.

Herzegovina [hə:tsigə'vi:nə], *Pr.n. Hist:* herzégovine *f*.

Herzegovinian [hə:tsigə'viniən]. *Hist:* (*a*) *a.* herzégovinien; (*b*) *s.* Herzégovinien, -ienne.

Hesiod ['hi:siɔd], *Pr.n.m. Gr.Lit:* Hésiode.

hesione [he'saiəni], *s. Ann:* hésione *f*.

Hesionidae [hesi'ɔnidi:], *s.pl. Ann:* hésionidés *m*.

hesitancy ['hezitənsi], *s.* **1.** hésitation *f*, incertitude *f*, irrésolution *f*. **2. to speak with a certain h.,** parler avec hésitation.

hesitant ['hezitənt], *a.* hésitant, irrésolu, indécis; **he's a very h. speaker,** il hésite beaucoup en parlant; il a du mal à trouver ses mots.

hesitantly ['hezitəntli], *adv.* avec hésitation.

hesitate ['heziteit], *v.i.* (*a*) hésiter (en parlant, en agissant); **to h. for a word,** hésiter pour trouver un mot; **to h. about what to do,** hésiter sur ce qu'il faut faire; **to h. between two courses,** hésiter, balancer, entre deux partis; **he hesitated (about) whether he should . . .,** il hésitait, ne sachant s'il devait . . .; **to h. before taking a decision,** hésiter avant de prendre une décision; **he didn't h. a moment,** il n'a pas hésité un instant; **he who hesitates is lost,** celui qui hésite a perdu; **he hesitates at nothing,** il n'hésite, ne recule, devant rien; **without hesitating,** sans hésiter, sans balancer; **to h. over the price,** hésiter à payer le prix demandé; (*b*) (*to be reluctant*) **to h. to do sth.,** hésiter à faire qch.

hesitating ['heziteitiŋ], *a.* (air, propos) hésitant, incertain; **painted with a h. brush,** peint d'un pinceau qui tâtonne.

hesitatingly ['heziteitiŋli], *adv.* (parler, agir) avec hésitation, en hésitant.

hesitation [hezi'teiʃ(ə)n], *s.* hésitation *f*; **without (the slightest) h.,** sans (la moindre) hésitation; sans balancer; *F:* sans faire ni une ni deux; **there's no room for h.,** il n'y a pas à hésiter; **he had no h. about it,** il n'y hésitait pas du tout; **I have no h. in acknowledging that . . .,** je n'hésite pas à reconnaître que . . ..

hesperetin, hesperitin [hes'peritin], *s. Ch:* hespérétine *f*.

Hesperia [hes'piəriə], *Pr.n. A.Geog:* Hespérie *f*.

Hesperides [hes'peridi:z], *Pr.n.f.pl. Gr.Myth:* **1.** les Hespérides; **the Garden of the H.,** le Jardin des Hespérides. **2.** (*a*) le Jardin des Hespérides; (*b*) les Iles Fortunées.

hesperidin [hes'peridin], *s. Ch:* hespéridine *f*.

hesperis ['hespəris], *s. Bot:* hespéris *f*, julienne *f*.

hesperornis [hespə'rɔ:nis], *s. Paleont:* hespérornis *m*.

Hesperus ['hespərəs], *Pr.n. Poet:* vesper *m*; Vénus *f*, l'étoile *f* du berger.

Hessian ['hesiən]. **1.** (*a*) *s. Geog:* Hessois, -oise; (*b*) *a. Geog:* hessois; *A.Cost:* **h. boots, s. hessians,** bottes *f* à la Souvarov; *Ent:* **h. fly,** cécidomyie destructrice; mouche *f* de Hesse; (*c*) *s. U.S: Hist:* mercenaire, *esp.* mercenaire allemand. **2.** *s. Tex:* étoffe grossière de chanvre; toile *f* de jute.

hessite ['hesait], *s. Miner:* hessite *f*.

hessonite ['hesənait], *s. Miner:* essonite *f*.

Hesychasm ['hesikæzm], *s. Rel.H:* hésychasme *f*.

Hesychast ['hesikæst], *s. Rel.H:* hésychaste *mf*.

het [het], *a. F:* **h. up,** (i) chauffé; survolté; énervé; (ii) fâché; **don't get h. up about it,** ne t'en fais pas pour cela, pas la peine de t'énerver.

hetaera [he'tiərə], **hetaira** [he'tairə], *s. Gr.Ant: etc:* hétare *f*, hétaïre *f*, hétère *f*, courtisane *f*.

hetaeria [he'tiəriə], **hetairia** [he'tairiə], *s. Gr.Ant: etc:* hétairie *f*, hétérie *f*.

hetaerism [he'tiərizm], **hetairism** [he'tairizm], *s. Gr.Ant: etc:* hétairisme *m*, hétérisme *m*.

heterandrous [hetə'rændrəs], *a. Bot:* hétérandre.

heteratomic [hetərə'tɔmik], *a. Ch:* hétéroatomique.

hetero- ['hetərou, hetə'rɔ], *comb.fm.* hétéro-.

heteroatom ['hetərouætəm], *s. Ch:* hétéroatome *m*.

heteroatomic [hetərouə'tɔmik], *a. Ch:* hétéroatomique.

heteroblastic [hetərou'blæstik], *a.* hétéroblastique.

heterocarpic [hetərou'kɑ:pik], *a. Bot:* hétérocarpe.

heterocentric [hetərou'sentrik], *a.* **1.** *Psy:* (pensées, etc.) tournées vers le dehors. **2.** *Opt:* (rayons) diffus.

Heterocera [hetə'rɔsərə], *s.pl. Ent: O:* hétérocères *m*.

heterocercal [hetərou'sə:kəl], *a. Ich:* (queue) hétérocerque.

heterocercality [hetərousə:'kæliti], *s. Ich:* hétérocercie *f*, hétérocerquie *f*.

heterochromosome [hetərou'krouməsoum], *s. Biol:* hétérochromosome *m*.

heterochromous [hetərou'krouməs], *a. Bot:* hétérochrome.

heterochronism, heterochrony [hetə'rɔkrənizm, -'rɔkrəni], *s. Biol:* hétérochronie *f*.

heteroclite ['hetərouklait], *a. & s. Gram:* hétéroclite (*m*).

Heterococcales [hetəroukɔ'keili:z], *s.pl. Algae:* hétérococcales *f*.

heterocyclic [hetərou'saiklik], *a. Ch:* hétérocyclique.

heterodactyl(ous) [hetərou'dæktil(əs)], *a. Orn:* hétérodactyle.

heterodon ['hetəroudɔn], *s. Rept:* hétérodon *m*.

heterodont ['hetəroudɔnt], *a. & s. Z:* hétérodonte (*m*).

Heterodonta [hetərou'dɔntə], *s.pl. Moll:* hétérodontes *m*.

heterodox ['hetəroudɔks], *a.* hétérodoxe.

heterodoxy ['hetəroudɔksi], *s.* hétérodoxie *f*.

heterodromous [hetərou'drouməs], *a. Mec:* hétérodrome.

heterodynamic [hetəroudai'næmik], *a. Nat.Hist:* hétérodyname.

heterodyne ['hetərədain], *a. & s. W.Tel:* hétérodyne (*m*).

heterogametism, heterogamety [hetərou'gæmitizm, -'gæmiti], *s. Nat.Hist:* hétérogamétie *f*.

heterogamous [hetə'rɔgəməs], *a. Nat.Hist:* hétérogame.

heterogamy [hetə'rɔgəmi], *s. Nat.Hist:* hétérogamie *f*.

heterogeneity [hetəroudʒi'ni:iti], *s.* hétérogénéité *f*.

heterogeneous [hetərə'dʒi:niəs], *a.* hétérogène.

heterogeneousness [hetərou'dʒi:niəsnis], *s.* hétérogénéité *f*.

heterogenesis [hetərou'dʒenəsis], *s. Biol:* hétérogénèse *f*.

heterogenite [hetə'rɔdʒinait], *s. Miner:* hétérogénite *f*.

heterogeny [hetə'rɔdʒini], *s. Biol:* hétérogénie *f*.

heterogony [hetə'rɔgəni], *s. Biol:* hétérogonie *f*.

heterograft ['hetərougrɑ:ft], *s. Biol: Surg:* hétérogreffe *f*.

heterogynous [hetə'rɔdʒinəs], *a. Biol:* hétérogyne.

hetero-infection [hetərouin'fekʃ(ə)n], *s.* hétéro-infection *f*.

heterolysin(e) [hetərou'laisin], *s. Bio-Ch:* hétérolysine *f*.

Heteromera [hetə'rɔmərə], *s.pl. Ent:* hétéromères *m*.

heteromerous [hetə'rɔmərəs], *a.* hétéromère.

heterometabolic, heterometabolous [hetəroume'tæbəlik, -me'tæbələs], *a. Ent:* hétérométabole.

heteromorphic, heteromorphous [hetərou'mɔ:fik, -'mɔ:fəs], *a. Nat.Hist: Ch:* hétéromorphe.

heteromorphism [hetərou'mɔ:fizm], *s. Nat.Hist: Ch:* hétéromorphie *f*, hétéromorphisme *m*.

heteromorphite [hetərou'mɔ:fait], *s. Miner:* hétéromorphite *f*.

heteromorphosis [hetərou'mɔ:fəsis], *s. Biol:* hétéromorphose *f*.

Heteromyidae [hetərou'maiidi:], *s.pl. Z:* hétéromyidés *m*.

Heteroneura [hetərou'nju:rə], *s.pl. Ent:* hétéroneures *m*.

heteronomous [hetə'rɔnəməs], *a.* hétéronome.

heteronomy [hetə'rɔnəmi], *s.* hétéronomie *f*.

heteronym ['hetərənim], *s. Ling:* **1.** *A:* hétéronyme *m*. **2.** homographe *m*; homogramme *m*.

heteronymous [hetə'rɔniməs], *a. Ling: A:* hétéronyme.

heterophile ['hetəroufail], *a. Biol:* hétérophile.

heterophoria [hetərou'fɔ:riə], *s. Opt:* hétérophorie *f*.

heterophthalmus [hetərɔf'θælməs], *s.* hétérophtalmie *f*.

heterophyllous [hetərou'filəs], *a. Bot:* hétérophylle.

heterophylly ['hetərəfili], *s. Bot:* hétérophyllie *f*.

heterophyte ['hetərəfait], *s. Bot:* plante *f* hétérophytique.

heterophytic [hetərou'fitik], *a. Bot:* hétérophytique.

heteroplasia [hetərou'pleiziə], *s. Med:* hétéroplasie *f*.

heteroplastic [hetərou'plæstik], *a.* hétéroplastique.

heteroplasty [hetərou'plæsti], *s. Surg:* hétéroplastie *f*; greffe *f* hétéroplastique, hétérogreffe *f*.

heteropod ['hetərəpɔd], *s. Moll:* hétéropode *m*.

Heteropoda [hetə'rɔpədə], *s.pl. Moll:* hétéropodes *m*.

heteropolar [hetərou'poulər], *a. Ch:* hétéropolaire.

Heteroptera [hetə'rɔptərə], *s.pl. Ent:* hétéroptères *m*.

heteropterous [hetə'rɔptərəs], *a. Ent:* hétéroptère.

heterosexual [hetərou'seksjuəl], *a. & s.* hétérosexuel, -elle.

heteroside ['hetərousaid], *s. Ch:* hétéroside *m*.

heterosis [hetə'rousis], *s. Biol:* hétérosis *f*.

heterosporic, heterosporous [hetərou'spɔ:rik, -'spɔ:rəs], *a. Bot:* hétérosporé.

heterospory [hetə'rɔspəri], *s. Bot:* hétérosporie *f*.

heterostatic [hetərou'stætik], *a. El:* hétérostatique.

heterostylism, heterostyly [hetərou'stailizm, -'staili], *s. Bot:* hétérostylie *f*.

heterosuggestion [hetərousə'dʒestʃən], *s. Psy:* hétérosuggestion *f*.

heterotaxis, heterotaxy [hetərou'tæksis, -'tæksi], *s. Anat: Bot: etc:* hétérotaxie *f*.

heterotrophic [hetərou'troufik], *a. Nat.Hist:* hétérotrophe.

heterotrophism [hetərou'troufizm], *s. Nat.Hist:* hétérotrophie *f*.

heterotypic(al) [hetərou'tipik(l)], *a.* hétérotypique.

heterozygote [hetərou'zaigout], *s. Nat.Hist:* hétérozygote *m*.

heterozygotic [hetərouzai'gɔtik], **heterozygous** [hetərou'zaigəs], *a. Nat.Hist:* hétérozygote.

heuchera ['hju:kərə], *s. Bot:* heuchère *f*.

heulandite ['hju:ləndait], *s. Miner:* heulandite *f*.

heuristic [hju'ristik], *a. & s.* heuristique (*f*).

hevea ['hi:viə], *s. Bot:* hévéa *m*.

hew [hju:], *v.* (*p.t.* **hewed;** *p.p.* **hewed, hewn** [hju:n]) **1.** *v.tr.* (*a*) couper, tailler (avec une hache, un ciseau, etc.); **to h. a stone,** tailler, dégrossir, dresser, équarrir, une pierre; **to h. coal,** piquer la houille; **to h. one's way,** se frayer, se tailler, un passage (à coups de hache); **to h. out a rock tomb,** creuser, tailler, une tombe dans le rocher; (*b*) **to h. down a tree,** abattre un arbre; **to h. off, away, a branch,** abattre, élaguer, une branche. **2.** *v.i. U.S:* **to h. to the line,** conformer, adhérer, à une ligne de conduite.

hewer ['hju:ər], *s.* **1.** tailleur *m,* coupeur *m* (de pierres, etc.); *Min:* piqueur *m* (de houille); haveur *m;* **to be hewers of wood and drawers of water,** (i) *B:* être employés à couper le bois et à puiser l'eau, (ii) *Fig: O:* mener une vie de forçat, de galérien. **2.** abatteur *m* (d'arbres).

hewgag ['hju:gæg], *s. U.S:* mirliton *m.*

hewing ['hju:iŋ], *s.* (*a*) taille *f,* coupe *f,* équarrissage *m* (de pierres, de bois); piquage *m* (de la houille); (*b*) abattage *m* (d'un arbre).

hex[1] [heks], *s. NAm: F:* **1.** sortilège *m,* (mauvais) sort; guigne *f.* **2.** sorcière *f.*

hex[2], *NAm: F:* **1.** *v.i.* pratiquer la sorcellerie. **2.** *v.tr.* jeter un sort, un maléfice, sur (qn, qch.).

hexa- ['heksə, hek'sæ], *comb.fm.* hexa-.

hexacanthous [heksə'kænθəs], *a.* hexacanthe.

hexachloride [heksə'klɔ:raid], *s. Ch:* hexachloride *m.*

hexachord ['heksəkɔ:d], *s. Mus:* hexacorde *m.*

hexacontane [heksə'kɔntein], *s. Ch:* hexacontane *m.*

Hexacorall(i)a [heksəkə'rɑ:l(i)ə], *s.pl. Coel:* hexacoralliaires *m.*

hexacosane [heksə'kousein], *s. Ch:* hexacosane *m.*

Hexactinellida [heksækti'nelidə], *s.pl. Spong:* hexactinellidés *m.*

hexad ['heksæd], *s.* série *f* de six; *Ch:* atome, ion, radical, hexavalent.

hexadecane [heksə'dekein], *s. Ch:* hexadécane *m.*

hexadecimal [heksə'desim(ə)l], *a.* hexadécimal, -aux.

hexadic [heks'ædik], *a. Ch:* (atome, etc.) hexavalent.

hexafluoride [heksə'flu:əraid], *s. Ch:* hexafluorure *m.*

hexagon ['heksəgən], *s. Mth:* hexagone *m; Mec.E:* **h. nut,** écrou *m* (à) six pans.

hexagonal [hek'sægən(ə)l], *a.* hexagone, hexagonal, -aux; *Mth: Cryst:* **h. pyramid,** dihexaèdre *m;* **h. nut,** écrou *m* (à) six pans.

hexagynian [heksə'dʒiniən], **hexagynous** [hek'sædʒinəs], *a. Bot:* hexagyne.

hexahedral [heksə'hi:dr(ə)l], *a. Mth:* hexaèdre, hexaédrique.

hexahedron [heksə'hi:drən], *s. Mth:* hexaèdre *m.*

hexamerous [hek'sæmərəs], *a. Nat.Hist:* à six parties, à six divisions.

hexameter [hek'sæmitər], *s. Pros:* hexamètre *m.*

hexametric(al) [heksə'metrik(l)], *a. Pros:* hexamètre.

hexanchus [hek'sæŋkəs], *s. Ich:* hexanche *m.*

hexandrous [hek'sændrəs], *a. Bot:* hexandre.

hexane ['heksein], *s. Ch:* hexane *m.*

hexapla ['heksəplə], *s.pl. B.Lit:* hexaples *m.*

hexapod ['heksəpɔd], *s. & a. Ent:* hexapode (*m*).

Hexapoda [hek'sæpədə], *s.pl. Ent:* hexapodes *m.*

hexapody [hek'sæpədi], *s. Pros:* hexapodie *f.*

hexastyle ['heksəstail], *a. & s. Arch:* hexastyle (*m*).

hexasyllabic [heksəsi'læbik], *a. Pros:* hexasyllabe.

hexatetrahedron ['heksə'tetrə'hi:drən], *s. Cryst:* hexatétraèdre *m.*

Hexateuch (the) [ðə'heksətjuk], *s. B.Lit:* l'Hexateuque *m.*

hexatomic [heksə'tɔmik], *a. Ch:* hexatomique.

hexavalent [heksə'veilənt], *a. Ch:* hexavalent.

hexene ['heksi:n], *s. Ch:* hexène *m.*

hexoctahedral ['heksɔktə'hi:dr(ə)l], *a. Cryst: Mth:* hexoctaèdre.

hexoctahedron ['heksɔktə'hi:drən], *s. Cryst: Mth:* hexoctaèdre *m.*

hexosan ['heksousæn], *s. Ch:* hexosane *m.*

hexose ['heksous], *s. Ch:* hexose *m.*

hextetrahedral ['hekstetrə'hi:dr(ə)l], *a.* hextétraèdre.

hextetrahedron ['hekstetrə'hi:drən], *s.* hextétraèdre *m.*

hexyl ['heksil], *s. Ch:* hexyle *m;* **h. alcohol,** alcool *m* hexylique.

hexylene ['heksili:n], *s. Ch:* hexylène *m.*

hexylic [hek'silik], *a. Ch:* hexylique.

hexyne ['heksain], *s. Ch:* hexyne *m.*

hey [hei], *int.* **1.** hé! holà! **2.** hein? **3.** *A:* **h. for the greenwoods!** en route pour les bois! **4. h. presto!** passez muscade!

heyday ['heidei], *s.* apogée *m,* beaux jours (de ses forces, de la prospérité); **to be in the h. of youth,** être en pleine jeunesse, dans, à, la fleur de l'âge, au printemps de la vie; **to be in the h. of one's glory,** être à l'apogée de sa gloire.

hey-ho [hei'hou], *int.* = HEIGH-HO.

Hezekiah [hezi'kaiə], *Pr.n.m.* Ézéchias.

hi [hai], *int.* (*a*) hé! là-bas! ohé! (*b*) *esp. NAm:* bonjour!

hiatal ['haiət(ə)l], *a.* hiatal, -aux.

hiatus, *pl.* **-uses** [hai'eitəs, -əsiz], *s.* **1.** lacune *f* (dans une série, un récit, etc.); *Med:* hiatus *m* (de Fallope, etc.). **2.** *Gram:* hiatus; heurtement *m* de voyelles. **3.** *A:* brèche *f.*

hibernaculum [haibə'nækjuləm], *s. Nat.Hist:* hibernacle *m.*

hibernal [hai'bə:n(ə)l], *a.* (temps, soleil) hivernal, -aux; (sommeil) hibernal.

hibernant ['haibənənt], *a. & s.* **1.** *Z:* hibernant. **2.** *A:* (*of pers.*) hivernant, -ante.

hibernate ['haibəneit], *v.i.* hiberner, hiverner; (*b*) *A:* (*of pers.*) (*to winter*) hiverner.

hibernating ['haibəneitiŋ], *a. Z:* hibernant.

hibernation [haibə'neiʃ(ə)n], *s. Z:* hibernation *f;* sommeil hibernal.

Hibernian [hai'bə:niən], *Lit:* (*a*) *a.* hibernien, irlandais; (*b*) *s.* Hibernien, -ienne; Irlandais, -aise.

Hibernianism [hai'bə:niənizm], **Hibernicism** [hai'bə:nisizm], *s. Ling:* locution irlandaise, idiotisme irlandais; tour de phrase irlandais.

hibiscus [hi'biskəs], *s. Bot:* ketmie *f,* hibiscus *m.*

hiccough[1], **hiccup**[1] ['hikʌp], *s.* hoquet *m;* **to have the hiccoughs,** avoir le hoquet.

hiccough[2], **hiccup**[2]. **1.** *v.i.* avoir le hoquet; hoqueter; *Aut: F:* **the engine's hiccupping,** le moteur marche irrégulièrement, fait des hoquets. **2.** *v.tr.* **he hiccuped out an apology,** il s'est excusé entre deux hoquets.

hick [hik], *NAm: F:* (*a*) *s.* paysan *m,* rustaud *m,* cambrousard *m;* (*b*) *a.* **a h. town,** un bled.

hickory ['hikəri], *s.* (*tree or wood*) noyer (blanc) d'Amérique; hickory *m.*

hidden ['hid(ə)n], *a.* caché; **h. treasure,** trésor caché; *Fin: etc:* **h. reserves,** réserve latente; **h. light,** vue dérobée; *Carp: etc:* **h. joint,** joint dérobé; *Fig:* **h. hand,** influence *f* occulte.

hiddenite ['hidənait], *s. Miner:* hiddénite *f.*

hide[1] [haid], *s.* affût *m* (de chasseur).

hide[2], *v.* (*p.t.* **hid;** *p.p.* **hid, hidden** ['hidn]) **1.** *v.tr.* (*a*) cacher (**from,** à); enfouir (qch. dans la terre); **to h. s.o. from justice,** soustraire qn à la justice, aux recherches de la justice; **where has he hidden himself?** où est-il allé se fourrer? **great treasures lie hidden within the earth,** la terre recèle de grands trésors; **to h. one's face,** (i) se cacher la figure, se voiler la face; (ii) *B:* détourner, cacher, sa face (**from,** de); **I didn't know where to h. my head,** je ne savais où me fourrer, où me mettre; **to h. one's light under a bushel,** mettre la lampe sous le boisseau; enfouir son talent; **he doesn't h. his light under a bushel,** la modestie est son moindre défaut; **to h. one's faults,** dissimuler, recouvrir, ses défauts; **to h. one's joy,** dissimuler sa joie; **to h. sth. from s.o.,** (i) cacher qch. à qn; (ii) taire qch. à qn; **to h. a scandal,** tenir un scandale secret; étouffer un scandale; **to h. (away) a treasure,** mettre un trésor dans une cache; (*b*) **to h. sth. from sight,** dérober, soustraire, qch. aux regards; **wall that hides the view,** mur *m* qui dérobe la vue; **clouds hid the sun,** des nuages voilaient le soleil; **his face was hidden by a beard,** une barbe cachait son visage; **the wall is hidden under the ivy,** la muraille disparait sous le lierre; **cottage hidden in a wood,** petite maison tapie, nichée, dans un bois. **2.** *v.i.* se cacher; (i) se tenir caché; se blottir (dans un coin, etc.); (ii) aller se cacher; (*of boars, deer*) prendre buisson, buissonner; **I didn't know where to h.,** je ne savais où me fourrer; **to h. (away) from s.o.,** se cacher de qn.

hide[3], *s.* **1.** peau *f,* dépouille *f* (d'un animal); *Com:* cuir *m;* **h. rope,** corde *f* en cuir. **2.** *F:* peau (de qn); **to save one's h.,** sauver sa peau; **to take, tan, the h. off (s.o.),** tanner le cuir à (qn).

hide[4], *v.tr. P: O:* tanner le cuir à (qn), administrer une tripotée à (qn).

hide[5], *s. A.Agr: Meas:* charruage *m* (= *approx.* 48 hectares).

hide-and-seek, *U.S:* **hide and go seek** ['haidən(gou)'si:k], *s. Games:* cache-cache *m.*

hideaway ['haidəwei]. **1.** *s.* cachette *f;* retraite *f.* **2.** *a.* secret, dissimulé.

hidebound ['haidbaund], *a.* **1.** (*a*) (*of cattle*) dont la peau adhère aux flancs; qui n'a que la peau et les os; (*b*) *Hort: Arb:* (arbre) serré dans son écorce. **2.** *F:* (*of pers.*) aux vues étroites; plein de préjugés; systématique; **h. opinions,** idées étroites, opiniâtres; **h. etiquette,** étiquette *f* rigide. **3.** (*bound with hide*) (livre) relié en peau; (bouclier, etc.) recouvert de peau.

hideous ['hidiəs], *a.* hideux, affreux, effroyable; d'une laideur repoussante; (crime) horrible, odieux; **in its most h. aspect,** dans toute sa laideur; **h. noise,** bruit *m* terrible, cacophonie *f; F:* **h. price,** prix affreux, salé; **what a h. picture!** quelle peinture repoussante, abominable!

hideously ['hidiəsli], *adv.* hideusement, affreusement; *F:* **it's h. expensive,** c'est excessivement cher.

hideousness ['hidiəsnis], *s.* hideur *f,* laideur *f,* horreur *f.*

hideout ['haidaut], *s. F:* cachette *f;* planque *f.*

hider ['haidər], *s.* **1.** dissimulateur, -trice. **2.** fugitif, -ive (qui se dérobe à la justice).

hiding[1] ['haidiŋ], *s.* (*a*) dissimulation *f* (de la joie, etc.); *Jur:* recel *m* (d'un criminel); **to go into h.,** se cacher, se soustraire aux regards; **to be in h.,** se tenir caché; **to come out of h.,** sortir de sa cachette; *Ven:* (*of animal*) débusquer; (*b*) *attrib.* **h. place,** cachette *f;* retraite *f;* **h. power,** opacité *f* (d'une couche de peinture, etc.).

hiding[2], *s. F:* raclée *f,* rossée *f,* trempée *f,* volée *f;* **to give s.o. a good h.,** flanquer, administrer, une raclée à qn; tanner le cuir à qn.

hidradenitis [hidrədi'naitis], **hidrosadenitis** [hidrousædi'naitis], *s. Med:* hidrosadénite *f.*

hidrosis [hi'drousis], *s. Med:* éphidrose *f.*

hidyhole ['haidihoul], *s. F:* cache *f* (d'enfant, etc.).

hie [hai], *v.i. & pr. A: & Lit:* **to h. to a place,** se hâter de se rendre dans un lieu; se rendre au plus vite, courir, à un endroit.

hierarch ['haiərɑ:k], *s. Ecc:* hiérarque *m,* grand prêtre.

hierarchal ['haiərɑ:k(ə)l], *a. Ecc:* hiérarchique.

hierarchic(al) [haiə'rɑ:kik(l)], *a.* hiérarchique; **in h. order,** par ordre hiérarchique.

hierarchically [haiə'rɑ:kik(ə)li], *adv.* hiérarchiquement.

hierarchization [haiərɑ:kai'zeiʃ(ə)n], *s.* hiérarchisation *f.*

hierarchize ['haiərɑ:kaiz], *v.tr.* hiérarchiser.

hierarchy ['haiərɑ:ki], *s.* hiérarchie *f.*

hieratic [haiə'rætik], *a.* (écriture *f,* style *m,* papier *m*) hiératique.

hieratically [haiə'rætik(ə)li], *adv.* hiératiquement.

hiero- ['haiərou, haiə'rɔ], *comb.fm.* hiéro-.

hierocracy [haiə'rɔkrəsi], *s.* hiérocratie *f.*

hieroglyph ['haiərəglif], *s.* hiéroglyphe *m.*

hieroglyphic(al) [haiərə'glifik(l)], *a.* hiéroglyphique.

hieroglyphically [haiərə'glifik(ə)li], *adv.* par (des) hiéroglyphes.

hieroglyphics [haiərə'glifiks], *s.pl.* hiéroglyphes *m,* signes *m* hiéroglyphiques.

hierogram ['haiərəgræm], *s.* hiérogramme *m.*

hierograph ['haiərəgræf], *s. Ant:* inscription *f* hiérographique.

hierographic(al) [haiərou'græfik(l)], *a.* hiérographique.

hierography [haiə'rɔgrəfi], *s.* hiérographie *f.*

Hieronymite [haiə'rɔnimait], *s. Rel.H:* hiéronymite *m.*

Hieronymus [haiə'rɔniməs], *Pr.n.m.* **1.** *Gr.Hist:* Hiéronyme. **2.** *Rel.H:* Hiéronyme, Jérôme.

hierophant ['haiəroufænt], *s. Gr.Ant:* hiérophante *m.*

Hierosolymitan [haiərousɔli'maitən], **Hierosolymite** [haiərou'sɔlimait], (*a*) *a.* hiérosolymite, hiérosolymitain, de Jérusalem; (*b*) *s.* Hiérosolymite *mf,* Hiérosolymitain, -aine.

hi-fi ['hai'fai], *a. & s. Rec: etc: F:* (de) haute fidélité.

higgle[1] ['higl], *s.* marchandage *m.*

higgle[2], *v.i.* **1.** marchander, marchandailler. **2.** *A:* colporter.

higgledy-piggledy ['higldi'pigldi], *adv. F:* sans ordre, en pagaïe, pêle-mêle; **tools thrown down h.-p. on the floor,** outils jetés en vrac sur le plancher.

higgler ['higlər], *s.* **1.** marchandeur, -euse, marchandailleur, -euse. **2.** *A:* colporteur *m,* marchand ambulant.

higgling[1] ['higliŋ], *a.* qui marchande; marchandeur.

higgling[2], *s.* **1.** marchandage *m.* **2.** *A:* colportage *m.*

high [hai], *a., adv. & s.*

I. *a.* **1.** (*a*) haut; **h. mountain,** haute montagne; **the mountain is 3,000 metres h.,** la montagne a trois mille mètres d'altitude; **the highest point in the range,** le point culminant de la chaîne; **house built on h. ground,** maison construite sur un terrain élevé; **wall two metres h.,** mur haut de deux mètres, qui a une hauteur de deux mètres; **how h. is that tree?** quelle est la hauteur de cet arbre? **the little chap was only** *so* **h.,** le gamin n'était pas plus grand que ça; **ship h. out of the water,** navire haut de franc-bord; **at h. water, h. tide,** à la marée haute; **perched on a h. seat,** haut assis(e); (*b*) *Cost:* (corsage, col) montant; (col) haut; **h.-necked dress,** robe montante; *A:* **wearing a h. stock,** haut cravaté, *pl.* haut cravatés; (*c*) **h. cheek bones,** pommettes saillantes; **h. shoulders,** épaules montantes, remontées; *Typ:* **h. letter,** caractère *m* à baisser. **2.** haut, élevé; (*a*) **the sun is getting higher (above the horizon),** le soleil remonte; **sun h. above the horizon,** soleil haut sur l'horizon; **the clouds are h.,** les nuages sont hauts; **h.-flying,** haut vol; *Av:* vol à grande hauteur; *Ecc:* **glory to God in the highest,** gloire à Dieu au plus haut des cieux; **higher up the river,** en amont; **with one's head h.,** la tête haute; **horse that holds his head h.,** cheval qui tire au vent; *Equit:* **h. action,** allure relevée (d'un cheval); *Mil:* **h. step,** pas *m* de l'oie; *Nau:* **with colours h.,** pavillon haut; (*b*) **of h. rank,** de haut rang; **h. ranking official,** haut fonctionnaire; **h., higher, executives,** cadres supérieurs; **to be in a h. position,** être haut placé; remplir de hautes fonctions; **higher posts,** postes, emplois, supérieurs; **the higher ranks of the secretariat,** la haute direction du secrétariat; *Sch:* **the higher forms,** les classes supérieures; **higher education,** études supérieures; **higher mathematics,** mathématiques supérieures; **the h. table,** la table d'honneur; *Sch:* la table des professeurs; **the higher animals,** les animaux supérieurs; **h. and mighty,** haut et puissant; **in a h. and mighty manner,** avec de grands airs, des airs de grand seigneur; d'un air important; **don't be so h. and mighty,** ne le prenez pas de si haut; (*c*) **h. thoughts,** pensées élevées, nobles; grandes pensées; **h. ideals,** haut idéalisme; (*d*) **h. prices,** prix élevés; **the h. price of food,** le prix élevé, la cherté, de la vie; **to fetch a h. price,** se vendre cher; **highest price,** chiffre *m* maximum; **to make a higher bid,** faire une offre supérieure; **h.-rate of interest,** taux d'intérêt élevé; gros intérêt; **to set a h. value on sth.,** estimer qch. haut; **to play for h. stakes,** jouer gros (jeu); **h. percentage,** gros pourcentage; forte, grande, proportion; *Cards:* **h. cards,** cartes hautes; **flush with king h.,** flux *m* au roi; **ore with a h. mineral content,** minerai à haute teneur, d'un haut titre; **anthracite with a h. ash content,** anthracite à teneur en cendres élevée; **historians put the number as h. as 1200,** les historiens portent le nombre à douze cents; **h. latitudes,** les hautes latitudes; **h. speed,** grande vitesse; marche *f* rapide; **highest speed,** vitesse maximum; vitesse de pointe; (*e*) **to have a h. opinion of s.o.,** tenir qn en haute estime; avoir une haute opinion de qn; **to speak of s.o. in the highest terms,** parler de qn en termes flatteurs; **to a h. degree,** à un haut degré; **to, in, the highest degree,** au suprême, au dernier, au plus haut, degré; au plus haut point; par excellence; **of the highest importance,** de première importance; **the highest efficiency,** (i) la plus haute compétence; (ii) le rendement maximum; **the highest knowledge,** le plus haut degré du savoir; **h. respect,** respect profond; *Rec: etc:* **h. fidelity,** haute fidélité; (*f*) **h. fever,** forte, grosse, fièvre; **h. wind,** vent fort, violent; grand, gros, vent; **there is a h. sea running,** la mer est grosse, houleuse; il y a de la mer; **h. treason,** haute trahison; *Pol:* **h. Tory,** conservateur *m* à outrance, d'extrême droite; *Pharm: etc:* **h. dilution,** dilution extrêmement étendue; (*g*) **h. colour,** (i) couleur vive; (ii) vivacité *f* du teint; **h. diet,** forte nourriture; **too h. a soil,** sol *m* trop riche; **h. spirits,** entrain *m*; **the h. spot of the match,** le point culminant du match; **there were no h. spots,** il n'y avait point de grands moments, d'incidents palpitants; *F:* **to hit the h. spots,** (i) marquer; toucher les hauteurs; (ii) fréquenter des endroits gais; (*h*) **h. voice,** (i) voix élevée, haute; (ii) voix grêle; *Mus:* **one tone higher,** un ton au-dessus; **to set a song half a tone higher,** hausser un chant d'un demi-ton. **3.** (*principal*) (*a*) **the H. Street,** la Grand-rue, la Grande rue; *Ecc:* **h. mass,** la grand-messe, la grande messe; **h. altar,** maître autel; (*b*) **h. day,** fête solennelle; jour de fête; **h. festival,** fête carillonnée. **4.** (*far advanced*) (*a*) **h. noon,** plein midi; **it is h. day,** il fait grand jour; **it's h. time he went to school,** il est grand, grandement, temps qu'il aille à l'école; **it's h. time we decided,** il est grand temps de décider; (*b*) (*of meat, etc.*) avancé, gâté; (*of game*) faisandé; (*of game*) **to get h.,** se faisander; **to smell h.,** avoir une forte odeur; (*c*) *F:* (*of pers.*) **to be h.,** (i) être ivre; avoir sa cuite; (ii) être dans un état d'euphorie; être sous l'influence des drogues; planer. **5.** (*of ship*) **h. and dry,** échoué au plein; à sec (sur la plage, etc.); *F:* (*of pers.*) **to be left h. and dry,** être laissé en plan.

II. *adv.* **1.** (*a*) haut; en haut; **higher (up),** plus haut; **higher and higher,** de plus en plus haut; **h. up in the skies,** haut dans les airs; **to aim h.,** (i) viser haut; (ii) *Fig:* avoir de hautes visées; **to aim too h.,** être trop ambitieux; **to fly h.,** voler haut; **to rise h. in the public esteem,** monter très haut dans l'estime publique; **this question was h. on the agenda,** cette question figurait dans les premières à l'ordre du jour; **to hunt h. and low for sth.,** chercher qch. de haut en bas, de la cave au grenier, partout, dans tous les coins (et recoins); (*b*) **higher up the river,** en amont; en remontant vers la source de la rivière; **there are summer pastures higher up the mountain,** les pâturages d'été sont plus hauts dans la montagne. **2. to go as h. as £2000,** aller jusqu'à £2000; *Cards: etc:* **to play, stake, h.,** jouer gros jeu; **to trump h.,** couper haut. **3.** fort, fortement; (*of wind*) **to blow h.,** souffler avec violence, en tempête; **to run h.,** (i) (*of sea*) être grosse, houleuse; **the sea is running h.,** il y a de la mer; (ii) (*of feeling*) s'échauffer; (iii) (*of prices*) être élevés; **expenditure is running h.,** les dépenses montent haut; **tempers, words, were running h.,** la querelle s'échauffait; **his voice rose h.,** sa voix s'éleva.

III. *s.* **1.** (*a*) **the Most H.,** le Très-Haut, le Tout-Puissant; (*b*) **on h.,** en haut; dans le ciel; **glory be to God on h.,** gloire à Dieu dans les hauteurs; **from on h.,** d'en haut; de là-haut; **a voice from on h.,** une voix dans les airs. **2.** *Meteor:* aire anticyclonique, anticyclonale. **3.** *St.Exch:* **highs and lows,** hausses *f* et baisses *f*; **prices have reached a new h.,** les prix ont atteint un nouveau maximum; **all-time h.,** record le plus élevé.

high-angle ['hai'æŋgl], *a.* *Artil: etc:* **h.-a. fire,** tir *m* courbe, tir sous de grands angles.

highball[1] ['haibɔ:l], *s.* *NAm:* **1.** *Rail:* (*a*) signal vert; (*b*) train qui file rapidement. **2.** grand verre de whisky, d'eau de vie, etc. à l'eau et à la glace.

highball[2], *v.i.* *NAm:* *F:* filer rapidement.

highbinder ['haibaindər], *s.* *U.S:* *F:* **1.** gangster *m*, assassin *m*, bandit *m*. **2.** escroc *m*, filou *m*.

high-born ['haibɔ:n], *a.* de famille noble; de sang noble; de haute naissance; de haute lignée; de noble extraction.

highboy ['haibɔi], *s.* *Furn:* *NAm:* commode *f* de hauteur double.

highbred ['haibred], *a.* **1.** (*a*) de parentage noble, de haute naissance; (*b*) (cheval *m*) bon sang, de race. **2.** parfaitement élevé; élevé dans le grand monde; **h.-b. manners,** manières parfaites, aristocratiques.

highbrow ['haibrau], *s.* *F:* **1.** intellectuel, -elle; grosse tête. **2.** *a.* **h. literature,** littérature *f* pour les intellectuels; **I don't care for h. music,** la musique classique ne me dit rien.

high-browed ['haibraud], *a.* **1.** (personne) à front élevé. **2.** *F:* intellectuel, calé.

highchair ['haitʃeər], *s.* chaise haute (de bébé).

high-class ['hai'klɑ:s], *a.* (marchandises, etc.) de premier ordre, de première qualité; **h.-c. hotel,** hôtel *m* de première classe; **h.-c. cooking,** la haute cuisine.

high-energy ['hai'enədʒi], *attrib.* **h.-c. physics,** physique *f* des hautes énergies.

highfalutin(g) ['haifə'lu:tin, -iŋ], *a.* *F:* (style, discours) ampoulé, prétentieux, pompeux, déclamatoire; **h. language,** langage pompeux.

high-fidelity ['haifi'deliti], *a.* *Rec: etc:* de haute fidélité.

highflier, highflyer ['hai'flaiər], *s.* **1.** (*of hawk, etc.*) haut voleur. **2.** *F:* extravagant, -ante; ambitieux, -ieuse.

highflown ['haifloun], *a.* (style, discours) ampoulé, pompeux, déclamatoire; **h. narrative,** récit *m* enthousiaste; **to write in a h. style,** écrire avec emphase, dans un style ambitieux.

high-flying ['hai'flaiiŋ], *a.* (oiseau, etc.) qui vole haut; (faucon) haut voleur; (avion) volant haut, à haute altitude.

high-frequency ['hai'fri:kwənsi], *a.* *El:* (courant, lampe) à haute fréquence; **h.-f. amplifier,** amplificateur *m* de haute fréquence; *Med:* **h.-f. current,** courant alto-fréquent.

high-gain ['hai'gein], *a.* *Elcs:* **h.-g. amplifier,** amplificateur *m* à gain élevé.

high-grade ['hai'greid], *a.* (*a*) (minerai, etc.) à haute teneur, d'un haut titre; (marchandises) de première qualité, de (premier) choix; **h.-g. petrol,** supercarburant *m*; (*b*) *Husb:* (bétail) métis, de premier croisement.

high-handed ['hai'hændid], *a.* (action *f*) arbitraire; (autorité *f*) tyrannique; **h.-h. government,** gouvernement *m* à poigne; **to be h.-h. with s.o.,** traiter qn d'une façon arbitraire.

high-handedly ['hai'hændidli], *adv.* arbitrairement; tyranniquement; d'une façon arbitraire.

high-hat[1] ['hai'hæt], *a.* & *s.* *F:* dédaigneux (*m*); arrogant (*m*); snob (*m*).

high-hat[2], *v.* (**high-hatting**) *F:* **1.** *v.i.* se donner de grands airs. **2.** *v.tr.* traiter (qn) de haut en bas.

highjack, highjacker, highjacking ['haidʒæk, -jækər, -jækiŋ], *v.tr.*, *s.* = HIJACK, HIJACKER, HIJACKING.

highland ['hailənd]. **1.** *s.* pays montagneux; *Geog:* **the Highlands,** (la) Haute Écosse; les Highlands *m*. **2.** *a.* (*a*) des montagnes; montagnard; (*b*) de la Haute Écosse, des Highlands; **h. cattle,** race bovine des Highlands.

highlander ['hailəndər], *s.* **1.** montagnard, -arde. **2.** **Highlander,** (i) Highlander *m*; habitant, -ante, de la Haute Écosse; (ii) soldat *m* d'un régiment écossais; **the Royal Highlanders,** le 42e régiment écossais.

high-level ['hai'levl], *a.* (*a*) au niveau supérieur; **h.-l. staff,** (i) *Ind: etc:* les cadres supérieurs; (ii) *Mil: etc:* les officiers supérieurs; **h.-l. decision,** décision prise à un niveau supérieur; (*b*) à haute altitude; **h.-l. station,** (i) *Rail:* gare *f* en contre-haut (lorsqu'il y a aussi une gare souterraine); (ii) station *f* de montagne (d'une garnison, etc.); (*c*) *Cmptr:* **h.-l. language,** langage évolué.

high-lift ['hai'lift], *a.* *Av:* à grande portance, hypersustentateur; **h.-l. device,** dispositif hypersustentateur; **h.-l. flap,** volet hypersustentateur; **h.-l. wing,** voilure *f* à grande portance.

highlight[1] ['hailait], *s.* **the highlights of a painting,** les rehauts *m*, les clairs *m*, d'une peinture; (*b*) grand moment; clou *m* (de la fête, de la représentation, etc.); point culminant (d'un match, etc.).

highlight[2], *v.tr.* (**highlighted**) mettre en vedette; mettre (un problème) au premier plan.

highly ['haili], *adv.* **1.** (*a*) **h. placed official,** haut fonctionnaire; (*b*) *A:* **to be h. descended,** être de haute naissance, de haute extraction, de haute lignée, de parentage noble. **2. his services are h. paid,** ses services sont largement rétribués; on paie très cher ses services; **to think h. of s.o.,** avoir une haute opinion de qn; tenir qn en grande estime; faire grand cas, grand état, de qn; **to think too h. of oneself,** avoir une trop haute opinion de soi; se trop priser. **3.** fort, très, bien, fortement; **h. amusing,** fort, très, amusant; **h. pleased,** extrêmement content; **h. displeased,** fort, très, mécontent; **h. seasoned,** fortement assaisonné; **h. polished table,** table *f* d'un beau poli; **to feel h. flattered,** se sentir très flatté; **h. coloured,** (tableau, style) haut en couleur; (récit) coloré; (*of pers.*) **h. strung,** nerveux, impressionnable.

high-mettled ['hai'metld], *a.* (cheval) fougueux, ardent, plein d'ardeur, plein de fougue; (cavalier *m*) intrépide.

high-minded ['hai'maindid], *a.* **1.** à l'esprit élevé; aux sentiments nobles, généreux; (action *f*, nature *f*) magnanime. **2.** *B:* orgueilleux.

high-mindedness ['hai'maindidnis], *s.* élévation *f* d'esprit, noblesse *f* de sentiments; magnanimité *f*; générosité *f* (de cœur); grandeur *f* d'âme.

high-muck-a-muck, high-muckety-muck ['hai'mʌkəmʌk, -'mʌkətimʌk], *s.* *esp.* *U.S:* *P:* gros bonnet, grosse légume.

highness ['hainis], *s.* **1.** (*a*) élévation *f* (des prix, etc.); (*b*) grandeur *f* (d'âme); (*c*) force *f*, violence *f* (du vent). **2.** (*title*) Altesse *f*; *Hist:* (*of the Sultan*) Hautesse *f*; **His, Her, Royal H.,** son Altesse Royale; **Your H.,** votre Grandeur.

high-octane ['hai'ɔktein], *a.* **h.-o. fuel, petrol,** essence *f* à haut indice d'octane; supercarburant *m*; **h.-o. aviation fuel,** carburant d'aviation à degré d'octane élevé.

high-pass ['haipɑ:s], *a.* *El:* **h.-p. filter,** filtre *m* passe-haut *inv*.

high-pitched ['haipitʃt], *a.* **1.** (*of sound*) aigu, -uë; **h.-p. voice,** voix aiguë, criarde, clairette; **h.-p. piano,** piano accordé à un diapason haut. **2.** *Const:* **h.-p. roof,** comble *m* à forte inclinaison, à forte pente; **h.-p. arch,** arche surhaussée.

high-powered ['hai'pauəd], *a.* de haute puissance; (*a*) gros (moteur); (auto) de haute puissance; *El:* (arc) à haute intensité; *W.Tel: etc:* (poste) de haute puissance, de grande portée; (*b*) *Opt:* (jumelles) à fort grossissement.

high-pressure ['hai'preʃər], *a.* (*a*) (cylindre, machine) à haute pression, à haute tension; *Meteor:* **h.-p. area,** aire anticyclonique, anticyclonale; (*b*) **h.-p. salesman,** vendeur importun, agressif, qui vous force la main; **h.-p. salesmanship,** l'art *m* de vendre coûte que coûte, en forçant la main.

high-principled ['hai'prinsipld], *a.* aux principes élevés; qui a de bons principes.

high-proof ['hai'pru:f], *a.* *Dist:* à forte teneur en alcool.

high-rise ['hai'raiz], *a.* **h. r. building,** gratte-ciel *m inv*.

high riser ['hai'raizər], *s.* gratte-ciel *m inv*.

highroad ['hairoud], *s.* grande route, route nationale.

high roller ['hai'roulər], *s.* *U.S:* *F:* (*a*) dépensier, -ière; (*b*) homme aventureux au jeu.

high-sounding ['hai'saundiŋ], *a.* **1.** (instrument) sonore, retentissant. **2.** (titre, éloge) pompeux, prétentieux; **h.-s. phrases,** expressions ronflantes.

high-speed ['hai'spi:d], *a.* (*a*) *Veh: etc:* ultra-rapide, capable d'une grande vitesse; (machine *f*) à marche rapide; (moteur *m*) grande vitesse; **h.-s. lathe,** tour *m* à marche rapide; (*b*) *Cmptr:* **h.-s. memory, store,** mémoire *f* rapide; **h.-s. printer,** imprimante *f* rapide; **h.-s. format,** forme absolue; **h.-s. carry,** report rapide, simultané; (*c*) *Cin:* **h.-s. shooting,** accélération *f* à la prise de vues; ralentissement *m* à la projection; (*d*) *Phot:* **h.-s. lens,** objectif *m* à très grande ouverture.

high-spirited ['hai'spiritid], *a.* intrépide; plein de courage, d'ardeur, de feu; **h.-s. horse,** cheval fougueux, vif, plein d'ardeur.

high-stepper ['hai'stepər], *s.* **1.** *Equit:* steppeur *m*; cheval *m* qui trousse, qui a de l'action, qui marche d'un pas relevé. **2.** (*a*) *O:* homme, femme, remarquable; (*b*) personne qui cherche toujours le divertissement.

high-stepping ['hai'stepiŋ], *a.* **1.** *Equit:* (cheval) à hautes actions, qui trousse, qui marche d'un pas relevé.

2. (*of pers.*) qui cherche le plaisir, le divertissement; **h.-s. town,** ville où il y a beaucoup de divertissements.

high-strung ['haistrʌŋ], *a.* (tempérament) nerveux, impressionnable, exalté; (personne) au tempérament nerveux.

hight [hait], *p.p. A:* appelé, dénommé, dit.

hightail ['haiteil], *v.tr. & i. F:* **to h. (it),** allonger le pas; ficher le camp.

high-tensile ['hai'tensail], *a.* (tôle d'acier) à haute résistance.

high-toned ['hai'tound], *a.* **1.** (livre *m*, journal *m*) d'un ton élevé. **2.** *F: often Pej:* supérieur, élégant; prétentieux.

high-up ['haiʌp], *s. F:* personnage important; haut fonctionnaire; gros bonnet, grosse légume.

highway ['haiwei], *s.* (*a*) grande voie de communication; grande route; artère *f*; *NAm:* **divided h., dual h.,** route à deux voies, à deux pistes, à deux chaussées; route jumelée; **h. patrolman,** motard *m*; *U.S:* **P type h.,** grande route à circulation réservée aux voitures servant au transport de personnes; **T type h.,** grande route à circulation réservée plus particulièrement aux camions; **through h.,** voie directe, route directe; **highways and byways,** chemins et sentiers; **the King's h.,** (i) le grand chemin; (ii) *Can:* = route nationale; *A:* **to take to the h.,** devenir un voleur de grand(s) chemin(s); **the h. to India,** la grande route des Indes; **to be on the h. to success, to ruin,** être en bonne voie de réussir; marcher inévitablement vers la ruine; (*b*) *Adm:* voie publique; **the Highways Department,** le service de la voirie; = les ponts et chaussées; **h. surveyor,** inspecteur *m* des routes, des ponts et chaussées; agent *m* voyer; **h. engineer** = ingénieur *m* des ponts et chaussées; **the H. Code,** le Code de la Route; (*c*) *U.S:* **community h.,** chemin vicinal; **belt h., encircling h.,** route de ceinture, d'encerclement.

highwayman, *pl.* **-men** ['haiweimən], *s.m.* voleur de grand(s) chemin(s); détrousseur.

hijack ['haidʒæk], *v.tr. F:* (*a*) s'emparer de force de (marchandises de contrebande, marchandises volées); (*b*) arrêter (un véhicule) et en voler le contenu; s'emparer de force (d'un véhicule, d'un avion); dérouter (un avion en vol) (en menaçant l'équipage); **hijacked aircraft,** avion capturé, détourné (de sa route), par des bandits armés.

hijacker ['haidʒækər], *s. F:* (*a*) bandit armé qui s'attaque aux contrebandiers; (*b*) pirate *m* de la route (qui s'empare d'un véhicule et de son contenu); (*c*) pirate de l'air.

hijacking ['haidʒækiŋ], *s. F:* (*a*) vol armé de marchandises de contrebande ou de marchandises volées; (*b*) vol armé d'un véhicule et de son contenu; (*c*) déroutement *m* d'un avion en vol; piraterie *f* de l'air, aérienne.

hike[1] [haik], *s. F:* **1.** *A:* vagabondage *m*; **to be on the h.,** vagabonder; être sur le trimard; battre le trimard. **2.** (longue) promenade *f* à pied; randonnée *f*. **3.** *NAm:* augmentation *f* (de prix, de salaire); hausse *f* (de prix).

hike[2]. *F:* **1.** *v.i.* (*a*) *A:* vagabonder, trimarder; (*b*) faire une (longue) promenade à pied; (*c*) **to h. off,** partir, filer, décamper. **2.** *v.tr.* (*a*) **to h. oneself up out of one's chair,** s'extraire de son fauteuil; **to h. oneself up on to sth.,** grimper (avec difficulté) jusqu'à qch.; (*b*) *NAm:* augmenter (les prix, les salaires); (*c*) **to h. a cheque,** falsifier un chèque.

hiker ['haikər], *s. F:* randonneur, -euse (à pied).

hiking ['haikiŋ], *s. F:* excursions *f*, tourisme *m*, à pied.

hilar ['hailər], *a. Bot:* hilaire.

hilarious [hi'lɛəriəs], *a.* gai, joyeux, hilare; *F:* rigoleur, -euse; **h. laughter,** grands éclats de rire; **it was h.!** c'était à se tordre de rire!

hilariously [hi'lɛəriəsli], *adv.* gaiement, joyeusement, avec hilarité; **to laugh h.,** rire aux éclats; se tenir les côtes de rire.

hilariousness [hi'lɛəriəsnis], **hilarity** [hi'læriti], *s.* hilarité *f*, gaieté *f*.

Hilary ['hiləri], *Pr.n.mf.* Hilaire; *Jur:* **H. term, session,** session *f* de la Saint-Hilaire (commençant en janvier).

hill[1] [hil], *s.* **1.** (*a*) colline *f*, coteau *m*; **rounded h.,** ballon *m*, (*small*) mamelon *m*; **up h. and down dale; over h. and dale,** par monts et par vaux; **h. country,** pays *m* de montagne(s); (*in India*) **h. station,** station *f* de montagne; **to spend the summer in the hills,** passer l'été dans une station de montagne; **h. sheep,** moutons *m* des montagnes; **h. people, h. folk,** montagnards *m*; **h. road,** route *f* de montagne; (*b*) éminence *f*; monticule *m*; (*c*) *Mil: Surv:* **h. 304,** la cote 304. **2.** (*on road*) côte *f*; (i) montée *f*; (ii) descente *f*; **dangerous h.,** descente dangereuse; **sharp h., steep h.,** (i) montée, (ii) descente, abrupte; *Aut:* **speed up h.,** vitesse *f* en côte; **h. start,** départ *m* en côte; **h. climbing,** montée des côtes; **h.-climbing efficiency,** rendement *m* en côte; **to take a h. in top,** attaquer une côte en prise directe; **to go down the h.,** (i) descendre la colline; descendre la côte; (ii) *F:* baisser, décliner; perdre ses forces.

hill[2], *v.tr. Hort:* **1.** remblayer, terrasser, amonceler (la terre). **2.** butter, terrer, chausser (une plante).

hill-and-dale ['hil(ə)n'deil], *a. Rec:* **h.-a.-d. recording,** enregistrement *m* (sur disque) en profondeur.

hillbilly ['hilbili], *s. U.S: F:* montagnard *m*, rustaud *m*; **h. songs,** (i) chants *m* populaires des ranchs des États du Sud; (ii) chants imitant le folklore.

hilliness ['hilinis], *s.* montuosité *f*; nature montueuse, accidentée (d'un pays).

hilling ['hiliŋ], *s. Hort:* **1.** remblai *m*, remblayage *m*. **2.** buttage *m* (des plantes, etc.).

hillman, *pl.* **-men** ['hilmæn, -men], *s.m.* montagnard.

hillock ['hilək], *s.* petite colline; monticule *m*, butte *f*, tertre *m*; (*rounded*) mamelon *m*; (*in plain*) mondrain *m*; **sand hillocks,** buttes de sable.

hill-robin ['hil'rɔbin], *s. Orn:* leiothrix *m* (jaune).

hillside ['hilsaid], *s.* flanc *m* de coteau; penchant *m*, versant *m*, d'une colline; coteau *m*.

hilltop ['hiltɔp], *s.* **1.** sommet *m* de (la) colline; hauteur *f*, éminence *f*. **2.** le haut de la côte.

hilly ['hili], *a.* **1.** (pays) montagneux, montueux; (terrain) accidenté. **2.** (chemin) montueux, à fortes pentes.

hilt[1] [hilt], *s.* **1.** poignée *f*, garde *f* (d'épée); **he ran his sword through him up to the h.,** il lui enfonça son épée à travers le corps jusqu'à la garde; **to prove an assertion up to the h.,** prouver et archiprouver son dire; démontrer surabondamment une assertion; *F:* **right up to the h.,** jusqu'à la gauche; **mortgaged up to the h.,** fortement grevé d'hypothèques. **2.** manche *m* (de dague, de couteau, etc.); crosse *f* (de pistolet).

hilt[2], *v.tr.* **1.** mettre une poignée à (une épée). **2.** mettre un manche à (un couteau, etc.).

hilum ['hailəm], *s.* **1.** *Bot:* hile *m*, ombilic *m*, cicatricule *f*. **2.** *Anat:* hile (du rein, etc.).

him [him], *pers.pron.m., objective case.* **1.** (*unstressed*) (*a*) (*direct*) le, (*before a vowel sound*) l'; (*indirect*) lui; **I hate h.,** je le déteste, je le hais; **do you love h.?** l'aimez-vous? **I obey h.,** je lui obéis; **I shall tell h. so,** je le lui dirai; **call h.,** appelez-le; **tell h. I have come,** dites-lui que je suis là; **give it (to) h.,** donnez-le-lui; **write h. a letter,** écrivez-lui une lettre; (*b*) (*refl.*) lui, soi; **he took his luggage with h.,** il a pris ses bagages avec lui; **he closed the door behind h.,** il a refermé la porte derrière lui; (*c*) (*refl.*) *A: & Lit:* **he bethought h. of the peril,** il s'avisa du danger; **he laid h. down to sleep,** il se coucha pour dormir. **2.** (*stressed*) (*a*) lui; **I found h. and his friend in the park,** je les ai trouvés, lui et son ami, dans le parc; **go with h.,** allez avec lui; **she is thinking of h.,** elle pense à lui; (*b*) (*with dem. force*) celui; **the prize goes to h. who comes in first,** le prix est pour celui qui arrivera le premier. **3.** (*as complement of v.* **to be**) **it's h.!** c'est lui; **just see if it isn't h.,** voyez donc si ce n'est pas lui; **it's h. I admire,** c'est lui que j'admire.

Himalaya [himə'leiə], *Pr.n. Geog:* **the H. mountains, the Himalayas,** l'Himalaya *m*.

Himalayan [himə'leiən], *a. Geog:* himalayen, -enne.

himself [him'self], *pers.pron. m.* (*a*) (*emphatic*) lui-même; **I saw David h.,** j'ai vu David lui-même, en personne; **he doesn't want to do it h.,** il ne veut pas le faire lui-même; **could he do it h.?** est-ce qu'il sait, pourrait, le faire? (*after illness*) **he's not (quite) h. again yet,** il n'est pas encore complètement remis; (*b*) (*refl.*) se; **he hurt h.,** il s'est fait mal; **he doesn't take care of h.,** il se soigne mal; **he keeps h. to h.,** il est très casanier, peu accueillant; **he lives by h.,** il vit seul; (*c*) (*used impersonally*) soi(-même); **everyone for h.,** chacun pour soi; **a man has to consider h.,** on est obligé de s'occuper de ses propres intérêts.

hind[1] [haind], *s. Z:* biche *f*; **h. calf,** faon *m* femelle.

hind[2], *s. A:* **1.** (*a*) valet *m* de ferme; (*b*) *Scot:* valet de ferme marié, qui a sa chaumière; (*c*) régisseur *m* (d'une ferme). **2.** (*a*) paysan *m*; (*b*) rustre *m*.

hind[3], **hinder**[1] [haindər], *a.* de derrière; postérieur. **1.** (*usu.* **hinder**) **hinder part,** partie postérieure, partie arrière; *F:* **hind(er) part foremost, hind(er) side before,** sens devant derrière. **2.** (*always* **hind**) **hind legs, feet,** jambes *f*, pattes *f*, de derrière; *Equit:* bipède postérieur; les gigots *m*; **horse strong in the h. legs,** cheval gigoté; *F:* **to get on one's h. legs,** se lever, se mettre debout (pour prononcer un discours); **h. quarters** (*of a horse*), arrière-main *m*, arrière-train *m*; *Veh: A:* **hind wheel,** roue *f* (d')arrière; **h. carriage,** arrière-train.

hindbrain ['haindbrein], *s. Anat:* = cerveau postérieur.

hinder[2] ['hindər], *v.tr.* **1.** (*impede*) gêner, embarrasser, arrêter (qn); dresser, susciter, des obstacles à (qn); retarder, entraver (qch.); faire obstacle à (un mouvement); **what's hindering you?** qu'est-ce qui vous arrête? vous y trouvez un obstacle? **2.** (*prevent*) empêcher, retenir, arrêter (**s.o. from doing sth.,** qn de faire qch.).

hindermost ['haindəmoust], *a.* = HINDMOST.

Hindi ['hindi:], *s. Ling:* hindî *m*.

hindmost ['haindmoust], *a.* dernier; **everyone for himself and the devil take the h.,** chacun pour soi et Dieu pour tous; sauve qui peut.

hindrance ['hindrəns], *s.* empêchement *m*, obstacle *m*, entrave *f*; **to act without (let or) h.,** agir sans entrave(s), sans encombre, en toute liberté.

hindsight ['haindsait], *s.* **1.** hausse *f* (de fusil). **2.** sagesse *f* d'après coup.

Hindu [hin'du:], (*a*) *a.* hindou; (*b*) *s.* Hindou, -oue.

Hinduism ['hindu:izm], *s.* (h)indouisme *m*.

Hindu-Kush ['hindu:'kuʃ], *Pr.n. Geog:* l'Indou-Koh *m*, l'Indou-Kouch *m*.

Hindustan [hindu'stɑ:n], *Pr.n. Geog:* Hindoustan *m*.

Hindustani [hindu'stɑ:ni], *a. & s. Ling:* hindoustani (*m*).

hinge[1] [hindʒ], *s.* **1.** (*a*) gond *m* (de porte); paumelle *f*; (**stamp**) **h.,** charnière *f*; **H-h.,** paumelle double; **hook and h.,** penture *f* et gond; *Nau:* **port hinges,** pentures de sabord; **door off its hinges,** porte *f* hors de ses gonds; **h. post,** barreau *m* de côtière (d'une grille); (*b*) (**butt**) **h.,** charnière *f*; **male, female, h.,** patte *f* mâle, femelle, de charnière; **loose-butt h.,** fiche *f* à vase; **pin h.,** charnière à fiche, à broche; **loose pin h.,** fiche à nœud; **h. pin,** broche *f*, cheville *f*, goujon *m*, axe *m*, de charnière; rivure *f*; **h. joint,** assemblage *m* à charnière; **flap h.,** briquet *m*; (**gemel h.,** gond *m* à piton); **strap h.,** couplet *m*, penture; (*c*) **ball-joint h.,** genou *m* de Cardan; charnière à rotule. **2.** (*a*) *Anat:* charnière, ginglyme *m*; **h. joint,** articulation *f* à charnière; (*b*) *Nat.Hist:* charnière (d'un bivalve); *Moll:* **h. jointed,** cardinifère; **h. line,** ligne cardinale. **3.** pivot *m* (d'une entreprise, etc.); point principal, nœud *m* (d'un argument).

hinge[2]. **1.** *v.tr.* (i) monter (une porte, etc.) sur ses gonds; (ii) mettre les charnières à (une boîte, etc.). **2.** *v.i.* (*a*) tourner, pivoter (**on,** autour de); **bone that hinges with another,** os *m* qui s'articule avec un autre; (*of seat, etc.*) **to h. forward,** basculer vers l'avant; (*b*) (*in novel, etc.*) **the character on whom everything hinges,** le pivot de l'action; **everything hinges on his answer,** tout dépend de sa réponse.

hinged [hindʒd], *a.* (porte, couvercle, etc.) à charnière(s); **h. flap,** (i) (*of counter, etc.*) battant *m*, planchette *f*, rabattable, relevable; (ii) (*of aircraft*) volet articulé; **h. connection,** assemblage *m* par articulation; **h. side (of box, etc.),** paroi *f* à rabattement; **h. sides of a lorry,** cloisons basculantes d'un camion; **h. girder,** poutre articulée; *Nau:* **h. funnel,** cheminée *f* à rabattement.

hinny[1] ['hini], *s. Z:* bardot *m*, bardeau *m*.

hinny[2], *s. Dial:* (*esp. Scot: & N.Eng:*) ma petite; chérie.

hinny[3], *v.i.* (*of horse*) hennir.

hint[1] [hint], *s.* **1.** (*a*) insinuation *f*; allusion indirecte; avis *m* à mots couverts; **broad h.,** (i) allusion évidente, claire; (ii) avis peu voilé, assez clair; **that's a straight h.!** à bon entendeur . . .! **that was a pretty broad h.!** c'était parler clairement! **to give, drop, s.o. a h.,** toucher un mot à qn; mettre qn sur la voie; donner l'éveil à qn; suggérer qch. à qn, laisser entrevoir qch. à qn; **if you had given me the slightest h. about it,** si vous m'en aviez donné le moindre soupçon; **gentle h.,** allusion discrète; **I'll give, drop, him a gentle h.,** je vais lui en toucher un mot tout doucement; **to throw out, drop, let fall, a h. that . . .,** donner à entendre, laisser entendre, que . . .; **to know how to take, to be able to take, a h.,** entendre (qn) à demi-mot; savoir ce que parler veut dire; **he took the h.,** il se l'est tenu pour dit; (*b*) (*sign*) signe *m*, indication *f*, suggestion *f*; **not a h. of surprise,** pas une ombre de surprise; **not the slightest h. of . . .,** pas le moindre soupçon de . . .; **a h. of a Belgian accent,** une pointe d'accent belge. **2. hints for housewives,** conseils *m* aux ménagères; **to jot down a few hints for s.o.,** noter quelques indications pour aider qn; **can you give me some hints?** (i) pouvez-vous me donner quelques conseils? (ii) pouvez-vous me mettre sur la voie? **driving hints,** recommandations *f* pour la conduite d'une voiture; **maintenance hints,** conseils et indications pour l'entretien (d'un appareil, etc.).

hint[2], *v.tr. & i.* insinuer (qch.); suggérer, faire, dire, (qch.) à mots couverts; **to h. to s.o. that. . .,** faire entendre à qn que . . .; **to h. at sth.,** laisser entendre qch., suggérer qch., à mots couverts, par sous-entendus; faire une allusion voilée à qch.; **to h. at the truth,** laisser entrevoir la vérité.

hinterland ['hintəlænd], *s.* hinterland *m*; arrière-pays *m inv.*

hip[1] [hip], *s.* **1.** *Anat:* hanche *f*; **h. measurement,** tour *m* de hanches; **h. bone,** os coxal, iliaque; **h. joint,** articulation coxo-fémorale, de la hanche; **h. bath,** bain *m* de siège; **h. pocket,** poche fessière; poche revolver; **to**

sway one's hips (in walking), se déhancher en marchant; se dandiner; **to have s.o. on the h.,** (i) *Wr:* avoir l'adversaire chargé sur l'une de ses hanches; (ii) *F:* tenir qn; avoir l'avantage sur qn; *A:* **to smite s.o. h. and thigh,** anéantir qn; **to be beaten h. and thigh,** être battu à plate couture. **2.** *Const:* **h. (piece, rafter),** arêtier *m*, arête *f*, chevron *m* d'arête (d'un comble); **h. slate,** ardoise cornière; **h.-tile,** arêtière *f*, enfaîteau *m*; tuile cornière; **h. lead** [led], **h. sheet,** bavette *f*; (*of sheet lead*) **h. bead,** arêtier; **h. roof,** comble *m*, toit *m*, en croupe.

hip[2], *s. Bot:* cynor(r)hodon *m*, fruit *m* du rosier; *Pharm:* **rose h. syrup,** sirop *m* de cynor(r)hodon.

hip[3], *s. F: A:* (*hypochondria*) mélancolie *f*, spleen *m*; *O:* **to have the h.,** avoir le cafard; broyer du noir.

hip[4], *v.tr. F: O:* attrister (qn); donner le spleen, le cafard, à (qn).

hip[5], *a. F:* **1.** à la page, dans le vent. **2.** fanatique de jazz.

hip[6], *int.* **1.** hep! **2. h.! h.! h.! hurrah!** hip! hip! hip! hourra!

hipe [haip], *s. Wr:* prise *f* avec enlacement de jambe.

hipparch ['hipɑ:k], *s. Gr.Ant:* hipparque *m*.

Hipparchus [hi'pɑ:kəs], *Pr.n.m. Gr.Hist:* Hipparque.

hipparion [hi'pɛəriən], *s. Paleont:* hipparion *m*.

hipped[1] [hipt], *a.* **1.** *Vet:* (cheval) déhanché, éhanché, épointé. **2.** (*a*) (*with adj. prefixed*) **broad-h.,** à fortes hanches; (*b*) *Arch:* **h. roof,** toit pourvu d'un arêtier; comble *m* en croupe.

hipped[2], *a. F:* **1.** *O:* crevé d'ennui. **2.** obsédé (par qch.). **3.** au courant; à la page.

hippic ['hipik], *a.* (concours *m*) hippique.

hippie ['hipi], *s. F:* hippie *mf*, hippy *mf*.

hippo ['hipou], *s. F:* hippopotame *m*.

hippoboscid [hipou'bɔsid], *s. Ent:* hippobosque *m*.

hippocampus [hipou'kæmpəs], *s.* **1.** *Gr.Myth: Ich:* hippocampe *m*. **2.** *Anat:* **h. major, minor,** grand, petit, hippocampe.

Hippocastanaceae [hipoukæstə'neisii:], *s.pl. Bot:* hippocastanacées *f*.

hippocras ['hipəkræs], *s.* hypocras *m*.

Hippocrates [hi'pɔkrəti:z], *Pr.n.m. Med.Hist:* Hippocrate.

Hippocratic [hipə'krætik], *a. Med:* hippocratique; **H. face,** facies *m* hippocratique; **H. fingers,** doigts *m* hippocratiques; **H. oath,** serment *m* d'Hippocrate.

hippocratism [hi'pɔkrətizm], *s. Med:* hippocratisme *m*.

Hippocrene ['hipəkri:n], *Pr.n. Gr.Ant:* Hippocrène *f*.

hippodrome ['hipədroum], *s.* **1.** hippodrome *m*. **2.** *NAm:* arène *f* (où on donne des spectacles équestres).

hippogriff ['hipəgrif], *s. Myth:* hippogriffe *m*.

hippolith ['hipəliθ], *s. Vet:* hippolithe *f*.

hippology [hi'pɔlədʒi], *s.* hippologie *f*.

Hippolytus [hi'pɔlitəs], *Pr.n.m. Gr.Lit:* Hippolyte.

hippophaë [hi'pɔfaii:], *s. Bot:* argousier *m*, hippophaé *m*.

hippophagous [hi'pɔfəgəs], *a.* hippophage.

hippophagy [hi'pɔfədʒi], *s.* hippophagie *f*.

hippopotamus, *pl.* **-muses, -mi** [hipə'pɔtəməs, -məsiz, m(a)i], *s. Z:* hippopotame *m*.

Hippotraginae [hipə'trædʒini:], *s.pl. Z:* hippotraginés *m*.

hippuric [hi'pju:rik], *a. Physiol:* (acide) hippurique.

hippus ['hipəs], *s. Med:* hippus *m*; athétose *f* pupillaire.

hippy ['hipi], *s. F:* hippie *mf*, hippy *mf*.

hipshot ['hipʃɔt], *a. Vet:* (cheval) déhanché, éhanché, épointé.

hipster ['hipstər], *s. P:* **1.** (*a*) fanatique *mf* de la musique pop; (*b*) membre *m* d'un groupe pop. **2.** hippie *mf*. **3.** type *m* nouvelle vague, qui est dans le vent. **4.** initié(e) à la drogue. **5.** *Cost:* (pantalon *m*, etc.) taille basse.

hirable ['haiərəbl], *a.* = HIREABLE.

hircine ['hə:sain, -si:n], *a.* hircin.

hire[1] [haiər], *s.* **1.** (*a*) *NAm:* louage *m* (d'un domestique); embauchage *m* (de main-d'œuvre); location *f* (d'une maison); **on h.,** à louer; (*b*) location (d'une voiture, d'une salle); **cars for h.,** voitures *f* en location, à louer; (*taxi sign*) **for h.,** libre; (*c*) **h. purchase,** (i) vente *f*, (ii) achat *m*, à crédit, à tempérament; **to buy sth. on the h.-purchase system,** acheter qch. à crédit. **2.** *esp. NAm:* (i) salaire *m*, gages *mpl*; (ii) loyer *m*; *Lit:* **the labourer is worthy of his h.,** toute peine, tout travail, mérite salaire.

hire[2], *v.tr.* **1.** (*a*) *esp. NAm:* engager (un ouvrier, un employé); prendre à son service (un domestique); (*b*) soudoyer (un assassin); (*c*) louer (une voiture, une salle, etc.); prendre (qch.) en location. **2.** *esp. NAm:* **to h. (sth.) (out),** louer (qch.), donner (qch.) en location (à qn). **3.** *v.pr. & i. NAm:* **to h. (oneself) out, to h. in,** accepter un emploi; (*of farmland*) se louer pour la saison.

hireable ['haiərəbl], *a.* qu'on peut louer; à louer.

hired ['haiərd], *a.* **1.** (*pers.*) (*a*) *NAm:* **h. man,** (i) domestique *m*; homme *m* à tout faire; (ii) (*also* **h. hand**) garçon *m* de ferme; ouvrier *m* agricole; **h. girl, h. help,** (i) bonne *f*; femme *f* de ménage; (ii) fille *f* de ferme; (*b*) **h. assassin,** assassin *m* à gages, à la solde de qn; *Hist:* **h. troops,** mercenaires *m*. **2.** (*thg*) **h. car,** voiture *f* de location.

hireling ['haiərliŋ], *s.* **1.** *usu. Pej:* mercenaire *m*, stipendié *m*, stipendiaire *m*. **2.** cheval *m* à louer.

hirer ['haiərər], *s.* **1.** (*a*) *NAm:* locataire *mf* (d'une chambre, etc.); (*b*) personne *f* qui prend (une voiture, etc.) en location, qui loue (une voiture, etc.). **2.** *NAm:* **h. (out),** loueur, -euse.

hiring ['haiəriŋ], *s.* **1.** (*a*) *NAm:* louage *m* (d'un domestique); embauchage *m* (d'un ouvrier); (*b*) louage (d'une voiture, etc.). **2.** *pl. Agr: A:* **hirings,** foire *f* de louage.

hirsute ['hə:sjut], *a.* hirsute, velu; *Bot:* (feuille) âpre; (arbuste) cilié.

hirsuteness ['hə:sjutnis], *s.* nature hirsute, velue.

hirsutism ['hə:sjutizm], *s.* hirsutisme *m*.

hirudiniculture [hi'ru:dinikʌltjər], *s.* hirudiniculture *f*; élevage *m* des sangsues.

Hirudinidae [hiru:'dinidi:], *s.pl. Ann:* Hirudinées *f*; *F:* sangsues *f*.

Hirundinidae [hirən'dinidi:], *s.pl. Orn:* hirundinidés *m*, les hirondelles *f*.

his[1] [hiz], *poss.a.* (*denoting a m. possessor*) (*a*) son, *f.* sa, *pl.* ses; **h. hat and gloves,** son chapeau et ses gants; **h. opinion,** son opinion *f*; **h. friend, h. friends,** son ami, *f.* son amie; ses amis, *f.* ses amies; **one of h. friends,** un de ses amis, un sien ami, un ami à lui; **h. father and mother,** son père et sa mère; *Adm:* ses père et mère; **the date and place of h. birth,** ses date et lieu de naissance; **h. own son,** son propre fils; **he fell on h. back,** il est tombé sur le dos; **I hurt h. arm,** je lui ai fait mal au bras; **he has hurt h. hand,** il s'est fait mal à la main; **h. eyes are brown,** il a les yeux bruns; (*emphatic*) **his idea would be to . . .,** son idée à lui serait de . . .; (*b*) **H. Majesty,** sa Majesté; **H. Lordship,** Monsieur (le comte, etc.). **2. he knew h. Homer from beginning to end,** il savait son Homère d'un bout à l'autre.

his[2], *poss.pron.* (*denoting a m. possessor*) le sien, la sienne, les siens, les siennes; **he took my pen as well as h.,** il a pris mon stylo avec le sien; **this book is h.,** ce livre est à lui, lui appartient; c'est son livre à lui; **here are my shoes, h. are near the fire,** voici mes souliers, les siens sont près du feu; **a friend of h.,** un de ses amis; un ami à lui; **a soldier friend of h.,** un militaire de ses amis; **it is no business of h.,** ce n'est pas son affaire; **no effort of h.,** aucun effort de sa part; **every action of h. was . . .,** tous ses actes étaient . . .; **I remember a remark of h.,** je me rappelle une remarque de lui; **that pride of h.,** son orgueil; cet orgueil dont il ne peut se défaire.

Hispania [hi'spæniə], *Pr.n. Geog: A: Lit:* Hispanie *f*.

Hispanic [hi'spænik], *a.* hispanique.

Hispanicism [hi'spænisizm], *s.* hispanisme *m*, espagnolisme *m*.

Hispanicize [hi'spænisaiz], **Hispaniolize** [hi'spæniəlaiz], *v.tr.* espagnoliser.

Hispano-American [hi'spænouə'merik(ə)n]. (*a*) *a.* hispano-américain; (*b*) *s.* Hispano-américain, -aine, *pl.* Hispano-américains, -aines.

Hispano-Moorish [hi'spænou'mɔ:riʃ], **Hispano-Moresque** [hi'spænoumɔ'resk], *a. Art:* hispano-moresque, *pl.* hispano-moresques.

hispid ['hispid], *a. Nat.Hist:* hispide.

hiss[1] [his], *s.* **1.** sifflement *m*; **h. of the gas,** sifflement du gaz; *Th: etc:* **applause and hisses,** applaudissements *m* et sifflets *m*. **2.** *Ling:* fricative sourde; sifflante *f*; chuintante *f*.

hiss[2], *v.tr. & i.* (*of pers., serpent, steam, etc.*) siffler; (*of arc lamp*) bruire; (*of steam, gas*) chuinter; **"you'll pay for that," he hissed,** "tu me le revaudras," dit-il d'une voix sifflante; **to h. (at) an actor, a play,** siffler un acteur, une pièce de théâtre; **to h. s.o. off the stage,** chasser qn à coups de sifflets; **to be hissed,** être sifflé.

hissing[1] ['hisiŋ], *a.* **h. noise,** sifflement *m*; chuintement *m*; bruissement *m*; *Med:* **h. respiration,** respiration sibilante; **h. gas,** gaz qui chuinte.

hissing[2], *s.* sifflement *m*; chuintement *m*; (*of arc lamp*) bruissement *m*; *I.C.E: etc:* **h. of the admission,** chuintement dans les tubulures d'admission.

hist [(p)st, hist], *int.* **1.** (*to enjoin silence*) chut! **2.** (*to attract attention*) pst! psitt!

histamin(e) ['histəmin, -mi:n], *s. Physiol:* histamine *f*.

hister ['histər], *s. Ent:* hister *m*, escarbot *m*.

Histeridae [his'teridi:], *s.pl. Ent:* histéridés *m*, histérides *m*.

histidine ['histədi:n], *s. Biol:* histidine *f*.

histiocyte ['histiousait], *s. Biol:* histiocyte *m*, cellule *f* histioïde.

histioid ['histiɔid], *a. Biol:* histioïde.

histo- ['histou], *comb.fm.* histo-.

histoblast ['histoublæst], *s. Ent:* histoblaste *m*.

histogene ['histoudʒi:n], *s. Biol:* histogène *m*.

histogenesis [histou'dʒenisis], **histogeny** [his'tɔdʒini], *s. Biol:* histogénèse *f*.

histogenetic [histoudʒə'netik], **histogenic** [histou'dʒi:nik], *a. Biol:* histogénique.

histogram ['histougræm], *s.* histogramme *m*.

histoid ['histɔid], *a. Biol:* hist(i)oïde.

histological [histə'lɔdʒikl], *a. Biol:* histologique.

histologist [his'tɔlədʒist], *s. Biol:* histologiste *mf*.

histology [his'tɔlədʒi], *s. Biol:* histologie *f*.

histolysis [his'tɔlisis], *s. Physiol:* histolyse *f*.

histone ['histoun], *s. Ch:* histon *m*, histone *f*.

histopathology [histoupə'θɔlədʒi], *s.* histopathologie *f*.

histoplasmosis [histouplæz'mousis], *s. Med:* histoplasmose *f*.

historian [his'tɔ:riən], *s.* historien, -ienne.

historiated [his'tɔ:rieitid], *a.* (manuscrit) historié, enjolivé d'ornements.

historic [his'tɔrik], *a.* **1.** historique; (événement) marquant; **h. building,** monument *m* historique; **h. battlefields,** champs *m* de bataille historiques; **an h. occasion,** une occasion mémorable. **2.** *Gram:* **h. tense,** temps *m* historique; *Gr.Gram:* temps second; **h. present,** présent historique, narratif, de narration; *Lt. & Fr.Gram:* **h. infinitive,** infinitif *m* de narration; **past h.,** passé simple.

historical [his'tɔrikl], *a.* **1.** historique, de l'histoire; **h. criticism,** critique *f* des sources; **h. event,** événement *m* historique, marquant; **h. character,** personnage *m* historique; **h. accuracy,** exactitude *f* historique; **h. record, account,** historique *m*. **2. h. painting,** tableau *m* d'histoire; **h. play, novel,** *s. NAm:* **historical,** pièce *f*, roman *m*, historique. **3. h. linguistics,** linguistique *f* historique.

historically [his'tɔrik(ə)li], *adv.* historiquement.

historicism [his'tɔrisizm], *s.* historicisme *m*.

historicity [histə'risiti], *s.* historicité *f*, caractère *m* historique (d'un fait).

historico- [his'tɔrikou], *comb.fm.* historico-.

historicophilosophic(al) [his'tɔrikoufilə'zɔfik(l)], *a.* historico-philosophique.

historicopolitical [his'tɔrikoupə'litikl], *a.* historico-politique.

historiographer [histɔ:ri'ɔgrəfər], *s.* historiographe *m*.

historiographic(al) [histɔriou'græfik(l)], *a.* historiographique.

historiography [histɔ:ri'ɔgrəfi], *s.* historiographie *f*.

history ['hist(ə)ri], *s.* **1.** (*a*) l'histoire *f*; **French, European, h.,** l'histoire de France, de l'Europe; **ancient, modern, h.,** l'histoire ancienne, moderne; *F:* **that's ancient h.,** c'est de l'histoire ancienne; ça c'est une vieille histoire; c'est vieux comme Adam; **sidelights on h.,** les à-côtés de l'histoire; **we're making h.,** nous faisons l'histoire; ce que nous faisons (en ce moment) restera, marquera, dans l'histoire, fera date; (*b*) **nation with a h.,** nation *f* avec un passé; **this ship has an interesting h.,** l'histoire de ce navire est intéressante; **this penknife has a h.,** je pourrais vous raconter toute une histoire sur ce canif; (*c*) *Sch:* **h. (book),** manuel *m*, livre *m*, d'histoire; **bring your French histories,** apportez vos histoires de France; (*d*) historique *m*; **regimental h.,** historique du régiment. **2.** *Th: A:* pièce *f*, drame *m*, historique. **3. natural h.,** histoire naturelle; sciences naturelles. **4.** (*a*) *Mil: etc:* **h. sheet,** feuille *f* matriculaire; état *m* signalétique et des services (d'un homme); (*b*) *Med:* **case h.,** dossier médical (d'un malade).

histotomy [his'tɔtəmi], *s. Med:* histotomie *f*.

histotoxic [histou'tɔksik], *a. Biol:* histotoxique.

histotoxin [histou'tɔksin], *s. Biol:* histotoxique *m*.

histozyme ['histouzaim], *s. Bio-Ch:* histozyme *m*.

histrion ['histriən], *s. A:* **1.** comédien *m*. **2.** *Pej:* histrion *m*, cabotin *m*.

histrionic(al) [histri'ɔnik(l)], *a.* **1.** théâtral, -aux. **2.** histrionique; peu sincère.

histrionically [histri'ɔnik(ə)li], *adv.* **1.** théâtralement. **2.** d'une manière histrionique.

histrionics [histri'ɔniks], *s.pl.* **1.** l'art *m* du théâtre. **2.** *Pej:* démonstrations *f* peu sincères; parade *f* d'émotion, d'affection, de colère, etc.; **it is mere h. on her part,** c'est une comédie qu'elle nous joue.

hit[1] [hit], *s.* **1.** (*a*) coup *m*; **a h. from a stone had scratched the paint,** un coup de pierre avait éraflé la peinture; *F:* **to have, make, a sly h. at s.o.,** représenter qn d'une manière satirique; décocher un trait satirique à qn; donner un coup de patte à qn; **a h. at doctors,** un coup de patte, un sarcasme, à l'adresse des médecins; **that's a h. at you,** c'est à vous que s'adresse l'allusion, c'est vous qui êtes visé; c'est une pierre dans votre jardin; (*b*) *Artil: etc:* (i) impact *m*; (ii) coup au but; (*c*) *Fenc:* touche *f*, coup; **a h.!** touché! **stop h.,** coup d'arrêt; **exchanged h., double h.,** coup fourré; **to score a h.,** toucher; **to score a h. on the arm,** porter un coup au bras; (*d*) *Bill:* touche; (*e*) (*hockey*) coup de crosse; **free h.,** coup franc; (*f*) (*baseball*) coup de batte; frappe *f*. **2.** (*a*) coup réussi; succès *m*; **lucky h.,** (i) coup heureux; (ii) trouvaille *f*; **to make a lucky h.,** (i) avoir de la chance; (ii) (*in guessing, etc.*) rencontrer juste; **to make, be, a h.,** (*of thg*) réussir en plein; (*of pers.*) faire sensation; (*b*) *Th: T.V: etc:* pièce *f*, chanson *f*, spectacle *m*, à succès; **it was a great h.,** c'était un succès fou; *T.V: etc:* **h. parade,** palmarès *m*.

hit[2], *v.* (**hit; hit; hitting**)

I. *v.tr. & i.* **1.** *v.tr.* (*a*) frapper; **to h. s.o. in the face,** frapper qn au visage; **a stone h. him on the forehead,** une pierre l'a attrapé au front; **to h. s.o. a blow,** porter, donner, un coup à qn; **to h. sth. sharply with a hammer,** donner un coup de marteau sec à qch.; *v.i.* **to h. hard,** frapper fort; cogner fort; *Cr:* **to h. (off, up) a hundred runs,** faire, marquer, cent courses, cent points; (*b*) **to h. one's leg,** s'attraper à la jambe; **to h. against sth.,** s'attraper à qch.; **to h. one's foot against a stone,** se heurter, se cogner, le pied contre une pierre; buter contre une pierre; **his head h. against the pavement,** sa tête a porté, a donné, sur le trottoir; *Nau:* **to h. a rock,** heurter un récif; (*c*) atteindre; *Fenc: Bill:* toucher; **to h. the mark,** atteindre le but; frapper juste; *Artil: etc:* toucher le but; *Mus:* **to h. the wrong note,** (i) frapper à faux (sur le piano, etc.); (ii) attaquer faux; **to h. s.o. with a stone,** atteindre qn avec une pierre; **to be h. by a bullet,** être atteint par une balle; (*of animal shot at*) **he's h.!** il en a! *F:* **he couldn't h. an elephant, a haystack, a barn door,** il raterait un éléphant dans un couloir; *Aut: F:* **to h. the hundred mark,** taper le 100; (*of allusion, etc.*) **to h. home,** porter (coup); piquer (qn) au vif; **to be hard h.,** (i) être sérieusement touché, être fortement, gravement, atteint (par ses pertes, etc.); (ii) être très épris de qn; avoir succombé aux charmes de qn; **we were hard h. by the war,** nous avons beaucoup souffert de la guerre; **heavily h. by a bankruptcy,** gravement atteint par une faillite; **he has been especially hard h.,** il a eu particulièrement à souffrir; ç'a été pour lui un coup particulièrement dur; **the strike has h. several factories,** la grève a atteint plusieurs usines; (*d*) **here goes, h. or miss!** allons-y, à tout hasard! vaille que vaille! **to strike out, to answer, h. or miss,** frapper, répondre, au hasard, au petit bonheur; **it's h. or miss!** c'est tout ou rien! *Mec.E:* **h.-or-miss governor, h.-and-miss governor,** régulateur *m* par tout ou rien; (*e*) *I.C.E:* **the engine is hitting on only three cylinders,** il n'y a que trois cylindres qui fonctionnent; (*f*) *U.S: F:* **he h. his friend for 100 dollars,** il a tapé son ami de 100 dollars. **2.** (*a*) *v.tr. & i.* **to h. on sth.,** découvrir, trouver (un moyen); rencontrer (un indice, un filon d'or, etc.); **to h. the right path,** rencontrer le bon chemin; **to h. (on) the right word,** trouver le mot juste; **you've h. it!** vous avez deviné juste! vous y êtes! vous avez mis le doigt dessus! *F:* en plein dans le mille! **he h. on it himself,** c'est lui qui l'a imaginé; *Journ: F:* **to h. the headlines,** défrayer la chronique; **to h. the headlines again,** retrouver la vedette; **to h. the nail on the head,** tomber juste; *F:* **to h. the roof, the ceiling,** être furieux; *F:* **to h. the high spots,** (i) voir, visiter, les choses les plus importantes; (ii) faire le tour des boîtes de nuit, etc.; *F:* **to h. it up,** faire la vie; *P:* **to h. the bottle,** boire (trop); *P:* **to h. the hay,** *U.S:* **the sack,** se coucher, se mettre au pieu; *esp. U.S: P:* **to h. the silk,** parachuter; *F:* **to h. the deck,** tomber à plat ventre; (*b*) *v.tr. U.S:* arriver à (un endroit); **to h. the trail, the road,** se mettre en route; (*c*) *v.tr.* rencontrer (qch.) (tout d'un coup, par accident); **after losing ourselves in the fog we suddenly h. the right road,** après nous être perdus dans le brouillard nous avons tout d'un coup retrouvé notre chemin; **we h. a terrible snowstorm,** nous nous sommes trouvés dans une tempête de neige terrible; (*d*) *v.tr. F:* **how did it h. you?** quelle impression cela vous a-t-il fait? **he didn't know what had h. him,** il se demandait ce qui lui était arrivé.

II. (*compound verbs*) **1. hit back,** *v.i.* se défendre; rendre coup pour coup (à qn).

2. hit off, *v.tr.* (*a*) imiter (qn); faire un portrait (satirique) de (qn, qch.); **you've h. him off perfectly, to a T,** c'est lui tout craché; (*b*) **to h. it off with s.o.,** s'accorder, s'entendre, avec qn; **they've never h. it off,** ils s'entendent, ils ont toujours vécu, comme chien et chat.

3. hit out, *v.i.* (*a*) **to h. out at s.o.,** décocher un coup à qn; détacher des coups à qn; **to h. out blindly,** se débattre comme un diable dans un bénitier; **when he is attacked he hits out,** quand on l'attaque il a la riposte rude; (*b*) *Cr: Ten:* retourner dru la balle; jouer un jeu vigoureux (mais sans finesse).

hit-and-run ['hitn(d)'rʌn], *a.* **killed by a h.-a.-r. driver,** tué par un chauffard qui ne s'est pas arrêté, qui a pris la fuite.

hitch[1] [hitʃ], *s.* **1.** (*a*) saccade *f*, secousse *f*; **to give one's trousers a h.,** remonter son pantalon (d'un mouvement sec); (*b*) (*of horse*) léger boitement. **2.** (*a*) *Nau:* nœud *m*; **half h.,** demi-clef *f*; **clove h.,** nœud de batelier; **blackwall h.,** nœud de croc; **marling-spike h.,** nœud de trésillon; **timber h.,** barbouquet *m*; (*b*) *N.Am:* (dispositif *m* d')attelage *m*; accrochage *m*; attache *f*; **trailer h.,** crochet *m*, système *m*, d'attelage (de remorque); sellette *f* (de semi-remorque); (*c*) **h. pin,** cheville *f* (de piano). **3.** (*a*) *Min:* légère faille; (*b*) empêchement *m*, anicroche *f*, contretemps *m*, accroc *m*, *F:* os *m*; **there's a h. somewhere,** il y a quelque chose qui cloche; **I've found the h.,** je vois ce qui cloche; **there was a serious h. in the negotiations,** les négociations ont accroché sérieusement; **without a h.,** sans à-coup, sans accroc, sans anicroche, *F:* tout de go; *W.Tel: T.V: etc:* **technical h.,** panne *f* d'émission, incident *m* technique. **4.** *N.Am: F:* (*a*) service *m* militaire; (*b*) **to do a three-year h. in prison,** faire trois ans de prison; **while waiting for a better job, he put in a h. with a builder,** en attendant un meilleur emploi il s'est embauché chez un entrepreneur. **5.** *F:* **to thumb a h.,** faire de l'autostop, du stop.

hitch[2]. **1.** *v.tr.* remuer (qch.) par saccades; **to h. up one's trousers,** remonter son pantalon (d'un coup sec). **2.** (*a*) *v.tr.* accrocher, attacher, fixer, *Nau:* amarrer (**sth. to sth.,** qch. à qch.); **to h. one's horse to a tree,** attacher son cheval à un arbre; **to h. a carriage on to a train,** accrocher une voiture à un train; *Fig:* **to h. one's wagon to a star,** attacher son char à une étoile; (*b*) *v.i.* faire de l'auto-stop, du stop; *v.tr.* **we hitched a ride to Bath,** on nous a pris en stop jusqu'à Bath. **3.** *v.i.* (*a*) **to h. on to sth.,** s'accrocher, s'attacher, s'atteler, à qch.; (*b*) *Mec.E:* (*of lathe tool*) s'enfoncer dans la pièce à travailler. **4.** *v.i. P:* **to get hitched (up),** se marier.

hitch-hike[1] ['hitʃhaik], *v.i.* faire de l'auto-stop, du stop; **to h.-h. to Paris,** aller à Paris en stop.

hitch-hike[2], *s.* voyage *m* en auto-stop, en stop.

hitch-hiker ['hitʃhaikər], *s.* auto-stoppeur, -euse.

hitch-hiking ['hitʃhaikiŋ], *s.* auto-stop *m*.

hitching ['hitʃiŋ], *s.* attache *f* (de qch. à qch.); *Nau:* amarrage *m*; **h. post, rail,** poteau *m*, rail *m*, d'attache (de chevaux).

hither ['hiðər]. **1.** *adv.* ici (exprimant la venue); **h. and thither,** çà et là. **2.** *a. A:* (*nearer*) le plus rapproché; de ce côté-ci; **on this h. side of the river,** de ce côté-ci du fleuve; *A.Geog:* **H. Gaul,** la Gaule citérieure.

hitherto ['hiðə'tu:], *adv.* jusqu'ici, jusqu'à présent; **as h.,** comme par le passé.

hitherward ['hiðəwəd], *adv. A:* de ce côté-ci, par ici.

Hitler ['hitlər], *Pr.n.m.* Hitler; **H. government,** gouvernement hitlérien.

Hitlerism ['hitlərizm], *s.* hitlérisme *m*.

Hitlerite ['hitlərait], *a. & s.* hitlérien, -ienne.

hitter ['hitər], *s.* frappeur *m*; *Box:* cogneur *m*; **to be a hard h.,** cogner, frapper, dur.

Hittite ['hitait], *A.Hist:* (*a*) *a.* hittite; (*b*) *s.* Hittite *mf*; (*c*) *s. Ling:* hittite *m*.

Hittitologist [hitai'tɔlədʒist], *s.* hittitologue *mf*.

hive[1] [haiv], *s.* **1.** ruche *f*; **frame h.,** ruche démontable; ruche à cadres; **h. of industry,** ruche d'industrie; vraie fourmilière. **2.** (*swarm*) essaim *m*.

hive[2]. **1.** *v.tr.* (*a*) mettre (des abeilles) dans une ruche; **to h. a swarm,** (re)cueillir un essaim dans une ruche; (*b*) *O:* amasser, accumuler (des vivres, etc.). **2.** *v.i.* (*a*) (*of swarm*) prendre possession de, entrer dans, la ruche; (*b*) *O:* vivre ensemble (comme des abeilles dans une ruche); (*c*) **to h. off,** essaimer.

hive[3], *s.* **1.** *pl. Med:* **hives,** (i) éruption *f*; urticaire *f*; (ii) strophulus *m*; (iii) varicelle pustuleuse; (iv) croup *m*; *F: A:* **bowel hives,** entérite *f*. **2.** *Pharm: A:* **h. syrup,** sirop *m* de scille composé (contre le croup).

hiveful ['haivful], *s.* ruchée *f*.

h'm [hm], *int.* (*expressing doubt*) heu! hum!

hmph [(h)m], *int.* expiration atone d'air par les narines, pour exprimer le mépris, l'indifférence.

ho[1] [hou], *int.* **1.** (*expressing surprise, amusement, etc.*) ho! **2.** (*to attract attention*) hé! ohé! *Nau:* **land ho!** la terre en vue! **sail ho!** navire en vue! **3. westward ho!** en route pour l'Ouest!

ho[2], *int.* (*to horse*) ho!

hoacin [wɔ'si:n], *s. Orn:* hoa(t)zin *m*.

hoar [hɔ:r]. **1.** *a. A:* = HOARY. **2.** *s. Lit:* **the h. of years,** le frimas des ans.

hoard[1] [hɔ:d], *s.* amas *m*, approvisionnement secret, accumulation secrète (de vivres, etc.); **h. of money,** trésor *m*, *F:* magot *m*; **h. of gold, of jewels,** trésor (secret) d'or, de bijoux.

hoard[2], *v.tr.* amasser, accaparer (le blé, etc.); accumuler (de l'argent); **to h. supplies,** pratiquer la resserre des vivres; **to h. up treasure,** *v.i.* **to h.,** thésauriser (des capitaux).

hoarder ['hɔ:dər], *s.* amasseur, -euse, accumulateur, -trice; **h. of provisions,** spéculateur *m* (pratiquant la resserre); **h. of money,** thésauriseur, -euse.

hoarding[1] ['hɔ:diŋ], *s.* **1.** resserre *f*, amassage *m* (de provisions); thésaurisation *f* (de capitaux). **2.** *pl.* **hoardings,** amas *m*, accumulation *f* (de vivres, de trésors).

hoarding[2] ['hɔ:diŋ], *s.* (*a*) clôture *f* en planches; palissade *f* (de chantier, etc.); (*b*) panneau *m* publicitaire, à affiches; panneau-réclame *m*, *pl.* panneaux-réclame.

hoarfrost ['hɔ:frɔst], *s.* gelée blanche.

hoarhound ['hɔ:haund], *s.* = HOREHOUND.

hoariness ['hɔ:rinis], *s.* **1.** blancheur *f* (des cheveux). **2.** vieillesse *f*.

hoarse [hɔ:s], *a.* (*of voice, etc.*) enroué, rauque; **to be h.,** être enroué; avoir la voix enrouée; **to shout oneself h.,** s'enrouer à force de crier; **h. sound,** graillement *m*.

hoarsely ['hɔ:sli], *adv.* d'une voix rauque, enrouée; avec un son rauque.

hoarsen ['hɔ:sn]. **1.** *v.tr.* enrouer (la voix). **2.** *v.i.* devenir enroué; s'enrouer; prendre un son rauque.

hoarseness ['hɔ:snis], *s.* (*a*) enrouement *m*; (*b*) raucité *f* (d'un son).

hoar-stone ['hɔ:stoun], *s. A:* borne *f* (de frontière).

hoary ['hɔ:ri], *a.* **1.** (*a*) (*of hair*) blanchi, chenu; **h.-headed old man,** vieillard *m* aux cheveux blancs; **h. old sinner,** vieux paillard; (*b*) (*of colour*) blanchâtre; (*c*) *Bot: Ent:* (feuillage, insecte) couvert de poils blancs, d'un duvet blanc. **2.** vénérable, séculaire.

hoatzin [wɔ(t)'si:n], *s. Orn:* hoatzin *m*, hoazin *m*, sasa *m*.

hoax[1] [houks], *s.* mystification *f*, supercherie *f*, mauvaise plaisanterie, farce *f*, tour *m*, attrape *f*, *Journ: F:* canard *m*; *Sch: F:* canular *m* (d'étudiants); **to play a h. on s.o.,** (i) mystifier qn; (ii) jouer un tour, faire une farce, à qn.

hoax[2], *v.tr.* mystifier, attraper (qn); jouer un tour à (qn); *F:* acheter, berner (qn); monter un bateau à (qn).

hoaxer ['houksər], *s.* mystificateur, -trice.

hoaxing ['houksiŋ], *s.* mystification *f*.

hob[1] [hɔb], *s.* **1.** *A:* rustre *m*, manant *m*. **2.** *A:* lutin *m*. **3.** furet *m* mâle; belette *f* mâle.

hob[2], *s.* **1.** plaque *f* de côté (d'une grille de cheminée, où l'on peut tenir les aliments, etc. au chaud). **2.** patin *m* (de traîneau). **3.** *Mec.E:* **h. (tap),** maîtresse-matrice *f*, *pl.* maîtresses-matrices; fraise-mère *f*, *pl.* fraises-mères; taraud-mère *m*, *pl.* tarauds-mères. **4.** = HOBNAIL[1] 1. **5.** *Games:* fiche *f* de but (au jeu de palets).

hob[3], *v.tr.* (**hobbed**) **1.** (*a*) *Mec.E:* fraiser, tailler (une taraudeuse, etc.); (*b*) *Metalw:* **to h. out,** estamper (à froid). **2.** ferrer (un soulier).

hobber ['hɔbər], *s. Mec.E:* = HOB[2] 3.

hobbing ['hɔbiŋ], *s.* **1.** fraisage *m* (d'une taraudeuse); taille *f* (d'engrenages); **h. machine,** machine *f* à tailler les engrenages. **2.** ferrage *m* (d'un soulier); *Dial:* **h. foot,** enclume universelle (pour cordonnerie).

hobble[1] ['hɔbl], *s.* **1.** boitillement *m*, clochement *m*; **to walk with a h.,** clopiner, boitiller, en marchant. **2.** (*a*) entrave *f*, abot *m* (pour chevaux, etc.); (*b*) *F: A:* embarras *m*; **to get into a h.,** se mettre dans le pétrin; (*c*) *A.Cost:* **h. skirt,** jupe entravée; jupe fourreau.

hobble[2]. **1.** *v.i.* boitiller, clocher, clopiner; **to h. along,** marcher en boitillant; avancer clopin-clopant; traîner la jambe; **to h. in, out,** entrer, sortir, clopin-clopant. **2.** *v.tr.* (*a*) entraver (un cheval, etc.); mettre un abot aux paturons (d'un cheval); **hobbled horse,** cheval entravé, enjarreté; (*b*) *F: A:* embarrasser (qn).

hobbledehoy ['hɔbldi'hɔi], *s.* jeune homme gauche; grand dadais.

hobby[1] ['hɔbi], *s.* **1.** *A:* bidet *m*, petit cheval de selle. **2.** passe-temps (favori); violon *m* d'Ingres; **to paint as a h.,** se distraire à faire de la peinture; **my main h. is photography,** ma principale distraction, mon violon d'Ingres, c'est la photographie; *esp. N.Am:* **to ride a h.,** s'adonner trop à son passe-temps favori (au détriment de son travail).

hobby[2], *s. Orn:* (faucon *m*) hobereau *m*; falquet *m*.

hobbyhorse ['hɔbihɔ:s], *s.* **1.** dada *m*; cheval *m* de bois; *Th: etc:* cheval-jupon *m*, *pl.* chevaux-jupons; (*in morris dance, etc.*) cheval frou. **2.** *A:* draisienne *f*, célérette *f*.

hobgoblin ['hɔbgɔblin], *s.* lutin *m*, farfadet *m*, gobelin *m*, esprit follet.

hobnail[1] ['hɔbneil], *s.* **1.** caboche *f*; clou *m* à ferrer (les souliers); becquet *m*, béquet *m*. **2.** *F: A:* = HOB[1] 1.

hobnail[2], *v.tr.* ferrer (un soulier).

hobnailed ['hɔbneild], *a.* (soulier) ferré, à gros clous; **h. boot,** godillot *m*; *Med: F:* **h. liver,** foie *m* cirrhotique.

hobnob ['hɔbnɔb], *v.i.* **(hobnobbed)** *(a) A:* boire, trinquer **(with s.o.,** avec qn); *(b)* **to h. with s.o.,** être de pair à compagnon avec qn; être à tu et à toi avec qn; **to h. with the great,** frayer avec les grands; être admis dans la familiarité des grands; fréquenter les grands.

hobo[1] ['houbou], *s. NAm: (a)* ouvrier ambulant; *(b)* chemineau *m*, trimardeur *m*, vagabond *m*, clochard *m*.

hobo[2], *v.i. NAm:* mener une vie de chemineau, de clochard.

hoboism ['houbouizm], *s.* vagabondage *m*.

hob-out ['hɔbaut], *s. Metalw:* estampe *f* à froid.

Hobson ['hɔbsən], *Pr.n.m.* **Hobson's choice,** choix *m* qui ne laisse pas d'alternative; **it's (a case of) Hobson's choice,** il n'y a pas d'alternative; c'est à prendre ou à laisser; c'est la carte forcée.

hoc [hɔk], *s. Cards:* hoc *m*.

hock[1] [hɔk], *s.* jarret *m* (de quadrupède).

hock[2], *v.tr.* couper le jarret à (un cheval, etc.).

hock[3], *s.* vin *m* du Rhin.

hock[4], *s. NAm: F:* gage *m*; **in h.,** (i) *(of watch, etc.),* au clou; (ii) *(of pers.)* en prison; **to be in h. to s.o.,** devoir de l'argent à qn; **h. shop** = crédit municipal; **in the h. shop,** au clou.

hock[5], *NAm: F:* engager (sa montre, etc.); mettre (sa montre, etc.) au clou.

Hock[6], *s. A:* **H. Monday, H. Tuesday** *(also* **Hockday, Hokeday),** le lundi, le mardi, de la Quasimodo.

hocket ['hɔkit], *s. A.Mus:* hoquet *m*.

hockey ['hɔki], *s.* **hockey,** *U.S:* **field h.,** *Can:* **grass h.,** (jeu *m* de) hockey *m*; **ice h.,** *NAm:* **hockey,** hockey sur glace, *Fr.C:* hockey; **h. stick,** crosse *f* de hockey.

hocus[1] ['houkəs], *s.* boisson narcotisée.

hocus[2], *v.tr.* **(hocussed) 1.** attraper, duper (qn); mystifier (qn); *F:* monter un bateau à (qn). **2.** *(a)* stupéfier (qn, un animal) au moyen d'un narcotique; droguer (qn, un cheval); *(b)* narcotiser, droguer (une boisson).

hocus-pocus[1] ['houkəs'poukəs], *s.* **1.** *(a)* passe-passe *m* (formule du prestidigitateur); **there's no h.-p. about it,** ce n'est pas un tour de passe-passe; *(b)* tour *m* de passe-passe. **2.** tromperie *f*, supercherie *f*, mystification *f*.

hocus-pocus[2], *v.* **(-pocussed) 1.** *v.i.* faire des tours de passe-passe. **2.** *v.tr.* *(a)* berner, mystifier (qn); *(b)* escamoter (qch.).

hod [hɔd], *s.* **1.** oiseau *m*, auge *f*, augette *f*, hotte *f* (de maçon). **2.** seau *m*, caisse *f* (à charbon).

hodden ['hɔdən]. **1.** *s. A:* gros drap (tissé au métier à main). **2.** *a. Scot:* **h. grey,** gros drap beige.

hodful ['hɔdful], *s.* hottée *f* (de briques, de mortier); seau *m* (de charbon).

hodgepodge ['hɔdʒpɔdʒ], *s. Cu: etc:* = HOTCHPOTCH.

Hodgkin ['hɔdʒkin], *Pr.n. Med:* **Hodgkin's disease,** lymphogranulomatose *f* maligne.

hodiernal [houdi'ə:nəl, hɔd-], *a. A. & Lit:* (vie *f*, progrès *m*) d'aujourd'hui.

hodman, *pl.* **-men** ['hɔdmən], *s.* aide-maçon *m*, *pl.* aides-maçons; porte-auge *m inv*.

hodograph ['hɔdəgræf], *s.* odographe *m*.

hodometer [hɔ'dɔmitər], *s.* odomètre *m*; (i) compte-pas *m inv*; (ii) compteur *m* (kilométrique); compteur enregistreur.

hodoscope ['hɔdəskoup], *s. Elcs:* hodoscope *m*.

hoe[1] [hou], *s.* *(a) Hort: Agr:* houe *f*, binette *f*, binot *m*, raclette *f*; **small h.,** houette *f*; **two-pronged h.,** binoche *f*; **double-headed h.,** bêchard *m*; **weeding h.,** sarcloir *m*; piochon *m*; **combined h. and fork,** serfouette *f*; **Dutch h., thrust h., push h.,** griffe-bineuse *f*, *pl.* griffes-bineuses; ratissoire *f* (à pousser); **draw h.,** ratissoire à tirer; **Canterbury h.,** croc *m* à pommes de terre; **mechanical h.,** motobineuse *f*; **rotary h.,** rotobineuse *f*; *(b)* **miner's h.,** sape *f*; *(c) Civ.E:* **back h.,** pelleteuse *f*; **back-h. loader,** chargeuse-pelleteuse *f*, *pl.* chargeuses-pelleteuses.

hoe[2], *v.tr.* **(hoed; hoeing)** houer, biner (le sol); sarcler (les mauvaises herbes); serfouir (les plantes potagères); ratisser (une allée); *O:* **a hard row to h.,** une tâche difficile, ingrate; **he has had a hard row to h.,** il a eu la vie dure.

hoe[3], *s. A: (used in place names)* promontoire *m*.

hoeing ['houiŋ], *s.* houement *m*, binage *m* (du sol); sarclage *m* (de mauvaises herbes); serfouissage *m* (de plantes potagères); **surface h.,** raclage *m*; raclée *f*.

hoer ['houər], *s. (pers.)* houeur *m*; bineur, -euse.

hoernesite ['hə:nisait], *s. Miner:* hœrnésite *f*.

hog[1] [hɔg], *s.* **1.** *(a)* porc châtré; *(b)* porc, cochon *m*, pourceau *m*; *Vet:* **h. cholera,** peste porcine; *F:* **to go the whole h.,** aller jusqu'au bout; tout risquer; **why not go the whole h., and . . .,** tant qu'à faire, pourquoi ne pas . . .; *(c) Z:* **Indian h., horned h.,** babiroussa *m*; **Mexican h.,** pécari *m*; **giant forest h.,** hylochère *m*; **h. deer,** (i) cerf *m* du Gange; daim *m* du Bengale; cerf-cochon *m*, *pl.* cerfs-cochons; (ii) babiroussa *m*; *(d)* **h. in armour,** (i) *F:* homme mal endimanché dans des vêtements trop raides; empoté *m*; (ii) *Z:* tatou *m* (du Brésil). **2.** *(pers.) F:* *(a)* goinfre *m*, glouton *m*, pourceau, goret *m*; *(b)* sale cochon; vache *f*, charogne *f*. **3.** *Husb:* agneau antenais. **4.** *Bot:* **hog's bane,** ansérine *f*; patte *f* d'oie; **h. plum,** spondias *m*, monbin *m*; prunier *m* d'Espagne, d'Amérique. **5.** *Nau: A: (brush)* goret. **6.** *Tchn:* *(a)* déchiqueteuse *f* (de matériaux de rebut, etc.); *(b) Paperm:* agitateur *m* (de cuvier à pâte).

hog[2], *v.* **(hogged) 1.** *v.i.* *(a) (of ship, keel)* s'arquer; avoir de l'arc; prendre de l'arc; *(of pipes, etc.)* cintrer; *(b) F: (of pers.)* prendre plus que sa part; faire le goinfre, le glouton. **2.** *v.tr.* *(a) Nau:* goreter (la carène); *(b) Nau:* donner de l'arc à (un navire); casser (un navire); *(c) Tchn:* déchiqueter (des matériaux de rebut, etc.); *(d)* anglaiser, couper en brosse (la crinière d'un cheval); *(e) F:* **to h. the limelight,** accaparer la vedette; **the X Company is hogging (all) the films,** la compagnie X se réserve le monopole des films; *Aut:* **to h. the road,** tenir toute la route; **don't h. all the cake!** laisse-moi un petit morceau de gâteau! **he hogged down his lunch and went,** après avoir avalé rapidement son déjeuner il est parti.

hogan ['hougən], *s.* hutte *f*, cabane *f* (de Peau-Rouge).

hogback ['hɔgbæk], *s.* *(a)* dos arqué; *(b) Geog:* dos *m* d'âne; ligne *f* de crête; route *f* formant ligne de crête.

hogbacked ['hɔgbækt], *a.* (pont, etc.) en dos d'âne.

hogfish ['hɔgfiʃ], *s. Ich:* *(a)* scorpène *f*, rascasse *f*, truie *f*; *F:* diable *m* de mer; *(b)* lachnolème *m*, *F:* capitaine *m*.

hogged [hɔgd], *a.* **1.** *(a)* (navire) arqué, cassé, ayant de l'arc; *(b)* (route) en dos d'âne, fortement bombée. **2.** (crinière de cheval) en brosse.

hogger ['hɔgər], *s. Tchn:* **1.** *(pers.)* déchiqueteur, -euse. **2.** *(machine)* = HOG 6.

hoggery ['hɔgəri], *s.* **1.** *esp. U.S:* porcherie *f*. **2.** *F:* goinfrerie *f*.

hogget ['hɔgit], *s. Husb:* agneau antenais.

hoggin ['hɔgin], *s.* gravier criblé, sableux.

hogging ['hɔgiŋ], *s.* **1.** *Nau:* *(a)* arc *m* (de la carène); *(b) A:* goretage *m*; nettoyage *m* de la carène. **2.** anglaisage *m* (de la crinière d'un cheval).

hoggish ['hɔgiʃ], **hoglike** ['hɔglaik], *a. F:* **1.** de cochon, de glouton. **2.** (individu) (i) glouton, (ii) grossier, malpropre.

hoggishness ['hɔgiʃnis], *s. F:* (i) gloutonnerie *f*; (ii) grossièreté *f*, malpropreté *f*.

hoghouse ['hɔghaus], *s. esp. U.S:* porcherie *f*.

hogling ['hɔgliŋ], *s. O:* cochon *m* de lait.

hogman, *pl.* **-men** ['hɔgmən], *s.m.* (i) éleveur, (ii) gardeur, de cochons.

Hogmanay ['hɔgmənei], *s. Scot:* la Saint-Sylvestre.

hog-nosed ['hɔgnouzd], *a.* **h.-n. snake,** hétérodon *m*; **h.-n. viper,** bothrops *m*; **h.-n. skunk,** conépate *m*.

hognut ['hɔgnʌt], *s. Bot: U.S:* *(a)* fruit *m* du carya; *(b)* arachide *f*.

hogpen ['hɔgpen], *s. esp. U.S:* porcherie *f*.

hog's back ['hɔgzbæk], *s.* = HOGBACK.

hogshead ['hɔgzhed], *s.* **1.** tonneau *m*, barrique *f*, foudre *m*; *A:* muid *m*. **2.** *Meas:* fût *m* de 52½ gallons, de 240 litres.

hog-tie ['hɔgtai], *v.tr. U.S:* *(a)* lier ensemble les quatre pattes (d'un animal); *F:* **to h.-t. a prisoner,** lier les poignets d'un prisonnier à ses chevilles; *(b)* **financial institutions that h.-t. the economy of a region,** institutions financières qui entravent l'économie d'une région.

hogwash ['hɔgwɔʃ], *s.* *(a)* eaux grasses (que l'on donne aux porcs); *(b) F:* rinçures *fpl*, lavasse *f*; **it's all h.,** c'est de la foutaise; *(c) F:* vin *m* fade; vinasse *f*.

hogweed ['hɔgwi:d], *s. Bot:* *(a)* berce commune; berce branc-ursine; *(b)* centinode *f*; (renouée *f*) traînasse *f*; *(c)* laiteron *m*; lait *m* d'âne; *(d)* pas-d'âne *m inv*.

hog-wild ['hɔgwaild], *a. NAm: F:* (enthousiasme, etc.) outré, exagéré, excessif; **to go h.-w. on spending,** dépenser sans compter, d'une manière extravagante.

hoi(c)k[1] [hɔik], *s.* *(a)* coup sec, saccade *f*; *(b) Av:* décollage *m* en chandelle.

hoi(c)k[2]. **1.** *v.tr. F:* *(a)* lever, tirer, arracher, (qch.) d'un coup sec; *(b)* faire monter (un avion) en chandelle; *(c)* redresser, cabrer (l'avion). **2.** *v.i. F: (of aircraft)* monter en chandelle.

hoicks [hɔiks], *int. Ven:* = taïaut!

hoi polloi ['hɔipə'lɔi], *s.pl.* **the h. p.,** la foule, les masses, le peuple.

hoise [hɔiz], *v.tr. A:* **(hoist; hoist)** = HOIST[2]; *still used in the phr.* **to be hoist with one's own petard,** être pris à son propre piège, dans ses propres lacets, dans son propre traquenard; s'enferrer.

hoist[1] [hɔist], *s.* **1.** *(a)* levage *m*; coup *m* de treuil; *Mec.E:* **h. bracket,** étrier *m* de levage; **h. drum,** tambour *m* de levage; **h. engine,** moteur *m* de levage; **h. eye,** anneau *m* de levage; **h. hook,** crochet *m* de levage; *(b)* **to give s.o. a h. (up),** aider qn à monter; faire la courte échelle à qn. **2.** *(a)* appareil *m*, engin *m*, de levage; treuil *m*, grue *f*, palan *m*; *Min:* bourriquet *m*; **double-drum h.,** treuil à deux tambours; *(b) (for goods)* monte-charge *m inv*; ascenseur *m* (de marchandises); *(for cars)* monte-voiture *m*, *pl.* monte-voitures; *(for persons)* ascenseur; **service h., plate h.,** monte-plats *m inv*; **h. hole,** *(through floor of warehouse, etc.),* tracas *m*. **3.** *Nau:* guindant *m* (de pavillon, de voile).

hoist[2], *v.tr.* *(a)* **to h. boats in, out,** embarquer, débarquer, les canots; **to h. a boat, a sail,** hisser une embarcation, une voile; **to h. a signal close up,** hisser un signal à bloc; **to h. a sail home, taut,** étarquer une voile; **h. away!** hissez! *(b) F:* **to h. s.o. on to his horse,** hisser qn sur son cheval; **to h. oneself up a wall, up to the window,** se hisser le long d'un mur, jusqu'à la fenêtre.

hoisting ['hɔistiŋ], *s.* *(a) Civ.E: etc:* levage *m*, hissage *m*; *(by windlass)* guindage *m*; **h. engine, h. gear, h. tackle,** appareil *m*, engin *m*, de levage, de hissage; *Min:* appareil, treuil *m*, d'extraction; **h. appliances, h. machinery,** appareils de levage, de hissage; guindages; **h. equipment,** dispositif *m*, matériel *m*, de levage; **h. gin,** bigue *f*; **h. cable,** chable *m*; **h. lug,** anneau *m* de levage; **h. strap,** courroie *f*, sangle *f*, de levage; *(b) Min:* remontée *f*, remonte *f*, extraction *f* (du minerai); **h. shaft,** puits *m* d'extraction; *(c) Nau:* **h. in of the boats,** embarquement *m* des canots; *(d) Mil:* **h. the colours,** lever *m* des couleurs.

hoistman, *pl.* **-men** ['hɔistmən], *s.m. Civ.E: etc:* machiniste d'extracteur.

hoistway ['hɔistwei], *s. (through floor of warehouse, etc.)* tracas *m*.

hoity-toity ['hɔiti'tɔiti]. **1.** *int.* ta, ta, ta! taratata! turlututu! **2.** *a.* *(a)* qui se donne des airs; qui fait l'important; *(b)* qui se froisse facilement; susceptible; **don't be so h.-t.!** prenez-le sur un autre ton! il n'y a aucune raison de vous froisser!

hokum ['houkəm], *s. F:* **1.** *Th:* jeu destiné (i) à faire rire le parterre, (ii) à faire appel à la sensiblerie du parterre. **2.** bêtises *fpl*, balivernes *fpl*.

holandric [hɔ'lændrik], *a. Biol:* holandrique.

holarctic [hɔ'lɑ:ktik], *a. Geog: etc:* holarctique.

holcus ['hɔlkəs], *s. Bot:* houlque *f*.

hold[1] [hould], *s.* **1.** *(a)* prise *f*; **to have h. of s.o., sth.,** tenir qn, qch.; **to catch, grip, get, lay, take, h. of s.o., sth.,** saisir, empoigner, qn, qch.; se saisir de, s'emparer de, qn, qch.; s'assurer de qch., (de la personne) de qn; mettre la main, *F:* mettre le grappin, sur qn, qch.; **if I could only get a h.,** si je pouvais trouver prise; **to get, catch, h. of s.o. again,** rempoigner qn; **where did you get h. of that?** où vous êtes-vous procuré cela? *F:* où avez-vous pêché ça? **it is difficult to get h. of this book,** ce livre est difficile à trouver, à se procurer; *(in library)* ce livre est toujours sorti; **to get h. of a secret,** découvrir un secret; **to get h. of s.o.,** se mettre en contact avec qn; **I can never get h. of him,** il n'est jamais là; **to keep h. of s.o.,** retenir qn; ne pas lâcher qn; **to keep h. of sth.,** ne pas lâcher, ne pas abandonner, qch.; **he kept h. of, retained his h. on, the rope,** il ne lâcha pas la corde; **to keep tight h. of, a firm h. on, sth.,** tenir qch. serré; se cramponner à qch.; **we must keep our h. on, must not lose h. of, this privilege,** c'est un privilège auquel il ne faut à aucun prix renoncer, qu'il faut défendre à tout prix, auquel il faut tenir ferme; **to relax one's h.,** relâcher son étreinte *f*; **to leave, lose, h. of sth.,** lâcher qch.; **to lose, let go, one's h.,** lâcher prise; **to lose one's h. on reality,** perdre le sens des réalités; *(b)* **to have a h. on, over, s.o.,** tenir qn; avoir prise sur qn, *F:* avoir barres, barre, sur qn; **no one has any h. over him,** nul n'a prise sur lui; **to gain a firm h. over s.o.,** acquérir un grand empire, un grand pouvoir, sur qn; **I haven't any h. on him,** je n'ai pas d'influence sur lui; **to keep a tight h. on s.o.,** tenir qn de court, de près; **the government maintained its h. over the province,** le gouvernement a gardé la région sous son autorité; *(c) Box:* tenu *m*; *Wr:* prise; **to get into holds,** en venir aux prises; **no holds barred,** toutes prises autorisées; **the election is being fought with no holds barred,** au cours de cette élection tous les coups sont permis. **2.** soutien *m*; point *m* d'appui; **the rock gives no h. for hand or foot,** le rocher n'offre de prise ni pour les mains ni pour les pieds; *Mec.E:* **to provide a h. for the babbit,** donner de la tenue au régule. **3.** *Civ.E:* fiche *f* (d'un pieu). **4.** *Mus:* point d'arrêt, point d'orgue; repos *m*. **5.** *(a)* tanière *f*, repaire *m* (de bêtes fauves); *(b) A:* place forte; *(c) A:* prison *f*. **6.** *esp. NAm:* *(a)* délai *m*; **there was a h. in the takeoff,** on a dû attendre le départ, le décollage; (*b*) **there will be a h. on all takeoffs until the fog has dispersed,** il est interdit à tous les avions de décoller avant que le brouillard (ne) se dissipe; **they put a h. on all hotel rooms still unoccupied,** ils ont donné l'ordre de leur réserver toutes les chambres d'hôtel libres.

hold[2], *v.* (*p.t.* **held** [held], *p.p.* **held,** *A:* **holden** ['hould(ə)n])

I. *v.tr.* **1.** tenir; (*a*) **to h. sth. in one's hand, in one's arms,** tenir qch. à, dans, la main, dans, entre, les bras; **would you h. this for me please?** voulez-vous prendre ceci un instant, vous charger de ceci? **to h. sth., s.o., tight(ly),** serrer qch., qn; tenir qch., qn, serré; **to h. s.o. fast,** tenir solidement qn; se cramponner à qn; **he held his head in his hands,** il se tenait la tête dans les mains; **to h. hands,** se donner la main; **they held each other's hands,** ils se tenaient (par) la main; **to h. one's sides with laughter,** se tenir les côtes de rire; **to h. sth. over s.o.,** menacer qn de qch.; **to h. one's nose,** se boucher le nez; (*b*) **to h. the key to the puzzle,** tenir le mot de l'énigme. **2.** (*a*) **to h. sth. in position,** tenir qch. en place; retenir qch.; **to h. sth. fast,** (main)tenir qch. en place; **the screws that h. the lock,** les vis qui fixent la serrure; (*b*) **to h. s.o. at bay, in check,** tenir qn aux abois, en échec, en respect; **to h. s.o. prisoner,** tenir, garder, qn prisonnier; **he was held on a charge of theft,** il fut arrêté sous l'inculpation de vol; **to h. s.o. as hostage,** retenir qn en otage; **to h. stocks as security,** détenir des titres en garantie; **to h. stocks for a rise,** conserver des valeurs en vue d'une hausse; **the farmers are holding their wheat,** les fermiers gardent leur blé; **to h. oneself ready, in readiness,** se tenir prêt; **to h. a horse to the pace,** soutenir un cheval; **to h. s.o. to his promise,** obliger, contraindre, qn à tenir sa promesse. **3.** (*a*) **to h. one's ground,** tenir bon, tenir ferme, ne pas lâcher pied; **to h. one's own,** se maintenir, se défendre; **he can h. his own against anyone,** il sait défendre ses idées, maintenir sa position, envers et contre tous; **the patient is holding his own,** le malade se maintient, se défend; **this product is still holding its own after all these years,** ce produit, lancé depuis des années, se vend toujours bien; **to h. a wager,** tenir un pari; *Mil:* **to h. a fort, a position,** défendre une forteresse, tenir une position; **don't worry! I can h. the fort while you are away,** ne vous inquiétez pas! je m'occuperai de tout, de la maison, des affaires, etc., pendant votre absence; **to be able to h. one's drink,** avoir la tête solide, bien porter le vin; **to h. the stage,** (i) (*of actor*) retenir l'attention de l'auditoire; (ii) (*of play*) tenir l'affiche (pendant longtemps); (*b*) *Nau: etc:* **to h. course,** tenir la route; *Tp:* **h. the line!** ne quittez pas! ne (me) coupez pas! *Aut:* **car that holds the road well,** voiture *f* qui tient bien la route. **4.** porter; **to h. one's head high,** porter la tête haute; **to h. oneself upright, erect,** se tenir droit; **to h. oneself well,** avoir de la tenue; **to h. oneself like a king,** avoir un port de roi. **5.** (*a*) (*contain*) contenir, renfermer (une quantité de qch.); **barrel that holds, will h., is capable of holding, twenty litres,** tonneau *m* d'une contenance de vingt litres, qui tient vingt litres; **car that holds six people,** voiture *f* à six places; **this car cannot h. five persons,** on ne peut pas tenir à cinq, on ne tient pas cinq, dans cette voiture; (*b*) **what the future holds,** ce que l'avenir nous réserve; *Lit:* **who knows what tomorrow holds?** les jours se suivent et ne se ressemblent pas. **6.** tenir (une séance, un conseil de guerre); avoir (une consultation); célébrer (une fête, etc.); **the Motor Show is held in October,** le Salon de l'automobile se tient au mois d'octobre; **to h. an auction,** faire, procéder à, une vente aux enchères; **the meeting will be held at 8 p.m.,** la réunion aura lieu à 8 heures du soir; **an inquiry will be held about, into, the causes of the accident,** on procédera à une enquête sur les causes de l'accident; **to h. a conversation with s.o.,** s'entretenir avec qn; **to h. a parley with s.o.,** parlementer avec qn. **7.** retenir; arrêter; empêcher; (*a*) **to h. one's breath,** retenir son haleine, son souffle; **to h. the car with the (hand) brake,** retenir, immobiliser, la voiture avec le frein à main; **can you h. the bus until my friend arrives?** pouvez-vous retenir le départ du car en attendant l'arrivée de mon ami? **it takes four (men) to h. him,** il faut le tenir à quatre; **there's no holding him,** (une fois lancé) il n'y a pas moyen de l'arrêter, de l'empêcher; **to h. one's tongue, one's peace,** se taire; garder, observer, le silence; **he can't h. his tongue,** il ne sait pas, ne peut pas, se taire; il a la langue trop longue; il est terriblement bavard; **h. your tongue!** taisez-vous! **to pay s.o. to h. his tongue,** payer à qn son silence; **to h. one's hand,** arrêter (de faire qch.); **h. it! h. your horses!** arrêtez! attendez! (une) minute! attention! stop! n'allez pas plus vite que les violons! **h. (hard)!** arrêtez! halte là! *Nau:* baste! *Row:* **h. (water)!** les avirons dans l'eau! endurez! (*at photographer's*) **h. it!** ne bougez plus! *F:* **h. your hat!** quelque chose de terrible (i) va arriver, (ii) vient d'arriver! (*b*) **to h. water,** (i) (*of cask, etc.*) tenir l'eau, être étanche; (ii) (*of theory, etc.*) tenir debout; **cask that does not h. water,** tonneau *m* qui laisse échapper l'eau, qui n'est pas étanche; **story that won't h. water,** récit plein d'invraisemblances; (*of accumulator*) **to h. the charge,** conserver sa charge; (*c*) retenir (l'attention); **to h. one's audience,** retenir l'attention de l'auditoire; *F:* empoigner son auditoire; (*d*) *Mil:* **to h. the enemy,** contenir l'ennemi. **8.** avoir, posséder (un titre, un emploi); détenir (une charge); occuper (une terre, une position); *Ecc:* **to h. a living,** jouir d'un bénéfice; **to h. a medal,** être titulaire d'une médaille; **to h. shares,** détenir des actions; **holding company,** société *f* de portefeuille; trust *m* de valeurs; **I take thee to my wedded wife to have and to h.,** je te prends pour ma femme et mon épouse afin de t'avoir et de te garder. **9.** (*consider*) (*a*) **to h. sth. lightly,** faire peu de cas, faire bon marché, de qch.; attacher peu d'importance à qch.; **to h. sth. sacred,** considérer, regarder, qch. comme sacré; tenir qch. pour sacré; **this is held to be true,** ceci passe pour vrai; **to h. s.o. to be very clever,** tenir qn pour très intelligent; **to h. s.o. responsible,** tenir qn responsable; **you are held to be liable,** vous êtes considéré comme responsable; *F:* **to h. the baby,** être responsable; payer les pots cassés; **he was left holding the baby,** on l'a laissé payer les pots cassés; **to h. s.o. in respect,** avoir du respect, de la déférence, pour qn; **to be held in respect,** être respecté de tous; (*b*) avoir, professer (une opinion); **he holds that . . .,** il soutient que . . ., il est d'avis que . . .; **the court held that . . .,** le tribunal a posé en principe que . . ., a décidé que . . .. **10.** (*sustain*) *Mus:* **to h. a note,** tenir, prolonger, une note; filer une note.

II. *v.i.* **1.** (*a*) (*of rope, nail, etc.*) tenir (bon); être solide; **the anchor holds,** l'ancre mord, croche, est en prise; **to h. tight, firm, fast,** tenir bon, tenir ferme; (*on bus, etc.*) **h. tight!** = attention au départ! (*b*) (*in riveting, etc.*) **to h. (up) against the hammer,** tenir coup aux chocs. **2.** durer, persister; continuer; (*of weather*) se maintenir; **if your luck holds,** si votre chance dure. **3. to h. (good, true),** être vrai, valable; demeurer vrai; **the comparison does not h. (good),** la comparaison n'est pas juste; **this holds (good) in every case,** cela s'applique dans tous les cas; **the same holds good, true, in respect of . . .,** il en est de même pour . . .; **treaty, promise, that still holds good,** traité *m*, promesse *f*, qui est toujours valable; **the order holds good,** cette ordonnance reste valable, reste en vigueur; **the bet holds good,** le pari tient; **the objection holds,** cette objection subsiste. **4. to h. to a belief, to h. by a principle,** rester attaché à une croyance, à un principe; ne pas renoncer à une croyance, à un principe; **to h. to one's promise,** tenir sa promesse; **to h. by, to, one's opinion, one's decision,** adhérer à, tenir pour, son opinion; s'en tenir à, maintenir, sa décision.

III. (*compound verbs*) **1. hold back.** (*a*) *v.tr.* retenir (qn, la foule, ses larmes); concentrer (ses sentiments, etc.); cacher, dissimuler, taire (la vérité); garder pour soi (un détail, etc.); (*b*) *v.i.* rester en arrière, se tenir au second plan; hésiter, montrer peu d'empressement; **to h. back from doing sth.,** se retenir de faire qch.; **buyers are holding back,** les acheteurs s'abstiennent; **to h. back for sth.,** se réserver pour qch.

2. hold down, *v.tr.* (*a*) baisser (la tête); (*b*) **to h. a man down,** maintenir un homme à terre; **you can't h. him down,** rien ne l'empêchera de réussir; **to h. down a job,** (i) se montrer à la hauteur d'un emploi; (ii) occuper un emploi; (*c*) **to h. prices down,** maintenir le niveau des prix.

3. hold forth, *v.i. F:* disserter, pérorer; laïusser; piquer un laïus; **to h. forth at length on sth.,** disserter longuement sur qch.

4. hold in. *v.tr.* serrer la bride à (un cheval); tenir en bride, contenir, retenir, maîtriser, parer (un cheval); réprimer (ses désirs); maîtriser (une passion); **to h. oneself in,** se contenir, se retenir.

5. hold off. (*a*) *v.tr.* tenir (qn, qch.) à distance; (*b*) *v.i.* (i) se tenir à distance (**from,** de); *Nau:* tenir le large; (ii) **the rain is holding off,** jusqu'ici il ne pleut pas; **the storm may h. off,** il est possible que l'orage n'éclate pas; (iii) s'abstenir; se réserver; montrer peu d'empressement (**from doing sth.,** à faire qch.).

6. hold on, *v.i.* (*a*) **to h. on to sth.,** (i) s'accrocher, se cramponner, se maintenir, se tenir, à qch.; (ii) ne pas lâcher, ne pas abandonner, qch.; **to h. on tight to one's chair,** se cramponner à sa chaise; *F:* **to h. on by one's eyebrows,** se maintenir tout juste; **h. on (a minute)!** (i) tenez bon! tenez ferme! *Nau:* étalez! (ii) *Tp:* ne quittez pas! (iii) attendez (un instant)! **to h. on to shares,** garder, ne pas lâcher, des actions; **if he can h. on for another two days,** (i) s'il a encore deux jours; (ii) s'il peut se tenir encore deux jours; **how long can you h. on?** combien de temps pouvez-vous tenir? (*b*) **h. on!** pas si vite! arrêtez (un moment)! (*c*) *Ind:* (*riveting*) faire contre-coup.

7. hold out. (*a*) *v.tr.* tendre, offrir, présenter (la main, etc.); offrir, laisser voir (des espérances); **to h. out a hand to s.o. (in difficulties),** aider qn qui se trouve dans une situation difficile, tendre la perche à qn; **to h. out good prospects to s.o.,** faire miroiter l'avenir aux yeux de qn; **to h. out sth. at arm's length,** tenir qch. à bout de bras; (*b*) *v.i.* durer; **to h. out against an attack,** soutenir une attaque; résister à une attaque; tenir bon contre une attaque; **it was impossible to h. out any longer,** (i) la position n'était plus tenable; (ii) on ne pouvait résister, refuser, plus longtemps; **if only the civilians h. out,** pourvu que les civils tiennent; **to h. out to the end,** tenir jusqu'au bout; **to h. out for a higher price, a higher wage offer,** exiger un prix, des salaires, plus élevés.

8. hold over, *v.tr.* remettre (à plus tard); ajourner (une décision, etc.); différer (une question); réserver (une coupe en forêt, etc.); **bills held over,** effets *m* en souffrance, en suspens.

9. hold together. (*a*) *v.tr.* maintenir (deux choses) ensemble; **we want a man who can h. the country together,** il nous faut un homme qui puisse rallier toute la nation, qui sache parer à un effondrement général; **a good manager knows how to h. his staff together,** un bon chef sait assurer la cohésion de son personnel; (*b*) *v.i.* tenir (ensemble); garder de la cohésion; ne pas se disjoindre; **garments that no longer h. together,** vêtements *m* qui ne tiennent plus, *F:* qui s'en vont; **we must h. together,** il faut rester unis; il faut nous sentir les coudes; il faut faire bloc; **the story doesn't h. together,** l'histoire *f* ne tient pas debout.

10. hold up. (*a*) *v.tr.* (i) soutenir (qn, qch.); *Metalw: etc:* contre-tenir (un rivet, etc.); (ii) lever (qch.) (en l'air); **to h. up one's head (again),** relever, redresser, la tête; **he will never h. up his head again,** jamais plus il n'osera relever la tête; **to h. sth. up to the light,** exposer qch. à un bon jour; tenir qch. à contre-jour; (iii) **to h. s.o. up as an example,** citer, offrir, proposer, qn comme exemple; **to h. s.o. up to ridicule,** tourner qn en ridicule; (iv) arrêter (qn, un train, une voiture, etc.); entraver, gêner, embarrasser, bloquer (la circulation, etc.); immobiliser (qn, qch.); **we were held up at the airport by the fog,** nous avons dû attendre, nous avons été immobilisés, à l'aéroport à cause du brouillard; **the car was held up at the traffic lights,** la voiture a dû s'arrêter au feu rouge; **our trip was held up by John's illness,** nous avons dû remettre notre voyage à cause de la maladie de Jean; **the plan was held up by, for, lack of money,** le manque de fonds a empêché la réalisation du projet; **to be held up by the immigration authorities,** être détenu par le service de surveillance de l'immigration; **goods held up at the customs,** marchandises *f* en consigne, en souffrance, à la douane; **payment has been held up pending enquiries,** on a refusé de régler en attendant de plus amples informations; **to h. up (s.o., a train, a lorry, a bank, etc.),** attaquer (qn, une banque), arrêter (un train, un camion), à main armée; (*b*) *v.i.* (i) se soutenir; **the children held up well until the last lap,** les enfants ont tenu le coup jusqu'à la dernière étape; (ii) (*of weather*) se maintenir; (iii) *esp. NAm:* **to h. up on the money,** ne pas débourser.

11. hold with, *v.i.* (*usu. neg.*) **I don't h. with his opinions,** je ne partage pas ses opinions; **I don't h. with such behaviour,** je désapprouve, je n'approuve pas, une telle conduite.

hold[3], *s. Nau:* cale *f*; **foremost h.,** cale avant; **after h.,** cale arrière; **the goods in the h.,** les marchandises *f* à fond de cale; **we have cargo in three holds,** nous avons des marchandises dans trois panneaux; **h. depth,** creux *m* de cale.

holdall ['houldɔːl], *s.* sac *m* de voyage; fourre-tout *m inv.*

hold back ['houldbæk], *s.* **1.** empêchement *m*, obstacle *m*. **2.** (*a*) cotisation *f*; (*b*) *Const:* retenue *f* de garantie.

hold-down ['houlddaun], *a.* **h.-d. nut,** écrou *m* de serrage; **h.-d. cotter,** goupille *f* de retenue; **h.-d. bolts,** boulons *m* d'assujettissement.

holder ['houldər], *s.* **1.** (*pers.*) (*a*) teneur, -euse (de qch.); *Metalw:* **h.-on, -up,** teneur de tas; (*b*) détenteur, -trice (*Fin:* de titres, d'une lettre de change; *Sp:* du record, d'une coupe); tenant *m* (d'un championnat); porteur, -euse (*Fin:* de titres, d'un effet); titulaire *mf* (d'un droit, d'un poste, d'un permis, d'une médaille); concessionnaire *mf* (d'un brevet); tenancier, -ière (d'une ferme); propriétaire *mf* (d'une terre); détenteur *m* (d'un terrain, etc., hypothéqué); **h. of a banking account,** titulaire d'un compte en banque; *Bank:* **the h. of our letter of**

credit, notre accrédité(e); *Jur:* **h. (on trust) of s.o.'s securities,** dépositaire *mf* des valeurs de qn; **holders of debt claims,** créanciers *m.* **2.** (*device*) support *m*, monture *f*, patte *f*; (*a*) (*expressed by* porte-, *e.g.*) **drill h., bit-h.,** porte-foret *m*, *pl.* porte-forets; **bell h.,** porte-timbre *m inv*; **tool h.,** porte-outil(s) *m*; chariot *m* (porte-outil) (d'un tour); (*b*) **curtain h.,** embrasse *f* de rideau; **saw-blade h.,** agrafe *f* de scie; **globe h., glass h.,** griffe *f* (de bec de lampe); **toothbrush h.,** (i) porte-brosses *m inv* à dents; (ii) étui *m* à brosse à dents; **cigarette h.,** porte-cigarette *m inv.* **3.** (*vessel*) récipient *m*; **gas h.,** cloche *f* à gaz; gazomètre *m.* **4.** poignée *f* (pour fer à repasser, etc.).

holdfast ['houldfɑːst], *s.* **1.** crampon *m*; serre-joint *m*, *pl.* serre-joints; sergent *m*, crochet *m*, patte *f*; patte-fiche *f*, *pl.* pattes-fiches; brabant *m* à patte; clameaux *mpl*; **bench h.,** valet *m*, pélican *m*, presse *f* à main (de menuisier). **2.** *Bot:* crampon (de plante grimpante); *Algae:* bulbe *m.*

holding ['houldiŋ], *s.* **1.** (*a*) tenue *f* (d'un objet, d'un crayon, etc., à la main); (*b*) tenue (d'un congrès, d'une séance, etc.); (*c*) *Nau:* **good, bad, h. ground,** fond *m* de bonne, de mauvaise, tenue. **2.** (*a*) *Mec.E:* fixation *f*, serrage *m*, assemblage *m*; maintien *m* (en position); arrêt *m* (d'un mouvement); **h. bolt,** boulon *m* d'assemblage; **h.-down bolt,** boulon de fixation; **h. device,** dispositif *m*, outil *m*, de serrage; **h. dog,** cliquet *m* d'arrêt, de retenue; *Mch.Tls:* **h. collet,** pince *f* de serrage; *Tp:* **h. circuit,** circuit *m* de maintien (en position de travail); **h. coil,** bobine *f* de maintien; (*b*) *Surg:* contention *f*; **h. of a fractured bone,** contention d'un os fracturé; **h. apparatus, h. appliance,** appareil *m* de contention; (*c*) *Mil:* **h. operation,** opération *f* de fixation (de l'adversaire); **h. attack, h. battle,** bataille *f* d'arrêt; **h.-up line, position,** ligne *f*, position *f*, d'arrêt. **3.** conservation *f*; prolongation *f* (d'un état de choses, d'un mouvement, d'une action); (*a*) *Mil:* **h. of a captured position,** conservation du terrain conquis; (*b*) *Mus:* prolongation (d'une note); **h. note,** tenue *f*; (*c*) *Av:* attente (imposée à un avion avant d'atterrir); **h. fix,** balise *f* d'attente; **h. flight path, h. pattern,** circuit *m* d'attente; **h. point,** point *m* d'attente; **h. sequence,** ordre *m* d'attente. **4.** (*a*) *Hist:* possession *f* (de terres), tenure *f*; (*b*) *Agr:* terre affermée; ferme *f*. **5.** *Fin:* avoir *m* (en actions); effets *mpl* en portefeuille; portefeuille *m* effets; dossier *m*; holding *m*; **he has holdings in several companies,** il est actionnaire de plusieurs sociétés; **h. company,** holding *m*, société *f* à portefeuille, trust financier. **6.** *Jur:* **h. of the courts (on a question),** jurisprudence *f* (d'un cas de droit).

holding up ['houldiŋʌp], *s.* (*a*) soutènement *m*; (*b*) *Tls:* *Metalw:* **h.-up hammer,** appuyeur *m*.

holdover ['houldouvər], *s. esp. NAm:* restant *m* (d'une ancienne croyance); survivance *f* (des temps passés).

holdup ['houldʌp], *s.* **1.** (*a*) arrêt *m*, embarras *m* (de voitures); entrave *f* à la circulation; suspension *f* de la circulation; (*b*) panne *f* (du métro, etc.). **2.** attaque *f* (d'un train, etc.); attaque, agression *f*, hold-up *m*, à main armée (dirigé(e) contre une banque, un bureau de poste, etc.).

hole[1] [houl], *s.* trou *m*. **1.** (*a*) trou, creux *m*, cavité *f*, fosse *f*; **to dig a h.,** creuser un trou; *F:* **to find oneself in a h.,** se trouver dans l'embarras, dans le pétrin, dans un mauvais pas, dans une impasse; (*b*) *Golf:* trou; **nine-h. course,** parcours *m* de neuf trous; **we were on the third h. when it began to rain,** nous jouions le troisième trou quand il a commencé à pleuvoir; (*c*) terrier *m*, accul *m* (de lapin); terrier (de blaireau); tanière *f* (de renard); catiche *f* (de loutre); trou (de souris, etc.); (*d*) *F:* **what a h.!** (i) (*of room, etc.*) quel (sale) trou! (ii) (*of house*) quel taudis! quel nid à rats! (iii) (*of town*) quel trou (mort)! quel bled! **2.** trou; orifice *m*, ouverture *f*; perforation *f* (dans une plaque de métal, du carton, etc.); point *m* (d'une courroie); perce *f* (d'une flûte); (*in bread, cheese*) **holes,** yeux *m*; (*a*) *Tchn:* **punched h.,** trou poinçonné; **reamed h.,** trou alésé; **tapped h.,** trou taraudé; *Mec.E: etc:* **drain h., emptying h.,** trou de vidange; **feed h., filling h.,** orifice de remplissage; **indexing h.,** trou de repère; **lubricating h., oil h.,** trou de graissage; lumière *f* (d'un coussinet); **inspection h.,** orifice, trou, de visite; fenêtrelle *f* d'inspection; regard *m* (d'un fourneau, etc.); *Mch: etc:* **sludge h., mud h., wash-out h.,** trou de sel; **blind h.,** trou borgne; **through h.,** trou traversant; **bleed h.,** trou de purge; **back-off h.,** trou de dégagement; *Const:* **weep h.,** trou d'écoulement; *Min:* **blast h., drill h.,** trou de mine; (*b*) *Cmptr:* **(punch) h.,** perforation; **sprocket h., feed h.,** perforation marginale, d'entraînement; **function h.,** perforation fonctionnelle; **code h.,** perforation significative (d'un code); (*c*) *Ph: Elcs: Cryst:* trou; **beam h.,** trou de faisceau; (*d*) *Med:* *F:* **h. in the heart,** trou dans le cœur; communication *f* (i) interventriculaire, (ii) inter-auriculaire; (*e*) **to bore a h.,** percer un trou; **to make, cut, pierce, a h. in a wall,** pratiquer une ouverture, un jour, dans un mur; **to stop (up) a h.,** boucher un trou; **to make a h. (in sth.),** faire un trou (à qch.); percer (qch.); trouer (un vêtement); faire une brèche (dans une paroi); **to make a h. in one's capital,** écorner, ébrécher, entamer, son capital; **I've made, worn, a h. in my stocking,** j'ai troué mon bas, fait un trou à mon bas; **this jersey is full of holes, in holes,** ce tricot est tout troué; **to pick holes in a theory, an argument,** relever, démontrer, les points faibles d'une théorie, d'un argument; **to knock holes in a theory,** démolir une théorie; *F:* **to drill holes in s.o.,** transpercer qn de coups de revolver.

hole[2]. *v.* **1.** *v.tr.* (*a*) trouer, percer (qch.); pratiquer, faire, un trou dans (qch.); *Navy:* **to h. a ship,** faire une brèche dans un navire; **the bow was holed,** l'avant était troué; *F:* **to h. s.o.,** transpercer qn d'une balle; *Min:* **to h. a mass of coal,** haver, souchever, un massif de houille; (*b*) percer (un tunnel); (*c*) faire entrer, mettre, (qch.) dans un trou; *Bill:* bloquer, blouser (la bille); *Golf:* **to h. the ball,** *v.i.* **to hole (out),** envoyer, mettre, la balle dans le trou; *F:* **holed in one!** vous tombez juste! vous avez deviné juste! **2.** *v.i.* (*a*) (*of stockings, etc.*) se trouer, se percer; (*b*) (*of animal*) (se) terrer.

hole-and-corner ['houln(d)'kɔːnər], *a.* *F:* clandestin, secret; **h.-a.-c. dealings,** affaires traitées en cachette; **h.-a.-c. deal,** affaire conclue en sous-main.

hole-in-the-wall ['houlinðə'wɔːl], *a.* *F:* **a h.-in-t.-w. business,** une petite affaire, un petit commerce, de rien du tout.

holeproof ['houlpruːf], *a.* introuable; (tissu, etc.) indéchirable; (bas, etc.) inusable.

holey ['houli], *a.* tout troué; plein de trous.

holiday[1] ['hɔlidi, -dei], *s.* **1.** (*a*) (jour *m* de) fête *f*; jour férié; **legal, official, national, public, bank, h.,** fête légale; *Ecc:* **h. of obligation,** fête d'obligation; **it's a h. tomorrow,** c'est fête demain; **the whole village was on h.,** tout le village était en fête; (*b*) (jour de) congé *m*; jour de sortie; *Sch:* **half h.,** après-midi *m* de congé; **I'm going to take a h. today,** je vais chômer, prendre un congé, aujourd'hui; **to take a h. from housework, from gardening,** se libérer des travaux ménagers, du jardinage, pendant quelque temps; (*c*) **a month's h.,** un mois de vacances; **holidays with pay,** congé payé; **the summer holidays,** les grandes vacances; **the Easter h.,** les fêtes de Pâques; *esp. Sch.* **to go home for the Easter holidays,** rentrer dans sa famille pour les vacances de Pâques; **when are you going on h.?** quand est-ce que vous allez prendre vos vacances? **where are you going for your holiday(s)?** où est-ce que vous allez passer vos vacances? **fishing h., camping h.,** vacances passées à pêcher, à faire du camping; **h. camp,** (i) grand établissement (au bord de la mer, etc.) où on peut passer des vacances organisées; (ii) (*for children*) = colonie *f* de vacances; **the h. season,** la période des vacances; **the beach was full of h. crowds,** il y avait une foule d'estivants sur la plage; **h. wear, clothes,** vêtements *m* pour les vacances; tenue *f* de loisir(s); **h. reading,** lecture *f* de vacances; *Sch:* **h. task,** devoir *m* de vacances; **h. course,** cours *m* de vacances. **2.** *Paint:* *U.S:* défaut *m* d'enrobage, dimanche *m*.

holiday[2] ['hɔlidei], *v.i.* passer les vacances (au bord de la mer, etc.); **where are you holidaying this year?** où passerez-vous vos vacances cette année?

holidaymaker ['hɔlideimeikər], *s.* villégiaturiste *mf*, vacancier, -ière; estivant, -ante.

holier-than-thou ['houliəðən'ðau], *a.* (*of attitude, etc.*) hypocritement pieux.

holily ['houlili], *adv.* saintement; pieusement.

holiness ['houlinis], *s.* (*a*) sainteté *f*; (*b*) (*of the Pope*) **His, Your, H.,** Sa, Votre, Sainteté.

holing ['houliŋ], *s.* **1.** *Min:* percement *m*, havage *m*, souchevage *m*. **2.** *Golf:* **within h.(-out) distance,** assez près pour envoyer la balle dans le trou.

holism ['houlizm], *s.* *Phil:* holisme *m*.

Holland ['hɔlənd]. **1.** *Pr.n. Geog:* Hollande *f*. **2.** *s.* (*a*) *Tex:* toile *f* de Hollande; hollande *f*; toile bise, toile écrue; (*b*) **hollands,** gin *m* de Hollande.

hollandaise ['(h)ɔlən'dez, -'deiz], *a.* & *s.* *Cu:* **h. (sauce),** sauce hollandaise.

Hollander ['hɔləndər], *s.* **1.** *A:* & *NAm:* Hollandais, -aise. **2.** (*in S. Africa*) colon hollandais. **3.** brique hollandaise (pour carrelage). **4.** *Paperm:* pile défileuse.

hollandite ['hɔləndait], *s.* *Miner:* hollandite *f*.

holler ['hɔlər], *v.i.* *P:* crier à tue-tête; brailler.

hollo(a)[1] [hɔ'lou], *int.* **1.** hé! **2.** *Ven:* taïaut!

hollo(a)[2], *v.i.* **1.** crier à tue-tête; hurler. **2.** *Ven:* crier taïaut; houper.

hollow[1] ['hɔlou], *a., adv.,* & *s.*

I. *a.* **1.** creux, caverneux, évidé; **h. tooth,** dent creuse; **h. lung,** poumon caverneux; **h. cheeks,** joues creuses, rentrées; **h. eyes,** yeux caves, enfoncés, rentrés; **h. features,** figure évidée; **h. road,** chemin creux; cavée *f*; *Const:* **h. partition,** mur *m* à double cloison; *Mil:* **h. square,** carré *m*; *F:* **to feel h.,** avoir un creux dans l'estomac; avoir faim; *F:* **he's got h. legs,** il boit comme un trou. **2.** (son) sourd; **with a h. sound,** avec un bruit sourd; sourdement; **in a h. voice,** d'une voix caverneuse; **h. cough,** toux creuse; **to give a h. cough,** tousser creux. **3.** (*of promise, friendship, etc.*) faux *f.* fausse; trompeur, -euse; vain; **h. peace,** paix fourrée; **h. victory,** victoire *f* à la Pyrrhus.

II. *adv.* **1. to sound h.,** sonner creux; **the box rang h.,** la boîte rendit un son creux. **2. to beat s.o. h.,** l'emporter complètement sur qn; battre qn à plate couture; **horse that beats the other runners h.,** cheval *m* qui tord les autres concurrents.

III. *s.* (*a*) creux *m* (de la main, d'un arbre, de la mer, d'un lit, etc.); cavité *f* (d'une dent); excavation *f*; évidure *f* (d'une moulure, etc.); (*b*) enfoncement *m*, dépression *f* (du sol); bas-fond *m*, *pl.* bas-fonds; creux de terre (entre hauteurs); cuvette *f*; **town situated in a h.,** ville située dans une vallée ou dans une cuvette; **the ground forms a deep h. here,** ici la terre s'enfonce profondément.

hollow[2]. **1.** *v.tr.* **to h. (out),** creuser, évider; canneler (une rainure); échancrer (le col d'une robe, etc.); (*undermine*) caver (un rocher, etc.); (*of water*) **to h. out the ground,** raviner le terrain; **hollowed-out stone,** pierre évidée, échancrée.

hollow-cheeked ['hɔlou'tʃiːkt], *a.* aux joues creuses.

hollow-eyed ['hɔlou'aid], *a.* aux yeux caves, enfoncés, creux.

hollow-ground ['hɔlou'graund], *a.* (rasoir) évidé (à la meule).

hollowing (out) ['hɔlouiŋ(aut)], *s.* creusement *m*; évidement *m*, évidage *m* (d'une vallée); ravinement *m* (du terrain); *Tls:* **h. knife,** plane creuse.

hollowness ['hɔlounis], *s.* **1.** creux *m*, concavité *f* (d'un arbre, d'une pierre, etc.); cavernosité *f* (d'un rocher). **2.** timbre caverneux (de la voix). **3.** manque *m* de sincérité (d'une promesse, d'une trêve, etc.); fausseté *f* (de cœur).

hollow-spun ['hɔlou'spʌn], *a.* (*of hollow concrete mouldings, pipes, etc.*) centrifugé.

hollow ware ['hɔlouwɛər], *s.* *Dom.Ec:* vaisselle *f* en faïence, en métal; bols *mpl*; **glass h. w.,** vaisselle en verre.

holluschick(ie) ['hɔləstʃik(i)], *s.* *Z:* jeune phoque *m* mâle.

holly ['hɔli], *s.* **1.** *Bot:* (*a*) **h. (tree),** houx *m*; **h. berry,** cenelle *f*; **h. grove, plantation,** houssaie *f*; (*b*) **knee h.,** fragon épineux; petit houx; housson *m*; houx-frelon *m*; faux buis, buis piquant; (*c*) **sea h.,** panicaut *m* maritime; **Alpine sea h.,** panicaut des Alpes, chardon bleu; (*d*) **h. fern,** lonchite *f*; (*e*) **h. oak,** yeuse *f*. **2.** *Ent:* **h. blue,** argus bleu.

hollyhock ['hɔlihɔk], *s.* *Bot:* rose trémière; passe-rose *f*, *pl.* passe-rose(s); alcée *f* (des jardins); bâton *m* de Saint-Jacques.

holm[1] [houm], *s.* **1.** petite île, îlot *m* (de rivière). **2.** rive plate (d'une rivière); terrain *m* d'alluvion.

holm[2], *s.* *Bot:* **h. (oak),** yeuse *f*.

holmia ['hɔlmiə], *s.* *Ch:* oxyde *m* de holmium.

holmium ['hɔlmiəm], *s.* *Ch:* holmium *m*.

holo- ['hɔlou], *comb.fm.* holo-.

holoaxial [hɔlou'æksiəl], *a.* *Cryst:* holoaxe.

holoblastic [hɔlou'blæstik], *a.* *Nat.Hist:* holoblastique.

holobranchiate [hɔlou'bræŋkieit], *a.* *Ich:* holobranche.

holocarpic [hɔlou'kɑːpik], **holocarpous** [hɔlou'kɑːpəs], *a.* *Bot:* holocarpe.

holocaust ['hɔləkɔːst], *s.* holocauste *m*.

Holocene ['hɔləsiːn], *a.* & *s.* *Geol:* holocène (*m*).

Holocephala, Holocephali [hɔlou'sefələ, -li], *s.pl.* *Ich:* holocéphales *m*.

holocephalan [hɔlou'sefələn], **holocephalian** [hɔlousə'feiliən], *a.* & *s.* *Ich:* holocéphale (*m*).

holocephalous [hɔlou'sefələs], *a.* *Ich:* holocéphale.

holocrine ['hɔləkrain], *a.* *Anat:* (glande *f*) holocrine.

holocrystalline [hɔlou'kristəl(a)in], *a.* *Miner:* holocristallin.

holoenzyme [hɔlou'enzaim], *s.* *Biol:* holoenzyme *f*.

Holofernes [hɔlə'fɔːniːz], *Pr.n.m. B.Hist:* Holopherne.

hologamy [hɔ'lɔgəmi], *s.* *Biol:* hologamie *f*.

hologram ['hɔləgræm], *s.* *Phot:* hologramme *m*.

holograph ['hɔləgræf]. **1.** *a.* (document *m*, testament *m*) (h)olographe. **2.** *s.* (*a*) (h)olographie *f*; document, testament, olographe; (*b*) **to write one's will in h.,** (h)olographier son testament.

holographic [hɔlə'græfik], *a.* *Phot:* holographique.

holography [hɔ'lɔgrəfi], *s.* **1.** olographie *f.* **2.** *Phot:* holographie *f.*
hologynic [hɔlou'dʒainik], *a. Med:* hologynique.
holohedral [hɔlou'hi:drəl], *a. Cryst:* holoédrique, holoèdre.
holohedrism [hɔlou'hi:drizm], *s. Cryst:* holoédrie *f.*
holohedron [hɔlou'hi:drən], *s. Cryst:* holoèdre *m.*
Holometabola [hɔloumi'tæbələ], *s.pl. Ent:* holométaboles *mpl.*
holometabolous [hɔloumi'tæbələs], *a. Ent:* holométabole.
holometer [hɔ'lɔmitər], *s. Astr: etc:* holomètre *m.*
holomorphic [hɔlou'mɔ:fik], *a. Mth:* holomorphe; *Cryst:* holoèdre.
holomorphosis, *pl.* **-es** [hɔlou'mɔ:fəsis, -i:z], *s. Biol:* holomorphose *f.*
holoparasite [hɔlou'pærəsait], *s. Nat.Hist:* holoparasite *m.*
holoparasitic [hɔloupærə'sitik], *a. Nat.Hist:* holoparasite.
Holophernes [hɔlə'fə:ni:z], *Pr.n. m. B.Hist:* Holopherne.
holophote ['hɔləfout], *s. Opt:* lampe *f* (de phare) avec lentilles à échelons.
holophrastic [hɔlou'fræstik], *a. Ling:* (langue *f*) holophrastique.
holoplankton [hɔlou'plæŋktən], *s. Biol:* holoplancton *m.*
holopneustic [hɔlou'nju:stik], *a. Ent:* holopneustique.
holoptic [hɔ'lɔptik], *a. Ent:* holophtalme.
holoptychius [hɔlɔp'tikiəs], *s. Ich:* holoptychius *m.*
holoside ['hɔləsaid], *s. Bio-Ch:* holoside *m.*
holosiderite [hɔlou'sidərait], *s. Miner:* holosidère *m.*
Holostei [hɔ'lɔstiai], *s.pl. Ich:* holostéens *m.*
holosteous [hɔ'lɔstiəs], *a. Nat.Hist:* holosté.
holosteric [hɔlə'sterik], *a.* (baromètre *m*) holostérique.
holosteum [hɔ'lɔstiəm], *s. Bot:* holostée *f.*
holosymmetry [hɔlou'simitri], *s. Cryst:* holoédrie *f.*
Holothuriae, Holothur(i)oidea [hɔlə'θju:rii:, -θjur(i)'ɔidiə], *s.pl. Echin:* holothurides *m,* holothuridés *m,* holothuries *f.*
holothurian, holothurioid [hɔlə'θju:riən, -riɔid], *s. Echin:* holothuridé *m;* holothurie *f; F:* concombre *m,* cornichon *m,* boudin *m,* de mer.
Holotricha [hɔ'lɔtrikə], *s.pl. Prot:* holotriches *m.*
holotype ['hɔlətaip], *s. Biol:* holotype *m.*
hols [hɔlz], *s.pl. Sch: F:* vacances *f.*
holster ['houlstər], *s.* fonte *f* (de selle); étui *m* de revolver (de selle, de ceinturon).
holt[1] [hoult], *s. Lit:* (*a*) bois *m,* taillis *m;* (*b*) colline boisée.
holt[2], *s.* (*of otter*) catiche *f.*
holus-bolus ['houləs'bouləs], *adv. F: O:* tout d'un coup; sans hésiter; en vitesse, en toute hâte; (avaler qch.) d'un (seul) trait.
holy ['houli]. **1.** *a.* **(holier, holiest)** (*a*) saint, sacré; **holiest,** très saint; sanctissime; **the H. Trinity,** la Sainte Trinité; **the H. Ghost, Spirit,** le Saint-Esprit, l'Esprit Saint, le Sanctificateur; **the H. Father,** le Saint-Père; le Pape; **the H. Name (of Jesus),** le saint nom de Jésus; **H. Writ,** les Écritures saintes, l'Écriture sainte; **the H. Land,** la Terre Sainte; **H. Cross Day,** fête *f* de l'Exaltation de la Sainte Croix; **H. Day of Obligation,** fête *f* d'obligation; **a h. war,** une guerre sainte; **h. bread, water,** pain bénit, eau bénite; **h. place,** lieu saint; **h. ground,** terre sacrée; **to keep the Sabbath day h.,** sanctifier le dimanche; **to swear by all that is h.,** jurer ses grands dieux; *F:* **to have a h. fear of sth.,** avoir une crainte salutaire de qch; (*b*) (*of pers.*) saint, pieux. **2.** *s.* **the H. of Holies,** le saint des saints.
holystone[1] ['houlistoun], *s. Nau:* brique *f* à pont, à briquer.
holystone[2], *v.tr. Nau:* briquer (le pont).
homage ['hɔmidʒ], *s.* **1.** *Hist:* (*a*) hommage *m;* (*b*) *coll.* les hommes *m,* les vassaux *m* (du seigneur). **2.** hommage; **to pay, do, h. to s.o.,** rendre, faire, hommage à qn.
Homalonotus [hɔmələlou'noutəs], *s. Paleont:* homalonotus *m.*
Homaridae [hou'mæridi:], *s.pl. Crust:* homaridés *m.*
homatropine [hɔ'mætrəpi(:)n, -pain], *s. Ch:* homatropine *f.*
Homburg ['hɔmbə:g]. **1.** *Pr.n.Geog:* Hombourg. **2.** *s.* **h. (hat),** chapeau mou; feutre *m* souple.
home[1] [houm], *s. & adv.*
I. *s.* **1.** (*a*) chez-soi *m inv;* logis *m;* foyer (familial, domestique); domicile conjugal; intérieur *m;* **a second h. (in the country),** une résidence secondaire (à la campagne); **I've come straight from h.,** je viens (directement) de chez moi; **the few houses near his h.,** les quelques maisons voisines de chez lui; **a village with (only) fifty homes,** village *m* de cinquante maisons, de cinquante feux; **a simple h.,** un intérieur simple; **the Ideal H. Exhibition,** *U.S:* **the H. Show** = le Salon des Arts Ménagers; **in the privacy of the h.** = dans l'intimité du chez-soi; **he is very pleasant in his own h.,** il est très aimable dans le particulier; **to have a h. of one's own,** avoir un chez-soi; être dans ses meubles; **I love my h.,** j'aime mon chez-moi; **television brings the world into your own h.,** la télévision vous apporte le monde à domicile; **she went back to live in the family h.,** elle est rentrée vivre dans la maison familiale, sous le toit paternel; **to return to one's old h.,** revenir au gîte; **to get prisoners back to their homes,** rendre des prisonniers à leurs foyers; **to give s.o. a h., to make a h. for s.o.,** recueillir qn; recevoir qn chez soi; **a friend offered me a h. with him,** un ami a offert de m'héberger; **I shall find a h. with my daughter,** je me caserai chez ma fille; j'irai habiter chez ma fille; **to make one's h. in France,** s'établir en France, *Adm:* élire domicile en France; *Lit:* **the mountains where Freedom made her h.,** les montagnes où la Liberté avait trouvé asile; **it's a h. from h.,** (cet hôtel, etc.), c'est un second chez-soi; on y est comme chez soi; *O:* **to go to one's last h.,** partir pour l'autre monde, pour sa dernière demeure; (*b*) **love of h.,** amour *m* du foyer; **there's no place like h.,** on n'est nulle part si bien que chez soi; **to leave h.,** (i) quitter la maison; (ii) partir (définitivement); quitter la famille; **he leaves h. at eight in the morning,** il quitte la maison à huit heures du matin; **his sons have left h.,** ses fils n'habitent plus chez lui, ont quitté la maison familiale; **to be away from h.,** être parti, absent, en voyage; **at h.,** (i) à la maison, chez soi; (ii) *Sp:* (jouer) sur le terrain du club; **jeweller working at h.,** bijoutier *m* en chambre; **to stay at h.,** garder la maison, rester chez soi, à la maison; **how are things at h.?** comment ça va chez vous? **is Mr. X at h.?** M. X est-il chez-lui? est-ce que je puis voir M. X? M. X peut-il me recevoir? **to find no one at h.,** trouver porte close; trouver visage de bois; **Mrs X is not at h. today,** Mme X (i) est en ville, (ii) ne reçoit pas, aujourd'hui; *O:* **she is at h. on Tuesdays,** elle reçoit le mardi; son jour est le mardi; **to be not at h., not to be at h. to anyone,** n'y être pour personne; ne pas être visible; défendre sa porte; consigner la porte à tout le monde; **I am always at h. to you,** j'y suis toujours pour vous; **to feel at h. with s.o.,** se sentir en pays de connaissance chez qn; se sentir à l'aise avec qn; **I feel quite at h. with them,** avec eux je me sens en famille; **I don't feel quite at h.,** je me sens un peu dépaysé; **to be at h. in the saddle,** avoir de l'assiette; **I am, feel, at h. in this town,** dans cette ville je suis en pays de connaissance; je me plais dans cette ville; **he is at h. on, in, with, any topic,** tous les sujets lui sont familiers; **to feel perfectly at h. on a subject,** bien connaître un sujet; être ferré sur un sujet; **to make oneself at h.,** (i) s'installer (dans un fauteuil, etc.); (ii) faire comme chez soi; **make yourself at h.,** (i) faites comme chez vous; (ii) *Iron:* ne vous gênez pas! **he's at h., makes himself at h., anywhere,** il est, se sent, partout chez lui. **2.** (*a*) patrie *f;* pays (natal); terre natale; **places nearer h.,** endroits moins éloignés de la patrie; (*of exile*) **to long for h.,** languir après la patrie; **we are exiles from h.,** nous sommes exilés loin de la patrie, loin du pays natal; **at h. and abroad,** chez nous, notre pays, et à l'étranger; **our policy at h. and abroad,** notre politique intérieure et extérieure; (*b*) **to take an example nearer h.,** sans aller chercher si loin; **when the question comes nearer h., they will think differently,** quand la question les touchera de plus près, ils changeront d'avis; (*c*) **Greece, the h. of the arts,** la Grèce, patrie des beaux-arts. **3.** *Nat.Hist:* (*a*) habitat *m* (d'un animal, d'une plante); **the tundra is the h. of the musk ox,** la toundra est l'habitat du bœuf musqué; **the h. of fishes is water,** l'élément *m* des poissons c'est l'eau; **the original h. of this plant was North America,** l'habitat original de cette plante était l'Amérique du Nord; (*b*) **a beaver builds his h. at the water's edge,** le castor établit son abri sur la rive d'un cours d'eau; **this island provides a h. for, affords a h. to, myriads of birds,** cette île abrite des myriades d'oiseaux. **4.** asile *m,* refuge *m,* hospice *m;* **sailors' h.,** foyer, abri, du marin; **old people's h.,** maison de retraite (pour les vieillards); **rest h.,** maison de repos; **h. for the blind,** hospice d'aveugles; **nursing h.,** clinique *f;* **convalescent h.,** maison de convalescence; **children's h.,** home *m* d'enfants; **(boarding) h. for dogs,** garderie *f* pour chiens; **she's quite likely to leave all her money to a cats' h.!** ça ne m'étonnerait pas si elle léguait tout son argent à une œuvre de bienfaisance pour chats! **5.** (*in games*) le but. **6.** *attrib.* (*a*) **h. circle, h. life,** cercle *m,* vie *f,* de famille; **the joys of h. life,** les joies, les plaisirs, du foyer; **the h. folk(s),** (i) la famille, les parents *m;* (ii) les gens de chez nous, du village; *O:* **to keep the h. fires burning,** entretenir nos foyers; assurer la sécurité de la patrie; **h. address,** adresse personnelle; **h. cinema,** cinéma *m* d'amateur, de famille; **h. brew,** bière, boisson, etc., faite, préparée, à la maison; **h.-brewed,** (bière) brassée, fabriquée, à la maison; (vin, etc.) fait à la maison; (cidre, etc.) de ménage; *NAm:* **h. economics,** économie *f* domestique; (*b*) **h. farm,** ferme attachée au domaine (qui fournit aux besoins du château); *Ven:* **the h. coverts,** les fourrés les plus près du château; (*c*) **the H. Counties,** les comtés *m* avoisinant Londres; *Sp:* **h. side,** équipe *f* qui reçoit; **h. ground,** terrain *m* du club; **h. match,** match *m* à domicile; *Rac:* **the h. stretch,** la fin du parcours; la ligne droite; *NAm: Ind: etc:* **h. office,** siège social (d'une compagnie); (*d*) **h. journey, freight,** voyage *m,* fret *m,* de retour; (*e*) (coup, etc.) qui porte; (question) qui touche au vif; **h. thrust,** (i) *Fenc:* botte *f;* coup *m* de fond; grand coup; (ii) pointe *f,* critique *f,* qui va droit au but, qui porte; **to tell s.o. a few h. truths,** dire son fait, ses quatre vérités, à qn; (*f*) **h. town,** ville natale; (*g*) (*of the nation*) **h. trade,** (i) commerce intérieur; (ii) cabotage national; **h. market,** marché intérieur; **h. products,** produits nationaux, du pays; **h. news,** nouvelles *f* de l'intérieur; **the H. Fleet,** la flotte métropolitaine; **h. army, h. forces,** armée métropolitaine; **the H. Guard** = la milice; **h. defence,** défense nationale, de la patrie; **h. service,** (i) *Mil: etc:* service *m* dans la métropole; (ii) *W.Tel: A:* = chaîne nationale; **the H. Office** = le Ministère de l'Intérieur; **the H. Secretary** = le Ministre de l'Intérieur; (*h*) *Hist: Pol:* **h. rule,** autonomie *f;* indépendance législative; **h. ruler,** partisan *m* de l'autonomie (*esp.* en Irlande); (*i*) *Cmptr:* **h. address,** adresse *f* piste; **h. position,** position initiale, de repos (d'un organe).
II. *adv.* **1.** (*a*) à la maison, chez soi, au logis; **to go, come, h.,** (i) rentrer (à la maison); s'en retourner chez soi; (ii) (*after period of absence*) rentrer dans sa famille; *F: O:* **to go h.,** mourir; partir pour l'autre monde; **on his way h.,** en retournant (chez lui); en rentrant, en revenant, chez lui; **let's walk h.,** retournons à pied; nous allons rentrer à pied; **to take a child h.,** ramener un enfant chez ses parents; **I took him h.,** je l'ai reconduit chez lui; **to get h.,** regagner la maison, son chez-soi; **the train h.,** le train du retour, du soir; **to bring work h.,** emporter du travail à faire à la maison; (*b*) au pays; **to go, come, h.,** retourner au pays; (*of soldier, etc.*) rentrer dans ses foyers; **to send s.o. h. (from abroad),** rapatrier qn; (*c*) *Nau:* **the anchor is coming h.,** l'ancre *f* ne tient pas; l'ancre chasse; (*d*) **to be h.,** être de retour; **so you're h. again!** vous voilà donc de retour! **2.** (*a*) (*of bullet, etc.*) **to go h.,** porter (coup); **the blow went h.,** le coup a porté; *F:* **his speech went h.,** son discours fit impression; **the reproach, the shaft, went h., came h. to him,** le reproche le piqua au vif, le toucha au vif; le reproche porta (coup); **it will come h. to him some day,** il s'en rendra compte un jour; **to strike h.,** frapper juste; porter coup; **to bring sth. h. to s.o.,** faire sentir qch. à qn; ouvrir les yeux à qn; **to bring h. to s.o. what he has lost,** faire comprendre à qn ce qu'il a perdu; **air raids bring war h. to the people,** les bombardements font comprendre aux gens ce que c'est que la guerre; **to bring a charge h. to s.o.,** prouver une accusation contre qn; **to bring a crime, a lie, h. to s.o.,** convaincre qn d'un crime, d'un mensonge; (*b*) à fond; **to thrust, push, press, an attack h.,** pousser une attaque à fond; **to screw a piece h.,** visser, serrer, une pièce à fond, à bloc; **to push a cartridge h.,** enfoncer une cartouche à bloc; *Nau:* **the sheets are h.,** les écoutes sont rendues, sont à bloc.
home[2], *v.* **1.** *v.i.* (*a*) retourner à son gîte; (*of pigeon*) revenir au colombier; (*b*) (*of aircraft*) revenir à, rallier, sa base; **an aircraft homing to its carrier,** un appareil revenant vers son porte-avions d'attache; (*c*) (*of aircraft, missile, etc.*) **to h. on, towards . . .,** mettre le cap sur . . ., se diriger vers, sur . . .; **to h. on a beam towards an objective,** se diriger sur faisceau vers un objectif. **2.** *v.tr.* diriger (un avion, un missile, etc., sur un point ou un objectif déterminé) par radioguidage ou autoguidage; **radar installations that h. aircraft to emergency airfields,** installations radar qui dirigent les avions sur des aérodromes de secours.
home-baked ['houm'beikt], *a.* (pain, gâteau) fait, cuit, à la maison; (pain) de ménage, de cuisson.
homebird ['houmbə:d], *s. F:* (*pers.*) casanier, -ière.
homebody ['houmbɔdi], *s. esp. U.S: F:* casanier, -ière.
homeborn ['houmbɔ:n], *a. esp. NAm:* du pays, de la localité; indigène.
homebound[1] ['houmbaund], *a.* (malade) obligé de rester à la maison.
homebound[2], *a.* (voyageur) qui rentre chez lui.
homebred ['houmbred], *a.* (*a*) du pays, élevé au pays; indigène; (*b*) élevé à la maison; (*c*) *A:* **with a h. courtesy,** avec une courtoisie naturelle, native, rustique.

homecoming ['houmkʌmiŋ]. 1. *a.* qui rentre, qui revient, au domicile, au foyer, dans sa patrie; **h. prisoners,** prisonniers rapatriés. 2. *s.* retour *m* au foyer, à la maison; rentrée *f.*

homecraft ['houmkrɑ:ft], *s.* les arts ménagers.

homegrown ['houm'groun], *a.* (denrée) du pays; (produit) indigène; (vin) du cru; (fruits, légumes) du jardin.

homeland ['houmlænd], *s.* 1. patrie *f.* 2. pays *m* où l'on a son chez-soi, sa famille.

homeless ['houmlis], *a.* sans foyer; sans asile; sans abri; sans feu ni lieu; **to be h.,** n'avoir pas d'asile; être sur le pavé; *s.pl.* **the h.,** les sans-gîte *m*, les sans-logis *m.*

homelike ['houmlaik], *a.* qui ressemble au foyer domestique; qui rappelle le chez-soi; **hotel with a h. atmosphere,** hôtel *m* où on se sent chez soi; **h. meal,** repas simple mais bien préparé; **his study is more h. than the drawing room,** son petit bureau est plus intime que le salon.

homeliness ['houmlinis], *s.* 1. simplicité *f* (de nourriture, de mobilier, de manières); bourgeoisie *f* (de goûts). 2. *NAm:* manque *m* de beauté; rudesse *f* (des traits).

homelover ['houmlʌvər], *s.* casanier, -ière; homme *m*, femme *f*, d'intérieur.

homeloving ['houmlʌviŋ], *a.* casanier, -ière.

homely ['houmli], *a.* 1. (nourriture *f*) simple, ordinaire; (goûts) bourgeois, modestes; (réception *f*) sans faste; **plain h. people,** gens *m* tout à fait simples, sans façon; **a (nice) h. woman,** une bonne ménagère; une femme d'intérieur; **h. dinner,** dîner *m* modeste, sans apprêt; **to do things in a h. way,** faire les choses simplement; **h. style,** (i) style *m* simple, sans apprêt; (ii) *Pej:* style sans élégance. 2. *NAm:* (*of pers.*) sans beauté; plutôt laid; **h. features,** traits *m* sans distinction, quelconques; **h. face,** visage ingrat.

homemade ['hou(m)'meid], *a.* 1. (*a*) (vêtement, gâteau) fait à la maison; (pain) de ménage, de cuisson; (*b*) (dispositif, etc.) de fortune; **h. bomb,** bombe *f* de fabrication artisanale. 2. (marchandises) du pays.

homemaker ['hou(m)'meikər], *s.* (*a*) ménagère *f*; femme *f* d'intérieur; mère *f* de famille; (*b*) aide familiale.

homeo- ['houmiou, 'hɔm-], *pref.* homéo-, homœo-.

homeomorphic [houmiou'mɔ:fik, hɔm-], *a. Cryst: Mth:* homéomorphe.

homeomorphism [houmiou'mɔ:fizm, hɔm-], *s. Cryst: Mth:* homéomorphie *f.*

homeopath ['houmioupæθ], *s. Med:* homéopathe *m.*

homeopathic [houmiou'pæθik], *a.* homéopathe; homéopathique.

homeopathy [houmi'ɔpəθi], *s. Med:* homéopathie *f.*

homeostasis [houmiou'steisis, hɔm-], *s.* homéostasie *f.*

homeostatic [houmiou'stætik, -hɔm], *a.* homéostatique.

homeotherm ['houmiouθə:m], *s.* homéotherme *m.*

homeothermic [houmiou'θə:mik], *a.* homéothermique.

homeotypic(al) [houmiou'tipik(l), hɔm-], *a.* homéotypique.

Homer[1] ['houmər], *Pr.n.m.* Homère.

homer[2], *s.* 1. *Orn:* pigeon voyageur. 2. *Sp:* shoot *m* au but; (*baseball*) homer *m*, tour complet. 3. *Av: Ball:* appareil, dispositif, autodirecteur; autodirecteur *m.*

Homeric [hou'merik], *a.* (poème *m*, rire *m*, etc.) homérique.

Homerid ['houmərid], *s. Gr.Ant:* Homéride *m.*

homesick ['houmsik], *a.* nostalgique; qui a le mal du pays; **to be h.,** être en proie à la nostalgie; **it makes me h.,** ça me donne le cafard.

homesickness ['houmsiknis], *s.* mal *m* du pays; nostalgie *f*; regret *m* de la patrie.

homespun ['houmspʌn]. 1. *a.* (*a*) (tissu *m* de laine) de fabrication domestique; (drap) fait, filé, à la maison; **h. linen,** toile *f* de ménage; (*b*) *O:* simple, sans apprêt, rustique, rude. 2. *s.* tissu fait à la maison; gros drap (tissé au métier à main); brouelle *f.*

homestead ['houmsted], *s.* 1. ferme *f* (avec dépendances); exploitation rurale. 2. *NAm:* bien *m* de famille; la concession statutaire de 160 acres; homestead *m.*

homesteader ['houmstedər], *s. NAm:* concessionnaire *m* d'un homestead.

homeward ['houmwəd]. 1. *a.* qui se dirige (i) vers sa maison, vers sa demeure; (ii) (*from abroad*) vers son pays; (*of ship*) vers son port d'attache, vers la métropole; **h. way,** chemin *m* qui mène à la maison; **h. voyage,** voyage *m* de retour. 2. *adv.* = HOMEWARDS 1.

homeward-bound ['houmwəd'baund], *a. Nau:* (navire) à destination de son port d'attache, retournant au port, retournant au pays, sur le retour; (cargaison) de retour.

homewards ['houmwədz], *adv.* 1. vers sa maison, vers sa demeure; (*from abroad*) vers son pays; **he hurried h.,** il se pressa de rentrer; il reprit en toute hâte le chemin de la maison; **ship coming h.,** navire *m* à destination de son port d'attache; *Nau:* **loading h.,** chargement *m* pour le retour; chargement de retour; **cargo h.,** cargaison *f* de retour. 2. *Min:* **h. method,** méthode *f* rétrograde; **h. working,** exploitation *f* en retour, en battant en retraite.

homework ['houmwə:k], *s.* 1. *Ind:* travail fait à la maison; travail (fait) en chambre. 2. *Sch:* les devoirs *m* (et les leçons *f*); **h. book,** cahier *m* de textes; *F:* **it was plain that the chairman had done, had not done, his h.,** il était évident que le président avait bien préparé, n'avait pas préparé, son discours.

homeworker ['houmwə:kər], *s. Ind:* ouvrier façonnier; ouvrier, -ière, en chambre.

homey ['houmi], *a.* = HOMELIKE.

homicidal [hɔmi'saidl], *a.* homicide, meurtrier.

homicide[1] ['hɔmisaid], *s.* (*pers.*) homicide *mf*, meurtrier *m.*

homicide[2], *s.* (*crime*) homicide *m*; *Jur:* **wilful, culpable, h.,** homicide volontaire; meurtre *m*; **felonious h.,** homicide prémédité; assassinat *m*; **justifiable h., h. in self defence,** homicide par légitime défense; *Scot:* **culpable h.,** homicide sans préméditation; **excusable h., h. by misadventure, by misfortune,** homicide par accident, par imprudence; homicide accidentel, involontaire.

homiletic [hɔmi'letik]. 1. *a.* homilétique. 2. *s.pl.* (*usu. with sg.const.*) **homiletics,** homilétique *f.*

homiliary [hɔ'miliəri], *s.* homiliaire *m.*

homilist ['hɔmilist], *s.* 1. auteur *m* d'homélies. 2. prédicateur *m.*

homily ['hɔmili], *s.* homélie *f.*

homing[1] ['houmiŋ], *a.* (*a*) *Orn:* **h. pigeon,** pigeon voyageur; (*b*) *Tchn:* directionnel, de radioguidage; **h. beacon,** balise *f* de radioguidage; **h. indications,** indications directionnelles; (*c*) autodirecteur, -trice; à tête chercheuse; **h. device, h. system,** appareil, dispositif, équipement, autodirecteur; autodirecteur *m*; *Av: Ball:* **h. eye,** cellule autodirectrice; *Ball: etc:* **h. head,** tête autodirectrice, tête chercheuse; *Navy:* **h. torpedo,** torpille autodirectrice, à tête chercheuse.

homing[2], *s.* (*a*) *Nat.Hist:* retour *m* au gîte; (*of pigeon*) retour *m* au colombier; (*b*) (*of aircraft*) (radio-)ralliement *m*; retour à la base, au terrain, au porte-avions d'attache; **h. to base,** retour sur le terrain, retour à la base; **h. aids,** moyens de ralliement; **h. procedure,** procédure *f* de ralliement, de retour à la base; **h. vector,** cap *m* de ralliement; (*c*) *Av: Ball:* autoguidage *m.*

hominid ['hɔminid], **hominoid** ['hɔminɔid], *a.* & *s. Z:* hominide (*m*), hominien (*m*).

Hominidae [hɔ'minidi:], *s.pl. Z:* hominiens *m.*

Hominoidea [hɔmi'nɔidiə], *s.pl. Z:* anthropoïdes *m.*

hominy ['hɔmini], *s. Cu: NAm:* bouillie *f* de farine de maïs à l'eau ou au lait; semoule *f* de maïs.

homo ['houmou], *s. F:* homosexuel *m*, pédé *m.*

homo- [-houmou, hɔ'mɔ], *comb.fm.* homo-.

homocentric [houmou'sentrik], *a. Mth: Opt:* homocentrique.

homocercal [houmou'sə:k(ə)l], *a. Ich: Z:* (animal *m*, queue *f*) homocerque.

homocercy [houmou'sə:si], *s. Ich:* homocerquie *f.*

homocyclic [hɔmou'saiklik], *a. Ch:* homocyclique.

homodromal, homodromous [hə'mɔdrəml, -məs], *a. Bot: etc:* homodrome.

homodynamic [houmoudai'næmik], *a. Ent:* homodyname.

homoeo- ['houmiou, 'hɔm-], *comb.fm.* = HOMEO-.

homofocal [houmou'fouk(ə)l], *a. Opt:* homofocal, -aux.

homogametic [houmougə'metik], *a. Biol:* homogamétique.

homogamous [hə'mɔgəməs], *a. Nat.Hist:* homogame.

homogamy [hə'mɔgəmi], *s. Nat.Hist:* homogamie *f.*

homogeneity [hɔmoudʒi'ni:iti], *s.* homogénéité *f*; *Tex:* **h. test,** épreuve *f* de texture.

homogeneous [hɔmou'dʒi:niəs], *a.* homogène; *Mth:* **h. co-ordinates,** coordonnées *f* homogènes.

homogeneously [hɔmou'dʒi:niəsli], *adv.* homogènement.

homogeneousness [hɔmou'dʒi:niəsnis], *s.* homogénéité *f*; nature *f* homogène (**of,** de).

homogenesis [hɔmou'dʒenisis], *s. Biol:* homogénésie *f.*

homogenization [hɔmɔdʒənai'zeiʃ(ə)n], *s.* homogénéisation *f.*

homogenize [hɔ'mɔdʒənaiz], *v.tr.* homogénéiser; **homogenized milk,** lait homogénéisé.

homogenizer [hɔ'mɔdʒənaizər], *s.* homogénéisateur, -trice.

homogeny [hɔ'mɔdʒəni], *s.* homogénie *f.*

homograft ['hɔmougrɑ:ft], *s. Surg:* homogreffe *f.*

homograph ['hɔməgræf], *s.* homographe *m.*

homographic [hɔmə'græfik], *a.* homographique, homographe.

homography [hɔ'mɔgrəfi], *s.* homographie *f.*

homoio- ['houmiou], *pref.* = HOMEO-.

homologate [hɔ'mɔləgeit], *v.tr. Jur: Scot:* homologuer, ratifier, légaliser, confirmer (un contrat, un testament, etc.).

homologation [hɔmələ'geiʃ(ə)n], *s. Jur: Scot:* homologation *f*, légalisation *f* (d'un document).

homologative [hɔmə'lɔgətiv], *a. Jur:* homologatif.

homological [hɔmə'lɔdʒik(ə)l], *a. Biol: Mth: etc:* homologique.

homologize [hə'mɔlədʒaiz]. 1. *v.i.* être homologue, correspondre (**with, to,** à). 2. *v.tr.* rendre homologue (**with, to,** à).

homologous [hə'mɔləgəs], *a. Biol: Mth: etc:* homologue.

homologue ['hɔməlɔg], *s. Biol: Mth: etc:* homologue *m.*

homology [hə'mɔlədʒi], *s. Biol: Mth: etc:* homologie *f.*

Homoneura [hɔmə'nju:rə], *s.pl. Ent:* homoneures *m.*

homonomy [hɔ'mɔnəmi], *s. Biol:* homonomie *f.*

homonym ['hɔmənim], *s. Ling:* homonyme *m.*

homonymic [hɔmə'nimik], **homonymous** [hɔ'mɔniməs], *a. Ling: etc:* homonyme.

homonymy [hɔ'mɔnimi], *s. Ling:* homonymie *f.*

homopetalous [hɔmou'petələs], *a. Bot:* homopétale.

homophone ['hɔməfoun], *s. Ling:* homophone *m.*

homophonic [hɔmə'fɔnik], *a. Ling: Mus:* homophone.

homophonous [hɔ'mɔfənəs], *a. Ling: Mus:* homophone.

homophony [hɔ'mɔfəni], *s. Ling: Mus:* homophonie *f.*

homoplasty ['hɔmouplæsti], *s. Physiol:* homoplastie *f.*

homopolar [hɔmou'poulər], *a. El: Biol:* homopolaire, unipolaire.

Homoptera [hɔ'mɔptərə], *s.pl. Ent:* homoptères *m.*

homopterous [hɔ'mɔptərəs], *a. Ent:* homoptère.

homosexual [hɔmou'seksjuəl], *a.* & *s.* homosexuel, -uelle.

homosexuality [hɔmouseksju'æliti], *s.* homosexualité *f.*

homothermal [hɔmou'θə:m(ə)l], *a. Ph:* homothermal, -aux.

homothermous [hɔmou'θə:məs], *a. Biol:* homotherme; homothermal, -aux.

homothetic [hɔmou'θetik], *a. Mth:* homothétique.

homotopic [hɔmou'tɔpik], *a. Mth:* homotope.

homotopy [hɔ'mɔtəpi], *s. Mth:* homotopie *f.*

homotransplantation [hɔmoutrænsplæn'teiʃ(ə)n], *s. Surg:* homogreffe *f*, greffe *f* homoplastique.

homotype ['hɔmətaip], *s. Biol:* homotype *m*, homologue *m.*

homotypic(al) [hɔmou'tipik(l)], *a. Biol:* homotype.

homozygosis, homozygosity [hɔmouzai'gousis, -'gɔsiti], *s. Biol:* homozygotie *f.*

homozygote [hɔmou'zaigout], *s. Biol:* homozygote *m.*

homozygous [hɔmou'zaigəs], *a. Biol:* homozygote.

homunculus [hɔ'mʌŋkjuləs], *s.* homuncule *m*, homoncule *m*; petit homme; nabot *m.*

homy ['houmi], *a. F:* = HOMELIKE.

Honduran [hɔn'dju:rən], **Honduranean** [hɔndju'reiniən], *Geog:* (*a*) *a.* hondurien; (*b*) *s.* Hondurien, -ienne.

hone[1] [houn], *s.* pierre *f* à aiguiser, à morfiler; pierre à huile; pierre à rasoir; affiloire *f*, affiloir *m.*

hone[2], *v.tr.* (*a*) aiguiser, affiler; passer (un outil) à la pierre à huile; repasser (un rasoir); (*b*) rectifier (un outil, une pièce).

honest ['ɔnist], *a.* 1. (*a*) (*of pers.*) honnête, probe, droit; loyal, -aux (en affaires); (juge *m*) intègre; **he charged me a price that was hardly h.,** il me l'a fait payer un prix tout juste honnête; **thoroughly h. man,** homme *m* d'une honnêteté à toute épreuve, d'une probité avérée; **h. straightforward nature,** nature droite et franche; **he has an h. face,** il a une figure d'honnête homme, d'honnête garçon; (*b*) vrai, sincère, de bonne foi; **the h. truth,** la pure vérité, la vérité vraie, l'exacte vérité; **tell us your h. opinion,** dites-nous de bonne foi votre opinion; **he made an h. attempt,** il s'y est appliqué de bonne foi; **h. confession,** confession *f* sincère, de bonne foi; **an h. piece of work,** un travail consciencieux; *P:* **I couldn't help it, h.,** c'était plus fort que moi, vraiment; (*c*) juste, légitime; **h. means,** moyens *m* légitimes; **to give h. weight,** donner bon poids; **to earn an h. living,** gagner honnêtement sa vie. 2. (*a*) *A:* (*of woman*) honnête, chaste; *now only in the phr.* **to make an h. woman of s.o.,** rendre l'honneur à une femme (en l'épousant); (*b*) *O:* (*usu. used condescendingly*) brave, honnête; **born of poor but h. parents,** né de parents pauvres mais honnêtes; **they are h. folk,** ce sont de braves gens.

honestly ['ɔnistli], *adv.* (*a*) honnêtement, loyalement; avec probité; de bonne foi; **to earn money h.,** gagner de l'argent honnêtement; (*b*) sincèrement; **quite h., h.**

speaking, à vrai dire; **I h. believed that . . .,** je pensais, en toute bonne foi, que . . .; **h., I can assure you . . .,** en toute sincérité je puis vous assurer . . .; **I can h. say that . . .,** je peux dire, la main sur le cœur, que . . ..

honesty [ˈɔnisti], *s.* **1.** (*a*) honnêteté *f*, probité *f*; loyauté *f* (en affaires); intégrité *f*; **tradesman of doubtful h.,** commerçant *m* d'une moralité douteuse; **he always put h. first,** il s'est toujours attaché à se montrer probe; *Prov:* **h. is the best policy,** l'honnêteté est la meilleure des tactiques; **h. pays,** l'honnêteté est toujours récompensée; on trouve avantage à se montrer honnête; (*b*) véracité *f*, sincérité *f*, bonne foi; franchise *f*, sans-façon *m* (d'un discours); **in all h.,** en toute sincérité. **2.** *Bot:* lunaire *f*; *F:* monnaie *f* du pape; satin blanc; médaille *f* (de Judas).

honey [ˈhʌni], *s.* **1.** (*a*) miel *m*; **clear h.,** miel liquide; **thick h.,** miel grenu; **virgin h., white h.,** miel vierge, miel de goutte; **comb h., h. in the comb,** miel en rayon; **h. bag, sac,** sac *m* à miel, premier estomac (des abeilles); **h. gathering,** butinement *m*; **h.-gathering insect,** insecte butineur; **h. making,** mellification *f*; **h.-making insect,** insecte mellifique; **to remove, extract, the h. from a hive,** démieller une ruche; **h. extractor, separator,** mello-extracteur *m*, *pl.* mello-extracteurs; **h. cake,** pain *m* d'épice au miel, nonnette *f*; **sweetened with h.,** miellé; **taste of h.,** goût mielleux; **h. wine,** bergerette *f*, œnomel *m*; **h. season, h. flow,** miélaison *f*; *Pharm:* **h. preparation,** mellite *m*; **borax h.,** mellite de borax; *Prov:* **daub yourself with h. and you'll never want for flies,** qui se fait brebis le loup le mange; faites-vous miel, les mouches vous mangeront; (*b*) douceur *f* (de mots, de caresses); **he was all h.,** il a été tout sucre et tout miel; **life is not all h.,** dans la vie tout n'est pas rose; **his words were h. to my soul,** il m'a versé du baume dans le cœur. **2.** (*term of endearment*) chéri, *f.* chérie; mignon, *f.* mignonne; mon petit chou. **3.** (*a*) *Bot:* **h. tree,** hovenia *m*; **h. locust,** gleditschia *m*; févier *m* à trois épines; acacia *m* à trois épines; *Fung:* **h. agaric, h. fungus, h. mushroom,** agaric miellé, tête-de-méduse *f*, *pl.* têtes-de-méduse; (*b*) *Z:* **h. bear,** kinkajou *m*; (*c*) *Orn:* **h. bird, h. guide,** indicateur *m*; **h. buzzard,** bondrée *f* (apivore).

honey-bearing [ˈhʌnibɛəriŋ], *a.* mellifère.

honeybee [ˈhʌnibiː], *s. Ent:* abeille *f* (domestique); **the honeybees,** les mellifères *m*.

honeyberry [ˈhʌniberi], *s. Bot: F:* mélicoque *m*.

honey-coloured [ˈhʌnikʌləd], *a.* miellé.

honeycomb¹ [ˈhʌnikoum], *s.* **1.** (*a*) rayon *m* de miel; gaufre *f* de miel; (*b*) gâteau *m* de miel; (*c*) *Tex:* nid d'abeilles *m*; **h.-weave towel,** serviette *f* nid d'abeilles; *Mec.E: etc:* **h. material,** matériau *m* (en) nid d'abeilles; *Aut:* **h. radiator,** radiateur *m* alvéolaire; nid d'abeilles; *Geol:* **h. structure, formation,** structure, formation, alvéolée, alvéolaire; *Z:* **h. bag, stomach,** deuxième estomac *m*, bonnet *m* (des ruminants). **2.** (*in metal*) chambre *f*, soufflure *f*.

honeycomb². **1.** *v.tr.* (*a*) cribler (de petits trous); affouiller; **the army was honeycombed with disaffection,** la désaffection ravageait l'armée; (*b*) marquer en nid d'abeilles. **2.** *v.i.* (*of metal*) se chambrer, s'affouiller.

honeycombed [ˈhʌnikoumd], *a.* **1.** alvéolé. **2.** (métal) chambré, crevassé, criblé de trous; (canon de fusil) affouillé; (bois) chambré (par les insectes).

honeycombing [ˈhʌnikoumiŋ], *s.* affouillement *m* (du sous-sol; d'un canon de fusil).

honeycreeper [ˈhʌnikriːpər], *s. Orn:* sucrier *m*, guit-guit *m*, dacnis *m*; **red-legged h.,** guit-guit saï; **blue h.,** guit-guit bleu.

honeycup [ˈhʌnikʌp], *s. Bot:* nectaire *m*.

honeydew [ˈhʌnidju], *s.* **1.** miellée *f*, miellure *f* (exsudée par les plantes). **2.** tabac sucré à la mélasse; honey-dew *m*. **3. h. melon,** gros melon à chair verdâtre.

honey-eater [ˈhʌniiːtər], *s. Orn:* méliphage *m*; **blue-faced h.-e.,** entomyzon *m*; **white-throated h.-e.,** méliphage à gorge blanche.

honey-eating [ˈhʌniiːtiŋ], *a. Z:* mellivore.

honeyed [ˈhʌnid], *a.* (*a*) (em)miellé; couvert de miel; (*b*) doucereux, mielleux, melliflu; **h. words,** paroles doucereuses, mielleuses; paroles de miel; **with h. words,** mielleusement.

honeyflower [ˈhʌniflauər], *s. Bot:* **(Cape) h.,** mélianthe *m*.

honeymoon¹ [ˈhʌnimuːn], *s.* (*a*) lune *f* de miel; **their marriage was an endless h.,** leur mariage fut une lune de miel sans fin; (*b*) **h. (trip),** voyage *m* de noces; **they're on their h.,** ils sont en voyage de noces; **h. couple,** couple *m* en voyage de noces.

honeymoon², *v.i.* aller, partir, être, en voyage de noces.

honeymooner [ˈhʌnimuːnər], *s. F:* **honeymooners,** couple *m* en voyage de noces.

honeysuckle [ˈhʌnisʌkl], *s.* **1.** *Bot:* chèvrefeuille *m*; **common h.,** chèvrefeuille des bois; **fly h.,** chèvrefeuille des haies, des buissons; **French h.,** sainfoin *m* d'Espagne; sainfoin à bouquets. **2.** *Arch:* gousse *f*, tigette *f*.

honeywort [ˈhʌniwəːt], *s. Bot:* mélinet *m*, cérinthe *m*.

honied [ˈhʌnid], *a.* = HONEYED.

honing [ˈhouniŋ], *s.* (*a*) repassage *m*, affilage *m* (d'un rasoir, etc.); (*b*) rectification *f*.

Honiton [ˈhɔnit(ə)n], *Pr.n.* **H. lace,** application *f* d'Angleterre (originaire de Honiton, Devon).

honk¹ [hɔŋk], *s.* **1.** (*a*) *A:* grognement *m* (du porc); (*b*) cri *m* de l'oie sauvage. **2.** *Aut: O:* cornement *m* (de l'avertisseur); **honk! honk!** couin! couin!

honk², *v.* **1.** *v.i.* (*a*) (*of goose, seal, etc.*) pousser un cri; (*b*) (*of foghorn, etc.*) retentir. **2.** *v.tr.* **to h. the horn,** faire retentir l'avertisseur.

honky-tonk [ˈhɔŋkiˈtɔŋk], *a.* & *s. NAm: F:* **h.-t. (joint),** bouge *m*, trou *m* borgne, bastringue *m*, boui-boui *m*.

Honolulu [hɔnəˈluːluː], *Pr.n. Geog:* Honolulu *m*.

Honolulan [hɔnəˈluːlən], *s.* originaire *mf*, habitant, -ante, de Honolulu.

honorarium, *pl.* **-ia, -iums** [ɔnəˈrɛəriəm, -iə, -iəmz], *s.* honoraires *mpl*, *occ.* honoraire (d'un docteur, d'un avocat).

honorary [ˈɔnərəri], *a.* **1.** (*a*) (emploi, service) honoraire, non rétribué, bénévole; **h. duties,** fonctions *f* sans rétribution, à titre gratuit; fonctions bénévoles; (*b*) **h. president,** président *m* d'honneur; **h. member,** membre *m* honoraire; associé, -ée (d'un cercle, etc.); **h. membership,** honorariat *m*; (*c*) *Mil:* **h. rank,** grade *m* honorifique; *Sch:* **h. degree,** grade honorifique, grade honoris causa; (*d*) **h. monument,** cénotaphe *m*. **2.** (*depending on honour*) (engagement *m*, contrat *m*) d'honneur.

honorific [ɔnəˈrifik]. **1.** *a.* (épithète *f*) honorifique. **2.** *s.* phrase *f* honorifique, mot *m* honorifique; formile *f* de politesse.

honorifically [ɔnəˈrifik(ə)li], *adv.* honorifiquement.

honour¹ [ˈɔnər], *s.* honneur *m*. **1.** (*high esteem*) **to hold s.o. in great h.,** honorer qn; avoir, montrer, beaucoup de respect, de l'estime, de la vénération, pour qn; **to bring a custom into h.,** mettre une coutume en honneur; **in the seat of h.,** assis à la place d'honneur; **to put up a statue in h. of s.o.,** ériger une statue à la gloire de qn; **a banquet was held in h. of his arrival,** on donna un banquet en l'honneur de son arrivée; **dinner in your h.,** dîner *m* en votre honneur, à votre intention; **to pay, do, h. to s.o.,** faire honneur à qn; **all h. to him!** honneur à lui! (*book published to honour a professor*) **studies in h. of Professor X,** hommage *m* au Professeur X; *Prov:* **h. to whom h. is due, h. where h. is due,** à tout seigneur tout honneur; à chaque saint sa chandelle. **2.** (*privilege*) (*a*) **to consider it an h. to do sth.,** tenir à honneur de faire qch.; **the h. of being first,** l'honneur d'être le premier; **to whom have I the h. of speaking?** à qui ai-je l'honneur de parler? **the Queen did me the h. of speaking to me,** la Reine me fit l'honneur de m'adresser la parole. **I have not the h. to belong to your profession,** je n'ai pas l'honneur d'appartenir à votre profession; *Com: O:* **I have the h. to submit to you . . .,** j'ai l'avantage de vous soumettre . . .; (*b*) *Games:* **to have the h.,** (*at bowls*) avoir la boule; (*at golf*) avoir l'honneur; **to throw a quoit, a bowl, etc., for the h.,** abut(t)er; *Golf:* **your h.!** à vous l'honneur! **3.** (*good name*) (*a*) **one's country's h.,** l'honneur de sa patrie; **for honour's sake,** pour (sauvegarder) l'honneur; **to come out of an affair with h.,** se tirer galamment d'une affaire; **to lose one's h.,** perdre son honneur; se déshonorer; **to fling away one's h.,** faire banqueroute à l'honneur; **to make (it) a point of h. to do sth.,** se piquer d'honneur de faire qch.; mettre son (point d')honneur à faire qch.; **to be in h. bound to . . .,** être obligé par l'honneur à . . .; **man of h.,** homme *m* d'honneur; *A:* **as I am a man of h.!** foi d'homme d'honneur! foi de gentilhomme! **he is the soul of h.,** il est l'honneur incarné, personnifié; il est la probité même; **debt of h.,** dette *f* d'honneur; **I cannot in h. accept this money,** je ne peux pas, en tout honneur, accepter cet argent; **to state on one's h. that . . .,** déclarer sur l'honneur que . . .; **to swear on one's h.,** jurer sur, par, sa foi; **word of h.,** parole *f* d'honneur; **to give one's word of h.,** engager sa parole (d'honneur); **on my (word of) h.!** je vous donne ma parole! sur l'honneur! *F: O:* **h. bright,** (i) foi d'honnête homme! (ma) parole d'honneur! sans mentir! (ii) bien sûr? vrai de vrai? parole d'honneur? **to be on one's h.,** être sur l'honneur; être engagé d'honneur; **I put you on your h.,** vous vous engagez d'honneur (to, à); je me fie à vous; **h. is satisfied,** l'honneur est satisfait; (*b*) **a woman's h.,** l'honneur, la réputation, d'une femme. **4.** distinction *f* honorifique; **academic honours,** distinctions académiques; **to aspire to honours,** aspirer aux honneurs; **to carry off the honours,** remporter la palme; **New Year's honours,** décorations *f* et promotions *f* du jour de l'an; *Sch:* **Honours list,** palmarès *m*; tableau *m* d'honneur. **5.** *Sch:* **honours course,** programme *m* d'études spécialisées du niveau de la licence; **honours degree** = licence; **first class honours** = licence avec mention (très) bien. **6.** (*a*) *usu. pl.* (*civilities*) **to receive s.o. with all due h., with full honours,** recevoir qn avec tous les honneurs qui lui sont dus; **to do the honours (of one's house),** faire les honneurs (de sa maison); **to pay the last honours to s.o.,** rendre les derniers honneurs à qn; *Mil:* **to render, pay, give, honours,** rendre les honneurs; **to leave a fortress with all the honours of war,** se retirer d'une forteresse avec tous les honneurs de la guerre; (*b*) *pl. Cards:* (*bridge etc.*) honneurs (as, roi, dame, et valet d'atout); **honours are even,** (i) *Cards:* les honneurs sont répartis également, sont partagés; (ii) nous sommes à deux de jeux. **7.** (*of pers.*) (*a*) **to be an h. to one's country, to one's sex,** faire honneur à sa patrie, à son sexe; **an h. to his native town,** la gloire de sa ville natale; (*b*) **Your H., His H.,** Monsieur le juge, Monsieur le président. **8.** *Com:* **acceptance for h.,** acceptation *f* par intervention, par honneur, sous protêt; intervention *f* à protêt; **the acceptor for h.,** l'avaliste *m*; le donneur d'aval; **act of h.,** acte *m* d'intervention; intervention *f*; **for (the) h. of. . .,** pour l'honneur de. . ..

honour², *v.tr.* **1.** (*a*) honorer (qn, la mémoire de qn); **I h. you for it,** cela vous fait honneur; *B:* **h. thy father and thy mother,** tes père et mère honoreras; (*b*) **to h. s.o. with one's confidence, a title, an invitation,** honorer qn de sa confiance, d'un titre, d'une invitation; **to h. a ceremony with one's presence,** honorer une cérémonie de sa présence; **a custom more honoured in the breach than in the observance,** (i) coutume à laquelle on ferait mieux de déroger; (ii) coutume à laquelle on fait le plus souvent l'honneur de déroger. **2. to h. one's signature,** faire honneur à sa signature; *Com:* **to h. a bill,** faire honneur à un effet; payer, accepter, accueillir, un effet; **honoured bill,** traite payée, acquittée.

honourable [ˈɔnərəbl], *a.* **1.** (conduite, famille) honorable; **he is an h. man,** c'est un homme d'honneur; il a les mains nettes; **h. action,** action *f* qui fait honneur à (qn); **h. peace,** paix *f* honorable; **all work is h.,** il n'y a pas de sot métier; tout travail est honorable. **2.** (*a*) **the H.,** *abbrev.* **the Hon.,** l'honorable . . . (titre donné aux fils cadets des *earls* et aux fils et filles des pairs au-dessous du rang de marquis; aux dames et demoiselles d'honneur de la Cour et à celles en ayant exercé les fonctions; aux juges de la Haute Cour qui n'ont pas droit au titre de *Lord*; *A:* aux membres des Gouvernements et des Conseils des Indes et des Colonies; aux membres de la Chambre des Communes; *U.S:* aux membres des deux Chambres, des Législatures d'État, et de la magistrature); **the Hon. member for Caithness,** l'honorable membre représentant Caithness; **the Hon. member has omitted to . . .,** mon honorable collègue a omis de . . .; (*b*) **the Most H.,** le très honorable (titre donné aux marquis, à l'Ordre du Bain, au Conseil privé de la Couronne); (*c*) **The Right H.,** le très honorable (titre donné aux pairs au-dessous du rang de marquis, aux Conseillers privés de la Couronne, au Lord Maire de Londres, et à certains autres dignitaires).

honourableness [ˈɔnərəbəlnis], *s.* caractère *m* honorable; honorabilité *f* (des intentions, etc.).

honourably [ˈɔnərəbli], *adv.* honorablement.

honoured [ˈɔnəd], *a.* honoré; **h. old age,** vieillesse honorée; **to bear an h. name,** porter un grand nom, un nom honorable.

hooch [huːtʃ], *s. P:* gnôle *f*, gniole *f* (de contrebande, de fabrication illicite).

hood¹ [hud], *s.* **1.** *Cost:* (*a*) capuchon *m* (de moine, d'agent de police, etc.); capuce *m* (de moine); cagoule *f* (de pénitent, de bandit); capuche *f* (de femme); capeline *f* (de femme, d'enfant); *A.Cost:* **French h.,** attifet *m*; (*b*) *Sch:* chaperon *m* (de toge universitaire) (= épitoge *f*); (*c*) *Hatm:* forme *f* (de chapeau); (*d*) *Ven:* chaperon (de faucon); *Harn:* camail *m*, béguin *m* (de cheval); (*e*) *Nat.Hist:* casque *m* (de fleur, d'insecte); manteau *m* (de lézard); coiffe *f*, capuchon (de cobra). **2.** (*a*) *Veh: etc:* **(folding, extensible) h.,** capote *f*, soufflet *m* (de voiture); tendelet *m* (de canot à vapeur); capote (de voiturette d'enfants); (*b*) *Nau:* capot *m* (d'écoutille, d'habitacle, de claire-voie); (*c*) *Phot:* abat-jour *m inv* (de mise au point); parasoleil *m* (d'objectif); (*d*) hotte *f*, auvent *m* (de forge, de laboratoire); tablier *m* (d'âtre) en trapèze; chapeau *m* (de lampe, de pieu); capuchon (de lampe, de meule); parapluie *m*, chapeau (de cheminée); *El:* cloche *f* (d'isolateur); *Aut: NAm:* capot (du moteur); (*e*) *Artil: Navy:* **armoured h.,** masque blindé; (*f*) **acoustic h.,** cabine *f* d'écoute, d'audition.

hood², *v.tr.* **1.** *Ven:* chaperonner (un faucon). **2.** capoter (une voiture, etc.); encapuchonner (une cheminée, etc.).

hood³, *s. NAm: P:* = HOODLUM.

hooded ['hudid], *a.* **1.** (*a*) (*of pers.*) encapuchonné; **hooded men,** cagoulards *m*; (*b*) (vêtement) à capuchon; (oiseau, etc.) mantelé; (fleur) capuchonnée; **h. (wicker) chair,** guérite *f* (de plage, etc.). **2.** (*a*) *Poet:* couvert, caché; (*b*) aux yeux bandés.

hoodie ['hudi], *s. Orn: F:* corneille mantelée.

hoodlum ['hu:dləm], *s. F:* (*a*) voyou *m*; (*b*) gangster *m*.

hoodman-blind ['hudmən'blaind], *s. Games: A:* colin-maillard *m*.

hoodmould(ing) ['hudmould(iŋ)], *s. Arch:* larmier *m*.

hoodoo¹ ['hu:du:], *s.* **1.** (*a*) vaudou *m*; envoûtement *m*; **h. priest,** sorcier *m*; (*b*) *F:* porteur, -euse, de malheur, de guigne; (*c*) *F:* malheur *m*, guigne *f*; (*d*) *attrib. F:* qui porte malheur. **2.** *Geol: NAm:* cheminée *f* des fées.

hoodoo², *v.tr. F:* ensorceler (qn); porter malheur à (qn).

hood-shaped ['hudʃeipt], *a. Nat.Hist:* cuculliforme.

hoodwink ['hudwiŋk], *v.tr.* **1.** *A:* mettre un bandeau à (qn); bander les yeux à, de (qn). **2.** *F:* tromper (qn); donner le change à (qn); en mettre plein les yeux à (qn); **to be completely hoodwinked,** n'y voir que du feu.

hooey ['hu:i], *F:* (*a*) *s.* bêtises *fpl*; (*b*) *int.* (tout ça c'est des) bêtises, (de la) foutaise!

hoof¹, *pl.* **-s, hooves** [hu:f, -s, hu:vz], *s.* (*a*) sabot *m* (de cheval, etc.); botte cornée; **beef on the h.,** bétail *m* sur pied; *Vet:* **h. rot,** fourchet *m*, piétin *m*; (*b*) *F:* pied *m*.

hoof², *v. F:* **1.** (*a*) *v.tr. & i.* **to h. (it),** aller à pied, à pattes, à pinces; prendre le train onze; (*b*) *v.i. NAm:* danser. **2.** *v.tr.* **to h. s.o. out,** chasser qn à coups de pied; sortir qn à coups de botte.

hoofbound ['hu:fbaund]. *Vet:* **1.** *a.* encastelé. **2.** *s.* encastelure *f*.

hoofed [hu:ft], *a.* (*a*) *Z:* (quadrupède) ongulé, à sabots, pourvu de sabots; (*b*) *Her:* onglé.

hoofer ['hu:fər], *s. NAm: P:* **1.** danseur, -euse (de cabaret, etc.). **2.** cabotin, -ine.

hoof-pick ['hu:fpik], *s. Farr:* cure-pied *m*, *pl.* cure-pieds.

hoofprint ['hu:fprint], *s.* empreinte *f*, marque *f*, trace *f*, de sabot.

Hoogly (the) [ðə'hu:gli]. *Pr.n. Geog:* le (fleuve) Hougli.

hoo-ha ['hu:hɑ:], *s. F:* **what's (all) the hoo-ha about?** qu'est-ce qu'il y a de cassé? qu'est-ce qui se passe?

hook¹ [huk], *s.* **1.** crochet *m*; croc *m*; griffe *f*; (*a*) pendoir *m*; **butcher's h.,** croc de boucherie, allonge *f* de boucher; **wall h.,** crampillon *m*; **chimney h., pot h.,** crémaillère *f*; **curtain (loop) h.,** rinceau *m*; **to hang one's coat on a h.,** pendre son manteau à une patère; **h.(-on) ladder,** échelle *f* à crochet(s); (*for door, etc.*) **h. and eye,** crochet à œillet; *Carp:* **cabin h.,** bourdonnière *f*; grain *m*; pivot *m*; **h. scarf,** écart *m* à dent, à crochet; **h. of a well chain,** main *f*; *Mec.E:* **h. at end of a chain,** clef *f*; **h. block,** poutre *f* à croc; **h. bolt,** crampon fileté; **h. nail,** (i) clou *m* à croc, à crochet; (ii) clou barbelé; crampon; (*b*) croc (pour happer qch.); **handled h.,** main *f* de fer; crochet *m*; **bench h.,** crochet d'établi; **glassworker's h.,** cornard *m*; **tanner's h.,** bouloir *m*; *Mec.E:* **pawl h.,** croc à déclic; *Veh:* **shaft h., breeching h.,** ragot *m*; *Av: Nau:* **arrester h.,** crosse *f* d'appontage; **catapulting h.,** crochet de catapultage; **chain h.,** croc à chaînes; **cargo h.,** croc de charge; **sister h.,** croc à ciseaux; **pelican h.,** croc à échappement; **h. rope,** vérine *f*; **by h. or (by) crook,** d'une manière, d'une façon, ou d'une autre; de manière ou d'autre; coûte que coûte; (*c*) *Cost:* agrafe *f*; crochet de couturière; **h. and eye,** agrafe et œillet, agrafe et porte; crochet et porte; (*d*) **h. and hinge, h. and ride,** gond *m* et penture; *F: A:* **to be off the hooks,** ne plus avoir toute sa raison; *F: A:* **to drop, slip, off the hooks,** mourir. **2.** (*a*) *Fish:* hameçon *m*; **gaff h.,** gaffeau *m*; **fly h.,** mouche montée sur hameçon; **to be caught, get, on the h.,** (i) (*of fish*) prendre le hameçon; (ii) *F:* (*of pers.*) se laisser prendre à l'amorce, au piège; gober le morceau; **baited h.,** (i) hameçon garni; (ii) *F:* piège; attrape-nigaud *m inv*; *NAm: F:* **to get s.o. off the hooks,** tirer qn d'affaire, sortir qn d'un mauvais pas; *F:* **on one's own h.,** tout seul; sans aide; à son propre compte; (*b*) *F:* (i) *A:* **the hooks,** la main; (ii) **if he gets his hooks into that,** s'il y met la patte. **3.** (*a*) **(reaping) h.,** faucille *f*; **thistle h., weed h.,** échardonnet *m*, échardonnette *f*; **pruning h.,** émondoir *m*, ébranchoir *m*; (*b*) **(painter's) shave h.,** grattoir *m*, ébardoir *m*; **rave h.,** bec-de-corbin, *pl.* becs-de-corbin, bec-corbeau *m*, *pl.* becs-de-corbeau. **4.** *Mus:* crochet (d'une croche, d'une double croche, etc.). **5.** (*a*) *Box:* **right h., left h.,** crochet du droit, du gauche; (*b*) *Golf: Cr:* coup tourné à gauche; *Golf:* coup tiré. **6.** cap *m*; pointe *f* de terre; coude *m* (d'une rivière); crochet (d'un chemin); *Geog:* **the H. (of Holland),** Hoek van Holland. **7.** *F:* **to sling, take, one's h.,** décamper, plier bagage; prendre ses cliques et ses claques; *NAm:* **to get the h.,** être congédié, saqué, mis à la porte.

hook², *v.*

I. *v.tr.* **1.** courber (le doigt). **2.** (*a*) **to h. sth. (on, up) to sth.,** accrocher, suspendre, qch. à qch.; raccorder (qch. à qch.); (*with passive force*) **the rods all h. together,** les tiges s'accrochent les unes aux autres; (*b*) *Typ:* **to h. in a word (at the end of a line),** crocheter un mot (au bout d'une ligne); **I hooked my arm in his,** je lui ai pris le bras; je me suis cramponnée à son bras. **3. to h. (up) a curtain, a dress, etc.,** agrafer un rideau, une robe, etc.; **dress that hooks up at the back,** robe qui s'agrafe par derrière. **4.** (*a*) crocher, gaffer (un bateau, un objet flottant); (*b*) *F:* voler (qch.), mettre le grappin sur (qch.); **he found the boys hooking apples from the tree,** il a trouvé les garçons qui volaient des pommes sur l'arbre. **5.** (*a*) *Fish:* prendre (un poisson) à l'hameçon; accrocher (un poisson); (*b*) *F:* amorcer, attraper (un mari, etc.); **if only you can get him to listen, he's hooked,** si seulement tu réussis à le faire écouter, tu l'auras; (*c*) *F:* **he got hooked on morphine,** il est devenu morphinomane. **6.** (*a*) **to h. the ball,** *Cr: etc:* renvoyer (la balle) d'un coup tourné à gauche; *Golf:* faire un coup tiré; *Rugby Fb:* **to h. the ball,** s'emparer du ballon avec le pied (dans la mêlée); (*b*) *Box:* donner un coup en crochet à (son adversaire). **7.** *F:* **to h. it,** filer, décamper, déguerpir.

II. (*compound verb*) **hook up,** *v.tr. & i.* (*a*) atteler (un cheval); (*b*) assembler (les pièces d'un appareil); installer (un appareil, etc.); *Cmptr:* (inter)connecter; *esp. U.S:* **we've finished hooking up the new bathroom,** l'installation de la nouvelle salle de bains est terminée; (*c*) *P:* (i) **to get hooked up,** se marier; (ii) **to be hooked up with s.o.,** être de mèche avec qn.

hook³, *s. Husb:* hanche *f* (de vache).

hookah ['hukə], *s.* narghileh *m*, narguilé *m*.

hook-billed ['huk'bild], *a. Orn:* oncirostre.

Hooke [huk], *Pr.n. Mec.E:* **Hooke's coupling,** joint *m* de Hooke; joint à articulation en croix; accouplement articulé.

hooked [hukt], *a.* **1.** (bec) crochu, recourbé. **2.** muni de crochets, d'hameçons, etc. **3.** *NAm:* **h. rug,** tapis *m* à points noués simples.

hooker¹ ['hukər], *s.* (*pers.*) **1.** *Min:* accrocheur *m* de wagons. **2.** *Rugby Fb:* talonneur *m*.

hooker², *s. Nau:* **1.** hourque *f*. **2.** *F: occ. Pej:* **an old h.,** une baille, une vieille barque.

hookey ['huki], *s.* **1.** *F:* **to play h.,** faire l'école buissonnière. **2.** *Cards:* **blind h.,** jeu *m* semblable au baccarat; *F:* **to play (blind) h. with the national resources,** (i) mettre en danger, (ii) gaspiller, les ressources nationales.

hooking ['hukiŋ], *s.* **1. h. on,** accrochage *m*; attelage *m* (d'un cheval de renfort, etc.). **2. h. up,** (i) accrochage (d'un rideau, etc.); (ii) agrafage *m* (d'une robe).

hooklike ['huklaik], *a. Nat.Hist:* unciforme, uncinulé.

hooknose ['huknouz], *s.* (*also* **hooked nose**) **1.** nez crochu; nez en bec-de-corbin. **2.** nez busqué, aquilin.

hook-nosed ['huknouzd], *a.* **1.** au nez crochu. **2.** au nez busqué, aquilin.

hookup ['hukʌp], *s.* **1.** combinaison *f* (d'intérêts financiers, etc.). **2.** *Tchn:* liaison *f*; *Mec.E:* liaison mécanique, conjugaison *f*; *W.Tel:* conjugaison de postes; postes conjugués; *Cmptr:* (inter)connexion *f*, liaison.

hookworm ['hukwə:m], *s. Ann:* ankylostome *m*; uncinaire *f*; *Med:* **h. (disease),** ankylostomiase *f*; anémie *f* des mineurs, uncinariose *f*.

hooligan ['hu:ligən], *s.* voyou *m*.

hooliganism ['hu:ligənizm], *s.* voyouterie *f*, voyoutisme *m*.

hoop¹ [hu:p], *s.* **1.** (*a*) *Coop:* cercle *m*, cerceau *m* (de tonneau); **double h.,** sommier *m*; **h. iron,** fer *m* feuillard; feuillard *m* (de fer); fer en rubans, en bandes; fer plat; cercles *mpl* de barrique; **h. cramp,** traitoir *m*; (*b*) cercle, cerceau (de mât, etc.); frette *f*, embrassure *f* (de pieu, de canon); virole *f*, anneau *m* (de moyeu, etc.); cerce *f* (de tamis, etc.); *Av:* cerce (de fuselage); *Mec.E: etc:* **h. ring,** frette; *Mch:* **eccentric h.,** bague *f*, collier *m*, d'excentrique; *El.E:* **commutator h.,** frette du collecteur; *Turf:* **white and cerise hoops,** casaque cerclée blanc et cerise; (*c*) jante *f*, bandage *m* (de roue); (*d*) *Mus:* cercle, vergette *f* (de tambour); **flesh h.,** vergette de roulage; (*e*) forme *f* (à fromage). **2.** cerceau (d'enfant, de cirque); (*in circus*) **paper h.,** ballon *m*; **to trundle, drive, a h.,** jouer au cerceau; faire courir, faire rouler, un cerceau; **to go through the h.,** (i) (*of equestrienne, dog, etc.*) passer à travers le cerceau; franchir le cerceau; (ii) *F:* sauter le bâton; **to put s.o. through the h.,** rendre la vie dure à qn. **3.** *A.Cost:* cercle de baleine, vertugadin *m* (de jupon); **h. (skirt, petticoat),** (i) vertugadin; (ii) jupe *f* à paniers; panier *m*. **4.** *Lap:* **h. (ring),** anneau, bague, jonc *m* (d'or, de diamants). **5.** (*half hoop*) (*a*) cerceau (de tente de voiture, etc.); (*b*) (*croquet*) arceau *m*; **to run the h.** passer l'arceau. **6. h. net,** (*for fish*) truble *f*, verveux *m*, pantène *f*, pantenne *f*; (*small*) trubleau *m*; (*for lobsters*) casier *m* à homards; (*for birds*) nasse *f*; (*for butterflies*) freloche *f*.

hoop², *v.tr.* **1.** (*a*) *Coop:* cercler, relier (un tonneau); (*b*) fretter, cercler (un canon, un mât, etc.); bander (une penture); **hooped concrete,** béton cerclé, fretté; (*c*) garnir (une roue) de jantes. **2.** *A: Cost:* mettre un cercle de baleine à (une jupe).

hooper ['hu:pər], *s. Coop:* (*also* **hoop maker**) cerclier *m*.

hooping ['hu:piŋ], *s.* (*a*) *Coop:* cerclage *m*, reliage *m* (de tonneaux); **h. machine,** machine *f* à cercler; (*b*) frettage *m* (d'un canon, etc.); bandage *m* (d'une poutre, etc.).

hoop-la ['hu:plɑ:], *s.* **1.** (*at fairs*) jeu *m* des anneaux. **2.** *NAm: F:* brouhaha (joyeux); tapage *m*; boucan *m*.

hoopoe ['hu:pou], *s. Orn:* huppe *f* (d'Europe); *A:* **wood h.,** irrisor *m*, moqueur *m* d'Afrique.

hoopwood ['hu:pwud], *s. Coop: etc:* feuillard *m*.

hoosegow ['hu:sgau], *s. U.S: P:* prison *f*, taule *f*, violon *m*.

hoosh [hu:ʃ], *s. A:* soupe *f* de pemmican et de biscuit de mer (aliment des explorateurs polaires).

Hoosier ['hu:ʒər], *s. U.S: F:* (*a*) habitant, -ante, originaire *mf*, de l'Indiana; (*b*) personne gauche, maladroite; rustre *m*.

hoot¹ [hu:t], *s.* **1.** (*a*) ululation *f*, (h)ululement *m* (de hibou); (*b*) huée *f* (de dérision, etc.); (*c*) *F:* **what a h.!** c'est marrant! c'est à se tordre (de rire)! (*d*) *Aut:* coup *m* de klaxon; coup *m* de sifflet (d'une locomotive, d'une usine); coup de sirène (de bateau, d'une usine); mugissement *m* (d'une sirène). **2.** *F:* **not to care a h., not to give two hoots (about s.o., sth.),** se ficher (royalement) (de qn, de qch.).

hoot². **1.** *v.i.* (*a*) (*of owl*) (h)ululer, chuinter, huer; (*b*) (*of pers.*) huer; **to h. at, after, s.o.,** poursuivre qn de huées; conspuer qn; *F:* **to h. with laughter,** rire aux éclats; (*c*) *Aut:* klaxonner, donner un coup de klaxon; (*d*) (*of locomotive, etc.*) siffler; lancer un coup de sifflet; (*of siren*) mugir; (*of ship*) faire marcher la sirène; lancer un coup de sirène. **2.** *v.tr.* huer, conspuer (qn); accueillir (qn) par des huées; poursuivre (qn) de cris, de huées; siffler (une pièce de théâtre); **to h. s.o. down,** faire taire qn (par des huées); **to h. a play off the stage,** (faire) tomber une pièce; **he was hooted off the stage,** il quitta la scène au milieu des huées.

hoot³, *s. N.Z: Austr: F:* argent *m*, pognon *m*.

hootch [hu:tʃ], *s. P:* = HOOCH.

hooter ['hu:tər], *s.* (*a*) *Nau: Ind:* sirène *f*; sifflet *m*; (*b*) *Aut: etc:* avertisseur *m*; klaxon *m*; (*c*) *P:* grand nez, trompette *f*.

hooting ['hu:tiŋ], *s.* (*a*) (h)ululement *m* (de hibou); (*b*) (*of pers.*) huées *fpl*; (*c*) *Aut:* coups *mpl* de klaxon.

hoots [hu:ts], *int. Scot:* allons donc! chansons!

hoove [hu:v], *s. Vet:* météorisation *f*, météorisme *m*, ballonnement *m*, empansement *m*.

Hoover¹ ['hu:vər], *s. R.t.m:* aspirateur *m* de la marque Hoover (souvent utilisé pour n'importe quel aspirateur).

hoover², *v.tr. F:* passer l'aspirateur sur (un plancher, etc.) (verbe dérivé de Hoover, *R.t.m.*).

hop¹ [hɔp], *s.* **1.** (*a*) *Bot:* houblon *m*; *Brew:* **hops,** le houblon; **h. growing,** culture *f* du houblon; **h.(-growing) area,** région houblonnière; **h. grower,** houblonnier *m*; **h. field, garden,** houblonnière *f*; **h. pole,** perche *f* à houblon; *F:* (*of pers.*) **what a h. pole!** quelle grande perche! **h. picking,** cueillette *f* du houblon; **h. picker,** cueilleur, -euse, de houblon; **h. kiln,** four *m*, séchoir *m*, à houblon; *O:* **h. pillow,** oreiller somnifère (rempli de houblon); (*b*) *Bot:* **h. hornbeam,** charme-houblon *m*, *pl.* charmes-houblon; **h. tree,** orme *m* à trois feuilles; **h. clover,** trèfle *m* jaune; luzerne-houblon *m*; lupuline *f*. **2.** *U.S: P:* stupéfiant *m*, *esp.* opium *m*.

hop², *v.* **(hopped** [hɔpt]) **1.** *v.tr.* (*a*) houblonner (la bière); (*b*) *U.S: P:* **to be hopped up,** être sous l'influence d'un stupéfiant; être drogué, camé. **2.** *v.i.* cueillir le houblon.

hop³, *s.* **1.** (*a*) petit saut; sautillement *m*; (*b*) saut à cloche-pied; *Sp:* **h., skip and jump,** triple saut; **he went off with a h., (a) skip and a jump,** il s'en est allé sur une gambade, en sautillant; *F:* **to catch s.o. on the h.,** surprendre qn; prendre qn au pied levé; *F:* **to keep s.o. on the h.,** faire valser qn; ne pas laisser chômer qn; (*c*) *Av:* étape *f*; **to do the journey in one h.,** faire le voyage d'un trait, sans étapes. **2.** *F:* (*dance*) sauterie *f*.

hop⁴, **1.** *v.i.* (*a*) sauter, sautiller; **to h. on one leg,** sauter à cloche-pied; **to h. away,** (i) s'éloigner à cloche-pied; (ii) (*of sparrow, etc.*) s'éloigner en sautillant; **the sparrows come hopping up to us,** les moineaux *m* s'approchent en sautillant; *F:* **to h. off,** filer; ficher le camp; (*b*) *F:* danser; (*c*) **to h. over a ditch,** sauter un fossé; **to h. out of bed, off one's bicycle,** sauter à bas de son lit, à bas de son vélo; **to h. on a bus,** sauter dans l'autobus; *F:* **to h. over to Paris,** faire un saut à Paris. **2.** *v.tr. F:* sauter (un obstacle); *P: A:* **to h. the twig, the perch,** (i) s'en aller; filer; décamper; (ii) mourir, sauter le pas, lâcher la rampe, casser sa pipe; *F:* **to h. it,** filer, ficher le camp, se débiner; **h. it!** allez, ouste! allez hop! va-t'-en! **3.** *v.tr. esp. U.S: F:* **to h. a ride (on a train),** voyager (en chemin de fer) sans payer.

hopbind, hopbine ['hɔpbain(d)], *s.* sarment *m*, tige *f*, liane *f*, de houblon.

hopcalite ['hɔpkəlait], *s. Ch:* hopcalite *f*.

hope[1] [houp], *s.* **1.** (*a*) espérance *f*, espoir *m*; **between h. and fear,** entre l'espérance et la crainte; **to be full of h.,** avoir bon espoir; **to lose h.,** perdre (l')espoir; **to have lost h.,** être désespéré, complètement découragé; **to h. against h.,** espérer contre toute espérance; **past all h.,** perdu sans retour, sans espoir; **he is past h.,** on désespère de le sauver; **when one is young there is always h.,** la jeunesse revient de loin; **there is no h. of his being appointed,** il n'y a aucun espoir qu'il soit nommé; **to put one's h. in the future,** compter sur l'avenir; **he will be carrying the hopes of America in the Olympic Games,** il portera les espoirs olympiques américains; **to set one's hopes on s.o., on sth.,** mettre tout son espoir en qn, en qch.; **to set one's hopes on doing sth.,** nourrir l'espoir de faire qch.; *Geog:* **the Cape of Good H.,** le cap de Bonne Espérance; (*b*) **in the h. of . . .,** dans l'attente de . . ., dans l'espoir de . . .; **to be, live, in h. of doing sth.,** avoir l'espoir de faire qch.; **I live in the certain h. of seeing him again,** je nourris la ferme espérance de le revoir. **2. he is the h. of his country,** il est l'espoir de son pays; **the young h. of an ancient family,** l'espoir d'une vieille famille; **my last h.,** mon dernier espoir; ma dernière planche de salut; **to have hopes of sth., of doing sth.,** avoir qch. en vue; avoir l'espoir de faire qch.; **I have good hopes of finding it again,** j'ai bon espoir de le retrouver; **I have hopes of seeing him tomorrow,** je pense le voir demain; **to live, be, in hopes that . . .,** caresser l'espoir, avoir l'espoir, oser espérer, que . . .; *Iron:* **what a h.! some h.!** si vous comptez là-dessus!

hope[2]. **1.** *v.i.* espérer; **he no longer hopes,** il n'espère plus; il n'a plus d'espoir; **we must h. against h.,** il faut espérer quand même, contre toute espérance; il ne faut jamais désespérer; **to h. on,** continuer d'espérer; se bercer d'espérances; **to h. for sth.,** espérer qch.; **that is not the result I had hoped for,** ce n'est pas là le résultat que j'avais rêvé; **hoped-for victory,** victoire attendue, espérée, désirée; victoire en espérance; **to h. for the best,** ne pas désespérer; avoir bon espoir; **to h. in God,** mettre son espoir en Dieu. **2.** *v.tr.* (*a*) **I h. and pray, expect, that . . .,** j'espère avec confiance que . . .; **what can one h. to gain by this?** qu'espère-t-on gagner à cela? **I h. to see you again,** j'espère vous revoir; **I had hoped to tell you myself,** je comptais vous l'apprendre moi-même; *Iron:* **I h. I may (be considered to) know something about my job,** je connais mon affaire peut-être! **I only h. you may get it!** je vous en souhaite! *Corr:* **hoping to hear from you,** dans l'attente de vos nouvelles; dans l'espoir de vous lire; (*b*) **I h. your brother is better,** j'espère que votre frère va mieux; **I h. he doesn't miss his train,** j'espère qu'il ne va pas manquer son train; **I h. you may succeed, may be right,** je souhaite que vous réussissiez, que vous ayez raison; **a day will come, I h., when . . .,** un jour viendra, je l'espère, où . . .; **you've done your work, I h.?** tu as fait ton travail, au moins?

hope[3], *s.* **1.** *A:* champ cultivé, terrain cultivé (entouré de terres incultes); **osier h.,** champ d'osier; oseraie *f*. **2.** *Scot:* vallon encaissé, sans issue. **3.** *Dial:* bras *m* de mer; petite baie.

hopeful ['houpful], *a.* **1.** plein d'espoir; **inclined to be h., in h. mood,** disposé à l'espérance; **we must remain h.,** il faut continuer d'espérer; **to be h. that . . .,** avoir bon espoir que . . .; **to be of a h. disposition,** être d'un naturel optimiste; voir tout en rose. **2.** (*a*) (avenir, carrière) qui donne de belles, de grandes, espérances, qui promet; *s. F:* (*usu. Iron:*) **young h.,** l'espoir de la famille; **this is my young h.,** voici mon fils; **young H. was spending a lot of money,** le fils à papa dépensait pas mal d'argent; (*b*) **the situation looks more h.,** la situation s'annonce meilleure, est plus encourageante; il y a un changement pour le mieux; les choses se présentent sous un meilleur jour.

hopefully ['houpfuli], *adv.* **1.** (travailler, etc.) avec bon espoir, avec confiance. **2. things were turning out h.,** les choses prenaient une tournure encourageante; *F:* **h. the snow will be gone by tomorrow,** espérons que la neige aura fondu demain.

hopefulness ['houpfulnis], *s.* **1.** bon espoir; confiance *f*. **2.** bons présages, bons indices (de la situation, etc.).

hopeite ['houpait], *s. Miner:* hopéite *f*.

hopeless ['houplis], *a.* **1.** sans espoir; désespéré; **h. grief,** noir chagrin; douleur *f* inconsolable. **2.** (*a*) qui ne permet aucun espoir; (maladie *f*, passion *f*, etc.) incurable; (situation) désespérée, sans issue; (projet *m*) qui n'a aucune chance de réussir; (excuse *f*) qui n'en imposerait à personne; (*of patient, etc.*) **to be in a h. state,** être dans un état désespéré; **the doctors say his case is h.,** les médecins l'ont condamné; **it's a h. job,** c'est désespérant; c'est à désespérer de jamais réussir; **to give sth. up as h.,** renoncer à faire qch.; **I know it is h. appealing to you,** je sais qu'il est parfaitement inutile de m'adresser à vous; **it is h. to try to . . .,** on aurait beau essayer de . . .; (*b*) *F:* **h. dunce, drunkard,** cancre *m* indécrottable, ivrogne *m* incorrigible; **you're h.!** vous êtes décourageant, désespérant!

hopelessly ['houplisli], *adv.* **1.** (vivre) sans espoir; (regarder qn) avec désespoir. **2.** (vaincu) irrémédiablement; (amoureux) sans retour; **h. poor,** pauvre irrémédiablement; **h. drunk,** soûl perdu.

hopelessness ['houplisnis], *s.* **1.** désespoir *m*. **2.** état désespéré, nature désespérante (d'une situation).

hophead ['hɔphed], *s. U.S: P:* toxicomane *mf*; drogué, -ée; camé, -ée.

hoplite ['hɔplait], *s. Gr.Ant:* hoplite *m*.

Hop-o'-my-thumb ['hɔpəmai'θʌm]. **1.** *Pr.n.* le Petit Poucet. **2.** *s. F: O:* petit bout d'homme.

hopper[1] ['hɔpər], *s.* **1.** (*a*) (*pers., animal*) sauteur, -euse; (*b*) *F:* sauterelle *f*; (*c*) (*of piano*) échappement *m* (du marteau); (*d*) **h. light, casement, frame,** fenêtre *f* à bascule, à charnière. **2.** (*a*) trémie *f*, huche *f*, hotte *f* (de moulin); (*b*) *Agr:* semoir *m*; (*c*) *Husb:* mangeoire *f*; trémie (pour poulets, etc.); (*d*) *Sm.a:* **cartridge h.,** auget *m* (de répétition); (*e*) *Cmptr:* magasin *m* d'alimentation (de cartes). **3.** *Nau:* **h. (barge),** marie-salope *f*, *pl.* maries-salopes; chaland *m*; allège *f*; *Rail:* **h. car,** wagon *m* tombereau.

hopper[2], *s.* cueilleur, -euse, de houblon.

hopping[1] ['hɔpiŋ], *s.* **1.** cueillette *f* du houblon. **2.** houblonnage *m*.

hopping[2], *s.* sautillement *m*, sauts *mpl*.

hopping[3], *adv. F:* **to be h. mad,** être fou de colère.

hopple[1] ['hɔpl], *s.* entrave *f* (pour chevaux, etc.).

hopple[2], *v.tr.* entraver (un cheval, etc.).

hopsack ['hɔpsæk], *s.* **1.** sac *m* à houblon. **2.** *Tex:* cheviote grossière.

hopscotch ['hɔpskɔtʃ], *s. Games:* la marelle.

hopvine ['hɔpvain], *s.* = HOPBIND.

hopyard ['hɔpjɑːd], *s.* houblonnière *f*.

horary ['hɔːrəri], *a. Astr: etc:* horaire.

Horatian [hə'reiʃ(ə)n], *a. Lt.Lit:* d'Horace; d'après Horace.

Horatii (the) [ðəhə'reiʃiai, -iiː], *Pr.n.m.pl. Rom.Hist:* les Horaces.

horde [hɔːd], *s.* horde *f* (de barbares, etc.).

hordein ['hɔːdiin], *s. Bio-Ch:* hordéine *f*.

hordenine ['hɔːdəniːn], *s. Pharm:* hordénine *f*.

hordeolum [hɔː'diːələm], *s. Med:* orgelet *m*.

hordeum ['hɔːdiəm], *s. Bot:* hordeum *m*.

horehound ['hɔːhaund], *s. Bot:* **(common, white) h.,** marrube *m*; **black h.,** ballote *f*.

horizon [hə'raiz(ə)n], *s.* **1.** horizon *m*; (*a*) **apparent, natural, visible, h.,** horizon apparent, visible, visuel; **clear h.,** horizon dégagé; **h. line,** ligne *f* d'horizon, niveau *m* de l'horizon; **on the h.,** à l'horizon, au-dessus de l'horizon; *Av: etc:* **h. lights,** feux *m* d'horizon; **this discovery opens up new horizons,** cette découverte ouvre de nouveaux horizons; (*b*) *Astr: Av: Nau:* **celestial h.,** horizon astronomique; **rational h.,** horizon vrai; **sensible h.,** horizon sensible; *Av:* **artificial h., bubble h.,** horizon artificiel; **gyro h.,** horizon gyroscopique; **h. bar,** barre *f* d'horizon (du directeur de vol). **2.** *Geol:* horizon (du sol).

horizontal [hɔri'zɔnt(ə)l]. **1.** *a.* horizontal, -aux; *U.S:* **h. increase in salaries of ten per cent,** augmentation *f* uniforme de dix pour cent sur toutes les rétributions. **2.** *s.* horizontale *f*.

horizontality [hɔrizɔn'tæliti], *s.* horizontalité *f*.

horizontally [hɔri'zɔntəli], *adv.* horizontalement.

horminum ['hɔːminəm], *s. Bot:* horminum *m*.

hormonal [hɔː'mounl], *a. Physiol:* hormonal, -aux.

hormone ['hɔːmoun], *s. Physiol:* hormone *f*; **h. dependent,** à dépendance endocrinienne, sous contrôle hormonal.

hormonotherapy [hɔːmounou'θerəpi], *s. Med:* hormonothérapie *f*.

horn[1] [hɔːn], *s.* **1.** (*a*) corne *f* (de bétail, de bélier, de bouc, de girafe, du diable, etc.); **horns of a stag,** bois *m* d'un cerf; (*of stag*) **to shed, cast, its horns,** perdre, poser, mettre bas, son bois; muer; **to remove, break, the horns of an animal,** écorner un animal; (*b*) *Nat.Hist:* antenne *f* (de cerf-volant); corne (de calao); aigrette *f* (de hibou); **horns of a snail,** cornes, *F:* antennes, d'un limaçon; *F:* **to draw in one's horns,** (i) rentrer les cornes; rentrer dans sa coquille; (ii) restreindre son ardeur, rabattre (de) ses prétentions, en rabattre; *F:* mettre de l'eau dans son vin; (*c*) *P:* (*not in polite use*) **to have the h.,** bander; (*d*) corne (d'un croissant, de la lune, d'une planète); branche *f* (d'un estuaire); antenne (de mine sous-marine); bigorne *f* (d'enclume); poignée *f* (de rabot); *Nau:* oreille *f* (de taquet); *El:* **horns of a switch,** cornes d'un disjoncteur, d'un commutateur; **h.-gap switch,** disjoncteur à cornes; **h. (lightning) arrester, h. gap,** éclateur *m*, parafoudre *m*, à cornes; (*e*) *Log:* corne (d'un dilemme); **on the horns of a dilemma,** enfermé dans un dilemme; (*f*) *Geog:* **Cape H., the H.,** le cap Horn; **the h. of Africa,** la péninsule des Somalis. **2.** (*horny matter*) corne; (*a*) **h. comb,** peigne *m* en corne; **h. spoon,** cuiller *f* de, en, corne; **to tip a bow with h.,** encorner un arc; (*b*) *Farr: etc:* corne (de sabot de cheval, d'âne, etc.); *Vet:* (*of horse's pumiced foot*) **spongy h.,** fourmilière *f*. **3.** *Mus:* (*a*) cor *m*, cornet *m*; **French h.,** cor d'harmonie; **hunting h.,** cor, trompe *f*, de chasse; **shepherd's h.,** buccin *m* de bouvier; **coach h.,** buccin de mail-coach; **h. player,** cor, corniste *m*; **to sound, wind, blow, the h.,** donner, sonner, du cor; (*b*) (*tenor oboe*) **English h.,** cor anglais; (*c*) **bass h.,** (i) tuba *m*; (ii) modification *f* russe du serpent. **4.** *Aut:* klaxon *m*, avertisseur *m*; **to sound one's h.,** klaxonner, donner un coup de klaxon. **5.** pavillon *m* (de haut-parleur, etc.). **6.** *A:* **drinking h.,** corne à boire; **h. of plenty,** corne d'abondance.

horn[2], *v.tr.* **1.** mettre des cornes à (qch.). **2.** écorner (un bœuf). **3.** (*of animals*) encorner (qn); donner un coup de corne à (qn); attaquer (qn) à coups de corne. **4.** *N.Arch:* **to h. the frame,** balancer les couples. **5.** *v.i. F:* **to h. in,** intervenir sans façon (dans une conversation, etc.).

hornbeam ['hɔːnbiːm], *s.* charme *m*; hêtre blanc; **h. plantation,** charmoie *f*.

hornbill ['hɔːnbil], *s. Orn:* calao *m*; **dwarf h.,** petit calao, tock *m*; **ground h.,** calao terrestre; **Malabar pied h.,** calao pie de Malabar; **red-billed h.,** tock à bec rouge; **rhinoceros h.,** oiseau-rhinocéros *m*, *pl.* oiseaux-rhinocéros.

hornblende ['hɔːnblend], *s. Miner:* hornblende *f*; **white h.,** calamite *f*.

hornblendite ['hɔːnblendait], *s. Miner:* hornblendite *f*.

hornblower ['hɔːnblouər], *s.* (*pers.*) corneur, -euse; sonneur *m* de cor, de trompe.

hornbook ['hɔːnbuk], *s. A:* abécédaire (monté derrière une plaque de corne).

horned [hɔːnd; *Lit:* 'hɔːnid], *a.* **1.** (*a*) (animal *m*) à cornes, cornu; (serpent, pavot, etc.) cornu; **the h. moon,** le croissant de la lune; **long-h.,** à longues cornes; **single-h.,** unicorne; *Rept:* **h. snake, viper,** vipère cornue; **h. toad,** phrynosome *m*; (*b*) *Her:* accorné. **2.** *Log:* **h. syllogism,** argument cornu.

horneophyton [hɔːniou'faitɔn], *s. Paleont:* hornéophyton *f*.

horner ['hɔːnər], *s.* **1.** préparateur, -trice, de corne; cornetier *m*. **2.** *occ.* = HORNBLOWER.

hornet ['hɔːnit], *s. Ent:* (*a*) frelon *m*; guêpe-frelon *f*, *pl.* guêpes-frelons; **to bring a hornet's nest about one's ears, to stir up a nest of hornets,** donner, tomber, se fourrer, dans un guêpier; (*b*) **h. fly,** asile *m* frelon.

hornfels ['hɔːnfelz], *s. Miner:* corne *f*, cornéenne *f*.

hornfish ['hɔːnfiʃ], *s. Ich:* orphie *f*.

hornful ['hɔːnful], *s.* pleine corne (de poudre, etc.).

horniness ['hɔːninis], *s.* (*a*) nature cornée (d'une substance); (*b*) callosité *f* (des mains).

hornist ['hɔːnist], *s. Mus:* cor *m*, joueur, -euse, de cor, *esp.* de cor d'harmonie.

hornless ['hɔːnlis], *a.* (*a*) (bête) sans cornes, (chèvre) mousse; (*b*) *Ent:* (insecte) acère; (*c*) (lune) sans cornes.

hornmeal ['hɔːnmiːl], *s. Com:* poudre *f* de corne.

hornpipe ['hɔːnpaip], *s. Danc: Mus:* matelote *f*.

horn-rimmed ['hɔːnrimd], *a.* (lunettes *fpl*) à monture en corne.

hornrims ['hɔːnrimz], *s.pl. O:* lunettes *f* à monture en corne.

horn silver ['hɔːn'silvər], *s. Miner:* argent corné; cérargyrite *f*, cérargyre *m*, kérargyre *m*.

hornstone ['hɔːnstoun], *s. Miner:* pierre *f* de corne; silex noir, silex corné.

hornswoggle ['hɔːnswɔgl], *v.tr. U.S: F:* duper, frauder (qn).

horntail ['hɔːnteil], *s. Ent:* sirex *m*.

hornwork ['hɔːnwɔːk], *s.* **1.** *Fort:* ouvrage *m* à cornes, en queue d'aronde. **2.** articles *mpl* de corne.

hornwort ['hɔːnwəːt], *s. Bot:* cératophylle *m*, cornifle *f.*

horny ['hɔːni], *a.* (*a*) corné; (bec *m*, etc.) de corne, en corne; **h. stone,** pierre cornée; (*b*) (*of hand, etc.*) calleux; **to grow h.,** se racornir; **to make one's hands h.,** se racornir les mains; **h.-handed,** aux mains calleuses.

horographer [hɔ'rɔgrəfər], *s.* horographe *m.*

horography [hɔ'rɔgrəfi], *s.* horographie *f.*

horologe ['hɔrəlɔdʒ], *s.* horologe *f.*

horologer, horologist [hɔ'rɔlədʒər, -dʒist], *s.* horloger *m.*

horological [hɔrə'lɔdʒik(ə)l], *a.* **1.** d'horloge, d'horlogerie. **2.** qui se rapporte à la mesure du temps.

horologian [hɔrə'loudʒiən], *s. Gr.Orthodox Ch:* horologe *m.*

horology [hɔ'rɔlədʒi], *s.* **1.** horlogerie *f.* **2.** horométrie *f.*

horopter [hɔ'rɔptər], *s. Opt:* horoptère *m.*

horopteric [hɔrɔp'terik], *a. Opt:* horoptérique.

horoscope ['hɔrəskoup], *s.* horoscope *m*; **to cast s.o.'s h.,** faire, dresser, tirer, l'horoscope de qn.

horoscopy [hɔ'rɔskəpi], *s.* horoscopie *f.*

horrendous [hɔ'rendəs], *a. F:* terrible, affreux, horrible.

horrible ['hɔrəbl], *a.* horrible, affreux, atroce, effroyable; **h. noise,** bruit *m* épouvantable; **it was h. to see,** cela faisait horreur à voir; **h. weather,** temps *m* abominable.

horribleness ['hɔrəblnis], *s.* caractère *m* horrible, effroyable (de qch.); affreuseté *f.*

horribly ['hɔrəbli], *adv.* horriblement, affreusement; **it's h. cold,** il fait un froid terrible.

horrid ['hɔrid], *a.* **1.** horrible, affreux; **h. sight,** chose *f* horrible à voir. **2.** *F:* méchant; **to be h. to s.o.,** être méchant envers qn; **to say h. things about s.o.,** dire des horreurs, des méchancetés, de qn; **what a h. man, woman!** quelle horreur d'homme, de femme! **don't be h.!** (i) ne dites pas, ne faites pas, des horreurs pareilles! (ii) ne faites pas le vilain! **how perfectly h. of you!** ce n'est pas du tout chic de votre part! **you h. thing!** oh, le vilain! oh, la vilaine!

horridly ['hɔridli], *adv.* **1.** affreusement. **2.** *F:* (se conduire) méchamment, abominablement.

horridness ['hɔridnis], *s.* **1.** horreur *f*, caractère *m* horrible (de qch.). **2.** *F:* méchanceté *f* (de conduite).

horrific [hɔ'rifik], *a.* horrifique; horrible.

horrification [hɔrifi'keiʃ(ə)n], *s.* horreur *f.*

horrify ['hɔrifai], *v.tr.* (*a*) horrifier (qn); faire horreur à (qn); (*b*) scandaliser (qn); **to be horrified,** être horrifié; être saisi, pénétré, d'horreur; **I was horrified at the idea,** (i) cette idée me faisait horreur; (ii) rien que d'y songer me faisait sauter.

horrifying ['hɔrifaiiŋ], *a.* horrifiant.

horripilate [hɔ'ripileit], *v.tr.* horripiler (qn); *F:* donner la chair de poule à (qn).

horripilation [hɔripi'leiʃ(ə)n], *s. Med:* horripilation *f*; *F:* chair *f* de poule.

horror ['hɔrər], *s.* **1.** horreur *f*; **paralysed with h.,** glacé d'horreur; **to my (unspeakable) h.,** à ma grande horreur; à mon grand effroi; **I fled in h.,** je m'enfuis horrifié; **to have a h. of s.o., of sth., of doing sth.,** avoir horreur de qn, de qch.; avoir qn, qch., en horreur; avoir horreur de faire qch.; **h. film,** film *m* d'épouvante, d'horreur. **2.** (*a*) chose horrible, affreuse; horreur; **what a h.!** quelle horreur! **the horrors of war, of death,** les horreurs de la guerre; les affres *f* de la mort; **to be suffering from the horrors of seasickness,** être en proie aux affres du mal de mer; **Chamber of Horrors,** Chambre *f* des Horreurs (d'un musée); (*b*) **that child's a little h.,** cet enfant est un petit poison; (*c*) *F:* **to have the horrors,** (i) grelotter de peur; (ii) être en proie au délire alcoolique, au delirium tremens; **it gives me the horrors,** cela me donne le frisson; ça me met les nerfs en pelote. **3.** *Med:* frisson *m* (symptomatique).

horrorstricken, horrorstruck ['hɔrəstrikn, -strʌk], *a.* saisi d'horreur; pénétré, glacé, frappé, d'horreur; atterré.

hors concours ['ɔːkɔŋ'kuər], *prep.phr.* hors-concours.

hors de combat [ɔːdə'kɔmbæt], *prep.phr.* hors de combat.

hors-d'œuvre [ɔː'dəːvr], *s.* (*pl.* **hors-d'œuvres**) *Cu:* hors-d'œuvre *m inv*; **h.-d'o. dish,** ravier *m*, plat *m* à hors-d'œuvre.

horse[1] [hɔːs], *s.* **1.** cheval, -aux *m*; (*a*) **draught h.,** cheval de trait; cheval de harnais, d'attelage; carrossier *m*; **heavy draught h.,** (cheval de) gros trait; **dray h.,** cheval de charrette; **plough h.,** cheval de labour, de labeur; **saddle h.,** cheval de selle; monture *f*; **carriage h.,** cheval de voiture, d'attelage; **led h.,** cheval en main; **head h. (of a team),** cheval de flèche; **school(ed) h.,** cheval d'école, de manège; **one-h., two-h., carriage,** voiture *f* à un cheval, à deux chevaux; *F:* **one-h. town,** petite ville de rien du tout; trou perdu; bled *m*; **one-h. show,** (i) spectacle *m* à deux sous; (ii) affaire *f* de quatre sous; **to mount a h.,** *A:* **to take h.,** monter à cheval; monter, enfourcher, un cheval; *A:* **to h.!** à cheval! **to fall off one's h.,** tomber de cheval; faire une chute de cheval; *A:* **to ride h. to h.,** aller de pair (à cheval); **to ride the high h., to get on one's high h.,** monter sur ses grands chevaux; se dresser sur ses ergots; le prendre de haut; faire l'important; *A:* **to change horses,** relayer; prendre des relais; changer de cheval, de chevaux; **one shouldn't change, swap, horses in midstream,** on ne change pas d'attelage au milieu du gué; *O:* **that's a h. of another colour,** ça c'est une autre paire de manches; **to talk horse(s),** parler chevaux; parler courses; **dead h.,** (i) cheval mort; (ii) *F:* travail payé d'avance; *Prov:* **it's a good h. that never stumbles,** il n'y a si bon cheval qui ne bronche; il n'y a bon charretier qui ne verse; *F:* **to eat like a h.,** manger comme un ogre; **I could eat a h.!** j'ai une faim de loup! *attrib.* **h. blanket, cloth, rug,** couverture *f* de cheval; **h. collar,** collier *m* de cheval; **h. dung,** (i) crottin *m*, (ii) fumier *m*, de cheval; **h. litter,** (i) litière *f* (de cheval); (ii) *A. Veh:* litière portée par deux chevaux; **h. block,** montoir *m*; *A:* **h. pistol,** pistolet *m* d'arçon; **h. path,** piste cavalière; **h. barge,** chaland remorqué par un cheval, à traction chevaline; *Vet:* **h. drench, draught,** breuvage *m*, purge *f* (pour chevaux); médecine *f* de cheval; *F:* **h. medicine,** remède *m* de cheval; *F: Pej:* **h. doctor,** (i) mauvais vétérinaire; (ii) toubib *m* qui ne vaut pas cher; **h. laugh,** gros rire bruyant; **h. sense,** gros bon sens; **h. coper, dealer, trader,** marchand de chevaux; (*often Pej:*) maquignon *m*; **h. dealing, h. trade,** commerce *m* de chevaux; (*often Pej:*) maquignonnage *m*; **h. mart,** marché *m* aux chevaux; **h. fair,** foire *f* aux chevaux; **h. show,** concours *m* hippique; **h. box,** (i) *Rail:* wagon *m* à chevaux; wagon-écurie *m*, *pl.* wagons-écuries; (ii) *Veh:* van *m*; **h. butcher,** boucher chevalin, hippophagique; **h. butchery,** boucherie chevaline; **h. thief, stealer, rustler,** voleur *m* de chevaux; (*b*) *Breed:* cheval mâle, cheval entier; **stud h.,** étalon *m*; **to take a mare to h.,** faire couvrir une jument; (*of mare*) **to take the h.,** souffrir l'étalon; (*c*) (i) *Z: F:* **horned h.,** gnou *m*; (ii) *Ich:* **sea h.,** hippocampe *m*; **h. mackerel,** caranx *m*, carangue *f*, saurel *m*; maquereau bâtard, balaou *m*, chinchard *m*, trachure *m*; (iii) *Ent:* **witches' h.,** phasme *m*, phasmidé *m*; **h. bot,** larve *f* d'œstre; (iv) *Bot:* **h. chestnut,** marron *m* d'Inde, *F:* châtaigne amère; **h. chestnut (tree),** marronnier *m* d'Inde; **h. bean,** (i) féverole *f*; fève *f* à chevaux; (ii) *U.S:* parkinsonia *m*; **h. parsley,** maceron potager, *F:* persil noir; (*d*) **white horses,** vagues *f* à crêtes d'écume; moutons *m*; (*e*) *Astr:* **the Flying H.,** Pégase *m*; (*f*) *F:* **horse's neck,** boisson *f* (alcoolique) au gingembre et au citron. **2.** *coll. Mil:* cavalerie *f*; troupes montées; **a regiment of five hundred h.,** un régiment de cinq cents chevaux; **h. soldier,** soldat monté; soldat de cavalerie; **h. artillery,** artillerie montée; **the (Royal) H. Guards,** la Garde du corps (à cheval); la cavalerie de la Garde. **3.** (*a*) **wooden h.,** (i) (*toy*) cheval de bois; (ii) *Ind:* chevalet *m* de montage; (iii) *Mil: A:* chevalet de torture; **rocking h.,** cheval à bascule; (*b*) *Gym:* cheval de bois, d'arçons; cheval-arçons *m*, *pl.* chevaux-arçons; **exercises on the h.,** (exercices *m* de) volte *f*; (*c*) *F: O:* **iron h.,** (i) bicyclette *f*; (ii) locomotive *f*. **4.** (*a*) **towel h.,** porte-serviettes *m inv* (mobile); **clothes h.,** chevalet pour linge; séchoir *m*; (*b*) *Tchn:* chevalet, tréteau *m*, chèvre *f*; **Slater's h.,** bourriquet *m*; *Leath:* **stitching h.,** étau *m*. **5.** *Geol: Min:* cheval de terre; nerf *m* (dans le filon); (*of lode*) **to take h.,** s'embrancher. **6.** *Metall:* **(old) h.,** cochon *m*. **7.** *Nau:* (*a*) (*footrope*) marchepied *m*; (*b*) barre *f* d'écoute; (*c*) (*jackstay*) filière *f* d'envergure.

horse[2]. **1.** *v.tr.* (*a*) fournir un cheval, des chevaux, à (qn); **to be well horsed,** être bien monté; avoir un bon cheval; (*b*) *F: A:* faire porter à dos (qn qui va être fouetté); (*c*) (i) faire couvrir (une jument); (ii) (*of stallion*) couvrir (la jument). **2.** *v.i. NAm: F:* **to h. (around),** faire des bêtises; **he doesn't h. around much with women,** il ne court pas après les filles.

horseback ['hɔːsbæk], *s.* **on h.,** à (dos de) cheval; sur un cheval; **to ride on h.,** aller à cheval; *Equit:* **to perform on h.,** faire de la voltige, de la haute école; **to look well on h.,** être beau cavalier, belle cavalière; se bien tenir à cheval; **young man on h.,** jeune cavalier; *F: A:* **a beggar on h.,** un parvenu.

horsebreaker ['hɔːsbreikər], *s.* dompteur *m*, dresseur *m*, de chevaux.

horsecar ['hɔːskɑːr], *s. U.S:* **1.** *A.Veh:* tramway *m* à chevaux, à traction animale. **2.** *Rail:* wagon *m* à chevaux.

horse-drawn ['hɔːsdrɔːn], *a.* **h.-d. vehicle,** véhicule *m* (à traction) hippomobile; véhicule attelé.

horseflesh ['hɔːsfleʃ], *s.* **1.** chair *f*, viande *f*, de cheval. **2.** *coll.* chevaux *mpl*; **to be a judge of h.,** s'y connaître en chevaux.

horsefly ['hɔːsflai], *s. Ent:* **1.** taon *m*. **2.** hippobosque *m*. **3.** œstre *m*.

horsehair ['hɔːsheər], *s.* crin *m* (de cheval); *Tex:* tissu *m* de crin; **vegetable h.,** crin végétal; **h. mattress,** matelas *m* de crin; **h. furniture,** meubles recouverts en crin; **h. plume,** crinière *f* (de casque).

horseheal ['hɔːshiːl], *s. Bot:* aunée *f* hélène.

horsehide ['hɔːshaid], *s.* peau *f*, cuir *m*, de cheval.

horse(-)leech ['hɔːsliːtʃ], *s.* **1.** *A:* vétérinaire *m*. **2.** *Ann:* grosse sangsue, *F:* voran *m*.

horseless ['hɔːslis], *a.* **1.** sans cheval, sans chevaux; (cavalier) sans monture. **2.** *A:* **h. carriage,** voiture *f* à propulsion mécanique, automobile *f*.

horseload ['hɔːsloud], *s.* charge *f* d'un cheval.

horseman, *pl.* **-men** ['hɔːsmən], *s.m.* **1.** cavalier, écuyer; **born h.,** homme de cheval; **to be a good h.,** bien monter à cheval; être bon cavalier. **2.** *Ich:* chevalier *m*. **3.** *Orn:* gros pigeon voyageur; pigeon cavalier.

horsemanship ['hɔːsmənʃip], *s.* équitation *f*, manège *m*; talent *m* d'écuyer; l'art de monter à cheval.

horsemeat ['hɔːsmiːt], *s.* viande *f* de cheval.

horsemint ['hɔːsmint], *s. Bot:* (i) menthe *f* aquatique; (ii) menthe sauvage.

horseplay ['hɔːsplei], *s.* jeu brutal, jeu de main(s); badinerie grossière; **no h.!** doucement! pas de brutalité!

horsepond ['hɔːspɔnd], *s.* abreuvoir *m* (pour chevaux).

horsepower ['hɔːspauər], *s. Mec:* (i) puissance *f* en chevaux, force *f* en chevaux, force motrice; (ii) *Meas:* cheval-vapeur *m* (britannique, = 33,000 pieds-livres par minute, = 1.0139 ch.-v. français); *pl.* chevaux-vapeur; **indicated h.,** puissance indiquée; chevaux indiqués; **nominal h.,** cheval nominal; **estimated h.,** puissance prévue; **brake h., actual h.,** puissance effective en chevaux; puissance au frein; chevaux au frein; cheval effectif; **shaft h.,** puissance au frein; *Aut:* **h. at road wheels,** rendement *m* à la jante; **h. hour,** cheval-heure *m*, *pl.* chevaux-heures; **h. formula,** formule *f* de puissance (d'une automobile); *O:* **a fifteen h. car,** une quinze chevaux.

horsepox ['hɔːspɔks], *s. Vet:* variole équine.

horseradish ['hɔːsrædiʃ], *s. Bot:* raifort *m*, cran *m*; cranson *m* de Bretagne; *Cu:* **h. sauce,** raifort à la crème.

horseshoe ['hɔː(s)ʃuː], *s.* **1.** (*a*) fer *m* à cheval; **h. iron,** fer *m* de maréchalerie; *Farr:* **h. gauge,** podomètre *m*; **h. nail,** clou *m* à cheval, à chevaux; clou de maréchal; (*b*) *attrib.* (table *f*, broche *f*, etc.) en (forme de) fer à cheval; **h. curve (of double staircase),** arcade *f*; (*c*) *Bot:* **h. vetch,** hippocrépide *f*; (*d*) *Z:* **h. bat,** rhinolophe *m*; fer-à-cheval *m*, *pl.* fers-à-cheval. **2.** (*a*) *Crust:* **h. crab,** crabe *m* des Moluques; limule *m*; (*b*) *Moll:* **h. clam,** lutraire *f*.

horseshoeing ['hɔː(s)ʃuːiŋ], *s.* ferrage *m*, ferrure *f*, des chevaux.

horsetail ['hɔːsteil], *s.* **1.** queue *f* de cheval; *Hist:* (*in Turkey*) **h. (ensign),** toug *m*. **2.** *Bot:* prêle *f* (des marais); equisetum *m*; *F:* queue-de-cheval *f*, *pl.* queues-de-cheval; **shrubby h.,** éphèdre *f*; uvette *f*; raisin *m* de mer; **water h.,** girandole *f* d'eau. **3.** *Anat:* nerfs rachidiens postérieurs; *F:* queue de cheval.

horseweed ['hɔːswiːd], *s. Bot:* érigéron *m* du Canada.

horsewhip[1] ['hɔːs(h)wip], *s.* cravache *f*.

horsewhip[2], *v.tr.* (**horsewhipped**) cravacher, sangler (qn); administrer une cravachée à (qn).

horsewhipping ['hɔːs(h)wipiŋ], *s.* coups *mpl* de cravache; cravachée *f*.

horsewoman, *pl.* **-women** ['hɔːswumən, -wimin], *s.f.* amazone, cavalière, écuyère.

horsfordite ['hɔːsfədait], *s. Miner:* horsfordite *f*.

horsiness ['hɔːsinis], *s.* (*a*) affectation *f* du genre jockey, du genre palefrenier; (*b*) amour exagéré de l'équitation, des chevaux.

horsing, *s. A:* fouettée *f*.

horst [hɔːst], *s. Geol:* horst *m*.

horsy ['hɔːsi], *a.* (*also* **horsey**) **1.** chevalin. **2.** (*of pers.*) (*a*) hippomane; (*b*) qui affecte le langage, le costume, des grooms et des jockeys; **she's terribly h.,** elle ne parle que chevaux; elle est toujours à se promener à cheval, à fréquenter des gymkhanas, etc.; (*c*) **h. face,** visage long au nez aquilin; profil chevalin.

hortative ['hɔːtətiv], *Lit:* **1.** *a.* exhortatif. **2.** *s.* exhortation *f*.

hortatory ['hɔːtət(ə)ri, hɔː'teit(ə)ri], *a. Lit:* exhortatif.

hortensia [hɔː'tensiə], *s. Bot:* hortensia *m*.

horticultural [hɔːti'kʌltjər(ə)l], *a.* (outil *m*) horticole, d'horticulture; **h. show,** exposition *f* d'horticulture.

horticulturally [hɔːti'kʌltjərəli], *adv.* **h. speaking,** parlant du point de vue de l'horticulture; **h. superior,** supérieur en fait d'horticulture.

horticulture ['hɔːtikʌltjər], *s.* horticulture *f*.

horticulturist [hɔːti'kʌltjərist], *s.* horticulteur *m.*
hortonolite [hɔː'tɔnəlait], *s. Miner:* hortonolite *f.*
hosanna [hou'zænə]. **1.** *int.* hosanna! **2.** *s.* hosanna *m.*
hose[1] [houz], *s.* **1.** *coll. pl. Cost:* (*a*) *A:* (i) chausses *fpl*; (ii) haut-de-chausses *m, pl.* hauts-de-chausses; **his h. were torn,** son haut-de-chausses était troué; (*b*) *Com:* bas *mpl.* **2.** (*pl.* **hoses**) (*a*) *Tchn:* tuyau *m* souple, tuyauterie *f* souple; boyau *m*; manche *f* (d'arrosage, etc.); **canvas h.,** manche en toile; **leather h.,** manche en cuir; **rubber h.,** tuyau en caoutchouc; **fire h.,** tuyau de pompe à incendie; boyau; **h. of a fire engine,** garniture *f* d'une pompe à incendie; **garden h., street h.,** manche, tuyau, d'arrosage; *Nau:* **washing h.,** manche de lavage; **h. reel,** chariot *m* à tuyaux; (*b*) *Mec.E:* (**flexible**) **h.,** tuyau flexible, durite *f*; **h. clamp,** collier *m* de durite; (**flexible**) **h. coupling,** accouplement *m* flexible; **h. pipe coupling,** tuyau d'accouplement flexible; **air h.,** tuyau d'air flexible.
hose[2], *v.tr.* (*a*) laver (qch.) à grande eau; **to h.** (**down**) **the car,** laver la voiture au jet d'eau; (*b*) arroser (un gazon, etc.) (au jet d'eau).
Hosea [hou'ziə], *Pr.n.m. B.Hist:* Osée.
hosepipe ['houzpaip], *s.* tuyau *m,* flexible *m* (de lavage, d'incendie, etc.).
hosier ['houziər], *s.* bonnetier, -ière.
hosiery ['houziəri], *s.* **h.** (**trade**), bonneterie *f*; **h. counter, department,** rayon *m* des bas et chaussettes.
hospice ['hɔspis], *s.* **1.** hospice *m* (pour voyageurs, du mont St Bernard, etc.). **2.** *A:* hospice; maison *f* de charité; asile *m* (pour vieillards, etc.).
hospitable [hɔs'pitəbl], *a.* hospitalier; accueillant; **it's a very h. house,** c'est une demeure hospitalière, une maison accueillante; *F:* c'est la maison du bon Dieu; **h. speech,** discours *m* de bienvenue; **mind h. to new ideas,** esprit ouvert aux idées nouvelles.
hospitably [hɔs'pitəbli], *adv.* hospitalièrement; avec hospitalité.
hospital ['hɔspitl], *s.* **1.** hôpital, -aux *m*; **to admit s.o.** (**in**)**to h.,** admettre qn à l'hôpital; **to send s.o. to h.,** hospitaliser qn; **two of the injured died in h.,** deux des victimes sont mortes à l'hôpital; **teaching h.** = centre hospitalier universitaire; *A:* (*of student*) **to walk the hospitals,** faire les hôpitaux; assister aux leçons cliniques; (*in wartime*) **Red Cross h.,** hôpital auxiliaire; **h. orderly,** (i) = aide soignante; (ii) *esp.Mil:* ambulancier, -ière; **h. train,** train *m* sanitaire; **h. ship,** navire-hôpital *m, pl.* navires-hôpitaux; *A:* **h. fever,** fièvre *f* des hôpitaux. **2.** (*a*) *Hist:* hospice *m* (des hospitaliers); (*b*) (*as Pr.n.*) **Greenwich H.,** l'Hospice de Greenwich (pour les invalides de la marine).
hospitalism [hɔs'pitəlizm], *s.* hospitalisme *m.*
hospitality [hɔspi'tæliti], *s.* hospitalité *f*; **to show s.o. h.,** accorder l'hospitalité à qn; héberger qn; faire à qn un accueil hospitalier; **to give h. to a pilgrim,** recueillir un pèlerin; *F:* **to enjoy His, Her, Majesty's h.,** faire de la prison.
hospitalization [hɔspitəlai'zeiʃ(ə)n], *s.* hospitalisation *f* (des malades).
hospitalize ['hɔspitəlaiz], *v.tr.* hospitaliser (un malade).
hospitaller [hɔs'pitələr], *s.* **1.** *Hist:* hospitalier *m*; **Knights Hospitallers,** chevaliers hospitaliers; **Order of the Knights Hospitallers,** Ordre *m* de l'Hôpital. **2.** *A:* (*in certain London hospitals*) aumônier *m.*
host[1] [houst], *s.* (*a*) *A: & Poet:* armée *f,* multitude *f,* foule *f*; **the heavenly hosts,** les célestes phalanges *f*; les troupes *f* célestes; les milices *f* célestes; **the Lord God of Hosts,** le Dieu des armées; le Seigneur, l'Éternel, des armées; **he was a h. in himself,** à lui seul il valait une armée; (*b*) **a** (**whole**) **h. of children, servants,** une ribambelle, un bataillon, d'enfants; (toute) une foule, (toute) une armée, de domestiques; **a h. of enemies,** une foule, une nuée, d'ennemis.
host[2], *s.* (*a*) hôte *m*; maître *m* de maison; **a pleasant h.,** un hôte accueillant; (*b*) hôtelier *m,* aubergiste *m*; *Hum:* **mine h.,** mon hôte; **to reckon without one's h.,** compter sans son hôte; (*c*) *Biol:* hôte (porteur d'un parasite ou d'un commensal); **intermediate, intermediary, h.,** hôte intermédiaire; (*d*) *Cmptr:* **h. computer,** ordinateur principal.
host[3], *v.tr. esp. U.S:* recevoir (qn), donner l'hospitalité à (qn).
host[4], *s. Ecc:* hostie *f*; **unconsecrated h.,** pain *m* à chanter, pain d'autel, pain azyme.
hosta ['hɔstə], *s. Bot:* hosta *m.*
hostage ['hɔstidʒ], *s.* **1.** otage *m*; **as** (**a**) **h.,** en otage, pour otage. **2.** gage *m*; *A:* **my hostages to fortune,** ma femme et mes enfants.
hostel ['hɔstəl], *s.* **1.** *A:* hôtellerie *f.* **2.** (*a*) pension *f,* maison *f* de famille, foyer *m* (sous la direction d'une œuvre sociale, etc.); **the Canadian H.,** la Maison du Canada (de la Cité Universitaire de Paris); (*b*) **youth h.,** auberge *f* de la jeunesse.
hosteller ['hɔstələr], *s.* (**youth**) **h.,** ajiste *mf.*
hostelling ['hɔstəliŋ], *s.* (**youth**) **h.,** ajisme *m.*
hostelry ['hɔstəlri], *s. A: & Lit:* hôtellerie *f*; auberge *f.*
hostess ['houstis], *s.f.* (*a*) hôtesse; maîtresse de maison; **good h.,** femme accueillante, qui sait recevoir; (*b*) hôtelière, aubergiste *f*; (*c*) *Av:* **air h.,** hôtesse de l'air; **ground h.,** hôtesse au sol.
hostile ['hɔstail]. **1.** *a.* (*a*) hostile, adverse, ennemi; **the h. army,** l'armée ennemie; **h. act,** acte *m* d'hostilité; **to make a h. demonstration against s.o.,** conspuer qn; (*b*) hostile, opposé (to, à); ennemi (to, de); **to be h. to s.o.,** être hostile à, envers, qn. **2.** *s. U.S:* ennemi *m*; *esp. Hist:* Peau-Rouge ennemi.
hostility [hɔs'tiliti], *s.* **1.** hostilité *f* (**to,** contre); animosité *f*; **to feel no h. towards s.o.,** n'avoir aucune animosité contre qn; **to show persistent h. to s.o.,** se montrer acharné après, contre, qn. **2.** *pl.* **hostilities,** hostilités; état *m* de guerre; **outbreak of hostilities,** ouverture *f* des hostilités; **at the beginning of hostilities,** au début des hostilités; **cessation of hostilities,** cessation *f* des hostilités, suspension *f* d'armes.
hostler ['ɔslər], *s.m. A:* valet *m* d'écurie; palefrenier *mf.*
hot[1] [hɔt], *a.* (**hotter, hottest**) **1.** (*a*) chaud; **steaming h., sizzling h.,** tout chaud, tout bouillant; **boiling h.,** (tout) bouillant; **burning h.,** brûlant; **to be very h.,** (*of thg*) être très chaud; être brûlant; (*of pers.*) avoir très chaud; (*of weather*) faire très chaud; **it was a h. day,** il faisait chaud; **it is unbearably h. in the Sahara,** il fait une chaleur étouffante dans le Sahara; **it was suffocatingly h.,** il faisait chaud à étouffer; on étouffait; **room as h. as an oven,** pièce *f* où il fait chaud comme dans un four, où l'on étouffe; **to get, grow, h.,** (i) (*of thg*) devenir chaud, chauffer; (ii) (*of pers.*) s'échauffer, commencer à avoir chaud; (iii) (*of weather*) commencer à faire chaud; (iv) (*of person, discussion, contest*) s'échauffer; (*of bearings*) **to run, get, h.,** chauffer, s'échauffer; gripper; **to make s.o. h.,** donner chaud à qn; **to keep a dish h.,** tenir un plat au chaud; mettre un plat au réchaud; **to serve food h.,** servir un plat tout chaud; *Comest:* **h. dog,** petit pain fourré d'une saucisse chaude; **during the h. weather,** pendant la chaleur; pendant les grandes chaleurs; **h. sun,** soleil ardent; **h. countries,** pays chauds; **h. fire,** feu vif; *Ind:* feu intensif; **h. water,** eau chaude; eau bouillante; **h. water bottle,** bouillotte *f*; (*earthenware, metal*) cruchon *m, F:* moine *m*; *F:* **to be in h. water,** avoir des ennuis; être dans le pétrin, dans l'embarras; **to get into h. water,** s'attirer, se créer, des ennuis; s'attirer une mauvaise affaire; **to get s.o. into h. water,** susciter des ennuis à qn; **h. air,** air chaud; **h.-air engine,** moteur *m,* machine *f,* à air chaud; moteur pyropneumatique; aéromoteur *m*; **h.-air dryer,** séchoir *m* à air chaud; **h.-air pipe,** tuyau *m* de chaleur; gaine *f* de chauffe; **h.-air jacket,** chambre *f* de réchauffe; **h.-air bath, cabinet,** étuve sèche; sudatoire *m*; *Metall:* **h.-air blast,** courant *m* d'air chaud; **h.-air vent,** bouche *f* de chaleur; *F:* **he was letting off a lot of h. air,** il parlait pour ne rien dire; il débitait des platitudes; *Mch:* **h. well,** bâche *f,* citerne *f* (de condenseur); réservoir *m* d'alimentation; **h.-blast stove,** four *m* à air chaud; **h. spot,** (i) *Metall:* point chaud; (ii) *I.C.E:* point d'inflammation; réchauffeur *m* (des gaz); (iii) *F:* boîte *f* de nuit; (iv) *F:* endroit *m* où on peut s'attendre à des troubles, de la bagarre; **it was h. work,** on s'y échauffait; *adv.* **the wind was blowing h.,** le vent était embrasé; **to blow h. and cold,** (i) souffler le chaud et le froid; (ii) parler, agir, de façons contradictoires; changer d'idées à chaque instant; *F:* **to get all h. and bothered,** s'échauffer; se faire du mauvais sang; *F:* **to get h. under the collar,** (i) être embarrassé; (ii) se mettre en colère, en rogne; **to go h. all over,** avoir une bouffée de chaleur; **to go h. and cold all over,** avoir le frisson; **how are you?—not so h.!** comment ça va?—comme ci, comme ça! je ne suis pas exactement dans mon assiette! (*b*) brûlant, cuisant; **h. fever,** fièvre brûlante; **h. blush,** rougeur brûlante, vive rougeur; **h. tears,** larmes cuisantes; (*c*) (poivre) cuisant; (moutarde) piquante; (assaisonnement) épicé; **h. sauce,** sauce très relevée; **this mustard is very h.,** cette moutarde vous emporte la bouche; *P: A:* **h. coppers,** la gueule de bois; *F:* **he's h. stuff,** (i) il est très fort, il roule tout le monde; (ii) c'est un viveur; **he's h. stuff at tennis,** au tennis c'est un as; *F:* **that's not so h.!** ce n'est pas si merveilleux que ça! ce n'est pas très intelligent! **h. player, opponent,** joueur *m,* adversaire *m,* de première force; (*d*) (*of colour*) trop vif. **2.** (*a*) **cakes h. from the oven,** gâteaux *m* sortant du four; **h. news,** nouvelles toutes fraîches; **news h. from the press,** nouvelles *fpl* sortant tout droit de la presse; nouvelles de la dernière heure; (*b*) *Ven:* **h. scent,** odeur forte; **h. trail,** voie chaude; **to be h. on the scent, on the trail,** être sur la bonne piste (d'un animal, d'un criminel); *F:* brûler; *Games:* **you're getting h.,** tu brûles. **3.** (*a*) violent, chaleureux; **the h. blood of youth,** la chaleur, la fougue, de la jeunesse; **to have a h. temper,** avoir le caractère emporté; s'emporter facilement; **h. words,** paroles violentes; mots vifs; (*b*) acharné; **h. contest,** chaude dispute; **h. argument,** discussion vive, violente; **at the hottest of the fray,** au plus fort du combat; **h. pursuit,** poursuite acharnée; **to be in h. pursuit, to be h. on the track, of s.o.,** poursuivre, presser, qn de près; **the resistance was h. and strong,** la résistance a été vigoureuse; *adv.* **they went at it h. and strong,** ils y allaient avec acharnement, de toutes leurs forces; (*c*) *F:* **I'm not h. on it,** ça ne m'emballe point; *Turf:* **h. favourite,** grand favori; **h. tip,** tuyau *m* increvable; (*d*) (*of animal*) en chaleur; *P:* **she's a h. piece, h. pants,** c'est une femme à coucher; (*e*) *Cost: F:* **h. pants,** un short-short; (*f*) *F:* **h. rod,** voiture gonflée; bolide *m*; **h. rodder,** amateur *m* de bolides; conducteur *m* casse-cou; *U.S: Av:* **h. rock,** pilote *m* casse-cou (mais habile). **4.** *F:* (*a*) **to make a place too h. for s.o.,** rendre la situation intenable à qn (dans un endroit); **the place was getting too h. for me,** je me trouvais dans un véritable guêpier; j'avais tout le monde contre moi; **to make things, it, too h. for s.o.,** rendre la vie intolérable, intenable, à qn; **I'll make it h. for him!** il lui en cuira! **to give it** (**to**) **s.o. h.,** laver la tête à qn; attraper qn de la belle façon; **to catch it h., get it h.,** recevoir un savon, recevoir un bon coup sur les ongles; **you'll get it h.!** tu vas la danser; **we're going to have a h. time,** il va y avoir du grabuge; ça va chauffer; *Mil:* il va y avoir du tabac; (*b*) **h. job,** travail urgent, prioritaire; *Tp:* **h. line,** ligne directe; (*U.S.A to Kremlin*) ligne rouge; (*Élysée to Kremlin*) ligne verte; (*c*) **h. car, etc.,** voiture, etc., recherchée par la police; (*d*) *Fin:* **h. money,** capitaux flottants, errants; **h. bills,** valeurs brûlantes. **5.** *Atom.Ph:* radio-actif; **h. lab**(**oratory**), laboratoire *m* de recherches radio-actives.
hot[2], *v.tr. F:* (*a*) **to h. sth. up,** (i) chauffer qch.; (ii) (faire) réchauffer (du potage, etc.); (*b*) *Aut:* **to h. up an engine,** gonfler un moteur; **hotted-up engine,** moteur gonflé; **to get s.o. all hotted up,** mettre qn en colère, en rogne; (*c*) *v.i.* **the air raids began to h. up,** et puis ce n'a été qu'une série de bombardements.
hotbed ['hɔtbed], *s.* **1.** *Hort:* couche *f* (de fumier, de terreau); couche à fumier; couche chaude; couche de forçage; germoir *m,* meule *f.* **2. h. of corruption, of intrigue,** foyer (ardent) de corruption, d'intrigue; officine *f* d'intrigue.
hot-blooded ['hɔt'blʌdid], *a.* emporté, ardent, passionné; **h.-b. race,** race *f* au sang fougueux.
hotbox ['hɔtbɔks], *s. Rail:* coussinet échauffé.
hotchpot ['hɔtʃpɔt], *s. Jur:* masse successorale; **bringing into h.,** rapport *m* (d'une donation, etc.) à la succession, à la masse successorale.
hotchpotch ['hɔtʃpɔtʃ], *s.* **1.** *Cu:* ragoût *m* (de légumes et de viande). **2.** mélange confus; méli-mélo *m, pl.* mélis-mélos.
hotel [(h)ou'tel], *s.* hôtel *m*; **private, residential, h.** = pension *f* de famille; **h. keeper,** hôtelier, -ière; **the h. trade,** l'industrie hôtelière; l'hôtellerie *f.*
hôtelier [(h)ou'teliei], *s.* hôtelier *m.*
hotfoot[1] ['hɔt'fut], *adv.* (s'en aller, arriver) à toute vitesse, en (toute) hâte, précipitamment; **to follow h. on the enemy,** talonner l'ennemi en fuite.
hotfoot[2], *v.i. & tr. U.S:* **to h.** (**it**) **after s.o.,** s'élancer à la poursuite de qn.
hothead ['hɔthed], *s.* exalté, -ée; tête ardente; tête chaude, emballée; **young hotheads,** jeunes impétueux.
hotheaded ['hɔt'hedid], *a.* **1.** exalté, impétueux, à la tête chaude. **2.** emporté, violent; prompt à se fâcher; **he's h.,** il est vif, prompt, à s'irriter; il a la tête près du bonnet.
hothouse ['hɔthaus], *s.* **1.** serre chaude; **h. plant,** (i) plante *f* de serre chaude; (ii) *F:* (*pers.*) plante de serre; **h. grapes,** raisin *m* de serre. **2.** *F:* = HOTBED 2.
hotly ['hɔtli], *adv.* **1.** (répondre, protester) vivement, avec chaleur. **2.** (poursuivre) avec acharnement, de près.
hotness ['hɔtnis], *s.* **1.** chaleur *f*; fougue *f,* violence *f* (des passions, du tempérament, etc.). **2.** force *f* (d'une moutarde, d'un assaisonnement).
hotplate ['hɔtpleit], *s. Dom.Ec:* (*a*) plaque chauffante; (*b*) chauffe-plats *m inv.*
hotpot ['hɔtpɔt], *s. Cu:* ragoût de viande aux pommes de terre, cuit à l'étuvée.
hot-press[1] ['hɔtpres], *s.* **1.** *Tex: etc:* calandre *f*; presse *f* à catir, à satiner. **2.** étuve *f* à linge.
hot-press[2], *v.tr.* calandrer, catir (le drap); satiner (le papier).
hot-pressing ['hɔt'presiŋ], *s.* calandrage *m*; catissage *m* (du drap); satinage *m* (du papier).
hot-short ['hɔt'ʃɔːt], *a.* (fer) cassant à chaud; (fer)

rouverain, rouverin.

hotshot ['hɔtʃɔt], *a. & s. U.S:* (*a*) **h. (freight train),** train *m* de marchandises (ultra-)rapide; (*b*) voiture *f*, avion *m*, ultra-rapide; (*c*) *F:* (joueur, chirurgien, etc.) spectaculaire, flamboyant (mais capable).

hotspur ['hɔtspəːr], *s. F:* tête chaude; cerveau brûlé; homme emporté; soupe *f* au lait.

hot-tempered ['hɔt'tempəd], *a.* colérique, coléreux; emporté, vif.

Hottentot ['hɔtntɔt]. **1.** *Ethn:* (*a*) *a.* hottentot; (*b*) *s.* Hottentot, -ote; (*c*) *s. F: A:* (i) personne *f* d'intelligence bornée; (ii) personne de peu de culture ou qui manque d'usage. **2.** *s. Bot:* **hottentot('s) bread,** testudinaire *f*; pied *m* d'éléphant.

hot-wire ['hɔt'waiər], *a.* **h.-w. voltmeter, etc.,** voltmètre *m, etc.,* thermique, à fil chaud.

hough [hɔk], *s. & v.tr.* = HOCK[1,2].

hound[1] [haund], *s.* (*a*) chien *m*; **Arabian gazelle h.,** sloughi *m*, lévrier persan, arabe; **Ibizan h.,** charnigue *m*; (*b*) *Ven:* chien de meute, de chasse à courre; chien courant; chien chasseur; braque *m*; **the pack of hounds, the hounds,** la meute, l'équipage *m*; **master of hounds,** maître *m* d'équipage; grand veneur; **to ride to hounds,** chasser (le renard); chasser à courre; **to hunt with hounds and horn,** chasser à cor et à cri; (*c*) *Sp:* coureur *m*, poursuivant *m* (dans un rallye-paper); (*d*) *Bot:* **hound's tongue,** cynoglosse *f*, *F:* langue-de-chien *f, pl.* langues-de-chien; (*e*) *F: Pej:* (*pers.*) canaille *f*.

hound[2], *v.tr.* **1.** (*a*) *Ven:* chasser (le gibier) au chien courant; (*b*) **to h. s.o. down,** poursuivre qn avec acharnement, sans relâche; s'acharner après, contre, sur, qn; traquer qn; **hounded from place to place,** pourchassé d'un lieu à l'autre; **he was hounded out of France,** il fut chassé de France par l'indignation publique. **2. to h. (a dog) at, on, s.o.,** exciter, pousser, (un chien) contre qn; **to h. the dogs on,** exciter les chiens à la poursuite.

hound[3], *s. Nau:* (*usu. pl.*) **hounds,** jottereaux *mpl*, épaulettes *fpl*, de capelage (de mât); noix *fpl* (du mât de hune).

houndfish ['haundfiʃ], *s.* (*a*) chien *m* de mer, cagnot *m*, roussette *f*; (*b*) aiguille *f* de mer, belone *f*, orphie *f*.

hounding ['haundiŋ], *s. Nau:* guindant *m* (d'un mât).

houndstooth ['haundztuːθ], *a. & s. Tex:* **h. (check),** pied-de-poule *m*.

hour ['auər], *s.* heure *f*. **1. an h. and a half,** une heure et demie; **half an h.,** une demi-heure; **a quarter of an h.,** un quart d'heure; **he gave me a bad quarter of an h.,** il m'a fait passer un mauvais quart d'heure; **to take sth. every h.,** prendre qch. d'heure en heure; **h. by h.,** d'heure en heure; heure par heure; **to pay s.o. by the h.,** payer qn à l'heure; **to be paid £2 an h.,** être payé £2 de l'heure; **to walk (at the rate of) five miles an h.,** faire cinq milles à l'heure; *Ind: etc:* **output per h.,** puissance *f* horaire; rendement *m* à l'heure; **it is nearly two hours' walk,** il y en a pour près de deux heures de marche; **at an hour's notice,** (i) avec préavis d'une heure; (ii) sans préavis; **to take hours over sth.,** mettre un temps interminable, mettre des heures, à faire qch.; **eight-h. day,** journée *f* (de travail) de huit heures; **office hours,** heures de bureau, heures de présence; **I do this work out of hours,** je fais ce travail en dehors de mes heures de bureau, d'atelier, etc.; **to work long hours,** faire de longues journées (de travail); *W.Tel: A:* **Children's H.,** l'Heure enfantine; (*b*) *attrib. Astr:* **h. circle,** cercle *m* horaire; **h. angle,** angle *m* horaire; **easterly, westerly, h. angle,** angle horaire oriental, occidental; *Chr:* **h. zone,** fuseau *m* horaire; **h. lines,** lignes *f* horaires (de cadran solaire); **h. hand,** petite aiguille (de montre, de pendule); *Nau: etc:* **h. ball,** boule *f* horaire, d'observatoire. **2.** (*a*) l'heure, le moment; *A:* **at the h. of seven,** à sept heures; **at the h. stated,** à l'heure dite; **the auspicious h.,** l'heure propice; (*for lovers*) l'heure du berger; **questions of the h.,** les questions *f* de l'heure (actuelle); les actualités *f*; **in the h. of need, of peril, of death,** à l'heure du besoin, du péril, de la mort; **in an evil h.,** en une heure néfaste; un jour de malheur; **the h. has come,** le moment est venu; il est l'heure; c'est l'heure; **his h. has come, has struck,** son heure est venue, a sonné; (*b*) **the small hours,** les premières heures (après minuit); **in the small hours (of the morning),** au beau milieu de la nuit; avant le point du jour; **he comes home in the small hours,** il rentre à des heures indues; il rentre fort avant dans la nuit; **well on into the small hours,** fort avant, bien avant, très avant, dans la nuit; **to keep late hours,** (i) rentrer à des heures indues; (ii) se coucher fort tard; veiller tard; **to keep early hours,** (i) rentrer toujours de bonne heure, à des heures raisonnables; (ii) se coucher de bonne heure; (iii) se lever tôt; **to keep regular hours,** se coucher et se lever à des heures régulières; mener une vie réglée; (*c*) *Ecc:* **Book of Hours,** livre *m* d'Heures.

hourglass ['auəglɑːs], *s.* sablier *m*; *MecE:* **h. screw, worm,** vis globoïdale, vis globique; *F: O:* **h. figure, waist,** taille *f* de guêpe.

houri ['huəri], *s.f.* houri.

hourly ['auəli]. **1.** *a.* (*a*) de toutes les heures; (service de trains, etc.) à chaque heure; **the mixture should be taken in h. doses of one teaspoonful,** la médecine doit être prise par doses d'une cuillerée chaque heure, d'une cuillerée par heure; **three-h. doses,** une dose toutes les trois heures; (*b*) (débit, rendement) par heure, à l'heure, horaire; (salaire) à l'heure; (*c*) continuel, de chaque instant; **his h. dread of death,** sa crainte perpétuelle de la mort. **2.** *adv.* (*a*) toutes les heures; d'heure en heure; (*b*) constamment, continuellement; (*c*) **we expect him h.,** nous l'attendons d'un moment à l'autre.

house[1], *pl.* **houses** [haus, 'hauziz], *s.* **1.** maison *f*; logis *m*, habitation *f*; **town h.,** (i) *A:* hôtel (particulier); (ii) maison de ville; **town houses,** pavillons groupés; **detached h.,** maison séparée; **semi-detached houses,** maisons doubles, jumelles, jumelées; **suburban h.,** maison de banlieue; **h. in the country,** (i) maison de campagne; (ii) résidence *f* secondaire à la campagne; **country houses open to the public,** châteaux ouverts au public; **small h.,** maisonnette *f*; *NAm:* **apartment h.,** immeuble divisé en appartements; maison de rapport; **private h.,** maison particulière; **one's private h.,** son domicile particulier; **bachelor's h.,** ménage *m* de garçon; **the White H.,** la Maison Blanche; **at, to, in, my h.,** chez moi; **we invited him to our h.,** nous l'avons invité à venir chez nous; **to pass s.o.'s h.,** passer devant la maison de qn, devant chez qn; **he lives in this very h.,** il demeure ici même; **from h. to h.,** de porte en porte; **to be confined to the h.,** être confiné au logis; **to keep (to) the h.,** ne pas sortir; rester chez soi; garder la maison; **to keep h.,** tenir la maison; **to keep h. for s.o.,** tenir, diriger, la maison de qn; **they keep h. together,** ils font ménage ensemble; **to keep open h.,** tenir table ouverte; **dolls' h.,** maison de poupée; **to play at keeping h.,** jouer au ménage; **to set up h.,** entrer en ménage; s'établir; s'installer; se mettre dans ses meubles; **to have a h. of one's own,** avoir sa propre maison, son chez-soi; être propriétaire d'une maison; **the son, daughter, of the h.,** le fils, la fille, de la maison; **to move h.,** déménager; **to have neither h. nor home,** n'avoir ni feu ni lieu; **to find the h. empty,** trouver maison nette; **h. of cards,** château de cartes; *attrib.* **h. property,** immeubles *mpl*; **to invest in h. property,** placer son argent en immeubles; **h. letting,** baux *mpl* à loyer; **h. duty, tax,** impôt *m* sur les propriétés bâties; **inhabited h. duty,** taxe *f* d'habitation; **h. agent,** agent immobilier; **h. agency,** agence immobilière; **h. painter,** peintre *m* en bâtiments, en décor; peintre décorateur; **h. coal,** charbon *m* de ménage; **h. telephone,** téléphone intérieur. **2.** (*a*) **the h. of God,** la maison de Dieu; **h. of prayer, of worship,** église *f*, temple *m*; **h. of correction,** maison de correction; **religious h.,** maison religieuse; **mother h.,** maison mère; **the H. of Commons,** la Chambre des Communes; **h. of call,** (i) *A:* bureau *m* de groupage de commandes et de colis; (ii) auberge *f*, hôtellerie *f*; (iii) lieu *m* de rendez-vous (amoureux); maison de passe; pied-à-terre *m inv*; (*b*) *Com: etc:* maison; **publishing h.,** maison d'éditions; **h. style,** genre *m*, style *m*, maison; (*in restaurant*) **h. speciality,** *F:* **h. special,** spécialité *f* de la maison; **h. charge,** couvert *m*; **to have a drink on the h.,** prendre une consommation aux frais du cafetier, du patron; *Fin:* **h. bill,** lettre de change creuse; *Nau:* **h. flag,** pavillon *m* d'armateur, de compagnie (de navigation); (*c*) *F:* **the H.,** (i) la Chambre des Communes ou des Lords; (ii) le collège de Christ Church à Oxford; (iii) la Bourse; *Parl:* **bill before the H.,** loi *f* en cours de vote; *St.Exch:* **members of the H.,** agents *m* de change; (*d*) *Sch:* (i) (*in boarding school*) maison d'élèves; (ii) (*in day school*) groupe *m* d'élèves (qui rivalise avec un autre); **h. match,** match *m* entre deux *houses;* (*e*) *Med:* **h. surgeon, physician,** interne *m* en chirurgie, en médecine (d'un hôpital); (*f*) *Astrol:* maison. **3.** (*a*) **hen h.,** poulailler *m*; *F: O:* **the little h.,** les cabinets *m*, les lieux *m*, le petit endroit; (*b*) *Tchn:* cabine *f* (d'une grue); *Nau:* rouf *m* (sur le pont); kiosque *m* (de la barre, etc.); (*c*) *Com: Ind:* salle *f*, bâtiment *m*; **counting h.,** (bureau *m*, service *m*, de) la comptabilité; **packing h.,** (i) salle, service, d'emballage; (ii) conserverie *f*, fabrique *f* de conserves. **4.** (*a*) (*members of household*) maison, *F:* maisonnée *f*; **the whole h. was down with influenza,** toute la maison avait la grippe; *Parl: etc:* (*of assembly*) **to make a h.,** être en nombre; avoir, réunir, le quorum; (*b*) famille *f*, maison, dynastie *f*; **the H. of Stuart, of Bourbon,** les Stuarts *m*, les Bourbons *m*; **the H. of Lancaster,** la Maison de Lancastre. **5.** *Th:* salle *f*, auditoire *m*, assistance *f*, chambrée *f*; **a good, full, h.,** une salle pleine; **to play to an empty h.,** jouer devant les banquettes (vides); *Cin:* **the first h.,** la première séance. **6.** (variété de) jeu *m* de loto.

house[2] [hauz], *v.tr.* (*a*) loger, héberger, recevoir (qn); pourvoir au logement de (la population); (*b*) faire rentrer (les troupeaux); rentrer, emmagasiner, engranger (le blé); mettre (la récolte) à l'abri; rentrer, mettre en serre (les fleurs); (*c*) mettre à l'abri, à couvert, rentrer (une locomotive, etc.); emmagasiner (un avion, etc.); garer (une voiture); loger, caser (un ustensile); *Nau:* rentrer (une voile); (*d*) enchâsser (un essieu, etc.); *Nau:* caler (un mât).

houseboat ['hausbout], *s.* péniche aménagée en habitation.

housebound ['hausbaund], *a.* (*of invalid*) obligé de garder la maison; immobilisé à la maison.

housebreak ['hausbreik], *v. NAm:* **1.** *v.tr.* dresser (un chien, un enfant) aux habitudes de propreté. **2.** *v.i.* cambrioler (une maison, etc.).

housebreaker ['hausbreikər], *s.* **1.** voleur *m* avec effraction; cambrioleur *m*. **2.** *Const:* démolisseur *m*, tombeur *m*; **housebreaker's yard,** chantier *m* de démolitions.

housebreaking ['hausbreikiŋ], *s.* **1.** effraction *f*, escalade *f*, violation *f* de domicile, cambriolage *m*; **h. tools,** attirail *m* de cambrioleur. **2.** démolition *f*; **h. contractor,** entrepreneur *m* de démolitions.

housebroken ['hausbroukn], *a. NAm:* (chien, chat) dressé à des habitudes de propreté.

housebuilder ['hausbildər], *s.* entrepreneur *m* de, en, bâtiments; entrepreneur de constructions.

housebuilding ['hausbildiŋ], *s.* entreprise *f* de bâtiments, de constructions.

houseclean ['hausklìːn], *v.i. esp. NAm:* faire le ménage.

housecoat ['hauskout], *s.* robe *f* d'intérieur.

housecraft ['hauskrɑːft], *s.* les arts ménagers.

housefly ['hausflai], *s.* mouche domestique, commune.

houseful ['hausful], *s.* maisonnée *f*; pleine maison (d'invités, etc.).

household ['haushould], *s.* **1.** (membres *mpl* de la) maison; famille *f*; ménage *m*; **he's one of the h.,** il est de la maison; *attrib.* **h. articles,** articles ménagers; **h. expenses,** frais *m* de, du, ménage; le budget domestique; dépense *f* de bouche; **h. duties,** (affaires *f* du) ménage; **h. bread,** pain *m* de ménage; **h. goods,** meubles *m*, mobilier *m*; **h. gods,** pénates *m*, lares *m*, dieux *m* domestiques; **h. word,** mot *m* d'usage courant; **his name is a h. word,** son nom est connu de tous, est dans toutes les bouches. **2.** (*a*) les domestiques; **to have a large h.,** avoir une nombreuse domesticité; (*b*) **the H.,** la Maison du souverain; **the H. troops,** la Garde. **3.** *Com:* **household(s),** farine *f* de seconde qualité.

householder ['haushouldər], *s.* (i) propriétaire *mf*, (ii) locataire *mf*, de maison; chef *m* de famille, de maison.

housekeeper ['hauskiːpər], *s.* **1.** homme, femme chargé(e) du soin et de la surveillance d'un bâtiment (surtout des bureaux sans occupants pendant la nuit); concierge *mf*. **2.** femme *f* de charge; gouvernante *f* (d'un prêtre, etc.); économe *f*, intendante *f* (d'un château, etc.); gouvernante (d'un hôtel); **working h.,** bonne *f* avec fonctions de gouvernante. **3.** ménagère *f*; femme d'intérieur; **my wife is a good h.,** ma femme est bonne ménagère.

housekeeping ['hauskiːpiŋ], *s.* **1.** le ménage; **to set up h.,** se mettre, entrer, en ménage; **to give up h.,** cesser de tenir maison, d'avoir un ménage. **2.** économie *f* domestique; les soins *m* du ménage; **to be good at h.,** s'entendre bien aux affaires du ménage, être bonne ménagère; **she knows nothing of h.,** ce n'est pas une femme d'intérieur; **h. book,** carnet *m* de dépenses.

housel ['hauzl], *v.tr. Ecc: A:* administrer le saint Sacrement à (qn); **to be houselled,** recevoir le saint Sacrement.

houseleek ['hausliːk], *s. Bot:* joubarbe *f*, barbajou(e) *m*; *F:* herbe *f* du tonnerre, artichaut *m* sauvage, artichaut des toits.

houseless ['hauslis], *a.* sans domicile, sans abri, sans asile.

houseline ['hauslain], *s. Nau:* luisin *m*, merlin *m*.

housemaid ['hausmeid], *s.f.* **1.** bonne; femme de chambre; *F:* **housemaid's knee,** hygroma *m* du genou; hydarthrose *f* du genou; épanchement *m* de synovie. **2.** *Furn:* entrebâilleur *m* (de porte).

houseman, *pl.* **-men** ['hausmən], *s.m.* (*a*) domestique; (*b*) employé de casino; (*c*) détective d'hôtel, etc.; (*d*) *Med:* interne *m* (d'un hôpital).

housemaster, housemistress ['hausmɑːstər, -mistris], *s.* professeur chargé de la surveillance (i) d'un internat, (ii) (*in day school*) d'un groupe d'élèves (nommé *house*).

house-parlourmaid ['haus'pɑːləmeid], *s.f.* femme de chambre qui fait aussi le service de table.

houseparty ['hauspɑ:ti], *s.* les invités *m* qui passent quelques jours à une maison (surtout à la campagne).

housephone ['hausfoun], *s.* téléphone intérieur.

houseproud ['hauspraud], *a.* fier de son chez-soi.

houseroom ['hausru:m], *s.* place *f* (pour loger qn, qch.); logement *m*; **there's h. for everybody,** il y a de la place pour loger tout le monde; *F:* **I wouldn't give it h.,** je n'en voudrais pas quand (bien) même on me le donnerait.

house-to-house ['haustə'haus], *a.* (quête *f*, vente *f*, etc.) à domicile; **h.-to-h. canvassing,** le porte à porte; **the police made a h.-to-h. search,** la police a fait une fouille maison par maison.

housetop ['haustɔp], *s.* toit *m*; *F:* **to proclaim, cry, sth. from the housetops,** publier, crier, qch. sur les toits; annoncer qch. à son de caisse.

housetrain ['haustrein], *v.tr.* dresser (un chien, etc.) à la propreté.

housetrained ['haustreind], *a.* (chien, etc.) propre, dressé à la propreté.

housewares ['hauswɛəz], *s.pl. U.S:* équipement ménager; articles *mpl* de ménage.

housewarming ['hauswɔ:miŋ], *s.* pendaison *f* de la crémaillère; **to give, have, a h.,** pendre la crémaillère; **when will the h. (party) be?** à quand la crémaillère?

housewife, *pl.* **-wives. 1.** *s.f.* ['hauswaif, -waivz] maîtresse de maison; mère de famille; ménagère. **2.** *s.* ['hʌzif, -vz] *O:* trousse *f* de couture; nécessaire *m* à ouvrage; cousette *f.* **3.** *attrib.* ['hauswaif] **h. style pillowcase,** taie *f* d'oreiller à rabat rentré.

housewifely ['hauswaifli], *a.* de ménagère, de maîtresse de maison.

housewifery ['hauswif(ə)ri], *s.* économie *f* domestique; connaissances ménagères; travaux *m* domestiques; soin *m* du ménage.

housework ['hauswə:k], *s.* travaux *m* domestiques, de ménage; **to do the h.,** faire le ménage.

houseworker ['hauswə:kər], *s. U.S:* bonne *f* (à tout faire); femme *f* de ménage.

housewrecker ['hausrekər], *s. U.S: Const:* démolisseur *m.*

housey-housey ['hausi'hausi], *s.* (jeu de) loto *m.*

housing[1] ['hauziŋ], *s.* **1.** (*a*) logement *m* (de personnes); **the h. problem, question, shortage,** le problème, la crise, la question, du logement; (*b*) rentrée *f* (des troupeaux, du blé, etc.); emmagasinage *m*, mise *f* en grange (du blé); rentrage *m* (du bois de chauffage, etc.); (*c*) mise à l'abri, à couvert (d'une locomotive, etc.); garage *m* (d'une auto); *Nau:* rentrée (d'une voile). **2.** (*a*) enchâssure *f* (d'un essieu, etc.); *Nau:* calage *m* (d'un mât); **drop keel h.,** puits *m* de dérive; (*b*) *Nau:* partie *f* (du mât) au-dessous du pont; partie (du beaupré) en dedans de l'étrave. **3.** (*a*) *Carp:* logement, ruinure *f* (d'une poutre, etc.); (*b*) *Mch: Mec.E: etc:* logement, bâti *m*, cage *f*, colonne *f* (d'un laminoir); montant *m*, jumelle *f* (d'une machine à raboter); coquille *f* (de moteur); carter *m*, boîte *f* (de l'engrenage); **chain h.,** logement de chaîne; *Aut:* **differential-gear h.,** carter du différentiel; **ball-shaped h.,** calotte *f* sphérique; **flexible h.,** gaine *f* flexible; **tubular h.,** tube *m* de protection; *Av: etc:* **filter h.,** boîtier *m* de crépine; **gastight h.,** enceinte *f* étanche aux gaz.

housing[2], *s. usu.pl.* housse *f* de cheval; caparaçon *m.*

houstonia [hus:'tounia], *s. Bot:* houstonia *f.*

Hova ['houvə], *Ethn:* (*a*) *a.* hova; (*b*) *s.* Hova *mf.*

hovel ['hɔv(ə)l], *s.* **1.** *A:* appentis *m*; hangar ouvert. **2.** taudis *m*, bouge *m*, masure *f*; **miserable h.,** cabane *f* à l'air miséreux; taudis; nid *m* à rats. **3.** *Cer:* four *m* à alandiers.

hoven ['houvn], *a. Vet:* météorisé.

hovenia [hou'vi:niə], *s. Bot:* hovenia *m.*

hover ['hɔvər], *v.i.* **1.** (*a*) (*of bird, insect*) planer, se balancer; **a smile hovered over her lips,** un sourire pointait, errait, glissait, sur ses lèvres; **danger is hovering over him,** le danger le menace, plane sur lui; (*b*) (*of aircraft*) planer, effectuer un vol stationnaire; (*c*) *F:* **I've been hovering,** j'ai fait un vol, une traversée, en aéroglisseur, en hovercraft. **2.** (*of pers.*) (*a*) **to h. round s.o.,** errer, rôder, autour de qn; (*b*) **to h. between two courses,** hésiter, balancer, entre deux partis.

hovercraft ['hɔvəkrɑ:ft], *s. inv.* véhicule *m* sur coussin d'air; aéroglisseur *m*; naviplane *m*, *F:* hovercraft *m.*

hoverfly ['hɔvəflai], *s. Ent:* bombyle *m.*

hovering ['hɔvəriŋ], *s. Av:* vol *m* stationnaire, à faible vitesse; (*of bird, etc.*) vol en suspension.

hoverplane ['hɔvəplein], *s. F:* hélicoptère *m.*

hoverport ['hɔvəpɔ:t], *s.* hoverport *m*; gare *f* aéroglisseur.

hovership ['hɔvəʃip], *s.* aéroglisseur marin.

hovertrain ['hɔvətrein], *s.* aérotrain *m.*

how[1] [hau], *adv.* **1.** (*a*) (*in what way, by what means*) comment; **h. can I do that?** comment puis-je faire cela? **h. does one spell this word?** comment écrit-on ce mot? **h. do you like your potatoes (done)?** comment aimez-vous mieux les pommes de terre? *F:* **h. the devil. . ., h. the dickens. . ., h. ever. . ., h. on earth. . ., h. in the world. . .?** comment diable. . .? **he managed it, the Lord knows h.,** il y est arrivé, Dieu sait comment; **tell me h. he did it,** dites-moi comment il l'a fait; **I enquired h. to send a postal order,** je me suis renseigné sur la manière d'envoyer un mandat; **look h. he holds his bow,** regardez de quelle façon il tient son archet; **I don't know h. it happened,** je ne sais comment cela s'est fait; **h. are you?** comment allez-vous? *F:* comment ça va? **h. do you, d'you, do?** (i) comment allez-vous? (ii) (*on being introduced*) enchanté (de faire votre connaissance); **h. is the market?** comment va le marché? **h. are bullocks today?** à quel prix sont les bœufs, combien les bœufs, aujourd'hui? **h. are plums selling?** combien vend-on les prunes? **h. is it that. . .?** comment se fait-il que. . .? d'où vient que. . .? **h. so?** comment ça? **h. now?** eh bien? qu'est-ce donc? qu'y a-t-il? **how's that?** (i) comment ça? (ii) *Cr:* appel à l'arbitre, pour savoir si le guichet est sauf, ou si la balle a été bien attrapée; *F:* **and h.!** et comment! **Mary answered him, and h.!** c'est Marie qui lui a répondu, et comment! **I see h. it is,** je vois ce qui en est; **I fail to see h. this affects you,** je ne vois pas en quoi cela vous intéresse; **h. can you!** vous n'avez pas honte? **h. could you!** vous n'avez pas eu honte? **h. can one laugh when one is penniless?** il s'agit bien de rire quand on n'a pas le sou; **h. to be happy,** comment s'y prendre pour être heureux; le moyen d'être heureux; **to learn h. to do sth.,** apprendre comment faire qch.; apprendre à faire qch.; **I know h. to swim,** je sais nager; **I was puzzled h. to answer,** j'étais embarrassé pour répondre; **I showed him h. to do it,** je lui ai enseigné à le faire; je lui ai montré comment faire; (*b*) **h. do you like, h. do you find, this wine?** comment trouvez-vous ce vin? qu'est-ce que vous dites de ce vin? **h. do you like this chicken?** aimez-vous ce poulet? **2.** (*to what extent*) (*a*) **h. much, h. many,** combien (de); **h. many times? h. often?** combien de fois? **h. many are there of you?** vous êtes combien de personnes? **you see h. little he cares,** vous voyez combien peu il s'en soucie, combien ça lui est égal; **you know h. useful he is to me,** vous savez combien, à quel point, il m'est utile; **you don't know h. right you are,** vous ne savez pas combien vous dites vrai; **you can imagine h. angry I was,** songez si j'étais furieux! **h. wide? h. long?** de quelle largeur? de quelle longueur? **h. long, wide, is this room?** quelle est la longueur, la largeur, de cette pièce? **h. old are you?** quel âge avez-vous? **I asked him h. old he was,** je lui ai demandé son âge; (*b*) (*in exclamations*) comme, que; **h. pretty she is!** comme elle est jolie! qu'elle est jolie! **h. dirty he is!** comme le voilà sale! **h. kind!** comme, que, c'est aimable (de votre part)! **h. he snores!** comme il ronfle! **h. strange it is that. . .!** comme c'est étrange que. . .! **h. sorry I am to disturb you!** combien je regrette de vous déranger! **h. I loved her!** comme je l'ai aimée! **h. small the world is!** que le monde est petit! **h. she has changed!** ce qu'elle a changé! **you know h. I love you,** vous savez si je vous aime; **h. I wish I could!** si seulement je pouvais! **h. often we went there!** que de fois nous y sommes allés! **h. great was his surprise, h. surprised he was, when. . .!** quelle ne fut pas sa surprise lorsque. . .! **3.** (*introducing indirect statement,* = *that*) que; **I told him h. there had been a great storm,** je lui ai dit qu'il y avait eu un grand orage; *F:* **he told me his grievances, and h. that you'd chucked him out,** il m'a raconté ses griefs, et comme quoi vous l'avez mis à la porte. **4.** *s.* **the hows and the whys,** les comment et les pourquoi; *U.S: F:* **that's about the h. of it,** je crois que c'est comme ça que c'est arrivé; **the h., the when, and the wherefore,** tous les détails.

how[2], *s. Dial:* (*N. of Eng.*) **1.** colline *f*, tertre *m*. **2.** tumulus *m.*

howbeit ['hau'bi:it], *adv. A:* néanmoins; quoi qu'il en soit; au demeurant.

howdah ['haudə], *s.* howdah *m.*

how-de-do, how-d'y(e)-do, howdy-do ['haudi'du:], *s. F: O:* **here's a (pretty) how-de-do!** en voilà une affaire! en voilà du joli! en voici d'une belle! quelle histoire! quel pétrin! quel aria! nous voilà bien!

howdy ['haudi], *int. NAm: F:* bonjour!

howea [hau'wi:ə], *s. Bot:* howea *m.*

howel ['hauəl], *s. Tls:* herminette *f.*

however [hau'evər], *adv.* **1.** (*in poetry sometimes* **howe'er** [hau'ɛər]) (*a*) de quelque manière que. . .; **h. he may do it,** de quelque manière qu'il le fasse; **do it h. you can,** faites-le comme vous le pourrez; **h. that may be,** quoi qu'il en soit; (*b*) quelque. . . que. . ., si. . . que. . .; **h. unhealthy it may be,** si malsain que ce soit; **h. artful she may be,** (i) si rusée qu'elle soit; (ii) toute rusée qu'elle est; **h. good his work is,** quelque excellent que soit son ouvrage; **your method, h. perfect in itself,** votre méthode, si parfaite soit-elle; **he has his moments, h. rare, of kindly feeling,** il a ses heures de bonté, si rares soient-elles; **h. closely I listened,** quelque attentivement que j'aie écouté; **h. loudly you ring no one will come,** quelque fort que vous sonniez personne ne viendra; **h. much he may admire you,** si fort qu'il vous admire; **h. much money you spend,** quelque argent que vous dépensiez; **h. much they boast,** quelque haut qu'ils se vantent; quoi qu'ils se vantent; quelque haut qu'ils se vantent; **h. little,** si peu qu'il soit; si peu que ce soit; **h. little he earns he always saves something,** si peu qu'il gagne il met toujours de l'argent de côté. **2.** toutefois, cependant, pourtant, d'ailleurs, du reste, au surplus; **the scheme h. failed,** pourtant le projet échoua; **if h. you don't agree,** si toutefois cela ne vous convient pas; si toutefois vous n'en convenez pas; **the troops h. arrived too late,** cependant les troupes arrivèrent trop tard.

howitzer ['hauitsər], *s. Artil:* obusier *m*; canon court; **field h.,** obusier de campagne.

howl[1] [haul], *s.* **1.** (*a*) hurlement *m* (de loup, de chien, etc.); clameurs *fpl*, mugissement *m* (du vent); **to give a h. of rage,** pousser un hurlement, un cri prolongé, de rage; hurler de rage; **there were howls of laughter,** on riait à gorge déployée; (*b*) huée *f*; **there was a h. from the crowd,** la foule, furieuse, a poussé des hurlements. **2.** *W.Tel:* réaction *f* dans l'antenne.

howl[2], *v.i. & tr.* **1.** (*of animals, people*) hurler; pousser des hurlements; (*of wind*) mugir, rugir, gronder; **to h. with pain,** hurler de douleur; *F:* **to h. with laughter,** rire à gorge déployée; **to h. dismally,** pousser des hurlements lugubres; **to h. with the pack,** hurler avec les loups; **to h. defiance at s.o.,** hurler, vociférer, des défis à l'adresse de qn; **to h. down a speaker,** faire taire un orateur en poussant des huées. **2.** *F:* beugler (une chanson, etc.). **3.** *W.Tel:* (*of set*) réactionner, rayonner, dans l'antenne.

howler ['haulər], *s.* **1.** (*a*) hurleur, -euse; (*b*) *Z:* (*monkey*) hurleur *m*; stentor *m*; **mantled h. (of Panama),** hurleur du Panama. **2.** *F:* grosse gaffe, bourde *f* énorme, erreur *f* comique; **schoolboy h.,** bourde *f* d'écolier; perle *f.*

howlet ['haulit], *s. Orn: Dial:* hulotte *f.*

howling[1] ['hauliŋ], *a.* **1.** (enfant *m*) qui hurle; (foule) hurlante; **h. tempest,** tempête furieuse; **h. dervish,** derviche hurleur, hurlant; **h. monkey,** singe hurleur. **2.** *F:* (*intensive*) très grand; énorme; **h. mistake,** bourde *f* énorme; **h. success,** succès fou; **a h. wilderness,** un désert affreux; **h. injustice, shame,** injustice criante; **it's a h. shame that. . .,** il est scandaleux que + *sub.*

howling[2], *s.* **1.** hurlement *m*; **h. of the wind, of the storm,** le mugissement, le grondement, les clameurs *f*, du vent, de la tempête. **2.** *W.Tel:* réaction *f* dans l'antenne.

howlite ['haulait], *s. Miner:* howlite *f.*

howsoever [hausou'evər], *adv. A: & Lit:* = HOWEVER 1.

how-to ['hautu:], *a. F:* **h.-to books,** petits manuels pratiques.

hoy[1] [hɔi], *s. Nau:* bugalet *m*; heu *m*; vaisseau côtier.

hoy[2], *int.* hé! holà! ohé!

hoya ['hɔiə], *s. Bot:* hoya *m*, hoyer *m.*

hoyden ['hɔidn], *s.f.* jeune fille à allures de garçon; jeune fille garçonnière; **she's a regular h.,** c'est un garçon manqué.

hoydenish ['hɔidniʃ], *a.* (*of manner, etc.*) garçonnier, -ière.

huanaco [hwæ'nɑ:kou], *s. Z:* guanaco *m.*

hub [hʌb], *s.* **1.** moyeu *m* (de roue, d'hélice, de poulie); **ball-bearing h.,** moyeu à billes; **swivel h.,** moyeu pivotant; *Cy:* **change-speed h.,** moyeu à changement de vitesse; **h. body,** corps *m* de moyeu; **h. brake,** frein *m* de moyeu; **h. flange,** disque *m*, flasque *m*, de moyeu; **h. extractor,** arrache-moyeu *m inv*; *Av:* **h. barrel,** logement *m* de pied de pale (de l'hélice); **up to the h. in sand, in mud,** enlisé, embourbé, jusqu'au moyeu. **2.** centre *m* d'activité; **London is the h. of the financial world,** Londres est le centre du monde financier; **the h. of the universe,** le pivot, le centre, de l'univers; *U.S: F:* **the H.,** la ville de Boston.

hubble-bubble ['hʌblbʌbl], *s. F:* **1.** gargouillement *m* (de l'eau qui court); glouglou *m* (de l'eau qui sort). **2.** bruit confus de voix. **3.** houka(h) *m*, narguilé *m* (de forme primitive).

hubhub ['hʌbʌb], *s.* remue-ménage *m*, bruit *m*, tumulte *m*, vacarme *m*, clameur *f*, tintamarre *m*, tohu-bohu *m*; **h. of voices,** brouhaha *m* de voix; des voix confuses.

hubby ['hʌbi], *s. F:* mari *m.*

hubcap ['hʌbkæp], *s. Veh:* couvre-moyeu *m*, *pl.* couvre-moyeux; *Aut:* chapeau *m* de moyeu, de roue; enjoliveur *m*; **nut-type h.,** écrou-chapeau *m*, *pl.* écrouschapeaux.

hübnerite ['hju:bnərait], *s. Miner:* hubnérite *f.*

hubris ['hju:bris], *s.* outrecuidance *f,* présomption *f,* orgueil *m.*

hubristic [hju'bristik], *a.* outrecuidant, orgueilleux.

huckaback ['hʌkəbæk], *s.* **h. (linen),** (grosse) toile ouvrée (pour serviettes, essuie-mains); toile (à) grain d'orge.

huckleberry ['hʌklberi], *s. Bot: NAm:* airelle *f* myrtille; bluet *m* du Canada; *F:* coussinet *m.*

huckster[1] ['hʌkstər], *s.* (*a*) *A:* revendeur, -euse; (*b*) colporteur *m*; (*c*) *esp. U.S:* publicitaire *m* (*esp.* pour les programmes de radio, de télévision); (*d*) mercanti *m,* profiteur, *m*; **political h.,** trafiquant *m* politique.

huckster[2], *v.tr. & i.* (*a*) marchander; (*b*) colporter; faire le porte à porte; (*c*) faire l'article (d'un produit); (*d*) faire trafic de (son influence, etc.).

huckstering ['hʌkstəriŋ], *s.* (*a*) marchandage *m*; (*b*) colportage *m*; (*c*) **political h.,** politicailleries *fpl,* trafics *mpl.*

huddle[1] ['hʌdl], *s.* (*b*) tas confus, pêle-mêle *m,* méli-mélo *m,* fouillis *m,* ramassis *m,* entassement *m* (de choses); **a h. of roofs,** un enchevêtrement de toits; (*b*) *F:* **to go into a h.,** entrer en conférence.

huddle[2], *v.tr. & i.* **1. to h. things (up, together),** entasser des choses pêle-mêle, sans ordre; **houses huddled together in the valley,** maisons serrées dans la vallée; **passengers huddled on the after deck,** passagers entassés sur l'arrière-pont; **to h. together,** s'entasser, se tasser; se serrer les uns contre les autres. **2.** (*of pers.*) **to h. (oneself) up,** se ramasser, se replier, sur soi-même; se pelotonner; **huddled (up) in bed,** couché en chien de fusil; **huddled (up) in a corner,** blotti dans un coin. **3.** *A:* **to h. over, through, a piece of work,** bâcler un travail. **4. to h. on one's clothes,** s'habiller à la hâte, à la va-vite.

hue[1] [hju:], *s.* teinte *f,* couleur *f,* nuance *f*; **his face has the h. of death,** la mort se peint sur son visage; **thoughts of a sombre h.,** pensées *f* d'un coloris sombre.

hue[2], *s.* **h. and cry,** clameur *f* de haro; *Jur:* clameur publique; proclamation *f* (désignant un criminel); **to raise a h. and cry against s.o.,** crier haro sur qn; crier tollé contre qn; **a h. and cry was raised against this reform,** cette réforme provoqua un tollé général; **to pursue s.o. with h. and cry,** poursuivre, chasser, qn à cor et à cri; courir sus à qn.

huebnerite ['hju:bnərait], *s. Miner:* hubnérite *f.*

huemal ['(h)weiməl], *s. Z:* huemal *m,* cerf *m* andin.

huerta ['(h)wεətə], *s. Geog:* huerta *f.*

huff[1] [hʌf], *s.* **1. to be in a h.,** être froissé, fâché; **to take (the) h.,** s'offenser, se froisser, s'offusquer; prendre la mouche; **he went off in a h.,** il prit la mouche et s'en alla. **2.** (*draughts*) soufflage *m* (d'un pion).

huff[2]. **1.** *v.i.* (*a*) *A:* souffler, haleter; (*still used in*) **he puffed and he huffed,** il soufflait et haletait; (*b*) s'offenser, s'offusquer, se fâcher, se formaliser; prendre la mouche. **2.** *v.tr.* (*a*) froisser (qn); **to be, feel, huffed,** être offensé, fâché; **he was very much huffed,** il a très mal pris la chose; (*b*) (*draughts*) souffler (un pion, son adversaire).

huffily ['hʌfili], *adv.* avec mauvaise humeur; d'un ton bourru, d'un ton de dépit.

huffiness ['hʌfinis], *s.* **1.** susceptibilité *f.* **2.** mauvaise humeur, pétulance *f.*

huffing ['hʌfiŋ], *s.* (*draughts*) soufflage *m* (d'un pion); **h. is not reckoned a move,** souffler n'est pas jouer.

huffish ['hʌfiʃ], *a.* susceptible.

huffy ['hʌfi], *a.* **1.** (*a*) susceptible; **in a h. tone of voice,** d'un ton pincé; (*b*) irascible. **2.** fâché, vexé; **he was very h. about it,** il a très mal pris la chose.

hug[1] [hʌg], *s.* **1.** étreinte *f,* embrassement *m,* embrassade *f*; **to give s.o. a h.,** étreindre qn. **2.** (*a*) étreinte (de l'ours); (*b*) *Wr:* prise *f*; **Cornish h.,** ceinture *f* de devant.

hug[2], *v.tr.* (**hugged**) **1.** (*a*) étreindre, embrasser, serrer, (qn) dans, entre, ses bras; serrer (qn) sur son cœur; prendre (qn) à pleins bras; se pendre, sauter, se jeter, au cou de (qn); (*b*) (*of bear*) étouffer, enserrer (sa victime); *F:* **to h. s.o. to death,** embrasser qn à l'étouffer; (*c*) chérir (ses défauts); **to h. a prejudice,** tenir à un préjugé; choyer un préjugé; **to h. a belief,** ne pas démordre d'une conviction; (*d*) **to h. oneself for doing sth.,** se féliciter, s'applaudir, d'avoir fait qch. **2.** (*a*) *Nau:* **to h. the land, the shore,** serrer la terre (de près); raser, ranger, longer, border, la côte; naviguer près de (la) terre; se rallier à terre; côtoyer; **to h. the wind,** tâter, serrer, pincer, chicaner, le vent; (*b*) **to h. the wall,** raser, longer, serrer, le mur; se couler au ras du mur; *Aut:* **to h. the nearside, the kerb,** serrer le trottoir; (*of pedestrian*) **to h. the edge of the kerb,** tenir le bord du trottoir; (*c*) *F:* **to h. the chimney corner, the fire,** se blottir, se tenir blotti, au coin du feu.

huge [hju:dʒ], *a.* immense, énorme, gigantesque; (bâtiment) énorme, vaste; (succès) immense, formidable, colossal, -aux, monstre; (bête) énorme; (homme) colossal, d'immense stature; **h. difference,** différence énorme, capitale; **h. collection of samples,** vaste collection *f* d'échantillons; **h. undertaking,** vaste entreprise *f*; **furs that fetch h. prices,** fourrures *f* qui se vendent à prix d'or, à des prix colossaux.

hugely ['hju:dʒli], *adv.* énormément; extrêmement.

hugeness ['hju:dʒnis], *s.* énormité *f,* immensité *f.*

huggable ['hʌgəbl], *a.* (enfant, poupée, etc.) qu'on voudrait embrasser, gentil(le) à croquer.

hugger-mugger[1] ['hʌgəmʌgər]. **1.** *s.* (*a*) désordre *m,* confusion *f,* pagaille *f,* pagaïe *f*; **to live in a h.-m. fashion,** (i) vivre cahin-caha, sans ordre, sans méthode; (ii) vivre dans le désordre matériel; (*b*) *A:* **in h.-m.,** en secret, clandestinement. **2.** *a.* (collection *f*) sans ordre; (arrangement) confus, de fortune. **3.** *adv.* (*a*) en désordre, confusément, pêle-mêle; (*b*) *A:* en cachette.

hugger-mugger[2]. **1.** *v.tr. A:* étouffer (un scandale, etc.). **2.** *v.i.* patauger; faire du gâchis; agir sans méthode, sans ordre; **to h.-m. together,** vivre entassés ensemble; **they're hugger-muggering along,** leur ménage va cahin-caha.

Hugh [hju:], **Hugo** ['hju:gou], *Pr.n.m.* Hugues.

Huguenot ['hju:gənɔt, -nou], *s. Rel.H:* Huguenot, -ote; **H. party, faction,** *A:* huguenoterie *f*; **his H. ancestors,** ses ancêtres huguenots.

huia ['hu:jə], *s. Orn:* huia *m.*

huisache [(h)wi:'su:tʃi], *s. Bot:* cassie *f.*

hulk [hʌlk], *s.* **1.** *Nau:* (*a*) carcasse *f* de navire; ponton *m*; vaisseau rasé; **mooring h.,** ponton d'amarrage; *Navy:* **receiving h.,** ponton-caserne *m, pl.* pontons-casernes; caserne flottante; (*b*) *F:* (*of ship*) **unwieldy old h.,** vieille carcasse, vieux sabot; (*c*) *pl. A:* **hulks,** navire pénitencier, bagne flottant; pontons. **2.** *F:* (*of pers.*) gros pataud; lourdaud *m,* mastoc *m.*

hulking ['hʌlkiŋ], *a.* gros, lourd; **big h., h. great, creature,** gros pataud; lourdaud *m,* mastoc *m*; grand balourd.

hull[1] [hʌl], *s.* **1.** (*a*) cosse *f,* gousse *f* (de pois, de fève); coque *f,* coquille *f,* écale *f,* brou *m* (de noix); (*b*) enveloppe *f* (de chrysalide, etc.). **2.** (*a*) *N.Arch:* coque (de navire); **strengthened h.,** coque renforcée; **welded h.,** coque soudée; **height above the h.,** hauteur *f* au-dessus du plat-bord; **h. down,** coque noyée; (*b*) *M.Ins:* corps *m*; **h. insurance,** assurance *f* sur corps; **h. underwriter,** assureur *m* sur corps; (*c*) *Av:* coque (d'hydroplane); coque-fuselage *f, pl.* coques-fuselages; (*d*) *Mil:* (*of tank*) coque; **h. plates,** plaques *f,* blindage *m,* de coque; **h. down position,** position *f* à défilement de coque.

hull[2], *v.tr.* **1.** écosser (des pois); écaler, ébrouer (des noisettes); monder (de l'orge); baller (de l'avoine); décortiquer (le riz, l'orge); **hulled barley,** orge mondé. **2.** *Nau:* percer la coque (d'un navire); *A:* canonner (un navire) en plein bois.

hullabaloo [hʌləbə'lu:], *s.* tintamarre *m,* vacarme *m*; remue-ménage *m inv*; **to make a h.,** (i) faire du vacarme, du chambard, du boucan; faire un brouhaha de tous les diables; (ii) éclater en protestations; réclamer à grands cris.

huller ['hʌlər], *s.* écosseur, -euse.

hulling ['hʌliŋ], *s.* décorticage *m,* décortication *f.*

hullo(a) [hʌ'lou], *int.* (*a*) (*calling attention*) ohé! holà! **h. you!** hé, là-bas! eh, là-bas! (*b*) (*expressing surprise*) **h. old chap!** tiens, c'est toi, mon vieux! **h.! that's curious!** tiens! tiens! c'est curieux; (*c*) (*greeting*) bonjour! **h. everybody!** salut à tous! (*d*) *Tp:* allô! *F: A:* **the h. girl,** la standardiste.

hum[1] [hʌm], *s.* bourdonnement *m* (d'abeille); ronflement *m* (de machine); ronron *m* (d'un moteur); vrombissement *m* (d'un avion, d'une toupie); brondissement *m,* ronflement (de toupie); murmure *m* (d'approbation); bruit sourd (de voix); *W.Tel: etc:* bourdonnement, ronflement; **mains h.,** ronflement du secteur; **h. of conversation,** brouhaha *m* de conversation; **the busy h. of a large city,** le bourdonnement d'une grande ville; *Med:* **venous h.,** (bruit *m* de) souffle *m*; bruit de rouet.

hum[2], *v.* (**hummed**) **1.** *v.i.* (*a*) (*of insect, etc.*) bourdonner; (*of top*) ronfler, vrombir; (*of aircraft*) vrombir; (*of millstone, etc.*) bruire; *W.Tel:* (*of set*) ronronner, ronchonner, ronfler; **town humming with activity,** ville bourdonnante d'activité; *F.* **to make things h., to keep things humming,** faire marcher rondement, faire ronfler, les choses; **things are beginning to h.,** ça chauffe; ça va chauffer; ça ronfle; (*b*) (*of pers.*) (i) dire hum; (ii) hésiter, ânonner (en parlant); **to h. and haw,** (i) toussoter (en commençant un discours), bredouiller, bafouiller; (ii) hésiter (à prendre un parti); tourner autour du pot. **2.** *v.tr.* fredonner, chantonner, baryton(n)er (un air); *v.i.* fredonner, chantonner; *Mus:* vocaliser (un air) à bouche fermée; **hummed accompaniment,** accompagnement *m* pour voix en sourdine; accompagnement à bouche fermée.

hum[3], *int.* hmm! hum!

hum[4], *v.i.* (**hummed**) *P:* puer, gazouiller, fouetter, boucaner, schlinguer, cocoter.

human ['hju:mən]. **1.** *a.* humain; **h. being,** être humain; **h. nature,** la nature humaine; **the h. race,** la race humaine; **a very h. error,** erreur bien humaine; **one can tell the h. hand,** on reconnaît la main de l'homme; **one must be less than h. not to have pity on them,** il faudrait être moins qu'humain, ne rien avoir d'humain, pour ne pas les prendre en pitié. **2.** *s.* être humain; **humans,** les humains *m*; **in humans,** dans l'espèce humaine.

humane [hju'mein], *a.* **1.** (*a*) humain, compatissant; accessible à la pitié; **h. task,** œuvre *f* humanitaire; **h. measures,** mesures bienfaisantes, humanitaires; **the Royal H. Society,** la Société de sauvetage, de secours aux noyés; (*b*) clément; qui évite de faire souffrir. **2.** *A:* **h. studies,** les humanités *f.*

humanely [hju'meinli], *adv.* humainement, avec humanité, avec bonté.

humaneness [hju'meinnis], *s.* bonté *f,* humanité *f.*

humanism ['hju:mənizm], *s. Lit: Phil:* humanisme *m.*

humanist ['hju:mənist], *s.* humaniste *m.*

humanistic [hjumə'nistik], *a.* humaniste; **h. studies,** les humanités *f,* les études *f* classiques.

humanitarian [hjumæni'tεəriən], *a. & s.* humanitaire (*mf*).

humanitarianism [hjumæni'tεəriənizm], *s.* humanitarisme *m.*

humanity [hju'mæniti], *s.* humanité *f.* **1.** (*a*) nature humaine; (*b*) le genre humain; les hommes *m.* **2. to treat s.o. with h.,** traiter qn avec humanité. **3.** (*a*) *pl. Lit: Phil:* **the humanities,** les humanités, les lettres *f*; *Sch: A:* **h. classes,** classes *f* de lettres; (*b*) *Sch: Scot:* **professor of h.,** professeur *m* de latin.

humanization [hju:mənai'zeiʃ(ə)n], *s.* humanisation *f.*

humanize ['hju:mənaiz], *v.tr.* humaniser; *F:* **he is beginning to get humanized,** il commence à s'humaniser; il devient plus sociable, moins ours.

humankind ['hju:mən'kaind], *s.* le genre humain; (les) humains *m*; (l')humanité *f.*

humanly ['hju:mənli], *adv.* humainement; en être humain; **h. speaking,** humainement parlant; **to do everything h. possible to help,** faire tout ce qu'il est humainement possible pour aider.

humanness ['hju:mənnis], *s.* qualité tout humaine (**of,** de); **the h. of some of these apes,** la ressemblance à l'homme qu'offrent certains de ces grands singes.

humble[1] ['hʌmbl], *a.* humble. **1.** (*lowly, meek*) **h. prayer,** humble prière *f*; **in my h. opinion,** à mon humble avis, **h. of heart, h.-hearted,** au cœur humble. **2.** (*a*) (*unpretentious*) modeste; **to be of h. origin, stock,** être d'origine modeste, d'une famille humble; (*b*) *Bot:* **h. plant,** sensitive *f.*

humble[2], *v.tr.* humilier, mortifier (qn); **to h. oneself,** s'humilier, s'abaisser; s'aplatir, se faire tout petit (**before,** devant); **God humbles the proud,** Dieu abaisse les superbes; *Lit:* **to h. s.o. to, in, the dust,** faire souffrir à qn les dernières humiliations; faire rentrer qn en terre; **to h. s.o.'s pride,** (r)abattre, rabaisser, mater, aplatir, l'orgueil, la fierté, de qn.

humble[3], *s.* (*a*) *A:* **h. pie,** pâté *m* de mou de cerf; (*b*) **to eat h. pie,** s'humilier (devant qn); présenter d'humbles excuses; se rétracter; faire amende honorable; avouer être dans son tort; s'aplatir; filer doux; en rabattre; **to make s.o. eat h. pie,** forcer qn à s'humilier, à se rétracter.

humble bee ['hʌmbəlbi:], *s. Ent:* bourdon *m.*

humbleness ['hʌmbəlnis], *s.* humilité *f.*

humbling[1] ['hʌmbliŋ], *a.* humiliant.

humbling[2], *s.* humiliation *f* (de qn); abaissement *m* (des grands, etc.).

humbly ['hʌmbli], *adv.* **1.** (parler) humblement, avec humilité; **most h.,** en toute humilité. **2.** (vivre) modestement; **h. born,** d'origine modeste, obscure.

humbug[1] ['hʌmbʌg], *s.* **1.** (*a*) *A:* mystification *f,* fumisterie *f*; (*b*) patelinage *m,* charlatanisme *m*; blagues *fpl*; **there's no h. about him,** c'est un homme franc et sincère; ce n'est pas un blagueur, un farceur, celui-là; ce n'est pas lui qui vous en contera; **(that's all) h.!** tout cela c'est de la blague. **2.** (*pers.*) (*a*) *A:* farceur *m*; (*b*) blagueur *m*; truqueur, -euse; (*c*) donneur, -euse, d'eau bénite; enjôleur, -euse; (*d*) charlatan *m.* **3.** (*a*) *Comest:* berlingot *m*; = bêtise *f* de Cambrai; (*b*) *Atom.Ph:* **h.-shaped magnetic field,** champ *m* magnétique en forme de berlingot.

humbug[2], *v.tr.* (**humbugged**) conter des blagues à (qn); en faire accroire à (qn); enjôler, attraper (qn); mettre (qn) dedans; payer (un créancier) en monnaie de singe;

mystifier (le public); *v.i.* blaguer; conter des balivernes; faire le malin; **to h. s.o. into doing sth.,** amener qn à faire qch. en abusant de son innocence; enjôler, embobeliner, qn.

humbugging ['hʌmbʌgiŋ], *s.* duperie *f,* blagues *fpl.*

humdinger ['hʌmdiŋər], *s. esp. U.S: F:* quelque chose d'extraordinaire, de fantastique.

humdrum ['hʌmdrʌm]. **1.** *a.* monotone; banal, -als; **h. people,** des gens peu intéressants, ennuyeux, routiniers, pot-au-feu *inv*; **h. work,** travail monotone, endormant; **h. existence,** existence *f* monotone, d'une monotonie endormante; **h. daily life,** le train-train quotidien. **2.** *s.* (*a*) (*pers.*) homme, femme, pot-au-feu, qui ne sort jamais de ses habitudes; (*b*) monotonie *f* (de l'existence, etc.).

humdrumness ['hʌmdrʌmnis], *s.* monotonie *f,* banalité *f* (de l'existence, d'un discours).

humectation [hju:mek'teiʃ(ə)n], *s.* humectation *f.*

humeral ['hju:mər(ə)l], *a.* (*a*) *Anat:* huméral, -aux; (*b*) *Ecc:* **h. (veil),** voile huméral.

humero-cubital ['hju:mərou'kju:bitl], *a. Anat:* brachio-cubital, -aux; huméro-cubital, -aux.

humerometacarpal ['hju:məroumetə'ka:pl], *a. Anat:* huméro-métacarpien, *pl.* huméro-métacarpiens.

humerus, *pl.* -i ['hju:mərəs, -ai, -i:], *s. Anat:* humérus *m.*

humic ['hju:mik], *a.* (*a*) humeux; (*b*) *Ch:* **h. acid,** acide *m* humique, ulmique; humine *f.*

humid ['hju:mid], *a.* humide; (*of heat, skin*) moite.

humidification [hjumidifi'keiʃ(ə)n], *s.* humidification *f.*

humidifier [hju'midifaiər], *s.* **1.** *Ind: Tex:* appareil *m* à humecter; *Dom.Ec: etc:* humidificateur *m.* **2.** produit humidifiant.

humidify [hju'midifai], *v.tr.* humidifier (l'air, etc.).

humidity [hju'miditi], *s.* humidité *f*; *Ind: Meteor:* état *m* hygrométrique (de l'air); hygrométricité *f* (de l'atmosphère).

humidor ['hju:midɔ:r], *s.* **1.** humidificateur *m* (d'atelier de filature, etc.). **2.** *NAm:* (*a*) hall *m* de dépôt (pour cigares); (*b*) boîte à cigares (pourvue d'un humidificateur).

humification [hjumifi'keiʃ(ə)n], *s.* humification *f.*

humified ['hju:mifaid], *a.* (*of soil*) humifié.

humifuse ['hju:mifjuz], *a. Bot:* humifuse.

humiliate [hju(:)'milieit], *v.tr.* humilier, mortifier (qn); *F:* donner un coup de caveçon à (qn).

humiliating [hju'milieitiŋ], *a.* humiliant, mortifiant.

humiliation [hjumili'eiʃ(ə)n], *s.* humiliation *f,* affront *m,* mortification *f*; aplatissement *m* (de qn); **to suffer all sorts of h.,** subir toute sorte d'affronts, d'humiliations.

humility [hju'militi], *s.* humilité *f*; **with, in, all h.,** en toute humilité.

humite ['hju:mait], *s. Miner:* humite *f.*

hummel ['hʌml], *s.* cerf *m* sans bois.

humming[1] ['hʌmiŋ], *a.* bourdonnant; **h. top,** toupie ronflante, vrombissante; toupie d'Allemagne.

humming[2], *s.* (*a*) = HUM[1]; fredonnement *m* (d'un air); **h. noise,** bourdonnement *m*; (*b*) **h. and hawing,** hésitation *f.*

hummingbird ['hʌmiŋbə:d], *s.* **1.** *Orn:* colibri *m,* oiseau-mouche *m, pl.* oiseaux-mouches; **the h. family, the hummingbirds,** les trochilidés *mpl*; **Anna h., Anna's h.,** colibri d'Anna; **bee h.,** oiseau-mouche Hélène; **broad-tailed h.,** oiseau-mouche tricolore; **comet h.,** colibri Sapho; **coquette h.,** colibri huppe-col; **crimson topaz h.,** grand topaze; **emerald h.,** colibri orvert; **giant h.,** oiseau-mouche patagon; **jacobin h.,** jacobine *f*; **purple-throated Carib h.,** oiseau-mouche grenat; **Rivoli's h.,** oiseau-mouche Rivoli; **ruby and topaz h.,** rubis-topaze *m*; **sabre-winged h.,** colibri à larges ailes; **slender shear-tail h.,** oiseau-mouche énicure; **sword-bill(ed) h.,** colibri, oiseau-mouche, porte-épée; **black-chinned h.,** colibri à gorge noire; **calliope h.,** colibri calliope; *Fr.C:* colibri de Calliope; **ruby-throated h.,** petit rubis de la Caroline, *Fr.C:* colibri à gorge rubis; **rufous h.,** colibri sasin, *Fr.C:* colibri roux. **2.** *Ent:* **h. hawkmoth,** moro(-)sphinx *m inv.,* sphinx *m* du caille-lait.

hummock ['hʌmək], *s.* **1.** tertre *m,* mamelon *m* (de terre); monticule *m.* **2.** monticule de glace; hummock *m.*

hummocky ['hʌməki], *a.* **1.** (terrain) couvert de tertres, de mamelons. **2. h. ice,** glace *f* en monticules, en hummocks.

humoral ['hju:mərəl], *a. A.Med:* humoral, -aux.

humoralism ['hju:mərəlizm], *s. A.Med:* humorisme *m.*

humoralist ['hju:mərəlist], *s. A.Med:* humoriste *m.*

humoralistic [hjumərə'listik], *a. A.Med:* humoriste.

humorist ['hju:mərist], *s.* **1.** (*a*) farceur *m,* plaisant *m*; (*b*) comique *m.* **2.** écrivain *m* humoristique; humoriste *m.*

humoristic [hjumə'ristik], *a.* humoristique.

humorous ['hju:m(ə)rəs], *a.* (*of pers.*) plein d'humour; plaisant, comique, drôle; (*of writer, etc.*) humoriste, humoristique; (*of drawing, etc.*) humoristique; **he is very h.,** il a beaucoup d'humour.

humorously ['hju:mərəsli], *adv.* plaisamment, drôlement, comiquement; humoristiquement, d'une façon humoristique.

humorousness ['hju:m(ə)rəsnis], *s.* humeur facétieuse; drôlerie *f.*

humour[1] ['hju:mər], *s.* **1.** (*a*) *A.Med:* humeur *f*; **the cardinal humours,** les quatre humeurs principales; (*b*) *Anat:* **aqueous h., vitreous h.,** humeur aqueuse, vitrée (de l'œil). **2.** (*mood, temper*) humeur, disposition *f*; **to be in the h. for doing sth.,** être en (bonne) disposition, en humeur, de faire qch., pour faire qch.; être disposé à faire qch.; **good h.,** bonne humeur; **to be in a good, bad, h.,** être de bonne, de mauvaise, humeur; être bien, mal, disposé; *F:* être bien, mal, luné; **to be in no h. for laughing, in no laughing h.,** ne pas être en train de rire; ne pas avoir envie de rire; ne pas se sentir d'humeur à rire, en humeur de rire; ne pas être en veine de plaisanter; *O:* **to be out of h.,** être maussade, grognon; **to be out of h. with s.o.,** être mécontent de qn; bouder qn. **3.** (*a*) humour *m*; **broad h.,** grosse gaieté, grosse jovialité; **grim h., black h.,** humour macabre, noir; (*b*) **the h. of the situation,** le côté plaisant, comique, de la situation; **I don't see the h. of it,** il n'y a pas de quoi rire; (*c*) sens *m* de l'humour; **to be lacking in h., to have no sense of h.,** ne pas avoir le sens de l'humour.

humour[2], *v.tr.* (*a*) **to h. s.o.,** complaire à qn; se prêter, se plier, à tous les caprices de qn; se soumettre aux exigences, aux caprices, de qn; ménager qn; **to h. a horse,** ménager, laisser aller, un cheval; **man who must be humoured,** homme *m* qu'il faut mitonner, qu'il ne faut pas contrarier; **to h. s.o.'s fancy,** passer une fantaisie à qn; flatter le caprice, la manie, de qn; (*b*) (*in carving, etc.*) **to h. the wood,** flatter le bois; se prêter à la nature du bois.

humourless ['hju:məlis], *a.* dépourvu d'humour, du sens de l'humour.

humous ['hju:məs], *a.* (*of acid, etc.*) humeux.

hump[1] [hʌmp], *s.* **1.** (*a*) bosse *f* (de bossu, de chameau); **to have a h.,** être bossu; *F:* **dowager's h.,** bosse de bison; (*b*) *F:* **h.(-backed) whale,** mégaptère *f,* jubarte *f*; (*c*) **h. in the road,** bosse de route; dos *m* d'âne; (*d*) *Rail:* butte *f* de triage, de gravité; (*e*) *Av:* **h. speed,** vitesse *f* au déjauger (d'un hydravion). **2.** *F:* **to have the h.,** avoir le cafard; broyer du noir; **that gives me the h.,** ça me donne le cafard; cela m'embête.

hump[2]. **1.** *v.tr.* (*a*) courber, arquer, cambrer; (*of pers., animal*) **to h. the back,** arrondir, arquer, bomber, le dos; faire le gros dos; (*in anticipation of a blow*) tendre le dos (à un coup); **to h. one's shoulders,** voûter les épaules; rentrer la tête dans les épaules; (*b*) *F:* mettre, hisser, porter, (un fardeau) sur son dos; *Austr:* **h. your swag! h. it!** prends ton baluchon! décampe! roule ta bosse! **2.** *v.i. & refl. NAm: F:* **to h. (oneself),** se fouler (la rate); se la fouler.

humpback ['hʌmpbæk], *s.* **1.** (*a*) bossu, -ue; (*b*) **to have a h.** [hʌmp'bæk], être bossu; *F:* porter son paquet, sa malle. **2. h. (whale),** mégaptère *f,* jubarte *f.*

humpbacked ['hʌmpbækt], *a.* bossu, gibbeux; **h. bridge,** pont en dos d'âne.

humped ['hʌmpt], *a.* (dos, animal) bossu; (dos) voûté; (animal, insecte) gibbeux; (toit) en bosse.

humph [hʌmf, hm], *int.* hum! hmm! (d'incrédulité ou de doute).

humpty ['hʌm(p)ti], *s. F:* **1.** *Furn:* pouf *m.* **2.** (*from the nursery rhyme*) **h. dumpty,** petite personne boulotte, ronde comme un œuf.

humulene ['hju:mjuli:n], *s. Ch:* humulène *m.*

humus ['hju:məs], *s. Agr: Hort:* humus *m*; terreau *m*; terre végétale; **h.-bearing,** humifère.

Hun [hʌn], *s.* **1.** (*usu. pl.*) *Hist:* hun(s) *m(pl).* **2.** *F:* (*in 1914–18 War*) boche *m.*

hunch[1] [hʌn(t)ʃ], *s.* **1.** bosse *f.* **2.** gros morceau (de pain, de fromage); **h. of bread,** quignon *m,* chicot *m,* chanteau *m,* de pain; michon *m.* **3.** (*a*) *NAm: F:* poussée *f* du coude; (*b*) **to have a h. that . . .,** soupçonner que . . .; **what makes you think that?—just a h.,** qu'est-ce qui vous a donné cette idée-là?—j'en ai le pressentiment.

hunch[2], *v.tr.* **1.** arrondir (le dos); voûter (les épaules); **with hunched shoulders,** la tête enfoncée dans les épaules; **to sit hunched up,** se tenir accroupi le menton sur les genoux. **2.** *NAm: F:* (*a*) pousser (qn) du coude; (*b*) passer un tuyau à (qn); tuyauter (qn).

hunchback ['hʌn(t)ʃbæk], *s.* bossu, -ue.

hunchbacked ['hʌn(t)ʃbækt], *a.* bossu.

hundred ['hʌndrəd]. **1.** *num. a. & s.* (*a*) cent (*m*); **a h. and one,** cent un; **page a h. and one,** page *f* cent un; **about a h. houses,** une centaine de maisons; **a h. of them were rotten,** il y en avait cent de pourris; **two h. apples,** deux cents pommes; **two h. and one pounds,** deux cent une livres; **in nineteen h.,** en dix-neuf cent, mil neuf cent; **not one in a h.,** pas un sur cent; **to live to be a h.,** atteindre la centaine; **they were dying in hundreds,** ils mouraient par centaines; **hundreds and thousands of people,** des milliers *m* de gens; **they died in hundreds of thousands,** ils mouraient par centaines de mille; **many h. thousand prisoners,** des prisonniers par centaines de mille; *Cu:* **hundreds and thousands** = vermicelles *fpl,* perlages *mpl*; *U.S:* **the Four H.,** la crème de la société; **to have fifteen h. a year,** avoir un revenu de quinze cents livres; **to drive at a h. kilometres an hour,** faire du cent à l'heure; **a h. per cent,** cent pour cent; **a h. per cent efficient,** de la plus haute capacité; **a h. per cent American,** Américain cent pour cent, corps et âme; **a h. per cent useless,** sans aucune valeur; *Hist:* **the H. Days,** les Cent-Jours *m*; **the H. Years' War,** la Guerre de Cent Ans; *Com:* **the long h., the great h.,** le grand cent; cent vingt; **a h. eggs,** un cent d'œufs; **to sell by the h.,** vendre au cent; *Sp:* **the h. metre race, the h. metres,** le cent mètres; (*b*) **not a h. miles away,** pas si loin d'ici; **a h. and one dangers,** mille dangers; **a h. and one details,** les mille et un détails; **I've told you hundreds of times,** je vous l'ai dit je ne sais combien de fois; **the odds are, it's, a h. to one that. . .,** il y a cent contre un à parier que . . .; **a h. to one it will be a failure,** ça fera four presque à coup sûr. **2.** *s. Hist:* (ancienne) division administrative du comté.

hundredfold ['hʌndrədfould]. **1.** *a.* centuple; *Opt:* **h. magnification,** grossissement *m* cent (fois). **2.** *adv.phr.* **a h.,** cent fois autant; **to be repaid a h.,** être payé au centuple; **to increase a h.,** centupler.

hundredth ['hʌndrədθ]. **1.** *num.a. & s.* centième (*mf*); **two h.,** deux centième; *Th:* **h. performance,** centième *f*; **in the h. place,** centièmement; *Ecc:* **the Old H.,** (i) le psaume *Jubilate Deo*; (ii) l'air sur lequel se chante ce psaume. **2.** *s.* (*fractional*) centième *m*; **three hundredths,** trois centièmes.

hundredweight ['hʌndrədweit], *s. Meas:* (*a*) poids *m* de 112 livres, = 50 kg 802; (*approx.* =) quintal *m*; (*b*) *U.S:* poids de 100 livres, = 45 kg 359.

Hungarian [hʌŋ'geəriən]. **1.** *Geog:* (*a*) *a.* hongrois; (*b*) *s.* Hongrois, -oise. **2.** *s. Ling:* hongrois *m.* **3.** *a. Bot:* **H. grass,** panic *m* d'Italie.

Hungary ['hʌŋgəri], *Pr.n. Geog:* Hongrie *f*; *Toil: A:* **H. water,** eau *f* de la reine de Hongrie.

hunger[1] ['hʌŋgər], *s.* (*a*) faim *f*; **to be faint with h.,** défaillir de faim; mourir de faim; *F:* avoir l'estomac dans les talons; **h. is the best sauce,** il n'est chère, n'est sauce, n'est viande, que d'appétit; la faim assaisonne tout; à bon appétit il ne faut point de sauce; **pang of h.,** fringale *f*; *Med:* **morbid h.,** faim-valle, boulimie *f*; **h. pains,** tiraillements *m* d'estomac; **h. cure,** diète (absolue); **h. march,** marche *f* de la faim; **h. marcher,** marcheur, -euse, de la faim; **h. strike,** grève *f* de la faim; **h. striker,** gréviste *mf* de la faim; **h. for sth.,** ardent désir de qch.; désir de posséder qch.; soif *f* de qch.; (*b*) *Bot:* **h. grass,** vulpin *m* agreste, *F:* chiendent *m* queue-de-renard.

hunger[2]. *esp. Lit:* **1.** *v.i.* (*a*) avoir faim; (*b*) **to h. after, for, sth.,** être affamé de, avoir soif de, qch.; désirer ardemment qch.; **to h. after praise,** avoir soif de louanges; **he hungered for her,** il avait faim de la revoir; **hungering for romance,** avide d'aventures romanesques. **2.** *v.tr. A:* affamer (qn); *esp.* **to h. s.o. into submission,** contraindre, mater, qn par la faim; **to h. a garrison out of a place,** faire sortir une garnison par la famine.

hungered ['hʌŋgəd], *a. A: & Lit:* affamé.

hungering, *s.* faim *f,* soif *f* (**after, for,** de).

hunger-strike ['hʌŋgəstraik], *v.i.* (*p.t.* **-struck**; *p.p.* **-struck**) faire la grève de la faim.

hungerweed ['hʌŋgəwi:d], *s. Bot:* **1.** renoncule *f* des champs. **2.** vulpin *m* agreste, *F:* chiendent *m* queue-de-renard.

hungrily ['hʌŋgrili], *adv.* avidement, voracement, avec voracité; **he looked h. at her,** il la regardait d'un œil avide.

hungry ['hʌŋgri], *a.* **1.** affamé, qui a faim; **to be, feel, h.,** avoir faim; sentir la faim; être affamé; **to be ravenously h., as h. as a hunter,** avoir une faim de loup, une faim dévorante; *F:* avoir l'estomac dans les talons; **to make s.o. h.,** donner faim à qn; **to go h.,** souffrir de la faim; **to remain h.,** rester sur sa faim; **I was getting h.,** je commençais à avoir faim; **to look h.,** avoir l'air famélique; *s.* **the h.,** ceux qui ont faim; les miséreux *m*; *Hist:* **the H. Forties,** les années de disette de 1840–50; *Vet:* **h. evil,** faim-valle *f.* **2.** (regard *m,* œil *m*) avide; **to be h. for knowledge,** être affamé de savoir; être avide d'apprendre. **3.** (terre *f*) pauvre, maigre; (rivière *f*) pauvre, peu poissonneuse.

hunk [hʌŋk], *s.* gros morceau (de gâteau, de fromage, etc.); quignon *m* (de pain).

hunkers ['hʌŋkəz], *s.pl. F:* (*used only in*) **on one's h.,** à croupetons, accroupi; **to sit down on one's h.,** s'accroupetonner, s'accroupir les fesses sur les talons.
hunks [hʌŋks], *s. F: O:* **stingy old h.,** vieil avare; grippe-sou *m,pl.* grippe-sou(s); ladre *m*; **he's an old h.,** c'est un rat.
Hunky ['hʌŋki], *s. U.S: usu. Pej:* immigrant, -ante, de l'Europe centrale.
hunky-dory ['hʌŋki'dɔ:ri], *a. F:* excellent, en bon ordre.
Hunnish ['hʌniʃ], *a.* (*a*) *Hist:* (férocité, etc.) digne des Huns; (*b*) d'une cruauté sauvage.
Hunnishness ['hʌniʃnis], *s.* férocité *f*, cruauté *f*.
hunt[1] [hʌnt], *s.* **1.** (*a*) chasse *f*; *esp.* chasse à courre, aux fauves; **fox h., tiger h.,** chasse au renard, au tigre; (*b*) équipage *m* de chasse; **the h. went past here,** la chasse a passé par ici; (*c*) terrain *m* de chasse; (*d*) *in Pr.n.* Rallye *m*. **2.** recherche *f*; **to go on a h. for sth.,** aller à la recherche de qch.; **there was a h. for the missing book,** on cherchait le livre perdu; **he continued his h. for work,** il continuait à chercher un emploi. **3.** = HUNTING[2] 3.
hunt[2], *v.*
I. *v.i. & tr.* **1.** *v.i.* (*a*) *Ven:* chasser au chien courant; chasser à courre; (*b*) **to h. (about) for sth., s.o.,** chercher (à découvrir) qch., qn; **to h. for treasure,** aller à la recherche d'un trésor; **to h. through the shops,** courir les magasins; (*c*) *Mch: El:* (*of engine, alternator, etc.*) pomper; s'affoler par instants; **the regulator is hunting,** le régulateur pompe. **2.** *v.tr.* (*a*) chasser (le cerf, etc.); **to h. whales,** pêcher la baleine; (*b*) **to h. a thief,** (i) poursuivre un voleur; (ii) être à la recherche d'un voleur; (iii) suivre la piste d'un voleur; (*c*) parcourir, battre (un terrain); (*d*) **to h. a horse,** monter un cheval à la chasse; **to h. the pack,** diriger, conduire, la meute.
II. (*compound verbs*) **1. hunt down,** *v.tr.* (*a*) traquer, forcer (une bête); *F:* mettre (qn) aux abois, à l'accul; **the police hunted down the murderer,** la police est arrivée à mettre la main sur l'assassin. (*b*) *F:* persécuter (qn); rendre la vie intenable à (qn).
2. hunt out, *v.tr.* (*a*) (i) chasser, expulser (qn); chasser (un chien); **to be hunted out of society,** être mis au ban de la société; (ii) **the artillery soon hunted them out,** l'artillerie eut bientôt fait de les débusquer; (*b*) déterrer, dénicher (qch.) (à force de recherches); découvrir (la vérité); arriver à retrouver (qn, qch.).
3. hunt up, *v.tr.* (*a*) déterrer (des faits, des renseignements); (*b*) aller relancer (qn).
hunter ['hʌntər], *s.* **1.** (*a*) chasseur *m*; tueur *m* (de lions, etc.); **the hunter's moon,** la lune de la chasse (qui suit la lune des moissons); (*b*) *F:* pourchasseur *m* (**of,** de); **curio h.,** dénicheur *m* d'antiquités; **dowry h.,** coureur *m* de dots. **2.** cheval *m* de chasse; hunter *m*. **3.** (montre *f* à) savonnette *f*; **half h.,** montre à guichet.
hunter-killer ['hʌntə'kilər], *s. Navy:* (avion *m*, bâtiment *m*, sous-marin *m*) chasseur *m* de sous-marins; **h.-k. operation,** opération aéronavale ayant pour objet la destruction des sous-marins ennemis.
hunting[1] ['hʌntiŋ], *a.* **h. man,** fervent *m* de la chasse à courre; grand chasseur.
hunting[2], *s.* **1.** (*a*) chasse *f* (à courre); poursuite *f* (du gibier); **fox h.,** chasse au renard; chasse à courre; **h. lodge, box,** pavillon *m* de chasse; maison *f*, rendez-vous *m*, de chasse; **h. crop,** stick *m* de chasse; **h. horn,** cor *m* de chasse; **h. song,** (air *m* de) chasse; **h. ground, field,** terrain *m* de chasse; **the Happy H. Grounds,** le Paradis des Peaux-Rouges; **in the h. field,** à la chasse; **h. coat, knife,** habit *m*, couteau *m*, de chasse; **h. belt,** ceinture cartouchière; **h. cries,** cris *mpl* de chasse; **h. terms,** termes *m* de vénerie; (*b*) **house h.,** recherche *f* d'une maison, d'un logement, *F:* la chasse au logement; **bargain h.,** la chasse aux soldes; *F:* **husband h.,** la chasse au mari; **a happy h. ground for collectors,** un paradis pour les collectionneurs. **2. (science of) h.,** vénerie *f*. **3.** *I.C.E:* irrégularité *f* de marche au ralenti (due à un mélange trop riche); *Mch:* mouvement *m* de galop (de locomotive); *Magn:* affolement *m* (de l'aiguille aimantée); *W.Tel: Cin:* pulsation *f* du son.
huntress ['hʌntris], *s.f.* chasseuse; *Poet:* chasseresse; **Diana the H.,** Diane chasseresse.
huntsman, *pl.* **-men** ['hʌntsmən], *s.m.* **1.** chasseur (à courre). **2.** veneur, piqueur.
huntsmanship ['hʌntsmənʃip], *s.* **1.** l'art *m* de la vénerie. **2.** adresse *f* à la chasse; talents *mpl* de chasseur.
hunt's-up ['hʌntsʌp], *s. Ven: A:* aubade *f*.
hunt-the-slipper ['hʌntðə'slipər], *s. Games:* jeu *m* du furet.
hup [hʌp], *int.* (*to a horse*) hue!
hurdle[1] ['hə:dl], *s.* **1.** (*a*) *Agr:* claie *f*, clôture *f*; (*b*) *Fort:* ouvrage *m* à claire-voie; (*c*) *Sp:* barrière *f*, obstacle *m*, barrage *m*; *Turf:* haie *f*; **h. race, the hurdles,** course *f* d'obstacles; *Equit:* course de haies; (*d*) *A:* claie de supplice; **to be drawn on a h.,** être traîné sur la claie. **2.** (*for sorting, drying, fruit, etc.*) claie, clayon *m*.
hurdle[2], *v.tr.* **1.** garnir, entourer, (qch.) de claies; **to h. off the ground,** entourer le terrain de claies. **2.** *Sp:* (*a*) sauter (un obstacle); (*b*) *v.i.* courir une course d'obstacles; courir une course de haies.
hurdler ['hə:dlər], *s.* **1.** fabricant *m* de claies. **2.** *Sp:* sauteur *m* d'obstacles, de barrière; *Turf:* (i) jockey *m*, (ii) cheval *m*, de courses de haies.
hurdling ['hə:dliŋ], *s. Sp:* saut *m* d'obstacles, de barrières, *Turf:* de haies.
hurdy-gurdy ['hə:digə:di], *s.* **1.** (*a*) *A:* vielle *f*; **h.-g. grinder,** vielleur, -euse; (*b*) *Hyd.E: U.S:* **h.-g. wheel,** roue *f* Pelton. **2.** *F:* orgue *m* de Barbarie.
hurl[1] [hə:l], *s.* **1.** lancée *f*, lancement *m*; *esp. U.S:* **a h. of angry water,** un torrent impétueux d'eau. **2.** *Sp:* crosse *f* de *hurling*.
hurl[2], *v.*
I. *v.tr. & i.* **1.** *v.tr.* lancer (qch.) avec force, avec violence (**at,** contre); **to h. stones at s.o.,** lancer une grêle de pierres à qn; **the explosion hurled them far and wide,** l'explosion les a projetés au loin, de tous côtés; **to h. oneself at sth., at s.o.,** se ruer sur qch., sur qn; **to h. oneself into the fray,** se jeter à corps perdu dans la mêlée; **hurled into the chasm,** précipité dans le gouffre, dans l'abîme; **to h. sarcasm, reproaches, at s.o.,** lancer des sarcasmes, des reproches, à qn; cribler, accabler, darder, qn de sarcasmes, de reproches; *F:* flanquer des reproches à qn; jeter des reproches à la tête de qn; **to h. abuse,** vociférer, cracher, des injures. **2.** *v.i. Sp:* jouer au *hurling*.
II. (*compound verbs*) **1. hurl back,** *v.tr.* refouler, repousser, rejeter (l'ennemi, etc.); rétorquer (une accusation).
2. hurl down, *v.tr.* précipiter; jeter bas.
hurler ['hə:lər], *s.* **1.** lanceur, -euse. **2.** *Sp:* joueur, -euse, de *hurling*.
hurley ['hə:li], *s. Sp:* = HURLING 2.
hurling, *s.* **1.** lancée *f*, lancement *m* (d'un projectile); jet *m* (d'une pierre, etc.); lancement (d'injures). **2.** *Sp:* (*a*) (*Cornwall*) forme primitive du football; (*b*) (*Ireland*) variété de jeu de hockey.
hurly-burly ['hə:libə:li], *s.* brouhaha *m*, tintamarre *m*, charivari *m*, tohu-bohu *m*; **to be out of the h.-b.,** se trouver loin de la vie trépidante de la ville; être à la campagne, en villégiature.
Huron ['hjuərən], *Ethn:* (*a*) *a.* huron; (*b*) *s.* Huron, onne.
Huronian [hju'rouniən], *a. Geol:* huronien.
hurrah[1] [hu'rɑ:], **hurray**[1] [hu'rei], *int. & s.* hourra (*m*); **h. for the Prince!** vive le prince! **h. for the holidays!** vive(nt) les vacances!
hurrah[2], **hurray**[2]. **1.** *v.i.* pousser un hourra, des hourras. **2.** *v.tr.* acclamer (qn) par des hourras.
hurricane ['hʌrikən, -kein], *s.* (*a*) *Meteor:* ouragan *m*; (*in W. Indies*) hurricane *m*; **it was blowing a h.,** le vent soufflait en ouragan; **h. lamp, lantern,** lampe-tempête *f*, lanterne-tempête *f*, *pl.* lampes-, lanternes-tempête; (*b*) *Orn:* **h. bird,** frégate *f*; (*c*) **the noise rose to a h.,** le bruit a atteint le volume d'un ouragan; **a h. of abuse,** une tornade d'injures.
hurried ['hʌrid], *a.* **1.** (pas) pressé, précipité; (ouvrage) fait à la hâte; hâtif; (mot) écrit à la hâte; **a few h. words,** quelques paroles dites à la hâte; **h. reading is unprofitable,** une lecture trop hâtive ne profite point; **to take a h. lunch,** expédier, dépêcher, son déjeuner. **2. I was h. when I wrote that letter,** j'étais très pressé, un peu bousculé, au moment où j'ai écrit cette lettre; je n'ai pas écrit à tête reposée; **on Mondays I'm always h.,** le lundi c'est toujours une bousculade.
hurriedly ['hʌridli], *adv.* à la hâte, en toute hâte; précipitamment; vivement.
hurriedness ['hʌridnis], *s.* précipitation *f* (des préparatifs, etc.).
hurry[1] ['hʌri], *s.* **1.** hâte *f*, précipitation *f*; **to write in a h.,** écrire à la hâte; **to go out in a h.,** sortir à la hâte, en courant; **to be always in a h.,** être toujours pressé, *F:* avoir le feu au derrière; **to be in too great a h. to make money,** avoir trop hâte, être trop pressé, de gagner de l'argent; **don't do anything in a h.,** ne faites rien qu'à tête reposée; **in my h. I forgot it,** dans ma précipitation je l'ai oublié; **to be in no h.,** ne pas être pressé; avoir le temps; *F:* **what's your h.?** qu'est-ce qui vous presse? **what a h. you are in!** (i) comme vous êtes pressé! (ii) comme vous êtes impatient! **is there any h.?** est-ce pressé? est-ce que cela presse? **there's no (special) h.,** rien ne presse; il n'y a rien qui presse; *F:* le feu n'est pas à la maison; la foire n'est pas sur le pont; **you won't see him again in a h.,** vous ne le reverrez pas de sitôt; **I shan't do it again in a h.,** on ne m'y reprendra pas de sitôt; **you won't beat that in a h.!** faites donc mieux que ça! **2.** empressement *m*; **he was in no h. to leave,** il était peu empressé de partir.
hurry[2], *v.*
I. *v.tr. & i.* **1.** *v.tr.* (*a*) hâter, presser (qn); **don't h. me,** ne me pressez pas; ne me bousculez pas; **to h. oneself,** se hâter, se dépêcher; se presser; faire diligence; (*b*) hâter, activer, presser (le travail); **work that cannot be hurried,** travail qui demande du temps, qu'il faut faire à tête reposée; *Th:* **to h. the ending,** brusquer le dénouement; (*c*) **to h. s.o. to a place,** entraîner qn en toute hâte vers un endroit; **troops were hurried to the spot,** on amena au plus vite des troupes sur les lieux; **to h. s.o. into a car,** faire monter qn en voiture en toute hâte, en le bousculant; **to h. s.o. into doing sth.,** entraîner qn à faire qch. sans lui donner le temps de réfléchir. **2.** *v.i.* (*a*) se hâter, se presser; se dépêcher; **to h. through one's lunch,** expédier son déjeuner; **don't h.,** ne vous pressez pas; **to h. over a job, etc.,** expédier, dépêcher, un ouvrage, etc.; **not to h. over sth.,** prendre son temps pour faire qch.; **there's no need to h.,** on a tout son temps; (*b*) presser le pas; **she hurried home,** elle s'est dépêchée de rentrer; **to h. into, out of, a room,** entrer dans une pièce, sortir d'une pièce, en toute hâte; **people were hurrying to get on the bus,** on se pressait pour monter dans l'autobus; **to h. after s.o.,** courir après qn, se hâter de suivre qn; **to h. up to s.o.,** accourir, se précipiter, vers qn; **to h. up, down, the stairs, upstairs, downstairs,** monter, descendre, l'escalier en toute hâte; (*c*) **to h. into one's clothes,** s'habiller en toute hâte.
II. (*compound verbs*) **1. hurry along.** (*a*) *v.tr.* entraîner (qn) précipitamment; (*b*) *v.i.* marcher d'un pas pressé; (*to moving crowd*) **h. along now!** dépêchez-vous!
2. hurry away. (*a*) *v.tr.* emmener, entraîner, (qn) précipitamment; (*b*) *v.i.* s'en aller bien vite, partir précipitamment; **I must h. away,** il faut que je me sauve.
3. hurry back. (*a*) *v.tr.* faire revenir, faire rentrer, (qn) en toute hâte; (*b*) *v.i.* revenir, retourner, bien vite, à la hâte; se presser de revenir.
4. hurry down. (*a*) *v.tr.* faire descendre (qn) à la hâte; (*b*) *v.i.* descendre en courant, précipitamment, à toute vitesse; se presser de descendre.
5. hurry forward, *v.i.* s'avancer vivement, en toute hâte.
6. hurry in, *v.i.* entrer précipitamment, en toute hâte.
7. hurry off, *v.i.* partir précipitamment, en toute hâte.
8. hurry on. (*a*) *v.tr.* faire hâter le pas à (qn); pousser (qn) en avant; pousser (la besogne); avancer (un travail); précipiter (une affaire); activer (une commande); accélérer (la livraison d'un article); presser (le départ de qn); **to be hurried on by the police,** (i) être talonné par la police; (ii) être entraîné par la police; (*b*) *v.i.* presser le pas; continuer sa route à vive allure.
9. hurry out. (*a*) *v.tr.* entraîner vivement (qn) dehors; (*b*) *v.i.* sortir vivement, précipitamment, avec précipitation, à la hâte, en toute hâte; se presser, se hâter, de sortir.
10. hurry up. (*a*) *v.tr.* faire avancer en toute hâte (des renforts, etc.); (*b*) *v.i.* (i) monter précipitamment; se presser de monter; arriver précipitamment, en toute hâte; (ii) se dépêcher, se hâter; hâter, presser, le pas; **now then, h. up!** allons, dépêchez-vous! plus vite que ça! pressez-vous un peu!
hurry-scurry[1], **-skurry** ['hʌri'skʌri]. **1.** *adv.* pêle-mêle, en désordre; (s'enfuir) à la débandade. **2.** *s.* confusion *f*, désordre *m*, bousculade *f*.
hurry-scurry[2], *v.i.* faire les choses à la hâte; courir en désordre, à la débandade.
hurst [hə:st], *s.* **1.** colline sablonneuse. **2.** (*a*) bouquet *m* d'arbres; bosquet *m*; (*b*) butte boisée. **3.** banc *m* de sable (formant gué).
hurt[1] [hə:t], *s.* mal *m*. **1.** blessure *f*; *O:* **to do s.o. (a) h.,** faire du mal à qn; blesser qn; *Mil: Navy:* **h. certificate,** certificat médical; certificat d'origine de blessure. **2.** tort *m*, détriment *m*, préjudice *m*, dommage *m*; **what h. can it do you?** quel tort cela peut-il vous faire? en quoi cela peut-il vous nuire? **3.** *Her:* tourteau *m* d'azur.
hurt[2], *v.tr.* (**hurt; hurt**) **1.** faire (du) mal à, blesser (qn); **to h. oneself,** se faire (du) mal; **to h. one's foot,** se blesser au pied; **his foot was permanently h. by his fall,** il est resté boiteux, estropié, de cette chute; **to get h.,** (i) être blessé; recevoir une blessure; (ii) (*at the hands of a criminal, etc.*) recevoir un mauvais coup; (iii) se faire du mal; **take care you don't get h.,** prenez garde (i) de vous blesser, (ii) de vous faire blesser; **my wound hurts (me),** ma blessure me fait mal; ma blessure cuit; **that hurts,** ça fait mal; **that doesn't h.,** cela ne fait pas mal. **2.** faire de la peine à (qn); **to h. s.o.'s feelings,** blesser, froisser, peiner, qn; offenser qn; mortifier qn; **her coldness h. me,** sa froideur m'a blessé, m'a froissé;

nothing hurts like the truth, il n'y a que la vérité qui offense; **the thing that hurts him most,** la chose qui lui tient au cœur. 3. (*to injure*) (*of things*) nuire à, gâter, abîmer, endommager (qch.); **too much water hurts plants,** trop d'eau nuit aux plantes; **to h. s.o.'s interests,** léser les intérêts de qn; léser qn; nuire aux intérêts de qn; (*with passive force*) **this material doesn't h. if it gets wet,** ce tissu ne s'abîme pas à être mouillé.

hurter ['hə:tər], *s.* 1. *Rail: etc:* heurtoir *m* (de voie en cul-de-sac). 2. *Veh:* heurtequin *m* (d'essieu).

hurtful ['hə:tf(u)l], *a.* 1. (*a*) nuisible, nocif; pernicieux; (*b*) préjudiciable (**to,** à); **it is h. to my interests,** cela porte atteinte à mes intérêts; cela lèse mes intérêts; **h. rumours,** bruits *m* préjudiciables. 2. **h. to the feelings,** froissant, blessant; **there is nothing so h. as ingratitude,** il n'y a rien qui blesse comme l'ingratitude.

hurtfully ['hə:tfuli], *adv.* 1. d'une manière nuisible, pernicieuse, préjudiciable. 2. d'une manière mortifiante, blessante.

hurtfulness ['hə:tf(u)lnis], *s.* nature nuisible, pernicieuse (de qch.); nocivité *f*.

hurtle ['hə:tl]. 1. *v.tr.* (*a*) heurter, faire choquer; (*b*) **to h. (down) rocks on the enemy,** lancer, faire dévaler, des rochers sur l'ennemi. 2. *v.i.* (*a*) se précipiter, s'élancer (avec bruit, comme un bolide); (*of car, etc.*) **to h. along,** dévorer la route; **to h. into sth.,** entrer en collision avec qch.; (*b*) **the rocks hurtled down,** les rochers dévalaient avec fracas; **the shells hurtled through the air,** les obus passaient en trombe.

hurtleberry ['hə:tlb(ə)ri], *s. Bot: A:* airelle *f* myrtille.

hurtling ['hə:tliŋ], *a.* bruyant, retentissant; qui passe, tombe, avec fracas.

husband[1] ['hʌzbənd], *s.* 1. mari *m*, époux *m*; **h. and wife,** les (deux) époux, les conjoints *m*; **to live as h. and wife,** vivre maritalement; *Jur:* **husband's authorization,** autorisation maritale; *F: O:* **husband's tea,** thé bon pour le mari (qui arrive toujours en retard); les rinçures *f* de la théière. 2. *A:* **a good h. of his money,** un bon administrateur de sa fortune; *Nau: A:* **ship's h.,** (i) gérant *m* (à bord); (ii) capitaine *m* d'armement; agent *m* d'affaires d'un navire.

husband[2], *v.tr.* 1. *O:* cultiver (la terre, etc.). 2. ménager, épargner, économiser (ses ressources, son argent, ses forces); bien gouverner (ses ressources). 3. *A: Hum:* marier, trouver un mari pour (une femme).

husbanding ['hʌzbəndiŋ], *s.* 1. *O:* culture *f* (de la terre). 2. ménagement *m* (de ses ressources, etc.).

husbandman, *pl.* **-men** ['hʌzbən(d)mən], *s.m. O:* 1. cultivateur, agriculteur. 2. laboureur.

husbandry ['hʌzbəndri], *s.* 1. agronomie *f*, industrie *f* agricole, économie rurale, agriculture *f*; **animal h.,** l'élevage *m*. 2. (*a*) **good h.,** bonne gestion; sage administration *f* (de son bien); **bad h.,** gaspillage *m*, maladministration *f*; (*b*) économie, frugalité *f*.

hush[1] [hʌʃ], *s.* 1. silence *m*, calme *m*; **the h. of the night,** le silence de la nuit; **the h. before the storm,** l'accalmie *f*, le calme, avant la tempête. 2. **h. money,** argent donné à qn pour acheter son silence; prime *f* au silence; prix *m* du silence (de qn), pot-de-vin *m*.

hush[2], *v.*

I. *v.tr. & i.* 1. *v.tr.* (*a*) calmer, faire taire (un enfant, les vents); imposer silence à (qn); apaiser (un enfant); **all nature is hushed,** toute la nature se tait; (*b*) étouffer (un bruit); **hushed conversation,** conversation étouffée, discrète; chuchotements *mpl*. 2. *v.i.* se taire, faire silence.

II. (*compound verb*) **hush up,** *v.tr.* étouffer (un scandale, etc.).

hush[3], *int.* chut! silence! du silence! **to say h.,** chuter.

hushaby(e) ['hʌʃəbai], *int.* **h. baby!** fais dodo, mon bébé.

hush-hush ['hʌʃhʌʃ], *F:* 1. *a.* archi-secret, -ète; **the latest type of h.-h. deterrent,** la plus récente des armes de dissuasion secrètes; **h.-h. assignment,** mission secrète. 2. *s.* politique *f* de silence.

hushing up ['hʌʃiŋʌp], *s.* étouffement *m* (d'un scandale, etc.).

husk[1] [hʌsk], *s.* cosse *f*, gousse *f* (de pois, etc.); pelure *f* (d'oignon, de fève de cacao); brou *m*, écale *f* (de noix); hérisson *m*, bogue *f* (de châtaigne); coque *f* (de grain de café); tégument *m*, pellicule *f*, écalure *f*, balle *f* (de grain); enveloppe *f* (de l'épi du maïs); **rice in the h.,** riz non décortiqué; *Husb:* **husks,** vannure *f*.

husk[2], *v.tr.* décortiquer; écosser (des pois); ébrouer, écaler, cerner (des noix); écorcer, perler, monder (le riz, l'orge); éplucher (le maïs); vanner (le grain).

husk[3], *s. Vet:* bronchite vermineuse (du bétail).

husked ['hʌskt], *a.* 1. *Bot: A:* cossu; à cosse. 2. écossé, mondé; (maïs) épluché; **h. barley,** orge mondé.

huskily ['hʌskili], *adv.* (parler) d'une voix enrouée (par la fatigue), d'une voix altérée, voilée (par l'émotion, par la colère).

huskiness ['hʌskinis], *s.* enrouement *m*, raucité *f* (de la voix, d'un son); empâtement *m* (de la voix).

husking ['hʌskiŋ], *s.* 1. décorticage *m*; écorçage *m* (du riz); épluchage *m* (du maïs). 2. *U.S:* réunion *f*, veillée *f*, pour l'épluchage du maïs.

husky[1] ['hʌski], *a.* 1. (pois, etc.) cossu. 2. **h. voice,** (i) voix enrouée, voilée; (*of drunkard*) voix de rogomme; (ii) voix altérée (par l'émotion). 3. *a. & s. F:* (homme) fort, costaud.

husky[2], *s.* 1. chien *m* esquimau, chien de traîneau. 2. (*a*) *Ethn:* **a H.,** un, une, Esquimau; (*b*) *Ling:* esquimau *m*.

huso ['hju:sou], *s. Ich:* huso *m*.

huss [hʌs], *s. Ich: Dial: Com:* chien *m* de mer; cagnot *m*, roussette *f*; squale *m*.

hussar [hu'zɑ:r], *s. Mil:* hussard *m*; *Hist:* **the Black Hussars,** les Hussards de la Mort.

Hussite ['hʌsait], *s. Rel.H:* hussite *m*.

hussy ['hʌzi], *s.f. F: A:* 1. coquine, friponne, mâtine, péronelle *f*; **you little h.!** petite effrontée, petite coquine! **sly h.,** fine lame. 2. drôlesse, garce.

hustings ['hʌstiŋz], *s.pl. A.Pol:* 1. estrade *f*, tribune *f* (où étaient nommés les candidats d'une élection politique et d'où ceux-ci haranguaient la foule). 2. élection *f*; **to mount the h.,** se présenter aux élections (pour la Chambre des Communes).

hustle[1] ['hʌsl], *s.* 1. bousculade *f*. 2. hâte *f*, promptitude *f*, activité *f* énergique; *F:* **to get a h. on,** se dépêcher.

hustle[2]. 1. *v.tr.* (*a*) bousculer, pousser, presser (qn); **to h. one another,** se bousculer; **to be hustled out of the way,** être repoussé vivement pour déblayer le chemin; être relégué vivement dans un coin; **to h. s.o.,** bousculer qn; (*c*) **to h. things on,** pousser le travail; *F:* mener les choses tambour battant; (*b*) **to h. s.o. into a decision,** forcer qn à se décider sans lui donner le temps de respirer; **I won't be hustled,** je ne veux pas qu'on me bouscule; on ne me fera pas agir sans réflexion; (*c*) (*of pickpocket*) bousculer (qn); voler (qn) à l'esbroufe. 2. *v.i.* (*a*) se dépêcher, se presser; **we must h. a bit,** il faut nous dépêcher un peu, que ça ronfle; (*b*) **to h. against s.o.,** bousculer qn; (*c*) **to h. through the crowd,** se frayer un passage, jouer des coudes pour passer, à travers la foule.

hustler ['hʌslər], *s.* 1. (*a*) bousculeur, -euse; (*b*) esbroufeur *m*. 2. débrouillard *m*, homme expéditif, homme d'expédition; brasseur *m*, remueur *m*, d'affaires; abatteur *m*, bâcleur *m*, de besogne; **you're a bit of a h.,** vous allez vite en besogne; vous ne traînez pas en affaires.

hustling ['hʌsliŋ], *s.* 1. = HUSTLE[1]. 2. vol *m* à l'esbroufe.

hut[1] [hʌt], *s.* hutte *f*, cabane *f*, cassine *f*; baraquement *m*; *Mil:* **Y.M.C.A. h.,** foyer *m* du soldat (sous les auspices de la *Young Men's Christian Association*); **Alpine h.,** chalet-refuge *m*, *pl.* chalets-refuges; **h. builder,** constructeur *m* de baraques; *Archeol:* **h. circle,** trace *f* d'habitation circulaire.

hut[2], *v.* **(hutted)** 1. *v.tr. Mil:* baraquer (des troupes). 2. *v.i.* (se) baraquer; loger dans des baraquements.

hutch [hʌtʃ], *s.* 1. (*a*) coffre *m*, huche *f*; (*b*) *NAm:* dressoir *m*, étagère *f*. 2. (*a*) **(rabbit) h.,** clapier *m*, lapinière *f*; cage *f*, cabane *f*, à lapins; (*b*) *F:* petite cabane, logis étroit. 3. *Tchn:* (*a*) **(baker's) h.,** pétrin *m*, huche *f*, maie *f*; (*b*) *Min:* benne (roulante); berline *f*; wagon *m* à minerai; wagonnet *m*; **h. runner,** traîneur *m* de wagonnets.

hutia ['hju:tiə], *s. Z:* capromys *m*, hutia *m*; **h. conga,** pilori *m* de Cuba.

hutments ['hʌtmənts], *s.pl.* baraquements *m*; camp *m* de baraques; baraques *f*; **temporary h.,** baraquements provisoires.

huzza[1] [hʌ'zɑ:, hu'zɑ:], *int. & s.* hourra (*m*), vivat (*m*).

huzza[2]. 1. *v.i.* crier hourra, vivat; pousser des hourras. 2. *v.tr.* acclamer, applaudir (qn); saluer (qn) de vivats.

hyacinth ['haiəsinθ], *s.* 1. *Miner:* hyacinthe *f*. 2. *Bot:* jacinthe *f*; **wood, wild, h.,** jacinthe des bois; **water h.,** eichornia *m*; *Hort:* **Roman h.,** jacinthe romaine; **Cape h., Peruvian h.,** jacinthe, scille *f*, du Pérou; **grape h.,** muscari *m*. 3. *a. & s.* (*colour*) (*a*) *occ.* rouge orangé *inv* (de l'hyacinthe); (*b*) bleu jacinthe *inv*, bleu violet *inv*.

hyacinthine [haiə'sinθain], *a.* 1. beau comme Hyacinthe. 3. bleu jacinthe *inv*.

Hyacinthus [haiə'sinθəs], *Pr.n.m. Myth:* Hyacinthe.

Hyades (the) [ðə'haiədi:z], *Pr.n.pl. Astr: Myth:* les Hyades *f*.

hyaena [hai'i:nə], *s.* = HYENA.

hyaenarctos [haii'nɑ:ktəs], *s. Paleont:* hyænarctos *m*.

Hyaenidae [hai'i:nidi:], *s.pl. Z:* hyénidés *m*.

hyaenodon [hai'i:nədɔn], *s. Paleont:* hyænodon *m*.

Hyaenodontidae [haii:nə'dɔntidi:], *s.pl. Paleont:* hyænodontidés *m*.

hyaline ['haiəlin]. 1. *a. Anat: Biol: Miner:* hyalin, transparent, diaphane. 2. *s. Poet:* (*a*) mer *f* de cristal; (*b*) ciel pur.

hyalite ['haiəlait], *s. Miner:* hyalite *f*.

hyalithe ['haiəliθ], *s. Glassm:* hyalite *f*.

hyalogen [hai'ælədʒ(ə)n], *s. Ch:* hyalogène *m*.

hyaloid ['haiəlɔid]. *Anat: etc:* 1. *a.* (*a*) (membrane, etc.) hyaloïde; (*b*) (*of artery, canal*) hyaloïdien. 2. *s.* membrane *f* hyaloïde; membrane du corps vitré.

hyalonema [haiəlou'ni:mə], *s. Spong:* hyalonème *f*.

hyalophane [hai'æləfein], *s. Miner:* hyalophane *f*.

hyaloplasm(a) [hai'ælouplæzm, haiælou'plæzmə], *s. Biol:* hyaloplasme *m*.

hyalosiderite [haiælou'sidərait], *s. Miner:* hyalosidérite *f*.

Hyalospongiae [haiælou'spɔndʒii:], *s.pl. Spong:* hexactinellidés *m*.

hyalotekite [haiælou'ti:kait], *s. Miner:* hyalotékite *f*.

hyaluronic [haiælju'rɔnik], *a. Bio-Ch:* = **h. acid,** acide *m* hyaluronique.

hyaluronidase [haiəlju'rɔnideis], *s. Biol:* hyaluronidase *f*.

Hyblaean [hi'bli:ən], *a. A.Geog:* hybléen.

hybrid ['haibrid]. *Biol: Hort: Ling: etc:* 1. *s.* (*a*) hybride *m*; **single-cross h.,** hybride simple; (*b*) (*of pers.*) métis, -isse. 2. *a.* (*a*) hybride; *Hort:* **h. variety,** variété hybride, adultérine; **h. plant,** plante hybride, métisse; **h. character,** hybridité *f* (d'un mot, etc.); *Bio-Ch:* **h. orbit(al),** orbitale *f* hybride; (*b*) hétérogène.

hybridism ['haibridizm], *s.* hybridisme *m*.

hybridity [hai'briditi], *s.* hybridité *f*.

hybridization [haibridai'zeiʃ(ə)n], *s. Biol:* hybridation *f*; *Bio-Ch:* **nuclear h.,** hybridation cellulaire.

hybridize ['haibrida:iz]. 1. *v.tr.* hybrider. 2. *v.i.* s'hybrider.

hydantoic [haidæn'touik], *a. Ch:* **h. acid,** acide *m* hydantoïque.

hydantoin [hai'dæntəwin], *s. Ch:* hydantoïne *f*.

hydatic [hai'dætik], *a. Med:* hydatique.

hydatid ['haidətid], *s. Med:* 1. kyste *m* hydatique. 2. hydatide *f*; *Vet: F:* ver-coquin *m*, *pl.* vers-coquins.

hydatidocele [haidə'tidousi:l], *s. Med:* hydatidocèle *f*.

hydatism ['haidətizm], *s. Med:* hydatisme *m*.

hydnum ['hidnəm], *s. Fung:* hydne *m*.

hydra ['haidrə], *s.* 1. (*a*) *Gr.Myth:* Hydre *f* (de Lerne); **h.-headed,** à têtes d'hydre, à sept têtes; **the h. of anarchy,** l'hydre de l'anarchie; (*b*) *Her:* hydre; **argent, a h. vert,** d'argent à une hydre de sinople. 2. *Astr:* l'Hydre (femelle). 3. *Coel:* (*pl.* **hydrae** ['haidri]) hydre.

hydrachnid [hai'dræknid], *s. Arach:* hydrachne *f*.

Hydrachnidae [hai'dræknidi:], *s.pl. Arach:* hydrachnidés *m*.

hydracid [hai'dræsid], *s. Ch:* hydracide *m*.

hydraemia [hai'dri:miə], *s. Med:* hydrémie *f*.

hydragogue ['haidrəgɔg], *a. & s. Med:* hydragogue (*m*).

hydramnion [hai'dræmniɔn], **hydramnios** [hai'dræmniɔs], *s. Med:* hydramnios *m*.

hydrangea [hai'dreindʒə], *s. Bot:* hortensia *m*, hydrangée *f*, hydrangea *f*, hydrangelle *f*.

Hydrangeaceae [haidrein'dʒeisii:], *s.pl. Bot:* hydrangées *f*.

hydrant ['haidrənt], *s.* prise *f* d'eau; bouche *f* d'eau; *esp.* **fire h.,** bouche d'incendie; *Fr.C:* borne-fontaine *f*; *Th:* grand secours.

hydranth ['haidrænθ], *s. Coel:* hydrante *m*.

hydrargillite [haidrɑ:dʒilait], *s. Miner:* hydrargillite *f*.

hydrargyric [haidrɑ:rdʒirik], *a. Pharm:* (onguent) hydrargyrique, mercuriel.

hydrarthrosis [haidrɑ:'θrousis], *s. Med:* hydarthrose *f*.

hydrastine [hai'dræsti:n], *s. Pharm:* hydrastine *f*.

hydratable [hai'dreitəbl], *a.* hydratable.

hydrate[1] ['haidreit], *s. Ch:* hydrate *m*; **h. of lime, calcium h.,** chaux hydratée, hydrate de chaux.

hydrate[2], *v.tr. Ch:* hydrater; **to become hydrated,** *v.i.* **to h.,** s'hydrater.

hydration [hai'dreiʃ(ə)n], *s. Ch:* hydratation *f*.

hydraulic [hai'drɔ:lik], *a.* 1. (force *f*, frein *m*, ascenseur *m*, turbine *f*, roue *f*, commande *f*, vérin *m*, circuit *m*, etc.) hydraulique; **h. engineer** = HYDRAULICIAN; **h. engineering,** hydraulique *f*, technique *f* hydraulique; travaux *m* hydrauliques. 2. *Const:* (ciment, chaux, mortier) hydraulique.

hydraulically [hai'drɔ:lik(ə)li], *adv.* 1. hydrauliquement; **h. controlled, h. operated,** à commande hydraulique; commandé, fonctionnant, hydrauliquement; **h. driven,** actionné, mû, hydrauliquement. 2. **h. speaking,** en termes d'hydraulique.

hydraulician [haidrɔ:'liʃ(ə)n], *s.* hydraulicien *m*; ingénieur *m* en hydraulique.

hydraulicity [haidrɔ:'lisiti], *s. Const:* hydraulicité *f*.

hydraulics [hai'drɔ:liks], *s.pl.* (*usu. with sg. const.*) hydraulique *f*, hydromécanique *f*.

hydrazide ['haidrəzaid], *s. Ch:* hydrazide *f.*
hydrazine ['haidrəzain], *s. Ch:* hydrazine *f.*
hydrazoate [haidrə'zoueit], *s. Ch:* azoture *m.*
hydrazoic [haidrə'zouik], *a. Ch:* azothydrique.
hydrazone ['haidrəzoun], *s. Ch:* hydrazone *f.*
hydrazotoluene [haidrəzou'tɔljui:n], *s.* hydrazotoluène *m.*
hydria ['haidriə, 'hidriə], *s. Gr.Ant:* hydrie *f.*
hydric ['haidrik], *a. Ch:* -hydrique; **h. chloride,** acide *m* chlorhydrique.
hydride ['haidraid], *s. Ch:* hydrure *m.*
hydrindene [hai'drindi:n], *s. Ch:* hydrindène *f,* indane *f.*
hydriodic [haidri'ɔdik], *a. Ch:* iodhydrique.
hydriodide [hai'draiədaid], *s. Ch:* iodhydrate *m.*
Hydriote ['haidriət]. *Geog:* **1.** hydriote; de l'île d'Hydra. **2.** *s.* Hydriote *mf.*
hydro[1] ['haidrou], *s.* établissement *m* hydrothérapique.
hydro[2], *s. Can:* (hydro-)électricité *f.*
hydro- ['haidrou], *comb.fm.* **1.** hydro-. **2.** *Ch:* -hydrique; -hydrate.
hydroa [hai'drouə], *s. Med:* hydroa *m.*
hydroaeric [haidrou'ɛərik], *a. Med:* hydroaérique.
hydro-aeroplane [haidrou'ɛərəplein], *s. A:* hydravion *m,* hydroaéroplane *m.*
hydroaromatic [haidrouærə'mætik], *a. Ch:* hydroaromatique.
Hydrobatidae [haidrou'bætidi:], *s.pl. Orn:* hydrobatidés *m,* les oiseaux-tempête *m.*
hydrobromic [haidrou'broumik], *a. Ch:* (acide *m*) bromhydrique.
hydrobromide [haidrou'broumaid], *s. Ch:* bromhydrate *m.*
hydrocarbide [haidrou'kɑ:baid], *s. Ch:* carbure *m* d'hydrogène.
hydrocarbon [haidrou'kɑ:bən], *s. Ch:* hydrocarbure *m;* carbure *m* d'hydrogène; **benzene hydrocarbons,** hydrocarbones *m* benzéniques; **a h.(-containing) mixture,** un mélange carburant.
hydrocarbonate [haidrou'kɑ:bəneit], *s. Ch:* hydrocarbonate *m.*
hydrocarbonic [haidroukɑ:'bɔnik], *a. Ch:* hydrocarboné.
hydrocele ['haidrousi:l], *s. Med:* hydrocèle *f.*
hydrocellulose [haidrou'seljulouz], *s. Ch:* hydrocellulose *f.*
hydrocephalic [haidrouse'fælik], *a. & s.,* **hydrocephalous** [haidrou'sefələs], *a. Med:* hydrocéphale (*mf*).
hydrocephalus [haidrou'sefələs], **hydrocephaly** [haidrou'sefəli], *s. Med:* hydrocéphalie *f.*
hydroceramic [haidrousə'ræmik], *a. Cer:* hydrocéramique; **h. vessel,** hydrocérame *m.*
hydrocerus(s)ite [haidrousə'rʌsait], *s. Miner:* hydrocérusite *f.*
Hydrocharitaceae [haidroukæri'teisii:], *s. Bot:* hydrocharidacées *f.*
hydrochloric [haidrou'klɔ(:)rik], *a. Ch:* (acide *m*) chlorhydrique.
hydrochloride [haidrou'klɔ(:)raid], *s. Ch:* chlorhydrate *m.*
Hydrochoeridae [haidrou'kiəridi:], *s.pl. Z:* hydrochœridés *m.*
hydrochore ['haidroukɔ:ər], *a. Bot:* hydrochore.
hydrocolloid [haidrou'kɔlɔid], *s. Dent:* hydrocolloïde *m.*
Hydrocorallia [haidroukə'ræliə], **Hydrocorallina** [haidroukɔrə'lainə], **Hydrocorallinae** [haidroukə'rælini:], *s.pl. Coel:* hydrocoralliaires *f.*
hydrocortisone [haidrou'kɔ:tizoun], *s. Physiol: Pharm:* cortisol *m,* hydrocortisone *f.*
hydrocotyle [haidrou'kɔtili], *s. Bot:* hydrocotyle *f; F:* écuelle *f* d'eau.
hydrocyanic [haidrousai'ænik], *a. Ch:* cyanhydrique.
hydrocyon [hai'drɔsiən], *s. Ich:* hydrocyon *m,* chien *m* d'eau, de fleuve.
hydrodesulphurization [haidroudi:sʌlfərai'zeiʃ(ə)n], *s. Petr:* hydrodésulfuration *f.*
hydrodynamic [haidroudai'næmik], *a.* hydrodynamique.
hydrodynamics [haidroudai'næmiks], *s.pl.* (*usu. with sg. const.*) hydrodynamique *f.*
hydroelectric [haidroui'lektrik], *a.* hydro(-)électrique; **h. power,** énergie hydraulique, houille blanche.
hydroelectricity [haidrouilek'trisiti], *s.* hydro(-)électricité *f.*
hydro-extractor [haidrouek'stræktər], *s. Ind:* hydro-extracteur *m, pl.* hydro-extracteurs; toupie *f* mécanique.
hydrofluoric [haidrouflu'ɔrik], *a. Ch:* fluorhydrique.
hydrofoil ['haidroufɔil], *s.* hydrofoil *m.*
hydrogel ['haidroudʒel], *s. Ch: Ph:* hydrogel *m.*
hydrogen ['haidrədʒen], *s. Ch:* hydrogène *m;* **heavy h.,** hydrogène lourd; deutérium *m;* **h. bomb,** bombe *f* à hydrogène, bombe H.
hydrogenate [hai'drɔdʒəneit], **hydrogenize** [hai'drɔdʒənaiz], *v.tr.* hydrogéner; combiner avec l'hydrogène.
hydrogenated [hai'drɔdʒəneitid], **hydrogenized** [hai'drɔdʒənaizd], *a.* (gaz, atome) hydrogéné.
hydrogenation [haidrɔdʒə'neiʃ(ə)n], *s.* hydrogénation *f.*
hydrogenous [hai'drɔdʒənəs], *a.* hydrogénique.
hydrogeology [haidroudʒi:'ɔlədʒi], *s.* hydrogéologie *f.*
hydroglider ['haidrouglaidər], *s. Av:* hydroglisseur *m.*
hydrograph ['haidrougræf], *s.* courbe *f* de débit d'un fleuve.
hydrographer [hai'drɔgrəfər], *s.* (ingénieur *m*) hydrographe *m.*
hydrographic(al) [haidrou'grafik(l)], *a.* hydrographique.
hydrography [hai'drɔgrəfi], *s.* hydrographie *f.*
hydroid ['haidrɔid], *a. & s. Coel:* hydroïde (*m*); *s.pl.* **hydroids,** hydraires *m.*
Hydroida [hai'drɔidə], **Hydroidea** [hai'drɔidiə], *s.pl. Coel:* hydraires *m.*
hydrokinetic [haidroukai'netik], *a.* qui appartient, se rapporte, à la cinétique des liquides.
hydrokinetics [haidroukai'netiks], *s.pl.* (*usu. with sg. const.*) cinétique *f* des liquides.
hydrolaccolith [haidrou'lækəliθ], *s. Geol:* hydrolaccolithe *m.*
hydrolase ['haidrouleis], *s. Bio-Ch:* hydrolase *f.*
hydrolith ['haidrouliθ], *s. Ch:* hydrolithe *f.*
hydrolize ['haidroulaiz], *v.tr.* hydrolyser.
hydrological [haidrə'lɔdʒik(ə)l], *a.* hydrologique.
hydrologist [hai'drɔlədʒist], *s.* hydrologue *mf.*
hydrology [hai'drɔlədʒi], *s.* hydrologie *f;* **ground-water h.,** hydrogénèse *f.*
hydrolysate [hai'drɔliseit], *s.* hydrolysat *m.*
hydrolyse ['haidroulaiz], *v.tr.* hydrolyser.
hydrolysis [hai'drɔlisis], *s. Ch:* hydrolyse *f;* **h. by fermentation,** zymohydrolyse *f.*
hydrolytic [haidrə'litik], *a.* qui appartient, se rapporte, à l'hydrolyse; qui agit par hydrolyse.
hydromagnesite [haidrou'mægnisait], *s. Miner:* hydromagnésite *f,* hydrocarbonate *m* de magnésie.
hydromancy ['haidrəmænsi], *s.* hydromancie *f.*
hydromantes ['haidroumænti:z], *s. Amph:* hydromante *f.*
hydromechanics [haidroumi'kæniks], *s.pl.* (*usu. with sg. const.*) hydromécanique *f.*
hydromedusa [haidroumi'dju:zə], *s. Coel:* hydroméduse *f.*
hydrometallurgy [haidroumi'tælədʒi], *s.* hydrométallurgie *f.*
hydrometeor [haidrou'mi:tiər], *s. Meteor:* hydrométéore *m.*
hydrometer [hai'drɔmitər], *s.* **1.** *Ph: Ind:* densimètre *m;* aréomètre *m;* hydromètre *m;* **Baumé h.,** aréomètre de Baumé; **acid h.,** pèse-acide *m inv,* acidimètre *m;* **h. syringe,** pipette *f* pèse-acide. **2.** *Hyd.E:* hydromètre; moulinet *m.*
hydrometric(al) [haidrou'metrik(l)], *a.* hydrométrique.
hydrometrograph [haidrou'metrougræf], *s. Hyd.E:* hydromètre *m;* moulinet *m.*
hydrometry [hai'drɔmitri], *s. Ph:* hydrométrie *f,* aréométrie *f.*
hydromorphic [haidrou'mɔ:fik], *a. Geol:* hydromorphe.
hydromotor ['haidroumoutər], *s.* hydromoteur *m.*
hydromys ['haidrəmis], *s. Z:* hydromys *m.*
hydronephrosis [haidroune'frousis], *s. Med:* hydronéphrose *f.*
hydronymy [hai'drɔnimi], *s.* hydronymie *f.*
hydropathic [haidrou'pæθik], *Med:* **1.** *a.* (*a*) (établissement *m*) hydrothérapique; (*b*) (médecin *m*) hydropathe. **2.** *s.* établissement *m* hydrothérapique; établissement thermal.
hydropathy [hai'drɔpəθi], *s.* hydropathie *f.*
hydropericardium ['haidrouperi'kɑ:diəm], *s. Med:* hydropéricarde *m.*
hydrophane ['haidroufein], *s. Miner:* hydrophane *f,* œil-du-monde *m, pl.* œils-du monde.
hydrophanous [hai'drɔfənəs], *a.* hydrophane.
Hydrophi(i)dae [hai'drɔfidi:, haidrou'fi:idi:], *s.pl. Rept:* hydrophidés *m,* les serpents marins.
Hydrophilidae [haidrou'filidi:], *s.pl. Ent:* hydrophilides *m.*
hydrophilite [hai'drɔfilait], *s. Miner:* hydrophilite *f.*
hydrophilizing [hai'drɔfilaiziŋ], *s. Tex:* hydrophilisation *f.*
hydrophilous [hai'drɔfiləs], *a.* **1.** *Nat.Hist:* hydrophile. **2.** *Bot:* hydrogame.
hydrophily [hai'drɔfili], *s. Bot:* hydrogamie *f,* pollinisation *f* par l'eau.
hydrophis ['haidrɔfis], *s. Rept:* hydrophis *m.*
hydrophobia [haidrə'foubiə], *s.* **1.** *Med:* hydrophobie *f, F:* la rage. **2.** phobie *f* de l'eau.
hydrophobic [haidrə'foubik], *a.* hydrophobe, hydrophobique; **h. patient,** hydrophobe *mf; Ch:* (*of molecule, etc.*) **h. property,** hydrophobie *f.*
hydrophone ['haidrəfoun], *s.* hydrophone *m.*
Hydrophoria [haidrou'fɔ:riə], *s.pl. Gr.Ant:* hydrophories *f.*
hydrophoric [haidrou'fɔrik], *a.* hydrophore.
hydrophthalmia [haidrɔf'θælmiə], **hydrophthalmos** [haidrɔf'θælmɔs], *s. Med:* hydrophtalmie *f.*
Hydrophyllaceae [haidroufi'leisii:], *s.pl. Bot:* hydrophyllacées *f.*
hydrophyllum [haidrou'filəm], *s. Bot:* hydrophylle *f.*
hydrophyte ['haidroufait], *s. Bot:* hydrophyte *f;* plante *f* d'eau.
hydrophyton [haidrou'faitən], *s. Coel:* hydrophyton *m.*
hydropic [hai'drɔpik], *a. Med:* hydropique.
hydroplane[1] ['haidrəplein], *s.* **1.** *Av:* hydravion *m.* **2.** *Nau:* (*a*) hydroplane *m;* (*b*) hydroglisseur *m.* **3.** *Nau:* barre *f* de plongée.
hydroplane[2], *v.i. Av:* hydroplaner.
hydropneumatic [haidrounju'mætik], *a.* (frein *m*) hydropneumatique.
hydroponic [haidrou'pɔnik], *a.* hydroponique.
hydroponics [haidrou'pɔniks], *s.pl.* culture *f* hydroponique, culture sans sol.
hydropsy ['haidrɔpsi], *s. Med:* hydropisie *f.*
hydropsyche [haidrou'saiki], *s. Ent:* hydropsyché *f.*
hydroquinone [haidroukwi'noun, -'kwainoun], *s. Ch: Phot:* hydroquinone *f.*
hydrorrhea [haidrə'ri:ə], *s. Med:* hydrorrhée *f.*
hydroscope ['haidrouskoup], *s. Opt: Oc:* loupe utilisée pour examiner, étudier, les hauts-fonds.
hydroscopist [hai'drɔskəpist], *s. O:* hydroscope *m.*
hydrosilicate [haidrou'silikeit], *s. Ch:* hydrosilicate *m.*
hydroski ['haidrouski:], *s. Navy:* hydroski *m.*
hydrosol ['haidrousɔl], *s. Ch:* hydrosol *m.*
hydrosome ['haidrousoum], *s. Coel:* hydrosome *m.*
hydrosphere ['haidrousfi:r], *s.* hydrosphère *f.*
hydrospinning ['haidrouspiniŋ], *s.* fluotournage *m,* repoussage *m* au tour.
hydrostat ['haidroustæt], *s.* hydrostat *m.*
hydrostatic(al) [haidrou'stætik(l)], *a.* hydrostatique.
hydrostatics [haidrou'stætiks], *s.pl.* (*usu. with sg. const.*) hydrostatique *f;* **h. engineer,** hydrostaticien *m*
hydrosulphide [haidrou'sʌlfaid], *s. Ch:* sulfhydrate *m,* hydrosulfate *m.*
hydrosulphite [haidrou'sʌlfait], *s. Ch:* hydrosulfite *m.*
hydrosulphurous [haidrou'sʌlfərəs], *a. Ch:* **h. acid,** acide hydrosulfureux.
hydrotalcite [haidrou'tælsait], *s. Miner:* hydrotalcite *f.*
hydrotaxis [haidrou'tæksis], *s.* hydrotaxie *f.*
hydrotechny [haidrou'tekni], *s.* hydrotechnique *f.*
hydrotheca [haidrou'θi:kə], *s. Coel:* hydrothèque *f.*
hydrotherapeutic [haidrouθerə'pju:tik], *a. Med:* hydrothérapique.
hydrotherapeutics ['haidrouθerə'pju:tiks], **hydrotherapy** [haidrou'θerəpi], *s. Med:* hydrothérapie *f.*
hydrotherapist [haidrou'θerəpist], *s.* hydrothérapiste *mf.*
hydrothermal [haidrou'θə:m(ə)l], *a.* hydrothermique; hydrothermal, -aux.
hydrothorax [haidrou'θɔ:ræks], *s. Med:* hydrothorax *m.*
hydrotimetry [haidrou'timitri], *s. Ch:* hydrotimétrie *f.*
hydro-treating ['haidroutri:tiŋ], *s. Petr:* hydrotraitement *m.*
hydrotropism [haidrou'troupizm], *s. Bot:* hydrotropisme *m.*
hydrotype ['haidroutaip], *s. Phot:* hydrotypie *f.*
hydrous ['haidrəs], *a. Ch:* hydrique, hydraté, aqueux.
hydroxamic [haidrɔk'sæmik], *a. Ch:* **h. acid,** acide *m* hydroxamique.
hydroxide [hai'drɔksaid], *s. Ch:* hydroxyde *m,* hydrate *m;* **aluminium h.,** hydrate d'aluminium; **sodium h.,** hydrate de soude; **calcium h.,** hydrate de chaux, de calcium.
hydroxy-acid [hai'drɔksiæsid], *s. Ch:* oxacide *m.*
hydroxyl [hai'drɔksil], *s. Ch:* hydroxyle *m,* oxhydrile *m.*
hydroxylamine [haidrɔk'siləmain], *s. Ch:* hydroxylamine *f.*
hydroxylated [hai'drɔksileitid], *a. Ch:* hydroxylé.
hydrozoon, *pl.* **-zoa** [haidrə'zouɔn, -'zouə], *s. Coel:* hydrozoaire *m;* hydroméduse *f.*
hyena [hai'i:nə], *s. Z:* hyène *f;* **laughing h.,** hyène moqueuse; **spotted h.,** hyène tachetée; **striped h.,** hyène

rayée; **painted h., h. dog,** lycaon *m*; loup peint.
Hygeia [hai'dʒi(:)ə]. *Pr.n.f. Gr. Myth:* Hygie.
hygiene ['haidʒi:n], *s.* hygiène *f.*
hygienic [hai'dʒi:nik], *a.* hygiénique.
hygienically [hai'dʒi:nikli], *adv.* hygiéniquement.
hygienics [hai'dʒi:niks], *s.pl.* (*usu. with sg. const.*) hygiène *f* (en tant que science).
hygienist ['haidʒi:nist], *s.* hygiéniste *mf.*
hygro- ['haigrou, hai'grɔ], *comb.fm.* hygro-.
hygrograph ['haigrougræf], *s.* hygrographe *m*, hygromètre enregistreur.
hygrology [hai'grɔlədʒi], *s. Ph:* hygrologie *f.*
hygroma [hai'groumə], *s. Med:* hygroma *m.*
hygrometer [hai'grɔmitər], *s. Ph:* hygromètre *m*; **hair h.,** hygromètre à cheveu; **dew-point h.,** hygromètre à condensation.
hygrometric(al) [haigrou'metrik(əl)], *a. Ph:* hygrométrique.
hygrometry [hai'grɔmitri], *s.* hygrométrie *f*, hygroscopie *f.*
hygronasty ['haigrounæsti], *s. Bot:* hygronastie *f.*
hygrophilous [hai'grɔfiləs], *a. Bot: Geog:* hygrophile.
hygroscope ['haigrəskoup], *s. Ph:* hygroscope *m.*
hygroscopic(al) [haigrə'skɔpik(əl)], *a.* hygroscopique.
hygroscopy [hai'grɔskəpi], *s. Ph:* hygroscopie *f.*
hygrostat ['haigroustæt], *s.* hygrostat *m.*
hygrotropism [haigrou'troupizm], *s. Ent: etc:* hygrotropisme *m.*
hylemya [hailə'mi:ə], *s. Ent:* hylémyie *f.*
Hylidae ['hailidi:], *s.pl. Amph:* hylidés *m*, les rainettes *f.*
hylo- [hailou, hai'lɔ], *comb.fm.* hylo-.
Hylobates [hai'lɔbəti:z], *s.pl. Z:* hylobatidés *m.*
hylogeny [hai'lɔdʒəni], *s.* hylogénie *f.*
hylotomous [hai'lɔtəməs], *a.* hylotome.
hylozoic [hailou'zouik], *a. Phil:* hylozoïque.
hylozoism [hailou'zouizm], *s. Phil:* hylozoïsme *m.*
Hymen ['haimən]. **1.** *Pr.n.m. Myth:* Hymen, Hyménée. **2.** *s. Anat:* hymen *m.*
hymenal ['haimən(ə)l], *a. Anat:* hymén(é)al, -aux.
hymeneal [haime'ni:əl], *a.* hyménéen.
hymenium, *pl.* **-a** [hai'mi:niəm, -ə], *s. Fung:* hyménium *m.*
hymenomycetes ['haimənoumai'si:ti:z], *s.pl. Fung:* hyménomycètes *m.*
Hymenophyllaceae [haimenoufi'leisii:], *s.pl. Bot:* hyménophyllées *f.*
Hymenoptera [haimen'ɔptərə], *s.pl. Ent:* hyménoptères *m.*
hymenopterist [haimen'ɔptərist], **hymenopterologist** [haimenɔptə'rɔlədʒist], *s.* hyménoptérologue *mf.*
Hymenopteroidea [haimenɔptə'rɔidiə], *s.pl. Ent:* hyménoptéroïdes *m.*
hymenopterology [haimənɔptə'rɔlədʒi], *s. Ent:* hyménoptérologie *f.*
hymenopterous [haimen'ɔptərəs], *a. Ent:* hyménoptère.
Hymettian [hai'metiən], *a. Geog:* du mont Hymette.
Hymettus [hai'metəs]. *Pr.n. Geog:* le mont Hymette; l'Hymette *m.*
hymn[1] [him], *s.* **1.** *Ecc:* hymne *f*, cantique *m*; **h. writer,** hymnographe *m*; **h. book,** recueil *m* d'hymnes, de cantiques; hymnaire *m.* **2.** hymne *m* (national, de guerre, etc.).
hymn[2], *v.tr. Lit:* **1.** chanter des hymnes en honneur de (Dieu, etc.). **2.** chanter les louanges de (qn).
hymnal ['himnəl]. *Ecc:* **1.** *a.* qui se rapporte à un cantique, aux cantiques. **2.** *s.* (*also* **hymnary** ['himnəri]) recueil *m* d'hymnes, de cantiques; hymnaire *m.*
hymnist ['himnist], **hymnodist** ['himnədist], *s.* (*a*) chanteur *m* d'hymnes; (*b*) hymnographe *m.*
hymnody ['himnədi], *s.* **1.** (*a*) pratique *f* du chant des cantiques; (*b*) hymnographie *f.* **2.** *coll.* hymnologie *f* (d'un pays, d'une Église).
hymnographer [him'nɔgrəfər], *s.* hymnographe *m.*
hymnology [him'nɔlədʒi], *s.* hymnologie *f*; hymnographie *f.*
Hynobiidae [hainou'baiidi:], *s.pl. Amph:* hynobiidés *m.*
hyoglossal [haiou'glɔs(ə)l], *a. Anat:* hyoglosse.
hyoglossus [haiou'glɔsəs], *s. Anat:* hyoglosse *m.*
hyoid ['haiɔid], *a.* & *s.* (os *m*) hyoïde *m.*
hyoidean [hai'ɔidiən], *a. Anat:* hyoïdien.
hyomandibula [haioumæn'dibjulə], *s.* (os *m*) hyomandibulaire *m.*
hyomandibular [haioumæn'dibjulər], *a.* & *s.* hyomandibulaire *m.*
hyoscine ['haiəsain], *s. Ch:* hyoscine *f.*
hyoscyamine [haiou'saiəmin], *s. Pharm:* hyosciamine *f.*
Hyotherium [haiou'θiəriəm], *s. Paleont:* hyotherium *m.*
hypabyssal [haipə'bisəl], *a. Geol:* hypabyssal.
hypaesthesia [hipes'θi:ziə], *s. Med:* hypoesthésie *f.*
hypaethral [hai'pi:θrəl, hi-], *a. Archeol:* hypèthre.
hypallage [hai'pælədʒi], *s. Rh:* hypallage *m.*
Hypapante [haipə'pænti], *s. Eastern Orthodox Ch:* hy(pa)panté *f.*
Hypatia [hai'peiʃjə]. *Pr.n.f. Hist:* Hypatie.
hype [haip], *s. P:* **1.** seringue *f* hypodermique. **2.** drogué, -ée.
hyped up ['haipt'ʌp], *a. P:* excité, *esp.* dopé.
hyper- ['haipər, hai'pə:r], *pref.* **1.** hyper-. **2.** exagéré, outré; à l'excès.
hyperacidity [haipərə'siditi], *s.* **gastric h.,** hyperchlorhydrie *f.*
hyperacousia [haipərə'ku:ziə], *s.* hyperacousie *f.*
hyperactive [haipə'ræktiv], *a.* hyperactif.
hyperactivity [haipəræk'tiviti], *s.* hyperactivité *f.*
hyperaemia [haipə'ri:miə], *s. Med:* hyperémie *f.*
hyperaesthesia [haipəris'θi:ziə], *s. Med:* hyperesthésie *f.*
hyperalgesia [haipəræl'dʒi:ziə], *s. Med:* hyperalgésie *f.*
hyperalgesic [haipəræl'dʒi:zik], *a. Med:* hyperalgésique.
hyperbar ['haipəbɑ:r], *s. Meteor:* courbe *f* isobarique de haute pression.
hyperbaric [haipə'bærik], *a. Med:* **h. therapy,** barothérapie *f.*
hyperbaton [hai'pə:bətɔn], *s. Rh:* hyperbate *f.*
hyperbola [hai'pə:bələ], *s. Mth:* hyperbole *f.*
hyperbole [hai'pə:bəli], *s. Rh:* hyperbole *f.*
hyperbolic(al) [haipə'bɔlik(əl)], *a. Mth: Rh:* hyperbolique; *Mth:* **h. curve,** hyperbole *f.*
hyperbolically [haipə'bɔlik(ə)li], *adv.* hyperboliquement.
hyperbolism [hai'pə:bəlizm], *s.* hyperbolisme *m.*
hyperbolist [hai'pə:bəlist], *s.* personne portée à l'hyperbole.
hyperbolize [hai'pə:bəlaiz], *v.i.* hyperboliser, exagérer.
hyperboloid [hai'pə:bəlɔid], *s. Mth:* hyperboloïde *m.*
hyperboloidal [haipəbə'lɔidl], *a. Mth:* hyperboloïde.
hyperborean [haipə'bɔ:riən], *a.* hyperboréen; du nord; *s. Myth:* **the hyperboreans,** les peuples hyperboréens.
hyperchlorhydria [haipəklɔ'(h)aidriə], *s. Med:* hyperchlorhydrie *f.*
hypercritic [haipə'kritik], *s.* hypercritique *m.*
hypercritical ['haipə'kritik(ə)l], *a.* (d')hypercritique, **to be h.,** être hypercritique, *F:* chercher la petite bête.
hypercriticism ['haipə'kritisizm], *s.* hypercritique *f*; critique *f* d'un rigorisme exagéré.
hypercriticize [haipə'kritisaiz], *v.tr.* & *i.* critiquer outre mesure, d'une façon exagérée.
hyperdermosis [haipədə:'mousis], *s. Vet:* hyperdermose *f.*
hyperdulia [haipədu'laiə], *s. R.C.Ch:* hyperdulie *f.*
hyperemotivity [haipəri:mou'tiviti], *s. Psy:* hyperémotivité *f.*
hyperenergy [haipər'enədʒi], *s. Med:* hyperénergie *f.*
hyperexcitation ['haipəreksi'teiʃ(ə)n], *s. Med:* surexcitation *f.*
hyperfine ['haipəfain], *a. Opt:* hyperfin.
hyperfocal [haipə'fouk(ə)l], *a. Opt: Phot:* hyperfocal, -aux; *esp.* **h. distance,** distance hyperfocale.
hypergenesis [haipə'dʒenəsis], *s. Med: Biol:* hypergénèse *f.*
hyperglycaemia [haipəglai'si:miə], *s. Med:* hyperglycémie *f.*
hyperglycaemic [haipəglai'si:mik], *a. Med:* hyperglycémiant.
hypergol ['haipəgɔl], *s. Space:* hypergol *m.*
Hypericaceae [haipəri'keisii:], *s.pl. Bot:* hypéricacées *f.*
hyperinsulinism [haipər'insjulinizm], *s. Med:* hyperinsulinisme *m.*
hyperkeratosis ['haipəkerə'tousis], *s. Med:* hyperkératose *f.*
hyperlordosis [haipəlɔ:'dousis], *s. Med:* hyperlordose *f.*
hypermarket ['haipəmɑ:kit], *s.* hypermarché *m.*
Hypermastigina [haipəmæs'tidʒinə], *s.pl. Prot:* trichonymphines *m.*
hypermetamorphosis ['haipəmetə'mɔ:fəsis], *s. Ent:* hypermétamorphose *f.*
hypermeter [hai'pə:mitər], *s. A.Pros:* hypermètre *m.*
hypermetric(al) [haipə'metrik(l)], *a. A.Pros:* hypermètre.
hypermetropia ['haipəme'troupiə], *s. Opt:* hypermétropie *f.*
hypermetropic ['haipəme'trɔpik], *a.* (personne *f*, œil *m*) hypermétrope.
hypermnesia [haipə'ni:ziə], *s. Psy:* hypermnésie *f.*
hyperon ['haipərɔn], *s. Atom.Ph:* hypéron *m.*
hyperoodon ['haipər'ouodɔn], *s. Z:* hyperoodon *m.*
hyperoxide [haipə'rɔksaid], *s.* hyperoxyde *m.*
hyperparasite [haipə'pærəsait], *s. Biol:* hyperparasite *m.*
hyperparasitic [haipəpærə'sitik], *a. Biol:* hyperparasite.
hyperphysical [haipə'fizik(ə)l], *a.* hyperphysique, surnaturel.
hyperpiesis [haipəpai'i:sis], *s. Med:* hyperpiésie *f*; hypertension artérielle.
hyperpituitarism [haipəpi'tju:itərizm], *s. Med:* hyperpituitarisme *m.*
hypersecretion [haipəsi'kri:ʃ(ə)n], *s. Med:* hypersécrétion *f.*
hypersensitive [haipə'sensitiv], *a.* hypersensible.
hypersensitivity [haipəsensi'tiviti], *s.* hypersensibilité *f.*
hypersensitizing ['haipə'sensitaiziŋ], *s. Phot:* hypersensibilisation *f* (de la pellicule).
hypersonic [haipə'sɔnik], *a. Av:* hypersonique.
hyperspace ['haipəspeis], *s. Mth:* hyperespace *m.*
hypertely [hai'pə:təli], *s. Z:* hypertélie *f.*
hypertension [haipə'tenʃ(ə)n], *s. Med:* hypertension (artérielle, etc.).
hypertensive [haipə'tensiv], *a.* **h. patient,** hypertendu, -e.
hyperthermia [haipə'θə:miə], *s. Med:* hyperthermie *f.*
hyperthyroidism [haipə'θairɔidizm], **hyperthyr(e)osis** *pl.* **-es,** [haipə'θair(i)ousis, -i:z], *s. Med:* hyperthyroïdie *f*; thyréose *f*, thyréotoxicose *f.*
hypertonic [haipə'tɔnik], *a. Ph: Ch:* hypertonique; **h. salt solution,** solution *f* hypertonique.
hypertonicity [haipətɔ'nisiti], **hypertonus** [haipə'tounəs], *s. Ch: Physiol:* hypertonie *f.*
hypertrichosis [haipətri'kousis], *s.* hypertrichose.
hypertrophic [haipə'trɔfik], **hypertrophous** [hai'pə:trəfəs], *a. Med:* hypertrophique.
hypertrophied [hai'pə:trəfid], *a.* (organe) hypertrophié.
hypertrophy[1] [hai'pə:trəfi], *s. Med:* hypertrophie *f.*
hypertrophy[2], *v.i.* s'hypertrophier.
hyperventilation [haipəventi'leiʃ(ə)n], *s. Med:* hyperventilation *f.*
hypervitaminosis, *pl.* **-es** [haipəvitəmi'nousis, -i:z], *s.* hypervitaminose *f.*
hypethral [hai'pi:θrəl, hi-], *a. Archeol:* hypèthre.
hypha, *pl.* **-ae** ['haifə, -i:], *s. Fung:* hyphe *m.*
hyphaene [hai'fi:ni], *s. Bot:* hyphaene *m*, hyphène *m.*
hyphen[1] ['haif(ə)n], *s.* trait *m* d'union; *Typ:* division *f.*
hyphen[2], **hyphenate** ['haifəneit], *v.tr.* mettre un trait d'union à (un mot); écrire (un nom) avec un trait d'union; **hyphenated word,** mot *m* à trait d'union; *U.S:* **hyphenated American,** étranger naturalisé (Germano-américain, Hispano-américain, etc.).
hyphening ['haif(ə)niŋ], *s.* emploi *m* d'un trait d'union.
hypholoma [haifə'loumə], *s. Fung:* hypholome *m.*
hyphomycetes [haifoumai'si:ti:z], *s.pl. Fung:* hyphomycètes *m*; *F:* moisissures *f.*
hyphydrogamy [haifi'drɔgəmi], *s. Bot:* hyphydrogamie *f.*
hypnagogic [hipnə'gɔdʒik], *a. Psy:* hypnagogique.
hypnea ['hipniə], *s. Moss:* hypne *f.*
hypnoid ['hipnɔid], **hypnoidal** [hip'nɔidl], *a.* (sommeil, etc.) hypnoïde.
hypnopedia [hipnou'pi:diə], *s.* hypnopédie *f*, enseignement *m* pendant le sommeil.
hypnosis [hip'nousis], *s.* hypnose *f.*
hypnotherapy [hipnou'θerəpi], *s. Med:* **1.** guérison *f* par l'hypnose. **2.** cure *f* de sommeil.
hypnotic [hip'nɔtik]. **1.** *a. Psy: Pharm:* hypnotique; **h. sleep,** sommeil *m* hypnotique; somnose *f*; **h. state,** état *m* d'hypnose; somnambulisme provoqué. **2.** *s.* (*a*) *Psy:* (*pers.*) hypnotique *mf*; (*b*) *Pharm:* hypnotique *m.*
hypnotism ['hipnətizm], *s.* hypnotisme *m.*
hypnotist ['hipnətist], *s.* hypnotiseur, -euse.
hypnotize ['hipnətaiz], *v.tr.* hypnotiser.
hypnotizer ['hipnətaizər], *s.* hypnotiseur *m.*
hypnotizing ['hipnətaiziŋ], *a.* hypnotiseur, -euse.
hypnotoxin [hipnou'tɔksin], *s. Biol:* hypnotoxine *f.*
hypo ['haipou], *s. Phot: F:* = HYPOSULPHITE.
hypo- ['haipou, hai'pɔ], *pref.* hypo.
hypoacidity [haipouə'siditi], *s.* **gastric h.,** hypochlorhydrie *f.*
hypoblast ['haipoublæst], *s. Biol:* hypoblaste *m.*
hypocaust ['haipoukɔ:st], *s. Rom.Ant:* hypocauste *m.*
hypocentre ['haipousentər], *s.* hypocentre *m.*
hypocephalus [haipou'sefələs], *s. Archeol:* hypocéphale *m.*
hypochlorate [haipou'klɔ:reit], *s. Ch:* hypochlorate *m.*
hypochlorhydria [haipouklɔ:haidriə], *s. Med:* hypochlorhydrie *f.*
hypochloric [haipou'klɔrik], *a. Ch:* hypochlorique.
hypochlorite [haipou'klɔ:rait], *s. Ch:* hypochlorite *m.*
hypochlorous [haipou'klɔ:rəs], *a. Ch:* **h. acid,** acide hypochloreux.
hypochloruria [haipouklɔ'ru:riə], *s. Med:* hypochlorurie *f.*
hypochondria [haipə'kɔndriə], *s. Med:* hypocondrie *f.*

hypochondriac [haipə'kɔndriæk], *a. & s.* hypocondriaque (*mf*); *s.* hypocondre *mf.*
hypochondriacal [haipəkɔn'draiək(ə)l], *a.* hypocondriaque.
hypochondrium [haipou'kɔndriəm], *s. Anat:* hypocondre *m.*
hypocorism [hai'pɔkərizm], *s.* hypocoristique *m.*
hypocoristic [haipoukɔ'ristik]. **1.** *a.* (nom) hypocoristique, diminutif. **2.** *s.* hypocoristique *m.*
hypocrisy [hi'pɔkrisi], *s.* hypocrisie *f*; **piece of h.,** *F:* tartuferie *f.*
hypocrite ['hipəkrit], *s.* hypocrite *mf, F:* tartufe *m*; (*of a woman*) sainte nitouche.
hypocritical [hipə'kritik(ə)l], *a.* hypocrite.
hypocritically [hipə'kritikli], *adv.* hypocritement.
hypocycloid ['haipou'saiklɔid], *s. Mth:* hypocycloïde *f*; épicycloïde intérieure.
hypocycloidal [haipousai'klɔidəl], *a.* hypocycloïdal, -aux.
hypoderm ['haipoudə:m], **hypoderma** [haipou'də:mə], *s.* **1.** *Anat: Bot: etc:* hypoderme *m.* **2.** *Ent:* **hypoderma,** hypoderme.
hypodermic [haipə'də:mik], *a.* **1. h. syringe,** *s.* **h.,** seringue *f* hypodermique, seringue à injections, de Pravaz; **h. theory,** hypodermie *f.* **2.** *Anat:* sous-cutané.
hypodermis [haipou'də:mis], *s. Biol:* hypoderme *m.*
hypodermosis [haipoudə:'mousis], *s. Vet:* hypodermose *f.*
hypoferric [haipou'ferik], *a. Med:* **h. anaemia,** anémie *f* ferriprive.
hypogastric [haipou'gæstrik], *a. Anat:* hypogastrique.
hypogastrium [haip'ougæstriəm], *s. Anat:* hypogastre *m.*
hypogeal, -gean, -geous [haipou'dʒi:əl, -'dʒi:ən, -'dʒi:əs], *a. Bot: Geol:* hypogé.
hypogene ['haipədʒi:n], *a. Geol:* hypogène.
hypogeum, -a [haipə'dʒi:əm, -ə], *s. Archeol: etc:* hypogée *m.*
hypoglossal [haipou'glɔsəl], *a. & s. Anat:* (nerf) hypoglosse *m.*
hypoglycaemia [haipouglai'si:miə], *s. Med:* hypoglycémie *f.*
hypoglycaemic [haipouglai'si:mik], *a. Pharm:* **h. drug,** hypoglycémiant *m*; *Med:* **h. coma,** coma *m* hypoglycémique.
hypogonadism [haipou'gounædizm], *s. Path:* hypogonadisme *m.*
hypogynous [hai'pɔdʒinəs, hi-], *a. Bot:* (étamine *f*, fleur *f*) hypogyne.
hypoid ['haipɔid], *a. Mec.E:* (engrenage *m*) hypoïde.
hypologia [haipou'loudʒiə], *s. Med:* hypologie *f.*
hypomania [haipou'meiniə], *s. Psy:* hypomanie *f.*
hyponitric [haipou'naitrik], *a. Ch:* hypoazotique.
hyponitrous [haipou'naitrəs], *a. Ch:* hypoazoteux, hyponitreux.
hypoparathyroidism ['haipoupærə'θairɔidizm], *s. Path:* hypoparathyroïdie *f.*
hypopharynx [haipou'færiŋks], *s. Anat: Ent:* hypopharynx *m.*
hypophosphate [haipou'fɔsfeit], *s. Ch:* hypophosphate *m.*
hypophosphite [haipou'fɔsfait], *s. Ch:* hypophosphite *m.*
hypophosphoric [haipoufɔs'fɔrik], *a. Ch:* hypophosphorique.
hypophosphorous [haipou'fɔsfərəs], *a. Ch:* hypophosphoreux.
hypophyseal [haipoufi'zi:əl], *a. Anat: Med:* hypophysaire.
hypophysis [hai'pɔfisis], *s. Anat:* hypophyse *f.*
hypopituitarism [haipoupi'tju:itərizm], *s.* hypopituitarisme *m.*
hyposcenium [haipou'si:niəm], *s. Gr.Ant: Th:* hyposcenium *m.*
hyposecretion [haipousi'kri:ʃ(ə)n], *s. Med:* hyposécrétion *f.*
hypostasis [hai'pɔstəsis], *s.* **1.** *Phil: Theol:* hypostase *f.* **2.** *Med:* (*a*) hypostase, hyperémie *f*, congestion *f* hypoastique; (*b*) dépôt *m* (dans l'urine, etc.).
hypostatic(al) [haipou'stætik(l)], *a. Phil: Theol: Biol:* hypostatique.
hypostyle ['haipoustail], *a. Arch:* hypostyle.
hyposulphate [haipou'sʌlfeit], *s. Ch: A:* hyposulfate *m.*
hyposulphite [haipou'sʌlfait], *s. Ch:* **1.** hyposulfite *m*, hiosulfate *m.* **2.** *U.S:* hydrosulfite *m.*
hypotension [haipou'tenʃ(ə)n], *s. Med:* hypotension *f* (vasculaire); *Surg:* **controlled h.,** hypotension contrôlée.
hypotensive [haipou'tensiv], *a.* **h. patient,** hypotendu, -e.
hypotenuse [hai'pɔtənju:z], *s. Mth:* hypoténuse *f*; **the square on the h.,** le carré de l'hypoténuse.
hypothalamus [haipou'θæləməs], *s. Anat:* hypothalamus *m.*
hypothec [hai'pɔθik, hi-], *s. Jur: Scot:* hypothèque *f*; *F:* **the whole h.,** toute l'affaire; tout le tremblement.
hypothecary [hai'pɔθikəri, hi-], *a. Jur: Scot:* hypothécaire.
hypothecate [hai'pɔθikeit, hi-], *v.tr. Jur:* hypothéquer (une terre); déposer (des titres) en nantissement.
hypothecation [haipɔθi'keiʃ(ə)n, hi-], *s.* fait *m* d'hypothéquer; inscription *f* hypothécaire; **letter of h.,** lettre *f* hypothécaire.
hypothenar [hai'pɔθənər], *s. Anat:* éminence *f* hypothénar.
hypothermal [haipou'θə:m(ə)l], *a. Geol:* hypothermal, -aux.
hypothermia [haipou'θə:miə], *s. Med:* hypothermie *f.*
hypothesis [hai'pɔθəsis], *s.* hypothèse *f*; **to assume the very worst h.,** envisager la pire des hypothèses; **working h.,** principe *m.*
hypothesize [hai'pɔθəsaiz], *v.i. & tr.* supposer (une notion); faire des hypothèses, des suppositions; admettre comme hypothèse (**that,** que).
hypothetic(al) [haipə'θetik(l)], *a.* hypothétique, supposé.
hypothetically [haipə'θetik(ə)li], *adv.* hypothétiquement, par hypothèse.
hypothyroidism [haipou'θairɔidizm], *s. Med:* hypothyroïdie *f.*
hypotonia [haipou'touniə], *s. Med:* hypotonie *f* (musculaire).
hypotonic [haipou'tɔnik], *a. Med: Ch:* hypotonique.
hypotonicity [haipoutɔ'nisiti], **hypotonus** [haipou'tounəs], *s. Med: Ch:* hypertonure *f.*
hypotrophy [hai'pɔtrəfi], *s. Med:* hypotrophie *f.*
hypotyposis [haipoutai'pousis], *s. Rh:* hypotypose *f.*
hypovitaminosis ['haipouvitəmi'nousis], *s.* hypovitaminose *f.*
hypoxanthine [haipɔ'sænθain], *s. Ch:* sarcine *f.*
Hypsidae ['hipsidi:], *s.pl. Ent:* hypsides *m.*
hypsography [hip'sɔgrəfi], *s.* hypsographie *f.*
hypsometer [hip'sɔmitər], *s.* hypsomètre *m*; thermo-baromètre *m, pl.* thermo-baromètres.
hypsometric(al) [hipsə'metrik(əl)], *a.* hypsométrique; *Mapm:* **h. layer, tint,** teinte *f* hypsométrique.
Hyracoidea [hairə'kɔidiə], *s.pl. Z:* hyracoïdes *m.*
hyrax ['hairæks], *s. Z:* hyrax *m*; daman *m* des rochers; **tree h.,** daman arboricole, des arbres.
Hyrcania [hə:'keiniə]. *Pr.n. A.Geog:* Hyrcanie *f.*
Hyrcanian [hə:keinən], *a.* hyrcanien.
hyson [haisn], *s. Com:* hys(s)on *m*; thé vert.
hyssop ['hisəp], *s. Bot:* hysope *f*; **hedge h.,** gratiole officinale; *F:* herbe *f* au pauvre homme; **false hedge h.,** ilysanthes *m.*
hysteralgia [histə'rældʒiə], *s. Med:* hystéralgie *f.*
hysterectomy [histə'rektəmi], *s. Surg:* hystérectomie *f.*
hysteresis [histə'ri:sis], *s. Magn:* hystérésis *f*, hystérèse *f* (magnétique); traînée *f* magnétique; attardement *m.*
hysteretic [histə'retik], *a. Magn:* (perte *f*, etc.) par hystérésis; **h. curve, h. diagram,** boucle *f* d'hystérésis.
hysteria [his'tiriə], *s.* **1.** *Med:* hystérie *f*; **mass h.,** hystérie collective; *Vet:* **canine h.,** hystérie canine. **2.** *F:* crise *f* d'exaltation.
hysteriac [his'tiəriæk], *s. Psy:* hystérique *mf.*
hysteric [his'terik], *a.* hystérique.
hysterical [his'terik(ə)l], *a.* **1.** *Med:* hystérique; atteint(e) d'hystérie. **2.** (*a*) sujet à des attaques de nerfs; d'une émotivité morbide; **h. sobs,** sanglots convulsifs; **h. speech,** discours *m* de détraqué; **h. laugh,** rire nerveux, énervé; (*b*) en proie à une attaque de nerfs; **to become h.,** avoir une attaque, une crise, de nerfs; **don't get h.,** ne vous mettez pas dans des états pareils; **she was h.,** elle était dans tous ses états.
hysterically [his'terik(ə)li], *adv.* sans pouvoir maîtriser ses émotions; **to weep h.,** avoir une crise de larmes; **to laugh h.,** être pris d'un rire nerveux; rire nerveusement; avoir le fou rire.
hystericism [his'terisizm], *s.* hystérisme *m* (dans la littérature, etc.).
hysterics [his'teriks], *s.pl.* **1.** attaque *f* de nerfs; crise *f* de nerfs; **to go, fall, into h.,** avoir une attaque, une crise, de nerfs; **it almost sent her into h.,** cela a failli lui donner une attaque de nerfs. **2.** fou rire; sanglots convulsifs.
hysteriform [his'terifɔ:m], *a. Psy:* hystériforme.
hysteritis [histə'raitis], *s. Med:* hystérite *f*, métrite *f.*
hysterocele ['histərousi:l], *s. Med:* hystérocèle *f*; hernie *f* de l'utérus.
hysterogenic [histərou'dʒenik], **hysterogenous** [histə'rɔdʒənəs], *a. Med:* hystérogène.
hysterography [histə'rɔgrəfi], *s. Med:* hystérographie *f.*
hysterotomy [histə'rɔtəmi], *s. Surg:* hystérotomie *f.*
Hystricidae [hi'strisidi:], *s.pl. Z:* hystricidés *m.*
Hystricomorpha [histrikou'mɔ:fə], *s.pl. Z:* histricomorphes *m.*

I

I[1], **i** [ai], *s.* **1.** (la lettre) I, i *m*; *Tp:* **I for Isaac,** I comme Irma; *F:* **to dot one's i's (and cross one's t's),** observer les longues et les brèves; mettre les points sur les i. **2.** *Tchn:* **I bar, I iron,** fer *m* (en) double T; fer en I; **I rail,** rail *m* à double champignon.

I[2]. **1.** *pers.pron;* (*a*) (*unstressed*) je *mf,* (*joined to vowel*) j'; **I sing,** je chante; **I accuse,** j'accuse; **here I am,** me voici; *F:* **he thinks he's the great I am,** il se croit le bon Dieu en personne; **what have I said?** qu'ai-je dit? **have I written?** ai-je écrit? (*b*) (*stressed*) moi *mf*; **he and I are great friends,** lui et moi, nous sommes de grands amis; **as tall as I (am),** aussi grand que moi; **it is I,** c'est moi; **I too,** moi aussi; **I who am speaking,** moi qui parle; **I'll help you,** c'est moi qui vous aiderai; *P:* (*in error for* **me**) **between you and I,** entre vous et moi; entre nous. **2.** *s.* **another I,** un autre moi(-même).

iamb ['aiæm(b)], *s. Pros:* ïambe *m.*

iambelegus [aiæm'beligəs], *s. A.Pros:* vers *m* ïambélégiaque.

iambic [ai'æmbik]. *Pros:* **1.** *a. & s.* **i. (foot),** ïambe *m*; **poem written in iambics,** poème écrit en vers ïambiques. **2.** *s.* (*poem*) ïambe.

iambus, *pl.* **-uses, -i** [ai'æmbəs, -əsiz, -ai], *s. Pros:* ïambe *m.*

Iapygia [aiə'pidʒiə]. *Pr.n. A.Geog:* Iapygie *f.*

Iapygian [aiə'pidʒiən]. *A.Geog:* (*a*) *a.* iapyge; (*b*) *s.* Iapyge *mf.*

iatrochemistry [iætrou'kemistri], *s. A.Med:* chimiatrie *f,* iatrochimie *f.*

iatrogenicity [iætroudʒe'nisiti], *s. Med:* iatrogénie *f.*

iatron [i'ætrɔn], *s. Cmptr:* mémoire *f* à tube cathodique.

iatrophysics [iætrou'fiziks], *s.pl.* (*usu. with sg. const.*) iatrophysique *f.*

Iberia [ai'biːriə]. *Pr.n. Geog:* Ibérie *f.*

Iberian [ai'biːriən]. **1.** *a.* (peuple) ibérien, ibérique; **the I. peninsula,** la Péninsule ibérique; **specialist in I. studies,** ibériste *mf.* **2.** *s.* Ibérien, -ienne; **the Iberians,** les Ibères *m.*

iberite ['aibərait], *s. Miner:* ibérite *f.*

Ibero-American [ai'biərouə'merikən], *a.* ibéro-américain, *pl.* ibéro-américains.

Ibero-Celtic [ai'biərou'keltik], *a. Ethn:* ibéro-celtique, *pl.* ibéro-celtiques.

ibex, *pl.* **-exes** ['aibeks, -eksiz], *s. Z:* ibex *m*; bouquetin *m* (des Alpes); **Siberian i.,** bouquetin de l'Himalaya.

ibidem, ibid, ib. [i'baidem, 'ibidem, 'ibid, ib], *adv.* ibidem, ibid, ib.; au lieu cité.

ibidorhyncha [aibidou'rinkə], *s. Orn:* ibidorhynque *m.*

ibis, *pl.* **-ises** ['aibis, -isiz], *s. Orn:* ibis *m*; **sacred i.,** ibis sacré; **scarlet i.,** ibis rouge; **glossy i.,** ibis falcinelle; **eastern glossy i.,** *Fr.C:* ibis luisant; **white-faced glossy i.,** *Fr.C:* ibis à face blanche; **wood i.,** tantale *m* d'Amérique, *Fr.C:* cigogne américaine.

ibisbill ['aibisbil], *s. Orn:* ibidorhynque *m.*

Ibo ['iːbou], *s. Ethn:* (*pl.* **Ibo**(**s**)) Ibo *m inv.*

iboga ['i'bougə], *s. Bot:* iboga *m.*

Ibsenism ['ibsənizm], *s. Lit:* ibsénisme *m.*

Ibsenite ['ibsənait], *s. Lit:* ibsénien, -ienne.

icaco [i'kɑːkou], *s. Bot:* (*a*) (*tree*) icaquier *m*; icaque *m*; (*b*) (*fruit*) icaque; prune *f* coton, des Andes.

Icaria [i'kɛəriə, ai-]. *Pr.n. Geog:* Icarie *f.*

Icarian [i'kɛəriən, ai-], *a. Geog:* icarien; **the I. Sea,** la mer Icarienne.

Icarus ['ikərəs]. *Pr.n.m. Gr.Myth:* Icare.

ice[1] [ais], *s.* glace *f.* **1.** (*a*) **my feet are as cold as i.,** j'ai les pieds comme de la glace, glacés; **this room is as cold as, like, i.,** on gèle dans cette pièce; **to break the i.,** rompre la glace; *Fig:* (i) faire cesser la contrainte; (ii) entamer un sujet, une affaire; *Fig:* **to get on to thin i.,** s'engager sur un terrain glissant; **to be on, skate on, thin i.,** être sur, toucher à, un sujet délicat, un sujet scabreux; *F:* **to cut no i. with s.o.,** être sans effet, ne faire aucune impression, sur qn; **explanations that cut no i.,** explications oiseuses, qui ne mènent pas loin; (*b*) *Dom.Ec:* glace (à rafraîchir); **broken i., crushed i.,** glace pilée; **bit, piece, of i.,** morceau *m* de glace; glaçon *m*; **to keep food on i.,** conserver des aliments sur la glace; *F:* **to put a project on i.,** mettre un projet en veilleuse, en suspens; différer un projet; *NAm:* **it's on i.,** l'affaire est dans le sac; *P:* **to put a criminal on i.,** mettre un criminel en prison, *P:* en taule; (*c*) *Geog:* **the i. of the Arctic,** les glaces de l'Arctique; **the i. regions, seas,** les régions, mers, glaciales; **anchor i., bottom i., ground i.,** glace(s) de fond; **broken i. (on river, etc.),** glaçons; **cat i.,** glace pourrie; **drifts of i.,** glaces, glaçons, en dérive; **drift i., floating i.,** glace(s) flottante(s); glaçons en dérive; **fast i.,** glace compactée; **field i.,** glace côtière, de banquise; **hummocky i.,** glace moutonnée; **pack i.,** glace de banquise; pack *m*; **pancake i.,** glace en crêpe; *Nau:* **gâteaux** *mpl* de glace; **slob i.,** glace morcelée; **young i.,** glace nouvelle; (*d*) *Meteor:* givre *m*; **black i., glazed i.,** verglas *m* (sur les routes); **i. accretion,** dépôt *m,* formation *f,* de givre; givrage *m*; *Av:* **i.-warning indicator, i. detector,** indicateur *m* de givrage; (*e*) *attrib. Geol:* **i. age,** époque *f* glaciaire; période *f* glaciaire; ère *f* glaciaire; *Mount:* **i. axe,** piolet *m*; *Hyd.E:* **i. apron,** brise-glace(s) *m* (d'un pont); *Med:* **i. bag,** vessie *f* (en caoutchouc) à glace; sac *m,* poche *f,* à glace; *Geog:* **i. bank, barrier,** banquise *f*; **the Great I. Barrier,** la Banquise; **i. floe,** banquise, banc *m* de glace; glaces flottantes; floe *m*; *Nau:* **i. beam,** brise-glace(s); **i. cap, i. sheet,** calotte *f* glaciaire; inlandsis *m*; *Med:* **i. blindness,** cécité *f* des neiges; **i. blue,** bleu glacier; *Meteor:* **i. break,** bris *m* de glace; **i. bucket, i. pail,** seau *m* à glace, à rafraîchir; *Rail: NAm:* **i. car,** wagon *m* frigorifique; **i. cave,** (i) caverne *f* dans la glace; (ii) glacière *f* domestique; **i. chamber,** (i) récipient *m* pour la glace; (ii) réfrigérant *m*; appareil *m* frigorifique; glacière; **i. chest,** glacière (domestique); buffet *m* glacière; armoire *f* frigorifique; **i. closet,** étuve froide; **i.-cold,** froid comme la glace; glacé, glacial; **i.-cold water,** eau glacée; **i.-cold wind,** vent glacial; **i. cube,** glaçon *m*; *Geog:* **i. fall,** cascade *f* (d'un glacier); **i. fender,** (i) *Nau:* paraglace *m*; brise-glace(s); (ii) souillard *m* (d'un pont); **i. field,** champ *m* de glace; icefield *m*; calotte *f,* banc *m,* de glace; *Geog:* **i. flow,** fleuve *m* de glace; glacier; *Meteor:* **i. fog,** brouillard givrant; *Geog:* **i. foot,** banquise; banc de glace; *Av:* **i. guard,** filtre *m* anti-givre; *Sp:* **i. hockey,** hockey *m* sur glace, *Fr.C:* hockey; **i.-hockey player,** hockeyeur *m*; *Mount:* **i. hook,** marteau *m* d'escalade; *Geog:* **i. jam,** embâcle *m* (de glaçons); **i. machine, i.-maker,** machine *f* à glace; congélateur *m*; **i. pack,** (i) embâcle (de glaçons); (ii) *Geog:* banquise; amas *m* de glace(s); pack *m*; (iii) *Med:* enveloppement glacé; **to put an i. pack on a patient's head,** mettre de la glace sur la tête d'un malade; *Nau:* **i. patrol,** service *m* de surveillance des glaces; **i.-patrol ship,** bâtiment *m,* navire *m,* de surveillance des glaces; **i. pick,** (i) *Mount:* pioche *f* à glace; (ii) *Dom.Ec:* poinçon *m* à glace; **i. pit,** glacière; *Geog:* **i. quake,** tremblement *m* qui accompagne la rupture des glaces; fracas *m* des glaces; **i. remover,** décongeleur *m*; *Nau:* **i. room,** glacière; *Sp:* **i. run,** piste artificielle de toboggan; *Sp:* **i. sailing,** (i) yachting *m* sur glace; (ii) patinage *m* à voile; **i. rink,** salle *f,* stade *m,* de patinage sur glace (artificielle); *Geog:* **i. shed,** ligne *f* de partage des glaciers; *Dial:* **the I. Saints,** les saints de glace (Mamert, Pancrace et Servais); **i. water,** (i) eau glacée, frappée; (ii) eau de glace fondue; *Sp:* **i. yacht,** bateau *m* à patins, à roulettes. **2.** *Cu:* **strawberry i., chocolate i.,** glace à la fraise, au chocolat; **i. pudding,** bombe glacée; **i. brick,** esquimau *m*; **water i.,** sorbet *m*; **to eat ices,** prendre des glaces. **3.** *Ch:* **dry i.,** neige *f* carbonique. **4.** *P:* diamants *mpl,* diam(e)s *mpl.*

ice[2]. **1.** *v.tr.* (*a*) congeler, geler; **to i. (up) the wings of an aircraft,** givrer les ailes d'un avion; **the ship was completely iced up,** le vaisseau était entièrement pris dans les glaces; (*b*) rafraîchir (l'eau, un melon, etc.) avec de la glace; frapper (du champagne); (*c*) glacer, surglacer (un gâteau). **2.** *v.i.* (*of pond, etc.*) **to i. (up, over),** geler; **the pond (was) soon iced over,** l'étang a rapidement gelé d'un bout à l'autre; (*of windscreen, propeller, etc.*) **to i. (up),** se givrer; *NAm: P.N:* **bridge ices,** danger de verglas sur le pont.

iceberg ['aisbəːg], *s.* **1.** iceberg *m.* **2.** *F:* homme, femme, de glace; homme glacial, femme glaciale; glaçon *m.*

iceblink ['aisbliŋk], *s.* reflet *m,* clarté *f,* des neiges (sur l'horizon).

iceboat ['aisbout], *s.* **1.** *Sp:* bateau *m* à patins; ice-boat *m, pl.* ice-boats. **2.** *Nau:* bateau brise-glace(s).

icebound ['aisbaund], *a.* (i) (navire) retenu, bloqué, par les glaces, pris dans les glaces; (ii) (port, etc.) fermé par les glaces.

icebox ['aisbɔks], *s.* **1.** glacière *f* (domestique); armoire *f* frigorifique. **2.** *NAm:* réfrigérateur *m.* **3.** *P:* (*in prison*) cellule individuelle, mitard *m.*

ice cream ['aiskriːm], *s.* glace *f* (à la crème); crème glacée; *Fr.C:* crème à la glace; **i. c. man,** glacier *m*; **i. c. parlour,** salon *m* de dégustation de glaces; café glacier; **i. c. spoon,** cuillère *f* à glace.

iced [aist], *a.* **1.** (*of cream*) glacé, à la glace; (melon) rafraîchi; (champagne) frappé; **i. coffee,** café glacé; **jug of i. water,** carafe frappée. **2.** (gâteau) glacé, surglacé.

icehouse ['aishaus], *s.* glacière *f*; **this room is like an i.,** c'est une glacière ici; on gèle dans cette salle.

Iceland ['aislənd]. *Pr.n. Geog:* Islande *f*; *Bot:* **I. moss, I. lichen,** mousse *f* d'Islande; **I. poppy,** pavot *m* d'Islande; *Miner:* **I. spar,** spath *m,* cristal *m,* d'Islande.

Icelander ['aisləndər], *s. Geog:* Islandais, -aise.

Icelandic [ais'lændik]. **1.** *a.* islandais, d'Islande. **2.** *s. Ling:* islandais *m.*

iceman, *pl.* **-men** ['aismæn, -men], *s.m.* **1.** homme rompu à l'exploration polaire, à l'alpinisme. **2.** fabricant, marchand, de glace. **3.** glacier, marchand de glaces. **4. the (three) Icemen,** les saints de glace (Mamert, Pancrace, Servais).

Iceni [ai'si:nai]. *Pr.n.pl. Hist:* Icènes *m*, Icéniens *m*.
Icenian [ai'si:niən], *a. Hist: Geol:* icénien.
iceplant ['aisplɑ:nt], *s.* **1.** *Bot:* (ficoïde) cristalline *f*; (ficoïde) glaciale *f*; ficoïde glacière. **2.** *Ind:* fabrique *f* de glace.
icer ['aisər], *s.* pâtissier-glacier *m*, *pl.* pâtissiers-glaciers.
Ichabod ['ikəbɔd]. **1.** *Pr.n. B.Hist:* Icabod. **2.** *int. O:* sa gloire s'est évanouie! son étoile a pâli! son éclat s'est terni!
ichneumon [ik'nju:mən], *s.* **1.** *Z:* ichneumon *m*; rat *m* de Pharaon, d'Égypte. **2.** *Ent:* **i. (fly),** ichneumon; vipio *m*.
Ichneumonidae [iknju:'mɔnidi:], *s. pl. Ent:* ichneumonidés *m*.
ichnograph ['iknəgræf], *s. Arch:* ichnographie *f*.
ichnographic(al) [iknə'græfik(l)], *a. Arch:* ichnographique.
ichnography [ik'nɔgrəfi], *s.* ichnographie *f*; plan géométral.
ichnology [ik'nɔlədʒi], *s.* ichnologie *f*.
ichor ['aikɔ:r], *s. Gr.Myth: Med:* ichor *m*.
ichorous ['aikərəs], *a. Med:* ichoreux.
ichthammol ['ikθæmɔl], *s. Pharm:* ichtyol *m* (sulfate d'ammonium).
ichthus ['ikθəs], *s. Ecc:* ichthys *m*.
ichthyic ['ikθi:ik], *a.* icht(h)yique.
ichthyo- [ikθiou, -ə, ikθi'ɔ], *comb.fm.* icht(h)yo-.
ichthyobdella [ikθioub'delə], *s. Ann:* ichtyobdelle *f*.
ichthyocol(la) [ikθiə'kɔl(ə)], *s.* icht(h)yocolle *f*; colle *f* de poisson.
ichthyodont ['ikθiədɔnt], *s. Paleont:* icht(h)yodonte *f*.
ichthyodorulite [ikθiə'dɔrjulait], **ichthyodorylite** [ikθiə'dɔrilait], *s. Paleont:* icht(h)yodorulite *f*.
ichthyoid ['ikθiɔid], *a.* icht(h)yoïde.
Ichthyol ['ikθiɔl], *s. R.t.m:* Ichtyol *m*.
ichthyologic(al) [ikθiə'lɔdʒik(l)], *a.* icht(h)yologique.
ichthyologist [ikθi'ɔlədʒist], *s.* icht(h)yologiste *mf*; icht(h)yologue *mf*.
ichthyology [ikθi'ɔlədʒi], *s.* icht(h)yologie *f*.
ichthyomorphic [ikθiə'mɔ:fik], *a.* icht(h)yomorphe.
Ichthyophagi [ikθi'ɔfədʒai], *s.pl.* icht(h)yophages *m*.
ichthyophagist [ikθi'ɔfədʒist], *s.* icht(h)yophage *m*.
ichthyophagous [ikθi'ɔfəgəs], *a.* icht(h)yophage.
ichthyophagy [ikθi'ɔfədʒi], *s.* icht(h)yophagie *f*.
Ichthyopterygia [ikθiɔptə'ridʒiə], *s.pl. Paleont:* icht(h)yoptérygiens *m*.
ichthyopterygium, *pl.* **-ia** [ikθiɔptə'ridʒiəm, -iə], *s. Ich:* icht(h)yoptérygie *f*.
ichthyornis [ikθi'ɔ:nis], *s. Paleont:* icht(h)yornis *m*.
Ichthyosauria [ikθiou'sɔ:riə], *s.pl. Paleont:* Ichtyosaures *m*.
ichthyosaur(us) [ikθiou'sɔ:r(əs)], *s. Paleont:* icht(h)yosaure *m*.
ichthyosis [ikθi'ousis], *s. Med:* icht(h)yose *f*.
ichthyotoxin [ikθiou'tɔksin], *s.* ichtyotoxine *f*.
ichthys ['ikθis], *s. Ecc:* ichthys *m*.
icicle ['aisikl], *s.* **1.** petit glaçon; chandelle *f* de glace. **2.** *Fig:* (*of pers.*) glaçon.
icily ['aisili], *adv.* **1.** d'un air glacial; d'une façon glaciale. **2. it's i. cold,** il fait un froid glacial.
iciness ['aisinis], *s.* **1.** froid glacial (du vent, etc.); **the i. of the roads,** l'état verglacé des routes. **2.** *Fig:* froideur glaciale (d'un accueil, etc.).
icing ['aisiŋ], *s.* **1.** (*a*) congélation *f*; (*b*) givrage *m*; **i. atmosphere conditions,** tendance givrante, au givrage, de l'atmosphère; **i. layer,** couche givrante; (*c*) glaçage *m*, surglaçage *m* (d'un gâteau); **i. sugar,** sucre *m* farine; sucre glace, à glacer. **2.** glacé *m*, glace *f* (de sucre). **3.** *Med:* **i. heart,** péricardite séreuse; **i. liver,** cirrhose *f* (du foie).
icon ['aikɔn], *s. Ecc:* icône *f*.
iconic [ai'kɔnik], *a.* (statue, etc.) iconique.
icono- [ai'kɔnə, aikə'nɔ], *comb.fm.* icono-.
iconoclasm [ai'kɔnəklæzm], *s.* iconoclas(t)ie *f*, iconoclasme *m*.
iconoclast [ai'kɔnəklæst], *s.* iconoclaste *mf*.
iconoclastic [aikɔnə'klæstik], *a.* iconoclaste.
iconographer [aikə'nɔgrəfər], *s.* iconographe *mf*.
iconographic(al) [aikɔnə'græfik(l)], *a.* iconographique.
iconography [aikə'nɔgrəfi], *s.* iconographie *f*.
iconolater [aikə'nɔlətər], *s. Rel.H:* iconolâtre *mf*.
iconolatry [aikə'nɔlətri], *s.* iconolâtrie *f*.
iconological [aikɔnə'lɔdʒikl], *a.* iconologique.
iconologist [aikə'nɔlədʒist], *s.* iconologiste *mf*, iconologue *mf*.
iconology [aikə'nɔlədʒi], *s.* iconologie *f*.
iconomania [aikɔnə'meiniə], *s.* iconomanie *f*.
iconometer [aikə'nɔmitər], *s. Phot:* iconomètre *m*; chercheur *m* focimétrique.
iconometry [aikə'nɔmitri], *s. Phot:* iconométrie *f*.
iconophile ['aikɔnəf(a)il], *s.* iconophile *mf*.
iconoscope [ai'kɔnəskoup], *s. T.V:* iconoscope *m*.
iconostasis [aikə'nɔstəsis], *s. Ecc.Arch:* iconostase *f*.
icosagon [ai'kɔsəgən], *s. Mth:* icosagone *m*.
icosagonal [aikə'sægən(ə)l], *a. Mth:* icosagone.
icosahedral [aikəsə'hedr(ə)l, -'hi:d-], *a. Mth:* icosaèdre.
icosahedron [aikəsə'hedr(ə)n, -'hi:d-], *s. Mth:* icosaèdre *m*.
icositetrahedron [aikousitetrə'hedron, -'hi:d-], *s. Mth:* polyèdre *m* à vingt-quatre faces.
icteric [ik'terik], *a. & s. Med:* ictérique (*mf*).
icterical [ik'terik(ə)l], *a. Med:* ictérique.
Icteridae [ik'teridi:], *s.pl. Orn:* ictéridés *m*.
icterogenic [iktərə'dʒenik], *a. Med:* ictérigène.
icterus ['iktərəs], *s.* **1.** *Med:* ictère *m*; jaunisse *f*. **2.** *Bot:* ictère. **3.** *Orn:* ictère, icterus *m*.
icticyon [ik'tisiən], *s. Z:* icticyon *m*.
Ictidosauria [iktidou'sɔ:riə], *s.pl. Paleont:* ictidosauriens *m*.
ictus ['iktəs], *s.* **1.** *Pros:* ictus *m*. **2.** *Med:* (*a*) ictus *m*; coup *m* (de sang, de chaleur); crise *f* (d'épilepsie); (*b*) battement *m* (du pouls).
icy ['aisi], *a.* **1.** couvert de glace; glacial, -als; **i. road,** route verglacée. **2.** glacial, glacé; **i. hands,** mains glacées; **i. wind,** vent glacial; vent à vous couper la figure; **this room is i. cold,** on gèle dans cette pièce; *Fig:* **i. welcome, smile,** accueil, sourire, glacial; sourire glacé; **i. answer,** réponse glacée; **to have an i. look,** avoir un air de glace.
id[1] [id], *s. Biol:* ide *m*.
id[2], *s. Psy:* **the id,** le ça.
Idaean [ai'di:ən], *a. & s. Gr.Ant:* idéen; du mont Ida.
idalia [ai'deiliə], *s. Ent:* idalie *f*.
Idalian [ai'deiliən], *a. Gr.Ant:* d'Idalie.
Idalium [ai'deiliəm], *s. A.Geog:* Idalie, Idalium.
idant ['aidənt], *s. Biol:* idante *m*.
ide [aid], *s. Ich:* ide *m*; able *m* jesse.
idea [ai'di:ə], *s.* **1.** idée *f*: (*a*) **general i.,** idée générale: **to give a general i. of a book,** donner un aperçu d'un livre; **worried, upset, by the i. of an accident,** agité par l'image d'un accident; **I can't bear the i. (of it),** je ne peux pas en souffrir l'idée; l'idée m'en est trop pénible; **I have an i. that I've seen him before,** j'ai l'impression, j'ai (l')idée, de l'avoir déjà vu; **I don't quite get the i.,** je ne saisis pas; **it's not my i. of pleasure,** ce n'est pas là ma conception du plaisir; **I had no i. that . . .,** je ne soupçonnais pas que . . .; j'étais loin de me douter que . . .; j'ignorais absolument que . . .; je n'avais aucune idée que . . .; **I had no i. he was there,** je ne me doutais aucunement qu'il fût là; **you have no i. how anxious I was,** vous ne vous faites pas idée combien j'étais inquiet; **I have no i. what a battle is like,** je n'ai aucune idée de ce que peut être une bataille; **I have no i. why . . .,** je ne saurais dire pourquoi . . .; **I haven't any i. what you mean,** je ne comprends pas du tout ce que vous voulez dire; *F:* **now don't get any ideas,** (i) il n'y a rien encore de décidé; ce n'est pas encore le moment d'agir; ne me prenez pas au pied de la lettre; (ii) ne vous croyez pas encore là; (iii) je ne suis pas une fille comme ça; **to have a clear i. of sth.,** se représenter clairement qch. par la pensée; **he has some i. of chemistry,** il a des notions de chimie; (*b*) **a bright i. strikes me,** il me vient une idée lumineuse; **what a funny i.!** quelle drôle d'idée! **what a good i. of yours to come here!** quelle bonne idée à vous de venir ici! bien vous a pris de venir ici; **to be full of ideas,** avoir de l'idée; **man of ideas,** homme à idées; **idea(s) man,** remueur *m* d'idées; **to hit upon the i. of doing sth.,** avoir la bonne inspiration, l'idée, de faire qch.; **he hasn't an i. in his head,** il a la tête absolument vide; **to get an i. that . . .,** s'imaginer que . . .; **to get ideas into one's head,** se faire des idées; **where did you get that i. (from)?** où avez-vous pris cela? **what put that i. into your head?** qu'est-ce qui vous a donné cette idée? **you may dismiss that i. from your mind,** vous pouvez chasser cette idée de votre esprit; *F:* **what an i.!** en voilà une idée! y pensez-vous! vous n'y pensez pas! **the (very) i.!** quelle idée! par exemple! a-t-on jamais vu, entendu, chose pareille! *F:* **what's the great, big, i.?** à quoi vise tout cela? *F:* **get the idea?** vous comprenez? (*c*) **to have a poor i. of s.o.'s abilities,** ne pas avoir une bien haute idée de la capacité de qn; **to force one's ideas on s.o.,** tâcher d'imposer ses idées, ses opinions, à qn; **to be dominated by one i.,** être sous l'empire d'une idée fixe; **a man who has only one i.,** l'homme d'une seule idée; un monomane; **my i. is to plant some trees here,** mon idée serait de planter ici quelques arbres; **I had some i. of going as far as Paris,** j'avais la pensée, j'avais quelque idée, de pousser jusqu'à Paris; **I studied French with the i. of going abroad,** j'ai étudié le français dans, avec, l'idée d'aller à l'étranger. **2.** *A: & Lit:* **the young i.,** l'âme *f* de l'enfant; l'esprit *m* de l'enfant; les jeunes.
ideal [ai'diəl]. **1.** *a.* (*a*) idéal, *pl.* idéaux; **i. personage,** personnage idéal; **it's i.!** c'est le rêve! c'est l'idéal! **our i. house,** la maison de nos rêves; **the I. Home Exhibition,** le Salon des arts ménagers; (*b*) *Mec.E: etc:* **i. efficiency,** rendement *m* optimum; *I.C.E:* **i. cycle,** cycle *m* théorique. **2.** *s.* idéal *m*, *pl.* -als, -aux; (*a*) **the i. of beauty,** le beau idéal, la beauté idéale; l'idéal de la beauté; (*b*) **a man with no ideals,** un homme sans idéal; **his high ideals,** sa hauteur de vues; (*c*) *Mth:* idéal.
idealism [ai'diəlizm], *s.* idéalisme *m*.
idealist [ai'diəlist], *s.* idéaliste *mf*.
idealistic [aidiə'listik], *a.* idéaliste.
idealistically [aidiə'listik(ə)li], *adv.* d'une manière, façon, idéaliste.
ideality [aidi'æliti], *s.* idéalité *f*.
idealization [aidiəlai'zeiʃ(ə)n], *s.* idéalisation *f*.
idealize [ai'diəlaiz], *v.tr.* idéaliser.
idealizing [ai'diəlaiziŋ], *s.* idéalisation *f*.
ideally [ai'diəli], *adv.* **1.** en idée. **2.** idéalement (beau, etc.); **she was i. beautiful,** elle était l'idéal de la beauté, la beauté en personne; **i., everyone should share alike,** l'idéal serait le partage égal pour tout le monde.
idealness [ai'diəlnis], *s.* idéalité *f*.
ideate[1] [ai'dieit]. *Psy:* **1.** *v.tr.* idéer; imaginer: concevoir l'idée de (qch.). **2.** *v.i.* concevoir, se faire, une idée, des idées.
ideate[2], *s. Psy:* idéat *m*.
ideation [aidi'eiʃ(ə)n], *s. Psy:* idéation *f*.
ideational [aidi'eiʃ(ə)n(ə)l], *a. Psy:* idéationnel.
idée-force [i:dei'fɔ:s], *s. Psy:* idée-force *f*, *pl.* idées-forces.
idem ['aidem], *adv.* idem.
idempotent [ai'dempətənt]. *Mth:* **1.** *a.* idempotent. **2.** *s.* quantité idempotente.
idem sonans ['aidem'sounænz]. *Lt.phr. Jur:* **name i. s. with another,** nom qui se prononce de la même manière qu'un autre; noms homophones.
identic [ai'dentik], *a. Dipl:* **i. notes,** notes *f* identiques, de la même teneur.
identical [ai'dentik(ə)l]. **1.** *a.* identique (**with,** à); même; **our tastes are i.,** nous avons les mêmes goûts; **the two concepts are i.,** les deux concepts sont mêmes; **i. copy (of a text),** copie textuelle; *Biol:* **i. twins,** jumeaux univitellins, monozygotes; *F:* vrais jumeaux. **2.** *s.* **the principle of the i.,** le principe des identiques *mpl*.
identifiable [aidenti'faiəbl], *a.* identifiable.
identification [aidentifi'keiʃ(ə)n], *s.* **1.** identification *f*; (*a*) **i. of sth. with sth.,** identification de qch. avec qch.; (*b*) **i. of a dead body, of a criminal,** identification d'un cadavre, d'un malfaiteur; **i. parade,** confrontation *f* d'un témoin avec un groupe de personnes dans lequel se trouve un individu suspecté par la police; *Mil: Av:* **i. friend or foe,** matériel *m*, dispositif *m*, électronique d'identification; **i. friend or foe radar,** radar identificateur; **i. papers, card,** pièces *fpl*, carte *f*, d'identité; **i. mark,** marque *f* d'identification, d'identité; signe distinctif; *Adm: etc:* estampille *f*; *Av: Nau:* **i. marks,** (lettres *f* et numéros *m* d')immatriculation *f*; lettres et numéros d'identification; *Adm: Aut:* **i. plate,** plaque *f* d'identité, plaque matricule; *Mil:* **i. disk,** plaque d'identité; **i. bracelet,** bracelet *m* d'identité; *Av:* **i. beacon, i. light,** phare *m*, feu *m*, d'identification; *Cmptr:* **file i.,** identification, indicatif *m*, nom *m*, de fichier; (*c*) *Psy:* identification. **2.** *Nat.Hist:* détermination *f* (d'un spécimen).
identificatory [aidentifi'keitəri], *a.* identificateur, -trice.
identifier [ai'dentifaiər], *s.* **1.** personne *f* qui constate l'identité de quelqu'un. **2.** *Cmptr:* identificateur *m*.
identify [ai'dentifai], *v.tr.* **1.** identifier; (*a*) **to i. sth. with sth.,** identifier qch. avec qch.; **to i. oneself with a cause, a party,** s'identifier à, avec, s'assimiler à, une cause, un parti politique; (*of party*) **to i. itself with a majority,** s'intégrer dans une majorité; **the reader identifies himself with the hero of the novel,** le lecteur s'identifie avec le héros du roman; (*b*) **to i. s.o., sth.,** identifier qn, qch.; constater, établir, l'identité de qn, qch.; reconnaître qn, qch.; *Nau:* **to i. a (strange) ship,** reconnaître un navire; (*c*) *v.i. F:* **to i. with s.o.,** être en rapport avec qn; **I can't i.,** ça n'a rien à voir avec moi. **2.** *Nat.Hist:* déterminer (un spécimen).
identifying [ai'dentifaiiŋ], *s.* identification *f*; *Cmptr:* **i. code,** code *m* d'identification.
identikit [ai'dentikit], *s.* photo-robot *m*, *pl.* photos-robots; portrait-robot *m*, *pl.* portraits-robots.
identity [ai'dentiti], *s.* **1.** identité *f*; (*a*) **to establish the i. between two things,** établir l'identité entre deux choses, de deux choses; (*b*) **to establish the i. of s.o.,** identifier qn; **to prove one's i.,** établir son identité; **payable on proof of i.,** payable contre preuve d'identité, sur présentation de pièces d'identité, contre légitimation; **mistaken i.,** erreur *f* sur la personne; *Adm:* **i. card,** carte

f d'identité; *Jur:* **i. certificate,** acte *m* de notoriété; *Mil:* **i. disk,** plaque *f* d'identité; **i. bracelet,** bracelet *m* d'identité; (*c*) *Mth:* **algebraic identities,** identités algébriques; (*d*) *Phil:* **i. principle,** principe *m* d'identité. **2.** *Austr: & N.Z:* **an old i. of the district,** une des personnalités de la région; **he's quite an i.,** c'est un original.

ideogram [ˈidiəgræm], **ideograph** [ˈidiəgræf], *s.* idéogramme *m.*

ideographic(al) [idiəˈgræfik(əl)], *a.* idéographique.

ideography [idiˈɔgrəfi], *s.* idéographie *f.*

ideologic(al) [aidiəˈlɔdʒik(ə)l], *a. Phil: etc:* idéologique.

ideologist [aidiˈɔlədʒist], **ideologue** [ˈaidiəlɔg], *s. Phil:* idéologue *mf.*

ideology [aidiˈɔlədʒi], *s. Phil:* idéologie *f*; *F:* **the i. of a political party,** l'idéologie d'un parti politique.

ideomotor [aidiouˈmoutər], *a. Psy:* idéo-moteur, -trice; *pl.* idéo-moteurs, -trices.

ides [aidz], *s.pl. Rom.Ant:* ides *f*; **the i. of March,** les ides de mars.

idiacanthus [idiəˈkænθəs], *s. Ich:* idiacanthus *m*, idiacanthe *m.*

idioblast [ˈidioublæst], *s. Biol:* idioblaste *m.*

idiochromatic [ˈidioukrouˈmætik], *a.* idiochromatique.

idiochromosome [ˈidiouˈkrouməsoum], *s. Biol:* idiochromosome *m.*

idiocy [ˈidiəsi], *s.* **1. (congenital) i.,** idiotie (congénitale); idiotisme *m.* **2.** bêtise *f*, stupidité *f*; **the sheer i. of this plan,** la bêtise sans nom de ce projet.

idiocyclophanous [ˈidiousaiˈklɔfənəs], *a. Cryst:* idiocyclophane.

idio-electric [ˈidiouiˈlektrik], *a. El: A:* idio-électrique, *pl.* idio-électriques.

idiogamous [idiˈɔgəməs], *a. Bot:* idiogame.

idiogamy [idiˈɔgəmi], *s. Bot:* idiogamie *f.*

idioglossia [idiouˈglɔsiə], *s. Med:* idioglossie *f.*

idiogram [ˈidiəgræm], *s. Biol:* idiogramme *m.*

idiolect [ˈidiəlekt], *s. Ling:* idiolecte *m.*

idiom [ˈidiəm], *s.* **1.** (*a*) dialecte *m*; idiome *m* (d'une région); (*b*) langue *f*, idiome (d'un pays). **2.** idiotisme *m*, locution *f* (d'une langue); **a French i.,** un gallicisme; **an English i.,** un anglicisme. **3.** *Mus:* manière *f* de s'exprimer (d'un compositeur).

idiomatic(al) [idiəˈmætik(əl)], *a.* **1.** idiomatique; **i. phrase,** idiotisme *m*; expression *f* idiomatique. **2.** qui appartient à la langue courante, à la langue familière; **his French is not very idiomatic,** son français n'est pas le français tel qu'on le parle.

idiomatically [idiəˈmætik(ə)li], *adv.* **to speak, write, express oneself, i.,** (i) parler, écrire, s'exprimer, d'une façon idiomatique, en se servant d'idiotismes; (ii) s'exprimer dans une langue étrangère avec autant de facilité et de correction que dans sa langue maternelle.

idiomorphic [idiouˈmɔːfik], *a. Miner:* idiomorphe, automorphe.

idiomuscular [idiouˈmʌskjulər], *a. Anat:* idiomusculaire.

idiopathic(al) [idiouˈpæθik(l)], *a. Med:* (maladie) idiopathique, essentielle.

idiopathy [idiˈɔpəθi], *s. Med:* idiopathie *f.*

idiophanous [idiˈɔfənəs], *a. Cryst:* idiocyclophane.

idiophone [ˈidiəfoun], *s. Mus:* idiophone *m.*

idioplasm [ˈidiəplæzm], *s. Biol:* idioplasme *m.*

idiorrhythmism [idiouˈriðmizm], **idiorrhythmy** [idiouˈriðmi], *s. Rel:* idiorrythmie *f.*

idiosome [ˈidiousoum], *s. Biol:* idiosome *m.*

idiostatic [idiouˈstætik], *a. El:* idiostatique.

idiosyncrasy [idiouˈsiŋkrəsi], *s.* **1.** *Med: etc:* idiosyncrasie *f.* **2.** habitude *f* propre à qn; petite manie; tic *m*; **idiosyncrasies of style,** particularités *f* de style; **professional i.,** déformation professionnelle.

idiosyncratic [idiousiŋˈkrætik], *a.* **1.** idiosyncrasique. **2.** qui est dans les habitudes de qn.

idiot [ˈidiət], *s.* **1.** *Med:* idiot, -ote; imbécile *mf*; **congenital i.,** idiot congénital; **i. child,** enfant idiot; **village i.,** idiot du village. **2.** imbécile; **to behave like an i., play the i.,** se conduire comme un imbécile, comme un idiot; faire l'imbécile; **what an i. I've been!** comme j'ai été bête! **he's a perfect i.,** il est bête à manger du foin; **you i.!** espèce d'imbécile, d'idiot! *F:* **the i. box,** la télé(vision).

idiothermous [idiouˈθəːməs], *a. Z:* (animal) à sang chaud.

idiotic [idiˈɔtik], *a.* **1.** *Med:* (esprit) idiot, inepte; (existence) d'imbécile. **2.** bête; **that's i.,** c'est stupide; **don't be i.!** ne fais pas l'idiot!

idiotically [idiˈɔtikəli], *adv.* **1.** *Med:* idiotement; ineptement. **2.** bêtement; (se conduire) en imbécile.

idiotism [ˈidiətizm], *s. NAm:* idiotisme *m*, locution *f* (d'une langue).

idiozome [ˈidiouzoum], *s. Biol:* idiozome *m.*

idite [ˈidait], **iditol,** *s. Ch:* idite *f*, iditol *m.*

idle[1] [ˈaidl], *a.* **1.** (*a*) (*of pers.*) inoccupé, oisif, désœuvré; **to be, stand, i.,** rester à ne rien faire; rester les bras croisés; **in my i. moments,** à mes heures perdues; dans mes moments de loisir, d'oisiveté; (*b*) (*of machinery, employees*) qui chôme, en chômage; (*of machine*) au repos, arrêté; **factory lying i.,** usine inactive, qui chôme; **to run i.,** (i) (*of machine*) marcher à vide; (ii) *I.C.E:* (*of engine*) tourner au ralenti; **i. speed,** ralenti; **i. range,** plage *f* de ralenti; (*of money*) **to lie i.,** dormir; **capital lying i.,** fonds dormants, inemployés, improductifs, morts, *F:* croupissants; capital osif; **to let one's money lie i.,** laisser dormir son argent; (*c*) *Mec.E:* **i. motion,** mouvement perdu; **i. period,** période *f* d'inactivité; (*in mechanical cycle*) temps mort; **i. side of a belt,** brin mou; **i. wheel,** roue folle, décalée, parasite, intermédiaire; **i. gear,** pignon fou, intermédiaire; **i. pulley,** (i) poulie-guide *f*, *pl.* poulies-guides; (ii) galet tendeur, poulie *f* de tension; (iii) galet, poulie, de renvoi; *Cin:* **i. rollers,** galets guide-film, galets presseurs; (*d*) *El:* **i. current,** courant déwatté. **2.** (*of pers.*) paresseux, fainéant, indolent; **the i. rich,** les riches désœuvrés; **to acquire i. habits,** se laisser aller à la paresse; prendre des habitudes de paresse. **3.** (*of actions, feelings, etc.*) inutile, vain, oiseux, futile; sans motif; **i. tears,** larmes *f* inutiles; **i. wish,** vain désir; **i. pretext,** prétexte *m* futile; **i. notions, threats,** idées *f*, menaces *f*, en l'air; **i. rumours,** rumeurs *f* sans fondement; **out of i. curiosity,** par curiosité désœuvrée.

idle[2], *v.i.* **1.** fainéanter, muser, musarder, paresser; **to i. about the streets for an hour,** flâner dans les rues pendant une heure; **to i. along the street,** descendre la rue en flânant; *v.tr.* **to i. one's time away,** perdre son temps à ne rien faire, à paresser, à flâner; passer des heures de fainéantise. **2.** *Aut:* (*of engine*) **to i. (over),** tourner, marcher, au ralenti.

idleness [ˈaidlnis], *s.* **1.** (*a*) inaction *f*, oisiveté *f*, désœuvrement *m*; (*b*) chômage *m* (involontaire) (des ouvriers, d'une fabrique, etc.). **2.** futilité *f* (d'une menace, d'un projet, etc.). **3.** (*of pers.*) paresse *f*, fainéantise *f*, indolence *f*, musardise *f*, musarderie *f*; **to live in i.,** *Lit:* **to eat the bread of i.,** vivre dans l'oisiveté, sans travailler; *Prov:* **i. is the root of all evil,** l'oisiveté est (la) mère de tous les vices.

idler [ˈaidlər], *s.* **1.** (*a*) oisif, -ive; désœuvré, -ée; flâneur, -euse; (*b*) fainéant, -ante; paresseux, -euse. **2.** (*a*) *Mec.E:* (i) roue folle, décalée, parasite, intermédiaire; (ii) pignon fou, intermédiaire; (iii) poulie-guide *f*, *pl.* poulies-guides; (iv) galet tendeur, poulie *f* de tension; (v) galet, poulie, de renvoi; (*b*) *Cin:* galet presseur; galet guide-film *inv.*

idling[1] [ˈaidliŋ], *a. I.C.E:* (moteur *m*) au ralenti.

idling[2], *s.* **1.** (*a*) musardise *f*, musarderie *f*, muserie *f*; **a piece of i.,** une perte de temps; (*b*) fainéantise *f.* **2.** *I.C.E:* (marche *f* au) ralenti *m*; **i. jet,** gicleur *m* de ralenti.

idly [ˈaidli], *adv.* **1.** sans rien faire, sans travailler; **to stand i. by,** rester là à ne rien faire, sans bouger. **2.** inutilement; d'une façon futile; sans motif; **to talk i.,** parler en l'air. **3.** (*a*) paresseusement; en paresseux; (*b*) nonchalamment; **to do sth. i.,** faire qch. pour passer le temps, d'une manière distraite, d'un air absent.

Ido [ˈiːdou], *s. Ling:* ido *m.*

idocrase [ˈiːdoukreis], *s. Miner:* idocrase *f*, vésuvianite *f.*

Idoist [ˈiːdouist], *s. Ling:* idiste *mf.*

Idoistic [iːdouˈistik], *a. Ling:* idiste.

idol [ˈaidl], *s.* **1.** idole *f*; (*a*) **to worship idols,** adorer des idoles; idolâtrer; **i. worship,** idolâtrie *f*, adoration *f* des idoles; (*b*) **to make an i. of wealth,** faire son idole de l'argent; **the i. of the day,** l'idole, le saint, du jour; **the i. of the family,** l'amour *m* de la famille. **2.** = IDOLUM.

idolater [aiˈdɔlətər], *f.* **idolatress** [aiˈdɔlətris], *s.* **1.** idolâtre *mf.* **2.** *F:* admirateur, -trice, adorateur, -trice (of, de).

idolatrous [aiˈdɔlətrəs], *a.* (vénération *f*) idolâtre; (culte *m*) idolâtrique.

idolatrously [aiˈdɔlətrəsli], *adv.* d'une manière idolâtre.

idolatry [aiˈdɔlətri], *s.* idolâtrie *f*; culte *m* des idoles; **to practise i.,** idolâtrer.

idolize [ˈaidəlaiz], *v.tr.* idolâtrer, adorer (qn, qch.); faire une idole de (qn, l'argent); être idolâtre de (qn); aimer (qn) jusqu'à l'idolâtrie.

idolizer [ˈaidəlaizər], *s.* admirateur, -trice; passionné, -ée (of, de).

idolizing[1] [ˈaidəlaiziŋ], *a.* (regard, etc.) plein d'adoration, d'admiration; **his i. mother,** sa mère qui l'adore.

idolizing[2], *s.* idolâtrie *f.*

idolum, *pl.* **-a** [aiˈdouləm, -ə], *s.* **1.** (*a*) illusion *f*, fantôme *m*, spectre *m*, ombre *f*; (*b*) idée *f*, conception *f.* **2.** conception fausse, erreur *f* (dans la philosophie de Bacon).

Idomeneus [aiˈdɔminjuːs]. *Pr.n.m. Gr.Lit:* Idoménée.

idoneity [aidəˈniːiti], *s. Ecc:* idonéité *f.*

idonic [aiˈdɔnik], *a. Ch:* (acide *m*) idonique.

idosaccharic [aidouˈsækərik], *a. Ch:* idosaccharique.

idose [ˈaidous], *s. Ch:* idose *m.*

idothea [aiˈdouθiə], *s. Crust:* idothée *f.*

idrialite [ˈidriəlait], *s. Miner:* idrialite *f.*

Idumaea [aidju(ː)ˈmi(ː)ə]. *Pr.n. A.Geog:* Idumée *f.*

Idumaean [aidju(ː)ˈmi(ː)ən]. *A.Geog:* (*a*) *a.* iduméen; (*b*) *s.* Iduméen, -éenne.

idyll [ˈ(a)idil], *s.* idylle *f.*

idyllic [(a)ˈdilik], *a.* idyllique.

idyllically [(a)iˈdilik(ə)li], *adv.* d'une façon idyllique; en idylle.

idyllist [ˈ(a)idilist], *s.* idylliste *mf*; auteur *m* d'idylles.

if [if], *conj.* si. **1.** (*conditional*) (*a*) **if I am late, I apologize,** si je suis en retard, je fais mes excuses; **if I wanted him, I rang,** si j'avais besoin de lui, je sonnais; **if I feel any doubt, I ask,** si je suis dans le doute, je demande; (*b*) **if he does it, he will be punished,** s'il le fait, il sera puni; **if he did it, he would be punished,** s'il le faisait, il serait puni; **if the weather is fine and (if) I am free, I shall go out,** s'il fait beau et si je suis libre, je sortirai; **if it is fine, and (if it is) not too windy, we shall go for a walk,** s'il fait beau et qu'il ne fasse pas trop de vent, nous irons nous promener; **if it had been fine, and (if) it had not been too windy, we should have gone for a walk,** s'il avait, s'il eût, fait beau et qu'il n'ait, n'eût, pas fait de vent, nous aurions, eussions, été en promenade; **if they had a capable leader and a man of energy,** s'ils avaient un chef capable, et qui eût de l'énergie; **if he has forgotten me and refuses to see me,** s'il m'a oublié et refuse de me recevoir; **if anybody should call, let me know,** s'il vient quelqu'un, faites-le-moi savoir; s'il venait quelqu'un, vous me le feriez savoir; **let him do it if he dare(s)!** qu'il le fasse s'il l'ose! **if records are to be trusted, there was no famine that year,** s'il faut en croire, à en croire, les documents, il n'y eut pas, il n'y aurait pas eu, de famine cette année-là; **if they are to be believed, nobody was saved,** à les en croire, personne n'aurait survécu; **if you hesitate (at all),** pour peu que vous hésitiez; **if the slightest hitch occurs,** survienne le moindre accroc; **if (it is) necessary,** s'il est nécessaire; s'il le faut; au besoin; **if (it is) possible,** si c'est possible; si possible; s'il se peut; **if (it be) so,** s'il en est ainsi; **the debts, if any, recovered,** les dettes qui auraient été recouvrées; **modifications if any will have to be made later,** les modifications éventuelles devront être apportées plus tard; **if anything she is a little more stupid than he (is),** si on peut les différencier, on peut dire qu'elle est un peu plus bête que lui; **he'll give you a pound for it, if that,** il vous en donnera une livre et encore! **if not,** sinon; si ce n'est; **leave him alone, if not, you will regret it,** laissez-le tranquille, sinon, vous allez le regretter; **nobody, if not he,** personne, sinon lui, si ce n'est lui; **I shouldn't wonder if it rains, if it rained,** cela ne m'étonnerait pas qu'il pleuve; **go and see him, if only to please me,** allez le voir, ne fût-ce, ne serait-ce, que pour me faire plaisir; **I'll do it if and when I like,** je le ferai si cela me plaît, et à mon heure; **I'll see you if and when I get back,** je vous reverrai à mon retour; **it would be strange if that were done,** il serait étrange que cela se fît; (*c*) **if I were you,** si j'étais vous; à votre place; *F:* si j'étais que de vous; **if it were so,** quand (même) il en serait ainsi, même s'il en était ainsi; **even if he did say so,** quand même il l'aurait dit; **(even) if I were given a hundred pounds, I wouldn't do it,** on me donnerait cent livres, me donnerait-on cent livres, que je ne le ferais pas; même si on me donnait cent livres, quand même on me donnerait cent livres, lors même qu'on me donnerait cent livres, je ne le ferais pas; **if I had been given a hundred pounds, I wouldn't have done it,** on m'aurait, on m'eût, donné cent livres que je ne l'aurais pas fait, que je ne l'eusse pas fait; quand on m'aurait, m'eût, donné cent livres, je ne l'aurais, je ne l'eusse, pas fait; **if we did not ask these questions, they would crop up of themselves,** ces questions, nous ne les poserions pas qu'elles se poseraient d'elles-mêmes; **if anyone had foretold these events, we should have said he was mad,** qui aurait prédit ces événements, on l'aurait traité de fou; (*d*) (*exclamatory*) **if I had only known!** si seulement je l'avais su! **if only he comes in time!** pourvu qu'il vienne à temps! *F:* **if I haven't lost my key!** c'est bien moi de perdre ma clef! (*e*) **as if,** comme si; **he talks as if he were drunk,** il parle comme s'il était ivre; **he looks as if he were drunk,** il a l'air d'être ivre; **it isn't as if I were leaving for ever,** ce n'est pas comme si je partais pour toujours; **he stood there as if thunderstruck,** il demeura là comme foudroyé; **as if to show it,** comme pour le montrer; **as if by chance,** comme par hasard; **as if I would allow it!** comme si je le permettrais! *F:* avec ça que je le permettrais! **2.** (*concessive*) **if they are poor,**

they are at any rate happy, s'ils sont pauvres, ils sont du moins heureux, ils sont du moins sont-ils heureux; **pleasant weather, if rather cold,** temps agréable, bien qu'un peu froid, encore qu'un peu froid; **well-paid, if uninteresting, work,** travail bien rémunéré à défaut d'être intéressant. **3.** (*introducing a noun clause,* = WHETHER) **do you know if he is at home?** savez-vous s'il est chez lui? **I asked if it was true,** j'ai demandé si c'était vrai. **4.** *s.* si *m inv*; **your ifs and buts make me tired,** je suis fatigué de vos si et de vos mais; **it is a very big if,** c'est une condition qui n'est pas aisément remplie; *Prov:* **if ifs and ans were pots and pans, there'd be no trade for tinkers,** avec des si on mettrait Paris en bouteille, dans une bouteille. **5.** *Turf: NAm:* **if bet,** pari *m* avec report; **if betting,** paris avec report.

if-then [if'ðen], *a. Cmptr:* **if.-t. operation,** opération conditionnelle; implication *f.*

igloo ['iglou], *s.* igloo *m.*

Ignatian [ig'neiʃən], *s. Rel H:* ignacien *m.*

Ignatius [ig'neiʃəs]. *Pr.n.m.* Ignace; **I. Loyola,** Ignace de Loyola.

igneous ['igniəs], *a.* igné; **i. rock,** roche éruptive, ignée.

ignescent [ig'nes(ə)nt]. **1.** *a.* ignescent. **2.** *s.* corps ignescent.

igniferous [ig'nifərəs], *a.* ignifère.

ignigenous [ig'nidʒənəs], *a.* ignigène.

ignimbrite [ig'nimbrait], *s. Geol:* ignimbrite *f.*

ignipuncture ['ignipʌŋktjər], *s. Med:* pointes *fpl* de feu; ignipuncture *f.*

ignis fatuus ['ignis'fætjuəs], *s.* feu follet.

ignitability [ignaitə'biliti], *s.* inflammabilité *f.*

ignitable [ig'naitəbl], *a.* inflammable, allumable.

ignite [ig'nait]. **1.** *v.tr.* mettre feu à (qch.); mettre (qch.) en ignition; allumer (une charge de mine); enflammer (un mélange explosif, le grisou). **2.** *v.i.* prendre feu, s'enflammer, s'allumer.

igniter [ig'naitər], *s.* dispositif *m* d'allumage; *Artil:* allumeur *m*, inflammateur *m*, boutefeu *m*; déflagrateur *m*; *Av:* allumeur; *El:* igniteur *m* (d'ignitron); **electric i.,** allumeur électrique; *I.C.E:* interrupteur *m*, rupteur *m*; **gas i.,** allume-gaz *m inv*; *Exp:* **push i.,** amorceur *m* à percussion; **pull i.,** amorceur à tirette.

ignitibility [ignaiti'biliti], *s.* inflammabilité *f.*

ignitible [ig'naitibl], *a.* inflammable, allumable.

igniting [ig'naitiŋ], *s.* ignition *f*, inflammation *f*, allumage *m*; **i. device,** allumeur *m*; *Exp:* **i. wire,** fil *m* d'allumage.

ignition [ig'niʃ(ə)n], *s.* **1.** ignition *f*, inflammation *f* (d'une charge de mine, etc.); **i. temperature,** température *f* d'ignition; **i. rod,** igniteur *m.* **2.** *I.C.E:* allumage *m*; **to cut, switch, off the i.,** couper l'allumage; **battery i., coil i.,** allumage par batterie, par bobine; **burner i.,** allumage par brûleur; **dynamo i.,** allumage par dynamo; **magneto i.,** allumage par magnéto; **direct-spark i.,** allumage par magnéto (à haute tension); **hot-bulb i.,** allumage par incandescence; **spark (plug) i.,** allumage par bougie; **spontaneous i.,** allumage spontané; **high-tension i.,** allumage haute tension; **low-tension i.,** allumage basse tension; **single i.,** allumage simple; **dual i.,** double allumage; **twin i.,** allumage jumelé; **advanced i.,** avance *f* à l'allumage; allumage avancé; **to advance the i.,** mettre de l'avance à l'allumage; **to advance the i. fully,** mettre toute l'avance; **delayed i., retarded i.,** retard *m* à l'allumage; allumage retardé; *attrib.* **i. cable, lead, wire,** fil *m* d'allumage, de bougie; **i. circuit,** circuit *m* d'allumage; **i. coil,** bobine *f* d'allumage; **i. diagram,** schéma *m* d'allumage; **i. key,** clef *f* de contact; **i.(-advance) lever,** levier *m* d'avance (à l'allumage); manette *f* d'allumage; **i. point,** foyer *m* d'allumage; **i. spark,** étincelle *f* d'allumage; **i. switch,** bouton *m*, commutateur *m*, contact *m*, d'allumage; **i. system,** dispositif *m*, système *m*, d'allumage; **i. timing,** (i) distribution *f*, réglage *m*, de l'allumage; (ii) point *m*, d'allumage; **i.-timing gear,** distributeur *m* d'allumage; **i. tower,** distributeur et commande *f* d'allumage. **3.** *El:* amorçage *m* (de tube à vide); **i. delay, i. lag,** délai *m*, retard *m*, d'amorçage.

ignitor [ig'naitər], *s. El:* igniteur *m.*

ignitron ['ignitrən], *s. El:* ignitron *m.*

ignivomous [ig'nivəməs], *s.* (volcan, dragon, etc.) ignivome.

ignivorous [ig'nivərəs], *a.* ignivore.

ignobility [ignə'biliti], **ignobleness** [ig'noublnis], *s.* ignobilité *f.*

ignoble [ig'noubl], *a.* **1.** *A:* (*of pers.*) plébéien, roturier; de basse naissance; **noble or i. followers,** adhérents nobles ou obscurs. **2.** (*of act, etc.*) ignoble, bas, *f.* basse; infâme, vil, indigne. **3.** *Ven: A:* (faucon) ignoble, de basse volerie, bas voleur.

ignobly [ig'noubli], *adv.* **1.** *A:* **to be i. born,** être de basse naissance. **2.** d'une façon ignoble; ignoblement, indignement.

ignominious [ignə'miniəs], *a.* **1.** ignominieux, honteux; **an i. death,** une mort ignominieuse; **an i. peace,** une paix honteuse. **2.** *A:* infâme.

ignominiously [ignə'miniəsli], *adv.* ignominieusement, avec ignominie; honteusement.

ignominiousness [ignə'miniəsnis], *s.* caractère ignominieux, honteux (de qch.).

ignominy ['ignəmini], *s.* **1.** ignominie *f*, honte *f*, grand déshonneur. **2.** *A:* infâmie *f.*

ignorable [ig'nɔːrəbl], *a.* qu'on peut feindre d'ignorer; **the opposition is not i.,** l'opposition est trop forte pour qu'on n'en tienne pas compte.

ignoramus [ignə'reiməs], *s.* ignorant, -ante; ignare *mf*; **he's a proper i.,** c'est le roi des ignorants.

ignorance ['ignər(ə)ns], *s.* ignorance *f.* **1.** inconnaissance *f*; **through i.,** par ignorance; **to keep s.o. in i. of sth.,** laisser ignorer qch. par qn; laisser qn dans l'ignorance de qch.; **I am in complete i. of his intentions,** j'ignore tout de ses intentions; **i. is bliss,** qui ne rien sait de rien ne doute; *Jur:* **i. of the law is no excuse,** nul n'est censé ignorer la loi; **to plead i.,** prétendre cause d'ignorance. **2. crass i.,** ignorance crasse; *F:* ânerie *f*; **his i. is phenomenal,** il ne sait rien de rien.

ignorant ['ignər(ə)nt], *a.* ignorant. **1.** (*unaware*) **to be i. of a fact,** ignorer un fait; *Jur:* être ignorant du fait; **to be i. of what is happening,** être ignorant de, ignorer, ce qui se passe; ne pas être informé, ne pas être au courant, de ce qui se passe. **2.** (*a*) (*unlearned*) **to be i. of history,** être ignorant en histoire; connaître fort mal l'histoire; **i. of art,** ignorant, incompétent, en matière d'art; **he is i. of the world,** il ne connaît pas le monde; **he is i. of our customs,** il est étranger à nos usages; (*b*) **an i. question,** une question qui trahit l'ignorance; **an i. person,** *s.m.* ignorant.

Ignorantine [ignə'ræntain], *a.* & *s. R.C.Ch:* **I. (friar),** (frère) ignorantin (*m*).

ignorantism ['ignər(ə)ntizm], *s.* ignorantisme *m*, obscurantisme *m.*

ignorantist ['ignər(ə)ntist], *s.* ignorantiste *m.*

ignorantly ['ignər(ə)ntli], *adv.* **1.** (se tromper) par ignorance. **2.** (discourir, etc.) avec ignorance.

ignore [ig'nɔːr], *v.tr.* **1.** feindre d'ignorer (qch.); ne tenir aucun compte de (qch.); se désintéresser de (qch.); passer (qch.) sous silence; **this action could not be ignored by the public,** cette action s'imposait à l'attention du public; **to i. one's own feelings,** refouler ses propres sentiments; **to i. s.o., s.o.'s existence,** ne pas vouloir reconnaître qn; ignorer qn; ne pas arrêter ses regards sur qn; feindre de ne pas voir qn; faire comme si qn n'existait pas; méconnaître qn; **to i. the facts,** méconnaître les faits; ne tenir aucun compte des faits; **to i. an invitation,** ne pas répondre à une invitation; **to i. an insult,** ne pas relever une injure; **to i. a rule,** sortir d'une règle, **to i. an objection,** passer à l'ordre du jour sur une objection; **to i. a prohibition,** passer outre à une interdiction; **to i. an order,** ne tenir aucun compte d'un ordre; *Rail:* **to i. a signal,** brûler un signal; **ignoring custom he marched in unannounced,** au mépris de l'usage il entra sans se faire annoncer. **2.** *Jur:* **to i. a bill,** rendre une fin de non-recevoir; prononcer un non-lieu; **to i. a complaint,** rejeter une plainte.

ignore character [ig'nɔː'kærəktər], *s. Cmptr:* caractère *m* de suppression, d'omission.

ignorer [ig'nɔːrər], *s.* contempteur, -trice (**of,** de); **to be an i. of the rules, of custom,** ne tenir aucun compte des règles, de l'usage.

ignoring [ig'nɔriŋ], *s.* méconnaissance *f.*

iguana [i'gwɑːnə], *s. Rept:* iguane *m*; **land i.,** conolophe *m*; **sea i.,** lézard *m* de mer; **Galapagos sea i.,** lézard marin des Galapagos; **keeltail i.,** iguane à queue carénée; **spinytail i.,** iguane à queue épineuse.

Iguania [i'gwɑːniə], *s.pl. Rept:* iguaniens *m.*

iguanian [i'gwɑːniən], *a.* & *s. Rept:* iguanien (*m*).

Iguanidae [i'gwɑːnidiː], *s.pl. Rept:* iguanidés *m.*

iguanodon [i'gwɑːnədən], *s. Paleont:* iguanodon *m.*

ijolite ['iːəlait], *s. Geol:* ijolit(h)e *f.*

Ike [aik], *s. T.V: P:* iconoscope *m.*

Ikey ['aiki]. *P:* **1.** *Pr.n.m.* Isaac. **2.** *s.m. Pej:* juif; *esp.* prêteur d'argent; *P:* youpin. **3.** *a.* (*a*) rusé; malin, -igne; astucieux; (*b*) *O:* prétentieux; gourmé.

ikon ['aikɔn], *s. Ecc:* icône *f.*

il- [il], *pref.* il-; **illiterate,** illettré.

ilang-ilang [i'læŋilæŋ], *s. Bot: Toil:* ilang ilang *m*, ylang-ylang *m.*

ileitis [ili'aitis], *s. Med:* iléite *f.*

ileo-caecal [iliou'siːk(ə)l], *a. Anat:* iléo-cæcal, -aux; **i.-c. valve,** valvule iléo-cæcale.

ileo-colic [iliou'kɔlik], *a. Anat:* iléo-colique, *pl.* iléo-coliques.

ileocolostomy [ilioukə'lɔstəmi], *s. Surg:* iléo-colostomie *f*, *pl.* iléo-colostomies.

ileocystoplasty [iliou'sistouplæsti], *s. Surg:* iléo-cystoplastie *f*, *pl.* iléo-cystoplasties.

ileo-ileostomy [ilioui li'ɔstəmi], *s. Surg:* iléo-iléostomie *f*, *pl.* iléo-iléostomies.

ileosigmoidostomy [iliousigmɔi'dɔstəmi], *s. Surg:* iléo-sigmoïdostomie *f*, *pl.* iléo-sigmoïdostomies.

ileostomy [ili'ɔstəmi], *s. Surg:* iléostomie *f.*

ilesite ['ailzait], *s. Miner:* ilésite *f.*

ileum ['iliəm], *s. Anat:* iléon *m*, iléum *m.*

ileus ['iliəs], *s. Med:* iléus *m*; passion *f* iliaque; coliques *fpl* de miséréré; **paralytic i.,** iléus paralytique.

ilex, *pl.* **-exes** ['aileks, -eksiz], *s. Bot:* ilex *m*; (i) yeuse *f*; chêne vert; (ii) houx *m.*

ilia ['iliə], *s.pl. Anat:* iles *m.*

iliac[1] ['iliæk], *a.* **1.** *A: Med:* **i. passion,** iléus *m*; passion *f* iliaque; coliques *fpl* de miséréré. **2.** *Anat:* (os *m*, artère *f*) iliaque.

Iliac[2], *a. Gr.Ant:* iliaque, d'Ilion.

iliacus, *pl.* **-ci** [i'laikəs, -sai], *s. Anat:* muscle *m* iliaque.

Iliad ['iliæd], *s. Gr.Lit:* **the I.,** l'Iliade *f.*

Ilian ['iliən], *a. A.Geog:* iliaque, d'Ilion.

Ilicaceae [aili'keisiiː], *s. pl. Bot:* ilicacées *f*, ilicinées.

iliolumbar [iliou'lʌmbər], *a. Anat:* ilio-lombaire, *pl.* ilio-lombaires.

iliopectineal [ilioupek'tiniəl], *a. Anat:* ilio-pectiné, *pl.* ilio-pectiné(e)s.

iliopubic [iliou'pjuːbik], *a, Anat:* ilio-pubien, *pl.* ilio-pubien(ne)s.

ilium[1], *pl.* **ilia** ['iliəm, 'iliə], *s. Anat:* ilion *m*, ilium *m.*

Ilium[2] ['ailiəm, 'il-]. *Pr.n.* Ilion *f*, Troie *f.*

ilk [ilk]. **1.** *a. Scot: A:* même. **2.** *s.* (*a*) *Scot:* (*of landowner bearing the name of his property*) **Moray of that i.,** Moray du domaine de Moray; (*b*) *Pej:* **and others of that i.,** et d'autres gens du même acabit; et d'autres du même genre.

ill [il], *a., adv., & s.* (*comp.* **worse,** *sup.* **worst**)

I. *a.* **1.** (*a*) mauvais; **i. name, i. manners,** mauvaise réputation, mauvaises manières; **i. effects,** effets pernicieux; *Prov:* **it is an i. wind that blows nobody any good,** à quelque chose malheur est bon; **i. turn,** mauvais service, méchant service; **to do s.o. an i. turn,** desservir qn; (*b*) méchant, mauvais; **i. deed,** mauvaise action, méchante action; méfait *m*; **i. tongues,** méchantes langues, mauvaises langues. **2.** (*a*) malade, souffrant; **to be, feel, i.,** être malade; se sentir souffrant; **to fall i., get i., be taken i.,** tomber malade; **to be i. with a fever,** souffrir d'un accès de fièvre; **to be very i. indeed, dangerously i.,** être au plus mal; **he was seriously i. last year,** il a fait une grave maladie l'année dernière; **he was more i. than we thought,** il était plus malade que nous ne l'avions supposé; **to look i.,** avoir mauvaise mine; avoir l'air malade; (*b*) *F:* **to be (violently) i.,** vomir; avoir mal au cœur. **3.** *A: & Scot:* **i. to please,** difficile à contenter, à satisfaire.

II. *adv.* mal. **1. to behave i.,** se mal conduire; **to take sth. i.,** prendre qch. en mauvaise part; savoir mauvais gré à qn de qch.; **it will go i. with them,** il leur en cuira; **you would have fared i., it would have gone i. with you, but for . . .,** les choses auraient mal tourné pour vous sans . . .. **2. to be i. provided with sth.,** être mal pourvu de qch.; **i.-deserved praise,** louanges peu méritées; **I can i. afford the expense,** je peux difficilement supporter cette dépense; **it i. becomes you to . . .,** il vous sied mal, il vous messied, de . . .; **to be critically i.,** être dangereusement malade. **3. to be, feel, i. at ease,** (i) être mal à l'aise; *F:* être dans ses petits souliers; (ii) être, se sentir, inquiet (**about,** au sujet de).

III. *s.* **1.** mal *m*; **I know no i. of him,** je ne sais rien contre lui; **to do i.,** faire du mal, faire le mal; **to speak, think, i. of s.o.,** dire du mal de qn; avoir une mauvaise opinion de qn; **speak no i. of the dead,** il ne faut pas troubler la cendre des morts; **for i. or well, we have . . .,** que ce soit un bien ou un mal, nous avons . . .. **2.** (*a*) dommage *m*, tort *m*; **I have suffered no i. at his hands,** il ne m'a fait aucun tort; (*b*) *pl.* maux *m*, malheurs *m*; **to suffer great ills,** souffrir de grands maux, de grandes misères; **the ills which God sends us,** les adversités que Dieu nous envoie; **the ills that came upon the country,** les calamités qui se sont abattues sur le pays.

ill-acquired ['ilə'kwaiəd], *a.* mal acquis.

ill-advised ['iləd'vaizd], *a.* **1.** (*of pers.*) malavisé; **you would be i.-a. to protest,** vous seriez malavisé à protester. **2.** (*of action*) impolitique, antipolitique, peu judicieux.

ill-advisedly ['iləd'vaizidli], *adv.* impolitiquement; peu judicieusement.

Illano [i'ljɑːnou], *s. Ethn:* Illano *m.*

ill-assorted ['ilə'sɔːtid], *a.* mal assorti; disparate.

illation [i'leiʃ(ə)n], *s.* illation *f*, inférence *f*, déduction *f*, conclusion *f.*

illative [i'leitiv], *a.* **1.** *Gram:* (*of particle, etc.*) illatif. **2.** (raisonnement, etc.) déductif.

ill-balanced ['il'bælənst], *a.* (esprit) mal équilibré; **i.-b. sentences,** phrases mal agencées.

ill-behaved ['ilbi'heivd], *a.* qui se conduit, se tient, mal; malhonnête; grossier.

ill-bred ['il'bred], *a.* **1.** mal élevé, malappris; de mauvaise compagnie. **2.** (cheval) de race mêlée; (chien) métis.

ill breeding ['il'bri:diŋ], *s.* manque *m* d'éducation, de politesse, de savoir-vivre; mauvais ton; mauvais genre; mauvaises manières.

ill-concealed ['ilkən'si:ld], *a.* mal dissimulé.

ill-considered ['ilkən'sidəd], *a.* (*of action, view, etc.*) peu réfléchi; **i.-c. measures,** mesures hâtives.

ill-defined ['ildi'faind], *a.* mal défini; indéfini; flou.

ill-disposed ['ildis'pouzd], *a.* **1.** malintentionné, malveillant; **i.-d. people,** esprits mal lunés; **i.-d. towards s.o.,** mal disposé envers qn; indisposé contre qn. **2. to be i.-d. to do sth.,** être peu disposé, mal disposé, à faire qch.

ill-doer ['il'duər], *s. O:* malfaiteur, -trice; propre à rien *mf.*

Illecebraceae [ilesi'breisii:], *s.pl. Bot:* caryophyllacées *f.*

illecebrum [i'lesibrəm], *s. Bot:* illecebrum *m.*

illegal [i'li:g(ə)l], *a.* **1.** illégal, -aux; *Jur:* **i. operation,** avortement provoqué par manœuvres criminelles. **2.** *Cmptr:* (caractère) interdit, invalide.

illegality [ili(:)'gæliti], *s.* illégalité *f.*

illegalize [i'li:gəlaiz], *v.tr.* rendre (qch.) illégal.

illegally [i'li:gəli], *adv.* illégalement.

illegibility [iledʒi'biliti], *s.* illisibilité *f.*

illegible [i'ledʒibl], *a.* illisible.

illegibly [i'ledʒibli], *adv.* illisiblement.

illegitimacy [ili'dʒitiməsi], *s.* illégitimité *f.*

illegitimate [ili'dʒitimət], *a.* **1.** (conclusion *f*) illégitime; **i. statement,** déclaration non autorisée. **2.** contre les règles; illégal, -aux; *Turf:* **i. racing,** courses *f* d'obstacles. **3.** *Jur:* (enfant) illégitime, bâtard.

illegitimately [ili'dʒitimətli], *adv.* illégitimement.

ill-famed ['il'feimd], *a.* mal famé.

ill-fated ['il'feitid], *a.* (enfant) infortuné, condamné au malheur; (jour) fatal, de malheur, néfaste; (effort) malheureux; **Troy, the i.-f.,** Troie, la malheureuse.

ill-favoured ['il'feivəd], *a.* **1.** (*of pers.*) laid; de mauvaise mine, de mauvais air; **i.-f. woman, girl,** laideron *f*; **he's certainly i.-f.,** il ne paie pas de mine. **2.** (mot) répugnant, désagréable.

ill(-)feeling ['il'fi:liŋ], *s.* ressentiment *m*, rancune *f*; **to do sth. to show there's no i.-f.,** faire qch. pour ne pas désobliger qn, par complaisance; **no i.-f.!** sans rancune!

ill-found ['il'faund], *a.* (navire) mal équipé, mal fourni, mal pourvu.

ill-founded ['il'faundid], *a.* (*of rumour*) mal fondé, sans fondement.

ill-gotten ['il'gɔtn], *a.* (bien) mal acquis.

ill humour [il'hju:mər], *s.* mauvaise humeur; humeur acariâtre; **to be in an i. h.,** être de mauvaise humeur.

ill-humoured [il'hju:məd], *a.* de mauvaise humeur; maussade, grincheux.

illiberal [i'libər(ə)l], *a.* peu libéral, -aux; (*a*) grossier; mal élevé; sans distinction; (*b*) borné, petit (d'esprit); (esprit) illibéral, -aux; (*c*) ladre, peu généreux, illibéral, mesquin.

illiberality [ilibə'ræliti], *s.* illibéralité *f*; (*a*) petitesse *f* (d'esprit); étroitesse *f* (de pensée); (*b*) manque *m* de générosité; ladrerie *f.*

illiberally [i'lib(ə)rəli], *adv.* sans libéralité, sans générosité; mesquinement.

illicit [i'lisit], *a.* illicite; **i. betting,** paris clandestins; **i. profits,** profits *m* illicites; *P:* rabiot *m.*

illicitly [i'lisitli], *adv.* illicitement.

illicitness [i'lisitnis], *s.* caractère *m*, nature *f*, illicite (d'un commerce).

illimitable [i'limitəbl], *a.* illimitable, illimité; sans bornes, sans limites.

illimitableness [i'limitəbəlnis], *s.* caractère illimité; immensité *f* (de qch.).

illimitably [i'limitəbli], *adv.* sans bornes, sans limites, sans mesure.

ill-informed [ilin'fɔ:md], *a.* **1.** mal renseigné. **2.** peu instruit; (*of criticism, etc.*) ignorant.

Illinoian [ili'nɔiən], *a.* & *s. Geol:* illinoisien (*m*).

Illinoi(s)an [ili'nɔi(z)(ə)n], *a.* & *s. Geog:* natif, -ive, originaire (*mf*), de l'Illinois.

ill-intentioned ['ilin'tenʃ(ə)nd], *a.* malintentionné (**towards,** envers).

illipe ['ilipi:], *s. Bot:* illipé *m*; **i. butter,** beurre *m*, huile *f*, d'illipé.

illiquid [i'likwid], *a.* (substance, argent, etc.) non liquide.

illiquidity [ili'kwiditi], *s. Fin:* non-liquidité *f.*

illite ['ilait], *s. Geol:* illite *f.*

illiteracy [i'lit(ə)rəsi], *s.* **1.** manque *m* d'instruction; analphabétisme *m.* **2.** faute *f* (de prononciation, etc.) qui indique le manque d'instruction, l'analphabétisme.

illiterate [i'lit(ə)rət], *a.* & *s.* illettré, -ée; analphabète (*mf*).

illiterately [i'lit(ə)rətli], *adv.* en illettré, en ignorant.

ill-judged ['il'dʒʌdʒd], *a.* (*of action*) malavisé; peu sage.

ill-kempt ['il'kempt], *a.* **1.** (*of hair, etc.*) mal peigné, inculte, hirsute; (*of pers., appearance, etc.*) hirsute, dépeigné. **2.** (*of garden, etc.*) peu soigné; mal tenu; négligé; en désordre.

ill-mannered ['il'mænəd], *a.* malhonnête, grossier, malappris; **to be i.-m.,** avoir de mauvaises manières; être mal élevé.

ill-matched ['il'mætʃt], *a.* mal assorti, disparate; **i.-m. couple,** époux mal assortis; ménage mal assorti, mal attelé.

ill-meaning ['il'mi:niŋ], *a.* (*of pers.*) malintentionné.

ill nature ['il'neitʃər], *s.* mauvais caractère; méchant caractère; méchanceté *f.*

ill-natured ['il'neitʃəd], *a.* d'un mauvais caractère; méchant; désagréable; mauvais; *F:* rosse; **to look i.-n.,** avoir l'air mauvais; **i.-n. jest,** plaisanterie méchante; **to say i.-n. things about s.o.,** dire des méchancetés sur qn.

ill-naturedly [il'neitʃədli], *adv.* méchamment; avec méchanceté; mauvaisement.

illness ['ilnis], *s.* maladie *f*; (*a*) **to have a long i.,** faire une longue maladie; **he had a slight i.,** il a fait une petite maladie; il s'est trouvé indisposé; **diplomatic i.,** maladie diplomatique; **severe i.,** maladie grave; **to be absent through i.,** être absent pour cause de, par suite de, maladie; **he has never had a day's i.,** il n'a jamais eu une heure de maladie; (*b*) **children's illnesses,** maladies, maux *m*, de l'enfance.

ill-nourished ['il'nʌriʃt], *a.* mal nourri.

illogical [i'lɔdʒik(ə)l], *a.* illogique; peu logique.

illogicality [ilɔdʒi'kæliti], **illogicalness** [i'lɔdʒik(ə)lnis], *s.* illogisme *m.*

illogically [i'lɔdʒikəli], *adv.* illogiquement; contrairement à la logique.

ill-omened ['il'oumend], *a.* de mauvais présage; de mauvais augure.

ill-qualified ['il'kwɔlifaid], *a.* incompétent; **i.-q. to do sth.,** peu qualifié pour faire qch.; peu apte à faire qch.

ill-spent ['il'spent], *a.* (temps, etc.) mal employé.

ill-starred ['il'stɑ:d], *a.* né sous une mauvaise étoile; (prince) infortuné; (jour) malheureux, néfaste; **i.-s. enterprise,** entreprise néfaste, vouée à l'insuccès.

ill-taught ['il'tɔ:t], *a.* **1.** (*of pers.*) sans instruction; illettré; ignorant. **2.** (*of subject*) mal enseigné.

ill-tempered ['il'tempəd], *a.* (*a*) (*of pers.*) de mauvais caractère; de méchant caractère; hargneux, maussade, grincheux, de mauvaise humeur; (*b*) (*of animal*) de méchant caractère.

ill-timed ['il'taimd], *a.* mal à propos, hors de propos; malencontreux, déplacé; **i.-t. arrival,** arrivée inopportune, intempestive; **i.-t. joke,** plaisanterie *f* hors de saison.

ill-tongued ['il'tʌŋd], *a.* (*a*) qui a une mauvaise langue; médisant; (*b*) grossier; mal embouché.

ill-treat ['il'tri:t], *v.tr.* maltraiter, brutaliser (qn, un chien); rudoyer (un cheval).

ill treatment ['il'tri:tmənt], *s.* mauvais traitements.

illume [i'lju:m], *v.tr. Poet:* illuminer, éclaircir (l'esprit).

illuminable [i'l(j)u:minəbl], *a.* illuminable.

illuminance [i'l(j)u:minəns], *s. Ph:* éclairement *m.*

illuminant [i'l(j)u:minənt]. **1.** *a.* éclairant, illuminant. **2.** *s.* (*a*) source *f* de lumière; (*b*) *Ch:* composition éclairante.

illuminate[1] [i'l(j)u:mineit], *s.* illuminé *m.*

illuminate[2], *v.tr.* **1.** éclairer (une salle, *Rad:* une cible, *W.Tel:* un réflecteur d'antenne). **2.** (*a*) illuminer (un édifice à l'occasion d'une fête); (*b*) *Fig:* **the joy that illuminated her countenance,** la joie qui illuminait son visage. **3.** enluminer (un manuscrit); enluminer, colorier (une carte, une gravure). **4.** (*a*) éclairer, élucider, porter de la lumière dans (un sujet, une question); (*b*) *Rel: Phil:* illuminer (l'esprit). **5.** embellir, jeter de l'éclat sur (une action).

illuminated [i'l(j)u:mineitid], *a.* **1.** éclairé; **brightly i.,** fortement éclairé; **i. sign,** enseigne lumineuse; **i. dial,** cadran éclairé, lumineux. **2.** (manuscrit) enluminé; **i. capital,** lettre *f* d'apparat; lettrine *f.*

Illuminati [ilumi'nɑ:ti:], *s.pl. Rel.H:* illuminés *m.*

illuminating[1] [i'l(j)u:mineitiŋ], *a.* **1.** éclairant, qui éclaire; **i. effect,** effet lumineux; *Mil:* **i. bomb,** bombe éclairante. **2. i. talk,** entretien *m* qui a éclairé la situation.

illuminating[2], *s.* **1.** éclairage *m*; **i. power,** pouvoir éclairant (du gaz, etc.); **i. apparatus,** appareil *m* d'éclairage; **i. engineer,** éclairagiste *m*; **i. engineering,** éclairagisme *m*; technique *f* de l'éclairage; **i. gas,** gaz *m* d'éclairage; **i. oil,** (i) huile *f* d'éclairage; huile lampante; (ii) pétrole lampant. **2.** illumination *f*, embrasement *m* (d'un édifice à l'occasion d'une fête, etc.). **3.** enluminement *m* (d'un manuscrit); coloriage *m* (d'une carte, d'une gravure). **4.** élucidation *f* (d'un sujet, d'une question). **5.** embellissement *m* (d'une action, etc.).

illuminatingly [il(j)umi'neitiŋli], *adv.* d'une manière illuminante, éclairante; de manière à éclairer (un sujet), à éclaircir (une question).

illumination [il(j)umi'neiʃ(ə)n], *s.* **1.** (*a*) éclairage *m* (d'une salle, d'une cible par un radar, d'un réflecteur d'antenne, etc.); **artificial i.,** éclairage artificiel; (*b*) illumination *f* (d'un édifice); (*c*) enluminement *m* (d'un manuscrit). **2.** (*a*) **to go out to see the illuminations,** sortir voir les illuminations; (*b*) **illuminations of a manuscript,** enluminures *f* d'un manuscrit. **3.** *Ph:* (*a*) **(degree of) i.,** éclairement *m*; **i. meter,** luxmètre *m*; (*b*) *Opt:* éclat *m* (d'une lentille, d'un objectif). **4.** *Theol:* illumination.

illuminative [i'l(j)u:minətiv], *a.* **1.** *Theol:* illuminatif. **2.** (discours, entretien, etc.) qui éclaire la situation. **3. i. art,** l'art *m* d'enluminer; enluminure *f.*

illuminator [i'l(j)u:mineitər], *s.* **1.** (*pers.*) (*a*) illuminateur, -trice; (*b*) *Art:* enlumineur, -euse. **2.** (*a*) dispositif *m* d'éclairage; *Med:* **X-ray i.,** négatoscope *m*; (*b*) *Nau:* verre *m* de hublot.

illumine [i'l(j)u:min], *v.tr.* = ILLUMINATE[2].

Illuminee [il(j)u:mi'ni:], *s. Rel.H:* illuminé, -ée.

illuminer [i'l(j)u:minər], *s.* **1.** illuminateur *m.* **2.** *A:* enlumineur *m* (de manuscrits).

illuminism [i'l(j)u:minizm], *s. Rel.H:* illuminisme *m.*

illuminometer [il(j)umi'nɔmitər], *s.* illuminomètre *m*; luxmètre *m*; photomètre portatif.

ill-use ['il'ju:z], *v.tr.* (*a*) maltraiter (un enfant, une femme); malmener (un adversaire); **the child, the dog, had been ill-used,** l'enfant, le chien, avait subi de mauvais traitements; (*b*) mal agir envers (qn); faire une injustice à (qn).

ill-used ['il'ju:zd], *a.* (*a*) maltraité, malmené; (*b*) **to think oneself i.-u.,** se croire (la) victime d'une injustice, d'un passe-droit; **to answer in an i.-u. tone of voice,** répondre d'une voix chagrine.

illusion [i'lu:ʒ(ə)n], *s.* **1.** illusion *f*; tromperie *f*; **optical i.,** (i) illusion d'optique; (ii) truc *m* d'optique; **to be, labour, under an i.,** être (la) victime, le jouet, d'une illusion; s'illusionner; se faire illusion; **to cherish an i.,** se bercer d'une illusion; **to cherish, entertain, illusions,** nourrir, entretenir, des illusions; se nourrir d'illusions; **to have illusions about oneself,** se faire illusion sur soi-même; **I have no illusions on this point,** je ne me fais aucune illusion sur ce point; **I am under no illusions (about this),** je ne m'illusionne pas, je ne me fais pas d'illusions (là-dessus, à ce sujet); **to lose one's illusions about sth.,** perdre ses illusions au sujet de qch.; se désabuser de qch.; **to have lost one's illusions,** avoir perdu ses illusions; être désabusé; être revenu de toutes ses illusions; **to work off an i. on s.o.,** illusionner qn. **2.** *Tex:* tulle *m* illusion.

illusioned [i'lu:ʒ(ə)nd], *a.* illusionné; qui se fait des illusions.

illusionism [i'lu:ʒ(ə)nizm], *s.* **1.** *Phil:* doctrine *f* que le monde de la matière n'est que pure illusion. **2.** *Art:* trompe-l'œil *m.* **3.** (*conjuring*) illusionnisme *m.*

illusionist [i'lu:ʒənist], *s.* **1.** *Phil:* adhérent, -ente, de la doctrine que le monde de la matière n'est que pure illusion. **2.** *Art:* peintre *m* de trompe-l'œil. **3.** prestidigitateur *m*, illusionniste *mf.*

illusive [i'lu:siv], *a.* illusoire, trompeur, mensonger.

illusively [i'lu:sivli], *adv.* illusoirement, trompeusement.

illusiveness [i'lu:sivnis], *s.* caractère illusoire, trompeur (de qch.).

illusorily [i'lu:s(ə)rili], *adv.* illusoirement.

illusory [i'lu:s(ə)ri], *a.* illusoire; qui ne se réalise point; sans effet; **i. profits,** bénéfices illusoires, mensongers.

illustrate ['iləstreit], *v.tr.* **1.** éclairer, expliquer, démontrer, (une règle, ce qu'on veut dire) par des exemples; **to i. the definition of a word with quotations,** illustrer la définition d'un mot par des citations; **in order to i. these facts,** afin de mettre ces faits en lumière; **lectures illustrated by slides,** conférences illustrées par des projections. **2.** illustrer; orner de gravures, de dessins (le texte d'un livre, d'un journal); **profusely illustrated,** abondamment illustré. **3.** *A:* illustrer, rendre illustre (une vie, etc.).

illustrated ['iləstreitid], *a.* & *s.* (journal, magazine) illustré (*m*).

illustrating ['iləstreitiŋ], *s.* **1.** explication *f* (d'un principe, d'une règle, etc.) au moyen d'exemples. **2.** illustration *f* (d'un livre, etc.).

illustration [iləs'treiʃ(ə)n], *s.* **1.** explication *f*, exemple *m*, preuve *f* (d'un principe, d'une règle); **by way of i.,** à titre d'exemple. **2.** illustration *f*; (*a*) action *f*, art *m* d'illustrer (les livres, etc.); (*b*) illustration, gravure *f*, image *f* (dans le texte d'un livre, d'un journal); **coloured i.,** illustration en couleur; **text i.,** vignette *f*.

illustrative ['iləstreitiv], *a.* éclairant; qui sert à éclairer, à expliquer; éclaircissant; **i. of sth.,** qui fournit un exemple de qch., qui explique qch.

illustrator ['iləstreitər], *s.* illustrateur *m* (d'un ouvrage).

illustrious [i'lʌstriəs], *a.* illustre, fameux, célèbre; (*as title*) **most i.,** très illustre; illustrissime.

illustriously [i'lʌstriəsli], *adv.* illustrement, d'une manière illustre, éclatante; avec éclat.

illustriousness [i'lʌstriəsnis], *s.* éclat *m*; gloire *f*, distinction *f*.

illutate [i'lu:teit], *v.tr. Med:* illuter.

illuvial [i'lu:viəl], *a. Geol:* illuvial, -aux.

illuviation [ilu:vi'eiʃ(ə)n], *s. Geol:* illuviation *f*.

illuvium, *pl.* **-iums, -ia** [i'lu:viəm, -iəmz, -iə], *s. Geol:* illuvium *m*.

ill will ['il'wil], *s.* mauvais vouloir; malveillance *f*, rancune *f*; **to bear no i. w. towards s.o.,** ne pas garder rancune à qn.

ill-willed ['il'wild], *a.* malveillant, rancunier.

ill-wisher ['il'wiʃər], *s.* malveillant, -ante; **he has no ill-wishers,** personne ne lui veut du mal, de mal.

illy ['illi], *adv. NAm:* mal.

Illyria [i'liriə]. *Pr.n. Hist:* Illyrie *f*.

Illyrian [i'liriən]. *Hist:* **1.** *a.* illyrien; **the I. movement,** l'illyrisme *m*. **2.** *s.* Illyrien, -ienne.

Illyric [i'lirik], *a. Hist:* illyrique.

ilmenite ['ilmənait], *s. Miner:* ilménite *f*.

ilvaite ['ilvəait], *s. Miner:* ilvaïte *f*.

im- [im], *pref.* im-.

image[1] ['imidʒ], *s.* **1.** (*a*) image (sculptée); représentation *f*, statue *f*, simulacre *m* (d'un dieu, etc.); (*for worship*) idole *f*; **i. breaker,** briseur *m* d'idoles; iconoclaste *mf*; **i. carver,** tailleur *m* d'images; **i. maker,** statuaire *m*; fabricant *m* d'images de piété; **i. worship,** culte *m* des idoles; idolâtrie *f*, iconolâtrie *f*; (*b*) *Num:* image. **2.** *Opt:* image; (*a*) **real i.,** image réelle; **virtual i.,** image virtuelle; **ghost i.,** image blanche; **inverted i.,** image renversée; **clear i., sharp i.,** image nette; *Phot:* **latent i.,** image latente; **false i.,** spectre *m* secondaire; (*b*) *Elcs: T.V:* **echo i., ghost i., double i.,** image double, image fantôme; **i. distortion,** distorsion *f* d'image; **i. frequency, i. response,** fréquence *f* image; **i. impedance,** impédance *f* image; **i. converter (tube),** tube transformateur d'images; **i. dissector,** dissecteur *m* optique, analyseur *m* optique; **i. reproducer,** tube à rayons cathodiques; (*c*) *Cmptr:* **card i.,** image de carte; **i. file,** fichier *m* vidéo. **3.** Image; portrait *m*; **God created man in his own i.,** Dieu créa l'homme à son image; **he's the very, living,** *F:* **spitting, i. of his father,** c'est l'image vivante, le portrait vivant, tout le portrait, de son père; *F:* c'est son père tout craché; **I've just met a man who is your very i.,** je viens de rencontrer votre sosie *m*; *Fig:* **he's the i. of discretion,** il est la sagesse même, incarnée. **4.** (*a*) image; idée *f*, conception *f*; **the images that swept through his mind,** les idées qui lui traversaient l'esprit; **he dismissed her i. from his mind,** il chassa son image de sa pensée; il ne songea plus à elle; **after i.,** image persistante, consécutive; (*b*) *Com:* **brand i.,** image de marque; (*of politician, etc.*) **(public) i.,** image (de marque). **5.** image, métaphore *f*; **style full of images,** style imagé, plein de métaphores; **to speak in images,** s'exprimer par métaphores; métaphoriser.

image[2], *v.tr.* **1.** (*a*) représenter (qn, qch.) par une image; tracer le portrait de (qn) (au crayon ou à la plume); (*b*) **the mountains are imaged in the lake,** les montagnes se reflètent dans le lac. **2. to i. sth. to oneself,** se figurer, s'imaginer, se représenter, qch.

image orthicon ['imidʒ'ɔ:θikɔn], *s. T.V:* image-orthicon *m*, *pl.* images-orthicons.

imagery ['imidʒ(ə)ri], *s.* **1.** *coll.* images sculptées; idoles *fpl*. **2.** figures *fpl* de rhétorique; langage figuré; images; **style full of i.,** style imagé, plein d'images.

imaginable [i'mædʒinəbl], *a.* imaginable; **the highest degree i.,** le plus haut degré imaginable; **the finest thing i.,** la plus belle chose qu'on puisse imaginer; tout ce qu'on peut imaginer de plus beau; **there's no i. reason why I shouldn't do it,** il n'y a pas la moindre raison qui m'empêche de faire; quelle raison pourrait-il y avoir pour que je ne le fasse pas?

imaginably [i'mædʒinəbli], *adv.* d'une manière imaginable, concevable; à ce qu'on peut s'imaginer; **he may i. have stayed at home,** il est imaginable, fort possible, qu'il soit resté chez lui.

imaginal [i'mædʒin(ə)l], *a. Ent:* imaginal, -aux; **i. disks, buds,** disques imaginaux.

imaginary [i'mædʒin(ə)ri], *a.* imaginaire; de pure fantaisie; **to create i. difficulties,** se créer des difficultés imaginaires; se faire des fantômes de rien; *Mth:* **i. quantity,** quantité *f* imaginaire; imaginaire *f*.

imagination [imædʒi'neiʃ(ə)n], *s.* imagination *f*; **to have a lively, an ardent, i.,** avoir l'imagination vive, une imagination fougueuse; **to have no i.,** manquer d'imagination; **the public has little i.,** le public est peu imaginatif; **to see one's youth in i.,** revoir sa jeunesse en imagination, en idée; rêver sa jeunesse; **the land of i.,** le pays des chimères; **that's your i.!** vous l'avez rêvé!

imaginational [imædʒin'neiʃn(ə)l], *a.* (connaissance) par l'imagination.

imaginative [i'mædʒinətiv], *a.* **1.** (*of pers., faculty, etc.*) imaginatif. **2.** (poème *m*, etc.) d'imagination.

imaginativeness [i'mædʒinətivnis], *s.* **1.** nature imaginative (d'un poème, dessin, etc.). **2.** don *m*, faculté *f*, d'imagination.

imagine [i'mædʒin], *v.tr.* **1.** (*a*) imaginer, concevoir (qch.); se figurer, se représenter (qch.); se faire une idée de (qch.); **I can i. nothing worse than poverty,** je ne saurais rien imaginer de pire que la pauvreté; **try to i. our position,** essayez de vous faire une idée de notre position; **he already imagined himself lost,** il se voyait déjà perdu; **i. yourself in Paris,** supposez-vous à Paris; **i. yourself as a soldier,** figurez-vous que vous êtes, que vous soyez, soldat; **nothing funnier could be imagined,** rien de plus drôle ne saurait s'imaginer; **as may (well) be imagined,** comme on peut (se) l'imaginer; **I can i. it happening,** je m'imagine fort bien que cela puisse arriver; **can you i. my making love to her?** me voyez-vous lui faisant la cour? **i. meeting you here!** qui aurait jamais pensé vous rencontrer ici! **just i. my despair,** représentez-vous, figurez-vous, imaginez(-vous) un peu, mon désespoir; **just i. what would happen!** songez donc à ce qui arriverait! **I leave you to i. what was the result,** je vous laisse à penser ce qui en résulta; **you can i. how angry I was!** pensez, songez, si j'étais furieux! **you can i. what it was (is, would be) like,** vous voyez ça d'ici; **you can't i. how happy we are,** vous n'imaginez pas comme nous sommes heureux; **you can't i. it!** on ne s'en fait pas idée! **can you i. it?** a-t-on idée d'une chose pareille? **I can't i. why you should allow it,** je ne vois pas pourquoi vous le permettriez; (*b*) (*suppose*) **I i. I have met you before,** j'imagine que je vous ai déjà rencontré; **I i. them to be fairly rich,** je les crois assez riches; **I know something about it, I i.!** j'en sais quelque chose, peut-être! **don't i. that I'm satisfied,** n'allez pas croire, ne croyez pas, que je sois satisfait; **I i. myself to have made a discovery,** je me flatte d'avoir fait une découverte. **2.** s'imaginer, se figurer; **to i. all sorts of things, to be always imagining things,** se faire des imaginations, des idées; **everywhere people imagined they saw spies,** partout on croyait voir des espions; **I imagined I heard a knock at the door,** j'ai cru entendre frapper à la porte.

imaginer [i'mædʒinər], *s.* imaginateur, -trice.

imagining [i'mædʒiniŋ], *s.* **1.** imagination *f*, conception *f*. **2. these are all vain imaginings,** chimères *f* que tout cela.

imagism ['imədʒizm], *s. Lit:* imagisme *m*.

imagist ['imədʒist], *s. Lit:* imagiste *mf*.

imago, *pl.* **imagos, imagines** [i'meigou, -'mɑ:-, i'meidʒini:z, i'mɑ:gini:z], *s.* **1.** *Ent:* imago *f*; image *f*; insecte parfait. **2.** *Psy:* imago; image affective (du père, de la mère).

ima(u)m [i'mɑ:m], *s. Rel:* imam *m*, iman *m*.

imamate [i'mɑ:meit], *s. Rel:* imamat *m*, imanat *m*.

imbalance [im'bæləns], *s.* déséquilibre *m*.

imbecile ['imbisi:l, -sail]. **1.** *a.* imbécile; (*a*) faible d'esprit; (*b*) *F:* d'une stupidité crasse, outrée; **i. remark,** remarque *f* imbécile. **2.** *s.* (*a*) imbécile *mf*; (*b*) *F:* imbécile; **you i!,** espèce *f* d'idiot, d'idiote!

imbecilic [imbi'silik], *a.* (sourire, etc.) imbécile.

imbecility [imbi'siliti], *s.* **1.** (*a*) imbécillité *f*; faiblesse *f* d'esprit; (*b*) faiblesse, ineptie *f* (d'une administration, etc.). **2.** action *f* inepte; imbécillité.

imbed [im'bed], *v.tr.* = EMBED.

imbedment [im'bedmənt], *s.* =EMBEDMENT.

imbibe [im'baib]. **1.** *v.tr.* (*a*) (*of pers.*) absorber, s'assimiler (des connaissances, des idées); s'imprégner de (connaissances, préjugés); **to i. sound principles from infancy,** sucer de bons principes avec le lait; (*b*) (*of pers.*) boire, avaler (une boisson); absorber (de la bière, etc.); aspirer (l'air frais); (*c*) (*of thg*) imbiber (qch.); s'imprégner, se pénétrer, de (créosote, etc.); **the water that the earth imbibes,** l'eau *f* que la terre imbibe, absorbe; **the cake imbibes the rum,** le gâteau s'imbibe de rhum. **2.** *v.i.* (*a*) boire des boissons alcooliques; (*b*) boire trop; être adonné à la boisson.

imbiber [im'baibər], *s.* **1.** (*pers.*) (*a*) buveur, -euse (**of,** de); (*b*) ivrogne *m*; buveur, -euse. **2.** (*thg*) absorbant *m* (**of,** de).

imbibing [im'baibiŋ], *s.* absorption *f*; imbibition *f* (de l'eau par les racines, etc.).

imbibition [imbi'biʃ(ə)n], *s.* imbibition *f*.

imbriago [imbri'ɑ:gou], *s. Ich:* imbriago *m*.

imbricate[1], **imbricated** ['imbrikeit(id)], *a. Arch: Nat.Hist:* imbriqué; **i. work,** imbrication *f*; *Geol:* **imbricate structure,** structure imbriquée; *Bot:* **imbricate leaves, petals,** feuilles, pétales, imbriquées; **imbricate aestivation,** (préfloraison) imbriquée (*f*).

imbricate[2], **1.** *v.tr.* imbriquer (des tuiles, etc.). **2.** *v.i.* (*of fish scales, etc.*) s'imbriquer.

imbrication [imbri'keiʃ(ə)n], *s. Nat.Hist: etc:* imbrication *f*.

imbricative ['imbrikeitiv], *a. Nat.Hist:* imbricatif.

imbroglio [im'brouliou], *s.* imbroglio *m*, embrouillement *m*; **to unravel an i.,** démêler un imbroglio.

imbrue [im'bru:], *v.tr. Lit:* **to i. (sth.) in, with, blood,** tremper (son épée, ses mains) dans le sang; souiller (ses mains) de sang; **imbrued with blood,** ensanglanté.

imbrute [im'bru:t], *A: & Lit:* **1.** *v.tr.* abrutir (qn); ravaler (qn) au niveau de la brute. **2.** *v.i.* s'abaisser au niveau de la brute; s'abrutir.

imbue [im'bju:], *v.tr.* **1.** *A:* **to i. sth. (with sth.),** imbiber qch. (d'un liquide); imprégner qch. (de teinture, etc.). **2.** *Lit:* **to i. s.o. with an idea,** pénétrer qn d'une idée; **to become imbued with prejudices, with new ideas,** s'imbiber, se pénétrer, de préjugés; s'imprégner d'idées nouvelles; **imbued with prejudices,** imbu de préjugés; **imbued with false principles,** pénétré, imprégné, de faux principes.

imidazol(e) [imi'dæzoul], *s. Ch:* imidazole *m*.

imide ['imaid], *s. Ch:* imide *m*.

imido ['imidou], *a. Ch:* **i. compound,** imide *m*; **i. acid,** imidoacide *m*; **i. ether,** imidoéther *m*.

imidogen [i'midədʒən], *s. Ch:* imidogène *m*.

imin ['imin], **imine** [i'mi:n], *s. Ch:* imine *f*.

imino ['iminou], *a. Ch:* imino-; **i. ether,** iminoéther *m*.

imipramine [i'miprəmain], *s. Pharm:* imipramine *f*.

imitable ['imitəbl], *a.* imitable.

imitate ['imiteit], *v.tr.* imiter, (*a*) copier; suivre l'exemple de (qn); **to i. s.o.'s style,** attraper la manière de qn; *Art: Lit: Mus:* pasticher le style de qn; **he has seldom been imitated,** il n'a rencontré que de rares imitateurs; **to i. a plan,** suivre un dessin; (*b*) singer, mimer (qn); contrefaire (le cri d'un oiseau, etc.); **a child imitates what it sees,** un enfant imite ce qu'il voit; **he could i. the master to the life,** il imitait le maître à s'y méprendre; (*c*) (*of insect, etc.*) **to i. its surroundings,** prendre l'aspect de son milieu; **paintings that i. mosaic,** peintures qui imitent la mosaïque.

imitation [imi'teiʃ(ə)n], *s.* **1.** imitation *f*; **to defy i.,** défier toute imitation; **in i. of s.o., sth.,** à l'imitation de, imitant, qn, qch.; à l'instar de (Paris, etc.); *Rel.Lit:* **the I. of Christ,** l'Imitation de Jésus-Christ. **2.** (*a*) copie *f*, imitation; *Com:* contrefaçon *f*; article contrefait; **beware of imitations,** méfiez-vous des contrefaçons; **weak i. of Carlyle,** mauvaise imitation, mauvais pastiche, de Carlyle; du Carlyle en détrempe; (*b*) *attrib.* factice; simili-; **i. leather,** cuir artificiel; similicuir *m*; **i. morocco, pigskin,** cuir genre maroquin; cuir façon porc; **i. sealskin coat,** manteau *m* (en) imitation loutre; **i. silver, gold,** similargent *m*, similor *m*; **i. bronze, marble,** similibronze *m*, similimarbre *m*; **i. stone,** similipierre *f*; **i. jewellery,** bijouterie fausse; bijoux *mpl* en faux, en simili, en toc, en imitation; **to wear i. jewellery,** porter du faux; **i. pearl,** perle fausse, perle postiche; **i. mineral water,** eau minérale artificielle; **i. joint,** joint simulé. **3.** *Mus:* **exact i.,** imitation régulière, canonique, contrainte; **i. by augmentation, in contrary motion,** imitation par augmentation, par mouvement contraire.

imitative ['imitətiv], *a.* **1.** (*a*) (son, etc.) imitatif; **i. arts,** arts imitatifs, arts d'imitation; (*b*) **manner, style, i. of s.o.,** manière *f*, style *m*, qui imite qn. **2.** (*of pers., etc.*) porté à imiter; imitateur, -trice; singe; (esprit *m*) copiste.

imitatively ['imitətivli], *adv.* en imitation.

imitativeness ['imitətivnis], *s.* tendance *f* à imiter; esprit imitatif, d'imitation.

imitator ['imiteitər], *s.* **1.** (*a*) imitateur, -trice; **the disciples and imitators of a great man,** les disciples et les imitateurs d'un grand homme; (*b*) *Com:* contrefacteur *m*; (*c*) *Lit: etc:* pasticheur, -euse. **2.** *F:* singe *m*; singeur, *f.* singeuse, singeresse.

immaculacy [i'mækjuləsi], *s.* état immaculé, pur; pureté parfaite.

immaculate [i'mækjulət], *a.* **1.** immaculé; sans tache;

Theol: **the I. Conception,** l'Immaculée Conception. **2.** (*of dress*) irréprochable, impeccable. **3.** *Nat.Hist:* non tacheté.

immaculately [i'mækjulətli], *adv.* **1.** sans tache, sans défaut. **2.** (vêtu) irréprochablement.

immaculateness [i'mækjulətnis], *s.* **1.** pureté parfaite, sans tache; état immaculé. **2.** impeccabilité *f* (de la tenue).

immanence ['imənəns], **immanency** ['imənənsi], *s.* immanence *f.*

immanent ['imənənt], *a.* immanent.

immanentism ['imənəntizm], *s. Phil: Theol:* immanentisme *m.*

immanentist ['imənəntist], *a. & s. Phil: Theol:* immanentiste.

Immanuel [i'mænjuəl]. *Pr.n.m. B.Lit:* Emmanuel.

immarginate [i'mɑ:dʒineit], *a. Bot:* émarginé.

immaterial [imə'tiəriəl], *a.* **1.** (esprit, etc.) immatériel, incorporel. **2.** (*a*) peu important; sans conséquence; **that fact is (quite) i.,** cela n'a point d'importance, n'a aucune importance; cela ne fait rien; **that is quite i. to me,** cela m'est indifférent; (*b*) **i. to the subject,** qui n'a aucun rapport avec la question.

immaterialism [imə'tiəriəlizm], *s. Phil:* immatérialisme *m.*

immaterialist [imə'tiəriəlist], *s. Phil:* immatérialiste *mf.*

immateriality [imətiəri'æliti], *s.* **1.** immatérialité *f.* **2.** insignifiance *f,* peu *m* d'importance (d'un fait).

immaterialize [imə'tiəriəlaiz], *v.tr.* immatérialiser.

immaterially [imə'tiəriəli], *adv.* immatériellement.

immature [imə'tjuər], *a.* **1.** (*a*) (qui n'est) pas mûr; **emotionally i. adults,** adultes dont les émotions manquent de maturité; (*b*) **the project is i.,** le projet n'est pas suffisamment mûri; **i. work,** œuvre *f* de jeunesse, d'apprenti; (*c*) *Biol:* immature; (*d*) *Geol: esp. U.S:* (vallée, etc.) au stade infantile. **2.** *A:* prématuré.

immaturely [imə'tjuəli], *adv.* **1.** avant la complète maturité. **2.** *A:* prématurément.

immatureness [imə'tjuənis], **immaturity** [imə'tjuəriti], *s.* immaturité *f*; **the i. of these projects,** le défaut de maturité de ces projets.

immeasurability [imeʒ(ə)rə'biliti], **immeasurableness** [i'meʒərəb(ə)lnis], *s.* incommensurabilité *f*; immensité *f.*

immeasurable [i'meʒ(ə)rəbl], *a.* (espace, abîme) incommensurable; (temps) immesurable, immense, infini; **to my i. joy,** à ma joie infinie; à ma grande joie.

immeasurably [i'meʒ(ə)rəbli], *adv.* démesurément, infiniment; outre mesure.

immediacy [i'mi:diəsi], *s.* **1.** relation directe, intime (**of sth. with sth.,** entre qch. et qch.). **2.** caractère immédiat (of, de); imminence *f* (d'un danger); urgence *f* (d'un besoin); **the i. of our peril,** notre péril pressant. **3.** *Phil: A.Jur:* immédiateté *f.*

immediate [i'mi:diət], *a.* immédiat. **1.** (*a*) sans intermédiaire; direct; **i. cause,** cause directe, prochaine; **my i. object,** mon premier but; **what are your i. plans?** que proposez-vous faire d'abord? **the i. future,** l'avenir prochain; le proche avenir; **in the i. future,** dans un avenir immédiat; dans l'immédiat; **it does not touch my i. interests,** cela ne me touche pas directement; *A.Jur:* **i. fief,** fief immédiat; *Phil:* **i. knowledge,** connaissance immédiate; (*b*) **my i. neighbour,** mon voisin immédiat; mon voisin le plus proche; **in the i. vicinity,** dans le voisinage immédiat; **the i. family, relations,** les proches parents. **2.** instantané; sans retard; **i. answer, delivery,** réponse immédiate, livraison immédiate; **for i. delivery,** urgent; à livrer de suite; **house for sale with i. possession,** maison à vendre avec jouissance immédiate; **house to let with i. possession,** maison à louer présentement; **to rent a house with i. possession,** louer une maison clefs en main. **3.** (besoin, danger) pressant, urgent; **work of i. urgency,** travail de première urgence.

immediately [i'mi:diətli]. **1.** *adv.* immédiatement; (*a*) directement; sans intermédiaire; **it does not affect me i.,** cela ne me touche pas directement; (*b*) tout de suite; sans délai; toute affaire cessante; toutes choses cessantes; **please answer i.,** veuillez nous répondre incessamment, sans délai; **please send i. . . . ,** veuillez (bien) envoyer d'urgence . . .; **i. on his return I wrote to him,** aussitôt son retour, dès son retour, je lui ai écrit; **i. after,** aussitôt après. **2.** *conj.* **i. he received the money, he paid me,** aussitôt l'argent reçu, dès qu'il eut reçu l'argent, il me paya.

immediateness [i'mi:diətnis], *s.* **1.** proximité immédiate. **2.** = IMMEDIACY 2.

immedicable [i'medikəbl], *a.* incurable.

immemorial [imi'mɔ:riəl], *a.* immémorial, -aux; **their i. privileges,** leurs privilèges immémoriaux; **from time i.,** de toute antiquité; de toute ancienneté; de temps immémorial; de toute éternité; **i. elms,** ormes *m* séculaires.

immemorially [imi'mɔ:riəli], *adv.* de temps immémorial; depuis un temps immémorial; de toute antiquité.

immense [i'mens], *a.* **1.** (étendue *f*) immense, vaste; (quantité *f*) énorme; **he is an i. eater,** il mange énormément; il a un appétit féroce. **2.** magnifique; **it was an i. success,** c'était un succès fou.

immensely [i'mensli], *adv.* **1.** immensément (vaste); énormément (riche). **2. to enjoy oneself i.,** s'amuser énormément.

immenseness [i'mensnis], **immensity** [i'mensiti], *s.* **1.** immensité *f* (de l'univers, d'une fortune, etc.). **2.** énormité *f* (d'un crime).

immensurable [i'menʃərəbl], *a.* immensurable.

immerge [i'mə:dʒ]. **1.** *v.tr.* = IMMERSE. **2.** *v.i. Astr: A:* immerger.

immergence [i'mə:dʒ(ə)ns], *s.* = IMMERSION.

immerse [i'mə:s], *v.tr.* **1.** (*a*) immerger, submerger, plonger (qn, qch.) (dans un liquide); *Bot:* **immersed plant,** plante immergée; (*b*) baptiser (qn) par immersion. **2. to i. oneself (again) in daydreams,** se (re)plonger dans une rêverie; **he immersed himself in conversation with his neighbour,** il se plongea dans la conversation avec son voisin; **to be immersed in one's work, in one's thoughts,** être plongé, absorbé, dans son travail, dans ses pensées.

immersion [i'mə:ʃ(ə)n], *s.* **1.** (*a*) immersion *f,* submersion *f*; **electric i. heater,** chauffe-liquides *m inv* électrique; thermoplongeur *m*; **i. (water) heater,** chauffe-eau *m inv* à immersion; *Nau:* **i. scale,** échelle *f* de tirant d'eau; *Opt:* **i. objective,** objectif *m* à immersion (d'un microscope); (*b*) baptême *m* par immersion. **2.** absorption *f* (d'esprit) (**in,** dans). **3.** *Astr:* immersion (d'un astre).

immigrant ['imigrənt], *a. & s.* immigrant, -ante; immigré, -ée; **country open to immigrants,** pays *m* d'immigration.

immigrate ['imigreit]. **1.** *v.i.* immigrer. **2.** *v.tr.* **to i. foreign labour into a country,** introduire dans un pays de la main-d'œuvre étrangère.

immigration [imi'greiʃ(ə)n], *s.* immigration *f*; **i. officer,** agent *m* du service de l'immigration.

imminence ['iminəns], **imminency** ['iminənsi], *s.* imminence *f,* proximité *f* (**of,** de).

imminent ['iminənt], *a.* (danger, événement) imminent; **to be i.,** être imminent.

imminently ['iminəntli], *adv.* d'une manière imminente, menaçante.

immingle [i'miŋgl]. **1.** *v.tr.* mêler (**with,** à). **2.** *v.i.* se mêler.

immiscibility [imisi'biliti], *s.* immiscibilité *f.*

immiscible [i'misibl], *a.* immiscible; qui ne peut pas être mêlé.

immitigable [i'mitigəbl], *a.* **1.** (haine) implacable. **2.** (douleur) que l'on ne saurait adoucir.

immix [i'miks], *v.tr.* mêler (**sth. with sth.,** qch. à qch.).

immixture [i'mikstʃər], *s.* **1.** mélange *m* (de deux substances). **2.** immixtion *f* (de qn dans une affaire).

immobile [i'moubail], *a.* **1.** fixe; à demeure; que l'on ne peut déplacer. **2.** immobile; sans mouvement.

immobility [imə'biliti], *s.* **1.** fixité *f.* **2.** immobilité *f.*

immobilization [imoubilai'zeiʃ(ə)n], *s.* **1.** (*a*) immobilisation *f* (d'un bras cassé, etc.); (*b*) immobilisation, arrêt *m* (d'une armée, de la circulation). **2.** *Fin:* immobilisation (des capitaux, etc.).

immobilize [i'moubilaiz], *v.tr.* **1.** (*a*) immobiliser (un membre blessé, etc.); assujettir (un animal qu'on veut opérer); (*b*) immobiliser, arrêter (une armée, la circulation sur les routes, etc.). **2.** *Fin:* **to i. capital, specie,** rendre des capitaux indisponibles; immobiliser, retirer de la circulation, des espèces monnayées.

immoderate [i'mɔd(ə)rət], *a.* immodéré, intempéré, outré, extravagant; **i. appetite,** appétit déréglé, désordonné; **i. thirst,** soif démesurée; **i. mirth,** gaieté exubérante, excessive.

immoderately [i'mɔd(ə)rətli], *adv.* immodérément, excessivement, extravagamment; avec excès; (rire) à gorge déployée.

immoderateness [i'mɔd(ə)rətnis], **immoderation** [imɔdə'reiʃ(ə)n], *s.* immodération *f,* excès *m,* extravagance *f.*

immodest [i'mɔdist], *a.* **1.** *A:* présomptueux, impudent. **2.** (femme, tenue) impudique, sans pudeur.

immodestly [i'mɔdistli], *adv.* **1.** *A:* présomptueusement, impudemment. **2.** impudiquement.

immodesty [i'mɔdisti], *s.* **1.** *A:* impudence *f.* **2.** impudeur *f.*

immolate ['imouleit], *v.tr.* immoler (qn, qch.).

immolation [imou'leiʃ(ə)n], *s.* immolation *f.*

immolator ['imouleitər], *s.* immolateur *m.*

immoral [i'mɔrəl], *a.* immoral, -aux; (*a*) (*of pers.*) dissolu; **to lead an i. life,** mener une vie dissolue; **i. conduct,** débauche *f*; (*b*) (ouvrage) contraire à la morale; **i. literature,** littérature malsaine; **very i.,** d'une grande immoralité; (*c*) *Jur:* **for i. purposes,** aux fins de débauche; **i. offence,** attentat *m* aux mœurs; **the i. classes,** les milieux spéciaux; le milieu; **(the crime of) living on i. earnings,** (le délit de) vagabondage spécial.

immoralism [i'mɔrəlizm], *s. Phil:* immoralisme *m.*

immoralist [i'mɔrəlist], *a. & s. Phil:* immoraliste (*mf*).

immorality [imə'ræliti], *s.* immoralité *f*; (i) débauche *f*; (ii) acte immoral; **to incite to i.,** inciter à la débauche.

immorally [i'mɔrəli], *adv.* immoralement.

immortal [i'mɔ:tl], *a. & s.* immortel (*m*); **the i. gods, the immortals,** les (dieux) immortels; **the i. memory of . . .,** le souvenir impérissable de . . ..

immortality [imɔ:'tæliti], *s.* immortalité *f.*

immortalization [imɔ:təlai'zeiʃ(ə)n], *s.* immortalisation *f.*

immortalize [i'mɔ:təlaiz], *v.tr.* immortaliser (le nom d'un auteur, etc.); éterniser, perpétuer (la mémoire de qn).

immortalizer [i'mɔ:təlaizər], *s.* immortalisateur, -trice.

immortally [i'mɔ:təli], *adv.* immortellement, perpétuellement.

immortelle [imɔ:'tel], *s. Bot:* immortelle *f.*

immotile [i'moutail], *a. Nat.Hist:* (organe, etc.) incapable de mouvement.

immovability [imu:və'biliti], *s.* **1.** fixité *f* (d'une machine, etc.). **2.** immuabilité *f* (de la volonté). **3.** impassibilité *f.*

immovable [i'mu:vəbl]. **1.** *a.* (*a*) fixe; que l'on ne peut déplacer; qui ne peut se déplacer; *Ecc:* **i. feast,** fête *f* fixe; (*b*) (opinion, volonté) immuable, inébranlable, tenace; **man i. in his purposes,** homme immuable dans ses projets; (*c*) (visage) impassible; (*d*) *Jur:* **i. property,** biens immobiliers, biens immeubles; **seizure of i. property,** saisie immobilière. **2.** *s. usu. pl. Jur:* **immovables,** biens immobiliers, biens immeubles.

immovableness [i'mu:vəb(ə)lnis], *s.* = IMMOVABILITY.

immovably [i'mu:vəbli], *adv.* **1.** immobilement; sans se mouvoir, sans remuer. **2.** immuablement, inébranlablement. **3.** impassiblement; sans s'émouvoir.

immune [i'mju:n]. **1.** *a.* (*a*) *Med:* **i. from contagion,** à l'abri de la contagion; **i. against, from, to, a poison,** immun, immunisé, contre un poison; **to render s.o. i. from a poison,** immuniser qn contre un poison; **virus i. to an antibiotic,** virus résistant à un antibiotique; **i. body,** immunisine *f,* sensibilisatrice *f,* ambocepteur *m*; **i. reaction,** immuno-réaction *f, pl.* immuno-réactions; **i. serum,** immun-sérum *m, pl.* immun-sérums; (*b*) **to be i. from evil influences,** être inaccessible aux mauvaises influences; **i. from criticism,** à l'abri de la critique; **to have become i. to the inclemency of the climate,** être blindé, cuirassé, contre les intempéries du climat; **i. from arrest,** pas susceptible d'être arrêté; **i. from taxation,** exempt d'impôts. **2.** *s. Med:* immun *m.*

immunify [i'mju:nifai], *v.tr. Med:* immuniser (**s.o. against sth.,** qn contre qch.).

immunisin [i'mju:nisin], *s. Biol:* immunisine *f.*

immunist ['imjunist], *s. A.Jur:* immuniste *mf.*

immunity [i'mju:niti], *s.* **1.** exemption *f* (**from,** de); **to claim i. from certain taxes,** demander à être exempt, affranchi, dispensé, de certains impôts; **diplomatic i., parliamentary i.,** immunité *f* diplomatique, parlementaire. **2.** *Med:* immunité (**from a disease,** contre une maladie); **i. of a virus to an antibiotic,** résistance *f* d'un virus à un antibiotique.

immunization [imjunai'zeiʃ(ə)n], *s. Med:* immunisation *f* (**against,** contre).

immunize ['imjunaiz], *v.tr. Med:* immuniser (**s.o. against sth.,** qn contre qch.).

immunizer ['imjunaizər], *s. Med:* immunisant *m.*

immunizing ['imjunaiziŋ], *a. Med: Vet:* (sérum, etc.) immunisant; **i. power,** pouvoir *m* immunigène.

immunochemistry [i'mju:nou'kemistri], *s.* immunochimie *f.*

immunoelectrophoresis, *pl.* **-reses** [i'mju:nouilektroufə'ri:sis, -'ri:si:z], *s.* immunoélectrophorèse *f.*

immunogenetics [i'mju:noudʒə'netiks], *s. pl.* (*often with sg. const.*) *Med:* immunogénétique *f.*

immunogenic [imju:nou'dʒenik], *a. Med:* immunogène, immunigène.

immunological [imjunə'lɔdʒikl], *a. Med:* immunologique.

immunologist [imju'nɔlədʒist], *s. Med:* immunologiste *mf.*

immunology [imju'nɔlədʒi], *s. Med:* immunologie *f.*

immunopathology [i'mju:noupə'θɔlədʒi], *s. Med:* immuno-pathologie *f.*

immunoreaction [i'mju:nouri'ækʃ(ə)n], *s. Med:* immuno-réaction *f, pl.* immuno-réactions.

immunosuppression [i'mju:nousə'preʃ(ə)n], *s. Med:* immuno-suppression *f, pl.* immuno-suppressions.

immunosuppressive [i'mju:nousə'presiv], *a. Med:* immuno-suppressif, *pl.* immuno-suppressifs, -ives.

immunotherapy [i'mju:nou'θerəpi], *s. Med:* immunothérapie *f.*

immunotransfusion [i'mju:noutrænz'fju:ʒ(ə)n], *s. Med:* immuno(-)transfusion *f, pl.* immuno(-)transfusions.

immure [i'mjuər], *v.tr.* **1.** enfermer, cloîtrer (qn); **immured nuns,** religieuses cloîtrées, murées. **2.** emmurer (une victime).

immurement [i'mjuəmənt], **immuring** [i'mjuəriŋ], *s.* **1.** séparation *f* (d'une religieuse, etc.) du monde. **2.** emmurement *m* (d'une victime).

immutability [imju:tə'biliti], *s.* immu(t)abilité *f,* inaltérabilité *f.*

immutable [i'mju:təbl], *a.* immuable; inaltérable.

immutably [i'mju:təbli], *adv.* immuablement.

imp[1] [imp], *s.* **1.** *(a)* diablotin *m,* petit démon, lutin *m,* gobelin *m; (b) F: (of child)* petit espiègle, petit diable; petite maligne; petite espiègle. **2.** *Ph:* **Cartesian i.,** ludion *m.*

imp[2], *v.tr. Ven: A:* **to i. a falcon's wings,** (i) greffer, ajouter, des plumes aux pennes d'un faucon; (ii) renforcer le vol d'un faucon.

impact[1] ['impækt], *s.* **1.** choc *m,* impact *m,* collision *f,* percussion *f; (a) Ph: Mec:* **i. of one body on, against, another,** choc, impact, d'un corps contre un autre; **i. strength,** résistance *f* au choc; **i. value,** résilience *f;* **i. test,** essai *m* de résilience, de résistance, au choc; **i. bending,** flexion due au choc; **i. bending strength,** résistance de flexion au choc; **i. pressure,** pression *f* d'impact; *Av:* **i. load,** choc d'atterrissage; *Typ:* **i. printer,** imprimante *f* à percussion; *(b) Artil: Ball:* impact; point *m* de chute (d'un projectile); **on i.,** à l'impact, à l'arrivée; *Artil:* **i. (type) fuse,** fusée percutante; **point of i.,** point d'impact; **mean point of i.,** point moyen d'impact; **i. velocity,** vitesse restante (d'un projectile); *Mil.Av:* **i. area,** zone *f* d'impact, des points de chute (des bombes); *(c) El:* **i. excitation,** excitation *f* par choc, par impulsion; **i. excited,** excité par choc, par impulsion; à couplage direct; *W.Tel:* **i. transmitter,** émetteur *m* à impulsion; *(d) Atom.Ph:* **i. radiation,** rayonnement *m,* radiation *f,* par choc; **i. ionization,** ionisation *f* par choc; **i. electron, i. neutron,** électron *m,* neutron *m,* de choc; **i. parameter,** paramètre *m* d'impact, de choc. **2.** *Fig:* répercussion(s) *f(pl),* impact; **the i. of socialism on private enterprise,** les répercussions, l'impact, du socialisme sur l'entreprise privée; **the i. of high wages on production costs,** l'incidence *f* des hauts salaires sur les prix de revient; **the i. of a publicity campaign,** la force d'impact d'une campagne publicitaire; **the i. of the news was staggering,** l'impact de la nouvelle était atterrant; **his speech made a great i. on the audience,** son discours eut un effet retentissant sur l'auditoire.

impact[2] [im'pækt]. **1.** *v.tr.* encastrer **(into,** dans); loger, fixer (solidement) **(into,** dans). **2.** *v.i. (a)* **to i. with, against, sth.,** se heurter contre qch.; *(b)* **to i. on s.o., sth.,** avoir des répercussions, un impact, sur qn, qch.

impacted [im'pæktid], *a.* encastré; *Surg:* **i. fracture,** fracture *f* avec impaction; *Dent:* **i. tooth,** dent barrée.

impaction [im'pækʃ(ə)n], *s.* encastrement *m; Surg:* impaction *f* (d'un os); *Dent:* inclusion *f* (d'une dent); *Obst:* enclavement *m* (de la tête); *Med:* **i. of the bowel,** occlusion intestinale.

impactless ['impæktlis], *a.* sans percussion; *Typ:* **i. printer,** imprimante *f* du type sans percussion.

impair [im'pɛər], *v.tr.* affaiblir (la vue, l'esprit); altérer, abîmer, délabrer (la santé); faire perdre, diminuer (les forces); ébrécher (sa fortune); compromettre (l'autorité de qn); **to i. the complexion,** abîmer le teint; **seriously impaired health,** santé gravement délabrée, gravement atteinte, fortement ébranlée; **impaired digestion,** estomac délabré, détérioré, endommagé; **his health, his fortune, is impaired,** il a la santé ébranlée, sa fortune est ébréchée; *F:* il ne va, ne bat, plus que d'une aile; **to i. the running of a machine,** nuire au bon fonctionnement d'une machine; *Can:* **impaired driver,** conducteur, -trice, (d'automobile) en état d'ivresse ou sous l'empire d'un stupéfiant.

impairing [im'pɛəriŋ], **impairment** [im'pɛəmənt], *s.* affaiblissement *m* (de la vue, de la mémoire); altération *f,* ébranlement *m* (de la santé); dégradation *f* (de la chaussée, etc.); délabrement *m* (de l'estomac); diminution *f* (des forces); **i. of a law,** dérogation *f* à une loi.

impala [im'pɑ:lə], *s. Z:* impala *m.*

impale [im'peil], *v.tr.* **1.** *Her:* accoler (deux blasons); partager (des armes) par un pal. **2.** *(a)* **to be impaled,** être empalé, s'empaler (sur une grille, etc.); *(b) Hist:* empaler, infliger le supplice du pal à (qn). **3.** *A:* enclore (un terrain) d'une palissade.

impaled [im'peild], *a.* **1.** *Her:* (écu) partagé. **2.** (criminel) empalé.

impalement [im'peilmənt], *s.* **1.** *Her:* **arms marshalled by i.,** armoiries réunies sur un écu mi-parti. **2.** *(a)* empalement *m* (par accident); **he just avoided i. on the railings,** il a failli s'empaler sur la grille; *(b) Hist:* empalement; supplice *m* du pal.

impaling [im'peiliŋ], *s.* **1.** *Her:* partage *m* (des armes); accolement *m* (de blasons). **2.** = IMPALEMENT 2.

impalpability [impælpə'biliti], *s.* **1.** impalpabilité *f,* intangibilité *f.* **2.** caractère *m* insaisissable (d'une différence subtile, etc.).

impalpable [im'pælpəbl], *a.* **1.** impalpable, intangible. **2.** insaisissable (à l'esprit); **i. beauties of style and expression,** beautés *f* subtiles de style et d'expression.

impalpably [im'pælpəbli], *adv.* **1.** de façon impalpable. **2.** de façon insaisissable (à l'esprit).

impaludation [impæl(j)u'deiʃ(ə)n], *s. Med:* impaludation *f.*

impaludism [im'pæl(j)udizm], *s. Med:* (im)paludisme *m.*

impanate [im'peineit, 'impəneit], *a. Theol:* impané.

impanation [impæ'neiʃ(ə)n], *s. Theol:* impanation *f.*

impanel [im'pænl], *v.tr.* **(impanelled)** constituer (d'office) (un comité, etc.); *Jur:* **to i. a jury,** former, dresser, la liste du jury; constituer le jury; former un tableau; **to i. a juror,** inscrire un juré sur la liste du jury.

imparidigitate [impæri'didʒiteit], *a. Z:* imparidigité.

imparipinnate [impæri'pineit], *a. Bot:* imparipenné.

imparisyllabic [impærisi'læbik], *a. Lt. & Gr.Gram:* imparisyllabe, imparisyllabique.

imparity [im'pæriti], *s.* imparité *f.*

impark [im'pɑ:k], *v.tr.* **1.** emparquer (des cerfs, moutons). **2.** palissader, clôturer (un terrain).

imparkation [impɑ:'keiʃ(ə)n], **imparking** [im'pɑ:kiŋ], *s.* **1.** mise *f* (des animaux) dans un parc. **2.** palissadement *m* (d'un terrain).

impart [im'pɑ:t], *v.tr.* **1.** *(a)* donner (du courage, etc.), imprimer, communiquer (un mouvement) **(to,** à); *(b)* **the exercise had imparted colour to their cheeks,** l'exercice leur avait coloré les joues; **body that imparts heat,** corps qui communique, transmet, de la chaleur. **2.** communiquer (des connaissances); faire connaître, annoncer, confier (une nouvelle); faire part de (qch.); transmettre (la vérité) **(to,** à); **truths easy to i.,** vérités facilement transmissibles. **3.** accorder (une faveur) **(to,** à).

imparter [im'pɑ:tər], *s.* communicateur, -trice; transmetteur *m.*

impartial [im'pɑ:ʃ(ə)l], *a. (of pers., conduct)* impartial, -aux; juste, sans prévention **(towards,** envers); **to be i.,** être impartial, équitable; tenir la balance égale.

impartiality [impɑ:ʃi'æliti], *s.* impartialité *f* **(to,** envers).

impartially [im'pɑ:ʃəli], *adv.* impartialement; avec impartialité; (juger) équitablement.

impartible[1] [im'pɑ:tibl], *a. Jur:* (bien *m*) indivisible.

impartible[2], *a. (of news, etc.)* communicable, transmissible.

impartment [im'pɑ:tmənt], *s.* communication *f,* transmission *f* (de nouvelles, etc.).

impassability [impɑ:sə'biliti], **impassableness** [im'pɑ:səblnis], *s.* état *m* infranchissable (d'une rivière, etc.); impraticabilité *f* (d'une route).

impassable [im'pɑ:səbl], *a.* (rivière, marécage) infranchissable; (barrière) impassable; (route) impraticable.

impasse ['æmpɑ:s], *s.* impasse *f,* cul-de-sac *m, pl.* culs-de-sac; **to be in an i.,** se trouver dans une impasse; se trouver coincé.

impassibility [impæsi'biliti], *s.* impassibilité *f.*

impassible [im'pæsibl], *a.* impassible; (i) insensible à la douleur; (ii) insensible à la pitié; (iii) (visage) composé.

impassibly [im'pæsibli], *adv.* impassiblement.

impassion [im'pæʃ(ə)n], *v.tr.* passionner; émouvoir vivement; exalter; enivrer (de passion).

impassioned [im'pæʃənd], *a.* (orateur, discours) passionné, véhément; (style) chaleureux, plein d'exaltation.

impassive [im'pæsiv], *a.* impassible; (i) insensible aux émotions; (ii) (visage) composé.

impassively [im'pæsivli], *adv.* impassiblement; sans s'émouvoir.

impassiveness [im'pæsivnis], **impassivity** [impæ'siviti], *s.* impassibilité *f;* insensibilité *f;* stoïcisme *m.*

impastation [impæ'steiʃ(ə)n], *s.* impastation *f.*

impaste [im'peist], *v.tr.* **1.** couvrir (qch.) d'une couche de pâte. **2.** pétrir (l'argile, etc.). **3.** *Art:* empâter (un tableau).

impasto [im'pæstou], *s. Art:* empâtement *m;* **i. work,** travail *m* en pleine pâte.

impastoed [im'pæstoud], *a. Art:* (tableau) empâté, peint en pleine pâte.

impatience [im'peiʃ(ə)ns], *s. (a)* impatience *f;* **he was getting into a state of feverish i.,** une fièvre d'impatience le gagnait; il se sentait gagner par une impatience fiévreuse, fébrile; **fits of i.,** impatiences; *(b)* **i. of sth.,** aversion *f,* dégoût *m,* pour qch.; intolérance *f* de qch.; **his i. of contradiction was well known,** tout le monde savait qu'il ne pouvait pas supporter la contradiction; *(c)* **i. to do sth.,** désir impatient de faire qch.; hâte *f* (de partir, etc.); **to be all i. to do sth.,** avoir une grande impatience de faire qch.

impatiens [im'peiʃienz], *s. Bot:* balsamine *f,* impatiens *f,* impatiente *f.*

impatient [im'peiʃ(ə)nt], *a. (a)* impatient; **to get, grow, i.,** s'impatienter; *F:* se ronger les ongles; **to get i. with sth., s.o.,** s'impatienter de qch., contre qn; **i. answer,** réponse vive, emportée; *(b)* **to be i. of advice, control,** ne pas aimer, ne pas supporter, souffrir difficilement, les conseils, la contrainte; *(c)* **to be i. for sth.,** être désireux, avide, de qch.; avoir hâte d'obtenir qch.; **to be i. to have sth.,** attendre qch. avec impatience; **to be i. to do sth.,** être impatient, avoir une grande impatience, *F:* brûler, de faire qch.; désirer faire qch. avec impatience.

impatiently [im'peiʃ(ə)ntli], *adv.* (attendre) avec impatience; (répondre) d'un ton d'impatience; (agir) d'un air impatient; (souffrir) impatiemment.

impavid [im'pævid], *a. Lit:* impavide, intrépide.

impawn [im'pɔ:n], *v.tr. Lit:* **1.** mettre, donner, en gage; engager (son honneur, etc.). **2.** risquer, engager, hasarder (le salut de l'État, etc.).

impeach [im'pi:tʃ], *v.tr.* **1.** *(a)* attaquer, mettre en doute (la véracité, la probité, de qn); porter atteinte à (l'honneur de qn); **to i. s.o.'s honour,** attaquer l'honneur de qn; attaquer qn dans son honneur; *(b) Jur:* récuser, reprocher (un témoin); révoquer (un témoignage) en doute. **2.** *(a)* **to i. s.o. of, with, a crime,** accuser qn d'un crime; *(b) Jur:* **to i. s.o. for high treason,** mettre qn en accusation pour haute trahison; accuser qn de haute trahison. **3.** blâmer, censurer (les motifs, la conduite, de qn).

impeachable [im'pi:tʃəbl], *a.* **1.** *(a) (of motive, conduct)* attaquable, blâmable; susceptible d'être mis en doute; susceptible de blâme; *(b)* (témoin, témoignage) récusable, sujet à caution. **2.** *Jur: (a) (of pers.)* accusable; susceptible d'être mis en accusation; *(b)* (crime *m*) qui entraîne une mise en accusation (i) par la Chambre des Communes, (ii) *U.S:* par la Chambre des Représentants.

impeacher [im'pi:tʃər], *s. Jur:* **1.** récusant, -ante (d'un témoin). **2.** accusateur, -trice.

impeachment [im'pi:tʃmənt], *s.* **1.** *(a)* dénigrement *m,* dépréciation *f* (de l'honneur de qn); *(b)* reproche *m,* récusation *f* (d'un témoin). **2.** *Jur:* mise *f* en accusation (d'un ministre, etc.) (i) par la Chambre des Communes, (ii) *U.S:* par la Chambre des Représentants.

impearl [im'pɔ:l], *v.tr. Lit:* emperler.

impeccability [impekə'biliti], *s.* impeccabilité *f.*

impeccable [im'pekəbl], *a.* **1.** *(of pers.)* incapable de pécher. **2.** *(of behaviour, dress, etc.)* impeccable, irréprochable.

impeccably [im'pekəbli], *adv.* (vêtu, etc.) irréprochablement, impeccablement.

impecuniosity ['impikju:ni'ɔsiti], *s.* impécuniosité *f;* manque *m* d'argent.

impecunious [impi'kju:niəs], *a.* impécunieux, besogneux.

impedance [im'pi:dəns], *s. El:* impédance *f;* **acoustic(al) i.,** impédance acoustique; **blocked i., damped i.,** impédance de sortie (d'un transformateur électro-acoustique); **characteristic i., surge i.,** impédance caractéristique; **complex i.,** impédance complexe; **input i., output i.,** impédance d'entrée, de sortie; **iterative i.,** impédance itérative; **load i.,** impédance de charge, d'utilisation; **mechanical i.,** impédance mécanique; **motional i.,** impédance motionnelle, impédance électrique cinétique; **terminal i.,** impédance terminale, aux bornes; **transfer i.,** impédance de transfert; **wave i.,** impédance d'onde; **i. coil,** *U.S:* **i. bond,** bobine *f* d'impédance, d'arrêt; **i. coupling,** couplage *m,* liaison *f,* par impédance; **i. matching,** adaptation *f* d'impédance; **i. voltage,** tension *f* de court-circuit (d'un transformateur).

impede [im'pi:d], *v.tr.* mettre obstacle à, empêcher, entraver, gêner, retarder (le progrès, l'activité, la marche de qn, etc.); **to i. the traffic,** entraver la circulation; **nothing impeded our march,** rien ne troubla notre marche; **to i. the enemy's movements,** contrarier les mouvements de l'ennemi; **long skirts i. one's movements,** les jupes longues sont gênantes; **obstacle that impedes our plans,** obstacle qui arrête nos projets; *El:* **impeding force,** force contre-électromotrice.

impeder [im'pi:dər], *s.* empêcheur, -euse; gêneur, -euse.

impediment [im'pedimənt], *s.* **1.** (*a*) entrave *f*, empêchement *m* (**to,** à); obstacle *m* (**to,** à); **i. to traffic,** gêne *f* pour la circulation; **i. to a marriage,** empêchement à une union; (*b*) **speech i.,** trouble *m* de, difficulté *f* dans, la parole, l'élocution; **to have an i. in one's speech,** avoir la parole, la prononciation, embarrassée; bégayer. **2.** *pl.* = IMPEDIMENTA.

impedimenta [impedi'mentə], *s.pl.* impédimenta *m*; **all the i. of war,** *F:* **of fishing,** tout l'attirail de la guerre, de la pêche.

impeding [im'pi:diŋ], *s.* mise *f* d'un obstacle (**of,** à).

impedometer [impi'dɔmitər], *s. Ek:* inductancemètre *m*; impédancemètre *m*.

impel [im'pel], *v.tr.* (**impelled**) **1.** pousser, forcer, déterminer (**s.o. to do sth.,** qn à faire qch.); **impelled by secret motives,** poussé par des motifs secrets. **2.** pousser (en avant); faire marcher; **ship impelled by the wind,** navire poussé, chassé, par le vent; **force that impels a cannonball,** force *f* qui anime un boulet.

impellent [im'pelənt]. **1.** *a.* = IMPELLING. **2.** *s.* moteur *m*; force motrice.

impeller [im'pelər], *s.* **1.** (*pers.*) instigateur, -trice. **2.** (*a*) *Hyd.E: Mec.E:* roue *f* (à aubes); rouet *m* (de pompe); couronne *f* mobile; impulseur *m*; rotor *m*, roue (de compresseur, de turbine); turbine *f*; **i. eye,** entrée *f* du rouet (d'une pompe); **vane i.,** roue à ailettes, à palettes; (*b*) *I.C.E: Av:* (sur)compresseur *m*; **i. gear ratio,** rapport *m* des vitesses du compresseur.

impelling [im'peliŋ], *a.* (*a*) (*of force, etc.*) impulsif; moteur, -trice; (*b*) (besoin, etc.) harcelant, urgent.

impend [im'pend], *v.i.* **1.** être suspendu (**over,** sur). **2. the danger impending over him,** le danger qui le menaçait; **war was impending,** la guerre était imminente.

impendence [im'pendəns], **impendency** [im'pendənsi], *s.* imminence *f* (d'un danger); proximité *f* (d'un événement).

impendent [im'pendənt], **impending** [im'pendiŋ], *a.* (danger, etc.) imminent, menaçant; **the impending storm,** l'orage prochain; **her impending arrival,** son arrivée prochaine.

impenetrability [impenitrə'biliti], *s.* **1.** impénétrabilité *f* (d'un blindage, etc.). **2.** impénétrabilité, inscrutabilité *f* (d'un mystère). **3.** *Ph:* impénétrabilité (de la matière).

impenetrable [im'penitrəbl], *a.* impénétrable (**to, by,** à); (*a*) **cuirass i. to arrows,** cuirasse impénétrable aux flèches; (*b*) **i. mystery,** mystère insondable; **i. designs,** desseins inscrutables, impénétrables; (*c*) **mind i. to new ideas,** esprit inaccessible, impénétrable, aux idées nouvelles; **heart i. to pity,** cœur impénétrable, insensible.

impenetrableness [im'penitrəb(ə)lnis], *s.* = IMPENETRABILITY.

impenetrably [im'penitrəbli], *adv.* impénétrablement.

impenetrate [im'penitreit], *v.tr.* pénétrer intimement, profondément, dans (qch.).

impenitence [im'penit(ə)ns], **impenitency** [im'penit(ə)nsi], *s.* impénitence *f*; **to die in final impenitence,** mourir dans l'impénitence finale.

impenitent [im'penit(ə)nt], *a.* & *s.* impénitent, -ente; *B:* **the i. thief,** le mauvais larron.

impenitently [im'penitəntli], *adv.* dans l'impénitence; sans contrition.

impennate [im'peneit], *a. Orn:* impenne, impenné.

Impennes [im'peni:z], *s. pl. Orn:* impennes *m*.

imperata [impə'rɑ:tə], *s. Bot:* imperata *m*.

imperatival [imperə'taivl], *a. Gram:* impératif; de l'impératif.

imperative [im'perətiv]. **1.** *a.* & *s. Gram:* **i. (mood),** (mode) impératif (*m*); **in the i. (mood),** à l'impératif, au mode impératif. **2.** *a.* (*a*) (ton) impératif, impérieux, péremptoire; **in a quick i. voice,** d'une voix sèche et impérieuse; (*b*) urgent, impérieux; **i. need, reason,** besoin impérieux; raison impérieuse, majeure; **discretion is i.,** la discrétion s'impose; **enlargement of the school is i.,** l'agrandissement de l'école s'impose; **it is i. to . . .,** la nécessité s'impose de . . .; **it is i. for us all to . . .,** il nous incombe à tous de . . .; **it is i. that he should come,** il est de toute nécessité qu'il vienne. **3.** *s.* (*a*) impératif; exigence *f*; commandement *m*; (*b*) *Phil:* **moral i., categorical i.,** impératif catégorique.

imperatively [im'perətivli], *adv.* (parler) impérativement; (ordonner) d'un ton impérieux; (exiger) impérieusement.

imperativeness [im'perətivnis], *s.* **1.** caractère impérieux; ton impératif, péremptoire (de la voix). **2.** urgence *f*.

imperatoria [imperə'tɔ:riə], *s. Bot:* impératoire *f*.

imperatorial [imperə'tɔ:riəl], *a.* (titre) impérial; (air, ton) d'empereur.

imperceptibility ['impəsepti'biliti], *s.* imperceptibilité *f*.

imperceptible [impə'septibl], *a.* imperceptible; (bruit, différence) insaisissable; (différence) insensible; **i. to the eye,** inappréciable à l'œil.

imperceptibleness [impə'septib(ə)lnis], *s.* imperceptibilité *f*.

imperceptibly [impə'septibli], *adv.* imperceptiblement, insensiblement.

imperceptive [impə'septiv], **impercipient** [impə'sipiənt], *a.* qui manque de perception.

imperfect [im'pə:fikt, -fekt]. **1.** *a.* (*a*) imparfait; (i) incomplet; (ii) défectueux; *Bot:* **i. fungus,** champignon imparfait; **i. flower,** fleur unisexuée; *Jur:* **i. obligation,** obligation imparfaite; obligation morale, naturelle; *Mus:* **i. cadence,** cadence imparfaite; (*b*) *Arch:* **i. arch,** voûte, arche, surbaissée. **2.** *a.* & *s. Gram:* **i. (tense),** (temps) imparfait (*m*); **verb in the i.,** verbe *m* à l'imparfait.

imperfectibility ['impəfekti'biliti], *s.* imperfectibilité *f*.

imperfectible [impə'fektibl], *a.* imperfectible.

imperfection [impə'fekʃ(ə)n], *s.* **1.** imperfection *f*, défectuosité *f*; **structural imperfections in a building,** vices *m* de construction d'un bâtiment. **2.** (*a*) état incomplet; (*b*) (*usu. pl.*) **imperfections,** (i) *Bookb:* défets *m*; **i. note,** bulletin *m* d'assemblage; (ii) *Typ:* sortes *f* pour parer aux remplacements.

imperfective [impə'fektiv], *a. Gram:* (verbe) imperfectif.

imperfectly [im'pə:fiktli, -fektli], *adv.* imparfaitement; (i) incomplètement; (ii) défectueusement.

imperfectness [im'pə:fiktnis, -fekt-], *s.* imperfection *f*; caractère imparfait (de qch.).

imperforable [im'pə:fərəbl], *a.* qu'on ne peut perforer.

imperforate [im'pə:fərət], *a.* **1.** (nez, anus, test, etc.) imperforé. **2.** (timbre-poste, etc.) non perforé.

imperforation [impə:fə'reiʃ(ə)n], *s.* imperforation *f* (de l'anus, etc.).

imperial [im'piəriəl]. **1.** *a.* (*a*) (gouvernement, etc.) impérial; **the i. crown,** la couronne impériale; **His (Her) I. Majesty,** sa Majesté Impériale; (*b*) *O:* de l'Empire britannique; **I. Preference,** système *m* de tarifs de préférence entre les membres de la Communauté britannique; (*c*) (poids et mesures) qui ont cours légal dans le Royaume-Uni; **i. pint,** pinte légale; (*d*) majestueux, altier, auguste. **2.** *s.* (*a*) *A:* (i) impériale *f* (de diligence); (ii) coffre *m* (de diligence); (*b*) (*beard*) impériale; (*c*) (papier) grand jésus; (*d*) *pl. Hist:* **the Imperials,** les Impériaux *m* (de l'Empereur d'Allemagne). **3.** *a. Bot:* **crown i.,** couronne impériale; fritillaire impériale.

imperialism [im'piəriəlizm], *s.* impérialisme *m*; (i) césarisme *m*; (ii) colonialisme *m*.

imperialist [im'piəriəlist], *a.* & *s.* **1.** impérialiste (*mf*); (i) césariste (*mf*); (ii) colonialiste (*mf*). **2.** *German Hist:* **the Imperialists,** les Impériaux *m*.

imperialistic [impiəriə'listik], *a.* = IMPERIALIST 1.

imperially [im'piəriəli], *adv.* **1.** impérialement; en empereur. **2.** majestueusement, altièrement.

imperil [im'peril], *v.tr.* (**imperilled**) mettre en péril, en danger; exposer (sa vie, ses espérances, etc.) au danger; **to i. one's good name,** risquer, compromettre, sa réputation.

imperious [im'piəriəs], *a.* **1.** (homme, ton, caractère) impérieux, arrogant, dictatorial, -aux; (ton) impératif. **2.** urgent; **i. necessity,** besoin impérieux, impératif.

imperiously [im'piəriəsli], *adv.* (parler, agir) impérieusement; en maître; d'une façon impérieuse.

imperiousness [im'piəriəsnis], *s.* **1.** arrogance *f*; ton impérieux, impératif; air impérieux. **2.** urgence *f*.

imperishability [imperiʃə'biliti], **imperishableness** [im'periʃəblnis], *s.* caractère, nature, impérissable.

imperishable [im'periʃəbl], *a.* impérissable.

imperishably [im'periʃəbli], *adv.* impérissablement.

imperium [im'piəriəm], *s. Lit:* pouvoir absolu.

impermanence [im'pə:mənəns], **impermanency** [im'pə:mənənsi], *s.* impermanence *f*.

impermanent [im'pə:mənənt], *a.* impermanent, transitoire.

impermeability [impə:miə'biliti], *s.* imperméabilité *f*, imporosité *f*.

impermeable [im'pə:miəbl], *a.* imperméable; **i. to water,** imperméable, étanche, à l'eau.

impermissible [impə'misibl], *a.* qui n'est pas admissible; interdit, défendu.

imperscriptible [impə'skriptibl], *a. Jur:* (droit, privilège) non enregistré, non inscrit.

impersonal [im'pə:s(ə)nəl], *a.* **1.** (style, etc.) impersonnel. **2.** *Gram:* (verbe) impersonnel. **3.** *Com:* **i. account,** compte fictif, anonyme.

impersonality [impə:sə'næliti], *s.* impersonnalité *f*.

impersonally [im'pə:s(ə)nəli], *adv.* impersonnellement.

impersonate [im'pə'səneit], *v.tr.* **1.** personnifier (la vertu, etc.). **2.** (*a*) *Th:* représenter, jouer le rôle de (qn); (*b*) se faire passer pour (qn).

impersonation [impə:sə'neiʃ(ə)n], *s.* **1.** personnification *f*; **the very i. of good humour,** l'incarnation *f* même de la bonne humeur; la bonne humeur même. **2.** *Th:* (*a*) création *f*, interprétation *f* (d'un rôle); (*b*) **to give impersonations of the actors of the day,** donner des imitations *f*, des charges *f*, des acteurs du jour. **3.** *Jur:* supposition *f* de personne.

impersonator [im'pə:səneitər], *s.* **1.** celui, celle, qui se fait passer pour un(e) autre. **2.** *Th:* (*a*) créateur, -trice, interprète *mf* (d'un rôle); (*b*) imitateur, -trice (des vedettes du jour, etc.); **male i., female i.,** actrice, acteur, qui joue un rôle travesti.

impertinence [im'pə:tinəns], **impertinency** [im'pə:tinənsi], *s.* **1.** (*a*) impertinence *f*, insolence *f*; **it's the height of i.,** c'est se moquer du monde, des gens; (*b*) **an i., a piece of i.,** une impertinence. **2.** *A:* futilité *f*, extravagance *f*. **3.** *Jur:* impertinence; manque *m* de pertinence, de rapport avec la question.

impertinent [im'pə:tinənt], *a.* **1.** impertinent, insolent; **an i. fellow,** un impertinent; **to be i. to s.o.,** dire des impertinences à qn; être insolent envers qn; **i. remark,** remarque déplacée; **would it be i. to ask you . . .?** peut-on vous demander sans indiscrétion . . .? serait-il indiscret de vous demander . . .? **2.** *Jur:* (sujet, récit) impertinent, hors de propos, sans rapport avec la cause.

impertinently [im'pə:tinəntli], *adv.* **1.** impertinemment, insolemment; avec impertinence; d'un ton insolent. **2.** *Jur:* (répondre) en dehors de la question.

imperturbability [impə(:)tə:bə'biliti], *s.* imperturbabilité *f*; flegme *m*; sang-froid *m*.

imperturbable [impə(:)'tə:bəbl], *a.* imperturbable, flegmatique.

imperturbably [impə(:)'tə:bəbli], *adv.* imperturbablement; sans se déconcerter.

impervious [im'pə:viəs], *a.* **1.** (*a*) (forêt *f*, etc.) impénétrable; **forest i. to the sun's rays,** forêt inaccessible aux rayons du soleil; (*b*) (*of material, etc.*) **i. (to water),** imperméable, étanche; **i. to gas,** imperméable aux gaz; **i. to acids,** inattaquable par les acides; *Ph:* **i. to radiant heat,** athermane, athermique; *Geol:* **i. stratum,** couche *f* étanche. **2. i. to reason,** inaccessible, rebelle, à la raison; **heart i. to pity,** cœur *m* inaccessible, peu sensible, à la pitié; **he's i. to criticism,** il est vacciné contre la critique.

imperviously [im'pə:viəsli], *adv.* impénétrablement.

imperviousness [im'pə:viəsnis], *s.* (*a*) impénétrabilité *f*; (*b*) **i. to damp,** imperméabilité *f*; étanchéité *f* (à l'humidité).

impetiginous [impi'tidʒinəs], *a. Med:* impétigineux.

impetigo [impi'taigou], *s. Med:* impétigo *m*; (*in children*) impétigo larvé, *F:* gourme *f*.

impetrate ['impitreit], *v.tr.* impétrer, obtenir (une grâce, un bénéfice, etc.).

impetration [impi'treiʃ(ə)n], *s.* impétration *f* (d'une grâce, d'un bénéfice).

impetuosity [impetju'ɔsiti], **impetuousness** [im'petjuəsnis], *s.* **1.** impétuosité *f*, violence *f* (d'un torrent, etc.). **2.** impétuosité, fougue *f* (d'une personne).

impetuous [im'petjuəs], *a.* **1.** (torrent, etc.) impétueux, violent. **2.** (caractère) fougueux, emporté, impétueux.

impetuously [im'petjuəsli], *adv.* impétueusement, avec impétuosité.

impetus ['impitəs], *s.* vitesse acquise; élan *m*; force *f* de jet; **vital i.,** poussée vitale; **to give an i. to sth.,** donner l'impulsion, donner le branle, à qch.; **business has received fresh i.,** les affaires ont reçu une nouvelle impulsion; **carried away by my own i.,** emporté par mon propre élan.

imphee ['imfi], *s. Bot:* sorg(h)o sucré.

impi ['impi], *s.* corps *m*, détachement *m*, de guerriers cafres.

impiety [im'paiəti], *s.* impiété *f*.

imping ['impiŋ], *s. Ven:* greffage *m* de plumes (aux pennes d'un faucon).

impinge [im'pin(d)ʒ], *v.i.* **to i. on sth.,** (i) *O:* entrer en collision avec qch.; se heurter à, contre, qch.; (ii) empiéter sur (les droits d'autrui, etc.).

impingement [im'pin(d)ʒmənt], **impinging** [im'pin(d)ʒiŋ], *s.* **1.** *O:* collision *f*, heurt *m*. **2.** empiètement *m* (sur les droits de qn, etc.).

impious ['impiəs], *a.* impie; **to lay an i. hand on sth.,** porter une main sacrilège sur qch.; *s.* **the i.,** les impies *m*.

impiously ['impiəsli], *adv.* avec impiété; d'une manière impie; sacrilègement.

impish ['impiʃ], *a.* de petit diable; d'espiègle; **i. laughter,** rire espiègle, malicieux.

impishly ['impiʃli], *adv.* en espiègle; comme un petit diable.

impishness ['impiʃnis], *s.* espièglerie *f*.

impiteous [im'pitiəs], *a. Poet:* impitoyable; sans pitié.

implacability [implækə'biliti], **implacableness** [im'plækəb(ə)lnis], *s.* implacabilité *f*.

implacable [im'plækəbl], *a.* implacable (**towards,** à, pour, à l'égard de).

implacably [im'plækəbli], *adv.* implacablement.

implacental [implə'sentl], *a. Z:* implacentaire.

Implacentalia [implæs(ə)n'teiljə], *s.pl. Z:* implacentaires *m*.

implant[1] [im'plɑːnt], *v.tr.* implanter. **1.** (*of muscles, bones, minerals*) **to be implanted,** être implanté (**in,** dans). **2.** inculquer (**an idea, an opinion, in s.o.,** une idée, une opinion, à qn); implanter (**an idea in s.o.,** une idée dans la tête de qn); insinuer (**a principle in s.o.,** un principe à qn); inspirer (**a sentiment in s.o.,** un sentiment à qn); **nature has implanted fear in us all,** en nous tous la nature a implanté la peur; **to i. in s.o.'s mind the desire to do sth.,** inspirer à qn le désir de faire qch.; **doubt had been implanted in his mind,** le doute était entré dans son cœur; **from his youth this ideal had been implanted in his mind,** dès sa jeunesse il avait été pénétré de cet idéal. **3.** *Med:* implanter (un comprimé d'hormone, etc.).

implant[2] ['implɑːnt], *s. Surg:* implant *m*; **intraosseous i.,** implant endo-osseux; **subperiosteal i.,** implant souspériosté, juxta-osseux; *Dent:* **dental i.,** implant dentaire, prothétique, odontologique.

implantation [implɑːn'teiʃ(ə)n], *s.* **1.** (*a*) implantation *f* (d'une idée dans la tête de qn, etc.); (*b*) *Med: etc:* implantation (d'un comprimé d'hormone, etc.). **2.** *Biol:* nidation *f* (de l'œuf).

implanter [im'plɑːntər], *s.* personne qui implante, inculque (des idées, etc.).

implausibility [implɔːzi'biliti], *s.* manque *m* de plausibilité, invraisemblance *f* (d'une excuse, etc.).

implausible [im'plɔːzibl], *a.* peu plausible; invraisemblable.

implausibly [im'plɔːzibli], *adv.* invraisemblablement.

impledge [im'pledʒ], *v.tr. Lit:* mettre en gage; engager (sa foi, etc.).

implement[1] ['implimənt], *s.* **1.** outil *m*, instrument *m*, ustensile *m*; **agricultural implements,** instruments aratoires, d'agriculture; **gardening implements,** ustensiles de jardinage; **kitchen implements,** ustensiles de cuisine; batterie *f* de cuisine; **fishing implements,** attirail *m* de pêche; **implements of war,** attirail, matériel *m*, de guerre. **2.** *Jur: Scot:* exécution *f* (d'un engagement); mise *f* en œuvre (d'un accord).

implement[2] ['impliment], *v.tr.* **1.** rendre effectif (un traité, un contrat); exécuter, remplir (un engagement); mettre en œuvre, à effet (un accord); mettre à exécution (un projet); donner suite à (une décision); **to i. an obligation,** s'acquitter d'une obligation; **to i. one's promise,** accomplir sa promesse; ajouter l'action aux paroles. **2.** augmenter (qch.); suppléer à (qch.).

implementation [implimen'teiʃ(ə)n], **implementing** ['implimentiŋ], *s.* exécution *f* (d'un engagement); mise *f* en œuvre (d'un accord).

impletion [im'pliːʃ(ə)n], *s.* **1.** remplissage *m*. **2.** plénitude *f*.

implicate ['implikeit], *v.tr.* **1.** *A: & Lit:* (*entwine*) entrelacer, entremêler (**in, with,** avec). **2.** (*involve*) impliquer; (*a*) renfermer; **words implicating contradiction,** mots qui impliquent, qui renferment, une contradiction; (*b*) **to i. s.o. in a crime,** impliquer, mêler, qn dans un crime; **without implicating anyone,** sans mettre personne en cause; sans compromettre personne; (*c*) *Med:* **wound that implicates the lung,** blessure qui intéresse le poumon.

implication [impli'keiʃ(ə)n], *s.* **1.** implication *f*; **by i.,** implicitement; par induction; **he did not realize the full i. of these words,** il ne se rendait pas compte de la portée de ces paroles. **2.** insinuation *f*, sous-entendu *m, pl.* sous-entendus.

implicative [im'plikətiv], *a.* implicite; **i. of a fact,** qui implique un fait.

implicit [im'plisit], *a.* **1.** (condition *f*, etc.) implicite; **i. recognition of . . .,** reconnaissance *f* tacite de . . .; **his i. desires,** ses désirs inavoués; *Mth:* **i. function,** fonction *f* implicite; **this is i. in the agreement,** ceci est contenu dans le contrat d'une manière implicite; **the conceptions i. in this philosophy,** les conceptions contenues implicitement dans cette philosophie. **2. i. faith,** (i) *Theol:* foi *f* implicite; (ii) confiance *f* aveugle, sans réserve (**in,** dans); **i. obedience,** obéissance absolue; parfaite obéissance.

implicitly [im'plisitli], *adv.* **1.** implicitement, tacitement; par induction. **2. to trust s.o. i.,** avoir une confiance aveugle en qn; avoir une foi implicite en qn; **to obey i.,** obéir aveuglément; obéir (à qn) au doigt et à l'œil.

implicitness [im'plisitnis], *s.* caractère *m* implicite (de la foi, de l'obéissance).

implied [im'plaid], *a.* **1.** (consentement) implicite, tacite; **i. meaning,** signification impliquée; sous-entendu *m, pl.* sous-entendus; *Jur:* **i. contract,** contrat *m* implicite, tacite; quasi-contrat *m, pl.* quasi-contrats; **i. condition,** condition *f* implicite. **2.** *Cmptr:* **i. addressing,** adressage *m* à progression automatique avancée.

impliedly [im'plaiidli], *adv.* implicitement, tacitement; par induction.

implode [im'ploud]. **1.** *v.i.* (*of vacuum tube, etc.*) imploser, faire implosion. **2.** *v.tr. Cmptr:* condenser, regrouper (des données).

implore [im'plɔːr], *v.tr.* implorer; **to i. s.o.'s help,** implorer l'appui de qn; **to i. forgiveness,** implorer son pardon; **I implored his forgiveness,** je le suppliai de me pardonner; **to i. s.o. to do sth.,** conjurer, supplier, qn de faire qch.; **leave me alone, she implored,** laissez-moi, lui dit-elle d'un ton suppliant.

implorer [im'plɔːrər], *s.* implorateur, -trice.

imploring[1] [im'plɔːriŋ], *a.* (regard, etc.) implorant, suppliant; implorateur, -trice.

imploring[2], *s.* supplication *f*, adjuration *f*; *Lit:* imploration *f*.

imploringly [im'plɔːriŋli], *adv.* d'un ton, air, suppliant; d'un ton implorant.

implosion [im'plouʒ(ə)n], *s.* **1.** écrasement *m*, implosion *f* (d'un tube à vide, etc.). **2.** *Ling:* implosion.

implosive [im'plousiv]. *Ling:* **1.** *a.* (son) implosif. **2.** *s.* implosive *f*.

impluvium, *pl.* **-ia** [im'pluːviəm, -iə], *s. Rom.Ant:* impluvium *m*.

imply [im'plai], *v.tr.* **1.** impliquer; **smoke implies a fire,** la fumée implique du feu; la fumée ne va pas sans feu; **conclusion implied from the evidence,** conclusion *f* qui découle (implicitement) des dépositions; **regime that implies a certain severity,** régime *m* qui comporte une certaine rigueur, qui ne va pas sans une certaine rigueur; **every duty implies a right,** tout devoir emporte, suppose, un droit; **that implies courage on his part,** cela lui suppose du courage; *Log:* **to i. a contradiction,** impliquer contradiction; **the word** *vénération* **implies more than the word** *respect,* le mot *vénération* renchérit sur le mot *respect;* **the questions implied,** les questions *f* en jeu. **2.** donner à entendre; **do you mean to i. that . . .?** est-ce à dire que . . .? **you seem to i. that . . .,** ce que vous dites fait, ferait, supposer que . . ..

impolarizable [impoulə'raizəbl], *a. El:* (pile *f*) impolarisable.

impolder [im'pouldər], *v.tr.* enfermer (un marécage) dans un polder.

impolicy [im'pɔlisi], *s.* **1.** mauvaise politique; politique malhabile, inopportune. **2.** imprudence *f*, maladresse *f* (d'un discours, etc.).

impolite [impə'lait], *a.* impoli (**to, towards,** envers); **i. answer, behaviour,** réponse *f*, conduite *f*, malhonnête.

impolitely [impə'laitli], *adv.* (répondre) impoliment; (se conduire) d'une façon malhonnête.

impoliteness [impə'laitnis], *s.* impolitesse *f*; manque *m* de civilité, de politesse.

impolitic [im'pɔlitik], *a.* (*a*) (homme) impolitique, imprudent; (*b*) (*of measure, etc.*) impolitique, malavisé; contraire à la bonne politique.

impoliticly [im'pɔlitikli], *adv.* impolitiquement, imprudemment.

imponderability [impɔnd(ə)rə'biliti], **imponderableness** [im'pɔnd(ə)rəb(ə)lnis], *s.* impondérabilité *f*.

imponderable [im'pɔnd(ə)rəbl]. **1.** *a.* impondérable. **2.** *s.pl.* **imponderables,** impondérables *m*.

imporosity [impɔ'rɔsiti], **imporousness** [im'pɔːrəsnis], *s.* imporosité *f*.

imporous [im'pɔːrəs], *a.* non poreux; imperméable.

import[1] ['impɔːt], *s.* **1.** sens *m*, signification *f* (d'un mot); teneur *f* (d'un document); **what is the i. of this ceremony?** que signifie cette cérémonie? **2.** importance *f* (d'un événement); portée *f* (d'une observation); valeur *f* (d'une découverte, etc.); **I had not grasped the full i. of these words,** je ne m'étais pas rendu compte de toute la portée de ces mots; **matter of great i.,** affaire *f* de toute (*except when used attributively*) importance. **3.** *Com:* (*usu. pl.*) **imports** (i) (*collective imports*) importations *f*; (ii) (*individual imports*) articles *m* d'importation; **the imports and exports of a country,** les importations et les exportations d'un pays, **visible and invisible imports,** importations visibles et invisibles; **i. ban, prohibition,** interdiction *f* d'importation; prohibition *f* d'entrée; **i. duty,** droit *m* d'entrée, d'importation; **i. firm,** maison *f* d'importation; **i. licence, permit,** licence *f*, permis *m*, d'importation; **i. list,** (i) liste *f* des importations; (ii) tarif *m* d'entrée; **i. trade,** commerce *m* d'importation; commerce passif; **i.-export (trade),** import-export *f*.

import[2] [im'pɔːt], *v.tr.* **1.** *Com:* importer (des marchandises); **imported goods,** importations *f*; **imported from England,** de provenance anglaise; **to i. labour from another district,** importer de la main-d'œuvre d'une autre région; **to i. new ideas into a country,** importer des idées nouvelles dans un pays. **2.** *Lit:* indiquer; (*a*) signifier, vouloir dire; **what the word imports,** ce que le mot indique, veut dire; la portée du mot; (*b*) déclarer, faire connaître, faire savoir (**that,** que); **inscription importing that . . .,** inscription *f* qui déclare que . . .; (*c*) présager, augurer (des changements, le beau temps, etc.). **3.** *A:* (*concern*) (*used only in 3rd pers. and impers.*) importer; être d'importance; **questions that i. us nearly,** questions *f* qui nous importent fort, qui nous regardent de près; **it imports us to know whether . . .,** il nous importe de savoir, il est important que nous sachions, si . . ..

importable [im'pɔːtəbl], *a.* importable.

importance [im'pɔːt(ə)ns], *s.* (*a*) importance *f*; **the i. of the subject,** la dignité du sujet; **to give i. to a word,** mettre un mot en valeur; **to be of i.,** avoir de l'importance; **the matter is of some i.,** l'affaire est d'importance; **point of i.,** point important, qui a son importance, qui a de l'importance; **point of vital i.,** point d'une importance capitale; **letters of the first, last, i.,** lettres *f* de la plus grande importance, de la dernière conséquence; **question of first, capital, greatest, primary, i.,** question *f* d'importance primordiale, capitale, de toute (première) importance, de la plus haute importance, qui vient en première ligne; **business of first i.,** affaire majeure; **a machine in which lightness is of primary i.,** une machine où la légèreté est primordiale; **it is of i. to . . .,** il importe de . . .; **it is of the highest, the first, i. to remember that . . .,** il importe fort, il importe au premier chef, il est capital, de se souvenir que . . .; **it is of slight i., of no great i.,** cela importe peu, cela ne fait pas grand-chose; **detail without i., of no i.,** détail *m* négligeable, sans importance; **to be of no i. to s.o.,** n'avoir aucune importance pour qn; **to attach i. to sth.,** mettre, attacher, prêter, de l'importance à qch.; **to attach great, exaggerated, i. to sth.,** prêter, attacher, beaucoup d'importance à qch., prêter à qch. une importance excessive, exagérée; **to attach the greatest i. to a fact,** tenir le plus grand compte d'un fait; (*b*) (*of pers.*) importance; **people of i.,** personnages importants; *F:* gens *m* de poids; **to be full of one's own i.,** être pénétré de son importance; se donner de grands airs; **man of little, no, i.,** homme sans conséquence.

important [im'pɔːt(ə)nt], *a.* (*a*) important; (*of nation, etc.*) **to become more i.,** s'agrandir; **the i. men of the village,** les notables *m*, *F:* les hommes conséquents, les gros bonnets, du village; **it is i. for you to know that . . ., that you should know that . . .,** il est important, il importe, que vous sachiez que . . .; il importe de savoir que . . .; (*b*) (*of pers.*) important; plein d'importance; **to look i.,** prendre, se donner, des airs (d'importance), de grands airs; se prendre pour quelqu'un d'important.

importantly [im'pɔːt(ə)ntli], *adv.* (*a*) d'une manière importante; **to bear i. on a matter,** avoir beaucoup d'importance pour une affaire; (*b*) (parler, etc.) d'un air, ton, d'importance.

importation [impɔː'teiʃ(ə)n], *s.* **1.** importation *f* (de marchandises); **for temporary i.,** en franchise *f* temporaire. **2.** importation; article *m* d'importation.

importee [impɔː'tiː], *s. esp. U.S: F:* immigrant, -ante.

importer [im'pɔːtər], *s.* importateur, -trice.

importing[1] [im'pɔːtiŋ], *a.* importateur, -trice; **the i. countries,** les pays importateurs.

importing[2], *s.* importation *f* (de marchandises).

importunate [im'pɔːtjunit], *a.* (créancier) importun; (visiteur) excédant, ennuyeux.

importunately [im'pɔːtjunitli], *adv.* importunément; avec importunité.

importunateness [im'pɔːtjunitnis], *s.* importunité *f*.

importune [im'pɔːtjuːn], *v.tr.* importuner (qn); **to i. s.o. with requests,** assaillir, assiéger, qn de sollicitations; **to i. s.o. to do sth.,** solliciter, presser, qn de faire qch.

importunity [impɔː'tjuːniti], *s.* importunité *f*.

impose [im'pouz]. **1.** *v.tr.* (*a*) *Ecc:* (*of priest*) **to i. hands on s.o.,** imposer les mains à qn, sur qn; (*b*) *Typ:* imposer (une feuille), mettre (la matière) en pages; **badly imposed page,** feuille bambochée; (*c*) **to i. one thing on**

another, surimposer une chose à une autre. 2. *v.tr.* (*a*) **to i. conditions (up)on s.o.,** imposer des conditions à qn; **to i. silence on s.o.,** imposer le silence à qn; **his bearing imposes respect,** *abs.* **imposes,** son maintien impose le respect, inspire du respect, en impose; (*b*) **to i. a tax on sth., on s.o.,** imposer un impôt sur qch., à qn; **to i. a tax on sugar,** imposer, taxer, le sucre; frapper le sucre d'un impôt; **to i. a tax on the people,** imposer le peuple; **to i. a penalty on s.o.,** infliger une peine à qn; frapper qn d'une peine; **to i. the maximum penalty provided,** appliquer le maximum de la peine; (*c*) **to i. an object of no value on s.o.,** refiler, repasser; *P:* coller, à qn un objet sans valeur; (*d*) *O:* **he imposed his lackey upon them as a lord,** il leur fit prendre son laquais pour un grand seigneur. 3. *v.i.* **to i. on, upon, s.o.,** (i) en imposer à qn; en faire accroire à qn; tromper qn; (ii) abuser de l'amabilité de qn; **to (let oneself) be imposed upon,** se laisser duper; s'en laisser conter; se laisser monter le coup (par qn); **to i. upon s.o.'s kindness,** abuser de la bonté de qn.

imposer [im'pouzər], *s. Typ:* imposeur *m.*

imposing[1] [im'pouziŋ], *a.* (air, ton) imposant; (spectacle) grandiose.

imposing[2], *s.* = IMPOSITION 1.

imposingly [im'pouziŋli], *adv.* d'une manière imposante; d'un air, ton, imposant.

imposingness [im'pouziŋnis], *s.* caractère imposant; apparence imposante.

imposition [impə'ziʃ(ə)n], *s.* 1. (*a*) *Ecc:* imposition *f* (des mains); (*b*) *Typ:* imposition (d'une feuille); mise *f* en pages; (*c*) imposition (d'une tâche, etc.). 2. imposition, impôt *m*, taxe *f*; *pl.* contributions *f.* 3. abus *m* de la bonne volonté de qn; **this is an i. on your kindness,** c'est abuser de votre bonté. 4. *Sch:* pensum *m*; punition *f.* 5. supercherie *f*, tromperie *f*, imposture *f.*

impossibilism [im'pɔsibilizm], *s.* idéologie *f.*

impossibilist [im'pɔsibilist]. 1. *a.* (théorie, etc.) d'idéologues, de visionnaires. 2. *s.* idéologue *m*, visionnaire *mf.*

impossibility [impɔsi'biliti], *s.* 1. impossibilité *f* (de qch.). 2. chose *f* impossible; **physical i.,** chose matériellement impossible; **to ask for impossibilities,** demander l'impossible; **no one is expected to perform impossibilities,** à l'impossible nul n'est tenu.

impossible [im'pɔsibl]. 1. *a.* (*a*) impossible; **nothing is i. to him,** rien ne lui est impossible; il peut tout; **it is i. for me to do it,** il m'est impossible de le faire; il n'y a pas moyen de le faire; **it would be i. for anyone to say whether . . .,** on ne saurait dire si . . .; **it would be i. for me to do otherwise,** il me serait impossible de faire autrement; **it is quite i. for us, we find it i., to help you,** nous nous voyons dans l'impossibilité, nous sommes dans l'impossibilité (matérielle), de vous aider; il nous est tout à fait impossible de vous aider; **it is absolutely i. for him to come,** il lui est absolument impossible de venir; il est absolument impossible qu'il vienne; **to make it i. for s.o. to do sth.,** mettre qn dans l'impossibilité de faire qch.; **it is i. to foresee such things,** de tels événements se dérobent à toute prévision, ne se laissent pas prévoir; **plan i. to execute,** projet *m* impossible à exécuter, qu'il est impossible d'exécuter, qu'il n'est pas possible d'exécuter; (*b*) (histoire *f*, récit *m*) invraisemblable; (*c*) *F:* **i. hat,** chapeau *m* impossible, impayable, grotesque, inénarrable, invraisemblable; **i. person,** personne *f* difficile à vivre, impossible; **you're i.!** vous êtes impossible! **the country is quite i. from the tourist's point of view,** c'est un pays impossible du point de vue touristique. 2. *s.* **the i.,** l'impossible *m*; **if, to suppose the i., . . .,** si, par impossible, . . .; **to look for the i.,** chercher le mouton à cinq pattes.

impossibly [im'pɔsibli], *adv.* 1. **not i.,** peut-être bien; c'est dans le domaine des possibilités. 2. *F:* **i. dressed,** habillé d'une façon ridicule, impossible, grotesque.

impost[1] ['impoust], *s.* 1. *Hist:* (*a*) impôt *m*; taxe *f*; droit *m* d'entrée; droit d'octroi; (*b*) tribut *m.* 2. *Turf:* handicap *m*; surcharge *f.*

impost[2], *s. Arch:* imposte *f*, sommier *m* (d'arcade).

impostor [im'pɔstər], *s.* imposteur *m.*

impostume [im'pɔstju:m], *s. Med: A:* apostume *m*, apostème *m*, abcès *m.*

imposture [im'pɔstjər], *s.* imposture *f*, supercherie *f*, tromperie *f*, fourberie *f*, charlatanerie *f.*

impot ['impɔt], *s. Sch: O:* pensum *m*; punition *f.*

impotence ['impət(ə)ns], **impotency** ['impət(ə)nsi], *s.* 1. (*a*) impuissance *f*; **enemy reduced to i.,** ennemi hors d'état de nuire, réduit à l'impuissance; (*b*) faiblesse *f*, décrépitude *f*, impotence *f.* 2. *Jur: Med:* impuissance (sexuelle).

impotent ['impət(ə)nt], *a.* 1. (*a*) impuissant; (*b*) impotent, décrépit, faible, perclus. 2. *Med: Jur:* impuissant.

impotently ['impət(ə)ntli], *adv.* sans force, en vain.

impound [im'paund], *v.tr.* 1. (*a*) mettre (une bête, une voiture, etc.) en fourrière; (*b*) enfermer (qn, qch.); parquer (des moutons); *Hyd.E:* retenir, endiguer, capter (les eaux); **to i. the water in a dock,** maintenir l'eau dans un bassin. 2. *Jur:* (*a*) confisquer, saisir (des marchandises); (*b*) faire déposer (des documents) au greffe.

impounding [im'paundiŋ], *s.* 1. (*a*) mise *f*, envoi *m*, en fourrière (de bestiaux, etc.); (*b*) parcage *m* (de moutons); (*c*) endiguement *m*, captage *m* (des eaux). 2. *Jur:* (*a*) arrêt *m*, saisie *f* (de marchandises); (*b*) prise *f* de possession (de documents).

impoundment [im'paundmənt], *s.* 1. = IMPOUNDING. 2. eaux captées (par un endiguement).

impoverish [im'pɔv(ə)riʃ], *v.tr.* appauvrir (qn, un pays, le sang); fatiguer, dégraisser, amaigrir (le sol); affaiblir (un mélange, etc.); **to i. a people,** appauvrir, anémier, un peuple.

impoverishing[1] [im'pɔv(ə)riʃiŋ], *a.* appauvrissant, anémiant.

impoverishing[2], **impoverishment** [im'pɔv(ə)riʃmənt], *s.* appauvrissement *m* (de qn, d'un pays, d'une langue, du sang); **i. of the soil,** dégradation *f* du sol; **i. of the mind,** étiolement *m* de l'esprit, de l'intelligence.

impracticability [impræktikə'biliti], *s.* impraticabilité *f*; impossibilité *f.*

impracticable [im'præktikəbl], *a.* 1. infaisable, impraticable; (chemin) impraticable; (théorie *f*) inapplicable, irréalisable. 2. *A:* (*of pers.*) intraitable.

impracticableness [im'præktikəb(ə)lnis], *s.* = IMPRACTICABILITY.

impracticably [im'præktikəbli], *adv.* d'une manière impraticable.

impractical [im'præktik(ə)l], *a.* 1. (*of pers.*) peu pratique. 2. (projet, etc.) impraticable, irréalisable.

imprecate ['imprikeit], *v.tr. esp. Lit:* **to i. curses upon s.o., on s.o.'s head,** appeler des malédictions sur la tête de qn; lancer, proférer, des imprécations contre qn; accabler qn d'imprécations; maudire qn; **to i. s.o., sth.,** maudire qn, qch.

imprecation [impri'keiʃ(ə)n], *s.* imprécation *f*, malédiction *f.*

imprecatory ['imprikeitəri], *a.* imprécatoire.

imprecise [impri'sais], *a.* imprécis, vague.

imprecisely [impri'saisli], *adv.* vaguement, sans précision.

imprecision [impri'siʒ(ə)n], *s.* imprécision *f*; manque *m* de précision.

impregnability [impregnə'biliti], *s.* imprenabilité *f* (d'une forteresse).

impregnable[1] [im'pregnəbl], *a.* (*a*) (forteresse) imprenable, inexpugnable; (*b*) (vérité, honneur) invincible (to, par).

impregnable[2], *a.* imprégnable, qui peut être imprégné.

impregnably [im'pregnəbli], *adv.* d'une façon inattaquable; dans une situation inexpugnable; invinciblement.

impregnant [im'pregnənt], *s.* imprégnant *m.*

impregnate[1] ['impregneit], *v.tr.* 1. *Biol:* féconder (une femelle). 2. (*a*) imprégner, imbiber, saturer (**sth. with sth.,** qch. de qch.); **to i. wood,** injecter le bois; **to i. matches,** paraffiner des allumettes; (*b*) **to become impregnated with false principles,** s'imprégner, se pénétrer, de faux principes. 3. **water impregnates porous bodies,** l'eau pénètre les corps poreux.

impregnate[2] [im'pregnət], *a. Biol:* fécondé.

impregnated ['impregneitid], *a.* 1. *Biol:* fécondé. 2. imprégné, saturé (**with,** de); **i. matches,** allumettes paraffinées.

impregnating ['impregneitiŋ], *a.* imprégnant.

impregnation [impreg'neiʃ(ə)n], *s.* 1. *Biol:* fécondation *f.* 2. (*a*) imprégnation *f* (d'un tissu, etc.); *Tchn:* injection *f*, imbibition *f*, pénétration *f* (du bois, etc.); (*b*) **i. of wood by creosote,** imprégnation du bois par la créosote.

impresario [impre'sɑ:riou], *s.* impresario *m.*

imprescriptible [impri'skriptibl], *a. Jur:* (droit *m*) imprescriptible.

impress[1] ['impres], *s.* 1. (*a*) impression *f*, empreinte *f*; **i. on a coin,** impression sur une pièce de monnaie; **i. of the fingers,** empreintes digitales; (*b*) marque distinctive; cachet *m*; **work that bears the i. of genius,** œuvre qui porte la marque, le cachet, l'empreinte, du génie. 2. *Typ:* **i. copy,** copie *f* typographique.

impress[2] [im'pres], *v.tr.* 1. (*a*) **to i. sth. on, upon, sth.,** imprimer, empreindre, qch. sur qch.; **to i. a seal on wax,** imprimer un cachet sur la cire; empreindre un cachet dans de la cire; **to i. a figure on a medal,** frapper une médaille d'une empreinte; **she impresses her personality on everything she wears,** à tout ce qu'elle porte elle imprime sa personnalité; **to i. sth. on the mind,** graver qch. dans la mémoire; (*b*) *Mec:* **to i. motion (up)on a body,** imprimer un mouvement à un corps. 2. **to i. sth. upon s.o.,** faire bien comprendre qch. à qn; inculquer (une idée) à qn; pénétrer qn (d'une idée); **you must i. on him that . . .,** il faut bien lui faire sentir que . . .; **I must i. on you that. . .,** mettez-vous bien dans la tête que . . .; **i. upon your children that they must . . .,** inculquez à vos enfants qu'il faut . . .. 3. **to i. sth. with a seal,** faire une impression sur qch. avec un cachet, à l'aide d'un cachet; *Fig:* **to i. s.o. with the idea that. . .,** donner l'idée à qn que . . ., pénétrer qn de l'idée que . . .. 4. (*a*) faire une impression à (qn); **how did she i. you?** quelle impression vous a-t-elle faite? **he impressed me favourably,** il m'a fait une impression favorable; **that is how it impressed me,** voilà l'effet que cela m'a produit; (*b*) **to i. s.o.,** faire impression sur qn; frapper, impressionner, qn; **in order to i. the ignorant,** pour en imposer aux ignorants; **he tried to i. me with his importance,** il a voulu me faire sentir toute son importance, me convaincre de son importance; **his firmness impressed them,** sa fermeté leur en a imposé; **I was deeply impressed by it,** cela m'a fait une grande impression; j'en ai été profondément impressionné; *F:* **I'm not impressed (by him),** il ne m'emballe pas; *F:* **I'm not impressed,** cela ne me dit pas grand-chose; cela me laisse froid; *v.i.* **he doesn't i.,** il ne fait pas impression.

impress[3] [im'pres], *v.tr.* (*a*) enrôler d'office; réquisitionner (des hommes en âge de servir); *esp. Navy: A:* presser, enrôler de force (des matelots); (*b*) réquisitionner (des vivres, des wagons, etc.).

impressed [im'prest], *a.* 1. *Nat.Hist: etc:* (coquillage, dessin, etc.) gravé en creux; (galet, caillou) impressionné, à empreinte. 2. *El: Mec:* (voltage, etc.) imprimé; **i. force,** force imprimée (à un corps); **i. motion,** mouvement acquis.

impressibility [impresi'biliti], *s.* = IMPRESSIONABILITY.

impressible [im'presibl], *a.* = IMPRESSIONABLE 1.

impressing [im'presiŋ], *s.* impression *f.*

impression [im'preʃ(ə)n], *s.* 1. (*action*) impression *f* (d'un cachet sur la cire, etc.); *Typ:* impression (d'un livre, etc.). 2. (*a*) empreinte *f*, impression (d'un cachet); **to take an i. of sth.,** prendre l'empreinte, l'impression, de qch.; **impressions of plants and animals in rocks,** empreintes de plantes et d'animaux dans des roches; *Dent:* **denture i.,** empreinte pour prothèse; **i. taking,** prise *f* d'empreinte (pour prothèse); (*b*) **the i. of the (Holy) Stigmata (of St Francis),** l'impression des saints stigmates (de Saint François); (*c*) **a file makes no i. on it,** la lime glisse dessus. 3. (*a*) *Typ:* empreinte (des caractères sur le papier); foulage *m* (du papier par les caractères); **i. cylinder,** cylindre *m* de rotative, de foulage, de marge; **kiss i.,** impression au minimum de pression; **muddy i.,** impression galeuse; **smudged i.,** impression maculée; (*b*) *Needlew:* **i. paper,** dessin calqué. 4. *Publ:* tirage *m*, édition *f* (d'un livre, d'un journal); **second i.,** deuxième tirage, deuxième édition. 5. *Engr:* impression; **proof i.,** épreuve *f* avant la lettre; *Lith:* **transfer i.,** épreuve à report. 6. (*a*) impression (sur qn, sur les sens); **the town gives an i. of sadness,** la ville donne une impression de tristesse; **to make a good, bad, i. (on s.o.),** faire (une) bonne, mauvaise, impression (sur qn); donner bonne opinion, une pauvre opinion, de sa capacité; **he always gives a bad i.,** c'est un homme qui marque mal; **to make a painful i. on s.o.,** impressionner qn péniblement; **what i. did it make on him?** quel effet cela lui a-t-il produit? **his speech created a great i.,** son discours fit une grande impression; **to make an i.,** faire impression; **tell us your impressions,** dites-nous vos impressions; **to judge by one's impressions,** juger par sentiment; juger d'après ses impressions; (*b*) idée *f*; **I have an i., I'm under the i., that I've seen him before,** j'ai l'impression de l'avoir déjà vu; j'ai dans l'idée, je pense, je suis d'avis, que je l'ai déjà vu; **to create the i. that. . .,** donner, produire, l'impression que . . ..

impressionability [impreʃ(ə)nə'biliti], *s.* impressionnabilité *f*; sensibilité *f* (**to,** à).

impressionable [im'preʃ(ə)nəbl], *a.* 1. (*a*) impressionnable, susceptible, sensible, affectable; **to be i.,** avoir la fibre sensible; **to be at an i. age,** être à un âge impressionnable; (*b*) **eye not i. by light,** œil *m* insensible à la lumière. 2. (*of substance*) susceptible de recevoir une empreinte.

impressionism [im'preʃənizm], *s. Art:* impressionnisme *m.*

impressionist [im'preʃənist], *a. & s. Art:* impressionniste (*mf*).

impressionistic [impreʃə'nistik], *a.* (tableau, poème) impressionniste, dans le genre impressionniste.

impressionistically [impreʃə'nistikli], *adv.* 1. (peint) dans le genre impressionniste. 2. (s'exprimer) selon ses impressions.

impressive [im'presiv], *a.* (spectacle, langage) impressionnant, émouvant; **man of i. stature,** homme de stature impressionnante; **to look i.,** avoir grand air; **his speech was very i.,** son discours fit impression; **i. silence,** silence impressionnant, solennel.

impressively [im'presivli], *adv.* d'une manière impressionnante, émouvante; (parler) d'un ton émouvant, avec solennité, solennellement.

impressiveness [im'presivnis], *s.* nature impressionnante, ton solennel (d'un spectacle, d'un discours, etc.).

impressment [im'presmənt], *s.* **1.** (*a*) enrôlement *m* d'office; (*b*) *Navy: A:* droit *m* pour la Couronne de réquisitionner des matelots en cas de pénurie de volontaires; presse *f* (de matelots); enrôlement forcé. **2.** réquisition *f* (de vivres, etc.).

imprest ['imprest], *s. Adm:* avance *f* de fonds (à un fournisseur de l'État); **i. account,** compte *m* d'avances; **i. accounting,** régie *f* d'avances; **i. accountant, i. holder,** régisseur *m* d'avances; **i. system,** comptabilité *f* de prévision.

imprimatur [impri'meitər], *s. Publ: Ecc:* imprimatur *m inv*; *Fig:* **the scheme has the Prime Minister's i.,** le projet a été approuvé par le premier ministre.

imprimis [im'praimis], *adv. A:* premièrement; en premier lieu; tout d'abord.

imprint[1] ['imprint], *s.* **1.** (*a*) empreinte *f* (d'un cachet, des pattes d'un animal, etc.); **to take an i. of sth.,** prendre l'empreinte de qch.; (*b*) *Cmptr:* impression *f* en creux. **2. publisher's i.,** firme *f*, rubrique *f*, de l'éditeur (sur la page de titre d'un livre); **printer's i.,** nom *m* de l'imprimeur (en dernière page ou au verso du titre); grebiche *f*; **no i.,** sans indication d'éditeur ni d'imprimeur; *Fig:* **the author has set his own i. on the work,** l'auteur a imprimé sa marque sur cette œuvre.

imprint[2] [im'print], *v.tr.* imprimer; (*a*) **to i. sth. on sth.,** imprimer, empreindre, qch. sur qch.; **to i. sth. on the memory, in the mind,** graver, fixer, qch. dans la mémoire, dans l'esprit; (*b*) **to i. sth. with sth.,** marquer, empreindre, qch. de qch.; **sand imprinted with footmarks,** sable qui porte des empreintes de pas.

imprinted [im'printid], *a. Publ:* portant la rubrique de la maison.

imprinter [im'printər], *s.* dispositif *m* d'impression; *Com:* **credit card i.,** presse *f* à cartes de crédit.

imprinting [im'printiŋ], *s.* impression *f*; *Nat.Hist.* identification *f*.

imprison [im'priz(ə)n], *v.tr.* emprisonner, enfermer (qn); mettre (qn) en prison; **to keep s.o. imprisoned,** tenir qn en prison.

imprisonable [im'priz(ə)nəbl], *a.* incarcérable.

imprisoning [im'priz(ə)niŋ], *s.* emprisonnement *m*; mise *f* en prison.

imprisonment [im'prizənm(ə)nt], *s.* emprisonnement *m*; **ten days' i.,** dix jours de prison; **false, illegal, i.,** détention illégale, arbitraire; emprisonnement illégal; séquestration *f*; *A:* **i. for debt,** prison *f* pour dettes; *A:* contrainte *f* par corps; **to serve a sentence of i.,** faire de la prison.

improbability [imprɔbə'biliti], *s.* **1.** improbabilité *f*; invraisemblance *f*. **2. there are several improbabilities in his account,** il y a plusieurs invraisemblances dans son récit.

improbable [im'prɔbəbl], *a.* improbable; **it's highly i. that he'll come,** il est très improbable, très peu probable, qu'il vienne.

improbably [im'prɔbəbli], *adv.* improbablement; invraisemblablement; **not i.,** très probablement.

improbation [improu'beiʃ(ə)n], *s. Jur: Scot:* mise *f* à l'écart d'un acte argué de faux, d'une pièce arguée de faux.

improbity [im'proubiti], *s.* improbité *f*; manque *m* d'honnêteté.

impromptu [im'prɔm(p)tju:]. **1.** *adv.* (faire qch.) sans préparation, (à l')impromptu; **to speak i.,** parler à l'impromptu; parler d'abondance. **2.** *a.* (poème, discours) impromptu; (bal, etc.) improvisé; **to get up an i. dance, to make an i. speech,** improviser un bal, un discours; **i. raft,** radeau improvisé, de fortune. **3.** *s. Th: Mus:* impromptu *m*.

improper [im'prɔpər], *a.* **1.** (*a*) (partage) incorrect; (expression *f*, diphtongue *f*, dérivation *f*) impropre; (terme) inexact; **to use a word in an i. sense,** donner à un mot un sens abusif; *Aut: O:* **i. signalling,** avertissement intempestif; (*b*) *Mth:* **i. fraction,** expression *f* fractionnaire. **2.** malséant, malhonnête, indécent, inconvenant; (conte) scabreux; **there's nothing i. in the play,** la pièce n'a rien d'inconvenant. **3.** déplacé; **it would be i. to refuse,** il serait de mauvaise grâce de refuser; **it would be i. to detain you any longer,** il ne serait point séant de vous retenir plus longtemps.

Improperia [imprɔ'piəriə], *s.pl. R.C.Ch:* **the I.,** les impropères *m*.

improperly [im'prɔpəli], *adv.* **1.** (se servir d'une expression) improprement, incorrectement; **word i. used,** mot employé abusivement; *Aut:* **to overtake i.,** dépasser contrairement au code; *Mil:* **i. dressed,** avec sa braguette déboutonnée. **2.** (se conduire) d'une manière inconvenante, malséante; malhonnêtement. **3.** (parler, s'exprimer) d'une façon déplacée; contrairement à la bonne règle.

impropriate[1] [im'prouprieit], *v.tr. Ecc:* séculariser (un bénéfice, un bien d'Église); attribuer (des revenus ecclésiastiques) à un laïque ou à des laïques.

impropriate[2], **impropriated** [improupri'eitid], *a. Ecc:* (bénéfice, etc.) sécularisé.

impropriation [improupri'eiʃ(ə)n], *s. Ecc:* **1.** sécularisation *f* (d'un bénéfice, etc.); attribution *f* à des laïques. **2.** bénéfice sécularisé.

impropriator [im'prouprieitər], *s.* laïque mis en possession d'un bien d'Église.

impropriety [imprə'praiəti], *s.* (*a*) impropriété *f*, inexactitude *f* (de langage, d'une opinion); (*b*) inconvenance *f*, indécence *f* (de conduite, d'un geste, etc.).

improvable [im'pru:vəbl], *a.* **1.** *Agr:* (terre *f*, sol *m*) exploitable, bonifiable, amendable. **2.** (*of pers., etc.*) améliorable, perfectible.

improve [im'pru:v]. **1.** *v.tr.* (*a*) améliorer, rendre meilleur (qch.); perfectionner, apporter des perfectionnements à (une invention); (r)abonnir, bonifier (le vin, etc.); nourrir, cultiver (l'esprit); étendre, élargir, accroître (ses connaissances); affiner (son goût); *Agr:* bonifier, amender (le sol); **to i. the appearance of s.o., sth.,** embellir qn, qch.; **that dress improves her greatly,** cette robe l'avantage beaucoup; **to i. one's natural gifts by study,** développer ses dons naturels par l'étude; **nature is improved by art,** l'art perfectionne la nature; *A:* **to i. an acquaintance,** cultiver une connaissance; **to i. sth. out of existence,** détruire, ruiner, qch. à force d'améliorations; tenir qch. sur le métier jusqu'à ce qu'il n'en reste plus rien; faire disparaître qch. par excès de zèle; (*b*) **to i. the occasion, the opportunity,** *F:* **the shining hour,** (i) profiter, tirer parti, de l'occasion; utiliser l'occasion; mettre l'occasion à profit; (ii) tirer une morale de ce qui vient de se passer; prononcer là dessus quelques paroles édifiantes; (*c*) *v.ind.tr.* **to i. on, upon, s.o., on s.o.'s performance,** faire mieux que qn, surpasser qn; **to i. on sth.,** améliorer qch.; remédier aux imperfections de qch.; **to i. on s.o.'s ideas,** enchérir sur les idées de qn; apporter d'heureuses modifications aux projets de qn; **to i. on a tale,** renchérir sur un récit; ajouter du sien à un récit; *Com:* **to i. on s.o.'s offer,** enchérir sur l'offre de qn. **2.** *v.i.* (*a*) s'améliorer, devenir meilleur; (*of wine, etc.*) se bonifier, (s')abonnir, rabonnir; **to i. with use,** s'améliorer à l'usage; **wine improves with age,** le vin acquiert en vieillissant; **his mind had improved through study,** son esprit s'était fortifié par l'étude; **he has greatly improved,** il a fait de grands progrès; **he improves on acquaintance,** il gagne à être connu; **the situation has improved,** la situation s'est améliorée; **his business is improving,** son commerce est en voie de relèvement; **business is improving, things are improving,** il y a une amélioration dans les affaires; les affaires reprennent; *F:* ça va mieux; **his health is improving,** sa santé s'améliore, se raffermit, reprend; **to i. in health, in manners,** gagner en santé, en manières; **I found him greatly improved** (i) **(in health),** j'ai trouvé dans son état une amélioration sensible; (ii) je le trouve beaucoup plus sympathique qu'auparavant; je trouve qu'il a gagné; **she has greatly improved in looks,** elle a beaucoup embelli, elle est beaucoup embellie; **to i. in one's studies,** avancer, faire des progrès, dans ses études; **to i. in one's Latin,** se perfectionner en latin; (*b*) *Com:* (*of prices, markets*) monter; être en hausse.

improved [im'pru:vd], *a.* (*a*) (*of situation, position, etc.*) amélioré; (*of invention, method*) perfectionné; **i. site,** terrain *m*, propriété *f*, où l'on a fait des travaux; (*b*) *Com:* **i. offer,** offre supérieure.

improvement [im'pru:vmənt], *s.* **1.** (*a*) amélioration *f* (de la situation, d'un commerce, etc.); perfectionnement *m* (d'une invention, d'un outillage); embellissement *m* (d'une ville); culture *f*, affinage *m* (de l'esprit); avancement *m* (des études); **a great i.,** beaucoup d'amélioration; **open to i.,** susceptible d'amélioration; **i. in health,** amélioration de la santé; (*of patient*) progrès *mpl* vers le mieux; **his condition continues to show i.,** le mieux continue à se manifester; *Pol: etc:* **there is an i. in the situation,** une détente s'est produite; *For:* **i. felling,** coupe *f* d'amélioration; (*b*) **i. of the occasion,** mise *f* à profit de l'occasion (pour faire de la morale, pour prononcer quelques paroles édifiantes); (*c*) **the moral i. of the people,** l'édification du peuple; **books for moral i.,** livres édifiants. **2.** (*a*) (*usu. pl.*) **improvements,** améliorations, changements *m* utiles, embellissements (dans une propriété, etc.); **all these so-called improvements,** tous ces prétendus progrès; **to effect improvements in sth.,** apporter des améliorations à qch.; **improvements in house building,** les progrès du bâtiment; **improvements are being carried out,** on est en train d'exécuter des travaux d'amélioration; **i. lease,** bail *m* qui impose au preneur l'obligation de faire des travaux d'amélioration; **i. loan,** prêt destiné à la modernisation; (*b*) **improvements in pay,** améliorations de traitement; (*c*) **to be an i. on s.o., sth.,** surpasser qn, qch.; valoir mieux, être mieux, que qn, qch.; **my new car is a great i. on the old one,** ma nouvelle voiture est bien supérieure à l'ancienne.

improver [im'pru:vər], *s.* **1.** (*a*) réformateur, -trice; rénovateur, -trice; (*b*) **i. upon an offer,** enchérisseur *m* sur une offre. **2.** *Ind:* apprenti, -ie; élève *mf*; (*in millinery, etc.*) petite main; petite; *Adm:* stagiaire *mf*. **3.** *Cost: A:* **dress i.,** rembourrage *m*; *esp.* tournure *f*.

improvidence [im'prɔvid(ə)ns], *s.* imprévoyance *f*.

improvident [im'prɔvid(ə)nt], *a.* (*a*) imprévoyant; insouciant de l'avenir; (*b*) prodigue.

improvidently [im'prɔvidəntli], *adv.* sans prévoyance; sans se soucier de l'avenir.

improving[1] [im'pru:viŋ], *a.* **1.** (*a*) améliorant; qui rend meilleur; (*b*) (livre) instructif, édifiant; (conversation, etc.) édifiante, dont on tire profit. **2.** (santé) en voie de rétablissement; **with i. health he became more cheerful,** à mesure que sa santé se rétablissait il recouvrait sa sérénité.

improving[2], *s.* amélioration *f*; perfectionnement *m*.

improvisation [imprəvai'zeiʃ(ə)n], *s. Lit: Mus: etc:* improvisation *f*.

improvise ['imprəvaiz]. *Lit: Mus: etc:* **1.** *v.tr.* (*a*) improviser (des vers, un morceau de musique, un discours); **improvised speech,** discours improvisé, impromptu *inv*; (*b*) improviser (un bal, un brancard, etc.); **hastily improvised,** sommairement organisé; **improvised law,** loi *f* de circonstance; **i. raft,** radeau *m* de fortune. **2.** *v.i.* improviser; parler, jouer, sans préparation; **to i. on the piano,** improviser au piano.

improviser ['imprəvaizər], *s.* improvisateur, -trice.

improvising ['imprəvaiziŋ], *s.* improvisation *f*.

imprudence [im'pru:d(ə)ns], *s.* imprudence *f* ((i) caractère imprudent; (ii) action imprudente).

imprudent [im'pru:d(ə)nt], *a.* imprudent, malavisé; **i. action,** imprudence *f*; action inconsidérée; **how i. of you!** quelle imprudence de votre part!

imprudently [im'pru:d(ə)ntli], *adv.* imprudemment; avec imprudence; **to act i.,** agir avec imprudence; faire, commettre, une imprudence, des imprudences.

impuberal [im'pju:bərəl], *a.* impubère.

impuberty [im'pju:bəti], *s.* impuberté *f*.

impudence ['impjud(ə)ns], *s.* **1.** impudence *f*, effronterie *f*, insolence *f*, audace *f*; **with the utmost i.,** avec le plus grand aplomb; **none of your i.!** ne soyez pas insolent! **to have the i. to say, do, sth.,** avoir l'aplomb, le front, de dire qch., de faire qch.; **a piece of i.,** une insolence. **2.** *A:* impudeur *f*.

impudent ['impjud(ə)nt], *a.* **1.** effronté, audacieux, insolent; **i. reply,** réponse insolente; **you i. child,** *A:* **hussy!** (i) petite effrontée! (ii) insolente! **i. fellow,** insolent; impertinent; **to be i. to s.o.,** être insolent envers, avec, qn; dire des insolences à qn; **as i. as a cock sparrow,** effronté comme un page. **2.** *A:* éhonté, impudent.

impudently ['impjud(ə)ntli], *adv.* **1.** effrontément, insolemment; avec insolence; audacieusement; *O:* **to lie i.,** mentir avec effronterie. **2.** *A:* impudemment; avec impudeur.

impudicity [impju(:)'disiti], *s.* impudicité *f*, impudeur *f*.

impugn [im'pju:n], *v.tr.* attaquer, contester (une proposition, etc.); mettre en doute, en question (la véracité de qch., l'honneur de qn); *Jur:* **to i. the character of a witness,** attaquer la moralité, le crédit, d'un témoin; **to i. a piece of evidence,** récuser un témoignage.

impugnable [im'pju:nəbl], *a.* (déclaration) contestable; (témoignage) récusable.

impugner [im'pju:nər], *s.* adversaire *mf*, attaquant, -ante; *Jur:* récusant, -ante.

impugning [im'pju:niŋ], **impugnment** [im'pju:nmənt], *s.* attaque *f*, mise *f* en doute (d'une affirmation, etc.); *Jur:* récusation *f* (d'un témoignage, témoin).

impuissance [im'pwi:isəns], *s.* impuissance *f*, faiblesse *f*; manque *m* de forces.

impuissant [im'pwi:sənt], *a.* impuissant, faible; sans forces.

impulse ['impʌls], *s.* **1.** (*a*) impulsion *f*; poussée motrice; choc (propulsif); *Ph:* quantité *f* de mouvement; **i. of a hammer blow,** force impulsive d'un coup de marteau; **i. of recoil,** impulsion de recul; **angular i.,** impulsion angulaire; moment *m* d'inertie géométrique; *Mch:* **i. blades,** aubages *m* d'action (d'une turbine); **i. stage,** étage *m* d'action (d'une turbine); **i. wheel,** roue *f* à action, à impulsion; **i. turbine,** turbine à choc, à impulsion, à action, d'action; *I.C.E:* **i. starter,** impulseur *m*, lanceur *m*, vibreur *m* de départ; *Navy:* **i. tube,** tube *m* lance-torpilles; (*b*) *El:* **electrical impulses,** impulsions électriques; **current i.,** impulsion de courant; **break i.,** impulsion d'ouverture; **make i.,** impulsion de fermeture; **i. corrector,** filtre *m* d'impulsions; **i. recorder, i. counter,** compteur *m* d'impulsions; **i. generator,** générateur *m* d'impulsions; **i. repeater,** répéteur *m* d'impulsions; **i. period,** période *f* d'impulsion; **i. ratio,** rapport *m* entre la durée d'une impulsion et sa période; **i. signal,** signal *m* d'appel par impulsions; *Elcs:* **i. noise,** bruit impulsionnel, impulsion parasite; (*c*) *Fig:* **to give an i. to sth.,** donner une impulsion, de l'impulsion, à qch. (au commerce, à l'enseignement, etc.). **2.** (*a*) impulsion, mouvement spontané, mouvement de premier élan; élan *m*; **the vital i.,** l'élan vital; **stray i.,** velléité *f*; **to feel an i. to do sth.,** se sentir poussé à faire qch.; **his first i. was to . . .,** son premier mouvement fut de . . ., le premier mouvement qu'il eut fut de . . .; **kind i., good i.,** bon mouvement; **charitable i.,** élan de charité; **out of a common i.,** d'un commun élan; (mus) par le même désir irrésistible, par le même besoin, par la même inspiration; **on the, a, first i.,** tout d'abord; à première vue; **under the i. of the moment,** sous l'impulsion du moment; **rash, sudden, i.,** coup *m* de tête; **to do sth. on a sudden i.,** faire qch. par caprice, par coup de tête; **to act on i.,** agir par impulsion, spontanément; **to yield to i.,** céder à l'entraînement du moment; **i. buying,** achat *m* décidé sur le moment; **creature of i.,** être *m* d'impulsion; **man of i.,** homme impulsif, primesautier; homme de premier mouvement; (*b*) *Psy:* pulsion (sexuelle, etc.); **obsessive i.,** impulsion-obsession *f*, *pl.* impulsions-obsessions. **3.** *Physiol:* **nerve i.,** signal nerveux.

impulsion [im'pʌlʃ(ə)n], *s.* **1.** impulsion *f*; force impulsive. **2. to act at the i. of s.o.,** agir à l'instigation de qn.

impulsive [im'pʌlsiv], *a.* **1.** (*a*) *Mec:* impulsif, propulsif; **i. force,** force impulsive, projective; force d'impulsion; **i. moment,** moment *m* d'inertie géométrique; (*b*) *Elcs:* **i. noise,** bruit impulsionnel. **2.** (*a*) (geste, etc.) involontaire, irréfléchi, spontané; **i. action,** coup *m* de tête; (*b*) (*of pers.*) impulsif, velléitaire, primesautier; **to be i. in one's actions,** agir par impulsion; être un impulsif, une impulsive; **to be i. in one's friendships,** être très impulsif dans le choix de ses amis.

impulsively [im'pʌlsivli], *adv.* (agir) par impulsion, impulsivement; sous le coup d'une impulsion; spontanément.

impulsiveness [im'pʌlsivnis], **impulsivity** [impʌl'siviti], *s.* impulsivité *f*, caractère impulsif; **the i. of his feelings,** ses sentiments impulsifs.

impulsivist [im'pʌlsivist], *s.* personne primesautière; impulsif, -ive.

impunity [im'pju:niti], *s.* impunité *f*; **to do sth. with i.,** faire qch. impunément, sans subir de conséquence fâcheuse; **with complete i.,** en toute impunité.

impure [im'pjuər], *a.* **1.** (sang, air, lait) impur. **2.** *Rel: Poet:* (*of hands, etc.*) impur, souillé. **3.** (*of pers., desire, etc.*) impur, impudique; **i. thoughts,** pensées impures.

impurely [im'pjuəli], *adv.* impurement; d'une manière impure.

impurity [im'pju:riti], *s.* **1.** (*a*) impureté *f* (de l'air, de l'eau, etc.); **i. in the blood,** vice *m* du sang; (*b*) **moral i.,** souillure morale; impureté. **2.** corps étranger, impureté, saleté *f*; *Elcs:* **acceptor i.,** impureté acceptrice.

imputability [impju:tə'biliti], *s.* imputabilité *f*.

imputable [im'pju:təbl], *a.* **1.** imputable, attribuable (**to,** à). **2.** *Theol:* **the righteousness of Christ is i. to believers,** les mérites *m* du Christ sont imputables aux croyants.

imputation [impju(:)'teiʃ(ə)n], *s.* **1.** imputation *f*; (i) attribution *f* (d'un crime à qn); (ii) chose imputée (à qn); **libellous imputations,** imputations calomnieuses. **2.** *Theol:* imputation (des mérites de Jésus-Christ aux fidèles).

imputative [im'pju:tətiv], *a. Theol:* (mérite, etc.) imputatif.

imputatively [im'pju:tətivli], *adv.* par imputation.

impute [im'pju:t], *v.tr.* **1.** imputer, attribuer (une action, etc.) (**to s.o.,** à qn); **the actions imputed to him,** les faits qu'on lui impute; *Jur:* les faits à lui imputés; *Com:* **imputed payments,** paiements imputés. **2.** *Theol:* imputer (les mérites de Jésus-Christ à qn).

imputing [im'pju:tiŋ], *s.* imputation *f*, attribution *f* (de qch. à qn).

imputrescibility [impjutresi'biliti], *s.* imputrescibilité *f*.

imputrescible [impju'tresibl], *a.* imputrescible.

in[1] [in], *prep., adv. a. & s.*

I. *prep.* **1.** (*of place*) (*a*) en, à, dans; **in Europe,** en Europe; **in France,** en France; **in Japan, Canada, Portugal,** au Japon, au Canada, au Portugal; **in India,** dans l'Inde, aux Indes; **in the Netherlands,** dans les Pays-Bas; **in the United States,** aux États-Unis; **in Touraine,** en Touraine; **in Ceylon, Madagascar, Newfoundland,** à Ceylan, à Madagascar, à Terre-Neuve; **in Kent,** dans le Kent; **in Paris,** à Paris; **our conversations in Rome,** nos conversations de Rome; **in such and such a latitude,** sous telle ou telle latitude; **to live somewhere in London,** demeurer dans Londres; **in the provinces,** en province; **the streets in Paris,** les rues de Paris; **to be in town,** être en ville; **to spend a week in Town,** passer une semaine (i) à la ville, (ii) à Londres; **in the country,** à la campagne; **in his country,** dans son pays; **to take a walk in the avenue,** se promener sur l'avenue; *Mil:* **in the field,** en campagne; **in the firing line,** sur la ligne de feu; **in the press,** sous presse; **in prison,** en prison; **in school, in church,** à l'école, à l'église; **in bed,** au lit; **in heaven and hell,** au ciel et en enfer; **in earth as it is in Heaven,** sur la terre comme dans le ciel; **not a cloud in the sky,** pas un nuage dans le ciel; **in the house,** dans la maison; **in one's house,** chez soi; **in the water,** dans l'eau; **in that boat,** sur ce bateau; **in a taxi,** dans un taxi; **to take a drive in a car,** se promener en voiture; **the key is in the door, in the lock,** la clef est sur la porte, sur la serrure; **in this book,** dans ce livre; **I read it in the newspaper,** je l'ai lu dans, sur, le journal; **in (the works of) Shakespeare one finds . . .,** chez Shakespeare on trouve . . .; **in the second chapter,** au deuxième chapitre; **in my hand,** dans ma main; **my fate is in your hands,** mon sort est entre vos mains; **he went upstairs candle in hand,** il monta l'escalier la chandelle à la main; **with a cigar in his mouth,** le cigare à la bouche; **the sun was shining in my eyes,** le soleil me donnait dans les yeux; **in the distance,** au loin; **in your place,** à votre place; **wounded in the shoulder,** blessé à l'épaule; (*b*) (*among*) **in the crowd,** dans la foule; **disaster always in my thoughts,** désastre toujours présent à mes pensées; **he is the first, the last, the only one, in his class,** il est le premier, le dernier, le seul, de sa classe; **to be in a club,** être membre d'un cercle; **it is not done in our circle,** cela ne se fait pas parmi nous; **in the thirties,** (i) entre trente et quarante; (ii) dans les années trente; **he is in the, his, sixties,** il a passé la soixantaine. **2.** (*in respect of*) **blind in one eye,** aveugle d'un œil; **strong in logic,** fort en logique; **expert in economics,** expert en économie politique; **two metres in length,** long de deux mètres; qui a deux mètres de long, de longueur; **the books, three in number,** ces livres, au nombre de trois. **3.** (*of ratio*) **one in ten,** un sur dix; **to pay twenty pence in the pound,** payer vingt pence par livre sterling; **once in ten years,** une fois tous les dix ans; **road with a gradient of one in four,** route *f* à vingt-cinq pour cent de pente. **4.** (*in time*) (*a*) **in 1927,** en 1927; **in those days,** en ce temps-là; **in the reign of Queen Victoria,** sous le règne de la reine Victoria; **in the night, in the daytime,** pendant la nuit, pendant la journée; de nuit, de jour; **in the afternoon,** dans l'après-midi; **at four o'clock in the afternoon,** à quatre heures de l'après-midi; **in the evening,** le soir, pendant la soirée; **in summer, autumn, winter,** en été, en automne, en hiver; **in spring,** au printemps; **in the winter of 1812,** pendant l'hiver de 1812; **in (the month of) April,** au mois d'avril, en avril; **in my youth,** dans, pendant, ma jeunesse; **in our journey,** pendant, au cours de, notre voyage; **in the future,** à l'avenir; **in the past,** par le passé; **never in my life,** jamais de ma vie; **in my time,** de mon temps; (*b*) **to do sth. in three hours,** faire qch. en trois heures; **in less than seven days,** en moins de sept jours; **he'll be here in three hours,** il sera là dans trois heures; **in a little while,** sous peu; **he came back in a few minutes,** il est revenu au bout de quelques minutes; **it will happen in the next 48 hours,** cela arrivera dans les 48 heures; *F:* **I haven't seen you in years,** ça fait des années que je ne t'ai vu; **I haven't eaten oysters in years,** je n'ai pas mangé d'huîtres depuis des années; (*c*) (*introducing a gerund*) **in crossing the river,** en traversant la rivière. **5.** (*of condition, state*) **in good health,** en bonne santé; **in tears,** en larmes; **in chains,** enchaîné, dans les fers; **in sorrow,** chagriné, affligé; **in despair,** au désespoir; **cow in calf, in-calf cow, mare in foal, in-foal mare, ewe in lamb, in-lamb ewe,** vache, jument, brebis, pleine; **to cry out in surprise, in terror,** pousser un cri de surprise, de terreur; **any man in his senses,** tout homme jouissant de son bon sens; **in a blaze,** en feu; en train de flamber; **the person in question,** la personne en question; **in the crude state,** à l'état brut. **6.** (*clothed in*) **in his shirt,** en chemise; **in slippers,** en pantoufles; **in brown shoes,** chaussé de souliers jaunes; **in female attire,** en vêtements de femme; **a man in a blue suit,** un homme vêtu d'un complet bleu; **dressed in white, in silk,** habillé de blanc, de soie; **they were all in white,** elles étaient toutes en blanc; **what shall I go in?—go in your dinner jacket,** qu'est-ce que je vais mettre?—mettez votre smoking. **7. to go out in the rain, in the snow,** sortir par la pluie, par la neige; **in this warm weather,** par ce temps chaud; **I can't stay outside in this heat,** je ne peux pas rester dehors par, avec, cette chaleur; **put on your overcoat in this cold weather,** mettez votre pardessus par le froid qu'il fait; **to work in the rain,** travailler sous la pluie; **in the sun,** au soleil; **in the dark(ness),** dans l'obscurité; **you are in my light,** vous êtes dans mon jour; vous me faites ombre; **to appear in a favourable light,** paraître sous un jour favorable. **8.** (*engaged in*) **to be in the motor industry,** être dans l'industrie automobile; **there were four of us in the concern,** nous étions quatre dans l'affaire; **in politics,** dans la politique; **the devil's in it,** le diable s'en mêle; **killed in action,** tué à l'ennemi. **9.** (*according to*) **in my opinion,** à mon avis, à mon opinion; **in justice,** en toute justice; pour être juste; **in common decency he ought to have written to her,** le plus élémentaire savoir-vivre exigeait qu'il lui écrivît. **10.** (*a*) (*of manner*) **in a reproachful tone,** (parler) sur, avec, un ton de reproche; **in a gentle voice,** d'une voix douce; **in a businesslike manner,** en bon homme d'affaires; d'une façon sérieuse; **written in an unoriginal style,** écrit d'un, dans un, style peu original; **in the French style,** à la française; **to be in (the) fashion,** être à la mode; (*b*) (*of medium*) **to write in French,** écrire en français; **to write in ink, in pencil,** écrire à l'encre, au crayon; **in writing,** par écrit; **payment in kind,** paiement *m* en nature; **to talk in whispers,** parler en chuchotant; (*c*) (*of arrangement*) **material in folds,** étoffe *f* en plis; **to walk in groups,** se promener par groupes; **to stand in a row, in a circle,** se tenir en ligne, en cercle; **in alphabetical order,** par ordre alphabétique; **packed in dozens,** en paquets de douze; **they were shown in in threes,** on les faisait entrer par trois; (*d*) (*of material*) **dress in green velvet,** robe *f* en velours vert; (*e*) **I've nothing in your size,** je n'ai rien à votre taille; **what have you got in scarves?** qu'est-ce que vous avez en fait de, comme, foulards? (*f*) (*of form*) **in the form of a pill,** sous forme de pilule; **demon in human shape,** démon sous une forme humaine; **money in gold,** espèces *fpl* en or; (*g*) (*of degree, extent*) **in large quantities,** en, par, grandes quantités; **to die in hundreds,** mourir par centaines; **in part,** en partie; **in places,** par endroits. **11.** (*of purpose*) **in reply to . . .,** en réponse à . . .; **in honour of . . .,** en l'honneur de . . .; **in quest, in search, of. . .,** à la recherche de . . .; **in memory of. . .,** en mémoire de . . .; **in the cause of humanity,** pour la cause de l'humanité. **12.** (*a*) (*with reflexive pronoun*) **equation true in itself,** équation vraie par elle-même; **this product is not a poison in itself,** ce produit n'est pas un poison en lui-même; (*b*) **it is rather presumptuous in a man of his type to . . .,** c'est assez présomptueux de la part d'un homme comme lui de . . .; **a peculiarity in young people,** une particularité chez les jeunes gens; **I was sure he had something in him,** je savais bien qu'il avait quelque chose dans le ventre. **13. in that,** par ce que, puisque, vu que; **the laws did more harm than good in that they made progress impossible,** ces lois firent plus de mal que de bien en ce sens qu'elles rendaient tout progrès impossible; **suicide is the more likely in that nobody else was in the house,** le suicide est d'autant plus probable qu'il n'y avait personne d'autre à la maison.

II. *adv.* (*the uses of* in *as an adjunct to verbs, such as* **ask in, bring in, etc.,** *are illustrated under the respective verbs*) **1.** (*a*) (*at home*) à la maison, chez soi; **is your mother in?** est-ce que votre mère est chez elle, à la maison? **Mr Martin is in,** M. Martin y est; (*b*) *F:* en prison; **what is he in for?** pour quel crime est-il en prison? (*c*) *Agr:* **the harvest is in,** la moisson est rentrée; (*d*) (*of train, coach, steamer, mail*) **to be in,** être arrivé; **the train is in,** le train est en gare, à quai; **the mail is in,** le courrier est arrivé; (*e*) *Nau:* **the sails are in,** les voiles sont serrées, sont ferlées; (*f*) **is the fire still in?** est-ce que le feu brûle encore? (*g*) **in with it!** rentrez-le! **in with you!** (i) entrez! allons, arrivez! (ii) allez-y! (*h*) (*inside*) **coat with the fur side in,** manteau avec le côté poil en dedans; (*i*) *Ten:* **the ball is in,** la balle est bonne. **2.** (*a*) (*in power, in office*) élu; au pouvoir; **the Liberals were in,** le parti libéral était au pouvoir; **the Liberal candidate is in,** le candidat libéral est élu; (*b*) (*in season*) **strawberries are in,** c'est la saison des fraises; **football is over and tennis isn't in,** le football est fini et le tennis n'a pas encore commencé; **summer is in,** c'est l'été; (*c*) (*in fashion*) **stripes are in this year,** les rayures sont de vogue, à la mode, la rage, cette année; (*d*) (*in practice*) **I've got my hand in,** je suis bien en train; ma main (y) est faite; je suis en main (pour dessiner, jouer, etc.); (*e*) (*in favour*) **to be (well) in with s.o.,** être en bons termes avec qn; être bien avec qn, *F:* dans les bons papiers de qn; **to be well in (at headquarters, etc.),** être très protégé, avoir des protections (au Ministère, etc.); **he is in with all the best people,** il est en rapport avec toutes les personnalités; il a de belles relations; **those who are in,** ceux qui sont acceptés par la bonne société; (*f*) *Turf:* **horse that is well in,** cheval *m* qui a un handicap avantageux; *F:* **to be well in on a deal,** avoir toutes les chances de réussir une affaire; **my luck is in,** je suis en veine; (*g*) *Sp:* (*at cricket, baseball*) **to be in,** battre la balle; *F:* être à la batte; **the side that is in,** l'équipe *f* qui est à la batte; **Jones is in,** Jones est à la batte, au jeu; le tour est à Jones; c'est Jones qui est au guichet. **3.** (*a*) (i) **to be in for (the loss of) a thousand pounds,** en avoir, y être, pour (une perte de) mille livres; **we're in for a week of this,** nous en avons pour une semaine; **we're in for a period of prosperity,** nous sommes partis pour une période de prospérité; **I'm in for a big thing,** je suis lancé dans une grosse affaire; **we're in for a storm,** nous aurons sûrement de l'orage; **he's in for a prison sentence,** il est bon pour l'emprisonnement; **he's in for a surprise,** il va être surpris; *F:* **to be in for it,** être sûr de son affaire; **he's in for it,** son affaire est bonne; qu'est-ce qu'il va prendre! **(now) we're in for it!** pas moyen d'en sortir! voilà la danse qui va commencer! **I'm in for it again!** je suis encore de la revue! **to have it in for s.o.,** avoir une dent contre qn; la garder bonne à qn; (ii) **to be in for a competition,** être inscrit pour un concours; (*b*) **to be in on a secret,** être du secret, dans le secret; **I wasn't in on it,** je n'étais pas dans le coup. **4.** (*phrases*) (*a*) **day in, day out; week in, week out; year in, year out,** tout le long du jour, de la semaine, de l'année; du matin au soir; d'un bout de la semaine à l'autre; sans trêve; (*b*) **all in,** (i) tout compris; **it will cost you £100, all in,** cela vous coûtera cent livres tout compris, cent livres prix global; **the prices quoted are all in,** les prix cotés s'entendent tous frais compris; (ii) *F:* **I'm absolutely all in,** je suis absolument éreinté, fourbu, rendu, vanné, esquinté; (*c*) *Ten:* **advantage in,** avantage dedans, au servant; (*d*) *Husb:* **to breed in and in,** accoupler des animaux consanguins; **bred in and in,** consanguin; (*e*) (i) **in and out,** entrer et sortir; **he is always in and out of the house,** il entre et sort comme chez lui; **in-and-out bolt,** boulon *m* libre; *Cin:* **in-and-out movement of the claws,** engrènement *m* des griffes (dans la perforation); *Sp:* **in-and-out running,** alternation *f* de victoires et d'échecs; (ii) **to know s.o. in and out,** connaître qn à fond.

III. *a.* **1.** (*a*) **the in door,** la porte d'entrée; *Com:* **in tray,** entrées *fpl*; *Cmptr:* **in tape,** bande *f* entrée; *Fin:* **i. book,** livre *m* du dedans; livre, registre *m*, des chèques à rembourser; (*b*) **in patient,** (malade) hospitalisé, -ée; **in maintenance,** entretien *m* des pauvres hospitalisés; (*c*) *Cr:* **the in side,** l'équipe *f* qui est à la batte. **2. an in joke,** une plaisanterie de coterie; **it's the in thing these days,** c'est la rage aujourd'hui.

IV. *s.* **1. ins and outs;** (*a*) **ins and outs of a stream, of a path,** méandres *m* d'un cours d'eau, d'un sentier; *F:* **to know the ins and outs of a matter,** connaître tous les coins et recoins, tous les tenants et aboutissants, d'une affaire; connaître le fort et le fin, le fort et le faible, d'une affaire; connaître une affaire dans tous ses détails; **the ins and outs of a house,** les aîtres *m* d'une maison; **I know all the ins and outs of these ruins,** je connais tous les tours et détours de ces ruines; (*b*) **doss house ins and outs,** habitués, -ées, des asiles de nuit; *F:* chevaux *m* de retour. **2.** *Pol:* **the ins,** le parti au pouvoir. **3.** *U.S: F:* **to have an in,** avoir de l'influence; **he has an in with the senator,** il a ses entrées chez le sénateur.

in[2], *Lt. prep.* (*occurs in many phrases of which the following are frequent*) *Jur:* **sentenced in absentia,** condamné par contumace; **in articulo mortis,** à l'article de la mort; *Ecc: Jur:* **in commendam,** en commende; *Jur:* **in contumaciam,** (condamner qn) par contumace; **in esse,** existant; qui existe; au monde; **in extenso,** in extenso; sans rien omettre; **in extremis,** in extremis; à l'article de la mort; **in flagrante delicto,** en flagrant délit; *Jur:* **in forma pauperis,** (intenter une action) avec assistance judiciaire; **in loco,** en lieu (de); **to stand in loco parentis to a child,** être investi de la puissance paternelle vis-à-vis d'un enfant; **in medias res,** in medias res; en plein sujet; **in memoriam,** en mémoire (de); *R.C.Ch:* **bishop in partibus (infidelium),** évêque *m* in partibus (infidelium); évêque dans les pays occupés par les infidèles; **in perpetuum,** in perpetuum; à perpétuité; *Phil:* **in posse,** en puissance; **in propria persona,** en propre personne; **in puris naturalibus,** in naturalibus; dans l'état de nudité; **in situ,** in situ; en place; dans l'endroit même; **in statu pupillari,** en tutelle; **in statu quo,** in statu quo; dans le statu quo; tel quel; **to inflict punishment in terrorem,** infliger une punition pour l'exemple; **in toto,** en entier; entièrement; absolument; **to reject a proposal in toto,** rejeter, repousser, une proposition en bloc, entièrement; **in transitu,** en transit; **in vacuo,** dans le vide.

in- [in], *pref. expressing negation.* **1.** in-; **inaction,** inaction. **2.** peu; pas; sans; non; **inexpensive,** peu coûteux; **insincere,** peu sincère; **incompact,** non compact; **indiscoverable, ineradicable,** qu'on ne peut découvrir, extirper; **inglorious,** sans gloire; **inconformity,** manque *m* de conformité.

inability [inə'biliti], *s.* incapacité *f* **(to do sth.,** de faire qch.); impuissance *f* **(to do sth.,** à faire qch.); **he admitted his i. to concentrate,** il s'avoua incapable de, impuissant à, se concentrer.

inaccessibility [inæksesi'biliti], **inaccessibleness** [inæk'sesiblnis], *s.* inaccessibilité *f*; *Geog:* **pole of inaccessibility,** pôle *m* d'inaccessibilité.

inaccessible [inæk'sesibl], *a.* (*a*) (point, port) inaccessible (to, à); **people i. to pity, to any feeling for beauty,** gens inaccessibles à la pitié, fermés au sentiment du beau; (*b*) (personne) inabordable.

inaccuracy [in'ækjurəsi], *s.* **1.** inexactitude *f*, imprécision *f*; **i. of a translation,** infidélité *f* d'une traduction. **2. work full of inaccuracies,** ouvrage plein d'inexactitudes.

inaccurate [in'ækjurət], *a.* (calcul, esprit) inexact; (esprit) imprécis; (avis, sens) incorrect; **i. account,** récit *m* infidèle; *Mil:* **i. fire,** tir déréglé; **i. balance,** balance fausse, défectueuse.

inaccurately [in'ækjurətli], *adv.* (calculer) inexactement; (juger, citer) incorrectement; (traduire) infidèlement.

inactinic [inæk'tinik], *a. Ph:* inactinique.

inaction [in'ækʃ(ə)n], *s.* inaction *f*; inertie *f*; **reduced to i.,** réduit à l'inaction; immobilisé; **policy of i.,** politique *f* de laisser-faire.

inactivate [in'æktiveit], *v.tr.* **1.** *Ch: etc:* rendre (un produit chimique, un sérum) inactif; inactiver, neutraliser. **2.** *Mil:* dissoudre (une unité).

inactivation [inækti'veiʃ(ə)n], *s. Ch: etc:* inactivation *f*.

inactive [in'æktiv], *a.* **1.** inactif; (esprit) inerte; **i. habits,** habitudes *f* d'inaction. **2.** (fabrique, mine) en chômage. **3.** *Mil:* en non-activité, en disponibilité, hors cadre, non mobilisé; **i. list,** personnel *m* hors cadre, (personnel du) cadre de reserve; **i. unit,** unité *f* de formation (à la mobilisation), unité de réservistes. **4.** *Ch:* (corps) inerte, sans action; *El:* (courant) déwatté; *Ph:* **body optically i.,** corps optiquement inactif.

inactively [in'æktivli], *adv.* inactivement, dans l'inaction.

inactivity [inæk'tiviti], *s.* inactivité *f*; inertie *f*; passivité *f*; *Hum:* **masterly i.,** sage politique *f* de laisser-faire.

inadaptability [inədæptə'biliti], **inadaptation** [inædæp'teiʃ(ə)n], *s.* incapacité *f* de s'adapter **(to,** à); **inadaptability of the soil,** incapacité, impropriété *f*, du sol à la culture.

inadaptable [inə'dæptəbl], *a.* (*a*) (*of pers.*) incapable de s'adapter **(to,** à); (*b*) (*of thg*) qui ne peut être adapté, ajusté **(to,** à); **i. soil,** sol *m* impropre à la culture.

inadequacy [in'ædikwəsi], *s.* insuffisance *f* (d'un revenu); imperfection *f*, état incomplet, inadéquation *f* (d'un système, etc.); **to be fully conscious of one's own i.,** connaître bien son insuffisance, son incapacité **(for,** pour).

inadequate [in'ædikwət], *a.* **1.** inadéquat, insuffisant; **i. salary,** salaire insuffisant; **i. information,** renseignements incomplets; **i. arrangements,** défaut *m* d'organisation; **to decide on i. grounds,** se décider sur de maigres raisons; (*of thg*) **to be i. to a purpose, to do sth.,** être insuffisant pour qch., pour faire qch.; **my words are i. to express my gratitude,** mes paroles sont bien au-dessous de la reconnaissance que je voudrais vous exprimer. **2. i. style,** style inapproprié au sujet; style pauvre.

inadequately [in'ædikwətli], *adv.* insuffisamment.

inadequateness [in'ædikwətnis], *s.* = INADEQUACY.

inadherent [inəd'hiər(ə)nt], **inadhesive** [inəd'hi:siv], *a.* inadhérent, qui n'adhère pas.

inadmissibility ['inədmisi'biliti], *s.* inadmissibilité *f* (d'une supposition, preuve, etc.); *Jur:* irrecevabilité *f* (d'une réclamation, etc.).

inadmissible [inəd'misibl], *a.* (théorie, prétention) inadmissible; (demande) inaccordable; *Jur:* (réclamation, excuse) irrecevable.

inadvertence [inəd'və:t(ə)ns], **inadvertency** [inəd'və:t(ə)nsi], *s.* **1.** inattention *f*, manque *m* d'attention; **to do sth. through i.,** faire qch. par inadvertance, par mégarde, par méprise, par oubli, par étourderie. **2.** erreur commise par inadvertance; étourderie *f*; négligence *f*.

inadvertent [inəd'və:t(ə)nt], *a.* **1.** (*of pers.*) inattentif **(to,** à); négligent **(to, de). 2.** (*of mistake, etc.*) commis par inadvertance, par mégarde; **i. joke,** plaisanterie involontaire, faite sans le vouloir.

inadvertently [inəd'və:t(ə)ntli], *adv.* par inadvertance, par distraction, par mégarde; par oubli, par étourderie; sans y prendre garde; *Theol:* **to sin i.,** pécher sans advertence.

inadvisability [inədvaizə'biliti], *s.* imprudence *f*, inopportunité *f* (d'une action).

inadvisable [inəd'vaizəbl], *a.* (*of action*) peu sage; imprudent; **we think it i. for you to travel,** nous croyons devoir vous déconseiller de voyager; **alcohol is i. for people suffering from high blood pressure,** l'alcool est déconseillé aux hypertendus.

inalienability [ineiliənə'biliti], **inalienableness** [in'eiliənəbəlnis], *s. Jur:* inaliénabilité *f*, indisponibilité *f*, incessibilité *f* (d'un bien, d'un droit).

inalienable [in'eiliənəbl], *a.* (bien *m*, droit *m*) inaliénable, indisponible, incessible.

inalienably [in'eiliənəbli], *adv.* inaliénablement.

inalterability [ino:lt(ə)rə'biliti], *s.* **1.** immutabilité *f*. **2.** inaltérabilité *f* (d'une couleur, d'une épreuve photographique, etc.).

inalterable [in'o:lt(ə)rəbl], *a.* **1.** immuable; à quoi l'on ne saurait apporter de changement. **2.** (matière colorante, épreuve *f* photographique, etc.) inaltérable.

inamissible [inə'misibl], *a. Theol:* (*of grace, etc.*) inamissible.

inamorata [inæmə'rɑ:tə], *s.f.* amoureuse, amante.

inamorato [inæmə'rɑ:tou], *s.m.* amant, amoureux.

in-and-in ['inənd'in], *a. Husb:* **in-a.-in breeding,** suite *f* d'accouplements consanguins.

inane [i'nein], *a.* **1.** *A:* (*of space*) vide; *s.* **the (great) i.,** le grand vide; le néant. **2.** (*of pers., action*) inepte, stupide, bête, niais; **i. smile,** sourire bête, niais; **i. answer,** réponse inepte, saugrenue; **i. remark,** ineptie *f*; **an i. person,** une nullité; *F:* une croûte, une ganache.

inanely [i'neinli], *adv.* bêtement, stupidement, niaisement, absurdement; **to talk i.,** débiter des inepties.

inanimate [in'ænimət], *a.* (*a*) (corps, style, etc.) inanimé, sans vie; **i. nature,** le monde inanimé; (*b*) *Gram:* (genre) inanimé.

inanimateness [in'ænimətnis], **inanimation** [inæni'meiʃ(ə)n], *s.* inanimation *f*, manque *m* d'animation.

inanition [inæ'niʃ(ə)n], *s. Med:* inanition *f*.

inanity [i'næniti], *s.* inanité *f*, niaiserie *f* (d'une remarque, etc.); **to talk a lot of inanities,** débiter des inepties, des niaiseries.

inappeasable [inə'pi:zəbl], *a.* inapaisable.

inappellable [inə'peləbl], *a. Jur:* (jugement *m*) sans appel, qui ne souffre pas d'appel.

inappetence [in'æpit(ə)ns], *s. Med:* inappétence *f*, manque *m* d'appétit.

inapplicability ['inæplikə'biliti], *s.* inapplicabilité *f* **(to,** à).

inapplicable [in'æplikəbl], *a.* inapplicable **(to,** à); *Mth:* **i. solution to a problem,** solution étrangère d'un problème.

inapplication [inæpli'keiʃ(ə)n], *s.* **1.** inapplication *f*; manque *m* d'application; indolence *f*. **2.** inapplicabilité *f*; manque d'à-propos.

inapposite [in'æpəzit], *a.* (citation, titre) sans rapport **(to,** avec), inapplicable **(to,** à); (réponse) faite mal à propos, hors de propos.

inappositely [in'æpəzitli], *adv.* (répondre) mal à propos.

inappositeness [in'æpəzitnis], *s.* manque *m* d'à-propos (d'une remarque, etc.).

inappreciable [inə'pri:ʃiəbl], *a.* inappréciable (à l'œil, etc.).

inappreciably [inə'pri:ʃiəbli], *adv.* inappréciablement.

inappreciation ['inəpri:ʃi'eiʃ(ə)n], *s.* manque *m*, défaut *m*, d'appréciation.

inappreciative [inə'pri:ʃiətiv], *a.* (public) insensible; (compte rendu, etc.) peu appréciateur, peu favorable.

inapprehensible [inæpri'hensibl], *a.* (sentiment, signification) insaisissable, incompréhensible.

inapprehension [inæpri'henʃ(ə)n], *s.* manque *m*, défaut *m*, de compréhension.

inapprehensive [inæpri'hensiv], *a.* **1.** inintelligent; qui manque d'appréhension; (esprit) lourd, obtus. **2.** sans appréhension **(of, de); to be i. of danger,** ne pas appréhender, ne pas redouter, le danger; être insouciant, sans crainte, du danger.

inapproachable [inə'proutʃəbl], *a.* **1.** (*a*) (cime, etc.) inaccessible; (côte) inabordable; (*b*) (*of pers.*) inabordable, inaccostable; (i) distant; (ii) farouche. **2.** incomparable, suréminent; sans pareil.

inapproachably [inə'proutʃəbli], *adv.* incomparablement (mieux, etc.).

inappropriate [inə'proupriət], *a.* peu approprié, qui ne convient pas (**to,** à); (*of word*) impropre; (*of speech*) déplacé; **entirely i. to the existing situation,** absolument incompatible avec la situation actuelle.

inappropriately [inə'proupriətli], *adv.* d'une façon impropre, peu appropriée.

inappropriateness [inə'proupriətnis], *s.* manque *m* d'à-propos (d'une remarque, etc.); **the i. of the way she was dressed,** l'inconvenance *f* de sa tenue.

inapt [in'æpt], *a.* inapte. **1.** (*a*) incapable; (*b*) inhabile, inexpert. **2.** peu approprié (**to,** à).

inaptitude [in'æptitju:d], **inaptness** [in'æptnis], *s.* **1.** inaptitude *f* (**for,** à). **2.** incapacité *f.*

inaptly [in'æptli], *adv.* improprement; **i. described,** mal décrit; **not i. so called,** appelé ainsi avec justesse, avec beaucoup d'à-propos.

inarch [in'ɑ:tʃ], *v.tr. Hort:* greffer par approche.

inarching [in'ɑ:tʃiŋ], *s. Hort:* greffage *m*, greffe *f*, par approche.

inarguable [in'ɑ:gjuəbl], *a.* incontestable, indisputable.

inarticulacy [inɑ:'tikjuləsi], *s.* = INARTICULATENESS.

Inarticulata ['inɑ:tikju'leitə], *s.pl. Moll:* inarticulés *m.*

inarticulate [inɑ:'tikjulət], *a.* **1.** *Nat.Hist:* inarticulé, sans articulations. **2.** (*a*) (son) inarticulé; (son) imparfaitement prononcé; **i. desires,** désirs inexprimés; (*b*) (animal *m*, etc.) qui n'a pas le don de la parole; muet, -ette; **the i. masses,** les masses *f* qui souffrent en silence, qui ne savent pas formuler leurs plaintes; (*c*) (malade) incapable de parler; **i. with rage, with drink,** bégayant de colère, d'ivresse.

inarticulated [inɑ:'tikjuleitid], *a.* = INARTICULATE 1, 2 (*a*).

inarticulately [inɑ:'tikjulətli], *adv.* d'une manière inarticulée; indistinctement.

inarticulateness [inɑ:'tikjulətnis], *s.* **1.** défaut *m*, manque *m*, d'articulation; prononciation indistincte; balbutie *f.* **2.** (*a*) mutisme *m*, aphonie *f*; (*b*) perte *f* de la voix.

inartificial [inɑ:ti'fiʃ(ə)l], *a.* sans art; sans artifice; naturel.

inartistic [inɑ:'tistik], *a.* (*a*) (*of production, etc.*) peu artistique; sans valeur artistique; (*b*) (*of pers.*) dépourvu de sens artistique.

inasmuch as [inəz'mʌtʃəz], *conj.phr.* **1.** *Jur:* attendu que, vu que, considérant que, puisque; **i. as the owner has not claimed his rights, the said rights have now lapsed,** considérant que, vu que, attendu que, le propriétaire n'a pas réclamé ses droits, lesdits droits sont périmés. **2.** *A:* dans la mesure que; *B:* **i. as ye have done it unto one of the least of these my brethren ye have done it unto me,** en tant que vous avez fait ces choses à l'un de ces plus petits de mes frères, vous me l'avez fait à moi-même.

inassimilable [inə'similəbl], *a.* (*of food, idea, immigrant, etc.*) inassimilable.

inattention [inə'tenʃ(ə)n], *s.* inattention *f*; (*a*) distraction *f*; **to have fits of i.,** avoir des moments d'inattention, de distraction; **to punish a pupil for i.,** punir un élève pour son inapplication; (*b*) **i. to one's business,** négligence *f* de ses affaires; (*c*) manque *m* de prévenances, d'attentions (**to, towards, s.o.,** à l'égard de qn).

inattentive [inə'tentiv], *a.* **1.** inattentif, distrait; (élève) inappliqué. **2.** négligent (to, de). **3.** peu attentionné (**to, towards, s.o.,** pour qn); peu prévenant.

inattentively [inə'tentivli], *adv.* sans attention; distraitement.

inattentiveness [inə'tentivnis], *s.* inattention *f*; distraction *f*; inapplication *f* (d'un élève).

inaudibility [inɔ:di'biliti], *s.* imperceptibilité *f*, insaisissabilité *f* (d'un son); faiblesse *f* (de la voix); **the i. of a speaker,** l'incapacité *f* d'un orateur de se faire entendre.

inaudible [in'ɔ:dibl], *a.* inaudible; (son) imperceptible; (réponse) insaisissable; **i. voice,** voix *f* faible; **the noise rendered his words i. to us,** le tapage nous empêchait d'entendre, de saisir, ses paroles; **it, he, is almost i.,** on l'entend à peine.

inaudibly [in'ɔ:dibli], *adv.* (déposer qch.) sans bruit; (parler, prier) de manière à ne pas être entendu.

inaugural [i'nɔ:gjur(ə)l]. **1.** *a.* inaugural, -aux; **i. address,** discours *m* d'inauguration. **2.** *s. U.S:* discours d'inauguration.

inaugurate [i'nɔ:gjureit], *v.tr.* (*a*) inaugurer (un monument, un édifice); **to i. a fête,** faire l'inauguration d'une fête; (*b*) inaugurer, commencer (une ère nouvelle); mettre en application, en vigueur (un nouveau système); (*c*) installer (un chef d'état, etc.) (avec cérémonie).

inauguration [inɔ:gju'reiʃ(ə)n], *s.* (*a*) inauguration *f* (d'un édifice, etc.); (*b*) commencement *m*, mise en application, en vigueur (d'un nouveau système, etc.); (*c*) installation cérémonieuse (d'un chef d'état, etc.); *U.S:* **i. day,** le jour de l'inauguration du nouveau président.

inaugurator [i'nɔ:gjureitər], *s.* inaugurateur, -trice.

inauguratory [i'nɔ:gjureitəri], *a.* inaugural, -aux.

inauspicious [inɔ:s'piʃəs], *a.* peu propice; fâcheux; malheureux; néfaste; **at an i. moment,** à un moment malencontreux.

inauspiciously [inɔ:s'piʃəsli], *adv.* sous de mauvais auspices; peu favorablement; **the day started i.,** la journée a commencé mal.

inauspiciousness [inɔ:s'piʃəsnis], *s.* mauvais auspices *mpl* (d'une mauvaise étoile); caractère malheureux (de certains jours, d'un début, etc.).

inbalance ['inbæləns], *s. Psy:* déséquilibre *m.*

inband ['inbænd], *s. Const:* boutisse *f.*

inbeing ['inbi:iŋ], *s.* **1.** immanence *f.* **2.** nature essentielle; essence *f*, âme *f* (de qch.).

in-between [inbi'twi:n]. **1.** *a.* intermédiaire, au milieu; **to take an i.-b. stand on a question,** se placer au milieu à propos d'une question. **2.** *s.* **in the i.-b.,** dans l'entre-deux; **to look for an i.-b.,** chercher un entre-deux, quelque chose entre les deux.

inboard ['inbɔ:d], *a. Nau:* **1.** *adv.* à l'intérieur du bord, en abord; **to take the anchor i.,** rentrer l'ancre. **2.** *prep.* en abord de. **3.** *a.* de l'intérieur, à l'intérieur; **i. cabin,** cabine intérieure, *Navy:* chambre intérieure; *Av:* **i. engine,** moteur intérieur; **i. nacelle,** fuseau-moteur intérieur.

inborn ['inbɔ:n], *a.* (*a*) (instinct, mérite) inné, infus, naturel; (*b*) *Med:* congénital, -aux.

inbound ['inbaund], *a.* (navire) qui entre en rade, au port; qui remonte vers le port.

inbred ['inbred], *a.* **1.** inné, naturel. **2.** *Breed:* (*of horses, etc.*) consanguin.

inbreed ['inbri:d], *v.* (**inbred**) **1.** *v.tr.* **to i. horses,** accoupler des chevaux consanguins. **2.** *v.i.* (*of animals*) s'accoupler avec des consanguins; (*of people*) s'accoupler avec des membres de la même famille.

inbreeding ['inbri:diŋ], *s.* accouplement *m* d'animaux consanguins; inbreeding *m*; suite *f* d'accouplements, de mariages, consanguins; consanguinité *f.*

inbuilt ['inbilt], *a.* (placard, etc.) incorporé; *Cmptr:* **i. check,** contrôle *m* automatique.

Inca ['iŋkə]. *Hist:* **1.** *s.* Inca *mf, pl.* Inca(s). **2.** *a.* inca *inv.*

Incaic [iŋ'keiik], *a.* incasique.

incalculability [inkælkjulə'biliti], *s.* incalculabilité *f.*

incalculable [in'kælkjuləbl], *a.* **1.** incalculable; **i. loss,** perte *f* incalculable, inestimable. **2. i. temper,** humeur sur laquelle on ne peut compter, à laquelle on ne peut se fier.

incalculably [in'kælkjuləbli], *adv.* incalculablement.

incalescence [inkæ'les(ə)ns], *s.* incalescence *f.*

incameration [inkæmə'reiʃ(ə)n], *s. Ecc.Hist:* incamération *f.*

incandesce [inkæn'des]. **1.** *v.tr.* rendre incandescent; mettre (une lampe, etc.) en incandescence. **2.** *v.i.* entrer en incandescence.

incandescence [inkæn'des(ə)ns], *s.* incandescence *f*; *Metall:* chaleur blanche.

incandescent [inkæn'des(ə)nt], *a.* incandescent; **i. mantle,** manchon incandescent; **i. light,** lumière *f* à incandescence; **i. gas burner,** bec *m* de gaz à incandescence; bec Auer; *El:* **i. lamp,** lampe *f* à incandescence.

incantation [inkæn'teiʃ(ə)n], *s.* incantation *f*, conjuration *f*, charme *m.*

incantatory [inkæn'teitəri], *a.* incantatoire.

incapability [inkeipə'biliti], *s.* **1.** incapacité *f.* **2.** *Jur:* inéligibilité *f.*

incapable [in'keipəbl]. **1.** *a.* **i. of,** incapable de; (*a*) (*of pers.*) **i. of movement, of speech, of much exertion,** incapable de se mouvoir, de parler, de grand effort; **i. of pity,** inaccessible à la pitié; **i. of deception,** incapable de tromper; **he's i. of doing such a spiteful thing,** il ne ferait jamais, n'est pas capable de faire, une méchanceté pareille; **I found myself i. to help, of helping, him,** je me trouvais dans l'impossibilité de lui prêter secours; *Jur:* **declared i. of managing his own affairs,** en état d'incapacité légale; **to have s.o. declared i. to manage, of managing, his own affairs,** faire interdire qn; (*b*) (*of thg*) **i. of improvement, of being improved,** peu susceptible d'amélioration; incapable d'amélioration, d'être amélioré; **i. of proof,** non susceptible de preuve; (*c*) *Jur:* (*of pers.*) **i. of succeeding (to an estate, etc.),** incapable de succéder; **i. of being elected to a position,** inéligible à une fonction. **2.** *a. & s.* incapable (*mf*), incompétent, -ente; **he's completely i., he's a complete i.,** c'est un parfait incapable.

incapably [in'keipəbli], *adv.* **1. to act i.,** faire preuve d'incapacité. **2. i. drunk,** ivre à ne plus se tenir debout.

incapacitant [inkə'pæsitənt], *s. Mil:* incapacitant *m.*

incapacitate [inkə'pæsiteit], *v.tr.* **1.** rendre (qn) incapable (**from working, for work,** de travailler). **2.** *Jur:* priver (qn) de capacité légale; frapper (qn) d'incapacité.

incapacitated [inkə'pæsiteitid], *a.* **1.** incapable (**for work, from working,** de travailler); infirme. **2.** *Jur:* privé de capacité légale; frappé d'incapacité; *s.* **the (legally) i.,** les (majeurs) incapables *mf.*

incapacitation ['inkəpæsi'teiʃ(ə)n], *s.* **1.** *Jur:* privation *f* de capacité légale. **2. i. for, from, work,** incapacité *f* de travail; **since his i.,** depuis son infirmité *f*; **wounded soldiers who suffer permanent i.,** blessés de guerre frappés d'invalidité *f.*

incapacity [inkə'pæsiti], *s.* **1.** incapacité *f*, incompétence *f*; **i. for doing sth., to do sth.,** incapacité de faire qch.; **the i. of the staff,** l'insuffisance *f* du personnel; la nullité du personnel. **2.** *Jur:* incapacité légale; inhabilité *f* (**to inherit,** à succéder).

incapsulate [in'kæpsjuleit], *v.tr.* **1.** mettre (qch.) dans une capsule. **2.** *Ling:* introduire un infixe dans (un mot).

incapsulation [inkæpsju'leiʃ(ə)n], *s.* **1.** mise *f* (de qch.) dans une capsule. **2.** *Ling:* infixe *m.*

incarcerate [in'kɑ:səreit], *v.tr.* incarcérer, mettre en prison, emprisonner.

incarcerated [in'kɑ:səreitid], *a.* **1.** incarcéré, en prison. **2.** *Med: A:* (*of hernia*) incarcéré; **to become i.,** s'incarcérer.

incarceration [inkɑ:sə'reiʃ(ə)n], *s.* **1.** incarcération *f*, emprisonnement *m.* **2.** *Med: A:* incarcération (d'une hernie).

incardinate [in'kɑ:dineit], *v.tr. Ecc:* (*R.C.Ch.*) faire (qn) cardinal; élever (qn) au cardinalat.

incardinated [in'kɑ:dineitid], *a. Ecc:* (prêtre) incardiné.

incardination [inkɑ:di'neiʃ(ə)n], *s. Ecc:* incardination *f.*

incarnadine[1] [in'kɑ:nədain]. *Lit:* **1.** *a.* (*a*) incarnadin; incarnat; couleur de chair; rose pâle *inv*; (*b*) rouge sang *inv.* **2.** *s.* incarnadin *m*, incarnat *m.*

incarnadine[2], *v.tr. Lit:* teindre en incarnat, (i) en rose pâle, (ii) en rouge sang.

incarnant [in'kɑ:nənt], *a. & s. Med:* incarnatif (*m*).

incarnate[1] [in'kɑ:neit], *a.* **1.** *Theol:* **the Word I.,** le Verbe incarné; (*of Christ*) **to become i.,** s'incarner; *Fig:* **the devil i.,** le diable incarné; **wisdom i.,** la sagesse incarnée. **2.** *Bot:* incarnat.

incarnate[2] ['inkɑ:neit], *v.tr.* incarner, revêtir la forme humaine; **to i. a virtue,** incarner une vertu.

incarnation [inkɑ:'neiʃ(ə)n], *s.* **1.** *Theol: etc:* incarnation *f* (du Christ, d'une idée). **2.** (*of pers.*) **to be the i. of wisdom,** incarner la sagesse du monde; être la sagesse incarnée; **to be the i. of health,** respirer la santé.

incase [in'keis], *v.tr.* **1.** encaisser, enfermer (**in,** dans); mettre (un objet) dans un étui. **2.** (*a*) munir (qch.) d'une enveloppe; blinder (une partie de machine, etc.); (*b*) revêtir, recouvrir (**s.o. in sth.,** qn de qch.).

incasement [in'keismənt], *s.* **1.** revêtement *m*; enveloppe *f.* **2.** *Anat:* emboîtement *m* (de deux os).

incautious [in'kɔ:ʃəs], *a.* imprudent; inconsidéré; **i. use of a word,** emploi irréfléchi d'un mot; **i. words,** paroles imprudentes, peu mesurées; **in an i. moment,** dans un moment d'irréflexion.

incautiously [in'kɔ:ʃəsli], *adv.* imprudemment, sans réflexion, sans précaution.

incautiousness [in'kɔ:ʃəsnis], *s.* imprudence *f*; manque *m* de précaution; irréflexion *f.*

incavation [inkə'veiʃ(ə)n], *s.* **1.** excavation *f*, creusage *m*, creusement *m.* **2.** creux *m*, dépression *f.*

incendiarism [in'sendjərizm], *s.* **1.** incendie *m* volontaire; **i. is suspected,** on attribue le sinistre à la malveillance. **2.** politique *f* de dévastation par le feu. **3.** propagation *f* de principes incendiaires, de la sédition, d'une politique de guerre.

incendiary [in'sendjəri]. **1.** *a.* (*a*) (matériel, bombe, etc.) incendiaire; (*b*) (discours, propos) incendiaire, séditieux. **2.** *s.* (*a*) incendiaire *mf*; auteur *m* volontaire (d'un incendie); (*b*) incendiaire; séditieux *m*; brandon *m* de discorde; (*c*) *F:* bombe *f* incendiaire.

incense[1] ['insens], *s.* encens *m*; *Ecc:* **i. bearer,** thuriféraire *m*, encenseur *m*; **i. boat,** navette *f*; **i. burner,** (i) (*pers.*) brûleur, -euse, d'encens; (ii) (*thg*) cassolette *f*; brûle-parfums *m inv*; *Ecc:* encensoir *m.*

incense[2] ['insens], *v.tr.* (*a*) encenser (qn, qch.); (*b*) brûler de l'encens devant (un autel, une idole); (*c*) embaumer (une chambre, l'air); purifier (l'air).

incense[3] [in'sens], *v.tr.* exaspérer, courroucer, irriter (qn); **to i. s.o. against s.o.,** mettre qn en colère contre qn.

incensed [in'senst], *a.* enflammé de colère; exaspéré, courroucé; **to become, get, i. (against, at, with, s.o.),** s'irriter, se courroucer, s'animer (contre qn).

incentive [in'sentiv]. **1.** *a.* (*a*) provocant, excitant; (*b*) stimulant; *Com: Ind:* **i. pay,** primes *fpl* de rendement. **2.** *s.* stimulant *m*, aiguillon *m*, motif *m*, encouragement *m*; **the true i. to scientific research,** le véritable ressort, aiguillon, de la recherche scientifique; **unemployment is an i. to crime,** le chômage pousse au crime; *Com: Ind:* **monetary incentives,** incitations *f* monétaires; primes *f*; **production incentives,** primes de rendement.

incentre ['insentər], *s. Mth:* centre *m* du cercle inscrit (d'un triangle).

incept[1] [in'sept]. **1.** *v.tr.* (*a*) *Biol:* (*of cell, organism*) absorber; (*b*) *Lit:* entreprendre; commencer. **2.** *v.i. Sch:* passer sa licence, son doctorat (à l'Université de Cambridge).

incept[2] ['insept], *s. Bot: Physiol:* rudiment *m* (d'un organe).

inception [in'sepʃ(ə)n], *s.* **1.** commencement *m*, début *m* (d'une entreprise, etc.). **2.** *Sch:* cérémonie *f* de la collation du grade de docteur à l'Université de Cambridge. **3.** *Biol: Physiol:* absorption *f*.

inceptive [in'septiv]. **1.** *a.* initial, -aux. **2.** *a.* & *s. Gram:* (temps, verbe) inchoatif (*m*).

incertitude [in'sə:titju:d], *s.* incertitude *f*.

incessant [in'sesənt], *a.* (bruit) incessant, continuel; **i. worries,** soucis éternels; **to be i. in one's complaints about s.o.,** ne pas tarir de griefs contre qn; se plaindre de qn sans cesse.

incessantly [in'sesəntli], *adv.* sans cesse, sans relâche, continuellement; *A: & Lit:* incessamment.

incest ['insest], *s.* inceste *m*.

incestuous [in'sestjuəs], *a.* (désirs, couple) incestueux; **i. person,** incestueux, -euse.

incestuously [in'sestjuəsli], *adv.* incestueusement.

incestuousness [in'sestjuəsnis], *s.* caractère incestueux.

inch[1] [in(t)ʃ], *s. Meas:* pouce *m* (= 2 centimètres 54); **square i.,** pouce carré; **cubic i.,** pouce cube; **i. tape,** mesure *f* à ruban gradué en pouces; **I've still got several inches (of my knitting) to do,** il m'en reste quelques doigts *m* (de mon tricot) à faire; **he makes the most of his inches,** il ne perd pas un pouce de sa taille; **a man of his inches,** un homme de sa taille; **he couldn't see an i. in front of him, of his nose,** il n'y voyait pas à deux pas devant lui; **to dispute the ground i. by i.; to dispute, fight, every i. of the ground,** disputer le terrain pied à pied; se défendre avec ardeur; **he's every i. a Tory,** il est tory jusqu'au bout des ongles, des doigts; c'est un tory à tous crins; **he's every i. a gentleman,** c'est un gentleman dans toute l'acceptation du terme; **not to give way an i.,** ne pas reculer d'une semelle; **he did not depart an i. from his orders,** il ne s'est pas départi d'une ligne des ordres qu'il avait reçus; **by inches, i. by i.,** peu à peu, petit à petit; **to die by inches,** mourir à petit feu; **I know every i. of the neighbourhood,** je connais la région dans tous ses recoins, comme ma poche; **we were all within an i. of a fight,** on était sur le point de se battre; **give him an i. and he'll take an ell,** donnez-lui-en un pouce, grand comme le doigt, et il en prendra long comme le bras; donnez-lui un pied et il en prendra quatre; *A:* **an i. of cold iron, steel,** un coup de poignard, d'épée.

inch[2]. **1.** *v.i.* **to i. forward, along,** (s')avancer peu à peu, petit à petit, pouce par pouce; **to i. back,** reculer peu à peu, petit à petit, pouce par pouce; **he tried to i. into the group,** il essaya de s'introduire petit à petit dans le groupe. **2.** *v.tr.* **to i. sth. forward, back,** faire avancer, faire reculer, qch. peu à peu, petit à petit, pouce par pouce; *Mec.E:* **to i. the tool to the work,** avancer lentement l'outil à la pièce.

inch[3], *s. Scot:* petite île; îlot *m*.

inching ['in(t)ʃiŋ], *s.* **i. forward, i. back,** avance *f*, recul *m*, petit à petit, peu à peu; *Mec.E:* **i. of the tool to the work,** amenage *m* de l'outil à la pièce.

inchmeal ['in(t)ʃmi:l], *adv.* pouce à pouce, pied à pied, par petits morceaux; peu à peu, petit à petit; **to take a town i.,** prendre une ville pied à pied; **to die (by) i.,** mourir à petit feu.

inchoate[1] ['inkoueit], *a.* **1.** rudimentaire, fruste. **2.** incomplet, imparfait.

inchoate[2], *v.tr. A:* commencer (un discours); engendrer (un projet); occasionner (la ruine de qn).

inchoation [inkou'eiʃ(ə)n], *s.* inchoation *f*, commencement *m*.

inchoative ['inkoucitiv, in'kouətiv], *a.* **1.** initial, -aux; premier. **2.** *Gram:* (verbe) inchoatif.

inchworm ['in(t)ʃwə:m], *s. NAm: Ent:* arpenteuse *f*; chenille *f* géomètre.

incidence ['insid(ə)ns], *s.* **1.** incidence *f* (d'un événement, d'un impôt) **(on,** sur). **2. the high i. of robbery with violence,** la fréquence des vols à main armée; **the i. of cancer has increased,** les cas de cancer se sont multipliés. **3.** *Opt: Elcs: Av: etc:* **(angle of) i.,** angle *m* d'incidence (d'un rayon de lumière, d'une onde électromagnétique, d'une aile d'avion, etc.); *Ball: Opt:* **grazing i.,** incidence rasante; *Av:* **i. bracing,** croisillonnement *m* d'incidence.

incident[1] ['insid(ə)nt], *s.* **1.** incident *m*; **frontier i.,** incident de frontière; **diplomatic i.,** incident diplomatique; **journey full of incidents,** voyage mouvementé, plein de péripéties; **novel full of incident(s),** roman plein d'événements; roman étoffé; **the different incidents of a novel,** les épisodes *m* d'un roman. **2.** *Jur:* (i) servitude attachée, (ii) privilège attaché, à une tenure.

incident[2], *a.* **1.** qui arrive; qui appartient, qui tient (to, à); **dangers i. to travel,** dangers *m* que comporte un voyage; dangers auxquels on est sujet, auxquels on peut s'attendre, en voyage; *Jur:* **fee i. to a title,** taxe *f* qui tient à un titre; **right of pasturage i. to a piece of land,** droit *m* de pâturage attaché à une terre. **2.** (*a*) *Opt: Elcs:* (rayon, etc.) incident, d'incidence; **i. direction, i. plan,** direction *f*, plan *m*, d'incidence; **i. beam,** faisceau incident; *Atom.Ph:* **i. particle,** particule incidente; (*b*) **light i. on a picture,** lumière *f* qui tombe sur un tableau.

incidental [insi'dentl]. **1.** *a.* (*a*) (événement) fortuit, accidentel; (*of circumstance, etc.*) incidentel; (*of observation, question, etc.*) incident; **it produced some i. good,** cela lui a en même temps fait quelque bien; **i. expenses,** faux frais; dépenses imprévues; **i. music for a play,** la musique pour une pièce; *Gram:* **i. clause,** incidente explicative; incise *f*; *Jur:* **i. plea of defence,** exception *f*; (*b*) auquel on peut s'attendre; **i. to sth.,** qui résulte de qch.; qui est inséparable de qch.; **fatigue i. to a journey,** fatigues que comporte un voyage, auxquelles nous expose un voyage. **2.** *s.* (*a*) chose fortuite; éventualité *f*; (*b*) *pl.* **incidentals,** faux frais; dépenses imprévues; (*c*) *Cmptr:* **incidentals time,** temps *m* d'activités annexes, d'utilisation annexe.

incidentally [insi'dent(ə)li], *adv.* **1.** incidemment; **an important question was i. raised,** une question importante fut soulevée à ce propos. **2.** soit dit en passant, entre parenthèses, **and, i., I have no desire to do so,** par ailleurs, (soit dit) par parenthèse, entre parenthèses, je n'ai aucun désir de le faire.

incinerate [in'sinəreit], *v.tr.* incinérer, réduire en cendres, cinéfier, carboniser (une substance, les victimes d'un incendie, etc.).

incineration [insinə'reiʃ(ə)n], *s.* incinération *f*; *Ch: etc:* **i. dish,** capsule *f* à incinération.

incinerator [in'sinəreitər], *s.* incinérateur *m*; **garden i.,** incinérateur de jardin.

incipience [in'sipiəns], **incipiency** [in'sipiənsi], *s.* commencement *m* (de l'aube, d'une crise); origine *f* (d'un système).

incipient [in'sipiənt], *a.* naissant; qui commence; **i. madness,** folie naissante; **i. beard,** barbe naissante; **i. fracture,** amorce *f* de fissure; **i. rheumatism, i. indiscipline,** commencements *m* de rhumatisme, d'indiscipline.

incipiently [in'sipiəntli], *adv.* au commencement; à l'origine.

incipit ['insipit], *s. Lit: Mus:* incipit *m inv.*

incisal [in'saizl], *a.* (bord, etc.) incisif, tranchant; *Dent:* **i. inclination,** inclinaison incisive.

incise [in'saiz], *v.tr.* **1.** inciser, faire une incision dans (l'écorce d'un arbre, etc.); *Surg:* inciser, débrider (une plaie, un tissu). **2.** *Art: etc:* graver en creux (une inscription, etc.).

incised [in'saizd], *a.* **1.** *Nat.Hist:* incisé; (bec d'oiseau) ciselé. **2. stone i. with a cross,** pierre *f* avec croix gravée en creux. **3.** *Geog:* (méandre) encaissé.

incising [in'saiziŋ], *s.* incision *f*; *Surg:* débridement *m*.

incision [in'siʒ(ə)n], *s.* **1.** incision *f*, entaille *f*; **to make an i. in sth.,** inciser qch.; *Hort:* **i. for a graft,** enture *f*; *Surg:* **i. of an adhesion,** incision, débridement *m*, d'une adhérence; **buttonhole i.,** boutonnière *f*; **radiating i.,** incision rayonnante. **2.** *Nat.Hist:* découpure *f*.

incisive [in'saisiv], *a.* **1.** (instrument, ton, style) incisif, tranchant; (ton) mordant; (esprit, jugement) pénétrant. **2.** *Anat:* **i. teeth,** (dents) incisives (*f*); **i. bone,** os incisif, intermaxillaire.

incisively [in'saisivli], *adv.* incisivement; d'un ton tranchant, mordant.

incisiveness [in'saisivnis], *s.* ton incisif, mordant, tranchant; **the i. of his style,** son style tranchant.

incisor [in'saizər], *s. Anat:* (dent) incisive (*f*); **peg-shaped i.,** incisive coniforme, conoïde, **shovel-shaped i.,** incisive en forme de pelle.

incisura [insi'zjuərə], *s. Anat:* incisure *f*.

incisure [in'saiʒər], *s.* (*a*) *Anat:* incisure *f*; (*b*) *Surg:* incision *f*.

incitable [in'saitəbl], *a.* incitable (to, à).

incitant [in'saitənt], *s. Biol: etc:* incitant *m*.

incitation [insai'teiʃ(ə)n], *s.* **1.** incitation *f*, excitation *f* (to, à). **2.** stimulant *m*, aiguillon *m*.

incite [in'sait], *v.tr.* inciter, instiguer, aiguillonner, animer **(to sth., to do sth.,** à qch., à faire qch.); **to i. s.o. to revolt,** pousser, exciter, qn à la révolte, à se révolter; **to i. s.o. to do wrong,** inciter qn au mal; **to i. s.o. to crime,** pousser qn au crime; **to i. s.o. to work,** stimuler qn au travail; **to i. workmen against their employers,** monter les ouvriers contre le patronat.

incitement [in'saitmənt], *s.* **1.** incitation *f*, excitation *f*, instigation *f*, encouragement *m* (to, à). **2.** stimulant *m*, aiguillon *m*; mobile *m*, motif *m* (of, de).

inciter [in'saitər], *s.* **1.** (*pers.*) instigateur, -trice **(to,** de); incitateur, -trice (to, à). **2.** (*thg*) stimulant *m*, mobile *m*, motif *m*.

inciting[1] [in'saitiŋ], *a.* (*of agent*) incitateur, -trice, incitatif, incitant; (*of speech*) (i) encourageant, entraînant; (ii) provocatif.

inciting[2], *s.* incitation *f*, provocation *f* (to, à).

incivility [insi'viliti], *s.* incivilité *f* (de qn, d'une action); **(piece of) i.,** incivilité; **he subjected me to many incivilities,** il m'a fait toutes sortes de malhonnêtetés.

incivism ['insivizm], *s.* incivisme *m*.

in-clearer ['inkliərər], *s. Fin:* commis *m* d'un *clearing banker,* qui travaille à la banque et qui est chargé du livre du dedans; commis chargé d'inscrire les chèques à rembourser.

in-clearing ['inkliəriŋ], *a. Fin:* **i.-c. book,** livre *m* du dedans; livre, registre *m*, des chèques à rembourser.

inclemency [in'klemənsi], *s.* inclémence *f*, rigueur *f* (de climat, de température); inclémence (de qn); **the i. of the weather,** l'inclémence du temps; les intempéries *f*; le mauvais temps.

inclement [in'klemənt], *a.* (juge, sort, etc.) inclément; (climat, etc.) inclément, rigoureux, rude.

inclinable [in'klainəbl], *a.* **1.** (*of pers.*) (*a*) enclin, porté, inclinant (to, à); (*b*) favorable (à qn, à un parti). **2.** (*of table, stand, etc.*) inclinable.

inclination [inkli'neiʃ(ə)n], *s.* **1.** inclination *f* (de la tête, du corps). **2.** inclinaison *f* (d'un talus); pente *f* (d'un coteau); inclinaison (d'une droite, d'un plan, d'une aiguille aimantée); déversement *m*, dévers *m* (d'un mur); dévoiement *m* (d'un tuyau de cheminée); **i. compass,** boussole *f* d'inclinaison; *Ball:* **i. of line of sight to horizontal,** angle *m* de site. **3.** (*a*) inclination, penchant *m*, tendance naturelle **(to, for,** à, pour); **to follow only one's own i.,** ne faire que ce à quoi l'on se sent porté; n'en faire qu'à sa tête; **to have an i. for sth.,** avoir un penchant pour qch.; se sentir du goût pour qch.; **to have an i. towards s.o.,** se sentir de l'attrait pour qn; **to have lost all i. for sth.,** être revenu de qch.; **I have no i. to help him,** je n'éprouve aucun désir de l'aider; **to do sth. from i.,** faire qch. par goût; (*b*) **i. to stoutness,** tendance *f* à l'embonpoint; **car with an i. to skid,** voiture qui a tendance à déraper.

incline[1] ['inklain], *s.* **1.** pente *f*, déclivité *f*, inclinaison *f*, plan incliné; plongée *f* (du terrain); *Rail: Civ.E:* (i) (*acclivity*) rampe *f*; (ii) (*declivity*) pente. **2.** *Min:* **i. (shaft),** puits incliné. **3.** *Mil:* oblique *f* (à gauche, à droite).

incline[2] [in'klain], *v.* incliner. **1.** *v.tr.* (*a*) pencher, faire pencher (la tête, le corps, un vase); *Lit:* **to i. one's ear to s.o., to a prayer,** prêter l'oreille à qn, à une prière; (*b*) *Lit:* **to i. the heart, the mind, s.o., to sth., to do sth.,** incliner, porter, disposer, le cœur, l'esprit, qn, à qch., à faire qch.; *Ecc:* **i. our hearts to keep this law,** incline nos cœurs à garder ce commandement; **his heart inclined him to pity,** son cœur l'inclinait à la miséricorde; **to feel, be, inclined to do sth.,** pencher, avoir de l'inclination, incliner, à faire qch.; se sentir disposé, d'inclination, à faire qch.; être, se sentir, en humeur de faire qch.; **I am inclined to think that he's right,** je suis porté à croire qu'il a raison; **not to be inclined to, for, work,** ne pas être disposé à travailler; **to be favourably inclined towards sth.,** être favorable à qch.; **I feel very much inclined to accept,** j'ai bien envie d'accepter; **he is more than half inclined to accept,** il s'en faut de peu qu'il accepte; **I am anything but inclined to consent,** je suis fort éloigné de consentir; **I am rather inclined to take your advice,** je goûte assez votre conseil; **if you feel inclined,** si le cœur vous en dit; **if ever you should feel so inclined,** si jamais l'envie vous en prenait; **prices are inclined to fall,** les prix tendent à baisser; **he's inclined to put on weight,** il a une tendance à prendre de l'embonpoint; (*c*) *A: & Lit:* **to i. one's steps towards, to,**

a place, diriger ses pas vers un lieu. **2.** *v.i.* (*a*) *A: & Lit:* (*of pers.*) s'incliner, se pencher; **inclining forward to see better,** penché en avant pour mieux voir; (*b*) (*of thg*) incliner, pencher (**to, towards,** à, vers); se déverser; avoir un dévers; **the campanile inclines to one side,** le campanile penche d'un côté; **inclined at an angle of 45°,** incliné à un angle de 45°; *Nau:* (*of submarine*) **to i. at a steep angle,** rendre de la pointe; (*c*) avoir un penchant (**to,** pour qch., à faire qch.); être enclin, porté, disposé (**to,** à); **to i. to pity, to mercy, to believe,** incliner, être disposé, à la pitié, à la clémence, à croire; **to i. to(wards) indulgence,** pencher à, vers, l'indulgence; **to i. to the belief that . . .,** incliner à croire que . . .; **Louis inclined towards an alliance with Spain,** Louis inclinait vers, pour, une alliance avec l'Espagne; **to i. to atheism,** avoir un penchant, pencher, à l'athéisme; (*d*) **to i. to corpulence,** avoir une tendance à la corpulence; (*e*) **green that inclines to blue,** vert qui tire sur le bleu; (*f*) **to i. to the left,** tirer sur la gauche; *Mil:* obliquer à gauche; **right i.!** oblique à droite, marche!

inclined [in'klaind], *a.* **1.** *Mth: etc:* (plan, etc.) incliné; (mur, etc.) penchant; **axis of rotation i. to the normal,** axe de rotation incliné sur la normale. **2.** (*a*) (*momentarily*) disposé, porté (**to,** à); (*b*) (*permanently*) enclin, incliné; **i. to laziness, to be lazy,** enclin, incliné, à la paresse; **devotionally i., i. to devotion,** inclinant à la dévotion. **3.** (*with adv. prefixed, e.g.*) **a well-i. youth,** un jeune homme porté au bien; **to be well-i. towards s.o.,** être bien disposé envers qn; **over-i. to do sth.,** trop porté à faire qch.

inclining[1] [in'klainiŋ], *a.* **1.** penché, qui penche; inclinant; **i. dial,** cadran déclinant. **2.** (*a*) **i. to devotion,** inclinant à la dévotion; (*b*) (*of colours*) **dark brown i. to black,** brun foncé tirant sur le noir.

inclining[2], *s.* inclination *f* (de la tête, etc.); *Nau:* **i. experiment,** expérience *f* de stabilité (d'un navire).

inclinometer [inkli'nɔmitər], *s.* (*a*) *Av: etc:* clinomètre *m,* inclinomètre *m*; indicateur *m* de pente; clitographe *m*; (*b*) (*dip needle*) boussole *f* d'inclinaison.

inclose, inclosure, etc. [in'klouz, in'klouʒər], *see* ENCLOSE, ENCLOSURE, *etc.*

include [in'klu:d], *v.tr.* comprendre, renfermer, embrasser; **the county includes all the region from . . . to . . .,** le comté englobe, comprend, toute la région depuis . . . jusqu'à . . .; **property that includes a house, a workshop and a store,** immeuble qui comporte une maison, un atelier et un magasin; **men above seventy are not included,** les hommes de plus de soixante-dix ans ne sont pas compris; **there are five of us, not including the children,** nous sommes cinq, sans compter les enfants; **price including carriage,** prix y compris le port; **up to and including December 31st,** jusqu'à et y compris le 31 décembre; **up to and including page 5,** jusqu'à la page 5 incluse; **the genus includes the species,** le genre renferme l'espèce; **he included them all in his contempt,** il les englobait tous dans son mépris; **to i. the innocent with the guilty,** confondre les innocents parmi les coupables; **to i. s.o. among one's friends,** compter qn parmi ses amis; *F:* **i. me out,** vous pouvez m'exclure; je ne serai pas de la partie; je n'y serai pas.

included [in'klu:did], *a.* **1.** compris, y compris; **all his property was sold, his house i.,** tous ses biens furent vendus, y compris sa maison, sa maison comprise; (*at hotel, etc.*) **service i.,** service compris. **2.** *Bot:* **i. stamens,** étamines incluses.

inclusion [in'klu:ʒ(ə)n], *s.* **1.** inclusion *f.* **2.** *Geol: etc:* inclusion (gazeuse, liquide, etc.); (*of extraneous rock*) enclave *f.*

inclusive [in'klu:siv], *a.* qui comprend, qui renferme; **to be i. of sth.,** comprendre, renfermer, qch.; **five i. of the driver,** cinq y compris le chauffeur; **i. sum,** somme globale; (*at hotel, etc.*) **i. terms,** conditions, tout compris; *Tp:* **i. charge, rate,** tarif *m* à forfait, forfaitaire; **from the 4th to the 12th February i.,** du 4 au 12 février inclusivement; *Cmptr:* **i. OR,** OU inclusif; **i. OR operation,** disjonction *f.*

inclusively [in'klu:sivli], *adv.* inclusivement.

incoagulable [inkou'ægjuləbl], *a.* incoagulable.

incoercibility [inkouə:si'biliti], *s.* **1.** caractère *m* indomptable (de qn). **2.** *Ph:* incoercibilité *f* (d'un fluide).

incoercible [inkou'ə:sibl], *a.* **1.** (*of pers.*) qui vient à bout de toute contrainte; indomptable. **2.** *Ph:* incoercible.

incog [in'kɔg], *a., adv. & s. F:* incognito (*m*).

incognito, *f.* **-ta,** *pl.* **-ti** [in'kɔgnitou, inkɔg'ni:tou, -tə, -ti:]. **1.** *a. & adv.* **to be, travel, incognito, incognita,** être, voyager, incognito. **2.** *s.* (*a*) **the young i.,** le jeune inconnu, la jeune inconnue; (*b*) incognito *m*; **to preserve one's i.,** garder l'incognito; **to respect s.o.'s i.,** respecter l'incognito de qn.

incognizable [in'kɔgnizəbl], *a.* incognoscible; inconnaissable.

incognizance [in'kɔgniz(ə)ns], *s.* inconnaissance *f.*

incognizant [in'kɔ(g)niz(ə)nt], *a.* **i. of sth.,** sans connaissance, ignorant, de qch.

incoherence [inkou'hiər(ə)ns], **incoherency** [inkou'hiər(ə)nsi], *s.* incohérence *f* (de particules, d'un argument, de la parole, etc.).

incoherent [inkou'hiər(ə)nt], *a.* (*a*) *Ph:* **i. molecules,** molécules incohérentes; (*b*) **i. ideas,** idées incohérentes, sans cohérence, hétéroclites; **i. reasoning,** raisonnement incohérent, qui ne tient pas debout; **i. style,** style incohérent, décousu; **the i. speech of a madman,** les divagations *f* d'un fou; **to become i. (with drink),** *F:* déparler.

incoherently [inkou'hiər(ə)ntli], *adv.* sans cohérence, sans suite; d'une manière incohérente; avec incohérence.

incohesion [inkou'hi:ʒ(ə)n], *s.* incohésion *f* (des molécules, d'un parti, etc.).

incohesive [inkou'hi:siv], *a.* incohésif; sans cohésion.

incombustibility ['inkəmbʌsti'biliti], *s.* incombustibilité *f.*

incombustible [inkəm'bʌstibl]. **1.** *a.* (gaz, etc,) incombustible; (sel) anticombustible. **2.** *s.* anticombustible *m.*

income ['inkəm], *s.* **1.** revenu *m,* revenus *mpl*; **source of i.,** source(s) *f* de revenu; **earned i.,** (i) revenu(s) du travail; (ii) revenus salariaux; (iii) revenus professionnels; **unearned i., private i.,** rente(s) *f*(*pl.*); **to have a private, an unearned, i. of £3000 a year,** avoir trois mille livres de rente; **person living on a private, an unearned, i.,** rentier, -ière; **his wife has a private, an independent, i.,** sa femme a une fortune personnelle; **he has a large i.,** il a de gros revenus; *F:* il gagne gros; **to live on one's i.,** (i) vivre de ses revenus; (ii) (*unearned*) vivre de ses rentes; **to live up to one's i.,** dépenser (i) tout ce qu'on gagne, (ii) tout son revenu; **to exceed, spend more than, one's i.,** dépenser plus que son revenu, que ses revenus; **land that brings in a good i.,** terre de bon rapport; **i. group, i. bracket,** tranche *f* de salaire, de revenus; **higher-i., lower-i., middle-i., groups,** groupes *m* (de contribuables) à revenus élevés, faibles, moyens; *Pol:* **incomes policy,** politique *f* des revenus; *Pol.Ec:* **gross, net, national i.,** revenu national brut, net; **i. tax,** impôt *m* (cédulaire) sur le revenu; **graduated i. tax,** impôt progressif; **i.-tax return,** déclaration de revenu, d'impôt sur le revenu. **2.** *Com:* recettes *fpl,* revenus; rentrées *fpl.*

incoming[1] ['inkʌmiŋ], *a.* **1.** qui entre, qui arrive; (locataire, navire) entrant; **the i. council,** les conseillers entrants; **the i. year,** l'année qui commence, la nouvelle année; **i. mail,** courrier à l'arrivée; correspondance reçue; **i. tide,** marée montante; *Tp:* **i. call,** enregistrement *m* d'appel; communication *f* d'arrivée; *El:* **i. circuit,** circuit *m* d'arrivée; **i. feeder,** feeder *m* de sous-station; *Cmptr:* **i. data,** données *fpl* en entrée; **i. traffic,** trafic *m* en réception. **2. i. profit,** profits accrus, réalisés, à réaliser. **3.** *Ven:* **i. game,** gibier *m* qui se dirige droit sur le chasseur.

incoming[2], *s.* **1.** entrée *f,* arrivée *f*; **his incomings and outgoings,** ses entrées et ses sorties; **i. of the spring,** arrivée, venue *f,* du printemps; **the i. and outgoing of the tide,** le flux et le reflux; *Min:* **i. of water,** venue d'eau. **2.** *pl.* **incomings,** recettes *f,* revenus *m*; *Com:* rentrées *f*; **his incomings and outgoings,** ses recettes et ses dépenses.

incommensurability ['inkəmenʃ(ə)rə'biliti], *s.* incommensurabilité *f.*

incommensurable [inkə'menʃ(ə)rəbl], *a.* *Mth:* (*a*) incommensurable (**with,** avec); **to be i. with sth.,** (i) n'avoir aucune commune mesure avec qch.; (ii) *Fig:* n'être pas digne d'être comparé à qch., d'être mis en parallèle avec qch.; (*b*) **i. number,** nombre irrationnel.

incommensurably [inkə'menʃ(ə)rəbli], *adv.* incommensurablement.

incommensurate [inkə'menʃ(ə)rət], *a.* **1.** pas en rapport, pas en proportion (**with,** avec); disproportionné (**with,** à); **his means are i. with his wants,** ses ressources ne sont pas en rapport avec ses besoins. **2.** = INCOMMENSURABLE.

incommensurately [inkə'menʃ(ə)rətli], *adv.* disproportionnément.

incommode [inkə'moud], *v.tr.* incommoder, déranger (qn); gêner, empêcher (la marche, la respiration).

incommoding [inkə'moudiŋ], *a.* incommodant, incommode, gênant.

incommodious [inkə'moudiəs], *a.* (*a*) *O:* incommode; peu confortable; désagréable; (*b*) (appartement, etc.) où l'on est à l'étroit.

incommodiously [inkə'moudiəsli], *adv.* (*a*) *O:* incommodément; désagréablement; (*b*) (logé, etc.) à l'étroit.

incommodiousness [inkə'moudiəsnis], *s.* (*a*) *O:* incommodité *f,* caractère *m* désagréable (de qch.); (*b*) étroitesse *f* (d'un logement).

incommodity [inkə'mɔditi], *s.* **1.** = INCOMMODIOUSNESS. **2.** chose incommode, désagréable, gênante.

incommunicability [inkəmju:nikə'biliti], **incommunicableness** [inkə'mju:nikəblnis], *s.* **1.** incommunicabilité *f.* **2.** réticence *f,* taciturnité *f.*

incommunicable [inkə'mju:nikəbl], *a.* **1.** (*of feelings, etc.*) incommunicable. **2.** (*of pers.*) taciturne; peu communicatif.

incommunicado ['inkəmju:ni'kɑ:dou], *adv.* **to be held i.,** être tenu, gardé, au secret.

incommunicative [inkə'mju:nikətiv], *a.* peu communicatif; réservé; renfermé; taciturne.

incommutability ['inkəmju:tə'biliti], *s.* immu(t)abilité *f*; inaltérabilité *f.*

incommutable [inkə'mju:təbl], *a.* **1.** immuable; inaltérable. **2.** que l'on ne peut échanger; non-interchangeable.

incomparability [inkɔmp(ə)rə'biliti], *s.* incomparabilité *f.*

incomparable [in'kɔmp(ə)rəbl], *a.* incomparable (**to, with,** à); **i. artist,** artiste incomparable, hors ligne, hors de pair.

incomparableness [in'kɔmp(ə)rəb(ə)lnis], *s.* incomparabilité *f.*

incomparably [in'kɔmp(ə)rəbli], *adv.* incomparablement, infiniment.

incompatibility ['inkəmpæti'biliti], *s.* incompatibilité *f* (**with,** avec; **between,** entre); inconciliabilité *f* (de deux théories); **i. of temper,** incompatibilité d'humeur.

incompatible [inkəm'pætibl]. **1.** *a.* (*a*) incompatible, inconciliable (**with,** avec); (*of ideas, etc.*) inalliable. (*b*) (*of metals, fluids, etc.*) non, peu, alliable (**with,** avec); (*c*) *Pharm:* (médicaments) incompatibles. **2.** *s.pl.* **incompatibles,** (i) choses *f,* idées *f,* médicaments *m,* incompatibles; (ii) métaux *m* peu alliables.

incompatibly [inkəm'pætibli], *adv.* incompatiblement.

incompetence [in'kɔmpit(ə)ns], **incompetency** [in'kɔmpit(ə)nsi], *s.* **1.** *Jur:* incompétence *f* (d'un tribunal); incompétence, incapacité *f,* inhabilité *f* (d'une personne); **i. to succeed,** inhabilité à succéder. **2.** (*a*) incompétence (de qn); insuffisance *f* (du personnel, etc.); manque *m* de capacité; (*b*) *Med:* **aortic i.,** insuffisance aortique.

incompetent [in'kɔmpit(ə)nt], *a.* **1.** *Jur:* (juge, tribunal) incompétent (à connaître d'une cause); (personne *f*) inhabile (à accomplir un acte); **i. to make a will,** inhabile à tester; **I am i. to advise on this matter,** cette question n'est pas de mon ressort; **I am i. to act,** je n'ai pas qualité pour agir. **2.** incompétent, incapable; **to be thoroughly i. to do sth.,** être tout à fait incompétent à faire qch.; n'avoir pas la moindre compétence pour faire qch.; *s.* **to weed out the incompetents,** éliminer les incapables.

incompetently [in'kɔmpit(ə)ntli], *adv.* incompétemment, sans compétence.

incomplete [inkəm'pli:t], *a.* incomplet, inachevé; imparfait; partiel; *Biol:* **i. metamorphosis,** métamorphose incomplète; *Bot:* **i. flower,** fleur incomplète; *A.Chr:* **i. year,** année *f* cave.

incompletely [inkəm'pli:tli], *adv.* incomplètement, imparfaitement.

incompleteness [inkəm'pli:tnis], **incompletion** [inkəm'pli:ʃ(ə)n], *s.* imperfection *f,* inachèvement *m*; *Bot:* avortement *m* (d'un organe).

incomplex [in'kɔmpleks], *a.* (syllogisme, etc.) incomplexe.

incompliance [inkəm'plaiəns], *s.* **1. i. with instructions,** refus *m* de suivre les instructions, d'obéir aux ordres. **2.** intransigeance *f,* inflexibilité *f* (de caractère).

incompliant [inkəm'plaiənt], *a.* **1.** (personne) qui refuse d'obéir aux ordres, de suivre les instructions. **2.** (caractère) intransigeant, inflexible, intraitable.

incomprehensibility [inkɔmprihensi'biliti], **incomprehensibleness** [inkɔmpri'hensib(ə)lnis], *s.* incompréhensibilité *f.*

incomprehensible [inkɔmpri'hensibl], *a.* **1.** incompréhensible; indéchiffrable; **she is i. to me,** je n'arrive pas à la comprendre. **2.** *Theol:* **the Father I.,** le Père infini.

incomprehensibly [inkɔmpri'hensibli], *adv.* incompréhensiblement.

incomprehension [inkɔmpri'henʃ(ə)n], *s.* défaut *m,* manque *m,* de compréhension; incompréhension *f*; inintelligence *f* (d'un texte, etc.).

incomprehensive [inkɔmpri'hensiv], *a.* **1.** incomplet, -ète. **2.** incompréhensif.

incomprehensiveness [inkɔmpri'hensivnis], *s.* **1.**

caractère incomplet; défaut *m* d'intégralité. **2.** incompréhensibilité *f*; défaut *m*, manque *m*, de compréhension.

incompressibility ['inkəmpresi'biliti], *s.* incompressibilité *f.*

incompressible [inkəm'presibl], *a.* incompressible; *Ch:* **i. volume,** covolume *m.*

incomputable [inkəm'pju:təbl], *a.* (somme d'argent, nombre) incalculable, incomptable.

inconceivability ['inkənsi:və'biliti], *s.* inconcevabilité *f.*

inconceivable [inkən'si:vəbl], *a.* inconcevable; **it's i. that he should have acted like that,** il est inconcevable, ce n'est pas à croire, qu'il ait agi ainsi.

inconceivably [inkən'si:vəbli], *adv.* inconcevablement; **i. stupid,** d'une sottise inconcevable, invraisemblable.

inconclusive [inkən'klu:siv], *a.* (raisonnement, témoignage) peu concluant, non concluant, inconcluant; **a lame and i. peace,** une paix boiteuse et mal assise.

inconclusively [inkən'klu:sivli], *adv.* d'une manière peu conclusive; sans conclure.

inconclusiveness [inkən'klu:sivnis], *s.* caractère peu concluant (d'un raisonnement, etc.).

incondensable [inkən'densəbl], *a.* (gaz, vapeur) non condensable.

incondite [in'kɔndit], *a.* **1.** *Art: Lit:* (ouvrage) mal arrangé, mal fait; informe, fruste. **2.** grossier, impoli, fruste. **3. i. interjection,** interjection naturelle.

Inconel ['iŋkənel], *s. R.t.m: Metall:* Inconel *m.*

inconformity [inkən'fɔ:miti], *s.* inconformité *f* (**to, with,** avec).

incongruent [in'kɔŋgruənt], *a.* **1.** qui ne convient pas (**to,** à); qui ne va pas (**to,** avec). **2.** *Anat:* (*of joint surfaces*) incongruent.

incongruity [inkɔŋ'gru(:)iti], *s.* **1.** désaccord *m*; manque *m* d'harmonie (**with,** avec); inconséquence *f*; **i. of terms,** disconvenance *f* de mots. **2.** absurdité *f,* incongruité *f*; **writings full of incongruities,** écrits remplis d'incongruités. **3.** inconvenance *f*; faute *f* contre le savoir-vivre; incongruité.

incongruous [in'kɔŋgruəs], *a.* **1.** qui ne s'accorde pas (**with,** avec); qui détonne (**with,** avec); sans rapport (**to, with,** avec); **conduct quite i. with one's principles,** conduite qui ne s'accorde pas du tout avec ses principes; **i. colours,** couleurs *f* qui jurent ensemble; couleurs disparates; **i. medley,** mélange *m* hétéroclite; **a strangely i. figure,** une forme baroque. **2.** (*of remark*) incongru, déplacé, absurde.

incongruously [in'kɔŋgruəsli], *adv.* **1.** mal à propos; **not i.,** assez justement; **i. dressed,** (i) vêtu d'une façon qui ne convient pas à l'occasion; (ii) affublé d'un costume hétéroclite. **2.** (répondre, etc.) incongrûment, d'une manière malséante; (se conduire, etc.) absurdement.

incongruousness [in'kɔŋgruəsnis], *s.* = INCONGRUITY 1.

inconsecutive [inkən'sekjutiv], *a.* (nombres, etc.) qui ne se suivent pas.

inconsequence [in'kɔnsikwəns], *s.* **1.** inconséquence *f,* illogisme *m*; manque *m* de logique. **2. numerous inconsequences,** de nombreuses inconséquences.

inconsequent [in'kɔnsikwənt], *a.* **1.** inconséquent, illogique; **i. reasoning,** raisonnement *m* qui pèche par la logique; *F:* raisonnement biscornu; **i. way of reasoning,** manière *f* illogique de raisonner; **i. ideas,** idées *f* sans suite; **i. mind,** esprit inconséquent; *Geol:* **i. drainage,** système hydrographique (i) antécédent, (ii) surimposé. **2.** = INCONSEQUENTIAL 2.

inconsequential [inkɔnsi'kwenʃ(ə)l], *a.* **1.** = INCONSEQUENT 1. **2.** (circonstance, affaire) sans importance.

inconsequentiality ['inkɔnsikwenʃi'æliti], *s.* inconséquence *f.*

inconsequentially [inkɔnsi'kwenʃəli], *adv.* **1.** = INCONSEQUENTLY. **2.** sans importance.

inconsequently [in'kɔnsikwəntli], *adv.* (agir, répondre) inconséquemment; avec inconséquence.

inconsiderable [inkən'sid(ə)rəbl], *a.* peu considérable; insignifiant, petit, négligeable; **a not i. number of people,** un nombre considérable, un assez grand nombre, de personnes.

inconsiderate [inkən'sid(ə)rət], *a.* **1.** inconsidéré; irréfléchi, étourdi; **i. opinion,** opinion peu réfléchie. **2.** (personne) sans égards pour les autres, qui ne pense pas aux autres; **it would be i. to do so,** ce serait manquer d'égards que d'agir ainsi; **it was most i. of you to do that,** vous avez manqué d'égards en agissant ainsi.

inconsiderately [inkən'sid(ə)rətli], *adv.* **1.** sans considération, sans réflexion; inconsidérément, étourdiment; sans réfléchir; **to talk i.,** avoir la langue légère, **2. to behave i. to s.o.,** manquer d'égards envers qn.

inconsiderateness [inkən'sid(ə)rətnis], **inconsideration** [inkənsidə'reiʃ(ə)n], *s.* **1.** irréflexion *f.* étourderie *f,* imprudence *f,* inconsidération *f.* **2.** manque *m* d'égards.

inconsistence [inkən'sist(ə)ns], *s. A:* = INCONSISTENCY.

inconsistency [inkən'sistənsi], *s.* **1.** inconsistance *f,* contradiction *f,* incompatibilité *f* (**between two things,** entre deux choses); **there is no i. in his acting in this way,** il n'y a rien de contradictoire à ce qu'il agisse ainsi. **2.** inconséquence *f,* inconsistance, illogisme *m,* manque *m* d'esprit de suite (d'une personne); incohérence *f* (d'un argument). **3. a tissue of inconsistencies,** un tissu d'inconséquences, d'incohérences.

inconsistent [inkən'sist(ə)nt], *a.* **1.** incompatible, en contradiction, en désaccord (**with,** avec); contradictoire (**with,** à); *Mth:* **i. equations,** équations *f* incompatibles; *Log:* **propositions that are i.,** propositions *f* qui se contredisent; **his words are i. with his conduct,** il y a désaccord entre ses paroles et sa conduite; sa conduite ne cadre pas avec ses paroles. **2.** (*of pers.*) inconsistant, qui manque d'esprit de suite; inconséquent, illogique; **to be i. in one's replies,** varier dans ses réponses. **3.** (récit) incohérent, qui ne tient pas debout.

inconsistently [inkən'sistəntli], *adv.* d'une manière inconséquente, incohérente; inconséquemment, illogiquement.

inconsolable [inkən'souləbl], *a.* inconsolable (**for sth.,** de qch.); (*of grief, etc.*) inguérissable.

inconsolably [inkən'souləbli], *adv.* inconsolablement.

inconsonance [in'kɔnsənəns], *s.* manque *m* d'accord, d'harmonie.

inconsonant [in'kɔnsənənt], *a.* (*of thg*) **to be i. with sth.,** ne pas être conforme à qch., ne pas être d'accord avec qch.; être en désaccord avec (les faits, une promesse, etc.).

inconspicuous [inkən'spikjuəs], *a.* peu en vue, peu en évidence; peu apparent; inapparent, peu frappant, discret, -ète; peu voyant; **an i. little flower,** une petite fleur cachée, modeste, que l'on voit à peine; **i. life,** vie effacée; **to be, remain, i.,** rester dans l'obscurité, dans la pénombre.

inconspicuously [inkən'spikjuəsli], *adv.* (vêtu, etc.) d'une manière discrète, peu frappante.

inconspicuousness [inkən'spikjuəsnis], *s.* caractère peu frappant, peu remarquable, effacé (de qch.).

inconstancy [in'kɔnstənsi], *s.* inconstance *f* (d'une personne, de caractère); instabilité *f,* caractère changeant (du temps, etc.).

inconstant [in'kɔnstənt], *a.* **1.** (homme, caractère) inconstant, volage. **2.** (vent) mobile, variable.

inconstantly [in'kɔnstəntli], *adv.* avec inconstance.

inconsumable [inkən'sju:məbl], *a.* **1.** qui ne peut être consumé (par le feu); qui ne peut se consumer. **2.** *Pol.Ec:* (capitaux *m,* etc.) inconsommables.

incontestability [inkəntestə'biliti], *s.* incontestabilité *f*; *Ins:* **i. clause,** clause *f* d'incontestabilité.

incontestable ['inkən'testəbl], *a.* (preuve, vérité) incontestable, indéniable; (témoignage) irrécusable.

incontestably [inkən'testəbli], *adv.* incontestablement; irrécusablement.

incontinence [in'kɔntinəns], **incontinency** [in'kɔntinənsi], *s.* (*a*) incontinence *f*; **the sin of i.,** le péché de la chair, le péché d'impureté; (*b*) *Med:* **incontinence of urine,** incontinence d'urine; (*c*) **i. of speech, of tongue,** incontinence de langue, incontinence verbale.

incontinent [in'kɔntinənt], *a.* (*a*) (*unchaste*) incontinent; (*b*) *Med:* **i. of urine,** qui ne peut retenir son urine; *F:* qui ne peut se retenir; (*c*) *A:* **i. of secrets,** qui ne peut garder un secret; **i. of speech,** bavard.

incontinently[1] [in'kɔntinəntli], *adv.* incontinemment.

incontinently[2], *adv. A:* sur-le-champ; incontinent.

incontrollable [inkən'trouləbl], *a.* (enfant) ingouvernable; (mouvement) irréprimable; (désir) irrésistible, irrépressible, indomptable; **i. laughter,** fou rire; rire convulsif, inextinguible.

incontrollably [inkən'trouləbli], *adv.* irrésistiblement; **to laugh i.,** avoir le fou rire.

incontrovertible [inkɔntrə'və:tibl], *a.* (vérité) incontroversable, incontestable, indisputable; (preuve) irrécusable; (témoignage) qui défie toute contradiction.

incontrovertibly [inkɔntrə'və:tibli], *adv.* d'une manière indisputable; incontestablement; sans contredit.

inconvenience[1] [inkən'vi:njəns], *s.* (*a*) inconvénient *m,* incommodité *f,* embarras *m,* dérangement *m,* contretemps *m*; **to cause i., to be an i., to s.o.,** incommoder, déranger, qn; **we are sorry for any i. we may have caused you,** nous regrettons le dérangement que nous avons pu vous causer; **I am putting you to a great deal of i.,** je vous donne beaucoup de dérangement, beaucoup d'embarras; **I managed it at great personal i.,** j'en suis venu à bout au prix de dérangements personnels considérables; **without the slightest i.,** sans le moindre inconvénient; sans le moindre dérangement; (*b*) **the i. of living so far from town,** les inconvénients qu'il y a à vivre si loin de la ville; (*c*) **inconveniences of old age,** inconvénients, incommodités, de la vieillesse.

inconvenience[2], *v.tr.* déranger, incommoder, gêner (qn); **you will not i. me in the least,** vous ne me causerez aucune gêne.

inconvenient [inkən'vi:njənt], *a.* (*of house, etc.*) incommode, malcommode; (*of pers.*) gênant; (*of time*) inopportun; **it's very i.,** c'est très gênant; **if it is not i. to you,** si cela ne vous gêne pas; **he arrived at an i. time,** il est venu dans un mauvais moment; **it is i. arriving in London on a Sunday,** il est incommode d'arriver à Londres le dimanche.

inconveniently [inkən'vi:njəntli], *adv.* incommodément; **i. arranged,** arrangé d'une façon incommode, malcommode; **to arrive i.,** arriver à un moment inopportun.

inconvertible [inkən'və:tibl], *a.* **1.** (*of paper money, etc.*) inconvertible (**into,** en). **2.** *Log:* (*of proposition*) inconvertible, inconversible.

inconvincible [inkən'vinsibl], *a.* qui refuse de se laisser convaincre; difficile à convaincre.

incoordinate(d) [inkou'ɔ:dineit(id)], *a.* sans coordination, qui manque de coordination.

incoordination ['inkouɔ:di'neiʃ(ə)n], *s.* incoordination *f*; manque *m* de coordination.

incorporable [in'kɔ:pərəbl], *a.* incorporable.

incorporate[1] [in'kɔ:p(ə)rət], *a.* incorporel.

incorporate[2], *a.* incorporé (**in one body,** en un seul corps); faisant corps (**with others,** avec d'autres).

incorporate[3] [in'kɔ:pəreit]. **1.** *v.tr.* (*a*) incorporer, mêler, unir (**with,** à, avec); **to i. oil with wax,** incorporer de l'huile à, avec, dans, de la cire; **to i. eggs into a sauce,** incorporer des œufs à une sauce; **to i. one bank with another,** fusionner une banque avec une autre; **to i. a piece of land in an estate,** incorporer un terrain dans un domaine; **to i. a paragraph in a chapter,** incorporer un paragraphe dans un chapitre; (*b*) **work that incorporates all the latest discoveries,** ouvrage où se trouvent incorporées toutes les découvertes les plus récentes; ouvrage qui offre un exposé des découvertes les plus récentes; (*c*) *Com:* constituer (une association) en société commerciale; réunir (des banques) en société; (*d*) ériger (une ville) en municipalité, doter (une ville) d'une municipalité. **2.** *v.i.* (*a*) s'incorporer (**in one body,** en un seul corps; **with others,** avec, à, d'autres); (*b*) *U.S:* se constituer en société commerciale.

incorporated [in'kɔ:pəreitid], *a.* **1.** incorporé (**in one body,** en un seul corps); faisant corps (**with others,** avec d'autres). **2.** (*a*) *Com: Jur:* **i. company,** (i) association constituée en société commerciale; société constituée, autorisée; (ii) *U.S:* société anonyme; (*b*) **i. town,** ville administrée par un conseil municipal; municipalité *f.*

incorporation [inkɔ:pə'reiʃ(ə)n], *s.* **1.** incorporation *f* (**in, with, into,** à, avec, dans); **i. of recruits into a regiment,** incorporation des recrues dans un régiment; **i. of a piece of land into an estate,** incorporation d'un terrain à un domaine; **the i. of the vanquished with the victors,** l'incorporation des vaincus avec les vainqueurs. **2.** (*a*) (i) *Com: Jur:* constitution *f* (d'une association) en société commerciale; (ii) érection *f* (d'une ville) en municipalité; (*b*) société commerciale, *U.S:* = société anonyme. **3.** *Ling:* incorporation.

incorporator [in'kɔ:pəreitər], *s. U.S:* (i) fondateur *m,* (ii) membre *m,* d'une société commerciale constituée.

incorporeal [inkɔ:'pɔ:riəl], *a.* (être, *Jur:* droit) incorporel; *Jur:* **i. hereditaments,** biens incorporels transmissibles par héritage.

incorporeality [inkɔ:pɔ:ri'æliti], **incorporeity** [inkɔ:pə'ri:iti], *s.* incorporéité *f,* incorporalité *f* (des anges, *Jur:* d'un droit).

incorrect [inkə'rekt], *a.* **1.** (*a*) (*of statement, account, etc.*) inexact; **events have proved our views i.,** les événements ont donné tort à nos prévisions, ont prouvé l'inexactitude de nos prévisions; (*b*) **i. expression,** locution vicieuse; incorrection *f* de langage; *Com:* **i. endorsement,** endos défectueux; (*c*) **i. text,** texte fautif, rempli de fautes. **2.** (*of style, behaviour, etc.*) incorrect; **it is i. to . . .,** il est de mauvais ton de . . .; c'est contraire (i) à la politesse, (ii) à l'étiquette, au protocole, de . . ..

incorrectly [inkə'rektli], *adv.* **1.** inexactement; (parler) vicieusement; **letter i. addressed,** lettre mal adressée; **i.**

printed, imprimé fautivement. **2.** (se conduire, etc.) incorrectement.

incorrectness [inkə'rektnis], *s.* **1.** (*a*) inexactitude *f* (d'un calcul, etc.); (*b*) caractère fautif (d'un texte, etc.). **2.** incorrection *f* (de style, dans la tenue).

incorrigibility [inkɔridʒi'biliti], *s.* incorrigibilité *f.*

incorrigible [in'kɔridʒibl], *a.* (enfant, paresse, etc.) incorrigible; **he's an i. pessimist,** il est incorrigiblement pessimiste; **he's i.,** il est incorrigible, *F:* il est indécrottable; il mourra dans sa peau.

incorrigibly [in'kɔridʒibli], *adv.* incorrigiblement.

incorrodible [inkə'roudibl], *a.* incorrodible (**by acids, etc.,** par les acides, aux acides, etc.).

incorrupt [inkə'rʌpt], *a. A:* **1.** sain; non corrompu; pur. **2.** (texte) non corrompu, correct, fidèle. **3.** (juge) incorrompu, incorruptible.

incorruptibility [inkərʌpti'biliti], **incorruptibleness** [inkə'rʌptib(ə)lnis], *s.* incorruptibilité *f* (d'une substance, d'un fonctionnaire).

incorruptible [inkə'rʌptibl], *a.* (i) matière, (ii) juge incorruptible.

incorruptibly [inkə'rʌptibli], *adv.* incorruptiblement.

incorruption [inkə'rʌpʃ(ə)n], *s.* incorruption *f*; *B:* **the body is raised in i.,** le corps ressuscite incorruptible.

incorruptness [inkə'rʌptnis], *s.* incorruption *f.*

incrassate [in'kræsət], **incrassated** [in'kræseitid], *a. Nat.Hist:* épaissi, enflé; *Bot:* **incrassate leaf,** feuille charnue.

incrassation [inkræ'seiʃ(ə)n], *s.* épaississement *m.*

increasable [in'kri:səbl], *a.* augmentable; susceptible d'augmentation.

increase[1] ['inkri:s], *s.* (*a*) augmentation *f* (de prix, de recettes, etc.); accroissement *m* (de vitesse, d'un nombre, de santé, de pression); gain *m* (de vitesse); croît *m* (de valeur, de bétail); surcroît *m* (de besogne); renouvellement *m* (de zèle, d'attention); redoublement *m* (d'efforts, de gaieté); multiplication *f* (des êtres, de l'espèce); **the i. in crime,** la multiplication des crimes; **i. in price,** augmentation de prix; renchérissement *m*; **i. in the cost of living,** renchérissement (du coût) de la vie; **i. in value (of property, etc.),** plus-value *f* (d'une propriété, etc.); **i. in wages,** augmentation, relèvement *m*, de salaire; **I've had an i. in salary,** j'ai été augmenté; **i. in taxation of 10%,** relèvement de taxe de 10%; **i. in power,** agrandissement *m* de pouvoir; **the takings are £500, an i. of 30% on last week('s),** la recette est de 500 livres, en augmentation de 30%, ce qui représente une plus-value de 30%, sur (celle de) la semaine dernière; *Jur:* **i. of penalty,** aggravation *f* de peine; (*b*) *A: & B:* fruits *mpl*, produits *mpl*, récoltes *fpl* (de la terre); (*c*) *adv.phr.* **to be on the i.,** être en augmentation; aller croissant; **crime is on the i.,** les crimes se multiplient, le nombre des crimes augmente beaucoup; **unemployment is on the i.,** le chômage s'accentue.

increase[2] [in'kri:s]. **1.** *v.i.* (*a*) augmenter, s'augmenter; grandir, s'agrandir; croître, s'accroître; prendre de l'extension, (*in bulk*) grossir; **the speed increases,** la vitesse augmente, s'accroît, grandit; **the rain increased,** la pluie redoubla; **his efforts increased,** ses efforts redoublaient, se multipliaient; **Rome increased by Alba's fall,** Rome s'accrut de la ruine d'Albe; **to i. in size, value,** augmenter de grandeur, de valeur; **to i. in price,** renchérir; (*of earth, lime*) **to i. in volume,** foisonner; **to go on increasing,** aller toujours croissant; *Nau:* **the tides are increasing,** les marées rapportent; (*b*) se multiplier; **plants that i. rapidly,** plantes qui se multiplient rapidement; **the population is increasing,** la population grossit, augmente, se multiplie; (*c*) *Knit:* **i. two at the beginning of the next row,** augmenter de deux points au commencement du rang suivant. **2.** *v.tr.* augmenter (la vitesse, la production); grossir (le nombre); accroître (sa fortune); relever (les salaires, les prix); agrandir (l'importance); *Com:* majorer (les prix); **to i. the distance,** allonger la distance; **to i. the expenditure,** grossir la dépense; **to i. the cost of goods,** renchérir des marchandises; **to i. s.o.'s salary,** augmenter (le salaire de) qn; **to i. taxes,** augmenter, majorer, les impôts; **if you could i. the sum to £1000,** si vous pouviez porter la somme à mille livres; **to i. the dose (of a medicine),** forcer la dose (d'un médicament); **to i. one's pace,** allonger, presser, le pas; presser, activer, son allure; **to i. speed,** forcer, augmenter, la vitesse; forcer l'allure, forcer de vitesse; *Nau:* **to i. speed to twenty knots,** pousser l'allure à vingt nœuds; **i. speed,** plus vite; *Phot:* **to i. the exposure,** forcer la durée de pose; **to i. discontent,** accentuer le mécontentement; **to i. one's care, one's efforts,** redoubler de vigilance, d'efforts; **to require increased care,** demander un surcroît de soins, d'attentions; **increased wealth,** fortune accrue; **increased cost of living,** renchérissement *m* (du coût) de la vie.

increasing[1] [in'kri:siŋ], *a.* croissant; **ever-i. influence,** influence toujours plus étendue.

increasing[2], *s.* augmentation *f*, accroissement *m*, agrandissement *m* (de vitesse, d'volume, d'importance); redoublement *m* (d'efforts).

increasingly [in'kri:siŋli], *adv.* de plus en plus (difficile, grand, etc.).

increate [inkri(:)'eit], *a. Phil: Theol:* incréé.

incredibility [inkredi'biliti], *s.* incrédibilité *f.*

incredible [in'kredibl], *a.* incroyable; **with i. swiftness,** avec une rapidité incroyable, inconcevable, qu'on ne saurait imaginer; **to spend i. sums of money,** dépenser des sommes folles; *F:* **it's i.!** c'est renversant!

incredibly [in'kredibli], *adv.* incroyablement; **he's i. stupid,** il est d'une sottise incroyable, sans pareille.

incredulity [inkri'dju:liti], **incredulousness** [in'kredjuləsnis], *s.* incrédulité *f.*

incredulous [in'kredjuləs], *a.* incrédule (**of,** à l'égard de); **i. smile,** sourire *m* d'incrédulité; sourire sceptique.

incredulously [in'kredjuləsli], *adv.* d'une manière incrédule; avec incrédulité; sans y attacher foi.

increment[1] ['inkrimənt], *s.* **1.** (*a*) augmentation *f*; accroissement *m* (d'une forêt, etc.); *Mth:* **i. of a function,** accroissement (infiniment petit) d'une fonction; différentielle *f*; *Mec:* **dynamic i.,** accroissement dynamique; *For:* **average i.,** accroissement moyen; (*b*) *Her:* **moon in i.,** croissant tourné. **2.** profit *m*; (*of land, shares*) **unearned i.,** plus-value *f.* **3.** *Cmptr:* incrément *m*; valeur *f* de progression.

increment[2], *v.tr. Cmptr:* augmenter, faire progresser (le compteur).

incremental [inkri'ment(ə)l], *a.* d'augmentation, d'accroissement; par augmentation, par accroissement; *Cmptr:* **i. computer,** calculateur *m* par accroissements, à valeurs variables; **i. duplex,** duplex *m* par addition.

incrementation [inkrimen'teiʃ(ə)n], *s. Cmptr:* augmentation *f*, progression *f.*

increscent [in'kres(ə)nt], *a.* **1.** croissant; *Her:* **i. moon,** croissant tourné. **2.** *Bot:* (organe) increscent.

incriminate [in'krimineit], *v.tr.* **1.** accuser (qn) d'un crime. **2.** impliquer (un complice, etc.) (dans une accusation); mêler (qn) à une affaire.

incriminating[1] [in'krimineitiŋ], *a.* (circonstance, etc.) qui tend à prouver la culpabilité (de qn); **i. documents,** pièces *f* à conviction.

incriminating[2], *s.* incrimination *f.*

incrimination [inkrimi'neiʃ(ə)n], *s.* incrimination *f*; accusation *f* (de qn).

incriminatory [inkrimi'neitəri], *a.* qui tend à prouver la culpabilité (de qn).

incroyable [ɛ̃krwajabl], *s. Hist:* incroyable *mf.*

incrust [in'krʌst]. **1.** *v.tr.* (*a*) incruster; **to i. ebony with mother of pearl,** incruster de la nacre dans l'ébène; (*b*) couvrir d'une croûte, encroûter, incruster (**with,** de). **2.** *v.i.* se couvrir d'une croûte, s'encroûter, s'incruster (**with,** de); (*of boiler, etc.*) s'entartrer.

incrustation [inkrʌs'teiʃ(ə)n], *s.* **1.** (*a*) incrustation *f*; action *f* d'incruster; (*b*) *Mch:* entartrage *m* (des chaudières). **2.** (*a*) incrustation (de nacre, etc.); revêtement *m* (en mosaïque, etc.); (*b*) *Mch:* tartre *m*; dépôt *m* calcaire. **3.** *F:* encroûtement *m* (d'une habitude, etc.).

incrusted [in'krʌstid], *a.* encroûté; revêtu d'incrustations; (*of boiler*) incrusté de tartre; entartré.

incubate ['inkjubeit]. **1.** *v.tr.* couver, incuber (des œufs). **2.** *v.i.* (*a*) (*of eggs*) être soumis à l'incubation; (*b*) (*of disease*) couver.

incubating ['inkjubeitiŋ], *a.* (*of bird, apparatus*) incubateur, -trice.

incubation [inkju'beiʃ(ə)n], *s.* incubation *f*; *Husb:* **artificial i.,** accouvage *m*; *Med:* **i. period,** période *f* d'incubation (d'une maladie).

incubative ['inkjubeitiv], *a.* **1.** (instinct *m*) de couvaison. **2.** *Med:* **i. period,** période *f* d'incubation.

incubator ['inkjubeitər], *s.* (*a*) incubateur *m*; (i) *Husb:* couveuse artificielle; mère artificielle; couvoir *m* (pour volaille), poussinière *f*, éleveuse *f* (pour poussins); (ii) *Bac:* étuve *f* à incubation, à cultures; (iii) (*for premature babies*) couveuse; (*b*) *Orn:* **i. bird,** mégapode *m.*

incubatory ['inkjubeitəri], *a.* = INCUBATIVE.

incubous ['inkjubəs], *a. Bot:* (feuille) incube.

incubus ['inkjubəs], *s.* **1.** *Myth:* incube *m.* **2.** *Fig:* (*a*) (*of pers.*) **to be an i. on s.o.,** être un cauchemar pour qn; être le cauchemar de qn; (*b*) *O:* fardeau *m*, poids *m* (des impôts, etc.); **he was at last free from the i. of debt,** il se trouvait enfin libéré du poids de ses dettes.

incudectomy [inkju'dektəmi], *s. Surg:* ablation *f* de l'enclume (de l'oreille).

inculcate ['inkʌlkeit], *v.tr.* inculquer (une leçon, etc.); **to i. sth. on s.o., in s.o.'s mind,** inculquer qch. à qn, dans l'esprit de qn.

inculcation [inkʌl'keiʃ(ə)n], *s.* inculcation *f.*

inculpable [in'kʌlpəbl], *a.* innocent, sans blâme.

inculpate ['inkʌlpeit], *v.tr.* **1.** inculper, incriminer (qn). **2.** impliquer (un complice, etc.) (dans une accusation); mêler (qn) à une affaire.

inculpation [inkʌl'peiʃ(ə)n], *s.* inculpation *f.*

inculpatory [in'kʌlpətəri], *a.* (lettre, parole) qui tend à inculper, à incriminer; accusateur, -trice; dénonciateur, -trice.

incumbency [in'kʌmbənsi], *s.* **1.** (*a*) *Ecc:* (i) possession *f* d'un bénéfice; (ii) bénéfice; charge *f*; (*b*) *esp. NAm:* charge, fonction *f* (d'un fonctionnaire). **2.** période *f* d'exercice (d'une charge ecclésiastique, etc.); *NAm:* **during his i. as mayor,** pendant son exercice des fonctions de maire; pendant qu'il était maire.

incumbent[1] [in'kʌmbənt], *s.* **1.** *Ecc:* bénéficier *m*, bénéficiaire *m*, titulaire *m* (d'une charge). **2.** *esp. NAm:* titulaire (d'une fonction administrative); **the present i. of the constituency,** le député actuel.

incumbent[2], *a.* **1.** (*a*) *A:* couché, posé, appuyé (**on,** sur); (*b*) *Geol:* (*of stratum*) superposé (**on,** à). **2.** *Nat.Hist:* incombant; **i. cotyledons,** cotylédons incombants. **3. to be i. on s.o. to do sth.,** incomber, appartenir, à qn de faire qch.; être du devoir de qn de faire qch.; *A:* **it is i. on you to warn them,** il vous appartient, il est de votre devoir, il vous incombe, c'est une obligation pour vous, de les avertir; **economy is i.,** l'économie s'impose.

incumbrance [in'kʌmbrəns], *s.* **1.** embarras *m*, charge *f.* **2.** *Jur:* (*a*) charges (d'une succession); (*b*) servitude *f.*

incunable [in'kju:nəbl], *s.* = INCUNABULUM.

incunabular [inkju(:)'næbjulər], *a.* (livre, édition) incunable.

incunabulist [inkju(:)'næbjulist], *s.* collectionneur, -euse, d'incunables.

incunabulum, *pl.* **-a** [inkju(:)'næbjuləm, -ə], *s.* incunable *m.*

incur [in'kə:r], *v.tr.* (**incurred**) courir (un risque); encourir (un blâme); subir (une perte); s'attirer (le courroux de qn); contracter (des dettes); **to i. ridicule,** s'exposer au ridicule; **to i. hatred,** s'attirer la haine; **to i. s.o.'s suspicions,** devenir suspect à qn; **to i. large losses,** éprouver, subir, des pertes sensibles; **it was we who incurred the loss,** la perte a porté sur nous; **injuries incurred in an accident,** blessures reçues dans un accident; **to i. expenses,** encourir des frais; faire des dépenses; *Com:* (*on bill of exchange*) **i. no expenses,** sans frais, sans protêt, sans compte de retour; **incurred expenses,** dépenses faites.

incurable [in'kju:rəbl]. **1.** *a.* (maladie *f*) incurable, inguérissable, qui ne pardonne pas; (mal *m*) sans remède, irrémédiable; **i. drunkard,** ivrogne invétéré. **2.** *s.* (*usu. in pl.*) **home for incurables,** hospice *m* des incurables; les Incurables *m.*

incurably [in'kju:rəbli], *adv.* incurablement; **to be i. lazy,** être d'une paresse incurable.

incuriosity [inkju:ri'ɔsiti], **incuriousness** [in'kju:riəsnis], *s.* incuriosité *f*, indifférence *f.*

incurious [in'kju:riəs], *a.* incurieux, sans curiosité, indifférent.

incuriously [in'kju:riəsli], *adv.* sans curiosité; avec indifférence.

incurrent [in'kʌr(ə)nt], *a. Spong:* **i. pore,** pore inhalant.

incursion [in'kə:ʃ(ə)n], *s.* incursion *f* (d'un ennemi, d'une maladie); **to make incursions into the enemy's country,** faire des descentes dans le pays ennemi; *Fig:* **my only i. into the theatrical world,** ma seule incursion dans le monde du théâtre.

incursive [in'kə:siv], *a.* incursif, agressif.

Incurvariidae [inkə:və'ri:idi], *s.pl. Ent:* incurvariides *m.*

incurvate ['inkə:veit], *v.tr.* incurver.

incurvated ['inkə:veitid], *a.* incurvé; courbé en dedans.

incurvation [inkə:'veiʃ(ə)n], *s.* incurvation *f*; courbure *f*, arqûre *f* (en dedans).

incurve[1] ['in'kə:v]. **1.** *v.tr.* incurver. **2.** *v.i.* s'incurver, se courber en dedans.

incurve[2] ['inkə:v], *s. Sp:* (*baseball*) balle qui décrit une courbe vers le batteur.

incurved ['inkə:vd], *a.* incurvé, courbé en dedans; *Nat.Hist:* incurvé; **i. nail,** ongle recourbé; ongle en griffe; *Bot:* **i. ovule,** ovule *m* campylotrope.

incus, *pl.* **incudes** ['iŋkəs, iŋ'kju:di:z], *s.* **1.** *Anat:* enclume *f* (de l'oreille interne). **2.** *Meteor:* incus *m inv*; sommet *m* en enclume (d'un cumulonimbus).

incuse [in'kju:z]. *Num:* **1.** *a. & s.* **i. (medal),** (médaille) incuse (*f*). **2.** *s.* frappe *f* en creux.

incused [in'kju:zd], *a.* (médaille, monnaie) incuse, frappée en creux.

incut ['inkʌt]. **1.** *a. Ind:* (bâti) échancré. **2.** *a. & s. Typ:* **i. (note),** manchette enclavée.

indamine ['indəmi:n], *s. Ch:* indamine *f.*

indan ['indæn], *s. Ch:* indane *f* hydrindène *f.*

Indanthrene [in'dænθri:n], *s. R.t.m: Dy:* Indanthrène *m.*

indazine ['indəzi:n], *s. Ch:* indazine *f.*

indazole ['indəzoul], *s. Ch:* indazole *m.*

indebted [in'detid], *a.* **1.** endetté; **to be heavily i. to s.o.,** devoir une forte somme à qn. **2.** redevable **(to s.o. for sth.,** à qn de qch.); **I am indebted to Mr Martin for this information,** c'est à M. Martin que je dois ce renseignement.

indebtedness [in'detidnis], *s.* **1.** dette(s) *f(pl)*; **the amount of my i.,** le montant de ma dette; *Jur:* **proof of i.,** affirmation *f,* titre *m,* de créance. **2. our i. to Greece,** notre dette envers la Grèce; ce dont nous sommes redevables à la Grèce; **I must acknowledge my i. to my predecessors,** il me faut reconnaître ma dette envers mes prédécesseurs, tout ce que je dois à mes prédécesseurs.

indecency [in'di:sənsi], *s.* **1.** indécence *f,* inconvenance *f*; *Jur:* **(public act of) i.,** attentat *m* aux mœurs; outrage (public) aux mœurs. **2. to commit indecencies,** commettre des indécences.

indecent [in'di:s(ə)nt], *a.* peu décent, indécent, inconvenant; **i. behaviour,** attentat *m* aux mœurs; **i. assault,** attentat *m* à la pudeur; outrage *m* aux mœurs; **i. exposure,** délit puni par la loi sur les mœurs; outrage public à la pudeur; **to do sth. with i. haste,** faire qch. avec une hâte peu dissimulée, en grande hâte.

indecently [in'di:səntli], *adv.* indécemment; d'une manière indécente.

indeciduate [indi'sidjuət], *a. Z:* (femelle) qui n'expulse pas la membrane caduque.

indeciduous [indi'sidjuəs], *a. Bot:* (*of leaf, plant*) persistant.

indecipherable [indi'saif(ə)rəbl], *a.* indéchiffrable.

indecision [indi'siʒ(ə)n], *s.* indécision *f,* irrésolution *f.*

indecisive [indi'saisiv], *a.* **1.** (*of argument, etc.*) indécisif, peu concluant; (*of battle*) indécis. **2.** (homme) indécis, irrésolu.

indecisively [indi'saisivli], *adv.* indécisivement; d'une façon indécisive; sans aboutir à une conclusion.

indecisiveness [indi'saisivnis], *s.* **1.** manque *m* de décision; indécision *f.* **2.** caractère indécis (d'un combat, etc.).

indeclinable [indi'klainəbl], *a. Gram:* (nom) indéclinable.

indecomposable [indi:kəm'pouzəbl], *a.* (élément *m,* mot *m*) indécomposable; *Astr:* (amas *m* d'étoiles) non résoluble; *Ch:* **i. body,** corps *m* indédoublable.

indecorous [in'dekərəs], *a.* malséant; de mauvais goût; inconvenant; **i. behaviour,** conduite *f* peu convenable; **facetiousness is i. in a judge,** les facéties ne conviennent pas à un juge, sont mal venues de la part d'un juge.

indecorously [in'dekərəsli], *adv.* d'une manière peu convenable; d'une manière inconvenante.

indecorousness [in'dekərəsnis], **indecorum** [indi'kɔ:rəm], *s.* (*a*) inconvenance *f,* malséance *f*; (*b*) manque *m* de décorum, de maintien, d'usage.

indeed [in'di:d], *adv.* **1.** (*a*) en effet; en vérité; vraiment; de fait; effectivement; **he was i. a man of genius,** c'était en effet, vraiment, un homme de génie; **one may i. say so,** on peut bien le dire; **praise which i. was well deserved,** éloges qui de fait étaient bien mérités; **i. it's perfectly true,** mais c'est que c'est vrai! **i. he wouldn't do such a thing,** je vous assure que jamais il ne ferait une chose pareille; ah non! jamais il ne ferait cela! (*b*) (*intensive*) **I am very glad i.,** je suis très très content; **thank you very much i.,** merci infiniment; merci mille fois; **he spoke very well, very well i.,** il a parlé très bien, mais très très bien; (*c*) (*concessive*) **there are i. exceptions to this rule,** cette règle n'est pas sans exceptions, j'en conviens; **I may i. be wrong,** il se peut toutefois que j'aie tort. **2.** même, à vrai dire; **he asserted the fact, i. he proved it,** il a affirmé le fait, il l'a même prouvé; **I think so, i. I am sure of it,** je le pense et même j'en suis sûr; **it is past midnight, i. it is one o'clock,** il est minuit passé, à vrai dire il est une heure, il est même une heure; **come as you are; i. no one is dressing,** venez comme vous êtes; aussi bien personne ne fait de toilette; **I forget his name, if i. I ever knew it,** son nom m'échappe, si tant est que je l'aie jamais su. **3.** (*a*) (*with affirmation or negation*) **yes i.!** (i) mais certainement! ça oui! oui vraiment! pour sûr! (ii) (*contradicting*) si fait! **no i.!** ça non! non vraiment! certes non! **does that surprise you?—it does i.!** cela vous étonne?—dame, oui! bien sûr que oui! (*b*) (*interrogatively*) **I have lived in Paris—i.?** j'ai vécu à Paris—vraiment? (*c*) (*as interjection*) **silk dresses i.!** ah! bien oui, on vous en donnera, des robes de soie! **your brother will do it for you—my brother i.!** votre frère fera cela pour vous—mon frère? ah bien oui! comptez là-dessus!

indefatigability [indifætigə'biliti], *s.* infatigabilité *f.*

indefatigable [indi'fætigəbl], *a.* infatigable, inlassable; **he was i.,** il a fourni un effort immense.

indefatigableness [indi'fætigəb(ə)lnis], *s.* infatigabilité *f.*

indefatigably [indi'fætigəbli], *adv.* infatigablement; sans se lasser.

indefeasibility ['indifi:zi'biliti], *s.* irrévocabilité *f,* incommutabilité *f*; imprescriptibilité *f* (d'un droit).

indefeasible [indi'fi:zibl], *a.* (droit, bien) irrévocable, imprescriptible, incommutable; *Jur:* **i. interest,** intérêt *m* indestructible.

indefeasibly [indi'fi:zibli], *adv.* irrévocablement.

indefectibility ['indifekti'biliti], *s.* **1.** indéfectibilité *f* (de l'Église, etc.). **2.** impeccabilité *f.*

indefectible [indi'fektibl], *a.* **1.** (grâce, etc.) indéfectible. **2.** impeccable.

indefectibly [indi'fektibli], *adv.* indéfectiblement.

indefensible [indi'fensibl], *a.* (place *f,* théorie *f*) indéfendable, indéfensible; (conduite) inexcusable; (argument) insoutenable.

indefensibly [indi'fensibli], *adv.* d'une manière indéfensible, inexcusable, insoutenable.

indefinable [indi'fainəbl], *a.* **1.** indéfinissable. **2. an i. feeling of pleasure,** un sentiment vague de plaisir.

indefinably [indi'fainəbli], *adv.* **1.** d'une manière indéfinissable. **2.** vaguement.

indefinite [in'definit], *a.* **1.** (*of ideas, promises, etc.*) indéfini, vague; **i. particulars,** détails imprécis, peu précis; **to leave a point i.,** laisser un point dans l'imprécision. **2.** (*a*) (*of distance, time, number*) indéfini, indéterminé; **i. leave,** congé illimité, indéfini; (*b*) *Bot:* (*of inflorescence, etc.*) indéfini; (*c*) *Gram:* (article, pronom) indéfini.

indefinitely [in'definitli], *adv.* **1.** (promettre) indéfiniment, vaguement. **2. to postpone sth. i.,** remettre qch. indéfiniment, aux calendes grecques; **to prolong a line i.,** prolonger une ligne indéfiniment; **I could go on giving examples i.,** je pourrais citer des exemples à l'infini.

indefiniteness [in'definitnis], *s.* caractère indéfini, vague (de qch.); indétermination *f.*

indeformable [indi'fɔ:məbl], *a.* indéformable.

indehiscence [indi'hisəns], *s. Bot:* indéhiscence *f.*

indehiscent [indi'hisənt], *a. Bot:* indéhiscent.

indelibility [indeli'biliti], *s.* indélébilité *f.*

indelible [in'delibl], *a.* indélébile, ineffaçable; **i. pencil,** crayon violet, à encre indélébile.

indelibly [in'delibli], *adv.* indélébilement, ineffaçablement; **i. engraved on the mind,** gravé dans la mémoire en caractères indélébiles.

indelicacy [in'delikəsi], *s.* **1.** (*a*) indélicatesse *f*; manque *m* de délicatesse; (*b*) inconvenance *f,* grossièreté *f.* **2.** (*a*) **guilty of several indelicacies,** coupable de plusieurs indélicatesses; (*b*) **indelicacies of speech,** gaillardises *f*; propos risqués, peu délicats.

indelicate [in'delikət], *a.* (*a*) indélicat; qui manque de tact, de délicatesse; peu délicat; **i. action,** indélicatesse *f*; (*b*) inconvenant, qui frise l'indécence; **i. joke,** histoire grivoise, corsée, risquée; **i. word,** mot malsonnant, grossier; **i. action,** inconvenance *f.*

indelicately [in'delikətli], *adv.* (*a*) indélicatement, sans délicatesse; (*b*) d'une façon inconvenante.

indemnification [indemnifi'keiʃ(ə)n], *s.* **1.** indemnisation *f,* dédommagement *m* **(of s.o. for sth.,** de qn de qch.). **2.** indemnité *f,* dédommagement, compensation *f*; **to pay a sum of money by way of i.,** payer une somme à titre d'indemnité.

indemnify [in'demnifai], *v.tr.* **1.** garantir (qn) **(from, against,** contre); *Pol:* **to i. a minister,** accorder à un ministre un bill d'indemnité. **2.** indemniser, dédommager (qn) **(for a loss,** d'une perte); **to i. oneself,** se dédommager **(for, de)**; **to i. s.o. for disadvantages, hardships,** compenser les désavantages, les privations, de qn.

indemnity [in'demniti], *s.* **1.** garantie *f,* assurance *f* (contre une perte, etc.); *Pol:* **bill, act, of i.,** bill *m* d'indemnité; *Com:* **i. bond, (letter of) i.,** cautionnement *m,* (lettre *f* de) garantie *f* (d'indemnité); décharge *f.* **2.** indemnité *f,* dédommagement *m,* compensation *f*; **to pay full i. to s.o.,** indemniser totalement qn; **i. for expropriation,** indemnité pour cause d'expropriation; **war i.,** indemnité de guerre; **receiver of an i.,** indemnitaire *mf.* **3.** *Can:* **an M.P.'s i.,** l'indemnité parlementaire d'un député.

indemonstrable [in'deməns trəbl], *a.* indémontrable.

indene ['indi:n], *s. Ch:* indène *m.*

indent[1] ['indent, in'dent], *s.* **1.** (*a*) dentelure *f,* entaille *f,* découpure *f*; échancrure *f,* indentation *f,* indenture *f* (du littoral); (*b*) *Carp:* adent *m.* **2.** (*a*) *Adm:* ordre *m* de réquisition (pour approvisionnements); *Mil:* **ration i.,** bon *m* de vivres; (*b*) commande *f* de marchandises, ordre *m* d'achat; *esp.* commande reçue de l'étranger.

indent[2] [in'dent]. **1.** *v.tr.* (*a*) denteler, découper, entailler (le bord de qch.); découper, échancrer (le littoral); (*b*) *Carp:* adenter, endenter (une poutre); (*c*) *Typ:* renfoncer, (faire) rentrer, faire un rentré à (une ligne); faire un alinéa; (*d*) *Jur:* passer (un document) en partie double (*A:* et les séparer par une coupure en zigzag); (*e*) *Com: A:* (*of parts of the British Commonwealth*) passer une commande pour (des marchandises de source anglaise, etc.). **2.** *v.i.* **to i. on s.o. for sth.,** (i) réquisitionner qch. de qn; (ii) passer une commande à qn pour (une marchandise).

indent[3] ['indent], *s.* (*a*) empreinte creuse; marque (laissée par un coup, un poids); creux *m,* bosselure *f*; (*b*) *Metalw: etc:* brouture (laissée par l'outil).

indent[4] [in'dent], *v.tr.* empreindre (en creux); bosseler, bossuer (une surface).

indentation [inden'teiʃ(ə)n], *s.* **1.** (*a*) découpage *m* (des bords de qch.); (*b*) *Carp:* endentement *m* (de deux poutres); (*c*) impression *f,* foulage *m* (du sable par les roues, etc.). **2.** dentelure *f*; entaille *f,* découpure *f*; échancrure *f,* indentation *f,* indenture *f* (du littoral). **3.** = INDENT[3]. **4.** *Typ:* = INDENTION 1.

indented[1] [in'dentid], *a.* **1.** (bord) dentelé; (littoral) échancré, indenté; (mur) endenté; **i. wheel,** roue dentée; *Navy:* **in i. order,** en ordre endenté. **2.** *Typ:* **i. line,** ligne *f* en alinéa, en retrait; alinéa (rentrant). **3.** *Jur:* **deed i.,** contrat *m* synallagmatique. **4.** *Her:* denché.

indented[2], *a.* (*a*) empreint (en creux); bossué, bosselé; (*b*) *Metalw:* (pièce) qui porte des marques de broutage.

indenter [in'dentər], *s. Com:* client *m* qui passe une commande pour des marchandises de source étrangère.

indenting[1] [in'dentiŋ], *s.* (*a*) découpage *m* (des bords de qch.); (*b*) *Carp:* endentement *m* (de deux poutres).

indenting[2], *s.* impression *f,* foulage *m* (du sable par les roues, etc.).

indention [in'denʃ(ə)n], *s.* **1.** *Typ:* (*a*) renfoncement *m* (d'une ligne); rentré *m*; **reverse i., hanging i.,** composition *f* en sommaire; (*b*) faible *m* (dans un blanchet). **2.** dentelure *f,* entaille *f,* découpure *f*; échancrure *f.*

indenture[1] [in'dentʃər], *s. Jur:* contrat *m* synallagmatique; contrat bilatéral; **to be bound by an i.,** être lié par un engagement; (*b*) *pl.* **indentures,** contrat, brevet *m,* d'apprentissage; obligé *m* (entre maître et apprenti); **to take up, be out of, one's indentures,** recevoir, avoir reçu, son congé d'acquit.

indenture[2], *v.tr.* **1.** lier (qn) par contrat; **indentured labour,** main d'œuvre engagée à long terme. **2.** mettre (qn) en apprentissage **(to s.o.,** chez qn); engager (qn) par un brevet d'apprentissage.

independable [indi'pendəbl], *a.* sur lequel on ne peut pas compter; auquel on ne peut se fier; (renseignement, etc.) peu sûr, peu digne de foi.

independence [indi'pendəns], *s.* **1.** indépendance *f* **(of,** de, à l'égard de); autonomie *f* (d'un état); **to show i.,** faire preuve d'indépendance; **the American War of I.,** la Guerre de l'Indépendance (des États-Unis); *U.S:* **I. Day,** le quatre juillet (fête nationale). **2.** *O:* **he had acquired a modest i.,** il s'était acquis une modeste indépendance.

independency [indi'pendənsi], *s.* **1.** indépendance *f,* liberté *f.* **2.** état, pays, indépendant, autonome. **3.** *Rel:* non-conformisme *m* (des Indépendants). **4.** indépendance financière.

independent [indi'pendənt]. **1.** *a.* (*a*) indépendant; (état, pays) autonome; **to be i. of s.o., sth.,** ne pas dépendre de qn, qch.; **to be i.,** être indépendant, son maître; **to become i.,** s'affranchir; **i. witness,** témoin volontaire; *Adm:* **i. school** = école *f* libre; *Aut:* **i. (front-wheel) suspension,** roues (avant) indépendantes; *Mil:* **i. force,** armée *f* autonome; **i. battalion,** bataillon *m* formant corps; **i. firing,** tir *m* à volonté; *Mth:* **i. variable,** variable indépendante; (*b*) (i) **a gentleman, a man, of i. means, an i. gentleman,** un rentier, un monsieur renté; **to be i.,** *O:* **have an i. income,** avoir une fortune personnelle, indépendante; vivre de ses rentes; (ii) **his children are i. (of him) now,** ses enfants peuvent maintenant se suffire à eux-mêmes, pourvoir eux-mêmes à leurs besoins; (*c*) (caractère, air) indépendant; (homme) qui ne demande d'avis à personne. **2.** *s. Pol: etc:* indépendant, -ante; *Rel.H:* **the Independents,** les Indépendants.

independently [indi'pendəntli], *adv.* **1.** indépendamment **(of, de)**; **they found their pleasure i.,** ils s'amusaient séparément; (*of ships*) **to proceed i. to a rendezvous,** naviguer en route libre à un rendez-vous. **2.** avec indépendance; d'un air indépendant.

indescribable [indis'kraibəbl], *a.* (fureur, misère, scène) indescriptible; (joie) indicible; **her grief is i.,** sa douleur ne saurait se peindre; **the i. something,** le je ne sais quoi.

indescribably [indis'kraibəbli], *adv.* indescriptiblement, indiciblement.

indestructibility [indistrʌkti'biliti], **indestructibleness** [indis'trʌktib(ə)lnis], *s.* indestructibilité *f.*

indestructible [indis'trʌktəbl], *a.* indestructible; *Pol.Ec:* (capital) inconsommable.

indestructibly [indis'trʌktibli], *adv,* indestructiblement.

indetectible, -able [indi'tektəbl], *a.* que l'on ne peut découvrir; imperceptible.

indeterminable [indi'tə:minəbl], *a.* **1.** (distance, origine) indéterminable. **2.** (querelle, dispute) qu'on ne saurait terminer, régler.

indeterminacy [indi'tə:minəsi], *s. Ph:* **i. principle,** loi *f* d'indétermination.

indeterminate [indi'tə:minət], *a.* (*of space, etc.*) indéterminé; (*of thought*) vague, imprécis; *Mth:* **i. quantity,** quantité indéterminée; **i. problem,** (problème) indéterminé (*m*); problème qui comporte plusieurs solutions.

indeterminately [indi'tə:minətli], *adv.* indéterminément, vaguement.

indetermination [inditə:mi'neiʃ(ə)n], *s.* indétermination *f*; (i) (*of pers.*) irrésolution *f,* indécision *f*; défaut *m* de volonté; (ii) absence *f* de conditions qui déterminent; (iii) *Mth:* absence de solution.

indetermined [indi'tə:mind], *a.* **1.** (*of quantity, date, etc.*) indéterminé, incertain. **2.** (*of question*) indécis. **3.** (*of pers.*) irrésolu, indécis.

indeterminism [indi'tə:minizm], *s. Phil:* indéterminisme *m.*

indeterminist [indi'tə:minist], *a. & s. Phil:* indéterministe (*mf*).

indevotion [indi'vouʃ(ə)n], *s.* indévotion *f.*

indevout [indi'vaut], *a.* indévot.

index[1], *pl.* **indexes, indices** ['indeks, 'indeksiz, 'indisi:z], *s.* **1.** (*pl.* **indexes**) **i. (finger),** index *m*, premier doigt. **2.** *Tchn:* (*pl.* **indexes**) (*a*) aiguille *f* (de cadran, balance, etc.); style *m* (de cadran solaire); *Surv:* **i. (bar) (of plane table),** alidade *f* (à pinnules); **i. glass, i. mirror,** grand miroir (de sextant); **i. correction,** correction *f* du zéro; mise *f* au point zéro; **i. error,** erreur instrumentale, de lecture; (*b*) *Typ:* main *f.* **3.** (*pl.* **indices**) indice *m*, signe (indicateur); **i. to the state of s.o.'s feelings,** indication *f* des sentiments de qn; *Geol:* **i. fossils,** fossiles *m* stratigraphiques. **4.** (*pl.* **indexes**) (*a*) repère *m*; (dispositif) indicateur (*m*); **i. mark,** (marque *f*) repère, point *m* de repère; **i. line,** ligne *f* (de) repère; **mechanical i.,** repère mécanique; *Mec.E:* **i. pin,** goupille *f* de repérage, ergot *m* de guidage; *Mch.Tls:* **i. dial, i. plate,** plateau diviseur, plateau indicateur; **i. head,** diviseur *m*; **i. ring,** anneau diviseur, bague divisée; (*b*) *U.S:* **i. board,** tableau indicateur. **5.** (*a*) (*pl.* **indexes**) index; table *f* alphabétique, répertoire *m* (d'un livre); **to enter an item on, in, the i.,** répertorier un article; **i. book,** livre répertoire; classeur *m*; *Mapm:* **i. to adjoining sheets,** tableau d'assemblage (des feuilles); **i. to corresponding sheets,** tableau des feuilles correspondantes; (*b*) *R.C.Ch:* **the (Expurgatory) I.,** l'Index (expurgatoire); **to put a book on the I.,** mettre un livre à l'Index. **6.** (*pl.* **indices**) (*a*) *Mth:* exposant *m*; caractéristique *f* (des logarithmes); (*b*) coefficient *m*, indice; *Opt:* **i. of refraction, refractive i.,** indice de réfraction; *Anthr:* **cranial i.,** indice céphalique; *Anat:* **dental i.,** indice dentaire; *Ling:* **word-frequency i.,** coefficient d'usage d'un mot; (*c*) *Com: Pol.Ec:* **i. number,** chiffre indicateur; indice; **weighted i., unweighted i.,** indice pondéré, non pondéré; **consumer's price i.,** indice des prix à la consommation; **cost of living i.,** indice du coût de la vie; **retail price i., wholesale price i.,** indice des prix de détail, des prix de gros; **overall i.,** indice général; **linked, tied, to the i.,** indexé. **7.** *Cmptr:* **modulation i.,** indice de modulation; **quality i.,** indice de qualité; **i. word,** mot *m* d'index; **i. register,** registre *m* d'index; **i. point,** point *m* machine.

index[2], *v.tr.* **1.** (*a*) **to i. a book,** faire, dresser, l'index d'un livre; indexer un livre; **to i. a bundle of papers,** répertorier une liasse; (*b*) répertorier, classer (un article). **2.** *R.C.Ch:* mettre (un livre) à l'Index.

indexed ['indekst], *a. Cmptr:* **i. address,** adresse indexée, variable; **i. sequential,** séquentiel indexé.

indexer ['indeksər], *s.* dresseur *m*, auteur *m*, de l'index (d'un livre).

indexing ['indeksiŋ], *s.* **1.** (*a*) indexage *m*, indexation *f* (d'un livre); (*b*) mise *f* (d'un nom, etc.) à l'index (d'un livre). **2.** *Mch.Tls:* **i. head,** diviseur *m.*

index-linked ['indeks'liŋkt], **index-tied** ['indeks'taid], *a.* (*of wages, etc.*) indexé.

India ['indjə]. **1.** *Pr.n. Geog:* l'Inde *f*; **Further I.,** l'Inde au delà du Gange, l'Inde transgangétique; *Hist:* **British I.,** l'Inde anglaise; **the East I. Company,** la Compagnie anglaise des Indes. **2.** *s. P:* marihuana *f,* marijuana *f,* chanvre indien.

Indiaman, *pl.* **-men** ['indjəmən], *s. Hist:* navire *m* qui faisait le service des Indes orientales.

Indian ['indiən]. **1.** (*a*) *a.* de l'Inde; des Indes; indien; **the I. Ocean,** l'océan Indien; **the I. Archipelago,** l'archipel Indonésien; l'Insulinde *f*; *Bot:* **I. strawberry,** duchesnea *f*; (*b*) *s.* (i) Indien, -ienne; (ii) Anglo-Indien, -ienne. **2.** (*a*) *a.* indien; des Indiens (d'Amérique); amérindien; (*b*) *s.* Indien, -ienne (d'Amérique); Amérindien, -ienne; **Red Indians, copper Indians,** Peaux-Rouges; *Can:* **the I. list,** le registre officiel des Indiens dans les réserves; *F:* **he's on the I. list,** il lui est interdit (par la loi) d'acheter des boissons alcooliques; *F:* **I. gift,** cadeau *m* que le donneur demande qu'on lui rende; cadeau-hameçon *m, pl.* cadeaux-hameçons; **it's a case of all chiefs and no Indians,** c'est que chacun est le chef et personne l'ouvrier.

indianaite [indi'ænəait], *s. Miner:* indianaïte *f.*

Indianian [indi'æniən], *a. & s.* (originaire *mf,* habitant, -ante) de l'Indiana.

Indianism ['indiənizm], *s.* indianisme *m.*

Indianist ['indiənist], *s.* indianiste *mf.*

indianite ['indiənait], *s. Miner:* indianite *f.*

Indianization ['indiənai'zeiʃ(ə)n], *s.* indianisation *f.*

Indianize ['indiənaiz], *v.tr.* indianiser.

Indianologist [indiə'nɔlədʒist], *s.* indianiste *m.*

india rubber, indiarubber ['indiə'rʌbər], *s.* (*a*) **i. (eraser),** gomme *f* à effacer; (*b*) caoutchouc *m*; gomme élastique; **i. ball,** balle *f* en caoutchouc; balle élastique; **i. band,** (i) élastique *m*; (ii) courroie *f* en caoutchouc.

Indic[1] ['indik], *a. Ling:* (groupe, etc.) indo-aryen, *pl.* indo-aryens, -ennes.

indic[2], *a. Ch:* indique.

indican ['indikən], *s. Ch:* indican *m.*

indican(a)emia [indikə'ni:miə], *s. Med:* indicanémie *f.*

indicant ['indikənt]. **1.** *a.* indicateur, -trice. **2.** *s.* signe indicateur.

indicanuria [indikə'nju:riə], *s. Med:* indicanurie *f.*

indicate ['indikeit], *v.tr.* **1.** (*a*) indiquer, montrer; **to i. sth. with the hand, by gesture,** indiquer qch. de la main, d'un geste; désigner, montrer, qch. du doigt; **the thermometer indicates a rise in temperature,** le thermomètre accuse une élévation de température; *Av:* **indicated airspeed,** vitesse indiquée; **the exits must be clearly indicated by illuminated lettering,** la signalisation lumineuse des sorties est obligatoire; (*b*) **at the time indicated,** à l'heure dite, indiquée; **the above-indicated cheques,** les chèques sus-mentionnés, indiqués ci-dessus; (*c*) *Med:* **case in which a certain treatment is indicated,** cas pour lequel un certain traitement est indiqué, qui réclame un certain traitement; cas justiciable d'un certain traitement; **strong measures were clearly indicated,** il était évident que la situation appelait, demandait, des mesures rigoureuses. **2.** (*a*) indiquer, dénoter, témoigner, être un indice de (qch.); **nothing indicated that winter was at hand,** rien n'indiquait que l'hiver approchait; **face that indicates energy,** visage qui annonce, qui dénote, l'énergie; (*b*) faire savoir (qch.) en termes brefs.

indication [indi'keiʃ(ə)n], *s.* **1.** indication *f* (**of sth. to s.o.,** de qch. à qn). **2.** (*a*) indice *m*, signe *m*; **countless indications told me that it would be a failure,** à mille indices je me suis rendu compte que cela ne réussirait pas; **meeting which, according to all indications, would be a stormy one,** assemblée que tout annonçait devoir être orageuse; **not the least i. of shame,** aucune apparence de honte; **there is every i. of his speaking the truth,** il y a toute apparence qu'il dit vrai; **there are many indications that his mind is failing,** tout porte à croire qu'il n'a plus toute sa raison; **the sudden fall of the barometer is an i. of a storm,** la baisse subite du baromètre est une annonce de tempête; **i. of good weather,** marque *f* du beau temps; **he gave early indications of his talent,** il laissa de bonne heure entrevoir son talent; (*b*) **to give clear i. of one's intentions,** faire connaître clairement ses intentions; (*c*) *Min:* indice révélateur de la présence de l'or.

indicative [in'dikətiv]. **1.** *a. & s. Gram:* **i. (mood),** (mode) indicatif *m*; **in the i.,** au mode indicatif; à l'indicatif. **2.** *a.* (*also* ['indikeitiv]) indicatif (**of,** de); **smile i. of satisfaction,** sourire qui dénote la satisfaction; **facts i. of sth.,** faits indicateurs de qch.; *Cmptr:* **i. information,** indicatif(s).

indicator ['indikeitər], *s.* **1.** (*pers.*) indicateur, -trice (**of,** de). **2.** (*a*) table *f* d'orientation (au sommet d'une montagne, etc.); (*b*) **i. (panel),** tableau indicateur; *Rail:* **train i.,** tableau indicateur du service des quais, **3.** (*a*) index *m*, aiguille *f* (de baromètre, etc.); **visual i.,** indicateur lumineux; *Av:* affichage *m*; *Aut: A:* **wing i.,** témoin *m*, repère *m*, d'aile; **direction i.,** indicateur, flèche *f,* de direction; (*flashing*) clignotant *m*; (*b*) *Mec.E: Mch: etc:* indicateur; **deflection i.,** indicateur de flexion; **strain i.,** indicateur de contrainte; **pressure i., vacuum i.,** indicateur de pression, de vide; **revolution i.,** compteur *m* de tours, tachymètre *m*; **i. dial, dial i.,** cadran indicateur; **i. card, diagram,** diagramme *m*, tracé *m*, d'indicateur; **to take an i. card,** relever un tracé d'indicateur; **i. cylinder,** cylindre *m* porte-papier (d'indicateur); *Aut:* **distance i.,** compteur kilométrique; odomètre *m*; (*c*) *Nau:* **draught i.,** indicateur de tirant d'eau; **rudder-angle i.,** indicateur d'angle de barre; **trim i.,** indicateur d'assiette; (*d*) *Av:* **airspeed i.,** indicateur de vitesse relative; badin *m*; **bank i.,** indicateur de pente latérale; **bank-and-turn i.,** indicateur de pente latérale et de virage; contrôleur *m* de vol; **climb i.,** variomètre *m*; **direction i.,** indicateur (gyroscopique) de direction; **directional i.,** indicateur (gyroscopique) de cap; **drift i.,** indicateur de dérive, dérivomètre *m*; **flight i.,** contrôleur de vol; **fore-and-aft level i., pitch (altitude) i.,** indicateur de pente longitudinale, indicateur de piqué; **stall warning i.,** avertisseur *m* de décrochage; (*e*) *El.E:* **power-on i., power-off i.,** indicateur de mise en circuit, de mise hors circuit; **i. switch,** culbuteur *m*; **leakage i.,** indicateur des pertes; détecteur *m* de fuites, de défaut d'isolement; (*f*) *Tp: etc:* **i. board,** tableau indicateur; **i. drop,** (volet) annonciateur *m*, (volet) indicateur; **drop i. board,** tableau indicateur à volets (de sonnerie de téléphone, etc.); **ring-off i.,** indicateur, annonciateur, de fin de conversation; **chargeable-time i.,** indicateur de durée de conversation, de durée d'occupation; (*g*) *Rad:* **plan position i.,** indicateur panoramique; *Elcs: W.Tel:* **tuning i.,** indicateur d'accord; (*h*) *Atom.Ph:* **radiation i.,** indicateur, signaleur *m*, de rayonnement; **radioactive i.,** indicateur radioactif; **alpha, beta-gamma, contamination i.,** signaleur de contamination alpha, bêta-gamma; **failed-sheath i.,** indicateur, signaleur, de rupture de gaine. **4.** (*a*) *Ch:* indicateur chimique; **liquid i.,** index liquide; (*b*) *Min:* indice révélateur de la présence de l'or. **5.** *Com:* **retail-price i., wholesale-price i.,** indice *m* des prix de détail, des prix de gros; **all-items i.,** indice général des cours; *Pol.Ec:* **economic indicators,** indicateurs d'alerte, *F:* clignotants. **6.** *Orn:* indicateur; **the Indicators,** les indicateurs, les indicatoridés *m.*

Indicatoridae [indikə'tɔ:ridi:], *s.pl. Orn:* indicatoridés *m*; indicateurs *m.*

indicatory [in'dikətəri], *a.* **1.** indicateur, -trice (**of,** de); qui indique. **2.** (symptôme) indicatif (**of,** de).

indicatrix ['indikeitriks], *s. Mth:* indicatrice *f.*

indicia [in'diʃiə], *s.pl.* indices *m,* signes *m* (d'une révolte qui couve, etc.).

indicial [in'diʃ(ə)l], *a.* indiciaire.

indicolite [in'dikəlait], *s. Miner:* indicolite *f*; saphir *m* du Brésil.

indict [in'dait], *v.tr. Jur:* accuser, inculper (qn) (**for,** de); mettre (qn) en accusation; traduire, poursuivre, (qn) en justice (**for,** pour); **indicted for complicity, indicted on a charge of complicity,** inculpé, accusé, de complicité; **he was indicted as a traitor,** il fut traduit en justice, mis en accusation, comme traître; il fut inculpé de trahison; **to i. a statement as false,** s'inscrire en faux contre un témoignage.

indictable [in'daitəbl], *a. Jur:* **1.** (personne *f*) attaquable, traduisible, en justice; inculpable, passible de poursuites. **2.** (action) qui tombe sous le coup de la loi; **i. offence,** délit *m.*

indicter [in'daitər], *s.* accusateur, -trice; dénonciateur, -trice; *Jur:* partie civile.

indiction [in'dikʃ(ə)n], *s. Rom. & Ecc.Hist: etc:* indiction *f*; (**era, cycle, of**) **i.,** indiction; **first i., seventh i.,** indiction première, septième.

indictment [in'daitmənt], *s. Jur:* **1.** accusation *f,* incrimination *f,* inculpation *f*; (*by public prosecutor*) réquisitoire *m*; plaidoyer réquisitorial; **i. for theft,** inculpation de vol; **to prefer, bring in, lay, an i. against s.o.,** intenter une action au criminel contre qn; *Hist: & NAm:* (*of grand jury*) **to find an i.,** prononcer la mise en accusation; rendre une ordonnance de renvoi. **2.** (*a*) acte *m* d'accusation (au criminel); **to draw up an i.,** rédiger un acte d'accusation; (*b*) *Hist: & NAm:* **bill of i.,** acte d'accusation et résumé *m* de l'instruction (renvoyés à la Chambre des mises en accusation).

Indies (the) [ði'indiz]. *Pr.n.pl. Geog:* les Indes *f*; **the East I.,** l'Insulinde *f*; *A:* les Indes (orientales); les Grandes Indes; l'Inde; **the West I.,** les Antilles *f,* les Indes occidentales; *A:* **the Dutch East I.,** les Indes Néerlandaises.

indifference [in'dif(ə)rəns], *s.* **1.** *A:* impartialité *f.* **2.** indifférence *f,* manque *m* d'intérêt, apathie *f* (**to,**

towards, sth., s.o., pour qch., à l'égard de qn); **i. to wealth,** détachement *m* des richesses; **it's a matter of i. to me whether I do that or something else,** il m'est indifférent de faire cela ou autre chose; **it's a matter of perfect i. to me,** cela m'est parfaitement indifférent; cela ne me fait ni chaud ni froid; **to show complete i. to s.o.'s fate,** se montrer complètement indifférent au sort de qn. **3.** médiocrité *f* (de talent, etc.). **4.** *Ch: Ph:* indifférence ((i) d'un corps; (ii) d'un sel). **5.** *Pol.Ec:* **i. curve,** courbe *f* d'indifférence; **i. map,** carte *f*, diagramme *m*, d'indifférence.

indifferent [in'dif(ə)rənt], *a.* **1.** *A:* (juge) impartial; **with an i. eye,** d'un œil impartial, indifférent. **2.** indifférent (to, à); **matter that is i. to him,** sujet qui lui est indifférent; **I am, feel, i. about him,** il m'est indifférent; je ne sens ni chaud ni froid pour lui; **he is, feels, i. about me,** je lui suis indifférent; **i. to other people's troubles,** indifférent aux maux d'autrui; **his praise is i. to me,** *F:* ses éloges ne me font ni chaud ni froid; **he is i. to everything,** tout lui est indifférent, égal; **all that leaves me absolutely i.,** tout cela me laisse dans une profonde indifférence. **3.** médiocre, passable; **very i. quality,** qualité *f* quelconque, médiocre; **some good, some bad, some i.,** les uns bons, d'autres mauvais, d'autres ni bons ni mauvais; **to be an i. painter,** peindre pauvrement. **4.** *O:* **to talk about i. topics,** causer de choses indifférentes, de choses sans importance, *F:* de la pluie et du beau temps. **5.** *Ch: Ph:* (sel, etc.) indifférent, neutre; *Magn:* **i. line of a magnet,** ligne *f* neutre d'un aimant.

indifferentism [in'dif(ə)rəntizm], *s. Rel.H: Pol:* indifférentisme *m*.

indifferentist [in'dif(ə)rəntist], *s. Rel.H: Pol:* indifférentiste *mf*; gallioniste *m*.

indifferently [in'dif(ə)rəntli], *adv.* **1.** *A:* impartialement. **2.** indifféremment, avec indifférence, avec froideur. **3.** médiocrement, passablement, ni bien ni mal; **to speak French i. well,** parler plutôt mal le français; **very i. provided with sth.,** assez mal pourvu de qch.; **food i. cooked,** nourriture préparée d'une façon quelconque; **to paint i.,** peindre pauvrement.

indigence ['indidʒ(ə)ns], **indigency** ['indidʒ(ə)nsi], *s.* indigence *f*, pauvreté *f*; *F:* la misère.

indigene ['indidʒi:n], *s.* indigène *mf*.

indigenous [in'didʒinəs], *a.* (*of plant, product, etc.*) indigène (to, à); du pays.

indigent ['indidʒ(ə)nt], *a.* indigent, pauvre; nécessiteux.

indigently ['indidʒ(ə)ntli], *adv.* dans l'indigence; misérablement.

indigested [indi'dʒestid], *a.* (*of knowledge, etc.*) indigeste, confus.

indigestibility [indidʒesti'biliti], *s.* indigestibilité *f*.

indigestible [indi'dʒestibl], *a.* indigeste; difficile à digérer.

indigestion [indi'dʒestʃ(ə)n], *s.* **1.** dyspepsie *f*; apepsie *f*; mauvaise digestion; **to have an attack of i.,** avoir une indigestion; **touch of i.,** léger embarras gastrique. **2.** état indigéré (des aliments); défaut *m* d'assimilation.

indigitamenta [indidʒitə'mentə], *s.pl. Rom.Ant:* indigitamenta *m*.

indign [in'dain], *a. Lit:* indigne, honteux.

indignant [in'dignənt], *a.* (air) indigné; (cri) d'indignation; **to be, feel, i. at sth.,** être indigné, s'indigner, de qch.; **to be highly i. with s.o.,** être vivement indigné, éprouver une vive indignation, contre qn; **we are i. to hear that we were not consulted,** cela nous indigne, nous sommes indignés, d'apprendre que nous n'avons pas été consultés; **he was i. that everything went so slowly,** il s'indignait de ce que tout allait si lentement; **to make s.o. i.,** indigner qn.

indignantly [in'dignəntli], *adv.* avec indignation; d'un ton d'indignation, d'un ton indigné; d'un air indigné.

indignation [indig'neiʃ(ə)n], *s.* indignation *f*; **i. at sth.,** indignation devant qch., excitée, inspirée, par qch.; **to feel strong i. against, with, s.o.,** éprouver une vive indignation contre qn; **righteous i.,** une juste indignation; **burst of i. against sth.,** soulèvement *m* contre qch.; **to the i. of all decent people,** au grand scandale de tous les gens de bien; **i. meeting,** meeting *m*, réunion *f*, de protestation.

indignity [in'digniti], *s.* **1.** indignité *f*; **to treat s.o. with i.,** traiter qn d'une manière indigne; faire affront à qn; outrager qn; **the i. of begging,** la honte de mendier; **the i. of a refusal,** l'affront *m* d'un refus. **2. to suffer indignities,** souffrir des affronts.

indigo, *pl.* -o(e)s ['indigou, -ouz], *s.* **1.** *Dy: Com:* indigo *m*; inde *m*; **i. blue,** (i) (*colour*) (bleu) indigo *m inv*; (ii) *Dy:* indigo bleu; **i. brown,** brun *m* d'indigo; **i. purple,** phénicine *f*; **i. red,** indigo rouge; indirubine *f*; **i. white,** indigo blanc; blanc *m* d'indigo; **i. factory,** indigoterie *f*; **i. manufacturer,** indigotier *m*; **i. worker,** indigotier. **2.** *Bot:* **i. (plant),** indigotier; anil *m*; **i. plantation,** indigoterie. **3.** *Orn:* **i. bird, i. bunting,** passerine bleue. **4.** *Rept:* **i. snake,** serpent noir des États-Unis.

indigofera [indi'gɔfərə], *s. Bot:* indigofera *m*; indigotier *m*.

indigoid ['indigɔid], *a. Ch:* indigoïde.

indigolite [in'digəlait], *s. Miner:* indicolite *f*.

indigotin [in'digətin, 'ind-], *s. Ch:* indigotine *f*.

indirect [indi'rekt], *a.* **1.** (*of influence, consequence, result, route, etc.*) indirect; *Gram:* **i. speech,** discours indirect; **i. object,** complément indirect; *Jur:* **i. evidence,** témoignage indirect; *Com: Ind:* **i. charges, i. expenses,** frais généraux, dépenses indirectes; **i. selling,** vente indirecte; *Artil: etc:* **i. fire,** tir indirect; *Mec.E:* **i. control,** commande indirecte; **i.-drive box,** boîte *f* de vitesses à commande indirecte; *Ph:* **i. wave,** onde indirecte. **2.** (moyen, etc.) détourné, oblique.

indirection [indi'rekʃ(ə)n], *s.* **1. by i.,** indirectement, par des moyens détournés. **2.** tromperie *f*, déloyauté *f*. **3.** manque *m* de but, d'objectif. **4.** *Cmptr:* adressage indirect.

indirectly [indi'rektli], *adv.* indirectement; par des voies détournées; **to learn sth. i.,** apprendre qch. indirectement, par ricochet.

indirectness [indi'rektnis], *s.* manque *m* de droiture, d'honnêteté; déloyauté *f*.

indirubin(e) [indi'ru:bin], *s. Ch:* indirubine *f*.

indiscernibility [indisə:nə'biliti], *s.* indiscernabilité *f*.

indiscernible [indi'sə:nəbl]. **1.** *a.* (*a*) indiscernable; (*b*) imperceptible. **2.** *s. Phil:* **principle of (identity of) indiscernibles,** principe *m* (de l'identité) des indiscernables.

indisciplinable [in'disiplinəbl], *a.* indisciplinable, indocile.

indiscipline [in'disiplin], *s.* indiscipline *f*.

indiscoverable [indis'kʌv(ə)rəbl], *a.* indécouvrable, introuvable.

indiscreet [indis'kri:t], *a.* **1.** indiscret, -ète; **he doesn't realize that he's being i.,** il ne se rend pas compte qu'il est indiscret; **would it be i. to ask you what you are going to do?** est-il indiscret de vous demander, peut-on vous demander sans indiscrétion, ce que vous comptez faire? **2.** peu judicieux; imprudent; **i. step,** démarche inconsidérée.

indiscreetly [indis'kri:tli], *adv.* **1.** indiscrètement, sans discrétion. **2.** imprudemment; sans considération.

indiscreetness [indis'kri:tnis], *s.* indiscrétion *f*.

indiscrete [indis'kri:t], *a.* sans parties; indivisé; d'une seule pièce.

indiscretion [indis'kreʃ(ə)n], *s.* **1.** (*a*) manque *m* de discrétion; (*b*) indiscrétion *f*, **calculated i.,** révélation délibérée d'un secret officiel sous couleur d'une étourderie; indiscrétion calculée. **2.** (*a*) action inconsidérée; imprudence *f*; (*b*) écart *m* de conduite; faux pas; **to be guilty of an i.,** (i) commettre une inconséquence; (ii) se compromettre (avec qn); commettre une imprudence; **she's been guilty of some indiscretions,** elle s'est rendue coupable de quelques indiscrétions; **indiscretions of youth,** péchés *m*, erreurs *f*, de jeunesse; **he committed a certain number of indiscretions in his youth,** il a fait quelques bêtises quand il était jeune; *Hum:* **dietary indiscretions,** écarts *m* de régime, excès *m* de table.

indiscriminable [indis'kriminəbl], *a.* indiscernable (from, de).

indiscriminate [indis'kriminət], *a.* (charité, vengeance, admirateur) aveugle, qui ne fait pas de distinction; **i. reading,** lectures de toutes sortes faites sans discernement; **i. sexual indulgence,** plaisirs sexuels intempérés; **i. slaughter,** tuerie générale; **i. blows,** coups frappés à tort et à travers, au hasard.

indiscriminately [indis'kriminətli], *adv.* (louer, censurer, frapper) sans faire de distinction; à tort et à travers, au hasard; (admirer) aveuglément.

indiscriminating [indis'krimineitiŋ], *a.* (critique *m*) sans discernement; (bienfaisance) aveugle.

indiscrimination [indiskrimi'neiʃ(ə)n], *s.* manque *m* de discernement.

indispensability [indispensə'biliti], **indispensableness** [indis'pensəb(ə)lnis], *s.* indispensabilité *f*.

indispensable [indis'pensəbl], *a.* **1.** (loi, devoir, engagement) obligatoire, qu'on ne peut négliger. **2.** indispensable; de première nécessité (to s.o., à qn; **for sth.,** pour, à, qch.; **for doing sth.,** pour faire qch.); **i. articles,** objets *m* de première, de toute, nécessité; **to make oneself i. to s.o.,** se rendre indispensable, nécessaire, à qn; **no one is i.,** personne n'est indispensable; pour un moine l'abbaye ne chôme pas.

indispose [indis'pouz], *v.tr.* **1. to i. s.o. towards s.o.,** indisposer, prévenir, qn contre qn; rendre qn défavorable à qn; **to i. s.o. to do sth.,** rendre qn peu disposé à faire qch.; **to i. s.o. from a course of action,** éloigner, détourner, qn d'une ligne de conduite. **2. to i. s.o. for sth., for doing sth.,** rendre qn peu propre à qch.; rendre qn incapable, hors d'état, de faire qch.; rendre qn inapte à faire qch. **3.** *O:* rendre (qn) malade; indisposer (qn).

indisposed [indis'pouzd], *a.* **1.** peu enclin, peu disposé (to do sth., à faire qch.). **2. to be, feel, i.,** être indisposé, souffrant; se sentir mal en train; **to become i.,** avoir un malaise.

indisposition [indispə'ziʃ(ə)n], *s.* **1.** indisposition *f* (to, towards, s.o., à l'égard de qn); aversion *f* (envers, pour, qn; pour qch.). **2.** peu de disposition, peu d'inclination (to do sth., à faire qch.). **3.** indisposition, malaise *m*.

indisputability ['indispju:tə'biliti], **indisputableness** [indis'pju:təb(ə)lnis], *s.* indisputabilité *f*, incontestabilité *f*, indiscutabilité *f* (d'un fait).

indisputable [indis'pju:təbl], *a.* incontestable, indiscutable, indisputable; hors de controverse; incontroversable; *Log: Phil:* (jugement, etc.) apodictique.

indisputably [indis'pju:təbli], *adv.* indiscutablement, incontestablement, indisputablement; sans discussion possible; sans conteste.

indissociable [indi'souʃiəbl], *a.* indissociable (**from,** de).

indissolubility ['indisɔlju'biliti], *s.* **1.** indissolubilité *f* (d'une union). **2.** *A:* insolubilité *f* (d'un sel).

indissoluble [indi'sɔljubl], *a.* **1.** (union, amitié) indissoluble. **2.** *A:* (sel, etc.) insoluble, indissoluble.

indissolubly [indi'sɔlubli], *adv.* indissolublement.

indistinct [indis'tiŋ(k)t], *a.* (objet, bruit, etc.) indistinct, peu distinct; (bruit) confus; (souvenir) vague; **the haze made the outlines i.,** la brume estompait les contours.

indistinctive [indis'tiŋ(k)tiv], *a.* sans individualité; qui manque de caractère; sans particularité.

indistinctly [indis'tiŋ(k)tli], *adv.* (voir, parler) indistinctement; (sentir) vaguement, confusément; **to speak i.,** manger ses mots.

indistinctness [indis'tiŋ(k)tnis], *s.* indistinction *f*, vague *m*; manque *m* de netteté (d'un objet, d'un son, d'une pensée).

indistinguishable [indis'tiŋgwiʃəbl], *a.* **1.** indistinguible, indiscernable, que l'on ne peut distinguer (**from,** de); **they are i.,** ils ne font qu'un. **2.** (bruit, sensation) insaisissable; **i. to the naked eye,** imperceptible à l'œil nu.

indite [in'dait], *v.tr. A:* composer (un poème); rédiger (une lettre, une dépêche).

inditement [in'daitmənt], *s. A:* composition *f* (d'un poème); rédaction *f* (d'une lettre, etc.).

inditer [in'daitər], *s. Hum: A:* auteur *m* , rédacteur *m* (d'une lettre); **great i. of letters,** grand écrivain de lettres.

inditing [in'daitiŋ], *s. A:* = INDITEMENT.

indium ['indiəm], *s. Ch:* indium *m*.

indivertible [indi'və:tibl], *a.* (personne) qu'on ne saurait détourner (**from,** de); (opinion) qu'on ne saurait changer.

individual [indi'vidjuəl]. **1.** *a.* (*a*) individuel, particulier; **each child has his i. desk,** chaque enfant a son pupitre individuel, particulier; **i. tables,** tables individuelles; **his pupils get i. attention,** il s'occupe de ses élèves individuellement; **i. sounds,** sons isolés; *Mec.E:* **i. drive,** commande séparée; (*b*) qui se distingue des autres; **he's so i. in his views,** il a des idées si originales. **2.** *s.* (*a*) individu *m*; *F:* **shady i.,** individu louche; **a private i.,** un simple particulier; **to act merely as a private i.,** agir en tant que particulier, en (qualité de) simple particulier; *F:* **we have had a letter from some i.,** (un) je ne sais qui nous a écrit; (*b*) **the i. and the collective,** l'individu et le collectif.

individualism [indi'vidjuəlizm], *s. Pol: etc:* individualisme *m*.

individualist [indi'vidjuəlist], *s. Pol: etc:* individualiste *mf*.

individualistic [individjuə'listik], *a.* individualiste.

individualistically [individjuə'listik(ə)li], *adv.* du point de vue individualiste.

individuality [individju'æliti], *s.* **1.** individualité *f*; **he has never shown any i.,** il n'a jamais fait preuve de personnalité; **to assume, take on, an i.,** s'individualiser.

individualization [individjuəlai'zeiʃ(ə)n], *s.* individualisation *f*.

individualize [indi'vidjuəlaiz], **individuate** [indi'vidjueit], *v.tr.* individualiser; considérer (des choses) individuellement.

individually [indi'vidjuəli], *adv.* **1.** individuellement. **2.** personnellement; **I am speaking i.,** je ne parle que pour moi.

individuation [individju'eiʃ(ə)n], *s. Phil:* individuation *f*.

indivisibility [indivizi'biliti], *s.* indivisibilité *f*.

indivisible [indi'vizibl]. **1.** *a.* indivisible, insécable. **2.** *s. Phil: Mth:* **indivisibles,** insécables *m.*
indivisibly [indi'vizibli], *adv.* indivisiblement.
indivisum [indi'vaisəm], *s. Jur:* bien(s) indivis.
Indo- ['indou], *comb. fm. Ethn: Geog:* Indo-.
Indo-Afghan ['indou'æfgæn]. *Ethn:* **1.** *a.* indo-afghan. **2.** *s.* Indo-Afghan, -ane.
Indo-Aryan ['indou'ɛəriən]. **1.** *Ethn:* (*a*) *a.* indo-aryen; (*b*) *s.* Indo-Aryen, -enne. **2.** *s. Ling:* indo-aryen *m.*
Indochina ['indou'tʃainə]. *Pr.n. Geog:* Indochine *f.*
Indochinese ['indoutʃai'ni:z]. *Geog:* **1.** *a.* indochinois. **2.** *s.* Indochinois, -oise.
indocile [in'dousail], *a.* indocile.
indocility [indou'siliti], *s.* indocilité *f.*
indoctrinate [in'dɔktrineit], *v.tr.* endoctriner, instruire; to **i. s.o. with an idea,** inculquer une idée à qn.
indoctrination [indɔktri'neiʃ(ə)n], *s.* endoctrinement *m.*
indoctrinator [in'dɔktrineitər], *s.* endoctrineur, -euse.
Indo-European ['indoujuərə'pi:ən]. **1.** *Ling: Ethn:* (*a*) *a.* indo-européen; (*b*) *s.* Indo-Européen, -enne. **2.** *s. Ling:* indo-européen *m.*
Indo-Gangetic ['indougæn'dʒetik], *a. Geog:* indo-gangétique, *pl.* indo-gangétiques.
indogen ['indoudʒən], *s. Ch:* indogène *m.*
indogenid(e) [in'dɔdʒənid, -aid], *s. Ch:* indogénide *m.*
Indo-Germanic ['indoudʒə:'mænik], *a. Ling:* indo-germanique, *pl.* indo-germaniques.
Indo-Iranian ['indoui'reiniən]. *Ling:* **1.** *a.* indo-iranien. **2.** *s.* indo-iranien *m.*
indol ['indɔl], **indole** ['indoul], *s. Ch:* indol *m.*
indolence ['indələns], *s.* **1.** indolence *f*, paresse *f*; mollesse *f*; nonchalance *f.* **2.** *Med:* indolence, insensibilité *f* (d'une tumeur, etc.).
indolent ['indələnt], *a.* **1.** indolent, paresseux; fainéant, nonchalant. **2.** *Med:* (*of tumour, etc.*) indolore, indolent, insensible, sans douleur.
indolently ['indələntli], *adv.* indolemment, paresseusement.
indolin(e) ['indəlin, -i:n], *s. Ch:* indoline *f.*
indomitable ['indəmitəbl], *a.* indomptable; (courage, etc.) invincible.
indomitably [in'dəmitəbli], *a.* indomptablement; invinciblement.
indone ['indoun], *s. Ch:* indone *f*, indénone *f.*
Indonesia [indou'ni:ziə, -ʒə]. *Pr.n. Geog:* Indonésie *f.*
Indonesian [indou'ni:ziən, -ʒ(ə)n]. **1.** *Geog:* (*a*) *a.* indonésien; (*b*) *s.* Indonésien, -ienne. **2.** *s. Ling:* indonésien *m.*
indoor ['indɔ:r], *a.* (*a*) (robe, vie, travail) d'intérieur; (décoration) d'appartement; **i. photography,** photographie *f* en appartement; **i. games,** (i) jeux *m* de salle; (ii) jeux de salon, de société; *Sp:* **an i. game,** une partie en salle; **i. swimming pool,** piscine couverte; **i. plant,** plante *f* d'appartement; **i. staff,** gens *mpl* de maison; **i. sanitation,** w.c. dans la maison; (*b*) *Hist:* **i. relief,** assistance *f* des pauvres hospitalisés; secours *m* dans les maisons de charité; **the i. poor,** les pauvres hospitalisés; les pensionnaires *mf* d'un hospice.
indoors [in'dɔ:z], *adv.* à la maison; **i. and out,** dans la maison et dehors; **to go i.,** (r)entrer (dans la maison); **to stay i.,** garder la chambre; rester à la maison; **to live too much i.,** vivre trop enfermé; **it happened i.,** cela a eu lieu dans la maison.
indophenin [indou'fi:nin], *s. Ch:* indophénine *f.*
indophenol [indou'fi:nɔl], *s. Ch:* indophénol *m.*
Indo-Portuguese ['indoupɔ:tju'gi:z]. *Ling:* **1.** *a.* indo-portugais, *pl.* indo-portugais(es). **2.** *s.* indo-portugais *m.*
indoxyl [in'dɔksil], *s. Ch:* indoxyle *m.*
indoxylic [indɔk'silik], *a. Ch:* indoxylique.
indoxylsulphuric [in'dɔksilsʌl'fjurik], *a. Ch:* (acide *m*) indoxyle-sulfurique, indoxylsulfurique.
indoxyluria [indɔksi'ljuriə], *s. Med:* indoxylurie *f.*
indraught, indraft ['indrɑ:ft], *s.* **1.** appel *m* d'air, entrée *f* d'air, venue *f* du vent (d'une machine soufflante). **2.** courant *m* remontant (d'eau).
indrawn ['indrɔ:n], *a.* (air) aspiré; **i. breath,** aspiration *f.*
indri ['indri:], *s. Z:* indri(s) *m.*
Indridae ['indridi:], *s.pl. Z:* indrisidés *m.*
Induan ['indjuən], *s. Geol:* trias inférieur; grès bigarré.
indubitable [in'dju:bitəbl], *a.* indubitable; hors de doute, incontestable.
indubitably [in'dju:bitəbli], *adv.* indubitablement; sans aucune doute; incontestablement, sans contredit.
induce [in'dju:s], *v.tr.* **1.** to **i. s.o. to do sth.,** induire, amener, déterminer, qn à faire qch.; **I have induced him to accompany us,** j'ai obtenu (de lui) qu'il vienne, qu'il viendrait, avec nous; **nothing will i. him to change his mind,** rien ne le fera changer d'idée; **he was induced to enter this career,** il se laissa entraîner dans cette carrière. **2.** (*a*) amener, produire, occasionner, causer, faire naître; **to i. sleep, perspiration,** provoquer le sommeil, la sueur; **medicine that induces perspiration,** médicament *m* qui sollicite la transpiration; **to i. the belief, the hope, that . . .,** porter à croire, faire espérer, que . . .; donner lieu de croire, d'espérer, que . . .; faire naître l'espoir que . . .; (*b*) *El: etc:* amorcer (un courant, des vibrations, etc.); induire (un courant). **3.** (*a*) **to i. a law from the ascertained results,** induire une loi des résultats acquis; (*b*) *O:* induire, conclure (**that . . .,** que . . .).
induced [in'dju:st], *a.* (*a*) **i. hypnosis,** hypnose provoquée; (*b*) **i. draught,** tirage induit par aspiration; tirage par induction; aérage négatif; (*c*) *El:* **i. current,** courant induit, d'induction; **i. charge,** charge *f* d'induit; **i. circuit,** induit *m*; **i. coil,** induit; **i. electromotive force,** force électromotrice induite; **i. voltage,** tension induite; **i. winding,** bobinage induit; (*d*) *Atom.Ph:* **i. radioactivity,** (i) radioactivité artificielle; (ii) radioactivité induite; **i. fission,** fission provoquée; **i. nuclear reaction,** réaction nucléaire artificielle.
inducement [in'dju:smənt], *s.* **1.** (*a*) motif *m*, mobile *m*, raison *f*, cause *f*, qui décide, pousse, encourage, qn à faire qch.; **i. to sleep,** provocation *f* au sommeil; **to hold out inducements to s.o. to do sth.,** encourager qn à faire qch. par des offres attrayantes, avantageuses; **the inducements of a business career,** les attraits *m* d'une carrière dans le commerce; **the inducements of a large town,** (i) les attraits, (ii) les tentations *f*, d'une grande ville; (*b*) *Jur:* incitation *f* (to, à). **2.** *Jur:* motif (d'un acte judiciaire); cause (d'un contrat).
inducer [in'dju:sər], *s.* **1.** tentateur, -trice; provocateur, -trice. **2.** *Tchn:* dispositif *m* d'admission d'air.
inducible [in'dju:sibl], *a. Biol:* inductible.
inducing [in'dju:siŋ], *a. El:* (*of wire, current, etc.*) inducteur, -trice.
induct [in'dʌkt], *v.tr.* **1.** (*a*) *Ecc:* **to i. a clergyman to a living,** mettre un ecclésiastique en possession d'un bénéfice; installer un ecclésiastique dans sa paroisse; (*b*) installer (un fonctionnaire) dans sa charge; (*c*) *A:* conduire (**s.o. to his seat,** qn à son siège); installer (qn dans un fauteuil, etc.). **2.** initier (**s.o. to sth.,** qn à qch.). **3.** *U.S:* incorporer (des conscrits dans l'armée).
inductance [in'dʌktəns], *s. El:* **1.** inductance *f*; **distributed i., lumped i.,** inductance répartie, concentrée; **mutual i.,** inductance mutuelle; **i. bridge,** pont *m* d'induction; **i. coupling,** couplage inductif; **i. feedback,** réaction inductive; **i. load,** charge inductive. **2. i. (coil),** (bobine *f* de) self(-induction) *f*; (bobine d')inductance; **iron-core i.,** inductance à noyau de fer; **air-core i.,** inductance sans fer; *W.Tel:* **tuning i., variable i.,** inductance de syntonisation; self de réglage, d'accord.
inductee [indʌk'ti:], *s.m. U.S:* (conscrit) incorporé (dans l'armée).
inductile [in'dʌktail], *a. Metall:* inductile.
inductility [indʌk'tiliti], *s. Metall:* inductilité *f.*
inducting [in'dʌktiŋ], *s.* **1.** installation *f* (to, dans). **2.** initiation *f* (to, à).
induction [in'dʌkʃ(ə)n], *s.* **1.** installation *f* (d'un ecclésiastique, d'un fonctionnaire). **2. i. of facts,** énumération *f* des faits, mise *f* en avant des faits (pour prouver qch.); apport *m* de preuves. **3.** *Log: Mth:* induction *f*; **philosophical i.,** induction baconienne; **to reason, prove a theorem, by i.,** raisonner, prouver un théorème, par induction. **4.** *El:* induction; **electric, magnetic, electromagnetic, i.,** induction électrique, magnétique, électromagnétique; **mutual i.,** induction mutuelle; **static i.,** induction statique; **nuclear i.,** induction nucléaire; **i. coil,** bobine *f* d'induction, bobine de self; **i. field,** champ *m* d'induction; **i. machine,** machine *f* à induction, machine asynchrone; **i. motor,** moteur *m* à induction; **squirrel-cage i. motor,** moteur à induction à cage d'écureuil; **wound-rotor i. motor,** moteur à induction à rotor bobiné; **i. regulator,** régulateur *m* d'induction; survolteur *m* d'induction; **i. relay,** relai inductif; *Metall:* **i. heating,** chauffage *m* par induction; **i. furnace,** four *m* à induction; **i. welding,** soudage *m* par induction; *Atom.Ph:* **i. accelerator,** accélérateur *m* à induction; bétatron *m.* **5.** *Mch: I.C.E:* admission *f*, entrée *f* (de la vapeur, des gaz); aspiration *f* (des gaz); **i. manifold,** collecteur *m* d'admission; **i. passage,** conduit *m* d'admission; **i. pipe,** tuyau *m*, conduit, d'admission; **i. port,** lumière *f*, orifice *m*, d'admission; **i. stroke,** course *f*, temps *m*, d'admission; course aspirante; **the i. (system),** l'admission; *Av:* **i. drag,** résistance, traînée, induite. **6.** *Med:* **i. of anaesthesia,** induction de l'anesthésie; **i. of sleep,** amorçage *m* du sommeil; endormissement *m.* **7.** *Biol:* **i. of embryonic cells,** induction embryonnaire. **8.** *U.S: Mil:* incorporation *f* (des conscrits); **i. center, i. station,** centre *m* d'incorporation.
inductive [in'dʌktiv], *a.* **1.** *A: & Lit:* **pleasures i. to sin,** plaisirs qui induisent au péché. **2.** *Log: Mth:* **the i. method,** la méthode inductive, baconienne; le mécanisme inductif; **i. reasoning,** raisonnement inductif, par induction. **3.** *El:* (*a*) inducteur, -trice; **i. current,** courant inducteur, circuit inducteur; **specific i. capacity,** pouvoir inducteur spécifique; **i. feed-back,** réaction inductrice; **i. power,** pouvoir inducteur; (*b*) inductif; **i. load,** charge inductive; **i. coupling,** accouplement inductif; (*c*) *Cmptr:* **i. potentiometer,** potentiomètre bobiné.
inductively [in'dʌktivli], *adv. Log: El:* par induction.
inductivity [indʌk'tiviti], *s. El:* inductivité *f.*
inductometer [indʌk'tɔmitər], *s. El:* inductomètre *m*, inductancemètre *m.*
inductor [in'dʌktər], *s.* **1.** *Ecc:* installateur *m* (d'un ecclésiastique) (**to his living,** dans sa charge). **2.** *El:* inducteur *m*, rotor *m* (d'une machine d'induction); **earth i.,** inducteur de terre; **i. coil,** bobine *f* d'induction; *I.C.E:* **magneto i.,** rotor de la magnéto; **i. alternator,** alternateur *m* à fer tournant. **3.** *Biol:* inducteur.
indulge [in'dʌldʒ]. **1.** *v.tr.* (*a*) avoir, montrer, trop d'indulgence pour (qn); gâter (qn); se prêter aux caprices de (qn); **to i. oneself,** s'écouter, ne rien se refuser; **she is used to indulging all her whims,** elle est habituée à se passer tous ses caprices; **to i. s.o. in sth.,** permettre qch. à qn; **to i. s.o. with sth.,** donner, accorder, qch. à qn; **to i. s.o.'s fancies,** flatter les caprices de qn; **used to being indulged by his mother,** (i) accoutumé aux gâteries de sa mère; (ii) accoutumé à ce que sa mère lui permette tout; **he is indulged in all his fancies,** on lui souffre toutes sortes de fantaisies, toutes ses fantaisies; (*b*) s'abandonner à (une fantaisie); se laisser aller à (un penchant); nourrir (un espoir); se livrer, donner libre cours, libre carrière, à (une passion); **to i. a vain hope, a fond hope,** caresser un vain espoir; se leurrer d'un espoir; (*c*) *R.C.Ch:* accorder une indulgence à (qn) (*d*) *Com:* accorder un délai à (une lettre de change, au payeur d'une lettre de change). **2.** *v.i.* **to i. in a practice,** s'adonner, se livrer, à une habitude; **to i. too freely in sth.,** faire abus de qch., abuser de qch.; **to i. in extravagance,** se livrer à des actes extravagants; **to i. in pleasures,** s'octroyer des plaisirs, s'adonner à des plaisirs; **to i. in sin,** s'adonner au péché; se complaire au mal; **to i. in strong language,** lâcher des jurons, des gros mots; **to i. in a nap,** faire un somme; **to i. in vain imaginings,** se repaître de chimères; **to i. in a new suit,** s'offrir, se payer, un complet neuf; **to i. in tobacco,** être adonné au tabac; **to i. in a cigar,** se permettre un cigare; **to i. in a glass of sherry,** s'offrir (la douceur d')un verre de xérès; **I rather think he indulges too much,** j'ai idée qu'il boit trop, qu'il se livre à la boisson, qu'il aime à lever le coude.
indulgence[1] [in'dʌldʒ(ə)ns], *s.* **1.** indulgence *f*, complaisance *f* (to, envers); longanimité *f*; **to grant s.o. every i.,** accorder à qn toutes les faveurs; tout passer à qn; **this was an i. to a guest,** c'était un traitement de faveur pour un invité; **a mother's i. for her children,** faiblesse *f* d'une mère pour ses enfants. **2.** (*a*) **i. in sin,** abandon *m* au péché; **sexual i.,** plaisirs sensuels; (*b*) **to allow oneself the i. of a glass of port,** s'offrir (la douceur d')un verre de porto. **3.** *R.C.Ch:* indulgence; **plenary i.,** indulgence plénière; *Hist:* **sale of indulgences,** vente *f* d'indulgences; **to attach an i. to a rosary,** indulgencier un chapelet. **4.** *Com:* délai de paiement (accordé au payeur d'une lettre de change).
indulgence[2], *v.tr. R.C.Ch:* indulgencier (un chapelet, etc.).
indulgent [in'dʌldʒ(ə)nt], *a.* indulgent; (*a*) **i. to s.o.,** indulgent envers, pour, qn; **i. towards the failings of others,** indulgent aux faiblesses d'autrui; (*b*) faible; **to be i. towards one's children's faults, to look on one's children with an i. eye,** se montrer faible envers ses enfants; **over-i. father,** père par trop indulgent; **i. husband,** (i) mari indulgent; (ii) *Pej:* mari complaisant.
indulgently [in'dʌldʒəntli], *adv.* (traiter, écouter) avec indulgence, avec douceur.
indulger [in'dʌldʒər], *s.* **1.** gâteur, -euse (d'un enfant). **2.** adonné, -ée (**in a vice,** à un vice).
indulin(e) ['indjulin, -lain], *s. Ch:* induline *f.*
indult [in'dʌlt], *s. R.C.Ch:* indult *m.*
indumentum, *pl.* **-s, -ta** [indju'mentəm, -z, -tə], *s. Nat.Hist:* poils *mpl*; pubescence *f*; *Orn:* plumes *fpl*, plumage *m.*
induplicate [in'dju:plikət], *a. Bot:* (*of petal*) indupliqué; **i. aestivation,** préfloraison induplicative.
indurate ['indju(ə)reit]. **1.** *v.tr.* (*a*) endurcir (le corps); *Geol:* indurer (l'argile, etc.); *A: & Lit:* endurcir (l'âme, le cœur); *Lit:* **they had been indurated to exposure,** ils avaient été endurcis aux rigueurs des saisons; (*b*) *Med:* indurer (les tissus). **2.** *v.i.* (*a*) se durcir, durcir; (*of the feelings, etc.*) s'endurcir; (*b*) *Med:* s'indurer; (*c*) (*of a*

custom) s'invétérer.
indurated ['indju(ə)reitid], *a.* **1.** (*of substance*) endurci; *Geol:* induré; *Fig:* (cœur) endurci. **2.** *Med:* (ulcère, etc.) induré. **3.** (usage) invétéré.
induration [indju(ə)'reiʃ(ə)n], *s.* **1.** durcissement *m*; *Geol:* induration *f*; *Fig:* endurcissement *m* (du cœur, de l'âme, de la conscience). **2.** *Med:* (*a*) induration (des tissus, d'un chancre); (*b*) tissu induré; induration.
indurative ['indju(ə)reitiv], *a.* **1.** qui tend à endurcir; endurcissant. **2.** *Med:* qui tend à indurer.
Indus, the [ði'indəs]. *Pr.n. Geog:* l'Indus *m*.
indusial [in'dju:ziəl], *a. Geol:* **i. limestone,** calcaire *m* à induses.
indusiate(d) [in'dju:zieit(id)], *a. Bot:* indusié.
indusium, *pl.* **-ia** [in'dju:ziəm, -iə], *s. Bot: Ent:* indusie *f*, induse *f*.
industrial [in'dʌstriəl], *a.* industriel; (*a*) **i. centre,** centre industriel; **i. complex, estate,** complexe industriel; **i. exhibition,** salon *m* de l'industrie; **i. training,** formation *f* à l'usine, dans l'entreprise; **i. atomic, nuclear, power,** énergie nucléaire industrielle; (*b*) **i. dispute,** conflit ouvrier, du travail; **i. unrest,** agitation ouvrière; **i. action,** (i) grève *f*; (ii) action revendicative; **i. relations,** relations humaines dans l'entreprise; **i. disease,** maladie professionnelle; **i. injuries,** accidents *m* du travail; **i. insurance,** assurance ouvrière; (*c*) *Hist:* **i. school,** (i) école professionnelle; (ii) école professionnelle pour enfants en dépôt ou en garde; école pour enfants moralement abandonnés; (*d*) *Anthr: Pol.Ec:* **i. unit,** atelier *m*; (*e*) *Fin:* **i. bank,** banque industrielle; **i. shares,** *s. pl.* **industrials,** valeurs industrielles; (*f*) *T.V:* **i. television,** télévision *f* à circuit fermé.
industrialism [in'dʌstriəlizm], *s.* industrialisme *m*.
industrialist [in'dʌstriəlist], *s.* industriel *m*.
industrialization [indʌstriəlai'zeiʃ(ə)n], *s.* industrialisation *f*.
industrialize [in'dʌstriəlaiz]. **1.** *v.tr.* industrialiser; **the milk trade is becoming industrialized,** le commerce du lait s'industrialise, devient une industrie. **2.** *v.i.* s'industrialiser.
industrious [in'dʌstriəs], *a.* (*a*) travailleur, diligent, assidu; **to be very i.,** être très travailleur; (*b*) *A:* empressé, zélé, ardent (**in sth., to do sth.,** à qch., à faire qch.).
industriously [in'dʌstriəsli], *adv.* (*a*) industrieusement, diligemment, assidûment; (*b*) *A:* avec zèle, avec empressement.
industriousness [in'dʌstriəsnis], *s.* assiduité *f* (au travail); application *f*.
industry ['indʌstri], *s.* **1.** application *f*, assiduité *f* au travail; travail *m*; diligence *f*, zèle *m*; **i. begets wealth,** le travail engendre la richesse. **2.** industrie *f*; **basic i.,** industrie de base; **processing i.,** industrie de transformation; **growing, growth, i.,** industrie en plein essor; **consumer goods i.,** industrie de consommation; **cottage i.,** industrie artisanale; artisanat *m*; **heavy i., light i.,** l'industrie lourde, légère; **primary i.,** industrie primaire; secteur *m* primaire; **sector of i.,** secteur industriel; branche *f* d'industrie; **agricultural industries,** industries agricoles; **aircraft i.,** industrie aéronautique; **armament i.,** industrie de l'armement; **boot and shoe i.,** industrie de la chaussure; **building i.,** industrie du bâtiment, le bâtiment; **chemical i.,** industrie chimique; **engineering i.,** industrie mécanique; **mining i.,** industrie minière, industrie extractive; **metal i.,** industrie métallurgique; **motor car i.,** industrie automobile; **oil i., petroleum i.,** industrie pétrolière, pétrolifère; **the shipping i.,** l'armement *m*; **shipbuilding i.,** industrie de constructions navales.
induviae [in'dju:vii:], *s.pl. Bot:* induvies *f*.
induvial [in'dju:viəl], *a. Bot:* induvial, -aux.
induviate [in'dju:vieit], *a. Bot:* induvié.
indwell ['indwel], *v.tr. & i.* (**indwelt; indwelling**) *A: & Lit:* **to i. (in) a place,** demeurer, séjourner, dans un lieu; habiter un lieu.
indwelling ['indweliŋ], *a.* **1.** *Lit:* (principe, etc.) intérieur; du cœur, de l'âme; intime. **2.** *Med:* **i. catheter,** cathéter laissé dans un organe, dans une voie.
inebriant [in'i:briənt]. **1.** *a.* enivrant, grisant, inébriant. **2.** *s.* inébriant *m*.
inebriate[1] [in'i:briət]. **1.** *a.* ivre, gris, enivré. **2.** *s.* ivrogne, -esse; **home for inebriates,** maison *f* de santé pour alcooliques.
inebriate[2] [in'i:brieit], *v.tr.* enivrer, griser; *Lit:* **the cup that cheers but not inebriates,** la coupe qui réconforte sans enivrer (c.-à-d. la tasse de thé).
inebriated [in'i:brieitid], *a.* gris, ivre, enivré; *F:* pris de boisson; **to become i. with wine,** *Fig:* **with praise,** s'enivrer, se griser, de vin, d'éloges.
inebriating [in'i:brieitiŋ], *a.* (vin, plaisir) enivrant, qui grise.
inebriation [ini:bri'eiʃ(ə)n], *s.* **1.** envirement *m*, action *f* de s'enivrer. **2.** ivresse *f*, ébriété *f*.
inebriety [ini'braiəti], *s.* **1.** ivresse *f*, ébriété *f*. **2.** ivrognerie *f*; alcoolisme *m*.
inedible [in'edibl], *a.* **1.** immangeable. **2.** non comestible.
inedited [in'editid], *a.* **1.** (*not* (*previously*) *published*) inédit. **2.** (*of published work*) publié (i) intégralement, (ii) sans notes.
ineducable [in'edjukəbl], *a.* inéducable.
ineffability [inefə'biliti], **ineffableness** [in'efəb(ə)lnis], *s.* ineffabilité *f*.
ineffable [in'efəbl], *a.* **1.** (*of joy, etc.*) ineffable, indicible. **2.** (*of sacred name, etc.*) qu'on n'ose pas prononcer.
ineffably [in'efəbli], *adv.* ineffablement, indiciblement.
ineffaceable [ini'feisəbl], *a.* ineffaçable, indélébile.
ineffaceably [ini'feisəbli], *adv.* ineffaçablement, indélébilement.
ineffective [ini'fektiv], *a.* **1.** (moyen, remède) inefficace, ineffectif, sans résultat, sans action, sans effet. **2.** (travail, architecture) qui manque d'effet artistique, qui n'a rien de frappant; **i. phrase,** expression *f* qui manque son but; **i. retort,** réplique *f* qui ne porte pas; **i. speech,** discours *m* qui ne produit pas d'effet; **i. speaker,** orateur *m* terne, dont les paroles ne portent pas; **i. style,** style plat, terne. **3.** (*of pers.*) incapable.
ineffectively [ini'fektivli], *adv.* inefficacement, vainement, sans produire d'effet.
ineffectiveness [ini'fektivnis], *s.* **1.** inefficacité *f*. **2.** manque *m* d'effet; manque de force (d'un argument, etc.).
ineffectual [ini'fektjuəl], *a.* **1.** (*a*) (effort, raisonnement) inefficace, sans effet, vain; **i. attempt, action,** tentative *f*, action *f*, qui n'a pas abouti; **i. treatment,** traitement *m* sans résultat; (*b*) qui donne une impression de faiblesse; terne. **2. i. person,** personne dont les efforts n'aboutissent jamais; personne incapable; velléitaire *mf*.
ineffectuality [inifektju'æliti], **ineffectualness** [ini'fektjuəlnis], *s.* inefficacité *f*.
ineffectually [ini'fektjuəli], *adv.* inefficacement.
inefficacious [inefi'keiʃəs], *a.* (remède, etc.) inefficace, sans effet.
inefficaciousness [inefi'keiʃəsnis], **inefficacity** [inefi'kæsiti], **inefficacy** [in'efikəsi], *s.* inefficacité *f*.
inefficiency [ini'fiʃ(ə)nsi], *s.* **1.** inefficacité *f* (des mesures qu'on avait prises, etc.). **2.** incapacité (professionnelle); incompétence *f*, insuffisance *f*, inhabileté *f* (de qn); **i. of labour,** incapacité professionnelle de la main-d'œuvre.
inefficient [ini'fiʃ(ə)nt], *a.* (*of measure, etc.*) inefficace, ineffectif; *F:* inefficient. **2.** (*of pers.*) incapable, incompétent, insuffisant; *s.* **the inefficient,** les incapables.
inefficiently [ini'fiʃ(ə)ntli], *adv.* **1.** inefficacement. **2.** sans compétence.
inelastic [ini'læstik], *a.* **1.** sans élasticité; raide; qui ne prête pas. **2.** *Fig:* qui manque de souplesse d'esprit, de caractère; raide. **3.** *Com: etc:* (demande, etc.) fixe, qui ne change pas; inélastique.
inelasticity [inilæs'tisiti], *s.* **1.** manque *m* d'élasticité; rigidité *f*. **2.** raideur *f* (d'esprit, de caractère). **3.** *Com: etc:* inélasticité *f* (du marché, etc.).
inelegance [in'eligəns], **inelegancy** [in'eligənsi], *s.* **1.** inélégance *f*. **2. inelegancies of style,** inélégances de style.
inelegant [in'eligənt], *a.* **1.** (style) inélégant; (personne) sans élégance. **2.** (goût) peu délicat, fruste.
inelegantly [in'eligəntli], *adv.* sans élégance, inélégamment.
ineligibility [inelidʒi'biliti], *s.* **1.** inéligibilité *f* (d'un candidat, etc.). **2.** caractère *m* peu acceptable, peu désirable (d'un prétendant).
ineligible [in'elidʒibl], *a.* (*a*) (candidat) inéligible; (*b*) indigne d'être choisi; peu acceptable, peu désirable; inacceptable; **i. for military service,** inapte au service militaire; **as a son-in-law he was quite i.,** comme gendre ce n'était pas du tout un parti convenable, un parti sortable.
ineluctability [inilʌktə'biliti], *s.* inéluctabilité *f*.
ineluctable [ini'lʌktəbl], *a.* inéluctable; inévitable.
ineluctably [ini'lʌktəbli], *adv.* inéluctablement, inévitablement.
inept [in'ept], *a.* **1.** (*of remark, etc.*) (i) déplacé; mal à propos; (ii) inepte, absurde; de la dernière stupidité; **he's hopelessly i.,** c'est un parfait incapable. **2.** *Jur:* (contrat) nul, de nul effet.
ineptitude [in'eptitju:d], **ineptness** [in'eptnis], *s.* **1.** manque *m* de justesse, d'à-propos (d'une observation). **2. an ineptitude,** une ineptie, une sottise.
ineptly [in'eptli], *adv.* ineptement, stupidement.
inequable [in'ekwəbl], *a.* inégal, -aux; irrégulier.
inequality [ini(:)'kwɔliti], *s.* **1.** inégalité *f* (de rang, de caractère, d'une surface, de style); variabilité *f*, inégalité (du climat); **social inequalities,** inégalités sociales; *Mth:* **the i.** $x > y$, l'inégalité $x > y$; *Astr:* **first i.,** première inégalité (du mouvement d'une planète). **2. the inequalities in the surface of the ground,** les inégalités, les irrégularités *f*, les bosses *f*, du terrain.
inequation [ini'kweiʃ(ə)n], *s. Mth:* inéquation *f*.
inequitable [in'ekwitəbl], *a.* inéquitable, peu équitable, injuste.
inequitably [in'ekwitəbli], *adv.* inéquitablement, injustement.
inequity [in'eqwiti], *s.* injustice *f*.
inequivalve(d) [in'i:kwivælv(d)], *a.* (mollusque) à valves inégales.
ineradicable [ini'rædikəbl], *a.* indéracinable, inextirpable.
inerm(ous) [in'ə:m(əs)], *a. Bot:* inerme, sans épines.
inerrancy [i'nerənsi], *s.* inerrance *f*.
inert [i'nə:t], *a.* **1.** (*a*) (masse, substance) inerte; (*b*) (esprit) inexcitable, inerte, apathique. **2.** *Ch:* (*of chemical, etc.*) inactif, inerte; **the i. gases,** les gaz rares.
inertance [i'nə:t(ə)ns], *s. Ac:* inertance *f*.
inertia [i'nə:ʃiə], *s.* inertie *f*; (*a*) *Ph: Mec:* **high i., slight i.,** forte, faible, inertie; **mass i.,** inertie de masse; **(electro)magnetic i.,** inertie (électro)magnétique; retard *m* d'aimantation; **thermal i.,** inertie thermique; **law of i.,** loi *f* d'inertie; **axis of i.,** axe *m* d'inertie; **i. diagram,** diagramme *m* des forces d'inertie; **ellipsoid of i.,** ellipsoïde *m* d'inertie; **moment of i.,** moment *m* d'inertie; **i. relay,** relais *m* d'inertie; **i. stress,** effort *m* d'inertie; *Exp:* **i. block,** masselotte *f*; *I.C.E:* **i. starting,** lancement *m* par inertie; **i. starter,** démarreur *m* à inertie; *Aut:* **i. seat belt,** ceinture *f* de sécurité à enrouleur; (*b*) (*of pers.*) paresse *f*; veulerie *f*; **they strove to overcome the i. of the masses,** ils s'efforcèrent de vaincre l'inertie des masses; (*c*) *Med:* **(uterine) i.,** inertie utérine; (*d*) *Phot:* **i. of an emulsion,** inertie d'une émulsion; (*e*) *Com:* **i. selling,** vente *f* par obtention abusive, frauduleuse, de commande.
inertial [i'nə:ʃ(ə)l], *a.* inertiel; inertial, -aux; d'inertie; *Ph: Mec:* **i. force,** force *f* d'inertie; **i. mass,** masse inertiale, inerte; *Ball: Av:* **i. control,** commande inertielle, commande à inertie; **i. guidance, i. navigation,** guidage inertiel; navigation inertielle; guidage, navigation, à, par, inertie; **i. guidance equipment, i. system,** centrale *f* à inertie; système inertiel; **i. platform,** plate-forme inertielle, à inertie.
inertly [i'nə:tli], *adv.* inertement, sans mouvement; **her hands rested i. in her lap,** ses mains reposaient inertes sur ses genoux.
inertness [i'nə:tnis], *s.* **1.** inertie *f*, inactivité *f*. **2.** *Ch:* **i. of a body,** inactivité d'un corps.
inescapable [ini'skeipəbl], *a.* inéluctable, inévitable.
inescation [ini'skeiʃ(ə)n], *s.* (*witchcraft*) inescation *f*.
inesite [ai'nisait], *s. Miner:* inésite *f*.
inessential [ini'senʃ(ə)l]. **1.** *a.* qui n'est pas essentiel; négligeable. **2.** *s.* **to omit inessentials,** laisser de côté ce qui n'est pas essentiel; se borner à l'essentiel.
inestimable [in'estiməbl], *a.* **1.** (*of damage, etc.*) inestimable, incalculable, inévaluable. **2.** (*of help, etc.*) d'un grand prix; inappréciable.
inestimably [in'estiməbli], *adv.* inestimablement, incalculablement.
inevitability [inevitə'biliti], **inevitableness** [in'evitəb(ə)lnis], *s.* inévitabilité *f*.
inevitable [in'evitəbl], *a.* (*a*) inévitable, inéluctable; immanquable; **to resign oneself to the i.,** se résigner à ce qu'on ne peut pas éviter, à l'inévitable; en prendre son parti; **it is absolutely i.,** il faut passer par là (ou par la fenêtre); **the mistakes i. to youth,** les erreurs que la jeunesse ne saurait éviter; (*b*) fatal, -als; obligé; **this reform is i.,** cette réforme viendra sûrement; **his promotion is i.,** il va de soi qu'il sera promu; **the i. hour,** l'heure fatale; **the i. latecomer,** le retardataire fatal; *Lit:* (*of a play, novel*) **the i. conclusion,** le dénouement fatal.
inevitably [in'evitəbli], *adv.* inévitablement, inéluctablement; fatalement.
inexact [inig'zækt], *a.* (récit, esprit) inexact.
inexactitude [inig'zæktitju:d], **inexactness** [inig'zæktnis], *s.* **1.** inexactitude *f* (d'un recit, etc.). **2.** erreur *f*.
inexactly [inig'zæktli], *adv.* inexactement.
inexcitability [ineksaitə'biliti], *s. Physiol:* inexcitabilité *f*.
inexcitable [inek'saitəbl], *a. Physiol:* inexcitable.
inexcusability [inekskju:zə'biliti], **inexcusableness** [ineks'kju:zəb(ə)lnis], *s.* nature *f* inexcusable (d'un affront, etc.).
inexcusable [ineks'kju:zəbl], *a.* inexcusable; sans

excuse; impardonnable.
inexcusably [ineks'kju:zəbli], *adv.* inexcusablement, impardonnablement.
inexecutable [ineksi'kju:təbl], *a.* inexécutable.
inexecution [ineksi'kju:ʃ(ə)n], *s.* inexécution *f* (d'un contrat, etc.).
inexhaustibility ['inegzɔ:sti'biliti], **inexhaustibleness** [ineg'zɔ:stib(ə)lnis], *s.* nature *f* inépuisable (d'une source d'approvisionnement, etc.).
inexhaustible [ineg'zɔ:stibl], *a.* **1.** (bonté, approvisionnement) inépuisable, inexhaustible; (source) intarissable. **2.** (athlète, etc.) infatigable.
inexigible [in'eksidʒibl], *a.* (dette) inexigible.
inexistence [ineg'zist(ə)ns], *s.* inexistence *f*; défaut *m* d'existence.
inexorability [ineks(ə)rə'biliti], **inexorableness** [in'eks(ə)rəb(ə)lnis], *s.* inexorabilité *f* (du sort, etc.); caractère *m*, nature *f*, inexorable, inflexible, implacable (de qn).
inexorable [in'eks(ə)rəbl], *a.* (personne, destin) inexorable; (personne) inflexible, implacable.
inexorably [in'eks(ə)rəbli], *adv.* inexorablement; inflexiblement, implacablement.
inexpedience [ineks'pi:diəns], **inexpediency** [ineks'pi:diənsi], *s.* inopportunité *f* (**of,** de); **the i. of raising the taxes,** ce qu'il y aurait d'inopportun à augmenter les impôts.
inexpedient [ineks'pi:diənt], *a.* inopportun, malavisé; **it's i. to do anything at the moment,** il est hors de propos, peu avantageux, inopportun, de faire n'importe quoi en ce moment.
inexpensive [iniks'pensiv], *a.* peu coûteux; bon marché; (qui ne coûte) pas cher; **house i. to run,** maison *f* économique.
inexpensively [iniks'pensivli], *adv.* (à) bon marché, à bas prix, à peu de frais, à bon compte; **to live i.,** vivre économiquement, à peu de frais.
inexpensiveness [iniks'pensivnis], *s.* bon marché, bas prix (de qch.).
inexperience [iniks'piəriəns], *s.* inexpérience *f* (**of,** de).
inexperienced [iniks'piəriənst], *a.* **1.** inexpérimenté, sans expérience, manquant d'expérience; neuf dans son métier; **i. driver,** conducteur inexpérimenté; novice *m*; débutant, -ante; **he is still i.,** il est encore novice; **man i. in business,** homme nouveau aux affaires; **he's i. in handling staff,** il n'a pas l'habitude de ménager le personnel. **2.** inaverti; **i. eye,** œil inexercé.
inexpert [in'ekspə:t], *a.* **1.** inexpert, maladroit; peu habile (**in,** à). **2.** *A:* inexpérimenté.
inexpertly [in'ekspə:tli], *adv.* d'une manière inexperte; maladroitement.
inexpiable [in'ekspiəbl], *a.* **1.** (crime) inexpiable. **2.** *A: & Lit:* (ressentiment) implacable; (guerre) impitoyable.
inexpiably [in'ekspiəbli], *adv.* d'une manière inexpiable.
inexplicable [iniks'plikəbl], *a.* (mystère) inexplicable; (ingratitude) inconcevable.
inexplicably [iniks'plikəbli], *adv.* inexplicablement; inconcevablement.
inexplicit [iniks'plisit], *a.* imprécis; inexplicite.
inexplosive [iniks'plousiv], *a.* inexplosible; indétonant.
inexpressibility [inikspresi'biliti], **inexpressibleness** [iniks'presib(ə)lnis], *s.* nature *f* inexprimable, indicible (de qch.).
inexpressible [iniks'presibl], *a.* (plaisir) inexprimable; (charme) indicible; (sentiment) au delà de toute expression.
inexpressibly [iniks'presibli], *adv.* inexprimablement; indiciblement; au delà de toute expression.
inexpressive [iniks'presiv], *a.* (geste, mot) inexpressif; (œil, regard) qui manque d'expression, sans expression; **i. countenance,** visage fermé.
inexpressiveness [iniks'presivnis], *s.* inexpressivité *f*.
inexpugnable [ineks'pʌgnəbl], *a.* (forteresse) inexpugnable, imprenable; (raisonnement, dignité) inattaquable.
inextensible [iniks'tensibl], *a.* inextensible.
inextinguishable [iniks'tiŋgwiʃəbl], *a.* (feu, rire) inextinguible.
inextricability [inikstrikə'biliti], *s.* inextricabilité *f*.
inextricable [iniks'trikəbl, in'eks-], *a.* (labyrinthe, embarras) inextricable.
inextricably [iniks'trikəbli, i'neks-], *adv.* inextricablement.
infallibilist [in'fælibilist], *s. Theol:* infaillibiliste *mf*.
infallibility [infæli'biliti], **infallibleness** [in'fælib(ə)lnis], *s. Theol: etc:* infaillibilité *f* (du pape, d'un jugement).
infallible [in'fælibl], *a.* (jugement, remède, etc.) infaillible; sûr; **judges are not i.,** les juges ne sont pas infaillibles.
infallibly [in'fælibli], *adv.* infailliblement.
infamous ['infəməs], *a.* **1.** *(a)* (personne, conduite) infâme; (conduite) abominable; (endroit) mal famé; *(b)* (homme) noté d'infamie. **2.** *Jur:* **i. crime,** crime infamant.
infamously ['infəməsli], *adv.* d'une manière infâme.
infamy ['infəmi], *s.* **1.** infamie *f* (d'un crime, etc.). **2.** note *f* d'infamie. **3. to be guilty of an i.,** être coupable d'une infamie.
infancy ['infənsi], *s.* **1.** *(a)* première enfance, petite enfance; toute première jeunesse; bas âge; **from i.,** dès la plus tendre enfance; *(b)* débuts *mpl*, première période, enfance (d'un art, d'une industrie); **the stage in its i.,** le théâtre à ses débuts; **industry still in its i.,** industrie encore dans son enfance; **the disease is only in its i.,** la maladie ne fait que commencer. **2.** *Jur:* minorité *f*; **to plead i.,** appuyer sa défense sur sa minorité; plaider l'incapacité en tant que mineur.
infant[1] ['infənt], *s.* **1.** *(a)* enfant *mf* du premier âge, en bas âge, au berceau; tout(e) petit(e) enfant; nourrisson *m*; **i. sovereign,** souverain *m* en bas âge; **the i. Jesus,** l'enfant Jésus; le petit Jésus; **newly-born i.,** nouveau-né *m*, nouveau-née *f*; **the i. years,** les années d'enfance; **i. mortality,** mortalité *f* infantile; **i. feeding,** alimentation *f* des nourrissons; **i. weakness,** faiblesse *f* d'enfant; *Sch:* **i. class, the infants,** la classe enfantine; **i. school,** école *f* pour les enfants de cinq à huit ans; *(b)* *F:* novice *m* (en politique, etc.); **i. country,** jeune pays *m*, pays dans son enfance; **i. navy,** marine naissante. **2.** *Jur:* mineur, -eure.
infant[2], *s. Spanish Hist:* infant *m*, infante *f*.
infanta [in'fæntə], *s.f. Spanish Hist:* infante.
infante [in'fænti], *s.m. Spanish Hist:* infant.
infanticidal [in'fæntisaidl], *a.* infanticide.
infanticide[1] [in'fæntisaid], *s.* (*pers.*) infanticide *mf*.
infanticide[2], *s.* (crime *m* d')infanticide *m*.
infantile ['infəntail], *a.* **1.** *(a)* (esprit, imagination) d'enfant; *(b)* (raisonnement, etc.) enfantin; **i. remark,** remarque enfantine, puérile. **2.** *Med:* (maladie) infantile; *A:* **i. paralysis,** poliomyélite *f*; *A:* paralysie (spinale) infantile.
infantilism [in'fæntilizm], *s.* **1.** *Med:* infantilisme *m*; arrêt *m* de croissance. **2.** puérilité *f*, enfantillage *m*.
infantine ['infəntain], *a.* enfantin; d'enfant.
infantry ['infəntri], *s. Mil:* *(a)* infanterie *f*; **fortress i., garrison i.,** infanterie de forteresse; **i. of the Guards,** infanterie de la Garde, la Garde à pied; *A:* **i. of the line, line i.,** infanterie de ligne; *F:* la ligne: *A:* les lignards *m*; **airborne i.,** infanterie aéroportée; **air-transported i.,** infanterie aérotransportée; **lorry-borne i., lorried i.,** infanterie portée (en camions); **mechanized i.,** infanterie mécanisée; **motorized i.,** infanterie motorisée; *A:* **mounted i.,** infanterie montée; **unmounted i.,** infanterie à pied, non motorisée; **close-support i.,** infanterie d'accompagnement; **divisional i.,** infanterie divisionnaire; *(b)* fantassins *mpl*; **four hundred i.,** quatre cents fantassins.
infantryman, *pl.* **-men** ['infəntrimən], *s.m.* soldat d'infanterie; fantassin.
infarct ['infɑ:kt], *s. Med:* infarctus *m*.
infarcted [in'fɑ:ktid], *a. Med:* (tissu) atteint d'un infarctus.
infarction [in'fɑ:kʃ(ə)n], *s. Med:* **1.** infiltration *f* du tissu (par un épanchement sanguin). **2.** infarctus *m*; **myocardial i.,** infarctus du myocarde.
infatuate [in'fætjueit], *v.tr.* **1.** affoler (qn); faire perdre l'esprit à (qn). **2.** inspirer une passion folle à (qn) (**with,** pour); enticher, engouer (qn) (**with,** de); **to i. s.o. with an idea,** enticher, *F:* embéguiner, qn d'une idée.
infatuated [in'fætjueitəd], *a.* infatué, entiché; **to become i. with s.o., sth.,** s'infatuer, s'affoler, s'engouer, s'enticher, de qn, de qch; **she has become i. with him,** il lui a tourné la tête; **to be i. with s.o., sth.,** aimer éperdûment qn; raffoler de qn, de qch.; avoir un béguin, une toquade, pour qn; être coiffé, toqué, de qn; *P:* en pincer pour qn; avoir qn dans la peau; **i. by her beauty,** ensorcelé par sa beauté.
infatuation [infætju'eiʃ(ə)n], *s.* engouement *m*; **to have an i. for s.o.,** avoir le béguin pour qn; **it is a case of mutual i.,** ils sont entichés l'un de l'autre; **he persists in his i.,** il persiste dans son aveuglement, dans son aberration; **to get over one's i. for s.o.,** se désengouer de qn; **to have lost one's i. for sth.,** être revenu de qch.
infeasible [in'fi:zibl], *a.* infaisable.
infect [in'fekt], *v.tr.* **1.** infecter, corrompre, vicier (l'air, les mœurs, etc.); **to i. the mind with an evil doctrine,** infecter l'esprit d'une mauvaise doctrine. **2.** *(a)* *Med:* contaminer, contagionner (qn); infecter (une plaie, une ville); **to i. s.o. with a disease,** communiquer une maladie à qn; (*of pers.*) **to become infected,** se contagionner; **infected with the plague,** atteint de la peste; **the lungs are infected,** les poumons sont atteints; **infected clothing,** vêtements porteurs de germes, contagifères; *(b)* **to i. s.o. with one's laziness, with one's high spirits,** communiquer sa paresse, sa gaieté, à qn; **the laughter infected all the guests,** ce rire contagieux gagna, se communiqua à, tous les convives. **3.** *Jur:* **contract infected with fraud,** contrat entaché de fraude. **4.** *Ling:* (*of vowel*) modifier (une autre voyelle).
infecting[1] [in'fektiŋ], *a.* infectant, qui infecte.
infecting[2], *s.* infection *f*.
infection [in'fekʃ(ə)n], *s.* **1.** *(a)* *Med:* infection *f*, contamination *f*, contagion *f*; **bacterial i.,** infection microbienne, bactérienne; **cross i.,** hospitalisme *m*; **focal i.,** infection focale; **latent i.,** infection latente; **primary i.,** primo-infection *f*, *pl.* primo-infections; **virus i.,** infection virale; **liable to i.,** en état de réceptivité; **centre, source, of i.,** foyer *m* d'infection; **to spread i.,** répandre l'infection; *(b)* **the i. of his enthusiasm,** la contagion de son enthousiasme. **2.** *Jur:* viciation *f* (d'un contrat par la fraude, etc.). **3.** *Ling:* modification *f* (d'une voyelle par une autre).
infectious [in'fekʃəs], *a.* **1.** (air) infect, pestilentiel. **2.** *(a)* *Med:* (*of disease*) (i) infectieux; **i. anaemia,** anémie infectieuse; **i. hepatitis, i. jaundice,** hépatite, jaunisse, infectieuse; **i. sinusitis,** sinusite infectieuse; (ii) contagieux; **is it an i. disease?** est-ce que c'est une maladie contagieuse, une maladie qui s'attrape? *(b)* **i. laughter,** rire contagieux, communicatif; **i. good humour,** bonne humeur contagieuse.
infectiousness [in'fekʃəsnis], *s.* *(a)* nature infectieuse (d'une maladie); *(b)* contagion *f* (du rire, etc.).
infective [in'fektiv], *a.* **1.** *Med:* (germe) infectieux, infectant. **2.** (rire, etc.) contagieux.
infectiveness [in'fektivnis], **infectivity** [infek'tiviti], *s. Med:* infectiosité *f*.
infelicitous [infi'lisitəs], *a.* **1.** (mariage, etc.) malheureux; (événement) fâcheux. **2.** (*of expression*) mal trouvé; malheureux; qui manque d'à-propos.
infelicitously [infi'lisitəsli], *adv.* maladroitement; gauchement; **he spoke rather i.,** il a fait un discours assez maladroit, un peu gauche.
infelicity [infi'lisiti], *s.* **1.** *(a)* défaut *m* de félicité, nature fâcheuse, *Lit:* infélicité *f* (d'un événement); *(b)* mauvaise fortune. **2.** *(a)* manque *m* de justesse, manque d'à-propos (d'une expression, etc.); *(b)* expression peu juste, malheureuse; gaffe *f*; **he was guilty of several infelicities,** (dans son discours) il a commis plus d'une gaffe.
infer [in'fə:r], *v.tr.* **(inferred) 1. to i. sth. from sth.,** inférer, déduire, conclure, arguer, qch. de qch.; **to i. a general rule from sth.,** tirer une règle générale de qch.; **I i. from that that he's guilty,** je conclus de cela qu'il est coupable; **it is inferred that he doesn't know what happened,** on suppose qu'il ne sait pas ce qui est arrivé. **2.** impliquer; **a picture infers the existence of a painter,** un tableau implique l'existence d'un peintre.
inference ['inf(ə)rəns], *s. Log: etc:* **1.** inférence *f*; **by i.,** par induction. **2.** inférence, déduction *f*, conclusion *f*; **to draw an i. from sth.,** tirer une conclusion, une conséquence, de qch.; **to make an i.,** formuler une conclusion; **I have known you make inferences quite as wild,** je vous ai vu arriver à des conclusions aussi extravagantes.
inferential [infə'renʃ(ə)l], *a.* déductif; **i. proofs,** preuves fondées sur certaines déductions.
inferentially [infə'renʃəli], *adv.* **1.** par déduction, par induction. **2. i. he's not to be trusted,** on peut conclure de là qu'on ne peut se fier à lui.
inferior [in'fiəriər]. **1.** *a.* *(a)* inférieur; **i. goods,** marchandises inférieures; **i. piece of work,** ouvrage *m* de second ordre; **i. quality,** qualité inférieure; basse qualité; **i. minds,** les esprits *m* subalternes; **to be in an i. position,** être dans une position inférieure, subordonnée; **to be i. to s.o. in learning, in merit,** être inférieur à qn en science, par le mérite; **greatly i. to the others,** très inférieur aux autres, bien au-dessous des autres; **to be in no way i. to s.o., sth.,** ne le céder en rien à qn, qch.; **he's very i. to his brother,** il est loin de valoir son frère; *(b)* *Astr:* **the i. planets,** les planètes inférieures; **i. conjunction,** conjonction inférieure; *(c)* *Bot:* (calice, ovaire) infère; *(d)* *Typ:* **i. letter, i. numeral,** *s.* **i.,** petite lettre inférieure, petit chiffre inférieur. **2.** *s.* *(a)* (*in school position*) inférieur, -eure; *(b)* (*in rank, grade*) inférieur, subordonné, -ée, subalterne *m*.
inferiority [infiəri'ɔriti], *s.* infériorité *f* (**to,** par rapport à); **numerical i., i. in numbers,** infériorité numérique, en nombre; *Psy:* **i. complex,** complexe *m* d'infériorité.
inferiorly [in'fiəriəli], *adv.* inférieurement, d'une manière inférieure.
infernal [in'fə:nl], *a.* **1.** infernal, -aux; de l'enfer; des enfers; **the i. regions,** les régions infernales; l'enfer *m*;

Lt.Lit: l'Averne *m*; **the i. powers,** les puissances infernales. 2. *F:* (*a*) infernal, abominable, diabolique; **i. machine,** machine infernale; (*b*) (*intensive*) (chaleur, etc.) d'enfer; **i. row,** bruit infernal; **it's an i. nuisance,** c'est diablement embêtant; **i. cheek,** fichu toupet; toupet infernal.

infernally [in'fəːnəli], *adv. F:* (*intensive*) **it's i. hot,** il fait une chaleur d'enfer; **an i. busy street,** une rue diablement mouvementée.

inferno, *pl.* **-os** [in'fəːnou, -ouz], *s.* enfer *m*; *Lit:* **Dante's I.,** l'Enfer de Dante; **the building had been burning for two hours and was a raging i.,** la maison brûlait depuis deux heures et formait un véritable brasier; *Hist:* **the i. of Stalingrad,** l'enfer de Stalingrad.

inferobranch ['inf(ə)roubræŋk], *s. Moll:* inférobranche *m.*

Inferobranchiata ['inf(ə)roubræŋki'eitə], *s.pl. Moll:* inférobranches *m.*

inferring [in'fəːriŋ], *s.* 1. déduction *f*, conclusion *f*, inférence *f*. 2. implication *f*.

infertile [in'fəːtail], *a.* (*a*) (terrain) stérile, infertile, infécond; (esprit) stérile; (*b*) (œuf) clair, non fécondé; *Ser:* (œuf) morfondu.

infertility [infəː'tiliti], *s.* infertilité *f*, infécondité *f*, stérilité *f*.

infest [in'fest], *v.tr.* (*of vermin, etc.*) infester; **country infested with mosquitoes, mosquito-infested country,** pays infesté de moustiques; **the roads were infested with highwaymen,** des brigands infestaient les routes.

infestation [infes'teiʃ(ə)n], *s.* invasion *f* (des plantes par les parasites, etc.); *Med:* infestation *f* (d'un organe par les parasites).

infeudation [infju(ː)'deiʃ(ə)n], *s. A.Jur:* inféodation *f*.

infibulate [in'fibjuleit], *v.tr.* infibuler.

infibulation [infibju'leiʃ(ə)n], *s.* infibulation *f*.

infidel ['infid(ə)l], *a. & s.* 1. *Hist:* infidèle (*mf*); mécréant, -ante. 2. *Pej:* incrédule (*mf*), incroyant, -ante (en matière de religion).

infidelity [infi'deliti], *s.* 1. incroyance *f* (en matière de religion). 2. (*a*) infidélité, déloyauté *f* (d'un serviteur, etc.); **conjugal i.,** infidélité conjugale; (*b*) **his frequent infidelities,** ses fréquentes infidélités.

infield ['infiːld], *s.* 1. (*a*) champs attenants aux bâtiments de la ferme; (*b*) *A:* terre *f* arable. 2. *Sp:* (*a*) *Cr:* terrain *m* près des guichets; (*b*) (*baseball*) intra-champ *m*, *pl.* intra-champs.

infielder ['infiːldər], *s. Sp:* (*baseball*) joueur *m* dans l'intra-champ.

infighting ['infaitiŋ], *s.* 1. *Box:* combat *m* corps à corps; corps-à-corps *m*. 2. guerre intestine (entre les membres d'un groupe, etc.).

infilling ['infiliŋ], *s.* (*a*) *Const:* blocaille *f*; (*b*) *Min:* remplissage *m* (d'un filon).

infiltrate[1] ['infiltreit, in'filtreit], *s.* (*a*) infiltration *f*; substance infiltrée, (*b*) *Med:* infiltrat *m*.

infiltrate[2] ['infiltreit]. 1. *v.tr.* (*a*) faire pénétrer (un liquide, etc.) dans (qch.); (*b*) (*of liquid*) s'infiltrer, pénétrer, dans (une substance); imprégner (une substance); **infiltrated with mineral salts,** imprégné de sels minéraux; (*c*) (*of troops*) s'infiltrer dans (l'ennemi, etc.); *Pol: etc:* (*of subversionists, etc.*) noyauter (un syndicat, etc.). 2. *v.i.* (*of fluid*) s'infiltrer (**into,** dans; **through,** à travers).

infiltration [infil'treiʃ(ə)n], *s.* 1. (*a*) infiltration *f* (d'un liquide, etc.) (**through,** à travers); *Geol:* **the i. theory,** la théorie de l'infiltration; *Min:* **i. vein,** filon *m* d'incrustation; *Med:* **fatty i.,** dégénérescence graisseuse; **i. anaesthesia,** anesthésie locale; **round cell i.,** infiltration, envahissement *m* par des cellules rondes; (*b*) (*of troops, etc.*) **to advance, progress, by i.,** avancer par infiltration, s'infiltrer; *Pol:* **the i. of communists into the trade unions,** l'infiltration, le noyautage, des syndicats par les communistes. 2. (*a*) **infiltrations,** infiltrations; incrustations *f*; (*b*) *Med:* infiltration, infiltrat *m*.

infiltrator ['infiltreitər], *s.* agent qui s'infiltre (dans un parti politique, etc.).

infinite ['infinit]. 1. *a.* infini; (*a*) illimité, sans bornes; **space is i.,** l'espace est infini; **i. mercy,** miséricorde infinie; *Mth:* **i. series,** série infinie; (*b*) (*very great*) **truth of i. importance,** vérité *f* d'une très grande, d'une vaste, importance; **to have i. trouble in doing sth.,** avoir une peine infinie, avoir infiniment de peine, à faire qch.; (*c*) (*with s. in pl.*) **i. ways of doing sth.,** une infinité de façons de faire qch.; **i. varieties,** variétés *f* sans nombre; (*d*) [in'fainait] *Gram:* **i. verb, verb i.,** formes substantives du verbe; **i. parts of the verb,** modes indéfinis, impersonnels, du verbe. 2. *s.* (*a*) *Theol:* **the I.,** l'infini *m*; (*b*) *Mth:* **the i.,** l'infini.

infinitely ['infinitli], *adv.* infiniment; **i. small,** infiniment petit; **i. numerous elements,** éléments *m* en quantité infinie; **i. more intelligent,** infiniment plus intelligent.

infinitesimal [infini'tesim(ə)l]. 1. *s. Mth:* (*a*) quantité infiniment petite; infinitésime *f*; (*b*) *pl.* **infinitesimals,** analyse infinitésimale. 2. *a.* infinitésimal, -aux; (*a*) *Mth:* **i. calculus,** calcul infinitésimal; (*b*) **an i. amount of impurity,** une quantité infinitésimale d'impuretés; **i. majority,** majorité *f* infime.

infinitesimally [infini'tesiməli], *adv.* infiniment (petit, etc.).

infinitive [in'finitiv], *a. & s. Gram:* infinitif (*m*); **i. clause,** proposition infinitive; **i. (mood),** (mode) infinitif; **to split an i.,** intercaler un adverbe entre to et le verbe (p.ex. **to utterly disbelieve, to deliberately ignore**); **in the i.,** à l'infinitif.

infinitude [in'finitjuːd], *s.* 1. infinité *f*, infinitude *f* (de l'espace, etc.). 2. *Lit:* **an i. of misfortunes,** une infinité de malheurs.

infinity [in'finiti], *s.* 1. (*a*) infinité *f*, infinitude *f* (de l'espace, etc.); (*b*) **an i. of ills,** une infinité de maux. 2. *Mth: etc:* infini *m*; **to i.,** à l'infini; **lines that meet at i.,** lignes qui se rencontrent à l'infini; *Phot:* **to focus on, for, i.,** mettre au point sur l'infini; régler, accrocher, à l'infini.

infirm[1] [in'fəːm], *a.* 1. (*of pers.*) infirme, faible, maladif, débile. 2. (esprit, jugement) irrésolu, flottant; *Lit:* **to be i. of purpose,** être irrésolu; avoir une volonté flottante, débile. 3. *Jur: A:* (document, etc.) invalide.

infirm[2], *v.tr. Jur:* infirmer, invalider, déclarer nul (un privilège, etc.).

infirmary [in'fəːməri], *s.* 1. infirmerie *f* (d'une école, prison, etc.). 2. hôpital *m*, -aux.

infirmity [in'fəːmiti], *s.* 1. (*a*) infirmité *f*, débilité *f*, faiblesse *f* (du corps, de l'esprit); (*b*) infirmité; affection particulière; **to suffer from an i.,** souffrir d'une infirmité; **the infirmities of old age,** les infirmités de la vieillesse. 2. **i. of purpose,** faiblesse de caractère; irrésolution *f*; manque *m* de volonté. 3. *Jur: A:* invalidité *f* (d'un titre, d'un argument).

infix[1] ['infiks], *s. Ling:* infixe *m*.

infix[2] [in'fiks], *v.tr.* 1. implanter (qch. dans qch.); **to i. sth. in the mind,** inculquer, graver, qch. dans l'esprit. 2. *Ling:* infixer, insérer (une lettre, une syllabe).

infixing [in'fiksiŋ], *s. Ling:* infixion *f* (d'une lettre, syllabe).

inflame [in'fleim]. 1. *v.tr.* (*a*) mettre le feu à, enflammer, allumer (une substance); (*b*) enflammer (le courage); allumer (la cupidité, les désirs); **alcohol inflames the blood,** l'alcool échauffe, enflamme, le sang; **to i. discord,** attiser la discorde; **to i. a quarrel,** envenimer une querelle; (*c*) *Med:* enflammer (une plaie, une muqueuse); envenimer (une plaie). 2. *v.i.* (*a*) s'enflammer, prendre feu; **hay inflames very easily,** le foin s'enflamme, prend feu, facilement; (*b*) *Med:* (*of wound, tissue*) s'enflammer; (*of wound*) s'envenimer.

inflamed [in'fleimd], *a.* 1. enflammé (**with,** de); **i. with passion,** brûlant d'amour. 2. *Med:* (*of wound, eye, etc.*) enflammé; (œil) injecté; **to become i.,** s'enflammer; s'envenimer. 3. *Her:* enflammé.

inflamer [in'fleimər], *s.* excitateur, -trice (des passions, des esprits).

inflaming [in'fleimiŋ], *s.* inflammation *f*.

inflammability [inflæmə'biliti], **inflammableness** [in'flæməb(ə)lnis], *s.* inflammabilité *f*.

inflammable [in'flæməbl]. 1. *a.* (*a*) (substance, etc.) inflammable; (*b*) (*of pers., crowd*) prompt à s'échauffer, à se prendre de passion; inflammable. 2. *s.pl.* **inflammables,** substances *f* inflammables.

inflammation [inflə'meiʃ(ə)n], *s.* 1. (*a*) inflammation *f* (d'un combustible); (*b*) inflammation, excitation *f* (des esprits). 2. *Med:* inflammation (d'une plaie, du cerveau); **i. of the chest, lungs,** fluxion *f* de poitrine; **i. of the eyelids,** inflammation du bord des paupières; blépharite *f*, *F:* cocotte *f*; **to cause i.,** amener l'inflammation; **to reduce the i. in a wound,** désenflammer une plaie.

inflammatory [in'flæmət(ə)ri], *a.* 1. (discours, brochure) incendiaire, provocateur, -trice. 2. *Med:* (fièvre, papule) inflammatoire. 3. (*of projectile, etc.*) inflammateur, -trice; incendiaire.

inflatable [in'fleitəbl], *a.* gonflable; **i. lifejacket,** gilet *m* de sauvetage gonflable; **i. raft,** radeau *m* pneumatique.

inflate [in'fleit], *v.tr.* 1. (*a*) gonfler, insuffler (un ballon); gonfler, faire enfler (le ventre); souffler (une vessie); gonfler (une voile); **to i. a tyre hard,** gonfler un pneu à bloc; **to i. the inner tube before fitting the outer cover,** mettre la chambre à air au rond avant de monter l'enveloppe; **to i. the lungs with air,** remplir les poumons d'air; *Med:* souffler dans les poumons; (*b*) **to i. s.o. with pride,** gonfler, bouffir, qn d'orgueil. 2. (*a*) *Com:* grossir, charger (un compte); (*b*) hausser, faire monter (les prix); (*c*) *Pol.Ec:* **to i. the currency,** accroître artificiellement la circulation fiduciaire; recourir à l'inflation.

inflated [in'fleitid], *a.* 1. (*a*) (ballon, etc.) gonflé, enflé; **to become i.,** s'enfler, se gonfler (d'air); (*b*) (*of pers.*) **i. with pride,** bouffi, gonflé, d'orgueil. 2. (*a*) *Com:* (prix) exagéré; (*b*) *Pol.Ec:* **i. currency,** circulation fiduciaire artificiellement accrue. 3. *Lit:* (style) enflé, ampoulé, déclamatoire.

inflater [in'fleitər], *s. Cy: etc:* pompe *f* à pneu (matique)s; **mechanical i.,** pompe à pneus automatique.

inflating [in'fleitiŋ], *s.* gonflement *m*, gonflage *m* (d'un ballon, pneu, etc.).

inflation [in'fleiʃ(ə)n], *s.* 1. (*a*) = INFLATING; (*b*) *Med:* inflation *f* (de l'estomac); (*c*) *Pol.Ec:* (i) hausse *f*, gonflement *m* (des prix, des salaires); (ii) inflation; **galloping i.,** inflation galopante; **pent-up i.,** inflation contenue, jugulée; **rate of i.,** taux *m* d'inflation; **the danger of i.,** le danger inflationniste; **monetary i.,** inflation monétaire; **i. of the currency,** inflation fiduciaire; **to resort to i.,** avoir recours à l'inflation. 2. *Lit:* enflure *f*, emphase *f* (du style).

inflationary [in'fleiʃ(ə)nəri], *a.* (politique, etc.) inflationniste, d'inflation; **i. tendency,** tendance *f* inflationniste, à l'inflation.

inflationism [in'fleiʃənizm], *s. Pol.Ec:* inflationnisme *m*.

inflationist [in'fleiʃənist], *a. & s. Pol.Ec:* inflationniste (*mf*).

inflator [in'fleitər], *s.* = INFLATER.

inflect [in'flekt], *v.tr.* 1. fléchir, courber (en dedans); **to i. a ray,** infléchir un rayon; **the wind often inflects its course,** le vent change souvent de direction. 2. *Gram:* donner (i) des inflexions, (ii) des flexions, à (un mot); conjuguer (un verbe). 3. (*a*) moduler (la voix); (*b*) *Mus:* altérer (une note).

inflected [in'flektid], *a.* 1. **i. position,** position courbée; *Arch:* **i. arch,** arc renversé; *Opt:* **i. ray,** rayon infléchi. 2. *Ling:* **i. language,** langue *f* à flexions, flexionnelle; **i. vowel,** voyelle infléchie; **i. forms of the verb,** inflexions *f* du verbe. 3. *Mus:* **i. note,** note altérée.

inflection [in'flekʃ(ə)n], *s.* = INFLEXION.

inflectional [in'flekʃən(ə)l], *a.* = INFLEXIONAL.

inflective [in'flektiv], *a. Ling:* (i) inflectif; (ii) flexionnel.

inflexed [in'flekst], *a. Nat.Hist:* courbé, infléchi; *Bot:* **i. stamen,** étamine infléchie; **to become i.,** s'infléchir.

inflexibility [infleksi'biliti], *s.* inflexibilité *f*, rigidité *f*.

inflexible [in'fleksibl], *a.* inflexible; **i. virtue,** vertu *f* intraitable, inflexible; **i. courage,** courage *m* inébranlable; **i. code of morals,** morale *f* rigide.

inflexibly [in'fleksibli], *adv.* inflexiblement, rigidement.

inflexion [in'flekʃ(ə)n], *s.* 1. (*a*) inflexion *f* (du corps, d'une route, etc.); fléchissement *m* (du corps, d'un ressort); *Carp:* **angle of i. of a plane,** basile *m* d'un rabot; (*b*) *Opt: Mth:* inflexion; **point of i., i. point,** point *m* d'inflexion (d'une courbe); changement *m* de direction (d'une ligne, d'un rayon). 2. *Ling:* (i) inflexion, (ii) flexion *f* (d'un mot); **the inflexions of the verb,** les flexions du verbe. 3. (*a*) inflexion (de la voix); **voice with musical inflexions,** voix aux modulations musicales; (*b*) *Mus:* altération *f* (d'une note).

inflexional [in'flekʃən(ə)l], *a.* (*of language*) flexionnel; à flexions.

inflict [in'flikt], *v.tr.* infliger (**sth. on s.o.,** qch. à qn); **to i. defeat on the enemy,** infliger une défaite à l'ennemi; **to i. a wound on s.o.,** faire une blessure à qn; **to i. suffering on s.o.,** faire subir, occasionner, du chagrin, une douleur, à qn; *Jur:* **to i. a punishment, a penalty, a fine, on s.o.,** infliger une punition, une peine, une amende, à qn; faire subir une peine à qn; *F:* **to i. oneself, one's company, on s.o.,** imposer sa compagnie à qn; s'imposer; **he inflicted himself on us,** il nous a infligé sa présence.

infliction [in'flikʃ(ə)n], *s.* 1. *Jur:* infliction *f* (d'une peine, d'un châtiment). 2. (*a*) peine infligée; châtiment *m*; (*b*) **the inflictions put upon this people,** les vexations *f* que subit ce peuple; *F:* **what an i. he is to us all!** comme il nous embête tous!

inflictive [in'fliktiv], *a. Jur:* (*of penalty*) inflictif.

inflorescence [inflə'res(ə)ns], *s. Bot:* 1. inflorescence *f*; **centrifugal i., centripetal i.,** inflorescence centrifuge, centripète. 2. (*a*) floraison *f*; (*b*) fleurs *fpl* (d'un arbre, etc.).

inflorescent [inflə'res(ə)nt], *a. Bot:* fleurissant; en fleurs.

inflow ['inflou], *s.* 1. (*a*) entrée *f*, affluence *f* (d'un cours d'eau); **the i. of the water,** la venue des eaux; la montée des eaux (dans un réservoir); **i. pipe,** arrivée *f* d'eau; (*b*) affluence *f*, afflux *m* (de gens, de marchandises); invasion *f* (d'idées nouvelles). 2. vitesse *f* d'appel (d'air).

inflowing[1] ['inflouiŋ], *s.* = INFLOW 1.

inflowing[2], *a.* entrant; qui entre; **i. air,** air *m* qui entre; **i. waters,** eaux affluentes; **i. current,** courant *m* d'entrée (dans un détroit, etc.).

influence[1] ['influəns], *s.* **1.** (*a*) influence *f*, action *f* (**upon, on,** sur); **to exert, exercise, an i., to bring i. to bear, on s.o.,** exercer une influence sur qn; influencer qn; agir sur qn; **to bring every i. to bear,** mettre tout en jeu (**in order to,** pour); **to use one's i. with s.o.,** user de son influence auprès de qn; **to have great i. over s.o.,** avoir beaucoup d'influence sur qn; (*of thg*) **to have an i., exercise i., on sth.,** agir, influer, sur qch.; **hormones have an i. on the whole body,** les hormones influencent l'organisme tout entier; **the sphere of i. of French culture,** la sphère d'influence, le rayonnement, de la culture française; **i. of a drug,** effet *m* d'une drogue; **to take a decision under the i. of fear,** prendre une résolution sous le coup de la peur; **under the i. of drink,** *F:* **under the i.,** sous l'empire de la boisson; *F:* dans les vignes du Seigneur; *Jur:* **undue i.,** intimidation *f*; **to exert undue i. on s.o.,** user d'intimidation envers qn; **undue i. upon a minor,** abus *m* de mineur; **to use undue i. with the maker of a will,** suggérer un testament; (*b*) (*of pers.*) **to have i.,** (i) avoir de l'influence, de l'autorité; (ii) avoir de la protection, des protections, du crédit (**with s.o.,** auprès de qn); **to have far-reaching i.,** avoir le bras long; **man of i.,** homme influent; **his i. in his native town,** son crédit dans sa ville natale; **outside i.,** influence étrangère; *F:* piston *m*; **he owes his position to i.,** il doit sa situation au piston, au pistonnage; **to use one's i. in favour of s.o.,** appuyer, *F:* pistonner, qn; **he is beginning to make his i. felt, recognized,** il commence à s'imposer; **he is an i. in his country,** c'est une puissance dans son pays. **2.** *El:* induction *f*; **i. machine,** machine *f* à influence; *Ball:* **i. fuse,** fusée *f* à influence, fonctionnant par influence. **3.** *Civ.E:* **i. line,** ligne *f* d'influence.

influence[2], *v.tr.* (*of pers.*) influencer (qn); (*of thg*) influer sur (qch., qn); **to i. one's friends,** influencer, exercer une influence sur, ses amis; **to i. s.o. in favour of doing sth.,** incliner qn à faire qch.; **factors that i. the tides,** facteurs qui influent sur les marées.

influent ['influənt]. **1.** *a.* qui afflue; **the i. tide,** la marée montante. **2.** *s. Geog:* affluent *m* (d'un cours d'eau).

influential [influ'enʃ(ə)l], *a.* influent; **to be i.,** avoir de l'influence; avoir le bras long; **to have i. friends,** avoir des amis influents, des amis en haut lieu.

influentially [influ'enʃəli], *adv.* **1.** (*a*) par influence; (*b*) avec une grande influence. **2.** *El:* par induction.

influenza [influː'enzə], *s. Med:* grippe *f*; **gastric i.,** grippe gastro-intestinale; **i. cold,** catarrhe grippal; **he has got, is down with, i.,** il a la grippe; *F:* il est grippé.

influenzal [influː'enz(ə)l], **influenzic** [influː'enzik], *a. Med:* grippal, -aux.

influx ['inflʌks], *s.* **1.** (*a*) entrée *f*, affluence *f* (d'un cours d'eau, etc.); **the i. of the water,** la venue des eaux; **the i. of Greek into the English language,** la pénétration du grec dans la langue anglaise; (*b*) affluence *f*, afflux *m* (de gens, de marchandises); afflux (de gaz); invasion *f* (d'idées nouvelles); **an i. of water,** une inondation; *Pol.Ec:* **i. of gold,** entrée, afflux, d'or. **2.** embouchure *f* (d'un cours d'eau).

info ['infou], *s. F:* informations *fpl*, renseignements *mpl*; *F:* rencard *m*; **bit of i.,** un renseignement; *F:* un tuyau; **to slip s.o. the i.,** tuyauter qn.

infold [in'fould], *v.tr.* envelopper (**sth. in sth.,** qch. dans qch.).

infolded [in'fouldid], *a. Nat.Hist:* replié en dedans.

in-folio [in'fouliou], *a.* **i.-f. volume,** (volume) in-folio (*m inv*).

inform[1] [in'fɔːm]. **1.** *v.tr.* (*a*) **to i. s.o. of sth.,** informer, avertir, aviser, prévenir, qn de qch.; apprendre, faire savoir, qch. à qn; faire part de qch. à qn; renseigner qn sur qch.; donner connaissance de qch. à qn; donner communication de qch. à qn; porter qch. à la connaissance de qn; **he informed me of his position,** il m'a mis au courant de sa situation; **to keep s.o. informed of what is happening,** tenir qn au courant de ce qui se passe; **to i. the administration of a decision,** saisir l'administration d'une décision, lui faire connaître une décision; **to i. the police,** avertir la police; **we are writing to i. you of the dispatch of . . .,** nous vous avisons de l'envoi de . . .; *Com:* **I am pleased to i. you that . . .,** j'ai l'avantage de vous informer que . . .; **I regret to have to i. you that . . .,** j'ai le regret de vous annoncer, de vous faire savoir, que . . .; **we are informed that . . .,** on nous apprend, nous fait savoir, que . . .; **I have come to help you, he informed me,** je viens vous aider, me dit-il; **he is dead, so I am informed,** il est mort, à ce que j'apprends; (*b*) **to i. s.o. on, about, sth.,** renseigner qn sur qch.; **until we are better informed,** jusqu'à plus ample information; **there is nobody better informed,** il n'y a personne de mieux renseigné; **to be fully informed, you should know that . . .,** pour votre édification, sachez que . . .. **2.** *v.i. Jur:* **to i. against s.o.,** dénoncer qn.

inform[2], *a. Lit:* (masse) informe.

informal [in'fɔːml], *a.* **1.** (*a*) *Jur:* (i) en dehors des règles; irrégulier; qui n'est pas rédigé dans les formes légales; (document) informe; (ii) *N.Z:* **i. vote,** bulletin *m* de vote nul; (*b*) (réunion *f*, séance *f*) en dehors des statuts; (renseignement) officieux; **i. step,** démarche officieuse; **i. commission,** commission officieuse. **2.** (dîner, etc.) sans cérémonie, en famille; **we shall be an i. gathering,** nous serons en petit comité; **i. clothes,** tenue *f* de sport, de loisirs, de campagne.

informality [infɔː'mæliti], *s.* **1.** *Jur:* vice *m* de forme; irrégularité *f* (de rédaction, etc.). **2.** absence *f* de formalité, de cérémonie; **the i. of these monthly dinners,** le caractère intime de ces dîners mensuels.

informally [in'fɔːməli], *adv.* **1.** (*a*) en dehors des règles; irrégulièrement; (*b*) officieusement; **the committee met i.,** le bureau s'est réuni à titre non officiel. **2.** sans cérémonie; sans formalités; *F:* à la bonne franquette; en famille.

informant [in'fɔːmənt], *s.* **1.** informateur, -trice; **who is your i.?** qui vous a appris cela? de qui tenez-vous cela? **I have it from a reliable i.,** je le tiens de bonne source. **2.** *Jur: Adm:* déclarant, -ante.

informatics [infə'mætiks], *s.pl.* (*usu. with sg. const.*) (science *f* de l')informatique *f*.

information [infə'meiʃ(ə)n], *s.* **1.** renseignement(s) *m(pl)*, information(s) *f(pl)*; (*a*) **all (the) needful i.,** tous (les) renseignements utiles; **I am sending you for your i., by way of i. . . .,** je vous envoie à titre d'information, pour votre gouverne . . .; *Adm:* **i. copy,** copie *f* pour information; **(strictly) confidential i.,** renseignements (strictement) confidentiels; **piece of i.,** renseignement, indication *f*; **collection of i.,** (i) recherche *f* de renseignements; rassemblement *m* d'informations; constitution *f* d'une documentation; (ii) recueil *m* de renseignements; **request for i.,** demande *f* de renseignements; **to ask for i. on, about, s.o., sth.,** demander des renseignements sur qn, qch.; se renseigner sur qch., qn; **to ask for detailed i. on sth.,** demander des détails, des renseignements détaillés, sur qch.; **to get, obtain, i. about s.o., sth.,** obtenir des renseignements sur qn, qch.; aller aux informations, aux nouvelles, au sujet de qn; **from whom did you get your i.?** par qui vous êtes-vous fait renseigner? **to give, furnish, i. (bearing) on, about, sth.,** donner, fournir, des renseignements sur, concernant, qch.; **to have no i. about sth.,** n'avoir aucune information, aucun renseignement, sur qch.; être sans avis de qch.; **for further i. apply to the head office,** pour (de) plus amples renseignements s'adresser au bureau central; *Cards:* **to convey i. to one's partner,** éclairer son partenaire; *Mil:* **i. on the enemy,** renseignements sur l'ennemi; **an item of i.,** un renseignement (particulier); un indice; **processing of i.,** exploitation *f* des renseignements; *Adm:* **i. bureau,** bureau *m* de renseignements, d'adresses; centre *m* d'information; **Central Office of I.** = Commissariat *m* à l'Information; *Hist:* **Ministry of I.,** Ministère *m* de l'Information; *Tp:* **i. call,** demande de renseignements; **i. desk,** table *f* de renseignements; (*b*) *Cmptr:* **i. processing industry,** l'informatique *f*; **handling, processing, of i.,** manipulation *f*, traitement *m*, de l'information; **i. processing centre,** centre *m* de traitement de l'information; centre de calcul; **i. processing department,** service *m* (de l')informatique; **i. engineer,** ingénieur informaticien; **i. engineering, science, technology,** (la science de) l'informatique; **i. network,** réseau *m* informatique; **i. specialist, technologist,** informaticien, -ienne; **i. theory,** théorie *f* de l'information. **2.** instruction *f*, savoir *m*, connaissances *fpl*; **man full of i.,** homme qui a beaucoup d'instruction, de savoir; **for my own i.,** pour mon instruction. **3.** *Jur:* dénonciation *f* (**against s.o.,** contre qn); délation *f* (**against s.o.,** de qn); **to lay (an) i. against s.o. with the police,** dénoncer qn à la police; informer contre qn.

informational [infə'meiʃənl], *a.* **1.** instructif, informant. **2.** *Cmptr:* informationnel; sur le plan information.

informative [in'fɔːmətiv], *a.* instructif; **i. books,** livres éducatifs; **i. influence,** influence informante.

informatory [in'fɔːmət(ə)ri], *a.* informatif; qui fait part (de qch. à qn); *Cards:* **i. bid,** enchère faite dans le but d'éclairer son partenaire; annonce *f* d'indication.

informed [in'fɔːmd], *a.* bien renseigné; **i. public opinion,** l'opinion publique bien renseignée, bien au courant; **i. observers say he'll be asked to resign,** ceux qui ont le mot de l'affaire disent, en lieu compétent on dit, qu'on va lui demander sa démission; **i. estimate,** une évaluation bien renseignée.

informer [in'fɔːmər], *s.* dénonciateur, -trice; informateur, -trice; indicateur, -trice; *P:* mouchard *m*; *Jur:* **common i.,** délateur, -trice; **to turn i.,** dénoncer ses complices; *P:* moucharder.

informing [in'fɔːmiŋ], *a.* **1.** (esprit, énergie) qui inspire, qui anime. **2.** (*a*) (auteur, livre) instructif, qui informe, qui instruit; (*b*) *Navy:* **i. gun,** coup *m* (de canon) de semonce.

infra- ['infrə], *pref.* infra-, sous-.

infra-axillary ['infrəæk'siləri], *a.* infra-axillaire, *pl.* infra-axillaires.

infrablack ['infrə'blæk], *a. T.V:* infra-noir, *pl.* infra-noirs.

infraclavicular [infrəklə'vikjulər], *a. Anat:* sous-claviculaire, *pl.* sous-claviculaires.

infraclusion [infrə'kluːʒ(ə)n], *s. Dent:* infraclusion *f*.

infracostal [infrə'kɔstl], *a. Anat:* sous-costal, *pl.* sous-costaux.

infract [in'frækt], *v.tr.* transgresser (la loi, etc.).

infraction [in'frækʃ(ə)n], *s.* **1.** infraction *f* (d'un droit); transgression *f*; **i. of the law,** violation *f* de la loi, infraction à la loi; **minor i. of the law, i. of regulations,** contravention *f*. **2.** *Med:* fêlure *f*.

infra dig ['infrə'dig], *adj.phr.* (*from Lt. phr.* **infra dignitatem**) *F:* **it would be i. d. for us to reply,** ce ne serait pas convenable de notre part, ce serait audessous de notre dignité, au-dessous de nous, de répondre; ce serait déchoir, nous manquer à nous-mêmes, que de répondre.

infradyne ['infrədain], *s. W.Tel:* infradyne *m*.

infralapsarian [infrəlæp'sɛəriən], *s. Rel.H:* infralapsaire *m*.

infralapsarianism [infrəlæp'sɛəriənizm], *s. Rel.H:* infralapsarisme *m*.

inframaxillary [infrəmæk'siləri], *a. Anat:* sous-maxillaire, *pl.* sous-maxillaires.

infrangible [in'fræn(d)ʒibl], *a.* infrangible; (i) (barre, etc.) incassable; (ii) (pacte) inviolable.

infraorbital [infrə'ɔːbitəl], *a. Anat:* sous-orbitaire, *pl.* sous-orbitaires.

infraposition [infrəpə'ziʃ(ə)n], *s.* infraposition *f*.

infrared [infrə'red], *a. Ph:* infra(-)rouge; **i. radiation, rays,** radiation *f* infra(-)rouge; infra(-)rouge *m*; (les) infra(-)rouges; **i. detector,** détecteur *m* d'infra(-)rouge; *Atom.Ph:* **i. maser,** maser *m* à infra(-)rouges; laser *m*; *Aut: Com:* **i. drying,** séchage *m* à l'infra(-)rouge; *Med:* **i. therapy,** traitement *m* par les radiations infra (-)rouges; **i. lamp,** lampe *f* à rayons infra(-)rouges; *Phot:* **i. photography,** photographie *f* à l'infra(-)rouge.

infrasonic ['infrə'sɔnik], *a.* infrasonore; **i. vibration,** infra(-)son *m*, *pl.* infra(-)sons.

infraspecific ['infrəspə'sifik], *a. Nat.Hist:* inclus dans une espèce.

infraspinator ['infrəspi'neitər], *s. Anat:* muscle sous-épineux.

infraspinous ['infrə'spainəs], *a. Anat:* (muscle) sous-épineux.

infrastructure ['infrəstrʌktjər], *s.* **1.** *Pol.Ec: Adm:* infrastructure *f*. **2.** *Trans: Mil:* infrastructure.

infrequency [in'friːkwənsi], *s.* rareté *f*, infréquence *f*.

infrequent [in'friːkwənt], *a.* rare, infréquent, peu fréquent.

infrequently [in'friːkwəntli], *adv.* rarement; **not i.,** assez souvent.

infringe [in'frindʒ]. **1.** *v.tr.* enfreindre, violer (une loi, une règle, un serment, une promesse); transgresser (la loi, une règle); **to i. a patent,** (i) contrefaire un objet breveté; (ii) empiéter sur un brevet; **to i. an author's, artist's, copyright,** violer, empiéter sur, les droits d'un auteur, d'un artiste. **2.** *v.ind.tr.* **to i. on s.o.'s rights,** empiéter sur les droits de qn.

infringement [in'frindʒmənt], *s.* **1.** infraction *f* (d'un règlement); violation *f* (d'une loi, d'un droit); **i. of a treaty,** infraction à un traité; **i. of s.o.'s rights,** infraction, atteinte *f*, aux droits de qn; empiètement *m* sur les droits de qn. **2. i. of a patent,** contrefaçon *f* (d'un brevet); **i. of (literary) copyright,** contrefaçon (littéraire); *Jur:* **i. suit, action for i.,** poursuites *fpl* en contrefaçon; **to bring an action for i. of patent against s.o.,** assigner qn en contrefaçon.

infringer [in'frindʒər], *s.* contrefacteur *m* (d'un brevet, etc.); violateur, -trice (des droits de qn).

infringing [in'frindʒiŋ], *s.* **1.** infraction *f*, violation *f* (d'une règle, etc.). **2.** empiètement *m* (**of s.o.'s rights,** sur les droits de qn).

infructescence [infrʌk'tes(ə)ns], *s. Bot:* infrutescence *f*.

infructuous [in'frʌktjuəs], *a.* infructueux.

infula, *pl.* **-ae** ['infjulə, -iː], *s. Rom. Ant: Ecc:* infule *f*.

infundibular [infʌn'dibjulər], **infundibuliform** [infʌn'dibjulifɔːm], *a. Nat.Hist:* infundibuliforme, infondibuliforme; en forme d'entonnoir.

infundibulum, *pl.* **-a** [infʌn'dibjuləm, -ə], *s. Anat:* infundibulum *m*.

infuriate [in'fjuːrieit], *v.tr.* rendre (qn, un taureau, etc.) furieux.

infuriated [in'fjuːrieitid], *a.* furieux, en fureur; **to become i.,** entrer en fureur.

infuriating [in'fjuːrieitiŋ], *a.* qui rend furieux; exaspérant; **at times I find him i.,** des fois il me met hors des gonds.

infuriatingly [in'fjuːrieitiŋli], *adv.* à rendre furieux; **he's i. polite,** il est d'une politesse exaspérante.

infuse [in'fjuːz], *v.tr.* **1.** (*a*) **to i. courage, new life, into s.o.,** infuser du courage, une nouvelle vie, à qn; (*b*) **to i. s.o. with ardour,** inspirer de l'ardeur à qn; **the corporate spirit with which the staff is infused,** l'esprit *m* de corps dont le personnel est pénétré. **2.** infuser, faire infuser (du thé, des herbes); *Pharm:* macérer.

infuser [in'fjuːzər], *s.* infusoir *m*; **tea i.,** œuf *m* à thé; boule *f* à thé; cuiller *f* automatique à thé.

infusibility [infjuːzi'biliti], *s.* infusibilité *f.*

infusible [in'fjuːzibl], *a.* infusible, non fusible.

infusing [in'fjuːziŋ], *s.* infusion *f* (d'herbes, etc.).

infusion [in'fjuːʒ(ə)n], *s.* **1.** *Theol:* infusion *f* (de la vérité, etc.). **2.** (*a*) infusion (d'une tisane); (*b*) tisane, infusion (de camomille, etc.); *Pharm:* infusé *m*. **3.** *Ecc:* **baptism by i.,** baptême *m* par infusion.

Infusoria [infjuː'zɔːriə], *s.pl. Prot:* protozoaires ciliés; *O:* infusoires *m.*

infusorial [infjuː'zɔːriəl], *a.* **i. earth,** (i) *Geol:* terre *f* à infusoires; farine *f* fossile; tripoli siliceux; kieselguhr *m*; (ii) *Com:* terre d'infusoires.

infusorian [infju'zɔːriən]. **1.** *s. Prot: O:* infusoire *m*. **2.** *a.* = INFUSORIAL.

infusory [in'fjuːzəri]. **1.** *a.* = INFUSORIAL. **2.** *s. Prot: O:* infusoire *m.*

ingate ['ingeit], *s. Metall:* attaque *f* de coulée.

ingenious [in'dʒiːnjəs], *a.* (homme, mécanisme) ingénieux; **i. answer,** réponse ingénieuse; **to be i. in doing sth.,** être ingénieux à faire qch.

ingeniously [in'dʒiːnjəsli], *adv.* ingénieusement.

ingeniousness [in'dʒiːnjəsnis], *s.* = INGENUITY.

ingénue [ɛ̃ʒei'njuː], *s.f. Th:* ingénue.

ingenuity [indʒi'nju(ː)iti], *s.* ingéniosité *f* (de qn, d'une invention); **technical i.,** habileté *f* technique; **to tax one's i. in order to do sth.,** s'ingénier à faire qch.

ingenuous [in'dʒenjuəs], *a.* **1.** franc, *f.* franche; sincère. **2.** ingénu, simple, candide; naïf, *f.* naïve.

ingenuously [in'dʒenjuəsli], *adv.* **1.** franchement, sincèrement. **2.** ingénument, naïvement; avec candeur; **remark made quite i.,** remarque faite en toute ingénuité, en toute candeur.

ingenuousness [in'dʒenjuəsnis], *s.* ingénuité *f*, naïveté *f*, candeur *f.*

ingerence ['indʒərəns], *s.* ingérence *f*, intervention *f*, intrusion *f* (dans les affaires d'autrui, d'un autre pays).

ingest [in'dʒest], *v.tr. Physiol:* ingérer (un aliment).

ingesta [in'dʒestə], *s.pl. Physiol:* ingesta *m.*

ingestion [in'dʒestʃ(ə)n], *s. Physiol:* ingestion *f.*

ingle ['iŋgl], *s. Lit:* feu *m* (qui brûle sur l'âtre); foyer *m* (domestique); **i. bench,** banc *m* sous le manteau de la cheminée.

inglenook ['iŋglnuk], *s.* coin *m* du feu.

inglorious [in'glɔːriəs], *a.* **1.** (*of pers.*) humble, modeste, obscur, inconnu. **2.** (combat, etc.) déshonorant, honteux.

ingloriously [in'glɔːriəsli], *adv.* **1.** (vivre, etc.) humblement, modestement. **2.** (s'acquitter) sans gloire; ignominieusement.

ingloriousness [in'glɔːriəsnis], *s.* ignominie *f* (d'un combat).

ingluvial [in'gluːviəl], *a. Orn:* ingluvial, -aux.

ingluvies [in'gluːviiːz], *s. Orn:* jabot *m.*

ingluvitis [ingluː'vaitis], *s. Vet:* inflammation *f* du jabot (des oiseaux domestiques).

in-goal [in'goul], *s. Rugby Fb:* en-but *m inv.*

ingoing[1] ['ingouiŋ], *a.* qui entre, entrant; **the i. crowd,** la foule qui entre; **i. tenant,** nouveau locataire.

ingoing[2], *s.* entrée *f.*

ingot ['iŋgət], *s.* lingot *m* (d'or, d'argent); saumon *m* (d'étain); **i. gold,** or *m* en lingot; **i. iron,** fer fondu, fer homogène; **i. steel,** acier en lingots; **i. mould,** moule *m* à lingots; lingotière *f.*

ingrain[1] ['ingrein], *a. Tex:* (*of wool*) teint en laine; (*of cotton*) teint avant la filature.

ingrain[2] [in'grein], *v.tr.* **1.** *Tex: A:* teindre (un tissu, etc.) grand teint. **2.** fixer; **certain habits are ingrained in one's nature,** certaines habitudes constituent une partie essentielle de sa nature; **prejudices that become ingrained,** préjugés qui s'incrustent.

ingrained [in'greind], *a.* (*a*) **hands i. with coal dust,** mains encrassées de poussier; **skin i. with dye,** peau imprégnée de teinture; **i. dirt,** charbon, etc., qui est entré dans les pores; (*b*) **i. prejudices,** préjugés enracinés; **i. habits,** habitudes invétérées; **i. rogue,** coquin invétéré; parfait coquin; **i. Tory,** conservateur à outrance, intransigeant.

ingrate ['ingreit], *a.* & *s. O:* ingrat, -e.

ingratiate [in'greiʃieit], *v.tr.* **to i. oneself with s.o.,** s'insinuer dans les bonnes grâces de qn; capter la confiance de qn; se faire bien venir de qn; se rendre agréable à qn; s'accréditer auprès de qn.

ingratiating [in'greiʃieitiŋ], *a.* insinuant, prévenant; (sourire) engageant; **to act, speak, in an i. manner,** agir, parler, d'une manière insinuante; pateliner.

ingratiatingly [in'greiʃieitiŋli], *adv.* d'une manière insinuante, prévenante, engageante.

ingratiatory [in'greiʃiət(ə)ri], *a.* (sourire, ton) insinuant, engageant.

ingratitude [in'grætitjuːd], *s.* ingratitude *f*; **to show i. to s.o.,** faire preuve d'ingratitude à l'égard de qn, envers qn; **to repay s.o. with i.,** payer qn d'ingratitude; **to reap i.,** semer en terre ingrate; être payé d'ingratitude.

ingravescent [ingrə'ves(ə)nt], *a.* (maladie) qui s'aggrave, qui va de mal en pis.

ingredient [in'griːdiənt], *s.* ingrédient *m*, élément *m*, partie constituante (d'un médicament, d'une boisson, etc.); *Ch:* principe *m* (d'un composé).

ingress ['ingres], *s.* **1.** (*a*) entrée *f*; *Jur:* **free i., egress and regress,** (servitude *f* du) droit de libre accès et de libre sortie; (*b*) admission *f* (d'un gaz, etc.). **2.** *Astr:* ingression *f.*

ingression [in'greʃ(ə)n], *s.* ingression *f*, incursion *f.*

ingressive [in'gresiv], *a. Gram:* ingressif.

ingrowing[1] ['ingrouiŋ], *a. Med:* **i. (toe)nail,** ongle incarné, qui s'incarne.

ingrowing[2], *s. Med:* incarnation *f* (des ongles).

ingrown ['ingroun], *a.* **1.** *Med:* (ongle) incarné. **2.** (préjugé, etc.) invétéré.

inguinal ['iŋgwin(ə)l], *a. Anat:* inguinal, -aux; inguinaire.

ingulf [in'gʌlf], *v.tr.* engloutir, engouffrer; **to be ingulfed in the sea,** être englouti par les flots; s'engouffrer, sombrer, s'abîmer, dans les flots.

ingurgitate [in'gəːdʒiteit], *v.tr.* (*a*) ingurgiter, avaler; (*b*) *Lit:* engloutir.

ingurgitation [ingəːdʒi'teiʃ(ə)n], *s.* ingurgitation *f.*

inhabit [in'hæbit], *v.tr.* **1.** habiter, habiter dans (une maison, une ville). **2.** *Cmptr:* occuper, avoir un encombrement de (tant d'octets).

inhabitable [in'hæbitəbl], *a.* habitable.

inhabitancy [in'hæbit(ə)nsi], *s. Jur:* habitation *f*, séjour *m* (dans une maison); résidence *f* (pendant la période requise pour devenir électeur, etc.).

inhabitant [in'hæbit(ə)nt], *s.* habitant, -ante.

inhabitation [inhæbi'teiʃ(ə)n], *s.* habitation *f* (d'un immeuble).

inhabited [in'hæbitid], *a.* (quartier, appartement) habité.

inhabiting [in'hæbitiŋ], *s.* habitation *f.*

inhalant [in'heilənt]. **1.** *a. Nat.Hist:* (pore, etc.) inhalant. **2.** *s. Med:* inhalation (gazeuse, liquide, etc.).

inhalation [in(h)ə'leiʃ(ə)n], *s.* (*a*) *Med: etc:* inhalation *f* (de chloroforme, d'oxygène, etc.); **i. mask,** masque *m* d'inhalation; (*b*) aspiration *f* (d'un parfum).

inhalator ['in(h)əleitər], *s. Med:* inhalateur *m.*

inhale [in'heil]. **1.** *v.tr.* (*a*) *Med:* inhaler (de l'éther, etc.); (*b*) aspirer, humer (un parfum); (*c*) respirer, avaler (la fumée d'une cigarette). **2.** *v.i.* avaler la fumée.

inhalent [in'heilənt], *a.* (pore, etc.) inhalant.

inhaler [in'heilər], *s.* **1.** (*pers.*) fumeur *m* qui a l'habitude d'avaler la fumée de sa cigarette. **2.** (*device*) (*a*) *Med:* inhalateur *m*; **atomizing i.,** inhalateur pulvérisateur; (*b*) *Ind:* respirateur *m*; masque *m* respiratoire.

inhaling [in'heiliŋ], *s.* inhalation *f*; **i. apparatus,** inhalateur *m.*

inharmonic [inhɑː'mɔnik], *a. Mus:* inharmonique.

inharmonious [inhɑː'mounjəs], *a. Mus: etc:* (son, accord) inharmonieux, sans harmonie, peu harmonieux.

inharmoniousness [inhɑː'mounjəsnis], **inharmony** [in'hɑːməni], *s.* manque *m* d'harmonie.

inhaul(er) ['inhɔːl(ə)r], *s. Nau:* hale-bas *m inv*; hale-dedans *m inv*; hale-à-bord *m inv.*

inhere [in'hiər], *v.i.* (*a*) (*of qualities, etc.*) exister (**in,** dans); être inhérent (**in,** à); (*b*) (*of rights, function*) appartenir, être assigné (**in,** à).

inherence [in'hiərəns], **inherency** [in'hiərənsi], *s.* inhérence *f* (**in,** à).

inherent [in'hiərənt], *a.* **1.** inhérent, naturel, propre (**in,** à); **i. laziness,** paresse inhérente; **i. defect, i. vice,** vice *m* propre; **i. moisture,** humidité *f* interne; **i. safety,** sûreté *f* intrinsèque; **i. stability,** stabilité *f* propre (d'un avion, d'un navire, etc.). **2. power i. in an office,** pouvoir assigné, qui appartient, à une fonction. **3.** *Cmptr:* **i. error,** erreur héritée, propre; **i. store,** mémoire inhérente, interne.

inherently [in'hiərəntli], *adv.* par héritance; **i. lazy,** né paresseux.

inherit [in'herit]. **1.** *v.tr.* (*a*) hériter de (qch.); **to i. a house, a title,** hériter d'une maison, d'un titre; **to i. a fortune,** succéder à une fortune; (*b*) **to i. sth. from s.o.,** hériter qch. de qn; **he inherited this furniture from his mother,** ce mobilier lui vient de sa mère; il a eu ce mobilier de sa mère; **to i. a characteristic, a taste, from one's father,** tenir un trait caractéristique, un goût, de son père; **he has inherited all his shortcomings,** il a hérité tous ses défauts; **problems inherited from the previous government,** problèmes légués, laissés, par le gouvernement antérieur. **2.** *v.i.* **to i. equally,** hériter de parts égales; **to i. jointly,** cohériter.

inheritable [in'heritəbl], *a.* **1.** (*a*) (titre) dont on peut hériter; **where the crown was i. by females,** là où les femmes pouvaient hériter de la couronne; (*b*) (maladie *f*) transmissible à ses descendants. **2.** *Jur:* (*of pers.*) apte à hériter (**to an estate,** d'une terre).

inheritage [in'heritidʒ], *s.* héritage *m*, patrimoine *m.*

inheritance [in'herit(ə)ns], *s.* **1.** succession *f*; **linear i.,** succession en ligne directe; **right of i.,** droit *m* de succession; **law of i.,** droit successif. **2.** patrimoine *m*, héritage *m*; *Jur:* hoirie *f*; **to come into an i.,** faire un héritage; recueillir une succession; **this property was a family i.,** ce bien lui est venu de famille; **the common i. of a nation,** le patrimoine commun d'une nation; *NAm:* **i. tax,** droits *mpl* de succession. **3.** *Biol:* patrimoine héréditaire.

inherited [in'heritid], *a.* (bien, trait, goût) hérité; **i. taint,** tache originelle, héréditaire; *Cmptr:* **i. error,** erreur héritée, propre.

inheritor [in'heritər], *s.* héritier *m.*

inheritress [in'heritris], *A:* **inheritrix** [in'heritriks], *s.f.* héritière.

inhesion [in'hiːʒ(ə)n], *s.* inhérence *f.*

inhibit[1] [in'hibit], *v.tr.* **1.** (*a*) *Jur: etc:* **to i. s.o. from doing sth.,** empêcher qn de faire qch.; interdire, défendre, à qn de faire qch.; (*b*) *Ecc:* suspendre, interdire (un prêtre); frapper (un prêtre) d'interdiction; **inhibited priest,** prêtre suspens. **2.** (*a*) *Med:* paralyser (une sécrétion, etc.); (*b*) *Psy:* inhiber (un sentiment); **inhibited person,** inhibé(e). **3.** *Ch: etc:* **to i. a reaction,** inhiber une réaction; *Petr:* **inhibited oil,** huile inhibée.

inhibit[2], *s. Cmptr:* **i. pulse,** impulsion *f* de blocage; **i. signal,** signal *m* d'interdiction.

inhibiting [in'hibitiŋ], *a.* (*of influence, etc.*) inhibiteur, -trice; **i. cause,** cause inhibitive, inhibitrice; *Cmptr:* **i. pulse,** impulsion *f* de blocage; **i. signal,** signal *m* d'interdiction; **i. circuit,** circuit inhibiteur.

inhibition [in(h)i'biʃ(ə)n], *s.* **1.** (*a*) *Jur. etc.* défense expresse; prohibition *f*; (*b*) *Ecc:* (i) suspense *f*, interdiction *f* (d'un prêtre); (ii) interdit *m*. **2.** *Med: Psy:* inhibition *f*; (i) **death from i.,** mort *f* par inhibition; **i. of blood,** absorption *f* de sang; (ii) **person with inhibitions,** inhibé(e). **3.** *Ch:* inhibition.

inhibitive [in'hibitiv], *a.* (mandat) prohibitif; (jugement) inhibitoire.

inhibitor [in'hibitər], *s.* **1.** *Ch: Bio-Ch: etc:* inhibiteur *m*; **corrosion i., oxidation i.,** inhibiteur de corrosion, d'oxydation; *Ind:* **pickling i.,** inhibiteur de décapage. **2.** *Cmptr:* (circuit) inhibiteur (*m*).

inhibitory [in'hibit(ə)ri], *a.* **1.** (mandat) prohibitif; (jugement) inhibitoire. **2.** *Anat:* **i. nerve,** nerf inhibiteur, d'inhibition. **3.** *Psy: Med:* **i. reflex,** réflexe inhibiteur. **4.** *Ch:* **i. phase,** colloïde protecteur.

inhomogeneity [inhɔmoudiʒ'niːiti], *s.* inhomogénéité *f*; non-homogénéité *f.*

inhomogeneous [inhɔmou'dʒiːniəs], *a.* inhomogène, non homogène.

inhospitable [inhɔ'spitəbl, in'hɔs-], *a.* inhospitalier; **i. shore,** terre inhospitalière; **i. fare,** mauvaise chère; *F:* chasse-cousin(s) *m.*

inhospitableness [inhɔ'spitəb(ə)lnis, in'hɔs-], **inhospitality** [inhɔspi'tæliti], *s.* inhospitalité *f.*

inhospitably [inhɔ'spitəbli, in'hɔs-], *adv.* d'une façon peu hospitalière.

in-house [in'haus], *a.* interne, intérieur; **binding can be an in-h. or outside operation,** la reliure peut se faire dans la maison ou en dehors; *Cmptr:* **in-h. data processing,** traitement *m* de l'information sur place, chez l'utilisateur; **in-h. software,** software *m* maison.

inhuman [in'hjuːmən], *a.* **1.** (père, maître) inhumain; insensible; brutal, -aux; (coutume) barbare. **2. human and i.,** humain et non humain; **an i. cry,** un cri inhumain.

inhumane [inhju(ː)'mein], *a.* inhumain, cruel, inaccessible à la pitié.

inhumanely [inhju(ː)'meinli], *adv.* (traiter qn) inhumainement; (massacrer) cruellement.

inhumanity [inhju(ː)'mæniti], *s.* inhumanité *f*, cruauté *f*, barbarie *f* (d'une personne, d'une action); **the i. of the**

troops, la brutalité des soldats.

inhumanly [in'hju:mənli], *adv.* **1.** = INHUMANELY. **2.** d'une façon non humaine; **i. strong,** fort comme un bœuf.

inhumation [inhju(:)'meiʃ(ə)n], *s.* inhumation *f*, enterrement *m* (d'un cadavre).

inhume [in'hju:m], *v.tr.* inhumer, enterrer (un cadavre).

inimical [i'nimik(ə)l], *a.* (*a*) (peuple) ennemi, hostile; **to be i. to s.o.,** être ennemi de qn, être hostile à qn; (*b*) défavorable, contraire, adverse (**to,** à); **practices i. to health,** habitudes mauvaises pour la santé.

inimically [i'nimikəli], *adv.* d'une manière hostile; hostilement, en ennemi.

inimitability [inimitə'biliti], **inimitableness** [i'nimitəb(ə)lnis], *s.* caractère *m* inimitable, nature *f* inimitable (de qch.).

inimitable [i'nimitəbl], *a.* inimitable.

inimitably [i'nimitəbli], *adv.* d'une manière inimitable; **it's i. funny,** c'est d'une drôlerie inimitable.

inion ['iniən], *s. Anat:* inion *m.*

iniquitous [i'nikwitəs], *a.* inique; **an i. deed,** un forfait, un crime, une iniquité.

iniquitously [i'nikwitəsli], *adv.* iniquement.

iniquitousness [i'nikwitəsnis], *s.* iniquité *f.*

iniquity [i'nikwiti], *s.* iniquité *f*; (i) **to be steeped in i.,** être perdu de vices; (ii) **to commit iniquities,** commettre des iniquités.

initial[1] [i'niʃ(ə)l]. **1.** *a.* (*a*) initial, -aux; premier; **i. phase, stage,** phase initiale, stade initial, premier stade (d'un événement, etc.); **the disease is only in the i. stages,** la maladie n'en est qu'à ses débuts, ne fait que commencer; **the i. difficulties,** les difficultés du début, du commencement; les premières difficultés; *Th:* **i. performance,** première (représentation); **i. adjustment, i. setting,** mise *f* au (point) zéro (d'un instrument de mesure, etc.); *Av: Nau:* **i. stability,** stabilité initiale; *Ball:* **i. mass,** masse initiale (d'un missile, etc.); **i. velocity,** vitesse initiale (d'un projectile); *Com: Fin:* **i. capital,** capital initial, d'apport; **i. (capital) expenditure, i. expenses, investment, outlay,** frais *mpl* de premier établissement; **i. cost,** coût initial; (*of manufactured product*) prix *m* de revient; **i. value,** valeur *f* de départ; *El:* **i. charge,** charge principale (d'un accumulateur); **i. voltage,** tension initiale (de décharge); *Ind:* **i. test,** essai *m* à la sortie d'usine, à la sortie de fabrication; *Mec.E:* **i. pitch,** pas *m* d'entrée (d'une vis, etc.); *Metall:* **i. creep,** fluage *m* primaire; *Mil:* **i. headquarters,** quartier général, poste de commandement, de départ, initial; **i. point,** point initial (de passage d'un convoi, *Av:* de largage des bombes); (*b*) *Atom.Ph:* **i. (radio)activity,** radioactivité initiale; **i. nucleus,** noyau original, primitif; **i. particle,** particule originale, primitive, primordiale; (*c*) *Bot:* **i. cell,** *s.* **initial,** (cellule) initiale (*f*); (*d*) *Typ:* **i. letter,** *s.* **initial,** lettre initiale; lettrine *f*; **illuminated i. (letter),** lettre ornée. **2.** *s. usu.pl.* **initials,** initiales *f*; (*to alteration of cheque, etc.*) paraphe *m*; (*of supervisor, etc.*) visa *m*; (*for sewing on garment, etc.*) monogramme *m*; **the U.N.E.S.C.O. initials,** le sigle de l'U.N.E.S.C.O.; **to put one's initials to sth.,** apposer son paraphe, son visa, à qch.

initial[2], *v.tr.* (**initialled**) parapher (un traité, une correction); viser (un acte, etc.); mettre son paraphe au bas (d'un acte); apposer son paraphe, son visa, ses initiales, à (un acte); **slip initialled by the cashier,** bordereau pourvu des initiales du caissier, visé par le caissier.

initialese [iniʃə'li:z], *s. F:* langage *m* des sigles.

initialization [iniʃəlai'zeiʃ(ə)n], *s. Cmptr:* initialisation *f.*

initialize [i'niʃəlaiz], *v.tr.* **1.** désigner (qn) par ses initiales. **2.** *Cmptr:* mettre (un programme) à la valeur initiale; *abs.* **to i. to a value,** initialiser à une valeur.

initialling [i'niʃəliŋ], *s.* apposition *f* de son paraphe (à un document).

initially [i'niʃəli], *adv.* au commencement; au début; initialement.

initiand [i'niʃiænd], *s.* aspirant, -ante, à une initiation; *F:* catéchumène *mf.*

initiate[1] [i'niʃiət], *s.* initié, -ée.

initiate[2] [i'niʃieit], *v.tr.* **1.** (*a*) commencer, ouvrir (des négociations, une ère nouvelle); jeter les bases (d'une amitié); lancer, amorcer (une entreprise, une mode); instaurer (des mesures, une méthode); instituer (une expérience, etc.); **to i. a deal,** entamer une affaire; **the relations which have been initiated between us,** les rapports que nous avons entamés; **to i. a new policy,** inaugurer une politique nouvelle; **to i. a reform,** prendre l'initiative, être l'initiateur, d'une réforme; *Jur:* **to i. proceedings against s.o.,** instituer des poursuites, introduire une instance, contre qn; (*b*) *Cmptr:* lancer, faire démarrer (un programme); déclencher (une opération). **2.** initier (qn); (*a*) **to i. s.o. into a secret,** initier qn à un secret; **to i. s.o. in a science, in an art,** initier qn à une science, aux procédés d'un art; (*b*) **to i. s.o. into a secret society,** initier qn à, admettre qn dans, une société secrète.

initiated [i'niʃieitid], *a.* initié; *s.* **the i.,** les initiés.

initiating[1] [i'niʃieitiŋ], *a.* primordial, -aux; qui déclenche, suscite, l'action, le phénomène; *Atom.Ph:* **i. electron,** électron *m* germe; **i. particle,** particule germe, primordiale; *El:* **i. relay,** relais *m* primaire.

initiating[2], *s.* initiation *f* (**into,** à; **in,** dans).

initiation [iniʃi'eiʃ(ə)n], *s.* **1.** (*a*) commencement(s) *m*, début(s) *m* (d'une entreprise); instauration *f*, inauguration *f* (d'un usage); (*b*) *Cmptr:* lancement *m*, déclenchement *m* (d'un programme, etc.). **2.** initiation *f* (de qn) (**into,** à); **i. rites,** rites *m* d'initiation. **3.** *Ch:* initiation (d'une réaction).

initiative [i'niʃiətiv]. **1.** *s.* initiative *f*; (*a*) **to take the i. in doing sth.,** prendre l'initiative pour faire qch.; **to have the i. with respect to sth.,** avoir l'initiative, le droit d'initiative, de qch.; *Mil:* **to have, keep, the i.,** avoir, garder, l'initiative; (*b*) **to have large powers of i.,** disposer d'une grande initiative; **to do sth. on one's own i.,** faire qch. de sa propre initiative, par soi-même; **to show, to lack, i.,** faire preuve, manquer, d'initiative, d'allant *m*; **lack of i.,** manque *m*, défaut *m*, d'initiative; **person with plenty of i.,** personne entreprenante. **2.** *a.* premier, introductoire, initiatique.

initiator [i'niʃieitər], *s.* **1.** initiateur, -trice; lanceur *m* (d'une mode, etc.). **2.** *Ch:* substance *f* qui amorce une réaction.

initiatory [i'niʃiət(ə)ri], *a.* **1.** premier, introductoire; **i. steps,** démarches *f* préparatoires, préliminaires. **2.** (*of rite, ceremony*) initiateur, -trice; d'initiation; initiatique.

inject [in'dʒekt], *v.tr.* (*a*) **to i. a fluid into a cavity, into a vein,** injecter un liquide dans une cavité, dans une veine; **to i. cocaine into the gum,** cocaïniser la gencive; **to i. capital into a business,** injecter du capital dans une entreprise; (*b*) **to i. a cavity with a fluid,** injecter une cavité d'un, avec un, liquide; **to i. an animal with antitoxin,** injecter une antitoxine à une bête; **to i. s.o. with morphia,** faire une piqûre de morphine à qn.

injectable [in'dʒektəbl], *a.* injectable.

injected [in'dʒektid], *a. Med:* (tissu, œil, etc.) injecté; **to become i. (with blood),** s'injecter (de sang).

injection [in'dʒekʃ(ə)n], *s.* injection *f.* **1.** (*a*) *Const:* **i. of cement by compressed air,** injection de ciment à l'air comprimé; *Mch:* **refrigerant i.,** injection de refroidissement; **water i.,** injection d'eau; **i. cock,** robinet *m* d'injection; prise *f* (de vapeur, etc.); **i. pipe,** tuyau *m* d'injection; **i. pump,** pompe *f* à injection; *Min:* pompe de charge; *I.C.E:* **fuel i.,** injection de carburant; **(fuel-) i. pump,** pompe d'injection (de carburant); **i. engine,** moteur *m* à injection; **i. nozzle,** tubulure *f* d'injection; injecteur *m*; *Ind:* **i. moulding (of plastics),** moulage *m* (du plastique) par injection; **i.-moulding press,** presse *f* à injection (pour le moulage du plastique); *Atom.Ph:* **electron i.,** injection d'électrons; **i. point,** point *m* d'injection; **i. moment,** moment *m* d'injection; (*b*) *Geol:* **i. of granite into gneiss,** injection du granit dans le gneiss. **2. i. of capital into a business,** injection, apport *m*, du capital dans une entreprise. **3.** *Med:* (*a*) **i. of the capillaries,** injection des capillaires; (*b*) **antitetanus i.,** injection, piqûre *f*, antitétanique; **hypodermic i., subcutaneous i.,** injection, piqûre, hypodermique, sous-cutanée; **intramuscular i.,** injection, piqûre, intramusculaire; **intravenous i.,** injection intraveineuse; **spinal i.,** injection spinale, rachidienne; **course of injections,** série *f* de piqûres; **to give s.o. an i.,** faire une injection, une piqûre, à qn; piquer qn; (*c*) **rectal i.,** lavement *m.* **4.** *Space:* **i. of a satellite into orbit,** insertion *f*, mise *f*, d'un satellite sur l'orbite.

injectivity [indʒek'tiviti], *s.* capacité *f* d'injection.

injector [in'dʒektər], *s. Mec.E:* injecteur *m* (d'eau dans une chaudière, de carburant dans la chambre de combustion d'un moteur à réaction, etc.); *I.C.E:* gicleur *m*; *Min:* pompe *f* de charge; *Const:* **cement i.,** injecteur de ciment; *Mec.E:* **grease i.,** injecteur à graisse, injecteur de lubrifiant; **lifting, non-lifting, i.,** injecteur aspirant, non aspirant; **i. pump,** pompe d'injection; *Atom.Ph:* **electron i.,** injecteur d'électrons.

injudicious [indʒu(:)'diʃəs], *a.* peu judicieux, malavisé; inconsidéré.

injudiciously [indʒu(:)'diʃəsli], *adv.* inconsidérément; d'une façon peu judicieuse.

injudiciousness [indʒu(:)'diʃəsnis], *s.* imprudence *f*; manque *m* de jugement; caractère peu judicieux (d'une action).

Injun ['indʒən], *s. F:* (*a*) *NAm:* Indien, -ienne (d'Amérique); (*b*) **honest I.?** (est-ce) bien sûr? parole d'honneur? sans blague? **honest I.!** vrai de vrai! sans blague! **to play I.,** se tenir caché; se dérober; s'esquiver.

injunction [in'dʒʌŋ(k)ʃ(ə)n], *s.* **1.** injonction *f*, ordre *m*, recommandation *f*; **to give s.o. strict injunctions to do sth.,** enjoindre strictement, formellement, à qn de faire qch.; **my parting injunctions to him were that he should be careful,** au moment de partir je lui ai enjoint de ne pas commettre d'imprudences. **2.** *Jur:* arrêt *m* de suspension; arrêt de sursis; (un) avant faire droit; **i. against s.o., restraining him from doing sth.,** injonction à qn de s'abstenir de faire qch.; **I shall ask for an i.,** je vais mettre opposition.

injunctive [in'dʒʌŋ(k)tiv], *a.* (*a*) *Jur:* injonctif; (*b*) *Gram:* **i. mood,** injonctif *m.*

injure ['indʒər], *v.tr.* **1.** nuire à, faire tort à, faire du mal à (qn, la réputation de qn); endommager (la réputation de qn); léser (qn); *Jur:* porter préjudice à (qn); **to i. oneself,** se faire du tort; se nuire à soi-même; **to i. s.o.'s interests,** compromettre, léser, les intérêts de qn. **2.** (*a*) blesser (qn); faire mal à (qn); **to be injured on duty,** être blessé en service commandé; **to i. oneself,** se blesser; se faire du mal; **fatally injured,** blessé mortellement; **his foot is permanently injured,** il en restera estropié du pied; **the blow has injured a nerve, the lung,** le coup a lésé un nerf, le poumon; **to i. s.o.'s pride,** léser l'amour-propre de qn; blesser qn dans son amour-propre; (*b*) endommager, abîmer, gâter (qch.); *Com:* avarier (des marchandises); (*of goods, etc.*) **to be injured,** souffrir (de la gelée, d'un voyage, etc.); s'avarier; **to i. one's health,** s'abîmer la santé; altérer, déranger, sa santé.

injured ['indʒəd], *a.* **1.** (*of pers.*) offensé, outragé; à qui on a fait tort; **i. wife,** femme trompée, trahie; **the i. party,** l'offensé, -ée; *Jur:* la partie lésée; **in an i. tone (of voice),** d'une voix offensée. **2.** (*a*) (bras, etc.) blessé, estropié; *s.* **the i.,** les blessés *m*; (*from accident*) les accidentés *m*; (*b*) (blé, etc.) endommagé, gâté, avarié.

injurer ['in(d)ʒərər], *s.* offenseur *m*, auteur *m* d'un tort, d'un mal.

injuria [in'dʒuəriə], *s. Jur:* violation *f* de droits.

injurious [in'dʒuəriəs], *a.* **1.** (*a*) nuisible, pernicieux, préjudiciable (**to,** à); **that would prove i. to my interests,** cela léserait mes intérêts; (*b*) **i. to (the) health,** nocif; nuisible à la santé. **2.** (langage) injurieux, offensant, outrageant.

injuriously [in'dʒuəriəsli], *adv.* **1.** injustement; à tort. **2. to affect s.o., sth., i.,** avoir un mauvais effet, un effet pernicieux, sur qn, sur qch. **3.** (parler) injurieusement.

injuriousness [in'dʒuəriəsnis], *s.* nuisibilité *f*, nocivité *f*; caractère nocif, nuisible (de qch.).

injury ['indʒ(ə)ri], *s.* **1.** tort *m*, mal *m*, préjudice *m*; *Jur:* lésion *f*; **to do s.o. an i.,** porter, causer, préjudice à qn; faire du tort à qn; porter atteinte à la réputation de qn; **doubts that do i. to one's faith,** doutes *m* qui entament la foi, qui portent atteinte à la foi; **to suffer i.,** subir un préjudice; **to the i. of s.o.,** au détriment de qn; **forgiveness of injuries,** pardon *m* des injures. **2.** (*a*) blessure *f* (au corps); *Med:* lésion; **to do oneself an i.,** (i) se blesser; se faire du mal; (ii) s'estropier; **he sustained no i., escaped without i.,** il n'a eu aucun mal; **to receive severe injuries,** recevoir de graves blessures; **internal injuries,** lésions internes; **there were no personal injuries,** il n'y a pas eu d'accident de personne; **industrial injuries,** accidents *m* du travail; (*b*) (*damage*) dommage *m*, dégât *m*; *Nau: Mch:* avarie *f*; **i. to the plant,** avaries de matériel; **injuries to a building due to the wet,** dégradation d'un bâtiment due à l'humidité.

injustice [in'dʒʌstis], *s.* **1.** injustice *f* (d'une loi, etc.); **I hate i.,** je déteste les injustices; **flagrant cases of i.,** des injustices flagrantes. **2. you do him an i.,** vous êtes injuste envers lui.

ink[1] [iŋk], *s.* **1.** encre *f*; (*a*) **writing i.,** encre à écrire; **written in i.,** écrit à l'encre; *F:* **to sling i.,** (i) (*also* **spill i.**) noircir du papier; scribouiller; (ii) *Journ:* écrire des articles injurieux; **bulky i.,** encre volumineuse; **heavy i.,** encre lourde; **opaque i.,** encre opaque; **stiff i.,** encre ferme; **oily i.,** encre grasse; **tacky i.,** encre poissante; **chalky i.,** encre terreuse; **glossy i.,** encre brillante; **metallic i.,** encre métallique; **indelible i., waterproof i.,** encre indélébile; **Indian i.,** encre de Chine; **coloured i.,** encre de couleur; **copying i., duplicating i.,** encre à copier; encre copiante, communicative; **copying-i. pencil,** crayon *m* à copier, à encre; **drawing i.,** encre à dessin; **i. for rubber stamps,** encre à tampon; **marking i.,** encre à marquer le linge; **printing i., printer's i.,** encre d'imprimerie, d'impression; **lithographic i.,** encre litho(graphique); **crayon i.,** encre litho à report; **litho writing i.,** encre d'écrivain litho; **phototransfer i.,** encre à report photo; **stumping i.,** encre pour reports de dessins litho; *Cmptr:* **conductive i.,** encre conductrice; **magnetic i.,** encre magnétique; (*b*) *attrib.* **i. blot, i. spot, i. stain,** tache *f* d'encre; *Psy:* **i.-blot test,** klecksographie *f*; test *m* de la tache d'encre; **i. bottle,** (i) bouteille *f* à encre; encrier *m*; (ii) bouteille d'encre; *Typ: etc:* **i. cylinder,** cylindre *m*, table *f*, à encrer; **i. feed,** conduit *m* (de stylo); **i. duct, i. fountain,** encrier *m*; **i. fountain roller,** rouleau *m* d'encrier; **i. pad,** tampon encrier; **i. recorder,** enregistreur *m* à stylet; **i. resisting,** repoussant l'encre; **i. retentive,** retenant l'encre; **i. slab,** table à encrer; **i. trough,** (i) *Tg:* capsule *f* d'encrage; (ii) *Typ:* encrier (des rouleaux encreurs); *Tg:* **i. writer,** récepteur-imprimeur *m*, *pl.* récepteurs-imprimeurs, à l'encre; appareil *m* à molette. **2.** *Moll:* noir *m*, encre (de seiche); sépia *f*; **i. bag, i. sac,** glande *f*, poche *f*, du noir. **3.** (*a*) *Fung:* **(shaggy) i. cap,** coprin (chevelu); (*b*) *Bot:* **i. disease,** maladie *f* de l'encre.

ink[2], *v.*

I. *v.tr.* **1.** noircir d'encre, barbouiller d'encre, tacher d'encre; **to i. one's fingers, one's face,** se couvrir les doigts d'encre; se barbouiller le visage d'encre. **2.** *Typ:* encrer (les lettres); toucher (la forme).

II. (*compound verbs*) **1. ink in,** *v.tr.* tracer à l'encre (des lignes faites au crayon); **to i. in a drawing,** mettre une épure à l'encre; repasser un dessin à l'encre.

2. ink out, *v.tr.* oblitérer, rayer, biffer (un mot, etc.) à l'encre.

3. ink over, *v.tr.* (*a*) = INK IN; (*b*) = INK OUT.

4. ink up, *v.tr.* imprégner, couvrir, d'encre; **to i. up an engraved plate,** tamponner une plaque gravée.

inker ['iŋkər], *s.* **1.** *Tg:* (*a*) récepteur-imprimeur *m*, *pl.* récepteurs-imprimeurs; récepteur *m* à encre; télégraphe écrivant; appareil *m* à molette; (*b*) molette *f* d'encrage. **2.** *Typ:* (rouleau) encreur *m*; (rouleau) toucheur *m*.

inkfish ['iŋkfiʃ], *s.* *Moll:* **1.** seiche *f*. **2.** calmar *m*, encornet *m*.

inkholder ['iŋkhouldər], *s.* réservoir *m* (de stylo).

inkhorn ['iŋkhɔːn], *s.* *A:* encrier *m* de corne.

inkiness ['iŋkinis], *s.* noirceur *f* (d'encre).

inking ['iŋkiŋ], *s.* *Typ:* encrage *m* (des rouleaux); **to increase the i.,** charger une couleur; **i. pad,** tampon *m* à impression; tampon encreur; **i. roller,** (i) *Typ:* (rouleau) encreur *m*; (rouleau) toucheur *m*; (ii) *Tg:* molette *f* d'encrage; **i. table,** encrier *m*.

inking in ['iŋkiŋ'in], *s.* mise *f* à l'encre.

inkling ['iŋkliŋ], *s.* soupçon *m*; **to give s.o. an i. of sth.,** faire pressentir qch. à qn; **if you had given me the slightest i. about it,** si vous m'en aviez donné le moindre soupçon; **he didn't let slip one word that might have given you an i. as to his feelings,** il ne lui est pas échappé une parole qui pût laisser deviner ses émotions; **he had an i. of the truth,** il entrevit, entrevoyait, la vérité; **I had an i. of his intention,** j'ai eu vent de son intention, **he has no i. of the matter,** il ne se doute de rien; **without having the least i. of what we intended,** sans se douter le moins du monde de nos intentions; **he hadn't an i. of, about, the subject under discussion,** il n'avait pas la moindre idée de ce qu'on discutait.

inkpot ['iŋkpɔt], *s.* encrier *m*.

ink-slinger ['iŋksliŋər], *s.* *F:* (*a*) gratte-papier *m inv*; scribouillard, -arde; (*b*) *Journ:* journaliste de bas étage; *esp.* journaliste calomniateur, -trice.

ink-slinging[1] ['iŋksliŋiŋ], *a.* *F:* (journaliste) calomniateur, -trice, diffamateur, -trice; (journalisme) calomnieux.

ink-slinging[2] *s.* journalisme calomnieux; calomnies *fpl*, médisance *f*.

inkstained ['iŋksteind], *a.* taché, barbouillé, d'encre.

inkstand ['iŋkstænd], *s.* grand encrier (avec poseplumes).

inkwell ['iŋkwel], *s.* encrier *m* (pour table percée).

inky[1] ['iŋki], *a.* **1.** taché d'encre; **i. fingers,** doigts barbouillés d'encre, couverts d'encre. **2. i. (black),** noir comme (de) l'encre; **the night was i. black,** il faisait noir comme dans un four. **3.** *Fung:* *NAm:* **i. cap,** coprin (chevelu).

inky[2], *s.* *Cin:* *F:* lampe *f* à incandescence.

inlaid ['inleid, in'leid], *a.* **1.** incrusté, marqueté; (plancher) parqueté; **i. floor,** parqueterie *f* en mosaïque; **i. linoleum,** linoléum incrusté; **i. work,** marqueterie *f*; pièces rapportées; **i. enamel work,** nielle *f*, niellage *m*; *Bookb:* **i. leather,** reliure *f* mosaïque. **2.** *Bookb:* (*of illustration*) encarté.

inland ['inlænd]. **1.** *s.* (l')intérieur *m* (d'un pays); **to explore the i.,** explorer l'intérieur des terres. **2.** *a.* (*a*) intérieur; **i. sea,** mer intérieure; **i. waterway,** voie d'eau intérieure; voie fluviale; **i. water transport,** transport *m* par voie d'eau intérieure, par voie fluviale; **i. water craft,** bâtiment fluvial; **i. navigation,** navigation intérieure, fluviale; *Geol:* **i. ice,** calotte *f* glaciaire; glacier continental; inlandsis *m*; (*b*) du pays; **i. trade,** commerce intérieur; **i. produce,** produits *m* indigènes, du pays; **i. telegram, i. parcel,** télégramme *m*, colis *m*, à destination de l'intérieur; **i. postage rates,** (tarif *m* d')affranchissement *m* en régime intérieur; **i. money order,** mandat *m* sur l'intérieur; **i. bill,** traite *f* sur le pays; effet *m*, lettre *f* de change, sur l'intérieur; **i. revenue,** contributions (directes et indirectes); **the (Commissioners of) I. Revenue, the I. Revenue (Department),** le fisc; **i. revenue stamp,** timbre fiscal. **3.** *adv.* **to go, march, i.,** pénétrer vers l'intérieur, dans les terres.

inlander ['inləndər], *s.* habitant, -ante, de l'intérieur (d'un pays).

in-laws [in'lɔːz], *s.pl.* parents *m* par alliance; alliés *m*; belle-famille *f*; beaux-parents.

inlay[1] ['inlei], *s.* **1.** (*a*) incrustation *f* (de nacre, etc.); **marquetry i.,** marqueterie *f*; *Bookb:* **leather i.,** applique *f*; reliure *f* mosaïque; (*b*) *NAm:* *Dent:* inlay *m*, incrustation (de métal, en or, en céramique, etc.); (*c*) *Dressm:* soufflet *m*; **lace i.,** incrustation de dentelle. **2.** *Bookb:* encartage *m*.

inlay[2] ['inlei, in'lei], *v.tr.* **(inlaid) 1.** incruster **(with,** de); marqueter (une table, etc.); parqueter (un plancher) en mosaïque; *Metalw:* damasquiner (une épée, etc.); **to i. with enamel,** nieller; **table inlaid with mother-of-pearl,** table incrustée de nacre, avec incrustations de nacre. **2.** *Bookb:* encarter (des illustrations).

inlayer ['inleiər], *s.* (ouvrier) marqueteur *m*.

inlaying ['inleiiŋ], *s.* **1.** incrustation *f*; (*of floor*) parqueterie *f* en mosaïque; *Metalw:* damasquinage *m* (d'une épée, etc.). **2.** *Bookb:* encartage *m*.

inlet[1] ['inlet], *s.* **1.** entrée *f*, arrivée *f*, admission *f* (d'air, de gaz, de vapeur, d'essence, etc.); *I.C.E:* *Mch:* **i. connection, i. feed pipe,** tubulure *f* d'admission; **i. duct,** (conduite *f* d')admission; **i. fitting,** raccord *m* d'entrée; **i. pipe,** tuyau *m* d'arrivée, d'admission (de vapeur, etc.); *Civ.E:* **tapered i. pipe,** cône *m* d'entrée (d'un pipe-line); *Hyd.E:* **i. tunnel,** galerie *f* d'amenée (d'eau); **i. velocity,** vitesse *f* d'entrée (de l'eau dans une turbine). **2.** (*a*) *Tchn:* (orifice *m* d')entrée, (orifice d')admission (d'air, de gaz, de vapeur, d'essence, etc.); ouïe *f* (de ventilateur, de pompe centrifuge); **i. for oil, for steam,** orifice d'admission de l'huile, de la vapeur; **water i.,** entrée d'eau; *El.E:* **cable i.,** entrée de câble; (*b*) *Geog:* goulet *m* (d'entrée dans un port, etc.); **i. of a channel,** entrée d'une passe; **inlets into a lake,** débouchés *m* d'un lac. **3.** *Geog:* petit bras de mer; crique *f*, anse *f*. **4.** *Dressm:* *etc:* pièce rapportée; incrustation *f*.

inlet[2], *a.* *Needlew:* **bodice i. with hand-made lace,** corsage *m* à entre-deux de dentelle à la main.

inlier ['inlaiər], *s.* *Geol:* enclave (rocheuse).

inline [in'lain], *a.* *Cmptr:* **i. sub routine,** sous programme *m*, *pl.* sous-programmes, ouvert, relogeable.

inlying ['inlaiiŋ], *a.* de l'intérieur (du pays).

inmate ['inmeit], *s.* (*a*) habitant, -ante (d'une maison); **all the inmates were awakened by the noise,** toute la maisonnée fut réveillée par le bruit; (*b*) pensionnaire *mf* (d'une maison de santé); hôte *m* (d'un hospice); (*c*) détenu, -ue (dans une prison).

inmost ['inmoust], *a.* le plus profond; **in the i. recesses of the woods,** au plus profond des bois; **the i. recesses of the soul, of the heart,** les replis les plus profonds, les plus secrets, de l'âme; les recoins *m* les plus intimes du cœur; **our i. thoughts, feelings,** nos pensées les plus secrètes, nos sentiments les plus intimes; **our i. being,** le tréfonds, l'arrière-fond *m*, de notre être.

inn [in], *s.* **1.** (*a*) auberge *f*; (*fashionable*) hôtellerie *f*, hostellerie *f*; **to put up at an i.,** descendre à une auberge, dans une hôtellerie; (*b*) (*restaurant*) hôtellerie, hostellerie. **2.** *Jur:* **Inns of Court,** les quatre Écoles de droit de Londres qui seules confèrent le droit d'être avocat.

innards ['inədz], *s.pl.* *P:* (= INWARDS) entrailles *f*, intestins *m*, viscères *m*; **pain in the i.,** mal *m* au ventre.

innate [i'neit], *a.* **1.** inné, infus; **i. common sense,** bon sens foncier, naturel; *Phil:* **i. ideas,** idées innées. **2.** *Biol:* endogène. **3.** *Bot:* (anthère) attachée à l'extrémité du filet.

innately [i'neitli], *adv.* (méchant, etc.) de naissance.

innateness [i'neitnis], *s.* *Phil:* *etc:* innéité *f* (des idées); caractère foncier (d'une qualité, etc.).

innatism [i'neitizm], *s.* *Phil:* innéisme *m*.

inner ['inər]. **1.** *a.* intérieur; (écorce *f*, etc.) interne, de dedans; **i. side,** côté *m* interne; **on the i. side,** à l'intérieur, en dedans; *Anat:* **the i. ear,** l'oreille *f* interne; **i. harbour,** arrière-port *m*, *pl.* arrière-ports; **i. dock,** arrière-bassin *m*, *pl.* arrière-bassins; **i. court,** cour intérieure (d'un immeuble); **i. radius (of railway-line),** petit rayon; **our i. life,** notre vie intérieure; **his i. conscience told him that he was wrong,** dans l'intimité de la conscience il se rendait compte qu'il avait tort; **the i. workings of the mind,** les opérations secrètes de l'esprit; **i. meaning,** sens *m* intime, fond *m* (d'un passage); **the i. circle,** le cercle intime (d'amis); le groupe dirigeant (d'un parti politique); *Fin:* **i. reserves,** réserves latentes. **2.** *s.* premier cercle autour de la mouche (d'une cible).

innermost ['inəmoust], *a.* **1.** = INMOST. **2. the i. satellite of Jupiter,** le satellite le plus proche de Jupiter.

innervate ['inəːveit], *v.tr.* *Physiol:* innerver.

innervation [inəː'veiʃ(ə)n], *s.* *Physiol:* innervation *f*.

innings ['iniŋz]. **1.** *s.pl.* (*a*) *Jur:* terres abandonnées par la mer; relais *m* de mer; accrue *f*; (*b*) *Civ.E:* terrains conquis sur les eaux marines. **2.** *s.sg.* (*pl. inv. or F:* **inningses**; *NAm: also* **inning**) *Sp:* (*Cr: baseball*) tournée *f*, tour *m* de batte ((i) de chaque équipe, (ii) de chaque membre de l'équipe); **he had a long i.,** (i) il est resté longtemps au guichet; (ii) *F:* il a vécu longtemps; il a fourni une longue carrière; **to have had a good i.,** (i) avoir vécu longtemps; (ii) avoir eu de la chance; *F:* *O:* **it's my i. now!** à mon tour! **wait till the opposition get their i.!** attendez que ce soit le tour de l'opposition!

innkeeper ['inkiːpər], *s.* aubergiste *mf*; hôtelier, -ière.

innocence ['inəs(ə)ns], *s.* **1.** (*a*) innocence *f* (d'un accusé); (*b*) **the i. of a holy life,** l'innocence d'une sainte vie; (*c*) naïveté *f*, simplicité *f*, innocence, candeur *f*; **to take advantage of s.o.'s i.,** abuser de l'innocence de qn; **the age of i.,** l'âge *m* d'innocence; **to pretend i.,** faire l'innocent; **to assume an air of i.,** prendre un air naïf, innocent; **to lose one's i.,** perdre son innocence; *F:* se déniaiser; **in all i.,** en toute innocence. **2.** *A:* innocence (d'une plaisanterie, d'un médicament, etc.).

innocent ['inəs(ə)nt], *a.* **1.** (*a*) innocent; pas coupable; **i. of a crime,** innocent d'un crime; **an i. person,** un(e) innocent(e); (*b*) dépourvu, vierge **(of,** de); **windows i. of glass,** fenêtres dépourvues de vitres, sans vitres; **to be quite i. of Latin,** ne pas savoir un mot de latin. **2.** (*a*) pur; sans péché; innocent; **as i. as a newborn babe,** innocent comme un enfant qui vient de naître; d'une candeur de nouveau-né; *s.* *B.Hist:* **the Holy Innocents,** les (saints) Innocents; **Holy Innocents' Day,** la fête des saints Innocents; **the Slaughter of the Innocents,** le Massacre des Innocents; *Parl:* *F:* *O:* **the Massacre of the Innocents,** le massacre, en fin de session, des projets de loi pour la considération desquels le temps a manqué; (*b*) naïf, *f.* naïve; sans malice; innocent; **i.-looking person,** personne *f* à l'air naïf; **to put on an i. air,** faire l'innocent(e); n'avoir pas l'air d'y toucher; avoir l'air de ne pas y toucher; *s.* *O:* **the village i.,** l'idiot *m*, l'innocent, du village. **3.** (*a*) (jeu, remède) innocent, inoffensif; (*b*) *Med:* **i. tumour,** tumeur bénigne; (*c*) (commerce) légitime, permis, autorisé; *Jur:* **i. purchase,** acquisition *f* de bonne foi.

innocently ['inəsəntli], *adv.* innocemment; en toute innocence; **to look i. at s.o.,** regarder qn d'un air naïf, d'innocence.

innocuity [inɔ'kju(ː)iti], *s.* innocuité *f*.

innocuous [i'nɔkjuəs], *a.* inoffensif, anodin; **the i. character of a book,** l'innocuité *f* d'un livre; **i. complaint,** maladie bénigne; **i. microbes,** microbes non pathogènes, banaux.

innocuously [i'nɔkjuəsli], *adv.* inoffensivement.

innocuousness [i'nɔkjuəsnis], *s.* innocuité *f*.

innominate [i'nɔminət], *a.* **1.** *Anat:* (os) innominé, iliaque; (artère) innominée, brachiocéphalique. **2.** *Jur:* (contrat) innom(m)é.

innovate ['inəveit], *v.i.* innover **(in,** à, en, dans).

innovating[1] ['inəveitiŋ], *a.* innovateur, -trice.

innovating[2], *s.* innovation *f*.

innovation [inə'veiʃ(ə)n], *s.* **1.** innovation *f*, changement *m* (dans une méthode, en politique, en littérature, etc.); **to make innovations in sth.,** apporter des changements, des innovations, à qch.; **old people dislike innovations,** la nouveauté répugne aux vieillards. **2.** *Jur:* *Scot:* novation *f*.

innovative ['inəveitiv], *a.* innovateur, -trice; qui sait innover.

innovator ['inəveitər], *s.* innovateur, -trice; novateur, -trice.

innoxious [i'nɔkʃəs], *a.* inoffensif.

innoxiously [i'nɔkʃəsli], *adv.* inoffensivement.

innoxiousness [i'nɔkʃəsnis], *s.* nature inoffensive (de qch.); innocuité *f*.

innuendo, *pl.* **-o(e)s** [inju(ː)'endou, -ouz], *s.* **1.** *Jur:* insinuation *f*, mot couvert (en apparence inoffensif, mais en réalité destiné à atteindre qn dans son honneur). **2.** allusion (malveillante); **to throw out innuendoes against s.o.,** *F:* jeter des pierres dans le jardin de qn; **to discredit s.o. by i.,** discréditer qn par sous-entendus.

Innuit, *pl.* **-uit(s)** ['injuit, -it(s)], *s.* **1.** *Ethn:* Unnuit *m*, Esquimau *m*. **2.** *Ling:* esquimau *m*

innumerable [i'njuːm(ə)rəbl], *a.* innombrable; (*usu. with* *pl. s.*) **i. books, books i.,** des livres innombrables, sans nombre; **the successes have been i.,** les réussites ne se comptent plus.

innumerably [i'nju:m(ə)rəbli], *adv.* sans nombre; innombrablement.

inobservance [inəb'zə:v(ə)ns], *s.* **1.** inattention *f.* **2.** inobservance *f* (d'une loi, du jeûne, d'une coutume, etc.); inobservation *f* (d'une promesse).

inobservant [inəb'zə:v(ə)nt], *a.* **1.** peu observateur, -trice. **2. those who are i. of the law,** ceux qui violent la loi.

inoccupation [inɔkju'peiʃ(ə)n], *s.* inoccupation *f.*

inoceramus [inou'serəməs], *s. Paleont:* inocérame *m*, inoceramus *m*; *F:* moule *f* de la craie.

inoculability [i'nɔkjuləbiliti], *s. Med:* inoculabilité *f.*

inoculable [i'nɔkjuləbl], *a. Med:* (matière, virus, personne) inoculable.

inoculate [i'nɔkjuleit], *v.tr.* **1.** *Hort:* greffer (un œil, une tige) **(into, on, upon,** sur). **2.** *Med:* (*a*) **to i. s.o. with a virus, to i. a virus into s.o.,** inoculer un virus à qn; *F:* **to i. s.o. with evil doctrines,** inoculer à qn de mauvaises doctrines; (*b*) **to i. s.o. (against a disease),** inoculer, vacciner, qn (contre une maladie); **to get inoculated before going abroad,** se faire vacciner avant de partir pour l'étranger.

inoculation [inɔkju'leiʃ(ə)n], *s.* **1.** *Hort:* greffe *f*, greffage *m.* **2.** *Med:* inoculation *f*; **protective i.,** vaccination préventive, immunisante; **curative i.,** inoculation curative.

inoculator [i'nɔkjuleitər], *s.* inoculateur, -trice.

inoculum [i'nɔkjuləm], *s. Med:* vaccin *m.*

inodorous [in'oudərəs], *a.* (gaz, etc.) inodore, sans odeur.

in-off [in'ɔf], *s. Bill:* coup dans lequel le joueur fait blouser sa bille après qu'elle a touché une autre.

inoffensive [inə'fensiv], *a.* **1.** (homme, médicament, animal) inoffensif. **2.** (odeur, etc.) sans rien de désagréable; (observation, etc.) qui n'a rien d'offensant.

inoffensively [inə'fensivli], *adv.* inoffensivement.

inoffensiveness [inə'fensivnis], *s.* caractère inoffensif (d'un remède, d'une observation, etc.).

inofficiosity [inəfiʃi'ɔsiti], *s. Jur:* inofficiosité *f* (d'un testament, etc.).

inofficious [inə'fiʃəs], *a. Jur:* **1.** (testament) inofficieux. **2.** (règlement, etc.) inopérant.

inofficiously [inə'fiʃəsli], *adv.* inofficieusement.

inoperable [in'ɔp(ə)rəbl], *a.* **1.** *Med:* (malade, cancer) inopérable. **2. machine in an i. condition,** machine *f* dans l'impossibilité de fonctionner.

inoperative [in'ɔp(ə)rətiv], *a.* **1.** *Jur:* (*of law, etc.*) inopérant. **2.** (machine, etc.) qui ne fonctionne pas.

inoperculate [ino'pə:kjulət], *a. Fung:* (casque) sans opercule.

inopportune [in'ɔpətju:n], *a.* inopportun; intempestif; **i. remarks,** propos *m* hors de saison.

inopportunely [in'ɔpətju:nli], *adv.* inopportunément; mal à propos; à contretemps; **to arrive, happen, i.,** tomber mal.

inopportuneness [in'ɔpətju:nnis], **inopportunity** [inɔpə'tju:niti], *s.* inopportunité *f.*

inordinacy [i'nɔ:dinəsi], *s.* nature démesurée, désordonnée; excès *m.*

inordinate [i'nɔ:dinət], *a.* **1.** démesuré, excessif, immodéré, désordonné; **neck of i. length,** cou démesuré. **2.** qui n'est pas réglé; *O:* **to keep i. hours,** rentrer, se coucher, à des heures indues.

inordinately [i'nɔ:dinətily], *adv.* **1.** démesurément, excessivement, immodérément. **2.** sans règle, sans mesure.

inordinateness [i'nɔ:dinətnis], *s.* nature démesurée, désordonnée; excès *m.*

inorganic [inɔ:'gænik], *a.* inorganique; (*a*) **i. bodies,** corps bruts, inorganiques, non organisés; (*b*) **i. chemistry,** chimie minérale; (*c*) *Ling:* **i. sound, i. letter,** son *m*, lettre *f*, inorganique.

inorganically [inɔ:'gænik(ə)li], *adv.* d'une façon inorganique; par des moyens inorganiques.

inornate [inɔ:'neit], *a.* (langage) inorné, sans ornement.

inosculate [i'nɔskjuleit]. **1.** *v.i. Anat:* (*of blood vessels*) s'aboucher, s'anastomer **(with,** avec); (*of fibres*) s'unir **(with,** à). **2.** *v.tr. Surg:* aboucher (des vaisseaux sanguins, etc.); unir par anastomose.

inosculation [inɔskju'leiʃ(ə)n], **inosculosis** [inɔskju'lousis], *s.* **1.** *Anat:* inosculation *f*, anastomose *f.* **2.** *Surg:* abouchement *m* (de vaisseaux sanguins).

inosine ['ainəsi:n], *s. Ch:* inosine *f.*

inosite ['ainəsait], **inositol** [ai'nousitɔl], *s. Ch:* inosite *f*; inositol *m.*

inostensible [inɔs'tensibl], *a.* inostensible.

inostensibly [inɔs'tensibli], *adv.* inostensiblement.

inotropic [inou'trɔpik], *a. Physiol:* inotrope.

inoxidizable [in'ɔksidaizəbl], *a.* inoxydable.

in pace [in'peisi], *s. Archeol:* cul *m* de basse-fosse; in(-)pace *m inv.*

in-plant ['in'plɑ:nt], *a. Ind: etc:* intérieur, interne; **in-p. course,** cours donné sur place.

input[1] ['input], *s.* **1.** (*a*) *Scot:* somme contribuée; (*b*) *pl. Adm:* (*VAT*) **inputs,** dépenses *f*, frais *mpl.* **2.** (*a*) consommation *f* (d'une usine, d'une machine); énergie absorbée, puissance absorbée; *Mch:* **water i.,** injection *f* d'eau; (*b*) *El: Elcs:* (i) puissance *f* à l'entrée, d'alimentation; tension *f* d'entrée, d'alimentation; (ii) entrée *f*; (iii) borne *f* d'entrée; **i. circuit,** circuit *m* d'entrée; **i. current,** courant *m* d'entrée; **i. signal,** signal *m* d'entrée; **i. terminal,** borne d'entrée; **i. transformer,** transformateur *m* d'entrée; **i. tube,** lampe *f* d'entrée; *W.Tel:* **aerial i.,** puissance reçue, collectée, par l'antenne; puissance d'alimentation de l'antenne; *Cin:* **i. control,** contrôle *m* de la modulation (à l'enregistrement). **3.** *Cmptr:* (i) entrée, introduction *f* (des données); (ii) **i. (data),** données introduites, données en entrée; **i. area, i. block,** zone *f* (d')entrée, d'introduction; **i. card,** carte *f* (d')entrée; **i. device,** organe *m*, périphérique *m*, d'entrée; **i. equipment,** matériel *m*, périphérique, d'entrée; **i. hopper,** magasin *m* d'alimentation (de cartes); **i. keyboard,** clavier *m* d'entrée, d'introduction; **i. programme,** programme *m* d'introduction; **i. tape,** bande entrée, émettrice, en lecture; **i. transaction,** mouvement *m* entrée; **i. work queue,** file *f* de travaux en entrée; **i./output control,** contrôle *m* des entrées/sorties; **i./output-limited,** subordonné, asservi, au temps d'entrée/sortie; **i./output typewriter,** machine à écrire émettrice/réceptrice, d'entrée/sortie. **4.** *Mch:* **i. of steam,** prise *f* de vapeur.

input[2], *v.tr.* **(inputted)** *Cmptr:* **to i. data,** introduire, entrer, des données (en mémoire, dans un ordinateur, etc.).

inquartation [inkwɔ:'teiʃ(ə)n], *s. Metall:* inquart *m*, inquartation *f.*

inquest ['inkwest], *s.* **1.** enquête *f*; *esp.* **coroner's i.,** enquête judiciaire par-devant jury (en cas de mort violente ou suspecte); **to hold an i. on a body,** procéder à une enquête pour déterminer la cause de la mort du décédé; *F:* **to hold an i. on a hand (of cards),** faire une analyse rétrospective sur un jeu de cartes. **2.** (*a*) jury *m*; (*b*) conclusions *fpl*, verdict *m* (du jury). **3.** *Theol:* **the Great I., Last I.,** le jugement dernier.

inquietude [in'kwaiətju:d], *s.* **1.** *Med:* agitation *f* (du corps). **2.** *Lit:* malaise *m*, agitation (de l'esprit); anxiété *f*, inquiétude *f.*

inquiline ['iŋkwilain], *Nat.Hist:* **1.** *a.* inquilin. **2.** *s.* inquilin *m.*

inquilinism [iŋ'kwilinizm], *s. Nat.Hist:* inquilinisme *m.*

inquilinous [inkwi'lainəs], *a. Nat.Hist:* inquilin.

inquire [in'kwaiər]. **1.** *v.tr.* **to i. the price of sth.,** s'informer du prix de qch.; **to i. the way of s.o.,** demander son chemin à qn; **to i. of s.o. what is happening,** s'informer auprès de qn de ce qui se passe; **I did not i. what he intended to do,** je ne me suis pas informé de ce qu'il comptait faire; **to i. whether the train has left, how to operate the lift,** demander si le train est parti, comment on fait marcher l'ascenseur. **2.** *v.i.* s'enquérir, se renseigner, se faire renseigner **(about,** sur); prendre des informations, des renseignements **(about,** sur); aller aux informations; **i. within,** s'adresser ici; **everybody is inquiring about her,** (i) tout le monde pose des questions à son sujet; (ii) tout le monde demande de ses nouvelles, demande ce qu'elle devient; **to i. after s.o., after s.o.'s health, for s.o.,** s'informer de la santé de qn; demander des nouvelles de qn; *F:* demander après qn; **to i. for s.o., sth.,** demander qn, qch.; demander si qn est là; demander à voir qn, qch.; **to i. into sth.,** faire des recherches, des investigations, sur qch.; examiner (une question, une affaire); *Jur:* enquêter, faire une enquête, sur (une affaire); **to i. into s.o.'s position,** s'informer de la situation de qn; **to i. into the assets of a debtor,** discuter un débiteur; **to i. into a crime,** informer d'un crime, sur un crime.

inquirer [in'kwaiərər], *s.* **1.** investigateur, -trice; **to be an i. about, into, sth.,** s'informer de qch., faire des recherches sur qch. **2. there have been many inquirers after, about, the job,** il y a eu beaucoup de candidats pour l'emploi.

inquiring [in'kwaiəriŋ], *a.* investigateur, -trice; curieux; **i. glance,** coup d'œil interrogateur; **ours is an i. age,** c'est un siècle investigateur que le nôtre; **he is of an i. disposition,** il est curieux par nature; c'est un esprit chercheur.

inquiringly [in'kwaiəriŋli], *adv.* d'un air, d'un ton, interrogateur; **to look, glance, i. at s.o.,** interroger qn du regard.

inquiry [in'kwaiəri], *s.* **1.** enquête *f*; recherche *f*; investigation *f*; **to conduct, hold, an i. into sth.,** procéder, se livrer, à une enquête sur qch.; **those conducting the i.,** les enquêteurs *m*; **to open an i.,** ouvrir une enquête, *Jur:* une instruction; **the facts established by the i.,** les faits qui résultent des informations; **to remand a case for further i.,** renvoyer une affaire à plus ample informé; **without i.,** sans investigation; *Jur:* **public i., administrative i.,** enquête de commodo et incommodo; **writ of i.,** mandat qui ordonne une enquête sur la mort de quelqu'un; *Theol:* **free i.,** libre examen *m.* **2.** demande *f* de renseignements; **after many inquiries,** à force de questions; **to make inquiries,** aller aux informations, aux renseignements; **he had made inquiries everywhere,** il s'était informé partout; **to make inquiries about s.o.,** prendre des renseignements sur qn; s'informer, se renseigner, sur qn; **private i. agent,** détective (privé); **to make inquiries after s.o.,** s'enquérir de qn; **to make inquiries into sth.,** faire des recherches, des investigations, sur qch.; **on i. we learnt that he had absconded,** en s'informant on a appris qu'il s'était enfui; renseignements pris, après enquête, il est apparu qu'il s'était enfui; **the i. office, (the) inquiries,** le bureau, *Adm:* le service, des renseignements; (les) renseignements; *Cmptr:* **i. character,** caractère *m* d'interrogation; **i. station,** poste *m* d'interrogation, de consultation.

inquisition [inkwi'ziʃ(ə)n], *s.* (*a*) recherche *f*, investigation *f*; (*b*) *Jur:* enquête *f*, perquisition *f*; (*c*) *Rel.H:* **the I.,** l'Inquisition *f.*

inquisitional [inkwi'ziʃ(ə)nl], *a.* inquisitorial, -aux; inquisitif.

inquisitive [in'kwizitiv], *a.* (*a*) investigateur, -trice; curieux; **i. look,** regard inquisiteur; (*b*) *Pej:* curieux, questionneur; indiscret, *F:* fouinard; **little children are so i.,** les petits enfants sont si questionneurs.

inquisitively [in'kwizitivli], *adv.* (*a*) avec curiosité; **to look at s.o. i.,** regarder qn d'un œil inquisiteur; (*b*) *Pej:* indiscrètement.

inquisitiveness [in'kwizitivnis], *s.* (*a*) **i. of mind,** curiosité *f* d'esprit; (*b*) curiosité indiscrète.

inquisitor [in'kwizitər], *s.* **1.** *Jur:* officier public chargé d'instruire et d'enquérir; enquêteur *m.* **2.** *Rel.H:* inquisiteur *m*; **the Grand I.,** le grand inquisiteur.

inquisitorial [inkwizi'tɔ:riəl], *a.* inquisitorial, -aux.

inroad ['inroud], *s.* (*a*) *Mil:* incursion *f*, invasion *f*, irruption *f*; **to make inroads upon the enemy,** harceler l'ennemi; (*b*) empiètement *m* (sur la liberté, les droits, de qn); **to make inroads on s.o.'s time,** prendre le temps de qn; **to make inroads on one's capital,** entamer, ébrécher, son capital.

inrush ['inrʌʃ], *s.* irruption *f* (d'eau, de voyageurs, etc.); entrée soudaine (d'air, de gaz).

insalivate [in'sæliveit], *v.tr. Physiol:* imprégner (les aliments) de salive.

insalivation [insæli'veiʃ(ə)n], *s. Physiol:* insalivation *f.*

insalubrious [insə'lu:briəs], *a.* insalubre, malsain.

insalubrity [insə'lu:briti], *s.* insalubrité *f.*

insalutary [in'sæljutəri], *a.* (état d'esprit, etc.) malsain.

insane [in'sein], *a.* **1.** (*of pers.*) fou, *f.* folle; (esprit) dérangé, aliéné; **to become i.,** tomber en démence *f*; perdre la raison; *NAm:* **i. asylum, i. hospital,** hospice *m*, asile *m*, d'aliénés; maison *f* de fous; *s.* **the i.,** les aliénés *m.* **2.** (désir, etc.) insensé, fou; **an i. imperialism,** un impérialisme forcené.

insanely [in'seinli], *adv.* follement; comme un fou, comme un insensé.

insaneness [in'seinnis], *s.* caractère insensé (d'une action, d'un désir, etc.).

insanitariness [in'sænit(ə)rinis], *s.* insalubrité *f* (d'une maison, etc.).

insanitary [in'sænit(ə)ri], *a.* insalubre; qui manque d'hygiène; malsain; antihygiénique.

insanity [in'sæniti], *s.* **1.** *Med:* folie *f*, démence *f*, insanité *f*; aliénation mentale. **2.** (*a*) folie (d'une démarche, etc.); (*b*) démarche folle; folie.

insatiability [inseiʃiə'biliti], **insatiableness** [in'seiʃiəb(ə)lnis], *s.* insatiabilité *f.*

insatiable [in'seiʃiəbl], *a.* (faim, désir, etc.) insatiable, inassouvissable; **i. for glory,** insatiable de gloire, irrassasiable de gloire; **i. in his ambition,** insatiable dans ses ambitions.

insatiably [in'seiʃiəbli], *adv.* insatiablement.

insatiate [in'seiʃieit], *a.* insatiable, inassouvissable; **i. fury,** rage inassouvie.

insaturable [in'sætʃərəbl], *a.* insaturable.

insaturated [in'sætʃəreitid], *a.* insaturé.

inscape ['inskeip], *s. Phil: etc:* essence *f.*

inscribable [in'skraibəbl], *a. Mth:* inscriptible **(in,** dans).

inscribe [in'skraib], *v.tr.* **1.** (*a*) inscrire, graver **(sth. on stone, etc.,** qch. sur la pierre, etc.); **to i. a name in a**

register, inscrire un nom dans un registre; (*b*) **to i. a tomb with a name,** graver un nom sur un tombeau. **2.** dédier (une œuvre littéraire) (**to,** à). **3.** *Mth:* inscrire (un polygone, etc.) (**in,** dans).

inscribed [in'skraibd], *a.* inscrit (**on,** sur; **in,** dans); *Fin:* **i. stock,** actions inscrites; rente inscrite (au Grand-Livre).

inscriber [in'skraibər], *s.* **1.** graveur *m* (d'une inscription). **2.** auteur *m* de la dédicace (d'un livre, etc.). **3.** *Cmptr:* dispositif *m* d'inscription.

inscribing [in'skraibiŋ], *s.* inscription *f.*

inscription [in'skripʃ(ə)n], *s.* **1.** (*a*) **i. of a name on a stone, in a register,** inscription *f* d'un nom sur une pierre, dans un registre; (*b*) inscription (sur un monument, etc.); inscription, légende *f* (d'une pièce de monnaie). **2.** dédicace *f* (d'un livre, etc.). **3.** *Fin:* (*a*) inscription au Grand-Livre; (*b*) **the inscriptions,** la rente inscrite.

inscriptive [in'skriptiv], *a.* qui se rapporte à une inscription; **i. lines,** lignes inscrites.

inscrutability [inskru:tə'biliti], **inscrutableness** [in'skru:təb(ə)lnis], *s.* inscrutabilité *f*; impénétrabilité *f* (d'un mystère, d'un visage).

inscrutable [in'skru:təbl], *a.* (dessein) impénétrable, inscrutable; (visage) fermé.

inscrutably [in'skru:təbli], *adv.* inscrutablement, impénétrablement.

insect ['insekt], *s.* (*a*) insecte *m*; *attrib.* **i. eater,** insectivore *m*; **i. killer,** insecticide *m*; **i. powder,** poudre *f* insecticide; **i. repellent,** insectifuge *m*; *Aut: O:* **i. deflector,** pare-insectes *m inv*; *For: etc:* **i. trench,** fossé *m* d'arrêt (contre les chenilles); (*b*) *F: O:* personne *f* méprisable; zéro *m*; **this miserable i.,** ce petit rien du tout.

Insecta [in'sektə], *s.pl.* insectes *m.*

insectarium, *pl.* **-ia** [insek'tεəriəm, -iə], *s.* insectarium *m.*

insecticidal [insekti'saidl], *a.* insecticide.

insecticide [in'sektisaid], *a. & s.* insecticide (*m*); **household i., domestic i.,** insecticide ménager.

insectifuge [in'sektifju:dʒ], *a. & s.* insectifuge (*m*).

Insectivora [insek'tivərə], *s.pl. Z:* insectivores *m.*

insectivore [in'sektivɔ:r], *s. Bot: Z:* insectivore *m.*

insectivorous [insek'tivərəs], *a. Bot: Z:* insectivore.

insectology [insek'tɔlədʒi], *s.* insectologie *f.*

insecure [insi'kjuər], *a.* **1.** (verrou, etc.) peu sûr; (glace, etc.) peu solide; (terrain) dangereux; (pont) mal affermi; (espoir) incertain, peu ferme. **2.** exposé au danger; (*of pers.*) **to be in an i. position,** être dans une position critique; *F:* branler dans le manche; **the monarchy was very i.,** la monarchie branlait; **to feel i.,** éprouver un manque de sécurité, d'assurance.

insecurely [insi'kjuəli], *adv.* peu solidement; sans sûreté; sans sécurité; **i. fastened door,** porte mal fermée.

insecurity [insi'kjuəriti], *s.* insécurité *f*; danger *m* (d'une position); **to have a feeling of i.,** éprouver un manque de sécurité, d'assurance; **to lead a life of i.,** mener une vie hasardeuse.

inselberg, *pl.* **-bergs, -berge** ['inzelbə:g, -bə:gz, -bə:gə], *s. Geog:* inselberg *m*, *pl.* -bergs, -berge.

inseminate [in'semineit], *v.tr.* **1.** *Agr:* ensemencer (une terre). **2.** *Biol:* inséminer; *Breed:* **to i. (artificially),** ensemencer (artificiellement).

insemination [insemi'neiʃ(ə)n], *s. Biol:* insémination *f*; *Breed:* **artificial i.,** insémination (artificielle); fécondation artificielle.

inseminator [in'semineitər], *s. Breed:* inséminateur, -trice.

insensate [in'senseit], *a.* **1.** (corps, matière) insensible; (homme) dépourvu de sensibilité. **2.** (projet, désir) insensé; **i. rage,** colère folle.

insensibility [insensi'biliti], *s.* **1.** défaillance *f*; **to fall into a state of i.,** perdre connaissance; s'évanouir; tomber en syncope; *Lit:* tomber en pâmoison; **after several hours of i.,** après être resté plusieurs heures sans connaissance. **2.** insensibilité *f* (**to,** à); indifférence *f* (**to,** pour).

insensibilization [insensibili'zeiʃ(ə)n], *s. Med:* insensibilisation *f.*

insensibilize [in'sensibilaiz], *v.tr. Med:* insensibiliser (un malade, un membre, etc.).

insensible [in'sensibl], *a.* **1.** insensible, imperceptible; **i. transition,** transition *f* à peine sensible; **by i. degrees,** insensiblement. **2.** sans connaissance; évanoui; **to become i.,** perdre connaissance; s'évanouir; tomber en syncope. **3.** insensible, indifférent (**to pain, etc.,** à la douleur, etc.); **i. to the beauties of art,** insensible aux beautés de l'art; *Lit:* **I am not i. of your kindness,** je ne suis pas insensible à votre bonté; **I am not i. how much I owe to him,** je ne suis pas sans reconnaître de combien je lui suis redevable; **he was quite i. of the danger he was in,** il ne se doutait pas du danger qui le menaçait.

insensibly [in'sensibli], *adv.* insensiblement; petit à petit; peu à peu.

insensitive [in'sensitiv], *a.* **1.** (*a*) insensible (**to,** à); **on the retina is a spot i. to light,** sur la rétine se trouve une tache insensible à la lumière; (*b*) *W.Tel: O:* **i. spot of a crystal,** plage insensitive d'une galène. **2.** (*of pers.*) **i. to shame, to friendship,** insensible à la honte, à l'amitié; **he remains i. and cold,** il reste insensible et froid; rien ne lui fait impression.

insensitively [in'sensitivli], *adv.* sans sensibilité.

insensitiveness [in'sensitivnis], **insensitivity** [insensi'tiviti], *s.* insensitivité *f.*

insentient [in'senʃ(ə)nt], *a.* insensible; qui n'éprouve aucune sensation.

inseparability [insep(ə)rə'biliti], **inseparableness** [in'sep(ə)rəb(ə)lnis], *s.* inséparabilité *f.*

inseparable [in'sep(ə)rəbl], *a.* inséparable (**from,** de); (*of pers.*) **they are i.,** *s.* **they are inseparables,** ils sont inséparables; ce sont deux inséparables; ils sont rivés l'un à l'autre; ils ne font qu'un; c'est l'ombre et le corps; c'est saint Roch et son chien; *Gram:* **i. particles,** particules *f* inséparables.

inseparably [in'sep(ə)rəbli], *adv.* inséparablement.

inseparate [in'sepərət], *a.* inséparable (**from,** de); indivisible.

insequent [in'si:kwənt], *a.* *Geol:* (réseau hydrographique) inséquent.

insert[1] ['insə:t], *s.* **1.** *Typ: etc:* insertion *f* (dans une épreuve). **2.** (*a*) pièce rapportée; *Cin:* scène-raccord *f*, *pl.* scènes-raccords; *Aut:* **cork inserts of the clutch plate,** pastilles *f* en liège du plateau d'embrayage; (*b*) garniture intérieure (en caoutchouc, en ruban d'acier, etc.); (*c*) **washer i.,** entre-rondelle *f*, *pl.* entre-rondelles; *Aut:* **spring-leaf i.,** entrelame *f*; (*d*) *Publ:* encartage *m.*

insert[2] [in'sə:t], *v.tr.* **1.** insérer (une page dans un livre, une annonce dans un journal); **to i. a bud under the bark,** insérer une greffe sous l'écorce; **to i. blotting paper between the sheets,** insérer, intercaler, du papier brouillard entre les feuilles; **to i. sth. in a catalogue,** porter qch. sur un catalogue; **to i. a clause, a condition, in an act,** insérer, introduire, apposer, une clause, une condition, dans un acte; *El:* **to i. a condenser in the circuit,** intercaler un condensateur dans le circuit; *Typ:* **to i. a line,** intercaler une ligne. **2.** introduire, enfoncer (une clef dans une serrure, une fiche dans un jack); encocher (une cheville); *Artil:* **to i. the charge,** introduire la charge; **wheel with inserted teeth,** roue *f* à dents rapportées; **inserted wooden cogs,** alluchons en bois rapportés. **3.** *Space:* **to i. a satellite into orbit,** injecter un satellite en orbite. **4.** *Bot:* **stamens inserted on the ovary,** étamines insérées sur l'ovaire.

insertable [in'sə:təbl], *a.* insérable.

inserting [in'sə:tiŋ], *s.* = INSERTION 1.

insertion [in'sə:ʃ(ə)n], *s.* **1.** insertion *f*, introduction *f* (de qch. dans qch.); **i. of an announcement in a paper,** insertion d'une annonce, d'un faire-part, dans un journal; **i. of a probe in a wound,** introduction d'une sonde dans une blessure; *Artil:* **i. of the charge,** introduction de la charge; *El:* **i. of a transformer into a network,** insertion d'un transformateur dans un réseau; **i. gain, i. loss,** gain *m*, affaiblissement *m*, d'insertion. **2.** *Anat: Bot:* insertion (d'un tendon sur un os, d'une feuille sur la tige). **3.** (*a*) *Typ:* insertion; **i. mark,** renvoi *m*; (*b*) *Needlew:* entre-deux *m inv*, entretoile *f* (de dentelle, etc.); (*c*) *Dressm:* incrustation *f*; **to make up a garment with insertions,** incruster un vêtement; (*d*) *Ind:* pièce *f* d'insertion; pièce d'épaisseur; *Mec.E:* garniture *f* (de joint); **i. joint,** joint *m* à bague de garniture.

inset[1] ['inset], *s.* **1.** flux *m* (de la marée). **2.** *Bookb:* (*a*) encart *m*, carton *m* (de 4 ou 8 pages); **to insert insets in a book,** encarter, cartonner, un livre; (*b*) (*leaf, advertisement*) encartage *m*; feuillet *m* intercalaire. **3.** *Typ:* gravure *f* hors texte; hors-texte *m inv*; hors-d'œuvre *m inv*; figurine *f*; médaillon *m* (en coin de page); *Mapm:* carton *m.* **4.** *Dressm:* incrustation *f.* **5.** *pl. Geol:* **insets,** phénocristaux *m.*

inset[2] ['in'set], *v.tr.* (*p.t. & p.p.* **inset, insetted**) **1.** *Bookb:* encarter (des feuillets, des annonces). **2.** *Typ:* insérer en cartouche, en médaillon; **map with three smaller plans i.,** carte *f* avec trois cartons, médaillons. **3.** *Dressm:* insérer (une pièce d'étoffe, etc.); faire des incrustations de (dentelle, etc.). **4.** *Typ:* renfoncer (les lignes, un alinéa).

inset[3] ['inset], *a.* **1. i. map,** carton *m*, papillon *m* (dans le coin d'une carte); **i. portrait,** portrait *m* en médaillon. **2.** *Mec.E:* **i. bearing,** coussinet rentrant.

insetting ['insetiŋ], *s.* **1.** *Bookb:* encartage *m.* **2.** *Typ:* insertion *f* en cartouche, en médaillon. **3.** *Dressm:* insertion (d'une pièce d'étoffe); incrustation *f.* **4.** *Typ:* renfoncement *m.*

inshore. *Nau:* **1.** *adv.* [in'ʃɔ:r] près de terre; (dirigé) vers la côte; **close i.,** tout près de terre; **to keep close i.,** naviguer près de terre; serrer la terre. **2.** *a.* ['inʃɔ:r], **i. navigation, fishery,** navigation, pêche, côtière; **i. tack,** bordée *f* de terre; **i. wind,** vent *m* du large.

inside *s., a., adv. & prep.*

I. *s.* [in'said], (*a*) dedans *m*, (côté) intérieur (*m*) (d'un habit, etc.); **the door opens from (the) i.,** la porte s'ouvre de dedans; **on the i.,** en, au, dedans; **the door was bolted on the i.,** la porte était verrouillée à l'intérieur; **to walk on the i. (of the pavement),** prendre le côté du mur; *Rail:* **the i. of the road,** le dedans de la voie; **the i. of the foot,** le dedans du pied; *F:* **to know the i. of an affair,** connaître les dessous *m* d'une affaire; *adv.phr.* **i. out** ['insaid'aut], à l'envers; **to turn sth. i. out,** mettre qch. à l'envers; retourner qch. comme un gant; **stockings turned i. out,** bas *m* à l'envers, *F:* en peau de lapin; *Fig:* **to turn everything i. out,** mettre tout sens dessus dessous; **the wind has blown my umbrella i. out,** le vent a retourné mon parapluie; *Fig:* **to know sth. i. out,** savoir qch. à fond, comme le fond de sa poche; connaître (un sujet) de A à Z; **to know Paris i. out,** connaître Paris comme le fond de sa poche, de fond en comble, dans ses tours et détours; (*b*) intérieur (d'une maison, d'une voiture, etc.); (*c*) *F:* les entrailles *f*; **to have pains in one's inside(s),** avoir mal (i) au ventre, (ii) à l'estomac; (*d*) **I'll finish this work in the i. of a week,** il ne me reste de travail que pour cinq ou six jours, que pour six jours au plus; (*e*) *pl. Paperm:* **insides,** le bon papier (à l'intérieur de la rame); (*f*) *Typ:* côté *m* de seconde (d'une feuille); (*g*) *Fb:* **the insides,** les inters *m.*

II. *a.* ['insaid], (*a*) intérieur; d'intérieur; (mesure, etc.) dans œuvre; **i. seat,** (i) place *f* à côté du couloir central (d'un avion, d'un autobus, etc.); (ii) *A:* place d'intérieur (d'un coche, etc.); **i. diameter,** diamètre *m* interne; **i. stair,** escalier *m* dans œuvre; **i. paint,** peinture *f* pour travaux d'intérieur; **i. work,** travaux d'intérieur; **to have an i. accomplice,** avoir un complice intérieur, dans la maison; **the theft must have been an i. job,** le vol a dû être commis par un des habitants de la maison; **to be on the i. track,** (i) *Rac:* être à la corde; tenir la corde; (ii) *F:* être avantagé; *F:* tenir la corde; *Fb:* **i. left,** intérieur, *F:* inter, gauche; **the i. forwards,** les inters; *Box:* **i. fighting,** combat *m* corps à corps; corps-à-corps *m inv*; (*b*) **i. information,** renseignements privés; **I speak with i. knowledge,** ce que je dis je le sais de bonne source, de haute source; **to know the i. story,** connaître le dessous des cartes; **the i. ring,** les initiés *m.*

III. *adv.* [in'said], (*a*) intérieurement; (fermé) en dedans; (propre) à l'intérieur; **with the fur i.,** le côté poil en dedans; **the purse is empty, there is nothing i.,** la bourse est vide, il n'y a rien dedans; **handbag with mirror i.,** sac *m* avec glace intérieure; **i. and out** ['insaidənd'aut], au dedans et au dehors; à l'intérieur et à l'extérieur; (*b*) dans la maison, la chambre, la salle, etc.; **to push s.o. i.,** pousser qn à l'intérieur, dedans; **come i.!** entrez! rentrez! **somebody called me from i.,** une voix à l'intérieur m'a appelé; *P:* **to put s.o. i.,** mettre qn sous les verrous, en taule; (*c*) *N.Am: F:* **to be i. on a matter,** connaître les dessous d'une affaire; être bien tuyauté; être de ceux qui sont au courant; être avantagé; *F: & N.Am:* **to do sth. i. of three hours,** faire qch. en moins de trois heures.

IV. *prep.* [in'said] **1.** à l'intérieur de, dans l'intérieur de, dans (la maison, etc.); *Th: F:* **to get right i. a part,** entrer dans la peau d'un personnage. **2. i. a week, an hour, a year,** en moins d'une semaine, d'une heure, d'une année; **he was back i. the hour,** il était de retour en moins d'une heure.

insider [in'saidər], *s.* **1.** initié, -iée; celui qui connaît le dessous des cartes. **2.** *A:* voyageur, -euse, à l'intérieur (de la voiture).

insidious [in'sidiəs], *a.* (ennemi, projet, etc.) insidieux; (raisonnement) captieux, astucieux; **i. offer,** proposition insidieuse, astucieuse; **i. disease,** maladie astucieuse; **an i. wine,** un petit vin traître.

insidiously [in'sidiəsli], *adv.* insidieusement, astucieusement, captieusement.

insidiousness [in'sidiəsnis], *s.* caractère insidieux (d'une maladie, etc.); astuce *f* (d'une question, etc.).

insight ['insait], *s.* **1.** perspicacité *f*, pénétration *f*; **mind of deep i.,** esprit pénétrant; **poet of great i.,** poète de grande intuition; **work that shows flashes of i.,** ouvrage où il y a des aperçus très fins; **i. into character,** finesse *f* psychologique; **he has an i. into character,** il sait pénétrer les caractères; **his thorough i. into the human heart,** sa connaissance intime du cœur humain. **2.** aperçu *m*; **to get an i. into sth.,** prendre un aperçu de qch.

insignia [in'signiə], *s.pl.* **1.** insignes *m* (de la royauté, etc.); *Mil:* **i. of rank,** signes distinctifs de grade. **2.** *U.S:*

s. sg. with pl. **insignia(s),** insigne.

insignificance [insig'nifikəns], *s.* insignifiance *f.*

insignificant [insig'nifikənt], *a.* **1.** (mot, geste) insignifiant, qui ne signifie rien. **2.** (perte, etc.) de peu d'importance; (affaire, etc.) de rien (du tout); **i. person,** personne sans importance; **to occupy an i. place in society,** occuper un rang infime dans la société; **of i. extraction,** de naissance infime.

insincere [insin'siər], *a.* (*a*) peu sincère; *Lit:* insincère; de mauvaise foi; (*b*) (*of smile, etc.*) faux, *f.* fausse.

insincerely [insin'siəli], *adv.* sans sincérité; d'un ton faux.

insincerity [insin'seriti], *s.* manque *m* de sincérité; fausseté *f.*

insinuate [in'sinjueit], *v.tr. & i.* insinuer. **1. to i. sth., oneself, into a place,** insinuer, glisser, qch. dans un endroit; s'insinuer, se glisser, dans un endroit; **to i. oneself into s.o.'s favour,** s'insinuer dans les bonnes grâces de qn. **2.** donner adroitement à entendre, à comprendre (qch.); laisser (sous-)entendre (qch.); **do you mean to i. that I am not to be trusted?** voulez-vous donner à entendre que je ne suis pas digne de foi? **to i. something nasty,** lancer une insinuation méchante.

insinuating [in'sinjueitiŋ], *a.* **1.** (*of manner, air, etc.*) insinuant. **2.** (*of statement, etc.*) suggestif.

insinuatingly [in'sinjueitiŋli], *adv.* d'une manière insinuante; d'un ton câlin.

insinuation [insinju'eiʃ(ə)n], *s.* **1.** insinuation *f,* introduction *f* (**of sth. into sth.,** de qch. dans qch.). **2.** insinuation; mot couvert; sous-entendu *m, pl.* sous-entendus.

insinuative [in'sinjueitiv], *a.* **1.** insinuant, câlin. **2.** (propos) suggestif.

insipid [in'sipid], *a.* (mets, conversation) insipide, fade, sans saveur; (sourire) bête; (style) décoloré; **i. compliments,** compliments *m* fades.

insipidity [insi'piditi], **insipidness** [in'sipidnis], *s.* insipidité *f*; fadeur *f.*

insipidly [in'sipidli], *adv.* insipidement, fadement.

insist [in'sist], *v.tr. & i.* insister. **1.** *v.i.* (*a*) **to i. on a point, on a fact,** insister, appuyer, s'appesantir, sur un point, sur un fait; **to i. upon one's innocence; to i. (on it) that one is innocent,** affirmer son innocence avec insistance; protester hautement de son innocence; **this is not a point to be insisted on,** ce n'est pas là un point sur lequel on doive insister; **I won't i.,** glissons là-dessus; (*b*) **to i. on sth., on doing sth.,** mettre une grande insistance à qch., à faire qch.; insister pour faire qch.; vouloir absolument, à toute force, faire qch.; **to i. on s.o.'s doing sth.,** exiger de qn qu'il fasse qch.; **he insists on your coming,** il insiste pour que vous veniez; il veut absolument, à toute force, que vous veniez; **you mean to i. on his apologizing personally?** vous tenez absolument à ce qu'il fasse des excuses en personne? **he insists on being paid at once,** il exige qu'on le paie sur-le-champ; **I i. on it,** je le veux absolument; **he insists on it,** il ne veut pas en démordre; **I i. on obedience,** je veux être obéi; **to i. on payment,** exiger le paiement; **to i. on one's rights,** revendiquer ses droits; **I'll have some more if you i.,** je vais reprendre si vous insistez. **2.** *v.tr.* **people insisted that they had seen him,** on prétendait qu'on l'avait vu; on affirmait avec insistance l'avoir vu; **he insisted that it was so,** il maintenait, soutenait, qu'il en était ainsi; **you must apologize, he insisted,** il faut faire des excuses, dit-il avec insistance.

insistence [in'sist(ə)ns], *s.* insistance *f*; (*a*) **in the face of his i.,** devant son insistance; **his i. upon his innocence,** ses protestations *f* d'innocence; **the doctor's i. on the necessity of staying in bed,** l'insistance du médecin sur la nécessité de garder le lit; (*b*) **i. on doing sth.,** insistance à faire qch.; **his i. on strict obedience,** l'importance qu'il attachait à une obéissance absolue.

insistent [in'sist(ə)nt], *a.* **1.** qui insiste, insistant; (*of thought, etc.*) obsédant; (*of creditor*) importun; **i. demands,** réclamations instantes; **to be very i.,** insister très fort; **these facts are very i.,** ces faits s'imposent à l'attention; **don't be too i.,** n'appuyez pas trop, n'insistez pas trop; **to be i. that sth. shall be done,** tenir à ce qu'on fasse qch. **2.** *Orn:* **i. hind toe,** pouce insistant.

insistently [in'sist(ə)ntli], *adv.* instamment; avec insistance, avec instance; **to call i. for action,** réclamer d'urgence une action immédiate.

insobriety [insə'braiəti], *s.* intempérance *f*; *A:* insobriété *f.*

insociability [insouʃə'biliti], *s.* insociabilité *f.*

insociable [in'souʃəbl], *a.* insociable.

insolate ['insəleit], *v.tr.* insoler; exposer (qn, qch.) au soleil.

insolation [insou'leiʃ(ə)n], *s.* **1.** *Meteor:* insolation *f*; ensoleillement *m.* **2.** *Med:* (*a*) coup *m* de soleil; insolation; *F:* coup de bambou; (*b*) cure *f,* bain *m,* de soleil; héliothérapie *f.*

insole ['insoul], *s. Bootm:* (*a*) première semelle; (*b*) semelle intérieure (de liège, feutre, etc.).

insolence ['insələns], *s.* insolence *f,* effronterie *f* (to, envers); **enough of your i.!** trêve d'insolences!

insolent ['insələnt], *a.* insolent (to, envers); **to be extremely i.,** être d'une extrême insolence; **an i. boy,** un (jeune) insolent.

insolently ['insələntli], *adv.* insolemment; avec insolence.

insolidity [insə'liditi], *s.* insolidité *f.*

insolubility [insəlju'biliti], **insolubleness** [in'səljub(ə)lnis], *s.* **1.** insolubilité *f* (d'un sel). **2.** insolubilité (d'un problème).

insoluble [in'səljubl], *a.* **1.** (sel *m,* etc.) insoluble; **i. in water,** insoluble dans l'eau. **2.** (problème) insoluble, irrésoluble; **problem i. to, for, the human mind,** problème insoluble à l'esprit humain.

insolvability [insəlvə'biliti], *s.* insolubilité *f* (d'un problème).

insolvable [in'səlvəbl], *a.* (problème *m,* etc.) insoluble, irrésoluble.

insolvency [in'səivənsi], *s.* (*a*) insolvabilité *f*; *Jur:* carence *f*; **to be in a state of i.,** être en état de cessation de paiements; (*b*) déconfiture *f*; faillite *f.*

insolvent [in'səlv(ə)nt]. **1.** *a.* (débiteur) insolvable; *Com:* (débiteur, société) en (état de) faillite, en déconfiture; **to become i.,** devenir insolvable; *Com:* faire faillite; **to declare oneself i.,** se déclarer insolvable; *Com:* déposer son bilan. **2.** *s.* débiteur *m* insolvable; *Com:* failli *m.*

insomnia [in'səmniə], *s.* insomnie *f*; **frequent bouts of i.,** fréquentes insomnies; **sufferer from i.,** insomnieux, -euse.

insomniac [in'səmniæk], *s.* insomniaque *mf*; insomnieux, -euse.

insomuch [insou'mʌtʃ]. *Lit: conj.phr.* **1. i. as** = INASMUCH AS. **2. i. that . . .,** à un tel point, au point, tellement, que . . ..

insouciance [in'su:siəns], *s.* insouciance *f.*

insouciant [in'su:siənt], *a.* insouciant.

inspan [in'spæn], *v.tr.* (**inspanned**) (*in S. Africa*) atteler (un wagon, une paire de bœufs).

inspect [in'spekt], *v.tr.* **1.** (*a*) examiner (qch.), regarder (qch.) de près; (*b*) inspecter (une école, une fabrique); contrôler, vérifier, compulser (les livres d'un négociant); visiter, vérifier, inspecter (une machine, etc.); *Mil:* **the frontier will be inspected,** il sera procédé à une reconnaissance de la frontière; *Sp:* **to i. the pitch,** visiter le terrain (avant le match). **2. to i. a regiment,** passer l'inspection, faire la revue, faire l'inspection, d'un régiment; passer un régiment en revue; inspecter un régiment; (*of troops*) **to be inspected,** passer en revue.

inspecting[1] [in'spektiŋ], *a.* **i. officer,** inspecteur *m.*

inspecting[2], *s.* inspection *f*; **i. order,** ordre *m* d'inspection.

inspection [in'spekʃ(ə)n], *s.* **1.** (*a*) examen *m*; vérification *f* (de documents, de titres de propriété, etc.); **to subject sth. to close i.,** soumettre qch. à un examen minutieux; **on close, closer, i.,** à y regarder de près; en y regardant de plus près; **to buy goods on i.,** acheter des marchandises sur examen; *Jur:* **right of i.,** droit *m* de regard; **deed of i.,** convention *f* entre un failli et ses créanciers pour la nomination des syndics; *Publ:* **i. copy,** spécimen *m*; (*b*) inspection *f,* visite *f* (d'un établissement, etc.); contrôle *m* (des billets, du personnel, du matériel, etc.); **periodical i. of factories,** visite périodique des fabriques; **tour of i.,** inspection; **general i.,** inspection générale; **the I. of Mines,** le Service du Contrôle des Mines; **sanitary i.,** visite, contrôle, sanitaire; **medical i.,** visite médicale; **physical i.,** examen, contrôle, médical; **to make, hold, an i.,** passer, effectuer, une inspection; (*of doctor*) **to make a medical i.,** faire, effectuer, passer, une visite médicale; **to undergo an i.,** (*of factory, etc.*) subir une inspection, être inspecté; *Med:* (*of patient*) subir, passer, une visite médicale; **second i., check i.,** contre-visite *f, pl.* contre-visites; **i. committee,** comité *m* de contrôle, de surveillance; *Cust:* **i. order,** bon *m* de visite; *Adm:* **i. stamp,** (i) cachet *m* de vérification; (ii) (*punch*) poinçon *m* de contrôle; *Tchn:* **i. cover(-plate), i. plate, i. panel,** panneau *m* de visite; **i. door,** porte *f* de visite; **i. hole, port,** orifice *m,* trou *m,* regard *m,* de visite; fenêtrelle *f*; **i. pit,** fosse *f* de visite, d'inspection; *El:* **i. box,** boîte *f* de visite (d'une canalisation électrique); *Tls:* **i. gauge,** calibre *m* de contrôle. **2.** *Mil:* revue *f*; **equipment i.,** revue de détail; **kit i.,** revue d'habillement; **i. of barracks,** revue de casernement; **to make, hold, an i.,** passer une revue, une inspection; **to undergo an i.,** être passé en revue; se présenter à une revue; subir une inspection.

inspectional [in'spekʃənl], *a.* (rapport, circonscription) d'inspection.

inspector [in'spektər], *s.* inspecteur *m* (des écoles, de police, etc.); *Rail:* surveillant *m*; (**woman**) **i.,** inspectrice *f*; **detective i.,** inspecteur de la Sûreté; **i. of taxes,** inspecteur, contrôleur *m,* des contributions directes; **boiler i.,** vérificateur *m,* visiteur *m,* de chaudières; **i. of mines,** inspecteur des mines; **i. of weights and measures,** vérificateur des poids et mesures; *Mil: etc:* **i. general,** inspecteur général.

inspectoral [in'spekt(ə)rəl], **inspectorial** [inspek'tɔ:riəl], *a.* (fonction, etc.) d'inspecteur.

inspectorate [in'spekt(ə)rət], *s.* (*a*) charge *f* d'un inspecteur; inspectorat *m,* inspection *f*; (*b*) territoire *m* d'un inspecteur; (*c*) **the i.,** le corps d'inspecteurs; *F:* l'inspection.

inspectorship [in'spektəʃip], *s.* **1.** inspectorat *m.* **2.** *Jur:* **deed of i.,** convention *f* entre un failli et ses créanciers pour la nomination des syndics.

inspectress [in'spektris], *s.f.* inspectrice.

inspiration [inspi'reiʃ(ə)n], *s.* **1.** aspiration *f,* inspiration *f* (d'air, d'oxygène, etc.). **2.** inspiration; (*a*) **divine i., mystical i.,** inspiration divine, mystique; **under the i. of their leader,** sous l'inspiration de leur chef; **to do sth. by i.,** faire qch. d'inspiration; **to take one's i. from s.o.,** s'inspirer de qn; **he is the i. of the movement,** c'est l'âme *f* du mouvement; **poetic i.,** la veine poétique; (*of poet*) **to lack i.,** manquer d'inspiration; *F:* manquer de souffle; (*b*) **to have a sudden i.,** avoir une inspiration subite.

inspirational [inspi'reiʃ(ə)nl], *a.* **1.** inspirateur, -trice. **2.** inspiré.

inspirator ['inspireitər], *s. Mch: Ind:* injecteur aspirant.

inspiratory [in'spaiərət(ə)ri], *a. Physiol:* (*of muscles, etc.*) inspirateur, -trice; (*of breath*) aspiratoire.

inspire [in'spaiər], *v.tr.* **1.** aspirer, inspirer (l'air, etc.). **2.** inspirer; (*a*) **to be inspired to do sth.,** être inspiré de faire qch.; **inspired by the example of his ancestors,** inspiré, aiguillonné, par l'exemple de ses ancêtres; **tales inspired by animal life,** contes inspirés de la vie des animaux; **the sea inspired him to produce his masterpiece,** la mer lui inspira son chef-d'œuvre; **to i. a thought, a feeling, in, into, s.o.,** inspirer une pensée, un sentiment, à qn; **to i. s.o. with confidence, with fear,** inspirer (de la) confiance, de la erreur, à qn; **to i. s.o. with respect,** imposer le respect à qn; **to i. s.o. with hope,** donner de l'espoir à qn; **inspired with hope,** animé d'espoir; **to i. respect,** inspirer, imprimer, le respect; (*b*) **I don't know what inspired me to turn back,** je ne sais pas ce que c'est qui m'a donné l'inspiration de revenir sur mes pas.

inspired [in'spaiəd], *a.* **1.** (air, oxygène) aspiré, inspiré. **2.** (*a*) (*of poet, verse, etc.*) inspiré, plein d'inspiration; **like one i.,** comme un inspiré; **to make an i. guess,** bien tomber; tomber juste; (*b*) (*of rumour, etc.*) officieux; *Journ:* **i. paragraph,** note *f* d'origine officieuse; **i. article,** article inspiré (en haut lieu).

inspirer [in'spaiərər], *s.* inspirateur, -trice (d'une œuvre, etc.).

inspiring [in'spaiəriŋ], *a.* (discours, etc.) inspirant; **i. influence,** influence vivifiante; **it's i. to know that there are people like that today,** cela donne du courage, cela encourage, de savoir qu'il est des gens comme ça aujourd'hui.

inspirit [in'spirit], *v.tr. O:* animer, encourager (**s.o. to do sth.,** qn à faire qch.); **he inspirited us to renewed efforts,** il nous encouragea à de nouveaux efforts.

inspissate [in'spiseit], *v.tr.* épaissir (un liquide); **to become inspissated,** *v.i.* **to i.,** s'épaissir; se condenser; *Lit:* **inspissated gloom,** ténèbres épaisses.

inspissation [inspi'seiʃ(ə)n], *s.* épaississement *m* (du sang, d'un liquide, etc.).

instability [instə'biliti], *s.* instabilité *f.* **1.** (*a*) *Ph: Mec:* **i. of a body in equilibrium,** instabilité d'un corps en équilibre; **dimensional i.,** instabilité dimensionnelle; **thermal i.,** instabilité thermique; **i. constant,** constante *f* d'instabilité; **i. region,** région *f,* zone *f,* d'instabilité (d'un système dynamique équilibré); (*b*) *Mec.E:* (i) déséquilibrage *m*; (ii) manque *m* d'assiette; *Av:* **inherent i.,** manque de stabilité propre; (*c*) *Meteor:* instabilité (atmosphérique); **i. line,** ligne *f* de grain, d'instabilité; **conditional i.,** instabilité conditionnelle; **convective i.,** instabilité de convection. **2.** (*a*) mobilité *f,* instabilité (de caractère); **the i. of human affairs,** la muabilité, la fragilité, des choses humaines; *Psy: Med:* **mental i.,** instabilité mentale; *Fin:* **monetary i.,** instabilité monétaire; (*b*) *Biol:* **i. of type,** inconstance *f* des types; (*c*) *Ch:* instabilité (d'un composé). **3.** manque *m* de solidité (d'un pont, etc.).

instal(l) [in'stɔ:l], *v.tr.* **1.** (*a*) installer (un évêque, qn dans une fonction); (*b*) **to i. oneself in a place,** s'installer dans un endroit; **she installed herself in an armchair,** elle s'installa dans un fauteuil. **2.** installer, monter, poser (une machine, etc.); installer (l'électricité, etc.); **to i. a workshop in a shed,** monter un atelier dans un hangar; *Mec.E:* **part installed in production, factory-installed part,** pièce *f* d'origine.

installation [instə'leiʃ(ə)n], *s.* **1.** installation *f* (d'un évêque, juge, etc.). **2.** *(a)* installation (du chauffage central dans la maison, etc.); *(b)* installation, montage *m*, pose *f* (d'une machine, etc.); mise *f* en place (d'un téléviseur, etc.); **the i. of the aerial is free,** l'installation de l'antenne est gratuite. **3.** installation; **electrical installations,** installations électriques; **ship, shore, installations,** installations à bord, à terre.

installer [in'stɔːlər], *s.* **1.** installateur *m* (du chauffage central, etc.). **2.** *NAm:* monteur *m* (d'une machine, etc.).

installing [in'stɔːliŋ], *s.* = INSTALLATION 1, 2.

instalment (*NAm: also* **installment**) [in'stɔːlmənt], *s.* **1.** *Com: etc:* fraction *f* (de paiement); acompte *m*; paiement *m* à compte; versement partiel; traite *f*; **to pay an i.,** verser un acompte, faire un versement; **final i.,** paiement pour solde; versement de libération; **to pay in, by, instalments,** échelonner, fractionner, les paiements, payer; **to pay a subscription in instalments,** fractionner le paiement d'un abonnement; **to pay in small instalments,** payer par parcelles *f*; payer sou à sou; **payable in two instalments,** payable en deux fois; **payable in monthly instalments,** payable par mensualités *f*; **repayable by instalments,** remboursable par acomptes, par paiements à termes, par versements échelonnés, en plusieurs versements; **to pay, buy, on the i. system, plan,** payer par abonnement; acheter à tempérament. **2.** tranche *f*; **to issue a loan, to vote credits, in instalments,** émettre un emprunt, voter des crédits, par tranches; **please return the proofs by instalments,** prière de renvoyer les épreuves par tranches, par sections. **3.** *Publ:* fascicule *m*, livraison *f* (d'un ouvrage à paraître en fascicules); **i. selling,** vente *f* par fascicules; *(b) Journ: W.Tel: T.V:* feuilleton *m*.

instance[1] ['instəns], *s.* **1.** *A:* sollicitation pressante; *now only used in the phr.* **at the i. of (s.o.),** sur l'instance, à la demande, à l'instigation, de (qn). **2.** exemple *m*, cas *m*; **an isolated i.,** un cas isolé; **in many instances,** dans bien des cas; **this is a good i.,** en voici un bon exemple; **for i.,** par exemple; **as an i. of his honesty I may mention this incident,** en témoignage de son intégrité je pourrais citer cet incident. **3.** *(a) Jur:* procès *m*, poursuite *f*, instance *f*; *(b)* **in the first i.,** en (tout) premier lieu; **in the present i., in this i.,** dans le cas actuel; dans cette circonstance; *Jur:* dans l'espèce. **4.** *Psy:* instance.

instance[2], *v.tr.* **1.** citer (qch., qn) en exemple; **i. the Dreyfus case,** citons l'affaire Dreyfus, témoin l'affaire Dreyfus. **2.** (*usu. in passive*) **his cruelty is well instanced by his treatment of his brother,** sa cruauté est bien illustrée, démontrée, par la manière dont il a traité son frère.

instancy ['instənsi], *s.* **1.** instance *f* (d'une requête). **2.** urgence *f* (d'un besoin, etc.). **3.** imminence *f* (du danger, de l'arrivée de qn).

instant[1] ['instənt], *a.* **1.** *(a)* instant, pressant, urgent; **he has i. need of you,** il a grand besoin de vous; *(b) A:* **to be i. with s.o. to do sth.,** prier instamment qn de faire qch. **2.** (*abbr.* **inst.**) courant; de ce mois; **on the 5th inst.,** le 5 courant; *Com:* **my letter of the 5th inst.,** ma lettre du 5 courant, du 5 ct. **3.** *(a)* immédiat; **this calls for i. remedy,** cela demande à ce qu'on y apporte immédiatement remède; il faut y remédier sur-le-champ; *(b)* (i) **i. water heater,** chauffe-eau instantané; **i. coffee,** café *m* soluble, en poudre; (ii) **i. beard,** barbe factice; *(c)* (risque, etc.) imminent. **4. the i. case,** le cas présent, actuel.

instant[2], *s.* instant *m*, moment *m*; **I expect him every i.,** je l'attends d'un instant à l'autre; **come this i.,** venez à l'instant, sur-le-champ; **I am going this i.,** j'y vais de ce pas; **I went that i., on the i.,** j'y suis allé immédiatement; **not an i. too soon,** juste à temps; **he was not an i. too soon,** il n'était que temps; **I wouldn't stand it for an i.,** je ne le tolérerais pas pendant un moment; **the i. he arrived,** (i) au moment où il arriva; (ii) dès, aussitôt, qu'il fut arrivé; *Mth:* **magnitude at an i.,** valeur instantanée.

instantaneity [instəntə'niːiti], **instantaneousness** [inst(ə)n'teinjəsnis], *s.* instantanéité *f*.

instantaneous [inst(ə)n'teinjəs], *a.* instantané; *El:* **i. value,** valeur instantanée; *Phot:* **i. exposure,** pose instantanée; instantané *m*.

instantaneously [inst(ə)nteinjəsli], *adv.* instantanément.

instanter [in'stæntər], *adv. A:* immédiatement; sur-le-champ.

instantly ['instəntli]. **1.** *adv. A:* instamment; avec instance; **they besought him i.,** ils l'en prièrent avec instance. **2.** *(a) adv.* tout de suite; immédiatement; sur-le-champ; à l'instant; **to catch an allusion i.,** saisir une allusion à la volée; *(b) conj. A: & Lit:* aussitôt que . . ., dès que . . ..

instar ['instɑːr], *s. Ent:* mue *f*; **second larval i.,** deuxième stade *m* larvaire.

instate [in'steit], *v.tr. Jur:* **to i. s.o. in, into, to, his rights,** établir, installer, qn dans ses droits.

instauration [instɔː'reiʃ(ə)n], *s.* restauration *f*, rénovation *f*.

instaurator ['instɔːreitər], *s.* restaurateur, -trice, rénovateur, -trice (d'une science, etc.).

instead [in'sted]. **1.** *prep.phr.* **i. of sth.,** au lieu de qch.; en guise de qch.; **to stand i. of sth.,** tenir lieu de qch.; **i. of s.o.,** à la place de qn; **I acted i. of the boss during his illness,** j'ai remplacé, représenté, le patron pendant sa maladie; j'ai assuré l'intérim pendant la maladie du patron; **i. of doing sth.,** au lieu de faire qch.; **i. of Peter coming in it was John who appeared,** au lieu que ce fût Pierre qui entrât, ce fut Jean qui apparut; **i. of (our) having profited we lost by it,** au lieu que nous y ayons gagné quelque chose, nous y avons perdu; **i. of diminishing, crime has increased,** loin que les crimes aient diminué ils ont augmenté; **now the house belongs to Guy i. of to all of us,** maintenant la maison appartient à Guy au lieu de nous appartenir à tous; **we have lunch in the garden i. of in the dining room,** nous déjeunons au jardin au lieu de nous tenir dans la salle à manger; **they help to lower i. of raise the standard of morality,** ils contribuent à abaisser le niveau des mœurs, au lieu de l'élever; **by methods of justice and peace i. of by arbitrary force,** par des méthodes équitables et pacifiques, remplaçant le recours à la force arbitraire. **2.** *adv.* au lieu de cela; **if John can't come take me i.,** si Jean ne peut pas venir, emmenez-moi à sa place; **he did not go to Rome but went to Venice i.,** au lieu d'aller à Rome il alla à Venise; **he is not allowed wine, and drinks tea i.,** comme le vin ne lui est pas permis il le remplace par du thé; **don't cry, laugh i.,** ne pleurez pas, riez plutôt.

instep ['instep], *s.* **1.** *(a)* cou-de-pied *m*, *pl.* cous-de-pied; **foot with a high i.,** pied, cou-de-pied, très cambré; **i. raiser,** cambrure *f* orthopédique; *(b) Bootm:* cambrure (d'un soulier). **2.** *Z:* face antérieure du canon (d'un cheval).

instigate ['instigeit], *v.tr.* **1.** inciter, pousser, provoquer (**s.o. to do sth.,** qn à faire qch. de mal); **to i. an offender,** inciter, suborner, un malfaiteur. **2. to i. revolt,** inspirer, susciter, la révolte.

instigation [insti'geiʃ(ə)n], *s.* instigation *f*, incitation *f* (to a crime, etc., à un crime, etc.); **at s.o.'s i.,** à l'instigation de qn.

instigator ['instigeitər], *s.* **1.** instigateur, -trice (d'un crime, etc.). **2.** susciteur, -trice, auteur *m* (d'une révolte, etc.); fauteur, -trice (d'une émeute).

instil(l) [in'stil], *v.tr.* (**instilled**) **1.** instiller (un liquide) (**into sth.,** dans qch.). **2.** faire pénétrer (goutte à goutte); **to i. courage into s.o.,** instiller le courage à qn; **to i. a quality, a feeling, an idea, into s.o.,** inculquer lentement une qualité à qn; inspirer un sentiment à qn; faire pénétrer une idée, infiltrer une idée, dans l'esprit de qn; **to i. a new doctrine into the people,** inoculer au peuple une nouvelle doctrine; **to i. good principles into s.o.,** insinuer de bons principes à qn; **these principles had been instilled into him from his boyhood,** dès sa jeunesse il avait été imprégné de ces principes.

instillation [insti'leiʃ(ə)n], *s.* **1.** instillation *f* (de gouttes dans les yeux, etc.). **2.** inspiration *f* (d'une idée, d'un sentiment); inculcation *f* (d'une vertu, etc.).

instiller [in'stilər], *s.* celui, celle, qui fait pénétrer (une idée, etc.); **i. of life into a scheme,** animateur, -trice, d'un projet.

instilling [in'stiliŋ], *s.* = INSTILLATION.

instinct[1] ['instiŋ(k)t], *s.* instinct *m*; **animals have the i. of self preservation,** les animaux ont l'instinct de (leur propre) conservation; **by i., from i.,** d'instinct, par instinct; **to act on (pure) i.,** agir par (pur) instinct; **to have an i. for business, for doing the right thing,** avoir l'instinct des affaires, de la chose à faire.

instinct[2] [in'stiŋ(k)t], *a. A: & Lit:* **i. with life,** doué de vie, plein de vie; **face i. with kindness,** visage respirant la bonté, pétri de bonté.

instinctive [in'stiŋ(k)tiv], *a.* instinctif.

instinctively [in'stiŋ(k)tivli], *adv.* instinctivement; d'instinct; par (pur) instinct; *F:* machinalement.

instinctual [in'stiŋ(k)tjuəl], *a.* instinctuel.

institute[1] ['institjuːt], *s.* **1.** *(a)* institut *m* (scientifique, littéraire, etc.); **the I. of Actuaries** = l'Institut de l'Actuariat; **the I. of London Underwriters,** l'Institut d'Assurances Maritimes de Londres; **i. for the blind,** établissement *m* pour aveugles; *(b)* cercle *m*, foyer *m*; *(c)* **mechanics' i.,** maison *f* de l'artisanat; **sailors' i.,** cercle, foyer, maison, du marin. **2.** *A:* institution *f*; ordre établi; **the institutes and customs of civil life,** les institutions et les usages de la vie civile. **3.** *pl. Jur:* **the Institutes of Justinian,** les Institutes *f* de Justinien.

institute[2], *v.tr.* **1.** instituer, établir (un ordre, une loi); fonder, constituer (une société); **newly instituted office,** poste *m* de création récente. **2.** *Jur:* **to i. an inquiry,** ordonner, instituer, une enquête; procéder à une enquête; **to i. (legal) proceedings, an action, against s.o.,** intenter un procès à qn; entamer, engager, instituer, des poursuites contre qn; **to i. an action at law,** porter plainte en justice. **3.** *(a) Ecc:* **to i. s.o. to a benefice,** investir qn d'un bénéfice; *(b) Jur:* **to i. s.o. as heir,** instituer qn héritier.

instituting ['institjuːtiŋ], *s.* = INSTITUTION 1.

institution [insti'tjuːʃ(ə)n], *s.* **1.** *(a)* institution *f*, établissement *m* (d'une loi, etc.); constitution *f* (d'un comité); création *f* (d'un État); fondation *f* (d'une banque); *(b)* commencement *m*, établissement (d'une enquête, etc.); *(c) Ecc:* investiture *f* (d'un ecclésiastique); *(d) Jur:* institution (d'un héritier). **2.** institution; chose établie; pratique passée dans les mœurs; **savings banks are a useful i.,** les caisses d'épargne sont une institution utile; **television has become an i.,** la télévision est passée dans les mœurs; **the Gilbert and Sullivan operas are a national i.,** les opérettes de Gilbert et Sullivan font partie du patrimoine national. **3.** *(a)* institution (d'éducation, d'utilité publique, etc.); **charitable i.,** établissement, œuvre *f*, de charité, de bienfaisance; *Adm:* établissement d'intérêt public (qui ne paie pas d'impôts); *A:* **our maid is an i. girl,** notre bonne nous est venue de l'Assistance publique; *(b)* établissement (public, financier, etc.); **military i.,** établissement militaire; *Fin:* **credit i.,** établissement de crédit; **investment i.,** société *f* de placement; *(c)* association *f* (d'ingénieurs, etc.).

institutional [insti'tjuːʃənl], *a.* **1.** qui se rapporte à une institution, à une œuvre de charité, etc.; institutionnel; **i. life,** la vie dans un établissement de charité. **2.** *NAm:* *(a)* **i. advertising,** publicité de prestige; *(b)* **i. investors,** organismes *m* de placement collectif.

institutionalism [insti'tjuːʃ(ə)nəlizm], *s. A:* **1.** la vie dans les établissements de charité. **2.** régime social qui comporte des établissements de charité. **3.** *Pol.Ec:* institutionnalisme *m*.

institutionalization ['institjuːʃ(ə)nəlai'zeiʃ(ə)n], *s. A:* institutionnalisation *f*.

institutionalize [insti'tjuːʃ(ə)nəlaiz], *v.tr.* **1.** *(a)* faire une institution de (qch.); institutionnaliser (qch.); *(b)* faire passer (qch.) dans les mœurs. **2.** *A:* faire entrer (qn) dans un établissement de charité, de l'Assistance publique.

institutionalized [insti'tjuːʃ(ə)nəlaizd], *a.* **1.** *A:* (enfant) (i) dans un établissement de charité, de l'Assistance publique; (ii) qui a été élevé par l'Assistance publique. **2. i. bribery,** corruption *f* qui a passé dans les mœurs.

institutor ['institjuːtər], *s.* instituteur, -trice (d'un ordre religieux, etc.); fondateur, -trice; organisateur, -trice.

instruct [in'strʌkt], *v.tr.* **1.** instruire (qn); **to i. s.o. in sth., how to do sth.,** instruire qn en, dans, qch.; enseigner qch. à qn; instruire qn à faire qch.; **to i. s.o. in Latin,** enseigner, apprendre, le latin à qn; **to i. a clerk in book-keeping,** instruire un commis à tenir les livres. **2.** *(a)* **to i. s.o. of a fact, of what is going on,** instruire qn d'un fait, de ce qui se passe; **he was instructed that it was safe for him to proceed,** on l'informa qu'il pouvait continuer son chemin sans danger; *(b) Jur:* **to i. a solicitor,** donner ses instructions à un avoué; **to i. counsel,** constituer avocat. **3. to i. s.o. to do sth.,** charger qn de faire qch.; mander à qn de faire qch.; donner des instructions à qn pour faire qch.; **I am instructed by the Board to inform you that . . .,** la Direction me charge de vous faire savoir que . . .; **the Committee had not been instructed to deal with this question,** la Commission n'avait pas été saisie de cette question; *Pol: U.S:* **to i. a representative,** donner des directives à son représentant à la Chambre.

instruction [in'strʌkʃ(ə)n], *s.* **1.** instruction *f*, enseignement *m*; **medical i.,** (i) enseignement de la médecine; (ii) études *fpl* de médecine; **practical i.,** instruction pratique; *Mil: etc:* **school of i.,** école *f* d'application; (*for N.C.O.'s*) **i. squad,** peloton *m* d'instruction; *Aut:* **driving i.,** leçons *fpl* de conduite. **2.** *usu.pl.* instructions, indications *f*, directives *f*; *(a)* ordres *m*; (*to sentry, etc.*) consigne *f*; (*to representative, etc.*) mandat *m*; **oral, written, instructions,** instructions verbales, écrites; **official instructions,** directives officielles; prescriptions légales; **service instructions,** consignes, circulaires *f*, de service; (*on printed form*) mentions *f* de service; (**book**

of) standing instructions, règlement *m*; *F:* guide-âne *m*, *pl.* guide-âne(s); *Nau:* **sailing instructions,** instructions nautiques; **he is provided with exact instructions,** il a reçu des directives précises; **to give s.o. strict instructions,** donner des instructions, directives, formelles, des ordres formels, à qn; **to carry out instructions,** exécuter des instructions, des ordres; appliquer des directives, des consignes; **to act in accordance with, contrary to, one's instructions,** se conformer, ne pas se conformer, aux directives, aux instructions, reçues, aux ordres reçus, à son mandat; **to act in accordance with, contrary to, s.o.'s instructions,** se conformer, ne pas se conformer, aux instructions, aux ordres, de qn; *Mil: etc:* **to act according to instructions,** suivre, se conformer à, la consigne; **to follow s.o.'s instructions,** suivre les directives, les instructions, de qn; **to obey s.o.'s instructions,** obéir aux ordres de qn; **to go beyond one's instructions,** aller au delà des ordres reçus; sortir du cadre de ses instructions, de son mandat; *Adm:* **under instructions from the Board,** d'ordre du Ministère; *Com: etc:* **we await your instructions,** nous attendons vos instructions, vos ordres; (*b*) **to give instructions how to use sth.,** donner des indications, des instructions, sur la manière de se servir de qch., sur le mode d'emploi de qch.; **instructions for use,** mode, notice *f*, d'emploi; **i. manual, i. book(let),** brochure *f*, livret *m*, d'instruction(s); manuel *m* d'entretien (d'une machine, etc.); (*c*) *Cmptr:* instruction (du programme); **basic i.,** instructions sous forme initiale; **extract i.,** instruction de rassemblement; **i. area,** zone (de mémoire) réservée aux instructions; **i. code,** instruction-machine *f*, *pl.* instructions-machines; **i. fetch(ing),** prise *f* en charge de l'instruction; **i. format,** structure *f* de l'instruction; **i. repertory,** répertoire *m* des instructions (d'un ordinateur); (*d*) *Jur:* **to give instructions to a solicitor, a counsel,** donner ses instructions à un avoué; constituer un avocat.

instructional [in'strʌkʃən(ə)l], *a.* (voyage) d'instruction; (école) d'application; (ordinateur, etc.) utilisé pour l'enseignement; *Cin:* **i. film,** film éducatif.

instructive [in'strʌktiv], *a.* instructif.

instructively [in'strʌktivli], *adv.* d'une manière instructive, éducative.

instructor [in'strʌktər], *s.* **1.** maître enseignant; précepteur *m*; *Mil:* instructeur *m*; **sergeant i.,** sergent instructeur; **naval i.,** professeur *m* à l'École navale; *Aut:* **driving i.,** moniteur *m* de conduite; *Sp:* **ski(ing) i., physical education i.,** moniteur de ski, d'éducation physique; **swimming i.,** professeur de natation; maître-nageur *m*, *pl.* maîtres-nageurs. **2.** *Sch: NAm:* chargé *m* de cours.

instructress [in'strʌktris], *s.f.* maîtresse; professeur *m* (de conduite, etc.); monitrice (de ski, d'éducation physique).

instrument[1] ['instrumənt], *s.* instrument *m*. **1.** (*means, agent*) **to serve as the i. of s.o.'s vengeance,** servir d'instrument à la vengeance de qn; **the government learnt of the plot through its instruments,** le gouvernement a pris connaissance du complot par ses organes; **he was a mere i. in the hands of the Cardinal,** il était l'âme damnée du Cardinal; **inventions that can easily become instruments of death,** inventions susceptibles de se transformer en instruments de mort. **2.** (*a*) **scientific i., precision i.,** instrument scientifique, de précision; **measuring i.,** instrument de mesure; **drawing i.,** instrument de dessin (artistique); **mathematical i.,** instrument de dessin (graphique); **optical i.,** instrument d'optique; **carving i.,** instrument à modeler; **cutting i.,** instrument tranchant; **single-bevelled cutting i., double-bevelled, bi-bevelled, cutting i.,** instrument tranchant à biseau unique, à double biseau; **surgical i.,** instrument de chirurgie, chirurgical; **grinding i.,** instrument abrasif, à meuler; **diamond grinding i.,** instrument abrasif diamanté; *Surv:* **surveying i.,** instrument de levés, topographique; **levelling i.,** instrument de nivellement; *Sm.a: Artil:* **aiming i.,** instrument de pointage; **navigation(al) i.,** instrument de navigation; **nautical i.,** instrument nautique; **i. maker,** constructeur *m* d'instruments; (*b*) **dial i.,** instrument à cadran; **aircraft instruments,** instruments de bord; **flying, landing, on instruments, i. flying, i. landing,** vol *m*, atterrissage *m*, aux instruments, sans visibilité; **i. flight rules,** règles *f* de vol aux instruments; **i. landing system,** dispositif *m* d'atterrissage sans visibilité; **i. board, i. panel,** (i) *Av: Aut:* tableau *m* de bord; (ii) tableau de commande, de contrôle; panneau *m*, tableau, des instruments (d'une installation industrielle, etc.); **i. panel light,** lampe *f*, éclairage *m*, de tableau de bord; (*c*) **musical i.,** instrument de musique; **wind, reed, stringed, i.,** instrument à vent, à anche, à cordes; **to play an i.,** jouer d'un instrument. **3.** (*a*) *Jur:* acte *m* juridique (de cession, de transmission, etc.); instrument, document officiel; **i. in writing,** acte instrumentaire; **i. of appeal,** acte d'appel; (*b*) **i. of commerce, of credit,** instrument de commerce, de crédit; *Com:* **negotiable i.,** effet *m* de commerce; titre *m* au porteur.

instrument[2] ['instrumənt, instru'ment]. **1.** *v.i. Jur:* instrumenter. **2.** *v.tr.* (*a*) *Mus:* orchestrer, instrumenter (un opéra, etc.); (*b*) équiper, munir, (un atelier, etc.) d'instruments; **well instrumented,** bien équipé.

instrumental [instru'mentl], *a.* **1.** contributif (**to,** à); **to be i. to a purpose, in doing sth.,** contribuer à un but, à faire qch.; **your friend was i. in getting me appointed,** c'est à votre ami que je dois ma nomination; **he was largely i. in the matter,** il a été pour beaucoup, a joué un rôle déterminant, décisif, dans l'affaire. **2.** *Tchn:* de l'instrument, d'instruments; **i. equipment,** équipement *m* en instruments; **i. error,** erreur (de lecture) due à l'instrument. **3.** *Mus:* **i. and vocal music,** musique instrumentale et vocale; **i. performer,** instrumentiste *mf*. **4.** *Gram:* **the i. case,** le cas instrumental; l'instrumental *m*.

instrumentalism [instru'mentəlizm], *s. Phil:* instrumentalisme *m*.

instrumentalist [instru'mentəlist], *s. Mus:* instrumentiste *mf*.

instrumentality [instrumen'tæliti], *s.* **to obtain an appointment through the i. of s.o.,** obtenir une nomination avec le concours, par l'intermédiaire, à l'aide, de qn.

instrumentally [instru'mentəli], *adv.* **1.** (*a*) (se servir de qch.) comme instrument; (*b*) (agir) comme instrument, en qualité d'intermédiaire. **2.** (*a*) au moyen d'un instrument (scientifique); (*b*) *Mus:* **Te Deum performed i. and vocally,** Te Deum pour chœurs et orchestre. **3.** *Jur:* (transmettre qch.) par acte juridique, par instrument légal. **4.** *Gram:* au sens instrumental.

instrumentary [instru'mentəri], *a. Jur: Scot:* **i. witness,** témoin *m* instrumentaire.

instrumentation [instrumen'teiʃ(ə)n], *s.* **1.** *Mus:* instrumentation *f*. **2.** (*a*) *coll.* (les) instruments *m*, (l')appareillage *m*; **aircraft i.,** instruments de bord d'un avion; (*b*) fabrication *f*, technologie *f*, des instruments, de l'appareillage; (*c*) mise *f* au point, réglage *m*, des appareils (de mesure, etc.). **3.** = INSTRUMENTALITY.

insubmersibility ['insʌbmə:si'biliti], *s.* insubmersibilité *f*.

insubmersible [insʌb'mə:sibl], *a.* insubmersible.

insubordinate [insə'bɔ:dinət], *a.* insubordonné, insoumis; (soldat, etc.) mutin.

insubordination ['insəbɔ:di'neiʃ(ə)n], *s.* insubordination *f*, insoumission *f*.

insubstantial [insəb'stænʃ(ə)l], *a.* insubstantiel; (*a*) imaginaire, chimérique; (*b*) (i) (corps) immatériel; (ii) qui manque de substance; **i. food,** aliments creux; **i. arguments,** arguments *m* vides, sans substance.

insubstantiality ['insəbstænʃi'æliti], *s.* manque *m* de substance; (i) irréalité *f*; (ii) manque de solidité.

insufferable [in'sʌf(ə)rəbl], *a.* insupportable, intolérable, insouffrable.

insufferably [in'sʌf(ə)rəbli], *adv.* insupportablement, intolérablement; **he's i. bumptious,** il est d'une suffisance insupportable.

insufficiency [insə'fiʃ(ə)nsi], *s.* insuffisance *f*; (i) **i. of food,** nourriture insuffisante; *Med:* **aortic i.,** insuffisance aortique; (ii) **unaware of his own insufficiencies,** ignorant de ses propres insuffisances, déficiences *f*.

insufficient [insə'fiʃ(ə)nt], *a.* insuffisant; **i. food supplies,** manque *m*, défaut *m*, de vivres.

insufficiently [insə'fiʃəntli], *adv.* insuffisamment.

insufflate ['insʌfleit], *v.tr.* insuffler ((i) une vessie, *Med:* un asphyxié; (ii) un gaz dans une vessie, etc.).

insufflation [insʌ'fleiʃ(ə)n], *s.* insufflation *f*; *Med:* **mouth-to-mouth i.,** respiration artificielle bouche à bouche; bouche-à-bouche *m*.

insufflator ['insʌfleitər], *s. Med:* insufflateur *m*.

insulance ['insjuləns], *s. El:* résistance *f* d'isolement.

insulant ['insjulənt], *s.* isolant *m*, isolateur *m*.

insular ['insjulər]. **1.** *a.* (*a*) (climat, etc.) insulaire; (*b*) (vie, etc.) d'insulaire; **i. mind,** esprit étroit, borné; **to be very i. in one's views,** avoir les idées très bornées. **2.** *s.* insulaire *mf*.

insularism ['insjulərizm], **insularity** [insju'læriti], *s.* insularité *f*; *esp.* **the i. of the English,** l'esprit borné, l'étroitesse *f* d'esprit, des Anglais.

insulate ['insjuleit], *v.tr.* **1.** faire une île, un îlot, de (qch.); **before Britain was insulated from the mainland,** avant que la Bretagne fût détachée du continent; **to i. sth. from its proper surroundings,** isoler qch. de, d'avec, son (propre) milieu. **2.** (*a*) *El:* isoler (un fil, etc.); **insulated with mica,** isolé au mica; (*b*) **to i. a steam pipe,** calorifuger une conduite; (*c*) **to i. against vibration,** protéger contre les vibrations; *W.Tel: etc:* **to i. a studio,** insonoriser un studio.

insulated ['insjuleitid], *a.* isolé; (*a*) *El:* étanche; (i) isolé; **i. wire,** fil isolé, étanche; **rubber-i.,** isolé au caoutchouc; (ii) isolant; **i. pliers,** pinces isolantes; (*b*) **(heat-)i.,** calorifugé; (*of ship's hold, train, etc.*) frigorifique; (*c*) **(sound-)i.,** insonore, insonorisé.

insulating ['insjuleitiŋ], *a.* isolant; isolateur, -trice; (*a*) *El:* **i. material,** matériau isolant; matière isolante; isolant *m* électrique; diélectrique *m*; **i. bead,** perle isolante; **i. compound,** pâte isolante; compound *m*; **i. ferrule,** virole isolante; **i. oil,** huile isolante; **i. varnish,** vernis isolant; **i. stool,** tabouret isolant; isoloir *m*; **i. tape,** ruban isolant; chatterton *m*; (*b*) **(heat-)i.,** calorifuge; **i. board,** matériau de placage calorifuge, isolant; **i. lagging,** enveloppe *f* calorifuge; (*c*) **(sound-)i.,** insonore; étanche, imperméable, au bruit; **sound-i. material,** matériau, matière, insonore; isolant *m* acoustique, phonique.

insulation [insju'leiʃ(ə)n], *s.* **1.** détachement *m* (d'une île d'avec un continent, etc.); isolement *m* (**from,** de). **2.** (*action, state*) isolation *f*, isolement; (*a*) **i. (testing) set,** appareil *m*, dispositif *m*, pour vérifier l'isolement (diélectrique, thermique, acoustique); **poor i.,** mauvais isolement; **faulty i., i. fault,** défaut *m*, panne *f*, d'isolement; **i. materials,** matériaux isolants, matières isolantes; isolants *m* (électriques, thermiques, acoustiques); (*b*) *El:* isolement (par rapport à la terre); **i. breakdown,** faux contact; **i. resistance,** résistance *f* d'isolement; (*c*) **heat i., thermal i.,** isolation thermique; calorifugeage *m*; **i. plate,** plaque *f* de protection; (*d*) **sound i., noise i.,** isolation contre le bruit; isolation acoustique, phonique; insonorisation *f* (d'une salle, d'un appareil, etc.). **3.** (*substance*) isolant (électrique, thermique, acoustique); *El:* diélectrique *m*; *El:* **bakelite i.,** isolant bakélisé; **burnt i.,** isolement corrodé.

insulator ['insjuleitər], *s.* **1.** *El:* (*a*) (*substance*) isolant *m*; diélectrique *m*; **spark plug i.,** isolant pour bougies d'allumage; (*b*) (*device*) isolateur *m*; godet *m* de support (de fil électrique, téléphonique, etc.); **high-tension i.,** isolateur haute tension; **radio-frequency i.,** isolateur haute fréquence; *Tg: Tp:* **line i.,** isolateur de ligne; *W.Tel:* **lead-in i.,** isolateur d'entrée (de poste, de bâtiment); **glass, porcelain, i.,** isolateur en verre, en porcelaine; **bobbin i.,** isolateur poulie (pour antenne); **cleat i.,** isolateur à gorges; **disc i.,** isolateur à disques; **petticoat i., cup i.,** isolateur à cloche; **single-, double-, petticoat i.,** isolateur à simple, double, cloche; **oil (-type) i.,** isolateur à huile; **pin(-type) i.,** isolateur à tige; **stand-off i.,** isolateur d'écartement; **suspension i.,** isolateur à suspension. **2.** (*a*) **heat i.,** isolant thermique; matériau *m*, matière *f*, calorifuge; (*b*) **sound i., noise i.,** isolant acoustique, phonique; matériau, matière, insonore. **3.** isolateur; tampon amortisseur (de moteur, etc.); *Mus:* godet de support, amortisseur *m* (de piano); **i. plate,** plaque isolante; **i. tube,** tube isolé.

insulin ['insjulin], *s. Med:* insuline *f*; **i. coma,** coma *m* insulinique; **i. shock,** choc *m* insulinique; **i. treatment,** insulinothérapie *f*.

insulinase ['insjulineis], *s. Ch: Biol:* insulinase *f*.

insulinization [insjulinai'zeiʃ(ə)n], *s. Med:* insulinothérapie *f*.

insult[1] ['insʌlt], *s.* **1.** insulte *f*, affront *m*, indignité *f*, avanie *f*; **an i. to one's honour,** un affront à l'honneur; **to offer an i. to s.o.,** faire (une) injure, faire (une) insulte, à qn; **to suffer, pocket, an i.,** boire un affront; *F:* avaler un crapaud, une couleuvre; **to add i. to injury,** doubler ses torts d'un affront; **it's an i. to one's intelligence, (good) taste,** c'est un outrage à l'intelligence, au bon goût. **2.** *NAm: Med:* choc *m*, blessure *f*, lésion *f* (du corps); **the insults of malnutrition,** les dommages causés par la sous-alimentation.

insult[2] [in'sʌlt], *v.tr.* **1.** insulter (qn); faire (une) insulte à (qn); faire affront, faire injure, à (qn); outrager (qn); **to feel insulted by a refusal,** tenir un refus pour une injure; **to i. s.o.'s intelligence,** faire outrage à l'intelligence de qn. **2.** *NAm: Med:* **foods that i. the body,** nourriture qui nuit à la santé; nourriture nocive.

insulter [in'sʌltər], *s.* **1.** insulteur, -euse. **2.** *Rom.Ant:* insulteur *m*.

insulting [in'sʌltiŋ], *a.* (geste, mot) offensant, injurieux; **to use i. language to s.o.,** dire des injures, lancer des insultes, à qn; injurier qn; *F:* invectiver qn; **to be guilty of i. behaviour towards s.o.,** (i) s'être conduit insolemment à l'égard de qn; (ii) *Jur:* être coupable d'outrages (à un agent, un magistrat).

insultingly [in'sʌltiŋli], *adv.* insolemment, d'une façon insultante, offensante.

insuperability [insju:p(ə)rə'biliti], *s.* nature *f* insurmontable, caractère *m* insurmontable (d'un obstacle, d'une

difficulté).
insuperable [in'sju:p(ə)rəbl], *a.* (difficulté, etc.) insurmontable; (obstacle) infranchissable.
insuperably [in'sju:p(ə)rəbli], *adv.* insurmontablement.
insupportable [insə'pɔ:təbl], *a.* (douleur, etc.) insupportable, intolérable.
insupportableness [insə'pɔ:təb(ə)lnis], *s.* nature *f* insupportable (de qch.).
insupportably [insə'pɔ:təbli], *adv.* insupportablement, intolérablement.
insurable [in'ʃuərəbl], *a.* assurable; **i. interest,** intérêt *m* pécuniaire.
insurance [in'ʃuərəns], *s.* assurance *f.* **1.** *Com:* (*a*) **to take out, effect, an i. on sth., against a risk,** contracter, prendre, une assurance, s'assurer, se faire assurer, sur qch., contre un risque; **accident i.,** assurance contre les accidents; assurance accidents *f, pl.* assurances-accidents; **baggage i.,** assurance-bagages *f, pl.* assurances-bagages; **burglary i., theft i.,** assurance contre le vol; **burst water pipes i.,** assurance dégâts des eaux; **disablement i.,** assurance-invalidité *f, pl.* assurances-invalidité; **employers' liability i.,** assurance (des) employeurs contre les accidents du travail; **fire i.,** assurance contre l'incendie; assurance-incendie *f, pl.* assurances-incendie; **life i.,** assurance sur la vie; assurance-vie *f, pl.* assurances-vie; **whole life i.,** assurance-décès *f, pl.* assurances-décès; **livestock i.,** assurance sur le bétail; **motor, car, i.,** assurance-auto *f, pl.* assurances-auto; **old age i.,** assurance-vieillesse *f, pl.* assurances-vieillesse; **plate-glass i.,** assurance contre le bris de glace; **personal liability i.,** assurance responsabilité civile; **third-party i.,** assurance vis-à-vis des tiers, aux tiers, contre les accidents causés aux tiers; **war-risk i.,** assurance contre les risques de guerre; **workmen's compensation i.,** assurance contre les accidents du travail; **all risks i., all-in i., comprehensive i.,** assurance tous risques; **collective i., group i.,** assurance collective; **double i.,** assurance cumulative; **index(-linked) i.,** assurance indexée; **time i.,** assurance à temps, à terme; **voluntary i.,** assurance facultative; (*b*) **marine i.,** assurance maritime; **i. against sea risks,** assurance contre les risques maritimes; **cargo i.,** assurance de la cargaison; **freight i.,** assurance du, sur, frêt; assurance-frêt *f, pl.* assurances-frêt; **i. on hull; i. on, of, ship,** assurance du, sur, navire; **assurance sur** corps; **i. for the voyage,** assurance au, pour le, voyage; (*c*) *attrib.* **i. agent,** agent *m* d'assurance(s); **i. broker,** courtier *m* d'assurance(s); **i. charges,** frais *m* d'assurance; **i. money,** indemnité *f* d'assurance; **the children got his i. money,** les enfants ont touché son assurance-vie; **i. policy,** police *f* d'assurance; **i. premium,** prime *f* d'assurance; (*d*) *F:* prime d'assurance; **to pay the i. on a car,** payer l'assurance, la prime d'assurance, d'une voiture; (*e*) **he's in i.,** il est dans les assurances; **i. shares,** valeurs *f* d'assurances. **2.** *Adm:* **state i., national i., social i.,** prévoyance sociale; assurances sociales; **unemployment i.,** assurance chômage.
insurant [in'ʃuərənt], *s. Com:* assuré, -ée.
insure [in'ʃuər], *v.tr.* **1.** *Com: etc:* (i) assurer, (ii) faire assurer (des marchandises, un vaisseau, un mobilier); **to i. one's life,** s'assurer, se faire assurer, sur la vie; **to i. sth. against all risks,** faire assurer qch. contre tous risques; *v.i.* **to i. against a risk,** s'assurer, se faire assurer, contre un risque. **2.** (*a*) *A:* garantir, assurer (le succès, l'exécution d'un projet, etc.); (*b*) *v.i.* **to i. against a danger,** se garantir d'un danger; parer à un danger.
insured [in'ʃuə:d], *a. & s.* assuré, -ée; **the property was i.,** il y a assurance; *Ins:* **i. value,** valeur assurée; *Post:* **i. letter,** lettre chargée; **parcel i. for five pounds,** colis chargé avec valeur déclarée cinq livres.
insurer [in'ʃuərər], *s. Com:* assureur *m.*
insurgency [in'sə:dʒ(ə)nsi], *s.* insurgence *f,* révolte *f.*
insurgent [in'sə:dʒ(ə)nt]. **1.** *a.* (*a*) insurgé, révolté, révolutionnaire; en état de rébellion, d'insurrection; **the i. army,** l'armée *f* des insurgés; (*b*) *Poet:* **the i. sea,** la mer qui avance, qui monte. **2.** *s.* insurgé, -ée; révolté, -ée; rebelle *mf; U.S: Hist:* **the insurgents,** les insurgents *m* (de la Guerre de l'Indépendance).
insuring [in'ʃuəriŋ], *s.* assurance *f.*
insurmountable [insə(:)'mauntəbl], *a.* (difficulté, obstacle) insurmontable; (obstacle) infranchissable.
insurmountably [insə(:)'mauntəbli], *adv.* insurmontablement.
insurrection [insə'rekʃ(ə)n], *s.* insurrection *f;* soulèvement *m,* émeute *f,* rébellion *f;* **to be in i. against s.o.,** être insurgé contre qn; **to be in open i. against s.o.,** être en pleine insurgence contre qn; **to rise in i.,** s'insurger, se soulever.
insurrectional [insə'rekʃənl], **insurrectionary** [insə'rekʃənəri], *a.* insurrectionnel.
insurrectionist [insə'rekʃənist], *s.* émeutier, -ière; insurgé, -ée; rebelle *mf.*
insusceptible [insə'septibl], *a.* **1.** insusceptible, non susceptible (**of,** de); *Lit:* **heart i. of pity,** cœur fermé à la pitié, inaccessible à la pitié. **2.** insensible (**to,** à); **a mind i. to flattery,** un esprit insensible à la flatterie. **3.** *Med:* **i. to a disease,** sans prédisposition à une maladie; peu susceptible d'attraper une maladie.
insweep ['inswi:p], *s.* courbure *f* en dedans; *Aut: A:* étranglement *m* (du châssis).
inswept ['inswept], *a.* courbé en dedans; *Aut: A:* (châssis) étranglé, à avant rétréci, rétréci à l'avant; à longerons coudés; **i. side member,** longeron cintré à l'avant.
intact [in'tækt], *a.* intact, indemne; **to keep one's reputation i.,** conserver sa réputation entière; *Fin:* **to maintain the capital i.,** maintenir le capital en état.
intagliated [in'tɑ:lieitid], *a. Lap: etc:* intaillé; travaillé à l'intaille.
intaglio[1] [in'tɑ:liou], *s. Lap: etc:* intaille *f;* **i. engraving,** gravure *f* en creux.
intaglio[2], *v.tr.* intailler.
intake ['inteik], *s.* **1.** (*a*) prise *f,* appel *m* (d'air, de vapeur); prise (d'eau, *El:* de courant); arrivée *f,* adduction *f,* amenée *f,* admission *f* (de vapeur); *I.C.E:* entrée *f* (d'air); **i. valve,** soupape *f* d'admission; *Av:* **nacelle i. ring,** entrée d'air de fuseau; *Min:* **i. airway,** galerie *f* d'appel d'air; (*b*) ouïe *f* (de ventilateur); œillard *m* (de pompe centrifuge); (*c*) *Hyd.E:* aire *f* d'alimentation; bassin *m* hydrographique. **2.** *Physiol:* **caloric i.,** ration *f* calorique; **food i.,** ration alimentaire. **3.** (*a*) diminution de diamètre (d'un tuyau); (*b*) *Const:* retraite *f* (d'un mur). **4.** (*a*) *Mil:* contingent *m;* (*b*) *Sch:* **the i.,** les élèves entrant(e)s; les nouveaux *m.*
intangibility [intæn(d)ʒi'biliti], **intangibleness** [in'tæn(d)ʒib(ə)lnis], *s.* **1.** intangibilité *f.* **2.** inviolabilité *f* (d'un traité, etc.).
intangible [in'tæn(d)ʒibl], *a.* **1.** intangible, impalpable; imperceptible; **the i. factors,** les impondérables *m; Com:* **i. assets,** *s.* **intangibles,** valeurs immatérielles; actif incorporel; *Jur:* **i. property,** biens incorporels. **2.** (traité, etc.) inviolable, *F:* sacro-saint, *pl.* sacro-saints.
intascale ['intəskeil], *s.* (*abbr. of* **inter tanker nominal freight scale**) barème mondial des taux de fret nominaux.
integer ['intidʒər], *s.* **1.** *Mth:* (nombre) entier (*m*). **2.** *Lit:* entier, tout *m,* totalité *f.*
integrable ['intigrəbl], *a. Mth:* (équation *f*) intégrable.
integral ['intigrəl]. **1.** *a.* (*a*) intégrant; **to be, form, an i. part of sth.,** faire partie intégrante de qch.; faire corps avec qch.; **to become an i. part of sth.,** s'intégrer dans qch.; **i. part of a contract,** partie intégrante d'un contrat; (*b*) *Mth:* **i. number,** nombre entier; **i. calculus,** calcul intégral; **i. function,** fonction intégrale; (*c*) *Tchn:* (i) d'une seule pièce; en un seul bloc; **crankcase cast i. with cylinder, crankcase and cylinder cast i.,** carter venu de fonte, venu de fonderie, avec le cylindre; carter et cylindre fondus en un seul bloc; **forged i. with sth.,** venu de forge, forgé d'une seule pièce, avec qch.; (ii) incorporé (**with,** à); structural, -aux; qui fait partie intégrante (**with,** de); **i. garage,** garage *m* qui fait corps avec la maison; *Av:* **i. wing fuel tank,** réservoir structural de voilure; **i. nacelles,** fuseaux-moteurs structuraux (de voilure). **2.** *s. Mth:* intégrale *f;* **general i.,** intégrale générale; **surface i.,** intégrale de surface; **line i.,** intégrale linéaire; **Fourier i.,** intégrale de Fourier; **i. sign,** signe *m* d'intégration.
integrality [inti'græliti], *s.* intégralité *f.*
integrally ['intigrəli], *adv.* intégralement; en totalité.
integrand ['intigrænd], *s. Mth:* fonction *f* à intégrer.
integrant ['intigrənt]. **1.** *a.* (*of part, etc.*) intégrant. **2.** *s.* partie intégrante; élément *m.*
integraph ['intigræf], *s. Mth:* intégraphe *m.*
integrate[1] ['intigrət], *a.* intégral, -aux; entier; **to keep sth. i.,** conserver qch. entier.
integrate[2] ['intigreit], *v.tr.* **1.** compléter, rendre entier (qch. d'incomplet). **2.** intégrer (une minorité dans un groupe); **to become integrated,** *v.i.* **to i.,** s'intégrer (dans un milieu social, ethnique, etc.); **federation that would i. the economies of the member nations,** une fédération dans laquelle les économies des pays membres seraient intégrées. **3.** *Mth:* intégrer (une fonction, équation différentielle, surface); déterminer l'intégrale (d'une fonction); **to i. by parts,** intégrer par parties.
integrated ['intigreitid], *a.* intégré; (*a*) **i. minorities,** minorités intégrées; (*b*) *Elcs:* **i. circuits, circuitry,** circuits intégrés; *Cmptr:* **i. data processing,** traitement intégré des données; *Atom.Ph:* **i. (neutron) flux,** flux (neutronique) intégré.
integrating ['intigreitiŋ], *a.* intégrateur; totalisateur; **i. instrument,** (appareil) intégrateur *m;* **i. metre,** compteur intégrateur; compteur totalisateur; **i. photometer,** photomètre *m* à intégration; *Ball:* **i. accelerometer,** accéléromètre intégrateur; *Cmptr:* **i. circuit,** circuit *m,* montage *m,* intégrateur.
integration [inti'greiʃ(ə)n], *s.* intégration *f;* (*a*) **the i. of ethnic minorities,** l'intégration des minorités ethniques; **sociological i.,** intégration sociale, insertion sociale; *Pol.Ec:* **vertical i., horizontal i.,** intégration, concentration, verticale, horizontale; *Ph: Elcs:* **i. of pulses,** intégration d'impulsions; *Cmptr:* **numerical i., trapezoidal i.,** intégration numérique, trapézoïdale; (*b*) *Mth:* **i. by parts,** intégration par parties; **asymptotic i.,** intégration asymptotique.
integrationist [inti'greiʃ(ə)nist], *s.* intégrationniste *mf.*
integrator ['intigreitər], *s. Mth: Elcs: Atom.Ph:* intégrateur *m; Atom.Ph:* **ion current i.,** intégrateur de courant ionique; *Mth:* **surface i.,** planimètre *m.*
integrifolious [integri'fouliəs], *a. Bot:* intégrifolié.
integrity [in'tegriti], *s.* **1.** intégrité *f,* état entier, intact (d'un texte, d'une somme d'argent, etc.); **in its i.,** en entier. **2.** intégrité, honnêteté *f,* probité *f* (de qn, d'un motif, etc.); rectitude *f* (de conduite); **man of i.,** homme intègre, probe.
integument [in'tegjumənt], *s. Nat.Hist:* tégument *m;* enveloppe *f; occ.* intégument *m;* **egg i.,** coquille *f* d'œuf.
integumental, integumentary [integju'mentl, -'mentəri], *a.* (enveloppe, surface, etc.) tégumentaire.
integumented [in'tegjumentid], *a. Nat.Hist:* à tégument; pourvu d'un tégument, d'une enveloppe.
intellect ['intilekt], *s.* **1.** intelligence *f,* esprit *m,* entendement *m,* intellect *m;* **the march of i.,** le mouvement des esprits; **man of i.,** homme intelligent, à l'esprit éclairé; **he was one of the best intellects of his time,** c'était une des meilleures intelligences de son époque. **2.** *coll.* **the i. of the country,** tous les meilleurs esprits du pays.
intellection [inti'lekʃ(ə)n], *s. Phil:* intellection *f.*
intellective [inti'lektiv], *a. Phil:* intellectif.
intellectual [inti'lektjuəl]. **1.** *a.* intellectuel; **i. pastimes,** jeux *m* d'esprit. **2.** *s.* intellectuel, -elle.
intellectualism [inti'lektjuəlizm], *s. Phil:* intellectualisme *m.*
intellectualist [inti'lektjuəlist], *a. & s. Phil:* intellectualiste (*mf*).
intellectuality ['intilektju'æliti], *s.* intellectualité *f.*
intellectualization ['intilektjuəlai'zeiʃ(ə)n], *s.* intellectualisation *f.*
intellectualize [inti'lektjuəlaiz]. **1.** *v.tr.* intellectualiser (un sujet, une philosophie); rationaliser (un sujet). **2.** *v.i.* discuter (à un niveau intellectuel).
intellectually [inti'lektjuəli], *adv.* intellectuellement.
intelligence [in'telidʒəns], *s.* **1.** intelligence *f;* (*a*) esprit *m;* **an i. superior to his own,** une intelligence supérieure à la sienne; (*b*) entendement *m,* sagacité *f;* **person of good i.,** personne intelligente, d'une réelle intelligence; *Psy:* **i. test,** test *m* d'intelligence; **i. quotient,** quotient intellectuel. **2.** renseignement(s) *m(pl);* (*a*) avis *m,* nouvelle(s) *f(pl);* **to give, receive, i. of sth.,** donner, avoir, avis de qch.; **i. office,** (i) bureau *m* de renseignements; (ii) *U.S:* bureau, agence *f,* de placement (de domestiques); *Journ:* **latest i.,** dernières nouvelles; informations *fpl* de la dernière heure; **shipping i.,** événements *m* maritimes; mouvement *m* maritime; mouvements des navires; nouvelles maritimes; (*b*) *Mil: etc:* **combat i.,** renseignements, documents *mpl,* du champ de bataille; **i. map,** carte renseignée, de renseignements; **i. photograph,** photographie (aérienne, etc.) de renseignements; **i. (service),** service *m* des renseignements; **i. officer,** officier *m* de renseignements, le deuxième Bureau. **3.** *Cmptr:* **artificial i.,** intelligence artificielle.
intelligent [in'telidʒənt], *a.* **1.** (*of child, animal, etc.*) intelligent; (*of answer, etc.*) avisé, intelligent; **to take an i. interest in sth.,** s'intéresser d'une manière intelligente à qch. **2.** *A: & Lit:* **to be i. of a fact,** être conscient d'un fait; être au courant d'une affaire; **to be i. of a subject,** être versé dans une matière.
intelligential [inteli'dʒenʃ(ə)l], *a.* **1.** intelligentiel. **2.** doué d'intelligence.
intelligently [in'telidʒəntli], *adv.* intelligemment; avec intelligence.
intelligentsia [inteli'dʒentsiə], *s.* intelligentsia *f,* intelligentzia *f.*
intelligibility [intelidʒi'biliti], **intelligibleness** [in'telidʒib(ə)lnis], *s.* intelligibilité *f.*
intelligible [in'telidʒibl], *a.* intelligible; **he spoke so quickly that he was hardly i.,** il parlait si vite qu'on le comprenait à peine.
intelligibly [in'telidʒibli], *adv.* intelligiblement; clairement.
intemperance [in'temp(ə)rəns], *s.* intempérance *f;* (*a*) **i. of speech,** intempérance de langue; (*b*) **given to i.,**

adonné à l'intempérance, *esp.* à l'alcoolisme.

intemperate [in'temp(ə)rət], *a.* **1.** (*of pers.*) intempérant; (*a*) immodéré; **to be i. in one's speech,** être peu mesuré dans son langage; **i. zeal,** excès *m* de zèle; (*b*) **i. habits,** habitudes *f* d'intempérance; **person of i. habits,** personne intempérante; intempérant, *esp.* adonné à la boisson; buveur, -euse. **2.** (climat) peu clément, inclément; (vent) immodéré, violent.

intemperately [in'temp(ə)rətli], *adv.* intempéramment; (*a*) (rire) immodérément; (*b*) (boire) à l'excès.

intemperateness [in'temp(ə)rətnis], *s.* intempérance *f* (de langue, etc.).

intend [in'tend], *v.tr.* **1.** (*a*) **to i. doing sth., to i. to do sth., to i. sth.,** avoir l'intention de faire qch.; se proposer, avoir en vue, de faire qch.; songer à faire qch.; compter faire qch.; **I did not i. to insult you, I intended no insult,** je n'avais pas l'intention de vous insulter; **we intended no harm,** nous l'avons fait sans mauvaise intention; **I don't i. you any harm,** je ne vous veux pas de mal; **was that intended?** était-ce fait avec intention, à dessein? **measure intended to secure peace,** mesure ayant pour but d'assurer la paix; **you don't i. me to believe that?** vous ne voulez pas me faire croire cela? (*b*) **I i. to be obeyed,** je prétends qu'on m'obéisse; je veux être obéi. **2. to i. s.o., sth., for sth.,** destiner qn, qch., à qch.; **we i. our son to be a schoolmaster,** nous destinons notre fils au professorat; **book intended for students,** livre destiné à l'usage des étudiants; **I intended this present for you,** je vous destinais ce cadeau; **I had not intended this novel to be filmed, for the screen,** je n'avais pas destiné ce roman à être filmé, à l'écran; **this remark is intended for you,** c'est à vous que cette observation s'adresse. **3.** (*a*) **I intended it for, as, a compliment,** mon intention était de vous faire un compliment; **this portrait is intended for Mr Martin,** ce portrait représente M. Martin; **he made a gesture which was intended to indicate a polite refusal,** il fit un geste qui voulait être un refus poli; (*b*) *O:* vouloir dire; entendre; **what exactly do you i. by that remark?** qu'entendez-vous exactement par cette observation?

intendance [in'tendəns], **intendancy** [in'tendənsi], *s. Hist:* intendance *f*; **junior i.,** sous-intendance *f*, *pl.* sous-intendances.

intendant [in'tendənt], *s. Hist:* intendant *m*; **junior i.,** sous-intendant *m*, *pl.* sous-intendants.

intended [in'tendid], *a.* **1.** (*a*) (voyage, etc.) projeté, en perspective; **my i. husband, bride,** *s. P:* **my i.,** mon fiancé, ma fiancée; mon prétendu, ma prétendue; *P:* mon futur, ma future; (*b*) **the i. effect,** l'effet voulu. **2.** intentionnel; fait avec intention.

intendedly [in'tendidli], *adv.* avec intention; à dessein; intentionnellement.

intending [in'tendiŋ], *a.* **i. purchasers, subscribers,** acheteurs *m*, abonnés *m*, en perspective; personnes *f* qui ont l'intention d'acheter, de s'abonner; acheteurs éventuels.

intendment [in'tendmənt], *s. Jur:* intention *f* véritable (du testateur, etc.); esprit *m* (d'un texte par opposition à la lettre).

intense [in'tens], *a.* (*a*) vif, *f.* vive; fort, intense; **i. heat,** chaleur intense; *Meteor:* fortes chaleurs; **i. blue,** bleu intense, saturé; **i. anxiety,** vive inquiétude; **i. hatred,** haine profonde, acharnée; **i. pain,** douleur vive, aiguë; **i. pleasure,** plaisir *m* intense; **i. stupidty,** bêtise *f* extrême; *Phot:* **i. negative,** cliché *m* intense; (*b*) **her i. expression,** son expression tendue; **i. young woman,** (i) jeune fille d'un sérieux exagéré; (ii) exaltée *f*; **the most i. moments of one's life,** les moments les plus intenses de la vie.

intensely [in'tensli], *adv.* (*a*) excessivement; **it was i. hot,** il faisait une chaleur intense; **i. cold weather,** (temps *m* d'un) froid intense; **i. blue eyes,** yeux *m* d'un bleu très vif; **to hate s.o. i.,** haïr qn profondément; (*b*) (vivre, regarder) avec intensité; intensément.

intenseness [in'tensnis], *s.* intensité *f* (du froid, d'un son, d'une émotion); force *f* (d'une passion); violence *f* (d'une douleur); **i. of thought,** contention *f* d'esprit.

intensification [intensifi'keiʃ(ə)n], *s.* **1.** intensification *f*, amplification *f* (d'un son, etc.). **2.** *Phot:* renforcement *m*, renforçage *m* (d'un cliché).

intensifier [in'tensifaiər], *s.* **1.** (*a*) amplificateur *m*, renforçateur *m*, renforceur *m*; **i. of sound,** amplificateur (acoustique); **i. telephone,** téléphone *m* haut-parleur; *Hyd.E:* **head i.,** renforceur de chute; (*b*) *El:* **spark i.,** amplificateur; **i. electrode,** électrode post(-)accélératrice, électrode de post(-)accélération; (*c*) *Hyd.E:* multiplicateur *m* de pression. **2.** *Phot:* renforçateur; **copper bromide i.,** renforçateur au bromure de cuivre; **iodine, lead, i.,** renforçateur à l'iode, au plomb.

intensify [in'tensifai]. **1.** *v.tr.* (*a*) intensifier, augmenter, accroître, rendre plus fort, plus vif (un son, un sentiment); amplifier (un son); renforcer (une couleur); **to i. the action of a drama,** corser l'action d'un drame; (*b*) *Phot:* renforcer (un cliché faible). **2.** *v.i.* s'augmenter, s'accroître; devenir plus fort, plus vif, plus intense.

intensifying[1] [in'tensifaiiŋ], *a.* amplifiant, amplificateur, renforçateur, de renforcement; *X Rays:* **i. screen,** écran renforçateur; *Phot:* **i. agent,** renforçateur *m*; **i. bath,** bain *m* de renforcement.

intensifying[2], *s.* intensification *f*, augmentation *f*, renforcement *m* (d'une action mécanique, administrative, psychologique, etc.); amplification *f* (d'un son, etc.); **i. of propaganda,** intensification de la propagande; *Phot:* **i. of a negative,** renforcement d'un cliché.

intensimeter [in'tensimi:tər], **intensitometer** [intensi'təmitər], *s. X Rays:* intensi(to)mètre *m*; dosimètre *m*; posemètre *m*.

intension [in'tenʃ(ə)n], *s.* **1.** *Log:* **i. and extension,** compréhension *f* et extension *f*. **2.** *Lit:* **i. of mind,** tension *f*, contention *f*, d'esprit; attention soutenue.

intensity [in'tensiti], *s.* **1.** = INTENSENESS; **with i.,** intensément. **2.** *Ph: etc:* intensité *f*, puissance *f* (d'une action mécanique, d'une vibration, d'un son, etc.); **i. of light,** intensité de la lumière, du flux lumineux; **luminous i.,** intensité lumineuse (d'une source de lumière); *Atom.Ph:* **radiation i.,** intensité de rayonnement; **neutron i.,** intensité neutronique; **i. waves,** ondes *f* d'intensité; *El:* **i. of current,** intensité du courant; **i. armature,** induit enroulé à haute tension; *W.Tel:* **i. distortion,** distorsion *f* d'amplitude; **i. modulation,** modulation *f* en intensité; **i. of magnetization,** intensité d'aimantation; **i. of field,** intensité du champ; *Mch: etc:* **i. of combustion, of draught,** intensité de la combustion, du tirage (dans un fourneau, etc.); *Mec:* **i. of compression,** compression *f* par unité de surface; **i. of gravity,** intensité, accélération *f*, de la pesanteur; **i. of stress,** charge *f*, tension *f*; **i. of shear stress,** charge de cisaillement; **i. of tensile stress,** charge, tension, de traction; **i. of torsional stress,** charge, tension, de torsion; *Trans: Tp: etc:* **i. of traffic,** intensité du trafic (routier, ferroviaire, téléphonique, etc.); (*b*) *Ch:* énergie *f* (d'une réaction); (*c*) *Phot:* **i. of a negative,** densité *f* d'un cliché; **graduation of i.,** graduation *f* des nuances; **i. range,** intervalle *m* d'intensité.

intensive [in'tensiv], *a.* (*of work, cultivation, etc.*) intensif; **i. study of a text,** étude serrée d'un texte; **i. propaganda,** propagande intensive, intense; *Med:* **i. care unit, ward,** service *m* de soins intensifs; *Gram:* **i. verb, pronoun,** (verbe, pronom) intensif (*m*).

intensively [in'tensivli], *adv.* intensivement, intensément.

intent[1] [in'tent], *s.* **1.** intention *f*, dessein *m*, but *m*; **with good i.,** dans une bonne intention; **with i. to defraud,** dans l'intention, dans le but, de frauder; **with no ill i., without evil i.,** sans mauvaise intention; sans songer à mal; **to do sth. with i.,** faire qch. de propos délibéré; *Jur:* **to put the question of i. to the jury; to ask the jury whether the act was committed with i.,** poser au jury la question intentionnelle; **with malicious i.,** avec intention délictueuse. **2. to all intents and purposes,** virtuellement; moralement parlant; en fait; de fait; à tous égards; **to all intents and purposes he is cured,** il est quasiment guéri; **to all intents and purposes he is the master,** il est censément le maître; **the business is settled, to all intents and purposes,** l'affaire est réglée, ou autant vaut.

intent[2], *a.* **1.** (*a*) **to be i. on sth.,** être tout entier à qch., être absorbé par qch.; **i. on business, on pleasure,** tout entier aux affaires, aux plaisirs; **to be i. on one's work,** être absorbé par, dans, son travail; **to be i. on doing sth.,** être résolu, déterminé, à faire qch.; **he was i. on acquiring these goods,** il tenait absolument, il était résolu, il était bien décidé, à s'emparer de ces marchandises; (*b*) **to stand silent and i.,** se tenir silencieux et attentif. **2.** (*of faculties, etc.*) ardent, acharné; **mind i. on learning,** esprit acharné à l'étude; **i. gaze,** regard profond; **i. application,** application soutenue.

intention [in'tenʃ(ə)n], *s.* intention *f*. **1.** (*a*) **I've no i. of disturbing you,** je n'ai pas la moindre intention de vous déranger; **I had no i., not the slightest i., of accepting,** je n'avais aucunement, nullement, l'intention, je n'avais pas la moindre intention, d'accepter; **I have no i. of ignoring his rights,** je n'entends aucunement méconnaître ses droits; **the letter was written with the i. of irritating him,** cette lettre a été écrite avec, dans, l'intention de l'irriter; **she accompanied him with the firm i. of its being the last time,** elle l'accompagna dans la ferme intention que ce serait pour la dernière fois; **he acted with the best and most honourable intentions,** il a agi en tout bien (et) tout honneur; **my intentions for the future,** mes intentions au sujet de l'avenir; **to grasp s.o.'s i.,** saisir la pensée de qn; **to look for an evil i. in everything,** chercher à tout de sinistres interprétations; *Prov:* **it is the i. that counts,** c'est l'intention qui fait l'action; **the road to hell is paved with good intentions,** l'enfer est pavé de bonnes intentions; (*b*) *pl. O:* **to court a woman with honourable intentions,** courtiser une femme pour le bon motif; **his intentions are honourable,** il a le mariage en vue; il a l'intention de l'épouser; **to make known one's intentions,** se déclarer. **2.** *Surg:* **healing (of a wound) by first, second, i.,** réunion *f* par première, deuxième, intention. **3.** *Ecc:* **to celebrate mass for a special, particular, i.,** dire une messe à l'intention spéciale (de qn, qch.).

intentional [in'tenʃən(ə)l], *a.* intentionnel, voulu; fait à dessein, fait exprès.

intentionality [intenʃə'næliti], *s. Psy:* intentionnalité *f*.

intentionally [in'tenʃənəli], *adv.* avec intention; à dessein; exprès; intentionnellement, délibérément; de propos délibéré.

intently [in'tentli], *adv.* (écouter) attentivement; (regarder) fixement; avec une attention soutenue; (réfléchir) profondément.

intentness [in'tentnis], *s.* contention *f* d'esprit; attention soutenue (du regard, etc.); **i. on one's work,** application *f* à son travail.

inter[1] [in'tə:r], *v.tr.* (**interred**) enterrer, ensevelir, inhumer (un mort).

inter[2] ['intər], *s. Sch: F: A:* examen *m* à la fin de la première année des études universitaires.

inter- [intər], *pref.* **1.** inter-. **2.** entre-. **3.** réciproque.

interact[1] ['intərækt], *s. Th:* **1.** (*period*) entracte *m*. **2.** (*entertainment*) entracte, intermède *m*.

interact[2] [intər'ækt], *v.i.* réagir réciproquement; agir l'un sur l'autre; interagir.

interacting [intər'æktiŋ], *a.* à action réciproque; à action conjuguée; **i. brakes,** freins conjugués; freinage conjugué.

interaction [intər'ækʃ(ə)n], *s.* action mutuelle, réciproque; *Ph: etc:* interaction *f* (des éléments d'un tout, etc.); **i. component,** composante *f* d'interaction; **i. cross-section,** section *f* efficace d'action réciproque, d'interaction; **i. energy,** énergie *f* d'action réciproque, d'action mutuelle; énergie d'interaction; *Mth:* **cylindrical i. space,** espace *m* d'interaction de révolution; *Atom.Ph:* **particle i.,** interaction de particules; **tensor i.,** interaction tensorielle.

interactive [intər'æktiv], *a. Cmptr:* interactif.

interactively [intər'æktivli], *adv. Cmptr:* interactivement.

interallied [intər'ælaid], *a.* interallié.

interambulacral ['intəræmbju'leikrəl], *a. Echin:* interambulacraire.

interambulacrum, *pl.* **-cra** ['interæmbju'leikrəm, -krə], *s. Echin:* interambulacre *m*.

inter-American ['intərə'merik(ə)n], *a.* interaméricain.

inter-Andean ['intər'ændiən], *a. Geog:* interandin.

interarticular [intərɑ:'tikjulər], *a. Anat:* interarticulaire.

interatomic [intərə'təmik], *a.* (espace, etc.) interatomique, entre les atomes.

interauricular ['intərɔ:'rikjulər], *a. Anat:* (communication, etc.) inter-auriculaire.

interbank ['intə(:)bæŋk], *a.* (opération, etc.) entre banques, entrebancaire; **i. loans,** prêts *m* de banque à banque.

interbedded [intə(:)'bedid], *a. Geol:* **i. strata,** couches intercalées.

interblend [intə(:)'blend]. **1.** *v.tr.* mélanger, entremêler (qch. avec qch.). **2.** *v.i.* se mêler, s'entremêler, se mélanger.

interblending [intə(:)'blendiŋ], *s.* mélange *m*, entremêlement *m*.

interblock ['intə(:)blək], *a. Cmptr:* **i. space,** espace *m* interbloc.

interbranch [intə(:)'brɑ:n(t)ʃ], *a.* (opérations) entre succursales (d'une même entreprise).

interbreed [intə(:)'bri:d], *v.* (**interbred**) **1.** *v.tr.* (*a*) croiser, entrecroiser (des races); *Husb:* accoupler (des animaux de races différentes); (*b*) *Husb:* accoupler (des animaux consanguins). **2.** *v.i.* (*a*) se reproduire par croisement; s'entrecroiser; (*b*) se reproduire par (i) mariages consanguins, (ii) accouplements consanguins.

interbreeding [intə(:)'bri:diŋ], *s.* **1.** croisement *m*, entrecroisement *m* (d'individus de races différentes). **2.** (i) mariages consanguins; (ii) accouplements consanguins.

intercadence [intə(:)'keid(ə)ns], *s. Med:* intercadence *f* (du pouls).

intercadent [intə(:)'keid(ə)nt], *a. Med:* (pouls) intercadent.

intercalare ['intə(:)'kæləri], *s. Z:* intercentre *m*.

intercalary |'intə(:)'kæləri|, *a.* **1.** *Chr:* (jour, mois, année) intercalaire. **2.** *Bot:* (entre-nœud, etc.) intercalaire; *Geol:* **i. strata,** couches intercalées; *Mapm:* **i. contour,** courbe *f* intercalaire.

intercalate |in'tə:kəleit|, *v.tr.* intercaler; **to i. a day in a month, a sentence in a text,** intercaler un jour dans un mois, une phrase dans un texte; *Geol:* **in this formation strata of different kinds are intercalated,** cette formation comprend des couches de nature différente intercalées.

intercalation |intə(:)kə'leiʃ(ə)n|, *s.* intercalation *f.*

intercapillary |intə(:)kæ'piləri|, *a. Anat:* intercapillaire.

intercarrier |intə(:)'kæriər|, *a. W.Tel:* (bande) entre deux ondes porteuses; **i. noise suppressor,** dispositif *m* de réglage silencieux; *T.V:* **i. sound system,** réception *f* par battement.

intercede |intə(:)'si:d|, *v.i.* **1.** *A:* intervenir. **2.** intercéder; s'entremettre (en faveur de qn); **to i. (with s.o.) for s.o.,** intercéder, plaider, (auprès de qn) en faveur de qn, pour qn; demander grâce pour qn.

interceder |intə(:)'si:dər|, *s.* intercesseur *m*; médiateur, -trice.

interceding |intə(:)'si:diŋ|, *s.* = INTERCESSION.

intercellular |intə(:)'seljulər|, *a.* intercellulaire; *Bot:* **i. space,** méat *m* intercellulaire.

intercensal |intə(:)'sens(ə)l|, *a.* (période) intercensitaire, entre deux recensements.

intercentrum |intə(:)'sentrəm|, *s. Z:* intercentre *m.*

intercept[1] |'intə(:)sept|, *s.* **1.** *Mth:* partie *f* d'une ligne entre deux points. **2.** *W.Tel: etc:* message intercepté. **3.** *U.S:* = INTERCEPTION.

intercept[2] |intə(:)'sept|, *v.tr.* **1.** intercepter (la lumière, la chaleur, une lettre, un navire, etc.); arrêter (qn) au passage; *W.Tel: etc:* capter, intercepter (un message); **to i. s.o.'s retreat,** couper la retraite à qn; **wall that intercepts the view,** mur qui dérobe la vue; *Fb:* **to i. a pass,** *v.i.* **to i.,** intercepter une passe; faire une interception. **2.** *Mth:* **the part of a line intercepted between two radii,** la partie d'une ligne comprise entre deux rayons.

intercepting |intə(:)'septiŋ|, *s.* = INTERCEPTION; *Civ.E:* **i. trap,** siphon *m* d'égout.

interception |intə(:)'sepʃ(ə)n|, *s.* interception *f* (de rayons lumineux, de lettres, d'un avion ennemi, etc.); *W.Tel: etc:* captation *f,* interception (de messages, de conversations, etc.); *Fb:* interception (d'une passe); *Mil:* **i. aircraft,** appareil *m,* avion *m,* d'interception; intercepteur *m.*

interceptive |intə(:)'septiv|, *a.* qui intercepte (la lumière, etc.); qui fait obstacle (à la vue, etc.).

interceptor |intə(:)'septər|, *s.* **1.** personne qui intercepte (un message, etc.). **2.** *Av:* (*a*) intercepteur *m* (d'aile); (*b*) *Mil:* intercepteur *m* (d'un avion ennemi, etc.); **i. aircraft,** appareil *m,* avion *m,* d'interception; intercepteur. **3.** *Civ.E:* siphon *m* d'égout.

intercession |intə(:)'seʃ(ə)n|, *s.* intercession *f*; **to make i. for s.o.,** intercéder en faveur de, pour, qn.

intercessor |intə(:)'sesər|, *s.* intercesseur *m*; médiateur, -trice; *F:* avocat *m.*

intercessory |intə(:)'sesəri|, *a.* (prière) d'intercession, de médiation.

interchange[1] |'intətʃein(d)ʒ|, *s.* **1.** échange *m* (de compliments, de notes diplomatiques, d'objets, de signaux, d'idées); communication *f* (d'idées). **2.** *Rail:* **i. service,** correspondance *f*; **i. station,** gare *f* de correspondance, de jonction; station *f* de correspondance (de métro). **3.** *Civ.E: Adm:* échangeur *m* (d'autoroute), **directional i.,** jonction *f* à circulation dirigée. **4.** succession alternative, alternance *f* (du jour et de la nuit, de monts et vallées, etc.). **5.** *El: etc:* interversion *f* (d'attaches de câbles, etc.). **6.** *Biol:* interchange *m* (entre chromosomes).

interchange[2] |intə(:)'tʃein(d)ʒ|. **1.** *v.tr.* (*a*) échanger (des compliments, des commodités, des signaux) (**with,** avec); **they had interchanged hats,** ils avaient fait un échange de chapeaux; (*b*) échanger (des parties d'une machine, etc.); **all parts of these machines can be interchanged,** toutes les pièces de ces machines sont interchangeables; (*c*) **to i. the position of two things,** changer deux choses de place; mettre l'une à la place de l'autre; *El: etc:* intervertir (des attaches de câbles, etc.). **2.** *v.i.* (*a*) s'interchanger; (*b*) se succéder alternativement.

interchangeability |'intə(:)tʃein(d)ʒə'biliti|, **interchangeableness** |intə(:)'tʃein(d)ʒəblnis|, *s.* interchangeabilité *f,* permutabilité *f*; amovibilité *f* (des parties d'une machine).

interchangeable |intə(:)'tʃein(d)ʒebl|, *a.* interchangeable, permutable; **machine with i. parts,** machine *f* à pièces interchangeables, amovibles; **i. letters, symbols,** lettres *f,* symboles *m,* permutables; *Cmptr:* **i. type bar,** barre *f* d'impression à caractères amovibles.

interchangeably |intə(:)'tʃein(d)ʒəbli|, *adv.* alternativement.

interchanger |intə(:)'tʃein(d)ʒər|, *s. Tchn:* échangeur *m* (de chaleur, etc.).

interchannel |intə(:)'tʃænl|, *a. W.Tel: Cmptr: etc:* entre voies; entre canaux; intercanal, -aux; *W.Tel:* **i. interference,** interférence *f* entre voies, entre canaux.

intercity |intə(:)'siti|, *a. Trans:* (service, etc.) interurbain, intervilles *inv.*

interclavicular |intə(:)klə'vikjulər|, *a. Anat:* interclaviculaire.

interclub |'intə(:)'klʌb|, *a.* (rencontre, etc.) interclubs *inv.*

intercolonial |intə(:)kə'louniəl|, *a.* (commerce) intercolonial, -aux.

intercolumnar |intə(:)kə'lʌmnər|, *a.* **1.** *Arch:* (espace) d'entrecolonnement. **2.** *Anat:* (fibre) intercolumnaire.

intercolumniation |'intə(:)kəlʌmni'eiʃ(ə)n|, *s. Arch:* entrecolonnement *m.*

intercom |'intə(:)kɔm|, *s. Tp: F:* intercom *m.*

intercommunicate[1] |intə(:)kə'mju:nikeit|, *v.i.* **1.** (*of rooms, etc.*) communiquer. **2. the prisoners can i.,** les prisonniers peuvent communiquer entre eux, peuvent s'entrecommuniquer, sont en rapport les uns avec les autres.

intercommunicate[2] |intə(:)kə'mju:nikət|, *a.* avec communication réciproque; (chambres, etc.) en communication.

intercommunication |'intə(:)kəmjuni'keiʃ(ə)n|, *s.* **1.** intercommunication *f* (entre deux chambres, *Rail:* entre wagons, etc.). **2.** intercommunication, rapports *mpl* (entre prisonniers, etc.); *Tp:* **i. system,** *F:* intercom *m.*

intercommunion |intə(:)kə'mju:njən|, *s.* **1.** intimité *f* de rapports, rapports *m* intimes (**between,** entre). **2.** *Ecc:* intercommunion *f* (de plusieurs églises).

intercommunity |intə(:)kə'mju:niti|, *s.* communauté *f* (de biens).

interconfessional |intə(:)kən'feʃənl|, *a. Ecc:* interconfessionnel.

interconnect [intə(:)kə'nekt]. *El: Cmptr:* **1.** *v.tr.* interconnecter (des circuits, des calculateurs). **2.** *v.i.* être interconnectés.

interconnected |intə(:)kə'nektid|, *a.* **1.** (chambres) en communication réciproque. **2.** *Tchn:* **i. controls,** commandes conjuguées; *El:* **i. circuits,** circuits interconnectés, *Cmptr:* **i. computers,** compteurs interconnectés. **3. i. facts,** faits intimement liés.

interconnecting[1] |intə(:)kə'nektiŋ|, *a.* = INTERCONNECTED 1, 2, *El:* **i. cables,** câbles *m* d'interconnexion.

interconnecting[2], *s.* **1.** ouverture *f* d'un accès (entre deux pièces, etc.). **2.** *El:* interconnexion *f* (de centrales, etc.).

interconnection |intə(:)kə'nekʃ(ə)n|, *s. El:* interconnexion *f* (de centrales, etc.).

intercontinental |intə(:)kɔnti'nentl|, *a.* intercontinental, -aux; **i. ballistic missile,** fusée intercontinentale; engin intercontinental.

interconvertible |intə(:)kən'və:tibl|, *a.* interchangeable (**with,** avec); réciproquement convertibles.

intercooler |intə(:)'ku:lər|, *s. Atom.Ph: etc:* refroidisseur *m* intermédiaire.

intercostal |intə(:)'kɔst(ə)l|, *a. Anat:* intercostal, -aux.

intercourse |'intəkɔ:s|, *s.* **1.** commerce *m,* relations *fpl,* rapports *mpl*; **our i. with other nations,** nos relations avec d'autres nations; **social i.,** la fréquentation du monde; **human i.,** relations humaines; commerce du monde. **2. (sexual) i.,** rapports sexuels; commerce charnel; **to have i. with a woman,** avoir des relations avec une femme; **adulterous i.,** commerce adultère. **3. i. with God,** communion *f* avec Dieu.

intercrop[1] |'intəkrɔp|, *s. Agr:* **1.** culture semée entre les lignes d'une autre culture. **2.** récolte dérobée.

intercrop[2] |intə(:)'krɔp|, *v.tr.* (**intercropped**) *Agr:* semer (deux cultures) en lignes alternantes.

intercross |intə(:)'krɔs|. **1.** (*a*) *v.tr.* entrecroiser; entrelacer; (*b*) *v.i.* (*of lines*) s'entrecroiser; s'entrelacer. **2.** *v.i. & tr. Breed:* = INTERBREED.

intercrossed |intə(:)'krɔst|, *a.* entrelacé, entrecroisé.

intercrossing |'intəkrɔsiŋ|, *s.* **1.** entrecroisement *m*; entrelacement *m.* **2.** = INTERBREEDING.

intercurrence |intə(:)'kʌrəns|, *s.* **1.** *Med: etc:* (*a*) intercurrence *f* (d'une maladie); (*b*) récurrence *f* (d'une fièvre, etc.). **2.** intervention *f* (d'un fait).

intercurrent |intə(:)'kʌrənt|, *a.* **1.** *Med:* (*of disease, etc.*) (*a*) intercurrent; (*b*) récurrent. **2.** (*a*) (fait, etc.) intervenu, survenu (dans l'intervalle); (*b*) (temps) écoulé (entre deux événements).

intercut |'intəkʌt|, *s. Cin:* scène-raccord *f, pl* scènes-raccords.

intercycle |'intəsaikl|, *s. Cmptr:* **1.** cycle *m* opératoire. **2.** intercycle *m.*

interdenominational |'intədinɔmi'neiʃənl|, *a. Ecc:* interconfessionnel.

interdenominationalism |'intədinɔmi'neiʃ(ə)nəlizm|, *s. Ecc:* interconfessionnalisme *m.*

interdental |intə(:)'dentl|, *a.* **1.** *Anat:* (espace, etc.) interdentaire. **2.** *Ling:* **i. consonant,** (consonne) interdentale (*f*).

interdepartmental |'intə(:)di:pɑ:t'mentl|, *a.* interdépartemental, -aux; *Adm: etc:* **i. questions,** questions communes à plusieurs services.

interdepartmentally |intə(:)di:pɑ:t'mentəli|, *adv.* interdépartementalement; entre services.

interdepend |intə(:)di'pend|, *v.i.* dépendre l'un de l'autre; être solidaires (l'un de l'autre).

interdependence |intə(:)di'pendəns|, *s.* interdépendance *f*; solidarité *f*; **i. of two processes of manufacture,** enclenchement *m* de deux opérations de la fabrication.

interdependent |intə(:)di'pendənt|, *a.* interdépendant; solidaire (**with,** de); **all these facts are i.,** tous ces faits s'enchaînent; **these two factors are i.,** ces deux facteurs s'entrepénètrent.

interdict[1] |'intədikt|, *s.* **1.** *Jur:* défense *f,* interdiction *f*; *Scot:* arrêt *m* de suspension; arrêt de sursis; (un) avant faire droit. **2.** *Ecc:* interdit *m*; **the Papal interdicts,** les interdits pontificaux; **to lay a church, a priest, under an i.,** mettre en interdit, frapper d'interdit, frapper d'interdiction, interdire, une église, un prêtre; **to raise, remove, the i.,** lever l'interdit.

interdict[2] |intə(:)'dikt|, *v.tr.* **1.** *Jur:* interdire, prohiber (le commerce avec l'étranger, etc.); **to i. s.o. from doing sth.,** interdire à qn de faire qch.; faire défense à qn de faire qch. **2.** *Ecc:* frapper d'interdiction, d'interdit (un prêtre, une ville); interdire (un prêtre); mettre (un pays) en interdit.

interdiction |intə(:)'dikʃ(ə)n|, *s.* **1.** interdiction *f* (des rites religieux, etc.). **2.** *Jur:* **to impose judicial i. on an insane person,** frapper un aliéné d'interdiction judiciaire. **3.** *Ecc:* = INTERDICT[1] 2. **4.** *Mil:* interdiction; **i. bombing,** bombardement *m* d'interdiction.

interdictory |intə(:)'diktɔri|, *a.* (loi) d'interdiction; (système) prohibitif.

interdiffuse |'intədi'fju:z|, *v.i.* (*of gases, etc.*) se mêler intimement.

interdigital |intə(:)'didʒit(ə)l|, *a. Anat:* interdigital, -aux,

interdigitate |intə(:)'didʒiteit|, *v.i. Anat:* s'entrecroiser.

interdigitation |intə(:)didʒi'teiʃ(ə)n|, *s. Anat:* entrecroisement *m* (des nerfs optiques, etc.).

inter-electrode |intəri'lektroud|, *a. El:* **i.-e. capacity,** capacité *f* entre (les) électrodes (d'un tube thermionique).

interest[1] |'int(ə)rest|, *s.* intérêt *m.* **1.** (*a*) participation *f*; **to have an i. in the profits,** participer aux bénéfices; **to have a direct i. in sth.,** avoir un intérêt personnel dans qch.; **I have no money i., financial i., in the business,** je n'ai pas de capitaux, je ne suis pas intéressé, dans cette entreprise; **the i. of each partner in the profits,** le tantième de chaque associé dans les bénéfices; **his i. in the company is £10,000,** sa commandite est de dix mille livres sterling; **to give the staff a financial i. in the business,** intéresser les employés dans l'entreprise; **to give s.o. a joint i. in an undertaking,** coïntéresser qn dans une affaire; (*b*) **the brewing i.,** la brasserie; les brasseurs *m*; **the shipping i.,** les armateurs *m*; le commerce maritime; **the Conservative i.,** le parti conservateur; **the landed i.,** les propriétaires terriens; **agreement between a foreign company and British interests,** arrangement *m* entre une compagnie étrangère et un groupe de capitalistes anglais. **2.** avantage *m,* profit *m*; **community of interest(s),** communauté *f* d'intérêts; **the public i.,** l'intérêt public; **one's own (personal) i.,** son propre intérêt; **to act in, against, one's (own) interest(s),** agir dans, contre, son propre intérêt; **to act in s.o.'s i.,** agir dans l'intérêt, pour le compte, de qn; **to act in s.o.'s best interest(s),** agir au mieux des intérêts de qn; **to prejudice s.o.'s interests,** nuire aux intérêts de qn; **to promote s.o.'s i.,** prendre les intérêts de qn; **it's in my i. to do this,** il est de mon intérêt de, j'ai intérêt à, faire ceci; **his own i. comes before everything else,** il ne tient compte que de son propre intérêt; son propre intérêt compte par-dessus tout; il ne connaît que ses intérêts; **everyone has an eye to his own i.,** chacun cherche son propre intérêt; *F:* chacun prêche pour son saint, pour sa paroisse; **in the interest(s) of truth,** dans l'intérêt de la vérité. **3.** *A:* crédit *m,* influence *f*; **to use one's i. on s.o.'s behalf,** user de son influence, intervenir, en faveur de qn; **to have i. with s.o.,** avoir du crédit auprès de qn; **to make i. with s.o.,** user de son crédit auprès de qn. **4.** (*a*) **the audience showed con-**

siderable i., l'assistance a témoigné beaucoup d'intérêt; **this may be of i. to you,** ceci peut vous intéresser; **to take, feel, an i. in s.o., sth.,** s'intéresser, porter intérêt, à qn; ressentir de l'intérêt pour qn; prendre de l'intérêt à qch.; **the i. which I take in you,** l'intérêt que je vous porte; **to take no (further) i. in sth.,** se désintéresser de qch.; **to take a fresh i. in life,** reprendre goût à la vie; **to take all the i. out of a play,** affadir une pièce; **these questions have no i. for me,** ces questions ne m'intéressent pas; **questions of world-wide i.,** questions qui intéressent le monde entier; (*b*) **I have many interests outside my work,** beaucoup de choses m'intéressent en dehors de mon travail; **to have an i. in politics,** avoir de l'intérêt pour la politique. **5.** *Fin:* intérêt(s) (de l'argent); **simple i., compound i.,** intérêts simples, composés; **i. due, payable,** intérêts exigibles; **fixed i.,** intérêt fixe; **back i.,** arrérages *mpl* (d'une rente, etc.); **to allow the (back) i. to accumulate,** laisser courir les arrérages; **i. on capital,** intérêt du capital; **i. on loan,** intérêt sur prêt; **i. on £100,** intérêt rapporté par 100 livres sterling; **to put one's money out at i.,** placer son argent; *F:* faire travailler son argent; **to borrow at i.,** emprunter à intérêt; **to lend (out) at i.,** prêter à intérêt; **to lend at short i.,** prêter à la petite semaine; **to lend at fair i.,** prêter à un intérêt honnête; **to bear, yield, i.,** porter intérêt, des intérêts; **loan bearing i., loan at i.,** prêt à intérêt; **to bear i. at 5%,** porter intérêt à 5%; **to yield 5% i.,** rapporter du 5%, un intérêt de 5%; **shares that yield (a) high i.,** actions *f* à gros rendement; **money earning no i.,** argent improductif, dormant; *Fig:* **to repay an injury with i.,** rendre le mal avec usure; *attrib.* **i. table,** table *f* des intérêts; **i. charges,** service *m* des intérêts; **i. warrant,** coupon *m* d'intérêt; **i.-bearing investment,** placement productif d'intérêt, qui porte intérêt; **i.-bearing securities,** valeurs *f* à intérêts. **6.** *Ins:* aliment *m,* risque *m,* intérêt; **each i. is to form the subject of a separate policy,** chaque aliment, risque, fera l'objet d'une police distincte.

interest², *v.tr.* **1.** intéresser (**s.o. in a business,** qn à, dans, une affaire); **to become interested in an enterprise,** s'intéresser à une entreprise. **2.** éveiller l'intérêt de (qn); **to i. s.o. in an event, in a cause,** intéresser qn à un événement, à une cause; **to i. a pupil in literature,** orienter un élève vers les belles-lettres; **your story interests me,** votre récit m'intéresse; **to i. oneself, to be interested, in s.o., in sth., in doing sth.,** s'intéresser à qn, à qch., à faire qch.; **to be interested in painting, music,** s'intéresser à la peinture, à la musique; **to feel interested in s.o.,** ressentir de l'intérêt pour qn; **he's interested in my family,** il prend un intérêt à ma famille; **subject that interests me greatly, in which I am greatly interested,** sujet qui m'intéresse beaucoup; **one cannot be too interested in it,** on ne saurait trop s'y intéresser; **to be interested in sth. being done,** être intéressé à ce que qch. se fasse; **I am not interested,** cela ne m'intéresse pas; cela est sans intérêt pour moi; **I am not interested in whether you approve or not,** que vous approuviez ou non, cela ne m'intéresse pas; **I should be interested to hear the end of the story,** je serais curieux d'apprendre la fin de l'histoire; **work that interests,** ouvrage intéressant, qui captive l'esprit.

interested |'int(ə)rəstid|, *a.* intéressé. **1.** *Com:* **the i. parties,** les parties intéressées; *Jur:* **i. party,** ayant droit *m, pl.* ayants droit. **2. i. motives,** motifs intéressés; **to act from i. motives,** agir par calcul, pour des motifs intéressés; **I'm not speaking from i. motives,** je parle sans intérêt. **3. i. audience,** auditoire intéressé; **with an i. look,** (i) d'un air intéressé; (ii) avec un regard d'intérêt.

interestedly |'int(ə)rəstidli|, *adv.* **1.** (regarder qch.) avec intérêt. **2. I don't speak i.,** je ne parle pas par intérêt; je parle sans calcul.

interesting |'int(ə)rəstiŋ|, *a.* intéressant; **i. book,** livre intéressant, attachant; **absorbingly i. work,** (i) œuvre passionnante à lire; (ii) travail passionnant à faire.

interface¹ |'intəfeis|, *s.* **1.** *Ch: Ph: etc:* interface *f*; *Petr:* (i) interface; (ii) contaminant *m* (entre produits dans un pipeline); *Cmptr:* **standard i.,** interface normalisée; *attrib.* **i. layer,** couche interface, isolante; **i. level,** niveau interfacial; **i. region,** région interfaciale. **2.** connexion *f,* liaison *f* (entre deux éléments hétérogènes).

interface², *v.tr. Cmptr:* **to i. a machine with a computer,** connecter, relier, une machine à un ordinateur.

interface³, *v.tr. Tail: Dressm:* garnir (un parement) d'une doublure intermédiaire.

interfacial |intə(:)'feiʃ(ə)l|, *a. Ph: Ch: etc:* interfacial, -aux; *Geom: Cryst:* (angle *m*) dièdre, entre deux faces; *Ph:* **i. tension,** tension interfaciale.

interfacing |intə(:)'feisiŋ|, *s. Tail: Dressm:* doublure *f* intermédiaire (d'un parement).

interfascicular |'intə(:)fæ'sikjulər|, *a. Anat: Bot:* interfasciculaire.

interfenestration |'intə(:)fenis'treiʃ(ə)n|, *s. Arch:* espacement *m* des fenêtres (d'un bâtiment).

interfere |intə'fiər|, *v.i.* **1.** (*a*) (*of pers.*) s'ingérer, s'immiscer, intervenir (**in a matter,** dans une affaire); s'interposer (dans une querelle); **he didn't i.,** il a laissé faire; **to i. with s.o., with s.o.'s affairs,** contrecarrer qn; se mêler des affaires, s'immiscer dans les affaires, de qn; **I don't like to be interfered with,** je n'aime pas qu'on se mêle de mes affaires, qu'on me contrecarre; **the state should not i. with private business,** l'État ne doit pas s'ingérer dans les affaires des particuliers; **to i. with the established government,** toucher au gouvernement établi; **don't i. with, in, what doesn't concern you,** ne vous mêlez pas de ce qui ne vous regarde pas; **don't i.!** (i) ne vous mêlez de rien! (ii) *F:* mêlez-vous de vos affaires, de ce qui vous regarde! **don't i. in family quarrels,** ne vous mêlez pas des querelles de famille; entre l'arbre et l'écorce ne mettez pas le doigt; **he's always interfering,** il fourre son nez partout; (*b*) toucher à (qch.); **someone has interfered with the clock,** on a touché à la pendule; **don't i. (with it)!** n'y touchez pas! **don't i. with the children!** laissez les enfants tranquilles! (*at inquest, etc.*) **she had not been interfered with,** il n'y a pas eu trace de viol; (*c*) (*of thg*) to **i. with (sth.),** gêner, contrarier (les projets de qn); gêner (la navigation, la circulation, etc.); entraver (la marche des affaires); masquer (la vue); **to i. with the operation of a regulation,** gêner l'application d'un règlement; **nothing must i. with the course of justice,** rien ne doit entraver le cours de la justice; **pleasure should not be allowed to i. with business,** il ne faut pas que les plaisirs empiètent sur les affaires; **sedentary occupations often i. with health,** les emplois sédentaires portent souvent atteinte à la santé; **that interferes with my interests,** cela porte atteinte à mes intérêts; **it interferes with my plans,** cela dérange mes projets; **there is a risk that their interests will i. with each other,** leurs intérêts risquent d'interférer; *Sp:* **to i. with an opponent is against the rules,** l'obstruction d'un adversaire est illégale. **2.** (*a*) *Ph: etc:* (*of light waves, etc.*) interférer; **to i. with a phenomenon,** perturber un phénomène; *Ch:* **traces of acid which i. with a reaction,** traces *f* d'acide qui perturbent une réaction; (*b*) *Elcs: W.Tel:* **to i. with a signal,** brouiller, parasiter, un signal. **3.** (*of horse*) se couper, s'entretailler; se friser.

interference |intə'fiərəns|, *s.* **1.** (*a*) intervention *f*; intrusion *f,* ingérence *f* (**in,** dans); *Jur:* **unwarrantable i.,** immixtion *f* (**with,** dans); (*b*) *Sp:* obstruction *f* (d'un adversaire). **2.** *Mec.E:* arc-boutement *m* (des engrenages). **3.** (*a*) *Ph:* interférence *f* (des ondes lumineuses, etc.); perturbation *f* (d'un phénomène physico-chimique); *Opt:* **i. bands, fringes,** bandes *f,* franges *f,* d'interférence; **i. figure, pattern,** figure *f* d'interférence; **i. filter,** filtre interférentiel; **i. microscopy,** microscopie interférentielle; **i. refractometer,** réfractomètre interférentiel; *Atom.Ph:* **electron i.,** interférence électronique; (*b*) *Elcs: W.Tel:* interférence(s), parasite(s) *m(pl),* brouillage *m*; **atmospheric i.,** parasites atmosphériques; **i. area,** zone *f* de brouillage; **i. clearance, elimination,** élimination *f* des interférences, des parasites, du brouillage; **i. eliminator, i. suppressor, i. filter,** dispositif éliminateur de parasites, filtre *m* antiparasites; **i. guard band,** espace réservé, espace libre, entre deux canaux; *Rad:* **i. unit,** générateur *m* de bruit(s); *El:* **i. current,** courant perturbateur; *Magn:* **i. field,** champ perturbateur, champ d'interférence; (*c*) *Aedcs:* interaction *f*; **i. drag,** traînée (générale) (d'un avion, d'un véhicule). **4.** *Dent:* **cuspal i.,** interférence des cuspides. **5.** *Farr: Vet:* entretaillure *f.*

interferential |intə(:)fə'renʃ(ə)l|, *a. Ph:* interférentiel.

interfering¹ |intə(:)'fiəriŋ|, *a.* **1.** (*of pers.*) importun; qui se mêle à ce qui ne le regarde pas; **he's so i.,** il fourre son nez partout. **2.** (*a*) *Ph: etc:* (*of waves*) interférent; (*of chemical reagent, etc.*) perturbateur, -trice; (*b*) *Elcs: W.Tel:* qui brouille; parasite; **i. signal,** signal parasite, perturbateur.

interfering², *s.* = INTERFERENCE 1, 5.

interferometer |intəf:iə'rɔmitər|, *s. Ph:* interféromètre *m.*

interferometry |intə(:)fiə'rɔmitri|, *s. Ph:* interférométrie *f.*

interferon |intə(:)'fiərɔn|, *s. Biol:* interféron *m.*

interfibrillar |intə(:)'fibrilər|, *a. Biol:* interfibrillaire.

interfluve |'intə(:)flu:v|, *s. Geog:* interfluve *m.*

interfold |'intəfould|, *v.tr.* plier l'un(e) dans l'autre.

interfoliaceous |'intə(:)fouli'eiʃəs|, *a. Bot:* (organe, etc.) interfoliaire, interfoliacé.

interfrontal |intə(:)'frʌnt(ə)l|, *a. Anat:* **i. suture,** suture *f* métopique.

interfuse |intə(:)'fju:z|. **1.** *v.tr.* (*a*) parsemer (**with,** de); **speech interfused with quotations,** discours parsemé, entrelardé, de citations; (*b*) mélanger, pénétrer (**with,** de); confondre (**with,** avec). **2.** *v.i.* se mélanger, se confondre, se marier.

interfusion |intə(:)'fju:ʒ(ə)n|, *s.* mélange *m,* fusion *f* (**with,** avec).

intergalactic |intə(:)gæ'læktik|, *a. Astr:* intergalactique.

intergeneric |intə(:)dʒə'nerik|, *a. Biol:* **i. hybrid,** hybride *m* de genres.

interglacial |intə(:)'gleiʃ(ə)l|, *a. & s. Geol:* (dépôt, etc.) interglaciaire; **i. (age, period),** interglacial *m.*

intergovernmental |'intə(:)gʌvən'mentl|, *a.* intergouvernemental, -aux.

intergradation |'intə(:)grə'deiʃ(ə)n|, *s. Biol:* rapprochement *m* par gradations (de deux formes).

intergrade¹ |'intə(:)greid|, *v.i. Biol:* se rapprocher par gradations (**with another form,** d'une autre forme).

intergrade², *s. Biol:* forme *f* de transition.

intergranular |intə(:)'grænjulər|, *a.* **1.** *Geol:* (texture) granulitique. **2.** *Metall:* (*of corrosion, etc.*) intergranulaire.

interheater |'intəhi:tər|, *s. Mch:* échauffeur *m* intermédiaire.

interim |'intərim|. **1.** *adv.* entre temps, en attendant; *adv.phr.* **ad i.,** par intérim, provisoirement; **duties ad i.,** intérimat *m.* **2.** *s.* intérim *m*; *Pol:* intérimat; **in the i.,** dans l'intérim, sur ces entrefaites; **to take over the duties of a post in the i.,** assurer l'intérim pendant une vacance. **3.** *a.* (rapport, etc.) intérimaire; **i. secretary,** secrétaire intérimaire, par intérimat; **i. copyright,** protection *f* intérimaire d'un ouvrage; *Jur:* **i. order,** avant faire droit *m inv.*

interionic |intərai'ɔnik|, *a. Ph:* **i. distance,** distance *f* qui sépare deux ions.

interior |in'tiəriər|. **1.** *a.* (*a*) (côté) intérieur; (terres, etc.) de l'intérieur; **i. trade,** commerce intérieur; *Mec.E:* **i. screw,** vis *f* femelle; *Mth:* **i. angle,** angle *m* interne; (*b*) **i. decoration,** décoration intérieure, de l'intérieur; (*c*) (*of sentiment, etc.*) intime; *Lit:* **i. monologue,** monologue intérieur. **2.** *s.* (*a*) intérieur *m* (du pays, des terres); **the i. of a building,** l'intérieur, les dedans *m,* d'un édifice; (*b*) *Art:* (tableau *m* d')intérieur; **(picture of a) forest i.,** sous-bois *m inv*; (*c*) *F: O:* **to have pains in one's i.,** avoir des douleurs d'entrailles.

interiority |intiəri'ɔriti|, *s.* intériorité *f.*

interiorization |intiəriərai'zeiʃ(ə)n|, *s. Psy:* intériorisation *f.*

interiorize |in'tiəriəraiz|, *v.tr. Psy:* intérioriser.

interiorly |in'tiəriəli|, *adv.* intérieurement, en dedans.

interjacent |intə(:)'dʒeis(ə)nt|, *a.* (angle, intervalle) intermédiaire, interjacent.

interjaculatory |intə(:)'dʒækjulət(ə)ri|, *a.* interjectif, exclamatif.

interject |intə(:)'dʒekt|, *v.tr.* **to i. a remark, a protest,** lancer une remarque; émettre une protestation; **"nonsense!" he interjected,** "sottises que tout cela!" s'exclama-t-il.

interjection |intə(:)'dʒekʃ(ə)n|, *s.* **1.** action *f* de lancer (une remarque, etc.), d'émettre (une protestation). **2.** *Gram:* interjection *f.*

interjectional |intə(:)'dʒekʃənl|, *a.* interjectionnel, interjectif.

interjectionally |intə(:)'dʒekʃənəli|, *adv.* interjectivement.

interjectory |intə(:)'dʒektəri|, *a.* interjectif.

interkinesis |'intə(:)kai'ni:sis|, *s. Biol:* intercinèse *f.*

interknit¹ |intə(:)'nit|, *v.* (*p.p. & p.t.* **interknit(ted)** **1.** *v.tr.* entrelacer. **2.** *v.i.* s'entrelacer.

interknit¹ |intə(:)'nit|, *v.* (*p.p. & p.t.* **interknit(ted)**) **1.** *v.tr.*

interlace |intə(:)'leis|. **1.** *v.tr.* (*a*) entrelacer (des branches, etc.); entrecroiser (des fils); (*b*) entremêler (**with,** de). **2.** *v.i.* s'entrelacer, s'entrecroiser; s'entremêler.

interlaced |intə(:)'leist|, *a.* entrelacé; *T.V:* **i. scanning,** entrelacement *m.*

interlacement |intə(:)'leismənt|, *s.* entrelacement *m* (de branches, etc.); entrecroisement *m* (de fils).

interlacing¹ |intə(:)'leisiŋ|, *a. Arch:* intersecté.

interlacing², *s.* **1.** = INTERLACEMENT. **2.** *Needlew: Arch:* entrelacs *m.* **3.** *T.V:* entrelacement *m,* exploration entrelacée.

interlap |intə(:)'læp|, *v.i.* s'imbriquer.

interlard |intə(:)'lɑ:d|, *v.tr.* (entre)larder, bigarrer, entremêler, *F:* piquer (un discours, ses récits) (**with,** de); **speech interlarded with Latin,** discours entrelardé de latin.

interlarding |intə(:)'lɑ:diŋ|, *s.* entrelardement *m.*

interleaf¹, *pl.* **-leaves** |'intəli:f, -li:vz|, *s.* **1.** feuille blanche (intercalée dans un livre); *Typ:* macule *f.* **2.** *Bot:* entrefeuille *f.*

interleaf² (*p.t. & p.p.* **interleaved**), **interleave**

|intə(:)ˈli:v|, *v.tr.* **1.** interfolier (un livre); *Typ:* intercaler (des feuilles); mettre (des feuilles) en macules. **2.** *Cmptr:* imbriquer (des programmes).

interleaved |intə(:)ˈli:vd|, *a.* **1.** *Bookb:* (livre) interfolié; *Typ:* **i. sheet,** feuille intercalée, intercalaire, mise en macule; *Typew:* **i. carbon (paper),** carbone *m* intercalaire; *Cmptr:* **i. carbon set,** liasse carbonée. **2.** *Cmptr:* **i. programmes,** programmes imbriqués.

interleaving |intə(:)ˈli:viŋ|, *s.* **1.** *Bookb:* interfoliage *m* (d'un livre); *Typ:* intercalage *m*, mise *f* en macule (d'une feuille). **2.** *Cmptr:* imbrication *f* (de programmes). **3.** *T.V:* intercalation *f* des signaux de chrominance dans les signaux de luminance.

interline[1] |intə(:)ˈlain|, *v.tr.* (*a*) interligner (un document, manuscrit); (*b*) écrire (une traduction, etc.) entre les lignes.

interline[2], *v.tr. Tail: etc:* mettre une doublure intermédiaire à (un vêtement, etc.).

interlinear |intə(:)ˈliniər|, *a.* **1.** (traduction, etc.) interlinéaire. **2.** (texte) à traduction interlinéaire.

interlineation |ˈintə(:)liniˈeiʃ(ə)n|, *s.* **1. i. of a text,** intercalation *f* de mots, de lignes, dans un texte. **2.** interlinéation *f*, interligne *m*; *Typ:* surcharge *f*.

interlingual |intə(:)ˈliŋgwəl|, *a.* interlinguistique.

interlinguistic |intə(:)liŋˈgwistik|, *a.* interlinguistique.

interlinguistics |intə(:)liŋˈgwistiks|, *s.pl.* (*usu. with sg. const.*) interlinguistique *f*.

interlining[1] |intə(:)ˈlainiŋ|, *s.* = INTERLINEATION.

interlining[2], *s. Tail:* doublure *f* intermédiaire.

interlink |intə(:)ˈliŋk|. **1.** *v.tr.* enchaîner, relier, rattacher (**with,** à); **to i. two chains,** relier deux chaînes; **to i. several facts,** relier entre eux plusieurs événements; **one sees how things are interlinked,** on voit comme les choses s'enchaînent; **with hands interlinked,** les mains entrelacées. **2.** *v.i.* se relier; s'agrafer.

interlinking |intə(:)ˈliŋkiŋ|, *s.* raccordement *m*, jonction *f*.

interlobar |intə(:)ˈloubər|, *a. Anat:* interlobaire; *Med:* **i. pleurisy,** pleurésie *f* interlobaire; interlobite *f*.

interlobular |intə(:)ˈlɔbjulər|, *a. Anat:* interlobulaire.

interlock[1] |intə(:)ˈlɔk|. **1.** *v.tr.* (*a*) entrecroiser, entrelacer (des fils, les doigts, etc.); (*b*) enclencher (un mécanisme); engrener (des roues dentées); emboîter, relier, rendre solidaires (les parties d'un tout, d'un mécanisme); bloquer, verrouiller (un système de fermeture, un dispositif de sécurité); (*c*) *Cin:* rendre solidaires, synchroniser (les appareils enregistreurs). **2.** *v.i.* (*a*) (*of threads, etc.*) s'entrecroiser, s'entrelacer, s'entremêler; (*b*) (*of mechanism*) s'enclencher; (*of pinions*) s'engrener, mordre; (*of parts*) s'emboîter; (*of closing device, safety device, etc.*) se bloquer, se verrouiller.

interlock[2], *s.* **1.** (*a*) = INTERLOCKING[2]; (*b*) système *m*, dispositif *m*, de sécurité à clef. **2.** *Tex:* (*a*) tissu interlock, entrecroisé; (*b*) **i. machine,** (machine *f* à tricoter) interlock (*m*). **3.** *El:* interlock.

interlocking[1] |intə(:)ˈlɔkiŋ|, *a.* (*a*) entrecroisé, entrelacé, entremêlé; **i. grate bars,** barreaux *m* de grille en zigzag; (*b*) **i. gear wheels,** roues *f* qui s'engrènent, s'enclenchent; **i. milling cutter,** fraise composée.

interlocking[2], *s.* (*a*) entrelacement *m*, entremêlement *m* (des fils d'un tissu, etc.); (*b*) enclenchement *m* (d'un mécanisme); engrènement *m* (de roues dentées); emboîtement *m*, liaison *f* (de différentes parties entre elles); blocage *m*, verrouillage *m* (d'un système de fermeture, d'un dispositif de sécurité); **i. device,** système *m* de verrouillage; dispositif de blocage; **i. gear,** appareil *m* d'enclenchement; mécanisme *m* à action solidarisée; (*c*) *Cin: etc:* synchronisation *f* (d'appareils enregistreurs, etc.).

interlocution |intə(:)ləˈkju:ʃ(ə)n|, *s.* interlocution *f*.

interlocutor[1] |intə(:)ˈlɔkjutər|, *s.* (*pers.*) interlocuteur, -trice.

interlocutor[2], *s. Jur: Scot:* interlocutoire *m*; (i) jugement *m* interlocutoire; (ii) jugement motivé; décision motivée.

interlocutory |intə(:)ˈlɔkjutəri|, *a. Jur:* (arrêt) interlocutoire, préjudiciel; **i. decree, i. judgment,** interlocutoire *m*; **to award an i. decree in a case,** interloquer une affaire; **to pronounce an i. decree against s.o.,** interloquer qn.

interloper |ˈintəloupər|, *s.* **1.** (*a*) intrus, -use; (*b*) commerçant marron. **2.** *A.Com: Nau:* (navire) interlope (*m*).

interlude |ˈintə(:)lu:d|, *s.* **1.** intermède *m* (entre deux scènes de théâtre, deux batailles, etc.); **musical i.,** interlude *m*; intermède musical. **2.** *Cmptr:* tête *f* de programme.

interlunar(y) |intəˈlu:nə(ri)|, *a.* (période, etc.) interlunaire.

intermarriage |intə(:)ˈmæridʒ|, *s.* **1.** *Jur:* mariage *m* (de deux personnes). **2.** intermariage *m* (i) entre les membres de différentes familles, tribus, castes, (ii) entre les membres d'une même famille.

intermarry |intə(:)ˈmæri|, *v.i.* **1.** *Jur:* se marier (**with,** avec). **2.** (*a*) (*of different tribes, etc.*) se marier les uns avec les autres, entre eux; **two races that often i.,** deux races qui s'allient souvent.

intermat |intə(:)ˈmæt|, *v.tr. Tex:* emmêler, feutrer (le poil, etc.).

intermaxillary |intə(:)mækˈsiləri|, *a. Anat: Z:* (os, etc.) intermaxillaire.

intermediacy |intə(:)ˈmi:diəsi|, *s.* **1.** entremise *f* (d'un négociateur, etc.). **2.** position *f* intermédiaire.

intermediary |intə(:)ˈmi:diəri|, *a. & s.* (*a*) intermédiaire (*m*); **to act as i.,** servir d'intermédiaire; (*b*) **in its i. state,** dans son état intermédiaire.

intermediate[1] |intə(:)ˈmi:diət|. **1.** *a.* intermédiaire; (*in time*) intermédiat; (*a*) **to pass from one state to another without any i. stage,** passer d'un état à un autre sans aucune transition; **i. stops,** arrêts *m* intermédiaires (au cours d'un voyage); *Av:* **i. landing,** escale *f*; *Nau:* **i. port,** port *m* d'escale, intermédiaire; *Rail:* **i. station,** gare *f* de passage; **i. points of the compass,** points collatéraux du compas; **i. gear,** *Mec.E:* engrenage *m* de transmission; *Aut:* vitesse *f* intermédiaire; **i. wheel,** roue *f* intermédiaire, roue parasite (d'un engrenage); *Mch:* **i. shaft,** arbre *m* intermédiaire, secondaire; *El:* **i. circuit,** circuit *m* intermédiaire; **i. switch,** interrupteur *m* va-et-vient; *Tp:* **i. distribution frame,** répartiteur *m* intermédiaire; **i. exchange,** bureau *m* intermédiaire; **circuit with i. receiving station,** ligne *f* à embrochage; (*b*) **i. size,** taille *f* intermédiaire; **i. hue,** teinte *f* intermédiaire; *El:* **i. frequency,** fréquence moyenne, intermédiaire; *Ball:* **i. range,** portée moyenne, intermédiaire; **i.-range ballistic missile,** missile *m* balistique à portée moyenne; *Mch:* **i. cylinder,** cylindre *m* à moyenne pression; *Sch:* **i. course,** cours moyen (d'algèbre, etc.); *A:* **i. (examination),** examen *m* de première année d'études universitaires; **i. school,** *U.S:* école *f* qui comprend jusqu'à la neuvième classe; *A:* (*in Wales*) = lycée *m*; *Fin:* **i. credit,** crédit *m* à moyen terme; (*c*) *Ch: Ind:* **i. (product),** produit *m* intermédiaire; demi-produit *m*, *pl.* demi-produits; *Geol:* **i. lava,** lave *f* neutre; **i. rocks,** roches *f* neutres, intermédiaires. **2.** *s.* (*pers.*) intermédiaire *m*.

intermediate[2] |intə(:)ˈmi:dieit|, *v.i.* s'entremettre; servir de médiateur (**between,** entre).

intermediately |intə(:)ˈmi:diətli|, *adv.* **1.** par intermédiaire; indirectement. **2.** (situé) dans une position intermédiaire.

intermedium, *pl.* **-iums, -ia** |intə(ː)ˈmi:diəm, -iəmz, -iə|, *s. Anat:* intermédiaire *m*.

intermenstrual |intə(:)ˈmenstruəl|, *a. Physiol:* intermenstruel.

interment |inˈtə:mənt|, *s.* enterrement *m*, inhumation *f*.

intermesh |intə(:)ˈmeʃ|, *v.i. NAm: Mec.E:* (s')engrener.

intermetallic |intə(:)miˈtælik|, *a. Metall:* intermétallique.

intermezzo, *pl.* **-os, -i** |intə(:)ˈmetsou, -ouz, -i|, *s. Mus:* intermezzo *m*.

intermigration |intə(:)maiˈgreiʃ(ə)n|, *s.* migration *f* réciproque.

interminable |inˈtə:minəbl|, *a.* (discussion, voyage) interminable, sans fin; (histoires) à n'en plus finir.

interminably |inˈtə:minəbli|, *adv.* interminablement, sans cesse.

intermingle |intə(:)ˈmiŋgl|. **1.** *v.tr.* entremêler; mélanger; **to i. colours,** mélanger des couleurs; **they intermingled their tears,** ils entremêlaient leurs larmes; **to i. jokes among facts,** entremêler des plaisanteries parmi les faits; **race in which diverse elements are intermingled,** race où se confondent des éléments divers. **2.** *v.i.* s'entremêler, se mêler, se confondre (**with,** avec).

intermingling |intə(:)ˈmiŋgliŋ|, *s.* entremêlement *m* (**with,** à, avec, de).

interministerial |intə(:)minisˈtiəriəl|, *a.* interministériel.

intermission |intə(:)ˈmiʃ(ə)n|, *s.* **1.** interruption *f*, relâche *f*, trêve *f*, pause *f*; *Med:* intermission *f*, rémission *f* (de la fièvre); intermittence *f* (du pouls); **without i.,** sans intermission, sans arrêt, sans discontinuer; **to work without i.,** travailler sans relâche, sans désemparer; *Med:* **days of i. (of a fever),** jours *m* intercalaires. **2.** *Th:* entracte *m*.

intermit |intə(:)ˈmit|, *v.* (**intermitted**) **1.** *v.tr. Lit:* interrompre, suspendre (ses travaux, etc.). **2.** *v.i. Med: etc:* (*of pulse, fever, etc.*) s'interrompre momentanément; avoir des intermittences.

intermittence |intə(:)ˈmit(ə)ns|, *s.* **1.** intermittence *f* (d'une source, etc.). **2.** intervalle *m* de repos; pause *f*; arrêt momentané.

intermittency |intə(:)ˈmit(ə)nsi|, *s.* intermittence *f* (d'une source, etc.).

intermittent |intə(:)ˈmit(ə)nt|, *a.* (*of stream, gunfire, etc.*) intermittent; **i. fever,** fièvre intermittente; fièvre doublée; **i. pulse,** pouls intermittent; *El:* **i. current,** courant intermittent; *Cin:* **i. feeding,** mouvement intermittent, saccadé; **i. mechanism,** mécanisme *m* d'escamotage.

intermittently |intə(:)ˈmit(ə)ntli|, *adv.* par intervalles, avec des intermissions, par intermittence.

intermix |intə(:)ˈmiks|. **1.** *v.tr.* entremêler, mélanger. **2.** *v.i.* s'entremêler, se mélanger.

intermixture |intə(:)ˈmikstʃər|, *s.* **1.** mixtion *f*. **2.** mélange *m*.

intermodulating |intə(:)ˈmɔdjuleitiŋ|, *s. W.Tel:* **i. distortion,** distorsion due à l'intermodulation.

intermodulation |intə(:)mɔdjuˈleiʃ(ə)n|, *s. W.Tel:* intermodulation *f*.

intermolecular |intə(:)məˈlekjulər|, *a. Ph:* intermoléculaire.

intermontane |intə(:)ˈmɔntein|, *a.* (plateau, etc.) entre montagnes.

intermundane |intə(:)ˈmʌndein|, *a.* **i. space,** intermonde *m*.

intermuscular |intə(:)ˈmʌskjulər|, *a.* (tissu, etc.) intermusculaire.

intern[1] |inˈtə:n|, *v.tr.* interner (des étrangers, etc.).

intern[2], **interne** |ˈintə:n|, *s. NAm:* interne *m* (des hôpitaux).

internal |inˈtə:n(ə)l|, *a.* **1.** (*a*) intérieur, interne; **i. friction,** frottement intérieur; **i. strain, stress,** tension *f* interne; **i. attachment,** fixation intérieure; *Mec.E:* **i. blower,** compresseur *m*; **i. supercharger,** compresseur interne; **i. gear,** engrenage intérieur, à dents intérieures; *El:* **i. current,** courant intérieur; **i. resistance,** résistance intérieure; **i. shield(ing),** écran intérieur; blindage *m* interne; **i. circuit,** circuit intérieur; *Atom.Ph:* **i. conversion,** conversion *f* interne (du noyau atomique); **i. energy,** énergie *f* interne; **i. exposure, irradiation,** irradiation *f* interne; *Metall:* **i. heating,** chauffage *m* à cœur; *Cmptr:* **i. store, storage,** mémoire *f* interne; **i. format,** format *m* interne; (*b*) *Med:* **i. disease, i. haemorrhage,** maladie *f*, hémorragie *f*, interne; **i. medicament, medicine,** médicament *m* interne; **to have i. pains,** souffrir de douleurs internes; (*c*) *Tp:* **i. cable,** câble *m* d'immeuble; **i. telephone,** téléphone intérieur. **2.** (*a*) (valeur, preuve) intrinsèque; (*b*) secret, intime; **the i. workings of the mind,** les opérations secrètes de l'esprit. **3.** (*a*) **i. trade,** commerce intérieur; **i. law,** droit *m* interne; **i. legislation,** législation nationale, interne; **i. revenue,** recettes fiscales; **i. security,** sécurité intérieure; **to maintain i. peace,** maintenir la paix intérieure, la paix à l'intérieur (du pays); **to be a prey to i. wars,** être en proie aux guerres intestines; (*b*) *Sch:* **i. student,** étudiant, -ante, d'une université. **4.** *s.pl. F:* **internals,** les entrailles *f*, les intestins *m*.

internally |inˈtə:nəli|, *adv.* intérieurement; (*a*) **i. fired boiler,** chaudière *f* à chauffage, à foyer, intérieur; *Cmptr:* **i. stored programme,** programme enregistré (par l'ordinateur); (*b*) *Med:* **not to be taken i.,** pour usage externe; (*c*) **i. he was none too happy,** il n'était pas trop content dans son for intérieur.

international |intə(:)ˈnæʃən(ə)l|. **1.** *a.* international, -aux; **i. law,** droit international; *Nau:* **i. rule,** règle *f* de jauge internationale; **the I. Working Men's Association,** *s.* **the I.,** l'Internationale *f*. **2.** *Sp:* (*a*) (joueur) international (*m*); (*b*) concours international.

Internationale (the) |ði:intənæʃiəˈnɑ:l|, *s.* l'Internationale *f*.

internationalism |intə(:)ˈnæʃ(ə)nəlizm|, *s.* internationalisme *m*.

internationalist |intə(:)ˈnæʃ(ə)nəlist|, *s.* internationaliste *mf*.

internationality |ˈintə(:)næʃəˈnæliti|, *s.* internationalité *f*.

internationalization |ˈintənæʃənəlaiˈzeiʃ(ə)n|, *s.* internationalisation *f* (d'un territoire, etc.).

internationalize |intə(:)ˈnæʃənəlaiz|, *v.tr.* internationaliser (un territoire, etc.).

internationally |intə(:)ˈnæʃənəli|, *adv.* internationalement.

internecine |intə(:)ˈni:sain|, *a.* (*a*) *A:* meurtrier; (*b*) **i. war,** guerre *f* d'extermination réciproque.

internee |intə:ˈni:|, *s.* interné, -ée.

internment |inˈtə:nmənt|, *s.* **1.** internement *m*; **i. camp,** camp *m* d'internement. **2. penal i.,** réclusion *f*.

internodal |intə(:)ˈnoudl|, *a. Bot:* internodal, -aux.

internode |ˈintənoud|, *s.* **1.** *Bot:* entre-nœud *m*, *pl.* entre-nœuds. **2.** *Anat:* phalange *f*.

internormal |intə(:)ˈnɔ:ml|, *a. Cryst:* (angle) dièdre, entre deux faces.

internship |ˈintə:nʃip|, *s. NAm: Med:* internat *m*.

internuclear |intə(:)'nju:kliər|, *a.* internucléaire.

internuncio |intə(:)'nʌnʃiou|, *s.* **1.** *Ecc:* internonce *m.* **2.** intermédiaire *m*, messager *m* (entre deux groupes, etc.).

internuncioship |intə(:)'nʌnʃiouʃip|, *s. Ecc:* internonciature *f.*

interoceanic |'intərouʃi'ænik|, *a.* interocéanique.

interoceptive |intərou'septiv|, *a. Physiol:* intérocepteur, -trice; intéroceptif.

interoceptor |intərou'septər|, *s. Physiol:* intérocepteur *m.*

interocular |intər'ɔkjulər|, *a.* (*of antennae, etc.*) interoculaire.

interopercle |intə'rɔpə:kl|, **interoperculum** |intərə'pəkjuləm|, *s. Ich:* interoperculaire *m.*

interosculate |intə'rɔskjuleit|, *v.i.* **1.** s'entremêler; se confondre. **2.** *Biol:* (*of species*) avoir des caractères communs.

interosseous |intə'rɔsiəs|, *a. Anat:* interosseux.

interpage |intə(:)'peidʒ|, *v.tr.* **1.** interfolier (un livre) de feuillets blancs. **2.** insérer entre deux pages; imprimer (des notes) sur une page intermédiaire.

interpapillary |intə(:)pə'piləri|, *a.* interpapillaire.

interparietal |intə(:)pə'raiət(ə)l|, *a. Anat:* interpariétal, -aux.

interparliamentary |intə(:)pɑ:l(j)ə'ment(ə)ri|, *a. Pol:* interparlementaire.

interparticle |intə(:)'pɑ:tikl|, *a. Atom.Ph:* interparticulaire.

interpeduncular |intə(:)pe'dʌŋkjulər|, *a. Anat:* interpédonculaire.

interpellant |intə(:)'pelənt|, *s. Parl:* interpellateur, -trice.

interpellate |in'tə:peleit|, *v.tr. Parl:* (*in Fr. Chamber*) interpeller (un ministre).

interpellation |intə(:)pe'leiʃ(ə)n|, *s.* interpellation *f.*

interpellator |in'tə:peleitər|, *s.* interpellateur, -trice.

interpenetrant |intə(:)'penitrənt|, *a.* qui s'entrepénètrent; *Cryst:* **i. twin,** macle *f* par entrecroisement.

interpenetrate |intə(:)'penitreit|. **1.** *v.tr.* pénétrer dans tous les interstices (d'un tissu, etc.); se répandre dans (un pays, l'air); pénétrer (l'air, etc.). **2.** *v.i.* (*of two thgs*) se pénétrer réciproquement, mutuellement; s'entrepénétrer, s'interpénétrer.

interpenetration |'intə(:)peni'treiʃ(ə)n|, *s.* **1.** pénétration *f* (**of,** dans). **2.** pénétration réciproque; interpénétration *f.*

interphase |'intəfeiz|, *s. Biol:* interphase *f.*

interphone |'intəfoun|, *s.* téléphone intérieur (d'un immeuble, avion, etc.); téléphone privé; *R.t.m:* **Interphone,** Interphone *m.*

interplait |intə(:)'plæt|, *v.tr.* entrelacer.

interplane |'intəplein|, *a. Av:* **i. strut,** montant *m* de cellule.

interplanetary |intə(:)'plænitəri|, *a.* (espace, etc.) interplanétaire.

interplay |'intəplei|, *s.* interaction *f*; effet *m* réciproque; effets combinés; **i. of colours,** effets de couleurs combinées.

interpleader |intə(:)'pli:dər|, *s. Jur:* **1.** action pétitoire incidente (pour décider l'attribution de propriété d'un bien réclamé par plusieurs plaideurs). **2.** (*in a case of distraint*) revendication *f* par un tiers des biens saisis.

Interpol |'intəpɔl|, *s.* Interpol *m.*

interpolar |intə(:)'poulər|, *a. El:* (circuit, etc.) interpolaire.

interpolate |in'tə:pəleit|, *v.tr.* (*a*) interpoler, intercaler (un mot, une phrase, un passage); *Gram:* **interpolated clause,** incise *f*; proposition intercalée; *Bookb:* **interpolated sheet,** feuille *f* intercalaire; *Mth:* **to i. a function,** interpoler une fonction; (*b*) altérer (un texte) par des interpolations.

interpolation |intə:pə'leiʃ(ə)n|, *s.* interpolation *f.*

interpolator |in'tə:pəleitər|, *s.* **1.** interpolateur, -trice. **2.** *Cmptr:* interclasseuse *f.*

interposal |intə(:)'pouzl|, **interposition** |intə(:)pə'ziʃ(ə)n|, *s.* **1.** interposition *f.* **2.** intervention *f.*

interpose |intə(:)'pouz|. **1.** *v.tr.* (*a*) interposer (un objet entre deux autres); (*b*) **to i. one's veto,** interposer son veto; **to i. one's authority to have sth. done,** interposer, faire intervenir, son autorité pour faire faire qch.; (*c*) **to i. a remark,** *abs.* **to i.,** faire une observation, interrompre (dans une conversation); placer son mot. **2.** *v.i.* s'interposer, intervenir (**between two opponents,** entre deux adversaires).

interpret |in'tə:prit|, *v.tr.* **1.** interpréter (une loi, un songe, etc.); interpréter, expliquer (un texte); déchiffrer, interpréter (des signaux); interpréter (un renseignement militaire, une photographie aérienne, etc.); **how do you i. the facts?** comment interprétez-vous les faits? **to i. s.o.'s words as a threat,** interpréter les paroles de qn comme, pour, une menace. **2.** (*a*) traduire (un discours, etc.); (*b*) *v.i.* faire l'interprète; (*c*) *Cmptr:* (i) traduire, interpréter (une carte); (ii) décoder (une instruction). **3.** *Th: Mus:* interpréter (un rôle, une composition musicale).

interpretable |in'tə:pritəbl|, *a.* interprétable.

interpretation |intə:pri'teiʃ(ə)n|, *s.* **1.** interprétation *f* (d'un texte, d'un songe, d'un signal, d'un renseignement militaire, d'un rôle); **to put a wrong i. on sth., on s.o.'s actions,** donner une fausse interprétation à qch., aux actions de qn; *Jur:* **i. clause,** clause interprétative (d'une loi). **2.** traduction orale. **3.** *Cmptr:* (i) traduction (d'une carte perforée); (ii) décodage *m* (d'une instruction, etc.).

interpretative |in'tə:priteitiv|, *a.* interprétatif, qui explique.

interpreter |in'tə:pritər|, *s.* **1.** interprète *mf*; truchement *m*; **to act as i. to s.o., to a meeting,** servir d'interprète à qn, auprès d'une assemblée; *Mil:* **i. with, to, a division,** interprète auprès d'une division; **a literary masterpiece needs no i.,** un chef-d'œuvre littéraire n'a besoin d'aucun truchement. **2.** *Cmptr:* (*machine*) traductrice *f.*

interpretership |in'tə:pritəʃip|, *s.* interprétariat *m.*

interpreting |in'tə:pritiŋ|, *s.* **1.** interprétation *f* (d'un texte, etc.). **2.** traduction *f* (d'un discours).

interpretive |in'tə:pritiv|, *a. Cmptr:* (programme) interprétatif; **i. programming,** programmation *f* en pseudo-instructions; **i. code,** pseudo-code *m, pl.* pseudo-codes.

interprofessional |intə(:)prə'feʃən(ə)l|, *a.* interprofessionnel.

interprovincial |intə(:)prə'vinʃ(ə)l|, *a.* (communication, etc.) entre provinces; commun à plusieurs provinces.

interracial |intə(:)'reiʃəl|, *a.* (logement, etc.) commun à plusieurs races; (mariages) entre des races différentes.

interradium, *pl.* **-ia** |intə(:)'reidiəm, -iə|, *s. Z:* interradius *m.*

interregnum, *pl.* **-ums, -a** |intə(:)'regnəm, -əmz, -ə|, *s.* interrègne *m.*

interrelate |'intə(:)ri'leit|. **1.** *v.tr.* mettre en communication (réciproque). **2.** *v.i.* se mettre en relation mutuelle.

interrelated |'intə(:)ri'leitid|, *a.* **1.** en communication. **2.** (faits) intimement reliés, étroitement reliés entre eux, en relation mutuelle, en corrélation.

interrelation |'intə(:)ri'leiʃ(ə)n|, *s.* relation mutuelle; corrélation *f.*

inter-resist |'intə(:)ri'zist|, *v.i.* (*of forces, etc.*) se résister (mutuellement); s'opposer (l'un(e) à l'autre).

interrogate |in'terəgeit|, *v.tr.* interroger, questionner (qn); interroger (un prisonnier de guerre), faire subir un interrogatoire à (un prévenu); interroger, consulter (un appareil enregistreur, un ordinateur, etc.); *Cmptr:* tester (un indicateur).

interrogating |in'terəgeitiŋ|, *a. Cmptr:* **i. pulse,** impulsion *f* de test; **i. typewriter,** machine *f* à écrire d'interrogation, d'entrée/sortie.

interrogation |interə'geiʃ(ə)n|, *s.* **1.** interrogation *f* (d'un candidat, etc.); interrogatoire *m* (d'un prévenu); *Mil:* **i. centre,** centre *m* d'interrogation (des prisonniers de guerre). **2.** *Gram:* **mark, note, of i., i. mark,** *NAm:* **i. point,** point *m* d'interrogation. **3.** question *f.*

interrogative |intə'rɔgətiv|. **1.** *a.* (*of tone, look, etc.*) interrogateur, -trice. **2.** *a. & s. Gram:* **i. (pronoun, etc.),** (pronom, etc.) interrogatif (*m*); **i. form of a verb,** forme interrogative d'un verbe.

interrogatively |intə'rɔgətivli|, *adv.* interrogativement; **to look at s.o. i.,** regarder qn d'un air interrogateur; lancer un regard interrogateur à qn.

interrogator |in'terəgeitər|, *s.* **1.** (*pers.*) interrogateur, -trice; questionneur, -euse. **2.** *W.Tel: Elcs:* (appareil) interrogateur-répondeur *m, pl.* interrogateurs-répondeurs; émetteur-récepteur *m, pl.* émetteurs-récepteurs; **i.-responder, i.-responser,** interrogateur-répondeur; émetteurpilote *m, pl.* émetteurs-pilotes, d'impulsion.

interrogatory |intə'rɔgət(ə)ri|. **1.** *a.* (*of look, etc.*) interrogateur, -trice. **2.** *s. Jur:* (*a*) question (posée à l'accusé); (*b*) interrogatoire *m.*

interrupt[1] |intə'rʌpt|, *v.tr.* **1.** interrompre (une action, un discours, une discussion); **to i. s.o.,** interrompre qn; couper la parole à qn; *F:* couper qn; **don't i.!** veuillez bien ne pas nous interrompre! pas d'interruptions s'il vous plait! n'interronpez pas! **to i. a private conversation,** interrompre une conversation privée. **2.** (*a*) suspendre, interrompre (la circulation); couper (les communications); interrompre (un circuit électrique); rompre (la cadence); **the war interrupted his studies,** la guerre marqua un temps d'arrêt dans ses études; (*b*) intercepter, former obstacle à (la vue, etc.); **nothing interrupted the march of the battalion,** rien ne troubla la marche du bataillon.

interrupt[2], *s. Cmptr:* interruption *f* (de programme).

interrupted |intə'rʌptid|, *a.* interrompu; **i. conversation,** conversation interrompue; *Mec.E:* **i. screw,** vis *f* à filets interrompus; *El:* **i. ringing,** sonnerie rythmée; *Elcs:* **i. continuous waves,** ondes modulées; *Metalw:* **i. spot welding,** soudage *m* par points à impulsions.

interrupter |intə'rʌptər|, *s.* **1.** (*pers.*) interrupteur, -trice. **2.** *El:* interrupteur *m*; coupe-circuit *m inv*; rupteur *m* de courant; (*switch*) disjoncteur *m*, disrupteur *m*; (*spark gap*) éclateur *m.*

interrupting[1] |intə'rʌptiŋ|, *a.* interrupteur, -trice.

interrupting[2], *s.* **1.** interruption *f* (d'une discussion, etc.). **2.** rupture *f* (d'un circuit, etc.); *El:* **i. capacity,** pouvoir *m* de rupture, intensité maximale de rupture.

interruption |intə'rʌpʃ(ə)n|, *s.* **1.** (*a*) interruption *f*; dérangement *m* (de qn); **to work six hours without i.,** travailler six heures sans interruption, d'affilée, (tout) d'une traite; (*b*) **interruptions came from all parts of the audience,** des interruptions venaient de toutes parts dans l'auditoire. **2. i. in continuity,** solution *f* de continuité.

interruptive |intə'rʌptiv|, **interruptory** |intə'rʌptəri|, *a.* interrupteur, -trice.

interscapular |intə(:)'skæpjulər|, *a. Anat:* (région, etc.) interscapulaire.

interscapulothoracic |'intə(:)skæpjulouθə'ræsik|, *a. Med:* interscapulothoracique.

interscholastic |'intə(:)skə'læstik|, **inter-school** |'intə(:)'sku:l|, *a.* (concours, etc.) interscolaire.

interscrew |'intə(:)skru:|, *s.* vis *f* de reliure.

intersect |intə(:)'sekt|. **1.** *v.tr.* entrecouper, intersecter, entrecroiser (**with, by,** de); croiser; *Mth:* couper, intersecter; **land intersected with ravines,** terrain (entre)coupé de ravins; **line that intersects another,** ligne qui en coupe une autre; (*of lines, surfaces*) **to i. one another,** se couper, s'intersecter; *Geol:* **intersected lode,** filon croisé. **2.** *v.i. Mth: etc:* (*of lines, surfaces*; *of roads*) se couper, s'intersecter, se croiser; s'entrecouper, s'entrecroiser; **intersecting point,** point *m* d'intersection; **streets that i.,** rues qui s'entrecroisent.

intersecting |intə(:)'sektiŋ|, *a.* entrecroisé; (lignes) qui se croisent; *Arch:* **i. arches,** arcs intersectés.

intersection |intə(:)'sekʃ(ə)n|, *s.* **1.** *Geom:* intersection *f* (de deux plans, etc.); *Surv:* recoupement *m*, intersection. **2.** (*a*) **(point of) i.,** point *m* d'intersection, de recoupement; point de section; (*b*) (*crossroads*) carrefour *m*; croisement *m* de chemins; **hidden i.,** intersection masquée; *NAm:* **braided i., multiple bridge i.,** croisement à niveaux multiples; **flared i.,** croisement à chaussée élargie; **four-way i.,** croisement à quatre branches; **rotary i.,** croisement à circulation giratoire.

intersectional |intə(:)'sekʃənl|, *a.* (ralentissement, etc.) aux croisements.

intersertal |intə(:)'sə:t(ə)l|, *a. Geol:* intersertal, -aux.

interservice |'intə(:)'sə:vis|, *a.* (match, etc.) entre les forces armées.

intersex |'intəseks|, *s. Biol:* intersexué, -ée.

intersexual |intə(:)'seksjuəl|, *a.* **1.** *Biol:* intersexué, hermaphrodite; bisexué. **2.** (hostilité, etc.) entre les deux sexes.

intersexualism |intə(:)'seksjuəlizm|, **intersexuality** |intə(:)seksju'æliti|, *s. Biol:* intersexualité *f.*

intershot |intə(:)'ʃɔt|, *a.* moiré; **blue i. with purple,** bleu moiré de violet.

intersidereal |'intə(:)sai'diəriəl|, *a. Astr:* intersidéral, -aux.

interspace[1] |'intə(:)speis|, *s.* **1.** espacement *m* (entre deux corps); entre-deux *m inv*; (*in time*) intervalle *m.* **2.** espace *m* (interplanétaire, interstellaire).

interspace[2] *v.tr.* espacer (des caractères, ses visites, etc.).

interspecific |intə(:)spi'sifik|, *a.* (hybride, etc.) interspécifique.

intersperse |intə(:)'spə:s|, *v.tr.* entremêler (**between, among,** entre; **with,** de); **to i. shrubs and trees,** entremêler des arbustes et des arbres; **poppies interspersed among the wheat,** coquelicots répandus parmi les blés; **countryside interspersed with farms,** contrée parsemée de fermes; **to i. a speech with quotations,** intercaler des citations dans un discours, émailler un discours de citations.

interspersion |intə(:)'spə:ʃ(ə)n|, *s.* entremêlement *m.*

interspinal |intə(:)'spain(ə)l|, *a. Anat:* interépineux.

interspinalis |intə(:)'spainəlis|, *s. Anat:* muscle interépineux.

interstadial |intə(:)'steidiəl|, *s. Geol:* interstadiaire *m.*

interstage |'intəsteidʒ|, *a.* (i) intermédiaire; (ii) entre étages, interétages; *Cmptr:* **i. punching,** perforation intercalée; *Mec.E:* **i. bearing,** palier *m* intermédiaire; **i. cooler,** radiateur *m* intermédiaire; **i. coupling,** couplage *m*, liaison *f*, entre étages; *El:* **i. transformer,** transformateur *m* de liaison, intermédiaire; *Elcs:* **i. amplifier,** amplificateur *m* interétages.

interstate |ˈintə(:)ˈsteit|, *a.* (commerce, chemin de fer, etc.) entre États (des États-Unis, de l'Australie, etc.).

interstellar |ˈintə(:)ˈstelər|, *a. Astr:* (espace, matière, etc.) interstellaire; (espace) intersidéral, -aux, interastral, -aux.

interstice |inˈtə:stis|, *s.* **1.** (*a*) interstice *m*; (*b*) alvéole *m* (de grillage d'accu, etc.). **2.** *pl. R.C.Ch:* **interstices,** interstices (entre la réception des divers ordres sacrés).

interstitial |intə(:)ˈstiʃ(ə)l|, *a.* (espace, *Anat:* tissu) interstitiel; *Med:* **i. nephritis,** néphrite interstitielle; *Cryst:* **i. atom,** atome *m* en position interstitielle.

interstratification |ˈintə(:)strætifiˈkeiʃ(ə)n|, *s. Geol:* interstratification *f.*

interstratify |intə(:)ˈstrætifai|. *Geol:* **1.** *v.tr.* interstratifier. **2.** *v.i.* (*of strata*) s'interstratifier.

intersubjective |intə(:)səbˈdʒektiv|, *a. Psy:* **i. communication,** communication intersubjective.

intersubjectivity |ˈintə(:)sʌbdʒekˈtiviti|, *s. Psy:* intersubjectivité *f.*

intertanglement |intə(:)ˈtæŋglmənt|, *s.* embrouillement *m*, emmêlement *m*.

intertexture |intə(:)ˈtekstʃər|, *s.* **1.** entrelacement *m*, entremêlement *m*. **2.** tissu *m*.

intertidal |ˈintə(:)ˈtaidl|, *a. Geog:* intertidal, -aux.

intertie[1] |ˈintətai|, *s.* **1.** *Const:* lierne *f* (entre deux montants). **2.** *El:* interconnexion *f.*

intertie[2] |intə(:)ˈtai|, *v. tr. El:* interconnecter.

intertrace |ˈintətreis|, *a. Elcs:* **i. period,** période située entre deux balayages.

intertrade |ˈintə(:)treid|, *s.* commerce *m* réciproque.

intertransversal |ˈintə(:)trænzˈvə:sl|, **intertransversary** |ˈintə(:)trænzˈvə:səri|, **intertransverse** |intə(:)ˈtrænzvə:s|, *a. Anat:* intertransversaire.

intertribal |intə(:)ˈtraib(ə)l|, *a.* commun à plusieurs tribus; **i. wars,** guerres *f* de tribus.

intertriginous |intə(:)ˈtridʒinəs|, *a. Med:* intertrigineux.

intertrigo |intə(:)ˈtraigou|, *s. Med:* intertrigo *m*.

intertropical |intə(:)ˈtrɔpik(ə)l|, *a.* intertropical, -aux.

intertwine |intə(:)ˈtwain|. **1.** *v.tr.* entrelacer. **2.** *v.i.* s'entrelacer, s'accoler.

intertwinement |intə(:)ˈtwainmənt|, *s.* entrelacement *m*.

intertwining[1] |intə(:)ˈtwainiŋ|, *a.* entrelacé(s).

intertwining[2], *s.* entrelacement *m*.

intertwist |intə(:)ˈtwist|, *v.tr.* entrelacer.

Intertype |ˈintətaip|, *s. Typ: R.t.m:* Intertype *f.*

interurban |intərˈə:bən|, *a.* interurbain.

interval |ˈintəv(ə)l|, *s.* intervalle *m*. **1.** (*time*) (*a*) **lucid i.,** intervalle lucide; **at intervals,** par intervalles; par à-coups; **visits at long intervals,** visites à de longs intervalles; **I see him at long intervals,** je le vois de loin en loin, **meetings held at short intervals,** séances très rapprochées; **ten years' i. between two events,** distance *f* de dix ans entre deux événements; **after an i. of time,** après un laps de temps; **the intervals between our visits are becoming longer,** nos visites s'espacent; **i. between the starting times of trains, between two lectures,** battement *m* des trains, entre deux conférences; **an hour's i. between two meetings,** une heure de battement entre deux séances; **the competitors start at intervals of one minute, at minute intervals,** les concurrents partent de minute en minute; **short i. of fair weather,** échappée *f* de beau temps; **sunny i.,** aperçue *f* de soleil; **bright intervals,** belles éclaircies; **rainy weather with bright intervals,** temps pluvieux avec éclaircies; *Tg:* **spacing i.,** intervalle de manipulation; (*b*) *Sch:* (période *f* de) récréation *f*; *Ind: etc:* **meal i.,** pause *f*; (*c*) (i) *Th:* entracte *m*; **in the i.,** à l'entracte; (ii) *Fb: etc:* mi-temps *f inv*, pause. **2.** (*a*) (*space*) **I. between two platoons,** intervalle entre deux sections; **i. between two beams,** écartement *m* de deux poutres; **at intervals there are telephone, call, boxes,** de distance en distance se trouvent des cabines téléphoniques; **trees growing at regular intervals along the road,** arbres qui jalonnent la route; **to place objects at regular intervals,** échelonner des objets; (*b*) *Mus:* **concordant i., discordant i.,** intervalle consonant, dissonant; (*c*) *Mapm:* **contour i.,** équidistance *f* des courbes; **vertical i.,** distance verticale.

intervarietal |intə(:)vəˈraiit(ə)l|, *a. Biol:* **i. cross,** hybride *m* de variétés; métis, -isse.

intervein |intə(:)ˈvein|, *v.tr.* veiner, strier (**with,** de).

intervene |intə(:)ˈvi:n|, *v.i.* **1.** (*of pers., thg*) intervenir, s'interposer, se jeter à la traverse; **to i. in s.o.'s defence,** intervenir pour prendre la défense de qn; **to i. in a quarrel,** intervenir dans une querelle; **to i. in the affairs of a neighbouring country,** intervenir dans un pays voisin; *Jur:* **to i. in an agreement,** intervenir dans un contrat. **2.** (*of event*) survenir, arriver. **3.** (*in time and space*) **ten years intervened,** dix ans s'écoulèrent; **ten miles intervened between the two towns,** dix milles séparaient les deux villes.

intervener, -or |intə(:)ˈvi:nər|, *s.* personne *f* qui intervient (dans une querelle, etc.); *Jur:* intervenant, -ante.

intervening[1] |intə(:)ˈvi:niŋ|, *a.* **1.** (*of pers.*) intervenant; *Jur:* **the i. party,** l'intervenant, -ante, **2.** (événement) survenu. **3.** (époque *f*, distance *f*) intermédiaire; **during the i. week,** pendant la semaine qui s'écoula.

intervening[2], **intervention** |intə(:)ˈvenʃ(ə)n|, *s.* intervention *f* (d'une personne, de la force armée, d'une nation étrangère, d'un tiers dans un procès); interposition *f* (d'un corps); *Com:* **intervention on protest,** intervention à protêt; *Med:* **surgical intervention,** intervention chirurgicale.

interventionism |intə(:)ˈvenʃ(ə)nizm|, *s. Pol: etc:* interventionnisme *m*.

interventionist |intə(:)ˈvenʃ(ə)nist|, *s. Pol: etc:* interventionniste *mf.*

interventricular |intə(:)venˈtrikjulər|, *a. Anat:* interventriculaire.

intervertebral |intə(:)ˈvə:tibrəl|, *a. Anat:* (disque, etc.) intervertébral, -aux.

interview[1] [ˈintə(:)vju:], *s.* **1.** (*a*) entrevue *f*; **to arrange an i. for s.o. with s.o.,** ménager à qn une entrevue avec qn; *Adm:* **to invite s.o. to an i.,** convoquer qn; (*b*) interview *f* (d'un candidat pour un poste). **2.** *Journ: etc:* interview; (*a*) **i. with the Minister,** interview du Ministre; (*b*) **to publish a series of interviews,** publier une série d'interviews.

interview[2], *v.tr.* **1.** (*a*) avoir une entrevue avec (qn); (*b*) **to i. candidates for a post,** examiner les candidats, donner des interviews aux candidats, à un poste. **2.** *Journ: etc:* (*of reporter, broadcaster*) interviewer (qn).

interviewee |intə(:)vju:ˈi:|, *s.* interviewé, -ée.

interviewer |ˈintəvju:ər|, *s. Journ: etc:* interviewer *m*, intervieweur *m*; (*for research*) enquêteur, -euse.

intervivos |intə(:)ˈvaivous, -ˈvi:vous|, *a. Jur:* entre vifs; **disposition i. v.,** donation *f* entre vifs.

intervocalic [intə(:)vəˈkælik], *a. Ling:* intervocalique.

inter-war [ˈintə(:)ˈwɔ:r], *a.* **the i.-w. years, period,** l'entre-deux-guerres *m or f*; l'interguerre *f.*

Interweave |intə(:)ˈwi:v|, *v.* (*p.t.* **interwove** [intə(:)wouv] *p.p.* **interwoven** [intə(:)ˈwouvn]) **1.** *v.tr.* (*a*) tisser ensemble (des fils d'or et de laine, etc.); entrelacer (des branches); *Tex:* **interwoven fabric,** tissu *m* droit fil; **material interwoven with gold threads,** tissu broché d'or; **interwoven with brass,** laitonné; (*b*) entremêler (des sentiments, des idées, etc.); **to i. foreign phrases in one's conversation,** entremêler des locutions étrangères dans sa conversation; **closely interwoven systems,** systèmes étroitement liés l'un à l'autre. **2.** *v.i.* s'entrelacer, s'entremêler.

Interweaving |intə(:)ˈwi:viŋ|, *s.* entrelacement *m*; entremêlement *m*.

interwind |intə(:)ˈwaind|, *v.tr.* (*p.t. & p.p.* **interwound** |-ˈwaund|) enrelacer; enrouler ensemble; *F:* mêler intimement.

interwork |intə(:)ˈwə:k|, *v.* (*p.t. & p.p.* **interworked** |-ˈwə:kt|) **1.** *v.tr.* entremêler, entrelacer (**with,** de); ouvrer l'un dans l'autre. **2.** *v.i.* réagir réciproquement.

interzonal |intə(:)ˈzounl|, **interzone** |intə(:)ˈzoun|, *a.* interzonal, -aux.

intestacy |inˈtestəsi|, *s. Jur:* fait *m* de mourir intestat; absence *f* de testament.

intestate |inˈtesteit|. **1.** *a.* (*a*) intestat *inv*; **she died i.,** elle est morte intestat; (*b*) **i. estate, i. succession,** succession *f* ab intestat; **to succeed to an i. estate,** hériter ab intestat. **2.** *s.* intestat *mf*; **the i.,** les intestats.

intestinal |inˈtestinl|, *a. Anat:* intestinal, -aux; **the i. tube,** le conduit intestinal.

intestine[1] |inˈtestin|, *a.* intestin; **i. wars,** guerres intestines.

intestine[2], *s. Anat:* intestin *m*; **the large i.,** le gros intestin; **the small i.,** l'intestin grêle.

intima, *pl.* **-mae, -mas** |ˈintimə, -mi:, -məz|, *s. Anat:* intima *m*, tunique *f* interne (des vaisseaux sanguins, etc.).

intimacy |ˈintiməsi|, *s.* **1.** intimité *f*; (*a*) **in the i. of the family,** dans l'intimité de la famille; (*b*) **the i. of a mixture,** l'intimité d'un mélange. **2.** *Jur:* **i. took place,** il y a eu relations charnelles; **evidence that i. took place,** preuve *f* de relations intimes.

intimate[1] |ˈintimət|. **1.** *a.* intime; (*a*) **i. friendship, friend,** amitié *f*, ami *m*, intime; **to be very i. with s.o.,** être très intime avec qn, *F:* être à tu et à toi avec qn; **to become i. with s.o.,** se lier (d'amitié) avec qn; **to be i. with the aristocracy,** être admis dans la familiarité de l'aristocratie; **to dine with a few i. friends,** dîner en petit comité; **only i. friends had been asked,** on n'avait invité que quelques intimes; **the i. nature of their conversation,** l'intimité de leur conversation; (*b*) **i. little restaurant,** petit restaurant intime; (*c*) **to be on i. terms with a woman,** avoir des relations intimes avec une femme; (*d*) **i. diary,** journal *m* intime; (*e*) **to have an i. knowledge of sth.,** avoir une connaissance approfondie de qch.; **i. connexion,** rapport intime, étroit; **i. mixture,** mélange *m* intime. **2.** *s.* (*usu. pl.*) intime *mf*; **his intimates,** ses intimes, ses familiers *m*.

intimate[2] |ˈintimeit|, *v.tr.* **1.** intimer (un ordre); signifier (ses intentions); **to i. sth. to s.o.,** signifier, notifier, qch. à qn; **I intimated to him that he had to meet his debts,** je lui ai signifié, lui ai fait savoir, qu'il devrait faire face à ses créances, qu'il eût à faire face à ses créances. **2.** donner à entendre, indiquer, suggérer (**sth. to s.o.,** qch. à qn); **he intimated that he had failed,** il a indiqué qu'il avait échoué.

intimately |ˈintimətli|, *adv.* intimement; à fond; **we know him i.,** nous le connaissons particulièrement; **I know Paris i.,** je connais Paris comme (le fond de) ma poche; **this question is i. connected with another,** cette question a un rapport très étroit avec une autre.

intimation |intiˈmeiʃ(ə)n|, *s.* **1.** avis *m* (de décès, etc.); **at the first i.,** au premier avis; **friends will please accept this, the only i.,** le présent avis tiendra lieu de faire-part. **2.** (*a*) avis à mots couverts; suggestion *f*; **I have often had intimations in dreams,** les rêves m'ont souvent apporté des prémonitions *f*; bien des événements m'ont été annoncés en rêve; (*b*) **intimations of immortality,** indications *f*, signes *m*, de l'immortalité.

intimidate |inˈtimideit|, *v.tr.* intimider; faire peur à (qn); **easily intimidated,** intimidable; timide.

intimidating |inˈtimideitiŋ|, *a.* intimidateur, -trice; intimidant.

intimidation |intimiˈdeiʃ(ə)n|, *s.* intimidation *f*; *Jur:* menaces *fpl*; **guilty of i.,** coupable de menaces; **i. of witnesses,** subornation *f* de témoins; **system of i.,** système *m* d'intimidation.

intimidator |inˈtimideitər|, *s.* intimidateur, -trice.

intimidatory |intimiˈdeitəri|, *a.* intimidateur, -trice.

intimism |ˈintimizm|, *s. Lit: Art:* intimisme *m*.

intimist |ˈintimist|, *a. & s. Lit: Art:* intimiste (*mf*).

intimity |inˈtimiti|, *s. O:* **1.** caractère *m* intime. **2.** la vie privée; le privé.

intinction |inˈtiŋ(k)ʃ(ə)n|, *s. Ecc:* intinction *f.*

intine |ˈinti:n|, *s. Bot:* intine *f*, endhyménine *f.*

into [ˈintu(:), ˈintə], *prep.* dans, en. **1.** (*motion, direction*) (*a*) **to go i. a house,** entrer dans une maison; *F:* **a little more and my car was i. him,** un peu plus et je lui rentrais dedans; **to go i. France,** passer en France; **to climb i. the boxing ring,** monter sur le ring; **to fall i. the hands of the enemy,** tomber entre les mains de l'ennemi; **the window opens i. the garden,** la fenêtre donne sur le jardin; **he took an apricot and bit i. it,** il a pris un abricot et y a mordu; **to come i. a property,** hériter d'un bien, **to get i. difficulties,** s'attirer des désagréments, des ennuis; se mettre dans le pétrin; *F:* **he was i. his third beer,** il avait commencé à boire, avait entamé, sa troisième bière; **to work far i. the night,** travailler bien avant dans la nuit; **to look i. the future,** voir dans l'avenir; pénétrer l'avenir; (*b*) *F:* **to be i. sth.,** être absorbé par qch.; **I'm not really i. that sort of thing,** ces choses-là ne me disent rien. **2.** (*change, result*) **to change sth. i. sth.,** changer qch. en qch.; **he was changed, turned, i. a serpent,** il fut transformé en serpent; **to grow i. a man,** devenir un homme; **to collect i. heaps,** amasser en tas; **to divide i. four,** diviser en quatre; **to break sth. i. pieces,** briser qch. en morceaux; **to burst i. tears,** fondre en larmes; **to thrash s.o. i. obedience,** faire obéir qn à force de coups de bâton; **to laugh s.o. i. silence,** réduire qn au silence sous un torrent de ridicule. **3.** *Mth:* **three i. six goes two, twice,** six divisé par trois fait deux.

intoed |ˈintoud|, *a.* **1.** (pied) tourné en dedans. **2.** aux pieds tournés en dedans.

intolerability |intɔl(ə)rəˈbiliti|, **intolerableness** |inˈtɔl(ə)rəblnis|, *s.* intolérabilité *f* (d'une douleur, etc.).

intolerable |inˈtɔl(ə)rəbl|, *a.* intolérable, insupportable.

intolerance |inˈtɔlər(ə)ns|, *s.* intolérance *f* (**of,** de); (*a*) **religious i., political i.,** intolérance en matière de religion, de politique; intolérantisme *m*; (*b*) *Med:* **i. of a drug,** intolérance d'un remède.

intolerant |inˈtɔlər(ə)nt|, *a.* **1.** intolérant; **to be very i.,** être d'une extrême intolérance; **he is i. of opposition,** il ne sait pas supporter l'opposition; **to be too i. of s.o.'s failings,** avoir trop d'intolérance pour les faiblesses de qn. **2.** *Med:* **to be i. of a drug,** ne pas supporter un médicament.

intolerantly |inˈtɔlər(ə)ntli|, *adv.* sans tolérance, avec intolérance.

intonate |ˈintəneit|, *v.tr.* = INTONE.

Intonation |intəˈneiʃ(ə)n|, *s.* **1.** *Mus:* (*a*) intonation *f* (d'une note); **right i., wrong i.,** intonation juste, fausse; (*b*) *Ecc. Mus:* (i) intonation (d'un plain-chant, etc.); (ii) psalmodie *f*. **2.** intonation, cadence *f*, modulation *f*, ton *m* (de la voix).

intone [in'toun], *v.tr. Ecc:* **1.** psalmodier (des litanies, etc.). **2.** entonner (le chant).

intorsion [in'tɔ:ʃ(ə)n], *s. Bot: etc:* intorsion *f.*

intoxicant [in'tɔksikənt]. **1.** *a.* enivrant, grisant, capiteux. **2.** *s.* boisson *f* alcoolique; spiritueux *m.*

intoxicate [in'tɔksikeit], *v.tr.* enivrer, griser, rendre ivre; **drink that intoxicates,** boisson enivrante, qui enivre; **scent that intoxicates,** parfum capiteux, qui grise.

intoxicated [in'tɔksikeitid], *a.* ivre, gris, pris de boisson; *Jur:* en état d'ébriété, d'ivresse; **slightly i.,** légèrement ivre; **to become i.,** s'enivrer (**with,** de); **i. with praise, with pride,** enivré, grisé, d'éloges, d'orgueil.

intoxicating [in'tɔksikeitiŋ], *a.* (vin, parfum) enivrant, grisant, capiteux; **i. liquors,** boissons *f* alcooliques; spiritueux *m*; *Fig:* **an i. woman,** une femme capiteuse.

intoxication [intɔksi'keiʃ(ə)n], *s.* **1.** *Med:* intoxication *f* (par un poison). **2.** (*a*) ivresse *f*; (*b*) griserie *f,* enivrement *m,* intoxication (du plaisir).

intra- ['intrə], *pref.* intra-.

intra-arterial ['intrəɑ:'tiəriəl], *a.* intra-artériel, *pl.* intra-artériel(le)s.

intra-articular ['intrəɑ:'tikjulər], *a.* intra-articulaire, *pl.* intra-articulaires.

intra-atomic ['intrəə'tɔmik], *a. Ph:* intra-atomique, *pl.* intra-atomiques.

intra-aural ['intrə'ɔ:rəl], *a.* intra-aural, -aux.

intrabony ['intrə'bouni], *a.* intra-osseux.

intracardiac, intracardial ['intrə'kɑ:diæk, -iəl], *a.* intracardiaque.

intracellular ['intrə'seljulər], *a. Biol:* intracellulaire.

intracerebral ['intrə'seribrəl], *a. Anat:* intracérébral, -aux.

intracervical ['intrə'sə:vikl], *a.* intracervical, -aux.

intracranial ['intrə'kreiniəl], *a.* intracrânien.

intractability [intræktə'biliti], **intractableness** [in'træktəbəlnis], *s.* indocilité *f* (d'un enfant, d'un animal); nature *f* incultivable (d'un terrain, etc.).

intractable [in'træktəbl], *a.* (enfant, animal) intraitable, indisciplinable, insoumis, indocile, obstiné; (cheval) rebours; (maladie) opiniâtre, invétérée, intraitable; (terrain) incultivable; (bois, etc.) difficile à travailler; **i. material,** matériaux ingrats, rebelles; **i. problem,** problème *m* très difficile.

intractably [in'træktəbli], *adv.* d'une façon intraitable.

intrada [in'trɑ:də], *s. Mus:* entrée *f.*

intradermal, intradermic [intrə'də:m(ə)l, -mik], *a. Med:* intradermique; **intradermal reaction,** intradermo-réaction *f, pl.* intradermo-réactions; *F:* intradermo *f.*

intrados [in'treidɔs], *s. Arch:* intrados *m.*

intra-epithelial ['intrəepi'θi:liəl], *a. Anat:* intraépithélial, -aux.

intraglacial ['intrə'gleiʃ(ə)l], *a. Geol:* intraglaciaire.

intrahepatic ['intrəhe'pætik], *a. Anat:* intrahépatique.

intramedullary ['intrəme'dʌləri], *a. Anat:* intramédullaire.

intra-mercurial ['intrəmə:'kju:riəl], *a. Astr:* intramercuriel.

intramolecular ['intrəmɔ'lekjulər], *a. Ph:* intramoléculaire.

intramontane ['intrə'mɔntein], *a. Geog:* intramontagnard, intramontagneux.

intramural [intrə'mju:r(ə)l], *a.* intra-muros *inv.*

intramurally [intrə'mju:rəli], *adv.* intra-muros.

intramuscular [intrə'mʌskjulər], *a.* intramusculaire.

intransigence [in'trænsidʒəns], *s.* intransigeance *f.*

intransigent [in'trænsidʒ(ə)nt], *a.* intransigeant.

intransigentism [in'trænsidʒəntizm], *s. Pol:* intransigeance *f.*

in-transit [in'trænsit], *a. Cmptr:* **in-t. storage,** mémoire *f* de transit.

intransitive [in'trænsitiv], *a. & s. Gram:* **i.** (**verb**), (verbe) intransitif (*m*).

intransitively [in'trænsitivli], *adv.* intransitivement.

intransitiveness [in'trænsitivnis], **intransitivity** [intrænsi'tiviti], *s.* intransitivité *f.*

intransmissible [intrænz'misibl], *a.* intransmissible.

intransmutable [intrænz'mju:təbl], *a.* intransmuable, intransmutable, non-transmuable.

intrant ['intrənt], *s. A:* débutant, -ante (dans une profession, etc.); nouveau membre (d'une société, etc.); fonctionnaire entrant.

intranuclear ['intrə'nju:kliər], *a.* intranucléaire.

intraocular ['intrə'ɔkjulər], *a. Anat: etc:* intra-oculaire, *pl.* intra-oculaires; **i. end of the optic nerve,** papille *f* optique.

intra-osseous ['intrə'ɔsiəs], *a.* intra-osseux; *Med:* **i.-o. implant,** implant endo-osseux.

intrapelvic ['intrə'pelvik], *a. Anat:* intrapelvien.

intrapleural [intrə'pluər(ə)l], *a. Anat:* intrapleural, -aux.

intrasolar [intrə'soulər], *a.* intrasolaire.

intraspecific [intrəspi'sifik], *a.* intraspécifique.

intraspinal [intrə'spainl], *a. Anat:* intra-rachidien, *pl.* intra-rachidiens.

intra-storage [intrə'stɔ:ridʒ], *a. Cmptr:* **i.-s. transfer,** transfert *m* interne.

intratelluric ['intrəte'lju:rik], *a. Geol:* intratellurique.

intrathecal [intrə'θi:kl], *a. Anat:* intra-rachidien, *pl.* intra-rachidiens.

intrathoracic ['intrəθɔ'ræsik], *a. Anat:* intrathoracique.

intra-uterine ['intrə'ju:tərain], *a. Anat:* intra-utérin, *pl.* intra-utérins.

intravaginal ['intrəvə'dʒain(ə)l, -'vædʒin(ə)l], *Anat:* intravaginal, -aux.

intravascular ['intrə'væskjulər], *a.* (circulation, etc.) intravasculaire.

intravascularly ['intrə'væskjuləli], *adv.* (injecté) dans les vaisseaux sanguins.

intravenous ['intrə'vi:nəs], *a. Physiol:* intraveineux.

intravert ['intrəvə:t], *s. Psy:* introverti, -ie.

intrazonal [intrə'zounl], *a. Geog:* (sol) intrazonal, -aux.

intreat [in'tri:t], *v.tr.* **to i. s.o. to do sth.,** prier, implorer, supplier, qn de faire qch.; demander en grâce à qn de faire qch.; demander instamment à qn de faire qch.; **they intreated him to stay,** ils le prièrent, ils lui demandèrent avec instance, de rester; **leave me alone, I i. you,** laissez-moi tranquille, je vous en prie; **I i. your indulgence,** je réclame votre indulgence; *Lit:* **to i. sth. of s.o.,** demander (en grâce) qch. à qn.

intrench [in'tren(t)ʃ]. **1.** *v.tr. Mil:* retrancher (un camp, une ville); *v.i.* faire des retranchements; **to i. oneself behind, in, (sth.),** se retrancher, se terrer, derrière (des remparts, *Fig:* un prétexte); se cantonner (dans un travail, etc.); *Geog:* **intrenched meander,** méandre encaissé. **2.** *v.i.* **to i. (up)on,** empiéter sur, enfreindre (un privilège, etc.).

intrepid [in'trepid], *a.* intrépide, brave, courageux; sans crainte.

intrepidity [intre'piditi], *s.* intrépidité *f*; courage *m*; fermeté *f* inébranlable.

intrepidly [in'trepidli], *adv.* intrépidement, courageusement.

intricacy ['intrikəsi], *s.* (*a*) complexité *f,* nature compliquée (d'un mécanisme, d'un problème, d'un dessin); caractère embrouillé (d'une affaire); (*b*) **the intricacies of the law,** les dédales de la loi.

intricate ['intrikət], *a.* (*a*) (modèle, mécanisme) compliqué; (question, affaire) difficile à démêler; **i. pattern, design,** dessin intriqué; **the i. streets,** le dédale des rues; (*b*) (*of thoughts, statements*) enchevêtré, embrouillé, confus; **i. details,** détails compliqués; (*c*) *Nat.Hist:* (*of fibres, etc.*) intriqué.

intricately ['intrikətli], *adv.* d'une manière compliquée, embrouillée.

intrication [intri'keiʃ(ə)n], *s. Nat.Hist:* intrication *f.*

intrigue[1] [in'tri:g], *s.* **1.** intrigue *f,* cabale *f,* machination *f*; **a court i.,** une intrigue de cour; **spirit of i.,** esprit *m* d'intrigue. **2.** *O:* intrigue, liaison *f,* aventure *f* (avec une femme). **3.** *Th:* intrigue (d'un drame, etc.); **comedy of i.,** comédie *f* d'intrigue.

intrigue[2]. **1.** *v.i.* (*a*) intriguer; mener des intrigues; **to i. with s.o.,** intriguer avec qn; **to i. on s.o.'s behalf,** intriguer pour qn; **to i. against s.o.,** intriguer, travailler, contre qn; **to i. to get s.o. an appointment,** machiner, intriguer, pour obtenir la nomination de qn; (*b*) *O:* avoir une intrigue, une liaison (**with,** avec). **2.** *v.tr.* intriguer (qn); éveiller, piquer, la curiosité de (qn); **I'm greatly intrigued by the idea,** l'idée m'intrigue énormément; **what I am most intrigued by is the colour,** ce qui m'intéresse avant tout c'est la couleur; **intrigued by all this whispering,** intrigué par tous ces chuchotements.

intriguer [in'tri:gər], *s.* intrigant, -ante; homme *m* de cabale.

intriguing[1] [in'tri:giŋ], *a.* **1.** (politicien, etc.) intrigant. **2.** **i. words,** paroles mystérieuses, intrigantes; **all this is very i.,** tout cela nous intrigue beaucoup, excite fort notre curiosité.

intriguing[2], *s.* machinations *fpl,* intrigues *fpl.*

intrinsic [in'trinsik], *a.* intrinsèque. **1.** *Anat:* **i. muscle,** muscle *m* intrinsèque. **2.** **i. defect,** vice *m* intrinsèque; **i. value,** valeur *f* intrinsèque; *El:* **i. semiconductor,** semiconducteur *m* (*pl.* semi-conducteurs) intrinsèque.

intrinsically [in'trinsik(ə)li], *adv.* intrinsèquement; *El:* **i. safe,** de sécurité intrinsèque.

intro ['introu], *s. F:* **1.** (i) présentation *f* (de qn à qn); (ii) lettre *f* de présentation, de recommandation. **2.** *Mus:* introduction *f* (d'un morceau, *esp.* d'un morceau de jazz).

intro- [intrə-, introu], *pref.* intro-.

introduce [intrə'dju:s], *v.tr.* **1.** introduire; (*a*) faire entrer; **to i. s.o. into a country, into a room,** introduire, faire entrer, qn dans un pays, dans une chambre; **reindeer were introduced into Scotland,** on a introduit le renne dans l'Écosse; **to i. a key into a lock,** introduire, faire entrer, une clef dans une serrure; **to i. a subject, a question,** amener un sujet, une question; mettre une question sur le tapis; **to i. a subject into the conversation,** introduire un sujet dans la conversation; amener la conversation sur un sujet; (*b*) **to i. s.o. into s.o.'s presence,** introduire qn auprès de qn; (*c*) établir, faire adopter (une loi, un usage); **to i. the use of sth.,** introduire l'emploi de qch.; **this fashion was introduced in the fifteenth century,** cette mode fut introduite, s'introduisit, entra en vogue, au quinzième siècle; (*d*) **to i. a bill (before Parliament),** déposer, présenter, un projet de loi; (*e*) (*of conjunction, adverb*) commencer (une phrase); (*f*) *Com:* lancer (une marchandise); *St.Exch:* introduire (des actions). **2.** (*a*) présenter; **to i. s.o. to s.o.,** présenter qn à qn; **to i. oneself to s.o.,** se présenter à qn; **to i. oneself (by name),** se faire connaître; **I shall i. her to you,** je vous la ferai connaître; je vous la présenterai; **I shall i. you to her,** je vous présenterai à elle; **who is going to i. us?** qui est-ce qui va faire les présentations? (*b*) (*of débutante*) **to be introduced to society,** faire son entrée dans le monde; **it was I who introduced her into society,** c'est moi qui l'ai produite dans le monde. **3.** **to i. s.o. to a process, etc.,** faire connaître un procédé, etc., à qn; initier qn à un procédé; **he introduced me to Greek,** il m'a initié au grec.

introducer [intrə'dju:sər], *s.* **1.** introducteur, -trice; présentateur, -trice. **2.** **i. of new ideas,** remueur, -euse, d'idées; innovateur, -trice.

introduction [intrə'dʌkʃ(ə)n], *s.* **1.** introduction *f* (**of sth. into sth.,** de qch. dans qch.); **i. of goods into a country, to the market,** introduction de marchandises dans un pays, lancement *m* de marchandises sur le marché. **2.** présentation *f* (**of s.o. to s.o.,** de qn à qn); **to do the introductions,** faire les présentations; **letter of i.,** (lettre d')introduction; lettre recommandative; lettre de recommandation, de présentation; **to give s.o. an i. to s.o.,** donner à qn une lettre de recommandation auprès de qn. **3.** avant-propos *m inv*; introduction, exorde *m* (d'un livre); *Mus:* introduction (d'un morceau). **4.** manuel *m* élémentaire (**to,** de); introduction (**to,** à). **5.** **this shrub is an i. from China,** cet arbuste a été introduit de la Chine, est de provenance chinoise.

introductive [intrə'dʌktiv], *a. occ.* = INTRODUCTORY.

introductory [intrə'dʌktəri], *a.* (qui sert) d'introduction; **i. page, epistle,** page *f,* épître *f,* liminaire; **after a few i. words,** après quelques mots d'introduction; *Com:* **i. price,** prix *m* de lancement.

introflexed [introu'flekst], *a.* introfléchi; recourbé en dedans.

introflexion [introu'flekʃ(ə)n], *s.* recourbement *m* en dedans.

introgression [introu'greʃ(ə)n], *s.* entrée (solennelle).

introgressive [introu'gresiv], *a. Biol:* introgressif; **i. hybridization,** hybridation introgressive.

introit ['introit], *s. Ecc:* introït *m.*

introitus [in'troitəs], *s. Anat:* orifice *m* (*esp.* du vagin).

introjection [intrə'dʒekʃ(ə)n], *s. Psy:* introjection *f.*

intromission [introu'miʃ(ə)n], *s.* **1.** *Ph: Bot:* intromission *f* (d'air, d'eau, d'un corps dans un autre). **2.** *Jur: Scot:* **i. into s.o.'s affairs,** immixtion *f,* ingérence *f,* dans les affaires d'autrui; **vicious i.,** ingérence vexatoire.

intromit [introu'mit], *v.* (**intromitted**) **1.** *v.tr.* admettre, faire entrer (qch. dans qch.). **2.** *v.i. Scot:* (s')immiscer, s'ingérer dans les affaires d'autrui; intervenir.

introrse [in'trɔ:s], *a. Bot:* (anthère) introrse.

introspect [introu'spekt], *v.i.* se livrer à l'introspection; s'introspecter; s'examiner soi-même.

introspection [introu'spekʃ(ə)n], *s.* introspection *f.*

introspective [introu'spektiv], *a.* introspectif.

introsuscept [introusə'sept], *v.i.* (*of intestine, etc.*) s'invaginer.

introsusception [introusə'sepʃ(ə)n], *s.* **1.** *Biol:* intussusception *f.* **2.** *Med:* intussusception, invagination *f* (de l'intestin).

introversion [introu'və:ʃ(ə)n], *s.* **1.** recueillement *m* (d'esprit); retour *m* sur soi-même; *Psy:* introversion *f.* **2.** *Med:* invagination *f*; **i. of the eyelid,** entropion *m.*

introvert[1] ['intrəvə:t], *s.* introverti, -ie.

introvert[2] [intrə'və:t], *v.tr.* **1.** **to i. one's mind, one's thoughts,** se recueillir (en soi-même). **2.** *Med:* retourner (un viscère) en dedans.

introverted [intrə'və:tid], *a.* **1.** (esprit) recueilli, *Psy:* introverti. **2.** (*a*) (viscère) retourné en dedans; (*b*) (pied, etc.) tourné en dedans. **3.** *Pros:* **i. rhymes,** rimes embrassées.

intrude [in'tru:d]. **1.** *v.tr.* (*a*) **to i. sth. into sth.,** introduire qch. de force dans qch.; (*b*) **to i. sth. on, upon, s.o.,** imposer qch. à qn; importuner qn de qch.; **he tries to i.**

himself, his presence, on us, il voudrait s'imposer. 2. *v.i.* faire intrusion (**on s.o.,** auprès de qn); être importun; **I am afraid of intruding,** je crains de vous être importun, de vous déranger, d'être de trop; **I hope I am not intruding,** j'espère que je ne vous importune pas; **I don't want to i. into your affairs,** je ne voudrais pas m'ingérer dans vos affaires; **to i. on s.o.'s privacy,** empiéter sur la solitude de qn.

intruded |in'tru:did|, *a. Geol:* **i. rock,** roche intrusive.

intruder |in'tru:dər|, *s.* 1. intrus, -use; gêneur, -euse; importun, -une; (*at reception*) *F:* resquilleur, -euse. 2. *Mil.Av:* chasseur *m* de pénétration.

intrusion |in'tru:ʒ(ə)n|, *s.* 1. (*a*) intrusion *f*; **to make an i. upon s.o.,** faire (une) intrusion auprès de qn; **i. on a company,** intrusion dans une société; *F:* resquillage *m*; (*b*) **I hope I am not guilty of an i.,** j'espère que je ne suis pas indiscret, que je ne dérange pas. 2. *Geol:* (*a*) (i) intrusion, injection *f* (volcanique, de porphyre), (ii) roche intrusive; (*b*) **i. of the sea,** ingression *f* de la mer. 3. *Jur:* usurpation *f* (**on,** de); empiètement *m* (**on,** sur).

intrusive |in'tru:siv|, *a.* 1. (*of pers.*) importun, indiscret; **i. fellow,** fâcheux *m*. 2. (*a*) *Ling: etc:* intrusif; (*b*) *Geol:* **i. rocks,** roches intrusives, d'intrusion.

intrusively |in'tru:sivli|, *adv.* importunément; en importun.

intrusiveness |in'tru:sivnis|, *s.* caractère importun, indiscret; indiscrétion *f*; importunité *f*.

intrust |in'trʌst|, *v.tr.* (= ENTRUST) charger (qn d'une tâche, etc.); confier (un secret, un enfant, etc., à qn); charger (qn de s'occuper de qch.); remettre (en confiance) (de l'argent à qn).

intubate |'intjubeit|, *v.tr. Surg: Vet:* intuber (le larynx, etc.).

intubation |intju'beiʃ(ə)n|, *s. Surg: Vet:* intubation *f*, tubage *m* (du larynx, etc.).

intuition |intju(:)'iʃ(ə)n|, *s.* (*a*) intuition *f*; **to have an i. of sth.,** avoir l'intuition de qch.; **to know sth. by i.,** savoir qch. par intuition; (*b*) *Theol:* science infuse.

intuitional |intju(:)'iʃən(ə)l|, *a.* intuitif.

intuition(al)ism |intju(:)'iʃən(əl)izm|, *s.* intuitionnisme *m*.

intuition(al)ist |intju(:)'iʃən(əl)ist|, *s.* intuitionniste *mf*.

intuitive |in'tju:itiv|, *a.* intuitif; (*a*) **i. truth,** vérité intuitive; **i. method,** méthode intuitive; **i. ideas,** idées *f* autodidactes; **i. knowledge,** connaissances intuitives, infuses. (*b*) (*of pers.*) intuitif.

intuitively |in'tju:itivli|, *adv.* intuitivement, par intuition.

intumesce |intju(:)'mes|, *v.i. Med:* s'enfler, se boursoufler, se gonfler.

intumescence |intju(:)'mesəns|, *s.* intumescence *f* (de la rate, etc.); enflure *f*; boursouflure *f*.

intumescent |intju(:)'mesənt|, *a.* intumescent; tuméfié; boursouflé; enflé.

inturned |'intə:nd|, *a.* tourné en dedans; *Med:* (*of club-foot*) varus, *f.* vara.

intussusception |intəssə'sepʃ(ə)n|, *s.* 1. *Biol:* intussusception *f*. 2. *Med:* intussusception, invagination *f* (de l'intestin).

inula |'injulə|, *s. Bot:* inule *f*, inula *f*, au(l)née *f*.

inulase |'injuleis|, *s. Bio-Ch:* inulase *f*.

inulin |'injulin|, *s. Ch:* inuline *f*.

inunction |in'ʌŋkʃ(ə)n|, *s.* 1. *Ecc:* onction *f*. 2. mise *f* d'un onguent, de l'huile (**of a wound,** sur une plaie).

inundate |'inʌndeit|, *v.tr.* inonder (**with,** de); **to be inundated with letters, requests,** être débordé de lettres, de requêtes.

inundation |inʌn'deiʃ(ə)n|, *s.* inondation *f*; débordement *m* (d'eau).

inurbane |inə:'bein|, *a.* peu courtois; incivil.

inurbanity |inə:'bæniti|, *s.* manque *m* de courtoisie, d'urbanité; incivilité *f*.

inure |i'njuər|. 1. *v.tr.* accoutumer, habituer, rompre, endurcir, aguerrir (**to,** à); **to i. oneself to fatigue,** se rompre, s'endurcir, à la fatigue; **inured to hardships, to fatigue,** habitué aux privations; dur à la fatigue; **to become inured to ridicule,** s'aguerrir au ridicule. 2. *v.i.* (*a*) *Jur:* (*of law, etc.*) entrer en vigueur; (*b*) **the profits i. to the benefit of members,** les profits reviennent aux membres.

inurement |i'njuəmənt|, *s.* aguerrissement *m*, endurcissement *m* (**to,** à); accoutumance *f* (à l'opium, etc.); habitude *f* (de l'opium, etc.).

inuring |i'njuəriŋ|, *s.* 1. aguerrissement *m* (**to,** à). 2. *Jur:* mise *f* en vigueur (d'une loi, etc.).

invade |in'veid|, *v.tr.* 1. (*a*) envahir; faire une invasion dans (un pays, etc.); (*b*) **to i. s.o.'s house,** faire invasion chez qn; **to i. s.o.'s privacy,** violer la retraite de qn; troubler l'intimité de qn. 2. empiéter sur (les droits de qn); porter atteinte à (un privilège).

invader |in'veidər|, *s.* 1. envahisseur *m*. 2. transgresseur *m* (d'un droit).

invading[1] |in'veidiŋ|, *a.* envahissant; **i. army,** armée envahissante, d'invasion.

invading[2], *s.* 1. envahissement *m*, invasion *f*. 2. empiétement *m* (**of a right,** d'un droit).

invaginate[1] |in'vædʒineit|. 1. *v.tr.* (*a*) engainer; (*b*) *Med: etc:* invaginer. 2. *v.i. Med: Biol:* (*of bowl, membrane*) s'invaginer.

invaginate[2], **invaginated** |in'vædʒineitid|, *a. Med: etc:* invaginé.

invagination [invædʒi'neiʃ(ə)n], *s. Biol: Med:* invagination *f*.

invalid[1] |in'vælid|, *a.* (*a*) *Jur:* (mariage *m*) invalide, non valide; (clause) non-valable; (décision) nulle et non avenue, nulle et de nul effet, nulle et sans effet; **i. assignment,** cession atteinte de nullité, qui devient nulle; **i. letter of credit,** lettre de crédit épuisée, périmée; (*b*) (*of argument, etc.*) peu valable; *Cmptr:* (*of address, code*) erroné, invalide.

invalid[2] |'invəli(:)d|. 1. *a. & s.* (*suffering from illness*) malade (*mf*); (*from infirmity or disability*) infirme (*mf*); (*from ill health*) valétudinaire (*mf*); **hopeless, complete, i.,** invalide impotent, grand invalide; **how are the invalids?** comment se portent les malades? **she has an i. sister,** elle a une sœur (i) infirme, (ii) d'une santé délicate, valétudinaire; **i. chair,** (i) fauteuil *m* de malade; (ii) voiture *f* d'infirme. 2. *s. Mil: etc:* (*disabled man*) invalide *m*.

invalid[3] |'invəli:d|. 1. *v.tr.* (*a*) rendre malade, infirme; **wound which invalided me for several months,** blessure qui me mit hors de combat pendant plusieurs mois; **invalided for life,** infirme pour la vie; (*b*) *Mil:* **to i. a man out of the army,** mettre un homme à la réforme, réformer un homme; **he was invalided home,** il fut renvoyé dans ses foyers pour cause de maladie. 2. *v.i. Mil: A:* (*a*) se faire porter malade; (*b*) être réformé.

invalidate |in'vælideit|, *v.tr. Jur:* 1. invalider, rendre nul (un testament); vicier (un acte, un contrat). 2. casser, infirmer (un jugement).

invalidating |in'vælideitiŋ|, *a. Jur:* infirmatif.

invalidation |invæli'deiʃ(ə)n|, *s. Jur:* 1. invalidation *f* (d'un document, d'un contrat). 2. infirmation *f*, cassation *f* (d'un jugement).

invalidism |'invəli(:)dizm|, *s.* valétudinarisme *m*; invalidité *f*.

invalidity |invə'liditi|, *s.* 1. invalidité *f* (d'un passeport, d'un contrat, etc.). 2. = INVALIDISM.

invalidly |in'vælidli|, *adv.* invalidement; sans validité; illégalement.

invaluable |in'væljuəbl|, *a.* inestimable; (trésor) d'un prix incalculable; (aide) impayable; **it's i.,** cela ne se paie pas; c'est inestimable, inappréciable.

invaluableness |in'væljuəb(ə)lnis|, *s.* valeur *f* inestimable, incalculable.

invaluably |in'væljuəbli|, *adv.* **i. precious,** d'une valeur inestimable.

invar |'invɑ:r|, *s. Metall:* invar *m*; **i. steel, i. tape, i. wire,** acier *m*, ruban *m*, fil *m*, invar *inv.*

invariability |invεəriə'biliti|, **invariableness** |in'vεəriəblnis|, *s.* invariabilité *f*.

invariable |in'vεəriəbl|, *a.* invariable; *Gram:* **i. particle,** particule *f* invariable.

invariance |in'vεəriəns|, *s. Mth:* invariance *f*.

invariant |in'vεəriənt|. 1. *a. & s. Mth:* invariant (*m*). 2. *a. Ph: Ch:* (système) invariant, nullivariant.

invasion |in'veiʒ(ə)n|, *s.* 1. (*a*) invasion *f*, envahissement *m*; (*b*) invasion; **the i. period falls later,** la période des invasions vient plus tard; **these invasions of my privacy, of my sanctum,** ces intrusions *f* dans mon intimité; ces violations *f* de ma retraite. 2. *Med:* invasion, début *m* (d'une maladie); **i. stage (of an illness),** période *f* d'invasion (d'une maladie). 3. **i. of s.o.'s rights,** violation des droits, empiètement *m* sur les droits, atteinte *f* aux droits, de qn.

invasive |in'veisiv|, *a.* envahissant; **i. war,** guerre *f* d'invasion.

invected |in'vektid|, *a. Her:* cannelé.

invective |in'vektiv|, *s.* invective *f*; **a torrent of invective(s),** un flot d'invectives, d'injures; une bordée d'injures; **past master of i.,** passé maître en matière d'invective.

inveigh |in'vei|, *v.i.* invectiver, déclamer, tonner, fulminer (**against,** contre); **to i. against the weather,** maudire le mauvais temps; **to be for ever inveighing against s.o.,** être perpétuellement déchaîné contre qn.

inveigle |in'veigl, -'vi:-|, *v.tr.* attirer, séduire, leurrer, enjôler (qn); **to i. s.o. into a place, into doing sth.,** attirer, entraîner, qn dans un endroit; entraîner, amener, qn à faire qch.; **to become inveigled in politics,** se laisser entraîner dans la politique.

inveiglement [in'veiglmənt, -'vi:-], *s.* 1. séduction *f*, enjôlement *m*. 2. leurre *m*, appât *m*, séduction; **he was proof against all inveiglements,** il a résisté à toutes les séductions, à tous les leurres; rien n'a pu le séduire.

inveigler |in'veiglər, -'vi:-|, *s.* séducteur, -trice; enjôleur, -euse; *Jur:* captateur, -trice.

inveigling |in'veigliŋ, -'vi:-|, *s.* séduction *f*, enjôlement *m*.

invent |in'vent|, *v.tr.* inventer (une machine, une histoire, etc.); **recently invented process,** procédé *m* d'invention récente; **to i. a plausible explanation for sth.,** inventer une explication vraisemblable de qch.

invention |in'venʃ(ə)n|, *s.* 1. invention *f* (d'une machine, d'une histoire, etc.); **he told me a story of his own i.,** il m'a raconté une histoire de son cru. 2. (*a*) chose inventée; invention; **a most useful i.,** une invention des plus utiles; (*b*) invention, mensonge *m*; **this is pure i.,** c'est une pure invention; c'est une histoire inventée de toutes pièces; (*c*) *Mus:* invention. 3. *A:* découverte *f*, invention (de reliques, etc.); *still used in Ecc:* **the I. of the Cross,** (la fête de) l'Invention de la (Sainte) Croix.

inventive |in'ventiv|, *a.* (esprit) inventif, trouveur.

inventiveness |in'ventivnis|, *s.* fécondité *f* d'invention; don *m* d'invention; inventivité *f*.

inventor |in'ventər|, *s.* inventeur, -trice.

inventorize |in'ventəraiz|, *v.tr.* inventorier (des marchandises); *v.i.* faire un inventaire; faire l'inventaire.

inventory[1] |'invənt(ə)ri|, *s.* 1. *Com:* inventaire *m*; **to take, draw up, an i.,** faire, dresser, un inventaire; **i. of fixtures,** état *m* des lieux; **i. book,** livre *m* d'inventaires; *Book-k:* **book i.,** inventaire comptable; **ingoing i.,** inventaire d'entrée (dans un immeuble); **outgoing i.,** inventaire de sortie (d'un immeuble); **i. with valuation,** inventaire avec prisée; *Nau:* **ship's i.,** inventaire de bord. 2. *NAm:* (*a*) stocks(s) *m*(*pl*); réserves *fpl*; **i. management, control,** gestion *f* des stocks, du stock; (*b*) (établissement *m*, levée *f*, d')inventaire.

inventory[2], *v.tr.* inventorier (les biens de qn); dresser l'inventaire (des biens de qn); *with passive force:* **furniture that inventories at £1000,** meubles dont l'inventaire se monte à £1000.

Inverness |invə'nes|. *Pr.n. Geog:* Inverness; *Cost: O:* **I. cloak, overcoat,** manteau *m* à pèlerine détachable; **I. cape,** macfarlane *m*.

inverse [in'və:s|. 1. *a.* inverse; **i. process,** processus *m* inverse; **in i. order,** en sens inverse; *Navy:* en ordre (de ligne) renversé; **i. correlation,** corrélation négative; *Mth:* **i. function,** fonction *f* inverse; **i. ratio,** raison *f* inverse; rapport *m* réciproque; **in i. ratio, proportion,** en raison, proportion, inverse (**to,** de); **i. square law,** loi *f* de l'inverse carré; *El:* **i. current,** courant *m* inverse; **i. coupling, feedback,** contre-réaction *f*, *pl.* contre réactions; réaction négative. 2. *s.* (*a*) inverse *m*, contraire *m* (**of,** de); (*b*) *Log: Mth:* inverse *f*.

inversely |in'və:sli|, *adv.* inversement; **i. proportional,** inversement proportionnel (**to,** à); **when y varies i. as x,** lorsque y varie en raison inverse de x.

inversion |in'və:ʃ(ə)n|, *s.* 1. renversement *m* (d'une image, d'une fraction, de l'utérus, etc.); *Mus:* **i. of a chord,** (i) renversement d'un accord; (ii) accord dérivé; *Geol:* **i. of a stratum,** déversement *m*, renversement, d'une couche; **i. of relief,** inversion *f* de relief; *Meteor:* **temperature i.,** inversion de température. 2. inversion (des mots d'une phrase, etc.); *Rh:* hyperbate *f*; *Log:* renversement (d'une proposition); *Mth:* **i. of an integral,** inversion d'une intégrale; *El:* **phase i.,** inversion de phase; **polarity i.,** inversion des pôles. 3. *Biol:* **chromosome i.,** inversion chromosomique. 4. *Ch:* inversion (du sucre, des hydrates de carbone). 5. *Psy:* **sexual i.,** inversion sexuelle; homosexualité *f*.

invert[1] |'invə:t|. 1. *a. & s.* **i. (sugar),** sucre inverti; sucrase *f*; invertase *f*; invertine *f*. 2. *s. Hyd.E:* radier *m* (d'un sas d'écluse, etc.). 3. *s. Psy:* inverti, -ie.

invert[2] |in'və:t|, *v.tr.* 1. renverser, retourner (un objet) (le haut en bas); *Mus:* **to i. a chord, an interval,** renverser un accord, un intervalle. 2. (*a*) invertir, intervertir, renverser (l'ordre, les positions); *Gram:* inverser (le sujet, etc.); apporter une inversion à (une phrase); (*b*) *Ch: Ph:* invertir (la lumière polarisée, le sucre). 3. retourner; mettre à l'envers; *Med:* **to i. the stomach,** vider l'estomac à l'aide d'un émétique.

invertase |in'və:teis|, *s. Bio-Ch:* invertase *f*; invertine *f*; saccharase *f*.

Invertebrata |invə:ti'breitə|, *s.pl. Z:* invertébrés *m*.

invertebrate |in'və:tibrət|. 1. *a.* (*a*) invertébré; (*b*) *F:* (*of pers.*) faible, flasque, mollasse. 2. *s.* (*a*) *Z:* invertébré *m*; (*b*) *F:* personne *f* de faible caractère; poule mouillée; nouille *f*.

inverted |in'və:tid|, *a.* 1. (*a*) inversé, renversé; **i. (gas) burner, mantle,** bec (de gaz), manchon, renversé; *Av:* **i. flight,** vol renversé, sur le dos; *I.C.E:* **i. (cylinder) engine,** moteur inversé, à cylindres inversés; *Cmptr:*

etc: **i. file,** fichier inversé; (*b*) *Dressm:* **i. pleat,** pli inverti, creux; double pli; (*c*) *Mus:* (accord, intervalle) renversé; (*d*) *Geol:* (pli) déversé, renversé; **i. relief,** inversion *f* de relief; (*e*) *Opt:* (image) renversée. **2.** (ordre, siphon) inverse; *Hyd.E:* (accumulateur) de sens contraire. **3.** *Psy:* (instinct) inverti.

inverter |in'vəːtər|, *s. El:* (i) redresseur *m*, convertisseur *m*, de courant; onduleur *m*; (ii) inverseur *m* (de polarité).

invertin |in'vəːtin|, *s. Bio-Ch:* = INVERTASE.

inverting |in'vəːtiŋ|, *s.* **1.** renversement *m* (d'une image, etc.); *Bio-Ch:* **i. enzyme,** invertase *f*, invertine *f*; *Cmptr:* **i. amplifier,** inverseur *m* de signe; *Opt:* **i. telescope,** lunette *f* astronomique. **2.** inversion *f* (d'une phrase). **3.** *Sug.-R:* inversion.

invest |in'vest|, *v.tr.* **1.** revêtir **(with,** de); (*a*) *A:* **to i. oneself in one's coat,** se revêtir, se vêtir, de son habit; (*b*) **to i. oneself in a character,** se mettre dans un rôle; **to i. a subject with interest,** rendre un sujet intéressant. **2.** investir (qn de l'autorité, etc.); **to i. s.o. with an office,** investir qn d'une fonction; pourvoir qn d'une charge; mettre qn en possession d'un emploi; **to i. the management of a bank in s.o.,** confier la direction d'une banque à qn. **3.** *Mil:* investir, cerner, bloquer (une place forte); **to i. a town closely,** serrer une ville de près; **the investing army,** le corps d'investissement. **4.** (*a*) *Fin:* placer, investir (son argent, des fonds); **to i. money,** faire des placements; **to i. money in a business,** mettre de l'argent, placer des fonds, dans un commerce; **to i. one's fortune in life annuities,** placer sa fortune en rentes viagères; **to i. one's money in real estate,** mettre son argent en biens-fonds; **I have invested funds in the scheme,** je suis intéressé à cette opération; **to i. one's money to good account,** faire valoir son argent; **money invested in an annuity,** argent constitué en viager; **capital invested,** mise *f* de fonds; capital engagé, investi; *Ind:* capital d'établissement; *v.i.* **to i. in house property,** faire des placements en immeubles; (*b*) *v.i. F:* **to i. in a new refrigerator,** acheter, se payer, s'offrir, un nouveau réfrigérateur.

investigate |in'vestigeit|, *v.tr.* examiner, étudier, sonder, remuer (une question); **to i. a crime,** faire une enquête sur, informer sur, enquêter sur, un crime; **I wish to i. this personally,** je veux m'en rendre compte par moi-même; **to i. the facts more thoroughly,** revenir avec plus d'attention sur les faits; reprendre les faits de plus haut; *v.i. F:* **I'll go and i.,** j'irai voir ce qui se passe.

investigating[1] |in'vestigeitiŋ|, *a.* (esprit, etc.) investigateur, -trice.

investigating[2], *s.* investigation *f*; recherches *fpl*; **i. committee,** commission *f* d'enquête.

investigation |investi'geiʃ(ə)n|, *s.* investigation *f*; recherches minutieuses; approfondissement *m* **(of,** de); enquête *f* **(of,** sur); **question under i.,** question *f* à l'étude; **preliminary investigations with a view to doing sth.,** études *f* préparatoires en vue de faire qch.; **scientific i.,** enquête scientifique; **analytical i.,** recherche *f* analytique; **accusation that will not bear i.,** accusation *f* insoutenable, qui ne supporte pas l'examen; **on i.,** après recherches; **on further i.,** en poursuivant mes recherches; *Jur:* **i. of a title,** examen *m* des titres (pour établir l'origine de propriété); **i. of a case,** instruction *f* d'un litige, d'un crime; **the police made investigations,** la police a procédé aux constatations, à une enquête.

investigative |in'vestigeitiv|, *a.* investigateur, -trice.

investigator |in'vestigeitər|, *s.* investigateur, -trice; chercheur, -euse; rechercheur, -euse; enquêteur, -euse.

investigatory |investi'geitəri|, *a.* investigateur, -trice.

investing |in'vestiŋ|, *s.* **1.** *Mil:* investissement *m.* **2.** *Fin:* placement *m* (de fonds).

investiture |in'vestitʃər|, *s.* **1.** (*a*) investiture *f* (d'un évêque, etc.); (*b*) remise *f* de décorations; **to hold an i.,** procéder à une remise de décorations. **2.** (*a*) *A: & Lit:* vêtement *m*; revêtement *m*; (*b*) *Z:* revêtement.

investment |in'vestmənt|, *s.* **1.** *Mil:* investissement *m*, cernement *m* (d'une place forte). **2.** (*a*) *Fin:* placement *m* (de fonds); mise *f* de fonds; investissement (des capitaux); **fixed i.,** (montant *m* des) immobilisations *fpl*; **good i.,** placement avantageux; **safe i.,** placement sûr; valeur *f* de tout repos; **long-term, short-t., i.,** placement à long, court, terme; **i. in real estate,** placements, investissements, immobiliers; **investments in securities,** placements en valeurs; **employee i. in the capital of a business,** actionnariat ouvrier; **to make, place, investments,** faire des investissements; **(list of) investments,** portefeuille *m* titres; valeurs en portefeuille; dossier *m*; **i. company,** société *f* de portefeuille, d'investissement, de placement; **i. credit,** crédit d'investissement; **i. market,** marché *m* des capitaux; **i. securities, i. stock,** valeurs en portefeuille, de placement; valeurs classées; (*b*) *Psy:* investissement (dans une activité, etc.). **3.** revêtement *m*; **asbestos i.,** revêtement à l'amiante; *Metall:* **casting i.,** revêtement pour coulée.

investor |in'vestər|, *s.* actionnaire *mf*, investisseur *m*, capitaliste *mf*; **small investors,** petits capitalistes, petits rentiers; l'épargne privée; la petite épargne; **i. in stocks (and shares), in real estate,** acheteur *m* de valeurs, de biens immobiliers.

inveteracy |in'vetərəsi|, *s.* caractère invétéré (d'un mal, etc.).

inveterate |in'vetərət|, *a.* (*a*) (mal, défaut) invétéré, enraciné; (*of disease, bad habit*) **to become i.,** s'invétérer, s'enraciner; (*b*) (ivrogne) invétéré; (fumeur) incorrigible, acharné, enragé; (ennemi) implacable, acharné; (haine) implacable, vivace; **i. gambler,** joueur invétéré; joueur dans l'âme.

inveterately |in'vetərətli|, *adv.* (*a*) dans le fond; foncièrement; (*b*) avec acharnement, opiniâtrement.

invidious |in'vidiəs|, *a.* **1.** haïssable, odieux; **i. task,** tâche ingrate, peu agréable. **2.** (i) qui incite l'envie, la haine; (ii) qui suscite la jalousie; **i. comparison,** comparaison désobligeante.

invidiously |in'vidiəsli|, *adv.* odieusement; de manière à susciter la jalousie; désobligeamment.

invidiousness |in'vidiəsnis|, *s.* caractère *m* haïssable, blessant (de qch.); odieux *m*, injustice *f* (d'une mesure).

invigilate |in'vidʒileit|, *v.i. Sch:* surveiller les candidats (à un examen).

invigilation |invidʒi'leiʃ(ə)n|, *s. Sch:* surveillance *f* (des candidats à un examen).

invigilator |in'vidʒileitər|, *s.* **1.** *Sch:* surveillant, -ante (des candidats à un examen). **2.** *Cmptr:* contrôleur *m* de séquence.

invigorant |in'vigərənt|, *s. Med:* fortifiant *m*, tonique *m.*

invigorate |in'vigəreit|. **1.** *v.tr.* (*a*) fortifier (qn), donner, communiquer, de la vigueur à (qn); (*b*) (*of the air, etc.*) vivifier, tonifier. **2.** *v.i.* (*a*) se fortifier; forcir; (*b*) reprendre ses forces.

invigorating |in'vigəreitiŋ|, *a.* (aliment, etc.) fortifiant; (air, temps, etc.) vivifiant, tonifiant.

invigoration |invigə'reiʃ(ə)n|, *s.* invigoration *f.*

invigorative |in'vigərətiv|, *a.* = INVIGORATING.

invigorator |in'vigəreitər|, *s.* fortifiant *m*, tonifiant *m.*

invincibility |invinsi'biliti|, *s.* invincibilité *f.*

invincible |in'vinsibl|, *a.* invincible.

inviolability |invaiələ'biliti|, **inviolableness** |in'vaiələblnis|, *s.* inviolabilité *f.*

inviolable |in'vaiələbl|, *a.* inviolable.

inviolably |in'vaiələbli|, *adv.* inviolablement.

inviolacy |in'vaiələsi|, **inviolateness** |in'vaiələtnis|, *s.* état inviolé, virginité *f* (d'un lieu sacré, etc.).

inviolate |in'vaiəleit|, *a.* (sanctuaire, secret, mont) inviolé; (mont) vierge; **i. tomb,** tombe qui n'a jamais été profanée; tombe restée intacte.

inviscid |in'visid|, *a.* (fluide) sans viscosité.

invisibility |invizi'biliti|, **invisibleness** |in'vizibəlnis|, *s.* invisibilité *f.*

invisible |in'vizibl|. **1.** *a.* (*a*) invisible; **i. to the naked eye,** invisible, indiscernable, à l'œil nu; **i. darn(ing),** reprise perdue; **i. ink,** encre *f* sympathique; *Pol.Ec:* **i. exports,** exportations *f* invisibles; (*b*) *F:* **when I called she was i.,** quand je me suis présenté chez elle, elle n'était pas visible. **2.** *s.pl. Pol.Ec:* **invisibles,** invisibles *m.*

invisibly |in'vizibli|, *adv.* invisiblement.

invitation |invi'teiʃ(ə)n|, *s.* (*a*) invitation *f* **(to do sth.,** à faire qch.); **to come at s.o.'s i.,** venir sur l'invitation de qn; **i. to lunch, to tea,** invitation à déjeuner, à prendre le thé; **i. card,** billet *m*, lettre *f*, d'invitation; **admission by i. only,** seuls les invités seront admis; *NAm:* **i. tournament,** concours réservé aux participants invités; *Fin:* **i. to the public to subscribe to a loan,** appel *m* au public pour la subscription d'un emprunt; **i. of tenders,** appel d'offres; (*b*) **speech that is an i. to criticism,** discours qui invite à, provoque, appelle, la critique, qui est une invite à la critique.

invitatory |in'vaitətəri|, *a. & s. Ecc:* **the i. (psalm),** l'antienne invitatoire.

invite[1] |in'vait|, *v.tr.* **1.** inviter; convier (des amis à dîner); **to i. s.o. in,** inviter qn à entrer; prier qn d'entrer; **to i. oneself,** venir sans invitation; s'inviter soi-même; **the invited guests,** les invités *m*; (*at table*) les convives *m.* **2.** engager, convier, inviter, appeler **(s.o. to do sth.,** qn à faire qch.); **to i. s.o.'s attention,** solliciter l'attention de qn; **to i. tenders for a bridge,** faire appel d'offres, solliciter des soumissions, pour la construction d'un pont; *Fin:* **to i. shareholders to subscribe the capital,** faire appel aux actionnaires pour souscrire le capital. **3.** provoquer (le danger, le malheur, la critique); **his accent invited laughter,** son accent prêtait à rire; **to i. discussion,** inviter à, appeler, la discussion; **he's inviting trouble,** il fait tout ce qu'il faut pour s'attirer une affaire; il se prépare des ennuis.

invite[2] |'invait|, *s.* **1.** *F:* invitation *f.* **2.** *Fenc:* invite *f.*

invitee |invai'tiː|, *s.* invité, -ée.

inviter |in'vaitər|, *s.* **1.** hôte, hôtesse. **2.** provocateur, -trice (de critiques, rires, etc.).

inviting |in'vaitiŋ|, *a.* invitant, attrayant, tentant; (mets) appétissant, ragoûtant; (dîner) engageant; **not very i.,** peu invitant, peu attrayant; **this armchair looks i.,** ce fauteuil vous tend les bras; **i. gesture,** geste *m* d'encouragement.

invitingly |in'vaitiŋli|, *adv.* d'une manière attrayante, tentante; **the door was i. open,** la porte ouverte invitait à entrer; **he drew up a chair i.,** il approcha une chaise en guise d'invitation.

invocation |invə'keiʃ(ə)n|, *s.* invocation *f*; **the i. of Saints,** l'invocation des Saints; **church under the i. of St Peter,** église *f* sous l'invocation, le vocable, de saint Pierre.

invocatory |in'vɔkətəri|, *a.* (formule, etc.) invocatoire.

invoice[1] |'invɔis|, *s. Com:* facture *f* (de débit); note *f* (de frais); **shipping i.,** facture d'expédition; **i. of origin, original i.,** facture d'origine, facture originale; **to make out an i.,** établir une facture; **as per i.,** suivant la facture; **i. book,** facturier *m*; copie *f* des factures; livre *m* des achats; **i. clerk,** facturier, -ière; **typist i. clerk,** dactylo-facturière *f*, *pl.* dactylos-facturières; **i. price,** prix *m* de facture; **i. work,** travaux *mpl* de facturation.

invoice[2], *v.tr.* facturer (des marchandises).

invoicing |'invɔisiŋ|, *s.* facturation *f* (de marchandises, de frais d'emballage, etc.); **i. machine,** machine *f* à facturer; facturière *f.*

invoke |in'vouk|, *v.tr.* **1.** (*a*) invoquer (Dieu, le nom du Seigneur, la Muse, la mémoire de qn); (*b*) **to i. s.o.'s aid,** appeler qn à son secours; **to i. vengeance on s.o.,** appeler la vengeance sur qn; **to i. a blessing on an undertaking,** demander à Dieu de bénir une entreprise. **2.** évoquer (un esprit) par des incantations; invoquer (un esprit). **3.** *Cmptr:* appeler (un programme, etc.). **4.** *Jur:* **documents invoked in a suit,** documents invoqués dans un litige.

invoker |in'voukər|, *s.* invocateur, -trice.

invoking |in'voukiŋ|, *s.* invocation *f.*

involucel |in'vɔljusel|, *s. Bot:* involucelle *m.*

involucellate |invɔlju'seleit|, *a. Bot:* involucellé.

involucral |invə'ljuːkrəl|, *a. Bot:* involucral, -aux.

involucrate |invə'ljuːkreit|, *a. Bot:* involucré.

involucre |'invəljuːkər|, *s.* **1.** *Anat:* enveloppe membraneuse (d'un organe). **2.** *Bot:* involucre *m*; collerette *f* (d'ombellifère); fane *f* (de renoncule).

involucrum, *pl.* **-a** |invə'ljuːkrəm, -ə|, *s. Anat:* = INVOLUCRE 1.

involuntarily |in'vɔlənt(ə)rili|, *adv.* involontairement.

involuntariness |in'vɔlənt(ə)rinis|, *s.* caractère *m*, nature *f*, involontaire (d'un mouvement, etc.).

involuntary |in'vɔlənt(ə)ri|, *a.* involontaire; *Anat:* **i. muscle,** muscle *m* lisse.

involute[1] |'invəluːt|. **1.** *a.* (*a*) spiral, -aux, en spirale; **i. spring,** (ressort) spiral (*m*); *Mec.E:* **i. spline,** cannelure *f* femelle; (*b*) *Bot:* **i. leaf,** feuille involutée, involutive; (*c*) *Geom: Mec.E:* (arc *m*) de développante; (engrenage *m*) à développante; **a 15° i. system,** un tracé en développant à 15°. **2.** *s. Geom: Mec.E:* développante *f*; **i. of a circle,** développante de cercle.

involute[2], *v.i. Med:* régresser.

involuted |'invəluːtid|, *a. Bot:* (*of leaf*) involuté, involutif.

involution |invə'luːʃ(ə)n|, *s.* **1.** (*a*) complication *f*; tours *mpl* et détours; ambages *mpl*, tortuosité *f*; (*b*) enchevêtrement *m*, embrouillement *m*; embarras *m.* **2.** *Nat.Hist:* involution *f* (d'une feuille, etc.). **3.** (*a*) *Mth:* **points in i.,** points *m* en involution; (*b*) *Mth:* élévation *f* à une puissance donnée d'un nombre quelconque, réel ou imaginaire. **4.** (*a*) involution (sénile, etc.); (*b*) *Med:* **i. of the womb,** involution utérine. **5.** *Biol:* involution, dégénérescence *f*; **i. form,** forme régressive; **i. period,** diapause *f* (d'une graine).

involutional |invə'luːʃ(ə)n(ə)l|, *a. Psy:* **i. melancholia, psychosis,** psychose *f* d'involution.

involutive |invə'luːtiv|, *a.* involutif.

involve |in'vɔlv|, *v.tr.* **1.** (*a*) *Lit:* envelopper, entortiller (in, dans); (*b*) *A: & Lit:* enrouler, replier (en spirale); (*c*) **to get involved with a rope,** s'empêtrer, s'empêcher, dans un cordage; (*d*) compliquer, entortiller (un récit); **to become involved in one's speech,** s'embrouiller (dans son discours). **2.** (*a*) **to i. s.o. in a quarrel,** engager qn dans une querelle; mêler qn à, dans, une querelle; **this involved him in great difficulties,** cela lui a attiré, l'a plongé dans, de grandes difficultés; **to i. s.o. in a charge, in a crime,** impliquer qn dans une accusation, dans un crime; **he involved his friend in his ruin,** il entraîna son ami dans sa ruine; **to i. oneself in trouble,** se créer des ennuis; *F:* se mettre dans le pétrin; **to i. oneself in debt,** s'endetter; (*b*) **to be involved in sth.,** être entraîné, enveloppé, dans qch.; **to be involved in a failure,** être enveloppé, pris, entraîné, dans une faillite; **we were involved in his disgrace,** sa honte a rejailli sur nous; **he is involved in a bad business,** il est mêlé dans une mauvaise affaire; **he is involved in the plot,** il est compromis, il a trempé, dans le complot; **the vehicle involved,** le véhicule impliqué, en cause (dans l'accident); **his honour is involved,** son honneur est engagé; **are your interests involved?** est-ce que cela touche, concerne, vos intérêts? **the forces involved,** les forces *f* en jeu; **a theory that involves, involving, gravitation,** une théorie qui fait intervenir la gravitation; (*c*) **she was involved in her knitting and did not reply,** préoccupée, absorbée, par son tricotage, elle n'a pas répondu; **to become involved in charitable work,** s'adonner aux œuvres de bienfaisance; **I cannot remain impartial because I am emotionally involved,** je ne peux rester impartial parce que cela me concerne de trop près, me touche trop; (*d*) **he got involved with his friend's wife,** il a eu une affaire avec la femme de son ami. **3.** (*include, entail*) comporter, impliquer, comprendre, entraîner; **to i. much expense,** nécessiter, entraîner, de grands frais; **expenses involved,** dépenses *f* à prévoir; **questions involved in a transaction,** questions liées à une transaction; **difficulties involved in a theory,** difficultés impliquées dans une théorie; **the difficulties which this would i.,** les difficultés que cela comporterait; **it involves trouble,** cela ne va pas sans peine; **it would i. living in London,** cela nécessiterait que j'aille vivre à Londres. **4.** *Mth: A:* élever (un nombre) à une puissance donnée.

involved [in'vɔlvd], *a.* **1.** (*a*) (style, discours) embrouillé, entortillé, embarrassé, compliqué, filandreux, touffu; (*b*) (*of pers.*) fermé, secret. **2.** (bien, domaine) grevé de dettes; *A:* **to be in i. circumstances,** être dans la gêne; faire de mauvaises affaires.

involvement [in'vɔlvmənt], *s.* **1.** (*a*) mise *f* en jeu (de forces, etc.); (*b*) *Med:* **meningeal i.,** complication méningée. **2.** implication *f*, *Pej:* empêtrement *m* (de qn dans une affaire); **on account of my i. with him,** parce que j'étais lié avec lui. **3.** *A:* embarras *m* pécuniaires. **4.** confusion *f*, imbroglio *m*.

invulnerability [invʌlnərə'biliti], *s.* invulnérabilité *f*.

invulnerable [in'vʌlnərəbl], *a.* (*of pers.*) invulnérable; (*of position, etc.*) inattaquable, invincible.

invulnerably [in'vʌlnərəbli], *adv.* invinciblement.

invultuation [invʌltju'eiʃ(ə)n], *s.* envoûtement *m*.

inwall [in'wɔ:l], *v.tr. NAm:* entourer d'un mur.

inward ['inwəd]. **1.** *a.* (*a*) intérieur; interne; **i. bleeding,** hémorragie *f* interne; **longing for i. peace,** soupirant la paix intérieure, soupirant la paix dans son for intérieur; (*b*) (orienté, se dirigeant) vers l'intérieur; d'entrée; (i) *Mch:* **i.-flow turbine,** turbine *f* centripète; (ii) **i. traffic of a port,** trafic *m* d'entrée, mouvement *m* à l'entrée (d'un port); **i. charges,** frais *m* à l'entrée (d'un navire dans un port); **i. bill of lading,** connaissement *m* d'entrée; **i. manifest,** manifeste *m* d'entrée; *Book-k:* **i. payment,** paiement reçu; encaissement *m*. **2.** *s.pl. P:* **inwards** ['inədz], entrailles *f*, intestins *m*, viscères *m*; **pain in one's inwards,** mal *m* au ventre. **3.** *adv.* = INWARDS; **i. opening door,** porte qui s'ouvre vers l'intérieur.

inwardly ['inwədli], *adv.* en dedans, intérieurement; **to bleed i.,** avoir une hémorragie interne; **I was i. pleased,** intérieurement, dans mon for intérieur, j'étais content; **he was not so calm i.,** il n'était pas si calme en dedans.

inwardness ['inwədnis], *s.* **1.** caractère intérieur, essence *f*, signification *f* intime (de qch.); **the true i. of a remark,** le sens profond d'une observation. **2.** spiritualité *f*; nature spirituelle.

inwards ['inwədz], *adv.* **1.** (*a*) vers l'intérieur; en dedans; (*b*) *Com: Nau:* pour l'importation; **clearance i.,** (i) déclaration *f*, (ii) permis *m*, d'entrée. **2.** dans l'âme, en dedans de nous; intérieurement.

inweave ['in'wi:v], *v.tr.* (**inwove** ['in'wouv]; **inwoven** ['in'wouvən]) **to i. a pattern into a fabric,** tisser un dessin dans une étoffe; **to i. a fabric with gold thread,** brocher une étoffe de fils d'or.

inworker ['inwɔ:kər], *s.* ouvrier, -ière, qui travaille à la fabrique, à l'usine.

inwrought ['in'rɔ:t], *a.* (*of fabric, design*) broché, incrusté, ouvragé (**with,** de); **patter i.** [in'rɔ:t] **into a fabric,** dessin ouvragé dans une étoffe; *A:* **mantle i. with beads,** manteau tissé de perles.

inyoite ['injouait], *s. Miner:* inyoite *f*.

iodargyrite [aiou'da:dʒirait], *s. Miner:* iodargyrite *f*, iodite *f*, iodyrite *f*.

iodate[1] ['aiədeit], *s. Ch:* iodate *m*; **potassium i.,** iodate de potasse.

iodate[2], *v.tr. Med: Phot:* (*with iodine*) ioder; (*with iodide*) iodurer.

iodation [aiə'deiʃ(ə)n], *s. Med: Phot:* ioduration *f*.

iodhydrate [aiəd'haidreit], *s. Ch:* iodhydrate *m*.

iodhydric [aiəd'haidrik], *a. Ch:* iodhydrique.

iodhydrin [aiəd'haidrin], *s. Ch:* iodhydrine *f*.

iodic [ai'ɔdik], *a. Ch.* (acide, etc.) iodique.

iodide ['aiədaid], *s. Ch:* iodure *m* (d'argent, etc.); **mercuric i.,** iodure de mercure.

iodiferous [aiə'difərəs], *a.* iodifère.

iodinate ['aiədineit], *v.tr. Ch:* iodurer.

iodine ['aiədi:n], *s. Ch:* iode *m*; *Pharm:* (**tincture of**) **i.,** teinture *f* d'iode; **i. water,** eau iodée; **i. liniment,** liniment ioduré; *Ch:* **i. value, number,** indice *m* d'iode; *Med:* **radio i.,** iode 131.

iodipin [ai'ɔdipin], *s. Pharm:* iodipine *f*.

iodism ['aiədizm], *s. Med:* iodisme *m*.

iodite ['aiədait], *s. Miner:* iodite *f*, iodyrite *f*, iodargyrite *f*.

iodization [aiədai'zeiʃ(ə)n], *s. Med: Phot:* ioduration *f*.

iodize ['aiədaiz], *v.tr. Med: Phot:* (*with iodine*) ioder; (*with iodide*) iodurer.

iodobenzene [aiədou'benzi:n], *s. Ch:* iodobenzène *m*.

iodobromite [aiədou'broumait], *s. Miner:* iodobromite *f*.

iodoform [ai'ɔdoufɔ:m], *s. Ch: Pharm:* iodoforme *m*; **i. gauze,** gaze (à l')iodoforme, iodoformée; **i. powder, pill,** poudre, pilule, iodoformée.

iodoformized [ai'ɔdoufɔ:maizd], *a.* (*of gauze, etc.*) iodoformé.

iodohydrin [aiədou'haidrin], *s. Ch:* iodhydrine *f*.

iodomercurate [aiədou'mə:kjureit], *s. Ch:* iodomercurate *m*.

iodometric [aiədou'metrik], *a. Ch:* iodométrique.

iodometry [aiə'dɔmitri], *s. Ch:* iodométrie *f*.

iodonium [aiə'douniəm], *s. Ch:* iodonium *m*.

iodophilia [aiədou'filiə], *s. Med:* iodophilie *f*.

iodoso- [aiə'dousou], *comb.fm.* iodoso-.

iodosobenzene [aiə'dousou'benzi:n], *s. Ch:* iodosobenzène *m*.

iodotannic [aiədou'tænik], *a. Pharm:* iodotannique.

iodothyrin [aiədou'θairin], *s. Med:* iodothyrine *f*.

iodous ['aiədəs], *a. Ch:* (acide) iodeux.

iodyrite [ai'ɔdirait], *s. Miner:* iodargyrite *f*, iodite *f*, iodyrite *f*.

iolite ['aiəlait], *s. Miner:* iolite *f*.

ion ['aiən], *s. Ph: Ch: El.* ion *m*; (*a*) **hydrogen i.,** ion d'hydrogène; **primary, secondary, i.,** ion primaire, secondaire; **gaseous i.,** ion gazeux; **lattice i.,** ion du réseau; (*b*) *attrib.* **i. accelerator,** accélérateur *m* d'ions; **i. beam,** faisceau *m* ionique; **i. bombardment,** bombardement *m* ionique; **i. burn,** tache *f* ionique; **i. chamber,** chambre *f* d'ionisation; **i. cloud,** nuage *m* d'ions; **i. cluster,** essaim *m*, groupe *m*, d'ions; **i. counter,** compteur *m* d'ions; **i. current,** courant *m* ionique; **i. density,** densité *f* ionique; **i. emission,** émission *f* d'ions; **i. engine,** moteur *m* ionique; **i. exchange,** échange *m* d'ions; **i. exchanger,** échangeur *m* d'ions; **i. flow,** flux *m* ionique; **i. gun,** canon *m* ionique; **i. impact,** choc *m* d'ions; **i. microscope,** microscope *m* ionique; **i. migration,** migration *f* d'ions; **i. mobility,** mobilité *f* ionique; **i. pair,** paire *f* d'ions; **i.(-pair) yield,** rendement *m* en paires d'ions; **i. propulsion,** propulsion *f* ionique; **i. rocket,** moteur-fusée *m* (*pl.* moteurs-fusées) ionique; **i. source,** source *f* d'ions; **i. spectrum,** spectre *m* ionique; **i. spot,** tache *f* ionique; **i. strength,** intensité *f* ionique; **i. trap,** piège *m* à ions; **i. tube,** tube *m* ionique.

Ionia [ai'ounjə]. *Pr.n. A.Geog:* Ionie *f*.

Ionian [ai'ounjən]. **1.** *a. Geog:* ionien; **the I. Sea,** la mer Ionienne; *Mus:* **I. mode,** mode ionien; *Phil:* **I. school,** école ionienne. **2.** *s. Geog:* Ionien, -ienne.

Ionic[1] [ai'ɔnik]. **1.** *a.* (*a*) *Arch: Pros:* (ordre, vers) ionique; (*b*) *Ling: Mus:* (dialecte, mode) ionien. **2.** *s.* (*a*) *Ling:* le dialecte ionien; (*b*) *Pros:* pied *m* ionique; vers *m* ionique.

ionic[2], *a. Ph: Ch: El:* (*of* (i) *gas, crystal, etc.,* (ii) *conductivity, mobility, propulsion, tube, etc.*) ionique; **i. bonds, bindings, links,** liens *m* ioniques; **i. heating,** chauffage *m* (par bombardement) ionique; **i. quantimeter,** dosimètre *m* d'ions.

ionium [ai'ouniəm], *s. Atom.Ph:* ionium *m*.

ionizable ['aiənaizəbl], *a.* ionisable.

ionization [aiənai'zeiʃ(ə)n], *s.* **1.** *Ph: El:* ionisation *f*; **collision, impact, i.,** ionisation par choc; **radiation i.,** ionisation par rayonnement; **thermal i.,** ionisation (d'origine) thermique; **columnar i.,** ionisation colonnaire; **primary, secondary, i.,** ionisation primaire, secondaire; **volume i.,** ionisation volumétrique; **i. current,** courant *m* d'ionisation; **i. potential,** potentiel *m* d'ionisation; **i. chamber,** chambre *f* d'ionisation; **capacitor i. chamber,** chambre d'ionisation à condensateur; **fission i. chamber,** chambre d'ionisation à fission; **pulse i. chamber,** chambre d'ionisation à impulsions; **gas-flow i. chamber,** chambre d'ionisation à courant gazeux; **liquid-wall i. chamber,** chambre d'ionisation à paroi liquide; **wall-less i. chamber,** chambre d'ionisation sans paroi; **i. counter,** compteur *m* à ionisation; **i. gauge, manometer,** jauge *f*, manomètre *m*, à ionisation. **2.** *Med:* (traitement *m* par) ionisation.

ionize ['aiənaiz]. *Ph: El:* **1.** *v.tr.* ioniser (l'air, un gaz). **2.** *v.i.* (*of acid, etc.*) s'ioniser.

ionized ['aiənaizd], *a.* (atome, gaz, etc.) ionisé; **i.-gas anemometer,** anémomètre *m* à ionisation.

ionizer ['aiənaizər], *s. Ph: El:* ionisant *m*, ionisateur *m*.

ionizing[1] ['aiənaiziŋ], *a.* (*of particle, radiation, etc.*) ionisant.

ionizing[2], *s. Ph: El:* ionisation *f* (d'un gaz, etc.); **i. potential,** potentiel *m* d'ionisation.

ionogen [ai'ɔnədʒən], *s. El:* électrolyte *m*.

ionometer [aiə'nɔmitər], *s. Ph:* ionomètre *m*.

ionometric [aiənə'metrik], *a.* ionométrique.

Ionone ['aiənoun], *s. R.t.m: Toil:* Ionone *f*.

ionophoresis, *pl.* **-eses** [aiənoufɔ'ri:sis, -i:si:z], *s. Ph:* électrophorèse *f*.

ionosphere [ai'ɔnəsfiər], *s.* ionosphère *f*; **i. layer,** couche *f* ionosphérique; **i. storm,** tempête *f* ionosphérique.

ionospheric [aiənou'sferik], *a.* (onde, perturbation, etc.) ionosphérique; **i. propagation,** propagation *f* dans l'ionosphère, dans l'atmosphère; **i. recorder,** enregistreur *m* ionosphérique.

iontophoresis, *pl.* **-eses** [aiɔntoufɔ'ri:sis, -i:si:z], *s. Med:* ionophorèse *f*.

iota [ai'outə], *s.* **1.** *Gr.Alph:* iota *m*; **i. subscript,** iota souscrit. **2.** iota, rien *m*; **we will not yield one i. of our privileges,** nous ne céderons pas le moindre petit privilège, pas un iota de nos privilèges.

iotacism [ai'outəsizm], *s. Ling:* iotacisme *m*.

IOU, *pl.* **IOU's** ['aiou'ju:, -ju:z], *s.* (**I owe you**) reconnaissance *f* (de dette); **I'll give you an IOU,** je vais vous faire un petit billet.

Iowan ['aiouən], *a. & s. Geog:* (habitant, -ante, originaire) de l'Iowa.

ipecacuanha [ipikækju'ænə], *F:* **ipecac** ['ipikæk], *s. Bot: Pharm:* ipécacuana *m*; *F:* ipéca *m*.

Iphigenia [ifidʒi'naiə], *Pr.n.f.* Iphigénie.

ipomoea [ipə'miə], *s. Bot:* ipomée *f*.

iproniazid [iprə'naiəzid], *s. Pharm:* iproniazide *f*.

ipseity ['ipsi:iti], *s. Phil:* ipséité *f*.

irade [i'rɑ:dei], *s. Hist:* iradé *m*.

Irak [i'rɑ:k]. *Pr.n. Geog:* Irak *m*.

Iraki [i'rɑ:ki], **Irakian** [i'rɑ:kiən]. **1.** *a.* (*a*) *Geog:* irakien; (*b*) *Ling:* relatif à, caractéristique de, l'irakien. **2.** *s.* (*a*) *Geog:* Irakien, -ienne; (*b*) *Ling:* irakien.

Iran [i'rɑ:n]. *Pr.n. Geog:* Iran *m*.

Irani [i'reini], **Iranian** [i'reinjən]. **1.** *a. Geog:* iranien. **2.** *s.* (*a*) *Geog:* Iranien, -ienne; (*b*) *Ling:* iranien.

Iraq [i'rɑ:k]. *Pr.n. Geog:* Irak *m*.

Iraqi [i'rɑ:ki], **Iraqian** [i'rɑ:kiən], *a. & s.* = IRAKI.

irascibility [iræsi'biliti], *s.* irascibilité *f*; tempérament *m* colérique, irritable.

irascible [i'ræsibl], *a.* (homme) irascible, coléreux; (tempérament) colérique.

irate [ai'reit], *a.* courroucé, en colère, furieux, irrité.

irately [ai'reitli], *adv.* avec colère, avec courroux; d'un ton irrité.

Irawad(d)i (the) [ði:i:rə'wɔdi]. *Pr.n. Geog:* l'Iraouaddy *m*.

ire ['aiər], *s. A: & Lit:* courroux *m*, colère *f*; *A:* ire *f* (des dieux).

ireful ['aiəful], *a. A: & Lit:* courroucé; (regard) plein de colère, irrité.

irefully ['aiəfuli], *adv. A: & Lit:* avec colère, avec courroux; d'un ton irrité.

Ireland ['aiələnd]. *Pr.n. Geog:* Irlande *f*; **Northern I.,** l'Irlande du Nord; **the Republic of I.,** la République d'Irlande.

irena [ai'ri:nə], *s. Orn:* irène *f*.

Irenaeus [airi'niəs]. *Pr.n.m.* (saint) Irénée.

irenarch [ai'ri:nɑ:k], *s. Rom.Hist:* irénarque *m*.

Irene [ai'ri:ni]. *Pr.n.f.* Irène.

irenic(al) [ai'ri:nik(əl)], *a. Ecc:* (écrit, etc.) irénique.

irenicism [ai'ri:nisizm], *s. Rel:* irénisme *m*.

irenicist [ai'ri:nisist], *s. Rel:* iréniste *m*.

irenikon [ai'ri:nikɔn], *s. Rel:* proposition *f* irénique.

Iridaceae [airi'deisii:], *s.pl. Bot:* iridacées *f*.

iridaceous [airi'deiʃəs], *a. Bot:* iridacé.

iridal ['airid(ə)l], *a. Anat:* irien.

iridectomy [airi'dektəmi], *s. Surg:* iridectomie *f*.

iridencleisis [airiden'kli:sis], *s. Med:* iridencleisis *m*.

iridescence [iri'desəns], *s.* irisation *f*, iridescence *f*; aspect irisé, chatoiement *m* (d'un plumage, d'une écaille, etc.).

iridescent [iri'desənt], *a.* irisé, iridescent; chatoyant; **to become i.,** s'iriser, se chromatiser; **to make i.,** iriser.

iridiagnosis ['airidaiəg'nousis], *s. Med:* irido-diagnostic *m.*

iridial [ai'ridiəl], **iridian** [ai'ridiən], *a. Anat:* iridien, irien; de l'iris.

iridic[1] [ai'ridik], *a.* (*a*) *Metall:* iridié; (*b*) *Ch:* iridique.

iridic[2], *a. Anat:* iridien, irien; de l'iris.

iridio-platinum [ai'ridiou'plætinəm], *s. Metall:* platine iridié.

iridite ['airidait], *s. Ch:* iridite *f.*

iridium [i'ridiəm], *s. Ch:* iridium *m*; **i.-pointed screw,** vis iridiée.

iridize[1] ['airidaiz, 'ir-], *v.tr.* iridier (une pointe de vis, etc.).

iridize[2] ['iridaiz], *v.tr.* iriser.

iridochoroiditis ['airidoukɔrɔi'daitis], *s. Med:* iridochoroïdite *f.*

iridocyclitis ['airidousai'klaitis], *s. Med:* iridocyclite *f.*

iridodiagnosis ['airidoudaiəg'nousis], *s. Med:* irido-diagnostic *m.*

iridodialysis ['airidoudai'ælisis], *s. Med:* iridodialyse *f.*

iridodonesis ['airidoudə'ni:sis], *s. Med:* iridodonèse *f,* iridodonésis *f.*

iridokeratitis ['airidoukerə'taitis], *s. Med:* irido-kératite *f.*

iridomyrmex ['airidou'mə:meks], *s. Ent:* iridomyrmex *m.*

iridoparalysis ['airidoupə'rælisis], **iridoplegia** ['airidou'pli:dʒiə], *s. Med:* iridoplégie *f.*

iridosclerectomy ['airidouskle'rektəmi], *s. Surg:* iridosclérectomie *f.*

iridosmine [iri'dɔzmi:n], **iridosmium** [iri'dɔzmiəm], *s. Miner:* iridosmine *f*; osmiridium *m.*

iridotomy [airi'dɔtəmi], *s. Surg:* iridotomie *f.*

iris[1] ['aiəris]. **1.** *Pr.n.f. Myth:* **Iris,** Iris. **2.** *s.* (*pl.* **irides** ['aiəridi:z]) *Anat:* iris *m* (de l'œil); *Med:* **i. diagnosis,** irido-diagnostic *m.* **3.** *s.* (*pl.* **irises** ['aiərisiz]) *Bot:* iris *m*; **yellow i.,** iris jaune, des marais; **Florentine i.,** iris de Florence; **stinking i.,** iris fétide; iris gigot; *Pharm: Toil:* **i. root,** racine *f* d'iris. **4.** *s.* (*pl.* **irises**) reflets irisés; chatoiement *m*; (*b*) *Opt:* iris; *Phot:* **i. diaphragm,** diaphragme *m* iris; *Cin:* **i. vignetter,** iris extérieur pour fondus; (*c*) *Elcs:* diaphragme (de guide d'ondes); **i.-equipped wave guide,** guide *m* d'ondes à diaphragme(s); (*d*) *Miner:* pierre *f* d'iris; quartz irisé; iris.

iris[2], *v.tr.* **1.** iriser. **2.** *Cin:* faire partir (une scène) dans un fondu (au moyen du diaphragme).

irisated ['airiseitid], *a.* irisé.

irisation [airi'seiʃ(ə)n], *s.* irisage *m,* irisation *f.*

Irish ['aiəriʃ]. **1.** *a.* (*a*) (peuple, etc.) irlandais; (beurre, etc.) d'Irlande; *Hist:* **the I. Free State,** l'État *m* libre d'Irlande; **I. boy, girl,** jeune Irlandais, Irlandaise; **I. American, Australian,** Américain, -aine, Australien, -ienne, d'origine irlandaise; **I. coffee,** café noir au whiskey irlandais couronné de crème Chantilly; **I. setter,** setter irlandais; **I. terrier,** terrier irlandais; Irish terrier; **I. wolfhound,** lévrier irlandais, d'Irlande; (*b*) *Civ.E:* **I. bridge,** gué *m*; (*c*) *F:* **the reasoning sounds a bit I. to me,** le raisonnement me semble assez illogique, absurde. **2.** *s.* (*a*) *Ling:* irlandais *m*; (*b*) *pl.* **the I.,** les Irlandais; (*c*) *P:* **to get one's I. up,** se mettre en colère, en boule.

Irishism ['aiəriʃizm], *s.* **1.** locution irlandaise. **2.** inconséquence *f,* naïveté *f,* calinotade *f.*

Irishman, *pl.* **-men** ['aiəriʃmən], *s.m.* Irlandais; *F:* **he's had an Irishman's rise,** d'évêque il s'est fait meunier.

Irishwoman, *pl.* **-women** ['aiəriʃwumən, -wimin], *s.f.* Irlandaise.

irising ['airisiŋ], *s. Cin:* rétrécissement progressif du champ.

iritis [ai'raitis], *s. Med:* iritis *f.*

irk [ə:k], *v.tr.* ennuyer (qn); *impers.* **it irks me to have to go there every week,** cela m'impatiente, m'est pénible, il m'en coûte, d'être obligé d'y aller chaque semaine.

irksome ['ə:ksəm], *a.* (travail) ennuyeux, ingrat.

irksomely ['ə:ksəmli], *adv.* d'une manière ennuyeuse.

irksomeness ['ə:ksəmnis], *s.* caractère ennuyeux, ingrat (d'une tâche, etc.).

Irkutsk [ə:'kutsk]. *Pr.n. Geog:* Irkoutsk.

iron[1] ['aiən], *s.* fer *m.* **1. old i.,** vieux fers; ferraille *f*; **(made) of i.,** de, en, fer; *Fig:* **he's made of i., has a constitution of i., an i. constitution,** il a une santé de fer, une carcasse d'acier, est solide comme un roc, est bâti à chaux et à sable; **man of i.,** homme dur, sans pitié; cœur *m* de pierre; **will of i.,** volonté *f* de fer; *Metall:* **cast i.,** (fer de) fonte *f*; fonte de fer; **crude i.,** fer cru, brut; fonte crue, brute; **soft i.,** fer doux; **brittle, short, i.,** fer aigre; **steely i.,** fer aciérain, aciéreux; acier extra doux; **forged, wrought, i.,** fer forgé; **(sheet) i.,** tôle *f*; **corrugated i.,** tôle ondulée, ridée; **bar i.,** fer en barres; **round (bar) i.,** fer rond, en rondins; **rod i.,** fer en verge(s); **slit i.,** côtes *fpl* de vache; **finished, merchant, i.,** fer marchand; **sectional i.,** (fer) profilé; **U i., T i.,** fer en U, en, à, T; **H i.,** fer en H, à double T. **2.** *attrib.* (*a*) **i. bar,** barre *f* de fer; **i. bridge,** pont *m* en fer; **i. (pulley) block,** poulie ferrée; **i. fittings, mountings,** ferrures *f*; **i. filings,** limaille *f* de fer; (*b*) *Miner: Ch:* **i. clay,** argile ferrugineuse; **i. sand,** sable ferrugineux; **i. garnet,** grenat ferreux; **i. ore,** minerai *m* de fer; **brown i. ore,** hématite brune, limonite *f*; **red i. ore,** hématite rouge, ferret *m* d'Espagne; *Geol:* **i. cap,** chapeau ferrugineux, de fer (d'une couche métallifère); **i. pan,** alios (ferrugineux); (*c*) *Metall:* **i. founder,** fondeur *m* de fonte, en fer; **i. foundry,** fonderie *f* de fonte; usine *f* métallurgique; **the i. and steel industry,** l'industrie *f* sidérurgique, la sidérurgie; *St Exch:* **i. and steel shares,** valeurs *f* métallurgiques; (*d*) *Fig:* **i. discipline,** discipline *f* de fer; **i. will,** volonté de fer; *Hist:* **the I. Duke,** le Duc de fer (Wellington); *Pol.Ec: etc:* **the i. law of necessity,** la loi d'airain de la nécessité; **Lassalle's i. law of wages,** la loi d'airain de Lassalle; (*e*) *Med:* **i. lung,** poumon *m* d'acier; (*f*) *U.S:* **i. man,** pièce *f* d'un dollar. **3.** *Med:* **to take i.,** prendre du fer; **i. deficiency,** manque *m* de fer; **i.-deficiency anaemia,** anémie *f* ferriprive. **4.** (*a*) *Hairdr: A:* **curling i.,** fer à friser; *Mch:* **clinkering i.,** ringard *m*; *Vet:* **firing i.,** cautère actuel; **to have several, too many, irons in the fire,** s'occuper de plusieurs, de trop de, choses à la fois; mener plusieurs affaires, trop d'affaires, de front; avoir trop d'affaires en main, sur les bras; **one shouldn't have too many irons in the fire,** il ne faut pas courir deux lièvres à la fois; (*b*) *F:* revolver *m*; pistolet *m*; (*c*) *Dom.Ec:* **(flat) i., laundry i.,** fer à repasser; **electric i.,** fer électrique; **travelling i.,** fer de voyage; **i. holder,** (i) *O:* poignée *f* de fer à repasser; (ii) (*also* **i. stand**) repose-fer *m, pl.* repose-fers; (*d*) *Carp:* **plane i.,** fer, couteau *m,* de rabot; **back i.,** contre-fer *m, pl.* contre-fers; (*e*) *Equit:* **(stirrup) i.,** étrier *m*; (*f*) *Golf:* (crosse *f* en) fer; **i. shot,** coup *m* de fer; (*g*) *Nau:* ferrure (de gouvernail). **5.** *Const:* poutre *f* de fer. **6.** (*a*) (i) **irons,** fers, chaînes *f*; *A:* **to be in irons,** être dans les fers; avoir les fers aux pieds; (ii) *Fig:* **the i. had entered his soul,** il s'était aigri; (*b*) *Med:* **to put a child's leg in irons,** faire porter des attelles en fer à un enfant; (*c*) *Nau:* (*of ship*) **to be in irons,** faire chapelle.

iron[2], *v.tr.* **1.** garnir (une porte, etc.) de fer, de ferrures; ferrer (une porte, etc.). **2.** mettre les fers à (qn); mettre (qn) aux fers. **3.** repasser (le linge); **to i. a collar,** donner un coup de fer à un col; **to i. out a crease,** faire disparaître un faux pli au fer chaud; *Fig:* **to i. out the difficulties in the way of an agreement,** aplanir les difficultés qui empêchent un accord; **to i. out an opponent,** battre un adversaire à plates coutures.

iron-banded ['aiən'bændid], *a. Const:* (ciment) fretté.

ironbark ['aiənba:k], *s.* **1.** *Bot:* eucalyptus résineux; gommier *m.* **2.** bois *m* de gommier.

iron-bearing ['aiən'bɛəriŋ], *a.* (terrain, etc.) ferrifère, ferreux.

ironbound ['aiənbaund], *a.* **1.** (tonneau, etc.) cerclé de fer, fretté de fer; **i. mallet,** marteau *m* à têtes rapportées. **2.** (*of regulations, etc.*) inflexible, sévère; (*of convictions, etc.*) inébranlable.

iron-cased ['aiən'keist], *a.* (électro-aimant, etc.) cuirassé; (conduite, etc.) à enveloppe de fonte.

ironclad ['aiənklæd]. **1.** *a.* (*a*) à enveloppe de fer; (vaisseau, électro-aimant) cuirassé; (puits) blindé; *El:* **i. panel,** panneau blindé; (*b*) *NAm:* (serment, contrat, etc.) strict; (règlement) rigoureux. **2.** *s. Navy: A:* cuirassé *m.*

irone ['airoun], *s. Ch:* irone *f.*

ironer ['aiənər], *s.* repasseur, -euse; **fine i.,** repasseuse de linge fin.

iron-grey ['aiən'grei], *a.* & *s.* gris (de) fer (*m inv*); **i.-g. beard,** barbe *f* gris fer, barbe poivre et sel.

ironhanded ['aiən'hændid], *a.* à la main de fer; sévère, inflexible.

ironic(al) [ai'rɔnik(l)], *a.* ironique; (*in debate*) **the ironic method,** l'ironisme *m.*

ironically [ai'rɔnik(ə)li], *adv.* ironiquement; (parler) avec ironie; **i., I happened to be there,** par ironie, ironiquement, le hasard a voulu que je sois là.

ironing ['aiəniŋ], *s.* repassage *m*; *A:* **his mother took in i.,** sa mère était repasseuse (à domicile); **i. machine,** machine *f* à repasser; repasseuse *f.*

ironist ['airənist], *s.* ironiste *mf.*

ironmaster ['aiənma:stər], *s.m.* maître de forges; métallurgiste.

ironmonger ['aiənmʌŋgər], *s.* quincaillier *m,* ferronnier *m*; **ironmonger's shop,** quincaillerie *f,* ferblanterie *f.*

ironmongery ['aiənmʌŋg(ə)ri], *s.* (*a*) (*goods*) quincaillerie *f*; (marchandise *f* de) quincaille *f*; (i) ferronnerie *f*; (ii) ferblanterie *f*; (*shop*) quincaillerie, ferblanterie.

ironmould ['aiənmould], *s.* (*a*) tache *f* de rouille; (*b*) vieille tache d'encre.

ironshod ['aiənʃɔd], *a.* (*of walking-stick, etc.*) ferré.

Ironside ['aiənsaid], *s. Eng.Hist:* (*a*) Côte *f* de fer (surnom du roi Edmond II); (*b*) *pl.* **Ironsides,** Côtes de Fer (surnom de la cavalerie d'Olivier Cromwell).

ironsmith ['aiənsmiθ], *s.* chaudronnier *m* en fer.

ironstone ['aiənstoun], *s.* **(clay) i.,** minerai *m* de fer (argileux); **i. china, ware,** porcelaine (anglaise) opaque.

ironware ['aiənwɛər], *s.* ferronnerie *f.*

ironweed ['aiənwi:d], *s. Bot:* (*a*) jacobée *f*; herbe *f* de Saint-Jacques; (*b*) *NAm:* (i) centaurée noire; chardon bénit; (ii) vipérine *f.*

iron-willed ['aiən'wild], *a.* à la volonté de fer.

ironwood ['aiənwud], *s. Bot:* bois *m* de fer; sidéroxyle *m*; ferréol *m*; **bastard i.,** xanthoxylum *m.*

ironwork ['aiənwə:k], *s.* **1.** construction *f* en fer; (*a*) (*work in wrought iron*) serrurerie *f*; (travail *m* de) ferronnerie *f*; **i. constructor, contractor,** serrurier *m* en bâtiments; (*b*) **heavy i., constructional i.,** charpente *f* en fer, grosse serrurerie, profilés *mpl* pour constructions; (*c*) (*parts made of iron*) ferrure(s) *f(pl)*; ferrerie *f*; ferrements *mpl* (d'un navire, d'un wagon); dentelle *f* (d'une balustrade, etc.). **2.** *pl.* (*often with sg. const.*) **ironworks;** (*a*) fonderie *f* de fonte; usine *f* métallurgique; (*b*) usine sidérurgique; forges *f.*

ironworker ['aiənwə:kər], *s.* **1.** (*worker in wrought iron*) (ouvrier) serrurier *m.* **2.** (*worker in heavy iron*) charpentier *m* en fer.

ironworking ['aiənwə:kiŋ], *s.* serrurerie *f*; charpenterie *f* en fer.

ironwort ['aiənwə:t], *s. Bot:* sidérite *f,* crapaudine *f*; *F:* thé *m* de campagne.

irony[1] ['airəni], *s.* ironie *f*; **by an i. of fate,** par une ironie du sort.

irony[2] ['aiəni], *a.* de fer; qui ressemble au fer.

Iroquois ['irəkwɔi]. *Ethn:* **1.** *a.* iroquois. **2.** *s.* Iroquois, -oise.

irradiance [i'reidiəns], **irradiancy** [i'reidiənsi], *s.* **1.** rayonnement *m,* éclat *m.* **2.** *Rad.-A:* radiance *f*; éclairement *m* énergétique.

irradiant [i'reidiənt], *a.* **1.** rayonnant. **2.** *Rad.-A:* irradiant.

irradiate [i'reidieit], *v.tr.* **1.** (*a*) (*of light, heat*) irradier (la terre, etc.), rayonner sur (la terre); (*of light rays*) illuminer (une surface); (*b*) *Rad.-A:* irradier (une substance, etc.); *Med:* **to i. a patient,** traiter un malade par irradiation, *F:* par les rayons. **2.** *Lit:* (*a*) éclairer, illuminer, rendre compréhensible (un sujet, le passé); (*b*) illuminer (l'âme, l'esprit). **3.** émettre comme des rayons; **presence that irradiates strength and courage,** présence d'où irradient la force et le courage. **4.** faire rayonner (le visage, etc.); **good humour irradiated his face,** la bonne humeur faisait rayonner son visage. **5.** *v.i.* irradier, rayonner.

irradiated [i'reidieitid], *a.* **1.** rayonnant; (*a*) *Ph:* **i. heat,** chaleur rayonnante; (*b*) **face i. with happiness,** visage rayonnant de bonheur. **2.** *Atom.Ph:* (combustible, etc.) irradié.

irradiation [ireidi'eiʃ(ə)n], *s.* **1.** (*a*) *Ph: Opt: Physiol:* irradiation *f*; (*b*) *Atom.Ph:* irradiation; *Med:* (traitement *m* par) irradiation; radiothérapie *f*; **contact i.,** irradiation par contact; **surface i.,** irradiation superficielle; **neutron i.,** irradiation neutronique; **fuel i.,** irradiation du combustible (dans le cœur du réacteur); **i. field,** champ *m* d'irradiation; **i. source,** source *f,* émetteur *m,* d'irradiation; **i. time,** durée *f* d'exposition; *Med:* **(deep) X-ray i.,** irradiation (profonde) par rayons X; **i. disease, sickness,** maladie *f* des irradiations, *F:* des rayons; radiotoxémie *f.* **2.** rayonnement *m,* éclat *m* (d'une source de lumière). **3.** illumination (spirituelle).

irradiative [i'reidiətiv], *a.* **1.** irradiateur, -trice. **2.** *Lit:* illuminant (pour l'âme, pour l'esprit).

irradiator [i'reidieitər], *s.* (*a*) *Atom.Ph:* irradiateur *m*; émetteur *m,* source *f,* de rayonnement; (*b*) *Med:* (appareil) émetteur de rayons X.

irrational [i'ræʃən(ə)l]. **1.** *a.* (*a*) (animal, etc.) dépourvu de raison, irraisonnable; (*b*) (*of fear, conduct, etc.*) déraisonnable, absurde, irrationnel; (*c*) *Mth:* (nombre) irrationnel. **2.** *s.* (*a*) être *m* irraisonnable; (*b*) *Mth:* quantité irrationnelle.

irrationalism [i'ræʃənəlizm], *s. Phil:* irrationalisme *m.*

irrationalist [i'ræʃənəlist], *a.* & *s. Phil:* irrationaliste (*mf*).

irrationality [iræʃə'næliti], *s.* **1.** déraison *f*; manque *m* de raison; irrationalité *f.* **2.** absurdité *f.*

irrationally [i'ræʃənəli], *adv.* d'une manière irraisonnable; déraisonnablement; irrationnellement.

Irrawad(d)y (the) [ðiːirə'wɔdi]. *Pr.n. Geog:* l'Iraouaddy *m.*

irrealizable |iriə'laizəbl|, *a.* (*of plan, Fin: funds, etc.*) irréalisable.

irrebuttable |iri'bʌtəbl|, *a. Jur:* (témoignage, etc.) irréfragable; **i. presumption,** présomption absolue.

irreclaimability |irikleimə'biliti|, *s.* **1.** incorrigibilité *f* (d'un toxicomane, etc.). **2.** incultivabilité *f* (d'un terrain).

irreclaimable |iri'kleiməbl|, *a.* **1.** (toxicomane, etc.) incorrigible; (ivrogne) invétéré. **2.** (terrain) incultivable.

irrecognizable |i'rekəgnaizəbl|, *a.* méconnaissable.

irrecognizably |i'rekəgnaizəbli|, *adv.* (changé) au point d'être méconnaissable.

irreconcilability |irekənsailə'biliti|, *s.* **1.** irréconciliabilité *f* (de deux personnes). **2.** inconciliabilité *f* (de deux croyances, etc.).

irreconcilable |irekən'sailəbl|, *a.* **1.** (*a*) (ennemi) irréconciliable; (haine) implacable; *Pol: etc:* **i. group,** groupe intransigeant; (*b*) *s. Pol: etc:* intransigeant, -ante. **2.** (croyance, témoignage) incompatible, inconciliable (**with,** avec); **to try to reconcile the i.,** vouloir concilier l'inconciliable.

irreconcilably |irekən'sailəbli|, *adv.* **1.** irréconciliablement. **2.** inconciliablement.

irrecoverable |iri'kʌv(ə)rəbl|, *a.* (créance) irrécouvrable; (perte) irréparable, irrémédiable.

irrecoverably |iri'kʌv(ə)rəbli|, *adv.* (endommagé) irrémédiablement, irréparablement; (ruiné) à tout jamais.

irrecusable |iri'kjuːzəbl|, *a.* (témoignage, preuve) irrécusable.

irrecusably |iri'kjuːzəbli|, *adv.* de manière irrécusable.

irredeemability |iridiːmə'biliti|, *s.* **1.** caractère irrachetable (d'un placement). **2.** incorrigibilité *f* (d'un malfaiteur).

irredeemable |iri'diːməbl|, *a.* **1.** (*a*) (faute) irrachetable; (*b*) *Fin:* (fonds) irrachetable, irréalisable, irremboursable; (papier) non convertible; **i. bonds,** *s.* **irredeemables,** obligations *f* non amortissables. **2.** (*a*) (désastre, tristesse, bassesse) irrémédiable; (*b*) (escroc) incorrigible.

irredeemably |iri'diːməbli|, *adv.* (condamné) sans recours; **i. bad system,** système mauvais de fond en comble.

irredentism |iri'dentizm|, *s. Pol:* irrédentisme *m.*

irredentist |iri'dentist|, *a. & s. Pol:* irrédentiste (*mf*).

irreducibility |'iridjuːsi'biliti|, **irreducibleness** |iri'djuːsiblnis|, *s.* irréductiblilité *f.*

irreducible |iri'djuːsibl|, *a.* (minimum, équation, fraction, hernie, luxation) irréductible.

irreformable |iri'fɔːməbl|, *a.* irréformable.

irrefragability |i'refrəgə'biliti|, *s.* irréfragabilité *f.*

irrefragable |i'refrəgəbl|, *a.* (réponse, témoignage, autorité) irréfragable; (réponse, témoignage) irrécusable, irréfutable.

irrefutability |irifjuːtə'biliti|, *s.* irréfutabilité *f.*

irrefutable |iri'fjuːtəbl|, *a.* (témoignage, déclaration) irréfutable; (témoignage) irrécusable.

irrefutably |iri'fjuːtəbli|, *adv.* irréfutablement; **to prove i. that one is right,** prouver sans conteste, sans réplique, qu'on a raison.

irregular |i'regjulər|, *a.* irrégulier. **1.** (*a*) contraire aux règles; **i. order, conduct,** ordre irrégulier, conduite irrégulière; **i. life,** vie déréglée; **i. household,** faux ménage; ménage irrégulier; *Jur:* **i. document,** document *m* informe; (*b*) *Nat.Hist:* anormal, -aux; (*c*) *Gram:* **i. plurals, verbs,** pluriels, verbes, irréguliers. **2.** asymétrique; (*of outline, etc.*) anfractueux; (*of surface*) raboteux; inégal, -aux; **i. shape,** forme irrégulière; **i. features,** traits irréguliers. **3.** (*uneven in duration, order, etc.*) **i. intervals,** intervalles irréguliers; **i. pulse,** pouls irrégulier, déréglé, inégal, intermittent; **i. breathing,** respiration saccadée; **i. action of a machine,** boitement *m* d'une machine; **i. rhymes,** rimes irrégulières. disposées d'une manière capricieuse; **i. verse,** vers irréguliers, libres. **4.** *Mil:* **i. troops,** *s.* **irregulars,** troupes irrégulières; irréguliers *m.* **5.** *s.pl. Com: NAm:* **irregulars,** articles *m* de deuxième qualité, de qualité moyenne.

irregularity |iregju'læriti|, *s.* **1.** (*a*) irrégularité *f* (de conduite, etc.); (*b*) *Adm: etc:* **to commit irregularities,** commettre des irrégularités (dans les comptes, les écritures). **2.** (*a*) irrégularité (des traits); (*b*) **irregularities of the ground,** aspérités *f,* accidents *m,* irrégularités, de terrain. **3.** arythmie *f* (des battements du cœur, etc.); *I.C.E:* dissymétrie *f* (des temps moteurs); **i. of the pulse,** dérèglement *m* du pouls.

irregularly |i'regjuləli|, *adv.* irrégulièrement; (i) d'une façon irrégulière, déréglée; (ii) **i. shaped,** d'une forme irrégulière; **i. shaped pearl,** perle *f* baroque.

irrelative |i'relətiv|, *a.* sans rapport (**to,** avec), étranger (**to,** à).

irrelevance |i'relivəns|, **irrelevancy** |i'relivənsi|, *s.* **1.** inapplicabilité *f* (**to,** à). **2.** inconséquence *f*; manque *m* d'à-propos. **3. speech full of irrelevancies,** discours rempli d'à-côtés qui n'ont rien à voir avec la question.

irrelevant |i'relivənt|, *a.* non pertinent; (*of remark, etc.*) hors de propos; qui manque d'à-propos; **i. to the subject,** étranger au sujet, sans rapport avec le sujet; **i. questions,** questions *f* hors de cause; **to make i. remarks,** divaguer; **that is i.,** cela n'a aucun rapport, n'a rien à voir, avec la question.

irrelevantly |i'relivəntli|, *adv.* mal à propos; hors de propos.

irrelievable |iri'liːvəbl|, *a.* qu'on ne peut soulager, alléger, adoucir; sans remède.

irreligion |iri'lidʒ(ə)n|, **irreligiousness** |iri'lidʒəsnis|, *s.* irréligion *f,* indévotion *f.*

irreligiosity |irilidʒi'ɔsiti|, *s.* irréligiosité *f.*

irreligious |iri'lidʒəs|, *a.* irréligieux.

irreligiously |iri'lidʒəsli|, *adv.* irréligieusement.

irremediable |iri'miːdiəbl|, *a.* (mal, faute, etc.) irrémédiable; sans remède; (perte, etc.) irrécupérable.

irremediably |iri'miːdiəbli|, *adv.* irrémédiablement; sans secours, sans remède; (ruiné) sans ressource.

irremissible |iri'misibl|, *a.* **1.** (faute) irrémissible; (péché) impardonnable. **2.** (devoir) irrémissible, dont on ne saurait se relâcher.

irremissibly |iri'misibli|, *adv.* sans rémission, irrémissiblement; sans miséricorde, implacablement.

irremission |iri'miʃ(ə)n|, *s.* irrémission *f.*

irremovability |irimuːvə'biliti|, *s.* (*a*) fixité *f* (d'une machine, etc.); (*b*) inamovibilité *f* (d'un fonctionnaire).

irremovable |iri'muːvəbl|, *a.* (*a*) qu'on ne saurait déplacer; ancré en place; fixe; (*b*) (fonctionnaire) inamovible.

irremovably |iri'muːvəbli|, *adv.* fermement, fixement.

irreparability |irepərə'biliti|, **irreparableness** |i'repərəblnis|, *s.* irréparabilité *f.*

irreparable |i'repərəbl|, *a.* (mal, perte) irréparable; (perte) irrémédiable, irrécupérable.

irreparably |i'repərəbli|, *adv.* (abîmer) irréparablement, irrémédiablement.

irreplaceable |iri'pleisəbl|, *a.* (trésor, ami) irremplaçable.

irreprehensible |irepri'hensibl|, *a.* irrépréhensible.

irreprehensibly |irepri'hensibli|, *adv.* irrépréhensiblement.

irrepressibility |'iripresi'biliti|, **irrepressibleness** |iri'presiblnis|, *s.* caractère *m,* nature *f,* irrépressible (d'une force, d'un rire).

irrepressible |iri'presibl|, *a.* (bâillement) irrésistible, irréprimable; (force) irrépressible; **i. impulse,** mouvement *m* qu'on ne saurait réprimer; **i. laughter,** rire *m* inextinguible; **i. child,** enfant *mf* (i) qui a le diable au corps, (ii) qu'on ne saurait faire taire; **i. spirits,** verve endiablée.

irrepressibly |iri'presibli|, *adv.* irrépressiblement.

irreproachability |iriproutʃə'biliti|, **irreproachableness** |iri'proutʃəbəlnis|, *s.* irréprochabilité *f.*

irreproachable |iri'proutʃəbl|, *a.* irréprochable; **i. dress,** vêtement *m* impeccable; **work i. in style,** ouvrage *m* irréprochable de style; **he was always i. in his conduct,** il a toujours été irréprochable dans sa conduite.

irreproachably |iri'proutʃəbli|, *adv.* irréprochablement.

irreproducible |iriprə'djuːsibl|, *a.* impossible à reproduire.

irresistance |iri'zistəns|, *s.* absence *f,* manque *m,* de résistance.

irresistibility |irizisti'biliti|, **irresistibleness** |iri'zistiblnis|, *s.* irrésistibilité *f.*

irresistible |iri'zistibl|, *a.* irrésistible.

irresistibly |iri'zistibli|, *adv.* irrésistiblement.

irresoluble |iri'zɔljubl|, *a.* (problème, etc.) insoluble.

irresolute |i'rezəl(j)uːt|, *a.* **1.** indécis; **to be i.,** être indécis; hésiter; ne savoir que faire. **2.** (caractère) irrésolu; (homme) qui manque de résolution; (esprit) vacillant, hésitant.

irresolutely |i'rezəl(j)utli|, *adv.* d'une manière indécise; irrésolument.

irresoluteness |i'rezəl(j)utnis|, **irresolution** |i'rezəl(j)uʃ(ə)n|, *s.* indécision *f* (de caractère); irrésolution *f*; manque *m* de résolution; **the i. of the human heart,** les flottements *m* du cœur humain; *Med:* **morbid i.,** maladie *f* du scrupule.

irresolvability |'irizɔlvə'biliti|, *s.* insolubilité *f* (d'un problème).

irresolvable |iri'zɔlvəbl|, *a.* **1.** (problème, question) insoluble. **2.** (corps) indécomposable, irréductible; **i. nebula,** nébuleuse *f* irrésoluble.

irrespective |iri'spektiv|. **1.** *a.* indépendant (**of,** de); **interest that is i. of all practical considerations,** intérêt qui ne dépend d'aucune considération pratique. **2.** *adv.* **i. of sth.,** indépendamment, sans tenir compte, de qch.; **promotion goes by ability i. of seniority,** l'avancement se fait selon les capacités indépendamment de l'ancienneté; **they go to the cinema i. of what film is being shown,** ils vont au cinéma sans se soucier du film qu'on donne.

irrespirable |iri'spaiərəbl|, *a.* irrespirable.

irresponsibility |'irispɔnsi'biliti|, *s.* **1.** (*a*) *Jur:* irresponsabilité *f* (d'un aliéné, etc.); (*b*) irresponsabilité (d'un dictateur, etc.). **2.** étourderie *f,* manque *m* de sérieux; irréflexion *f.*

irresponsible |iri'spɔnsibl|, *a.* **1.** (*a*) *Jur:* (*of mental defective, etc.*) irresponsable; (*b*) (agent, etc.) irresponsable; qui ne relève de personne. **2.** (*a*) (*of pers.*) étourdi, irréfléchi; brouillon, évaporé, peu sérieux; à la tête légère; **to be quite i.,** n'être pas maître de ses actes; **their i. gaiety,** leur insouciante gaieté; *s.* **to entrust serious business to irresponsibles,** confier des affaires sérieuses à des gens qui n'ont pas de plomb dans la tête; (*b*) (*of action*) irréfléchi. **3.** *Com:* insolvable.

irresponsibly |iri'spɔnsibli|, *adv.* **1.** irresponsablement. **2.** étourdiment; **to act i.,** agir à l'étourdie, à la légère; **so i. lighthearted,** si ingénument gai.

irresponsive |iri'spɔnsiv|, *a.* (*of pers.*) flegmatique, peu émotif, froid; (visage) fermé; **to be i. to s.o.'s advances,** être insensible, ne pas répondre, aux avances de qn; **i. to entreaties,** sourd aux prières.

irresponsiveness |iri'spɔnsivnis|, *s.* flegme *m,* réserve *f,* froideur *f*; **i. to s.o.'s advances,** insensibilité *f* aux avances de qn.

irretentive |iri'tentiv|, *a.* (mémoire) qui ne retient pas, peu fidèle.

irretentiveness |iri'tentivnis|, *s.* manque *m* de fidélité (de la mémoire).

irretractable |iri'træktəbl|, *a.* (*of confession, etc.*) irrétractable.

irretrievability |'iritriːvə'biliti|, *s.* irréparabilité *f.*

irretrievable |iri'triːvəbl|, *a.* irréparable, irrémédiable; **i. step,** démarche sur laquelle on ne saurait revenir, sur laquelle il n'y a pas à revenir.

irretrievably |iri'triːvəbli|, *adv.* irréparablement; irrémédiablement; (ruiné) à tout jamais.

irreverence |i'rev(ə)rəns|, *s.* irrévérence *f*; manque *m* de respect (**towards,** envers, pour).

irreverent |i'rev(ə)rənt|, *a.* (*in religious matters*) irrévérent; (*in social intercourse*) irrévérencieux.

irreverently |i'rev(ə)rəntli|, *adv.* irrévérencieusement.

irreversibility |irivəːsi'biliti|, *s.* **1.** irrévocabilité *f* (d'une décision). **2.** irréversibilité *f* (d'une machine).

irreversible |iri'vəːsibl|, *a.* **1.** (*of decision, etc.*) irrévocable. **2.** (*of process, gear, etc.*) irréversible.

irreversibly |iri'vəːsibli|, *adv.* sans retour; irrévocablement.

irrevocability |irevəkə'biliti|, **irrevocableness** |i'revəkəbəlnis|, *s.* irrévocabilité *f.*

irrevocable |i'revəkəbl|, *a.* irrévocable; *Jur:* (décision) irréformable.

irrevocably |i'revəkəbli|, *adv.* irrévocablement.

irrigable |'irigəbl|, **irrigatable** |iri'geitəbl|, *a.* (terre) irrigable.

irrigate |'irigeit|, *v.tr.* **1.** (*a*) *Agr:* irriguer (des champs); (*b*) (*of river*) arroser (un bassin, une région). **2.** *Med:* irriguer (une plaie, etc.); injecter (une cavité). **3.** *v.i. U.S: F:* boire.

irrigation |iri'geiʃ(ə)n|, *s.* **1.** irrigation *f* (des champs); arrosement *m,* arrosage *m* (des prés, etc.); baignage *m* (des prés); **i. canal, ditch,** canal *m* d'irrigation; **i. pump,** pompe *f* d'arrosage. **2.** *Med:* irrigation (du côlon, etc.).

irrigator |'irigeitər|, *s.* **1.** *Agr:* (*a*) (*pers.*) arroseur *m*; (*b*) machine *f* à arroser; arroseuse *f*; irrigateur *m.* **2.** *Med:* irrigateur, injecteur *m*; seringue *f* à injection; bock *m.*

irrisor |i'raizər|, *s. Orn:* irrisor *m.*

irritability |iritə'biliti|, *s.* irritabilité *f* (d'une personne, d'un muscle, du protoplasme).

irritable |'iritəbl|, *a.* **1.** (caractère, esprit) irritable, irascible; **she's very i. today,** elle a les nerfs en pelote aujourd'hui. **2.** *Biol:* (nerf, protoplasme) irritable.

irritableness |'iritəbəlnis|, *s.* irritabilité *f* (de caractère).

irritancy[1] |'iritənsi|, *s.* = IRRITATION.

irritancy[2], *s. Jur: Scot:* annulation *f* (d'un acte, d'une clause).

irritant[1] ['iritənt], *a. & s. Med:* irritant (*m*).

irritant[2], *a. Jur: Scot:* **clause i.,** clause irritante, article annulatif.

irritate[1] |'iriteit|, *v.tr.* **1.** irriter, mettre en colère, agacer (qn, un animal); exciter (un animal); **to become irritated,** s'irriter, s'agacer; **to be very much irritated,** être en proie à une vive irritation. **2.** (*a*) *Med:* irriter (un organe); aviver, envenimer (une plaie); **to i. the nerves,**

irriter, *F:* agacer, les nerfs; (*b*) *Physiol: Biol:* stimuler, irriter (un organe).

irritate[2], *v.tr. Jur: Scot:* rendre nul et de nul effet.

irritating |'iriteitiŋ|, *a.* **1.** irritant, agaçant; **an i. laugh,** un rire agaçant, *F:* empoisonnant. **2.** *Med:* irritant, irritatif.

irritatingly |'iriteitiŋli|, *adv.* d'une façon agaçante, irritante.

irritation |iri'teiʃ(ə)n|, *s.* **1.** irritation *f*; **a constant (source of) i.,** une cause continuelle d'irritation; **momentary i.,** contrariété passagère; **state of nervous i.,** état d'énervement. **2.** (*a*) *Med:* irritation (de la gorge, de l'estomac); *F:* agacement *m* (des nerfs); (*b*) *Physiol:* irritation, stimulation *f* (d'un organe).

irritative |'iritetiv|, *a. Med:* irritatif.

irrotational |irə'teiʃ(ə)nl|, *a. Ph: Mth:* (mouvement) irrotationnel.

irrupt |i'rʌpt|, *v.i.* **1.** (*of crowd, etc.*) faire irruption (dans une pièce, etc.). **2.** (*of population, etc.*) se multiplier sans contrôle.

irruption |i'rʌpʃ(ə)n|, *s.* irruption *f*; *Hyd.E:* **i. of water,** venue *f* d'eau.

Irvingite |'ə:viŋait|, *s. Ecc:* Irvingien, -ienne.

Isaac |'aizək|. *Pr.n.m.* Isaac.

Isabel |'izəbel|, **Isabella** |izə'belə|. **1.** *Pr.n.f.* Isabelle. **2.** *a.* & *s.* (couleur) isabelle (*m*) *inv*; gris jaune (*m*) *inv.*

isabelline |izə'belin, -ain|, *a.* isabelle *inv.*

isadelphous |aisə'delfəs|, *a. Bot:* isadelphe.

Isaeus |ai'zi(:)əs|. *Pr.n.m. Gr.Hist:* Isée.

isagogic |aisə'gɔdʒik|. **1.** *a.* isagogique. **2.** *s.pl.* (*usu. with sg. const.*) **isagogics,** isagogique *f.*

Isaiah |ai'zaiə|. *Pr.n.m. B.Hist:* Isaïe.

isallobar |ai'sæləbɑ:r|, *s. Meteor:* isallobare *f.*

isallobaric |aisælə'bɑ:rik, -'bærik|, *a. Meteor:* isallobarique.

isallotherm |ai'sæləθə:m|, *s. Meteor:* isallotherme *f.*

isanemone |ai'sænimoun|, *s. Meteor:* isanémone *f.*

isanomal |aisə'nouməl|, *s. Meteor:* isanomale *f.*

isanomalous |aisə'nɔmələs|, *a. Meteor:* **i. lines,** isanomales *f.*

isatic |'aisətik|, *a. Ch:* isatique.

isatin |'aisətin|, *s. Ch:* isatine *f.*

isatis |'aisətis|, *s. Bot:* isatide *m,* isatis *m.*

isatogenic |aisətou'dʒenik|, *a. Ch:* isatogénique.

Isauria |i'sɔ:riə|. *Pr.n. A.Geog:* Isaurie *f.*

Isaurian |i'sɔ:riən|. **1.** *a. Hist:* (*of dynasty, etc.*) isaurien. **2.** *s. A.Geog:* **the Isaurians,** les Isauriens *m.*

isba(h) |'izbɑ|, *s.* izba *f*; chaumière *f* russe.

Iscariot |is'kæriət|. *Pr.n.m. B.Hist:* Iscariote; **Judas I.,** Judas Iscariote.

Iscariotism |is'kæriətizm|, *s.* iscariotisme *m.*

ischæmia |is'ki:miə|, *s. Med:* ischémie *f.*

ischæmic |is'ki:mik|, *a. Med:* ischémique.

ischial |'iskiəl|, **ischiadic** |iski'ædik|, **ischiatic** |iski'ætik|, *a. Anat:* ischiatique, sciatique.

ischiocavernosus |'iskioukævə'nousəs|, *s. Anat:* ischio-caverneux *m.*

ischiocavernous |'iskiou'kævənəs|, *a. Anat:* ischio-caverneux.

ischium, *pl.* **-ia** |'iskiəm, -iə|, *s. Anat:* ischion *m.*

ischuria |is'kjuəriə|, *s. Med:* ischurie *f.*

isenthalpic |aizen'θælpik|, *a. Ph:* qui est d'égale enthalpie.

isentropic |aisen'trɔpik|, *a. Ph:* isentropique.

iserine |'aisəri:n|, *s. Miner:* isérine *f.*

isethionic |aisi'θaiɔnik|, *a. Ch:* iséthionique.

Iseult |i'su:lt|. *Pr.n.f.* Yseult, Iseult.

Isfahan |isfə'hɑ:n|. *Pr.n. Geog:* Ispahan, Isfahan.

Ishmael |'iʃmei(ə)l|. **1.** *Pr.n.m. B.Hist:* Ismaël. **2.** *s.* (*a*) paria *m,* déshérité *m*; (*b*) ennemi *m* de la communauté.

Ishmaelite |'iʃmiəlait|, *s.* **1.** *B.Hist:* Ismaélite *m,* Ismaïlite *m.* **2.** = ISHMAEL 2.

Isiac |'aisiæk|, *a.* & *s.* isiaque (*m*).

Isiacal |'aisiəkl|, *a.* isiaque.

isidium |ai'sidiəm|, *s. Bot:* isidium *m,* isidie *f.*

Isidorian |izi'dɔ:riən|, *a. Ecc.Hist:* de saint Isidore.

Isidorus |izi'dɔ:rəs|. *Pr.n.m.* (saint) Isidore.

isinglass |'aiziŋglɑ:s|, *s.* **1.** (*a*) colle *f* de poisson, ichtyocolle *f,* isinglass *m*; **leaf i.,** ichtyocolle en cœur; gros cordon; **lyre i.,** ichtyocolle en lyre; petit cordon; **book i.,** ichtyocolle en livre; (*b*) gélatine *f* (pour gelées, etc.); (*c*) **Bengal i.,** agar-agar *m.* **2.** *Miner: F:* mica *m.*

Islam |'izlɑ:m|, *s.* (i) (*religion*) Islam; (ii) (*people*) l'Islam; **to go over to I.,** embrasser l'islamisme.

Islamic |iz'læmik|, *a.* islamique.

Islamism |'izləmizm|, *s.* islamisme *m.*

Islamist |'izləmist|, *s.* **1.** *Rel:* islamite *mf.* **2.** *Sch:* islamisant *m.*

Islamite |'izləmait|. **1.** *s.* islamite *mf*; **the Islamites,** l'Islam *m.* **2.** *a.* islamique.

Islamitic |izlə'mitik|, *a.* islamique.

Islamization |izləmai'zeiʃ(ə)n|, *s.* islamisation *f.*

Islamize |'izləmaiz|, *v.tr.* islamiser.

island |'ailənd|, *s.* **1.** île *f*; **small i.,** îlot *m*; **a rock i.,** un rocher isolé (dans la mer); **barrier i.,** île de cordon libre; **tied i.,** île rattachée; **coral i.,** île madréporique, coralienne; **floating i.,** (i) île flottante; (ii) *Cu:* œufs *mpl* à la neige; île flottante; **i. arc,** îles en arc, en guirlande; **the Pacific Islands,** les îles du Pacifique; **the I. Princess,** la Princesse de l'île, des îles; **our i. story,** l'histoire de notre île; **i. kingdom,** royaume *m* insulaire. **2.** (*a*) îlot (de maisons, etc.); **i. building site,** terrain *m* à bâtir formant îlot; *Rail:* **i. platform,** quai *m* d'entre-voie; quai entre voies; (*b*) (**street**) **i., safety i., traffic i.,** refuge *m* (pour piétons); île de sécurité; **centre i.,** îlot central; (*c*) (*in supermarket*) gondole *f*; **i. showcase,** vitrine centrale (de salle de musée, etc.); (*d*) *Navy:* îlot, superstructure *f* (d'un porte-avions); (*e*) *Fig:* **i. of resistance,** ilot de résistance. **3.** *Biol: Med:* **the islands of Langerhans,** les ilots pancréatiques de Langerhans.

islander |'ailəndər|, *s.* insulaire *mf*; **Channel Islanders,** habitants *m* des îles de la Manche.

isle |ail|, *s.* **1.** (*a*) (*poet. except in certain proper names*) île *f*; **the British Isles,** les Iles britanniques; **the I. of Man,** l'île de Man; **the I. of Wight,** l'île de Wight; (*b*) petite île, îlot *m*; (*c*) péninsule *f*; **the I. of Whithorn,** la péninsule de Whithorn. **2.** îlot (de maisons).

islet |'ailit|, *s.* **1.** îlot *m.* **2.** *Biol:* **the islets of Langerhans,** les îlots pancréatiques de Langerhans.

ism |izm|, *s. F: Pej:* doctrine *f,* théorie *f*; **he'll support any "ism",** il tient pour n'importe quelle doctrine.

Ismaili [ismɑ:'i:l], **Ismailian** [ismɑ:'i:liən]. **1.** *s.* Ismaélien *m,* Ismaïlien *m.* **2.** *a.* (doctrine, etc.) des Ismaéliens; **I. Moslems,** musulmans ismaéliens, ismaïliens.

Ismailism |ismɑ'i:lizm|, *s.* ismaélisme *m,* ismaïlisme *m.*

iso- |'aisə, 'aisou, ai'sɔ|, *pref.* iso-.

isoagglutination |'aisouəglu:ti'neiʃ(ə)n|, *s. Physiol: Med:* isoagglutination *f.*

isoagglutinin |'aisouə'glu:tinin|, *s. Physiol: Med:* isoagglutinine *f.*

isoamyl |aisou'æmil|, *s. Ch:* isoamyle *m.*

isoamylic |'aisouæ'milik|, *a. Ch:* isoamylique.

isoantibody |'aisou'æntibɔdi|, *s. Physiol: Med:* isoanticorps *m.*

isoantigen |aisou'æntidʒen|, *s. Physiol: Med:* isoantigène *m.*

isoapiol(e) |aisou'æpiɔl|, *s. Ch:* isoapiol *m.*

isobar |'aisoubɑ:r|, *s.* **1.** *Meteor: Ph:* isobare *f*; courbe *f* isobare; ligne *f* isobare. **2.** *Atom.Ph:* isobare.

isobaric |aisou'bærik|. **1.** *a.* (*a*) *Meteor: Ph:* (ligne) isobare; (carte) isobarique, isobarométrique; **i. curve,** (courbe, ligne) isobarique (*f*); **i. surface,** surface *f* isobare; (*b*) *Atom.Ph:* **i. spin,** spin *m* isobarique, isotopique. **2.** *s. Meteor:* (ligne) isobare.

isobarometric |aisoubærou'metrik|, *a. Meteor:* (carte) isobarique, isobarométrique.

isobase |'aisoubeis|, *s. Geol:* isobase *f.*

isobath |'aisoubæθ|, *s. Oc:* isobathe *f.*

isobathic |aisou'bæθik|, *a. Oc:* isobathe.

isobilateral |aisoubai'lætərəl|, *a. Bot:* (*of leaf*) bifacial, -aux.

isoborneol |aisou'bɔ:niɔl|, *s. Ch:* isobornéol *m.*

isobront(on) |'aisoubrɔnt, aisou'brɔnt(ə)n|, *s. Meteor:* isobronte *f.*

isobutane |aisou'bju:tein|, *s. Ch:* isobutane *m.*

isobutyl |aisou'bju:til|, *s. Ch:* isobutyle *m.*

isobutylene |aisou'bju:tili:n|, *s. Ch:* isobutène *m,* isobutylène *m.*

isocaloric |aisoukæ'lɔrik|, *a. Med:* (régime) isocalorique.

isocandle |'aisoukændl|, *a. Ph:* (diagramme, ligne) isabougie.

isocardia |aisou'kɑ:diə|, *s. Moll:* isocarde *f*; *F:* cœur-de-bœuf *m, pl.* cœurs-de-bœuf.

isocephalic |aisouse'fælik|, *a.* isocéphalique.

isocephaly |aisou'sefəli|, *s.* isocéphalie *f.*

isocheim |'aisoukaim|, *s. Meteor:* (ligne) isochimène *f.*

isocheimal |aisou'kaiməl|, **isochimenal** |aisou'kaimənl|, *a. Meteor:* (ligne) isochimène.

isochore |'aisoukɔ:r|, *s. Ph:* (courbe *f*) isochore (*f*).

isochoric |aisou'kɔrik|, *a.* isochore.

isochromatic |aisoukrou'mætik|, *a. Opt: Phot:* (ligne, courbe) isochromatique; *Mec.* isochromes.

isochronal |ai'sɔkrənəl|, **isochronic** |aisou'krɔnik|, *a.* = ISOCHRONOUS.

isochrone |'aisoukroun|, *s. Geol: Meteor:* isochrone *f.*

isochronism |ai'sɔkrənizm|, *s. Mec: Physiol:* isochronisme *m.*

isochronous |ai'sɔkrənəs|, *a. Mec: etc:* isochrone, isochronique; **i. curve,** ligne *f,* courbe *f,* isochrone, tautochrone; *Mch:* **i. governor,** régulateur *m* isochrone.

isocinchomeronic |'aisousiŋkoume'rɔnik|, *a. Ch:* isocinchoméronique.

isoclasite |ai'sɔkləsait|, *s. Miner:* isoclase *m or f,* isoclasite *m or f.*

isoclinal |aisou'klainl|, *a.* & *s.* **1.** *Geol:* (pli, etc.) isoclinal, -aux. **2.** *Magn: etc:* **i. (line),** ligne *f* isoclinique, isocline; isocline *f.*

isocline ['aisəklain], *s. Geol:* isocline *f.*

isoclinic |aisou'klinik|, *a. Geol: Magn:* (ligne) isoclinique, isocline.

isocolloid |aisou'kɔlɔid|, *s. Ph:* isocolloïde *m.*

isocolon |aisou'koulən|, *s. Rh:* isocolon *m.*

isocracking |'aisoukrækiŋ|, *s. Petr:* isocraquage *m,* craquage isomérisant.

Isocrates |ai'sɔkrəti:z|. *Pr.n.m. Gr.Hist:* Isocrate.

isocyanate |aisou'saiəneit|, *s. Ch:* isocyanate *m.*

isocyanic |aisousai'ænik|, *a. Ch:* isocyanique.

isocyanide |aisou'saiənaid|, *s. Ch:* carbylamine *f,* isonitrile *m.*

isocyclic |aisou'saiklik|, *a. Ch:* isocyclique.

isodactylism [aisou'dæktilizm], *s. Z:* isodactylie *f.*

isodactylous [aisou'dæktiləs], *a. Z:* isodactyle.

isodiabatic |'aisoudaiə'bætik|, *a. Ph:* isodiabatique.

isodiapheres |aisou'daiəfi:əz|, *s.pl. Atom.Ph:* noyaux *m* isodiaphères.

isodimorphic, isodimorphous |aisoudai'mɔ:fik, -fəs|, *a. Cryst:* isodimorphe.

isodimorphism |aisoudai'mɔ:fizm|, *s. Cryst:* isodimorphisme *m.*

isodomic, isodomous |ai'sɔdəmik, -məs|, *a. Arch:* isodome.

isodomon |ai'sɔdəmən|, **isodomum,** *pl.* **-a** |ai'sɔdəməm, -ə|, *s. Arch:* isodomon *m.*

isodont |'aisoudɔnt|, **isodontal, isodontous** |aisou'dɔntl, -təs|, *a. Z:* isodonte.

isodose |'aisou'dous|, *s. Atom.Ph: Med: etc:* isodose *f*; **i. curve, line,** courbe *f,* ligne, *f,* isodose, isodosique; **i. chart,** carte *f* d'isodoses; **i. diagram,** *U.S:* **i. pattern,** diagramme *m* d'isodoses; **i. map,** carte *f* d'isodoses; *Atom.Ph:* **i. recorder,** enregistreur *m* d'isodoses.

isodynamia |aisoudai'neimiə|, *s. Mec: Physiol:* isodynamie *f.*

isodynamic |aisoudai'næmik|, *a.* **1.** *Mec: Magn:* **i. curve, line,** courbe *f,* ligne *f,* isodynamique. **2.** *Physiol:* **i. foods,** aliments *m* isodynamiques, isodynames.

isoelectric |aisoui'lektrik|, *a. Ch:* (point, etc.) isoélectrique.

isoelectronic |aisouilek'trɔnik|, *a.* isoélectronique.

isoelectronically |aisouilek'trɔnik(ə)li|, *adv.* isoélectroniquement.

isoetes |ai'souiti:z|, *s. Bot:* isoète *m.*

isoeugenol |aisou'ju:dʒinɔl|, *s. Ch:* isoeugénol *m.*

isogamic |aisou'gæmik|, **isogamous** |ai'sɔgəməs|, *a. Bot:* isogame.

isogamy |ai'sɔgəmi|, *s. Bot:* isogamie *f.*

isogeotherm |aisou'dʒi:ouθə:m|, *s.* (ligne) isogéotherme (*f*).

isogeothermal |aisoudʒi:ou'θə:ml|, *a.* & *s.* (ligne) isogéotherme (*f*).

isogloss |'aisouglɔs|, *s. Ling:* ligne *f* isoglosse.

isoglossal |aisou'glɔsəl|, *a. Ling:* isoglosse.

isogonal [ai'sɔgənəl]. **1.** *a.* = ISOGONIC 1(*a*). **2.** *s.* = ISOGONIC 2.

isogonic [aisou'gɔnik]. **1.** *a.* (*a*) *Mth: Magn:* (ligne) isogone, isogonique; **transformation by i. conjugates,** transformation arguésienne inverse; conjugué isogonal; (*b*) *Biol:* (organe) isogonique, isométrique. **2.** *s. Mth: Magn:* ligne *f* isogone.

isogram |'aisougræm|, *s.* ligne *f* isoplèthe.

isohaline |aisou'heilain|, **isohalsine** |aisou'hælsain|, *s.* isohaline *f.*

isohel |'aisouhel|, *a.* (courbe) isohèle.

isohyet |aisou'haiət|, *s. Meteor:* isohyète *m.*

isohyetal |aisou'haiətəl|, *a. Meteor:* isohyète.

isohypse |aisou'hips|, *s. Mapm:* isohypse *f.*

isoionic |aisouai'ɔnik|, *a. Ch: Ph:* isoïonique.

isolable |'aisələbl|, *a. Ch: etc:* isolable.

isolate[1] |'aisəleit|, *v.tr.* **1.** (*a*) isoler (un malade, un fil électrique, etc.) (**from,** de, d'avec); **to i. sick cattle,** cantonner des bestiaux malades; *Mth:* **to i. the unknown quantity,** dégager l'inconnue; *Tchn:* **to i. a fault,** localiser une panne; (*b*) faire le vide autour de (qn). **2.** *Ch:* isoler, dégager (un corps simple); *Biol:* isoler (une culture). **3.** *El:* = INSULATE 2(*a*).

isolate[2], *s.* isolat *m.*

isolated |'aisəleitid|, *a.* (hameau) isolé, écarté, détaché, relégué; **i. instance,** cas isolé; **i. farm,** ferme isolée, détachée; *El:* **i. plant,** installation isolée.

isolating[1] |'aisəleitiŋ|, *a.* isolant; *esp. Ling:* **i. languages,** langues isolantes.

isolating[2], *s.* isolement *m*; **i. of sick animals,** cantonnement *m* des bêtes malades; *Mil:* **complete i. of an enemy position,** isolement complet d'une position ennemie; *El:* **i. condenser,** condensateur *m* d'isolement; **i. switch,** interrupteur *m* d'isolement (de ligne); sectionneur *m*; **i. circuit,** circuit *m* d'isolement; *Mch: etc:* **i. valve,** robinet *m* d'isolement (de conduite de vapeur, etc.).

isolation |aisə'leiʃ(ə)n|, *s.* **1.** (*a*) isolement *m* (d'un malade); **i. hospital,** hôpital *m* d'isolement; hôpital de contagieux; **i. ward,** service *m* des contagieux; (*b*) *El: Ac: etc:* = INSULATION 2. **2.** isolement, solitude *f*; **policy of splendid i.,** politique *f* du splendide isolement.

isolationism |aisə'leiʃənizm|, *s. Pol:* isolationnisme *m.*

isolationist |aisə'leiʃənist|, *a. & s. Pol:* isolationniste (*mf*).

isolator |'aisəleitər|, *s. El:* (*a*) isolant *m*, isolateur *m*, isoloir *m*; tabouret isolant; (*b*) (*switch*) interrupteur *m* (de ligne); sectionneur *m.*

Isolde |i'zɔldə|. *Pr.n.f.* Yseu(l)t, Iseu(l)t.

isolette |aisə'let|, *s. Med: NAm:* incubateur *m* (pour nouveau-né).

isoleucine |aisou'lju:si:n|, *s. Ch:* isoleucine *f.*

isoline |'aisoulain|, *s. Meteor:* ligne *f* isoplèthe.

isolog(ue) |'aisəlɔg|, *s. Ch:* isologue *m.*

isologous |ai'sɔləgəs|, *a. Ch:* (corps) isologue.

isomagnetic |aisoumæg'netik|, *a.* (ligne) isomagnétique.

isomer |'aisəmər|, *s. Ch: Ph:* isomère *m.*

isomere |'aisəmiər|, *s. Anat:* portion *f* homologue (d'un membre).

isomeric |aisou'merik|, *a.* **1.** *Ch:* (corps simple) isomère, isomérique. **2.** *Bot:* (fleur) isomère, isomérique. **3.** *Anat:* (portion) homologue (d'un membre).

isomerism |ai'sɔmərizm|, *s. Ch: Bot:* isomérie *f*; **cis-trans i., syn-anti i.,** isomérie cis-trans.

isomerization |'aisoumərai'zeiʃ(ə)n|, *s. Ch: etc:* isomérisation *f.*

isomerous |ai'sɔmərəs|, *a.* **1.** *Bot:* isomère. **2.** *Ch: etc:* = ISOMERIC 1.

isometric(al) |aisou'metrik(l)|, *a.* **1.** (projection, perspective) isométrique; **i. drawing,** dessin *m* isométrique, en perspective; **i. drafting machine,** machine *f* à dessiner en perspective. **2.** *Cryst:* isométrique; tesséral, -aux. **3.** *Physiol:* (contraction musculaire) isométrique.

isomorph |'aisoumɔ:f|, *s. Cryst: etc:* isomorphe *m.*

isomorphic |aisou'mɔ:fik|, **isomorphous** |aisou'mɔ:fəs|, *a.* isomorphe.

isomorphism |aisou'mɔ:fizm|, *s. Cryst: Mth: etc:* isomorphisme *m.*

isoneph |'aisounef|, *s. Meteor:* isonèphe *f.*

isonephelic |aisou'nefəlik|, *a. Meteor:* isonèphe.

isoniazid |aisou'naiəzid|, *s. Med:* isoniazide *m.*

isonicotinic |'aisounikə'tinik|, *a. Ch:* isonicotinique.

isonitrile |aisou'naitrail|, *s. Ch:* isonitrile *m.*

isonomy |ai'sɔnəmi|, *s. Pol: Cryst:* isonomie *f.*

isooctane |aisou'ɔktein|, *s. Ch:* isooctane *m.*

isopachyte |aisou'pækait|, *s. Geol:* isopache *f.*

isoparaffin |aisou'pærəfin|, *s.* isoparaffine *f.*

isopelletierine |aisoupeli'tiəri:n|, *s. Ch:* isopelletiérine *f.*

isopentane |aisou'pentein|, *s. Ch:* isopentane *m.*

isoperimeter |aisoupə'rimitər|, *s. Mth:* isopérimètre *m.*

isoperimetrical |'aisouperi'metrikl|, *a. Mth:* isopérimètre.

isophanal |'aisoufein(ə)l|, *a. Biol:* isophane, isophène.

isophane |'aisoufein|, **isophene** |'aisoufi:n|, *s. Biol:* isophène *m*, isophane *m.*

isophotal |aisou'foutl|, *a. Opt:* (ligne) isophote.

isophthalic |aisɔf'θælik|, *a. Ch:* (acide) isophtalique.

isopleth |'aisoupleθ|, *s.* ligne *f* isoplèthe.

isopod, *pl.* **-pods, -poda** |'aisəpɔd, -pɔdz, ai'sɔpədə|, *s. Crust:* isopode *m*; **the Isopoda,** les isopodes.

isopodan |ai'sɔpəd(ə)n|, *a. & s. Crust:* isopode (*m*).

isopodous |ai'sɔpədəs|, *a. Crust:* isopode.

isoprene |'aisoupri:n|, *s. Ch:* isoprène *m.*

isopropenyl |aisou'proupenil|, *s. Ch:* isopropényle *m.*

isopropyl |aisou'proupil|, *s. Ch:* isopropyle *m*; **i. alcohol,** alcool *m* isopropylique.

Isoptera |ai'sɔptərə|, *s.pl. Ent:* isoptères *m*; (les) termites *m.*

isoquinoline |aisou'kwinəli:n|, *s. Ch:* isoquinoléine *f.*

isosceles |ai'sɔsili:z|, *a. Mth:* (triangle) isocèle.

isoseismal |aisou'saizməl|, *a. & s. Geol:* **i. (line),** (ligne *f*) isoséiste (*f*), isosiste (*f*).

isoseismic |aisou'saizmik|, *a. Geol:* isoséiste, isosiste.

isoseist |'aisousaist|, *s. Geol:* isoséiste *f*, isosiste *f.*

isospin |'aisouspin|, *s. Ch: Ph:* spin *m* isotopique, isobarique; isospin *m.*

Isospondyli |aisou'spɔndilai|, *s.pl. Ich:* isospondyles *m.*

isosporous |ai'sɔspərəs|, *a. Bot:* isospore.

isostasy |ai'sɔstəsi|, *s. Geol:* isostasie *f.*

isostatic |aisou'stætik|, *a. Geol:* (mouvement, etc.) isostatique.

isostemonous |aisou'stemənəs|, *a. Bot:* isostémone.

isosteric |aisou'sterik|, *a. Ch:* isostère.

isosterism |ai'sɔstərizm|, *s. Ch:* isostérie *f.*

isotheral |aisou'θiərəl|, *a. & s. Meteor:* **i. (line),** ligne *f* isothère.

isotherm |'aisouθə:m|, *s. Meteor:* isotherme *f.*

isothermal |aisou'θə:m(ə)l|, **isothermic** |aisou'θə:mik|, *a. Ph: Meteor:* (transformation, ligne) isotherme, isothermique.

isotone |'aisoutoun|, *s. Ph:* isotone *m*; **i. nuclides,** nucléides *m* isotones.

isotonic |aisou'tɔnik|, *a. Ph: etc:* isotonique; *Med:* **i. solution,** soluté *m* isotonique; *Physiol:* **i. contraction,** contraction *f* isotonique (d'un muscle).

isotonicity |aisoutə'nisiti|, *s. Ph: Physiol:* isotonie *f.*

isotope |'aisoutoup|, *s. Ch: Ph:* isotope *m*; **parent i.,** isotope père, isotope précurseur; **tracer i.,** isotope indicateur, traceur; **abundance ratio of isotopes,** rapport *m* isotopique; **i. nuclides,** nucléides *m* isotopes; **i. exchange,** échange *m* isotopique; **i. separation,** séparation *f* des isotopes, isotopique; **i. technology,** technologie *f* des isotopes.

isotopic |aisou'tɔpik|, *a. Ph: Ch:* (effet, courant, déplacement, nombre, masse) isotopique; **i. datation,** datation *f* isotopique, par les isotopes; **i. spin,** spin *m* isotopique, isobarique; isospin *m*; *Atom.Ph:* **i. indicator, tracer,** indicateur *m*, traceur *m*, isotopique.

isotopy |ai'sɔtəpi|, *s. Ch:* isotopie *f.*

isotron |'aisoutrɔn|, *s. Atom.Ph:* isotron *m*; **i. separator,** séparateur *m* isotron.

isotropic |aisou'trɔpik|, *a. Ph: Cryst:* isotrope, isotropique; *Biol:* (œuf) isotrope; **optically i.,** monoréfringent; **i. medium,** milieu *m* isotropique, isotrope; *Atom.Ph:* **i. scattering of neutrons,** diffusion *f* isotropique des neutrons.

isotropism |ai'sɔtrəpizm|, **isotropy** |ai'sɔtrəpi|, *s. Ch: Ph:* isotropie *f.*

isotype |'aisoutaip|, *s. Nat.Hist:* isotype *m.*

isotypic(al) |aisou'tipik(l)|, *a. Cryst:* isotype.

isovaleric |'aisouvæ'lerik|, *a. Ch:* isovalérique, isovalérianique.

isoxazole |ais'ɔksəzoul|, *s. Ch:* isoxazole *m.*

Israel |'izreiəl|. *Pr.n. Geog: B.Hist:* Israël *m.*

Israeli |iz'reili|. *Geog:* **1.** *a.* israélien. **2.** *s.* (*pl.* **Israeli(s)**) Israélien, -ienne.

Israelite |'izriəlait|. **1.** *a.* israélite. **2.** *s.* Israélite *mf.*

Israelitic |izriə'litik|, *a.* (histoire, etc.) israélite.

Israelitish |'izriəlaitiʃ|, *a.* israélite.

issuable |'isjuəbl|, *a.* **1.** *Jur:* **i. matter,** matière *f* à litige. **2.** *Fin:* (*of bonds, etc.*) émissible, susceptible d'être émis. **3. his resignation is i.,** sa démission pourra en résulter.

issuance |'isjuəns|, *s. NAm:* délivrance *f* (d'un brevet, d'un permis de conduire).

issuant |'isjuənt|, *a. Her:* (lion, etc.) issuant.

issue[1] |'isju:|, *s.* **1.** sortie *f*, décharge *f* (de fumée, etc.). **2.** *Med:* (*a*) épanchement *m*, perte *f*, décharge, saillie *f* (de sang, etc.); écoulement *m*, décharge (de pus); (*b*) *O:* **running i.,** cautère *m* en plein écoulement; exutoire *m*; **i. pea,** pois *m* à cautère. **3.** (*way out*) (*a*) issue *f*, sortie, débouché *m* (**out of,** de); **the issues from the Underground,** les sorties du Métro; **to find an i. out of one's difficulties,** trouver un moyen de sortir de ses difficultés; (*b*) embouchure *f* (d'un fleuve); déversoir *m* (d'un barrage, etc.). **4.** issue, résultat *m*, fin *f*, dénouement *m*, aboutissement *m*; **whatever the i. of the combat may be,** quelle que soit l'issue du combat; **to await the i. (of events),** attendre la fin, le résultat; **to abide the i.,** attendre l'issue; **in the i., nothing was decided,** à la fin, en fin de compte, il n'y avait rien de décidé; **what will be the i. of it all?** que sortira-t-il de tout cela? **to bring the matter to an i.,** faire aboutir la question; en finir avec la question; **to bring sth. to a happy i.,** mener qch. à bonne fin, à bien; faire aboutir qch.; **favourable, unfavourable, i.,** bon, mauvais, résultat; bonne, mauvaise, fin. **5.** progéniture *f*, descendance *f*, postérité *f*; **to leave i.,** laisser postérité; **to die without i.,** mourir sans postérité, sans laisser de postérité; **died without i.,** mort sine prole; **his numberless i.,** ses innombrables descendants *m*. **6.** (*a*) *Jur:* **i. (of fact, of law),** (i) question *f*, point *m* (de fait, de droit); (ii) conclusion *f*; **main i. of a suit,** fond *m* d'un procès; **side i.,** question d'intérêt secondaire; **to plead the general i.,** plaider non coupable; **to state an i.,** poser une question; *Fig:* **I don't want to make an i. of it,** je n'en fais pas une affaire; (*b*) **to join i.,** accepter les conclusions; **to join i. with s.o. about sth.,** discuter l'opinion, le dire, de qn au sujet de qch.; **here I join i. with you,** ici je me sépare entièrement de vous; **the i. joined,** la cause en état; **the case at i.,** le cas en litige; **the point at i.,** la question pendante, contestée; **matters at i.,** matières *f* en contestation, en discussion; **the business at i.,** l'affaire dont il s'agit; **the interests at i.,** les intérêts en jeu; **the case is at i. on its merits,** le fond de la cause est en état; **to be at i. on a question,** être en débat sur une question; **to be at i., take i., with s.o.,** être (i) en désaccord, (ii) en contestation, avec qn; **to put a claim in i.,** contester une réclamation; **to obscure the i.,** (i) obscurcir la question; *F:* embrouiller l'écheveau; (ii) *Fig:* faire du camouflage autour de la question; **to evade the i.,** user de fuites, de subterfuge, de faux-fuyants; **to confuse the i.,** masquer le but à atteindre; empêcher de prendre des résolutions; brouiller les cartes; (*c*) *P:* **and the whole bloody i.,** et tout le bataclan, et toute la sacrée bande. **7.** (*a*) *Adm: Fin:* émission *f* (de mandats, d'un emprunt, de billets de banque, d'actions, etc., *Post:* de timbres-poste); **to make a new i. of capital, a new loan i.,** procéder à une nouvelle augmentation de capital, à un nouvel emprunt; **home currency issues,** billets émis à l'intérieur du pays; **i. price,** taux *m* d'émission; *Bank:* **i. department,** service *m* des émissions; (*b*) *Adm: Mil: etc:* distribution *f*, *Mil:* versement *m*, sortie (de matériel, vivres, etc.); **free i.,** distribution, délivrance *f*, à titre gratuit; **i. in kind,** prestation *f* en nature; *Com: Cmptr:* **i. card,** carte *f* (de) sortie de stock; *Mil: etc:* **i. boots, shirts,** brodequins *m*, chemises *f*, réglementaires, de l'armée; *U.S:* **government i. equipment,** matériel *m* réglementaire de l'armée; *Navy:* (*on ship*) **i. room,** soute *f* à provisions, aux vivres; coqueron *m*; cambuse *f*; (*c*) (i) parution *f*, publication *f* (d'un livre); lancement *m* (d'un prospectus, etc.); **in course of i.,** en cours de publication; (ii) *Mil:* **i. of orders,** publication des ordres; (*d*) *Rail: etc:* délivrance (de billets, de passeports, etc.); *Th:* contrôle *m* (des billets); (*in library*) **i. of books,** communication *f* de livres. **8.** édition *f* (d'un livre); édition, numéro *m* (d'un journal).

issue[2]. **1.** *v.i.* (*a*) **to i. (out, forth),** (i) *A:* (*of pers.*) sortir; (ii) (*of blood, water*) jaillir, s'écouler, découler (**from,** de); **a smell of garlic is issuing from the kitchen,** de la cuisine se dégage une odeur d'ail; *Lit:* **spring that issues from the earth,** source qui sort de la terre; (*b*) provenir, dériver (**from,** de); **income issuing out of land,** revenu provenant d'une propriété; **the children issuing from this marriage,** les enfants provenant, provenus, de ce mariage; (*c*) **to i. in sth.,** avoir (qch) pour résultat; se terminer par, aboutir à (qch.). **2.** *v.tr.* (*a*) émettre, mettre en circulation (des billets de banque, etc.); créer (un effet de commerce); (*b*) publier, donner (une nouvelle édition, etc.); lancer (un prospectus, etc.); *Jur:* **to i. a summons, a warrant for the arrest of s.o.,** décerner, lancer, une citation, un mandat d'arrêt contre qn; **to i. a decree,** rendre un arrêt, *Fin:* **to i. a letter of credit,** fournir une lettre de crédit; **to i. a draft on s.o.,** fournir une traite sur qn; *Com:* **bill issued for value received in goods,** billet causé en valeur reçue en marchandises; *Mil:* **to i. an order,** publier, donner, un ordre; (*c*) verser, distribuer (des provisions, etc.); délivrer (des billets de chemin de fer, des passeports, etc.); (*of library*) communiquer (des livres); **no rifles have been issued yet,** on n'a pas encore touché de fusils; **each man will be issued with two uniforms,** chaque homme touchera deux tenues; **to i. s.o. with sth.,** délivrer qch. à qn; **pensioners are issued with a special card,** on délivre une carte spéciale aux retraités; *Navy: A:* **to i. the ship's company with rum,** distribuer du rhum à l'équipage.

issueless |'isjulis|, *a.* **1.** (défunt) sans enfants, sans descendance; **to die i.,** mourir sans laisser d'enfants, sans postérité. **2.** (démarche, etc.) qui ne produit rien; (discussion, etc.) sans résultat.

issuer |'isjuər|, *s.* **1.** *Fin:* émetteur *m* (d'un billet de banque); créateur, -trice (d'un effet de commerce). **2.** délivreur *m*, distributeur, -trice (de billets de chemin de fer, de provisions, etc.).

issuing[1] |'isjuiŋ|, *a.* **1.** (fumée) qui sort; (sang, eau) qui jaillit. **2.** émetteur, -trice; distributeur, -trice; *Post:* **i. office,** bureau *m* d'émission, *Fin:* **i. banker,** banquier émetteur; **i. company,** société émettrice; **i. house,** banque *f* de placement.

issuing[2], *s.* **1.** émission *f* (d'un emprunt, etc.); publication *f* (d'un livre, d'un journal). **2.** délivrance *f* (de billets); distribution *f* (de vivres); (*in library*) communication *f* (des livres).

Istanbul |istæn'bu:l|. *Pr.n. Geog:* Istanb(o)ul *m*, Istamb(o)ul *m.*

isthmian |'is(θ)miən|. **1.** *a.* (*a*) *Geog:* (terrain, canal, etc.), isthmique; *U.S:* **the I. canal,** le canal de Panama; (*b*) *Gr.Ant:* **i. games, i. festival,** jeux *m* isthmiques; **i. odes,** odes *f* isthmiques; isthmiques *f*. **2.** *s. Geog:* **Isthmian,** habitant, -ante, d'un isthme; *U.S:* habitant de l'isthme de Panama; Panaméen, -éenne; *A.Hist:* habitant de l'isthme de Corinthe.

isthmus, *pl.* **-muses** [ˈis(θ)məs, -məsiz], *s. Geog: Anat:* isthme *m*; **the I. of Suez,** l'isthme de Suez; *Anat:* **i. of the fauces,** isthme du gosier, bucco-pharyngien, *pl.* bucco-pharyngiens.

istle [istli], *s. Bot:* ixtle *m*; *Com:* **i. (fibre),** tampico *m.*

Istria [ˈistriə]. *Pr.n. Geog:* Istrie *f.*

Istrian [ˈistriən]. *Geog:* **1.** *a.* istrien. **2.** *s.* Istrien, -ienne.

it[1] [it], *pers.pron.* **1.** (*referring to inanimate objects, animals, and colloquially to children, but in French taking the gender of the noun for which* it *stands*) (*a*) (*nom.*) il, *f.* elle; **the house is small but it is my own,** la maison est petite mais elle est à moi; **where is your hat?—it's in the cupboard,** où est votre chapeau?—il est dans l'amoire; (*b*) (*acc.*) le, *f.* la; **he took her hand and pressed it,** il lui prit la main et la serra; **I don't believe it,** je ne le crois pas; **I do not remember it,** je ne me le rappelle pas; je ne m'en souviens pas; **and my cake, have you tasted it?** et mon gâteau, y avez-vous goûté? **he had felt the charm and still felt it,** il s'était senti sous le charme, il y était encore; *P: Hum:* (*of pers., to express contempt*) **this is my boy friend—where did you find it?** c'est mon flirt—où l'as-tu ramassé? où as-tu ramassé ça? (*c*) (*dat.*) lui *mf*; **fetch the dog and give it something to eat,** allez chercher le chien et donnez-lui à manger; (*d*) (*reflexive*) **the Committee has devoted much care to the task before it,** le comité a donné beaucoup d'attention à la tâche qui lui incombait; (*e*) (*stressed*) *F:* **he thinks he's it** [hiːzˈit], il se croit sorti de la cuisse de Jupiter; **this book is absolutely** ***it!*** c'est un livre épatant! **she's got** ***it,*** elle a du chien; **it's the it of its,** c'est le nec plus ultra; **this is** ***it,*** nous y voilà! ça y est! on est fait! *Games:* (*at blind man's buff, etc.*) **to be** ***it,*** être le chasseur, le chercheur; **he's going to be** ***it,*** il le sera. **2.** (*a*) (*as vague object of a verb*) **to face it,** faire front; **hang it!** zut! sapristi! **I haven't got it in me to hurt him,** je ne suis pas capable de lui faire mal; **I didn't think he had it in him,** je ne pensais pas qu'il possédait cette qualité; *for* **come it, foot it, lord it, rough it, etc.,** *see the verbs*; (*b*) (*as vague object of a preposition*) **now for it!** et maintenant allons-y! **there is nothing for it but to run,** il n'y a qu'une chose à faire, c'est de filer; *F:* **he's (in) for it,** son affaire est bonne; je ne le vois pas blanc; **to have a bad time of it,** souffrir; en voir de dures; **the worst of it is that he's unashamed,** le plus mauvais de la chose c'est qu'il n'a pas honte. **3.** ce, cela, il; **who is it?** qui est-ce? **that's it,** (i) c'est ça; (ii) ça y est! **that's not it,** ce n'est pas cela; **it was John who told me so,** c'est Jean qui me l'a dit; **it was the French army that made the assault,** ce fut l'armée française qui donna l'assaut; **it was here that it happened,** c'est ici que c'est arrivé; **it frightens me,** cela me fait peur; **it doesn't matter,** cela ne fait rien; **it's raining,** il pleut; **it's ten o'clock,** il est dix heures; **it's Monday,** c'est aujourd'hui lundi; **it was the seventh of March,** on était au sept mars. **4.** (*anticipatory*) (*a*) (*provisional subject*) **it only remains to thank the reader,** il ne me reste qu'à remercier le lecteur; **it's nonsense talking like that,** il est absurde de parler comme ça; **a more heinous offence it is hard to imagine,** il est difficile d'imaginer une offense plus grave; **it is impossible to work in this heat,** il est impossible de travailler par cette chaleur; **it relieved him to accuse himself,** cela le soulageait de s'accuser; **it makes one shudder to look down,** cela vous fait frémir de regarder en bas; **it appears that he lost his way,** il paraît qu'il s'est égaré; **it is only rarely that we see him,** ce n'est que rarement que nous le voyons; **how is it that you are still here?** d'où vient que vous êtes encore ici? **it is said that he was very mean,** on dit qu'il était très avare; **it says in the regulations that all passengers must have tickets,** on lit dans les règlements que chaque voyageur doit être muni d'un billet; **it is laid down that the guilty must be punished,** il est écrit que les coupables doivent être punis; (*b*) (*provisional object*) **they believe it their duty to look after our morals,** ils croient de leur devoir de surveiller nos mœurs; **the fog made it difficult to calculate the distance,** le brouillard rendait difficile l'estimation des distances; **I thought it well to warn you,** j'ai jugé bon de vous avertir; **I hardly think it likely that he'll come,** je ne crois guère qu'il vienne; **I leave it to others to answer,** je laisse à d'autres le soin de répondre; **she took it into her head that he was angry,** elle s'est mis dans la tête qu'il était fâché; **you may rely upon it that he will do his best,** vous pouvez compter qu'il fera de son mieux. **5.** (*with prepositions*) **at it, in it, to it,** y; **to consent to it,** y consentir; **look to it,** faites-y attention; **to fall in it,** y tomber; **the box and the negatives contained in it,** la boîte et les clichés y contenus; **my consignment and the invoice relating to it,** mon envoi *m* et la facture y relative; **above it, over it,** au-dessus; dessus; **a courtyard with a glazed roof over it,** une cour avec un vitrage au-dessus; **someone has spilt ink over it,** on a répandu de l'encre dessus; **below it, under(neath) it,** au-dessous; dessous; **for it,** en, y; pour lui, pour elle, pour cela; **he loved his country and died for it,** il aimait sa patrie et mourut pour elle; **I feel the better for it,** je m'en trouve mieux; **from it,** en; **he's not bad, far from it,** il n'est pas méchant, loin de là, tant s'en faut, il s'en faut; **of it,** en, y; **give me half of it,** donnez-m'en la moitié; **I'll speak of it,** j'en parlerai; **think of it,** pensez-y; **on it,** y, dessus; **don't tread on it,** ne marchez pas dessus; **when I got up from the table I left my letter on it,** en quittant la table j'y ai laissé ma lettre; **with it,** avec cela, avec lui, avec elle; *F:* avec; **the river carries everything along with it,** la rivière entraîne tout avec elle; **I seized a stone and cracked his head with it,** j'ai saisi une pierre et lui ai fendu la tête avec.

It[2], *s. F:* (*abbr. of* **Italian**) vermouth italien; **a gin and It,** un gin vermouth.

ita [ˈiːtə], *s. Bot:* **i. (palm),** mauritia *f.*

itabirite [itæˈbairait], *s. Miner:* itabirite *f.*

itacism [ˈiːtəsizm], *s. Ling:* itacisme *m.*

itacolumite [aitəˈkɔlumait], *s. Geol:* itacolumite *f.*

itaconic [aitəˈkɔnik], *a. Ch:* (acide) itaconique.

Italian [iˈtæliən]. **1.** *a.* (*a*) *Geog:* italien; **I. sky,** ciel *m* d'Italie; (*b*) **I. cooking,** cuisine italienne; **I. blind,** store *m* à l'italienne; **I. hand,** écriture anglaise; **I. cloth,** percaline *f* pour doublures. **2.** *s.* (*a*) Italien, -ienne; (*b*) *Ling:* italien *m*; (*c*) *F:* vermouth italien.

Italianate[1] [iˈtæliəneit], *a.* italianisé.

Italianate[2], *v.tr.* italianiser.

Italianism [iˈtæliənizm], *s.* **1.** *Ling:* italianisme *m.* **2.** (*a*) italianisme, caractère italien; (*b*) amour *m* de l'Italie, des choses italiennes.

Italianist [iˈtæliənist], *s.* **1.** italianisant, -e. **2.** amateur *m* de l'Italie, des choses italiennes.

Italianization [itæliənaiˈzeiʃ(ə)n], *s.* italianisation *f.*

Italianize [iˈtæliənaiz], *v.tr.* italianiser; **to become Italianized,** s'italianiser.

Italic [iˈtælik]. **1.** *a. A.Geog: Ling:* italique. **2.** *Typ:* **italic:** (*a*) *a.* (caractère *m*) italique; **i. capitals,** capitales penchées; (*b*) *s. usu. pl.* **to print in italic(s),** imprimer en italique(s); **the italics are mine,** c'est moi qui souligne.

Italicism [iˈtælisizm], *s.* italianisme *m*; tour *m* de phrase italien.

italicization [itælisaiˈzeiʃ(ə)n], *s. Typ:* mise *f* en italique(s).

italicize [iˈtælisaiz], *v.tr. Typ:* imprimer, mettre, en italiques; (*in manuscript*) souligner; **italicized words,** mots italiqués; mots en italiques.

Italiot [iˈtæliət]. *Ethn:* **1.** *a.* italiote. **2.** *s.* Italiote *mf.*

Italo- [ˈitəlou], *comb.fm.* italo-; **Italo-Byzantine,** italo-byzantin, *pl.* italo-byzantins; **I.-Celtic,** italo-celtique, *pl.* italo-celtiques.

Italy [ˈitəli]. *Pr.n. Geog:* Italie *f.*

itch[1] [itʃ], *s.* **1.** démangeaison *f*; *F:* **to have an i. for sth., to do sth.,** avoir une démangeaison de qch., de faire qch.; brûler, mourir d'envie, de faire qch.; **to have an i. for money, gain,** être âpre au gain; *F:* **the seven year i.,** l'écueil *m* des sept ans de mariage; la démangeaison de la septième année. **2.** *Med: F:* gale *f*; psore *f*, psora *f*; (*of animals*) gale, rogne *f*; (*slight*) *F:* grattelle *f*; **person suffering from the i.,** personne gratteleuse; **bricklayer's i.,** gale du ciment; **barber's i.,** sycosis *m*, mentagre *f*; **baker's i.,** psoriasis *m*; **i. ointment,** onguent *m* parasiticide; *Arach:* **i. mite,** démodex *m*; sarcopte *m*, acarus *m*, de la gale.

itch[2], *v.i.* **1.** (*a*) démanger; (*of pers.*) éprouver des démangeaisons; **my hand itches,** la main me démange; *impers.* **where does it i.?** où est-ce que cela vous démange? **garment that makes one i.,** vêtement qui irrite la peau; (*b*) **bites that i.,** morsures qui font éprouver des démangeaisons. **2.** *F:* **to i. to do sth.,** brûler, griller, mourir, d'envie de faire qch.; **my fingers are itching to thrash him,** les mains me démangent, me brûlent, de lui donner une raclée; **I was itching to speak,** la langue me démangeait (de parler); je mourais d'envie de prendre la parole; **she is itching to be off,** les pieds lui brûlent; **he's itching for trouble,** la peau lui démange.

itchiness [ˈitʃinis], *s.* démangeaison *f*, picotement *m* (à la peau).

itching[1] [ˈitʃiŋ], *a.* (plaie, peau) qui démange; *F:* **to have an i. palm,** être âpre au gain.

itching[2], *s.* **1.** démangeaison *f*; *Med:* prurit *m*; *F:* **I've an i. under my foot,** j'ai quelque chose qui m'asticote, me gratte, sous le pied. **2.** grande envie, *F:* démangeaison (de faire qch.).

itchweed [ˈitʃwiːd], *s. Bot:* vératre *m*, ellébore blanc.

itchy [ˈitʃi], *a.* **1.** *Med:* galeux. **2.** *F:* **I've got an i. elbow,** le coude me démange; j'ai des démangeaisons au coude; **to have i. feet,** brûler de (i) partir, (ii) se déplacer.

itea [ˈitiə], *s. Bot:* itea *m.*

item [ˈaitəm]. **1.** *adv. Com: Book-k:* de même; de plus; en outre; item. **2.** *s.* (*a*) *Com:* article *m*; **please send us the following items,** prière de nous envoyer les articles suivants; (*b*) *Book-k;* écriture *f*, article, poste *m*, détail *m*; **cash i.,** article de caisse; **i. of expenditure, expense i.,** article, chef *m*, de dépense; **credit i.,** poste créditeur; **balance sheet items,** détails du bilan; **to give the items on an invoice,** donner les détails d'une facture, détailler une facture; **this i. does not appear in our books,** cette écriture ne figure pas dans nos livres; (*c*) **the second i. of the contract,** l'article deux du contrat; **the items on the agenda,** les questions *f* à l'ordre du jour; **the last i. on the programme,** (i) *Th: etc:* le dernier numéro du programme; (ii) *Adm: etc:* la dernière rubrique du programme (de travaux publics, etc.); (*d*) *Journ:* **did you read that i. about the exhibition?** avez-vous lu cet entrefilet au sujet de l'exposition? **news items,** faits divers, échos *m*; (*e*) *Cmptr:* élément *m* d'information.

itemize [ˈaitəmaiz], *v.tr.* détailler (une facture, etc.); **itemized account,** compte spécifié.

iterance [ˈitərəns], *s.* répétition *f*, réitération *f* (d'une phrase).

iterate [ˈitəreit]. **1.** *v.tr.* réitérer; répéter (constamment) (un mot, une accusation). **2.** *v.tr. & i. Mth: Ph: Cmptr:* itérer; *v.i.* procéder par itération; *Cmptr:* effectuer des itérations.

iterated [ˈitəreitid], *a.* **1.** réitéré, répété. **2.** *Mth: Ph: Cmptr:* itéré; *Mth:* **i. integral,** intégrale itérée; *Atom.Ph:* **i. fission,** fission itérée, multiple.

iteration [itəˈreiʃ(ə)n], *s.* **1.** réitération *f*, répétition *f.* **2.** *Mth: Ph: Cmptr:* itération *f*; **i. methods,** méthodes *f* d'itération; *Cmptr:* **i. loop,** boucle *f* d'itérations.

iterative [ˈitərətiv], *a. Gram: Mth: Ph: etc:* itératif; *Mth:* **i. solution,** solution itérative; *El:* **i. impedance,** impédance itérative; *Cmptr:* **i. process, operation,** processus itératif, opération itérative; itération *f.*

Ithaca [ˈiθəkə]. *Pr.n. A.Geog:* Ithaque *f.*

ithagine [ˈiθədʒain], *s. Orn:* ithaginis *m.*

Ithomiidae [iθouˈmiːidiː], *s.pl. Ent:* ithomiides *m.*

ithyphallic [iθiˈfælik], *a. Gr.Ant: Pros:* ithyphallique.

itineracy [aiˈtinərəsi, it-], **itinerancy** [aiˈtinərənsi, it-], *s.* **1.** vie ambulante; vagabondage *m.* **2. itinerancy,** déplacements *mpl* (d'un prédicateur, etc.).

itinerant [iˈtinərənt, ai-], *a.* **1.** (marchand, comédien, musicien) ambulant; **i. vendor,** marchand forain; **i. gang of workmen,** brigade ambulante; **i. life,** vie vagabonde. **2. i. judges,** juges qui vont en tournée; juges ambulants.

itinerary [aiˈtinərəri]. **1.** *a.* itinéraire. **2.** *s.* (*route, guide book, map, record*) itinéraire *m.*

itinerate [iˈtinəreit, ai-], *v.i. O:* voyager; aller d'un endroit à un autre.

itineration [aitinəˈreiʃ(ə)n], *s.* voyages *mpl* de lieu en lieu; déplacements *mpl.*

its [its]. **1.** *poss.a.* son, *f.* sa, *pl.* ses; (*in the fem. before a vowel sound*) son; (*of animal*) **its nose, mouth, and eyes,** son nez, sa bouche, et ses yeux; (*of forest, etc.*) **its extent,** son étendue *f*; **do you know its extent?** est-ce que vous en connaissez l'étendue? **when the adder appeared again I cut off its head,** quand la vipère a reparu je lui ai coupé la tête; **a charm of its own,** un charme qui lui appartient; un charme qui est à lui seul, à elle seule. **2.** *occ. poss.pron.* (*stressed*) **the body has its function also, without which the soul could not fulfil** ***its,*** le corps aussi a sa fonction, sans laquelle l'âme ne saurait remplir la sienne.

itself [itˈself], *pers.pron.* lui-même, elle-même, soi-même; (*a*) (*emphatic*) **the child i. is quite normal,** l'enfant lui-même, elle-même, est tout à fait normal(e); **it would be simplicity i.,** ce serait tout ce qu'il y a de plus simple; **she is kindness i.,** elle est la bonté même, en personne; (*b*) (*reflexive*) **the dog hurt i.,** le chien s'est fait mal; **door that opens i.,** porte qui s'ouvre (d')elle-même, toute seule; **the house looks i. again after the repairs,** la maison reprend son aspect normal après les réparations; (*c*) (*after prepositions*) **the dog, child, was left by i.,** le chien, l'enfant, était laissé(e) tout(e) seul(e); **by i. the thing is not important,** toute seule la chose n'a pas d'importance; **the thing in i.,** la chose en elle-même; **frankness is attractive in i.,** la franchise est attirante en, de, soi; **an accident trifling in i.,** un accident sans importance en soi; **the cup wouldn't crack by i.,** la tasse ne se fendrait pas toute seule.

itsy-bitsy [ˈitsiˈbitsi], *a. F:* (*a*) (style) décousu; (*of room, etc.*) (i) meublé de bric et de broc; (ii) encombré de bibelots; (*b*) tout petit.

itty-bitty [ˈitiˈbiti], *a. NAm: F:* tout petit, mignon.

Iulus[1] [aiˈjuːləs]. *Pr.n.m. Lt.Lit:* Iule.

iulus[2], *s.* **1.** *Myr:* iule *m*; mille-pieds *m inv.* **2.** *Bot: A:* iule; chaton *m*.
iva |'aivə|, *s. Bot:* ive *f*, ivette *f*.
Ivanhoe |'aivənhou|. *Pr.n.m. Eng. Lit:* Ivanhoé.
ivied |'aivid|, *a.* couvert de lierre.
ivoried |'aivərid|, *a.* (teint, etc.) d'ivoire.
ivorine |'aivəri:n|, *s. Com:* ivorine *f*.
ivory |'aivəri|, *s.* **1.** (*a*) ivoire *m*; **raw, live, i.,** morfil *m*, ivoire vert; **imitation i.,** éburine *f*; ivorine *f*; **vegetable i.,** ivoire végétal; corozo *m*; **worker in i.,** ivoirier *m*; *F: A:* **black i.,** les esclaves noirs; *P:* le bois d'ébène; **the black i. trade,** la traite des noirs; (*b*) (objet *m* d')ivoire; **a collection of ivories,** une collection d'ivoires; (*c*) *pl. F:* **ivories:** (i) *Bill:* billes *f*; (ii) dés *m*; (iii) dents *f*; (iv) *Mus: A:* **to tickle the ivories,** jouer du piano; *F:* taquiner les touches, *A:* l'ivoire. **2.** *attrib.* (*a*) d'ivoire, en ivoire; **i. casket,** coffret *m* en ivoire, d'ivoire; **i. dealer,** marchand *m* d'ivoire; **i. trade,** ivoirerie *f*; **i. work,** ivoirerie; **i.-backed brush,** brosse *f* à dos d'ivoire; *Com:* **i. black,** noir *m* d'ivoire; *Lit:* **i. tower,** tour *f* d'ivoire; *P:* **i. dome,** intellectuel *m*; *F:* grosse tête; (*b*) **i. complexion,** teint *m* d'ivoire; **i.-white teeth,** dents *f* d'une blancheur d'ivoire; (*c*) *Bot:* **i. nut,** corozo *m*; **i. palm,** arbre *m* à ivoire; (*d*) *Geog:* **the I. Coast,** la Côte d'Ivoire; (*e*) *Paperm:* **i. paper,** (papier *m*) bristol *m*.
ivory-towered |'aivəri'tauəd|, *a. Lit:* (savant, etc.) reclus, qui vit en anchorite, en ermite.
ivy |'aivi|, *s. Bot:* **1.** lierre *m*; *Art: etc:* **i. leaf,** feuille *f* de lierre. **2. poison i.,** sumac vénéneux; *Fr.C:* herbe *f* à la puce; **American i.,** vigne *f* vierge; **ground i.,** lierre terrestre, rampant; rondelote *f*. **3.** *attrib. U.S:* **I. League,** qui fait partie, est caractéristique, porte le cachet, du cercle des vieilles universités prestigieuses des états de l'est; *Com:* **I. League suit,** complet très élégant et de bon ton.
ivy-clad, -covered, -mantled |'aiviklæd, -kʌvəd, -mæntld|, *a.* tapissé, couvert, de lierre.
ivy-leaved |'aivili:vd|, *a. Bot:* à feuilles de lierre; **i.-l. geranium,** géranium *m* lierre.
ixia |'iksiə|, *s. Bot:* ixia *f*, ixie *f*.
ixiolite |'iksioulait|, *s. Miner:* ixio(no)lite *f*.
ixodes |ik'soudi:z|, *s. Arach:* ixodes *m*.
ixodid |ik'soudid|, *s. Arach:* ixode *m*.
Ixodidae |ik'soudidi:|, *s.pl. Arach:* ixodidés *m*.
ixtle |'ikstli|, *s. Bot:* ixtle *m*.
izard |'izəd|, *s. Z:* isard *m*, izard *m*; antilope *f* chamois.
izba ['izbɑ:], *s.* isba *f*, chaumière *f* russe.
izzard |'izəd|, *s. U.S: A: & Dial:* (la lettre) Z, z.

J

J, j [dʒei], *s.* (la lettre) J, j *m*; *Tp:* **J for Jack,** J comme Joseph; **J pen,** plume J.

jab[1] [dʒæb], *s.* **1.** (*a*) coup *m* du bout de quelque chose; coup de pointe; (*b*) *Med: F:* piqûre *f*; **have you had your jabs?** tu les as eues, tes piqûres? **2.** *Box:* coup sec; un jab.

jab[2], *v.tr. & i.* **(jabbed; jabbing) 1. to j. s.o., sth., with sth.,** piquer qn, qch., du bout de qch.; **to j. a penknife into sth.,** enfoncer un canif, donner un coup de canif, dans qch.; **to j. s.o.'s eye out with an umbrella, to j. one's umbrella into s.o.'s eye,** crever un œil à qn avec un parapluie; **to j. at s.o., at sth.,** lancer un coup sec à qn, qch.; *Med: F:* **to j. s.o.,** faire une piqûre à qn. **2.** *Box:* donner un coup sec, un jab, à (qn).

jabber[1] ['dʒæbər], *s.* **1.** baragouin *m*, baragouinage *m*, bredouillage *m*. **2.** bavardage *m*, jacasserie *f*, jabotage *m*.

jabber[2]. **1.** *v.i.* (*a*) bredouiller, baragouiner; (*b*) jacasser; **she never stops jabbering,** elle jacasse comme une pie borgne. **2.** *v.tr.* **to j. French,** baragouiner le français.

jabberer ['dʒæbərər], *s.* **1.** baragouineur, -euse; bredouilleur, -euse. **2.** jaboteur, -euse; jacasseur, -euse; bavard, -arde; jacasse *f*.

jabbering, *s.* = JABBER[1].

Jabez ['dʒeibiz], *Pr.n.m. B.Hist: etc:* Jabbets *m*.

jabiru ['dʒæbiru:], *s. Orn:* jabiru *m*; **African j.,** jabiru d'Afrique.

jaborandi [dʒæbə'rændi], *s. Bot: Pharm:* jaborandi *m*.

jabot ['ʒæbou], *s. Cost:* jabot *m*.

jacal [hæ'kɑ:l], *s. U.S:* hutte mexicaine.

jacamar ['dʒækəmɑ:r], *s. Orn:* jacamar *m*.

jacana ['dʒækənə], *s. Orn:* jacana *m*.

Jacanidae [dʒæ'kænidi:], *s.pl. Orn:* jacanidés *m*.

jacaranda [dʒækə'rændə], *s. Bot:* jacaranda *m*; **j. wood,** faux palissandre.

jacarini [dʒækə'ri:ni], *s. Orn:* jacarini *m*.

jacinth ['dʒæsinθ]. **1.** *s. Miner: Lap:* jacinthe *f*, hyacinthe *f*. **2.** *a. & s.* (*colour*) rouge orangé *inv*.

Jack, jack[1] [dʒæk], *Pr.n. & s.*

I. *Pr.n.m.* (*dim. of* **John**) **1.** Jean, Jeannot; **he was off before you could say J. Robinson,** il est parti sans qu'on ait le temps de faire, de dire, ouf; crac, le voilà parti! *F:* **I'm all right, J.,** je m'en tire bien (et tant pis pour les autres); *O:* **J. Ketch,** le bourreau (= M. Deibler); **J. Sprat,** un petit bout d'homme; **J. the Giant Killer,** Jean le tueur de géants; *Prov:* **there are more Jacks than one at the fair,** il y a à la foire plus d'un âne qui s'appelle Martin. **2. J. (tar),** un marin; **when Jack's ashore,** quand le marin tire une bordée; **an old j. tar,** un vieux marsouin; un loup de mer. **3.** *Bot: F:* **J. by the hedge,** alliaire *f*; **J. go to bed at noon,** salsifis *m* des prés.

II. *s.* **1.** (*pers.*) (*a*) *A:* (i) valet *m*; (ii) manœuvre *m*; (*b*) **j. in office,** bureaucrate *m* (qui fait l'important); petit employé qui se donne des airs de chef; **j. of all trades,** touche-à-tout *m inv*; *Prov:* **a j. of all trades is master of none,** qui est propre à tout n'est propre à rien; **every man j.,** tout le monde; *A:* **j. in the green,** homme qui est entouré d'un cadre de feuillage (dans les jeux du premier mai); *O:* **j.-a-dandy,** fat *m*, dandy *m*; *A:* **j. pudding,** pitre *m*, paillasse *m*, bouffon *m*; *Toys:* **j. in the box,** diable *m* (à ressort); boîte *f* à surprise, à malice; diablotin *m*. **2.** *Cards:* valet *m*. **3.** *Clockm:* jaquemart *m*. **4.** *Ich:* (*a*) brocheton *m*; **j. crevalle,** cavaille; (*b*) **j. salmon,** saumoneau *m*, jeune saumon *m*. **5.** (*a*) (*pour indiquer le mâle de l'espèce*) âne *m*; **j. hare,** bouquin *m*; **j. rabbit,** (i) lapin (mâle); (ii) gros lièvre américain; (*b*) *Orn:* (i) (*pour indiquer les petites espèces*) **j. snipe,** bécassine sourde; (ii) *F:* choucas *m* des tours, corneille *f* (des clochers).

III. *s.* (*terme qui s'applique à nombre d'organes, d'outils, de dispositifs auxiliaires*) **1.** (*a*) **(roasting) j.,** tournebroche *m*; (*b*) **(chimney) j.,** mitre *f* (de cheminée) à tête mobile; girouette *f* à fumée; tambourin *m*; tourne-vent *m inv*; gueule-de-loup *f*, *pl.* gueules-de-loup. **2.** support *m*; (*a*) *Ind:* **assembling j.,** support d'assemblage; (*b*) **sawyer's j.,** chèvre *f*, chevalet *m* (de scieur); (*c*) *Mec.E:* (i) cric *m*; **hand j.,** cric à main; **car j., wheel j.,** cric pour voiture, lève-auto *m inv.*; lève-roue *m inv.*; **garage j., wheeled j.,** cric de garage, cric roulant; **rail j.,** lève-rail(s) *m inv*; **rack (and pinion) j.,** cric à crémaillère; **j. and circle,** cric sur crémaillère circulaire; **ratchet j.,** cric à rochet; **body of a j.,** corps *m* d'un cric; **bearing j. plate,** semelle *f* d'un cric; **head of a j.,** tête *f* d'un cric; **claws, spikes, of a j.,** griffes *f* d'un cric; (ii) vérin *m*; **lifting j.,** vérin de levage; **oil j.,** vérin à huile; **strut j.,** *Min:* **tool j.,** vérin de serrage; **hydraulic j.,** vérin hydraulique; **pneumatic j.,** vérin pneumatique; **telescopic j.,** vérin télescopique; **bottle j.,** vérin à bouteille; **roller j.,** vérin à galet; **traversing j.,** vérin à chariot; **levelling j.,** vérin de mise à niveau; **pulling j.,** vérin de tirage; *Av:* **(undercarriage) retracting j.,** vérin d'escamotage (du train d'atterrissage); **jacks actuating the variable-area nozzle,** vérins actionnant la tuyère à section variable. **3. black j.,** (i) *A:* valise noire; (ii) *F:* matraque *f*, assommoir *m*, nerf *m* de bœuf; (iii) *Miner: F:* blende *f*. **4.** *El: Tp:* jack *m*; fiche *f* femelle; **annunciator j.,** jack à volet; **spring j.,** jack de liaison, de jonction; conjoncteur *m*; **listening j.,** jack d'écoute; **key j.,** jack de manipulation; **transfer j.,** jack de renvoi; **j. bush,** douille *f* de jack; **j. plug,** fiche de jack; **j. panel,** panneau *m* de jacks, de commutation; tableau *m* de connexions; tableau commutateur, manuel; **j. strip,** réglette *f* de jacks. **5.** *Games:* (*bowls*) cochonnet *m*; **j. high,** à la même hauteur que le cochonnet. **6.** *Mus: A:* sautereau *m* (de clavecin). **7.** *Nau:* **j. (cross tree),** barre *f* de cacatois. **8.** *U.S: F:* argent *m*, pognon *m*.

jack[2], *v.tr.* **1.** mettre sur cric, sur vérins. **2. to j. up,** (i) mettre à niveau, soulever, au moyen de vérins; (ii) soulever (une voiture, etc.) avec un cric; (iii) *F:* augmenter (des prix, etc.); (iv) *v.i.* (*also* **j. in**) *F:* céder; abandonner, renoncer à, une entreprise, etc.

jack[3], *s. Nau:* pavillon *m* beaupré; **the Union J.,** le pavillon britannique, du Royaume-Uni; **black j.,** le pavillon noir (des pirates); **j. staff,** mât *m*, bâton *m*, de (pavillon de) beaupré; **pilot j.,** signal *m* pour pilote.

jack[4], *s. Hist:* **1.** *Cost:* jaque *f*, grippon *m*, hoqueton *m*. **2.** broc *m*, hanap *m*, en cuir; **black J.,** outre en cuir vernie de noir.

jack[5], *s. Bot:* **1. j. (fruit),** jaque *m*. **2. j. (tree),** jaquier *m* (de Malaisie).

jackal ['dʒækɔ:l], *s.* **1.** *Z:* chacal *m*, *pl.* chacals. **2.** *F: A:* chacal, âme damnée (d'un homme politique, etc.).

jackanapes ['dʒækəneips], *s.* **1.** *A:* singe *m*. **2.** *F:* (*a*) *A:* impertinent *m*, fat *m*, freluquet *m*; (*b*) petit vaurien, petite vaurienne.

jackaroo [dʒækə'ru:], *s. Austr: F: O:* colon récemment venu d'Angleterre; nouveau débarqué.

jackass ['dʒækæs], *s.* **1.** (*a*) âne (mâle) *m*; baudet *m*; (*b*) **j. deer,** (i) singsing *m*; (ii) cerf *m* à queue noire; (*c*) idiot; -ote, imbécile *mf*. **2.** *Orn:* martin-pêcheur (*pl.* martins-pêcheurs) géant (d'Australie).

jackboots ['dʒækbu:ts], *s.pl.* **1.** bottes *f* de cavalier, à genouillères. **2.** *Nau: etc:* bottes cuissardes; cuissardes *f*.

jackdaw ['dʒækdɔ:], *s. Orn:* choucas *m* des tours, *F:* corneille *f* (des clochers); **East European j.,** choucas de Russie.

jacket[1] ['dʒækit], *s.* **1.** (*a*) *Cost:* veste *f*; veston *m* (d'homme); **single-breasted, double-breasted, j.,** veston droit, croisé; **dinner j.,** smoking *m*; **smoking j.,** veston d'intérieur; **Eton j.,** veste noire et courte terminée en pointe dans le dos (comme portent les jeunes élèves d'Eton); **sheepskin j.,** canadienne *f*; **lumber(man's) j.,** blouson *m*; **wool(len) j.,** gilet *m* de laine; **bed j.,** liseuse *f*; **fencing j.,** veste d'escrime; *Artil: A:* **to get, obtain, one's j.,** être admis dans la *Royal Horse Artillery* (régiment d'élite); (*b*) robe *f* (d'un animal); pelure *f* (de fruit, etc.); **potatoes cooked in their jackets,** pommes *f* de terre en robe de chambre. **2.** (*a*) **(filing) j.,** chemise *f*; (*b*) jaquette *f*, liseuse (de livre); protège-livre *m*, *pl.* protège-livres; pochette *f* (de disque); (*c*) *Mec.E: etc:* **cooling j.,** chemise, enveloppe *f*, manchon *m*, de refroidissement (d'un cylindre, d'un tuyau, d'un canon de mitrailleuse, etc.); **water j.,** chemise d'eau (d'un four à cuve), radiateur *m* à eau (d'une mitrailleuse, etc.); **j. cock,** robinet *m* de purge, de vidange, de la chemise d'eau, du radiateur à eau; **j. water,** eau de refroidissement, de radiateur, de chemise; *Aut: etc:* **spring j.,** gaine *f* de ressort; (*d*) *Atom.Ph:* gaine, chemise (enveloppant les éléments fissiles dans un réacteur); (*e*) *Artil:* **barrel j., gun j.,** jaquette *f* de canon; *Ball:* **bullet j.,** chemise, enveloppe, de la balle; (*f*) *Dent:* **porcelain j.,** couronne *f* de céramique.

jacket[2], *v.tr.* **(jacketed) 1.** *O:* habiller (un homme) d'un veston, (une femme) d'une jaquette. **2.** garnir, envelopper, (un cylindre, une chaudière, etc.) d'une chemise; chemiser. **3.** classer (un document).

jacketed ['dʒækitid], *a.* **1.** garni d'une chemise ou d'une couverture mobile; à chemise; **water-j. cylinder,** cylindre *m* à chemise. **2.** *Artil:* (canon *m*) à manchon. **3.** (*pers.*) vestonné.

jacketing ['dʒækitiŋ], *s.* chemisage *m* (d'un cylindre, etc.); *Atom.Ph:* chemisage, gainage *m* (des éléments fissiles dans un réacteur).

jacking ['dʒækiŋ], *s.* **1.** mise *f* sur cric, sur vérins; levage *m* au cric; **j. pad,** patin *m* de levage; **j. points,** points *m* de levage; *Nau:* **j. engine, j. gear,** vireur *m*. **2. j. up,** (i) mise *f* à niveau, soulèvement *m*, au moyen de vérins; (ii) soulèvement (d'une voiture, etc.) au moyen d'un cric.

jack(-)knife[1] ['dʒæknaif], *s.* **1.** couteau *m* de poche; couteau pliant, fermant; surin *m*. **2.** *Swim:* **j.-k. dive,** saut *m* de carpe.

jack(-)knife[2]. **1.** *v.tr. U.S: P:* suriner (qn). **2.** *v.i.* (*a*) se plier en deux (pour entrer, sortir de, quelque part); (*b*)

Swim: faire un saut de carpe; (*c*) *Aut:* (*esp. of vehicle with trailer*) se mettre en zigzag en travers de la route.

jack-leg ['dʒækleg], *a. U.S:* (*a*) peu habile; (*b*) peu scrupuleux; **j.-l. lawyer,** avocassier *m*, chicaneur *m*.

jackline ['dʒæklain], *s. Nau:* **1.** filin mince. **2.** chemin *m* de fer (de mât ou de gui). **3.** filière *f* d'envergure.

jackman, -men ['dʒækmən, -men], *s. Hist:* suivant *m* (d'un noble).

jack-o'-lantern ['dʒækə'læntə:n], *s.* **1.** *A:* homme qui porte une lanterne. **2.** feu follet; furolle *f*. **3.** *esp. NAm:* potiron, illuminé de l'intérieur et décoré d'un visage humain.

jackpot ['dʒækpɔt], *s.* (*a*) *Cards:* (*poker*) (jack-)pot *m*; (*b*) **to hit the j.,** gagner le coquetier, le gros lot.

jackrabbit ['dʒæk'ræbit], *s.* gros lièvre américain.

jackscrew ['dʒækskru:], *s.* cric *m*, vérin *m*, à vis; vérin de calage; *Carp:* viole *f*.

jackshaft ['dʒækʃɑ:ft], *s. Aut:* arbre *m* secondaire, arbre de renvoi (de la boîte des vitesses).

Jacksonian [dʒæk'souniən], *a. Med:* (*of epilepsy, etc.*) Jacksonien.

Jack-Spaniard ['dʒæk'spæniəd], *s. Ent:* poliste *f*.

jackstay ['dʒækstei], *s. Nau:* = JACKLINE.

jackstraw ['dʒæk'strɔ:], *s.* **1.** *A:* homme *m* de paille; faquin *m*. **2.** *Games:* fiche *f* de jonchets; **jackstraws,** (jeu *m* de) jonchets *m*.

Jacky ['dʒæki], *Pr.n.* (*dim.*) (*a*) *m* Jeannot; (*b*) *f*; Jacqueline.

Jacob ['dʒeikəb], *Pr.n.m.* Jacob; **Jacob's ladder,** (i) *B:* l'échelle *f* de Jacob; (ii) *Bot:* polémonie bleue; valériane grecque; échelle de Jacob; (iii) *Nau:* échelle de revers; échelle de pilote; (iv) *Hyd.E:* (pompe *f* à) chapelet *m*; **Jacob's staff,** (i) *Surv:* piquet *m* (d'équerre d'arpenteur); (ii) *Bot:* molène commune; bouillon-blanc *m*, *pl.* bouillons-blancs.

jacobaea [dʒækə'biə], *s. Bot:* jacobée *f*.

Jacobean [dʒækə'biən], *a.* **1.** (*a*) *Arch: Furn: etc:* de l'époque de Jacques Ier; du dix-septième siècle; (*b*) *Furn: Com:* en chêne patiné. **2.** *Rel.H:* de saint Jacques le Mineur. **3.** *Mth:* **J. (determinant),** déterminant jacobien, fonctionnel.

Jacobin[1] ['dʒækəbin], *a.* & *s. Rel.H: Fr.Hist:* Jacobin, -ine.

jacobin[2], *s. Orn:* **1.** colibri *m* jacobine. **2.** jacobin *m*; pigeon *m* à capuchon.

Jacobinical [dʒækə'binikl], *a. Fr.Hist.* jacobin; jacobinisant.

Jacobinism ['dʒækəbinizm], *s. Fr.Hist:* jacobinisme *m*.

Jacobite ['dʒækəbait], *a.* & *s. Eng.Hist:* jacobite (*mf*); partisan *m* de Jacques II, des Stuarts (après 1688).

Jacobus [dʒə'koubəs], **1.** *Pr.n.m. Lit.Hist:* **J. a Voragine,** Jacques de Voragine. **2.** *s. Num:* jacobus *m*.

jaconet ['dʒækənet], *s. Tex:* **1.** jaconas *m*. **2. glazed j.,** brillanté *m* (pour doublures).

Jacquard [dʒə'kɑ:d], *Pr.n. Tex:* **J. loom,** métier *m* Jacquard; jacquard *m* or *f*, jacquart *m* or *f*; **J. woven,** à la Jacquard.

jactation, jactitation [dʒæk(ti)'teiʃ(ə)n], *s.* **1.** (*a*) *A:* & *Lit:* jactance *f*; (*b*) *Jur:* **j. of marriage,** imposture *f* (consistant à se faire passer pour l'époux ou l'épouse d'une autre personne). **2.** *Med:* jactation *f*, jactitation *f*, anxiété *f*; agitation *f*.

jade[1] [dʒeid], *s.* **1.** (*of horse*) (*a*) rosse *f*, haridelle *f*; vieux carcan; (*b*) cheval vicieux, rétif, méchant, difficile, cabochard. **2.** *A:* (*of woman*) (*a*) drôlesse *f*; coureuse *f*; (*b*) *F:* pendarde *f*; **you little j.,** petite coquine! petite effrontée! petite scélérate! friponne! **she's a fickle j.,** c'est un oiseau volage.

jade[2]. **1.** *v.tr.* (*a*) surmener, éreinter (un cheval, etc.); (*b*) fatiguer, harasser (qn, l'esprit de qn); excéder, éreinter (qn). **2.** *v.i.* (*of interest, attention, etc.*) languir, fléchir.

jade[3], *s. Miner:* **1.** jade *m*, néphrite *f*; **oriental j.,** jade oriental. **2.** = JAD(E)ITE. **3. j. (green),** vert *m* de jade; vert olivâtre.

jaded ['dʒeidid], *a.* (*a*) (*of horse*) surmené, éreinté, esquinté; (*b*) (*of pers.*) fatigué, excédé, harassé, esquinté; **he looks j.,** il a l'air fatigué, esquinté; **j. palate,** goût blasé; palais fatigué.

jad(e)ite ['dʒeidait], *s. Miner:* jadéite *f*.

jaeger ['jeigər], *s. Orn: NAm:* **long-tailed j.,** labbe *m* longicaude, labbe à longue queue; **parasitic j.,** labbe parasite; **pomarine j.,** labbe pomarin.

Jael ['dʒeiel], *Pr.n.f. B.Hist:* Jahel, Jaël.

jag[1] [dʒæg], *s. O:* **1.** (*a*) pointe *f*, saillie *f*, dent *f*, arête *f* (de rocher, etc.); (*b*) *Cost: O:* crevé *m*, taillade *f*. **2.** *Carp: etc:* adent *m*.

jag[2], *v.tr.* (**jagged** [dʒægd]) **1.** déchiqueter (une robe, la peau, etc.); denteler (le bord d'une étoffe); ébrécher (un couteau); **the waves have jagged the coast,** les vagues ont découpé la côte. **2.** *Cost:* taillader (une manche), pour y faire des crevés.

jag[3], *s.* **1.** *U.S: Dial:* petit fardeau; petite charge (de bois, foin, etc.). **2.** *P:* (*a*) **to have a j. on,** (i) être soûl, avoir sa cuite; (ii) être camé; (*b*) bombe *f*; orgie *f*; **crying j.,** orgie de pleurs; **to go on a weekend j.,** passer un weekend à (i) faire la bombe, (ii) se soûler, (iii) se camer.

jagged[1] ['dʒægid], *a.* (*of line, edge, etc.*) déchiqueté, entaillé, dentelé, ébréché; (feuille) découpée, laciniée; (contour, rocher) haché; **j. stone,** pierre *f* aux arêtes vives; **j. wound,** plaie mâchée; **j. rocks,** rochers pointus, dentelés; **j. outline of a coast,** dentelures *fpl* d'une côte.

jagged[2] [dʒægd], *a. P:* (*a*) soûl; (*b*) camé.

jaggedness ['dʒægidnis], *s.* état déchiqueté, dentelé (d'une arête, d'un rocher, etc.).

jagger ['dʒægər], *s.* **1.** *Cu:* coupe-pâte *m inv*, videlle *f*. **2.** *Stonew:* gradine *f*.

jaggery ['dʒægəri]. *s. Sug.-R:* jagré *m*.

jagging ['dʒægiŋ], *s.* découpage *m*, entaillage *m*; *Cu:* **j. iron,** videlle *f*.

jaggy ['dʒægi], *a.* = JAGGED[1].

jaguar ['dʒægjuər, -ɑ:r], *s. Z:* jaguar *m*.

jaguarondi, jaguarundi [dʒægwə'rɔndi, -'rʌndi], *s. Z:* jaguarondi *m*, jaguarundi *m*.

Jahveh ['jɑ:vei], *Pr.n.m. B.Hist:* Jahvé, Jéhovah.

Jahvism ['jɑ:vizm], *s. B.Hist:* jéhovisme *m*.

jail [dʒeil], *s.* prison *f*; maison *f* d'arrêt; **to be in j.,** être en prison.

jail[2], *v.tr.* mettre (qn) en prison.

jailbird ['dʒeilbə:d], *s. F:* échappé, -ée, de prison; gibier *m* de potence.

jailer ['dʒeilər], *s.* gardien *m* de prison.

Jain(a) ['dʒein(ə)]. *Rel:* **1.** *s.* (d)jaïn(a) *m*. **2.** *a.* (d)jaïn, -e.

Jainism ['dʒeinizm], *s. Rel:* (d)jaïnisme *m*.

Jairus ['dʒaiərəs, dʒei'aiərəs], *Pr.n.m. B:* Jaïr(e); **the raising of Jairus's daughter,** la résurrection de la fille de Jaïr(e).

Jake [dʒeik]. **1.** *Pr.n.m. F:* Jacob. **2.** *s.m. U.S:* **country j.,** rustaud. **3.** *s.pl.* (*usu. with sg. const.*) *F:* **the jakes,** le petit endroit, les chiottes *f*.

jalap ['dʒæləp], *s. Bot: Pharm:* jalap *m*.

jalop(p)y [dʒə'lɔpi], *s. F:* vieux tacot; vieille guimbarde.

jalouse [dʒæ'lu:z], *v.tr. Scot:* soupçonner; se douter de (qch.).

jalpaite ['dʒælpəait], *s. Miner:* jalpaïte *f*.

jam[1] [dʒæm], *s.* **1.** (*a*) blocage *m*; coincement *m*; enrayement *m* (d'une mitrailleuse, etc.); **j. free,** qui ne peut se bloquer, s'enrayer; *Mec.E:* **j. nut,** contre-écrou *m*, *pl.* contre-écrous; (*b*) *Mus: F:* **j. session,** jam session *f*, séance de jazz improvisé; bœuf *m*. **2.** (*a*) foule *f*, presse *f* (de gens); (*b*) **(traffic) j.,** encombrement *m*, arrêt *m*, embouteillage *m* (de circulation); *F:* **to be in a j.,** être dans le pétrin; (*c*) embâcle *m* (de glaçons, de bûches, dans une rivière); enchevêtrement (de bûches); prise *f* de billes; **to break a j.,** débâcler la rivière, etc.; *Sm.a: etc:* **to clear the j.,** désenrayer le fusil, etc.

jam[2], *v.* (**jammed**) **1.** *v.tr.* (*a*) serrer, presser; **crowd jammed into a room,** foule serrée, pressée, comprimée, dans une salle; **to j. sth. into a box,** fourrer, enfoncer de force, qch. dans une boîte; *U.S:* **to j. a bill through (Congress),** faire passer un projet de loi à la hâte; (*b*) **to get one's finger jammed between two weights,** avoir le doigt coincé, écrasé, entre deux poids; **to j. one's hat on one's head,** enfoncer son chapeau sur sa tête; **to j. on the brakes,** bloquer les freins; freiner brusquement; donner un brusque coup de frein; serrer les freins à bloc; (*c*) coincer, caler, engager (une machine, etc.); enrayer (une mitrailleuse, une roue, etc.); *Nau:* **to j. a cable,** étriver, étrangler, un câble; **to j. the helm,** coincer, engager, la barre; **to get jammed,** (se) coincer; (*d*) **people were jamming the corridor,** des gens, une foule de gens, obstruaient, bloquaient, le couloir; causaient un encombrement dans le couloir; (*e*) *W.Tg:* brouiller (un message, un signal). **2.** *v.i.* (*a*) (*of drawer, etc.*) se coincer, se caler; (*of machine part*) (se) coincer, s'engager, gommer; (*of machine*) prendre; (*of rifle*) s'enrayer; (*of machine gun, wheel*) se caler, s'enrayer; (*of brake*) se bloquer; (*of bearings*) (se) gripper; (*of gear-wheels*) s'arc-bouter; (*of pistons, etc.*) (se) gommer; *Aut:* (*of cutout*) rester collé; *Cin:* (*of film in its channel*) bourrer; *Nau:* (*of rope*) étriver; genoper; **the lift has jammed,** l'ascenseur est coincé, en panne; **the cable is jammed,** le câble est mordu; (*b*) *Mus: F:* jouer en jam-session.

jam[3], *adv.* **the bus was j. full,** l'autobus *m* était comble et archicomble; **to screw up a nut j. tight,** serrer un écrou à refus.

jam[4], *s.* confiture(s) *f* (*pl*); **strawberry j.,** confiture(s) de fraises; **j. dish,** confiturier *m*; **j. manufacturer,** confiturier, -ière; **j. factory,** fabrique *f* de confitures; **my wife's a wonderful j. maker,** ma femme fait d'excellentes confitures, *Cu.* **J. puff,** puits *m* d'amour; *F:* **it's not all j.,** ce n'est pas si facile que ça; **it's money for j.,** c'est donné; **what d'you want, j. on it? j. on both sides?** ça ne te suffit pas?

jam[5], (**jammed**) (*a*) *v.i.* faire des confitures; (*b*) *v.tr.* mettre de la confiture sur (une tartine).

Jamaica [dʒə'meikə], *Pr.n. Geog:* la Jamaïque; **J. pepper,** piment *m*, poivre *m*, de la Jamaïque; poivron *m*; toute-épice *f*, *pl.* toutes-épices; **J. rum,** rhum *m* de la Jamaïque; **J. wood,** brésillet *m*; jamaïque *m*; **J. cedar,** cèdre *m* acajou; **J. ebony,** grenadille *f*; **J. plum,** prunier *m* d'Amérique.

Jamaican [dʒə'meikən], *Geog:* (*a*) *a.* jamaïquain; (*b*) *s.* Jamaïquain, -aine.

jamb [dʒæm], *s.* jambage *m*, montant *m*, chambranle *m* (de porte, de cheminée); battée *f*, dosseret *m* (de porte); poteau *m* d'huisserie.

jambolan ['dʒæmbəlæn], *s. Bot:* **j. (plum),** jamelongue *f*, jambul *m*.

jamboree [dʒæmbə'ri:], *s.* **1.** réjouissances tapageuses, bombance *f*, noce *f*. **2.** (*a*) *Scout:* jamboree *m*; (*b*) *F:* réunion générale (d'une association).

jambosa [dʒæm'bouzə], *s. Bot:* jambosier *m*, jambose *f*.

James [dʒeimz], *Pr.n.m.* Jacques; *B.Hist:* **J. the Greater,** Jacques le Majeur; **J. the Less,** Jacques le Mineur.

jamesonite ['dʒeimsənait], *s. Miner:* jamesonite *f*; **fibrous j.,** plumosite *f*.

Jamestown ['dʒeimztən], *Pr.n. Bot: O:* **J. weed, lily,** chasse-taupe *m*, *pl.* chasse-taupes.

jamjar ['dʒæmdʒɑ:r], *s.* confiturier *m*; pot *m* à confitures.

jammer ['dʒæmər], *s. W.Tel: etc:* brouilleur *m*.

jamming ['dʒæmiŋ], *s.* **1.** (*a*) serrement *m*, pressage *m*; **j. of one's finger,** coincement *m*, écrasement *m*, du doigt; **j. (on) of a brake,** blocage *m* (d'un frein); freinage brusqué; (*b*) arrêt *m* de fonctionnement (d'une machine, etc.); coincement (d'une soupape, etc.); calage *m*, enrayage *m*, enrayement *m* (d'une mitrailleuse, etc.); étranglement *m* (d'un câble); arc-boutement *m*, *pl.* arc-boutements (des dents d'un engrenage); grippage *m* (des coussinets); collage *m* (des pistons); *Cin:* **j. of the film,** bourrage *m* du film; (*c*) *W.Tel: etc:* brouillage *m* (d'un signal); **noise j., spot j.,** brouillage aléatoire, étroit; **barrage j.,** brouillage de barrage; **j. station, transmitter,** brouilleur *m*, poste, émetteur, brouilleur, station de brouillage. **2.** tassement *m* (de glaçons, etc.).

jammy ['dʒæmi], *a.* **1.** couvert de confiture; collant, gluant. **2.** *F: O:* épatant, bath. **3.** *F:* veinard.

jampot ['dʒæmpɔt], *s.* = JAMJAR.

Jane [dʒein]. **1.** *Pr.n.f.* Jeanne. **2.** *s.f. F:* femme, fille; **a plain J.,** une fille sans attraits.

Jan(e)ite ['dʒeinait], *s.* admirateur, -trice, des romans de Jane Austen.

Janet ['dʒænit], *Pr.n.f.* Jeannette.

jangle[1] ['dʒæŋgl], *s.* **1.** *A:* querelle *f*, chamaille *f*. **2.** sons discordants; cliquetis *m*.

jangle[2]. **1.** *v.i.* (*a*) *A:* se quereller, se chamailler; (*b*) rendre des sons discordants; cliqueter; s'entrechoquer. **2.** *v.tr.* faire rendre des sons discordants à (de la ferraille, etc.); faire entrechoquer (des clefs, etc.); **jangled nerves,** nerfs ébranlés, agacés, à vif, en pelote; **state of jangled nerves,** état *m* d'énervement *m*.

jangling ['dʒæŋgliŋ], *a.* aux sons discordants; cacophonique; **j. machinery,** mécanique criarde; **j. piano,** piano discordant, démantibulé, qui ferraille.

janiceps ['dʒæniseps], *s. Ter:* janiceps *m*.

janissary ['dʒænisəri], *s. Hist:* janissaire *m*.

janitor ['dʒænitər], *s.* portier *m*, concierge *m*.

janitress ['dʒænitris], *s.f.* portière *f*; concierge *f*.

janizary ['dʒænizəri], *s. Hist:* janissaire *m*.

jankers ['dʒæŋkəz], *s.pl. Mil: P:* piquet *m* des punis; la pelote, le bal; **j. brigade,** peloton *m* de chasse.

jannock ['dʒænək], *a. F: esp. N.Eng:* loyal, -aux; équitable; comme il faut; **it wouldn't be j.,** ce ne serait pas loyal, juste.

Jansenism ['dʒænsənizm], *s. Rel.H:* jansénisme *m*.

Jansenist ['dʒænsənist], *a.* & *s. Rel.H:* janséniste (*mf*).

janthina ['dʒænθinə], *s. Moll:* janthine *f*.

Janthinidae [dʒæn'θinidi:], *s.pl. Moll:* janthinidés *m*.

Januarius [dʒænju'ɛəriəs], *Pr.n.m. Rel.H:* Janvier.

January ['dʒænju(ə)ri], *s.* janvier *m*; **in J.,** en janvier; (on) **the first, the seventh, of J.,** le premier, le sept, janvier.

Janus ['dʒeinəs], *Pr.n.m. Rom.Myth:* Janus; **J.-faced,** à deux visages.

Jap [dʒæp]. (*a*) *s.* (*often Pej:*) japonais, -aise; **the Japs,** les Japonais; (*b*) *a. Tex:* **J. cloth, silk,** pongée *m* du Japon; *Pej:* **one of those J. motor bikes,** une de ces motos japonaises.

Japan[1] [dʒə'pæn] **1.** *Pr.n. Geog:* Japon *m*, **in J.,** au Japon; *attrib. Bot:* **J. laurel,** aucuba *m*; **J. clover,**

lespedeza *m*; *Oc:* **J. Current,** Kouro-sivo *m*. **2.** *s.* (*a*) laque *m* (de Chine); vernis japonais; vernis du Japon; vernis-émail *m*, *pl.* vernis-émaux; (*b*) **black j.,** vernis à l'asphalte, laque à l'asphalte. **3.** *Cer:* Japon.

japan[2], *v.tr.* (**japanned**) laquer (un métal, etc.); vernisser avec du laque; **to j. in black,** laquer noir.

Japanese [dʒæpə'ni:z]. **1.** *Geog:* (*a*) *a.* japonais; **the J. ambassador,** l'ambassadeur *m* du Japon; **J. vellum,** papier *m* du Japon; *Bot:* **J. laurel,** aucuba *m*; **J. moss,** helxine *f*; **J. clover,** lespedeza *m*; **J. raisin tree,** hovenia *m*; **J. rubber plant, J. laurel,** crassule *f*; (*b*) *s.* Japonais, -aise. **2.** *s. Ling:* japonais *m*.

japanned [dʒə'pænd], *a.* laqué; **j. leather,** cuir verni; **j. sheet iron,** tôle vernie.

japanner [dʒə'pænər], *s.* laqueur *m*, vernisseur *m*.

japanning [dʒə'pæniŋ], *s.* **1.** vernissage *m*, vernissure *f*, au laque. **2.** laque *m* (de Chine).

jape[1] [dʒeip], *s. O:* plaisanterie *f*, badinerie *f*, raillerie *f*.

jape[2], *v.i. O:* plaisanter, badiner, railler.

Japhet(h) ['dʒeifet], *Pr.n.m. B.Hist:* Japhet.

Japhetic [dʒə'fetik], *a. Ethn: etc:* japhétique.

japonic [dʒə'pɔnik], *a.* **1.** japonais. **2.** *Ch:* **j. acid,** acide *m* japonique. **3.** *Pharm:* **j. earth,** cachou *m*.

japonica [dʒə'pɔnikə], *s. Bot:* **1.** cognassier *m* du Japon. **2.** (**camellia**) **j.,** camélia *m*; rose *f* du Japon.

japonism ['dʒæpənizm], *s. Art:* japonisme *m*.

japyx ['dʒeipiks], *s. Ent:* japyx *m*.

jar[1] [dʒɑ:r], *s.* **1.** dissonance *f*; son discordant, dur. **2.** (*a*) ébranlement *m*; trépidation *f*; choc *m*; secousse *f*; coup sec; contrecoup *m*; **jar(s) of a machine,** à-coup(s) *m*, secousse(s), battement(s) *m*, d'une machine; **his fall gave him a nasty j.,** sa chute l'a fortement ébranlé; **it was a nasty j. for him,** cela a été pour lui une vilaine surprise, une forte secousse; **j. to the nerves,** secousse nerveuse; (*b*) manque *m* d'accord; choc (d'intérêts, etc.); (*c*) *O:* querelle *f*. **3.** *Min:* coulisse *f* (de perforateur); **drilling j.,** glissière *f* de forage.

jar[2], *v.* (**jarred**) **1.** *v.i.* (*a*) rendre un son discordant, dur; **noise that jars (on the ear),** bruit *m* qui déchire, choque, l'oreille; (*b*) heurter, cogner; (*of machine part, etc.*) **to j. on sth.,** se cogner à qch.; cogner sur qch.; heurter contre qch.; **to j. on s.o.'s feelings,** froisser, choquer, les sentiments de qn; **the noise jarred on my nerves,** le bruit m'agaçait, m'ébranlait, les nerfs; le bruit me donnait, me portait, me tapait, sur les nerfs; le bruit me crispait les nerfs; (*c*) (*of door, window, etc.*) vibrer, trembler; (*of machine*) marcher par à-coups; (*of screw, etc.*) **to j. loose,** se desserrer; (*of car door, etc.*) **to j. open,** s'ouvrir par contre-coup, sous l'effet de la vibration; (*d*) être en désaccord (**with sth.,** avec qch.); **opinions that j.,** opinions *f* qui ne s'accordent pas, qui se heurtent; **colours that j.,** couleurs *f* qui jurent (**with,** avec); couleurs qui détonnent; (*e*) *Mus:* (*of note*) détonner; (*f*) *A:* se quereller, se disputer, se chamailler. **2.** *v.tr.* (*a*) choquer, heurter, cogner; **the fall jarred his spine,** la chute lui a ébranlé la colonne vertébrale; **machine that jars the whole house,** machine *f* qui ébranle toute la maison; (*b*) choquer (l'oreille, etc.); agacer (les nerfs, etc.); froisser (les sentiments).

jar[3], *s.* (*a*) récipient *m*; pot *m* (à confitures, etc.); jarre *f* (d'huile); (**glass**) **j.,** bocal *m*; *Com:* **family(-sized) j.,** pot familial; (*b*) *El:* verre *m*, vase *m* (de pile électrique); **accumulator j.,** bac *m* d'accumulateur; **Leyden j.,** bouteille *f* de Leyde; (*c*) **to have a j.,** boire un coup.

jar[4], *v.tr.* conserver (des fruits, etc.) en bocal.

jar[5], *s. A:* (*of door, etc.*) **on the j.,** entrouvert, entrebâillé.

jararaca [ʒærə'rɑ:kə], *s. Rept:* jararaca *m*.

jardinière [ʒɑ:dini'ɛər], *s.* **1.** jardinière *f*; cache-pot *m*. **2.** *Cu:* jardinière, macédoine *f* (de légumes).

jargon[1] ['dʒɑ:gən], *s.* **1.** jargon *m*, langage *m* (d'une profession, etc.); **to know the j. of the stage,** posséder l'argot des coulisses; **lawyer's j.,** style *m* de pratique; jargon du Palais. **2.** baragouin *m* (inintelligible); charabia *m*; *Med:* **j. aphasia,** jargonaphasie *f*. **3.** *Lit: A:* piaillerie *f*, piaulement *m*, gazouillement *m* (des oiseaux).

jargon[2], jargoon [dʒɑ:'gu:n], *s. Miner:* jargon *m*; hyacinthe *f* citrine.

jargonelle [dʒɑ:gə'nel], *a. & s.* **j. pear,** jargonelle *f*.

jargonist ['dʒɑ:gənist], *s.* jargonneur, -euse.

jargonize ['dʒɑ:gənaiz]. **1.** *v.i.* s'exprimer en jargon; jargonner. **2.** *v.tr.* mettre en jargon; jargonner.

jarl [jɑ:l], *s. Hist:* jarl *m* (scandinave).

jarosite ['dʒærəsait, dʒə'rousait], *s. Miner:* jarosite *f*.

jarrah ['dʒærə], *s. Bot:* jarrah *m*; **j. (wood),** bois *m* de jarrah.

jarring[1] ['dʒɑ:riŋ], *a.* **1.** (*of sound*) discordant, dur; qui déchire l'oreille; *Mus:* (*on 'cello, etc.*) **j. string,** corde *f* qui sonne le tambour; **j. note,** note *f* qui détonne; **his remark, attitude, struck a j. note,** sa remarque, son attitude, a troublé l'harmonie (de la réunion, etc.). **2.** (*of blow, etc.*) qui ébranle tout le corps; (*of incident, behaviour, etc.*) qui produit une impression désagréable. **3.** (*of door, window, etc.*) vibrant, tremblant. **4.** en désaccord, opposé; **j. colours,** couleurs *f* disparates, qui jurent, qui détonnent; **j. interests,** intérêts *m* incompatibles.

jarring[2], *s.* **1.** sons discordants. **2.** cognement *m*; trépidation *f*, vibration *f*, secousse(s) *f*, battement(s) *m* (d'une machine); **j. of the nerves,** irritation *f*, agacement *m*, des nerfs. **3.** manque *m* d'accord, entrechoquement *m* (d'opinions, etc.). **4.** *O:* querelles *fpl*; discorde.

jarvey ['dʒɑ:vi], *s. F: A:* cocher *m* (de fiacre); collignon *m*, automédon *m*.

jasione [dʒæsi'ouni, dʒei-], *s. Bot:* jasione *f*.

jasmin(e) ['dʒæzmin, 'dʒæs-], *s. Bot:* **1.** (**common, white**) **j.,** jasmin *m*; **Spanish j.,** jasmin d'Espagne; **winter j.,** jasmin d'hiver. **2. red j.,** frangipanier *m* à fleurs rouges; **night j.,** arbre *m* triste; **Cape j.,** jasmin du Cap; **bastard j.,** (i) jasmin bâtard; (ii) cestrum *m*; **star j., confederate j.,** trachélospermum *m*; **rock j.,** androsace *m*.

jasmone ['dʒæzmoun], *s. Ch:* jasmone *f*.

Jasper[1] ['dʒæspər], *Pr.n.m.* Gaspard.

jasper[2], *s. Miner:* (*a*) jaspe *m*; **banded j., striped j., ribbon j.,** jaspe rubané; **agate j.,** agate jaspée, jaspagate *f*; **Egyptian j.,** caillou *m* d'Égypte; **red-tinged j.,** jaspe sanguin; (*b*) **j. opal,** opale *f* jaspe.

jasperize ['dʒæspəraiz], *v.tr.* jasper.

jasperizing ['dʒæspəraiziŋ], *s.* jaspage *m*.

jasperoid ['dʒæspərɔid], *a.* jaspoïde.

jaspilite, jaspilyte ['dʒæspilait], *s. Miner:* jaspilite *f*.

Jassidae ['dʒæsidi:], *s.pl. Ent:* jassidés *m*.

jaundice ['dʒɔ:ndis], *s.* **1.** *Med:* jaunisse *f*, ictère *m*; **true j.,** ictère vrai; ictère biliphéique; **blue j.,** cyanose *f*; ictère bleu; **malignant j.,** ictère grave. **2.** *A: & Lit:* prévention *f*; vues faussées par l'envie.

jaundiced ['dʒɔ:ndist], *a.* **1.** *Med:* ictérique, bilieux; **j. eyes,** yeux injectés de bile. **2. to look on the world with a j. eye,** (i) voir tout en noir; (ii) tout regarder d'un œil jaloux, envieux.

jaunt[1] [dʒɔ:nt], *s.* (petite) excursion, sortie *f*; **on a j.,** en excursion; *F:* **he may call it a business trip but to my mind it's just a j.,** il a beau parler de voyage d'affaires; pour moi il est parti s'amuser.

jaunt[2], *v.i.* faire une (petite) excursion, se balader; **they're out jaunting,** ils sont partis en excursion, s'amuser.

jauntily ['dʒɔ:ntili], *adv.* **1.** d'une manière désinvolte; avec insouciance; cavalièrement. **2.** d'un air effronté, suffisant.

jauntiness ['dʒɔ:ntinis], *s.* **1.** (*a*) désinvolture *f*, insouciance *f*; air dégagé; (*b*) air effronté; suffisance *f*. **2.** fantaisie piquante (d'un chapeau).

jaunty[1] ['dʒɔ:nti], *a.* **1.** (*of manner, etc.*) (*a*) insouciant, cavalier, dégagé, désinvolte; **with a j. air,** d'un air dégagé; (*b*) effronté, suffisant. **2.** enjoué, vif, sémillant; **j. step,** démarche vive, preste; **j. little hat,** petit chapeau coquin.

jaunty[2], *s.m. Navy: F:* capitaine d'armes.

Java ['dʒɑ:və]. **1.** *Pr.n. Geog:* Java; *Prehist:* **J. (ape) man,** pithécanthrope *m*; *Orn:* **J. peacock,** spicifère *m*; **J. sparrow,** calfat *m*, moineau *m* de Java; *Bot:* **J. plum,** jamelongue *f*. **2.** *s. NAm: P:* café *m*, jus *m*.

Javanese [dʒɑ:və'ni:z], *Geog:* (*a*) *a.* javanais; (*b*) *s.* Javanais, -aise.

javelin ['dʒævlin], *s.* javelot *m*; *Sp:* **j. throwing,** lancement *m* du javelot.

jaw[1] [dʒɔ:], *s.* **1.** (*a*) mâchoire *f*; **upper j., lower j.,** mâchoire supérieure, inférieure; **the jaws,** la mâchoire, les mâchoires; *P:* **I'll break your j.!** je vais te casser la gueule! *F:* **jaws of a chasm,** gueule *f* d'un gouffre; **to snatch s.o. from the jaws of death,** arracher qn des bras de la mort; *F:* **his j. dropped,** il a fait une drôle de tête; (*b*) *Tchn:* mâchoire, mors *m*, mords *m*, mordache *f* (de tenailles, d'un étau, etc.); branles *mpl* (d'un étau); gorge *f* (d'une poulie); mâchoire, bec *m* (d'une clef anglaise); **sliding j. of a wrench,** mâchoire mobile de clef à molette; **j. of sliding callipers,** pied *m*, branche *f*, d'un pied à coulisse; **holding j.,** mors, mâchoire, de serrage; **gripping jaws, vice jaws,** mordaches; **meshing j.,** mâchoire dentelée, striée; *attrib.* **three-j., four-j.,** à trois, à quatre, mordaches, griffes; (*c*) *Nau:* **j. of the boom, of a gaff,** mâchoire de gui, de corne. **2.** (*a*) *F:* bavardage *m*; **to have a good j.,** bien bavarder, tailler une bonne bavette; *P:* **hold your j.!** ta gueule! la ferme! (*b*) *esp. Sch: F:* sermon *m*, prêche *m*, laïus *m*; *O:* **he gave me a good old j.,** il m'a flanqué un de ces sermons! il m'a bien engueulé!

jaw[2]. *F:* **1.** *v.i.* (*a*) bavarder; (*b*) *Sch:* laïusser, piquer un laïus. **2.** *v.tr. esp. Sch:* sermonner, réprimander (qn); faire la morale à (qn); engueuler (qn).

jawbone ['dʒɔ:boun], *s.* os *m* maxillaire; mâchoire *f*.

jawbreaker, jawbuster ['dʒɔ:breikər, -bʌstər], *s.* (*a*) mot *m* à vous décrocher la mâchoire; (*b*) bonbon dur.

jawing ['dʒɔ:iŋ], *s.* = JAW[1] 2.

jay [dʒei], *s.* **1.** *Orn:* (*a*) geai *m* (des chênes); **blue j.,** geai bleu; **ground j.,** geai coureur; **gray, Canada, Oregon, j.,** mésangeai *m* du Canada, *Fr.C:* geai gris; **Steller's j.,** geai de Steller; **Siberian j.,** mésangeai imitateur; (*b*) **j. thrush,** garrulax *m*, grive-geai *f*. **2.** *NAm: F:* (*a*) bavard, -arde, moulin *m* à paroles; (*b*) idiot, -ote; nouille *f*. **3.** *P:* cigarette *f* de marijuana, stick *m*. **3.** *a. U.S: F:* bête; ignorant, rustre.

jaywalk ['dʒeiwɔ:k], *v.i. F:* traverser (la rue) (i) d'une manière imprudente, distraite, (ii) en dehors du passage clouté.

jaywalker ['dʒeiwɔ:kər], *s. F:* piéton distrait, imprudent.

jaywalking ['dʒeiwɔ:kiŋ], *s.* inattention *f* de la part des piétons; traversée illégale (d'une chaussée).

jazz[1] [dʒæz]. **1.** *s.* (*a*) *Mus:* jazz *m*; **hot j.,** jazz-hot *m*; **j. band,** jazz-band *m*; (*b*) *Tex: O:* étoffe bariolée; (*c*) vacarme *m*, tapage *m*. **2.** *a. F:* (*of sound*) discordant; (*of colour*) tapageur; *O:* **j.-patterned,** (étoffe) bariolée.

jazz[2]. **1.** *v.i.* danser le jazz. **2.** *v.tr.* **to j. (up) a tune,** tourner une mélodie en jazz; *F:* **to j. s.o. up,** animer, émoustiller, qn; **to j. up a colour scheme,** barioler un coloris; **jazzed up,** (i) *Pej:* modernisé; (ii) (*of pers.*) endimanché; sur son trente-et-un; (iii) *P:* drogué, camé.

jazzman, *pl.* **-men** ['dʒæzmæn, -men], *s. Mus:* jazzman *m*, *pl.* jazzmen.

jazzy ['dʒæzi], *a.* **1.** (air) de jazz. **2.** = JAZZ[1] 2. **3.** *F:* tape-à-l'œil. **4.** *P:* vieux jeu.

jealous ['dʒeləs], *a.* **1.** jaloux (**of,** de); **to be j. of s.o.,** être jaloux de qn; jalouser qn; **to be j. of one's good name, one's authority,** être jaloux de sa réputation, de son autorité; **j. because her friend has a new fur coat,** jalouse, envieuse, du nouveau manteau de fourrure de son amie. **2.** (*zealous*) **j. care,** soin jaloux; **j. enquiries,** enquêtes faites avec un soin jaloux; **to keep a j. watch over s.o.,** surveiller qn avec un soin jaloux.

jealously ['dʒeləsli], *adv.* **1.** jalousement. **2.** soigneusement; avec zèle; avec méfiance.

jealousy ['dʒeləsi], *s.* jalousie *f*.

Jean[1] [dʒi:n], *Pr.n.f.* Jeanne.

jean[2], *s. Tex:* **1.** coutil *m*, treillis *m*. **2.** *pl. Cost:* **jeans,** (i) jean *m*, blue-jean *m*, *pl.* blue-jeans; (ii) (*also* **blue jeans**) cotte (américaine); (iii) *U.S: F:* pantalon *m*.

jean(n)ette [dʒə'net], *s. Tex:* gros coutil.

jeep[1] [dʒi:p], *s. Aut:* jeep *f*.

jeep[2], *v. esp. U.S:* **1.** *v.tr.* transporter (qch.) en jeep. **2.** *v.i.* voyager en jeep.

jeepable ['dʒi:pəbl], *a.* (route) praticable (seulement) en jeep, en (véhicule) tout-terrain.

jeepers ['dʒi:pəz], *int. U.S: F:* **j. (creepers)!** mon Dieu! sapristi!

jeez(e) ['dʒi:z], *int. esp. U.S: F:* mon Dieu!

jeer[1] [dʒiər], *s.* **1.** raillerie *f*, moquerie *f*, brocard *m*. **2.** huée *f*; **greeted with jeers,** accueilli par des huées, par des lazzi(s).

jeer[2], *v.i.* **1. to j. at sth.,** se moquer de qch.; se railler de qch; **to j. at misfortune,** insulter au malheur. **2. to j. at s.o.,** (i) se moquer de qn; railler qn; narguer qn; (ii) huer, conspuer, qn; *v.tr.* **to j. s.o. off the stage,** forcer qn à quitter la scène sous les huées.

jeerer ['dʒiərər], *s.* railleur, -euse, moqueur, -euse.

jeering[1] ['dʒiəriŋ], *a.* railleur, -euse, moqueur, -euse.

jeering[2], *s.* raillerie *f*, moquerie *f*.

jeeringly ['dʒiəriŋli], *adv.* d'une manière railleuse, moqueuse; d'un ton railleur.

jeers [dʒiəz], *s.pl. Nau:* drisses *f* de basses vergues.

jefferisite ['dʒefərisait], *s. Miner:* jefferisite *f*.

jeffersonite ['dʒefəsənait], *s. Miner:* jeffersonite *f*.

Jeffrey ['dʒefri], *Pr.n.m.* Geoffroi.

jehad [dʒi'hɑ:d], *s.* = JIHAD.

Jehoshaphat [dʒi'hɔʃəfæt], *Pr.n.m. B.Hist:* Jéhosaphat, Josaphat; **the Valley of J.,** la vallée de Josaphat; *F: A:* **jumping J.!** mon Dieu!

Jehosheba [dʒi:'hɔʃibə]. *Pr.n.f. B.Hist:* Josabeth.

Jehovah [dʒi'houvə], *Pr.n.m.* **1.** *B:* Jéhovah. **2.** *Rel:* **Jehovah's Witness,** témoin *m* de Jéhovah.

Jehovist [dʒi'houvist], *s. B.Hist:* auteur *m* des livres jéhovistes.

Jehovistic [dʒi:hou'vistik], *a. B.Hist:* jéhoviste.

Jehu ['dʒi:hju:]. **1.** *Pr.n.m.* Jéhu. **2.** *s. A:* (*a*) cocher qui va un train d'enfer, qui conduit à fond de train; (*b*) automédon *m*, collignon *m*.

jejune [dʒi'dʒu:n], *a.* (*of land, author, etc.*) stérile, aride; (*of studies, etc.*) aride, improductif, ingrat; (*of land*) maigre.

jejunely [dʒi'dʒu:nli], *adv.* maigrement, stérilement; **to treat a subject j.,** traiter un sujet sèchement.

jejuneness [dʒi'dʒu:(n)nis], *s.* stérilité *f*, aridité *f* (d'une terre, d'un auteur); improductivité *f*, aridité, sécheresse

f (d'un sujet); maigreur *f* (de la terre).
jejunostomy [dʒidʒu:n'ɔstəmi], *s. Surg:* jéjunostomie *f.*
jejunum [dʒi'dʒu:nəm], *s. Anat:* jéjunum *m.*
jell [dʒel], *v.i.* **1.** se prendre en gelée; se congeler. **2.** *F:* se cristalliser; réussir; **my idea didn't j.,** mon idée n'a pas cristallisé; **we didn't j.,** on n'était pas sur la même longueur d'ondes.
jellaba ['dʒeləbə], *s. Cost:* djellaba *f.*
jellification [dʒelifi'keiʃ(ə)n], *s.* congélation *f*; prise *f* en gelée.
jellify ['dʒelifai]. **1.** *v.tr.* faire prendre (un jus, etc.) en gelée; congeler. **2.** *v.i.* se prendre en gelée; se congeler.
jelloped ['dʒeləpt], *a. Her:* (*cock, dolphin*) **j. or,** barbé d'or.
jelly[1] ['dʒeli], *s.* **1.** *Cu:* (*a*) **table j.,** gelée *f*; **red-currant j.,** gelée de groseille(s); **j. bag,** chausse *f* (à filtrer la gelée); **j. baby,** (i) bonbon *m* (en forme d'un petit bonhomme); (ii) *P:* amphétamine *f*; *F:* **to beat, pound, s.o. into a j.,** battre qn comme plâtre; mettre qn en capilotade, en compote; réduire qn en bouillie, en marmelade; (*b*) **meat j.,** glace *f*; gelée de viande. **2.** (*a*) *A:* **hectograph j.,** pâte *f* à copier; (*b*) *Petr:* gels *mpl* de pétrole; *Exp:* plastic *m*; **mineral j., petroleum j.,** graisse minérale; vaseline *f*; *Ch:* **vegetable j.,** pectine *f.* **3.** *Ap:* **royal j.,** gelée royale.
jelly[2]. **1.** *v.tr.* (*a*) faire prendre (un jus, etc.) en gelée; (*b*) *Cu:* mettre en gelée, en aspic; **jellied eels,** anguilles *f* en gelée; aspic *m* d'anguilles; **cold jellied chicken,** chaud-froid *m* de poulet. **2.** *v.i.* se prendre en gelée; se congeler.
jellyfish ['dʒelifiʃ], *s. Coel:* méduse *f.*
jemadar ['dʒemədɑ:r], *s.m. A.Mil:* (*in India*) sous-lieutenant *m* indigène (entre sous-officiers et officiers ayant la "King's commission," *Viceroy's Commissioned officer*).
jemima [dʒi'maimə], *s. F:* **1.** *A:* nœud de cravate tout fait. **2.** *pl. A:* **jemimas,** bottines *f* à élastiques. **3.** pot *m* de chambre, Jules *m*, Thomas *m.*
Jemmy ['dʒemi]. **1.** *Pr.n.m.* (*a*) *O:* (*dim. of James*) Jacquot; (*b*) **a dismal J.,** un broyeur de noir. **2.** *s. Tls:* broche-levier *f*, *pl.* broches-leviers; **(burglar's) j.,** pince-monseigneur *f*, *pl.* pinces-monseigneur. **3.** *s. Cu: F: O:* tête *f* de mouton. **4.** *s. F: A:* pardessus *m.*
Jena ['jeinə], *Pr.n. Geog:* Iéna *m*; *Glassm:* **J. glass,** verre *m* d'Iéna.
Jennerian [dʒe'niəriən], *a. Med:* (vaccin, etc.) jennérien.
jennet ['dʒenit], *s.* **1.** (*horse*) genet *m.* **2.** (*a*) ânesse *f*; (*b*) bardot *m.*
Jenny ['dʒeni]. **1.** *Pr.n.f.* (*dim. of Jane*) Jeannette, Jeanneton. **2.** *s.* (*a*) **j. wren,** roitelet *m*; (*b*) (*indicating the female*) **j. owl,** hibou *m* femelle; **j. robin,** rouge-gorge *m* femelle, *pl.* rouges-gorges femelles; **j. (ass),** ânesse *f*; (*c*) *Ent: A:* **j. spinner,** tipule *f.* **3.** *s. Bot:* **creeping j.,** lysimaque *f*, lysimachie *f*; nummulaire *f*; herbe *f* aux écus. **4.** *s. Mec.E:* chariot *m* de roulement (d'un pont roulant). **5.** *s. Tex:* **(spinning) j.,** métier *m* à filer; **cotton j.,** métier à filer le coton.
jeopard ['dʒepəd], *v.tr. NAm:* = JEOPARDIZE.
jeopardize ['dʒepədaiz], *v.tr.* exposer (qn, qch.) au danger; mettre (qn, qch.) en danger, en péril; **to j. one's honour, one's life,** compromettre, hasarder, son honneur, sa vie; **to j. one's business,** (i) faire péricliter, (ii) laisser péricliter, ses affaires; **to j. one's finances,** se mettre dans l'embarras.
jeopardy ['dʒepədi], *s.* danger *m*, péril *m*; **to be in j., (of one's life),** être en danger, en péril; **(of one's honour, happiness, etc.)** être compromis; **(of business, etc.)** péricliter.
Jephthah ['dʒefθə], *Pr.n.m. B.Hist:* Jephté.
jequirity [dʒe'kwiriti], *s. Bot:* abrus *m* à chapelet; liane *f* réglisse; **j. beans,** pois *m* d'Amérique; pois de bedeau.
jerboa [dʒə:'bouə], *s. Z:* gerboise *f*; souris sauteuse; souris de montagne; rat sauteur.
jeremiad [dʒeri'maiæd], *s.* jérémiade *f*, plainte *f*; **to go through a long j.,** conter ses doléances.
Jeremiah [dʒeri'maiə], **Jeremy** ['dʒerəmi]. **1.** *Pr.n.m.* Jérémie. **2.** *s.m. F:* **Jeremiah,** geigneur, geignard, prophète de malheur.
Jerez ['hɛəreθ], *Pr.n. Geog:* Xérès, Jérez.
Jericho ['dʒerikou], *Pr.n. Geog:* Jéricho *m*; *F: O:* **to send s.o. to J.,** envoyer qn au diable, à tous les diables; envoyer paître qn; envoyer qn à la balançoire; **go to J.!** va t'asseoir! fiche-moi le camp!
jerk[1] [dʒə:k], *s.* **1.** saccade *f*, secousse *f*, à-coup *m*, saut *m* (d'une corde, etc.); *Nau:* coup *m* de fouet; **to give a cord a j.,** donner une secousse à une corde; **he pulled himself up with a j.,** (i) il s'est levé d'un mouvement sec; (ii) il s'est arrêté net (en se rendant compte que . . ., etc.); **with one j.,** tout d'une tire; (*of car, etc.*) **to move by jerks,** avancer par saccades, par à-coups. **2.** *Physiol:* secousse, trémoussement *m* (d'un membre); tic *m*; *Med:* réflexe tendineux; *F: O:* **to have the jerks,** avoir la danse de Saint-Guy; se trémousser; *Med:* **muscle j.,** secousse musculaire; **ankle j.,** réflexe tendineux de la cheville; **knee j.,** réflexe patellaire, rotulien. **3.** *Gym:* jeté *m* (de l'haltère); **two-hands j.,** jeté à deux bras; *F:* **put a j. into it!** grouille-toi! *F:* **physical jerks,** la gymnastique. **4.** *NAm: F:* zéro *m*; type (complètement) nul; idiot *m*, farfelu *m*, nouille *f.*
jerk[2]. **1.** *v.tr.* (*a*) donner une secousse à (qch.); donner une saccade, des saccades, à (qch.); secouer (qn, qch.); tirer (qch.) d'un coup sec; **to j. sth. out of s.o.'s hand,** arracher qch. de la main de qn (d'un coup sec); **to j. the bedclothes off s.o.,** découvrir qn d'une secousse; **he jerked himself free,** il s'est dégagé d'une secousse; **he jerked out a few words,** il a proféré quelques mots d'un ton bref; *Equit:* **to j. a horse's mouth,** saccader un cheval; (*b*) lancer brusquement, vivement (une pierre, etc.). **2.** *v.i.* se mouvoir soudainement; **the door jerked open,** la porte s'ouvrit brusquement; **to j. along,** avancer par saccades, par à-coups.
jerk[3], *v.tr.* dessécher (des lanières de viande) au soleil; charquer (la viande); **jerked beef,** charqui *f*, charque *f.*
jerkily ['dʒə:kili], *adv.* d'une manière saccadée; par saccades; par à-coups.
jerkin ['dʒə:kin], *s. A.Cost:* justaucorps *m*; **buff-j.,** collet *m* de buffle; pourpoint *m* de cuir épais.
jerkiness ['dʒə:kinis], *s.* (*a*) décousu *m* (du style); (*b*) **the j. of his movements was due to his illness,** ses mouvements saccadés témoignaient sa maladie.
jerking ['dʒə:kiŋ], *s.* secousses *fpl*; saccades *fpl*; *Nau:* coup *m* de fouet.
jerkwater ['dʒə:kwɔ:tər], *a. NAm: F:* (*a*) **j. train,** train *m* de petite ligne; (*b*) éloigné, perdu; **j. town,** trou *m*, bled *m*; (*c*) piètre, méprisable, minable, de rien du tout; **a j. show,** un piètre spectacle; **j. politician,** politicien *m* méprisable.
jerky ['dʒə:ki], *a.* **1.** (*of gesture, step, voice, etc.*) saccadé; (*of style*) décousu. **2.** *U.S: F:* bête, cave, nouille.
Jeroboam [dʒerə'bouəm]. **1.** *Pr.n.m. B.Hist:* Jéroboam. **2.** *s.* (*a*) *A:* grande coupe (à boire, à punch); (*b*) grosse bouteille pansue (de champagne, etc.); jéroboam *m.*
Jerome [dʒə'roum], *Pr.n.m.* Jérôme.
jerque [dʒə:k], *v.tr. Cust: A:* visiter (un navire).
jerquer ['dʒə:kər], *s. A:* vérificateur *m* (de douane).
jerrican ['dʒerikæn], *s.* jerrycan *m*; bidon *m.*
Jerry[1] ['dʒeri]. **1.** *Pr.n.m.* (*dim. of Jeremy, Jeremiah*) Jérémie. **2.** *s. F:* (*a*) *Typ: A:* roulance *f*; (*b*) *A:* **j. (shop),** cabaret *m*, caboulot *m*, bistro *m*; (*c*) pot *m* de chambre, Thomas *m*, Jules *m.*
Jerry[2], *s.* (*dim. of German*) *F: Pej: O:* boche *m*, Fritz *m*, Fridolin *m.*
jerry-build ['dʒeribild]. (*a*) *v.tr.* bâtir (une maison) avec du matériau de camelote, sans souci de la solidité; (*b*) *v.i.* bâtir des maisons de boue et de crachat, des maisons en carton.
jerry-builder ['dʒeribildər], *s. Pej:* constructeur *m* de maisons de carton, de camelote, de mauvaises bâtisses.
jerry-built ['dʒeribilt], *a. Pej:* (maison *f*) de camelote, de carton, de boue et de crachat.
jerrycan ['dʒerikæn], *s.* = JERRICAN.
Jersey ['dʒə:zi]. **1.** *Geog:* (*a*) (Ile de) Jersey *m*; (*b*) **J. (cow),** vache *f* de Jersey. **2.** *s.* (*a*) *Cost:* jersey *m*; chandail *m*; tricot *m* (de laine); **(sailor's) j.,** vareuse *f*; **(football, etc.) j.,** maillot *m*; (*b*) *Tex:* jersey; tricot de laine, de soie, etc.
Jerseyman, *pl.* **-men** ['dʒə:zimən], *s.m.* **1.** Jersiais. **2.** *U.S:* habitant *m*, originaire *m*, de New Jersey.
Jerusalem [dʒə'ru:sələm]. *Pr.n. Geog:* Jérusalem; *Bot:* **J. thorn,** (i) argalon *m*; (ii) parkinsonia *m*; (iii) acacia *m* à catéchu; *Hort:* **J. artichoke,** topinambour *m.*
jess[1] [dʒes], *s. Ven:* jet *m* (pour faucon).
jess[2], *v.tr. Ven:* attacher (le faucon) avec le jet.
jessamine ['dʒesəmin], *s. Bot:* = JASMIN(E).
Jesse ['dʒesi], *Pr.n.m.* **1.** *B.Hist:* Jessé *m*; **the tree of J.,** l'arbre *m* de Jessé; *Ecc.Art:* **J. window,** verrière dans laquelle est représenté l'arbre de Jessé. **2.** *U.S: F:* **to give s.o. J.,** tancer qn.
Jessie ['dʒesi]. *Pr.n.f.* (*dim. of Jane*) Jeannette.
jest[1] [dʒest], *s.* **1.** raillerie *f*, plaisanterie *f*, badinage *m*, badinerie *f*, farce *f*; **to make a j. of sth.,** tourner qch. en plaisanterie; **to turn everything into a j.,** badiner de tout; blaguer sur tout; tout tourner en blague, à la blague; **to say sth. in j.,** dire qch. en plaisantant, pour rire, pour s'amuser, par plaisanterie; **there's many a true word spoken in j.,** on dit souvent la vérité en riant; **half in j., half in earnest,** moitié plaisantant, moitié sérieux. **2.** bon mot, facétie *f.* **3.** objet *m* de risée; risée *f.*
jest[2], *v.i.* plaisanter (**about sth.,** sur qch.); badiner, railler, se moquer; **you're jesting,** vous voulez rire; vous plaisantez.
jester ['dʒestər], *s.* **1.** railleur, -euse; plaisant *m*; farceur, -euse; moqueur, -euse. **2.** *Hist:* (*a*) ménestrel *m*, jongleur *m*; (*b*) bouffon *m*; **the King's j.,** le bouffon du roi.
jesting[1] ['dʒestiŋ], *a. O:* railleur, -euse; moqueur, -euse.
jesting[2], *s. O:* raillerie *f*, plaisanterie *f*, badinage *m*; **this is no j. matter,** il n'y a pas de quoi rire.
jestingly ['dʒestiŋli], *adv. O:* d'un ton moqueur, railleur; en plaisantant; pour rire.
Jesu ['dʒi:zju:]. *Pr.n.m. Poet:* Jésus.
Jesuit ['dʒeʒjuit], *s.* (*a*) *R.C.Ch:* jésuite *m*; (*b*) *Pej:* **he's a proper J.,** c'est un vrai jésuite; *Pharm: A:* **Jesuit's bark,** quinquina *m.*
jesuitic(al) [dʒeʒju'itik(l)], *a. often Pej:* jésuitique.
jesuitically [dʒeʒju'itik(ə)li], *adv. usu. Pej:* jésuitiquement.
Jesuitism ['dʒeʒjuitizm], *usu. Pej:* **Jesuitry** ['dʒeʒjuitri], *s.* jésuitisme *m.*
Jesus ['dʒi:zəs]. *Pr.n.m.* Jésus; **J. Christ,** Jésus-Christ; *Ecc:* **the Society of J.,** la Compagnie de Jésus.
jet[1] [dʒet]. **1.** *s. Miner:* jais *m*, *A:* jaïet *m*; **j. brooch,** broche *f* en jais, de jais; **j. glass,** jais artificiel. **2.** (*a*) **j. (black),** (i) *a.* noir comme du jais; noir (de) jais *inv*; (ii) *s.* noir *m* de jais; (*b*) *s.* **j. coal,** houille grasse; cannel(-coal) *m.*
jet[2], *s.* **1.** jet *m* (d'eau, de vapeur, de gaz, etc.); giclée *f* (de sang); *Ph:* veine *f* fluide (d'eau, de gaz); **j. of flame,** jet, dard *m*, de flamme; **thin j. of water,** filet *m* d'eau; **flat j. of water,** lame *f* d'eau; **(vertical) water j. (of fountain),** cierge *m* d'eau (d'une fontaine); *Mch:* **j. condensation,** condensation *f* par injection; *Min:* **abrasive j.,** jet abrasif. **2.** (*a*) ajutage *m*, jet (de tuyau d'arrosage, d'incendie, etc.); **spreader j.,** jet en éventail; lance *f* à éventail; (*b*) *I.C.E:* **(carburetter) j.,** gicleur *m*; **starting j., warming-up j.,** gicleur de départ; **idle j., slow-running j., slow-speed j.,** gicleur de ralenti; **j. carrier, j. holder,** porte-gicleur *m inv*; **main j., power j.,** gicleur principal; **auxiliary j.,** gicleur auxiliaire; **acceleration j.,** gicleur d'accélération; **economizer j.,** gicleur d'économie; **high-speed j.,** gicleur de grande vitesse, de grande puissance; **j. plug,** bouchon *m* de gicleur; (*c*) brûleur *m* (de foyer à mazout). **3.** *Metall:* (*a*) trou *m* de coulée; (*b*) jet de coulée (attenant à une pièce); coulée *f.* **4.** *I.C.E:* (*a*) buse *f*, tuyère *f* (d'éjection des gaz); *Space:* **attitude control j.,** buse, tuyère, de contrôle en attitude (d'un véhicule spatial); **roll control j.,** buse de contrôle en roulis; **j. gun,** pistolet *m* de manœuvre (permettant aux astronautes de se déplacer individuellement dans l'espace); (*b*) jet *m* (de gaz d'échappement); gaz *mpl* d'échappement; **j. deflection,** déviation *f* du jet; **j. deflector,** déviateur *m* de jet; **j. pipe, j. nozzle,** tuyère, buse, d'éjection; **j.-pipe, j.-nozzle, diameter,** diamètre *m*, section *f*, (de l'orifice) de sortie (des gaz); **j. propulsion,** propulsion *f* par réaction, par fusée(s); **j. thrust,** poussée *f* statique; (*c*) *Av: etc:* **j. (engine),** moteur *m* à réaction, réacteur *m*; **j. turbine,** turbine *f* à réaction; **j. turbine engine,** turboréacteur *m*; **continuous j.,** stato-réacteur *m*, *pl.* stato-réacteurs; **intermittent j.,** pulso-réacteur *m*, *pl.* pulso-réacteurs; **j. pods,** fuseaux *m* réacteurs; **j. power plant, unit,** groupe *m* réacto-propulseur; **j. fuel,** carburéacteur *m*, carburant *m* pour moteur à réaction; **j.-propelled aircraft, j. (plane),** avion *m* à réaction, *F:* jet; **twin j. (aircraft),** biréacteur *m*; **three j., tri-j.,** triréacteur *m*; **four j., quadri-j.,** quadriréacteur *m*; **j. liner,** avion commercial, avion de ligne, à réaction; **j. transport (aircraft),** avion de transport à réaction; **j. cargo aircraft,** avion cargo à réaction; **j. fighter, bomber,** chasseur *m*, bombardier *m*, à réaction; **j. bomb,** bombe volante, bombe à réaction; **j. car,** voiture *f* à turbine. **5.** *Meteor:* **j. stream,** jet-stream *m*, courant-jet *m.*
jet[3], *v.* **(jetted; jetting) 1.** *v.i.* (*of fluid*) s'élancer en jet; gicler. **2.** *v.tr.* (*a*) faire s'élancer, faire gicler (un fluide); (*b*) émettre un jet de (fluide); (*c*) *Petr:* (i) dévier (un puits) par jet de boue; (ii) nettoyer (un puits) au jet. **3.** *v.i. F:* faire un voyage en avion à réaction, en jet.
jeté [ʒətei], *s. Danc:* jeté *m.*
jetsam ['dʒetsəm], *s. Jur:* **1.** marchandise jetée à la mer (pour alléger le navire). **2.** épaves jetées à la côte; épaves rejetées (par la mer).
jetted ['dʒetid], *a. Tail:* **j. pocket,** poche *f* en fente sans patte.
jetting ['dʒetiŋ], *s. Petr:* (i) déviation *f* par jet de boue; (ii) nettoyage *m* au jet; **abrasive j.,** perforation *f* par jet abrasif.
jettison[1] ['dʒetis(ə)n], *s.* (*a*) *Jur: Nau:* jet *m* (de marchandises) à la mer; **j. of cargo,** jet de cargaison, de marchandises (à la mer); **j. of deck cargo,** jet de pontée (à la mer); (*b*) *Av:* largage *m* par-dessus bord, délestage *m* (des bombes, du carburant, du matériel, du fret, pour des raisons de sécurité); **j. device, j. gear,** dispositif *m*

de largage rapide (du siège du pilote, du matériel, etc.); **j. system, j. valve,** vide-vite *m inv* (du carburant); **j. tank,** réservoir *m* largable.

jettison[2], *v.tr.* **(jettisoned)** *(a) Jur: Nau:* jeter à la mer, se délester de (la cargaison); **to j. the cargo, the deck cargo,** jeter la cargaison, la pontée, à la mer; se délester de la cargaison, de la pontée; **goods jettisoned,** marchandises jetées à la mer; *(b) Av:* larguer par-dessus bord, se délester (des bombes, du carburant, du matériel, du frêt, pour des raisons de sécurité); *(c)* **to j. a bill,** se délester d'un projet de loi; jeter par-dessus bord un projet de loi.

jettisoning ['dʒetisəniŋ], *s.* **1.** *(a) Jur: Nau:* jet *m* (de marchandises) à la mer, par-dessus bord; *(b) Av:* largage *m* par-dessus bord; délestage *m.* **2.** renonciation *f* **(of,** à).

jetty[1] ['dʒeti], *s. (a)* jetée *f,* môle *m,* digue *f;* **j. head,** musoir *m* (de jetée); *(b) (on piles)* estacade *f,* appontement *m;* **landing j.,** embarcadère *m,* débarcadère *m; (c) (leading down to ferry)* cale *f.*

jetty[2], *a. (a)* noir comme le jais; *(b)* en jais.

Jew[1] [dʒu:], *s.* **1.** *(a)* juif *m;* **black Jews,** falaschas *m;* **the Wandering J,** le Juif errant; Ahasvérus; **J. baiting,** persécution *f* des Juifs; *Pej:* **J. boy,** youpin *m,* youtre *m; (b) Pej:* **an old J.,** un vieil usurier. **2.** *(a)* **Jew's harp,** (i) *Mus:* guimbarde *f;* (ii) *Nau:* manille *f,* cigale *f* (de chaîne d'ancre); *(b) Bot:* **wandering J.,** ruine-de-Rome *f;* **Jew's ear,** hirnéole *f,* oreille de Judas; **Jew's mallow,** guimauve potagère.

jew[2], *v.tr. Pej:* **1.** duper, frauder (qn); mettre (qn) dedans. **2. to j. down,** marchander (le prix de qch.).

Jewdom ['dʒu:dəm], *s.* la Juiverie.

jewel[1] ['dʒu:əl], *s.* **1.** *(a)* bijou *m,* joyau *m;* **the brightest j. in my crown,** le plus beau joyau de mon écrin, le plus beau fleuron de ma couronne; **the jewels of the Crown,** (i) les joyaux de la Couronne; (ii) *F: A:* nos colonies *f;* **j. case,** coffret *m,* écrin *m* à bijoux; **j. stand,** porte-bijoux *m inv; F:* **she's a j.,** c'est une perle, un trésor; **what a j. of a child!** quel bijou d'enfant! *(b) pl.* pierres précieuses; gemmes *f;* pierreries *f.* **2.** *Clockm:* rubis *m.*

jewel[2], *v.tr.* **(jewelled) 1.** orner, parer, (qn) de bijoux. **2.** *Clockm:* monter (un rouage) sur rubis.

jewel(l)ed ['dʒu:əld], *a.* **1.** orné, paré, de bijoux. **2.** *Clockm:* monté sur rubis; à rubis.

jeweller ['dʒu:ələr], *s.* bijoutier *m,* joaillier *m.*

jewel(le)ry ['dʒu:əlri], *s. (trade or jewels)* bijouterie *f,* joaillerie *f.*

jewel-thrush ['dju:əlθrʌʃ], *s. Orn:* brève *f* superbe, grive *f* superbe.

Jewess ['dʒu:es, -is], *s.f.* Juive.

jewfish ['dʒu:fiʃ], *s.* poisson juif; **spotted j.,** poisson juif tacheté.

jewing ['dʒu:iŋ], *s.* morilles *fpl* (du bec d'un pigeon).

Jewish ['dʒu:iʃ], *a.* juif, *f.* juive.

Jewry ['dʒuəri], *s.* **1.** la Juiverie. **2.** *Geog: A:* la Judée.

Jezebel ['dʒezəbel]. *Pr.n.f.* **1.** *B.Hist:* Jézabel. **2.** *F: O: (a)* femme éhontée, dévergondée; messaline; *(b)* **painted J.,** vieille femme fardée, vieux tableau.

jib[1] [dʒib], *s.* **1.** *Nau:* foc *m;* **outer j.,** grand foc; **inner j.,** petit foc; **flying j.,** clinfoc *m,* dragon *m;* **storm j.,** trinquette *f,* tourmentin *m;* **j. boom,** bout-dehors *m, pl.* bouts-dehors, de foc; **flying j. boom,** baïonnette *f* de clinfoc; **j. stay,** draille *f; F: O: (of pers.)* **I don't like the cut of his j.,** il a une sale binette, une vilaine coupe, une sale coupe; sa découpure ne me revient pas; **I know him by the cut of his j.,** je le reconnais à sa tournure. **2.** *Mec.E:* **(crane) j., derrick j.,** volée *f,* flèche *f,* bec *m,* bras *m,* potence *f,* écharpe *f,* rancher *m* (de grue); **flexible j.,** bec élastique; **j. crane,** grue *f* à volée, à flèche, à bras; **j. post,** arbre *m,* fût *m* (de grue).

jib[2], *v.i.* **(jibbed)** *(a) (of horse)* regimber **(at sth.,** devant qch.); refuser; se dérober; *(b) (of pers.)* se regimber, récalcitrer; **to j. at sth.,** regimber contre qch.; répugner à qch.; se cabrer contre qch.; **to j. at a job,** renâcler, se refuser, à une besogne; **he won't j.,** il marchera; **to j. at doing sth.,** rechigner, répugner, à faire qch.

jibber[1] ['dʒibər], *s.* **1.** cheval rétif, quinteux; cheval qui se dérobe. **2.** *F: (of pers.)* récalcitrant, -ante; regimbeur, -euse.

jibber[2], *v.i. (a)* faire des sons inarticulés (comme un singe); *F:* **he was gibbering with rage,** il bégayait de rage; *(b)* baragouiner.

jibbing[1] ['dʒibiŋ], *a.* (cheval) rétif, quinteux.

jibbing[2], *s. (a)* regimbement *m,* refus *m; Equit:* acculement *m; (b)* rechignement *m* (devant la besogne, etc.).

jib door ['dʒib'dɔ:r], *s.* porte dérobée; fausse porte; porte perdue.

jibe [dʒaib], *v.i. NAm:* être en accord, s'accorder, s'harmoniser (avec qch.).

Jibuti [dʒi'bu:ti]. *Pr.n. Geog:* Djibouti *m.*

jiff [dʒif], **jiffy** ['dʒifi], *s. F:* **in (half) a j.,** en un instant; en moins de rien; en un clin d'œil; *F:* en cinq sept, en cinq sec; **I'll have it done in a j.,** je vais vous faire ça en deux temps trois mouvements; **I'll be down in a j.,** je descends dans un instant.

jig[1] [dʒig], *s.* **1.** *(a) Danc: Mus:* gigue *f; (b) esp. NAm: F:* **the jig's up,** c'est fichu, c'est dans le lac; *(c) esp. U.S: F:* **in j. time,** vite, rapidement. **2.** *(a) Mec.E:* calibre *m,* gabarit *m* (de forme, de réglage, d'usinage); bâti *m* (de montage); montage *m;* **assembly j.,** gabarit, bâti, de montage; tréteau *m* de montage; **centring j.,** gabarit de centrage, montage à centrer; **drill j.,** gabarit de perçage; **hinged reversing j.,** gabarit réversible à charnière; *(b) Mch.Tls:* **j. borer, j. boring machine,** machine *f* à pointer et à aléser, à pointer et à percer; **j. drill,** machine à pointer et à percer; **j. mill,** machine à pointer et à fraiser. **3.** *Min: (a)* plan automoteur (de crible à minerai); jig *m; (b)* = JIGGER[1] 3 *(b), (c).* **4.** *Tex:* laineuse *f.*

jig[2], *v.* **(jigged) 1.** *v.i. (a)* danser la gigue; *(b) F:* sautiller; **to j. up and down,** se trémousser (en dansant). **2.** *v.tr. (a)* secouer légèrement; *(b) Min:* cribler, passer au crible, sasser (le minerai); laver (le minerai) au jig; *(c) Mec.E:* travailler sur montage, sur gabarit.

jigger[1] ['dʒigər], *s.* **1.** danseur, -euse, de gigue. **2.** *(a) F:* machin *m,* truc *m,* chose *f; (b)* bicyclette *f;* vélomoteur *m; (c) Bill: O:* chevalet *m;* appui-queue *m, pl.* appuis-queue; *(d) Bootm:* fer *m; (e) El: W.Tel:* jigger *m;* transformateur *m* d'oscillations; *(f) NAm:* petite mesure à whisky, à gin, etc. **3.** *Min: (a) (pers.)* cribleur, -euse; *(b)* crible *m* (pour minerai); classeur-pulsateur *m; (dry)* sasseur *m; (c)* tenaille *f* d'accrochage; pince *f* d'accrochage (de wagon). **4.** *Nau: (tackle)* palan *m* à fouet; cartahu *m.* **5.** *Cer:* **j. machine,** tour *m* à calibre.

jigger[2], *v.tr. Cer:* mouler au tour (à calibre); calibrer.

jigger[3], *s. Ent:* puce pénétrante, *F:* chique *f.*

jigger[4], *v.tr. F:* **1.** *O: (used only in passive)* **I'm jiggered if I'll do it,** du diable si je le fais; je veux bien être changé en bourrique si je le fais; **well, I'm jiggered!** (i) pas possible! non, mais des fois! (ii) zut alors! **2.** *(a)* **to j. sth. up,** bousiller (une montre, etc.); gâcher (une affaire); *(b) O:* **to be jiggered up,** être éreinté, fourbu.

jiggerer ['dʒigərər], *s. Cer:* calibreur *m.*

jiggery-pokery ['dʒigəri'poukəri], *s. F:* **1.** manigances *fpl.* **2.** eau bénite de cour.

jigging[1] ['dʒigiŋ], *a. Min: (of washers, etc.)* oscillant, à secousses.

jigging[2], *s.* **1.** *Min:* criblage *m,* sassement *m* (du minerai). **2.** *Mec.E: (a)* montage *m;* gabarit *m* de montage; *(b)* pose *f* sur gabarit.

jiggle ['dʒigl], *v.tr. & i.* secouer, balancer, légèrement; **to j. about,** sautiller.

jigsaw[1] ['dʒigsɔ:], *s. Carp:* machine alternative à découper; scie *f* à chantourner; scie anglaise; sauteuse *f; Games:* **j. (puzzle),** puzzle *m,* jeu *m* de patience *f;* **j. map,** carte *f* de patience.

jigsaw[2], *v.tr. Carp:* chantourner.

jigsawing ['dʒigsɔ:iŋ], *s. Carp:* chantournage *m.*

jihad [dʒi'hɑ:d], *s. (a) Rel.H:* djihad *m; (b) A:* croisade *f* (contre une opinion, etc.); guerre *f* à outrance.

Jill [dʒil]. **1.** *Pr.n.f. (dim. of Gillian) (a)* Julie; *(b) A:* (i) jeune femme; jeune fille; (ii) amoureuse; **Jack and J.,** les deux amoureux; = Jeannot et Colette. **2.** *s.* furet *m* femelle; belette *f* femelle.

jillion ['dʒiliən], *num.a. & s. U.S: F:* des millions *m* (et des millions); **I've climbed those stairs a j. times,** j'ai monté cet escalier des millions de fois.

jilt[1] [dʒilt], *s.f.* coquette; lâcheuse.

jilt[2], *v.tr.* laisser là, délaisser, *F:* planter (là), plaquer (un amoureux); **after being engaged for two years he (she) was jilted,** après avoir été fiancé(e) pendant deux ans, sa fiancée l'a lâché (son fiancé s'est dérobé).

Jim [dʒim], *Pr.n.m.* **1.** *(dim. of James)* Jacquot, Jim. **2.** *U.S: (a) Pej: A:* **J. Crow,** nègre *m; (b) Hist:* **J. Crow (law),** la ségrégation des noirs. **3. j. crow,** (i) *Mec.E:* pince *f* pied-de-biche; (ii) *Rail:* presse *f* (à cintrer les rails).

jim-jams ['dʒimdʒæmz], *s.pl. F: O:* **1.** delirium *m* tremens; folie *f* des ivrognes. **2. to have the j.-j.,** avoir le frisson; avoir les nerfs en pelote; **he gives me the j.-j.,** il me donne le frisson.

Jimmy ['dʒimi]. **1.** *Pr.n.m. (dim. of James)* Jacquot, Jimmy; *F: A:* **J. (Grant),** émigrant *m.* **2.** *s.* = JEMMY 2.

jimp [dʒimp], *a. Scot:* **1.** *(of pers.)* svelte, mince. **2.** *(of dress, measure, etc.)* trop juste.

jim(p)son weed ['dʒimsən'wi:d], *s. NAm: Bot:* chasse-taupe *m, pl.* chasse-taupes; pomme épineuse.

jingle[1] ['dʒiŋgl], *s.* **1.** tintement *m* (d'un grelot, etc.); bruit *m* d'anneaux; cliquetis *m* (de fourchettes, de verres, etc.); **j. of verse,** tintement des vers, des rimes; *Com:* **j. (of advertisement),** ritournelle *f* publicitaire; **I heard only a meaningless j.,** je n'ai entendu que des mots confus et dépourvus de sens. **2.** *Austr:* carriole *f.*

jingle[2]. **1.** *v.i. (of bells)* tinter, tintinnabuler, carillonner; *(of keys, etc.)* cliqueter; **to j. together,** s'entrechoquer; **the carriage jingled past,** la voiture passa avec un bruit de grelots. **2.** *v.tr.* faire tinter (des grelots, etc.); faire sonner (son argent, ses clefs); agiter (ses clefs).

jinglet ['dʒiŋglit], *s.* bille *f* (d'un grelot).

jingling[1] ['dʒiŋgliŋ], *a.* qui tinte; tintant, tintinnabulant; *Mus: F:* **j. Johnnie,** chapeau chinois; lyre-carillon *f, pl.* lyres-carillons.

jingling[2], *s.* tintement *m;* carillonnement *m* (de cloches); cliquetis *m* (de clefs, etc.); **the j. of glasses,** le tintement, le carillon, des verres.

jingo ['dʒiŋgou]. **1.** *int. O: (a)* **by j.!** nom de nom! nom d'un petit bonhomme! nom d'une pipe! *(b)* **by j., you're right!** tiens! mais vous avez raison! **2.** *(a) s. (pl. jingoes)* chauvin, -ine; patriotard *m; (b) a.* **the j. party,** le parti chauvin.

jingoism ['dʒiŋgouizm], *s.* chauvinisme *m.*

jingoist ['dʒiŋgouist], *s.* chauvin, -ine.

jingoistic [dʒiŋgou'istik], *a.* chauviniste, cocardier.

jink[1] [dʒiŋk], *s.* **1.** *Scot: & Fb:* évite *f,* esquive *f;* **to give s.o. the j.,** esquiver qn. **2.** *pl. F:* **high jinks,** (i) *A:* soirée *f* folâtre; (ii) rigolade *f.*

jink[2], *v. esp. Scot: U.S:* **1.** *v.i. (a)* s'esquiver; *esp. Av:* **to j. about,** faire des manœuvres d'évitement; *(b)* s'élancer, se précipiter **(into,** dans; **out of,** hors de). **2.** *v.tr. (a)* esquiver, éviter (qn); *(b)* duper (qn); mettre (qn) dedans; rouler (qn).

jinnee, *pl.* **jinn,** *F:* **jinns** [dʒini:, dʒin, dʒinz], *s. (Jinn is often used erroneously as sg.)* djinn *m;* génie *m* (des Mille et une Nuits).

Jinny ['dʒini]. **1.** *Pr.n.. (dim. of Jane)* Jeanneton, Jeannette. **2.** *s. (a) Min:* **J. (road),** plan automoteur; *(b) Mec.E: etc:* chariot *m* de roulement (d'un pont roulant).

jinricksha, jinrickshaw [dʒin'rikʃɔ:], *s.* djiraricha *f,* pousse-pousse *m inv.*

jinx[1] [dʒiŋks], *s. F:* **1.** porte-malheur *m inv.* **2.** maléfice *m;* **this diamond has a j. on it,** ce diamant est ensorcelé, porte malheur; **to break the j.,** échapper à la guigne.

jinx[2], *v.tr. F:* **1.** porter malheur, porter la guigne, à (qn); **to be jinxed,** avoir la guigne. **2.** jeter un sort sur (qn).

jipijapa ['hi:pi'hɑ:pə], *s. U.S:* **j. hat,** panama *m.*

jird [dʒə:d], *s. Z:* mérione *m.*

jitney ['dʒitni], *s. U.S:* **1.** pièce *f* de cinq cents. **2. j. (bus),** autobus *m* à itinéraire fixe et à prix modique. **3.** *a.* bon marché et de mauvaise qualité; en toc.

jitter[1] ['dʒitər], *s.* **1.** *F:* **the jitters,** la frousse; **to give (s.o.) the jitters,** flanquer la trouille (à qn), donner les jetons à qn. **2.** *Rad:* décrochage *m,* instabilité *f; T.V: Cin:* sautillement *m* (de l'image).

jitter[2], *v.* **1.** *v.i. (a) F:* se démener; s'exciter; se trémousser; *(b) Rad:* sauter, être instable; *T.V: Cin:* sautiller, sauter. **2.** *v.tr. F:* flanquer la trouille à (qn).

jitterbug ['dʒitəbʌg], *s. O:* **1.** *(a)* danse désordonnée; *(b)* danseur, -euse, du *jitterbug.* **2.** *F:* défaitiste *mf,* paniquard, -arde.

jittery ['dʒitəri], *a. F:* **to be j.,** avoir la frousse.

jiu-jitsu [dʒu:'dʒitsu:], *s.* jiu-jitsu *m.*

jive[1] [dʒaiv], *s. Danc:* jive *m.*

jive[2], *v.i. Danc:* faire du jive.

Joan [dʒoun], *Pr.n.f.* Jeanne; **J. of Arc,** Jeanne d'Arc.

Joanna [dʒou'ænə], *Pr.n.f.* Jeanne.

Joash ['dʒouæʃ], *Pr.n.m. B.Hist:* Joas(h).

job[1] [dʒɔb], *s.* **1.** tâche *f,* besogne *f,* ouvrage *m,* travail *m* (particulier); *(a)* **to do a j.,** exécuter un travail, faire une besogne; **I have a little j., a j. of work, for you,** j'ai un petit travail pour vous, j'ai de quoi vous occuper un peu; **I like doing little jobs like that,** j'aime bien ce genre de petits travaux, ce genre de bricolage; **my special j. is to . . .,** je m'occupe surtout de . . ., mon rôle consiste surtout à . . .; **to have a big j. on one's hands,** avoir une tâche difficile; avoir de quoi faire; *F: (child's language)* **to do a big j.,** faire caca; **I'm getting on with the j. now,** je suis en train de le faire; **materials fit, unfit, for the j.,** matériaux *m* propres, impropres, à cet ouvrage, à cet usage; **odd jobs,** (i) petits travaux; brocantes *f;* bricoles *f;* (ii) les à-côtés *m* de l'industrie; les métiers à part; **odd-j. man,** (i) homme *m* de corvée, de peine; (ii) homme à tout faire; **to work by the j., to do j. work,** (i) travailler à la tâche, à la pièce, aux pièces; (ii) travailler à façon; (iii) *(by contract)* travailler à forfait; **j. worker,** ouvrier, -ière, aux pièces, à la tâche; **j. wage,** salaire *m* à forfait; *(b) Ind:* opération *f;* travail (particulier); **precision j.,** travail de précision; **j. clock,** pendule *f* de pointage; **j. ticket,** bon *m* de travail; **j. engineering,** organisation *f* du travail; **j. sequencing,** décomposition *f* du travail; **j. scheduling,** planification *f* du travail; **j. specification,** données *fpl* d'exécution; **to be on the j.,** (i) être sur le tas; (ii) travailler avec acharnement, d'arrache-pied; *F:* turbiner; (iii) *Turf:* (*of horse*) fournir un gros effort; (iv) *F:* être à la hauteur de sa tâche; savoir comment s'y prendre; **on-the-j. training,** apprentissage *m*, formation *f*, sur le tas; **on-the-j. testing,** essais *mpl* sur le tas; (*c*) **to make a good j. of sth.,** bien faire, réussir, qch.; **you've made a lovely j. of that,** vous vous en êtes tiré à merveille, *F:* vous avez fait du bon boulot; **to make a bad j. of sth.,** mal faire, *F:* bousiller, qch.; **it's a good j. that . . .,** il est fort heureux que . . .; **that's a good j.! and a good j. too!** tant mieux! à la bonne heure! **that's, it's, a bad j.,** c'est une mauvaise affaire! c'est bien malheureux! *Iron:* je vous plains! **to give sth. up as a bad j.,** renoncer à faire qch.; y renoncer; (*d*) *Cmptr:* travail, job *m*; **j. bank,** banque *f* de l'emploi; **j. deck,** paquet *m* de cartes (d'un travail); **j. clock,** pendule *f* de pointage; **j. mix,** groupe *m* de travaux; **j. scheduler,** programmateur *m* de travaux; **j.-oriented terminal,** terminal spécialisé; **j. shop,** atelier (i) travaillant à la demande, (ii) organisé en sections homogènes; (*e*) *F:* **my new car's a lovely j.,** ma nouvelle voiture, c'est du beau travail; **that's just the j.,** ça fait juste l'affaire; *P:* **the blonde j. sitting near the bar,** la petite blonde assise près du bar; (*f*) tâche difficile; corvée *f*; **I had a j. to do it,** j'ai eu du mal, *F:* un sacré boulot, à le faire; **it's quite a j. to get, getting, there,** c'est toute une affaire que d'y aller; **I had quite an easy j. fitting the machine together,** je n'ai pas eu de peine à, ce n'était pas difficile de, monter l'appareil; **moving is an awful j.!** quelle corvée que de déménager! (*g*) **this pin isn't good enough for the j.,** cette épingle, cette goupille, ne tiendra pas le coup; **the pill did its j.,** la pilule a rempli son office. **2.** emploi *m*, place *f*, poste *m*; fonctions *fpl*; situation *f*; *F:* job; **to look for a j.,** chercher un emploi, du travail; **to lose one's j.,** perdre son emploi; **to resign, throw up, one's j.,** donner sa démission; lâcher sa position, son travail; **to be out of a j.,** chômer; se trouver en chômage, sans travail; **he's got a good j.,** il a une belle situation, *F:* un bon job; **he likes his j.,** il aime son métier, son travail; *Adm:* **j. analysis, description,** analyse *f*, description *f*, de la fonction; **his j. is to repair fences,** son métier est de remettre les clôtures en état; **it's her j. to sweep the room,** c'est à elle de balayer la pièce; **this trade isn't everybody's j.,** ce métier n'est pas l'affaire de tout le monde; **he knows his j.,** il connaît son métier, son affaire; il s'y entend; **every man to his j.,** (à) chacun son métier; *F:* **there was a rush to find jobs for the boys,** ce fut une ruée pour la distribution des planques, vers l'assiette au beurre. **3.** *attrib. Com:* **j. lot, line,** soldes *mpl*; articles *mpl*, marchandises *fpl*, d'occasion, articles dépareillés; bloc *m* de marchandises; **to buy a j. lot of books,** acheter des livres en vrac; **to buy, sell, sth. as a j. lot,** acheter, vendre, qch. à forfait; **j.-lot quantities,** petites séries (de fabrication); *F:* **I'd get rid of the whole j. lot,** moi, je bazarderais tout! **4.** (i) intrigue *f*; (ii) affaire illégale, *esp.* cambriolage *m*; **put-up j.,** coup monté; **inside j.,** acte illégal, cambriolage, perpétré avec des complices intérieurs. **5.** *Typ:* **j. (printing, work),** travail, -aux, de ville; **j. printer,** imprimeur *m* de travaux de ville; **j. compositor,** ouvrier *m* en conscience; **j. chase,** ramette *f*.

job[2] [dʒɔb], *v.* (**jobbed**) **1.** *v.i.* (*a*) faire des petits travaux; bricoler; (*b*) travailler à la tâche, à la pièce; (*c*) *Com: Ind:* (i) faire du marchandage; (ii) vendre en demi-gros; (iii) vendre et acheter; (*d*) *St.Exch:* agioter, spéculer; **to j. in bills, to j. in and out,** faire la navette; (*e*) intriguer, tripoter; se livrer à des tripotages. **2.** *v.tr.* (*a*) *F:* exécuter (une tâche); **that job's jobbed,** voilà mon boulot fini; (*b*) louer (un cheval, une voiture); (*c*) *Com: Ind:* marchander (une entreprise); (i) prendre (un travail) à forfait; (ii) donner (un travail) à forfait; (*d*) *St.Exch:* **to j. shares,** faire le négoce (en bourse) d'actions (en gros et en détail); (*e*) exploiter (un emploi); *O:* **to j. s.o. into a post,** user d'influences occultes pour faire nommer qn à un poste; **to j. s.o. off,** se débarrasser (déloyalement) de qn.

Job[3] [dʒoub], *Pr.n.m.* Job; **Job's comforter,** (i) consolateur *m* pessimiste; ami *m* de Job; (ii) *F:* clou *m*, furoncle *m*; **Job's news,** nouvelles *f* de malheur; *Bot:* **Job's tears,** larme-de-Job *f*, larme-du-Christ *f*; larmille *f*.

jobber ['dʒɔbər], *s.* **1.** ouvrier, -ière, à la tâche; tâcheron *m*; **odd j.,** bricoleur *m*. **2.** *A:* loueur *m* de chevaux et de voitures; remiseur *m* (de voitures). **3.** intermédiaire *m* revendeur; (*in contract work*) marchandeur *m*, sous-traitant *m*, *pl.* sous-traitants. **4.** *St.Exch:* **(stock) j.,** marchand *m* de titres (en gros et en détail) qui exécute les ordres que lui donnent les agents de change). **5.** *Pej: O:* tripoteur, -euse; intrigueur, -euse; exploiteur, -euse (d'une fonction).

jobbery ['dʒɔbəri], *s.* **1.** *F: O:* maquignonnage *m*; **political j.,** intrigues *f* politiques; tripotages *mpl*; prévarication *f*; **it's all j.,** tout se fait par compère et par commère. **2.** *St.Exch:* agiotage *m*, agio *m*, tripotage.

jobbing[1] [dʒɔbiŋ], *a.* **1.** qui travaille à la tâche, à la pièce; **j. workman,** (ouvrier) façonnier (*m*); ouvrier à la tâche, à façon; **j. tailor,** tailleur *m* à façon; **j. cabinet maker,** ébéniste *m* à façon; **j. gardener,** jardinier *m* à la journée. **2.** *Typ:* **j. hand,** homme *m* en conscience; **j. work,** ouvrage *m* de ville. **3.** *O:* tripotier.

jobbing[2], *s.* **1.** ouvrage *m* à la tâche; *Tail:* travail *m* à façon, *F:* à la pompe. **2.** *A:* louage *m* de voitures, de chevaux. **3.** *Ind: Com:* commerce *m* d'intermédiaire; vente *f* en demi-gros. **4.** *St.Exch:* (*a*) courtage *m* (de titres en gros et en détail); *Pej:* **stock j.,** agiotage *m*; (*b*) **j. in contangoes,** arbitrage *m* de reports. **5.** *Typ:* travaux *mpl* de ville.

jobless ['dʒɔblis], *a.* sans travail; en chômage.

Jocasta [dʒɔ'kæstə]. *Pr.n.f. Gr.Lit:* Jocaste.

Jock [dʒɔk]. **1.** *Pr.n.m.* (*dim. of John*) *Scot:* Jean. **2.** *s. F: O:* (*a*) soldat écossais; (*b*) Écossais *m*.

jockey[1] ['dʒɔki], *s.* **1.** (*a*) *Turf:* jockey *m*; **probable starters and jockeys,** partants *m* et montes *f* probables; **amateur j.,** gentleman-rider *m*, *pl.* gentlemen-riders; **j. cap,** casquette *f* de jockey; **j. club,** jockey-club *m*; (*b*) *T.V: etc:* **disc j.,** présentateur *m* de disques. **2.** *Mec.E:* **j. pulley, j. wheel,** (i) poulie *f*, galet *m*, de guidage; galopin *m*; (ii) galet de tension (de courroie); pignon tendeur.

jockey[2]. **1.** *v.tr.* (*a*) (i) tromper, duper, rouler, refaire (qn); (ii) mener (qn) par le bout du nez; **to j. s.o. out of sth.,** soutirer, escamoter, qch. à qn; **to j. s.o. out of ten pounds,** refaire qn de dix livres; **to j. s.o. out of a job,** évincer qn; **to j. s.o. into an office,** user d'influences occultes pour faire nommer qn à un office; **to j. s.o. into doing sth.,** amener sournoisement qn à faire qch.; (*b*) **to j. a transaction,** maquignonner une affaire. **2.** *v.i.* (*a*) manœuvrer; **the yachts were jockeying for the breeze,** les yachts *m* manœuvraient pour avoir le vent; (*b*) *Pej:* (*of pers.*) **to j. for sth.,** intriguer pour obtenir qch. **3.** *v.tr. Turf:* monter (un cheval).

jockeying ['dʒɔkiiŋ], *s.* **1.** *Turf:* métier *m* de jockey. **2.** tricherie *f*; duperie *f*, fourberie *f*; intrigue *f*, maquignonnage *m*.

jocko ['dʒɔkou], *s. Z:* chimpanzé *m*, jocko *m*.

jockstrap ['dʒɔkstræp], *s. Cost:* slip *m* de soutien (pour sportifs), support *m* athlétique.

jocose [dʒə'kous], *a.* facétieux; jovial, -aux; goguenard, gouailleur.

jocosely [dʒə'kousli], *adv.* facétieusement, jovialement; d'un ton goguenard, gouailleur; en plaisantant.

jocoseness [dʒə'kousnis], *s.* jocosité *f*; humeur joviale.

jocosity [dʒə'kɔsiti], *s.* **1.** = JOCOSENESS. **2.** facétie *f*, plaisanterie *f*.

jocular ['dʒɔkjulər], *a.* facétieux, jovial, -aux; enjoué; **in a j. vein,** d'un ton rieur.

jocularity [dʒɔkju'læriti], *s.* jovialité *f*, jocosité *f*, enjouement *m*.

jocularly ['dʒɔkjuləli], *adv.* facétieusement; jovialement.

jocund ['dʒɔkənd], *a. Lit:* jovial, -aux; badin, gai, enjoué.

jocundity [dʒə'kʌnditi], *s. Lit:* jovialité *f*, badinage *m*, enjouement *m*, gaieté *f*.

jocundly ['dʒɔkʌndli], *adv. Lit:* jovialement; d'un air badin, enjoué.

jodhpurs ['dʒɔdpə:z], *s.pl. Cost:* pantalon *m* d'équitation (serré à la cheville).

Joe [dʒou]. **1.** *Pr.n.m.* (*dim. of Joseph*) Joseph; *F: O:* **not for J.!** pour rien au monde! on ne me la fait pas! je ne coupe pas là-dedans! **2.** *s. F:* (*a*) *esp. NAm:* homme *m*, type *m*; **a couple of good joes,** deux bons types; **G.I. Joe,** soldat américain; (*b*) *Pej:* **a holy J.,** (i) un ecclésiastique; (ii) un dévot; (*c*) **J. Soap,** poire *f*, homme qui s'attire toutes les corvées; (*d*) **J. Miller,** (i) recueil *m* de plaisanteries; (ii) vieille plaisanterie; plaisanterie usée. **3.** *s. U.S: Bot: F:* **J.-Pye weed,** eupatoire pourpée.

joey ['dʒoui], *s.* **1.** *Austr:* jeune kangourou *m*. **2.** *F: A:* pièce *f* de trois pence.

jog[1] [dʒɔg], *s.* **1.** (*a*) coup *m* (de coude, etc.); **to give s.o.'s memory a j.,** rafraîchir la mémoire de qn; (*b*) secousse *f*, cahot *m* (d'une voiture, etc.). **2.** petit trot; **to go along at an easy j.,** aller son petit bonhomme de chemin; trottiner.

jog[2], *v.* (**jogged**) **1.** *v.tr.* (*a*) pousser (d'un coup sec); **to j. s.o.'s elbow,** pousser le coude à qn; **to j. s.o. with one's elbow,** donner un coup de coude à qn; **to j. s.o.'s memory,** donner le branle à la mémoire de qn; rafraîchir la mémoire à qn; donner des points de repère à qn; (*b*) (*of vehicle*) secouer, cahoter (les voyageurs); (*c*) **to j. one's horse on, to j. s.o. on,** serrer les côtes à son cheval, à qn; (*d*) *Tchn:* taquer (des feuilles de papier); *Cmptr:* battre (un paquet de cartes). **2.** *v.i.* (*a*) **to j. along,** (i) trottiner (à cheval); aller au petit trot; (ii) aller, faire, son petit bonhomme de chemin; aller cahin-caha; **we must be jogging (on, along),** il faut nous remettre en route; **we're jogging along,** les choses *f* vont leur train; (*b*) *Sp:* faire du jogging.

jogger ['dʒɔgər], *s.* **1.** *Tchn:* taqueuse *f*. **2.** *F:* **memory j.,** pense-bête *m*, *pl.* pense-bêtes. **3.** *Sp:* joggeur, -euse.

jogging[1] ['dʒɔgiŋ], *a.* **1.** (*of vehicle, etc.*) cahotant. **2. j. pace,** petit trot.

jogging[2], *s.* **1.** (*a*) coups *mpl* de coude; (*b*) taquage *m*, alignement *m* (de feuilles); *Cmptr:* battage *m* (de cartes); **j. machine,** taqueuse *f*. **2.** cahotage *m*, cahotement *m* (d'une voiture); cahots *mpl*, secousses *fpl*. **3.** petit trot. **4.** *Sp:* jogging *m*.

joggle[1] ['dʒɔgl], *s. F:* petite secousse.

joggle[2]. **1.** *v.tr.* (*a*) *F:* secouer légèrement; **to j. sth. in, out,** faire entrer, faire sortir, qch. par petites secousses; (*b*) *Tchn:* taquer (des feuilles); *Cmptr:* battre (des cartes). **2.** *v.i.* (*a*) branler; (*b*) **to j. along,** (i) avancer par saccades; (ii) avancer cahin-caha.

joggle[3], *s.* **1.** (*a*) *Carp:* embrèvement *m*; (*b*) *Carp: Mec.E:* adent *m*, crémaillère *f*, gradin *m*. **2.** (*a*) *Carp:* goujon *m* (d'assemblage, d'assujettissement, de pied de poteau, etc.); *Const:* **j. piece, post,** poinçon *m* (de comble); (*b*) *Const:* goujon (prisonnier) (pour assembler deux pierres). **3. j. (joint),** (i) *Carp:* assemblage *m*, joint *m*, à embrèvement; (ii) *Carp: Mec.E:* assemblage à adent, à crémaillère, à gradin; (iii) *Corp:* assemblage, joint, à goujon; *Const:* assemblage (de pierres) à goujon (prisonnier). **4.** *N.Arch:* (*a*) épaulement *m*; (*b*) jogglinage *m*.

joggle[4], *v.tr.* **1.** (*a*) *Carp:* embrever; (*b*) *Carp: Mec.E:* assembler en adent, en crémaillère, en gradin; (*c*) *Metalw:* former (un adent, une crémaillère, un gradin). **2.** (*a*) *Carp:* goujonner (des pièces de bois); (*b*) *Const:* goujonner (des pierres). **3.** *N.Arch:* (*a*) épauler; **joggled joint,** joint, clin, épaulé; **joggled frame,** membrure épaulée; (*b*) joggliner.

joggling ['dʒɔgliŋ], *s.* **1.** = JOGGLE[3] 3; **j. machine,** machine *f* à former les adents, les crémaillères. **2.** *N.Arch:* jogglinage *m*; **j. machine,** presse *f* à joggliner.

jogtrot ['dʒɔgtrɔt], *s.* (*a*) petit trot; **at a j.,** au petit trot; (*b*) vie routinière.

Johanna [dʒou'(h)ænə], *Pr.n.f.* Jeanne.

Johannine [dʒou'(h)ænain], *a. Theol:* johannique; de saint Jean.

johannite [dʒou'(h)ænait], *s. Miner:* johannite *m*.

John [dʒɔn]. **1.** *Pr.n.m.* Jean; **St J. the Baptist,** saint Jean Baptiste; *Hist:* **J. of Gaunt,** Jean de Gand; **J. Lackland,** Jean sans Terre; **Don J. of Austria,** Juan d'Autriche. **2.** *Pr.n.m.* **J. Bull,** John Bull, l'Anglais typique; *F:* **J. Blunt,** l'homme qui dit carrément son fait; *Hist: F:* **J. Company,** la Compagnie (anglaise) des Indes; *NAm: Jur:* **J. Doe** = M. Dupont; *NAm: F:* **J. Henry,** *U.S: F:* **J. Hancock,** sa signature. **3.** *s. esp. U.S:* (*a*) *F:* homme *m*, type *m*; (*b*) *P:* client *m* d'une prostituée; (*c*) (*also Austr:*) **the johns,** la police, les flics *m*. **4.** *s.* (*a*) *Ich:* **J. Dory,** dorade *f*; (*b*) *F:* **J. Barleycorn,** le whisky; (*c*) *Cost: F:* **long johns,** caleçon long. **5.** *s. esp. NAm: F:* **the j.,** les cabinets *m*, la toilette *f*.

johnboat ['dʒɔnbout], *s. esp. U.S:* bateau plat (de rivière).

Johne [dʒɔn], *Pr.n. Vet:* **Johne's disease,** paratuberculose *f*.

Johnnie, Johnny ['dʒɔni]. **1.** *Pr.n.m.* (*dim. of* **John**) Jeannot; *F:* **Johnny come lately,** nouveau venu; *Mil: F:* **Johnny Raw, Johnny Newcome,** bleu *m*, morveux *m*; *Nau: P:* **Johnny Armstrong,** la force des bras. **2.** *s. F:* (*a*) type *m*, individu *m*; **what does the inspector j. want?** ce type-là, l'inspecteur, qu'est-ce qu'il veut? (*b*) petit crevé; gommeux *m*. **3.** *s. Orn: F:* manchot *m*.

johnnycake ['dʒɔnikeik], *s. Cu:* galette *f* (i) *U.S:* de farine de maïs, (ii) *Austr:* de farine de froment.

Johnsonese [dʒɔnsə'ni:z], *s.* langage *m*, style *m*, à la docteur Johnson; style johnsonien.

Johnsonian [dʒɔn'souniən], *a.* (langage, etc.) johnsonien, à la docteur Johnson.

join[1] [dʒɔin], *s.* joint *m*, jointure *f*; soudure *f* (d'os, de chambre à air de pneu, etc.); habillure *f* (de treillis métallique, etc.); ligne *f* de jonction (de deux feuilles d'une carte, etc.).

join[2], *v.*

I. *v.tr. & i.* **1.** *v.tr.* (*a*) joindre, unir, réunir (deux morceaux de drap, etc.); relier, assembler (deux madriers, etc.); rapprocher (les lèvres d'une plaie); souder (un os fracturé); **to j. (two things) end to end,** joindre (deux choses) bout à bout; ajoindre, rabouter, raboutir (des planches); raccorder (des tuyaux); **beams joined side by side,** poutres accolées; **to j. panels edge to edge, face to face,** affronter des panneaux; **to j.**

(together) the fragments of sth., joindre, réunir, les morceaux de qch.; **to j. (together) the broken ends of a cord,** (re)nouer les bouts cassés d'un cordon; **to j. sth. with sth.,** réunir qch. à qch.; **to j. sth. (on) to sth.,** rapporter, ajouter, attacher, qch. à qch.; **to j. sth. to the end of sth.,** attacher qch. au bout de qch.; **to j. hands with s.o.,** (i) prendre qn par la main; (ii) s'unir à qn, se joindre à qn (pour faire qch.); **they joined hands to ford the stream,** ils se sont donné la main pour traverser la rivière; **the nations must j. hands and co-ordinate their efforts,** les nations *f* doivent se tendre la main, faire cause commune, et coordonner leurs efforts; *Mil:* **the two regiments joined hands,** les deux régiments *m* opérèrent une jonction; **joined in, by, marriage,** unis par le mariage; **to j. (forces) with s.o. in doing sth.,** se joindre à qn pour faire qch.; **to j. company with s.o.,** se joindre à qn; rejoindre qn; (*b*) ajouter; **to j. threats with, to, remonstrances,** ajouter les menaces aux remontrances; accompagner des remontrances de menaces; **to j. strength of body with strength of mind,** réunir, associer, la force du corps à celle de l'âme; **the documents joined to the report,** les documents annexés au procès-verbal; (*c*) **the neck joins the head to the body,** le cou unit, joint, relie, réunit, la tête au corps; **straight line that joins two points,** droite *f* qui joint deux points. **2.** *v.tr.* (*a*) se joindre à, s'unir à (qn); rejoindre (qn); **he joined us on our way,** il nous a rejoints en route; **will you j. us, j. our party?** voulez-vous vous joindre à nous? voulez-vous vous mettre des nôtres? voulez-vous être de la partie? **I will j. you at . . .,** je vous (re)joindrai à . . .; **let us j. the ladies,** allons retrouver, rejoindre, les dames; **to j. the procession,** se mêler au cortège; **to j. s.o. in sth.,** se joindre à qn dans (une entreprise, etc.); **to j. s.o. in a bottle of port,** partager une bouteille de porto avec qn; (*b*) *Mil:* **to j. one's unit,** rallier, rejoindre, son unité; *Nau: Navy:* **to j. one's ship,** rejoindre son navire, le bâtiment; rallier le bord; (*c*) entrer dans (un club, un régiment, etc.); **to j. a religious order,** entrer dans un ordre; **to j. a (political) party,** prendre rang dans un parti; adhérer à, s'affilier à, un parti; **to j. a company, an association,** se mettre d'une société; entrer dans une société; devenir membre d'une société; **to j. evening classes,** s'inscrire pour un cours du soir; **to j. a band of robbers,** s'affilier, s'associer, à une bande de voleurs; **to j. the army,** s'engager, s'enrôler, dans l'armée. **3.** *v.tr.* (*a*) se joindre, s'unir, à (qch.); **the place where the footpath joins the road,** l'endroit *m* où le sentier rejoint la route; (*b*) **to be joined to, to j., sth.,** être contigu à qch.; **in the past England was joined to France,** dans le passé l'Angleterre tenait à la France. **4.** *v.i.* se joindre, se rejoindre, s'unir (**with sth., with s.o.,** à qn, à qch.); (*of the lips of wound*) s'agglutiner; **parallel lines never j.,** les lignes *f* parallèles ne se rencontrent jamais, ne se rejoignent jamais; **to j. together,** (*of thgs*) se souder; (*of pers.*) se réunir (pour faire qch.); **to j. together in liability, in responsibility,** se solidariser; **to j. with s.o. in doing sth.,** se joindre à qn pour faire qch.

II. (*compound verbs*) **1. join in,** *v.i.* se mettre de la partie; s'associer à, s'affilier à (un projet, etc.); prendre part à (une querelle, etc.); **to j. in the protest,** joindre sa voix aux protestations.

2. join up, *v.i. Mil: F:* s'engager, s'enrôler.

joinder [ˈdʒɔindər], *s.* réunion *f,* union *f*; *esp. Jur:* **j. of actions,** jonction *f* d'instances; **j. of issue,** mise *f* en état de la cause.

joiner [ˈdʒɔinər], *s.* **1.** menuisier *m*; **joiner's shop,** une menuiserie. **2.** *F:* personne *f* de caractère grégaire, qui aime s'associer aux clubs et aux œuvres en commun; **I'm a non-j.,** je n'aime pas les associations.

joinering [ˈdʒɔinəriŋ], **joinery** [ˈdʒɔinəri], *s.* menuiserie *f*; **a piece of j.,** une menuiserie, une pièce menuisée.

joining [ˈdʒɔiniŋ], *s.* **1.** (*a*) jonction *f,* (ré)union *f,* assemblement *m,* assemblage *m* (des morceaux de qch., etc.); suture *f* (d'os, etc.); liaison *f* (de sons, etc.); **j. of two beams side by side,** accolement *m* de deux poutres; **j. edge to edge,** affrontement *m* (de panneaux, etc.); **j. of battle,** entrée *f* en bataille; (*b*) *El:* **j. up,** connexion *f*; **j. up in parallel,** connexion en parallèle; **j. up in series,** connexion en série, en tension. **2.** entrée (dans un club, etc.); **j. (up),** engagement *m,* enrôlement *m* (dans l'armée).

joint[1] [dʒɔint], *s.* **1.** (*a*) joint *m,* jointure *f*; *Const:* **joints in masonry,** joints de la maçonnerie; **j. filled with plaster,** solin *m*; **channelled j.,** anglet *m*; *Mec.E: etc:* **soldered j., welded j.,** soudure *f*; assemblage soudé; **cramp j.,** joint à agrafes; **cotter j.,** agrafe *f* à clavette; **flange(d) j.,** joint à collerette, à brides; **pap j.,** joint à téton; **screw(ed) j.,** joint, assemblage, à vis; joint vissé; **union j.,** (joint) union *f*; joint à manchon, à raccord fileté; **rivet j.,** assemblage à rivets, par rivets; **sleeve j.,** emmanchement *m*; **slip j.,** joint glissant; **j. pin,** goupille *f*; **j. pipe,** tuyau *m* de jonction; **j. flange,** bride *f* de raccord; **face-to-face j.,** joint sec; **flush j.,** assemblage affleuré; joint lisse, à franc bord; **covering j., lap(ped) j., overlap j.,** joint à recouvrement, à clin; joint chevauché; **staggered joints,** joints alternés, croisés, décalés; **moving j., working j.,** joint mobile; **sliding j.,** joint coulissant, glissant; **asbestos j.,** joint d'amiante, au carton d'amiante; **copper-asbestos j.,** joint métalloplastique; **hydraulic j.,** joint hydraulique; **yoke j.,** chape *f,* étrier *m*; **close, tight, j.,** joint étanche; **oil j.,** joint à huile; **oiltight, steamtight, watertight, j.,** joint étanche à l'huile, à la vapeur, à l'eau; *Plumb:* **wiped j.,** soudure *f* à nœud; nœud *m* de soudure; *Rail:* **rail j.,** joint de rail; assemblage; **emergency rail j.,** assemblage d'urgence, de secours; **supported, unsupported, rail j.,** joint (de rail) appuyé, en porte à faux; (*b*) *El:* épissure *f*; **straight j.,** épissure droite; **shielded j.,** épissure cuirassée; **j. box,** boîte *f* de jonction (de câbles); (*c*) *Mec.E: etc:* **hinged j.,** articulation *f,* assemblage, à charnière; **flexible j.,** transmission *f* flexible; **knuckle j.,** joint articulé, en charnière; **knee j.,** joint articulé; rotule *f*; jarret *m* (de tuyau); **Cardan j., gimbal j., universal j.,** joint de, à la, Cardan; cardan *m*; joint articulé, brisé; joint universel, charnière universelle; **cross-pin Cardan j.,** joint de Cardan à croisillon; **cup(-and-ball) j.,** joint à rotule, à calotte sphérique, à genou; **toggle j.,** rotule; (joint à) genou *m*; (*d*) *Bookb:* mors *m*; (*e*) *Carp:* assemblage, empatture *f*; **mortise-and-tenon j.,** assemblage à tenon et (à) mortaise; assemblage à emboîtement; **dovetail j.,** assemblage à queue d'aronde; **notch(ed) j.,** joint à, en, adent; endente *f,* trave *f*; **scarf j.,** assemblage à mi-bois, à trait de Jupiter; joint biseauté; **step j.,** (i) assemblage, joint, à recouvrement; (ii) assemblage, entaille *f,* à mi-bois; **lap j.,** assemblage, joint, à recouvrement; assemblage à clin; **rabbet j.,** assemblage à feuillure. **2.** *Anat:* (point *m* d')articulation; joint, jointure (du genou, etc.); **hip, knee, j.,** articulation de la hanche, du genou; **elbow j.,** articulation du coude; **rheumatism in, of, the joints,** rhumatisme *m* articulaire; **out of j.,** (i) (bras, etc.) disloqué, démis, déboîté, luxé; (ii) *F:* (système, mécanisme, etc.) désorganisé, dérangé, détraqué; **to put one's arm out of j.,** se démettre, se disloquer, le bras; *F:* **to put s.o.'s nose out of j.,** jouer un mauvais tour à qn; dégoter qn; (*of shoulder, etc.*) **to come out of j.,** se déboîter; *F:* **the times are out of j.,** le monde est désaxé, désorienté, à l'envers; tout va de travers. **3.** (*a*) partie *f* (du corps, d'une chose articulée) entre deux articulations; virole *f,* phalange *f* (du doigt); **three-j. fishing rod,** canne *f* à pêche à trois corps; (*b*) *Cu:* morceau *m,* quartier *m,* pièce *f,* de viande; **(roast) j.,** rôti *m*; **cut off the j.,** tranche *f* de rôti. **4.** (*a*) *Bot:* nœud *m,* articulation (de tige); (*b*) *Bot:* entrenœud *m*; *Bot: Ent:* article *m.* **5.** *Geol:* joint, diaclase *f,* cassure *f,* délit *m*; **contraction j.,** synclase *f.* **6.** *P:* endroit *m*; logement *m*; **(low) j.,** boîte *f* (louche); bouge *m*; **(gambling) j.,** tripot *m*; **clip j.,** boîte, maison *f,* tire-pognon; **it's not a bad j.,** (i) c'est pas mal comme niche; (ii) on s'y amuse pas mal; **I don't like those slap-up joints,** ça ne me va pas, ces endroits mondains, trop chics. **7.** *P:* cigarette *f* de marijuana, joint *m,* stick *m.*

joint[2], *v.tr.* **1.** (*a*) joindre, assembler (des pièces de bois, etc.); emmancher (des tuyaux, etc.); (*b*) articuler; **bone that is jointed with another,** os *m* qui s'articule avec un autre. **2.** découper, démembrer, dépecer (un poulet, etc.). **3.** *Const:* jointoyer (un mur, etc.). **4.** *Carp:* varloper (deux planches, etc.).

joint[3], *a.* **1.** (*of work, etc.*) commun, en commun, combiné, coordonné; **j. efforts,** efforts réunis, en commun; **j. action,** action combinée, collective; **j. use,** cojouissance *f*; mitoyenneté *f* (d'un mur, d'une haie); **j. report,** rapport collectif; **j. commission,** commission *f* mixte; **j. military commission,** commission militaire interalliée; **j. committee,** (i) comité *m* mixte; (ii) *Pol:* commission interparlementaire; **j. undertaking,** entreprise *f* en participation; *Bank:* **j. account,** compte conjoint, compte à demi, compte en participation; **deal on j. account,** opération *f* en participation; *Fin:* **j. shares,** actions indivises; **j. stock,** capital social; **j.-stock bank,** société *f* de dépôt; *Jur:* **j. estate,** communauté *f*; *Publ:* **edition published at the j. expense of publisher and author,** édition faite en participation; *Com: etc:* **j. orders, ordering,** groupage *m* de commandes. **2.** co-, associé; **j. author,** coauteur *m*; collaborateur, -trice; **j. editor, editress,** corédacteur, -trice; **j. director, directress,** codirecteur, -trice; **j. directorship,** codirection *f*; **j. guardian,** cotuteur, -trice; **j. guardianship,** cotutelle *f*; **j. sponsorship,** copaternité *f*; **j. heir, heiress,** cohéritier, -ière; copartageant, -ante; codétenteur, -trice (d'un héritage); **j. legatee,** colégataire *mf*; **j. beneficiaries,** bénéficiaires conjoints, indivis; **j. holder,** codétenteur, -trice (d'une succession); coporteur *m,* porteur associé, porteur indivis (d'un titre); **j. mandatory, proxy,** comandataire *m*; **j. manager, manageress,** codirecteur, -trice; cogérant, -ante; **j. management,** codirection *f,* cogérance *f*; **j. partner,** coassocié, -ée; **j. partnership,** coassociation *f*; **j. owner, proprietor,** (i) copossesseur *m,* copropriétaire *mf*; *Jur:* communiste *mf,* indivisaire *m,* propriétaire indivis; (ii) co-armateur *m,* quirataire *m* (d'un navire); **j. ownership,** (i) copossession *f,* copropriété *f*; mitoyenneté *f* (d'un mur mitoyen, etc.); *Jur:* indivision *f*; (ii) quirat *m* (d'un navire); **to have j. ownership of sth.,** coposséder qch.; **j. tenant,** colocataire *mf*; **j. tenancy,** location indivise; **j. creditor,** cocréancier *m*; **j. debtor,** codébiteur, -trice; **j. obligation,** coobligation *f*; **j. defendant,** codéfendeur *m*; **j. plaintiff,** codemandeur, -eresse; **j. purchasers,** coacquéreurs *m*; acheteurs associés; **j. purchase,** coacquisition *f*; **j. seller,** covendeur, -euse; **j. regent,** corégent *m*; **j. regency,** corégence *f*; **j. rule,** synarchie *f.*

jointed [ˈdʒɔintid], *a.* **1.** (*a*) articulé; jointif; **j. doll,** poupée articulée; **delicately j. limbs,** membres *m* aux fines attaches; **j. walking stick,** canne jointée; *Bot:* **j. stalk,** tige articulée; *Z:* **many-j.,** multiarticulé; *Mec.E: etc:* **j. coupling,** accouplement *m* à articulation; **lock-j.,** à emboîtement; **lap-j.,** à recouvrement à clin; (*b*) (poulet, etc.) démembré, dépecé; coupé par les joints; (*c*) *Geol:* (roche *f*) à joints. **2.** (*of horse*) **short-j.,** court-jointé, *pl.* court-jointés; **long-j.,** long-jointé.

jointer [ˈdʒɔintər], *s.* **1.** (*pers.*) assembleur, -euse. **2.** (*thg*) (*a*) *Carp:* (i) *Tls:* varlope *f*; (ii) machine *f* à rainer; (*b*) *Const:* mirette *f* (de maçon); tire-joint *m inv.*

jointing [ˈdʒɔintiŋ], *s.* **1.** jointement *m,* jointure *f,* assemblage *m* (de planches, etc.); emmanchage *m* (de tuyaux); **steam j.,** joints *mpl* étanches à la vapeur; **j. rivets,** rivets *m* d'attache; **j. compound,** lut *m,* mastic *m,* compound *m* de fermeture (pour joints). **2.** démembrement *m,* découpage *m* (d'un poulet, etc.). **3.** *Const:* (*a*) jointoiement *m* (d'un mur, etc.); (*b*) joints (d'un mur). **4.** *Carp:* (*a*) varlopage *m*; **j. plane,** (i) *Carp:* varlope *f*; (ii) *Geol:* plan *m* de séparation, de diaclase; (*b*) entaillage *m.*

jointless [ˈdʒɔintlis], *a.* sans joints. **1.** sans articulations; *Z: etc:* inarticulé; *Bot:* (tige *f*) sans nœuds. **2.** fait tout d'une pièce.

jointly [ˈdʒɔintli], *adv.* ensemble, conjointement; **to start a company j. with . . .,** créer une société en commun avec . . .; **to possess sth. j.,** posséder qch. conjointement, indivisément, par indivis; **to inherit j.,** copartager une succession; *Jur:* **j. liable, responsible,** solidaire; **acting j.,** agissant solidairement; **to render j. liable, responsible,** solidariser; **you are j. liable for the damage,** vous êtes solidaire des dégâts; **j. and severally liable,** responsables conjointement et solidairement; **to manage a firm j.,** cogérer une maison, être cogérants d'une maison.

jointress [ˈdʒɔintris], *s.f. Jur:* douairière.

jointure[1] [ˈdʒɔintjər], *s.* (*a*) propriété indivise entre mari et femme; (*b*) douaire *m.*

jointure[2], *v.tr.* assigner un douaire à (une femme).

joist[1] [dʒɔist], *s. Const:* solive *f,* soliveau *m,* poutre *f,* poutrelle *f*; **beams and joists,** solivure *f* (d'un édifice); **main j., binding j.,** traverse *f* de plancher; solive de plafond; **intermediate j.,** solive de remplissage; **bridging j.,** lambourde *f*; **floor j.,** lambourde, gîte *m,* de plancher; **trimmed j.,** solive enchevêtrée, boiteuse.

joist[2], *v.tr.* **1.** poser le solivage de (la maison, etc.). **2.** assujettir (les ais, etc.) sur le solivage.

joisting [ˈdʒɔistiŋ], *s.* solivage *m,* poutrage *m,* poutraison *f.*

joke[1] [dʒouk], *s.* (*a*) plaisanterie *f,* farce *f, F:* blague *f*; **to say, do, sth. for a j., by way of a j.,** dire, faire, qch. par plaisanterie, en plaisantant, pour s'amuser, pour rire; **I did it for a j.,** je l'ai fait histoire de rire; **you mean this for a j.,** vous voulez rire; **to make a j. of everything,** tourner tout en badinage, en blague; badiner de tout; blaguer de tout; **the j. is that . . .,** le comique de l'histoire, c'est que . . .; **the best of the j. is that . . .,** le plaisant de l'affaire, c'est que . . .; **it's all a huge j.,** tout ça n'est pas sérieux; **it's no j. waiting for hours,** ce n'est pas amusant d'attendre des heures; **it will be no j. to . . .,** ce ne sera pas une petite affaire (que) de . . .; **practical j.,** (i) mauvais tour, mauvaise plaisanterie, mystification *f,* farce; (ii) brimade *f*; **to play a practical j. on s.o.,** mystifier qn; faire une farce, une attrape, à qn; **the joke's on me,** c'est à vous, à eux, de rire; **it's a silly j.,** c'est une mauvaise plaisanterie; **that's a good j.!** en voilà une bonne! **that's a poor j.!** je la trouve mauvaise! **he knows how to take a j.,** il entend la plaisanterie; (*b*) bon mot; facétie *f*, plaisanterie; **he is always ready with a j.**, il a toujours le mot pour rire; **he must have his little j.**, il aime à plaisanter; (*c*) sujet *m* de plaisanterie; risée *f*; **he's the j. of the town**, il est en butte aux railleries de toute la ville.

joke². **1.** *v.i.* plaisanter, railler, badiner; **to j. at, about, sth.**, plaisanter de qch.; **I was only joking**, je l'ai dit pour badiner, en badinant; je l'ai dit histoire de rire; **you're joking! you must be,** *F:* **you've got to be, joking!** vous voulez rire! **I'm not joking**, je ne plaisante pas; **without joking**, blague à part; **to j. with s.o.**, plaisanter avec qn. **2.** *v.tr.* plaisanter, railler (qn); se moquer de (qn).

joker ['dʒoukər], *s.* **1.** farceur, -euse; plaisant *m*; *F:* blagueur, -euse; loustic *m*; **practical j.**, mauvais plaisant; plaisantin *m*; malavisé *m*. **2.** *F: Pej:* type *m*, individu *m*; **some joker's pinched my umbrella**, c'est un petit rigolard qui m'a chipé mon parapluie. **3.** *Cards:* joker *m*. **4.** *U.S: F:* petite clause insérée dans un projet de loi, dans un contrat, dont l'effet est d'en infirmer les articles essentiels; subtilité *f*, échappatoire *f*.

joking¹ ['dʒoukiŋ], *a.* (ton, air) moqueur, de plaisanterie; **half j., half angry**, moitié plaisantant, moitié en colère; moitié figue moitié raisin.

joking², *s.* plaisanterie *f*, badinage *m*, *F:* blague *f*.

jokingly ['dʒoukiŋli], *adv.* en plaisantant; pour rire; d'un ton moqueur, railleur.

jollier ['dʒɔliər], *s. U.S: F:* railleur, -euse; plaisant *m*.

jollification [dʒɔlifi'keiʃ(ə)n], *s. F:* réunion joyeuse, gaie; partie *f* de plaisir.

jollify ['dʒɔlifai]. *F: O:* **1.** *v.i.* s'amuser; faire la noce. **2.** *v.tr.* émoustiller, agaillardir.

jolliness ['dʒɔlinis], **jollity** ['dʒɔliti], *s.* **1.** gaieté *f*; **to be in no mood for jollity**, ne pas avoir le cœur à se réjouir. **2.** *O:* **jollities**, gaietés, réjouissances *f*.

jolly¹ ['dʒɔli]. **1.** *a.* (*a*) (*pers.*) joyeux, gai; (*b*) *F:* (i) (*pers.*) *A:* agréable; (ii) *O:* **what a j. little room!** quelle pièce charmante! (*c*) *F: O:* éméché, gris, pompette; (*d*) *F: A:* (*intensifying*) fameux; considérable; **what a j. liar!** quel menteur! **It's a j. shame!** bien sûr que ce n'est pas chic! **2.** *adv. F:* rudement, fameusement, joliment, énormément; **I'll take j. good care**, je ferai rudement attention; **and a j. good job too!** tant mieux (pour ça)! **I j. well am right!** je vous assure que j'ai bien raison! **I'll do what I j. well please!** tu n'as rien à dire, je ferai ce qui me plaira; **he did it j. quickly**, il l'a fait bien vite. **3.** *s. F:* soldat *m* d'infanterie de marine; marsouin *m*.

jolly², *v.tr.* plaisanter, railler (qn); **to j. s.o. along**, encourager qn par des plaisanteries, des flatteries, etc.

jolly³, *s. Nau:* **j. (boat)**, (petit) canot (à bord d'un navire).

jolt¹ [dʒoult], *s.* **1.** (*a*) cahot *m*, choc *m*, secousse *f*, soubresaut *m*, tressaut *m*; **the jolts of the road**, les cahots, les secousses, de la route; (*b*) *Mec.E:* à-coup *m*, *pl.* a coups; *Aut:* coup *m* de raquette. **2.** surprise *f*, choc; **it gave me a bit of a j.**, cela m'a donné un coup; cela m'a fait quelque chose. **3.** *P:* (*a*) petit coup de gniole; (*b*) piqûre *f* d'héroïne, etc.

jolt². **1.** *v.tr.* cahoter, ballotter, secouer; imprimer une (brusque) secousse à (qch.); **to be jolted**, être cahoté; tressauter; subir des chocs; **the basket was jolted out of the cart**, un cahot de la charrette a fait tomber le panier; **the journey had jolted down my meal**, les cahots du voyage avaient fait descendre mon déjeuner. **2.** *v.i.* (*a*) (*of vehicle*) cahoter, ballotter, tressauter, soubresauter; **to j. along**, avancer avec des cahots, en cahotant; avancer cahin-caha; **we jolted over the stone**, d'un cahot nous avons franchi la pierre; (*b*) *Mec.E:* avoir, donner, des à-coups; *Aut:* donner des coups de raquette.

joltiness ['dʒoultinis], *s.* inégalité *f* (d'une route, etc.); roulement dur (d'une charrette, etc.).

jolting¹ ['dʒoultiŋ], *a.* cahotant.

jolting², *s.* **1.** cahotement *m*, cahotage *m*, ballottement *m*, ébranlement *m* (d'une voiture, etc.). **2.** *Mec.E:* à coups *mpl*; *Aut:* coups *mpl* de raquette.

jolty ['dʒoulti], *a.* (véhicule, etc.) cahotant; (chemin) cahoteux, raboteux.

Jonah ['dʒounə]. **1.** *Pr.n.m. B.Hist:* Jonas. **2.** *s.* guignard *m*, malchanceux *m*; porte-malheur *m inv.*

Jonathan ['dʒɔnəθən]. **1.** *Pr.n.m.* (*a*) *B.Hist:* Jonathan; (*b*) *P:* **Brother J.**, les États-Unis. **2.** *s.* (variété de) pomme *f* à couteau.

jonquil ['dʒɔŋkwil]. **1.** *s. Bot:* jonquille *f*. **2.** *a. & s.* (couleur *f*) jonquille (*m*) *inv.*

Jonsonian [dʒɔn'souniən], *a. Lit.Hist:* (théâtre *m*, etc.) de Ben Jonson.

Joppa ['dʒɔpə], *Pr.n.A.Geog:* Joppé.

Jordan¹ ['dʒɔ:d(ə)n], *Pr.n. Geog:* **1.** (*river*) le Jourdain; *O:* **this side of J.**, de ce côté de la tombe. **2.** (*country*) Jordanie *f*.

jordan², *s. F: O:* pot *m* de chambre; Jules *m*, Thomas *m*.

Jordan³, *attrib.* **J. almond**, amande *f* de Malaga.

Jordanian [dʒɔ'deiniən], *Geog:* (*a*) *a.* jordanien; (*b*) *s.* Jordanien, -ienne.

jordanon ['dʒɔ:dənɔn], *s. Bot:* jordanon *m*, petite espèce.

jorum ['dʒɔ:rəm], *s.* **1.** *A:* coupe *f*, hanap *m*. **2.** bol *m*, bolée *f* (de punch, etc.).

Joseph ['dʒouzif], *Pr.n.m.* Joseph; *F: A:* **not for J.**, pour rien au monde!

Josephine ['dʒouzifi:n], *Pr.n.f.* Joséphine.

josephinite [dʒouzi'fi:nait], *s. Miner:* joséphinite *f*.

Josephus [dʒou'si:fəs], *Pr.n.m. Hist:* Josèphe.

josh¹ [dʒɔʃ], *s. F:* plaisanterie *f*, raillerie *f*.

josh², *v.tr. F:* plaisanter, railler (qn); se moquer de (qn); taquiner (qn).

josher ['dʒɔʃər], *s. F:* farceur, -euse; plaisant *m*; gausseur, -euse.

Joshua ['dʒɔʃjuə], *Pr.n.m. B.Hist:* Josué.

Josiah [dʒə'saiə], *Pr.n.m. B.Hist:* Josias.

joss [dʒɔs], *s.* (*in China*) idole *f*; **j. house**, temple (chinois); **j. stick**, bâton *m* d'encens.

josser ['dʒɔsər], *s. F: O:* **1.** type *m*, individu *m*; **old j.**, vieille baderne. **2.** *Mil: Austr:* aumônier *m*.

jostle¹ ['dʒɔsl], *s.* bousculade *f*, presse *f* (d'une foule); coudoiement *m*.

jostle². **1.** *v.i.* jouer des coudes; **to j. against, with, s.o. in a crowd**, bousculer, presser, qn dans une foule; **to j. (one's way) to the front**, jouer des coudes pour arriver au premier rang, pour se faire jour. **2.** *v.tr.* (*a*) bousculer, presser, coudoyer (qn); **to be jostled by the crowd**, être bousculé par la foule; être pressé dans la foule; **to be jostled about**, se faire bousculer; être houspillé; **to j. s.o. out of the way**, écarter qn en jouant des coudes; (*b*) *Rac:* serrer (un concurrent).

jostling ['dʒɔsliŋ], *s.* **1.** = JOSTLE¹. **2.** *Rac:* action *f* de serrer un concurrent.

jot¹ [dʒɔt], *s.* (*a*) *A:* iota *m*; (*b*) **not a j., not one j. or tittle**, pas un iota; **not a j. of truth**, pas un atome de vérité.

jot², *v.tr.* (**jotted**) **to j. sth. down**, noter qch.; prendre note de qch.; prendre qch. en note; jeter qch. sur le papier.

jotter ['dʒɔtər], *s.* bloc-notes *m*, *pl.* blocs-notes.

jotting ['dʒɔtiŋ], *s.* **1.** **j. down (of a note)**, prise *f* (d'une note). **2.** *pl.* **jottings**, notes *f*, mémorandum *m*.

Joule [dʒu:l]. **1.** *Pr.n.m.* Joule; *Ph:* **Joule's law**, la loi de Joule; **Joule's equivalent**, équivalent *m* mécanique de la chaleur. **2.** *s. Ph.Meas:* joule *m*; **a million joules**, mégajoule *m*; **j.-second**, joule-seconde *m*, *pl.* joules-seconde.

journal¹ ['dʒə:n(ə)l], *s.* **1.** journal, -aux *m*; *Nau:* journal de bord; livre *m* de loch; *Book-k:* (livre) journal; *Pol:* **the Journals**, le compte rendu des débats; le procès-verbal (des séances). **2.** journal; feuille (quotidienne); revue (savante); **fashion j.**, journal de modes. **3.** *Mec.E:* tourillon *m* (d'arbre); fusée *f* (d'essieu); **main journals of the crankshaft**, portées *fpl*, portage *m*, du vilebrequin; **vertical j.**, pivot *m*; **j. bearing**, (i) palier *m*; (ii) portée *f* de fusée; (iii) coussinet *m* de palier; **j. box**, (i) *Mec.E:* palier; boîte *f* des coussinets, boîte à tourillons; (ii) *Rail:* boîte d'essieu; boîte à graisse, à huile.

journal², *v.tr. Mec.E:* **1.** **to j. a shaft**, tourner les fusées, les tourillons, d'un arbre; tourillonner un arbre. **2.** **spindle journaled in a plate**, broche *f* dont le tourillon est monté dans une plaque.

journalese [dʒə:nə'li:z], *s. F:* style *m* de journaliste, de journal.

journalism ['dʒə:nəlizm], *s.* journalisme *m*.

journalist ['dʒə:nəlist], *s.* **1.** journaliste *mf*; **he is a j.**, il fait du journalisme. **2.** auteur *m* d'un journal (particulier).

journalistic [dʒə:nə'listik], *a.* journalistique.

journalize ['dʒə:nəlaiz]. **1.** *v.tr.* (*a*) tenir un journal de (ses voyages, etc.); (*b*) *Book-k:* porter (un article) au journal; journaliser (un article). **2.** *v.i.* (*a*) écrire dans les journaux; faire du journalisme; (*b*) tenir un journal.

journalizer ['dʒə:nəlaizər], *s. Book-k:* journaliste *mf*.

journey¹, *pl.* **-eys** ['dʒə:ni, -iz], *s.* **1.** (*a*) voyage *m*; trajet *m*; parcours *m* (entre deux endroits); **sea j.**, voyage sur mer; **return j.**, *Nau: Av:* **inward j.**, (voyage de) retour *m*; *Nau: Av:* **outward j.**, (voyage d')aller *m*; **j. there and back**, (voyage) aller et retour; **to go on, make, undertake, a j.**, faire un voyage; voyager; **to start, set out, on a j.**, partir en voyage; se mettre en route; **to set out again on one's j.**, se remettre en route; **he's just come back from a j.**, il revient de voyage; **to wish s.o. a good, pleasant, j.**, souhaiter bon voyage, bonne route, à qn; **bus j.**, trajet d'autobus; **a two hours' train j.**, un trajet, un voyage, de deux heures en chemin de fer; **he didn't stop talking (for) the whole of the j.**, il a parlé pendant tout le trajet, tout le parcours; **I had my j. for my pains, trouble, for nothing**, j'en ai été pour mon voyage; *Com:* (*of traveller*) **to be on j.**, être en tournée; *O:* **to go on one's last j.**, faire le grand voyage; partir pour l'autre monde; **to be at one's journey's end**, (i) être arrivé à destination; (ii) être à la fin de sa carrière, de sa vie; (*b*) *A:* **(day's) j.**, journée *f*, étape *f*. **2.** *A:* journée (de combat, de travail). **3.** *Min:* rame *f* (de wagons).

journey², *v.i.* (**journeyed; journeying**) voyager.

journeyman, *pl.* **-men** ['dʒə:nimən], *s.* **1.** (*a*) *Ind:* compagnon *m*; **j. carpenter**, compagnon charpentier; **j. baker**, ouvrier boulanger; garçon boulanger; (*b*) *A:* homme *m* de peine; *F:* cheval *m* de bât. **2.** pendule, horloge, distributrice (d'un système de pendules électriques).

journeywork ['dʒə:niwə:k], *s.* **1.** travail *m* à la journée; travail à gages. **2.** labeur *f*; dure besogne.

joust¹ [dʒaust], *s.* joute *f*.

joust², *v.i.* jouter.

Jove [dʒouv], *Pr.n.m.* Jupiter; **Jove's thunderbolts**, les traits *m* de Jupiter; *F: O:* **by J.!** (i) parbleu! (ii) mâtin! nom d'un tonnerre! **by J., it's cold!** mon Dieu, qu'il fait froid!

jovial ['dʒouvjəl], *a.* jovial, -aux; enjoué, gai; **j. smile**, sourire jovial; **he's in a j. mood today**, il est bien gai, en bonne humeur, aujourd'hui.

joviality [dʒouvi'æliti], *s.* jovialité *f*, enjouement *m*, gaîté *f*; bonne humeur.

jovially ['dʒouviəli], *adv.* jovialement, gaiement.

Jovian¹ ['dʒouviən], *a.* (*a*) jupitérien; (*b*) *Astr:* jovien.

Jovian², **Jovianus** [dʒouvi'einəs], *Pr.n.m. Rom.Hist:* Jovien.

jowl [dʒaul], *s.* (*a*) mâchoire *f*; (*b*) joue *f*, bajoue *f* (d'homme, de porc, etc.); (*c*) fanon *m* (de bœuf, de dindon); jabot *m* (d'oiseau); (*d*) hure *f*, tête *f* (de saumon, d'esturgeon, etc.).

joy¹ [dʒɔi], *s.* joie *f*, allégresse *f*; **face beaming with j.**, visage rayonnant d'allégresse, de joie; **to be full of j.**, être en joie, être plein de joie; **to leap for j.**, sauter de joie; **to laugh from sheer j.**, rire d'aise; *O:* **oh j.!** quel bonheur! quel plaisir! *F:* **any j.?** ça a marché? *F:* **no j.!** pas de chance! **to my great j.**, à ma grande joie; **to be s.o.'s j.**, faire la joie de qn; **a thing that is a j. to see**, une chose qui fait plaisir à voir; **to give s.o. j.**, faire plaisir à qn; *A:* **God give you j.!** que Dieu vous garde en sa sainte joie; (*also Iron:*) **I wish you j. of it!** je vous en félicite! **the joys of the countryside**, les charmes *m* de la campagne; *Ecc:* **the Seven Joys of Mary**, les sept Allégresses de la Vierge.

joy². *A: & Lit:* **1.** *v.i.* se réjouir (**in sth.**, de qch.); **to j. to do sth.**, prendre du plaisir à faire qch. **2.** *v.tr.* réjouir; rendre joyeux.

joybells ['dʒɔibelz], *s.pl. O: & Lit:* carillon *m* (de fête); **the joybells were ringing**, les cloches *f* sonnaient la joie à toute volée; les cloches carillonnaient.

joyful ['dʒɔiful], *a.* joyeux, heureux; (*a*) **to be j.**, être allègre, être en joie, être plein de joie; (*b*) **j. news**, bonnes nouvelles.

joyfully ['dʒɔifuli], *adv.* joyeusement, heureusement, allégrement.

joyfulness ['dʒɔifulnis], *s.* **1.** joie *f*, allégresse *f*. **2.** caractère joyeux.

joygirl ['dʒɔigə:l], *s.f. esp. U.S: P:* prostituée, poule.

joyhouse ['dʒɔihaus], *s. esp. U.S: P:* bordel *m*.

joyless ['dʒɔilis], *a.* sans joie; triste.

joylessly ['dʒɔilisli], *adv.* tristement, sans joie.

joylessness ['dʒɔilisnis], *s.* manque *m* de joie; absence *f* de joie; tristesse *f*.

joyous ['dʒɔiəs], *a.* joyeux, heureux; (*of pers.*) allègre.

joyously ['dʒɔiəsli], *adv.* joyeusement, heureusement, allégrement.

joyousness ['dʒɔiəsnis], *s.* (*a*) joie *f*, allégresse *f*; (*b*) humeur joyeuse.

joypop¹ ['dʒɔipɔp], *s. P:* emploi intermittent d'une drogue (par un non-initié); piqûre *f* de remonte-pente.

joypop², *v.i.* (**joypopped**) *P:* se droguer (mais pas régulièrement); se donner une piqûre de remonte-pente.

joypopper ['dʒɔipɔpər], *s. P:* personne qui se drogue (mais pas régulièrement); saccadeur *m*.

joyride¹ ['dʒɔiraid], *s.* **1.** *F:* (*a*) balade en voiture (faite à l'insu du propriétaire); (*b*) balade en voiture, à motocyclette, etc.; **to have a j.**, faire une balade, se balader, en voiture (avec ou sans l'assentiment du propriétaire); (*c*) *Av:* vol *m* de plaisir; virée *f*. **2.** *P:* expérience de drogues faite par un non-initié; saccade *f*.

joyride², *v.i. F:* se balader (en voiture, etc.).

joyrider ['dʒɔiraidər], *s.* **1.** *F:* baladeur, -euse (en voiture, etc.). **2.** *P:* = JOYPOPPER.

joystick ['dʒɔistik], *s. Av:* levier *m* de commande; *F:* manche *m* à balai; **to pull on the j.**, redresser l'avion (avant l'atterrissage).

jube ['dʒu:bi], *s. Ecc.Arch:* jubé *m.*

jubilance ['dʒu:biləns], *s. Lit:* réjouissance *f*, jubilation *f*.

jubilant ['dʒu:bilənt], *a.* (*a*) (*of pers.*) réjoui (**at sth.,** de qch.); exultant; (*b*) (cri, etc.) joyeux, de joie; **j. face,** visage épanoui.

jubilantly ['dʒu:biləntli], *adv.* avec joie.

jubilate[1] ['dʒu:bileit], *v.i.* se réjouir; exulter.

Jubilate[2] [dʒu:bi'lɑ:ti], *s.* **1.** *Ecc:* le Jubilate Deo. **2.** chant *m* de triomphe.

jubilation [dʒu:bi'leiʃ(ə)n], *s.* (*a*) joie *f*, allégresse *f*; exultation *f*; jubilation *f*; (*b*) réjouissance *f*, fête *f*.

jubilee ['dʒu:bili:], *s.* **1.** *Jew.Rel: R.C.Ch:* jubilé *m.* **2.** jubilé; (fête *f* du) cinquantième anniversaire (d'un événement); **to celebrate one's j.,** célébrer la cinquantaine; **silver j.,** fête du vingt-cinquième anniversaire (du couronnement du roi, etc.); **golden j.,** fête du cinquantième anniversaire (du couronnement d'un souverain, etc.); **diamond j.,** fête du soixantième anniversaire; noces de diamant; **j. celebrations,** fêtes jubilaires; **j. year,** année *f* jubilaire.

Judaea [dʒu:'diə], *Pr.n. B.Geog:* Judée *f*.

Judaean [dʒu'di:ən], *a. & s. B.Geog:* (habitant, originaire) de la Judée.

Judaeo-Christian ['dʒu:deiou'kristjən], *a.* judéo-chrétien, -ienne, *pl.* judéo-chrétiens, -iennes.

Judaeo-Christianity ['dʒu:deioukristi'æniti], *s.* judéo-christianisme *m.*

Judaeo-Spanish ['dʒu:deiou'spæniʃ], *s. Ling:* judéo-espagnol *m.*

Judah ['dʒu:də]. *Pr.n. B.Hist:* Juda *m.*

Judaic(al) [dʒu:'deiik(l)], *a.* judaïque.

Judaism ['dʒu:deiizm], *s.* judaïsme *m.*

Judaist ['dʒu:deiist], *s.* judaïsant, -ante.

Judaize ['dʒu:deiaiz]. **1.** *v.i.* judaïser. **2.** *v.tr.* (*a*) enjuiver; (*b*) convertir au judaïsme.

Judas ['dʒu:dəs]. **1.** *Pr.n.m. B.Hist:* (*a*) **J. (Iscariot),** Judas (Iscariote); **J. kiss,** baiser *m* de Judas; (*b*) **J., the brother of James,** Jude, frère de Jacques; **J. of Galilee,** Judas le Galiléen; **J. surnamed Barsabas,** Judas surnommé Barsabas; **J. Maccabaeus,** Judas Macchabée. **2.** *s.* (*a*) **j. (hole, trap),** judas *m* (dans une porte); (*b*) *attrib.* (i) **J.-coloured,** (cheveux) roux, de Judas; (ii) *Bot:* **J. tree, J. thorn,** arbre *m* de Judée; arbre d'amour; gaînier *m*; cercis *m*; **J. ear,** hirnéole *f* oreille de Judas.

judcock ['dʒʌdkɔk], *s. Orn:* bécassin *m.*

judder[1] ['dʒʌdər], *s. Aut:* trépidation *f* (du frein, etc.).

judder[2], *v.i.* (*of brakes, etc.*) trépider; (*of tool*) brouter.

Judeo- ['dʒu:deiou], *comb.fm.* = JUDAEO-.

judge[1] [dʒʌdʒ], *s.* **1.** (*a*) juge *m*; **circuit j.,** juge en tournée; **presiding j.,** président *m* du tribunal; **j. of appeal,** conseiller *m* à la cour (d'appel, de cassation); **the judges,** la magistrature assise; *B:* **(the Book of) Judges,** le livre des Juges; les Juges; (*b*) *U.S:* magistrat *m.* **2.** *Sp: etc:* arbitre *m*, juge; *Rac:* commissaire *m* à l'arrivée; membre *m* du jury (d'une exposition canine, d'horticulture, etc.). **3.** connaisseur, -euse; **to be a good j. of wine,** être connaisseur en vin; s'y connaître, s'y entendre, en vin; être gourmet; **good j. of music,** bon juge en matière de musique; **I'm no j. of horseflesh,** je ne me connais pas, ne m'y connais pas, en chevaux.

judge[2], *v.tr.* **1.** (*a*) juger (un prisonnier, une affaire); **to j. which party is in the wrong,** juger quelle partie a tort; **a man is judged by his actions,** un homme se juge par ses actions; **to j. in favour of sth.,** conclure à qch.; *v.i.* **God must j. between us,** Dieu en jugera entre nous; (*b*) **to leave it to the country to j.,** s'en remettre au verdict de l'opinion publique; **to j. others by oneself,** mesurer les autres à son aune; **to j. by appearances,** juger sur, par, d'après, les apparences; **to j. sth. by sth. else,** juger qch. sur qch.; **judging by . . .,** à en juger par . . .; (*c*) *v.i.* arbitrer (à un comice agricole, etc.); faire fonction de juge. **2.** apprécier, estimer (une distance, etc.); **to j. distance by the eye,** mesurer la distance à la vue. **3. to j. it necessary to do sth.,** juger nécessaire de faire qch.; **it was judged better to begin at once,** on décida qu'il valait mieux se mettre à l'œuvre immédiatement; **I j. it to be a small town,** je suis d'avis, j'estime, que c'est une petite ville; à mon avis c'est une petite ville; **it is for you to j.,** c'est à vous d'en juger; **as far as I can j.,** à ce qu'il me paraît; autant que j'en puis juger; **j. for yourself,** jugez(-en) par vous-même. **4.** *v.ind.tr.* **j. of my surprise!** jugez de ma surprise! jugez quelle fut ma surprise! jugez combien je fus surpris! *O:* **to j. well, ill, of s.o.,** penser du bien, du mal, de qn.

judge advocate ['dʒʌdʒ'ædvəkeit], *s.* (*pl.* **judge advocates**) *Mil: etc:* (i) assesseur *m* auprès d'un tribunal militaire; rapporteur *m*; (ii) *U.S:* = Commissaire *m* du Gouvernement; **j. a. substitute,** subrogateur *m*; **Judge Advocate General** (*pl.* **Judge Advocate Generals**), Président *m* du Tribunal militaire de cassation; **Deputy Judge Advocate General** = Commissaire rapporteur.

judg(e)ment ['dʒʌdʒmənt], *s.* jugement *m.* **1.** (*a*) **the Last J., J. day,** le jugement dernier; *Jur:* **j. on the merits,** jugement au fond; **j. in rem,** jugement en matière immobilière; **to enter into j. with s.o.,** entrer en jugement avec qn; *B:* **to sit in j.,** être assis dans le siège de la justice; **to sit in j. on s.o.,** juger qn; se poser en juge de qn; (*b*) décision *f* judiciaire; arrêt *m* (d'une cour de cassation, etc.); sentence *f* (d'une cour inférieure); **j.-at-law,** jugement passé en force de chose jugée; **j. by consent,** jugement d'accord; **enforceable j.,** jugement exécutoire; **j. provisionally enforceable,** jugement exécutoire par provision; **j. debt,** dette entérinée par la cour; **to pass, give, deliver, j.,** prononcer, rendre, un jugement; rendre un arrêt; statuer sur une affaire; **to pass j. on a prisoner,** juger un accusé; **to pass j. on a criminal,** condamner un criminel; **to pass j. on a work,** porter un jugement sur une œuvre; juger une œuvre; **it is not for me to pass j. on him,** ce n'est pas à moi de le juger; **to suspend j.,** suspendre son jugement; **to accept, acquiesce in, the j. pronounced on one,** subir sa condamnation; **it is a j. on you, on him,** (i) c'est une punition, un châtiment, de Dieu; c'est le doigt de Dieu! (ii) *F:* ça vous apprendra! ça lui apprendra! **2.** opinion *f*, avis *m*; **to form a j. on sth.,** former un jugement, une opinion, d'après qch.; **to give one's j. on sth.,** exprimer son avis, son sentiment, sur qch.; **in the j. of many people,** au jugement de bien des gens; de l'avis de bien des gens; **in my j.,** à mon avis; **to reverse one's j.,** changer d'avis; se déjuger; **against our better j.,** contrairement à notre opinion délibérée; à notre jugement délibéré. **3.** bon sens; discernement *m*; **to have a sound, clear, good, j.,** avoir le jugement sain, le sens droit; **to show (sound) j.,** montrer du jugement; **to use j. in sth.,** faire preuve de discernement; **by j.,** au sentiment, au jugé.

judgeship ['dʒʌdʒʃip], *s.* (*a*) fonctions *fpl* de juge; (*b*) *U.S:* fonctions de magistrat, magistrature *f*.

judging ['dʒʌdʒiŋ], *s.* **1.** (*a*) jugement *m*; (*b*) arbitrage *m.* **2.** appréciation *f* (des distances, etc.).

judicature ['dʒu:dikətjər], *s.* **1.** judicature *f*; **court of j.,** cour *f* de justice; **the J. Acts (of 1873–75),** les lois *f* organisant le système judiciaire anglais. **2.** période *f* d'exercice (d'un juge). **3.** *coll.* la magistrature.

judicial [dʒu'diʃ(ə)l], *a.* **1.** (*a*) judiciaire; juridique; **j. inquiry,** enquête *f* judiciaire; **j. proof,** preuves *fpl* en justice; **j. murder,** assassinat légal, juridique; (*b*) **to be invested with j. powers,** être investi de pouvoirs judiciaires; **to aim at high j. office,** viser à la haute judicature; **the J. Committee of the Privy Council,** la Section judiciaire du Conseil privé (fait fonction de Cour d'appel à l'égard des tribunaux coloniaux, des tribunaux ecclésiastiques, et de la Cour de l'Amirauté); *A:* **j. combat,** combat *m* judiciaire; combat en champ clos. **2.** (*a*) de bonne justice; **j. fairness,** impartialité *f*; (*b*) **j. faculty,** faculté *f* judiciaire; sens *m* critique; discernement *m.* **3.** *Theol:* **j. blindness, j. infatuation,** aveuglement *m* qui est une punition de Dieu.

judicially [dʒu'diʃəli], *adv.* **1.** judiciairement, juridiquement. **2.** impartialement. **3.** avec discernement.

judiciary [dʒu'diʃiəri]. **1.** *a.* judiciaire. **2.** *s.* la magistrature; **officials of the j.,** fonctionnaires *m* de l'ordre judiciaire.

judicious [dʒu'diʃəs], *a.* (*of pers., thought, etc.*) judicieux; d'un jugement sain, sensé; **j. purchases,** emplettes judicieuses; **a j. policy,** une politique sage.

judiciously [dʒu'diʃəsli], *adv.* judicieusement; avec sagesse.

judiciousness [dʒu'diʃəsnis], *s.* discernement *m*; bon sens.

judo ['dʒu:dou], *s.* judo *m.*

judoka [dʒu'doukə], *s. inv.* judoka *mf.*

Judy ['dʒu:di], *Pr.n.f.* **1.** *F:* Judith. **2.** (*a*) la femme de Guignol, de Polichinelle; (*b*) *s.f. F:* femme, fille.

jug[1] [dʒʌg], *s.* **1.** (*a*) cruche *f*, broc *m*; (*for milk, etc.*) pot *m*; **small j.,** cruchon *m*, pichet *m*, cruchette *f*; **pewter j.,** pichet d'étain; **j. and bottle department,** comptoir d'un café réservé aux boissons à emporter; (*b*) (*jug and contents*) **j. of milk, etc.,** pot de lait, etc.; **j. of wine,** pichet de vin. **2.** *F:* prison *f*, violon *m*, taule *f*; **to put s.o. in j.,** mettre qn dedans.

jug[2], *v.tr.* (**jugged**) **1.** *Cu:* étuver, braiser; **jugged hare** = civet *m* de lièvre. **2.** *F:* emprisonner, coffrer (qn); **to be jugged,** être mis en prison; être coffré.

jug[3], *s.* note *f* du chant du rossignol; **the j. j. of the nightingale,** le chant du rossignol.

jug[4], *v.i.* (**jugged**) (*of nightingale*) chanter.

jug[5], *v.i.* (**jugged**) (*of partridges*) se former en compagnie.

jugal ['dʒu:gəl], *a. Anat:* jugal, -aux; malaire, zygomatique.

jugate ['dʒu:geit], *a.* **1.** *Bot:* (*of leaves, etc.*) conjugué. **2.** *Num:* **j. heads,** têtes conjuguées, accolées.

jug-eared ['dʒʌg'iəd], *a. F:* aux oreilles protubérantes.

jugful ['dʒʌgful], *s.* cruchée *f*; potée *f*; pleine cruche, plein pot, plein broc (**of,** de); *U.S: F:* **not by a j.,** tant s'en faut.

Juggernaut ['dʒʌgənɔ:t], *s.* **1.** *Rel.H:* Djaggernat *m.* **2.** (*a*) poids écrasant; roues meurtrières; (*b*) *Veh:* mastodonte *m* (de la route).

juggins ['dʒʌginz], *s. F:* idiot, -ote; nouille *f*; cruche *f*.

juggle[1] ['dʒʌgl], *s.* **1.** (*a*) jonglerie *f*; **he did a j. with some balls,** il a jonglé avec des boules; (*b*) tour *m* de passe-passe, d'escamotage. **2.** *F:* supercherie *f*, fourberie *f*, imposture *f*; **financial j.,** tripotage financier.

juggle[2]. **1.** *v.i.* (*a*) jongler (avec des boules, etc.); (*b*) faire des tours de passe-passe; **to j. with facts, with figures,** jongler avec les faits, avec les chiffres; **to j. with s.o.'s feelings,** jouer avec les sentiments de qn; **to j. with s.o.,** berner, mystifier, qn; (*c*) **to j. with words,** jongler avec les mots. **2.** *v.tr.* **to j. sth. away,** escamoter qch.; *F:* **to j. sth. out of s.o.,** escamoter, escroquer, qch. à qn.

juggler ['dʒʌglər], *s.* **1.** (*a*) jongleur, -euse; bateleur *m*; (*b*) escamoteur, -euse; prestidigitateur *m.* **2.** *F:* homme *m* de mauvaise foi.

jugglery ['dʒʌgləri], **juggling** ['dʒʌgliŋ], *s.* **1.** (*a*) jonglerie *f*; (*b*) tours *mpl* de passe-passe; escamotage *m.* **2.** fourberie *f*; mauvaise foi; imposture *f*.

jug-handled ['dʒʌghændld], *a. U.S: F:* inéquitable; (contrat) unilatéral.

jughead ['dʒʌghed], *s. U.S: F:* **1.** (*a*) idiot, -ote; nouille *f*; (*b*) cabochard, -arde; personne entêtée, têtue. **2.** (*a*) mulet *m*; (*b*) (i) mauvais cheval, haridelle *f*; (ii) cabochard, cheval entêté.

Juglandaceae [dʒʌglæn'deisii:], *s.pl. Bot:* juglandacées *f.*

jugular ['dʒʌgjulər], *a. & s. Anat:* jugulaire (*f*).

jugulate ['dʒʌgjuleit], *v.tr.* (*a*) égorger (qn); (*b*) étrangler (qn).

jugulum ['dʒʌgjuləm], *s.* **1.** *Anat:* clavicule *f.* **2.** *Orn:* gorge *f*.

juice[1] [dʒu:s], *s.* **1.** jus *m*, suc *m*, pressis *m* (de la viande, d'un fruit); eau *f* (d'un fruit); **fruit j.,** jus de fruit(s); *Sug.-R:* **cane j.,** jus de canne. **2.** suc, sève *f*, essence *f* (d'une science, d'un récit). **3.** (*a*) *Aut:* essence *f*, jus; **to step on the j.,** mettre les gaz; (*b*) *El:* courant *m*, jus; (*c*) *P:* whisky *m*; gnôle *f*.

juice[2], *v.tr. esp. U.S:* (*a*) extraire le jus (des fruits); (*b*) ajouter du jus à (un plat); (*c*) *P:* **juiced (up),** ivre, soûl.

juiceless ['dʒu:slis], *a.* **1.** sans jus, sans suc. **2.** (*of narrative, etc.*) sec, *f.* sèche; aride, sans intérêt.

juicer ['dʒu:sər], *s. U.S:* presse-fruits *m inv.*

juiciness ['dʒu:sinis], *s.* nature juteuse, succulence *f* (d'un fruit, etc.).

juicy ['dʒu:si], *a.* **1.** (*a*) succulent, juteux; plein de jus; fondant; (rôti) qui jute; (*b*) *F:* **j. pipe,** pipe *f* qui supe; (*of pipe*) **to get j.,** super. **2.** (*a*) *U.S:* (temps) pluvieux, humide; (*b*) (récit, style) plein de suc, savoureux; (*c*) *Art:* (tableau) d'un coloris chaud et transparent, d'une transparence juteuse; (*d*) *F:* qui fait scandale; **a nice j. scandal,** un scandale tout frais, tout juteux.

juju ['dʒu:dʒu:], *s.* **1.** fétiche *m*; grigri *m.* **2.** tabou *m.*

jujube ['dʒu:dʒu:b], *s.* **1.** *Bot:* (*a*) jujube *f*, gingeole *f*; (*b*) **j. (tree),** jujubier *m*, gingeolier *m.* **2.** (*a*) *Pharm:* (pâte *f* de) jujube; (*b*) boule *f* de gomme.

juke (box) ['dʒu:k(bɔks)], *s.* (*a*) juke-box *m*; (*b*) *Cmptr:* **j. storage,** mémoire *f* à disques.

julep ['dʒu:lep], *s.* **1.** *Pharm:* julep *m.* **2. (mint) j.,** whisky frappé à la menthe.

Julia ['dʒu:liə], *Pr.n.f.* Julie, Julia.

Julian[1] ['dʒu:ljən], *Pr.n.m. Ecc.Hist:* Julien.

Julian[2], *a.* Julien, de Jules César; *Chr:* **J. year,** année julienne; *Geog:* **J. Alps,** Alpes Juliennes.

Juliana [dʒu:li'ɑ:nə], *Pr.n.f.* Julienne.

julienite ['dʒu:liənait], *s. Miner:* juliénite *f*.

julienne [ʒu:li'en], *s. Cu:* **j. soup,** (potage *m* à la) julienne.

Juliet ['dʒu:liet], *Pr.n.f.* Juliette.

Julius ['dʒu:liəs], *Pr.n.m.* Jules; **J. Caesar,** Jules César.

July, *pl.* **-ys** [dʒu'lai, -aiz], *s.* juillet *m*; **in (the month of) J.,** en juillet, au mois de juillet; **(on) the first, the seventh, of J., on J. (the) first, (the) seventh,** le premier, le sept, juillet.

jumbal ['dʒʌmbl], *s.* = JUMBLE[3].

jumble[1] ['dʒʌmbl], *s.* **1.** brouillamini *m*, pêle-mêle *m*, méli-mélo *m*, fouillis *m*, fatras *m*, culbutis *m* (d'objets hétéroclites); entremêlement *m*, embrouillement *m* (d'idées); enchevêtrement *m* (de mots). **2.** *A:* cahot *m* (d'une voiture); ballottement *m* (de la mer). **3.** objets usagés, de rebut; **j. sale,** vente *f* d'objets usagés, etc. (pour une œuvre de charité).

jumble[2]. **1.** *v.tr.* brouiller, mêler confusément, mettre pêle-mêle; **jumbled story,** histoire *f* sans queue ni tête; **to j. up one's papers,** mêler, embrouiller, ses papiers; **to j. everything up, together,** tout mettre en salade. **2.** *v.i.* (*a*) se mêler confusément, se brouiller, se mettre pêle-mêle; (b) A: **to j. along,** avancer en cahotant.

jumble[3], s. Cu: gimb(e)lette f.

jumbo ['dʒʌmbou], s. **1.** (a) (i) éléphant m célèbre de la ménagerie de Barnum; (ii) F: éléphant; (b) (nickname for fat pers.) F: gros lourdaud; = Patapouf. **2.** Metall: manchon m de refroidissement (de tuyère). **3.** Min: jumbo m. **4.** a. F: énorme; colossal, -aux; a. & s. R.t.m. **J. (jet),** (avion) gros porteur.

jumboism ['dʒʌmbouizm], s. U.S: F: culte m du colossal.

jumboization [dʒʌmbouai'zeiʃ(ə)n], s. N.Arch: allongement m (d'un navire); F: jumboïsation f.

jumboize ['dʒʌmbouaiz], v.tr. N.Arch: allonger (un navire).

jumby ['dʒʌmbi], s. (a) (in W. Indies) spectre m, fantôme m; (b) **j. bird,** oiseau m de mauvais augure.

Jumna (the) [ðə'dʒʌmnə], Pr.n. Geog: la Jumna, la Yamuna.

jump[1] [dʒʌmp], s. **1.** (a) saut m, bond m; **to clear sth. at one j.,** franchir qch. de plein saut; **to take a j.,** faire un saut; sauter; Sp: **high j.,** saut en hauteur; **long j.,** saut en longueur (avec élan); **flying j., running j.,** saut avec élan, saut précédé d'une course; P: **go (and) take a running j. (at yourself)!** va te faire voir! va te faire foutre! **triple j.,** triple saut; **standing j.,** saut sans élan, de pied ferme, à pieds joints; **j. from a height,** saut en profondeur; Bill: **j. shot,** coup m qui fait sauter la bille; **j. in prices,** brusque hausse f des prix; **rents have gone up with a j.,** les loyers ont fait un bond; (b) lacune f, vide m (dans une série, etc.). **2.** sursaut m, haut-le-corps m inv; Equit: (of horse) contre-coup m, pl. contre-coups; **that gave me a j.,** cela m'a fait sursauter; F: **to keep s.o. on the j.,** ne pas laisser le temps de souffler à qn; F: **he's always on the j.,** il n'est jamais tranquille; F: **to have the jumps,** (i) avoir les nerfs en pelote; (ii) avoir la bougeotte, être sur une pile électrique; (iii) O: avoir la danse de Saint-Guy; (iv) A: avoir le delirium tremens; F: **he's for the high j.!** (i) O: il va être pendu; (ii) qu'est-ce qu'il va prendre! son affaire est bonne! F: **to get the j. on s.o., to be a j. ahead of s.o.,** devancer qn; prendre l'avantage sur qn. **3.** (a) Ball: angle m d'écart initial; (b) Artil: relèvement; **angle of j.,** angle de relèvement. **4.** Tchn: anomalie f, discontinuité f, saut (dans un phénomène, un processus, etc.); Hyd.E: ressaut m; Atom.Ph: **negative, positive, j.,** saut négatif, positif; El: **j. spark,** étincelle disruptive, sautante; Mec.E: etc: **j. coupling,** assemblage m à manchon taraudé; **j. weld(ing),** soudure f, soudage m, bout par bout, par rapprochement; **j.-welded,** soudé par, à, rapprochement; soudé bout à bout. **5.** Cmptr: branchement m, renvoi m (sur une séquence, un sous-programme, etc.); **j. instruction,** instruction f de branchement. **6.** Turf: Equit: obstacle m; **to put a horse at, over, a j.,** diriger un cheval vers un obstacle; faire sauter un obstacle à son cheval; **racecourse with jumps,** piste f à obstacles.

jump[2], v.

I. v.i. **1.** (a) sauter; bondir; Av: sauter (en parachute); (to dog) **j.!** allons, hop! houp là! **the children were jumping about,** les enfants sautaient, sautillaient; **to j. for joy,** sauter de joie; **to j. at a bargain,** saisir une occasion; **to j. at an offer,** sauter sur une offre; **to j. at the opportunity, chance,** sauter sur l'occasion; F: **j. to it!** allez-y! plus vite que ça! grouillez-vous! **to j. from one subject to another,** sauter d'un sujet à un autre; **to j. to a conclusion,** arriver (i) immédiatement, (ii) prématurément, à une conclusion; juger trop vite; conclure à la légère; **prices have jumped 10%,** les prix ont monté de 10% d'un coup; **the car hit a tree but the driver jumped clear,** la voiture a heurté un arbre mais le conducteur s'est sauvé en sautant; **to make a table j.,** donner une brusque secousse à une table; **it made the cups j.,** cela a fait sauter les tasses; (b) **he jumped across, over, the flower bed,** d'un saut il a franchi la plate bande; **to j. over a hedge,** franchir, sauter par-dessus, une haie; **to j. off, down from, a wall,** sauter à bas d'un mur; **to j. down (on to the ground),** sauter à terre; **to j. down a flight of stairs,** sauter du haut en bas d'un escalier; F: **to j. down s.o.'s throat,** rembarrer, rabrouer, qn; **to j. in to save s.o. from drowning,** se jeter, plonger, dans l'eau pour sauver qn; Aut: Rail: **j. in!** montez vite! **to j. out of bed,** sauter à bas du lit; **he jumped out on to the platform,** il a sauté sur le quai; **to j. out on s.o.,** bondir sur qn; F: **I nearly jumped out of my skin,** cela m'a fait sursauter; **his eyes were jumping out of his head,** ses yeux lui sortaient de la tête; **the dogs were jumping up at me,** les chiens sautaient après moi; (c) El: (of spark) jaillir. **2.** (a) sursauter, soubresauter, tressauter; **you needn't j.!** ne tiquez pas! **the price made me j.,** le prix m'a fait sauter; **my heart jumped when I heard the news,** (i) mon cœur a bondi, (ii) j'ai eu un serrement de cœur, lorsque j'ai appris la nouvelle; (b) Mec.E: etc: (of tool) brouter; (c) El: **the brushes are jumping,** les balais m soubresautent; (d) (of gun) se cabrer; (of gun carriage) ruer.

II. v.tr. **1.** (a) franchir, sauter (une haie, etc.); **to j. a passage (in a book),** sauter un passage (d'un livre); (of train) **to j. the metals, the rails,** dérailler; sortir des rails, quitter les rails; Rec: **to j. the sound groove,** dérailler; **the chain has jumped the sprockets,** la chaîne a sauté les pignons; esp. U.S: **to j. a town,** quitter une ville au plus vite; Biol: **characteristics that j. several generations,** caractéristiques f qui sautent plusieurs générations; **to j. the queue,** passer avant son tour, F: resquiller; Aut: F: **to j. the lights,** brûler, griller, le feu (rouge); F: **to j. the gun,** (i) Sp: voler le départ; partir en balance; (ii) commencer à faire quelque chose prématurément, avant son tour; prendre les devants; (b) (at draughts) **to j. a man,** sauter un pion. **2.** (to cause to jump) (a) **to j. a horse,** faire sauter un cheval; Ven: **to j. (a deer),** débûcher, débusquer (un cerf); (b) Bill: **to j. a ball off the table,** faire sauter une bille; (c) **to j. a child (up and down) on one's knees,** faire sauter un enfant sur ses genoux; (d) F: O: **I won't be jumped into doing it,** je ne le ferai pas avant d'avoir le temps de réfléchir; il ne faut pas me bousculer; **he jumped a question on me,** il m'a posé une question à brûle-pourpoint, sans me donner le temps de réfléchir. **3.** (a) saisir (qch.) à l'improviste; voler (qch.); **to j. a stronghold,** saisir une place forte par un coup de main; **to j. a claim,** (i) Min: s'emparer d'une concession (en l'absence de celui qui l'a délimitée); (ii) usurper les droits de qn; F: O: **to j. s.o.,** (i) refaire, voler, attraper, qn; (ii) circonvenir qn; prendre qn de vitesse; couper l'herbe sous le pied à qn; (b) NAm: **to j. a train,** (i) monter dans un train en marche; (ii) descendre d'un train en marche. **4.** Metalw: (a) refouler (une barre de métal, etc.); aplatir, écraser, refouler (un rivet, etc.); (b) = JUMP-WELD. **5.** Min: forer (la pierre, etc.) au fleuret.

III. (compound verbs) **1. jump back,** v.i. sauter en arrière; reculer brusquement; (of spring, etc.) reprendre sa position initiale.

2. jump off, v.i. Sp: esp. Equit: faire un barrage.

3. jump up, v.i. se (re)lever d'un saut; **j. up!** allons! debout!

jump[3], s., **Jumps,** s.pl. A.Cost: camisole f.

jumped-up ['dʒʌmpt'ʌp], a. F: (bourgeois, etc.) parvenu.

jumper[1] ['dʒʌmpər], s. **1.** (a) (pers.) (i) sauteur, -euse; Sp: **high j.,** sauteur, -euse, en hauteur; **long j.,** sauteur, -euse, en longueur; (ii) Rail: F: O: contrôleur m de billets (sur un train en marche); (b) U.S: Com: F: livreur m; (c) Equit: jumper m; cheval m à obstacles; hunter m. **2.** Ent: F: sauteur. **3.** El: Tp: Tg: cavalier m, bretelle f, liaison volante; **j. lead,** connexion volante; **j. wire,** fil volant. **4.** Min: **j. (bar),** barre f de mine ou de carrière; fleuret m. **5.** Metalw: refouloir m. **6.** Nau: (preventer rope) attrape f de mauvais temps.

jumper[2], s. Cost: **1.** vareuse f, chemise f (de marin, etc.). **2.** tricot m (de femme), pull-over m, F: pull m. **3.** NAm: (a) robe f à bretelles, Fr.C: jumper m; (b) barboteuse f (pour enfants).

jumpiness ['dʒʌmpinis], s. F: **1.** nervosité f, agitation f. **2.** instabilité f (du marché, etc.).

jumping[1] ['dʒʌmpiŋ], a. (a) sauteur, -euse; (b) Toys: **j. jack,** pantin m; F: **political j. jack,** pantin, fantoche m, politique; (c) Bot: F: **j. betty,** balsamine f (des jardins).

jumping[2], s. **1.** (a) saut(s) m (pl); bond(s) m (pl); Av: **j. hole,** trappe f d'évacuation; **j. off place,** point m de départ, base avancée (d'une expédition, etc.); (b) El: jaillissement m (d'une étincelle), (c) Mec.E: broutage m, broutement m (d'un outil). **2.** (a) franchissement m (d'une haie); Equit: monte f à l'obstacle; jumping m; Turf: **j. race,** course f d'obstacles; Sp: **hurdle j.,** saut m de barrière, de haie; Rail: **j. of the metals,** déraillement m; (b) cahotage m (d'un appareil, etc.). **3.** appropriation f (d'une concession, etc.). **4.** Metalw: (a) refoulement m; **j. hammer,** refouloir m; (b) soudure f, soudage m, bout à bout, par refoulement. **5.** Min: forage m au fleuret.

jump-off ['dʒʌmpɔf], s. Sp: (a) départ m (d'une course); (b) Equit: barrage m.

jump-weld ['dʒʌmpweld], v.tr. souder par encollage, par rapprochement; souder bout à bout.

jumpy ['dʒʌmpi], a. F: **1.** (of pers.) agité, nerveux; **to be j.,** avoir les nerfs agacés, à vif; **to feel j. about sth.,** avoir le trac, la frousse, à propos de qch. **2.** (a) (of market, etc.) instable; (b) (of style) sautillant, saccadé.

Juncaceae [dʒʌŋ'keisii:], s.pl. Bot: joncacées f.

junco ['dʒʌŋkou], s. Orn: **slate-coloured j.,** bruant ardoisé, pinson m niverolle; Fr.C: junco ardoisé; **Oregon j.,** junco de l'Oregon, Fr.C: junco à dos roux.

junction ['dʒʌŋ(k)ʃ(ə)n], s. **1.** jonction f, confluence f (de deux rivières, etc.); raccordement m, abouchement m (de tuyaux); El: connexion f, prise f, raccordement; Anat: Bot: Arch: etc: **line of j.,** commissure f; (of two armies) **to effect a j.,** opérer une jonction; se donner la main. **2.** (a) (point m de) jonction; carrefour m (em)branchement m, bifurcation f (de route, de voie de chemin de fer); nœud m (de voies ferrées, etc.); (b) Rail: gare f, station f, de bifurcation, d'embranchement, de jonction; **facing j.,** bifurcation en pointe; **trailing j.,** bifurcation par le talon; **j. within station limits,** bifurcation, embranchement, en gare; **j. outside station limits, j. between stations,** bifurcation, embranchement, en pleine voie, en dehors des gares; **j. line,** voie f d'embranchement, de raccordement; branchement m; (c) Metalw: etc: joint m, soudure f, raccord m; **cold j.,** soudure froide; **butt j.,** abouchement m (de deux tuyaux); Civ.E: **j. plate,** bande f (de jonction); (d) El: **j. box,** boîte f de dérivation, de jonction, de raccordement, de branchement; boîte à barres; manchon m de jonction.

juncture ['dʒʌŋ(k)tjər], s. **1.** jointure f (de deux plaques, etc.). **2.** conjoncture f (de circonstances); **at this j.,** (i) à ce moment (critique); sur ces entrefaites; en l'occurrence; (ii) dans les circonstances actuelles.

June [dʒu:n], s. **1.** juin m; **in (the month of) J.,** en juin, au mois de juin; **(on) the first, the seventh, of J., (on) J. (the) first, (the) seventh,** le premier, le sept, juin. **2.** (a) Bot: **J. berry,** amélanchier m à grappes; **J. grass,** pâturin m des prés; (b) Ent: **J. beetle, bug,** hanneton m.

jungle ['dʒʌŋgl], s. **1.** (a) jungle f, fourré m, brousse f; **tangled j. of facts,** embrouillamini confus de faits; **the j. growth of legal procedure,** le maquis de la procédure; Sch: F: **blackboard j.,** pétaudière f scolaire contestataire et anticonformiste; (b) Z: **j. bear,** ours jongleur, lippu; **j. cat,** lynx m des marais; Orn: **j. fowl,** coq m sauvage; Austr: mégapode m; **green j. fowl,** coq de Java; **red j. fowl,** coq bankiva. **2.** pl. St.Exch: F: **jungles,** valeurs ouest-africaines.

jungli ['dʒʌŋgli]. **1.** s. indigène m des jungles. **2.** a. qui habite la jungle.

junior ['dʒu:njər], a. & s. **1.** (in age) cadet, -ette; plus jeune; Sp: junior m, esp. U.S: F: le benjamin; **he is three years my j., three years j. to me, my j. by three years,** il est mon cadet de trois ans; il est plus jeune que moi de trois ans; **Martin J.,** Martin (i) le jeune, (ii) fils; U.S: **come on J.!** viens, mon fils! Sch: **the juniors, the J. school,** les petits; Sp: **j. event,** épreuve f des cadets; U.S: **j. students,** les étudiants de troisième année (du cours de quatre années). **2.** (in rank) moins ancien; subalterne (m); **j. partner,** associé en second, second associé, dernier associé; **j. officer,** officier m subalterne; A: **the J. Service,** l'armée f; Jur: **j. counsel,** avocat m en second; Fin: **j. stocks,** actions f de dividende; Cards: **j. (hand),** joueur m à droite du déclarant. **3.** (of civilization, etc.) postérieur. **4.** Tan: **j. (split),** croûte f (d'une peau fendue).

juniority [dʒu:ni'ɔriti], s. **1.** infériorité f d'âge. **2.** position moins élevée (d'un fonctionnaire, etc.). **3.** postériorité f (d'une civilisation, etc.).

juniper ['dʒu:nipər], s. Bot: **j. (tree),** genévrier m, genièvre m; **dwarf j.,** genévrier nain, des Alpes; **Virginian j.,** genévrier de Virginie; **Spanish j.,** cade m; **j. berry,** baie f de genièvre; Pharm: **j. oil,** essence f de genièvre; **j.-tar oil,** huile de cade.

junk[1] [dʒʌŋk], s. **1.** (a) vieux cordages mpl; vieux filin; étoupe f, chènevotte f, fourrure f; (b) (choses fpl de) rebut m; déchet m; camelote f; Com: rossignols mpl; **piece of j.,** rossignol; **j. heap,** dépotoir m; tas m de ferraille; **j. dealer,** marchand m de ferraille, de chiffons; brocanteur m; (c) F: **that's all j.,** tout ça c'est des bêtises; (d) U.S: P: narcotiques mpl, stupéfiants mpl, came f. **2.** Nau: bœuf salé. **3.** blanc m de baleine. **4.** Mch: **j. ring,** (i) couronne f, couvercle m, de piston; (ii) garniture f de piston; cercle m d'étoupe.

junk[2], v.tr. **1.** O: couper (qch.) en gros morceaux. **2.** F: mettre (qch.) au rebut.

junk[3], s. Nau: jonque f.

junk[4], s. Surg: éclisse faite de joncs.

junket[1] ['dʒʌŋkit], s. **1.** Cu: (a) A: (cream cheese) jonchée f; (b) lait caillé (souvent parfumé). **2.** F: (a) festin m, banquet m; (b) esp. U.S: partie f de plaisir; (c) esp. U.S: voyage officiel aux frais de la princesse.

junket[2], v.i. F: **1.** banqueter, festoyer. **2.** esp. U.S: faire une partie de plaisir. **3.** esp. U.S: voyager aux frais de la princesse.

junkie ['dʒʌŋki], s. P: (a) toxicomane mf, drogué, -ée; camé, -ée; (b) revendeur, -euse, de came.

junkman, pl. **-men** ['dʒʌŋkmən], s. marchand m de ferraille, de chiffons; brocanteur m.

junkroom ['dʒʌŋkru:m], s. (pièce f de) débarras m.

junkshop [ˈdʒʌŋkʃɔp], *s.* boutique *f* de marchand de ferraille, de brocanteur; *F:* **I got it in a j.,** je l ai acheté chez un brocanteur.

junky [ˈdʒʌŋki], *s.* = JUNKIE.

junkyard [ˈdʒʌŋkjɑːd], *s.* entrepôt *m* de marchand de ferraille.

Juno [ˈdʒuːnou]. **1.** *Pr.n.f. Rom.Myth: Astr:* Junon. **2.** *s.* (*of a woman*) une Junon.

Junonian [dʒuˈnouniən], *a.* junonien.

junta [ˈdʒʌntə], *s.* **1.** *Hist: Pol:* (*in Spain, Italy, etc.*) junte *f.* **2.** = JUNTO.

junto, *pl.* **-os** [ˈdʒʌntou, -ouz], *s.* cabale *f*, ligue *f*, faction *f.*

Jupiter [ˈdʒuːpitər]. **1.** *Pr.n.m. Rom.Myth: Astr:* Jupiter. **2.** *s. Bot:* **Jupiter's beard,** (i) anthyllide *f* barbe-de-Jupiter; (ii) joubarbe *f* des toits; artichaut *m* sauvage; (iii) valériane *f* rouge, barbe-de-Jupiter *f*, *pl.* barbes-de-Jupiter.

Jura [ˈdʒuːrə], *Pr.n. Geog:* **the J. Mountains, the Juras,** le Jura.

jural [ˈdʒuːrəl], *a.* **1.** juridique; qui a rapport au droit. **2.** qui a rapport aux obligations morales.

Jurassic [dʒəˈræsik], *Geol:* **1.** *a.* jurassique. **2.** *s.* **Upper J.,** Jura blanc; **Middle J.,** Jura brun.

jurat[1] [ˈdʒuːræt], *s. Hist:* **1.** jurat *m* (des villes du Midi). **2.** officier municipal (des Cinq Ports, etc.).

jurat[2], *s. Jur:* formule *f* à la fin d'une déclaration sous serment indiquant les noms des parties et de l'officier qui l'a dressée, et la date et le lieu de sa rédaction.

juratory [ˈdʒuːrət(ə)ri], *a.* (déclaration *f*, etc.) sous serment; (obligation *f*) juratoire.

juridical [dʒəˈridik(ə)l], *a.* **1.** juridique, judiciaire. **2. j. person,** personne morale.

juridically [dʒəˈridik(ə)li], *adv.* juridiquement.

jurisconsult [dʒuːrisˈkɔnsʌlt], *s.* jurisconsulte *m*, juriste *m.*

jurisdiction [dʒuːrisˈdikʃ(ə)n], *s.* juridiction *f*; (*a*) **to have j. over s.o.,** avoir la juridiction sur qn; **area within, under, the j. of . . .,** territoire soumis à l'autorité judiciaire, à la juridiction, de . . ., territoire relevant de . . .; **he comes under my j.,** c'est un de mes justiciables; (*b*) compétence *f*; **general j. of a court,** compétence générale d'une cour; (*of a question*) **to come within the j. of a court,** rentrer dans la juridiction, dans la compétence, d'une cour; être du ressort d'une cour; compéter, ressortir, à une cour; tomber sous la juridiction d'une cour; **this matter does not come within our j.,** cette matière n'est pas de notre compétence.

jurisdictional [dʒuːrisˈdikʃən(ə)l], *a.* juridictionnel.

jurisprudence [dʒuːrisˈpruːd(ə)ns], *s.* jurisprudence *f*; **medical j.,** médecine légale.

jurisprudential [dʒuːrispruˈdenʃ(ə)l], *a.* jurisprudentiel.

jurist [ˈdʒuːrist], *s.* **1.** (*a*) juriste *m*, jurisconsulte *m*, légiste *m*; (*b*) *U.S:* homme *m* de loi; avocat *m*, etc. **2.** étudiant, -ante, en droit.

juror [ˈdʒuːrər], *s.* **1.** (*a*) *Jur:* juré *m*; membre *m* du jury; **petty j.,** membre du petit jury, du jury de jugement; *A:* **grand j.,** membre du jury d'accusation; (*b*) membre du jury (d'une exposition, d'un comice, etc.). **2.** *Hist:* prêtre assermenté (après la Révolution de 1688).

jury[1] [ˈdʒuːri], *s.* **1.** *Jur:* jury *m*; jurés *mpl*; **petty j., trial j., common j.,** jury de jugement; petit jury; *Hist: & U.S:* **grand j.,** jury d'accusation, = chambre *f* des mises en accusation; **to be, serve, on the j.,** être du jury; **foreman of the j.,** chef *m* du jury; **gentlemen of the j.!** messieurs les jurés! **j. process,** convocation *f* des jurés. **2.** jury (d'un concours, d'une exposition, etc.).

jury[2], *a. Nau:* de fortune, improvisé; **j. mast, rudder,** mât *m*, gouvernail *m*, de fortune; **j. rig(ging),** gréement *m* de fortune; **to rig up a j. mast and sail,** improviser un mât et une voile; **j. strut,** chandelle *f*; montant *m* auxiliaire de renforcement.

juryman, *pl.* **-men, -woman,** *pl.* **-women** [ˈdʒuːrimən, -wumən, -wimin], *s.* = JUROR 1; *s.* juré *m*; membre *m* du jury.

jussive [ˈdʒʌsiv], *a. & s. Gram:* impératif (*m*).

just [dʒʌst], *a. s. & adv.*

I. *a. & s.* **1.** *a.* (*a*) (homme *m*, jugement *m*, etc.) juste, équitable; impartial, -aux; **he was a j. man,** c'était un juste; **to be j. to s.o.,** être juste envers, pour, qn; *Jur:* **a j. and lawful decision, sentence, verdict,** un bien-jugé; **j. reward of his actions,** juste récompense *f*, récompense bien méritée, de ses actions; **it is only j.,** ce n'est que justice; **as was only j.,** comme de juste; **j. wrath,** colère *f* juste, légitime; **to speak in a j. cause,** plaider en faveur d'une juste cause; **to show j. cause for . . .,** donner une raison valable de . . .; (*b*) **a j. remark,** une observation juste, judicieuse, à propos; **he gives us a j. picture of . . .,** il nous donne un tableau exact de . . .. **2.** *s.pl.* **the j.,** les justes *m*; **to sleep the sleep of the j.,** dormir du sommeil du juste.

II. *adv.* **1.** (*a*) juste, justement, précisément; **j. at that spot, at that time,** juste à cet endroit, à ce moment; **j. here,** juste ici; **j. by the gate,** tout près de la porte; **it is j. a week ago that . . .,** il y a juste, précisément, une semaine que . . .; **it is j. twelve o'clock,** il est midi juste; **it was j. five years ago on this very day,** voilà de cela cinq ans aujourd'hui même; **j. then,** juste alors; **not ready j. yet,** pas encore tout à fait prêt; **j. five pounds,** cinq livres (tout) juste; **j. how many are there?** combien y en a-t-il au juste? **j. how many are they?** combien sont-ils au juste? **she's j. ten,** elle a juste, exactement, dix ans; *F:* **she's j. on ten,** elle aura bientôt dix ans; **he's j. the man you want,** c'est précisément l'homme qu'il vous faut; c'est votre homme; **that's j. what you want,** c'est justement ce que vous désirez; cela fera tout juste votre affaire; **that's j. what happened,** voilà justement, c'est bel et bien, ce qui est arrivé; **that's j. what I was about to say,** c'est précisément, c'est juste, ce que j'allais dire; **I thought you were French—that's j. what I am,** je pensais que vous étiez Français—je le suis précisément; c'est bien vrai; **that's j. it,** (i) c'est bien cela; (ii) justement! **j. so!** c'est bien cela! parfaitement! précisément! justement! *F:* (*of pers.*) **very j. so,** très correct; **it's j. the same,** c'est tout un; *F:* c'est tout comme; **he did it j. for a joke,** il l'a fait simplement histoire de rire; **j. when the door was opening,** au moment même où la porte s'ouvrait; **I cannot say j. when he arrived,** je ne peux vous dire précisément quand il est arrivé; (*b*) **j. as;** (i) **I can do it j. as well as he (can),** je peux le faire tout aussi bien que lui; **he's j. as clever as you,** il est tout aussi intelligent que vous; **it would be j. as well if he came,** il y aurait avantage à ce qu'il vienne; **that's j. as good,** c'est tout comme; **j. as often as you wish,** tout aussi souvent que vous voudrez; **I would j. as soon have this one,** j'aimerais tout autant celui-ci; **he told me not to pay him back, which was j. as well because I hadn't any money,** il m'a dit de ne pas lui rendre l'argent, ce qui était pour le mieux puisque je n'en avais pas; **j. as you please!** comme vous voudrez! à votre aise! **I will take it j. as it is,** je le prends tel qu'il est, tel quel; **leave my things j. as they are,** laissez mes affaires telles quelles; **she came j. as she was,** elle est venue telle qu'elle était; **do it j. as I showed you,** faites-le absolument comme je vous l'ai indiqué; **j. as . . . so . . .,** de même que . . . de même . . ., comme . . . ainsi . . .; (ii) **j. as he was starting out,** au moment (même) de partir; au moment où il partait; (*c*) **j. now;** (i) **business is bad j. now,** actuellement, à l'heure actuelle, les affaires vont mal; (ii) **I can't do it j. now,** je ne peux pas le faire en ce moment, pour le moment; (iii) **he came in j. now,** il est rentré tout à l'heure, il y a peu de temps; il rentre à l'instant; il vient de rentrer; (iv) *Dial:* dans un instant; (*d*) (*intensive*) **they were j. starving,** ils mouraient littéralement de faim; **it was j. splendid,** c'était ni plus ni moins que merveilleux; **that's j. everything,** (i) tout est là; (ii) cela fait toute la différence du monde; *P:* **won't you catch it j.! won't you j. catch it!** tu (ne) vas rien écoper! **didn't they beat us j.!** quelle raclée! *F:* **you remember?—don't I j.!** vous vous en souvenez?—si je m'en souviens! **didn't we j. enjoy ourselves!** on a bien rigolé; **did you enjoy yourselves?—I should j. say we did!** vous vous êtes amusés?—pour sûr! **j. you wait!** tu n'as qu'à attendre! **2.** (*a*) **j. before I came,** immédiatement avant mon arrivée; **j. after,** immédiatement après; (*b*) **he has j. written to you,** il vient de vous écrire; **I had (only) j. sat down when . . .,** je venais à peine de m'asseoir lorsque . . .; **he has (only) j. come,** il arrive à l'instant; il ne fait que d'arriver; **I have only j. heard of it,** je l'apprends à l'instant même; je viens seulement de l'apprendre; **I have j. finished my meal,** je sors de table; **he has j. left,** il sort d'ici; **he has j. left school,** il sort du collège; **he has j. come out of prison,** il sort de prison; **j. cooked,** fraîchement, nouvellement, cuit; (*of book*) **j. out,** vient de paraître. **3. to be j. doing sth.,** être justement en train de faire qch.; **hair j. turning grey,** cheveux qui commencent à grisonner; **he was j. beginning,** il ne faisait que de commencer; **I was j. finishing my dinner,** j'achevais de dîner; **I'm j. coming!** j'arrive! je viens à l'instant! **he is j. going out,** il est sur le point de sortir. **4. he j. managed to do it,** c'est tout juste s'il est arrivé à le faire; c'est à peine s'il a pu le faire; **I j. missed being appointed,** il s'en est fallu de peu, d'un rien, que je ne sois nommé; **I was only j. saved from drowning,** j'ai failli me noyer; j'allais me noyer quand on m'a repêché; **they j. missed the train,** ils ont manqué de peu le train; **I've only j. enough to live on,** j'ai tout juste de quoi vivre; **you're j. in time to . . .,** vous arrivez juste à temps pour . . .. **5.** (*a*) seulement; **j. once,** seulement une fois; rien qu'une fois; **j. one,** un seul, rien qu'un; **I had had a glass of beer, j. one,** j'avais consommé un demi, rien qu'un; **j. a little bit,** un tout petit peu; **he is j. an ordinary man,** c'est tout simplement un homme ordinaire; **j. you and you alone,** vous seul et rien que vous; **I'll j. see whether . . .,** j'irai voir si . . .; **I'll j. make sure that . . .,** un instant, je vais vérifier que . . .; *F:* **I'll j. pop in,** je ne ferai qu'entrer et sortir; **I'd j. punch his head,** je lui flanquerais une taloche et voilà tout; **j. give her a pair of gloves,** donnez-lui tout simplement une paire de gants; **I j. told him that . . .,** je lui ai dit tout bonnement que . . .; **if there is too much, we must j. leave some,** s'il y en a trop, on en sera pour en laisser; **he had gone out j. to get a breath of air,** il était sorti pour respirer un peu; **I have come j. to see you,** je viens uniquement pour vous voir; **they will travel fifty miles j. to go to a dance,** ils font cinquante milles rien que pour aller à un bal; **he told me the secret, only j. to me,** il m'a confié le secret, rien qu'à moi; (*b*) **j. sit down, please,** veuillez donc vous asseoir; **j. tell Mary to bring in the tea!** dites donc à Marie de servir le thé; **j. listen!** écoutez donc! écoutez un peu! **j. look!** regardez-moi ça! **j. read that!** lisez donc ça! **j. taste that!** goûtez cela, vous m'en direz des nouvelles! *F:* **j. (you) shut up!** vous, taisez-vous!

justaucorps [ˈdʒʌstoukɔər], *s. A.Cost:* justaucorps *m.*

justice [ˈdʒʌstis], *s.* **1.** justice *f*; (*a*) **to dispute the j. of a claim, of a sentence,** contester le bien-fondé, la justice, d'une réclamation, d'un jugement; **he complained with j. of his treatment,** il s'est plaint à juste titre de la manière dont il a été traité; **methods of j. and peace,** méthodes *f* équitables et pacifiques; (*b*) **in j. to him it must be admitted that . . .,** pour lui rendre justice il faut avouer que . . .; **I am bound in j. to . . .,** je suis obligé, pour être juste, de . . .; **in all j. we must allow him to . . .,** en toute justice il faut lui permettre de . . .; **poetic j.,** justice idéale; **to dispense j.,** rendre la justice; **to do j. to s.o., to do s.o. j.,** rendre, faire, justice à qn; **to do j. to one's talent,** faire valoir son talent; **to do oneself j.,** se faire valoir; **he does not do himself j.,** il reste au-dessous de lui-même; **to do j. to a meal,** faire honneur à un repas; (*c*) **to bring s.o. to j.,** traduire qn en justice; conduire qn devant la justice; **the murderer was quickly brought to j.,** on fit prompte justice du meurtrier; *Hist:* **bed of j.,** lit *m* de justice. **2.** magistrat *m*; (*a*) juge *m* (d'un tribunal d'ordre supérieur); **Mr Justice Long,** M. le juge Long; **the Lord Chief J.** (*pl.* **Lord Chief Justices**)**, the Chief J. of England,** le président du Tribunal du Banc du Roi; **the Lords Justices,** les juges de la cour de cassation; (*b*) *U.S:* **Chief J.,** président d'une cour suprême; (*c*) *Scot:* **J. Clerk,** assesseur *m* du président du tribunal; (*d*) **the Justices,** les juges (du tribunal d'instance).

justicer [ˈdʒʌstisər], *s. A:* justicier *m.*

justiciability [dʒʌstisiəˈbiliti], *s.* justiciabilité *f.*

justiciable [dʒʌsˈtiʃiəbl], *a. & s.* justiciable (*mf*) (d'un tribunal, etc.).

justiciar [dʒʌsˈtiʃiər], *s. Hist:* grand justicier (sous les rois normands et les Plantagenets).

justiciary [dʒʌsˈtiʃiəri], *a. & s.* **1.** justicier (*m*). **2.** *Jur: Scot:* **High Court of J.,** tribunal *m* suprême en matière criminelle; **Circuit Court of J.,** tribunal suprême en tournée.

justifiability [ˈdʒʌstifaiəˈbiliti], **justifiableness** [dʒʌstiˈfaiəblnis], *s.* caractère *m* justifiable (d'une accusation, etc.).

justifiable [ˈdʒʌstifaiəbl], *a.* (crime, etc.) justifiable, justifié, défendable; (acte, colère) légitime; **hardly j. remark,** observation peu justifiée; **j. refusal,** refus motivé.

justifiably [dʒʌstiˈfaiəbli], *adv.* justifiablement, légitimement.

justification [dʒʌstifiˈkeiʃ(ə)n], *s.* **1.** (*a*) justification *f*; raison *f* d'être; **it can be said in his j. that . . .,** on peut dire pour le justifier, pour le disculper, que . . .; **there is no j. for such an action,** une pareille action est injustifiable; **written j.,** apologie *f* (de sa vie, de sa conduite); (*b*) *Jur:* (*in libel suit*) **to plead j.,** établir la défense sur la vérité des faits allégués par le défendeur. **2.** *Typ:* (*a*) justification (des caractères, des lignes); (*b*) parangonnage *m* (de caractères de corps différents).

justificative [dʒʌstifiˈkeitiv], **justificatory** [dʒʌstifiˈkeitəri], *a.* justificatif; justificateur, -trice.

justified [ˈdʒʌstifaid], *a.* justifié; **fully j. decision,** décision bien fondée.

justifier [ˈdʒʌstifaiər], *s.* **1.** justificateur, -trice. **2.** *Typ:* justificateur *m.*

justify [ˈdʒʌstifai], *v.tr.* **1.** justifier (qn, sa conduite, etc.); légitimer, motiver (une action); **to j. a statement,** justifier, prouver le bien-fondé de, son dire; **to j. s.o. before s.o.,** faire l'apologie de qn devant qn; **nothing can j. a soldier (in) disobeying an order,** rien ne saurait justifier le soldat qui désobéit à un ordre; **he was**

justified in the event, l'événement lui a donné raison; **are you justified in refusing?** avez-vous le droit de refuser? *Jur:* **to j. bail,** justifier de sa solvabilité (avant de fournir caution). **2.** *Typ:* (*a*) justifier (une ligne); (*b*) parangonner (des caractères de corps différents).
justifying ['dʒʌstifaiiŋ], *a.* justificatif; justificateur, -trice; *Theol:* **j. faith, grace,** foi, grâce, justifiante.
Justinian [dʒʌs'tiniən]. **1.** *Pr.n.m. Hist:* Justinien. **2.** *a.* **the J. Code,** le Code Justinien.
Justinianian [dʒʌstini'einiən], *a.* = **JUSTINIAN** 2.
justly ['dʒʌstli], *adv.* **1.** justement; avec justice; **to deal j. with s.o.,** (i) traiter qn équitablement; (ii) faire justice à qn; **to be j. punished for one's sins,** être puni par où l'on a péché; **famous, and j. so,** célèbre à juste titre, à bon droit. **2.** avec justesse; **he j. remarked that . . .,** avec juste raison, avec justesse, il fit remarquer que . . ..
justness ['dʒʌstnis], *s.* **1.** justice *f* (d'une cause, etc.). **2.** justesse *f* (d'une idée, d'une observation, etc.).
jut[1] [dʒʌt], *s.* saillie *f,* avancement *m,* projection *f* (d'un toit, etc.).
jut[2], *v.i.* **(jutted) to j. (out),** être en saillie, faire saillie, (s')avancer; **balcony that juts out,** balcon qui forme avance *f*; **to j. out from sth.,** sortir de qch.; déborder qch.; **to j. out over sth.,** surplomber qch.; **a cape juts out into the sea,** un cap s'avance dans la mer.
jute[1] [dʒu:t], *s. Bot: Tex:* jute *m.*
Jute[2], *s. Hist:* Jute *mf.*
Jutish ['dʒu:tiʃ], *a. Hist:* jute.
Jutlander ['dʒʌtləndər], *s. Geog:* Jutlandais, -aise.
jutting[1] ['dʒʌtiŋ], *a.* **j.(-out),** saillant, en saillie, débordant.
jutting[2], *s.* saillie *f.*
Juvenal ['dʒu:vən(ə)l], *Pr.n. Lt.Lit:* Juvénal.
juvenescence [dʒu:vi'nes(ə)ns], *s. Lit:* passage *m* de la jeunesse à l'adolescence *f*; adolescence *f.*
juvenescent [dʒu:vi'nes(ə)nt], *a. Lit:* en train de passer de la jeunesse à l'adolescence; adolescent.
juvenile ['dʒu:vənail]. **1.** *a.* (*a*) juvénile; **j. strength,** force *f* juvénile; force de la jeunesse; **j. production,** œuvres *f* de jeunesse; **j. books,** *s.,* **juveniles,** livres *m* pour enfants, pour la jeunesse; **j. literature,** littérature enfantine; **j. court,** tribunal *m* pour enfants et adolescents; **j. offender,** accusé mineur; **j. offenders,** l'enfance délinquante; (*b*) *Geol:* **j. water,** eau juvénile, tellurique, hypogée. **2.** *s.* jeune *mf.*
juvenilely ['dʒu:vənailli], *adv.* juvénilement.
juvenilia [dʒu:və'niliə], *s.pl.* juvenilia *m,* œuvres *f* de jeunesse.
juvenility [dʒu:və'niliti], *s.* juvénilité *f,* jeunesse *f.*
juxta- ['dʒʌkstə], *pref.* juxta-.
juxtalinear [dʒʌkstə'liniər], *a.* (traduction *f*) juxtalinéaire.
juxtapose ['dʒʌkstəpouz], *v.tr.* juxtaposer.
juxtaposed ['dʒʌkstəpouzd], *a.* juxtaposé; en juxtaposition.
juxtaposition [dʒʌkstəpə'ziʃ(ə)n], *s.* juxtaposition *f*; **to be in j.,** se juxtaposer.
jynx [dʒinks], *s. Orn:* torcol *m,* torcou *m.*

K

K, k [kei], *s.* (la lettre) K, k, *m*; *Tp:* **K for King,** K comme Kléber.

Kaaba ['kɑːbə], *s. Rel:* Kaaba *f.*

kaama ['kɑːmə], *s. Z:* caama *m*; antilope *f* de l'Afrique du Sud.

kabaragoya [kə'bɑːrə'gɔiə], *s. Rept:* varan *m* à bandes.

Kabard(in) ['kæbɑːd(in)], *s.* **1.** *Geog:* Kabardien, -ienne; Kabardin, -ine. **2.** *Ling:* (*also* **Kabardian**) kabarde *m.*

Kabardinian [kæbɑː'diniən], *a. Geog:* karbarde, kabardien, kabardin.

Kabul ['kɔːbul]. *Pr.n. Geog:* Kaboul.

Kabyle [kə'bail, 'kæbil]. **1.** *Ethn:* (*a*) *a.* kabyle; (*b*) *s.* Kabyle *mf.* **2.** *s. Ling:* kabyle *m.*

Kabylia [kæ'biliə]. *Pr.n. Geog:* Kabylie *f.*

kaddish ['kædiʃ], *s. Jew.Rel:* kaddisch *m.*

Kaffir ['kæfər]. **1.** *Ethn:* (*a*) *a.* caf(f)re; (*b*) *s.* Caf(f)re *mf.* **2.** *s. St.Exch: F:* **Kaffirs,** kaffriques *m*, sud-africaines *f.*

Kaffraria [kæ'frɛəriə], *s. Geog:* Cafrerie *f.*

kagu ['kægu:], *s. Orn:* kagou *m.*

kail [keil], *s.* = KALE.

kailyard ['keiljɑːd], *s.* (*a*) *Scot:* (jardin) potager *m*; (*b*) *Lit.Hist:* **the k. school,** l'école des romanciers qui ont décrit la vie des petites gens des *Lowlands* d'Écosse (J. M. Barrie, etc.).

kainite ['kainait, 'kei-], *s. Miner:* kaïnite *f.*

kainosite ['kainousait, 'kei-], *s. Miner:* kaïnosite *f.*

kaiser ['kaizər], *s.* kaiser *m.*

kaiserism ['kaizərizm], *s. Pol: usu. Pej:* césarisme prussien.

kaka ['kɑːkə], *s. Orn:* nestor méridional.

kakapo ['kɑːkəpou], *s. Orn:* kakapo *m*, perroquet-hibou *m*, *pl.* perroquets-hiboux.

kakemono [kæki'mounou], *s. Art:* kakémono *m.*

kale [keil], *s.* **1.** *Hort:* **curly k., green k.,** chou frisé; **Scotch k.,** chou rouge. **2.** *Scot:* soupe *f* aux choux, aux légumes.

kaleidoscope [kə'laidəskoup], *s.* kaléidoscope *m.*

kaleidoscopic [kəlaidə'skɔpik], *a.* kaléidoscopique.

kaleidoscopically [kəlaidə'skɔpik(ə)li], *adv.* d'une manière kaléidoscopique; comme un kaléidoscope.

kalends ['kæləndz], *s.pl.* kalendes *f*, calendes *f.*

kali ['keili, 'kæli], *s.* **1.** *Bot:* kali *m.* **2.** *Ch: A:* alcali végétal.

kaliborite [kæli'bɔːrait], *s. Miner:* kaliborite *f.*

kalinite ['kælinait], *s. Miner:* kalinite *f.*

kaliophilite [kæli'ɔfilait], *s. Miner:* kaliophilite *f.*

kalmia ['kælmiə], *s. Bot:* kalmie *f.*

Kalmu(c)k ['kælmʌk]. **1.** *Ethn:* (*a*) *a.* kalmouk; (*b*) *s.* Kalmouk *mf.* **2.** *s. Ling:* kalmouk *m*, oïrat *m.* **3.** *s. Tex:* kalmouk *m.*

kalong ['kɑːlɔŋ], *s. Z:* roussette *f* comestible (de la Malaisie); kalong *m.*

Kamakura [kæmə'kuːrə]. *Pr.n. Geog:* Kamakoura.

kamarezite [kɔ'mærizait], *s. Miner:* kamarézite *f.*

kamari [kə'mɑːri], *s. Bot:* calophyllum *m.*

Kamchatka [kæm'tʃætkə]. *Pr.n. Geog:* Kamtchatka *m.*

kame [keim], *s. Geol:* kame *m.*

kamichi [kɑːmiki], *Orn:* horned screamer.

kamikaze [kɑːmi'kɑːzi], *s. Japanese Hist:* kamikaze *m.*

kanaka [kə'nɑːkə, 'kænəkə]. *Ethn:* (*a*) *a.* canaque; (*b*) *s.* canaque *mf.*

Kandahar [kændə'hɑːr]. *Pr.n. Geog:* Kandahar *m.*

kangaroo [kæŋgə'ruː], *s.* **1.** (*a*) *Z:* kangourou *m*; **k. rat,** (i) bettongie *m*, kangourou-rat; (ii) dipodomys *m*, kangourou-rat; **filander k.,** kangourou philander, lapin *m* d'Aroe; (*b*) *Z:* **k. bear,** koala *m*; **musk k.,** rat musqué kangourou; *Ent:* **k. beetle,** sagra *m.* **2.** *St.Exch: F:* **kangaroos,** (i) actions minières de l'Australie occidentale; (ii) joueurs *m* sur ces actions. **3.** (*a*) *Parl:* **k. closure,** clôture *f* par tranches; (*b*) **k. court,** tribunal irrégulier.

Kansan ['kænz(ə)n]. **1.** *a. & s. Geog:* (originaire *mf*, habitant, -ante) du Kansas. **2.** *a. & s. Geol:* kansanien (*m*).

Kantian ['kæntiən]. *Phil:* **1.** *a.* kantien, kantiste. **2.** *s.* (*also* **Kantist**) kantiste *mf.*

Kant(ian)ism ['kænt(iən)izm], *s.* kantisme *m.*

kaolin ['keiəlin], *s.* kaolin *m.*

kaolinic [keiə'linik], *a.* kaolinique.

kaolinite ['keiəlinait], *s. Miner:* kaolinite *f.*

kaolinization [keiəlinai'zeiʃ(ə)n], *s.* kaolinisation *f.*

kaolinize ['keiəlinaiz], *v.tr.* kaoliniser.

kaon [keiɔn], *s. Atom.Ph:* kaon *m.*

kapok ['keipɔk], *s.* kapok *m*; **k. tree,** kapokier *m*, fromager *m.*

kappa ['kæpə], *s. Gr.Alph:* kappa *m.*

kaput [kə'put], *a. F:* kapout *inv*, fichu.

karagan ['kɑːrəgən], *s. Z:* karagan *m*; renard *m* de Tartarie.

karakul ['kærək(u)l], *s.* karakul *m*, caracul *m.*

karatas [kæ'reitəs], *s. Bot:* karatas *m.*

karate [kæ'rɑːti], *s. Sp:* karaté *m.*

karite, kariti ['kæriti], *s. Bot:* karité *m*; **k. (nut) butter,** beurre *m* de karité.

karma ['kɑːmə], *s. Rel:* karma *m.*

karri [kari], *s. Bot:* karri *m.*

karroo [kə'ruː], *s. Geog:* karrou *m*; **Great, Little, K.,** Grand, Petit, Karrou.

karst [kɑːst]. *Geog:* (*a*) *s.* karst *m*; (*b*) *attrib.* karstique; **k. country,** pays *m*, région *f*, karstique.

karstic ['kɑːstik], *a. Geog:* karstique.

karstland ['kɑːstlænd], *s. Geog:* région *f* karstique.

kart [kɑːt], *s.* kart *m*; **k. racing,** karting *m.*

karting ['kɑːtiŋ], *s.* karting *m.*

karyogamic [kæriou'gæmik], *a.* caryogamique.

karyogamy [kæri'ɔgəmi], *s. Biol:* caryogamie *f.*

karyokinesis [kærioukai'niːsis], *s. Biol:* caryocinèse *f*, karyokinèse *f*, karyocinèse *f.*

karyokinetic [kærioukai'netik], *a. Biol:* caryocinétique, karyokinétique, karyocinétique.

karyolitic [kæriou'litik], *a.* caryolitique.

karyolymph ['kærioulimf], *s. Biol:* caryolymphe *f.*

karyolysis [kæri'ɔlisis], *s. Med: etc:* caryolyse *f.*

karyorrhexis [kæriɔ'reksis], *s. Med:* caryorrhexis *f.*

karyosome ['kæriousoum], *s. Biol:* caryosome *m.*

karyotyping ['kærioutaipiŋ], *s. Biol:* analyse *f* des chromosomes.

kasbah ['kæzbə], *s.* casba(h) *f.*

Kashmir [kæʃ'miər]. *Pr.n. Geog:* Cachemire *m.*

Kashmiri [kæʃ'miəri]. **1.** *Geog:* (*a*) *a.* cachemirien; (*b*) *s.* Cachemirien, -ienne. **2.** *s. Ling:* cachemirien *m.*

kasolite ['kæsəlait], *s. Miner:* kasolite *f.*

Kassite ['kæsait]. *A.Hist:* (*a*) *a.* kassite; (*b*) *s.* Kassite *mf.*

kat [kæt], *s. Bot:* kat *m*, qat *m.*

katabatic [kætə'bætik], *a. Meteor:* (courant) descendant; **k. wind,** vent *m* catabatique.

katabolism [kə'tæbəlizm], *s. Biol:* catabolisme *m.*

katadromous [kætə'drouməs], *a. Ich:* thalassotoque.

Katanga [kə'tæŋgə]. *Pr.n. Geog:* Katanga *m.*

Katangan [kə'tæŋgən], *a. Geog:* katangais.

katathermometer [kætəθəː'mɔmitər], *s.* katathermomètre *m.*

katazone ['kætəzoun], *s. Geol:* catazone *f.*

Katharine, Katherine, Kathryn ['kæθ(ə)rin]. *Pr.n.f.* Catherine.

katydid ['keiti'did], *s. U.S: Ent: F:* sauterelle verte (d'Amérique).

kauri ['kauəri], *s.* **1.** *Bot:* **k. (pine),** dammara *m* austral; kauri *m.* **2. k. resin, gum, copal,** résine *f* fossile de kauri; dammar austral, kauri.

kava ['kɑːvə], **kawa** ['kɑːwə], *s.* kava *f*, kawa *f* (plante ou boisson).

kayak ['kaiæk], *s. Nau:* kayac *m*, kayak *m.*

kayaker ['kaiəkər], *s. Nau:* kayakiste *mf.*

kazoo [kə'zuː], *s. Mus: F:* mirliton *m*; bigophone *m.*

kea ['kiːə], *s. Orn:* nestor *m*, kéa *m.*

Keatsian ['kiːtsiən], *a. Lit.Hist:* de Keats; à la manière de Keats.

kebab ['kebæb, kə'bæb], *s. Cu:* chiche-kebab *m*, *pl.* chiche-kebabs.

keck[1] [kek], *s.* hoquet *m* de nausée.

keck[2], *v.i.* avoir envie de vomir; faire des efforts pour vomir; avoir des hauts-le-cœur, des hoquets de nausée.

kedge[1] [kedʒ], *s. Nau:* **k. (anchor),** ancre à jet.

kedge[2]. *Nau:* **1.** *v.tr.* haler, touer (un navire) sur une ancre à jet. **2.** *v.i.* se touer sur une ancre à jet.

kedgeree [kedʒə'riː], *s. Cu:* (*a*) (*in India*) mets épicé à base de riz avec légumes, œufs, etc.; (*b*) restes de poisson accommodés avec du riz, des œufs et du beurre.

kedging ['kedʒiŋ], *s. Nau:* halage *m*, touage *m*, touée *f* (sur une ancre à jet).

Kedron ['kiːdrɔn]. *Pr.n. B.Hist:* (**the Brook**) **K.,** le Cédron.

keef [kiːf], *s. P:* marijuana *f*, kif *m.*

keek[1] [kiːk], *s. Scot:* coup d'œil furtif.

keek[2], *v.i. Scot:* **to k. at s.o., sth.,** jeter un coup d'œil furtif sur qn, qch.

keel[1] [kiːl], *s.* **1.** (*a*) *N.Arch:* quille *f*; **to lay down a k.,** monter, poser, la quille d'un bateau, d'un navire; **bilge k.,** quille latérale, de bouchain, de roulis; aileron (de sous-marin); **drop k.,** dériveur *m*, aile *f*, quille, de dérive; **docking k., grounding k.,** quille d'échouage; **false k., outer k.,** fausse quille; **k. blocks,** tins *m* de cale sèche; **even k., uneven k.,** tirant d'eau égal, inégal; **on an even k.,** (i) *Nau:* sans différence de tirant d'eau, de calaison; (ii) *Av:* dans une position horizontale; en ligne de vol; (*of ship*) **to be, sail, on an even k.,** être dans ses lignes d'eau; avancer sans roulis ni tangage; (*b*) *Aer:* quille (d'hydravion, etc.); **k. surface,** surface *f* de quille; **k. fairing,** carénage *m* de la quille; (*c*) *Lit:* navire *m.* **2.** *Nat.Hist:* carène *f* (de feuille, de pétale, de mandibule, etc.).

keel[2]. **1.** *v.tr.* (*a*) mettre (un navire) en carène; (*b*) **to k. over a ship,** faire chavirer un navire. **2.** *v.i.* (*a*) (*of ship*) rouler sur sa quille; renvoyer; (*b*) **to k. over,** (i) (*of ship*) faire le tour; chavirer; (ii) *F:* (*of pers.*) s'évanouir, tomber dans les pommes.

keel[3], *s. A:* (*a*) *Nau:* chaland charbonnier; (*b*) *Meas:* chaland de charbon (21518 kilos).

keel[4], *s. Scot:* ocre *f* rouge (pour marquer les moutons).

keel[5], *v.tr. Scot:* marquer (un mouton) à l'ocre rouge.

keeled [ki:ld], *a.* **1.** *N.Arch:* (navire) à quille. **2.** *Nat.Hist: etc:* caréné; *Prehist:* **k. scraper,** grattoir caréné.

keelhaul ['ki:lhɔ:l], *v.tr. Nau: A:* donner la cale humide, la grande cale, à (un matelot).

keelson ['ki:lsən, 'kel-], *s. N.Arch:* carlingue *f*; contre-quille *f, pl.* contre-quilles; **bilge k.,** carlingue de bouchain; **middle-line k.,** carlingue centrale.

keen[1] [ki:n], *s. Dial:* (*Irish*) lamentation *f* funèbre; mélopée funèbre (chantée en veillant le corps).

keen[2], *v.tr. Dial:* (*Irish*) **to k. a corpse,** chanter une mélopée en veillant un corps.

keen[3], *a.* **1.** (couteau, etc.) affilé, aiguisé; **k. edge,** fil tranchant; **k. point,** pointe acérée, pointe aiguë; **k. grindstone,** meule ardente; **as k. as a razor,** affilé comme un rasoir. **2.** (froid, vent, air) vif, piquant, aigre; (son) aigu; (froid) perçant. **3.** (chagrin) aigu; (regret) poignant; (remords) cuisant; **k. pleasure,** vif plaisir; plaisir sensible; **k. pain,** douleur vive, aiguë, poignante; **k. appetite,** rude appétit; **k. satire,** satire mordante, âpre, piquante, acerbe. **4.** (*a*) (*of pers.*) ardent, assidu, zélé; **he is a k. businessman,** il est âpre aux affaires; **k. sportsman,** ardent sportif; **k. golfer,** enragé *m* de golf; **they are k. competitors,** ils se font une concurrence acharnée; ce sont des concurrents acharnés; **he's as k. as mustard,** il brûle de zèle; *F:* **to be k. on sth.,** être enthousiaste de qch.; être amateur enthousiaste de qch.; être porté sur qch.; être emballé pour qch.; avoir la passion de qch.; raffoler de qch.; *F:* **to be k. on s.o.,** être emballé pour qn; être très ami avec qn; être amoureux de qn; **he's k. on maths, on sport,** il mord bien aux math; le sport le passionne; **are you k. on going?** tenez-vous beaucoup à y aller? **he's not k. on it,** il n'y tient pas beaucoup; **I'm not very k. on it,** ça ne me dit pas grand-chose; ça ne m'emballe pas; **you won't always be so k.,** vous en reviendrez; **k. to enjoy life,** épris, curieux, de toutes les jouissances; (*b*) **k. interest,** vif intérêt; **k. competition,** concurrence acharnée, âpre; **there is a k. demand for these stocks,** ces fonds sont activement recherchés; *Com:* **k. prices,** prix *m* au plus bas, prix étudiés. **5.** (œil, regard) perçant, pénétrant, vif; **to have a k. eye for a bargain,** être prompt à reconnaître une bonne affaire; **to have a k. ear,** avoir l'oreille fine, l'ouïe fine; **he is a k. judge of men,** il juge les hommes avec pénétration; **k. observer of contemporary affairs,** curieux observateur des événements contemporains; **dog k. of scent,** chien *m* qui a un bon flair. **6.** (esprit) fin, pénétrant, vif, perçant.

keen-edged ['ki:nedʒd], *a.* bien affilé; aiguisé, tranchant; **k.-e. satire,** satire acérée, mordante.

keen-eyed ['ki:n'aid], *a.* **1.** aux yeux perçants; au regard perçant. **2.** perspicace.

keenly ['ki:nli], *adv.* **1. the wind was blowing k.,** il faisait un vent âpre. **2. it touched me k.,** cela me toucha profondément, douloureusement. **3.** âprement, vivement, avidement; **k. disputed point,** question âprement discutée; **k. fought match,** partie âprement contestée; **k. criticized,** vivement critiqué; **to listen k.,** écouter avidement; **to be k. interested in . . .,** s'intéresser vivement à. . . .

keenness ['ki:nnis], *s.* **1.** finesse *f*, acuité *f* (du tranchant d'un outil). **2.** âpreté *f*, rigueur *f* (du froid); **there is a k. in the air,** il y a de l'aigre dans l'air. **3.** ardeur *f*, vivacité *f*, empressement *m*, zèle *m* (de qn); mordant *m* (des troupes, etc.); **to show much k. in doing sth.,** mettre beaucoup d'âpreté, d'empressement, à faire qch.; **k. on doing sth.,** grand désir de faire qch. **4. k. of sight,** acuité visuelle; acuité de la vision; **k. of hearing,** finesse de l'ouïe. **5.** pénétration *f*, finesse (d'esprit).

keen-scented ['ki:n'sentid], *a.* (chien) qui a un bon flair.

keen-set ['ki:n'set], *a. O:* qui se sent de l'appétit (**for,** pour); affamé (**for,** de).

keen-sighted ['ki:n'saitid], *a.* à la vue perçante.

keen-witted ['ki:n'witid], *a.* à l'esprit délié; à l'esprit perçant.

keep[1] [ki:p], *s.* **1.** donjon *m* (d'un château fort). **2.** nourriture *f*, subsistance *f*; entretien *m*; frais *mpl* de subsistance; **to earn one's k.,** subvenir à ses besoins; **so much a day and one's k.,** tant par jour logé et nourri; **he isn't worth his k.,** il ne gagne pas sa nourriture. **3.** *F:* **for keeps,** pour de bon; **you can have it for keeps,** vous pouvez le garder; je vous le donne; **he seems to be here for keeps,** on dirait qu'il est installé ici pour de bon, à tout jamais. **4.** *Mec:* chapeau *m* (de palier). **5.** *Min:* **keeps,** clichages *m*, taquets *m* (de cage).

keep[2], *v.* (**kept** [kept]; **kept**)

I. *v.tr.* **1.** (*observe*) observer, suivre (la loi, une règle); obéir à (la loi); tenir, remplir (une promesse); rester fidèle à (un vœu); tenir, respecter, observer (un traité); **to k. late hours,** se coucher tard; **to k. one's word,** tenir (sa) parole; **to k. s.o. to his promise,** exiger de qn qu'il tienne sa promesse; **to k. to the truth,** ne pas se départir de la vérité; **to k. an appointment,** ne pas manquer, être exact, à un rendez-vous; *Ecc:* **to k. the commandments,** observer les commandements. **2.** (*celebrate, observe*) célébrer (une fête); **to k. a saint's day,** fêter un saint; **to k. one's birthday,** fêter, célébrer, son anniversaire; **to k. a fast,** observer le jeûne; **to k. Sunday, Lent,** observer le dimanche, le carême; **to k. Christmas in the old style,** fêter Noël à l'ancienne mode; *Sch: O:* **to k. chapel,** assister à l'office (à la chapelle). **3.** (*protect*) (*a*) **God k. (you)!** Dieu vous garde! **God k. his soul!** (que) Dieu ait son âme! *A:* **God will k. us,** Dieu nous protégera; (*b*) préserver (**s.o. from evil,** qn du mal); *F:* **Heaven k. me out of his clutches!** que le ciel m'empêche de tomber sous sa patte! (*c*) *Mil:* défendre (une forteresse, etc.); *A:* **to k. the gates (of the town),** garder les portes (de la ville); (*d*) *Sp:* **to k. goal,** garder le but; *Cr:* **to k. wicket,** garder le guichet. **4.** (*a*) garder (des moutons, des troupeaux); (*b*) entretenir (un jardin, etc.); **well kept, badly kept, road,** route bien, mal, entretenue; (*c*) tenir (un journal, des comptes); **to k. note of sth.,** tenir note de qch.; *Com:* **to k. the books,** tenir les livres, les écritures; (*d*) subvenir aux besoins de (qn); **he doesn't earn enough to k. himself,** il ne gagne pas de quoi vivre; **he has his parents to k.,** il a ses parents à sa charge; **to k. s.o. in clothes, in food,** fournir de l'habillement, de la nourriture, à qn; *F:* **I'd rather k. him a week than a fortnight!** il mange comme un ogre! (*e*) avoir (une voiture, etc.); élever (des abeilles, de la volaille); **they k. a dog to guard the house,** ils ont un chien de garde; **to k. a mistress,** entretenir une maîtresse; *O:* **kept woman,** maîtresse, femme entretenue; (*f*) tenir (une école, un magasin, une pension de famille); **to k. an inn,** tenir auberge; (*g*) *Com:* tenir, avoir en magasin (des marchandises); **do you k. nails?** est-ce que vous vendez des clous? **5.** (*a*) maintenir (l'ordre); garder (le silence, un secret); **to k. one's composure,** garder son sang-froid; **to k. one's countenance,** garder son sérieux; *F:* **they k. themselves to themselves,** ils font bande à part; *F:* **k. the party clean!** (i) pas de grossièretés! (ii) soyons honnêtes! pas de sales tours! (iii) pas de scandales! (*b*) **it's too warm to k. the central heating on,** il fait trop chaud pour maintenir le chauffage central; (*c*) *Navy:* **to k. the speed of the fleet,** soutenir la vitesse de la flotte; (*d*) **to k. a good table,** faire bonne chère; **to k. open house,** tenir maison ouverte. **6.** (*detain*) **to k. s.o. in prison,** tenir, retenir, qn en prison; **to k. a boy at school until he is eighteen,** laisser un enfant au lycée jusqu'à dix-huit ans; **I kept him at home,** je l'ai gardé à la maison; **the doctor kept him in bed,** le médecin l'a obligé de garder le lit; **to k. s.o. for dinner,** retenir qn à dîner; **he kept me late,** il m'a attardé; il m'a mis en retard; **there was nothing to k. me in England,** il n'y avait rien pour me retenir en Angleterre; **don't let me k. you!** je ne vous retiens pas! **what's keeping you?** qu'est-ce qui vous retient? **7.** (*restrain; prevent*) **the dykes k. the river in its bed,** les digues contiennent la rivière dans son lit; **to k. back an army,** retenir une armée; **the police were trying to k. the crowd back,** la police essayait de contenir, de retenir, la foule; **to k. back one's tears,** refouler, retenir, ses larmes; s'empêcher de pleurer; **to k. prices down,** empêcher les prix de monter, d'augmenter; **to k. s.o. from falling,** empêcher qn de tomber; **to k. fruit from rotting,** empêcher les fruits de pourrir; **I don't know what kept me from slapping his face,** je ne sais pas ce qui m'a retenu de le gifler; **it kept me from going,** cela m'a empêché d'y aller; **the wind will k. the rain off, away,** le vent empêchera la pluie; **she carried a parasol to k. off the sun,** elle portait une ombrelle pour se protéger, s'abriter, du soleil; **k. your hands off (that)!** n'y touchez pas! **k. your hands off (me), k. your hands to yourself,** (à) bas les mains, les pattes! **to draw the curtains to k. the light out,** fermer les rideaux pour empêcher la lumière d'entrer; **if you put on your coat it will k. out the cold,** si vous mettez votre manteau vous n'aurez pas froid; **you can't k. a good man down,** under, quoi qu'il lui arrive un homme de valeur sait le surmonter. **8.** (*reserve*) garder (**sth. for s.o., for oneself,** qch. pour qn, pour soi); **k. me some food if I'm late,** gardez-moi de quoi manger si je suis en retard; **to k. sth. for later,** garder, conserver, réserver, qch. pour plus tard; **is this seat being kept?** est-ce que cette place est retenue? **to k. sth. back from s.o.'s wages,** retenir une somme sur le salaire de qn. **9.** (*a*) garder (des provisions, etc.); **the cupboard where I k. the crockery,** l'armoire où je mets la vaisselle; **the drawers in which I k. my papers,** les tiroirs où je range mes papiers; **she keeps her letters under lock and key,** elle garde ses lettres sous clef; **to k. matches away from the children,** tenir les allumettes hors de la portée des enfants; **to k. the archives,** veiller à la conservation des archives; (*b*) **to k. fruit until it is ripe,** garder des fruits jusqu'à ce qu'ils mûrissent. **10.** (*retain*) (*a*) garder (qch.); conserver (son emprise sur qch.); retenir (l'attention de qn); garder (la page dans un livre); **you can k. the book I lent you,** vous pouvez garder le livre que je vous ai prêté; **I can make money but I can't k. it,** je sais gagner de l'argent mais je ne sais pas le conserver; **this child can't k. a thing in his head,** cet enfant ne retient rien; (*b*) **I'll k. my coat on,** je vais garder mon manteau; **it was so windy I couldn't k. my hat on,** le vent était si fort que je ne pouvais pas empêcher mon chapeau de s'envoler; **I can't k. my food down,** je ne peux pas garder ma nourriture; chaque fois que je mange je vomis. **11. to k. sth. to oneself,** taire qch.; **I kept my impressions to myself,** j'ai gardé mes impressions pour moi; *F:* **you can k. your remarks to yourself!** j'en ai assez de vos observations! **to k. sth. from s.o.,** cacher, taire, qch. à qn. **12. to k. (on) one's course, one's route,** continuer, poursuivre, son chemin, sa route; **to k. (in) the middle of the road,** garder le milieu de la route. **13. to k. (to) one's bed, one's room, the house,** garder le lit, la chambre; rester à la maison. **14.** (*a*) **to k. the field,** tenir la campagne (en temps de guerre); **to k. the field against the enemy,** se maintenir contre les attaques de l'ennemi; **to k. the stage,** tenir la scène; *Equit:* **to k. one's seat,** rester en selle; garder son assiette; *Nau:* **to k. the sea,** tenir la mer; (*b*) **to k. one's seat,** rester assis; (*c*) **to k. one's figure,** garder la ligne; **to k. one's looks,** conserver sa beauté; rester belle; (*of thg*) **to k. its shape, its colour,** conserver sa forme, sa couleur. **15.** (*a*) **to k. sth. clean, warm, secret,** tenir qch. propre, chaud, secret; **to k. oneself warm,** (i) se tenir au chaud; (ii) s'habiller chaudement; **to k. sth. intact,** maintenir qch. intact; **to k. the door open, shut,** garder, laisser, la porte ouverte, fermée; **the noise kept me awake,** le bruit m'a empêché de dormir; **try to k. him interested,** tâchez de maintenir son attention, son intérêt; **she had kept her innocence,** elle avait conservé son innocence; **k. Wednesday free for dinner,** je vous retiens à dîner mercredi; **to k. s.o. waiting,** faire attendre qn; **he kept us standing two hours,** il nous a tenus debout pendant deux heures; **she always keeps the radio going, on,** elle fait jouer la radio sans arrêt; (*b*) **to k. one's hands in one's pockets,** garder les mains dans ses poches; **to k. one's eyes fixed on sth.,** fixer qch. du regard; **to k. s.o. at work,** *F:* **at it,** faire travailler qn sans cesse; serrer les côtes à qn; **to k. sth. ready, in readiness,** avoir toujours qch. prêt; **to k. sth. in reserve, in store,** tenir qch. en réserve; **to k. s.o. in a state of fear,** entretenir qn dans l'effroi, la crainte; *Nau:* **k. her so,** gouvernez comme ça.

II. *v.i.* **1.** rester, se tenir; **to k. close to the door,** se tenir près de la porte; **she told the children to k. away from the river,** elle a dit aux enfants de ne pas s'approcher de la rivière; **k. away (from me), k. back!** n'approchez pas! éloignez-vous! n'avancez pas! **k. off the grass!** défense de marcher sur le gazon! **k. out of this!** mêlez-vous de ce qui vous regarde! **to k. out of danger,** rester à l'abri du danger; **to k. to the left, to the right,** tenir la gauche, la droite; **to k. together,** rester ensemble; ne pas se séparer; **to k. well, in good health,** se maintenir, rester, en bonne santé; **how are you keeping?** comment allez-vous? **to k. quiet,** se tenir, rester, tranquille; se tenir coi; **to k. awake, calm,** rester éveillé, calme; **to k. smiling,** garder le sourire; **k. smiling! k. your pecker up!** bon courage! **the weather is keeping cool, fine,** le temps reste frais, se maintient au beau. **2.** *Sch: F: O:* (*esp. at Cambridge*) habiter, loger. **3.** continuer; (*a*) **to k. at work, working,** continuer de travailler; continuer son travail; **to k. hard at it,** travailler sans relâche; **to k. straight on,** suivre, continuer, tout droit; **to k. on the right track,** suivre, garder, la bonne voie; *F:* **to k. (on) at s.o. with appeals for money,** harceler, bombarder, qn de demandes d'argent; **to k. close to the river, alongside the river,** suivre le bord de la rivière; (*b*) **to k. (on) doing sth.,** ne pas cesser de faire qch.; **don't k. (on) asking questions,** ne posez pas tout le temps des questions; **he keeps (on) changing his plans,** il modifie continuellement ses projets; *F:* **to k. on at s.o.,** être toujours sur le dos de qn; harceler, tracasser, qn; **this thought kept coming back to him,** cette pensée lui venait sans cesse à l'esprit. **4.** (*with passive force*) (*of food, etc.*) se garder, se conserver; **butter that will k.,** beurre *m* qu'on peut conserver; **I'll tell you the story later; it will k.,** je vous raconterai l'histoire plus tard;

elle n'y perdra rien.

III. (*compound verbs*) **1. keep in.** (*a*) *v.tr.* (i) empêcher (qn) de sortir; *Sch:* **to k. a pupil in,** mettre un élève en retenue; consigner un élève; (ii) entretenir (un feu); (iii) **to k. one's hand in,** s'entretenir la main; se tenir en haleine; (*b*) *v.i.* (i) (*of fire*) rester allumé; (ii) *F:* **to k. in with s.o.,** cultiver qn; entretenir de bonnes relations avec qn; rester en bons termes avec qn.

2. keep up. (*a*) *v.tr.* (i) entretenir (un bâtiment, une route, un feu); **it requires a great deal of money to k. up such an establishment,** il faut avoir une grosse fortune pour entretenir une maison, un établissement, semblable; (ii) conserver (un usage); entretenir (une correspondance, son français, etc.); **they have kept up their friendship,** ils sont restés amis; **we must k. it up,** il nous faut continuer nos efforts; **I couldn't k. it up any longer,** j'ai dû y renoncer; **k. it up!** allez toujours! continuez! (iii) soutenir (l'intérêt, etc.); soutenir, maintenir (son courage); **to k. up appearances,** garder, sauver, les apparences; (iv) **I mustn't k. you up,** je ne veux pas vous empêcher de vous coucher, vous faire coucher tard; **we kept the children up later last night,** hier soir nous avons couché les enfants plus tard que d'habitude; (*b*) *v.i.* (i) **the weather is keeping up,** le temps se maintient; (ii) **to k. up with s.o.,** marcher de front avec qn; aller de pair avec qn; **I can't k. up with you,** vous marchez, parlez, etc., trop vite pour moi; *F:* **to k. up with the Joneses,** faire concurrence aux voisins; rivaliser de standing avec ses voisins; ne pas se laisser distancer par les voisins; **to k. up with the times,** être de son temps; être à la page.

keeper ['ki:pər], *s.* **1.** (*pers.*) (*a*) garde *m*, gardien *m*; surveillant *m*, gardien (de prison); gardien (d'un aliéné); conservateur *m* (de musée, etc.); gardeur, -euse (de troupeaux); *Metall:* garde-feu *m, pl.* gardes-feu (de haut fourneau); **park k., lighthouse k.,** gardien de parc, de phare; **K. of the Seals,** Garde des sceaux; (*b*) garde-chasse *m, pl.* gardes-chasse(s); (*c*) tenancier, -ière (d'un établissement); préposé, -ée (de bibliothèque, de chemin de fer, etc.); **boarding-house k.,** patron, -onne, propriétaire *mf,* d'une pension de famille; (*d*) entreteneur *m* (d'une femme); (*e*) dépositaire *m* (d'un secret). **2.** *Tchn:* (*device*) (*a*) (*pawl, click*) détente *f,* cliquet *m*; (*b*) (*lock nut*) contre-écrou *m, pl.* contre-écrous; (*c*) *Locksm:* gâche *f* (de serrure); (*d*) mentonnet *m* (de loquet); auberon *m* (de verrou); (*e*) arrêtoir *m*, bosse *f* (de chaine); *Nau:* bosse *f* (de cordage); (*f*) *Harn:* passant *m*; **sliding k.,** coulant *m*; (*g*) *El:* armature *f,* armure *f,* contact *m* (d'un aimant). **3.** bague *f* de sûreté (portée au doigt pour en empêcher une autre de glisser); jonc *m*. **4. apples that are good keepers,** pommes *f* de bonne garde, qui se conservent.

keeping ['ki:piŋ], *s.* **1.** (*a*) observation *f* (d'une règle, d'une promesse); (*b*) célébration *f* (d'une fête). **2.** conservation (de fruits, etc.); **good k. wine,** vin *m* de garde. **3.** garde *f*; **to have s.o., sth., in one's k.,** avoir qn, qch., en garde, sous sa garde; **in God's k.,** à la garde de Dieu. **4. in k. with . . .,** en harmonie, en accord, en rapport, avec . . .; à l'unisson de . . .; qui s'accorde avec . . .; qui convient à . . .; **in k. with his principles,** conforme à ses principes; **carpet in k. with the curtains,** tapis assorti aux rideaux; **out of k. with . . .,** peu en harmonie, en désaccord, avec . . ..

keg [keg], *s.* caque *f* (de harengs); barillet *m*, baricaut *m* (d'eau-de-vie, etc.); tonnelet *m* (d'eau); **powder k.,** baril *m* de poudre.

kelly[1] ['keli], *s. U.S: F:* chapeau *m* (d'homme).

kelly[2], *s. Petr:* tige carrée d'entraînement; **hexagonal k.,** tige hexagonale.

keloid ['kelɔid], **keloma** [ke'loumə], *s. Med:* chéloïde *f.*

kelp [kelp], *s.* **1.** *esp. Scot:* varech *m*; **k. gatherer,** ramasseur, -euse, de varech. **2.** *Ch:* **k. ash,** kelp *m*.

kelpie[1] ['kelpi], *s. Scot:* **(water) k.,** esprit *m* des eaux.

kelpie[2], *s. Austr: F:* chien métis.

kelp pigeon ['kelp'pidʒin], *s. Orn:* chionis *m*.

kelson ['kelsən], *s. Nau:* = KEELSON.

kelt [kelt], *s. Scot:* (*salmon*) charognard *m*, kelt *m*, ravalé *m*.

Kelvin ['kelvin]. *Pr.n.* (*a*) *El:* **K. effect,** effet *m* de Kelvin, effet pelliculaire, de peau; (*b*) *Ph:* **K. scale,** échelle Kelvin, échelle absolue (de température).

kemp [kemp], *s. Tex:* jarre *m* (dans la laine).

kempite ['kempait], *s. Miner:* kempite *f.*

ken[1] [ken], *s.* **within s.o.'s k.,** (i) à portée de la vue de qn; (ii) dans les connaissances, dans la compétence, de qn; **out of, beyond, s.o.'s k.,** hors de (i) la vue, (ii) la compétence, de qn; **that's beyond my k.,** cela dépasse ma compétence, me dépasse; *Lit:* **a new star swam into his k.,** une nouvelle étoile apparut à son horizon.

ken[2], *v.* (*p.t.* **kenned, kent;** *p.p.* **kent;** *pr.p.* **kenning**) **1.** *v.i. A:* **as far as I could k.,** aussi loin que je pouvais voir. **2.** *v.tr. A: & Scot:* connaître (qn); savoir (qch.).

kennedya [keni'di:ə, kə'ni:diə], *s. Bot:* kennedya *m*.

kennel[1] ['kenl], *s.* **1.** (*a*) chenil *m* (de chiens de chasse); **the hunt kennel(s),** le chenil de la meute; **k. management,** la conduite du chenil; (*b*) *usu. pl.* établissement *m* d'élevage de chiens; **kennels that have produced many champions,** établissement qui a produit beaucoup de champions; **to buy a dog from a good k.,** acheter un chien chez un bon éleveur; **to put a dog into kennels,** mettre un chien en pension; (*c*) *F: O:* bouge *m*, taudis *m*, trou *m*, chenil. **2.** (*a*) loge *f,* niche *f* (de chien de garde, etc.); (*b*) *Ven:* terrier *m* (de renard). **3.** *Ven:* (*a*) **the k.,** la meute; (*b*) **k. of wolves,** bande *f* de loups.

kennel[2], *v.* **(kennelled) 1.** *v.i.* (*a*) (*of dog*) se nicher, se loger; (*b*) (*of fox*) se terrer. **2.** *v.tr.* **to k. the hounds,** mettre la meute dans le chenil.

kennel[3], *s. A:* ruisseau *m* (de rue).

kennelmaid ['kenlmeid], *s.f.* employée d'éleveur de chiens, de chenil.

kennelman, *pl.* **-men** ['kenlmən], *s.m.* valet de chenil; employé d'éleveur de chiens.

kenogenesis [kenou'dʒenəsis], *s.* cénogénèse *f.*

kenosis [ke'nousis], *s. Theol:* kénôse *f.*

kenotoxin [kenou'tɔksin], *s. Physiol:* cénotoxine *f,* kénotoxine *f.*

kenotron [ke'noutrɔn], *s.* kénotron *m*.

kentia ['kentiə], *s. Bot:* kentia *m*.

Kentish ['kentiʃ], *a. Geog:* du comté de Kent; *Geol:* **K. rag,** calcaire *m* du Kent; *Ent:* **K. glory,** endromis *m*; *A: & Lit:* **K. fire,** applaudissements prolongés (souvent ironiques).

kentledge ['kentlidʒ], *s. Nau:* lest (permanent) en gueuses; gueuse *f* (de fer); saumon *m* (de fonte).

kentrolite ['kentrəlait], *s. Miner:* kentrolite *f.*

Kentuckian [ken'tʌkiən], *a. & s. Geog:* (originaire *mf,* habitant, -ante) du Kentucky.

Kenya ['ki:njə]. *Pr.n. Geog:* Kenya *m*.

Kenyan ['ki:njən]. *Geog:* (*a*) *a.* kenyan; (*b*) *s.* Kenyan, -ane.

Keplerian [kep'lɛəriən], *a. Astr:* képlérien.

keraphyllocele [kerə'filousi:l], *s. Vet:* kéraphyllocèle *m*.

keratectomy [kerə'tektəmi], *s. Surg:* kératectomie *f.*

keraterpeton [kerə'tə:pitɔn], *s. Paleont:* kératerpéton *m*.

keratic [ke'rætik], *a. Physiol:* kératique; **k. reaction,** réaction *f* kératique.

keratin ['kerətin], *s. Ch: Physiol:* kératine *f.*

keratinization [kerætinai'zeiʃ(ə)n], *s. Physiol:* kératinisation *f.*

keratinized ['kerətinaizd], *a. Physiol:* kératinisé.

keratinous [ke'rætinəs], *a.* kératinique.

keratitis [kerə'taitis], *s. Med:* kératite *f.*

keratoconjunctivitis ['kerətoukəndʒʌŋ(k)ti'vaitis], *s. Med:* kérato-conjonctivite *f.*

keratoconus [kerətou'kounəs], *s. Med:* kératocône *m*.

keratodermia [kerətou'də:miə], *s. Med:* kératodermie *f.*

keratogenous [kerə'tɔdʒənəs], *a.* kératogène.

keratoid ['kerətɔid], *a.* kératoïde.

keratolysis [kerə'tɔlisis], *s. Med:* kératolyse *f.*

keratomalacia [kerətoumə'leisiɑ], *s. Med:* kératomalacie *f.*

keratomycosis [kerətoumai'kousis], *s. Med:* kératomycose *f.*

keratoplasty [kerətou'plæsti], *s. Surg:* kératoplastie *f.*

keratoscope [ke'rætouskoup], *s. Med:* kératoscope *m*.

keratoscopy [kerə'tɔskəpi], *s. Med:* kératoscopie *f.*

keratose ['kerətous], *a.* kératique.

keratosed ['kerətouzd], *a.* kératinisé.

keratosis [kerə'tousis], *s. Med: Vet:* kératose *f*; **senile k.,** kératose sénile, crasse *f* sénile.

keratotomy [kerə'tɔtəmi], *s. Surg:* kératotomie *f.*

kerb[1] [kə:b], *s.* **1.** (*a*) bordure *f,* bord *m*, de trottoir; garde-pavé *m inv*; **stone k.,** bordage *m* de pierres; **the edge of the k.,** l'arête vive du trottoir; **to slip off the k.,** glisser au défaut du trottoir; **car drawn up at the k.,** voiture en stationnement (le long du trottoir); (*b*) *St.Exch: F:* **business done on the k.,** opérations *fpl* après clôture de Bourse. **2.** margelle *f* (de fontaine, de puits).

kerb[2], *v.tr.* border (un puits, un trottoir); mettre la bordure à (un trottoir).

kerbstone ['kə:bstoun], *s.* (*a*) pierre *f* de parement (d'un trottoir); (*b*) *St.Exch: F:* **k. market,** la coulisse; **k. broker,** coulissier *m*, courtier *m* en valeurs mobilières.

kerchief ['kə:tʃif], *s. Cost: O:* (*a*) (*for head*) fanchon *f,* marmotte *f*; mouchoir *m* de tête; (*b*) fichu *m*; (*c*) *A:* mouchoir *m*.

kerf [kə:f], *s.* **1.** (*a*) trait *m* de scie; voie *f* de scie; (*b*) *Metalw:* **(torch-cut) k.,** trait de chalumeau. **2.** bout coupé, surface *f* de coupe (d'un arbre abattu). **3.** *Min:* havage *m*; saignée *f.*

kerfuffle [kə'fʌfl], *s. F:* remue-ménage *m*, tohu-bohu *m*; **they made a great k. about it,** ils en ont fait toute une histoire.

kerma ['kə:mə], *s. Atom.Ph:* kerma *m*.

kermes ['kə:miz], *s.* **1.** (*a*) *Ent: Dy:* kermès (animal); (*b*) *Bot:* **k. (oak),** chêne *m* kermès. **2.** *A.Pharm:* kermès (minéral).

kermesite ['kə:mizait], *s. Miner:* kermésite *f.*

kermess, kermis ['kə:mes, -mis], *s.* (*a*) kermesse *f,* foire annuelle de Flandres; (*b*) kermesse, fête *f* de charité.

kern[1] [kə:n], *s. Typ:* crénage *m* (d'un caractère).

kern[2], *v.tr. Typ:* créner (un caractère); **kerned letter,** lettre crénée.

kern(e) [kə:n], *s. Hist:* fantassin irlandais.

kernel ['kə:n(ə)l], *s.* **1.** (*a*) amande *f* (de noisette, de noyau); pignon *m* (de pomme de pin); (*b*) grain *m* (de céréale); graine *f* de légumineuse; (*c*) *Cu:* noix *f* (de veau). **2.** *Med: Dial:* glande engorgée. **3.** (*a*) *Atom.Ph: Ch:* noyau, cœur *m*, intérieur *m* (d'une structure, d'une réaction, etc.); **diffusion k.,** noyau de l'intégrale de diffusion; **slowing-down k.,** noyau de l'intégrale de ralentissement; (*b*) noyau (d'une organisation, etc.); fond *m*, essentiel *m* (d'un problème, etc.).

kerning ['kə:niŋ], *s. Typ:* crénage *m*.

kerogen ['kerədʒən], *s. Geol:* kérogène *m*.

kerosene ['kerəsi:n], *s.* **1.** *Ch:* kérosène *m*. **2.** *NAm:* pétrole lampant; **vaporizing k.,** pétrole pour moteur.

kerria ['keriə], *s. Bot:* kerria *m*, kerrie *f* (du Japon).

kersey ['kə:zi], *s. Tex:* créseau *m*.

kerseymere ['kə:zimiər], *s. Tex:* casimir *m*.

kerygma [ke'rigmə], *s. Theol:* kérygme *m*.

kerygmatic [kerig'mætik], *a. Theol:* kérygmatique.

keryl ['keril], *s. Ch:* kérosène chloré.

kestrel ['kestrəl], *s. Orn:* (faucon *m*) crécerelle *f*; **lesser k.,** faucon crécerellette; **fox k.,** faucon renard; **grey k.,** faucon ardoisé.

ketazine ['ketəzain], *s. Ch:* cétazine *f.*

ketch [ketʃ], *s. Nau:* **1.** *A:* quaiche *f.* **2.** ketch *m*, dundee *m*, dindet *m*.

ketchup ['ketʃəp], *s.* **tomato k., mushroom k.,** sauce piquante à base de tomates, de champignons; ketchup *m*.

ketene ['ki:ti:n], *s. Ch:* cétène *m*.

ketmia ['ketmiə], *s. Bot:* ketmie *f.*

ketogenesis [ki:tou'dʒenəsis], *s. Bio-Ch:* cétogénèse *f.*

ketogenetic [ki:tou'dʒenətik], *a. Bio-Ch:* cétogène.

ketol ['ki:təl], *s. Ch:* indol(e) *m*.

ketone ['ki:toun], *s. Ch:* cétone *f.*

ketonic [ki:'tɔnik], *a. Ch:* cétonique.

ketose ['ki:tous], *s. Bio-Ch:* cétose *m*.

ketosis [ki:'tousis], *s. Med:* cétose *f*; *Vet:* acétose *f,* toxémie *f* de gestation (de la brebis).

ketoxime [ki:'tɔksi:m], *s. Ch:* cétoxime *f.*

kettle [ketl], *s.* **1.** (*a*) (*for boiling water*) bouilloire *f*; **k. holder,** poignée *f* de bouilloire (en drap, etc.); (*b*) (*for cooking*) chaudron *m*; chaudière *f*; **fish k.,** saumonnière *f*; **camp k.,** marmite *f*; *Mil:* **mess k.,** gamelle *f*; *F:* **here's a pretty, a fine, a nice, k. of fish!** en voilà une belle besogne, une jolie affaire, un beau gâchis! nous voilà dans de beaux draps! **and that's another k. of fish!** en voilà bien une autre! **2.** *Geol:* **giant's k.,** marmite, chaudière, de géant(s).

kettledrum ['ketldrʌm], *s. Mus:* timbale *f*; **to play the k.,** battre des timbales.

kettledrummer ['ketldrʌmər], *s. Mus:* timbalier *m*.

ketupa [ke't(j)u:pə], *s. Orn:* kétupa *m*, kétupu *m*.

Keuper ['kɔipər], *a. & s. Geol:* keuper (*m*).

key[1] [ki:], *s.* **1.** (*a*) clef *f,* clé *f* (de serrure, de porte, etc.); **pin k.,** clef bénarde; **piped k.,** clef forée; **paracentric k.,** clef paracentrique, clef de sûreté (pour serrure à barillet); **skeleton k.,** passe-partout *m inv*; **k. bit,** panneton *m* de clef; **k. drop,** cache-entrée *f inv* (de serrure); **k. pin,** broche *f* de serrure; **k. ring,** porte-clefs *m inv*; anneau brisé (pour clefs); **k. chain,** chainette *f* porte-clefs; **k. case,** étui *m* porte-clefs; (*in hotel, etc.*) **k. rack,** tableau *m* (pour clefs); **k. plate,** (i) écusson *m*; entrée *f* de serrure; (ii) *Lith:* planche *f* de trait (dans un report de couleurs); *Lith:* **k. transfer,** faux décalque; **k. money,** arrhes *fpl, F:* pas *m* de porte; **to put the k. in the lock,** introduire la clef dans la serrure; **to turn the k. (in the lock),** donner un tour de clef (à la porte); *F:* **to have the k. to the door,** atteindre sa majorité; *F:* **to get the k. of the street,** être mis à la porte; se trouver sans asile, sans abri; **Gibraltar, the k. to the Mediterranean,** Gibraltar, clef de la Méditerranée; **it was the k. to his success,** cela lui a ouvert les portes du succès; (*b*) *attrib.* d'une importance capitale, vitale; **k. factor,** facteur *m* clef; **k. post,** poste *m* clef; **k. industry,** industrie *f* clef; **k. man,** cheville ouvrière, pilier *m*, pivot *m* (d'un établissement, d'une organisation); **k. point, k. position,** position *f* clef; verrou *m*; *Mil: etc:* point vital, point qui commande une position, une zone; **k. per-**

sonnel, workers, staff, personnel *m* de base; *Ball:* **k. range,** distance *f* repère, de référence; *Ch:* **k. substance,** substance *f* de base; (*c*) *Theol:* **power of the keys,** pouvoir *m* des clefs; (*d*) **the (House of) Keys,** le Parlement de l'Ile de Man; **the House of the Keys,** la Maison de la Vallée (d'Andorre). **2.** (*a*) clef (d'une énigme, d'un mystère, etc.); **k. to a cipher,** clef d'un chiffre; *Chess:* **k. move,** premier coup (de la solution d'un problème); **I've got the k. to the puzzle,** je tiens le mot de l'énigme; (*b*) légende *f* (d'une carte, etc.); (*on squared map*) **k. numbers,** numéros *m* de repérage; (*c*) *Sch:* corrigé *m*; livre *m* du maître; traduction *f* (d'un texte au programme); solutions *fpl* (des problèmes); (*d*) *Cmptr:* indicatif *m*, critère *m* (de tri, d'identification, etc.). **3.** (*a*) *Mus:* **major, minor, k.,** ton majeur, mineur; **the k. of C,** le ton d'ut; **relative minor k.,** ton relatif mineur; **to transpose a piece to a higher k.,** élever le ton d'un morceau; **to speak in a high k.,** parler sur un ton aigu; *Mus:* **k. signature,** armature *f* (de la clef); signes accidentels, constitutifs; **to put the k. signature to a piece of music,** armer la clef; (*b*) *Art: etc:* caractéristique de luminosité (d'un tableau, d'une image); **landscape in a light k.,** paysage *m* d'une tonalité claire; **picture painted in a low k.,** tableau peint dans des tons sombres; *Cin:* **high-k., low-k., picture,** image lumineuse, sombre; **middle-k. picture,** image normale. **4.** (*a*) touche *f* (de piano, d'orgue); **k. action,** mécanisme *m* des touches (d'un piano); *Fig:* **to touch the right k.,** toucher la corde sensible; (*b*) touche (de machine à écrire, etc.); *Tp: Tg:* clef, touche (d'appel, etc.); *El:* manette *f*; *Tp: Tg:* **lever k.,** clef de commutation à bascule; **listening k.,** clef d'écoute; **speaking k.,** clef de conversation; **combined listening and speaking k.,** clef combinée d'écoute et de conversation; **interruption k.,** clef de rupture; **locking k.,** clef à enclenchement; **non-locking k.,** clef à retour automatique; **(current-)reversing k.,** clef d'inversion de courant; *Tg:* **(sending, signalling) k.,** manipulateur *m*; **Morse k.,** clef, manipulateur, Morse; **to work the k.,** manipuler; **k. jack,** jack *m* de manipulation; **k. clicks,** claquements *m* de manipulation; *Artil:* **firing k.,** détente *f*; (*c*) clef (d'un instrument à vent); plateau (d'une flûte Boehm, etc.). **5.** *Tchn:* (*a*) clef, carotte *f* (de robinet); (*b*) (*spanner*) **box k.,** clef à douille; **screw k.,** clef à écrous, clef de serrage; (*c*) remontoir *m* (de pendule, de jouet mécanique, etc.). **6.** (*a*) *Carp:* clef; **through-tenon joint with k.,** assemblage *m* à tenon passant avec clef; (*b*) *Mec.E: etc:* clavette *f*; cale *f*, coin *m*, clavette (d'arbre); *Rail:* coin (de coussinet de rail); **set k.,** coin prisonnier; **feather k.,** clavette linguiforme, languette *f* (d'arbre); **k. and gib,** clavette et contre-clavette; **gib-head k.,** clavette à mentonnet, à tête; **gib-heel k.,** clavette à talon; **flat k.,** clavette plate; **spring k.,** clavette fendue, à ressort; **sunk k.,** clavette encastrée, noyée; **tangent k.,** clavette tangentielle; **Woodruff k.,** clavette disque, Woodruff; **locking k.,** clavette de verrouillage; **retaining k.,** clavette de fixation; **tightening k.,** clavette de serrage; **k. drift,** chasse-clavette *m*, *pl.* chasse-clavettes; chasse-clef *m*, *pl.* chasse-clefs; **k. bolt,** boulon *m* à clavette, boulon freiné; **k. groove, k. slot, k. seat,** rainure *f* de clavette, de clavetage, de cale; logement *m* de clef; chemin *m*, mortaise *f*, de clavette; cannelure *f*; *Tls:* **k.-seat rule,** règle cornière pour tracer les rainures de clavetage; règle pour transmissions; (*c*) *El:* fiche *f*. **7.** (*a*) *Const:* rappointis *m*; **to rough brickwork and give the plaster a k.,** piquer la maçonnerie pour donner de la prise au plâtre; (*b*) *Carp:* adent *m* (pour empêcher une poutre, etc., de glisser). **8.** *Bot:* samare *f* (de frêne, d'érable).

key[2], *v.tr.* **1.** (*a*) *Mec.E:* clavet(t)er, coincer, caler (**a pulley on, to, a spindle,** une poulie sur un arbre); **to k. sth. with sth.,** lier qch. à qch.; rendre qch. solidaire de qch.; **keyed on,** clavet(t)é; monté à clavette(s); **keyed to . . .,** clavet(t)é, lié, à . . .; solidaire de . . .; *Rail:* **to k. the rails,** coincer les rails; (*b*) *Carp:* adenter (une planche). **2.** (*a*) *Mus:* **to k. (up) the strings of an instrument,** accorder un instrument; (*b*) **to k. s.o. up to doing sth.,** donner du cœur à qn pour l'amener à faire qch.; **crowd keyed up for the match,** foule tendue dans l'attente du match; **he was all keyed up,** il était crispé, tendu; (*c*) *Tg:* manipuler. **3.** *Arch:* **to k. (in) an arch,** bander une voûte. **4.** *Cmptr:* coder (l'information); **to k. in (a value),** introduire par l'intermédiaire d'un clavier, introduire manuellement, imposer (une valeur). **5.** *Com:* **to k. one's publicity,** assurer le repérage de sa publicité (par des particularités dans les annonces, etc.).

key[3], *s. Geog:* caye *f*, îlot *m* à fleur d'eau.

keyboard[1] ['ki:bɔ:d], *s.* **1.** clavier *m* (de piano, de machine à écrire, à calculer, etc.); clavecin *m* (de carillon); **pedal k.,** clavier des pédales (d'un orgue); *Typew:* **four-bank k.,** clavier à quatre rangées de touches; **k.-controlled, k.-operated,** commandé par clavier; **k. computer,** ordinateur *m* comptable (à clavier); **k. printer,** imprimante *f* à clavier; **k. perforator, k. punch,** perforatrice *f* à clavier. **2.** (*in hotel*) porte-clefs *m inv*; tableau *m*.

keyboard[2], *v.tr. Cmptr:* introduire par clavier (des textes).

key-driven ['ki:drivn], *a.* commandé par clavier, par touche; **k.-d. computer,** ordinateur *m* comptable (à clavier).

keyed [ki:d], *a.* **1.** *Mus:* (instrument) à touches. **2.** *Mec.E:* (assemblage, boulon) à clavette; **k. plates,** plaques goujonnées. **3.** *Tg:* manipulé; **k. continuous wave,** onde entretenue manipulée. **4.** *Arch:* **k. arch,** arc *m*, arche *f*, à clef.

keyhole ['ki:houl], *s.* (*a*) entrée *f* de (la) clef; trou *m* de (la) serrure; **to look through the k.,** regarder par le trou de la serrure; **k. saw,** scie *f* à guichet; scie d'entrée; (*b*) trou de clef (de pendule, de montre).

keying ['ki:iŋ], *s.* **1.** *Mec.E:* clavet(t)age *m*, calage *m*, coinçage *m*; **k. hammer,** marteau *m* chasse-coins; **k. wedge,** coin *m* de calage. **2.** *Mus:* accordage *m* (d'un piano). **3.** *Tg:* manipulation *f*; **k. wave,** onde *f* de manipulation, de travail; **k. cable, k. line,** câble *m*, ligne *f*, de télécommande, de télémanipulation. **4.** *Cmptr:* **k. (in),** introduction *f*, imposition *f*, au clavier; **k. equipment,** matériel *m* de perforation; **k. error,** erreur *f* de perforation; **k. speed,** vitesse *f* de frappe. **5.** *Arch:* **k. (in) of an arch,** clavage *m* d'une voûte.

keyless ['ki:lis], *a.* sans clef.

keynote ['ki:nout], *s. Mus:* tonique *f*; **this was the k. of his speech,** cela a été la note dominante, l'idée dominante, de son discours; **k. of a policy,** mot *m* d'ordre d'une politique; **quality was the k. of the exhibition,** l'exposition *f* a eu lieu sous le signe de la qualité.

keypunch[1] ['ki:pʌn(t)ʃ], *s. Cmptr:* perforatrice *f* à clavier; poinçonneuse *f*; **k. centre, department, section,** atelier *m* de perforation; **k. operator, girl,** perforatrice, perforeuse *f*; **k. supervisor,** monitrice *f* de perforation.

keypunch[2], *v.tr. Cmptr:* perforer (une carte, etc. au moyen d'un clavier).

keypuncher ['ki:pʌn(t)ʃər], *s. Cmptr:* (*pers.*) perforatrice *f*, perforeuse *f*.

keypunching ['ki:pʌn(t)ʃiŋ], *s. Cmptr:* perforation *f* (à l'aide d'un clavier); **k. error,** erreur *f* de perforation.

keysort ['ki:sɔ:t], *attrib. Cmptr:* **k. card,** carte *f* à perforations marginales.

keystone ['ki:stoun], *s.* clef *f* de voûte; claveau droit; clausoir *m*; voussoir *m* de clef; **ornamental k.,** agrafe *f*; **hanging k.,** clef pendante; **to put the k. in place,** fermer la voûte; **considerations which are the k. of a policy,** considérations qui constituent la clef de voûte, le pivot, d'une politique; *Cin:* **k. effect,** distorsion due à un angle de projection excessif; **k. picture,** image raccourcie vers le haut ou vers le bas.

keystroke ['ki:strouk], *s. Cmptr:* frappe *f* (d'une touche).

keyway ['ki:wei], *s.* **1.** entrée *f* de serrure. **2.** *Mec.E: etc:* rainure *f* de clavette, de clavetage, de cale; logement *m* de clef; chemin *m*, mortaise *f*, de clavette; cannelure *f*; **k. cutting machine,** (i) machine *f* à tailler, à mortaiser, les rainures de cale; (ii) machine à fraiser les rainures de cale; **k. cutter, k. cutting tool,** outil *m* à tailler les rainures, à rainurer, à rainer; machine à canneler portative; **k. milling machine,** machine à fraiser les rainures de cale.

keyword ['ki:wə:d], *s.* mot-clef *m*, mot-clé *m*, *pl.* mots-clefs, -clés.

Kezia(h) [ki'zaiə]. *Pr.n.f. B.Hist:* Ketsia.

khaki ['kɑ:ki]. **1.** *s. Tex:* kaki *m*. **2.** kaki *inv*.

Khalkidike [kælki'di:ki]. *Pr.n. Geog:* Chalcidique *f*.

khamsin ['kæmsin], *s. Meteor:* khamsin *m*.

khan[1] [kɑ:n], *s.* (*inn*) kan *m*; caravansérail *m*.

khan[2], *s.* (*chief*) khan *m*, kan *m*.

khanate ['kɑ:neit], *s.* khanat *m*.

Kharbin ['kɑ:bin]. *Pr.n. Geog:* Kharbine *m*.

kharif [kə'ri:f], *s.* saison *f* des pluies (au Soudan).

khat [kæt], *s. Bot:* kat *m*, qat *m*.

khedive [ke'di:v], *s.* khédive *m*.

khediv(i)ate [ke'di:v(i)eit], *s.* khédivat *m*, khédiviat *m*.

Khivan ['ki:vən]. *Geog:* (*a*) *a.* kivien; (*b*) *s.* Kivien, -ienne.

Khyber ['kaibər]. *Pr.n. Geog:* **the K. Pass,** le Khaïber; la Passe de Khaïber.

kiang [kjæŋ], *s. Z:* hémione *m*.

kibble[1] ['kibl], *s. Min:* benne *f*, cuf(f)at *m*, tonne *f*, tine *f*.

kibble[2], *v.tr.* égruger (le blé, etc.).

kibbling ['kibliŋ], *s.* égrugeage *m*; **k. mill,** moulin *m* à égruger.

kibbutz, *pl.* **-zim** [ki'buts, kibut'si:m], *s. Agr:* kibboutz, *pl.* kibboutzim.

kibe [kaib], *s. O:* engelure *f*, gerçure *f* (surtout au talon); mule *f*.

kibitz ['kibits], *v.i. F:* (*a*) suivre une partie de cartes en donnant son avis; (*b*) donner des conseils non sollicités, se mêler de ce qui ne vous regarde pas.

kibitzer ['kibitsər], *s.* celui, celle, qui donne des conseils non sollicités, qui se mêle de tout; canule *f*, casse-pieds *m inv*.

kibosh[1] ['kaibɔʃ], *s. F:* **1.** bêtises *fpl*; de la blague. **2. to put the k. on sth.,** esquinter, bousiller, qch.; mettre fin à qch.

kibosh[2], *v.tr. F:* faire avorter (une affaire); mettre fin à (une affaire).

kick[1] [kik], *s.* **1.** (*a*) coup *m* de pied; *Fb: etc:* **free k.,** coup de pied franc; **goal k.,** coup de pied de but; **overhead k.,** coup de pied retourné; **cross k.,** coup de pied croisé; *Ski:* **k. turn,** conversion *f*; virage *m* en plaine; (*of motor cycle*) **k. starter,** pédale *f* de mise en marche; lanceur *m*; démarreur *m* au pied, kick(-starter) *m*; *F:* **to get more kicks than ha'pence,** recevoir plus de coups que de pain, que de caresses; *F:* **to get the k.,** être saqué, mis à la porte; *F:* **it's better than a k. in the pants,** ça vaut mieux qu'un coup de pied au cul, au derrière; (*b*) ruade *f* (d'un cheval, etc.). **2.** (*a*) vigueur *f*, énergie *f*; **if that horse had any k. in him,** si ce cheval était plus fringant; *F:* **he's got no k. left in him,** il est complètement à plat, vide, pompé; (*b*) *F:* **a drink with a k. in it,** une boisson qui vous remonte, qui gratte; **to get a k. out of (doing) sth.,** prendre plaisir à qch.; être tout excité de faire qch.; **I get quite a k. out of skiing,** ça me remonte de faire du ski; **I don't get much of a k. out of it,** ça ne me fait pas grand effet; **to do sth. for kicks,** faire qch. pour s'amuser; faire ce qui vous chante; (*c*) *F:* résistance *f*, opposition *f*; **to have a k. at sth.,** regimber contre qch.; (*d*) *P:* plainte(s) *f(pl)*, grogne *f*, rouspétance *f*; (*e*) *P:* **to go on a k.,** se lancer dans la drogue, prendre le pied, aller à la défonce; **bum kicks,** mauvaise expérience d'une drogue, mauvais voyage. **3.** (*a*) recul *m*, réaction *f*, repoussement *m*, bourrade *f* (d'un fusil); cahot *m*, secousse *f* (d'un mécanisme, etc.); (*b*) *I.C.E:* = KICKBACK; (*c*) *Nau:* (*order to engine room*) **one k. ahead, astern!** un tour en avant, en arrière! **4.** *Fb:* **a good, bad, k.,** joueur *m* qui a un bon, un mauvais, coup de pied.

kick[2], *v.*

I. *v.i.* & *tr.* **1.** *v.i.* (*a*) donner un coup de pied, des coups de pied; (*of animal*) ruer, lancer des ruades; (*b*) *Sp:* (*of athlete*) démarrer; (*c*) (*of pers.*) *F:* grogner, rouspéter; **to k. at, against, sth.,** regimber contre qch.; répugner à qch.; **to k. at fate,** se cabrer contre son destin; **to k. at doing sth.,** rechigner à faire qch.; **he didn't (even) k. at it,** il s'est laissé faire; il n'a pas rouspété; (*d*) (*of gun*) reculer, repousser. **2.** *v.tr.* (*a*) donner un coup de pied, des coups de pied, à (qn, qch.); pousser (qn, qch.) du pied; (*of horse, etc.*) détacher un coup de pied à (qn); **to get kicked,** recevoir des coups de pied; *Fb:* **to k. the ball,** botter le ballon; **to k. a goal,** marquer un but; **he kicked the ball in through the window,** d'un coup de pied il a fait entrer le ballon par la fenêtre; **he kicked the ball (up) into the air,** d'un coup de pied il a fait rebondir le ballon (dans l'air); **to k. a ball about,** donner des coups de pied à un ballon; **to k. sth. away, aside,** repousser qch. du pied; écarter qch. à coups de pied, d'un coup de pied; **to k. s.o. downstairs,** faire dégringoler l'escalier à qn; *F:* **to k. s.o.'s behind,** botter qn; flanquer à qn un coup de pied au cul, au derrière; *P:* **to k. the bucket,** mourir, casser sa pipe, lâcher la rampe, claquer; **to k. a man when he's down,** donner le coup de pied de l'âne à qn; **he could have kicked himself for being so shy,** il s'en voulait de sa timidité; **I felt like kicking myself,** je me serais donné des claques; (*b*) **the gun kicked my shoulder,** j'ai reçu le recul du fusil sur l'épaule.

II. (*compound verbs*) **1. kick around,** *F:* (*a*) *v.i.* traîner; rouler sa bosse; **there are plenty of people like that kicking around,** des gens comme ça, ce n'est pas ça qui manque; (*b*) *v.tr.* **to k. s.o. around,** traiter qn sans ménagements.

2. kick back. (*a*) *v.i.* (i) *I.C.E:* (*of engine*) donner des retours en arrière; (ii) rendre un coup de pied (à qn); *F:* (*of pers.*) réagir; regimber; **if you do him a wrong he'll k. back,** faites-lui du tort et il vous le rendra; (*b*) *v.tr.* relancer (un ballon); **to k. sth. back into place,** remettre qch. à sa place avec un mouvement, un coup, de pied.

3. kick in. (*a*) *v.tr.* **to k. (the door, etc.) in,** enfoncer (la porte, etc.) à coups de pied, d'un coup de pied; (*b*) *v.i. F:* payer sa part, son écot.

4. kickoff. (*a*) *v.tr.* enlever (qch.) d'un coup de pied; **to k. off one's shoes,** enlever, se débarrasser de, ses chaussures d'un mouvement brusque du pied; (*b*) *v.i.* (i) *Fb:* donner le coup d'envoi; mettre le ballon en jeu; (ii)

F: démarrer, partir, lever l'ancre.

5. kick out. (*a*) *v.tr.* chasser (qn) à coups de pied; *F:* **to be kicked out,** être mis à la porte, être saqué; *Fb:* **to k. (the ball) out,** renvoyer (le ballon); *Cmptr:* sortir (des données) de la mémoire; (*b*) *v.i.* (*of horse, etc.*) lancer des ruades.

6. kick over, *v.tr.* renverser (qch.) d'un coup de pied.

7. kick up, *v.tr. F:* **to k. up a fuss,** faire des embarras; **to k. up a dust,** faire une scène; **to k. up a row, a racket, a shindy,** faire du tapage, du boucan.

kick[3], *s.* **1.** culot *m* (d'une bouteille); cône *m* (de fond de bouteille). **2.** mentonnet *m* (d'une lame de couteau pliant).

kickback ['kikbæk], *s.* (*a*) *I.C.E:* retour *m* en arrière; *Aut:* **starting-handle k.,** retour de manivelle; (*b*) *F:* réaction violente, coup *m* en boomerang; (*c*) *F:* ristourne *f*, dessous-de-table *m inv*; (*d*) *P:* récidive *f* dans la drogue, rebranchage *m.*

kickdown ['kikdaun], *s. Aut:* (*automatic gearbox*) **k. switch,** rétro-contact *m*, *pl.* rétro-contacts.

kicker ['kikər], *s.* **1.** (*a*) donneur *m* de coups de pied; (*b*) *Fb:* joueur *m*; (*c*) *F:* **high k.,** (i) *Th:* danseuse *f* de cancan, de chahut; (ii) chahuteur, -euse. **2.** (*a*) cheval *m*, etc., qui rue; rueur, -euse; (*b*) *esp. U.S: F:* (*pers.*) ronchonot *m*; rouspéteur, -euse.

kicking[1] ['kikiŋ], *a.* **1.** (enfant *m*) qui gigote; (cheval *m*) qui rue. **2.** *Cr: Ten:* (balle *f*) qui rebondit vivement.

kicking[2], *s.* **1.** coups *mpl* de pied; (*of animal*) ruades *fpl.* **2.** *Harn:* **k. strap,** plate-longe *f*, *pl.* plates-longes. **3.** recul *m*, repoussement *m* (d'un fusil).

kick-off ['kikɔf], *s.* **1.** *Fb:* coup *m* d'envoi; coup de pied de départ; *Fig: F:* démarrage *m*; **k.-o. at two o'clock,** la partie commence à deux heures. **2. a good k.-o. from the springboard,** un bon coup d'appel sur le tremplin.

kickshaw ['kikʃɔ:], *s. A:* **1.** *Cu:* friandise *f*. **2.** bagatelle *f*, colifichet *m.*

kickstand ['kikstænd], *s.* béquille *f* (de bicyclette).

kick-up ['kikʌp], *s.* **1.** *F:* tapage *m*, boucan *m*, chahut *m*. **2.** *Mec.E:* butée *f*. **3.** (*a*) *Mth: etc:* **k.-up of a curve,** saut *m* brusque d'une courbe; (*b*) *Aut: O:* courbure *f* du châssis; **k.-up chassis,** châssis à arrière relevé.

kid[1] [kid], *s.* **1.** (*a*) *Z:* chevreau *m,f.* chevrette; **goat in k.,** chèvre pleine; (*b*) (peau *f* de) chevreau, cabron *m*; **k. gloves,** *Com:* **kids,** gants *m* (en peau) de chevreau; **you can't fight your way through life with k. gloves,** la vie ne se prend pas avec des gants; **to handle s.o. with k. gloves,** ménager qn. **2.** *F:* (*a*) mioche *mf*, gosse *mf*, gamin, -ine; **my k. brother,** mon petit frère; (*b*) *U.S: F:* **say, k.!** dis-moi, mon petit, ma petite.

kid[2], *v.* (**kidded**) **1.** *v.tr.* (*of goat*) mettre bas (un chevreau). **2.** *v.i.* (*of goat*) chevroter, chevretter, biqueter; mettre bas.

kid[3], *v.tr. F:* raconter des histoires à (qn); en conter à (qn); bonimenter (qn); faire marcher (qn); **you're kidding us,** tout ça c'est des blagues; **no kidding!** sans blague! **to k. s.o. that. . .,** faire accroire à qn que. . .; **to k. oneself,** se bercer d'espoirs; s'en faire accroire; se faire des illusions; **she kids herself that she's musical,** elle s'imagine être musicienne; **who are you trying to k.?** tu te fiches de moi? **are you kidding?** tu me fais marcher?

kid[4], *s. Nau:* (**mess**) **k.,** gamelle *f*, écuelle *f*, gamelot *m.*

kidder ['kidər], *s. F:* blagueur, -euse: conteur, -euse; bonimenteur, -euse.

kiddie, kiddy ['kidi], **kiddywink** ['kidiwiŋk], *s. F:* petit(e) gosse; mioche *mf.*

kiddiecar ['kidika:r], *s.* (*a*) voiture *f* à pédales (pour enfant); (*b*) *U.S:* tricycle *m* (pour enfant).

kiddle ['kidl], *s. Fish:* **1.** gord *m*, guideau *m* (de rivière). **2.** parc *m* (de pêche côtière).

kid-glove ['kid'glʌv], *a. F:* **to give s.o. the k.-g. treatment,** ménager qn; traiter qn avec beaucoup de considération, beaucoup de soin.

kidling ['kidliŋ], *s. F:* jeune chevreau *m*; cabri *m*, biquet *m.*

kidnap ['kidnæp], *v.tr.* (**kidnapped**) enlever (qn) de vive force; voler (un enfant); kidnapper (qn).

kidnapper ['kidnæpər], *s.* auteur *m* d'un enlèvement; voleur, -euse, ravisseur, -euse (d'enfant); kidnapper *mf*, kidnappeur, -euse.

kidnapping ['kidnæpiŋ], *s.* kidnapping *m*; enlèvement *m*; vol *m* (d'enfant); *Jur:* (délit *m* de) rapt *m* (d'enfant).

kidney ['kidni], *s.* **1.** (*a*) *Anat:* rein *m*; *Med:* **floating k.,** rein mobile, flottant; néphroptose *f*; **stone in the kidneys,** calcul rénal; (*b*) **two people of the same k.,** deux personnes du même acabit, du même tonneau, de (la) même farine; **men of that k.,** hommes de cet acabit; **a man of his k.,** un homme de sa trempe; (*c*) *Med:* **k. tray,** cuvette *f* à pansements réniforme, *F:* haricot *m*. **2.** (*a*) *Cu:* rognon *m*; **devilled kidneys,** rognons à la diable; (*b*) *Geol:* rognon (de silex, etc.); **k. ore,** hématite *f* rouge en rognons; **k. stone,** néphrite *f*; rognon de silex; (*c*) *Hort:* **k. bean,** (i) haricot nain; (ii) haricot d'Espagne, à grappes; **k. potato,** vitelotte *f*; *Bot:* **k. vetch,** (anthyllide *f*) vulnéraire *f*; trèfle *m* jaune.

kidneyroot ['kidniru:t], *s. U.S: Bot:* eupatoire pourprée.

kidney-shaped ['kidniʃeipt], *a.* (table, etc.) en forme de haricot; *Nat Hist:* réniforme; *Geol:* **k.-s. concretion,** rognon *m.*

kidskin ['kidskin], *s.* peau *f* de chevreau; cabron *m*; *attrib.* en peau de chevreau.

kier[1] ['kiər], *s. Tex:* autoclave *m* à blanchiment; cuve à débouillir.

kier[2], *v.tr. Tex:* blanchir à l'autoclave.

kieselguhr ['ki:zlguər], *s. Miner:* kieselguhr *m.*

kieserite ['ki:zərait], *s. Miner:* kiesérite *f.*

kike [kaik], *s. U.S: P: Pej:* juif *m*, youpin *m.*

kilampere ['kilæmpɛər], *s. El.Meas:* kiloampère *m.*

kilderkin ['kildəkin], *s. Com:* baril *m* (de 72 à 80 litres).

kilerg ['kilə:g], *s. Ph.Meas:* kiloerg *m.*

Kilkenny [kil'keni], *Pr.n. Geog:* Kilkenny; **to fight like K. cats,** se battre comme chien et chat; se battre (l'un contre l'autre) en furieux; se combattre avec acharnement.

kill[1], *s.* **1.** *Ven:* (*a*) mise *f* à mort (du renard, du cerf, etc.); (*b*) gibier tué; le tableau. **2.** (*a*) *Mil: etc:* destruction *f*, élimination *f* (de l'ennemi); **k. potential,** potentiel *m* de destruction; **k. probability,** probabilité *f*, chances *fpl*, de destruction; **single-shot k. probability,** probabilité, chances, de destruction par un coup isolé; (*b*) *F:* assassinat *m*; descente *f* (d'avion ennemi); coulée *f* (d'un navire ennemi). **3.** *Ten:* smash *m.*

kill[2], *v.*

I. *v.tr.* **1.** (*a*) tuer, faire mourir (qn, une plante); faire périr (qn); *Mil:* détruire, éliminer (l'ennemi); tuer, abattre (un animal); descendre (une perdrix, un homme); **Marius attacked them and killed a hundred thousand of their men,** Marius les attaqua et leur tua cent mille hommes; **thou shalt not k.,** tu ne tueras point; **k. or cure remedy,** remède *m* héroïque; **to be hard to k.,** avoir l'âme chevillée au corps, chevillée dans le corps; avoir la vie dure; **this superstition will be hard to k.,** cette superstition aura la vie dure; *F:* **to k. a bottle,** sécher une bouteille; **to k. two birds with one stone,** faire d'une pierre deux coups; faire coup double; **to k. s.o. with kindness,** faire du mal à qn par excès de bonté; **you're killing me with suspense, you're killing me by inches,** vous me faites mourir d'impatience, vous me faites mourir à petit feu; *F:* **he was laughing fit to k. himself,** il crevait de rire; **to k. oneself (with work),** se tuer à (force de) travailler; se donner un mal de chien; *F:* **to be out to k.,** se donner, prendre, des airs de conquérant; **to be dressed to k.,** porter une toilette irrésistible, ébouriffante; être en grand tralala; (*b*) (*of butcher*) abattre, tuer (un bœuf, etc.); (*with passive force*) (*of beast*) **to k. well,** donner un bon rendement (de viande); (*c*) **to k. the nerve of a tooth,** tuer le nerf d'une dent; (*d*) *Ven:* servir la bête. **2. to k. time,** tuer le temps; **to k. ambition,** éteindre l'ambition; **to k. all feelings of humanity,** détruire, étouffer, tout sentiment d'humanité; *Pol:* **to k. a bill,** couler un projet de loi; **the carpet kills the curtains,** le tapis fait passer les rideaux inaperçus, enlève tout effet aux rideaux; le tapis tue les rideaux; *Publ: Journ:* **to k. a passage,** supprimer un passage; **killed matter,** matière restée sur le marbre; *Typ:* **to k. type,** distribuer de la composition. **3.** (*a*) amortir (le son); **room that kills sound,** (i) pièce sourde; (ii) pièce insonorisée; (*b*) *Ch:* neutraliser (un acide, etc.); *Plumb: etc:* décomposer, neutraliser (l'esprit de sel); **to k. lime,** éteindre, amortir, la chaux; **to k. smells,** neutraliser les odeurs; (*c*) *Petr:* **to k. a well,** arrêter une éruption dans un puits (de pétrole); (*d*) *Metall:* débarrasser (la fonte) des gaz dissous; calmer (l'acier); (*e*) *Soapm:* **to k. the goods,** empâter le corps gras; (*f*) *Tan:* dégraisser (une peau). **4.** *Sp:* (*a*) *Fb:* bloquer (le ballon); (*b*) *Ten:* tuer, massacrer (la balle).

II. (*compound verb*) **kill off,** *v.tr.* (*a*) exterminer (toute une population, etc.); (*b*) **the author kills off his hero in the last chapter,** l'auteur fait mourir son héros, se débarrasse de son héros, au dernier chapitre.

killdeer ['kildi:ər], *s. Orn:* gravelot *m* à double collier, *Fr.C:* pluvier *m* kildir.

killed [kild], *a.* **1.** tué, abattu; *F:* descendu; *Mil:* (*of the enemy*) détruit, éliminé. **2.** *Tchn:* (*a*) *Ch:* (*of acid, etc.*) neutralisé; *Plumb: etc:* **k. spirits,** acide saturé; esprit de sel décomposé, neutralisé; *F:* eau *f* à souder; (*b*) *Metall:* **k. steel,** acier calmé; **semi-k. steel,** acier demi-calmé.

killer ['kilər], *s.* **1.** (*a*) tueur, -euse, meurtrier *m*; **k. disease,** maladie meurtrière; (*b*) *Z:* **k. (whale),** épaulard *m*. **2.** (*in slaughtering*) **humane k.,** revolver *m* d'abattage. **3. insect k., fly k.,** insecticide *m.*

killick ['kilik], *s. Nau:* **1.** petite ancre; grosse pierre servant à ancrer. **2.** *F:* matelot breveté de première classe; *F:* **to dip the k.,** être dégradé.

killing[1] ['kiliŋ], *a.* **1.** (*a*) meurtrier, assassin; **k. frost,** gelée meurtrière; (*b*) (*in compounds*) **germ-k.,** microbicide. **2.** (*a*) (métier) tuant, assommant, écrasant; (*b*) **k. anxiety,** inquiétude mortelle; **all this anxiety is k.,** toutes ces inquiétudes me font mourir. **3.** *F:* **it's too k. for words,** c'est à mourir de rire; c'est à se tordre les côtes; **to have a k. time,** s'amuser follement; **k. story,** histoire crevante.

killing[2], *s.* **1.** (*a*) tuerie *f*, abattage *m* (d'animaux); (*in bullfight*) mise *f* à mort; (*b*) meurtre *m*; (*c*) *Mil:* destruction *f*, élimination *f* (de l'ennemi); (*d*) *attrib.* **k. power of a shell,** effet meurtrier d'un obus; (*of shotgun*) **k. circle,** gerbe *f* de plombs efficaces; **k. bottle,** flacon *m* de cyanure de potassium (d'entomologiste); (*e*) *F:* **to make a k.,** faire un bénéfice énorme, une affaire à tout casser. **2.** *Tchn:* (*a*) amortissement *m* (des sons); (*b*) *Petr:* arrêt *m* de l'éruption (d'un puits de pétrole); (*c*) *Ch:* neutralisation *f* (d'un acide, etc.); *Plumb: etc:* décomposition *f*, neutralisation (de l'esprit de sel); (*d*) *Metall:* élimination des gaz dissous (de la fonte); calmage *m* (de l'acier); (*e*) *Soapm:* empâtement *m* (du corps gras); (*f*) *Tan:* dégraissage *m* (des peaux).

killingly ['kiliŋli], *adv. F:* **k. funny story,** histoire *f* à mourir de rire, à crever de rire; histoire tordante.

killjoy ['kildʒɔi], *s.* rabat-joie *m inv*, empêcheur *m* de danser en rond, trouble-fête *m inv*; **k. expression,** face *f* de carême, d'enterrement.

kiln[1] [kiln], *s.* **1.** (*a*) four *m* (céramique); **brick k.,** four à briques; **lime k.,** four à chaux, chaufour *m*; **cement k.,** four à ciment; **coke k.,** four à coke; **cracking k.,** four de craquage; **roasting k.,** four de grillage; (*b*) séchoir *m*, sécherie *f*, étuve *f*; **humidity-regulated k.,** étuve, séchoir, à réglage d'humidité; **water-spray k.,** four de séchage à projection, à vaporisation, d'eau; **hop k.,** four, séchoir, à houblon; *Brew:* **malt k.,** touraille *f*; **hemp k.,** haloir *m*, hâloir *m*; *Hort:* **seed k.,** four à sécher; sécherie; **k. drying, seasoning,** séchage *m* au four; étuvage *m*; *Brew:* touraillage *m* (du malt). **2. charcoal k.,** meule *f* (de charbon de bois).

kiln[2], *v.tr.* **1.** (*a*) cuire (des briques); (*b*) étuver (l'émail, la laque). **2. to k. (dry),** étuver; sécher (le houblon, etc.) au four, (des graines) à l'étuve; *Brew:* tourailler (le malt).

kilning ['kilniŋ], *s.* **1.** (*a*) *Cer: etc:* cuisson *f*; (*b*) étuvage *m* (de l'émail). **2.** séchage *m* au four; étuvage *m*; *Brew:* touraillage *m* (du malt).

kilo ['ki:lou], *s. Meas: F:* (= KILOGRAMME) kilo *m.*

kilo- ['kilə, -ou], *pref.* kilo-.

kilocalorie [kilou'kæləri], *s. Ph.Meas:* kilocalorie *f*, millithermie *f.*

kilocycle ['kiləsaikl], *s. Ph: El:* kilocycle *m*; kilohertz *m.*

kiloerg ['kilouə:g], *s. Ph.Meas:* kiloerg *m.*

kilogram(me) ['kiləgræm], *s. Meas:* kilogramme *m.*

kilogrammetre [kilə'græmitər], *s. Ph.Meas:* kilogrammètre *m*; mètre-kilogramme *m*, *pl.* mètres-kilogrammes.

kiloherz ['kilouhə:ts], *s. Meas:* kilohertz *m.*

kilojoule ['kiloudʒu:l], *s. Meas:* kilojoule *m.*

kilolitre ['kiləli:tər], *s. Meas:* kilolitre *m.*

kilometre ['kiləmi:tər, *esp. NAm:* ki'ləmitər], *s. Meas:* kilomètre *m*; **to measure in kilometres,** kilométrer (une route, etc.); **length in kilometres,** kilométrage *m*; **distance in kilometres,** distance *f* kilométrique; *Rail:* **ton kilometres,** tonnes-kilomètres marchandises; **passenger kilometres,** voyageurs kilomètres.

kilometric [kilə'metrik], *a.* kilométrique; **k. grid,** carroyage *m*, quadrillage *m*, kilométrique; *Ph:* **k. wave,** onde *f* kilométrique.

kiloton ['kiloutʌn], *s. Meas:* kilotonne *f*; **a twenty k. atomic bomb,** une bombe atomique de vingt kilotonnes.

kilovar ['kilouva:r], *s. El.Meas:* kilovar *m*; **k.-hour,** kilovar-heure *m*, *pl.* kilovar-heures.

kilovolt ['kiləvoult], *s. El.Meas:* kilovolt *m*; **k.-ampere,** kilovolt-ampère *m*, *pl.* kilovolts-ampères; **k.-ampere-hour,** kilovolt-ampère-heure *m*, *pl.* kilovolt-ampère-heures.

kilowatt ['kiləwɔt], *s. El.Meas:* kilowatt *m*; **k.-hour,** kilowatt-heure *m*, *pl.* kilowatt-heures.

kilt[1] [kilt], *s. Cost:* (*a*) kilt (écossais); (*b*) fustanelle *f* (de soldat grec).

kilt[2], *v.tr.* **1.** *O:* **to k. (up) one's skirts,** retrousser ses jupes. **2.** plisser (l'étoffe).

kilted ['kiltid], *a.* **1.** portant le kilt. **2.** (*a*) *O:* (*of skirt*) retroussé; (*b*) (*of cloth, garment*) plissé.

kilter ['kiltər], *s. NAm: F:* bonne condition; **out of k.,** (i) en panne; (ii) en porte à faux.

kilting ['kiltiŋ], *s.* **1.** (*a*) *O:* retroussement *m* (de jupes);

(*b*) (i) plissement *m* (de l'étoffe); (ii) plissure *f*. **2.** plissé *m*.

kimberlite ['kimbəlait], *s. Geol: Min:* kimberlite *f*.

Kimeridgian [kimə'ridʒiən], *a.* & *s. Geol:* kiméridgien (*m*).

kimono [ki'mounou], *s. Cost:* kimono *m*.

kin [kin], *s.* **1.** (*a*) *Dial:* race *f*; (*b*) souche *f* (d'une famille). **2.** (*a*) parents *mpl*; **his k.,** ses parents, sa parenté; **lineal k.,** parent(s) en ligne directe; **collateral k.,** parent(s) en ligne collatérale; (*b*) **to be of k. to s.o.,** être parent de qn, apparenté avec qn, allié à qn; **we are k.,** nous sommes parents; **he is no k. to me,** il ne m'est rien; **next of k.,** la famille, le parent le plus proche; **to inform the next of k.,** prévenir la famille.

kinaes- (*e.g.* **kinaesthesia**) *See* KINES-.

kinase ['kineis, 'kaineis], *s. Biol: Ch:* kinase *f*.

kinchin ['kintʃin], *s. P: A:* gosse *mf*; **k. lay,** vol *m* de l'argent confié aux enfants envoyés faire des commissions.

kind[1] [kaind], *s.* **1.** (*race*) espèce *f*, genre *m*. **2.** (*a*) (*class, sort*) genre, espèce, sorte *f*; **(of) what k. is it?** de quelle sorte (est-ce)? **the best kinds of books,** les meilleurs livres; **what k. of tree is this?** quelle sorte d'arbre est-ce? **what k. of man is he?** quel genre d'homme est-ce? **what k. of man do you take me for?** pour qui me prenez-vous? **he is the k. of man who will hit back,** il est homme à se défendre, à se venger; **people of all kinds,** des gens de toutes sortes; **of the same k.,** du même genre; **perfect of its k.,** parfait dans son genre; **something of the k.,** quelque chose de pareil, de semblable; quelque chose de ce genre; **he said something of the k.,** il a dit quelque chose d'approchant; **nothing of the k.,** rien de la sorte; rien de semblable; **he did nothing of the k.,** il n'a rien fait de pareil; **do nothing of the k.!** gardez-vous-en bien! **we had coffee of a k.,** nous avons bu quelque chose qui pouvait passer pour du café; **in a k. of a way,** en quelque façon; **that's the k. of thing I mean,** c'est à peu près ce que je veux dire; **he felt a k. of compunction,** il ressentait comme des remords; **she was with them as a k. of maid,** elle était comme qui dirait leur bonne; **the trees formed a k. of arch,** les arbres formaient comme une arche; **a k. of sour taste,** un goût assez âpre; *Theol:* **communion in both kinds,** communion *f* sous les deux espèces; (*b*) (i) **this k. of man,** ce genre d'hommes; les hommes de cette sorte; **I can't bear these kinds of things,** je ne peux pas supporter ces choses-là; (ii) *P:* **k. of** (*occ. written* **kinda** ['kaində]); **he k. of sniffed,** il a reniflé ou presque; **I k. of expected it,** je m'en doutais presque; **it's k. of chilly,** il fait plutôt froid; **he looks k. of stupid,** il a l'air plutôt bête. **3.** *A:* (*nature*) **the law of k.,** la loi de la nature. **4.** *A:* (*character*) **they act after their k.,** ils agissent conformément à leur nature. **5. in k.:** (*a*) **they differ in k., not merely in degree,** ils diffèrent en nature et non seulement en degré; **difference in k.,** différence *f* spécifique; (*b*) **payment in k.,** paiement *m*, livraison *f*, en nature; **to repay s.o. in k.,** (i) rembourser qn en nature; (ii) payer qn de la même monnaie; rendre à qn la monnaie de sa pièce.

kind[2], *a.* **1.** bon, aimable, bienveillant, bienfaisant, prévenant; **a k. heart,** un bon cœur; **they are k. people,** ce sont des gens aimables; ce sont de braves gens; **k. words,** bonnes paroles, paroles bienveillantes; **k. invitation,** aimable invitation *f*; **to give s.o. a k. reception,** faire bon accueil à qn; **to give a project a k. reception,** recevoir une proposition favorablement; **give him my k. regards,** faites-lui mes amitiés; **to be k. to s.o.,** se montrer bon pour, envers, qn; être plein de bontés pour qn; **it's very k. of you,** c'est bien aimable de votre part, **it's very k. of you to . . .,** c'est bien aimable de votre part, à vous, de. . .; **(would you) be k. enough to, so k. as to . . .,** soyez assez bon pour . . .; ayez la bonté de . . .; ayez la complaisance de . . .; voulez-vous être assez aimable pour . . .; voulez-vous avoir l'amabilité de. . .; veuillez (bien). . .; **you are really too k.,** vous êtes vraiment trop aimable; **k. wind,** vent ami. **2.** *A:* tendre, aimant. **3.** (*a*) *A:* (*of soil, metals, etc.*) favorable, propice, facile à travailler; **k. strata,** couches *f* favorables; (*b*) **detergents are not k. to my skin,** ma peau supporte mal les détergents.

kinda ['kaində], *adv. P: see* KIND[1] 2 (*b*).

kindergarten ['kindəgɑ:tn], *s. Sch:* jardin *m* d'enfants; école maternelle.

kind-hearted ['kaind'hɑ:tid], *a.* (qui a le cœur) bon; bienfaisant; **he is a k.-h. man,** c'est un bon cœur.

kindheartedly ['kaind'hɑ:tidli], *adv.* avec bonté, avec bienveillance.

kind-heartedness ['kaind'hɑ:tidnis], *s.* bonté *f* de cœur; bienveillance *f*.

kindle ['kindl]. **1.** *v.tr.* (*a*) allumer (une flamme, un feu); enflammer, embraser (du charbon, une forêt); (*b*) allumer (la haine); faire naître, susciter (les passions); enflammer (le courage, les désirs); embraser (le cœur); aviver (les soupçons, le chagrin); exciter (le zèle). **2.** *v.i.* (*a*) (*of fire, wood, etc.*) s'allumer, s'enflammer, prendre feu; (*b*) (*of passions*) s'allumer, s'enflammer; **his eyes kindled,** ses yeux *m* s'allumèrent, (*with anger*) s'enflammèrent.

kindler ['kindlər], *s.* **1.** *Lit:* excitateur, -trice (de désirs, etc.). **2.** allume-feu *m inv*.

kindliness ['kaindlinis], *s.* **1.** bonté *f*, bienveillance *f*. **2.** (*a*) douceur *f* (de climat); (*b*) *Ind: O:* tractabilité *f* (des matériaux).

kindling ['kindliŋ], *s.* **1.** allumage *m*, embrasement *m*, enflammement *m*. **2. k. (wood),** bois *m* d'allumage, petit bois; allume-feu *m inv*.

kindly[1] ['kaindli], *adv.* avec bonté; favorablement; **he spoke very k. to me,** (i) il m'a dit des choses bien aimables; (ii) il m'a parlé avec (une grande) bonté; **he spoke very k. of you,** il a dit des choses très aimables à votre égard; **he very k. spoke to me,** il a eu la bonté de me parler; **to be k. disposed towards s.o.,** éprouver de la sympathie pour qn; être bien disposé envers qn; **would you k. close the door,** (i) voulez-vous avoir la bonté de, veuillez (bien), voulez-vous bien, fermer la porte; (ii) (*in exasperation*) mais fermez la porte, je vous en prie! **k. sit down!** mais asseyez-vous donc! *Com:* **k. remit by cheque,** prière de nous couvrir par chèque; **to take sth. k.,** bien prendre qch.; prendre qch. en bonne part; **I should take it k. if. . .,** cela me ferait bien plaisir si . . .; **to take k. to s.o., to sth.,** prendre qn en amitié; trouver qn sympathique; s'adonner volontiers à qch.; **not to take k. to s.o., to sth.,** ne pas aimer qn, qch.; trouver qn peu sympathique; ne pas s'accommoder de qch.

kindly[2], *a.* **1.** (*a*) bon, bienveillant; bienfaisant; **to have a k. feeling towards s.o.,** ressentir de la sympathie pour qn; **k. tone, advice,** ton, conseil, paternel; (*b*) (climat) doux; (terrain) favorable; **k. wind,** vent ami; (*c*) *Ind:* (matière *f*) ouvrable, (facilement) traitable. **2.** *A:* (*a*) **a k. Scot,** un Écossais de naissance; (*b*) *Ecc:* **the k. fruits of the earth,** les fruits divers de la terre.

kindness ['kaindnis], *s.* **1.** bonté *f* **(towards s.o.,** pour qn); bienveillance *f*, amabilité *f* **(towards,** envers); prévenance *f*; **prompted by feelings of k.,** animé de sentiments bienveillants; **thanks for your k.,** merci de votre complaisance *f*; **they are k. itself,** ces gens-là sont la bonté même; **to show k. to s.o.,** témoigner de la bonté à qn; **will you have the k. to . . .?** voulez-vous avoir la bonté de . . .? **the milk of human k.,** le lait de la tendresse humaine. **2.** *A:* amitié *f*, indulgence *f* **(for,** pour); **to have a k. for s.o.,** avoir de l'indulgence pour qn. **3. a k.,** un service (rendu); un bienfait; **to do s.o. a k.,** rendre service à qn; **will you do me a great k.?** voulez-vous me rendre un grand service? **to heap, shower, k. on s.o.,** combler qn de bienfaits, de bontés; **a k. is never wasted,** un bienfait n'est jamais perdu.

kindred ['kindrid]. **1.** *s.* (*a*) (i) parenté *f* (de qn avec qn); **the ties of k.,** les liens *m* du sang; (ii) affinité *f* **(with,** avec); **(table of) k. and affinity,** degré *m* de consanguinité (qui constitue un empêchement au mariage); (*b*) *coll.* parents *mpl*; famille *f*; **all her k. lie there,** c'est là que reposent tous ses parents. **2.** *a.* (*a*) *A:* de la même famille; (*b*) de la même nature; du même genre; analogue; **k. souls,** âmes *f* sœurs; **he has found a k. spirit,** il a trouvé une âme qui a des affinités avec la sienne.

kine [kain], *s.pl. A:* vaches *f*.

kinematic [kinə'mætik, kain-], *a. Ph:* cinématique; **k. chain,** chaîne *f* cinématique; **k. viscosity,** viscosité *f* cinématique.

kinematics [kinə'mætiks, kain-], *s.pl.* (*usu. with sg. const.*) *Ph:* cinématique *f*.

kinesalgia [kini'sældʒiə, kain-], *s. Med:* cinésalgie *f*.

kinescope ['kinəskoup], *s. T.V:* **1.** vidéo-enregistreur *m* sur film, *pl.* vidéo-enregistreurs; *F:* kinéscope *m*. **2.** cinégramme *m*.

kinesiatrics [kini:zi'ætriks, kai-], *s. Med:* kinésithérapie *f*, cinésithérapie *f*.

kinesic [ki'ni:zik, kai-], *a.* kinésique.

kinesi(o)meter [kini:'zimitər, kini:zi'ɔmitər; kai-], *s. Med:* kinésimètre *m*.

kinesipath(ist) [ki'ni:zipæθ(ist), kai-], *s. Med:* kinésithérapeute *mf*.

kinesitherapy [kini:zi'θerəpi, kai-], *s. Med:* kinésithérapie *f*, cinésithérapie *f*.

kinesthesia [kini:s'θi:ziə, kai-], **kinesthesis** [kini:s'θi:sis, kai-], *s.* kinesthésie *f*.

kinesthetic [kini:s'θetik, kai-], *a.* kinesthésique, kinésique.

kinetic [ki'netik, kai-], *a.* cinétique; (*a*) *Hyd.E:* **k. head,** (i) hauteur *f* de chute d'eau; (ii) pression *f* dynamique; *El:* **k. equation circuit,** circuit *m* des équations cinétiques; *Ph:* **k. energy,** énergie *f* cinétique; **k. potential,** potentiel *m* cinétique; (*b*) **k. art,** art *m* cinétique.

kinetically [ki'netik(ə)li, kai-], *adv.* cinétiquement.

kinetics [ki'netiks, kai-], *s.pl.* (*usu. with sg. const.*) cinétique *f*.

kinetin ['kinətin, 'kai-], *s. Bio-Ch:* kinétine *f*.

kinetochore [ki'ni:toukɔər, kai-], *s. Biol:* cinétochore *m*.

kinetogenesis [kini:tou'dʒenəsis, kai-], *s. Biol:* cinétogénèse *f*.

kinetograph [ki'netəgræf, kai-], *s. Cin:* kinétographe *m*.

kinetoscope [ki'netəskoup, kai-], *s. Cin:* kinétoscope *m*.

king[1] [kiŋ], *s.* **1.** roi *m*; (*a*) **K. Albert,** le roi Albert; **K. Emperor,** roi et empereur; **the kings and queens of England,** les souverains *m* britanniques; **puppet k.,** roi fantoche; *B:* **K. of Kings,** Roi des rois; **the three Kings,** les (trois) Rois Mages; **the Book of Kings,** le livre des Rois; **to crown s.o. k.,** couronner qn roi; **dish fit for a k.,** morceau *m* de roi; **he wouldn't call the k. his cousin,** le roi n'est pas son oncle, son cousin; (*b*) *Her:* **K. of Arms,** roi d'armes; **Garter K. of Arms,** le chef des trois rois d'armes d'Angleterre; (*c*) *Myth:* **the Erl K.,** le Roi des Aulnes; (*d*) *Ind: etc:* magnat *m*; **one of the oil kings,** un des rois du pétrole; (*e*) *Ich:* **k. carp,** reine *f* des carpes; *Crust:* **k. crab,** limule *m*, crabe *m* des Moluques; *Rept:* **k. cobra,** hamadryade *f*; *Orn:* **k. crow,** drongo royal; **k. vulture,** catharte *m*; condor *m* papa; *Bot:* **king's rod,** asphodèle *m* rameau; **king's spear,** asphodèle blanc; bâton royal. **2.** (*a*) *Chess: Cards:* roi; (*b*) (*at draughts*) dame *f*.

king[2], *v.tr. F:* **to k. it,** faire le roi; trancher du roi.

kingbird ['kiŋbə:d], *s. Orn:* tyran *m*; **western, Arkansas, k.,** tyran occidental; **tropical, Couch's, k.,** tyran mélancolique; **eastern k.,** tyran savana, *Fr.C:* tyran tritri; **gray k.,** tyran gris.

kingbolt ['kiŋboult], *s.* **1.** *Const: Mec.E:* cheville maîtresse, cheville ouvrière; pivot central; boulon *m* formant pivot. **2.** *Const:* poinçon *m*, aiguille *f* (d'une ferme de comble).

kingcraft ['kiŋkrɑ:ft], *s.* (*a*) l'art *m* de régner; (*b*) le métier de roi.

kingcup ['kiŋkʌp], *s. Bot:* **1.** bouton *m* d'or. **2.** populage *m*, souci *m* d'eau.

kingdom ['kindəm], *s.* **1.** royaume *m*; **the United K.,** le Royaume-Uni; **I wouldn't do it for a k.,** je ne le ferais pas pour un empire; **the k. of heaven,** le royaume des cieux; **to come into one's k.,** se faire reconnaître, s'imposer. **2.** règne (animal, végétal, minéral); **in the animal k.,** chez les animaux. **3.** (*a*) *Theol:* règne; **Thy k. come,** que Ton règne arrive, vienne; (*b*) *F:* **k. come,** le paradis; **to send s.o. to k. come,** expédier qn dans l'autre monde; envoyer qn *ad patres*; **to knock s.o. into k. come,** flanquer une volée à qn; **he'll talk until k. come,** il parlerait jusqu'à l'éternité.

kingfish ['kiŋfiʃ], *s. Ich:* **1.** lampris tacheté. **2.** sériole *f*.

kingfisher ['kiŋfiʃər], *s. Orn:* martin-pêcheur *m*, *pl.* martins-pêcheurs; **pied k.,** alcyon *m* pie; **belted k.,** alcyon à collier; **three-toed k.,** ceyx *m*; **racket-tailed k.,** tanysiptère; **stork-billed k.,** alcyon *m* à grand bec; **wood k.,** martin-chasseur *m*.

kinglet ['kiŋlit], *s.* **1.** (*petty king*) roitelet *m*. **2.** *Orn:* roitelet; **golden-crowned k.,** roitelet d'Amérique, *Fr.C:* roitelet à couronne dorée; **ruby-crowned k.,** roitelet de Pennsylvanie, *Fr.C:* roitelet à couronne rubis.

kinglike ['kiŋlaik]. **1.** *a.* de roi; royal, -aux. **2.** *adv.* en roi, comme un roi.

kingliness ['kiŋlinis], *s.* air *m* de roi; noblesse *f* de maintien.

kingly ['kiŋli], *a.* de roi; royal, -aux; **k. act,** action *f* digne d'un roi; **k. bearing,** prestance royale.

kingmaker ['kiŋmeikər], *s.* faiseur *m* de rois.

kingpin ['kiŋpin], *s.* **1.** (*a*) axe *m* de rotule; (*b*) = KINGBOLT[1]; (*c*) cheville ouvrière (d'une organisation, d'une entreprise). **2.** *Games:* quille *f* du milieu.

kingpost ['kiŋpoust], *s.* **1.** *Const:* (*also* **king truss**) poinçon *m*, aiguille *f* (d'une ferme de comble); **k. truss,** ferme simple. **2.** *Av:* (*a*) pylône *m*, guignol *m*; mât *m* de cabane; (*b*) contre-fiche *f*, *pl.* contre-fiches; support *m*.

kingship ['kiŋʃip], *s.* royauté *f*.

king-size(d) ['kiŋ'saizd], *a. Com:* géant; **k.-s. cigarettes,** cigarettes *f* grand format.

kingsman, *pl.* **-men** ['kiŋzmən, -men], *s.m.* **1.** partisan du roi; royaliste. **2.** *A:* douanier *m*. **3.** étudiant de King's College, Cambridge.

kingwood ['kiŋwud], *s. Com:* bois violet; bois d'amarante; bois de violette.

kink[1] [kiŋk], *s.* **1.** (*a*) vrillage *m*; nœud *m*, tortillement *m* (dans un fil, dans une corde); plissement *m* (du drap); grigne *f* (dans le feutre); jarret *m*, faux pli (dans le fil de fer); *Nau:* coque *f* (dans un cordage); *Tex:* vrille *f*, boucle *f*, *Mec.E: etc:* pliure *f* (d'un matériau, d'une pièce mécanique); (*b*) *Cryst:* pliage *m*; (*c*) crampe *f*; torticolis *m*. **2.** *F:* lubie *f*, manie *f*, point *m* faible (de qn); **he's got a k.,** (i) il est un peu timbré; (ii) il a des goûts sexuels excentriques.

kink[2]. **1.** *v.i.* (*of rope*) se nouer, se tortiller, vrillonner; *Nau:* former une coque; faire des coques; (*of thread*) vriller. **2.** *v.tr.* nouer, tortiller (un fil); faire une coque à (un cordage).

kinkajou ['kiŋkədʒu:], *s. Z:* kinkajou *m*; **pale-faced k.,** olingo *m*.

kinking ['kiŋkiŋ], *s.* (*a*) vrillage *m*; nouement *m*; coques *fpl*; (*b*) *Cryst:* pliage *m*.

kinky ['kiŋki], *a.* (*a*) (*of rope, etc.*) noué; (*of hair*) crépu; (*b*) *F:* (*of pers.*) (i) fantasque, extravagant, excentrique; timbré; (ii) qui a des goûts sexuels excentriques; (*c*) *F:* (*of clothes, etc.*) extravagant; (*d*) *P:* volé, chipé.

kinless ['kinlis], *a.* sans parents; sans famille.

kino ['ki:nou], *s. Pharm: etc:* kino *m*.

kinoplasm ['kainouplæzm], *s. Biol:* kinoplasma *m*.

Kinosternidae [kainou'stə:nidi:], *s.pl. Rept:* kinosternidés *m*.

kinosternon [kaino'stə:nɔn], *s. Rept:* kinosternon *m*.

kinsfolk ['kinzfouk], *s.pl.* parents *mpl* et alliés *mpl*; parenté *f*, famille *f*.

kinship ['kinʃip], *s.* parenté *f*; **the call of k.,** la voix du sang.

kinsman, *pl.* **-men** ['kinzmən], *s.m.* parent; *Jur:* affin; **kinsmen by marriage,** parents par alliance; alliés.

kinswoman, *pl.* **-women** ['kinzwumən, -wimin], *s.f.* parente; alliée.

kiosk ['kiɔ:sk], *s.* kiosque *m*; **newspaper k.,** kiosque à journaux.

kip[1] [kip], *s. Leath:* peau *f* de veau, d'agneau.

kip[2], *s.* **1.** *A:* bordel *m*. **2.** *P:* (*a*) asile *m* de nuit; (*b*) lit *m*, pieu *m*, pajot *m*, plumard *m*; (*c*) **to have a k.,** piquer un roupillon.

kip[3], *v.i.* (**kipped**) *P:* (*a*) coucher (dans tel ou tel endroit); **to k. down,** se pieuter; (*b*) dormir, roupiller.

kip[4], *s. Meas: U.S:* mille livres *f* (unité de charge).

kipper[1] ['kipər], *s.* **1.** *Com:* hareng légèrement salé et fumé; hareng doux; kipper *m*. **2.** *Fish:* saumon *m* mâle (pendant la fraieson). **3.** *P: A:* (*a*) individu *m*, type *m*; (*b*) gosse *mf*.

kipper[2], *v.tr.* saler et fumer (des harengs); **kippered herring** = KIPPER[1] 1.

kipperer ['kipərər], *s.* préparateur *m* de harengs doux; saleur *m* et fumeur *m*.

kirk [kə:k], *s. Scot:* (*a*) église *f*; (*b*) **the K.,** l'Église (presbytérienne) d'Écosse; **k. assembly,** assemblée *f*, consistoire *m*, de l'Église d'Écosse; **k. session,** tribunal ecclésiastique composé du pasteur et des anciens de la paroisse.

kirkman, *pl.* **-men** ['kə:kmən], *s.m. Scot:* membre de l'Église d'Écosse.

kirkyard ['kə:kjɑ:d], *s. Scot:* cimetière *m*.

kirombo [ki'rɔ:mbou], *s. Orn:* couroll *m*.

kirtle ['kə:tl], *s. A.Cost:* **1.** (*for men*) tunique *f*. **2.** (*for women*) jupe *f* (pour protéger une robe); cotte *f*.

kirtled ['kətld], *a. A:* **1.** portant une tunique. **2.** portant une jupe, une cotte.

kirving ['kə:viŋ], *s. Min:* havage *m*, souchevage *m*.

kish [kiʃ], *s. Metall:* graphite *m* de fourneau.

kishy ['kiʃi], *a. Metall:* graphiteux.

kiskadee ['kiskədi:], *s. Orn:* pitanga *m*, pitagua *m*, tyran *m* bentevi.

kismet ['kizmet], *s.* le sort; la destinée; le destin.

kiss[1] [kis], *s.* **1.** baiser *m*; accolade *f*; **to give s.o. a k.,** donner un baiser à qn; **to send, blow, s.o. a k.,** envoyer un baiser à qn avec le bout des doigts; **to steal a k. from s.o.,** dérober un baiser à qn; **to snatch a k.,** voler, cueillir, un baiser; (*to child*) **give mother a k.!** fais (une) bise à maman! *Ecc: etc:* **k. of peace,** baiser de paix; *Med: F:* **k. of life,** bouche-à-bouche *m*. **2.** *Bill:* contrecoup *m*; contre *m*; bosse *f*. **3.** (*a*) petit bonbon; (*b*) pâté de cire à cacheter (tombé sur l'enveloppe). **4.** *Typ:* **k. impression,** impression *f* au minimum de pression.

kiss[2], *v.tr.* **1.** donner un baiser à, embrasser (qn); (NOTE: **baiser qn** *is strictly literary and never used in normal conversation*) baiser (le front, la main, de qn, un objet sacré); (*ceremonially*) accolader; donner l'accolade à (qn); **he kissed the Queen's hand,** il baisa la main de la reine; (*of minister, etc.*) **to k. hands,** baiser la main du souverain, être admis au baisemain (en entrant en fonction, pour prendre congé); **he kissed her forehead, he kissed her on the forehead,** il l'embrassa sur le front; **they kissed (each other),** ils se sont embrassés; *F:* **they were kissing away,** ils étaient en train de se bécoter; *F:* **to k. and be friends,** se réconcilier; **to k. the Pope's toe,** baiser la mule du Pape; **to k. the Book,** baiser la Bible (pour prêter serment); *Lit:* **to k. the dust,** mordre la poussière; **to k. the rod,** se soumettre humblement au châtiment; lécher, baiser, la main qui vous frappe; **one should never k. and tell,** il ne faut jamais se vanter de sa bonne fortune; **to k. one's hand to s.o.,** envoyer un baiser à qn de la main; **to k. s.o. goodbye,** dire adieu à qn en l'embrassant; **I soon kissed away her tears,** avec quelques baisers j'eus bientôt fait de sécher ses larmes; *Lit:* **the sunbeams kissed her hair,** les rayons de soleil caressaient, effleuraient, ses cheveux. **2.** *Bill:* (*a*) (*of ball*) frapper (une autre) par contrecoup, par contre; (*b*) *v.i.* (*of balls*) se frapper par contrecoup.

kissable ['kisəbl], *a. F:* qu'on voudrait embrasser.

kiss-curl ['kiskə:l], *s.* accroche-cœur *m*, *pl.* accroche-cœurs.

kisser ['kisər], *s.* **1.** embrasseur, -euse. **2.** *P:* bouche *f*, museau *m*; **one right in the k.,** une pêche en pleine poire.

kissing ['kisiŋ], *s.* (*a*) baisers *mpl*, embrassade *f*, embrassement *m*; *Ecc:* baisement *m* (de la mule du Pape); **k. of hands,** baisemain *m*; **I know her quite well but we're not on k. terms,** je la connais assez bien mais on ne s'embrasse pas; (*b*) **k. gate,** portillon *m* (avec battant entre chicanes).

kiss-in-the-ring ['kisinðə'riŋ], *s.* ronde enfantine (avec embrassades).

kit[1] [kit], *s.* **1.** (*a*) seau *m*; tinette *f* (à beurre, etc.); (*b*) bourriche *f* (pour poisson). **2.** (*a*) effets *mpl*, bagages *mpl*; *Mil: etc:* petit équipement; effets (personnels); **I've brought my overnight k.,** j'ai apporté un sac de nuit; **to pack up one's k.,** plier bagage, faire ses paquets; *Mil: etc:* **k. inspection,** revue *f* de détail, d'inspection; *F:* **the whole k. and caboodle, and boiling,** tout le bataclan; (*b*) trousseau *m*, trousse *f* (d'outils, etc.); **repair k.,** nécessaire *m*, trousse, de réparations; **model construction k.,** boîte *f* de construction; **first-aid k.,** trousse de première urgence; (*c*) **riding k.,** tenue *f* de cheval; **troops in full battle k.,** troupes en tenue de campagne.

kit[2], *v.tr.* (**kitted**) équiper, fournir son équipement à (un soldat, etc.); **(all) kitted up,** complètement équipé; *Mil:* **to be kitted out, up,** toucher son paquetage.

kit[3], *s.* (*a*) chaton *m*; (*b*) **fox k.,** renardeau *m*; petit renard.

kit[4], *v.i.* (**kitted**) (*of cat*) mettre bas, chatonner.

kit[5], *s. Mus: A:* pochette *f* (de maître de danse).

Kit[6]. *Pr.n.* (*dim.*) **1.** *Pr.n.f.* Catherine. **2.** *Pr.n.m.* Christophe. **3.** (*a*) *Hist:* **K.-Cat Club,** club *m* du Kit-Cat (XVIIIe siècle; ses membres se réunissaient dans une taverne tenue par Christopher Cat ou Catling); (*b*) *Art:* **k.-cat (portrait),** portrait *m* en buste qui laisse voir les mains.

kitbag ['kitbæg], *s.* sac *m* de voyage; sac (de) marin; *Mil:* sac à paquetage, sac de grande monture.

kitbox ['kitbɔks], *s. Mil:* cantine *f* (à bagages).

kitchen ['kitʃin], *s.* **1.** (*a*) cuisine *f*; **back k.,** arrière-cuisine *f*, *pl.* arrière-cuisines; **in the k.,** à la cuisine; **mobile k.,** cuisine roulante (de l'armée); **communal k.,** cuisine partagée entre plusieurs familles; *A:* **soup k.,** fourneau *m* économique; soupe *f* populaire; *F:* **thieves' k.,** (i) repaire *m* de voleurs; (ii) officine *f* (d'affaires véreuses, d'intrigues); (*b*) (*esp. in hotel*) **the k.,** le personnel, la brigade, de cuisine; **the k. sent us up a meal,** on nous a fait monter un repas de la cuisine; (*c*) *Scot:* cuisine, aliments *mpl*. **2.** *attrib.* (*a*) de cuisine; **k. table, chairs,** table *f*, chaises *f*, de cuisine; **k. unit,** bloc-cuisine *m*, *pl.* blocs-cuisines; **k. utensils, k. equipment,** batterie *f* de cuisine; **k. stove,** cuisinière *f*; **k. range,** fourneau *m* de cuisine; cuisinière à charbon; **k. sink,** évier *m*; *F:* **k.-sink literature,** littérature *f* boîte à ordures; *F:* **everything but the k. sink,** tout, y compris la cage aux serins; **k. towel,** essuie-mains *m inv* (pour la cuisine); **k. staff,** personnel de cuisine; **k. garden,** (jardin) potager *m*; **k. gardener,** personne *f* qui cultive des légumes; (*b*) *Prehist:* **k. midden,** kjœkken-mœdding *m*; débris *mpl*, déchets *mpl*, de cuisine.

kitchener ['kitʃənər], *s.* **1.** cuisinier *m* (de monastère). **2.** fourneau *m* de cuisine; cuisinière *f* à charbon.

kitchenette [kitʃin'et], *s.* petite cuisine.

kitchenmaid ['kitʃinmeid], *s.f.* fille de cuisine.

kitchenware ['kitʃinwɛər], *s.* faïence *f*, vaisselle *f*, de cuisine.

kite[1] [kait], *s.* **1.** (*a*) *Orn:* milan *m*; **brahminy k.,** milan-pêcheur; **Cayenne k.,** autour *m* de Cayenne; **Everglade k., snail k.,** buse *f* des coquillages; **pariah k., black k.,** milan noir; **swallow-tailed k.,** naucler-martinet *m*, *Fr.C:* milan à queue fourchue; **black-winged k.,** élanion blanc; (*b*) *F: O:* (*pers.*) vautour *m*, usurier *m*. **2.** (*a*) (i) cerf-volant, *pl.* cerfs-volants; (ii) *Fin: F:* cerf-volant; traite *f* en l'air; billet *m* de complaisance; **k. balloon,** ballon captif, observateur; ballon cerf-volant; *F:* saucisse *f*; **k. flyer,** (i) lanceur, -euse, de cerf(s)-volant(s); (ii) *Fin: F:* tireur *m* en l'air, à découvert; **k. flying,** (i) lancement *m* de cerfs-volants; (ii) ballon(s) d'essai; (iii) *Fin: F:* tirage *m* en l'air, en blanc; **to fly, send up, a k.,** (i) lancer, enlever, faire voler, un cerf-volant; (ii) *F:* tâter le terrain; lancer un ballon d'essai; se rendre compte d'où vient le vent; (iii) *Fin: F:* tirer en l'air; tirer en blanc; (*b*) *F:* **as high as a k.,** (i) ivre, soûl; (ii) drogué, chargé, camé. **3.** (*a*) *pl. Nau:* **(flying-)kites,** voiles supérieures au perroquet; (*b*) *Navy:* **mine-sweeping kites,** panneaux *m* de dragage. **4.** *Av: F:* avion *m*, taxi *m*.

kite[2]. **1.** *v.i.* (*a*) voler comme un cerf-volant; (*b*) *U.S: F:* **to k. (off),** filer, ficher le camp. **2.** *v.tr.* (*a*) faire voler (qn, qch.) comme un cerf-volant; (*b*) *Fin:* **to k. (paper),** tirer en l'air, tirer en blanc.

kith [kiθ], *s. A:* amis *mpl*, voisins *mpl* et connaissances *fpl*; *still used in* **our k. and kin,** nos parents et amis; **all one's k. and kin,** tout le cousinage; **to be of the same k. and kin,** être de même parenté; **to have neither k. nor kin,** être seul sur la terre.

kitool [ki'tu:l], *s.* = KITTUL.

kitsch [kitʃ], *s. F:* art, etc., populaire et sentimental.

kitten[1] ['kitn], *s.* **1.** (*a*) chaton *m*; petit(e) chat(te); **cat in, with, k.,** chatte pleine; **a cat and her kittens,** une chatte et ses petits; *F:* (*of pers.*) **to have kittens,** être dans tous ses états; avoir le trac; (*b*) *esp. NAm:* jeune lapin; jeune hamster *m*; (*c*) (*as term of endearment*) ma petite, ma mignonne. **2.** *U.S: F:* **kittens,** moutons *m* (sous les meubles).

kitten[2], *v.tr. & i.* (*of cat*) mettre bas (des petits); avoir des petits; chatonner.

kittenish ['kitəniʃ], *a.* **1.** (*of girl, disposition*) (*a*) coquette, chatte; (*b*) enjouée. **2. k. grace,** grâce féline.

kittiwake ['kitiweik], *s. Orn:* mouette *f* tridactyle; **red-legged k.,** mouette à pattes rouges.

kittle ['kitl], *a. esp. Scot:* difficile à arranger, à manier; **k. cattle,** gens d'humeur chatouilleuse, difficile; **women are k. cattle,** les femmes sont fantasques et changeantes; les femmes sont difficiles à manier; **k. points of law,** points de droit épineux, délicats.

kittul [ki'tu:l], *s.* **1.** *Bot:* caryote brûlant. **2.** *Com:* kitool *m*.

kitty[1] ['kiti], *s.* chaton *m*.

kitty[2], *s.* **1.** (*a*) *Cards: etc:* cagnotte *f*; (*b*) cagnotte, caisse commune (d'un groupe). **2.** (*at bowls*) cochonnet *m*.

Kitty[3]. *Pr.n.f.* (*dim.*) Catherine.

kiwi ['ki:wi:], *s.* **1.** *Orn:* aptéryx *m*; kiwi *m*. **2.** *Av: F:* membre *m* du personnel de terre (d'un corps d'aviation); *F:* rampant. **3.** *F:* Néo-Zélandais(e), Kiwi. **4. k. fruit,** souris végétale.

Klansman, *pl.* **-men** ['klænzmən], *s. U.S:* membre *m* du Ku-Klux-Klan.

klaprothite ['klæprouθait], **klaprotholite** [klæ'prɔθoulait], *s. Miner:* klaprothite *f*.

klepht [kleft], *s. Hist:* clephte *m*, klephte *m*.

kleptomania [kleptə'meiniə], *s.* kleptomanie *f*.

kleptomaniac [kleptə'meiniæk], *a. & s.* kleptomane (*mf*).

klipdassie ['klipdæsi:], *s. Z:* daman *m* (du Cap).

klippe ['klipə], *s. Geol:* klippe *m*.

klipspringer ['klipspriŋər], *s. Z:* oréotrague *m*.

Klondyke[1] ['klɔndaik], *Pr.n.* **1.** *Geog:* Klondike *m*. **2.** *Scot:* pêcherie *f* de harengs au large du littoral ouest de l'Écosse.

klondyke[2], *v.tr. Scot:* exporter (des harengs) tout frais.

Klondyker ['klɔndaikər], *s.* **1.** chercheur *m* d'or au Klondike. **2.** *Scot:* exportateur *m* de harengs tout frais.

kloof [klu:f], *s.* (*in S. Africa*) ravin *m*, gorge *f*.

Klydonograph [klai'dɔnəgræf], *s. El: R.t.m:* Klydonographe *m*.

klystron ['klistrɔn], *s. Elcs: W.Tel:* klystron *m*; tube *m* (électronique) à modulation de vitesse; **drift-tube k.,** klystron à glissement; **k. drift space,** espace *m* de glissement du klystron; **k. with external cavity,** klystron à cavité externe; **reflex k.,** klystron réflexe; **underbunching, overbunching, k.,** klystron en soustention, en sustension.

knack [næk], *s.* tour *m* de main; talent *m*, *F:* truc *m*, chic *m*; **to have the k. of doing sth., a k. for doing sth.,** avoir le talent de faire qch.; avoir le coup, le tour de main, pour faire qch.; savoir s'y prendre pour faire qch.; **to acquire, get into, the k. of sth.,** attraper le coup pour, la façon de, faire qch.; se faire la main à qch.; **I haven't got into the k. of it yet,** je n'ai pas encore attrapé le coup; **to lose the k. of sth.,** perdre la pratique de qch.; **to have lost the k. of sth.,** n'avoir plus l'habitude de qch.; **it's a matter of k.,** c'est une affaire d'habitude, de tour de main; **the k. of pleasing,** le don, l'art *m*, de plaire; **he has a happy k. of saying the right thing,** il a le don de l'à-propos.

knacker ['nækər], *s.* **1.** abatteur *m* de chevaux; équarrisseur *m*; **knacker's yard** = KNACKERY. **2.** (*a*) entrepreneur *m* de démolitions; (*b*) démolisseur *m* de vieux navires. **3.** *pl. P:* **knackers,** testicules *f,* balloches *f.*

knackery ['nækəri], *s.* abattoir *m* de chevaux; chantier *m* d'équarrissage; équarrissoir *m,* écorcherie *f.*

knackered ['nækəd], *a. P:* crevé, vidé, vanné.

knag [næg], *s.* nœud *m* (dans le bois).

knaggy ['nægi], *a.* (bois) noueux.

knap[1] [næp], *s. Dial:* éminence *f,* colline *f.*

knap[2], *v.tr.* (**knapped**) faire craquer (qch.); briser (qch.); **to k. stone,** casser des pierres (pour la réfection des routes); **knapping hammer,** casse-pierres *m inv.*

knapper ['næpər], *s.* casseur *m* de pierres.

knapsack ['næpsæk], *s.* (*a*) havresac *m,* sac *m* (porté sur le dos); sac alpin, tyrolien; (*b*) *Mil:* sac d'ordonnance.

knapweed ['næpwid], *s. Bot:* (**black**) **k.,** centaurée (noire); chardon bénit; **brown radiant k.,** jacée *f*; **brown k.,** tête-de-moineau *f, pl.* têtes-de-moineau.

knar [nɑːr], *s.* **1.** = KNAG. **2.** nœud saillant (de tronc d'arbre).

knautia ['nautiə], *s. Bot:* knautia *m.*

knave [neiv], *s.* **1.** (*a*) *O:* fripon *m,* coquin *m, A:* fourbe *m*; *F: A:* **you little k.!** petit diable! petit espiègle! (*b*) *A:* serviteur *m,* valet *m, A:* varlet *m.* **2.** *Cards:* valet; **k. of clubs,** valet de trèfle; (*at loo, etc.*) mistigri *m.*

knavery ['neivəri], *s.* **1.** *O:* friponnerie *f,* coquinerie *f,* fourberie *f.* **2.** *A:* espièglerie.

knavish ['neiviʃ], *a.* **1.** *O:* de fripon, de coquin, fourbe, malin, malicieux; **k. fellow,** coquin *m,* fourbe *m*; **k. trick,** tour *m* de coquin; coquinerie *f,* friponnerie *f.* **2.** *A:* espiègle.

knavishness ['neiviʃnis], *s. O:* = KNAVERY.

knead [niːd], *v.tr.* **1.** pétrir, malaxer, travailler (la pâte, l'argile); fraiser, fraser (la pâte); **to k. together the various elements of a society,** réunir, mélanger, amalgamer, les éléments divers d'une société. **2.** *Med:* masser, pétrir (les muscles). **3.** *v.i.* (*of cat*) faire son pain.

kneader ['niːdər], *s.* **1.** (*pers.*) pétrisseur, -euse. **2.** pétrin *m* mécanique; pétrisseuse *f.*

kneading ['niːdiŋ], *s.* **1.** pétrissage *m* (de la pâte); malaxage *m* (de l'argile, etc.); **k. machine, trough,** pétrin *m.* **2.** *Med:* massage *m,* foulage *m* (des muscles).

knebelite ['neibəlait], *s. Miner:* knébélite *f.*

knee[1] [niː], *s.* **1.** (*a*) genou, -oux *m*; **to have knock knees,** être cagneux, avoir les genoux en dedans; *Anat:* **k. reflex, k. jerk,** réflexe patellaire, rotulien; **to be k. deep in mud,** être enfoncé dans la boue jusqu'aux genoux; *A.Cost:* **k. breeches,** culotte courte; **to hold sth. on one's knees,** tenir qch. sur ses, les, genoux; **to bend, bow, the k. to, before, s.o.,** mettre un genou en terre devant qn; fléchir le genou devant qn; **to ask for sth. on one's (bended) knees, on bended k.,** demander qch. à genoux; **to receive sth. on bended k.,** mettre un genou en terre pour recevoir qch.; recevoir qch. un genou à terre; **on one k.,** un genou en terre, à terre; **to drop on one's k., on one k.,** mettre un genou en terre; fléchir le genou; **to go down, fall, drop, on one's knees,** s'agenouiller; se mettre, se jeter, à genoux; tomber à genoux; fléchir les genoux; **on your knees!** à genoux! **to go down on one's knees to s.o.,** se jeter, se traîner, aux genoux de qn; **to bring s.o. to his knees,** (i) mettre qn à genoux; forcer qn à s'agenouiller; (ii) obliger qn à capituler; **without getting off his knees,** sans se relever; **to learn sth. at one's mother's k.,** apprendre qch. auprès de sa mère; (*b*) *F:* genou malade; **tennis k.,** foulure du genou (due au tennis); (*c*) *Vet:* (*of horse*) **broken knees,** couronnement *m*; **to break its knees,** se couronner; **ox k.,** genou de bœuf; **thick k.,** genou de veau; **sheep k., hollow k.,** genou de mouton, genou creux; **calf k.,** jambes cagneuses; **horse (that stands) over at the knees,** cheval brassicourt; (*d*) *Orn: F:* **thick k.,** courlis *m* de terre; (*e*) *Bot:* pneumatophore *m*; (*f*) *F:* **to make knees in one's trousers,** faire des poches *f,* des ronds *m* aux genoux (de son pantalon). **2.** (*a*) *Mec.E: Const:* genou, équerre *f,* sabot *m*; genouillère; **iron k.,** genouillère en fer; **k. lever,** levier *m* à genouillère; **wooden k.,** console *f* en bois; **k. bracket,** console-équerre *f, pl.* consoles-équerres; (*b*) *Carp: etc:* **k. timber,** bois courbant, coudé, courbe; (*c*) **k. swell,** genouillère (d'un harmonium); (*d*) *N.Arch:* courbe *f* (de consolidation); **dagger k., racking k.,** courbe oblique; **hanging k.,** courbe verticale; **lodger, lodging, k.,** courbe horizontale; **standard k.,** courbe renversée; **head k., k. of the head,** éperon *m,* guibre *f*; **k. (plate),** gousset *m* (de charpente); **beam k.,** gousset de barot; **flanged k.,** gousset à bord tombé.

knee[2], *v.tr.* **1.** pousser (qch., qn) du genou. **2.** *Carp:* assujettir au moyen d'un genou, d'une équerre.

kneecap ['niːkæp], *s.* **1.** genouillère *f* (d'armure, de cheval, etc.). **2.** *Anat:* rotule *f.*

kneed [niːd], *a.* **1.** (*with adj. prefixed, e.g.*) **weak-k.,** faible des genoux, du jarret; faible. **2.** *Bot:* (*also* **knee-jointed**) géniculé. **3.** *Tchn:* coudé.

knee-high [niː'hai], *a. & adv.* à hauteur du genou; *F:* **when I was k.-h. to a grasshopper,** dans mon enfance; *F:* **he's only k.-h. to a grasshopper, to a mosquito, to a bumble bee,** c'est un tout petit (de rien du tout), un petit poucet.

kneehole ['nihoul], *s. Furn:* trou *m* (dans un bureau) pour l'entrée des genoux; **k. desk,** bureau *m* ministre.

kneel [niːl], *v.i.* (*p.t. & p.p.* **knelt** [nelt], *occ.* **kneeled**) **to k. (down),** s'agenouiller; se mettre à genoux; **to k. to s.o.,** se mettre à genoux devant qn; **to k. on one knee,** mettre un genou en terre.

knee-length ['niːleŋθ], *a.* (robe, etc.) qui descend jusqu'au genou.

kneeler ['niːlər], *s.* **1.** personne à genoux, personne agenouillée. **2.** agenouilloir *m*; coussin *m* pour s'agenouiller.

kneeling[1] ['niːliŋ], *a.* agenouillé, à genoux.

kneeling[2], *s.* agenouillement *m.*

kneepad ['niːpæd], *s.* genouillère *f* (de parqueteur, etc.).

kneepan ['niːpæn], *s. Anat:* rotule *f.*

kneepiece ['niːpiːs], *s.* genouillère *f* (d'armure).

kneesies ['niːziz], *s.pl. F:* **to play k.,** faire du genou.

knee-sprung ['niːsprʌŋ], *a. Farr:* **k.-s. horse,** (cheval) brassicourt (*m*).

knell[1] [nel], *s.* glas *m*; **to toll the k.,** sonner le glas; **this rang the death k. of his hopes,** cette nouvelle, ce refus, etc., sonnait le glas de ses espérances.

knell[2]. *A:* **1.** *v.i.* sonner le glas, tinter. **2.** *v.tr.* sonner (le requiem de qn).

knickerbocker ['nikəbɔkər]. **1.** *s.pl.* **knickerbockers,** culotte (bouffante). **2.** *Tex:* **k. yarn,** fil moucheté.

knickers ['nikəz], *s.pl.* **1.** *F: O:* = KNICKERBOCKERS. **2.** (*undergarment*) culotte *f* (de femme).

knick-knack ['niknæk], *s.* colifichet *m,* babiole *f,* bibelot *m.*

knick-knackery ['niknækəri], *s.* bibelots *mpl,* bimbeloterie *f.*

knife[1], *pl.* **knives** [naif, naivz], *s.* **1.** (*a*) couteau *m*; **kitchen k.,** couteau de cuisine; **cook's k.,** tranchelard *m*; **table k.,** couteau de table; **carving k.,** couteau à découper; **fish k., dessert k., fruit k.,** couteau à poisson, à dessert, à fruits; **k. and fork,** couvert *m*; **k.-and-fork meal,** repas substantiel (qui comprend un plat de viande, etc., qu'on mange avec un couteau et une fourchette); **k. rest,** porte-couteau *m, pl.* porte-couteaux; **k. basket,** panier *m* ramasse-couverts; **k. box, case,** boîte *f* à couteaux; **k. sharpener,** affiloir *m* (pour couteaux); **k. grinder,** (i) (*pers.*) rémouleur *m*; repasseur *m* de couteaux; (ii) (*instrument*) meule *f* à aiguiser; *O:* **k. polish, cleaner,** poudre *f* à nettoyer les couteaux; nettoie-couteaux *m inv*; **before you could say k.,** en un rien de temps; en moins de rien; avant que vous n'eussiez pu dire ouf! (*b*) **pocket k.,** couteau de poche, canif *m*; **Norwegian k.,** couteau de chasse et de pêche; (*c*) couteau; poignard *m*; **to get, have, one's k. into s.o.,** poursuivre qn avec acharnement; s'acharner après, contre, sur, qn; en vouloir à qn; avoir la tête montée contre qn; (*d*) *Surg:* bistouri *m*; scalpel *m*; inciseur *m*; **we shall have to have recourse to the k.,** il va falloir opérer; **he was under the k. for two hours,** l'opération a duré deux heures; (*e*) *Tchn:* **coopers' hollowing k.,** plane creuse de tonnelier; (*for marking barrels*) **razing k.,** rouanne *f*; **putty k.,** spatule *f* de vitrier; couteau à palette, à mastiquer; *Cmptr:* **feed k.,** couteau d'alimentation (de cartes); **punch k.,** poinçon *m* de perforation. **2.** couteau, lame *f* (d'un hache-paille, etc.); couperet *m* (de la guillotine); *Tex:* rasoir *m* (de tondeuse). **3.** *El:* **contact k.,** couteau de contact; **k. switch,** interrupteur *m,* commutateur *m,* à couteau, à lame(s).

knife[2], *v.tr.* **1.** donner un coup de couteau à (qn); poignarder (qn). **2.** *U.S:* dégringoler (un homme politique) (par des moyens déloyaux, occultes).

knifeboard ['naifbɔːd], *s.* **1.** planche *f* à couteaux. **2.** *A:* **k. omnibus,** omnibus *m* à impériale; **k. seat,** banquette *f* de l'impériale.

knife-boy ['naifbɔi], *s.m. A:* petit domestique chargé de nettoyer les couteaux.

knife-edge ['naifedʒ], *s.* **1.** (*a*) arête *f* (de montagne) en lame de couteau; (*b*) *Tchn:* bord tranchant; pièce *f* (mécanique, etc.) en lame de couteau; couteau *m* (de balance, etc.); arête *f* (de couteau de balance, etc.). **2.** *attrib.* (*a*) *W.Tel:* *O:* **k.-e. tuning,** réglage *m* à sélectivité très poussée; (*b*) **trousers with a k.-e. crease,** pantalon au pli cassant.

knife-edged ['naifedʒd], *a.* (*a*) **k.-e. file,** lime *f* à couteau; (*b*) **k.-e. pleats,** plis cassants; **k.-e. wit,** esprit mordant.

knife-shaped ['naifʃeipt], *a. Nat.Hist:* cultellaire.

knight[1] [nait], *s.* **1.** chevalier *m*; (*a*) *Lit:* **the Knights of the Round Table,** les Chevaliers de la Table Ronde; **the K. of the Sorrowful, Rueful, Woeful, Countenance,** le Chevalier de la Triste-Figure; *A: & Lit:* **k. of the pestle,** apothicaire *m*; *F: A:* **k. of the road,** (i) commis voyageur; (ii) vagabond *m*; (*b*) *Hist:* **k. service,** service *m* de haubert; **knight's fee,** fief *m* de haubert; **k. errant** (*pl.* **knights errant**), chevalier errant; paladin *m*; **k. errantry,** chevalerie errante; *Pol.Hist:* **K. of the Shire,** représentant *m* du comté au Parlement; (*c*) **K. of the Garter,** chevalier de l'Ordre de la Jarretière; **k. bachelor,** chevalier (n'appartenant à aucun ordre); *A:* **k. banneret,** chevalier banneret. **2.** *Chess:* cavalier *m.*

knight[2], *v.tr.* **1.** *Hist:* armer chevalier (un écuyer, etc.). **2.** faire, créer, (qn) chevalier; donner l'accolade *f* à (qn).

knightage ['naitidʒ], *s.* corps *m* des chevaliers.

knighthead ['naithed], *s. N.Arch:* apôtre *m.*

knighthood ['naithud], *s.* **1.** chevalerie *f.* **2. he has just been given a k.,** il vient d'être créé chevalier; **to decline a k.,** refuser le titre de chevalier.

knighting ['naitiŋ], *s.* élévation (de qn) à l'ordre de la chevalerie.

knightliness ['naitlinis], *s.* devoirs *mpl* d'un chevalier; caractère *m* chevaleresque; aspect *m* chevaleresque.

knightly ['naitli], *a.* (conduite *f,* etc.) chevaleresque, de chevalier; (ordre *m*) de la chevalerie.

knit[1] [nit], *s.* tricot *m,* tricotage *m*; **scarf of a loose k.,** cache-col *m* à mailles lâches; **fisherman k.,** tricot sport.

knit[2], *v.* (*p.t. & p.p.* **knitted** *or* **knit**) **1.** *v.tr.* (*a*) tricoter (un vêtement); (*b*) faire les mailles à l'endroit; **k. two, purl two,** deux à l'endroit, deux à l'envers; (*c*) **to k. one's brows,** froncer, serrer, le(s) sourcil(s); renfrogner sa mine, son front; prendre un air sourcilleux; (*d*) faire souder (les os); lier (un liquide, un ciment); (*e*) joindre, unir, lier (des personnes); **knit (together) by close friendship,** liés d'une étroite amitié; (*f*) **to k. up a garment,** assembler un vêtement, les bords d'un vêtement (en les tricotant); **to k. up an argument,** rassembler les fils d'un argument. **2.** *v.i.* (*a*) tricoter, faire du tricot; (*b*) (*of bones*) se souder, se nouer, se recoller, se rejoindre; (*of liquid, cement*) se lier, prendre; (*of fruit*) (se) nouer.

knit[3], **knitted** ['nitid], *a.* **1. knit(ted) scarf,** écharpe tricotée; écharpe de, en, tricot; **knitted lace,** dentelle *f* au tricot; **knitted fabric,** tricot *m*; **knitted wear,** tricot; **knit(ted) goods,** bonneterie *f.* **2. knit(ted) eyebrows,** sourcils froncés. **3. close-knit,** étroitement lié; **closely knit sentences,** phrases *f* d'une structure serrée.

knitter ['nitər], *s.* **1.** tricoteur, -euse. **2.** (*machine*) tricoteuse *f,* machine *f* à tricoter.

knitting ['nitiŋ], *s.* **1.** (*a*) tricotage *m*; **k. needle,** aiguille *f* à tricoter; **k. machine,** machine *f* à tricoter; tricoteuse *f*; **k. frame,** tricoteur *m*; (*b*) soudure *f* (des os). **2.** tricot *m*; **plain k.,** (tricot en) point *m* mousse; **I've brought my k.,** j'ai apporté mon tricot.

knittle(-stuff) ['nitl(stʌf)], *s. Nau:* commande *f,* aiguillette *f,* hanet *m.*

knitwear ['nitweər], *s.* tricots *mpl*; bonneterie *f.*

knob[1] [nɔb], *s.* **1.** (*a*) (*on surface, forehead, etc.*) bosse *f,* protubérance *f*; (*on tree*) loupe *f*; (*b*) pomme *f* (de canne, de balustrade); pommeau *m* (de crosse de revolver); bouton *m,* olive *f,* poignée *f* (de porte, de tiroir, etc.); (*c*) *Mec.E:* (**knurled**) **k.,** bouton (moleté) (d'appareil, etc.); molette *f* (de réglage, etc.); **control k.,** bouton, molette, de réglage; *Elcs: T.V: W.Tel:* **tuning k.,** bouton de réglage du son, de la tonalité; bouton d'accord (d'un appareil radio, d'un électrophone, etc.); (*d*) *El:* poulie isolante (à gorge(s)); **k. and tube wiring,** câblage *m* sur taquets; (*e*) *Elcs:* tube *m* électronique en forme d'oignon; (*f*) *P:* tête *f,* caboche; (*g*) *P:* **with knobs on,** et le pouce, et mèche, et le rab; **the same to you with knobs on!** que le diable t'emporte! **2.** *NAm:* = KNOLL. **3.** morceau *m* (de charbon, de sucre); *Cu:* noix *f,* noisette *f* (de beurre).

knob[2], *v.* (**knobbed**) **1.** *v.tr.* bosseler (une surface). **2.** *v.i.* **to k. out,** bomber; former une bosse.

knobbed [nɔbd], *a.* **1.** (*of surface*) plein de bosses; (*of tree*) loupeux. **2.** (*of stick*) à pommeau.

knobble[1] ['nɔbl], *s.* petite bosse.

knobble[2], *v.tr. Metall:* cingler, tringler (le fer).

knobbly ['nɔbli], *a.* plein de bosses; couvert de protubérances; (*of tree*) loupeux.

knobby ['nɔbi], *a.* **1.** = KNOBBLY. **2.** en forme de bosse.

knobkerrie ['nɔbkeri], *s.* massue *f* à grosse tête non dégrossie (employée par les Cafres).

knobstick ['nɔbstik], *s.* **1.** (*a*) canne *f* à pommeau; (*b*) = KNOBKERRIE. **2.** *Ind: P: A:* ouvrier non syndiqué; jaune *m.*

knock[1] [nɔk], *s.* **1.** coup *m,* heurt *m,* choc *m*; **to give s.o. a k. on the head,** (i) porter à qn un coup à la tête; (ii) assommer qn; **to get a nasty k.,** attraper un vilain coup; *F:* **to take the k.,** essuyer de grosses pertes; être fortement atteint (dans ses finances); *Aut.Ins:* **k.-for-k.**

agreement, convention entre compagnies d'assurance, par laquelle chacune s'engage à dédommager son client, en cas d'accident, sans chercher à départager les responsabilités. **2. k. at the door,** coup à la porte; coup de marteau; **there was a k. at the door,** on a frappé à la porte; **he heard a k.,** il a entendu frapper; **he gave a loud k.,** il a frappé très fort; **I know him by his k.,** je le reconnais à sa manière de frapper; **k., k.!** toc, toc! pan, pan! **3.** (*a*) *Mec.E: etc:* cognement *m*, cliquetis *m*; **engine k., piston k.,** cognement du moteur, du piston; (*b*) *I.C.E:* détonation *f* (du carburant dans le moteur); **k. intensity,** intensité *f* de détonation; **k. rating,** indice *m* de détonation. **4.** *Games: etc: F:* **your k.!** c'est ton tour; c'est ta passe.

knock[2], *v.*

I. *v.tr. & i.* **1.** *v.tr.* (*a*) frapper, heurter, cogner; **to k. s.o. on the head,** (i) frapper qn sur la tête; (ii) assommer qn; **our plans have been knocked on the head, knocked into a cocked hat,** nos projets sont tombés dans l'eau; **to k. one's head against sth.,** (i) heurter de la tête, se cogner la tête, contre qch.; (ii) *Fig:* se heurter à, buter contre, un obstacle; **it's like knocking your head against a brick wall,** c'est peine perdue; **he was knocked senseless, silly, by the blow,** le coup lui a fait perdre connaissance; *F:* **to k. s.o. for six, into the middle of next week,** battre qn à plates coutures; démolir, assommer, qn; **to k. s.o. cold,** assommer qn raide; **to k. one's leg,** s'attraper à la jambe; **to k. sth. out of s.o.'s hand,** faire tomber qch. de la main de qn; (*b*) **to k. a hole in, through, sth.,** faire un trou dans qch.; percer qch.; **to k. a nail in, into, a wall,** enfoncer un clou dans un mur; *F:* **that'll k. a bit of sense into him!** ça le lui apprendra! **to k. two things together,** frapper deux choses l'une contre l'autre; *Nau:* **to be knocked off course,** être chassé à la dérive; **to k. a book off the table,** faire tomber un livre de la table; **she knocked the handle off the jug,** elle a cassé l'anse de la cruche; **I managed to get something knocked off the price,** j'ai réussi à faire rabattre quelque chose du prix; **he knocked my hat off,** il a fait tomber mon chapeau; *F:* **to k. s.o.'s head, block, off,** flanquer une taloche à qn; battre qn à plates coutures; **to k. sth., s.o., over,** faire tomber, renverser, qch., qn; *Rugby Fb:* **to k. (the ball) on,** projeter le ballon en avant (avec la main); (*c*) *F:* épater (qn); **that knocks you!** ça te la coupe! **to k. s.o. sideways,** renverser, abasourdir, stupéfier, qn; (*d*) *F:* critiquer (qn, qch.); (*e*) *P:* faire l'amour à, coïter avec (une femme). **2.** *v.i.* (*a*) frapper, heurter (**at,** à); taper (**at,** sur); **to k. at the door,** frapper à la porte; (*b*) **to k. against sth.,** se donner un coup, se heurter, se cogner, contre qch.; buter contre qch.; (*c*) *I.C.E:* (*of engine*) cogner, cliqueter, taper, pilonner; (*of bearings*) tambouriner.

II. (*compound verbs*) **1. knock about** (*esp. U.S:* *also* **knock around**) (*a*) *v.tr.* bousculer, maltraiter, malmener, rudoyer, houspiller (qn); **the furniture has been badly knocked about,** les meubles ont été fort maltraités, sérieusement endommagés; **they were knocking each other about,** ils se cognaient, se battaient; (*b*) *v.i.* **to k. about (the world),** rouler sa bosse; parcourir le monde; bourlinguer; **I spent an hour knocking about waiting for him,** j'ai flâné pendant une heure en l'attendant.

2. knock back, *v.tr. F:* **1. to k. back a drink,** s'enfiler un pot; s'envoyer, lamper, un verre; **k. it back!** cul sec! **2.** coûter; **it knocked me back £200,** ça m'a coûté £200.

3. knock down, *v.tr.* (*a*) renverser (qch., qn); jeter (qch., qn) par terre; étendre (qn) par terre (d'un coup de poing); abattre (un mur, etc.); **he was knocked down by a car,** il a été renversé par une voiture; *F:* **a smell fit to k. you down,** une odeur à vous renverser; (*b*) adjuger, vendre (un article aux enchères); **to k. sth. down to s.o.,** adjuger qch. à qn.

4. knock off, (*a*) *v.tr.* (i) achever (un travail); expédier (une besogne); **he can k. off an article in no time,** il peut écrire un article en un rien de temps; (ii) *P:* voler, faucher (qch.); (iii) *P:* assassiner, zigouiller (qn); (*b*) *v.i. Ind: etc:* s'arrêter de travailler; (*at end of day*) cesser le travail, débrayer; **we k. off at six,** nous finissons à six heures; **let's k. off for a few minutes,** arrêtons pendant quelques minutes.

5. knock out, *v.tr.* (*a*) (i) chasser, repousser (un rivet); **to k. s.o.'s eye, brains, out,** crever un œil, faire sauter la cervelle, à qn; **I'll k. those stupid ideas out of your head,** je vais te débarrasser de ces idées stupides; (ii) **to k. out a pipe,** débourrer une pipe; (*b*) **to k. s.o. out,** assommer qn raide; *Box:* **to k. one's opponent out,** mettre son adversaire knock-out; knockouter son adversaire; **to be knocked out,** être assommé par le coup; (*c*) *Sp:* (*in tournament, etc.*) **to be knocked out,** être éliminé.

6. knock together, *v.tr.* assembler à la hâte (un abri, un radeau, etc.); **that furniture's just been knocked together,** ça, c'est des meubles de pacotille, de camelote.

7. knock under, *v.i. A:* se rendre, se soumettre.

8. knock up, (*a*) *v.tr.* (i) construire (un hangar, etc.) à la hâte; **to k. up a garage out of an old hen house,** se faire un garage de fortune d'un vieux poulailler; **to k. up a meal,** improviser un repas; (ii) *v.tr. & i. Ten:* **to k. up (a few balls),** faire des balles (avant la partie); (iii) *Cr:* **to k. up a century,** faire cent points; (iv) réveiller, faire lever (qn); (v) éreinter, épuiser (qn); **I'm quite knocked up,** je n'en peux plus; je suis vanné, éreinté; **knocked up,** (i) épuisé, éreinté; (ii) *P:* enceinte; (vi) *Bookb: etc:* **to k. up a sheaf of papers,** tapoter une liasse de papiers (pour en faire coïncider les bords); (*b*) *v.i.* **to k. up against sth.,** se heurter contre qch.; **to k. up against s.o.,** (i) se heurter contre qn; (ii) rencontrer qn par hasard, à l'improviste; tomber sur qn.

knockabout ['nɔkəbaut]. **1.** (*a*) *a.* (jeu, etc.) violent, bruyant; (*b*) *a. & s.* **k. (comedian),** bateleur *m*; clown *m*; **k. (act, performance),** tour *m* de bateleur; clownerie *f* (avec échange de bourrades); (*c*) *a.* vagabond, errant; **k. life,** vie errante, *F:* de bâton de chaise; (*d*) *a.* **k. clothes,** (i) tenue *f* de loisir, de sport; (ii) vêtements usagés (qu'on met pour faire du jardinage, du bricolage, etc.). **2.** *s.* (*a*) **a secondhand car that will serve as a k.,** une voiture d'occasion qui servira pour les petits trajets. (*b*) petit yacht.

knockdown ['nɔkdaun], *a.* **1.** (*a*) **k. blow,** coup *m* d'assommoir; (*b*) (machine *f*, etc.) démontable; (*c*) **k. argument,** argument irréfutable. **2. k. price,** prix *m* minimum; prix de réclame.

knocker ['nɔkər], *s.* **1.** (*pers.*) (*a*) frappeur, -euse; **k. up,** réveilleur, -euse; (*b*) *F:* critique hargneux. **2.** (*a*) **(door)k.,** marteau *m* (de porte); heurtoir *m*; (*b*) *P: A:* **not to feel up to the k.,** ne pas être dans son assiette; **to be dressed up to the k.,** être sur son trente et un, en grand tralala. **3.** *pl. P:* seins *m*, nichons *m*.

knock-free ['nɔkfri:], *a. I.C.E:* (carburant) antidétonant.

knocking ['nɔkiŋ], *s.* **1.** coups *mpl* (à la porte, etc.). **2.** (*of engine*) tapage *m*, pilonnage *m*; cognement *m*.

knock-kneed ['nɔk'ni:d], *a.* cagneux; qui a les genoux en dedans; qui a les jambes en x; **k.-k. horse,** cheval serré du devant; cheval panard.

knock-off ['nɔkɔf], *s.* **1.** *Mec.E:* butée *f* (de déclenchement); déclenchement *m*; **k.-o. motion,** arrêt *m* de secours (de presse, etc.). **2.** *Ind: etc:* **k.-o. (time),** débauchée *f*; (heure de) fermeture *f* (des ateliers, des bureaux).

knock-on ['nɔkɔn], *s. Atom.Ph:* collision *f* de neutrons.

knockout ['nɔkaut]. **1.** *a.* (*a*) (coup *m*) de grâce; **k. drops,** soporifique (*esp.* ajouté à une boisson); coup d'assommoir; (*b*) **k. price,** prix *m* imbattable, qui défie toute concurrence; (*c*) **k. competition,** concours *m* avec (épreuves) éliminatoires; (*d*) *F:* magnifique, mirobolant. **2.** *s.* (*a*) coup de grâce; *Box:* knock-out *m*, *pl.* knock-outs; (*b*) *F:* (*pers. or thg*) merveille *f*; phénomène *m*; **she's a k.!** ce qu'elle est belle! c'est un prix de Diane! *P:* **it's a fair k.!** c'est renversant! (*c*) (*at auction*) entente *f* (entre concurrents pour baisser les prix); revidage *m*; (*d*) *Sp:* élimination progressive (des concurrents, des équipes).

knockup ['nɔkʌp], *s. Ten:* **to have a k.,** faire quelques balles (avant la partie, pour se faire la main).

knoll [noul], *s.* mamelon *m*, tertre *m*, monticule *m*, butte *f*.

knop [nɔp], *s. A:* bouton *m*, boucle *f*; *Tex:* **k. wool, yarn,** laine boutonnée, bouclée; bouclette *f*.

knopite ['nɔpait], *s. Miner:* knopite *f*.

Knossian ['(k)nɔsiən], *a. A.Hist:* de Cnosse, de Cnossos.

Knossos ['(k)nɔsɔs]. *Pr.n. Geog: A.Hist:* Cnosse, Cnossos.

knot[1] [nɔt], *s.* **1.** (*a*) nœud *m*; **to tie a k.,** faire, serrer, former, un nœud; **to untie a k.,** défaire un nœud; **to make, tie, a k. in a piece of string,** faire un nœud à, nouer, une ficelle; *F:* **to tie a k. in one's handkerchief,** faire un nœud à son mouchoir (afin de se souvenir de qch.); faire un pense-bête; **reef k.,** nœud plat; **slip k.,** nœud coulant; **figure of eight k.,** nœud d'arrêt; **granny k.,** nœud de vache, de soldat; **Turk's head k.,** bonnet turc, pomme de tire-veille, de tournevire; **manrope k., wall and crown k.,** tête *f* de More, d'alouette; (*b*) nœud (de rubans); **sailor's k.,** nœud régate (marine); **true lover's k.,** lacs *m* d'amour (en 8 couché); (*c*) **k. of hair,** chignon *m*; (*d*) *Needlew:* **French k.,** point d'armes tortillé. **2.** *Nau:* (*a*) nœud, division *f*, de la ligne de loch; (*b*) **so many knots,** tant de nœuds (= tant de milles marins par heure); (*of ship*) **to make 10 knots,** filer 10 nœuds; **ship capable of 20 knots at the most,** navire donnant tout au plus 20 nœuds. **3.** nœud (d'une question, d'un problème). **4. the marriage k.,** les nœuds du mariage; le lien conjugal; *F:* (*of priest*) **to tie the k.,** prononcer le conjungo. **5.** (*a*) nœud (d'une tige, d'un ligament, etc.); nodus *m* (d'un ligament, etc.); nodosité *f* (arthritique, etc.); *Bot:* bracelet *m* (de graminée); *Tex:* **k. in raw silk yarn,** bouchon *m*; (*b*) nœud (du bois); **dead k.,** nœud vicieux; **loose k.,** nœud tombant; **k. hole,** trou *m* provenant d'un nœud; (*c*) *Geol: etc:* concrétion *f*, nodule *m*. **6.** groupe *m*, troupe *f*, noyau *m* (de personnes); groupe (d'objets); **k. of trees,** bouquet *m* d'arbres; **they stood in a k. at the door,** ils se tenaient groupés à la porte. **7. porter's k.,** surdos *m*, torche *f*, tortillon *m*. **8.** *Bot:* **k. grass,** renouée *f* des oiseaux; centinode *f*, traînasse *f*; herbe *f* à cochon; cochonnée *f*; **seaside k. grass,** renouée maritime; **whorled k. grass,** illécèbre *f*.

knot[2], *v.* (**knotted**) **1.** *v.tr.* (*a*) nouer; faire un nœud, des nœuds, à (une ficelle); **to k. together two ropes,** attacher deux cordages ensemble; abouter deux cordages; (*b*) (*of gout, etc.*) nouer (les membres); (*c*) *Needlew:* exécuter (des franges, etc.) au macramé; *abs.* faire du macramé; (*d*) *Paint:* masquer les nœuds (d'une boiserie, etc.). **2.** *v.i.* (*of spring*) se nouer, faire des nœuds; (*of joints*) se nouer.

knot[3], *s. Orn:* bécasseau *m* maubèche, canut *m*, *Fr.C:* bécasseau à poitrine rousse.

knotted ['nɔtid], *a.* **1.** (corde *f*, fouet *m*) à nœuds. **2.** = KNOTTY 3. **3.** *Geol:* (schiste, etc.) noduleux. **4.** *Algae:* **k. wrack,** goémon *m*.

knotter ['nɔtər], *s.* **1.** *Tchn:* noueur, -euse (de franges, etc.). **2.** *Nau:* **a thirty k.,** un navire de trente nœuds.

knottiness ['nɔtinis], *s.* **1.** nodosité *f* (d'une plante); caractère noueux, raboteux (d'une planche). **2.** difficulté *f*, complexité *f* (d'un problème).

knotting ['nɔtiŋ], *s.* **1.** nouement *m* (de cordes); **k. and splicing,** école *f* de nœuds. **2.** *Needlew:* macramé *m*. **3.** *Paint:* vernis *m*, mastic *m*, pour masquer les nœuds.

knotty ['nɔti], *a.* **1.** (*of rope, etc.*) plein de nœuds. **2.** (*of question, problem, etc.*) épineux, embrouillé; **k. point,** question difficile, épineuse, ardue. **3.** (*a*) (*of wood, etc.*) noueux, raboteux, racheux, râcheux; (*b*) **k. hands,** mains noueuses.

knotwork ['nɔtwə:k], *s.* **1.** *Arch:* entrelacs *m*. **2.** *Needlew:* macramé *m*.

knout[1] [naut], *s.* **1.** knout *m*. **2.** (supplice *m* du) knout.

knout[2], *v.tr.* knouter.

know[1] [nou], *s. F:* **to be in the k.,** avoir le mot de l'affaire; être au courant (de l'affaire); être dans le secret, du secret, à la page; connaître, voir, le dessous des cartes; *Rac: etc:* avoir des tuyaux; **those who are in the k.,** les initiés.

know[2], *v.* (**knew** [nju:]; **known** [noun])

I. *v.tr. & i.* **1.** *a.* (*a*) (*recognize*) reconnaître; **don't you k. me?** est-ce que vous ne me reconnaissez pas? **she knew him at a distance,** elle l'a reconnu de loin; **I'd k. him a mile off, anywhere,** je le reconnaîtrais à des kilomètres, n'importe où; **I didn't k. you when you came forward,** je ne vous ai pas reconnu quand vous vous êtes avancé; **I knew him by his walk,** je l'ai reconnu à son allure, à sa démarche; **he is easily known by his scar,** il est facilement reconnaissable à sa balafre; **I knew him for a German,** je l'ai reconnu comme Allemand; j'ai reconnu en lui un Allemand; (*b*) distinguer (**from,** de, d'avec); **to k. good from evil,** connaître le bien d'avec le mal; **I didn't k. the one from the other,** je ne pouvais pas les distinguer l'un de l'autre; **you wouldn't k. him from an Englishman,** vous le prendriez pour un Anglais. **2.** (*a*) (*be acquainted with*) connaître (qn, un lieu); **to be in surroundings one knows,** être en pays de connaissance; **to get, come, to k. s.o.,** faire la connaissance de qn; **to get to k. s.o. better,** faire plus ample connaissance avec qn; **when I first knew him,** quand je fis sa connaissance; **I had known him as a poor man,** je l'avais connu pauvre; **k. thyself,** connais-toi toi-même; **to k. s.o. like a book,** connaître qn comme le fond de sa poche; (*b*) **he doesn't k. what fear is,** il ne sait pas ce que c'est que d'avoir peur; **he has never known trouble,** il n'a jamais su ce que c'est que la peine; **his zeal knows no bounds,** son zèle ne connaît pas de bornes; (*c*) **to k. about sth.,** être informé de qch.; être au courant; **do they k. about it?** est-ce qu'ils sont informés? sont-ils au courant (de l'affaire)? **nobody knows anything about it,** personne n'en sait rien; **he knows all about it,** il sait tout; il s'y connaît; il sait le fonds et le tréfonds de l'affaire; **he knows all about ships, all about machines,** il est très calé sur la marine, sur les machines; **I see you k. all about it,** je vois que vous êtes de la partie; **I should like to k. all about it,** j'aimerais en savoir le fin mot; **he knows nothing at all about it,** il ne sait rien de rien (de l'affaire); **he knows nothing whatever about . . .,** il ignore tout de . . .; **I k. (even) less about it than you,** j'en sais (encore) moins que vous; **I k. nothing about it,** je n'en sais pas un mot; **I don't k. about that!** reste à savoir! je n'ai pas encore décidé! je n'en suis pas bien sûr! **I don't k. so much about that,** je n'en suis pas si sûr que ça; *F:* **what d'you k. about that?** qu'avez-vous à dire à cela? (*d*) **to k. of s.o.,** connaître qn de réputation; avoir entendu parler de qn; **I k. of a good watchmaker,** je connais un bon horloger; **to get to k. of sth.,** apprendre qch.; **when did you k. of it?** quand l'avez-vous su? **we knew nothing of it,** nous l'ignorions; *F:* **not that I k. of,** pas que je sache. **3.** (*to be intimate with*) connaître, fréquenter (qn); **they are neighbours of ours but we do not k. them,** ils sont nos voisins mais nous ne les fréquentons pas; **he is not a man to k.,** ce n'est pas un homme à fréquenter. **4.** *A:* **to k. a woman,** connaître une femme (charnellement). **5.** savoir, connaître, posséder (un sujet, une langue); **to k. sth. by heart,** savoir qch. par cœur; **to k. how to do sth.,** savoir faire qch.; s'entendre à faire qch.; **to k. how to read, swim,** savoir lire, nager; **to k. how to behave,** savoir se conduire; **I don't k. how to do it,** je ne sais comment m'y prendre, comment (il faut) le faire; **they k. how to fight,** ils savent se battre; **a patron who knows how to appreciate art,** un patron juste appréciateur des arts. **6.** (*a*) (*to have cognizance of*) savoir (qch.); **to k. more than one says,** en savoir plus long qu'on n'en dit; **I k. that well enough,** je ne le sais que trop; **now I k.!** je sais à quoi m'en tenir! me voilà fixé! j'y suis! **if youth but knew!** si jeunesse savait! **had I known,** si j'avais su; **as far as I k., for all I k.,** autant que je sache; *F:* **I wouldn't k.,** je ne saurais dire; **what do you k.?** quoi de neuf? **well, what do you k.!** sans blague! **I knew it (would happen)!** ça y est! **he knows a good thing when he sees it,** il sait ce qui est bon; c'est un connaisseur; **he'll k. the answer,** il pourra nous aider; il s'y connaît; **he knows all the answers,** il a réponse à tout; **you don't k. much,** (i) vous ne savez pas grand-chose; (ii) vous n'êtes guère au courant; **not to k. sth.,** ne pas savoir qch.; ignorer qch.; **certain things which you cannot fail to k.,** certaines choses que vous ne pouvez pas ignorer; *F:* **to k. a thing or two, to k. one's way about, around,** être malin, roublard; **he doesn't seem to k. the value of time,** il semble ignorer le prix du temps; **is his father rich?—I don't k.,** son père est-il riche?—je ne sais pas; je n'en sais rien; je l'ignore; **as everyone knows,** comme tout le monde le sait; au su de tous; **what three people k. the whole world knows,** ce que trois personnes savent est public; **they k. everything that's going on,** ils n'ignorent rien de ce qui se passe; **he says it's a good thing, and he knows,** il dit que c'est une bonne affaire, et il est de la partie, il s'y connaît; **don't prophesy unless you k.,** il ne faut prophétiser qu'à bon escient; **he knows his own mind,** il sait ce qu'il veut; **I would have you k. that . . .,** sachez que . . .; *Jur:* **be it known that . . .,** il est fait à savoir que . . .; **everyone knows that . . .,** personne n'ignore que . . .; **I k. that the earth is round,** je sais que la terre est ronde; **I don't k. that he understands much about it,** je doute, je ne crois pas, qu'il y entende grand-chose; **I don't k. that he has any relatives,** je ne lui connais pas de parents; **I knew (that) he had talent,** je lui connaissais du talent; **how do you k. (that) he will come?** qui vous dit qu'il viendra? **how do I k., how am I to k., whether you will pay me?** qu'est-ce qui me dit que vous me payerez? **I don't k. whether he agrees with me (or not),** je ne sais (pas) s'il est de mon avis (ou non, ou pas); **do you k. when . . ., why . . .?** savez-vous quand . . ., pourquoi . . .? **heaven (only) knows when I shall get back,** Dieu sait quand je serai de retour; **he got out of it Heaven knows how!** il s'en est tiré Dieu sait comme! **he didn't quite k. what to say,** il ne savait trop que dire; **he knows what he's talking about,** il est sûr de son fait; **he knows what's what,** il est bien renseigné; il sait de quoi il retourne; il la connaît; **I k. what I k.,** je sais ce que je sais; **I k. not what,** je ne sais quoi; **when under the influence of drink he doesn't k. what he's doing,** quand il est ivre il ne se connaît plus; **now I k. what I wanted to k.,** maintenant je suis fixé; **I'll let them k. what stuff I'm made of,** on verra de quel bois je me chauffe; *F: A:* **it's such a bore, don't you k.,** c'est tellement assommant, quoi! (*b*) **I k. him to be a liar,** je sais que c'est un menteur; **I did not k. him to be one of their accomplices,** j'ignorais qu'il fût, qu'il était, un de leurs complices; **a little woman whom I knew by instinct to be Mrs X,** une petite femme que j'ai reconnue d'instinct pour Mme X; **he is known to be a good father,** on le sait bon père; **he is not known to have any fixed address,** on ne lui connaît pas de domicile; **I have known it (to) happen, it has been known to happen,** c'est une chose que j'ai vue, qu'on a vue, se produire; **I have known stranger things happen,** j'ai vu arriver des choses encore plus singulières; **I have known people die of it,** je sais des gens qui en sont morts; **I have known educated people make this mistake,** j'ai vu commettre cette erreur à des gens instruits; **I have known him do many a kind action,** je l'ai vu, je lui ai vu, accomplir mainte bonne action; **I have never known him (to) do it before,** c'est la première fois, à ma connaissance, qu'il agit ainsi; **I have never known him tell a lie,** je ne sache pas qu'il ait jamais menti; **have you ever known me (to) tell a lie?** m'avez-vous jamais entendu dire un mensonge? m'avez-vous jamais surpris à mentir? **he had never been known to laugh,** on ne l'avait jamais vu rire; **criminals have been known to jest even on the scaffold,** on a vu des criminels plaisanter jusque sur l'échafaud. **7. to get to k. sth.,** apprendre qch.; **I knew it yesterday,** je l'ai appris hier; je l'ai su hier; **how did you get to k. that?** comment avez-vous appris cela? **to get to k. the details of a business,** s'initier aux détails d'un commerce; **I am glad to k. it,** je suis content de le savoir, de l'apprendre; **I don't want to k. any more,** je ne cherche pas à en savoir plus long; **please let us k. whether . . .,** veuillez nous faire savoir si . . .; **everything gets known,** tout se sait; **I don't want it known,** je ne veux pas que cela se sache; **how did it get known?** comment cela s'est-il su? **it is bound to become known,** cela se saura forcément. **8.** *F:* **don't I k. it!** à qui le dites-vous! **not if I k. it!** pour rien au monde! je m'en garderai bien! **she is pretty and well she knows it, and doesn't she k. it!** elle est jolie et elle le sait bien; **a firm that reduces its advertising soon knows it,** une maison qui diminue sa publicité ne tarde pas à s'en ressentir. **9. to k. better,** avoir trop d'expérience, trop de savoir-faire, pour commettre un faux pas ou mal juger; **to k. better than to . . .,** se bien garder de . . .; **I k. better (than that),** (i) je sais bien que non; j'en sais plus long; je sais à quoi m'en tenir; je m'y connais mieux que ça; (ii) on ne m'y prendra pas; je suis plus malin que ça; *F:* pas si bête! à d'autres! **he knows better than to do that,** il est trop fin, trop expérimenté, trop avisé, pour faire cela; il n'est pas assez niais, assez simple, pour faire cela; il se garderait bien de faire cela; **they k. no better, don't k. any better,** ils ne peuvent (pas) faire mieux; *Iron:* **he knows better!** il s'y connaît! **they k. better than to make these concessions,** ils sont trop avisés pour accorder ces concessions; **you ought to k. better at your age,** vous devriez avoir plus de sagacité, de clairvoyance, être plus raisonnable, à votre âge; **he is old enough to k. better,** à son âge il devrait être plus raisonnable; **you ought to have known better,** (i) vous n'auriez pas dû vous y laisser prendre; vous auriez dû faire preuve de plus de jugement; vous auriez dû être plus prudent; (ii) vous n'auriez pas dû vous conduire comme ça; **I thought you would have known better,** je vous croyais plus de raison; **another time you'll k. better,** vous êtes averti pour une autre occasion; **you k. best,** vous en êtes le meilleur juge; **you k. best what should be done,** vous savez mieux que personne ce qu'il faut faire.

knowable ['nouəbl], *a.* **1.** connaissable. **2.** reconnaissable (**by,** à).

know-all ['nouwɔ:l], *s. F:* (*U.S: also* **know-it-all**) je-sais-tout *m*; **k.-a. manner,** air omniscient, d'omniscience.

know-how ['nouhau], *s. F:* savoir-faire *m* (technique); recette *f*; tour *m* de main; connaissances *fpl* techniques; technique opérationnelle; habileté *f*.

knowing[1] ['nouiŋ], *a.* **1.** (facultés *fpl*) de compréhension. **2.** intelligent, instruit. **3.** fin, habile, malin, rusé, déluré; **a k. smile,** un sourire entendu; **to look k., pretend to be k.,** prendre un (petit) air entendu, rusé, un air connaisseur; faire l'entendu; *F:* **she's a k. one,** elle est roublarde. **4.** *esp. U.S: F:* (*of hat, etc.*) chic, coquet.

knowing[2], *s.* compréhension *f*, connaissance *f* (**of,** de).

knowingly ['nouiŋli], *adv.* **1.** sciemment; à bon escient; en connaissance de cause; **I have never k. injured him,** je ne lui ai jamais fait de mal sciemment. **2.** finement, habilement; d'un air rusé; **he smiled k.,** il sourit d'un air entendu.

knowledge ['nɔlidʒ], *s.* **1.** (*a*) connaissance *f* (d'un fait, d'une personne); **to get k. of sth.,** apprendre qch.; **it has come to my k. that . . .,** il est venu, arrivé, parvenu, à ma connaissance que . . .; j'ai appris que . . .; **to keep sth. from s.o.'s k.,** cacher qch. à qn; **I had no k. of it,** je ne le savais pas; je l'ignorais; **lack of k.,** ignorance *f* (**of,** de); **people of whom I had no k.,** des gens que je ne connaissais pas, dont je ne soupçonnais pas l'existence; **her k. of him,** ce qu'elle savait de lui; **this is within the k. of all,** cela, tout le monde le sait; **it is a matter of common k. that . . .,** c'est un fait notoire, il est de notoriété publique, que . . .; **to the k. of everyone, to everyone's k.,** au su de tout le monde; **to (the best of) my k., as far as my k. goes,** à ma connaissance; (autant) que je sache; (à ce) que je sache; **to my certain k.,** à mon vu et su; **to my certain k. they have . . .,** je sais pertinemment qu'ils ont . . .; **not to my k.,** pas que je sache; **without my k.,** à mon insu; **to speak from (one's own) k.,** parler par expérience (personnelle); **to speak with full k. (of the facts),** parler en connaissance de cause, en pleine connaissance des faits; **with a full k. of what would result,** sachant parfaitement ce qui en résulterait; (*b*) **he had grown out of all k.,** il était tellement grandi qu'on ne le reconnaissait plus; il avait grandi au point d'être méconnaissable. **2.** savoir *m*, science *f*, connaissance(s); **to have a k. of several languages,** connaître plusieurs langues; **he has a little k., a working k., of Latin,** il a quelques connaissances en latin; **to have no k. of a subject,** être ignorant d'un sujet; **to have a thorough k. of a subject,** posséder, connaître, un sujet à fond; **his k. is immense,** ses connaissances sont immenses, très étendues; **he has a working k. of politics,** il a fait son apprentissage de la politique; **he left school with little or no k.,** il a quitté l'école avec un mince bagage; **wanted: a representative with a good k. of grocery,** on demande un représentant connaissant bien l'épicerie; **k. of the world, of the heart,** la science du monde, du cœur; **to have no k. of the ways of the world,** ne pas avoir l'usage du monde; **k. of the law that everyone ought to possess,** les connaissances en droit que chacun devrait posséder; **k. is power,** savoir c'est pouvoir; **the advance of k.,** les progrès *m* de la science; *B:* **the tree of k. of good and evil,** l'arbre de la science du bien et du mal. **3. carnal k.,** connaissance charnelle; **unlawful carnal k.,** rapports sexuels illicites.

knowledgeable ['nɔlidʒəbl], *a.* bien informé.

known [noun], *a.* **1.** connu, reconnu, su; **k. fact,** fait bien connu; fait reconnu; **such are the k. facts,** tels sont les faits constatés; **the k. talent of X,** le talent bien connu de X; **a k. enemy, thief,** un ennemi, voleur, avéré. **2.** *Mth:* **k. quantity,** quantité connue.

know-nothing ['nounʌθiŋ]. **1.** *a. & s.* ignorant, -ante. **2.** *s.* agnostique *mf*.

knoxvillite ['nɔksvilait], *s. Miner:* knoxvillite *f*.

knuckle[1] ['nʌkl], *s.* **1.** articulation *f*, jointure *f*, du doigt; **to rap s.o. over the knuckles, to give s.o. a rap on the knuckles,** donner sur les doigts, sur les ongles, à qn. **2.** *Cu:* **k. of a leg of lamb, mutton,** (i) (*bone*) manche *m*, (ii) (*meat*) souris *f* (d'un gigot); **k. of veal, of pork,** jarret *m* de veau, de porc; **k. of ham,** jambonneau *m*; *F:* **that's getting rather near the k.,** cela frise l'indécence; *Games:* **to play at k. bones,** jouer aux osselets. **3.** (*a*) *Mec.E. etc.* **k. (joint),** articulation à genouillère, joint *m* en charnière; agrafe articulée; charnière universelle; **k. end,** chape *f*; **k. pin,** (i) *Mec.E:* axe *m* d'articulation, à rotule; cheville *f* d'attelage; (ii) *Mch:* axe de pied de bielle secondaire; (*b*) *N.Arch:* vive arête; angle *m* de couple; (*c*) charnon *m* (d'une charnière).

knuckle[2], *v.*

I. *v.tr.* **1.** frapper ou frotter (qch.) avec le poing; **to k. one's eyes,** se frotter les yeux avec le poing. **2.** (*at marbles*) caler (la bille).

II. (*compound verbs*) **1. knuckle down,** *v.i.* (*a*) (*at marbles*) appuyer la main à terre (en lançant la bille); (*b*) s'y mettre sérieusement.

2. knuckle over, *v.i.* (*of horse, leg*) être bouleté.

3. knuckle under, *v.i.* se soumettre; céder; mettre les pouces; **I won't k. under to him,** il ne va pas me faire la loi.

knuckleduster ['nʌkldʌstər], *s.* coup de-poing (américain), *pl.* coups-de poing.

knucks [nʌks], *s.pl. U.S: F:* **to play k.,** jouer aux billes.

knur [nɔ:r], *s.* nœud *m* (dans un tronc d'arbre).

knurl[1] [nɔ:l], *s.* **1.** nœud *m* (du bois). **2.** *Metalw:* (*a*) *Tls:* molette *f*, godronnoir *m*; (*b*) molet(t)age *m*; **straight k.,** moletage droit; **spiral k.,** moletage incliné; **diamond k.,** moletage croisé; **k. holder,** porte-outil *m inv* à molet(t)er; porte-molette *m*, *pl.* porte-molettes.

knurl[2], *v.tr. Metalw:* molet(t)er, godronner.

knurled ['nɔ:ld], *a.* (écrou) moleté, à molette, godronné.

knurling ['nɔ:liŋ], *s.* molet(t)age *m*, godronnage *m*.

koa ['kouə], *s. Bot:* koa *m*.

koala [kou'ɑ:lə], *s. Z:* koala *m*.

kob(a) [kɔb, koubə], *s. Z:* kob *m*.

kobellite ['koubəlait], *s. Miner:* kobellite *f*.

kobold ['kɔbɔld, bould], *s. Myth:* kobold *m*; lutin *m*; gnome *m*.

koechlinite ['kɔklinait], *s. Miner:* kœchlinite *f*.

koel ['kouəl], *s. Orn:* koel *m*.

koettigite, köttigite ['kɔtigait], *s. Miner:* köttigite *f*.

kogia ['koudʒiə], *s. Z:* kogia *m*.

kohl [koul], *s. Toil:* khôl *m*, kohol *m*.

kohlrabi [koul'ræbai, -'rɑ:bi], *s. Bot:* chou-rave *m*, *pl.* choux-raves; turnep(s) *m*.

kola [ˈkoulə], *s. Bot:* cola *m*, kola *m*, **k. (tree),** kolatier *m*; **k. nut,** noix *f* de cola, de kola.

kolkhoz [ˈkɔlkɔz], *s.* kolkhoze *m*, ferme collective.

Komodo [kəˈmoudou], *Pr.n. Rept:* **K. dragon, lizard,** monitor, varan, géant.

konel metal [ˈkounlˈmetəl], *s.* konel *m*.

konickite [ˈkɔnikait], *s. Miner:* konickite *f*.

kookaburra [ˈkukəbʌrə], *s. Orn:* martin-pêcheur géant d'Australie.

koolah [ˈku:lə], *s. A:* = KOALA.

kopje [ˈkɔpi], *s. Geol:* kopje *m*.

koppite [ˈkɔpait], *s. Miner:* koppite *f*.

Koran (the) [ðəkɔ:ˈrɑ:n], *s. Rel:* le Koran, le Coran.

Koranic [kɔ:ˈrænik], *a.* coranique; du Koran, du Coran.

Korea [kəˈriə]. *Pr.n. Geog:* Corée *f*; **North K., South K.,** Corée du Nord, du Sud.

Korean [kəˈriən], *Geog:* (*a*) *a.* coréen; **North K., South K.,** nord-coréen, sud-coréen; *Hist:* **the K. War,** la Guerre de Corée; (*b*) *s.* Coréen, -enne.

kornelite [ˈkɔ:nilait], *s. Miner:* kornélite *f*.

kornerupine [kɔ:nəˈru:pi:n], *s. Miner:* kornérupine *f*.

kosher [ˈkɔʃər, ˈkouʃər], *a.* (*a*) *Jew. Rel:* cacher, -ère; kascher, -ère; (*b*) *F:* légitime, comme il faut, au poil, impec.

koto [ˈkoutou], *s. Mus:* koto *m*.

kotow [kouˈtau], *s. & v.i.* = KOWTOW[1,2].

kouprey [ˈkouprei], *s. Z:* kouprey *m*.

kowtow[1] [kauˈtau], *s.* prosternation *f*, prosternement *m* (à la chinoise).

kowtow[2], *v.i.* **1.** se prosterner, se courber (à la chinoise) (to, devant); saluer à la chinoise. **2. to k. to s.o.,** faire des courbettes devant qn; s'aplatir devant qn; courber l'échine devant qn.

kraal [krɑ:l], *s.* kraâl *m* (village ou corral).

kraft [krɑ:ft], *s. Paperm:* papier *m* d'emballage fort, papier kraft.

krait [krait], *s. Rept:* bungare *m*.

kraken [ˈkrɑ:k(ə)n, ˈkreik(ə)n], *s. Moll:* craken *m*, kraken *m*.

Krakow [ˈkrɑ:kɔf]. *Pr.n. Geog:* Cracovie *f*.

krameria [kræˈmiəriə], *s. Bot:* krameria *m*.

Krarup [ˈkrærəp]. *Pr.n. El:* **K. loading,** krarupisation *f*.

krater [ˈkreitər], *s. Gr.Ant:* cratère *m*.

kraurosis [krauˈrousis], *s. Med:* kraurosis *m*.

krausite [ˈkrausait], *s. Miner:* krausite *f*.

Kraut [kraut], *s. P: Pej:* Allemand *m*, Boche *m*.

Krebs [krebz]. *Pr.n. Bio-Ch:* **K. cycle,** cycle *m* de Krebs, de l'acide citrique.

kreittonite [ˈkraitənait], *s. Miner:* creittonite *f*.

kremersite [ˈkreməzait], *s. Miner:* krémersite *f*.

Kremlin (the) [ðəˈkremlin], *s.* le Kremlin.

Kremlinologist [kremliˈnɔlədʒist], *s.* kremlinologiste *mf*.

Kremlinology [kremliˈnɔlədʒi], *s.* kremlinologie *f*.

krennerite [ˈkrenərait], *s. Miner:* krennérite *f*.

kriegspiel [ˈkri:gʃpi:l], *s.* kriegspiel *m*.

krill [kril], *s. Crust:* krill *m*.

krimmer [ˈkrimər], *s. Com:* (variété *f* de) caracul *m*.

kris(s) [kri:s], *s.* kriss *m*.

kroehnkite, kröhnkite [kreŋkait], *s. Miner:* kröhnkite *f*.

kromeski, kromesky [krɔˈmeski], *s. Cu:* cromesquis *m*.

krummhorn [ˈkrumhɔ:n], *s. Mus: A:* cromorne *m*, tournebout *m*.

kryokonite [kraiˈɔkənait], *s. Geol:* kryokonite *f*.

krypton [ˈkriptɔn], *s. Ch:* krypton *m*.

Ks(h)at(t)riya [(kə)ˈʃætriə], *s.* kshatriya *m*.

ksi [ksai], *s. Gr.Alph:* ksi.

kudos [ˈkju:dɔs], *s.* (*a*) prestige *m*; (*b*) célébrité *f*.

kudu [ˈku:du:], *s. Z:* koudou *m*, coudou *m*; **greater k.,** grand koudou; **lesser k.,** petit koudou.

kudzu [ˈkudzu:], *s. Bot:* **k. (vine),** ku-dzu *m*.

kufi [ˈkoufi], *s. Rept:* vipère *f* du Levant.

kuk(e)ri [ˈku:k(ə)ri], *s.* koukri *m*; coutelas *m* (des Gurkhas).

Ku-Klux Klan [ˈk(j)u:klʌksˈklæn], *s.* le Ku-Klux Klan (association secrète qui se forma dans les États du Sud après la guerre civile, pour lutter contre l'influence des noirs).

Ku-Kluxer, Ku-Klux Klanner, Klansman [ˈk(j)u:ˈklʌksər, -klʌksˈklænə, -ˈklænzmən], *s.* membre *m* du Ku-Klux Klan.

kulak [ˈku:læk], *s.* koulak *m*.

kümmel [ˈkyməl, ˈkiməl], *s. Dist:* kummel *m*.

kumquat [ˈkʌmkwɔt], *s. Bot:* k(o)umquat *m*.

kupfernickel [ˈkupfənikl], *s. Miner:* kupfernickel *m*, nickéline *f*.

Kupffer [ˈkupfər]. *Pr.n. Anat:* **Kupffer('s) cells,** cellules *f* de Kupffer.

Kurd [kə:d], *Ethn:* (*a*) *a.* k(o)urde; (*b*) *s.* K(o)urde *mf*.

Kurdish [ˈkə:diʃ]. **1.** *a. Ethn:* k(o)urde. **2.** *s. Ling:* k(o)urde *m*.

Kurdistan [kə:diˈstɑ:n]. *Pr.n. Geog:* K(o)urdistan *m*.

kurgan [ˈkə:gən], *s. Archeol:* kourgane *m*.

Kuril(e) [ˈkju:ril]. *Pr.n. Geog:* **the K. Islands,** les îles Kouriles.

Kuro Siwo [ˈku:rouˈsi:wou, -ˈʃi:-], *Pr.n. Oc:* **the K. S. (current),** le Kouro-sivo, Kuro-shio.

kurtosis [kə:ˈtousis], *s. Stat:* kurtosis *m*.

kusimanse(l) [kusiˈmænsə(l)], *s. Z:* crossarque *m*.

Kuweit [ku:ˈweit]. *Pr.n. Geog:* Koweït *m*.

Kuweiti [ku:ˈweiti], *Geog:* (*a*) *a.* koweïtien; (*b*) *s.* Koweïtien, -ienne.

kvass [kvæs], *s.* kwas *m*; bière *f* de seigle (de la Russie).

kyang [kjæŋ], *s. Z:* hémione *m*.

kyanite [ˈkaiənait], *s. Miner:* cyanite *m*.

kyanization [kaiənaiˈzeiʃ(ə)n], *s.* kyanisation *f*.

kyanize [ˈkaiənaiz], *v.tr.* kyaniser; imprégner (le bois) de sublimé corrosif.

kyle [kail], *s. Scot:* détroit *m*; **the Kyles of Bute,** les détroits de Bute.

kylix [ˈkailiks], *s.* kylix *f*.

kymograph [ˈkaimougræf], *s. Med: etc:* kymographe *m*.

kymography [kaiˈmɔgrəfi], *s. Med:* kymographie *f*.

Kymric [ˈkʌmrik, ˈkim-], *a.* cymrique.

kyphosis [kaiˈfousis], *s. Med:* cyphose *f*.

kyphotic [kaiˈfɔtik], *a. Med:* cyphotique.

kyrie [ˈkiriei], *s. Ecc:* **k. (eleison** [eˈlei(i:)sɔn]**),** kyrie *m inv* (eleïson).

kyriologic [kiriouˈlɔdʒik], *a.* (écriture) kyriologique, curiologique.

kyte [kait], *s. Scot:* estomac *m*.